1983 HIGHLIGHTS

GENERAL INDEX

—J—

— S —

Democrats Gain in 1982 Elections, But Fall Short of Clear Defeat of Reagan Policy

Urged by Pres. Ronald Reagan to "stay the course" for another two years, American voters did not give the president a clear mandate in the 1982 mid-term elections. With unemployment a major issue, as indicated by exit polls, voters gave the Democrats at least 25 new seats in the House of Representatives and control of two-thirds of the nation's state houses, but left the Republicans with a slim margin in the Senate.

The larger-than-expected Democratic gains in the House signaled a threat to Pres. Reagan's economic policies. Losers included at least 24 Republican incumbents and at least 14 freshman representatives who had swept into office on Pres. Reagan's coattails in 1980.

In the races for governor, Democrats captured 27 governorships, but lost the coveted leadership of the state house in California as Thomas Bradley failed in his bid to become the nation's first black governor.

Despite several extremely close races in the East and Midwest, the Republicans managed to maintain their 54-46 margin in the senate, possibly salvaging chances for passage of the president's economic policies in the congress.

Addenda, Late News, Changes

Nations of the World (p. 497-582)

Bolivia: The Bolivian Congress, meeting for the first time in more than two years of military rule, elected, Oct. 5, Hernan Siles Zuazo as president of a civilian government.

Italy: Prime Minister Giovanni Spadolini's 14-month-old government was brought down, Aug. 7, but on Aug. 23, the Prime Minister formed Italy's 42d postwar Cabinet with the same parties and ministers as the previous one.

Netherlands: Prime Minister Andreas van Agt resigned, Oct. 13. He was replaced by former Economics Minister Ruud Lubbers.

Swaziland: King Sobhuza II died, Aug. 21, at his palace near the capital, Mbabane.

West Germany: Helmut Kohl was elected Chancellor, Oct. 1. He suceeded Helmut Schmidt.

Awards (p. 410-412)

Nobel Prize in Physics: Kenneth G. Wilson, U.S., was awarded about $157,000 for his method of analyzing the basic changes in matter under the influence of pressure and temperature (p. 410).

Nobel Prize in Chemistry: Aaron Klug, South-African-born scientist working in Cambridge, England, was awarded about $157,000 for his research revealing the most detailed structures of viruses and some of the most important components within all living things (p. 410).

Nobel Prize in Medicine or Physiology: Sune Bergstrom and Bengt Samuelsson, both Sweden, split $157,000 prize with John R. Vane, U.K., for discoveries in controlling prostaglandins, a natural substance implicated in a wide range of human and animal illnesses (p. 411).

Nobel Prize in Literature: Gabriel Garcia Marquez, a Colombian who lives in Mexico, won $157,000 for novels of breadth and epic richness (p. 411).

Nobel Peace Prize: Alva Myrdal, Sweden, and Alfonso Garcia Robles, Mexico, split $157,000 for their efforts to promote disarmament (p. 411).

Nobel Memorial Prize in Economics: George J. Stigler, U.S., for research on the working of industry and the role of government regulation in the economy (p. 412).

Broadcasting and Theater (pp. 418)

Emmy Awards, by Academy of Television Arts and Sciences, for nighttime programs, 1981-82: Dramatic series: *Hill Street Blues;* actor: Daniel J. Travanti, *Hill Street Blues;* actress: Michael Learned, *Nurse;* supporting actor: Michael Conrad, *Hill Street Blues;* supporting actress: Nancy Marchand, *Lou Grant;* director: Harry Harris, *Fame;* writing: *Hill Street Blues.* Comedy series: *Barney Miller;* actor: Alan Alda, *M*A*S*H;* actress: Carol Kane, *Taxi;* supporting actor: Christopher Lloyd; *Taxi;* supporting actress: Loretta Swit, *M*A*S*H;* director: Alan Rafkin, *One Day at a Time;* writing: *Taxi.* Limited series or special: *A Woman Named Golda; Marco Polo;* actor: Mickey Rooney, *Bill;* actress: Ingrid Bergman, *A Woman Named Golda;* supporting actor: Laurence Olivier, *Brideshead Revisited;* supporting actress: Penny Fuller, *The Elephant Man;* director: Marvin J. Chomsky, *Inside the Third Reich;* writing: Corey Blechman, Barry Morrow, *Bill.* Variety, music, or comedy: *Night of 100 Stars;* director: *Goldie and Kids.*

Arts and Media (pp. 427-428)

Debra Sue Maffett, of Anaheim, Cal., was chosen **Miss America 1983** (p. 428).

National Defense (p. 329)

Adm. Wesley L. McDonald replaced Adm. Harry D. Train as NATO's supreme allied commander in the Atlantic.

The Reagan Administration (p. 318)

Martin Stuart Feldstein was selected by Pres. Reagan, Aug. 6, as the new chairman of the Council of Economic Advisers.

Sports (pp. 822-917)

Boston Marathon: Alberto Salazar of Eugene, Ore. covered the traditional distance of 26 miles 385 yards in the record time of 2 hours 8 minutes 51 seconds to win the 86th annual Boston Marathon. Dick Beardsley of Rush City, Minn. finished second. Charlotte Teske of W. Germany placed first among the women in 2 hours 29 minutes 33 seconds.

New York Marathon: Alberto Salazar of Eugene, Ore. covered the 26 mile-385-yard course in a world record 2 hours 9 minutes 29 seconds to win the New York Marathon for the third consecutive year. Rodolfo Gomez of Mexico finished second. Grete Waitz of Norway won her fourth woman's title with a time of 2 hours 27 minutes 14 seconds.

115th ANNIVERSARY EDITION

The World Almanac

and Book of Facts for 1983

The Top 10 News Stories of 1982

The state of the U.S. economy, especially the year-long rise in the unemployment rate, engrossed the nation as Pres. Ronald Reagan defended his economic policies, including a $98.3 billion tax bill, by citing the decrease in interest rates and a stock market rally as harbingers of better times.

Hurling the Middle East back into open warfare, Israel invaded Lebanon, leading to the ouster of the PLO leadership from Lebanon.

Argentina seized the British-held Falkland Islands, but went down to defeat in face of the military superiority of the task force deployed to reassert British control over the islands.

Not willing to resign themselves to martial law, the Polish people protested its imposition and continued to support the Solidarity movement, even after the labor union was officially banned.

Keeping the pressure on until the very end, supporters of the Equal Rights Amendment finally admitted defeat when they lost several key votes before the ratification deadline.

Yielding his stewardship at Foggy Bottom, Secretary of State Alexander Haig surprised the nation with his decision, apparently over policy disagreement, to resign.

Over half a million demonstrators against nuclear arms marched to New York City's Central Park, highlighting the growth in the U.S. of the worldwide anti-nuclear movement.

Unexpectedly, a Washington, D.C., jury found John W. Hinckley, Jr. not guilty by reason of insanity on charges of shooting Pres. Ronald Reagan and 3 others in 1981.

Victory seemed closer for Iran in its war with Iraq when it invaded Iraq in July, but, after several weeks of intensive fighting, the war once again stood at a deadlock.

Broadening sanctions on sales of U.S. equipment for the Soviet pipeline to include U.S. licensees, Pres. Ronald Reagan outraged the nation's European allies.

The First Annual World Almanac High School Records Contest Picks Winners in Academic, Sports, Miscellaneous Categories

Peacemakers and scientists have the Nobels, journalists the Pulitzers, and athletes the Olympic medals, but high school students have never had their own special awards recognizing their achievements.

The World Almanac felt that this was a serious omission and, to remedy the situation, has established The World Almanac High School Records. The results listed below represent the first annual selection. The World Almanac Records will now be a permanent feature of The World Almanac.

Earlier this year, we sent out the word that we were seeking records in 3 categories — academic, sports, and miscellaneous. We divided each of the categories into 2 sections, individual and group. We set a deadline and waited for the submissions to come in. We then asked a distinguished writer, Paula Danziger, the author of *The Cat Ate My Gymsuit* and *There's a Bat in Bunk Five,* and a distinguished editor, Elizabeth Geiser, a senior vice president of the Gale Research Company, to join our editor in judging the entries. They took the judging very seriously and, as the results below show, decided to make awards only in certain categories. Although the submissions in the other categories were notable, the judges did not feel any one record merited selection over the others.

New Submissions Welcome

The winners for 1982 appear below. We offer them our congratulations on their fine achievements. At the same time, we offer a challenge to all other high school students across the United States and Canada to top the 1982 winners. If you think you can better the 1982 records or have submissions in the vacant categories, please let us know and you may be a winner in 1983 and find your name in the 1984 edition of *The World Almanac & Book of Facts.*

The rules are simple. You must currently be a high school student and hold an achievement in one of the categories below. For example, if you think your school has the most recipients of National Merit Scholarships for one year, then you can enter your school in the Academic Group category. If you think you can pole vault higher than any other high school student, then enter the Sports Individual category. If your talents are a bit more offbeat, enter the Miscellaneous categories. Let us know, for instance, if you think you can eat more hamburgers at lunch than your friends or you and your friends have played the longest running games of "Dungeons and Dragons."

Once you've decided to enter, send us a postcard or letter, specifying the category you are entering and describing the achievement. Have the entry endorsed by either your principal, teacher, school coach, or a parent and send it to: RECORDS, The World Almanac, 200 Park Avenue, New York, NY 10166.

Good Luck!

1982 World Almanac High School Records

Academic

Individual: no winner chosen.

Group: Antilles High School, Fort Buchanan, Puerto Rico

Achievement: Five members of the class of 1982, out of a class of 119, received confirmed appointments to the U.S. Military Academy at West Point.

Sport

Individual: Danielle Strieter, Alexandria, Va.

Achievement: Playing number one on the Groveton High School tennis team in her freshmen, sophomore, and junior years, she did not lose one match or one set in any high school district match. She lost only 15 out of 411 games in those three years of undefeated play.

Group: no winner chosen.

Miscellaneous

Individual: Gary Beltowski, Rockville, Md.

Achievement: Holds a Pac-Man score of 3,179,020 playing alone. He is also the author of "Win at Pac-Man" and has a contract for a second book.

Group: The students of Julesburg, Colorado Junior High School, with the help of the elementary school.

Achievement: Made a paper chain totaling 1,135 feet to decorate the halls of the junior high school.

Winners of the 1982 Red Line/World Almanac National BMX Skills Competition

The 1982 Red Line/World Almanac National BMX Skills Competition Tour was held in 40 shopping centers across the United States during the summer of 1982. The competition was comprised of 5 skill events. The winners in these events, the first nationwide BMX skills competition and one of the largest in BMX history, are listed below.

The Rules of the Game

The competition was open to both amateurs and professionals 5 years or older. The average age of the competitors was 17 years and ranged up to 56 years old. Competitors were required to use an official BMX-style bicycle. Such a bicycle is distinguished by its 20-inch wheels and high-rise handlebars. Brand new BMX bicycles were provided for participants who wished to use them.

Safety was stressed throughout the competition. All contestants were required to wear proper safety equipment and clothing. Helmets and other safety gear were made available to anyone who needed them. A free BMX safety manual was distributed at all competition locations. The skills events were held on a portable track that was transported from town to town and set on the existing asphalt in the shopping center parking lots.

The first event, the 25-meter dash, was conducted from a dead-start against the clock. In the 25-meter slalom, the contestants were required to negotiate, in the designated order, the outside perimeter of 6 cones on a 25-meter course, also against the clock.

The ramp jump was from a one-foot high ramp measured to the landing spot of the contestant's back wheels. For the "Wheelie" event, a wheelie was defined as the act of lifting the front wheel off the ground for a sustained period of time. The contestant was given one minute to begin the wheelie; timing began when the front wheel was lifted from the ground and ended when the front wheel or any part of the contestant's body touched the ground.

In the bunny hop, the contestants cleared a horizontal crossbar set above the ground at various heights. In clearing the crossbar, the contestant was required to completely lift his bicycle off the ground without placing either foot on the ground during the approach. After clearing the crossbar and upon landing, the two bicycle wheels had to touch the ground before any part of the contestant's body touched the ground. The contestants were judged by the greatest heights reached.

For more information about the competition and the schedule for 1983, please write to Jane Flatt, Publisher, The World Almanac, 200 Park Avenue, New York, NY 10166.

The Events	Final Results	
25-Meter Dash	Jeff Kosmala Panorama City, CA	3.22 seconds
25-Meter Slalom	Steve Gorski Troy, MI	7.24 seconds
Ramp Jump	Martin Aparijo Buena Park, CA	15 ft. 9½ in.
Wheelie	Brian Scura Garden Grove, CA	42:23.35
Bunny Hop (2 winners)	Tim Tracy Thousand Oaks, CA	41 in.
	Vance Hubersberger Beulah, CO	41 in.

Heroes of Young America: The Third Annual Poll

The World Almanac's® Annual Poll to discover the heroes of America's youth had a new look in 1982 and, when the results were all tabulated, a new winner as the top hero.

Alan Alda, the actor who for over 10 years has played one of TV's quintessential anti-heroes, "Hawkeye" Pierce on "M*A*S*H," was selected as the top hero by high school students across the United States. Alda also gained the most votes as the top male hero in the Comedy category.

In winning the Top Hero category, Alda ousted the reigning top hero, Burt Reynolds, who had swept the balloting during the first two years of polling by The World Almanac®.

Poll Has New Look

The poll's new look is reflected in the division of the balloting into 9 separate categories. In past years, the students had chosen the winners from a straight alphabetical listing of names. As a result, the winners had come primarily from the worlds of entertainment and sports and had also been primarily male. In order to encourage the students to select those they admire in all walks of life, the balloting in this year's poll was conducted in 8 specific categories in addition to the selection of a top hero. The students were also asked to select at least one male and one female in each of the specific categories. In the final selection, the male and female who received the most votes in each category were named the winners.

In addition, The World Almanac® broadened the age range of the students participating in the poll, from 8th graders only to grades 8 through 12. As in the past two years, the schools chosen to participate through the World Almanac co-sponsoring newspapers represented a geographic cross-section of the United States and both suburban and intercity schools.

Results Are Mixed Bag

The final results, which are listed below, are a mixed bag, representing both young, up-and-coming individuals and well-established figures who would probably also rank high as heroes of parents of the students who participated in the poll. Alan Alda, Carol Burnett, Sandra Day O'Connor, Neil Armstrong, Walter Cronkite, and Barbara Walters certainly fall into the latter category. Whereas the Sports category, with Tracy Austin and Sugar Ray Leonard, and several of the entertainment categories, especially the music and dance category, with Rick Springfield and Pat Benatar, include winners who appeal specifically to the younger generation in the United States.

This year, in marked contrast to the two previous years of polling, women did very well in the overall voting. Although the division into categories makes it impossible to compare the total votes gained by an individual in a scientific manner, the results do show the top three vote-getters in the categories were women: Pat Benatar, Sandra Day O'Connor, and Judy Blume. The highest vote-getter in the categories was Pat Benatar.

Selleck Runner-Up

Although only one top hero was chosen in the first category, the tabulation showed Tom Selleck as the runner-up. It is also interesting to note, in view of the number of votes women received in the category voting, that no woman placed in the top eight in the contest for Top Hero.

The voting for Top Hero in the Newsmaker category showed no politicians among the winners. However, Pres. Ronald Reagan did poll the second highest number votes overall in that category.

Also of interest is the showing made by Burt Reynolds, the top winner for the past two years. Reynolds was the third runner-up in the Top Hero category. In the Movie Performers/Noncomedy category, Reynolds was runner-up for top male hero, although in overall voting he came in third after Bo Derek.

Top Hero

Alan Alda, TV and movie actor, is best known for his role as "Hawkeye" Pierce on the TV series "M*A*S*H"; won Emmy for best actor in 1982.

Movie Performers/Noncomedy

Clint Eastwood, actor, most recently starred in *Every Which Way but Loose,* and *Firefox.*

Bo Derek, actress, gained fame in *10* and recently appeared in *Tarzan, the Ape Man.*

Television Performers/Noncomedy

Tom Selleck, actor, stars in the weekly series "Magnum, P.I."

Stefanie Powers, actress, stars weekly in "Hart to Hart."

Comedy

Alan Alda, TV and movie actor, long-time star of the TV series "M*A*S*H."

Carol Burnett, TV and movie actress, appeared recently in *The Four Seasons* and the movie version of *Annie.*

Music and Dance

Rick Springfield, pop singer; appears on the soap opera "General Hospital."

Pat Benatar, cabaret singer turned rock singer.

Sports

Sugar Ray Leonard, WBC and WBA welter-weight boxing champion.

Tracy Austin, tennis player, 1979 and 1981 U.S. Open champion.

News and Sports Media

Walter Cronkite, former anchorman, "CBS Evening News."

Barbara Walters, TV journalist, ABC-TV.

Artists and Writers

Jim Davis, cartoonist, creator of the lasagna-loving cat "Garfield."

Judy Blume, author, primarily of young adult novels, including *Superfudge* and *Tiger Eyes.*

Newsmakers

Neil Armstrong, former astronaut, was the first man to walk on the moon.

Sandra Day O'Connor, jurist, is the first woman to serve on the U.S. Supreme Court.

The Ninety-Eighth Congress

With 1982 Election Results

The Senate

Terms are for 6 years and end Jan. 3 of the year preceding name. Annual salary $60,662.50. To be eligible for the U.S. Senate a person must be at least 30 years of age, a citizen of the United States for at least 9 years, and a resident of the state from which he is chosen. The Congress must meet annually on Jan. 3, unless it has, by law, appointed a different day.

Address: Washington, DC 20510

Senate officials (97th Congress): President Pro Tempore Strom Thurmond; Majority Leader Howard H. Baker Jr.; Majority Whip Ted Stevens; Minority Leader Robert C. Byrd; Minority Whip Alan Cranston.

Rep., 54; Dem., 46; Total, 100. *Served in Senate during 97th Congress.
Preliminary returns

Term ends	Senator (Party, home)	1982 Election
	Alabama	
1985	Howell Heflin* (D, Tuscumbia)	
1987	Jeremiah Denton* (R, Mobile)	
	Alaska	
1985	Ted Stevens* (R, Anchorage)	
1987	Frank H. Murkowski* (R, Anchorage)	
	Arizona	
1987	Barry M. Goldwater* (R, Scottsdale)	
1989	Dennis DeConcini* (D, Tucson)	413, 951
	Pete Dunn (R, Phoenix)	292, 638
	Arkansas	
1985	David Pryor* (D, Little Rock)	
1987	Dale Bumpers* (D, Charleston)	
	California	
1987	Alan Cranston* (D, Palm Springs)	
1989	Pete Wilson (R, San Diego)	3,897,771
	Edmund G. Brown (D, Sacramento)	3,431,030
	Colorado	
1985	William L. Armstrong* (R, Aurora)	
1987	Gary Hart* (D, Denver)	
	Connecticut	
1987	Christopher J. Dodd* (D, Norwich)	
1989	Lowell P. Weicker Jr.* (R, Mystic)	538,678
	Anthony Toby Moffett (D, Litchfield)	493,237
	Delaware	
1985	Joseph R. Biden Jr.* (D, Wilmington)	
1989	William V. Roth Jr.* (R, Wilmington)	105,472
	David N. Levinson (D, Middletown)	83,722
	Florida	
1987	Paula Hawkins* (R, Winter Park)	
1989	Lawton Chiles* (D, Holmes Beach)	1,609,936
	Van B. Poole (R, Fort Lauderdale)	995,421
	Georgia	
1985	Sam Nunn* (D, Perry)	
1987	Mack Mattingly* (R, St. Simons Is.)	
	Hawaii	
1987	Daniel K. Inouye* (D, Honolulu)	
1989	Spark M. Matsunaga* (D, Honolulu)	245,386
	Clarence J. Brown (R, Kamuela)	52,071
	Idaho	
1985	James A. McClure* (R, Payette)	
1987	Steven D. Symms* (R, Boise)	
	Illinois	
1985	Charles H. Percy* (R, Wilmette)	
1987	Alan J. Dixon* (D, Belleville)	
	Indiana	
1987	Dan Quayle* (R, Huntington)	
1989	Richard G. Lugar* (R, Indianapolis)	967,638
	Floyd Fithian (D, Lafayette)	819,403
	Iowa	
1985	Roger W. Jepsen* (R, Davenport)	
1987	Charles E. Grassley* (R, New Hartford)	
	Kansas	
1985	Nancy Landon Kassebaum* (R, Wichita)	
1987	Robert J. Dole* (R, Russell)	
	Kentucky	
1985	Walter D. Huddleston* (D, Elizabethtown)	
1987	Wendell H. Ford* (D, Owensboro)	
	Louisiana	
1985	J. Bennett Johnston* (D, Shreveport)	
1987	Russell B. Long* (D, Baton Rouge)	
	Maine	
1985	William S. Cohen* (R, Bangor)	
1989	George J. Mitchell* (D, Waterville)	278,568
	David F. Emery (R, Rockland)	179,886
	Maryland	
1987	Charles McC. Mathias Jr.* (R, Frederick)	
1989	Paul S. Sarbanes* (D, Baltimore)	691,358
	Lawrence J. Hogan (R, Landover)	412,610
	Massachusetts	
1985	Paul E. Tsongas* (D, Lowell)	
1989	Edward M. Kennedy* (D, Barnstable)	1,249,014
	Raymond Shamie (R, Walpole)	784,062
	Michigan	
1985	Carl Levin* (D, Detroit)	
1989	Donald W. Riegle Jr.* (D, Flint)	1,713,300
	Philip E. Ruppe (R, Houghton)	1,221,743

Term ends	Senator (Party, home)	1982 Election
	Minnesota	
1985	Rudolph E. Boschwitz* (R, Wayzata)	
1989	David Durenberger* (R, Minneapolis)	903,625
	Mark Dayton (D, Minneapolis)	794,251
	Mississippi	
1985	Thad Cochran* (R, Jackson)	
1989	John C. Stennis* (D, DeKalb)	400,531
	Haley Barbour (R, Yazoo City)	226,741
	Missouri	
1987	Thomas F. Eagleton* (D, St. Louis)	
1989	John C. Danforth* (R, Newburg)	780,276
	Harriett Woods (D, University City)	753,835
	Montana	
1985	Max Baucus* (D, Missoula)	
1989	John Melcher* (D, Forsyth)	164,223
	Larry Williams (R, Kalispell)	126,142
	Nebraska	
1985	J. James Exon* (D, Lincoln)	
1989	Edward Zorinsky* (D, Omaha)	357,602
	Jim Keck (R, Omaha)	151,727
	Nevada	
1987	Paul Laxalt* (R, Carson City)	
1989	Chic Hecht (R, Las Vegas)	120,354
	Howard W. Cannon* (D, Las Vegas)	114,736
	New Hampshire	
1985	Gordon J. Humphrey* (R, Swapee)	
1987	Warren Rudman* (R, Nashua)	
	New Jersey	
1985	Bill Bradley* (D, Denville)	
1989	Frank R. Lautenburg (D, Montclair)	1,115,283
	Millicent Fenwick (R, Bernardsville)	1,043,144
	New Mexico	
1985	Pete V. Domenici* (R, Albuquerque)	
1989	Jeff Bingaman (D, Sante Fe)	217,191
	Harrison "Jack" Schmitt* (R, Silver City)	186,014
	New York	
1987	Alphonse M. D'Amato* (R, C, RTL, Island Park)	
1989	Daniel Patrick Moynihan* (D, Oneonta)	3,141,145
	Florence Sullivan (R, C, RTL, Brooklyn)	1,665,320
	North Carolina	
1985	Jesse A. Helms* (R, Raleigh)	
1987	John P. East* (R, Greenville)	
	North Dakota	
1987	Mark Andrews* (R, Mapleton)	
1989	Quentin N. Burdick* (D, Fargo)	152,247
	Gene Knorr (R, Minot)	82,484
	Ohio	
1987	John Glenn* (D, Grandview Hts.)	
1989	Howard M. Metzenbaum* (D, Lyndhurst)	1,935,327
	Paul E. Pfeifer (R, Bucyrus)	1,392,658
	Oklahoma	
1985	David Lyle Boren* (D, Okla. City)	
1987	Don Nickles* (R, Ponca City)	
	Oregon	
1985	Mark O. Hatfield* (R, Salem)	
1987	Bob Packwood* (R, Lake Oswego)	
	Pennsylvania	
1987	Arlen Specter* (R, Philadelphia)	
1989	John Heinz* (R, Pittsburgh)	2,125,797
	Cyril H. Wecht (D, Pittsburgh)	1,393,941
	Rhode Island	
1985	Claiborne Pell* (D, Newport)	
1989	John H. Chafee* (R, Warwick)	169,362
	Julius C. Michaelson (D, Providence)	160,639
	South Carolina	
1985	Strom Thurmond* (R, Aiken)	
1987	Ernest Fritz Hollings* (D, Columbia)	
	South Dakota	
1985	Larry Pressler* (R, Humboldt)	
1987	James Abdnor* (R, Mitchell)	
	Tennessee	
1985	Howard H. Baker Jr.* (R, Huntsville)	
1989	James R. Sasser* (D, Nashville)	777,250
	Robin L. Beard (R, Franklin)	479,893
	Texas	
1985	John G. Tower* (R, Wichita Falls)	
1989	Lloyd Bentsen* (D, Houston)	1,782,700
	James M. Collins (R, Dallas)	1,234,477
	Utah	
1987	Jake Garn* (R, Salt Lake City)	
1989	Orrin G. Hatch* (R, Salt Lake City)	309,547
	Ted Wilson (D, Salt Lake City)	218,895
	Vermont	
1987	Patrick J. Leahy* (D, Burlington)	
1989	Robert T. Stafford* (R, Rutland)	83,259
	James A. Guest (D, Waitsfield)	78,447
	Virginia	
1985	John William Warner* (R, Middleburg)	
1989	Paul S. Trible Jr. (R, Newport News)	723,988
	Richard J. Davis (D, Portsmouth)	689,818
	Washington	
1987	Slade Gorton* (R, Olympia)	
1989	Henry M. Jackson* (D, Everett)	850,289
	Doug Jewett (R, Seattle)	299,758
	West Virginia	
1985	Jennings Randolph* (D, Charleston)	
1989	Robert C. Byrd* (D, Sophia)	382,028
	Cleve Benedict (R, Lewisburg)	171,432
	Wisconsin	
1987	Robert W. Kasten Jr.* (R, Thiensville)	
1989	William Proxmire* (D, Madison)	986,718
	Scott McCallum (R, Fond du Lac)	526,133
	Wyoming	
1985	Alan Kooi Simpson* (R, Cody)	
1989	Malcolm Wallop* (R, Big Horn)	94,863
	Roger McDaniel (D, Cheyenne)	72,352

The House of Representatives

Members' terms to Jan. 3, 1985. Annual salary $60,662.50; house speaker $79,125. To be eligible for membership, a person must be at least 25, a U.S. citizen for at least 7 years, and a resident of the state from which he or she is chosen.

Address: Washington, DC 20515

House Officials (97th Congress): Speaker Thomas P. O'Neill; Majority Leader James Wright; Majority Whip Thomas S. Foley; Minority Leader Robert H. Michel; Minority Whip Trent Lott.

C-Conservative; D-Democratic; DFL-Democrat Farmer-Labor; I-Independent; L-Liberal; Libert- Libertarian; R-Republican; S-Statesmen's Party; U-Unopposed; RTL-Right to Life.

Democrats, 268, Republicans, 165, undecided, 2. Total 435.

Note: Two contests in Georgia were delayed because of undecided reapportionment.

(Those marked * served in the 97th Congress.)

Bold face denotes the winner.

Preliminary returns.

Dist.	Representative (Party, Home)	1982 Election
	Alabama	
1.	**Jack Edwards*** (R, Mobile)	**84,968**
	Steve Gudac (D, Mobile)	51,507
2.	**William L. Dickinson*** (R, Montgomery)	**83,026**
	Billy Joe Camp (D, Montgomery)	79,809
3.	**Bill Nichols*** (D, Sylacauga)	**100,657**
	Richard Landers Jr. (Libert., Wetumpka)	3,945
4.	**Tom Bevill*** (D, Florence)	**Unopposed**
5.	**Ronnie G. Flippo*** (D, Florence)	**107,701**
	Leopold Yambrek (R, Killen)	23,950
6.	**Ben Erdreich** (D, Birmingham)	**87,540**
	Albert Lee Smith (R, Birmingham)	73,682
7.	**Richard C. Shelby*** (D, Woodstock)	**111,881**
	James Jones (Libert., Tuscaloosa)	4,195
	Alaska At Large	
	Don Young* (R, Fort Yukon)	**94,595**
	Dave Carlson (D, Anchorage)	39,102
	Arizona	
1.	**John McCain** (R, Tempe)	**88,879**
	William E. Hegarty (D, Tempe)	41,174
2.	**Morris K. Udall*** (D, Tucson)	**74,161**
	Roy B. Laos (R, Tucson)	28,713
3.	**Bob Stump*** (D, Tolleson)	**100,959**
	Pat Bosch (D, Tolleson)	58,267
4.	**Eldon Rudd*** (R, Scottsdale)	**95,378**
	Wayne O. Earley (D, Phoenix)	43,972
5.	**Jim McNulty** (D, Bisbee)	**83,820**
	Jim Kolbe (R, Tucson)	82,317
	Arkansas	
1.	**Bill Alexander*** (D, Osceola)	**112,480**
	Chuck Banks (R, Osceola)	60,668
2.	**Ed Bethune*** (R, Searcy)	**96,529**
	Charles L. George (D, Cahot)	82,625
3.	**John Paul Hammerschmidt*** (R, Harrison)	**132,047**
	Jim McDougal (D, Kingston)	68,571
4.	**Beryl Anthony Jr.*** (D, El Dorado)	**117,798**
	Bob Leslie (R, Redfield)	61,525
	California	
1.	**Douglas H. Bosco** (D, Occidental)	**106,379**
	Don H. Clausen* (R, Crescent City)	100,500
2.	**Gene Chappie*** (R, Chico)	**114,672**
	John A. Newmeyer (D, Napa)	80,343
3.	**Robert T. Matsui*** (D, Sacramento)	**191,172**
	Bruce A. Daniel (Libert., Newcastle)	15,880
4.	**Vic Fazio*** (D, West Sacramento)	**112,706**
	Roger B. Canfield (R, Citrus Heights)	66,059
5.	**Phillip L. Burton*** (D, San Francisco)	**101,747**
	Milton Marks (R, San Francisco)	70,593
6.	**Barbara Boxer** (D, Greenbrae)	**95,592**
	Dennis McQuaid (R, Novato)	87,118
7.	**George Miller*** (D, Martinez)	**126,376**
	Paul E. Vallely (R, (Walnut Creek)	56,565
8.	**Ronald V. Dellums*** (D, Berkeley)	**119,436**
	Claude B. Hutchison (R, Lafayette)	93,704
9.	**Fortney H. (Pete) Stark*** (D, Oakland)	**103,073**
	William J. Kennedy (R, Pleasanton)	66,357
10.	**Don Edwards*** (D, San Jose)	**75,922**
	Bob Herriott (R, Milpitas)	40,687
11.	**Tom Lantos** (D, Woodside)	**109,035**
	Bill Royer* (R, Redwood City)	75,847
12.	**Ed Zschau** (R, Los Altos)	**111,549**
	Emmett Lynch (D, Los Altos)	59,786
13.	**Norman Y. Mineta*** (D, San Jose)	**109,785**
	Tom Kelly (R, San Jose)	52,119
14.	**Norman D. Shumway*** (R, Stockton)	**130,274**
	Baron Reed (D, Roseville)	75,359
15.	**Tony Coelho*** (D, Merced)	**82,901**
	Ed Bates (R, Coarsegold)	44,022
16.	**Leon E. Panetta*** (D, Carmel Valley)	**140,602**
	G. Richard Arnold (R, Santa Cruz)	24,068
17.	**Charles Pashayan Jr.*** (R, Fresno)	**78,584**
	Gene Tackett (D, McFarland)	66,203
18.	**Richard Lehman** (D, Sanger)	**90,943**
	Adrian C. Fondse (R, Ripon)	58,546
19.	**Robert J. Lagomarsino*** (R, Ojai)	**110,241**
	Frank Frost (D, Santa Barbara)	65,074
20.	**William M. Thomas** (R, Bakersfield)	**113,893**
	Robert J. Bethea (D, Bakersfield)	53,428
21.	**Bobbi Fiedler*** (R, Northridge)	**135,808**
	George Henry Margolis (D, Simi Valley)	45,705
22.	**Carlos J. Moorhead*** (R, Glendale)	**142,504**
	Harvey L. Goldhammer (D, La Crescenta)	45,649
23.	**Anthony C. Beilenson*** (D, Los Angeles)	**118,533**
	David Armor (R, Tarzana)	80,299
24.	**Henry A. Waxman*** (D, Los Angeles)	**86,902**
	Jerry Zerg (R, Los Angeles)	44,151
25.	**Edward R. Roybal*** (D, Los Angeles)	**69,638**
	Daniel John Gorham (Libert., Los Angeles)	11,687
26.	**Howard L. Berman** (D, Studio City)	**95,853**
	Hal Phillips (R, Burbank)	64,756
27.	**Mel Levine** (D, Santa Monica)	**106,200**
	Bart W. Christensen (R, Santa Monica)	65,895
28.	**Julian C. Dixon*** (D, Los Angeles)	**101,574**
	David Goerz (R, Los Angeles)	23,955
29.	**Augustus F. Hawkins*** (D, Los Angeles)	**96,017**
	Milton MacKaig (R, Downey)	24,212
30.	**Matthew G. "Marty" Martinez** (D, Monterey Park)	**60,033**
	John H. Rousselot* (R, San Gabriel)	51,058
31.	**Mervyn M. Dymally** (D, Compton)	**85,307**
	Henry C. Minturn (R, Hawthorne)	32,384
32.	**Glenn M. Anderson*** (D, Hawthorne)	**83,755**
	Brian Lungren (R, Long Beach)	56,958
33.	**David Dreier*** (R, La Verne)	**110,344**
	Paul Servelle (D, Whittier)	54,764

Dist.	Representative (Party, Home)	1982 Election
34.	**Esteban Torres** (D, La Puente)	**67,569**
	Paul R. Jackson (R, Pico Rivera)	50,180
35.	**Jerry Lewis*** (R, San Bernardino)	**111,293**
	Robert E. Erwin (D, Chino)	51,774
36.	**George E. Brown Jr.*** (D, Riverside)	**76,096**
	John Paul Stark (R, San Bernardino)	64,005
37.	**Al McCandless** (R, Palm Desert)	**103,392**
	Curtis P. "Sam" Cross (D, Indio)	67,551
38.	**Jerry M. Patterson*** (D, Garden Grove*)	**72,853**
	William F. Dohr (R, Santa Ana)	60,349
39.	**William E. Dannemeyer*** (R, Fullerton)	**127,376**
	Frank G. Verges (D, Fullerton)	46,129
40.	**Robert E. Badham*** (R, Newport Beach)	**141,112**
	Paul Haseman (D, Laguna Niguel)	51,900
41.	**Bill Lowery*** (R, San Diego)	**137,212**
	Tony Brandenburg (D, Encinitas)	57,793
42.	**Don Lungren*** (R, Long Beach)	**139,890**
	James P. Spellman (D, Long Beach)	57,893
43.	**Roy "Pat" Archer** (D, Escondido)	**56,754**
	Johnnie Crean (R, San Juan Capistrano)	54,838
44.	**Jim Bates** (D, San Diego)	**77,339**
	Shirley M. Gissendanner (R, San Diego)	37,637
45.	**Duncan Hunter*** (R, Coronado)	**115,186**
	Richard Hill (D, El Centro)	49,343

Colorado

Dist.	Representative (Party, Home)	1982 Election
1.	**Patricia Schroeder*** (D, Denver)	**78,749**
	Arch Decker (R, Denver)	48,624
2.	**Timothy E. Wirth*** (D, Boulder)	**98,735**
	John C. Buechner (R, Boulder)	57,840
3.	**Ray Kogovsek*** (D, Pueblo)	**89,762**
	Tom Wiens (R, Dillon)	75,382
4.	**Hank Brown*** (R, Greeley)	**102,841**
	Charles L. "Bud" Bishop (D, Fort Collins)	44,964
5.	**Ken Kramer*** (R, Colorado Springs)	**81,278**
	Tom Cronin (D, Colorado Springs)	55,343
6.	**Jack Swigert** (R, Denver)	**93,585**
	Steve Hogan (D, Aurora City)	54,038

Connecticut

Dist.	Representative (Party, Home)	1982 Election
1.	**Barbara B. Kennelly*** (D, Hartford)	**126,601**
	Herschel A. Klein (R, Windsor)	58,332
2.	**Samuel Gejdenson*** (D, Bozrah)	**96,202**
	Tony Guglielmo (R, Stafford)	73,283
3.	**Bruce A. Morrison** (D, Hamden)	**89,848**
	Lawrence J. DeNardis* (R, Hamden)	88,384
4.	**Stewart B. McKinney*** (R, Westport)	**87,205**
	John Aristotle Phillips (D, Norwalk)	66,321
5.	**William R. Ratchford*** (D, Danbury)	**99,029**
	Neal B. Hanlon (R, Naugatuck)	70,054
6.	**Nancy L. Johnson** (R, New Britain)	**99,263**
	William E. Curry Jr. (D, Farmington)	92,063

Delaware At Large

Dist.	Representative (Party, Home)	1982 Election
	Thomas R. Carper (D, New Castle)	**98,672**
	Thomas B. Evans Jr.* (R, Wilmington)	87,063

Florida

Dist.	Representative (Party, Home)	1982 Election
1.	**Earl Hutto*** (D, Panama City)	**79,755**
	J. Terry Bechtol (R, Pensacola)	27,369
2.	**Don Fuqua*** (D, Altha)	**76,792**
	Ron McNeil (R, Havana)	47,635
3.	**Charles E. Bennett*** (D, Jacksonville)	**71,551**
	George Grimsley (R, Jacksonville)	13,359
4.	**Bill Chappell*** (D, Ocala)	**79,777**
	Larry Gaudet (R, Middleburg)	39,633
5.	**Bill McCollum*** (R, Altamonte Springs)	**98,691**
	Dick Batchelor (D, Orlando)	65,276
6.	**Kenneth H. "Buddy" MacKay** (D, Ocala)	**84,884**
	Ed Havill (R, Eustis)	53,474
7.	**Sam Gibbons*** (D, Tampa)	**83,290**
	Ken Ayers (R, Tampa)	28,711
8.	**C. W. Bill Young*** (R, St. Petersburg)	**Unopposed**
9.	**Michael Bilirakis** (R, Palm Harbor)	**91,940**
	George H. Sheldon (D, Tampa)	88,543
10.	**Andy Ireland*** (D, Winter Haven)	**Unopposed**
11.	**Bill Nelson*** (D, Melbourne)	**98,132**
	Joel Robinson (R, Melbourne)	39,962
12.	**Tom Lewis** (R, North Palm Beach)	**81,171**
	Brad Culverhouse (D, Fort Pierce)	73,259
13.	**Connie Mack** (R, Cape Coral)	**116,491**
	Dana N. Stevens (D, Sarasota)	69,744
14.	**Daniel A. Mica*** (D, West Palm Beach)	**128,567**
	Steve Mitchell (R, West Palm Beach)	47,534
15.	**Clay Shaw Jr.*** (R, Fort Lauderdale)	**89,128**
	Edward J. Stack (D, Pompano Beach)	67,058
16.	**Larry Smith** (D, Hollywood)	**91,601**
	Maurice Berkowitz (R, Plantation)	43,261
17.	**William Lehman*** (D, North Miami Beach)	**Unopposed**
18.	**Claude Pepper*** (D, Miami)	**69,853**
	Ricardo Nunez (R, Coral Gables)	28,460
19.	**Dante B. Fascell*** (D, Miami)	**72,174**
	Glenn Rinker (Coral Gables)	49,946

Georgia

Dist.	Representative (Party, Home)	1982 Election
1.	**Lindsay Thomas** (D, Screven)	**67,015**
	Herb Jones (R, Savannah)	36,315
2.	**Charles Hatcher*** (D, Albany)	**Unopposed**
3.	**Richard Ray** (D, Perry)	**73,837**
	Tyron Elliott (R, Woodbury)	30,253
4.	**Elliott H. Levitas*** (D, Atlanta)	**(A)**
	Dick Winder (R, Dunwoody)	
5.	**Wyche Fowler Jr.*** (D, Atlanta)	**(A)**
	Doug Steele (R, Atlanta)	
6.	**Newt Gingrich*** (R, Carrollton)	**59,284**
	Jim Wood (D, Forest Park)	49,093
7.	**Larry P. McDonald*** (D, Marietta)	**71,441**
	Dave Sellers (R, Marietta)	45,405
8.	**J. Roy Rowland** (D, Dublin)	**Unopposed**
9.	**Ed Jenkins*** (D, Jasper)	**82,688**
	Charles Sherwood (R, Cornelia)	25,518
10.	**Doug Barnard Jr.*** (D, Augusta)	**Unopposed**

(A) Election delayed until Nov. 30, 1982.

Hawaii

Dist.	Representative (Party, Home)	1982 Election
1.	**Cecil (Cec) Heftel*** (D, Honolulu)	**134,779**
	Rockne H. Johnson (Libert., Honolulu)	15,128
2.	**Daniel K. Akaka*** (D, Honolulu)	**132,072**
	Amelia Oy Fritts (Libert., Kaneohe)	7,245

Idaho

Dist.	Representative (Party, Home)	1982 Election
1.	**Larry E. Craig*** (R, Midvale)	**86,165**
	Larry LaRocco (D, Boise)	74,423
2.	**George Hansen*** (R, Pocatello)	**83,910**
	Richard Stallings (D, Roxburg)	76,601

Illinois

Dist.	Representative (Party, Home)	1982 Election
1.	**Harold Washington*** (D, Chicago)	**154,042**
	Charles A. Taliaferro (R, Chicago)	5,327
2.	**Gus Savage*** (D, Chicago)	**119,763**
	Kevin Walker Sparks (R, Harvey)	17,206
3.	**Marty Russo*** (D, South Holland)	**104,693**
	Richard D. Murphy (R, Chicago)	24,550
4.	**George M. O'Brien*** (R, Joliet)	**59,936**
	Michael A. Murer (D, Joliet)	50,077
5.	**William O. Lipinski** (D, Chicago)	**94,134**
	Daniel J. Partyka (R, Chicago)	26,272
6.	**Henry J. Hyde*** (R, Bensenville)	**88,493**
	Leroy E. Kennel (D, Lombard)	40,939
7.	**Cardiss Collins*** (D, Chicago)	**102,845**
	Dansby Cheeks (R, Oak Park)	15,350
8.	**Dan Rostenkowski*** (D, Chicago)	**113,536**
	Bonnie Hickey (R, Chicago)	21,717
9.	**Sidney R. Yates*** (D, Chicago)	**98,883**
	Catherine Bertini (R, Chicago)	46,447

Dist.	Representative (Party, Home)	1982 Election
10.	**John E. Porter*** (R, Evanston)	**85,968**
	Eugenia S. Chapman (D, Arlington Heights)	60,633
11.	**Frank Annunzio*** (D, Chicago)	**121,808**
	James F. Moynihan (R, Chicago)	44,733
12.	**Philip M. Crane*** (R, Mt. Prospect)	**80,478**
	Daniel G. DeFosse (D, Antioch)	37,027
13.	**John N. Erlenborn*** (R, Glen Ellyn)	**108,614**
	Robert Bily (D, Lemont)	46,749
14.	**Tom Corcoran*** (R, Ottawa)	**98,267**
	Dan McGrath (D, Ottawa)	53,862
15.	**Edward R. Madigan*** (R, Lincoln)	**97,590**
	Tim L. Hall (D, Dwight)	47,085
16.	**Lynn Martin*** (R, Rockford)	**89,405**
	Carl R. Schwerdtfeger (D, Elizabeth)	66,777
17.	**Lane Evans** (D, Rock Island)	**91,896**
	Kenneth G. McMillan (R, Bushnell)	82,603
18.	**Robert H. Michel*** (R, Peoria)	**92,354**
	G. Douglas Stephens (D, Peoria)	87,936
19.	**Daniel B. Crane*** (R, Danville)	**94,539**
	John Gwinn (D, Champaign)	86,956
20.	**Richard J. Durbin** (D, Springfield)	**100,758**
	Paul Findley* (R, Pittsfield)	99,345
21.	**Melvin Price*** (D, East St. Louis)	**88,660**
	Robert H. Gaffner (R, Greenville)	46,224
22.	**Paul Simon*** (D, Makanda)	**121,545**
	Peter G. Prineas (R, Carbondale)	62,456

Indiana

Dist.	Representative (Party, Home)	1982 Election
1.	**Katie Hall** (D, Gary)	**89,369**
	Thomas H. Krieger (R, Whiting)	66,921
2.	**Philip R. Sharp*** (D, Muncie)	**106,475**
	Ralph Van Natta (R, Shelbyville)	82,690
3.	**John Hiler*** (R, LaPorte)	**85,774**
	Richard C. Bodine (D, Mishawaka)	81,671
4.	**Dan R. Coats*** (R, Fort Wayne)	**107,266**
	Roger M. Miller (D, Huntington)	58,692
5.	**Elwood Hillis*** (R, Kokomo)	**105,238**
	Allen B. Maxwell (D, Kokomo)	66,729
6.	**Dan Burton** (R, Indianapolis)	**129,363**
	George E. Grabianowski (D, Zionsville)	70,421
7.	**John T. Myers*** (R, Covington)	**97,052**
	Stephen S. Bonney (D, West Lafayette)	55,431
8.	**Francis X. McCloskey** (D, Bloomington)	**99,978**
	Joel Deckard* (R, Evansville)	93,671
9.	**Lee H. Hamilton*** (D, Nashville)	**120,217**
	Floyd E. Coates (R, Lexington)	58,346
10.	**Andrew Jacobs Jr.*** (D, Indianapolis)	**110,443**
	Michael A. Carroll (R, Indianapolis)	55,421

Iowa

Dist.	Representative (Party, Home)	1982 Election
1.	**Jim Leach*** (R, Davenport)	**89,499**
	William E. Gluba (D, Davenport)	61,681
2.	**Thomas J. Tauke*** (R, Dubuque)	**98,420**
	Brent Appel (D, Dubuque)	68,536
3.	**Cooper Evans*** (R, Grundy Center)	**103,973**
	Lynn G. Cutler (D, Waterloo)	83,517
4.	**Neal Smith*** (D, Altoona)	**118,354**
	Dave Readinger (R, Des Moines)	60,583
5.	**Tom Harkin*** (D, Ames)	**92,982**
	Arlyn E. Danker (R, Minden)	65,184
6.	**Berkley Bedell*** (D, Spirit Lake)	**101,407**
	Al Bremer (R, Mason City)	56,553

Kansas

Dist.	Representative (Party, Home)	1982 Election
1.	**Pat Roberts*** (R, Dodge City)	**111,785**
	Kent Roth (D, Great Bend)	49,460
2.	**Jim Slattery** (D, Topeka)	**86,175**
	Morris Kay (R, Lawrence)	64,164
3.	**Larry Winn Jr.*** (R, Overland Park)	**82,007**
	William L. Kostar (D, Westwood)	53,218
4.	**Dan Glickman*** (D, Wichita)	**106,157**
	Gerald Caywood (R, Wichita)	35,311
5.	**Bob Whittaker*** (R, Augusta)	**102,974**
	Lee Rowe (D, Emporia City)	47,520

Kentucky

Dist.	Representative (Party, Home)	1982 Election
1.	**Carroll Hubbard Jr.*** (D, Mayfield)	**Unopposed**
2.	**William H. Natcher*** (D, Bowling Green)	**49,568**
	Mark T. Watson (R, Elizabethtown)	17,561
3.	**Romano L. Mazzoli*** (D, Louisville)	**91,379**
	Carl Brown (R, Louisville)	45,169
4.	**Gene Snyder*** (R, Brownsboro Farms)	**73,572**
	Terry L. Mann (D, Newport)	61,576
5.	**Harold Rogers*** (R, Somerset)	**52,941**
	Doye Davenport (D, Greensburg)	28,228
6.	**Larry J. Hopkins*** (R, Lexington)	**68,895**
	Don Mills (D, Lexington)	49,846
7.	**Carl D. Perkins*** (D, Hindman)	**81,770**
	Tom Hamby (R, Ewing)	21,482

Louisiana

1. **Bob Livingston*** (R, New Orleans)
2. **Lindy (Mrs. Hale) Boggs*** (D, New Orleans)
3. **W.J. "Billy" Tauzin** (D, Thibodaux)
4. **Buddy Roemer** (D, Bossier City)
5. **Jerry Huckaby*** (D, Ringgold)
6. **W. Henson Moore*** (R, Baton Rouge)
7. **John B. Breaux*** (D, Crowley)
8. **Gillis W. Long*** (D, Alexandria)

Louisiana did not have an election in November 1982. Under the state's unique election law, candidates of all parties run together on a single non-partisan ballot in each district. If no candidate wins a majority, the top two finishers regardless of party oppose each other in a November runoff. This year, all eight incumbents easily won majorities in the September 11 balloting and thus were elected to Congress.

Maine

Dist.	Representative (Party, Home)	1982 Election
1.	**John R. McKernan Jr.** (R, Cumberland)	**125,215**
	John M. Kerry (D, Old Orchard Beach)	119,019
2.	**Olympia J. Snowe*** (R, Auburn)	**134,473**
	James Patrick Dunleavy (D, Presque Isle)	67,967

Maryland

Dist.	Representative (Party, Home)	1982 Election
1.	**Roy Dyson*** (D, Great Mills)	**87,292**
	C. A. Porter Hopkins (R, Cambridge)	38,414
2.	**Clarence D. Long*** (D, Ruxton)	**82,184**
	Helen D. Bentley (R, Lutherville)	73,923
3.	**Barbara A. Mikulski*** (D, Baltimore)	**107,970**
	H. Robert Scherr (R, Baltimore)	37,623
4.	**Majorie S. Holt*** (R, Severna Park)	**73,431**
	Patricia O'Brien Aiken (D, Annapolis)	47,200
5.	**Steny H. Hoyer*** (D, Berkshire)	**82,466**
	William P. Guthrie (R, Cheverly)	21,044
6.	**Beverly B. Byron*** (D, Frederick)	**99,780**
	Roscoe Bartlett (R, Frederick)	34,685
7.	**Parren J. Mitchell*** (D, Baltimore)	**102,508**
	M. Leonora Jones (R, Baltimore)	13,881
8.	**Michael D. Barnes*** (D, Kensington)	**117,722**
	Elizabeth W. Spencer (R, Gaithersburg)	47,386

Massachusetts

Dist.	Representative (Party, Home)	1982 Election
1.	**Silvio O. Conte*** (R, Pittsfield)	**Unopposed**
2.	**Edward P. Boland*** (D, Springfield)	**118,320**
	Thomas P. Swank (R, West Brookfield)	44,536
3.	**Joseph D. Early*** (D, Worcester)	**Unopposed**
4.	**Barney Frank*** (D, Newton)	**121,632**
	Margaret M. Heckler (R, Wellesley)	82,862
5.	**James M. Shannon** (D, Lawrence)	**140,029**
	Angelo Laudani (Libert., Lexington)	25,298
6.	**Nicholas Mavroules*** (D, Peabody)	**117,565**
	Thomas H. Trimarco (R, Beverly)	85,755
7.	**Edward J. Markey*** (D, Malden)	**150,414**
	David Basile (R, Woburn)	43,043

Dist.	Representative (Party, Home)	1982 Election
8.	**Thomas P. O'Neill Jr.*** (D, Cambridge)	**123,121**
	Frank Luke McNamara Jr. (R, Boston)	41,239
9.	**Joe Moakley*** (D, Boston)	**102,452**
	Deborah R. Cochran (R, Dedham)	55,378
10.	**Gerry E. Studds*** (D, Cohasset)	**137,379**
	John E. Conway (R, Cohasset)	62,985
11.	**Brian J. Donnelly*** (D, Boston)	**Unopposed**
	Michigan	
1.	**John Conyers Jr.*** (D, Detroit)	**126,241**
	Bill Krebaum (Libert., Detroit)	3,253
2.	**Carl D. Pursell*** (R, Plymouth)	**106,379**
	George Wahr Sallabe (D, Ann Arbor)	52,427
3.	**Howard Wolpe*** (D, Lansing)	**96,871**
	Richard L. Milliman (R, Lansing)	73,224
4.	**Mark D. Siljander*** (R, Three Rivers)	**87,499**
	David A. Masiokas (D, Niles)	56,954
5.	**Howard S. Sawyer*** (R, Rockford)	**98,287**
	Stephen V. Monsma (D, Grand Rapids)	87,091
6.	**Bob Carr** (D, Okemas)	**84,526**
	Jim Dunn* (R, East Lansing)	78,233
7.	**Dale E. Kildee*** (D, Flint)	**118,538**
	George R. Darrah (R, Flint)	36,303
8.	**Bob Traxler*** (D, Bay City)	**113,664**
	Sheila M. Hart (Libert., Saginaw)	10,978
9.	**Guy Vander Jagt*** (R, Luther)	**112,419**
	Gerald D. Warner (D, Muskegon)	61,728
10.	**Donald Joseph Albosta*** (D, St. Charles)	**101,818**
	Lawrence W. Reed (R, Midland)	65,807
11.	**Robert W. Davis*** (R, Gaylord)	**106,085**
	Kent Bourland (D, Marquette)	69,193
12.	**David E. Bonior*** (D, Mt. Clemens)	**104,166**
	Ray Contesti (R, Mt. Clemens)	52,301
13.	**George W. Crockett Jr.*** (D, Detroit)	**108,396**
	Letty Gupta (R, Detroit)	13,848
14.	**Dennis M. Hertel*** (D, Detroit)	**115,344**
	Harold Dunn (Libert., Warren)	6,070
15.	**William D. Ford*** (D, Taylor)	**94,795**
	Mitchell Moran (R, Taylor)	33,815
16.	**John D. Dingell*** (D, Trenton)	**113,896**
	David K. Haskins (R, Dearborn)	39,277
17.	**Sander Levin** (D, Southfield)	**115,881**
	Gerald E. Rosen (R, Detroit)	55,462
18.	**William S. Broomfield*** (R, Birmingham)	**133,233**
	Allen J. Sipher (D, Farmington Hills)	46,603
	Minnesota	
1.	**Timothy J. Penny** (D, New Richland)	**105,412**
	Tom Hagedorn* (R, Truman)	98,075
2.	**Vin Weber*** (R, Slayton)	**116,776**
	James W. Nichols (D, Lake Benton)	99,075
3.	**Bill Frenzel*** (R, Golden Valley)	**155,761**
	Joel A. Saliterman (D, St. Louis Park)	58,523
4.	**Bruce F. Vento*** (D, St. Paul)	**151,009**
	Bill James (R, Vadnais Heights)	54,994
5.	**Martin Olav Sabo*** (D, Minneapolis)	**135,880**
	Keith W. Johnson (R, Bloomington)	61,012
6.	**Gerry Sikorski** (D, Stillwater)	**91,506**
	Arlen Erdahl* (R, Fridley)	86,703
7.	**Arlan Stangeland*** (R, Barnesville)	**104,510**
	Gene Wenstrom (D, Elbow Lake)	103,452
8.	**James L. Oberstar*** (D, Chisholm)	**144,841**
	Marjory L. Luce (R, Peguot Lakes)	45,009
	Mississippi	
1.	**Jamie L. Whitten*** (D, Charleston)	**80,001**
	Fran Fawcett (R, Oxford)	32,495
2.	**Webb Franklin** (R, Greenwood)	**73,588**
	Robert G. Clark (D, Ebenezer)	71,335
3.	**G. V. (Sonny) Montgomery*** (D, Meridian)	**101,742**
	James Bradshaw (I, Walters)	7,379
4.	**Wayne Dowdy*** (D, McComb)	**80,370**
	Liles Williams (R, Clinton)	69,100
5.	**Trent Lott*** (R, Pascagoula)	**82,681**

Dist.	Representative (Party, Home)	1982 Election
	Arlon (Blackie) Coate (D, Ocean Springs)	22,566
	Missouri	
1.	**William (Bill) Clay*** (D, St. Louis)	**102,605**
	William E. White (R, St. Louis)	52,545
2.	**Robert A. Young*** (D, Maryland Heights)	**100,773**
	Harold L. Dielmann (R, Creve Coeur)	77,436
3.	**Richard A. Gephardt*** (D, St. Louis)	**131,528**
	Richard Foristel (R, St. Louis)	37,450
4.	**Ike Skelton*** (D, Lexington)	**95,816**
	Wendell Bailey* (R, Jefferson City)	78,730
5.	**Alan Wheat** (D, Kansas City)	**96,059**
	John A. Sharp (R, Kansas City)	66,664
6.	**E. Thomas Coleman*** (R, Kansas City)	**88,514**
	Jim Russell (D, Savannah)	74,258
7.	**Gene Taylor*** (R, Sarcoxie)	**90,887**
	David A. Geisler (D, Springfield)	89,006
8.	**Bill Emerson*** (R, Cape Girardeau)	**85,453**
	Jerry Ford (D, Cape Girardeau)	79,976
9.	**Harold L. Volkmer*** (D, Hannibal)	**99,248**
	Larry E. Mead (R, Columbia)	63,949
	Montana	
1.	**Pat Williams*** (D, Helena)	**92,495**
	Bob Davies (R, Bozeman)	58,671
2.	**Ron Marlenee*** (R, Scobey)	**73,842**
	Howard Lyman (D, Great Falls)	59,898
	Nebraska	
1.	**Douglas K. Bereuter*** (R, Utica)	**135,354**
	Curt Donaldson (D, Lincoln)	45,156
2.	**Hal Daub*** (R, Omaha)	**91,900**
	Richard M. Fellman (D, Omaha)	69,914
3.	**Virginia Smith*** (R, Chappell)	**Unopposed**
	Nevada	
	Harry Reid (D, Las Vegas)	**60,329**
	Peggy Cavnar (R, Las Vegas)	44,337
	Marry Gojack (D, Reno)	51,947
	Barbara Vucanovich (R, Reno)	70,054
	New Hampshire	
1.	**Norman E. D'Amours*** (D, Manchester)	**76,881**
	Robert C. Smith (R, Wolfeboro)	61,876
2.	**Judd Gregg*** (R, Greenfield)	**92,218**
	Robert L. Dupay (D, Nashua)	37,726
	New Jersey	
1.	**James J. Florio*** (D, Camden)	**109,747**
	John A. Dramesi (R, Blackwood)	39,225
2.	**William J. Hughes*** (D, Ocean City)	**104,053**
	John J. Mahoney (R, Milmay)	47,490
3.	**James J. Howard*** (D, Spring Lake Heights)	**103,313**
	Marie Sheehan Muhler (R, Marlboro)	60,059
4.	**Christopher H. Smith*** (R, Old Bridge)	**85,448**
	Joseph P. Merlino (D, Trenton)	76,507
5.	**Marge Roukema*** (R, Ridgewood)	**104,411**
	Fritz Cammerzell (D, Hopewell)	53,641
6.	**Bernard J. Dwyer*** (D, Edison)	**100,441**
	Bertram L. Buckler (R, East Brunswick)	46,029
7.	**Matthew J. Rinaldo*** (R, Union)	**90,715**
	Adam K. Levin (D, Westfield)	70,398
8.	**Robert A. Roe*** (D, Wayne)	**88,279**
	Norm Robertson (R, Clifton)	35,952
9.	**Robert G. Torricelli** (D, New Milford)	**96,828**
	Harold C. Hollenbeck* (R, East Rutherford)	83,869
10.	**Peter W. Rodino Jr.*** (D, Newark)	**78,964**
	Timothy Lee Jr. (R, East Orange)	14,863
11.	**Joseph G. Minish*** (D, West Orange)	**105,530**
	Rey Redington (R, Montclair)	57,237
12.	**Jim Courter** (R, Hackettstown)	**117,020**
	Jeff Connor (D, Oldwick)	56,466

Dist.	Representative (Party, Home)	1982 Election
13.	**Edwin B. Forsythe*** (R, Moorestown)	**99,031**
	George S. Callas (D, Brielle)	65,866
14.	**Frank J. Guarini*** (D, Jersey City)	**90,442**
	Charles J. Catrillo (R, Jersey City)	27,379
	New Mexico	
1.	**Manuel Lujan Jr.*** (R, Albuquerque)	**74,598**
	Jan Alan Hartke (D, Albuquerque)	67,120
2.	**Joe Skeen*** (R, Picacho)	**71,247**
	Caleb Chandler (D, Clovis)	50,605
3.	**Bill Richardson** (D, Santa Fe)	**83,970**
	Marjorie Bell Chambers (R, Los Alamos)	46,392
	New York	
1.	**William Carney*** (R, C, RTL Hauppauge)	**80,223**
	Ethan C. Eldon (D, Stony Brook)	47,226
2.	**Thomas J. Downey*** (D, Amityville)	**85,301**
	Paul G. Costello (R, C, Islip)	48,978
3.	**Robert J. Mrazek** (D, Centerport)	**90,815**
	John LeBoutillier* (R, C, Old Westbury)	83,053
4.	**Norman F. Lent*** (R, C, East Rockaway)	**104,846**
	Robert P. Zimmerman (D, Great Neck)	63,161
5.	**Raymond J. McGrath*** (R, C, RTL, Valley Stream)	**100,115**
	Arnold J. Miller (D, L, Hempstead)	66,764
6.	**Joseph P. Addabbo*** (D, L, Ozone Park)	**94,327**
	Mark E. Scott (C, Ozone Park)	4,735
7.	**Benjamin S. Rosenthal** (D, L, Elmhurst)	**81,122**
	Albert Lemishow, (R, C, RTL, Flushing)	23,992
8.	**James H. Scheuer** (D, L, Queens)	**88,507**
	John T. Blume (R, C, Flushing)	10,900
9.	**Geraldine A. Ferraro*** (D, Forest Hills)	**73,840**
	John J. Weigandt (R, Richmond Hill)	19,917
10.	**Charles E. Schumer*** (D, L, Brooklyn)	**86,977**
	Stephen Marks (R, C, Brooklyn)	21,165
11.	**Edolphus Towns** (D, Brooklyn)	**38,314**
	James W. Smith (R, Brooklyn)	5,248
12.	**Major R. Owens** (D, L, Brooklyn)	**43,045**
	David Katam Sr. (R, Brooklyn)	3,102
13.	**Stephen J. Solarz*** (D, L, Brooklyn)	**66,610**
	Leon F. Nadrowski (R, RTL, Brooklyn)	14,067
14.	**Guy V. Molinari*** (R, C, Staten Island)	**66,781**
	Leo C. Zeferetti* (D, Brooklyn)	50,601
15.	**Bill Green*** (R, Manhattan)	**64,714**
	Betty G. Lall (D, L, Manhattan)	55,061
16.	**Charles B. Rangel** (D, L, Manhatten)	**72,999**
	Michael T. Berns (C, Manhattan)	1,225
17.	**Ted Weiss*** (D, L, Manhattan)	**109,090**
	Louis S. Antonelli (R, C, RTL, Manhattan)	19,527
18.	**Robert Garcia*** (D, R, L, Manhattan.	**54,852**
	Mario Pichler (C, Manhattan)	772
19.	**Mario Biaggi*** (D, L, RTL, Bronx	**112,220**
	Michael J. McSherry (C, Bronx)	6,935
20.	**Richard L. Ottinger*** (D, Mamaroneck)	**80,736**
	Jon S. Fossel (R, C, Katonah)	61,001
21.	**Hamilton Fish Jr.** (R, C, RTL, Millbrook)	**111,162**
	J. Morgan Strong (D, Cold Spring)	35,998
22.	**Benjamin A. Gilman*** (R, Middletown)	**89,687**
	Peter A. Peyser* (D, Irvington)	68,424
23.	**Samuel S. Stratton*** (D, Amsterdam)	**159,233**
	Frank Wicks (R, Nuclear Freeze, Schenectady)	38,966
24.	**Gerald B. H. Solomon** (R, C, RTL, Glen Falls)	**136,676**
	Roy Esiason (D, L, Granville)	47,988
25.	**Serwood L. Boehlert** (R, New Hartford)	**87,509**
	Anita Maxwell (D, Newport)	66,496
26.	**David O'B. Martin** (R, C, Canton)	**104,365**
	David P. Landy (D, Canton)	46,381
27.	**George C. Wortley*** (R, Fayetteville)	**91,942**
	Elaine Lytel (D, L, DeWitt)	77,272
28.	**Matthew F. McHugh*** (D, L, Ithaca)	**97,633**
	David F. Crowley (R, C, Binghamton)	73,463
29.	**Frank Horton*** (R, Rochester)	**115,370**
	William C. Larsen (D, Pittsford)	45,677
30.	**Barber B. Conable Jr.*** (R, Alexander)	**117,603**
	Bill Benet (D, Rochester)	48,090
31.	**Jack F. Kemp*** (R, C, Hamburg)	**131,710**
	James A. Martin (D, Gowanda)	43,318
32.	**John J. LaFalce*** (D, L, Buffalo)	**114,827**
	Raymond R. Walker (R, C, Lockport	8,391
33.	**Henry J. Nowak*** (D, L, Buffalo)	**124,632**
	Walter J. Pillich (R, C, Hamburg)	19,673
34.	**Stanley N. Lundine** (D, Jamestown)	**94,280**
	James J. Snyder (R, C, Olean)	61,674
	North Carolina	
1.	**Walter B. Jones*** (D, Farmville)	**80,049**
	James F. McIntyre III (R, Emerald Isle)	17,464
2.	**I.T. "Tim" Valentine Jr.** (D, Nashville)	**59,745**
	Jack Marin (R, Durham)	34,282
3.	**Charles O. Whitley*** (D, Mt. Olive)	**68,579**
	Eugene McDaniel (R, Bules Creek)	38,911
4.	**Ike Andrews*** (D, Cary)	**70,344**
	William Cobey Jr. (R, Chapel Hill)	65,050
5.	**Stephen L. Neal*** (D, Winston-Salem)	**88,220**
	Anne Bagnal (R, Winston-Salem)	57,283
6.	**Charles Robin Britt** (D, Greensboro)	**68,689**
	Eugene Johnston* (R, Greensboro)	58,234
7.	**Charles Rose***(D, Fayetteville)	**68,523**
	Edward Johnson (R, Lumberton)	27,135
8.	**W. G. (Bill) Hefner*** (D, Concord)	**70,900**
	Harris D. Blake (R, Pinehurst)	50,869
9.	**James G. Martin*** (R, Davidson)	**64,427**
	Preston Cornelius (D, Mooresville)	47,337
10.	**James T. Broyhill*** (R, Lenoir)	**81,176**
	Jhon Rankin (Libert., Gastonia)	6,399
11.	**James McClure Clarke** (D, Fairview)	**85,271**
	William M. (Bill) Hendon* (R, Asheville)	84,101
	North Dakota At Large	
	Byron L. Dorgan* (D, Bismarck)	**163,032**
	Kent H. Jones (R, Bismarck)	64,059
	Ohio	
1.	**Thomas A. Luken*** (D, Cincinnati)	**98,977**
	John "Jake" Held (R, Cincinnati)	52,571
2.	**Bill Gradison*** (R, Cincinnati)	**97,198**
	William Luttmer (D, Cincinnati)	53,091
3.	**Tony P. Hall*** (D, Dayton)	**119,468**
	Kathryn Brown (Libert., Dayton)	16,755
4.	**Michael Oxley*** (R, Findlay)	**104,995**
	Robert W. Moon (D, Conover)	57,529
5.	**Delbert L. Latta*** (R, Bowling Green)	**86,408**
	James R. Sherck (D, Fremont City)	70,118
6.	**Bob McEwen** (R, Hillsboro)	**91,957**
	Lynn Alan Grimshaw (D, Wheelersburg)	63,404
7.	**Michael Dewine** (R, Cedarville)	**87,763**
	Roger D. Tackett (D, So. Charleston)	65,602
8.	**Thomas N. Kindness*** (R, Hamilton)	**97,620**
	John W. Griffen (D, Miamisburg)	49,623
9.	**Marcy Kaptur** (D, Toledo)	**94,92[illegible]**
	Ed Weber* (R, Toledo)	64,503
10.	**Clarence E. Miller*** (R, Lancaster)	**99,595**
	John M. Buchanan (D, Newark)	57,850
11.	**Dennis E. Eckart*** (D, Concord Township)	**93,09[illegible]**
	Glen W. Warner (R, Ashtabula)	56,57[illegible]
12.	**John R. Kasich** (R, Westerville)	**88,60[illegible]**
	Bob Shamansky* (D, Bexley)	82,32[illegible]

Dist.	Representative (Party, Home)	1982 Election
13.	**Donald J. Pease*** (D, Oberlin)	**92,266**
	Timothy Paul Martin (R, Elyria)	53,256
14.	**John F. Seiberling*** (D, Akron)	**113,300**
	Louis A. Mangels (R, Fairlawn)	50,376
15.	**Chalmers P. Wylie*** (R, Worthington)	**104,416**
	Greg Kostelac (D, Columbus)	46,611
16.	**Ralph Regula*** (R, Navarre)	**109,408**
	Jeffrey R. Orenstein (D, N. Canton)	56,761
17.	**Lyle Williams*** (R, Warren)	**98,450**
	George D. Tablack (D, Campbell)	80,212
18.	**Douglas Applegate*** (D, Steubenville)	**Unopposed**
19.	**Edward F. Feighan** (D, Cleveland)	**111,459**
	Richard G. Anter II (R, Fairview Park)	72,503
20.	**Mary Rose Oakar*** (D, Cleveland)	**103,380**
	Paris T. LeJeune (R, Cleveland)	17,715
21.	**Louis Stokes*** (D, Warrensville Hts.)	**132,431**
	Alan G. Shatteen (R, Cleveland)	21,374

Oklahoma

Dist.	Representative (Party, Home)	1982 Election
1.	**James R. Jones*** (D, Tulsa)	**75,511**
	Richard C. Freeman (R, Tulsa)	61,416
2.	**Mike Synar*** (D, Muskogee)	**110,111**
	Lou Striegel (R, Broken Arrow)	41,866
3.	**Wes Watkins*** (D, Ada)	**120,490**
	Patrick M. Miller (R, Snow)	26,282
4.	**Dave McCurdy*** (D, Norman)	**84,075**
	Howard Rutledge (R, Norman)	44,282
5.	**Mickey Edwards*** (R, Oklahoma City)	**97,318**
	Dan Lane (D, Oklahoma City)	41,287
6.	**Glenn English*** (D, Cordell)	**102,306**
	Ed Moore (R, Yukon)	33,144

Oregon

Dist.	Representative (Party, Home)	1982 Election
1.	**Les AuCoin*** (D, Forest Grove)	**114,684**
	Bill Moshofsky (R, Portland)	97,911
2.	**Bob Smith** (R, Burns)	**101,321**
	Larryann Willis (D, Vale)	81,487
3.	**Ron Wyden*** (D, Portland)	**153,248**
	Thomas H. Phelan (R, Portland)	42,119
4.	**James Weaver*** (D, Eugene)	**112,401**
	Ross Anthony (R, Eugene)	77,747
5.	**Denny Smith*** (R, Salem)	**103,213**
	J. Ruth McFarland (D, Boring)	98,263

Pennsylvania

Dist.	Representative (Party, Home)	1982 Election
1.	**Thomas M. Foglietta*** (D, Philadelphia)	**100,426**
	Michael Marino (R, Philadelphia)	37,137
2.	**William H. Gray III*** (D, Philadelphia)	**117,765**
	Milton Street (I, Philadelphia)	34,293
3.	**Robert A. Borski** (D, Philadelphia)	**90,889**
	Charles F. Dougherty* (R, Philadelphia)	88,617
4.	**Joseph P. Kolter** (D, New Brighton)	**100,398**
	Eugene V. Atkinson* (R, Philadelphia)	64,464
5.	**Richard T. Schulze*** (R, Wayne)	**90,585**
	Bob Burger (D, Glen Mills)	44,131
6.	**Gus Yatron*** (D, Reading)	**107,976**
	Harry B. Martin (R, Boyertown)	42,129
7.	**Robert W. Edgar*** (D, Broomall)	**105,711**
	Steve Joachim (R, Springfield Township)	84,902
8.	**Peter H. Kostmayer** (R, Solebury)	**83,145**
	James K. Coyne (R, Newtown)	80,942
9.	**Bud Shuster*** (R, D, Everett)	**91,906**
	Eugene J. Duncan (D, Altoona)	48,760
10.	**Joseph M. McDade*** (R, Scranton)	**102,255**
	Robert J. Rafalko (D, Scranton)	49,198
11.	**Frank Harrison** (D, Wilkes-Barre)	**90,386**
	James L. Nelligan* (R, Forty-Fort)	78,379
12.	**John P. Murtha*** (D, Johnstown)	**95,479**
	William N. Tuscano (R, Greensburg)	53,607
13.	**Lawrence Coughlin*** (R, Villanova)	**108,898**
	Martin J. Cunningham Jr. (D, Norristown)	59,632
14.	**William J. Coyne*** (D, Pittsburgh)	**119,127**
	John R. Clark (Pittsburgh)	35,582
15.	**Don Ritter*** (R, Coopersburg)	**79,770**
	Richard J. Orloski (D, Allentown)	58,286
16.	**Robert S. Walker*** (R, E. Petersburg)	**92,897**
	Jean D. Mowery (D, Lancaster)	37,519
17.	**George W. Gekas** (R, Harrisburg)	**84,512**
	Larry J. Hochendoner (D, Harrisburg)	61,952
18.	**Doug Walgren*** (D, Pittsburgh)	**101,363**
	Ted Jacob (R, Pittsburgh)	84,406
19.	**William F. Goodling*** (R, Jacoby)	**100,935**
	Larry Becker (D, York)	41,779
20.	**Joseph M. Gaydos*** (D, McKeesport)	**125,720**
	Terry T. Ray (R, Monroeville)	37,875
21.	**Thomas J. Ridge** (R, Erie)	**79,822**
	Anthony Andrezeski (D, Erie)	79,340
22.	**Austin J. Murphy*** (D, Charleroi)	**122,640**
	Frank J. Paterra (R, N. Charleroi)	32,034
23.	**William F. Clinger Jr.*** (R, Warren)	**92,123**
	Joseph J. Calla (D, Johnsonburg)	48,753

Rhode Island

Dist.	Representative (Party, Home)	1982 Election
1.	**Fernand J. St Germain*** (D, Woonsocket)	**94,497**
	Burton Stallwood (R, Lincoln)	59,537
2.	**Claudine Schneider*** (R, Narragansett)	**91,116**
	James V. Aukerman (D, S. Kingstown)	72,077

South Carolina

Dist.	Representative (Party, Home)	1982 Election
1.	**Thomas F. Hartnett*** (R, Mt. Pleasant)	**62,677**
	Mullins McLeod (D, Walterboro)	51,525
2.	**Floyd Spence*** (R, Lexington)	**71,441**
	Ken Mosely (D, Orangeburg)	50,652
3.	**Butler Derrick*** (D, Edgefield)	**77,229**
	Gordon T. Davis (Libert., Westminster)	8,272
4.	**Carroll A. Campbell Jr.*** (R, Greenville)	**70,090**
	Marion E. Tyus (D, Greenville)	40,489
5.	**John Spratt** (D, York)	**69,226**
	John S. Wilkerson (R, Clover)	33,110
6.	**Robert M. Tallon Jr.** (D, Florence)	**61,183**
	John L. Napier* (R, Bennettsville)	55,744

South Dakota

Dist.	Representative (Party, Home)	1982 Election
1.	**Thomas A. Daschle*** (D, Aberdeen)	**144,013**
	Clint Roberts* (R, Presho)	133,986

Tennessee

Dist.	Representative (Party, Home)	1982 Election
1.	**James H. Quillen*** (R, Kingsport)	**90,286**
	Jessie J. Cable (D, Jonesboro)	27,614
2.	**John J. Duncan*** (R, Knoxville)	**Unopposed**
3.	**Marilyn Lloyd Bouquard*** (D, Chattanooga)	**84,082**
	Glen Byers (R, Cleveland)	49,847
4.	**Jim Cooper** (D, Shelbyville)	**93,502**
	Cissy Baker (R, Huntsville)	48,586
5.	**Bill Boner*** (D, Nashville)	**109,270**
	Laural Steinhice (R, Nashville)	27,109
6.	**Albert Gore Jr.*** (D, Carthage)	**Unopposed**
7.	**Don Sundquist** (R, Memphis)	**73,702**
	Bob Clement (D, Dickson)	72,230
8.	**Ed Jones** (D, Yorkville)	**93,818**
	Bruce Benson (R, Memphis)	31,525
9.	Harold E. Ford (D, Memphis)	112,245
	Joe Crawford (R, Memphis)	40,813

Texas

Dist.	Representative (Party, Home)	1982 Election
1.	**Sam B. Hall Jr.*** (D, Marshall)	**98,184**
	John Traylor (Libert., Longview)	2,584
2.	**Charles Wilson*** (D, Lufkin)	**90,195**
	Ed Richbourg (Libert., Bidor)	5,617
3.	**Steve Bartlett** (R, Dallas)	**94,870**
	James L. McNees Jr. (D, Dallas)	27,162
4.	**Ralph M. Hall*** (D, Rockwall)	**93,166**
	Peter J. Collumb (R, McKinney)	33,673

Dist.	Representative (Party, Home)	1982 Election
5.	**John Bryant** (D, Dallas)	**50,526**
	Joe Devany (R, Dallas)	26,298
6.	**Phil Gramm*** (D, College Station)	**83,067**
	Ron Hard (Libert., Conroe)	4,951
7.	**Bill Archer*** (R, Houston)	**108,635**
	Dennis Scoggins (D, Houston)	17,839
8.	**Jack Fields*** (R, Humble)	**50,583**
	Henry E. Allee (D, Houston)	37,983
9.	**Jack Brooks*** (D, Beaumont)	**78,960**
	John W. Lewis (R, Friendswood)	31,409
10.	**J. J. "Jake" Pickle*** (D, Austin)	**120,530**
	William G. Kelsey (Libert., Elgin)	8,727
11.	**Marvin Leath*** (D, Marlin)	**82,058**
	Tom Kilbride (Libert., Waco)	3,065
12.	**Jim Wright*** (D, Fort Worth)	**76,048**
	Jim Ryan (R, Euless)	32,937
13.	**Jack Hightower*** (D, Vernon)	**85,693**
	Ron Slover (R, Amarillo)	47,825
14.	**William N. "Bill" Patman** (D, Ganado)	**73,388**
	Joe Wyatt (R, Victoria)	47,037
15.	**E. "Kika" de la Garza*** (D, Mission)	**41,327**
	Frank L. Jones III (Libert., Ingelside)	1,882
16.	**Ronald Coleman** (D, El Paso)	**44,044**
	Pat B. Haggerty (R, El Paso)	36,064
17.	**Charles W. Stenholm*** (D, Stamford)	**106,148**
	James Cooley III (Libert., Winters)	3,352
18.	**Mickey Leland*** (D, Houston)	**67,932**
	C. Leon Pickett (R, Houston)	12,087
19.	**Kent Hance*** (D, Lubbock)	**89,552**
	E. L. Hicks (R, Denver City)	19,976
20.	**Henry B. Gonzalez*** (D, San Antonio)	**68,344**
	Roger V. Gary (Libert., San Antonio)	4,178
21.	**Tom Loeffler*** (R, Hunt)	**104,116**
	Charles S. Stough (D, Boerne)	34,113
22.	**Ron Paul*** (R, Lake Jackson)	**Unopposed**
23.	**Abraham "Chick" Kazen Jr.*** (D, Laredo)	**48,919**
	Jeff Wentworth (R, San Antonio)	40,154
24.	**Martin Frost*** (D, Dallas)	**58,471**
	Lucy P. Patterson (R, Dallas)	21,054
25.	**Mike Andrews** (D, Houston)	**63,903**
	Mike Faubion (R, Houston)	40,063
26.	**Jim Bradshaw** (R, Fort Worth)	**65,698**
	Tom Vandergriff (D, Arlington)	64,124
27.	**Solomon P. Ortiz** (D, Corpus Christi)	**66,548**
	Jason Luby (R, Corpus Christi)	35,198
	Utah	
1.	**James V. Hansen*** (R, Farmington)	**111,792**
	A. Stephen Dirks (D, Ogden)	66,029
2.	**Dan Marriott*** (R, Salt Lake City)	**91,599**
	Frances Farley (D, Salt Lake City)	78,633
3.	**Howard C. Nielson** (R, Provo)	**108,273**
	Henry A. Hursh (I, Orem)	32,601
	Vermont At Large	
1.	**James M. Jeffords*** (R, Montpelier)	**112,756**
	Mark A. Kaplan (D, Burlington)	37,922
	Virginia	
1.	**Herbert Bateman** (R, Newport News)	**76,928**
	John J. McGlennon (D, Williamsburg)	62,380
2.	**G. William Whitehurst*** (R, Virginia Beach)	**Unopposed**
3.	**Thomas J. Bliley Jr.*** (R, Richmond)	**92,867**
	John Waldrop Jr. (D, Richmond)	63,467
4.	**Norman Sisisky** (D, Petersburg)	**86,679**
	Robert W. Daniel Jr.* (D, (Spring Grove)	67,562
5.	**Dan Daniel*** (D, Danville)	**Unopposed**
6.	**James Olin** (D, Roanoke)	**68,098**
	Kevin Miller (R, Harrisonburg)	66,526
7.	**J. Kenneth Robinson*** (R, Winchester)	**76,650**
	Lindsay G. Dorrier Jr. (D, Scottsville)	46,458
8.	**Stan Parris*** (R, Springfield)	**69,445**
	Herbert E. Harris II (D, Mt. Vernon)	67,980
9.	**Frederick Boucher** (D, Abingdon)	**74,616**
	William C. Wampler (R, Bristol)	74,250
10.	**Frank R. Wolf*** (R, Vienna)	**86,389**
	Ira M. Lechner (D, Falls Church)	75,444
	Washington	
1.	**Joel Pritchard*** (R, Seattle)	**89,168**
	Brian Long (D, Seattle)	44,240
2.	**Al Swift*** (D, Bellingham)	**86,849**
	Joan Houchen (R, Camano Island)	60,216
3.	**Don Bonker*** (D, Tumwater)	**91,721**
	J.T. Quigg (R, Aberdeen)	56,267
4.	**Sid Morrison*** (R, Zillah)	**99,877**
	Charles D. Kilbury (D, Pasco)	40,152
5.	**Thomas S. Foley*** (D, Spokane)	**103,362**
	John Sonneland (R, Spokane)	57,601
6.	**Norman D. Dicks*** (D, Bremerton)	**76,913**
	Ted Haley (R, Tacoma)	39,523
7.	**Mike Lowry*** (D, Seattle)	**98,483**
	Bob Dorse (R, Seattle)	39,320
8.	**Rodney Chandler** (R, Redmond)	**49,456**
	Beth Bland (D, Mercer Island)	39,193
	West Virginia	
1.	**Allan B. Mollohan*** (D, Fairmont)	**79,289**
	John F. McCuskey (R, Bridgeport)	69,933
2.	**Harley O. Staggers Jr.** (D, Keyser)	**87,506**
	J. D. Hinkle Jr. (R, Buckhannon)	48,848
3.	**Bob Wise** (D, Charleston)	**81,669**
	David Michael Staton* (R, South Charleston)	58,914
4.	**Nick J. Rahall II *** (D, Beckley)	**90,679**
	Homer L. Harris (R, Huntington)	21,956
	Wisconsin	
1.	**Les Aspin*** (D, East Troy)	**94,445**
	Peter N. Jannson (R, Racine)	59,450
2.	**Robert Kastenmeier*** (D, Sun Prairie)	**113,204**
	Jim Johnson (R, Darlington)	72,290
3.	**Steven Gunderson*** (R, Osseo)	**99,078**
	Paul Offner (D, La Crosse)	75,021
4.	**Clement J. Zablocki*** (D, Milwaukee)	**129,006**
	John Gudenschwager (Consti., West Allis)	944
5.	**Jim Moody** (D, Milwaukee)	**98,958**
	Rod K. Johnston (R, Milwaukee)	54,521
6.	**Thomas E. Petri*** (R, Fond du Lac)	**110,375**
	Gordon E. Loehr (D, Ford du Lac)	59,741
7.	**David R. Obey*** (D, Wausau)	**121,998**
	Bernard A. Zimmerman (R, Marshfield)	57,483
8.	**Toby Roth*** (R, Appleton)	**100,056**
	Ruth C. Clusen (D, Green Bay)	73,545
9.	**F. James Sensenbrenner Jr.*** (R, Nashotah)	**Unopposed**
	Wyoming At Large	
	Richard B. Cheney* (R, Casper)	112,309
	Ted Hommel (D, Cheyenne)	46,079

Non-Voting Delegates

District of Columbia

Walter E. Fauntroy* (D, D.C.)

Guam

Antonio Borja Won Pat* (D, Agana)

Virgin Islands

Ron deLugo (D, St. Croix)

American Samoa

Fofo I. F. Sunia (I, Pago Pago)

Governors of States and Possessions

Reflecting Nov. 2, 1982 elections

State	Capital	Governor	Party	Term years	Term expires	Annual salary
Alabama	Montgomery	George C. Wallace	Dem.	4	Jan. 1987	$50,000
Alaska	Juneau	William Sheffield	Dem.	4	Dec. 1986	74,196
Arizona	Phoenix	Bruce Babbitt	Dem.	4	Jan. 1987	50,000
Arkansas	Little Rock	Bill Clinton	Dem.	2	Jan. 1985	35,000
California	Sacramento	George Deukmejian	Rep.	4	Jan. 1987	49,100
Colorado	Denver	Richard D. Lamm	Dem.	4	Jan. 1987	50,000
Connecticut	Hartford	William A. O'Neill	Dem.	4	Jan. 1987	42,000
Delaware	Dover	Pierre S. du Pont 4th	Rep.	4	Jan. 1985	35,000
Florida	Tallahassee	Robert Graham	Dem.	4	Jan. 1987	60,498
Georgia	Atlanta	Joe Frank Harris	Dem.	4	Jan. 1987	65,934
Hawaii	Honolulu	George R. Ariyoshi	Dem.	4	Dec. 1986	50,000
Idaho	Boise	John V. Evans	Dem.	4	Jan. 1987	40,000
Illinois	Springfield	James R. Thompson	Rep.	4	Jan. 1987	58,000
Indiana	Indianapolis	Robert D. Orr	Rep.	4	Jan. 1985	48,000
Iowa	Des Moines	Terry Branstad	Rep.	4	Jan. 1987	60,000
Kansas	Topeka	John Carlin	Dem.	4	Jan. 1987	45,000
Kentucky	Frankfort	John Y. Brown Jr.	Dem.	4	Dec. 1983	50,000
Louisiana	Baton Rouge	David C. Treen	Rep.	4	May 1984	73,440
Maine	Augusta	Joseph E. Brennan	Dem.	4	Jan. 1987	35,000
Maryland	Annapolis	Harry Hughes	Dem.	4	Jan. 1987	60,000
Massachusetts	Boston	Michael S. Dukakis	Dem.	4	Jan. 1987	40,000
Michigan	Lansing	James J. Blanchard	Dem.	4	Jan. 1987	70,000
Minnesota	St. Paul	Rudy Perpich	Dem.	4	Jan. 1987	66,500
Mississippi	Jackson	William Winter	Dem.	4	Jan. 1984	53,000
Missouri	Jefferson City	Christopher S. Bond	Rep.	4	Jan. 1985	55,000
Montana	Helena	Ted Schwinden	Dem.	4	Jan. 1985	43,360
Nebraska	Lincoln	Bob Kerrey	Dem.	4	Jan. 1987	40,000
Nevada	Carson City	Richard Bryan	Dem.	4	Jan. 1987	50,000
New Hampshire	Concord	John H. Sununu	Rep.	2	Jan. 1985	44,520
New Jersey	Trenton	Thomas H. Kean	Rep.	4	Jan. 1986	85,000
New Mexico	Santa Fe	Toney Anaya	Dem.	4	Jan. 1987	60,000
New York	Albany	Mario Cuomo	Dem.	4	Jan. 1987	85,000
North Carolina	Raleigh	James B. Hunt	Dem.	4	Jan. 1985	57,864
North Dakota	Bismarck	Allen I. Olson	Rep.	4	Jan. 1985	47,000
Ohio	Columbus	Richard Celeste	Dem.	4	Jan. 1987	50,000
Oklahoma	Oklahoma City	George Nigh	Dem.	4	Jan. 1987	48,000
Oregon	Salem	Victor Atiyeh	Rep.	4	Jan. 1987	55,423
Pennsylvania	Harrisburg	Richard Thornburgh	Rep.	4	Jan. 1987	66,000
Rhode Island	Providence	J. Joseph Garrahy	Dem.	2	Jan. 1985	49,500
South Carolina	Columbia	Richard W. Riley	Dem.	4	Jan. 1987	60,000
South Dakota	Pierre	William J. Janklow	Rep.	4	Jan. 1987	46,750
Tennessee	Nashville	Lamar Alexander	Rep.	4	Jan. 1987	68,226
Texas	Austin	Mark White	Dem.	4	Jan. 1987	71,400
Utah	Salt Lake City	Scott M. Matheson	Dem.	4	Jan. 1985	48,000
Vermont	Montpelier	Richard A. Snelling	Rep.	2	Jan. 1985	44,850
Virginia	Richmond	Charles S. Robb	Dem.	4	Jan. 1986	75,000
Washington	Olympia	John Spellman	Rep.	4	Jan. 1985	63,000
West Virginia	Charleston	Jay Rockefeller	Dem.	4	Jan. 1985	60,000
Wisconsin	Madison	Anthony S. Earl	Dem.	4	Jan. 1987	65,801
Wyoming	Cheyenne	Ed Herschler	Dem.	4	Jan. 1987	55,000
Amer. Samoa	Pago Pago	Peter Coleman	Rep.	4	Jan. 1985	—
Guam	Agana	Paul Calvo	Rep.	4	Jan. 1985	50,000
N. Mariana Isls.	Saipan	Pedro Tenorio	Rep.	4	Jan. 1986	20,000
Puerto Rico	San Juan	Carlos Romero Barcelo	N.P.	4	Jan. 1985	36,200
Virgin Islands	Charlotte Amalie	Juan Luis	Ind.	4	Jan. 1987	52,000

The Races for Governor

States	Democrats	Vote	Republicans	Vote
Alabama	George Wallace	640,148	Emory Folmar	433,028
Alaska	William Sheffield	67,314	Thomas A. Fink	55,451
Arizona	Bruce Babbit*	455,760	Leo Corbet	236,857
Arkansas	Bill Clinton	435,092	Frank D. White*	357,172
California	Tom Bradley	3,711,183	George Deukmejian	3,762,328
Colorado	Richard D. Lamm*	607,347	John Fuhr	295,441
Connecticut	William A. O'Neill*	570,476	Lewis B. Rome	497,561
Florida	Bob Graham*	1,711,946	Lewis A. Bafalis	930,845
Georgia	Joe Frank Harris	728,825	Robert H. Bell	432,680
Hawaii	George Ariyoshi*	141,043	D. G. Anderson	81,507
Idaho	John Evans*	164,851	Phil Batt	161,274
Illinois	Adlai E. Stevenson 3d	1,720,822	James R. Thompson*	1,753,057
Iowa	Roxanne Conlin	482,858	Terry Branstad	546,324
Kansas	John Carlin*	405,546	Sam Hardage	339,595
Maine	Joseph E. Brennan*	280,664	Charles L. Cragin	172,696
Maryland	Harry R. Hughes*	692,832	Robert A. Pascal	424,247
Massachusetts	Michael S. Dukakis	1,221,589	John W. Sears	749,306
Michigan	James J. Blanchard	1,562,477	Richard H. Headlee	1,358,237
Minnesota	Rudy Perpich	1,001,906	Wheelock Whitney	687,282

States	Democrats	Vote	Republicans	Vote
Nebraska	Bob Kerrey	272,812	Charles Thone*	264,534
Nevada	Richard Bryan	128,133	Robert F. List*	100,138
New Hampshire	Hugh Gallen*	132,503	John H. Sununu	145,650
New Mexico	Toney Anaya	215,481	John Irick	190,341
New York	Mario M. Cuomo	2,609,734	Lewis E. Lehrman	2,446,529
Ohio	Richard Celeste	1,978,635	Clarence J. Brown	1,302,583
Oklahoma	George Nigh*	545,987	Tom Daxon	330,889
Oregon	Ted Kulongoski	363,062	Victor G. Atiyeh	617,924
Pennsylvania	Allen E. Ertel	1,754,601	Dick Thornburgh*	1,868,240
Rhode Island	J. Joseph Garrahy*	237,807	Vincent J. Marzullo	76,076
South Carolina	Richard W. Riley*	466,347	William D. Workman Jr.	201,002
South Dakota	Michael O'Connor	81,487	William J. Janklow*	195,653
Tennessee	Randall Tyree	499,404	Lamar Alexander*	736,487
Texas	Mark White	1,664,528	William P. Clements Jr.*	1,426,920
Vermont	Madeleine M. Kunin	73,852	Richard A. Snelling*	91,383
Wisconsin	Anthony S. Earl	895,690	Terry J. Kohler	662,303
Wyoming	Ed Herschler*	106,377	Warren A. Morton	61,895

Mayors and City Managers of Larger North American Cities

Reflecting Nov. 2, 1982 elections

*Asterisk before name denotes city manager. All others are mayors. For mayors, dates are those of next election; for city managers, they are dates of appointment.

D, Democrat; R, Republican; N-P, Non-Partisan

City	Name	Term
Abilene, Tex.	Elbert E. Hall, N-P	**1984, Apr.**
Abington, Pa.	*Albert Herrmann	**1978, May**
Akron, Oh.	Roy L. Ray, R	**1983, Nov.**
Alameda, Cal.	*J. Bruce Rupp	**1980, Nov.**
Albany, Ga.	*Carl Leavy	**1980, Jan.**
Albany, N.Y.	Erastus Corning 2d, D	**1985, Nov.**
Albuquerque, N.M.	*Frank Kleinhenz	**1974, July**
Alexandria, Va.	*Douglas Harman	**1975, Nov.**
Alhambra, Cal.	*Andrew Lazzaretto Jr.	**1980, Jan.**
Allen Park, Mich.	Frank J. Lada, D.	**1983, Nov.**
Allentown, Pa.	Joseph S. Daddona, D	**1985, Nov.**
Alton, Ill.	Paul A. Lenz, N-P	**1985, Apr.**
Altoona, Pa.	Alan Hancock, R	**1983, Nov.**
Amarillo, Tex.	*John S. Stiff	**1963, Sept.**
Ames, La.	*John Elwell	**1980, Mar.**
Anaheim, Cal.	*William O. Talley	**1976, July**
Anchorage, Alas.	Tony Knowles, N-P	**1983, Oct.**
Anderson, Ind.	Thomas McMahan, R	**1983, Nov.**
Anderson, S.C.	*Richard Burnette	**1976, Sept.**
Ann Arbor, Mich.	*Terry V. Sprenkel	**1980, Jan.**
Appleton, Wis.	Dorothy Johnson, N-P	**1984, Apr.**
Arcadia, Cal.	*George J. Watts	**1981, Feb.**
Arlington, Mass.	*Donald R. Marquis	**1966, Nov.**
Arlington, Tex.	*Ross Calhoun	**1973, Mar.**
Arlington, Va.	*W.V. Ford	**1976, Mar.**
Arlington Hts., Ill.	*L.A. Hanson	**1958, Oct.**
Arvada, Col.	*Craig Kocian	**1977, Mar.**
Asheville, N.C.	*Kenneth Michalove	**1977, Apr.**
Atlanta, Ga.	Andrew Young, D	**1985, Nov.**
Atlantic City, N.J.	Michael Matthews, D	**1986, June**
Auburn, N.Y.	*Bruce Clifford	**1966, Aug.**
Augusta, Ga.	Edward McIntyre, D	**1984, Oct.**
Aurora, Col.	*Robert E. Broom	**1978, June**
Austin, Tex.	*Dan H. Davidson	**1972, Aug.**
Bakersfield, Cal.	*Philip Kelmar	**1981, Jan.**
Baldwin Park, Cal.	*Ralph Webb	**1981, Apr.**
Baltimore, Md.	William Schaefer, D	**1983, Nov.**
Bangor, Me.	*John W. Flynn	**1977, Feb.**
Baton Rouge, La.	Pat Screen, D	**1984, Nov.**
Battle Creek, Mich.	*Gordon Jaeger	**1976, Mar.**
Bay City, Mich.	*David D. Barnes	**1979, May**
Baytown, Tex.	*Fritz Lanham	**1972, May**
Beaumont, Tex.	*Ray A. Riley	**1978, Apr.**
Belleville, Ill.	Richard Brauer, N-P	**1985, Apr.**
Bellevue, Wash.	*Andrea Beatty	**1980, May**
Bellflower, Cal.	James Earle Christo, R	**1984, Apr.**
Beloit, Wis.	*H. Herbert Holt	**1971, Jan.**
Berkeley, Cal.	*Daniel Boggan Jr.	**1982, Jan.**
Berwyn, Ill.	Joseph Lanzillotti, D	**1985, Apr.**
Bessemer, Ala.	Ed Porter, N-P	**1986, July**
Bethlehem, Pa.	Paul M. Marcincin, D	**1985, Nov.**
Beverly Hills, Cal.	*Edward Kreins	**1979, Oct.**
Billings, Mont.	*Al Thelen	**1979, Nov.**
Biloxi, Miss.	Gerald Blessey, D	**1985, June**
Binghamton, N.Y.	Juanita M. Crabb, D.	**1984, Nov.**
Birmingham, Ala.	Richard Arrington Jr., D.	**1983, Oct.**
Bismarck, N.D.	Bus Leary, D.	**1986, Apr.**
Bloomfield, Minn.	*John Pidgeon	**1967, Dec.**
Bloomfield, N.J.	John W. Kinder, R	**1983, Nov.**
Bloomington, Ill.	Richard Buchanan, R	**1985, Feb.**
Bloomington, Ind.	Francis X. McCloskey, D	**1983, Nov.**
Bloomington, Minn.	*John Pidgeon	**1967, Sept.**
Boca Raton, Fla.	*James Zumwalt	**1980, May**
Boise, Ida.	Dick Eardley, N-P	**1985, Nov.**
Bossier City, La.	Marvin E. Anding, D	**1985, May**
Boston, Mass.	Kevin White, D	**1983 Nov.**
Boulder, Col.	*Robert Westdyke	**1976, Aug.**
Bowie, Md.	*G. Charles Moore	**1975, Aug.**
Bowling Green, Ky.	*Charles W. Coates	**1977, Feb.**
Bridgeport, Conn.	Leonard Paoletta, R.	**1983, Nov.**
Bristol, Conn.	Michael Werner, R	**1983, Nov.**
Brockton, Mass.	Paul V. Studenski, D	**1983, Nov.**
Brooklyn Center, Minn.	*Gerald G. Splinter	**1977, Oct.**
Brownsville, Tex.	Emilio Hernandez, N-P	**1983, Nov.**
Bryan, Tex.	*Ernest R. Clark	**1979, Feb.**
Buffalo, N.Y.	James D. Griffen, D	**1985, Nov.**
Burlington, Vt.	Bernard Sanders, N-P	**1983, Mar.**
Calumet City, Ill.	Robert C. Stefaniak, D	**1985, Apr.**
Cambridge, Mass.	*Robert Healey,	**1981, Dec.**
Camden, N.J.	Melvin Primas Jr., D	**1985, June**
Canton, Oh.	Stanley A. Cmich, R.	**1983, Nov.**
Cape Girardeau, Mo.	*Gary A. Eide	**1981, Mar.**
Carson, Cal.	*Raymond Meador	**1982, May**
Casper, Wyo.	*Kenneth Erickson	**1969, Oct.**
Cedar Rapids, Ia.	Donald J. Canney, N-P	**1983, Nov.**
Champaign, Ill.	*V. Eugene Miller	**1974, Sept.**
Charleston, S.C.	Joseph P. Riley Jr., D	**1983, Nov.**
Charleston, W. Va.	Joe F. Smith, D	**1983, Mar.**
Charlotte, N.C.	H. Edward Knox, D	**1983, Nov.**
Charlottesville, Va.	*Cole Hendrix	**1971, Jan.**
Chattanooga, Tenn.	Charles A. Rose, N-P	**1983, Mar.**
Chesapeake, Va.	*John T. Maxwell	**1978, Sept.**
Chester, Pa.	Joseph Battle, R	**1983, Nov.**
Cheyenne, Wyo.	Donald Erickson, R	**1984, Nov.**
Chicago, Ill.	Jane M. Byrne, D	**1983, Apr.**
Chicago Hts., Ill.	Charles Panici, R	**1983, Apr.**
Chicopee, Mass.	Robert Kumor Jr., D.	**1983, Nov.**
Chula Vista, Cal.	*Lane F. Cole	**1975, Feb.**
Cicero, Ill.	Henry J. Klosak, R	**1985, Apr.**
Cincinnati, Oh.	*Sylvester Murray	**1979, Sept.**
Clearwater, Fla.	*Anthony Shoemaker	**1977, June**
Cleveland, Oh.	George Voinovich, R	**1985, Nov.**
Cleveland Hgts., Oh.	*Richard Robinson	**1978, July**
Clifton, N.J.	*Joseph J. Lynn	**1982, Sept.**
Col. Spgs., Col.	*George H. Fellows	**1966, July**
Columbia, Mo.	*Richard Gray	**1980, Nov.**
Columbia, S.C.	*Graydon V. Olive Jr.	**1970, Mar.**
Columbus, Ga.	Undecided	**1986, Nov.**
Columbus, Oh.	Tom Moody, R	**1983, Nov.**
Commerce, Cal.	*Robert Hinderliter	**1973, Aug.**
Compton, Cal.	*Ronald D. Nelson	**1980, July**
Concord, Cal.	*Farrel A. Stewart	**1960, Apr.**
Coon Rapids., Minn.	*Richard Thistle	**1979, July**
Coral Gables, Fla.	*J. Martin Gainer	**1975, Jan.**
Corpus Christi, Tex.	*Edward A. Martin	**1982, Mar.**
Corvallis, Ore.	*Gary F. Pokorny	**1978, Nov.**
Costa Mesa, Cal.	*Fred Sorsabel	**1970, Nov.**
Council Bluffs, Ia.	*Michael G. Miller	**1978, Aug.**
Covington, Ky.	Bernard Moorman, N-P	**1983, Nov.**

City	Name	Term
Cranston, R.I.	Edward DiPrete, R	1986, Nov.
Crystal, Minn.	*John Irving	1963, Jan.
Culver City, Cal.	*Dale Jones	1969, Aug.
Cuyahoga Falls, Oh.	Robert Quirk, D	1985, Nov.
Dallas, Tex.	*Charles S. Anderson	1981, Oct.
Daly City, Cal.	*David R. Rowe	1969, July
Danbury, Conn.	James Dyer, D.	1983, Nov.
Danville, Ill.	David S. Palmer, N-P	1983, Apr.
Danville, Va.	*Charles Church	1981, June
Davenport, Ia.	*Michael Kadlecik, Act.	1982, Mar.
Dayton, Oh.	*Earl Sterzer	1979, Feb.
Daytona Bch., Fla.	*Howard D. Tipton	1978, Oct.
Dearborn Hgts., Mich.	Donald Bishop, D	1985, Nov.
Decatur, Ala.	Bill Dukes, D	1984, Aug.
Decatur, Ill.	*Leslie T. Allen	1972, Sept.
Denton, Tex.	*G. C. Hartung	1976, Oct.
Denver, Col.	William H. McNichols, D	1983, May
Des Moines, Ia.	*Richard Wilkey	1973, Oct.
Des Plaines, Ill.	John Seitz, R.	1985, Apr.
Detroit, Mich.	Coleman A. Young, N-P	1983, Nov.
Dotham, Ala.	Kenneth Everett, N-P	1985, July
Dover, Del.	Crawford J. Carroll, N-P	1983, Apr.
Downers Grove, Ill.	*James R. Griesemer	1972, Sept.
Downey, Cal.	James Quinn, R	1984, June
Dubuque, Ia.	*W. Kenneth Gearhart	1979, Aug.
Duluth, Minn.	John Fedo, N-P	1983, Nov.
Durham, N.C.	*Barry Del Castilho	1980, Oct.
E. Chicago, Ind.	Robert A. Pastrick, D	1983, Nov.
E. Cleveland, Oh.	*Frank Wise	1979, Jan.
E. Detroit, Mich.	*vacant	
E. Lansing, Mich.	*Jerry Coffman	1977, Jan.
E. Orange, N.J.	Thomas H. Cooke Jr., D	1985, Nov.
E. Providence, Mich.	*Earl Sandquist	1979, Sept.
E. St. Louis, Ill.	Carl E. Officer, D	1983, Apr.
Eau Claire, Wis.	*Stephen Atkins	1978, Sept.
Edina, Minn.	*Kenneth Rosland	1977, Nov.
Edison, N.J.	Anthony Yelencsics, D	1984, Nov.
El Cajon, Cal.	*Robert Acker	1982, July
El Monte, Cal.	*L.C. Bevington	1982, Sept.
El Paso, Tex.	Johnathan W. Rogers, N-P	1983, Apr.
Elgin, Ill.	*Leo Nelson	1972, Dec.
Elizabeth, N.J.	Thomas G. Dunn, D	1984, Nov.
Elkhart, Ind.	Eleanor Kesim, D	1983, Nov.
Elmhurst, Ill.	*Robert T. Palmer	1953, Aug.
Elmira, N.Y.	*Joseph E. Sartori	1972, June
Elyria, Oh.	Michael Keys, D	1983, Nov.
Enfield, Conn.	*Robert F. Ledger Jr.	1977, Mar.
Enid, Okla.	*Lyle Smith	1979, Feb.
Erie, Pa.	Louis J. Tullio, D	1985, Nov.
Escondido, Cal.	*Vernon Hazen	1982, July
Euclid, Oh.	Anthony Giunta, D	1983, Nov.
Eugene, Ore.	*Michael Gleason	1981, Jan.
Evanston, Ill.	*Joel Asprooth	1982, May
Evansville, Ind.	Michael Vandeveer, D	1983, Nov.
Everett, Mass.	Edward Connolly, D.	1983, Nov.
Everett, Wash.	William Moore, N-P	1985, Nov.
Fairborn, Oh.	*William Burns	1977, Feb.
Fairfield, Cal.	*B. Gale Wilson	1956, Mar.
Fair Lawn, N.J.	*Frank Peruggi	1977, July
Fall River, Mass.	Carlton Viveiros, N-P	1983, Nov.
Fargo, N.D.	Jon Lindgren, D	1984, Apr.
Farmington Hills, Mich.	*Lawrence Savage	1979, Feb.
Fayetteville, Ark.	*Donald Grimes	1972, Apr.
Fayetteville, N.C.	*John P. Smith	1981, Jan.
Fitchburg, Mass.	David Gilmartin, D	1983, Nov.
Flagstaff, Ariz.	*Frank Abeyta	1981, Jan.
Flint, Mich.	James Rutherford, N-P	1983, Nov.
Florissant, Mo.	James J. Eagan, N-P	1983, Apr.
Fond du Lac, Wis.	*Myron Medin Jr.	1967, Nov.
Ft. Collins, Col.	*John Arnold	1977, Oct.
Ft. Lauderdale, Fla.	*Constance Hoffmann	1980, Oct.
Ft. Lee, N.J.	Nicholas Corbiscello, R	1984, Nov.
Ft. Smith, Ark.	*William Faught	1981, July
Ft. Wayne, Ind.	Win Moses, D	1983, Nov.
Ft. Worth, Tex.	*Robert Herchert	1978, Aug.
Fountain Valley, Cal.	*Howard Stephens	1981, Oct.
Fremont, Cal.	*Charles Kent McClain	1981, May
Fresno, Cal.	*Gerald E. Newfarmer	1978, Sept.
Fullerton, Cal.	*William C. Winter	1979, Oct.
Gadsden, Ala.	Steve Means, D.	1986, July
Gainesville, Fla.	*George E. Morgan	1982, Sept.
Galesburg, Ill.	*Lawrence Asaro	1979, Sept.
Galveston, Tex.	*Stephen Huffman	1980, Apr.
Gardena, Cal.	*John Sheehan	1979, Oct.
Garden Grove, Cal.	*Delbert L. Powers	1980, July
Garfield Hts., Oh.	Theodore Holtz, D.	1983, Nov.
Garland, Tex.	*Fred Greene	1979, July
Gary, Ind.	Richard G. Hatcher, D	1983, Nov.
Gastonia, N.C.	*Gary Hicks	1973, Dec.
Glendale, Ariz.	*John Maltbie	1982, July
Glendale, Cal.	*Hugh McKinley	1978, June
Grand Forks, N.D.	H.C. Wessman, R	1984, Apr.
Gr. Prairie, Tex.	*Ted C. Willis	1981, Aug.
Gr. Rapids, Mich.	*Joseph G. Zainea	1976, Oct.
Great Falls, Mont.	*G. Allen Johnson	1981, Jan.
Greeley, Col.	*Peter Morrell	1973, Dec.
Green Bay, Wis.	Samuel Halloin, N-P	1983, Apr.
Greensboro, N.C.	*T.Z. Osborne	1973, Feb.
Greenville, Miss.	William Burnley Jr., D	1983, Dec.
Greenville, S.C.	*John Dullea	1971, Oct.
Greenwich, Conn.	Rebecca Breed, R.	1983, Nov.
Groton, Conn.	Catherine Kolnaski, D	1983, May
Gulfport, Miss.	Jack Barnett, R	1985, June
Hackensack, N.J.	*Joseph J. Squillace	1964, Oct.
Hagerstown, Md.	Donald Frush, R	1984, Mar.
Hamden, Conn.	Peter F. Villano, D	1983, Nov.
Hamilton, Oh.	*Jack Kirsch	1975, Dec.
Hammond, Ind.	Edward J. Raskosky, D.	1983, Nov.
Hampton, Va.	*Thomas Miller	1981, Mar.
Harrisburg, Pa.	Stephen Reed, D	1985, Nov.
Hartford, Conn.	*W. Wilson Gaitor	1980, July
Harvey, Ill.	James A. Haines, R	1983, Apr.
Hattiesburg, Miss.	Bobby L. Chain, R	1985, May
Haverhill, Mass.	William H. Ryan, R	1983, Nov.
Hawthorne, Cal.	*R. Kenneth Jue	1977, Jan.
Hayward, Cal.	*Donald Blubaugh	1979, Nov.
Hialeah, Fla.	Raul Martinez, D.	1983, Nov.
High Point, N.C.	*Cyrus L. Books	1976, Aug.
Highland Pk., Ill.	Robert Buhai, N-P	1983, Apr.
Hoboken, N.J.	Steve Cappiello, D	1985, May
Hollywood, Fla.	*James Chandler	1976, Nov.
Holyoke, Mass.	Ernest Proulx, D	1983, Nov.
Honolulu, Ha.	Eileen Anderson, D	1984, Nov.
Houston, Tex.	Kathryn Whitmire, N-P	1983, Nov.
Huntington, W. Va.	*Jean Kipp Dean	1982, Aug.
Huntington Beach, Cal.	*Floyd Belsito	1976, June
Huntsville, Ala.	Joe W. Davis, N-P	1984, July
Hutchinson, Kan.	*George Pyle	1967, Sept.
Idaho Falls, Ida.	Thomas Campbell, N-P	1985, Nov.
Independence, Mo.	*Keith Wilson Jr.	1980, July
Indianapolis, Ind.	William Hudnut, R	1983, Nov.
Inglewood, Cal.	*Paul Eckles	1975, Nov.
Inkster, Mich.	*Wylie Williams Jr.	1979, Mar.
Iowa City, Ia.	*Neal Berlin	1975, Feb.
Irving, Tex.	*Jack Huffman	1974, Jan.
Irvington, N.J.	Anthony T. Blasi, D	1986, May
Jackson, Mich.	*S.W. McAllister Jr.	1974, Mar.
Jackson, Miss.	Dale Danks, D	1985, May
Jackson, Tenn.	Bob Conger, D.	1983, June
Jacksonville, Fla.	Jake Godbold, D.	1983, May
Jamestown, N.Y.	Steve Carlson, D	1983, Nov.
Janesville, Wis.	*Philip L. Deaton	1976, Mar.
Jefferson City, Mo.	George Hartsfield, D	1983, Apr.
Jersey City, N.J.	Gerald McCann, N-P	1985, May
Johnson City, Tenn.	*Charles Tyson	1979, Jan.
Johnstown, Pa.	Herbert Pfuhl Jr., R	1985, Nov.
Joliet, Ill.	*Kenneth Murray	1981, Oct.
Joplin, Mo.	*James P. Berzina	1977, Mar.
Kalamazoo, Mich.	*Robert C. Bobb	1976, Nov.
Kansas City, Kan.	John Reardon, D	1983, Apr.
Kansas City, Mo.	Richard Berkley, R	1983, Mar.
Kenosha, Wis.	John Bilotti, N-P	1984, Apr.
Kettering, Oh.	*Robert Walker	1982, Oct.
Key West, Fla.	Dennis Wardlow, D	1983, Nov.
Killeen, Tex.	*Robert M. Hopkins	1982, Apr.
Knoxville, Tenn.	Randell L. Tyree, D	1983, Oct.
Kokomo, Ind.	Stephen Daily, D	1983, Nov.
LaCrosse, Wis.	Patrick Zielke, N-P	1983, Apr.
La Habra, Cal.	*Lee Risner	1970, Nov.
La Mesa, Cal.	*Ronald Bradley	1980, May
La Mirada, Cal.	*Gary K. Sloan	1981, Apr.
Lafayette, Ind.	James Riehle, D	1983, Nov.
Lafayette, La.	Dud Lastrapes, R	1984, Apr.
Lake Charles, La.	Paul Savoie, D	1985, Apr.
Lakeland, Fla.	*Robert V. Youkey	1960, Jan.
Lakewood, Cal.	*Howard L. Chambers	1976, May
Lakewood, Col.	*Bill Kirchhoff	1980, Nov.
Lakewood, Oh.	Anthony Sinagra, R	1983, Nov.
Lancaster, Pa.	Arthur E. Morris, R	1985, Nov.
Lansing, Mich.	Terry John McKane, N-P	1985, Nov.
Largo, Fla.	*D. Russell Barr	1980, June
Las Cruces, N.M.	*J.W. Harrison	1980, Aug.
Las Vegas, Nev.	William Briare, N-P	1983, June
Lawrence, Kan.	*Buford M. Watson Jr.	1970, Jan.

City	Name	Term
Lawrence, Mass.	Lawrence LeFebre, D.	**1983, Nov.**
Lawton, Okla.	*Robert Metzinger.	**1977, Jan.**
Lewiston, Me.	*Lucien Gosselin	**1980, July**
Lexington, Ky.	Scotty Baesler, N-P	**1985, Nov.**
Lima, Oh.	Harry Moyer, N-P	**1985, Nov.**
Lincoln, Neb.	Helen Boosalis, D	**1983, May**
Little Rock, Ark.	*Mahlon Martin	**1980, July**
Livermore, Cal.	*Leland Horner	**1978, Oct.**
Lombard, Ill.	*Paul Sharon	**1979, Nov.**
Long Beach, Cal.	*John Dever	**1977, Jan.**
Long Beach, N.Y.	*William McKenney	**1978, Jan.**
Longview, Tex.	*C. Ray Jackson	**1980, Apr.**
Lorain, Oh.	William Parker, R	**1983, Nov.**
Los Angeles, Cal.	Thomas Bradley, N-P	**1985, June**
Louisville, Ky.	Harvey Sloane, D	**1985, Nov.**
Lowell, Mass.	*B. Joseph Tully	**1979, June**
L. Merion, Pa.	*Thomas B. Fulweiler	**1968, Jan.**
Lubbock, Tex.	*Larry Cunningham	**1976, Sept.**
Lynchburg, Va.	*E. Allen Culverhouse	**1979, June**
Lynn, Mass.	Antonio J. Marino, D.	**1983, Nov.**
Lynwood, Cal.	*Charles Gomez.	**1982, Feb.**
Macon, Ga.	George Israel, R.	**1983, Nov.**
Madison, Wis.	Joel Skornicka, N-P	**1983, Apr.**
Malden, Mass.	Thomas Fallon, D	**1983, Nov.**
Manchester, Conn.	Stephen Penny, D.	**1983, Nov.**
Manchester, N.H.	Emile Beaulieu, D	**1983, Nov.**
Manitowoc, Wis.	Anthony V. Dufek, D	**1983, Apr.**
Mansfield, Oh.	Edward Meehan, R	**1983, Nov.**
Marion, Ind.	Fred Weagley, R	**1983, Nov.**
Marion, Oh.	Ronald Malone, D.	**1983, Nov.**
McAllen, Tex.	Othal Brand, N-P	**1985, Apr.**
McKeesport, Pa.	Lou Washowich, D	**1983, Nov.**
Medford, Mass.	*Carroll P. Sheehan.	**1980, Aug.**
Melbourne, Fla.	*Samuel Halter	**1978, July**
Memphis, Tenn.	Wyeth Chandler, N-P	**1983, Nov.**
Mentor, Oh.	*Edward Podojil	**1977, Nov.**
Meriden, Conn.	*Dana Miller	**1980, Feb.**
Meridian, Miss.	*Joel W. Forrester	**1959, July**
Mesa, Ariz.	*C.K. Luster	**1979, June**
Mesquite, Tex.	*C.K. Duggins	**1976, Feb.**
Miami, Fla.	*Howard V. Gary	**1981, Apr.**
Miami Beach, Fla.	Norman Ciment, N-P	**1983, Nov.**
Middletown, Oh.	*Dale F. Helsel	**1970, Oct.**
Midland, Tex.	G. Thane Akins, R.	**1983, Apr.**
Midwest City, Okla.	*Irving P. Frank	**1978, Apr.**
Milford, Conn.	Alberta Jagoe, D	**1983, Nov.**
Milwaukee, Wis.	Henry W. Maier, D.	**1984, Apr.**
Minneapolis, Minn.	Donald Fraser, D	**1985, Nov.**
Minnetonka, Minn.	*James F. Miller	**1979, Jan.**
Minot, N.D.	*R.A. Schempp	**1977, Nov.**
Mobile, Ala.	Gary Greenough, N-P.	**1985, July**
Modesto, Cal.	*Garth Lipsky	**1974, Jan.**
Monroe, La.	Robert Powell, D	**1984, Apr.**
Montclair, N.J.	*Bertrand Kendall	**1980, Sept.**
Montebello, Cal.	*Joseph Goeden	**1980, May**
Monterey Park, Cal.	*Lloyd de Llamas	**1976, Sept.**
Montgomery, Ala.	Emory Folmar, R	**1983, Nov.**
Mt. Prospect, Ill.	*Terrance Burghard.	**1978, Nov.**
Mt. Vernon, N.Y.	Thomas E. Sharpe, D.	**1983, Nov.**
Mountain View, Cal.	*Bruce Liedstrand.	**1976, Aug.**
Muncie, Ind.	Alan K. Wilson, R	**1983, Nov.**
Muskegon, Mich.	*William Gleason	**1979, June**
Muskogee, Okla.	*C. Clay Harrell	**1979, June**
Napa, Cal.	*William Bopf	**1977, Dec.**
Naperville, Ill.	*George Smith.	**1978, June**
Nashua, N.H.	Maurice Arel, D	**1983, Nov.**
Nashville, Tenn.	Richard Fulton, D	**1983, Aug.**
National City, Cal.	*Tom McCabe	**1979, Feb.**
New Bedford, Mass.	John Markey, N-P	**1983, Nov.**
New Britain, Conn.	William J. McNamara, D	**1983, Nov.**
New Castle, Pa.	Angelo Sands, D	**1983, Nov.**
New Haven, Conn.	Biagio DiLieto, D.	**1983, Nov.**
New London, Conn.	*C.F. Driscoll.	**1969, May**
New Orleans, La.	Ernest Morial, D	**1986, Mar.**
New Rochelle, N.Y.	*C. Samuel Kissinger	**1975, Apr.**
New York, N.Y.	Edward Koch, D	**1985, Nov.**
Newark, N.J.	Kenneth Gibson, D	**1986, July**
Newark, Oh.	Mary M. Lusk, D.	**1983, Nov.**
Newport, R.I.	*John Connors Jr.	**1981, Mar.**
Newport Beach, Cal.	*Robert L. Wynn.	**1971, Aug.**
Newport News, Va.	*Robert T. Williams	**1981, Feb.**
Newton, Mass.	Theodore Mann, R	**1985, Nov.**
Niagara Falls, N.Y.	*William Sdao	**1980, Mar.**
Norfolk, Va.	*Julian Hirst	**1976, July**
Norman, Okla.	*James D. Crosby.	**1975, Oct.**
Norristown, Pa.	*John Plonski	**1979, Apr.**
No. Charleston, S.C.	John Bourne, R	**1986, May**
North Chicago, Ill.	Leo F. Kukla, D	**1985, Apr.**
North Las Vegas.	*Michael Dyal	**1982, May**
No. Little Rock, Ark.	Reed Thompson, N-P	**1984, Nov.**
Norwalk, Cal.	Robert E. White, D	**1983, Apr.**
Norwalk, Conn.	Thomas O'Connor, R	**1983, Nov.**
Norwich, Conn.	*Charles Whitty	**1973, June**
Novato, Cal.	*Phillip J. Brown	**1974, May**
Oak Lawn, Ill.	*Richard E. O'Neill	**1966, Nov.**
Oak Park, Ill.	*Jack Gruber	**1976, Oct.**
Oak Ridge, Tenn.	*M. Lyle Lacy 3d	**1978, July**
Oakland, Cal.	*Henry L. Gardner	**1981, June**
Oceanside, Cal.	*Robert Bourcier	**1978, June**
Odessa, Tex.	*John Harrison	**1982, Aug.**
Ogden, Ut.	*Cowles Mallory.	**1981, Mar.**
Oklahoma City, Okla.	*Scott Johnson	**1981, Dec.**
Omaha, Neb.	Michael Boyle, D	**1985 May**
Ontario, Cal.	R.E. Ellingwood, N-P	**1984, Apr.**
Orange, Cal.	*Joseph Baker.	**1978, Dec.**
Orange, N.J.	Joel Shain, D.	**1984, May**
Orlando, Fla.	Bill Frederick, N-P	**1984, Sept.**
Oshkosh, Wis.	*W. O. Frueh.	**1976, Aug.**
Overland Park, Kan.	*Donald Pipes	**1977, June**
Owensboro, Ky.	*William Sequino	**1981, Apr.**
Oxnard, Cal.	*Stephen Cook	**1979, Apr.**
Pacifica, Cal.	*David Finigan	**1981, May**
Palm Springs, Cal.	*Norman R. King	**1979, Dec.**
Palo Alto, Cal.	*William Zaner.	**1979, Sept.**
Parma, Oh.	John Petruska, D	**1983, Nov.**
Pasadena, Cal.	*Donald F. McIntyre.	**1973, June**
Pasadena, Tex.	Johnny Isbell, D	**1985, Apr.**
Passaic, N.J.	Robert Hare, N-P	**1985, May**
Paterson, N.J.	Frank X. Graves Jr., D	**1986, May**
Pawtucket, R.I.	Henry Kinch, D.	**1983, Nov.**
Peabody, Mass.	Peter Torigian, D	**1983, Nov.**
Pekin, Ill.	Willard Birkmeier, D.	**1983, Apr.**
Pensacola, Fla.	*Steve Garman	**1978, May**
Peoria, Ill.	*James B. Daken	**1979, Jan.**
Petersburg, Va.	*John P. Bond 3d	**1979, Oct.**
Perth Amboy, N.J.	George J. Otlowski, D	**1984, May**
Philadelphia, Pa.	William Green, D	**1983, Nov.**
Phoenix, Ariz.	*Marvin Andrews	**1976, Oct.**
Pico Rivera, Cal.	*Robert L. Williams	**1981, Aug.**
Pine Bluff, Ark.	D.W. Wallis, D	**1984, Nov.**
Pittsburgh, Pa.	Richard S. Caliguiri, D.	**1985, Nov.**
Pittsfield, Mass.	Charles Smith, D	**1983, Nov.**
Plainfield, N.J.	Everett C. Lattimore, D	**1985, Nov.**
Plano, Tex.	Jack Harvard, N-P	**1983, Apr.**
Pocatello, Ida.	*Charles W. Moss.	**1970, Sept.**
Pomona, Cal.	*Ora E. Lampman.	**1978, July**
Pompano Beach, Fla.	*Daniel Olmetti	**1982, Apr.**
Pontiac, Mich.	Wallace Holland, N-P	**1985, Nov.**
Port Arthur, Tex.	*George Dibrell	**1962, Oct.**
Port Huron, Mich.	*Gerald R. Bouchard	**1965, June**
Portage, Mich.	*Donald Ziemke	**1974, Aug.**
Portland, Me.	Linda Abromson, R	**1983, May**
Portland, Ore.	Frank Ivancie, N-P.	**1984, Nov.**
Portsmouth, Oh.	*Barry Feldman	**1977, Jan.**
Portsmouth, Va.	*George Hanbury	**1982, June**
Poughkeepsie, N.Y.	*William J. Theysohn	**1982, Mar.**
Prichard, Ala.	John H. Smith, D	**1984, Aug.**
Providence, R.I.	Vincent A. Cianci, N-P	**1986, Nov.**
Provo, Ut.	Jim Ferguson, N-P	**1985, Nov.**
Pueblo, Col.	*Fred E. Weisbroad	**1967, Feb.**
Quincy, Ill.	C. David Neussen, R	**1985, Apr.**
Quincy, Mass.	Francis X. McCauley, R.	**1983, Nov.**
Racine, Wis.	Stephen Olson, N-P.	**1983, Apr.**
Raleigh, N.C.	G. Smedes York, N-P	**1983, Oct.**
Rapid City, S.D.	Arthur La Croix, R.	**1983, May**
Reading, Pa.	Karen Miller, D.	**1983, Nov.**
Redding, Cal.	*William Brickwood	**1970, Sept.**
Redlands, Cal.	*Chris Christiansen	**1978, Nov.**
Redondo Beach, Cal.	*Timothy Casey	**1981, Oct.**
Redwood City, Cal.	*James M. Fales Jr.	**1971, Aug.**
Reno, Nev.	*Chris Cherches.	**1979, Nov.**
Revere, Mass.	George V. Colella, D	**1983, Nov.**
Richardson, Tex.	Raymond Noah, R.	**1983, Apr.**
Richfield, Minn.	*Karl Nollenberger	**1979, July**
Richmond, Cal.	*Joseph Salvato.	**1980, July**
Richmond, Ind.	Clifford Dickman, R	**1983, Nov.**
Richmond, Va.	*Manuel Deese	**1979, Jan.**
Riverside, Cal.	*Douglas Weiford	**1980, Mar.**
Roanoke, Va.	*H. Bern Ewert	**1978, Jan.**
Rochester, Minn.	*Steven Kvenvold	**1979, June**
Rochester, N.Y.	*Peter Korn	**1980, Mar.**
Rock Hill, S.C.	*Joe Lanford	**1979, July**
Rockford, Ill.	John McNamara, D	**1985, Apr.**
Rockville, Md.	John Freeland, N-P	**1984, Apr.**
Rome, N.Y.	Carl Eilenberg, R	**1983, Nov.**
Rosemead, Cal.	*Frank Tripepi	**1975, Jan.**

City	Name	Term
Roseville, Mich.	*B. J. Nardelli	**1975, Nov.**
Roseville, Minn.	*James Andre	**1974, May**
Roswell, N.M.	*James Whitford Jr.	**1982, Aug.**
Royal Oak, Mich.	*William Baldridge.	**1975, Sept.**
Sacramento, Cal.	*Walter Slipe.	**1976, Mar.**
Saginaw, Mich.	*Thomas Dalton	**1978, Nov.**
St. Clair Shores, Mich.	*Roy Stype	**1982, May**
St. Cloud, Minn.	Robert Huston, N-P	**1984, Mar.**
St. Joseph, Mo.	*Anton Harwig	**1982, Sept.**
St. Louis, Mo.	Vincent Schoemehl, D	**1985, Apr.**
St. Louis Park, Minn.	*James Brimeyer	**1980, Aug.**
St. Paul, Minn.	George Latimer, D	**1983, Nov.**
St. Petersburg, Fla.	*Alan Harvey	**1980, Mar.**
Salem, Mass.	Jean Levesque, D.	**1983, Nov.**
Salem, Ore.	*Ralph Hanley	**1978, June**
Salina, Kan.	*Rufus L. Nye	**1979, May**
Salinas, Cal.	*Robert Christofferson	**1972, Dec.**
Salt Lake City, Ut.	Ted Wilson, D	**1983, Nov.**
San Angelo, Tex.	*Stephen Brown	**1982, Jan.**
San Antonio, Tex.	*Thomas Huebner.	**1977, Jan.**
San Bernardino, Cal.	W. R. Holcomb, N-P.	**1985, Mar.**
San Bruno, Cal.	*Gerald Minford	**1971, Dec.**
San Diego, Cal.	*Ray Blair Jr.	**1978, May**
San Francisco, Cal.	Dianne Feinstein, D	**1983, Nov.**
San Jose, Cal.	*Francis T. Fox	**1980, May**
San Leandro, Cal.	*Lee Riordan.	**1976, Jan.**
San Mateo, Cal.	*Richard Delong.	**1976, Sept.**
San Rafael, Cal.	Lawrence Mulryan, D	**1983, Nov.**
Sandusky, Oh.	*Frank Link.	**1972, Jan.**
Sandy, Ut.	Lawrence P. Smith, R.	**1986, Nov.**
Santa Ana, Cal.	*A. J. Wilson	**1980, July**
Santa Barbara, Cal.	*Richard Thomas	**1977, Jan.**
Santa Clara, Cal.	*Donald Von Raesfeld	**1962, Feb.**
Santa Cruz, Cal.	*Richard Wilson	**1981, June**
Santa Fe, N.M.	*Jerry Manzagol.	**1982, June**
Santa Maria, Cal.	*Robert Grogan	**1963, Jan.**
Santa Monica, Cal.	*vacant	
Santa Rosa, Cal.	*Kenneth Blackman.	**1970, July**
Sarasota, Fla.	*Kenneth Thompson	**1950, Feb.**
Savannah, Ga.	*Arthur A. Mendonsa	**1971, Sept.**
Schenectady, N.Y.	Frank J. Duci, R	**1983, Nov.**
Scottsdale, Ariz.	*Roy Pederson	**1980, Mar.**
Scranton, Pa.	James McNulty, D.	**1985, Nov.**
Seattle, Wash.	Charles Royer, N-P	**1985, Nov.**
Shaker Heights, Oh.	Walter C. Kelley, N-P	**1983, Nov.**
Sheboygan, Wis.	Richard Suscha, N-P	**1985, Apr.**
Shreveport, La.	John Hussey, N-P.	**1986, Sept.**
Simi Valley, Cal.	*Lin Koester	**1979, June**
Sioux City, Ia.	*J.R. Castner	**1982, Sept.**
Sioux Falls, S.D.	Rick Knobe, R	**1984, Apr.**
Skokie, Ill.	*Robert Eppley	**1979, Jan.**
Somerville, Mass.	Eugene Brune, D	**1983, Nov.**
South Bend, Ind.	Roger Parent, D	**1983, Nov.**
So. Gate, Cal.	*John Gottes, Act.	**1981, Aug.**
So. S.F., Cal.	*C. W. Birkelo	**1976, Dec.**
Southfield, Mich.	*Del Borgsdorf.	**1980, June**
Spartanburg, S.C.	*W. H. Carstarphen	**1975, Mar.**
Spokane, Wash.	*Terry Novak	**1978, July**
Springfield, Ill.	J. Michael Houston, N-P	**1983, Apr.**
Springfield, Mass	Theodore Dimauro, D	**1983, Nov.**
Springfield, Mo.	*Don G. Busch.	**1971, Oct.**
Springfield, Oh.	*Thomas M. Bay	**1978, Sept.**
Springfield, Ore.	John Lively, D	**1984, Nov.**
Stamford, Conn.	Louis A. Clapes, R	**1983, Nov.**
Sterling Hts., Mich.	*Barry Feldman	**1982, Feb.**
Stillwater, Okla.	*Lawrence Gish	**1966, Aug.**
Stockton, Cal.	*Ray Cezar	**1980, Dec.**
Stratford, Conn.	*Gloria Minie	**1980, Mar.**
Suffolk, Va.	*John Rowe Jr.	**1980, Mar.**
Sunnyvale, Cal.	*Thomas Lewcock	**1980, Oct.**
Syracuse, N.Y.	Lee Alexander, D	**1985, Nov.**
Tacoma, Wash.	*Erling O. Mork	**1975, June**
Tallahassee, Fla.	*Daniel A. Kleman.	**1974, Aug.**
Tampa, Fla.	Bob Martinez, N-P.	**1983, Mar.**
Taylor, Mich.	Cameron Priebe, D	**1983, Nov.**
Teaneck, N.J.	*Werner H. Schmid	**1959, Mar.**
Tempe, Ariz.	Harry E. Mitchell, D	**1984, Apr.**
Temple, Tex.	*Barney Knight	**1978, Dec.**
Terre Haute, Ind.	P. Pete Chalos, D	**1983, Nov.**
Thornton, Col.	*Gerald E. Hagman	**1979, July**
Thousand Oaks, Cal.	*Grant Brimhall	**1978, Jan.**
Titusville, Fla.	*Norman Hickey.	**1974, June**
Toledo, Oh.	*David A. Boston	**1981, Sept.**
Topeka, Kan.	William McCormick, R	**1983, Apr.**
Torrance, Cal.	*Edward J. Ferraro	**1964, Mar.**
Trenton, N.J.	Arthur Holland, D	**1986, May**
Troy, Mich.	*Frank Gerstenecker	**1970, Feb.**
Troy, N.Y.	*John P. Buckley	**1972, June**

City	Name	Term
Tucson, Ariz.	*Joel Valdez	**1974, May**
Tulsa, Okla.	James M. Inhofe, R	**1984, Apr.**
Tyler, Tex.	*Terry Childers	**1982, Sept.**
Union City, N.J.	William Musto, D.	**1986, May**
Univ. City, Mo.	*Frank Ollendorff	**1980, Mar.**
Upland, Cal.	*S. Lee Travers	**1974, June**
Upper Arlington, Oh.	*H. W. Hyrne	**1968, May**
Urbana, Ill.	Jeffrey Markland, R	**1985, Apr.**
Utica, N.Y.	Stephen Pawlinga, D	**1983, Nov.**
Vallejo, Cal.	*Ted McDonell.	**1979, Jan.**
Vancouver, Wash.	*Paul Grattet.	**1980, June**
Victoria, Tex.	*James J. Miller	**1980, June**
Vineland, N.J.	Patrick R. Fiorilli, N-P	**1984, May**
Virginia Beach, Va.	*Thomas Muelhenbeck	**1982, June**
Waco, Tex.	*David F. Smith Jr.	**1971, Sept.**
Walnut Creek, Cal.	*Thomas Dunne	**1972, May**
Waltham, Mass.	Arthur J. Clark, N-P	**1983, Nov.**
Warren, Mich.	James Randlett, N-P	**1983, Nov.**
Warren, Oh.	Daniel Sferra, D	**1983, Nov.**
Warwick, R.I.	Joseph W. Walsh, D	**1984, Nov.**
Wash, D.C.	Marion Barry, D	**1986, Nov.**
Waterbury, Conn.	Edward Bergin, D	**1983, Nov.**
Waterloo, Ia.	Leo Rooff, R	**1983, Nov.**
Wausau, Wis.	John Kannenberg, N-P	**1984, Apr.**
Wauwatosa, Wis.	James A. Benz, N-P.	**1984, Apr.**
W. Allis, Wis.	Jack Barlich, N-P	**1984, Feb.**
W. Covina, Cal.	*Herman Fast	**1976, Aug.**
W. Hartford, Conn.	*William Brady.	**1977, Sept.**
W. Haven, Conn.	Lawrence Minichino, R	**1983, Nov.**
W. New York, N.J.	Anthony DeFino, D	**1983, May**
W. Palm Beach, Fla.	*Richard Simmons	**1969, Nov.**
Westland, Mich.	Charles Pickering Jr., N-P	**1985, Nov.**
Wheaton, Ill.	*Donald Rose	**1980, Nov.**
Wheeling, W. Va.	*F. Wayne Barte.	**1979, Nov.**
White Plains, N.Y.	Alfred Del Vecchio, R	**1985, Nov.**
Whittier, Cal.	*Tom Mauk	**1980, Sept.**
Wichita, Kan.	*E. H. Denton	**1976, July**
Wichita Falls, Tex.	*Stuart A. Bach	**1980, Oct.**
Wilkes-Barre, Pa.	Thomas McLaughlin, D	**1983, Nov.**
Williamsport, Pa.	Stephen Lucasi, R.	**1983, Nov.**
Wilmington, Del.	William T. McLaughlin, D	**1984, Nov.**
Wilmington, N.C.	*Robert Cobb	**1977, Dec.**
Winston-Salem, N.C.	*Bryce A. Stuart	**1980, Jan.**
Woonsocket, R.I.	Gaston Ayotte Jr., D	**1983, Nov.**
Worcester, Mass.	*Francis J. McGrath.	**1951, Apr.**
Wyandotte, Mich.	James Wagner, N-P.	**1983, Apr.**
Wyoming, Mich.	*James Sheeran	**1976, Nov.**
Yakima, Wash.	*Richard Zais Jr.	**1979, Jan.**
Yonkers, N.Y.	*Sal Preziosa	**1982, Mar.**
York, Pa.	William Althaus, R.	**1985, Nov.**
Youngstown, Oh.	George Vukovich, D.	**1985, Nov.**
Zanesville, Oh.	Cameron R. Agin, D.	**1983, Nov.**

Canadian Cities

(as of Nov. 3, 1982)

Calgary, Alta.	Ralph Klein.	**1983, Nov.**
Charlottetown, P.E.I.	Frank Moran	**1982, Nov.**
Edmonton, Alta.	Cec Purves.	**1983, Oct.**
Fredericton, N.B.	Elbridge Wilkins	**1983, May**
Guelph, Ont.	Norman Jary.	**1982, Nov.**
Halifax, N.S.	Ronald Wallace	**1982, Oct.**
Hamilton, Ont.	Bill Powell	**1982, Nov.**
Hull, Que.	Michel Legere	**1982, Nov.**
Kingston, Ont.	John Gerretsen	**1982, Nov.**
Kitchener, Ont.	Morley Rosenberg	**1982, Nov.**
London, Ont.	Al Gleeson	**1982, Nov.**
Moncton, N.B.	Dennis Cochrane	**1983, May**
Montreal, Que.	Jean Drapeau	**1982, Nov.**
North York, Ont.	Mel Lastman	**1982, Nov.**
Oshawa, Ont.	Allan Pilkey.	**1982, Nov.**
Ottawa, Ont.	Mrs. Marion Dewar	**1982, Nov.**
Peterborough, Ont.	Bob Barker.	**1982, Nov.**
Quebec, Que.	Jean Pelletier	**1985, Nov.**
Regina, Sask.	Larry Schneider	**1982, Oct.**
Saint John, N.B.	Bob Lockhart	**1983, May**
St. John's, Nfld.	John Murphy.	**1985, Dec.**
Saskatoon, Sask.	Clifford Wright	**1982, Oct.**
Sault Ste. Marie	Don MacGregor	**1982, Nov.**
Sherbrooke, Que.	Jacques O'Bready	**1982, Nov.**
Sudbury, Ont.	Jim Gordon.	**1982, Nov.**
Toronto, Ont.	Art Eggleton	**1982, Nov.**
Vancouver, B.C.	Mike Harcourt	**1982, Nov.**
Victoria, B.C.	Peter Pollen	**1983, Nov.**
Waterloo, Ont.	Mrs. Marjorie Carroll	**1982, Nov.**
Windsor, Ont.	Bert Weeks	**1982, Nov.**
Winnipeg, Man.	Bill Norrie.	**1983, Oct.**

Off-Beat News Stories of 1982

That penned-in feeling — Betty Tennis, city clerk, resigned in the wake of a pen scandal that rocked the community of Ozark, Mo. It seems that Mrs. Tennis, when offered "a good deal on some pens," ordered six gross. Unfortunately, the pens kept coming well beyond the original order of six gross, and Mrs. Tennis, thinking she had no alternative, kept paying. By the time the city council was apprized of the error, 12,528 pens, valued at $7,000, had been delivered. While the city planned to return 24 gross of pens not yet paid for, the problem of what to do with the remaining pens was left unsolved. "We're going to do something," insisted city attorney Jim Eiffert. "We couldn't use this many pens in 20 years."

And make sure seats are in the upright position — Kelly Vail of Glastonbury, Conn., reported some unusual preflight instructions given to passengers on a recent flight to Milwaukee: "Smoking is permitted in aisles 17-22 only. No smoking is allowed in the first 16 aisles or in the lavatories. Anyone caught smoking in the lavatories or writing on the walls will be asked to leave."

The jury found a crack in his case — In a Fort Lauderdale, Fla., courtroom, Robert Infante was on trial for kicking a dent in his neighbor's car. His lawyer, Steve Jerome, evidently thinking things weren't going well for his client, decided their case needed some extra flair. He decided to sing his closing argument as an operatic aria. Jerome, his face flushed as he strained for notes, sang, "Innocent, or is this man guiiiiilty? He is not guiiiiilty," to the melody of "Vesti la giubba" from the opera *I Pagliacci*. The jury was at first stunned, then began to giggle, and returned a verdict of guilty. Although Infante wouldn't say that the singing had hurt his case, he did admit, "I don't think it helped, and I should have stuck by my decision not to let him do it."

The price one pays for fame — Included among the pension applications being investigated by Boston's chief lawyer Harold Carroll was a request from Barry Hynes, 47 years old and a city employee since 1963. Hynes was asking for a pension due to the poor health that both he and his doctor believed to be the result of job stress — particularly since staff cutbacks had increased his workload. Among his afflictions, Hynes claimed to suffer from "nightmares relating to City Council meetings gone out of control."

Hynes' plight seemed minor compared to that of another Boston official, Richard Sinnott. Sinnott's official function was the granting of entertainment licenses, a job which required his attendance at rock concerts by Rick James and The Who. As a result, he claimed he had been "reduced to a shell of myself, barely able to function."

She hardly played cricket — "I don't blame Mildred for what she has done," acknowledged Michael Rowley. "I told her from the beginning cricket would always come first." Rowley was referring to his wife's divorce, awarded to her on the grounds that her husband's obsession with cricket constituted unreasonable behavior — he was, in Mildred's words, "cricket mad." Rowley was unable to be in court during the proceedings; he was off keeping score for his favorite cricket team, the Worcestershire Marauders.

This ain't the Bronx, is it? — Motormen on the New York City subway system are used to seeing just about everything on the tracks, including pumpkins, people, tires, washing machines, basketballs and rabbits. But even the subway operators were stunned when a trainman on the Canarsie line in Brooklyn announced "I think there is a car out there." Unbelievably, a man from the neighboring borough of Queens had, in fact, managed to perch his car on the street-level tracks. To get there, he had driven his car through a chain-like fence, bounced through a gulley, and driven through yet another fence. At least he knew he was lost. His first words to the transit police on the scene were, "Hi. I'm from Rosedale. I don't know my way around here."

Scramble for a presidential breakfast — It's not easy to find freshly squeezed orange juice in Indianapolis, Ind., in February. But when the advance team for the president of the United States passes the word that the president likes fresh orange juice, and you're a legislative aide to Indiana House Speaker J. Robert Dailey, you do what has to be done. Thus John Coldren found himself wandering the streets in search of an ample supply of morning refreshment. His search finally took him to the Hyatt-Regency Hotel where he was able to get two quarts at the per-glass price. Total cost: $12.60, paid out of Coldren's own pocket. "... for security reasons, I couldn't tell them who it was for," Coldren explained. Virtue is not always rewarded, however. At the morning meeting of the State's General Assembly, Mr. Reagan asked for coffee — but no juice.

Is that clear? — The top booby prize of the Plain English Awards in London, England went to the following letter, written by the director of British Rail's catering division to a customer who had complained about the lack of a dining car on his train: "Whilst I can readily appreciate your frustration at the loss of breakfast, since in the circumstances you describe it is unfortunately true that in many cases where a catering vehicle becomes defective and both stores and equipment need to be transferred into a replacement car, this can only be done during the train's journey.

"It is not of course possible to make the transfer whilst vehicles are in the sidings and the intensity of coach workings is such that the train sets are not available to be put into a platform at other times to enable the transfer to be carried."

For its contribution, British Rail was awarded two pounds of Lancaster tripe and a plaque commemorating the railroad's contribution to "absolute tripe — official gibberish which no one should be expected to understand."

Our horses leave a lot to be desired — Thus read the headline of an ad in the May 13, 1982 edition of *The New York Times*, offering (can you guess?) "250,000 cubic yards of 'Thoroughbred manure." The ad noted that "These Thoroughbred horses are some of the best-fed animals in the world, and if you're a fertilizer user, you know what that means ... Whether you're a farmer, mushroom grower, fertilizer packager, or a quick-witted entrepreneur, call us, and we'll work out a deal you'll like."

All in the line of duty — As far as Marlene Willoughby was concerned, serving on a jury was a "bummer," but she acknowledged that every patriotic American must answer when duty calls. Marlene was a reigning queen of pornographic movies who, according to her own estimate, had appeared in over 100 sex movies. She also claimed to have worked as the "sexual advisor" to the movie "Raging Bull." As one might expect, Marlene's appearance in court caused quite a stir: "They all recognized me," she noted, referring to many of the clerks and officers at Manhattan Criminal Court. But what was really distracting was a fellow juror who kept pointing and whispering, "She's the porno star." Marlene solved the problem by telling him to "cool it." "There are a lot of perverts in this courthouse," she noted.

They shoot subterranean saurians, don't they? — From Sweden to Syracuse the letters kept coming, all asking the same question — Was it true that alligators resided in the sewer system of New York? A letter from Celoron, N.Y. was typical: "I disagree with a co-worker whom (sic) insists that an alligator which had lived in a sewer system over a long period of time does not change color. I said I believe the pigmentation of the alligator would become much lighter and in some cases turn almost white." To this and all letters, John T. Flaherty, chief of design in the New York City Bureau of Sewers (who was also charged with the occasional details of maintaining a 6,500-mile sewer system), responded, "No Virginia, there are no alligators in the New York City sewer system." Mr. Flaherty explained that there were no alligators because there was not enough space and there were floods that would drown even a full-sized crocodile. Also the food supply was insufficient — "the vast majority of it has been, to put it as delicately as possible, predigested," said Flaherty.

CONSUMER SURVIVAL KIT

Your Federal Income Tax: Facts on Filing

Source: Internal Revenue Service, U.S. Treasury Department.

Who Must File

Every individual under 65 years of age who resided in the United States and had a gross income of $3,300 or more during the year must file a federal income tax return. Anyone 65 or older on the last day of the tax year is not required to file a return unless he had gross income of $4,300 or more during the year. A married couple, both 65 or older, need not file unless their gross income is $7,400 or more.

A taxpayer with gross income of less than $3,300 (or less than $4,300 if 65 or older) should file a return to claim the refund of any taxes withheld, even if he is listed as a dependent by another taxpayer.

If you are married, you must file a tax return if your combined gross income was $5,400 or more, provided you are eligible to file a joint return and are living together at the close of the tax year. The requirement is $6,400 if one spouse is 65 or older, and $7,400 if both of you are 65 or older. If you are married and your spouse files a separate return, or you did not share the same household at the end of the year, you must file a tax return if your gross income was $1,000 or more.

Forms to Use

A taxpayer may, at his election, use form 1040, form 1040A or form 1040EZ. However, those taxpayers who choose to itemize deductions must use the longer form 1040.

Deductions

A taxpayer may either itemize deductions or choose the zero bracket amount. For single taxpayers the zero bracket amount is $2,300. For married taxpayers filing a joint return it is $3,400. For married taxpayers filing separate returns the deduction is $1,700 each.

New Tax Changes for 1982 and After

The changes most likely to affect millions of tax payers include:

- **Tax Rate Cuts Will Continue.** Tax rates fell by about another 10 percent on July 1, 1982, and will drop another 10 percent on July 1, 1983, adding to a total of approximately 23 percent.
- **Top Tax Rate Drops.** The maximum rate for high-bracket individuals (formerly as much as 70 percent on unearned income such as interest, dividends, rent, and royalties) falls to 50 percent.
- **"Marriage Penalty" Decreases.** If both spouses work outside the home, they are allowed a deduction from their gross income of 5 percent of whichever salary is lower, with the maximum deduction being $1,500. Next year, the percentage will rise to 10 and the maximum to $3,000.
- **Higher Tax Credits for Child Care.**
- **Individual Retirement Accounts (IRAs) Will Broaden.** Even those persons covered by company pension plans can now open IRAs. The tax-free investment in an IRA has increased from $1,500 to $2,000. Self-employed people are allowed to shelter as much as $15,000 (up from $7,500) of their income in a Keogh Retirement Plan.
- **Interest Exclusion to Drop.** The $200 exclusion for the single tax payer ($400 for married couples) for tax-free interest and dividends has been cut in half and applys only to dividends.
- **Charitable Contributions Deductible on All Forms.** Even the taxpayer who does not itemize may write off 25 percent of the first $100 donated to charitable organizations. By 1986, non-itemizers will be able to deduct all charitable contributions.

Dates for Filing Returns

For individuals using the calendar year, Apr. 15 is final date (unless it falls on a Saturday, Sunday, or a legal holiday) for filing income tax returns and for payment of any tax due, and the first quarterly installment of the estimated tax. Other installments of estimated tax to be paid June 15, Sept. 15, and Jan. 15.

Apr. 15 is final date for filing declaration of estimated tax. Amended declarations may be filed June 15, Sept. 15, and Jan. 15.

Instead of paying the 4th installment a final income return may be filed by Jan. 31. Farmers may file a final return by Mar. 1 to satisfy estimated tax requirements.

Joint Return

A husband and wife may make a return jointly, even if one has no income personally.

One provision stipulates that if one spouse dies, the survivor may compute his tax using joint return rates for the first two taxable years following, provided he or she was also entitled to file a joint return the year of the death, and furnishes over half the cost of maintaining in his household a home for a dependent child or stepchild. If the taxpayer remarries before the end of the taxable year these privileges are lost but he is permitted to file a joint return with his new spouse.

Estimated Tax

If total tax exceeds withheld tax by at least $200, declarations of estimated tax are required from (1) single individuals, heads of a household or surviving spouses, or a married person entitled to file a joint return whose spouse does not receive wages, who expects a gross income over $20,000; (2) married individuals with over $10,000 where both spouses receive wages; (3) married individuals with over $5,000 not entitled to file a joint return; and (4) individuals whose gross income can reasonably be expected to include more than $500 from sources other than wages subject to withholdings.

Exemptions

Personal exemption is $1,000.

Every individual has an exemption of $1,000, to be deducted from gross income. A husband and a wife are each entitled to a $1,000 exemption. A taxpayer 65 or over on the last day of the year gets another exemption of $1,000. A person blind on the last day of the year gets another exemption of $1,000.

Exemption for dependents, over one-half of whose total support comes from the taxpayer and for whom the other dependency tests have been met, is $1,000. This applies to a child, stepchild, or adopted child as well as certain other relatives with less than $1,000 gross income; also to a child, stepchild, or adopted child of the taxpayer who is under 19 at the end of the year or was a full-time student during 5 months of the year even if he makes $1,000 or more. A dependent can be a non-relative if a member of the taxpayer's household and living there all year.

Taxpayer gets the exemption for his child who is a student regardless of the student's age or earnings, provided the taxpayer provides over half of the student's total support. If the student gets a scholarship, this is not counted as support.

Child and Disabled Dependent Care

To qualify, a taxpayer must be employed and provide over one-half the cost of maintaining a household for a dependent child under 15, a disabled dependent of any age, or a disabled spouse.

Taxpayers may be allowed a credit based on a percentage of employment related expenses.

For further information consult your local IRS office or the instructional material attached to your return form.

Life Insurance

Life insurance paid to survivors is not taxed as income. Interest on life insurance left with the insurance company and paid to survivors at intervals is taxable when available. Surviving spouse has an exclusion of the prorata amount of principal payable at death plus up to $1,000 per year of interest earned when life insurance proceeds are payable in installments.

Regular payments under the Railroad Retirement Act, and those received as social security, are exempt.

Dividends

The first $100 in dividends can be excluded from income. If husband and wife both receive $100 on their joint return they can exclude $200. An individual is also entitled to exclude up to $750 ($1,500 on a joint return) for certain dividends received from qualifying public utilities.

The exclusion does not apply to dividends from tax-exempt corporations, mutual savings banks, building and loan associations, and several others.

Dividends paid in stock or in stock rights are generally exempt from tax, except when paid in place of preferred stock dividends of the current or preceding year, or when the stockholder has an option to take stock or property or when the stock distribution is disproportionate.

Deductible Medical Expenses

Expenses for medical care, not compensated for by insurance or other payment for taxpayer, spouse, and dependents, in excess of 3% of adjusted gross income are deductible. There is no limit to the maximum amount of medical expenses that can be deducted.

Medical care includes diagnosis, treatment and prevention of disease or for the purpose of affecting any structure or function of the body, and amounts paid for insurance to reimburse for hospitalization, surgical fees and other medical expenses.

Only medicine and drugs in excess of 1% of adjusted gross income may be deducted.

One-half the cost of medical care insurance premiums up to $150 can be deducted without regard to the 3% limitation. The other half plus any excess over $150 is included with other medical expenses subject to the 3% limit.

Medical expenses for a decedent paid by his estate within one year after his death may be treated as expenses of the decedent taxpayer.

Medical and hospital benefits provided by the employer may be exempt from individual income tax.

Disability income payments are excludable only if the payee is totally and permanently disabled and under age 65 at the end of the tax year. Up to $5,200 can be excluded but must be reduced by income above certain limits.

Deductions for Contributions

Deductions up to 50% of taxpayers' adjusted gross income may be taken for contribution to most publicly supported charitable organizations, including churches or associations of churches, tax-exempt educational institutions, tax-exempt hospitals, and medical research organizations associated with a hospital. The deduction is generally limited to 20% for such organizations as private nonoperating foundations, and certain organizations that do not qualify for the 50% limitation.

Taxpayers also are permitted to carry over for five years certain contributions, generally to publicly supported organizations, which exceed the 50% allowable deduction the year the contribution was made.

Also permissible is the deduction as a charitable contribution of unreimbursed amounts up to $50 a school month spent to maintain an elementary or high school student, other than a dependent or relative, in taxpayer's home. There must be a written agreement between you and a qualified organization.

For changes applying to 1982 income tax and thereafter see box this page and page 55.

Don't Forget These Changes from Last Year

The following tax code provisions that affected 1981 returns are still in effect.:

- **Sale of a Home.** Two new provisions, both of which apply to the sale of a principal residence only, may shield some of the gains made on the sale from taxes.

1. For those 55 or older, the tax exclusion on profit on selling a home rises from $100,000 to $125,000 on all sales made after July 20, 1981.
2. The period during which payment of income tax on the profit from selling a home can be delayed if the profit is reinvested in another principal residence increases from 18 months to 2 years.

- **Tax Incentives for Savings.** The taxpayer has the option of investing in the new All Savers Certificates only until Dec. 31, 1982. Up to $1,000 (single taxpayers) or $2,000 (married, filing jointly) in interest from these certificates is tax-exempt.
- **Capital Gains Tax Reduced.** The tax rate on long-term capital gains (profits from the sale of an asset such as stocks or real estate held for more than a year) decreases from a maximum of 28 percent to no more than 20 percent on sales and exchanges that took place after June 9, 1981.
- **Windfall Profit Tax Credit.** For those who own a royalty in oil production, the credit against the Crude Oil Windfall Profit Tax in 1981 rose from $1,000 to $2,500.
- **Tougher Penalties for Late Taxes.** If you face the possibility of filing late, closely examine the new penalties—the IRA can, as of Jan. 1, 1982 charge the full prime lending rate (the rate banks often charge their best customers) on taxes paid late.

Deductions for Interest Paid

Interest paid by the taxpayer is deductible.

To deduct interest on a debt, you must be legally liable for that debt. No deduction will be allowed for payments you make for another person if you were not legally liable to make them.

Prizes and Awards

All prizes and awards must be reported in gross income, except when received without action by the recipient. To be exempt, awards must be received primarily in recognition of religious, charitable, scientific, educational, artistic, literary, or civic achievement. (Nobel and Pulitzer prizes exempt.)

Deductions for Employees

An employee may use the zero bracket amount and deduct as well the following if in connection with his employment: transportation, except commuting; automobile expense, including gas, oil, and depreciation; however, meals and lodging are deductible as traveling expense only if the employee is away from home overnight.

An outside salesman—a salesman who works fulltime outside the office, using the latter only for incidentals—may use the zero bracket amount and deduct all his business expenses.

An employee who is reimbursed and is required to account to his employer for his business expenses will not be required to report either the reimbursement or the expenses on his tax return. Any allowance to the employee in excess of his expenses must be included in gross income. If he claims a deduction for an excess of expenses over reimbursement he will have to report the reimbursement and claim actual expenses.

An employee who is not required to account to his employer must report on his return the total amounts of reimbursements and expenses for travel, transportation, entertainment, etc., that he incurs under a reimbursement arrangement with his employer.

The expense of moving to a new place of employment may be deducted under certain circumstances regardless of whether the taxpayer is a new or continuing employee, or whether he pays his own expenses or is reimbursed by his employer. Reimbursement must be reported as income.

Tax Credit for the Elderly

Subject to certain rules or exclusions, taxpayers 65 or older may claim a credit which varies according to filing status. Taxpayers should read IRS instructions carefully for full details. You may also be eligible for a credit if you are under age 65 and receive a taxable pension from a public retirement system.

The credit is limited to 15% of $2,500 for single taxpayers; 15% of $2,500 for married taxpayers filing a joint return when only one taxpayer is 65 or older; 15% of $3,750 for married taxpayers both 65 or older filing a joint return; and 15% of $1,875 for a married taxpayer filing a separate return.

Net Capital Losses

An individual taxpayer may deduct capital losses up to $3,000 against his ordinary income. However, it takes $2 of net long-term capital loss to get $1 of offset against other income. He may carry the rest over to subsequent years at the same rate, no legal limit on the number of years.

Income Averaging

Individuals with large fluctuations in their annual income may be able to take advantage of averaging provisions available to taxpayers whose income for a particular year exceeds 120% of their average income for the prior 4 years, if the excess is more than $3,000.

Individual Income Tax Returns for 1980

(Money Amounts are in Thousands of Dollars)

Size of adjusted gross income	All returns: Number of returns	Percent of total	Adjusted gross income less deficit: Amount	Average	Returns with itemized deductions: Number	Total deductions
All returns, total	93,616,278	100.0	1,606,265,685	17.158	28,791,240	214,784,413
No adjusted gross income	626,582	0.7	-10,630,438	-16.966	—	—
$1 under $1,000	3,013,967	3.2	1,754,919	582	16,271	66,653
$1,000 under $2,000	4,268,874	4.6	6,375,661	1.494	99,108	122,549
$2,000 under $3,000	4,381,185	4.7	10,889,840	2.486	83,763	205,285
$3,000 under $4,000	3,925,807	4.2	13,726,981	3.497	118,945	370,002
$4,000 under $5,000	3,735,373	4.0	16,790,231	4.495	131,605	462,656
$5,000 under $6,000	3,841,183	4.1	21,090,752	5.491	163,435	827,076
$6,000 under $7,000	3,783,388	4.0	24,587,805	6.499	238,043	1,184,510
$7,000 under $8,000	3,787,354	4.0	28,408,098	7.501	274,996	1,223,019
$8,000 under $9,000	3,540,525	3.8	30,122,406	8.508	305,151	1,616,109
$9,000 under $10,000	3,417,185	3.7	32,447,593	9.495	335,386	1,682,545
$10,000 under $11,000	3,204,017	3.4	33,604,648	10.488	450,997	2,178,635
$11,000 under $12,000	2,927,049	3.1	33,646,764	11.495	458,390	2,142,622
$12,000 under $13,000	2,892,089	3.1	36,134,580	12.494	474,703	2,446,392
$13,000 under $14,000	2,734,286	2.9	36,901,558	13.496	582,633	2,831,862
$14,000 under $15,000	2,521,221	2.7	36,517,995	14.484	585,576	3,077,230
$15,000 under $20,000	11,083,032	11.8	193,185,494	17.431	3,586,976	18,943,695
$20,000 under $25,000	9,127,402	9.7	204,801,408	22.438	4,631,122	26,994,568
$25,000 under $30,000	6,779,115	7.2	185,637,441	27.384	4,406,243	28,088,020
$30,000 under $40,000	7,911,046	8.5	271,671,598	34.341	6,227,012	45,703,175
$40,000 under $50,000	3,034,287	3.2	134,048,970	44.178	2,723,716	24,517,020
$50,000 under $75,000	2,009,790	2.1	118,613,662	59.018	1,868,245	22,140,864
$75,000 under $100,000	524,031	0.6	44,937,942	85.754	499,492	8,622,629
$100,000 under $200,000	434,041	0.5	57,232,819	131.860	417,883	10,578,647
$200,000 under $500,000	97,232	0.1	27,338,930	281.172	95,495	5,169,415
$500,000 under $1,000,000	12,105	(1)	8,059,284	665.781	11,983	1,677,220
$1,000,000 or more	4,112	(1)	8,368,749	2,278.392	4,071	1,912,017
Total taxable returns	73,739,632	78.8	1,547,392,960	20.985	27,629,821	204,283,458
Total nontaxable returns	19,876,646	21.2	58,872,725	2.962	1,161,419	10,500,955

Size of adjusted gross income	Taxable income: Number of returns	Amount	Total income tax: Number of returns	Percent of all returns (Col. 1)	Amount	Average (dollars)
All returns, total	87,891,993	1,273,558,005	73,739,632	78.8	248,400,602	3,369
No adjusted gross income	—	—	6,825	1.1	58,699	8,601
$1 under $1,000	9,268	8,460	2,157	(1)	*1,907	884
$1,000 under $2,000	3,559,909	2,027,505	130,734	3.1	9,009	69
$2,000 under $3,000	3,870,137	5,520,194	132,132	3.0	21,005	159
$3,000 under $4,000	3,569,791	7,986,091	1,908,315	48.6	115,135	60
$4,000 under $5,000	3,589,644	10,500,606	2,510,372	67.2	414,642	165
$5,000 under $6,000	3,744,443	13,600,471	2,538,658	66.1	720,873	284
$6,000 under $7,000	3,711,604	16,890,038	2,636,511	69.7	1,141,385	433
$7,000 under $8,000	3,753,115	20,216,901	2,940,189	77.6	1,551,568	528
$8,000 under $9,000	3,506,671	22,026,260	3,091,478	87.3	1,940,926	628
$9,000 under $10,000	3,392,197	24,404,965	3,214,979	94.1	2,466,828	767
$10,000 under $11,000	3,180,877	25,726,057	3,074,294	96.0	2,846,114	926
$11,000 under $12,000	2,913,474	26,184,233	2,845,961	97.2	3,068,226	1,078
$12,000 under $13,000	2,882,668	28,294,649	2,828,424	97.8	3,499,231	1,237

Size of adjusted gross income	Taxable income: Number of returns	Taxable income: Amount	Total income tax: Number of returns	Total income tax: Percent of all returns (Col. 1)	Total income tax: Amount	Total income tax: Average (dollars)
$13,000 under $14,000. . .	2,732,315	29,149,355	2,678,425	98.0	3,776,272	1,410
$14,000 under $15,000. . .	2,510,858	28,865,653	2,469,278	97.9	3,845,424	1,557
$15,000 under $20,000. . .	11,065,186	155,126,174	10,949,245	98.8	22,755,952	2,078
$20,000 under $25,000. . .	9,116,162	164,742,449	9,061,231	99.3	26,703,075	2,947
$25,000 under $30,000. . .	6,772,544	150,121,298	6,755,904	99.7	26,617,113	3,940
$30,000 under $40,000. . .	7,902,815	220,228,768	7,872,143	99.5	44,214,063	5,617
$40,000 under $50,000. . .	3,031,539	108,469,219	3,023,613	99.6	25,427,064	8,409
$50,000 under $75,000. . .	2,007,282	95,864,221	1,999,782	99.5	26,992,266	13,498
$75,000 under $100,000 . .	523,150	36,114,502	522,463	99.7	12,344,777	23,628
$100,000 under $200,000 .	433,142	46,488,456	433,138	99.8	19,116,073	44,134
$200,000 under $500,000 .	97,042	22,156,743	97,180	99.9	11,062,659	113,837
$500,000 under $1,000,000	12,060	6,385,506	12,099	99.9	3,642,673	301,072
$1,000,000 or more.	4,100	6,459,230	4,102	99.8	4,047,642	986,748
Total taxable returns.	73,719,865	1,245,868,163	73,739,632	100.0	248,400,602	3,369
Total nontaxable returns . . .	14,172,128	27,689,842	—	—	—	—

(1) Less than 0.05 percent.

State Individual Income Taxes: Rates, Exemptions

Source: Tax Foundation, Inc. Data as of Sept. 1, 1982
Footnotes at end of table.

State	Taxable income	Percentage rates	Taxable income	Percentage rates	Personal exemp.: Single	Personal exemp.: Married family head	Credit per depend.
Alabama[1]	First $1,000	2	$3,001-$5,000	4.5	$1,500	$3,000	$300
	1,001-3,000	4	Over 6,000	5			
Arizona[1 2 4]	First 1,000	2	3,001-4,000	5	1,589	3,178	954
	1,001-2,000	3	4,001-5,000	6			
	2,001-3,000	4	5,001-6,000	7	Over 6,000	8	
Arkansas[3]	First 2,999	1	9,000-14,999	4.5	17.50 (tax credit)	35	6
	3,000-5,999	2.5	15,000-24,999	6			
	6,000-8,999	3.5	25,000 and over	7			
California[1 2 4 6] . .	First 2,850	1	11,431-13,580	6	(tax credit) 35	70	11
	2,851-4,990	2	13,581-15,710	7			
	4,991-7,130	3	15,711-17,860	8	Heads of households have slightly lower tax rates.		
	7,131-9,290	4	17,861-20,000	9			
	9,291-11,430	5	20,001-22,140	10	Over 22,140	11	
Colorado[1 4 6] . . .	First 1,335	2.5	8,012-9,346	5.5	1,135	2,270	1,135
	1,336-2,670	3	9,347-10,681	6			
	2,671-4,006	3.5	10,682-12,017	6.5	Surtax on intangible income over $15,000, 2%. A credit equal to ½ of 1% of net taxable income is allowed for income under $9,000.		
	4,007-5,341	4	12,018-13,352	7.5			
	5,342-6,676	4.5	13,352 and over	8			
	6,677-8,011	5					
Connecticut. . . .	7% capital gains tax; tax on dividends earned if federal adjusted gross income is greater than or equal to $20,000; tax ranges from 1% on $20,000 through 9% on $100,000 and over.				100	200	
Delaware[3]	First 1,000	1.4	10,001-15,000	8.2	Exemptions apply only to adjusted gross incomes of more than $20,000 and net capital gains more than $100 (or $200 on joint returns).		
	1,001-2,000	2.0	15,001-20,000	8.4	600	1,200	600
	2,001-3,000	3.0	20,001-25,000	8.8			
	3,001-4,000	4.2	25,001-30,000	9.4			
	4,001-5,000	5.2	30,001-40,000	11.0			
	5,001-6,000	6.2	40,001-50,000	12.2			
	6,001-8,000	7.2	Over 50,000	13.5			
	8,000-10,000	8.0					
Dist. of Col.[1 4] . . .	First 1,000	2	5,001-10,000	7	750	1,500	750
	1,001-2,000	3	10,001-13,000	8			
	2,001-3,000	4	13,001-17,000	9			
	3,001-4,000	5	17,001-25,000	10			
	4,001-5,000	6	Over 25,000	11			
Georgia[3 5]	First 1,000	1	5,000-6,999	4	1,500	3,000	700
	1,001-2,999	2	7,000-10,000	5			
	3,000-4,999	3	Over 10,000	6	For married persons filing separately, rates range from 1% on the first $500 to 6% on $5,000 or more. For single persons rates range from 1% on first $750 to 6% on $7,000 or more.		

State	Taxable income	Percentage rates	Taxable income	Per-centage rates	Personal exemp. Single	Personal exemp. Married family head	Credit per depend.
Hawaii[1]	First 1000	**0**	5,001-7,000	**6.5**	1,000	2,000	1,000
	1,001-2,000	**2.25**	7,001-11,000	**7.5**	Special tax rates for heads of households.		
	2,001-3,000	**3.25**	11,001-21,000	**8.5**			
	3,001-4,000	**4.5**	21,001-29,000	**9.5**	41,001-61,000	**10.5**	
	4,001-5,000	**5**	29,001-41,000	**10**	Over 61,000	**11**	
Idaho[2,3,4]	First 1,000	**2**	3,001-4,000	**5.5**	Federal exemptions		
	1,001-2,000	**4**	4,001-5,000	**6.5**	Each person (husband and wife filing jointly are deemed one person) filing return pays additional $10.		
	2,001-3,000	**4.5**	Over 5,000	**7.5**			
Illinois	Total net income		**2.5**		1,000	2,000	1,000
Indiana[4]	Adjusted gross	**1.9**			1,000	*2,000	500
*Lesser of $1,000 or adjusted gross income of each spouse, but not less than $500.							
Iowa[3,6]	First 1,023	**0.5**	3,070-4,092	**3.5**	(tax credit) 15	30	10
	1,024-2,046	**1.25**	4,093-7,161	**5**	Net incomes $5,000 or less are not taxable.		
	2,047-3,069	**2.75**	7,162-9,207	**6**	On up to **13%** over $76,725		
Kansas[2,4]	First 2,000	**2**	5,001-7,000	**5**	1,000	2,000	1,000
	2,001-3,000	**3.5**	7,001-10,000	**6.5**	20,001-25,000 **8.5**		
	3,001-5,000	**4**	10,001-20,000	**7.5**	Over 25,000 **9.0**		
Kentucky[3]	First 3,000	**2**	4,001-5,000	**4**	(tax credit)		
	3,001-4,000	**3**	5,001-8,000	**5**	20	40	20
			Over 8,000	**6**			
Louisiana[1,2]	First 10,000	**2**	Over 50,000	**6**	6,000	12,000	1,000
	10,001-50,000	**4**					
Credits are allowed new income which is taxed at 2%; additional $1,000 exemp. for blindness allowed for dependents.							
Maine[1,3]	First 2,000	**1**	8,001-10,000	**7**	1,000	2,000	1,000
	2,001-4,000	**2**	10,001-15,000	**8**			
	4,001-6,000	**3**	15,001-25,000	**9.2**			
	6,001-8,000	**6**	Over 25,000	**10**			
Maryland[1,3,4]	First 1,000	**2**	2,001-3,000	**4**	800	1,600	800
	1,001-2,000	**3**	Over 3,000	**5**			
An additional exemption of $800 is allowed for each dependent 65 or over.							
Massachusetts	Earned and business income:	**5***			2,000	4,000	700
	Interest, divs., capital gains on intangibles:	**10***	The exemptions shown are those allowed against business income, including salaries and wages. A specific exemption of $2,000 is allowed for each taxpayer. In addition, a dependency exemption of $600 is allowed for a dependent spouse who has income from all sources of less than $2,000. In the case of a joint return, the exemption is the smaller of (1) $4,600 or (2) $2,600 plus the income of the spouse having the smaller income.				
*Plus 7.5% surtax.							
Michigan[4]	All taxable income	**4.6**			1,500	3,000	1,500
Minnesota[1,3,4,6]	First 654	**1.6**	6,533-9,144	**10.2**	66	132	66
	655-1,308	**2.2**	9,145-11,756	**11.5**			
	1,309-2,614	**3.5**	11,757-16,327	**12.8**			
	2,615-3,920	**5.8**	16,328-26,121	**14**			
	3,921-5,226	**7.3**	26,122-35,915	**15**	An additional tax credit of $66 is allowed for each unmarried taxpayer aged 65 or older.		
	5,227-6,532	**8.8**	Over 35,915	**16**			
Mississippi[3]	First 5,000	**3**	Over 5,000	**4**	6,000	9,500	1,500
Missouri[4]	First 1,000	**1.5**	5,001- 6,000	**4**	1,200	2,400	400
	1,001-2,000	**2**	6,001- 7,000	**4.5**			
	2,001-3,000	**2.5**	7,001- 8,000	**5**	An additional $800 exemption is allowed unmarried head of household.		
	3,001-4,000	**3**	8,001-9,000	**5.5**			
	4,001-5,000	**3.5**	Over 9,000	**6**			
Montana[3]	First 1,100	**2**	8,801-11,000	**7**	880	1,760	880
	1,101-2,200	**3**	11,001-15,300	**8**			
	2,201-4,400	**4**	15,301-21,900	**9**	Additional surtax of 10% on tax liability.		
	4,401-6,600	**5**	21,901-38,400	**10**			
	6,601-8,800	**6**	Over 38,400	**11**			
Nebraska[3,4]					Federal exemptions		
The tax is imposed as a % of the taxpayer's Fed. income tax liability (not including surtax) before credits, with limited adjustments. The rate is 17%.							

State	Taxable income	Percentage rates	Taxable income	Percentage rates	Personal exemp. Single	Personal exemp. Married family head	Credit per depend.
New Hampshire	Interest and dividends (except interest on savings accounts).	5	4% commuter tax		$1,200 each income is exempt; additional $1,200 exemptions are allowed to persons who are 65 or older, blind or handicapped and unable to work.		
New Jersey[3]	First 20,000	2			1,000	2,000	1,000
	Over 20,000	2.5			Additional credit of $1,000 allowed for the elderly, and disabled.		
Commuter tax from 2% on net income under $1,000 to 14% on income over $23,000. (Will cease after 12/31/90)							
New Mexico[2,3,4]	First 2,000	0.5	12,001-14,000	2.8			
	2,001-3,000	0.6	14,001-16,000	3.3	Federal exemptions		
	3,001-4,000	0.8	16,001-18,000	3.7			
	4,001-5,000	0.9	18,001-20,000	4.2	The income classes reported are for individuals. For joint returns and heads of households, a separate rate schedule is provided. A credit is allowed for state and local taxes for gross income of less than $9,000		
	5,001-6,000	1.0	20,001-25,000	4.6			
	6,001-7,000	1.2	25,001-35,000	5.0			
	7,001-8,000	1.5	35,001-50,000	5.3			
	8,001-10,000	1.9	50,001-100,000	5.7			
	10,000-12,000	2.3	Over 100,000	6.0			
New York[1,4]	First 1,000	2	13,001-15,000	9	800	1,600	800
	1,001-3,000	3	15,001-17,000	10	Income from unincorporated business is taxed at 4%. The following credit is allowed: $100 tax or less, full amount; $100 to $200 difference between $200.00 and amount of tax; $200 or more, no credit.		
	3,001-5,000	4	17,001-19,000	11			
	5,001-7,000	5	19,001-21,000	12			
	7,001-9,000	6	21,001-23,000	13			
	9,001-11,000	7	Over 23,000	14			
The maximum tax rate on personal service income is 10%.							
North Carolina[3,4]	First 2,000	3	6,001-10,000	6	1,100	2,200*	800
	2,001-4,000	4	Over 10,000	7			
	4,001-6,000	5					
*An additional exemption of $1,100 is allowed the spouse having the lower income; joint returns are not permitted.							
North Dakota[3]	First 3,000	1	8,001-12,000	5	Federal exemptions		
	3,001-5,000	2	12,001-30,000	7.5	A credit of 25% of income liability is allowed up to a maximum of $100.		
	5,001-8,000	3	Over 30,000	4			
Ohio[4]	First 5,000	0.5	15,001-20,000	2.5	650	1,300	650
	5,001-10,000	1	20,001-40,000	3			
	10,001-15,000	2	over 40,000	3.5			
Taxpayers age 65 or older are allowed a $25 credit, or if they have received a lump sum distribution from a pension, retirement or profit sharing plan during the tax year, they are allowed a credit equal to $25 times the taxpayer's expected remaining life. Credit may not exceed tax otherwise due. Credit is also allowed for an amount paid during the school year for elementary and secondary education or instruction or training of dependents who do not have a high school diploma.							
Oklahoma[1,4]	First 2,000	0.5	10,001-12,500	4	1,000	2,000	1,000
	2,001-5,000	1	12,501-15,000	5	Rates for single persons, married couples filing separately, and estates and trusts range from .5% on the first $1,000 to 6% over $7,500.		
	5,001-7,500	2	Over 15,000	6			
	7,501-10,000	3					
Non-resident aliens are taxed at a flat rate of 6% of Oklahoma taxable income.							
Oregon[3,4]	First 500	4.2	3,001-4,000	8.7	1,000	2,000	1,000
	501-1,000	5.3	4,001-5,000	9.8	A credit is provided in an amount and equal to 25% of the federal retirement income tax credit to the extent that such a credit is based on Oregon taxable income.		
	1,001-2,000	6.5	Over 5,000	10.8			
	2,001-3,000	7.6					
Pennsylvania	2.2% of specified classes of taxable income						
Rhode Island	21.9% of modified federal income tax liability				Federal Exemptions		
South Carolina[1]	First 2,000	2	6,001-8,000	5	800	1,600	800
	2,001-4,000	3	8,001-10,000	6			
	4,001-6,000	4	Over 10,000	7			
Tennessee	Interest and dividends	6			Dividends from corporations, 75% of whose property is taxable in Tenn., are taxed at 4%.		
Utah[1]	First 1,500	2.25	4,501-6,000	5.75	750	1,000	750
	1,501-3,000	3.75	6,001-7,500	6.75	Married taxpayers filing separately, single taxpayers, estates and trusts, pay rates ranging from 2.75% on first $750 of taxable income to 7.75% on taxable income over $3,750.		
	3,001-4,500	4.75	Over 7,500	7.75			
Vermont[4]	Federal exemptions.						
The tax is imposed at a rate of 24% of the fed. income tax liability of the taxpayer for the taxable year after certain credits (retirement income, investment, foreign tax, child and dependent care, and tax-free covenant bonds) but before any surtax on fed. liability, reduced by a % equal to the % of the taxpayer's adjusted gross income for the taxable year which is not Vermont income.							
Virginia[3]	First 3,000	2	5,001-12,000	5	600	1,200	600
	3,001-5,000	3	Over 12,000	5.75			

State	Taxable income	Percentage rates	Taxable income	Percentage rates	Personal exemp. Single	Married family head	Credit depend.
West Virginia[1,3]	First 2,000	2.1	26,001-32,000	6.5	600	1,200	600
	2,001-4,000	2.3	32,001-38,000	6.8	For joint returns and a return of a surviving spouse, a separate rate schedule is provided.		
	4,001-6,000	2.8	26,001-32,000	6.5			
	6,001-8,000	3.2	32,001- 38,000	6.8			
	8,001-10,000	3.5	38,001-44,000	7.2			
	10,001-12,000	4	44,001-50,000	7.5			
	12,001-14,000	4.6	50,001-60,000	7.9	90,001-100,000	9.1	
	14,001-16,000	4.9	60,001-70,000	8.2	100,001-150,000	9.3	
	16,001-18,000	5.3	70,001-80,000	8.6	150,001-200,000	9.5	
	18,001-20,000	5.4	80,001-90,000	8.8	Over 200,000	9.6	
Wisconsin[1,4]	First 3,600	3.4	14,501-18,100	8.7	(Tax Credit)		
	3,601-7,200	5.2	18,101-24,100	9.1	20	40	20
	7,201-10,900	7.0	24,101-48,200	9.5			
	10,901-14,500	8.2	Over $48,200	10.0			

(1) A standard deduction and optional tax table are provided. In Louisiana, standard deduction is incorporated in tax tables. (2) Community property state in which, in general, one-half of the community income is taxable to each spouse. (3) A standard deduction is allowed. (4) A limited general tax credit for taxpayers filing joint returns and a credit for home improvements is allowed in Ohio; a limited tax credit is allowed for sales taxes in Colorado, Massachusetts, Nebraska, and Vermont; for property taxes and city income taxes in Michigan; for personal property taxes in Maryland and Wisconsin; for property taxes in D.C. if household income is less than $10,000, and in N.Y. if household income is less than $12,000; for installation of solar energy devices in Arizona, California, Kansas, New Mexico, North Carolina, and Oregon; for property taxes paid on pollution control property in Colorado; for installation of insulation in residences in Idaho; and for making an existing building accessible to the handicapped in Kansas. (5) Tax credits are allowed: $15 for single person or married person filing separately if AGI is $3,000 or less. (For each dollar by which the federal AGI exceeds $3,000 the credit is reduced by $1 until no credit is allowed if federal AGI is $3,015 or more.) $30 for heads of households or married persons filing jointly with $6,000 or less AGI. (For each dollar by which federal AGI exceeds $6,000, credit is reduced by $1 until no credit is allowed if federal AGI is $6,030 or more.) (6) Tax bracket adjusted for inflation.

State Estate Tax Rates and Exemptions

Source: Compiled by Tax Foundation from Commerce Clearing House data

As of Sept. 1, 1982. *See index for state inheritance tax rates and exemptions.*

State (a)	Rates (on net estate after exemptions) (b)	Maximum rate applies above	Exemption
Alabama	Maximum federal credit (c, d)	$10,040,000	$60,000
Alaska	Maximum federal credit (c, d)	10,040,000	60,000
Arizona	Maximum federal credit (c, d)	10,000,000	60,000 (e)
Arkansas	Maximum federal credit (c, d)	10,040,000	60,000 (e)
California	Maximum federal credit (c, d)	10,040,000	60,000
Colorado	Maximum federal credit (c, d)	10,040,000	60,000
Florida	Maximum federal credit (c, d)	10,040,000	60,000
Georgia	Maximum federal credit (c, d)	10,040,000	60,000
Massachusetts	5% on first $50,000 to 16%	4,000,000	30,000 (e, f)
Minnesota	7% on first $75,000 to 12%	975,000	225,000 (e)
Mississippi	1% on first $60,000 to 16% (g)	10,000,000	175,625 (e)
Missouri	Maximum federal credit (c, d)	10,040,000	60,000
New Mexico	Maximum federal credit (c, d)	10,040,000	60,000
New York	2% on first $50,000 to 21% (g, h)	10,100,000	(e,i,j)
North Dakota	Maximum federal credit (c, d)	10,040,000	60,000 (e)
Ohio	2% on first $40,000 to 7% (g)	500,000	10,000 (e, k)
Oklahoma	1% on first $10,000 to 10% (g)	10,000,000	60,000 (e,l,m)
Rhode Island	2% on first $25,000 to 9% (c, g)	1,000,000	25,000 (e, n)
South Carolina	5% on first $40,000 to 7% (g)	100,000	120,000 (e, n)
Texas	Maximum federal credit (c, d)	10,040,000	60,000
Utah	Maximum federal credit (c, d)	10,040,000	60,000 (e)
Vermont	Maximum federal credit (c, d)	10,040,000	60,000 (e)
Virginia	Maximum federal credit (c, d)	10,040,000	60,000 (e)
Washington	Maximum federal credit (c, d)	10,040,000	60,000

(a) Excludes states shown in table on page 64 which levy an estate tax, in addition to their inheritance taxes, to assure full absorption of the federal credit. (b) The rates generally are in addition to graduated absolute amounts. (c) Maximum federal credit allowed under the 1954 code for state estate taxes paid is expressed as a percentage of the taxable estate (after $60,000 exemption) in excess of $40,000, plus a graduated absolute amount. In Rhode Island on net estates above $250,000. (d) A tax on nonresident estates is imposed on the proportionate share of the net estate which the property located in the state bears to the entire estate wherever situated. (e) Transfers to religious, charitable, educational, and municipal corporations generally are fully exempt. Limited in Mississippi to those located in United States or its possessions. (f) Applies to net estates above $60,000. Otherwise, exemption is equal to Massachusetts net estate. (g) An additional estate tax is imposed to assure full absorption of the federal credit. In New York, this applies only to residents. In Rhode Island on net estates above $250,000. (h) On net estate before exemption. Marital deduction is one-half of adjusted gross estate or $250,000, whichever is greater. Orphans under age 21 receive deduction. (i) Insurance receives special treatment. (j) The specific exemptions are $20,000 of the net estate transferred to spouse and $5,000 to lineal ancestors and descendants and certain other named relatives. The credit is variable, ranging from the full amount of tax if estate tax is $2,750 or less to $500 if estate tax is $5,000 or more. (k) Property is exempt to the extent transferred to surviving spouse, not exceeding $60,000; for a child under 18, $14,000; and for each child 18 years of age and older, $6,000. (l) An estate valued at $100 or less is exempt. (m) Exemption is a total aggregate of $175,000 for father, mother, child, and named relatives. (n) Marital deduction is $175,000 in Rhode Island. In South Carolina, marital deduction is one-half of adjusted gross estate up to $250,000.

State Retail Sales Taxes: Types and Rates

Sept. 1, 1982.

State	Tangible personal property	Admissions	Selected service: Rest. meals	Selected service: Transient lodging	Selected service: Public utilities	Rates on other services and nonretail business
Alabama[2]	4%[3]	4%	4%	4%	...	Gross rcpts of amus't operators, 4%, agric., mining and mfg. mach., 1.5%
Arizona[2]	4	4	4	3	4	Timbering, 1.5%; storage, apt., office rental, 3%.
Arkansas[2]	3	3	3	3	3	Printing, photographic services; rcpts. from coin-operated dev.; repair services incl. auto and elect., 3%.
California[2]	4.75[5]	...	4.75	...	[14]	Renting, leasing, producing, fabricating, processing, pringting, 4.75%
Colorado[2]	3	...	3	3[10]	3	
Connecticut	7.5	...	7[7]	7[10]	7[13]	Storing for use or consumption of persor property items, 7%.
D. of C.	6	5	6	6	5	Duplicating, mailing, addressing and public stenographic services, 5%; sales of food for off-premise consumption, nonprescription medicines, 2%.
Florida	5	5	5	5	...	Rental income of amus't mach., 5%.
Georgia	3	3	3	3 3		Levies on amus's dev., 3%.
Hawaii[1]	4	4	4	4	...	Sugar processors, pineapple farmers an selected businesses, 0.5%; insur. solicitors, 2% contractors, sales rep., professions, radio stations, 4%.
Idaho[6]	3	3	3	3	...	Closed circuit TV boxing, wrestling, 5%.
Illinois[2]	4	...	4	...	...	Property sold in connection with a sale o service, 4%, remodeling repairing and reconditioning of tangible personal property, 4%.
Indiana	4	...	4	4	4	
Iowa	3	3	3	3	3	Laundry, dry cleaning, automobile and cold storage, photography, printing, repairs, barber and beauty parlor services, advt., dry cleaning equip. rentals and gross rcpt from amus't dev., 3%.
Kansas[2]	3	3	3	3	3	Gross rcpts. from operation of coin-operated devices; commer. amus't, 3%.
Kentucky[2]	5	5	5	5	5	Storage, sewer services, photog. a photo fin., 5%; ticket sales to boxing or wrestling on closed circuit TV, 5% of gross rcpts; tax also applies to pay'ts for right broadcast matches.
Louisana[2]	3	3	3	3	...	Food and prescpt'n. drugs, exempt.
Maine	5	...	5	5	5	Proceeds from closed circuit TV, 5%.
Maryland[2]	5[3]	[11]	5[7]	5	5	Farm equip., 2%; mfg. equip., includi that used in generation of electricity or in R.&S. sold to mfrs., 2%; watercra 3%
Mass.	5	...	[7]	5.7[9]	...	
Michigan	4	...	4	4	4	
Minnesota[2]	5[3]	5	5	5	5	Food, medicines and clothing are exemp coin-operated vending mach., 3% of gross sale
Mississippi[1]	5[3]	...	5	5	5	Wholesaling, 0.125% (0.5% on sales of meat for human consumption; 5% on beer, alc. bevs., soft drinks and motor fuel); extracting or mining of minerals, specifi miscellaneous bus. incl. bowling, pool halls, warehouses, laundry and dry cleaning, pest control services, specified repair se ices, 5%; cotton ginning, 15c per bale; sales of materials to railroads for use in track structures, 3%; tractors, indust. fuel a mfg. mach. sales over $500, 1%.
Missouri[2]	3.125	3.125	3.125	3.125	3.125	
Nebraska[2]	3	3	3	3	3	
Nevada[2]	3.5[10]	...	3.5	...	...	
New Jersey[1 2]	5	5[11]	5	5[9]	...	
New Mexico[1 2]	3.5[3]	3.5	3.5	3.5	3.5	
New York[2]	4	4[11]	4[7]	4[9]	4	Safe deposit rentals, 4%.
North Carolina[2]	3[3]	...	3	3	...	Farm and industrial machinery, 1% ($80 max.); airplanes, boats and locomotives, 2% ($120 max.); sales of horses and mules, 1%

State	Tangible personal property	Admissions	Selected service: Rest. meals	Selected service: Transient lodging	Selected service: Public utilities	Rates on other services and nonretail business
North Dakota	3[3]	3	3	3	3	Severance of sand or gravel from the soil, 3%.
Ohio[2]	5	...	5	5	...	
Oklahoma[2]	2[3]	2	2	2	2	Advert. (exclusive of newspapers, periodicals, billboards), printing, auto storage, gross proceeds from amusement dev., 2%.
Pennsylvania[2]	6	...	6[7]	6	6	Cleaning, polishing, lubr. and insp. motor vehicles, rental income of coin-operated amuse. dev., 6%.
Rhode Island	6	...	6	6	6	
South Carolina	4	...	4	4	4	
South Dakota[1 2]	4	4	4	3	3	Farm mach. and agric. irrigation equip., 2%; gross rcpts. from professions (other than medical), 4%.
Tennessee[2]	4.5	...	4.5	4.5	4.5	Vending machines, 1.5% (except tobacco products, 2.5%); industrial, farm equipment and machinery, 1%.
Texas[2]	4[3]	...	4	...	4	
Utah[2]	4	4	4	4	4	
Vermont	3	3	[12]	[12]	3	
Virginia[2]	3[3]	...	3	3	...	
Washington[1 2]	4.5	4.5	4.5	4.5	...	Rentals, auto, parking, other specified services, amusements, recreations, 4.5% (unless subject to county or city adm. taxes, when they remain taxable under the state business, occupation levy, 1%).
West Virginia[1]	5[3]	5	5	5	...	All services except public util. and personal and professional services, 5%.
Wisconsin[2]	5	5[11]	5	5	5	
Wyoming[2]	3	3	3	3	3	

(1) All but a few states levy sales taxes of the single-stage retail type. Ha. and Miss. levy multiple-stage sales taxes. The N.M. and S.D. taxes have broad bases with respect to taxable services but they are not multiple-stage taxes. Wash. and W.Va. levy gross receipts taxes on all business, distinct from their sales taxes. Alaska also levies a gross receipts tax on businesses. The rates applicable to retailers, with exceptions, under these gross receipts taxes are as follows: Alaska 0.5% on gross receipts of $20,000-$100,000 and 0.25% on gross receipts in excess of $100,000; Wash., 0.44%, plus a 6% surtax; and W.Va., 0.55%. N.J. imposes a tax of 0.05% on retail stores with income in excess of $150,000, and an unincorporated business tax at the rate of 0.25% of 1% if gross receipts exceed $5,000.

(2) In addition to the State tax, sales taxes are also levied by certain cities and/or counties.

(3) Motor vehicles are taxed at the general sales tax rates with the following exceptions: Ala., 1.5%; Miss., 3%; and N.C., 2% ($120 maximum). Motor vehicles are exempt from the general sales and use taxes but are taxed under motor vehicle tax laws in Md., 4%; Minn., 4%; N.M., 2%; N.D. 4%; Okla., 2%; S.D. and W.Va., 3%; Tex., 4%; Va., 2%; and the D.C., 4%.

(4)Ariz. and Miss. also tax the transportation of oil and gas by pipeline. Ga., Mo., Okla., and Utah do not tax transportation of property. Miss. taxes taxicab transportation at the rate of 2%. Okla. does not tax fares of 15¢ or less on local transportation. Utah does not tax street railway fares.

(5) "Lease" excludes the use of tangible personal property for a period of less than one day for a charge of less than $10 when the privilege of using the property is restricted to use on the premises or at a business location of the grantor.

(6) A limited credit (or refund) in the form of a flat dollar amount per personal exemption is allowed against the personal income tax to compensate for (1) sales taxes paid on food in Col., D.C., and Neb.; and (2) all sales taxes paid in Ida., Mass., and Vt. Low-income taxpayers (adjusted gross income not over $6,000) are allowed a credit against D.C. tax liability ranging from $2 to $6 per personal exemption, depending on taxpayer's income bracket. A refund is allowed if credit exceeds tax liability.

(7) Restaurant meals below a specified price are exempt: Conn. and Md. less than $1; N.Y. less than $1 (when alcoholic beverages are sold, meals are taxable regardless of price); and Pa., 50¢ or less. In Mass., restaurant meals ($1 or more) which are taxed at 8% under the meals excise tax are exempt.

(8) Conn., exempts clothing for children under 10 years of age. Pa. and Wisc. exempt clothing with certain exceptions.

(9) In Col. and Conn., the first 30 consecutive days of rental or occupancy of rooms is taxable. Over 30 days is exempt. In Mass., transient lodging (in excess of $2 a day) is subject to a 5.7% (5% plus 1.4% surtax) room occupancy excise tax. In N.J. and N.Y., rooms which rent for $2 a day or less are exempt.

(10) Includes a statewide mandatory 1% county sales tax collected by the state and paid to the counties for support of local school districts.

(11) Md. taxes at 0.5% gross receipts derived from charges for rentals of sporting or recreational equipment, and admissions, cover charges for tables, services or merchandise at any roof garden or cabaret. In N.J., admissions to a place of amusement are taxable if the charge is in excess of 75¢. N.Y. taxes admissions when the charge is over 10¢; exempt are participating sports (such as bowling and swimming), motion picture theaters, race tracks, boxing, wrestling, and live dramatic or musical performances. In Wis., sales of admissions to motion picture theaters costing 75¢ or less are exempt.

(12) Meals and rooms are exempt from sales tax, but are subject to a special excise tax of 5%.

(13) Gas, water, electricity, telephone and telegraph services provided to consumers through mains, lines or pipes are exempt. Gas and electric energy used for domestic heating are exempt. Interstate telephone calls are exempt, as are calls from coin-operated telephones.

(14) Beginning Jan. 1, 1975, a surcharge for efficiency is imposed at the rate of 1/10th mill ($0.0001) per kwh.

State Inheritance Tax Rates and Exemptions

Source: Compiled by Tax Foundation from Commerce Clearing House data.
As of Sept. 1, 1982

State (a)	Rates (b) (percent)			Max. rate applies above ($1,000)	Exemptions (c) ($1,000)			
	Spouse, child, or parent	Brother or sister	Other than relative		Spouse	Child or parent	Brother or sister	Other than relative
Connecticut (d)	2-8	4-10	8-14	1,000	100	20	6	1
Delaware	1-6	5-10	10-16	200	70	3	1	None
District of Columbia	1-8	5-23	5-23	1,000	5	5	1	1
Hawaii	2-7	3-10	3-10	200	100	50	5	5
Idaho	2-15	4-20	8-30	500	50(e)	30(f)	10	10
Illinois	2-14	2-14	10-30	500	40(g)	20(g)	10	0.1
Indiana	1-10	7-15	10-20	1,500	All	10(f)	0.5	0.1
Iowa	1-8	5-10	10-15	150	120	50(f)	None	None
Kansas	0.5-5	3-12.5	10-15	500	250	30	5	None
Kentucky	2-10	4-16	6-16	500	50	5	1	0.5
Louisiana	2-3	5-7	5-10	25	5(e)	5	1	0.5
Maine (h)	5-10	8-14	14-18	250(j)	50	25	1	1
Maryland (k)	1	10	10	(h)	.15	.15	0.15	0.15
Michigan	2-10 (m)	2-10 (m)	12-17 (m)	750	65(f)	10	10	None
Montana	2-8	4-16	8-32	100	All	7	1.0	None
Nebraska	1	1	6-18	60	All	10	10	0.5
New Hampshire	(o)	15	15	(h)	(o)	(o)	None	None
New Jersey	2-16	11-16	15-16	3,200	15	15	0.5	0.5
North Carolina	1-12	4-16	8-17	3,000	3-15(p)	(q)	None	None
Oregon	12	12	12	(h)	(r,s)	(r,s)	(r)	None
Pennsylvania	6	15	15	(h)	None	None	None	None
South Dakota (u)	(v)	4-16	6-24	100	All	30(f)	0.5	0.1
Tennessee	5.5-9.5	5.5-9.5	6.5-16	440	120(w)	120	120	10
West Virginia	3-13	4-18	10-30	1,000	30	10	None	None
Wisconsin	2.5-12.5	5-25	10-30(u)	500	All	10	1	0.5
Wyoming	2	2	6	All	200	33	33	None

(a) In addition to an inheritance tax, all states listed also levy an estate tax, generally to assure full absorption of the federal credit. Exception is S.D.

(b) Rates generally apply to excess above graduated absolute amounts.

(c) Generally, transfers to governments or to solely charitable, educational, scientific, religious, literary, public, and other similar organizations in the U.S. are wholly exempt. Some states grant additional exemptions either for insurance, homestead, joint deposits, support allowance, disinherited minor children, orphaned, incompetent or blind children, and for previously or later taxed transfers. In many states, exemptions are deducted from the first bracket only.

(d) There is a marital deduction equal to the greater of $250,000 or 50% of the value of the gross estate.

(e) Community property state in which, in general, either all community property to the surviving spouse is exempt, or only one-half of the community property is taxable on the death of either spouse.

(f) Exemption for child (in thousands); $20 in Iowa; and $30 in S.D.; $10 in Indiana ($5,000 per parent). Exemption for minor child is (in thousands): $50 in Idaho; $20 in Ky. In Mich. a widow receives $5,000 for every minor child to whom no property is transferred in addition to the normal exemption for a spouse.

(g) Additional credit of $1,200

(h) For persons dying after 6/30/81 but before 7/1/82 tax liability is 85% of calculated tax; 75% between 6/30/82 and 7/1/83; 65% between 6/30/83 and 7/1/84; 55% between 6/30/84 and 7/1/85; 45% between 6/30/85 and 7/1/86. Tax is scheduled to be replaced after 6/30/86.

(i) On estates an additional inheritance tax equal to 30% of the basic tax is imposed.

(j) In Maine the maximum rate for any other relative applies above $150,000.

(k) Where property of a decedent subject to administration in Md. is $7,500 or less, no inheritance taxes are due.

(l) Rate applies to entire share.

(m) No exemption if share exceeds amounts stated.

(n) There is no tax on the share of any beneficiary if the value of the share is less than $100.

(o) Spouse entitled to another $10,000 exemption.

(p) Spouses, minor children, parents, and minor adopted children in the decedent's line of succession are entirely exempt.

(q) Credit.

(r) Credits allowed on pro rata basis according to tax liability on the amount of credit unused by surviving spouse or beneficiaries.

(s) Net taxable estates are allowed an exemption of $100,000 if the decedent died in 1982, $200,000 if death occurs in 1983 or 1984 and $500,000 if death occurs in 1985 or 1986.

(t) Credit is allowed to surviving spouse, child or stepchild under 18 years who is incapable of self support. The credit is $48,000 in 1982, $36,000 in 1983 and 1984 and zero thereafter. Estates of decedents dying after 1/1/87 are not subject to inheritance tax.

(u) Primary rate. If value of share exceeds $15,000 but less than $50,000, the tax liability is 2½ times the primary rate; between $50,000 and $100,000, 4 times the primary rate; over $100,000, 5 times the primary rate.

(v) However, the $2,000 family exemption is specifically allowed as a deduction.

(w) The rates range from 3-6% for a spouse or a child and from 3-12% for parents. Parent exemption is $3,000. Spouses exempt from tax.

Federal Estate and Gift Tax

Source: Tax Foundation, Inc.

Estate Tax

As a result of the Economic Recovery Tax Act of 1981, e lifetime unified credit against combined estate and gift xes is increased in steps from $47,000 in 1981 to $62,800 1982, $79,300 in 1983, $96,300 in 1984, $121,800 in 1985, 55,800 in 1986, and $192,800 in 1987. Thus, cumulative nsfers exempt from estate and gift taxes are increased m $175,625 in 1981, to $225,000 in 1982, $275,000 in 83, $325,000 in 1984, $400,000 in 1985, $500,000 in 1986, d $600,000 in 1987 and thereafter. The act also reduced e maximum estate and gift tax rate over a four-year period m 70 percent in 1981, decreasing to 50 percent in 1985 d thereafter. The schedules for 1982 through 1985 are own below.

Estate taxes are computed by applying the unified rate edule, shown below, to the total estate minus allowable ductions, such as funeral expenses, administrative exnses, debts and charitable contributions, plus taxable gifts de after 1976. Gift taxes paid are subtracted from tax e, and credit also may be taken for state death taxes. The ount of the state tax credit is determined by the schedule own in the table below or the actual state taxes paid, ichever is less. No state tax credit is available to an adstable taxable estate (i.e., taxable estate minus $60,000) aller than $40,000. Transfers to a surviving spouse are nerally tax exempt.

The law provides for real property passed on to family embers for use in a closely held business, such as farming, be valued in basis of such use, rather than fair market value on basis of highest and best use. In no case may this special valuation reduce the gross estate by more than $600,000 in 1981, $700,000 in 1982, and $750,000 in 1983 and thereafter.

Generation-skipping transfers that occur after April 30, 1976, in general are now subject to taxes substantially equivalent to those that would have been imposed had the property been transferred outright to each successive generation. However, an exclusion is provided for transfers to grandchildren up to $250,000 for each child of the decedent who serves as a conduit for the transfer (not for each grandchild).

A return must be filed for the estate of every U.S. citizen or resident whose gross estate exceeds $225,000 in 1982 ($60,000 for the estate of a nonresident not a citizen). The return is due nine months after death unless an extension is granted.

Gift Tax

Any citizen or resident alien whose gifts to any one person exceed $3,000 ($10,000 after 1981) within a calender year will be liable for payment of a gift tax, at rates determined under the unified estate and gift tax schedule. Gift tax returns are filed on an annual basis and ordinarily are due by April 15 of the following year.

Gifts made by a husband and wife to a third party may be considered as having been made one-half by each, provided both spouses consent to such division.

Unified Rate Schedule for Estate and Gift Tax for 1982

If the amount with respect to which the tentative tax to be computed is:	The tentative tax is:		
t over $10,000	18 percent of such amount.		
ver $10,000 but not over $20,000	$1,800, plus 20%	of the excess over	$10,000.
ver $20,000 but not over $40,000	$3,800, plus 22%	of the excess over	$20,000.
ver $40,000 but not over $60,000	$8,200, plus 24%	of the excess over	$40,000.
ver $60,000 but not over $80,000	$13,000, plus 26%	of the excess over	$60,000.
ver $80,000 but not over $100,000	$18,200, plus 28%	of the excess over	$80,000.
ver $100,000 but not over $150,000	$23,800, plus 30%	of the excess over	$100,000.
ver $150,000 but not over $250,000	$38,800, plus 32%	of the excess over	$150,000.
er $250,000 but not over $500,000	$70,800, plus 34%	of the excess over	$250,000.
ver $500,000 but not over $750,000	$155,800, plus 37%	of the excess over	$500,000.
ver $750,000 but not over $1,000,000	$248,300, plus 39%	of the excess over	$750,000.
ver $1,000,000 but not over $1,250,000	$345,800, plus 41%	of the excess over	$1,000,000.
ver $1,250,000 but not over $1,500,000	$448,300, plus 43%	of the excess over	$1,250,000.
ver $1,500,000 but not over $2,000,000	$555,800, plus 45%	of the excess over	$1,500,000.
ver $2,000,000 but not over $2,500,000	$780,800, plus 49%	of the excess over	$2,000,000.
ver $2,500,000 but not over $3,000,000	$1,025,800, plus 53%	of the excess over	$2,500,000.
er $3,000,000 but not over $3,500,000	$1,290,800, plus 57%	of the excess over	$3,000,000.
ver $3,500,000 but not over $4,000,000	$1,575,800, plus 61%	of the excess over	$3,500,000.
ver $4,000,000	$1,880,000, plus 65%	of the excess over	$4,000,000.
Rates remain the same for subsequent years except for the maximums:			
82: Over $4,000,000	$1,880,000, plus 65%	of the excess over	$4,000,000
83: Over $3,500,000	$1,575,800, plus 60%	of the excess over	$3,500,000
84: Over $2,500,000	$1,025,800, plus 55%	of the excess over	$2,500,000
85: Over $2,500,000	$1,025,800, plus 50%	of the excess over	$2,500,000

State Death Tax Credit for Estate Tax

Adjusted taxable estate from	to	Credit = +	%	Of excess over	Adjusted taxable estate from	to	Credit = +	%	Of excess over
$ 0	$ 40,000	0	0	$ 0	2,540,000	3,040,000	146,800	8.8	2,540,000
40,000	90,000	0	.8	40,000	3,040,000	3,540,000	190,800	9.6	3,040,000
90,000	140,000	400	1.6	90,000	3,540,000	4,040,000	238,800	10.4	3,540,000
140,000	240,000	1,200	2.4	140,000	4,040,000	5,040,000	290,800	11.2	4,040,000
240,000	440,000	3,600	3.2	240,000	5,040,000	6,040,000	402,800	12	5,040,000
440,000	640,000	10,000	4	440,000	6,040,000	7,040,000	522,800	12.8	6,040,000
640,000	840,000	18,000	4.8	640,000	7,040,000	8,040,000	650,800	13.6	7,040,000
840,000	1,040,000	27,600	5.6	840,000	8,040,000	9,040,000	786,800	14.4	8,040,000
1,040,000	1,540,000	38,800	6.4	1,040,000	9,040,000	10,040,000	930,800	15.2	9,040,000
1,540,000	2,040,000	70,800	7.2	1,540,000	10,040,000		1,082,800	16	10,040,000
2,040,000	2,540,000	106,800	8	2,040,000					

The adjusted taxable estate equals the taxable estate minus $60,000.

City Income Tax in U.S. Cities over 50,000

Compiled by Tax Foundation from Commerce Clearing House data and other sources.

City	Rates % 1982	Rates % Orig.	Year began
Cities with 500,000 or more inhabitants			
Baltimore, Md.	(50% of state tax)	1.0	1966
Cleveland, Oh.	2.0	0.5	1967
Columbus, Oh.	1.5	0.5	1947
Detroit, Mich.	3.0	1.0	1965
Kansas City, Mo.	1.0	0.5	1964
New York, N.Y.	.9-4.3	0.4-2.0	1966
Philadelphia, Pa.	4.3125	1.5	1939
Pittsburgh, Pa.	2.125	1.0	1954
St. Louis, Mo.	1.0	.25	1948
Cities with 100,000 to 499,999 inhabitants			
Akron, Oh.	2.0	1.0	1962
Allentown, Pa.	1.0	1.0	1958
Birmingham, Ala.	1.0	1.0	1970
Canton, Oh.	1.9	0.6	1954
Cincinnati, Oh.	2.0	1.0	1954
Dayton, Oh.	1.75	0.5	1949
Erie, Pa.	1.0	1.0	1948
Flint, Mich.	1.0	1.0	1965
Grand Rapids, Mich.	1.0	1.0	1967
Lansing, Mich.	1.0	1.0	1968
Lexington, Ky.	2.0	1.0	1952
Louisville, Ky.[1]	2.2	0.75	1948
Parma, Oh.	1.5	0.5	1967
Scranton, Pa.	2.6	1.0	19
Toledo, Oh.	1.5	1.0	19
Youngstown, Oh.	2.0	0.3	19
Cities with 50,000 to 99,999 inhabitants			
Altoona, Pa.	1.0	1.0	19
Bethlehem, Pa.	1.0	1.0	19
Chester, Pa.	2.0	1.0	19
Covington, Ky.	2.5	1.0	19
Euclid, Oh.	1.5	0.5	19
Gadsden, Ala.	2.0	1.0	19
Hamilton, Oh.	1.5	0.8	19
Harrisburg, Pa.	1.0	1.0	19
Lakewood, Oh.	1.0	1.0	19
Lancaster, Pa.	0.5	0.5	19
Lima, Oh.	1.0	.75	19
Lorain, Oh.	1.0	0.5	19
Pontiac, Mich.	1.0	1.0	19
Reading, Pa.	1.0	1.0	19
Saginaw, Mich.	1.0	1.0	19
Springfield, Oh.	2.0	1.0	19
Warren, Oh.	1.0	0.5	19
Wilkes-Barre, Pa.	1.0	1.0	19
Wilmington, Del.	1.0	0.5	197
York, Pa.	1.0	1.0	19

(1) Includes rates for Jefferson City and school board.

Understanding the Economy: A Glossary of Terms

Balance of payments: The difference between all payments made to foreign countries and all payments coming in from abroad over a set period of time. A *favorable* balance exists when more payments are coming in than going out and an *unfavorable* balance exists when the reverse is true. Payments include gold, the cost of merchandise and services, interest and dividend payments, money spent by travelers, and repayment of principal on loans.

Balance of trade (trade gap): The difference between exports and imports, both in actual funds and credit. A nation's balance of trade is *favorable* when exports exceed imports and *unfavorable* when the reverse is true.

Cost of living: The cost of maintaining a particular standard of living measured in terms of purchased goods and services. The rise in the cost of living is the same as the rate of inflation.

Cost-of-living benefits: Benefits that go to those persons whose money receipts increase automatically as prices rise.

Credit crunch (liquidity crisis): The period when cash for lending to business and consumers is in short supply.

Deficit spending: The practice whereby a government goes into debt to finance some of its expenditures.

Depression: A long period of little business activity when prices are low, unemployment is high, and purchasing power decreases sharply.

Devaluation: The official lowering of a nation's currency, decreasing its value in relations to foreign currencies.

Disposable income: Income after taxes which is available to persons for spending and saving.

Federal Reserve System: The entire banking system of the U.S., incorporating 12 Federal Reserve banks (one in each of 12 Federal Reserve districts), and 24 Federal Reserve branch banks, all national banks and state-chartered commercial banks and trust companies that have been admitted to its membership. The system wields a great deal of influence on the nation's monetary and credit policies.

Gross National Product (GNP): The total dollar value of all goods that have been bought for final use and services during a year. The GNP is generally considered to be the most comprehensive measure of a nation's economic activity. The *Real* GNP is the GNP adjusted for inflation.

GNP price deflator: A statistical measure that shows changes, both up and down, in the price level of the GNP over a span of years. It covers a larger segment of the economy than is usually covered by other price indexes.

Inflation: An increase in the average level of prices; double-digit inflation occurs when the percent increase rises above 10.

Key leading indicators: A series of a dozen indicators from different segments of the economy used by the Commerce Department to try to foretell what will happen in the economy in the near future.

Money supply: The currency held by the public plus checki accounts in commercial banks and savings institutions.

National debt: The debt of the central government as disti guished from the debts of the political subdivisions of the natic and private business and individuals.

National debt ceiling:—Limit set by Congress beyond which t national debt cannot rise. This limit is periodically raised by Co gressional vote.

Per capita income: The nation's total income divided by the nur ber of people in the nation.

Prime interest rate: The rate charged by banks on short-ter loans to their large commercial customers with the highest cre rating.

Producer price index (formerly the wholesale price index): A stat tical measure of the change in the price of wholesale goods. It reported for 3 different stages of the production chain: crude, int mediate, and finished goods.

Public debt: The total of the nation's debts owed by state, loc and national government. This is considered a good measure how much of the nation's spending is financed by borrowing rath than taxation.

Recession: A mild decrease in economic activity marked by a d cline in real GNP, employment, and trade, usually lasting months to a year, and marked by widespread decline in many se tors of the economy. Not as severe as a depression.

Seasonal adjustment: Statistical changes made to compensate f regular fluctuations in data that are so great they tend to distc the statistics and make comparisons meaningless. For instan seasonal adjustments are made in mid-winter for a slowdown housing construction and for the rise in farm income in the fall ter the summer crops are harvested.

Stagflation (slumpflation): The combination in the economy which a high rate of inflation coincides with a high rate of une ployment.

Supply-side economics: The school of economic thinking wh stresses the importance of the costs of production as a means revitalizing the economy. Advocates policies that raise capital a labor output by increasing the incentives to produce.

Wage-price controls: A policy under which the level of wag salaries and prices are set by law or the administration.

Wage-price spiral: The phenomenon that takes place when wo ers succeed in obtaining pay raises greater than their increase productivity. Since the higher wages mean increased cost to t employers, prices tend to increase; the resulting higher prices g workers an incentive to bargain for even higher wages.

Windfall profits tax: A tax on the profits received by oil prod ers as a result of the decontrol of oil prices and their resulting ris

How Much Do You Really Make? Is Your Salary Keeping Up With Inflation?

The Consumer Price Index (CPI) is a measure of the average change in prices over time in a fixed market basket of goods and services. From Jan. 1978, the Bureau of Labor Statistics began publishing CPI's for two population groups: (1) a new CPI for All Urban Consumers (CPI-U) which covers about 80% of the total noninstitutional civilian population; and (2) a revised CPI for Urban Wage Earners and Clerical Workers (CPI-W) which represents about half the population covered by the CPI-U. The CPI-U includes, in addition to wage earners and clerical workers, groups that had been excluded from CPI coverage, such as professional, managerial, and technical workers, the self-employed, retirees and others not in the labor force.

The CPI is based on prices of food, clothing, shelter, and fuels, transportation fares, charges for doctors' and dentists' services, drugs, and the other goods and services bought for day-to-day living. The index measures price changes from a designated reference date—1967—which equals 100.0. An increase of 122%, for example, is shown as 222.0. This change can also be expressed in dollars as follows: The price of a base period "market basket" of goods and services in the CPI has risen from $10 in 1967 to $22.00.

Which Index For You?

Which index should you use to calculate the impact of inflation on your life? If your income is near the poverty level, or if you are retired on a moderate income, you should probably use the new CPI-U. Otherwise, even if you are moderately rich, the CPI-W will probably be the best indicator for you.

The CPI (W and U) emerges each month as single numbers. At the end of the year an average is computed from the monthly figures. (Averaging does away with fluctuations caused by special situations that have nothing to do with inflation.)

For example, the average CPI for 1981 was 272.3. This means that the value of goods and services, which was set at 100% in 1967, cost 172.3% more in 1981.

Changes in prices and how they affect you can be calculated by comparing the CPI of one period against another. The 1981 CPI reading of 272.3 can be compared to the 1980 reading of 247.0 Dividing by 247.0, the excess over 1 is the percentage increase for the year 1981; in this case, 10.2%.

Did your income increase by enough to keep up with this inflation? To make the comparison, dig out your old W-2 or income tax return forms, or find your old paycheck stubs. Both gross and takehome pay comparisons will be of interest to you, but take care to compare equals. Overtime pay should not be counted. Also, watch out for changes in deductions such as those for tax exemptions, credit union payments, payroll bonds, and the like. These have nothing to do with inflation and should be added back to your take home pay.

Measuring Your Paycheck

A. To compare year-to-year earnings in percent form, divide your 1981 earnings by those of 1980 and express the result as a percentage. For example, if you earned the gross wages of the average U.S. worker, your paychecks in 1980 showed about $235.10 per week as compared with $255.20 per week in 1981, an increase of 10.85%. Since prices rose by 10.2% during 1981, the average worker gained .65% in real gross income that year. You can do the same kind of calculation on your total 1980 and 1981 earnings by using your total annual income figures in place of weekly earnings figures.

B. Another way to handle the same figures takes a dollar form. For this calculation, assume your wage was $235.10 at the end of 1980. During 1981, prices increased by 10.2%. To match that price increase, your wages should have gone up to $259.08 (235.10 times 1.102) by the end of 1981.

While readings on a monthly basis may be misleading, you may want a rough idea of how much you are being affected by inflation right now. For example, if you had weekly earnings of $265.52 in May of 1982, compared to earnings of $262.24 in December, 1981, your income went up 7.35% (The difference, $13.28, divided by 262.24). The CPI-W went from 281.1 to 286.5 during the same period, a gain of .01%. This means you kept pace with inflation in the first 5 months of 1982. You can make the same calculation for any month by using the latest CPI figures as they are issued by the Department of Labor and published in your local newspaper.

Consumer Price Indexes, 1982

Source: Bureau of Labor Statistics, U.S. Labor Department

	December 1981		January		March		May	
(1967=100)	CPI-U	CPI-W	CPI-U	CPI-W	CPI-U	CPI-W	CPI-U	CPI-W
All Items	—	—	—	—	—	—	—	—
Food, beverages	272.1	272.4	274.1	274.6	274.9	275.3	277.8	278.1
Housing	305.9	305.5	306.7	306.2	306.9	306.4	313.7	313.5
Apparel, upkeep	189.4	188.5	189.3	188.5	190.9	190.6	191.0	190.0
Transportation	292.5	294.2	291.9	293.7	287.1	288.8	283.8	285.3
Medical care	310.5	309.2	312.9	311.8	318.1	316.7	324.2	322.6
Entertainment	228.2	225.5	229.7	226.5	232.3	228.8	233.6	230.2
Other goods, services	246.2	243.0	247.6	244.4	252.2	249.3	256.1	253.2
Services	322.9	323.4	324.4	324.8	325.7	326.0	331.8	332.4
Rent, for home	216.5	216.0	217.8	217.4	219.6	219.1	221.8	221.3
Household, less rent	392.2	396.5	393.7	397.8	393.3	397.4	402.8	408.0
Transportation	284.4	283.7	286.7	286.0	288.6	287.6	291.2	289.9
Medical care	335.8	333.9	338.7	337.0	344.2	342.2	350.8	348.7
Other services	249.2	247.8	251.2	249.6	253.9	252.3	256.6	255.1
All items less food	281.6	281.5	282.3	282.3	282.2	281.9	285.5	285.0
Commodities	259.6	260.0	259.9	260.5	259.1	259.6	260.7	260.9
Commodities less food	247.5	248.2	247.2	248.0	245.9	246.5	246.9	247.1
Nondurables	272.3	273.5	272.4	273.5	269.9	270.5	269.4	270.1
Energy[1]	414.6	417.6	416.4	419.0	406.1	407.9	402.1	403.1
All items less energy[1]	271.1	269.9	272.1	270.9	273.6	272.3	278.3	277.0

(1) Not seasonally adjusted

Average Consumer Price Indexes

Source: Bureau of Labor Statistics, U.S. Labor Department

The Consumer Price Index (CPI-W) measures the average change in prices of goods and services purchased by urban wage earners and clerical workers. (1967 = 100)

	1975		1976		1977		1978		1979		1980		1981	
	Index	%+	Index	%+	Index	%+	Index	%+	Index	%+	Index	%+	Index	%+
All items	161.2	9.1	170.5	5.8	181.5	6.5	195.3	7.6	217.7	11.5	247.0	13.5	282.5	8.4
Food, drink	172.1	8.4	177.4	3.1	188.0	6.0	206.2	9.7	228.7	10.9	248.7	8.7	274.1	4.7
Housing	164.5	10.6	174.6	6.1	186.5	6.8	202.6	8.6	227.5	12.3	263.2	12.3	306.7	9.7
Apparel, upkeep	142.3	4.5	147.6	3.7	154.2	4.5	159.5	3.4	166.4	4.3	177.4	6.6	189.3	3.4
Transportation	150.6	9.4	165.5	9.9	177.2	7.1	185.8	4.9	212.8	14.5	250.5	17.7	291.9	9.5
Medical care	168.6	12.0	184.7	9.5	202.4	9.6	219.4	8.4	240.1	9.4	267.2	11.3	312.9	12.1
Entertainment	152.2	8.9	159.8	5.0	167.7	4.9	176.2	5.1	187.7	6.5	203.7	8.5	229.7	6.9
Other	153.9	8.4	162.7	5.7	172.2	5.8	183.2	6.4	196.3	7.2	213.6	8.8	247.6	9.8

Consumer Price Index by Cities

(1967-100, except Anchorage and Miami

City[1]	1978 avg.	1979 avg.	1980 avg.	March, 1982 CPI-U	March, 1982 CPI-W	June, 1982 CPI-U	June, 1982 CPI-W
Anchorage, Alas. (10/67=100)	187.5	207.0	228.2	260.0	254.5	—	—
Atlanta, Ga.	192.6	212.7	242.3	—	—	291.1	293.1
Baltimore, Md.	199.6	218.8	250.3	281.9	282.2	—	—
Boston, Mass.	193.1	212.9	240.0	269.8	269.8	—	—
Buffalo, N.Y.	193.0	211.3	235.6	—	—	265.8	264.1
Chicago, Ill.-Northwest Ind.	190.7	214.6	245.5	276.4	276.5	291.8	291.5
Cincinnati, Ohio-Ky.-Ind.	199.1	223.8	254.0	284.9	287.2	—	—
Cleveland, Ohio	193.9	219.5	252.9	—	—	297.8	297.0
Dallas-Ft. Worth, Tex.	194.0	218.6	255.6	—	—	304.8	300.5
Denver-Boulder, Col.	202.1	233.5	261.5	309.2	315.0	—	—
Detroit, Mich.	194.1	218.8	252.1	278.2	275.1	289.1	286.0
Honolulu, Ha.	184.1	204.6	228.5	—	—	269.5	269.5
Houston, Tex.	208.2	235.7	265.4	—	—	313.9	310.9
Kansas City, Mo.-Kan.	191.8	219.2	248.1	—	—	281.6	280.1
Los Angeles-Long Beach, Anaheim, Cal.	192.8	213.7	247.3	286.6	290.4	290.1	293.9
Miami, Fla. (11/77=100)	104.8	114.8	130.8	155.1	156.4	—	—
Milwaukee, Wis.	192.3	218.8	251.5	289.3	292.5	—	—
Minneapolis-St. Paul, Minn-Wis.	199.7	222.6	247.8	—	—	304.1	303.8
New York, N.Y.-Northeast N.J.	196.1	213.1	237.2	267.4	265.9	276.7	275.3
Northeast Pa. (Scranton)	191.9	210.7	237.1	267.2	268.4	—	—
Philadelphia, Pa.-N.J.	194.3	213.6	241.4	274.7	274.3	279.7	279.1
Pittsburgh, Pa.	195.5	217.3	247.2	—	—	285.1	285.9
Portland, Ore.-Wash.	198.4	225.4	255.4	286.7	283.9	—	—
St. Louis, Mo.-Ill.	191.5	215.8	244.9	280.7	279.3	—	—
San Diego, Cal.	200.1	233.1	268.5	319.0	313.9	—	—
San Francisco-Oakland, Cal.	197.8	214.6	247.3	—	—	304.6	303.4
Seattle-Everett, Wash.	194.8	216.3	252.1	293.4	289.6	—	—
Washington, D.C.-Md.-Va.	197.0	218.6	244.7	278.8	283.8	—	—

(1) The area listed includes the entire Standard Metropolitan Statistical Area, except New York and Chicago, which include the Standard Consolidated Area.

Annual Percent Change in Productivity and Related Data, 1970-81

Source: Bureau of Labor Statistics, U.S. Labor Department

Item	1970	1971	1972	1973	1974	1975	1976	1977	1978	1979	1980	198
Private business sector:												
Output per hour of all persons	0.8	3.6	3.5	2.6	-2.4	2.2	3.3	2.4	0.6	-0.9	-0.7	1.
Real compensation per hour	1.3	2.2	3.1	1.6	-1.4	0.5	2.6	1.2	0.9	-1.4	-2.8	-0.
Unit labor cost	6.4	2.9	2.9	5.3	12.1	7.3	5.1	5.1	8.0	10.7	11.2	7.
Unit nonlabor payments	0.7	7.6	4.5	5.9	4.4	15.1	4.0	6.4	6.7	5.7	5.8	13.
Implicit price deflator	4.5	4.4	3.4	5.5	9.5	9.8	4.7	5.6	7.5	9.0	9.4	9.
Nonfarm business sector:												
Output per hour of all persons	0.3	3.3	3.7	2.4	-2.5	2.0	3.2	2.2	0.6	-1.3	0.9	1.
Real compensation per hour	1.0	2.2	3.3	1.3	-1.4	0.4	2.2	1.0	0.9	-1.7	-2.9	-0.
Unit labor cost	6.6	3.2	2.9	5.0	12.2	7.5	4.7	5.2	8.0	10.7	11.2	8.
Unit nonlabor payments	1.1	7.4	3.2	1.3	5.9	16.7	5.7	6.9	5.3	4.7	8.0	13.
Implicit price deflator	4.8	4.5	3.0	3.8	10.2	10.3	5.0	5.7	7.1	8.8	10.2	9.
Manufacturing:												
Output per hour of all persons	-0.2	6.1	5.0	5.4	-2.4	2.9	4.4	2.5	0.9	0.7	0.2	2.
Real compensation per hour	0.8	1.8	2.0	0.9	-0.3	2.5	2.1	1.8	0.6	-1.4	-1.6	-0
Unit labor cost	7.0	0.0	0.3	1.7	13.3	8.8	3.4	5.7	7.4	9.0	11.6	7
Unit nonlabor payments	-2.5	11.2	0.8	-3.3	-1.8	25.9	7.4	6.7	2.5	-2.6	-2.7	12.
Implicit price deflator	4.3	3.1	0.5	0.3	9.0	13.1	4.6	6.0	6.0	5.7	7.8	8.

Consumer Price Index (CPI-U) by Region and City Size

Source: Bureau of Labor Statistics, U.S. Labor Department

(City sizes: A=1.25 million or more; B=385,000 to 1.25 million; C=75,000 to 385,000; D=75,000 or less.)

June, 1982 (Dec. 1977 = 100)	All items	Food and beverages	Housing	Apparel, upkeep	Transportation	Medical care	Entertainment	Other goods and services
Northeast								
Size A	147.7	145.9	151.6	118.6	157.2	147.5	136.5	139.8
Size B	155.5	144.1	165.2	122.8	164.6	150.2	137.5	142.1
Size C	163.5	148.8	182.1	128.3	162.2	152.7	136.4	146.7
Size D	156.9	142.9	169.3	123.4	161.2	155.4	141.1	144.0
North Central								
Size A	159.6	144.1	175.1	114.0	165.1	153.0	137.1	141.4
Size B	155.3	142.8	163.3	123.0	163.2	155.2	129.5	152.5
Size C	155.2	145.0	162.1	124.7	165.7	155.6	139.2	141.2
Size D	156.4	148.7	164.0	120.5	163.1	158.3	131.5	148.3
South								
Size A	156.3	146.7	165.2	124.9	163.4	152.8	132.0	144.1
Size B	158.4	146.9	167.2	123.6	167.0	154.5	143.1	143.3
Size C	157.6	146.0	167.0	118.6	165.1	162.5	142.7	144.5
Size D	156.5	147.7	164.6	109.4	163.3	166.6	145.2	150.4
West								
Size A	160.8	146.4	170.1	120.0	167.7	164.4	138.5	147.0
Size B	158.6	148.9	165.6	125.2	165.9	159.5	139.4	149.1
Size C	149.7	145.1	150.3	122.3	163.5	159.6	134.2	139.9
Size D	159.9	149.9	165.5	140.5	162.8	166.2	150.6	153.3

The Northeast region includes cities from Boston to Pittsburgh; the North Central, cities from Cleveland to Grand Island, Neb. and from Minneapolis to St. Louis and Cincinnati; the South, cities from Baltimore to Dallas; the West, cities from Alamogordo, N. Mex., to Butte, Mont. Anchorage, and Honolulu.

Annual Average Purchasing Power of the Dollar

Source: Bureau of Labor Statistics, U.S. Labor Department

Obtained by dividing the index for 1967 (100.00) by the index for the given period and expressing the result in dollars and cents. Beginning 1961, wholesale prices include data for Alaska and Hawaii; beginning 1964, consumer prices include them.

Year	As measured by— Wholesale prices	Consumer prices	Year	Wholesale prices	Consumer prices	Year	Wholesale prices	Consumer prices
1940	$2.469	$2.381	1969	$ .939	$ .960	1976	$ .546	$ .587
1950	1.222	1.387	1970	.906	.860	1977	.515	.551
1955	1.139	1.247	1971	.878	.824	1978	.478	.493
1960	1.054	1.127	1972	.840	.799	1979	.463	.461
1965	1.035	1.058	1973	.744	.752	1980	.405	.406
1967	1.000	1.000	1974	.625	.677	1981	.371	367
1968	.976	.960	1975	.572	.620	1982, June	.357	.344

Average Weekly Earnings of Production Workers[1]

Source: Bureau of Labor Statistics, U.S. Labor Department

Year and month	Manufacturing workers						Private nonagricultural workers					
	Gross average weekly earnings		Spendable average weekly earnings[2]				Gross average weekly earnings		Spendable average weekly earnings[2]			
			Worker with no dependents		Worker with 3 dependents				Worker with no dependents		Worker with 3 dependents	
	Current dollars	1977 dollars	Current dollars	1977 dollars	Current dollars	1977 dollars	Current dollars	1977 dollars	Current dollars	1977 dollars	Current dollars	1977 dollars
1973	166.46	227.09	132.57	180.86	143.50	195.77	145.39	198.35	117.71	160.31	143.50	173.78
1974	176.80	217.20	140.19	172.22	151.56	186.19	154.76	190.12	124.37	152.79	151.56	165.37
1975	190.79	214.85	151.61	170.73	166.29	187.26	163.53	184.16	132.49	149.20	166.29	164.02
1976	209.32	222.92	167.83	178.73	181.32	193.10	175.45	186.85	143.30	152.61	181.32	166.00
1977	228.90	228.90	183.80	183.80	200.06	200.06	189.00	189.00	155.19	155.19	200.06	169.93
1978	249.27	231.66	197.40	183.46	214.87	199.69	203.70	189.31	165.39	153.71	214.87	167.95
1979	268.94	224.64	212.70	177.40	232.38	193.81	219.91	183.41	178.00	148.46	194.82	162.49
1980	288.62	212.64	225.79	165.90	247.01	181.49	235.10	172.74	188.82	138.74	206.40	151.65
1981	318.00	212.00	244.09	163.73	267.36	178.24	255.20	170.13	202.00	134.67	220.57	147.05
1982 Jan. . .	312.38	201.02	—	—	—	—	255.95	164.70	—	—	—	—
Feb. . .	326.93	209.70	—	—	—	—	269.39	168.31	—	—	—	—
Mar. . .	327.27	210.33	—	—	—	—	261.99	168.37	—	—	—	—
Apr. . .	325.85	167.80	—	—	—	—	262.27	167.80	—	—	—	—
May . .	329.55	208.71	—	—	—	—	265.52	168.16	—	—	—	—
June .	334.05	209.09	—	—	—	—	267.40	167.33	—	—	—	—

(1) Data relate to production workers in mining and manufacturing; to construction workers in contract construction; and to nonsupervisory workers in transportation and public utilities; wholesale and retail trade; finance, insurance, and real estate; and services. (2) Spendable average weekly earnings are based on gross average weekly earnings less the estimated amount of the worker's Federal, social security, and income taxes. Figures are no longer available after 1981. (p)—preliminary.

Interest Laws and Consumer Finance Loan Rates

Source: Revised by Christian T. Jones. Editor Consumer Finance Law Bulletin, Prospect Heights, Ill.

Most states have laws regulating interest rates. These laws fix a legal or conventional rate which applies when there is no contract for interest. They also fix a general maximum contract rate, but in many states there are so many exceptions that the general contract maximum actually applies only to exceptional cases. Also, federal law has preempted state limits on first home mortgages and, over $1,000, business and agricultural credit, subject to each state's right to reinstate its own law.

Legal rate of interest. The legal or conventional rate of interest applies to money obligations when no interest rate is contracted for and also to judgments. The rate is usually somewhat below the general interest rate.

General maximum contract rates. General interest laws in most states set the maximum rate between 8% and 16% per year. The general maximum is fixed by the state constitution at 10% per year in Arkansas. Loans to corporations are frequently exempted or subject to a higher maximum. In recent years, it has also been common to provide special rates for home mortgage loans and variable rates that are indexed to federal rates.

Specific enabling acts. In many states special statutes permit industrial loan companies, second mortgage lenders, and banks to charge 1.5% a month or more. Laws regulating revolving loans, charge accounts and credit cards generally limit charges to 1.5% per month plus annual fees for credit cards. Rates for installment sales contracts in most states are somewhat higher. Credit unions may generally charge 1% to 1½% a month. Pawnbrokers' rates vary widely. Savings and loan associations, and loans insured by federal agencies, are also specially regulated. A number of states allow regulated lenders to charge any rate agreed to with the customer.

Consumer finance loan statutes. Most consumer finance loan statutes are based on early models drafted by the Russell Sage Foundation (1916-42) to provide small loans to wage earners under license and other protective regulations. Since 1969 the model has frequently been the Uniform Consumer Credit Code which applies to credit sales and loans for consumer purposes. In general, licensed lenders may charge 3% a month for loans of smaller amounts and reduced rates for additional amounts. A few states permit add-on rates of 17% to 20% to $300 and lower rates for additional amounts. An add-on of 17% ($17 per $100) per year yields about 2.5% per month if paid in equal monthly installments. Discount rates produce higher yields than add-on rates of the same amount. In the table below unless otherwise stated, monthly and annual rates are based on reducing principal balances, annual add-on rates are based on the original principal for the full term, and two or more rates apply to different portions of balance or original principal.

States with consumer finance loan laws and the rates of charge as of Oct. 1, 1982:

Maximum monthly rates computed on unpaid balances, unless otherwise stated.

Ala. . . . Annual add-on: 15% to $750, 10% to $2,000, 8% over $2,000 (min. 1.5% on unpaid balances), plus 2% fee (max. $20). Higher rates for loans up to $749. To 7/1/87, over $5,000, any agreed rate.

Alas. . . 3% to $850, 2% to $10,000, flat rate to $25,000. Over $10,000, any agreed rate.

Ariz. . . To $1,000: 3% to $300, 2% to $600, 1.5% over $600. Over $1,000: 2.5% to $300, 2% to $1,000, 1.5% to $1,500, 1% to $10,000; (1.625% min.): 1% fee to $1,500. Over $10,000, any agreed rate.

Cal.. . . 2.5% to $225, 2% to $900, 1.5% to $1,650, 1% to $10,000 (1.6% min.). Over $10,000, any agreed rate.

Colo.. . 36% per year to $630, 21% to $2,100, 15% to $25,000 (21% min.).

Conn. . Annual Add-on: 17% to $600, 11% to $5,000; 11% over $1,800 to $5,000 for certain secured loans.

Del.. . . Any agreed rate.

Fla.. . . 30% per year to $500, 24% to $1,000, 18% to $2,500; 18% per year on any amount over $2,500 to $25,000.

Ga. . . . 10% per year discount to 18 months, add-on to 36½ months; 8% fee to $600, 4% on excess plus $2 per month; max. $3,000.

Ha. . . . 3.5% to $100, 2.5% to $300; 2% on entire balance over $300 (temporary rate to 7/1/85).

Ida.. . . 36% per year to $840, 24% to $2,800, 18% to $70,000 (21% min.).

Ill.. . . . Any agreed rate.

Ind.. . . 36% per year to $660, 21% to $2,200, 15% to $55,000 (21% min.).

Ia. . . . 3% to $500, 2% to $1,200, 1.5% to $2,000; or equivalent flat rate. Over $2,000, 10% per year discount.

Kan. . . 36% per year to $540, 21% to $1,800, 14.45% to $25,000 (18% min.).

Ky. . . . 3% to $1,000, 2% to $3,000. Over $3,000, 2%.

La. . . . 36% per year to $1,400, 27% to $4,000, 24% to $7,000, 21% over $7,000, plus $25 fee.

Me.. . . 30% per year to $540, 21% to $1,800, 15% to $45,000 (18% min.).

Md.. . . 2.75% to $500, 2% to $2,000. Over $2,000, 2% to $6,000.

Mass. . 23% per year plus $20 fee to $6,000.

Mich.. . 31% per year to $500, 13% to $3,000 (18% min.).

Minn.. . 33% per year to $350, 19% to $35,000 (21.75% min.).

Miss.. . 36% per year to $800, 33% to $1,800, 24% to $4,500, 12% over $4,500.

Mo.. . . 2.218% to $800, 1.25% to $2,500, 10% per year over $2,500, plus 5% fee (max. $15).

Mont.. . Annual add-on; 20% to $500, 16% to $1,000, 12% to $7,500. 2% per mo. over $7,500 to $25,000.

Neb. . . 24% per year to $1,000. 23% over, plus fee of 7% to $2,000 and 5% over.

Nev. . . Any agreed rate.

N.H. . . 2% to $600, 1.5% to $1,500; Any agreed rate to $10,000.

N.J.. . . 30% per year to $5,000.

N.M. . . Any agreed rate.

N.Y. . . Any agreed rate.

N.C. . . 3% to $600, 1.25% to $3,000.

N.D. . . 2.5% to $250, 2% to $500, 1.75% to $750, 1.5% to $1,000; any agreed rate on entire amount over $1,000 to $15,000.

Ohio . . 28% per year to $1,000, 22% to $3,000; 21% on entire amount over $3,000.

Okla.. . 30% per annum to $600, 21% to $2,000, 15% to $45,000. (21% min.). Special rates to $100.

Ore. . . Any agreed rate.

Pa. . . . 9.5% per year discount to 36 months, 6% for remaining time plus 2% fee (min. 2%) to $5,000.

P.R. . . Annual Add-on: 20% to $300, 7% to $600.

R.I. . . . 3% to $300, 2.5% for loans between $300 and $800; 2% for larger loans to $2,500.

S.C. . . Any agreed rate.

S.D. . . Any agreed rate.

Tenn.. . 7.5% per year discount plus fees; no size limit (max. 18% per year on unpaid balances).

Texas . Annual add-on: 18% to $810, 8% to $6,750 or formula rate (max. 24% per year on unpaid balances.)

Utah . . 36% per year to $840, 21% to $2,800, 15% to $55,000 (18% min.) or, by rule, 21%.

Vt. . . . 2% to $1,000, 1% to $3,000 (min. 1.5%).

Va. . . . 3% to $500, 2.25% to $1,500, 1.5% to $2,500; or annual add-on of 21% to $500, 17% to $1,500, 13% to $2,500; 2% fee.

Wash. . 2.5% to $500, 1.5% to $1,000, 1% to $2,500.

W.Va. . 36% per year to $500, 24% to $1,500, 18% to $1,600.

Wis. . . 23% per year to $3,000; 21% on entire balance over $3,000; or variable rates.

Wyo.. . 36% per year to $300, 21% to $1,000, 15% to $25,000 (21% min.).

Shopping for Credit: Ask the Right Questions

Source: New York State Banking Department

Under federal law, all institutions that extend or arrange for the extension of consumer credit must give the borrower meaningful information about the cost of each loan. The cost must be expressed as the dollar amount of the interest or finance charge, and as the annual percentage rate computed on the amount financed.

To be sure the loan or credit agreement you are considering suits both your budget and your individual needs, shop around. And ask questions to compare and evaluate a lender's rate and services. For instance:

1. What is the annual percentage rate?
2. What is the total cost of the loan in dollars?
3. How long do you have to pay off the loan?
4. What are the number, amounts, and due dates of payments?
5. What is the cost of deferring or extending the time period of the loan?
6. What is the cost of late charges for overdue payments?
7. If you pay the loan off early, are there any prepayment penalties?
8. Does the loan have to be secured? If so, what collateral is required?
9. What is the cost of credit life or other insurance that is being offered or may be required?
10. Are there any other charges you may have to pay?

Fair Credit: What You Should Know

Source: Federal Trade Commission

Federal legislation has made it easier for you to be treated fairly in credit-related areas:

Billing. Don't let the anonymous computer get you down. The Fair Credit Billing Act states that, if you find an error in the amount of $50 or more in your credit card statement or department store revolving charge statement and you write to the company about it (on a separate sheet of paper, not the bill), the company must acknowledge your letter within 30 days and must resolve the dispute within 90 days.

Equal Credit. The Equal Credit Opportunity Act (ECOA) bans any discrimination according to sex or marital status in the granting of credit. Discrimination is also prohibited on the basis of age, race, color, religion, national origin, or receipt of public assistance payments.

However, the creditor may ask questions relating to these areas if they have bearing on your credit worthiness. The creditor does have the right to determine whether you are willing and able to repay your debts. For instance, the creditor can ask you if you are "married," "unmarried," or "separated" if, and only if, (1) you are applying jointly with your spouse; (2) your spouse will be an authorized user of the account; (3) you live in a community property state or you list assets located in a community property state. Similarly, a creditor may ask about alimony, child support, and separate maintenance if, and only if, you are depending on these as sources to establish your ability to repay your debts. In this case, the creditor may ask whether there is a court order that requires the payments or may inquire about the length of time and regularity of the payments, as well as your ex-spouse's credit history.

The ECOA also requires that if you are turned down for credit, the creditor must tell you the reason you were turned down.

Mail-Order Merchandise. By law, you have the right to receive merchandise ordered through the mail within 30 days, unless another deadline has been specified. Promises such as "one week" or "4 to 6 weeks" must be met. If either the seller's or the FTC's deadline is missed, you have the right to cancel and have all your money returned. If you run into a problem with late or non-delivery, contact the Federal Trade Commission for help.

Managing Credit: How Much Debt is Safe?

Source: Citibank

With the current rate of inflation, it is extremely important for consumers to keep close track of their individual use of credit and debt.

Before you make any new purchases, which involve moving income from the optional spending part of your budget to your fixed budget as a loan to be repaid, you must be sure you have those extra dollars and that you can do without them each month.

How Much Average Debt is Safe?

Once you've decided to apply for credit, you face the most-asked question about consumer debt: how much is safe?

There is no simple answer that applies to each consumer's situation. Most experts, today, avoid general rules of thumb. Don't be misled by the percents of gross income that lenders may use to decide how much institutional risk they run in any specific application for a loan. The lending institution can use only gross income and loan-commitment averages to estimate its own average risk, and cannot know how any individual consumer will actually repay. Only you can gauge that, based on your own habits, values, and needs.

How do you determine what you can handle? To help decide, you must know at a given time how many dollars you have for optional spending, and then how many of those dollars you can move into fixed repayments.

Here's one technique for determining how many optional dollars you have:

1. Write down your annual take-home income after deductions (for taxes, etc.) and divide by 12 to get your monthly take-home income.
2. From the monthly figure, subtract all your current monthly fixed expenses—those to which you are currently committed or must cover over the next year. Include your gasoline and car costs, other transportation, heating, utilities, food, rent, or mortgage (but no other loan repayments), real estate taxes, insurance, etc.
3. Next, total your monthly nonmortgage loan repayments and subtract them from the previous amount.

The total figure you're left with is your monthly optional spending amount. Now you must consider how comfortably you're managing with this amount. Consider that amount less the new monthly repayment. Can you still manage on the remaining amount, or should you wait until your take-home income goes up or your present debt loan goes down?

Are You Headed for Financial Trouble?

Although there is no dependable formula for determining your individual debt ratio, there are certain clear warning signals that you may have reached or have already passed it.

Consider the following signals and, if several of them describe your financial situation, it may be time to look for help.

1. Your checkbook balance is getting lower and lower each month.
2. You don't seem to be able to make it from month to month without writing overdrafts on your checking account.
3. You pay only the minimum due or even less on your charge accounts each month.
4. You have borrowed on your life insurance and see little possibility of paying it back soon.
5. Your savings account is slowly disappearing or has completely disappeared, and you're not able to put any of your regular income into savings.
6. You manage to get through each month by depending on undependable extra income like overtime or odd jobs.
7. You find yourself depending on credit cards for day-to-day living expenses and using cash advances to pay off other debts.
8. You are behind on one or more of your installment payments.
9. You don't really know how much money you owe.
10. You are receiving overdue notices or phone calls from creditors.
11. Family disputes over money are growing.
12. You occasionally juggle paying bills, paying one creditor while giving excuses to another.
13. You've had to ask creditors for extensions on due dates.
14. You've taken out loans to pay debts, or taken out a debt consolidation loan.
15. You are at or near the limit on the credit lines allowed on your credit cards.
16. When you use credit, you try to get it for the longest time period and the lowest payments without considering how much more this will cost you in interest.
17. You must borrow money to pay bills you can anticipate, like quarterly property taxes.
18. Although you regularly pay all of your debts, you are forced to continue living on credit and, as a result, your debt loan never really shrinks or is even increasing.

What can you do if you find yourself in financial trouble? The first step is to drastically cut your optional spending. Put yourself and your family on a crash tight-cash program until you can stabilize your financial situation. Also, you may need to turn some assets into cash and apply it to your debts.

If these attempts fail, get in touch with your creditors. Candidly, explain your situation. Some of them may agree to a longer repayment schedule which will insure that they get their money back and that they will keep you as a customer. You may pay more in interest, but you'll have a better credit record.

If you're still in trouble, you probably need good financial counseling.

How to Find Credit Counseling

In the U.S., there are hundreds of free volunteer-staffed credit counseling sources. Others, staffed by professionals, charge a fee.

Look up Consumer Credit Counseling in your local phone book. Call the Consumer Affairs Department of your city for referrals. Contact community-centered organizations, church, local banks, consumer finance company, credit union, labor union, or your employer's personnel department.

If you can't find a local agency, write to the Family Service Association of America (44 E. 23rd St., New York, NY 10010) or the National Foundation for Consumer Credit (1819 H Street N.W., Washington, DC 20006).

Consumer Installment Credit

Source: Federal Reserve System (estimates of amounts outstanding, millions of dollars)

		By holder					By type			
End of year or month	Total	Commercial banks	Finance companies	Credit unions	Retailers	Savings—loans and other	Automobile	Mobile homes	Revolving	All others
1974	164,594	80,054	36,087	21,895	18,114	8,444	54,266	14,642	13,681	82,005
1975	171,996	82,936	35,995	25,666	18,201	9,198	57,242	14,434	15,019	85,301
1976	193,525	93,728	38,918	31,169	19,260	10,450	67,707	14,573	17,189	94,056
1977	230,564	112,373	44,868	37,605	23,490	12,228	82,911	14,945	39,274	93,434
1978	273,645	136,016	54,298	44,334	25,987	13,010	101,647	15,235	48,309	108,454
1979	312,024	154,177	68,318	46,517	28,119	14,893	116,362	16,838	56,937	121,887
1980	313,472	147,013	76,756	44,041	28,448	17,214	116,838	17,322	58,352	120,960
1981	333,375	149,300	89,818	45,954	29,551	18,752	126,431	18,486	63,049	125,409
1982, June	331,851	146,775	93,009	45,882	26,645	19,540	128,415	18,543	59,302	125,591

Mortgages: New Alternatives to the Long-term Fixed-rate Loan

Source: Federal Home Loan Bank Board

Until quite recently the only type mortgage generally available in most parts of the country was the long-term fixed-rate mortgage. This mortgage had identical monthly payments and a term of 25 to 30 years. In the past several years, new mortgage forms have been developed, which have more flexible payment schedules and/or adjustable interest rates. These mortgages include:

• **Graduated-Payment Mortgage:** The graduated-payment mortgage (GPM) has a fixed interest rate, but the payments start out at a lower level than on a fixed-rate mortgage. The payments on a GPM increase at a known rate during the early years of the loan. On the most popular GPM plan, the payments increase at 7½ percent each year for the first 5 years of the loan. Payments on a GPM ultimately rise to a level higher than on a comparable fixed-payment mortgage.

Because the payments on a GPM start out at a low level, they may be insufficient to pay all the interest owed. That portion of the monthly interest in excess of the monthly payment is added to the loan balance. The outstanding balance on most GPM's actually increases for the first several years. This addition to the loan balance is called negative amortization.

A GPM is advantageous for a first-time homeowner who

cannot, at the outset, handle the payments of a conventional loan, but hopes to be able to when his income rises.

Pledged-Account Mortgage: The pledged-account mortgage (PAM) is a special type of GPM. On most GPM plans the low initial payments are insufficient to pay all the interest owed. On a PAM, that portion of the interest due that is not covered by the monthly payment is deducted from a savings account pledged by the borrower. A part of the borrower's down payment is used to establish the savings account which is then pledged over to the lender. Some, but not all graduated payment mortgages have the pledged account feature.

Adjustable Mortgages: Adjustable mortgages are the newest and most complex of the new mortgage forms. The common feature of adjustable mortgages is that the interest rate is not fixed and will vary according to some interest rate index that is selected at the time the loan is originated. Lenders are not required to increase the interest rate on the mortgage as the index increases, but they are required to lower the interest rate if the index decreases. Adjustable mortgage contracts may contain limitations on the minimum and maximum size of an interest rate change.

Depending upon a particular lender's adjustable mortgage plan, a change in the interest rate may result in a change in the monthly payment, the term of the loan, the outstanding balance of the loan, or some combination of these. A number of lenders offer plans in which the interest rate can change every 3 or 6 months, but the payment changes every 3 years. Under such a plan an increase in the interest rate may mean that the monthly payment is insufficient to pay all the interest due that month. When this happens the unpaid interest will be added to the loan balance. Negative amortization can occur on adjustable mortgages if payments are adjusted less frequently than the interest rate.

Some lenders have adjustable mortgage plans with interest rate caps, that is, limitations on the amount by which payments may change. The adjustable mortgages made by federal savings and loan associations are known as AML's (adjustable mortgage loans) and the adjustable mortgages made by national banks are known as ARM's (adjustable rate mortgages). Variable-rate mortgages (VRM) and renegotiable-rate mortgages (RRM) are specific types of adjustable mortgages.

Graduated-Payment Adjustable Mortgage: The graduated-payment adjustable mortgage (GPAM) combines the scheduled payment increase feature of the GPM with an adjustable interest rate. All of the variations involve a deferral of some of the interest owed during the early years of the loan. Some plans have payments rising by a set amount each year for the first several years; other plans fix the low payments

Savings by Individuals in the U.S.

Source: Federal Reserve System

(annual flow in billions of dollars)

	1970	1975	1977	1978	1979	1980	1981
Increase in financial assets	81.5	171.7	234.3	270.5	286.0	303.8	327.7
Currency and demand deposits	8.9	6.9	21.3	22.3	23.4	11.0	22.0
Savings accounts	43.6	83.4	107.5	100.1	79.2	131.2	69.9
Money market fund shares	—	1.3	.2	6.9	34.4	29.2	107.5
Securities	.2	25.5	17.0	40.1	55.2	17.5	4.2
U.S. Savings Bonds	.3	4.0	4.7	3.9	−.8	−7.3	−4.3
Other U.S. Treasury securities	−11.3	15.7	6.4	19.2	32.5	18.1	19.6
U.S. Govt. agency securities	6.4	−1.0	5.7	7.6	20.1	9.7	15.4
State & local obligations	−.9	6.2	−1.5	1.8	2.4	3.0	14.9
Corporation & foreign bonds	· 10.7	8.9	−3.8	−2.9	10.3	3.6	−10.4
Open market paper	−3.8	−4.4	9.8	16.3	7.5	−7.6	0.3
Mutual fund shares	2.6	−.3	.4	−.5	−.6	4.4	7.8
Other corporate equities	−4.3	−3.5	−4.8	−5.2	−16.2	−6.3	−39.0
Private life insurance reserves	5.4	8.5	11.3	11.7	12.3	11.4	9.7
Private insured pension reserves	2.8	8.1	14.9	18.3	16.2	20.0	28.3
Private noninsured pension reserves	6.9	11.8	17.4	15.9	14.0	22.3	22.5
Government ins. & pension reserves	8.9	15.1	22.5	27.9	24.4	35.3	37.4
Miscellaneous financial assets	5.4	11.1	22.0	27.3	26.9	25.7	26.1
Gross investment in tangible assets	144.7	222.3	320.7	366.4	398.7	381.6	412.7
Owner-occupied homes	25.7	45.6	80.7	97.1	106.6	93.8	96.2
Other fixed assets	33.2	42.1	58.6	67.7	75.9	79.5	81.6
Consumer durables	85.2	133.2	178.8	199.3	212.3	211.9	232.0
Inventories	.5	2.4	2.5	2.3	−3.9	−3.5	2.8
Capital consumption allowances	99.6	166.6	203.7	229.5	260.0	292.1	324.1
Owner-occupied homes	12.1	22.2	28.6	33.6	39.1	45.6	52.9
Other fixed assets	22.3	38.7	46.5	52.9	61.0	68.4	73.6
Consumer durables	65.2	105.7	128.6	143.1	159.9	178.1	197.6
Net investment in tangible assets	45.1	55.7	117.0	137.0	138.7	89.5	88.6
Owner-occupied homes	13.6	23.5	52.1	63.6	67.5	48.2	43.3
Other fixed assets	10.9	3.4	12.2	14.9	14.8	11.0	8.1
Consumer durables	20.0	26.5	50.2	56.3	52.4	33.8	34.4
Inventories	.5	2.4	2.5	2.3	3.9	−3.5	2.8
Net increase in debt	34.4	63.5	169.2	203.2	210.8	142.1	138.3
Mortgage debt on nonfarm homes	14.1	38.0	93.0	107.6	114.6	83.4	65.3
Other mortgage debt	8.4	7.0	16.7	17.8	20.0	18.1	15.1
Consumer credit	5.4	9.6	40.2	47.6	46.3	2.3	25.3
Security credit	−1.8	.7	1.3	1.3	−1.2	5.0	0.2
Policy loans	2.3	1.6	1.7	2.6	4.7	6.7	7.4
Other debt	5.9	6.5	16.3	26.3	26.3	26.6	25.0
Individuals' saving	92.2	164.0	182.1	204.2	213.9	251.2	277.9
Less Govt. ins. & pen. reserves	8.9	15.1	22.5	27.9	24.4	35.3	37.4
Net inv. in consumer durables	20.0	26.5	50.2	56.3	52.4	33.8	34.4
Capital gains dividends from mutual funds	.9	.2	.6	.7	.9	1.7	2.7
Net savings by farm corps.	−.1	.1	−.2	−.2	−.2	−.5	−0.6
Equals pers. saving, F/F basis	62.5	122.1	109.0	119.6	136.4	180.9	204.0
Personal saving, NIPA basis	55.8	94.3	74.1	76.3	86.2	101.3	107.6
Difference	6.8	27.8	34.9	43.3	50.3	79.6	96.4

for the first 3 or 5 years. There are a limitless number of possible GPAM variations. Very few lenders are now offering this form of loan.

Wraparound Mortgages: The wraparound mortgage is a technique by which a homebuyer can assume a low interest rate mortgage from the seller. Suppose a buyer needs a $50,000 mortgage and the previous owner has an assumable mortgage with a relatively low interest rate and a remaining balance of $30,000. The buyer might obtain a wraparound mortage for $50,000. The payments to the wraparound lender must be large enough to continue to make payments on the assumed mortgage and to amortize the additional $20,000 loan. The advantage to the buyer is that the "blended" interest rate is lower than the new mortgage rates and the payments to the wraparound lender are lower than the payments on a new $50,000 mortgage at current interest rates.

Shared-Appreciation Mortgage: A shared-appreciation mortgage (SAM) is a mortgage loan in which the borrower agrees to share the appreciation, or increase in value, of the property with the lender in return for an interest rate lower than that on a standard mortgage. SAMs have a contingent interest feature; a portion of the total interest due is contingent upon the appreciation of the property. At either the sale or transfer of the property, or the refinancing or maturity of the loan, the borrower must pay the lender a share of the appreciation of the property securing the loan. Payments on SAMs are based on a long amortization schedule, but the loan may become due at the end of 5 to 10 years.

The borrower and the lender jointly determine the size of the interest rate discount, the term of the loan, and the share of the appreciation due to the lender. The amount of appreciation is unknown at the time of origination, hence the total interest due and the effective interest rate are also uncertain. Although SAMs have a relatively low initial payment, the household's mortgage payment could increase very significantly if the lender's share of the appreciation and remaining principal balance had to be refinanced at market rate. At the current time, SAMSs are offered by relatively few lenders.

Investment: A Basic Glossary

Source: Merrill, Lynch, Pierce, Fenner & Smith, Inc.

The investment possibilities in securities for you as an individual are extremely varied. If you are beginning to consider what is best for your personal needs and find the world of securities somewhat bewildering, we hope the following glossary may offer some help.

Bear Market: A market in which prices are falling.

Bond: A written promise or IOU by the issuer to repay a fixed amount of borrowed money on a specified date and to pay a set annual rate of interest in the meantime, generally at semi-annual intervals. Bonds are generally considered safe because the lender (whether a company or the government) must make interest payments before their money is spent on anything else. Some of the most common bonds include:

Commercial Paper: An extremely short-term corporate IOU, generally due in 270 days or less. Available in face amounts of $100,000, $250,000, $500,000, $1,000,000 and combinations thereof. Yield in recent years has averaged from 12 to 17 percent.

Convertible Bond: A corporate bond (see below) which may be converted into a stated number of shares of the corporations common stock. Its price tends to fluctuate along with fluctuations in the price of the stock as well as with changes in interest rates. Average yield in recent years has ranged from 8 to 12 percent.

Corporate Bond: Evidence of debt by a corporation. Differs from a municipal bond in various ways, but particularly in taxability of interest. Considered safer than the common or preferred stock of the same company. Yield has averaged in recent years from 12 to 17 percent.

Government Bond: An IOU of the U.S. Treasury, considered the safest security in the investment world. They are divided into two categories, those that are not marketable and those that are. *Savings Bonds* cannot be bought and sold once the original purchase is made. These include the familiar Series E bonds. You buy them at 75 percent of their face value and when they mature, 5 years later, they will pay you back 100 percent of face value if you cash them in. Recently they have been paying about 6 percent interest compounded semiannually to maturity. Another type, Series H, are not discounted, but issued in amounts of $500, $1,000, $5,000, and $10,000 and pay their interest in semiannual checks. They pay 8 percent the first year of their 10-year life, 5.8 percent for the next 4 years, and 6 percent for the last 5 years. Marketable bonds fall into 3 categories. *Treasury Bills* are short-term U.S. obligations, maturing in 3, 6, or 12 months. They are sold at a discount of the face value, and the minimum denomination is $10,000. Yield in recent years has ranged from 7½ percent to 16½ percent. *Treasury Notes* mature in up to 10 years. Denominations range from $500, $1,000 to $5,000, $10,000 and up. In recent years the yield has ranged from 8¼ percent to 15 percent. *Treasury Bonds* mature in 10 to 30 years. The minimum investment is $1,000 and yield has ranged from 8⅜ to 12⅝ percent in recent years.

Municipal Bond: Issued by governmental units such as states, cities, local taxing authorities and other agencies. Interest is exempt from U.S. — and sometimes state and local — income tax. Yield in recent years has averaged from 18 to 15 percent.

Bull Market: A market in which prices are on the rise.

Stock: *Common Stocks* are shares of ownership in a corporation; they are the most direct way to participate in the fortunes of a company. The sometimes wide swings in the prices of this kind of stock may mean a chance for big profits (or equally big losses). *Preferred Stock* is a type of stock on which a fixed dividend must be paid before holders of common stock are issued their share of the issuing corporation's earnings. Prices are higher and yields lower than comparable bonds and are, consequently, not the best investment for individuals. Payments are usually made quarterly. They are especially attractive to corporate investors because 85 percent of preferred dividends are tax exempt to corporations. Many high-grade preferreds currently pay about 10¾ percent to 11¼ percent interest. *Convertible Preferred Stock* can be converted into the common stock of the company that issued the preferred. This stock has the advantage of producing a higher yield than common stock and it also has appreciation potential. *Over-the-Counter Stock* is not traded on the major or regional exchanges, but rather through dealers from whom you buy directly. These stocks tend to belong to smaller companies. Prices of OTC stocks are based on the dealer's supply, what he paid for them, the demand for them, and the prices of competitive dealers. *Blue Chip* stocks are so called because they have been leading stocks for a long time. They do not show dramatic growth, but yield good dividends over time. *Growth* stocks are stocks which grow yearly by a growing percentage; they do well even in bad times.

Dow-Jones Industrial Average: A measure of stock market prices, based on the 30 leading manufacturing companies on the New York Stock Exchange.

Mutual Fund: A portfolio, or selection, of professionally bought and managed stocks in which you pool your money along with thousands of other people. A share price is based on net asset value, or the value of all the investments owned by the funds, less any debt, and divided by the total number of shares. The major advantage is less risk — it is spread out over many stocks and, if one or two do badly, the remainder may shield you from the losses. *Bond Funds* are mutual funds that deal in the bond market exclusively. *Money Market Mutual Funds* buy in the so-called "Money Market" — institutions that need to borrow large sums of money for short terms. Usually the individual investor cannot afford the denominations required in the "Money Market" (i.e. treasury bills, commercial paper, certificates of deposit), but through a money market mutual fund he can take advantage of these money makers when interest rates are high. These funds offer special checking account advantages, as you can generally write a check against your investment at any time in amounts of $500 or more. The minimum investment is generally $1,000. Average yield over recent years has been from 12 to 17 percent.

Top 20 Stocks of the Decade

Of all the stocks of the FORTUNE 500, investors reaped the highest returns from 1971 to 1981 in these 20. The benchmark against which the top 20 can be compared, at the bottom of the table, is the median for the 500 in all but two categories: the standards for dividend payout and price-earnings ratios are those of Standard & Poor's 400 industrials.

Company	Total return, 1971-81 average	Growth in earnings per share 1971-81 average	Dividend payout[1] 1981
Teledyne	31.6%	41.7%	0%
Intel	30.3%	35.2%	0%
NVF	30.1%	0.1%	60.4
Oak Industries	29.7%	26.1%	10.8
Nucor	29.6%	26.5%	9.6%
Moore McCormack	29.5%	40.5%	15.5%
Cooper Industries	27.8%	49.2%	21.8%
Northrop	27.2%	12.9%	54.4%
Trinity Industries	26.8%	31.6%	12.7%
Dorchester Gas	26.3%	34.3%	8.4%
Handy & Harman	26.2%	31.6%	30.7%
Marion	26.0%	*	7.7%
Storage Tech.	25.8%	*	0%
NL Industries	25.3%	52.3%	17.9%
Consol. Papers	25.2%	26.5%	39.6%
Dean Foods	24.2%	22.2%	21.3%
Wang Labs	23.9%	29.8%	8.8%
Colt Industries	23.8%	25.3%	38.3%
Carpenter Tech.	23.3%	27.2%	38.5%
Freeport-McMo Ran	23.1%	27.0%	19.6%
Top 20 (median)	**26.3%**	**27.1%**	**20.8%[2]**
Benchmark	**8.5%**	**13.4%**	**42.7**

*Loss in 1971. (1) As percent of earnings. (2) Average.

Individual Retirement Accounts

All wage earners under the age of 70 1/2 became eligible to set up their own tax-sheltered Individual Retirement Account (IRA) in 1982. Prior to 1982, only those workers not covered by another plan, such as a company pension or profit sharing program, could set up an IRA.

Those who elect to open an IRA can choose from a wide variety of investment options offered by banks, insurance companies, credit unions, mutual funds, brokerage firms, and other financial institutions. However, the new law prohibits investment in life insurance and collectibles such as gems, art works, antiques, stamps, etc.

Congress cited two major reasons for making more people eligible for IRAs. Because IRAs provide an extra cushion for retirement, Congress hoped to relieve some of the pressure on the financially troubled Social Security system. In addition, Congress hoped that the IRAs would encourage people to save more. The increased savings, which will be accumulated by banks and other lending institutions, can be loaned to business and industry and play a key role in the revitalization of the U.S. economy.

What is an IRA?

An IRA is a tax-deferred investment plan that allows almost anyone who earns wages to save a portion of their income for retirement and to legally shelter that income from taxes. Each individual employee can set aside in an IRA any portion of his income up to a maximum of $2,000, or $2,250 if he or she has a non-working spouse: A married couple, when both are wage earners, can set aside $4,000. The couple may then apportion the money between them in any way they choose, so long as neither one receives more than $2,000.

A person is under no obligation to contribute the maximum $2,000 each year. In fact, if a person chooses, no yearly contribution need be made at all. The money may be invested in different kinds of investment vehicles.

Tax Advantage

The full amount that is contributed to an IRA each year is deducted from the wage earner's taxable income. No taxes are paid on the money invested or the interest it earns until the money is withdrawn from the account. It should be stressed that an IRA is not tax-free, but tax-deferred. The taxes must be paid when the money begins to be withdrawn at retirement when the wage earner will presumably be in a much lower tax bracket and pay less tax.

Withdrawals from an IRA *may* be made without penalty in the year that a person turns 59 1/2, and *must* be made in the year that a person turns 70 1/2. Withdrawals may be made in installments over a period of years or in a single lump sum.

The minimum amount that *must* be withdrawn from an IRA at age 70 1/2 is based on a person's life expectancy, or the combined life expectancy of both spouses in the case of a married couple. Actuarial tables show that a man at age 70 1/2 has a life expectancy of 12 years; therefore, enough should be taken from his IRA in steady yearly withdrawals to empty the account in 12 years. At age 70 1/2, a women's life expectancy is 14 years.

When a wage earner dies, the money left in an IRA goes to the named beneficiary. The beneficiary may take the money and pay tax on it, or move the money into the beneficiary's own IRA to prolong its tax-deferred status. The $2,000 ceiling does not apply in this situation, nor does it apply to persons who transfer accumulated pension benefits into an IRA.

Establishing an IRA

A person may establish an account at any time during the

calendar year up until they file their tax return for that year—no later than April 15 unless an extension has been granted. To start an IRA, a person need only complete a form and provide the money, either in a single sum or in smaller contributions during the year.

While the funds in an IRA cannot be withdrawn before age 59 1/2 without a penalty, they may be moved from one investment vehicle to another. The funds may also be moved from one financial institution to another if the wage earner is not happy with the earnings performance of the account, or as individual objectives or economic conditions change. However, this may only be done once a year.

Early Withdrawal

If a person decides to remove funds from an IRA before reaching the age of 59 1/2, the amount withdrawn is taxable that year. In addition, the person will be subject to a 10% IRS tax penalty.

Growth or Stability?

Because IRA income can be placed in a wide range of investment vehicles, individuals should give careful consideration to their objectives before committing their money.

Some may feel more comfortable with a highly stable investment with a fixed rate of return. In this case, an investor should shop around for the best rate of return. The difference of 1/2% over a 20-year period can be substantial.

Others may feel that they can afford to invest their money in something that has the potential to grow more rapidly. They may decide to invest in stocks, corporate bonds, or a mutual fund. They should be aware that such investment vehicles tend to fluctuate and contain an element of risk.

An individual will have to decide if preservation of the original investment is more important than potential growth. Before making a decision, a person might find it helpful to consult with his or her banker, accountant, or financial advisor.

Computer Language

The personal computer, once considered a hobbyist's gadget, is in the early stages of becoming a fixture in the American home. Over one million units were sold in 1981 and an estimated three million more will be brought into American homes by the end of 1982. The following is a glossary of key words or terms that consumers should learn if they are considering buying their own personal computer.

Acoustic coupler: a device that allows other electronic devices to communicate by making, and also listening to sounds made over an ordinary telephone. See **Modem.**

Address: designates the location of an item of information stored in the computer's memory. Without this, finding stored information would be an insurmountable task.

BASIC: a popular computer language that is used by many small and personal computer systems. It means—Beginner's All-purpose Symbolic Instruction Code.

Bit: short for binary digit, the smallest unit of information stored in a computer. It always has the binary value of "O" or "1." Bits are usually grouped to form nibbles (4 bits) and bytes (8 bits).

Boot, Booting, or Bootstrap: the program, or set of commands, that gets the computer to move into action.

Bug: a mistake that occurs in a program within a computer or in the unit's electrical system. When a mistake is found and corrected, it's called debugging.

Cassette: units used to store information for mini and microcomputers. They are similar in size and shape to audio recording cassettes.

CPU: the Central Processing Unit within the computer that executes the instructions that the user gives the system.

Chip: a term for the integrated circuit and its package which contains coded signals.

Crunch: to make a certain amount of information fit into a smaller amount of space than normally required.

Cursor: the symbol on the computer monitor that marks the place where the operator is working.

Disk: a revolving plate on which information and programs are stored. See also Floppy Disk.

Disk Drive: a peripheral machine that stores information on disks.

Documentation: user or operator instructions that come with some hardware and software that tells how to use the material.

DOS: "Disk Operating System," a collection of programs designed to facilitate the use of a disk drive and floppy disk.

Error Message: a statement by the computer indicating that the user has done something incorrectly.

File: a logical group of pieces of information labelled by a specific name; considered a single unit by the computer. It is used commonly on microcomputers and word processors.

Floppy disk: a small inexpensive disk used to record and store information. It must be used in conjunction with a disk drive.

Graphics: the pictures or illustrations in the computer program.

Hardware: the physical apparatus or "nuts and bolts" that make up a computer. It includes silicon chips, transformers, boards and wires, etc. Also used to describe various pieces of equipment including the computer, printer, modem, etc.

Interface: the hardware or software necessary to connect one device or system to another.

K: abbreviation for Kilo-byte used to denote 1,024 units of stored matter.

Language: any set of compiled, unified, or related commands or instructions that are acceptable to a computer.

Load: the actual operation of putting information and data into the computer or memory.

Memory: the internal storage of information.

Microcomputer: a small, complete computer system. Most personal computers now in use are microcomputers.

Minicomputer: an intermediate computer system sized between the very small microcomputer and the large computer.

Modem: short for modulating-demodulating. An acoustic or non-acoustic coupler, used either with a telephone or on a direct-line, for transmitting information from one computer to another.

Monitor: the screen on which the material from the computer appears and can be read. Looks like a small TV screen but produces more vivid characters than a home TV.

Printer: a computer output device that, when attached to a computer, will produce printed copy on paper.

Program: coded instructions telling a computer how to perform a specific function.

RAM: abbreviation for random-access-memory. A type of microchip, its patterns can be changed by the user and the information it generates stored on tape, disk, or in printed form.

ROM: abbreviation for read-only-memory. A type of microchip that is different from RAM in that it cannot be altered by the user.

Software: the programs, or sets of instructions, procedural rules, and, in some cases, documentation that make the computer function.

Terminal: a work station away from the main computer that allows several people to have access to a single, main computer.

User friendly: hardware or software designed to help people become familiar with their computer. Usually includes simple and easy to follow instructions.

Word Processor: a text-editing program or system that allows electronic writing and correcting of articles, books, etc.

Features of Selected Personal Computers

	Commodore "64"	Apple II +®	IBM®	Tandy TRS-80® III	Atari 800®
Base price[1]	$595	$1,530	$1,565	$999	$899
Advanced personal computer features					
Built-in user memory[2]	64K	48K	16K	16K	16K
Programmable	yes	yes	yes	yes	yes
Real typewriter keyboard	yes (66 keys)	yes (52 keys)	yes (83 keys)	yes (65 keys)	yes (61 keys)
Graphics characters (from keyboard)	yes	no	no	no	yes
Upper and lower case letters	yes	upper only	yes	yes	yes
Maximum 5 1/4" disk capacity per drive[2]	170K/1000K	143K	160K	178K	96K
Audio features					
Sound generator	yes	yes	yes	no	yes
Music synthesizer	yes	no	no	no	no
Hi-fi output	yes	no	no	no	no
Video features					
TV output	yes	extra	extra	no	yes
Input/output features					
"Smart" peripherals	yes	no	no	no	yes
Software features					
CP/M® option (over 1,000 packages)	yes	yes	yes	yes	no
Game machine features					
Cartridge game slot	yes	no	no	no	yes
Game controllers	yes	yes	yes	no	yes

(1) Manufacturer's suggested retail price as of mid 1982. Disk drives and printers are not included in prices. Prices are subject to change.
(2) Each "K" equals 1,024 characters or digits of information.

Directory of Consumer and Information Offices

Source: Office of Consumer Affairs, U.S. Department of Health and Human Services

Advertising:
National Advertising Division, Council of Better Business Bureaus, 845 Third Avenue, New York, New York 10022; (212) 754-1320.
Political advertising on TV and radio
Fairness/Political Broadcast Br., Broadcast Bureau, Federal Communications Commission, Washington, DC 20554; (202) 632-7586.

Aging:
Director, National Clearinghouse on Aging, Department of Health and Human Services, Washington, DC 20201; (202) 245-0188.

Air Travel:
Fares and routes
Office of Congressional, Community and Consumer Affairs, Civil Aeronautics Board, Washington, DC 20428; (202) 673-6047.
Safety
Chief, Community and Consumer Liaison Division, Federal Aviation Administration, Department of Transportation; (202) 426-1960.

Alcohol and Alcoholism:
Distilled Spirits Council of the U.S., Inc., 425 13th St., N.W., Suite 1300, Washington, DC 20004; (202) 628-3544.

Appliances:
Major Appliance Consumer Action Panel (MACAP), 20 No. Wacker Dr., Chicago, IL 60606; (312) 984-5858.
Product Safety
Public Inquiries Office, Consumer Product Safety Commission, Washington, DC 20207; (800) 638-8326; (800) 492-8363 in Maryland; (800) 638-8333 in Puerto Rico, Virgin Islands, Alaska, Hawaii.
Radiation
Director, Technical Information Staff (HFX-25), Bureau of Radiological Health, Food and Drug Administration, Department of Human Services, 5600 Fishers Lane, Rockville, MD 20857; (301) 443-3434.

Automobiles:
Safety and recalls
Administrator, National Highway Traffic Safety Administration, Department of Transportation, Washington, DC 20590; (800) 424-9393; (202) 426-1023 in Washington, DC.
Fuel-saving devices and additives
Fuel-Saving Device Evaluation Coordinator, Vehicle Emission Laboratory, Environmental Protection Agency, 2565 Plymouth Rd., Ann Arbor, MI 48105; (313) 668-4299.
Office of Consumer Affairs, Department of Energy, Washington, DC 20585; (202) 252-5373.

Banking:
American Bankers Association, 1120 Connecticut Ave., NW, Washington, DC 20036; (202) 467-4000.

Child Abuse:
National Center on Child Abuse and Neglect, P.O. Box 1182, Washington, DC 20013; (202) 245-2840.
Parents Anonymous, Suite 208, 22330 Hawthorne Blvd., Torrance, CA 90505; (800) 421-0353; (800) 352-0386 in California.

Child Support:
Office of the Deputy Director, Office of Child Support Enforcement, Department of Health and Human Services, 6110 Executive Blvd., Rockville, MD 20852; (301) 443-4442.

Civil Rights:
Civil Rights Division, Department of Justice, Main Justice Bldg., Washington, DC 20530; (202) 633-3847.
Employment
Office of Executive Director, Equal Employment Opportunity Commission, Washington, DC 20506; (202) 634-6814.
Housing
Office of Fair Housing and Equal Opportunity, Department of Housing and Urban Development, Washington, DC 20410; (800) 424-8590; (202) 426-3500 in Washington, DC.
Unfair Labor Practices
Offices of Executive Secretary, National Labor Relations Board, Washington, DC 20570; (202) 254-9430.

Consumer Information:
For a copy of the free Consumer Information Catalog, a listing of more than 200 Federal consumer publications, write to: Consumer Information Center, Pueblo, CO 81009. An annual listing of Federal consumer publications in Spanish can also be obtained from the same address.

Copyrights:
Information and Publication Section, Copyright Office, Library of Congress, Washington, DC 20559; (202) 287-8700.

Cosmetics:
Office of Consumer Affairs (HFE-88), Food and Drug Administration, Department of Health and Human Services, 5600 Fishers Lane, Rockville, MD 20857; (301) 443-3170.

Credit Counseling:
Executive Director, National Foundation for Consumer Credit, 8701 Georgia Ave., Suite 601, Silver Springs, MD 20910.

Drugs, Drug Abuse:
Abuse
Office of Consumer-Affairs, HFE-88, Food and Drug Administration, Department of Health and Human Services, 5600 Fishers Lane, Rockville, MD 20857, (301) 443-3170.

Education:
Office of Public Participation and Special Concerns, Department of Education, Washington, DC 20202; (202) 447-9043.
National Education Association of the United States, 1201 16th St. NW, Washington, DC 20036; (202) 833-4000.

Employment:
Coordinator of Consumer Affairs, Department of Labor, Washington, DC 20210; (202) 523-6060.
Discrimination
Director, Equal Opportunity Employment Commission, Washington, DC 20506; (202) 634-6814.
Safety and Health
Hazards Evaluation and Technical Assistance Branch, National Institute of Occupational Safety and Health, 4676 Columbia Parkway, Cincinnati, OH 45226; (513) 684-2176.
Training
For information on employment and training programs, such as the Comprehensive Employment and Training Act (CETA) programs, most of which are handled by state and local governments, check with state or local employment offices listed in the white pages of the phone book, or your mayor's office. General information can be obtained from the Director, Employment and Training Administration, Department of Labor, Washington, DC 20213; (202) 376-6905.

Energy:
Conservation and Renewable Energy Referral Service; (800) 523-2929; (800) 462-4983 in Pennsylvania.
Nuclear regulation
Office of Public Affairs, Nuclear Regulatory Commission, Washington, DC 20555; (301) 492-7715.

Environment:
Public Inquiries Center (A-107), Environmental Protection Agency, Washington, DC 20460; (202) 755-0707.

Federal Regulations:
Federal Register
Office of the Federal Register, General Information, Washington, D.C. 20405; (202) 523-5240. The *Federal Register*, published five days a week, informs the public about proposed and new government regulations. It includes Presidential proclamations, Executive Orders, and other Presidential documents. It may be ordered from the Superintendent of Documents, U.S. Government Printing Office, Washington, DC 20402 for $1.00 per copy, $45.00 for six months, or $75.00 per year. Contact the Library, Office of the Federal Register, National Archives, Washington, DC 20408; (202) 633-6930.

Food:
General inquiries and labeling, quality, and safety (all foods except meat and poultry products)
Office of Consumer Affairs (HFE-88), Food and Drug Administration, Department of Health and Human Services, 5600 Fishers Lane, Rockville, MD 20857; (301) 443-3170.
Labeling, quality, and safety (meat and poultry products)
Food and Safety Inspection Service, Department of Agriculture, Washington, DC 20250; (202) 472-4485.
Food Stamps and Food Assistance Programs
Contact local or state Welfare Office, or local health department.

Freight Shipments:
Office of Consumer Protection, Interstate Commerce Commission, Washington, DC 20423; (800) 424-9312; (202) 275-0860 in Washington, DC.
Office of Consumer Affairs, Federal Maritime Commission, Washington, DC 20573; (202) 523-5807.
Community and Consumer Liaison Division (APA-400), Federal Aviation Administration, Department of Transportation, Washington, DC 20591; (202) 426-1960.
Office of Public Affairs (ROA-30), Federal Railroad Administration, Department of Transportation, Washington, DC 20590; (202) 426-0881.

Handicapped:
Clearinghouse on the Handicapped, Department of Education Services, Washington, DC 20202; (202) 245-0080.
Architectural barriers
National Center for a Barrier-Free Environment, 1140 Connecticut Ave. NW, Washington, DC 20036; (800) 424-2809; (202) 466-6896 in Washington, DC.
Employment
President's Committee on Employment of the Handicapped, 1111 20th St. NW, Washington, DC 20036; (202) 653-5044.
Reading material for the blind and physically handicapped
Director, National Library Service for the Blind and Physically Handicapped, 1291 Taylor St. NW, Washington, DC 20542; (800) 424-8567; (202) 287-5100, in Washington, DC.

Health:
National Health Information Clearinghouse, Department of Health and Human Services, P.O. Box 1133, Washington, DC 20013; (800) 336-4797; (703) 522-2590 in Washington, DC, Virginia, Alaska, and Hawaii.
Division of Program Promotion, Office of Health Maintenance Organizations, Department of Health and Human Services, 12420 Parklawn Dr., Rockville, MD 20857; (301) 443-2300.

Housing:
Information Center, Department of Housing and Urban Development, Washington, DC 20410; (202) 755-6420.
FHA Loans
Federal Housing Administration, Department of Housing and Urban Development, Washington, DC 20410; (202) 755-6600.
FmHA Insured Loans
Farmers Home Administration, Department of Agriculture, Washington, DC 20250; (202) 447-4323.
Mobile Homes
Office of Mobile Home Standards, Department of Housing and Urban Development, Washington, DC 20410; (202) 755-6920.
Real Estate Settlement Procedures
Office of Real Estate Practices, Department of Housing and Urban Development, Washington, DC 20410; (202) 755-6524.

Insurance:
Flood insurance
Federal Insurance Administrator, Federal Emergency Management Agency, Washington, DC 20472; (800) 434-8372; (202) 287-0750.

Mail:
Fraud
Check with your local postmaster, or Consumer Advocate, U.S. Postal Service, Washington, DC 20260; (202) 245-4514.
Mail orders
Mail Order Action Line, 6 E. 43rd St., New York, New York 10017; (212) 689-4977.
Unordered merchandise and *late delivery*
Check with your local postmaster, or Enforcement, Federal Trade Commission, Washington, DC 20580.
Unsolicited mail
To remove your name from a mailing list, contact the Mail Preference Service, Name-Removal Program, 6 E. 43rd St., New York, New York 10017; (212) 689-4977.

Medicaid:
Contact your local Welfare or social services offices.

Medicare:
Contact your local Social Security Office, or your area Medicare carrier, by looking under Medicare in the local telephone directory. Or contact Medicare Inquiries, Health Care Financing Administration, Department of Health and Human Services, 6325 Security Blvd., Baltimore, MD 21207; (301) 594-9086.

Moving and Movers:
Office of Consumer Protection, Interstate Commerce Commission, Washington, DC 20423; (800) 424-9312; (202) 275-0860 in Washington, DC.

Nursing Homes:
Division of Long-Term Care, Health Care Financing Ad-

ministration, Department of Health and Human Services, 1849 Gwyn Oak Ave., Dogwood East Bldg., Baltimore, MD 21207; (301) 594-3642.
Consumer Services, American Health Care Association, 1200 15th St. NW, Washington, DC 20005; (202) 833-2050.

Passports:
Citizens Counselor Services, Department of State, Room 4811, Washington, DC 20520; emergencies (202) 632-5225; non-emergencies (202) 632-3444.

Patents and Trademarks:
Commissioner of Patents and Trademarks, Washington, DC 20231; (703) 557-3428.

Pensions:
Pension Benefit Guaranty Corp., 2020 K Street NW, Washington, DC 20006; (202) 254-4317.

Product Quality:
Office of Consumer Affairs, Department of Commerce, Washington, DC 20230; (202) 377-5001.

Product Safety:
Public Inquiries, Consumer Product Safety Commission, Washington, DC 20207; (800) 638-8326; (800) 492-8363 in Maryland; (800) 638-8333 in Alaska, Hawaii, Puerto Rico, Virgin Islands.

Social Security:
Local Social Security Office.

Stocks and Bonds:
Director, Office of Consumer Affairs, Securities and Exchange Commission, Washington, DC 20549; (202) 523-3952.

Taxes:
The Internal Revenue Service (IRS) has 58 district offices that provide tax assistance by toll-free telephone. Toll-free numbers are listed in IRS tax packages and in local telephone directories. Taxpayers may also use the toll-free network to clarify bills and notices, and to contact the Problem Resolution Officer for complaints unresolved through normal channels.

Train Travel:
Amtrak, Office of Customer Relations, P.O. Box 2709, Washington, DC 20013; (202) 383-2121.
Office of Consumer Protection, Interstate Commerce Commission, Washington, DC 20423; (800) 424-9312; (202) 275-0860 in Washington, DC.
Consumer Affairs Officer, Federal Railroad Administration, Department of Transportation, Washington, DC 20590; (202) 426-0881.

Veterans:
Medical Care
The Inquiries Unit (101B3), Veterans Administration, Washington, DC 20420; (202) 389-3314.
Vocational Rehabilitation
Veterans Assistance Service (27), Veterans Administration, Washington, DC 20420; (202) 389-2567.

Warranties:
Federal Trade Commission, Washington, DC 20420; (202) 389-2567.

Canadian Consumer Associations

Consumers' Association of Canada

The Consumers' Association of Canada (CAC) is a voluntary, non-profit organization founded in 1947 to represent consumer interests. It also provides members with information on consumer legislation and the results of its research and tests on consumer goods and services. The national office is at 2660 Southvale Cres., Level 3, Ottawa, Ont. K1B 5C4; branch offices are in each province and territory. CAC publishes monthly, bilingual magazines, *Canadian Consumer* and *Le Consommateur Canadien* (circulation 180,000). Annual membership fee is $16.

Automobile Protection Association

The Automobile Protection Association (APA) is a non-profit, independently-financed consumer group founded in 1969 to advise motorists on the quality of automotive products and services, to publicize and encourage legal action against what it considers dishonest or dangerous practices in the automobile industry, and to press federal and provincial governments for protective legislation. For a $20 annual fee members receive periodic APA bulletins as well as free legal consultation when needed. Accredited garage service is provided in Montreal and Ottawa. Headquarters are at 292 St-Joseph West, Montreal, Quebec H2V 2N7. Branch office at 448 Kent, Ottawa, Ont. K2P 2B5.

Employment and Training Services and Unemployment Insurance

Source: Employment and Training Administration, U.S. Labor Department

Employment Service

The Federal-State Employment Service consists of the U.S. Employment Service and affiliated state employment services with their network of about 2,000 local offices. During fiscal year 1981, these offices made 5.7 million placements, 5.2 million in nonagricultural and 457,000 in agricultural industries. Overall, 3.7 million different individuals were placed in employment.

The employment service refers employable applicants to job openings that use their highest skills and helps the unemployed obtain services or training to make them employable. It also provides special attention to older workers, youth, minorities, the poor, handicapped workers, migrants, seasonal farmworkers, and workers who lose their jobs because of foreign trade competition.

Veterans receive priority services including referral to jobs and training at all employment service offices. During fiscal year 1981, these offices placed over 507,000 veterans in jobs.

Comprehensive Employment and Training Services

The Comprehensive Employment and Training Act (CETA) of 1973 set up a community system to give people training and job-related services and place them in jobs. Under this system all states and cities, counties, and combinations of local units with populations of 100,000 or more received federal grants to plan and run comprehensive training programs in their localities. Under the Private Sector Initiative Program, every program sponsor set up a Private Industry Council to help involve businesses in hiring and training economically disadvantaged workers. A major inducement for employers to hire certain disadvantaged workers is the Targeted Jobs Tax Credit, amounting to $3,000 for each eligible worker paid $6,000 or more for the first year of employment.

National Activities

The federal role under CETA was to provide support and technical assistance to local programs, insure proper use of federal money, and serve groups with special job disadvantages.

In addition to continuing programs for Indians and migrant and seasonal farmworkers, there were continuing efforts for youth. These efforts include the Job Corps, which was training 44,000 disadvantaged youths at 106 residential centers at the end of fiscal year 1981, and the Summer Youth Employment Programs which supported about 900,000 part-time jobs in 1981. CETA was scheduled to expire Sept. 30, 1982, and replacement legislation has been under consideration in the Congress. The Employment and Training Administration also has programs to promote apprenticeship and to help employable people on Aid to Families with Dependent Children find jobs.

Unemployment Insurance

Unlike old-age and survivors insurance, entirely a federal program, the unemployment insurance program is a Federal-State system that provides insured wage earners with partial replacement of wages lost during involuntary unemployment. The program protects most workers. During fiscal year 1981, an estimated 88.2 million workers in commerce, industry, agriculture, and government, including the armed forces, were covered under the Federal-State system. In addition, an estimated 500,000 railroad workers were insured against unemployment by the Railroad Retirement Board.

Each state, as well as the District of Columbia, Puerto Rico, and the Virgin Islands, has its own law and operates its own program. The amount and duration of the weekly benefits are determined by state laws, based on prior wages and length of employment. States are required to extend the duration of benefits when unemployment rises to and remains above specified state levels; costs of extended benefits are shared by the state and federal governments.

Under the Federal Unemployment Tax Act, as amended in 1976, the tax rate is 3.4% on the first $6,000 paid to each employee of employers with one or more employees in 20 weeks of the year or a quarterly payroll of $1,500. A credit of up to 2.7% is allowed for taxes paid under state unemployment insurance laws that meet certain criteria, leaving the federal share at 0.7% of taxable wages.

Social Security Requirement

The Social Security Act requires, as a condition of such grants, prompt payment of due benefits. The Federal Unemployment Tax Act provides safeguards for workers' right to benefits if they refuse jobs that fail to meet certain labor standards. Through the Unemployment Insurance Service of the Employment and Training Administration, the Secretary of Labor determines whether states qualify for grants and

Employment Security

Selected unemployment insurance data by state. Calendar year 1980, state programs only.

	Insured claimants[1] (1,000)	Beneficiaries[2] (1,000)	Exhaustions[3] (1,000)	Initial claims[4] (1,000)	Benefits paid[5] (1,000)	Avg. weekly benefit for total unemployment[p]	Funds available for benefits Dec. 31, 1980[6] (millions)	Employers subject to state law Dec. 31, 1980 (1,000)
Alabama	240	210	54	507	$176,024	$76.76	$83	67
Alaska	35	32	9	62	44,134	85.13	90	11
Arizona	99	72	17	184	71,151	83.44	269	53
Arkansas	157	118	31	316	113,321	88.95	3	44
California	1,479	1,068	337	2,892	1,357,892	86.41	3,038	584
Colorado	103	77	22	181	86,363	110.99	125	72
Connecticut	169	137	20	312	163,744	102.73	109	81
Delaware	37	31	6	79	42,442	108.47	7	14
District of Columbia	37	26	11	40	55,146	122.22	23	17
Florida	235	185	66	393	153,013	74.49	797	210
Georgia	316	248	70	614	176,268	78.68	471	100
Hawaii	45	33	7	75	40,991	106.11	102	22
Idaho	54	50	15	127	54,101	97.46	87	23
Illinois	650	555	232	1,116	1,205,902	114.60	77	249
Indiana	383	297	111	748	319,084	84.96	244	93
Iowa	161	142	32	265	188,528	117.02	114	66
Kansas	98	88	22	166	113,832	105.84	224	54
Kentucky	239	185	63	467	255,589	101.33	42	62
Louisiana	177	135	42	284	207,890	108.52	221	77
Maine	77	72	19	191	56,774	85.55	34	30
Maryland	172	149	38	338	178,487	91.72	385	78
Massachusetts	314	246	62	580	315,789	97.38	238	117
Michigan	649	650	308	1,996	1,141,476	101.87	276	160
Minnesota	185	159	54	316	284,145	117.72	12	86
Mississippi	118	100	22	250	85,066	69.26	237	43
Missouri	312	244	83	704	278,426	88.41	125	112
Montana	42	36	12	80	41,194	98.11	18	23
Nebraska	63	44	13	83	43,823	93.78	79	37
Nevada	52	45	10	103	53,230	100.09	130	20
New Hampshire	54	45	3	81	30,199	84.82	82	23
New Jersey	485	424	157	861	675,735	100.69	134	165
New Mexico	41	30	9	80	33,465	82.74	91	29
New York	794	611	213	1,756	1,007,601	93.07	514	393
North Carolina	432	304	48	973	230,529	87.09	600	103
North Dakota	27	24	8	47	32,424	105.94	16	20
Ohio	655	556	182	1,461	1,075,705	124.95	57	196
Oklahoma	84	59	18	150	63,171	99.75	193	63
Oregon	181	163	35	431	202,748	98.86	345	67
Pennsylvania	783	678	156	1,890	1,164,447	115.56	151	207
Puerto Rico	144	69	42	294	83,677	53.29	67	46
Rhode Island	85	68	25	178	76,174	89.04	27	24
South Carolina	199	171	31	502	124,314	82.19	198	53
South Dakota	17	16	3	34	16,584	96.87	11	18
Tennessee	287	228	65	661	233,519	78.04	200	79
Texas	370	256	90	553	251,261	86.22	277	263
Utah	60	48	13	94	61,728	105.70	61	30
Vermont	32	27	5	58	28,077	90.13	18	14
Virginia	227	145	39	404	154,388	95.54	67	92
Virgin Islands	3	4	1	6	3,194	69.44	3	2
Washington	248	205	44	530	299,588	110.43	357	96
West Virginia	124	120	26	189	158,148	105.92	1	36
Wisconsin	386	293	69	655	451,009	117.47	257	93
Wyoming	29	12	2	24	16,014	107.51	73	15
TOTAL	**12,448**	**9,992**	**3,072**	**25,411**	**$13,777,521**	**$98.85**	**$11,464**	**4,730**

(p.) Preliminary. (1) Claimants whose base-period earnings or whose employment — covered by the unemployment insurance program — was sufficient to make them eligible for unemployment insurance benefits as provided by state law. (2) Based on number of first payments. (3) Based on final payments. Some claimants shown, therefore, actually experienced their final week of compensable unemployment toward the end of the previous calendar year but received their final payments in the current calendar year. Similarly, some claimants who served their last week of compensable unemployment toward the end of the current calendar year did not receive their final payment in this calendar year and hence are not shown. A final week of compensable unemployment in a benefit year results in the exhaustion of benefit rights for the benefit year. Claimants who exhaust their benefit rights in one benefit year may be entitled to further benefits in the following benefit year. (4) Excludes intrastate transitional claims to reflect more nearly instances of new unemployment. Includes claims filed by interstate claimants in the Virgin Islands. (5) Adjusted for voided benefit checks and transfers under interstate combined wage plan. (6) Sum of balance in state clearing accounts, benefit payment accounts, and unemployment trust fund accounts in the U.S. Treasury.

for tax offset credit for employers.

Benefits are financed solely by employer contributions, except in Alaska, Alabama, and New Jersey, where employees also contribute. Benefits are paid through the states' public employment offices, at which unemployed workers must register for work and to which they must report regularly for referral to a possible job during the time when they are drawing weekly benefit payments. During the 1981 calendar year, $15.3 billion in benefits was paid under state unemployment insurance programs to 9.4 million beneficiaries. They received an average weekly payment of $106.48 for total unemployment for an average of 15.8 weeks.

Federal Worker Benefits

Benefits for unemployed federal workers and ex-servicemen are financed by the federal government but are paid by the state agencies.

During calendar year 1981, $169 million was paid to 87,000 unemployed federal civilian workers. The average weekly payment was $102.41 and was paid for an average of 19.2 weeks. A total of $256 million was paid to 100,000 unemployed ex-servicemen. The average weekly benefit was $108.27 and was paid for an average of 23.8 weeks.

Jobs: Job Openings to 1990 and Current Earnings

Source: Bureau of Labor Statistics, U.S. Labor Department. For more detailed information on job categories, see the Occupational Outlook Handbook, 1982-83 Edition.

Occupation	Est. no. of Jobs, 1980 (000)	% Change 1978-90 (est.)	Median Earnings[1] (dollars)
Industrial			
Assemblers	1,670	19-31	236
Blue-collar worker supv.	1,300	16-25	236
Compositors	128	−2 to −10	394
Machine tool oper.	1,020	18-21	274
Machinist, all-round	303	16-29	356
Photographic process workers	77	6-16	230
Printing press oper.	178	9-17	320
Tool-and-die makers	166	8-24	433
Welders	573	22-37	334
Office			
Accountants	900	25-34	379
Bank officers, mgrs.	400	26-33	411
Bank tellers	480	25-29	189
Bookkeepers	1,700	15-24	227
Cashiers	1,600	28-36	168
Collection workers	89	22-34	233
Computer operating pers.	558	22-30	260
Computer programmers	228	49-60	422
Computer systems analysts	205	68-80	519
Insurance claim reps.	210	39-43	270
Lawyers	425	25-39	546
Librarians	135	3-5	320
Library assistants	154	3-4	203
Personnel & labor relations	178	15-22	402
Postal clerks	265	−29	400
Purchasing agents	172	16-24	390
Receptionists	635	22-31	230
Secretaries	2,500	28-37	229
Stenographers	280	−2 to −8	275
Telephone operators	340	4-15	240
Typists	1,100	18-25	213
Service Occupations			
Barbers	112	7-22	327[2]
Bartenders	382	19-26	195
Correction officers	103	47-49	313[3]
Cooks and chefs	1,100	22-28	171
Cosmetologists	515	14-29	179
Firefighters	27	17-19	362
Food counter workers	426	48	141
Guards	650	23-24	232
Meatcutters	190	11-18	316
Police officers	495	17-19	363
Waiters and waitresses	1,700	21-28	150
Educational and related occupations			
K-6 teachers	1,600	18-19	322
Second. school teach.	1,237	−14	351
Coll., univ. faculty	691	−9	444
Sales occupations			
Advertising workers	100	NA	334
Auto. sales workers	157	26-36	179
Real estate agents, brokers	580	34-46	326
Retail trade sales workers	3,300	19-27	178
Construction occupations			
Carpenters	970	18-27	325
Constr. laborers	2,100	NA	250
Electricians (constrs.)	560	20-28	419
Painters	382	14-25	271
Plumbers, pipefitters	407	20-28	404
Roofers	113	15-24	267
Transportation occupations			
Airplane mechanics	109	15-22	427
Airplane pilots	82	15-23	530
Airline reser. agts.	86	0-7	339[2]
Flight attendants	56	15-22	365[2]
Busdrivers (local)	97	27-29	298
Truckdrivers (local)	1,700	23-31	314
Truckdrivers (long-dist.)	575	23-31	517
Scientific and technical occupations			
Aerospace engineers	68	43-52	NA
Chemical engineers	55	23-32	575
Chemists	113	18-24	467
Civil engineers	165	26-31	505
Drafters	322	20-39	343
Electrical engineers	325	35-47	549
Industrial engineers	115	26-38	530
Mathematicians	40	11-14	508[4]
Mechanical engineers	213	29-41	540
Mechanics and repairers			
Appliance repairers	77	16-29	385[5]
Automobile mechanics	845	24-33	285
Bus. machine operators	55	60-74	327
Computer serv. technicians	83	93-112	395
Indust. machinery repairers	507	17-26	334[5]
Shoe repairers	16	12-17	200[2]
Telephone, PBX installers and repairers	130	15-30	412
TV, radio serv. technicians	83	31-43	336
Health and medical occupations			
Dentists	126	23	1,057[2]
Dental assistants	140	38-42	183
Dental hygienists	36	67	300[2]
Dietitians	44	38-46	304[6]
Health serv. administrators	220	43-53	431
Medical laboratory workers	205	35-43	304[7]
Nurses, registered	1,105	40-47	332
Nurses, licensed practical	550	42	227
Operating room technicians	31.5	39-45	
Pharmacists	141	10-20	463
Physical therapists	34	51-59	305
Physicians, osteopaths	424	32	501
Radiologic technologists	106	36-43	290
Veterinarians	36	31-43	656[3]
Social scientists			
Economists	44	26-32	536
Political scientists	15	14	413[8]
Psychologists	106	22-27	394
Sociologists	21	6-8	500[9]
Social service occupations			
School counselors	53	0	396
Social workers	345	20-24	309
Design occupations			
Architects	79.5	33-41	428
Interior designers	35	25	(10)
Communications occupations			
Newspaper reporters	57	22-32	351
Public relations workers	87	18-26	402

(1) Average median weekly earnings of wage and salary workers employed full-time, annual averages in 1981. (2) 1980 annual average based on reports in Occupational Outlook Handbook, 1982-83 edition. (3) 1980 average for federal government workers. (4) Average starting salary for Ph.D. holders in 1980. (5) 1980 average salary based on 35-hour week. (6) 1980 average salary for entry level workers in hospitals. (7) 1980 average salary for medical technologists working in hospitals, medical centers, and medical schools. (8) 1979-80 average salary for associate professors. (9) 1979 average salary for doctoral sociologists. (10) 1980 average salary ranged from $15,000 to $25,000 for moderately experienced workers.

Quality of Life in U.S. Metropolitan Areas: A Comparative Table

Source: For personal per capita income, *Survey of Current Business,* April 1982; for unemployment rate, Bureau of Labor Statistics; for projected growth in employment and in personal income, Chase Econometrics Regional Forecasting Service; for average purchase price of a home, Federal Home Loan Bank Board; for crime rate, *Uniform Crime Reports 1980,* Federal Bureau of Investigation; for weather data, *Comparative Climatic Data for the United States Through 1980,* National Oceanic and Atmospheric Administration. Data given is for Standard Metropolitan Statistical Area (SMSAs) whenever possible; in all other cases, data given is for segment of SMSA for which data is available.

	Per capita personal income 1980	% Jobless June 1982	Projected annual % growth in jobs 1979-1990	Projected annual % growth in income 1979-1990	Average price of a home July 1982 (prel.) $000	Crime rate per 100,000 1980[8]	Mean no. of days[9] clr.—cldy.—pt. cldy.	Mean no. of days temp. below 32°F	Normal daily max. temp. August °F
Anaheim-Santa Ana Garden Gr. Cal.	11,857	7.0	3.4	3.2	130.4	6,847.0	NA	NA	NA
Atlanta, Ga.	9,997	6.6	2.1	2.8	90.2	7,575.2	107—110—148	60	86.4
Baltimore, Md.	10,016	10.5	1.0	2.0	75.4	7,473.0	109—108—148	99	85.1
Birmingham, Ala.	8,909	13.0	2.1	2.8	NA	7,079.0	99—111—155	61	89.7
Boston-Lowell-Brockton-Lawrence-Haverhill, Mass.-N.H.	10,803	7.9[1]	1.1	2.1	74.9	6,493.3	100—105—160	99	79.3
Bridgeport-Stamford-Norwalk-Danbury, Ct.	14,197	7.7[2]	1.3	1.6	NA	6,183.0	100—107—158	100	80.4
Buffalo, N.Y.	9,458	12.2	0.2	1.3	NA	5,305.8	55—102—208	135	77.6
Chicago, Ill.	11,394	11.0	0.6	1.4	88.1	5,721.8	86—107—172	132	82.3
Cincinnati, Oh., Ky., Ind.	9,877	8.0[3]	1.4	1.9	NA	5,774.2	NA	110	85.8
Cleveland, Oh.	11,236	10.8	0.3	1.2	84.9	5,634.4	69— 98—198	125	80.4
Columbus, Oh.	7,326	9.3	1.3	2.0	90.8	7,541.4	74—106—185	121	83.7
Dallas-Ft. Worth, Tex.	11,041	7.2	3.2	3.6	88.5	8,270.7	141— 93—131	41	96.1
Dayton, Oh.	9,639	11.4	0.8	1.6	NA	7,430.2	80—102—183	118	83.4
Denver-Boulder, Col.	11,301	6.3	3.0	3.6	87.1	8,356.9	118—128—119	159	85.8
Detroit, Mich.	11,208	14.4	0.4	1.8	69.0	7,582.3	77—105—183	124-139	81.6-82.0
Ft. Lauderdale-Hollywood, Fla.	10,737	6.5	NA	4.3	NA	9,345.4	NA	NA	NA
Hartford-New Britain-Bristol, Ct.	11,395	6.4[4]	1.4	2.0	NA	6,606.9	80—110—175	137	81.9
Honolulu, Ha.	10,492	7.1	2.0	2.6	114.9[6]	7,574.3	88—176—101	0	87.4
Houston, Tex.	11,861	7.1	4.1	4.5	95.8	6,900.1	97—110—158	26	94.3
Indianapolis, Ind.	10,082	9.1	0.9	1.7	68.7[7]	6,009.2	91— 99—175	121	84.0
Kansas City, Mo.-Kan.	10,550	8.4	1.3	2.2	68.7	7,720.3	119—102—144	104	88.7
Los Angeles-Long Beach, Cal.	11,350	8.8	1.5	2.2	130.4	8,418.7	165—114— 91	0-1	75.8-84.0
Louisville, Ky.-Ind.	9,275	8.7[3]	1.1	2.2	70.0	5,570.3	94—103—168	92	86.8
Memphis, Tenn.-Ark.-Miss.	8,696	9.9	1.4	2.3	NA	6,492.3	120— 96—149	59	90.6
Miami, Fla.	9,598	7.8	2.6	3.1	84.9	11,581.8	73—173—119	0	89.9
Milwaukee, Wis.	10,906	10.3	1.5	2.2	87.7	5,364.2	94—100—171	145	79.7
Minneapolis-St. Paul, Minn.-Wis.	11,329	6.3	2.0	2.6	82.7	6,137.1	99—102—164	157	80.8
Nashville-Davidson, Tenn.	8,821	8.7	2.8	3.3	NA	5,761.7	102—108—155	77	89.2
Newark, N.J.	11,689	8.2	0.6	0.9	97.2	6,990.4	95—112—158	87	83.7
New Orleans, La.	9,791	10.6	2.1	3.0	NA	7,890.2	108—119—138	13	90.6
New York, N.Y.-N.J.	11,087	9.9	0.1	1.3	97.2	8,592.8	100—122—143	80	82.5
Philadelphia, Pa.-N.J.	10,142	8.5	0.5	1.2	63.3	5,357.8	93—110—162	100	84.8
Phoenix, Ariz.	9,637	8.0	3.7	4.2	85.3	9,308.4	213— 82— 70	11	102.2
Pittsburgh, Pa.	10,253	12.0	0.8	1.6	69.0	3,485.3	58—103—204	124	80.9
Portland, Ore.-Wash.	10,650	9.9	2.8	3.2	85.1	7,324.9	69— 69—227	44	78.1
Providence-Warwick-Pawtucket, R.I.	9,457	9.8	0.7	1.5	NA	5,859.4	103—103—159	123	79.8
Riverside-San Bernadino- Ontario, Cal.	9,011	11.6	2.6	3.1	NA	8,231.9	NA	NA	NA
Rochester, N.Y.	10,812	7.0	1.1	2.0	67.0	6,111.2	61—108—196	135	80.1
Sacramento, Cal.	10,185	10.8	1.9	2.8	NA	9,373.1	190— 75—100	17	91.3
St. Louis, Mo.-Ill.	10,300	9.5	0.4	1.7	70.2	6,488.0	104—101—160	106	87.2
Salt Lake City-Odgen, Ut.	8,347	7.1	3.3	3.9	NA	7,247.1	127—104—134	130	90.2
San Antonio, Tex.	8,445	8.9	2.8	3.5	NA	6,411.1	107—120—138	23	95.9
San Diego, Cal.	9,962	9.5	3.4	3.7	112.2	7,038.4	148—118— 99	0	77.3
San Francisco-Oakland, Cal.	12,998	7.6	1.0	2.0	123.3	8,540.6	161—102—102	1.5	68.2
San Jose, Cal.	12,297	7.5	3.2	3.4	123.3	7,612.2	NA	NA	NA
Seattle-Everett, Wash.	11,882	11.0	2.4	3.1	118.0	7,862.0	65— 86—215	24	74
Tampa-St. Petersburg, Fla.	8,731	7.0	3.2	3.7	86.1	8,071.1	95—143—127	4	90.4
Washington D.C.-Md.-Va.	12,871	6.3	1.5	2.3	120.6	6,938.8	101—103—162	95	86

(1) Boston only; Lowell, 8.2; Brockton, 11.5; Lawrence-Haverhill, 9.8. (2) Bridgeport only; Stamford, 3.5. (3) June 1981. (4) Hartford only; New Britain 9.6. (5) Worcester only. (6) June 1982. (7) May 1982. (8) Includes all crime. (9) Categories are determined for daylight hours only; clear denotes zero to 0.3 sky cover; partly cloudy denotes 0.4 to 0.7 average sky cover; cloudy denotes 0.8 to complete sky cover. Figures may not add to 365 days in all cases; discrepancy is due to averaging based on several reporting sites in the area.

Social Security Programs: After the Paychecks Stop

Source: Social Security Administration, U.S. Department of Health and Human Services

Old-Age, Survivors, and Disability Insurance; Medicare; Supplemental Security Income

New Legislation

On August 13, 1981, President Reagan signed into law the Omnibus Budget Reconciliation Act of 1981 (Public law 97-35). Following are some of the provisions under the new law that affect Social Security:

(1) Elimination of the minimum Social Security benefit for both current and future beneficiaries and payment instead of a wage-related benefit based on the worker's average earnings. Legislation signed into law on Dec. 29, 1981 (Public Law 97-123) restored the minimum benefit for people eligible for benefits before 1982.

(2) Phasing out of student benefits for persons aged 19 or over or in postsecondary schools.

(3) Payment of the lump-sum death benefit only when there is a spouse who was living with the worker or a spouse or child eligible for immediate monthly survivor benefits.

(4) Offset of Social Security disability benefits when total public plan benefits based on disability exceed 80% of certain predisability earnings—a "Megacap" provision.

Old-Age, Survivors, and Disability Insurance

Old-Age, Survivors, and Disability Insurance covers almost all jobs in which people work for wages or salaries, as well as most work of self-employed persons, whether in a city job, or in business, or on a farm.

Old-Age, Survivors, and Disability Insurance is paid for by a tax on earnings (for 1982, up to $32,400; the taxable earnings base is now subject to adjustment when cost-of-living benefit increases have been made). The employed worker and his or her employer share the tax equally (cash tips count as covered wages if they amount to $20 or more from one place of employment. The worker reports them to the employer, who includes them in the social security tax reports, but only the worker pays contributions on the amount of the tips).

The employer deducts the tax each payday and sends it, with an equal amount (the employer's share), to the District Director of Internal Revenue. The collected taxes are deposited in the Federal Old-Age and Survivors Insurance Trust Fund and the Federal Disability Insurance Trust Fund; they can be used only to pay benefits, the cost of rehabilitation services, and administrative expenses.

Benefit Increase, June 1982

Social Security checks delivered to beneficiaries in the first week of July 1982 reflected the eighth automatic cost-of-living increase in cash benefits under legislation enacted in 1972 and 1973. The 7.4% increase, which became effective for June, applied to benefits for all persons eligible for benefits in 1982.

Automatic increases are initiated whenever the Consumer Price Index (CPI) of the Bureau of Labor Statistics for the first calendar quarter of a year exceeds by at least 3 percent the CPI for the base quarter, which is either the first calendar quarter of the preceding year or the quarter in which an increase was legislated by Congress. In this case, the base quarter was the first quarter of 1981. The size of the benefit increase is determined by the actual percentage rise of the CPI during the quarters measured.

As a result of the benefit increase, average monthly benefits payable to retired workers rose to $465.30 for men and $359.78 for women. Average amounts for disabled workers were $487.46 for men and $351.39 for women.

Social Security benefits are based on a worker's primary insurance amount (PIA), which is related by law to the average indexed monthly earnings (AIME) on which social security contributions have been paid. The full PIA is payable to a retired worker who becomes entitled to benefits at age 65 and to an entitled disabled worker at any age. Spouses and children of retired or disabled workers and survivors of deceased workers receive set proportions of the PIA subject to a family maximum amount. The PIA is calculated by applying varying percentages to succeeding parts of the AIME. The formula is adjusted annually to reflect changes in average annual wages in the economy.

Amount of Work Required

To qualify for benefits, the worker must have worked in covered employment long enough to become insured. Just how long depends on when the worker reaches age 62 or, if earlier, when he or she dies or becomes disabled.

A person is fully insured if he or she has one quarter of coverage for every year after 1950 (or year age 21 is reached) up to but not including the year in which the worker reaches age 62, dies, or becomes disabled.

Certain provisions in the law permit special monthly payments under the Social Security program to persons aged 72 and over who are not eligible for regular social security benefits since they had little or no opportunity to earn social security work credits during their working lifetime.

To get disability benefits, in addition to being fully insured, the worker must also have credit for 5 out of 10 years before he or she becomes disabled. A disabled blind worker need meet only the fully insured requirement. Persons disabled before age 31 can qualify with a briefer period of coverage. Certain survivor benefits are payable if the deceased worker had 6 quarters of coverage in the 13 quarters preceding death.

Work Years Required

The following table shows the number of work years required to be fully insured for Old-Age or Survivors benefits, according to the year worker reaches retirement age or dies.

Work credit for retirement benefits

If you reach 62 in	Years you need	If you reach 62 in	Years you need
1974	6*	1979	7
1975	6	1981	7½
1976	6¼	1983	8
1977	6½	1987	9
1978	6¾	1991 or later	10

*For 1974 a woman needs only 5¾ years.

Work credit for survivors and disability benefits

Born after 1929, die or become disabled at age	Born before 1930, die or become disabled before age 62 in	Years needed
32		2½
34		3
36		3½
38		4
40		4½
42		5
44		5½
45		5¾
46		6
48		6½
50	1979	7
52	1981	7½
54	1983	8
56	1985	8½
58	1987	9
60	1989	9½
62 or older	1991 or later	10

Contribution and benefit base

Calendar year	Current base
1977	$16,500
1978	17,700
1979	22,900
1980	25,900
1981	29,700
1982	32,400

Tax-rate schedule
[Percent of covered earnings]

Year	Total	OASDI	HI
	Employees and employers, each		
1977	5.85	4.95	0.90
1978	6.05	5.05	1.00
1979-80	6.13	5.08	1.05
1981	6.65	5.35	1.30
1982-84	6.70	5.40	1.30
1985	7.05	5.70	1.35
1986-89	7.15	5.70	1.45
1990 and after	7.65	6.20	1.45
	Self-employed		
1977	7.90	7.00	0.90
1978	8.10	7.10	1.00
1979-80	8.10	7.05	1.05
1981	9.30	8.00	1.30
1982-84	9.35	8.05	1.30
1985	9.90	8.55	1.35
1986-89	10.00	8.55	1.45
1990 and after	10.75	9.30	1.45

What Aged Workers Get

When a person has enough work in covered employment and reaches retirement age (65 for full benefit, 62 for reduced benefit), he or she may retire and get monthly old-age benefits. If a person aged 65 or older continues to work and has earnings of more than $6,000 in 1982, $1 in benefits will be withheld for every $2 above $6,000. The annual exempt amount for people under age 65 is $4,440 in 1982. The annual exempt amount and the monthly test are raised automatically or according to the rise in general earnings levels. (The annual exempt amount for retirees 65 or older increases to $6,000 in 1982). The eligible worker who is 72 (age 70 beginning in 1983) receives the full amount of benefit regardless of earnings.

A worker's benefit will be raised by 3% for each year after 1970 for which the worker between 65 and 72 did not receive benefits because of earnings from work or because the worker had not applied for benefits. The delayed retirement credit is increased to 1 percent a year for workers reaching age 62 before 1978. No increases are to be paid to the worker's dependents or survivors under this provision.

In January, 1982, the special benefit for persons aged 72 or over who do not meet the regular coverage requirements is $117.00 a month (175.70 for a couple if both members are eligible). Like the monthly benefits, these payments are now subject to cost-of-living increases. For benefits payable for the month of June 1982, the benefit for an individual is $125.60 and for a couple is $188.60. The special payment is not made to persons on the public assistance or supplemental security income rolls.

Social Security benefits are not subject to income taxes.

Workers retiring before age 65 have their benefits permanently reduced by 5/9 of 1% for each month they receive benefits before age 65. Thus, people entitled to benefits in the month they reach age 62 receive 80% of the benefit that would be payable at age 65. The nearer to age 65 the worker is when he or she begins collecting a benefit, the larger the benefit will be.

Benefits for Worker's Spouse

The spouse of a worker who is getting social security retirement or disability payments may become entitled to a spouse's insurance benefit in a reduced amount when he or she reaches 65 of one-half of the worker's benefit. Reduced spouse's benefits are available at age 62 (25/36 of 1% reduction for each month of entitlement before age 65). Benefits are also payable to the divorced spouse of an insured worker if he or she was married to the worker for at least 20 years (10 years eff. Jan. 1979).

Benefits for Children of Retired or Disabled Workers

If a worker has a child under 18 when he or she retires or becomes disabled the child will get a benefit that is half of the worker's unreduced benefit, and so will his or her spouse, even if he or she is under 62 if he or she is caring for a child of the worker who is under 16 or disabled. Total benefits paid on a worker's earnings record are subject to a maximum and if the total paid to a family exceeds that maximum, the individual dependents' benefits are adjusted downward. (Total benefits paid to the family of a worker who retired in June 1982 at age 65 and who always had the maximum amount of earnings creditable under Social Security can be no higher than $1,276.00.)

When entitled children reach 18, their benefits will stop, except that a child permanently and totally disabled before 22 may get a benefit as long as his or her disability meets the definition in the law. Benefits may now be paid to a grandchild or step-grandchild of a worker or of his or her spouse, in special circumstances. Additionally, benefits will be paid to a child until age 19 if the child is in full-time attendance at an elementary or secondary school.

OASDI	July 1982	July 1981	July 1980
Monthly beneficiaries, total (in thousands)	**35,375**	**35,698**	**35,146**
Aged 65 and over, total	24,626	24,036	23,437
Retired workers	18,244	17,734	17,213
Survivors and dependents	6,314	6,220	6,124
Special age-72 beneficiaries	68	82	100
Under age 65, total	10,749	11,662	11,709
Retired workers	2,197	2,121	2,008
Disabled workers	2,682	2,827	2,861
Survivors and dependents	5,870	6,714	6,840
Total monthly benefits (in millions)	**$13,089**	**$12,054**	**$10,466**

What Disabled Workers Get

If a worker becomes so severely disabled that he or she is unable to work, he or she may be eligible to receive a monthly disability benefit that is the same amount that would have been received for a retired-worker benefit if he or she were 65 at the start of the disability. When he or she reach 65, the disability benefit becomes a retired-worker benefit.

Benefits like those provided for dependents of retired-worker beneficiaries may be paid to dependents of disabled beneficiaries.

Survivor Benefits

If a worker should die while insured, one or more types of benefits would be payable to survivors.

1. A cash payment to cover burial expenses that amounts to $255. Payment is made only when there is a spouse who was living with the worker or a spouse or child eligible for immediate monthly survivor benefits.

2. At age 65, the surviving spouse will receive a benefit that is 100% of the deceased worker's basic amount. The surviving spouse may choose to get the benefit as early as age 60, but the benefit is then reduced by 19/40 of 1% for each month it is paid before age 65. However, for those aged 62 and over whose spouses claimed their benefits before 65, the benefit is the reduced amount the worker would be getting if alive but not less than 82 1/2% of the basic benefit.

Disabled widows and widowers qualify for benefits at age 50 at reduced rates that depend on age at entitlement. The widow or widower must have become totally disabled before or within 7 years after the spouse's death.

3. A benefit for each child until the child reaches 18. The monthly benefit of each child of a worker who has died is three-quarters of the amount the worker would have received if he or she had lived and drawn retirement benefits. A child with a permanent disability that began before age 22 may receive his or her benefit after that age. Also, a child may receive student's benefits until age 19 if he or she is in full-time attendance at an elementary or secondary school.

4. A mother's or father's benefit for the widow(er), if children of the worker under 16 are in his or her care. The benefit is 75% of the basic benefit and he or she draws it until the youngest child reaches 16. Payments stop then even if the child's benefit continues because he or she is attending school. They may start again when he or she is 60 unless he or she marries. If he or she marries and the marriage is

ended, he or she regains benefit rights. If he or she has a disabled child beneficiary aged 16 or over in care, benefits also continue. This benefit is also paid to the divorced spouse, if the marriage lasted for at least 10 years. (20 years prior to January 1979)

5. Dependent parents may be eligible for benefits, if they have been receiving at least half their support from the worker before his or her death, have reached age 62, and (except in certain circumstances) have not remarried since the worker's death. Each parent gets 75% of the basic benefit except that if only one parent survives the benefit is 82 1/2%.

Self-Employed

A self-employed person who has earnings of $400 or more in a year must report such earnings for social security tax purposes. The person reports net returns from the business. Income from real estate, savings, dividends, loans, pensions or insurance policies may not be included unless they are part of the business.

A self-employed person who has net earnings of $400 or more in a year gets a quarter of coverage for each $340 (for 1982), up to a maximum of 4 quarters of coverage. If earnings are less than $400 in a year they do not count toward social security credits. The nonfarm self-employed person must make estimated payments of his or her social security taxes, on a quarterly basis, for 1982, if combined estimated income tax and social security tax amount to at least $200.

The nonfarm self-employed have the option of reporting their earnings as ⅔ of their gross income from self-employment but not more than $1,600 a year and not less than their actual net earnings. This option can be used only if actual net earnings from self-employment income is less than $1,600 and may be used only 5 times. Also, the self-employed person must have actual net earnings of $400 or more in 2 of the 3 taxable years immediately preceding the year in which he or she uses the option.

When a person has both taxable wages and earnings from self-employment, only as much of the self-employment income as will bring total earnings up to the current taxable maximum is subject to tax for social security purposes. A self-employed person pays the tax at a lower rate than the combined rate for an employee and his employer — about 1 ½ times what the employee alone pays.

Farm Owners and Workers

Self-employed farmers whose gross annual earnings from farming are under $2,400 may report ⅔ of their gross earnings instead of net earnings for social security purposes. Farmers whose gross income is over $2,400 and whose net earnings are less than $1,600 can report $1,600. Cash or crop shares received from a tenant or share farmer count if the owner participated materially in production or management. The self-employed farmer pays contributions at the same rate as other self-employed persons.

Agricultural employees. Earnings from farm work count toward benefits (1) if the employer pays $150 or more in cash during the year; (2) if the employee works on 20 or more days for cash pay figured on a time basis. Under these rules a person gets credit for one calendar quarter for each $340 in cash pay in 1982 up to four quarters.

Foreign farm workers admitted to the United States on a temporary basis are not covered.

Household Workers

Anyone working as maid, cook, laundress, nursemaid, baby-sitter, chauffeur, gardener and at other household tasks in the house of another is covered by social security if he or she earns $50 or more in cash in a calendar quarter from any one employer. Room and board do not count, but carfare counts if paid in cash. The job does not have to be regular or fulltime. The employee should get a card at the social security office and show it to the employer.

The employer deducts the amount of the social security tax from the worker's pay, adds an identical amount as the employer's own tax and sends the total amount to the federal government, with the number of the employee's social security card.

Medicare

Under Medicare, protection against the costs of hospital care is provided for social security and railroad retirement beneficiaries aged 65 and over and, for persons entitled for 24 months to receive a social security disability benefit, certain persons (and their dependents) with end-stage renal disease, and, on a voluntary basis with payment of a special premium, persons aged 65 and over not otherwise eligible for hospital benefits; all those eligible for hospital benefits may enroll for medical benefits and pay a monthly premium and so may persons aged 65 and over who are not eligible for hospital benefits.

Persons eligible for both hospital and medical insurance may choose to have their covered services provided through a Health Maintenance Organization.

Hospital insurance.—From October 1981 to September 1982, about $33.7 billion was withdrawn from the hospital insurance trust fund for hospital and related benefits.

As of January 1982, the hospital insurance program paid the cost of covered services for hospital and posthospital care as follows:

- Up to 90 days of hospital care during a benefit period (spell of illness) starting the first day that care as a bed-patient is received in a hospital or skilled-nursing facility and ending when the individual has not been a bed-patient for 60 consecutive days. For the first 60 days, the hospital insurance pays for all but the first $260 of expenses; for the 61st day to 90th day, the program pays all but $65 a day for covered services. In addition, each person has a 60-day lifetime reserve that can be used after the 90 days of hospital care in a benefit period are exhausted, and all but $130 a day of expenses during the reserve days are paid. Once used, the reserve days are not replaced. (Payment for care in a mental hospital is limited to 190 days.)
- Up to 100 days' care in a skilled-nursing facility (skilled-nursing home) in each benefit period. Hospital insurance pays for all covered services for the first 20 days and all but $32.50 daily for the next 80 days. At least 3 days' hospital stay must precede these services, and the skilled-nursing facility must be entered within 14 days after leaving the hospital. (The 1972 law permits more than 14 days in certain circumstances.)
- Unlimited visits by nurses or other health workers (not doctors) from a home health agency in the 365 days after release from a hospital or extended-care facility.

Medical insurance. Aged persons can receive benefits under this supplementary program only if they sign up for them and agree to a monthly premium ($12.20 beginning July 1982). The Federal Government pays the rest of the cost. In December of each year the Secretary of Health and Human Services announces the premium payable starting in July of the following year. The premiums are to be increased only when there is a general benefit increase in the year and it will rise no more than the percent by which the cash benefits have been increased since the last premium increase.

About 142 million bills were reimbursed under the medical insurance program from October 1981 to September 1982 for a total of $14.9 billion. As of September 1982, about 28.2 million persons were enrolled — 2.7 million of them disabled persons under age 65.

The medical insurance program pays 80% of the reasonable charges (after the first $75 in each calendar year) for the following services:

- Physicians' and surgeons' services, whether in the doctor's office, a clinic, or hospital or at home (but physician's charges for X-ray or clinical laboratory services for hospital bed-patients are paid in full and without meeting the deductible).
- Other medical and health services, such as diagnostic tests, surgical dressings and splints, and rental or purchase of medical equipment. Services of a physical therapist in independent practice, furnished in his office or the patient's home. A hospital or extended-care facility may provide covered outpatient physical therapy services under the medical insurance program to its patients who have exhausted their hospital insurance coverage.
- Physical therapy services furnished under the supervision

of a practicing hospital, clinic, skilled nursing facility, or agency.

- Certain services by podiatrists.
- All outpatient services of a participating hospital (including diagnostic tests).
- Outpatient speech pathology services, under the same requirements as physical therapy.
- Services of licensed chiropractors who meet uniform standards, but only for treatment by means of manual manipulation of the spine and treatment of subluxation of the spine demonstrated by X-ray.
- Supplies related to colostomies are considered prosthetic devices and payable under the program.
- Home health services even without a hospital stay (up to 100 visits a year) are paid up to 100%.

To get medical insurance protection, persons approaching age 65 may enroll in the 7-month period that includes 3 months before the 65th birthday, the month of the birthday, and 3 months after the birthday, but if they wish coverage to begin in the month they reach 65 they must enroll in the 3 months **before** their birthday. Persons not enrolling within their first enrollment period may enroll later, during the first 3 months of each year but their premium is 10% higher for each 12-month period elapsed since they first could have enrolled.

The monthly premium is deducted from the cash benefit for persons receiving social security, railroad retirement, or civil service retirement benefits. Income from the medical premiums and the federal matching payments are put in a Supplementary Medical Insurance Trust Fund, from which benefits and administrative expenses are paid.

Medicare card. Persons qualifying for hospital insurance under social security receive a health insurance card similar to cards now used by Blue Cross and other health agencies. The card indicates whether the individual has taken out medical insurance protection. It is to be shown to the hospital, skilled-nursing facility, home health agency, doctor, or whoever provides the covered services.

Payments are made only in the 50 states, Puerto Rico, the Virgin Islands, Guam, and American Samoa, except that hospital services may be provided in border areas immediately outside the U.S. if comparable services are not accessible in the U.S. for a beneficiary who becomes ill or is injured in the U.S.

Supplemental Security Income

On Jan. 1, 1974, the Supplemental Security Income (SSI) program established by the 1972 Social Security Act amendments replaced the former federal grants to states for aid to the needy aged, blind, and disabled in the 50 states and the District of Columbia. The program provides both for federal payments based on uniform national standards and eligibility requirements and for state supplementary payments varying from state to state. The Social Security Administration administers the federal payments financed from general funds of the Treasury—and the state supplements as well, if the state elects to have its supplementary program federally administered. The states may supplement the federal payment for all recipients and must supplement it for persons otherwise adversely affected by the transition from the former public assistance programs. In July 1982, the number of persons receiving federal payments and federally administered state payments was 3,927,733, and the amount of these payments was $782.5 million.

As a result of the 7.4% benefit increase, the maximum federal SSI payment for an individual with no other countable income, living in his own household, rises from $264.70 to $284.30, and that for a couple, similarly situated, goes from $397.00 to $426.40.

Minimum and maximum monthly retired-worker benefits payable to individuals who retired at age 65, 1960—82[1]

Year of attainment of age 65[2]	Minimum benefit: Payable at the time of retirement	Minimum benefit: Payable effective June 1982	Maximum benefit: Payable at the time of retirement, Men[3]	Maximum benefit: Payable at the time of retirement, Women	Maximum benefit: Payable effective June 1982, Men[3]	Maximum benefit: Payable effective June 1982, Women
1960	$33.00	$182.90	$119.00	...	$472.50	...
1961	33.00	182.90	120.00	...	476.20	...
1962	40.00	182.90	121.00	$123.00	480.50	$488.60
1963	40.00	182.90	122.00	125.00	484.50	496.00
1964	40.00	182.90	123.00	127.00	488.60	504.20
1965	44.00	182.90	131.70	135.90	488.60	504.20
1966	44.00	182.90	132.70	135.90	492.20	504.20
1967	44.00	182.90	135.90	140.00	504.20	530.10
1968	[4]55.00	182.90	[4]156.00	[4]161.60	511.90	530.10
1969	55.00	182.90	160.50	167.30	526.90	549.10
1970	64.00	182.90	189.80	196.40	541.50	560.50
1971	70.40	182.90	213.10	220.40	552.60	571.20
1972	70.40	182.90	216.10	224.70	560.50	582.60
1973	84.50	182.90	266.10	276.40	575.00	597.30
1974	84.50	182.90	274.60	284.90	593.20	615.60
1975	93.80	182.90	316.30	333.70	615.60	649.30
1976	101.40	182.90	364.00	378.80	655.50	682.30
1977	107.90	182.90	412.70	422.40	698.60	714.90
1978	114.30	182.90	459.80	...	734.80	...
1979	121.80	182.90	503.40	...	755.40	...
1980	133.90	182.90	572.00	...	780.90	...
1981	153.10	182.90	677.00	...	808.60	...
1982	[5]170.30	182.90	[5]679.30	...	729.50	...

(1) Assumes retirement at beginning of year. (2) The final benefit amount payable after SMI premium or any other deductions is rounded to next lower $1 (if not already a multiple of $1). (3) Benefit for both men and women are shown in men's columns except where women's benefit appears separately. (4) Effective for February 1968. (5) Derived from transitional guarantee computation based on 1978 PIA table.

Examples of monthly benefit awards for selected beneficiary families with first eligibility in 1981, by average monthly earnings, effective June 1981

Beneficiary family	Average monthly covered earnings of insured worker: $76 or less	$100	$300	$550	$750	$900	$1,100	$1,475	$2,158
Retired worker claiming benefits at age 65, or disabled worker:									
Worker alone	$170.30	$219.10	$388.70	$580.30	$712.60	$773.10	$849.70	$971.50	$1,156.60
Worker with spouse claiming benefits at—									
Age 65 or older	255.50	328.70	583.10	870.50	1,068.90	1,159.70	1,274.60	1,457.30	1,734.90
Age 62	234.20	301.30	534.50	798.00	979.90	1,063.10	1,168.40	1,335.90	1,590.40
Worker, spouse, and 1 child	255.50	328.70	637.20	1,050.10	1,247.00	1,352.70	1,486.50	1,700.00	2,024.10
Widow or widower claiming benefits at—									
Age 65 or older[1]	170.30	219.10	388.70	580.30	712.60	773.10	849.70	971.50	1,156.60
Age 60	121.80	156.70	278.00	415.00	509.60	552.80	607.60	694.70	827.00
Disabled widow or widower claiming benefits at age 50	85.20	109.60	194.40	290.20	356.30	386.60	424.90	485.80	578.30
1 surviving child	[2]170.30	[2]170.30	291.60	435.30	534.50	579.90	637.30	728.70	867.50
Widow or widower aged 65 or older and 1 child[1]	255.50	328.70	637.20	1,015.60	1,247.00	1,352.70	1,486.50	1,700.00	2,024.10
Widowed mother or father and 1 child	255.50	328.70	583.20	870.60	1,069.00	1,159.80	1,274.60	1,457.40	1,735.00
Widowed mother or father and 2 children	255.50	328.70	637.20	1,050.10	1,247.00	1,352.70	1,486.50	1,700.00	2,024.10
Maximum family benefits	255.50	328.70	637.20	1,050.10	1,247.00	1,352.70	1,486.50	1,700.00	2,024.10

(1) Widow's or widower's benefit limited to amount spouse would have been receiving if still living but not less than 82½ percent of the PIA. (2) Sole survivor. **NOTE:** The higher average monthly earnings shown in column headings on the right are not, in general, possible now since earnings in some of the earlier years—when the maximum amount creditable was lower—must be included in the average. The benefit amounts shown in these columns are not currently payable. (Effective June 1981, the highest average monthly creditable earnings possible for a worker retiring at age 65 without a previous period of disability is $846.)

Social Security Trust Funds

Old-Age and Survivors Insurance Trust Fund, 1937-81

[in millions]

Calendar year	Receipts: Net contrib. inc., reimbursements from gen'l rev.	Receipts: Net interest received	Expenditures: Cash benefit payments, rehabilitation services	Expenditures: Transfers to Railroad Retirement acct.	Expenditures: Administrative expenses	Total assets at end of year
1937	$765	$2	$1	...	...	$766
1940	325	43	35	...	$26	2,031
1950	2,667	257	961	...	61	13,721
1960	10,866	516	10,677	$318	203	20,324
1970	30,705	1,515	28,798	579	471	32,454
1976	63,976	2,300	65,705	1,212	959	35,388
1978	76,085	2,008	80,361	1,589	1,115	27,520
1980	103,996	1,845	105,082	1,442	1,154	22,823
1981	123,301	2,060	123,804	1,585	1,307	21,490
Cum, 1937-81	1,029,373	36,310	1,010,858	17,599	15,471	21,490

Disability Insurance Trust Fund, 1957-81

Calendar year	Receipts: Net contrib. inc., reimbursements from gen'l rev.	Receipts: Net interest received	Expenditures: Cash benefit payments, rehabilitation services	Expenditures: Transfers to Railroad Retirement acct.	Expenditures: Administrative expenses	Total assets at end of year
1957	$702	$7	$57	...	$3	$649
1960	1,010	53	568	$ –5	36	2,289
1970	4,497	277	3,085	10	164	5,614
1976	8,336	422	10,055	26	285	5,745
1977	9,266	304	11,547	...	399	3,370
1978	13,555	256	12,599	30	325	4,226
1979	15,232	358	13,786	30	371	5,630
1980	13,385	485	15,515	12	368	3,629
1981	16,906	172	17,275	29	436	3,049
Cum, 1957-81	131,782	5,386	129,388	438	4,428	3,049

Hospital Insurance Trust Fund, 1966-82

[In thousands]

Fiscal year:	Receipts: Net contribution income[1]	Receipts: Transfers from railroad retirement account[2]	Receipts: Reimbursements from general revenues[3]	Receipts: Net interest[4]	Expenditures: Net hospital and related service benefits[5]	Expenditures: Administrative expenses[6]	Total assets at end of period
1966	$908,797	...	...	$5,970	...	$63,564	$851,204
1967	2,688,684	$16,200	$337,850	45,903	$2,507,773	88,848	1,343,221
1970	4,784,789	61,307	628,262	139,423	4,804,242	148,660	2,677,401
1975	11,296,773	126,749	529,353	614,989	10,355,390	256,134	9,870,039
1977	13,659,042	...	944,000	770,966	14,912,370	294,762	11,114,685
1978	16,689,361	196,506	830,938	797,209	17,415,132	417,537	11,796,031
1979	19,943,084	175,600	874,849	883,158	19,898,459	411,565	13,362,700
1980	23,260,335	221,800	837,906	1,061,433	23,793,420	460,841	14,489,913
1981	30,445,979	246,700	800,000	1,324,834	28,909,081	305,416	18,092,929
Cum. 1966-81	175,414,803	1,693,440	9,849,582	7,507,983	172,579,414	3,793,470	18,092,929

(1) Represents amounts appropriated (estimated tax collections with suitable subsequent adjustments) after deductions for refund of estimated amount of employee-tax overpayment; and, beginning July 1973, premiums for coverage of uninsured individuals aged 65 and over. (2) Transfers (principal only) from the railroad retirement account with respect to contributions for hospital insurance coverage of railroad workers. (3) Represents Federal Government transfers from general funds appropriations to meet costs of benefits for persons not insured for cash benefits under OASDHI or railroad retirement and for costs of benefits arising from military wage credits. (4) Interest and profit on investments after transfers of interest or reimbursed administrative expenses (see footnote 6) and interest on amounts transferred from railroad retirement account (see footnote 3). (5) Represents payment vouchers on letters of credit issued to fiscal intermediaries under sec. 1816 and direct payments to providers of services under sec. 1815 of the Social Security Act. (6) Subject to subsequent adjustment among all four Social Security trust funds for allocated cost of each operation. Fiscal year 1966 includes "tool-up" period from date of enactment of Social Security Amendments of 1965 (July 20).

Supplementary Medical Insurance Trust Fund: Status, 1967-82

[In thousands]

Fiscal year:	Receipts: Premium income[1]	Receipts: Transfers from general revenues[2]	Receipts: Net interest[3]	Expenditures: Net medical service benefits[4]	Expenditures: Administrative expenses[5]	Total assets at end of period
1967	$646,682	$623,000	$14,052	$664,261	$133,682	$485,791
1970	936,000	928,151	11,536	1,979,287	216,993	57,181
1975	1,886,962	2,329,590	105,539	3,765,397	404,458	1,424,413
1976	1,951,221	2,939,338	103,645	4,671,847	528,214	1,218,555
1977	2,192,903	5,052,944	136,710	5,866,922	474,717	2,279,426
1978	2,431,133	6,385,503	228,848	6,852,252	504,234	3,968,425
1979	2,635,492	6,840,785	362,787	8,259,077	554,496	4,993,913
1980	2,927,711	6,931,713	415,510	10,143,930	593,327	4,531,591
1981	3,319,607	8,747,430	384,348	12,344,913	895,374	3,742,690
Cum. 1967-1981	26,791,611	49,344,695	1,978,772	68,406,337	5,966,049	3,742,690

(1) Represents voluntary premium payments from and in behalf of the insured aged and (beginning July 1973) disabled. (2) Represents Federal Government transfers from general funds appropriations to match aggregate premiums paid. (3) Represents interest and profit on investments, after transfers of interest on reimbursed administrative expenses (see footnote 5). (4) Represents payment vouchers on letters of credit issued to carriers under sec. 1842 of the Social Security Act. (5) Subject to subsequent adjustments among all four Social Security trust funds for allocated cost of each operation. Fiscal year 1966 includes "tool-up" period from date of enactment of Social Security Amendments of 1965 (July 30).

Tips on Cutting Energy Costs in Your Home

Source: Con Edison Conservation Services

Heating

In many homes, in areas where temperatures drop during the winter, more energy is used for heating than anything else. Conservation measures pay off in a home which is losing heat excessively. Installing the right amount of insulation, storm windows and doors, caulking and weatherstripping are important. Also consider the following advice:

- Make sure the thermostat and heating system are in good working order. An annual checkup is recommended.
- Set the thermostat no higher than 68 degrees. When no one is home, or when everyone is sleeping, the setting should be turned down to 60 degrees or lower. An automatic setback thermostat can raise and lower your home's temperature at times you specify.
- Close off and do not heat unused areas.
- If you do not have conventional storm windows or doors use kits to make plastic storm windows.
- Keep the outside doors closed as much as possible.
- Special glass fireplace doors help keep a room's heat from being drawn up the chimney when the fire is burning low. In any case, close the damper when a fireplace is not in use.
- Use the sun's heat by opening blinds and draperies closed at night or on cold cloudy days to reduce heat loss.
- Keep radiators and warm air outlets clean. Do not block them with furniture or draperies.

Water Heater

In many homes, the water heater ranks second only to the heating system in total energy consumption. It pays to keep the water heater operating efficiently, and not to waste hot water.

- Put an insulation blanket on your water heater when you go on vacation, or turn it to a minimum setting if there is danger of freezing pipes.
- If you have a dishwasher, set the water heater thermostat no higher than 140 degrees. If not, or if you have a separate water heater for baths, a setting as low as 110 degrees may be sufficient.
- Run the dishwasher and clothes washer only when you have a full load. Use warm or cold water cycles for laundry when you can.
- Take showers instead of tub baths. About half as much hot water is used for a shower.
- Install a water-saver shower head.
- Do not leave the hot water running when rinsing dishes or shaving. Plug and partially fill the basin, or fill a pan with water.
- Use the right size water heater for your needs. An oversized unit wastes energy heating unneeded water. An undersized unit will not deliver all the hot water you want when you need it.
- When shopping for a water heater, look for the yellow-and-black federal EnergyGuide label to learn the estimated yearly energy cost of a unit.

Air Conditioning

- Clean or replace the filter in an air conditioner at the beginning of the cooling season. Then check it once a month and clean or change the filter if necessary. A dirty filter blocks the flow of air and keeps the air conditioner from doing its best job of cooling.
- Adjust the temperature control setting to provide a room temperature no lower than 78 degrees. Since most air conditioner thermostats are not marked in degrees but by words such as "cold" and "colder," use a good wall thermometer to tell which setting will provide the desired temperature.
- Close windows and doors when the air conditioner is running.
- When the outside temperature is 78 degrees or cooler turn off the air conditioner and open windows to cool your home.
- Always keep your air conditioner turned off when you are away from home or not using the areas that it cools. An air conditioner timer can be set to turn it off when family members go to work, and to turn it on just before the first one arrives home. These timers are available at hardware stores.
- Close draperies and shades to block out the sun's heat.
- When shopping for a new room air conditioner, look for the yellow-and-black federal EnergyGuide label to learn the Energy Efficiency Rating (EER) and the estimated yearly operating cost. The higher the EER, the less electricity will be used for a cooling job.
- Read the manufacturer's instructions and follow them closely.
- If you have a central air conditioning system, run your hands along the ducts while it is operating to check for air leaks. Repair leaks with duct tape. Make sure the duct system is properly insulated.

Refrigerators and Freezers

The refrigerator operates 24 hours a day, every day, so it is important to make sure your refrigerator is working efficiently. It is one of the biggest users of energy in the home all year round.

- Keep the condenser coils clean. The coils are on the back or at the bottom of the refrigerator. Carefully wipe, vacuum or brush the coils to remove dust and dirt at least once a year.
- Examine door gaskets and hinges regularly for air leaks. The doors should fit tightly. To check, place a piece of paper between the door and the cabinet. Close the door with normal force, then try to pull the paper straight out. There will be a slight resistance. Test all around the door including the hinge side. If there are any places where the paper slides out easily, you need to adjust the hinges or replace the gasket, or both.
- Pause before opening your refrigerator door. Think of everything you will need before you open the door so you do not have to go back several times. When you open the door, close it quickly to keep the cool air in.
- Adjust the temperature-setting dial of the refrigerator as the manufacturer recommends. Use a thermometer to check the temperature (38 to 40 degrees is usually recommended for the refrigerator; zero degrees for the freezer). Settings that are too cold waste electricity and can ruin foods.
- If you have a manual-defrost refrigerator, do not allow the ice to build up more than ¼ inch thick.
- For greatest efficiency, keep your refrigerator well stocked but allow room for air to circulate around the food.
- The freezer, on the other hand, should be packed full. If necessary, fill empty spaces with bags of ice cubes or fill milk cartons with water and freeze.
- When you are going to be away from home for a week or more, turn off and unplug the refrigerator, empty and clean it, and prop the door open.

- If you are buying a new refrigerator, look for one with a humid-dry ("power-saver") switch. This switch is used to turn off "anti-sweat" heaters in the doors to save electricity when the heaters are not needed.
- When shopping for a new refrigerator or freezer, look for the federal EnergyGuide label to help you select an efficient unit.

Cooking

There are many ways to save electricity or gas by careful use of the range or oven.

- Cook as many dishes in the oven at one time as you can instead of cooking each separately. If recipes call for slightly different temperatures, say 325, 350, and 375 degrees, pick the middle temperature of 350 to cook all 3 dishes and remove each dish as it's done.
- Don't preheat the oven unnecessarily. Usually, any food that takes more than an hour of cooking can be started in a cold oven.
- Turn off your oven or range just before the cooking is finished. The heat that is left will usually finish the cooking.
- Whenever you peek into an oven by opening a door, the temperature drops about 25 degrees. So open the oven door as little as possible.
- Use the lowest possible heat setting to cook foods on top of the range.
- Match the pot to the size of the surface unit. Putting a small pot on a large surface unit wastes energy without cooking the food any faster.
- On gas ranges, the flame should burn in a firm, blue cone. If the flame is not blue, the range is probably not working efficiently. Get a service representative to check it.

Lighting

The first rule is to turn off lights no one is using. There also are ways to improve your home's lighting level and save energy at the same time.

- Get all family members in the habit of turning off lights when they leave a room, even if they will be gone only for a short time.
- During the day, try to get along with as few lights as possible. Let the daylight do the work. White or lightcolored walls make a room seem brighter.
- Use bulbs of lower wattage where you don't need strong light.
- When you need strong light, use one large bulb instead of several smaller ones. One 100-watt incandescent bulb produces more light than 2 60-watt bulbs, with 20 percent less energy consumption. But never use bulbs of a higher wattage than a fixture was designed to take.
- Use 3-way bulbs where possible, so you can choose the amount of light you need.
- Modern solid-state dimmer controls let you save energy by reducing your lighting level and wattage. Many are easy to install.
- Consider changing to fluorescent lighting, especially in kitchens, bathrooms, and work areas. Fluorescent tubes give more light at lower energy cost than incandescent bulbs with the same wattage. Plug-in fluorescent fixtures are available at hardware stores, or an electrician can install permanent fixtures.

Fuel Economy in 1983 Autos; Comparative Miles per Gallon

Source: U.S. Environmental Protection Agency

The mileage numbers and rankings below refer to testing completed through September 3, 1982. The testing of several major model types had not been completed when these data were released.

Make, model	Cu. in. displcmt.	Cylinders	Trans.[1]	Mileage
Alfa Romeo Spider	120	4	m	23
AMC Concord	258	4	m	21
AMC Spirit	258	6	a	21
Audi 4000	97	4	m	39
Audi 5000	131	5	a	19
BMW 320	108	4	m	25
BMW 633 CSI	196	6	m	19
BMW 733 I	196	6	a	18
Buick Century	263	6	a	26
Buick Electra	252	6	a	18
Buick LeSabre	252	6	a	18
Buick Regal	263	6	a	26
Buick Riviera	252	6	a	17
Buick Skyhawk	121	4	a	25
Buick Skylark	173	6	m	21
Cadillac Deville/Brougham	350	8	a	22
Cadillac Eldorado, Seville	249	8	a	17
Chevrolet Celebrity	151	4	m	26
Chevrolet Cavalier	121	4	m	25
Chevrolet Chevette	98	4	m	31
Chev. Chevette Diesel	111	4	a	37
Chevrolet Citation	173	6	a	22
Chevrolet Impala/Caprice	350	8	a	17
Chevrolet Malibu	305	8	a	18
Chevrolet Monte Carlo	229	6	a	20
Chrysler Cordoba/300	305	8	a	18
Chrysler LeBaron	318	8	a	17
Chrysler New Yorker	135	4	a	24
Datsun 2-Seater 280zx	168	6	m	19
Datsun Nisson Sentra	91	4	m	40
Datsun 200SX	133	4	a	25
Datsun Pulsar	168	6	m	20
Datsun 810	170	6	m	30
Dodge Aries	135	4	a	28
Dodge Challenger	156	4	a	23
Dodge Colt	86	4	m	39
Dodge Charger	105	4	m	32
Dodge Diplomat	225	6	a	19
Dodge Miranda	225	6	a	17
Dodge Omni	135	4	a	29
Dodge 400 Convertible	140	4	m	26
Fiat Spider 2000	122	4	a	22
Fiat X1/9	91	4	m	26
Ford Escort	98	4	m	33
Ford Fairmont Futura	140	4	a	21
Ford EXP	98	4	m	29
Ford LTD	140	4	a	21
Ford Mustang	140	4	m	26
Ford Thunderbird	231	6	a	21
Honda Accord	107	4	a	29
Honda Civic	8	4	m	46
Jaguar XJ	258	6	a	17
Mazda GLC	91	4	m	34
Mazda Rx7	70	2	m	20
Mercury Capri	140	4	m	22
Mercury Cougar	231	6	a	21
Mercury Lynx	98	4	a	27
Mercury Marquis	140	4	a	21
Mercury Zephyr	200	6	a	19
Olds. Cutlass Sup.	307	8	a	18
Oldsmobile Delta 88	307	8	a	17
Oldsmobile 98	307	8	a	17
Oldsmobile Omega	151	4	m	27
Oldsmobile Toronado	307	8	a	16
Plymouth Colt	86	4	m	39
Plymouth Gran Fury	225	6	a	19
Plymouth Horizon	135	4	m	28
Plymouth Reliant	135	4	m	29
Plymouth Sapporo	156	4	m	24
Plymouth Turismo	105	4	m	32
Pontiac Bonneville	305	8	a	18
Pontiac Grand Prix	231	6	a	21
Pontiac 2000	110	4	a	28
Pontiac Phoenix	173	6	m	21
Porsche 911	183	6	m	16
Porsche 944	151	4	a	21
Subaru	109	4	m	30
Toyota Celica	144	4	m	25
Toyota Celica Supra	168	6	m	21
Toyota Corolla	97	4	a	31
Toyota Cressida	168	6	a	22
Toyota Starlet	79	4	m	42
Toyota Tercel	89	4	a	32
Volkswgn Diesl. Rbt.	97	4	m	48
Volkswgn Jetta	105	4	m	30
Volkswgn Rabbit	105	4	m	32
Volkswgn Scirocco	105	4	m	29

1) Type of transmission: a = automatic; m = manual.

Measuring Energy

Source: Energy Information Administration, U.S. Energy Dept.

The following tables of equivalents contain those figures commonly used to compare different types of energy sources and their various measurements.

Btu — a British thermal unit — the amount of heat required to raise one pound of water one degree Fahrenheit. Equivalent to 1,055 joules or about 252 gram calories. A therm is usually 100,000 Btu but is sometimes used to refer to other units.

Calorie — The amount of heat required to raise one gram of water one degree Centigrade; abbreviated cal.; equivalent to about .003968 Btu. More common is the kilogram calorie, also called a kilocalorie and abbreviated Cal. or Kcal; equivalent to about 3.97 Btu. (One Kcal is equivalent to one food calorie.)

Btu Values of Energy Sources

(These are conventional or average values, not precise equivalents.)

Coal (per 2,000 lb. ton of U.S. production):
Anthracite = 22.9×10^6 Btu
Bituminous coal and lignite = 22.6×10^6
Average heating value of coal used to generate electricity in 1979 was 21.4 x 10^6 Btu per metric ton.

Natural Gas:
Dry (per cubic foot) = 1,021 Btu
Liquefied Natural Gas (Methane) (per barrel) = 3.0×10^6

Electricity — 1 kwh = 3,412 Btu

Petroleum (per barrel):
Crude oil = 5.80×10^6 Btu
Residual fuel oil = 6.29×10^6
Distillate fuel oil = 5.83×10^6
Gasoline (including aviation gas) = 5.25×10^6
Jet fuel (kerosene) = 5.67×10^6
Jet fuel (naphtha) = 5.36×10^6
Kerosene = 5.67×10^6

Nuclear — (per kilowatt hour) = 10,769

The Btu and calorie, being small amounts of energy, are usually expressed as follows when large numbers are involved.

1×10^3 Btu = 1,000
1×10^6 = 1,000,000
1×10^9 = 1,000,000,000
1×10^{12} = 1 trillion
1×10^{15} = 1 quadrillion
1×10^{18} = 1 quintillion or 1 Q unit
One Q unit = 44.3 billion short tons of coal
= 172.4 billion tons of oil
= 980 trillion cubic feet of natural gas

Other Conversion Factors

Electricity — 1 kwh = 0.3 pounds of coal
= 0.25 gallon of crude oil
= 3.3 cubic feet of natural gas

Natural gas — 1 tcf (trillion cubic feet) = 45×10^6 short tons of bituminous and lignite coal produced
= 176×10^6 barrels of crude oil

Coal — 1 mstce (million short tons of coal equivalent) = 3.9×10^6 barrels of crude oil
= 1.7×10^6 short tons of crude oil
= 22.1×10^9 cubic feet of natural gas

Oil — 1 million short tons (6.65×10^6 barrels)
= 4×10^9 kwh of electricity (when used to generate power)
= 12×10^9 kwh uncoverted
= 1.7×10^6 short tons of coal
= 37×10^9 cubic feet of natural gas

Approximate Conversion Factors for Oils

To convert	Barrels to metric tons	Metric tons to barrels	Barrels/ day to tons/ year	Tons/year to barrels/ day
	Multiply by:			
Crude oil[1] . .	.136	7.33	49.8	.0201
Gasoline . .	.118	8.45	43.2	.0232
Kerosene . .	.128	7.80	46.8	.0214
Diesel fuel .	.133	7.50	48.7	.0205
Fuel oil . . .	.149	6.70	54.5	.0184

(1) Based on world average gravity (excluding natural ga liquids).

Removing Common Spots and Stains

By Polly Fisher, Syndicated Columnist, "Polly's Pointers," Newspaper Enterprise Association

Precaution: The following stain removal techniques are primarily intended for use on washable fabrics and surfaces, unles otherwise noted. If your fabric is labeled "dry clean only," consult a professional dry cleaner for safe treatment of the stain Before treating any stain, be sure the remedy is safe for the fabric or finish of the stained surface. Always test the recom mended cleaning solution at the recommended temperature (and this includes water, soap, and detergent) on a hidden part c the garment or other item: a seam allowance, a collar facing, a turned-under hem. While these remedies are all considered rea sonably safe for most fabrics, the colorfastness of commercial dyes varies greatly. Be especially alert for any bleeding c change of color when you make your test. Above all, follow the care-label instructions and use common sense when dealin with any cleaning method. All products mentioned here can be obtained at local supermarkets, drug stores, or hardwar stores.

Beverages (Alcoholic Drinks, Coffee, Fruit Juice, Soda, Tea, Wine)

When spills first occur, pour, sponge, or otherwise wet the fabric with ordinary club soda or any unflavored carbonated or sparkling water. Blot with a clean cloth, napkin, tissue, or paper towel. In most cases, this will clean up the spot without leaving any stain.

When such stains have set, stretch the stained area of fabric over a large bowl and hold it taut with a large rubber band. Then pour boiling water over the stain. If any stain remains, sponge with lemon juice. If the fabric is white, leave the lemon juice-treated fabric out in the sun to dry and bleach.

Blood

Wash fresh blood stains in cold water and a mild soap c detergent. Hand soap or dishwashing liquid is fine. Neve wash blood stains with warm or hot water.

If stains have dried and set, sponge with a little hydroge peroxide until the stain disappears.

On mattresses and other large items that are difficult t wash, spread a thick paste of cornstarch and water over th stained area. Let dry thoroughly, then vacuum off.

Candle Wax

With a dull knife, gently scrape off as much wax as poss

ble. Sandwich the fabric between two thick layers of paper towels and iron over the spot with a hot iron. Frequently change the towels for fresh ones as the wax melts and soaks into the paper. If any colored stain remains after all wax has been removed, sponge with rubbing alcohol.

Chewing Gum

On flat, smooth fabrics, harden gum by rubbing with an ice cube, then peel gum off. If any stain remains, sponge with alcohol or dry cleaning fluid (often sold as "spot remover.")

On knits, particularly fuzzy, loose sweaters, massage vegetable shortening into the gummy area. This will loosen the gum and lift it from the fibers. Wash out with cool water and mild soap or detergent. Repeat if necessary until all gum is gone.

Chocolate

Rub with a mild detergent and warm water. If stain remains, sponge lightly with dry cleaning fluid.

Glue

To remove plastic cement, apply nail-polish remover (acetone) sparingly. This will dissolve the cement. Blot with a clean cloth. Nail-polish remover and other acetone-based products will also dissolve "super" glues. Do not use on acetates and acetate blends.

White all-purpose glue should be soaked in warm water, then sponged with ammonia. Rinse, then launder.

The glue left by price tags and labels on bottles, plastics, or almost any surface, can be easily removed by rubbing with vegetable oil and a clean cloth. Rinse or wash the oil off after removing the glue. (Not recommended for use on fabrics.)

Grease and Oil Stains

Rub fresh stains with hand soap and wash vigorously with warm water.

On fabrics that cannot be washed, sprinkle fresh grease stains liberally with cornstarch. Let set for fifteen minutes, then brush or vacuum thoroughly. The cornstarch will absorb the grease. Safe for velvets and furs if brushed out gently.

Apply waterless handcleaner to grease, oil, or tar stains. Rub in gently, then launder as usual. Place paper towels under the fabric to absorb the grease as you're working the handcleaner into the fabric.

Greying (All-Over)

Greying of fabrics may be caused by soap left in the fabric after laundering. Add one cup of white vinegar to the final rinse water of your machine's cycle. This will break up and rinse away soap buildup and soften the fabric.

Ink

Ballpoint pen ink on fabrics and vinyl can be sprayed with hairspray. The hairspray will dissolve the ink which should be blotted up and wiped away with a clean cloth or paper towels.

Sponge stains caused by printer's ink or carbon paper with rubbing alcohol, then rinse.

Mildew

Saturate light mildew stains on white and pastel fabrics with lemon juice and bleach in the sun for several hours. (Don't apply the juice to any other part of the fabric.) Launder as usual.

If mildew stains are heavy or remain after treating with lemon juice, sponge with hydrogen peroxide. Again, launder afterwards.

Paint

Dab paint spots with turpentine. When paint softens, blot up with clean paper towels. Rinse, then launder.

To remove paint from your skin, rub the spots with ordinary vegetable oil.

Perspiration

Soak stained fabric in warm white vinegar for thirty minutes, then launder as usual.

Yellowing (All-Over)

Use chlorine bleach (on cottons and other bleachable fabrics only) in laundering, according to bottle directions. Do not use chlorine bleach on nylon fabrics. Chlorine bleach can *cause* yellowing on nylon.

Restore whiteness to delicate fabrics and items that you don't want to treat with harsh chemicals by soaking in a cream of tartar solution. Add one tablespoon cream of tartar to one gallon of hot water, then soak garments overnight. Good for baby clothes, diapers, linen handkerchiefs, and delicate synthetic knits.

Life Insurance: Facts You Need to Know

Source: American Council of Insurance

One of the most important purchases you can make—and one you need to be well-informed about—is life insurance.

Most insurance companies are currently simplifying their life insurance plans in order that consumers might have a better idea of what they're really buying. In addition to making policies easier to read and understand, the companies are developing new premium payment methods to lower the financial burden of insurance purchase. Since almost one-third of all life insurance is bought by people aged 25-43, with over 60% paying more than $260 annually for insurance, such innovations as monthly payment plans (instead of annual or semi-annual, lump sum payments) are becoming common.

There are 3 basic types of insurance policies: (1) whole life—a policy that continues in effect as long as you pay the fixed premium; (2) endowment—a policy that will pay you or your beneficiary its face amount after a designated time; and (3) term—the policy pays your beneficiary the face amount if you die while the policy is in force.

Life Insurance as an Investment?

There's a good deal of controversy about the value of insurance as an investment, especially in times of double-digit inflation. Whole life policies, with their fixed premiums and cash value that grows over the course of the years (that can be collected when you decide to terminate the policy or borrowed against up to the current value of the policy) are considered by many to be an effective way to protect a family financially, while also having money wisely invested. Term insurance, on the other hand, is a much less expensive type of insurance, and achieves much the same purpose as whole life (of course, only during the "term" of its existence). But there is no cash surrender value or borrowing privilege.

Since both current protection and a good future investment are necessary, the consumer must carefully weigh the advantages of life insurance before making a purchase.

How to Read a Life Insurance Policy

All life insurance policies, regardless of type, can be divided into 3 parts:

1. **Summary**—This is the basic agreement of the policy. It includes the name of the insured, the face amount of the policy, the beneficiary's name, and premium amount, as well as the type of policy, any riders (additions to the policy you might have bought), and whether or not the cost of the insurance has been figured on a guaranteed basis or a participating basis.
2. **Details**—Approximately 10 clauses giving the specifics of the policy's operation, such as due date of premium, value of the policy when you surrender it for either cash or a loan, the amount paid on your death, options for how your beneficiary can receive that money.

3. **Application**—A two-fold section that gives personal information about you and it lets you make some decisions about how the policy will work. Among typical items covered are what happens in the event of your suicide, whether you engage in dangerous sports or occupations, what your rights are under the policy, etc.

As with any legal document, it is important to read and understand what you are purchasing. If you need further information, a good source is the American Council of Insurance, 1850 K St. N.W., Washington, DC 20006.

How Is Your Life Insurance Dollar Used?

Source: American Council of Life Insurance, 1980 figures.

Of each dollar of income received by U.S. insurance companies, $ .71 comes from premiums and $ .29 from net investment earning and other income.

The following breakdown shows how each premium dollar received from insurance purchasers is spent:

Benefit payments to policy holders	$ .498
Additions to policy reserve funds	$ .296
Additions to special reserves & surplus funds	$ .021
Commissions to agents	$ .056
Home and field office expenses	$ .09[illegible]
Taxes	$ .02[illegible]
Dividends to shareholders	$ .01[illegible]
Total	$ 1.00[illegible]

Stress: How Much Can Affect Your Health?

Source: Reprinted with permission from the *Journal of Psychosomatic Research,* Vol. 11, pp. 213-218, T.H. Holmes, M.D.; The Social Readjustment Rating Scale © 1967, Pergamon Press, Ltd.

Change, both good and bad, can create stress and stress, if sufficiently severe, can lead to illness. Drs. Thomas Holmes and Minoru Masudu, psychiatrists at the University of Washington in Seattle, have developed the Social Readjustment Rating Scale. In their study, they gave a point value to stressful events. The psychiatrists discovered that in 79 percent of the persons studied major illness followed the accumulation of stress-related changes totaling over 300 points in one year. The scale follows:

The Social Readjustment Rating Scale

Life Event	Value
Death of Spouse	100
Divorce	73
Marital separation from mate	65
Detention in jail or other institution	63
Death of a close family member	63
Major personal injury or illness	53
Marriage	50
Being fired at work	47
Marital reconciliation with mate	45
Retirement from work	45
Major change in the health or behavior of a family member	44
Pregnancy	40
Sexual difficulties	39
Gaining a new family member (e.g., through birth, adoption, oldster moving in, etc.)	39
Major business readjustment (e.g., merger, reorganization, bankruptcy, etc.)	39
Major change in financial state (e.g., a lot worse off or a lot better off than usual)	38
Death of a close friend	37
Changing to a different line of work	36
Major change in the number of arguments with spouse (e.g., either a lot more or a lot less than usual regarding child-rearing, personal habits, etc.)	35
Taking out a mortgage or loan for a major purchase (e.g. for a home, business, etc.)	31
Foreclosure on a mortgage or loan	30
Major change in responsibilities at work (e.g., promotion, demotion, lateral transfer)	29
Son or daughter leaving home (e.g., marriage, attending college, etc.)	29
In-law troubles	29
Outstanding personal achievement	28
Wife beginning or ceasing work outside the home	26
Beginning or ceasing formal schooling	26
Major change in living conditions (e.g., building a new home, remodeling, deterioration of home or neighborhood)	25
Revision of personal habits (dress, manners, association, etc.)	24
Troubles with the boss	23
Major change in working hours or conditions	20
Change in residence	20
Changing to a new school	20
Major change in usual type and/or amount of recreation	19
Major change in church activities (e.g., a lot more or a lot less than usual)	19
Major change in social activities (e.g., clubs, dancing, movies, visiting, etc.)	18
Taking out a mortgage or loan for a lesser purchase (e.g., for a car, TV, freezer, etc.)	17
Major change in sleeping habits (a lot more or a lot less sleep, or change in part of day when asleep)	16
Major change in number of family get-togethers (e.g., a lot more or a lot less than usual)	15
Major change in eating habits (a lot more or a lot less food intake, or very different meal hours or surroundings)	15
Vacation	13
Christmas	12
Minor violations of the law (e.g., traffic tickets, jaywalking, disturbing the peace, etc.)	11

Effects of Commonly Abused Drugs

Source: National Institute on Drug Abuse

Tobacco

Effects and dangers: Nicotine, the active ingredient in tobacco, acts as a stimulant on the heart and nervous system. When tobacco smoke is inhaled the immediate effects on the body are a faster heart beat and elevated blood pressure. These effects, however, are quickly dissipated. Tar (in the smoke) contains many carcinogens. These compounds, many of which are in polluted air but are found in vastly greater quantities in cigarette smoke, have been identified as major causes of cancer and respiratory difficulties. Even relatively young smokers can have shortness of breath, nagging cough, or develop cardiovascular and respiratory difficulties. A third principal component of cigarette smoke, carbon monoxide, is also a cause of some of the more serious health effects of smoking. Carbon monoxide can reduce the blood's ability to carry oxygen to body tissues and can promote the development of arteriosclerosis (hardening of the arteries). Long-term effects of smoking cigarettes are emphysema, chronic bronchitis, heart disease, lung cancer, and cancer in other parts of the body.

Risks during pregnancy: Women who smoke during pregnancy are more likely to have babies that weigh less, and more frequently lose their babies through stillbirth or death soon after birth.

Alcohol

Effects: Like sedatives, it is a central nervous system depressant. In small doses, it has a tranquilizing effect on most people, although it appears to stimulate others. Alcohol first acts on those parts of the brain which affect self-control and other learned behaviors; lowered self-control often leads to the aggressive behavior associated with some people who drink.

Dangers: In large doses, alcohol can dull sensation and impair muscular coordination, memory, and judgment. Taken in larger quantities over a long period time, alcohol can damage the liver and heart and can cause permanent brain damage. A large dose of alcohol, which can be as little as a pint or less of whiskey consumed at once, can interfere with the part of the brain that control breathing. The respiratory failure which results can bring death. Delirium tremens, the most extreme manifestation of alcohol withdrawal, can also cause death. On the average, heavy drinkers shorten their life span by about 10 years.

Risks during pregnancy: Women who drink heavily during pregnancy (more than 3 ounces of alcohol per day or about 2 mixed drinks) run a higher risk than other women of delivering babies with physical, mental and behavioral abnormalities.

Dependence: Repeated drinking produces tolerance to the drug's effects and dependence. The drinker's body then needs alcohol to function. Once dependent, drinkers experience withdrawal symptoms when they stop drinking.

Marijuana ("grass", "pot", "weed")

What is it?: A common plant (*Cannabis sativa*), its chief psychoactive ingredient is delta-9-tetrahydrocannabinol, or THC. The amount of THC in the marijuana cigarette (joint) primarily determines its psychoactive potential.

Effects: Most users experience an increase in heart rate, reddening of the eyes, and dryness in the mouth and throat. Studies indicate the drug temporarily impairs short-term memory, alters sense of time, and reduces the ability to perform tasks requiring concentration, swift reactions, and coordination. Many feel that their hearing, vision, and skin sensitivity are enhanced by the drug, but these reports have not been objectively confirmed by research. Feelings of euphoria, relaxation, altered sense of body image, and bouts of exaggerated laughter are also commonly reported.

Dangers: Scientists believe marijuana can be particularly harmful to lungs because users typically inhale the filtered smoke deeply and hold it in their lungs for prolonged periods of time. Marijuana smoke has been found to have more cancer-causing agents than are found in cigarette smoke (see above). Because marijuana use increases heart rate as much as 50% and brings on chest pain in people who have a poor blood supply to the heart (and more rapidly than tobacco smoke does), doctors believe people with heart conditions or who are at high risk for heart ailments, should not use marijuana. Findings also suggest that regular use may reduce fertility in women and that men with marginal fertility or endocrine functioning should avoid marijuana use and that it is especially harmful during adolescence, a period of rapid physical and sexual development.

Risks during pregnancy: Research is limited, but scientists believe marijuana which crosses the placential barrier, may have a toxic effect on embryos and fetuses.

Dependence: Tolerance to marijuana, the need to take more and more of the drug over time to get the original effect, has been proven in humans and animals. Physical dependence has been demonstrated in research subjects who ingested an amount equal to smoking 10 to 20 joints a day. When the drug was discontinued, subjects experienced withdrawal symptoms—irritability, sleep disturbances, loss of appetite and weight, sweating, and stomach upset.

Bad reactions: Most commonly reported immediate adverse reaction to marijuana use is the "acute panic anxiety reaction," usually described as an exaggeration of normal marijuana effects in which intense fears of losing control and going crazy accompany severe anxiety. The symptoms often disappear in a few hours when the acute drug effects have worn off.

Hallucinogens ("psychodelics")

What are they?: Drugs which affect perception, sensation, thinking, self-awareness, and emotion.

(1) **LSD (lysergic acid diethylamide),** a synthetic, is converted from lysergic acid which comes from fungus (ergot).

Effects: Vary greatly according to dosage, personality of the user, and conditions under which the drug is used. Basically, it causes changes in sensation. Vision alters; users describe changes in depth perception and in the meaning of the perceived object. Illusions and hallucinations often occur. Physical reactions range from minor changes such as dilated pupils, a rise in temperature and heartbeat, or a slight increase in blood pressure, to tremors. High doses can greatly alter the state of consciousness. Heavy use of the drug may produce flashbacks, recurrences of some features of a previous LSD experience days or months after the last dose.

Dangers: After taking LSD, a person loses control over normal thought processes. Although many perceptions are pleasant, others may cause panic or may make a person believe that he or she cannot be harmed. Longer-term harmful reactions include anxiety and depression, or "breaks from reality" which may last from a few days to months. Heavy users sometimes develop signs of organic brain damage, such as impaired memory and attention span, mental confusion, and difficulty with abstract thinking. It is not known yet whether such mental changes are permanent.

(2) **Mescaline:** Comes from peyote cactus and its effects are similar to those of LSD.

Phencyclidine (PCP or "angel dust")

What is it?: A drug that was developed as a surgical anesthetic for humans in the late 1950s. Because of its unpleasant and unusual side effects, PCP was soon restricted to its only current legal use as a veterinary anesthetic and tranquilizer.

Effects: Vary according to dosage. Low doses may provide the usual releasing effects of many psychoactive drugs. A floaty euphoria is described, sometimes associated with a feeling of numbness (part of the drug's anesthetic effects). Increased doses produce an excited, confused intoxification, which may include muscle rigidity, loss of concentration and memory, visual disturbances, delirium, feelings of isolation, convulsions, speech impairment, violent behavior, fear of death, and changes in the user's perceptions of their bodies.

Dangers: PCP intoxication can produce violent and bizarre behavior even in people not otherwise prone to such behavior. Violent actions may be directed at themselves or others and often account for serious injuries and death. More people die from accidents caused by the erratic behavior produced by the drug than from the drug's direct effect on the body. A temporary, schizophrenic-like psychosis, which can last for days or weeks, has also occurred in users of moderate or higher doses.

Stimulants ("Uppers")

What are they?: A class of drugs which stimulate the central nervous system and produce an increase in alertness and activity.

(1) **Amphetamines** promote a feeling of alertness and increase in speech and general physical activity. Under medical supervision, the drugs are taken to control appetite.

Effects and dangers: Even small, infrequent doses can produce toxic effects in some people. Restlessness, anxiety, mood swings, panic, circulatory and cardiac disturbances, paranoid thoughts, hallucinations, convulsions, and coma have all been reported. Heavy, frequent doses can produce brain damage which results in speed disturbances and difficulty in turning thoughts into words. Death can result from injected amphetamine overdose. Long-term users often have acne resembling a measles rash; trouble with teeth, gums and nails, and dry lifeless hair. As heavy users who inject amphetamines accumulate larger amounts of the drug in their bodies, the resulting toxicity can produce amphetamine psychosis. People in this extremely suspicious, paranoid state, frequently exhibit bizarre, sometimes violent behavior.

Dependence: People with a history of sustained low-dose use quite often become dependent and feel they need the drug to get by.

(2) **Cocaine** is a stimulant drug extracted from the leaves of the coca plant. Street cocaine is a powder that is most commonly inhaled, though some users ingest, inject, or smoke a form of the drug called freebase.

Effect: Increases heart rate and blood pressure.

Dangers: Paranoia is not an uncommon response to heavy doses. Psychosis may be triggered in users prone to mental instability. Repeated inhalation often results in nostril and nasal membrane irritation. Some regular users have reported feelings of restlessness, irritability, and anxiety. Others have experienced hallucinations of touch, sight, taste, or smell. When people stop using cocaine after taking it for a long time, they frequently become depressed. They tend to fight off this depression by taking more cocaine, just as in the up/down amphetamine cycle. Cocaine is toxic. Although few people realize it, overdose deaths, though rare, from injected, oral and even snorted cocaine have occurred. The deaths are a result of seizures followed by respiratory arrest and coma, or sometimes by cardiac arrest.

Dependence: It's not a narcotic; no evidence suggests that it produces a physical dependence, but psychological dependence can clearly result from heavy or continuous use.

Sedatives (Tranquilizers, sleeping pills)

What are they?: Drugs which depress the central nervous system, more appropriately called sedative-hypnotics because they include drugs which calm the nerves (the sedation effect) and produce sleep (the hypnotic effect). Of drugs in this class, barbiturates ("barbs", "downers," "reds") have the highest rate of abuse and misuse. The most commonly abused barbiturates include pentobarbital (Nembutal), secobarbital (Seconal), and amobarbital (Amytal). These all have legitimate use as sedatives or sleeping aids. Among the most commonly abused nonbarbiturate drugs are glutethimide (Doriden), meprobamate (Miltown), methyprylon (Noludar), ethchlorvynol (Placidyl), and methaqualone (Sopor, Quaalude). These are prescribed to help people sleep. Benzodiazepines, especially diazepam (Valium), prescribed to relieve anxiety, are commonly abused, and their rate of abuse and misuse is increasing.

Dangers: These can kill. Barbiturate overdose is implicated in nearly one-third of all reported drug-induced deaths. Accidental deaths may occur when a user takes an unintended larger or repeated dose of sedatives because of confusion or impairment in judgment caused by initial intake of the drug. With lesser, but still large doses, users can go into coma. Moderately large doses often produce an intoxicated stupor. Users' speech is often slurred, memory vague, and judgment impaired. Taken along with alcohol, the combination can be fatal. Tranquilizers act somewhat differently than other sedatives and are considered less hazardous. But even by themselves, or in combination with other drugs (especially alcohol and other sedatives) they can be quite dangerous.

Dependence: Potential for dependence is greatest with barbiturates, but all sedatives, tranquilizers, can be addictive. Barbiturate withdrawal is often more severe than heroin withdrawal.

Narcotics

What they are?: Drugs that relieve pain and often induce sleep. The opiates, which are narcotics, include opium and drugs derived from opium, such as morphine, codeine, and heroin. Narcotics also include certain synthetic chemicals that have a morphine-like action, such as methadone.

Which are abused?: Heroin ("junk," "smack") accounts for 90% of narcotic abuse in the U.S. Sometimes medicinal narcotics are also abused, including paregoric containing codeine, and methadone, meperidine, and morphine.

Dependence: Anyone can become heroin dependent if he or she takes the drug regularly. Although environmental stress and problems of coping have often been considered as factors that lead to heroin addiction, physicians or psychologists do not agree that some people just have an "addictive personality" and are prone to dependence. All we know for certain is that continued use of heroin causes dependence.

Dangers: Physical dangers depend on the specific drug, its source, and the way it is used. Most medical problems are caused by the uncertain dosage level, use of unsterile needles and other paraphernalia, contamination of the drug, or combination of a narcotic with other drugs, rather than by the effects of the heroin (or another narcotic) itself. The life expectancy of a heroin addict who injects the drug intravenously is significantly lower than that of one who does not. An overdose can result in death. If, for example, an addict obtains pure heroin and is not tolerant of the dose, he or she may die minutes after injecting it. Infections from unsterile needles, solutions, syringes, cause many diseases. Serum hepatitis is common. Skin abscesses, inflammation of the veins and congestion of the lungs also occur.

Withdrawal: When a heroin-dependent person stops taking the drug, withdrawal begins within 4-6 hours after the last injection. Full-blown withdrawal symptoms—which include shaking, sweating, vomiting, a running nose and eyes, muscle aches, chills, abdominal pains, and diarrhea—begin some 12-16 hours after the last injection. The intensity of symptoms depends on the degree of dependence.

Immunization Schedule for Children

Age	Type of Vaccination	Disease Immunized Against
2 months	DPT	Diphtheria, Tetanus (Lockjaw), Pertussis (Whooping Cough)
	Oral Polio Vaccine	Polio Myelitis
3 months	DPT	
4 months	DPT	
	Oral Polio Vaccine	
6 months	Oral Polio Vaccine	

Age	Type of Vaccination	Disease Immunized Against
12 months	Live Measles Vaccine	Measles
	Rubella Vaccine	German Measles
	Mumps Vaccine	Mumps
	Tuberculin Test	
18 months	DPT Booster	
	Oral Polio Vaccine	
5 years	DPT Booster	
	Oral Polio Vaccine	

Heart Disease

Warning Signs

Source: American Heart Association

Of Heart Attack
- Prolonged, oppressive pain or unusual discomfort in the center of the chest
- Pain may radiate to the shoulder, arm, neck or jaw
- Sweating may accompany pain or discomfort
- Nausea and vomiting may also occur
- Shortness of breath may accompany other signs

The American Heart Association advises immediate action at the onset of these symptoms. The Association points out that over half of heart attack victims die before they reach the hospital and that the average victim waits 3 hours before seeking help.

Of Stroke
- Sudden temporary weakness or numbness of face or limbs on one side of the body
- Temporary loss of speech, or trouble speaking or understanding speech
- Temporary dimness or loss of vision, particularly in one eye
- An episode of double vision
- Unexplained dizziness or unsteadiness
- Change in personality, mental ability
- New or unusual pattern of headaches

Major Risk Factors

Blood pressure— systolic pressure under 120 is normal; systolic pressure over 150
= 2 times the risk of heart attack
= 4 times the risk of stroke

Cholesterol— level under 194 is normal; level of 250 or over
= 3 times the risk of heart attack or stroke

Cigarettes— with non-smoking considered normal; smoking one pack a day
= 2 times the risk of heart attack
= 4 times the risk of stroke

U.S. DEATHS DUE TO CARDIOVASCULAR DISEASES BY MAJOR TYPE OF DISORDER, 1980

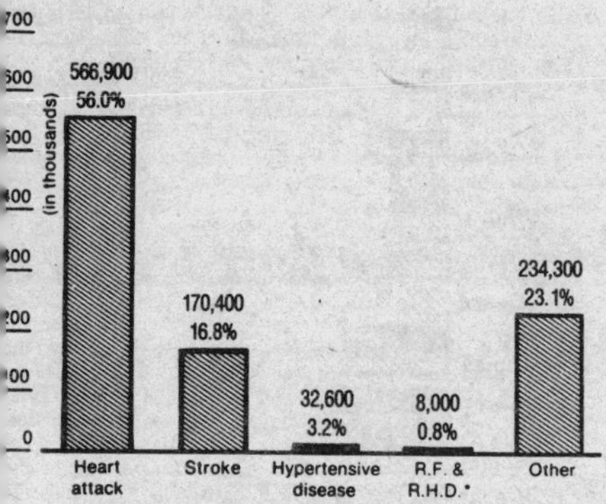

*Rheumatic Fever and Rheumatic Heart Disease
Source: National Center for Health Statistics
U.S. Department of Health and Human Services

ESTIMATED ECONOMIC COSTS IN BILLIONS OF DOLLARS OF CARDIOVASCULAR DISEASES BY TYPE OF EXPENDITURE, 1983

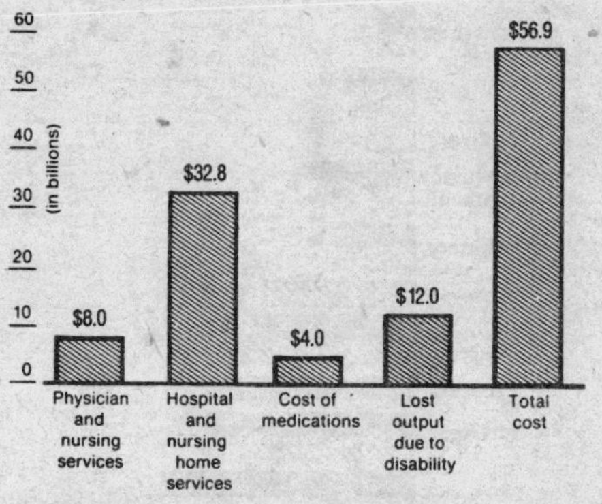

Source: American Heart Association

Cardiovascular Disease Statistical Summary

Cost — $56.9 billion (AHA est.) in 1983.

Prevalence — 42,330,000 Americans have some form of heart and blood vessel disease.
- hypertension — 37,000,000 (nearly one in 4 adults).
- coronary heart disease — 4,540,000
- rheumatic heart disease — 1,970,000.
- stroke — 1,830,000.

Mortality — 988,569 in 1978 (51% of all deaths). 1980: 1,012,150 (51%).
- nearly one-fourth of all persons killed by CVD are under age 65.

Congenital or inborn heart defects — 35 recognizable types of defects.
- about 25,000 babies are born every year with heart defects.
- post-natal mortality from heart defects was estimated to be 6,500 in 1980.

Heart attack — caused 566,900 deaths in 1980.
- 4,540,000 alive today have history of heart attack and/or angina pectoris.
- 350,000 a year die of heart attack before they reach hospital.
- As many as 1,500,000 Americans will have a heart attack this year and about 550,000 of them will die.

Stroke — killed 170,400 in 1980; afflicts 1,830,000.

CCU — most of the 7,000 general hospitals in U.S. have coronary care capability.
Hypertension (high blood pressure) — 37,000,000 adults.
- easily detected and usually controllable, but only a minority have it under adequate control.

Rheumatic heart disease — 100,000 children; 1,870,000 adults.
- killed 13,402 in 1978, 8,000 in 1980.

Note: 1980 mortality data are estimates based on 1980 provisional data as published by USDHHS.

Cancer Information

Source: American Cancer Society

Cancer Warnings

Site	Warning signal— see your doctor	Comment
Breast	Lump or thickening in the breast, or unusual discharge from nipple.	The leading cause of cancer death in women.
Colon and rectum	Change in bowel habits; bleeding.	Considered a highly curable disease when digital and procto-scopic examinations are included in routine checkups.
Lung	Persistent cough, or lingering respiratory ailment.	The leading cause of cancer death among men and rising mortality among women.
Oral (including pharynx)	Sore that does not heal; difficulty in swallowing.	Many more lives should be saved because the mouth is easily accessible to visual examination by physicians and dentists.
Skin	Sore that does not heal, or change in wart or mole.	Skin cancer is readily detected by observation, and diagnosed by simple biopsy.
Uterus	Unusual bleeding or discharge.	Uterine cancer mortality has declined 70% during the last 40 years with wider application of the Pap test. Postmenopausal women with abnormal bleeding should be checked.
Kidney and bladder	Urinary difficulty, bleeding.	Protective measures for workers in high-risk industries are helping to eliminate one of the important causes of these cancers.
Larynx	Hoarseness, difficulty in swallowing.	Readily curable if caught early.
Prostate	Urinary diffculty.	Occurs mainly in men over 60, the disease can be detected by palpation at regular checkup.
Stomach	Indigestion.	An 80% decline in mortality in 50 years, for reasons yet unknown.
Leukemia	Leukemia is a cancer of blood-forming tissues and is characterized by the abnormal production of immature white blood cells. Acute lymphocytic leukemia strikes mainly children and is treated by drugs which have extended life from a few months to as much as 10 years. Chronic leukemia strikes usually after age 25 and progresses less rapidly.	
Lymphomas (including multiple myeloma)	These cancers arise in the lymph system and include Hodgkin's disease and lymphosarcoma. Some patients with lymphatic cancers can lead normal lives for many years. Five-year survival rate for Hodgkin's disease increased from 25% to 54% in 20 years.	

CANCER INCIDENCE BY SITE AND SEX, 1982 ESTIMATES*

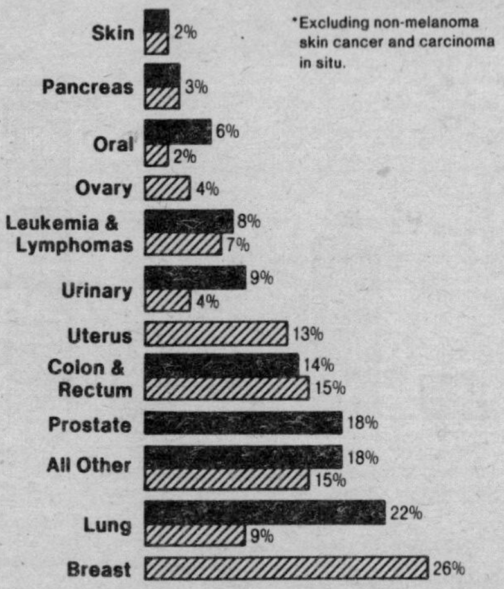

*Excluding non-melanoma skin cancer and carcinoma in situ.

CANCER DEATHS BY SITE AND SEX, 1982 ESTIMATES

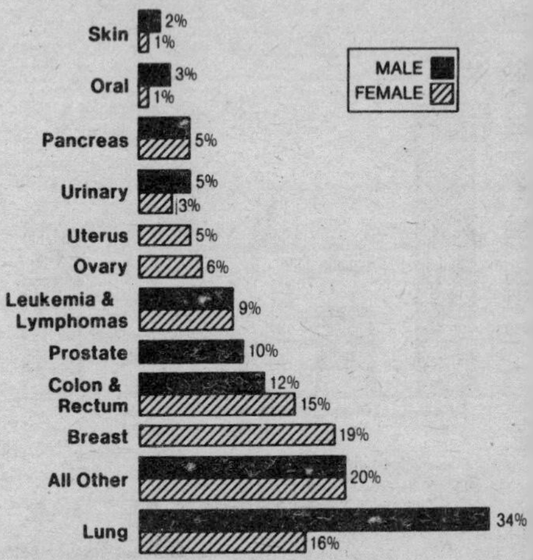

Basic First Aid

First aid experts stress that knowing what to do for an injured person until a doctor or trained person gets to an accident scene can save a life, especially in cases of stoppage of breath, severe bleeding, and shock.

People with special medical problems, such as diabetes, cardiovascular disease, epilepsy, or allergy, are also urged to wear some sort of emblem identifying it, as a safeguard against use of medication that might be injurious or fatal in an emergency. For instance, there are many epileptics, as well as diabetics, who can mistakenly be taken for drunk or ill, according to Medic Alert, a nonprofit organization which pioneered the wearing of an informative emblem. Emblems may be obtained from Medic Alert Foundation, Turlock, CA 95380.

Most accidents occur in homes. National Safety Council figures show that home accidents annually far outstrip those in other locations, such as in autos, at work, or in public places.

Measures for some of the most frequent emergencies fol low:

Animal bites — Wounds should be washed with soap unde running water and animal should be caught alive for ra bies test. Call doctor or take patient to him.

Asphyxiation — Start mouth-to-mouth resuscitation imme diately after getting patient to fresh air. Call physician.

Bleeding — Elevate the wound above the heart if possibl Press hard on wound with sterile compress until bleedin stops. Send for doctor if it is severe.

Burns — If mild, with skin unbroken and no blisters, plung into ice water until pain subsides. Apply mild burn oin ment or petroleum jelly if pain persists. Send for physicia if burn is severe. Apply sterile compresses and keep pa tient quiet and comfortably warm until doctor's arriva Do not try to clean burn, or to break blisters.

Chemicals in eye — With patient lying down, pour cupful of water immediately into corner of eye, letting it run other side to remove chemicals thoroughly. Cover with sterile compress and call doctor.

'hoking — Get behind the victim, wrap your arms about him above his waist. Make a fist with one hand and place it, with large thumb knuckle pressing inward, just below the point of the "V" of the rib cage. Grasp the fist with the other hand and give several hard upward thrusts or hugs. As last resort, lean victim forward and slap back between shoulder blades. Start mouth-to-mouth resuscitation if breathing stops. Send for physician or rush victim to hospital.

'onvulsions — Place person on back on bed or rug so he can't hurt himself. Loosen clothing. Turn head to side. Put thick wad of cloth between jaws so patient can't bite tongue. Raise and pull lower jaw forward. Sponge head and neck with cool water if convulsions do not stop. Send for doctor.

:uts (minor) — Apply mild antiseptic and sterile compress after washing with soap under warm running water.

:lectric shock — If possible, turn off power. Don't touch victim until contact is broken; pull him from contact with rope, wooden pole, or loop of dry cloth. Start artificial respiration if breathing has stopped. Send for doctor.

'oreign body in eye — Touch object with moistened corner of handkerchief if it can be seen. If it cannot be seen or does not come out after a few attempts, take patient to doctor. Do not rub eye, since this may force item in deeper.

'ainting — Seat patient and fan his face if he feels faint. Lower head to knees. Lay him down with head turned to side if he becomes unconscious. Loosen clothing and open windows. Wave aromatic spirits of ammonia or smelling salts under nose. Keep patient lying quietly for at least 15 minutes after he regains consciousness. Call doctor if faint lasts for more than a few minutues.

'alls — Send for physician if patient has continued pain. Cover wound with sterile dressing and stop any severe bleeding. Do not move patient unless absolutely necessary — as in case of fire — if broken bone is suspected. Keep patient warm and comfortable.

'oisoning — Call doctor. Use antidote listed on label if container is found. Call local Poison Control Center if possible. Except for lye, other caustics, and petroleum products, induce vomiting unless victim is unconscious. Give milk if poision or antidote is unknown.

;hock (injury-related) — Keep the victim lying down; if uncertain as to his injuries, keep the victim flat on his back. Maintain the victim's normal body temperature; if the weather is cold or damp, place blankets or extra clothing over and under the victim; if weather is hot, provide shade. Get medical care as soon as possible.

Snakebites — Immediately get victim to a hospital. If there is mild swelling or pain, apply a consticting band 2 to 4 inches above the bite. Keep the victim calm and immobilize the bitten extremity, keeping it at or below heart level. Cold therapy is not recommended. If the snake can be killed without risk or delay, it should be brought, with care, to the hospital for identification. If symptoms such as rapid swelling and severe pain develop, a ½-inch incision over the fang marks and suction should be performed immediately. The cut should be made with a sharp sterilized blade just through the skin and suction done for 30 minutes with a suction cup or mouth.

Stings from insects — If possible, remove stinger and apply solution of ammonia and water, or paste of baking soda. Call physician immediately if body swells or patient collapses. Prevent recurrence of severe allergic reaction via desensitization treatment from doctor.

Unconsciousness — Send for doctor and place person on stomach with his head turned to side. Start resuscitation if he stops breathing. Never give food or liquids to an unconscious person.

Mouth-to-Mouth Resuscitation

Stressing that your breath can save a life, the American Red Cross gives the following directions for mouth-to-mouth resuscitation if the victim is not breathing:

- Turn victim on his back and begin artificial respiration at once.
- Wipe out quickly any foreign matter visible in the mouth, using your fingers or a cloth wrapped around your fingers.
- Tilt victim's head back.
- Pull or push jaw into jutting-out position.
- If victim is a small child, place your mouth tightly over his mouth and nose and blow gently into his lungs about 20 times a minute. If victim is adult, cover the mouth with the mouth, pinch his nostrils shut, and blow vigorously about 12 times a minute.
- If unable to get air into lungs of victim, and if head and jaw positions are correct, suspect foreign matter in the throat. To remove it, suspend a small child momentarily by the ankles or hold child with head down for a moment and slap sharply between shoulder blades.
- If victim is an adult, turn him on his side and use same procedure.
- Again, wipe mouth to remove foreign matter.
- Repeat breathing, removing mouth each time to allow for escape of air. Continue until victim breathes for himself.

A Patient's Bill of Rights

Source: American Hospital Association, © copyright 1972.

Often, as a hospital patient, you feel you have little con-rol over your circumstances. You do, however, have some mportant rights. They have been enumerated by the Ameri-an Hospital Association.

1. The patient has the right to considerate and respectful care.
2. The patient has the right to obtain from his physician complete current information concerning his diagnosis, treatment, and prognosis in terms the patient can be reasonably expected to understand. When it is not medically advisable to give such information to the patient, the information should be made available to an appropriate person in his behalf. He has the right to know, by name, the physician responsible for coordinating his care.
3. The patient has the right to receive from his physician information necessary to give informed consent prior to the start of any procedure and/or treatment. Except in emergencies, such information for informed consent should include but not necessarily be limited to the specific procedure and/or treatment, the medically significant risks involved, and the probable duration of incapacitation. Where medically significant alternatives for care or treatment exist, or when the patient requests information concerning medical alternatives, the patient has the right to such information. The patient also has the right to know the name of the person responsible for the procedures and/or treatment.
4. The patient has the right to refuse treatment to the extent permitted by law and to be informed of the medical consequences of his action.
5. The patient has the right to every consideration of his privacy concerning his own medical care program. Case discussion, consultation, examination, and treatment are confidential and should be conducted discreetly. Those not directly involved in his care must have the permission of the patient to be present.
6. The patient has the right to expect that all communications and records pertaining to his care should be treated as confidential.
7. The patient has the right to expect that within its capacity a hospital must make reasonable response to the request of a patient for services. The hospital must provide evaluation, service, and/or referral as indicated by the urgency of the case. When medically permissable, a patient may be transferred to another facility only after he has received complete information and explanation concerning the need for and alternatives to such a transfer. The institution to which the patient is to be transferred must first have accepted the patient for transfer.
8. The patient has the right to obtain information as to any relationship of his hospital to other health care and edu-

cation institutions insofar as this care is concerned. The patient has the right to obtain information as to the existence of any professional relationships among individuals, by name, who are treating him.

9. The patient has the right to be advised if the hospital proposes to engage in or perform human experimentation affecting his care or treatment. The patient has the right to refuse to participate in such research projects.
10. The patient has the right to expect reasonable continuity of care. He has the right to know in advance what appointment times and physicians are available and wher The patient has the right to expect that the hospital w provide a mechanism whereby he is informed by his ph sician of the patient's continuing health care requir ments following discharge.
11. The patient has the right to examine and receive an e planation of his bill, regardless of the source of paymen
12. The patient has the right to know what hospital rul and regulations apply to his conduct as a patient.

Common Food Additives: How Safe Are They?

Source: Reprinted from "Chemical Cuisine" which is available from Center for Science in the Public Interest, 1755 S St., N.W., Washington, D.C. 20009, f $2.50, copyright 1978.

Avoid

Artificial Colorings: Most are synthetic chemicals not found in nature. Some are safer than others, but names of colorings are not liste on label. Used mostly in foods of low nutritional value, usually indicating that fruit or natural ingredient omitted.

Additive	Use	Comment
Blue No. 1	In beverages, candy, baked goods.	Very poorly tested.
Blue No. 2	Pet food, beverages, candy.	Very poorly tested.
Citrus Red No. 2	Skin of some Florida oranges.	May cause cancer. Does not seep through into pulp.
Green No. 3	Candy, beverages.	Needs better testing.
Orange B	Hot dogs.	Causes cancer in animals.
Red No. 3	Cherries in fruit cocktail, candy, baked goods.	May cause cancer.
Red. No. 40	Soda, candy, gelatin, desserts, pastry, pet food, sausage.	Causes cancer in mice. Widely used.
Yellow No. 5	Gelatin dessert, candy, pet food, baked goods.	Poorly tested; might cause cancer. Some people allergic to it. Widely used.
Brominated Vegetable Oil (BVO)	Emulsifier, clouding agent. Citrus-flavored soft drinks.	Residue found in body fat; safer substitutes available.
Butylated Hydroxytoluene (BHT)	Antioxidant. Cereals, chewing gum, potato chips, oils, etc.	May cause cancer; stored in body fat; can cause allergic reaction. Safer alternatives.
Caffeine	Stimulant. Naturally in coffee, tea cocoa; added to soft drinks.	Causes sleeplessness; may cause miscarriages or birt defects.
Quinine	Flavoring. Tonic water, quinine water, bitter lemon.	Poorly tested; some possibility that may cause birth defects.
Saccharin	Noncaloric sweetener. "Diet" products.	Causes cancer in animals.
Sodium Nitrite, Sodium Nitrate	Preservative, coloring, flavoring. Bacon, ham, frankfurters, luncheon meats, smoked fish, corned beef.	Prevents growth of botulism bacteria but can lead to formation of small amounts of cancer-causing nitrosamines, particularly in fried bacon.

Caution

Additive	Use	Comment
Artificial Coloring: Yellow No. 6	Beverages, sausage, baked goods, candy, gelatin.	Appears safe, but can cause allergic reactions.
Artificial Flavoring	Soda, candy, breakfast cereals, gelatin deserts.	Hundreds of chemicals used to mimic natural flavors, almost exclusively in "junk" foods; indicates "real thing" is left out. May cause hyperactivity in some children.
Butylated Hydroxyanisole (BHA)	Antioxidant. Cereals, chewing gum, potato chips, oils.	Appears safer than BHT but needs better testing. Safe substitutes available.
Heptyl Paraben	Preservative. Beer.	Probably safe, has not been tested in presence of alcohol.
Monosodium Glutamate (MSG)	Flavor enhancer. Soup, seafood, poultry, cheese, sauces, stews, etc.	Damages brain cells in infant mice, causes "Chinese restaurant syndrome" (headache and burning or tightness in head, neck, arms) in some sensitive adults.
Phosphoric Acid; Phosphates	Acidifier, chelating agent, buffer, emulsifier, nutrient, discoloration inhibitor. Baked goods, cheese, powdered foods, cured meat, soda, breakfast cereals, dried potatoes.	Useful chemicals that are not toxic, but their widesprea use creates dietary imbalance that may be causing osteoporosis.
Propyl Gallate	Antioxidant. Oil, meat products, potato stocks, chicken soup base, chewing gum.	Not adequately tested, use in frequently unnecessary.
Sulfur Dioxide Sodium Bisulfite	Preservative, bleach. Sliced fruit, wine, grape juice, dried potatoes, dried fruit.	Can destroy vitamin B-1, but otherwise safe.

Safe

The following common food additives are rated as safe by the Center for Science in the Public Interest. Space restrictions prohibit a detailed description of each additive. The additives are: Alginate, Propylene & Glycol Alginate, Alpha Tocopherol, Ascorbic Acid, Erythorbic Acid, Beta Carotene, Calcium (Sodium) Propionate, Calcium (or Sodium) Stearoyl Lactylate, Carrageenan, Casein, Sodium Caseinate, Citric Acid, Sodium Citrate, EDTA, Ferrous Gluconate, Fumaric Acid, Gelatin, Glycerin (Glycerol), gums (Locus Bean, Guar, Furcelleran, Arabic, Karaya, Tragacanth, Ghatti), Hydrolyzed Vegetable Protein (HVP), Lactic Acid, Lactose, Lecithin, Mannitol, Mon-and-Diglycerides, Polysorbate 60, 65 and 80, Sodium Benzoate, Sodium Carboxymethylcellulose (CMC), Sorbic Acid, Potassium Sorbate, Sorbitan Monostearate, Sorbitol, Starch and Modified Starch, Vanillan, Ethyl Vanillan.

Special Considerations

Additive	Use	Comment
Salt (Sodium chloride)	Flavoring. Most processed foods: soup, potato chips, crackers, cured meat, etc.	Large amounts of sodium may cause high blood pressure in susceptible persons and increase risk of heart attack and stroke.
Sugars: Corn Syrup, Dextrose, Glucose, Invert Sugar, Sugar	Sweeteners. Candy, soft drinks, cookies, syrups, toppings, sweetened cereals and many other foods.	Mostly in foods with low, if any, nutritional value. Excess sugars may promote tooth decay and precipitate diabetes in susceptible persons; condensed sources of calories.

Food and Nutrition

Food contains proteins, carbohydrates, fats, water, vitamins and minerals. Nutrition is the way your body takes in and uses these ingredients to maintain proper functioning. If you aren't eating foods that your body needs, you suffer from poor nutrition and, sooner or later, your health will deteriorate.

Protein

Proteins are composed of amino acids and are indispensable in the diet. They build, maintain, and repair the body. Best sources: eggs, milk, soybeans, nuts, fish, meat, poultry. No one of these foods will supply all the necessary proteins.

Fats

Fats provide energy by furnishing calories to the body, and by carrying vitamins A, D, E, and K. They are the most concentrated source of energy in the diet. Best sources: butter, margarine, salad oils, nuts, cream, eggs, most cheeses, lard, meat.

Carbohydrates

Carbohydrates provide energy for body function and activity by supplying immediate calories. The 3 forms of carbohydrates are sugars, starches, and cellulose. Best sources: wheats and cereals, legumes, nuts, potatoes (with skin), fruits, honey.

Water

Water dissolves and transports other nutrients throughout the body aiding the process of digestion, absorption, circulation, and excretion. It also helps regulate body temperature. We get water from all foods.

Vitamins

Vitamin A—promotes good eyesight and helps keep the skin and mucous membranes resistant to infection. Best sources: liver, carrots, sweet potatoes, kale, collard greens, turnips, whole milk.

Vitamin B_1 (thiamine)—essential to the nervous system, heart, liver. Best sources: meat, fish, poultry, wheat germ, brewers' yeast, brown rice, whole grain cereals.

Vitamin B_2 (riboflavin)—an aid to healthy eyes. Best sources: liver, almonds, wheat germ, mushrooms, turnip greens, whole milk, milk products.

Vitamin B_6 (pyridoxine)—important in the regulation of the central nervous system. Best sources: whole grains, meats, nuts, brewers' yeast.

Vitamin B_{12} (cobalamin)—necessary for the formation of red blood cells. Best sources: meat, fish, eggs, soybeans.

Niacin—maintains the health of skin, tongue, and digestive system. Best sources: poultry, peanuts, fish, organ meats, milk and milk products, eggs.

Other B vitamins are—biotin, choline, folic acid (folacin), inositol, PABA (para-aminobenzoic acid), and pantothenic acid.

Vitamin C (ascorbic acid)—maintains collagen, a protein necessary for the formation of skin, ligaments, and bones. It helps heal wounds and mend fractures, and aids in resisting some types of virus and bacterial infections. Best sources: citrus fruits and juices, turnips, broccoli, Brussels sprouts, potatoes and sweet potatoes, tomatoes, cabbage.

Vitamin D—important for bone development. Best sources: sunlight, fortified milk and milk products, fish, egg yolks, organ meats.

Vitamin E (tocopherol)—helps protect red blood cells. May aid the circulatory system and counteract the aging process. Best sources: wheat germ, whole grains, eggs, peanuts, organ meats, margarine, vegetable oils, green leafy vegetables.

Vitamin K—necessary for formation of prothrombin, which helps blood to clot. Best sources: green leafy vegetables, tomatoes, egg yolks, oats, wheat, rye.

Minerals

Calcium—the most abundant mineral in the body, works with phosphorus in building and maintaining bones and teeth. Best sources: whole sesame seeds, cheese, milk and milk products, and blackstrap molasses.

Phosphorus—the 2d most abundant mineral, performs more functions than any other mineral, and plays a part in nearly every chemical reaction in the body. Best source: wheat germ, brewers' yeast, powdered skim milk.

Iron—the 2d most essential trace element in the body, it is necessary for the formation of myoglobin, which transports oxygen to muscle tissue, and hemoglobin, which transports oxygen in the blood. Best sources: organ meats, molasses, beans, green leafy vegetables, and shellfish.

Other minerals—chromium, cobalt, copper, fluorine, iodine, magnesium, manganese, molybdenum, potassium, selenium, sodium, sulfur, and zinc.

Recommended Daily Dietary Allowances

Source: Food and Nutrition Board, National Academy of Sciences—National Research Council (Revised 1980)

The allowances are amounts of nutrients recommended as adequate for maintenance of good nutrition in almost all healthy persons in the U.S. Diets should be based on a variety of common foods in order to provide other nutrients for which human requirements have been less well defined.

				Fat soluble Vitamins			Water soluble Vitamins							Minerals					
	Age (years)	Weight (lbs.)	Protein (grams)	Vitamin A[1]	Vitamin D[2]	Vitamin E[3]	Vitamin C (mg.)	Thiamin (mg.)	Riboflavin (mg.)	Niacin (mg.)[4]	Vitamin B_6 (mg.)	Folacin (micrograms)	Vitamin B_{12} (micrograms)	Calcium (mg.)	Phosphorus (mg.)	Magnesium (mg.)	Iron (mg.)	Zinc (mg.)	Iodine (micrograms)
Infants. . .	to 6 mos.	13	kg × 2.2	420	10	3	35	0.3	0.4	6	0.3	30	0.5	360	240	50	10	3	40
	to 1 yr.	20	kg × 2.0	400	10	4	35	0.5	0.6	8	0.6	45	1.5	540	360	70	15	5	50
Children. .	1-3	29	23	400	10	5	45	0.7	0.8	9	0.9	100	2.0	800	800	150	15	10	70
	4-6	44	30	500	10	6	45	0.9	1.0	11	1.3	200	2.5	800	800	200	10	10	90
	7-10	62	34	700	10	7	45	1.2	1.4	16	1.6	300	3.0	800	800	250	10	10	120
Males . . .	11-14	99	45	1000	10	8	50	1.4	1.6	18	1.8	400	3.0	1200	1200	350	18	15	150
	15-18	145	56	1000	10	10	60	1.4	1.7	18	2.0	400	3.0	1200	1200	400	18	15	150
	19-22	154	56	1000	7.5	10	60	1.5	1.7	19	2.2	400	3.0	800	800	350	10	15	150
	23-50	154	56	1000	5	10	60	1.4	1.6	18	2.2	400	3.0	800	800	350	10	15	150
	51 +	154	56	1000	5	10	60	1.2	1.4	16	2.2	400	3.0	800	800	350	10	15	150
Females .	11-14	101	46	800	10	8	50	1.1	1.3	15	1.8	400	3.0	1200	1200	300	18	15	150
	15-18	120	46	800	10	8	60	1.1	1.3	14	2.0	400	3.0	1200	1200	300	18	15	150
	19-22	120	44	800	7.5	8	60	1.1	1.3	14	2.0	400	3.0	800	800	300	18	15	150
	23-50	120	44	800	5	8	60	1.0	1.2	13	2.0	400	3.0	800	800	300	18	15	150
	51 +	120	44	800	5	8	60	1.0	1.2	13	2.0	400	3.0	800	800	300	10	15	150
Pregnant			+30	+200	+5	+2	+20	+0.4	+0.3	+2	+0.6	+400	+1.0	+400	+400	+150	[5]	+5	+25
Lactating			+20	+400	+5	+3	+40	+0.5	+0.5	+5	+0.5	+100	+1.0	+400	+400	+150	[5]	+10	+50

(1) Retinol equivalents. (2) Micrograms of cholecalciferol. (3) Milligrams alpha-tocopherol equivalents. (4) Niacin equivalents. (5) The use of 30-60 milligrams of supplemental iron is recommended.

Nutritive Value of Food (Calories, Proteins, etc.)

Source: Home and Garden Bulletin No. 72; available from Supt. of Documents, U. S. Government Printing Office, Washington, DC 20402

Food	Measure	Food Energy (calories)	Protein (grams)	Fat (grams)	Saturated fats (grams)	Carbohydrate (grams)	Calcium (milligrams)	Iron (milligrams)	Vitamin A (I.U.)	Thiamin (milligrams)	Riboflavin (milligrams)	Niacin (milligrams)	Ascorbic acid
Dairy products													
Cheese, cheddar	1 oz.	115	7	9	6.1	T	204	.2	300	.01	.11	T	[illegible]
Cheese, cottage, small curd	1 cup	220	26	9	6.0	6	126	.3	340	.04	.34	.3	[illegible]
Cheese, cream	1 oz.	100	2	10	6.2	1	23	.3	400	T	.06	T	[illegible]
Cheese, Swiss	1 oz.	105	8	8	5.0	1	272	T	240	.01	.10	T	[illegible]
Cheese, pasteurized process spread, American	1 oz.	82	5	6	3.8	2	159	.1	220	.01	.12	T	[illegible]
Half-and-Half	1 tbsp.	20	T	2	1.1	1	16	T	20	.01	.02	T	[illegible]
Cream, sour	1 tbsp.	25	T	3	1.6	1	14	T	90	T	.02	T	[illegible]
Milk, whole	1 cup	150	8	8	5.1	11	291	.1	310	.09	.40	.2	[illegible]
Milk, nonfat (skim)	1 cup	85	8	T	.3	12	302	.1	500	.09	.37	.2	[illegible]
Buttermilk	1 cup	100	8	2	1.3	12	285	.1	80	.08	.38	.1	[illegible]
Milkshake, chocolate	10.6 oz.	355	9	8	5.0	63	396	.9	260	.14	.67	.4	[illegible]
Ice Cream, hardened	1 cup	270	5	14	8.9	32	176	.1	540	.05	.33	.1	[illegible]
Sherbet	1 cup	270	2	4	2.4	59	103	.3	190	.03	.09	.1	[illegible]
Yogurt, fruit-flavored	8 oz.	230	10	3	1.8	42	343	.2	120	.08	.40	.2	[illegible]
Eggs													
Fried in butter	1	85	5	6	2.4	1	26	.9	290	.03	.13	T	[illegible]
Hard-cooked	1	80	6	6	1.7	1	28	1.0	260	.04	.14	T	[illegible]
Scrambled in butter (milk added)	1	95	6	7	2.8	1	47	.9	310	.04	.16	T	[illegible]
Fats & oils													
Butter	1 tbsp.	100	T	12	7.2	T	3	T	430	T	T	T	[illegible]
Margarine	1 tbsp.	100	T	12	2.1	T	3	T	470	T	T	T	[illegible]
Salad dressing, blue cheese	1 tbsp.	75	1	8	1.6	1	12	T	30	T	.02	T	[illegible]
Salad dressing, French	1 tbsp.	65	T	6	1.1	3	2	.1	-	-	-	-	[illegible]
Salad dressing, Italian	1 tbsp.	85	T	9	1.6	1	2	T	T	T	T	T	[illegible]
Mayonnaise	1 tbsp.	100	T	11	2.0	T	3	.1	40	T	.01	T	[illegible]
Meat, poultry, fish													
Bluefish, baked with butter or margarine	3 oz.	135	22	4	-	0	25	0.6	40	.09	.08	1.6	[illegible]
Clams, raw, meat only	3 oz.	65	11	1	-	2	59	5.2	90	.08	.15	1.1	[illegible]
Crabmeat, white or king, canned	1 cup	135	24	3	.6	1	61	1.1	-	.11	.11	2.6	[illegible]
Fish sticks, breaded, cooked, frozen	1 oz.	50	5	3	-	2	3	.1	0	.01	.02	.5	[illegible]
Salmon, pink, canned	3 oz.	120	17	5	.9	0	167	.7	60	.03	.16	6.8	[illegible]
Sardines, Atlantic, canned in oil	3 oz.	175	20	9	3.0	0	372	2.5	190	.02	.17	4.6	[illegible]
Shrimp, French fried	3 oz.	190	17	9	2.3	9	61	1.7	-	.03	.07	2.3	[illegible]
Tuna, canned in oil	3 oz.	170	24	7	1.7	0	7	1.6	70	.04	.10	10.1	[illegible]
Bacon, broiled or fried crisp	2 slices	85	4	8	2.5	T	2	.5	0	.08	.05	.8	[illegible]
Ground beef, broiled, 10% fat	3 oz.	185	23	10	4.0	0	10	3.0	20	.08	.20	5.1	[illegible]
Roast beef, relatively lean	3 oz.	165	25	7	2.8	0	11	3.2	10	.06	.19	4.5	[illegible]
Beef steak, lean and fat	3 oz.	330	20	27	11.3	0	9	2.5	50	.05	.15	4.0	[illegible]
Beef & vegetable stew	1 cup	220	16	11	4.9	15	29	2.9	2,400	.15	.17	4.7	[illegible]
Lamb, chop, lean and fat	3.1 oz.	360	18	32	14.8	0	8	1.0	-	.11	.19	4.1	[illegible]
Liver, beef	3 oz.	195	22	9	2.5	5	9	7.5	45,390	.22	3.56	14.00	[illegible]
Ham, light cure, lean and fat	3 oz.	245	18	19	6.8	0	8	2.2	0	.40	.15	3.1	[illegible]
Pork, chop, lean and fat	2.7 oz	305	19	25	8.9	0	9	2.7	0	.75	.22	4.5	[illegible]
Bologna	1 slice	85	3	8	3.0	T	2	.5	-	.05	.06	.7	[illegible]
Frankfurter, cooked	1	170	7	15	5.6	1	3	.8	-	.08	.11	1.4	[illegible]
Sausage, pork link, cooked	1 link	60	2	6	2.1	T	1	.3	0	.10	.04	.5	[illegible]
Veal, cutlet, braised or boiled	3 oz.	185	23	9	4.0	0	9	2.7	-	.06	.21	4.6	[illegible]
Chicken, drumstick, fried, bones removed	1.3 oz.	90	12	4	1.1	T	6	.9	50	.03	.15	2.7	[illegible]
Chicken, half broiler, broiled, bones removed	6.2 oz.	240	42	7	2.2	0	16	3.0	160	.09	.34	15.5	[illegible]
Chicken a la king	1 cup	470	27	34	12.7	12	127	2.5	1,130	.10	.42	5.4	[illegible]
Chicken potpie, baked, 1/3 of 9 in. diam. pie	1 piece	545	23	31	11.3	42	70	3.0	3,090	.34	.31	5.5	[illegible]
Fruits & products													
Apple, raw, 2-3/4 in. diam.	1	80	T	1	-	20	10	.4	120	.04	.03	.1	[illegible]
Applejuice	1 cup	120	T	T	-	30	15	1.5		.02	.05	.2	[illegible]
Applesauce, canned, sweetened	1 cup	230	1	T	-	61	10	1.3	100	.05	.03	.1	[illegible]
Apricots, raw	3	55	1	T	-	14	18	.5	2,890	.03	.04	.6	[illegible]
Banana, raw	1	100	1	T	-	26	10	.8	230	.06	.07	.8	[illegible]
Cherries, sweet, raw	10	45	1	T	-	12	15	.3	70	.03	.04	.3	[illegible]
Fruit cocktail, canned, in heavy syrup	1 cup	195	1	T	-	50	23	1.0	360	.05	.03	1.0	[illegible]
Grapefruit, raw, medium, white	1/2	45	1	T	-	12	19	.5	10	.05	.02	.2	[illegible]
Grapes, Thompson seedless	10	35	T	T	-	9	6	.2	50	.03	.02	.2	[illegible]
Lemonade, frozen, diluted	1 cup	105	T	T	-	28	2	.1	10	.01	.02	.2	[illegible]
Cantaloupe, 5-in. diam.	1/2	80	2	T	-	20	38	1.1	9,240	.11	.08	1.6	[illegible]
Orange, 2-5/8 in. diam.	1	65	1	T	-	16	54	.5	260	.13	.05	.5	[illegible]
Orange juice, frozen, diluted	1 cup	120	2	T	-	29	25	.2	540	.23	.03	.9	[illegible]
Peach, raw, 2-1/2 in. diam.	1	40	1	T	-	10	9	.5	1,330	.02	.05	1.0	[illegible]
Peaches, canned in syrup	1 cup	200	1	T	-	51	10	.8	1.100	.03	.05	1.5	[illegible]
Pear, raw, Bartlett, 2-1/2 in. diam.	1	100	1	1	-	25	13	.5	30	.03	.07	.2	[illegible]
Pineapple, heavy syrup pack, crushed, chunks	1 cup	190	1	T	-	49	28	.8	130	.20	.05	.5	[illegible]
Raisins, seedless	1 cup	420	4	T	-	112	90	5.1	30	.16	.12	.7	[illegible]
Strawberries, whole	1 cup	55	1	1	-	13	31	1.5	90	.04	.10	.9	[illegible]
Watermelon, 4 by 8 in. wedge	1 wedge	110	2	1	-	27	30	2.1	2,510	.13	.13	.9	[illegible]
Grain products													
Bagel, egg	1	165	6	2	.5	28	9	1.2	30	.14	.10	1.2	[illegible]
Biscuit, 2 in. diam., from home recipe	1	105	2	5	1.2	13	34	.4	T	.08	.08	.7	[illegible]
Bread, raisin	1 slice	65	2	1	.2	13	18	.6	T	.09	.06	.6	[illegible]
Bread, white, enriched, soft-crumb	1 slice	70	2	1	.2	13	21	.6	T	.10	.06	.8	[illegible]
Bread, whole wheat, soft-crumb	1 slice	65	3	1	.1	14	24	.8	T	.09	.03	.8	[illegible]
Oatmeal or rolled oats	1 cup	130	5	2	.4	23	22	1.4	0	.19	.05	.2	[illegible]
Bran flakes (40% bran), added sugar, salt, iron, vitamins	1 cup	105	4	1	-	28	19	12.4	1,650	.41	.49	4.1	[illegible]
Corn flakes, added sugar, salt, iron, vitamins	1 cup	95	2	T	-	21	*	0.6	1,180	.29	.35	2.9	[illegible]
Rice, puffed, added iron, thiamin, niacin	1 cup	60	1	T	-	13	3	.3	0	.07	.01	.7	[illegible]

(continued)

(continued)

Food	Measure	Food Energy (calories)	Protein (grams)	Fat (grams)	Saturated fats (grams)	Carbohydrate (grams)	Calcium (milligrams)	Iron (milligrams)	Vitamin A (I.U.)	Thiamin (milligrams)	Riboflavin (milligrams)	Niacin (milligrams)	Ascorbic acid (milligrams)
Wheat, shredded, plain, 1 biscuit or 1/2 cup	1 serving	90	2	1	-	20	11	.9	0	.06	.03	1.1	0
Cake, angel food, 1/12 of cake	1	135	3	T	-	32	50	.2	0	.03	.08	.3	0
Coffeecake, 1/6 cake	1	230	5	7	2.0	38	44	1.2	120	.14	.15	1.3	T
Cupcake, 2-1/2 in. diam., with chocolate icing	1	130	2	5	2.0	21	47	.4	60	.05	.06	.4	T
Boston cream pie with custard filling, 1/12 of cake	1	210	3	6	1.9	34	46	.7	140	.09	.11	.8	T
Fruitcake, dark, 1/30 of loaf	1	55	1	2	.5	9	11	.4	20	.02	.02	.2	T
Cake, pound, 1/17 of loaf	1	160	2	10	2.5	16	6	.5	80	.05	.06	.4	0
Brownies, with nuts, from commercial recipe	1	85	1	4	.9	13	9	.4	20	.03	.02	.2	T
Cookies, chocolate chip, from home recipe	4	205	2	12	3.5	24	14	.8	40	.06	.06	.5	T
Vanilla wafers	10	185	2	6	-	30	16	.6	50	.10	.09	.8	0
Crackers, graham	2	55	1	1	.3	10	6	.5	0	.02	.08	.5	0
Crackers, saltines	4	50	1	1	.3	8	2	.5	0	.05	.05	.4	0
Danish pastry, round piece	1	275	5	15	4.7	30	33	1.2	200	.18	.19	1.7	T
Doughnut, cake type	1	100	1	5	1.2	13	10	.4	20	.05	.05	.4	T
Macaroni and cheese, from home recipe	1 cup	430	17	22	8.9	40	362	1.8	860	.20	.40	1.8	T
Muffin, corn	1	125	3	4	1.2	19	42	.7	120	.10	.10	.7	T
Noodles, enriched, cooked	1 cup	200	7	2	-	37	16	1.4	110	.22	.13	1.9	0
Pancake, plain, from home recipe	1	60	2	2	.5	9	27	.4	30	.06	.07	.5	T
Pie, apple, 1/7 of pie	1	345	3	15	3.9	51	11	.9	40	.15	.11	1.3	2
Pie, banana cream, 1/7 of pie	1	285	6	12	3.8	40	86	1.0	330	.11	.22	1.0	1
Pie, cherry, 1/7 of pie	1	350	4	15	4.0	52	19	.9	590	.16	.12	1.4	T
Pie, lemon meringue, 1/7 of pie	1	305	4	12	3.7	45	17	1.0	200	.09	.12	.7	4
Pie, pecan, 1/7 of pie	1	495	6	27	4.0	61	55	3.7	190	.26	.14	1.0	T
Pie, pumpkin, 1/7 of pie	1	275	5	15	5.4	32	66	1.0	3,210	.11	.18	1.0	T
Pizza, cheese, 1/8 of 12 in. diam. pie	1	145	6	4	1.7	22	86	1.1	230	.16	.18	1.6	4
Popcorn, popped, plain	1 cup	25	1	T	T	5	1	.2	-	-	.01	.1	0
Pretzels, stick	10	10	T	T	-	2	1	T	0	.01	.01	.1	0
Rice, white, enriched, instant, cooked	1 cup	180	4	T	T	40	5	1.3	0	.21	**	1.7	0
Rolls, enriched, brown & serve	1	85	2	2	.4	14	20	.5	T	.10	.06	.9	T
Rolls, frankfurter & hamburger	1	120	3	2	.5	21	30	.8	T	.16	.10	1.3	T
Spaghetti with meat balls & tomato sauce, from home recipe	1 cup	330	19	12	3.3	39	124	3.7	1,590	.25	.30	4.0	22
Legumes, nuts, seeds													
Beans, Great Northern, cooked	1 cup	210	14	1	-	38	90	4.9	0	.25	.13	1.3	0
Peanuts, roasted in oil, salted	1 cup	840	37	72	13.7	27	107	3.0	-	.46	.19	24.8	0
Peanut butter	1 tbsp.	95	4	8	1.5	3	9	.3	-	.02	.02	2.4	0
Sunflower seeds	1 cup	810	35	69	8.2	29	174	10.3	70	2.84	.33	7.8	-
Sugars & sweets													
Candy, caramels	1 oz.	115	1	3	1.6	22	42	.4	T	.01	.05	.1	T
Candy, milk chocolate	1 oz.	145	2	9	5.5	16	65	.3	80	.02	.10	.1	T
Fudge, chocolate	1 oz.	115	1	3	1.3	21	22	.3	T	.01	.03	.1	T
Candy, hard	1 oz.	110	0	T	-	28	6	.5	0	0	0	0	0
Honey	1 tbsp.	65	T	0	0	17	1	.1	0	T	.01	.1	T
Jams & Preserves	1 tbsp.	55	T	T	-	14	4	.2	T	T	.01	T	T
Sugar, white, granulated	1 tbsp.	45	0	0	0	12	0	T	0	0	0	0	0
Vegetables													
Asparagus, canned, spears	4 spears	15	2	T	-	3	15	1.5	640	.05	.08	.6	12
Beans, lima, thick-seeded	1 cup	170	10	T	-	32	34	2.9	390	.12	.09	1.7	29
Beans, green, from frozen, cuts	1 cup	35	2	T	-	8	54	.9	780	.09	.12	.5	7
Beets, canned, diced or sliced	1 cup	65	2	T	-	15	32	1.2	30	.02	.05	.2	5
Broccoli, cooked	1 stalk	45	6	1	-	8	158	1.4	4,500	.16	.36	1.4	162
Cabbage, raw, coarsely shredded or sliced	1 cup	15	1	T	-	4	34	.3	90	.04	.04	.02	33
Carrots, raw, 7-1/2 by 1-1/8 in.	1	30	1	T	-	7	27	.5	7,930	.04	.04	.4	6
Cauliflower, raw	1 cup	31	3	T	-	6	29	1.3	70	.13	.12	.8	90
Celery, raw	1 stalk	5	T	T	-	2	16	.1	110	.01	.01	.1	4
Collards, cooked	1 cup	65	7	1	-	10	357	1.5	14,820	.21	.38	2.3	144
Corn, sweet, cooked	1 ear	70	2	1	-	16	2	.5	310	.09	.08	1.1	7
Corn, cream style	1 cup	210	5	2	-	51	8	1.5	840	.08	.13	2.6	13
Cucumber, with peel	6-8 slices	5	T	T	-	1	7	.3	70	.01	.01	.1	3
Lettuce, Iceberg, chopped	1 cup	5	T	T	-	2	11	.3	180	.03	.03	.2	3
Mushrooms, raw	1 cup	20	2	T	-	3	4	.6	T	.07	.32	2.9	2
Onions, raw, chopped	1 cup	65	3	T	-	15	46	.9	T	.05	.07	.3	17
Peas, frozen, cooked	1 cup	110	8	T	-	19	30	3.0	960	.43	.14	2.7	21
Potatoes, baked, peeled	1	145	4	T	-	33	14	1.1	T	.15	.07	2.7	31
Potatoes, frozen, French fried	10	110	2	4	1.1	17	5	.9	T	.07	.01	1.3	11
Potatoes, mashed, milk added	1 cup	135	4	2	.7	27	50	.8	40	.17	.11	2.1	21
Potato chips	10	115	1	8	2.1	10	8	.4	T	.04	.01	1.0	3
Potato salad	1 cup	250	7	7	2.0	41	80	1.5	350	.20	.18	2.8	28
Sauerkraut, canned	1 cup	40	2	T	-	9	85	1.2	120	.07	.09	.5	33
Spinach, chopped, from frozen	1 cup	45	6	1	-	8	232	4.3	16,200	.14	.31	.8	39
Squash, summer, cooked	1 cup	30	2	T	-	7	53	.8	820	.11	.17	1.7	21
Sweet potatoes, baked in skin, peeled	1	160	2	1	-	37	46	1.0	9,230	.10	.08	.8	25
Tomatoes, raw	1	25	1	T	-	6	16	.6	1,110	.07	.05	.9	28
Tomato catsup	1 tbsp.	15	T	T	-	4	3	.1	210	.01	.01	.2	2
Tomato juice	1 cup	45	2	T	-	10	17	2.2	1,940	.12	.07	1.9	39
Miscellaneous													
Beer	12 fl. oz.	150	1	0	0	14	18	T	-	.01	.11	2.2	-
Gin, rum, vodka, whisky, 86 proof	1-1/2 fl. oz.	105	-	-	0	T	-	-	-	-	-	-	-
Wine, table	3-1/2 fl. oz.	85	T	0	0	4	9	.4	-	T	.01	.1	-
Cola-type beverage	12 fl. oz.	145	0	0	0	37	-	-	0	0	0	0	0
Ginger ale	12 fl. oz	115	0	0	0	29	-	-	0	0	0	0	0
Gelatin dessert	1 cup	140	4	0	0	34	-	-	-	-	-	-	-
Mustard, prepared	1 tsp.	5	T	T	-	T	4	.1	-	-	-	-	-
Olives, pickled, green	4 medium	15	T	2	.2	T	8	.2	40	-	-	-	-
Pickles, dill, whole	1	5	T	T	-	1	17	.7	70	T	.01	T	4
Popsicle, 3 fl. oz.	1	70	0	0	0	18	0	T	0	0	0	0	0
Soup, cream of chicken, prepared with milk	1 cup	180	7	10	4.2	15	172	.5	610	.05	.27	.7	2
Soup, cream of mushroom, prepared with milk	1 cup	215	7	14	5.4	16	191	.5	250	.05	.34	.7	1
Soup, tomato, prepared with water	1 cup	90	2	3	.5	16	15	.7	1,000	.05	.05	1.2	12

T — Indicates trace * — Varies by brand

Birthstones

Source: Jewelry Industry Council

Month	Ancient	Modern
January	Garnet	Garnet
February	Amethyst	Amethyst
March	Jasper	Bloodstone or Aquamarine
April	Sapphire	Diamond
May	Agate	Emerald
June	Emerald	Pearl, Moonstone, or Alexandrite
July	Onyx	Ruby
August	Carnelian	Sardonyx or Peridot
September	Chrysolite	Sapphire
October	Aquamarine	Opal or Tourmaline
November	Topaz	Topaz
December	Ruby	Turquoise or Zircon

Wedding Anniversaries

The traditional names for wedding anniversaries go back many years in social usage. As such names as wooden, crystal, silver, and golden were applied it was considered proper to present the married pair with gifts made of these products or of something related. The list of traditional gifts, with a few allowable revisions in parentheses, is presented below, followed by modern gifts in **bold face.**

1st-Paper, **clocks**
2d-Cotton, **china**
3d-Leather, **crystal & glass**
4th-Linen (silk), **electrical appliances**
5th-Wood, **silverware**
6th-Iron, **wood**
7th-Wool (copper), **desk sets**
8th-Bronze, **linens & lace**
9th-Pottery (china), **leather**
10th-Tin (aluminum), **diamond jewelry**
11th-Steel, **fashion jewelry, accessories**
12th-Silk, **pearls or colored gems**
13th-Lace, **textiles & furs**
14th-Ivory, **gold jewelry**
15th-Crystal, **watches**
20th-China, **platinum**
25th-Silver, **sterling silver jubliee**
30th-Pearl, **diamond**
35th-Coral (jade), **jade**
40th-Ruby, **ruby**
45th-Sapphire, **sapphire**
50th-Gold, **gold**
55th-Emerald, **emerald**
60th-Diamond, **diamond**

Canadian Marriage Information

Source: Compiled from information provided by the various provincial government departments and agencies concerned.

Marriageable age, by provinces, for both males and females with and without consent of parents or guardians. In some provinces, the court has authority, given special circumstances, to marry young couples below the minimum age. Most provinces waive the blood test requirement and the waiting period varies across the provinces.

Province	With consent		Without consent		Blood test	other province	Wait for license	Wait after license
	Men	Women	Men	Women	Required	Accepted		
Newfoundland	16	16	19	19	None	None	4 days	4 days
Prince Edward Island	16	16	18	18	Yes	Yes	5 days	None
Nova Scotia	(1)	(1)	19	19	None	None	5 days	None
New Brunswick	16	14	18	18	None	None	5 days	None
Quebec	14	12	18	18	None	—	—	None
Ontario	16	16	18	18	None	—	None[2]	3 days
Manitoba	16	16	18	18	Yes	Yes	None	24 hours
Saskatchewan	15	15	18	18	Yes	Yes	5 days	24 hours
Alberta	16[8]	16[8]	18	18	Yes[3]	Yes[4]	None[5]	None
British Columbia	16[6]	16[6]	19	19	None	None	2 days[7]	None
Yukon Territory	15	15	19	19	None	None	None	24 hours
Northwest Territories	15	15[9]	19	19	None	Yes	None	None

(1) There is no statutory minimum age in the province. Anyone under the age of 19 years must have consent for marriage and no person under the age of 16 may be married without authorization of a Family Court judge and in addition must have the necessary consent of the parent or guardian. (2) Special requirements applicable to nonresidents. (3) Applies only to applicants under 60 years of age. (4) This is upon filing of negative lab report indicating blood test was taken within 14 days preceding date of application for license. (5) Exception where consent is required by mail; depending receipt of divorce documents, etc. (6) Persons under 16 years of age (no minimum age specified) may also be married if they have obtained, in addition to the usual consent from parents or guardian, an order from a judge of the Supreme or County Court in this province. (7) Including day of application, e.g., a license applied for on a Monday cannot be issued until Wednesday. (8) Under 16 allowed if pregnant or the mother of a living child. (9) Under 15 allowed if pregnant or with the written permission of the Commissioner of the NWT.

Grounds for Divorce in Canada

Source: Government of Canada Divorce Act

The grounds for divorce in Canada are the same for all the provinces and its territories. There are two categories of offense

A. Marital Offense:
- Adultery
- Sodomy
- Bestiality
- Rape
- Homosexual act
- Subsequent marriage
- Physical cruelty
- Mental cruelty

B. Marriage breakdown by reason of:
- Imprisonment for aggregate period of not less than 3 years
- Imprisonment for not less than 2 years on sentence of death or sentence of 10 years or more
- Addiction to alcohol
- Addiction to narcotics
- Whereabouts of spouse unknown
- Non-consummation
- Separation for not less than 3 years
- Desertion by petitioner for not less than 5 years

Residence time: Domicile in Canada. Time between interlocutory and final decree: normally 3 months before final can be applied for.

Marriage Information

Source: Compiled by William E. Mariano, Council on Marriage Relations, Inc., 110 E. 42d St., New York, NY 10017 (as of Aug. 24, 1982)

Marriageable age, by states, for both males and females with and without consent of parents or guardians. But in most states, the court has authority to marry young couples below the ordinary age of consent, where due regard for their morals and welfare so requires. In many states, under special circumstances, blood test and waiting period may be waived.

State	With consent		Without consent		Blood test*		Wait for license	Wait after license
	Men	Women	Men	Women	Required	Other state accepted		
Alabama(b)	14	14	18	18	Yes	Yes	none	none
Alaska	16	16	18	18	Yes	No	3 days	none
Arizona	16(i)	16	18	18	Yes	Yes	none	none
Arkansas	17	16(j)	18	18	Yes	No	3 days	none
California	18(i)	18	18	18	Yes (n)	Yes	none	none
Colorado	16	16	18	18	Yes (n)	...	none	none
Connecticut	16	16(l)	18	18	Yes	Yes	4 days	none
Delaware	18	16(o)	18	18	Yes	Yes	none	24 hrs. (c)
District of Columbia	16	16	18	18	Yes	Yes	3 days	none
Florida	18	18	18	18	Yes	Yes	3 days	none
Georgia	16	16	18	18	Yes	Yes	none (k)	none
Hawaii	16	16	18	18	Yes	Yes	none	none
Idaho	16	16	18	18	Yes (n)	Yes	none (k)	none
Illinois (a)	16	16	18	18	Yes (p)	Yes	none	1 day
Indiana	17(o)	17(o)	18	18	Yes (p)	No	72 hours	none
Iowa	16(o)	16(o)	18	18	Yes	Yes	3 days	none
Kansas	14	12	18	18	Yes	Yes	3 days	none
Kentucky	—(o)	—(o)	18	18	Yes	No	3 days	none
Louisiana (a)	18(o)	16(j)	18	16	Yes	No	none	72 hours
Maine	16(j)	16(j)	18	18	No	No	5 days	none
Maryland	16	16	18	18	none	none	48 hours	none
Massachusetts	—(o)	—(o)	18	18	Yes	Yes	3 days	none
Michigan (a)	18	16	18	18	Yes	No	3 days	none
Minnesota	16(e)	16(e)	18	18	none	...	5 days	none
Mississippi (b)	17(q)	15(q)	21	21	Yes	...	3 days	none
Missouri	15	15	18	18	none	Yes	3 days	none
Montana	15	15	18	18	Yes (n)	Yes	none	3 days
Nebraska	17	17	18	18	Yes (n)	Yes	2 days	none
Nevada	16	16	18	18	none	none	none	none
New Hampshire (a)	14(e)	13(e)	18	18	Yes	Yes	5 days	none
New Jersey (a)	—	12	18	18	Yes	Yes	72 hours	none
New Mexico	16	16	18	18	Yes	Yes	none	none
New York	16	14	18	18	Yes (p)	No	none	24 hrs.(g)
North Carolina (a)	16	16	18	18	Yes (p)	Yes	none	none
North Dakota (a)	16	16	18	18	Yes	...	none	none
Ohio (a)	18	16	18	18	Yes	Yes	5 days	none
Oklahoma	16	16	18	18	Yes	No	none (f)(h)	none
Oregon	17	17	18	18	Yes	No	3 days	none
Pennsylvania	16	16	18	18	Yes	Yes	3 days	none
Rhode Island (a) (b)	18	16	18	18	Yes (n)	No	none	none
South Carolina	16	14	18	18	none	none	24 hrs.	none
South Dakota	16	16	18	18	Yes	Yes	none	none
Tennessee (b)	16	16	18	18	Yes	Yes	3 days	none
Texas	14	14	18	18	Yes	Yes	none	none
Utah (a)	14	14	18	18	none	Yes	none	none
Vermont (a)	18	16	18	18	Yes	...	none	5 days
Virginia (a)	16	16	18	18	Yes	Yes (m)	none	none
Washington	17	17	18	18	(d)	...	3 days	none
West Virginia	18	16	18	18	Yes	No	3 days	none
Wisconsin	16	16	18	18	Yes	Yes	5 days	none
Wyoming	16	16	19	19	Yes	Yes	none	none
Puerto Rico	18	16	21	21	(f)	none	none	none
Virgin Islands	16	14	18	18	none	none	8 days	none

***Many states have additional special requirements; contact individual state.** (a) Special laws applicable to non-residents. (b) Special laws applicable to those under 21 years; Ala., bond required if male is under 18, female under 18. (c) 24 hours if one or both parties resident of state; 96 hours if both parties are non-residents. (d) None, but both must file affidavit. (e) Parental consent plus court's consent required. (f) None, but a medical certificate is required. (g) Marriage may not be solemnized within 10 days from date of blood test. (h) If either under 18, 72 hrs. (i) Statute provides for obtaining license with parental or court consent with no state minimum age. (j) Under 16, with parental and court consent. (k) If either under 18, wait 3 full days. (l) If under stated age, court consent required. (m) Va. blood test form must be used. (n) Applicant must also supply a certificate of immunity against German measles (rubella). (o) If under 18, parental and/or court consent required. (p) Statement whether person is carrier of sickle-cell anemia may be required. (q) Both parents' consent required for men age 17, women age 15; one parent's consent required for men 18-20 years, women ages 16-20 years.

How to Obtain Birth, Marriage, Death Records

The United States government has published a series of inexpensive booklets entitled: Where to Write for Birth & Death Records; Where to Write for Marriage Records; Where to Write for Divorce Records; Where to Write for Birth and Death Records of U. S. Citizens Who were Born or Died Outside of the U. S.; Birth Certifications for Alien Children Adopted by

U. S. Citizens; You May Save Time Proving Your Age and Other Birth Facts. They tell where to write to get a certified cop of an original vital record. Supt. of Documents, Government Printing Office, Washington, DC 20402.

Grounds for Divorce

Source: Compiled by William E. Mariano, Council on Marriage Relations, Inc., 110 E. 42d St., New York, NY 10017 (as of Aug. 24, 1982)

Persons contemplating divorce should study latest decisions or secure legal advice before initiating proceedings since differ ent interpretations or exceptions in each case can change the conclusion reached.

State	Breakdown of marriage/ incompatibility	Cruelty	Desertion	Non-support	Alcohol &/or drug addiction	Felony	Impotency	Insanity[1]	Living separate and apart	Other grounds	Residence time	Time between interlocut and final decrees
Alabama	X	X	X	X	X	X	X	X	2 yrs.	A-B-E	6 mos.	none-M
Alaska	X	X	X	...	X	X	X	X		B-C-F	1 yr.	none
Arizona	X	...	...	...	...	...	...	...			90 days	none
Arkansas	...	X	X	X	X	X	X	X	3 yrs.	C-I	3 mos.	none
California[2]	X	...	...	...	...	...	...	X			6 mos.	6 mos.
Colorado[2]	X	...	...	...	...	...	...	...			90 days	none
Connecticut	X	X	X	X	X	X	...	X	18 mos.	B	1 yr.	none
Delaware	X[4]	...	...	...	...	...	...	...	6 mos.		6 mos.	none
Dist. of Columbia	...	...	...	...	...	...	...	...	6 mos.-1 yr.		6 mos.	none
Florida	X	...	...	...	...	...	...	X			6 mos.	none
Georgia	X	X	X	...	X	X	X	X		A-B-F	6 mos.	L
Hawaii	X	...	...	...	...	...	...	...	2 yrs.	K	3 mos.	none
Idaho	X	X	X	X	X	X	...	X	5 yrs.	H	6 wks.	none
Illinois	...	X	X	...	X	X	X	...		I-J	90 days	none
Indiana	X	...	...	...	...	X	X	X			6 mos.	none
Iowa	X	...	...	...	...	...	...	...			1 yr.	none-N
Kansas	X	...	...	...	...	...	...	...		H	60 days	none-M
Kentucky	X	...	...	...	...	...	...	...	1 yr.		180 days	none
Louisiana	...	X	X	X	X	X	...	...	1 yr.	C-J-K	12 mos.	none-N
Maine	X	X	X	X	X	...	X	X		H	6 mos.	none
Maryland	...	X	X	...	...	X	X	X	1-3 yrs.	D-I	1 yr.	none
Massachusetts	X[4]	X	X	X	X	X	X	...	6 mos.-1 yr.		1 yr.	6 mos.
Michigan	X	...	...	...	...	...	...	...			180 days	none
Minnesota	X	...	...	...	...	...	...	...		K	180 days	none-O
Mississippi	X	X	X	...	X	X	X	X		A	6 mos.	none-P
Missouri	X[4]	...	...	...	...	...	...	...			90 days	none
Montana	X	...	...	...	...	...	...	...			90 days	none
Nebraska	X	...	...	...	...	...	...	...			1 yr.	6 mos.
Nevada	X	...	...	...	...	...	...	X	1 yr.		6 wks.	none
New Hampshire[3]	X	X	X	X	X	X	X	...	2 yrs.	K	1 yr.	none
New Jersey	...	X	X	...	X	X	...	X	18 mos.	E-K	1 yr.	none
New Mexico	X	X	X	...	...	...	...	...			6 mos.	none
New York	...	X	X	...	...	X	...	...	1 yr.	K	1 yr.	none
North Carolina	...	...	...	...	...	...	X	X	1 yr.	A-E	6 mos.	none
North Dakota	X	X	X	X	X	X	X	X		H-K	12 mos.	none
Ohio	X	X	X	...	X	X	X	X	2 yrs.	B-G-H-I	6 mos.	none
Oklahoma	X	X	X	X	X	X	X	X		A-B-G-H	6 mos.	none
Oregon[2]	X	...	...	...	...	...	...	...		B	6 mos.	30 days
Pennsylvania	X	X	X	...	...	X	X	X	3 yrs.	C-D-I	6 mos.	none
Rhode Island	X	X	X	X	X	X	X	...	3 yrs.		1 yr.	3 mos.
South Carolina	...	X	X	...	X	...	...	...	1 yr.		3 mos.	none
South Dakota	...	X	X	X	X	X	...	...			none	none
Tennessee	X	X	X	X	X	X	X	...		A-H-I-J-K	6 mos.	none
Texas	X	X	X	...	...	X	...	X	3 yrs.		6 mos.	none-O
Utah	...	X	X	X	X	X	X	X		K	3 mos.	3 mos.
Vermont	...	X	X	X	...	X	...	X	6 mos.		6 mos.	3 mos.
Virginia	...	X	X	...	...	X	...	...	6 mos.-1 yr.	E	6 mos.	none-P
Washington	X	...	...	...	...	...	...	...			none	none-R
West Virginia	X	X	X	...	X	X	...	X	1 yr.	U	1 yr.	none
Wisconsin	X	...	...	...	...	...	...	...	1 yr.	K	6 mos.	none-O
Wyoming	X	...	...	...	...	...	...	X	2 yrs.		60 days	none

Adultery is either grounds for divorce or evidence of irreconcilable differences and a breakdown of the marriage in all states. Th plaintiff can invariably remarry in the same state where he or she procured a decree of divorce or annulment. Not so the defenda who is barred in certain states for some offenses. After a period of time has elapsed even the offender can apply for permission.

(1) Generally 5 yrs. insanity but: permanent insanity in Ut.; incurable insanity in Col.; 1 yr. Wis.; 18 mos. Alas.; 2 yrs. Ga., Ha., In Nev., N.J., Ore., Wash., Wy.; 3 yrs. Ark., Cal., Fla., Md., Minn., Miss., N.C., Tex., W. Va.; 6 yrs. Ida.; Kan: Incompability by reason mental illness or incapacity. (2) Cal., Colo., and Ore., have procedures whereby a couple can obtain a divorce without an attorney a without appearing in court provided certain requirements are met. (3) Other grounds existing only in N.H. are: Joining a religious orc disbelieving in marriage, treatment which injures health or endangers reason, wife without the state for 10 years, and wife in state yrs. husband never in state and intends to become a citizen of a foreign country. (4) Provable only by fault grounds, separation some period, generally a year, proof of marital discord or commitment for mental illness. (A) Pregnancy at marriage. (B) Fraudule contract. (C) Indignities. (D) Consanguinity. (E) Crime against nature. (F) Mental incapacity at time of marriage. (G) Procurement out-of-state divorce. (H) Gross neglect of duty. (I) Bigamy. (J) Attempted homocide. (K) Separation by decree in Conn.; after decre one yr. in La., N.Y., Wis.; 18 mos. in N.H.; 2 yrs. in Ala., Ha., Minn., N.C. Tenn.; 3 yrs. in Ut.; 4 yrs. in N.J., N.D.; 5 yrs. in Md. (L) Dete mined by court order. (M) 60 days to remarry. (N) One yr. to remarry except Ha. one yr. with minor child; La. 90 days. (O) 6 mos. remarry. (P) Adultery cases, remarriage in court's discretion. (Q) Plaintiff, 6 mos.; defendant 2 yrs. to remarry. (R) No remarriage if appeal is pending. (S) Actual domicile in adultery cases. (U) Abuse and neglect of child; physical or mental injury to child. **Enoch A den Laws.** disappearance and unknown to be alive - Conn., S.C., Va., Vt., 7 yrs. absence; Ala., Ark., N.Y. 5 yrs. (called dissolutio N.H. 2 yrs.

N.B. Grounds not recognized for divorce may be recognized for separation or annulment. Local laws should be consulted.

Who Owns What: Familiar Consumer Products

'he following is a list of familiar consumer products and their parent companies. If you wish to register a complaint beyond the local l, the address of the parent company can be found on pages 106-112.

niral appliances: Magic Chef
: cleanser: Colgate-Palmolive
tate Insurance Co.: Sears, Roebuck
cin: American Home Products
a Velva: Nabisco
y's restaurants: Royal Crown
nour meats: Greyhound
d anti-perspirant: Carter-Wallace
ow shirts: Cluett, Peabody
ri home computers: Warner Communications
s car rental: Norton Simon
s reducing products: Purex

gies: Colgate-Palmolive
anti-perspirant: Bristol-Myers
er aspirin: Sterling Drug
ch Aircraft: Raytheon
son & Hedges cigarettes; Philip Morris
ty Crocker products: General Mills
s Eye frozen foods: General Foods
ck & White scotch: Heublein
o pads: Purex
t toiletries: Faberge
get Rent A Car: Transamerica
weiser beer: Anheuser-Busch
ferin: Bristol-Myers
nble Bee canned fish: Castle & Cooke
ger King restaurants: Pillsbury
iness Week magazine: McGraw-Hill
ter Brown shoes: Brown Group

dillac pet foods: U.S. Tobacco
'n Crunch cereal: Quaker Oats
rier air conditioners: United Technologies
ap Stick: A.H. Robins
ef Boy-ar-dee products: American Home Products
eerios cereal: General Mills
cken Of the Sea tuna: Ralston Purina
rol hair products: Bristol-Myers
d Power detergent: Colgate-Palmolive
: 45 malt liquor: Heileman Brewing
umbia Pictures: Coca Cola
enhagen snuff: U.S. Tobacco
er Girl cosmetics: Noxell
cker Jack: Borden
st toothpaste: Procter & Gamble
co shortening: Procter & Gamble
cura skin care products: Purex
le dog food: General Foods

h detergent: Procter & Gamble
: Rite Cola: Royal Crown
e Cups: American Can
n's Pills: Purex
e pineapple products: Castle & Cooke
tan: American Home Products
acell batteries: Dart & Kraft
y-Off oven cleaner: American Home Products
abeth Arden cosmetics: Eli Lilly
an Allen furniture: Interco
eady batteries: Union Carbide
edrin: Bristol-Myers

detergent: Colgate-Palmolive
er Price toys: Quaker Oats
gg Bros. shoe stores: Genesco
my shaving cream: Gillette
ger coffee: Procter & Gamble
mula 409 spray cleaner: Clorox
nco-American foods: Campbell Soup
ndly Ice Cream restaurants: Hershey Foods
kies pet foods: Carnation
-Lay snacks: PepsiCo

orade: Stokely-Van Camp
itol: Nabisco
em toothpaste: Procter & Gamble
od Seasons salad dressing: General Foods
en Giant vegetables: Pillsbury

ston fashions: Norton Simon
milton Beach appliances: Scovill
dy Wipes: Colgate-Palmolive
rah's resorts, casinos: Holiday Inns
d and Shoulders shampoo: Procter & Gamble
man's mayonnaise: CPC International
: fruit drinks: Coca Cola
t-Wesson foods: Norton Simon

Ivory soap products: Procter & Gamble
Jack in the Box restaurants: Ralston Purina
Jell-o: General Foods
Jim Beam whiskey: American Brands
Johnnie Walker scotch: Norton Simon
Karastan rugs: Fieldcrest Mills
Ken-L-Ration pet foods: Quaker Oats
Kentucky Fried Chicken: Heublein
Kinney shoe stores: F.W. Woolworth
Knorr soups: CPC International
Kool Aid soft drinks: General Foods
Ladies' Home Journal magazine: Charter
Lestoil: Noxell
Log Cabin syrup: General Foods

Magic Pan restaurants: Quaker Oats
Magnavox products: North American Philips
Marlboro cigarettes: Philip Morris
Max Factor cosmetics: Norton Simon
Maxwell House coffee: General Foods
Mazola oil: CPC International
Michelob beer: Anheuser-Busch
Miller beer: Philip Morris
Minute Maid frozen juices: Coca-Cola
Minute Rice: General Foods
Mountain Dew soda: PepsiCo
NBC broadcasting: RCA
National Car Rental: Household International
Newsweek magazine: Washington Post
9-Lives cat food: H.J. Heinz
Norge appliances: Magic Chef
Noxzema skin products: Noxell
Ore-Ida frozen foods: H.J. Heinz
Oreo cookies: Nabisco
Oscar Mayer meats: General Foods

Pall Mall cigarettes: American Brands
Paper Mate pens: Gillette
Paul Masson wines: Seagram
People magazine: Time
Pepperidge Farms products: Campbell Soup
Pizza Hut restaurants: PepsiCo
Playtex products: Esmark
Prell shampoo: Procter & Gamble
Prince Matchabelli fragrances: Chesebrough-Pond's
Q-Tips: Chesebrough-Pond's
Radio Shack retail outlets: Tandy
Ragu foods: Chesebrough-Pond's
Rawlings sporting goods: Figgie International
Red Devil paints: Insilco
Red Lobster Inns: General Mills
Right Guard deodorant: Gillette
Rise shave lathers: Carter-Wallace
Ritz crackers: Nabisco

Samsonite luggage: Beatrice Foods
Sanka coffee: General Foods
Sergeant's pet care products: A.H. Robins
7-Eleven stores: Southland
Seven-Up: Philip Morris
Smirnoff vodka: Heublein
Smith & Wesson handguns: Bangor Punta
Sports Illustrated magazine: Time
Steak and Ale restaurants: Pillsbury
Sunkist orange soda: General Cinema

Taco Bell restaurants: PepsiCo
Tang soft drink: General Foods
Thom McAn shoe stores: Melville
Tide detergent: Procter & Gamble
Tiffany jewelry: Avon
Tiparillo's: Culbro
Tropicana foods: Beatrice Foods
Tupperware products: Dart & Kraft
Tylenol: Johnson & Johnson
Ultra Brite toothpaste: Colgate-Palmolive
V-8 vegetable juice: Campbell Soup
Virginia Slims cigarettes: Philip Morris
Vitalis hair tonic: Bristol-Myers

Wall Street Journal: Dow Jones
Weight Watchers: H.J. Heinz
Wheaties cereal: General Mills
White Owl cigars: Culbro
White Rain shampoo: Gillette
Wizard air freshener: American Home Products
Wyler's drink mixes: Borden
Yuban coffee: General Foods

Business Directory

Listed below are major U.S. corporations, and major foreign corporations with their U.S. headquarters, **whose opera tions—products and services—directly concern the American consumer.** At the end of each listing is a **representative samp** of some of the company's products.

Should you, as a dissatisfied consumer, wish to register a complaint beyond the local level, address your correspondence the attention of the Consumer Complaint Office of the individual company. Be as specific as possible about the dealer's nar and address, purchase date or date of service, price, name and serial number (if any) of the product, and places you may ha sought relief, with dates. Include copies of receipts and guarantees and/or warranties. Don't forget your name and comple address and telephone number with area code.

Company. . .Address. . .Chief executive officer. . .Business.

AMF Inc.. . .777 Westchester Ave., White Plains, NY 10604. . .W.T. York. . .producer bowling equip., industrial prods.

AMR Corp.. . .PO Box 61616, Dallas/Ft. Worth Airport, TX 75261. . .Albert V. Casey. . .Air transportation (American Airlines).

Abbott Laboratories. . . Abbott Park, No. Chicago, IL 60064. . .R.A. Schoellhorn. . .health care prods.

Aetna Life & Casualty Co.. . .151 Farmington Ave., Hartford, CT. . .W.O. Bailey. . .insurance.

Alberto-Culver Co.. . .2525 Armitage Ave., Melrose Park, IL 60160. . .Leonard H. Lavin. . .hair care preparations, feminine hygiene products, household and grocery items.

Albertson's Inc.. . .250 Parkchester Blvd., Boise, ID 83726. . .W.E. McCain. . .supermarkets.

Alcan Aluminium Ltd.. . .1 Place Ville Marie, Montreal, Que., Canada H3C 3H2. . .D.M. Culver. . .aluminum producer.

Allegheny International, Inc.. . .2 Oliver Plaza, Pittsburgh, PA 15230. . .Robert J. Buckley. . .steel specialty metals & materials, consumer products.

Allied Corp.. . . Box 2245R, Morristown, NJ 07960. . .Edward L. Hennessy Jr.. . .oil, gas, chemicals, fibers & plastics, electrical products, auto safety restraints.

Allied Stores Corp.. . .1114 Ave. of the Americas, N.Y., NY 10036. . .Thomas M. Macioce. . .dept. stores incl. Bonwit Teller; Plymouth Shops; Gertz; Garfinckel's.

Allis Chalmers Corp.. . .1205 S. 70th St., West Allis, WI 53214. . .David C. Scott. . .manuf. of processing equip., electrical power equip., industrial trucks, farm machinery.

Aluminum Co. of America. . .1501 Alcoa Bldg., Pittsburgh, PA 15219. . .W.H. Krome George. . .mining, refining, & processing of aluminum.

AMAX Inc.. . .AMAX Center, Greenwich, CT 06836. . .J. Towers. . .natural resources and mineral development.

Amerada Hess Corp.. . .1185 Ave. of the Americas, N.Y., NY 10036. . .Leon Hess. . .integrated petroleum co.

American Bakeries Co.. . .10 Riverside Plaza, Chicago, IL 60606. . .N.S. Leist. . .wholesale bakery goods.

American Brands, Inc.. . .245 Park Ave., N.Y., NY 10017. . .E.H. Whittemore. . .tobacco (Pall Mall, Carlton, Lucky Strike cigarettes; Half and Half, Paleden pipe tobacco); whiskey (Jim Beam); snack foods, golf equipment, office supplies, toiletries, insurance.

American Broadcasting Companies Inc.. . .1330 Ave. of the Americas, N.Y., NY 10019. . .L.H. Goldenson. . .broadcasting, publishing.

American Can Co.. . . American Lane, Greenwich, CT 06830. . .William S. Woodside. . .manuf. containers and packaging prods.

American Cyanamid Co.. . . One Cyanamid Plaza, Wayne, NJ 07470. . .J.G. Affleck. . .medical, agricultural prods., specialty chemicals.

American Greetings Corp.. . .10500 American Rd., Cleveland, OH 44144. . .Irving I. Stone. . .greeting cards.

American Hoist & Derrick Co.. . .63 S. Robert, St. Paul, MN 55107. . .Robert P. Fox. . .heavy equip.

American Home Products Corp.. . .685 3d Ave., N.Y., NY 10017. . .J. W. Culligan. . .prescription drugs, household prods. (Woolite, Easy-Off oven cleaner); food (Chef Boy-ar-dee); drugs (Anacin, Dristan).

American Motors Corp.. . .2777 Franklin Rd., Southfield, MI 48034. . .W.P. Tippett Jr.. . .passenger vehicles, service parts; Jeep Corp.

American Standard Inc.. . .40 W. 40th St., N.Y., NY 10018. . .William A. Marquard. . .building, transportation, industrial, security, and graphic prods., construction and mining equip.

American Sterilizer Co.. . .2222 W. Grandview Blvd., Erie, PA 16512. . .H.E. Fish. . .health care equip.

American Stores Co.. . .709 East South Temple, Salt La City, UT 84127. . .L.S. Skaggs. . .retail food markets, dept. drug stores, restaurants.

American Telephone & Telegraph Co.. . .195 Broadway, N. NY 10007. . .Charles L. Brown. . .communications. . .Weste Electric.

Amstar Corp.. . .1251 Ave. of Americas, N.Y., NY 10020. . .F bert T. Quittmeyer. . .sweeteners, industrial tools and equip.

Anchor Hocking Corp.. . .109 N. Broad, Lancaster, (43130. . .G.C. Barber. . .glass containers, metal and plas closures.

Anheuser-Busch, Inc.. . .721 Pestalozzi St., St. Louis, M 63118. . .A.A. Busch 3d. . .brewing (Budweiser, Michelob, N ural Light).

Armstrong Rubber Co.. . .500 Sargent Dr., New Haven, 06507. . .James A. Walsh. . .tires.

Armstrong World Industries. . .W. Liberty St. Lancaster, 17604. . .Harry A. Jensen. . .interior furnishings.

Arvin Industries, Inc.. . .1531 13th St., Columbus, 47201. . .J.K. Baker. . .auto exhaust systems, record players

Ashland Oil, Inc.. . .1401 Westchester Ave., Ashland, 41114. . .J.R. Hall. . .petroleum refiner; chemicals, coal, ins ance.

Atlantic Richfield Co.. . .515 S. Flower St., Los Angeles, 90071. . .Robert O. Anderson. . .petroleum, chemicals.

Automatic Data Processing, Inc.. . .405 Route 3, Clifton, 07015. . .F.R. Lautenberg. . .computer services.

Avco Corp.. . .1275 King St., Greenwich, CT 06830. . .J Kerr. . .consumer finance, insurance and management s vices.

Avery International Corp.. . .150 N. Orange Grove Blvd., Pa dena, CA 91103. . .Charles D. Miller. . .self-adhesive labels.

Avon Products, Inc.. . .9 West 57th St., N.Y., NY 10019. . .I vid W. Mitchell. . .cosmetics, fragrances, toiletries; Tiffany Co.

Ball Corp.. . .345 S. High St., Muncie, IN 47302. . .R.M. Rin en. . .packaging and industrial prods.

Bally Manufacturing Corp.. . .2640 W. Belmont Ave., Chica IL 60618. . .R.E. Mullane. . .coin-operated amusement gaming equip.; hotel-casino operator.

Bangor Punta Corp.. . .1 Greenwich Plaza, Greenwich, 06830. . .J.E. Stewart. . .general aviation (Piper), handg (Smith & Wesson), sailboats (O'day; Cal; Ranger), rec ational prods.

Bausch & Lomb. . . One Lincoln First Square, Rochester, 14601. . .D.E. Gill. . .manuf. of vision care products, acces ries.

Baxter Travenol Labs Inc.. . . One Baxter Pky., Deerfield, 60015. . .Vernon R. Loucks Jr.. . .medical care prods.

Beatrice Foods Co.. . .2 LaSalle St., Chicago, 60602. . .James L. Dutt. . .foods (Tropicana); recreatio travel, home prods.

Bell & Howell Co.. . .7100 McCormick Rd., Chicago, 60645. . .R.B. Huff. . .audio-visual instruments, business eq and supplies, electronics.

Bendix Corp.. . . Bendix Center, Southfield, MI 48034. . .W Agee. . .automotive, aerospace, industrial prods.

Best Products Co.. . . Box 26303, Richmond, VA 23260. . .S ney Lewis. . .catalog/showroom merchandiser.

Bethlehem Steel Corp.. . .8th & Eaton Ave., Bethlehem, 18016. . .D.H. Trautlein. . .steel & steel prods.

Black & Decker Mfg. Co.. . .701 E. Joppa Rd., Towson, 21204. . .Francis P. Lucier. . .manuf. power tools.

H & R Block, Inc.. . .4410 Main St., Kansas City, 64111. . .Henry W. Block. . .tax preparation.

Blue Bell, Inc.. . .335 Church Ct., Greensboro, NC 27420. . . Mann. . .manuf. western wear, sportswear.

eing Company...7755 E. Marginal Way So., Seattle, WA 98108...T.A. Wilson...aircraft manuf.
ise Cascade Corp... One Jefferson St., Boise, ID 83728...J.B. Fery...timber, paper, wood prod.
rden, Inc...277 Park Ave., N.Y., NY 10172...E.J. Sullivan...food, cheese and cheese products, snacks (Cracker Jack), beverages.
rg-Warner Corp...200 S. Michigan Ave., Chicago, IL 60604...J.F. Bere...air conditioning, plastics, chemicals, industrial prods., financial & protection services.
istol-Myers Co...345 Park Ave., N.Y., NY 10154...Richard L. Gelb...toiletries (Ban anti-perspirant), hair items (Clairol, Vitalis), drugs (Bufferin, Excedrin), household prods., infant formula (Enfamil).
own Group, Inc...8400 Maryland Ave., St. Louis, MO 63105...W.L.H. Griffin...manuf. and wholesaler of women's and children's shoes (Buster Brown).
unswick Corp... One Brunswick Plaza, Skokie, IL 60077...K.B. Abernathy...marine, medical, recreation prods.
cyrus-Erie Co...P.O. Box 56, S. Milwaukee, WI 53172...N.K. Elstrom...mining, construction equip.
rlington Industries, Inc...3330 W. Friendly Ave., Greensboro, NC...W. A. Klopman...textile mfg.
rlington Northern Inc...176 E. 5th St., St. Paul, MN 55101...R.M. Bressler...rail transportation, natural resources.
rroughs Corp... Burroughs Place, Detroit, MI...W.M. Blumenthal...business equipment.

S Inc...51 W. 52d St., N.Y., NY 10019...W. S. Paley...-broadcasting, publishing, recorded music, leisure prods.
C International, Inc... International Plaza, Englewood Cliffs, NJ 07632...J.W. McKee Jr...branded food items (Hellman's; Best Foods; Mazola; Skippy; Knorr Soups), corn wet milling prods.
mpbell Soup Co... Campbell Pl., Camden, NJ 08101...R. G. McGovern...canned soups, spaghetti (Franco-American), vegetable juice (V-8), pork and beans; pet foods, restaurants, confections.
mpbell Taggart, Inc...6211 Lemmon Ave., Dallas, TX 75222...C.B. Lane...bakeries, food prods., Mexican restaurants, canned and frozen Mexican foods.
pital Cities Communications, Inc...485 Madison Ave., New York, NY 10022...T.S. Murphy...operates television and radio stations, newspapers.
rnation Co...5045 Wilshire Blvd., Los Angeles, CA 90036...H.E. Olson...canned evaporated milk, tomato prods., pet foods (Friskies).
rter-Wallace, Inc...767 5th Ave., New York, NY 10153...H.H. Hoyt Jr...personal care items, anti-perspirant (Arrid), shave lathers (Rise), laxative (Carter's Pills), pet products.
stle & Cooke, Inc... Financial Plaza of the Pacific, P.O. Box 2990, Honolulu, HI 96802...D.J. Kirchhoff...food processing...Dole, Bumble Bee.
terpillar Tractor Co...100 N.E. Adams St., Peoria, IL 61629...Robert E. Gilmore...heavy duty earth-moving equip., diesel engines.
lanese Corp...1211 Ave. of the Americas, N.Y., NY 10036...John D. Macomber...chemicals, fibers, plastics, and specialties.
ssna Aircraft Co...5800 East Pawnee Rd., Wichita, KS 67201...Russell W. Meyer Jr...general aviation aircraft, accessories, fluid power systems.
ampion International Corp...1 Champion Plaza, Stamford, CT 06921...A.C. Sigler...forest prods.
ampion Spark Plug Co...900 Upton Ave., Toledo, OH 43661...R.A. Stranahan Jr...ignition devices.
arter Co...208 Laura St., Jacksonville FL 32202...R.K. Mason...oil refining & marketing, magazine publishing (Redbook; Ladies' Home Journal).
esebrough-Pond's Inc...33 Benedict Pl., Greenwich, CT 06830...Ralph E. Ward...cosmetics, toiletries, clothing, food prods., footwear...Adolph's; Health-Tex; Vaseline; Q-Tips; Pertussin; Prince Matchabelli; Ragu.
romalloy American Corp...120 S. Central Ave., St. Louis, MO 63105...F.P. Nykiel...agricultural equip., metal fabrication, petroleum services, transportation, apparel, industrial/-commercial equip.
rysler Corp...1200 Lynn Townsend Dr., Detroit, MI 48231...Lee Iacocca...cars, trucks.
urch's Fried Chicken, Inc...355A Spencer Lane, San Antonio, TX 78284...R.A. Harvin...fried chicken restaurants.
Cincinnati Milacron Inc...4701 Marburg Ave., Cincinnati, OH 45209...J.A.D. Grier...machine tools.
Clorox Co...1221 Broadway, Oakland, CA 94612...Edwin H. Shutt Jr...retail consumer prods.
Cluett, Peabody & Co...510 5th Ave., New York, NY 10036...H.H. Henley Jr...apparel (Arrow; RPM Fashions).
Coastal Corp...9 Greenway Plaza East, Houston, TX 77046...O. S. Wyatt Jr...petroleum products, and natural gas.
Coca-Cola Co...310 North Ave., Atlanta, GA 30313...R.C. Goizueta...soft drink (Coca Cola; MelloYellow), syrups, citrus and fruit juices (Minute Maid, Hi-C), wines (Taylor), films (Columbia Pictures).
Coleman Co., Inc...250 N. St. Francis Ave., Wichita, KS 67202...S. Coleman...outdoor recreation prods., heating & air conditioning equip.
Colgate-Palmolive Co...300 Park Ave., N.Y., NY 10022...Keith Crane...soaps (Palmolive; Irish Spring), detergents (Fab; Ajax; Cold Power), tooth paste (Colgate; Ultra Brite), household prods. (Baggies; Handy Wipes; Curad bandages), restaurants (Ranch House; Lum's).
Collins & Aikman Corp...210 Madison Ave., N.Y., NY 10016...Donald F. McCullough...textiles.
ConAgra, Inc...1 Central Park Plaza, Omaha, NE 68102...Charles M. Harper...grain processing & merchandising, poultry products.
Consolidated Foods Corp...3 First National Plaza, Chicago, IL 60602...John H. Bryan Jr...foods, housewares, appliances, clothing...Electrolux; Fuller Brush; Hanes; Gant; Popsicle; Sara Lee; Shasta; Tyco.
Continental Air Lines, Inc...7300 World Way West, Los Angeles, CA 90009...R. F. Six...commercial air carrier, hotel operator.
Continental Group, Inc... One Harbor Plaza, Stamford, CT 06902...S. B. Smart Jr...natural resources, financial services, packaging, insurance.
Control Data Corp...8100-34th Ave. South, Minneapolis, MN 55420...Wm. C. Norris...computer services and systems, financial and insurance services.
Adolph Coors Co... East of Town, Golden, CO 80401...W. K. Coors...brewery.
Corning Glass Works... Houghton Park, Corning, NY 14831...Amory Houghton Jr...glass mfg.
Cox Broadcasting Corp...1601 W. Peachtree St. NE, Atlanta, GA 30309...C.M. Kirtland...broadcasting, publishing.
Crane Co...300 Park Ave., N.Y., NY 10022...Thomas M. Evans...fluid & pollution controls, steel, aircraft and aerospace, building prods.
Crown Cork & Seal Co...9300 Ashton Rd., Phila., PA 19136...J.F. Connelly...cans, packaging machinery & equip.
Crown Zellerbach Corp... One Bush St., San Francisco, CA 94104...W.T. Creson...pulp and paper products; forest products.
Culbro Corp...605 3rd Ave., New York, NY 10016...E. M. Cullman...cigars (Corina; Robert Burns; White Owl; Tiparillo's), snack foods.

Dan River, Inc...107 Frederick St., Greenville, SC 29606...D. W. Johnson Jr...textiles.
Dana Corp...4500 Dorr St., Toledo, OH 43697...Gerald B. Mitchell...truck and auto parts supplies.
Dart & Kraft, Inc...2211 Sansters Rd., Northbrook, IL 60062...J. R. Richmond...food prods. (cheese, mayonnaise), direct selling (Tupperware), consumer products (Duracell batteries; West Bend appliances).
Data General Corp... Southboro, MA 01772...E. D. deCastro...digital computers.
Dayton-Hudson Corp...777 Nicollet Mall, Minneapolis, MN 55402...W. A. Andres...department, specialty, book stores; B. Dalton; Mervyn's.
Deere & Company... John Deere Rd., Moline, IL 61265...Robert A. Hanson...farm, industrial, and outdoor power equip.
Delta Air Lines, Inc... Hartsfield Atlanta Intl. Airport, Atlanta, GA 30320...David C. Garrett Jr...air transportation.
Denny's Inc...14256 E. Firestone Blvd., La Mirada, CA 90637...V.O. Curtis...restaurants.
Diamond International Corp...733 3d Ave., N.Y., NY 10017...William J. Koslo...mfg. lumber, matches, pulp & paper, packaging, specialty printing.
Diamond Shamrock Corp...717 North Harwood St., Dallas, TX 75201...W.H. Bricker...energy, technology, and chemicals.
Diebold, Inc... Canton, OH 44711...E.F. Wearstier...bank

systems, equip.

DiGiorgio Corp.... One Maritime Plaza, San Francisco, CA 94111. . .R. DiGiorgio. . .food processing and distribution.

Digital Equipment Corp....146 Main St., Maynard, MA 01754. . .Kenneth H. Olsen. . .small computers.

Walt Disney Productions...500 S. Buena Vista St., Burbank, CA 91505. . .E. Cardon Walker. . .motion pictures, amusement parks. . .Disneyland, Walt Disney World, Epcot Center.

Dr Pepper Co....5523 E. Mockingbird Lane, Dallas, TX 75265. . .W.W. Clements. . .soft drinks (Dr. Pepper; Canada Dry).

Dow Chemical Co....2020 Dow Center, Midland, MI 48640. . .P.F. Oreffice. . .chemicals, plastics, metals, consumer prods.

Dow Jones & Co....22 Courtlandt St., New York, NY 10007. . .W. H. Phillips. . .financial news service, publishing (Wall Street Journal; Barron's; Ottaway Newspapers).

Dresser Industries, Inc.... The Dresser Bldg., Dallas, TX 75201. . .J. V. James. . .supplier of technology and services to energy related industries.

E.I. du Pont de Nemours & Co...1007 Market St., Wilmington, DE 19898. . .E. G. Jefferson. . .chemicals, petroleum, consumer prods., coal.

Dun & Bradstreet Corp....299 Park Ave., New York, NY 10171. . .H. Drake. . .business information and computer services, publishing, broadcasting.

Eastern Air Lines Inc.... Miami International Airport, Miami, FL 33148. . .Frank Borman. . .air transportation.

Eastman Kodak Co....343 State St., Rochester, NY 14650. . .Walter A. Fallon. . .photographic prods.

Jack Eckerd Corp....8333 Dryan Dairy Rd., Clearwater, FL 33518. . .S. Turley. . .drug store chain, department stores, optical & video equip. stores.

Emerson Electric Co....8100 W. Florissant Ave., St. Louis, MO 63136. . .C.F. Knight. . .electrical/electronics products.

Emery Air Freight Corp.... Old Danbury Rd., Wilton, CT 06897. . .John C. Emery Jr.. . .air freight forwarder.

Esmark, Inc....55 E. Monroe St., Chicago, IL 60603. . .Donald P. Kelly. . .food (Swift processed meats), personal products (Playtex), auto products (STP), hosiery, knitwear.

Ethyl Corp....330 S. 4th St., Richmond, VA 23217. . .Floyd D. Gottwald Jr.. . .petroleum and industrial chemicals, plastics, aluminum, energy-related prods.

Ex-Cell-O Corp....2855 Coolidge Rd., Troy, MI 48084. . .E. Paul Casey. . .precision parts and tools for aircraft, auto markets.

Exxon Corp....1251 Ave. of the Americas, N.Y., NY 10020. . .C.C. Garvin Jr.. . .world's largest oil co.

FMC Corp...200 E. Randolph Dr., Chicago, IL 60601. . .R.H. Malott. . .machinery, chemicals.

Fabergé, Inc....1345 Ave. of the Americas, N.Y., NY 10019. . .George Barrie. . .cosmetics, toiletries (Brut; Babe; Farrah Fawcett).

Fairchild Industries, Inc....20301 Century Blvd., Germantown, MD 20767. . .E.G. Uhl. . .aircraft manuf.

Federal Express Corp....2990 Airways Blvd., Memphis, TN 38194. . .F.W. Smith. . .small package delivery service.

Federated Department Stores, Inc....7 W. 7th St., Cincinnati, OH 45202. . .H. Goldfeder. . .dept. stores. . .Abraham & Straus; Bloomingdale's; Boston Store; Burdines; Foley's; Lazarus; Rich's; Rike's; Sanger-Harris.

Fieldcrest Mills, Inc....326 East Stadium Dr., Eden, NC 27288. . .William C. Battle. . .household textile prods., rugs (Karastan, Laurelcrest).

Figgie International Inc....4420 Sherwin Dr., Willoughby, OH 44094. . .H. E. Figgie Jr.. . .serves consumer, industrial, technical, service markets; Rawlings Sporting Goods.

Firestone Tire & Rubber Co....1200 Firestone Pkwy., Akron, OH 44317. . .Richard A. Riley. . .tires, rubber and metal prods.

Fleetwood Enterprises, Inc....3125 Myers St., Riverside, CA 92523. . .John C. Crean. . .mobile homes, recreational vehicles.

Fluor Corp....3333 Michelson Dr., Irvine, CA 92730. . .J. R. Fluor. . .engineering and construction.

Ford Motor Co.... The American Rd., Dearborn, MI 48121. . .Philip Caldwell. . .motor vehicles, Ford Tractor; Lincoln-Mercury.

Fort Howard Paper Co....1919 S. Broadway, Green Bay, WI 54305. . .P.J. Schierl. . .disposable paper prods.

Fruehauf Corp....PO Box 238, Detroit, MI 48232. . .R. D. Rowen. . .transportation equip.

GAF Corp....140 W. 51st St., New York, NY 10020. . .Je Werner. . .chemicals, bldg. materials.

GTE Corp.... One Stamford Forum, Stamford, 06904. . .Theodore F. Brophy. . .operates largest U.S. ir pendent telephone system.

Gannett Co., Inc.... Lincoln Tower, Rochester, 14604. . .A.H. Neuharth. . .newspaper publishing, TV stati outdoor advertising.

General Cinema Corp....27 Boylston St., Chestnut Hill, 02167. . .R. A. Smith. . .movie exhibitor, soft drinks (Sunkis

General Dynamics Corp.... Pierre Laclede Ctr., St. Louis, 63105. . .D. S. Lewis. . .military and commercial aircraft, t cal missiles.

General Electric Co....3135 Easton Ave., Fairfield, 06431. . .J. F. Welch Jr.. . .electrical, electronic equip.

General Foods Corp....250 North, White Plains, 10625. . .J.L. Ferguson. . .packaged foods (Maxwell Ho Yuban; Sanka; Jell-O; Post cereals; Birds Eye frozen fo Gaines, Cycle dog foods; Tang, Kool Aid soft drinks; Mi Rice; Oscar Mayer meats.

General Instruments Corp....1775 Broadway, New York, 10019. . .F. G. Hickey. . .race track betting systems, CA semiconductors, electronic equip.

General Mills, Inc....9200 Wayzatta Blvd., Minneapolis, 55440 . . .H.B. Atwater Jr.. . .foods, toys, restaurants, fas and specialty retailing. . .Wheaties; Cheerios; Betty Croc Red Lobster Inns).

General Motors Corp.... Gen. Motors Bldg., Detroit, 48202. . .R. B. Smith. . .world's largest auto manuf.

General Tire & Rubber Co.... One General St., Akron, 44329. . .M.G. O'Neil. . .tires, rubber prods.

Genesco Inc.... Genesco Park, Nashville, TN 37202. . . Hanigan. . .footwear and men's clothing. . .Hardy; Cover Jarman; Flagg Bros.; Bell Bros.; Johnston & Murphy.

Georgia-Pacific Corp....900 S.W. 5th Ave., Portland, 97204. . .Robert F. Flowerree. . .building prods., pulp, pa chemicals.

Gerber Products Co....445 State St., Fremont, MI 49412. . thur J. Frens. . .baby foods, clothing, nursery accessories insurance.

Getty Oil Co....3810 Wilshire Blvd., Los Angeles, 90010. . .Sidney R. Petersen. . .petroleum exploration & duction.

Gillette Co.... Prudential Tower Bldg., Boston, MA 02199. . man M. Mockler Jr.. . .razors, pens (Paper Mate; Flair), t ries (Right Guard, Dri, Soft deodorants; Foamy shaving cr Earth Born shampoo), hair products (Toni; Adorn; White R

Global Marine, Inc....811 W. 7th St., Los Angeles, 90017. . .C. R. Luigs. . .offshore oil and gas drilling.

B.F. Goodrich Company...500 S. Main St., Akron, 44318. . .John D. Ong. . .rubber, chemical, plastic prods.

Goodyear Tire & Rubber Co....1144 E. Market St., Akron, 44316. . .Charles J. Pilliod Jr.. . .tires, rubber prods.

Gould Inc....10 Gould Center, Rolling Meadows, 60008. . .W.T. Ylvisaker. . .electrical and industrial prods.

W.R. Grace & Co.... Grace Plaza, 1114 Ave. of the Amer N.Y., NY 10036. . .J. Peter Grace. . .chemicals, natura sources, consumer prods. and services, restaurants. . . C nel Home Centers; Herman's World of Sporting Goods.

Great Atlantic & Pacific Tea Co....2 Paragon Dr., Mont NJ 07645. . .James Wood. . .retail food stores.

Greyhound Corp.... Greyhound Tower, Phoenix, 85077. . .R.C. Batastini. . .meat and poultry packer (Arm bus transportation, soap prods., food, financial services.

Grumman Corp....111 Stewart, Bethpage, NY 11714. . . C. Bierwirth. . .aerospace, truck bodies.

Gulf Oil Corp.... Gulf Blvd., Pittsburgh, PA 15230. . .J.E. Le production and marketing of petroleum and related produ

Gulf + Western Industries, Inc.... One Gulf & Western P N.Y., NY 10023. . .David N. Judelson. . .diversified manufa ing, financial services, consumer and food products, na resources, home furnishings, entertainment (Paramount tures; Madison Square Garden).

Halliburton Co....2600 Southland Center, Dallas, 75201. . .J. P. Harbin. . .oil field services, engineering, struction.

Hart Schaffner & Marx...101 N. Wacker Dr., Chicag 60606. . .Jerome S. Gore. . .apparel manufacturer and ret (Hickey-Freeman).

Heileman (G.) Brewing Co....100 Harborview Plaza, Crosse, WI 54601. . .R. G. Cleary. . .brewery (Tuborg C Schmidt; Carling Black Label; Colt 45 Malt Liquor).

H.J. Heinz Co....P.O. Box 57, Pittsburgh, PA 15230...Anthony J.F. O'Reilly...foods (Star-Kist; Ore-Ida; '57 Varieties), 9-Lives cat food, Weight Watchers.
Hershey Food Corp...100 Manson Rd., Hershey, PA 17033...William Dearden...chocolate & confectionery prods., pasta (San Giorgio); restaurants (Friendly Ice Cream).
Heublein, Inc... Farmington, CT 06032...Hicks B. Waldron...alcoholic beverages (Smirnoff Vodka; Black & White Scotch; Lancers Portuguese wines); food (Kentucky Fried Chicken).
Hewlett-Packard Co...1501 Page Mill Rd., Palo Alto, CA 94304...John A. Young...electronic instruments.
Hillenbrand Industries, Inc... Highway 46, Batesville, IN 47006...W.A. Hillenbrand...manuf. burial caskets, electronically operated hospital beds.
Hilton Hotels Corp...9880 Wilshire Blvd., Beverly Hills, CA 90210...Barron Hilton...hotels, casinos.
Holiday Inns, Inc...3742 Lamar Ave., Memphis, TN 38195...Roy E. Winegardner...hotels, motels, casinos (Harrah's).
Honeywell, Inc... Honeywell Plaza, Minneapolis, MN 55408...E.W. Spencer...industrial systems & controls, aerospace guidance systems, information systems.
Hoover Universal Inc...P.O. Box 1003, Ann Arbor, MI 41806...D. T. Carroll...aluminum, steel, plastic prods.
Hoover Co...101 E. Maple St., No. Canton, OH 44720...M. R. Rawson...manuf. vacuum cleaners, washing machines, dryers.
Geo. A. Hormel & Co...501 16th Ave. N.E., Austin, MN 55912...R.L. Knowlton...meat packaging, pork and beef prods.
Household International Inc...2700 Sanders Rd., Prospect Heights, IL 60070...G.R. Ellis...financial and insurance services, merchandising, manufacturing, transportation...King-Seeley Thermos; National Car Rental; Household Finance.
Hughes Tool Co...5425 Polk Ave., Houston, TX 77023...J.R. Lesch...supplier of products and services to the oil, gas, & mining industries; mfg. of rock drilling bits & tool joints.
Humana, Inc...P.O. Box 1438, Louisville, KY 40201...D. A. Jones...operates hospitals.

IC Industries, Inc... One Illinois Ctr., 111 E. Wacker Dr., Chicago, IL 60601...William B. Johnson...diversified prods. and services...railroads, consumer products, food, auto products.
Imperial Oil Ltd...111 St. Clair Ave. W., Toronto, Ont., Canada...D.M. Ivor...Canada's largest oil co.
Insilco Corp...1000 Research Pkwy., Meriden, Ct 06450...Durand B. Blatz...diversified manufacturer...International Silver; Red Devil Paints and Chemicals; Rolodex; Taylor Publishing.
Intel Corp...3065 Bowers Ave., Santa Clara, CA 95051...G. E. Moore...semiconductor memory components.
Interco Inc...P.O. Box 8777, St. Louis, MO 63102...J.K. Riedy...apparel, footwear mfg.; specialty apparel shops, home furnishings (Ethan Allen).
International Business Machines Corp... Old Orchard Rd., Armonk, NY 10504...Frank T. Cary...information-handling systems, equip., and services.
International Harvester Co...401 N. Michigan Ave., Chicago, IL 60611...L. W. Menk...manuf. farm tractors and machinery, truck and construction equip.
International Paper Co...77 W. 45th St., New York, NY 10036...E. A. Gee...paper, wood prods.
International Telephone and Telegraph Corp...320 Park Ave., N.Y., NY 10022...R.V. Araskog...world's largest manuf. of telecommunications equip.

Johnson & Johnson...501 George St., New Brunswick, NJ 08903...James E. Burke...surgical dressings, pharmaceuticals, health and baby prods.
Jonathan Logan, Inc...50 Terminal Rd., Secaucus, NJ 07094...Richard J. Schwartz...female apparel.
Jostens, Inc...5501 Norman Center Dr., Minneapolis, MN 55437...H. W. Lurton...school rings, yearbooks.

Kaiser Aluminum & Chemical Corp...300 Lakeside Dr., Oakland, CA 94643...Cornell C. Maier...aluminum, agricultural chemicals.
Kaiser Steel Corp...P.O. Box 5050, Fontana, CA 92335...S. A. Girard...steelmaker.
Kane-Miller Corp...555 White Plains Rd., Tarrytown, NY 10591...Stanley B. Kane...food processing.
Kaufman and Broad, Inc...10801 National Blvd., Los Angeles, CA 90064...Eli Broad...home builder.
Kellogg Co...235 Porter, Battle Creek, MI 49016...William E. LaMothe...ready to eat cereals & other food prods...Mrs. Smith's Pie Co.; Salada Foods.
Kerr-McGee Corp...P.O. Box 25861, Oklahoma City, OK 73125...Dean A. McGee...oil, natural gas, uranium, coal.
Kidde, Inc...9 Brighton Rd., Clifton, NJ 07015...Fred R. Sullivan...mfgr. safety, security, protection, industrial, commercial, consumer and recreation prods. and services.
Kimberly-Clark Corp...N. Lake St., Neenah, WI 54956...Darwin E. Smith...paper and lumber prods.
K mart Corp...3100 W. Big Beaver Rd., Troy, MI 48084...B. M. Fauber...chain of discount stores.
Knight-Ridder Newspapers, Inc... One Harold Plaza, Miami, FL 33101...J.K. Batten...largest U.S. newspaper co.; broadcasting, publishing.
Koppers Co., Inc... Koppers Bldg., Pittsburgh, PA 15219...C. R. Pullin...diversified manuf.
Kroger Co...1014 Vine St., Cincinnati, OH 45201...Lyle Everingham...grocery chain, drugstores (SupeRx), amusement parks.

LTV Corporation...P.O. Box 225003, Dallas, TX 75265...Paul Thayer...steel, aerospace, meat & food prods. (Wilson Foods), shipping, energy-oriented prods.
Lanier Business Products, Inc...1700 Chantilly Dr., Atlanta, GA 30324...G. W. Milner...office equip., business prods.
Lenox, Inc... Old Princeton Pike, Lawrenceville, NJ 08648...J. S. Chamberlin...fine china dinnerwear, glasswear, jewelry.
Levi Strauss & Co...2 Embarcadero Center, San Francisco, CA 94106...R. T. Grohman...blue denim jeans, other apparel.
Levitz Furniture Corp...1317 NW 167th St., Miami, FL 33169...Robert M. Elliott...furniture stores.
Libbey-Owens-Ford Co...811 Madison Ave., Toledo, OH 43695...Don T. Mc Kone...glass and fabricated prods.
Eli Lilly & Company...307 E. McCarty St., Indianapolis, IN 46285...Richard D. Wood...mfg. human health and agricultural products, cosmetics (Elizabeth Arden).
Litton Industries, Inc...360 N. Crescent, Beverly Hills, CA 90210...Charles B. Thornton...industrial systems & services, advanced electronic systems, electronic & electrical prods., marine engineering, printing & publishing.
Lockheed Corp...2555 N. Hollywood Way, Burbank, CA 91520...Lawrence O. Kitchen...commercial and military aircraft, missiles.
Loews Corp...666 5th Ave., N.Y., NY 10019...Laurence A. Tisch...tobacco prods., motion picture theaters, hotels, real estate, insurance.
M. Lowenstein Corp...1430 Broadway, N.Y., NY 10018...R. Bendheim...textiles.
Lucky Stores, Inc...6300 Clark Ave., Dublin, CA 94566...S. D. Ritchie...supermarkets, restaurants, dept., fabric, and automotive stores.

MCA Inc...100 Universal City Plaza, Universal City, CA 91608...Lew R. Wasserman...motion pictures, television; music publishing, mail order, novelty, and gift merchandise.
MEI Corp...710 Marquette Ave., Minneapolis, MN 55402...Donald E. Benson...soft drink bottler, distributor.
MacMillian, Inc...866 3d Ave., New York, NY 10022...E. P. Evans...book printing and publishing; information (Berlitz; Katharine Gibbs).
R. H. Macy & Co. Inc...151 W. 34th St., New York, NY 10001...E. S. Finkelstein...department stores.
Magic Chef, Inc...740 King Edward Ave., Cleveland, TN 37311...S.B. Rymer Jr...major household appliances, heating and air conditioning equip., soft drink vending equip...Admiral; Norge; Gaffers & Sattler; Johnson; Dixie-Narco.
MAPCO, Inc...1800 South Baltimore Ave., Tulsa, OK 74119...W. H. Thompson Jr...coal, gas, natural gas liquids.
Marriott Corp... Marriott Dr., Wash., DC 20058...J. Willard Marriott Jr...restaurants (Roy Rogers; Big Boy), hotels, food services.
Martin Marietta Corp...6801 Rockledge Dr., Bethesda, MD 20034...J. D. Rauth...aluminum, aerospace, cement, chemicals.
Mary Kay Cosmetics, Inc...8787 Stemmon Freeway, Dallas, TX 75247...Mary Kay Ash...cosmetics, toiletries.
Masonite Corp...29 N. Wacker Dr., Chicago, IL 60606...R. N. Rasmus...building materials.

Mattell, Inc....5150 Rosecrans Ave., Hawthorne,CA 90250...A. S. Spear...toy & hobby prods. (Barbie dolls), electronics (Intelevision), publishing, entertainment...Circus World theme park.
Maytag Co....403 W. 4th St. N., Newton, IA 50208...Daniel J. Krumm...manuf. home laundry equip.
McCormick & Co., Inc....11350 McCormick Rd., Hunt Valley, MD 21031...H. K. Wells...world's leading manuf. of seasoning & flavoring prods.
McDonald's Corp.... McDonald's Plaza, Oak Brook, IL 60521...F. L. Turner...fast service restaurants.
McDonnell Douglas Corp....P.O. Box 516, St. Louis, MO 63131...Sanford N. McDonnell...commercial & military aircraft, space systems & missiles.
McGraw-Edison Co....333 W. River Rd., Elgin, IL 60120...E.J. Williams...electrical and mechanical prods.
McGraw-Hill, Inc....1221 Ave. of the Americas, New York, NY 10020...H. W. McGraw Jr...book, magazine publishing (Business Week), information & financial services (Standard and Poor's), TV stations.
Mead Corp.... Courthouse Plaza N.E., Dayton, OH 45463 ...B. K. Roberts...pulp, paper, school and office prods., furniture.
Medtronic, Inc....3055 Hway 8, Minneapolis, MN 55440...D. R. Olseth...heart pacemakers and support systems.
Melville Corp....3000 Westchester Ave., Harrison, NY 10528...Francis C. Rooney Jr...shoe stores (Thom McAn), apparel, drug stores.
Merck & Co., Inc....P.O. Box 2000, Rahway, NJ 07065...John L. Huck...human & animal health care prods.
Merrill Lynch & Co., Inc.... One Liberty Plaza, N.Y., NY 10080...R. E. Birk...securities broker, financial services, real estate.
Metromedia, Inc.... One Harmon Plaza, Secaucus, NJ 07094...J. W. Kluge...television & radio broadcasting, publishing, entertainment (Ice Capades; Harlem Globetrotters).
Milton Bradley Co....1500 Main St., Springfield, MA 01101...James J. Shea Jr...board and card games, electronic games, toys (Playskool), school supplies.
Mobil Corp....150 E. 42d St., N.Y., NY 10017...Rawleigh Warner Jr...international oil co.; chemicals, dept. stores (Montgomery Ward).
Mohasco Corp....57 Lyon St., Amsterdam, NY 12010...S. I. Landgraf...home furnishings.
Monsanto Company...800 N. Lindbergh Blvd., St. Louis, MO 63166...John W. Hanley...chemicals, plastics, agricultural prods., textiles.
Morton Norwich...110 N. Wacker Dr., Chicago, IL 60606...Charles S. Locke...pharmaceuticals, (Pepto-Bismol), salt (Morton), household cleaning prods. (Fantastik; Spray 'n Wash), specialty chemicals.
Motorola, Inc....1303 E. Algonquin Rd., Schaumburg, IL 60196...R. W. Galvin...electronic equipment and components.
Murray Ohio Manuf. Co....219 Franklin Rd., Brentwood, TN 37027...W. M. Hannon...bicycles, power mowers.

NCR Corp....1700 S. Patterson Blvd., Dayton, OH 45479...Charles E. Exley Jr...business information processing systems.
NL Industries...1230 Ave. of the Americas, New York, NY 10020...Ray C. Adam...petroleum services & equipment, specialty chemicals, fabricated metal products.
Nabisco Brands, Inc.... DeForest Ave., E. Hanover, NJ 07936...Robert M. Schaeberle...crackers (Ritz; Premium), cookies (Oreo; Fig Newton), toiletries (Aqua Velva), pharmaceutical prods. (Geritol), candy (Baby Ruth; Butter Finger).
National Distillers & Chemical Corp....99 Park Ave., N.Y., NY 10016...Drummond C. Bell...wines and liquors, chemicals, insurance...Almaden Vineyards.
National Medical Care, Inc.... Hancock Tower, Boston, MA 02116...C. L. Hampers...medical services and prods.
National Semiconductor Corp....2900 Semiconductor Dr., Santa Clara, CA 95051...Charles E. Sporck...manuf. of semiconductors.
North American Philips Corp....100 E. 42d St., N.Y., NY 10017...P. C. Vink...consumer prods., electrical, electronic prods., professional equip...Magnavox; Norelco.
Northrop Corp....1800 Century Park E., Los Angeles, CA 90067...Thomas V. Jones...aircraft, electronics, communications.
Northwest Airlines, Inc.... Minneapolis-St. Paul Intl. Airport, St. Paul, MN 55111...M. J. Lapensky...air transportation.
Northwest Industries, Inc....6300 Sears Tower, Chicago, IL 60606...Ben W. Heineman...industrial & chemical prods., consumer prods., oil and gas drilling supplies.
Norton Simon Inc....277 Park Ave., N.Y., NY 10017...David J. Mahoney...foods (Hunt-Wesson), beverages (Johnnie Walker Scotch; Tanqueray Gin), cosmetics & fashions (Max Factor; Halston), car rental (Avis).
Noxell Corp....11050 York Rd., Cockeysville, MD...G. L. Bunting Jr...toiletry, household, consumer prods. (Noxzema; Rain Tree; Lestoil; Cover Girl).

Occidental Petroleum Corp....10889 Wilshire Blvd., Los Angeles, CA 90024...Dr. Armand Hammer...oil, gas, chemicals, coal.
Ogden Corp....277 Park Ave., New York NY 10017...R. E. Ablon...transportation, foods, metals.
Olin Corp....120 Long Ridge Rd., Stamford, CT 06904...John M. Henske...chemicals, metals, paper, sporting and defense ammunition.
Outboard Marine Corp....100 Sea Horse Dr., Waukegan, IL 60085...C.D. Strang...outboard motors, mowers (Lawn Boy).
Owens-Corning Fiberglas Corp.... Fiberglas Tower, Toledo, OH 43659...W.W. Boeschenstein...glass fiber and related prods.
Owens-Illinois, Inc.... One SeaGate Toledo, OH 43666...Edwin D. Dodd...glass, corrugated, and plastic containers.

Pabst Brewing Co....1000 Market St., Milwaukee, WI 53201...W.F. Smith Jr...brewery.
Pan American World Airways... Pan Am Bldg., 200 Park Ave., N.Y., NY 10017...C. Edward Acker...air transportation.
Pargas, Inc....P.O. Box 67, Waldorf, MD 20601...N. L. Langley...distributes liquified petroleum gas; coal mining.
Parker Drilling Co.... Parker Bldg., Tulsa, OK 74103...R. L. Parker Jr...oil and gas drilling services.
Parker Pen Co....1 Parker Place, Janesville, WI 53545...J. R. Peterson...writing instruments, recreational equip., temp. help service (Manpower, Inc.).
J.C. Penney Co., Inc....1301 Ave. of the Americas, N.Y., NY 10019...Donald V. Seibert...dept. stores, catalog sales, food, drugs, insurance.
Pennwalt Corp.... Pennwalt Bldg., 3 Pkwy., Phila., PA 19102...Edwin E. Tuttle...chemicals, health prods., precision equip.
Pennzoil Co.... Pennzoil Pl., Houston, TX 77001...B. P. Kerr...Integrated oil and gas co.
PepsiCo, Inc.... Anderson Hill Rd., Purchae, NY 10577...D. M. Kendall...soft drinks, (Pepsi-Cola; Mountain Dew), snack foods (Frito-Lay; Doritos) restaurants (Pizza Hut; Taco Bell), sporting goods (Wilson), transportation (North American Van Lines).
Pfizer Inc....235 E. 42d St., N.Y., NY 10017...E.T. Pratt Jr...pharmaceutical, hospital, agricultural, chemical prods.
Philip Morris Inc....100 Park Ave., N.Y., NY 10017...George Weissman...cigarettes (Marlboro, Benson & Hedges, Merit, Virginia Slims); beer (Miller High Life, Lite; Lowenbrau brands); soft drinks (Seven-up); specialty chemicals, paper, packaging materials, real estate.
Phillips-Van Heusen Corp....1290 Ave. of the Americas, New York, NY 10019...L. S. Phillips...men, boys apparel.
Pillsbury Co....608 2d Ave. So., Minneapolis, MN 55402...W. H. Spoor...canned & frozen vegetables (Green Giant), bakery, flower mixes, restaurants (Burger King; Steak and Ale)
Pinkerton's, Inc....100 Church St., New York, NY 10007...E. C. Fey...security and investigative services.
Pitney Bowes, Inc.... Walter H. Wheeler Dr., Stamford, CT 06904...Fred T. Allen...postage meters, mail handling equip., office equipment, retail systems.
Playboy Enterprises, Inc....919 N. Michigan Ave., Chicago, IL 60691...Hugh Hefner...magazine publishing, hotels and casinos, CATV.
Polaroid Corp....549 Technology Sq., Cambridge, MA 02139...photographic equip., supplies and optical goods.
Ponderosa System, Inc....P.O. Box 578, Dayton, OH 45401...G. S. Office Jr...steakhouse restaurants.
Potlatch Corp.... Golden Gateway Center, San Francisco, CA 94119...R. B. Madden...lumber, paper prods.
Procter & Gamble Co....301 E. 6th St., Cincinnati, OH 45202...E.G. Harness...soap & detergent (Ivory; Dash; Tide; Spic and Span), shortenings (Crisco; Fluffo), toiletries (Crest and Gleem toothpastes; Prell, and Head and Shoulders shampoos), pharmaceuticals (Pepto-Bismol), Pampers disposable

diapers, Folger coffee.

Purex Corp....5101 Clark Ave., Lakewood, CA 90712...William R. Tincher...household cleaning prods. (Brillo; Old Dutch Cleanser; Purex), drugs & toiletries (Ayds; Doan's Pills; Cuticura).

Purolator, Inc....255 Old New Brunswick Rd., Piscataway, NJ 08854...F. H. Cook...auto equip., courier and guard services.

Quaker Oats Co.... Merchandise Mart Plaza, Chicago, IL 60654...Robert D. Stuart Jr....foods, cereal (Life; Cap'n Crunch; Puffed Wheat; Puffed Rice), foods (Aunt Jemima; Celeste), pet foods (Ken-L-Ration; Puss 'n Boots), Fisher Price toys, Magic Pan restaurants.

Quaker State Oil Refining Corp....255 Elm St., Oil City, PA 16301...Q.E. Wood...refining, marketing petroleum prods., filters, mining & marketing coal.

RCA Corp....30 Rockefeller Plaza, N.Y., NY 10020...T. F. Bradshaw...radio, television (NBC), electronics, communications, financial services.

Ralston Purina Co.... Checkerboard Sq., St. Louis, MO 63164...W. R. Stritz...pet and livestock food, Jack In the Box restaurants.

Ramada Inns, Inc....3838 E. Van Buren, Phoenix, AZ 85008...Richard Snell...hotel operation, casinos.

Raytheon Company...141 Spring St., Lexington, MA 02173...Thomas L. Phillips...electronics, aviation, appliances...Amana Refrigeration; Beech Aircraft.

Revere Copper & Brass Inc....605 3d Ave., N.Y., NY 10158...William F. Collins...fabricator of nonferrous metals.

Revlon, Inc....767 5th Ave., N.Y., NY 10153...Michael C. Bergerac...cosmetics, pharmaceuticals.

Reynolds Metals Co....6601 W. Broad St., Richmond, VA 23261...D. P. Reynolds...aluminum prods.

R.J. Reynolds Industries, Inc.... Reynolds Blvd., Winston-Salem, NC 27102...J. P. Sticht...crude oil, petroleum, transportation, tobacco (Camels; More), food, and beverage prods.

Richardson-Vicks Inc....10 Westport Rd., Wilton, CT 06897...J.S. Scott...health and personal care prods., drugs, specialty chemicals.

Rite Aid Corp.... Shiremanstown, PA 17011...A. Glass...discount drug stores.

Robertshaw Controls Co....P.O. Box 26544, Richmond, VA 23261...Ralph S. Thomas...controls, control systems.

A.H. Robins Co., Inc....1407 Cummings Dr., Richmond, VA 23220...E.C. Robins Jr....health care, consumer prods. (Chap Stick; Quencher), Sergeant's pet care prods.

Rockwell Intl. Corp....600 Grant St., Pittsburgh, PA 29029...D. R. Beall...aerospace, electronic, automotive prods.

Roper Corp....1905 W. Court St., Kankakee, IL 60901...C.M. Hoover...appliances, home and lawn prods.

Rorer Group Inc....500 Virginia Dr., Ft. Washington, PA 19034...J. W. Eckman...pharmaceuticals (Maalox; Ascriptin; Emetrol).

Royal Crown Cos., Inc....41 Perimeter Center East, Atlanta, GA 30346...D.A. McMahon...soft drinks (Nehi; RC Cola; Diet Rite Cola), restaurants (Arby's), citrus prods., home furnishings.

Rubbermaid Inc....1147 Akron Rd., Wooster, OH 44691...S. C. Gault...rubber and plastic consumer prods.

Ryder System, Inc....3600 NW 82d Ave., Miami, FL 33166...L. D. Barnes...truck leasing service.

SCM Corp....299 Park Ave., N.Y., NY 10171...Paul H. Elicker...typewriters, appliances, food, chemicals, paper prods.... Smith Corona; Proctor-Silex.

Safeway Stores, Inc.... Oakland, CA 94660...P. A. Magowan...retail food stores.

St. Regis Paper Co....150 E. 42d St., N.Y., NY 10017...William R. Haselton...pulp and paper, building prods.

Santa Fe Industries, Inc....224 S. Michigan Ave., Chicago, IL 60604...J. S. Reed...transport, real estate, construction, natural resources...Atchison, Topeka and Santa Fe Railway.

Savin Corp.... Columbus Ave., Valhalla, NY 10595...R. K. Low...office copiers, word processing equip.

Schering-Plough Corp....1000 Galloping Hill Rd., Kenilworth, NJ 07033...R. P. Luciano...pharmaceuticals, consumer prods.

Jos. Schlitz Brewing Co....235 W. Galena St., Milwaukee, WI 53212...Frank Sellinger...brewery (Schlitz; Old Milwaukee; Erlanger).

Schlumberger Ltd....277 Park Ave., New York, NY 10172...Jean Riboud...oilfield services, electronics, measurement and control devices.

Scientific-Atlanta, Inc....1 Technology Pkwy., Atlanta, GA 30348...S. Topol...communications & instrumentation prods.

Scott Paper Co.... Scott Plaza, Phila., PA 19113...Charles D. Dickey Jr....paper prods.

Scovill Inc....500 Chase Pkwy., Waterbury, CT 06708...W. F. Andrews...automotive, security, housing prods., sewing aids, small appliances (Hamilton Beach).

Seagram Co. Ltd....1430 Peel St., Montreal, Que., Canada H3A 1S9...E. M. Bronfman...distilled spirits & wine (Seven Crown; Chivas Regal; Calvert; Wolfschmidt Vodka; Paul Masson; Christian Brothers; Gold Seal).

G.D. Searle & Co....P.O. Box 1045, Skokie, IL 60076...Donald Rumsfeld...pharmaceutical/consumer, medical, optical prods., vision centers.

Sears, Roebuck & Co.... Sears Tower, Chicago, IL 60684...Edward R. Telling...merchandising, insurance (Allstate), financial services (Dean Winter).

Shell Oil Co....P.O. Box 2463, Houston, TX 77001...John F. Bookout...oil, gas, chemicals.

Sherwin-Williams Co....101 Prospect Ave. N.W., Cleveland, OH 44115...John G. Breen...world's largest paint producer; drug stores.

Simplicity Pattern Co., Inc....200 Madison Ave., New York, NY 10016...G. F. Lacey...paper patterns for home sewing.

Singer Co....30 Rockefeller Plaza, N.Y., NY 10020...Joseph B. Flavin...sewing prods., power tools.

Skyline Corp....2520 By-Pass Rd., Elkhart, IN 46515...Arthur J. Decio...mfg. housing and recreational vehicles.

A.O. Smith...3533 N. 27th St., Milwaukee, WI 53201...L.B. Smith...auto and truck frames.

Smithkline Corp.... One Franklin Plaza, Phila., PA 19101...H. Wendt...pharmaceuticals, animal health prods., diagnostic instruments, cosmetics.

Snap-on Tools Corp....2801 80th St., Kenosha, WI 53140...E. C. Schindler...manuf. mechanic's tools, equip.

Sony Corp.... Tokyo, Japan...A. Morita...manuf. televisions, radios, tape recorders, audio equip., video tape recorders.

Southland Corp....2828 N. Haskell Ave., Dallas, TX 75204...J. P. Thompson...convenience stores (7-Eleven; Gristede's), auto parts stores.

Southern Pacific Co.... One Market Plaza, San Francisco, CA 94105...B.F. Biaggini...railroad, leasing, communications, real estate, natural resources.

Sperry Corp....1290 Ave. of the Americas, N.Y., NY 10104...J. Paul Lyet...computers and data processing, farm, guidance & control equip.

Squibb Corp....40 W. 57th St., N.Y., NY 10019...Richard M. Furlaud...drugs, confectionery, household prods....Charles of the Ritz; Life Savers.

A.E. Staley Manufacturing Co....2200 E. Eldorado, Decatur, IL 62525...Donald E. Nordlund...corn and soybean processing, consumer prods (Sta-Puff softeners).

Standard Oil Co. of California...225 Bush, San Francisco, CA 94104...J.R. Grey...integrated oil co.

Standard Oil Co. (Indiana)...200 E. Randolph Dr., Chicago, IL 60601...John E. Swearingen...oil and gas exploitation & prod., chemicals, fertilizers.

Standard Oil Co. (Ohio)... Midland Bldg., Cleveland, OH 44115...Alton W. Whitehouse Jr....oil & natural gas.

Stanley Works...195 Lake St., New Britain, CT 06050...D.W. Davis...hand tools, hardware, door opening equipment.

Sterling Drug Inc....90 Park Ave., N.Y., NY 10016...W. Clarke Wescoe...pharmaceuticals, cosmetics & toiletries, household, proprietary prods., chemicals, environmental control (Bayer Aspirin, Lysol Dorothy Gray; Parfums Givenchy).

J.P. Stevens & Co., Inc....1185 Ave. of the Americas, N.Y., NY 10036...W. Stevens...fabrics, carpets, other textile home furnishings.

Stokely-Van Camp, Inc....941 N. Meridian, Indianapolis, IN 46206...W.B. Stokely III...canned fruits, vegetables, and frozen foods, soft drinks (Gatorade).

Storer Broadcasting Co....1177 Kane Concourse, Miami Beach, FL 33154...P. Storer...television & radio broadcasting, CATV.

Sun Company, Inc....100 Matsonford Rd., Radnor, PA 19087...T. A. Burtis...petroleum.

Supermarkets General Corp....301 Blair Rd., Woodbridge, NJ 07095...H. Brody...supermarkets (Pathmark); Rickel Home Centers.

Taft Broadcasting Co....1718 Young St., Cincinnati, OH 45210...D. S. Taft...radio, TV broadcasting, TV cartoons (Hanna-Barbera), amusement parks.
Tandy Corp....1800 One Tandy Center, Fort Worth, TX 76102...Phil R. North...consumer electronics retailing & mfg...Radio Shack.
Teledyne, Inc....1901 Ave. of the Stars, Los Angeles, CA 90067...H. E. Singleton...electronics, aerospace prods., industrial prods., insurance, finance.
Tenneco, Inc....P.O. Box 2511, Houston, TX 77001...J. L. Ketelsen...oil, natural gas pipelines, construction and farm equip.
Texaco Inc....2000 Westchester Ave., White Plains, NY 10650...Maurice F. Granville...petroleum and petroleum prods.
Texas Instruments Inc....13500 North Central, Dallas, TX 75265...Mark Shepherd Jr...electrical & electronics mfg.
Textron Inc....40 Westminster St., Providence, RI 02903...Robert P. Straetz...aerospace, consumer, industrial, metal prods.
3M...3M Center, St. Paul, MN 55144...Lewis W. Lehr...abrasives, adhesives, building services & chemicals, electrical, health care, photographic, printing, recording materials.
Tidewater Inc....1440 Canal St., New Orleans, LA 70112...J. P. Laborde...marine equip. for oil industry.
Time Inc....Time & Life Bldg., New York, NY 10020...R. P. Davidson...magazine publisher (Time; Sports Illustrated; Fortune; Money; People), CATV (Home Box Office), forest prods.
Toro Co....8009-34th Ave. South, Minneapolis, MN 55420...K. B. Melrose...lawn, snow removal equip.
Toys "R" Us...395 W. Passaic St., Rochelle, NJ 07662...Charles Lazarus...toy retailer.
Trane Co., The...3600 Pammel Creek Rd., La Crosse, WI 54601...W. G. Roth...air conditioning and heat transfer equip.
Transamerica Corp....600 Montgomery St., San Francisco, CA 94111...John R. Beckett...insurance, financial, leisure, business services (Occidental Life Ins.; Budget Rent A Car).
Trans World Corp....605 3d Ave., N.Y., NY 10158...L. Edwin Smart...holding co...Trans World Airlines; Hilton International; Spartan Food Systems, Century 21 real estate corp.
Travelers Corp....One Tower Sq., Hartford, CT 06115...E. H. Budd...insurance.

UAL, Inc....1200 Algonquin Rd., Elk Grove Township, IL 60007...R. J. Ferris...holding co. United Airlines, Westin Hotels.
Union Carbide Corp....Old Ridgebury Rd., Danbury, CT 06817...W. M. Anderson...chemicals.
Union Oil Co. of California...Union Oil Center, Los Angeles, CA 90017...F. L. Hartley...integrated oil co., mining, chemicals.
Union Pacific Corp....345 Park Ave., N.Y., NY 10022...J.H. Evans...railroad, natural resources.
Uniroyal, Inc....Middlebury, CT 06749...Joseph P. Flannery...tires, chemical, plastic prods.
United States Gypsum Co....101 S. Wacker Dr., Chicago, IL 60606...G. J. Morgan...largest U.S. producer of gypsum & related prods.
United States Steel Corp....600 Grant St., Pittsburgh, PA 15230...David M. Roderick...largest U.S. steel co., chemicals, transportation, oil.
United States Tobacco Co....100 W. Putnam Ave., Greenwich, CT 06830...L.F. Bantle...smokeless tobacco (Copenhagen; Skoal; Happy Days), pipes & pipe tobacco, pet foods (Cadillac).
United Technologies...United Technologies Bldg., Hartford, CT 06101...Harry J. Gray...aerospace, industrial prods. & services...Carrier Corp.; Otis Elevator; Pratt & Whitney, Sikorsky Aircraft.
Upjohn Co....7000 Portage Rd., Kalamazoo, MI 49001...R.T. Parfet Jr...pharmaceuticals, chemicals, agricultural and health care prods.
USAir, Inc....Washington National Airport, Wash., DC 20001...Edwin I. Colodny...air transportation.
U.S. Home Corp....1177 West Loop South, Houston, TX 77001...G. R. Odom...manuf. single family homes.

VF Corp....1047 No. Park Rd., Wyomissing, PA 19610...L.R. Pugh...apparel...Vanity Fair; Kay Windsor; Lee.
Vulcan Materials Co....One Metroplex Dr., Birmingham, AL 35209...B. A. Monagham...construction materials, chemicals, metals.

Walgreen Co....200 Wilmot Rd., Deerfield, IL 60015...Charles R. Walgreen 3d...retail drug chain, restaurants.
Wang Laboratories, Inc....One Industrial Ave., Lowell, MA 01851...A. Wang...word processors.
Warnaco Inc....350 Lafayette St., Bridgeport, CT 06601...James C. Walker...apparel...Hathaway, Puritan, High Tide, White Stag.
Warner Communications Inc....75 Rockefeller Plaza, N.Y., NY 10019...Steven J. Ross...filmed entertainment, records & music publishing, book publishing, CATV system, consumer prods., Atari, Franklin Mint.
Warner-Lambert Co....201 Tabor Rd., Morris Plains, NJ 07950...Ward S. Hagan...health care, optical prods., candy.
Washington Post Co....1150 15th St., N.W., Washington, DC 20071...Katharine Graham...newspapers, magazines (Newsweek), TV stations.
Wendy's Intl., Inc....PO Box 256, Dublin, OH 43017...R. L. Barney...quick service hamburger restaurants.
Western Air Lines, Inc....6060 Avion Dr., Los Angeles, CA 90045...N. G. Bergt...air transportation.
Western Union Corp....One Lake St., Upper Saddle River, NJ 07458...Robert M. Flanagan...telecommunications.
Westinghouse Electric Corp....Westinghouse Bldg., Gateway Center, Pittsburgh, PA 15222...R.E. Kirby...manuf. electrical, mechanical equip., radio and television stations.
West Point-Pepperell Inc....400 W. 10th St., West Point, GA 31833...J. L. Lanier Jr...apparel, industrial & household fabrics.
Weyerhaeuser Co....Tacoma, WA 98477...George H. Weyerhaeuser...manuf., distribution forest prods.
Wheelabrator-Frye Inc....Liberty Lane, Hampton, NH 03842...M. D. Dingman...environmental, energy, engineered prods., chemicals and specialty prods., railroad freight cars and equip.
Whirlpool Corp....Administrative Center, Benton Harbor, MI 49022...John H. Platts...major home appliances.
White Consolidated Industries, Inc....11770 Berea Rd., Cleveland, OH 44111...R.H. Holdt...major home appliances (Kelvinator, Frigidaire), industrial equip. and machinery.
Willamette Industries, Inc....3800 1st Interstate Tower, Portland, OR 97201...Gene D. Knudson...building materials and paper prods.
Williams Cos....One Williams Center, Tulsa, OK 74172...J. H. Williams...fertilizer, energy, metals.
Winn-Dixie Stores, Inc....5050 Edgewood Ct., Jacksonville, FL 32203...B.L. Thomas...retail grocery chain.
Wometco Enterprises, Inc....306 N. Miami Ave., Miami, FL 33128...M. Wolfson...television broadcasting, CATV, soft drink bottler.
F.W. Woolworth Co....233 Broadway, N.Y., NY 10007...Edward F. Gibbons...variety stores, dept. stores, shoestores...Woolco, Kinney.
Wm. Wrigley Jr. Co....410 N. Michigan Ave., Chicago, IL 60611...William Wrigley...chewing gum.

Xerox Corp....Stamford, CT 06904...C. Peter McColough...equip. for reproduction, reduction, and transmission of printed information.

Zale Corp....3000 Diamond Park, Dallas TX 75247...... D. Zale...jewelry retailer.
Zayre Corp....Framingham, MA 01701...S. L. Feldberg...self-service discount dept. stores, specialty shops.
Zenith Radio Corp....100 Milwaukee Ave., Glenview, IL 60025...R. W. Kluckman...consumer electronic prods.
Zurn Industries, Inc....One Zurn Place, Erie, PA 16512...D. M. Zurn...pollution control, energy, mechanical systems, leisure prods.

U.S. Budget Receipts and Outlays—1978-1981

Source: U.S. Treasury Department, Bureau of Govt. Financial Operations
(Fiscal years end Sept. 30)
(thousands of dollars)

Classification	Fiscal 1978	Fiscal 1979	Fiscal 1980	Fiscal 1981
Net Receipts				
Individual income taxes	180,987,773	217,840,966	244,068,898	285,550,802
Corporation income taxes	59,951,865	65,676,588	64,599,673	61,137,136
Social insurance taxes and contributions:				
Federal old-age and survivors insurance	73,140,779	83,409,910	95,580,645	117,757,091
Federal disability insurance	12,250,395	14,583,743	16,639,155	12,418,490
Federal hospital insurance	16,679,867	19,890,684	23,233,135	30,360,679
Railroad retirement taxes	1,822,006	2,189,887	2,311,977	2,457,238
Total employment taxes and contributions	**103,893,048**	**120,074,224**	**138,764,911**	**162,993,498**
Other insurance and retirement:				
Unemployment	13,849,597	15,386,733	15,335,788	15,398,386
Federal supplementary medical insurance	2,431,133	2,636,005	2,927,711	3,319,094
Federal employees retirement	3,174,262	3,428,322	3,659,505	3,908,270
Civil service retirement and disability	62,323	66,042	59,228	76,148
Total social insurance taxes and contributions	**123,410,366**	**141,591,326**	**160,747,143**	**186,426,256**
Excise taxes	18,376,183	18,744,953	24,329,156	40,839,143
Estate and gift taxes	5,285,401	5,410,556	6,389,480	6,786,537
Customs duties	6,572,717	7,438,533	7,173,836	8,082,808
Deposits of earnings-Federal Reserve Banks	6,641,091	8,326,930	11,767,143	12,833,713
All other miscellaneous receipts	771,976	910,317	980,682	955,899
Net Budget Receipts	**401,997,000**	**465,940,168**	**520,056,012**	**602,612,295**
Net Outlays				
Legislative Branch	1,048,776	1,077,101	1,217,983	1,208,819
The Judiciary	435,124	479,665	564,144	637,279
Executive Office of the President:				
The White House Office	16,571	16,159	18,967	21,078
Office of Management and Budget	29,299	29,788	34,963	35,122
Total Executive Office	**74,566**	**79,589**	**95,385**	**95,635**
Funds appropriated to the President:				
Appalachian regional development	261,674	304,337	340,531	336,795
Disaster relief	470,290	284,220	573,760	400,547
Foreign assistance-security	2,019,665	1,786,014	3,903,034	3,546,682
Foreign assistance-bilateral	434,972	593,058	1,372,452	1,489,325
Int. narcotics control assistance	34,987	46,702	26,875	NA
Total funds appropriated to the President	**4,475,091**	**2,536,618**	**7,507,055**	**7,009,908**
Agriculture Department:				
Food stamp program	5,498,774	6,821,746	9,117,136	11,252,902
Child Nutrition Program	2,526,732	2,879,668	3,377,056	3,438,238
Total Agriculture Department	**20,368,401**	**20,633,725**	**24,554,916**	**26,029,802**
Commerce Department	5,252,159	4,071,765	3,103,596	2,226,045
Defense Department:				
Military personnel	27,075,347	28,407,171	30,841,732	36,408,884
Retired military personnel	9,171,474	10,279,058	11,919,776	13,729,065
Operation and maintenance	33,577,970	36,424,304	44,770,126	51,863,633
Procurement	19,975,553	25,404,254	29,020,667	35,191,231
Research and development	10,507,963	11,152,177	13,126,878	15,277,593
Military construction	1,931,504	2,079,987	2,449,521	2,458,186
Family housing	1,404,772	1,467,517	1,680,174	1,720,887
Corps of Engineers and civil functions	2,611,625	2,886,226	3,204,436	3,124,375
Total Defense Department	**105,677,084**	**117,921,453**	**136,137,929**	**159,183,160**
Education Department	8,763,618	10,713,037	13,124,205	15,087,770
Energy Department	6,429,745	7,888,792	6,463,498	11,631,087
Health and Human Services Department:				
Food and Drug Administration	275,971	299,834	325,736	337,167
National Institutes of Health	2,675,703	2,869,565	3,222,304	3,603,805
Public Health Service	NA	6,928,528	7,817,750	8,378,623
Old-age and survivors benefits	81,205,460	87,591,968	100,621,850	119,413,467
Social Security Administration	108,221,236	118,041,422	134,353,608	159,500,955
Human Development Services	5,252,264	5,718,598	5,343,312	5,090,101
Total Health and Human Services Dept.	**162,809,429**	**181,185,638**	**194,690,800**	**230,303,851**
Housing and Urban Development Department	7,760,944	9,218,091	12,582,279	14,032,380
Interior Department	3,677,605	4,087,007	4,376,994	4,427,690
Justice Department:				
Federal Bureau of Investigation	552,001	585,991	609,181	691,176
Total Justice Department	**2,397,372**	**2,521,715**	**2,631,677**	**2,682,472**
Labor Department:				
Unemployment Trust Fund	11,169,127	11,172,982	16,440,284	18,739,096
Total Labor Department	**22,902,043**	**22,650,336**	**29,724,001**	**30,083,819**
State Department	1,251,536	1,548,046	1,938,405	1,897,364
Transportation Department	13,451,791	15,485,569	19,614,572	22,554,054
Treasury Department:				
Internal Revenue Service	3,325,766	3,422,178	4,331,945	5,033,188
Interest on the public debt	48,694,855	59,837,203	74,860,226	95,589,367
General revenue sharing	6,854,924	6,847,709	6,828,835	5,136,892
Total Treasury Department	**56,309,144**	**64,595,923**	**76,690,723**	**92,632,962**

Classification	Fiscal 1978	Fiscal 1979	Fiscal 1980	Fiscal 1981
Net Outlays (cont'd)				
Environmental Protection Agency	4,071,472	4,799,768	5,601,883	5,231,851
General Services Administration	117,042	172,761	169,331	185,562
National Aeronautics and Space Administration	3,980,022	4,187,232	4,849,924	5,421,388
Veterans Administration	18,962,152	19,887,171	21,134,538	22,904,006
Independent agencies:				
ACTION	203,163	211,325	133,319	150,164
Arms Control and Disarmament Agency	13,990	14,653	17,256	15,888
Board for International Broadcasting	65,451	82,692	98,372	88,199
Civil Aeronautics Board	101,359	99,336	116,657	147,151
Commission on Civil Rights	10,464	10,257	12,035	12,137
Community Services Administration	767,918	778,894	2,166,279	689,228
Consumer Product Safety Commission	40,058	39,270	44,177	40,861
Corporation for Public Broadcasting	119,200	120,200	152,000	162,000
District of Columbia	370,968	393,151	424,694	492,231
Equal Employment Opportunity Commission	74,160	92,453	130,788	134,212
Export-Import Bank of the United States	−105,904	200,052	1,836,003	2,066,222
Federal Communications Commission	64,065	69,542	75,804	80,892
Federal Deposit Insurance Corporation	−566,610	−1,218,370	−922,130	−1,725,994
Federal Emergency Management Agency	259,290	417,422	660,106	372,135
Federal Home Loan Bank Board	−403,045	−488,357	552,046	369,931
Federal Trade Commission	58,815	62,605	68,474	70,081
Intragovernmental Agencies	153,247	88,911	104,927	69,152
International Communications Agency	352,116	373,463	432,752	436,926
Interstate Commerce Commission	64,899	54,797	155,682	74,190
Legal Services Corporation	157,429	254,307	320,308	324,314
Merit Systems Protection Board	NA	6,476	13,086	20,569
National Foundation on the Arts and Humanities	247,261	283,630	320,702	314,172
National Labor Relations Board	90,414	97,190	108,867	114,450
National Science Foundation	802,783	869,647	911,907	975,009
National Transportation Safety Board	15,513	15,515	17,754	18,296
Nuclear Regulatory Commission	270,862	309,475	377,872	416,844
Office of Personnel Management	10,962,658	12,654,562	15,052,426	18,088,914
Postal Service	1,778,240	1,786,509	1,676,878	1,343,217
Railroad Retirement Board	4,074,556	4,365,399	4,788,046	5,307,621
Securities and Exchange Commission	61,302	65,978	74,140	78,025
Small Business Administration	2,766,028	1,631,142	1,898,932	1,912,527
Smithsonian Institution	125,239	132,182	138,758	166,875
Tennessee Valley Authority	1,412,228	1,884,141	1,869,233	1,927,758
U.S. Railway Association	753,725	737,150	672,055	191,250
Other Independent agencies	177,152	186,299	287,139	464,643
Total independent agencies	**25,078,715**	**26,681,897**	**34,931,166**	**35,567,788**
Undistributed offsetting receipts	−15,722,226	−18,488,845	−21,932,702	−30,306,097
Net Budget Outlays	**450,758,000**	**493,221,018**	**579,602,970**	**660,544,033**
Less net receipts	401,997,000	465,940,168	520,056,012	602,612,295
Deficit	**−48,761,000**	**−27,280,850**	**−59,546,958**	**57,931,739**

(NA) Not available.

U.S. Net Receipts and Outlays

Source: U.S. Treasury Department; annual statements for year ending June 30[3] (thousands of dollars)

Yearly average	Receipts	Expenditures	Yearly average	Receipts	Expenditures	Yearly average	Receipts	Expenditures
1789-1800[1]	5,717	5,776	1871-1875	336,830	287,460	1916-1920[6]	3,483,652	8,065,333
1801-1810[2]	13,056	9,086	1876-1880	288,124	255,598	1921-1925	4,306,673	3,578,989
1811-1820[2]	21,032	23,943	1881-1885	366,961	257,691	1926-1930	4,069,138	3,182,807
1821-1830[2]	21,928	16,162	1886-1890	375,448	279,134	1931-1935[4]	2,770,973	5,214,874
1831-1840[2]	30,461	24,495	1891-1895	352,891	363,599	1936-1940[4]	4,960,614	10,192,367
1841-1850[2]	28,545	34,097	1896-1900	434,877	457,451	1941-1945[4]	25,951,137	66,037,928
1851-1860	60,237	60,163	1901-1905	559,481	535,559	1946-1950[5,7]	39,047,243	42,334,534
1861-1865	160,907	683,785	1906-1910	628,507	639,178			
1866-1870	447,301	377,642	1911-1915	710,227	720,252			

Fiscal year	Receipts	Expenditures	Fiscal year	Receipts	Expenditures	Fiscal year	Receipts	Expenditures
1955	60,389,744	64,569,973	1972[8]	215,262,639	238,285,907	1978	401,997,000	450,758,000
1960	77,763,460	76,539,413	1973	232,191,842	246,603,359	1979	465,954,656	493,607,095
1964	89,458,664	97,684,375	1974	264,847,484	268,342,952	1980	520,056,012	579,602,970
1965	93,071,797	96,506,904	1975	281,037,466	324,641,586	1981	602,612,295	660,544,033
1968[9]	153,675,705	172,803,186	1976	300,005,077	365,610,129			
1970	193,843,791	194,968,258	1976 Trans[3]	81,772,766	94,472,996			
1971	188,332,129	210,652,667	1977[3]	356,861,331	401,896,376			

(1) Average for period March 4, 1789, to Dec. 31, 1800. (2) Years ended Dec. 31, 1801 to 1842; average for 1841-1850 is for the period Jan. 1, 1841, to June 30, 1850. (3) Effective fiscal year 1977, fiscal year is reckoned Oct. 1-Sept. 30; transition quarter covers July 1, 1976-Sept. 30, 1976. (4) Expenditures for years 1932 through 1946 have been revised to include Government corps. (wholly owned) etc. (net). (5) Effective January 3, 1949, amounts refunded by the Government, principally for the overpayment of taxes, are being reported as deductions from total receipts rather than as expenditures. Also, effective July 1, 1948, payments to the Treasury, principally by wholly owned Government corporations for retirement of capital stock and for disposition of earnings, are excluded in reporting both budget receipts and expenditures. Neither of these changes affects the size of the budget surplus or deficit. Beginning 1931 figures in each case have been adjusted accordingly for comparative purposes. (6) Figures for 1918 through 1946 are revised to exclude statutory debt retirement (sinking fund, etc.). (7) Excludes $3 billion transferred to Foreign Economics Corporation Trust Fund and includes $3 billion representing expenditures made from the FEC Trust Fund. (8) Effective fiscal year 1972 loan repayments and loan disbursements will be netted against expenditures and known as outlays. (9) From 1968, figures include trust funds (e.g. Social Security).

Summary of U.S. Receipts by Source and Outlays by Function

Source: U.S. Treasury Department, Bureau of Govt. Financial Operations

(in millions)

Net Receipts	Fiscal 1978	Fiscal 1979	Fiscal 1980	Fiscal 1981[1]
Individual income taxes	$180,988	$217,800	$244,069	$285,551
Corporation income taxes	59,952	65,700	64,600	61,137
Social insurance taxes and contributions	117,743	141,600	160,747	186,426
Excise taxes	18,376	18,700	24,329	40,839
Estate and gift taxes	5,285	5,400	6,389	6,787
Customs duties	6,572	7,400	7,174	8,083
Miscellaneous receipts	7,400	9,200	12,748	13,790
Total	**401,997**	**465,900**	**520,056**	**602,612**
Net outlays				
National defense	105,200	117,700	135,880	159,699
International affairs	5,900	6,100	10,472	11,051
General science, space, and technology	4,700	5,000	5,999	6,422
Energy	5,900	6,900	6,623	10,642
Natural resources and environment	10,900	12,100	14,130	13,783
Agriculture	7,700	6,200	4,951	5,598
Commerce and housing credit	3,300	2,600	7,795	3,995
Transportation	15,400	17,500	20,840	23,312
Community and regional development	11,000	9,500	9,917	9,265
Education, training, employment and social services	26,500	29,700	31,399	30,563
Health	43,700	49,600	58,165	69,324
Income security	146,200	160,200	192,133	225,599
Veterans benefits and services	19,000	19,900	21,167	22,937
Administration of justice	3,800	4,200	4,554	4,721
General government	3,800	4,200	4,641	4,730
General purpose fiscal assistance	9,600	8,400	8,306	6,621
Interest	44,000	52,600	64,564	82,590
Undistributed offsetting receipts	−15,800	−18,500	−21,933	−30,306
Total	**450,800**	**493,700**	**579,603**	**660,544**

(1) Estimate

U.S. Direct Investment Abroad, Countries and Industries

Source: Bureau of Economic Analysis, U.S. Commerce Department

(millions of dollars)

	Direct investment position		Equity and intercompany account outflows (inflows (−))		Reinvested earnings		Fees and royalties		Income	
	1980	1981	1980	1981	1980	1981	1980	1981	1980	1981
All areas	215,578	227,342	2,221	-4,287	17,017	12,978	5,780	5,867	37,149	31,873
Petroleum	47,595	52,107	-2,596	-1,939	4,633	4,033	239	209	13,185	13,168
Manufacturing	89,160	92,480	3,628	-617	6,066	3,550	4,068	4,007	11,053	8,212
Other	78,822	82,756	1,189	-1,731	6,317	5,395	1,473	1,651	12,911	10,493
Developed countries	158,350	167,112	5,618	-2,232	12,395	7,675	4,841	4,805	24,642	18,790
Petroleum	34,677	37,348	164	-2,514	3,932	2,710	253	296	8,636	7,131
Manufacturing	71,385	73,164	3,170	-962	4,220	2,345	3,655	3,510	8,374	5,901
Other	52,289	56,600	2,284	1,244	4,243	2,620	933	999	7,632	5,758
Canada	44,978	46,957	161	-2,385	3,589	1,770	931	980	5,855	4,072
Petroleum	10,800	10,705	446	-2,484	1,358	406	67	62	1,986	999
Manufacturing	18,876	19,658	319	-300	1,037	691	713	747	1,835	1,756
Other	15,302	16,593	-605	399	-1,194	673	151	171	2,034	1,317
Europe	96,539	101,318	5,670	-37	7,610	4,625	3,176	3,035	15,994	11,874
Petroleum	20,157	22,458	136	247	2,236	2,038	156	189	5,882	5,345
Manufacturing	45,332	45,534	2,796	-805	2,822	1,014	2,459	2,264	5,645	2,983
Other	31,050	33,326	2,738	521	2,552	1,573	561	582	4,468	3,546
Other	16,833	18,837	-213	191	1,196	1,280	734	790	2,792	2,844
Petroleum	3,720	4,184	-418	-276	338	266	30	44	767	787
Manufacturing	7,176	7,971	54	143	361	640	483	499	894	1,161
Other	5,937	6,681	151	324	498	374	221	246	1,130	895
Developing countries	53,277	56,109	-3,378	-1,614	4,429	4,692	1,227	1,331	11,894	12,283
Petroleum	10,271	12,132	-2,812	1,087	654	899	278	188	4,138	5,468
Manufacturing	17,775	19,317	458	345	1,846	1,206	413	497	2,679	2,311
Other	24,749	24,660	-1,041	-3,046	1,928	2,586	536	645	5,077	4,505
Latin America	38,882	38,883	-631	-3,312	3,366	3,254	581	669	6,968	5,844
Petroleum	4,331	4,499	11	-137	289	295	48	67	961	1,052
Manufacturing	14,550	15,762	516	337	1,483	847	265	288	2,136	1,727
Other	20,001	18,622	-1,158	-3,511	1,594	2,112	268	314	3,872	3,065
Other	14,395	17,226	-2,747	1,698	1,063	1,438	646	662	4,926	6,439
Petroleum	5,935	7,633	-2,908	1,224	365	604	230	121	3,176	4,416
Manufacturing	3,226	3,555	-59	8	363	359	149	209	544	583
Other	5,299	6,038	209	465	335	475	267	331	1,206	1,440
International	3,951	4,122	-19	-441	193	612	-288	-268	614	799

State Finances

Revenues, Expenditures, Debts, Taxes, U.S. Aid, Military Contracts

For fiscal 1980 (year ending June 30, 1980, except: Alabama and Michigan, Sept. 30; New York, Mar. 31; Texas, Aug. 31
*Military prime contracts. Taxes are State income and sales (or gross receipts) taxes, and vehicle, etc., fees.

Sources: Census Bureau, U.S. Treasury and Defense Depts.

State	Receipts (thousands)	Outlays (thousands)	Total debt (thousands)	Per cap. debt	Per cap. taxes	Per cap. U.S. aid	Military contracts (thousands)*
Alabama	$4,153,588	$4,001,856	$1,032,338	$265.38	$477.32	$407	$746,415
Alaska	3,229,513	2,032,718	1,544,554	3,861.38	3,594.02	1,462	257,355
Arizona	3,187,080	2,637,287	94,007	34.59	619.72	308	729,656
Arkansas	2,295,172	2,147,542	362,579	158.68	507.99	411	172,384
California	36,087,253	32,812,199	8,361,705	353.28	818.23	371	13,914,411
Colorado	3,365,513	2,804,770	460,497	159.40	516.06	344	518,300
Connecticut	3,472,328	3,341,266	3,879,197	1,248.13	591.92	372	3,879,061
Delaware	970,333	886,151	1,044,499	1,755.46	866.75	426	243,828
Florida	8,222,693	7,386,754	2,626,926	269.70	493.25	293	2,053,198
Georgia	5,194,061	4,900,734	1,404,635	257.07	499.44	434	960,992
Hawaii	1,895,329	1,660,028	1,864,213	1,931.83	1,034.59	480	315,410
Idaho	1,107,804	1,041,287	327,334	346.75	519.43	416	28,115
Illinois	12,729,900	12,428,758	6,277,201	549.76	619.47	392	1,006,783
Indiana	4,794,271	4,866,803	607,581	110.67	491.03	292	1,297,786
Iowa	3,479,012	3,411,812	380,999	130.79	599.67	341	303,102
Kansas	2,418,808	2,254,031	438,137	185.42	537.31	346	806,245
Kentucky	4,168,415	4,569,135	3,035,267	829.08	585.89	401	277,519
Louisiana	5,412,417	4,886,708	2,977,031	708.14	570.22	372	694,643
Maine	1,369,397	1,325,879	730,266	649.13	550.36	464	459,418
Maryland	5,564,324	5,434,815	3,502,248	830.70	654.84	437	1,795,406
Massachusetts	7,457,128	7,336,101	5,784,878	1,008.35	684.56	503	3,743,171
Michigan	12,356,577	12,633,601	2,916,082	314.98	642.43	424	1,701,749
Minnesota	5,700,144	5,417,876	2,069,902	507.70	785.52	408	1,070,273
Mississippi	2,884,870	2,690,817	815,045	323.30	498.98	472	808,291
Missouri	4,257,652	3,996,072	1,017,862	207.01	425.98	391	3,264,063
Montana	1,153,208	1,004,971	309,533	393.31	553.69	618	35,241
Nebraska	1,505,994	1,392,220	199,341	126.97	520.23	348	103,631
Nevada	1,220,521	1,097,558	527,969	660.79	596.50	419	50,396
New Hampshire	893,832	889,448	899,050	976.17	290.44	375	306,481
New Jersey	8,822,117	8,536,848	6,526,797	886.31	579.28	384	1,532,102
New Mexico	2,183,291	1,744,172	707,783	544.45	712.34	514	294,87
New York	27,199,172	24,977,939	23,640,088	1,346.48	724.31	545	5,678,789
North Carolina	6,201,827	5,732,542	1,265,720	215.48	547.39	328	676,759
North Dakota	1,013,327	909,915	219,276	335.80	569.47	531	73,156
Ohio	12,180,344	11,397,371	4,014,977	371.86	441.48	318	1,633,33
Oklahoma	3,433,126	3,248,996	1,525,740	504.38	587.12	350	466,886
Oregon	4,040,741	3,455,956	4,886,286	1,855.79	552.74	469	196,182
Pennsylvania	14,004,267	12,644,004	6,347,873	534.92	610.16	380	2,215,92
Rhode Island	1,392,699	1,361,003	1,463,092	1,544.98	581.61	504	261,79
South Carolina	3,484,289	3,325,311	1,937,234	621.11	538.01	342	331,44
South Dakota	762,190	739,503	714,274	1,035.18	392.06	642	20,97
Tennessee	4,028,047	3,873,736	1,405,948	306.24	411.02	442	533,40
Texas	12,924,347	11,486,851	2,468,627	173.50	475.03	278	5,413,35
Utah	1,888,807	1,754,804	537,074	367.61	537.82	391	251,35
Vermont	711,123	675,867	654,159	1,280.15	521.17	635	125,13
Virginia	5,655,917	5,393,220	1,926,291	360.32	513.15	332	3,366,84
Washington	6,323,963	5,714,612	1,600,407	387.51	706.40	405	2,316,80
West Virginia	2,640,308	2,678,563	1,816,478	931.53	625.38	487	123,89
Wisconsin	6,587,518	6,074,117	2,445,967	519.87	715.48	430	377,56
Wyoming	937,196	797,449	362,895	770.48	824.04	625	33,29
Total or average	**$276,961,733**	**$257,811,981**	**$121,957,862**	**$539.95**	**$606.88**	**$441**	**$68,069,56**

U.S. Customs and Internal Revenue Receipts

Source: U.S. Treasury Department, Bureau of Govt. Financial Operations

Gross. Not reduced by appropriations to Federal old-age and survivors insurance trust fund or refunds or receipts.

Fiscal year	Customs	Internal Revenue	Fiscal year	Customs	Internal Revenue	Fiscal year	Customs	Internal Revenue
1930	$587,000,903	$3,039,295,014	1955	$606,396,634	$66,288,691,586	1977	$5,150,151,000	$358,139,000,00
1935	343,353,034	3,277,690,028	1960	1,123,037,579	91,774,802,823	1978	6,728,612,000	399,776,000,00
1940	348,590,635	5,303,133,988	1965	1,477,548,820	114,428,991,753	1979	7,639,620,000	460,412,185,00
1945	354,775,542	43,902,001,929	1970	2,429,799,000	195,700,000,000	1980	7,481,593,000	519,375,273,00
1950	422,650,329	39,448,607,109	1975	3,675,532,000	293,800,000,000	1981	8,523,275,124	606,799,103,00

Note: Through 1976 the fiscal year ended June 30. From 1977 on, fiscal year ends Sept. 30.

U.S. Business Indexes

Source: Federal Reserve System; F.W. Dodge Div., McGraw-Hill; U.S. Labor Department; U.S. Commerce Department

(1967=100, except as noted)

Period	Industrial production: Total	Market Products: Total	Final: Total	Consumer goods	Equipment	Intermediate	Materials	Industry: Manufacturing	Capacity utilization in mfg.[1]	Construction contracts	Nonagricultural employment—Total[2]	Manufacturing: Employment[3]	Manufacturing: Payrolls	Total retail sales[4]	Prices[4]: Consumer	Prices[4]: Producer finished goods
1963	76.5	76.4	75.5	81.3	67.5	79.9	76.7	75.8	83.5	86.1	86.1	87.7	76.0	79	91.8	93.8
1965	89.8	88.2	87.6	92.6	80.7	90.6	92.4	89.7	89.5	93.2	92.3	93.9	88.1	90	94.5	95.7
1970	107.8	106.9	105.3	109.0	100.1	112.9	109.2	106.4	79.3	123.1	107.7	98.0	114.1	119	116.3	110.3
1975	117.8	119.3	118.2	124.0	110.2	123.1	115.5	116.3	72.9	162.3	116.9	91.3	157.3	185	161.2	163.4
1978	146.1	144.8	142.2	149.1	132.8	154.1	148.3	146.8	84.4	174.3	130.3	102.1	222.4	248	195.4	194.6
1979	152.5	150.0	147.2	150.8	142.2	160.5	156.4	153.6	85.7	121.0[5]	136.5	105.3	249.0	282	217.4	217.7
1980	147.0	146.7	145.3	145.4	145.2	151.9	147.6	146.7	79.1	106.0[5]	137.6	99.4	264.3	304	246.8	247.0
1981	151.0	150.6	149.5	147.9	151.8	154.4	151.6	150.4	78.5	107.0[5]	139.1	98.5	288.1	331	272.4	269.8
1982	138.2	141.1	141.1	143.7	137.6	140.8	133.7	137.1	69.7	118.0[5]	136.6	89.9	288.2	336	290.6	279.9

(1) Ratios of indexes of production to indexes of capacity. (2) Employees only, excluding personnel in Armed Forces. (3) Production workers only. (4) Without seasonal adjustment. (5) 1977-100.

Producer Price Indexes

Source: Bureau of Labor Statistics, U.S. Labor Department

Producer Price Indexes measure average changes in prices received in primary markets of the U.S. by producers of commodities in all stages of processing.

Commodity group (1967 = 100)	Annual Avg. 1979	Annual Avg. 1980	1981 Jan.	1981 June	1982 Jan.	1982 June
All commodities	**235.6**	**268.8**	**284.8**	**294.8**	**298.3**	**299.4**
Farm products processed foods and feeds	**229.8**	**244.7**	**257.9**	**254.3**	**246.0**	**255.3**
Farm products	241.4	249.4	264.5	260.7	242.2	252.7
Processed foods and feeds	222.5	241.2	253.3	249.9	247.1	255.8
Industrial commodities	**236.5**	**274.8**	**291.5**	**305.1**	**311.8**	**310.7**
Textile products and apparel	168.7	183.5	193.1	200.1	205.0	204.5
Hides, skins, leathers, and related products	252.4	248.9	258.2	261.6	261.8	262.7
Fuels and related products and power	408.1	574.0	634.6	707.6	705.1	677.4
Chemicals and allied products	222.3	260.3	274.3	290.5	292.9	293.5
Rubber and plastic products	194.3	217.4	224.8	233.4	237.3	243.3
Lumber and wood products	300.4	288.9	296.5	298.1	285.5	288.7
Pulp, paper, and allied products	219.0	249.2	264.4	272.9	285.5	289.3
Metals and metal products	259.3	286.4	294.0	298.4	304.7	300.1
Machinery and equipment	213.9	239.8	253.3	262.1	274.1	278.4
Furniture and household durables	171.3	187.7	194.0	197.3	203.5	206.6
Nonmetallic mineral products	248.6	283.0	296.6	313.6	315.6	318.7
Transportation equipment (Dec. 1968 = 100)	188.1	207.0	227.4	234.3	248.6	249.6
Miscellaneous products	208.7	258.8	264.3	266.3	268.3	271.6

Indexes of Manufacturing, Industrial Countries

Source: Bureau of Labor Statistics, U.S. Labor Department (1977=100)

Output per hour

Country	1960	1965	1970	1975	1976	1978	1979	1980	1981
United States	60.0	74.5	79.1	93.4	97.5	100.9	101.5	101.7	104.5
10 Foreign countries	37.6	49.5	69.0	89.1	95.7	105.1	111.6	115.6	NA
Canada	50.4	62.9	77.0	91.2	96.7	101.6	103.3	101.3	101.9
Japan	22.0	33.1	61.4	85.3	93.3	107.9	117.4	125.4	129.1
Belgium	31.8	39.8	58.6	85.0	93.7	106.7	112.8	117.6	NA
Denmark	34.5	44.9	61.9	89.5	96.4	104.4	106.9	108.7	115.1
France	39.8	51.3	70.2	88.0	95.2	105.3	111.0	111.7	114.3
West Germany	40.0	53.5	68.5	89.3	95.0	103.8	108.9	110.1	113.0
Italy	36.5	52.9	72.7	91.1	98.9	103.0	110.5	116.9	119.2
Netherlands	31.7	41.3	63.0	85.2	96.1	105.7	111.3	112.5	NA
Sweden	43.0	59.4	82.0	100.5	101.6	104.3	112.7	113.4	112.8
United Kingdom	55.6	67.0	80.5	94.6	98.4	103.2	106.7	107.2	113.4
8 European countries	41.1	54.0	71.2	90.3	96.6	104.2	109.8	112.7	NA
Original EEC	39.0	52.1	69.4	89.1	95.9	104.3	110.0	111.9	NA

Unit Labor Costs in U.S. dollars

Country	1960	1965	1970	1975	1976	1978	1979	1980	1981
United States	61.1	57.5	57.6	91.5	94.6	107.4	117.1	130.6	140.0
10 Foreign countries	35.7	41.8	46.7	94.6	91.0	119.5	129.1	140.0	NA
Canada	59.3	51.0	62.0	90.3	101.1	197.9	103.2	116.2	125.1
Japan	30.2	37.4	41.3	90.4	88.2	126.2	117.9	113.8	121.8
Belgium	30.8	38.7	42.1	90.7	88.5	115.4	125.9	133.0	NA
Denmark	31.4	38.5	46.4	93.7	92.1	115.1	130.6	132.9	109.4
France	40.7	48.0	48.3	100.6	95.2	117.0	133.6	156.2	138.7
West Germany	26.0	32.6	42.4	89.8	88.4	121.0	136.1	148.1	125.3
Italy	32.5	41.2	50.6	104.3	90.5	115.6	129.5	141.0	126.1
Netherlands	24.9	35.0	41.4	93.5	89.0	116.8	128.9	134.9	NA
Sweden	29.6	34.9	40.5	82.9	92.4	105.6	110.9	124.3	114.1
United Kingdom	44.9	51.8	55.1	102.1	93.4	124.0	158.4	213.5	202.0
8 European countries	34.0	41.0	46.8	95.7	91.1	118.7	135.9	154.6	NA
Original EEC	30.4	38.1	45.0	94.9	90.4	118.6	133.4	147.2	NA

Gross National Product, National Income, and Personal Income

Source: Bureau of Economic Analysis, U.S. Commerce Department includes Alaska and Hawaii beginning in 1960 (millions of dollars)

	1950	1960	1970	1975	1980	1981
Gross national product	**286,172**	**505,978**	**982,419**	**1,528,833**	**2,633,108**	**2,937,716**
Less: Capital consumption allowances	23,853	47,712	90,827	161,954	293,204	330,096
Equals: Net national product	**262,319**	**458,266**	**894,592**	**1,366,879**	**2,339,904**	**2,607,620**
Less: Indirect business tax and nontax liability	23,422	45,389	94,027	139,246	213,004	251,292
Business transfer payments	778	1,974	3,983	7,599	11,390	12,395
Statistical discrepancy	2,030	−683	−2,076	7,371	3,904	−1,883
Plus: Subsidies minus current surplus of government enterprises	114	422	2,716	2,339	5,478	6,647
Equals: National income	**236,203**	**412,008**	**798,374**	**1,215,002**	**2,117,084**	**2,352,463**
Less: Corporate profits and inventory valuation adjustment	2,272	9,760	37,549	95,902	181,619	190,630
Net interest	...	...	...	78,615	187,699	235,653
Contributions for social insurance	7,058	21,058	58,712	110,579	203,983	238,120
Wage accruals less disbursement	24	0	0	0	−40	42
Plus: Government transfer payment to persons	14,404	26,966	75,898	170,567	285,847	323,939
Personal interest income	8,929	23,284	64,284	115,529	263,421	328,982
Dividends	8,803	12,890	22,884	31,885	55,920	62,510
Business transfer payments	778	1,974	3,983	7,599	11,390	12,395
Equals: Personal income	**226,102**	**399,724**	**801,271**	**1,255,486**	**2,160,401**	**2,415,844**

National Income by Type of Income

(millions of dollars)

	1960	1965	1970	1975	1979	1980	1981
Compensation of employees	**294,932**	**396,543**	**609,150**	**931,079**	**1,459,234**	**1,596,500**	**1,767,602**
Wages and salaries	271,932	362,005	546,453	805,872	1,227,397	1,343,600	1,493,964
Private	222,782	292,145	430,481	630,431	993,910	1,090,000	1,210,858
Government	49,150	69,860	115,972	175,441	233,487	253,600	283,106
Supplements to wages, salary	23,000	34,538	62,697	125,207	231,837	252,900	273,638
Employer contrib. for social ins.	11,780	16,698	30,680	60,079	109,147	115,800	133,219
Other labor income	11,220	17,840	32,017	65,128	122,690	137,100	140,419
Proprietors' income	**46,978**	**56,674**	**65,140**	**86,980**	**130,775**	**130,600**	**124,700**
Business and professional	35,558	44,106	51,208	63,509	97,965	107,200	100,745
Inventory valuation adj.	91	-198	-506	-1,164	-2,974	-3,700	-1,589
Farm	11,420	12,568	13,932	23,471	32,810	23,400	23,955
Rental income of persons	**13,758**	**17,117**	**18,644**	**22,426**	**26,908**	**31,800**	**33,878**
Corp. prof., with inv. adjust.	**46,580**	**77,096**	**67,891**	**95,902**	**178,158**	**182,700**	**190,630**
Corp. profits before tax	48,540	75,209	71,485	120,378	236,638	245,500	232,076
Corp. profits tax liability	22,696	30,876	34,477	49,811	92,531	82,300	81,175
Corp. profits after tax	25,844	44,333	37,008	70,567	144,107	163,200	150,901
Dividends	12,890	19,120	22,884	31,885	52,735	56,000	65,097
Undistributed profits	12,954	25,213	14,124	38,682	91,372	107,200	85,804
Inventory valuation adj.	327	-1,865	-5,067	-12,432	-41,769	-45,700	-24,614
Net interest	**9,760**	**18,529**	**37,549**	**78,615**	**129,741**	**179,800**	**235,653**
National income	**412,008**	**565,959**	**798,374**	**1,215,002**	**1,924,814**	**2,121,400**	**2,352,463**

Appropriations by the Federal Government

Source: U.S. Treasury Department, Bureau of Govt. Financial Operations (fiscal year)

Year	Appropriations	Year	Appropriations	Year	Appropriations	Year	Appropriations
1890	$395,430,284.26	1940	$13,349,202,681.73	1959	$82,055,863,758.58	1972	$247,638,104,722.57
1895	492,477,759.97	1944	118,411,173,965.24	1960	80,169,728,902.87	1973	275,554,945,383.88
1900	698,912,982.83	1945	73,067,712,071.39	1961	89,229,575,129.94	1974	311,728,034,120.95
1905	781,288,215.95	1950	52,867,672,466.21	1962	91,447,827,731.00	1975	374,124,469,875.62
1910	1,044,433,622.64	1952	127,788,153,262.97	1963	102,149,886,566.52	1976	403,740,395,600.61
1915	1,122,471,919.12	1953	94,916,821,231.67	1965	107,555,087,622.62	1977	466,559,809,964.06
1920	6,454,596,649.56	1954	74,744,844,304.88	1967	140,861,235,376.56	1978	507,782,291,489.99
1925	3,748,651,750.35	1955	54,761,172,461.58	1969	203,049,351,090.91	1979	563,960,833,788.25
1930	4,665,236,678.04	1956	63,857,731,203.86	1970	222,200,021,901.52	1980	690,391,124,920.77
1935	7,527,559,327.66	1958	77,145,934,082.25	1971	247,623,820,964.75	1981	744,409,241,781.90

Note: Through 1976 the fiscal year ended June 30. From 1977 on, fiscal year ends Sept. 30.

Public Debt of the U.S.

Source: U.S. Treasury Department, Bureau of Govt. Financial Operations

Fiscal year	Gross debt	Per cap.	Fiscal year	Gross debt	Per cap.	Fiscal year	Gross debt	Per cap.
1870	$2,436,453,269	$61.06	1930	$16,185,309,831	$131.51	1975	$533,188,976,772	$2,496.90
1880	2,090,908,872	41.60	1940	42,967,531,038	325.23	1977	698,839,928,356	3,215.59
1890	1,132,396,584	17.80	1950	256,087,352,351	1,688.30	1978	771,544,478,952	3,521.78
1900	1,263,416,913	16.60	1960	284,092,760,848	1,572.31	1979	826,519,096,841	3,736.86
1910	1,146,939,969	12.41	1965	313,818,898,984	1,612.70	1980	907,701,290,900	3,969.55
1920	24,299,321,467	228.23	1970	370,093,706,950	1,807.09	1981	997,854,525,000	p4,329.52

(p) Preliminary. Note: Through 1976 the fiscal year ended June 30. From 1977 on, fiscal year ends Sept. 30.

National Income by Industry

Source: Bureau of Economic Analysis, U.S. Commerce Department
(millions of dollars)

	1960	1965	1970	1975	1979	1980	1981
Agricul., forestry, fisheries	**17,468**	**20,366**	**24,455**	**42,827**	**65,822**	**58,455**	**68,708**
Farms	16,452	18,805	22,191	39,379	59,296	51,549	61,067
Agri. services, forestry, fisheries	1,016	1,561	2,264	3,448	6,526	6,906	7,641
Mining	**5,613**	**6,013**	**7,810**	**18,149**	**30,089**	**37,383**	**44,933**
Metal mining	807	856	1,179	1,635	2,759	3,067	3,535
Coal mining	1,286	1,372	2,231	6,228	8,382	9,531	9,655
Crude petroleum, natural gas	2,606	2,670	3,099	8,075	15,674	21,001	27,968
Nonmetallic min. & quar.	914	1,115	1,301	2,211	3,274	3,784	3,775
Contract construction	**20,972**	**29,840**	**43,821**	**61,795**	**104,262**	**108,454**	**113,351**
Manufacturing	**125,448**	**170,361**	**215,388**	**312,467**	**508,887**	**525,575**	**580,780**
Nondurable goods	**51,818**	**65,416**	**88,088**	**127,942**	**198,300**	**216,157**	**235,991**
Food, kindred products	12,150	14,232	19,579	30,020	38,090	41,384	46,794
Tobacco manufactures	1,020	1,096	1,696	2,155	3,849	4,401	5,114
Textile mill products	4,484	5,872	7,525	8,754	13,673	13,599	14,549
Apparel, other fabric prod.	4,933	6,494	8,722	10,773	15,284	15,761	17,058
Paper, allied products	4,706	6,005	7,968	11,833	19,285	19,666	21,238
Printing, pub., allied industry	6,666	8,725	11,883	16,672	26,010	28,247	30,684
Chemicals, allied products	9,106	12,398	16,042	23,820	35,451	33,749	42,652
Petroleum and coal products	4,396	4,811	6,632	12,893	28,298	36,394	35,809
Rubber, misc. plastic products	2,751	3,939	5,804	8,661	15,098	15,151	18,024
Leather, leather products	1,606	1,844	2,237	2,361	3,262	3,805	4,069
Durable goods	**73,630**	**104,945**	**127,300**	**184,525**	**310,587**	**309,418**	**344,789**
Lumber, wood, except furn.	3,362	4,534	5,537	8,936	17,046	15,246	15,068
Furniture and fixtures	2,098	2,904	3,715	4,588	7,727	7,791	8,405
Stone, clay, glass products	4,620	5,654	6,891	9,858	17,104	16,457	16,885
Primary metal industries	11,066	14,491	15,757	24,231	38,428	38,434	43,251
Fabricated metal products	8,124	11,475	14,812	24,300	39,917	40,819	44,751
Machinery, except electrical	11,919	18,239	24,353	36,801	63,790	67,572	75,681
Electric and electronic equipment	10,496	14,855	20,132	26,646	45,004	48,413	53,571
Transport equip. exc. autos	8,266	11,330	14,480	15,715	26,259	29,666	32,548
Motor vehicles and equipment	8,399	14,455	12,086	19,045	32,424	19,568	25,365
Instruments	2,948	4,128	5,797	9,006	15,317	17,564	20,121
Misc. manufacturing	2,332	2,880	3,740	5,399	7,571	7,888	9,143
Transportation	**18,141**	**23,069**	**30,308**	**44,455**	**75,739**	**81,174**	**86,985**
Railroad	6,710	7,016	7,612	9,987	15,937	16,789	18,127
Local; interurban passenger transit	1,619	1,897	2,308	2,933	3,841	4,291	4,475
Motor freight trans., warehousing	5,886	8,396	11,830	18,935	32,046	33,512	35,903
Water transportation	1,635	1,982	2,503	3,323	5,384	6,148	6,854
Air transportation	1,370	2,636	4,358	7,062	12,518	13,730	14,404
Pipeline transportation	350	390	528	820	1,745	1,919	1,987
Transportation service	571	752	1,169	1,935	4,268	4,785	5,235
Communication	**8,228**	**11,497**	**17,600**	**27,066**	**43,367**	**48,884**	**55,337**
Telephone and telegraph	7,293	10,255	15,887	24,358	38,315	43,240	49,139
Radio broadcasting, television	935	1,242	1,713	2,708	5,052	5,644	6,198
Electric, gas, sanitary services	**8,923**	**11,442**	**14,864**	**24,302**	**35,793**	**41,037**	**48,569**
Wholesale and retail trade	**64,737**	**84,662**	**122,213**	**194,227**	**296,595**	**315,613**	**353,227**
Wholesale trade	23,420	30,469	44,860	80,564	126,333	137,350	155,768
Retail trade	41,317	54,193	77,353	113,663	170,262	178,263	197,459
Finance, ins. and real estate	**48,608**	**63,987**	**92,625**	**140,375**	**261,597**	**295,501**	**324,201**
Banking	7,255	8,943	16,448	20,109	39,629	44,354	48,518
Credit agencies, other than banks	−1,076	−1,617	−1,981	−4,729	4,650	3,183	1,270
Security, commodity brokers	1,219	1,942	2,733	4,144	6,804	8,773	11,693
Insurance carriers	4,816	5,880	9,269	12,751	26,978	29,092	29,749
Insurance agents, brokers, service	2,070	2,957	4,223	6,704	11,151	12,476	13,754
Real estate	33,940	45,741	61,812	100,078	172,749	198,300	221,221
Holding and other investment cos.	384	141	121	1,318	−364	−677	−2,004
Services	**44,648**	**64,142**	**103,304**	**168,516**	**273,986**	**309,941**	**349,358**
Hotels, other lodging places	2,114	2,964	4,659	6,952	12,623	14,203	16,302
Personal services	4,608	5,965	7,436	8,329	12,454	13,360	14,342
Misc. business services	5,091	8,399	14,051	23,928	46,527	53,859	61,861
Automobile repair, serv., garages	1,746	2,402	3,616	5,944	10,425	11,013	12,099
Misc. repair services	1,094	1,494	2,149	3,478	5,811	6,739	7,494
Motion pictures	891	1,201	1,581	1,842	4,106	4,272	4,758
Amusement, recreation services	1,662	2,201	3,321	5,268	8,120	8,524	9,582
Medical, other health services	10,636	15,790	29,472	54,075	86,109	99,249	114,021
Legal services	2,695	4,197	6,691	11,828	18,443	21,347	23,376
Education services	2,419	4,145	6,688	10,014	14,029	15,388	17,000
Social Services	—	—	—	5,003	8,286	9,518	10,699
Nonprofit membership org.	4,176	5,787	8,912	11,016	14,148	15,584	16,660
Misc. professional services	3,719	5,629	9,673	15,030	26,444	30,300	34,127
Private households	3,797	3,968	5,055	5,809	6,461	6,585	7,037
Government, government enterprises	**52,707**	**75,374**	**127,421**	**199,875**	**277,060**	**306,157**	**335,988**
Federal	25,303	33,303	53,093	72,007	93,301	102,677	113,597
General Government	21,676	28,298	44,723	58,976	75,672	82,879	92,313
Government enterprises	3,627	5,005	8,370	13,031	17,629	19,798	21,284
State & local	27,404	42,071	74,328	127,868	183,759	203,480	222,391
General Government	25,470	39,294	69,964	119,641	171,772	189,929	207,392
Government enterprises	1,934	2,777	4,364	8,227	11,987	13,551	14,999
Domestic income	**415,493**	**560,753**	**799,809**	**1,234,054**	**1,973,197**	**2,128,174**	**2,361,437**
Rest of the world	**2,477**	**4,681**	**4,616**	**10,534**	**42,572**	**46,073**	**49,180**
All industries, total	**417,970**	**565,434**	**804,425**	**1,244,588**	**2,015,769**	**2,174,247**	**2,410,617**

U.S. Currency and Coin

Source: U.S. Treasury Department (June 30, 1982)

Amounts in Circulation and Outstanding

	Amounts in circulation	Add amounts held by: United States Treasury	Add amounts held by: Federal Reserve Banks	Amounts outstanding
Currency				
Federal Reserve Notes[1]	$134,234,239,456	$3,264,039	$19,795,479,602	$154,032,983,097
United States Notes	304,438,577	18,100,439	.....	322,539,016
Currency No Longer Issued	275,445,099	198,334	36,292	275,679,725
Total	**134,814,123,132**	**21,562,812**	**19,795,515,894**	**154,631,201,838**
Coin[2]				
Dollars[3]	$1,505,332,991	$362,978,399	$156,392,508	[3]$2,024,703,898
Fractional Coin	11,850,570,780	52,862,292	250,922,928	12,154,356,000
Total	**13,355,903,771**	**415,840,691**	**407,315,436**	**14,179,059,898**
Total currency and coin	**148,170,026,903**	**437,403,503**	**20,202,831,330**	**168,810,261,736**

Currency in Circulation by Denominations

Denomination	Total currency in circulation	Federal Reserve Notes[1]	United States Notes	Currency no longer issued
1 Dollar	$3,497,507,019	$3,343,184,850	$143,481	$154,178,688
2 Dollars	679,030,776	544,938,476	134,079,166	13,134
5 Dollars	4,556,750,255	4,403,064,500	113,722,410	39,963,345
10 Dollars	11,192,296,270	11,166,578,700	5,950	25,711,620
20 Dollars	42,470,808,160	42,450,470,080	3,380	20,334,700
50 Dollars	15,489,533,150	15,477,698,150	.....	11,835,000
100 Dollars	56,575,984,400	56,496,646,200	56,484,100	22,854,100
500 Dollars	160,461,500	160,268,500	.....	193,000
1,000 Dollars	186,416,000	186,205,000	.....	211,000
5,000 Dollars	1,835,000	1,785,000	.....	50,000
10,000 Dollars	3,500,000	3,400,000	.....	100,000
Fractional parts	487	.....	.....	487
Partial notes[4]	115	.....	90	25
Total currency	**134,814,123,132**	**134,234,239,456**	**304,438,577**	**275,445,099**

Comparative Totals of Money in Circulation — Selected Dates

Date	Amounts (in millions)	Per capita[5]	Date	Amounts (in millions)	Per capita[5]	Date	Amounts (in millions)	Per capita[5]
June 30, 1982	[6]$148,170.0	$638.77	June 30, 1955	$30,229.3	$182.90	June 30, 1930	$4,522.0	$36.74
June 30, 1981	138,080.2	600.86	June 30, 1950	27,156.3	179.03	June 30, 1925	4,815.2	41.56
June 30, 1975	81,196.4	380.08	June 30, 1945	26,746.4	191.14	June 30, 1920	5,467.6	51.36
June 30, 1970	54,351.0	265.39	June 30, 1940	7,847.5	59.40	June 30, 1915	3,319.6	33.01
June 30, 1965	39,719.8	204.14	June 30, 1935	5,567.1	43.75	June 30, 1910	3,148.7	34.07
June 30, 1960	32,064.6	177.47						

(1) Issued on and after July 1, 1929. (2) Excludes coin sold to collectors at premium prices. (3) Includes $481,781,898 in standard silver dollars. (4) Represents value of certain partial denominations not presented for redemption. (5) Based on Bureau of the Census estimates of population. (6) Highest amount to date.

The requirement for a gold reserve against U.S. notes was repealed by Public Law 90-269 approved Mar. 18, 1968. Silver certificates issued on and after July 1, 1929 became redeemable from the general fund on June 24, 1968. The amount of security after those dates has been reduced accordingly.

U.S. Money in Circulation, by Denominations

Source: U.S. Treasury Department, Bureau of Governmental Financial Operations

Outside Treasury and Federal Reserve Banks. (millions of dollars)

End of year	Total in circulation	Coin and small denomination: Total	Coin	$1	$2	$5	$10	$20	Large denomination currency: Total	$50	$100	$500	$1,000	$5,000	$10,000
1950	27,741	19,305	1,554	1,113	64	2,049	5,998	8,529	8,438	2,422	5,043	368	588	4	12
1960	32,869	23,521	2,427	1,533	88	2,246	6,691	10,536	9,348	2,815	5,954	249	316	3	10
1970	57,093	39,639	6,281	2,310	136	3,161	9,170	18,581	17,454	4,896	12,084	215	252	3	4
1975	86,547	54,866	8,959	2,809	135	3,841	10,777	28,344	31,681	8,157	23,139	175	204	2	4
1978	114,645	66,693	10,739	3,194	661	4,393	11,661	36,045	47,952	11,279	36,306	167	194	2	4
1979	125,600	70,693	11,658	3,308	671	4,549	11,894	38,613	54,907	12,585	41,960	164	192	2	4
1980	137,244	73,893	12,419	3,499	677	4,635	11,924	40,739	63,352	13,731	49,264	163	189	2	3

Seigniorage on Coin and Silver Bullion

Source: U.S. Treasury Department, Bureau of Govt. Financial Operations

Seigniorage is the profit from coining money; it is the difference between the monetary value of coins and their cost, including the manufacturing expense.

Fiscal year	Total	Fiscal year	Total
Jan. 1, 1935-June 30, 1965, cumulative	$2,525,927,763.84	1976	$769,722,066.00
1968	383,141,339.00[1]	1977	407,022,950.00
1970	274,217,884.01	1978	367,156,260.25
1972	580,586,683.00	1979	991,909,496.55
1974	320,706,638.49	1980	662,814,791.48
1975	660,898,070.69	1981	450,174,439.26
		Cumulative Jan. 1, 1935-Sept. 30, 1981	10,524,282,518.23

(1) Revised to include seigniorage on clad coins.

Bureau of the Mint

Source: Bureau of the Mint, U.S. Treasury Department

The first United States Mint was established in Philadelphia, Pa., then the nation's capital, by the Act of April 2, 1792, which provided for gold, silver, and copper coinage. Originally, supervision of the Mint was a function of the secretary of state, but in 1799 it became an independent agency reporting directly to the president. When the Coinage Act of 1873 was passed, all mint and assay office activities were placed under a newly organized Bureau of the Mint in the Department of the Treasury.

The Bureau of the Mint manufactures all U.S. coins and distributes them through the Federal Reserve banks and branches. The Mint also maintains physical custody of the Treasury's monetary stocks of gold and silver, moving, storing and releasing from custody as authorized. Functions performed by the Mint on a reimbursable basis include: the manufacture and sale of medals of a national character, the production and sale of numismatic coins and coin sets and, as scheduling permits, the manufacture of foreign coins.

The traditional 90% silver coinage was gradually phased out and cupronickel clad coinage introduced when the Coinage Act of 1965 removed all silver from the dime and quarter and reduced the silver content of the half dollar to 40%. P.L. 91-607, approved Dec. 31, 1970, removed the remaining silver from the half dollar, and in providing for the resumption of dollar coinage, directed that both denominations produced for circulation also be cupronickel clad metal. P.L. 95-447, approved Oct. 10, 1978, further amended the Coinage Act of 1965 to provide for changes in the design, weight and size of the $1 coin. Beginning in January 1979, the likeness of Susan B. Anthony has appeared on the obverse with the Apollo II Moon Landing on the reverse. The new small dollar weighs 8.1 grams and has a diameter of 26.5 millimeters.

The composition of the 5-cent coin continues to be 75% copper and 25% nickel. The traditional 95% copper cent is being replaced with a copper-plated zinc coin. Production commenced early in 1982. Both types are circulating simultaneously. The new cents are identical in size, shape, color and design to the predominantly copper cents but are somewhat lighter, having a standard weight of 2.50 grams as opposed to the 3.11 gram standard weight of the copper cent. They contain 2.4% copper and 97.6% zinc. The core is an alloy of zinc with 0.8% copper. The outer surface is barrel electroplated with copper.

P.L. 97-104, approved December 23, 1981, directed the production for public sale of up to 10 million 90% silver half dollars commemorating the 250th anniversary, in 1982, of the birth of George Washington. This is the first time a special commemorative coin has been issued for the government's own account in a design reserved solely for the commemorative issue and not intended for general circulation. It is also the first time since 1964 that a 90% silver coin has been produced by the U.S. Mint.

Special coinage commemorating the 1984 Olympic Games in Los Angeles will be issued in 1983 and 1984. P.L. 97-220, approved July 22, 1982, authorized two 90% silver $1 coins to be dated 1983 and 1984, and a 90% gold $10 coin dated 1984, marking the event.

Calendar year coinage production for 1981 follows:

Domestic Coinage Executed During Calendar Year 1981

Denomination	Philadelphia	Denver	San Francisco	Total value	Total pieces
Dollars—non-silver	**$ 3,000,000.00**	**$ 3,250,000.00**	**$ 3,492,000.00**	**$ 9,742,000.00**	**9,742,000**
Subsidiary					
Half dollars	$ 14,772,000.00	$ 13,919,766.50	-0-	$ 28,691,766.50	57,383,533
Quarter dollars	150,429,000.00	143,930,708.25	-0-	294,359,708.25	1,177,438,833
Dimes	67,665,000.00	71,228,414.30	-0-	138,893,414.30	1,388,934,143
Total subsidiary	**$232,866,000.00**	**$229,078,889.05**	**-0-**	**$461,944,889.05**	**2,623,756,509**
Minor					
Five-cent pieces	$ 32,875,200.00	$ 18,240,092.15	-0-	$ 51,115,292.15	1,022,305,843
One-cent pieces[1]	66,113,050.00	53,732,356.77	$ 8,804,450.00	128,649,856.77	12,864,985,677[1]
Total minor,	**$ 98,988,250.00**	**$ 71,972,448.92**	**$ 8,804,450.00**	**$179,765,148.92**	**13,887,291,152**
Total domestic coinage	**$334,854,250.00**	**$304,301,337.97**	**$12,296,450.00**	**$651,452,037.97**	**16,520,789,661**

Delivered by San Francisco Assay Office

1980 Proof sets	1,410,575
1981 Proof sets	4,063,083
Bicentennial 40% silver proof sets	156,117
Bicentennial 40% silver uncir. sets	46,623

Coinage Executed for Foreign Governments

Country	No. of pieces
Dominican Republic	13,520,000
Panama	10,000,000
Total	**23,520,000**

(1) Manufactured at West Point Depository—$18,824,000.00 (1,882,400,000 pieces)

Portraits on U.S. Treasury Bills, Bonds, Notes and Savings Bonds

Denomination	Savings bonds	Treas. bills	Treas. bonds	Treas. notes
25	Washington			
50	F.D. Roosevelt		Jefferson	
75	Truman			
100	Eisenhower		Jackson	
200	Kennedy			
500	Wilson		Washington	
1,000	T. Roosevelt	H. McCulloch	Lincoln	Lincoln
5,000	McKinley	J.G. Carlisle	Monroe	Monroe
10,000	Cleveland	J. Sherman	Cleveland	Cleveland
50,000		C. Glass		
100,000		A Gallatin	Grant	Grant
1,000,000		O. Wolcott	T. Roosevelt	T. Roosevelt
100,000,000				Madison
500,000,000				McKinley

Large Denominations of U.S. Currency Discontinued

The largest denomination of United States currency now being issued is the $100 bill. Issuance of currency in denominations of $500, $1000, $5,000 and $10,000 was discontinued in 1969 because their use had declined sharply over the previous two decades.

As large denomination bills reach the Federal Reserve Bank they are removed from circulation.

Because some of the discontinued currency is expected to be in the hands of holders for many years, the description of the various denominations below is continued:

Amt.	Portrait	Embellishment on back
$ 1	Washington	Great Seal of U.S.
2	Jefferson	Signers of Declaration
5	Lincoln	Lincoln Memorial
10	Hamilton	U.S. Treasury
20	Jackson	White House
50	Grant	U.S. Capitol

Amt.	Portrait	Embellishment on back
$ 100	Franklin	Independence Hall
500	McKinley	Ornate denominational marking
1,000	Cleveland	Ornate denominational marking
5,000	Madison	Ornate denominational marking
10,000	Chase	Ornate denominational marking
100,000*	Wilson	Ornate denominational marking

*For use only in transactions between Federal Reserve System and Treasury Department.

Gold Reserves of Central Banks and Governments

Source: IMF, *International Financial Statistics*
(Million fine troy ounces)

Year end	All countries[1]	Int'l Monetary Fund	United States	Canada	Japan	Belgium	France	Fed. Rep. of Germany	Italy	Netherlands	Switzerland	United Kingdom
1965	1,193.59	53.40	401.86	32.88	9.37	44.52	134.46	126.00	68.68	50.19	86.91	64.72
1966	1,165.65	75.77	378.14	29.87	9.40	43.56	149.66	122.62	68.97	49.45	81.17	55.44
1967	1,126.38	76.63	344.71	29.00	9.66	42.26	149.54	120.79	68.57	48.91	88.26	36.89
1968	1,107.37	65.37	311.20	24.66	10.17	43.53	110.77	129.69	83.52	48.51	74.97	42.10
1969	1,112.86	66.00	338.83	24.92	11.80	43.40	101.34	116.56	84.46	49.16	75.49	42.03
1970	1,057.88	123.97	316.34	22.59	15.20	42.01	100.91	113.70	82.48	51.06	78.03	38.54
1971	1,026.96	135.20	291.60	22.69	19.43	44.12	100.66	116.47	82.40	54.53	83.11	22.15
1972	1,017.98	153.43	275.97	21.95	21.11	43.08	100.69	117.36	82.37	54.17	83.11	21.05
1973	1,020.47	153.43	275.97	21.95	21.11	42.17	100.91	117.61	82.48	54.33	83.20	21.03
1974	1,018.91	153.40	275.97	21.95	21.11	42.17	100.93	117.61	82.48	54.33	83.20	21.03
1975	1,017.76	153.43	274.71	21.95	21.11	42.17	100.93	117.61	82.48	54.33	83.20	21.03
1976	1,012.90	149.51	274.68	21.62	21.11	42.17	101.02	117.61	82.48	54.33	83.28	21.03
1977	1,027.83	131.57	277.55	22.01	21.62	42.45	101.67	118.30	82.91	54.63	83.28	22.22
1978	1,034.84	118.20	276.41	22.13	23.97	42.59	101.99	118.64	83.12	54.78	83.28	22.82
1979	943.09	106.83	264.60	22.18	24.23	34.21	81.92	95.25	66.71	43.97	83.28	18.25
1980	950.82	103.43	264.32	20.98	24.23	34.18	81.85	95.18	66.67	43.94	83.28	18.84

(1) Covers IMF members with reported gold holdings, Switzerland and Netherlands Antilles. For countries not listed above, see *International Financial Statistics*, a monthly publication of the International Monetary Fund.

World Gold Production

Source: Bureau of Mines, U.S. Interior Department (in troy ounces)

Year	Estimated world prod.	Africa: South Africa	Africa: Ghana	Africa: Zaire	North and South America: United States	Canada	Mexico	Nicaragua	Colombia	Other: Australia	India	Japan	Philippines	All other
1970	47,522,342	32,164,107	707,900	180,590	1,743,322	2,408,574	198,241	115,173	201,519	619,922	104,200	225,189	602,715	8,220,890
1971	46,494,837	31,388,631	697,517	171,685	1,495,108	2,243,000	150,915	121,134	188,847	672,106	118,569	255,255	637,048	8,355,022
1972	44,843,374	29,245,273	724,051	140,724	1,449,943	2,078,567	146,061	112,340	188,137	754,866	105,776	243,027	606,730	9,047,879
1973	43,296,755	27,494,603	722,531	133,642	1,175,750	1,954,340	132,557	85,051	215,876	554,278	105,390	188,274	572,250	9,962,213
1974	40,124,290r	24,388,203	r614,007	130,603	1,126,886	1,698,392	134,454	82,639	265,195	r512,611	101,114	r139,719	r537,615	r10,392,852
1975	38,476,371r	22,937,820	523,889	103,217	1,052,252	r1,653,611	r144,710	70,281	r308,864	r526,821	r90,826	r143,503	r502,577	r10,418,000
1976	39,024,485r	r22,936,018	532,473	91,093	1,048,037	1,691,806	162,811	75,841	300,307	502,741	100,696	r137,643	501,210	10,943,809
1977	38,906,145r	22,501,886	480,884	80,418	1,100,347	1,733,609	212,709	65,764	r257,070	r624,270	96,902	r149,004	r558,554	r11,044,728
1978	38,983,019r	22,648,558	402,034	76,077	998,832	1,735,077	202,003	r73,947	r246,446	647,579	89,186	145,240	586,531	r11,131,509
1979	38,768,978r	r22,617,179	362,000	69,992	r964,390	1,644,265	r190,364	61,086	269,369	596,910	r84,781	127,626	r535,166	r11,245,850
1980p	39,141,041	21,669,468	r353,000	39,963	r969,782	r1,627,477	r195,991	e60,000	r510,439	r544,022	78,834	r102,339	r589,965	r12,399,761
1981e	40,784,803	21,121,157	330,000	70,000	1,377,946	1,512,526	185,000	50,000	535,000	530,000	80,000	99,314	670,000	14,223,860

(e) estimated (p) preliminary (r) revised

U.S. and World Silver Production

Source: Bureau of Mines, U.S. Interior Department

Largest production of silver in the United States in 1915—74,961,075 fine ounces.

Year (Cal.)	United States: Fine ozs.	United States: Value	World Fine ozs.
1930	50,748,127	$19,538,000	248,708,426
1935	45,924,454	33,008,000	220,704,231
1940	69,585,734	49,483,000	275,387,000
1945	29,063,255	20,667,200	162,000,000
1950	43,308,739	38,291,545	203,300,000
1955	36,469,610	33,006,839	224,000,000
1960	36,000,000	33,305,858	241,300,000
1965	39,806,033	51,469,201	257,415,000
1970	45,006,000	79,697,000	310,891,000
1975	34,938,000	154,424,000	303,112,000
1978	39,385,000	212,681,000	345,428,000
1979	33,896,000	420,261,000	344,821,000
1980	32,329,000	667,278,000	338,798,000
1981	40,685,000	427,943,000	364,912,000

50 Stocks Most Widely Held by Investment Companies

Source: Vickers Associates, Inc.

Publicly-held issues throughout the U.S. in order of number of institutions, etc., which held shares, as of Mar. 31, 1982.

IBM
A T & T
Schlumberger Ltd.
Philip Morris
Exxon Corp.
General Electric
Eastman Kodak
Digital Equip.
Smithkline Beckman
Atlantic Richfield
Minn. Mining & Manuf.
Warner Comm.
Union Carbide
Xerox Corp.
Union Oil of Cal.
Monsanto Co.
McDonald's Corp.
Halliburton Co.
Johnson & Johnson
General Motors
Gulf Oil Corp.
Pfizer Inc.
Hewlett Packard Co.
Citicorp
Texaco Inc.
Northwest Airlines
Royal Dutch Petrol.
Tandy Corp.
Phillips Petrol.
K Mart Corp.
PepsiCo Inc.
Bristol Myers Co.
Mobil Corp.
Travelers Corp.
Standard Oil of Ind.
R.J. Reynolds
AMP Inc.
Superior Oil Co.
JC Penney
Goodyear Tire
Syntex Corp.
Merck & Co. Inc.
Texas Oil & Gas Corp.
Toys R Us
Standard Oil of Cal.
Sterling Drug Inc.
J.P. Morgan
Procter & Gamble
General Tel. & Elec.
Amer. Express Co.

Corporations and Stocks

Stock Exchanges Trade 14.7 Billion Shares in U.S. Firms in 1981

The Securities and Exchange Commission reported in 1982 that 14.7 billion shares of stock were traded on the New York, American, and other U.S. stock exchanges in 1981.

The N.Y. Stock Exchange listed 2,214 issues of 1,547 companies for a total of 38.9 billion shares, valued on June 31, 1982, at $1.02 trillion. Average daily trading was 52.3 million through July 31, 1982, compared to 47.8 million in 1981.

The American Stock Exchange listed 959 issues of 828 companies. Average daily volume through Aug. 31, 1982, was 4.11 million shares.

A 1980 count indicated that 29.8 million persons owned shares in American corporations.

N.Y. Stock Exchange Transactions and Seat Prices

Source: New York Stock Exchange

Year	Yearly volumes: Stock shares	Yearly volumes: Bonds par values	Seat price: High	Seat price: Low
1900	138,981,000	$579,293,000	$47,500	$37,500
1905	260,569,000	1,026,254,000	85,000	72,000
1910	163,705,000	634,863,000	94,000	65,000
1915	172,497,000	961,700,000	74,000	38,000
1920	227,636,000	3,868,422,000	115,000	85,000
1925	459,717,623	3,427,042,210	150,000	99,000
1929	1,124,800,410	2,996,398,000	625,000	550,000
1930	810,632,546	2,720,301,800	480,000	205,000
1935	381,635,752	3,339,458,000	140,000	65,000
1940	207,599,749	$1,669,438,000	$60,000	$33,000
1950	524,799,621	1,112,425,170	54,000	46,000
1960	766,693,818	1,346,419,750	162,000	135,000
1970	2,937,359,448	4,494,864,600	320,000	130,000
1975	4,693,427,000	5,178,300,000	138,000	55,000
1979	8,155,914,000	4,087,890,000	210,000	82,000
1980	11,352,294,000	5,190,304,000	275,000	175,000
1981	*11,853,740,659	5,733,071,000	285,000	220,000

*Record high for trading in stocks.

American Stock Exchange Transactions and Seat Prices

Source: American Stock Exchange

Year	Yearly volumes: Stock shares	Yearly volumes: Bonds[1] princ. amts.	Seat price: High	Seat price: Low
1929	476,140,375	$513,551,000	$254,000	$150,000
1930	222,270,065	863,541,000	225,000	70,000
1940	42,928,337	303,902,000	7,250	6,900
1945	143,309,392	167,333,000	32,000	12,000
1950	107,792,340	47,549,000	11,000	6,500
1960	286,039,982	$32,670,000	$60,000	$51,000
1970	843,116,260	641,270,000	180,000	70,000
1975	457,610,360	259,128,000	72,000	34,000
1980	1,626,072,625	355,723,000	252,000	95,000
1981	1,343,400,220	301,226,000	275,000	200,000

(1) corporate

U.S. Industrials with Largest Annual Sales and Income

Source: Reprinted by permission from The FORTUNE Directory; © 1982 Time Inc.

Company	Sales (thousands)	Income (or loss) (thousands)
Exxon	$108,107,688	$5,567,481
Mobil	64,488,000	2,433,000
General Motors	62,698,500	333,400
Texaco	57,628,000	2,310,000
Standard Oil of California	44,224,000	2,380,000
Ford Motor	38,247,100	(1,060,100)
Standard Oil (Indiana)	29,947,000	1,922,000
International Business Machines	29,070,000	3,308,000
Gulf Oil	28,252,000	1,231,000
Atlantic Richfield	27,797,436	1,671,290
General Electric	27,240,000	1,652,000
E.I. du Pont de Nemours	22,810,000	1,401,000
Shell Oil	21,629,000	1,701,000
International Telephone & Telegraph	17,306,189	676,804
Phillips Petroleum	15,966,000	879,000
Tenneco	15,462,000	813,000
Sun	15,012,000	1,076,000
Occidental Petroleum	14,707,543	722,216
U.S. Steel	13,940,500	1,077,200
United Technologies	13,667,758	457,686
Standard Oil (Ohio)	13,457,091	1,946,898
Western Electric	13,008,000	711,300
Getty Oil	12,887,360	856,865
Dow Chemical	11,873,000	564,000
Procter & Gamble	$11,416,000	$ 593,000
Chrysler	10,821,600	(475,600)
Union Oil of California	10,745,900	791,400
Eastman Kodak	10,337,000	1,239,000
Dart & Kraft	10,211,000	347,500
Union Carbide	10,168,000	649,000
Boeing	9,788,200	473,000
R.J. Reynolds Industries	9,765,700	767,800
Ameranda Hess	9,396,219	212,591
Westinghouse Electric	9,367,500	438,000
Ashland Oil	9,262,076	90,032
Marathon Oil	9,219,991	343,059
Caterpillar Tractor	9,154,500	578,900
Goodyear Tire & Rubber	9,152,905	260,295
Cities Service	8,899,300	(49,200)
LTV	8,822,700	386,300
Beatrice Foods	8,772,804	304,211
Xerox	8,691,000	598,200
Philip Morris	8,306,600	676,200
RCA	8,004,800	54,000
McDonnell Douglas	7,384,900	176,600
International Harvester	7,327,165	(393,128)
Bethlehem Steel	7,298,000	210,900
Rockwell International	7,039,700	291,800
PepsiCo	7,027,443	333,456
Monsanto	6,947,700	445,100

Largest Losses by U.S. Industrials, 1981

Source: Reprinted by permission from The FORTUNE Director©; 1982 Time, Inc.

Company	Sales rank	Loss (000)
Ford Motor	6	$1,060,100
Chrysler	26	475,600
Kaiser Steel	310	437,455
International Harvester	46	393,128
Lockheed	57	288,800
AM International	342	245,051
Commonwealth Oil Refining	314	212,309
American Motors	162	136,563
Coastal	59	96,399
Gulf Resources & Chemical	459	77,929
U.S. Industries	285	62,671
Envirotech	484	55,987
Cities Service	39	49,200
McLouth Steel	385	40,000
Fiat-Allis	474	39,975
Allis-Chalmers	188	28,841
DPF	399	24,364
Pabst Brewing	397	23,536
J.P. Stevens	189	22,874
Jos. Schlitz Brewing	335	20,604
Hoover	376	18,778
Westmoreland Coal	480	14,775
Lever Brothers	281	11,500
Certain Teed	334	10,916
Rath Packing	491	9,582
American Bakeries	451	7,690
Scovill	331	4,534
Varian Associates	400	3,554

30 Largest Industrials Outside the U.S.

Source: Reprinted by permission from The FORTUNE World Business Directory; © 1981 Time Inc.

Company	Sales (thousands)	Income (or loss) (thousands)
Royal Dutch/Shell Group, N-B	$77,114,243	$5,174,282
British Petroleum, B	48,035,941	3,337,121
ENI, It	27,186,939	98,046
Fiat, It	25,155,000	NA
Française des Pétroles, F	23,940,355	946,772
Unilever, B-N	23,607,516	658,820
Renault, F	18,979,278	160,165
Petróleos de Venezuela, V	18,818,931	3,450,921
Elf Aquitaine, E	18,430,074	1,378,222
Philips' Gloeilampenfabrieken, N	18,402,818	165,210
Volkswagenwerk, G	18,339,046	170,964
Siemens, G	17,950,253	332,434
Daimler-Benz, G	17,108,100	605,149
Peugeot, F	16,846,434	(348,998)
Hoechst, G	16,480,551	251,605
Bayer, G	15,880,596	356,342
BASF, G	15,277,348	197,641
Thyssen, G	15,235,998	61,611
Petrobrás, Br	14,836,326	767,419
Pemex, M	14,813,514	17,316
Nestlé, S	14,615,187	407,785
Toyota Motor, J	14,233,779	616,051
Nissan Motor, J	13,853,503	461,647
Imperial Chemical Industries, B	13,290,347	(46,510)
Nippon Steel, J	13,104,996	496,205
Hitachi, J	12,871,328	503,385
Matsushita Electric Industrial, J	12,684,404	541,923
Mitsubishi Heavy Industries, J	10,997,586	100,659
BAT Industries, B	10,987,175	323,247
Genérale d'Electricite, 7	10,847,129	96,407

National headquarters: B, Britain; Br. Brazil; F, France; G, West Germany; Ir, Iran; It, Italy; J, Japan; M, Mexico; N, Netherlands; S, Switzerland; V, Venezuela. NA—not available.

All Banks in U.S.—Number, Deposits

Source: Federal Reserve System

Comprises all national banks in the United States and all state commercial banks, trust companies, mutual stock savings banks, private and industrial banks, and special types of institutions that are treated as banks by the federal bank supervisory agencies.

	Number of banks						Total deposits (millions of dollars)					
		F.R.S. members			Nonmembers			F.R.S. members			Nonmembers	
Year (As of June 30)	Total all banks	Total	Nat'l	State	Mutual savings	Other	Total all banks	Total	Nat'l	State	Mutual savings	Other
1925	**26,479**	9,538	8,066	1,472	621	18,320	**51,641**	32,457	19,912	12,546	7,089	12,095
1930	**23,855**	8,315	7,247	1,068	604	14,936	**59,828**	38,069	23,235	14,834	9,117	12,642
1935	**16,047**	6,410	5,425	985	569	9,068	**51,149**	34,938	22,477	12,461	9,830	6,381
1940	**14,955**	6,398	5,164	1,234	551	8,008	**70,770**	51,729	33,014	18,715	10,631	8,410
1945	**14,542**	6,840	5,015	1,825	539	7,163	**151,033**	118,378	76,534	41,844	14,413	18,242
1950	**14,674**	6,885	4,971	1,914	527	7,262	**163,770**	122,707	82,430	40,277	19,927	21,137
1955	**14,309**	6,611	4,744	1,867	525	7,173	**208,850**	154,670	98,636	56,034	27,310	26,870
1960	**14,006**	6,217	4,542	1,675	513	7,276	**249,163**	179,519	116,178	63,341	35,316	34,328
1965	**14,295**	6,235	4,803	1,432	504	7,556	**362,611**	259,743	171,528	88,215	50,980	51,889
1970	**14,167**	5,805	4,638	1,167	496	7,866	**502,542**	346,289	254,322	91,967	69,285	86,968
1975, Dec. 31	**15,108**	5,787	4,741	1,046	475	8,846	**896,879**	590,999	447,590	143,409	110,569	195,311
1979, Dec. 31	**15,171**	5,425	4,448	977	463	9,283	**1,241,591**	781,947	594,970	186,977	141,970	317,675
1980, Dec. 31	**15,145**	5,422	4,425	997	460	9,263	**1,333,399**	843,028	651,846	191,182	150,000	340,371
1981, Dec. 31	**15,141**	5,475	4,454	1,021	441	9,225	**1,412,843**	898,405	704,591	193,814	146,192	368,247

Bank Rates on Short-term Business Loans

Source: Federal Reserve System

Percent per annum. Short-term loans mature within one year.

		All size loans							Size of loan in $1,000				
		Ave. 35 cities	N.Y. C.	7 Other N.E.	8 No. Cent.	7 S.E.	8 S.W.	4 West	1-9	10-99	100 to 499	500 to 999	1,000 and over
1967	Aug. 1-15	5.95	5.66	6.29	5.92	5.92	6.01	6.02	6.58	6.46	6.16	5.89	5.72
1970	Aug. 1-15	8.50	8.24	8.89	8.47	8.49	8.53	8.54	9.15	9.07	8.75	8.46	8.25
1974	May	11.15	11.08	11.65	11.09	10.88	10.82	11.19	10.50	11.06	11.41	11.32	11.06
1975	May	8.16	7.88	8.37	8.00	8.70	8.34	8.33	9.57	9.10	8.52	8.18	7.90
1976	Aug.	7.80	7.48	8.18	7.70	7.95	7.75	8.15	8.85	9.41	8.65	9.33	9.26
	Nov.	7.28	6.88	7.62	7.28	7.51	7.33	7.52	8.56	9.22	8.45	9.13	8.69

		Size of Loan in $1,000[1]						
		All sizes	1-24	25-49	50-99	100-499	500-999	1,000 and over
1977	Feb.	7.50	9.03	8.46	8.47	7.67	7.17	6.58
	May	7.40	9.09	8.43	8.07	7.60	7.13	6.67
1978	Feb.	8.90	9.65	9.45	9.29	9.05	8.79	8.34
	May	8.96	9.81	9.63	9.40	9.08	8.90	8.53
1979	Feb.	12.27	12.14	12.01	12.83	12.55	12.63	11.99
	May	12.34	12.30	12.69	13.02	12.61	12.68	12.07
1980	Feb.	15.67	15.06	15.54	15.91	16.23	16.34	15.50
	May	17.75	17.90	18.78	18.95	18.49	19.13	17.10
1981	Feb.	19.91	19.59	19.53	19.77	20.18	20.87	19.83
	May	19.99	19.45	19.87	19.10	19.93	19.58	20.14

(1) In Feb. 1977, The Quarterly Interest Rate Survey was replaced by the Survey of Terms of Bank Lending (STBL). The STBL is conducted in the middle month of each quarter at about 340 member and nonmember banks. The regional breakdown was discontinued at that time. The last previous revision began with the survey period of Feb. 1971. It incorporated a number of technical changes in coverage, sampling, and interest rate calculations.

Federal Reserve System

The Federal Reserve System is the central bank for the United States. The system was established on December 23, 1913, originally to give the country an elastic currency, to provide facilities for discounting commercial paper, and to improve the supervision of banking. Since then, the system's responsibilities have been broadened and, through the monitoring of money and credit growth, it helps work toward the nation's overall economic objectives of growth, high employment, the maintenance of a stable dollar, and a long-run balance in international payments.

The Federal Reserve System consists of the Board of Governors; the 12 District Reserve Banks and their branch offices; the Federal Open Market Committee; and, the system member banks. Several advisory councils help the Board meet its varied responsibilities.

The hub of the system is the seven member Board of Governors in Washington. The members of the board are appointed by the President and confirmed by the Senate, to serve 14-year terms. The President also appoints the Chairman and Vice-Chairman of the Board from among the board members for 4-year terms that may be renewed. Currently, the board members are: Paul A. Volcker, Chairman; Preston Martin, Vice Chairman; Henry C. Wallich; J. Charles Partee, Nancy H. Teeters; Emmett J. Rice, and; Lyle E. Gramley.

The board is the policy-making body. In addition to monetary policy responsibilities, it supervises the budget and operations of the Reserve Banks, approves the appointments of their presidents and appoints 3 of each District Bank's directors, including the chairman and vice chairman of each Reserve Bank's board.

The 12 Reserve Banks and their branch offices serve as the decentralized portion of the system, carrying out day-to-day operations such as circulating currency and coin, providing fiscal agency functions and payments mechanism services. The District Banks are located in Boston, New York, Philadelphia, Cleveland, Richmond, Atlanta, Chicago, St. Louis, Minneapolis, Kansas City, Dallas and San Francisco.

The system's principal function is monetary policy, which it controls using three tools: reserve requirements, the discount rate and open market operations. Uniform reserve requirements, set by the board, are applied to the transaction accounts and nonpersonal time deposits of all depository institutions. Responsibility for setting the discount rate (the interest rate at which depository institutions can borrow money from the Reserve Banks) is shared by the Board of Governors and the Reserve Banks. Discount rates are set by the individual boards of directors of the Federal Reserve Banks, subject to approval by the Board of Governors. The most important tool of monetary policy is open market operations (the purchase and sale of government securities). Responsibility for influencing the cost and availability of money and credit through the purchase and sale of government securities lies with the Federal Open Market Committee (FOMC). This committee is composed of the 7 members of the Board of Governors, the president of the Federal Reserve Bank of New York, and 4 other Federal Reserve Bank presidents, who serve on a rotating basis as voting members of the committee. The committee bases its decisions on current economic and financial developments and outlook, setting yearly growth objectives for key measures of money supply and bank credit. The decisions of the committee are carried out by the Domestic Trading Desk of the Federal Reserve Bank of New York.

At the end of 1981, about 5,500 commercial banks—out of a total of nearly 15,000 in the country—were members of the Federal Reserve System. These banks accounted for 71 percent of all bank deposits. National banks, which are chartered by the Comptroller of the Currency, are required by law to be members of the system. Banks chartered by any of the 50 states may elect to become members if they meet the requirements established by the Board of Governors.

The Federal Reserve Act prescribes a Federal Advisory Council, consisting of one member from each Federal Reserve District, elected annually by the Board of Directors of each of the 12 Federal Reserve Banks. They meet with the Federal Reserve Board at least four times a year to discuss business and financial conditions and to make advisory recommendations.

The Consumer Advisory Council is a statutory body, including both consumer and creditor representatives, which advises the Board of Governors on its implementation of consumer regulations and other consumer-related matters. In addition, in 1980 Congress passed the Monetary Control Act which established the Thrift Institutions Advisory Council (TIAC) to provide information and views on the special needs and problems of thrifts.

This piece of legislation also extended access to Federal Reserve discount and borrowing privileges and other services to nonmember depository institutions. The act required the Federal Reserve to set a schedule of fees of its services. And, it was through this act that the Depository Institutions Deregulations Committee (DIDC) was formed to provide for the orderly elimination of the limitations on the maximum rate of interest and dividends which may be paid on deposits by commercial banks, mutual savings banks, and savings and loan associations. Congress intended that the phase-out be completed by March 31, 1986. DIDC consists of the Secretary of the Treasury, the Chairman of the Board of Governors of the Federal Reserve System, the Chairman of the Board of Directors of the Federal Deposit Insurance Corporation, the Chairman of the Federal Home Loan Bank Board, and the Chairman of the National Credit Union Administration Board, each of whom has one vote, and the Comptroller of the Currency who is a nonvoting members.

Largest Banks Outside the U.S.

Source: 500 Largest Banks in the Free World, compiled by the American Banker, New York. (Copyright 1982) Based on deposits Dec. 31, 1981, or nearest fiscal year-end. (thousands of U.S. dollars)

Bank, country	Deposits
Banque Nationale de Paris, France	93,864,493
Credit Lyonnais, Paris, France	85,227,142
Barclays Bank Plc, London, United Kingdom	82,069,943
Credit Agricole Mutuél, Paris, France	81,532,981
Deutsche Bank, Frankfurt, Germany	79,178,568
Societe Generale, Paris, France	78,872,023
National Westminster Bank Plc, London, United Kingdom	76,082,443
Midland Bank Plc, London, United Kingdom	72,325,167
Dai-Ichi Kangyo Bank Ltd., Tokyo, Japan	67,613,876
Royal Bank of Canada, Montreal, Canada	62,903,983
Fuji Bank, Ltd., Tokyo, Japan	62,839,955
Sumitomo Bank Ltd., Osaka, Japan	62,132,908
Mitsubishi Bank Ltd., Tokyo, Japan	59,128,752
Sanwa Bank Ltd., Osaka, Japan	56,181,590
Dresdner Bank, Frankfurt, Germany	54,999,850
Westdeutsche Landesbank Girozentrale, Duesseldorf, Germany	53,293,337
Industrial Bank of Japan, Ltd., Tokyo, Japan	49,538,080
Lloyds Bank Plc, London, United Kingdom	48,492,043
Norinchukin Bank, Tokyo, Japan	47,967,274
Canadian Imperial Bank of Commerce, Toronto, Canada	47,592,092
Hongkong and Shanghai Banking Corp., Hong Kong, Hong Kong	47,562,829
Barclays Bank International Ltd., London, United Kingdom	45,510,747
Bank of Montreal, Canada	45,393,559
Algemene Bank Nederland, Amsterdam, Netherlands	44,644,967
Union Bank of Switzerland, Zurich, Switzerland	44,543,816
Mitsui Bank, Ltd., Tokyo, Japan	44,386,642
Swiss Bank Corp., Basle, Switzerland	43,853,418
Bank of Tokyo, Ltd., Japan	43,591,185
Tokai Bank Ltd., Nagoya, Japan	43,300,812
Commerzbank, Duesseldorf, Germany	43,025,817
Long-Term Credit Bank of Japan Ltd., Tokyo, Japan	41,499,681
Bayerische Vereinsbank, Munich, Germany	41,134,951
Amsterdam-Rotterdam Bank, Amsterdam, Netherlands	39,419,280
Banca Nazionale del Lavoro, Rome, Italy	38,771,209
Bayerische Hypotheken-und Wechsel-Bank, Munich, Germany	38,370,278
Mitsubishi Trust & Banking Corp., Tokyo, Japan	38,063,196
Bayerische Landesbank Girozentrale, Munich	37,915,457

Largest U.S. Commercial Banks

Source: Largest Commercial Banks in U.S., compiled by the American Banker, New York. (Copyright 1981) Based on deposits Dec. 31, 1981.

Rank	Bank	Deposits
1	Bank of America NT&SA, San Francisco	95,985,514,000
2	Citibank NA, New York	72,471,147,000
3	Chase Manhattan Bank NA, New York	58,585,662,000
4	Manufacturers Hanover Trust Co., New York	42,166,528,000
5	Morgan Guaranty Trust Co., New York	37,688,690,000
6	Chemical Bank, New York	30,673,591,000
7	Continental Illinois NB&T Co., Chicago	29,881,262,000
8	First National Bank, Chicago	25,867,640,000
9	Security Pacific National Bank, Los Angeles	23,441,590,827
10	Bankers Trust Co., New York	23,276,946,000
11	Wells Fargo Bank NA, San Francisco.	17,226,231,000
12	Crocker National Bank, San Francisco	16,516,627,000
13	First Interstate Bank of Calif., Los Angeles	14,556,481,000
14	Marine Midland Bank NA, Buffalo, N.Y.	14,188,360,000
15	Mellon Bank NA, Pittsburgh	12,498,583,000
16	Irving Trust Co., New York	12,381,224,000
17	First National Bank, Boston	10,490,450,000
18	Seattle-First National Bank	8,131,220,000
19	Bank of New York	8,080,264,605
20	First National Bank, Dallas	7,544,952,000
21	National Bank of Detroit	7,536,248,000
22	RepublicBank Dallas NA	7,130,456,000
23	First City National Bank, Houston	6,762,474,000
24	Texas Commerce Bank NA, Houston	5,819,287,000
25	Republic National Bank, New York	5,313,908,922
26	North Carolina National Bank, Charlotte	5,232,583,000
27	Union Bank, Los Angeles	5,206,310,000
28	Valley National Bank, Phoenix	5,027,360,000
29	Southeast Bank NA, Miami	5,008,198,000
30	National Bank of North America, New York	4,725,764,000
31	Harris Trust & Savings Bank, Chicago	4,574,817,000
32	Wachovia B&T Co. NA, Winston-Salem, N.C.	4,490,414,717
33	Pittsburgh National Bank	4,441,283,330
34	Philadelphia National Bank	4,410,424,000
35	Rainier National Bank, Seattle	4,319,135,000
36	Northern Trust Co., Chicago	4,318,122,000
37	BancOhio National Bank, Columbus	4,009,985,000
38	United States National Bank, Portland, Ore.	3,929,451,000
39	Detroit Bank & Trust Co.	3,822,523,000
40	AmeriTrust Co., Cleveland	3,741,667,000
41	First Interstate Bank of Oregon NA, Portland	3,668,876,000
42	First Pennsylvania Bank NA, Philadelphia	3,560,527,000
43	California First Bank, San Francisco	3,496,975,000
44	Manufacturers National Bank, Detroit	3,492,007,000
45	First Union National Bank, Charlotte, N.C.	3,335,706,000

Bank Suspensions

Source: Federal Deposit Insurance Corp. Deposits in thousands of dollars. The figures represent banks which, during the periods shown, closed temporarily or permanently on account of financial difficulties; does not include banks whose deposit liabilities were assumed by other banks.

Year	Susp.	Deposits	Year	Susp.	Deposits	Year	Susp.	Deposits	Year	Susp.	Deposits
1929	659	230,643	1938	50	10,296	1963	2	23,444	1972	1	20,482
1930	1,352	853,363	1939	32	32,738	1964	7	23,438	1973	3	25,811
1931	2,294	1,690,669	1940	19	5,657	1965	3	42,889	1975	1	18,248
1932	1,456	715,626	1955(a)	4	6,503	1966	1	774	1976	3	18,859
1933*	4,004	3,598,975	1958	3	4,156	1967	4	10,878	1978	1	1,284
1934	9	1,968	1959	3	2,593	1969	4	9,011	1979	3	12,795
1935	24	9,091	1960	1	6,930	1970	4	34,040	1980	3	15,500
1936	42	11,241	1961	5	8,936	1971	5	74,605	1981	2	45,700
1937	50	14,960									

*Figures for 1933 comprise 628 banks with deposits of $360,413,000 suspended before or after the banking holiday (the holiday began March 6 and closed March 15) or placed in receivership during the holiday; 2,124 banks with deposits of $2,520,391,000 which were not licensed following the banking holiday and were placed in liquidation or receivership; and 1,252 banks with deposits of $718,171,000 which had not been licensed by June 20, 1933. (a) No suspensions in years 1945-1954, 1962, 1968, 1974, 1977.

Per Capita Personal Income, by States and Regions

Source: Bureau of Economic Analysis, U.S. Commerce Department (dollars)

State and Region	1970	1975	1979	1980	1981
United States	**3,893**	**5,861**	**8,773**	**9,521**	**10,491**
New England	**4,245**	**6,030**	**8,910**	**10,105**	**11,058**
Connecticut	4,871	6,779	10,129	11,720	12,816
Maine	3,250	4,766	7,039	7,925	8,535
Massachusetts	4,276	6,077	8,893	10,125	11,128
New Hampshire	3,720	5,417	8,351	9,131	9,994
Rhode Island	3,878	5,709	8,510	9,444	10,153
Vermont	3,447	4,924	7,329	7,827	8,723
Mideast	**4,384**	**6,380**	**9,112**	**10,192**	**11,301**
Delaware	4,468	6,547	9,327	10,339	11,095
District of Columbia	4,644	7,262	10,570	12,039	13,539
Maryland	4,267	6,403	9,331	10,460	11,477
New Jersey	4,684	6,794	9,747	10,924	12,127
New York	4,605	6,519	9,104	10,260	11,466
Pennsylvania	3,879	5,841	8,558	9,434	10,370
Great Lakes	**4,050**	**6,047**	**9,118**	**9,779**	**10,656**
Illinois	4,446	6,735	9,799	10,521	11,576
Indiana	3,709	5,609	8,570	8,936	9,720
Michigan	4,041	5,991	9,403	9,950	10,790
Ohio	3,949	5,778	8,715	9,462	10,313
Wisconsin	3,712	5,616	8,484	9,348	10,035
Plains	**3,657**	**5,719**	**8,628**	**9,338**	**10,270**
Iowa	3,643	5,894	8,772	9,358	10,474
Kansas	3,725	5,958	9,233	9,983	10,813
Minnesota	3,819	5,779	8,865	9,724	10,768
Missouri	3,654	5,476	8,251	8,982	9,651
Nebraska	3,657	5,882	8,684	9,365	10,366
North Dakota	3,077	5,888	8,231	8,747	10,213
South Dakota	3,108	5,009	7,455	7,806	8,833
Southeast	**3,208**	**5,028**	**7,624**	**8,111**	**9,014**
Alabama	2,892	4,635	6,962	7,488	8,219
Arkansas	2,791	4,510	6,933	7,268	8,044
Florida	3,698	5,631	8,546	8,996	10,165
Georgia	3,300	5,029	7,630	8,073	8,934
Kentucky	3,076	4,887	7,390	7,613	8,420
Louisiana	3,023	4,803	7,583	8,458	9,518
Mississippi	2,547	4,047	6,178	6,580	7,408
North Carolina	3,200	4,940	7,385	7,819	8,649
South Carolina	2,951	4,665	7,057	7,266	8,039
Tennessee	3,079	4,804	7,343	7,720	8,447
Virginia	3,677	5,772	8,587	9,392	10,349
West Virginia	3,038	4,962	7,372	7,800	8,377
Southwest	**3,465**	**5,469**	**8,627**	**9,284**	**10,405**
Arizona	3,614	5,391	8,423	8,791	9,754
New Mexico	3,045	4,843	7,560	7,841	8,529
Oklahoma	3,341	5,280	8,509	9,116	10,247
Texas	3,507	5,584	8,788	9,545	10,729
Rocky Mountain	**3,540**	**5,571**	**8,357**	**9,095**	**10,056**
Colorado	3,838	5,987	9,122	10,025	11,215
Idaho	3,243	5,179	7,571	8,056	8,937
Montana	3,395	5,388	7,684	8,536	9,410
Utah	3,169	4,900	7,197	7,649	8,313
Wyoming	3,672	6,123	9,922	10,898	11,665
Far West	**4,310**	**6,474**	**9,901**	**10,713**	**11,669**
California	4,423	6,575	10,047	10,938	11,923
Nevada	4,583	6,625	10,521	10,727	11,576
Oregon	3,677	5,769	8,938	9,317	10,008
Washington	3,997	6,298	9,565	10,309	11,277
Alaska	4,638	9,636	11,219	12,790	13,763
Hawaii	4,599	6,708	9,223	10,101	11,036

Civilian Employment of the Federal Government

Source: Workforce Analysis and Statistics Division, U.S. Office of Personnel Management as of June 30, 1981

Agency	All areas	United States: Total	United States: Full-time	United States: Part-time & intermittent	Outside United States: Total	Outside United States: Territories	Outside United States: Foreign countries
otal, all agencies[1]	**2,947,428**	**2,824,668**	**2,569,827**	**254,841**	**122,760**	**32,975**	**89,785**
Percent distribution	100	96	87	9	4	1	3
egislative branch	**40,467**	**40,381**	**39,222**	**1,159**	**86**	**15**	**71**
Congress	20,458	20,458	20,458	—	—	—	—
Senate	7,756	7,756	7,756	—	—	—	—
House of Representatives	12,689	12,689	12,689	—	—	—	—
Comm. on Security and Coop. in Europe	13	13	12	1	—	—	—
Architect of the Capitol	2,150	2,150	1,571	579	—	—	—
General Accounting Office	5,339	5,262	5,108	154	77	16	61
Government Printing Office	6,575	6,575	6,402	173	—	—	—
Library of Congress	5,278	5,269	4,920	349	9	—	9
Tax Court	237	237	234	3	—	—	—
Other	430	430	403	27	—	—	—
udicial branch	**15,340**	**15,168**	**14,242**	**926**	**172**	**172**	—
United States Courts	14,987	14,815	14,191	624	172	172	—
Supreme Court	353	353	323	30	—	—	—
xecutive branch	**2,891,621**	**2,769,119**	**2,516,363**	**252,756**	**122,502**	**32,797**	**89,705**
Executive Office of the President	1,800	1,795	1,665	130	5	—	5
White House Office	453	453	417	36	—	—	—
Office of the Vice President	25	25	24	1	—	—	—
Office of Management and Budget	674	674	643	31	—	—	—
Council of Economic Advisors	32	32	32	—	—	—	—
Council on Environmental Quality	19	19	19	—	—	—	—
Domestic Policy Staff	46	46	46	—	—	—	—
Executive Mansions and Grounds	87	87	87	—	—	—	—
Office of Special Representatives Trade Negotiations	155	150	121	29	5	—	5
Office of Science and Technology Policy	18	18	18	—	—	—	—
National Security Council	70	70	61	9	—	—	—
xecutive departments	**1,778,287**	**1,679,225**	**1,588,528**	**90,697**	**99,062**	**13,544**	**85,518**
State	23,853	8,330	7,910	420	15,523	—	15,523
Treasury	128,153	127,120	120,649	6,471	1,033	631	402
Defense	1,008,462	931,421	912,349	19,072	77,041	10,097	66,944
Department of the Army	365,892	329,366	321,155	8,211	36,526	3,815	32,711
Department of the Navy	327,138	305,008	298,848	6,160	22,130	5,033	17,097
Department of the Air Force	241,435	226,229	222,566	3,663	15,206	1,925	13,281
Defense Logistics Agency	48,089	47,715	47,098	617	374	55	319
Other Defense Activities	25,908	23,103	22,682	421	2,805	40	2,765
Justice	55,824	54,942	53,459	1,483	882	402	480
Interior	86,575	86,235	76,900	9,335	340	274	66
Agriculture	135,880	134,377	103,844	30,533	1,503	749	754
Commerce	44,173	43,400	37,509	5,891	773	282	491
Labor	22,238	22,134	21,240	894	104	64	40
Health and Human Services	158,708	157,718	144,761	12,957	990	937	53
Housing and Urban Development	16,323	16,136	15,831	305	187	187	—
Transportation	70,122	69,439	68,001	1,438	683	564	119
Department of Energy	21,039	21,036	20,104	932	3	—	3
Department of Education	6,937	6,937	5,971	966	—	—	—
dependent agencies	**1,111,534**	**1,088,099**	**926,170**	**161,929**	**23,435**	**18,116**	**5,319**
Action	1,991	1,484	1,402	82	507	23	484
Board of Governors, Fed. Res. System	1,525	1,525	1,485	40	—	—	—
Community Service Admin.	1,081	1,081	1,058	23	—	—	—
Environmental Protection Agency	13,579	13,562	11,261	2,301	17	17	—
Federal Communications Comm.	2,109	2,100	2,046	54	9	9	—
Federal Trade Commission	1,753	1,753	1,602	151	—	—	—
General Services Admin.	35,702	35,605	32,515	3,090	97	85	12
International Communications Agency	7,999	3,320	3,255	65	4,679	—	4,679
Interstate Commerce Commission	1,851	1,851	1,800	51	—	—	—
National Aeronautics and Space Admin.	24,245	24,225	23,999	226	20	1	19
National Labor Relations Board	3,004	2,981	2,923	58	23	23	—
Nuclear Regulatory Comm.	3,701	3,701	3,481	220	—	—	—
Office of Personnel Mgmt.	8,226	8,204	6,211	1,993	22	22	—
Panama Canal Commission	8,848	74	74	—	8,774	8,774	—
Securities and Exchange Comm.	1,984	1,984	1,945	39	—	—	—
Selective Service System	203	203	203	—	—	—	—
Small Business Admin.	5,470	5,372	5,259	113	98	98	—
Tennessee Valley Authority	53,320	53,316	52,954	362	4	—	4
U.S. Postal Service	664,691	661,782	541,058	120,724	2,909	2,909	—
Veterans Administration	234,040	231,682	201,686	29,996	2,358	2,124	234
All other agencies	36,212	32,294	29,953	2,341	3,918	1,097	2,821

(1) Excludes employees of Central Intelligence Agency, National Security Agency (not reported to the Office of Personnel Manage-ent) and uncompensated employees. June 1981 total includes 40,742 employees exempted from personnel ceilings in the Youth rograms and Worker Trainee Opportunities Program.

U.S. Labor Force, Employment and Unemployment

Source: Bureau of Labor Statistics, U.S. Labor Department

(numbers in thousands; seasonally adjusted)

Labor force	Annual average			1982				
	1977	1979	1981	Jan.	Mar.	May	Jun.	Jul.
Civilian labor force	99,009	104,962	108,670	108,879	109,346	110,666	110,191	110,52
Employed	92,017	98,824	100,397	99,581	99,492	100,117	99,764	99,73
Agriculture	3,283	3,347	3,368	3,411	3,349	3,488	3,357	3,46
Nonagricultural industries	88,734	95,477	97,030	96,170	96,144	96,629	96,406	96,27
Unemployed	6,991	6,137	8,273	9,298	9,854	10,549	10,427	10,79
Long term, 15 weeks & over	1,942	1,241	2,285	2,399	2,954	3,286	3,673	3,58
Unemployment rates (unemployment in each group as a percent of the groups' civilian labor force								
Total, 16 years and over	7.1	5.8	7.6	8.5	9.0	9.5	9.5	9.
Men, 20 years and over	5.2	4.2	6.3	7.5	7.9	8.4	8.7	8.
Women, 20 years and over	7.0	5.7	6.8	7.2	7.9	8.3	8.1	8.
Both sexes, 16 to 19 years	17.8	16.1	19.6	21.7	21.9	23.1	22.3	24.
White, total	6.2	5.1	6.7	7.5	7.9	8.5	8.4	8
Men, 20 years and over	4.7	3.6	5.6	6.6	7.0	7.5	7.7	7
Women, 20 years and over	6.2	5.0	5.9	6.3	6.9	7.3	7.1	7.
Both sexes, 16 to 19 years	15.4	14.0	17.3	19.6	19.0	20.3	19.4	21.
Black & other, total	13.1	11.3	14.2	15.1	16.6	17.2	17.1	17.
Men, 20 years and over	10.0	8.5	12.1	14.2	15.1	15.5	15.9	15.
Women, 20 years and over	11.7	10.2	12.4	12.4	14.2	14.5	14.1	14
Both sexes, 16 to 19 years	37.9	33.2	37.8	37.9	42.2	45.5	46.7	47
Married men, spouse present	3.6	2.8	4.3	5.3	5.5	6.1	6.5	6.
Married women, spouse present	6.5	5.1	6.0	6.2	7.1	7.4	7.0	7.
Women who head families	9.4	8.3	10.4	10.4	10.6	11.8	12.4	12.
Full-time workers	6.6	5.3	7.3	8.4	8.9	9.2	9.4	9
Part-time workers	9.9	8.8	9.4	9.6	10.0	10.5	9.8	11
White-collar workers	4.3	3.4	4.0	4.2	4.8	4.8	5.0	4
Blue-collar workers	8.1	7.0	10.3	12.5	12.9	13.5	13.9	14
Service workers	8.2	7.2	8.9	9.2	10.2	11.3	9.9	10
Farm workers	4.7	3.9	5.3	6.9	5.4	8.3	7.2	6.
Nonagricultural w/s workers	6.5	5.4	7.2	8.1	8.7	9.1	9.1	9
Construction	12.7	10.3	15.6	18.7	17.9	18.8	19.2	20
Manufacturing	6.7	5.6	8.3	10.4	10.8	11.6	12.3	12
Durable goods	6.2	5.0	8.2	11.0	10.8	12.2	13.2	12
Nondurable goods	7.4	6.5	8.4	9.5	10.8	10.7	11.0	11
Wholesale & retail trade	8.0	6.5	8.1	8.7	10.3	10.6	9.7	10
Finance & service ind.	6.0	4.9	5.9	5.9	6.9	6.9	6.8	7
Government workers	4.2	3.7	4.7	4.8	4.9	5.0	4.6	4

Note: Pre-1982 data have been revised to reflect 1980 census population controls.

Employed Persons by Major Occupational Groups and Sex

Annual averages 1981 Occupational group	Thousands of persons Both sexes	Males	Females	Percent distribution Both sexes	Males	Female
Total Employed	100,397	57,397	43,000	100.0	100.0	100.0
White-collar workers	52,949	24,608	28,341	52.7	42.9	65.9
Professional and technical	16,420	9,100	7,319	16.4	15.9	17.0
Managers and administrators, except farm	11,540	8,372	3,168	11.5	14.6	7.4
Sales workers	6,425	3,509	2,916	6.4	6.1	6.8
Clerical workers	18,564	3,626	14,938	18.5	6.3	34.7
Blue-collar workers	31,261	25,433	5,828	31.1	44.3	13.6
Craft kindred workers	12,662	11,859	802	12.6	20.7	1.9
Operatives, except transport	10,540	6,350	4,190	10.5	11.1	9.7
Transport equipment operatives	3,476	3,167	309	3.5	5.5	0.7
Nonfarm laborers	4,583	4,056	527	4.6	7.1	1.2
Service workers	13,438	5,097	8,342	13.4	8.9	19.4
Private household workers	1,047	38	1,010	1.0	0.1	2.3
Other service workers	12,391	5,059	7,332	12.3	8.8	17.1
Farm workers	2,749	2,260	490	2.7	3.9	1.1
Farm & farm managers	1,485	1,317	168	1.5	2.3	0.4
Farm laborers & supervisors	1,264	943	322	1.3	1.6	0.7

Note: Pre-1982 data have been revised to reflect 1980 census population controls.

Employment and Unemployment in the U.S.

Civilian labor force, persons 16 years of age and over (in thousands)

Year	Civilian labor force	Employed	Unemployed	Year	Civilian labor force	Employed	Unemploye
1940	52,705	45,070	7,635	1975	93,775	85,846	7,92
1950	62,208	58,918	3,288	1976	96,158	88,752	7,40
1960	69,628	65,778	3,852	1977	99,009	92,017	6,99
1965	74,455	71,088	3,366	1978	102,251	96,048	6,20
1970	82,771	78,678	4,093	1979	104,962	98,824	6,13
1973	89,429	85,064	4,365	1980	106,940	99,303	7,63
1974	91,949	86,794	5,156	1981	108,670	100,397	8,27

Average Salaries of Full-time Federal Civilian Employees

Source: Office of Personnel Management, Oct. 31, 1981

Occupation	Men No. of employees	Men Average salary	Women No. of employees	Women Average salary
Blue Collar				
Baker	188	$18,514	17	$18,580
Barber	28	18,381	—	—
Beautician	—	—	6	20,034
Boiler operator	4,852	21,355	21	17,326
Carpenter	8,155	20,869	73	18,194
Cook	3,728	20,258	1,033	18,001
Electrician	12,835	21,600	261	17,956
Elevator operator	57	13,472	109	13,926
Forklift operator	2,114	18,461	114	16,864
Janitor	14,396	14,630	5,585	14,446
Laborer	14,575	14,344	1,274	14,125
Locksmith	274	19,852	9	18,859
Locomotive engineer	125	21,354	—	—
Machinist	13,571	22,207	315	18,029
Mechanic, A/C	5,304	21,329	46	16,451
Mechanic, aircraft	15,409	22,289	243	19,109
Mechanic, general	9,965	20,322	107	17,178
Painter	9,423	20,231	326	17,648
Pipefitter	15,719	22,626	156	18,573
Plumber	2,417	20,190	19	17,153
Pressman	2,305	21,341	274	19,327
Sheet metal	12,638	21,203	649	18,695
Store worker	2,529	16,753	1,353	12,859
Toolmaker	994	24,903	6	20,533
Tractor operator	2,248	17,349	35	16,569
Vehicle operator	14,104	18,461	449	17,105
Warehouseman	22,534	17,715	2,296	16,500
Welder	6,883	20,946	147	17,741

Occupation	Men No. of employees	Men Average salary	Women No. of employees	Women Average salary
White-Collar				
Accountant	18,110	$31,261	3,555	$24,593
Architect	1,513	32,775	106	28,588
Attorney	13,056	40,092	4,062	34,578
Chaplain	521	31,948	10	16,789
Chemist	6,479	33,684	1,490	27,310
Clerk/Typist	3,575	11,703	59,679	11,593
Dental assistant	201	13,653	2,769	13,560
Editor/Writer	857	29,000	1,344	23,418
Editor, technical	1,085	28,278	691	24,038
Engineer, civil	15,731	33,197	480	24,417
Engineer, electrical	4,504	33,084	108	26,482
Engineer, mechanical	10,221	33,121	187	25,082
Law clerk	261	23,164	246	23,187
Librarian	1,117	30,728	2,296	27,473
Messenger	525	10,277	71	10,906
Nurse	2,598	21,498	32,931	22,840
Paralegal	815	30,042	1,288	23,501
Personnel mgmt.	5,356	33,306	4,053	26,868
Pharmacist	2,063	27,286	527	24,960
Public relations	1,878	33,531	1,122	26,654
Purchasing	1,172	17,022	3,844	15,723
Secretary	842	14,825	85,091	15,836
Social work	2,030	28,675	1,607	27,164
Statistician	1,889	33,817	755	28,770
Technician, medical	1,144	17,011	1,527	15,819
Therapist, occupational	81	23,274	597	21,943
Therapist, physical	245	23,842	437	21,748

U.S. Balance of International Payments

Source: Bureau of Economic Analysis, U.S. Commerce Department
(millions of dollars)

	1955	1960	1965	1970	1975	1978	1979	1980	1981
Exports of goods and services	**19,948**	**28,861**	**41,086**	**65,673**	**155,729**	**221,036**	**286,508**	**344,667**	**372,892**
Merchandise, adjusted	14,424	19,650	26,461	42,469	107,088	142,054	182,055	223,966	236,254
Transfers under U.S. military agency sales contracts	200	335	830	1,501	4,049	8,240	7,194	8,231	3,665
Receipts of income on U.S. investments abroad	2,817	4,616	7,436	11,746	25,351	42,972	65,970	75,936	95,258
Other services	2,507	4,261	6,359	9,957	19,242	27,772	31,289	36,534	50,693
Imports of goods and services	**−17,795**	**−23,729**	**−32,801**	**−60,050**	**−132,836**	**−230,240**	**−281,630**	**−333,888**	**−361,813**
Merchandise, adjusted	−11,527	−14,758	−21,510	−39,866	−98,041	−175,813	−211,524	−249,308	−264,143
Direct defense expenditures	−2,901	−3,087	−2,952	−4,855	−4,795	−7,354	−8,469	−10,746	—
Payments of income on foreign investments in the U.S.	−520	−1,237	−2,088	−5,516	−12,564	−22,073	−33,460	−43,174	−52,908
Other services	−2,847	−4,646	−6,251	−9,815	−17,436	−25,001	−28,178	−30,660	−44,762
Unilateral transfers, net	−2,498	−2,308	−2,854	−3,294	−4,613	−5,055	−5,666	−7,056	−6,608
U.S. official reserve assets, net	182	2,145	1,225	2,481	−849	−732	−1,107	−8,155	−5,175
U.S. Government assets, other than official reserve assets, net	−310	−1,100	−1,605	−1,589	−3,474	−4,644	−3,783	−5,165	−5,137
U.S. private assets, net	−1,255	−5,144	−5,335	−10,228	−35,380	−57,279	−56,858	−71,456	−98,982
Foreign official assets in the U.S., net		1,473	134	6,908	7,027	33,293	−14,271	15,492	4,785
Other foreign assets in the U.S., net		821	607	−550	8,643	30,804	51,845	34,769	73,136
Allocations of special drawing rights	—	—	—	867	—	—	1,139	1,152	1,093
Statistical discrepancy	371	−1,019	−458	−219	5,753	11,354	23,822	29,640	25,809
Memoranda:									
Balance on merchandise trade	2,897	4,892	4,951	2,603	9,047	−33,759	−29,469	−25,342	−27,889
Balance on goods and services	2,153	5,132	8,284	5,624	22,893	−9,204	4,878	10,779	11,079
Balance on goods, services, and remittances	1,556	4,496	7,238	4,066	21,175	−11,088	2,736	8,382	8,975
Balance on current account	−345	2,824	5,431	2,330	18,280	−14,259	1,414	3,723	4,471

Note.—Details may not add to totals because of rounding.

Federal Deposit Insurance Corporation (FDIC)

The primary purpose of the Federal Deposit Insurance Corporation (FDIC) is to insure deposits in all banks approved for insurance coverage benefits under the Federal Deposit Insurance Act. The major functions of the FDIC are to pay off depositors of insured banks closed without adequate provision having been made to pay depositors' claims, to act as receiver for all national banks placed in receivership and for state banks placed in receivership when appointed receiver by state authorities, and to prevent the continuance or development of unsafe and unsound banking practices. The FDIC's entire income consists of assessments on insured banks and income from investments; it receives no appropriations from Congress. It may borrow from the U.S. Treasury not to exceed $3 billion outstanding, but has made no such borrowings since it was organized in 1933. The FDIC surplus (Deposit Insurance Fund) as of Dec. 31, 1981 was $12.2 billion.

Foreign Direct Investment in the U.S.

(Millions of dollars)

	Position at year end[1]		Capital inflows (outflows (-))						Income[4]	
			1980			1981				
	1980	1981	Total	Equity and intercompany account inflows[2]	Reinvested earnings of incorporated affiliates[3]	Total	Equity and intercompany account inflows[2]	Reinvested earnings of incorporated affiliates[3]	1980	1981
Total	**68,351**	**89,759**	**13,666**	**7,500**	**6,167**	**21,301**	**17,201**	**4,099**	**9,470**	**7,807**
By area:										
Canada	10,074	12,212	2,811	1,246	1,565	1,656	1,593	63	1,795	247
Europe	45,731	57,705	8,262	4,890	3,371	12,403	9,528	2,875	5,757	5,561
Of which:										
France	2,960	5,844	668	527	140	2,878	2,995	−117	234	87
Germany	5,402	7,067	−255	−179	−75	1,662	1,596	65	45	136
Netherlands	16,909	20,177	4,167	1,969	2,198	3,733	1,702	2,030	3,360	3,346
Switzerland	3,870	4,368	428	466	−38	497	532	−35	238	288
United Kingdom	12,242	15,527	2,438	1,693	745	3,276	2,598	678	1,368	1,198
Japan	4,225	6,887	732	92	639	2,662	1,988	675	722	768
Other	8,322	12,955	1,862	1,271	591	4,579	4,092	487	1,195	1,231
Memorandum: OPEC[5]	664	3,524	285	275	10	2,864	2,869	−5	58	45
By industry:										
Petroleum	12,363	17,813	2,456	−276	2,732	5,448	3,060	2,388	3,467	3,407
Manufacturing	25,159	29,533	4,275	2,825	1,449	4,293	4,347	−54	2,390	1,012
Food products	4,187	4,791	1,578	117	1,462	599	346	253	1,549	372
Chemicals and allied products	8,017	8,488	805	639	165	468	313	156	327	384
Primary and fabricated metals	3,590	4,325	570	369	201	735	680	55	250	252
Machinery	4,195	4,626	615	753	−138	371	766	−395	−8	−199
Other manufacturing	5,170	7,303	706	948	−241	2,120	2,243	−122	271	204
Trade	14,296	17,734	2,726	1,760	965	3,428	2,388	1,040	1,410	1,576
Finance	5,000	7,448	1,435	1,088	347	2,451	2,042	409	966	1,170
Insurance	5,365	5,896	1,218	771	447	528	278	250	828	230
Real Estate	3,073	4,564	1,185	1,144	41	1,485	1,514	−30	207	171
Other	3,095	6,770	373	187	186	3,668	3,572	96	202	241

(1) Book value of foreign direct investor's equity in, and net outstanding loans to, their U.S. affiliates; a U.S. affiliate is a U.S. business enterprise in which a single foreign person owns, directly or indirectly, at least 10 percent of the voting securities, or the equivalent. (2) Net change in foreign parents' capital stock, including additional paid-in capital, in, and intercompany account balances with, incorporated U.S. affiliates, and in their claims on the net assets of unincorporated U.S. affiliates. (3) Foreign parents' shares in the net income of incorporated U.S. affiliates (net of U.S. income taxes), less their shares in the gross dividends of these affiliates. (4) Foreign parents' shares in the net income of U.S. affiliates (net of U.S. income taxes), plus net interest paid (net of withholding taxes) on intercompany accounts between parents and affiliates, less withholding taxes on dividends paid to parents by affiliates. (5) Countries in the Organization of Petroleum Countries (OPEC) are: Algeria, Ecuador, Gabon, Indonesia, Iran, Iraq, Kuwait, Libya, Nigeria, Qatar, Saudi Arabia, Venezuela, and United Arab Emirates.

Total Value of Canadian Construction Work

Source: Statistics Canada (thousands of Canadian dollars)

Province	1980 New	1980 Repair	1980 Total	1981 New	1981 Repair	1981 Total
Newfoundland	709,888	140,272	850,160	811,788	139,292	951,08
Prince Edward Island	135,169	40,380	175,999	108,897	42,619	151,51
Nova Scotia	929,505	253,812	1,183,317	1,200,275	300,394	1,500,66
New Brunswick	781,786	176,266	958,052	792,306	216,280	1,008,58
Quebec	7,493,127	1,859,247	9,352,374	8,608,560	2,069,564	10,678,12
Ontario	9,863,146	2,574,315	12,437,461	11,742,708	2,825,015	14,567,72
Manitoba	1,091,930	305,914	1,397,844	1,228,026	353,026	1,581,05
Saskatchewan	1,873,396	405,018	2,278,414	2,340,627	416,394	2,757,02
Alberta	10,334,773	1,358,704	11,693,477	12,241,618	1,577,442	13,819,06
British Columbia	6,939,752	1,059,956	7,999,708	8,725,579	1,216,882	9,942,46
Total	**40,152,472**	**8,174,334**	**48,326,806**	**47,800,384**	**9,156,908**	**56,957,29**

Canadian Pulpwood, Wood Pulp, and Newsprint

Source: Canadian Statistical Review, June 1982 (thousands of metric tons)

Year	Pulpwood production[1] (1,000 cu. meters)	Wood pulp production[2] Total	Mechanical	Chemical	Wood pulp exports[3]	Newsprint production	Newsprint shipments Total	Domestic	Exports[4]
1978	45,308	19,185.6	7,480.2	11,671.0	7,320	8,811	8,883	908	7,975
1979	48,729	19,571.6	7,441.1	12,104.6	7,828	8,710	8,730	948	7,781
1980	50,386	19,970.2	7,506.0	12,438.7	7,990	8,625	8,621	982	7,639
1981	52,688	19,294.7	7,629.4	11,646.5	7,442	8,946	8,916	1,042	7,877

(1) Pulpwood produced for domestic use, excluding exports, but including receipts of purchased roundwood. (2) Total pulp production covers "screenings" which are already included in exports. "Screenings" are excluded throughout from mechanical and chemical pulp. (3) Customs exports. (4) Mill shipments destined for export.

MANUFACTURES AND MINERALS

General Statistics for Major Industry Groups

Source: Bureau of the Census

The estimates for 1980 in the following table are based upon reports from a representative sample of about 70,000 manufacturing establishments.

Industry	All employees		Production workers			Value added by mfr.
	Number (1,000)	Payroll (millions)	Number (1,000)	Manhours (millions)	Wages (millions)	(millions)
Food and kindred products	1,537.4	23,221.5	1,090.1	2,152.7	14,797.3	75,301.6
Tobacco products	58.0	1,044.8	46.6	88.1	767.4	6,156.8
Textile mill products	817.4	9,253.1	707.1	1,393.4	7,228.2	19,056.3
apparel, oth. textile prods.	1,307.3	11,354.3	1,129.5	2,000.5	8,503.4	23,425.5
Lumber and wood products	698.1	8,904.8	581.7	1,097.7	6,719.9	18,079.0
Furniture and fixtures	472.7	5,623.2	383.8	727.0	3,926.0	11,631.1
Paper and allied products	645.1	11,699.3	492.8	1,004.0	8,187.5	29,673.0
Printing and publishing	1,262.8	18,843.1	716.0	1,325.2	9,592.0	44,374.7
Chemicals, allied products	909.7	18,269.0	544.7	1,080.4	9,482.6	73,385.3
Petroleum and coal products	148.9	3,615.1	99.8	199.7	2,135.0	24,815.6
Rubber, misc. plastics prod.	703.2	10,140.5	544.4	1,032.5	6,777.3	22,568.7
Leather, leather products	232.4	2,199.9	200.5	345.5	1,635.3	4,851.2
Stone, clay, glass products	613.3	10,062.3	479.7	945.5	7,190.3	24,051.0
Primary metal industries	1,096.1	23,556.4	854.2	1,638.6	17,306.2	47,619.2
Fabricated metal products	1,616.8	26,700.6	1,224.0	2,381.3	17,908.5	57,917.1
Machinery, except electric	2,410.8	44,603.7	1,595.7	3,149.1	25,771.3	99,435.4
Electric, electronic equip.	1,963.2	32,453.3	1,303.0	2,492.2	17,762.6	73,149.5
Transportation equipment	1,771.0	38,843.9	1,212.4	2,371.9	24,091.0	76,482.0
Instruments, related prods.	616.4	10,672.1	370.7	721.5	5,021.4	27,913.1
Misc. manufacturing indus.	429.0	5,374.0	321.7	603.8	3,321.2	12,704.0
Administrative and auxiliary[1]	1,335.3	33,916.3	—	—	—	—
All industries, total	**20,644.9**	**350,351.2**	**13,898.4**	**26,750.6**	**198,124.4**	**772,590.1**

(1) In addition to the employment and payroll for operating manufacturing establishments, manufacturing concerns reported separately for central administrative offices or auxiliary units (e.g., research laboratories, storage warehouses, power plants, garages, repair shops, etc.) which serve the manufacturing establishments of a company rather than the public.

Manufacturing Production Worker Statistics

Source: Bureau of Labor Statistics, U.S. Labor Department (p — preliminary)

Year	All employees	Production workers	Payroll index 1977=100	Avg. weekly earnings	Avg. hourly earnings	Avg. hrs. per wk.
1955	16,882,000	13,288,000	31.5	$75.30	$1.85	40.7
1960	16,796,000	12,586,000	35.4	89.72	2.26	39.7
1965	18,062,000	13,434,000	45.1	107.53	2.61	41.2
1970	19,367,000	14,044,000	58.6	133.33	3.35	39.8
1975	18,323,000	13,043,000	76.8	190.79	4.83	39.5
1977	19,647,000	14,110,000	100.0	228.90	5.68	40.3
1978	20,476,000	14,714,000	113.6	249.27	6.17	40.4
1979	21,040,000	15,068,000	125.2	269.34	6.70	40.2
1980	20,285,000	14,214,000	126.8	288.62	7.27	39.7
1981	20,173,000	14,021,000	137.7	318.00	7.99	39.8
1982, Jan.	19,353,000	13,200,000	127.3	312.38	8.42	37.1
Feb.	19,299,000	13,168,000	133.1	326.93	8.34	39.2
Mar.	19,207,000	13,093,000	132.2	327.27	8.37	39.1
Apr.	19,073,000	12,971,000	130.6	325.85	8.42	38.7
May.	19,043,000	12,958,000	132.0	329.55	8.45	39.0
June[p]	19,035,000	12,948,000	133.8	334.05	8.50	39.3
July[p]	18,720,000	12,671,000	130.3	332.60	8.55	38.9

Personal Consumption Expenditures for the U.S.

Source: Bureau of Economic Analysis, U.S. Commerce Department (billions of dollars)

	1976	1977	1978	1979	1980	1981
Durable goods	**156.8**	**178.2**	**200.2**	**213.4**	**214.3**	**234.6**
Motor vehicles and parts	72.6	84.8	95.7	96.6	89.7	98.6
Furniture and household equipment	59.1	65.7	72.8	81.8	86.3	93.4
Other	25.2	27.7	31.7	35.1	38.3	42.6
Nondurable goods	**441.7**	**478.8**	**528.2**	**600.0**	**670.4**	**734.5**
Food	230.6	249.8	275.9	311.6	343.7	375.3
Clothing and shoes	75.3	82.6	92.4	99.1	104.7	114.6
Gasoline and oil	44.0	48.1	51.2	66.6	87.0	96.8
Other nondurable goods	91.9	98.2	108.8	122.8	135.0	147.9
Fuel oil and coal	9.8	10.7	11.9	16.1	19.0	19.7
Other	82.1	87.6	96.9	106.6	116.0	128.2
Services	**485.7**	**547.4**	**618.0**	**693.7**	**782.5**	**874.1**
Housing	166.5	185.9	209.6	236.0	266.0	295.3
Household operation	71.6	81.1	90.1	99.3	111.7	128.9
Electricity and gas	32.9	38.5	42.9	47.8	56.6	66.8
Other	38.7	42.6	47.2	51.5	55.1	62.1
Transportation	38.6	46.4	51.2	56.3	62.9	65.4
Other	209.0	234.1	267.1	302.0	341.9	384.4
Total personal consumption expenditures	**1,084.3**	**1,204.4**	**1,346.5**	**1,507.2**	**1,667.2**	**1,843.2**

General Manufacturing Statistics for States

Source: Bureau of the Census, U.S. Commerce Department

1978 States	All employees: Number (1,000)	All employees: Payroll (millions)	Production workers: Number (1,000)	Production workers: Man-hrs. (millions)	Production workers: Wages (millions)	Value added by mfr. (millions)	Value of shipments (millions)	Capit[al] exper[nditures] (millior[ns])
U.S. total	**20,508.9**	**$299,142.6**	**14,231.0**	**27,681.8**	**$176,446.6**	**$657,245.8**	**$1,523,429.9**	**$55,243**
Alabama	346.7	4,233.8	277.0	541.4	3,018.0	9,745.9	23,351.3	1,610
Alaska	10.7	170.8	8.9	16.2	127.7	546.8	1,464.6	65
Arizona	123.2	1,739.4	79.6	155.6	923.8	3,959.6	8,051.9	318
Arkansas	205.5	2,186.2	166.1	322.0	1,580.2	5,500.0	13,963.1	606
California	1,903.1	28,486.4	1,240.0	2,376.8	15,112.2	62,510.4	135,765.2	4,493
Colorado	163.0	2,442.6	102.3	197.4	1,287.4	5,237.7	11,765.5	550
Connecticut	432.2	6,581.5	264.0	528.2	3,218.4	12,290.7	21,957.9	679
Delaware	66.8	1,308.7	33.3	67.2	466.8	2,011.6	6,427.3	186
District of Columbia	17.7	201.3	7.8	14.2	109.8	668.2	1,047.3	17
Florida	396.5	4,877.6	276.8	533.5	2,755.8	11,266.2	24,991.4	1,081
Georgia	511.6	5,819.3	392.9	770.4	3,830.8	13,944.6	35,812.2	1,459
Hawaii	23.7	285.2	17.4	30.9	173.0	782.9	2,063.1	46
Idaho	56.9	729.4	43.4	82.7	499.4	1,843.5	4,485.6	194
Illinois	1,310.7	20,613.4	870.0	1,705.1	11,899.8	44,854.4	103,858.1	2,975
Indiana	735.2	11,754.9	541.7	1,058.6	7,922.9	25,699.9	58,934.7	2,166
Iowa	246.6	3,725.4	175.6	338.5	2,430.5	9,846.1	26,547.5	840
Kansas	185.6	2,528.1	132.3	267.4	1,635.2	6,153.9	18,671.5	413
Kentucky	288.9	3,890.0	215.6	409.6	2,590.1	10,845.1	25,716.5	799
Louisiana	200.7	3,008.8	149.0	299.1	1,997.7	10,056.5	31,852.7	2,103
Maine	107.2	1,226.8	88.3	170.5	876.8	2,691.1	5,866.7	424
Maryland	252.6	3,786.5	169.7	327.0	2,218.8	7,739.2	17,780.3	508
Massachusetts	640.4	8,797.6	426.1	823.0	4,734.2	18,632.0	34,450.4	1,170
Michigan	1,180.7	22,892.8	822.7	1,671.5	14,240.9	41,804.6	104,920.7	4,742
Minnesota	365.5	5,385.2	228.2	438.2	2,785.0	10,908.1	25,838.6	788
Mississippi	221.7	2,276.8	178.7	344.2	1,628.6	5,986.6	13,863.9	512
Missouri	453.4	6,549.1	308.2	590.4	3,787.0	15,031.3	37,489.7	965
Montana	25.3	361.0	19.4	37.4	266.3	850.6	3,070.5	130
Nebraska	92.5	1,231.6	66.9	132.9	786.5	3,249.7	10,572.1	219
Nevada	17.6	233.1	12.5	23.7	141.1	660.1	1,216.2	68
New Hampshire	103.9	1,220.2	78.4	149.5	773.3	2,764.2	5,055.4	196
New Jersey	798.1	12,025.2	493.4	956.0	5,922.5	24,725.4	54,748.0	1,639
New Mexico	28.1	326.8	20.1	37.1	197.7	794.9	2,126.0	56
New York	1,537.5	22,886.1	964.8	1,845.3	11,261.3	48,309.8	94,296.5	2,917
North Carolina	789.1	8,430.4	626.1	1,213.8	5,655.1	20,616.6	45,259.2	1,513
North Dakota	14.1	181.3	9.7	19.6	110.7	485.1	1,376.0	58
Ohio	1,362.4	22,703.2	937.9	1,868.3	14,252.6	47,641.4	106,487.8	3,292
Oklahoma	172.5	2,381.1	115.9	224.6	1,353.1	5,237.3	14,011.8	445
Oregon	222.4	3,323.6	165.6	311.3	2,221.6	7,166.6	16,753.0	659
Pennsylvania	1,350.8	20,017.8	944.1	1,801.4	12,070.2	40,550.5	88,924.8	2,557
Rhode Island	129.5	1,479.2	98.4	184.7	904.2	2,998.0	5,987.9	217
South Carolina	387.1	4,251.6	308.1	607.0	2,942.9	9,476.8	21,124.6	978
South Dakota	23.9	301.3	17.7	35.1	203.5	726.1	2,154.2	46
Tennessee	509.9	5,863.3	389.0	743.2	3,884.8	14,045.8	31,750.2	1,156
Texas	960.4	13,719.4	647.2	1,287.1	7,736.2	36,496.4	104,646.8	4,601
Utah	79.8	1,037.5	56.2	105.8	633.8	2,380.2	5,935.9	248
Vermont	45.0	615.8	31.5	63.1	354.2	1,382.7	2,562.5	133
Virginia	406.2	4,929.0	309.2	597.9	3,231.8	11,961.1	27,069.5	1,046
Washington	286.0	4,873.2	195.8	365.9	2,847.2	10,424.6	25,604.1	943
West Virginia	123.9	1,910.0	91.9	176.4	1,275.4	4,426.8	9,743.7	51
Wisconsin	561.8	8,457.9	399.2	780.0	5,392.4	18,813.9	43,712.1	1,408
Wyoming	8.6	123.8	6.1	11.7	80.8	425.6	1,402.6	5

Employees in Non-Agricultural Establishments

Source: Bureau of Labor Statistics, U.S. Labor Department

(thousands)

Annual Average by Industry Division

Year	Total	Mining	Contr./construction	Manufacturing	Trans. and public utilities	Whole., retail trade	Finance, insur., real estate	Service, miscellaneous	Gove[rn]me[nt]
1955	50,641	792	2,839	16,882	4,141	10,535	2,298	6,240	6,9
1960	54,189	712	2,926	16,796	4,004	11,391	2,629	7,378	8,3
1965	60,765	632	3,232	18,062	4,036	12,716	2,977	9,036	10,0
1970	70,880	623	3,588	19,367	4,515	15,040	3,645	11,548	12,5
1975	76,945	752	3,525	18,323	4,542	17,060	4,165	13,892	14,6
1978	86,697	851	4,229	20,505	4,923	19,542	4,724	16,252	15,6
1979	89,823	958	4,463	21,040	5,136	20,192	4,975	17,112	15,9
1980	90,406	1,027	4,346	20,285	5,146	20,310	5,160	17,890	16,2
1981	91,105	1,132	4,176	20,173	5,157	20,551	5,301	18,592	16,0

Sales and Profits of Manufacturing Corporations by Industry Groups

Source: Federal Trade Commission

Industry Group (Amounts estimated in millions of dollars)	Sales 1Q 1981	Sales 4Q 1981	Sales 1Q 1982	Net profits after taxes 1Q 1981	Net profits after taxes 4Q 1981	Net profits after taxes 1Q 1982
All manufacturing corporations	**520,813**	**534,369**	**500,943**	**24,372**	**22,856**	**18,998**
Nondurable manufacturing corporations	286,713	291,325	274,644	14,228	14,315	12,170
Food and kindred products	69,579	73,051	68,662	2,106	2,446	2,120
Tobacco manufactures	4,397	4,951	4,715	577	538	536
Textile mill products	11,608	11,741	10,260	243	198	78
Paper and allied products	15,166	15,402	15,125	769	829	418
Printing and publishing	17,339	19,401	18,107	814	990	621
Chemicals and allied products	47,779	44,609	45,641	3,525	2,985	2,900
Industrial chemicals and synthetics	24,219	21,803	21,964	1,610	1,215	951
Drugs	6,432	6,330	6,608	658	784	899
Petroleum and coal products	95,001	94,169	85,982	5,395	5,464	4,935
Rubber and miscellaneous plastics products	11,287	11,393	11,172	423	317	304
Other nondurable manufacturing corporations	14,557	16,610	14,979	375	548	259
Durable manufacturing corporations	234,100	243,043	226,229	10,144	8,540	6,829
Stone, clay and glass products	10,218	10,881	9,090	238	267	-167
Primary metal industries	34,207	32,398	29,719	1,756	373	107
Iron and steel	23,216	22,084	20,025	921	5	25
Nonferrous metals	10,991	10,314	9,694	835	369	82
Fabricated metal products	25,390	25,984	24,848	1,022	760	786
Machinery, except electrical	46,429	51,331	46,807	2,745	3,492	2,657
Electrical and electronic equipment	37,701	40,211	37,964	2,164	1,745	1,781
Transportation equipment	49,591	50,276	48,454	727	568	646
Motor vehicles and equipment	28,849	27,481	27,554	-384	-139	1
Aircraft, guided missiles and parts	15,985	17,731	16,129	962	555	522
Instruments and related products	11,067	12,340	11,490	1,066	979	877
Other durable manufacturing corporations	19,497	19,622	17,928	426	356	142
All mining corporations	**15,870**	**19,591**	**19,076**	**1,712**	**1,646**	**1,581**
All retail trade corporations	**222,492**	**N/A**	**N/A**	**2,499**	**N/A**	**N/A**
All wholesale trade corporations	**273,591**	**267,277**	**N/A**	**3,886**	**4,332**	**N/A**

Annual Rates of Profit on Stockholders' Equity

Source: Federal Trade Commission

By Industry after taxes: by percent	1Q 1980	2Q 1980	3Q 1980	4Q 1980	1Q 1981	2Q 1981	3Q 1981	4Q 1981	1Q 1982
All manufacturing corporations	**15.4**	**13.6**	**12.5**	**14.1**	**13.6**	**15.6**	**13.4**	**12.0**	**10.1**
Nondurable manufacturing corporations	18.0	16.4	15.6	15.4	15.0	16.6	14.9	14.2	12.1
Food and kindred products	12.8	13.5	15.2	17.4	13.4	14.1	13.8	14.6	12.6
Tobacco manufacturers	21.3	20.3	22.3	15.3	21.7	19.6	19.4	18.6	18.4
Textile mill products	11.0	7.9	6.6	8.6	8.2	13.1	9.9	6.5	2.6
Paper and allied products	13.1	13.0	10.6	11.6	12.3	13.7	9.7	12.5	6.2
Printing and publishing	15.0	16.5	17.2	16.7	13.4	15.1	15.6	15.5	9.7
13.6 Chemicals and allied products	18.0	15.3	15.0	13.3	16.6	15.6	13.9	13.3	13.0
Industrial chemicals and synthetics	16.0	12.3	9.6	9.7	15.8	13.7	11.9	11.4	8.9
Drugs	21.6	18.3	22.6	16.9	16.5	16.3	16.1	18.6	20.8
Petroleum and coal products	23.7	21.1	17.8	17.5	16.3	19.8	17.4	15.4	13.9
Rubber and miscellaneous plastics products	7.3	4.9	5.4	9.2	12.5	14.9	11.4	9.1	8.7
Other nondurable manufacturing corporations	11.4	11.4	16.3	14.6	10.8	13.0	14.4	15.0	7.0
Durable manufacturing corporations	12.6	10.6	9.1	12.7	12.0	14.6	11.6	9.5	7.7
Stone, clay and glass products	5.9	11.5	14.4	11.5	5.3	12.4	11.9	5.8	-3.7
Primary metal industries	16.8	11.8	5.6	12.5	14.8	14.7	13.9	3.0	0.9
Iron and steel	12.8	8.2	3.4	11.7	12.5	15.3	18.4	0.1	0.4
Nonferrous metals	22.8	17.1	8.8	13.6	18.4	13.7	6.3	8.0	1.8
Fabricated metal products	16.6	13.3	12.3	13.5	13.1	16.5	14.1	9.4	9.8
Machinery, except electrical	14.1	15.4	13.7	16.6	13.4	15.3	14.1	15.5	11.8
Electrical and electronic equipment	16.0	14.8	14.1	15.6	16.3	15.9	12.9	12.3	12.6
Transportation equipment	3.8	-3.6	-6.2	3.4	4.9	12.7	1.9	3.8	4.3
Motor vehicles and equipment	-2.1	-14.0	-18.0	-3.0	-4.3	10.1	-6.9	-1.6	0.0
Aircraft, guided missiles and parts	16.6	16.6	15.4	15.5	21.5	17.0	13.9	11.7	10.8
Instruments and related products	16.3	17.8	17.8	17.9	17.5	17.4	17.7	14.9	13.3
Other durable manufacturing corporations	12.3	8.8	12.0	11.2	7.0	9.7	9.8	5.9	2.4
All mining corporations	**14.3**	**18.0**	**21.7**	**22.9**	**18.8**	**16.5**	**20.6**	**17.9**	**16.2**
All retail trade corporations	**8.5**	**11.7**	**12.6**	**20.2**	**9.3**	**13.8**	**11.0**	**N/A**	**N/A**
All wholesale trade corporations	**16.4**	**17.6**	**18.8**	**16.5**	**14.5**	**17.4**	**12.0**	**15.3**	**N/A**

Retail Store Sales

Source: Bureau of the Census, U.S. Commerce Department (millions of dollars)

Kind of business	1980	1981
All retail stores	**951,902**	**1,038,790**
Durable goods stores	**296,594**	**326,596**
Automotive group	162,309	180,772
Motor vehicle, other automotive dealers	144,257	151,707
Auto and home supply stores	18,052	20,145
Furniture and appliance group	43,416	45,701
Furniture, home furnishings stores	26,474	27,947
Household appliance, radio TV stores	13,182	14,313
Bldg. matl., hardware, garden supply, and mobile home dealers	49,616	53,164
Building matl. and supply stores	33,361	35,059
Hardware stores	8,224	9,432

Kind of business	1980	1981
Nondurable goods stores	**655,308**	**712,194**
Apparel group	44,426	47,755
Men's and boys' wear stores	7,830	7,786
Women's apparel, accessory stores	16,437	17,827
Shoe stores	7,849	8,613
Food group	217,047	237,586
Grocery stores	200,956	219,324
General merchandise group with stores	117,227	127,494
Department stores	94,705	103,609
Variety stores	8,694	8,960
Eating and drinking places	85,842	94,070
Gasoline service stations	93,624	101,665
Drug and proprietary stores	30,504	32,999
Liquor stores	17,083	17,461

Total retail stores sales (millions of dollars) — (1955) 183,851; (1958) 200,353; (1959) 215,413; (1960) 219,529; (1961) 218,992; (1962) 235,563; (1963) 246,666; (1964) 261,870; (1965) 284,128; (1966) 303,956; (1967) 292,956; (1968) 324,358; (1969) 346,717; (1970) 368,403; (1971) 406,234; (1972) 449,069; (1973) 509,538; (1974) 540,988; (1975) 588,146; (1976) 657,375; (1977) 725,220; (1978) 804,684; (1979) 894,343.

Cotton, Wool, Silk, and Man-Made Fibers Production

Source: Economics, Statistics, and Cooperatives Service, U.S. Agriculture Department

Cotton and wool from reports of the Agriculture Department; silk, rayon, and non-cellulosic man-made fibers from Textile Organon, a publication of the Textile Economics Bureau, Inc.

Year	Cotton[1] (million bales)[5]		Wool[2] (million pounds)		Silk	Man-made fibers[3] Cellulosic (million pounds)		Man-made fibers[3] Non-cellulosic[4] (million pounds)	
	U.S.	World	U.S.	World	World (mil. lbs.)	U.S.	World	U.S.[4]	World[6]
1940	12.6	31.2	434.0	4,180	130	471.2	2,485.3	4.6	4.6
1950	10.0	30.6	249.3	4,000	42	1,259.4	3,552.8	145.9	177.4
1960	14.2	46.2	298.9	5,615	68	1,028.5	5,749.1	854.2	1,779.1
1965	15.0	55.0	224.8	5,731	72	1,527.0	7,359.4	2,062.4	4,928.9
1970	10.2	53.6	176.8	6,107	90	1,373.2	7,573.9	4,053.5	10,361.7
1971	10.5	59.8	172.2	5,972	90	1,390.9	7,617.1	4,761.0	12,366.0
1972	13.7	62.9	168.2	5,560	93	1,394.3	7,846.0	5,927.3	14,057.8
1973	13.0	63.3	151.7	5,474	95	1,357.0	8,069.4	6,997.4	16,842.0
1974	11.5	64.3	137.1	5,769	99	1,198.8	7,786.7	6,906.5	16,505.2
1975	8.3	54.0	125.5	5,911	104	749.0	6,523.2	6,432.2	17,344.6
1976	10.6	57.4	116.0	5,827	123	840.9	7,075.9	7,302.6	20,448.7
1977	14.4	63.5	109.8	5,838	108	887.7	7,232.7	8,114.6	21,967.7
1978	10.9	60.2	103.9	5,975	113	904.5	7,314.4	8,706.3	24,123.3
1979	14.6	65.7	105.8	6,180	121	929.8	7,451.5	9,451.0	25,565.2
1980	11.1	65.6	106.5	6,296	123	806.0	7,148.2	8,759.8	25,122.3
1981	15.6	70.8	111.0	6,378	126	770.1	7,036.6	9,047.0	25,789.1

(1) Year beginning Aug. 1. (2) Grease basis. (3) Includes filament yarn and staple and tow fiber. (4) Includes textile glass fiber. (5) 480-pound net weight bales, U.S. beginning 1960 and world beginning 1965. (6) 1966 to date, excludes Olefin.

Work Stoppages (Strikes) in the U.S.

Source: Bureau of Labor Statistics, U.S. Labor Department

	Number stoppages	Workers involved (thousands)	Man days idle (thousands)
Average 1935-1939	2,862	1,130	16,900
War Period Dec. 8, 1941-Aug. 14, 1945	14,371	6,744	36,300
Year			
1950	4,843	2,410	38,800
1952	5,117	3,540	59,100
1953	5,091	2,400	28,300
1954	3,468	1,530	22,600
1955	4,320	2,650	28,200
1956	3,825	1,900	33,100
1957	3,673	1,390	16,500
1958	3,694	2,060	23,900
1959	3,708	1,880	69,000
1960	3,333	1,320	19,100
1961	3,367	1,450	16,300
1962	3,614	1,230	18,600
1963	3,362	941	16,100
1964	3,655	1,640	22,900
1965	3,963	1,550	23,300
1966	4,405	1,960	25,400
1967	4,595	2,870	42,100
1968	5,045	2,649	49,018
1969	5,700	2,481	42,869
1970	5,716	3,305	66,414
1971	5,138	3,280	47,589
1972	5,010	1,714	27,066
1973	5,353	2,251	27,948
1974	6,074	2,778	47,991
1975	5,031	1,746	31,237
1976	5,648	2,420	37,859
1977	5,506	2,040	35,822
1978	4,230	1,623	36,922
1979	4,827	1,727	34,754
1980	3,885	1,366	33,289
1981	2,568	1,081	24,730

Employment Status of Civilian Labor Force

Source: Bureau of Labor Statistics, U.S. Labor Department (thousands)

Employment status	Annual average				1982				
	1978	1979	1980	1981	Jan.	Mar.	May	June	July
Total noninstitutional pop.	164,027	166,951	169,848	172,272	173,495	173,843	174,201	174,364	174,544
Total labor force	104,368	107,050	109,042	110,812	111,038	111,521	112,841	112,364	112,702
Civilian noninstitutional pop.	161,910	164,863	167,745	170,130	171,335	171,667	172,026	172,190	172,364
Civilian labor force	102,251	104,962	106,940	108,670	108,879	109,346	110,666	110,191	110,522
Employed	96,048	98,824	99,303	100,397	99,581	99,492	100,117	99,764	99,732
Agriculture	3,387	3,347	3,364	3,368	3,411	3,349	3,488	3,357	3,460
Nonagricultural	92,661	95,477	95,938	97,030	96,170	96,144	96,629	96,406	96,272
Unemployed	6,202	6,137	7,637	8,273	9,298	9,854	10,549	10,427	10,790
Unemployment rate	6.1	5.8	7.1	7.6	8.5	9.0	9.5	9.5	9.8
Not in labor force	59,659	59,900	60,806	61,460	62,456	62,321	61,360	61,999	61,842
Men, 20 years & over									
Civilian noninstitutional population	68,268	69,709	71,138	72,419	73,120	73,287	73,499	73,585	73,685
Civilian labor force	54,471	55,615	56,455	57,197	57,368	57,554	58,164	58,016	58,084
Employed	52,143	53,308	53,101	53,582	53,047	53,006	53,260	52,985	52,996
Agriculture	2,394	2,387	2,396	2,384	2,390	2,377	2,464	2,424	2,474
Nonagricultural	49,749	50,920	50,706	51,199	50,657	50,629	50,796	50,561	50,522
Unemployed	2,328	2,308	3,353	3,615	4,322	4,548	4,904	5,031	5,088
Unemployment rate	4.3	4.2	5.9	6.3	7.5	7.9	8.4	8.7	8.8
Not in labor force	13,796	14,093	14,683	15,222	15,752	15,733	15,335	15,569	15,601
Women, 20 years & over									
Civilian noninstitutional pop.	76,948	78,496	80,065	81,497	82,260	82,478	82,707	82,811	82,926
Civilian labor force	38,128	39,708	41,106	42,485	42,868	43,243	43,683	43,904	44,076
Employed	35,836	37,434	38,492	39,590	39,764	39,807	40,075	40,350	40,392
Agriculture	594	600	584	604	649	636	634	581	600
Nonagricultural	32,241	36,834	37,907	38,986	39,115	39,172	39,441	39,769	39,791
Unemployed	2,292	2,276	2,615	2,895	3,104	3,435	3,608	3,554	3,684
Unemployment rate	6.0	5.7	6.4	6.8	7.2	7.9	8.3	8.1	8.4
Not in labor force	38,820	38,787	38,958	39,012	39,392	39,235	39,024	38,907	38,850

Industrial Minerals: Distribution, Resources, Reserves

Source: Organization for Economic Cooperation and Development

(Resource and reserve figures are based on average conservative estimates.)

Minerals	Distribution of reserves, 1977 (% of world total)	Resources[1] 1977 (million metric tons)	Reserves[2] 1977 (million metric tons)	Ratio of reserves to 1976 demand in years[3]	Ratio of reserves to total demand 1976-2000[4]
Iron	USSR(30.2) Brazil(17.5) Canada(11.7) Australia(11.5) India(5.8)	195,000	93,400	194	5.1
Copper	U.S.(18.5) Chile(18.5) USSR(7.9) Peru(7.0) Canada(6.8) Zambia(6.4)	726	456	54	1.4
Lead	U.S.(20.8) Australia(13.8) USSR(13.2) Canada(9.5) South Africa(4.1)	1,360	124	29	1.2
Tin	Indonesia(23.6) China(14.8) Thailand(11.8) Bolivia(9.7) Malaysia(8.2) USSR(6.1) Brazil(5.9)	37	10.2	42	1.5
Zinc	Canada(18.7) U.S.(14.5) Australia(12.6) USSR(7.3) Ireland(5.5)	1,800	150	27	0.9
Aluminum	Guinea(23.9) Australia(18.6) Brazil(10.3) Jamaica(6.2) India(5.8) Guiana(4.1) Cameroon(4.1)	7,600	5,000	over 200	6.2
Titanium	Brazil(26.3) India(17.5) Canada(15.2) South Africa(8.6) Australia(6.6) Norway(6.4) U.S.(6.0)	2,015	394	over 300	4.4
Chromium	S. Africa(74.1) Rhodesia(22.2) USSR(0.6) Finland(0.6) India(0.4) Madagascar(0.3) Brazil(0.3)	5,300	820	over 300	10.3
Cobalt	Zaire(30.3) New Caledonia(18.8) USSR(13.9) Philippines(12.8) Zambia(7.7) Cuba(7.3)	4.5	1.5	44	1.3
Columbium	Brazil(76.6) USSR(6.4) Canada(5.5) Zaire(3.8) Uganda(3.0) Niger(3.0)	14.6	10.7	over 800	17
Manganese	S. Africa(45.0) USSR(37.5) Australia(8.0) Gabon(5.0) Brazil(2.2)	3,265	1,814	185	4.6
Molybdenum	U.S.(38.4) Chile(27.8) Canada(8.1) USSR(6.6) China(6.0)	31.7	9.0	108	2.2
Nickel	New Caledonia(25.0) Canada(16.0) USSR(13.5) Indonesia(13.0) Australia(9.3) Philippines(9.0)	127.7	54.4	83	2.2
Tantalum	Zaire(55.0) Nigeria(11.0) North Korea(6.4) U.S.(6.1) USSR(2.9)	0.26	0.06	60	1.8
Tungsten	China(46.9) Canada(12.1) USSR(10.6) N. Korea(5.6) U.S.(5.4) Australia(2.7)	3.4	2.0	57	1.4
Vanadium	USSR(74.8) S. Africa(18.7) Chile(1.4) Australia(1.4) Venezuela(0.9) India(0.9)	56.2	9.7	over 300	8.2
Bismuth	Australia(20.7) Bolivia(16.3) U.S.(10.9) Canada(6.5) Mexico(6.5) Peru(5.4)	0.13	0.08	30	0.8
Mercury	Spain(38.4) USSR(18.2) Yugoslavia(8.6) U.S.(8.6) China(4.5) Mexico(4.5) Turkey(4.5) Italy(4.1)	0.80	0.24	30	0.9
Silver	USSR(26.2) U.S.(24.8) Mexico(13.9) Canada(11.6) Peru(10.0)	0.51	0.19	20	0.6
Platinum	S. Africa(82.3) USSR(15.6) Canada(1.6) Colombia(0.3) U.S.(0.1)	0.026	0.009	110	3.1
Asbestos	Canada(42.7) USSR(32.3) S. Africa(6.3) Rhodesia(6.3) U.S.(4.2)	135	87	22	0.5

(1) Seabed deposits not included; these are (in million metric tons): cobalt, 280; manganese, 36,425; nickel, 1,350; molybdenum, 78; vanadium, 107. Other minerals for which resource estimates are considerably increased if seabed deposits are included are titanium, aluminum, lead, copper, bismuth, silver and, to a lesser extent, zinc, iron, chromium, and tungsten. (2) Reserves are defined as that portion of the identified resources from which useable material can be economically and legally extracted at the time of determination. (3) Ie., iron will last 194 years if used at the 1976 rate. (4) Ie., there is 5.1 times more iron than total estimated demand between 1976 and 2000.

U.S. Nonfuel Mineral Production

Source: Bureau of Mines, U.S. Interior Department

Production as measured by mine shipments, sales, or marketable production (including consumption by producers)

Metals	1980 Quantity	1980 Value (thousands)	1981 Quantity	1981 Value (thousands)
Antimony ore and concentrate . . . . . short tons, antimony content	343	W	646	W
Bauxite . . . . thousand metric tons, dried equivalent	1,559	$23,353	1,510	26,489
Copper (recoverable content of ores, etc.) . . . . metric tons	[r]1,181,116	[r]2,666,931	1,538,160	2,886,440
Gold (recoverable content of ores, etc.). . . . . troy ounces	[r]969,782	[r]594,050	1,377,946	633,359
Iron ore, usable (excluding byproduct iron sinter) thousand long tons, gross weight	69,562	2,543,484	72,158	2,914,689
Iron oxide pigments, crude . . . . short tons	62,642	4,043	67,214	4,142
Lead (recoverable content of ores, etc.) . . . . metric tons	[r]550,366	[r]515,189	445,535	358,821
Manganiferous ore (5% to 35% Mn). . . . . short tons, gross weight	173,887	2,444	175,760	2,889
Mercury . . . . 76-pound flasks	30,657	11,939	27,904	11,549
Molybdenum (content of concentrate). . . . . thousand pounds	149,311	1,344,181	118,916	945,540
Nickel (content of ore and concentrate) . . . . short tons	14,653	W	12,099	W
Silver (recoverable content of ores, etc.) . . . thousand troy ounces	[r]32,329	[r]667,278	40,685	427,943
Titanium concentrate:				
Ilmenite . . . . short tons, gross weight	593,704	32,041	523,681	37,013
Tungsten ore and concentrate . . . . thousand pounds contained W	6,036	50,575	7,815	62,231
Vanadium (recoverable in ore and concentrate) . . . . . . short tons	4,806	64,370	5,126	71,496
Zinc (recoverable content of ores, etc.) . . . . metric tons	[r]317,103	[r]261,671	312,418	306,879
Combined value of beryllium, magnesium chloride for magnesium metal, platinum-group metals (1980), rare-earth metals, tin, titanium (rutile), zircon concentrate, and values indicated by symbol W	XX	141,492	XX	68,195
Total metals	**XX**	**[r]8,922,000**	**XX**	**8,758,000**
Nonmetals (except fuels)				
Abrasive stones[2] . . . . short tons	2,131	2,233	4,501	1,176
Asbestos. . . . . metric tons	80,079	30,599	75,618	30,685
Asphalt and related bitumens, native:				
bituminous limestone, sandstone, gilsonite . . thousand short tons	1,252	25,030	1,261	27,654
Barite. . . . . do	2,245	65,957	2,849	102,439
Boron minerals . . . . do	1,545	366,760	1,481	435,387
Bromine. . . . . thousand pounds	[r]380,400	[r]95,400	389,500	90,200
Calcium chloride . . . . short tons	581,012	47,950	704,691	61,692
Carbon dioxide, natural. . . . . thousand cubic feet	1,628,424	2,561	1,577,053	2,607
Cement:				
Portland . . . . thousand short tons	71,612	3,613,332	68,197	3,515,600
Masonry. . . . . do	3,040	188,456	2,738	161,819
Clays. . . . . do	48,790	898,947	44,379	988,845
Diatomite. . . . . do	689	100,610	687	113,010
Emery . . . . short tons	[r]W	[r]W	W	W
Feldspar . . . . do	[e]710,000	[e]23,200	[e]665,000	[e]21,000
Fluorspar . . . . do	92,635	12,611	115,404	18,412
Garnet (abrasive) . . . . do	26,909	[r]1,098	25,451	2,059
Gem stones(e)	NA	6,930	NA	7,625
Gypsum . . . . thousand short tons	12,376	[r]103,059	11,497	98,101
Helium:				
Crude . . . . million cubic feet	299	3,588	175	2,100
High-purity . . . . do	1,159	26,657	1,223	31,798
Lime . . . . thousand short tons	19,010	842,922	18,856	884,197
Mica:				
Scrap . . . . do	[r]116	[r]6,262	133	8,212
Peat . . . . do	788	16,190	757	18,783
Perlite . . . . short tons	638,000	16,500	591,000	17,418
Phosphate rock . . . . thousand metric tons	54,415	1,256,947	53,624	1,437,986
Potassium salts. . . . . thousand metric tons, K_2O equivalent	2,217	353,862	1,908	328,900
Pumice. . . . . thousand short tons	[r]543	[r]4,267	499	4,311
Pyrites . . . . thousand metric tons	847	13,812	797	49,160
Salt. . . . . thousand short tons	40,352	656,164	38,907	636,328
Sand and gravel . . . . do	[r]792,700	[r]2,289,000	[e]754,800	[e]2,290,000
Sodium carbonate (natural) . . . . do	W	W	W	W
Sodium sulfate (natural) . . . . do	583	[r]36,387	608	43,186
Stone[3] . . . . do	[r]984,856	[r]3,404,736	874,381	3,276,967
Sulfur, Frasch process . . . . thousand metric tons	7,400	720,511	5,910	715,683
Talc and pyrophyllite . . . . thousand short tons	1,473	25,626	1,343	31,497
Tripoli . . . . short tons	121,233	676	107,330	617
Vermiculite . . . . thousand short tons	337	23,483	320	26,181
Combined value of aplite, emery, graphite, iodine, kyanite, lithium minerals, magnesite, magnesium compounds, greensand marl, olivine, staurolite, wollastonite, and values indicated by symbol W	XX	[r]941,212	XX	933,515
Total nonmetals	**XX**	**[r]16,224,000**	**XX**	**16,415,000**
Grand total	**XX**	**[r]25,146,000**	**XX**	**25,173,000**

(e) Estimate. (r) Revised. (NA) Not available. (W) Withheld to avoid disclosing company proprietary data; included in "Combined value" figures. (XX) Not applicable.
(1) Production as measured by mine shipments, sales, or marketable production (including consumption by producers).
(2) Grindstones, pulpstones, grinding pebbles, sharpening stones, and tube mill liners.
(3) Excludes abrasive stone, bituminous limestone, bituminous sandstone, and soapstones, all included elsewhere in table.

U.S. Nonfuel Mineral Production—Leading States

Source: Bureau of Mines, U.S. Interior Department

1981 State	Value (thousands)	Percent of U.S. total	Principal minerals, in order of value
Arizona	$2,565,840	10.19	Copper, molybdenum, cement, silver.
Minnesota	2,151,871	8.55	Iron ore, sand and gravel, stone, lime.
California	1,975,016	7.85	Cement, boron minerals, sand and gravel, stone.
Florida	1,725,589	6.85	Phosphate rock, stone, cement, clays.
Texas	1,658,203	6.59	Cement, sulfur, stone, sand and gravel.
Michigan	1,438,355	5.71	Iron ore, cement, magnesium compounds, salt.
Colorado	965,766	3.84	Molybdenum, cement, sand and gravel, silver.
Missouri	870,326	3.46	Lead, cement, stone, lime.
Georgia	804,455	3.20	Clays, stone, cement, sand and gravel.
Utah	783,232	3.11	Copper, gold, molybdenum, pottasium salts.

Value of U.S. Mineral Production

(millons of dollars)

Production as measured by mine shipments sales or marketable production.

Year[1]	Fuels	Nonmetallic	Metals	Total[2]	Year[1]	Fuels	Nonmetallic	Metals	Total[2]
1930	2,500	973	501	3,980	1974	40,889	8,687	5,501	55,077
1940	2,662	784	752	4,198	1975	47,505	9,570	5,191	62,266
1950	8,689	1,882	1,351	11,862	1976	52,484	10,616	6,086	69,186
1960	12,142	3,868	2,022	18,032	1977	59,575	11,701	5,810	77,086
1965	14,047	4,933	2,544	21,524	1978	NA	13,525	6,298	NA
1970	20,152	5,712	3,928	29,792	1979	NA	15,438	8,536	NA
1972	22,061	6,482	3,642	32,185	1980	NA	16,224	8,922	NA
1973	24,949	7,476	4,362	36,787	1981	NA	16,415	8,758	NA

(1) Excludes Alaska and Hawaii, 1930-53. (2) Data may not add to total because of rounding figures. (P) Preliminary.

U.S. Pig Iron and Steel Output

Source: American Iron and Steel Institute (net tons)

Year	Total pig iron	Pig iron and ferro-alloys	Raw steel	Year	Total pig iron	Pig iron and ferro-alloys	Raw steel
1940	46,071,666	47,398,529	66,982,686	1975	101,208,000	103,345,000	116,642,000
1945	53,223,169	54,919,029	79,701,648	1976	86,870,000	88,780,000	128,000,000
1950	64,586,907	66,400,311	96,836,075	1977	81,328,000	83,082,000	125,333,000
1955	76,857,417	79,263,865	117,036,085	1978	87,679,000	89,351,000	137,031,000
1960	66,480,648	68,566,384	99,281,601	1979	87,003,000	88,906,000	136,341,000
1965	88,184,901	90,918,040	131,461,601	1980	68,721,000	70,329,000	111,835,000
1970	91,435,000	93,851,000	131,514,000	1981	73,570,000	75,096,000	120,828,000

Steel figures include only that portion of the capacity and production of steel for castings used by foundries which were operated by companies producing steel ingots.

Raw Steel Production

(thousands of net tons)

State	1979	1980	1981	State	1979	1980	1981
New York	4,035	2,675	3,147	Illinois	11,729	8,961	9,105
Pennsylvania	28,213	23,517	24,066	Michigan	10,922	7,877	8,943
R.I., Conn., N.J., Del., Md.	6,638	5,161	5,777	Minn., Mo., Okla., Texas	8,260	8,642	9,068
Va., W.Va., Ga., Fla., N.C., S.C.,	6,788	6,066	6,497	Ariz., Colo., Utah, Wash., Ore., Ha.	5,165	4,795	4,842
Kentucky	2,438	2,141	2,397	California	3,672	2,628	2,653
Ala., Tenn., Miss., Ark.	4,487	3,452	3,585				
Ohio	21,082	16,100	18,096				
Indiana	22,912	19,820	22,652	**Total**	**136,341**	**111,835**	**120,828**

U.S. Copper, Lead, and Zinc Production

Source: Bureau of Mines, U.S. Interior Department

Year	Copper		Lead[1]		Zinc	
	Mil. lbs.	$1,000	Short tons	$1,000	Short tons	Mil. dol.
1950	1,823	379,122	418,809	113,078	591,454	167
1960	2,286	733,708	228,899	53,562	334,101	87
1965	2,703	957,028	301,147	93,959	611,153	178
1970	3,439	1,984,484	571,767	178,609	534,136	164
1975	2,827	1,814,763	563,783	267,230	425,792	366

Year	Copper		Lead[1]		Zinc	
	Mil. lbs.	$1,000	Metric tons	$1,000	Metric tons	Mil. dol.
1977	3,008	2,009,297	537,499	363,789	407,889	309
1978	2,993	1,990,323	529,661	393,516	302,669	207
1979	3,182	2,960,675	525,569	609,929	267,341	220
1980	2,604	2,666,931	550,366	515,189	317,103	261
1981	3,391	2,886,440	445,535	358,821	312,418	306

(1) Production from domestic ores.

Labor Union Directory

Source: Bureau of Labor Statistics; World Almanac Questionnaire
(*) Independent union; all others affiliated with AFL-CIO.

Actors and Artistes of America, Associated (AAAA), 165 W. 46th St., New York, NY 10036; founded 1919; Frederick O'-Neal, Pres. (since 1971); no individual members, 9 affiliates.

Actors' Equity Association, 165 W. 46th St., New York, NY 10036; founded 1913; Ellen Burstyn, Pres.; 30,000 members.

Air Line Pilots Association, 1625 Massachusetts Ave. NW, Washington, DC 20036. John J. O'Donnell, Pres.; 33,000 members.

Aluminum Brick & Clay Workers International Union (AWIU), 3362 Hollenberg Drive, Bridgeton, MO 63044; founded 1953; Lawrence A. Holley, Pres. (since 1977); 50,000 members, 250 locals.

Automobile, Aerospace & Agricultural Implement Workers of America, International Union, United (UAW), 8000 E. Jefferson Ave., Detroit, MI 48214; founded 1935; Douglas Fraser, Pres. (since 1977); 1,200,000 members, 1,611 locals.

Bakery, Confectionery & Tobacco Workers International Union (BC&T), 10401 Connecticut Ave., Kensington, MD 20895; founded 1886; John DeConcini, Pres. (since 1978); 170,000 members, 201 locals.

Barbers, Beauticians, and Allied Industries, International Association, 7050 West Washington St., Indianapolis, IN 46214; Richard Plumb, Pres.; 41,000 members, 702 locals.

Boilermakers, Iron Shipbuilders, Blacksmiths, Forgers and Helpers, International Brotherhood of (BSF), 570 New Brotherhood Bldg., Kansas City, KS 66101; founded 1880; Harold J. Buoy, Pres. (since 1973); 150,000 members, 400 locals.

Bricklayers and Allied Craftsmen, International Union of, 815 15th St. NW, Washington, DC 20005; Thomas F. Murphy, Pres.; 147,715 members, 758 locals.

Carpenters and Joiners of America, United Brotherhood of, 101 Constitution Ave. NW, Washington, DC 20001; William Konyha, Pres.; 820,000 members, 2,301 locals.

Cement, Lime Gypsum and Allied Workers International Union, United (U.C.L.G.A.W.I.U.), 7830 West Lawrence Ave., Norridge, IL 60656; founded 1939; Thomas F. Miechur, Pres. (since 1970); 35,367 members, 318 locals.

Chemical Workers Union, International (ICWU), 1655 West Market St., Akron, OH 44313; founded 1944; Frank D. Martino, Pres. (since 1975); 70,000 members, 400 locals.

Clothing and Textile Workers Union, Amalgamated (ACTWU), 15 Union Square, New York, NY 10003; founded 1914; Murray H. Finley, Pres. (since 1972); 510,000 members, 900 locals.

Communications Workers of America, 1925 K St. NW, Washington, DC 20006; Glenn E. Watts, Pres.; 600,000 members, 900 locals.

Distillery, Wine & Allied Workers International Union (DWU), 66 Grand Ave., Englewood, NJ 07631; founded 1940; George J. Oneto, Pres. (since 1974); 25,000 members, 67 locals.

***Distributive Workers of America,** 13 Astor Place, New York, NY 10003; Cleveland Robinson, Pres.; 50,000 members, 40 locals.

***Education Association, National,** 1201 16th St. NW, Washington, DC 20036; Willard H. McGuire, Pres.; 1,700,000 members, 12,000 affiliates.

Electrical, Radio and Machine Workers, International Union of (IUE), 1126 16th St. NW, Washington, DC 20036; founded 1949; David J. Fitzmaurice, Pres. (since 1976); 225,000 members, 640 locals.

***Electrical, Radio & Machine Workers of America, United (UE),** 11 E. 51st St. New York, NY 10022; founded 1936; James Kane, Gen. Pres. (since 1981); 165,000 members, 200 locals.

Electrical Workers, International Brotherhood of (IBEW), 1125 15th St., NW, Washington, DC 20005; founded 1891; Charles H. Pillard, Pres. (since 1970); 1,000,000 members, 1,479 locals.

Farm Workers of America, United (UFW), La Paz, Keene, CA 93531; founded 1962; Cesar E. Chavez, Pres. (since 1973); 100,000 members.

***Federal Employees, National Federation of (NFFE),** 1016 16th St. NW, Washington, DC 20036; founded 1917; James M. Peirce Jr., Pres. (since 1976); 150,000 members, 600 locals.

Fire Fighters, International Association of, 1750 New York Ave. NW, Washington, DC 20006; John A. Gannon, Pres.; 171,674 members, 1,798 locals.

Firemen and Oilers, International Brotherhood of, VFW Bldg., 200 Maryland Ave. NE, Washington, DC 20002; George J. Francisco, Pres.; 40,000 members.

Food and Commercial Workers International Union, United, 1775 K St., NW, Washington, DC 20006; William H. Wynn, Pres.; 1.3 million members, 790 locals.

Furniture Workers of America, United, 700 Broadway, New York, NY 10003; Carl Scarbrough, Pres.; 29,967 members, 106 locals.

Garment Workers of America, United (UGWA), 200 Park Ave. So., New York, NY 10003; founded 1891; William O'Donnell, Gen. Pres. (since 1977); 25,000 members, 155 locals.

Glass Bottle Blowers Association (GBBA), 608 E. Baltimore Pike, Media, PA 19063; founded 1842; James E. Hatfield, Pres.; 82,000 members, 245 locals.

Glass and Ceramic Workers of North America, United, 556 E. Town St., Columbus, OH 43215; Joseph Roman, Pres.; 30,000 members, 181 locals.

Glass Workers Union, American Flint (AFGWU), 1440 So. Byrne Rd., Toledo, OH 43614; founded 1878; George M. Parker, Pres. (since 1961); 31,000 members, 238 locals.

Government Employees, American Federation of (AFGE), 1325 Massachusetts Ave. NW, Washington, DC 20005; founded 1932; Kenneth T. Blaylock, Natl. Pres. (since 1976); 300,000 members, 1,500 locals.

Grain Millers, American Federation of (AFGM), 4949 Olson Memorial Hwy., Minneapolis, MN 55422; founded 1948; Frank Hoese, Gen. Pres. (since 1979); 35,000 members, 204 locals.

Graphic Arts International Union (GAIU), 1900 L St., NW, Washington, DC 20036; founded 1882; Kenneth J. Brown, Pres. (since 1959); 120,000 members, 220 locals.

Hotel and Restaurant Employees International Union, 120 E. 4th St., Cincinnati, OH 45202; Edward T. Hanley, Pres.; 400,000 members, 225 locals.

Industrial Workers of America, International Union, Allied (AIW), 3520 W. Oklahoma Ave., Milwaukee, WI 53215; founded 1935; Dominick D'Ambrosio, Intl. Pres. (since 1975); 75,000 members, 405 locals.

Iron Workers, International Association of Bridge Structural and Ornamental, 1750 New York Ave. NW, Washington, DC 20006; John H. Lyons, Pres.; 181, 647 members, 318 locals.

Laborers' International Union of North America (LIUNA), 905 16th St. NW, Washington, DC 20006; founded 1903; Angelo Fosco, Gen. Pres. (since 1976); 650,000 members, 820 locals.

Ladies Garment Workers Union, International (ILGWU), 1710 Broadway, New York, NY 10019; founded 1900; Sol C. Chaikin, Pres. (since 1975); 322,505 members, 447 locals.

Leather Goods, Plastic and Novelty Workers' Union, International, 265 W. 14th St., New York, NY 10011; Frank Casale, Pres.; 40,000 members, 97 locals.

Letter Carriers, National Association of (NALC), 100 Indiana Ave. NW, Washington, DC 20001; founded 1889; Vincent R. Sombrotto, Pres. (since 1979); 240,000 members, 4,500 locals.

***Locomotive Engineers, Brotherhood of (BLE),** 1365 Ontario Ave., Cleveland, OH 44114; founded 1863; John F. Sytsma, Pres. (since 1976); 62,888 members, 727 divisions.

Longshoremen's Association, International, 17 Battery Pl., New York, NY 10004; Thomas W. Gleason, Pres.; 76,579 members, 367 locals.

***Longshoremen's & Warehousemen's Union, International (ILWU),** 1188 Franklin St., San Francisco, CA 94109; founded 1937; James R. Herman, Pres. (since 1977); 58,000 members, 78 locals.

Machinists and Aerospace Workers, International Association of, 1300 Connecticut Ave. NW, Washington, DC 20036; William W. Winpisinger, Pres.; 943,280 members, 1,904 locals.

Maintenance of Way Employes, Brotherhood of, 12050 Woodward Ave., Detroit, MI 48203; O. M. Berge, Pres.; 169,693 members, 966 locals.

Marine & Shipbuilding Workers of America, Industrial Union of (IUMSWA), 8121 Georgia Ave., Silver Springs, MD 20910; founded 1934; Frank Derwin, Pres. (since 1971); 25,000 members, 40 locals.

Maritime Union of America, National, 346 W. 17th St., New York NY 10011; Shannon Wall, Pres.; 35,000 members.

Mechanics Educational Society of America, 1421 First National Bldg., Detroit, MI 48226; Alfred J. Smith, Pres.; 25,000 members, 29 locals.

***Mine Workers of America, United (UMWA),** 900 15th St. NW, Washington, DC 20005; founded 1890; Sam Church Jr., Pres.; 250,000 members, 866 locals.

Molders' and Allied Workers' Union, International, 1225 E. McMillan St., Cincinnati, OH 45206; Carl W. Studenroth, Pres.;

75,000 members, 242 locals.

Musicians of the United States and Canada, American Federation of (AF of M), 1500 Broadway, New York, NY 10036; founded 1896; Victor W. Fuentealba, Pres. (since 1978); 280,000 members, 600 locals.

Newspaper Guild, The (TNG), 1125 15th St. NW, Washington, DC; founded 1933; Charles A. Perlik Jr., Pres. (since 1969); 32,000 members, 80 locals.

***Nurses Association, American,** 2420 Pershing Rd., Kansas City, MO 64108; Barbara Nichols, Pres.; 170,000 members, 53 affiliates.

Office and Professional Employees International Union, 265 W. 14th St., New York, NY 10011; John Kelly, Pres.; 125,000 members, 275 locals.

Oil, Chemical and Atomic Workers International Union, PO Box 2812, 1636 Champa St., Denver, CO 80201, A.F. Grospiron, Pres.; 177,433 members, 617 locals.

Operating Engineers, International Union of (IUOE), 1125 17th St. NW, Washington, DC 20036; founded 1896; J.C. Turner, Gen. Pres.; 420,000 members, 210 locals.

Painters and Allied Trades, International Brotherhood of (IBPAT), 1750 New York Ave. NW, Washington, DC 20006; founded 1887; S. Frank Raftery, Gen. Pres. (since 1965); 192,170 members, 809 locals.

Paperworkers International Union, United (UPIU), 702 Church St., P.O. Box 1475, Nashville, TN 37202; founded 1884; Wayne E. Glenn, Pres. (since 1978); 265,000 members, 1,250 locals.

***Plant Guard Workers of America, International Union, United (UPGWA),** 25510 Kelly Rd., Roseville, MI 48066; founded 1948; James C. McGahey, Pres. (since 1948); 29,243 members, 162 locals.

Plasterers' and Cement Mason's International Association of the United States & Canada; Operative, 1125 17th St. NW, Washington, DC 20036; Melvin H. Roots, Pres.; Robert J. Holton, Secy.-Treas.; 65,000 members, 365 locals.

Plumbing and Pipe Fitting Industry of the United States and Canada, United Association of Journeymen and Apprentices of the, 901 Massachusetts Ave. NW, Washington, DC 20001; Martin Ward, Pres.; 350,000 members.

***Police, Fraternal Order of,** 5613 Belair Rd., Baltimore, MD 21206; Leo V. Marchetti, Pres,; 157,909 members, 1,409 affiliates.

***Postal Supervisors, National Association of,** 490 L'Enfant Plaza SW, Washington, DC 20024; Donald N. Ledbetter, Pres.; 35,000 members, 460 locals.

Postal Workers Union, American (APWU), 817 14th St. NW, Washington, DC 20005; founded 1971; Moe Biller, Gen. Pres. (since 1980); 320,000 members, 5,000 locals.

Printing and Graphic Communications Union, International, 1730 Rhode Island Ave. NW, Washington, DC 20036; Sol Fishko, Pres.; 110,000 members, 556 locals.

Railway, Airline and Steamship Clerks, Freight Handlers, Express and Station Employees; Brotherhood of, 3 Research Place, Rockville, MD 20850; R. I. Kilroy, Pres.; 200,000 members, 800 locals.

Railway Carmen of the United States and Canada, Brotherhood, 4929 Main St., Kansas City, MO 64112; founded 1890; O.W. Jacobson, Gen. Pres.; 91,000 members, 600 locals.

Retail, Wholesale and Department Store Union, 30 E. 29th St., New York, NY 10016; Alvin E. Heaps, Pres.; 200,000 members, 315 locals.

Roofers, Damp and Waterproof Workers Association, United Slate, Tile and Composition, 1125 17th St. NW, Washington, DC 20036; Roy Johnson, Pres.; 28,000 members, 205 locals.

Rubber, Cork, Linoleum and Plastic Workers of America, United, 87 South High St., Akron, OH 44308; Milan Stone, Pres.; 130,000 members, 524 locals.

***Rural Letter Carriers' Association, National,** Suite 1204, 1750 Pennsylvania Ave. NW, Washington, DC 20006; Wilbur S. Wood, Pres.; 64,000 members.

Seafarers International Union of North America (SIUNA), 675 4th Ave., Brooklyn, NY 11232; founded 1938; Frank Drozak, Pres. (act.); 90,000 members.

Service Employees International Union (SEIU), 2020 K St. NW, Washington, DC 20006; founded 1921; John J. Sweeney, Pres. (since 1980); 650,000 members, 328 locals.

Sheet Metal Workers' International Association (SMWIA), 1750 New York Ave. NW, Washington, DC 20006; founded 1888; Edward J. Carlough, Gen. Pres. (since 1970); 160,000 members, 352 locals.

Shoe Workers of America, United, 120 Boylston St., Boston, MA 02116; George O. Fecteau, Pres.; 35,000 members, 125 locals.

State, County and Municipal Employees, American Federation of, 1625 L St. NW, Washington, DC 20036; Jerry Wurf, Pres.; 1,098,000 members, 2,950 locals.

Steelworkers of America, United (USWA), 5 Gateway Center, Pittsburgh, PA 15222; founded 1942; Lloyd McBride, Pres. (since 1977); 1,200,000 members, 4,843 locals.

Teachers, American Federation of (AFT), 11 Dupont Circle NW, Washington, DC 20036; founded 1916; Albert Shanker, Pres. (since 1974); 580,000 members, 2,010 locals.

***Teamsters, Chauffeurs, Warehousemen and Helpers of America, International Brotherhood of (IBT),** 25 Louisiana Ave. NW, Washington, DC 20001; founded 1903; Roy L. Williams, Gen. Pres. (since 1981); 2,000,000 members, 745 locals.

Television and Radio Artists, American Federation of, 1350 Ave. of the Americas, New York, NY; founded 1937; Bill Hillman, Pres.; 55,000 members, 38 locals.

Textile Workers of America, United (UTWA), 420 Common St., Lawrence, MA 01840; founded 1901; Francis Schaufenbil, Intl. Pres. (since 1972); 50,000 members, 221 locals.

Theatrical Stage Employees and Moving Picture Operators of the United States and Canada, International Alliance of, 1515 Broadway, New York, NY 10036; Walter Diehl, Pres.; 61,471 members, 870 locals.

Toys, Playthings, Novelties and Allied Products of the United States and Canada, International Union of Dolls, 147 E. 26th St., New York, NY 10010; Julius Isaacson, Pres.; 31,000 members, 23 locals.

Transit Union, Amalgamated (ATU), 5025 Wisconsin Ave. NW, Washington, DC 20016; founded 1892; John W. Rowland, Intl. Pres. (since 1981); 160,000 members, 295 locals.

Transport Workers Union of America, 1980 Broadway, New York, NY 10023; William G. Lindner, Pres.; 100,000 members, 105 locals.

Transportation Union, United (UTU), 14600 Detroit Ave., Cleveland, OH 44107; founded 1969; Fred A. Hardin, Pres. (since 1979); 210,000 members.

***Treasury Employees Union, National (NTEU),** 1730 K St. NW, Washington, DC 20006; founded 1938; Vincent L. Connery, Natl. Pres. (since 1966); 115,000 members, 201 chapters.

Typographical Union, International (ITU), PO Box 157, Colorado Springs, CO 80901; founded 1852; Joe Bingel, Pres. (since 1978); 88,200 members, 520 locals.

***University Professors, American Association of (AAUP),** 1 Dupont Circle, Washington, DC 20036; founded 1915; Henry T. Yost, Pres.; 75,000 members, 1,300 locals.

Upholsterers' International Union of North America (UIU), 25 N. 4th St., Philadelphia, PA 19106; founded 1882; John Serembus, Pres.; 38,513 members, 141 locals.

Utility Workers Union of America (UWUA), 815 16th St. NW, Washington, DC 20006; founded 1946; James Joy Jr., Natl. Pres. (since 1980); 60,000 members, 220 locals.

Woodworkers of America, International (IWA), 1622 N. Lombard St., Portland, OR 97217; founded 1937; Keith Johnson, Intl. Pres. (since 1973); 120,000 members, 207 locals.

Canadian Unions

Source: Labour Canada

Independent Unions (1982)

Nurses' Association, Ontario	31,000
Quebec Govt. Employees' Union	43,339
Teachers' Association, Alberta	26,000
Teachers' Association of Ontario, Fed. of Women	29,800
Teachers' Federation, British Columbia	31,379
Teachers' Federation, Ontario Secondary School	35,720
Teaching Congress, Quebec	82,122
Teamsters, Chauffeurs, Warehousemen and Helpers of America, International Brotherhood of	93,000

Canadian Labor Congress (CLC) (1980)

Automobile, Aerospace and Agricultural Implement Workers of America, International Union, United	121,829
Communication Workers of Canada	28,000
Energy and Chemical Workers Union	32,000
Govt. Employees, National Union of Provincial	230,000
Paperworkers Union, Canadian	66,210
Postal Workers, Canadian Union of	23,500
Public Employees, Canadian Union of	274,742
Public Service Alliance of Canada	157,633
Railway, Transport and General Workers, Canadian Brotherhood of	38,500

Confederation of National Trade Unions (CNTU) (1982)

Federation of Public Service Employees Inc.	28,000
National Federation of Building and Woodworkers Inc.	30,000
Social Affairs Federation	84,000

ENERGY

Nuclear Power Reactors in U.S.

Source: Technical Information Center, U.S. Energy Department
as of Dec. 31, 1980

State	Site	Plant name	Capacity (kilowatts)	Utility	Commercia operatio
Alabama	Decatur	Browns Ferry Unit 1	1,065,000	Tennessee Valley Authority	197
	Decatur	Browns Ferry Unit 2	1,065,000	Tennessee Valley Authority	197
	Decatur	Browns Ferry Unit 3	1,065,000	Tennessee Valley Authority	197
	Dothan	Joseph M. Farley Unit 1	829,000	Alabama Power Co.	197
Arkansas	Russellville	Arkansas Unit 1	850,000	Ark. Power & Light Co.	197
	Russellville	Arkansas Unit 2	912,000	Ark. Power & Light Co.	198
California	Eureka	Humboldt Bay Unit 3	63,000	Pacific Gas & Electric Co.	196
	San Clemente	San Onofre Unit 1	430,000	So. Calif. Ed. & San Diego Gas & El. Co.	196
	Diablo Canyon	Diablo Canyon Unit 1	1,084,000	Pacific Gas & Electric Co.	198
	Clay Station	Rancho Seco Station	918,000	Sacramento Munic. Utility District	197
Colorado	Platteville	Ft. St. Vrain Station	330,000	Public Service Co. of Colorado	197
Connecticut	Haddam Neck	Haddam Neck	575,000	Conn. Yankee Atomic Power Co.	196
	Waterford	Millstone Unit 1	660,000	Northeast Nuclear Energy Co.	197
	Waterford	Millstone Unit 2	870,000	Northeast Nuclear Energy Co.	197
Florida	Florida City	Turkey Point Unit 3	693,000	Fla. Power & Light Co.	197
	Florida City	Turkey Point Unit 4	693,000	Fla. Power & Light Co.	197
	Red Level	Crystal River Unit 3	825,000	Florida Power Corp.	197
	Ft. Pierce	St. Lucie Unit 1	802,000	Fla. Power & Light Co.	197
Georgia	Baxley	Edwin I. Hatch Unit 1	787,000	Georgia Power Co.	197
	Baxley	Edwin I. Hatch Unit 2	784,000	Georgia Power Co.	197
Illinois	Morris	Dresden Unit 1	200,000	Commonwealth Edison Co.	196
	Morris	Dresden Unit 2	794,000	Commonwealth Edison Co.	197
	Morris	Dresden Unit 3	794,000	Commonwealth Edison Co.	197
	Zion	Zion Unit 1	1,040,000	Commonwealth Edison Co.	197
	Zion	Zion Unit 2	1,040,000	Commonwealth Edison Co.	197
	Cordova	Quad-Cities Unit 1	789,000	Comm. Ed. Co.-Ia.-Ill. Gas & Elec. Co.	197
	Cordova	Quad-Cities Unit 2	789,000	Comm. Ed. Co.-Ia.-Ill. Gas & Elec. Co.	197
Iowa	Palo	Duane Arnold Unit 1	538,000	Iowa Electric Light and Power Co.	197
Maine	Wiscasset	Maine Yankee	790,000	Me. Yankee Atomic Power Co.	197
Maryland	Lusby	Calvert Cliffs Unit 1	845,000	Baltimore Gas & Electric Co.	197
	Lusby	Calvert Cliffs Unit 2	845,000	Baltimore Gas & Electric Co.	197
Massachusetts	Rowe	Yankee Station	175,000	Yankee Atomic Electric Co.	196
	Plymouth	Pilgrim Unit 1	655,000	Boston Edison Co.	197
Michigan	Big Rock Point	Big Rock Point	72,000	Consumers Power Co.	196
	South Haven	Palisades Station	805,000	Consumers Power Co.	197
	Bridgman	Donald C. Cook Unit 1	1,054,000	Ind. & Michigan Electric Co.	197
	Bridgman	Donald C. Cook Unit 2	1,100,000	Ind. & Michigan Electric Co.	197
Minnesota	Monticello	Monticello	545,000	Northern States Power Co.	197
	Red Wing	Prairie Island Unit 1	530,000	Northern States Power Co.	197
	Red Wing	Prairie Island Unit 2	530,000	Northern States Power Co.	197
Nebraska	Fort Calhoun	Ft. Calhoun Unit 1	457,000	Omaha Public Power District	197
	Brownville	Cooper Station	778,000	Neb. Pub. Power Dist.-Ia. Power & Light Co.	197
New Jersey	Toms River	Oyster Creek Unit 1	650,000	Jersey Central Power & Light Co.	196
	Salem	Salem Unit 1	1,090,000	Public Service Electric & Gas, N.J.	197
	Salem	Salem Unit 2	1,115,000	Public Service Electric & Gas, N.J.	198
New York	Buchanan	Indian Point Unit 2	873,000	Consolidated Edison Co.	197
	Buchanan	Indian Point Unit 3	965,000	Power Authority of State of N.Y.	197
	Ontario	R.E. Ginna Unit 1	470,000	Rochester Gas & Electric Co.	197
	Scriba	9-Mile Point Unit 1	620,000	Niagra Mohawk Power	196
	Scriba	James A. FitzPatrick	821,000	Power Authority of State of N.Y.	197
North Carolina	Southport	Brunswick Steam Unit 1	821,000	Carolina Power & Light Co.	197
	Southport	Brunswick Steam Unit 2	821,000	Carolina Power & Light Co.	197
	Cowans Ford Dam	Wm. B. McGuire Unit 1	1,180,000	Duke Power Co.	198
Ohio	Oak Harbor	Davis-Besse Unit 1	906,000	Toledo Edison-Cleveland El. Illum. Co.	197
Oregon	Prescott	Trojan Unit 1	1,130,000	Portland Gen. Electric Co.	197
Pennsylvania	Peach Bottom	Peach Bottom Unit 2	1,065,000	Philadelphia Electric Co.	197
	Peach Bottom	Peach Bottom Unit 3	1,065,000	Philadelphia Electric Co.	197
	Shippingport	Shippingport Station	60,000	Duquesne Light Co.	195
	Shippingport	Beaver Valley Unit 1	852,000	Duquesne Light Co.-Ohio Edison Co.	197
	Middletown	Three Mile Island Unit 1	819,000	Metropolitan Edison Co.	197
	Middletown	Three Mile Island Unit 2	906,000	Jersey Central Power & Light Co.	197
South Carolina	Hartsville	H. B. Robinson Unit 2	700,000	Carolina Power & Light Co.	197
	Seneca	Oconee Unit 1	887,000	Duke Power Co.	197
	Seneca	Oconee Unit 2	887,000	Duke Power Co.	197
	Seneca	Oconee Unit 3	887,000	Duke Power Co.	197
Tennessee	Daisy	Sequoyah Unit 1	1,148,000	Tennessee Valley Authority	198
Vermont	Vernon	Vermont Yankee Station	514,000	Vt. Yankee Nuclear Power Corp.	197
Virginia	Gravel Neck	Surry Unit 1	822,000	Va. Electric & Power Co.	197
	Gravel Neck	Surry Unit 2	822,000	Va. Electric & Power Co.	197
	Mineral	North Anna Unit 1	907,000	Va. Electric & Power Co.	197
	Mineral	North Anna Unit 2	907,000	Va. Electric & Power Co.	198
Washington	Richland	N-Reactor/WPPSS Steam	850,000	U.S. Energy Department	196
Wisconsin	La Crosse	Genoa Station	50,000	Dairyland Power Cooperative	196
	Two Creeks	Point Beach Unit 1	497,000	Wis. Mich. Power Co.	197
	Two Creeks	Point Beach Unit 2	497,000	Wis. Mich. Power Co.	197
	Carlton	Kewaunee Unit 1	535,000	Wis. Public Service Corp.	197

Nuclear plant capacity (kilowatts): operable 74,000,000; being built 84,000,000; planned 15,000,000; Total 173,000,000.

World Nuclear Power

Source: Energy Information Administration. Net Megawatts of Energy as of June 30, 1982

Country	Operable	Construction	Total (including those planned)
U.S.	61,916	77,485	146,961
France	21,626	40,950	90,936
Japan	16,615	9,183	34,575
USSR	15,886	28,420	71,506
Germany, W.	9,832	9,411	35,544
UK	7,597	5,533	15,580
Sweden	6,415	3,032	9,447
Canada	5,494	10,384	15,878
Taiwan	3,110	1,814	10,824
Finland	2,160		3,160
Spain	1,973	10,148	16,021
Switzerland	1,940	942	4,947
Germany, E.	1,694	3,264	6,590

Country	Operable	Construction	Total (including those planned)
Belgium	1,675	3,807	5,482
Italy	1,232	1,996	9,128
Bulgaria	1,224	2,420	9,644
Czechoslovakia	840	2,520	12,676
India	808	1,368	3,586
Yugoslavia	632		3,632
Brazil	626	2,490	10,586
Korea	564	6,694	10,858
Netherlands	499		499
Hungary	408	2,224	5,632
Argentina	335	1,298	3,433
Pakistan	125	937	1,062

World Electricity Production

Source: UN Monthly Bulletin of Statistics, March 1982 (1981 production, in million kilowatt-hours)

U.S.	2,513,096	Italy[3]	106,870	Czechoslovakia	74,265
USSR	1,454,000	Australia	103,564	Romania[4]	67,500
Japan	476,539	Sweden	99,924	Netherlands	62,246
W. Germany	368,772	Brazil	99,864	Yugoslavia	60,076
United Kingdom	278,028	E. Germany[4]	95,952	Mexico[4]	59,952
Canada[1]	276,757	Spain	92,971	Belgium	50,413
France	260,328	Norway	92,304	Switzerland	49,088
China[2]	120,000	S. Africa[4]	90,929	Austria	42,901
Poland	115,006	India[1]	89,730		

(1) Through September. (2) 1975 estimate. (3) Through July. (4) 1980 estimate.

Production of Electricity in the U.S. by Source

Source: Energy Information Administration, U.S. Energy Department
Amounts include both privately-owned and publicly-owned utilities.

Calendar Year	Net production million kwh	Percentage produced by source: Coal	Oil	Gas	Nuclear	Hydro	Other[1]	Fuel Consumption: Coal 1,000 sht. tns.	Oil 1,000 bbls.	Gas million cu. ft.
1971	1,612,593	44.3	13.6	23.2	2.4	16.5	0.05	327,887	396,468	3,975,971
1974	1,867,103	44.5	16.0	17.2	6.1	16.1	0.1	392,423	536,245	3,443,293
1976	2,037,775	46.4	15.7	14.4	9.4	13.9	0.2	448,456	555,937	3,081,286
1977	2,124,580	46.4	16.8	14.4	11.8	10.4	0.2	477,229	623,742	3,191,948
1978	2,206,515	44.2	16.5	13.8	12.5	12.7	0.2	481,254	635,600	3,188,306
1979	2,247,372	47.8	13.5	14.7	11.4	12.4	0.2	527,051	523,565	3,490,523
1980	2,286,439	50.8	10.7	15.1	10.9	12.0	0.2	569,274	420,214	3,681,495
1981	2,294,812	52.4	9.0	15.1	11.9	11.4	0.2	596,797	586,117	3,640,154

(1) Includes electricity produced from geothermal power, wood, and waste.

U.S. Petroleum Imports by Source

Source: Department of Energy (in thousands of barrels per day)

Nation	1977	1978	1979	1980	1981
Algeria	565.2	632.1	630.5	488	311
Indonesia	576.2	538.2	416.9	348	366
Iran	786.4	544.7	303.2	9	0
Libya	837.7	641.1	654.0	554	319
Nigeria	1,229.6	904.7	1,077.6	857	620
Saudi Arabia	1,523.8	1,137.2	1,346.8	1,261	1,129
United Arab Emirates	446.3	378.4	279.7	172	81
Venezuela	908.8	633.5	691.1	481	406
Other OPEC[1]	378.1	224.0	212.2	130	90
Total OPEC	**7,252.2**	**5,636.9**	**5,612.0**	**4,300**	**3,323**
Arab OPEC Members	3,636.5	2,920.8	3,037.4	2,551	1,848
Bahamas	168.0	158.4	147.7	78	74
Canada	502.8	468.6	532.5	455	447
Neth'lands Antilles	218.3	317.8	231.3	225	197
Puerto Rico	102.8	230.1	91.8	88	62
Trinidad/Tobago	286.0	89.4	186.3	176	133
Virgin Islands	468.7	251.0	431.5	388	327
Mexico	179.3	426.8	434.1	533	523
Other non-OPEC	657.1	649.9	744.0	491	534
Total non-OPEC	**2,583.0**	**2,591.5**	**2,799.1**	**2,609**	**2,672**
Total imports (avg.)	**8,714.0**	**10,843.7**	**NA**	**6,909**	**5,995**

(1) Ecuador, Gabon, Iraq, Kuwait, Qatar. (2) Imports do not add to totals because OPEC figures include petroleum transshipped through, and usually refined in, other countries and counted again as imports from those countries. NA-Not available.

U.S. Dependence on Petroleum Imports

Source: Department of Energy (million barrels per day average)

Source	1975	1976	1977	1978	1979	1980	1981
Arab nations	1.38	2.42	3.18	2.96	3.04	2.55	1,84
All OPEC	3.60	5.07	6.19	5.64	5.61	4.30	3.32
All nations	6.06	7.31	8.81	8.23	8.41	6.90	5.99
U.S. production	16.32	17.46	18.43	18.82	18.43	17.06	16.06

World Production of Crude Oil

Leading Nations

(thousands of barrels per day)
Source: Energy Information Administration, U.S. Energy Dept.
Monthly Energy Review, July, 1982

Nation	1980 Production	1980 % of total production
1. USSR	11,770	21.8%
2. Saudi Arabia	9,900	18.3
3. United States[1]	8,597	15.9
4. Iraq	2,514	4.7
5. Venezuela	2,167	4.0
6. China	2,114	3.8
7. Nigeria	2,055	3.6
8. Mexico	1,937	3.3
10. Libya	1,787	3.3
10. United Arab emirates	1,709	3.2
11. Iran	1,662	3.1
12. Kuwait	1,656	3.1
13. United Kingdom	1,622	3.0
14. Indonesia	1,577	2.9
15. Canada[1]	1,424	2.6
16. Algeria[1]	1,012	1.9
17. Qatar	472	0.9
Total	**53,975**	

Nation	1981 Production	1981 % of total production
1. USSR	11,800	23.5%
2. Saudi Arabia	9,815	19.6
3. United States	8,572	17.1
4. Mexico	2,310	4.6
5. Venezuela	2,100	4.2
6. China	2,025	4.0
7. United Kingdom	1,810	3.6
8. Indonesia	1,605	3.2
9. United Arab Emirates	1,500	3.0
10. Nigeria	1,430	2.9
11. Iran	1,380	2.8
12. Canada	1,285	2.6
13. Libya	1,140	2.3
14. Kuwait	1,125	2.4
15 Iraq	1,000	2.0
16. Algeria	805	1.6
17. Qatar	405	0.8
Total	**50,107**	

(1) Includes lease condensate

World Oil Supply and Demand Projections

Source: Central Intelligence Agency
(million barrels per day)

	1976	1977	1978	1979	1980	1985
Demand (non-Communist)	**48.4**	**49.8-50.5**	**51.2-52.2**	**52.5-54.1**	**54.9-56.7**	**68.3-72.6**
United States	16.7	17.8-18.3	18.2-19.0	18.4-19.7	19.3-20.7	22.2-25.6
West Europe	13.6	13.9-14.3	13.8-14.2	13.7-14.4	13.7-14.7	15.8-18.2
Japan	5.2	5.3-5.4	5.5-5.8	5.9-6.2	6.2-6.6	8.1-8.8
Canada	2.0	2.0-2.1	2.1-2.2	2.2-2.3	2.2-2.4	2.9-3.5
Other developed[1]	1.2	1.2	1.3	1.3	1.4	1.9
Non-OPEC LDCs[2]	6.7	7.1	7.5	7.8	8.5	12.0
OPEC[3] countries	2.1	2.3	2.5	2.8	3.0	4.0
Other demand[4]	0.9	0	0	0	0	0
Non-OPEC supply[5]	**17.5**	**18.5**	**20.1**	**21.2**	**22.0**	**20.4-22.4**
United States	9.7	9.6	10.2	10.2	10.0	10.0-11.0
West Europe	0.9	1.8	2.5	3.1	3.7	4.0-5.0
Japan	0	0	0	0	0	0.1
Canada	1.6	1.6	1.5	1.5	1.5	1.3-1.5
Other developed[1]	0.5	0.5	0.5	0.5	0.5	0.4
Non-OPEC LDCs	3.7	4.1	4.6	5.3	6.1	8.0-9.0
Net Communist trade[6]						
USSR-East Europe	0.9	0.7	0.5	0.2	−0.3	−3.5−4.5
China	0.2	0.2	0.3	0.4	0.5	0
Required OPEC production[7]	**30.9**	**31.3-32.0**	**31.1-32.1**	**31.3-32.9**	**32.9-34.7**	**46.7-51.2**

(1) Australia, Israel, New Zealand, South Africa. (2) LDCs: less developed countries. (3) OPEC: Organization of Petroleum Exporting Countries. (4) Including stock changes and statistical discrepancy. (5) Including natural gas liquids. (6) Difference of Communist countries' exports and imports; minus sign indicates net Communist imports. (7) OPEC production capacity will reach 27.5-29.4 million barrels per day by 1985, exclusive of Saudi Arabia; Saudi projections are uncertain.

U.S. Energy Consumption per GNP Dollar

Source: Energy Information Administration, U.S. Energy Dept.
(Average thousand Btu per 1972 constant dollar)

1974	58.3	**1979**/1st qtr	60.8	**1980**/1st qtr	57.0	**1981**/1st qtr	53.8
1975	57.3	2nd qtr	49.4	2nd qtr	48.0	2nd qtr	45.8
1976	57.3	3rd qtr	48.9	3rd qtr	47.3	3rd qtr	46.0
1977	55.6	4th qtr	53.5	4th qtr	52.6	4th qtr	49.9
1978	56.4	Average	53,2	Average	51.3	Average	48.9

U.S. Crude Oil Reserves

Source: American Petroleum Institute for figures through 1979; Energy Information Administration for later figures.

Estimates of proved reserves, which can be recovered under present economic relationships and known technology. Improved technology or higher world prices would increase estimates of reserves. Cumulative production for all years through Dec. 31, 1978 was 117,766,214 thousand barrels.

(thousands of 42-gallon barrels)

Year	Discoveries, revisions, extensions	Production	Proved reserves at end of year	Change from previous year[1]	Year	Discoveries, revisions, extensions	Production	Proved reserves at end of year	Change from previous year[1]
1948	3,795,207	2,002,448	23,280,444	1,792,759	1965	3,048,079	2,686,198	31,352,391	361,881
1949	3,187,845	1,818,800	24,649,489	1,369,045	1966	2,963,978	2,864,242	31,452,127	99,736
1950	2,562,685	1,943,776	25,268,398	618,909	1967	2,962,122	3,037,579	31,376,670	(75,457)
1951	4,413,954	2,214,321	27,468,031	2,199,633	1968	2,454,635	3,124,188	30,707,117	(669,553)
1952	2,749,288	2,256,765	27,960,554	492,523	1969	2,120,036	3,195,291	29,631,862	(1,075,255)
1953	3,296,130	2,311,856	28,944,828	984,274	1970	12,688,918	3,319,445	39,001,335	9,369,473
1954	2,873,037	2,257,119	29,560,746	615,918	1971	2,317,732	3,256,110	38,062,957	(938,378)
1955	2,870,724	2,419,300	30,012,170	451,424	1972	1,557,848	3,281,397	36,339,408	(1,723,549)
1956	2,974,336	2,551,857	30,434,649	422,479	1973	2,145,831	3,185,400	35,299,839	(1,039,569)
1957	2,424,800	2,559,044	30,300,405	(134,244)	1974	1,993,573	3,043,456	34,249,956	(1,049,883)
1958	2,608,242	2,372,730	30,535,917	235,512	1975	1,318,463	2,886,292	32,682,127	(1,567,829)
1959	3,666,745	2,483,315	31,719,347	1,183,430	1976	1,085,291	2,825,252	30,942,166	(1,739,961)
1960	2,365,328	2,471,464	31,613,211	(106,136)	1977	1,403,780	2,859,544	29,486,402	(1,455,764)
1961	2,657,567	2,512,273	31,758,505	145,294	1978	1,347,265	3,029,898	27,803,760	(1,682,642)
1962	2,180,896	2,550,178	31,389,223	(369,282)	1979	2,205,673	2,958,144	27,051,289	(752,471)
1963	2,174,110	2,593,343	30,969,990	(419,233)	1980	2,751,000	2,975,000	26,827,289	(224,000)
1964	2,664,767	2,644,247	30,990,510	20,520	1981	2,432,000	2,949,000	26,310,289	(517,000)

(1) Parenthesis indicate decline.

U.S. Crude Petroleum Production by Chief States

Source: Energy Information Administration, U.S. Energy Department (thousands of 42-gallon barrels)

Year	Alas.	Cal.	Col.	Fla.	Kan.	La.	Miss.	N.M.	Okla.	Tex.	Wyo.
1950 . .	0	327,607	23,303	487	107,586	208,965	38,236	47,367	164,599	829,874	61,631
1960 . .	559	305,352	47,469	369	113,453	400,832	51,673	107,380	192,913	927,479	133,910
1965 . .	11,128	316,428	33,511	1,462	104,733	594,853	56,183	119,166	203,441	1,000,749	138,314
1970 . .	83,616	372,191	24,723	12,999	84,853	906,907	65,119	128,184	223,574	1,249,697	160,345
1975 . .	69,834	322,199	38,089	41,877	59,106	650,840	46,614	95,063	163,123	1,221,929	135,943
1976 . .	63,398	326,021	38,992	44,460	58,714	606,501	46,072	92,130	161,426	1,189,523	134,149
1977 . .	169,201	349,609	39,460	46,641	57,496	562,905	43,022	87,223	156,382	1,137,880	136,472
1978 . .	448,620	347,181	36,797	47,536	56,586	532,740	39,494	83,365	150,456	1,074,050	137,385
1979 . .	511,538	352,465	32,251	47,170	56,995	494,462	38,286	79,379	143,642	1,013,255	124,553
1980 . .	591,684	356,644	29,565	42,846	60,152	466,964	36,533	75,456	151,960	975,239	214.161
1981 . .	828,300	544,100	14,700	10,900	37,100	298,500	20,900	55,500	95,000	809,300	84,000

Other chief states in 1981 were North Dakota and Michigan.

U.S. Petroleum and Natural Gas Production

Source: Energy Information Administration, U.S. Energy Department

Year	Crude oil		Natural gas liquids		Total oil	Natural gas	
	Production	Value	Production	Value	& N.G.L.	Marketed	Value
	1,000 bbls.	$1,000	1,000 bbls.	$1,000	1,000 bbls.	mil. cu. ft.	$1,000
1945	1,713,655	2,094,250	112,004	187,564	1,828,539	3,944,021	191,006
1950	1,973,574	4,963,380	181,961	419,605	2,155,693	6,282,060	408,521
1955	2,484,428	6,870,380	281,371	619,006	2,766,325	9,405,351	978,357
1960	2,574,933	7,420,181	340,157	808,385	2,915,365	12,771,038	1,789,970
1965	2,848,514	8,158,298	441,556	911,603	3,290,083	16,042,753	2,494,542
1970	3,517,450	11,173,726	605,916	1,275,112	4,123,366	21,920,642	3,745,680
1975	3,056,779	23,116,059	595,958	2,772,588	3,652,737	20,108,661	8,945,062
1976	2,976,180	24,229,540	587,045	3,284,089	3,563,225	19,952,438	11,571,776
1977	2,986,710	25,397,307	584,900	4,386,750	3,571,610	19,924,671	15,522,658
1978	3,178,216	28,476,815	572,320	NA	3,578,892	19,690,000	18,095,009
1979	3,121,480	39,051,332	578,160	NA	3,715,335	20,471,000	24,113,634
1980	3,137,905	66,492,206	574,145	NA	3,728,110	20,379,000	32,667,537

Average Consumer Cost of Fuels

Source: Department of Energy
(1972 constant dollars)

Fuel	1975	1976	1977	1978	1979	1980	1981
Leaded regular gasoline (cent/gal)	43.7	43.1	43.2	41.0	49.8	119.1	131.1
Residential heating oil (cent/gal)	29.3	30.2	31.2	31.7	40.8	97.8	120.5
Residential natural gas (cent/Mcf)	132.8	145.4	162.2	163.5	185.3	391.5	455.7
Residential electricity (cent/kWh)	2.73	2.77	2.81	2.76	2.66	5.36	6.20

Mcf=million cubic feet; kwh=million kilowatt hours.

U.S. Total Fuel Supply and Demand

Source: Energy Information Administration, U.S. Energy Department

(thousands of 42-gallon barrels)

Year	Gasoline[1] Production	Gasoline[1] Total demand	Kerosene[2] Production	Kerosene[2] Total demand	Distillate fuel oil Production	Distillate fuel oil Total demand	Residual fuel oil Production	Residual fuel oil Total demand
1950[3] . . .	1,024,181	1,019,011	118,512	119,922	398,912	75,435	425,217	570,021
1960. . . .	1,522,497	1,525,126	136,842	133,188	667,050	695,165	332,147	577,934
1965. . . .	1,733,258	1,756,419	201,788	219,932	765,430	779,644	268,567	601,893
1970. . . .	2,135,838	2,165,598	313,544	358,146	897,097	928,109	257,510	824,073
1971. . . .	2,231,157	2,246,025	306,847	365,308	912,097	974,077	274,684	851,262
1972. . . .	2,352,310	2,384,734	313,554	379,984	963,625	1,067,321	292,519	937,707
1974. . . .	2,371,004	2,436,681	290,780	346,706	974,025	1,076,771	390,491	968,185
1975. . . .	2,420,962	2,479,857	308,034	347,399	968,650	1,040,838	450,957	903,914
1976. . . .	2,549,627	2,597,305	323,114	350,565	1,070,209	1,146,695	503,953	1,025,148
1977. . . .	2,565,950	2,625,080	355,145	376,680	1,192,090	1,213,990	635,100	1,111,425
1978. . . .	2,612,670	2,702,095	354,415	386,900	1,153,765	1,242,825	615,390	1,103,395
1979. . . .	2,494,655	2,566,128	368,707	391,650	1,148,778	1,207,278	614,806	1,029,913
1980. . . .	2,369,580	2,567,410	369,380	392,740	971,995	1,208,515	575,605	1,031,490
1981. . . .	2,337,825	2,404,626	434,350	463,550	953,745	1,099,745	482,165	762,120

Demand usually exceeds the production; the difference is made up by dipping into stocks or imports. (1) Includes special naphtha production. (2) Includes kerosene type jet fuel. (3) 1950 figures are on a 48-state basis.

U.S. Natural Gas Reserves

Source: American Gas Association through 1979; as of 1980, Energy Information Administration, U.S. Energy Department

Estimates of proved reserves, which can be recovered under existing economic and operating conditions.

Year	Natural gas (millions of cu. ft.) Discoveries, revisions and extensions	Change in underground storage[1]	Production[4]	Proved reserves at end of year	Natural gas liquids (1,000 42-gallon barrels) Discoveries, revisions and extensions	Production[4]	Proved reserves at end of year
1946	17,632,864	(2)	4,915,774	159,703,813	(2)	129,262	3,163,219
1947	10,921,187	(2)	5,599,235	165,025,765	251,538	160,782	3,253,975
1948	13,823,090	51,202	5,975,001	172,925,056	470,557	183,749	3,540,783
1949	12,605,615	82,146	6,211,124	179,401,693	386,776	198,547	3,729,012
1950	11,985,361	52,935	6,855,244	184,584,745	766,062	227,411	4,267,663
1951	15,965,808	132,030	7,923,673	192,758,910	723,991	267,052	4,724,602
1952	14,267,606	197,766	8,592,716	198,631,566	556,838	284,789	4,996,651
1953	20,341,933	513,629[3]	9,188,365	210,298,763	743,969	302,698	5,437,922
1954	9,547,074	90,408	9,375,314	210,560,931	107,350	300,815	5,244,457
1955	21,897,616	87,164	10,063,167	222,482,544	514,508	320,400	5,438,565
1956	24,716,115	133,241	10,848,685	236,483,215	809,820	346,053	5,902,332
1957	20,008,051	178,761	11,439,890	245,230,137	137,392	352,364	5,687,360
1958	18,896,724	57,582	11,422,651	252,761,792	858,206	341,548	6,204,018
1959	20,621,249	160,453	12,373,063	261,170,431	703,444	385,154	6,522,308
1960	13,893,978	281,273	13,019,356	262,326,326	725,130	431,379	6,816,059
1961	17,166,421	159,544	13,378,649	266,273,642	694,686	461,649	7,049,096
1962	19,483,958	159,231	13,637,973	272,278,858	732,549	470,128	7,311,517
1963	18,164,667	253,733	14,546,025	276,151,233	878,120	515,659	7,673,978
1964	20,252,139	195,110	15,347,028	281,251,454	608,744	536,090	7,746,632
1965	21,319,279	150,483	16,252,293	286,468,923	832,312	555,410	8,023,534
1966	20,220,432	134,523	17,491,073	289,332,805	894,116	588,684	8,328,966
1967	21,804,333	151,403	18,380,838	292,907,703	929,758	644,493	8,614,231
1968	13,697,008	118,568	19,373,427	287,349,852	685,659	701,782	8,598,108
1969	8,375,004	107,169	20,723,190	275,108,835	281,028	735,962	8,143,174
1970	37,196,359	402,018	21,960,804	290,746,408	307,579	747,812	7,702,941
1971	9,825,421	310,301	22,076,512	278,805,618	347,720	746,434	7,304,227
1972	9,634,563	156,563	22,511,898	266,084,846	238,273	755,941	6,786,559
1973	6,825,049	(354,282)	22,605,406	249,950,207	408,979	740,831	6,454,707
1974	8,679,184	(178,424)	21,318,470	237,132,497	619,841	724,099	6,350,449
1975	10,483,688	302,561	19,718,570	228,200,176	618,504	701,123	6,267,830
1976	7,555,468	(187,550)	19,542,020	216,026,074	834,766	700,629	6,401,967
1977	11,851,924	446,930	19,447,050	208,877,878	291,171	698,773	5,994,365
1978	10,586,144	148,733	19,311,048	200,301,707	595,666	664,179	5,925,852
1979	14,285,947	293,323	19,910,353	194,916,624	389,805	660,334	5,655,323
1980	11,612,116	(2)	18,699,000	199,021,000	745,900	731,000	6,728,000

(1) Parentheses indicate decline. (2) Not estimated. (3) All native gas in storage reservoirs formerly classified as proved reserves is included in this figure. (4) Preliminary net production.

U.S. Passenger Car Efficiency

Source: Department of Energy

Year	Average fuel consumed per car Gal.	Index	Average miles traveled per car Miles	Index	Average miles per gallon Miles	Index
1969	718	105.0	9,782	102.6	13.63	97.8
1970	735	107.5	9,978	104.7	13.57	97.4
1971	746	109.1	10,121	106.2	13.57	97.4
1973	763	111.5	9,992	104.8	13.10	94.0
1974	704	102.9	9,448	99.1	13.43	96.4
1975	712	104.1	9,634	101.1	13.53	97.1
1977	706	103.2	9,839	103.2	13.94	100.1
1978	715	104.5	10,046	105.4	14.06	100.9
1979	664	97.1	9,485	99.5	14.29	102.6
1980	603	88.2	9,135	95.8	15.15	108.8

U.S. Motor Fuel Supply and Demand

Source: Energy Information Administration, U.S. Energy Department

(thousands of 42-gallon barrels)

Year	Supply: Production	Supply: Daily average	Demand: Domestic	Demand: Export
1945	793,431	2,174	696,333	88,059
1950	1,024,481	2,806	994,290	24,721
1955	1,373,950	3,764	1,329,788	34,521
1960[1]	1,522,497	4,171	1,511,670	13,456
1965	1,733,258	4,749	1,750,028	6,391
1970	2,135,838	5,852	2,162,642	2,956
1971	2,231,157	6,113	2,242,921	3,104
1972	2,352,310	6,445	2,382,569	2,165
1973	2,434,943	6,671	2,484,262	3,318
1974	2,371,004	6,496	2,434,368	2,313
1975	2,420,962	6,633	2,477,786	2,071
1976	2,549,627	6,966	2,597,305	3,807
1977	2,566,315	7,031	2,619,605	2,155
1978	2,615,955	7,167	2,706,840	1,250
1979	2,513,937	6,837	2,580,080	500
1980	2,374,690	6,506	2,401,335	1,000
1981	2,337,825	6,405	2,404,620	2,000

(1) Beginning with 1960 Alaska and Hawaii are included.

Coal and Coke Production in the U.S.

Source: Energy Information Administration, U.S. Energy Department

Year	Penn. anthracite: Production 1,000 net tons	Penn. anthracite: Value $1,000	Bituminous: Production 1,000 net tons	Bituminous: Value $1,000
1945	54,934	323,944	577,617	1,768,204
1950	44,077	392,398	516,311	2,500,374
1955	26,205	206,097	464,633	2,092,383
1960	18,817	147,116	415,512	1,950,421
1963	18,267	153,503	458,928	2,013,390
1964	17,184	148,648	486,998	2,165,582
1965	14,866	122,021	512,088	2,276,022
1966	12,941	100,663	533,881	2,421,293
1967	12,256	96,160	552,026	2,555,377
1968	11,461	97,245	545,245	2,546,340
1969	10,473	100,769	560,505	2,795,509
1970	9,729	105,341	602,932	3,772,662
1971	8,727	103,469	552,192	3,901,496
1972	7,106	85,251	595,386	4,561,983
1973	6,830	90,260	591,738	5,049,612
1974	6,617	144,695	603,406	9,502,347
1975	6,203	198,481	648,438	12,472,486
1976	6,228	209,234	678,685	13,189,481
1977	5,861	202,373	691,300	13,700,000
1978	5,370	352,260	665,127	14,500,000
1979	4,395	180,458	621,751	16,980,001
1980	6,003	NA	618,363	21,600,000

Coke production (1,000 net tons—value in $1,000)—(1968) 63,653, $1,157,359; (1969) 64,757, $1,355,260; (1970) 66,525, $1,849,160; (1971) 57,436, $1,745,693; (1972) 60,507, $2,012,486; (1973) 64,325, $2,442,151; (1974) 61,581, $4,510,150; (1975) 57,207, $4,835,654; (1976) 58,333, $5,021,616; (1977) 53,510, $4,652,776; (1978) 49,010, $5,634,847; (1979) 52,943, $5,458,568; (1980) 46,130, $3,882,471.

Coke exports (short tons)—(1968) 791,909; (1969) 1,629,000; (1970) 2,478,338; (1971) 1,508,639; (1972) 1,231,633; (1973) 1,394,980; (1974) 1,277,681; (1975) 1,272,906; (1976) 1,314,725; (1977) 1,240,577; (1978) 693,000; (1979) 1,440,000; (1980) 2,071,042. **Imports** —(1968) 94,085; (1969) 173,052; (1970) 152,879; (1971) 173,914; (1972) 185,023; (1973) 1,077,737; (1974) 3,540,326; (1975) 1,818,981; (1976) 1,311,472; (1977) 1,829,000; (1978) 5,722,000; (1979) 3,974,000; (1980) 658,532.

Anthracite exports (net tons)—(1966) 766,025; (1967) 594,797; (1968) 518,159; (1969) 627,492; (1970) 789,499; (1971) 671,024; (1972) 743,451; (1973) 716,546; (1974) 735,173; (1975) 639,601; (1976) 615,167; (1977) 624,908; (1978) 866,000; (1979) 1,233,000; (1980) 1,795,000.

NA = Not available.

Production of Energy by Type

Source: Energy Information Administration, U.S. Energy Department

Quadrillion (10^{15}) Btu

	Coal[1]	Crude oil[2]	NGPL[3]	Natural gas (dry)	Hydro-electric power[4]	Nuclear electric power	Other[5]	Total energy produced
1973 Total	14.366	19.493	2.569	22.187	2.861	0.910	0.046	62.433
1975	15.189	17.729	2.374	19.640	3.155	1.900	0.072	60.059
1976	15.853	17.262	2.327	19.480	2.976	2.111	0.081	60.091
1977	15.829	17.454	2.327	19.565	2.333	2.702	0.082	60.293
1978	15.037	18.434	2.245	19.485	2.958	2.977	0.068	61.204
1979	17.651	18.104	2.286	20.076	2.954	2.748	0.089	63.907
1980	19.209[R]	18.249[R]	2.254[R]	20.112[R]	2.890[R]	2.672[R]	0.114	65.499[R]
1981	18.987	18.146	2.298	19.929	2.732	2.901	0.127	65.120

Geographic coverage: the 50 United States and District of Columbia. Totals may not equal sum of components due to independent rounding. (1) Includes bituminous coal, lignite, and anthracite. (2) Includes lease condensate. (3) Natural gas plant liquids. (4) Includes industrial and utility production of hydropower. (5) Includes geothermal power and electricity produced from wood and waste. R=Revised data.

Consumption of Energy by Type

Quadrillion (10^{15}) Btu

	Coal[1]	Natural gas (dry)	Petroleum	Hydro-electric power[2]	Nuclear electric power	Net imports of coal coke[3]	Other[4]	Total Energy consumed
1973 Total	13.300	22.512	34.840	3.010	0.910	(0.008)	0.046	74,609
1975	12.823	19.948	32.731	3.219	1.900	0.014	0.072	70.707
1976	13.733	20.345	35.175	3.066	2.111	0.000	0.081	74.510
1977	13.965	19.931	37.122	2.515	2.702	0.015	0.082	76.332
1978	13.846	20.000	37.965	3.164	2.977	0.131	0.068	78.150
1979	15.109	20.666	37.123	3.166	2.748	0.066	0.089	78.968
1980	15.461[R]	20.394[R]	34.202[R]	3.107[R]	2.672[R]	(0.037)	0.114	75.913[R]
1981	16.039	19.762	32.113	2.970	2.901	(0.017)	0.127	73.895

Geographic coverage: the 50 United States and District of Columbia. Totals may not equal sum of components due to independent rounding. (1) Includes bituminous coal, lignite, and anthracite. (2) Includes industrial and utility production, and net imports of electricity. (3) Parentheses indicate exports are greater than imports. (4) Includes geothermal power and electricity produced from wood and waste. R=Revised data.

World's Largest Hydroelectric Plants

Source: Bureau of Reclamation, U.S. Dept. of The Interior

Rank order	Name, country	Rated capacity (present) MW	Rated capacity (ultimate) MW	Year of initial operation
1.	Itaipu, Brazil/ Paraguay	—	12600	UC(1983)
2.	Grand Coulee, U.S.A.	6430	10080	1942
3.	Guri (Raul Leoni), Venezuela	2800	10060	1968
4.	Tucuruí, Brazil	—	6480	UC(1982)
5.	Sayano-Shushensk, USSR	—	6400	1980
6.	Corpus-Christi, Argentina/Paraguay	—	6000	UC(1990)
7.	Krasnoyarsk, USSR	6096	6096	1968
8.	LaGrande 2, Canada	—	5328	UC(1982)
9.	Churchill Falls, Canada	5225	5225	1971
10.	Bratsk, USSR	4100	4600	1964
11.	Ust'-Ilimsk, USSR	3675	4500	1974
12.	Cabora Bassa, Mozambique	2075	4150	1974
13.	Yacyretá-Apipe, Argentina/Paraguay	—	4050	UC(1986)
14.	Rogun, USSR	—	3600	UC(1985)
15.	Randolph-Hunting, U.S.A.	—	3575	UC(1991)
16.	Paulo Afonso, Brazil	1524	3409	1955
17.	Pati (Chapéton), Argentina	—	3300	UC(1990)
18.	Brumley Gap, U.S.A.	3200	3200	1973
19.	Inga I, Zaire	360	2820	1974
20.	Gezhouba, China	—	2715	UC(1986)
21.	John Day, U.S.A.	2160	2700	1969
22.	Nurek, USSR	900	2700	1976
23.	Revelstoke, Canada	—	2700	UC(1983)
24.	Sao Simao, Brazil	2680	2680	1979
25.	Ilha Solteira, Brazil	2650	2650	1973
26.	LaGrande 4, Canada	—	2637	UC(1984)
27.	Mica, Canada	1736	2610	1976
28.	Volgograd-22nd Congress, USSR	2560	2560	1958
29.	Itaparica, Brazil	—	2500	UC(1985)
30.	Bennett W.A.C., Canada	2116	2416	1969
31.	Chicoasén, Mexico	—	2400	1980
32.	Atatürk, Turkey	—	2400	UC(1990)
33.	LaGrande 3, Canada	—	2304	UC(1982)
34.	Volga-V.I. Lenin, USSR	2300	2300	1955
35.	Iron Gates I, Romania/Yugoslavia	2300	2300	1970
36.	Fos do Areia, Brazil	2250	2250	UC(1983)
37.	Itumbiara, Brazil	—	2124	UC(1982)
38.	Bath County, U.S.A.	—	2100	UC(1985)
39.	High Aswan (Saad-el-Aali), Egypt	2100	2100	1967
40.	Tarbella, Pakistan	1400	2100	1977
41.	Piedra de Aquila, Argentina	—	2100	UC(1989)
42.	Chief Joseph, U.S.A.	2069	2069	1956
43.	Salto Santiago, Brazil	—	2031	1980
44.	McNary, U.S.A.	980	2030	1954
45.	Green River, U.S.A.	—	2000	1980
46.	Tehri, India	—	2000	UC(1990)
47.	Cornwall, U.S.A.	—	2000	1978
48.	Ludington, U.S.A.	1979	1979	1973
49.	Robert Moses-Niagara, U.S.A.	1950	1950	1961
50.	Salto Grande, Argentina/Uruguay	—	1890	1979
51.	Saunders-Moses, Canada/U.S.A.	1824	1824	1958
52.	The Dalles, U.S.A.	1119	1807	1957
53.	Karakaya, Turkey	—	1800	UC(1985)
54.	Dinorwic, Great Britain	—	1800	UC(1982)
55.	Grand'Maison, France	—	1800	1984
56.	Kayalaan, Philippines	—	1800	UC(1983)
57.	Inga II, Zaire	180	1750	1979

Largest Hydroelectric Plants in U.S.

Source: Energy Information Administration, U.S. Energy Department (Capacities as of Dec. 31, 1981)

Plant Name	State	Owner	Installed Capacity (KW)
Coulee Dam	Washington	USBR-Pacific NW Region	6,270,000
John Day	Oregon	USCE-North Pacific Div	2,160,000
Chf Joseph	Washington	USCE-North Pacific Div	2,069,000
LD Pump St	Michigan	Consumers Power Co	1,978,800
Moses Niag	New York	Power Authy of St of NY	1,950,000
Dalles Dam	Washington	USCE-North Pacific Div	1,806,800
Raccoon Mt	Tennessee	Tennessee Valley Auth	1,530,000
Castaic	California	Los Angeles (city of)	1,331,000
Rocky Reach	Washington	Chelan Pub Util Dist #1	1,213,950
Blenheim G	New York	Power Authy of St of NY	1,000,000
McNary	Oregon	USCE-North Pacific Div	980,000
Glen Canyon	Arizona	USBR-Upper Colorado Reg	950,000
Moses Pr Dm	New York	Power Authy of St of NY	912,000
Northfld Mt	Massachusetts	W Massachusetts Elec Co	846,000
Wanapum	Washington	Grant Pub Util Dist #2	831,250
Litle Goose	Washington	USCE-North Pacific Div	810,000
Monumental	Washington	USCE-North Pacific Div	810,000
Lwr Granite	Washington	USCE-North Pacific Div	810,000
Muddy Run	Pennsylvania	Philadelphia Elec Co	800,000
Priest Rpds	Washington	Grant Pub Util Dist #2	788,500
Wells	Washington	Douglas Pub Util Dist #1	774,300
Bonneville	Oregon	USCE-North Pacific Div	717,900
Hoover Dam	Nevada	USBR-Lower Colorado Reg	672,500
Hoover Dam	Arizona	USBR-Lower Colorado Reg	667,500
Edwrd Hyatt	California	California (State of)	644,250
Boundary	Washington	Seattle (city of)	634,600
Wilson Dam	Alabama	Tennessee Valley Auth	629,840
Rock Island	Washington	Chelan Pub Util Dist #1	622,500
Jocassee	South Carolina	Duke Power Co	610,000
Ice Harbor	Washington	USCE-North Pacific Div	603,000
Bear Swamp	Massachusetts	New England Elec System	600,000
Oahe	South Dakota	USCE-Omaha District	595,000
Brownlee	Idaho	Idaho Power Co	585,400
Shasta Dam	California	USBR-Mid Pacific Region	539,000
Smith Mtn	Virginia	Appalachian Power Co	537,250
Fairfield	South Carolina	So Carolina Elec & Gas Co	511,200

Major World Dams

Source: Int'l Commission on Large Dams. (1) Bureau of Reclamation, U.S. Interior Dept. *Replaces existing dam.
Volume in cubic yards. **Capacity** (gross) in acre feet. Year of completion. U.C. under construction.
Type: A—Arch. B—Buttress. E—Earthfill. G—Gravity. R—Rockfill. MA—Multi-arch.

Name of dam	Type	Year	River and basin	Country	Height Feet	Crest Length Feet	Volume (1,000 C.Y.)	Res. cap. (1,000 A.F.)
Afsluitdijk	E	1932	Zuider Zee	Netherlands	62	105,000	82,963	4,864
Akosombo-Main	R	1965	Volta	Ghana	463	2,100	10,400	120,000
Almendra	A	1970	Turmes-Douro	Spain	662	1,860	2,188	2,148
Alpe Gera	G	1965	Comor-Adda-Po	Italy	584	1,710	2,252	53
Bagdad Tailings	E	1973	Maroney Gulch	U.S.	121	2,601	37,304	40
Beas	G	1975	Beas-Indus	India	435	6,400	46,432	6,600
W.A.C. Bennett*	E	1967	Peace-Mackenzie	Canada	600	6,700	57,157	57,006
Bhakra	G	1963	Sutlend-Indus	India	742	1,700	5,400	8,000
Bratsk	GE	1964	Angara	USSR	410	16,864	18,283	137,220
Brouwershavense Gat	E	1972		Netherlands	118	20,341	35,316	466
Castaic	E	1973	Castaic Cr.	U.S.	340	5,200	44,002	432
Charvak	E	1970	Chirchik-Sir Darya	USSR	551	2,483	24,983	1,620
Chirkey	A	1975	Sulak-Caspian Sea	USSR	764	1,109	1,602	2,252
Chivor	R	1975	Bata	Colombia	778	919	14,126	661
Cochiti (1)	E	1975	Rio Grande	U.S.	250	28,000	62,128	724
Copper Cities Tailing 2	E	1973	Tinhorn Wash	U.S.	325	7,598	30,003	4
Cougar	R	1964	S.F. McKenzie	U.S.	519	1,600	13,000	219
Dartmouth	R	1978	Mitta-Mitta	Australia	591	2,200	18,312	3,232
Dneprodzerzhinsk	GE	1964	Dnieper	USSR	112	118,090	28,503	1,994
Don Pedro*	R	1971	Tuolume-San Joaquin	U.S.	585	1,900	16,760	2,030
Dworshak	G	1974	N. Fork Clearwater	U.S.	717	3,287	6,500	3,453
El Chocon	E	1974	Limay	Argentina	282	7,546	17,004	17,025
Emosson	A	1974	Barberine	Switz.	590	1,818	1,426	184
Esperanza Tailings	E	1973	Santa Cruz	U.S.	121	10,600	39,703	5
Fort Peck (1)	E	1940	Missouri	U.S.	250	21,026	125,628	19,100
Fort Randall (1)	E	1956	Missouri	U.S.	160	10,700	50,200	6,100
Gardiner*	E	1968	South Saskatchewan	Canada	223	16,700	85,592	8,000
Garrison (1)	E	1956	Missouri	U.S.	210	12,000	66,500	24,400
Gepatsch	R	1965	Faggenbach-Inn	Austria	500	1,908	9,810	113
Glen Canyon (1)	A	1964	Colorado	U.S.	710	156	4,901	27,000
Goscheneralp	E	1960	Goschener	Switz.	508	1,771	12,230	62
Grand Coulee (1)	G	1942	Columbia	U.S.	550	6,030	10,653	9,386
Grande Dixence	G	1962	Dixence-Rhone	Switz.	935	2,280	7,792	325
Guri	GE	1968	Caroni-Orinoco	Venezuela	348	2,264	4,917	14,349
Haringvliet	E	1970	Haringvliet	Netherlands	79	18,044	26,160	527
High Aswan (Sadd-El-Aali)	ER	1970	Nile	Egypt	364	12,565	55,745	137,000
Hirakud	GE	1956	Mahandi	India	202	15,748	25,100	6,600
Hoover (1)	AG	1936	Colorado	U.S.	726	1,244	4,400	28,537
Hungry Horse (1)	AG	1953	S. Fork Flathead	U.S.	564	2,115	3,086	3,468
Ilha Solteira	EG	1973	Parana Rio de la Plata	Brazil	295	20,308	29,454	27,730
Irkutsk	GE	1956	Angara	USSR	144	8,989	16,219	37,290
Iroquois	G	1958	St. Lawrence	Canada	76	2,665	175	24,288
Ivankova	EG	1937	Volga-Caspian S.	USSR	98	31,398	20,207	908
Jari	E	1967	Jari	Pakistan	234	5,700	42,378	400
Daniel Johnson*	MA	1968	Manicougan-St. Lawrence	Canada	703	4,311	2,950	115,000
Kakhovka	EG	1955	Dnieper	USSR	121	5,380	46,615	14,755
Kanev	E	1974	Dnieper	USSR	82	52,950	49,519	2,125
Kapchagay	E	1970	Ili	USSR	164	1,542	5,078	22,813
Kariba	A	1959	Zambesi	Rhod.-Zambia	420	2,025	1,350	130,000
Keban	ERG	1974	First (Euphrates)	Turkey	679	3,881	20,900	25,110
Kiev	E	1964	Dnieper	USSR	72	177,448	57,550	3,021
King Paul (Kremasta)	ER	1965	Acheloos	Greece	541	1,510	10,686	3,850
Kremenchug	EG	1961	Dnieper	USSR	108	39,844	41,190	10,945
Kurobegawa No. 4	A	1964	Kurobe	Japan	610	1,603	1,782	162
Lauwerszee	E	1969	Lauwerszee	Netherlands	75	42,650	46,530	40
Ludington	E	1973	Lake Michigan	U.S.	170	29,301	37,703	83
Luzzone	A	1963	Brenno di Luzzone	Switz.	682	1,738	1,739	71
Mangla	E	1967	Jhelum	Pakistan	380	11,000	85,868	5,150
Marimbondo	E	1975	Grande	Brazil	315	12,297	24,328	5,184
Mauvoisin	A	1957	Drance de Bagnes	Switz.	777	1,706	2,655	148
Mica	E	1974	Columbia	Canada	794	2,600	42,001	20,025
Mingechaur	E	1953	Kura	USSR	262	5,085	20,400	12,970
Navajo (1)	E	1963	San Juan	U.S.	402	3,648	26,841	1,709
New Bullards Bar	A	1970	North Yuba-Sacramento	U.S.	637	2,200	2,700	960
New Cornelia Tailings	E	1973	Ten Mile Wash, Ariz.	U.S.	98	35,600	274,016	20
New Melones (1)	R	1979	Stanislaus-San Joaquin	U.S.	625	1,650	15,708	2,400
Oahe (1)	E	1960	Missouri	U.S.	245	9,300	92,000	23,600
Okutadami	G	1961	Tadami	Japan	515	1,575	2,145	487
Oroville	E	1968	Feather-Sacramento	U.S.	770	6,920	78,005	3,538
Owen Falls	G	1954	Lake Victoria-Nile	Uganda	100	2,725		166,000
Place Moulin	AG	1965	Buthier-Dora Baltea	Italy	502	2,181	1,962	81
Reza Shah Kabir	A	1975	Karoun	Iran	656	1,247	1,570	2,351
Rybinsk	GE	1941	Volga-Caspian S.	USSR	98	2,060	3,329	20,590
Sakuma	G	1956	Tenryu	Japan	510	963	1,465	265
San Luis (1)	E	1967	San Luis-San Joaquin	U.S.	382	18,600	77,670	2,041
Saratov	E	1967	Volga-Caspian S.	USSR	131	37,204	52,843	10,458
Shasta (1)	AG	1945	Sacramento	U.S.	602	3,460	8,430	4,552
Swift	E	1958	Lewis-Columbia	U.S.	610	2,100	15,800	756
Tabka	E	1975	Euphrates	Syria	197	14,764	60,166	11,350
Talbingo	R	1971	Tamut	Australia	530	2,300	18,950	747
Tarbela	ER	1975	Indus	Pakistan	486	9,000	159,203	11,100
Trinity (1)	E	1962	Trinity-Klamath	U.S.	537	2,450	29,400	2,448
Tsimlyansk	EG	1952	Don	USSR	128	43,411	44,328	17,715
Tuttle Creek	E	1962	Big Blue-Missouri	U.S.	154	7,500	22,937	413
Twin Buttes (1)	E	1963	Mid and So. Concho R., Spring Cr.-Colorado, Texas	U.S.	134	42,460	21,442	641
Twin Buttes Tailings	E	1973	Santa Cruz	U.S.	239	11,299	38,604	209
Vilyui	ER	1967	Vilyui	USSR	246	2,297	3,793	29,104
Volga-22d congress USSR	ERG	1958	Volga-Caspian S.	USSR	144	13,108	33,020	27,160
Volga-V. I. Lenin	EG	1955	Volga-Caspian S.	USSR	148	12,405	44,299	47,020
Yellowtail (1)	A	1966	Bighorn-Missouri	U.S.	525	1,480	1,546	1,375
Zeya	G	1975	Zeya	USSR	369	2,343	3,139	55,452

Major U.S. Public and Private Dams and Reservoirs

Source: Corps of Engineers, U.S. Army
Heights over 350 feet.

Height—Difference in elevation in feet, between lowest point in foundation and top of dam, exclusive of parapet or other projections. **Length**—Overall length of barrier in feet, main dam and its integral features as located between natural abutments. **Volume**—Total volume in cubic yards of all material in main dam and its appurtenant works. **Year**—Date structure was originally completed for use. (UC) Under construction subject to revision. **River**—Mainstream. **Purpose**—I-Irrigation; C-Flood Control; H-Hydroelectric; N-Navigation; S-Water Supply; R-Recreation; D-Debris Control; O-Other. **Parentheses** after name indicate type of dam as follows: (RE)-Earth; (PG)-Gravity; (ER)-Rockfill; (CB)-Buttress; (VA)-Arch; (MV)-Multi-arch; (OT)-Other. †Replacing existing dam.

Name of dam	State	River	Ht.	Lgth.	Vol. (1,000)	Purpose	Year
Oroville (RE)	Cal.	Feather River	756	6800	78000	IR	1968
Hoover (VA)	Nev.	Colorado River	726	1242	4400	IHCO	1936
Dworshak (PG)	Ida.	North Fork of Clearwater	717	3287	6450	HCR	1973
Glen Canyon (VA)	Ariz.	Colorado River	710	1560	4901	HCSR	1966
New Bullards Bar (VA)	Cal.	North Yuba River	635	2200	2600	SD	1970
New Melones (ER)	Cal.	Stanislaus River	625	1560	16000	IH	1979
Swift Dam (RE)	Wash.	North Fork Lewis River	610	2100	15400	HR	1958
Mossyrock Dam (VA)	Wash.	Cowlitz River	606	1648	1270	HCR	1968
Shasta (PG)	Cal.	Sacramento River	602	3460	8711	ISHN	1945
Yankee Doodle Tailings (ER)	Mon.	Yankee Doodle and Silver Bow Cr.	570	13200	200000	O	1972
Don Pedro (RE)	Cal.	Tuolumne River	568	1800	16000	HI	1971
Hungry Horse (VA)	Mon.	South Fork of Flathead River	564	2115	3086	IHCN	1953
Grand Coulee (PG)	Wash.	Columbia River	550	4173	10585	IHCN	1942
Ross Dam (VA)	Wash.	Skagit River	540	1300	919	HR	1949
Trinity (RE)	Cal	Trinity River	537	2600	29410	IHCR	1962
John's Branch No. 2 (OT)	W.Va.	John's Branch of Toney Fork	534	2250	8218	O	1963
Yellowtail (VA)	Mon.	Bighorn River	525	1360	146	ICHR	1966
Cougar (ER)	Ore.	South Fork McKenzie River	519	1600	13000	HCIR	1964
Flaming Gorge (VA)	Ut.	Green River	502	1285	987	HCSR	1964
Stirrat No. 15 Waste Embank. (OT)	W.Va.	Rockhouse Br. of Island Cr.	500	1800	11000	O	1977
Fontana Dam (PG)	N.C.	Little Tennessee River	480	2365	3576	H	1944
New Exchequer (ER)	Cal.	Merced River	479	1240	5169	HI	1926
Wyco No. 2 Refuse Embank. (OT)	W.Va.	Guyandot River	469	1500	6453	O	1978
Morrow Point (VA)	Col.	Gunnison River	468	741	365	HCRO	1968
Dry Fork Slurry Impound (OT)	W.Va.	Trib. Dry Fork of Tug Fork	465	2100	14406	O	1960
Mill Branch Coal Refuse Dam (OT)	W.Va.	Crane Fork of Clear Fork	465	1584	4000	O	1963
Carters Main Dam (ER,RE)	Ga.	Coosawattee River	464	1950	15000	CHR	1974
Detroit (PG)	Ore.	North Santiam River	463	1580	1500	HCRI	1953
Anderson Ranch (RE)	Ida.	South Fork Boise River	456	1350	9653	IHCR	1950
Union Valley (RE)	Cal.	Silver Creek	453	1800	10000	SH	1963
Round Butte Dam (RE,ER)	Ore.	Deschutes River	440	1450	9600	HR	1964
Pine Flat Lake (PG)	Cal.	Kings River	440	1840	2400	CIRH	1954
Jocassee (ER)	S.C.	Keowee River	435	1800	11600	H	1973
O'Shaughnessy (PG)	Cal.	Moccasin Creek	430	900	663	H	1923
Mud Mountain Dam (ER)	Wash.	White River	425	700	2300	C	1948
Libby Dam (PG)	Mon.	Kootenai River	422	2890	375	HC	1973
Pacoima (VA)	Cal.	Pacoima Creek	420	640	226	C	1929
Owyhee Dam (VA)	Ore.	Owyhee River	417	833	538	ICR	1932
Lower Hell Hole (ER)	Cal.	Rubicon River	410	1550	8315	SD	1966
Castaic (RE)	Cal.	Castaic Creek	410	5200	44000	IR	1973
Mammoth Pool (RE)	Cal.	San Joaquin River	406	820	5355	HS	1960
San Gabriel No. 1 (ER)	Cal.	San Gabriel River	405	1520	10600	C	1939
Navajo (RE)	N.M.	San Juan River	402	3648	26840	IR	1963
Little Blue Run Dam (RE)	Pa.	Little Blue Run of Ohio River	400	2100	13000	O	1977
No name (RE)	S.C.	Jocassee River	400	1000		H	1972
Pyramid (ER)	Cal.	Piru Creek	400	1080	6952	IR	1973
Rockhouse Branch Refuse Bank	W.Va.	Rockhouse Br. of Cow Ck.	400	1350	11200	O	1973
Brownlee Dam (ER)	Ida.	Snake River	395	1380	6000	H	1958
Summersville Dam (ER)	W.Va.	Gauley River	390	2280	13565	CRSO	1965
Blue Mesa (RE)	Col.	Gunnison River	390	785	3093	HCRO	1966
Diablo Dam (VA)	Wash.	Skagit River	386	1180	350	HR	1929
San Luis (RE)	Cal.	San Luis Creek	382	18600	77664	ISHR	1967
Green Peter (PG)	Ore.	Middle Santiam River	378	1517	1142	CHRI	1967
Merriman Dam (RE)	N.Y.	Roundout Creek	375	2400	5800	S	1945
Jenkins Refuse Dam (OT)	Ky.	Elkhorn Creek	363	1700	12229	D	1974
Spruce Lick Fork Refuse Disp. (OT)	W.Va.	Spruce Lick Fk. of West Pond	360	400	17736	O	1977
Steel Trap Br. Refuse Dam (OT)	Ky.	Steel Trap Br. of Phillips Fk.	358	650	4250	O	1979
Abiquiu Dam (RE)	N.M.	Rio Chama	354	1540	11793	CD	1963
Arrowrock	Ida.	Boise River	350	1150	636	IDCR	1915

World's Largest Dams

Source: International Commission on Large Dans

Based on total volume of structure. All dams listed are predominantly earthfill or rockfill and may contain concrete section.

Name of dam	Cubic yards	Completed
New Cornelia Tailings, U.S.	274,015,735	1973
Tarbela, Pakistan	159,202,796	1975
Fort Peck, U.S.	125,627,386	1940
Oahe, U.S.	91,999,965	1963
Mangla, Pakistan	85,868,291	1967
Gardiner, Canada	85,592,313	1968
Afsluitdijk, Netherlands	82,963,331	1932
Oroville, U.S.	78,004,889	1968
San Luis, U.S.	77,668,746	1967
Garrison, U.S.	66,502,768	1956
Cochiti, U.S.	65,698,378	1975
Tabka, Syria	60,165,746	1975
Kiev, USSR	57,549,844	1964
W.A.C. Bennett, Canada	57,157,458	1967
High Aswan Sadd-El-Aili, Egypt	55,744,871	1970
Saratov, U.S.S.R.	52,841,220	1967
Mission Tailings, No. 2, U.S.	52,433,139	1973
Fort Randall, U.S.	50,199,159	1956
Kanev, USSR	49,519,024	1974
Kakhovka, USSR	46,615,373	1955
Itumbiara, Brazil	46,563,055	1980
Lauwerszee, Netherlands	46,530,356	1969
Beas, India	46,432,260	1975
Tsimlyansk, USSR	44,327,767	1952
Volga, V.I. Lenin, USSR	44,298,992	1955
Castaic, U.S.	44,002,087	1971
Jari, Pakistan	42,377,612	1967
Mica, Canada	42,000,922	1973
Kremeiychug, USSR	41,189,982	1961
Esperanza Tailings, USA	39,702,852	1973

TRADE AND TRANSPORTATION

Notable Steamships and Motorships

Source: Lloyd's Register of Shipping as of June 8, 1982

Gross tonnage is a measurement of enclosed space (1 gross ton=100 cu. ft.) Deadweight tonnage is the weight (long tons) of cargo, fuel, etc., which a vessel is designed to carry safely.

Oil Tankers

Name, registry	Dwght. ton.	Lgth. ft.	Bdth. ft.
Seawise Giant, Liber.	564,763	1504.0	209.0
Pierre Guillaumat, Fr.	555,051	1359.0	206.0
Prairial, Fr.	554,974	1359.0	206.0
Bellamya, Fr.	553,662	1359.0	206.0
Batillus, Fr.	553,662	1358.0	206.0
Esso Atlantic, Liber.	516,893	1333.0	233.0
Esso Pacific, Liber.	516,423	1333.0	233.0
Nanny, Swed.	491,120	1194.0	259.0
Nissei Maru, Jap.	484,337	1243.0	203.0
Globtik London, Liber.	483,933	1243.0	203.0
Globtik Tokyo, Liber.	483,662	1243.0	203.0
Burmah Enterprise, U.K.	457,927	1241.0	224.0
Burmah Endeavour, U.K.	457.841	1241.0	223.0
Robinson, Liber.	431,232	1236.0	226.0
Coraggio, It.	423,798	1240.0	226.0
Berge Empress, Nor.	423,700	1252.0	223.0
Berge Emperor, Nor.	423,700	1285.0	223.0
Hilda Knudsen, Nor.	423,639	1240.0	226.0
Esso Deutschland, W. Ger.	421,681	1240.0	226.0
Jinko Maru, Jap.	413,553	1200.0	229.0
David Packard, Liber.	413,115	1200.0	229.0
Aiko Maru, Jap.	413,012	1200.0	229.0
Chevron South America, Liber.	412,612	1200.0	229.0
Chevron No. Amer., Liber.	412,612	1200.0	229.0
World Petrobras, Liber.	411,508	1187.0	229.0
Nai Superba, It.	409,400	1253.0	207.0
Nai Genova, It.	409,400	1253.0	207.0
Al Rekkah, Kuw.	407,822	1200.0	229.0
Esso Japan, Liber.	406,640	1187.0	229.0
Esso Tokyo, Liber.	406,258	1187.0	229.0
U.S.T. Atlantic, U.S.	404,531	1188.0	228.0

Bulk, Ore, Bulk Oil, & Ore Oil Carriers

Name, registry	Dwght. ton.	Lgth. ft.	Bdth. ft.
World Gala, Liber.	282,462	1109.0	179.0
Weser Ore, Liber.	278,734	1099.0	170.0
Docecanyon, Liber.	275,589	1113.0	180.0
Jose Bonifacio Braz.	270,358	1106.0	179.0
Licorne Pacifique, Fr.	269,007	1111.0	176.0
Usa Maru, Jap.	268,767	1105.0	179.0
Cast Narwhal, Liber.	268,728	1101.0	176.0
Hitachi Venture, Liber.	267,889	1063.0	180.0
Rhine Ore, Pan.	264,999	1099.0	170.0
Alkisma Alarabia, Saud. Arab.	264,591	1101.0	176.0
Licorne Atlantique, Fr.	262,411	1101.0	176.0
Hoegh Hill, Nor.	249,259	1069.0	170.0
World Truth, Liber.	249,223	1069.0	170.0
Hoegh Hood, Nor.	248,604	1069.0	170.0
Seiko Maru, Jap.	247,867	1069.0	170.0
Konkar Dinos, Gr.	234,752	1075.0	160.0
World Recovery, Liber.	231,054	1075.0	161.0
Berge Brioni, Nor.	227,558	1030.0	165.0
Berge Adria, Nor.	227,558	1030.0	164.0
Rimula, U.K.	227,412	1091.0	149.0
Rapana U.K.	227,400	1091.0	149.0
Ruhr Ore, Liber.	227,086	1096.0	149.0
Alva Bay, U.K.	225,898	1091.0	149.0
Konkar Theodoros, Gr.	225,162	1091.0	164.0
Alva Sea U.K.	225,010	1090.0	149.0
Andros Atlas, Gr.	224,074	1061.0	158.0
Andros Antares, Liber.	223,888	1061.0	158.0
Andros Aries, Gr.	223,605	1061.0	158.0
World Lady, Liber.	219,080	1075.0	164.0
Donau Ore, Liber.	218,957	1075.0	164.0
Tantalus, U.K.	218,035	1075.0	164.0
Atsuta Maru, Jap.	271,451	1075.0	164.0
Tsurumi, Jap.	217,257	1075.0	164.0

World's Largest Passenger Ships

Name, registry	Dwght. ton.	Lgth. ft.	Bdth. ft.
Norway, Nor.	70,202	1035.0	110.0
Queen Elizabeth 2, U.K.	67,140	963.0	105.0
Oriana, U.K.	41,920	804.0	97.0
Rotterdam, Neth. Ant.	38,644	748.0	94.0
United States, U.S.	38,216	990.0	101.0
Europa, W. Ger.	33,819	654.0	98.0
Eugenio C., It.	30,567	713.0	96.0

Container, Liquefied Gas, Misc. Ships

Name, registry	Dwght. ton.	Lgth. ft.	Bdth. ft.
Hoegh Gandria, Nor.	95,683	943.0	142.0
Golar Spirit, Liber.	93,815	948.0	146.0
Golar Freeze, Liber.	85,158	943.0	142.0
Khannur, Liber.	84,855	963.0	136.0
Gimi, Liber.	84,855	963.0	136.0
Hilli, Liber.	84,855	961.0	136.0
Lake Charles, U.S.	83,744	936.0	149.0
Louisiana, U.S.	83,744	936.0	149.0
LNG Libra, U.S.	83,729	936.0	149.0
LNG Taurus, U.S.	83,729	936.0	149.0
LNG Virgo, U.S.	83,729	936.0	149.0
LNG Aires, U.S.	83,646	936.0	149.0
LNG Capricorn, U.S.	83,608	936.0	149.0
LNG Gemini, U.S.	83,608	936.0	149.0
LNG Leo, U.S.	83,608	936.0	149.0
LNG Aquarius, U.S.	83,102	936.0	143.0
Mostefa Ben-Boulaid, Alger.	82,243	914.0	134.0
Rhenania, W. Ger.	80,946	941.0	137.0
Bachir Chihani, Alger.	80,328	924.0	136.0
Larbi Ben M'Hidi, Alger.	80,328	924.0	136.0
Ben Franklin, Fr.	80,071	894.0	134.0
Nestor, Bermuda	78,915	902.0	138.0
Methania, Belg.	78,511	918.0	136.0
Edouard L.D., Fr.	78,212	920.0	136.0
Pollenger, U.K.	76,496	857.0	131.0
Norman Lady, U.K.	76,416	818.0	131.0
Mourad Didouche, Alger.	74,741	900.0	137.0
Ramdane Abane, Alger.	74,741	900.0	137.0
Golden Phoenix, U.S.	72,000	931.0	140.0
El Paso Savannah, U.S.	72,000	931.0	140.0
El Paso Southern, U.S.	69,472	948.0	135.0
El Paso Howard Boyd, U.S.	69,472	948.0	135.0
El Paso Arzew, U.S.	69,472	948.0	135.0
Gastor, Pan.	68,246	902.0	138.0
Tenaga Dua, Malays.	68,086	920.0	136.0
Tenaga Lima, Malays.	68,086	920.0	136.0
Tenaga Empat, Malays.	68,086	920.0	136.0
Tenaga Tiga, Malays.	66,808	920.0	136.0
El Paso Consolidated, Liber.	66,807	920.0	136.0
El Paso Sonatrach, Liber.	66,807	920.0	136.0
El Paso Paul Kayser, Liber.	66,807	920.0	136.0
Palace Tokyo, Jap.	64,378	807.0	131.0
Kurama Maru, Jap.	59,294	898.0	105.0
Nedlloyd Dejima, Neth.	58,716	941.0	106.0
Nedlloyd Delft, Neth.	58,613	941.0	106.0
Cardigan Bay, U.K.	58,497	950.0	106.0
Kowloon Bay, U.K.	58,496	950.0	106.0
Tokyo Bay, U.K.	58,496	950.0	106.0
Liverpool Bay, U.K.	58,496	950.0	106.0
Osaka Bay, U.K.	58,496	950.0	106.0
Kasuga Maru, Jap.	58,440	948.0	105.0
City of Edinburgh, U.K.	58,284	950.0	106.0
Benavon, U.K.	58,283	950.0	106.0
Benalder, U.K.	58,283	950.0	106.0
Hamburg Express, W. Ger.	58,087	943.0	106.0
Tokio Express, W. Ger.	57,995	943.0	106.0
Bremen Express, W. Ger.	57,535	949.0	106.0
Hongkong Express, W. Ger.	57,524	941.0	106.0
Korrigan, Fr.	57,249	946.0	105.0
Esso Fuji, Pan.	55,896	807.0	131.0
Esso Westernport, Liber.	54,056	838.0	116.0
City of Durban, U.K.	53,790	848.0	106.0
Table Bay, U.K.	53,784	848.0	106.0
Geomitra, U.K.	53,128	849.0	114.0
Genota, U.K.	53,128	849.0	113.0
S.A. Waterberg, So. Afr.	53,050	848.0	106.0
S.A. Winterberg, So. Afr.	53,050	848.0	106.0
S.A. Sederberg So. Afr.	53,023	848.0	106.0
S.A. Helderberg So. Afr.	53,023	848.0	106.0
Transvaal, W. Germ.	52,811	848.0	106.0

Nuclear Powered Merchant Ships

Name, registry	Dwght. ton.	Lgth. ft.	Bdth. ft.
Arktika, USSR	18,172	485.0	98.0
Otto Hahn, W. Ger.	16,871	564.0	76.0
Lenin, USSR	13,366	439.0	90.0
Mutsu, Jap.	8,214	428.0	62.0

Merchant Fleets of the World

Source: Maritime Administration, U.S. Commerce Department

Oceangoing steam and motor ships of 1,000 gross tons and over as of Jan. 1, 1981, excludes ships operating exclusively on the Great Lakes and inland waterways and special types such as channel ships, icebreakers, cable ships, etc., and merchant ships owned by any military force. Tonnage is in thousands. Gross tonnage is a volume measurement; each cargo gross ton represents 100 cubic ft. of enclosed space. Deadweight tonnage is the carrying capacity of a ship in long tons (2,240 lbs.).

Country of registry	Total no.	Total gross tons	Dwt. tons	Freighters Number	Freighters Dwt. tons	Bulk Carriers Number	Bulk Carriers Dwt. tons	Tankers Number	Tankers Dwt. tons
Total-All Countries	24,867	385,711	654,909	14,242	121,252	4,798	185,311	5,359	346,329
United States [1]	864	16,020	24,090	471	6,885	20	607	308	16,152
Privately-Owned	578	13,467	21,103	263	4,604	20	607	288	15,835
Government-Owned	286	2,554	2,987	208	2,281	—	—	20	317
Algeria	68	1,236	1,842	39	292	6	127	23	1,423
Argentina	203	2,206	3,336	115	1,148	25	955	62	1,230
Australia	74	1,460	2,276	30	353	30	1,329	14	593
Bangladesh	33	298	422	27	280	1	93	4	43
Belgium	74	1,677	2,639	33	474	27	1,473	13	677
Brazil	313	4,611	7,720	197	1,647	49	2,914	64	3,156
British Colonies	202	2,767	4,310	124	877	62	2,760	14	668
*Bulgaria	108	1,095	1,620	50	347	39	735	17	537
Canada	102	646	980	35	185	13	380	47	409
Chile	47	570	938	29	293	10	503	8	142
*China (People's Rep.)	695	6,706	10,129	495	5,004	95	3,238	87	1,817
China (Taiwan)	170	2,003	3,032	115	1,028	39	1,322	13	655
Colombia	41	272	356	34	282	—	—	4	46
*Cuba	90	687	935	70	745	7	83	10	90
Cyprus	395	1,719	2,507	344	1,914	25	390	19	186
*Czechoslovakia	16	154	229	11	67	5	163	—	—
Denmark	275	4,782	8,009	167	1,666	33	1,049	69	5,288
Ecuador	32	260	351	19	182	—	—	12	157
Finland	175	2,178	3,553	91	487	40	869	36	2,176
France	345	10,981	19,539	178	2,034	48	2,719	117	14,782
*German Dem. Repub.	158	1,282	1,776	129	1,046	19	399	8	325
Germany (Fed. Rep.)	473	7,381	11,863	359	3,651	47	2,762	64	5,441
Ghana	29	199	262	29	262	—	—	—	—
Greece	2,928	40,502	69,559	1,515	14,765	943	30,096	415	24,518
Honduras	45	175	230	37	199	—	—	7	22
*Hungary	21	72	101	21	101	—	—	—	—
India	370	5,704	9,221	230	2,826	102	4,346	31	2,009
Indonesia	254	1,053	1,490	196	1,048	10	158	36	220
Iran	55	1,062	1,759	39	505	—	—	16	1,253
Iraq	45	1,350	2,447	23	306	—	—	22	2,141
Ireland	25	138	207	15	35	6	159	4	14
Israel	39	471	634	28	303	11	331	—	—
Italy	622	10,256	17,269	229	1,638	144	6,851	230	8,687
Ivory Coast	19	180	236	19	236	—	—	—	—
Japan	1,762	36,730	62,001	717	6,503	511	22,057	526	33,408
*Korea (People's Dem.)	29	218	352	21	155	2	52	5	144
Korea (Republic of)	385	3,789	6,285	232	1,501	103	2,306	50	2,478
Kuwait	86	2,309	3,767	60	1,178	2	18	23	2,569
Lebanon	76	201	275	74	268	2	7	—	—
Liberia	2,271	78,743	153,342	522	5,876	853	41,520	889	105,890
Libya	27	836	1,530	13	46	—	—	14	1,484
Malaysia	73	651	949	55	375	11	476	4	91
Maldives	37	171	239	35	229	1	6	—	—
Malta	30	144	210	18	88	7	105	4	15
Mexico	61	836	1,278	14	96	5	144	42	1,038
Morocco	44	324	538	24	103	3	99	17	336
Netherlands	444	5,066	8,300	350	2,444	28	1,046	63	4,794
New Zealand	23	196	236	14	123	6	31	3	82
Nigeria	30	425	624	29	352	—	—	1	273
Norway	616	21,566	38,575	194	2,011	151	10,424	248	26,072
Pakistan	51	480	650	45	593	1	17	—	—
Panama	2,437	23,183	38,011	1,701	13,301	406	11,016	294	13,468
Peru	52	578	936	30	298	12	433	10	206
Philippines	235	1,731	2,757	153	1,017	29	1,088	39	630
Poland	318	3,175	4,686	220	1,686	81	2,023	13	965
Portugal	76	1,158	1,963	51	395	4	116	20	1,449
*Romania	191	1,625	2,408	139	821	44	1,156	7	429
Saudi Arabia	92	1,652	2,891	43	259	5	187	42	2,440
Singapore	622	7,148	11,754	431	3,912	85	3,118	98	4,696
South Africa	29	606	767	21	423	6	284	2	61
Spain	509	6,907	12,235	315	1,487	71	2,375	117	8,354
Sweden	232	3,751	6,225	133	1,324	30	1,150	67	3,746
Switzerland	30	287	437	17	146	8	277	5	15
Thailand	68	323	489	45	286	1	2	22	202
Tunisia	19	115	164	11	56	2	32	6	76
Turkey	178	1,346	2,093	116	574	22	785	29	709
*USSR [2]	2,530	16,550	21,757	1,847	11,235	161	3,140	467	7,248
United Arab Emirates	12	105	193	10	55	—	—	2	138
United Arab Rep.	87	413	552	61	338	1	2	14	154
United Kingdom	1,056	25,424	42,302	450	4,820	216	11,086	378	26,323
Uruguay	18	178	286	12	96	1	22	5	169
Venezuela	64	613	918	46	398	5	88	13	431
Vietnam	41	227	344	33	241	4	53	4	50
Yugoslavia	258	2,417	3,698	184	1,663	52	1,568	14	430
Zaire	8	77	116	7	101	—	—	—	—

*Source material limited. (1) Excludes 60 non-merchant type and/or Navy-owned vessels currently in the Natl. Defense Reserve Fleet. (2) Includes U.S. Government-owned ships transferred to USSR under lend-lease agreements and still under that registry.

U.S. Foreign Trade with Leading Countries

Source: Office of Planning and Research, U.S. Commerce Department

(millions of dollars)

Exports from the U.S. to the following areas and countries and imports into the U.S. from those areas and countries:	Exports			Imports		
	1979	1980	1981	1979	1980	1981
Total	**$181,816**	**$220,705**	**$233,739**	**$206,256**	**$240,834**	**$261,305**
Western Hemisphere	**61,555**	**74,114**	**81,667**	**68,509**	**78,489**	**85,436**
Canada	33,096	35,395	39,564	38,046	41,455	46,414
20 Latin American Republics	26,259	36,030	38,950	24,767	29,851	32,023
Central American Common Market	1,655	1,951	1,773	1,895	1,849	1,546
Dominican Republic	610	795	772	665	786	926
Panama	528	699	844	191	330	297
Bahamas	334	396	441	1,587	1,382	1,262
Jamaica	292	305	479	375	383	366
Netherlands Antilles	412	448	499	1,830	2,564	2,626
Trinidad and Tobago	462	680	688	1,559	2,378	2,215
Europe	**60,026**	**71,372**	**69,715**	**43,547**	**47,849**	**53,410**
OECD countries (excludes depend. and Yugo.)	53,514	66,654	64,548	41,272	45,952	51,399
Western Europe	54,342	67,512	65,377	41,681	46,416	51,855
European Economic Community	42,592	53,679	52,363	33,293	35,958	41,624
Belgium and Luxembourg	5,187	6,661	5,765	1,741	1,914	2,297
Denmark	732	863	887	707	725	850
France	5,587	7,485	7,341	4,768	5,247	5,851
Germany, Federal Republic of	8,478	10,960	10,277	10,955	11,681	11,379
Ireland	695	836	1,025	323	411	498
Italy	4,362	5,511	5,360	4,918	4,313	5,189
Netherlands	6,917	8,669	8,595	1,853	1,910	2,366
United Kingdom	10,635	12,694	12,439	8,028	9,755	12,835
European Free Trade Association	...	...	...	...	...	...
Austria	312	448	484	379	388	382
Finland	337	505	613	449	439	525
Iceland	48	79	71	226	200	198
Norway	688	843	892	1,267	2,632	2,477
Portugal	691	911	1,075	244	256	238
Sweden	1,515	1,767	1,842	1,652	1,617	1,714
Switzerland	3,660	3,781	3,022	2,076	2,787	2,448
Greece	812	922	676	183	292	359
Spain	2,506	3,179	3,397	1,303	1,209	1,533
Turkey	354	540	789	201	175	261
Yugoslavia	757	756	648	389	446	437
Eastern Europe	5,684	3,860	4,338	1,866	1,433	1,555
USSR	3,607	1,513	2,431	874	453	348
Asia	**48,771**	**60,168**	**63,849**	**66,739**	**78,848**	**92,033**
Near East	**11,030**	**11,900**	**14,964**	**14,989**	**17,280**	**18,543**
Iran	1,021	23	300	2,784	339	64
Iraq	442	724	914	618	352	164
Israel	1,855	2,045	2,521	750	943	1,243
Jordan	334	407	727	4	3	2
Kuwait	765	886	976	87	472	86
Lebanon	227	303	296	15	33	19
Saudi Arabia	4,875	5,769	7,327	7,983	12,509	14,391
Syria	229	239	143	165	26	83
Japan	**17,581**	**20,790**	**21,823**	**26,248**	**30,701**	**37,612**
East and South Asia	**20,160**	**27,478**	**27,062**	**25,502**	**30,867**	**35,878**
Bangladesh	204	292	158	88	85	85
China, People's Republic of	1,724	3,755	3,603	592	1,054	1,892
China, Republic of	3,272	4,337	4,305	5,902	6,850	8,049
Hong Kong	2,083	2,686	2,635	3,995	4,736	5,428
India	1,167	1,689	1,748	1,038	1,098	1,202
Indonesia	982	1,545	1,302	3,621	5,183	6,022
Korea, Republic of	4,190	4,685	5,116	4,047	4,147	5,141
Malaysia	932	1,337	1,537	2,146	2,577	2,183
Pakistan	529	642	492	120	128	174
Philippines	1,570	1,999	1,787	1,490	1,730	1,964
Singapore	2,330	3,033	3,003	1,467	1,920	2,114
Thailand	961	1,263	1,170	600	816	946
Oceania	**4,319**	**4,876**	**6,436**	**3,072**	**3,392**	**3,352**
Australia	3,617	4,093	5,242	2,164	2,509	2,465
New Zealand and Samoa	534	599	940	709	703	766
Africa	**6,299**	**9,060**	**11,097**	**24,382**	**32,251**	**27,071**
Algeria	404	542	717	4,943	6,577	5,038
Canary Islands	113	158	160	8	6	3
Egypt	1,433	1,874	2,159	381	458	397
Gabon	33	48	128	322	278	432
Ghana	91	127	154	225	206	246
Ivory Coast	128	185	130	363	288	344
Kenya	61	141	150	50	54	52
Liberia	108	113	128	136	128	113
Libya	468	509	813	5,256	7,124	5,301
Morocco	271	344	429	40	35	36
Nigeria	632	1,150	1,523	8,162	10,905	9,249
South Africa, Rep. of	1,413	2,464	2,912	2,616	3,321	2,445
Sudan	103	143	208	16	17	58
Tunisia	175	174	222	95	60	10
Zaire	113	155	141	286	361	423

U.S. Exports and Imports of Leading Commodities

Source: Office of Planning and Research, U.S. Commerce Department (millions of dollars)

Commodity	Exports 1979	Exports 1980	Exports 1981	Imports 1979	Imports 1980	Imports 1981
Food and live animals	**22,251**	**27,744**	**30,291**	**15,170**	**15,763**	**15,238**
Cattle, except for breeding	...	...	...	236	228	182
Meat and preparations	1,127	1,293	1,482	2,539	2,346	1,996
Cheese	...	...	...	293	NA	NA
Dairy products and eggs	161	255	433	304	318	357
Fish	1,029	915	1,083	2,639	2,612	2,962
Grains and preparations	14,454	18,079	19,457	178	NA	NA
Wheat, including flour	5,492	6,586	8,073	...	...	...
Rice	850	1,285	1,526	...	...	...
Grains and animal feed	2,318	2,878	2,739	298	331	381
Fruits and nuts }	2,130	2,930	3,314	859	859	995
Vegetables }				1,203	1,188	1,592
Sugar	...	...	...	974	1,988	2,142
Coffee, green	...	...	...	3,820	3,872	2,622
Cocoa or cacao beans	...	...	...	555	395	466
Tea	...	...	...	126	131	133
Spices	...	...	...	139	NA	NA
Beverages and Tobacco	**2,337**	**2,663**	**2,915**	**2,565**	**2,772**	**3,138**
Alcoholic beverages	...	...	...	2,013	2,220	2,399
Tobacco and manufactures	2,092	2,390	2,686	436	422	427
Beverages and other tobacco	245	273	...	117	NA	...
Crude materials, inedible, except fuels	**20,756**	**23,791**	**20,993**	**10,653**	**10,496**	**11,193**
Hides and skins	992	694	700	139	88	101
Soybeans, oilseeds, peanuts	5,708	5,883	6,200	...	...	428
Synthetic rubber	579	695	625	...	...	...
Rubber, including latex	...	...	...	897	816	778
Lumber and rough wood	2,797	2,675	2,059	2,913	2,134	2,033
Wood pulp and pulpwood	1,644	2,454	2,315	1,506	1,725	1,778
Textile fibers and wastes	2,198	2,864	2,260	231	242	344
Ores and metal scrap	3,324	4,518	2,718	3,249	3,696	3,838
Mineral fuels and related mat'ls	**5,621**	**7,982**	**10,279**	**59,998**	**79,058**	**81,417**
Coal	3,328	4,523	6,006	...	...	...
Petroleum and products	1,918	2,833	3,696	56,036	73,771	75,577
Natural gas	180	NA	...	3,526	5,155	5,720
Animal and vegetable oils and fats	**1,845**	**1,946**	**1,750**	**740**	**533**	**479**
Chemicals	**17,308**	**20,740**	**21,187**	**7,479**	**8,583**	**9,446**
Medicines and pharmaceuticals	1,591	1,932	2,165	441	508	583
Fertilizers, manufactured	1,404	2,265	1,735	976	1,104	1,181
Plastic materials and resins	3,241	3,884	3,809	626	NA	NA
Machinery and transport equip.	**70,495**	**84,629**	**95,736**	**53,677**	**60,546**	**69,627**
Machinery	44,745	55,790	62,946	28,044	31,904	38,212
Aircraft engines and parts	1,423	1,915	2,349	328	NA	NA
Auto engines and parts	1,631	1,688	1,975	1,949	NA	NA
Agricultural machinery	2,636	3,104	3,523	711	682	1,282
Tractors and parts	1,547	1,809	2,102	1,205	NA	643
Office machines and computers	6,475	8,709	9,810	2,500	2,929	3,563
Transport equipment	25,750	28,839	32,791	25,634	28,642	31,415
Road motor vehicles and parts	15,077	14,590	16,214	22,075	24,134	26,217
Aircraft and parts except engines	9,719	12,816	14,738	1,078	1,885	2,585
Other manufactured goods	**32,100**	**42,714**	**42,160**	**51,069**	**55,900**	**63,471**
Tires and tubes	353	511	584	1,136	1,143	1,331
Wood and manufactures, exc. furniture	2,797	2,675	2,059	855	632	705
Paper and manufactures	1,967	2,831	2,961	3,357	3,587	3,875
Glassware and pottery	...	...	...	1,097	1,224	1,349
Diamonds, excl. industrial	...	...	...	1,862	2,252	2,198
Nonmetallic mineral manuf.	1,948	2,209	2,194	...	...	...
Metals and manufactures	3,432	4,205	4,769	17,458	18,718	22,333
Pig iron and ferroalloys	2,342	3,123	2,880	702	NA	NA
Iron and steel-mill products	2,227	2,998	2,801	6,764	6,686	11,211
Platinum group metals	...	...	...	800	NA	NA
Nonferrous base metals	1,609	2,964	2,046	6,320	7,623	6,952
Other manuf. of metals	...	...	...	3,671	3,731	4,170
Textiles, other than clothing	3,189	3,632	3,619	2,216	2,493	3,046
Clothing	931	1,203	1,232	5,874	6,427	7,537
Footwear	...	...	...	2,861	2,808	3,019
Furniture	385	521	697	1,035	NA	NA
Scientific and photo equip., photo supplies	5,514	6,763	7,481	1,912	NA	NA
Printed matter	956	1,097	1,297	529	613	622
Clocks and watches	138	133	147	946	1,097	1,276
Toys, games, sporting goods	882	1,012	1,072	1,665	1,914	2,167
Artworks and antiques	...	...	...	1,487	2,672	2,056
Other transactions	**9,103**	**8,496**	**8,428**	**4,905**	**7,183**	**7,296**
Total	**181,816**	**220,705**	**233,739**	**206,256**	**240,834**	**261,305**

U.S. Merchandise Exports and Imports, by Continent

Source: Office of Planning and Research, U.S. Commerce Department (millions of dollars)

Year	Exports				General imports			
	Western Hemis.	Europe	Asia & Oceania	Africa	Western Hemis.	Europe	Asia & Oceania	Africa
1965	9,932	9,397	7,129	1,071	9,257	6,292	4,999	867
1970	15,611	14,817	11,294	1,502	16,928	11,395	10,515	1,090
1974	35,746	30,070	28,937	3,204	40,332	24,410	28,943	6,551
1975	38,843	32,732	31,246	4,266	37,773	21,465	28,590	8,277
1976	41,074	35,900	33,229	4,396	43,356	23,645	41,131	12,522
1977	43,751	37,304	35,295	4,564	50,697	28,801	51,210	16,950
1978	50,394	43,608	44,228	4,752	56,473	37,985	60,719	16,799
1979	61,555	60,026	53,090	6,299	68,509	43,547	69,811	24,382
1980	74,114	71,371	65,044	9,060	78,687	48,039	83,691	34,410
1981	81,667	69,715	70,285	11,097	85,436	53,410	95,385	27,071

Value of U.S. Exports, Imports, and Merchandise Balance

(millions of dollars)

Year	Principal Census trade totals					Other Census totals		
	U.S. exports and reexports excluding military grant-aid	U.S. general imports f.a.s. transaction values[1]	U.S. merchandise balance f.a.s.[1]	U.S. general imports c.i.f.	U.S. balance exports f.a.s. imports c.i.f.	Military grant-aid shipments	Exports of domestic merchandise	Re-exports
1950	9,997	8,954	1,043	—	—	282	10,146	133
1955	14,298	11,566	2,732	—	—	1,256	15,426	128
1960	19,659	15,073	4,586	—	—	949	20,408	201
1965	26,742	21,520	5,222	—	—	779	27,178	343
1970	42,681	40,356	2,325	42,833	−152	565	42,612	634
1975	107,652	98,503	9,149	105,935	1,716	461	106,622	1,490
1979	181,860	209,458	−27,598	222,228	−40,368	165	178,798	3,226
1980	220,626	244,871	−24,245	256,984	−36,358	156	216,668	4,115
1981	233,677	261,305	−27,628	273,352	−39,675	62	228,961	4,778

Note: Export values include both commercially-financed shipments and shipments under government-financed programs such as AID and PL-480. (1) Prior to 1974, imports are customs values, i.e. generally at prices in principal foreign markets.

U.S. Foreign Trade, by Economic Classes

(millions of dollars)

Economic class	1965	1970	1975	1978	1979	1980	1981
Exports, total	**29,128**	**45,114**	**106,622**	**141,228**	**178,798**	**216,672**	**228,961**
Excluding military grant-aid	**...**	**...**	**106,161**	**141,142**	**178,634**	**216,515**	**228,899**
Crude foods	2,587	2,748	11,804	12,723	15,782	9,695	10,662
Manufactured foods	1,590	1,921	4,221	6,690	7,625	13,197	13,064
Crude materials	2,887	4,492	10,883	15,603	20,030	18,776	20,314
Agricultural	1,942	2,524	5,747	12,090	15,025	...	...
Semimanufactures	4,114	6,866	12,815	18,904	30,844	37,312	44,836
Finished manufactures	16,008	26,563	66,379	87,234	104,296	126,518	140,086
Excluding military grant-aid	...	...	65,918	87,149	104,131	126,362	140,023
Imports, total[1]	**22,293**	**40,748**	**99,305**	**176,052**	**210,285**	**245,262**	**260,982**
Crude foods	2,008	2,579	3,642	7,241	7,748	7,737	7,318
Manufactured foods	1,877	3,519	5,953	8,127	9,615	10,385	10,841
Crude materials	3,709	4,126	23,570	41,141	57,674	76,380	75,475
Agricultural	864	797	1,280	1,956	2,377	2,336	2,425
Semimanufactures	4,964	7,263	17,326	27,575	31,767	34,072	37,712
Finished manufactures	8,871	22,464	46,411	89,204	100,327	112,620	129,636

(1) Customs values are shown for imports.

Total Exports and Exports Financed by Foreign Aid

(millions of dollars)

	1965	1970	1975	1978	1979	1980	1981
Exports, total	**27,530**	**43,224**	**107,592**	**143,663**	**181,816**	**220,783**	**233,739**
Agricultural commodities	6,306	7,349	22,097	29,777	35,212	41,757	43,815
Nonagricultural commodities	20,445	35,310	85,094	113,801	146,602	178,948	189,924
Manufactured goods (domestic)	17,439	29,343	70,950	94,535	116,678	143,971	154,335
Military grant—aid	779	565	461	85	165	156	62
Export financed under P.L.-480	1,323	1,021	1,181	1,144	1,239	1,094	1,276
Sales for foreign currency	899	276	—	—	—	—	—
Donations, including disaster relief	253	255	257	350	418	329	504
Long-term dollar credit sales	152	490	924	794	821	765	772
AID expend. for U.S. goods for export	—	—	665	988	710	673	588

Value of Principal Agricultural Exports

(millions of dollars)

Commodity	Avg. 1961-65	Avg. 1966-70	1965	1970	1975	1979	1980	1981
Wheat and wheat products	1,268	1,197	1,214	1,144	5,292	5,586	6,660	8,157
Feed grains	841	1,082	1,162	1,099	5,492	7,739	9,759	9,377
Rice	178	311	244	314	858	854	1,288	1,527
Fodders and feeds	179	386	278	496	987	838	1,126	1,066
Oilseeds and products	774	1,182	1,029	1,642	NA	8,886	9,393	9,555
Cotton, raw	639	408	495	377	991	2,198	2,864	2,260

Shortest Navigable Distances Between Ports

Source: Distances Between Ports. Defense Mapping Agency Hydrographic/Topographic Center

Distances shown are in nautical miles (1,852 meters or about 6,076.115 feet) To get statute miles, multiply by 1.15.

TO / FROM	New York	Montreal	Colon[1]
Algiers, Algeria	3,617	3,600	4,745
Amsterdam, Netherlands	3,438	3,162	4,825
Baltimore, Md.	417	1,769	1,901
Barcelona, Spain	3,714	3,697	4,842
Boston, Mass.	386	1,308	2,157
Buenos Aires, Argentina	5,817	6,455	5,472
Cape Town, S. Africa[2]	6,786	7,118	6,494
Cherbourg, France	3,154	2,878	4,541
Cobh, Ireland	2,901	2,603	4,308
Copenhagen, Denmark	3,846	3,570	5,233
Dakar, Senegal	3,335	3,566	3,694
Galveston, Tex.	1,882	3,165	1,492
Gibraltar[3]	3,204	3,187	4,332
Glasgow, Scotland	3,086	2,691	4,508
Halifax, N.S.	600	895	2,295
Hamburg, W. Germany	3,674	3,398	5,061
Hamilton, Bermuda	697	1,572	1,659
Havana, Cuba	1,186	2,473	998
Helsinki, Finland	4,309	4,033	5,696
Istanbul, Turkey	5,001	4,984	6,129
Kingston, Jamaica	1,474	2,690	551
Lagos, Nigeria	4,883	5,130	5,049
Lisbon, Portugal	2,972	2,943	4,152
Marseille, France	3,891	3,874	5,019
Montreal, Quebec	1,460		3,126
Naples, Italy	4,181	4,164	5,309
Nassau, Bahamas	962	2,274	1,166
New Orleans, La.	1,708	2,991	1,389
New York, N.Y.		1,460	1,974
Norfolk, Va.	294	1,700	1,779
Oslo, Norway	3,827	3,165	5,053
Piraeus, Greece	4,688	4,671	5,816
Port Said, Egypt	5,123	5,106	6,251
Rio de Janeiro, Brazil	4,770	5,354	4,367
St. John's, Nfld.	1,093	1,043	2,695
San Juan, Puerto Rico	1,399	2,445	993
Southampton, England	3,189	2,913	4,576

TO / FROM	San. Fran.	Vancouver	Panama[1]
Acapulco, Mexico	1,833	2,613	1,426
Anchorage, Alas.	1,872	1,444	5,093
Bombay, India	9,794	9,578	12,962
Calcutta, India	8,991	8,728	12,154
Colon, Panama[1]	3,298	4,076	44
Jakarta, Indonesia	7,641	7,360	10,637
Haiphong, Vietnam	6,496	6,231	9,673
Hong Kong	6,044	5,777	9,195
Honolulu, Hawaii	2,091	2,423	4,685
Los Angeles, Cal.	371	1,161	2,913
Manila, Philippines	6,221	5,976	9,347
Melbourne, Australia	6,970	7,343	7,928
Pusan, S. Korea	4,914	4,623	8,074
Ho Chi Min City, Vietnam	6,878	6,664	10,017
San Francisco, Cal.		812	3,245
Seattle, Wash.	807	126	4,020
Shanghai, China	5,396	5,110	8,566
Singapore	7,353	7,078	10,505
Suva, Fiji	4,749	5,183	6,325
Valparaiso, Chile	5,140	5,915	2,616
Vancouver, B.C.	812		4,032
Vladivostok, USSR	4,563	4,378	7,741
Yokohama, Japan	4,536	4,262	7,682

TO / FROM	Port Said	Cape Town[2]	Singapore
Bombay, India	3,049	4,616	2,441
Calcutta, India	4,695	5,638	1,649
Dar es Salaam, Tanzania	3,238	2,365	4,042
Jakarta, Indonesia	5,293	5,276	525
Hong Kong	6,462	7,006	1,454
Kuwait	3,360	5,176	3,833
Manila, Philippines	6,348	6,777	1,330
Melbourne, Australia	7,842	5,963	3,844
Ho Chi Min City, Vietnam	5,667	6,263	649
Singapore	5,018	5,614	
Yokohama, Japan	7,907	8,503	2,889

(1) Colon on the Atlantic is 44 nautical miles from Panama (port) on the Pacific. (2) Cape Town is 35 nautical miles northwest of the Cape of Good Hope. (3) Gibraltar (port) is 24 nautical miles east of the Strait of Gibraltar.

Notable Ocean Passages by Ships

Compiled by N.R.P. Bonsor

Sailing Vessels

Date	Ship	From	To	Nautical miles	Time D. H. M	Speed (knots)
1846	Yorkshire	Liverpool	New York	3150	16. 0. 0	8.46†
1853	Northern Light	San Francisco	Boston	—	76. 6. 0	—
1854	James Baines	Boston Light	Light Rock	—	12. 6. 0	—
1854	Flying Cloud	New York	San Francisco	15091	89. 0. 0	7.07†
1868-9	Thermopylae	Liverpool	Melbourne	—	63.18.15	—
—	Red Jacket	New York	Liverpool	3150	13. 1:25	10.05†
—	Starr King	50 S. Lat	Golden Gate	—	36. 0. 0	—
—	Golden Fleece	Equator	San Francisco	—	12.12. 0	—
1905	Atlantic	Sandy Hook	England	3013	12. 4. 0	10.32

Atlantic Crossing by Passenger Steamships

Date	Ship		From	To	Nautical miles	Time D. H. M	Speed (knots)
1819 (5/22 - 6/20)	Savannah (a)	US	Savannah	Liverpool	—	29. 4. 0	—
1838 (5/7 - 5/22)	Great Western	Br	New York	Avonmouth	3218	14.15.59	9.14
1840 (8/4 - 8/14)	Britannia (b)	Br	Halifax	Liverpool	2610	9.21.44	10.98†
1854 (6/28 - 7/7)	Baltic	US	Liverpool	New York	3037	9.16.52	13.04
1856 (8/6 - 8/15)	Persia	Br	Sandy Hook	Liverpool	3046	8.23.19	14.15†
1876 (12/16-12/24)	Britannic	Br	Sandy Hook	Queenstown	2882	7.12.41	15.94
1895 (5/18 - 5/24)	Lucania	Br	Sandy Hook	Queenstown	2897	5.11.40	22.00
1898 (3/30 - 4/5)	Kaiser Wilhelm der Grosse	Ger	Needles	Sandy Hook	3120	5.20. 0	22.29
1901 (7/10 - 7/17)	Deutschland	Ger	Sandy Hook	Eddystone	3082	5.11. 5	23.51
1907 (10/6 - 10/10)	Lusitania	Br	Queenstown	Sandy Hook	2780	4.19.52	23.99
1924 (8/20 - 8/25)	Mauretania	Br	Ambrose	Cherbourg	3198	5. 1.49	26.25
1929 (7/17 - 7/22)	Bremen*	Ger	Cherbourg	Ambrose	3164	4.17.42	27.83
1933 (6/27 - 7/2)	Europa	Ger	Cherbourg	Ambrose	3149	4.16.48	27.92
1933 (8/11 - 8/16)	Rex	It	Gibraltar	Ambrose	3181	4.13.58	28.92
1935 (5/30 - 6/3)	Normandie*	Fr	Bishop Rock	Ambrose	2971	4. 3. 2	29.98
1938 (8/10 - 8/14)	Queen Mary	Br	Ambrose	Bishop Rock	2938	3.20.42	31.69
1952 (7/11 - 7/15)	United States	US	Bishop Rock	Ambrose	2906	3.12.12	34.51
1952 (7/3 - 7/7)	United States* (e)	US	Ambrose	Bishop Rock	2942	3.10.40	35.59

Other Ocean Passages

Date	Ship	From	To	Nautical miles	Time D. H. M	Speed (knots)
1928 (June)	USS Lexington	San Pedro	Honolulu	2226	3. 0.36	30.66
1944 (Jul-Sep)	St. Roch (c) (Can)	Halifax	Vancouver	7295	86. 0. 0	—
1945 (7/16-7/19)	USS Indianapolis (d)	San Francisco	Oahu, Hawaii	2091	3. 2.20	28.07
1945 (11/26)	USS Lake Champlain	Gibraltar	Newport News	3360	4. 8.51	32.04
1950 (Jul-Aug)	USS Boxer	Japan	San Francisco	5000	7.18.36	26.80†

Date	Ship	From	To	Nautical miles	Time D. H. M	Speed (knots)
1951 (6/1-6/9)	USS Philippine Sea	Yokohama	Alameda	5000	7.13. 0	27.62†
1958 (2/25-3/4)	USS Skate (f)	Nantucket	Portland, Eng	3161	8.11. 0	15.57
1958 (3/23-3/29)	USS Skate (f)	Lizard, Eng	Nantucket	—	7. 5. 0	—
1958 (7/23-8/7)	USS Nautilus (g)	Pearl Harbor	Iceland (via N. Pole)	—	15. 0. 0	—
1960 (2/16-5/10)	USS Triton (h)	New London	Rehoboth, Del	41500	84. 0. 0	20.59†
1960 (8/15-8/20)	USS Seadragon (i)	Baffin Bay	NW Passage, Pac	850	6. 0. 0	—
1962 (10/30-11/11)	African Comet* (US)	New York	Cape Town	6786	12.16.22	22.03
1973 (8/20)	Sea-Land Exchange (k) (US)	Bishop Rock	Ambrose	2912	3.11.24	34.92
1973 (8/24)	Sea-Land Trade (US)	Kobe	Race Rock, BC	4126	5. 6. 0	32.75

† The time taken and/or distance covered is approximate and so, therefore, is the average speed.

* Maiden voyage. (a) The Savannah, a fully rigged sailing vessel with steam auxiliary (over 300 tons, 98.5 ft. long, beam 25.8 ft., depth 12.9 ft.) was launched in the East River in 1818. It was the first ship to use steam in crossing any ocean. It was supplied with engines and detachable iron paddle wheels. On its famous voyage it used steam 105 hours. (b) First Cunard liner. (c) First ship to complete NW Passage in one season. (d) Carried Hiroshima atomic bomb in World War II. (e) Set world speed record; average speed eastbound on maiden voyage 35.59 knots (about 41 m.p.h.). (f) First atomic submarine to cross Atlantic both ways submerged. (g) World's first atomic submarine also first to make undersea voyage under polar ice cap, 1,830 mi. from Point Barrow, Alaska, to Atlantic Ocean, Aug. 1-4, 1958, reaching North Pole Aug. 3. Second undersea transit of the North Pole made by submarine USS Skate Aug. 11, 1958, during trip from New London, Conn., and return. (h) World's largest submarine. Nuclear-powered Triton was submerged during nearly all its voyage around the globe. It duplicated the route of Ferdinand Magellan's circuit (1519-1522) 30,708 mi., starting from St. Paul Rocks off the NE coast of Brazil, Feb. 24-Apr. 25, 1960, then sailed to Cadiz, Spain, before returning home. (i) First underwater transit of Northwest Passage. (k) Fastest freighter crossing of Atlantic.

Commerce at Principal North American Ports

Handling 2,000,000 tons or more per year

Source: Corps of Engineers, Department of the Army (short tons); Statistics Canada. (metric tons); 1980.

New Orleans, La.	177,315,800
New York, N.Y.	166,991,220
Houston, Texas	108,937,268
Valdez Hrbr., Alaska	85,973,086
Baton Rouge	79,346,780
Norfolk Hrbr., Va.	54,217,591
Beaumont, Texas	52,260,728
Baltimore Hrbr., Md.	50,041,515
Tampa Harbor, Fla.	48,625,160
Philadelphia, Pa.	47,882,836
Corpus C. Ship Chnl	45,001,096
Duluth-Supr., Minn.	41,434,568
Corpus Christi, Tex.	39,107,016
Long Beach, Calif.	38,779,672
Mobile, Alabama	37,568,968
Pittsburgh, Pa.	36,586,155
Chicago, Ill.	32,993,244
Los Angeles, Calif.	30,151,053
Port Arthur, Texas	29,796,633
Portland, Ore.	29,314,059
Texas City, Tex.	25,948,936
Marcus Hook, Pa.	25,695,547
Pascagoula, Miss.	25,433,560
St. Louis, Metro.	24,528,760
Paulsboro, N.J.	22,789,580
Toledo Hrbr., Ohio	22,263,285
Boston, Mass, Port Of	22,033,922
Seattle, Wash.	21,288,838
Newport News, Va.	20,820,941
Lake Charles, La.	20,750,300
Freeport, Texas	20,131,067
Detroit, Mich.	19,268,443
Huntington, W. Va.	19,226,875
Conneaut Hrbr., Ohio	18,654,609
Richmond, Calif.	18,559,965
Tacoma Hrbr., Wash.	17,162,210
Indiana, Ind.	16,898,932
Jacksonville, Fla.	15,644,000
Cleveland, Ohio	14,045,151
Everglades, Fla.	13,287,691
Portland, Maine.	12,847,571
Savannah, Georgia	12,293,179
New Castle, Del.	11,457,204
Memphis, Tenn.	11,451,998
Escanaba, Mich.	11,240,618
Cincinnati, Ohio.	10,833,216
St. Paul, Minn.	10,528,472
San Juan, P.R.	10,087,394
Ashtabula, Ohio	10,074,956
Longview, Wash.	9,956,229
Galveston, Tex.	9,631,091
New Haven, Conn.	9,336,328
Anacortes, Wash.	9,165,812
Charleston, S.C.	9,096,714
Albany, N.Y.	8,711,672
Lorain Hrbr., Ohio	8,151,368
Presque Isle, Mich.	7,881,252
Wilmington, N.C.	7,826,488
Louisville, Ky.	7,694,745
Honolulu, Hawaii	7,646,270
Providence, R.I.	7,509,253
Calcite, Mich.	7,452,156
Stoneport, Mich.	7,354,310
Oakland, Calif.	7,313,533
Camden-Gloucester, N.J.	7,244,469
Taconite, Minn.	7,027,556
Gary Hrbr., Ind.	6,870,639
Coos Bay, Oreg.	6,803,966
Sandusky, Ohio	6,412,386
Buffalo, N.Y.	5,986,470
Harbor Island, Tex.	5,980,348
Oahu, Hawaii	5,725,722
Silver Bay, Minn.	4,871,456
Fall River, Mass.	4,804,481
Angeles Hrbr., Wash.	4,277,697
Milwaukee, Wis.	4,079,506
Mount Vernon, Ind.	4,013,027
Matagorda Ship, Tex.	3,991,089
Miami, Fla.	3,929,398
St. Clair, Mich.	3,726,267
Wilmington, Delaware	3,535,993
Vicksburg, Miss.	3,362,267
Victoria, Texas	3,303,122
Jefferson, N.Y.	3,301,718
Penn Manor, Pa.	3,279,466
Grays River, Wash.	3,248,960
Morehead City, N.C.	3,010,777
Port Inland, Mich.	3,005,691
Port Dolomite, Mich.	2,978,917
Vancouver, Wash.	2,911,452
Portsmouth, N.H.	2,783,781
Hempstead, N.Y.	2,769,267
Ketchikan, Alaska	2,767,173
Alpena, Mich.	2,737,030
Helena, Ark.	2,708,260
Canaveral, Fla.	2,706,932
Greenville, Miss.	2,706,791
Brownsville, Tex.	2,569,697
New London, Conn.	2,529,841
Pensacola, Fla.	2,458,151
Astoria, Oreg.	2,437,185
Green Bay, Wis.	2,299,001
Minneapolis, Minn.	2,246,839
San Diego, Calif.	2,188,859
Huron Hrbr., Ohio	2,129,061
Ludington, Mich.	2,129,001
Bellingham, Wash.	2,047,351

Commerce at Principal Canadian Ports

Vancouver, B.C.	50,711,625
Port Cartier, Que.	27,315,493
Montreal, Que.	25,536,934
Thunder Bay, Ont.	22,501,848
Sept-Isles, Que.	21,468,851
Saint John, N.B.	16,897,120
Quebec, Que.	14,884,170
Hamilton, Ont.	13,916,872
Halifax, N.S.	13,183,499

Sarnia, Ont.	8,441,052	Jervis Inlet, B.C.	3,529,216
Sorel, Que.	8,025,801	Toronto, Ont.	3,329,838
New Westminster, B.C.	7,343,965	Trois Rivieres, Que.	3,528,414
Baie Comeau, Que.	7,240,479	Crofton, B.C.	3,247,393
Nanticoke, Ont.	5,914,349	Fraser River, B.C.	3,094,575
Sault Ste. Marie, Ont.	5,782,079	Prince Rupert, B.C.	2,979,151
Port Alfred, Que.	4,665,191	Havre St-Pierre, Que.	2,702,756
Victoria, B.C.	4,441,838	Windsor, Ont.	2,577,087
Port Hawkesbury, N.S.	3,774,869	Levis, Que.	2,185,688
Port Noire, Que.	3,712,282	Clarkson, B.C.	2,036,241
Nanaimo, B.C.	3,671,650		

Commerce on U.S. Inland Waterways

Source: Corps of Engineers, Department of the Army 1980

Mississippi River System and Gulf Intracoastal Waterway

Waterway	Tons
Mississippi River, Minneapolis to the Gulf	441,544,078
Mississippi River, Minneapolis to St. Louis	76,394,879
Mississippi River, St. Louis to Cairo	92,914,550
Mississippi River, Cairo to Baton Rouge	146,271,193
Mississippi River, Baton Rouge to New Orleans	323,684,566
Mississippi River, New Orleans to Gulf	292,334,680
Gulf Intracoastal Waterway	97,512,197
Mississippi River System	584,212,076

Ton-Mileage of Freight Carried on Inland Waterways

System	Ton-miles
Atlantic Coast waterways	30,401,892
Gulf Coast waterways	36,641,483
Pacific Coast waterways	14,871,249
Mississippi River System, including Ohio River and tributaries	228,930,466
Great Lakes system, U.S. commerce only	96,034,192
Total:	**406,879,282**

Important Waterways and Canals

The St. Lawrence & Great Lakes Waterway, the largest inland navigation system on the continent, extends from the Atlantic Ocean to Duluth at the western end of Lake Superior, a distance of 2,342 miles. With the deepening of channels and locks to 27 ft., ocean carriers are able to penetrate to ports in the Canadian interior and the American midwest.

The major canals are those of the St. Lawrence Great Lakes waterway — the 3 new canals of the St. Lawrence Seaway, with their 7 locks, providing navigation for vessels of 26-foot draught from Montreal to Lake Ontario; the Welland Ship Canal by-passing the Niagara River between Lake Ontario and Lake Erie with its 8 locks, and the Sault Ste. Marie Canal and lock between Lake Huron and Lake Superior. These 16 locks overcome a drop of 580 ft. from the head of the lakes to Montreal. From Montreal to Lake Ontario the former bottleneck of narrow, shallow canals and of slow passage through 22 locks has been overcome, giving faster and safer movement for larger vessels. The new locks and linking channels now accommodate all but the largest ocean-going vessels and the upper St. Lawrence and Great Lakes are open to 80% of the world's saltwater fleet.

Subsidiary Canadian canals or branches include the St Peters Canal between Bras d'Or Lakes and the Atlantic Ocean in Nova Scotia; the St. Ours and Chambly Canals on the Richelieu River, Quebec; the Ste. Anne and Carillon Canals on the Ottawa River; the Rideau Canal between the Ottawa River and Lake Ontario, the Trent and Murrary Canals between Lake Ontario and Georgian Bay in Ontario and the St. Andrew's Canal on the Red River. The commercial value of these canals is not great but they are maintained to control water levels and permit the passage of small vessels and pleasure craft. The Canso Canal, completed 1957, permits shipping to pass through the causeway connecting Cape Breton Island with the Nova Scotia mainland.

The Welland Canal overcomes the 326-ft. drop of Niagara Falls and the rapids of the Niagara River. It has 8 locks each 859 ft. long, 80 ft. wide and 30 ft. deep. Regulations permit ships of 730-ft. length and 75-ft. beam to transit.

Fastest Scheduled Train Runs in U.S. and Canada

Source: Donald M. Steffee, figures are based on 1982 timetables

Passenger—(78 mph and over)

Railroad	Train	From	To	Dis. miles	Time min.	Speed mph.
Amtrak	Five trains	Wilmington	Baltimore	68.4	45	91.2
Amtrak	Metroliner	Wilmington	Baltimore	68.4	46	89.2
Amtrak	Four trains	Rennselear	Hudson	28.0	19	88.4
Amtrak	Three trains	Baltimore[1]	Wilmington	68.4	47	87.3
Amtrak	Six trains	Baltimore[1]	Wilmington	68.4	48	85.5
Amtrak	Palmetto	BWI Station	Beltway	19.7	14	84.4
Amtrak	Three trains	Wilmington	Baltimore	68.4	49	83.8
Amtrak	Valley Forge	Trenton	Newark	48.1	35	82.5
Amtrak	Cardinal	Baltimore	Wilmington	68.4	50	82.1
Amtrak	Southwest Limited	Garden City	Lamar	99.9	73	82.1
Via Rail Canada	Simco	Dorval	Kingston	165.8	122	81.5
Via Rail Canada	Executive	Kingston	Guildwood	145.1	107	81.4
Via Rail Canada	Three trains	Dorval[1]	Kingston	165.8	123	80.9
Via Rail Canada	Four trains	Kingston[1]	Guildwood	145.1	108	80.6
Amtrak	Four trains	Baltimore[1]	Wilmington	68.4	51	80.5
Amtrak	Three trains	Newark	Philadelphia	80.5	60	80.5
Amtrak	Three trains	Trenton	Newark	48.1	36	80.2
Via Rail Canada	Three trains	Cornwall[1]	Kingston	108.1	81	80.1
Amtrak	Cardinal	Wilmington	Aberdeen	38.7	29	80.1
Via Rail Canada	Renaissance	Kingston	Guildwood	145.1	109	79.9
Amtrak	Number 237	Trenton	No. Philadelphia	27.9	21	79.7
Conrail	Jersey Arrow	Princeton Jct.	Newark	38.4	29	79.4
Via Rail Canada	Simco	Kingston	Guildwood	145.1	110	79.1
Via Rail Canada	Simco	Kingston	Cornwall	108.1	82	79.1
Via Rail Canada	Meridian	Belleville	Cobourg	43.3	33	78.7
Via Rail Canada	Two trains	Dorval[1]	Cornwall	57.7	44	78.7
Amtrak	Four trains	Wilmington	Baltimore	68.4	52	78.9
Amtrak	Two trains	Metropark	Trenton	33.9	26	78.2
Via Rail Canada	Meridian	Cornwall	Kingston	108.1	83	78.1
Via Rail Canada	Two trains	Cobourg	Guildwood	57.2	44	78.0

(1) Runs listed in both directions

Freight — (62 mph and over)

Union Pacific	BASV	North Platte	Cheyenne	225.4	205	66.0
Union Pacific	Super Van	North Platte	Cheyenne	225.4	215	62.9
Santa Fe	Six trains	Gallup	Winslow	125.8	120	62.9
Santa Fe	No. 199	Seligman	Kingman	88.1	85	62.2

Fastest Scheduled Passenger Train Runs in Japan and European Countries

Country	Train	From	To	Dis. miles	Time min.	Speed mph.
France	TGV trains (2)	Lyon (Brotteaux)	Le Creusot	77.2	40	114.9
Japan	Hikari train	Nagoya	Yokohama	196.5	105	112.3
Great Britain	High Speed train	London	Chippenham	93.8	54	104.3
West Germany	Three trains	Hamm	Bielefeld	41.7	24	104.2
Italy	Rapido	Chiusi	Rome	91.9	65	84.8
Sweden	No. 142	Skvode	Laxa	52.2	41	77.4

Two New High Speed Lines Opened in Japan

On June 23, 1982 the Tohoku Shinkansen from Omiya (20 miles north of Tokyo) to Morioka, 288.9 miles was opened to traffic. "Yamabiko" trains, making only principal station stops, cover the distance in 3 hours 17 minutes averaging 88.0 mph. The Joetsu Shinkansen from Omiya to Niigata (167.4 miles) on the Sea of Japan was opened in November, 1982. "Asahi" trains make this run in 1 hour 50 minutes; averaging 91.3 mph, stops included. These are the first high speed lines running north and east of Tokyo.

Passenger Car Production, U.S. Plants

Source: Motor Vehicle Manufacturers Association of the U.S., Inc.

	1980	1981	1982 7 mos.
American Motors Corp.			
Spirit	54,223	35,143	10,969
Concord	68,344	49,480	13,799
Eagle	42,158	24,696	9,113
Alliance	—	—	6,046
Total American Motors Corp.	**164,725**	**109,319**	**39,927**
Chrysler Corp.			
Horizon	145,036	139,014	46,460
Reliant	75,822	216,901	99,140
Volare	51,735	—	—
Caravelle	6,277	2,139	—
Gran Fury	14,472	7,448	—
Total Plymouth	**293,342**	**365,502**	**145,600**
LeBaron	62,592	52,478	68,068
Chrysler	19,871	4,862	—
Total Chrysler-Plymouth	**375,805**	**422,842**	**213,668**
Omni	121,703	125,650	43,771
Aries	60,666	170,139	75,091
Aspen	36,881	—	—
Dodge 400	—	13,817	20,523
Diplomat	30,733	12,644	—
St. Regis	13,186	3,682	—
Total Dodge	**263,169**	**325,932**	**139,385**
Total Chrysler Corp.	**638,974**	**748,774**	**353,053**
Ford Motor Co.			
LTD (Ford)	91,135	40,886	—
Thunderbird	117,856	64,328	25,258
Escort	108,450	353,162	173,255
Granada	113,281	103,702	74,051
Fairmont	198,219	176,246	74,280
Pinto	68,179	—	—
Mustang	232,507	153,719	79,078
Total Ford	**929,627**	**892,043**	**425,922**
Marquis	55,524	65,720	45,268
Cougar XR-7	42,927	28,223	8,327
Cougar/Monarch	41,264	49,831	35,953
Zephyr	66,657	51,868	24,899
Lynx	37,641	117,991	53,929
Bobcat	12,445	—	—
Capri	68,070	50,336	21,097
Lincoln	22,781	26,651	25,352
Mark	28,146	25,640	18,792
Continental	—	11,894	11,692
Versailles	1,866	—	—
Total Lincoln-Mercury	**377,321**	**428,154**	**245,309**
Total Ford Motor Co.	**1,306,948**	**1,320,197**	**671,231**
General Motors Corp.			
Chevrolet	134,909	147,337	21,353
Corvette	44,190	27,990	17,580
Monte Carlo	125,474	139,899	41,865
Celebrity (Malibu)	231,594	213,628	100,909
Camaro	118,211	99,059	136,228
Citation	459,388	300,652	112,030
Cavalier/Monza	150,544	139,837	53,574
Chevette	454,068	376,951	138,608
Acadian	18,958	—	—
Total Chevrolet	**1,737,336**	**1,445,353**	**622,147**
Pontiac	50,512	10,064	—
Grand Prix	76,030	97,051	49,021
Bonneville (LeMans)	64,870	88,293	73,751
Firebird	79,568	48,961	82,188
Phoenix	136,210	96,597	32,963
J-2000 Sunbird	149,239	91,465	27,437
T-1000	—	88,871	32,168
Total Pontiac	**556,429**	**521,302**	**297,528**
Oldsmobile	233,845	276,452	163,422
Toronado	37,923	43,929	19,800
Supreme/Ciera (Cutlass)	395,784	385,674	178,994
Omega	115,673	132,268	50,285
Firenza	—	10	30,099
Total Oldsmobile	**783,225**	**838,333**	**442,600**
Buick	149,668	171,834	102,576
Riviera	44,525	58,275	21,206
Century/Regal	370,880	370,676	203,106
Skylark	218,502	239,175	87,390
Skyhawk	—	—	47,918
Total Buick	**783,575**	**839,960**	**462,198**
Cadillac	115,424	155,622	88,439
Eldorado	54,267	57,861	34,317
Seville	34,300	23,344	12,595
Cimarron	—	22,308	3,439
Total Cadillac	**203,991**	**259,135**	**138,790**
Total General Motors Corp.	**4,064,556**	**3,904,083**	**1,963,263**
Checker Motors Corp.	**3,197**	**3,010**	**2,000**
Volkswagen of America	**197,106**	**167,755**	**60,160**
Total Passenger Cars	**6,375,506**	**6,253,138**	**3,089,634**

Automobile Factory Sales

Source: Motor Vehicle Manufacturers Association, Detroit, Mich.—wholesale values

Year	Passenger cars		Motor trucks, buses		Total	
	Number	Value	Number	Value	Number	Value
1900	4,192	$4,899,433	...	...	4,190	$4,899,443
1910	181,000	215,340,000	6,000	9,660,000	187,000	225,000,000
1920	1,905,560	1,809,170,963	321,789	423,249,410	2,227,349	2,232,420,373
1930	2,787,456	1,644,083,152	575,364	390,752,061	3,362,820	2,034,853,213
1940	3,717,385	2,370,654,083	754,901	567,820,414	4,472,286	2,938,474,497
1950	6,665,863	8,468,137,000	1,337,193	1,707,748,000	8,003,056	10,175,885,000
1960	6,674,796	12,164,234,000	1,194,475	2,350,680,000	7,869,271	14,514,914,000
1970	6,546,817	14,630,217,000	1,692,440	4,819,752,000	8,239,257	19,449,969,000
1981	6,255,340	NA	1,700,908	NA	7,956,248	NA

After July 1, 1964 all tactical vehicles are excluded. Federal excise taxes are excluded in all years.

Motor Vehicle Registrations, Taxes, Motor Fuel, Drivers' Ages

Source: Federal Highway Adm.

State, 1981	Driver's age Jan. 1, 1982 (1) Regular	(2) Juvenile	Minimum age for purchase alcoholic beverage	Licensed drivers (1,000)	Registered autos, buses & trucks (1,000)	State gas tax per gal. cents	Motor fuel adjusted net total tax receipts $1,000	Motor fuel consumption Highway 1,000 gallons	Non-highway 1,000 gallons
Alabama	16		19	2,271	3,026	11	180,966	2,126,341	42,737
Alaska	16		19	221	259	8	14,851	180,049	40,655
Arizona	16		17	1,933	2,047	8	115,450	1,446,963	43,026
Arkansas	16		21	1,469	1,630	9.5	128,207	1,303,034	30,161
California	16/18	14	21	15,669	17,744	7	777,120	11,330,390	255,887
Colorado	21	16	21	2,048	2,370	7	124,493	1,528,776	61,052
Connecticut	16/18		19	2,174	2,189	11	150,708	1,327,964	30,333
Delaware	16/18		20	417	402	9	29,923	305,283	5,290
Dist. of Col.	18	16	21	344	279	11	21,188	175,291	2,330
Florida	16		19	7,268	7,882	8	385,472	4,838,540	161,972
Georgia	16		19	3,424	3,850	7.5	234,833	3,086,487	59,402
Hawaii	15		18	542	582	8.5	29,914	345,733	15,051
Idaho	16	14	19	631	861	9.5	56,301	504,578	43,199
Illinois	16/18		21	7,003	7,640	7.5	373,987	5,102,930	237,435
Indiana	16/18		21	3,631	3,859	8.5	296,706	3,054,646	80,790
Iowa	16/18	14	19	2,107	2,331	10	182,851	1,714,616	148,575
Kansas	16	14	21	1,675	2,038	8	115,104	1,443,548	80,945
Kentucky	16		21	2,055	2,604	9	182,522	1,867,177	32,284
Louisiana	15/17	15	18	2,259	2,863	8	177,114	2,211,334	39,952
Maine	15/17	15	20	730	744	9	46,742	532,013	14,372
Maryland	16/18	15¾	21	2,722	2,857	9	177,108	1,957,794	32,692
Massachusetts	17/18	16½	20	3,640	3,809	9.8	252,025	2,291,485	39,934
Michigan	16/18	14	21	6,400	6,582	11	431,810	4,108,255	132,324
Minnesota	16/18	15	19	2,336	3,142	11	267,197	2,139,238	104,364
Mississippi	15		21	1,587	1,635	9	121,628	1,317,197	28,713
Missouri	16		21	3,245	3,293	7	194,596	2,763,325	123,455
Montana	15/16		19	599	723	9	49,397	523,232	40,178
Nebraska	16	14	20	1,093	1,280	13.6	145,401	950,508	82,252
Nevada	16	14	21	626	687	6	44,875	533,054	21,813
New Hampshire	16/18	16	20	652	724	11	55,014	407,339	10,145
New Jersey	17	16	19	4,928	4,871	8	279,594	3,348,705	55,881
New Mexico	15/16		21	855	1,097	8	71,668	843,692	18,289
New York	17/18	16	18	9,240	7,988	8	462,868	5,569,766	174,955
North Carolina	16/18		21	3,777	4,617	9	326,952	3,086,132	94,782
North Dakota	16	14	21	419	638	8	34,393	455,518	74,157
Ohio	16/18	14	21	7,031	7,990	7	471,839	5,368,283	201,224
Oklahoma	16		21	1,965	2,729	6.5	127,883	2,013,945	57,403
Oregon	16	14	21	1,991	2,127	7	86,324	1,471,538	59,489
Pennsylvania	17/18	16	21	7,056	7,131	11	655,048	5,070,441	76,965
Rhode Island	16/18		20	587	640	10	43,718	380,232	19,992
South Carolina	16	15	21	1,953	2,020	11	195,418	1,674,770	38,410
South Dakota	16	14	21	481	608	12	66,839	463,754	71,791
Tennessee	16	14	19	2,810	3,335	7	214,714	2,623,250	61,645
Texas	16/18	15	19	9,288	10,787	5	459,259	8,735,415	262,742
Utah	16/18		21	845	1,000	9	79,259	788,209	21,697
Vermont	18	16	18	344	360	9	25,476	249,987	5,921
Virginia	16/18		21	3,461	3,704	11	276,552	2,717,465	56,101
Washington	16/18		21	2,663	3,306	12	253,413	1,970,632	61,060
West Virginia	16/18	16	18	1,506	1,384	10.5	94,248	903,712	14,132
Wisconsin	16/18	14	18	2,982	3,017	9	252,666	2,314,361	104,973
Wyoming	16	14	19	346	479	8	37,019	438,071	27,079
Total				**145,299**	**159,760**	—	**9,878,293**	**111,904,998**	**3,600,006**

(1) Unrestricted operation of private passenger car. When 2 ages are shown, license is issued at lower age upon completion of approved driver education course. (2) Juvenile license issued with consent of parent or guardian.

Auto Registrations, Motor Fuel, Drivers' Ages in Canada

Source: Statistics Canada

Province	Minimum driver's age (1982)	Registered road motor vehicles (1979)	Registered[4] road motor vehicles (1980)	Fuel consumption on roads and highways 1980[5] (thousands of litres) Gasoline	Diesel	Liquified petroleum
Newfoundland	17	197,670	212,198	620,629	111,252	1,091
Prince Edward Island	16[1]	68,361	68,750	186,148	14,763	42
Nova Scotia	16[1]	457,905	530,018	1,190,639	161,561	1,072
New Brunswick	16[1]	356,267	364,236	1,124,765	232,936	288
Quebec	16[2]	3,150,580	3,187,433	8,578,685	1,537,644	4,209
Ontario	16	4,645,706	4,647,820	13,013,890	2,001,627	967[6]
Manitoba	16	645,552	656,435	1,395,781	228,722	2,187
Saskatchewan	16	682,881	683,955	1,531,037	270,694	3,755
Alberta	16	1,530,118	1,659,079	n.a.	n.a.	n.a.
British Columbia	16	1,569,866	1,672,575	4,168,703	671,139	5,564
Yukon	16[1]	17,665	18,333	54,270	59,964	1,112
Northwest Territories	16[3]	16,129	16,320	33,500	23,670	—
Total		**13,338,700**	**13,717,152**	**31,898,047**	**5,313,972**	**20,286**

(1) Parental consent required under 18. (2) Min. driving age for public vehicles is 18. (3) Learner's permit at 15. (4) Registrations include: passenger automobiles (including taxis and for-hire cars) 10,255,511; trucks and truck tractors 2,902,730; school buses 24,241; other buses 38,328; motorcycles 388,680; registered mopeds 36,507; other road vehicles (ambulances, fire trucks, etc.) 50,155. (5) Based on road-use tax figures; no figures available for Alberta where the road-use tax was removed in 1978. (6) Up to Apr. 23, 1980 when the Ont. govt. removed the road tax on liquified petroleum gas.

Memorable Manned Space Flights

Sources: National Aeronautics and Space Administration and The World Almanac.

Crew, date	Mission name	Orbits[1]	Duration	Remarks
Yuri A. Gagarin (4/12/61)	Vostok 1	1	1h 48m.	First manned orbital flight.
Alan B. Shepard Jr. (5/5/61)	Mercury-Redstone 3	(2)	15m 22s	First American in space.
Virgil I. Grissom (7/21/61)	Mercury-Redstone 4	(2)	15m 37s	Spacecraft sank. Grissom rescued.
Gherman S. Titov (8/6-7/61)	Vostok 2	16	25h 18m.	First space flight of more than 24 hrs.
John H. Glenn Jr. (2/20/62)	Mercury-Atlas 6	3	4h 55m 23s	First American in orbit.
M. Scott Carpenter (5/24/62)	Mercury-Atlas 7	3	4h 56m 05s	Manual retrofire error caused 250 mi. landing overshoot.
Andrian G. Nikolayev (8/11-15/62)	Vostok 3	64	94h 22m.	Vostok 3 and 4 made first group flight.
Pavel R. Popovich (8/12-15/62)	Vostok 4	48	70h 57m.	On first orbit it came within 3 miles of Vostok 3.
Walter M. Schirra Jr. (10/3/62)	Mercury-Atlas 8	6	9h 13m 11s	Closest splashdown to target to date (4.5 mi.).
L. Gordon Cooper (5/15-16/63)	Mercury-Atlas 9	22	34h 19m 49s	First U.S. evaluation of effects on man of one day in space.
Valery F. Bykovsky (6/14-6/19/63)	Vostok 5	81	119h 06m.	Vostok 5 and 6 made 2d group flight.
Valentina V. Tereshkova (6/16-19/63)	Vostok 6	48	70h 50m.	First woman in space.
Vladimir M. Komarov, Konstantin P. Feoktistov, Boris B. Yegorov (10/12/64)	Voskhod 1	16	24h 17m.	First 3-man orbital flight: first without space suits.
Pavel I. Belyayev, Aleksei A. Leonov (3/18/65)	Voskhod 2	17	26h 02m.	Leonov made first "space walk" (10 min.)
Virgil I. Grissom, John W. Young (3/23/65)	Gemini-Titan 3	3	4h 53m 00s	First manned spacecraft to change its orbital path.
James A. McDivitt, Edward H. White 2d, (6/3-7/65)	Gemini-Titan 4	62	97h 56m 11s	White was first American to "walk in space" (20 min.).
L. Gordon Cooper Jr., Charles Conrad Jr. (8/21-29/65)	Gemini-Titan 5	120	190h 55m 14s	First use of fuel cells for electric power; evaluated guidance and navigation system.
Frank Borman, James A. Lovell Jr. (12/4-18/65)	Gemini-Titan 7	206	330h 35m 31s	Longest duration Gemini flight
Walter M. Schirra Jr., Thomas P. Stafford (12/15-16/65)	Gemini-Titan 6-A	16	25h 51m 24s	Completed world's first space rendezvous with Gemini 7.
Neil A. Armstrong, David R. Scott (3/16-17/66)	Gemini-Titan 8	6.5	10h 41m 26s	First docking of one space vehicle with another; mission aborted, control malfunction.
John W. Young, Michael Collins (7/18-21/66)	Gemini-Titan 10	43	70h 46m 39s	First use of Agena target vehicle's propulsion systems; rendezvoused with Gemini 8.
Charles Conrad Jr., Richard F. Gordon Jr. (9/12-15/66)	Gemini-Titan 11	44	71h 17m 08s	Docked, made 2 revolutions of earth tethered; set Gemini altitude record (739.2 mi.).
James A. Lovell Jr., Edwin E. Aldrin Jr. (11/11-15/66)	Gemini-Titan 12	59	94h 34m 31s	Final Gemini mission; record 5½ hrs. of extravehicular activity.
Vladimir M. Komarov (4/23/67)	Soyuz 1	17	26h 40m.	Crashed after re-entry killing Komarov.
Walter M. Schirra Jr., Donn F. Eisele, R. Walter Cunningham (10/11-22/68)	Apollo-Saturn 7	163	260h 09m 03s	First manned flight of Apollo spacecraft command-service module only.
Georgi T. Beregovoi (10/26-30/68)	Soyuz 3	64	94h 51m.	Made rendezvous with unmanned Soyuz 2.
Frank Borman, James A. Lovell Jr., William A. Anders (12/21-27/68)	Apollo-Saturn 8	10[3]	147h 00m 42s	First flight to moon (command-service module only); views of lunar surface televised to earth.
Vladimir A. Shatalov (1/14-17/69)	Soyuz 4	45	71h 14m.	Docked with Soyuz 5.
Boris V. Volyanov, Aleksei S. Yeliseyev, Yevgeny V. Khrunov (1/15-18/69)	Soyuz 5	46	72h 46m.	Docked with Soyuz 4; Yeliseyev and Khrunov transferred to Soyuz 4.
James A. McDivitt, David R. Scott, Russell L. Schweickart (3/3-13/69)	Apollo-Saturn 9	151	241h 00m 54s	First manned flight of lunar module.

(continued)

Crew, date	Mission name	Orbits[1]	Duration	Remarks
Thomas P. Stafford, Eugene A. Cernan, John W. Young (5/18-26/69)	Apollo-Saturn 10	31[4]	192h 03m 23s	First lunar module orbit of moon.
Neil A. Armstrong, Edwin E. Aldrin Jr., Michael Collins (7/16-24/69)	Apollo-Saturn 11	30[3]	195h 18m 35s	First lunar landing made by Armstrong and Aldrin; collected 48.5 lbs. of soil, rock samples; lunar stay time 21 h, 36m, 21 s.
Georgi S. Shonin, Valery N. Kubasov (10/11-16/69)	Soyuz 6	79	118h 42m	First welding of metals in space.
Anatoly V. Filipchenko, Vladislav N. Volkov, Viktor V. Gorbatko (10/12-17/69)	Soyuz 7	79	118h 41m	Space lab construction tests made; Soyuz 6, 7 and 8 — first time 3 spacecraft 7 crew orbited earth at once.
Charles Conrad Jr., Richard F. Gordon, Alan L. Bean (11/14-24/69)	Apollo-Saturn 12	45[3]	244h 36m 25s	Conrad and Bean made 2d moon landing; collected 74.7 lbs. of samples, lunar stay time 31 h, 31 m.
James A. Lovell Jr., Fred W. Haise Jr., John L. Swigart Jr. (4/11-17/70)	Apollo-Saturn 13	...	142h 54m 41s	Aborted after service module oxygen tank ruptured; crew returned safely using lunar module oxygen and power.
Alan B. Shepard Jr., Stuart A. Roosa, Edgar D. Mitchell (1/31-2/9/71)	Apollo-Saturn 14	34[3]	216h 01m 57s	Shepard and Mitchell made 3d moon landing, collected 96 lbs. of lunar samples; lunar stay 33 h, 31 m.
Vladimir A. Shatalov, Aleksei S. Yeliseyev, Nikolai Rukavishnikov (4/22-24/71)	Soyuz 10	32	47h 46m	Docked with prototype Salyut orbiting space station for 5½ hrs. then mission was aborted.
Georgi T. Dobrovolsky, Vladislav N. Volkov, Viktor I. Patsayev (6/6-30/71)	Soyuz 11	360	569h 40m	Docked with Salyut space station; and orbited in Salyut for 23 days; crew died during re-entry from loss of pressurization.
David R. Scott, Alfred M. Worden, James B. Irwin (7/26-8/7/71)	Apollo-Saturn 15	74[3]	295h 11m 53s	Scott and Irwin made 4th moon landing; first lunar rover use; first deep space walk; 170 lbs. of samples; 66 h, 55 m, stay.
Charles M. Duke Jr., Thomas K. Mattingly, John W. Young (4/16-27/72)	Apollo-Saturn 16	64[3]	265h 51m 05s	Young and Duke made 5th moon landing; collected 213 lbs. of lunar samples; lunar stay line 71 h, 2 m.
Eugene A. Cernan, Ronald E. Evans, Harrison H. Schmitt (12/7-19/72)	Apollo-Saturn 17	75[3]	301h 51m 59s	Cernan and Schmitt made 6th manned lunar landing; collected 243 lbs. of samples; record lunar stay of 75 h.
Charles Conrad Jr., Joseph P. Kerwin, Paul J. Weitz (5/25-6/22/73)	Skylab 2	...	672h 49m 49s	First American manned orbiting space station; made long-flights tests, crew repaired damage caused during boost.
Alan L. Bean, Jack R. Lousma, Owen K. Garriott (7/28-9/25/73)	Skylab 3	...	1,427h 09m 04s	Crew systems and operational tests, exceeded pre-mission plans for scientific activities; space walk total 13h, 44 m.
Gerald P. Carr, Edward G. Gibson, William Pogue (11/16/73-2/8/74)	Skylab 4	...	2,017h 16m 30s	Final Skylab mission; record space walk of 7 h, 1 m., record space walks total for a mission 22 h, 21 m.
Alexi Leonov, Valeri Kubason (7/15-7/21/75)	Soyuz 19	96	143h 31m	
Vance Brand, Thomas P. Stafford, Donald K. Slayton (7/15-7/24/75)	Apollo 18	136	217h 30m	U.S.-USSR joint flight. Crews linked-up in space, conducted experiments, shared meals, and held a joint news conference.
Boris Yolynov, Vitaly Zhobovov (7/26-8/24/76)	Soyuz 21	...	50 days	Conducted experiments aboard Salyut 5.
Vladimir Lyakhov, Varery Ryumin (2/26/-8/19/79)	Soyuz 32, 34	...	175 days	Docked with Salyut 6. Set new space endurance record.
Robert L. Crippen, John W. Young (4/12-14/81)	Columbia	36	54h 22m	First demonstration of re-usable winged spaceship.

Columbia (Nov. 12-14,, 1981); Joe Engle, Richard Truly pilots. Columbia (Mar. 22-30, 1982); Jack Lousma, C. Gordon Fullerton pilots. Soyuz T-5 launched May 13, 1982 carrying 2 cosmonauts who linked up with Salyut 7. Soyuz T-6 (June 24-July 2, 1982); 2 cosmonauts and French Air Force officer. Columbia (June 27-July 4, 1982); Thomas Mattingly 2d, Henry Hartsfield Jr. pilots.

(1) The U.S. measures orbital flights in revolutions while the Soviets use "orbits." (2) Suborbital. (3) Moon orbits in command module. (4) Moon orbits.

Fire aboard spacecraft Apollo I on the ground at Cape Kennedy, Fla. killed Virgil I. Grissom, Edward H. White and Roger B. Chaffee on Jan. 27, 1967. They were the only U.S. astronauts killed in space tests.

Notable Ocean and Intercontinental Flights

(Certified by the Federation Aeronautique Internationale as of Jan., 1982)

	From	To	Miles	Time	Date
		Dirigible Balloons			
British R-34(1)	East Fortune, Scot.	Mineola, N.Y.	.....	108 hrs.	July 2-6, 1919
	Mineola, N.Y.	Pulham, Eng.	.....	75 hrs.	July 9-13, 1919
Amundsen-Ellsworth-Nobile expedition	Spitsbergen	Teller, Alas.	.....	80 hrs.	May 11-14, 1926
Graf Zeppelin	Friedrichshafen	Lakehurst, N.J.	6,630	4d 15h 46m	Oct. 11-15, 1928
Hindenburg Zeppelin	Germany	Lakehurst, N.J.	.....	51h 17m	June 30-July 2, 1936
	Lakehurst, N.J.	Frankfort, Ger.	.....	42h 53m	Aug. 9-11, 1936
USN ZPG-2 Blimp	S. Weymouth, Mass.	Africa			
	Africa	Key West, Fla.	7,000	275h	Mar. 4-16, 1957
		Airplanes			
USN NC-4	Rockaway, N.Y.	Lisbon, Port.	.....	....	May 8-27, 1919
John Alcock-A.W. Brown (2)	St. John's, Nfld.	Clifden, Ireland	1,960	16h 12m	June 14-15, 1919
Richard E. Byrd (3)	Spitsbergen	North Pole	1,545	15h 30m	May 9, 1926
Charles Lindbergh (4)	Mineola, N.Y.	Paris	3,610	33h 29m 30s	May 20-21, 1927
C. Levin-	Roosevelt Field, N.Y.				
C. Chamberlin (5)	Mineola, N.Y.	Isleben, Germany	3,911	42h 31m	June 4-6, 1927
Baron G. von Huenefeld, crew (6)	Dublin	Greenly Isl., Lab.	.....	37 hrs.	Apr. 12-13, 1928
Sir Hubert Wilkins (9)	Point Barrow, Alaska	Spitsbergen	.....	....	Apr. 16, 1928
Sir Chas. Kingsford-Smith, crew (7)	Oakland, Cal.	Brisbane, Aust.	.....	....	May 31-June 8, 1928
Amelia Earhart Putnam, W. Stultz, L. Gordon	Trepassy, Nfld.	Burry Port, Wales	.....	20h 40m	June 17-18, 1928
Richard E. Byrd (8)	Bay of Whales	South Pole	.....	....	Nov. 28-29, 1929
D. Coste-M. Bellonte	Paris	Valley Stream, N.Y.	4,100	37h 18m 30s	Sept. 1-2, 1930
Wiley Post-Harold Gatty	Harbor Grace, Nfld.	England	2,200	16h 17m	June 23-24, 1931
Clyde Pangborn-Hugh Herndon Jr. (10)	Tokyo	Wenatchee, Wash.	4,458	41h 34m	Oct. 3-5, 1931
Amelia Earhart Putnam (11)	Harbor Grace, Nfld.	Ireland	2,026	14h 56m	May 20-21, 1932
James A. Mollison (12)	Portmarnock, Ire.	Pennfield, N.B.	.....	....	Aug. 18, 1932
China Clipper (Pan Am. Airways) (13)	San Francisco	Manila, P.I.	.....	....	Nov. 22-28, 1935
	Manila, P.I.	San Francisco	.....	....	Dec. 1-6, 1935
Gromoff, Yumasheff, Danilin (USSR)	Moscow, USSR	San Jacinto, Cal.	6,262	62h 02m	July 12-14, 1937
Douglas C. Corrigan	New York	Dublin, Ire.	.....	28h 13m	July 17-18, 1938
B-29 (C.J. Miller)	Honolulu	Washington, D.C.	4,640	17h 21m	Sept. 1, 1945
C-54 (Maj. G.E. Cain)	Tokyo	Washington, D.C.		31h 24m	Sept. 3, 1945
Col. David C. Schilling, USAF (14)	England	Limestone, Me.	3,300	10h 01m	Sept. 22, 1950
Chas. F. Blair Jr.	New York	London	3,500	7h 48m	Jan 31, 1951
Chas. F. Blair Jr. (15)	Bardufoss, Norway	Fairbanks, Alas.	3,300	10h 29m	May 29, 1951
Chas. F. Blair Jr.	Fairbanks, Alaska	New York	3,450	9h 31m	May 30, 1950
Canberra Bomber	England	Australia	.....	20h 20m	Mar. 16, 1952
Two U.S. S-55 Helicopters (16)	Westover AFB, Mass.	Prestwick, Scotland	3,410	42h 30m	July 15-31, 1952
Canberra Bomber (17)	Aldergrove, N.Ire.	Gander, Nfld.	2,073	4h 34m	Aug. 26, 1952
	Gander, Nfld.	Aldergrove, N.Ire.	2,073	3h 25m	Aug. 26, 1952
British Comet	London-Tokyo	Tokyo-London	20,400	74h 52m	Apr. 3-7, 1953
British Comet	London	Rio de Janeiro	6,000	12h 30m	Sept. 13-14, 1953
Max Conrad (solo)	New York	Paris	.....	22h 23m	Nov. 7, 1954
Canberra Bomber	London (round trip)	New York	6,920	14h 21m 45.4s	Aug. 23, 1955
Capt. William F. Judd	New York	Paris	.....	24h 11m	Jan. 29-30, 1956
Three USAF F-100Cs	London	Los Angeles	6,710	14h 5m	May 13, 1957
Spirit of St. Louis II (USAF F-100F jet)	McGuire AFB, N.J.	Le Bourget, Paris	.....	6h 38m	May 21, 1957
USAF KC-135	Tokyo	Lajes AFB, Azores	10,230	18h 48m	Apr. 7-8, 1958
Max Conrad (solo)	New York	Palermo, Sicily	4,440	32h 55m	June 22-23, 1958
USAF KC-135	Yokota AB, Japan	Washington, D.C.	7,100	12h 28m	Sept. 12, 1958
Max Conrad (solo)	Chicago	Rome	5,000	34h 3m	Mar. 5-6, 1959
Max Conrad (solo)	Casablanca, Mor.	Los Angeles	7,700	58h 36m	June 2-4, 1959
USSR TU-114 (18)	Moscow	New York	5,092	11h 6m	June 28, 1959
Boeing 707 airliner	San Francisco	Sydney, Australia	7,630	16h 10m	July 2, 1959
Boeing 707-320	New York	Moscow	c.5,090	8h 54m	July 23, 1959
Max Conrad (solo)	Casablanca, Mor.	El Paso, Tex.	6,911	56h 26m	Nov. 22-26, 1959
Col. J.B. Swindal	Washington, D.C.	Moscow	5,004	8h 39m 02.2s	May 19, 1963
Concorde GB	London	Washington, D.C.	1,023 mph	3h 34m 48s	May 29, 1976
Concorde	Paris	Washington, D.C.	1,071.86 mph	3h 35m 15s	Aug. 18, 1978
Concorde	Paris	New York	1,037.50 mph	3h 30m 11s	Aug. 22, 1978

Notable first flights: (1) Atlantic aerial round trip. (2) Non-stop transatlantic flight. (3) Polar flight. (4) Solo transatlantic flight in the Ryan monoplane the "Spirit of St. Louis." (5) Transatlantic passenger flight. (6) East-West transatlantic crossing. (7) U.S. to Australia flight. (8) South Pole flight. (9) Trans-Arctic flight. (10) Non-stop Pacific flight. (11) Woman's transoceanic solo flight. (12) Westbound transatlantic solo flight. (13) Pacific airmail and U.S. to Philippines crossing. (14) Non-stop jet transatlantic flight. (15) Solo across North Pole. (16) Transatlantic helicopter flight. (17) Transatlantic round trip on same day. (18) Non-stop between Moscow and New York.

International Aeronautical Records

Source: The National Aeronautic Association, 806 15th St. NW, Washington, DC 20005, representative in the United States of the Federation Aeronautique Internationale, certifying agency for world aviation and space records. The International Aeronautical Federation was formed in 1905 by representatives from Belgium, France, Germany, Great Britain, Spain, Italy, Switzerland, and the United States, with headquarters in Paris. Regulations for the control of official records were signed Oct. 14, 1905. World records are defined as maximum performance, regardless of class or type of aircraft used. Records to July, 1982.

World Air Records—Maximum Performance in Any Class

Speed over a straight course — 3,529.56 kph. (2,193.16 mph) — Capt. Elden W. Joersz, USAF, Lockheed SR-71; Beale AFB, Cal., July 28, 1976.

Speed over a closed circuit — 3,367.221 kph. (2,092.294 mph) — Maj. Adolphus H. Bledsoe Jr., USAF, Lockheed SR-71; Beale AFB, Cal., July 27, 1976.

Distance in a straight line — 20,168.78 kms (12,532.28 mi.) — Maj. Clyde P. Evely, USAF, Boeing B52-H; Kadena, Okinawa to Madrid, Spain, Jan. 11, 1962.

Distance over a closed circuit — 18,245.05 kms (11,336.92 mi.) — Capt. William Stevenson, USAF, Boeing B52-H; Seymour-Johnson, N.C., June 6-7, 1962.

Altitude — 37,650 meters (123,523.58 feet) — Alexander Fedotov, USSR, E-266M; Podmoskovnoye, USSR, Aug. 31, 1977.

Altitude in horizontal flight — 25,929.031 meters (85,068.997 ft.) — Capt. Robert C. Helt, USAF, Lockheed SR-71; Beale AFB, Cal., July 28, 1976.

Manned Space Craft

Duration — 175 days — Vladimir Lyakhov & Valery Ryumin, USSR, Salyut 6, Feb. 26—Aug. 19, 1979.

Altitude — 377,668.9 kms (234,672.5 mi.) — Frank Borman, James A. Lovell Jr., William Anders, Apollo 8; Dec. 21-27, 1968.

Greatest mass lifted — 127,980 kgs. (282,197 lbs.) — Frank Borman, James S. Lovell Jr., William Anders, Apollo 8; Dec. 21-27, 1968.

Distance — 92,941,650 kms. (57,751,264.59 mi.) — Vladimir Kovalyonok, Alexandre Ivan Chenkov, USSR; Soyuz 29, Salyut 6, Soyuz 31; June 15-Nov. 2, 1978.

World "Class" Records

All other records, international in scope, are termed World "Class" records and are divided into classes: airships, free balloons, airplanes, seaplanes, amphibians, gliders, and rotorplanes. Airplanes (Class C) are sub-divided into four groups: Group I — piston engine aircraft, Group II — turboprop aircraft, Group III — jet aircraft, Group IV — rocket powered aircraft. A partial listing of world records follows:

Airplanes (Class C-I, Group I—piston engine)

Distance, closed circuit — 14,441.26 kms (8,974 mi.) — James R. Bede, U.S.; BD-2, Columbus, Oh. to Kansas City course, Nov. 7-9, 1969.

Distance, straight line — 18,081.99 kms. (11,235.6 miles) — Cmdr. Thomas D. Davies, USN; Cmdr. Eugene P. Rankin, USN; Cmdr. Walter S. Reid, USN, and Lt. Cmdr. Ray A. Tabeling, USN; Lockheed P2V-1; from Pearce Field, Perth, Australia to Columbus, Oh., Sept. 29-Oct. 1, 1946.

Speed over 3-kilometer measured course — 803.138 kph. (499.04 mph) — Steve Hinton; P-51D; Tonopah, Nev., Aug. 14, 1979.

Speed for 100 kilometers (62.137 miles) without payload — 755.668 kph. (469.549 mph.) — Jacqueline Cochran, U.S.; North American P-51; Coachella Valley, Cal., Dec. 10, 1947.

Speed for 1,000 kilometers (621.369 miles) without payload — 693.78 kph. (431.09 mph.) — Jacqueline Cochran, U.S.; North American P-51; Santa Rosasummit, Cal. — Flagstaff, Ariz. course, May 24, 1948.

Speed for 5,000 kilometers (3,106.849 miles) without payload — 544.59 kph. (338.39 mph.) — Capt. James Bauer, USAF, Boeing B-29; Dayton, Oh., June 28, 1946.

Speed around the world — 327.73 kph (203.64 mph) — D.N. Dalton, Australia; Beechcraft Duke; Brisbane, Aust., July 20-25, 1975. Time: 5 days, 2 hours, 19 min., 57 sec.

Light Airplanes—(Class C-1.d)

Distance in a straight line — 12,341.26 kms. (7,668.48 miles) — Max Conrad, U.S.; Piper Comanche; Casablanca, Morocco to Los Angeles, June 2-4, 1959.

Speed for 100 kilometers — (62,137 miles) in a closed circuit — 519.480 kph. (322.780 mph.) — Ms. R. M. Sharpe, Great Britain; Vickers Supermarine Spitfire 5-B; Wolverhampton, June 17, 1950.

Helicopters (Class E-1)

Distance in a straight line — 3,561.55 kms. (2,213.04 miles) — Robert G. Ferry, U.S.; Hughes YOH-6A helicopter; Culver City, Cal., to Ormond Beach, Fla., Apr. 6-7, 1966.

Speed over 3-km. course — 348.971 kph. (216.839 mph.) — Byron Graham, U.S.; Sikorsky S-67 helicopter; Windsor Locks, Conn., Dec. 14, 1970.

Gliders (Class D-I—single place)

Distance, straight line — 1,460.8 kms. (907.7 miles) — Hans Werner Grosse, West Germany; ASK12 sailplane; Luebeck to Biarritz, Apr. 25, 1972.

Altitude above sea level — 14,102 meters (46,267 feet) — Paul F. Bikle, U.S.; Sailplane Schweizer SGS-123-E; Mojave, Lancaster, Cal., Feb. 25, 1961.

Airplanes (Class C-I, Group II—Turboprop)

Distance in a straight line — 14,052.95 kms. (8,732.09 miles) — Lt. Col. Edgar L. Allison Jr., USAF, Lockheed HC-130 Hercules aircraft; Taiwan to Scott AFB, Ill.; Feb. 20, 1972.

Altitude — 15,549 meters (51,014 ft.) — Donald R. Wilson, U.S.; LTV L450F aircraft; Greenville, Tex., Mar. 27, 1972.

Speed for 1,000 kilometers (621.369 miles) without payload — 871.38 kph. (541.449 mph.) — Ivan Soukhomline, USSR; TU-114 aircraft; Sternberg, USSR; Mar. 24, 1960.

Speed for 5,000 kilometers (3,106.849 miles) without payload — 877.212 kph. (545.072 mph.) — Ivan Soukhomline, USSR; TU-114 aircraft, Sternberg, USSR; Apr. 9, 1960.

Airplanes (Class C-1, Group III—Jet-powered)

Distance in a straight line — 20,168.78 kms. (12,532.28 mi.) — Maj. Clyde P. Evely, USAF, Boeing B-52-H, Kadena, Okinawa, to Madrid, Spain, Jan. 10-11, 1962.

Distance in a closed circuit — 18,245.05 kms. (11,336.92 miles) — Capt. William Stevenson, USAF, Boeing B-52-H, Seymour-Johnson, N.C., June 6-7, 1962.

Altitude — 36,650 meters (123,523.58 ft.) — Alexander Fedotov, USSR; E-226M airplane; Podmoskovnoye, USSR, Aug. 31, 1977.

Speed over a 3-kilometer course — 1,590.45 kph (988.26 mph) — Darryl G. Greenamyer, U.S.; F-104; Tonopah, Nev., Oct. 24, 1977.
Speed for 100 kilometers in a closed circuit — 2,605 kph. (1,618.7 mph.) — Alexander Fedotov, USSR; E-266 airplane, Apr. 8, 1973.
Speed for 500 kilometers in a closed circuit — 2,981.5 kph. (1,852.61 mph.) — Mikhail Komarov, USSR; E-266 airplane, Oct. 5, 1967.
Speed for 1,000 kilometers in a closed circuit — 3,367.221 kph (2,092.294 mph) — Maj. Adolphus H. Bledsoe Jr., USAF; Lockheed SR-71; Beale AFB, Cal., July 27, 1976.
Speed for 2,000 kilometers in closed circuit — 1,708.817 kph. (1,061.808 mph.) — Maj. H. J. Deutschendorf Jr., U.S.; Convair B-58 Hustler Bomber; Edwards AFB, Cal., Jan. 12, 1961.

Balloons-Class A

Altitude — 34,668 meters (113,739.9 feet) — Cmdr. Malcolm D. Ross, USNR; Lee Lewis Memorial Winzen Research Balloon; Gulf of Mexico, May 4, 1961.

Duration —137 hr., 5 min., 50 sec. — Ben Abruzzo and Maxie Anderson; Double Eagle II; Presque Isle, Maine to Miserey, France (3,107.61 mi.); Aug. 12-17, 1978.

FAI Course Records

Los Angeles to New York — 1,954.79 kph (1,214.65 mph) — Capt. Robert G. Sowers, USAF; Convair B-58 Hustler; elapsed time: 2 hrs. 58.71 sec., Mar. 5, 1962.
New York to Los Angeles — 1,741 kph (1,081.80 mph) — Capt. Robert G. Sowers, USAF; Convair B-58 Hustler; elapsed time: 2 hrs. 15 min. 50.08 sec., Mar. 5, 1962.
New York to Paris — 1,753.068 kph (1,089.36 mph) — Maj. W. R. Payne, U.S.; Convair B-58 Hustler; elapsed time: 3 hrs 19 min. 44 sec., May 26, 1961.
London to New York — 945.423 kph (587.457 mph) — Maj. Burl Davenport, USAF; Boeing KC-135; elapsed time: 5 hrs. 53 min. 12.77 sec.; June 27, 1958.
Baltimore to Moscow, USSR — 906.64 kph (563.36 mph) — Col. James B. Swindal, USAF; Boeing VC-137 (707); elapsed time: 8 hrs. 33 min. 45.4 sec., May 19, 1963.
Belfast to Gander, Newfoundland — 774.25 kph (481.099 mph) — Wing Commander R. P. Beamont, Great Britain; Canberra bomber, Aug. 31, 1951; elapsed time: 4 hrs. 18 min. 24.4 sec.
New York to London — 2,908.026 kph (1,806.964 mph) — Maj. James V. Sullivan, USAF; Lockheed SR-71; elapsed time 1 hr. 54 min. 56.4 sec., Sept. 1, 1974.
London to Los Angeles — 2,310.353 kph (1,435.587 mph) — Capt. Harold B. Adams, USAF; Lockheed SR-71; elapsed time: 3 hrs. 47 min. 39 sec., Sept. 13, 1974.

National Aviation Hall of Fame

The National Aviation Hall of Fame at Dayton, Oh., is dedicated to honoring aviation's outstanding pioneers.

Allen, William M.
Armstrong, Neil A.
Arnold, Henry "Hap"

Balchen, Bernt
Baldwin, Thomas S.
Beachey, Lincoln
Beech, Olive A.
Beech, Walter H.
Bell, Alexander Graham
Bell, Lawrence D.
Boeing, William E.
Byrd, Richard E.

Cessna, Clyde V.
Chamberlin, Clarence D.
Chanute, Octave
Chennault, Claire L.
Cochran (Odlum), Jacqueline
Conrad Jr., Charles
Cunningham, Alfred A.
Curtiss, Glenn H.

deSeversky, Alexander P.
Doolittle, James H.
Douglas, Donald W.
Draper, Charles S.

Eaker, Ira C.
Earhart, (Putnam), Amelia
Ellyson, Theodore G.
Ely, Eugene B.

Fairchild, Sherman M.
Fleet, Reuben H.
Fokker, Anthony H.G.
Foulois, Benjamin D.

Gabreski, Francis S.
Glenn Jr., John H.
Goddard, George W.
Goddard, Robert H.
Gross, Robert E.
Grumman, Leroy R.
Guggenheim, Harry F.

Hegenberger, Albert F.
Heinemann, Edward H.
Hughes, Howard R.

Johnson, Clarence L.

Kenney, George C.
Kettering, Charles F.
Kindelberger, James H.
Knabenshue, A. Roy

Langley, Samuel P.
Lahm, Frank P.
Lear, William P. Sr.
LeMay, Curtis E.
LeVier, Anthony W.
Lindbergh, Anne M.
Lindbergh, Charles A.
Link, Edwin A.
Loening, Grover
Luke Jr., Frank

Macready, John A.
Martin, Glenn L.
McDonnell, James S.
Mitchell, William "Billy"
Montgomery, John J.
Moss, Sanford A.

Northrop, John K.

Patterson, William A.
Piper Sr., William T.
Post, Wiley H.

Read, Albert C.
Reeve, Robert C.
Richardson, Holden C.
Rickenbacker, Edward V.
Rodgers, Calbraith P.
Rogers, Will
Ryan, T. Claude

Schriever, Bernard A.
Selfridge, Thomas E.
Shepard Jr., Alan B.
Sikorsky, Igor I.
Six, Robert F.
Smith, C.R.
Spaatz, Carl A.
Sperry Sr., Elmer A.
Sperry Sr., Lawrence B.

Taylor, Charles E.
Towers, John H.
Trippe, Juan T.
Turner, Roscoe
Twining, Nathan F.

Wade, Leigh
Walden, Henry W.
Wright, Orville
Wright, Wilbur

Yeager, Charles E.

The Busiest Airports, 1981

(Total take-offs and landings)

United States

Source: Federal Aviation Administration

Chicago O'Hare	645,586
Atlanta International	601,026
Long Beach	588,543
Van Nuys	558,918
Los Angeles International	502,884
Denver Stapleton	479,766
Dallas Ft. Worth	472,331
Santa Ana	469,133
Oakland International	436,905
Seattle-Boeing	410,072

Canada

Source: Aviation Statistics Centre, Statistics Canada

St. Hubert, Que.	263,414
Vancouver International, B.C.	262,658
Pitt Meadows, B.C.	251,048
Toronto International, Ont.	248,333
Calgary International, Alta.	233,205
Springbank, Alta.	232,058
Toronto Island, Ont.	214,651
St. Andrews, Man.	203,341
Buttonville, Ont.	199,982
Ottawa International, Ont.	199,928

Notable Trips Around the World

(Certified by Federation Aeronautique Internationale as of Jan., 1982)

Fast circuits of the earth have been a subject of wide interest since Jules Verne, French novelist, described an imaginary trip by Phileas Fogg in Around the World in 80 Days, assertedly occurring Oct. 2 to Dec. 20, 1872.

	Terminal	Miles	Time	Date
Nellie Bly	New York, N.Y.		72d 06h 11m	1889
George Francis Train	New York, N.Y.		67d 12h 03m	1890
Charles Fitzmorris	Chicago		60d 13h 29m	1901
J. W. Willis Sayre	Seattle		54d 09h 42m	1903
Col. Burnlay-Campbell			40d 19h 30m	1907
Andre Jaeger-Schmidt			39d 19h 42m 38s	1911
John Henry Mears			35d 21h 36m	1913
Two U.S. Army airplanes	Seattle (57 hops, 21 countries)	26,103	35d 01h 11m	1924
Edward S. Evans and Linton Wells (New York World) (1)	New York	18,400	28d 14h 36m 05s	June 16-July 14, 1926
John H. Mears and Capt. C.B.D. Collyer	New York		23d 15h 21m 03s	June 29-July 22, 1928
Graf Zeppelin	Friedrichshafen, Ger. via Tokyo, Los Angeles, Lakehurst, N.J.	21,700	20d 04h	Aug. 14-Sept. 4, 1929
Wiley Post and Harold Gatty (Monoplane Winnie Mae)	Roosevelt Field, N.Y. via Arctic Circle	15,474	8d 15h 51m	June 23-July 1, 1931
Wiley Post (Monoplane Winnie Mae) (2)	Floyd Bennett Field, N.Y. via Arctic Circle	15,596	115h 36m 30s	July 15-22, 1933
H. R. Ekins (Scripps-Howard Newspapers in race) (Zeppelin Hindenburg to Germany air planes from Frankfurt)	Lakehurst, N.J., via Frankfurt, Germany	25,654	18d 11h 14m 33s	Sept, 30-Oct. 19, 1936
Howard Hughes and 4 assistants	New York, Paris, Moscow, Siberia, Fairbanks	14,824	3d 19h 08m 10s	July 10-13, 1938
Mrs. Clara Adams (Pan American Clipper)	Port Washington, N.Y., return Newark, N.J.		16d 19h 04m	June 28-July 15, 1939
Globester, U.S. Air Transport Command	Washington, D.C.	23,279	149h 44m	Sept. 28-Oct. 4, 1945
Capt. William P. Odom (A-26 Reynolds Bombshell)	New York, via Paris, Cairo, Tokyo, Alaska	20,000	78h 55m 12s	Apr. 12-16, 1947
America, Pan American 4-engine Lockheed Constellation (3)	New York	22,219	101h 32m	June 17-30, 1947
Col. Edward Eagan	New York	20,559	147h 15m	Dec. 13, 1948
USAF B-50 Lucky Lady II (Capt. James Gallagher) (4)	Fort Worth, Tex.	23,452	94h 01m	Feb. 26-Mar. 2, 1949
Jean-Marie Audibert	Paris		4d 19h 38m	Dec. 11-15, 1952
Pamela Martin	Midway Airport, Chicago		90h 59m	Dec. 5-8, 1953
Three USAF B-52 Stratofortresses (5)	Merced, Cal., via Nfld., Morocco, Saudi Arabia, India, Ceylon, P.I., Guam	24,325	45h 19m	Jan. 15-18, 1957
Joseph Cavoli	Cleveland, Oh.		89h 13m 37s	Jan. 31-Feb. 4 1958
Peter Gluckmann (solo)	San Francisco	22,800	29d	Aug. 22-Sept. 20, 1959
Milton Reynolds	San Francisco		51h 45m 22s	Jan. 12-14, 1960
Sue Snyder	Chicago	21,219	62h 59m	June 22-24, 1960
Max Conrad (solo)	Miami, Fla.	25,946	8d 18h 35m 57s	Feb. 28-Mar. 8, 196
Sam Miller & Louis Fodor	New York		46h 28m	Aug. 3-4, 196
Robert & Joan Wallick	Manila, Philippines	23,129	5d 6h 17m 10s	June 2-7, 196
Arthur Godfrey, Richard Merrill Fred Austin, Karl Keller	New York	23,333	86h 9m 01s	June 4-7, 196
Trevor K. Brougham	Darwin, Australia	24,800	5d 05h 57m	Aug. 5-10, 197
Walter H. Mullikin, Albert Frink, Lyman Watt, Frank Cassaniti, Edward Shields	New York	23,137	1d 22h 50s	May 1-3,197
Arnold Palmer	Denver, Col.	22,985	57h 25m 42s	May 17-19, 197
Boeing 747 (6)	San Francisco	26,382	54h 7m 12s	Oct. 28-31, 197

(1) Mileage by train and auto, 4,110; by plane, 6,300; by steamship, 8,000. (2) First to fly solo around northern circumference of the world, also first to fly twice around the world. (3) Inception of regular commercial global air service. (4) First non-stop round-the-world flight, refueled 4 times in flight. (5) First non-stop global flight by jet planes; refueled in flight by KC-97 aerial tankers; average speed approx. 525 mph. (6) Speed record around the world over both the earth's poles.

U.S. Scheduled Airline Traffic

Source: Air Transport Association of America (thousands)

	1979	1980	1981
Passenger traffic			
Revenue passengers enplaned	316,683	296,903	285,72
Revenue passenger miles	262,023,375	255,192,114	248,756,78
Available seat miles	416,126,429	432,535,103	424,661,31
Cargo traffic (ton miles)	7,188,610	7,083,674	7,058,06
Freight	5,907,731	5,685,622	5,616,75
Express	56,194	55,945	67,97
U.S. Mail	1,206,298	1,318,496	1,347,49
Overall traffic and service			
Nonscheduled traffic—total ton miles	1,160,801	2,052,522	1,941,29
Total revenue ton miles—all services	34,550,922	34,655,516	33,875,09
Total available ton miles—all services	62,545,447	66,162,893	64,149,94

Air Distances Between Selected World Cities in Statute Miles

Point-to-point measurements are usually from City Hall

	Bangkok	Berlin	Cairo	Cape Town	Caracas	Chicago	Hong Kong	Honolulu	Lima	London
Bangkok	....	5,352	4,523	6,300	10,555	8,570	1,077	6,609	12,244	5,944
Berlin	5,352	....	1,797	5,961	5,238	4,414	5,443	7,320	6,896	583
Cairo	4,523	1,797	....	4,480	6,342	6,141	5,066	8,848	7,726	2,185
Cape Town	6,300	5,961	4,480	....	6,366	8,491	7,376	11,535	6,072	5,989
Caracas	10,555	5,238	6,342	6,366	....	2,495	10,165	6,021	1,707	4,655
Chicago	8,570	4,414	6,141	8,491	2,495	....	7,797	4,256	3,775	3,958
Hong Kong	1,077	5,443	5,066	7,376	10,165	7,797	....	5,556	11,418	5,990
Honolulu	6,609	7,320	8,848	11,535	6,021	4,256	5,556	....	5,947	7,240
London	5,944	583	2,185	5,989	4,655	3,958	5,990	7,240	6,316	....
Los Angeles	7,637	5,782	7,520	9,969	3,632	1,745	7,240	2,557	4,171	5,439
Madrid	6,337	1,165	2,087	5,308	4,346	4,189	6,558	7,872	5,907	785
Melbourne	4,568	9,918	8,675	6,425	9,717	9,673	4,595	5,505	8,059	10,500
Mexico City	9,793	6,056	7,700	8,519	2,234	1,690	8,788	3,789	2,639	5,558
Montreal	8,338	3,740	5,427	7,922	2,438	745	7,736	4,918	3,970	3,254
Moscow	4,389	1,006	1,803	6,279	6,177	4,987	4,437	7,047	7,862	1,564
New York	8,669	3,979	5,619	7,803	2,120	714	8,060	4,969	3,639	3,469
Paris	5,877	548	1,998	5,786	4,732	4,143	5,990	7,449	6,370	214
Peking	2,046	4,584	4,698	8,044	8,950	6,604	1,217	5,077	10,349	5,074
Rio de Janeiro	9,994	6,209	6,143	3,781	2,804	5,282	11,009	8,288	2,342	5,750
Rome	5,494	737	1,326	5,231	5,195	4,824	5,774	8,040	6,750	895
San Francisco	7,931	5,672	7,466	10,248	3,902	1,859	6,905	2,398	4,518	5,367
Singapore	883	6,164	5,137	6,008	11,402	9,372	1,605	6,726	11,689	6,747
Stockholm	5,089	528	2,096	6,423	5,471	4,331	5,063	6,875	7,166	942
Tokyo	2,865	5,557	5,958	9,154	8,808	6,314	1,791	3,859	9,631	5,959
Warsaw	5,033	322	1,619	5,935	5,559	4,679	5,147	7,366	7,215	905
Washington, D.C.	8,807	4,181	5,822	7,895	2,047	596	8,155	4,838	3,509	3,674

	Los Angeles	Madrid	Melbourne	Mexico City	Montreal	Moscow	New Delhi	New York	Paris	Peking
Bangkok	7,637	6,337	4,568	9,793	8,338	4,389	1,813	8,669	5,877	2,046
Berlin	5,782	1,165	9,918	6,056	3,740	1,006	3,598	3,979	548	4,584
Cairo	7,520	2,087	8,675	7,700	5,427	1,803	2,758	5,619	1,998	4,698
Cape Town	9,969	5,308	6,425	8,519	7,922	6,279	5,769	7,803	5,786	8,044
Caracas	3,632	4,346	9,717	2,234	2,438	6,177	8,833	2,120	4,732	8,950
Chicago	1,745	4,189	9,673	1,690	745	4,987	7,486	714	4,143	6,604
Hong Kong	7,240	6,558	4,595	8,788	7,736	4,437	2,339	8,060	5,990	1,217
Honolulu	2,557	7,872	5,505	3,789	4,918	7,047	7,412	4,969	7,449	5,077
London	5,439	785	10,500	5,558	3,254	1,564	4,181	3,469	214	5,074
Los Angeles	....	5,848	7,931	1,542	2,427	6,068	7,011	2,451	5,601	6,250
Madrid	5,848	....	10,758	5,643	3,448	2,147	4,530	3,593	655	5,745
Melbourne	7,931	10,758	....	8,426	10,395	8,950	6,329	10,359	10,430	5,643
Mexico City	1,542	5,643	8,426	....	2,317	6,676	9,120	2,090	5,725	7,753
Montreal	2,427	3,448	10,395	2,317	....	4,401	7,012	331	3,432	6,519
Moscow	6,068	2,147	8,950	6,676	4,401	....	2,698	4,683	1,554	3,607
New York	2,451	3,593	10,359	2,090	331	4,683	7,318	....	3,636	6,844
Paris	5,601	655	10,430	5,725	3,432	1,554	4,102	3,636	....	5,120
Peking	6,250	5,745	5,643	7,753	6,519	3,607	2,353	6,844	5,120	....
Rio de Janeiro	6,330	5,045	8,226	4,764	5,078	7,170	8,753	4,801	5,684	10,768
Rome	6,326	851	9,929	6,377	4,104	1,483	3,684	4,293	690	5,063
San Francisco	347	5,803	7,856	1,887	2,543	5,885	7,691	2,572	5,577	5,918
Singapore	8,767	7,080	3,759	10,327	9,203	5,228	2,571	9,534	6,673	2,771
Stockholm	5,454	1,653	9,630	6,012	3,714	716	3,414	3,986	1,003	4,133
Tokyo	5,470	6,706	5,062	7,035	6,471	4,660	3,638	6,757	6,053	1,307
Warsaw	5,922	1,427	9,598	6,337	4,022	721	3,277	4,270	852	4,325
Washington, D.C.	2,300	3,792	10,180	1,885	489	4,876	7,500	205	3,840	6,942

	Rio de Janiero	Rome	San Francisco	Singapore	Stockholm	Teheran	Tokyo	Vienna	Warsaw	Wash., D.C.
Bangkok	9,994	5,494	7,931	883	5,089	3,391	2,865	5,252	5,033	8,807
Berlin	6,209	737	5,672	6,164	528	2,185	5,557	326	322	4,181
Cairo	6,143	1,326	7,466	5,137	2,096	1,234	5,958	1,481	1,619	5,822
Cape Town	3,781	5,231	10,248	6,008	6,423	5,241	9,154	5,656	5,935	7,895
Caracas	2,804	5,195	3,902	11,402	5,471	7,320	8,808	5,372	5,559	2,047
Chicago	5,282	4,824	1,859	9,372	4,331	6,502	6,314	4,698	4,679	596
Hong Kong	11,009	5,774	6,905	1,605	5,063	3,843	1,791	5,431	5,147	8,155
Honolulu	8,288	8,040	2,398	6,726	6,875	8,070	3,859	7,632	7,366	4,838
London	5,750	895	5,367	6,747	942	2,743	5,959	771	905	3,674
Los Angeles	6,330	6,326	347	8,767	5,454	7,682	5,470	6,108	5,922	2,300
Madrid	5,045	851	5,803	7,080	1,653	2,978	6,706	1,128	1,427	3,792
Melbourne	8,226	9,929	7,856	3,759	9,630	7,826	5,062	9,790	9,598	10,180
Mexico City	4,764	6,377	1,887	10,327	6,012	8,184	7,035	6,320	6,337	1,885
Montreal	5,078	4,104	2,543	9,203	3,714	5,880	6,471	4,009	4,022	489
Moscow	7,170	1,483	5,885	5,228	716	1,532	4,660	1,043	721	4,876
New York	4,801	4,293	2,572	9,534	3,986	6,141	6,757	4,234	4,270	205
Paris	5,684	690	5,577	6,673	1,003	2,625	6,053	645	852	3,840
Peking	10,768	5,063	5,918	2,771	4,133	3,490	1,307	4,648	4,325	6,942
Rio de Janeiro	....	5,707	6,613	9,785	6,683	7,374	11,532	6,127	6,455	4,779
Rome	5,707	....	6,259	6,229	1,245	2,127	6,142	477	820	4,497
San Francisco	6,613	6,259	....	8,448	5,399	7,362	5,150	5,994	5,854	2,441
Singapore	9,785	6,229	8,448	....	5,936	4,103	3,300	6,035	5,843	9,662
Stockholm	6,683	1,245	5,399	5,936	....	2,173	5,053	780	494	4,183
Tokyo	11,532	6,142	5,150	3,300	5,053	4,775	....	5,689	5,347	6,791
Warsaw	6,455	820	5,854	5,843	494	1,879	5,689	347	....	4,472
Washington, D.C.	4,779	4,497	2,441	9,662	4,183	6,341	6,791	4,438	4,472	....

AGRICULTURE

World and Regional Food Production, 1976 to 1981

Source: UN Food and Agriculture Organization

Region	1976	1977	1978	1979	1980	1981[1]	Change 1980 to 1981	Annual rate of change 1971-80
	(1969-71 = 100)							
Food Production								
Developing market economies[2]	118	122	127	127	133	140	+ 7	3.3
Africa	111	109	113	114	120	123	+ 3	1.7
Far East	115	124	128	125	133	142	+ 9	3.5
Latin America	123	127	133	136	139	146	+ 7	3.9
Near East	128	125	131	132	138	141	+ 3	3.4
Asian centrally planned economies	122	122	129	137	136	141	+ 5	3.4
Total Developing Countries	**119**	**122**	**128**	**130**	**134**	**140**	**+ 6**	**3.3**
Developed market economies[2]	112	116	119	122	119	124	+ 5	2.0
North America	117	122	123	127	123	135	+ 12	2.4
Oceania	128	124	142	136	122	131	+ 9	2.9
Western Europe	108	111	116	120	123	120	− 3	1.9
Eastern Europe and the USSR	115	117	125	119	116	115	− 1	1.6
Total Developed Countries	**113**	**116**	**121**	**121**	**119**	**121**	**+ 2**	**1.9**
World	**116**	**119**	**124**	**125**	**125**	**129**	**+ 4**	**2.5**

Note: Food production covers crops and livestock only. (1) Preliminary. (2) Including countries in other regions not specified.

Food Production Per Capita in Developing Regions, 1976-81

Source: UN Food and Agriculture Organization

Region	1976	1977	1978	1979	1980	1981[1]	Change 1980 to 1981	Annual rate of change 1971-80
	(1969-71 = 100)							
Developing market economies[2]	100	101	105	102	104	107	+3	+0.7
Africa	93	89	90	88	90	90	0	−1.2
Far East	99	103	108	103	107	112	+5	+1.0
Latin America	101	103	107	107	108	111	+3	+1.2
Near East	107	102	106	105	105	104	−1	+0.6
Total developing countries	**103**	**103**	**107**	**107**	**108**	**110**	**+2**	**+1.1**

(1) Preliminary. (2) Including countries in other regions not specified.

Food Intake Below Critical Minimum Limit in Developing Regions

Source: UN Food and Agriculture Organization

(Estimated)

The critical minimum limit for food intake is 1.2 times the Basal Metabolic Rate (BMR).

Region	Total Population (millions)		Percentage below 1.2 BMR		Total number below 1.2 BMR (millions)	
	1969-71	1972-74	1969-71	1972-74	1969-71	1972-74
Africa	278	301	25	28	70	83
Far East	968	1,042	25	29	256	297
Latin America	279	302	16	15	44	46
Near East	167	182	18	16	31	29
MSA[1]	954	1,027	27	30	255	307
Other developing market economies	738	800	20	18	146	148
Total developing market economies	1,692	1,827	24	25	401	455

(1) Countries most severely affected by food shortages.

World Daily Dietary Energy Supply in Relation to Requirements

Source: UN Food and Agriculture Organization

Region	Dietary energy[1]				Supply as percent of requirement[2]			
	1966-68	1969-71	1972-74	1975-77	1966-68	1969-71	1972-74	1975-77
Developing market economies	2,122	2,206	2,193	2,219	81	85	84	85
Africa	2,136	2,194	2,174	2,208	82	84	84	85
Latin America	2,511	2,531	2,518	2,552	97	97	97	98
Near East	2,413	2,431	2,498	2,657	93	94	96	102
Far East	1,959	2,079	2,053	2,053	75	80	80	80
Others	2,268	2,326	2,371	2,345	87	89	91	90
Asian centrally planned econ.	2,087	2,224	2,317	2,420	80	86	89	93
Total developing countries	**2,110**	**2,211**	**2,233**	**2,282**	**81**	**85**	**86**	**88**
Developed market economies	3,200	3,275	3,323	3,329	123	126	128	128
North America	3,384	3,467	3,493	3,519	130	133	134	135
Western Europe	3,256	3,333	3,389	3,378	125	128	130	130
Oceania	3,288	3,360	3,365	3,418	126	129	129	131
Others	2,701	2,769	2,852	2,872	104	107	110	110
Eastern Europe and the U.S.S.R.	3,300	3,379	3,413	3,465	127	130	131	133
Total developed countries	**3,232**	**3,309**	**3,353**	**3,373**	**124**	**127**	**129**	**130**
World	**2,457**	**2,541**	**2,559**	**2,590**	**95**	**98**	**98**	**99**

(1) Calories per capita per day. (2) Daily calorie requirement is 3,000 for men, 2,200 for women.

Agricultural Products — U.S. and World Production and Exports

Source: Foreign Agricultural Service, U.S. Agriculture Department

1981/82 Commodity	Unit	Production U.S.	Production World	Production % U.S.	Exports[6] U.S.	Exports[6] World	Exports[6] % U.S.
Wheat	MMT	[1] 76.0	[2] 453.4	16.7	[3] 48.4	[3] 98.7	49.0
Oats	MMT	[1] 8.4	[2] 47.0	17.9	[1] 0.061	[2] 1.3	4.7
Corn	MMT	[4] 208.3	[2] 438.8	47.5	[4] 52.4	[2] 72.4	72.4
Barley	MMT	[1] 10.4	[2] 160.3	6.5	[1] 2.2	[2] 18.7	11.6
Rice[5]	MMT	[5] 8.4	[5] 410.9	2.0	[5] 2.9	[6] 12.1	23.8
Soybeans	MMT	55.3	[7] 87.3	63.3	24.8	29.1	85.2
Tobacco, unmfd.[8]	1,000 MT	[9] 935.2	[9] 5,664.0	16.5	265.1	1,328.2	20.0
Edible, Veg. Oils	MMT	11.4	41.5	27.5	[7,10] 1.2	[7] 12.0	10.0
Cotton[5,11]	Mil. Bales	15.6	71.3	21.9	6.6	20.3	32.5

(1) Year beginning June 1. (2) Year beginning July 1. (3) Includes wheat flour in grain equivalent. (4) Year beginning October 1. (5) Year beginning August 1. (6) Calendar Year 1982. (7) Year beginning September 1. (8) Calendar Year 1981. (9) Farm sales weight basis. (10) Includes oil equivalent of exported oilseed. (11) Bales of 480 lbs. net weight.

Grain, Hay, Potato, Cotton, Soybean, Tobacco Production

Source: Economic Research Service: U.S. Agriculture Department

1981 State	Barley 1,000 bushels	Corn, grain 1,000 bushels	Cotton lint 1,000 bales[1]	All hay 1,000 tons	Oats 1,000 bushels	Potatoes 1,000 cwt.	Soybeans 1,000 bushels	Tobacco 1,000 pounds	All wheat 1,000 bushels
Alabama	—	34,100	418	1,152	2,360	2,085	47,150	—	24,860
Alaska	—	—	—	—	—	—	—	—	—
Arizona	4,085	4,550	1,613	1,216	—	1,456	—	—	21,844
Arkansas	—	3,185	620	1,806	2,160	—	99,000	—	67,650
California	40,320	35,750	3,500	7,851	3,600	20,886	—	—	107,085
Colorado	18,900	108,230	—	3,303	1,750	13,904	—	—	87,394
Connecticut[2]	—	—	—	175	—	486	—	5,175	—
Delaware	1,300	15,023	—	45	—	1,248	7,020	—	1,720
Florida	—	17,985	18	483	—	6,565	11,040	22,834	—
Georgia	—	69,000	165	1,021	4,500	—	41,420	120,960	46,010
Hawaii	—	—	—	—	—	—	—	—	—
Idaho	63,130	6,820	—	4,343	2,760	80,040	—	—	89,780
Illinois	—	1,452,540	—	3,501	13,530	525	354,540	—	92,500
Indiana	—	654,000	—	2,256	5,525	887	151,800	16,280	62,100
Iowa	—	1,739,900	—	8,224	59,520	270	330,075	—	4,485
Kansas	1,664	158,760	—	6,070	8,500	—	45,300	—	305,000
Kentucky	2,016	149,000	—	3,304	288	—	50,150	510,226	28,560
Louisiana	—	2,409	735	805	—	128	65,730	45	11,550
Maine[2]	—	—	—	401	3,010	26,520	—	—	—
Maryland	5,040	72,450	—	551	1,100	312	11,100	29,900	5,617
Massachusetts[2]	—	—	—	278	—	743	—	1,818	—
Michigan	1,352	273,600	—	3,894	21,080	8,503	29,100	—	41,500
Minnesota	57,680	744,700	—	8,206	90,090	14,947	145,200	—	144,025
Mississippi	—	6,440	1,570	1,249	—	—	75,600	—	24,000
Missouri	—	213,400	161	6,750	4,590	—	159,075	6,580	115,500
Montana	56,760	850	—	4,808	4,840	1,739	—	—	172,830
Nebraska	897	802,700	—	7,165	15,405	2,472	82,680	—	106,200
Nevada	1,650	—	1.4	1,046	—	3,460	—	—	1,850
New Hampshire[2]	—	—	—	201	—	—	—	—	—
New Jersey	1,037	12,375	—	276	385	2,066	4,872	—	2,352
New Mexico	1,876	9,000	127	1,256	—	945	—	—	9,000
New York	—	74,400	—	5,273	17,920	12,240	—	—	7,040
North Carolina	3,410	140,910	94	636	4,399	2,542	47,000	793,315	15,990
North Dakota	105,600	41,553	—	4,761	44,160	20,125	6,440	—	331,700
Ohio	—	360,000	—	3,473	17,010	2,073	99,750	21,760	72,600
Oklahoma	1,550	3,850	410	3,307	3,780	—	6,480	—	172,800
Oregon	11,700	2,750	—	2,886	4,550	21,710	—	—	77,380
Pennsylvania	4,104	134,400	—	4,535	20,010	5,250	3,100	25,160	9,720
Rhode Island[2]	—	—	—	19	—	800	—	—	—
South Carolina	1,161	33,060	165	414	2,208	—	32,550	149,580	14,350
South Dakota	20,060	180,600	—	5,786	70,520	702	23,100	—	88,970
Tennessee	—	55,040	315	2,078	816	279	61,100	161,119	37,400
Texas	2,100	127,530	5,820	6,959	18,860	2,381	10,560	—	183,400
Utah	9,834	1,650	—	2,186	798	1,276	—	—	8,856
Vermont[2]		—	—	973	—	147	—	—	—
Virginia	5,917	56,250	0.4	1,640	940	2,320	17,145	155,139	17,160
Washington	44,080	12,875	—	2,542	1,600	52,380	—	—	168,350
West Virginia	550	6,256	—	817	618	—	—	2,250	360
Wisconsin	1,550	378,000	—	11,055	52,606	18,190	12,375	26,071	5,518
Wyoming	8,978	5,060	—	2,129	2,295	1,060	—	—	8,430
Total U.S.	**478,301**	**8,200,951**	**15,733**	**143,105**	**508,083**	**333,682**	**2,030,452**	**2,048,211**	**2,793,436**

(1) Equiv. to 480 lbs. (2) All harvested corn acreage is for silage.

Production of Chief U.S. Crops

Source: Economics, Statistics, and Cooperatives Service: U.S. Agriculture Department

Year	Corn for grain 1,000 bushels	Oats 1,000 bushels	Barley 1,000 bushels	Sorghums for grain 1,000 bushels	All wheat 1,000 bushels	Rye 1,000 bushels	Flax-seed 1,000 bushels	Cotton lint 1,000 bales	Cotton seed 1,000 tons
1970 . .	4,152,243	915,236	416,091	683,179	1,351,558	36,840	29,416	10,192	4,068
1975 . .	5,828,961	642,042	374,386	753,046	2,122,459	15,958	15,553	8,302	3,218
1977 . .	6,425,457	750,901	420,159	792,983	2,036,318	17,312	15,105	14,389	5,521
1978 . .	7,267,927	581,657	454,759	731,270	1,775,524	24,065	8,614	10,855	4,269
1979 . .	7,938,819	526,551	382,798	808,862	2,134,060	22,389	12,014	14,629	5,778
1980 . .	6,644,841	458,263	360,956	579,197	2,374,306	16,483	7,928	11,122	4,470
1981 . .	8,200,951	508,083	478,301	880,266	2,793,436	18,621	7,799	15,733	6,254

Year	Tobacco 1,000 lbs.	All hay 1,000 tons	Beans dry edible 1,000 cwt.	Peas dry edible 1,000 cwt.	Peanuts 1,000 lbs.	Soy-beans 1,000 bushels	Pota-toes 1,000 cwt.	Sweet pota-toes 1,000 cwt.
1970	1,906,453	126,969	17,399	3,315	2,983,121	1,127,100	325,716	13,164
1975	2,181,775	132,210	17,442	2,731	3,857,122	1,547,383	322,254	13,225
1977	1,912,759	131,313	16,610	1,023	3,726,015	1,761,755	354,576	12,395
1978	2,024,820	143,817	18,935	3,601	3,952,384	1,868,754	366,314	13,115
1979	1,526,549	147,847	20,476	2,039	3,968,485	2,267,901	342,497	13,370
1980	1,786,192	131,027	26,395	3,285	2,307,847	1,792,062	302,857	10,953
1981	2,048,211	143,105	31,814	2,290	3,948,985	2,030,452	333,682	12,622

Year	Five seed crops* 1,000 lbs.	Sugar and seed 1,000 tons	Sugar beets 1,000 tons	[1]Pecans million lbs.	Al-monds million lbs.	[1]Wal-nuts 1,000 tons	[1]Fil-berts 1,000 tons	Oranges** 1,000 boxes	Grape-fruit** 1,000 boxes
1970	251,934	23,996	26,378	77.6	124.0	111.8	9.3	189,970	53,910
1975	161,609	28,344	29,704	124.2	160.0	199.3	12.1	243,060	61,610
1977	139,101	26,830	25,007	118.3	156.5	192.5	11.8	248,720	74,600
1978	143,817	25,997	25,788	249.9	82.1	160	14.1	225,320	74,660
1979	147,847	26,532	21,996	210.6	376.0	208	13.0	216,000	67,380
1980	131,070	26,963	23,502	183.5	322.0	197	15.4	280,010	73,200
1981	159,195	27,408	27,271	339.1	407.0	225	14.7	251,140	67,860

*Fine seed crops include alfalfa, red clover, lespedeza, and timothy. **Crop year ending in year cited. (1) In shells.

Harvested Acreage of Principal U.S. Crops

Source: Economics, Statistics, and Cooperatives Service: U.S. Agriculture Department (thousands of acres)

State	1979	1980	1981	State	1979	1980	1981
Alabama	4,136	4,096	4,665	Nevada	562	571	534
Arizona	1,083	1,194	1,227	New Hampshire	116	118	117
Arkansas	8,333	8,398	9,658	New Jersey.	549	541	546
California	6,455	6,662	6,890	New Mexico	1,323	1,383	1,371
Colorado	6,262	6,928	6,669	New York.	4,311	4,331	4,240
Connecticut.	144	145	146	North Carolina	5,263	5,414	5,620
Delaware	519	526	547	North Dakota.	20,726	18,350	22,926
Florida.	1,537	1,522	1,549	Ohio	11,023	11,041	10,898
Georgia	5,374	5,635	6,391	Oklahoma	9,630	9,969	10,020
Hawaii.	108	105	106	Oregon	2,646	2,740	2,753
Idaho	4,594	4,681	4,918	Pennsylvania	4,496	4,564	4,648
Illinois	23,827	24,004	24,110	Rhode Island	18	18	18
Indiana	12,553	12,878	13,086	South Carolina	2,858	2,886	3,148
Iowa.	25,342	25,646	25,744	South Dakota.	15,121	14,898	15,812
Kansas	20,858	21,645	21,868	Tennessee	5,211	5,396	5,726
Kentucky	5,223	5,447	5,938	Texas	22,750	22,581	24,384
Louisiana	5,129	5,272	5,560	Utah.	1,149	1,144	1,127
Maine	411	405	407	Vermont.	544	549	540
Maryland	1,562	1,593	1,647	Virginia	2,849	3,009	3,165
Massachusetts.	162	164	164	Washington.	4,556	4,843	5,099
Michigan	6,909	7,086	7,369	West Virginia	714	721	755
Minnesota.	21,653	21,831	22,277	Wisconsin.	9,476	9,559	9,524
Mississippi	6,404	6,403	6,702	Wyoming	1,853	1,860	1,860
Missouri.	14,338	14,624	14,786	**Total U.S.**	**337,686**	**340,893**	**356,265**
Montana	8,813	8,566	9,719				
Nebraska	18,213	18,951	19,291				

Crop acreages included are corn, sorghum, oats, barley, wheat, rice, rye, soybeans, flaxseed, peanuts, sunflower, popcorn, cotton, all hay dry edible beans, dry edible peas, potatoes, sweet potatoes, tobacco, sugarcane and sugar beets; harvested acreages for winter wheat, rye, al hay, tobacco and sugarcane are used in computing total planted acreage.

U.S. Farms by State—Number, Acreage, and Value

Source: Census of Agriculture, U.S. Bureau of the Census

State	Farms (Number)		Average size of farm (acres)		Value of land and buildings (per acre)		Percent of land area in farms	
	1974	1978	1974	1978	1974	1978	1974	1978
Alabama	56,678	57,503	209	201	$ 364	639	36.5	35.6
Alaska	291	383	5,612	3,359	42	109	0.5	0.4
Arizona	5,803	7,660	6,539	5,047	111	199	52.3	53.3
Arkansas	50,959	58,959	287	265	419	770	44.0	46.9
California	67,674	81,706	493	405	653	1,186	33.4	33.1
Colorado	25,501	29,633	1,408	1,197	188	322	54.1	53.4
Connecticut	3,421	4,560	129	110	1,525	2,227	14.1	16.1
Delaware	3,400	3,632	185	187	971	1,500	49.7	53.5
Florida	32,466	44,068	407	302	685	1,149	38.1	38.4
Georgia	54,911	58,648	253	234	474	777	37.3	37.0
Hawaii	3,020	4,310	702	461	485	897	51.5	48.3
Idaho	23,680	26,478	603	562	339	585	27.0	28.1
Illinois	111,049	109,924	262	270	846	1,858	81.5	83.3
Indiana	87,915	88,427	191	193	720	1,589	72.7	73.7
Iowa	126,104	126,456	262	266	719	1,550	92.3	93.8
Kansas	79,188	77,129	605	619	296	501	91.6	91.2
Kentucky	102,053	109,980	141	137	427	861	56.9	59.3
Louisiana	33,240	38,923	275	247	512	1,001	31.7	33.4
Maine	6,436	8,158	237	197	341	538	7.7	8.1
Maryland	15,163	18,727	174	145	1,060	1,800	39.1	41.6
Massachusetts	4,497	5,891	134	115	961	1,443	12.0	13.6
Michigan	64,094	68,237	169	168	553	975	29.8	31.5
Minnesota	98,537	102,963	280	279	429	901	54.4	56.5
Mississippi	53,620	54,182	267	256	379	681	47.2	45.8
Missouri	115,711	121,955	258	253	396	726	67.5	69.9
Montana	23,324	24,469	2,665	2,545	112	196	66.7	66.8
Nebraska	67,597	65,916	683	702	282	525	94.3	94.5
Nevada	2,076	2,877	5,209	3,641	85	191	15.4	14.9
New Hampshire	2,412	3,288	210	164	564	919	8.8	9.4
New Jersey	7,409	9,895	130	106	1,807	2,701	20.0	21.8
New Mexico	11,282	14,253	4,170	3,389	78	143	60.5	62.2
New York	43,682	49,273	215	201	510	670	30.7	32.4
North Carolina	91,280	89,367	123	127	590	1,051	36.0	36.3
North Dakota	42,710	41,169	992	1,021	195	347	95.6	94.8
Ohio	92,158	95,937	170	168	706	1,483	59.7	61.3
Oklahoma	69,719	79,388	475	433	302	512	75.2	78.0
Oregon	26,753	34,642	682	532	250	504	29.6	29.9
Pennsylvania	53,171	59,942	154	146	734	1,273	28.4	30.4
Rhode Island	597	866	102	86	1,500	2,370	9.1	11.1
South Carolina	29,275	33,430	211	189	467	773	31.9	32.7
South Dakota	42,825	39,665	1,074	1,123	145	256	94.6	91.6
Tennessee	93,659	97,036	140	136	467	860	49.5	49.7
Texas	174,068	194,253	771	708	243	386	80.0	82.0
Utah	12,184	13,833	871	760	188	400	20.2	20.0
Vermont	5,906	7,273	282	241	462	660	28.1	29.6
Virginia	52,699	56,869	184	175	558	930	38.0	39.1
Washington	29,410	37,730	567	451	350	692	39.1	39.9
West Virginia	16,909	20,532	207	188	300	592	22.7	25.1
Wisconsin	89,479	89,945	197	201	434	856	50.6	51.9
Wyoming	8,018	8,495	4,274	3,969	80	144	55.1	54.2
Total	**2,314,013**	**2,478,642**	**440**	**415**	**336**	**628**	**44.9**	**45.4**

Livestock on Farms in the U.S.

Source: Economics, Statistics, and Cooperatives Service: U.S. Agriculture Department (thousands)

Year (On Jan. 1)	All cattle	Milk cows	All sheep	Hogs	Horses* and mules
1890	60,014	15,000	44,518	48,130	18,054
1900	59,739	16,544	48,105	51,055	21,004
1910	58,993	19,450	50,239	48,072	24,211
1920	70,400	21,455	40,743	60,159	25,742
1925	63,373	22,575	38,543	55,770	22,569
1930	61,003	23,032	51,565	55,705	19,124
1935	68,846	26,082	51,808	39,066	16,683
1940	68,039	24,940	52,107	61,165	14,478
1945	85,573	27,770	46,520	59,373	11,950
1950	77,963	23,853	29,826	58,937	7,781
1955	96,592	23,462	31,582	50,474	4,309
1960	96,236	19,527	33,170	59,026	3,089
1965	109,000	[2]15,380	25,127	57,030	

Year (On Jan. 1)	All cattle	Milk cows	All sheep	Hogs
1970	112,369	12,091	20,423	[3]57,046
1971	114,578	11,909	19,731	[3]67,285
1972	117,862	11,776	18,739	[3]62,412
1973	121,539	11,622	17,641	[3]59,017
1974	127,788	11,297	16,310	[3]60,614
1975	132,028	11,220	14,515	[3]54,693
1976	127,980	11,071	13,311	[3]49,267
1977	122,810	10,998	12,722	[3]54,934
1978	116,375	10,896	12,421	[3]56,539
1979	110,864	10,790	12,365	[3]60,356
1980	111,192	10,779	12,687	[3]67,353
1981	114,321	10,860	12,936	[3]64,512
1982[1]	115,691	10,998	13,116	[3]58,691

*Discontinued in 1960. (1) Total estimated value on farms as of Jan. 1, 1982, was as follows (avg. value per head in parentheses): cattle and calves $47,978,582 ($415); sheep and lambs $746,520,000 ($56.90); hogs and pigs $4,115,148,000 ($70.10). (2) New series, milk cows and heifers that have calved, beginning 1965. (3) As of Dec. 1 of preceding year.

Wool Production

Source: Economic Research Service: U.S. Agriculture Department

	Sheep shorn (1,000)	Shorn wool (1,000 lbs.)	Value ($1,000)	Price per lb. (cents)	Pulled wool (1,000 lbs.)	Total wool (1,000 lbs)
1970	19,163	161,587	57,162	35.4	15,200	176,787
1975	14,403	119,535	53,505	44.8	6,000	125,535
1976	13,536	111,100	73,332	66.0	4,850	115,950
1977	13,217	107,328	77,276	72.0	2,450	109,778
1978	12,719	102,942	76,690	74.5	1,000	103,942
1979	13,068	104,860	90,531	86.3	900	105,760
1980	13,249	105,452	92,862	88.1	1,050	106,502
1981	13,484	109,753	103,744	94.5	1,150	110,903

U.S. Meat and Lard Production and Consumption

Source: Economic Research Service: U.S. Agriculture Department (million lbs.)

	Beef		Veal		Lamb and mutton		Pork (exclud. lard)		All meats		Lard	
Year	Production	Consumption	Production	Consumption	Production	Consumption	Production	Consumption	Production	Consumption	Production	Consumption
1940	7,175	7,257	981	981	876	873	10,044	9,701	19,076	18,812	2,288	1,901
1950	9,534	9,529	1,230	1,206	597	596	10,714	10,390	22,075	21,721	2,631	1,891
1960	14,753	15,147	1,109	1,093	768	852	13,905	13,838	30,535	30,930	2,562	1,358
1970	21,685	22,926	588	581	551	657	14,699	14,661	37,523	38,825	1,913	939
1975	23,976	25,398	873	876	410	430	11,779	11,852	37,038	38,556	1,012	615
1980	21,664	23,321	400	412	318	350	16,615	16,562	38,979	40,645	1,207	540
1981	22,389	23,756	435	437	338	361	15,873	15,927	39,035	40,483	1,158	572

Grain Receipts at U.S. Grain Centers

Source: Chicago Board of Trade Marketing Information Department (thousands bushels)

1981	Wheat	Corn	Oats	Rye	Barley	Soybeans	Total
Chicago	16,603	90,705	3	—	4	13,002	117,323
Duluth*	—	—	—	—	—	—	—
Enid*	—	—	—	—	—	—	—
Hutchinson*	—	—	—	—	—	—	—
Indianapolis	—	—	—	—	—	—	—
Kansas	63,725	48,530	25,280	—	3	9,627	145,165
Milwaukee	3,051	44,950	33	—	17,595	962	66,593
Minneapolis	137,665	19,153	16,557	2,254	69,275	401	245,305
Omaha	36,564	55,664	1,628	—	—	9,833	103,689
Peoria	175	9,635	—	—	—	39	9,849
Sioux City	—	156	768	—	—	154	1,078
St. Joseph	1,988	6,482	1,092	—	—	388	9,950
St. Louis	—	24,228	—	—	—	—	24,228
Toledo	29,019	111,054	2,203	—	—	45,884	188,160
Witchita	27,984	236	—	—	174	1,190	29,584
Total	**316,774**	**410,793**	**47,564**	**2,254**	**87,051**	**79,480**	**940,924**

*Not available

Grain Storage Capacity at Principal Grain Centers in U.S.

Source: Chicago Board of Trade Marketing Information Department (bushels)

Cities	Capacity	Cities	Capacity
Atlantic Coast	36,800,000	Texas High Plains	76,800,000
Great Lakes		Enid	66,100,000
Toledo	4,330,000	Gulf Points	
Buffalo	8,200,000	South Mississippi	43,600,000
Chicago	48,835,000	North Texas Gulf	28,200,000
Milwaukee	9,100,000	South Texas Gulf	14,000,000
Duluth	75,800,000	Plains	
River Points		Wichita	60,300,000
Minneapolis	124,200,000	Topeka	61,600,000
Peoria	6,600,000	Salina	45,000,000
St. Louis	25,500,000	Hutchinson	42,000,000
Sioux City	11,600,000	Hastings-Grand Island	24,100,000
Omaha-Council Bluffs	35,300,000	Lincoln	39,600,000
Atchison	24,500,000	Pacific N.W.	
St. Joseph	20,600,000	Puget Sound	9,500,000
Kansas City, Mo.	72,400,000	Portland	24,900,000
Southwest		California Ports	14,300,000
Fort Worth	57,600,000		

Atlantic Coast — Albany, N.Y., Philadelphia, Pa., Baltimore, Md., Norfolk, Va. **Gulf Points** — New Orleans, Baton Rouge, Ama. Belle Chase, La., Mobile, Ala. **North Texas Gulf** — Houston, Galveston, Beaumont, Port Arthur, Texas. **South Texas Gulf** — Corpus Christi, Brownsville, Texas. **Pacific N.W.** — Seattle, Tacoma, Wash., Portland, Oreg., Columbia River **Calif. Ports** — San Francisco, Stockton, Sacramento, Los Angeles. **Texas High Plains** — Amarillo, Lubbock, Hereford, Plainview, Texas.

U.S. Egg Production

Source: Economic Research Service: U.S. Agriculture Department (millions of eggs)

State	1978	1979	1980	1981	State	1978	1979	1980	1981	State	1978	1979	1980	1981
Ala.	3,329	3,300	3,354	3,095	La.	603	601	553	510	Oh.	2,140	2,253	2,333	2,431
Alas.	4.7	6.7	4.4	6.7	Me.	1,912	1,913	1,793	1,607	Okla.	612	754	839	839
Ariz.	135	139	113	98	Md.	344	356	381	547	Ore.	563	616	638	665
Ark.	4,002	4,123	4,153	3,996	Mass.	341	339	326	321	Pa.	3,436	3,836	4,251	4,268
Cal.	8,412	8,713	8,796	8,400	Mich.	1,497	1,491	1,459	1,541	R.I.	51.0	59.2	84	88
Col.	534	484	464	552	Minn.	2,189	2,183	2,223	2,355	S.C.	1,411	1,561	1,679	1,613
Conn.	897	938	1,004	990	Miss.	1,696	1,653	1,584	1,717	S.D.	526	476	464	461
Del.	129	132	138	175	Mo.	1,320	1,376	1,460	1,431	Tenn.	974	999	962	922
Fla.	2,954	3,189	3,044	2,802	Mont.	193	[1]178	170	174	Tex.	2,630	2,795	3,092	3,224
Ga.	5,662	6,067	5,637	5,578	Neb.	780	802	847	802	Ut.	395	385	416	459
Ha.	218	229	222	221.3	Nev.	2.3	1.8	1.8	1.8	Vt.	110	99	100	81
Ida.	206	[1]192	202	228	N.H.	222	218	182	157	Va.	885	939	913	947
Ill.	1,380	1,347	1,267	1,262	N.J.	375	342	279	291	Wash.	1,121	1,172	1,295	1,332
Ind.	3,447	3,536	3,697	4,093	N.M.	359	368	378	347	W.Vir.	154	178	149	155
Ia.	1,914	1,849	1,784	1,920	N.Y.	1,845	1,767	1,776	1,858	Wis.	973	911	946	951
Kan.	511	483	427	416	N.C.	3,081	3,155	3,174	3,078	Wyo.	14.4	10.8	10.5	8.1
Ky.	553	583	536	509	N.D.	115	111	82	80	**Total**	**67,157**	**69,209**	**69,683**	**69,603**

Note: The egg and chicken production year runs from Dec. 1 of the previous year through Nov. 30. (1) Included are eggs destroyed because of possible PCB contamination.

Net Income per Farm by States

Source: Economic Research Service, U.S. Agriculture Department (dollars)

State	1978	1979	1980	State	1978	1979	1980
Alabama	9,563	10,115	4,426	Nebraska	9,409	14,098	1,987
Alaska	7,249	4,261	-4,680	Nevada	6,923	16,078	14,266
Arizona	54,894	64,644	56,180	New Hampshire	4,736	3,552	618
Arkansas	16,304	17,726	8,697	New Jersey	8,962	8,400	3,634
California	35,805	45,464	42,335	New Mexico	14,893	17,093	12,137
Colorado	12,801	18,509	15,302	New York	7,962	9,702	7,909
Connecticut	16,573	11,593	10,049	North Carolina	12,856	12,221	11,170
Delaware	29,105	28,492	13,708	North Dakota	12,102	9,448	2,215
Florida	34,174	37,653	28,636	Ohio	6,000	8,605	4,755
Georgia	10,286	11,454	705	Oklahoma	4,279	11,036	4,989
Hawaii	35,533	38,334	33,431	Oregon	6,291	9,025	7,259
Idaho	15,041	14,374	18,780	Pennsylvania	8,827	12,192	9,204
Illinois	11,011	17,906	1,951	Rhode Island	10,468	6,704	4,521
Indiana	8,304	11,411	6,355	South Carolina	2,691	8,028	1,097
Iowa	15,831	13,106	4,659	South Dakota	10,685	13,480	4,980
Kansas	9,274	16,655	7,165	Tenneesse	3,219	3,888	968
Kentucky	7,453	9,194	7,462	Texas	6,564	12,070	6,712
Louisiana	10,856	14,183	8,415	Utah	7,152	7,577	5,266
Maine	12,935	11,211	1,578	Vermont	14,499	15,478	12,288
Maryland	11,440	12,170	5,633	Virginia	5,886	6,170	3,750
Massachusetts	15,721	13,279	10,012	Washington	20,245	16,781	19,147
Michigan	7,556	8,903	7,810	West Virginia	866	1,623	1,440
Minnesota	13,660	13,820	11,120	Wisconsin	10,688	15,465	14,554
Mississippi	10,368	12,416	4,934	Wyoming	6,212	8,531	2,177
Missouri	7,028	10,118	2,553	**Total. U.S.**	**10,860**	**13,456**	**8,180**
Montana	11,190	4,209	4,595				

Note: Data based on the 1974 Census of Agriculture definition of a farm (sales of $1,000 or more).

Farm Income—Cash Receipts from Marketings

Source: Economic Research Service: U.S. Agriculture Department ($1,000)

1981 State	Crops	Live-stock	Gov't pay'ts	Total	1981 State	Crops	Live-stock	Gov't pay'ts	Total
Alabama	946,933	1,263,888	21,362	2,210,821	Nebraska	2,855,229	3,520,799	101,019	6,376,028
Alaska	8,122	4,928	352	13,050	Nevada	80,625	133,245	3,742	213,870
Arizona	979,223	727,354	5,860	1,706,577	New Hampshire	26,706	70,510	714	97,216
Arkansas	1,825,112	1,611,497	40,125	3,436,609	New Jersey	353,081	106,229	1,465	459,310
California	9,682,353	4,220,808	23,368	13,903,161	New Mexico	300,579	542,388	25,961	842,967
Colorado	1,072,942	2,012,335	47,597	3,085,277	New York	844,702	1,876,071	6,910	2,720,773
Connecticut	142,071	186,037	395	328,108	North Carolina	2,650,855	1,585,435	15,547	4,236,290
Delaware	120,967	271,539	1,751	392,506	North Dakota	2,208,798	594,031	130,659	2,802,829
Florida	3,009,125	1,029,384	10,992	4,038,509	Ohio	2,018,507	1,428,635	24,089	3,447,142
Georgia	1,537,682	1,739,818	38,055	3,277,500	Oklahoma	1,046,825	1,831,799	124,474	2,878,624
Hawaii	383,386	88,171	716	471,557	Oregon	1,143,940	570,718	19,336	1,714,658
Idaho	1,322,020	956,202	29,495	2,278,222	Pennsylvania	758,011	2,147,612	11,878	2,905,623
Illinois	5,419,988	2,224,893	49,236	7,644,881	Rhode Island	19,556	14,154	156	33,710
Indiana	2,615,650	1,701,855	27,890	4,317,505	South Carolina	718,767	398,576	15,930	1,117,343
Iowa	4,989,996	5,725,464	58,170	10,715,460	South Dakota	923,889	1,865,430	90,724	2,789,319
Kansas	2,314,656	3,177,414	231,760	5,492,070	Tennessee	996,903	838,733	20,674	1,835,636
Kentucky	1,423,900	1,358,683	14,346	2,782,583	Texas	4,631,083	5,423,442	321,365	10,054,525
Louisiana	1,261,207	452,465	15,435	1,713,672	Utah	142,084	412,821	7,817	554,905
Maine	184,775	279,936	2,345	464,711	Vermont	30,284	365,645	1,562	395,929
Maryland	364,151	697,142	2,961	1,061,293	Virginia	732,582	911,026	10,818	1,643,608
Massachusetts	195,937	136,853	837	332,790	Washington	2,009,061	896,004	37,297	2,905,065
Michigan	1,678,160	1,111,057	17,263	2,789,217	West Virginia	53,642	163,449	2,988	217,091
Minnesota	3,521,641	3,390,413	79,121	6,912,054	Wisconsin	1,096,450	4,146,475	16,877	5,242,925
Mississippi	1,382,504	863,677	19,522	2,246,181	Wyoming	153,032	462,768	10,702	615,800
Missouri	1,910,100	2,313,920	105,401	4,224,020	**U.S.**	**74,941,988[1]**	**68,480,786[1]**	**1,932,190**	**143,422,774[1]**
Montana	854,196	629,058	65,131	1,483,254					

(1) Not official.

Average Prices Received by U.S. Farmers

Source: Statistical Reporting Service: U.S. Agriculture Department

The figures represent dollars per 100 lbs. for hogs, beef cattle, veal calves, sheep, lamb, and milk (wholesale), dollars per head for milk cows; cents per lb. for milk fat (in cream), chickens, broilers, turkeys, and wool; cents for eggs per dozen.

Weighted calendar year prices for livestock and livestock products other than wool. 1943 through 1963, wool prices are weighted on marketing year basis. The marketing year has been changed (1964) from a calendar year to a Dec.-Nov. basis for hogs, chickens, broilers and eggs.

Year	Hogs	Cattle (beef)	Calves (veal)	Sheep	Lambs	Cows (milk)	All Milk	Milk fat (in cream)	Chickens (excl. broilers)	Broilers	Turkeys	Eggs	Wool
1930	8.84	7.71	9.68	4.74	7.76	74	2.21	34.5	...	...	20.2	23.7	19.5
1940	5.39	7.56	8.83	3.95	8.10	61	1.82	28.0	13.0	17.3	15.2	18.0	28.4
1950	18.00	23.30	26.30	11.60	25.10	198	3.89	62.0	22.0	27.4	32.9	36.3	62.1
1960	15.30	20.40	22.90	5.61	17.90	223	4.21	60.5	12.2	16.9	25.4	36.1	42.0
1970	22.70	27.10	34.50	7.51	26.40	332	5.71	70.0	9.1	13.6	22.6	39.1	35.5
1975	46.10	32.20	27.20	11.30	42.10	412	8.75	71.0	9.9	26.3	34.8	52.5	44.7
1978	46.60	48.50	59.10	21.80	62.80	675	10.60	102.0	12.4	26.3	43.6	52.2	74.5
1979	41.80	66.10	88.70	26.30	66.70	1,040	12.00	119.0	14.4	25.9	41.1	58.3	86.3
1980	38.00	62.40	76.80	21.10	63.60	1,190	13.00	—	11.0	27.7	41.3	56.3	88.1
1981	43.90	58.60	64.00	21.20	54.90	1,200	13.80	—	11.1	28.5	38.2	63.1	94.5

The figures represent cents per lb. for cotton, apples, and peanuts; dollars per bushel for oats, wheat, corn, barley, and soybeans; dollars per 100 lbs. for rice, sorghum, and potatoes; dollars per ton for cottonseed and baled hay.

Weighted crop year prices. Crop years are as follows: apples, June-May; wheat, oats, barley, hay and potatoes, July-June; cotton, rice, peanuts and cottonseed, August-July; soybeans, September-August; and corn and sorghum grain, October-September.

Crop year	Corn	Wheat	Upland cotton[1]	Oats	Barley	Rice	Soybeans	Sorghum	Peanuts	Cotton-seed	Hay	Potatoes	Apples
1930	.663	.550	9.46	0.31	.420	1.74	1.34	1.02	3.46	22.00	11.00	1.47	...
1940	.674	.601	9.83	0.30	.393	1.80	.892	.873	3.33	21.70	9.78	.850	...
1950	2.00	1.52	39.90	0.79	1.19	5.09	2.47	1.88	10.9	86.60	21.10	1.50	...
1960	1.74	.997	30.08	0.60	.838	4.55	2.13	1.49	10.0	42.50	21.70	2.00	4.79
1970	1.33	1.33	22.81	0.62	.973	5.17	2.85	2.04	12.8	56.50	26.10	1.21	6.97
1975	2.54	3.55	51.10	1.45	2.42	8.35	4.92	4.21	19.6	97.00	52.10	4.48	8.80
1978	2.25	2.97	58.10	1.20	1.92	8.16	6.66	3.59	21.1	114.00	49.80	3.38	13.90
1979	2.52	3.78	63.1	1.36	2.29	10.50	6.28	4.18	20.6	121.00	59.50	3.43	15.40
1980	3.11	3.91	74.4	1.79	2.85	12.80	7.57	5.25	25.1	129.00	71.00	6.55	12.1
1981	2.48	3.65	54.5	1.91	2.52	9.05	6.08	4.18	26.8	87.50	67.10	5.40	15.6

(1) Beginning 1964, 480 lb. net weight bales. (2) Series discontinued in 1980.

Index Numbers of Prices Received by Farmers

Source: Statistical Reporting Service; U.S. Agriculture Department (index 1910-14=100 per cent)

Year	All farm products	All crops	Livestock	Food grains	Feed grains and hay	Cotton	Tobacco	Oil-bearing crops	Fruit	Commercial vegetables	Potatoes sweetpot.[1]	Meat animals	Dairy products	Poultry and eggs
1910	104	105	102	109	96	118	84	120	100	...	83	101	100	104
1920	211	235	190	249	202	262	233	208	188	...	294	171	202	222
1930	125	115	134	93	106	104	140	111	149	128	162	133	142	128
1940	100	90	109	84	85	83	134	103	81	122	89	108	120	98
1950	258	233	280	224	193	282	402	276	194	211	166	340	249	186
1960	239	222	253	203	152	254	500	214	244	230	203	296	259	160
1970	274	225	325	162	179	183	604	265	217	292	218	405	350	147
1975	463	452	474	426	400	348	899	529	313	458	391	567	537	235
1980	614	539	691	452	417	583	1,219	664	458	562	469	878	798	254
1981	633	580	688	456	446	565	1,363	718	477	676	647	848	842	264

Ratio of prices[2] received to prices paid by farmers

Year	ratio
1968	79
1969	79
1970	77
1971	75
1972	79
1973	94
1975	76
1978	72
1980	65
1981	62

(1) Including dry edible beans. (2) Ratio of the index prices received by farmers, adjusted to reflect government payments to the index of prices paid, for commodities and services, interest, taxes and wage rates.

Food Stamps—Costs and Benefits

Fiscal year	Average persons participating per month	Value per year: Total purchase	Value per year: Bonus	Avg. bonus per participant per month
1962	142,817	$ 35,202,266	$ 13,152,695	7.67
1965	424,652	85,471,989	32,505,096	6.38
1970	4,340,030	1,089,960,761	549,663,811	10.55
1975	17,064,196	7,265,641,706	4,385,501,248	21.41
1979	17,669,985	7,223,375,000	6,478,066,000	30.55
1980	21,072,566	NA[1]	8,686,098,335	34.35
1981	22,430,562	NA[1]	10,629,972,724	39.49

(p) preliminary. (1) Not Applicable. The elimination of the purchase requirement began January 1979. The Food Stamp Program enables low-income families to buy more food of greater variety to improve their diets. If a household meets eligibility requirements it receives food stamps based on its net income and the number of people in the household. Over the past few years major reform measures went into effect. These include changes in the allowable deductions; eliminate the food stamp purchase requirement; streamline administration; and reduce the potential for fraud or abuse. County and city welfare departments administer the program locally.

Government Payments by Programs, by States

Source: Economic Research Service: U.S. Agriculture Department ($1,000)

1981 State	Conser-vation[1]	Feed grain program	Wheat program	Cotton program	Rice program	Drought & flood program	Misc. program[2]	Total
Alabama	5,431	1,405	1,908	2,000	0	0	10,618	21,362
Alaska	202	133	1	0	0	0	16	352
Arizona	2,706	339	1,748	83	0	0	984	5,860
Arkansas	3,643	808	10,168	6,355	125	0	19,026	40,125
California	5,733	3,710	9,505	145	1	0	4,274	23,368
Colorado	5,522	3,332	21,719	0	0	0	17,024	47,597
Connecticut	362	1	1	0	0	0	31	395
Delaware	239	814	265	0	0	0	433	1,751
Florida	3,635	3,118	233	20	0	0	3,986	10,992
Georgia	4,887	9,226	5,163	3,364	0	1	15,414	38,055
Hawaii	577	0	0	0	0	0	139	716
Idaho	2,535	7,741	13,068	0	0	2	6,149	29,495
Illinois	6,648	14,329	11,284	0	0	0	16,975	49,236
Indiana	4,547	9,392	7,566	0	0	0	6,385	27,890
Iowa	7,523	11,730	972	0	0	0	37,945	58,170
Kansas	5,136	22,630	147,924	0	0	0	56,070	231,760
Kentucky	4,857	4,773	3,383	0	0	0	1,333	14,346
Louisiana	3,172	168	1,303	5,247	793	0	4,752	15,435
Maine	2,111	3	3	0	0	0	228	2,345
Maryland	866	614	684	0	0	0	797	2,961
Massachusetts	577	8	0	0	0	0	252	837
Michigan	4,476	2,457	4,117	0	0	0	6,213	17,263
Minnesota	6,015	13,051	22,941	0	0	0	37,114	79,121
Mississippi	4,671	234	3,076	5,876	85	0	5,580	19,522
Missouri	6,865	19,897	31,241	5,403	1	0	41,994	105,401
Montana	5,572	9,801	38,980	0	0	0	30,778	85,131
Nebraska	4,927	16,260	20,975	0	0	0	58,857	101,019
Nevada	806	401	252	0	0	0	2,283	3,742
New Hampshire	619	0	0	0	0	0	95	714
New Jersey	592	452	217	0	0	0	204	1,465
New Mexico	2,660	2,615	7,446	2,777	0	0	10,463	25,961
New York	4,334	296	877	0	0	0	1,403	6,910
North Carolina	4,105	4,038	3,874	282	0	0	3,248	15,547
North Dakota	3,563	14,539	67,796	0	0	0	44,761	130,659
Ohio	4,881	7,724	8,102	0	0	0	3,382	24,089
Oklahoma	5,133	1,435	61,365	15,931	0	0	40,610	124,474
Oregon	3,599	1,203	9,517	0	0	0	5,017	19,336
Pennsylvania	4,159	4,383	771	0	0	0	2,565	11,878
Rhode Island	107	0	0	0	0	0	49	156
South Carolina	2,718	5,010	2,280	1,051	0	0	4,871	15,930
South Dakota	3,563	18,326	25,955	0	0	0	42,880	90,724
Tennessee	4,243	1,945	4,196	2,753	0	0	7,537	20,674
Texas	15,445	14,593	48,744	170,676	746	4	71,157	321,365
Utah	3,231	872	1,121	0	0	0	2,593	7,817
Vermont	1,085	18	3	0	0	0	456	1,562
Virginia	2,846	1,083	1,751	1	0	0	5,137	10,818
Washington	5,163	5,467	19,593	0	0	0	7,074	37,297
West Virginia	2,009	61	29	0	0	0	889	2,988
Wisconsin	5,598	1,933	627	0	0	0	8,719	16,877
Wyoming	1,691	582	1,804	0	0	0	6,625	10,702
Total	**185,585**	**242,950**	**624,548**	**221,964**	**1,751**	**7**	**655,385**	**1,932,190**

(1) Includes amounts paid under Agricultural and Conservation Programs. (2) Includes Sugar Act, National Wool Act, Milk Indemnity Program, Beekeepers Indemnity Program, Hay and Cattle Transportation Program, Cropland Adjustment Program, Forest Incentive Program, Water Bank Program, Emergency Livestock Feed Program, Great Plains and other miscellaneous programs.

Farm Employment—Annual Averages

Source: Economic Research Service: U.S. Agriculture Department (Index 1910-14=100 per cent)

Year	Total Aver. no. (1,000)	Total Index %	Family Aver. no. (1,000)	Family Index %	Hired Aver. no. (1,000)	Hired Index %
1920	13,432	99	10,041	99	3,391	100
1930	12,497	92	9,307	92	3,190	94
1940	10,979	82	8,300	81	2,679	79
1950	9,926	75	7,597	73	2,329	69
1960	7,057	52	5,172	52	1,885	55
1970	4,523	34	3,348	33	1,175	35
1979	3,774	28	2,501	25	1,273	37
1980	3,705	27	2,402	24	1,303	35

Average Farm Wages

Source: Economic Research Service, U.S. Agriculture Department

(dollars per hour)

Method of pay:	1978	1979	1980
All hired farm workers	3.09	3.39	3.66
Paid by piece-rate	3.76	4.07	4.61
Paid by other than piece-rate	3.04	3.34	3.59
Paid by hour only[1]	3.08	3.38	3.63
Paid cash wages only[2]	3.22	3.58	3.82
Paid by hour cash wages only[3]	3.10	3.41	3.67
Type of work performed:			
Field and livestock workers	2.81	3.11	3.45
Packinghouse workers	3.18	3.39	3.63
Machine operators	3.13	3.44	3.70
Supervisors	4.95	5.22	5.59
Other agricultural workers	3.60	3.82	4.06
Indexes[4]			
(1910-14=100)	2,044	2,242	2,421
(1967=100)	241	265	286

(1) May include perquisites such as room and board, includes only those paid by the hour. (2) Does not include perquisites, includes all methods of pay. (3) Does not include perquisites, includes only those paid by the hour. (4) Indexes are based on all hired farm workers and are adjusted for seasonal variation.

Federal Food Program Costs

Source: Food and Nutrition Service, U.S. Agriculture Department (millions of dollars)

Calendar year	Food stamps Total value	Food stamps Bonus	Food distribution[2] WIC[1]	Food distribution[2] Needy persons[3]	Food distribution[2] Schools	Food distribution[2] Institutions	Child nutrition School lunch	Child nutrition School bkfst.	Child nutrition Child care	Child nutrition Summer food	Child nutrition Special milk	Total costs
1971	3,105	1,523	—	324	215	25	532	19	21	20	91	2,770
1975	8,325	4,386	89	75	354	20	1,259	86	49	50	123	6,491
1977	8,272	5,067	256	46	565	18	1,674	148	111	126	153	8,164
1978	8,347	5,165	386	65	624	29	1,825	178	134	107	142	8,655
1979	6,478	6,478	527	89	709	51	2,010	224	164	112	141	10,505
1980	8,685	8,686	712	101	938	71	2,307	289	214	113	152	13,583
1981(p.)	—	10,630	888	137	904	75	2,397	339	296	104	100	15,870

(1) Special Supplemental Food Program for Women, Infants, and Children. (2) Cost of food delivered to state distribution centers. (3) Represents costs of the Needy Family Program, Supplemental Food Program, and the Nutrition Program for the Elderly. (p) preliminary.

Consumption of Major Food Commodities per Person

Source: Economic Research Service: U.S. Agriculture Department

Commodity[1]	1970	1980	1981[2]
Meats	151.2	147.6	144.5
Beef	84.0	76.5	77.2
Veal	2.4	1.5	1.6
Lamb and mutton	2.9	1.3	1.4
Pork	61.9	68.3	64.3
Fish (edible weight)	11.8	12.8	13.0
Poultry products:			
Eggs	39.1	34.6	33.6
Chicken (ready-to-cook)	40.4	50.1	51.7
Turkey (ready-to-cook)	8.0	10.5	10.7
Dairy products:			
Cheese	11.5	17.6	18.0
Condensed and evaporated milk	7.1	3.8	3.9
Fluid milk and cream (product weight)	277	250	245
Ice cream (product weight)	17.6	17.3	17.2
Fats and Oils—Total fat content	52.6	56.5	57.3
Butter (actual weight)	5.3	4.5	4.3
Margarine (actual weight)	10.8	11.3	11.2
Lard	4.6	2.4	2.5
Shortening	17.3	18.2	18.5
Other edible fats and oils	17.7	22.7	23.5
Fruits:			
Fresh	78.9	85.7	87.3
Citrus	27.9	28.1	24.6
Noncitrus	51.0	57.6	62.7

Commodity[1]	1970	1980	1981[2]
Processed:			
Canned fruit	23.4	17.4	16.6
Canned juice	14.5	16.7	19.1
Frozen (including juices)	9.9	13.0	12.9
Chilled citrus juices	4.7	5.8	4.2
Dried	2.7	2.4	2.4
Vegetables:			
Fresh[3]	91.4	99.5	95.2
Canned (excluding potatoes and sweet potatoes)	51.1	49.8	45.9
Frozen (excluding potatoes)	9.6	10.4	11.3
Potatoes[4]	117.4	112.8	110.1
Sweet potatoes[4]	5.6	5.4	4.7
Grains:			
Wheat flour[5]	111	117	117
Rice	6.7	9.4	11.0
Other:			
Coffee	10.4	7.8	7.1
Tea	.7	.7	.8
Cocoa	3.1	2.6	2.9
Peanuts (shelled)	5.8	5.5	6.1
Dry edible beans	6.2	4.6	4.2
Melons	21.1	16.9	18.9
Sugar (refined)	101.7	83.7	79.4

(1) Quantity in pounds, retail weight unless otherwise shown. Data on calendar year basis except for dried fruits, fresh citrus fruits, peanuts, and rice which are on a crop-year basis, and eggs which are on a marketing year basis. Data are as of August 1982. (2) Preliminary. (3) Commercial production for sale as fresh produce. (4) Including fresh equivalent of processed. (5) White, whole wheat, and semolina flour including use in bakery products.

Farm-Real Estate Debt Outstanding by Lender Groups

Source: Economic Research Service, U.S. Agriculture Department

Jan. 1	Total farm-real estate debt[1]	Amounts held by principal lender groups: Federal land banks[1]	Farmers Home Administration[2]	Life insurance companies[3]	All commercial banks	Other[4]
	$1,000	$1,000	$1,000	$1,000	$1,000	$1,000
1955	8,245,278	1,279,787	378,108	2,051,784	1,161,308	3,374.291
1960	12,082,409	2,335,124	676,224	2,819,542	1,523,051	4,728,468
1965	18,894,240	3,686,755	1,284,913	4,287,671	2,416,634	7,218,267
1970	29,182,766	6,671,222	2,279,620	5,733,900	3,545,024	10,953,000
1975	46,288,419	13,402,441	3,214,657	6,297,400	5,966,282	17,407,639
1976	51,068,946	15,949,720	3,368,747	6,726,000	6,296,286	18,728,193
1977	56,559,645	18,454,578	3,657,467	7,400,200	6,781,410	20,265,990
1978	63,641,566	21,391,162	3,982,054	8,819,400	7,780,261	21,668,689
1979	70,832,679	24,619,184	4,121,038	10,478,200	8,556,542	23,057,715
1980	82,677,505	29,641,784	7,110,613	12,165,300	8,623,281	25,136,527
1981	92,017,878	35,944,492	7,714,928	12,927,800	8,745,242	26,685,416
1982	102,045,484	43,563,819	8,744,181	13,100,252	8,387,232	28,250,000

(1) Includes data for joint stock land banks and Federal Farm Mortgage Corporations. (2) Includes loans made directly by FmHA fo farm ownership, soil and water loans to individuals, recreation loans to individuals, Indian tribe land acquisition, grazing associations, anc irrigation drainage and soil conservation associations. Also includes loans for rural housing on farm tracts and labor housing. (3) Taker from Life Insurance Institute Tally sheet. (4) Estimated by ERS, USDA.

Giant Trees of the U.S.

Source: The American Forestry Association

There are approximately 679 different species of trees native to the continental U.S., including a few imports that have become naturalized to the extent of reproducing themselves in the wild state.

The oldest living trees in the world are reputed to be the bristlecone pines, the majority of which are found growing on the arid crags of California's White Mts. Some of them are estimated to be more than 4,600 years old. The largest known bristlecone pine is the "Patriarch," believed to be 1,500 years old. The oldest known redwoods are about 3,500 years old.

Recognition as the National Champion of each species is determined by total mass of each tree, based on this formula: the circumference in inches as measured at a point 4 1/2 feet above the ground plus the total height of the tree in feet plus 1/4 of the average crown spread in feet. Trees are compared on the basis of this formula. Trees within five points of each other are declared co-champions. The Giant Sequoia champion has the largest circumference, 83 ft. 2 in., Gallberry Holly the smallest, 5 in. Following is a small selection of the 661 trees registered with the American Forestry Assn.

(Figure in parentheses is year of most recent measurement)

Species	Height (ft.)	Location
Acacia, Koa (1969)	140	Kau, Ha.
Ailanthus, Tree-of-Heaven (1972)	60	Long Island, N.Y.
Alder, European (1974)	68	Princeton, Ill.
Apple, Southern Crab (1981)	35.5	Swannanoa, N.C.
Ash, Blue (1970)	86	Danville, Ky.
Aspen, Bigtooth (1979)	92	Rocky, Md.
Bald Cypress, Common (1981)	83	St. Francisville, La.
Basswood, American (1971)	115	Grand Traverse Co. Mich.
Bayberry, Pacific (1972)	38	Siuslaw Natl. Forest, Ore.
Beech, American (1976)	161	Three Oaks, Mich.
Birch, River	92	Anne Arundel, Md.
Birch, Yellow (1978)	107	Huron Mtn. Club, Mich.
Birch, Yellow (1973)	114	Gould City, Mich.
Blackbead, Catclaw (1976)	88	Sarasota, Fla.
Blackhaw, Rusty (1961)	25	nr. Washington, Ark.
Bladdernut, American (1972)	36	nr. Utica, Mich.
Boxelder (1976)	110	Lenawee Co., Mich.
Buckeye, Painted (1972)	144	Union County, Ga.
Buckthorn, Cascara (1977)	37	Seaside, Ore.
Buckthorn (1977)	35	Coos County, Ore.
Buckwheat tree (1981)	44	Wash. County, Fla.
Buffaloberry, Silver (1975)	22	Malheur Co., Ore.
Bumelia, Gum (1977)	80	Robertson Co., Tex.
Butternut (1973)	102	Portland, Ore.
Buttonbush, Common (1977)	23	nr. High Springs, Fla.
Cajeput (1975)	66	Sarasota, Fla.
Camphor-tree (1977)	72	Hardee Co., Fla.
Casuarina, Horsetail (1968)	89	Olowalo, Maui, Ha.
Catalpa, Northern (1972)	94	Lansing, Mich.
Cedar, Port-Orford (1972)	219	Siskiyou Natl. Forest, Ore.
Cercocarpus, Birchleaf (1972)	34	Central Point, Ore.
Cherry, Black (1980)	132	Washtenaw Co., Mich.
Chestnut, American (1979)	82	Oregon City, Ore.
Chinaberry (1967)	75	Koahe, So. Kuona, Ha.
Chinkapin, Giant (1979)	75	Cottage Grove, Ore.
Chokecherry, Common (1972)	66	Ada, Mich.
Coconut (1979)	92.5	Hilo, Ha.
Coffeetree, Kentucky (1976)	110	Van Buren Co., Mich.
Cottonwood, Black (1981)	148	Rainbow Falls St. Park, Wash.
Cypress, Monterey (1975)	97	Brookings, Ore.
Dahoon (1975)	72	Osceola For., Fla.
Desert Willow (1976)	56	Gila Co., Ariz.
Devil's-walkingstick (1976)	51	San Felasco Hammock, Fla.
Devilwood (1972)	37	Mayo, Fla.
Dogwood, Pacific (1975)	50	nr. Clatskanie, Ore.
Douglas Fir (1972)	221	Olympic Natl. Pk., Wash.
Doveplum (1965)	45	Miami, Fla.
False-Mastic (1975)	70	Lignumvitae Key, Fla.
Fig, Florida Strangler (1973)	80	Old Cutler Hammock, Fla.
Fir, Noble (1972)	278	Gifford Pinchot Natl. Forest, Wash.
Gumbo-limbo (1973)	50	Homestead, Fla.
Hackberry, Common (1972)	118	Allegan Co., Mich.
Hawthorn, Scarlet, (1967)	50	Glenview, Ill.
Hemlock, Western (1978)	195	Tillamook, Ore.
Hercules-club (1961)	38	Little Rock, Ark.
Hickory, Pignut (1972)	125	nr. Brunswick, Ga.
Holly, American (1979)	99	Congaree Swamp, S.C.
Honeylocust, Thornless (1976)	130	Washtenaw Co., Mich.
Hophornbeam, Eastern (1976)	73	Traverse Co., Mich.
Hoptree, Common (1972)	31	Ada, Mich.
Hornbeam, American (1975)	65	Milton, N.Y.
Joshua-tree (1967)	32	San Bernardino Natl. Forest, Cal.
Juniper, Western (1954)	87	Stanislaus Natl. Forest, Cal.
Larch, Western (1980)	175	Libby, Mont.
Laurelcherry, Carolina (1972)	44	Dellwood, Fla.
Lebbek (1968)	65	Lahaina, Maui, Ha.
Loblolly-Bay (1972)	84	Ocala Natl. Forest, Fla.
Locust, Black (1974)	96	Dansville, N.Y.
Lysiloma, Bahama (1973)	79	Homestead, Fla.
Madrone, Pacific (1974)	79	Humboldt Co., Cal.
Magnolia, Cucumber tree (1979)	94	North Canton, Oh.
Mangrove, Red (1975)	75	Everglades Natl. Pk., Fla.
Maple, Red (1972)	125	nr. Armada, Mich.
Mesquite, Velvet (1952)	55	Coronado Natl. Forest, Ariz.
Mountain-Ash, Showy (1972)	58	nr. Gould City, Mich.
Mountain-Laurel (1981)	28	Oconee County, S.C.
Mulberry, White (1976)	82	Battle Creek, Mich.
Oak, Pin (1978)	134	Smithland, Ky.
Oak, Scarlet (1978)	150	Maud, Ala.
Osage-Orange (1972)	51	Charlotte Co., Va.
Palmetto, Cabbage (1978)	90	Highlands Hammock State Pk., Fla.
Paloverde, Blue (1976)	53	Riverside Co., Cal.
Paulownia, Royal (1969)	105	Philadelphia, Pa.
Pawpaw, Common (1981)	56	Pickens County, S.C.
Pear (1976)	57	Clawson, Mich.
Pecan (1980)	143	Cocke Co., Tenn.
Peppertree (1973)	47	San Juan Capistrano, Cal.
Pinckneya (1972)	21	nr. Mt. Pleasant, Fla.
Pine, Ponderosa (1974)	223	Plumas, Cal.
Plum, American (1972)	35	Oakland Co., Mich.
Poison Sumac (1972)	20	Robin's Island, N.Y.
Pondcypress (1972)	135	nr. Newton, Ga.
Poplar, Balsam (1976)	128	Champion, Mich.
Possumhaw (1981)	42	Congaree Swamp, S.C.
Redbay (1972)	58	Randolph Co., Ga.
Redwood, Coast (1972)	362	Humboldt Redwoods State Park, Cal.
Royalpalm, Florida (1973)	80	Homestead, Fla.
Sassafras (1972)	100	Owensboro, Ky.
Seagrape (1972)	57	Miami, Fla.
Sequoia, Giant (1975)	275	Sequoia Natl. Pk., Cal.
Serviceberry, Downy (1975)	50	New Philadelphia, Oh.
Silktree (1971)	41	Gilmer, Tex.
Silverbell, Two-wing (1971)	55	Tallahassee, Fla.
Smoketree, American (1974)	47	Lewiston, Ida.
Soapberry, Western (1979)	67	Newton County, Tex.
Sourwood (1972)	118	nr. Robbinsville, N.C.
Sparkleberry Tree (1977)	30	Pensacola, Fla.
Spruce, Sitka (1973)	216	Seaside, Ore.
Sugarberry (1976)	78	Society Hill, S.C.
Sumac, Shining (1974)	55	Grenada Co., Miss.
Sweetleaf, Common (1972)	55	Tallahassee, Fla.
Sycamore, Cal. (1945)	116	nr. Santa Barbara, Cal.
Tamarisk (1981)	34	Columbus, N.M.
Tesota (1972)	32	nr. Quartzsite, Ariz.
Torreya, Cal. (1945)	141	nr. Mendocino, Cal.
Trifoliate-Orange (1968)	26	Harrisburg, Pa.
Tupelo, Black (1969)	117	Harrison Co., Tex.
(1969)	139	nr. Houston, Tex.
Walnut, Cal. (1973)	116	nr. Chico, Cal.
Willow, Crack (1972)	112	nr. Utica, Mich.
Winterberry, Common (1971)	40	Wildwood, Fla.
Witch Hazel, Common (1976)	43	Muskegon, Mich.
Yaupon (1972)	45	nr. Devers, Tex.
Yellow-Poplar (1972)	124	Bedford, Va.
Yellowwood (1981)	76	Ann Arbor, Mich.
Yew, Pacific (1969)	60	nr. Mineral, Wash.
Yucca, Aloe (1972)	15	Lakeland, Fla.

EDUCATION

American Colleges and Universities

Student and Faculty Figures for Spring Term, 1982

Source: World Almanac questionnaires and U.S. Office of Education

(For Canadian Colleges and Universities, see Index)

All coeducational unless followed by (M) for men only, or (W) for women only. Even though marked (M) or (W) some are coeducational at graduate level and in evening and summer divisions. Asterisk (*) denotes landgrant college.

Governing official is president or chancellor unless otherwise designated. Year is that of founding. The word college is part of the name unless another designation is given.

Affiliation: IP-Independent (Private), IR (Independent-Religions affiliation), Pf-Public (federal), Ps-Public (state), Pl-Public (local), Psl-Public (state and local), Psr-Public (state related).

Highest Degree Offered: A-Associate's (2 yrs.), B-Bachelor's (4 yrs.), 1P-First Professional, M-Master's, S-Specialist, D-Doctorate.

Each institution listed has an enrollment of at least 200 students of college grade. Number of teachers is the total number of individuals on teaching staff. Enrollment and faculty in italics includes all full-time and part-time students and teachers on all branches and campuses.

(A) Designates colleges that have not provided up-to-date information.

(See Index for typical tuition fees)

Name, address	Year	Governing official, affiliation, and highest degree offered		Students	Teachers
Abilene Christian, Abilene, TX 79699	1906	William J. Teague	IR-M	4,456	180
Abraham Baldwin Agric. (A), Tifton, GA 31794	1908	Stanley R. Anderson	Ps-A	2,372	101
Adams, State (A), Alamosa, CO 81102	1923	William Fulkerson	Ps-M	2,000	115
Adelphi Univ. (A), Garden City, NY 11530	1896	Timothy Costello	IP-D	11,819	360
Adirondack Community (A), Glens Falls, NY 12801	1960	Charles R. Eisenhart	Psl-A	2,037	65
Adrian (A), Adrian, MI 49221	1859	Donald S. Stanton	IR-M	945	61
Aeronautics, Academy of, Flushing, NY 11371	1932	Walter M. Hartung	IP-A	1,900	85
Agnes Scott (W), Decatur, GA 30030	1889	Ruth A. Schmidt	IP-B	600	82
Aims Comm., Greeley, CO 80632	1969	George Conger	Pl-A	5,117	277
Akron, Univ. of, Akron, OH 44325	1870	Dominic J. Guzzetta	Ps-D	*25,820*	*2,231*
Alabama A&M Univ. (A), Normal, AL 35762	1875	Richard D. Morrison	Ps-S	*4,379*	*321*
Alabama Christian, Montgomery, AL 36193	1942	J. Walker Whittle	IP-A	*1,928*	*83*
Alabama State Univ., Montgomery, AL 36195	1874	Robert L. Randolph	Ps-S	4,034	237
Alabama, Univ. of (A), University, AL 35486	1831	Joab Thomas	Ps-D	17,918	994
at Birmingham (A), Birmingham, AL 35294	1966	S.R. Hill Jr.	Ps-D	13,799	1,417
at Huntsville (A), Huntsville, AL 35899	1960	John C. Wright	Ps-S	5,006	224
Alameda, Coll. of, Alameda, CA 94501	1970	Don Hongisto	Psl-A	7,014	113
Alaska, Univ. of*, Fairbanks, AK 99701	1917	Patrick J. O'Rourke	Ps-D	*5,086*	*400*
Albany Coll. of Pharmacy, Albany, NY 12208	1881	Walter Singer	IP-B	542	40
Albany Junior, Albany, GA 31707	1966	B.R. Tilley	Ps-A	1,919	94
Albany State, Albany, GA 31705	1903	Billy C. Black	Ps-M	1,979	127
Albany, Junior Coll. of, Albany, NY 12208	1957	William Kahl	IP-A	1,274	73
Albemarle, Coll. of the (A), Elizabeth City, NC 27909	1960	J.P. Chesson Jr.	Ps-A	1,118	43
Albertus Magnus (W), New Haven, CT 06511	1925	Sister Julia McNamara	IP-B	552	58
Albion, Albion, MI 49224	1835	Bernard Tagg Lomas	IR-B	1,853	120
Albright, Reading, PA 19603	1856	David G. Ruffer	IP-B	2,085	155
Albuquerque, Univ. of (A), Albuquerque, NM 87140	1920	Clifford Smith	IP-B	2,000	75
Alcorn State Univ., Lorman, MS 39096	1871	Walter Washington	Ps-M	2,418	162
Alderson-Broaddus, Philippi, WV 26416	1871	Richard E. Shearer	IR-B	794	74
Alexander City State Junior, Alexander City, AL 35010	1965	W. Byron Causey	Ps-A	*1,278*	*74*
Alfred Univ., Alfred, NY 14802	1836	Edward G. Coll, Jr.	IP-D	2,323	216
Alice Lloyd, Pippa Passes, KY 41844	1923	Jerry C. Davis	IP-A	*418*	*25*
Allan Hancock, Santa Maria, CA 93454	1920	Gary R. Edelbrock	Psl	*10,500*	*130*
Allegany Community, Cumberland, MD 21502	1961	Donald Alexander	Psl-A	2,050	135
Allegheny, Meadville, PA 16335	1815	David B. Harned	IP-M	1,864	131
Allen Co. Comm., Iola, KS 66749	1923	Bill R. Spencer	Psl-A	1,215	103
Allen Univ., Columbia, SC 29204	1870	David W. Williams	IR-B	331	34
Allentown Coll. of St. Francis de Sales, Center Valley, PA	1965	Rev. Daniel G. Gambet	IR-B	710	72
Alma, Alma, MI 48801	1886	Oscar E. Remick	IP-B	1,080	100
Alpena Community (A), Alpena, MI 49707	1952	Charles Donnelly	Pl-A	1,659	50
Alvernia, Reading, PA 19607	1960	Sister Mary Victorine	IR-B	654	71
Alverno (W), Milwaukee, WI 53215	1936	Sister Joel Read	IP-B	1,372	113
Alvin Comm., Alvin, TX 77511	1949	A.R. Allbright	Psl-A	3,160	169
Amarillo, Amarillo, TX 79178	1929	H.D. Yarbrough	Psl-A	5,600	250
American Academy of Art, Chicago, IL 60604	1923	I. Shapiro	IP-A	968	26
American Cons. of Music, Chicago, IL 60603	1886	Charles Moore	IP-D	335	120
Amer. Inst. of Business (A), Des Moines, IA 50321	1921	Keith Fenton	Pl-A	900	45
American International, Springfield, MA 01109	1885	Harry J. Courniotes	IP-M	2,254	145
American River (A), Sacramento, CA 95841	1955	Robert D. Jensen	Pl-A	*22,025*	*641*
American Univ. (A), Washington DC 20016	1893	Richard Berendzen	IP-D	12,500	1,050
Amherst (A), Amherst, MA 01002	1821	John William Ward	IP-B	1,475	150
Anderson, Anderson, IN 46012	1917	Robert H. Reardon	IR-1P	2,032	176
Anderson, Anderson, SC 29621	1911	Vacant	IR-A	1,061	61
Andrew, Cuthbert, GA 31740	1854	William T. Greer	IR-A	350	24
Andrews Univ., Berrien Springs, MI 49104	1874	Joseph Smoot	IR-S	3,083	220
Angelina, Lufkin, TX 75901	1968	Jack W. Hudgins	Psl-A	2,200	100
Angelo State Univ. (A), San Angelo, TX 76909	1928	Lloyd Vincent	Ps-M	5,600	231
Anna Maria (A), Paxton, MA 01612	1946	Bernadette Madore	IR-M	1,574	143
Anne Arundel Comm., Arnold, MD 21012	1961	Thomas E. Florestano	Psl-A	*6,600*	*180*
Anoka-Ramsey Comm. (A), Coon Rapids, MN 55433	1965	Neil Christenson	Ps-A	3,645	92
Anson Tech., Ansonville, NC 28007	1962	H.B. Monroe	Psl-A	*600*	*48*
Antelope Valley, Lancaster, CA 93534	1929	Clinton Stine	Psl-A	7,500	254
Antioch, Yellow Spgs., OH 45387	1852	William M. Birenbaum	IP-D	*3,584*	*482*
Appalachian Bible, Bradley, WV 25818	1950	Lester E. Pipkin	IP-B	212	15
Appalachian State Univ., Boone, NC 28608	1899	John E. Thomas	Ps-S	10,047	587
Aquinas (A), Grand Rapids, MI 49506	1922	Norbert J. Hruby	IR-M	2,172	78

Name, address	Year	Governing official, affiliation, and highest degree offered		Students	Teachers
Aquinas Junior, (W) Milton, MA 02186	1956	Sr. Mary Morgan	IR-A	400	26
Aquinas Junior, Nashville, TN 37205	1961	Sister Robert Ann Britton	IR-A	277	35
Arapahoe Community (A), Littleton, CO 80120	1965	Norman Lloyd	Ps-A	6,220	235
Arizona, (A), Univ., Tempe, AZ 85287	1885	J. Russell Nelson	Ps-D	36,246	1,677
Arizona, Univ. of*, Tucson, AZ 85721	1885	Henry Koffler	Ps-D	35,206	1,709
Arizona Western, Yuma, AZ 85364	1962	Kenneth E. Borland	Psl-A	4,532	125
Arkansas, Batesville, AR 72501	1872	Dan C. West	IR-B	514	57
Arkansas, Baptist (A), Little Rock, AR 72202	1884	J.C. Oliver	IR-B	271	26
Arkansas Tech, Russellville, AR 72801	1909	Kenneth Kersh	Ps-M	2,964	213
Arkansas State Univ. (A), State Univ., AR 72467	1909	Ray Thornton	Ps-S	7,615	360
Arkansas, Univ. of*, Fayetteville, AR 72701	1872	James E. Martin	Ps-D	31,574	1,919
at Little Rock (A), Little Rock, AR 72204	1927	G. Robert Ross	Ps-M	10,038	406
at Pine Bluff, Pine Bluff, AR 71601	1873	Lloyd V. Hackley	Pf-A	2,694	196
Armstrong (A), Berkeley, CA 94704	1918	John E. Armstrong	IP-M	452	52
Armstrong State, Savannah, GA 31406	1935	Henry L. Ashmore	Ps-M	2,950	185
Art Center Coll. of Design, Pasadena, CA 91103	1931	Donald R. Kubly	IP-M	1,176	175
Art Inst. of Chicago (A), Chicago, IL 60603	1866	Donald Irving	IP-M	1,832	170
Asbury, Wilmore, KY 40390	1890	Cornelius R. Hager	IP-B	1,151	101
Asheville-Buncombe Tech., Asheville, NC 28801	1958	Harvey L. Haynes	Psl-A	15,000	300
Ashland, Ashland, OH 44805	1878	Joseph R. Shultz	IP-S	2,760	200
Ashland Community, Ashland, KY 41101	1937	Robert L. Goodpaster, Dir.	Ps-A	1,572	50
Assumption, Worcester, MA 01609	1904	Joseph H. Hagan	IR-M	2,400	200
Athens State, Athens AL 35611	1822	James R. Chasteen	Ps-B	1,017	73
Atlanta College of Art, Atlanta, GA 30309	1928	William Voos	IP-B	270	31
Atlantic Christian, Wilson, NC 27893	1902	Harold C. Doster	IR-B	1,552	115
Atlantic Comm., Mays Landing, NJ 08330	1964	L.R. Winchell Jr.	Psl-A	8,794	160
Atlantic Union (A), So. Lancaster, MA 01561	1882	Larry Lewis	IR-B	630	90
Auburn Univ.*, Auburn, AL 36849	1856	H. Hanley Funderburk	Ps-D	15,390	1,538
Augsburg (A), Minneapolis, MN 55454	1869	Oscar A. Anderson	IR-B	1,625	85
Augusta, Augusta, GA 30910	1925	George A. Christenberry	Ps-S	3,791	156
Augustana, Rock Island, IL 61201	1860	J. Thomas Tredway	IP-M	2,277	185
Augustana, Sioux Falls, SD 57197	1860	William C. Nelson	IP-M	2,048	162
Aurora, Aurora, IL 60507	1893	Alan J. Stone	IR-M	1,310	100
Austin, Sherman, TX 75090	1849	Dr. Harry E. Smith	IR-M	1,140	109
Austin Comm., Austin, MN 55912	1940	Arlan Burmeister	Ps-A	950	52
Austin Peay State Univ., Clarksville, TN 37040	1927	Robert O. Riggs	Ps-S	5,200	250
Averett, Danville, VA 24541	1859	Howard W. Lee	IP-M	973	55
Avila, Kansas City, MO 64145	1916	Sister Olive Louise Dallavis	IP-M	1,974	200
Azusa Pacific Univ., Azusa CA 91702	1899	Paul E. Sago	IP-M	2,386	135
Babson (A), Babson Park, MA 02157	1919	Ralph Z. Sorenson	IP-M	2,800	89
Bacone, Muskogee, OK 74401	1880	Paul Moore	IR-A	384	35
Baker Jr. Col. of Business, Flint, MI 48507	1911	Edward J. Kurtz	IP-A	1,500	61
Baker Univ., Baldwin City, KS 66006	1858	Ralph Tanner	IR-M	834	80
Bakersfield, Bakersfield, CA 93305	1913	John J. Collins	Ps-A	11,940	525
Baldwin-Wallace, Berea, OH 44017	1845	Neal Malicky	IR-M	3,400	175
Ball State Univ., Muncie, IN 47306	1918	Robert Bell	Ps-D	17,175	900
Baltimore, Univ. (A), of Baltimore, MD 21201	1925	H. Melbane Turner	Pf-M	5,350	261
Baltimore, Comm. Col. of (A), Baltimore, MD 21215	1947	Rafael L. Cortada	Psl-A	11,490	584
Baptist Bible (A), Springfield, MO 65802	1950	William E. Dowell	IR-B	1,686	65
Baptist Bible College of Pa., Clarks Summit, PA 18411	1932	Mark Jackson	IR-M	830	45
Baptist Coll. at Charleston (A), Charleston, SC 29411	1960	John Hamrick	IR-B	2,500	105
Barat (A) (W), Lake Forest, IL 60045	1858	Sister Judith Cagney	IP-B	743	79
Barber-Scotia, Concord, NC 28025	1867	Mable McLean	IR-B	347	31
Bard, Annandale-on-Hudson, NY 12504	1860	Leon Botstein	IP-M	750	80
Barnard (W), New York, NY 10027	1889	Ellen Futter	IP-B	2,484	220
Barrington, Barrington, RI 02806	1900	David G. Horner	IP-B	402	22
Barry, Miami Shores, FL 33161	1940	Sister Jeanne O'Laughlin	IR-M	2,197	155
Barstow, Barstow, CA 92311	1962	J.W. Edwin Spear	Psl-A	1,750	74
Barton County Comm., Great Bend, KS 67530	1965	Jimmie Downing	Psl-A	3,272	244
Bates, Lewiston, ME 04240	1855	Thomas H. Reynolds	IP-B	1,425	133
Bay de Noc Comm. (A), Escanaba, MI 49829	1963	Edwin E. Wuehle	Psl-A	1,531	92
Baylor Univ., Waco, TX 76798	1845	Herbert H. Reynolds	IR-D	10,412	560
Bay Path Junior (W), Longmeadow, MA 01106	1897	Jeanette T. Wright	IP-A	712	33
Beal, Bangor, ME 04401	1891	David Tibbetts	IP-A	*450*	*40*
Beaufort Co. Comm., Washington, NC 27889	1968	James P. Blanton	Ps-A	1,035	55
Beaver (A), Glenside, PA 19038	1853	Edward D. Gates	IP-M	2,040	137
Beaver Co., Comm. Col. of Monaca, PA 15065	1966	Terry L. DiCianna	Psl-A	2,250	120
Becker Junior (A), Worcester, MA 01609	1784	Lloyd H. Van Buskirk	IP-A	*1,174*	*54*
Beckley, Beckley, WV 25801	1933	John Saunders	IP-A	1,484	63
Bee County, Beeville TX 78102	1967	Grady C. Hogue	Psl-A	2,023	114
Belhaven, Jackson, MS 39202	1883	Verne R. Kennedy	IR-B	1,034	60
Bellarmine, Louisville, KY 40205	1950	Eugene Petrik	IR-M	2,588	123
Belleville Area, Belleville, IL 62221	1946	Bruce R. Wissore	Psl-A	12,773	630
Bellevue, Bellevue, NE 68005	1966	Richard Winchell	IP-B	2,600	90
Bellevue Community (A), Bellevue, WA 98007	1966	Thos. O'Connell	Ps-A	10,582	114
Belmont, Nashville, TN 37203	1951	William Troutt	IR-B	1,793	156
Belmont Abbey, Belmont, NC 28012	1876	Dr. Dempsey	IR-B	765	60
Belmont Technical (A), St. Clairsville, OH 43950	1969	Paul R. Ohm	Ps-A	563	20
Beloit, Beloit, WI 53511	1846	Rogert Hull	IP-M	1,124	90
Bemidji State, Bemidji, NM 56601	1919	Richard R. Haugo	Ps-M	5,138	240
Benedict (A), Columbia, SC 29204	1870	Henry Ponder	IP-B	1,379	120
Benedictine (A), Atchison KS 66002	1858	Rev. Gerard Senecal	IP-B	1,100	90
Benjamin Franklin University, Wash. D.C. 20013	1907	Marthajane Kennedy	IP-M	460	37
Bennett (W), Greensboro, NC 27420	1926	Isaac H. Miller	IR-B	600	59
Bennington (A), Bennington, VT 05201	1925	Joseph S. Murphy	IP-M	594	77
Bentley (A), Waltham, MA 02154	1917	Gregory Adamian	IP-M	7,000	120
Berea (A), Berea, KY 40404	1855	W.D. Weatherford	IP-B	1,514	140
Bergen Community (A), Paramus, NJ 07652	1965	Alban E. Reid	Psl-A	11,533	519
Berkeley School, The (A), Little Falls, NJ 07424	1931	Larry L. Luing	IP-A	540	23
Berkshire Community (A), Pittsfield, MA 01201	1960	Jonathan M. Daube	Ps-A	2,896	180
Berry, Mount Berry, GA 30149	1902	Gloria M. Shatto	IP-M	1,413	112
Bethany, Lindsborg, KS 67456	1881	Arvin Hahn	IR-B	850	55
Bethany, Bethany, WV 26032	1840	Todd H. Bullard	IR-B	818	81
Bethany Bible, Scotts Valley, CA 95066	1919	Richard B. Foth	IR-B	618	42
Bethany Nazarene, Bethany, OK 73008	1899	John Knight	IR-M	1,368	88
Bethel (A), McKenzie, TN 38201	1842	William L. Odom	IR-B	360	20
Bethel, Mishawaka, IN 46545	1947	Albert J. Beutler	IP-M	438	47
Bethel, North Newton, KS 67117	1887	Harold Schultz	IR-B	747	75

Name, address	Year	Governing official, affiliation, and highest degree offered		Students	Teachers
Bethel, St. Paul, MN 55112	1947	George K. Brushaber	IR-A	2,200	160
Bethune-Cookman, Daytona Beach, FL 32015	1904	O.P. Bronson	IP-B	1,574	130
Big Bend Community, Moses Lake, WA 98837	1962	Peter DeVries	Ps-A	2,300	106
Biola, La Mirada, CA 90639	1908	Richard Chase	IR-D	3,258	268
Birmingham-Southern, Birmingham, AL 35254	1856	Neal R. Berte	IR-A	1,534	90
Biscayne (A), Miami, FL 33054	1952	Rev. Patrick H. O'Neill	IR-M	3,000	200
Bishop (A), Dallas, TX 75241	1881	Harry S. Wright	IP-B	985	60
Bishop State Jr., Mobile, AL 36690	1965	Yvonne Kennedy	Ps-A	1,633	60
Bismarck Junior, Bismarck, ND 58501	1939	Kermit Lidstrom	Pl-A	2,194	120
Black Hawk, Moline, IL 61265	1946	Richard J. Puffer	Psl-A	*7,450*	*283*
Blackhawk Technical Inst., Janesville, WI 53545	1968	O.L. Johnson (Dir.)	Pl-A	2,144	133
Black Hills State, Spearfish, SD 57783	1883	J. Gilbert Hause	Ps-M	*5,000*	*215*
Blackburn, Carlinville, IL 62626	1837	William F. Denman	IR-A	463	47
Bladen Tech., Dublin, NC 28332	1967	Geo. Resseguie	Psl-A	*550*	*34*
Blinn, Brenham, TX 77833	1883	James H. Atkinson	Psl-A	*2,900*	*138*
Bliss, Columbus, OH 43214	1899	James D. Tussing	IP-A	440	25
Bloomfield, Bloomfield, NJ 07003	1868	Merle F. Allshouse	IR-A	1,845	130
Bloomsburg State (A), Bloomsburg, PA 17815	1839	James McCormick	Ps-M	6,503	316
Bluefield, Bluefield, VA 24605	1922	Charles Tyer	IR-B	389	39
Bluefield State, Bluefield, WV 24701	1895	Jerold O. Dugger	Ps-B	2,300	102
Blue Mountain (W), Blue Mountain, MS 38610	1873	E. Harold Fisher	IR-B	415	32
Blue Mountain Comm., Pendleton, OR 97801	1962	Ronald L. Daniels	Pl-A	2,400	72
Blue Ridge Comm., Weyers Cave, VA 24486	1965	James A. Armstrong	Pf-A	2,225	105
Bluffton (A), Bluffton, OH 45817	1899	Elmer Neufeld	IR-B	662	55
Bob Jones Univ., Greenville, SC 29614	1927	Bob Jones Jr.	IR-D	6,300	409
Boca Raton, Coll. of (A), Boca Raton, FL 33431	1963	Donald E. Ross	IP-A	524	38
Boise State, Boise, ID 83725	1932	John Keiser	Ps-M	11,956	508
Boston, Chestnut Hill, MA 02167	1863	Rev. J. Donald Monan	IR-D	*14,000*	*1,000*
Boston State (A), Boston, MA 02115	1852	Kermit C. Morrissey	Ps-M	11,000	328
Boston Conserv. of Music, Boston, MA 02215	1867	William A. Seymour	IP-M	600	100
Boston Univ., Boston, MA 02215	1839	John Silber	IP-D	28,707	2,543
Bowdoin, Brunswick, ME 04011	1794	Arthur LeRoy Greason, Jr.	IP-B	1,373	104
Bowie State* (A), Bowie, MD 20715	1865	Rufus L. Barfield	Ps-M	2,664	137
Bowling Green State Univ., Bowling Green, OH 43403	1910	Paul J. Olscamp	Ps-D	*17,488*	*737*
Bradford, Bradford, MA 01830	1803	Arthur Levine	IP-B	375	45
Bradley Univ. (A), Peoria, IL 61625	1897	Martin G. Abegg	IP-M	5,600	400
Brainerd Comm., Brainerd, MN 56401	1938	Curtis Murton Jr.	Ps-A	556	37
Brandeis Univ., Waltham, MA 02254	1948	Marver Bernstein	IP-D	3,580	435
Brandywine (A), Wilmington, DE 19803	1965	Robert J. Bruce	IP-A	*891*	*43*
Brazosport, Lake Jackson, TX 77566	1948	W.A. Bass	Pl-A	3,500	165
Brenau, Gainesville, GA 30501	1878	James T. Rogers	IP-M	1,270	75
Brescia (A), Owensboro, KY 42301	1950	Sr. George Ann Cecil	IP-B	860	75
Brevard (A), Brevard, NC 28712	1953	J.C. Martinson Jr.	IR-A	750	67
Brevard Comm. (A), Cocoa, FL 32922	1960	Maxwell King	Ps-A	*10,934*	*600*
Brewton-Parker (A), Mt. Vernon, GA 30445	1904	William S. Miller	IR-A	930	115
Briar Cliff, Sioux City, IA 51104	1930	Charles Bensman	IP-B	1,150	65
Bridgeport Engineering Inst., Bridgeport, CT 06606	1924	William J. Owens	IP-B	*896*	*88*
Bridgeport, Univ. of, Bridgeport, CT 06601	1927	Leland Miles	IP-S	*7,000*	*450*
Bridgewater, Bridgewater, VA 22812	1880	Wayne F. Geisert	IP-B	966	77
Bridgewater State, Bridgewater, MA 02324	1840	Adrian Rondileau	Ps-M	7,600	253
Brigham Young Univ., Provo, UT 84602	1875	Jeffrey R. Holland	IR-D	37,166	1,530
Brigham Young Univ. (A), Laie, HI 96762	1955	J. Elliott Cameron	IR-B	1,736	78
Bristol College, Bristol, TN 37621	1895	Jack O. Anderson	IP-B	198	16
Bristol Community (A), Falls River, MA 02720	1966	Eileen T. Farley	Ps-A	2,205	130
Brookdale Comm (A), Lincroft NJ 07738	1967	Donald H. Smith	Psl-A	9,791	140
Brookhaven, Farmers Branch, TX 75234	1978	Deon Holt	Psl-A	6,200	252
Brooklyn Law School, Brooklyn, NY 11201	1901	Paul Windels	IP-1P	1,230	66
Brooks Inst., Santa Barbara, CA 93108	1946	Ernest Brooks Jr.	IP-M	800	40
Broome Community (A), Binghamton, NY 13902	1946	Vacant	Ps-A	5,556	155
Broward Community, Ft. Lauderdale, FL 33301	1960	Alfred H. Adams	Ps-A	*26,787*	*824*
Brown Univ., Providence, RI 02912	1764	Howard R. Swearer	IP-D	7,655	474
Brunswick Junior (A), Brunswick, GA 31520	1961	John W. Teel	Ps-A	1,200	59
Bryan, Dayton, TN 37321	1930	Theodore Mercer	IP-B	579	47
Bryant, Smithfield RI 02917	1863	William O'Hara	IP-M	6,235	262
Bryant & Stratton Business Inst. (A), Rochester, NY 14604	1973	Francis J. Gustina	IP-A	636	30
Bryn Mawr (A) (W), Bryn Mawr, PA 19010	1885	Mary Patterson McPherson	IP-D	1,784	150
Bucknell Univ., Lewisburg, PA 17837	1846	Dennis O'Brien	IP-M	3,312	229
Bucks County Comm. (A), Newtown, PA 18940	1964	Charles Rollins	Pl-A	8,100	190
Buena Vista, Storm Lake, IA 50588	1891	Keith G. Briscoe	IP-B	*1,386*	*100*
Butler County Comm., Butler, PA 16001	1965	Thomas Ten Hoeve Jr	Psl-A	1,250	115
Butler County Comm. (A), El Dorado, KS 67042	1927	Carl Heinrich	Pl-A	2,195	102
Butler Univ., Indianapolis, IN 46208	1855	John G. Johnson	Pl-S	3,985	220
Butte Community, Oroville, CA 95965	1968	Wendell Lee Reeder	Pl-A	12,000	420
Cabrillo, Aptos, CA 95003	1959	John C. Petersen	Psl-A	11,300	434
Cabrini, Radnor PA 19087	1957	Sr. Eileen Cuine	IR-B	653	60
Caldwell (A), Caldwell, NJ 07006	1939	Sr. Edith Magdalen Visic	IR-B	681	80
Caldwell Comm. Coll. & Tech. Inst. (A), Lenoir, NC 28645	1964	H. Edwin Beam	Psl-A	*1,300*	*120*
California Baptist, Riverside, CA 92504	1950	James R. Staples	IR-M	600	72
Cal. Coll. of Arts and Crafts, Oakland, CA 94618	1907	Harry Xavier Ford	IP-M	1,160	195
Cal. College of Podiatric Med., San Francisco, CA 94115	1914	Stanley Burnham	IP-D	*387*	*190*
Cal. Inst. of the Arts, Valencia, CA 91355	1962	Robert Fitzpatrick	IP-M	750	150
Cal. Inst. of Tech., Pasadena, CA 91125	1891	Marvin L. Goldberger	IP-D	1,760	375
Cal. Lutheran, Thousand Oaks, CA 91360	1960	Jerry H. Miller	IP-M	2,450	250
Cal. Maritime Academy, Vallejo, CA 94590	1929	R. Adm. Joseph Rizza	Ps-B	465	30
Cal. Polytechnic State Univ., San Luis Obispo, CA 93407	1901	Warren J. Baker	Ps-M	15,848	945
Cal. State, Bakersfield CA 93309	1970	Jacob Frankel	Ps-M	3,404	223
Cal. State, California, PA 15419	1852	John P. Watkins	Ps-M	4,384	304
Cal. State Univ., Dominguez Hills, CA 90747	1965	Donald Gerth	Ps-M	9,500	405
Cal. State, San Bernardino, CA 92407	1965	John Pfau	Ps-M	4,782	275
Cal. State Stanislaus, Turlock, CA 95380	1957	Walter Olson	Ps-M	4,298	232
Cal. State Polytechnic Univ., Pomona, CA 91768	1938	Hugh La Bounty Jr	Ps-M	16,170	800
Cal. State Univ., Chico, CA 95929	1887	Robin S. Wilson	Ps-M	14,276	790
Cal. State Univ., Fresno, CA 93704	1910	Harold H. Haak	Ps-M	16,000	990
Cal. State Univ., Fullerton, CA 92634	1957	Jewel Plummer Cobb	Ps-M	22,339	1,301
Cal. State Univ., Hayward, CA 94542	1957	Ellis McCune	Ps-M	10,463	592
Cal. State Univ. (A), Long Beach, CA 90840	1949	Stephen Horn	Ps-M	30,100	2,000
Cal. State Univ. (A), Los Angeles, CA 90032	1947	James M. Rosser	Ps-D	25,000	895
Cal. State Univ., Northridge, CA 91330	1958	James W. Cleary	Ps-M	25,438	1,588

Name, address	Year	Governing official, affiliation, and highest degree offered		Students	Teachers
Cal. State Univ., Sacramento, CA 95819	1947	W. Lloyd Johns	Ps-M	22,662	1,100
Cal. State Univ. (A), San Francisco, CA 94132	1899	Paul F. Romberg	Ps-D	24,120	1,812
Cal. Univ. of*, Berkeley, CA 94720	1868	David S. Saxon	Ps-D	*138,700*	*6,355*
Berkeley Campus (A), Berkeley, CA 94720	1873	Ira Michael Heyman	Ps-D	30,445	1,494
Davis Campus, Davis, CA 95616	1906	James Meyer	Ps-D	19,276	1,316
Irvine Campus, Irvine, CA 92717	1960	D.G. Aldrich	Ps-D	11,057	652
Los Angeles Campus, Los Angeles, CA 90024	1919	Charles Young	Ps-D	33,435	2,968
Riverside Campus (A), Riverside, CA 92502	1954	Tomas Rivera	Ps-D	4,700	416
San Diego Campus, La Jolla, CA 92093	1912	Richard C. Atkinson	Ps-D	12,319	850
San Francisco Campus, San Francisco, CA 94122	1899	Paul F. Romberg	Ps-D	23,227	1,654
Santa Barbara Campus, Santa Barbara, CA 93106	1944	Robert A. Huttenback	Ps-S	15,500	679
Santa Cruz Campus, Santa Cruz, CA 95064	1965	R.L. Sinsheimer	Ps-D	6,860	550
California Western School of Law, San Diego, CA 92101	1958	Robert K. Castetter	IP-1P	750	47
Calumet, Whiting, IN 46394	1951	Rev. Louis Osterhage	IR-B	1,316	87
Calvary Bible, Kansas City, MO 64147	1932	Leslie P. Madison	IP-M	495	40
Calvin, Grand Rapids, MI 49506	1876	Anthony Dickema	IR-M	3,723	262
Camden County (A), Blackwood, NJ 08012	1967	Otto R. Mauke	Psl-A	*7,466*	*335*
Cameron, Lawton, OK 73505	1927	Don Davis	Ps-B	5,178	178
Campbellsville, Campbellsville, KY 42718	1906	William Randolph	IR-B	712	45
Campbell Univ., Buies Creek, NC 27506	1887	Norman A. Wiggins	IR-JD	*3,174*	*175*
Canada, Redwood City, CA 94061	1968	Donald J. Macintyre	Psl-A	9,541	252
Canisius, Buffalo, NY 14208	1870	Rev. James Demske	IP-M	4,410	268
Canyons, Coll. of the, Valencia, CA 91355	1969	L.B. Newcomer	Psl-A	4,400	140
Cape Cod Comm., W. Barnstable, MA 02668	1960	James F. Hall	Ps-A	4,360	230
Cape Fear Tech. Inst., Wilmington, NC 28401	1959	M.J. McLeod	Psl-A	1,500	75
Capital City Jr. (A), Little Rock, AR 72204	1927	Perry Turnbull	IP-A	469	22
Capital Univ., Columbus, OH 43209	1850	Harvey A. Stegemoeller	IR-M	2,569	198
Capitol Inst. of Tech., Kensington, MD 20795	1964	G.W. Troxler	IP-B	836	43
Cardinal Stritch, Milwaukee, WI 53217	1937	Sister M. Kliebhan	IR-M	1,150	104
Carl Albert Junior (A), Poteau, OK 74953	1934	Joe E. White	Ps-A	1,710	60
Carl Sandburg, Galesburg, IL 61401	1966	William Anderson	Psl-A	4,065	129
Carleton, Northfield, MN 55057	1866	Robert Edwards	IP-B	1,700	175
Carlow (W), Pittsburgh, PA 15213	1929	Sister Jane Scully	IR-B	1,013	96
Carnegie-Mellon (A), Univ., Pittsburgh, PA 15213	1900	Richard M. Cyert	IP-D	4,772	417
Carroll, Helena, MT 59625	1909	Francis Kerins	IR-1P	1,358	110
Carroll, Waukesha, WI 53186	1846	Robert V. Cramer	IR-B	1,321	114
Carson-Newman, Jefferson City, TN 37760	1851	J. Cordell Maddox	IR-B	1,731	109
Carteret Tech., Morehead City, NC 28557	1963	Donald Bryant	Psl-A	937	58
Carthage, Kenosha, WI 53141	1847	Erno Dahl	IP-M	1,456	96
Case Western Reserve Univ., Cleveland OH 44106	1826	David V. Ragone	IP-D	8,488	1,482
Casper, Casper, WY 82601	1945	Lloyd H. Loftin	Psl-A	1,600	210
Castleton State (A), Castleton, VT 05735	1787	Thomas K. Meier	Ps-M	2,200	150
Catawba, Salisbury, NC 28144	1851	Stephen H. Wurster	IR-B	869	62
Catawba Valley Tech., Hickory, NC 28601	1958	Robert E. Paap	Pf-A	2,318	101
Catholic Univ. of America, Washington, DC 20064	1887	Dr. Edmund D. Pellegrino	IR-D	7,750	575
Cath. Univ. of Puerto Rico (A), Ponce, PR 00731	1948	F.J. Carreras	IR-M	*8,959*	*380*
Catonsville Comm., Baltimore, MD 21228	1957	John M. Kingsmore	Psl-A	*11,000*	*442*
Cayuga Co. Comm. (A), Auburn, NY 13021	1953	John Anthony	Psl-A	2,829	84
Cazenovia (W), Cazenovia, NY 13035	1824	Stephen Schneeweiss	Pl-A	603	54
Cecil Community, North East, MD 21901	1968	Robert L. Gell	Psl-A	1,300	125
Cedar Crest (A), Allentown, PA 18104	1867	Dr. Gene S. Cesari	IR-A	1,125	127
Cedarville, Cedarville, OH 45314	1887	Paul H. Dixon	IR-A	1,667	91
Centenary (A) (W), Hackettstown, NJ 07840	1873	Charles Dick	IP-B	593	80
Centenary Coll. of La, Shreveport, LA 71104	1825	Donald Webb	IP-M	1,261	110
Central, McPherson, KS 67460	1914	Dorsey Brause	IP-A	305	24
Central Arizona (A), Coolidge, AZ 85228	1969	Mel Everingham	Pl-A	*6,749*	*NA*
Central Bible, Springfield, MO 65803	1922	H. Maurice Lednicky	IR-B	1,022	49
Central Carolina Tech. Inst., Sanford, NC 27330	1962	James F. Hockaday	Ps-A	2,069	135
Central Connecticut State, New Britain, CT 06053	1849	F. Don James	Ps-M	12,407	643
Central Florida, Univ. of, Orlando, FL 32816	1963	Trevor Colbourn	Ps-D	13,093	500
Central Florida Comm., Ocala, FL 32678	1957	Henry E. Goodlett	Psl-A	3,118	100
Centralia, Centralia, WA 98531	1925	Robert Lorence	Ps-A	6,500	250
Central Methodist, Fayette, MO 65248	1854	Joe Howell	IR-B	700	61
Central Mich. Univ., Mt. Pleasant, MI 48859	1892	Harold Abel	Ps-D	16,477	740
Central Missouri St. Univ., Warrensburg, MO 64093	1871	James Horner	Ps-S	9,887	510
Central Nebr. Tech. Comm. (A), Grand Island, NE 68801	1966	Chester Guasman	Psl-A	*16,072*	*132*
Central New England, Worcester, MA 01610	1905	Edward Mattar III	IP-B	1,722	130
Central Ohio Tech., Newark, OH 43055	1971	Julius Greenstein	Ps-A	1,268	84
Central Oregon Comm. (A), Bend, OR 97701	1949	Frederick Boyle	Pl-A	1,896	69
Central Piedmont Comm., Charlotte, NC 28235	1963	Richard H. Hagemeyer	Psl-A	26,000	1,560
Central State Univ., Edmond, OK 73034	1891	Bill Lillard	Ps-M	12,000	475
Central State Univ., Wilberforce, OH 45384	1887	Lionel H. Newsom	Ps-B	2,487	136
Central Tech. Comm. (A), Grand Is., NE 68802	1966	Chester H. Gausman	Pl-A	11,525	127
Central Texas, Killeen, TX 76542	1967	L.M. Morton Jr.	Psl-A	*5,219*	*183*
Central University of Iowa, Pella, IA 50219	1853	Kenneth J. Weller	IR-B	1,572	99
Central Virginia Comm., Lynchburg, VA 24502	1967	Donald Puyear	Ps-A	3,208	158
Central Washington, Ellensburg, WA 98926	1891	Donald L. Garrity	Ps-M	6,511	369
Central Wesleyan (A), Central, SC 29630	1906	John Newby	IR-B	414	41
Central Wyoming (A), Riverton, WY 82501	1976	Richard St. Pierre	Psl-A	1,158	67
Central YMCA Comm. (A), Chicago, IL 60606	1960	Ralph H. Lee	IP-A	3,189	83
Centre Coll. of Ky., Danville, KY 40422	1819	Richard L. Mornill	IR-B	700	75
Cerritos, Norwalk, CA 90650	1956	Wilford Michael	Psl-A	22,713	750
Cerro Coso Comm. (A), Ridgecrest, CA 93555	1973	Raymond A. McCue	Ps-A	4,426	134
Chabot, Hayward, CA 94545	1961	Reed L. Buffington	Ps-A	*20,000*	*800*
Chadron State, Chadron, NE 69337	1911	Edwin Nelson	Pf-S	2,001	89
Chaffey, Alta Loma, CA 91701	1911	Samuel Ferguson	Psl-A	*12,700*	*400*
Chaminade Univ. of Honolulu, Honolulu, HI 96816	1955	Fr. Raymond A. Roesch	IP-M	2,305	186
Champlain, Burlington, VT 05401	1878	Robert A. Skiff	IP-A	1,140	55
Chapman, Orange, CA 92666	1861	G.T. Smith	IR-M	*27,082*	*2,308*
Charles Co. Comm., La Plata, MD 20646	1958	J.N. Carsey	Psl-A	3,916	273
Charles S. Mott Comm. (A), Flint, MI 48503	1923	Charles Pappas	Pl-A	8,457	220
Charleston, Coll. of, Charleston, SC 29424	1770	Edward M. Collins Jr.	Ps-M	5,000	285
Charleston, Univ. of, Charleston, WV 25304	1888	Thomas G. Voss	IP-M	2,122	133
Chatham (W), Pittsburgh, PA 15232	1890	Alberta Arthurs	IP-B	676	75
Chattanooga St. Tech. Comm. (A), Chattanooga, TN 37406	1963	Charles W. Branch	Ps-A	4,602	164
Chemeketa Comm., Salem, OR 97305	1969	Arthur A. Binnie	Ps-A	*7,543*	*280*
Chesapeake, Wye Mills, MD 21679	1967	Robert Schleiger	Psl-A	*1,500*	*144*
Chestnut Hill (W), Philadelphia, PA 19118	1924	Sister Matthew Anita McDonald	IR-M	820	99
Cheyney State (A), Cheyney, PA 19319	1837	Wade Wilson	Ps-M	2,262	202

Name, address	Year	Governing official, affiliation, and highest degree offered		Students	Teachers
Chicago, City Colleges of (A), Chicago, IL 60601	1911	Oscar Shabat	Psl-A	114,381	1,450
City College of Chicago, Chicago, IL 60601	1977	Salvatore G. Rotella	Psl-A	14,898	70
Daley (A), Chicago, IL 60652	1960	William P. Conway	Psl-A	7,388	125
Kennedy-King (A), Chicago, IL 60621	1934	Ewen Akin	Psl-A	9,444	225
Loop (A), Chicago, IL 60601	1962	Salvatore G. Rotella	Psl-A	7,428	200
Malcolm X. (A), Chicago, IL 60612	1911	James C. Griggs	Psl-A	7,627	175
Olive-Harvey, Chicago, IL 60628	1970	Homer D. Franklin	Psl-A	4,795	194
Truman (A), Chicago, IL 60640	1956	Wallace B. Appelson	Psl-A	11,504	225
Wright, Chicago, IL 60634	1935	Ernest Clements	Psl-A	10,000	185
Chicago, Univ. of (A), Chicago, IL 60637	1891	Hanna Gray	IP-D	9,034	1,040
Chicago Coll. of Osteopathic, Chicago, IL 60615	1900	Thaddeus Kawalek	IP-S	398	250
Chicago State Univ., Chicago, IL 60628	1867	Benjamin Alexander	Ps-M	7,091	300
Chicago Urban Skills Inst. (A), Chicago, IL 60609	1970	Peyton S. Hutchison	Psl-A	39,250	550
Chipola Junior, Marianna, FL 32446	1947	James R. Richburg	Ps-A	1,355	52
Chowan, Murfreesboro, NC 27855	1852	Bruce E. Whitaker	IR-A	1,141	71
Christian Brothers, Memphis, TN 38104	1871	Bro. Theodore Drahmann	IR-B	1,483	127
Christopher Newport (A), Newport News, Va 23606	1960	John E. Anderson	Ps-B	3,900	111
Cincinnati, Univ. of, Cincinnati, OH 45221	1819	Henry Winkler	Ps-D	*38,895*	*3,209*
Cisco Junior, Cisco, TX 76437	1941	Norman Wallace	Psl-A	1,423	95
Citadel, The (A), Charleston, SC 29409	1843	V. Adm. James Stockdale	Ps-M	3,277	155
Citrus, Azusa, CA 91702	1915	Dan Angel	Psl-A	9,901	344
City, Bellevue, WA 98008	1973	Michael A. Pastore	IP-M	2,290	150
City College of San Francisco, San Francisco, CA 94112	1935	Kenneth S. Washington	Psl-A	29,000	1,100
Clackamas Comm., Oregon City, OR 97045	1966	John Hakanson	Pl-A	9,200	320
Claflin (A), Orangeburg, SC 29115	1869	Hubert V. Manning	IR-B	739	62
Claremont McKenna, Claremont, CA 91711	1946	Jack Lee Stark	IP-B	820	90
Claremore (A), Claremore, OK 74017	1902	Richard Mosier	Psr-A	1,872	81
Clarendon, Clarendon, TX 79226	1898	Kenneth D. Vaughan	Ps-A	848	47
Clarion State, Clarion, PA 16214	1967	Thomas Bond	Ps-M	*4,700*	*280*
Clark (A), Atlanta, GA 30314	1869	Elias Blake Jr	IR-B	1,876	116
Clark, Indianapolis, IN 46202	1963	Don J. Williams	IP-A	*870*	*45*
Clark (A), Vancouver, WA 98663	1933	Richard A. Jones	Ps-A	4,500	416
Clark Co. Comm., N. Las Vegas, NV 89030	1971	Judith Eaton	Pf-A	9,039	400
Clark Tech., Springfield, OH 45501	1962	Richard Brinkman	Ps-A	3,000	162
Clark Univ. (A), Worcester, MA 01610	1887	Mortimer Appley	IP-D	2,495	135
Clarke, Dubuque, IA 52001	1843	Meneve Dunham	IP-M	850	83
Clarke, Newton, MS 39345	1908	Lewis Nobles	IR-M	175	28
Clarkson, Potsdam, NY 13676	1896	Robert A. Plane	IP-D	3,944	247
Clatsop Community, Astoria, OR 97103	1958	Philip Bainer	Psl-A	*1,990*	*200*
Clayton Junior, Morrow, GA 30260	1969	Harry S. Downs	Pf-A	3,248	120
Cleary, Ypsilanti, MI 48197	1883	Gilbert Bursley	Pl-B	649	47
Clemson Univ.*, Clemson, SC 29631	1889	Bill Lee Atchley	Ps-D	11,926	870
Cleveland Inst. of Art, Cleveland, OH 44106	1882	Joseph McCullough	IP-B	522	70
Cleveland Inst. of Music, Cleveland, OH 44106	1920	Grant Johannesen	IP-D	270	134
Cleveland State Comm., Cleveland, TN 37311	1967	L. Quentin Lane	Pf-A	3,500	150
Cleveland State Univ., Cleveland, OH 44115	1964	Walter Waetjen	Ps-S	17,711	713
Cleveland Tech., Shelby, NC 28150	1965	James Petty	Psl-A	1,323	93
Clinton Community, Clinton, IA 52732	1946	Charles C. Spence	Ps-A	*1,000*	*54*
Clinton Community (A), Plattsburgh, NY 12901	1966	Albert B. Light	Psl-A	1,400	31
Cloud County Comm., Concordia, KS 66901	1965	James P. Ihrig	Psl-A	1,912	220
Coahoma Junior (A), Clarksdale, MS 38614	1949	McKinley C. Martin	Psl-A	1,521	64
Coastal Carolina Comm., Jacksonville, NC 28540	1965	James Henderson Jr.	Psl-A	*2,540*	*147*
Cochise (A), Douglas, AZ 85607	1962	Vacant	Pl-A	*4,209*	*68*
Coe, Cedar Rapids, IA 52402	1851	John Brown	IP-B	1,224	82
Coffeyville Comm. Jr. (A), Coffeyville, KS 67337	1923	Russell Graham	Pl-A	1,600	51
Coker, Hartsville, SC 29550	1908	James Daniels	IP-B	250	45
Colby, Waterville, ME 04901	1813	William R. Cotter	IP-B	1,658	151
Colby Comm., Colby, KS 67701	1964	James Tangeman	Psl-A	*2,100*	*90*
Colby-Sawyer (A), New London, NH 03257	1837	H. Nicholas Muller	IP-B	700	69
Coleman (A), La Mesa, CA 92041	1963	Maurice Egan	IP-B	681	40
Colgate Univ., Hamilton, NY 13346	1819	George D. Langdon, Jr.	IP-M	2,488	165
Colorado, Colo. Spgs., CO 80903	1874	Gresham Riley	IP-M	*1,945*	*167*
Colorado Mountain, Glenwood Spgs., CO 81601	1968	Dean F. Lillie	Psl-A	*2,067*	*500*
Colorado Northwestern Comm. (A), Rangely, CO 81648	1962	James H. Bos	Psl-A	1,187	70
Colorado Sch. of Mines (A), Golden, CO 80401	1876	Guy McBride Jr.	Ps-D	2,543	176
Colorado State Univ.*, Fort Collins, CO 80523	1870	Ralph E. Christoffersen	Ps-S	18,651	1,200
Colorado, Univ. of (A), Boulder, CO 80302	1876	Arnold Weber	Ps-D	20,167	950
Colorado Springs, Colorado Springs, CO 80933	1965	Donald Schwartz	Ps-M	4,955	192
Colorado Women's (A) (W), Denver, CO 80220	1888	Sherry Manning	IP-B	509	42
Columbia (W), Columbia, SC 29203	1854	Ralph Mirse	IR-M	953	101
Columbia, Columbia, MO 65216	1851	Bruce B. Kelly	IP-B	2,400	195
Columbia Basin (A), Pasco, WA 99301	1955	Fred L. Esvelt	Ps-A	10,000	382
Columbia Bible, Columbia, SC 29230	1923	J. Robertson McQuilkin	IP-M	779	41
Columbia Greene Comm. (A), Hudson, NY 12534	1966	Edward J. Owen	Psl-A	1,218	37
Columbia Jr., Columbia, CA 95310	1968	W. Dean Cunningham	Psl-A	*3,600*	*130*
Columbia Jr., Columbia, SC 29202	1935	Michael Gorman	IP-A	510	39
Columbia State Comm., Columbia, TN 38401	1966	Harold S. Pryor	Ps-A	2,227	87
Columbia Union, Takoma Park, MD 20912	1904	William Loveless	IR-B	756	125
Columbia Univ., New York, NY 10027	1754	Michael I. Sovern	IP-D	18,700	4,600
Teachers College, New York, NY 10027	1887	L.A. Cremin	IP-D	4,500	150
Columbus, Columbus, GA 31993	1958	Francis J. Brooke	Pf-S	4,213	234
Columbus Coll. of Art & Design, Columbus, OH 43215	1879	Joseph Canzani	IP-B	1,107	65
Columbus Tech. Inst. (A), Columbus, OH 43215	1963	Clarence Schauer	Ps-A	4,966	264
Compton Comm., Compton, CA 90221	1927	Abel B. Sykes Jr.	Psl-A	6,700	278
Concord, Athens, WV 24712	1872	Meredith Freeman	Ps-B	2,362	117
Concordia, Ann Arbor, MI 48105	1963	Howard Kramer	IR-B	529	45
Concordia, Bronxville, NY 10708	1881	Ralph Schultz	IR-B	443	60
Concordia, Milwaukee, WI 53208	1881	R.J. Buuck	IR-B	*602*	*45*
Concordia, Moorhead, MN 56560	1891	Paul Dovre	IR-B	2,586	188
Concordia, Portland, OR 97211	1905	E.P. Weber	IR-B	263	47
Concordia, River Forest, IL 60305	1864	Paul A. Zimmerman	IR-M	1,200	95
Concordia, St. Paul, MN 55104	1893	Gerhardt Hyatt	IR-B	746	56
Concordia Lutheran, Austin, TX 78705	1926	Ray F. Martens	IR-B	428	39
Concordia Teachers, Seward, NE 68434	1894	M.J. Stelmachowicz	IR-M	1,027	95
Concordia Theological Seminary (A), Ft. Wayne, IN 46825	1846	Robert Preus	IR-D	571	35
Connecticut, New London, CT 06320	1911	Oakes Ames	IP-M	1,927	194
Connecticut, Univ. of (A), Storrs, CT 06268	1881	Edward V. Gant, Act.	Ps-D	*21,349*	*1,15*
Connors State (A), Warner, OK 74469	1908	Melvin Self	Ps-A	1,800	64
Contra Costa, San Pablo, CA 94806	1950	H. Rex Craig	Psl-A	9,547	300

Name, address	Year	Governing official, affiliation, and highest degree offered		Students	Teachers
Converse (W), Spartanburg, SC 29301	1889	Robert T. Coleman, Jr.	IP-M	1,052	91
Cooke County, Gainesville, TX 76240	1924	Alton Laird	Pl-A	1,549	82
Cooper Union, New York, NY 10003	1859	Bill N. Lacy	IP-M	900	162
Copiah-Lincoln Junior (A), Wesson, MS 39191	1928	Billy Thames	Isl-A	*1,500*	*NA*
Coppin State, Baltimore, MD 21216	1900	Calvin Burnett	Ps-M	2,279	180
Cornell, Mt. Vernon, IA 52314	1853	Philip Secor	IP-A	908	72
Cornell Univ., Ithaca, NY 14853	1865	Frank Rhodes	IP-D	*18,099*	*1,900*
Corning Community (A), Corning, NY 14830	1957	Donald H. Hangen	Psl-A	3,068	104
Cosumnes River College (A), Sacramento, CA 95823	1970	Vincent P. Padilla	Psl-A	6,000	121
Cottey (W), Nevada, MO 64772	1884	Evelyn Milam	IP-A	327	34
Covenant, Lookout Mt., TN 37350	1955	Martin Essenburg	IR-B	529	38
Cowley County Comm., Arkansas City, KS 67005	1922	Gwen Nelson	Ps-A	1,600	80
Crafton Hills, Yucaipa, CA 92399	1972	Donald L. Singer	Psl-A	4,564	250
Craven Comm., New Bern, NC 28560	1965	Thurman E. Brock	Ps-A	1,687	52
Creighton Univ., Omaha, NE 68178	1878	Rev. Michael G. Moinson	IP-D	5,766	900
Crowder (A), Neosho, MO 64850	1964	Dell Reed	P-A	1,257	70
Cuesta, San Luis Obispo, CA 93406	1964	Frank Martinez	Psl-A	6,300	218
Culver-Stockton, Canton, MO 63435	1853	Robert W. Brown	IR-B	643	51
Cumberland, Lebanon, TN 37087	1842	Ernest Stockton	IP-B	500	27
Cumberland, Williamsburg, KY 40769	1889	Jim Taylor	IR-M	2,033	112
Cumberland County, Vineland, NJ 08360	1966	Philip Phelon	Psl-A	2,427	94
Curry, Milton, MA 02186	1879	William Boyle	IP-M	1,211	103
Cuyahoga Community, Cleveland, OH 44115	1963	Nolen Ellison	Psl-A	*26,800*	*1,010*
Cypress, Cypress, CA 90630	1966	Jack A. Scott	Pl-A	*15,876*	*217*
Dabney S. Lancaster, Comm. (A), Clifton Forge, VA 24422	1964	John F. Backels	Ps-A	1,151	70
Daemen, Amherst, NY 14226	1947	R.S. Marshall	IP-B	1,522	115
Dakota State, Madison, SD 57042	1881	Carleton M. Opgaard	Pf-B	1,107	75
Dakota Wesleyan Univ., Mitchell, SD 57301	1885	James B. Beddow	IR-B	531	58
Dallas Baptist, Dallas, TX 75211	1896	W. Marvin Watson	IR-M	1,327	54
Dallas Univ., Irving, TX 75061	1958	Robert F. Sasseen	IR-D	2,815	182
Dallas Co. Comm. Col. System (A), Dallas, TX 75202	1965	Bill J. Priest	Ps-A	*32,790*	*2,412*
Dalton Jr., Dalton, GA 30720	1963	Derrell Roberts	Ps-A	1,533	84
Dana, Blair, NE 68008	1884	James Kallas	IR-B	595	50
Daniel Webster, Nashua, NH 03063	1966	Louis D'Allesandro	IP-B	1,011	30
Danville Area Comm., Danville, IL 61832	1946	Ronald K. Lingle	Psl-A	4,500	150
Dartmouth (A), Hanover, NH 03755	1769	John George Kemeny	IP-D	4,115	291
Davenport Coll. of Business, Grand Rapids, MI 49503	1866	Donald W. Maine	IP-A	*4,282*	*170*
David Lipscomb, Nashville, TN 37203	1891	G. Williard Collins	IR-B	2,375	142
Davidson County Comm., Lexington, NC 27292	1958	Grady Love	Psl-A	2,357	104
Davidson, Davidson, NC 28036	1837	Samuel R. Spencer Jr.	IP-B	1,404	108
Davis & Elkins (A), Elkins, WV 26241	1904	Gordon E. Hermanson	IR-B	980	81
Davis Jr. Coll. of Business (A), Toledo, OH 43604	1858	Ruth L. Davis	IP-A	450	35
Dawson Comm., Glendive, MT 59330	1940	Donald H. Kettner	Psl-A	610	35
Dayton, Univ. of, Dayton, OH 45469	1850	Bro. Raymond Fitz	IR-D	10,190	640
Daytona Beach Comm., Daytona Beach, FL 32015	1958	Charles Polk	Ps-A	8,803	205
Dean Junior, Franklin, MA 02038	1941	Richard Crockford	IP-A	2,159	120
DeAnza, Cupertino, CA 95014	1967	A. Robert DeHart	Pl-A	*25,000*	*850*
Defiance (A), Defiance, OH 43512	1850	Marvin J. Ludwig	IP-B	765	62
DeKalb Community (A), Clarkston, GA 30021	1964	W.W. Scott	Pl-A	18,333	280
Delaware, Univ. of*, Newark, DE 19711	1833	E.A. Trabant	Psr-D	*18,619*	*870*
Delaware State*, Dover, DE 19901	1891	Luna I. Mishoe	Ps-B	2,069	144
Delaware County Comm. of (A), Media, PA 19063	1967	Richard D. DeCosmo	Psl-A	5,880	100
Delaware Tech. and Comm. (A), Dover, DE 19901	1967	John R. Kotula	Ps-A	*7,022*	*195*
Del. Valley Coll. of S&A, Doylestown, PA 18901	1896	Joshua Feldstein	Pl-B	1,717	101
Delgado, New Orleans, LA 70119	1921	Harry J. Boyer	Psl-A	*11,617*	*265*
Del Mar (A), Corpus Christi, TX 78404	1935	Jean Richardson	Pl-A	13,155	309
Delta, University Ctr., MI 48710	1958	Donald Carlyon	Psl-A	13,500	450
Delta State Univ. (A), Cleveland, MS 38733	1924	Kent Wyatt	Ps-M	2,693	156
Denison Univ. (A), Granville, OH 43023	1831	Robert C. Good	IP-B	2,128	188
Denver, Univ. of, Denver, CO 80208	1864	Ross Pritchard	IP-D	8,475	523
Denver, Comm. Coll. of (A), Denver, CO 80218	1968	Robert E. Lahti	Ps-A	*14,308*	*304*
DePaul Univ., Chicago, IL 60604	1898	Rev. John T. Richardson	IR-D	13,300	762
DePauw Univ., Greencastle, IN 46135	1837	Richard Rosser	IP-M	2,431	206
Desert, Coll. of the, Palm Desert, CA 92260	1958	F.D. Stout	Psl-A	*11,769*	*383*
Des Moines Area Comm., Ankeny, IA 50021	1967	Joseph Borgen	Psl-A	*7,000*	*221*
Detroit Coll. of Business, Dearborn, MI 48126	1962	Frank Paone	IP-B	*2,789*	*177*
Detroit Coll. of Law, Detroit, MI 48201	1891	Ellsworth G. Reynolds	IP-B	867	61
Detroit Inst. of Tech. (A), Detroit, MI 48201	1877	H. Thompson	IP-B	1,443	31
Detroit, Univ. of, Detroit, MI 48221	1877	Rev. Robert A. Mitchell	IR-D	*6,375*	*455*
Diablo Valley (A), Pleasant Hill, CA 94523	1949	William P. Niland	Psl-A	18,742	580
Dickinson, Carlisle, PA 17013	1773	Samuel Banks	Pl-B	1,745	141
Dickinson School of Law (A), Carlisle, PA 17013	1834	Dale F. Shughart	IP-D	500	39
Dickinson State, Dickinson, ND 58601	1918	Albert Watrel	Ps-B	1,153	70
Dillard Univ. (A), New Orleans, LA 70122	1869	Samuel Cook	IR-B	1,208	92
District of Columbia, Univ. of (A), Washington, DC 20009	1851	Wendell Russell	Pl-M	*1,310*	*132*
Van Ness Campus, Washington, DC 20008	1976	Lisle C. Carter, Jr.	Pl-M	*14,115*	*581*
District One Tech. Ins., Eau Claire, WI 54701	1912	Norbert Wurtzel	Psl-A	*3,700*	*130*
Dixie (A), St. George, UT 84770	1911	Alton L. Wade	P-F	1,790	75
Doane (A), Crete, NE 68333	1872	Philip R. Heckman	IP-B	624	61
Dr. Martin Luther, New Ulm, MN 56073	1884	Lloyd O. Huebner	IR-B	750	72
Dodge City Community, Dodge City, KS 67801	1935	Charles M. Barnes	Pl-A	1,421	110
Dominican Coll. of Blauvelt (A), Blauvelt, NY 10962	1952	Sr. Eileen O'Brien	IP-B	1,343	78
Dominican Coll. of San Rafael, San Rafael, CA 94901	1890	Barbara Bundy	IR-M	831	139
Donnelly (A), Kansas City, KS 66102	1949	Rev. Raymond Davern	IR-A	978	35
Dordt, Sioux Center, IA 51250	1955	John B. Hulst	IR-B	1,060	70
Dowling, Oakdale, NY 11769	1965	V.P. Meskill	IP-M	2,150	172
Drake Univ., Des Moines, IA 50311	1881	Wilbur C. Miller	IP-D	6,627	384
Draughons Jr., Nashville, TN 37217	1884	C.W. Davidson	IP-A	*600*	*42*
Draughons Jr., Savannah, GA 31401	1889	John T. South, III	IP-A	*633*	*40*
Drew Univ., Madison, NJ 07940	1866	Paul Hardin	IR-D	1,946	119
Drexel Univ., Philadelphia, PA 19104	1891	William W. Hagerty	IP-D	12,594	740
Drury, Springfield, MO 65802	1873	Norman C. Crawford, Jr.	IP-M	*2,922*	*195*
Dubuque, Univ. of, Dubuque, IA 52001	1852	Walter F. Peterson	IR-1P	1,217	79
Duke Univ. (A), Durham, NC 27706	1838	Terry Sanford	IP-D	*9,900*	*1,385*
Dundalk Community (A), Baltimore, MD 21222	1970	John E. Ravekes	Pl-A	2,213	131
Du Page, Coll. of, Glen Ellyn, IL 60137	1967	Harold D. McAninch	Ps-A	*22,974*	*1,200*
Duquesne Univ., Pittsburgh, PA 15282	1878	Rev. Donald S. Nesti	IR-D	6,611	497
Durham Tech. Inst., Durham, NC 27703	1965	Phil Wynn Jr.	Psl-A	2,000	130

Name, address	Year	Governing official, affiliation, and highest degree offered		Students	Teachers
Dutchess Community (A), Poughkeepsie, NY 12601	1957	John J. Connolly	Psl-A	5,975	132
Dyersburg State Comm., Dyersburg, TN 38024	1969	Carl Christian Andersen	Ps-A	1,387	81
Dyke, Cleveland, OH 44114	1848	John Corfias	IP-A	1,456	125
D'Youville. Buffalo. NY 14201	1908	Sister Denise Roche	IP-M	1,400	100
Earlham, Richmond, IN 47374	1847	Franklin Wallin	IR-M	1,013	98
East Carolina Univ., Greenville, NC 27834	1907	John M. Howell	Ps-1P	*14,685*	*846*
East Central Junior (A), Decatur, MS 39327	1928	Charles V. Wright	Psl-A	785	50
East Central Junior, Union, MO 63084	1968	Donald D. Shook	Pl-A	1,978	81
East Central Oklahoma St. Univ., Ada, OK 74820	1909	Stanley Wagner	Ps-M	3,941	175
East Los Angeles (A), Monterey Park, CA 91754	1945	Arthur D. Avila, Act.	Psl-A	15,652	680
East Mississippi Jr. (A), Scooba, MS 39358	1927	C. Cheatham	Psl-A	*1,554*	*47*
East Stroudsburg State, E. Stroudsburg, PA 18301	1893	Dennis Bell	Ps-M	3,886	234
East Tennessee State Univ. (A), Johnson City, TN 37614	1911	Ronald E. Beller	Ps-D	9,153	530
East Texas Baptist, Marshall, TX 75670	1912	Jerry Dawson	IR-B	962	54
East Texas State Univ. (A), Commerce, TX 75428	1889	F.H. McDowell	Ps-D	*8,752*	*347*
Eastern (A), St. Davids, PA 19087	1952	Daniel E. Weiss	IR-B	700	72
Eastern Arizona, Thatcher, AZ 85552	1888	W.M. McGrath	Ps-A	4,039	235
Eastern Conn. State (A), Willimantic, CT 06226	1889	Charles Richard Webb	Ps-M	2,950	239
Eastern Illinois Univ., Charleston, IL 61920	1895	Daniel Marvin, Jr.	Ps-S	10,016	450
Eastern Iowa Comm. (A), Davenport, IA 52803	1966	Michael E. Crawford, Supt.	Psl-A	*2,900*	*155*
Eastern Kentucky Univ. (A), Richmond, KY 40475	1906	Julius Powell	Ps-M	13,714	650
Eastern Maine Voc. Tech. Inst. (A), Bangor, ME 04401	1966	Alan R. Campbell, Dir.	Pf-A	1,600	150
Eastern Mennonite, Harrisonburg, VA 22801	1917	Richard C. Detweiler	IR-M	936	80
Eastern Michigan Univ., Ypsilanti, MI 48197	1849	John W. Porter	Ps-S	19,156	774
Eastern Montana, Billings, MT 59101	1927	William A. Johnstone	Ps-M	4,035	200
Eastern Nazarene, Quincy, MA 02170	1918	Stephen W. Nease	IR-M	902	56
Eastern New Mexico Univ., Portales, NM 88130	1934	Warren Armstrong	Ps-S	*6,474*	*330*
Eastern Oklahoma State (A), Wilburton, OK 74578	1909	James Miller	Ps-A	*1,622*	*69*
Eastern Oregon State, LaGrande, OR 97850	1928	Rodney A. Briggs	Ps-M	*1,825*	*175*
Eastern Utah (A), Coll. Of, Price, UT 84501	1937	Dean McDonald	Ps-A	*1,250*	*35*
Eastern Washington Univ. Cheney, WA 99004	1882	H.G. Frederickson	Ps-D	*7,591*	*573*
Eastern Wyoming, Torrington, WY 82240	1948	Charles Rogers	Psl-A	1,190	117
Eastfield, Mesquite, TX 75150	1970	Eleanor Ott	Ps-A	*7,988*	*1,900*
Eckerd, St. Petersburg, FL 33733	1958	Peter Armacost	IP-A	1,031	69
Edgecliff (A), Cincinnati, OH 45206	1935	Sr. M. Molitor	IR-B	841	42
Edgecombe Tech. Inst., Tarboro, NC 27886	1968	Charles McIntyre	Psl-A	*1,250*	*65*
Edgewood (A), Madison, WI 53711	1927	Sister Alice O'Rourke	IR-B	680	80
Edinboro State, Edinboro, PA 16444	1857	Foster F. Diebold	Ps-M	5,848	360
Edison Community, Ft. Myers, FL 33907	1962	David G. Robinson	Psl-A	*5,145*	*227*
Edmonds Community, Lynnwood, WA 98036	1967	Thomas C. Nielsen	Ps-A	7,000	260
Edmondson Junior, Chattanooga, TN 37411	1914	J.L. Lasson	IP-A	367	22
Edward Waters (A), Jacksonville, FL 32209	1866	Cecil Wayne Cone	IR-B	703	35
Edward Williams (A), Hackensack, NJ 07601	1964	Jerome Pollack	IP-A	398	9
Eisenhower, Seneca Falls, NY 13148	1965	Thomas R. Plough, Dean	IP-A	535	60
El Camino, Torrance, CA 90506	1947	Stuart E. Marsee	Psl-A	31,000	700
El Centro, Dallas, TX 75202	1966	Queen F. Randall	Psl-A	6,738	325
El Paso County Community, El Paso, TX 79998	1969	Robert E. Shepack	Psl-A	*15,000*	*513*
El Reno Jr., El Reno, OK 73036	1938	Bill S. Cole	Pf-A	1,399	52
Elgin Community, Elgin, IL 60120	1949	Mark L. Hopkins	Psl-A	*6,500*	*348*
Elizabeth City State Univ. (A), Eliz. City, NC 27909	1891	Marion Thorpe, Chan.	Ps-B	1,560	114
Elizabeth Seton (A), Yonkers, NY 10701	1960	Sr. Mary Ellen Brosnan	IP-A	989	81
Elizabethtown, Elizabethtown, PA 17022	1899	Mark C. Ebersole	IR-B	1,380	135
Elizabethtown Comm., Elizabethtown, KY 42701	1964	James Owen, Dir.	Ps-A	1,927	61
Ellsworth Comm., Iowa Falls, IA 50126	1890	Duane R. Lloyd, Dean	Psl-A	950	54
Elmhurst, Elmhurst, IL 60126	1871	Ivan Frick	IR-B	3,560	249
Elmira, Elmira, NY 14901	1855	Leonart Grant	IP-M	2,651	150
Elon (A), Elon College, NC 27244	1889	J.F. Young	IR-B	2,577	84
Embry-Riddle Aero. Univ., Bunnell, FL 32010	1926	Jack R. Hunt	IP-M	*10,319*	*737*
Emerson, Boston, MA 02116	1880	Allan Koenig	IP-M	2,090	140
Emmanuel (W), Boston, MA 02116	1919	Sister Janet Eisner	IR-M	*1,083*	*130*
Emmanuel, Franklin Springs, GA 30639	1919	C.Y. Melton	IR-A	427	29
Emory & Henry, Emory, VA 24327	1836	Thomas F. Chilcote	IR-B	789	60
Emory Univ., Atlanta, GA 30322	1836	James T. Laney	IR-D	*8,164*	*1,250*
Emporia State, Emporia, KS 66801	1865	John Visser	Ps-S	5,553	320
Endicott (A) (W), Beverly, MA 01915	1939	Carol A. Hawkes	IP-A	837	70
Enterprise State Junior, Enterprise, AL 36331	1965	Joseph D. Talmadge	Ps-A	1,700	74
Erie Community (A), Buffalo, NY 14221	1946	Oscar Smuckler, Act.	Psl-A	10,296	325
Erskine, Due West, SC 29639	1839	Wm. Bruce Ezell Jr.	IR-IP	635	50
Essex Community, Baltimore, MD 21237	1957	John E. Ravekes	Psl-A	9,500	432
Essex County, Newark, NJ 07102	1968	A. Zachary Yamba	Psl-A	6,813	300
Eureka, Eureka, IL 61530	1855	Daniel Gilbert	IR-B	410	37
Evangel, Springfield, MO 65802	1955	Robert Spence	IP-B	1,779	126
Evansville, Univ. of, Evansville, IN 47714	1854	Wallace B. Graves	IR-M	*4,908*	*253*
Everett Comm., Everett, WA 98201	1941	Paul D. Walker	Ps-A	6,500	250
Evergreen State, Olympia, WA 98505	1970	Daniel Evans	Ps-M	2,475	125
Fairfield Univ., Fairfield, CT 06430	1942	Rev. Aloysius P. Kelly	IR-M	5,131	296
Fairleigh Dickinson Univ., Rutherford, NJ 07016	1942	Jerome Pollack	IP-D	*20,000*	*1,574*
Fairmount State (A), Fairmount, WV 26554	1867	Wendell G. Hardway	Ps-B	5,165	310
Faith Baptist Bible (A), Ankeny, IA 50021	1921	Gordon L. Shipp	IR-B	440	24
Fashion Inst. of Tech. (A), New York, NY 10001	1944	Marvin J. Peldman	Psl-B	8,444	164
Faulkner State Jr., Bay Minette, Al 36507	1965	Gary L. Branch	Ps-A	1,147	45
Fayetteville St. Univ., Fayetteville, NC 28301	1867	Charles Lyons Jr.	Pf-M	*2,850*	*190*
Fayetteville Tech. Inst., Fayetteville, NC 28303	1961	Howard Boudreau	Psl-A	5,328	247
Feather River, Quincy, CA 95971	1968	Joseph Brennan	Ps-A	1,793	77
Felician, Lodi, NJ 07644	1942	Sr. M. Hiltrude Koba	IP-B	656	75
Fergus Falls Comm., Fergus Falls, MN 56537	1960	W.A. Waage	Ps-A	666	41
Ferris State, Big Rapids, MI 49307	1884	Robert Ewigleben	Ps-1P	11,200	600
Ferrum, Ferrum, VA 24088	1913	Joseph T. Hart	IR-B	1,615	103
Findlay, Findlay, OH 45840	1882	Glen R. Rasmussen	IR-A	1,300	100
Finger Lakes, Comm. Coll. of (A), Canandaigua, NY 14424	1965	Charles Meder	Psl-A	2,800	85
Fisher Junior, Boston, MA 02116	1903	Richard A. Boudreau	IP-A	*4,170*	*263*
Fisk Univ. (A), Nashville, TN 37203	1865	Walter Leonard	IP-M	915	83
Fitchburg State, Fitchburg, MA 01420	1894	Vincent J. Mara	Pf-M	6,368	319
Flagler, St. Augustine, FL 32084	1967	William L. Proctor	IP-B	904	52
Flathead Valley Comm., Kalispell, MT 59901	1967	Donald A. Gatzke	Psl-A	1,734	83
Florida, Temple Terrace, FL 33617	1946	Bob F. Owen	IP-A	447	37
Florida A.&M. Univ.*, Tallahassee, FL 32307	1887	Walter L. Smith	Ps-M	4,964	400

ame, address	Year	Governing official, affiliation, and highest degree offered		Stu-dents	Teach-ers
lorida Atlantic Univ., Boca Raton, FL 33431	1961	Glenwood L. Creech	Ps-S	8,348	489
lorida Inst. of Tech. (A), Melbourne, FL 32901	1958	Jerome P. Keuper	IP-D	*3,899*	*180*
lorida Jr. (A), Jacksonville, FL 32202	1966	Benjamin R. Wygal	Pl-A	*38,524*	*335*
lorida Keys Comm. (A), Key West, FL 33040	1965	William A. Seeker	Ps-A	1,918	91
lorida Memorial, Miami, FL 33054	1879	Willie Robinson	IR-B	877	55
lorida Southern, Lakeland, FL 33802	1885	Robert Davis	IR-M	3,099	188
lorida State Univ., Tallahassee, FL 32306	1851	Bernard F. Sliger	Ps-D	22,363	1,546
lorida Tech. Univ. (A), Orlando, FL 32816	1963	Trevor Colbourn	Ps-M	10,605	397
lorida Univ. of* (A), Gainesville, FL 32611	1845	Robert Q. Marston	Ps-D	33,232	2,529
loyd Junior (A), Rome, GA 30161	1970	David McCorkle	Ps-A	1,445	55
ontbonne, St. Louis, MO 63105	1923	Sister Jane Hassett	IP-M	882	110
oothill, Los Altos Hills, CA 94022	1958	James S. Fitzgerald	Pl-A	16,200	332
ordham Univ. (A), Bronx, NY 10458	1841	Rev. James C. Finlay	IP-D	*14,653*	*499*
orsyth Sch. for Dental Hygienists, Boston, MA 02115	1916	John W. Hein,	IP-A	200	26
orsyth Tech. Inst. (A), Winston-Salem, NC 27103	1963	Harley Affeldt	Psl-A	2,679	104
t. Hays State, Hays, KS 67601	1902	Gerald W. Tomanek	Ps-S	5,607	271
t. Lauderdale, Ft. Lauderdale, FL 33301	1940	Douglas Devaux	IP-B	*1,115*	*45*
ort Lewis, Durango, CO 81301	1911	Rexer Berndt	IP-B	3,312	160
t. Scott Comm., Ft. Scott, KS 66701	1919	Wayne McElroy	Psl-A	1,248	60
t. Steilacoom Comm., Tacoma, WA 98498	1967	Robert H. Stauffer	Ps-A	8,334	302
ort Valley State* (A), Fort Valley, GA 31030	1895	Cleveland W. Pettigrew	Ps-M	1,748	142
ort Wayne Bible, Fort Wayne, IN 46807	1904	Harvey R. Bostrum	IR-B	500	35
ort Wright (A), Spokane, WA 99204	1907	Sister Sheila McEvoy	IR-M	413	72
ox Valley Tech. Inst. (A), Appleton, WI 54913	1967	William Sirek	Psl-A	4,782	240
ramingham State, Framingham, MA 01701	1839	D. Justin McCarthy	Ps-M	3,125	170
rancis Marion, Florence, SC 29501	1970	Walter D. Smith	Ps-M	2,728	138
rank Phillips, Borger, TX 79036	1948	Andy Hicks	Psl-A	927	62
ranklin, Franklin, IN 46131	1834	Edwin A. Penn	IR-B	596	67
ranklin Inst., Boston, MA 02116	1908	Michael C. Mazzola	IP-A	800	62
ranklin Univ., Columbus, OH 43215	1902	Frederick J. Bunte	IP-B	5,212	196
ranklin and Marshall, Lancaster, PA 17604	1787	Keith Spalding	IP-B	1,994	132
ranklin Pierce, Rindge, NH 03461	1962	Walter Peterson	IP-B	1,500	80
ranklin Pierce Law Center, Concord, NH 03301	1973	Robert H. Rines	IP-IP	347	29
reed-Hardeman, Henderson, TN 38340	1908	E. Claude Gardner	IR-B	1,224	88
ree Will Baptist Bible (A), Nashville, TN 37205	1942	Charles A. Thigpen	IR-B	600	26
resno City, Fresno, CA 93741	1910	Clyde C. McCully	Psl-A	15,645	450
resno Pacific, Fresno, CA 93727	1944	Edmund Janzen	IR-M	900	55
riends Univ., Wichita, KS 67213	1898	Richard Felix	IR-B	850	69
rontier Comm., Fairfield, IL 62837	1977	Richard L. Mason	Psl-A	1,034	347
rostburg State, Frostburg, MD 21532	1898	Nelson Guild	Ps-M	3,609	203
ullerton, Fullerton (A), CA 92634	1913	Philip W. Borst	Ps-A	19,062	567
ulton-Montgomery Comm. (A), Johnstown, NY 12095	1963	Hadley S. DePuy	Psl-A	1,565	57
urman Univ., Greenville, SC 29613	1826	John Edwin Johns	IR-M	2,485	155
iadsden State Junior, Gadsden, AL 35999	1965	Arthur W. Dennis	Ps-A	3,500	205
ainesville Junior, Gainesville, GA 30503	1964	Hugh M. Mills Jr.	Ps-A	1,585	58
allaudet (A), Washington, DC 20002	1864	Edward C. Merrill Jr.	IP-D	943	126
alveston (A), Galveston, TX 77550	1967	Melvin M. Plexco	Psl-A	*2,203*	*80*
annon, Erie, PA 16541	1933	Joseph P. Scottino	IP-M	4,200	250
iarden City Comm. (A), Garden City, KS 67846	1920	Thomas F. Saffell	Pl-A	1,800	90
iardner-Webb (A), Boiling Springs, NC 28017	1905	Dr. Craven E. Williams	IR-B	1,450	80
iaston (A), Dallas, NC 28034	1963	W. Wayne Scott	Psl-A	2,613	154
iateway Tech. Inst. (A), Kenosha, WI 53141	1911	Keith Stoehr	Psl-A	*20,000*	*785*
iavilan (A), Gilroy, CA 95020	1963	Rudy Melone	Psl-A	*2,400*	*83*
ieneral Motors Inst., Flint, MI 48502	1919	William B. Cottingham	IP-B	2,389	132
ienesee Community (A), Batavia, NY 14020	1966	Stuart Steiner	Psl-A	2,069	72
ieneva, Beaver Falls, PA 15010	1848	Donald W. Felker	IR-B	1,406	99
ieorge C. Wallace St. Comm. (A), Dothan, AL 36303	1947	Nathan L. Hodges	Ps-A	3,050	115
ieorge Fox, Newberg, OR 97132	1891	David Le Shana	IR-B	743	78
ieorge Mason Univ., Fairfax, VA 22030	1966	George W. Johnson	Ps-D	14,273	750
ieorge Washington Univ., Washington, DC 20052	1821	Lloyd H. Elliott	IP-D	21,416	2,759
ieorge Williams, Downers Grove, IL 60515	1890	Richard E. Hamlin	IP-M	1,175	100
ieorgetown, Georgetown, KY 40324	1829	Ben M. Elrod	IR-M	1,170	90
ieorgetown Univ., Washington, DC 20057	1789	Rev. Timothy Healy	IR-D	12,231	537
ieorgia, Milledgeville, GA 31061	1889	Edwin G. Speir, Jr.	Ps-M	3,440	145
ieorgia Inst. Of Tech.*, Atlanta, GA 30332	1885	Joseph M. Pettit	Ps-D	11,158	662
ieorgia Southern, Statesboro, GA 30460	1906	Vernon Crawford	Ps-S	6,336	350
ieorgia Southwestern (A), Americus, GA 31709	1906	William H. Capitan	Ps-M	2,101	114
ieorgia State Univ., Atlanta, GA 30303	1913	Noah N. Langdale Jr.	Ps-D	21,009	831
ieorgia, Univ. of*, Athens, GA 30602	1785	Fred C. Davison	Ps-D	23,657	2,000
ieorgian Court (A), Lakewood, NJ 08701	1908	Sister Barbara Williams	IP-M	1,358	111
iermanna Comm., Locust Grove, VA 22508	1970	William P. Briley	Ps-A	1,596	62
iettysburg, Gettysburg, PA 17325	1832	Charles E. Glassick	IR-B	1,941	166
ilassboro State, Glassboro, NJ 08028	1923	Mark M. Chamberlain	Ps-S	9,900	437
ilendale Comm. (A), Glendale, AZ 85032	1965	John Waltrip	Pl-A	12,291	180
ilendale Comm., Glendale, CA 91208	1927	John Grande	Psl-A	10,947	515
ilen Oaks Comm. (A), Centreville, MI 49032	1965	Justus Sundermann	Pl-A	900	66
ilenville State, Glenville, WV 26351	1872	William Simmons	Pf-A	1,998	100
iloucester County, Sewell, NJ 08080	1968	Gary L. Reddig	Pl-A	3,305	143
iogebic Community, Ironwood, MI 49938	1932	R. Ernest Dear	Pl-A	1,447	77
iolden Gate Univ., San Francisco, CA 94105	1901	Otto W. Butz	IP-D	*10,700*	*400*
iolden West, Huntgtn. Bch., CA 92647	1965	Lee A. Stevens	Psl-A	21,166	618
ioldey Beacom, Wilmington, DE 19808	1886	William R. Baldt	IP-B	1,780	85
ionzaga Univ., Spokane, WA 99258	1887	Bernard Coughlin	IR-D	3,454	369
iordon, Wenham, MA 01984	1889	Richard Gross	IP-B	1,094	80
iordon Junior, Barnesville, GA 30204	1852	Jerry M. Williamson	Pf-A	1,502	60
ioshen, Goshen, IN 46526	1894	J. Lawrence Burkholder	IR-B	1,208	95
ioucher (W), Towson, MD 21204	1885	Rhoda M. Dorsey	IP-M	1,055	145
iovernors State Univ., Park Forest South, IL 60466	1969	L. Goodman-Malamuth	Acs-M	5,017	332
irace (A), Winona Lake, IN 46590	1948	Homer Kent	IR-B	804	34
irace Coll. of the Bible, Omaha, NE 68108	1943	Robert W. Benton	IR-A	396	27
iraceland, Lamoni, IA 50140	1895	Joe E. Hanna	IP-B	1,296	88
irahm Junior (A), Boston, MA 02215	1950	Robert B. Vail	IP-A	541	59
irambling State Univ., Grambling, LA 71245	1901	Joseph B. Johnson	Ps-M	3,928	210
irand Canyon, Phoenix, AZ 85061	1949	Bill Williams	IR-B	1,227	75
irand Rapids Junior (A), Grand Rapids, MI 49502	1914	Richard Calkins	Pl-A	7,301	230
irand Valley State, Allendale, MI 49401	1960	Arend D. Lubbers	Ps-M	6,699	240
irand View, Des Moines, IA 50316	1896	Karl F. Langrock	IR-B	1,296	75
irays Harbor, Aberdeen, WA 98520	1930	Joseph A. Malik	Ps-A	2,900	120

Name, address	Year	Governing official, affiliation, and highest degree offered		Students	Teachers
Grayson County Junior, Denison, TX 75020	1964	Jim Williams	Psl-A	4,003	15
Greater Hartford Comm., Hartford, CT 06105	1967	Arthur C. Banks Jr.	Ps-A	3,302	9
Great Falls, Coll. of (A), Great Falls, MT 59405	1932	William A. Shields	IR-M	1,253	8
Greenbrier Comm., Lewisburg, WV 24901	1969	Vivian Crane, Dean.	Ps-A	400	2
Green Mountain, Poultney, VT 05764	1834	James M. Pollock	IP-B	410	5
Green River Comm., Auburn, WA 98002	1965	James P. Chadbourne	Ps-A	4,715	34
Greenfield Comm., Greenfield, MA 01301	1962	David George	Ps-A	2,448	15
Greensboro, Greensboro, NC 27401	1838	James S. Barrett	IR-B	630	6
Greenville, Greenville, IL 62246	1892	W. Richard Stephens	IR-B	835	6
Greenville Tech., Greenville, SC 29606	1962	Thomas Barton Jr.	Ps-A	33,369	52
Grinnell, Grinnell, IA 50112	1846	George A. Drake	IP-B	1,206	12
Grossmont, El Cajon, CA 92020	1961	Ivan Jones	Psl-A	15,200	55
Grove City, Grove City, PA 16127	1876	Charles S. MacKenzie	IP-B	2,256	12
Guilford, Greensboro, NC 27410	1837	William R. Rogers	IR-B	1,650	12
Guilford Tech. Inst., Jamestown, NY 27282	1958	Raymond Needham	Psl-A	4,413	23
Gulf Coast Bible (A), Houston, TX 77008	1953	John W. Conley	IR-B	351	1
Gulf Coast Comm. (A), Panama City, FL 32401	1957	Lawrence W. Tyree	Ps-A	4,117	18
Gustavus Adolphus, St. Peter, MN 56082	1862	John Kendall	IR-B	2,284	21
Gwynedd-Mercy, Gwynedd Valley, PA 19437	1948	Sister Isabelle Keiss	IP-B	2,169	18
Hagerstown Junior, Hagerstown, MD 21740	1946	Atlee Kepler	Psl-A	2,361	13
Hahnemann Medical, Philadelphia, PA 19102	1848	William Likoff	IP-D	1,800	45
Halifax Comm., Weldon, NC 27890	1967	Phillip W. Taylor	Psl-A	2,584	6
Hamilton, Clinton, NY 13323	1812	J.M. Carovano	IP-B	1,650	13
Hamline Univ., St. Paul, MN 55104	1854	Charles J. Graham	IR-M	1,850	15
Hampden-Sydney (M), Hampden-Syndey, VA 23943	1776	Josiah Bunting III	IR-A	770	6
Hampshire College, Amherst, MA 01002	1965	Adele S Simmons	IP-B	1,225	10
Hampton Institute, Hampton, VA 23668	1868	William R. Harvey	IP-M	3,351	24
Hanover, Hanover, IN 47243	1827	John E. Horner	IR-B	1,000	7
Harcum Junior (A), Bryn Mawr, PA 19010	1915	Michael A. Duzy	IP-A	930	7
Hardbarger Jr. of Bus (A), Raleigh NC 27602	1924	James W. Burnette	IP-A	750	3
Hardin-Simmons Univ., Abilene, TX 79698	1891	Dr. Jesse C. Fletcher	IR-M	2,049	12
Harding Univ., Searcy, AR 72143	1924	Clifton L. Ganus	IP-M	3,076	19
Harford Community, Bel Air, MD 21014	1957	A.C. O'Connell	Psl-A	4,300	22
Harris-Stowe State, St. Louis, MO 63103	1857	Henry Givens Jr.	Ps-B	1,281	9
Harrisburg Area Comm., Harrisburg, PA 17110	1964	James Odom Jr.	Psl-A	6,036	24
Hartford, Univ. of, W. Hartford, CT 06117	1877	Stephen Trachtenberg	IP-D	9,264	75
Hartford State Tech. (A), Hartford, CT 06106	1948	L. Barrell	Psl-A	1,423	4
Hartnell, Salinas, CA 93901	1920	Gibb R. Madsen	Ps-A	8,382	31
Hartwick, Oneonta, NY 13820	1928	Philip S. Wilder Jr	IP-B	1,370	10
Harvard Univ.**, Cambridge, MA 02138	1636	Derek Curtis Bok	IP-D	16,053	1,31
Harvey Mudd, Claremont, CA 91711	1955	Kenneth D. Baker	IP-M	510	7
Haskell Indian Junior, Lawrence, KS 66044	1884	Gerald E. Gipp	Pf-A	932	6
Hastings, Hastings, NE 68901	1882	Clyde B. Matters	IR-B	798	6
Haverford, Haverford, PA 19041	1833	Robert B. Stevens	IP-B	1,050	11
Hawaii, Univ. of (A), Honolulu, HI 96822	1907	Durwood Long, Chan.	Ps-D	*67,000*	*4,74*
Hawkeye Inst. of Tech., Waterloo, IA 50704	1966	John Hawse	Ps-A	1921	14
Haywood Tech. Inst. (A), Clyde, NC 28721	1964	J.H. Nanney	Ps-A	1,600	16
Hazard Community, Hazard, KY 41701	1968	J. Marvin Jolly	Ps-A	333	3
Heidelberg, Tiffin, OH 44883	1850	William C. Cossell	IP-B	780	8
Henderson Community, Henderson, KY 42420	1960	Marshall Arnold	Ps-A	983	5
Henderson Co. Jr., Athens, TX 75751	1946	William J. Campion	Psl-A	2,789	13
Henderson State Univ, Arkadelphia, AR 71923	1890	Martin B. Garrison	Ps-M	3,041	16
Hendrix, Conway, AR 72032	1884	Joe B. Hatcher	IR-B	1,017	6
Henry Ford Comm. (A), Dearborn, MI 48128	1938	Stuart M. Bundy	Pl-A	14,856	60
Herkimer Co. Comm. (A), Herkimer, NY 13350	1966	Robert McLaughlin	Psl-A	2,059	9
Hesston, Hesston, KS 67062	1909	Kirk Alliman	IP-A	657	6
Hibbing Comm., Hibbing, MN 55746	1916	Orville A. Olson	Ps-A	823	4
High Point, High Point, NC 27262	1924	Charles R. Lucht	IR-A	1,385	6
Highland Comm., Freeport, IL 61032	1966	Howard Sims	Ps-A	4,494	17
Highland Comm., Highland, KS 66035	1858	Jack D. Nutt	Psl-A	1,626	9
Highland Park Comm., Highland Park, MI 48203	1918	Chrystine R. Shack	Psl-A	2,706	12
Highline Comm., Midway, WA 98031	1961	Shirley B. Gordon	Ps-A	9,800	34
Hilbert, Hamburg, NY 14075	1957	Sister Edmunette Paczesny	IP-A	600	4
Hill Junior, Hillsboro, TX 76645	1923	Eblert C. Hutchins	Pl-A	1,100	6
Hillsborough Comm., Tampa, FL 33630	1968	Barbara Holmes	Ps-A	*12,142*	*5*
Hillsdale, Hillsdale, MI 49242	1844	George C. Roche III	IP-B	1,435	7
Hinds Junior, Raymond, MS 39154	1917	Clyde Muse	Psl-A	9,035	35
Hiram, Hiram, OH 44234	1850	Elmer Jagow	IP-B	1,165	9
Hiwassee (A), Madisonville, TN 37354	1849	Horace N. Barker	Pl-A	574	[illegible]
Hobart & William Smith, Geneva, NY 14456	1822	Carol Brewster	IP-B	1,800	15
Hocking Technical, Nelsonville, OH 45764	1968	John J. Light	Ps-A	2,532	16
Hofstra Univ., Hempstead, NY 11550	1935	James M. Shuart	IP-D	11,158	67
Hollins (W), Hollins Coll., VA 24020	1842	Paula P. Brownlee	IP-M	954	10
Holmes Junior, Goodman, MS 39079	1911	M. R. Thorne	Psl-A	1,197	5
Holy Cross, Coll. of the (A), Worcester, MA 01610	1843	Rev. John Brooks	IR-M	2,663	21
Holy Cross Jr., Notre Dame, IN 46556	1966	Brother John Driscoll	IR-A	300	2
Holy Family, Philadelphia, PA 19114	1954	Sister M. Francesca Onley	IP-B	1,287	15
Holy Names, Oakland, CA 94619	1868	Sister Lois MacGilliway	IR-S	750	11
Holyoke Community, Holyoke, MA 01040	1946	Winston H. Lavalle	Ps-A	3,000	17
Honolulu Comm., Honolulu, HI 96817	1920	C. Yoshioka	Ps-A	5,317	24
Hood, (W) Frederick, MD 21701	1893	Martha Church	IP-M	1,756	14
Hope, Holland, MI 49423	1866	Gordon J. Van Wylen	IP-B	2,458	14
Hopkinsville Comm., Hopkinsville, KY 42240	1965	Thomas Riley	Ps-A	1,080	[illegible]
Horry Georgetown Tech., Conway, SC 29526	1966	Kent Sharples	Ps-A	*5,500*	*1*
Houghton, Houghton, NY 14744	1883	D.R. Chamberlain	IR-B	*1,164*	*1*
Housatonic Comm., Bridgeport, CT 06608	1966	Vincent Darnowski	Ps-A	2,617	1
Houston Baptist Univ. (B), Houston, TX 77074	1960	William Hinton	IR-M	2,551	1
Houston Comm. Coll. (A), Houston, TX 77007	1971	J.B. Whiteley	Pl-A	*30,011*	*2*
Houston, Univ. of (A), Houston, TX 77004	1927	Philip G. Hoffman	Ps-D	*40,500*	*1,6*
Downtown College (A), Houston, TX 77002	1974	Alexander F. Schilt	Ps-B	4,927	25
Howard (A), Big Spring, TX 79720	1945	Charles Hays	Psl-A	1,047	[illegible]
Howard Community, Columbia, MD 21044	1969	Dwight A. Burill	Psl-A	3,330	1
Howard Payne Univ., Brownwood, TX 76801	1889	Ralph Phelps Jr	IR-B	1,172	[illegible]
Howard Univ. (A), Washington, DC 20059	1867	James E. Cheek	IP-D	10,709	1,0
Hudson Valley Comm. (A), Troy, NY 12180	1953	J. Fitzgibbons	Ps-A	6,932	2
Humboldt State Univ., Arcata, CA 95521	1913	Alistair McCrone	Ps-M	7,460	4
Humphreys (A), Stockton, CA 95207	1896	Robert G. Humphreys	IP-A	300	[illegible]
Huntingdon, Montgomery, AL 36106	1854	Allen K. Jackson	IR-A	680	[illegible]

Name, address	Year	Governing official, affiliation, and highest degree offered		Students	Teachers
Huntington, Huntington, IN 46750	1897	Eugene B. Habecker	IR-M	479	61
Huron (A), Huron, SD 57350	1883	Wendell L. Jahnke	IR-B	315	34
Husson, Bangor, ME 04401	1898	Delmont N. Merrill	IP-M	1,570	135
Huston-Tillotson, Austin, TX 78702	1876	John Q. Taylor King	IR-B	604	48
Hutchinson Comm., Hutchinson, KS 67501	1928	James Stringer	PsI-A	3,048	269
daho, Coll. of, Caldwell, ID 83605	1891	Arthur H. DeRosier Jr.	IP-M	757	72
daho State Univ. (A), (A), Pocatello, ID 83209	1901	Myron Coulter	Ps-D	10,747	449
daho, Univ. of.*, Moscow, ID 83843	1889	Richard D. Gibb	Pf-D	8,998	599
linois, Jacksonville, IL 62650	1829	Donald Mundinger	IR-B	758	79
linois, Univ. of* (A), Urbana, IL 61801	1867	Stanley Ikenberry	Ps-D	*62,703*	*8,497*
Chicago Circle* (A), Chicago, IL 60680	1965	Donald Riddle	Ps-D	20,285	1,500
Medical Center* (A), Chicago, IL 60680	1896	Joseph Begando	Ps-D	*4,923*	*729*
Urbana-Champaign*, Urbana, IL 61801	1867	John E. Cribbet	Ps-S	35,152	2,700
linois Benedictine, Lisle, IL 60532	1887	Richard Becker	IR-M	2,100	130
linois Central, E. Peoria, IL 61635	1967	Leon Perley	PI-A	14,048	641
linois Coll. of Optometry (A), Chicago, IL 60616	1955	Alfred Rosenbloom	IP-S	598	65
linois Coll. of Pod. Med. (A), Chicago, IL 60610	1912	John F. Briggs	IP-S	646	90
linois Eastern Comm., Olney, IL 62450	1962	Charles R. Novak	Ps-A	*1,070*	*174*
linois Inst. of Technology, Chicago, IL 60616	1890	Thomas L. Martin Jr.	IP-D	7,300	635
linois State Univ., Normal, IL 61761	1857	Lloyd I. Watkins	Ps-D	19,479	1,107
linois Valley Comm., Oglesby, IL 61348	1924	Alfred Wisgoski	PsI-A	3,945	173
linois Wesleyan Univ. (A), Bloomington, IL 61701	1851	Robert Eckley	IP-B	1,700	131
mmaculata, Immaculata (A), PA 19345	1920	Sister Marie Antoine	IR-B	1,303	99
mmaculate Heart (A), Los Angeles, CA 90027	1916	Nancy Heer	IR-B	701	40
mperial Valley, Imperial (A), CA 92251	1922	Dan Angel	PsI-A	5,076	275
ncarnate Word, San Antonio, TX 78209	1881	Sister Margaret Slattery	IR-M	1,463	116
ndependence Comm., Independence, KS 67301	1925	M. Leon Foster	PI-A	937	67
ndiana Central Univ., Indianapolis, IN 46227	1902	Gene Sease	IR-M	3,392	248
ndiana Inst. of Techn., Ft. Wayne, IN	1930	Thomas F. Scully	IP-B	600	39
ndiana State Univ., Terre Haute, IN 47809	1865	Richard Landini	Ps-D	15,677	870
ndiana Univ., Bloomington, IN 47405	1820	John W. Ryan	Ps-D	*80,586*	*3,301*
ndiana Vocational Tech., Indianapolis, IN 46206	1963	Myron E. Eicher	Ps-A	*24,428*	*1,639*
ndiana Univ. of Pa., Indiana, PA 15705	1875	John Worthen	Ps-D	*12,399*	*675*
ndian Hills Comm., Ottumwa, IA 52501	1966	Lyle A. Hellyer	PsI-A	1,582	162
ndian Hills Comm. (A), Centerville, IA 52544	1930	Lyle Hellyer	PsI-A	1,228	96
ndian River Comm. (A), Ft. Pierce, FL 33450	1959	Herman Heise	Ps-A	6,300	367
ndian Valley, Novato, CA 94947	1970	Constance M. Carroll	PsI-A	3,000	126
nsurance, Coll. of., New York, NY 10038	1962	A. Leslie Leonard	IP-M	3,500	255
nter Amer. Univ. of P.R., San Juan, PR 00753	1912	Frederico M. Mathew	IP-M	6,892	298
nternatl. (A), L.A., CA 90024	1970	Robert D. Fitzgerald	IP-D	350	127
nternatl. Fine Arts, Miami, FL 33132	1965	Edward Porter	IP-A	260	23
nternational Business, Ft. Wayne, IN 46804	1889	Anthony Conti	IP-A	700	22
nver Hills Comm., (A), Inver Grove Hts., MN 55075	1970	Wallace A. Simpson	PsI-A	3,500	64
ona, New Rochelle, NY 10801	1940	John Driscoll	IP-M	6,225	250
owa, Univ. of. (A), Iowa City, IA 52242	1847	Willard L. Boyd	Ps-D	25,100	1,577
owa State Univ.*, Ames, IA 50011	1858	W. Robert Parks	PS-D	24,474	2,068
owa Central Comm., Ft. Dodge, IA 50501	1966	Edwin Barbour	Ps-A	2,644	114
owa Lakes Comm. (A), Estherville, IA 51334	1967	Richard Blacker	PsI-A	*1,605*	*85*
owa Wesleyan, Mt. Pleasant, IA 52641	1842	Jerry L. Richards	IR-A	776	70
owa Western Comm., Council Bluffs, IA 51502	1966	Robert Looft	Ps-A	*2,600*	*193*
sothermal Comm., Spindale, NC 28160	1965	Ben E. Fountain Jr.	PsI-A	2,581	100
tasca Comm., Grand Rapids, MN 55744	1922	Philip J. Anderson	Ps-A	1,200	100
tawamba Junior, (A), Fulton, MS 38843	1948	W.O. Benjamin	PI-A	*3,710*	*123*
thaca, Ithaca, NY 14850	1892	James J. Whalen	IP-M	4,778	430
ackson Comm., Jackson, MI 49203	1928	Clyde E. LeTarte	PI-A	7,853	107
ackson State Comm., Jackson, TN 38301	1965	W.L. Nelms	Pf-A	2,700	113
ackson State Univ. (A), Jackson, MS 39217	1877	John A. Peoples Jr.	Ps-S	6,699	364
acksonville State Univ., Jacksonville, AL 36265	1883	Theron F. Montgomer	Ps-M	6,509	348
acksonville Univ., Jacksonville, FL 32211	1934	Frances Bartlett Kinne	IP-M	2,596	191
ames Madison Univ., Harrisonburg, VA 22807	1908	Ronald Carrier	Ps-S	8,970	444
amestown, Jamestown, ND 58401	1883	J.N. Anderson	IP-B	620	55
amestown Community (A), Jamestown, NY 14701	1950	David W. Petty, Act.	Ps-A	3,607	105
arvis Christian (A), Hawkins, TX 75765	1912	C.A. Berry	IR-B	555	48
efferson, Hillsboro, MO 63050	1963	Ray Henry	PI-A	5,000	200
efferson Community, Louisville, KY 40201	1968	Ronald Horvath	Ps-A	*6,256*	*320*
efferson Community (A), Watertown, NY 13601	1961	John Henderson	PsI-A	1,578	93
efferson Davis State Jr., Brewton, AL 36427	1965	George McCormick	Ps-A	879	40
efferson State Jr., Birmingham, AL 35215	1965	Judy Merritt	Ps-A	5,350	243
ersey City State, Jersey City, NJ 07305	1929	William Maxwell	Ps-M	8,810	298
ohn A. Logan, Carterville, IL 62918	1967	Harold O'Neil	PsI-A	2,400	85
ohn Brown Univ., Siloam Springs, AR 72761	1919	John E. Brown	IP-B	750	50
ohn Carroll Univ. (A), Cleveland, OH 44118	1886	Rev. Thomas P. O'Malley	IP-M	4,170	174
ohn C. Calhoun St. Comm., Decatur, AL 35602	1973	J.R. Chasteen	Ps-A	5,040	274
ohn F. Kennedy Univ., Orinda, CA 94563	1964	Robert Fisher	IP-M	1,600	400
ohn Marshall Law School, Chicago, IL 60604	1899	Fred F. Herzog	IP-M	1,597	113
ohn Tyler Comm. (A), Chester, VA 23831	1967	Freddie W. Nicholas	PsI-A	4,400	152
ohn Wesley (A), Owosso, MI 48867	1909	William H. Reid	IP-B	204	16
ohns Hopkins Univ., Baltimore, MD 21218	1876	Steven Muller	IP-D	*10,505*	*1,506*
ohnson County Comm., Overland Park, KS 66210	1969	Charles J. Carlsen	PsI-A	7,000	400
ohnson C. Smith Univ., Charlotte, NC 28216	1867	Wilbert Greenfield	IP-B	1,310	97
ohnson State (A), Johnson, VT 05656	1827	Edward Elmendorf	Ps-M	1,341	96
ohnson & Wales (A), Providence, RI 02903	1914	Morris J. Gaebe	IR-B	6,000	75
oliet Junior (A), Joliet, IL 60436	1901	Derek N. Nunney	PI-A	2,160	279
ones, Jacksonville, FL 32211	1918	Jack H. Jones	IP-B	1,364	53
ones County Junior Ellisville, MS 39437	1927	Thos. Terrell Tisdale	PsI-A	2,239	120
udson, Elgin, IL 60120	1963	Harm A. Weber	IR-B	426	47
** Oldest college in the United States					
udson (A), Marion, AL 36756	1838	N. McCrummen	IR-B	413	28
uilliard School The, New York, NY 10023	1905	Peter Mennin	IP-D	900	225
uniata, Huntingdon, PA 16652	1876	Frederick M. Binder	IP-B	1,307	94
alamazoo, Kalamazoo, MI 49007	1833	George N. Rainsford	IP-B	1,367	102
alamazoo Valley Comm., Kalamazoo, MI 49009	1966	Dale B. Lake	PsI-A	7,477	200
ankakee Comm., Kankakee, IL 60901	1966	Lilburn H. Horton	Ps-A	3,100	105
an. City Art Inst., Kansas City, MO 64111	1885	John W. Lottes	1P-B	578	50
an. City Coll. of Osteop. Med. (A), Kansas City, MO 64124	1916	Rudolph Bremen	IP-1P	617	57
an. City Kan. Comm., Kansas City, KS 66112	1923	Alton L. Davies	PsI-A	3,682	204

Name, address	Year	Governing official, affiliation, and highest degree offered		Stu- dents	Teach ers
Kansas Newman, Wichita, KS 67213	1933	Rev. Romans R. Galiardi	IR-B	700	65
Kansas State Univ.* (A), Manhattan, KS 66506	1863	Duane Acker	Ps-D	19,547	1,950
Kansas, Univ. of., Lawrence, KS 66045	1866	Gene Budig	Ps-D	*26,367*	*1,32*
Kansas Wesleyan, Salina, KS 67401	1886	Daniel Bratton	IR-B	450	49
Kapiolani Comm. Honolulu, HI 96814	1946	Dewey Kim	Psl-A	*5,000*	*20*
Kaskaskia, Centralia, IL 62801	1940	Paul Blowers	Psl-A	*3,190*	*14*
Katharine Gibbs School, New York, NY 10017	1917	Eleanor P. Vreeland	IP-A	2,389	116
Kauai Community, Lihue, HI 96766	1965	LeRoy J. King	Ps-A	1,069	51
Kean Coll. of New Jersey, Union, NJ 07083	1855	Nathan Weiss	Ps-M	13,458	385
Kearney State, Kearney, NE 68847	1903	Brendan McDonald	Ps-S	7,173	245
Keene State, Keene, NH 03431	1909	Barbara J. Seelye	Ps-M	3,470	223
Kellogg Community (A), Battle Creek, MI 49016	1956	Richard F. Whitmore	Psl-A	8,000	96
Kendall, Evanston, IL 60201	1934	Andrew Cothran	IP-B	386	36
Kennesaw, Marietta, GA 30061	1966	Betty Siegel	Pf-B	4,000	200
Kent State Univ., Kent, OH 44242	1910	Brage Golding	Ps-D	26,000	850
Kentucky, Univ. of*, Lexington, KY 40506	1865	Otis A. Singletary	Ps-D	23,047	1,842
Kentucky Jr., of Business (A), Lexington, KY 40576	1941	Joseph E. Hurn	IP-A	475	63
Kentucky State Univ.*, Frankfort, KY 40601	1886	W.A. Butts	Ps-M	2,158	101
Kentucky Wesleyan, Owensboro, KY 42301	1858	Luther W. White III	IR-B	936	87
Kenyon, Gambier, OH 43022	1824	Philip Jordan, Jr.	IP-B	1,450	123
Kettering Coll. of Med. Arts, Kettering, OH 45429	1967	Winton Beaven	IP-A	487	67
Keuka (W), Keuka Park, NY 14478	1890	Elizabeth Woods Shaw	IP-B	524	63
Keystone Junior, La Plume, PA 18440	1868	John B. Hibbard	IP-A	893	65
Kilgore (A), Kilgore, TX 75662	1935	Stewart McLaurin	Psl-A	4,095	173
King, Bristol, TN 37620	1867	Donald R. Mitchell	IR-B	332	4
King's, Briarcliff Manor, NY 10510	1938	Robert A. Cook	IP-A	794	5
King's (A), Charlotte, NC 28204	1901	Richard Poyner	IP-A	375	14
King's, Wilkes-Barre, PA 18711	1946	Rev. James Lackenmier	IP-B	2,263	15
King's River Comm. (A), Reedley, CA 93654	1926	Ray A. Cattani	Psl-A	3,330	13
Kirksville Coll. of Osteop. Med., Kirksville, MO 63501	1892	H. Charles Moore	IP-1P	513	8
Kirkwood Comm. (A), Cedar Rapids, IA 52406	1966	Bill F. Stewart	Ps-A	3,938	22
Kirtland Comm., Roscommon, MI 48653	1966	Raymond D. Homer	Psl-A	1,556	105
Kishwaukee, Malta, IL 60150	1967	Norman Jenkins	Psl-A	3,524	27
Knox, Galesburg, IL 61401	1837	John McCall	IP-B	1000	98
Knoxville (A), Knoxville, TN 37921	1875	Clinton M. Marsh	IR-B	432	4
Kutztown State, Kutztown, PA 19530	1866	Lawrence M. Stratton	Ps-M	5,259	34
Labette Comm. (A), Parsons, KS 67357	1923	Jerry L. Gallentine	Pl-A	2,350	9
Lackawanna Jr., Scranton, PA 18503	1894	John X. McConkey	IP-A	*1076*	*9*
Lafayette, Easton, PA 18042	1826	David W. Ellis	IP-B	2,323	17
LaGrange, LaGrange, GA 30240	1831	Walter Y. Murphy	IR-M	949	5
Lake City Comm. (A) Lake City, FL 32055	1947	Herbert E. Phillips	Ps-A	3,000	10
Lake County, Coll. of, Grayslake, IL 60030	1967	John O. Hunter	Psl-A	12,391	575
Lake Erie, Painesville, OH 44077	1856	Charles E.P. Simmons	IP-M	1,500	7
Lake Forest, Lake Forest, IL 60045	1857	Eugene Hotchkiss III	IP-M	1,120	8
Lake Land (A), Mattoon, IL 61938	1966	Robert D. Webb	Psl-A	3,500	9
Lakeland, Lakeland, FL 33802	1927	Eugene L. Roberts	IP-A	210	1
Lakeland, Sheboygan, WI 53081	1862	Richard E. Hill	IR-B	687	5
Lakeland Comm. (A), Mentor, OH 44060	1967	Wayne Rodehorst	Psl-A	6,158	10
Lake Michigan, Benton Harbor, MI 49022	1946	Walter Browe	Psl-A	3,013	25
Lake Region Comm., Devils Lake, ND 58301	1941	Dennis Michaelis	Psl-A	709	6
Lake-Sumter Comm., Leesburg, FL 32748	1962	Robert S. Palinchak	Ps-A	2,005	10
Lake Superior State, Sault Ste. Marie, MI 49783	1946	Kenneth Light	Ps-M	2,559	12
Lakeshore Tech Inst. (A), Cleveland, WI 53015	1967	Frederick Nierode	Psl-A	6,150	13
Lakewood Comm. (A), White Bear Lake, MN 55110	1967	N. Christenson, Act.	Ps-A	2,474	9
Lamar Community, Lamar, CO 81052	1937	Gordon Snowbarger	Ps-A	450	6
Lamar Univ., Beaumont, TX 77710	1923	C. Robert Kemble	Ps-D	13,700	38
Lambuth, Jackson, TN 38301	1843	Harry W. Gilmer	IR-B	753	6
Lander, Greenwood, SC 29646	1872	Larry Jackson	Pf-M	1,825	10
Lane, Jackson, TN 38301	1882	Herman Stone Jr.	IR-B	795	4
Lane Community, Eugene, OR 97405	1964	Eldon G. Schafer	Pl-A	8,500	42
Laney (A), Oakland, CA 94607	1953	Odell Johnson	Psl-A	11,316	20
Langston Univ.* (A), Langston, OK 73050	1897	Ernest L. Holloway	Ps-B	1,322	10
Lansing Community, Lansing, MI 48901	1957	Philip Gannon	Ps-A	19,749	1,15
Laramie County Comm., Cheyenne, WY 82001	1969	Harlan L. Heglar	Pl-A	2,793	17
Laredo Junior, Laredo, TX 78040	1946	Domingo Arechiga	Psl-A	3,229	15
LaRoche, Pittsburgh, PA 15237	1963	Sr. Margaret Huber	IR-M	1,548	12
La Salle (A), Philadelphia, PA 19141	1863	Bro. Patrick Ellis	IR-M	7,000	19
Lasell Junior (W) (A), Newton, MA 02166	1851	Arthur Griffin	IP-A	650	4
Lassen Comm. (A), Susanville, CA 96130	1925	Robert Theiler	Pl-A	3,100	21
Latter-Day Saints Bus., Salt Lake City, UT 84111	1886	R.F. Kirkham	IR-A	824	3
La Verne, La Verne, CA 91730	1891	Armen Sarafian	IP-D	3,500	35
Lawson State Comm. (A), Birmingham, AL 35020	1949	Jesse Lewis	Ps-A	1,740	8
Lawrence Inst. of Tech. (A), Southfield, MI 48075	1932	Richard E. Marburger	IP-1P	5,260	25
Lawrence Univ., Appleton, WI 54912	1847	Richard Warch	IP-B	1,142	11
Lebanon Valley, Annville, PA 17003	1866	Frederick P. Sample	IR-B	1,287	9
Lee, Baytown, TX 77520	1934	Robert Cloud	Ps-A	4,955	19
Lee, Cleveland, TN 37311	1918	Ray H. Hughes	IR-B	1,160	7
Lees Junior, Jackson, KY 41339	1927	Troy R. Eslinger	IR-A	310	2
Lees-McRae, Banner Elk, NC 28604	1900	H.C. Evans Jr.	IP-A	736	4
Lehigh County Comm. (A), Schnecksville, PA 18078	1966	John G. Berrier	Psl-A	3,312	13
Lehigh Univ., Bethlehem, PA 18015	1865	Peter Likins	IP-D	6,354	53
Leicester Jr. (A), Leicester, MA 01524	1784	L. Van Burkirk	IP-A	209	2
Le Moyne (A), Syracuse, NY 13214	1946	W. O'Halloran	IR-B	1,838	10
Le Moyne-Owen, Memphis, TN 38126	1870	Walter L. Walker	IR-B	973	7
Lenoir Comm., Kinston, NC 28502	1958	Jesse L. McDaniel	Pf-A	1,900	32
Lenoir-Rhyne (A), Hickory, NC 28601	1891	Albert Anderson	IR-M	1,386	10
Lesley (A) (W), Cambridge, MA 02238	1909	Don A. Orton	IP-M	1,870	32
LeTourneau, Longview, TX 75602	1946	Richard H. LeTourneau	IP-B	1,038	6
Lewis & Clark, Portland, OR 97219	1867	John R. Howard	IP-M	3,213	18
Lewis and Clark Comm., Godfrey, IL 62035	1970	Wilbur R.L. Trimpe	Psl-A	5,837	24
Lewis Univ., Romeoville, IL 60441	1930	David Delahanty	IR-M	2,776	20
Lexington Technical Inst. (A), Lexington, KY 40506	1965	William Price	Ps-A	2,074	6
Life Chiropractic, Marietta, GA 30060	1974	Sid E. Williams	IP-1p	1,520	11
Lima Technical, Lima, OH 45805	1971	James S. Biddle	Ps-A	2,073	14
Limestone, Gaffney, SC 29340	1845	William J. Briggs	IP-B	1,515	9
Lincoln (A), Lincoln, IL 62656	1865	Dale Brummet	IP-A	530	5
Lincoln Christian (A), Lincoln, IL 62656	1944	John P. Hasty	IP-M	611	3
Lincoln Land Comm., Springfield, IL 62708	1967	Robert L. Poorman	Psl-A	6,754	34

ame, address	Year	Governing official, affiliation, and highest degree offered		Stu-dents	Teach-ers
ncoln Memorial Univ., Harrogate, TN 37752	1897	Gary J. Burchett	IP-B	1,278	71
ncoln Trail, Robinson, IL 62454	1969	Richard Sanders	Psl-A	1,241	210
ncoln Univ. (A), Jefferson City, MO 65101	1866	James Frank	Ps-M	2,643	143
ncoln Univ. (A), Lincoln Univ., PA 19352	1854	Herman Branson	Psr-M	1,200	115
ncoln Univ. (A), San Francisco, CA 94118	1919	E. Barbara Jorss	IP-M	650	35
ndenwood, St. Charles, MO 63301	1827	Robert Johns	IP-M	*1,916*	*146*
ndsey Wilson Coll. (A), Columbia, KY 42728	1903	John B. Besley	IR-A	408	24
nfield, McMinnville, OR 97128	1849	Charles Walker	IP-M	1,242	85
nn Benton Comm. (A), Albany, OR 97321	1968	Raymond J. Needham	Pl-A	13,500	150
vingston Univ., Livingston, AL 35470	1835	Asa Green	Ps-S	1,280	74
vingstone, Salisbury, NC 28144	1879	F. George Shipman	IR-M	794	73
ck Haven State, Lock Haven, PA 17745	1870	Francis Hamblin	Ps-B	2,409	180
ma Linda Univ., Loma Linda, CA 92350	1905	V. Norskov Olsen	IR-D	*5,248*	*1,777*
n Morris, Jacksonville, TX 75766	1873	Faulk W. Landrum	IR-A	316	27
ng Beach City, Long Beach, CA 90808	1930	John McCuen	Psl-A	*30,559*	*1,166*
ng Island Univ. (A), Brooklyn, NY 11201	1926	Edward Clark	IP-D	6,851	456
C.W. Post (A), Greenvale, NY 11548	1954	Edward Cook	IP-M	10,803	331
ongview Community (A), Lee's Summit, MO 64063	1969	Aldo Leker	Pl-A	4,027	60
ongwood, Farmville, VA 23901	1839	Janet D. Greenwood	Ps-M	2,360	175
oop, Chicago, IL 60601	1962	Salvatore G. Rotella	Psl-A	7,923	165
orain County Comm., Elyria, OH 44035	1963	Omar Olson	Psl-A	6,312	205
oras, Dubuque, IA 52001	1839	Rev. James J. Byrne	IR-M	1,882	127
oretto Heights, Denver, CO 80236	1918	Adele Phelan	IP-B	904	99
os Angeles Baptist, Newhall, CA 91322	1927	John Dunkin	IR-B	375	40
s Angeles City, Los Angeles, CA 90029	1929	Stelle Feuers	Psl-A	20,142	892
s Angeles Harbor (A), Wilmington, CA 90744	1949	Leslie Koltai	Psl-A	11,000	200
os Angeles Pierce (A), Woodland Hills, CA 91364	1947	Herbert Ravetch	Pl-A	21,000	634
os Angeles Southwest, Los Angeles, CA 90047	1967	Walter C. McIntosh	Ps-A	7,908	225
A. Trade Technical, Los Angeles, CA 90015	1949	Thomas L. Stevens Jr.	Pl-A	20,000	600
os Angeles Valley, Van Nuys, CA 91401	1949	Mary Lee	Ps-A	*26,600*	*700*
uisburg (A), Louisburg, NC 27549	1787	J. Allen Norris Jr.	IR-A	576	39
ouisiana (A), Pineville, LA 71360	1906	Robert Lynn	IR-B	1,085	89
ouisiana St. Univ.* (A), Baton Rouge, LA 70803	1860	Martin Woodin	Ps-D	*48,049*	*2,241*
A & M, Baton Rouge, LA 70803	1860	James H. Wharton	Ps-D	*28,673*	*1,251*
at Alexandria, Alexandria, LA 71301	1960	H. Rouse Caffey	Ps-A	1,465	92
at Eunice, Eunice, LA 70535	1967	Anthony Mumphrey	Ps-A	1,528	70
Law Center (A), Baton Rouge, LA 70803	1906	Dr. William D. Hawkland, Chan.	Ps-D	876	27
Medical Center, New Orleans, LA 70112	1931	Allen Copping	Ps-D	2,500	2,000
New Orleans Campus (A), New Orleans, LA 70122	1956	Homer L. Hitt, Chan.	Ps-D	14,161	461
Shreveport Campus, Shreveport, LA 71115	1964	E. Grady Bogue	Ps-S	4,176	125
ouisiana Tech. Univ., Ruston, LA 71272	1894	F. Jay Taylor	Ps-D	11,019	435
uisville, Univ. of, Louisville, KY 40292	1798	Donald C. Swain	Ps-D	*20,057*	*1,713*
well, Univ. of, Lowell, MA 01854	1895	William T. Hogan	Ps-D	*16,121*	*989*
wer Columbia, Longview, WA 98632	1934	Vernon R. Pickett	Psl-A	4,200	125
yola, Baltimore, MD 21210	1852	Rev. J.A. Sellinger	IR-M	6,500	400
yola Marymount Univ., Los Angeles, CA 90045	1914	Rev. D.P. Merrifield	IR-M	*6,168*	*360*
yola Univ., Chicago, IL 60611	1870	Rev. R.C. Baumhart	IR-D	*16,140*	*1,285*
yola Univ., New Orleans, LA 70118	1912	Rev. James Carter	IR-M	4,356	336
bbock Christian, Lubbock, TX 79407	1957	H.M. Pruitt	IR-B	1,151	86
rleen B. Wallace St. Jr., Andalusia, AL 36420	1969	W.H. McWhorter	Ps-A	824	35
ther, Decorah, IA 52101	1861	H. George Anderson	IR-B	2,024	155
zerne County Comm., Nanticoke, PA 18634	1966	Thomas J. Moran	Psl-A	3,568	194
coming, Williamsport, PA 17701	1812	Frederick E. Blumer	IP-B	1,204	76
nchburg, Lynchburg, VA 24501	1903	Carey Brewer	IR-M	2,335	158
ndon State, Lyndonville, VT 05851	1911	Janet Gorman Murphy	Ps-M	1,117	88
acalester, St. Paul, MN 55105	1874	John B. Davis Jr	IR-B	1,730	165
acCormac Junior, Chicago, IL 60604	1904	Gordon Borchardt	IP-A	378	41
acMurray (A), Jacksonville, IL 62650	1846	B.G. Stephens	IP-B	673	65
acomb County Comm. (A), Warren, MI 48093	1954	Albert L. Lorenzo	Pl-A	*28,429*	*711*
acon Junior (A), Macon, GA 31206	1968	William Wright	Psl-A	2,382	77
adison Area Technical (A), Madison, WI 53703	1912	Norman P. Mitby, Dir.	Pl-A	*42,700*	*325*
adison Business (A), Madison, WI 53703	1856	Stuart E. Sears	IP-A	302	14
adonna, Livonia, MI 48150	1947	Sr. Mary F. Van de Vyver	IR-M	3,385	165
aine Maritime Academy (A), Castine, ME 04421	1941	E.A. Rodgers, Supt.	Ps-B	650	55
aine System, Univ. of* (A), Bangor, ME 04401	1865	P. McCarthy, Chan.	Ps-M	*26,750*	*1,136*
at Augusta, Augusta, ME 04330	1965	Hilton Power, Act.	Ps-B	3,515	238
at Farmington (A), Farmington, ME 04938	1863	Einar Olsen	Ps-B	2,100	83
at Ft. Kent (A), Ft. Kent, ME 04743	1878	Richard J. Spath	Ps-B	650	30
at Machias (A), Machias, ME 04654	1909	Arthur Buswell	Ps-B	729	35
at Orono* (A), Orono, ME 04469	1865	Kenneth W. Allen, Act.	Ps-D	11,574	611
at Portland-Gorham (A), Portland, ME 04103	1878	N.E. Miller	Ps-M	*7,602*	*544*
at Presque Isle (A), Presque Isle, ME 04769	1903	Constance Carlson, Act.	Ps-B	1,416	71
ainland, Coll. of the, Texas City, TX	1967	Justus D. Sunderman	Psl-A	2,700	165
alcolm X (A), Chicago, IL 60612	1911	Samuel Huffman	Ps-A	6,830	215
alone (A), Canton, OH 44709	1892	Lon D. Randall	IR-A	776	50
anatee Junior, Bradenton, FL 33506	1957	Stephen Korcheck	Ps-A	5,907	218
anchester (A), N. Manchester, IN 46962	1889	Alfred B. Helman	IR-M	1,253	110
anchester Comm., Manchester, CT 06040	1963	William E. Vixert	Ps-A	7,500	280
anhattan (A), Riverdale, NY 10471	1853	Brother J.S. Sullivan	IP-M	4,905	354
anhattan Sch. of Music (A), New York, NY 10027	1917	John O. Crosby	IP-D	870	171
anhattanville (A), Purchase, NY 10477	1841	Barbara K. Debs	IP-M	1,334	128
ankato State Univ. (A), Mankato, MN 56001	1867	Dr. Margaret R. Preska	Ps-S	11,616	496
annes Coll. of Music (A), New York, NY 10021	1916	Charles Kaufman	IP-D	550	110
anor Junior, Jenkintown, PA 19046	1947	Sr. Miriam Clare Kowal	IR-A	400	48
ansfield State(A), Mansfield, PA 16933	1857	Janet L. Travis	Pf-M	2,500	210
aple Woods Comm., Kansas City, MO 64156	1969	Stephen R. Brainard	Psl-A	*2,800*	*125*
aria, Albany, NY 12208	1958	Sr. L. Fitzgerald	IR-A	754	57
aria Regina (A), Syracuse, NY 13208	1963	Sr. Stella M. Zuccolillo	IR-A	416	42
arian (A), Indianapolis, IN 46222	1951	Louis C. Gatto	IP-B	880	85
arian Coll. of Fond du Lac (A), Fond du Lac, WI 54935	1936	Leo V. Krzywkowski	IR-B	525	70
aricopa Tech. Comm., Phoenix AZ 85034	1968	Charles A. Green	Pl-A	3,224	153
arietta (A), Marietta, OH 45750	1835	Sherrill Cleland	IP-M	1,475	135
arin, Coll. of (A), Kentfield, CA 94904	1926	I.P. Diamond	Ps-A	6,950	162
arion (A), Marion, IN 46952	1920	Robert Luckey	IR-M	1,097	91
arion Institute (A), Marion, AL 36756	1842	Maj. Gen. Barfield	IP-A	220	19
arist (A), Poughkeepsie, NY 12601	1946	Dennis J. Murray	IP-B	2,400	80
arlboro (A), Marlboro, VT 05344	1946	B. Ragle	IP-B	222	35
arquette Univ. (A), Milwaukee, WI 53233	1881	Rev. J.P. Raynor	IR-D	13,879	911

Name, address	Year	Governing official, affiliation, and highest degree offered		Students	Teach[ers]
Mars Hill (A), Mars Hill, NC 28754	1856	Fred Blake Bentley	IR-B	1,862	1
Marshall Univ. (A), Huntington, WV 25701	1837	Robert B. Hayes	Ps-M	11,883	5
Marshalltown Comm., Marshalltown, IA 50158	1927	Paul Kegel	Pf-A	*1,455*	*1*
Martin, Pulaski, TN 38478	1870	Bill Starnes	IR-A	315	
Martin Comm., Williamston, NC 27892	1968	Vacant	Ps-A	647	
Martin Tech. Inst. (A) Williamston, NC 27892	1968	Joseph B. Carter	Psl-A	1,250	
Mary Baldwin (A), Staunton, VA 24401	1842	Virginia Lester	IR-B	785	
Mary Hardin Baylor, Univ. of (A), Belton, TX 76513	1845	Bobby E. Parker	IR-B	1,037	
Mary Holmes, West Point, MS 39773	1892	Joseph A. Gore	IP-A	400	
Mary Washington (A), Fredericksburg, VA 22401	1908	Prince B. Woodard	Ps-B	2,292	1
Marycrest (A), Davenport, IA 52804	1939	A. Lynn Bryant	IP-M	1,196	
Marygrove (A), Detroit, MI 48221	1910	John E. Shay, Jr.	IR-M	1,059	
Maryland Inst. of Art (A), Baltimore, MD 21217	1826	Fred Lazarus IV	IP-M	1,650	1
Maryland, Univ. of*, Adelphi, MD 20783	1807	John S. Toll	Ps-D	*80,001*	*4,6*
Eastern Shore, Princess Anne, MD 21853	1886	William P. Aytche	Ps-O	1,129	
Marylhurst (A), Marylhurst, OR 97036	1893	Sr. V.A. Baxter	IR-B	740	
Marymount (A) (W), Tarrytown, NY 10591	1919	Sr. Brigid Driscoll	IP-B	1,254	1
Marymount Coll. of Ks., Salina, KS 67401	1922	John P. Murry	IP-B	758	
Marymount Coll. of Va., Arlington, VA 22207	1950	Sr. M. Majella Berg	IR-M	1,427	1
Marymount Manhattan, New York, NY 10021	1961	Colette Mahoney	IP-B	2,247	1
Marymount Palos Verdes, Rancho Palos Verdes, CA 90274	1975	Thomas D. Wood	1P-A	449	
Maryville (A), Maryville, TN 37801	1819	Wayne Anderson	IR-B	603	
Maryville (A), St. Louis, MO 63141	1872	Claudius Pritchard	IP-M	1,731	1
Marywood (A), (W), Scranton, PA 18509	1915	Sister M. Coleman Nee	IR-M	3,020	2
Mass. Bay Comm. (A), Watertown, MA 02181	1961	John McKenzie	Ps-A	4,096	2
Massachusetts Coll. Of Art, Boston, MA 02215	1873	John Nolan	Ps-M	2,000	1
Mass. Coll. of Pharmacy (A), Boston, MA 02115	1823	Raymond A. Gosselin	IP-D	*1,250*	
Mass. Institute of Tech.*, Cambridge, MA 02139	1861	Paul E. Gray	IP-D	9,510	1,9
Mass. Maritime Academy (A), Buzzards Bay, MA 02532	1892	Rr. Adm. John Aylmer	Ps-B	906	
Massachusetts, Univ. of* (A), Boston, MA 02135	1863	David C. Knapp	Ps-S	*34,000*	*2,0*
Amherst Campus, Amherst, MA 01003	1863	Loren Baritz	Ps-D	*24,903*	*1,2*
Harbor Campus (A), Boston, MA 02125	1965	Robert A. Corrigan	Ps-D	6,600	5
Massasoit Comm., Brockton, MA 02402	1966	George E. Ayers	Ps-A	3,758	1
Mater Dei, Ogdensburg, NY 13669	1960	John T. Burns	IR-A	339	
Mattatuck Comm., Waterbury, CT 06708	1967	N.P. Yarborough	Ps-A	3,514	1
Maui Community, Kahului, HI 96732	1965	Alma Cooper, Provost	Ps-A	2,019	
Mayland Technical (A), Spruce Pine, NC 28777	1971	O.M. Blake Jr.	Psl-A	572	
Maysville Comm., Maysville, KY 41056	1968	James C. Shires, Dir.	Ps-A	547	
Mayville State, Mayville, ND 58257	1889	James Schobel	Ps-B	700	
McCook Comm., McCook, NE 69001	1926	Elmer Kuntz	Psl-A	496	
McDowell Tech. Inst. (A), Marion, NC 28752	1964	John Price	Psl-A	568	
McHenry County, Crystal Lake, IL 60014	1967	Robert C. Bartlett	Psl-A	3,991	1
McKendree, Lebanon, IL 62254	1828	Gerrit J. TenBrink	IR-M	*695*	
McLennan Comm., Waco, TX 76708	1965	Wilbur Ball	Psl-A	4,049	
McMurry, Abilene, TX 79697	1923	Tom K. Kim	IR-B	1,550	1
McNeese State Univ., Lake Charles, LA 70609	1939	Jack V. Doland	Ps-S	6,980	2
McPherson, McPherson, KS 67460	1887	Paul Hoffman	1R-B	467	
Medaille, Buffalo, NY 14214	1875	Leo R. Downey	IP-B	791	
Medical Coll. of Ga., Augusta, GA 30912	1828	William Moretz	Ps-D	2,350	7
Medical Coll. of Pa. (A), Philadelphia, PA 19129	1850	Robert J. Slater	IP-D	836	4
Medical Univ. of S.C., Charleston, SC 29425	1824	William H. Knisely	Ps-D	2,560	7
Med. & Dentistry of NJ, Univ. of, Newark, NJ 07103	1956	Stanley S. Bergen Jr.	Ps-D	*2,096*	*1,*
Meharry Medical, Nashville, TN 37208	1876	David Stacher	IP-D	965	
Memphis Acad. of Arts (A), Memphis, TN 38112	1936	Jameson M. Jones	IP-D	219	
Memphis State Univ., Memphis, TN 38152	1912	Thomas Carpenter	Ps-D	20,183	9
Menlo, Menlo Park, CA 94025	1927	Richard O'Brien	IP-B	641	
Meramec Community (A), St. Louis, MO 63122	1962	Glynn E. Clark	Pl-A	7,070	3
Merced, Merced, CA 95340	1962	W.C. Martineson	Psl-A	*8,900*	
Mercer County Comm. (A), Trenton, NJ 08690	1966	John P. Hanley	Pl-A	*7,293*	
Mercer Univ., Macon, GA 31207	1833	R. Kirby Godsey	IR-D	*5,109*	
Mercy, Dobbs Ferry, NY 10522	1950	Donald Grunewald	IP-M	*9,547*	
Mercy Coll. of Detroit, Detroit, MI 48219	1941	Sister Agnes Mary Mansour	IR-M	2,214	
Mercyhurst (A), Erie, PA 16546	1926	William P. Garvey	IR-M	1,400	
Meredith (A), (W) Raleigh, NC 27611	1891	John Edgar Weems	IR-B	1,578	
Meridian Jr. (A), Meridian, MS 39301	1937	William F. Scaggs	Pl-A	2,880	
Merrih, Oakland, CA 94619	1953	John Greene	Psl-A	10,500	
Merrimack, No. Andover, MA 01845	1947	Rev. John E. Deegan	IR-A	3,495	1
Merritt Comm., Oakland, CA 94619	1953	John B. Greene	Psl-A	8,669	
Mesa, Grand Junction, CO 81502	1925	John Tomlinson	Ps-B	4,626	
Mesa Comm. (A), Mesa, AZ 85202	1965	Theo Heap	Pl-A	12,169	
Mesabi Comm. (A), Virginia, MN 55792	1918	Gilbert Staupe	Ps-A	949	
Messiah, Grantham, PA 17027	1909	D. Ray Hostetter	IR-B	*1,485*	
Methodist, Fayetteville, NC 28301	1956	Richard Pearce	IR-B	881	
Metropolitan Comm., Minneapolis, MN 55403	1965	Curtis W. Johnson	Ps-A	2,450	
Metropolitan Comm., Kansas City, MO 64111	1964	William J. Mann	Psl-A	*18,605*	
Metropolitan State, Denver, CO 80204	1965	Richard Fontera	Ps-B	15,500	
Miami, Univ. of (A), Coral Gables, FL 33124	1925	Edward T. Foote	IP-D	*15,970*	*1,*
Miami-Dade Comm., Miami, FL 33176	1960	Robert H. McCabe,	Psl-A	*43,822*	*1,*
Miami-Jacobs Jr. Coll. of Bus. (A), Dayton, OH 45401	1860	Charles P. Harbottle	IP-A	738	
Miami Univ. (A), Oxford, OH 45056	1809	Paul Pearson	Ps-D	*17,137*	
Michael J. Owens Tech. (A), Perrysburg, OH 43551	1967	Jacob H. See	Ps-A	2,991	
Michigan Christian (A), Rochester, MI 48063	1959	Milton B. Fletcher	IR-B	353	
Michigan State Univ. (A), East Lansing, MI 48824	1855	Cecil Mackey	Ps-D	44,576	3,
Michigan Tech Univ. (A), Houghton, MI 49931	1885	Dale F. Stein	Ps-D	7,865	
Michigan, Univ. of (A), Ann Arbor, MI 48109	1817	Harold T. Shapiro	Ps-D	*47,081*	*3,*
Mid-America Nazarene (A), Olathe, KS 66061	1966	R. Curtis Smith	IP-B	1,354	
Middle Georgia, Cochran, GA 31014	1884	Louis C. Alderman Jr.	Ps-A	1,410	
Middle Tenn. State Univ. (A), Murfreesboro, TN 37132	1911	Sam H. Ingram	Ps-D	11,275	
Middlebury (A), Middlebury, VT 05753	1800	Olin Robinson	IP-B	1,900	
Middlesex Comm., Beford, MA 01730	1970	James E. Houlihan, Jr.	Ps-A	6,500	
Middlesex Comm., Middletown, CT 06457	1966	Robert A. Chapman	Ps-A	2,605	
Middlesex County (A), Edison, NJ 08818	1966	Rose M. Channing	Psl-A	11,020	
Midland, Midland, TX 79701	1973	Jess Parrish	Psl-A	2,754	
Midland Lutheran (A), Fremont, NE 68025	1883	L. Dale Lund	IR-B	894	
Midlands Tech. (A), Columbia, SC 29202	1973	Robert Grigsby Jr.	Psl-A	*5,341*	
Midway (W), Midway, KY 40347	1847	Nelsen M. Hoffman	IR-A	338	
Mid Michigan Comm. (A), Harrison, MI 48625	1965	Eugene W. Gillaspy	Psl-A	2,800	
Mid-Plains Comm. (A), No. Platte, NE 69101	1974	Kenneth L. Aten	Psl-A	1,630	
Mid-State Tech. Inst., Wis. Rapids, WI 54494	1907	M.H. Schneeberg	Psl-A	*2,137*	

ame, address	Year	Governing official, affiliation, and highest degree offered		Stu-dents	Teach-ers
dwestern State Univ. (A), Wichita Falls, TX 76308	1922	Louis J. Rodriguez	Ps-M	4,400	144
les (A), Birmingham, AL 35208	1905	Clyde W. Williams	IR-B	1,265	97
les Comm., Miles City, MT 59301	1939	Judson H. Flower	Psl-A	1,097	43
llersville State (A), Millersville, PA 17551	1855	William Duncan	Ps-B	4,400	350
lligan (A), Milligan Coll, TN 37682	1881	Jess W. Johnson	IR-B	754	51
llikin Univ. (A), Decatur, IL 62522	1901	J. Roger Miller	IR-B	1,606	158
lls (W) (A), Oakland, CA 94613	1852	Barbara White	IP-B	973	87
llsaps (A), Jackson, MS 39210	1890	George M. Harmon	IP-M	1,099	93
lton (A), Milton, WI 53563	1844	Ronald J. Dickman	IP-B	431	35
lwaukee Area Tech., Milwaukee, WI 53203	1911	Russell Slicker	Psl-A	*28,000*	*1,200*
lwaukee Sch. of Eng. (A), Milwaukee, WI 53201	1903	Robert R. Spitzer	IP-M	2,564	133
lwaukee Stratton, Milwaukee, WI 53202	1863	Maritza Samoorian	IP-A	421	32
neral Area, Flat River, MO 63601	1922	Dixie Kohn	Pl-A	1,506	82
nneapolis Comm., Minneapolis, MN 55403	1965	Earl Bowman	Ps-A	3,050	100
ols. Coll. of Art. & Design (A), Minneapolis, MN 55404	1886	Jerome J. Hausman	IP-B	540	47
nnesota, Univ. of*, Minneapolis, MN 55455	1851	C.P. Magrath	Ps-D	*59,000*	*8,500*
Duluth Campus*, Duluth, MN 55812	1947	Robt. Heller, Prov.	Psr-M	7,524	500
Morris Campus* (A), Morris, MN 56267	1960	John Imholte, Prov.	Ps-B	*1,946*	*109*
not State, Minot, ND 58701	1913	Gordon Olson	Ps-M	2,550	130
ra Costa, Oceanside, CA 92056	1934	H. Dean Holt	Ps-A	6,300	363
sericordia (A), Dallas, PA 18612	1924	Joseph R. Fink	IR-M	1,217	98
ssion Comm., Santa Clara, CA 95054	1976	D. Candy Rose	Ps-A	9,556	290
ssissippi, Clinton, MS 39058	1826	Lewis Nobles	IR-D	*3,571*	*220*
ssissippi Delta Jr., Moorhead, MS 38761	1926	J.T. Hall	Psl-A	1,800	110
ssissippi Gulf Coast Jr. (A), Perkinston, MS 39573	1925	J.J. Hayden Jr.	Psl-A	*5,789*	*267*
ssissippi Industrial, Holly Springs, MS 38635	1905	J.V. Trice, Adm. Chair	IR-A	312	19
ss. Univ. for Women (W), Columbus, MS 39701	1884	James Strobel	Ps-S	1,857	170
ssissippi State Univ.*, Miss. State, MS 39762	1878	James McComas	Ps-D	12,454	717
ssissippi, Univ. of, University, MS 38677	1848	P.L. Fortune Jr.	Ps-D	*10,162*	*535*
ssissippi Valley State Univ., Itta Bena, MS 38941	1950	Joe L. Boyer	Ps-M	2,279	165
ssouri Baptist, St. Louis, MO 63141	1963	Robert Sutherland	IR-B	457	44
ssouri Inst. of Tech. (A), Kansas City, MO 64114	1931	C.R. LeValley	IP-B	953	19
ssouri Southern State, Joplin, MO 64801	1965	Donald C. Darnton	Ps-B	4,330	194
ssouri, Univ. of*, Columbia, MO 65211	1839	James Olson	Ps-D	*51,829*	*2,183*
at Columbia*, Columbia, MO 65211	1859	Barbara Uehling	Ps-D	*24,774*	*2,500*
at Kansas City*, Kansas City, MO 64110	1929	George Russell	Ps-S	11,771	750
at Rolla*, Rolla, MO 65401	1870	James M. Marchello	Ps-D	7,559	341
at St. Louis*, St. Louis, MO 63121	1963	Arnold Grobman	Ps-D	12,100	430
ssouri Valley (A), Marshall, MO 65340	1889	Robert J. Glass	IR-B	497	45
ssouri Western State, St. Joseph, MO 64507	1965	Marvin Looney	Ps-B	4,267	165
tchell (A), New London, CT 06320	1939	Robert C. Weller	IP-A	943	51
tchell Comm., Statesville, NC 28677	1856	Charles Poindexter	Psl-A	1,100	60
berly Junior (A), Moberly, MO 65270	1927	Andrew Komar Jr.	Ps-A	851	25
bile (A), Mobile, AL 36613	1961	William K. Weaver Jr.	IR-B	1,026	70
desto Junior (A), Modesto, CA 95350	1921	Kenneth Griffin	Psl-A	*15,038*	*221*
hawk Valley Comm. (A), Utica, NY 13501	1946	G.H. Robertson	Ps-A	6,800	175
hegan Comm., Norwich, CT 06360	1970	Wes Wright	Ps-A	2,455	121
lloy (W) (A), Rockville Ctre, NY 11570	1955	Sister Janet Fitzgerald	IR-1P	1,501	173
nmouth, Monmouth, IL 61462	1853	Bruce Haywood	IR-B	641	70
nmouth, W. Long Branch, NJ 07764	1933	Samuel H. Magill	IP-M	4,092	200
nroe Comm. (A), Rochester, NY 14623	1961	Moses Koch	Psl-A	10,234	285
nroe County Comm., Monroe, MI 48161	1964	Ronald Campbell	Pl-A	2,196	112
ntana Coll. of Mineral Science & Tech., Butte, MT 59701	1893	Fred W. DeMoney	Ps-M	2,016	100
ntana State Univ., Bozeman, MT 59717	1893	William J. Tietz Jr.	Ps-D	11,187	681
ntana, Univ. of, Missoula, MT 59812	1895	Neil S. Bucklew	Ps-D	8,869	487
ntcalm Comm., Sidney, MI 48885	1965	Herbert N. Stoutenburg	Psl-A	1,200	50
ntclair State (A), Upper Montclair, NJ 07043	1908	David W.D. Dickson	Ps-M	15,743	759
nterey Inst. of International Studies, Monterey, CA 93940	1955	William Craig	IP-M	439	74
nterey Peninsula (A), Monterey, CA 93940	1947	Max Tadlock	Ps-A	10,000	350
ntevallo, Univ. of (A), Montevallo, AL 35115	1896	James Vickrey	Ps-M	2,812	194
ntgomery Comm., Rockville, MD 20850	1946	Robert E. Parilla	Psl-A	*18,712*	*978*
ntgomery Co. Comm. (A), Blue Bell, PA 19422	1964	Leroy Brendlinger	Pl-A	7,200	150
ntreat-Anderson, Montreat, NC 28757	1916	Silas M. Vaughn	IR-A	400	33
ody Bible Institute, Chicago, IL 60610	1886	George Sweeting	IP-B	1,349	94
ore Coll. of Art (W) (A), Philadelphia, PA 19103	1844	H.J. Burgart	IP-B	674	73
orhead State, Moorhead, MN 56560	1885	Roland Dille	Ps-M	8,235	359
orpark, Moorpark, CA 93021	1967	W. Ray Hearon	Pl-A	9,346	430
rame Valley Comm., Palos Hills, IL 60465	1967	Fred Gaskin	Pl-A	13,000	400
ravian (A), Bethlehem, PA 18018	1742	Herman E. Collier Jr.	IR-B	1,814	125
rehead State Univ., Morehead, KY 40351	1922	Morris Norfleet	Ps-S	6,739	387
rehouse (M) (A), Atlanta, GA 30314	1867	Hugh Gloster	IP-B	1,678	105
rgan Comm. (A), Ft. Morgan, CO 80701	1970	Robert F. Datteri	Ps-A	813	84
rgan State (A), Baltimore, MD 21239	1867	Andrew Billingsley	Ps-D	5,151	352
rningside, Sioux City, IA 51106	1894	Miles Tommeraasen	IR-M	1,282	169
rris, Sumter, SC 29150	1908	Luns C. Richardson	IP-B	658	53
rris, County Coll. of, Randolph, NJ 07869	1968	Sherman H. Masten	Psl-A	11,999	196
rris Brown (A), Atlanta, GA 30314	1881	Robert Threatt	IP-B	1,611	113
rris Harvey (A), Charleston, WV 25304	1888	Thomas Voss	IP-B	2,156	80
rristown, Morristown, TN 37814	1881	Charles Wade	IP-A	300	23
rton, Cicero, IL 60650	1924	Robert V. Moritary	Psl-A	4,000	165
tlow State Comm., Tullahoma, TN 37388	1969	Harry D. Wagner	Ps-A	1,660	75
Aloysius Junior, Cresson, PA 16630	1897	J. Edward Pierce	IR-A	534	54
unt Holyoke (W), S. Hadley, MA 01075	1837	Elizabeth Kennan	IP-M	1,979	184
untain View (A), Dallas, TX 75211	1970	David Sims	Psl-A	*6,500*	*250*
Hood Comm., Gresham, OR 97030	1966	R.S. Nicholson	Psl-A	*11,000*	*410*
Ida Junior, Newton Centre, MA 02159	1899	Bryan E. Carlson	IP-A	1,164	93
Marty, Yankton, SD 57078	1936	William Tucker	IR-B	*612*	*73*
Mary (W), Milwaukee, WI 53222	1913	Sister Ellen Lorenz	IR-A	1,127	117
Mercy, Cedar Rapids, IA 52402	1928	Thomas R. Feld	IR-B	1,121	85
Olive (A), Mt. Olive, NC 28365	1951	Williams B. Raper	IR-A	678	55
St. Clare (A), Clinton, IA 52732	1928	Dan C. Johnson	IR-B	392	36
St. Joseph (W), Mt. St. Joseph, OH 45051	1920	Jean Patrice Harrington	IR-B	1,806	181
St. Mary (A), Newburgh, NY 12550	1959	Sr. Ann Sakac	IP-B	1,079	83
St. Mary's (W) (A), Los Angeles, CA 90036	1925	Sr. Magdalen Coughlin	IR-M	*1,144*	*142*
St. Mary's, Emmitsburg, MD 21727	1808	Robert Wickenheiser	IR-M	1,540	121
St. Vincent, Coll. of, Riverdale, NY 10471	1847	Sister Doris Smith	IP-B	1,230	90
San Antonio (A), Walnut, CA 91789	1945	John D. Randall	Psl-A	20,707	632
San Jacinto, San Jacinto, CA 92383	1963	Dennis Mayer	Pl-A	4,000	130
Senario, Ladysmith, WI 54848	1962	Robert E. Powless	IP-B	531	54

Name, address	Year	Governing official, affiliation, and highest degree offered		Students	Teache
Mt. Union, Alliance, OH 44601	1846	G. Benjamin Lantz Jr.	IP-B	1,077	
Mt. Vernon (W), Washington, DC 20007	1875	Jane Evans	IP-B	492	
Mt. Vernon Nazarene (A), Mount Vernon, OH 43050	1968	L. Guy Nees.	IR-B	1,005	
Mt. Wachusett Comm. (A), Gardner, MA 01440	1963	Arthur F. Haley	Ps-A	1,476	1
Muhlenberg, Allentown, PA 18104	1848	John H. Morey	IP-B	1,533	12
Multnomah Sch. of the Bible, Portland, OR 97220	1936	Joseph C. Aldrich	IP-M	704	4
Mundelein, Chicago, IL 60660	1930	Sr. Susan Rink	IP-M	1,500	12
Murray State (A), Tishomingo, OK 73460	1908	Clyde Kindell	Ps-A	1,357	
Murray State Univ. (A), Murray, KY 42071	1923	C. Curris	Ps-M	*8,158*	*3*
Muskegon Business, Muskegon, MI 49442	1885	Robert Jewell	IP-A	1,175	4
Muskegon Comm., Muskegon, MI 49442	1926	John G. Thompson	Psl-A	5,180	18
Muskingum, New Concord, OH 43762	1837	Arthur J. DeJong	IR-B	1,030	
Napa, Napa, CA 94558	1942	William H. Fedderson	Psl-A	6,033	41
Nash Tech. Inst., Rocky Mount, NC 27801	1968	J. Reid Parrott Jr.	Ps-A	1,400	6
Nassau Community (A), Garden City, NY 11530	1959	George Chambers	Psl-A	17,595	47
Nasson, Springvale, ME 04083	1912	Edgar B. Schick	IP-B	475	
Nathanial Hawthorne (A), Antrim, NH 03440	1962	Kenneth F. McLaughlin	IP-B	1,200	
National Buiness College, Roanoke, VA 24011	1886	Frank E. Longaker	IP-A	*850*	
National Coll. (A), Rapid City, SD 57709	1941	John Hauer	IP-B	1,277	
National Coll. of Chiropractic, Lombard, IL 60148	1906	Joseph Janse	IP-1P	980	
National Coll. of Education, Evanston, IL 60201	1886	Orley R. Herron	IP-M	*4,400*	
Navarro, Corsicana, TX 75110	1946	Kenneth Walker	Psl-A	2,000	
Nazareth Coll., Nazareth, MI 49074	1924	John E. Hopkins	IR-B	545	
Nazareth Coll. of Rochester, Rochester, NY 14610	1924	Robert Kidera	IP-M	2,687	2
Nebraska, Univ. of*, Lincoln, NE 68588	1869	Martin A. Massengale	Ps-D	24,786	1,2
at Omaha, Omaha, NE 68182	1908	Delbert Weber,	Ps-S	15,492	5
Nebraska Wesleyan Univ., Lincoln, NE 68504	1887	John White Jr.	IP-B	1,018	1
Nebraska Western, Scottsbluff, NE 69361	1926	John Harms	Psl-A	1,532	
Neosho County Comm. Jr., Chanute, KS 66720	1936	J.C. Sanders	Psl-A	985	
Neumann College, Aston, PA 19014	1965	Sr. M. Marie Cunningham	IR-B	715	
Nevada, Univ. of*, Reno, NV 89557	1864	Joseph Crowley	Ps-D	*9,600*	*3*
at Las Vegas, Las Vegas, NV 89154	1957	Leonard E. Goodall	Ps-P	10,544	4
New England (A), Henniker, NH 03242	1948	J.K. Cummiskey	IP-M	*1,650*	
New England, Univ. of, Biddeford, ME 04005	1978	Jack S. Ketchum	IP-1P	650	
New England Cons. of Music (A), Boston, MA 02115	1867	J.S. Ballinger	IP-M	750	1
New Hampshire, Manchester, NH 03104	1932	Edward Shapiro	IP-M	5,739	2
New Hampshire, Univ. of*, Durham, NH 03824	1866	Evelyn E. Handler	Pf-D	12,474	7
New Hampshire Tech. Inst., Concord, NH 03301	1965	D. Larrabee Sr.	Ps-A	1,233	1,
New Hampshire Voc. Tech., Manchester, NH 03102	1945	Richard Mandeville	Ps-A	373	
New Hampshire Voc. Tech., Portsmouth, NH 03801	1945	Daniel F. Forte	Ps-A	950	
New Haven, Univ. of* (A), New Haven, CT 06516	1920	Phillip Kaplan	IP-M	7,531	4
New Jersey Inst. of Tech., Newark, NJ 07102	1881	Saul K. Fenster	Ps-S	6,500	3
New Mexico Junior (A), Hobbs, NM 88240	1966	Robert A. Anderson	Psl-A	1,764	
New Mexico Highlands Univ., Las Vegas, NM 87701	1893	John Aragon	Ps-M	2,776	1
N. Mexico Inst. of Min. & Tech., Socorro, NM 87801	1889	Charles R. Holmes	Ps-S	1,291	
New Mexico Military Inst., Roswell, NM 88201	1891	Maj. Gen. G. Childress	Ps-A	900	
New Mexico State Univ.*, Las Cruces, NM 88003	1888	Gerald W. Thomas	Ps-D	*15,916*	*6*
New Mexico, Univ. of*, Albuquerque, NM 87131	1889	William Davis	Ps-D	*25,262*	*1,5*
New Orleans, Univ. of, New Orleans, LA 70148	1958	Leon J.V. Richelle,	Ps-D	15,595	6
Newport-Salve Regina (A), Newport, RI 02840	1947	Lucille McKillop	IR-M	1,700	
New River Community, Dublin, VA 24084	1969	H. Randall Edwards	Ps-A	3,241	1
New Rochelle, Coll. of (W)(A), New Rochelle, NY 10801	1904	Sister Dorothy Ann Kelly	IP-M	*4,613*	
New School for Soc. Research (A), New York, NY 10011	1919	John R. Everett	IP-D	25,000	1,5
New York City, Univ. of (A), New York, NY 10021	1847	Robert J. Kibbee, Chan.	Psl-B	*172,616*	*11,6*
Bernard M. Baruch (A), New York, NY 10010	1919	Joel Segall	Psl-D	14,592	6
Bronx Comm. (A), Bronx, NY 10453	1957	Roscoe C. Brown Jr.	Psl-A	6,818	5
Brooklyn (A), Brooklyn, NY 11210	1930	Robert L. Hess	Psl-D	16,691	1,4
City (A), New York, NY 10031	1847	Bernard Harleston	Psl-M	12,341	1,1
Medgar Evers (A), Brooklyn, NY 11225	1969	Richard D. Trent	Psl-B	2,708	3
Herbert H. Lehman (A), Bronx, NY 10468	1931	Leonard Lief	Psl-D	9,248	6
Hostos Comm. (A), Bronx, NY 10451	1968	Flora Mancuso Edwards.	Psl-A	2,673	2
Hunter (A), New York, NY 10021	1870	Donna E. Shalala	Psl-M	17,509	1,1
John Jay Coll. of Criminal Just (A), New York, NY 10019	1964	Gerald Lynch	Psl-D	6,172	3
Kingsborough Comm. (A), Brooklyn, NY 11235	1963	Israel Glasser, Act.	Psl-A	8,450	5
LaGuardia Comm. (A), Long Is. City, NY 11101	1968	Joseph Shenker	Psl-A	6,563	5
Manhattan Comm. (A), New York, NY 10019	1963	Joshua Smith	Psl-A	8,355	5
Mt. Sinai School of Med. (A), New York, NY 10029	1963	Thomas C. Chalmers	IP-1P	454	
New York City Tech. Comm. (A), Brooklyn, NY 11201	1947	Ursula Schwerin	Psl-B	13,147	9
Queens (A), Flushing, NY 11367	1937	Saul B. Cohen	Psl-M	18,127	1,3
Queensborough Comm. (A), Bayside, NY 11364	1958	Kurt R. Schmeller	Psl-A	11,643	9
Staten Island (A), Staten Island, NY 10301	1976	Edmond Volpe	Psl-M	10,608	6
York (A), Jamaica, NY 11451	1966	Milton G. Bassin	Psl-B	3,801	2
N.Y. Inst. of Technology, Old Westbury, NY 11568	1955	Alexander Schure	IP-D	*11,000*	
New York Law School, New York, NY 10013	1891	E. Donald Shapiro, Dean	IP-1P	1,466	1
New York Medical (A), Valhalla, NY 10590	1860	Joseph A. Cimino.	IP-D	756	5
New York, State Univ. of (A), Albany, NY 12210	1948	C.R. Wharton Jr., Chan.	Ps-D	*348,361*	*14,*
Agric. & Tech. Inst. (A), Alfred, NY 14802	1908	David H. Huntington	Ps-A	4,138	
" " " (A), Canton, NY 13617	1907	Earl MacArthur	Ps-A	2,329	
" " " (A), Cobleskill, NY 12043	1911	Walton A. Brown	Ps-A	2,683	
" " " (A), Delhi, NY 13753	1913	Seldon M. Kruger.	Ps-A	2,381	
" " " (A), Farmingdale, NY 11735	1912	F.A. Cipriani	Ps-A	13,049	
" " " (A), Morrisville, NY 13408	1908	Royson N. Whipple.	Ps-A	2,997	
State Univ. (A), Albany, NY 12222	1844	V.J. O'Leary	Ps-D	15,391	
" " Buffalo, NY 14260	1846	Steven B. Sample	Ps-D	*27,411*	*1,*
" " Binghamton, NY 13901	1946	Clifford D. Clark	Ps-D	11,592	
" " Stony Brook, NY 11794	1957	John H. Marburger III	Ps-D	15,723	1,
State Univ. Colleges, Brockport, NY 14420	1867	John E. Von de Wetering	Ps-S	8,800	
" " Buffalo, NY 14222	1867	D. Bruce Johnstone	Ps-M	11,783	
" " Cortland, NY 13045	1868	James M. Clark.	Ps-M	5,856	
" " Saratoga Spgs., NY 12866	1971	James Hall	Ps-B	5,125	
" " Fredonia, NY 14063	1867	Dallas K. Beal.	Ps-M	5,212	
" " Geneseo, NY 14454	1867	E.B. Jakubauskas	Ps-M	5,546	
" " New Paltz, NY 12561	1885	Alice Chandler	Ps-M	7,265	
" " Oneonta, NY 13820	1889	Clifford Craven	Ps-M	6,293	
" " Oswego (A), NY 13126	1861	Virginia Radley	Ps-M	7,554	
" " (A), Old Westbury, NY 11568	1965	John Maguire	Ps-B	2,850	
" " Plattsburgh, NY 12901	1889	Joseph C. Burke	Ps-M	6,266	
" " Potsdam, NY 13676	1816	James H. Young	Ps-M	4,899	

ame, address	Year	Governing official, affiliation, and highest degree offered		Students	Teachers
" " Purchase, NY 10577	1967	Sheldon N. Grebstein	Ps-B	3,601	185
" " College of Tech., Utica/Rome, NY 13502	1966	William Kunsela	Ps-M	3,533	207
Agri. & Tech. Coll. (A), Farmingdale, NY 11735	1948	Frank A. Cipriani	Ps-A	13,591	400
Buffalo Health Sciences Ctr. (A), Buffalo, NY 14214	1846	F.C. Pannill, V.P.	Ps-D	2,968	354
Env'm't'l. Sci. & Forestry, Syracuse, NY 13210	1911	Edward Palmer	Ps-D	1,750	110
Downstate Medical Center, Brooklyn, NY 11203	1860	Donald J. Scherl	Ps-D	1,456	717
Health Sciences Center, Stony Brook, NY 11794	1957	John H. Narburger III	Ps-D	1,449	350
Maritime (A), Bronx, NY 10465	1874	Sheldon Kinney	Ps-M	1,070	70
Upstate Medical Center (A), Syracuse, NY 13210	1834	Richard P. Schmidt	Ps-D	937	300
ew York Univ., New York, Ny 10003	1831	John Brademas	IP-D	33,366	5,300
ewberry, Newberry, SC 29108	1856	Glen E. Whitesides	IR-B	737	78
iagara County Comm. (A), Sanborn, NY 14132	1962	Jack C. Watson	Psl-A	3,835	123
iagara Univ., Niagara Univ., NY 14109	1856	Rev. John G. Mahoney	IR-M	3,845	276
icholls State Univ., Thibodaux, LA 70301	1948	Vernon Galliano	Ps-D	7,248	332
ichols, Dudley, MA 01570	1815	Lowell Smith	IP-M	1,072	60
orfolk State (A), Norfolk, VA 23504	1935	Harrison B. Wilson	Ps-M	7,286	421
ormandale Comm., Bloomington, MN 55431	1968	Dale A. Lorenz	Ps-A	5,800	250
orthampton Co. Area Comm., Bethlehem, PA 18017	1966	Robert J. Kopecek	Psl-A	4,217	268
orth Adams State, North Adams, MA 01247	1894	William P. Haas	Ps-M	2,215	125
orth Carolina Central U. (A), Durham, NC 27707	1910	A. Whiting, Chan.	P-1P	4,910	359
orth Carolina, Univ. of, Chapel Hill, NC 27514	1972	William Friday			
A&T State Univ., Greensboro, NC 27411	1891	Edward B. Fort	Ps-M	5,166	352
at Asheville (A), Asheville, NC 28814	1927	William Highsmith, Chan.	Pf-B	2,178	137
at Chapel Hill, Chapel Hill, NC 27514	1789	Christopher C. Fordham III,	Ps-D	21,575	2,006
at Charlotte, Charlotte, NC 28223	1946	E.K. Fretwell, Jr.,	Ps-M	9,574	672
at Greensboro, Greensboro, NC 27412	1891	William E. Moran,	Ps-D	10,201	533
at Wilmington, Wilmington, NC 28403	1947	Wm. H. Wagoner	Ps-M	5,100	290
C. School of the Arts, Winston-Salem, NC 27117	1965	Robert Suderburg,	Ps-M	470	89
C. State Univ. at Raleigh, NC 27650	1889	Bruce Poulton	Ps-D	*22,500*	*2,000*
orth Carolina Wesleyan, Rocky Mount, NC 27801	1956	S. Bruce Petteway	IR-B	887	53
orth Central, Naperville, IL 60566	1861	Gael D. Swing	IR-B	1,329	98
orth Central Bible, Minneapolis, MN 55404	1930	Don Argue	IR-A	836	40
orth Central Michigan, Petoskey, MI 49770	1958	A.D. Shankland	Pl-A	1,965	88
orth Central Tech. Inst. (A), Wausau, WI 54401	1912	Dwight E. Davis	Pl-A	*14,000*	*135*
orth County Comm. (A), Saranac Lake, NY 12983	1967	P.J. Cayan	Psl-A	1,376	48
Dak. St. Sch. of Science, Wahpeton, ND 58075	1903	Clair T. Blikre	Ps-A	3,422	183
orth Dakota State Univ., Fargo, ND 58105	1890	L.D. Loftsgard	Ps-D	*9,277*	*450*
Dak. St. Univ., Bottineau & Inst. of Forestry, Bottineau, ND 58318	1907	Michael Smith	Ps-A	436	28
orth Dakota, Univ. of*, Grand Forks, ND 58202	1883	Thomas Clifford	Ps-D	10,750	584
ortheast Alabama State Jr., Rainsville, AL 35986	1965	E.R. Knox	Ps-A	889	55
ortheastern Illinois Univ., Chicago, IL 60625	1961	Ronald Williams	Ps-M	*10,049*	*536*
ortheastern Junior (A), Sterling, CO 80751	1941	Marvin W. Weiss	Pl-A	2,111	69
ortheastern Okla. A&M, Miami, OK 74354	1919	D.D. Creech	Ps-A	2,953	143
ortheastern Okla. State (A), Tahlequah, OK 74464	1909	W. Roger Webb	Ps-M	6,100	250
ortheastern Univ. (A), Boston, MA 02115	1898	Kenneth Ryder	IP-D	*42,437*	*739*
ortheast Louisiana Univ., Monroe, LA 71209	1931	Dwight Vines	Ps-D	11,300	439
ortheast Miss. Junior, Booneville, MS 38829	1948	Harold T. White	Psl-A	2,105	100
ortheast Missouri State Univ., Kirksville, MO 63501	1867	Charles T. McClain	Ps-S	6,500	440
ortheast Neb. Tech. Comm., Norfolk, NE 68701	1928	Robert P. Cox	Psl-A	1,730	95
ortheast Wisc. Tech. Inst., Green Bay, WI 54303	1913	Gerald Prindiville	Psl-A	8,286	178
orthern Arizona Univ. (A), Flagstaff, AZ 86011	1899	Eugene M. Hughes	Ps-D	12,300	520
orthern Colorado, Univ. of, Greeley, CO 80639	1890	Robert C. Dickeson	Ps-D	9,145	557
orthern Essex Comm., Haverhill, MA 01830	1961	J.R. Dimitry	Ps-A	7,421	386
orthern Illinois Univ., DeKalb, IL 60115	1895	William Monat	Ps-D	25,000	1,150
orthern Iowa, Univ. of, Cedar Falls, IA 50614	1876	John Kamerick	Ps-D	10,185	669
orthern Kentucky Univ., Highland Hts., KY 41076	1968	A.D. Albright	Pf-M	8,290	307
orthern Michigan Univ. (A), Marquette, MI 49855	1899	John X. Jamrich	Ps-S	9,376	350
orthern Montana, Havre, MT 59501	1929	James H.M. Erickson	Ps-M	1,584	113
orthern Oklahoma, Tonkawa, OK 74653	1901	Edwin Vineyard	Ps-A	1,900	89
rthern State, Aberdeen, SD 57401	1901	Lester A. Clarke	Ps-M	2,706	114
rthern Virginia Comm., Annandale, VA 22003	1965	Richard Ernst	Ps-A	*35,282*	*1,428*
rth Florida, Univ. of (A), Jacksonville, FL 32216	1965	Thos. Carpenter	Ps-M	4,039	205
rth Florida Junior, Madison, FL 32340	1958	Gary P. Sims	Psl-A	900	60
rth Georgia, Dahlonega, GA 30597	1873	John H. Owen	Ps-M	1,956	105
rth Greenville, Tigerville, SC 29688	1892	James D. Jordan	IR-A	580	60
rth Harris County, Houston, TX 77073	1972	W.W. Thorne	Psl-A	7,787	310
rth Hennepin Comm., Minneapolis, MN 55445	1966	John F. Helling	Ps-A	4,785	173
rth Idaho, Coeur d'Alene, ID 83814	1939	Barry Schuler	Pl-A	2,348	154
rth Iowa Area Comm., Mason City, IA 50401	1918	Dave Buettner	Psl-A	1,900	260
rthland, Ashland, WI 54806	1892	Malcolm McLean	IR-B	630	52
rthland Comm., Thief River Falls, MN 56701	1965	Theodore Easton	Ps-A	600	33
rth Park (A), Chicago, IL 60625	1891	Lloyd Ahlem	IR-1P	1,092	77
rth Shore Community (A), Beverly, MA 01915	1965	George Traicoff	Ps-A	2,321	110
rth Texas State Univ., Denton, TX 76203	1890	Alfred F. Hurley	Ps-D	17,487	1142
rthrop Univ. (A), Inglewood, CA 90306	1942	B.J. Shell	IP-1P	1,452	123
rthwest Bible (A), Minot, ND 58701	1934	Edward L. Williams	IR-B	252	11
rthwest Christian, Eugene, OR 97401	1895	William E. Hays	IR-B	297	22
rthwest, Kirkland, WA 98033	1934	D.V. Hurst	IR-B	761	30
rthwest Community, Powell, WY 82435	1946	Sinclair Orendorff	Psl-A	1,664	120
rthwestern, Orange City, IA 51041	1882	Friedhelm Radandt	IR-B	903	62
rthwestern Conn. Comm., Winsted, CT 06098	1965	Regina Duffy	Ps-A	2,143	84
rthwestern Michigan, Traverse City, MI 49684	1951	George Miller	Psl-A	3,027	150
rthwestern State Univ. (A), Natchitoches, LA 71457	1884	René Bienvenu	Ps-D	*5,443*	*283*
rthwestern Okla. St. Univ., Alva, OK 73717	1897	Joe Struckle	Ps-M	2,200	75
rthwestern Univ., Evanston, IL 60201	1851	Robert Henry Strotz	IP-D	*15,471*	*1,500*
rthwest Miss. Junior (A), Senotobia, MS 38668	1927	Henry B. Koon	Ps-A	*2,743*	*130*
rthwest Missouri State Univ., Maryville, MO 64468	1905	B.D. Owens	Ps-S	4,485	236
rthwest Nazarene, Nampa, ID 83651	1913	Kenneth Pearsall	IR-M	1,352	85
rwalk Comm., Norwalk, CT 06854	1961	Mary W. Brackett, Act.	Ps-A	3,393	110
rwalk State Tech. (A), Norwalk, CT 06854	1961	William M. Krummel	Ps-A	1,481	44
rwich Univ., Northfield, VT 05663	1819	Maj. Gen. W. Russell Todd	IP-D	*2,110*	*179*
rthwood Inst., Midland, MI 48640	1959	David E. Fry	IP-B	*2,561*	*97*
tre Dame, Coll. of, Belmont, CA 94002	1851	Sr. Veronica Skillin	IP-M	1,421	165
tre Dame (W), Manchester, NH 03104	1950	Sr. Jeannette Vezeau	IP-M	740	87
tre Dame Coll. of Oh. (W), Cleveland, OH 44121	1923	Sister Mary Marthe	IR-B	*770*	*68*
tre Dame of Maryland, Baltimore, MD 21210	1873	Sister Kathleen Feeley	IP-A	1,660	88
tre Dame, Univ. of, Notre Dame, IN 46556	1842	Rev. T.M. Hesburgh	IP-D	9,023	725
va Univ. (A), Ft. Lauderdale, FL 33314	1964	Abraham Fischler	IP-D	*8,171*	*125*

Name, address	Year	Governing official, affiliation, and highest degree offered		Students	Teachers
Nyack, Nyack, NY 10960	1882	Thomas Bailey	IR-M	700	63
Oakland City (A), Oakland City, IN 47660	1885	J.W. Murray	IR-B	520	3
Oakland Comm. (A), Bloomfield Hills, MI 48013	1965	Robert F. Roelofs	PsI-A	*22,762*	*50*
Oakland Univ., Rochester, MI 48063	1957	Joseph Champagne	Ps-S	16,808	54
Oakton Comm. (A), Morton Grove, IL 60053	1969	William Koehnline	PI-A	5,795	14
Oakwood, Huntsville, AL 35896	1896	Calvin B. Rock	IR-B	1,320	9
Oberlin, Oberlin, OH 44074	1833	James L. Powell, Act.	IP-M	2,820	23
Occidental, Los Angeles, CA 90041	1887	Richard C. Gilman	IP-M	1,644	12
Ocean County, Toms River, NJ 08753	1964	Kenneth Kerr	PsI-A	5,600	27
Odessa, Odessa, TX 79762	1945	Philip Speegle	PsI-A	3,800	23
Oglethorpe Univ., Atlanta, GA 30319	1835	Manning Pattillo Jr.	IP-B	1,101	5
Ohio Dominican, Columbus, OH 43219	1911	Sister M. Andrew Matesich	IR-1P	956	7
Ohio Coll. of Podiatric Med. (A), Cleveland, OH 44106	1916	Abe Rubin	IP-B	585	2
Ohio Inst. of Technology (A), Columbus, OH 43209	1952	Richard A Czerniak	IP-B	2,718	5
Ohio Northern Univ., Ada, OH 45810	1871	DeBow Freed	IR-1P	2,700	19
Ohio State Univ.*, Columbus, OH 43210	1870	Edward H. Jennings	Ps-D	*57,604*	*3,18*
Ohio Univ., Athens, OH 45701	1804	Charles J. Ping	Ps-D	*20,311*	*1,16*
Ohio Wesleyan Univ. (A), Delaware, OH 43015	1842	Thomas Wenzlau	IR-B	2,392	16
Ohlone, Fremont, CA 94539	1965	Peter Blomerly	PI-A	8,200	39
Okaloosa-Walton Jr., Niceville, Fl 32578	1963	J.E. McCracken	PsI-A	3,847	17
Oklahoma Baptist Univ., Shawnee, OK 74801	1910	Vacant	IR-B	1,500	13
Oklahoma Christian, Oklahoma City, OK 73111	1950	J. Terry Johnson	IR-B	1,707	8
Oklahoma City Southwestern (A), Oklahoma City, OK 73127	1946	Scott T. Muse, Jr.	IR-A	693	2
Oklahoma City Univ., Oklahoma City, OK 73106	1904	Jerald C. Walker	IP-D	2,604	19
Oklahoma Panhandle St. Univ., Goodwell, OK 73939	1909	Thomas L. Palmer	Ps-B	1,213	6
Oklahoma Sch. of Business, Acctg. Law & Finance (A), Tulsa, OK 74103	1919	H. Everett Pope Jr.	IP-A	287	
Oklahoma State Univ.*, Stillwater OK 74078	1890	Lawrence Boger	Pf-D	*22,709*	*1,23*
Oklahoma, Univ. of, Norman, OK 73019	1890	William S. Banowsky	Ps-D	19,648	82
Okla. Univ. of Science & Arts, Chickasha, OK 73018	1908	Roy Troutt	Ps-B	1,406	8
Old Dominion Univ., Norfolk, VA 23508	1930	A.B. Rollins Jr.	Ps-D	17,023	62
Olivet, Olivet, MI 49076	1844	Donald A. Morris	IR-A	615	4
Olivet Nazarene, Kankakee, IL 60901	1907	Leslie Parrott	IR-M	2,059	11
Olney Central, Olney, IL 62450	1962	Charles R. Novak	PsI-A	1,070	17
Olympic, Bremerton, WA 98310	1946	Henry Milander	Ps-A	5,739	32
Onondaga Comm. (A), Syracuse, NY 13215	1962	A. Paloumpis	PI-A	7,000	21
Oral Roberts Univ., Tulsa, OK 74171	1965	Oral Roberts	IR-D	3,875	42
Orangeburg-Calhoun Tech, Orangeburg, SC 29115	1966	M. Rudy Groomes	PsI-A	2,077	12
Orange Coast, Costa Mesa, CA 92626	1947	Robert Moore	Ps-A	29,000	97
Orange County Comm. (A), Middletown, NY 10940	1950	Robert T. Novak	Ps-A	4,988	13
Oregon College of Educ. (A), Monmouth, OR 97361	1856	G. Leinwand	Ps-M	3,200	17
Oregon Inst. of Tech., Klamath Falls, OR 97601	1947	Kenneth Light	Ps-A	2,463	17
Oregon State Univ.*, Corvallis, OR 97331	1868	Robert MacVicar	Ps-D	17,460	1,65
Oregon, Univ. of, Eugene, OR 97403	1876	Paul Olum	Ps-D	16,948	1,59
Orlando, Orlando, FL 32810	1953	Donald C. Jones	IP-B	1077	5
Oscar Rose Junior, Midwest City, OK 73110	1970	Joe Packnett, Act.	Ps-A	8,912	30
Osteopathic Medicine and Health Sciences, Univ. of, Des Moines, IA 50312	1898	J.L. Azneer	IP-SD	735	35
Otero Junior, La Junta, CO 81050	1941	William L. McDivitt	Ps-A	823	4
Otis Art Inst., Los Angeles, CA 90057	1918	Neil Hoffman	IP-M	661	10
Ottawa Univ. (A), Ottawa, KS 66067	1865	Robert Shaw	IR-B	*535*	*5*
Otterbein (A), Westerville, OH 43081	1847	Thomas Jefferson Kerr	IR-B	1,677	10
Ottumwa Heights (A), Ottumwa, IA 52501	1925	Sr. Bernadine Pieper	IR-A	310	2
Ouachita Baptist Univ., Arkadelphia, AR 71923	1886	Daniel R. Grant	IR-M	1,576	11
Our Lady of Elms, Col. of (W), Chicopee, MA 01013	1928	Sr. Mary Dooley	IP-B	727	8
Our Lady of the Lake Univ., San Antonio, TX 78285	1911	Sr. Eliz. Sueltenfuss	IR-M	1,695	11
Owensboro Jr. Coll. of Business, Owensboro, KY 42302	1963	Lenda S. Voyles	IP-A	386	3
Ozarks, Coll. of the, Clarksville, AR 72830	1834	Fritz H. Ehren	IR-B	654	5
Ozarks, School of the (A), Pt. Lookout, MO 65726	1906	James Spainhower	IP-B	1,200	8
Pace, Univ. (A), New York, NY 10038	1906	Edward J. Mortola	IP-B	*21,523*	*3*
Pacific Christian, Fullerton, CA 92631	1928	Knofel Staton	IR-M	461	7
Pacific Lutheran Univ., Tacoma, WA 98447	1890	William Rieke	IR-M	3,652	28
Pacific States Univ. (A), Los Angeles, CA 90006	1928	Steven Kase	IP-B	700	2
Pacific Union, Angwin, CA 94508	1882	J.W. Cassel, Jr.	IP-M	1,744	12
Pacific Univ., Forest Grove, OR 97116	1849	James Miller	IR-M	1,035	10
Pacific, Univ. of the, Stockton, CA 95211	1851	Stanley McCaffrey	IP-D	6,000	42
Paducah Comm., Paducah, KY 42201	1932	Donald J. Clemens	Ps-A	1,859	5
Paine (A), Augusta, GA 30910	1882	J.S. Scott Jr.	IR-B	757	6
Palm Beach Atlantic, W. Palm Beach, FL 33401	1968	Claude H. Rhea	IR-B	652	7
Palm Beach Junior, Lake Worth, FL 33461	1933	Edward M. Eissey	PsI-A	11,300	50
Palomar Comm., San Marcos, CA 92069	1946	Omar H. Scheidt	PsI-A	18,438	27
Palo Verde Comm., Blythe, CA 92225	1947	Dan Radakovich	Ps-A	360	[illegible]
Pan American Univ., Edinburg, TX 78539	1927	Miguel A. Nevarez	Ps-M	*8,523*	*4*
Panola Junior, Carthage, TX 75633	1947	Gary McDaniel	PsI-A	987	4
Paris Junior, Paris, TX 75460	1924	Louis B. Williams	PsI-A	2,043	1
Park, Parkville, MO 64152	1875	Harold Condit	IR-A	*2,215*	*2*
Parkersburg Comm., Parkersburg, WV 26101	1971	Eldon L. Miller	Ps-A	3,365	17
Parkland, Champaign, IL 61820	1967	William M. Staerkel	PsI-A	9,300	55
Parsons School of Design (A), New York, NY 10011	1896	John R. Everett	IP-M	3,000	25
Pasadena City (A), Pasadena, CA 91106	1924	Richard S. Meyers	Ps-A	19,115	40
Pasadena Coll. of Chiropractic, Pasadena, CA 91103	1972	Arthur J. Garrow	IP-1P	200	[illegible]
Pasco-Hernando Comm. (A), Dade City, FL 33525	1972	Milton O. Jones	Ps-A	1,700	17
Passaic Co. Comm., Paterson, NJ 07509	1970	Gustavo Mellander	PI-A	4,113	[illegible]
Patrick Henry State Jr. (A), Monroeville, AL 36460	1965	Cecil Murphy	Ps-A	596	[illegible]
Paul D. Camp Comm., Franklin, VA 23851	1971	Johnnie E. Merritt	Ps-A	1,076	[illegible]
Paul Quinn, Waco, TX 76704	1872	Norman Hardy	IR-A	502	[illegible]
Paul Smith's Coll. of Arts & Sci., Paul Smiths, NY 12970	1937	T.N. Stainback	IP-A	1,146	[illegible]
Peabody Cons. of Music, Baltimore, MD 21202	1857	Vacant	IP-D	420	[illegible]
Peace (W), Raleigh, NC 27604	1857	S. David Frazier	IR-A	483	[illegible]
Pearl River Junior, Poplarville, MS 39470	1909	M.R. White	PsI-A	2,527	1
Peirce Junior, Philadelphia, PA 19102	1865	Raymond C. Lewin	IP-A	2,050	1
Pembroke St. Univ. (A), Pembroke, NC 28372	1887	English E. Jones	Ps-M	2,158	1
Peninsula, Port Angeles, WA 98362	1961	Paul G. Cornaby	Ps-A	2,439	1
Pennsylvania, Univ. of, Philadelphia, PA 19104	1740	Sheldon Hackney	IP-D	22,623	3,6
Penn Col. of Optometry (A), Philadelphia, PA 19141	1919	Melvin Wolfberg	IP-1P	586	[illegible]
Penn. Coll. of Podiatric Med., Phila., PA 19107	1963	James Bates	IP-D	475	1
Penn., Medical Col. of, Philadelphia, PA 19129	1850	Maurice Clifford	IP-D	531	6

ame, address	Year	Governing official, affiliation, and highest degree offered		Stu- dents	Teach- ers
enn. State Univ.*, University Park, PA 16802	1855	John W. Oswald	Psr-D	*63,800*	*2,632*
enn Valley Comm. (A), Kansas City, MO 64111	1915	Dorothy M. Wright	Pl-A	5,033	105
ensacola Jr. (A), Pensacola, FL 32504	1948	Horace Hartsell	Ps-A	*11,000*	*450*
epperdine Univ., Malibu, CA 90265	1937	Howard A. White	IR-D	*6,872*	*171*
eralta Comm. (A), Oakland, CA 94610	1964	Donald Godbold	Pl-A	*40,756*	*1,406*
eru State, Peru, NE 68421	1867	Larry Tangeman	Ps-B	852	47
eiffer, Misenheimer, NC 28109	1885	Cameron West	IR-B	*742*	*75*
hiladelphia, Comm., Coll. of, Philadelphia, PA 19107	1964	Allen T. Bonnell	Psl-A	*13,509*	*650*
hila. College of Art, Philadelphia, PA 19102	1876	Thomas Schutte	IP-M	*1,095*	*285*
hila. Coll. of Bible, Langhorne PA 19047	1913	W. Sherrill Babb	IP-B	575	29
hila. Coll. of Osteopathic Med., Philadelphia, PA 19131	1899	Thomas Rowland Jr.	IP-D	823	222
hila. Coll. of the Performing Arts, Phila., PA 19102	1870	Joseph Castaldo	IP-M	335	115
hila. Coll. of Pharm. & Science, Philadelphia, PA 19104	1821	William Thawley	IP-D	1,100	115
hila. Coll. of Textiles & Science, Philadelpia, PA 19144	1884	D.B. Partridge	IP-M	2,955	166
hilander Smith, Little Rock, AR 72203	1877	Grant S. Shockley	IR-B	637	52
hillips County Comm., Helena, AR 72342	1966	John Easley	Psl-A	1,500	80
hillips Univ., Enid, OK 73702	1906	Joe R. Jones	IR-M	1,177	92
hoenix (A), Phoenix, AZ 85013	1920	William Berry	Pl-A	13,495	190
iedmont, Demorest, GA 30535	1898	James E. Walter	IR-B	366	25
iedmont Bible, Winston-Salem, NC 27101	1945	Donald Drake	IP-B	411	31
iedmont Tech., Greenwood, SC 29646	1966	Lex Walters	Psl-A	1,657	141
iedmont Tech., Roxboro, NC 27573	1970	Edward W. Cox	Ps-A	*1,565*	*65*
iedmont Virginia Comm., Charlotte, VA 22901	1972	George B. Vaughan	Ps-A	3,715	200
ikes Peak Comm. (A), Colorado Springs, CO 80906	1968	Donald McInnis	Ps-A	5,439	300
ikeville, Pikeville, KY 41501	1889	Jackson Hall	IP-A	616	75
ima Comm., Tucson, AZ 85709	1970	S. James Manilla	Ps-A	*20,400*	*954*
ine Manor (W), Chestnut Hill, MA 02167	1911	Rosemary Ashby	IP-B	555	58
'ine Manor Junior (W)(A), Chestnut Hill, MA 02167	1911	Rosemary Ashby	IP-A	377	47
'itt Comm. (A), Greenville, NC 27834	1964	W.E. Fulford Jr.	Ps-A	2,455	148
'ittsburgh, Univ. of (A), Pittsburgh, PA 15260	1787	Wesley W. Posvar	IP-D	*29,315*	*2,333*
ittsburgh State U., Pittsburgh, KS 66762	1903	James Appleberry	Ps-S	5,122	304
itzer, Claremont, CA 91711	1963	Frank Ellsworth	IP-B	752	70
lymouth State, Plymouth, NH 03264	1871	Kasper Marking	Ps-M	3,376	162
oint Loma (A), San Diego, CA 92106	1902	Bill D. Draper	IR-M	1,806	133
oint Park, Pittsburgh, PA 15222	1960	John Hopkins	IP-M	2,795	160
olk Comm. (A), Winter Haven, FL 33880	1964	Frederick T. Lenfestey	Ps-A	5,600	150
olytechnic Institute of NY (A), Brooklyn, NY 11201	1854	George Bugliarello	IP-D	*4,560*	*357*
omona, Claremont, CA 91711	1887	David Alexander	IP-B	1,380	103
orterville (A), Porterville, CA 93257	1927	Paul D. Alcantra	Ps-A	2,304	110
ortland Comm., Portland, OR 97219	1961	John Anthony	Psl-A	*27,952*	*2,617*
ortland State Univ. (A), Portland, OR 97207	1955	Joseph Blumel	Ps-D	16,730	508
ortland, Univ. of, Portland, OR 97203	1901	Arthur A. Schulte, Act.	IR-M	2,800	165
ost, Waterbury, CT 06708	1890	Douglas Picht	IP-A	1,547	70
otomac State, Keyser, WV 26726	1901	J.L. McBee, Exec. Dean	Pf-A	*1,094*	*58*
rairie State (A), Chicago Hts., IL 60411	1958	Richard Creal	Ps-A	*5,434*	*98*
rairie View A & M Univ. (A), Prairie View, TX 77445	1878	Alvin Thomas	PS-M	5,125	306
ratt Community, Pratt, KS 67124	1938	John G. Waltney	Pl-A	367	31
ratt Institute, Brooklyn, NY 11205	1887	Richardson Pratt Jr.	IP-M	5,300	530
resbyterian (A), Clinton, SC 29325	1880	Kenneth B. Orr	IR-B	946	73
resentation, Aberdeen, SD 57401	1954	Sr. Lynn Marie Welbig	IR-A	352	45
restonburg Comm., Prestonburg, KY 41653	1964	Henry A. Campbell	Ps-A	783	48
rince George's Comm., Largo, MD 20772	1958	Robert Bickford	Psl-A	*22,000*	*300*
rinceton Univ., Princeton, NJ 08544	1746	William G. Bowen	IP-D	*5,981*	*636*
rincipia (A), Elsah, IL 62028	1898	Arthur F. Schulz Jr.	IP-B	884	96
rovidence, Providence, RI 02918	1919	Rev. T. R. Peterson	IR-S	6,000	254
uerto Rico, Univ. of*, San Juan, PR 00931	1903	Antonio M. Moutilla	Pf-D	*18,257*	*1,450*
uerto Rico Jr., Rio Piedras, PR 00928	1949	Domingo Marrero	IP-A	3,998	205
uget Sound, Univ. of (A), Tacoma, WA 98416	1888	Philip M. Phibbs	IP-M	5,378	294
urdue Univ.*, W. Lafayette, IN 47907	1869	Arthur G. Hansen	Ps-D	*44,796*	*4,985*
Queens (W), Charlotte, NC 28274	1857	Billy Wireman	IR-M	952	100
Quincy, Quincy, IL 62301	1860	Rev. G. Brinkman	IR-B	1,018	96
Quincy Jr., Quincy, MA 02169	1958	Edward Pierce	Pl-A	4,100	50
Quinebaug Valley Comm., Danielson, CT 06239	1971	Robert E. Miller	Ps-A	926	43
Quinnipiac (A), Hamden, CT 06518	1929	Richard A. Terry	IP-B	3,778	158
Quinsigamond Comm., Worcester, MA 01606	1963	Clifford S. Peterson	Ps-A	5,616	293
Radcliffe (W) (A), Cambridge MA 02138	1879	Matina Souretia Horner	IP-D	2,161	(a)
Radford (A), Radford, VA 24142	1910	Donald N. Dedman	Ps-M	5,693	300
Ramapo Coll. of N.J., Mahwah, NJ 07430	1969	George T. Potter	Ps-B	4,600	222
Randolph-Macon, Ashland, VA 23005	1830	Ladell Payne	IP-B	856	82
Randolph-Macon Woman's (W), Lynchburg, VA 24503	1891	Robert Spivey	IR-B	782	85
Randolph Tech., Asheboro, NC 27203	1962	M.H. Branson	Ps-A	1,141	39
Ranger Junior (A), Ranger TX 76470	1926	Jack Elsom	Ps-A	722	32
Reading Area Comm. (A), Reading, PA 19603	1971	Lewis Ogle	Psl-A	887	74
Redlands, Univ. of, Redlands, CA 92373	1907	Douglas R. Moore	IP-M	2,839	405
Redwoods, Coll. of the, Eureka, CA 95501	1964	Donald Weichert	Pl-A	*5,756*	*550*
Reed, Portland, OR 97202	1909	Paul Bragdon	IP-B	1,100	105
Regis, Denver, CO 80221	1877	Rev. David M. Clarke	IR-M	2,812	339
Regis (W) (A), Weston, MA 02193	1927	Sister Therese Higgins	IR-M	1,277	104
Reinhardt, Waleska, GA 30183	1883	Allen O. Jernigan	IR-A	453	41
Rend Lake (A), Ina, IL 62846	1967	Harry J. Braun	Psl-A	3,114	65
Rensselaer Poly. Inst., Troy, NY 12181	1824	George M. Low	IP-D	6,200	400
Rhode Island, Providence, RI 02908	1854	David E. Sweet	Ps-M	9,468	481
Rhode Island, Comm. Coll of (A), Warwick, RI 02886	1964	Edward J. Liston	Ps-A	*12,000*	*300*
R.I. School of Design, Providence, RI 02903	1877	Lee Hall	IP-M	1,519	198
Rhode Island, Univ. of*, Kingston, RI 02881	1892	Frank Newman	Ps-D	*13,821*	*734*
Rice Univ., Houston, TX 77251	1891	Norman Hackerman	IP-D	3,524	400
Richland, Dallas, TX 75243	1972	Stephen Mittlestet	Pl-A	12,500	600
Richland Comm., Decatur, IL 62526	1971	John Kirk	Psl-A	4,418	200
Richmond Tech., Rockingham, NC 28379	1964	R. Kenneth Melvin	Ps-A	*1,054*	*92*
Richmond, Univ. of, Richmond, VA 23173	1830	E. Bruce Heilman	IR-M	4,066	325
Ricks, Rexburg, ID 83440	1888	Bruce C. Hafen	IR-A	6,800	285
Rider (A), Lawrenceville, NJ 08648	1865	Frank N. Elliott	IP-M	5,583	188
Rio Grande, Rio Grande, OH 45674	1876	Paul Hayes	IP-B	1,273	60
Rio Hondo Comm., Whittier, CA 90608	1960	Herbert Sussman	Psl-A	12,400	218
Ripon, Ripon, WI 54971	1851	Bernard S. Adams	IP-B	952	95
Riverside City, Riverside, CA 92506	1916	Charles A. Kane	Ps-A	15,946	583
Rivier, Nashua, NH 03060	1933	Sister Jeanne Perreault	IP-M	2,024	149

Name, address	Year	Governing official, affiliation, and highest degree offered		Students	Teachers
Roanoke (A), Salem, VA 24153	1842	Norman Fintel	IR-B	1,250	7
Roanoke-Chowan Tech., Ahoskie, NC 27910	1967	Edward Wilson, Jr.	Psl-A	573	11
Robert Morris (A), Coraopolis, PA 15108	1921	Charles Sewall	IP-B	4,133	8
Robert Morris, Carthage, IL 62321	1965	J.R. McCartan	IP-A	1,350	7
Roberts Wesleyan, Rochester, NY 14624	1866	William C. Crothers	IR-B	613	5
Robeson Tech. Inst., Lumberton, NC 28358	1965	R. Craig Allen	Psl-A	*1,288*	*5*
Rochester Comm., Rochester, MN 55901	1915	Charles Hill	Ps-A	3,217	14
Rochester Inst. of Tech. (A), Rochester, NY 14623	1829	M. Richard Rose	IP-M	15,704	1,16
Rochester, Univ. of, Rochester, NY 14627	1850	Robert Sproull	IP-D	*8,965*	*1,05*
Rockford, Rockford, IL 61101	1847	Norman L. Stewart	IP-M	1,431	12
Rockhurst, Kansas City, MO 64110	1910	Rev. Robert Weiss	IR-M	3,623	21
Rockingham Comm., Wentworth, NC 27375	1966	Gerald B. James	Psl-A	8,260	15
Rockland Comm. (A), Suffern, NY 10901	1959	Seymour Eskow	Psl-A	7,456	12
Rock Valley, Rockford, IL 61101	1964	Karl Jacobs	Ps-A	10,566	54
Rocky Mountain, Billings, MT 59102	1878	Bruce Alton	IR-B	370	3
Roger Williams (A), Bristol, RI 02809	1948	Wm. Rizzini	IP-B	3,750	26
Rogue Comm., Grants Pass, OR 97526	1971	Howard P. Sims	Psl-A	1,850	26
Rollins, Winter Park, FL 32789	1885	Thaddeus Seymour	IP-M	2,835	12
Roosevelt Univ., Chicago, IL 60605	1945	Rolf A. Weil	IP-M	8,361	48
Rosary, River Forest, IL 60305	1918	Sister Jean Murray	IR-S	1,692	12
Rose-Hulman Inst. of Tech. (M), Terre Haute, IN 47803	1874	Samuel F. Hulbert	IP-M	1,213	8
Rosemont, Rosemont, PA 19010	1921	Dorothy Brown	IR-B	550	8
Rush Univ., Chicago, IL 60612	1972	James A. Campbell	IP-D	1,172	78
Russell Sage, Troy, NY 12180	1916	Willam Kahl	IP-M	*4,500*	*37*
Rust, Holly Spgs., MS 38635	1866	W.A. McMillan	IR-B	739	4
Rutgers Univ.*, New Brunswick, NJ 08903	1766	Edward J. Bloustein	Ps-D	*48,456*	*2,74*
Rutledge, Charleston, SC 29406	1911	George LaSalle	IP-A	585	1
Rutledge Coll. (A), Spartanburg, SC 29303	NA	Eugene Spiess	IP-A	300	1
Rutledge Coll. (A), Winston-Salem, NC 27101	1962	John R. Middleton	IP-A	310	2
Rutledge Coll. (A), Charlotte, NC 28202	1977	Carl Settle	IP-A	314	1
Sacramento City (A), Sacramento, CA 95822	1916	Douglas Burris	Pl-A	13,080	45
Sacred Heart, Univ. of the, Santurce, PR 00914	1935	Pedro Gonzalez Ramos	IR-B	7,032	33
Sacred Heart Univ., Bridgeport, CT 06606	1963	Anthony V. Pinciaro, Act.	IP-M	4,811	32
Saddleback Comm., Mission Viejo, CA 92692	1967	Vacant	Psl-A	*30,000*	*80*
Saginaw Valley State, Univ. Center, MI 48710	1964	Jack Ryder	Ps-M	4,355	121
St. Ambrose, Davenport, LA 52803	1882	William Bakrow	IP-M	2,060	13
St. Andrews Presbyterian, Laurinburg, NC 28352	1961	A.P. Perkinson Jr.	IR-B	742	5
St. Anselm, Manchester, NH 03102	1889	Rev. Joseph Gerry	IR-B	1,901	14
St. Augustine's (A), Raleigh, NC 27610	1867	Prezell R. Robinson	IP-B	1,761	8
St. Benedict, Coll. of (W), St. Joseph, MN 56374	1913	Sr. Emanuel Renner	IR-B	2,246	14
St. Bonaventure Univ., St. Bonaventure, NY 14778	1854	Rev. Mathias Doyle	IP-M	2,790	161
St. Catherine, Coll. of (W), St. Paul, MN 55105	1905	Catherine McNamee	IR-B	2,337	227
St. Clair County Comm. (A), Pt. Huron, MI 48060	1923	Richard Norris	Psl-A	3,549	20
St. Cloud State Univ., St. Cloud, MN 56301	1869	Brendan McDonald	Ps-S	11,500	50
St. Edward's Univ., Austin, TX 78704	1885	Bro. Stephen Walsh	IR-M	2,500	15
St. Elizabeth, Coll. of (W), Convent Station, NJ 07961	1899	Sister Jacqueline Burns	IR-B	858	95
St. Francis, Fort Wayne, IN 46808	1890	Sister M. Jo Ellen Scheetz	IR-M	1,288	8
St. Francis, Brooklyn, NY 11201	1884	Bro. Donald Sullivan	IP-B	2,816	68
St. Francis, Loretto, PA 15940	1847	Rev. Christian Oravec	IR-M	1,564	89
St. Francis, Coll. of (A), Joliet, IL 60435	1930	John Orr	IR-M	3,251	184
St. Gregory's (A), Shawnee, OK 74801	1875	Rev. Michael Roethier	IR-A	313	12
St. John Fisher, Rochester, NY 14618	1948	Rev. Patrick Braden	IP-B	2,182	185
St. John's, Annapolis, MD 21404	1696	Edwin J. Delattre	IP-B	386	5
St. John's, Winfield, KS 67156	1893	Gordon Beckler	IR-B	300	3
St. John's, Santa Fe, NM 87501	1969	Ed Delattre	IP-M	315	44
St. John's River Comm., Palatka, FL 32077	1958	Robert L. McLendon Jr.	Pf-A	*2,191*	*8*
St. John's Univ., Collegeville, MN 56321	1857	Fr. Hilary Thimmesh	IR-M	1,950	13
St. John's Univ., Jamaica, NY 11439	1870	Rev. Joseph T. Cahill	IR-D	*18,490*	*88*
St. Joseph, West Hartford, CT 06117	1932	Sr. Mary O'Connor	IR-M	1,284	131
St. Joseph's, Rensselaer, IN 47978	1889	Rev. Charles Banet	IR-M	982	66
St. Joseph's, Brooklyn, NY 11205	1916	Sr. G.A. O'Connor	IP-B	*1,700*	*20*
St. Joseph's, North Windham, ME 04062	1912	Anthony Santoro	IP-B	500	45
St. Joseph's, Philadelphia, PA 19131	1851	Rev. Donald MacLean	IR-M	5,947	328
St. Lawrence Univ., Canton, NY 13617	1856	W. Lawrence Gulick	IP-M	2,694	174
St. Leo, St. Leo, FL 33574	1963	Thomas Southard	IR-A	1,150	6
St. Louis Coll. of Pharmacy, St. Louis, MO 63110	1864	Charles C. Rabe	IP-B	650	4
St. Louis Community (A), St. Louis, MO 63110	1962	Richard Greenfield, Chan.	Pl-A	*27,110*	*1,38*
at Florissant Valley, St. Louis, MO 63135	1962	David Harris	Psl-A	12,000	45
at Forest Park, St. Louis, MO 63110	1962	Vernon Crawley	Psl-A	7,970	390
at Meramec, St. Louis, MO 63122	1963	Ralph R. Doty	Psl-A	12,136	397
St. Louis Univ. (A), St. Louis, MO 63103	1818	Rev. Thomas J. Fitzgerald	IP-D	*10,088*	*2,53*
Parks, Cahokia, IL 62206	1927	Paul A. Whelan	IR-B	620	51
St. Martin's (A), Lacey, WA 98503	1895	Fr. John C. Scott	IR-B	655	32
St. Mary, Coll. of, Omaha, NE 68124	1923	John Richert	IP-B	1064	119
St. Mary (W), Leavenworth, KS 66048	1923	Sr. Mary J. McGilley	IR-B	824	87
St. Mary of the Plains Coll., Dodge City, KS 67801	1952	Michael McCarthy	IR-B	621	68
St. Mary-of-the-Woods (W), St. Mary-of-the-Woods, IN 47876	1840	Sister Jeanne Knoerle	IR-B	691	84
St. Mary's (W) (A), Notre Dame, IN 46556	1844	John Duggan	IR-B	1,764	201
St. Mary's (W) (A), Raleigh, NC 27611	1842	John T. Rice	IR-A	510	32
St. Mary's (A), Winona, MN 55987	1912	Peter Clifford	IR-M	1,354	71
St. Mary's Jr. (A), Minneapolis, MN 55454	1964	Sr. Anne Joachim Moore	IR-A	770	10
St. Mary's Coll. of California, Moraga, CA 94775	1863	Bro. Mel Anderson	IR-M	2,674	216
St. Mary's Coll. of Maryland, St. Mary's City, MD 20686	1839	Richard D. Weigle	Ps-A	1,348	109
St. Mary's Dominican (W), New Orleans, LA 70118	1910	Sr. Mary Gerald Shea	IR-B	866	93
St. Mary's Univ., San Antonio, TX 78284	1852	Rev. David J. Paul	IR-M	3,268	167
St. Michael's, Winooski, VT 05404	1904	Edward L. Henry	IR-M	1,997	125
St. Norbert, DePere, WI 54115	1898	Neil Webb	IR-B	1,733	121
St. Olaf, Northfield, MN 55057	1874	Harlan Foss	IR-B	3,097	270
St. Paul Bible, Bible College, MN 55375	1916	L. J. Eagen	IR-B	654	47
St. Paul's (A), Lawrenceville, VA 23868	1888	S. Dallas Simmons	IP-A	693	47
St. Peter's, Jersey City, NJ 07306	1872	Rev. Edward Glynn	IR-M	*4,207*	*39*
St. Petersburg Junior, St. Petersburg, FL 33733	1927	Carl M. Kuttler, Jr.	Pl-A	*16,106*	*73*
St. Rose, Coll. of, Albany, NY 12203	1920	Thomas Manion	IP-M	2,875	177
St. Scholastica, Coll. of (A), Duluth, MN 55811	1912	Bruce Stender	IR-M	1,115	125
St. Teresa, Coll. of (W) (A), Winona, MN 55987	1907	Thomas Hamilton	IR-B	650	65
St. Thomas Aquinas (A), Sparkill, NY 10976	1952	Donald McNeils	IP-B	1,500	75
St. Thomas, Coll. of (A), St. Paul, MN 55105	1885	Msgr. Terrence Murphy	IP-S	4,681	295

Name, address	Year	Governing official, affiliation, and highest degree offered		Students	Teachers
St. Thomas, Univ. of, Houston, TX 77006	1947	Rev. William J. Young	IR-D	*1,939*	*120*
St. Vincent (M) (A), Latrobe, PA 15650	1846	Rev. Leopold Krul	IR-B	820	80
St. Xavier, Chicago, IL 60655	1847	Ronald O. Champagne	IR-M	2,311	202
Salem (W), Winston-Salem, NC 27108	1772	Thomas V. Litzenburg, Jr.	IR-B	635	66
Salem, Salem, WV 26426	1888	James C. Stam	IP-M	*1,248*	*77*
Salem Community, Penns Grove, NJ 08069	1972	Guy Altieri, Act.	Pl-A	1,222	60
Salem State, Salem, MA 01970	1854	James T. Amsler	Ps-M	8,192	274
Salisbury State, Salisbury, MD 21801	1925	Thomas Bellavance	Ps-M	4,349	247
Sam Houston State Univ. (A), Huntsville, TX 77341	1879	E.T. Bowers	Ps-S	9,532	464
Samford Univ. (A), Birmingham, AL 35209	1841	Leslie S. Wright	IR-M	3,674	218
Sampson Tech., Clinton, NC 28328	1965	C.W. Paderick	Ps-A	835	50
San Antonio (A), San Antonio, TX 78284	1925	Bob Barringer, Act.	Psl-A	21,038	978
San Bernardino Valley, San Bernardino, CA 92410	1926	Arthur Jensen	Psl-A	16,302	710
San Diego, Mesa, San Diego, CA 92111	1962	Allen Brooks	Psl-A	23,700	1050
San Diego, Univ. of, San Diego, CA 92110	1949	Author E. Hughes	IR-D	4,560	284
San Diego City, San Diego, CA 92101	1918	Allen Repashy	Psl-A	*22,850*	*853*
San Diego State Univ., San Diego, CA 92182	1897	Thomas Day	Ps-D	*33,330*	*1,550*
San Francisco Art Inst., San Francisco, CA 94133	1879	Stephen Goldstine	IP-M	600	60
San Francisco, Univ. of, San Francisco, CA 94117	1855	Rev. J. LoSchiavo	IP-D	5,699	440
Sangamon State Univ. (A), Springfield, IL 62708	1970	Alex B. Lacy	Ps-M	3,683	210
San Jacinto (A), Pasadena, TX 77505	1961	Thomas M. Spencer	Ps-A	12,000	300
San Joaquin Delta Comm. (A), Stockton, CA 95207	1935	Dale Parnell	Psl-A	20,710	549
San Jose City, San Jose, CA 95128	1921	Theodore I. Morquia	Psl-A	15,087	676
San Jose State Univ., San Jose, CA 95192	1857	Gail P. Fullerton	Ps-M	*24,945*	*1,008*
San Luis Obispo Co. Comm. (A), San Luis Obispo, CA 93406	1965	Merlin Eisenbise	Pl-A	5,504	200
San Mateo, Coll. of, San Mateo, CA 94402	1922	Lois A. Callahan	Pl-A	16,300	600
Sandhills Comm., Carthage, NC 28327	1963	Raymond A. Stone	Psl-A	1,800	115
Santa Ana, Santa Ana, CA 92706	1915	William Wenrich	Ps-A	*33,852*	*1400*
Santa Barbara City (A), Santa Barbara, CA 93109	1908	Glenn Gooder	Psl-A	8,613	243
Santa Clara, Univ. of, Santa Clara, CA 95053	1851	William Rewak	IP-D	6,774	401
Santa Fe, Coll. of (A), Santa Fe, NM 87501	1947	Bro. Cyprian Luke	IR-B	1,117	75
Santa Fe Community (A), Gainesville, FL 32602	1965	Alan Robertson	Ps-A	6,056	326
Santa Monica, Santa Monica, CA 90405	1929	Richard Moore	Ps-A	20,341	845
Santa Rosa Junior (A), Santa Rosa, CA 95401	1928	Roy Mikalson	Pl-A	18,788	188
Sarah Lawrence (A), Bronxville, NY 10708	1926	Charles DeCarlo	IP-M	1,060	120
Sauk Valley (A), Dixon, IL 61021	1965	Dr. Garner	Psl-A	4,600	225
Savannah State, Savannah, GA 31404	1890	Wendell G. Rayburn	Ps-M	2,103	160
Sayre Jr., Sayre, OK 73662	1938	Harry Patterson	Psl-A	522	19
Schenectady Co. Comm. (A), Schenectady, NY 12305	1968	Karl Zopf	Ps-A	2,120	69
Schoolcraft, Livonia, MI 48152	1961	Richard McDowell	Psl-A	*8,212*	*341*
Schreiner (A), Kerrville, TX 78028	1923	Sam Junkin	IR-A	500	31
Scott Community, Bettendorf, IA 52722	1966	John Blong	Ps-A	2,020	150
Scottsdale Comm., Scottsdale, AZ 85253	1970	Arthur W. DeCabooter	Psl-A	6,961	297
Scranton, Univ. of, Scranton, PA 18510	1888	Rev. William Byron	IP-M	4,216	203
Scripps (W), Claremont, CA 91711	1926	John Chandler	IP-B	575	85
S.D. Bishop State Jr. (A), Mobile, AL 36603	1965	Sanford Bishop	Ps-A	1,650	75
Seattle Central Comm., Seattle, WA 98122	1966	Donald Phelps	Ps-A	*8,568*	*335*
Seattle Pacific Univ., Seattle, WA 98119	1891	David C. LeShara	IR-M	2,851	206
Seattle Univ., Seattle, WA 98122	1891	Rev. William Sullivan	IR-D	4,633	175
Selma Univ., Selma, AL 36701	1878	M.C. Cleveland Jr.	IR-B	500	32
Seminole Comm. (A), Sanford, FL 32771	1965	E.S. Weldon	Psl-A	4,673	393
Sequoias, Coll. of the, Visalia, CA 93277	1925	Ivan Crookshanks	Psl-A	7,625	150
Seton Hall Univ. (A), S. Orange, NJ 07079	1856	E.R. D'Alessio	IR-D	9,557	647
Seton Hill (W), Greensburg, PA 15601	1883	Eileen Farrell	IR-B	973	86
Seward County Comm. (A), Liberal, KS 67901	1967	James Hooper	Psl-A	1,760	92
Shasta, Redding, CA 96099	1949	Kenneth B. Cerreta	Psl-A	11,988	460
Shaw Coll. at Detroit (A), Detroit, MI 48202	1936	Romallus Murphy	IP-B	895	41
Shaw Univ., Raleigh, NC 27611	1865	Stanley Smith	IR-B	1,572	60
Shelby State Comm. (A), Memphis, TN 38104	1970	Jess Parrish	Ps-A	*5,585*	*300*
Sheldon Jackson, Sitka, AK 99835	1878	Michael E. Kaelke	IR-B	210	25
Shenandoah Coll. of Music, Winchester, VA 22601	1875	James A. Davis	IR-M	911	150
Shepherd, Shepherdstown, WV 25443	1871	James Butcher	Ps-B	3,106	158
Sheridan, Sheridan, WY 82801	1948	Gordon Ward	Psl-A	1,217	102
Shippensburg State, Shippensburg, PA 17257	1871	Anthony F. Ceddia	Ps-M	5,589	308
Shoreline Comm. (A), Seattle, WA 98133	1964	Ronald Bell	Ps-A	8,177	360
Shorter, Rome, GA 30161	1873	George L. Balentine	IR-B	805	65
Siena, Loudonville, NY 12211	1937	Rev. Hugh F. Hines	IP-B	3,208	189
Siena Heights, Adrian, MI 49221	1919	Louis Vaccaro	IP-M	1,800	72
Sierra, Rocklin, CA 95677	1914	G.C. Angove	Psl-A	*12,056*	*393*
Simmons (W), Boston, MA 02115	1899	William J. Holmes	IP-D	2,800	250
Simpson, Indianola, IA 50125	1860	Robert McBride	IR-B	1,000	76
Simpson, San Francisco, CA 94134	1921	Mark W. Lee	IR-M	250	25
Sinclair Comm., Dayton, OH 45402	1887	David Ponitz	Psl-A	18,000	1,500
Sinte Gleska, Rosebud, SD 57570	1971	Lionel Bordeaux	Psl-A	336	48
Sioux Falls, Sioux Falls, SD 57105	1883	Owen Halleen	IR-M	911	75
Siskiyous, Coll. of the (A), Weed, CA 96094	1957	Ivan Crookshanks	Psl-A	7,556	310
Skagit Valley, Mt. Vernon, WA 98273	1926	James Ford	Ps-A	5,800	250
Skidmore, Saratoga Spgs., NY 12866	1922	Joseph C. Palamountian Jr.	IP-B	2,100	160
Skyline, San Bruno, CA 94066	1969	James C. Wyatt	Psl-A	8,500	350
Slippery Rock State, Slippery Rock, PA 16057	1889	Herb Reinhard Jr.	Ps-M	5,715	346
Smith (W), Northampton, MA 01063	1871	Jill Kerr Conway	IP-B	2,566	281
Snead State Jr., Boaz, AL 35957	1898	William H. Osborn	Ps-A	1,089	30
Snow, Ephraim, UT 84627	1888	J.M. Higbee	Ps-A	1,404	60
Solano Comm., Suisun City, CA 94590	1945	William H. Wilson Sr.	Psl-A	11,500	427
Somerset Comm., Somerset, KY 42501	1965	Roscoe Kelley	Psl-A	1,065	54
Somerset County, Somerville, NJ 08876	1968	S. Charles Irace	Ps-A	4,800	160
Sonoma State Univ. (A), Rohnert Park, CA 94928	1961	Peter Diamandopoulos	Pf-M	5,600	550
South, Univ. of the (A), Sewanee, TN 37375	1857	Robert Ayres Jr.	IR-1P	1,278	136
South Alabama, Univ. of, Mobile, AL 36688	1963	Frederick Whiddon	Ps-D	8,002	491
South Carolina St.*, Orangeburg, SC 29117	1896	M.M. Nance Jr.	Ps-M	3,720	260
South Carolina, Univ. of*, Columbia, SC 29208	1801	James B. Holderman	Ps-D	*36,045*	*2,074*
S.D. Sch. of Mines & Tech., Rapid City, SD 57701	1885	Richard Schleusener	Ps-D	2,718	123
South Dakota State Univ.*, Brookings, SD 57007	1881	Sherwood Berg	Ps-D	7,167	700
South Dakota, Univ. of, Vermillion, SD 57069	1862	Joseph McFadden	Ps-D	6,220	350
Southeast Comm., Fairbury, NE 68352	1941	Daniel Gerber	Psl-A	431	24
Southeast Comm. (A), of (A), KY 40823	1960	Larry Stanley	Ps-A	600	21
South Florida, Univ. of (A), Tampa, FL 33620	1956	John Lott Brown	Ps-D	*25,054*	*1,265*
South Florida Jr. (A), Avon Park, FL 33825	1965	William Stallard	Ps-A	938	28
South Georgia, Douglas, GA 31533	1908	W.C. Sitemore	Pf-A	1,074	53

Name, address	Year	Governing official, affiliation, and highest degree offered		Students	Teachers
South Oklahoma City, Oklahoma City, OK 73159	1972	Dale L. Gibson	Ps-A	7,891	99
South Plains, Levelland, TX 79336	1958	Marvin L. Baker	Psl-A	3,300	250
South Texas Coll. of Law, Houston, TX 77002	1923	G.R. Walker	IP-1P	1,200	50
Southeast Missouri St. Univ. (A), Cape Girardeau, MO 63701	1873	Bill Stacy	Ps-M	9,061	422
Southeastern (A), Lakeland, FL 33801	1935	Cyril Homer	IR-B	1,208	41
Southeastern Comm. (A), Burlington, IA 52655	1966	C.A. Callison, Supt.	Ps-A	*2,068*	*92*
Southeastern Comm., Keokuk, IA 52632	1953	C.W. Callison	Ps-A	453	24
Southeastern Comm., Whiteville, NC 28472	1965	Dan W. Moore	Pf-A	1,900	135
Southeastern Illinois (A), Harrisburg, IL 62946	1960	Harry Abell	Ps-A	2,400	65
Southeastern Louisiana Univ., Hammond, LA 70402	1925	J. Larry Crain	Ps-S	8,158	319
Southeastern Mass. Univ., N. Dartmouth, MA 02747	1895	Donald E. Walker	Ps-M	7,621	339
Southeastern Okla. St. Univ., Durant, OK 74701	1909	Leon Hibbs	Ps-M	4,333	175
Southeastern Univ., Washington, DC 20024	1879	Harry Miller	IP-M	1,757	150
Southern, Collegedale, TN 37315	1892	Frank Krittel	IR-B	*1,860*	*120*
Southern Arkansas Univ., Magnolia, AR 71753	1909	Harold Brinson	Ps-M	*1,978*	*145*
Southern Baptist (A), Walnut Ridge, AR 72476	1941	D.J. Nicholas	Psl-A	550	25
Southern California, Costa Mesa, CA 92626	1920	Wayne Kraiss	IP-B	777	64
Southern Cal., Univ. of (A), Los Angeles, CA 90007	1880	James Zumberge	IP-D	28,129	3,684
Southern Coll. of Optometry, Memphis, TN 38104	1932	Spurgeon B. Eure	IP-1P	560	32
Southern Colorado, Univ. of (A), Pueblo, CO 81001	1933	Richard Pesqueira	Ps-B	6,000	285
Southern Conn. State (A), New Haven, CT 06515	1893	Manson Van B. Jennings	Ps-M	11,720	396
Southern Idaho, Coll. of (A), Twin Falls, ID 83301	1965	James L. Taylor	Psl-A	3,700	109
Southern Illinois Univ., Edwardsville, IL 62025	1965	Earl Lazerson	Ps-D	10,205	650
Southern Illinois Univ., Carbondale, IL 62901	1869	Albert Somit	Ps-D	*23,991*	*1,475*
Southern Maine, Univ. of (A), Gorham, ME 04038	1878	Robert L. Woodbury	Ps-M	*8,203*	*502*
Southern Methodist Univ., Dallas, TX 75275	1911	L. Donald Shields	IR-D	9,292	602
Southern Missionary (A), Collegedale, TN 37315	1892	Frank Knittel	IR-B	*2,100*	*125*
Southern Miss., Univ. of, Hattiesburg, MS 39406	1910	Audrey Lucas	Ps-D	*9,747*	*658*
Southern Ohio (A), Cincinnati, OH 45202	1927	H.W. Nagel	IP-A	*1,600*	*60*
Southern Oregon State (A), Ashland, OR 97520	1926	Natale Sicuro	Ps-M	4,705	250
Southern Seminary Jr. (A), Buena Vista, VA 24416	1867	Bill J. Elkins	IR-A	237	20
Southern Tech. Inst. (A), Marietta, GA 30060	1948	Stephen Cheshier	Ps-A	2,500	120
Southern Univ. (A), Baton Rouge, LA 70813	1880	Jesse Stone Jr.	Psl-M	8,404	403
Southern Union State Jr. (A), Wadley, AL 36276	1922	Ray Jones	Ps-A	*1,413*	*31*
Southern Utah State, Cedar City, UT 84720	1897	Gerald R. Sherratt	Ps-B	2,106	119
Southern Vermont, Bennington, VT 05201	1926	Thomas Gee	Ps-B	715	46
Southwest Baptist Univ., Bolivar, MO 65613	1878	Harlan Spurgeon	IR-B	1,449	99
Southwestern, Chula Vista, CA 92010	1960	Jewell E. Stindt	Psl-A	12,829	499
Southwestern, Winfield, KS 67156	1885	Robert P. Sessions	IR-B	610	50
Southwestern Adventist, Keene, TX 76059	1893	Donald McAdams	IR-B	744	50
Southwestern Comm., Creston, IA 50801	1966	John A. Smith	Ps-A	605	38
Southwestern La., Univ. of, Lafayette, LA 70504	1898	Ray Authement	Ps-D	15,493	620
Southwestern at Memphis, Memphis, TN 38112	1848	James Daughdrill Jr.	Pl-B	1,050	126
Southwestern Michigan, Dowagiac, MI 49047	1966	David Briegel	Psl-A	2,500	175
Southwestern Okla. St. Univ., Weatherford, OK 73096	1901	Leonard Campbell	Ps-M	4,932	245
Southwestern Oregon Comm., Coos Bay, OR 97420	1961	Jack E. Brookins	Psl-A	3,700	250
Southwestern Univ., Georgetown, TX 78626	1840	Roy B. Shilling Jr.	IR-B	1,000	86
Southwest Mississippi Jr., Summit, MS 39666	1918	Horace Holmes	Psl-A	1,371	73
Southwest Mo. St. Univ., Springfield, MO 65804	1905	Duane Meyer	Ps-S	*15,361*	*679*
Southwest St. Univ., Marshall, MN 56208	1963	Jon Wefald	Ps-B	2,008	107
Southwest Texas Junior, Uvalde, TX 78801	1846	Wayne Matthews	Psl-A	1,996	126
Southwest Texas St. Univ., San Marcos, TX 78666	1899	Robert L. Hardesty	Pf-M	15,277	594
Southwest Virginia Comm., Richlands, VA 24641	1968	Charles King	Ps-A	3,912	150
Spalding, Louisville, KY 40203	1814	Sister Eileen Egan	IR-S	1,005	95
Spartanburg Methodist (A), Spartanburg, SC 29301	1911	George D. Fields, Jr.	Pl-A	1,035	40
Spartanburg Tech., Spartanburg, SC 29303	1962	Joe D. Gault	Psl-A	1,865	125
Spelman (W), Atlanta, GA 30314	1881	Donald Stewart	IP-B	1,447	109
Spokane Comm. (A), Spokane, WA 99207	1963	Raymond F. LaGrandeur	Ps-A	5,132	206
Spokane Falls Comm. (A), Spokane, WA 99204	1970	Gerald Saling	Ps-A	5,574	253
Spoon River, Canton, IL 61520	1959	Paul C. Gianini, Jr.	Psl-A	2,500	135
Spring Arbor, Spring Arbor, MI 49283	1873	Kenneth Coffman	IR-B	*901*	*45*
Spring Garden, Philadelphia, PA 19118	1851	Daniel DeLucca	IP-B	1,345	86
Spring Hill (A), Mobile, AL 36608	1830	Rev. Paul S. Tipton	IR-B	1,018	80
Springfield (A), Springfield, MA 01109	1885	Wilbert Locklin	IP-D	2,365	131
Springfield Tech. Comm., Springfield, MA 01105	1967	Leonard J. Collamore	Ps-A	6,900	400
Springfield Coll. in Illinois, Springfield, IL 62702	1929	Sr. Francis M. Thrailkill	IR-A	450	40
Stanford Univ. (A), Stanford, CA 94305	1885	Donald Kennedy	Psl-D	12,866	1,692
State Fair Comm., Sedalia, MO 65301	1966	Fred E. Davis	Pl-A	1,606	99
State Tech. Inst., Memphis, TN 38134	1967	Charles Whitehead	Pf-A	6,445	300
Stephen F. Austin State Univ., Nacogdoches, TX 75962	1921	William Johnson	Ps-D	10,153	440
Stephens (W), Columbia, MO 65243	1833	Arland Christ-Janer	IP-B	1,355	140
Sterling, Sterling, KS 67579	1887	Charles Schoenherr	IR-B	418	46
Stetson Univ., De Land, FL 32720	1883	Pope A. Duncan	IR-D	*2,934*	*199*
Steubenville, Univ. of, Steubenville, OH 43952	1946	Rev. M. Scanlon	IR-M	961	76
Stevens Inst. of Tech., Hoboken, NJ 07030	1870	Kenneth C. Rogers	IP-D	3,057	224
Stillman, Tuscaloosa, AL 35403	1876	Cordell Wynn	IR-B	640	47
Stockton State (A), Pomona, NJ 08240	1966	Peter Mitchell	Ps-B	4,600	163
Stonehill, N. Easton, MA 02356	1948	Rev. Bartley MacPhaidin	IR-B	2,645	217
Strayer (A), Washington, DC 20005	1904	Murray Donoho III	IP-B	1,800	50
Sue Bennett, London, KY 40741	1897	Earl F. Hays	IR-A	315	24
Suffolk County Comm. (A), Selden, NY 11784	1960	Albert M. Ammerman	Ps-A	21,000	600
Suffolk Univ., Boston, MA 02114	1906	Daniel H. Perlman	IP-S	6,136	255
Sullivan County Comm. (A), Loch Sheldrake, NY 12759	1962	Richard F. Grego	Ps-A	1,740	71
Sul Ross State Univ., Alpine, TX 79830	1917	C.R. Richardson	Pf-M	*2,048*	*94*
Sumter Area Tech (A), Sumter, SC 29150	1963	James Hudgins	Ps-A	3,306	69
Suomi, Hancock, MI 49930	1896	Ralph J. Jalkanen	IR-A	481	42
Surry Community, Dobson, NC 27017	1965	Swanson Richards	Psl-A	2,800	110
Susquehanna Univ., Selinsgrove, PA 17870	1858	Jonathan Messerli	IP-B	1,523	115
Swarthmore, Swarthmore, PA 19081	1864	Theodore Friend	IP-M	1,315	151
Sweet Briar (W), Sweet Briar, VA 24595	1901	Harold B. Whiteman Jr.	IP-B	642	100
Syracuse Univ., Syracuse, NY 13210	1871	Melvin A. Eggers	IP-D	21,313	1,202
Tabor, Hillsboro, KS 67063	1908	Vernon Janzen	IR-B	438	45
Tacoma Comm., Tacoma, WA 98465	1965	Larry P. Stevens	Ps-A	6,500	526
Taft, Taft, CA 93268	1922	David Cothrun	Psl-A	1,381	43
Talladega (A), Talladega, AL 35160	1867	Joseph Gayles	IP-B	698	46
Tallahassee Comm. (A), Tallahassee, FL 32304	1965	Marm Harris	Pl-A	3,303	126
Tampa, Tampa, FL 33607	1953	Donald C. Jones	IP-B	1,642	105
Tampa, Univ. of (A), Tampa, FL 33606	1931	Richard Cheshire	IP-M	2,068	146

Name, address	Year	Governing official, affiliation, and highest degree offered		Students	Teachers
Tarkio, Tarkio, MO 64491	1883	Roy McIntosh	IR-B	350	35
Tarleton State Univ., Stephenville, TX 76402	1899	W.O. Trogdon	Ps-M	3,728	142
Tarrant County Junior, Ft. Worth, TX 76102	1965	Joe B. Rushing	Pf-A	*23,000*	*900*
Taylor Univ., Upland, IN 46989	1846	Gregg Lehman	IR-B	1,488	100
Technical Career Inst., New York, NY 10001	1909	Samuel Steinman	IP-A	1,800	150
Tech. Coll. of Alamance, Haw River, NC 27258	1958	W. Ronald McCarter	Psl-A	1,583	75
Temple Junior, Temple, TX 76501	1926	Marvin Felder	Psl-A	2,397	107
Temple Univ., Philadelphia, PA 19122	1884	Peter J. Liacouras	Psr-D	*31,474*	*2,706*
Tennessee State Univ.*, Nashville, TN 37203	1912	F. Humphries	Ps-S	7,730	412
Tennessee System, Univ., of* (A), Knoxville, TN 37916	1794	Edward Boling	Psl-D	*45,402*	*3,392*
Ctr. for Health Sci.* (A), Memphis, TN 38103	1911	T. Farmer, Chan.	Ps-D	2,187	1,170
at Chattanooga*, Chattanooga, TN 37401	1886	Frederick W. Obear	Ps-M	7,480	415
at Knoxville*, Knoxville, TN 37916	1794	Jack Reese	Ps-D	28,601	1,458
at Martin*, Martin, TN 38238	1927	Charles Smith	Ps-M	5,583	261
at Nashville* (A), Nashville, TN 37203	1947	Vacant	Ps-M	5,419	120
Tennessee Tech. Univ., Cookeville, TN 38501	1915	Arliss Roaden	Ps-D	7,133	514
Tennessee Temple, Chattanooga, TN 37404	1946	J.R. Faulkner	IR-D	3,030	166
Tennessee Wesleyan, Athens, TN 37303	1857	George Naff Jr.	IR-B	505	55
Texarkana Comm., Texarkana, TX 75501	1927	Carl M. Nelson	Psl-A	3,653	210
Texas (A), Tyler, TX 75701	1894	Allen C. Hancock	IR-B	592	37
Texas A & I Univ., Kingsville, TX 78363	1925	Billy J. Franklin	Ps-D	4,657	251
Texas A & M Univ.*, College Station, TX 77843	1876	Frank W.R. Hubert	Ps-D	*35,146*	*2,074*
Texas Christian Univ. (A), Fort Worth, TX 76129	1873	William Tucker	IR-D	6,283	422
Texas Eastern Univ. (A), Tyler, TX 75701	1971	James Stewart Jr.	Ps-M	1,938	78
Texas Lutheran, Seguin, TX 78155	1892	Charles Oestreich	IR-B	1,043	75
Texas Southern Univ. (A), Houston, TX 77004	1947	Granville Sawyer	Ps-D	9,147	453
Texas Southmost, Brownsville, TX 78520	1926	Albert A. Besteiro	Pl-A	4,640	197
Texas System, Univ. of (A), Austin, TX 78701	1881	E. Don Walker			
at Arlington (A), Arlington, TX 76019	1895	Wendell Nedderman	Ps-D	19,135	829
at Austin, Austin, TX 78712	1883	Peter Flawn	Ps-D	48,156	3,000
at Dallas, Richardson, TX 75080	1969	Robert Rutford	Ps-D	6,628	349
at El Paso, El Paso, TX 79968	1913	Haskell Monroe	Ps-D	14,463	661
Health Science Center, Dallas, TX 75235	1948	Charles Sprague	Ps-D	1,313	988
at Houston, Houston, TX 77025	1972	Roger J. Bulger	Ps-D	2,733	792
at San Antonio, San Antonio, TX 78284	1959	Frank Harrison	Ps-S	2,212	505
Medical Branch, Galveston, TX 77550	1891	William Levin	Pf-D	1,599	450
at Permian Basin, Odessa, TX 79762	1969	V.R. Cardozier	Ps-M	1,640	87
at San Antonio, San Antonio, TX 78285	1969	James Wagener	Ps-M	9,575	457
at Tyler, Tyler, TX 75701	1971	George F. Hamm	Ps-M	2,048	125
Texas Tech. Univ., Lubbock, TX 79409	1923	Lauro Cavazos	Ps-D	23,500	1,500
Texas Wesleyan (A), Fort Worth, TX 76105	1891	Jon Fleming	IR-B	1,667	112
Texas Woman's Univ. (W), Denton, TX 76204	1901	Mary B. Huey	Ps-D	7,498	495
Thames Valley State Tech., Norwich, CT 06360	1963	Donald Welter	Ps-A	1,650	76
Thiel, Greenville, PA 16125	1866	Louis Almen	IR-B	948	80
Thomas, Waterville, ME 04901	1894	Paul G. Jenson	IP-M	874	67
Thomas A. Edison State, Trenton, NJ 08625	1972	Larraine Matusak	Ps-B	3,698	NA
Thomas Jefferson Univ. (A), Philadelphia, PA 19107	1824	Lewis Bluemle	IP-D	1,469	1,912
Thomas More (A), Ft. Mitchell, KY 41017	1921	Robert J. Giroux	IR-B	1,350	85
Thomas Nelson Comm., Hampton, VA 23670	1968	Thomas Kubala	Psl-A	5,568	283
Thornton Comm., So. Holland, IL 60473	1927	Nathan A. Ivey	Ps-A	12,000	325
Three Rivers Comm., Poplar Bluff, MO 63901	1966	J.L. Bottenfield	Psl-A	1,750	53
Tidewater Comm. (A), Portsmouth, VA 23703	1968	George Pass	Ps-A	*14,968*	*750*
Tiffin Univ., Tiffin, OH 44883	1888	George Kidd Jr.	IP-B	477	24
Tift, Forsyth, GA 31029	1847	Robert W. Jackson	IR-B	703	65
Toccoa Falls, Toccoa Falls, GA 30598	1907	Paul L. Alford	IP-B	661	50
Toledo, Univ. of, Toledo, OH 43606	1872	Glen R. Driscoll	Ps-D	21,170	1,254
Tomkins-Courtland Comm. (A), Groton, NY 13053	1967	Hushang Bahar	Ps-A	2,793	48
Tougaloo (A), Tougaloo, MS 39174	1869	George A. Owens	IR-B	886	76
Towson State Univ., Baltimore, MD 21204	1866	Hoke Smith	Pf-M	15,107	818
Transylvania Univ., Lexington, KY 40508	1780	Irvin E. Lunger	IP-B	750	72
Treasure Valley Comm., Ontario, OR 97914	1962	Emery Skinner	Psl-A	2,200	70
Trenton State, Trenton, NJ 08625	1855	Harold Eickhoff	Ps-M	6,913	380
Trevecca Nazarene, Nashville, TN 37203	1901	Homer Adams	IR-B	961	70
Tri-County Tech., Pendleton, SC 29670	1961	Don Garrison	Psl-A	*2,507*	*171*
Trident Tech (A), Charleston, SC 29405	1964	Charles F. Ward	Ps-A	*5,400*	*170*
Trinidad State Junior, Trinidad, CO 81082	1925	Thomas Sullivan	Ps-A	1,135	121
Trinity (A), Hartford, CT 06106	1823	Theodore Lockwood	IP-M	1,885	135
Trinity, Deerfield, IL 60015	1897	Harry Evans	IP-A	598	58
Trinity, Burlington, VT 05446	1925	Janice Ryan	IR-B	872	72
Trinity (A), Washington, DC 20017	1897	Sr. Rose Anne Fleming	IR-M	1,000	82
Trinity Univ., San Antonio, TX 78284	1869	Ronald Calgaard	IR-M	3,629	296
Tri-State Univ., Angola, IN 46703	1884	Carl Elliott	IP-B	1,058	80
Triton, River Grove, IL 60171	1965	Brent Knight	Psl-A	14,097	689
Trocaire (A), Buffalo, NY 14220	1958	Sr. M. Carmina Coppola	IP-A	911	35
Troy State Univ. System, Troy, AL 36081	1887	Ralph W. Adams	Ps-S	*12,718*	*626*
Truett-McConnell, Cleveland, GA 30528	1946	Ronald Weitman	IR-A	876	124
Tufts Univ., Medford, MA 02155	1852	Jean Mayer	IP-D	7,248	994
Tulane Univ., New Orleans, LA 70118	1834	Eamon Kelly	IP-D	10,321	837
Tulsa, Univ. of, Tulsa, OK 74104	1894	J. Paschal Twyman	IP-D	*6,382*	*293*
Tulsa Junior, Tulsa, OK 74119	1968	A.M. Philips	Psl-A	*13,751*	*550*
Tunxis Comm., Farmington, CT 06032	1970	Benjamin G. Davis	Ps-A	3,000	110
Tusculum, Greenville, TN 37743	1794	Earl R. Mezoff	IP-B	310	36
Tuskegee Institute, Tuskegee Inst., AL 36088	1881	Benjamin F. Payton	IP-S	3,562	350
Tyler Junior, Tyler, TX 75711	1926	Raymond Hawkins	Psl-A	6,916	329
Ulster County Comm. (A), Stone Ridge, NY 12484	1961	Robert T. Brown	Ps-A	2,681	87
Umpqua Comm., Roseburg, OR 97470	1964	I.S. Hakanson	Pl-A	4,377	100
Union, Barbourville, KY 40906	1879	Mahlon A. Miller	IR-M	1,030	70
Union (A), Cranford, NJ 07016	1933	Saul Orkin	IP-A	*6,200*	*230*
Union, Lincoln, NE 68506	1891	Dean L. Hubbard	IP-B	979	70
Union (A), Schenectady, NY 12308	1795	John Morris	IP-B	3,318	140
Union County Voc.-Tech. (A), Scotch Plains, NJ 07076	1960	Myron Corman, Act.	Pl-A	1,760	94
Union Univ., Jackson, TN 38301	1825	Robert E. Craig	IP-B	1,382	86
U.S. Air Force Academy, Col. Springs, CO 80840	1954	Maj. Gen. Robert Kelley,	Pf-B	4,417	574
U.S. Coast Guard Acad., New London, CT 06320	1876	R. Adm. Charles Larkin, Supt.	Pf-B	916	114
U.S. International Univ. (A), San Diego, CA 92131	1952	William Rust	IP-B	2,893	91
U.S. Merchant Marine Acad. (A), Kings Point, NY 11024	1938	Rear Adm. Thomas King, Supt.	Pf-B	1,150	83
U.S. Military Academy (A), West Point, NY 10996	1802	Lt. Gen. A. Goodpaster	Pf-B	4,067	636
U.S. Naval Academy, Annapolis, MD 21402	1845	V. Adm. E. C. Walker	Pf-B	4,500	600

Name, address	Year	Governing official, affiliation, and highest degree offered		Stu-dents	Teach-ers
Unity, Unity, ME 04988	1965	Louis Wilcox Jr.	IP-B	278	3
Upper Iowa Univ. (A), Fayette, IA 52142	1857	Darcy C. Coyle	IP-B	2,199	4
Upsala, E. Orange, NJ 07019	1893	Rodney Felder	IR-M	1,800	8
Urbana, Urbana, OH 43078	1850	A. Perry Whitmore	IR-B	590	7
Ursinus, Collegeville, PA 19426	1869	Richard Richter	IP-B	2,033	16
Ursuline, Pepper Pike, OH 44124	1871	Sister M. Kenan	IR-M	1,147	8
Utah State Univ.* (A), Logan, UT 84322	1888	Stanford Cazier	Ps-D	9,939	46
Utah, Univ. of, Salt Lake City, UT 84112	1850	David P. Gardner	Ps-D	23,373	3,26
Utica Junior (A), Utica, MS 39175	1903	J. Louis Stokes	Ps-A	950	6
Valdosta State (A), Valdosta, GA 31601	1906	Hugh C. Bailey	Ps-M	4,862	25
Valencia Comm., Orlando, FL 32802	1967	James F. Gollattscheck	Ps-A	*11,500*	*73*
Valley City State, Valley City, ND 58072	1890	Vacant	Ps-B	1,208	7
Valparaiso Univ., Valparaiso, IN 46383	1859	Robert V. Schnabel	IR-M	4,467	33
Vanderbilt Univ., Nashville, TN 37240	1873	Alexander Heard	IP-D	8,911	1,95
Vassar (A), Poughkeepsie, NY 12601	1861	Virginia Smith	IP-M	2,260	18
Ventura, Ventura, CA 93003	1925	Richard A. Glenn	Ps-A	14,000	80
Vermillion Comm., Ely, MN 55731	1922	Ray Kenney	Ps-A	474	3
Vermont, Comm. Coll. of (A), Montpelier, VT 05602	1970	Myrna R. Miller	Psr-A	2,000	39
Vermont, Univ. of*, Burlington, VT 05405	1791	Lattie Coor	Ps-D	11,100	1,31
Vermont Technical (A), Randolph Center, VT 05061	1962	James Todd	Ps-A	793	6
Victor Valley (A), Victorville, CA 92392	1961	B.W. Wadsworth	Pl-A	3,024	7
Victoria, Victoria, TX 77901	1925	Roland E. Bing	Psl-A	2,647	13
Villa Julie, Stevenson, MD 21153	1952	Carolyn Manuszak	Pl-A	821	9
Villa Maria (W), Erie, PA 16505	1925	Sr. M. Lawrence Antoun	IP-B	639	6
Villanova Univ., Villanova, PA 19085	1843	Rev. John M. Driscoll	IP-D	10,187	65
Vincennes Univ., Vincennes, IN 47591	1801	Phillip M. Summers	Ps-A	*5,661*	*30*
Virgin Islands, Coll. of the, St. Thomas, VI 00801	1962	Arthur A. Richards	Ps-M	*2,608*	*20*
Virginia, Univ. of, Charlottesville, VA 22906	1819	Frank Hereford Jr.	Ps-D	16,420	1,63
Virginia Commonwealth Univ., Richmond, VA 23284	1838	Edmund Ackell	Ps-D	*18,500*	*2,23*
Virginia Highlands Comm., Abingdon, VA 24210	1967	E Jean Walker	Pf-A	1,354	9
Virginia Intermont, Bristol, VA 24201	1884	Kenneth Glass	IR-B	817	5
Virginia Military Inst. (M), Lexington, VA 24450	1839	Gen. Sam S. Walker, Supt.	Ps-B	1,309	13
Virginia Poly. Inst. & State Univ.*, Blacksburg, VA 24061	1872	William Lavery	Ps-D	21,584	2,52
Virginia State*, Petersburg, VA 23803	1882	Curtis E. Bryan	Ps-M	4,564	22
Virginia Union Univ., Richmond, VA 23220	1865	David Shannon	IR-M	1,327	11
Virginia Western Comm., Roanoke, VA 24015	1967	Charles Downs	Ps-A	*6,450*	*25*
Virginia Wesleyan, Norfolk, VA 23502	1961	Lambuth M. Clarke	IP-B	826	7
Vista, Berkeley, CA 94704	1974	John Holleman	Psi-A	8,840	36
Viterbo, La Crosse, WI 54601	1890	Robert Gibbons	IR-B	1,113	11
Volunteer State Comm., Gallatin, TN 37066	1970	Hal R. Ramer	Ps-A	3419	16
Voorhees (A), Denmark, SC 29042	1897	George B. Thomas	IR-B	651	4
Wabash (M) (A), Crawfordsville, IN 47933	1832	Lewis S. Salter	IP-B	800	7
Wabash Valley, Mt. Carmel, IL 62863	1960	James B. Benedict	Psl-A	1,624	18
Wagner, Staten Island, NY 10301	1883	Sam H. Frank	IR-M	2458	18
Wake Forest Univ., Winston-Salem, NC 27109	1834	James R. Scales	IR-D	4,829	1,06
Wake Tech., Raleigh, NC 27603	1963	Bruce I. Howell	Ps-A	2,400	15
Waldorf, Forest City, IA 50436	1903	Arndt Braaten	IR-A	410	3
Walker, Jasper, AL 35501	1938	David J. Rowland	IP-A	701	4
Walla Walla, College Place, WA 99324	1892	N. Clifford Sorensen	IR-M	1,967	16
Walla Walla Comm., Walla Walla, WA 99362	1967	Wayland Dewitt	Ps-A	4,500	14
Walsh, North Canton, OH 44720	1958	Francis Blovin	IR-M	1,120	9
Walsh Coll. of Accountancy, Troy, MI 48084	1922	Jeffrey Barry	IP-M	1,700	8
Walters State Comm., Morristown, TN 37814	1970	Jack E. Campbell	Pf-A	3,166	18
Warner Pacific, Portland, OR 97215	1937	Marshall K. Christensen	IR-M	481	4
Warren Wilson, Swannanoa, NC 28778	1894	Reuben A. Holden	IR-B	566	12
Wartburg, Waverly, IA 50677	1852	Robert Vogel	IP-B	1,046	8
Washburn Univ. of Topeka, Topeka, KS 66621	1865	John L. Green, Jr.	Psr-M	6,200	24
Washington, Chestertown, MD 21620	1782	Douglas Cater	IP-M	688	6
Washington and Jefferson, Washington, PA 15301	1781	Howard J. Burnett	IP-A	1,077	9
Washington and Lee Univ., Lexington, VA 24450	1749	Robert Huntley	IP-1P	1,679	17
Washington State Comm. (A), Spokane, WA 92207	1963	Max M. Synder	Ps-A	*26,729*	*37*
Washington State Univ., Pullman, WA 99164	1890	Glenn Terrell	Ps-D	17,048	1,31
Washington Univ., St. Louis, MO 63130	1853	W.H. Danforth	IP-D	*10,900*	*2,44*
Washington, Univ. of*, Seattle, WA 98195	1861	William P. Gerberding	Ps-D	35,000	2,50
Washtenaw Comm., Ann Arbor, MI 48106	1965	Gunder Myran	Psl-A	8,500	50
Waterbury State Tech (A), Waterbury, CT 06708	1964	Charles A. Ekstrom	Ps-A	1,715	10
Waubonsee Comm., Sugar Grove, IL 60554	1967	John J. Swalec, Jr.	Psl-A	7,250	30
Waukesha Co. Tech. Inst., Pewaukee, WI 53072	1923	R. Anderson,	Psl-A	*5,000*	*21*
Wayland Baptist (A), Plainview, TX 79072	1908	David L. Jester	IR-B	1,468	5
Wayne Community, Goldsboro, NC 27530	1957	Clyde Erwin Jr.	Ps-A	2,166	14
Wayne County Comm. (A), Detroit, MI 48226	1967	Richard Simons Jr.	Ps-A	*21,000*	*90*
Wayne State, Wayne, NE 68787	1910	Lyle Seymour	Ps-S	2,312	13
Wayne State Univ., Detroit, MI 48202	1868	David Adamany	Ps-D	33,408	2,10
Waynesburg (A), Waynesburg, PA 15370	1849	Joseph Marsh	IP-B	871	7
Weber State (A), Ogden, UT 84408	1889	Rodney H. Brady	Ps-B	10,065	43
Webster, St. Louis, MO 63119	1915	Leigh Gerdine	IP-M	*5,400*	*85*
Wellesley (W), Wellesley, MA 02181	1875	Nannerl O. Keohane	IP-B	2,152	29
Wells (W) (A), Aurora, NY 13026	1868	Patti McGill Peterson	IP-B	527	5
Wentworth Institue of Technology (A), Boston, MA 02115	1904	Edward I. Kirkpatrick	IP-B	2,250	13
Wesley (A), Dover, DE 19901	1873	R.J. Cooke	IR-B	1,167	7
Wesleyan (W), Macon, GA 31297	1836	Fred Hicks	IP-B	420	7
Wesleyan Univ., Middletown, CT 06457	1831	Colin G. Campbell	IP-D	3,043	30
Westbrook (A), Portland, ME 04103	1834	Thomas B. Courtice	IP-B	920	8
Westchester Comm. (A), Valhalla, NY 10595	1946	Joseph N. Hankin	Psl-A	7,000	30
West Chester State, West Chester, PA 19380	1871	Charles Mayo	Ps-M	9,209	50
West Florida, Univ. of, Pensacola, FL 32504	1963	James Robinson	Pf-M	*5,350*	*1,20*
West Georgia, Carrollton, GA 30118	1933	Maurice Townsend	Pf-S	5,207	24
West Hills Comm., Coalinga, CA 93210	1932	Joseph M. Conte	Pf-A	2,352	18
West Liberty State, West Liberty, WV 26074	1837	James L. Chapman	Ps-B	2,632	15
West Los Angeles (A), Culver City, CA 90230	1968	M. Fujimoto	IP-M	10,041	40
West Oahu, Aica, HI 96782	1975	Ralph M. Miwa	Ps-B	346	1
West Shore Comm., Scottville, MI 49454	1967	John Eaton	Pl-A	940	4
West Texas State Univ., Canyon, TX 79016	1909	Gail Shannon	Ps-M	6,182	35
West Valley, Saratoga, CA 95070	1964	Frank Pearce, Supt.	Ps-A	14,979	50
W. Va. Inst. of Tech., Montgomery, WV 25136	1895	Leonard C. Nelson	Ps-M	3,316	19
West Virginia North, Comm., Wheeling, WV 26003	1972	Daniel B. Crowder	Ps-A	*3,858*	*24*
West Virginia State, Institute, WV 25112	1891	Thomas W. Cole, Jr.	Ps-B	4,485	20

Name, address	Year	Governing official, affiliation, and highest degree offered		Students	Teachers
West Virginia Univ.*, Morgantown, WV 26505	1867	E. Gordon Gee	Ps-D	*21,265*	*2,100*
W. Virginia Wesleyan (A), Buckhannon, WV 26201	1890	Hugh A. Latimer	IP-M	1,746	128
Western Carolina Univ., Cullowhee, NC 28723	1889	H.F. Robinson	Ps-S	6,659	369
Western Conn. State (A), Danbury, CT 06810	1903	Robert Bersi	Ps-M	*5,454*	*168*
Western Illinois Univ., Macomb, IL 61455	1899	Leslie F. Malpass	Ps-S	13,297	697
Western Iowa Tech. Comm., Sioux City, IA 51102	1966	Robert Kiser	Pf-A	1,350	110
Western Kentucky Univ., Bowling Green, KY 42101	1906	Donald Zacharias	Ps-S	13,500	585
Western Maryland, Westminster, MD 21157	1868	Ralph C. John	IP-M	1,867	167
Western Mich. Univ., Kalamazoo, MI 49008	1903	John T. Bernhard	Ps-D	20,269	850
Western Montana, Dillon, MT 59725	1893	Robert Thomas	Ps-M	850	43
Western New England, Springfield, MA 01095	1919	Beverly Miller	IP-M	*6,000*	*300*
Western New Mexico Univ., Silver City, NM 88062	1893	Robert E. Glennen	Ps-M	1,103	109
Western Okla. State, Altus, OK 73521	1926	W.C. Burris	Ps-A	1,784	80
Western Oregon State (A), Monmouth, OR 97361	1856	Gerald Leinwand	Ps-M	3,120	261
Western Piedmont Comm., Morganton, NC 28655	1964	James A. Richardson	Ps-A	1,850	125
Western State Col. of Colo., Gunnison, CO 81230	1911	John Melon	Ps-M	3,200	155
Western Texas, Synder, TX 79549	1970	Don Newbury	PsI-A	1,107	85
Western Washington Univ., Bellingham, WA 98225	1895	James L. Talbot, Act.	Ps-M	10,291	522
Western Wisc. Tech. Inst., LaCrosse, WI 54601	1917	Charles Richardson, Dir	PsI-A	5,000	250
Westfield State (A), Westfield, MA 01085	1838	Francis J. Pilecki	Ps-M	4,386	217
Westmar, Le Mars, IA 51031	1890	John F. Courter	IR-A	578	43
Westminster (A), Fulton, MO 65251	1851	J.H. Saunders	IP-B	746	59
Westminster, New Wilmington, PA 16142	1852	Robert E. Lauterbach	IR-M	1,685	144
Westminster, Salt Lake City, UT 84105	1875	James E. Petersen	IP-M	1,120	99
Westminster Choir, Princeton, NJ 08540	1926	Ray E. Robinson	IP-M	419	60
Westmont, Santa Barbara, CA 93108	1940	David Winter	IR-B	1,060	85
Wharton County Junior, Wharton, TX 77488	1946	Theodore Nicksick Jr.	PsI-A	2,219	142
Wheaton, Wheaton, IL 60187	1860	J. Richard Chase	IP-M	2,400	190
Wheaton (W), (A), Norton, MA 02766	1834	Alice F. Emerson	IP-B	1,140	84
Wheeling, Wheeling, WV 26003	1954	Fr. Thomas S. Acker	IP-M	1,050	85
Wheelock, Boston, MA 02215	1888	Gordon L. Marshall	IP-M	911	119
Whitman, Walla Walla, WA 99362	1859	Robert Skotheim	IP-B	1,160	112
Whittier, Whittier, CA 90602	1901	Eugene Mills	IP-M	*1,154*	*128*
Whitworth, Spokane, WA 99251	1890	Robert Mounce	IR-M	1,921	90
Wichita State Univ., Wichita, KS 67208	1895	Clark Ahlberg	Ps-D	16,954	810
Widener, Chester, PA 19013	1821	Robert Bruce	IP-M	3,466	268
Wilberforce Univ., Wilberforce, OH 45384	1856	Charles Taylor	IR-B	612	53
Wiley, Marshall, TX 75670	1873	Robert Hayes Sr.	IR-B	613	52
Wilkes, Wilkes-Barre, PA 18766	1933	Robert Capin	IP-M	3,200	190
Wilkes Community, Wilkesboro, NC 28697	1965	David E. Daniel	Ps-A	2,703	91
Willamette Univ. (A), Salem, OR 97301	1842	Jerry E. Hudson	IP-1P	1,886	183
William Carey, Hattiesburg, MS 39401	1906	J. Ralph Noonkester	IR-S	*1,537*	*90*
William Jewell, Liberty, MO 64068	1849	J. Gordon Kingsley	IR-B	1,746	166
Wm. and Mary, Coll. of, Williamsburg, VA 23185	1693	Thomas A. Graves Jr.	Ps-D	6,520	557
Wm. Mitchell Coll. of Law, St. Paul, MN 55105	1956	Geoffrey W. Peters, Dean	IP-D	1,150	117
Wm. Paterson (A), Wayne, NJ 07470	1855	Seymour C. Hyman	Ps-M	12,555	379
William Penn (A), Oskaloosa, IA 52577	1873	Gus Turbeville	IR-B	571	42
William Rainey Harper (A), Palatine, IL 60067	1965	Robert E. Lahti	PsI-A	19,575	933
William Woods (W), Fulton, MO 65251	1870	John M. Bartholomy	IR-B	821	69
Williams, Williamstown, MA 01267	1793	John W. Chandler	IP-M	2,000	160
Williamsburg Tech., Kingstree, SC 29556	1969	John T. Wynn	PsI-A	432	43
Williamsport Area Comm., Williamsport, PA 17701	1965	Robert Brueder	PsI-A	3,500	180
Willmar Comm., Willmar, NM 56201	1962	John Torgelson	Pf-A	820	57
Wilmington, New Castle, DE 19720	1965	Audrey K. Doberstein	IP-M	893	65
Wilmington, Wilmington, OH 45177	1870	Robert E. Lucas	IR-B	*1,200*	*85*
Wilson (W), Chambersburg, PA 17201	1869	Mary-Linda Meinan	IR-B	229	43
Wilson Co. Tech. Inst., Wilson, NC 27893	1958	Frank L. Eagles	PsI-A	1,347	55
Wingate, Wingate, NC 28174	1895	Thomas Corts	IR-B	1,518	76
Winona State Univ., Winona, MN 55987	1860	Robert A. Hanson	Ps-S	5,408	225
Winthrop, Rock Hill, SC 29733	1886	Charles Vail	Ps-S	4,960	314
Wisconsin, Univ. of (A), Madison, WI 53706	1971	Edwin Young	Ps-D	*150,629*	*7,036*
Eau Claire, Eau Claire, WI 54701	1916	Emily Hannah	Ps-S	10,963	567
Green Bay (A), Green Bay, WI 54302	1969	Edward W. Weidner	Ps-M	3,641	160
La Crosse (A), La Crosse, WI 54601	1909	Noel Richards	Ps-M	9,016	533
Madison (A), Madison, WI 53706	1849	Irving Shain	Ps-D	39,000	2,300
Milwaukee, Milwaukee, WI 53201	1956	Frank E. Horton	Ps-D	24,845	1,222
Oshkosh, Oshkosh, WI 54901	1871	Edward Penson	Ps-M	11,129	520
Parkside (A), Kenosha, WI 53141	1969	Alan Guskin	Ps-B	5,300	180
Platteville, Platteville, WI 53818	1866	Warren Carrier	Ps-M	5,200	300
River Falls, River Falls, WI 54022	1874	George Field	Ps-M	5,505	300
Stevens Point (A), Stevens Point, WI 54481	1894	Philip R. Marshall	Ps-M	8,942	430
Stout (A), Menomonie, WI 54751	1893	Robert Swanson	Ps-S	7,400	550
Superior, Superior, WI 54880	1893	Karl W. Myer	Ps-S	2,300	350
Whitewater, Whitewater, WI 53190	1868	James Connor	Ps-M	10,212	575
Wisconsin Center, Univ of (A),	1972	Edward Fort	Ps-A	*9,302*	*534*
at Baraboo (A), Baraboo, WI 53913	1968	Edward Fort, Chan.	Ps-A	399	28
at Barron Co., Rice Lake, WI 54868	1966	Robert Polk	Ps-A	353	25
at Fond du Lac, Fond du Lac, WI 54935	1968	Willard J. Henken, Dean	Ps-A	538	41
at Fox Valley, Menasha, WI 54952	1972	Rue C. Johnson	Ps-A	1,100	60
at Manitowoc, Manitowoc, WI 54220	1933	Chester F. Natunewicz, Dean	Ps-A	390	30
at Marathon, Wausau, WI 54401	1947	Robert Polk	Ps-A	1,052	70
at Marinette, Marinette, WI 54143	1846	William Schmidtke, Dean	Ps-A	435	24
at Marshfield/Wood, Marshfield, WI 54449	1963	Robert Polk	Ps-A	562	30
at Richland (A), Richland Ctr., WI 53581	1967	Marjorie Wallace, Dean	Ps-A	326	9
at Rock County, Janesville, WI 53545	1966	Robert Polk	Ps-A	865	40
at Sheboygan, Sheboygan, WI 53081	1933	K.M. Bailey, Dean	Ps-A	691	34
at Waukesha (A), Waukesha, WI 53186	1966	Kenneth D. Oliver, Dean	Ps-A	1,700	90
at Washington, West Bend, WI 53095	1967	R.O. Thompson, Dean	Ps-A	678	37
Wittenberg Univ. (A), Springfield, OH 45501	1845	W.A. Kinnison	IR-M	2,308	148
Wofford, Spartanburg, SC 29301	1854	J.M. Lesesne Jr.	IR-B	1,012	75
Wood Junior, Mathiston, MS 39752	1886	Felix Sutphin	IR-A	400	38
Wooster, Coll. of, Wooster, OH 44691	1866	Henry Copeland	IP-B	1,816	134
Worcester Jr. (A), Worcester, MA 01610	1888	E.P. Mattar III	IP-A	1,100	75
Worcester Polytechnic Inst., Worcester, MA 01609	1865	Edmund T. Cranch	IP-D	3,487	197
Worcester State, Worcester, MA 01602	1874	Vacant	Ps-M	5,865	219
Worthington Comm., Worthington, MN 56187	1936	Frederick A. Voda	Ps-A	665	50
Wright State Univ., Dayton, OH 45435	1967	Robert J. Kegerreis	Ps-D	*15,327*	*1,001*
Wyoming, Univ. of, Laramie, WY 82071	1886	Donald L. Veal	Ps-D	9,105	856
Xavier Univ. (A), Cincinnati, OH 45232	1831	Rev. Robert Mulligan	IR-M	7,209	350

Name, address	Year	Governing official, affiliation, and highest degree offered		Students	Teachers
Yakima Valley, Yakima, WA 98907	1928	Terrence R. Brown	Ps-A	3,467	250
Yale Univ., New Haven, CT 06520	1701	A.B. Giamatti	IP-D	10,098	1,731
Yankton, Yankton, SD 57078	1881	Orlan Mitchell	IR-B	244	48
Yavapai, Prescott, AZ 86301	1966	Joseph Russo	Ps-A	*5,844*	*311*
Yeshiva Univ., New York, NY 10033	1886	Norman Lamm	IP-D	*6,640*	*2,680*
York, York, NE 68567	1890	Gary Bartholomew	IR-A	409	27
York College of Pa., York, PA 17405	1789	Robert V. Iosue	IP-M	4,000	215
Young Harris, Young Harris, GA 30582	1886	Ray Farley	IP-A	527	40
Youngstown State Univ., Youngstown, OH 44555	1908	John J. Coffelt	Ps-M	15,664	761
Yuba Comm., Marysville, CA 95901	1927	Daniel G. Walker	PsI-A	*9,790*	*270*

Canadian Colleges and Universities

Source: Statistics Canada

Each institution listed has an enrollment of at least 200 students of college grade. Enrollment and faculty include all branches and campuses for the 1980-81 academic year. Number of full-time teachers is the total number of individuals on teaching staff. Governing official is the president unless otherwise designated. All institutions are co-educational. Indented colleges are degree-granting affiliates.

Name	Location	Established	Governing official	Students	Teachers
Acadia Univ.	Wolfville, N.S.	1838	G.R.C. Perkin	2,760	210
Alberta, Univ. of	Edmonton, Alta.	1906	M. Horowitz	18,270	1,580
Bishop's Univ.	Lennoxville, Que.	1843	G.I.H. Nicholl	750	80
Brandon Univ.	Brandon, Man.	1899	H.J. Perkins	940	150
British Columbia, Univ. of	Vancouver, B.C.	1908	Douglas T. Kenny	19,870	2,090
Brock Univ.	St. Catharines, Ont.	1964	A.J. Earp	2,300	210
Calgary, Univ. of	Calgary, Alta.	1945	Norman E. Wagner	11,080	1,110
Canadian Bible College	Regina, Sask.	1941	R.A. Boda	380	10
Canadian Union College	College Hts., Alta.	1919	N. Mathews	210	20
Carleton Univ.	Ottawa, Ont.	1942	William Beckel	8,430	620
Concordia Univ.	Montreal, Que.	1974	John O'Brien, Rector	10,780	700[1]
Dalhousie Univ.	Halifax, N.S.	1818	W.A. MacKay	7,070	810
King's Coll., Univ. of	Halifax, N.S.	1789	John F. Godfrey	370	10
Guelph, Univ. of	Guelph, Ont.	1964	Donald F. Forster	9,390	770
Lakehead Univ.	Thunder Bay, Ont.	1965	G.A. Harrower	2,690	240
Laurentian Univ. of Sudbury	Sudbury, Ont.	1960	Henry B.M. Best	2,390	290
Nipissing Univ. Coll.	North Bay, Ont.	1961	G. Zytaruk	230	30
Laval Universite	Quebec, Que.	1852	Jean-Guy Paquet, Rector	18,170	1,470[1]
Lethbridge, Univ. of	Lethbridge, Alta.	1967	John Woods	1,490	170
Manitoba, Univ. of	Winnipeg, Man.	1877	A. Haimark	12,650	1,289
St. Boniface, Coll. de	Winn., Man.	1871	N. Boisvert	210	30
McGill Univ.	Montreal, Que.	1821	David Johnston	16,400	1,250[1]
McMaster Univ.	Hamilton, Ont.	1887	A.A. Lee	9,910	900
Mem. Univ. of Newfoundland	St. John's, Nfld.	1925	L. Harris	6,740	830
Moncton, Univ. de	Moncton, N.B.	1963	G. Finn	2,940	280
Montreal, Univ. de	Montreal, Que.	1920	Paul Lacoste, Rector	14,730	1,460[1]
Ecole Polytechnique	Montreal, Que.	1876	M.J.B. Lavingueur	2,350	200[1]
Hautes Etudes Commerciales	Montreal, Que.	1907	P. Laurin	1,720	130[1]
Mount Allison Univ.	Sackville, N.B.	1840	G.R. MacLean	1,510	140
Mount St. Vincent Univ.	Halifax, N.S.	1925	Margaret Fulton	1,440	110
New Brunswick, Univ. of	Fredericton, N.B.	1785	J. Downey	6,070	570
Nova Scotia Coll. of Arts & Design	Halifax, N.S.	1887	Garry Neill Kennedy	430	40
Ottawa, Univ. of	Ottawa, Ont.	1848	Roger Guindon	11,710	1,010
Prince Edward Island, Univ. of	Charlottetown, P.E.I.	1969	Peter Meincke	1,320	120
Quebec, Univ. of	Ste-Foy, Que.	1969	Gilles Boulet	18,850	1,410[1]
Queen's Univ.	Kingston, Ont.	1841	R.L. Watts	11,000	930
Regina, Univ. of	Regina, Sask.	1974	Lloyd I. Barber	3,070	350
Campion College	Regina, Sask.	1924	J.B. Gavin	360	20
Luther College	Regina, Sask.	1926	M.A. Anderson	210	10
Royal Military Coll. of Can.	Kingston, Ont.	1876	Donald Tilley	680	150
Royal Roads Military Coll.	Victoria, B.C.	1942	E.S. Graham	250	40
Ryerson Polytechnical Inst.	Toronto, Ont.	1948	B. Segal	9,170	640
St. Francis Xavier Univ.	Antigonish, N.S.	1853	Rev. G.A. MacKinnon	2,120	150
Cape Breton, Coll. of	Sidney, N.S.	1974	D.F. Campbell	620	60
St. Mary's Univ.	Halifax, N.S.	1802	Kenneth L. Ozmon	2,270	190
St. Thomas Univ.	Fredericton, N.B.	1934	G.W. Martin	720	60
Saskatchewan, Univ. of	Saskatoon, Sask.	1907	L.F. Kristjansen	9,760	1,040
Sherbrooke, Univ. of	Sherbrooke, Que.	1954	C. Hamel	6,990	650[1]
Coll. Militaire Royal de St. Jean	Sherbrooke, Que.	1952	C.E. Sevard	200	70
Simon Fraser Univ.	Burnaby, B.C.	1965	George Pederson	5,040	490
Technical Univ. of N.S.	Halifax, N.S.	1907	J.C. Callaghan	790	70
Toronto, Univ. of	Toronto, Ont.	1827	James M. Ham	33,050	2,590
Ontario Inst. for Studies in Ed.	Toronto, Ont.	1965	B.J. Shapiro, dir.	680	150
St. Michael's Coll., Univ. of	Toronto, Ont.	1852	P.J.M. Swan	210	100
Trent Univ.	Peterborough, Ont.	1963	D.F. Theall	2,180	180
Trinity Western Coll.	Langley, B.C.	1969	R.N. Snider	610	NA
Victoria, Univ. of	Victoria, B.C.	1963	H.E. Petch	5,670	520
Waterloo, Univ. of	Waterloo, Ont.	1957	D. Wright	15,290	770
St. Jerome, Univ. of	Waterloo, Ont.	1866	N.L. Choate	460	30
Western Ontario, Univ. of	London, Ont.	1878	George E. Connell	14,820	1,320
Brescia College	London, Ont.	1919	D. Kuntz	350	20
Huron College	London, Ont.	1863	J.G. Morden	560	40
King's College	London, Ont.	1855	J.D. Morgan	1,100	40
Wilfrid Laurier Univ.	Waterloo, Ont.	1973	N.H. Tayler	3,890	220
Windsor, Univ. of	Windsor, Ont.	1857	Mervyn Franklin	6,780	520
Winnipeg, Univ. of	Winnipeg, Man.	1871	R. Farquhar	2,400	190
York Univ.	Downsview, Ont.	1959	H. Ian MacDonald	11,820	1,020

(1) Estimate.

Tuition Fees at Selected U.S. Colleges and Universities

Source: World Almanac Questionnaire

The College Entrance Examination Board has estimated that the average tuition per year in a 4-year private college for 1981-1982 was $3,709. The tuition at a 4-year public college averaged $819.

Fees for tuition charged per year by colleges and universities for courses, use of libraries, laboratories and other facilities are a major part of student expenses. Tuition varies considerably, depending on the type of institution, its control and location. The lowest tuition fees are those of state-controlled or other public-controlled institutions for residents of their state, city, etc. Students from other states or areas have to pay more. In the following list, such state or other public institutions are shown with two figures. The lower one is the tuition fee for residents, the higher one the tuition fee for students from other states or areas.

(Tuition does not include room, board, or other expenses.)

School	Tuition
Abilene Christian	$2,240
Akron Univ.	1,430-2,960
Alabama State Univ.	600-1,200
Alaska, Univ. of	600-780
Albion	4,716
Albright	5,660
Alma	4,399
Appalachian State Univ.	772-2,520
Arizona, Univ. of.	710-3,250
Arkansas, Univ. of	780-1,920
Auburn Univ.	990-2,280
Austin Peay State Univ.	720-2,478
Avila	3,100
Baldwin-Wallace	6,604
Ball State	1,116-2,460
Bates	8,100
Baylor	2,880
Bemidji State Univ.	850-1,300
Blue Mountain	1,650
Bob Jones	1,836
Boston	6,000
Brandeis Univ.	6,700
Brown	8,200
Bryan	2,750
Bucknell	7,350
Buena Vista	4,900
Cabrini	4,150
Cal. Inst. of Tech.	6,250
Cameron Univ.	500-1,325
Cardinal Stritch	3,600
Carleton	6,951
Case Western Reserve Univ.	6,200
Charleston, Univ. of	3,350-4,000
Chicago State Univ.	882-2,466
Clemson Univ.	1,210-2,488
Colgate Univ.	6,345
Columbia Univ.	7,000
Connecticut	8,000
Dakota State	925-1,800
Dallas, Univ. of	3,300-4,390
Davidson	7,700
Dayton, Univ. of	3,910

School	Tuition
Delaware, Univ. of	1,160-2,900
Denver, Univ. of	5,790
DePauw	6,250
Dordt	3,850
Drake	5,230
East Carolina Univ.	372-2,160
Eastern Arizona	156-1,306
Emmanuel	1,890
Eureka	3,750
Fairfield Univ.	5,025
Fort Lauderdale	1,820
Fort Lewis	598-2,632
Franklin	2,170
Georgetown Univ.	6,830
George Washington Univ.	4,900
Goucher	6,150
Green Mountain	4,475
Harvard Univ.	6,930
Hastings	3,590
Haverford	8,000
Hendrix	3,200
Hope	4,980
Hopkinsville Comm.	390-1,170
Idaho, College of	4,600
Indiana Univ.	1,328
Iowa State Univ.	1,040-2,580
Ithaca	5,526
Jacksonville State Univ.	700-1,050
Jersey City State	864-1,504
John Brown Univ.	4,400
Johns Hopkins	6,700
Kalamazoo	6,492
Kansas, Univ. of.	904-2,220
Kentucky, Univ. of.	846-2,470
Knox	6,350
Lake Michigan	345-465
Lock Haven State	1,250-2,190
Lowell, Univ. of	986-3,242
Lubbock Christian	2,600
Memphis State Univ.	832-2,590
Montana State	674-2,042
Muskingum	5,444

School	Tuition
Nebr. Wesleyan Univ.	3,616
New Mexico State	744-2,256
New Orleans, Univ. of	624-1,654
North Carolina State Univ.	682-2,506
Oberlin	7,500
Occidental	6,850
Ohio State Univ.	1,380-3,510
Penn., Univ. of	8,000
Peru State	690-1,200
Pfeiffer	3,450
Pittsburgh State	726-1,520
Portland Comm.	540-1,140
Purdue	1,350-3,800
Quincy	3,600
Randolph-Macon	5,000
Redlands, Univ. of	6,750
Rhode Island, Univ. of	1,082-3,552
Richmond, Univ. of	5,575
Ripon	6,020
Rochester, Univ. of.	6,850
St. Bonaventure Univ.	4,250
St. Leo	3,360
St. Olaf	4,970
St. Paul Bible	2,190
Selma Univ.	1,500
Southern Methodist Univ.	5,000
Tabor	3,200
Tampa, Univ. of	1,700
Temple Univ.	2,616-4,800
Tennessee, Univ. of.	867-2,628
Tiffin Univ.	2,400
Utah, Univ. of	960-2,727
Vanderbilt Univ.	6,100
Vermont, Univ. of	2,250-5,800
Virginia, Univ. of.	1,350-3,276
Washington Univ.	7,125
West Virginia Inst. of Tech.	594-1,794
Williams	7,800
Worcester State	845-2,792
Yale, Univ	8,190
Yankton	3,840

Federal Funds for Education, 1981

Source: National Center for Education Statistics, U.S. Department of Education

Includes grants, loans, and directly administered services. Estimated. (thousands of dollars)

Type of support, level, and program area	
Elementary-secondary education	**$7,737,276**
School asst.—federally affected areas	553,942
Educationally deprived/Economic Opportunity Programs	5,186,820
Supporting services	393,096
Teacher corps	14,638
Vocational education	461,013
Dependents' schools abroad	421,274
Public lands revenue for schools	373,482
Assistance in special areas	54,457
Emergency school asst.	226,698
Other	51,856
Higher education	**9,827,596**
Basic research	3,001,600
Research facilities	400,700
Training grants, fellowships, and traineeships	1,003,724
Facilities and equipment	86,424
Other institutional support	585,000
Other student assistance	4,750,148
Vocational-tech. and continuing ed.	**7,710,096**
Vocational-technical education	$7,230,264
Veterans' education	264,804
General continuing education	171,561
Training, federal, state, and local personnel	43,467
Grants, total	**25,274,968**
Loans, total	**1,495,607**
Student loan program, Nat. Def. Ed. Act.	1,474,970
College facilities loans	20,637
Total grants and loans	**26,770,575**
Other federal funds, total	**9,263,686**
Applied research and development	3,288,500
School lunch and milk programs	3,288,600
Training of federal personnel, military	1,299,594
Library services	**474,107**
Grants to public libraries	67,550
National library services	406,557
International education	**85,871**
Educational exchange program	NA
AID projects	84,893
ACTION (previously Peace Corps)	NA
Other international educ. and training	978
Other	**911,906**
Agricultural extension service	264,468
Educational television facilities	167,900
Other education; property transfers	395,624

Fall Enrollment and Teachers in Full-time Day Schools

Elementary and Secondary Day Schools, Fall 1980

Source: National Center for Education Statistics, U.S. Education Dept.

State	Local school districts			Enrollment			Classroor
	Total	Operating	Nonoperating	Total	Elementary	Secondary	teachers
United States	**15,912**	**15,601**	**311**	**40,984,093**	**27,664,973**	**13,319,120**	**2,183,53**
Alabama	127	127	—	758,721	527,753	230,968	36,17
Alaska	52	52	—	86,514	60,417	26,097	5,22
Arizona	229	217	12	513,790	357,112	156,678	25,71
Arkansas	370	370	—	447,700	309,909	137,791	24,07
California	1,036	1,036	—	4,118,022	2,760,725	1,357,297	193,84
Colorado	181	181	—	546,033	374,366	171,667	29,84
Connecticut	165	165	—	531,459	363,590	167,869	34,58
Delaware	16	16	—	99,403	57,045	42,358	5,62
Florida	67	67	—	1,510,225	1,041,859	468,366	73,98
Georgia	187	187	—	1,068,737	741,675	327,062	56,51
Hawaii	1	1	—	165,068	109,597	55,471	7,18
Idaho	115	115	—	203,247	143,759	59,488	9,93
Illinois	1,012	1,011	1	1,983,463	1,334,909	648,554	108,06
Indiana	305	304	1	1,055,589	708,419	347,170	53,09
Iowa	443	443	—	533,857	351,155	182,702	32,74
Kansas	307	307	—	415,291	282,725	132,566	26,36
Kentucky	181	181	—	669,798	463,804	205,994	32,89
Louisiana	66	66	—	777,560	543,598	233,962	43,93
Maine	283	227	56	222,497	152,642	69,855	11,77
Maryland	24	24	—	750,665	492,842	257,823	40,86
Massachusetts	403	348	55	1,021,885	676,314	345,571	64,98
Michigan	575	575	—	1,863,419	1,225,021	638,398	84,37
Minnesota	437	435	2	754,318	482,025	272,293	44,14
Mississippi	153	153	—	477,059	329,760	147,299	25,93
Missouri	551	551	—	844,648	567,198	277,450	48,87
Montana	568	554	14	155,193	105,680	49,513	9,37
Nebraska	1,089	1,035	54	280,430	189,029	91,401	16,79
Nevada	17	17	—	149,481	100,597	48,884	7,12
New Hampshire	168	157	11	167,232	111,902	55,330	8,44
New Jersey	606	585	21	1,246,008	819,567	426,441	76,55
New Mexico	88	88	—	271,198	185,874	85,324	14,08
New York	721	715	6	2,871,004	1,837,772	1,033,232	155,32
North Carolina	144	144	—	1,129,376	785,881	343,495	56,22
North Dakota	335	296	39	116,885	76,787	40,098	7,37
Ohio	615	615	—	1,957,381	1,312,353	645,028	100,52
Oklahoma	619	619	—	577,807	398,895	178,912	33,90
Oregon	311	310	1	464,599	319,129	145,470	22,59
Pennsylvania	504	504	—	1,909,292	1,231,428	677,864	109,92
Rhode Island	40	40	—	148,320	95,366	52,954	9,19
South Carolina	92	92	—	619,223	426,384	192,839	32,21
South Dakota	196	188	8	128,507	84,994	43,513	7,96
Tennessee	147	147	—	853,569	602,044	251,525	41,16
Texas	1,076	1,074	2	2,900,073	2,048,684	851,389	159,53
Utah	40	40	—	343,618	250,242	93,376	13,69
Vermont	273	247	26	95,815	66,359	29,456	6,47
Virginia	139	135	4	1,010,371	703,322	307,049	57,02
Washington	300	300	—	757,639	515,430	242,209	35,51
West Virginia	55	55	—	383,503	270,309	113,194	21,66
Wisconsin	433	433	—	830,247	527,655	302,592	48,49
Wyoming	49	49	—	98,305	70,093	28,212	6,36
District of Columbia	1	1	—	110,049	70,978	29,071	5,23

Public School Attendance, Teachers, Expenditures

Source: National Center for Education Statistics, U.S. Education Department

School year	Pop. 5 to 17 yrs.	Pupils		Teachers[1]				Total expend.
		Enrolled	Av. daily attend.	Male	Female	Total	Salary[2]	
1900	21,404,322	15,503,110	**10,632,772**	126,588	296,474	**423,062**	$325	**$214,964,61**
1910	24,239,948	17,813,852	**12,827,307**	110,481	412,729	**523,210**	485	**426,250,43**
1920	27,728,788	21,578,316	**16,150,035**	95,654	583,648	**679,302**	871	**1,036,151,20**
1930	31,571,322	25,678,015	**21,264,886**	141,771	712,492	**854,263**	1,420	**2,316,790,38**
1940	29,805,259	25,433,542	**22,042,151**	194,725	680,752	**875,477**	1,441	**2,344,048,92**
1950	30,788,000	25,111,427	**22,283,845**	194,968	718,703	**913,671**	3,010	**5,837,643,00**
1960	43,881,000	36,086,771	**32,477,440**	392,700	962,300	**1,355,000**	5,174	**15,613,255,00**
1970 (Fall)	52,435,000	45,909,088	**42,495,346**	649,250	1,411,865	**2,061,115**	9,570	**44,423,865,00**
1971 (Fall)	52,133,000	46,081,000	**42,544,000**	668,000	1,395,000	**2,063,000**	10,100	**48,513,986,00**
1972 (Fall)	51,637,000	45,744,000	**42,408,000**	702,000	1,400,000	**2,102,000**	10,608	**51,905,025,00**
1974 (Fall)	51,485,000	46,441,189	**41,438,054**	722,868	1,432,580	**2,155,448**	11,185	**56,970,355,00**
1975 (Fall)	50,372,000	44,790,946	**41,269,720**	741,000	1,455,000	**2,196,000**	*12,448	**70,629,000,00**
1976 (Fall)	49,853,000	44,317,000	**40,832,000**	*741,000	*1,445,000	**2,186,000**	*13,397	**75,014,000,00**
1977 (Fall)	49,010,000	43,576,906	**40,080,000**	*746,500	*1,462,070	**2,208,570**	*14,244	**80,844,366,00**
1978 (Fall)	48,046,000	42,611,000	**39,065,000**	*745,000	*1,454,000	**2,199,000**	*14,970	**86,711,615,00**
1980 (Fall)	47,400,000	40,984,093	**38,234,000**	*710,300	*1,473,200	**2,183,500**	*16,780	**95,961,561,00**

* Estimated. (1) Prior to 1954 includes other nonsupervisory instructional staff (librarians and guidance and psychological personnel). (2) Average annual salary per member of instructional staff, including supervisors and principals. Beginning in 1975, data are for classroom teachers only.

Canadian Fall Enrollment, Teachers, Expenditures in Day Schools

Full-time Public Elementary and Secondary Day Schools—1980-81

Source: Statistics Canada

	Enrollment			Teachers			School Board
	Elementary Kdgn.-Gr. 8	Secondary Gr. 9 and up	Total	Elementary Kdgn.-Gr. 8	Secondary Gr. 9 and up	Total	expenditure per pupil[1] 1979 (calendar year)[e]
Canada	**3,323,819**	**1,532,606**	**4,856,425**	**163,843[e]**	**100,937[e]**	**264,240[e]**	**2,293**
Nfld	112,718	35,815	148,533	5,921	1,817	7,738	1,711
P.E.I.	17,730	9,120	26,850	970	402	1,372	1,843
N.S.	129,270	56,298	185,568	7,427	3,172	10,599	1,760
N.B.	101,546	51,257	152,803	4,938	2,738	7,676	1,804
Que.	803,873	328,775	1,132,648	40,500[e]	32,500[e]	73,000[e]	2,655
Ont.	1,216,071	619,466	1,835,537	56,846	34,996	91,842	2,253
Man.	141,449	62,946	204,395	7,834	3,343	11,177	2,068
Sask.	141,055	63,919	204,974	7,303	3,521	10,824	2,170
Alta.	299,697	138,118	437,815	16,656	6,099	22,755	2,278
B.C.	345,860	163,945	509,805	14,695	11,600	26,295	2,275
Yukon	3,761	1,164	4,925	193	78	271	2,787
N.W.T.	10,789	1,783	12,572	560	131	691	3,076

(e) estimate. (1) Includes provincial expenditures made on behalf of school boards.

Cost per Pupil by State

Source: National Center for Education Statistics, U. S. Education Department

Expenditures per pupil in average daily attendance in public elementary and secondary day schools, 1979-80.

State	Expenditure per pupil: Total[1]	Current[2]	Capital outlay[3]	Interest on school debt
United States	**$2,494**	**$2,275**	**$170**	**$49**
Alabama	1,741	1,612	115	14
Alaska	5,146	4,728	151	267
Arizona	2,433	1,971	398	64
Arkansas	1,839	1,574	224	41
California	2,376	2,268	89	19
Colorado	2,826	2,421	330	75
Connecticut	2,520	2,425	47	48
Delaware	3,019	2,868	55	96
District of Columbia	3,265	3,259	6	0
Florida	2,082	1,889	160	33
Georgia	1,833	1,625	181	26
Hawaii	2,528	2,322	204	2
Idaho	1,914	1,659	215	40
Illinois	2,778	2,587	140	51
Indiana	2,166	1,910	248	7
Iowa	2,552	2,340	177	35
Kansas	2,422	2,205	175	42
Kentucky	1,847	1,701	91	55
Louisiana	2,017	1,794	172	52
Maine	1,947	1,824	82	41
Maryland	2,843	2,598	204	41
Massachusetts	2,952	2,819	54	79
Michigan	2,873	2,640	151	82
Minnesota	2,686	2,457	221	9
Mississippi	1,788	1,664	124	1
Missouri	2,071	1,936	98	37
Montana	2,882	2,476	363	43
Nebraska	2,403	2,150	199	54
Nevada	2,553	2,088	356	108
New Hampshire	2,069	1,917	115	37
New Jersey	3,379	3,191	116	72
New Mexico	2,396	2,034	339	23
New York	3,681	3,462	134	85
North Carolina	1,871	1,754	104	[3]13
North Dakota	2,071	1,927	121	23
Ohio	2,208	2,075	94	39
Oklahoma	2,176	1,926	229	21
Oregon	3,104	2,692	355	58
Pennsylvania	2,742	2,535	101	106
Rhode Island	2,670	2,601	17	52
South Carolina	1,996	1,752	209	35
South Dakota	1,932	1,911	1	19
Tennessee	1,825	1,635	175	14
Texas	2,309	1,916	316	77
Utah	2,208	1,657	491	60
Vermont	2,240	2,049	137	55
Virginia	2,211	1,970	191	51
Washington	3,073	2,568	446	58
West Virginia	2,160	1,920	219	21
Wisconsin	2,693	2,495	145	53
Wyoming	3,326	2,527	698	101

(1) Includes current expenditures for day schools, capital outlay, and interest on school debt. (2) Includes expenditures for day schools only; excludes adult education, community colleges, and community services. (3) Estimated by the National Center for Education Statistics. NOTE.—Because of rounding, details may not add to totals.

110 Years of Public Schools

Pupils and teachers (thousands)	1869-70	1899-1900	1909-10	1919-20	1929-30	1939-40	1949-50	1959-60	1969-70	1979-80
Total U.S. population	39,818	75,995	90,492	104,512	121,770	130,880	148,665	179,323	203,212	226,505
Population 5-17 years of age	12,055	21,573	24,009	27,556	31,417	30,150	30,168	43,881	52,490	47,400
Percent aged 5-17 years	30.3	28.4	26.5	26.4	25.8	23.0	20.3	24.5	25.8	20.9
Enrollment (thousands)										
Elementary and secondary	6,872	15,503	17,814	21,578	25,678	25,434	25,111	36,087	45,619	41,579
Percent pop. 5-17 enrolled	57.0	71.9	74.2	78.3	81.7	84.4	83.2	82.2	86.9	87.7
Percent in high schools	1.2	3.3	5.1	10.2	17.1	26.0	22.7	23.5	28.5	32.9
High school graduates	....	62	111	231	592	1,143	1,063	1,627	2,589	2,757
Average school term (in days)	132.2	144.3	157.5	161.9	172.7	175.0	177.9	178.0	178.9	178.8
Total instructional staff	....	....	....	678	880	912	962	1,464	2,253	2,438
Teachers, librarians: Men	78	127	110	93	140	195	195	402	691	781[4]
Women	123	296	413	565	703	681	719	985	1,440	1,516[4]
Percent men	38.7	29.9	21.1	14.1	16.6	22.2	21.3	29.0	33.4	34.0[4]
Revenue & expenditures (millions)										
Total revenue	....	$219	$433	$970	$2,088	$2,260	$5,437	$14,746	$40,267	$96,881
Total expenditures	$63	214	426	1,036	2,316	2,344	5,837	15,613[1]	40,683	95,962
Current elem. and secondary	....	179	356	861	1,843	1,941	4,687	12,329	34,218	86,984
Capital outlay	....	35	69	153	370	257	1,014	2,661	4,659	6,506
Interest on school debt	....	....	....	18	92	130	100	489	1,171	1,874
Other	....	....	....	3	9	13	35	132	636	598
Salaries and pupil cost				(Data in unadjusted dollars)						
Average annual teacher salary[2]	$189	$325	$485	$2,130	$3,869	$3,894	$5,928	$8,213	$10,917	$16,780[4]
Expenditure per capita total pop.	1.59	2.83	4.71	24.24	51.85	48.40	77.34	138.21	247.23	423.66
Current expenditure per pupil ADA[3]	....	16.67	27.85	130.41	236.25	238.05	411.29	595.50	1,007.65	2,275.05

(1) Because of a modification of the scope, "current expenditures for elementary and secondary schools" data for 1959-60 and later years are not entirely comparable with data for prior years. (2) Includes supervisors, principals, teachers and other non-supervisory instructional staff. (3) "ADA" means average daily attendance in elementary and secondary day schools. (4) Estimated.

Public Libraries in Selected North American Cities

Source: World Almanac questionnaire (1982)

First figure in parentheses denotes number of branches-2d figure indicates number of bookmobiles. (*) indicates county library system; (†) indicates state library system; (C) Canadian dollars; (A) library has not provided up-to-date information.

City	No. bound volumes	Circu- lation	Cost of operation
Akron, Oh.* (18-2)	1,084,246	2,012,535	$ 4,337,177
Albuquerque, N.M. (7-2)	350,000	1,550,000	2,515,000
Atlanta Ga.* (27-3) (A)	1,054,996	3,037,409	6,480,519
Austin, Tex. (15-0)	675,163	2,177,742	5,820,366
Baltimore, Md.† (32-2)	2,188,901	2,318,562	10,240,185
Birmingham, Ala.* (18-2)	1,010,237	2,041,084	4,113,000
Boston, Mass. (24-2)	4,878,195	1,670,418	9,753,094
Buffalo, N.Y.* (52-4)	3,337,124	5,781,970	13,348,085
Calgary, Alta. (20)	793,053	3,739,560	C8,145,777
Charlotte, N.C.* (15-0)	736,343	1,975,793	4,103,791
Chicago, Ill. (90-0)	6,354,072	7,811,071	41,600,000
Cincinnati, Oh.* (39-2)	3,337,442	6,045,487	11,127,803
Cleveland, Oh. (32-2)	2,332,702	3,368,808	14,500,000
Columbus, OH.* (20-2)	1,233,180	3,652,452	7,646,960
Dallas, Tex. (18-0)	1,706,262	3,714,591	8,775,389
Dayton, Oh.* (19-1)	1,412,551	4,692,202	5,858,125
Denver, Col. (21-1)	1,767,159	2,838,966	9,317,000
Detroit, Mich. (26-3)	2,500,000	1,719,000	14,000,000
Edmonton, Alta. (11-3) (A)	828,850	3,884,322	C10,211,000
El Paso, Tex. (8-3)	420,000	1,100,000	2,200,000
Ft. Worth, Tex. (8-2)	800,000	2,400,000	3,410,000
Hamilton, Ont. (9-2)	800,259	2,044,083	C8,404,000
Hartford, Conn. (9-1) (A)	486,000	432,000	2,103,800
Honolulu, Ha.† (47-6)	2,025,200	5,042,682	10,000,000
Houston, Tex. (27-2)	2,600,000	5,900,000	17,000,000
Indianapolis, Ind.* (22-2)	1,379,124	3,945,402	8,002,662
Jacksonville, Fla.* (11-1)	986,733	2,157,906	3,747,111
Kansas City, Mo. (17-0)	1,255,212	887,322	4,069,859
Kitchener, Ont. (4-4)	419,239	1,246,778	C2,545,879
London, Ont. (12-2)	580,867	1,941,182	4,709,942
Long Beach, Cal. (11-0)	702,692	1,969,904	5,389,528
Los Ang., Cal. (66-5) (A)	5,364,882	12,009,014	17,543,199
Louisville, Ky.* (20-3)	1,139,534	2,371,199	5,009,578
Memphis, Tenn.* (23-3)	1,429,361	2,545,404	6,619,878
Miami, Fla.* (25-6)	1,850,632	3,700,000	16,000,000
Milwaukee, Wis. (12-3)	2,335,485	3,237,348	10,966,762
Minneapolis, Minn. (14-0)	1,642,196	2,623,039	9,036,321
Mobile, Ala. (5-1)	389,538	880,314	2,198,048
Montreal, Que. (21-1)	1,408,127	3,496,615	C9,810,285
Nashville, Tenn.* (13-2)	519,717	1,779,349	4,050,097
Newark, N.J. (14-3)	1,216,335	1,594,264	5,235,060
New Haven, Conn. (8-0)	570,767	425,790	1,389,882
New Orleans, La. (11-0)	812,446	1,180,340	(A)
New York (resrch) (A)	5,027,455	none	23,192,000
N.Y.C. brches (82-2) (A)	3,572,056	8,600,017	29,948,000
Brooklyn* (57-0)	2,776,281	6,730,781	22,305,189
Queens* (58-0)	4,402,504	6,245,766	22,434,765
Norfolk, Va. (11-1)	695,690	1,050,842	2,759,983
Oakland, Cal. (15-3)	775,203	1,568,840	4,366,699
Okla. City, Okla.* (10-5) (A)	597,235	1,732,101	2,414,088
Omaha, Neb. (10-0)	555,789	1,713,021	(A)
Ottawa, Ont. (7-2)	666,404	2,150,404	6,429,897
Philadelphia, Pa. (51-0)	2,933,732	5,003,398	21,923,192
Phoenix, Ariz. (9-1)	1,172,000	3,700,000	5,945,000
Pittsburgh, Pa. (20-3)	1,932,817	2,897,392	9,730,420
Portland, Ore.* (14-2)	1,155,392	3,204,212	5,313,310
Québec, Que. (8-1)	197,797	700,000	C2,858,836
Richmond, Va. (6-1)	642,319	1,091,239	1,718,001
Rochester, N.Y. (10-2)	916,939	1,500,000	5,489,807
Sacramento, Cal.* (26-3) (A)	1,057,000	3,428,680	6,700,000
St. Catharines, Ont. (3-0)	322,351	1,005,350	C2,211,922
St. Louis, Mo.* (15-20)	1,600,000	7,615,727	6,550,000
St. Paul, Minn. (10-1)	847,830	1,841,426	4,110,622
San Antonio, Tex.* (12-4)	(A)	2,275,106	3,752,995
San Diego, Cal. (29-1)	1,684,719	4,235,888	6,151,302
San Fran., Cal. (26-1)	1,701,815	2,435,234	8,041,271
San Jose, Cal. (16-1)	1,182,000	2,300,000	5,700,000
Saskatoon, Sask. (4-3)	374,311	1,388,460	C3,369,500
Seattle, Wash. (22-3) (A)	1,525,636	4,465,128	8,618,988
Tampa, Fla.* (13-1) (A)	645,648	2,048,563	4,352,269
Toledo, Oh.* (17-2)	1,200,000	3,500,000	6,958,274
Toronto, Ont. (28-1)	1,354,512	5,223,757	C17,199,548
Tucson, Ariz.* (16-2)	687,200	3,500,000	5,943,900
Tulsa, Okla.* (20-2)	800,000	1,753,570	6,032,237
Vancouver, B.C. (20-1)	907,924	4,412,769	10,566,744
Wash. D.C.* (27-0) (A)	1,425,820	1,466,623	11,200,000
Wichita, Kan. (11-0) (A)	431,110	1,202,542	2,608,728
Windsor, Ont.(7-0)	491,493	1,103,635	C3,184,483
Winnipeg, Man. (21-4)	1,056,368	3,045,663	C6,167,231
Yonkers, N.Y. (5-1)	306,626	794,097	3,526,211

Major U.S. Academic Libraries

Source: World Almanac questionnaire (1982)

(A) library has not provided up-to-date information.

Institution	No. bound volumes	Microfilm units	Enroll- ment	Staff Prof.	Staff Total	Annual acquisition expense
U. of California, Berkeley	5,927,773	1,676,272	30,000	141	602	$3,600,000
U. of California, Los Angeles (A)	4,108,682	1,806,105	31,300	140	584	4,989,891
U. of Chicago	4,441,500	807,747	8,976	69	306	2,233,000
U. of Colorado, Boulder	1,900,000	2,152,000	19,704	42	175	1,278,910
Columbia U.	5,112,559	132,135	17,000	140	527	3,006,596
Cornell U.	4,431,429	89,400	16,810	138	431	3,695,318
Duke U.	3,006,026	789,409	9,369	88	252	2,347,076
U. of Florida	3,098,622	2,118,501	33,772	61	101	2,334,684
Harvard U.	10,260,571	2,387,994	17,833	282	947	5,728,552
U. of Illinois, Urbana-Champaign (A)	5,936,823	1,552,446	34,792	139	507	3,372,321
Indiana U., Bloomington (A)	3,735,523	898,879	76,394	121	471	2,433,500
U. of Iowa	2,356,096	1,618,967	25,000	71	114	2,752,175
Johns Hopkins U. (A)	2,300,000	1,100,000	8,000	46	153	1,700,000
U. of Kansas	2,100,000	1,000,000	22,000	57	152	1,850,000
U. of Michigan, Ann Arbor (A)	5,049,501	1,403,096	35,824	155	576	2,212,803
Michigan State U. (A)	2,613,447	1,117,363	41,374	77	303	1,739,402
U. of Minnesota	3,445,649	1,154,545	39,362	119	424	2,398,190
U. of Missouri, Columbia	2,068,788	2,328,526	23,000	58	220	1,724,444
New York U.	2,613,739	1,631,238	23,113	86	329	2,250,301
U. of No. Carolina, Chapel Hill	2,722,799	102,197	20,663	73	228	2,911,063
Northwestern U.	2,800,000	1,095,000	14,000	101	352	2,250,000
Ohio State U.	3,615,108	1,707,241	48,991	101	443	2,332,439
U. of Pennsylvania (A)	2,900,000	1,400,000	21,900	88	242	1,471,368
U. of Pittsburgh	2,339,242	1,382,354	29,206	75	313	1,864,082
Princeton U. (A)	3,260,396	1,396,298	5,877	94	394	2,588,531
Rutgers U. (A)	2,216,843	1,512,086	35,297	106	362	2,542,699
Stanford U.	4,771,643	128,663	12,870	143	565	4,044,000
Syracuse U.	1,952,594	1,970,813	16,329	58	276	1,675,388
U. of Texas, Austin	3,177,779	2,195,241	45,825	131	538	4,504,655
Tulane U. (A)	1,372,405	918,497	(A)	45	192	1,295,566
U. of Virginia	2,391,585	886,507	16,452	84	278	2,558,290
U. of Washington, Seattle	4,024,258	3,370,411	31,957	120	473	3,171,418
U. of Wisconsin, Madison	4,044,136	1,940,859	36,301	128	497	2,842,618
Yale U.	7,579,121	1,390,135	10,098	177	377	(A)

Educational Attainment by Age, Race, and Sex

Source: U.S. Bureau of the Census (Number of persons in thousands)

Race, age, and sex	Years of school completed: All persons	Less than high school, 4 years	High school, 4 years	College, 1 to 3 years	College, 4 years or more	Percent: All persons	Less than high school, 4 years	High school, 4 years	College, 1 to 3 years	College, 4 years or more
March 1980										
races										
to 24 years.	29,118	6,667	13,329	7,157	1,963	100.0	22.9	45.8	24.6	6.7
years and over	130,409	40,902	47,934	19,379	22,193	100.0	31.4	36.8	14.9	17.0
25 to 34 years	36,615	5,357	14,481	7,942	8,836	100.0	14.6	39.5	21.7	24.1
35 to 44 years	25,426	5,579	10,456	4,109	5,280	100.0	21.9	41.1	16.2	20.8
45 to 54 years	22,698	7,194	9,128	2,834	3,542	100.0	31.7	40.2	12.5	15.6
55 to 64 years	21,476	8,431	8,065	2,521	2,459	100.0	39.3	37.6	11.7	11.4
65 years and over	24,194	14,340	5,804	1,973	2,076	100.0	59.3	24.0	8.2	8.6
ale, 25 years and over . . .	61,389	18,885	20,080	9,593	12,832	100.0	30.8	32.7	15.6	20.9
male, 25 years and over .	69,020	22,018	27,854	9,786	9,362	100.0	31.9	40.4	14.2	13.6
hite										
to 24 years.	24,717	5,246	11,466	6,207	1,796	100.0	21.2	46.4	25.1	7.3
years and over	114,763	33,803	43,149	17,350	20,460	100.0	29.5	37.6	15.1	17.8
25 to 34 years	31,435	4,160	12,449	6,855	7,969	100.0	13.2	39.6	21.8	25.4
35 to 44 years	22,129	4,425	9,193	3,633	4,878	100.0	20.0	41.5	16.4	22.0
45 to 54 years	19,971	5,730	8,385	2,597	3,258	100.0	28.7	42.0	13.0	16.3
55 to 64 years	19,331	6,990	7,601	2,374	2,365	100.0	36.2	39.3	12.3	12.2
65 years and over	21,898	12,495	5,521	1,892	1,989	100.0	57.1	25.2	8.6	9.1
ale, 25 years and over . . .	54,389	15,756	18,026	8,609	11,998	100.0	29.0	33.1	15.8	22.1
male, 25 years and over .	60,374	18,047	25,124	8,741	8,462	100.0	29.9	41.6	14.5	14.0
ack										
to 24 years.	3,711	1,257	1,598	733	123	100.0	33.9	43.1	19.8	3.3
years and over	12,927	6,306	3,980	1,618	1,024	100.0	48.8	30.8	12.5	7.9
25 to 34 years	4,097	1,007	1,712	868	508	100.0	24.6	41.8	21.2	12.4
35 to 44 years	2,677	1,003	1,080	380	215	100.0	37.5	40.3	14.2	8.0
45 to 54 years	2,257	1,308	597	186	165	100.0	58.0	26.5	8.2	7.3
55 to 64 years	1,855	1,298	363	125	70	100.0	70.0	19.6	6.7	3.8
65 years and over	2,040	1,688	229	59	65	100.0	82.7	11.2	2.9	3.2
ale, 25 years and over . . .	5,717	2,797	1,706	774	440	100.0	48.9	29.8	13.5	7.7
male, 25 years and over .	7,209	3,509	2,274	844	583	100.0	48.7	31.5	11.7	8.1
anish Origin[1]										
to 24 years.	1,954	854	751	304	44	100.0	43.7	38.4	15.6	2.3
years and over	5,934	3,291	1,586	603	454	100.0	55.5	26.7	10.2	7.7
25 to 34 years	2,227	971	730	326	198	100.0	43.6	32.8	14.6	8.9
35 to 44 years	1,454	748	432	146	128	100.0	51.4	29.7	10.0	8.8
45 to 54 years	1,036	638	237	88	72	100.0	61.6	22.9	8.5	6.9
55 to 64 years	643	456	120	34	32	100.0	70.9	18.7	5.3	5.0
65 years and over	574	477	67	8	23	100.0	83.1	11.7	1.4	4.0
ale, 25 years and over . . .	2,825	1,556	677	332	261	100.0	55.1	24.0	11.8	9.2
male, 25 years and over .	3,109	1,736	909	271	193	100.0	55.8	29.2	8.7	6.2
March 1970										
l races										
to 24 years.	22,494	5,732	9,996	5,392	1,374	100.0	25.5	44.4	24.0	6.1
years and over	109,310	48,948	37,134	11,164	12,063	100.0	44.8	34.0	10.2	11.0
25 to 34 years	24,865	6,517	10,929	3,491	3,926	100.0	26.2	44.0	14.0	15.8
35 to 44 years	23,021	8,216	9,325	2,523	2,958	100.0	35.7	40.5	11.0	12.8
45 to 54 years	23,298	9,735	8,875	2,352	2,336	100.0	41.8	38.1	10.1	10.0
55 to 64 years	18,413	10,347	4,905	1,567	1,594	100.0	56.2	26.6	8.5	8.7
65 years and over	19,713	14,134	3,100	1,230	1,249	100.0	71.7	15.7	6.2	6.3
ale, 25 years and over . . .	51,784	23,311	15,571	5,580	7,321	100.0	45.0	30.1	10.8	14.1
male, 25 years and over .	57,527	25,638	21,563	5,584	4,743	100.0	44.6	37.5	9.7	8.2
hite										
to 24 years.	19,536	4,496	8,865	4,886	1,289	100.0	23.0	45.4	25.0	6.6
years and over	98,112	41,789	34,493	10,452	11,380	100.0	42.6	35.2	10.7	11.6
25 to 34 years	21,887	5,222	9,828	3,204	3,633	100.0	23.9	44.9	14.6	16.6
35 to 44 years	20,392	6,756	8,541	2,319	2,776	100.0	33.1	41.9	11.4	13.6
45 to 54 years	20,961	8,134	8,392	2,209	2,227	100.0	38.8	40.0	10.5	10.6
55 to 64 years	16,731	8,960	4,719	1,526	1,527	100.0	53.6	28.2	9.1	9.1
65 years and over	18,141	12,716	3,013	1,193	1,218	100.0	70.1	16.6	6.6	6.7
ale, 25 years and over . . .	46,606	19,963	14,410	5,259	6,972	100.0	42.8	30.9	11.3	15.0
male, 25 years and over .	51,506	21,825	20,083	5,191	4,408	100.0	42.4	39.0	10.1	8.6
ack										
to 24 years.	2,713	1,158	1,076	419	61	100.0	42.7	39.7	15.4	2.2
years and over	10,089	6,686	2,358	592	452	100.0	66.3	23.4	5.9	4.5
25 to 34 years	2,651	1,237	1,018	237	161	100.0	46.7	38.4	8.9	6.1
35 to 44 years	2,347	1,372	690	164	122	100.0	58.5	29.4	7.0	5.2
45 to 54 years	2,128	1,509	422	117	81	100.0	70.9	19.8	5.5	3.8
55 to 64 years	1,545	1,284	165	38	59	100.0	83.1	10.7	2.5	3.8
65 years and over	1,417	1,290	64	35	28	100.0	91.0	4.5	2.5	2.0
ale, 25 years and over . . .	4,619	3,120	1,025	261	212	100.0	67.5	22.2	5.7	4.6
emale, 25 years and over .	5,470	3,565	1,333	330	240	100.0	65.2	24.4	6.0	4.4

(1) Persons of Spanish origin may be of any race.

The Principal Languages of the World

Source: Sidney S. Culbert, Guthrie Hall NI — University of Washington

Total number of speakers of languages spoken by at least one million persons (midyear 1982)

Language	Millions
Achinese (Indonesia)	2
Afrikaans (S. Africa)	8
Albanian	4
Amharic (Ethiopia)	10
Arabic	155
Armenian	4
Assamese[1] (India)	15
Aymara (Bolivia; Peru)	1
Azerbaijani (USSR; Iran)	8
Bahasa (see Malay-Indonesian)	
Balinese	3
Baluchi (Pakistan; Iran)	3
Batak (Indonesia)	2
Bemba (S. Central Africa)	2
Bengali[1] (Bangladesh; India)	151
Berber[2] (N. Africa)	
Bhili (India)	4
Bihari (India)	8
Bikol (Philippines)	2
Bisaya (see Cebuano, Panay-Hiligaynon, and Samar-Leyte)	
Bugi (Indonesia)	3
Bulgarian	9
Burmese	26
Byelorussian (mainly USSR)	9
Cambodian (see Khmer)	
Canarese (see Kannada)	
Cantonese (China)	55
Catalan (Spain; France; Andorra)	6
Cebuano (Philippines)	9
Chinese[3]	
Chuang[7] (China)	
Chuvash (USSR)	2
Czech	11
Danish	5
Dayak (Borneo)	1
Dutch (see Netherlandish)	
Edo (W. Africa)	1
Efik	3
English	397
Esperanto	1
Estonian	1
Ewe (W. Africa)	3
Fang-Bulu (W. Africa)	2
Finnish	5
Flemish (see Netherlandish)	
French	107
Fula (W. Africa)	10
Galician (Spain)	3
Galla (see Oromo)	
Ganda (or Luganda)(E. Africa)	3
Georgian (USSR)	4
German	119
Gilaki (Iran)	2
Gondi (India)	2
Greek	10
Guarani (mainly Paraguay)	3
Gujarati[1] (India)	34
Hakka (China)	23
Hausa (W. and Central Africa)	23
Hebrew	3
Hindi[1,4]	254
Hindustani[4]	
Hungarian (or Magyar)	13
Ibibio (see Efik)	
Ibo (or Igbo)(W. Africa)	12
Ijaw (W. Africa)	2
Ilocano (Philippines)	4
Iloko (see Ilocano)	
Indonesian (see Malay-Indonesian)	
Italian	62
Japanese	119
Javanese	49
Kamba (E. Africa)	1
Kanarese (see Kannada)	
Kannada[1] (India)	32
Kanuri (W. and Central Africa)	3
Kashmiri[1]	3
Kazakh (USSR)	6
Khalkha (Mongolia)	2
Khmer (Kampuchea)	6
Kikongo (see Kongo)	
Kikuyu (or Gekoyo)(Kenya)	3
Kimbundu (see Mbundu-Kimbundu)	
Kirghiz (USSR)	2
Kituba (Congo River)	3
Kongo (Congo River)	2
Konkani (India)	2
Korean	60
Kurdish (S.W. of Caspian Sea)	7
Kurukh (or Oraon)(India)	1
Lao[5] (Laos, Asia)	3
Latvian (or Lettish)	2
Lingala (see Ngala)	
Lithuanian	3
Luba-Lulua (Zaire)	3
Luganda (see Ganda)	
Luhya (or Luhia)(Kenya)	1
Luo (Kenya)	2
Luri (Iran)	2
Macedonian (Yugoslavia)	2
Madurese (Indonesia)	9
Makua (S.E. Africa)	3
Malagasy (Madagascar)	8
Malay-Indonesian	115
Malayalam[1] (India)	31
Malinke-Bambara-Dyula (Africa)	7
Mandarin (China)	726
Marathi[1] (India)	57
Mazandarani (Iran)	2
Mbundu (Umbundu group)(S.Angola)	3
Mbundu (Kimbundu group)(Angola)	2
Mende (Sierra Leone)	1
Meo (see Miao)	
Miao (and Meo)(S.E.Asia)	3
Min (China)	42
Minankabau (Indonesia)	4
Moldavian (inc. with Romanian)	
Mongolian (see Khalkha)	
Mordvin (USSR)	1
Morê (see Mossi)	
Mossi (or Morê)(W. Africa)	3
Ndongo (see Mbundu-Kimbundu)	
Nepali (Nepal; India)	11
Netherlandish (Dutch and Flemish)	20
Ngala (or Lingala)(Africa)	3
Norwegian	5
Nyamwezi-Sukuma (S.E. Africa)	2
Nyanja (S.E. Africa)	3
Oraon (see Kurukh)	
Oriya[1] (India)	27
Oromo (Ethiopia)	8
Panay-Hiligaynon (Philippines)	4
Panjabi (see Punjabi)	
Pashto (see Pushtu)	
Pedi (see Sotho, Northern)	
Persian (Iran, Afghanistan)	
Polish	
Portuguese	1
Provencal (Southern France)	
Punjabi[1] (India; Pakistan)	
Pushtu (mainly Afghanistan)	
Quechua (S. America)	
Rajasthani (India)	
Romanian	[illegible]
Ruanda (S. Central Africa)	
Rundi (S. Central Africa)	
Russian (Great Russian only)	2
Samar-Leyte (Philippines)	
Sango (Central Africa)	
Santali (India)	
Sepedi (see Sotho, Northern)	
Serbo-Croatian (Yugoslavia)	[illegible]
Shan (Burma)	
Shona (S.E. Africa)	
Siamese (see Thai)	
Sindhi[1] (India; Pakistan)	
Sinhalese (Sri Lanka)	
Slovak	
Slovene (Yugoslavia)	
Somali (E. Africa)	
Sotho, Northern (S. Africa)	
Sotho, Southern (S. Africa)	
Spanish	2[illegible]
Sundanese (Indonesia)	
Swahili (E. Africa)	[illegible]
Swedish	
Tagalog (Philippines)	[illegible]
Tajiki (USSR)	
Tamil[1] (India; Sri Lanka)	[illegible]
Tatar (or Kazan-Turkic)(USSR)	
Telugu[1] (India)	[illegible]
Thai[5]	[illegible]
Thonga (S.E. Africa)	
Tibetan	
Tigrinya (Ethiopia)	
Tiv (E. Central Nigeria)	
Tswana (S. Africa)	
Tulu (India)	
Turkish	[illegible]
Turkoman (USSR)	
Twi-Fante (or Akan)(W.Africa)	
Uighur (Sinkiang, China)	
Ukrainian (mainly USSR)	[illegible]
Umbundu (see Mbundu-Umbundu)	
Urdu[1] (Pakistan; India)	[illegible]
Uzbek (USSR)	[illegible]
Vietnamese	[illegible]
Visayan (see Cebuano, Panay-Hiligaynon, and Samar-Leyte)	
White Russian (see Byelorussian)	
Wolof (W. Africa)	
Wu (China)	[illegible]
Xhosa (S. Africa)	
Yi (China)	
Yiddish[6]	
Yoruba (W. Africa)	[illegible]
Zhuang[7] (China)	
Zulu (S. Africa)	

(1) One of the fifteen languages of the Constitution of India. (2) Here considered a group of dialects. (3) See Mandarin, Cantones[illegible] Wu, Min and Hakka. The "national language" (Guoyu) or "common speech" (Putonghua) is a standardized form of Mandarin as sp[illegible] ken in the area of Peking. (4) Hindi and Urdu are essentially the same language, Hindustani. As the official language of India it is wr[illegible] ten in the Devanagari script and called Hindi. As the official language of Pakistan it is written in a modified Arabic script and call[illegible] Urdu. (5) Thai includes Central, Southwestern, Northern and Northeastern Thai. The distinction between Northeastern Thai and Lao[illegible] political rather than linguistic. (6) Yiddish is usually considered a variant of German, though it has its own standard grammar, dictiona[illegible] ies, a highly developed literature, and is written in Hebrew characters. (7) A group of Thai-like dialects with about 9 million speakers.

UNITED STATES POPULATION

The 1980 census figures in this section are taken from the report, *1980 Census of Population and Housing,* PHC 80-V-1 through 56, and ›m PC 80-S1-4, *Population and Households for Census Designated Places.* These figures are called "final counts" in the reports but some of em may be changed when the report, *Characteristics of the Population, Number of Inhabitants,* PC 80-1A, is released.

Population of the U.S., 1970-1980

Region, division, and state	1980 Census	1970 Census	Pct. + or −	1980 Urban	1980 Rural	Pct. urban	Rank 1980	Rank 1970
nited States	**226,504,825**	**203,302,031**	**11.5**	**166,965,380**	**59,539,445**	**73.7**	...	...
Regions:								
ortheast	49,136,667	49,060,514	0.2	38,904,486	10,232,181	79.2	...	...
orth Central	58,853,804	56,590,294	4.0	41,465,803	17,388,011	70.6	...	...
outh	75,349,155	62,812,980	20.0	50,382,409	24,966,746	66.9	...	...
/est	43,165,199	34,838,243	24.0	36,212,682	6,952,517	83.9	...	...
New England	**12,348,493**	**11,847,245**	**4.2**	**9,269,249**	**3,079,244**	**75.1**	...	...
aine	1,124,660	993,722	15.2	534,072	590,588	47.5	38	38
ew Hampshire	920,610	737,681	24.8	480,325	440,285	52.2	42	41
ermont	511,456	444,732	15.0	172,735	338,721	33.8	48	48
assachusetts	5,737,037	5,689,170	0.8	4,808,339	928,698	83.8	11	10
hode Island	947,154	949,723	-0.3	824,004	123,150	87.0	40	39
onnecticut	3,107,576	3,032,217	2.5	2,449,774	657,802	78.8	25	24
Middle Atlantic	**36,788,174**	**37,213,269**	**-1.1**	**29,635,237**	**7,152,937**	**80.6**	...	...
ew York	17,557,288	18,241,391	-3.8	14,857,202	2,700,086	84.6	2	2
ew Jersey	7,364,158	7,171,112	2.7	6,556,697	807,461	89.0	9	8
ennsylvania	11,866,728	11,800,766	0.6	8,221,338	3,645,390	69.3	4	3
East North Central	**41,669,738**	**40,262,747**	**3.5**	**30,483,799**	**11,185,939**	**73.1**	...	...
hio	10,797,419	10,657,423	1.3	7,916,181	2,881,238	73.3	6	6
diana	5,490,179	5,195,392	5.7	3,524,578	1,965,601	64.2	12	11
inois	11,418,461	11,110,285	2.8	9,474,939	1,943,522	83.0	5	5
ichigan	9,258,344	8,881,826	4.2	6,547,842	2,710,502	70.7	8	7
/isconsin	4,705,335	4,417,821	6.5	3,020,259	1,685,076	64.2	16	16
West North Central	**17,184,066**	**16,327,547**	**5.3**	**10,982,004**	**6,202,062**	**63.9**	...	...
innesota	4,077,148	3,806,103	7.1	2,725,270	1,351,878	66.8	21	19
wa	2,913,387	2,825,368	3.1	1,707,872	1,205,515	58.6	27	25
issouri	4,917,444	4,677,623	5.1	3,350,746	1,566,698	68.1	15	13
orth Dakota	652,695	617,792	5.6	318,263	334,432	48.8	46	45
outh Dakota	690,178	666,257	3.6	320,323	369,955	46.4	45	44
ebraska	1,570,006	1,485,333	5.7	983,731	586,275	62.7	35	35
ansas	2,363,208	2,249,071	5.1	1,575,899	787,309	66.7	32	28
South Atlantic	**36,943,139**	**30,678,826**	**20.4**	**24,798,027**	**12,145,112**	**67.1**	...	...
elaware	595,225	548,104	8.6	420,706	174,519	70.7	47	46
aryland	4,216,446	3,923,897	7.5	3,386,026	830,420	80.3	18	18
istrict of Columbia	637,651	756,668	-15.7	637,651	—	100.0	...	...
rginia	5,346,279	4,651,448	14.9	3,529,301	1,816,978	66.0	14	14
/est Virginia	1,949,644	1,744,237	11.8	705,319	1,244,325	36.2	34	34
orth Carolina	5,874,429	5,084,411	15.5	2,818,794	3,055,635	48.0	10	12
outh Carolina	3,119,208	2,590,713	20.4	1,686,135	1,433,073	54.1	24	26
eoriga	5,464,265	4,587,930	19.1	3,406,171	2,058,094	62.3	13	15
lorida	9,739,992	6,791,418	43.4	8,207,924	1,532,068	84.3	7	9
East South Central	**14,662,882**	**12,808,077**	**14.5**	**8,157,600**	**6,505,282**	**55.6**	...	...
entucky	3,661,433	3,320,711	13.7	1,859,478	1,801,955	50.8	23	23
ennessee	4,590,750	3,926,018	16.9	2,772,513	1,818,237	60.4	17	17
abama	3,890,061	3,444,354	12.9	2,332,804	1,557,257	60.0	22	21
ississippi	2,520,638	2,216,994	13.7	1,192,805	1,327,833	47.3	31	29
West South Central	**23,743,134**	**19,326,077**	**22.9**	**17,426,782**	**6,316,352**	**73.4**	...	...
rkansas	2,285,513	1,923,322	18.8	1,179,079	1,106,434	51.6	33	32
ouisiana	4,203,972	3,644,637	15.3	2,885,535	1,318,437	68.6	19	20
klahoma	3,025,266	2,559,463	18.2	2,035,009	990,257	67.3	26	27
exas	14,228,383	11,198,655	27.1	11,327,159	2,901,224	79.6	3	4
Mountain	**11,368,330**	**8,289,901**	**37.2**	**8,682,880**	**2,685,450**	**76.4**	...	...
ontana	786,690	694,409	13.3	416,402	370,288	52.9	44	43
aho	943,935	713,015	32.4	509,702	434,233	54.0	41	42
/yoming	470,816	332,416	41.6	295,898	174,918	62.8	49	49
olorado	2,888,834	2,209,596	30.7	2,328,876	559,958	80.6	28	30
ew Mexico	1,299,968	1,017,055	27.8	939,223	360,745	72.2	37	37
rizona	2,717,866	1,775,399	53.1	2,278,189	439,677	83.8	29	33
tah	1,461,037	1,059,273	37.9	1,232,908	228,129	84.4	36	36
evada	799,184	488,738	63.5	681,682	117,502	85.3	43	47
Pacific	**31,796,869**	**26,548,342**	**19.9**	**27,529,802**	**4,267,067**	**86.6**	...	...
/ashington	4,130,163	3,413,244	21.0	3,037,765	1,092,398	73.6	20	22
regon	2,632,663	2,091,533	25.9	1,787,912	844,751	67.9	30	31
alifornia	23,668,562	19,971,069	18.5	21,611,033	2,057,529	91.3	1	1
laska	400,481	302,583	32.4	258,191	142,290	64.5	50	50
awaii	965,000	769,913	25.3	834,901	130,099	86.5	39	40
uerto Rico	3,196,520	2,712,033	17.9	2,134,365	1,062,155	66.8	...	...

U.S. Population by Officia

(Members of the Armed Forces overseas o

State	1790	1800	1810	1820	1830	1840	1850	1860	1870	188
Ala. . .	......	1,250	9,046	127,901	309,527	590,756	771,623	964,201	996,992	1,262,50
Alas.. .	......	......	......	......	......	......	......	......	......	.....
Ariz. . .	......	......	......	......	......	......	......	......	9,658	40,44
Ark. . .	......	......	1,062	14,273	30,388	97,574	209,897	435,450	484,471	802,52
Cal. . .	......	......	......	......	......	......	92,597	379,994	560,247	864,69
Col. . .	......	......	......	......	......	......	......	34,277	39,864	194,32
Conn. .	237,946	251,002	261,942	275,248	297,675	309,978	370,792	460,147	537,454	622,70
Del. . .	59,096	64,273	72,674	72,749	76,748	78,085	91,532	112,216	125,015	146,60
D.C. . .	......	14,023	24,023	33,039	39,834	43,712	51,687	75,080	131,700	177,62
Fla. . .	......	......	......	......	34,730	54,477	87,445	140,424	187,748	269,49
Ga.. . .	82,548	162,686	252,433	340,989	516,823	691,392	906,185	1,057,286	1,184,109	1,542,18
Ha.. . .	......	......	......	......	......	......	......	......	......	.....
Ida. . .	......	......	......	......	......	......	......	......	14,999	32,61
Ill. . . .	......	......	12,282	55,211	157,445	476,183	851,470	1,711,951	2,539,891	3,077,87
Ind. . .	......	5,641	24,520	147,178	343,031	685,866	988,416	1,350,428	1,680,637	1,978,30
Ia. . . .	......	......	......	......	......	43,112	192,214	674,913	1,194,020	1,624,61
Kan. . .	......	......	......	......	......	......	......	107,206	364,399	996,09
Ky.. . .	73,677	220,955	406,511	564,317	687,917	779,828	982,405	1,155,684	1,321,011	1,648,69
La.. . .	......	......	76,556	153,407	215,739	352,411	517,762	708,002	726,915	939,94
Me. . .	96,540	151,719	228,705	298,335	399,455	501,793	583,169	628,279	626,915	648,93
Md. . .	319,728	341,548	380,546	407,350	447,040	470,019	583,034	687,049	780,894	934,94
Mass. .	378,787	422,845	472,040	523,287	610,408	737,699	994,514	1,231,066	1,457,351	1,783,08
Mich. .	......	......	4,762	8,896	31,639	212,267	397,654	749,113	1,184,059	1,636,93
Minn. .	......	......	......	......	......	......	6,077	172,023	439,706	780,77
Miss.. .	......	8,850	40,352	75,448	136,621	375,651	606,526	791,305	827,922	1,131,59
Mo. . .	......	......	19,783	66,586	140,455	383,702	682,044	1,182,012	1,721,295	2,168,38
Mon.. .	......	......	......	......	......	......	......	......	20,595	39,15
Neb.. .	......	......	......	......	......	......	......	28,841	122,993	452,40
Nev.. .	......	......	......	......	......	......	......	6,857	42,491	62,26
N.H. . .	141,885	183,858	214,460	244,161	269,328	284,574	317,976	326,073	318,300	346,99
N.J. . .	184,139	211,149	245,562	277,575	320,823	373,306	489,555	672,035	906,096	1,131,11
N.M.. .	......	......	......	......	......	......	61,547	93,516	91,874	119,56
N.Y. . .	340,120	589,051	959,049	1,372,812	1,918,608	2,428,921	3,097,394	3,880,735	4,382,759	5,082,87
N.C. . .	393,751	478,103	555,500	638,829	737,987	753,419	869,039	992,622	1,071,361	1,399,75
N.D. . .	......	......	......	......	......	......	......	......	*2,405	36,90
Oh. . .	......	45,365	230,760	581,434	937,903	1,519,467	1,980,329	2,339,511	2,665,260	3,198,06
Okla. .	......	......	......	......	......	......	......	......	......	....
Ore. . .	......	......	......	......	......	......	13,294	52,465	90,923	174,76
Pa.. . .	434,373	602,365	810,091	1,049,458	1,348,233	1,724,033	2,311,786	2,906,215	3,521,951	4,282,89
R.I.. . .	68,825	69,122	76,931	83,059	97,199	108,830	147,545	174,620	217,353	276,53
S.C. . .	249,073	345,591	415,115	502,741	581,185	594,398	668,507	703,708	705,606	995,57
S.D. . .	......	......	......	......	......	......	......	*4,837	*11,776	98,26
Tenn. .	35,691	105,602	261,727	422,823	681,904	829,210	1,002,717	1,109,801	1,258,520	1,542,35
Tex. . .	......	......	......	......	......	......	212,592	604,215	818,579	1,591,74
Ut. . . .	......	......	......	......	......	......	11,380	40,273	86,786	143,96
Vt. . . .	85,425	154,465	217,895	235,981	280,652	291,948	314,120	315,098	330,551	332,28
Va.. . .	821,287	880,200	974,600	1,065,366	1,211,405	1,239,797	1,421,661	1,596,318	1,225,163	1,512,56
Wash. .	......	......	......	......	......	......	1,201	11,594	23,955	75,11
W. Va..	......	......	......	......	......	......	......	......	442,014	618,45
Wis. . .	......	......	......	......	......	30,945	305,391	775,881	1,054,670	1,315,49
Wy. . .	......	......	......	......	......	......	......	......	9,118	20,78
U.S.[1] . .	**3,929,214**	**5,308,483**	**7,239,881**	**9,638,453**	**12,866,020**	**17,069,453**	**23,191,876**	**31,443,321**	**38,558,371**	**50,155,78**

*1860 figure is for Dakota Territory; 1870 figures are for parts of Dakota Territory. (1) U.S. total includes persons (5,318 in 1830 an 6,100 in 1840) on public ships in the service of the United States not credited to any region, division, or state.

Density of Population by States

(Per square mile, land area only)

State	1920	1960	1970	1980	State	1920	1960	1970	1980	State	1920	1960	1970	198
Ala.. .	45.8	64.2	67.9	76.6	La. . .	39.6	72.2	81.0	94.4	Okla. .	29.2	33.8	37.2	44.
Alas.*	0.1	0.4	0.5	0.7	Me.. .	25.7	31.3	32.1	36.3	Ore. .	8.2	18.4	21.7	27
Ariz. .	2.9	11.5	15.6	23.9	Md.. .	145.8	313.5	396.6	428.6	Pa. . .	194.5	251.4	262.3	264
Ark.. .	33.4	34.2	37.0	43.9	Mass.	479.2	657.3	727.0	733.3	R. I.. .	566.4	819.3	902.5	897
Cal.. .	22.0	100.4	127.6	151.4	Mich. .	63.8	137.7	156.2	162.8	S. C. .	55.2	78.7	85.7	103.
Col.. .	9.1	16.9	21.3	27.9	Minn. .	29.5	43.1	48.0	51.3	S. D. .	8.3	9.0	8.8	9
Conn..	286.4	520.6	623.6	637.9	Miss. .	38.6	46.0	46.9	53.4	Tenn..	56.1	86.2	94.9	111
Del.. .	113.5	225.2	276.5	308.0	Mo.. .	49.5	62.6	67.8	71.3	Tex. .	17.8	36.4	42.7	54
D. C. .	7,292.9	12,523.9	12,401.8	10,127.0	Mon. .	3.8	4.6	4.8	5.4	Ut. . .	5.5	10.8	12.9	17
Fla.. .	17.7	91.5	125.5	179.9	Neb. .	16.9	18.4	19.4	20.5	Vt. . .	38.6	42.0	47.9	55
Ga.. .	49.3	67.8	79.0	94.1	Nev. .	.7	2.6	4.4	7.3	Va. . .	57.4	99.6	116.9	134
Ha.* .	39.9	98.5	119.6	150.2	N. H. .	49.1	67.2	81.7	102.4	Wash.	20.3	42.8	51.2	62
Ida.. .	5.2	8.1	8.6	11.5	N. J. .	420.0	805.5	953.1	986.1	W. Va.	60.9	77.2	72.5	80
Ill.. . .	115.7	180.4	199.4	205.2	N. M..	2.9	7.8	8.4	10.7	Wis. .	47.6	72.6	81.1	86
Ind.. .	81.3	128.8	143.9	152.8	N. Y..	217.9	350.6	381.3	370.6	Wy.. .	2.0	3.4	3.4	4
Ia.. . .	43.2	49.2	50.5	52.1	N. C..	52.5	93.2	104.1	120.3	**U.S. .**	***29.9**	**50.6**	**57.4**	**64**
Kan. .	21.6	26.6	27.5	28.9	N. D..	9.2	9.1	8.9	9.4					
Ky. . .	60.1	76.2	81.2	92.3	Oh.. .	141.4	236.6	260.0	263.3					

*For purposes of comparison, Alaska and Hawaii included in above tabulation for 1920, even though not states then.

ensus from 1790 to 1980

her U.S. nationals overseas are not included.)

1890	1900	1910	1920	1930	1940	1950	1960	1970	1980
1,513,401	1,828,697	2,138,093	2,348,174	2,646,248	2,832,961	3,061,743	3,266,740	3,444,354	3,890,061
....	....	....	....	....	....	....	226,167	302,583	400,481
88,243	122,931	204,354	334,162	435,573	499,261	749,587	1,302,161	1,775,399	2,717,866
1,128,211	1,311,564	1,574,449	1,752,204	1,854,482	1,949,387	1,909,511	1,786,272	1,923,322	2,285,513
1,213,398	1,485,053	2,377,549	3,426,861	5,677,251	6,907,387	10,586,223	15,717,204	19,971,069	23,668,562
413,249	539,700	799,024	939,629	1,035,791	1,123,296	1,325,089	1,753,947	2,209,596	2,888,834
746,258	908,420	1,114,756	1,380,631	1,606,903	1,709,242	2,007,280	2,535,234	3,032,217	3,107,576
168,493	184,735	202,322	223,003	238,380	266,505	318,085	446,292	548,104	595,225
230,392	278,718	331,069	437,571	486,869	663,091	802,178	763,956	756,668	637,651
391,422	528,542	752,619	968,470	1,468,211	1,897,414	2,771,305	4,951,560	6,791,418	9,739,992
1,837,353	2,216,331	2,609,121	2,895,832	2,908,506	3,123,723	3,444,578	3,943,116	4,587,930	5,464,265
....	....	....	....	....	....	....	632,772	769,913	965,000
88,548	161,772	325,594	431,866	445,032	524,873	588,637	667,191	713,015	943,935
3,826,352	4,821,550	5,638,591	6,485,280	7,630,654	7,897,241	8,712,176	10,081,158	11,110,285	11,418,461
2,192,404	2,516,462	2,700,876	2,930,390	3,238,503	3,427,796	3,934,224	4,662,498	5,195,392	5,490,179
1,912,297	2,231,853	2,224,771	2,404,021	2,470,939	2,538,268	2,621,073	2,757,537	2,825,368	2,913,387
1,428,108	1,470,495	1,690,949	1,769,257	1,880,999	1,801,028	1,905,299	2,178,611	2,249,071	2,363,208
1,858,635	2,147,174	2,289,905	2,416,630	2,614,589	2,845,627	2,944,806	3,038,156	3,220,711	3,661,433
1,118,588	1,381,625	1,656,388	1,798,509	2,101,593	2,363,880	2,683,516	3,257,022	3,644,637	4,203,972
661,086	694,466	742,371	768,014	797,423	847,226	913,774	969,265	993,722	1,124,660
1,042,390	1,188,044	1,295,346	1,449,661	1,631,526	1,821,244	2,343,001	3,100,689	3,923,897	4,216,446
2,238,947	2,805,346	3,366,416	3,852,356	4,249,614	4,316,721	4,690,514	5,148,578	5,689,170	5,737,037
2,093,890	2,420,982	2,810,173	3,668,412	4,842,325	5,256,106	6,371,766	7,823,194	8,881,826	9,258,344
1,310,283	1,751,394	2,075,708	2,387,125	2,563,953	2,792,300	2,982,483	3,413,864	3,806,103	4,077,148
1,289,600	1,551,270	1,797,114	1,790,618	2,009,821	2,183,796	2,178,914	2,178,141	2,216,994	2,520,638
2,679,185	3,106,665	3,293,335	3,404,055	3,629,367	3,784,664	3,954,653	4,319,813	4,677,623	4,917,444
142,924	243,329	376,053	548,889	537,606	559,456	591,024	674,767	694,409	786,690
1,062,656	1,066,300	1,192,214	1,296,372	1,377,963	1,315,834	1,325,510	1,411,330	1,485,333	1,570,006
47,355	42,335	81,875	77,407	91,058	110,247	160,083	285,278	488,738	799,184
376,530	411,588	430,572	443,083	465,293	491,524	533,242	606,921	737,681	920,610
1,444,933	1,883,669	2,537,167	3,155,900	4,041,334	4,160,165	4,835,329	6,066,782	7,171,112	7,364,158
160,282	195,310	327,301	360,350	423,317	531,818	681,187	951,023	1,017,055	1,299,968
6,003,174	7,268,894	9,113,614	10,385,227	12,588,066	13,479,142	14,830,192	16,782,304	18,241,391	17,557,288
1,617,949	1,893,810	2,206,287	2,559,123	3,170,276	3,571,623	4,061,929	4,556,155	5,084,411	5,874,429
190,983	319,146	577,056	646,872	680,845	641,935	619,636	632,446	617,792	652,695
3,672,329	4,157,545	4,767,121	5,759,394	6,646,697	6,907,612	7,946,627	9,706,397	10,657,423	10,797,419
258,657	790,391	1,657,155	2,028,283	2,396,040	2,336,434	2,233,351	2,328,284	2,559,463	3,025,266
317,704	413,536	672,765	783,389	953,786	1,089,684	1,521,341	1,768,687	2,091,533	2,632,663
5,258,113	6,302,115	7,665,111	8,720,017	9,631,350	9,900,180	10,498,012	11,319,366	11,800,766	11,866,728
345,506	428,556	542,610	604,397	687,497	713,346	791,896	859,488	949,723	947,154
1,151,149	1,340,316	1,515,400	1,683,724	1,738,765	1,899,804	2,117,027	2,382,594	2,590,713	3,119,208
348,600	401,570	583,888	636,547	692,849	642,961	652,740	680,514	666,257	690,178
1,767,518	2,020,616	2,184,789	2,337,885	2,616,556	2,915,841	3,291,718	3,567,089	3,926,018	4,590,750
2,235,527	3,048,710	3,896,542	4,663,228	5,824,715	6,414,824	7,711,194	9,579,677	11,198,655	14,228,383
210,779	276,749	373,351	449,396	507,847	550,310	688,862	890,627	1,059,273	1,461,037
332,422	343,641	355,956	352,428	359,611	359,231	377,747	389,881	444,732	511,456
1,655,980	1,854,184	2,061,612	2,309,187	2,421,851	2,677,773	3,318,680	3,966,949	4,651,448	5,346,279
357,232	518,103	1,141,990	1,356,621	1,563,396	1,736,191	2,378,963	2,853,214	3,413,244	4,130,163
762,794	958,800	1,221,119	1,463,701	1,729,205	1,901,974	2,005,552	1,860,421	1,744,237	1,949,644
1,693,330	2,069,042	2,333,860	2,632,067	2,939,006	3,137,587	3,434,575	3,951,777	4,417,821	4,705,335
62,555	92,531	145,965	194,402	225,565	250,742	290,529	330,066	332,416	470,816
62,947,714	**75,994,575**	**91,972,266**	**105,710,620**	**122,775,046**	**131,669,275**	**150,697,361**	**179,323,175**	**203,302,031**	**226,504,825**

U.S. Center of Population, 1790-1980

Center of Population is that point which may be considered as center of population gravity of the U.S. or that point upon which the U.S. ould balance if it were a rigid plane without weight and the population distributed thereon with each individual being assumed to have ual weight and to exert an influence on a central point proportional to his distance from that point.

ear	N. Lat. °	'	"	W.Long. °	'	"	Approximate location
90	39	16	30	76	11	12	23 miles east of Baltimore, Md.
00	39	16	6	76	56	30	18 miles west of Baltimore, Md.
10	39	11	30	77	37	12	40 miles northwest by west of Washington, D.C. (in Va.)
20	39	5	42	78	33	0	16 miles east of Moorefield, W. Va.[1]
30	38	57	54	79	16	54	19 miles west-southwest of Moorefield, W. Va.[1]
40	39	2	0	80	18	0	16 miles south of Clarksburg, W. Va.[1]
50	38	59	0	81	19	0	23 miles southeast of Parkersburg, W. Va.[1]
60	39	0	24	82	48	48	20 miles south by east of Chillicothe, Oh.
70	39	12	0	83	35	42	48 miles east by north of Cincinnati, Oh.
80	39	4	8	84	39	40	8 miles west by south of Cincinnati, Oh. (in Ky.)
90	39	11	56	85	32	53	20 miles east of Columbus, Ind.
00	39	9	36	85	48	54	6 miles southeast of Columbus, Ind.
10	39	10	12	86	32	20	In the city of Bloomington, Ind.
20	39	10	21	86	43	15	8 miles south-southeast of Spencer, Owen County, Ind.
30	39	3	45	87	8	6	3 miles northeast of Linton, Greene County, Ind.
40	38	56	54	87	22	35	2 miles southeast by east of Carlisle, Sullivan County, Ind.
50 (Inc. Alaska & Hawaii)	38	48	15	88	22	8	3 miles northeast of Louisville, Clay County, Ill.
60	38	35	58	89	12	35	6 1/2 miles northwest of Centralia, Ill.
70	38	27	47	89	42	22	5 miles east southeast of Mascoutah, St. Clair County, Ill.
80	38	8	13	90	34	26	near DeSoto, Mo.

) West Vigini a was set off from Virginia Dec. 31, 1862, and admitted as a state June 20, 1863.

Congressional Apportionment

	1980	1970		1980	1970		1980	1970		1980	1970		1980	1970
Ala. . .	7	7	Ida. . .	2	2	Minn. .	8	8	N. D. .	1	1	Vt. . . .	1	1
Alas. .	1	1	Ill.. . .	22	24	Miss.. .	5	5	Oh. . .	21	23	Va.. . .	10	10
Ariz. .	5	4	Ind. . .	10	11	Mo. . .	9	10	Okla. .	6	6	Wash. .	8	7
Ark.. .	4	4	Ia.. . .	6	6	Mon.. .	2	2	Ore.. .	5	4	W. Va..	4	4
Cal.. .	45	43	Kan. .	5	5	Neb.. .	3	3	Pa. . .	23	25	Wis. . .	9	9
Col.. .	6	5	Ky. . .	7	7	Nev.. .	2	1	R. I.. .	2	2	Wy. . .	1	1
Conn..	6	6	La. . .	8	8	N. H.. .	2	2	S. C. .	6	6			
Del.. .	1	1	Me.. .	2	2	N. J.. .	14	15	S. D. .	1	2	**Totals.**	**435**	**435**
Fla.. .	19	15	Md.. .	8	8	N. M. .	3	2	Tenn. .	9	8			
Ga.. .	10	10	Mass..	11	12	N. Y.. .	34	39	Tex.. .	27	24			
Ha.. .	2	2	Mich. .	18	19	N. C.. .	11	11	Ut.. . .	3	2			

The chief reason the Constitution provided for a census of the population every 10 years was to give a basis for apportionment of representatives among the states. This apportionment largely determines the number of electoral votes allotted to each state.

The number of representatives of each state in Congress is determined by the state's population, but each state is entitled to one representative regardless of population. A Congressional apportionment has been made after each decennial census except that of 1920.

Under provisions of a law that became effective Nov. 15, 1941, apportionment of representatives is made by the method of equa proportions. In the application of this method, the apportionmen is made so that the average population per representative has th least possible variation between one state and any other. The firs House of Representatives, in 1790, had 65 members, or one repre sentative for each 30,000 of the estimated population, as provide by the Constitution. As the population grew, the number of repre sentatives was increased but the total membership has been fixed a 435 since 1912.

U.S. Area and Population: 1790 to 1980

Source: U.S. Bureau of the Census

Area figures represent area on indicated date including in some cases considerable areas not then organized or settled, and not covered by the census. Area figures have been adjusted to bring them into agreement with remeasurements made in 1940.

Census date	Area (square miles)			Population			
	Gross	Land	Water	Number	Per sq. mile of land	Increase over preceding census Number	%
1790 (Aug. 2)	888,811	864,746	24,065	3,929,214	4.5	(X)	(X)
1800 (Aug. 4)	888,811	864,746	24,065	5,308,483	6.1	1,379,269	35.1
1810 (Aug. 6)	1,716,003	1,681,828	34,175	7,239,881	4.3	1,931,398	36.4
1820 (Aug. 7)	1,788,006	1,749,462	38,544	9,638,453	5.5	2,398,572	33.1
1830 (June 1)	1,788,006	1,749,462	38,544	12,866,020	7.4	3,227,567	33.5
1840 (June 1)	1,788,006	1,749,462	38,544	17,069,453	9.8	4,203,433	32.7
1850 (June 1)	2,992,747	2,940,042	52,705	23,191,876	7.9	6,122,423	35.9
1860 (June 1)	3,022,387	2,969,640	52,747	31,443,321	10.6	8,251,445	35.6
1870 (June 1)	3,022,387	2,969,640	52,747	[1]39,818,449	[1]13.4	8,375,128	26.6
1880 (June 1)	3,022,387	2,969,640	52,747	50,155,783	16.9	10,337,334	26.0
1890 (June 1)	3,022,387	2,969,640	52,747	62,947,714	21.2	12,791,931	25.5
1900 (June 1)	3,022,387	2,969,834	52,553	75,994,575	25.6	13,046,861	20.7
1910 (Apr. 15)	3,022,387	2,969,565	52,822	91,972,266	31.0	15,977,691	21.0
1920 (Jan. 1)	3,022,387	2,969,451	52,936	105,710,620	35.6	13,738,354	14.9
1930 (Apr. 1)	3,022,387	2,977,128	45,259	122,775,046	41.2	17,064,426	16.1
1940 (Apr. 1)	3,022,387	2,977,128	45,259	131,669,275	44.2	8,894,229	7.2
1950 (Apr. 1)[2]	3,615,211	3,552,206	63,005	151,325,798	42.6	19,161,229	14.5
1960 (Apr. 1)[2]	3,615,123	3,540,911	74,212	179,323,175	50.6	27,997,377	18.5
1970 (Apr. 1)[2]	[3]3,618,467	[3]3,540,023	[3]78,444	[4]203,302,031	57.4	23,978,856	13.4
1980 (Apr. 1)[2]	3,618,770	3,539,289	79,481	226,504,825	64.0	23,202,794	11.4

(X) Not applicable. (1) Revised to include adjustments for underenumeration in Southern States; unrevised number is 38,558,371. (2) Includes Alaska and Hawaii. (3) Figures corrected after final reports were issued. (4) The official 1970 resident population count is 203,235,298; the difference of 23,372 is due to errors found after tabulations were completed.

Black and Hispanic Population by States

Source: U.S. Bureau of the Census (1980)

	Black	Hispanic		Black	Hispanic		Black	Hispanic
Ala.	995,623	33,100	La..	1,237,263	99,105	Okla.	204,658	57,41
Alas..	13,619	9,497	Me.	3,128	5,005	Ore..	37,059	65,83
Ariz..	75,034	440,915	Md.	958,050	64,740	Pa..	1,047,609	154,00
Ark.	373,192	17,873	Mass..	221,279	141,043	R.I..	27,584	19,70
Cal.	1,819,282	4,543,770	Mich.	1,198,710	162,388	S.C..	948,146	33,41
Col.	101,702	339,300	Minn.	53,342	32,124	S.D..	2,144	4,02
Conn..	217,433	124,499	Miss..	887,206	24,731	Tenn.	725,949	34,08
Del.	95,971	9,671	Mo.	514,274	51,667	Tex..	1,710,250	2,985,64
D.C..	448,229	17,652	Mon..	1,786	9,974	Ut..	9,225	60,30
Fla.	1,342,478	857,898	Neb..	48,389	28,020	Vt..	1,135	3,30
Ga.	1,465,457	61,261	Nev..	50,791	53,786	Va..	1,008,311	79,87
Ha.	17,352	71,479	N.H..	3,990	5,587	Wash..	105,544	119,98
Ida.	2,716	36,615	N.J.	924,786	491,867	W.Va.. . . .	65,051	12,70
Ill.	1,675,229	635,525	N.M..	24,042	476,089	Wis..	182,593	62,98
Ind.	414,732	87,020	N.Y..	2,401,842	1,659,245	Wy.	3,364	24,49
Ia.	41,700	25,536	N.C..	1,316,050	56,607	**Total**	**26,488,218**	**14,605,88**
Kan..	126,127	63,333	N.D..	2,568	3,903			
Ky..	259,490	27,403	Oh.	1,076,734	119,880			

Rankings of U.S. Standard Metropolitan Statistical Areas

Source: U.S. Bureau of the Census

Metropolitan areas are ranked by 1980 provisional population size based on new SMSA definitions and compared with a ranking of areas as defined in the 1970 census. Included are 141 of the 323 Standard Metropolitan Statistical Areas (SMSAs) as defined through June 30, 1981 by the Office of Federal Statistical Policy and Standards.

SMSA	1980 Rank	1980 Pop.	1970 Rank	1970 Pop.
New York, NY-NJ	1	9,119,737	1	9,973,716
Los Angeles-Long Beach, CA	2	7,477,657	2	7,041,980
Chicago, IL	3	7,102,328	3	6,974,755
Philadelphia, PA-NJ	4	4,716,818	4	4,824,110
Detroit, MI	5	4,352,762	5	4,435,051
San Francisco-Oakland, CA	6	3,252,721	6	3,109,249
Washington, DC-MD-VA	7	3,060,240	7	2,910,111
Dallas-Fort Worth, TX	8	2,974,878	12	2,377,623
Houston, TX	9	2,905,350	16	1,999,316
Boston, MA	10	2,763,357	8	2,899,101
Nassau-Suffolk, NY	11	2,605,813	9	2,555,868
St. Louis, MO-IL	12	2,355,276	10	2,410,884
Pittsburgh, PA	13	2,263,894	11	2,401,362
Baltimore, MD	14	2,174,023	13	2,071,016
Minneapolis-St. Paul, MN-WI	15	2,114,256	17	1,965,391
Atlanta, GA	16	2,029,618	18	1,595,517
Newark, NJ	17	1,965,304	15	2,057,468
Anaheim-Santa Ana-Garden Grove, CA	18	1,931,570	20	1,421,233
Cleveland, OH	19	1,898,720	14	2,063,729
San Diego, CA	20	1,861,846	23	1,357,854
Miami, FL	21	1,625,979	26	1,267,792
Denver-Boulder, CO	22	1,619,921	27	1,239,545
Seattle-Everett, WA	23	1,606,765	19	1,424,605
Tampa-St. Petersburg, FL	24	1,569,492	30	1,088,549
Riverside-San Bernardino-Ontario, CA	25	1,557,080	28	1,139,149
Phoenix, AZ	26	1,508,030	35	971,228
Cincinnati, OH-KY-IN	27	1,401,403	22	1,387,207
Milwaukee, WI	28	1,397,143	21	1,403,884
Kansas City, MO-KS	29	1,327,020	25	1,273,926
San Jose, CA	30	1,295,071	31	1,065,313
Buffalo, NY	31	1,242,573	24	1,349,211
Portland, OR-WA	32	1,242,187	34	1,007,130
New Orleans, LA	33	1,186,725	32	1,046,470
Indianapolis, IN	34	1,166,929	29	1,111,352
Columbus, OH	35	1,093,293	33	1,017,847
San Juan, PR	36	1,086,376	—	936,693
San Antonio, TX	37	1,071,954	38	888,179
Fort Lauderdale-Hollywood, FL	38	1,014,043	58	620,100
Sacramento, CA	39	1,014,002	42	803,793
Rochester, NY	40	971,879	36	961,516
Salt Lake City-Ogden, UT	41	936,255	49	705,458
Providence-Warwick-Pawtucket, RI-MA	42	919,216	37	908,887
Memphis, TN-AR-MS	43	912,887	41	834,103
Louisville, KY-IN	44	906,240	39	867,330
Nashville-Davidson, TN	45	850,505	50	699,271
Birmingham, AL	46	847,360	44	767,230
Oklahoma City, OK	47	834,088	51	699,092
Dayton, OH	48	830,070	40	852,531
Greensboro-Winston-Salem-High Point, NC	49	827,385	47	724,129
Norfolk-Virginia Beach-Portsmouth, VA-NC	50	806,691	46	732,600
Albany-Schenectady-Troy, NY	51	795,019	43	777,977
Toledo, OH-MI	52	791,599	45	762,658
Honolulu, HI	53	762,874	55	630,528
Jacksonville, FL	54	737,519	57	621,827
Hartford, CT	55	726,114	48	720,581
Orlando, FL	56	700,699	74	453,270
Tulsa, OK	57	689,628	63	549,154
Akron, OH	58	660,328	52	679,239
Gary, Hammond, E. Chicago, IN	59	642,781	54	633,367
Syracuse, NY	60	642,375	53	636,596
Northeast Pennsylvania	61	640,396	56	621,882
Charlotte-Gastonia, NC	62	637,218	62	557,785
Allentown-Bethlehem-Easton, PA-NJ	63	636,714	60	594,382
Richmond, VA	64	632,015	64	547,542
Grand Rapids, MI	65	601,680	67	539,225
New Brunswick-Perth Amboy-Sayreville, NJ	66	595,893	61	583,813
West Palm Beach, FL	67	573,125	96	348,993
Omaha, NE-IA	68	570,399	65	542,646
Greenville-Spartanburg, SC	69	568,758	71	473,454
Jersey City, NJ	70	556,972	59	607,839

SMSA	1980 Rank	1980 Pop.	1970 Rank	1970 Pop.
Austin, TX	71	536,450	93	360,463
Youngstown-Warren, OH	72	531,350	68	537,124
Tucson, AZ	73	531,263	95	351,667
Raleigh-Durham, NC	74	530,673	76	419,254
Springfield-Chicopee-Holyoke, MA	75	530,668	66	541,752
Oxnard-Simi Valley-Ventura, CA	76	529,899	85	378,497
Wilmington, DE-NJ-MD	77	524,108	70	499,493
Flint, MI	78	521,589	69	508,664
Fresno, CA	79	515,013	77	413,329
Long Branch-Asbury Park, NJ	80	503,173	72	461,849
Baton Rouge, LA	81	493,973	87	375,628
Tacoma, WA	82	485,643	78	412,344
El Paso, TX	83	479,899	94	359,291
Knoxville, TN	84	476,517	81	409,409
Lansing-East Lansing, MI	85	468,482	75	424,271
Las Vegas, NV	86	461,816	123	273,288
Albuquerque, NM	87	454,499	102	333,266
Paterson-Clifton-Passaic, NJ	88	447,585	73	460,782
Harrisburg, PA	89	446,072	80	410,505
Mobile, AL	90	442,819	86	376,690
Johnson City-Kingsport-Bristol, TN-VA	91	433,638	88	373,591
Charleston-North Charleston, SC	92	430,301	100	336,125
Chattanooga, TN-GA	93	426,540	90	370,857
New Haven, CT	94	417,592	79	411,287
Wichita, KS	95	411,313	84	389,352
Columbia, SC	96	408,176	107	322,880
Canton, OH	97	404,421	83	393,789
Bakersfield, CA	98	403,089	104	330,234
Bridgeport, CT	99	395,455	82	401,752
Little Rock, AR	100	393,494	106	323,296
Davenport-Rock I.-Moline, IA-IL	101	383,958	91	362,638
Fort Wayne, IN	102	382,961	92	361,984
York, PA	103	381,255	105	329,540
Shreveport, LA	104	376,646	101	336,000
Beaumont-Port Arthur-Orange, TX	105	375,497	97	347,568
Worcester, MA	106	372,940	89	372,144
Peoria, IL	107	365,864	98	341,979
Newport News-Hampton, VA	108	364,449	103	333,140
Lancaster, PA	109	362,346	108	320,079
Stockton, CA	110	347,342	113	291,073
Spokane, WA	111	341,835	115	287,487
Des Moines, IA	112	338,048	109	313,562
Vallejo-Fairfield, Napa, CA	113	334,402	135	251,129
Augusta, GA-SC	114	327,372	122	275,787
Corpus Christi, TX	115	326,228	118	284,832
Madison, WI	116	323,545	114	290,272
Lakeland-Winter Haven, FL	117	321,652	143	228,515
Jackson, MS	118	320,425	130	258,906
Utica-Rome, NY	119	320,180	99	340,477
Lexington-Fayette, KY	120	318,136	125	266,701
Colorado Springs, CO	121	317,458	139	239,288
Reading, PA	122	312,509	112	296,382
Huntington-Ashland, WV-KY-OH	123	311,350	116	286,935
Evansville, IN-KY	124	309,408	117	284,959
Huntsville, AL	125	308,593	119	282,450
Trenton, NJ	126	307,863	110	304,116
Binghamton, NY	127	301,336	111	302,672
Santa Rosa, CA	128	299,827	156	204,885
Santa Barbara-Santa Maria-Lompoc, CA	129	298,660	127	264,324
Appleton-Oshkosh, WI	130	291,325	121	276,948
Salinas-Seaside-Monterey, CA	131	290,444	136	247,450
Pensacola, FL	132	289,782	137	243,075
McAllen-Pharr-Edinburg, TX	133	283,229	162	181,535
Lawrence-Haverhill, MA-NH	134	281,981	131	258,564
South Bend, IN	135	280,772	120	279,813
Erie, PA	136	279,780	128	263,654
Rockford, IL	137	279,514	124	272,063
Kalamazoo-Portage, MI	138	279,192	132	257,723
Eugene-Springfield, OR	139	275,226	151	215,401
Lorain-Elyria, OH	140	274,909	134	256,843
Montgomery, AL	141	272,687	146	225,911

Cities—Growth and Decline

Source: U.S. Bureau of the Census (cities over 170,000 ranked by 1980 population)

Rank	City	1980	1970	1960	1950	1900	1850	1790
1	New York, N.Y.	7,071,030	7,895,563	7,781,984	7,891,957	3,437,202	696,115	49,401
2	Chicago, Ill.	3,005,072	3,369,357	3,550,404	3,620,962	1,698,575	29,963	...
3	Los Angeles, Cal.	2,966,763	2,811,801	2,479,015	1,970,358	102,479	1,610	...
4	Philadelphia, Pa.	1,688,210	1,949,996	2,002,512	2,071,605	1,293,697	121,376	28,522
5	Houston, Tex.	1,594,086	1,233,535	938,219	596,163	44,633	2,396	...
6	Detroit, Mich.	1,203,339	1,514,063	1,670,144	1,849,568	285,704	21,019	...
7	Dallas, Tex.	904,078	844,401	679,684	434,462	42,638	...	...
8	San Diego, Cal.	875,504	697,471	573,224	334,387	17,700	...	...
9	Baltimore, Md.	786,775	905,787	939,024	949,708	508,957	169,054	13,503
10	San Antonio, Tex.	785,410	654,153	587,718	408,442	53,321	3,488	...
11	Phoenix, Ariz.	764,911	584,303	439,170	106,818	5,544	...	...
12	Honolulu Co., Ha.	762,874	630,528	294,194	248,034	39,306	...	...
13	Indianapolis, Ind.	700,807	736,856	476,258	427,173	169,164	8,091	...
14	San Francisco, Cal.	678,974	715,674	740,316	775,357	342,782	34,776	...
15	Memphis, Tenn.	646,356	623,988	497,524	396,000	102,320	8,841	...
16	Washington, D.C.	637,651	756,668	763,956	802,178	278,718	40,001	...
17	San Jose, Cal.	636,550	459,913	204,196	95,280	21,500	...	...
18	Milwaukee, Wis.	636,212	717,372	741,324	637,392	285,315	20,061	...
19	Cleveland, Oh.	573,822	750,879	876,050	914,808	381,768	17,034	...
20	Columbus, Oh.	564,871	540,025	471,316	375,901	125,560	17,882	...
21	Boston, Mass.	562,994	641,071	697,197	801,444	560,892	136,881	18,320
22	New Orleans, La.	557,482	593,471	627,525	570,445	287,104	116,375	...
23	Jacksonville, Fla.	540,898	504,265	201,030	204,517	28,429	1,045	...
24	Seattle, Wash.	493,846	530,831	557,087	467,591	80,671	...	...
25	Denver, Col.	491,396	514,678	493,887	415,786	133,859	...	...
26	Nashville-Davidson, Tenn.	455,651	426,029	170,874	174,307	80,865	10,165	...
27	St. Louis, Mo.	453,085	622,236	750,026	856,796	575,238	77,860	...
28	Kansas City, Mo.	448,159	507,330	475,539	456,622	163,752	...	...
29	El Paso, Tex.	425,259	322,261	276,687	130,485	15,906	...	...
30	Atlanta, Ga.	425,022	495,039	487,455	331,314	89,872	2,572	...
31	Pittsburgh, Pa.	423,938	520,089	604,332	676,806	321,616	46,601	...
32	Oklahoma City, Okla.	403,213	368,164	324,253	243,504	10,037	...	...
33	Cincinnati, Oh.	385,457	453,514	502,550	503,998	325,902	115,435	...
34	Fort Worth, Tex.	385,141	393,455	356,268	278,778	26,688	...	...
35	Minneapolis, Minn.	370,951	434,400	482,872	521,718	202,718	...	...
36	Portland, Ore.	366,383	379,967	372,676	373,628	90,426	...	...
37	Long Beach, Cal.	361,334	358,879	344,168	250,767	2,252	...	...
38	Tulsa, Okla.	360,919	330,350	261,685	182,740	1,390	...	...
39	Buffalo, N.Y.	357,870	462,768	532,759	580,132	352,387	42,261	...
40	Toledo, Oh.	354,635	383,062	318,003	303,616	131,822	3,829	...
41	Miami, Fla.	346,931	334,859	291,688	249,276	1,681	...	...
42	Austin, Tex.	345,496	253,539	186,545	132,459	22,258	629	...
43	Oakland, Cal.	339,288	361,561	367,548	384,575	66,960	...	...
44	Albuquerque, N.M.	331,767	244,501	201,189	96,815	6,238	...	...
45	Tucson, Ariz.	330,537	262,933	212,892	45,454	7,531	...	...
46	Newark, N.J.	329,248	381,930	405,220	438,776	246,070	38,894	...
47	Charlotte, N.C.	314,447	241,420	201,564	134,042	18,091	1,065	...
48	Omaha, Neb.	311,681	346,929	301,598	251,117	102,555	...	...
49	Louisville, Ky.	298,451	361,706	390,639	369,129	204,731	43,194	200
50	Birmingham, Ala.	284,413	300,910	340,887	326,037	38,415	...	...
51	Wichita, Kan.	279,272	276,554	254,698	168,279	24,671	...	...
52	Sacramento, Cal.	275,741	257,105	191,667	137,572	29,282	6,820	...
53	Tampa, Fla.	271,523	277,714	274,970	124,681	15,839	...	...
54	St. Paul, Minn.	270,230	309,866	313,411	311,349	163,065	1,112	...
55	Norfolk, Va.	266,979	307,951	304,869	213,513	46,624	14,326	2,959
56	Virginia Beach, Va.	262,199	172,106	8,091	5,390	...	...	...
57	Rochester, N.Y.	241,741	295,011	318,611	332,488	162,608	36,403	...
58	Akron, Oh.	237,177	275,425	290,351	274,605	42,728	3,266	...
59	St. Petersburg, Fla.	236,893	216,159	181,298	96,738	1,575	...	...
60	Corpus Christi, Tex.	231,999	204,525	167,690	108,287	4,703	...	...
61	Jersey City, N.J.	223,532	260,350	276,101	299,017	206,433	6,856	...
62	Anaheim, Cal.	221,847	166,408	104,184	14,556	1,456	...	...
63	Baton Rouge, La.	219,486	165,921	152,419	125,629	11,269	3,905	...
64	Richmond, Va.	219,214	249,332	219,958	230,310	85,050	27,570	3,761
65	Fresno, Cal.	218,202	165,655	133,929	91,669	12,470	...	...
66	Colorado Springs, Col.	215,150	135,517	70,194	45,472	21,085	...	...
67	Shreveport, La.	205,815	182,064	164,372	127,206	16,013	1,728	...
68	Lexington-Fayette, Ky.	204,165	108,137	62,810	55,534	26,369	8,159	834
69	Santa Ana, Cal.	203,713	155,710	100,350	45,533	4,933	...	...
70	Dayton, Oh.	203,588	243,023	262,332	243,872	85,333	10,977	...
71	Jackson, Miss.	202,895	153,968	144,422	98,271	7,816	1,881	...
72	Mobile, Ala.	200,452	190,026	194,856	129,009	38,469	20,515	...
73	Yonkers, N.Y.	195,351	204,297	190,634	152,798	47,931	...	...
74	Des Moines, Ia.	191,003	201,404	208,982	177,965	62,139	...	...
75	Knoxville, Tenn.	183,139	174,587	111,827	124,769	32,637	2,076	...
76	Grand Rapids, Mich.	181,843	197,649	177,313	176,515	87,565	2,686	...
77	Montgomery, Ala.	178,157	133,386	134,393	106,525	30,346	8,728	...
78	Lubbock, Tex.	173,979	149,101	126,691	71,747	...	...	...
79	Anchorage, Alas.	173,017	48,081	44,237	11,254	...	...	...
80	Fort Wayne, Ind.	172,196	178,269	161,776	133,607	45,115	4,282	...
81	Lincoln, Neb.	171,932	149,518	128,521	98,884	40,169	...	...
82	Spokane, Wash.	171,300	170,516	181,608	161,721	36,848	...	...
83	Riverside, Cal.	170,876	140,089	84,332	46,764	7,973	...	...
84	Madison, Wis.	170,616	171,809	126,706	96,056	19,164	1,525	...
85	Huntington Beach, Cal.	170,505	115,960	11,492	5,237	...	...	...
86	Syracuse, N.Y.	170,105	197,297	216,038	220,583	108,374	22,271	...

City Population by Race and Spanish Origin

Source: U.S. Bureau of the Census

This table presents a summary of the final 1980 census population counts for cities over 200,000, classified by race and Spanish origin. Counts of the population by race as well as Spanish origin in this table are provisional.

	Total	White	Black	Am. Indian Eskimo & Aleut.	Asian & Pacific Islander	Other	Spanish origin[1]
Akron, Oh.	237,177	182,114	52,719	368	858	1,118	1,534
Albuquerque, NM	331,767	268,731	8,361	7,341	3,162	44,172	112,084
Anaheim, CA	221,847	190,679	2,557	1,686	8,913	18,012	38,015
Atlanta, GA	425,022	137,878	282,912	422	2,000	1,810	5,842
Austin, TX	345,496	261,166	42,118	1,003	3,642	37,567	64,766
Baltimore, MD	786,775	345,113	431,151	2,108	4,949	3,454	7,641
Baton Rouge, LA	219,486	135,766	80,119	288	1,603	1,710	3,985
Birmingham, AL	284,413	124,730	158,223	185	793	482	2,227
Boston, MA	562,994	393,937	126,229	1,302	15,150	26,376	36,068
Buffalo, NY	357,870	252,365	95,116	2,383	1,322	6,684	9,499
Charlotte, NC	314,447	211,980	97,627	1,039	2,367	1,434	3,418
Chicago, IL	3,005,072	1,490,217	1,197,000	6,072	69,191	242,592	422,061
Cincinnati, OH	385,457	251,144	130,467	425	2,216	1,205	2,988
Cleveland, OH	573,822	307,264	251,347	1,094	3,384	10,733	17,772
Colorado Springs, CO	215,150	189,113	11,961	1,100	3,144	9,832	18,268
Columbus, OH	564,871	430,678	124,880	924	4,714	3,675	4,651
Corpus Christi, TX	231,999	188,279	11,889	662	1,277	29,892	108,175
Dallas, TX	904,078	555,270	265,594	3,732	7,678	71,804	111,082
Dayton, OH	203,588	126,389	75,031	300	869	999	1,748
Denver, CO	491,396	367,344	59,252	3,847	7,007	53,946	91,937
Detroit, MI	1,203,339	413,730	758,939	3,420	6,621	20,629	28,970
El Paso, TX	425,259	249,214	13,466	1,251	3,544	157,784	265,819
Fort Worth, TX	385,141	265,428	87,723	1,227	2,340	28,423	48,696
Fresno, CA	218,202	156,501	20,665	2,097	6,111	32,828	51,489
Honolulu, HI (county)	762,874	252,293	16,831	2,182	456,873	34,695	54,777
Houston, TX	1,594,086	977,530	440,257	3,228	32,898	140,173	281,224
Indianapolis, IN	700,807	540,294	152,626	994	3,792	3,101	6,145
Jackson, MS	202,895	106,285	95,357	142	621	490	1,508
Jacksonville, FL	540,898	394,734	137,324	1,198	5,240	2,402	9,775
Jersey City, NJ	223,532	127,699	61,954	261	9,793	23,825	41,672
Kansas City, MO	448,159	312,836	122,699	1,622	3,499	7,503	14,703
Lexington-Fayette, KY	204,165	174,605	27,121	225	1,360	854	1,488
Long Beach, CA	361,334	269,953	40,732	2,982	19,609	28,058	50,700
Los Angeles, CA	2,966,763	1,816,683	505,208	16,595	196,024	432,253	815,989
Louisville, KY	298,451	212,102	84,080	336	931	1,002	2,005
Memphis, TN	646,356	333,789	307,702	530	2,701	1,634	5,225
Miami, FL	346,931	231,069	87,110	329	1,861	26,562	194,087
Milwaukee, WI	636,212	466,620	146,940	5,018	3,600	14,034	26,111
Minneapolis, MN	370,951	323,832	38,433	8,932	4,104	5,650	4,684
Mobile, AL	200,452	125,786	72,568	368	972	758	2,265
Nashville-Davidson, TN	455,651	344,886	105,942	529	2,202	2,092	3,627
New Orleans, LA	557,482	236,967	308,136	524	7,332	4,523	19,219
New York, NY	7,071,030	4,293,695	1,784,124	11,824	231,505	749,882	1,405,957
Newark, NJ	329,248	101,417	191,743	551	2,366	33,171	61,254
Norfolk, VA	266,979	162,300	93,987	885	7,149	2,658	6,074
Oakland, CA	339,288	129,690	159,234	2,199	26,341	21,824	32,491
Oklahoma City, OK	403,213	322,374	58,702	10,405	4,167	7,565	11,295
Omaha, NE	311,681	266,070	37,852	1,792	1,734	4,233	7,304
Philadelphia, PA	1,688,210	983,084	638,878	2,325	17,764	46,159	63,570
Phoenix, AZ	764,911	642,059	37,682	10,771	6,979	67,420	115,572
Pittsburgh, PA	423,938	316,694	101,813	482	2,596	2,353	3,196
Portland, OR	366,383	316,993	27,734	3,526	10,636	7,494	7,807
Richmond, VA	219,214	104,743	112,357	357	976	781	2,210
Rochester, NY	241,741	168,102	62,332	1,014	1,536	8,757	13,153
Sacramento, CA	275,741	186,477	36,866	3,322	24,017	25,059	39,160
St. Louis, MO	453,085	242,576	206,386	642	1,696	1,785	5,531
St. Paul, MN	270,230	243,226	13,305	2,538	2,695	8,466	7,864
St. Petersburg, FL	236,893	193,277	41,000	331	1,272	1,013	4,210
San Antonio, TX	785,410	617,636	57,654	1,782	5,086	103,252	421,774
San Diego, CA	875,504	666,829	77,700	5,065	57,207	68,703	130,610
San Francisco, CA	678,974	395,082	86,414	3,548	147,426	46,504	83,373
San Jose, CA	636,550	470,013	29,157	4,826	52,448	80,106	140,574
Santa Ana, CA	203,713	132,072	8,232	1,627	10,631	51,151	90,646
Seattle, WA	493,846	392,766	46,755	6,253	36,613	11,459	12,646
Shreveport, LA	205,815	119,529	84,627	292	773	594	2,769
Tampa, FL	271,523	200,741	63,835	545	1,903	4,499	35,982
Toledo, OH	354,635	283,920	61,750	661	1,653	6,651	10,667
Tucson, AZ	330,537	270,188	12,301	4,341	3,523	40,184	82,189
Tulsa, OK	360,919	298,114	42,594	13,740	2,813	3,658	6,189
Virginia Beach, VA	262,199	226,788	26,291	633	6,570	1,917	5,160
Washington, DC	637,651	171,796	448,229	1,031	6,635	9,960	17,652
Wichita, KA	279,272	235,818	30,200	2,579	3,895	6,780	9,902

(1) persons of spanish origin may be of any race

Jewish Population by Countries and Cities

Source: American Jewish Year Book

Europe (including Asiatic USSR and Turkey)	4,102,350
America, North, Central, and South	6,839,560
Asia	3,339,810
Africa	173,430
Australia and New Zealand	72,000
Total	**14,527,150**

Europe

Albania	300
Austria	13,000
Belgium	41,000
Bulgaria	7,000
Czechoslovakia	12,000
Denmark	7,500
Finland	1,000
France	650,000
Germany	38,000
Gibraltar	600
Great Britain	410,000
Greece	6,000
Hungary	80,000
Ireland	1,900
Italy	41,000
Luxembourg	1,000
Malta	50
Netherlands	30,000
Norway	900
Poland	6,000
Portugal	600
Romania	45,000
Spain	12,000
Sweden	17,000
Switzerland	21,000
Turkey	24,000
USSR	2,630,000
Yugoslavia	5,500

North America

Canada	305,000
Mexico	37,500
United States (P.R. 1,800; VI, 510)	5,920,890

Central America and West Indies

Barbados	70
Costa Rica	2,500
Cuba	1,500
Curaçao	700
Dominican Republic	200
El Salvador	350
Guatemala	2,000
Haiti	150
Honduras	200
Jamaica	350
Nicaragua	200
Panama	2,000
Trinidad	300

South America

Argentina	300,000
Bolivia	750
Brazil	150,000
Chile	30,000
Colombia	12,000
Ecuador	1,000
Paraguay	1,200
Peru	5,200
Surinam	500
Uruguay	50,000
Venezuela	15,000

Asia

Afghanistan	200
Burma	50
China	30
Cyprus	30
Hong Kong	250
India	8,000
Indonesia	100
Iran	70,000
Iraq	450
Israel	3,254,000
Japan	400
Lebanon	400
Pakistan	250
Philippines	200
Singapore	450
Syria	4,500
Yemen	500

Australia and New Zealand

Australia	67,000
New Zealand	5,000

Africa

Algeria	1,000
Egypt	400
Ethiopia	22,000
Kenya	450
Libya	20
Morocco	22,000
Rep. of South Africa	118,000
Tunisia	7,000
Zaire	200
Zambia	400
Zimbabwe	1,960

World Cities

Adelaide	1,600
Amsterdam	15,000
Antwerp	13,000
Athens	2,800
Auckland	1,500
Basel	2,300
Belgrade	1,500
Berlin (both sectors)	6,000
Bogota	5,500
Bombay (and district)	6,970
Bordeaux	6,400
Brisbane	1,200
Brussels	24,500
Bucharest	40,000
Budapest	65,000
Cape Town	25,650
Copenhagen	7,000
Durban	5,990
Geneva	3,250
Glasgow	13,000
Goteborg	1,600
Guatemala City	1,500
Haifa	210,000
Istanbul	20,000
Izmir	2,500
Jerusalem	290,000
Johannesburg	57,500
Kiev	170,000
Leeds	18,000
Leningrad	165,000
Lima	5,000
Liverpool	6,500
London (greater)	260,000
Lyons	20,000
Madrid	3,000
Malmo	1,930
Manchester (greater)	35,000
Marseilles	65,000
Melbourne	32,000
Mexico, D. F.	32,500
Milan	9,000
Montevideo	48,000
Montreal	100,000
Moscow	285,000
Nice	20,000
Ottawa	8,500
Paris	300,000
Perth	3,200
Porto Alegre	12,000
Prague	3,000
Rabat	2,500
Recife	3,000
Rio de Janeiro	55,000
Rome	10,000
Salisbury	1,100
San Jose	2,500
Santiago	28,000
Sao Paulo	75,000
Sofia	4,000
Stockholm	5,000
Strasbourg	12,000
Sydney	26,500
Teheran	50,000
Tel Aviv-Jaffa	394,000
Toronto	120,000
Toulouse	18,000
Vancouver	14,000
Valparaiso	4,000
Vienna	9,000
Warsaw	4,500
Winnipeg	18,000
Zurich	6,150

U.S. Cities and Counties

Alameda and Contra Costa Co., Cal.	28,000
Albany, NY	13,500
Alexandria, Va. (area)	20,000
Atlanta, Ga.	27,500
Atlantic City, NJ	11,800
Baltimore, Md.	92,000
Bergen Co., NJ.	100,000
Boston (inc. Brockton)	170,000
Bridgeport, Conn.	18,500
Buffalo, NY	21,000
Camden, NJ	26,000
Chicago Metro Area	253,000
Cincinnati, Oh.	21,500
Cleveland, Oh.	75,000
Columbus, Oh.	13,000
Dallas, Tex.	20,000
Denver, Col.	30,000
Detroit, Mich.	75,000
Essex Co., NJ	95,000
Fort Lauderdale, Fla.	75,000
Framingham, Mass.	16,000
Hartford (inc. New Britain	23,500
Hollywood, Fla.	55,000
Houston, Tex.	28,000
Indianapolis, Ind.	11,000
Kansas City, Mo.	20,000
Las Vegas, Nev.	16,000
Long Beach, Cal.	13,500
Los Angeles Metro	503,000
Lynn, Mass.	19,000
Miami, Fla.	225,000
Milwaukee, Wis.	23,900
Minneapolis, Minn.	23,200
Montgomery Co., Md.	70,000
Monmouth Co., NJ.	32,000
Morris-Sussex Cos. NJ	15,000
New Haven, Conn.	20,000
New Orleans, La.	10,600
New York, (greater)	1,998,000
New York City	1,228,000
Manhattan	171,000
Brooklyn	514,000
Bronx	143,000
Queens	379,000
Staten Island	21,000
Nassau-Suffolk	605,000
Westchester	165,000
Ocean Co., NJ	12,000
Orange Co., Cal.	40,000
Palm Beach Co., Fla. (excl. Boca Raton)	35,000
Philadelphia Metro.	295,000
Phoenix, Ariz.	29,000
Pittsburgh, Pa.	50,000
Prince George's Co., Md.	20,000
Raritan Valley, NJ	18,000
Richmond, Va.	10,000
Rochester, NY	21,500
Rockland Co., NY	25,000
San Diego, Cal.	32,500
San Francisco, Cal.	75,000
San Jose, Cal.	15,000
Seattle, Wash.	16,000
Springfield, Mass.	10,000
Stamford, Conn.	12,000
St. Louis, Mo.	60,000
Syracuse, NY	11,000
Union Co., NJ	39,500
Washington, DC (greater)	160,000
Worcester, Mass.	10,000

Population, Urban and Rural, by Race: 1960 and 1970

Source: U.S. Bureau of the Census

An urbanized area comprises at least one city of 50,000 inhabitants (central city) plus contiguous, closely settled areas (urban fringe). (thousands)

Year and area	1960			1970		
	Total	White	Negro and other	Total	White	Negro and other
Population, total	**179,323**	**158,832**	**20,491**	**203,212**	**177,749**	**25,463**
Urban	125,269	110,428	14,840	149,325	128,773	20,552
Inside urbanized areas	95,848	83,770	12,070	118,447	100,952	17,495
Central cities	57,975	47,627	10,348	63,922	49,547	14,375
Urban fringe	37,873	36,143	1,731	54,525	51,405	3,120
Outside urbanized areas	29,420	26,658	2,762	30,878	27,822	3,057
Rural	54,054	48,403	5,651	53,887	48,976	4,911

Immigration by Country of Last Residence 1820-1979

Source: U.S. Immigration and Naturalization Service (thousands)

Country	1820-1979, total	1951-1960, total	1961-1970, total	1975	1976	1977	1978	1979	Percent 1820-1979	Percent 1961-1970	Percent 1971-1979
All countries*	**49,023**	**2,515.5**	**3,321.7**	**386.2**	**398.6**	**462.3**	**601.4**	**460.3**	**100.0**	**100.0**	**100.0**
Europe	**36,248**	**1,325.6**	**1,123.4**	**72.8**	**73.0**	**74.0**	**76.2**	**64.2**	**73.9**	**33.8**	**17.7**
Austria[1]	4,316 (Austria and Hungary)	67.1	20.6	0.5	0.5	0.5	0.5	0.5	8.8 (Austria and Hungary)	0.6	0.2
Hungary		36.6	5.4	0.6	0.6	0.5	0.6	0.5		0.2	0.1
Belgium	204	18.6	9.2	0.4	0.5	0.5	0.6	0.6	0.4	0.3	0.1
Czechoslovakia	138	0.9	3.3	0.3	0.3	0.3	0.4	0.5	0.3	0.1	0.1
Denmark	364	11.0	9.2	0.3	0.4	0.4	0.4	0.4	0.7	0.3	0.1
Finland	33	4.9	4.2	0.2	0.2	0.2	0.3	0.3	0.1	0.1	0.1
France	753	51.1	45.2	1.8	2.0	2.7	2.7	2.9	1.5	1.4	0.6
Germany[1]	6,983	477.8	190.8	5.9	6.6	7.4	7.6	7.2	14.2	5.7	1.6
Great Britain[2]	4,911	195.5	210.0	12.2	13.0	14.0	16.4	15.5	10.0	6.3	3.0
Greece	659	47.6	86.0	9.8	8.6	7.8	7.0	5.9	1.3	2.6	2.0
Ireland[3]	4,731	57.3	37.5	1.1	1.0	1.0	0.9	0.8	9.7	1.1	0.3
Italy	5,298	185.5	214.1	11.0	8.0	7.4	7.0	6.0	10.8	6.4	2.8
Netherlands	360	52.3	30.6	0.8	0.9	1.0	1.2	1.2	0.7	0.9	0.2
Norway	856	22.9	15.5	0.4	0.3	0.3	0.4	0.4	1.7	0.5	0.1
Poland[1]	519	10.0	53.5	3.5	3.2	3.3	4.5	3.9	1.1	1.6	0.9
Portugal	450	19.6	76.1	11.3	11.0	10.0	10.5	7.1	0.9	2.3	2.3
Spain	261	7.9	44.7	2.6	2.8	5.6	4.3	3.3	0.5	1.3	0.9
Sweden	1,273	21.7	17.1	0.5	0.6	0.6	0.6	0.8	2.6	0.5	0.1
Switzerland	350	17.7	18.5	0.7	0.8	0.8	0.9	0.8	0.7	0.6	0.2
USSR[1,4]	3,374	0.6	2.3	4.7	7.4	5.4	4.7	1.9	6.9	0.1	0.8
Yugoslavia	115	8.2	20.4	2.9	2.3	2.3	2.2	1.7	0.2	0.6	0.7
Other Europe	308	10.8	9.2	1.3	2.0	2.0	2.5	2.0	0.6	0.3	0.4
Asia	**3,000**	**153.3**	**427.8**	**129.2**	**146.7**	**150.8**	**243.6**	**183.0**	**6.1**	**12.9**	**34.9**
China[5]	536	9.7	34.8	9.2	9.9	12.5	14.5	12.3	1.1	1.0	2.5
Hong Kong	[6]197	15.5	75.0	12.5	13.7	12.3	11.1	16.8	0.4	2.3	2.8
India	178	2.0	27.2	14.3	16.1	16.8	19.1	18.6	0.4	0.8	3.6
Iran	[6]47	3.4	10.3	2.2	2.6	4.2	5.9	8.3	0.1	0.3	0.9
Israel	[6]88	25.5	29.6	3.5	5.2	4.4	4.5	4.3	0.2	0.9	0.9
Japan	410	46.3	40.0	4.8	4.8	4.5	4.5	4.5	0.8	1.2	1.1
Jordan	[6]40	5.8	11.7	2.3	2.4	2.9	3.2	3.1	0.1	0.3	0.6
Korea	[6]269	6.2	34.5	28.1	30.6	30.7	28.8	28.7	0.5	1.0	6.2
Lebanon	[6]56	4.5	15.2	4.0	5.0	5.5	4.8	4.8	0.1	0.5	0.9
Philippines	[7]421	19.3	98.4	31.3	36.8	38.5	36.6	40.8	0.9	3.0	7.9
Turkey	386	3.5	10.1	1.1	1.0	1.0	1.0	1.3	0.8	0.3	0.3
Vietnam	[8]133	2.7	4.2	2.7	2.4	3.4	87.6	19.1	0.3	0.1	3.6
Other Asia	240	9.0	36.7	13.2	16.2	14.1	22.0	20.4	0.5	1.2	3.6
America	**9,203**	**996.9**	**1,716.4**	**174.7**	**169.2**	**223.2**	**266.5**	**197.1**	**18.8**	**51.7**	**44.8**
Argentina	[9]96	19.5	49.7	2.8	2.7	3.1	4.1	3.1	0.2	1.5	0.7
Brazil	[9]59	13.8	29.3	1.4	1.4	1.9	2.2	1.8	0.1	0.9	0.4
Canada	4,121	378.0	413.3	11.2	11.4	18.0	23.5	20.2	8.4	12.4	3.7
Colombia	[9]155	18.0	72.0	6.4	5.7	8.2	10.9	10.5	0.3	2.2	1.7
Cuba	[10]532	78.9	208.5	25.6	28.4	66.1	27.5	14.0	1.1	6.3	6.3
Dominican Rep.	[9]230	9.9	93.3	14.1	12.5	11.6	19.5	17.5	0.5	2.8	3.3
Ecuador	[9]90	9.8	36.8	4.7	4.5	5.2	5.7	4.4	0.2	1.1	1.1
El Salvador	[9]49	5.9	15.0	2.4	2.4	4.4	5.9	4.5	0.1	0.4	0.7
Guatemala	[9]43	4.7	15.9	1.9	2.0	3.7	4.1	2.6	0.1	0.5	0.6
Haiti	[10]88	4.4	34.5	5.0	5.3	5.2	6.1	6.1	0.2	1.0	1.2
Honduras	[9]37	6.0	15.7	1.4	1.3	1.6	2.7	2.5	0.1	0.5	0.4
Mexico	2,160	299.8	453.9	62.6	58.4	44.6	92.7	52.5	4.4	13.7	14.8
Panama	[9]50	11.7	19.4	1.7	1.8	2.5	3.3	3.5	0.1	0.6	0.5
Peru	[9]51	7.4	19.1	2.3	2.6	3.9	5.1	4.0	0.1	0.6	0.7
West Indies	744	29.8	133.9	22.3	19.6	27.1	34.6	24.8	1.5	4.0	5.7
Other America	701	99.2	106.2	8.9	9.2	16.1	18.6	25.0	1.4	3.2	3.0
Africa	**142**	**14.1**	**29.0**	**5.9**	**5.7**	**9.6**	**10.3**	**11.2**	**0.3**	**0.9**	**1.7**
Australia and New Zealand	**122**	**11.5**	**19.6**	**1.8**	**2.1**	**2.5**	**2.7**	**2.5**	**0.2**	**0.6**	**0.5**
Other Oceania	**308**	**14.0**	**5.7**	**1.8**	**1.8**	**2.1**	**2.2**	**2.4**	**0.6**	**0.2**	**0.4**

* Figures may not add to total due to rounding. (1) 1938-1945, Austria included with Germany; 1899-1919, Poland included with Austria-Hungary, Germany, and USSR. (2) Beginning 1952, includes data for United Kingdom not specified, formerly included with "Other Europe". (3) Comprises Eire and Northern Ireland. (4) Europe and Asia. (5) Beginning 1957, includes Taiwan. (6) Prior to 1951, included with "Other Asia". (7) Prior to 1951, Philippines included with "All other". (8) Prior to 1953, data for Vietnam not available. (9) Prior to 1951, included with "Other America". (10) Prior to 1951, included with "West Indies".

Poverty by Family Status, Sex, and Race

Source: U.S. Bureau of the Census
(In 1980, according to poverty level defined in table below. Thousands)

	1980		1979		1978		1977	
	No.	%*	No.	%*	No.	%*	No.	%*
Total poor	**29,272**	**13.0**	**26,072**	**11.7**	**24,497**	**11.4**	**24,720**	**11.6**
In families	22,601	11.5	19,964	10.2	19,062	10.0	19,505	10.2
Head	6,217	10.3	5,461	9.2	5,280	9.1	5,311	9.3
Related children	11,114	17.9	9,993	16.0	9,722	15.7	10,028	16.0
Other relatives	5,270	7.1	4,509	6.1	4,059	5.7	4,165	5.9
Unrelated individuals	6,227	22.9	5,743	21.9	5,435	22.1	5,216	22.6
In male-head families	**10,120**	**36.7**	**9,400**	**34.9**	**9,793**	**5.9**	**10,300**	**6.2**
Head	2,972	32.7	2,645	30.4	2,626	5.3	2,701	5.5
Related children	5,866	50.8	5,635	48.6	4,035	7.9	4,371	8.5
Other relatives	1,282	18.5	1,120	16.9	3,131	4.8	3,228	5.0
Unrelated male individuals	4,118	27.4	3,771	26.0	1,824	17.1	1,796	18.0
In female-head families	12,481	7.4	10,563	6.3	9,269	35.6	9,205	36.2
Head	3,245	6.3	2,816	5.5	2,654	31.4	2,610	31.7
Related children	5,248	10.4	4,358	8.5	5,687	50.6	5,658	50.3
Other relatives	3,988	5.9	3,389	5.1	928	14.6	938	15.8
Unrelated female individuals	2,109	17.4	1,972	16.9	3,611	26.0	3,419	26.1
Total white poor	**19,699**	**10.2**	**17,214**	**9.0**	**16,259**	**8.7**	**16,416**	**8.9**
In families	14,587	8.6	12,495	7.4	12,050	7.3	12,364	7.5
Head	4,195	8.0	3,581	6.9	3,523	6.9	3,540	7.0
Female	1,609	25.7	1,350	22.3	1,391	23.5	1,400	24.0
Related children	6,817	13.4	5,909	11.4	5,674	11.0	5,943	11.4
Other relatives	3,575	5.5	3,006	4.7	2,852	4.5	2,882	4.6
Unrelated individuals	4,760	20.4	4,452	19.7	4,209	19.8	4,051	20.4
Total black poor	**8,579**	**32.5**	**8,050**	**31.0**	**7,625**	**30.6**	**7,726**	**31.3**
In families	7,190	31.1	6,800	30.0	6,493	29.5	6,667	30.5
Head	1,826	28.9	1,722	27.8	1,622	27.5	1,637	28.2
Female	1,301	49.4	1,234	49.4	1,208	50.6	1,162	51.0
Related children	3,906	42.1	3,745	40.8	3,781	41.2	3,850	41.6
Other relatives	1,458	19.5	1,333	18.2	1,094	15.7	1,181	17.4
Unrelated individuals	1,314	41.0	1,168	37.3	1,132	38.6	1,059	37.0

*Percent of total population in that general category who fell below poverty level. For example, of all black female heads of households in 1978, 50.6% were poor.

Estimated Poverty Level, 1981, by Family Size and Sex of Head

		Non-Farm			Farm		
Numbers of family members	**Total**	**Total**	**Male**	**Female**	**Total**	**Male**	**Female**
1 member	$4,184	$4,190	$4,037	$4,379	$3,539	$3,392	$3,680
Under 65 yrs.	4,286	4,290	4,109	4,441	3,693	3,492	3,773
65 years and over	3,941	3,949	3,938	3,990	3,359	3,347	3,392
2 members	5,338	5,363	5,316	5,373	4,502	4,302	4,513
Head under 65 yrs.	5,518	5,537	5,415	5,568	4,714	4,497	4,721
Head 65 years and over	4,954	4,983	4,946	4,988	4,233	4,185	4,237
3 members	6,539	6,565	6,386	6,608	5,573	5,271	5,587
4 members	8,385	8,414	8,382	8,418	7,170	7,152	7,170
5 members	9,923	9,966	9,878	9,976	8,472	8,373	8,474
6 members	11,215	11,269	11,227	11,274	9,613	9,168	9,625
7 members	13,883	13,955	13,767	13,986	11,915	12,133	11,889

Poverty Level by Family Size 1980, 1981

	Estimated: 1981	Revised: 1980
1 persons	$ 4,620	$ 4,186
Under 65 years	4,730	4,284
65 years and over	4,360	3,950
2 persons	5,920	5,361
Householder under 65 years	6,110	5,537
Householder 65 years and over	5,500	4,982

	Estimated: 1981	Revised: 1980
3 persons	$ 7,250	$ 6,570
4 persons	9,290	8,415
5 persons	11,000	9,967
6 persons	12,440	11,272
7 persons	14,080	12,761
8 persons	15,670	14,199
9 persons or more	18,650	16,896

Income Distribution by Population Fifths

Families, 1980	Top income of each fifth				Average	Percent distribution of total income					
Race	**Lowest**	**Second**	**Third**	**Fourth**	**Top 5%**	**Lowest fifth**	**Second fifth**	**Third fifth**	**Fourth fifth**	**Highest fifth**	**Top 5%**
Total	10,286	17,390	24,630	34,534	54,060	5.1	11.6	17.5	24.3	41.6	15.3
White	11,310	18,442	25,481	35,400	55,200	5.6	11.9	17.6	24.0	40.9	15.1
Black and other	5,928	10,600	17,429	26,800	43,400	4.1	9.5	16.0	25.2	45.3	16.3
Black	5,556	9,901	16,000	24,877	39,125	4.2	9.6	16.1	25.4	44.8	15.5
Region											
Northeast	10,956	18,476	25,478	35,550	54,656	5.4	11.9	17.6	24.2	41.0	15.0
North Central	11,000	18,280	25,107	34,708	53,000	5.5	12.1	17.9	24.3	40.4	14.8
South	9,150	15,504	22,752	32,160	51,500	4.8	11.1	17.2	24.4	42.6	15.9
West	11,025	18,608	26,116	37,000	58,114	5.3	11.5	17.4	24.2	41.7	15.3

Aid to Families with Dependent Children

Source: Office of Research and Statistics, Social Security Administration

December, 1980	Number of recipients			Payments to recipients			% change from Dec., 1979	
State	No. of families	Total[1]	Children	Total amount	Average per family	Average per recipient	No. of recip.	Amount
Alabama	63,246	178,322	127,684	$6,967,928	$110.17	$39.07	-.4	.9
Alaska	6,606	15,931	10,882	2,590,514	392.15	162.61	5.5	31.3
Arizona	21,573	59,809	43,589	3,809,666	176.59	63.70	19.7	26.8
Arkansas	29,822	85,008	61,667	4,360,856	146.23	51.30	.4	3.1
California	511,486	1,498,216	996,054	220,451,580	431.00	147.14	10.1	27.8
Colorado	29,467	81,031	55,415	7,591,646	257.63	93.69	8.9	17.8
Connecticut	49,407	139,685	96,240	18,308,524	370.57	131.07	2.9	14.7
Delaware	12,404	34,243	23,555	2,817,520	227.15	82.28	5.1	5.9
Dist. of Columbia	30,278	81,985	56,556	7,661,257	253.03	93.45	-5.1	-4.4
Florida	103,315	279,392	199,015	18,229,236	176.44	65.25	12.8	16.0
Georgia	89,912	233,730	168,813	12,591,009	140.04	53.87	8.5	23.4
Guam	1,492	5,311	3,877	316,333	212.02	59.56	12.4	15.6
Hawaii	20,046	61,342	40,802	7,731,955	385.71	126.05	2.2	3.7
Idaho	7,503	20,326	13,845	2,064,949	275.22	101.59	-.9	3.0
Illinois	222,937	691,434	482,773	62,903,873	282.16	90.98	4.6	8.4
Indiana	60,229	170,239	119,431	12,351,154	205.07	72.55	11.8	23.5
Iowa	40,476	111,287	73,907	12,553,542	310.15	112.80	13.6	15.3
Kansas	27,720	71,956	50,828	7,817,479	282.02	108.64	11.3	19.3
Kentucky	67,159	175,071	122,437	12,478,662	185.81	71.28	6.7	22.5
Louisiana	72,163	218,966	160,212	11,254,465	155.96	51.40	4.1	19.1
Maine	21,466	57,700	39,504	4,954,190	230.79	85.86	-5.1	-.9
Maryland	80,823	220,316	148,989	19,304,624	238.85	87.62	5.0	17.5
Massachusetts	125,232	347,830	226,570	43,793,572	349.70	125.91	-1.2	7.2
Michigan	246,648	752,578	494,459	96,243,119	390.20	127.88	16.4	21.3
Minnesota	53,856	145,634	96,383	18,582,462	345.04	127.60	11.9	20.0
Mississippi	59,814	176,253	129,704	5,257,257	87.89	29.83	2.8	5.8
Missouri	73,506	215,682	144,865	16,795,310	228.49	77.87	12.9	24.1
Montana	7,136	19,883	13,621	1,646,790	230.77	82.82	8.7	12.0
Nebraska	13,573	37,541	25,900	3,890,757	286.65	103.64	10.6	24.8
Nevada	5,114	13,827	9,524	1,096,034	214.32	79.27	23.9	35.7
New Hampshire	8,647	23,648	15,636	2,377,068	274.90	100.52	9.7	17.2
New Jersey	152,383	469,010	322,034	49,908,100	327.52	106.41	2.8	13.1
New Mexico	19,550	56,157	38,657	3,705,145	189.52	65.98	7.8	21.9
New York	367,628	1,109,601	762,672	136,745,976	371.97	123.24	1.3	1.9
North Carolina	80,074	201,828	142,638	13,014,235	162.53	64.48	4.3	5.5
North Dakota	4,859	13,111	9,045	1,413,489	290.90	107.81	3.2	9.9
Ohio	200,243	572,347	380,365	50,348,940	251.44	87.97	16.9	16.9
Oklahoma	31,543	91,984	66,752	7,880,651	249.84	85.67	5.5	6.4
Oregon	35,440	93,993	60,731	9,315,930	262.86	99.11	-4.3	-23.5
Pennsylvania	218,713	637,387	435,408	64,712,837	295.88	101.53	2.6	9.1
Puerto Rico	46,245	169,697	118,368	2,812,545	60.82	16.57	-2.9	14.9
Rhode Island	18,772	53,950	36,563	7,613,825	405.59	141.13	7.3	8.7
South Carolina	57,643	156,080	110,573	6,685,505	115.98	42.83	4.5	21.8
South Dakota	6,946	18,753	13,120	1,555,186	223.90	82.93	-7.1	-1.8
Tennessee	65,958	173,854	122,637	7,448,916	112.93	42.85	10.2	10.7
Texas	106,104	320,002	232,384	11,490,205	108.29	35.91	4.5	4.6
Utah	13,954	43,710	27,335	4,504,653	322.82	103.06	25.9	33.8
Vermont	8,129	24,251	15,379	2,839,074	349.25	117.07	14.7	21.2
Virgin Islands	1,165	3,441	2,721	228,534	196.17	66.41	13.3	57.6
Virginia	65,272	175,927	121,821	14,487,213	221.95	82.35	7.8	19.1
Washington	61,639	173,339	108,234	23,434,682	380.19	135.20	20.9	27.2
West Virginia	28,026	79,971	60,820	4,970,373	177.35	62.15	3.8	5.6
Wisconsin	85,129	231,979	154,465	32,026,663	376.21	138.06	15.2	26.7
Wyoming	2,737	7,008	4,996	720,012	263.07	102.74	6.5	8.3
Total	**3,841,208**	**11,101,556**	**7,600,455**	**$1,106,656,020**	**$288.10**	**$99.68**	**7.0**	**14.8**

(e) Estimated. (1) Includes as recipients the children and one or both parents or one caretaker relative other than a parent in families in which the requirements of such adults were concerned in determining the amount of assistance. (2) Incomplete. Data for foster care not reported by Puerto Rico and the Virgin Islands.

Welfare Recipients and Payments, 1955-1980

Category		1955, Dec.	1965, Dec.	1970, Dec.	1975, Dec. (b)	1978, Dec.	1979, Dec.	1980, Dec.
Old age:	Recipients	2,538,000	2,087,000	2,082,000	2,333,685	1,967,900	1,871,716	1,807,776
	Total amt.	$127,003,000	$131,674,000	$161,642,000	$217,002,000	$197,630,000	$229,613,000	$221,303,000
	Avg. amt.	$50.05	$63.10	$77.65	$92.99	$100.43	$122.67	$128.20
	(a)Avg. real $	$62.41	$66.75	$66.78	$57.65	$49.47	$53.50	$49.61
AFDC:	Recipients	2,192,000	4,396,000	9,659,000	11,389,000	10,325,000	10,378,679	11,101,556
	Total amt.	$51,472,000	$144,355,000	$485,877,000	$824,648,000	$891,399,000	$963,929,242	$1,106,656,000
	Avg. amt.	$23.50	$32.85	$50.30	$72.40	$86.33	$92.88	$99.68
	(a)Avg. real $	$29.30	$34.76	$43.26	$44.89	$46.49	$45.58	$38.58
Blind:	Recipients	104,000	85,100	81,000	75,315	77,135	77,250	78,401
	Total amt.	$5,803,000	$6,922,000	$8,446,000	$11,220,000	$12,681,000	$16,398,000	$16,381,000
	Avg. amt.	$55.55	$81.35	$104.35	$148.97	$164.40	$212.27	$213.23
	(a)Avg. real $	$69.27	$86.07	$89.74	$92.36	$88.34	$92.25	$82.52
Disabled:	Recipients	241,000	557,000	935,000	1,950,625	2,171,890	2,200,609	2,255,840
	Total amt.	$11,750,000	$37,035,000	$91,325,000	$279,073,000	$336,256,000	$399,879,000	$444,322,000
	Avg. amt.	$48.75	$66.50	$97.65	$143.07	$154.82	$181.71	$197.90
	(a)Avg. real $	$60.79	$70.36	$83.98	$88.70	$83.19	$79.35	$76.59

(a) Dollar amounts adjusted to represent actual purchasing power in terms of average value of dollar during 1967. (b) Administration of the public assistance programs of Old-age Assistance, Aid to the Blind, and Aid to the Disabled was transferred to the Social Security Administration by Public Law 92-603 effective 1/1/74.

U.S. Places of 5,000 or More Population—With ZIP and Area Codes

Source: U.S. Bureau of the Census; U.S. Postal Service; N.Y. Telephone Co.

The listings below show the official urban population of the United States. "Urban population" is defined as all persons living in (a) places of 5,000 inhabitants or more, incorporated as cities, villages, boroughs (except Alaska), and towns (except in New England, New York, New Jersey, Pennsylvania and Wisconsin), but excluding those persons living in the rural portions of extended cities; (b) unincorporated places of 5,000 inhabitants or more; and (c) other territory, incorporated or unincorporated, included in urbanized areas.

The non-urban portion of an extended city contains one or more areas, each at least 5 square miles in extent and with a population density of less than 100 persons per square mile. The area or areas constitute at least 25 percent of the legal city's land area of a total of 25 square miles or more.

In New England, New York, New Jersey, Pennsylvania, and Wisconsin, minor civil divisions called "towns" often include rural areas and one or more urban areas. Only the urban areas of these "towns" are included here, except in the case of New England where entire town populations, which may include some rural population, are shown; these towns are indicated by italics. Boroughs in Alaska may contain one or more urban areas which are included here. Population in Hawaii is counted by county subdivisions.

(u) means place is unincorporated.

The ZIP Code of each place appears before the name of that place, if it is obtainable. Telephone Area Code appears in parentheses after the name of the state or, if a state has more than one number, after the name of the place.

CAUTION—Where an asterisk (*) appears before the ZIP Code, ask your local postmaster for the correct ZIP Code for a specific address within the place listed.

Alabama (205)

ZIP code	Place	1980	1970
35007	Alabaster	7,079	2,642
35950	Albertville	12,039	9,963
35010	Alexander City	13,807	12,358
36420	Andalusia	10,415	10,092
36201	Anniston	29,523	31,533
35016	Arab	5,967	4,399
35611	Athens	14,558	14,360
36502	Atmore	8,789	8,293
35954	Attalla	7,737	7,510
36830	Auburn	28,471	22,767
36507	Bay Minette	7,455	6,727
35020	Bessemer	31,729	33,428
*35203	Birmingham	284,413	300,910
35957	Boaz	7,151	5,635
36426	Brewton	6,680	6,747
35020	Brighton	5,308	2,277
35215	Center Point(u)	23,317	15,675
36611	Chickasaw	7,402	8,447
35044	Childersburg	5,084	4,831
35045	Clanton	5,832	5,868
35055	Cullman	13,084	12,601
35601	Decatur	42,002	38,044
36732	Demopolis	7,678	7,651
36301	Dothan	48,750	36,733
36330	Enterprise	18,033	15,591
36027	Eufaula	12,097	9,102
35064	Fairfield	13,040	14,369
36532	Fairhope	7,286	5,720
35555	Fayette	5,287	4,568
35630	Florence	37,029	34,031
35214	Forestdale(u)	10,814	6,091
35967	Fort Payne	11,485	8,435
36360	Fort Rucker(u)	8,932	14,242
35068	Fultondale	6,217	5,163
*35901	Gadsden	47,565	53,928
35071	Gardendale	7,928	6,537
36037	Greenville	7,807	8,033
35976	Guntersville	7,041	6,491
35565	Haleyville	5,306	4,190
35640	Hartselle	8,858	7,355
35209	Homewood	21,271	21,245
35226	Hoover	15,064	688
35020	Hueytown	13,309	7,095
*35804	Huntsville	142,513	139,282
35210	Irondale	6,521	3,166
36545	Jackson	6,073	5,957
36265	Jacksonville	9,735	7,715
35501	Jasper	11,894	10,798
36863	Lanett	6,897	6,908
35094	Leeds	8,638	6,991
35228	Midfield	6,536	6,621
*36601	Mobile	200,452	190,026
36460	Monroeville	5,674	4,846
*36104	Montgomery	178,157	133,386
35223	Mountain Brook	17,400	19,474
35660	Muscle Shoals	8,911	6,907
35476	Northport	14,291	9,435
36801	Opelika	21,896	19,027
36467	Opp	7,204	6,493
36203	Oxford	8,939	4,361
36360	Ozark	13,188	13,555
35124	Pelham	6,759	931
35125	Pell City	6,616	5,602
36867	Phenix City	26,928	25,281
36272	Piedmont	5,544	5,063
35127	Pleasant Grove	7,102	5,090
36067	Prattville	18,647	13,116
36610	Prichard	39,541	41,578
35901	Rainbow City	6,299	3,099
35809	Redstone Arsenal(u)	5,728	....
36274	Roanoke	5,896	5,251
35653	Russellville	8,195	7,814
36201	Saks(u)	11,118	....
36571	Saraland	9,833	7,840
35768	Scottsboro	14,758	9,324
36701	Selma	26,684	27,379
36701	Selmont-West Selmont(u)	5,255	2,270
35660	Sheffield	11,903	13,115
35150	Sylacauga	12,708	12,255
35160	Talladega	19,128	17,662
35217	Tarrant City	8,148	6,835
36582	Theodore(u)	6,392	....
36619	Tillman's Corner(u)	15,941	....
36081	Troy	12,587	11,482
35401	Tuscaloosa	75,143	65,773
35674	Tuscumbia	9,137	8,828
36083	Tuskegee	12,716	11,028
35216	Vestavia Hills	15,733	12,250
36201	West End-Cobb(u)	5,189	5,515

Alaska (907)

ZIP code	Place	1980	1970
*99502	Anchorage	173,017	48,081
99702	Eielson AFB(u)	5,232	6,149
99701	Fairbanks	22,645	14,771
99801	Juneau	19,528	6,050
99611	Kenai Peninsula borough	25,282	16,586
99901	Ketchikan	7,198	6,994
99835	Sitka	7,803	3,370

Arizona (602)

ZIP code	Place	1980	1970
85321	Ajo(u)	5,189	5,881
85220	Apache Junction	9,935	2,443
85323	Avondale	8,134	6,626
85603	Bisbee	7,154	8,328
86430	Bullhead City-Riviera(u)	10,364	....
85222	Casa Grande	14,971	10,536
85224	Chandler	29,673	13,763
85228	Coolidge	6,851	5,314
85707	Davis-Monthan AFB(u)	6,279	....
85607	Douglas	13,058	12,462
85205	Dreamland-VeldaRose(u)	5,969	....
85231	Eloy	6,240	5,381
86001	Flagstaff	34,641	26,117
85613	Fort Huachuca(u)	NA	6,659
85234	Gilbert	5,717	1,971
*85301	Glendale	96,988	36,228
85501	Globe	6,708	7,333
85614	Green Valley(u)	7,999	....
86025	Holbrook	5,785	4,759
86401	Kingman	9,257	7,312
86403	Lake Havasu City	15,737	4,111
85301	Luke(u)	NA	5,047
*85201	Mesa	152,453	63,049
85621	Nogales	15,683	8,946
86040	Page(u)	NA	1,439
85253	Paradise Valley	10,832	6,637
85345	Peoria	12,251	4,792
*85026	Phoenix	764,911	584,303
86301	Prescott	20,055	13,631
85546	Safford	7,010	5,493

ZIP code	Place	1980	1970
85631	San Manuel(u)	5,443	....
*85251	Scottsdale	88,364	67,823
85635	Sierra Vista	25,968	6,689
85350	Somerton	5,761	2,225
85713	South Tucson	6,554	6,220
85351	Sun City(u)	40,505	13,670
*85282	Tempe	106,743	63,550
86045	Tuba City(u)	5,045	....
*85726	Tucson	330,537	262,933
85364	West Yuma(u)	NA	5,552
86047	Winslow	7,921	8,066
85364	Yuma	42,433	29,007

Arkansas (501)

ZIP code	Place	1980	1970
71923	Arkadelphia	10,005	9,841
72501	Batesville	8,263	7,209
72015	Benton	17,437	16,499
72712	Bentonville	8,756	5,508
72315	Blytheville	24,314	24,752
71701	Camden	15,356	15,147
72830	Clarksville	5,237	4,616
72032	Conway	20,375	15,510
71635	Crossett	6,706	6,191
71639	Dumas	6,091	4,600
71730	El Dorado	26,685	25,283
72701	Fayetteville	36,604	30,729
71742	Fordyce	5,175	4,837
72335	Forrest City	13,803	12,521
72901	Fort Smith	71,384	62,802
72601	Harrison	9,567	7,239
72342	Helena	9,598	10,415
71801	Hope	10,290	8,830
71901	Hot Springs	35,166	35,631
72076	Jacksonville	27,589	19,832
72401	Jonesboro	31,530	27,050
*72201	Little Rock	158,461	132,483
71753	Magnolia	11,909	11,303
72104	Malvern	10,163	8,739
72360	Marianna	6,220	6,196
71654	McGehee	5,671	4,683
71953	Mena	5,154	4,530
71655	Monticello	8,259	5,085
72110	Morrilton	7,355	6,814
72653	Mountain Home	7,447	3,936
72112	Newport	8,339	7,725
*72114	North Little Rock	64,419	60,040
72370	Osceola	8,881	7,892
72450	Paragould	15,214	10,639
71601	Pine Bluff	56,576	57,389
72455	Pocahontas	5,995	4,544
72756	Rogers	17,429	11,050
72801	Russellville	14,000	11,750
72143	Searcy	13,612	9,040
72116	Sherwood	10,586	2,754
72761	Siloam Springs	7,940	6,009
72764	Springdale	23,458	16,783
72160	Stuttgart	10,941	10,477
75501	Texarkana	21,459	21,682
72472	Trumann	6,044	6,023
72956	Van Buren	12,020	8,373
71671	Warren	7,646	6,433
72390	West Helena	11,367	11,007
72301	West Memphis	28,138	26,070
72396	Wynne	7,805	6,696

California

ZIP code	Place	Area code	1980	1970
94501	Alameda	(415)	63,852	70,968
94507	Alamo(u)	(415)	8,505	14,059
94706	Albany	(415)	15,130	15,561
*91802	Alhambra	(213)	64,615	62,125
90249	Alondra Park(u)	(213)	12,096	12,193
92001	Alpine(u)	(714)	5,368	1,570
91001	Altadena(u)	(213)	40,510	42,415
95116	Alum Rock(u)	(408)	17,471	18,355
94590	American Canyon(u)	(707)	5,712	....
*92803	Anaheim	(714)	221,847	166,408
96007	Anderson	(916)	7,381	5,492
94509	Antioch	(415)	43,559	28,060
92307	Apple Valley(u)	(714)	14,305	6,702
95003	Aptos(u)	(408)	7,039	8,704
91006	Arcadia	(213)	45,994	45,138
95521	Arcata	(707)	12,338	8,985
95825	Arden-Arcade(u)	(916)	87,570	82,492
93420	Arroyo Grande	(805)	11,290	7,454
90701	Artesia	(213)	14,301	14,757
93203	Arvin	(805)	6,863	5,199
94577	Ashland(u)	(415)	13,893	14,810
93422	Atascadero	(805)	15,930	10,290
94025	Atherton	(415)	7,797	8,085
95301	Atwater	(209)	17,530	11,640
95603	Auburn	(916)	7,540	6,570
92505	August(u)	(209)	5,445	6,293
91746	Avocado Heights(u)	(213)	11,721	9,810
91702	Azusa	(213)	29,380	25,217
*93302	Bakersfield	(805)	105,611	69,515
91706	Baldwin Park	(213)	50,554	47,285
92220	Banning	(714)	14,020	12,034
92311	Barstow	(714)	17,690	17,442
93402	Baywood-Los Osos(u)	(805)	10,933	3,487
95903	Beale AFB East(u)	(916)	6,329	7,029
92223	Beaumont	(714)	6,818	5,484
90201	Bell	(213)	25,450	21,836
90706	Bellflower	(213)	53,441	52,334
90201	Bell Gardens	(213)	34,117	29,308
94002	Belmont	(415)	24,505	23,538
94510	Benicia	(707)	15,376	7,349
95005	Ben Lomond(u)	(408)	7,238	2,793
*94704	Berkeley	(415)	103,328	114,091
*90213	Beverly Hills	(213)	32,367	33,416
92314	Big Bear(u)	(714)	11,151	5,268
92316	Bloomington(u)	(714)	6,674	11,957
92225	Blythe	(714)	6,805	7,047
92002	Bonita(u)	(714)	6,257	....
95006	Boulder Creek(u)	(408)	5,662	1,806
92227	Brawley	(714)	14,946	13,746
92621	Brea	(714)	27,913	18,447
95605	Broderick-Bryte(u)	(916)	10,194	12,782
*90620	Buena Park	(714)	64,165	63,646
*91505	Burbank	(213)	84,625	88,871
94010	Burlingame	(415)	26,173	27,320
92231	Calexico	(714)	14,412	10,625
93725	Calwa(u)	(209)	6,640	5,191
93010	Camarillo	(805)	37,732	19,219
93010	Camarillo Heights(u)	(805)	6,341	5,892
95682	Cameron Park(u)	(916)	5,607	....
95008	Campbell	(408)	27,067	23,797
91351	Canyon Country(u)	(213)	15,728	....
92055	Camp Pendleton South(u)	(714)	7,952	13,692
92624	Capistrano Beach(u)	(714)	6,168	4,149
95010	Capitola	(408)	9,095	5,080
92007	Cardiff-by-the-Sea(u)	(714)	10,054	5,724
92008	Carlsbad	(714)	35,490	14,944
95608	Carmichael(u)	(916)	43,108	37,625
93013	Carpinteria	(805)	10,835	6,982
90744	Carson	(213)	81,221	71,150
92077	Casa De Oro-Mt. Helix(u)	(714)	19,651	....
92010	Castle Park-Otay(u)	(714)	21,049	15,445
94546	Castro Valley(u)	(415)	44,011	44,760
95307	Ceres	(209)	13,281	6,029
90701	Cerritos	(213)	52,756	15,856
91724	Charter Oak(u)	(213)	6,840	....
94541	Cherryland(u)	(415)	9,425	9,969
92223	Cherry Valley(u)	(714)	5,012	3,165
95926	Chico	(916)	26,601	19,580
95926	Chico North(u)	(916)	11,739	6,656
95926	Chico West(u)	(916)	6,378	4,787
91710	Chino	(714)	40,165	20,411
93610	Chowchilla	(209)	5,122	4,349
*92010	Chula Vista	(714)	83,927	67,901
95610	Citrus(u)	(916)	12,450	....
95610	Citrus Heights(u)	(916)	85,911	21,760
91711	Claremont	(714)	30,950	24,776
93612	Clovis	(209)	33,021	13,856
92236	Coachella	(714)	9,129	8,353
93210	Coalinga	(209)	6,593	6,161
92324	Colton	(714)	27,419	20,016
90022	Commerce	(213)	10,509	10,635
*90220	Compton	(213)	81,286	78,547
*94520	Concord	(415)	103,251	85,164
93212	Corcoran	(209)	6,454	5,249
91720	Corona	(714)	37,791	27,519
92118	Coronado	(714)	16,859	20,020
94925	Corte Madera	(415)	8,074	8,464
*92626	Costa Mesa	(714)	82,291	72,660
	Country Club(u)	(209)	9,585	....
*91722	Covina	(213)	33,751	30,395
92325	Crestline(u)	(714)	6,715	....
90201	Cudahy	(213)	17,984	16,998
90230	Culver City	(213)	38,139	34,451
95014	Cupertino	(408)	25,770	17,895
90630	Cypress	(714)	40,391	31,569
*94017	Daly City	(415)	78,519	66,922
94526	Danville(u)	(415)	26,446	....
92629	Dana Point(u)	(714)	10,602	4,745
95616	Davis	(916)	36,640	23,488
90250	Del Aire(u)	(213)	8,487	11,930
93215	Delano	(805)	16,491	14,559
92014	Del Mar	(714)	5,017	3,956
92240	Desert Hot Springs	(714)	5,941	2,738
91765	Diamond Bar(u)	(714)	28,045	10,576
93618	Dinuba	(209)	9,907	7,917
95620	Dixon	(916)	7,541	4,432
*90241	Downey	(213)	82,602	88,573
91010	Duarte	(213)	16,766	14,981
94566	Dublin(u)	(415)	13,496	13,641
90220	East Compton(u)	(213)	6,435	5,853
92343	East Hemet(u)	(714)	14,712	8,598
90638	East La Mirada(u)	(213)	9,688	12,339
90022	East Los Angeles(u)	(213)	110,017	104,881
94303	East Palo Alto(u)	(415)	18,191	18,727
93257	East Porterville(u)	(209)	5,218	4,042
92508	Edgemont(u)	(714)	5,215	....
93523	Edwards AFB(u)	(805)	8,554	10,331
*92020	El Cajon	(714)	73,892	52,273
92243	El Centro	(714)	23,996	19,272
94530	El Cerrito	(415)	22,731	25,190
95624	Elk Grove(u)	(916)	10,959	3,721

ZIP code	Place		1980	1970
*91734	El Monte	(213)	79,494	69,892
93446	El Paso de Robles	(213)	9,163	7,168
93030	El Rio(u)	(805)	5,674	6,173
90245	El Segundo	(213)	13,752	15,620
94803	El Sobrante(u)	(415)	10,535	....
92630	El Toro(u)	(714)	38,153	8,654
92709	El Toro Station(u)	(714)	7,632	6,970
92024	Encinitas(u)	(714)	10,796	5,375
*92025	Escondido	(714)	62,480	36,792
95501	Eureka	(707)	24,153	24,337
93221	Exeter	(209)	5,619	4,475
94930	Fairfax	(415)	7,391	7,661
94533	Fairfield	(707)	58,099	44,146
95628	Fair Oaks(u)	(916)	20,235	11,256
92028	Fallbrook(u)	(714)	14,041	6,945
93223	Farmersville	(209)	5,544	3,456
93015	Fillmore	(805)	9,602	6,285
90001	Florence-Graham(u)	(213)	48,662	42,900
95828	Florin(u)	(916)	16,523	9,646
95630	Folsom	(916)	11,003	5,810
92335	Fontana	(714)	37,109	20,673
95841	Foothill Farms(u)	(916)	13,700	....
95437	Fort Bragg	(707)	5,019	4,455
95540	Fortuna	(707)	7,591	4,203
94404	Foster City	(415)	23,287	9,522
92708	Fountain Valley	(714)	55,080	31,886
95019	Freedom(u)	(408)	6,416	5,563
*94536	Fremont	(415)	131,945	100,869
*93706	Fresno	(209)	218,202	165,655
*92631	Fullerton	(714)	102,034	85,987
95632	Galt	(209)	5,514	3,200
*90247	Gardena	(213)	45,165	41,021
95205	Garden Acres(u)	(213)	7,361	7,870
*92640	Garden Grove	(714)	123,351	121,155
92392	George AFB(u)	(714)	7,061	7,404
95020	Gilroy	(408)	21,641	12,684
92509	Glen Avon(u)	(714)	8,444	5,759
*91209	Glendale	(213)	139,060	132,664
91740	Glendora	(213)	38,654	32,143
92324	Grand Terrace	(714)	8,498	5,901
95945	Grass Valley	(916)	6,697	5,149
93308	Greenacres(u)	(805)	5,381	2,116
93433	Grover City	(805)	8,827	5,939
91745	Hacienda Heights	(213)	49,422	35,969
94019	Half Moon Bay	(415)	7,282	4,023
93230	Hanford	(209)	20,958	15,179
90716	Hawaiian Gardens	(213)	10,548	9,052
90250	Hawthorne	(213)	56,447	53,304
*94544	Hayward	(415)	94,167	93,058
95448	Healdsburg	(707)	7,217	5,438
92343	Hemet	(714)	23,211	12,252
94547	Hercules	(415)	5,963	252
90254	Hermosa Beach	(213)	18,070	17,412
92345	Hesperia(u)	(714)	13,540	4,592
92346	Highland(u)	(714)	10,908	12,669
94010	Hillsborough	(415)	10,451	8,753
95023	Hollister	(408)	11,488	7,663
91720	Home Gardens(u)	(714)	5,783	5,116
*92647	Huntington Beach	(714)	170,505	115,960
90255	Huntington Park	(213)	46,223	33,744
92032	Imperial Beach	(714)	22,689	20,244
92201	Indio	(714)	21,611	14,459
*90306	Inglewood	(213)	94,245	89,985
*92711	Irvine	(714)	62,134	7,381
94707	Kensington(u)	(415)	5,342	5,823
93930	King City	(408)	5,495	3,717
93631	Kingsburg	(209)	5,115	3,843
91011	La Canada-Flintridge	(213)	20,153	20,714
91214	La Crescenta-Montrose(u)	(213)	16,531	19,620
90045	Ladera Heights(u)	(213)	6,647	6,079
94549	Lafayette	(415)	20,879	20,484
*92651	Laguna Beach	(714)	17,860	14,550
92653	Laguna Hills(u)	(714)	33,600	13,676
92677	Laguna Niguel(u)	(714)	12,237	4,644
90631	La Habra	(213)	45,232	41,350
92352	Lake Arrowhead(u)	(714)	6,272	2,682
92040	Lakeside(u)	(714)	23,921	11,991
92330	Lake Elsinore	(714)	5,982	3,530
*90714	Lakewood	(213)	74,654	83,025
92041	La Mesa	(714)	50,342	39,178
90638	La Mirada	(714)	40,986	30,808
93241	Lamont(u)	(805)	9,616	7,007
93534	Lancaster	(805)	48,027	32,728
90624	La Palma	(714)	15,663	9,687
91747	La Puente	(213)	30,882	31,092
	La Riviera(u)	(916)	10,906	....
94939	Larkspur	(415)	11,064	10,487
91750	La Verne	(714)	23,508	12,965
90260	Lawndale	(213)	23,460	24,825
92045	Lemon Grove	(209)	20,780	19,794
93245	Lemoore	(209)	8,832	4,219
93245	Lemoore Station(u)	(209)	5,888	9,210
90304	Lennox(u)	(213)	18,445	16,121
92024	Leucadia(u)	(714)	9,478	....
95207	Lincoln Village(u)	(916)	6,476	6,112
95901	Linda(u)	(916)	10,225	7,112
93247	Lindsay	(209)	6,924	5,206
95062	Live Oak(u) (Santa Cruz)	(408)	11,482	6,443
94550	Livermore	(415)	48,349	37,703
95334	Livingston	(209)	5,326	2,588
95240	Lodi	(209)	35,221	28,691
92354	Loma Linda	(714)	10,694	7,651
90717	Lomita	(213)	17,191	19,784
93436	Lompoc	(805)	26,267	25,284
*90801	Long Beach	(213)	361,334	358,879
90720	Los Alamitos	(213)	11,529	11,346
94022	Los Altos	(415)	25,769	25,062
94022	Los Altos Hills	(415)	7,421	6,871
*90052	Los Angeles	(213)	2,966,763	2,811,801
93635	Los Banos	(209)	10,341	9,188
95030	Los Gatos	(408)	26,593	22,613
94903	Lucas Valley-Marinwood(u)	(415)	6,409	....
90262	Lynwood	(213)	48,548	43,354
93637	Madera	(209)	21,732	16,044
90266	Manhattan Beach	(213)	31,542	35,352
95336	Manteca	(209)	24,925	13,845
93933	Marina	(408)	20,647	8,343
90291	Marina Del Rey(u)	(213)	8,065	....
94553	Martinez	(415)	22,582	16,506
95901	Marysville	(916)	9,898	9,353
95655	Mather AFB(u)	(916)	5,245	7,027
91016	Mayflower Village(u)	(213)	5,017	....
90270	Maywood	(213)	21,810	16,996
93250	Mc Farland	(805)	5,151	4,177
95521	McKinleyville(u)	(707)	7,772	....
93023	Meiners Oaks-Mira Monte(u)	(805)	9,512	7,025
93640	Mendota	(209)	5,038	2,705
94025	Menlo Park	(415)	25,673	26,826
95340	Merced	(209)	36,499	22,670
94030	Millbrae	(415)	20,058	20,920
94941	Mill Valley	(415)	12,967	12,942
95035	Milpitas	(408)	37,820	26,561
91752	Mira Loma(u)	(714)	8,707	8,482
92675	Mission Viejo(u)	(714)	48,384	11,933
*95350	Modesto	(209)	106,105	61,712
91016	Monrovia	(213)	30,531	30,562
91763	Montclair	(714)	22,628	22,546
90640	Montebello	(213)	52,929	42,807
93940	Monterey	(408)	27,558	26,302
91754	Monterey Park	(213)	54,338	49,166
94556	Moraga	(415)	15,014	14,205
95037	Morgan Hill	(408)	17,060	5,579
93442	Morro Bay	(805)	9,064	7,109
*94042	Mountain View	(415)	58,655	54,132
92405	Muscoy(u)	(714)	6,188	7,091
94558	Napa	(707)	50,879	36,103
92050	National City	(714)	48,772	43,184
94560	Newark	(415)	32,126	27,153
91321	Newhall(u)	(805)	12,029	9,651
*92660	Newport Beach	(714)	63,475	49,582
93444	Nipomo(u)	(805)	5,247	3,642
91760	Norco	(714)	21,126	14,511
95603	North Auburn(u)	(916)	7,619	....
94025	North Fair Oaks(u)	(415)	10,294	9,740
95660	North Highlands(u)	(916)	37,825	31,854
90650	Norwalk	(213)	85,232	90,164
94947	Novato	(415)	43,916	31,006
95361	Oakdale	(209)	8,474	6,594
*94615	Oakland	(415)	339,288	361,561
92054	Oceanside	(714)	76,698	40,494
93308	Oildale(u)	(805)	23,382	20,879
93023	Ojai	(805)	6,816	5,591
95961	Olivehurst(u)	(916)	8,929	8,100
*91761	Ontario	(714)	88,820	64,118
95060	Opal Cliffs(u)	(408)	5,041	5,425
*92667	Orange	(714)	91,788	77,365
95662	Orangevale(u)	(916)	20,585	16,493
94563	Orinda (u)	(415)	16,825	6,790
95965	Oroville	(916)	8,683	7,536
93030	Oxnard	(805)	108,195	71,225
94044	Pacifica	(415)	36,866	36,020
93950	Pacific Grove	(408)	15,755	13,505
93550	Palmdale	(805)	12,277	8,511
92260	Palm Desert	(714)	11,801	6,171
92262	Palm Springs	(714)	32,271	20,936
94302	Palo Alto	(415)	55,225	56,040
90274	Palos Verdes Estates	(213)	14,376	13,631
95969	Paradise	(916)	22,571	14,539
90723	Paramount	(213)	36,407	34,734
95823	Parkway-Sacramento So.(u)	(916)	26,815	28,574
*91109	Pasadena	(213)	119,374	112,951
92370	Perris	(714)	6,740	4,228
94952	Petaluma	(707)	33,834	24,870
90660	Pico Rivera	(213)	53,459	54,170
94611	Piedmont	(415)	10,498	10,917
94564	Pinole	(415)	14,253	13,266
93449	Pismo Beach	(805)	5,364	4,043
94565	Pittsburg	(415)	33,034	21,423
92670	Placentia	(714)	35,041	21,948
95667	Placerville	(916)	6,739	5,416
94523	Pleasant Hill	(415)	25,124	24,610
94566	Pleasanton	(415)	35,160	18,328
91766	Pomona	(714)	92,742	87,384
93257	Porterville	(209)	19,707	12,602
93041	Port Hueneme	(805)	17,803	14,295
92064	Poway(u)	(714)	32,263	9,422
93534	Quartz Hill(u)	(213)	7,421	4,935
92065	Ramona(u)	(714)	8,173	3,554
95670	Rancho Cordova(u)	(916)	42,881	30,451
91730	Rancho Cucamonga	(714)	55,250	19,484

ZIP code	Place		1980	1970
92270	Rancho Mirage	(714)	6,281	2,767
90274	Rancho Palos Verdes	(213)	35,227	33,285
96080	Red Bluff	(916)	9,490	7,676
96001	Redding	(916)	41,995	16,659
92373	Redlands	(714)	43,619	36,355
*90277	Redondo Beach	(213)	57,102	57,451
*94064	Redwood City	(415)	54,965	55,686
93654	Reedley	(209)	11,071	8,131
92376	Rialto	(714)	35,615	28,370
*94802	Richmond	(415)	74,676	79,043
93555	Ridgecrest	(714)	15,929	7,629
95003	Rio Del Mar(u)	(408)	7,067	....
95673	Rio Linda(u)	(916)	7,359	7,524
95367	Riverbank	(209)	5,695	3,949
*92502	Riverside	(714)	170,876	140,089
95677	Rocklin	(916)	7,344	3,039
94572	Rodeo(u)	(415)	8,286	5,356
94928	Rohnert Park	(707)	22,965	6,133
90274	Rolling Hills Estates	(213)	9,412	6,735
95401	Roseland(u)	(707)	7,915	5,105
91770	Rosemead	(213)	42,604	40,972
95826	Rosemont(u)	(916)	18,888	....
95678	Roseville	(916)	24,347	18,221
90720	Rossmoor(u)	(213)	10,457	12,922
91745	Rowland Heights(u)	(213)	28,252	16,881
92509	Rubidoux(u)	(714)	16,763	13,969
*95813	Sacramento	(916)	275,741	257,105
93901	Salinas	(408)	80,479	58,896
94960	San Anselmo	(415)	11,927	13,031
*92403	San Bernardino	(714)	118,057	106,869
94066	San Bruno	(415)	35,417	36,254
...	San Buenaventura (*see Ventura*)	(805)		
94070	San Carlos	(415)	24,710	26,053
92672	San Clemente	(714)	27,325	17,063
*92109	San Diego	(714)	875,504	697,471
91773	San Dimas	(714)	24,014	15,692
*91340	San Fernando	(213)	17,731	16,571
*94101	San Francisco	(415)	678,974	715,674
91776	San Gabriel	(213)	30,072	29,336
93657	Sanger	(209)	12,558	10,088
92383	San Jacinto	(714)	7,098	4,385
95101	San Jose	(408)	636,550	459,913
92375	San Juan Capistrano	(714)	18,959	3,781
94577	San Leandro	(415)	63,952	68,698
94580	San Lorenzo(u)	(415)	20,545	24,633
93401	San Luis Obispo	(805)	34,252	28,036
92069	San Marcos	(714)	17,479	3,896
91108	San Marino	(213)	13,307	14,177
*94402	San Mateo	(415)	77,561	78,991
94806	San Pablo	(415)	19,750	21,461
*94901	San Rafael	(415)	44,700	38,977
94583	San Ramon(u)	(415)	22,356	4,084
*92711	Santa Ana	(714)	203,713	155,710
*93102	Santa Barbara	(805)	74,542	70,215
*95050	Santa Clara	(408)	87,746	86,118
95060	Santa Cruz	(408)	41,483	32,076
90670	Santa Fe Springs	(213)	14,559	14,750
93454	Santa Maria	(805)	39,685	32,749
*90406	Santa Monica	(213)	88,314	88,289
93060	Santa Paula	(805)	20,552	18,001
*95402	Santa Rosa	(707)	83,205	50,006
92071	Santee(u)	(714)	47,080	21,107
95070	Saratoga	(408)	29,261	26,810
91350	Saugus-Bouquet Canyon(u)	(213)	16,283	....
94965	Sausalito	(415)	7,090	6,158
95066	Scotts Valley	(408)	6,891	3,621
90740	Seal Beach	(213)	25,975	24,441
93955	Seaside	(408)	36,567	36,883
95472	Sebastopol	(707)	5,500	3,993
93662	Selma	(209)	10,942	7,459
93263	Shafter	(805)	7,010	5,327
91024	Sierra Madre	(213)	10,837	12,140
90806	Signal Hill	(213)	5,734	5,588
93065	Simi Valley	(805)	77,500	59,832
92075	Solana Beach(u)	(714)	13,047	5,023
93960	Soledad	(408)	5,928	4,222
95476	Sonoma	(707)	6,054	4,259
95073	Soquel(u)	(408)	6,212	5,795
91733	South El Monte	(213)	16,623	13,443
90280	South Gate	(213)	66,784	56,909
92677	South Laguna(u)	(714)	6,013	2,566
95705	South Lake Tahoe	(916)	20,681	12,921
95350	South Modesto(u)	(209)	12,492	7,889
95965	South Oroville(u)	(916)	7,246	4,111
91030	South Pasadena	(213)	22,681	22,979
94080	South San Francisco	(415)	49,393	46,646
91770	South San Gabriel(u)	(213)	5,421	5,051
91744	South San Jose Hills(u)	(213)	16,049	12,386
90605	South Whittier(u)	(213)	43,815	46,641
95991	South Yuba(u)	(916)	7,530	5,352
*92077	Spring Valley(u)	(714)	40,191	29,742
94305	Stanford(u)	(415)	11,045	8,691
90680	Stanton	(714)	21,144	18,186
*95204	Stockton	(209)	149,779	109,963
94585	Suisun City	(707)	11,087	2,917
92381	Sun City(u)	(714)	8,460	5,519
92388	Sunnymead(u)	(714)	11,554	6,708
*94086	Sunnyvale	(408)	106,618	95,976
96130	Susanville	(916)	6,520	6,608
93268	Taft	(805)	5,316	4,285
94806	Tara Hills-Montalvin Manor(u)	(415)	9,471	....
94941	Tamalpais-Homestead Valley(u)	(415)	8,511	....
91780	Temple City	(213)	28,972	31,034
*91360	Thousand Oaks	(805)	77,797	35,873
94920	Tiburon	(415)	6,685	6,209
*90510	Torrance	(213)	131,497	134,968
95396	Tracy	(209)	18,428	14,724
93274	Tulare	(209)	22,475	16,235
95380	Turlock	(209)	26,291	13,992
92680	Tustin	(714)	32,073	22,313
92705	Tustin-Foothills(u)	(714)	26,174	26,699
92277	Twentynine Palms(u)	(714)	7,465	5,667
92278	Twentynine Palms Base(u)	(714)	7,079	5,647
95482	Ukiah	(707)	12,035	10,095
94587	Union City	(415)	39,406	14,724
91786	Upland	(714)	47,647	32,551
95688	Vacaville	(707)	43,367	21,690
91355	Valencia(u)	(213)	12,163	4,243
91744	Valinda(u)	(213)	18,700	18,837
94590	Vallejo	(707)	80,188	71,710
92343	Valle Vista(u)	(714)	5,474	....
93437	Vandenberg AFB(u)	(805)	8,136	13,193
93436	Vandenberg Village(u)	(805)	5,839	....
*93001	Ventura	(805)	74,474	57,964
92392	Victorville	(714)	14,220	10,845
90043	View Park-Windsor Hills(u)	(213)	12,101	12,268
92667	Villa Park	(714)	7,137	2,723
94553	Vine Hill-Pacheco(u)	(415)	6,129	....
93277	Visalia	(209)	49,729	27,130
92083	Vista	(714)	35,834	24,688
91789	Walnut	(714)	9,978	5,992
*94596	Walnut Creek	(415)	53,643	39,844
94596	Walnut Creek West(u)	(415)	5,893	8,330
90255	Walnut Park(u)	(213)	11,811	8,925
93280	Wasco	(805)	9,613	8,269
95076	Watsonville	(408)	23,543	14,719
90044	West Athens(u)	(213)	8,531	13,311
90502	West Carson(u)	(213)	17,997	15,501
90247	West Compton(u)	(213)	5,907	5,748
*91793	West Covina	(213)	80,094	68,034
90069	West Hollywood(u)	(213)	35,703	34,622
92683	Westminster	(714)	71,133	60,076
95351	West Modesto(u)	(209)	NA	6,135
90047	Westmont(u)	(213)	27,916	29,310
94565	West Pittsburg(u)	(415)	8,773	5,969
91746	West Puente Valley(u)	(213)	20,445	20,733
95691	West Sacramento(u)	(916)	10,875	12,002
*90606	West Whittier-Los Nietos(u)	(213)	20,962	20,845
*90605	Whittier	(213)	68,872	72,863
90222	Willowbrook(u)	(213)	30,845	28,705
93286	Woodlake	(209)	5,375	3,371
95695	Woodland	(916)	30,235	20,677
94062	Woodside	(415)	5,291	4,734
92686	Yorba Linda	(714)	28,254	11,856
96097	Yreka City	(916)	5,916	5,394
95991	Yuba City	(916)	18,736	13,986
92399	Yucaipa(u)	(714)	23,345	19,284
92284	Yucca Valley(u)	(714)	8,294	3,893

Colorado (303)

80840	Air Force Academy	8,655	....
81101	Alamosa	6,830	6,985
80401	Applewood(u)	12,040	8,214
*80001	Arvada	84,576	49,844
80010	Aurora	158,588	74,974
*80302	Boulder	76,685	66,870
80601	Brighton	12,773	8,309
80020	Broomfield	20,730	7,261
81212	Canon City	13,037	9,206
.....	Castlewood	16,413	....
80110	Cherry Hills Village	5,127	4,605
81220	Cimarron Hills	6,597	....
81520	Clifton	5,223	....
*80901	Colorado Springs	215,150	135,517
80120	Columbine	23,523	....
80022	Commerce City	16,234	17,407
81321	Cortez	7,095	6,032
81625	Craig	8,133	4,205
*80202	Denver	491,396	514,678
80022	Derby(u)	8,578	10,206
81301	Durango	11,426	10,333
80214	Edgewater	5,714	4,910
80110	Englewood	30,021	33,695
80620	Evans	5,063	2,570
80439	Evergreen	6,376	2,321
80221	Federal Heights	7,846	1,502
80913	Fort Carson(u)	13,219	19,399
80521	Fort Collins	64,632	43,337
80701	Fort Morgan	8,768	7,594
80017	Fountain	8,324	3,515
80401	Golden	12,237	9,817
81501	Grand Junction	28,144	20,170
80631	Greeley	53,006	38,902
80110	Greenwood Village	5,729	3,095
80501	Gunbarrel	5,172	....
81230	Gunnison	5,785	4,613

ZIP code	Place	1980	1970
.....	Ken Caryl	10,661	....
80026	Lafayette	8,985	3,498
81050	La Junta	8,338	8,205
80215	Lakewood	112,848	92,743
81052	Lamar	7,713	7,797
80120	Littleton	28,631	26,466
80120	Littleton Southeast(u)	33,029	22,899
80501	Longmont	42,942	23,209
80027	Louisville	5,593	2,409
80537	Loveland	30,244	16,220
81401	Montrose	8,722	6,496
80233	Northglenn	29,847	27,785
*81003	Pueblo	101,686	97,774
80911	Security-Widefield(u)	18,768	15,297
80110	Sheridan	5,377	4,787
80221	Sherrelwood(u)	17,629	18,868
80122	Southglenn	37,787	....
80477	Steamboat Springs	5,098	2,340
80751	Sterling	11,385	10,636
80906	Stratmoor	5,519	....
80229	Thornton	40,343	13,326
81082	Trinidad	9,663	9,901
80229	Welby(u)	9,668	6,875
80030	Westminster	50,211	19,512
80221	Westminster East(u)	6,002	7,576
80033	Wheat Ridge	30,293	29,778

Connecticut (203)

See Note on Page 218

ZIP code	Place	1980	1970
06401	Ansonia	19,039	21,160
06001	*Avon*	11,201	8,352
06037	*Berlin*	15,121	14,149
06801	*Bethel*	16,004	10,945
06002	*Bloomfield*	18,608	18,301
06405	*Branford*	23,363	20,444
*06602	Bridgeport	142,546	156,542
06010	Bristol	57,370	55,487
06804	*Brookfield*	12,872	9,688
06013	Burlington	5,660	4,070
06234	Brooklyn	5,691	4,965
06019	*Canton*	7,635	6,868
06410	*Cheshire*	21,788	19,051
06413	*Clinton*	11,195	10,267
06415	*Colchester*	7,761	6,603
06340	Conning Towers-Nautilus Park(u)	9,665	9,791
06238	*Coventry*	8,895	8,140
06416	*Cromwell*	10,265	7,400
06810	Danbury	60,470	50,781
06820	Darien	18,892	20,336
06418	Derby	12,346	12,599
06422	Durham	5,143	4,489
06423	East Haddam	5,621	4,676
06424	*East Hampton*	8,572	7,078
06108	*East Hartford*	52,563	57,583
06512	*East Haven*	25,028	25,120
06333	*East Lyme*	13,870	11,399
06425	Easton	5,962	4,885
06016	*East Windsor*	8,925	8,513
06029	*Ellington*	9,711	7,707
06082	*Enfield*	42,695	46,189
06426	Essex	5,078	4,911
06430	*Fairfield*	54,849	56,487
06032	*Farmington*	16,407	14,390
06033	*Glastonbury*	24,327	20,651
06035	*Granby*	7,956	6,150
06830	*Greenwich*	59,578	59,755
06351	*Griswold*	8,967	7,763
06340	*Groton*	41,062	38,244
06340	Groton Borough	10,086	8,933
06437	*Guilford*	17,375	12,033
06438	Haddam	6,383	4,934
06514	*Hamden*	51,071	49,357
*06101	Hartford	136,392	158,017
06082	Hazardville(u)	5,436	....
06248	Hebron	5,453	3,815
06037	Kensington(u)	7,502	....
06239	*Killingly*	14,519	13,573
06339	*Ledyard*	13,735	14,837
06759	*Litchfield*	7,605	7,399
06443	*Madison*	14,031	9,768
06040	*Manchester*	49,761	47,994
06250	*Mansfield*	20,634	19,994
06450	Meriden	57,118	55,959
06762	*Middlebury*	5,995	5,542
06457	Middletown	39,040	36,924
06460	Milford	50,898	50,858
06468	*Monroe*	14,010	12,047
06353	*Montville*	16,455	15,662
06770	Naugatuck	26,456	23,034
*06050	New Britain	73,840	83,441
06840	*New Canaan*	17,931	17,451
06810	*New Fairfield*	11,260	6,991
*06510	New Haven	126,109	137,707
06111	*Newington*	28,841	26,037
06320	New London	28,842	31,630
06776	*New Milford*	19,420	14,601
06470	*Newtown*	19,107	16,942
06471	*North Branford*	11,554	10,778
06473	*North Haven*	22,080	22,194
06856	Norwalk	77,767	79,288
06360	Norwich	38,074	41,739
06779	Oakville(u)	8,737	....
06371	Old Lyme	6,159	4,964
06475	*Old Saybrook*	9,287	8,468
06477	*Orange*	13,237	13,524
06483	Oxford	6,634	4,480
02891	Pawcatuck(u)	5,216	5,255
06374	*Plainfield*	12,774	11,957
06062	*Plainville*	16,401	16,733
06782	*Plymouth*	10,732	10,321
06480	*Portland*	8,383	8,812
06712	*Prospect*	6,807	6,543
06260	Putnam	6,855	6,918
.....	*Putnam*	8,580	8,598
06875	*Redding*	7,272	5,590
06877	Ridgefield Center(u)	6,066	5,878
.....	*Ridgefield*	20,120	18,188
06067	*Rocky Hill*	14,559	11,103
06483	*Seymour*	13,434	12,776
06484	Shelton	31,314	27,165
06082	Sherwood Manor(u)	6,303	....
06070	*Simsbury*	21,161	17,475
06071	Somers	8,473	6,893
06488	*Southbury*	14,156	7,852
06489	*Southington*	36,879	30,946
06074	*South Windsor*	17,198	15,553
06082	Southwood Acres(u)	9,779	....
06075	*Stafford*	9,268	8,680
*06904	Stamford	102,453	108,798
06378	*Stonington*	16,220	15,940
06268	Storrs(u)	11,394	10,691
06430	Stratfield-Brooklawn(u)	8,890	....
06497	*Stratford*	50,541	49,775
06078	*Suffield*	9,294	8,634
06786	Terryville(u)	5,234	....
06787	*Thomaston*	6,272	6,233
06277	*Thompson*	8,141	7,580
06084	*Tolland*	9,694	7,857
06790	Torrington	30,987	31,952
06611	*Trumbull*	32,989	31,394
06060	*Vernon*	27,974	27,237
06492	*Wallingford*	37,274	35,714
*06701	Waterbury	103,266	108,033
06385	*Waterford*	17,843	17,227
06795	*Watertown*	19,489	18,610
06498	Westbrook	5,216	3,820
06107	*West Hartford*	61,301	68,031
06516	West Haven	53,184	52,851
06880	*Weston*	8,284	7,417
06880	*Westport*	25,290	27,318
06109	*Wethersfield*	26,013	26,662
06226	Willimantic	14,652	14,402
06897	*Wilton*	15,351	13,572
06094	*Winchester*	10,841	11,106
06280	*Windham*	21,062	19,626
06095	*Windsor*	25,204	22,502
06096	*Windsor Locks*	12,190	15,080
06098	Winsted	8,092	8,954
06716	*Wolcott*	13,008	12,495
06525	*Woodbridge*	7,761	7,673
06798	*Woodbury*	6,942	5,869
06281	Woodstock	5,117	4,311

Delaware (302)

ZIP code	Place	1980	1970
19711	Brookside(u)	15,255	7,856
19703	Claymont(u)	10,022	6,584
19901	Dover	23,512	17,488
19802	Edgemoor(u)	7,397	....
19805	Elsmere	6,493	8,415
19963	Milford	5,356	5,314
19711	Newark	25,247	21,298
19973	Seaford	5,256	5,537
19804	Stanton(u)	5,495	....
19803	Talleyville(u)	6,880	....
19899	Wilmington	70,195	80,386
19720	Wilmington Manor —Chelsea—Leedom	9,233	10,134

District of Columbia (202)

ZIP code	Place	1980	1970
*20013	Washington	637,651	756,668

Florida

ZIP code	Place	Area code	1980	1970
32701	Altamonte Springs	(305)	22,028	4,391
32703	Apopka	(305)	6,019	4,045
33821	Arcadia	(813)	6,002	5,658
32233	Atlantic Beach	(904)	7,847	6,132
33823	Auburndale	(813)	6,501	5,386
.....	Aventura(u)	(305)	10,162	....
33825	Avon Park	(813)	8,026	6,712
32807	Azalea Park(u)	(305)	8,304	7,367
33830	Bartow	(813)	14,780	12,891
.....	Bay Crest(u)	(813)	5,927	....

ZIP code	Place		1980	1970
.....	Bayonet Point(u)	(813)	16,455	....
33542	Bay Pines(u)	(813)	5,757	....
33505	Bayshore Gardens(u)	(813)	14,945	9,255
33589	Beacon Square(u)	(813)	6,513	2,927
32073	Bellair-Meadowbrook Terrace(u)	(904)	12,144	....
33430	Belle Glade	(305)	16,535	15,949
32506	Belleview(u)	(904)	15,439	916
32661	Beverly Hills(u)	(904)	5,024	....
33432	Boca Raton	(305)	49,505	28,506
33923	Bonita Springs(u)	(813)	5,435	1,932
33435	Boynton Beach	(305)	35,624	18,115
*33506	Bradenton	(813)	30,170	21,040
33511	Brandon(u)	(813)	41,826	12,749
32525	Brent(u)	(904)	21,872	....
33314	Broadview Park(u)	(305)	6,022	6,049
33313	Broadview-Pompano Park(u)	(305)	5,256	....
33512	Brooksville	(904)	5,582	4,060
33311	Browardale(u)	(305)	7,571	17,444
33142	Browns Village(u)	(305)	NA	23,442
33142	Brownsville(u)	(305)	18,058	....
33054	Bunche Park(u)	(305)	NA	5,773
32401	Callaway	(904)	7,154	3,240
32920	Cape Canaveral	(305)	5,733	4,258
33904	Cape Coral	(813)	32,103	11,470
33055	Carol City(u)	(305)	47,349	27,361
32707	Casselberry	(305)	15,247	9,438
33401	Century Village(u)	(305)	10,619	2,679
32324	Chattahoochee	(904)	5,332	7,944
*33515	Clearwater	(813)	85,450	52,074
32711	Clermont	(904)	5,461	3,661
33440	Clewiston	(813)	5,219	3,896
32922	Cocoa	(305)	16,096	16,110
32931	Cocoa Beach	(305)	10,926	9,952
32922	Cocoa West(u)	(305)	6,432	5,779
33060	Coconut Creek	(305)	6,288	1,359
33060	Collier City(u)	(305)	7135	....
33064	Collier Manor-Cresthaven(u)	(305)	7,045	7,202
33801	Combee Settlement(u)	(813)	5,400	4,963
32809	Conway(u)	(305)	23,940	8,642
33314	Cooper City	(305)	10,140	2,535
33134	Coral Gables	(305)	43,241	42,494
33065	Coral Springs	(305)	37,349	1,489
.....	Coral Terrace(u)	(305)	22,702	....
32536	Crestview	(904)	7,617	7,952
33803	Crystal Lake(u)	(813)	6,827	6,227
33157	Cutler(u)	(305)	15,593	....
33157	Cutler Ridge(u)	(305)	20,886	17,441
33880	Cypress Gardens(u)	(813)	8,043	3,757
.....	Cypress Lake(u)	(813)	8,721	....
33004	Dania	(305)	11,811	9,013
33314	Davie	(305)	20,877	5,859
*32015	Daytona Beach	(904)	54,176	45,327
33441	Deerfield Beach	(305)	39,193	16,662
32433	DeFuniak Springs	(904)	5,563	4,966
32720	De Land	(904)	15,354	11,641
33444	Delray Beach	(305)	34,325	19,915
33617	Del Rio(u)	(813)	7,409	....
32725	Deltona(u)	(904)	15,710	4,868
33528	Dunedin	(813)	30,203	17,639
33610	East Lake-Orient Park (u)	(813)	5,612	5,697
33940	East Naples(u)	(813)	12,127	6,152
32032	Edgewater	(904)	6,726	3,348
32542	Eglin AFB(u)	(904)	7,574	7,769
33614	Egypt Lake(u)	(813)	11,932	7,556
33531	Elfers(u)	(813)	11,396	....
33533	Englewood(u)	(813)	10,242	5,108
32504	Ensley(u)	(904)	14,422	....
32726	Eustis	(904)	9,453	6,722
32804	Fairview Shores(u)	(305)	10,174	....
32034	Fernandina Beach	(904)	7,224	6,955
32730	Fern Park(u)	(305)	8,890	....
32504	Ferry Pass(u)	(904)	16,910	....
33030	Florida City	(305)	6,174	5,133
32751	Forest City(u)	(305)	6,819	....
*33310	Fort Lauderdale	(305)	153,256	139,590
33841	Fort Meade	(813)	5,546	4,374
*33920	Fort Myers	(813)	36,638	27,351
33931	Fort Myers Beach(u)	(813)	5,753	4,305
33450	Fort Pierce	(305)	33,802	29,721
33452	Fort Pierce NW(u)	(305)	5,929	3,269
32548	Fort Walton Beach	(904)	20,829	19,994
*32601	Gainesville	(904)	81,371	64,510
33801	Gibsonia(u)	(813)	5,011	....
32960	Gifford(u)	(305)	6,240	5,772
.....	Gladeview(u)	(305)	18,919	....
33143	Glenvar Heights(u)	(305)	13,216	....
33055	Golden Glades(u)	(305)	23,154	....
32733	Goldenrod(u)	(305)	13,681	....
32560	Gonzalez(u)	(904)	6,084	....
32503	Goulding(u)	(904)	5,352	....
33170	Goulds(u)	(305)	7,078	6,690
33463	Greenacres City	(305)	8,843	1,731
32561	Gulf Breeze	(904)	5,478	4,190
33581	Gulf Gate Estates(u)	(813)	9,248	5,874
33737	Gulfport	(813)	11,180	9,976
33844	Haines City	(813)	10,799	8,956
33009	Hallandale	(305)	36,517	23,849
*33010	Hialeah	(305)	145,254	102,452
33455	Hobe Sound(u)	(305)	6,822	2,029
32805	Holden Heights(u)	(305)	13,840	6,206
33590	Holiday(u)	(813)	18,392	....
32017	Holly Hill	(904)	9,953	8,191
*33022	Hollywood	(305)	117,188	106,873
33030	Homestead	(305)	20,668	13,674
33030	Homestead Base(u)	(305)	7,594	8,257
33568	Hudson(u)	(813)	5,799	2,278
33934	Immokalee(u)	(813)	11,038	3,764
32937	Indian Harbour Beach	(305)	5,967	5,371
33880	Inwood(u)	(813)	6,668	....
33162	Ives Estates(u)	(305)	12,623	....
*32201	Jacksonville	(904)	540,898	504,265
32250	Jacksonville Beach	(904)	15,462	12,779
33568	Jasmine Estates(u)	(813)	11,995	2,967
33457	Jensen Beach(u)	(305)	6,639	....
33458	Jupiter	(305)	9,868	3,136
.....	Kendale Lakes(u)	(305)	32,769	....
33156	Kendall(u)	(305)	73,758	35,497
.....	Kendall Green(u)	(305)	6,768	....
33149	Key Biscayne(u)	(305)	6,313	....
33037	Key Largo(u)	(305)	7,447	2,866
33040	Key West	(305)	24,292	29,312
32303	Killearn(u)	(904)	8,700	....
.....	Kings Point(u)	(305)	8,724	....
32741	Kissimmee	(305)	15,487	7,119
33618	Lake Carroll(u)	(305)	13,012	5,577
32055	Lake City	(904)	9,257	10,575
*33802	Lakeland	(813)	47,406	42,803
33801	Lakeland Highlands(u)	(813)	10,426	....
.....	Lake Lorraine(u)	(904)	5,427	....
33054	Lake Lucerne(u)	(305)	9,762	....
33612	Lake Magdalene(u)	(813)	13,331	9,266
33403	Lake Park	(305)	6,909	6,993
....	Lakeside(u)	(904)	10,534	....
33853	Lake Wales	(813)	8,466	8,240
33460	Lake Worth	(305)	27,048	23,714
33460	Lantana	(305)	8,048	7,126
33540	Largo	(813)	58,977	24,230
33313	Lauderdale Lakes	(305)	25,426	10,577
33313	Lauderhill	(305)	37,271	8,465
33545	Laurel(u)	(813)	6,368	....
33717	Lealman(u)	(813)	19,873	....
32748	Leesburg	(904)	13,191	11,869
33936	Lehigh Acres(u)	(813)	9,604	4,394
33033	Leisure City(u)	(305)	17,905	....
33614	Leto(u)	(904)	9,003	8,458
33064	Lighthouse Point	(305)	11,488	9,071
.....	Lindgren Acres(u)	(305)	11,986	....
32060	Live Oak	(904)	6,732	6,830
32810	Lockhart(u)	(305)	10,571	5,809
33548	Longboat Key	(813)	8,221	2,850
32750	Longwood	(305)	10,029	3,203
33549	Lutz(u)	(813)	5,555	....
32444	Lynn Haven	(904)	6,239	4,044
32751	Maitland	(305)	8,763	7,157
33550	Mango-Seffner(u)	(813)	6,493	....
33050	Marathon(u)	(305)	7,568	4,397
33063	Margate	(305)	36,044	8,867
32446	Marianna	(904)	7,074	7,282
*32901	Melbourne	(305)	46,536	40,236
33314	Melrose Park(u)	(904)	5,725	6,111
33561	Memphis(u)	(813)	5,501	3,207
32952	Merritt Island(u)	(305)	30,708	29,233
*33152	Miami	(305)	346,931	334,859
33139	Miami Beach	(305)	96,298	87,072
33023	Miami Gardens —Utopia-Carver(u)	(305)	9,025	....
33014	Miami Lakes(u)	(305)	9,809	....
33153	Miami Shores	(305)	9,244	9,425
33166	Miami Springs	(305)	12,350	13,279
32570	Milton	(904)	7,206	5,360
32754	Mims(u)	(305)	7,583	8,309
33023	Miramar	(305)	32,813	23,997
32757	Mount Dora	(904)	5,883	4,646
32506	Myrtle Grove(u)	(904)	14,238	16,186
33940	Naples	(813)	17,581	12,042
33940	Naples Park(u)	(813)	5,438	1,522
33032	Naranja-Princeton(u)	(305)	10,381	....
32233	Neptune Beach	(904)	5,248	4,281
33552	New Port Richey	(813)	11,196	6,098
33552	New Port Richey East(u)	(813)	6,627	2,758
32069	New Smyrna Beach	(904)	13,557	10,580
32578	Niceville	(904)	8,543	4,155
33169	Norland(u)	(305)	19,471	....
33308	North Andrews Gardens(u)	(305)	8,967	7,082
33903	North Fort Myers(u)	(813)	22,808	8,798
33314	North Lauderdale	(305)	18,479	1,213
33161	North Miami	(305)	42,566	34,767
33160	North Miami Beach	(305)	36,481	30,544
33940	North Naples(u)	(813)	7,950	3,201
33408	North Palm Beach	(305)	11,344	9,035
33596	North Port	(813)	6,205	2,244
33169	Norwood(u)	(305)	NA	14,973
33308	Oakland Park	(305)	21,939	16,261
33860	Oak Ridge(u)	(813)	15,477	....
32670	Ocala	(904)	37,170	22,583
32548	Ocean City(u)	(904)	5,582	5,267
32761	Ocoee	(813)	7,803	3,937
33163	Oius(u)	(305)	17,344	....
33165	Olympia Heights(u)	(305)	33,112	....

ZIP code	Place		1980	1970
33558	Oneco(u)	(813)	6,417	3,246
33054	Opa-Locka	(305)	14,460	11,902
33054	Opa-Locka North(u)	(305)	5,721	....
32073	Orange Park	(904)	8,766	5,019
*32802	Orlando	(305)	128,394	99,006
32811	Orlovista(u)	(305)	6,474	....
32074	Ormond Beach	(904)	21,378	14,063
32074	Ormond By-The-Sea(u)	(904)	7,665	6,002
32570	Pace(u)	(904)	5,006	1,776
33476	Pahokee	(305)	6,346	5,663
32077	Palatka	(904)	10,175	9,444
33505	Palma Sola(u)	(813)	5,297	1,745
32905	Palm Bay	(305)	18,560	7,176
33480	Palm Beach	(305)	9,729	9,086
33403	Palm Beach Gardens	(305)	14,407	6,102
33561	Palmetto	(813)	8,637	7,422
33157	Palmetto Estates(u)	(305)	11,116	....
33563	Palm Harbor(u)	(813)	5,215	....
33619	Palm River-Clair Mel(u)	(813)	14,447	8,536
33460	Palm Springs	(305)	8,166	4,340
33012	Palm Springs North(u)	(305)	5,838	....
32401	Panama City	(904)	33,346	32,096
33023	Pembroke Pines	(305)	35,776	15,496
32502	Pensacola	(904)	57,619	59,507
33157	Perrine(u)	(305)	16,129	10,257
32347	Perry	(904)	8,254	7,701
32809	Pine Castle(u)	(305)	9,992	....
32808	Pine Hills(u)	(305)	35,771	13,882
33565	Pinellas Park	(813)	32,811	22,287
33168	Pinewood(u)	(305)	16,216	....
33566	Plant City	(813)	19,270	15,451
33314	Plantation	(813)	48,501	23,523
*33060	Pompano Beach	(305)	52,618	38,587
33064	Pompano Beach Highlands(u)	(305)	16,154	5,014
33950	Port Charlotte(u)	(813)	25,730	10,769
32019	Port Orange	(904)	18,756	3,781
33452	Port St. Lucie	(305)	14,690	330
*33950	Punta Gorda	(813)	6,797	3,879
32351	Quincy	(904)	8,591	8,334
33156	Richmond Heights(u)	(305)	8,577	6,663
33312	Riverland (u)	(305)	5,919	5,512
33404	Riviera Beach	(305)	26,596	21,401
33314	Rock Island(u)	(813)	5,022	....
32955	Rockledge	(305)	11,877	10,523
33570	Ruskin(u)	(813)	5,117	2,414
33572	Safety Harbor	(813)	6,461	3,103
32084	St. Augustine	(904)	11,985	12,352
32769	St. Cloud	(305)	7,840	5,041
*33730	St. Petersburg	(813)	236,893	216,159
33706	St. Petersburg Beach	(813)	9,354	8,024
33508	Samoset(u)	(813)	5,747	4,070
33432	Sandalfoot Cove(u)	(305)	5,299	....
32771	Sanford	(305)	23,176	17,393
*33578	Sarasota	(813)	48,868	40,237
33577	Sarasota Springs(u)	(813)	13,860	4,405
32937	Satellite Beach	(305)	9,163	6,558
.....	Scott Lake(u)	(305)	14,154	....
33870	Sebring	(813)	8,736	7,223
33578	Siesta Key(u)	(813)	7,010	4,460
32809	Sky Lake(u)	(305)	6,692	....
32703	South Apopka(u)	(305)	5,687	2,293
33505	South Bradenton(u)	(813)	14,297	....
32021	South Daytona	(904)	9,608	4,979
33579	Southgate(u)	(813)	7,322	6,885
33143	South Miami	(305)	10,884	11,780
33157	South Miami Heights(u)	(305)	23,559	10,395
32937	South Patrick Shores(u)	(305)	9,816	10,313
33595	South Venice(u)	(813)	8,075	4,680
32401	Springfield	(904)	7,220	5,949
33512	Spring Hill(u)	(813)	6,468	....
32091	Starke	(904)	5,306	4,848
33494	Stuart	(305)	9,467	4,820
33570	Sun City Center(u)	(813)	5,605	2,143
33160	Sunny Isles(u)	(305)	12,564	....
33304	Sunrise	(305)	39,681	7,403
33139	Sunset(u)	(305)	13,531	....
33144	Sweetwater	(305)	8,251	3,357
33614	Sweetwater Creek(u)	(813)	NA	19,453
*32303	Tallahassee	(904)	81,548	72,624
33313	Tamarac	(305)	29,142	5,193
33144	Tamiami(u)	(305)	17,607	....
*33602	Tampa	(813)	271,523	277,714
.....	Tanglewood(u)	(813)	8,229	....
33589	Tarpon Springs	(813)	13,251	7,118
33617	Temple Terrace	(813)	11,097	7,347
33905	Tice(u)	(813)	6,645	7,254
32780	Titusville	(305)	31,910	30,515
32505	Town 'n' Country(u)	(904)	37,834	....
33740	Treasure Island	(813)	6,316	6,120
32807	Union Park(u)	(305)	19,175	2,595
33620	University (Hillsborough)(u)	(813)	24,514	10,039
32580	Valparaiso	(904)	6,142	6,504
33595	Venice	(813)	12,153	6,648
33595	Venice Gardens(u)	(813)	6,568	....
32960	Vero Beach	(305)	16,176	11,908
32960	Vero Beach South(u)	(305)	12,636	7,330
33901	Villas(u)	(813)	8,724	....
32507	Warrington(u)	(904)	15,792	15,848
33314	Washington Park(u)	(305)	7,240	....
32703	Wekiva Springs(u)	(305)	13,386	....
33505	West Bradenton(u)	(813)	NA	6,162
33155	Westchester(u)	(305)	29,272	....
32446	West End(u)	(904)	NA	5,289
33138	West Little River(u)	(305)	32,492	....
32901	West Melbourne	(305)	5,078	3,050
33144	West Miami	(305)	6,076	5,494
*33401	West Palm Beach	(305)	62,530	57,375
32505	West Pensacola(u)	(904)	24,371	20,924
33168	Westview(u)	(305)	9,102	....
33880	West Winter Haven(u)	(813)	NA	7,716
33165	Westwood Lakes(u)	(305)	11,478	12,811
33305	Wilton Manors	(305)	12,742	10,948
33803	Winston(u)	(813)	9,315	4,505
32787	Winter Garden	(305)	6,789	5,153
33880	Winter Haven	(813)	21,119	16,136
32789	Winter Park	(305)	22,314	21,895
32707	Winter Springs	(305)	10,475	1,161
32548	Wright(u)	(904)	13,011	....
33599	Zephyrhills	(813)	5,742	3,369

Georgia

ZIP code	Place		1980	1970
31620	Adel	(912)	5,592	4,972
*31701	Albany	(912)	73,934	72,623
31709	Americus	(912)	16,120	16,091
*30601	Athens	(404)	42,549	44,342
*30304	Atlanta	(404)	425,022	495,039
*30901	Augusta	(404)	47,532	59,864
31717	Bainbridge	(912)	10,553	10,887
30032	Belvedere Park(u)	(404)	17,766	....
31723	Blakely	(912)	5,880	5,267
31520	Brunswick	(912)	17,605	19,585
30518	Buford	(404)	6,697	4,640
31728	Cairo	(912)	8,777	8,061
30701	Calhoun	(404)	5,335	4,748
31730	Camilla	(912)	5,414	4,987
30032	Candler-McAfee(u)	(404)	27,306	....
30117	Carrollton	(404)	14,078	13,520
30120	Cartersville	(404)	9,508	10,138
30125	Cedartown	(404)	8,619	9,253
30341	Chamblee	(404)	7,137	9,127
31014	Cochran	(912)	5,121	5,161
30337	College Park	(404)	24,632	18,203
*31902	Columbus	(404)	169,441	155,028
30027	Conley(u)	(404)	6,033	....
30207	Conyers	(404)	6,567	4,809
31015	Cordele	(912)	10,914	10,733
30209	Covington	(404)	10,586	10,267
30720	Dalton	(404)	20,743	18,872
31742	Dawson	(912)	5,699	5,383
*30030	Decatur	(404)	18,404	21,943
31520	Dock Junction(u)	(912)	6,189	6,009
30340	Doraville	(404)	7,414	9,157
31533	Douglas	(912)	10,980	10,195
30134	Douglasville	(404)	7,641	5,472
30333	Druid Hills(u)	(404)	12,700	....
31021	Dublin	(912)	16,083	15,143
30338	Dunwoody(u)	(404)	17,768	....
31023	Eastman	(912)	5,330	5,416
30344	East Point	(404)	37,486	39,315
30635	Elberton	(404)	5,686	6,438
30060	Fair Oaks(u)	(404)	8,486	....
30535	Fairview(u)	(404)	6,558	....
31750	Fitzgerald	(912)	10,187	8,187
30050	Forest Park	(404)	18,782	19,994
31905	Fort Benning South(u)	(404)	15,074	27,495
30905	Fort Gordon(u)	(404)	14,069	15,589
30741	Fort Oglethorpe	(404)	5,443	3,869
31313	Fort Stewart(u)	(912)	15,031	4,467
31030	Fort Valley	(912)	9,000	9,251
30501	Gainesville	(404)	15,280	15,459
31408	Garden City	(404)	6,895	5,790
30316	Gresham Park(u)	(404)	6,232	....
30223	Griffin	(404)	20,728	22,734
30354	Hapeville	(404)	6,166	9,567
31313	Hinesville	(912)	11,309	4,115
31545	Jesup	(912)	9,418	9,091
30144	Kennesaw	(404)	5,095	3,548
30728	La Fayette	(404)	6,517	6,044
30240	La Grange	(404)	24,204	23,301
30245	Lawrenceville	(404)	8,928	5,207
30057	Lithia Springs(u)	(404)	9,145	....
30059	Mableton(u)	(404)	25,111	....
*31201	Macon	(912)	116,860	122,423
30060	Marietta	(404)	30,805	27,216
30907	Martinez(u)	(404)	16,472	....
31034	Midway-Hardwick(u)	(912)	8,977	14,047
31061	Milledgeville	(912)	12,176	11,601
30655	Monroe	(404)	8,854	8,071
31768	Moultrie	(912)	15,708	14,400
30075	Mountain Park(u)	(404)	9,425	268
30263	Newnan	(404)	11,449	11,205
30319	North Atlanta(u)	(404)	30,521	....
30033	North Decatur(u)	(404)	11,830	....
30033	North Druid Hills(u)	(404)	12,438	....
30032	Panthersville(u)	(404)	11,366	....
30269	Peachtree City	(404)	6,429	793
31069	Perry	(912)	9,453	7,771
31643	Quitman	(912)	5,188	4,818

ZIP code	Place		1980	1970
*30274	Riverdale	(404)	7,121	2,521
30161	Rome	(404)	29,654	30,759
30075	Roswell	(404)	23,337	5,430
31522	St. Simons(u)	(912)	6,566	5,346
31082	Sandersville	(912)	6,137	5,546
30328	Sandy Springs(u)	(404)	46,877	....
*31401	Savannah	(912)	141,634	118,349
30079	Scottdale(u)	(404)	8,770	....
30080	Smyrna	(404)	20,312	19,157
30278	Snellville	(404)	8,514	1,990
30901	South Augusta(u)	(404)	51,072	....
30458	Statesboro	(912)	14,866	14,616
30401	Swainsboro	(912)	7,602	7,325
31791	Sylvester	(912)	5,860	4,226
30286	Thomaston	(404)	9,682	10,024
31792	Thomasville	(912)	18,463	18,155
30824	Thomson	(404)	7,001	6,503
31794	Tifton	(912)	13,749	12,179
30577	Toccoa	(404)	9,104	6,971
30084	Tucker(u)	(404)	25,399	....
31601	Valdosta	(912)	37,596	32,303
30474	Vidalia	(912)	10,393	9,507
31093	Warner Robins	(912)	39,893	33,491
31501	Waycross	(912)	19,371	18,996
30830	Waynesboro	(404)	5,760	5,530
30901	West Augusta(u)	(404)	24,242	....
31410	Wilmington Island(u)	(912)	7,546	3,284
30680	Winder	(404)	6,705	6,605

Hawaii (808)

See Note on Page 218

ZIP code	Place		1980	1970
.....	Ewa		190,037	132,299
.....	Hilo		37,017	28,412
.....	Honolulu		365,048	324,871
.....	Kahului		13,026	8,287
.....	Keaau-Mountain View		7,055	3,802
.....	Kekaha-Waimea		5,256	4,159
.....	Kihei		6,035	1,636
.....	Koolauloa		14,195	10,562
.....	Koolaupoko		109,373	92,219
.....	Kula		5,077	2,124
.....	Lahaina		10,284	5,524
.....	Makawao-Paia		10,361	5,788
.....	North Kona		13,748	4,832
.....	Papaikou-Wailea		5,261	5,503
.....	South Kona		5,914	4,004
.....	Wahiawa		41,562	37,329
.....	Waialua		9,849	9,171
.....	Waianae		32,810	24,077
.....	Wailua-Anahola		6,030	3,599
.....	Wailuku		10,674	9,084

Idaho (208)

ZIP code	Place		1980	1970
83221	Blackfoot		10,065	8,716
*83708	Boise City		102,451	74,990
83318	Burley		8,761	8,279
83605	Caldwell		17,699	14,219
83201	Chubbuck		7,052	2,924
83814	Coeur D'Alene		20,054	16,228
83401	Idaho Falls		39,590	35,776
83338	Jerome		6,891	4,183
83501	Lewiston		27,986	26,068
83642	Meridian		6,658	2,616
83843	Moscow		16,513	14,146
83647	Mountain Home		7,540	6,451
83648	Mountain Home AFB(u)		6,403	6,038
83651	Nampa		25,112	20,768
83661	Payette		5,448	4,521
83201	Pocatello		46,340	40,036
83854	Post Falls		5,736	2,371
83440	Rexburg		11,559	8,272
83350	Rupert		5,476	4,563
83301	Twin Falls		26,209	21,914

Illinois

ZIP code	Place		1980	1970
60101	Addison	(312)	28,836	24,482
60102	Algonquin	(312)	5,834	3,515
60658	Alsip	(312)	17,134	11,608
62002	Alton	(618)	34,171	39,700
62906	Anna	(618)	5,408	4,766
*60004	Arlington Heights	(312)	66,116	65,058
*60507	Aurora	(312)	81,293	74,389
60010	Barrington	(312)	9,029	8,581
60103	Bartlett	(312)	13,254	3,501
61607	Bartonville	(309)	6,110	7,221
60510	Batavia	(312)	12,574	9,060
62618	Beardstown	(217)	6,338	6,222
*62220	Belleville	(618)	42,150	41,223
60104	Bellwood	(312)	19,811	22,096
61008	Belvidere	(815)	15,176	14,061
60106	Bensenville	(312)	16,124	12,956
62812	Benton	(618)	7,778	6,833
60162	Berkeley	(312)	5,467	6,152
60402	Berwyn	(312)	46,849	52,502
62010	Bethalto	(618)	8,630	7,074
60108	Bloomingdale	(312)	12,659	2,974
61701	Bloomington	(309)	44,189	39,992
60406	Blue Island	(312)	21,855	22,629
60439	Bolingbrook	(312)	37,261	7,651
60538	Boulder Hill(u)	(312)	9,333	....
60914	Bourbonnais	(815)	13,280	5,909
60915	Bradley	(815)	11,008	9,881
60455	Bridgeview	(312)	14,155	12,506
60153	Broadview	(312)	8,618	9,623
60513	Brookfield	(312)	19,395	20,284
60090	Buffalo Grove	(312)	22,230	12,333
60459	Burbank	(312)	28,462	26,726
62206	Cahokia	(618)	18,904	20,649
62914	Cairo	(618)	5,931	6,277
60409	Calumet City	(312)	39,673	33,107
60643	Calumet Park	(312)	8,788	10,069
61520	Canton	(309)	14,626	14,217
62901	Carbondale	(618)	27,194	22,816
62626	Carlinville	(217)	5,439	5,675
62821	Carmi	(618)	6,264	6,033
60187	Carol Stream	(312)	15,472	4,434
60110	Carpentersville	(312)	23,272	24,059
60013	Cary	(312)	6,640	4,358
62801	Centralia	(618)	15,126	15,966
62206	Centreville	(618)	9,747	11,378
61820	Champaign	(217)	58,133	56,837
61920	Charleston	(217)	19,355	16,421
62629	Chatham	(217)	5,597	2,788
62233	Chester	(618)	8,027	5,310
*60607	Chicago	(312)	3,005,072	3,369,357
60411	Chicago Heights	(312)	37,026	40,900
60415	Chicago Ridge	(312)	13,473	9,187
61523	Chillicothe	(309)	6,176	6,052
60650	Cicero	(312)	61,232	67,058
60514	Clarendon Hills	(312)	6,857	6,750
61727	Clinton	(217)	8,014	7,581
62234	Collinsville	(618)	19,613	18,224
60477	Country Club Hills	(312)	14,676	6,920
60525	Countryside	(312)	6,538	2,864
60435	Crest Hill	(815)	9,252	7,460
60445	Crestwood	(312)	10,712	5,770
60417	Crete	(312)	5,417	4,656
61611	Creve Coeur	(309)	6,851	6,440
60014	Crystal Lake	(815)	18,590	14,541
61832	Danville	(217)	38,985	42,570
60559	Darien	(312)	14,968	7,789
*62521	Decatur	(217)	94,081	90,397
60015	Deerfield	(312)	17,430	18,876
60115	De Kalb	(815)	33,099	32,949
*60016	Des Plaines	(312)	53,568	57,239
61021	Dixon	(815)	15,659	18,147
60419	Dolton	(312)	24,766	25,990
60515	Downers Grove	(312)	39,274	32,544
62832	Du Quoin	(618)	6,594	6,691
62024	East Alton	(618)	7,123	7,309
60411	East Chicago Heights	(312)	5,347	5,000
61244	East Moline	(309)	20,907	20,956
61611	East Peoria	(309)	22,385	18,671
*62201	East St. Louis	(618)	55,200	70,169
62025	Edwardsville	(618)	12,460	11,070
62401	Effingham	(217)	11,270	9,458
62930	Eldorado	(618)	5,198	3,876
60120	Elgin	(312)	63,798	55,691
60007	Elk Grove Village	(312)	28,907	20,346
60126	Elmhurst	(312)	44,251	46,392
60635	Elmwood Park	(312)	24,016	26,160
*60204	Evanston	(312)	73,706	80,113
60642	Evergreen Park	(312)	22,260	25,921
62837	Fairfield	(618)	5,954	5,897
62208	Fairview Heights	(618)	12,414	10,050
62839	Flora	(618)	5,379	5,283
60422	Flossmoor	(312)	8,423	7,846
60130	Forest Park	(312)	15,177	15,472
60020	Fox Lake	(312)	6,831	4,511
60131	Franklin Park	(312)	17,507	20,348
61032	Freeport	(815)	26,406	27,736
60030	Gages Lake-Wildwood(u)	(312)	5,848	5,337
61401	Galesburg	(309)	35,305	36,290
61254	Geneseo	(309)	6,373	5,840
60134	Geneva	(312)	9,881	9,049
62034	Glen Carbon	(618)	5,197	1,897
60022	Glencoe	(312)	9,200	10,542
60137	Glendale Heights	(618)	23,163	11,406
60137	Glen Ellyn	(312)	23,649	21,909
60025	Glenview	(312)	30,842	24,880
60425	Glenwood	(312)	10,538	7,416
62040	Granite City	(618)	36,815	40,685
60030	Grayslake	(312)	5,260	4,907
62246	Greenville	(618)	5,271	4,631
60031	Gurnee	(312)	7,179	2,738
60103	Hanover Park	(312)	28,850	11,735
62946	Harrisburg	(618)	9,322	9,535
60033	Harvard	(815)	5,126	5,177
60426	Harvey	(312)	35,810	34,636
60656	Harwood Heights	(312)	8,228	9,060
60429	Hazel Crest	(312)	13,973	10,329
62948	Herrin	(618)	10,040	9,623
60457	Hickory Hills	(312)	13,778	13,176
62249	Highland	(618)	7,122	5,981

ZIP code	Place		1980	1970
60035	Highland Park	(312)	30,611	32,263
60040	Highwood	(312)	5,452	4,973
60162	Hillside	(312)	8,279	8,888
60521	Hinsdale	(312)	16,726	15,918
60172	Hoffman Estates	(312)	38,258	22,238
60456	Hometown	(312)	5,324	6,729
60430	Homewood	(312)	19,724	18,871
60942	Hoopeston	(217)	6,411	6,461
60143	Itasca	(312)	7,948	4,638
62650	Jacksonville	(217)	20,284	20,553
62052	Jerseyville	(618)	7,506	7,446
*60431	Joliet	(815)	77,956	78,827
60458	Justice	(312)	10,552	9,473
60901	Kankakee	(815)	30,141	30,944
61443	Kewanee	(309)	14,508	15,762
60525	La Grange	(312)	15,681	17,814
60525	La Grange Park	(312)	13,359	15,459
60045	Lake Forest	(312)	15,245	15,642
60102	Lake in the Hills	(312)	5,651	3,240
60047	Lake Zurich	(312)	8,225	4,082
60438	Lansing	(312)	29,039	25,805
61301	La Salle	(815)	10,347	10,736
62439	Lawrenceville	(618)	5,652	5,863
60439	Lemont	(312)	5,640	5,080
60048	Libertyville	(312)	16,520	11,684
62656	Lincoln	(217)	16,327	17,582
60645	Lincolnwood	(312)	11,921	12,929
60046	Lindenhurst	(312)	6,220	3,141
60532	Lisle	(312)	13,625	5,329
62056	Litchfield	(217)	7,204	7,190
60441	Lockport	(815)	9,017	9,861
60148	Lombard	(312)	37,295	34,043
61111	Loves Park	(815)	13,192	12,390
60534	Lyons	(312)	9,925	11,124
61455	Macomb	(309)	19,632	19,643
62060	Madison	(618)	5,915	7,042
62959	Marion	(618)	14,031	11,724
60426	Markham	(312)	15,172	15,987
60443	Matteson	(312)	10,223	4,741
61938	Mattoon	(217)	19,787	19,681
60153	Maywood	(312)	27,998	29,019
60050	McHenry	(815)	10,908	6,772
*60160	Melrose Park	(312)	20,735	22,716
61342	Mendota	(815)	7,134	6,902
62960	Metropolis	(618)	7,171	6,940
60445	Midlothian	(312)	14,274	14,422
61264	Milan	(309)	6,264	4,873
61265	Moline	(309)	45,709	46,237
61462	Monmouth	(309)	10,706	11,022
60450	Morris	(815)	8,833	8,194
61550	Morton	(309)	14,178	10,811
60053	Morton Grove	(312)	23,747	26,369
62863	Mount Carmel	(618)	8,908	8,096
60056	Mount Prospect	(312)	52,634	34,995
62864	Mount Vernon	(618)	16,995	16,270
60060	Mundelein	(312)	17,053	16,128
62966	Murphysboro	(618)	9,866	10,013
60540	Naperville	(312)	42,330	22,794
60451	New Lenox	(815)	5,792	2,855
60648	Niles	(312)	30,363	31,432
61761	Normal	(309)	35,672	26,396
60656	Norridge	(312)	16,483	17,113
60542	North Aurora	(312)	5,205	4,833
60062	Northbrook	(312)	30,735	25,422
60064	North Chicago	(312)	38,774	47,275
60093	Northfield	(312)	5,807	5,010
60164	Northlake	(312)	12,166	14,191
61111	North Park(u)	(815)	15,806	15,679
60546	North Riverside	(312)	6,764	8,097
60521	Oak Brook	(312)	6,641	4,164
60452	Oak Forest	(312)	26,096	19,271
*60454	Oak Lawn	(312)	60,590	60,305
*60301	Oak Park	(312)	54,887	62,511
62269	O'Fallon	(618)	10,217	7,268
62450	Olney	(618)	9,026	8,974
60462	Orland Park	(312)	23,045	6,391
61350	Ottawa	(815)	18,166	18,716
60067	Palatine	(312)	32,166	26,050
60463	Palos Heights	(312)	11,096	8,544
60465	Palos Hills	(312)	16,654	6,629
62557	Pana	(217)	6,040	6,326
61944	Paris	(217)	9,885	9,971
60466	Park Forest	(312)	26,222	30,638
60466	Park Forest South	(312)	6,245	1,748
60068	Park Ridge	(312)	38,704	42,614
61554	Pekin	(309)	33,967	31,375
*61601	Peoria	(309)	124,160	126,963
61614	Peoria Heights	(309)	7,453	7,943
61354	Peru	(815)	10,886	11,772
61764	Pontiac	(815)	11,227	10,595
61356	Princeton	(815)	7,342	6,959
60070	Prospect Heights	(312)	11,808	13,333
62301	Quincy	(217)	42,352	45,288
61866	Rantoul	(217)	20,161	25,562
60471	Richton Park	(312)	9,403	2,558
60627	Riverdale	(312)	13,233	15,806
60305	River Forest	(312)	12,392	13,402
60171	River Grove	(312)	10,368	11,465
60546	Riverside	(312)	9,236	10,357
60472	Robbins	(312)	8,119	9,641
62454	Robinson	(618)	7,285	7,178
61068	Rochelle	(815)	8,982	8,594
61071	Rock Falls	(815)	10,624	10,287
*61125	Rockford	(815)	139,712	147,370
61201	Rock Island	(309)	47,036	50,166
60008	Rolling Meadows	(312)	20,167	19,178
60441	Romeoville	(312)	15,519	12,888
60172	Roselle	(312)	16,948	6,207
62024	Rosewood Heights(u)	(217)	5,085	3,391
60073	Round Lake Beach	(312)	12,921	5,717
60174	St. Charles	(312)	17,492	12,945
62881	Salem	(618)	7,813	6,187
60411	Sauk Village	(312)	10,906	7,479
60172	Schaumburg	(312)	52,319	18,531
60176	Schiller Park	(312)	11,458	12,712
62225	Scott AFB(u)	(618)	8,648	7,871
62565	Shelbyville	(217)	5,259	4,887
61282	Silvis	(309)	7,130	5,907
60076	Skokie	(312)	60,278	68,322
60177	South Elgin	(312)	6,218	4,289
60473	South Holland	(312)	24,977	23,931
*62703	Springfield	(217)	99,637	91,753
61362	Spring Valley	(815)	5,822	5,605
60475	Steger	(312)	9,269	8,104
61081	Sterling	(815)	16,273	16,113
60402	Stickney	(312)	5,893	6,601
60103	Streamwood	(312)	23,456	18,176
61364	Streator	(815)	14,769	15,600
60501	Summit	(312)	10,110	11,569
62221	Swansea	(618)	5,347	5,432
60178	Sycamore	(815)	9,219	7,843
62568	Taylorville	(217)	11,386	10,644
60477	Tinley Park	(312)	26,171	12,572
61801	Urbana	(217)	35,978	33,976
62471	Vandalia	(618)	5,338	5,160
60061	Vernon Hills	(312)	9,827	1,056
60181	Villa Park	(312)	23,185	25,891
60555	Warrenville	(312)	7,519	3,281
61571	Washington	(309)	10,364	6,790
62204	Washington Park	(618)	8,223	9,524
60970	Watseka	(815)	5,543	5,294
60084	Wauconda	(312)	5,688	5,460
60085	Waukegan	(312)	67,653	65,134
60153	Westchester	(312)	17,730	20,033
60185	West Chicago	(312)	12,550	9,988
60558	Western Springs	(312)	12,876	13,029
62896	West Frankfort	(618)	9,437	8,854
60559	Westmont	(312)	16,718	8,832
61604	West Peoria(u)	(309)	5,219	6,873
60187	Wheaton	(312)	43,043	31,138
60090	Wheeling	(312)	23,266	13,243
60091	Wilmette	(312)	28,229	32,134
60093	Winnetka	(312)	12,772	14,131
60096	Winthrop Harbor	(312)	5,438	4,794
60097	Wonder Lake(u)	(312)	5,917	4,806
60191	Wood Dale	(312)	11,251	8,831
60515	Woodridge	(312)	22,322	11,028
62095	Wood River	(618)	12,449	13,186
60098	Woodstock	(815)	11,725	10,226
60482	Worth	(312)	11,592	11,999
60099	Zion	(312)	17,861	17,268

Indiana

ZIP code	Place		1980	1970
46001	Alexandria	(317)	6,028	5,600
46011	Anderson	(317)	64,695	70,787
46703	Angola	(219)	5,486	5,117
46706	Auburn	(219)	8,122	7,388
47421	Bedford	(812)	14,410	13,087
46107	Beech Grove	(317)	13,196	13,559
47401	Bloomington	(812)	51,646	43,262
46714	Bluffton	(219)	8,705	8,297
47601	Boonville	(812)	6,300	5,736
47834	Brazil	(812)	7,852	8,163
46112	Brownsburg	(317)	6,242	5,751
46032	Carmel	(317)	18,272	6,691
46303	Cedar Lake	(219)	8,754	7,589
47111	Charlestown	(812)	5,596	5,933
46304	Chesterton	(219)	8,531	6,177
47130	Clarksville	(812)	15,164	13,298
47842	Clinton	(317)	5,267	5,340
46725	Columbia City	(219)	5,091	4,911
47201	Columbus	(812)	30,292	26,457
47331	Connersville	(317)	17,023	17,604
47933	Crawfordsville	(317)	13,325	13,842
46307	Crown Point	(219)	16,455	10,931
46733	Decatur	(219)	8,649	8,445
46514	Dunlap(u)	(219)	5,397	....
46311	Dyer	(219)	9,555	4,906
46312	East Chicago	(219)	39,786	46,982
46514	Elkhart	(219)	41,305	43,152
46036	Elwood	(317)	10,867	11,196
*47708	Evansville	(812)	130,496	138,764
*46802	Fort Wayne	(219)	172,196	178,269
46041	Frankfort	(317)	15,168	14,956
46131	Franklin	(317)	11,563	11,477
*46401	Gary	(219)	151,953	175,415
46933	Gas City	(317)	6,370	5,742
46526	Goshen	(219)	19,665	17,871
46135	Greencastle	(317)	8,403	8,852

ZIP code	Place		1980	1970
46140	Greenfield	(317)	11,439	9,986
47240	Greensburg	(812)	9,254	8,620
46142	Greenwood	(317)	19,327	11,869
46319	Griffith	(219)	17,026	18,168
*46320	Hammond	(219)	93,714	107,983
47348	Hartford City	(317)	7,622	8,207
46322	Highland	(219)	25,935	24,947
46342	Hobart	(219)	22,987	21,485
47542	Huntingburg	(812)	5,376	4,794
46750	Huntington	(219)	16,202	16,217
*46206	Indianapolis	(317)	700,807	736,856
47546	Jasper	(812)	9,097	8,641
47130	Jeffersonville	(812)	21,220	20,008
46755	Kendallville	(219)	7,299	6,838
46901	Kokomo	(317)	47,808	44,042
*47901	Lafayette	(317)	43,011	44,955
46405	Lake Station	(219)	14,294	9,858
46350	La Porte	(219)	21,796	22,140
46226	Lawrence	(317)	25,591	16,353
46052	Lebanon	(317)	11,456	9,766
47441	Linton	(812)	6,315	5,450
46947	Logansport	(219)	17,899	19,255
46356	Lowell	(219)	5,827	3,839
47250	Madison	(812)	12,472	13,081
46952	Marion	(317)	35,874	39,607
46151	Martinsville	(317)	11,311	9,723
46410	Merrillville	(219)	27,677	15,918
46360	Michigan City	(219)	36,850	39,369
46544	Mishawaka	(219)	40,224	36,060
47960	Monticello	(219)	5,162	4,869
46158	Mooresville	(317)	5,349	5,800
47620	Mount Vernon	(812)	7,656	6,770
*47302	Muncie	(317)	77,216	69,082
46321	Munster	(219)	20,671	16,514
47150	New Albany	(812)	37,103	38,402
47362	New Castle	(317)	20,056	21,215
46774	New Haven	(219)	6,714	5,346
46060	Noblesville	(317)	12,056	7,548
46962	North Manchester	(219)	5,998	5,791
47265	North Vernon	(812)	5,768	4,582
47130	Oak Park(u)	(812)	5,871	....
46970	Peru	(317)	13,764	14,139
46168	Plainfield	(317)	9,191	8,211
46563	Plymouth	(219)	7,693	7,661
46368	Portage	(219)	27,409	19,127
47371	Portland	(219)	7,074	7,115
47670	Princeton	(812)	8,976	7,431
47374	Richmond	(317)	41,349	43,999
46975	Rochester	(219)	5,050	4,631
46173	Rushville	(317)	6,113	6,686
47167	Salem	(812)	5,290	5,041
46375	Schererville	(219)	13,209	3,663
47170	Scottsburg	(812)	5,068	4,791
47274	Seymour	(812)	15,050	13,352
46176	Shelbyville	(317)	14,989	15,094
*46624	South Bend	(219)	109,727	125,580
46383	South Haven(u)	(219)	6,679	....
46224	Speedway	(317)	12,641	14,523
47586	Tell City	(812)	8,704	7,933
*47808	Terre Haute	(812)	61,125	70,335
46072	Tipton	(317)	5,004	5,313
46383	Valparaiso	(219)	22,247	20,020
47591	Vincennes	(812)	20,857	19,867
46992	Wabash	(219)	12,985	13,379
46580	Warsaw	(219)	10,647	7,506
47501	Washington	(812)	11,325	11,358
47906	West Lafayette	(317)	21,247	19,157
46394	Whiting	(219)	5,630	7,054
47394	Winchester	(317)	5,659	5,493

Iowa

ZIP code	Place		1980	1970
50511	Algona	(515)	6,289	6,032
50009	Altoona	(515)	5,764	2,883
50010	Ames	(515)	45,775	39,505
50021	Ankeny	(515)	15,429	9,151
50022	Atlantic	(712)	7,789	7,306
52722	Bettendorf	(319)	27,381	22,126
50036	Boone	(515)	12,602	12,468
52601	Burlington	(319)	29,529	32,366
51401	Carroll	(712)	9,705	8,716
50613	Cedar Falls	(319)	36,322	29,597
*52401	Cedar Rapids	(319)	110,243	110,642
52544	Centerville	(515)	6,558	6,531
50616	Charles City	(515)	8,778	9,268
51012	Cherokee	(712)	7,004	7,272
51632	Clarinda	(712)	5,458	5,420
50428	Clear Lake City	(515)	7,458	6,430
52732	Clinton	(319)	32,828	34,719
50053	Clive	(515)	5,906	3,005
52240	Coralville	(319)	7,687	6,130
51501	Council Bluffs	(712)	56,449	60,348
50801	Creston	(515)	8,429	8,234
*52802	Davenport	(319)	103,264	98,469
52101	Decorah	(319)	7,991	7,237
51442	Denison	(712)	6,675	6,218
*50318	Des Moines	(515)	191,003	201,404
52001	Dubuque	(319)	62,321	62,309
51334	Estherville	(712)	7,518	8,108
52556	Fairfield	(515)	9,428	8,715
50501	Fort Dodge	(515)	29,423	31,263
52627	Fort Madison	(319)	13,520	13,996
51534	Glenwood	(712)	5,280	4,421
50112	Grinnell	(515)	8,868	8,402
51537	Harlan	(712)	5,357	5,049
50644	Independence	(319)	6,392	5,910
50125	Indianola	(515)	10,843	8,852
52240	Iowa City	(319)	50,508	46,850
50126	Iowa Falls	(515)	6,174	6,454
52632	Keokuk	(319)	13,536	14,631
50138	Knoxville	(515)	8,143	7,755
51031	Le Mars	(712)	8,276	8,159
52060	Maquoketa	(319)	6,313	5,677
52302	Marion	(319)	19,474	18,028
50158	Marshalltown	(515)	26,938	26,219
50401	Mason City	(515)	30,144	30,379
52641	Mount Pleasant	(319)	7,322	7,007
52761	Muscatine	(319)	23,467	22,405
50201	Nevada	(515)	5,912	4,952
50208	Newton	(515)	15,292	15,619
50662	Oelwein	(319)	7,564	7,735
52577	Oskaloosa	(515)	10,629	11,224
52501	Ottumwa	(515)	27,381	29,610
50219	Pella	(515)	8,349	6,668
50220	Perry	(515)	7,053	6,906
51566	Red Oak	(712)	6,810	6,210
51201	Sheldon	(712)	5,003	4,535
51601	Shenandoah	(712)	6,274	5,968
*51101	Sioux City	(712)	82,003	85,925
51301	Spencer	(712)	11,726	10,278
50588	Storm Lake	(712)	8,814	8,591
50322	Urbandale	(515)	17,869	14,434
52349	Vinton	(319)	5,040	4,845
52353	Washington	(319)	6,584	6,317
*50701	Waterloo	(319)	75,985	75,533
50677	Waverly	(319)	8,444	7,205
50595	Webster City	(515)	8,572	8,488
50265	West Des Moines	(515)	21,894	16,441
50311	Windsor Heights	(515)	5,632	6,303

Kansas

ZIP code	Place		1980	1970
67410	Abilene	(913)	6,572	6,661
67005	Arkansas City	(316)	13,201	13,216
66002	Atchison	(913)	11,407	12,565
67010	Augusta	(316)	6,968	5,977
66012	Bonner Springs	(913)	6,266	3,884
66720	Chanute	(316)	10,506	10,341
67337	Coffeyville	(316)	15,185	15,116
67701	Colby	(913)	5,544	4,658
66901	Concordia	(913)	6,847	7,221
67037	Derby	(316)	9,786	7,947
67801	Dodge City	(316)	18,001	14,127
67042	El Dorado	(316)	10,510	12,308
66801	Emporia	(316)	25,287	23,327
66442	Fort Riley North(u)	(913)	16,086	12,469
66701	Fort Scott	(316)	8,893	8,967
67846	Garden City	(316)	18,256	14,790
67735	Goodland	(913)	5,708	5,510
67530	Great Bend	(316)	16,608	16,133
67601	Hays	(913)	16,301	15,396
67060	Haysville	(316)	8,006	6,531
67501	Hutchinson	(316)	40,284	36,885
67301	Independence	(316)	10,598	10,347
66749	Iola	(316)	6,938	6,493
66441	Junction City	(913)	19,305	19,018
*66110	Kansas City	(913)	161,087	168,213
66043	Lansing	(913)	5,307	3,797
66044	Lawrence	(913)	52,738	45,698
66048	Leavenworth	(913)	33,656	25,147
66206	Leawood	(913)	13,360	10,645
66215	Lenexa	(913)	18,639	5,549
67901	Liberal	(316)	14,911	13,862
67460	McPherson	(316)	11,753	10,851
66502	Manhattan	(913)	32,644	27,575
66203	Merriam	(913)	10,794	10,955
66222	Mission	(913)	8,643	8,125
67114	Newton	(316)	16,332	15,439
66061	Olathe	(913)	37,258	17,917
66067	Ottawa	(913)	11,016	11,036
66204	Overland Park	(913)	81,784	77,934
67357	Parsons	(316)	12,898	13,015
66762	Pittsburg	(316)	18,770	20,171
66208	Prairie Village	(913)	24,657	28,378
67124	Pratt	(316)	6,885	6,736
66203	Roeland Park	(913)	7,962	9,760
67665	Russell	(913)	5,427	5,371
67401	Salina	(913)	41,843	37,714
*66203	Shawnee	(913)	29,653	20,946
*66603	Topeka	(913)	115,266	125,011
67152	Wellington	(316)	8,212	8,072
*67202	Wichita	(316)	279,272	276,554
67156	Winfield	(316)	10,736	11,405

Kentucky

ZIP code	Place		1980	1970
41101	Ashland	(606)	27,064	29,245
40004	Bardstown	(502)	6,155	5,816

ZIP code	Place		1980	1970
41073	Bellevue	(606)	7,678	8,847
40403	Berea	(606)	8,226	6,956
42101	Bowling Green	(502)	40,450	36,705
40218	Buechel(u)	(502)	6,912	5,359
42718	Campbellsville	(502)	8,715	7,598
42330	Central City	(502)	5,250	5,450
40701	Corbin	(606)	8,075	7,474
*41011	Covington	(606)	49,013	52,535
41031	Cynthiana	(606)	5,881	6,356
40422	Danville	(606)	12,942	11,542
41074	Dayton	(606)	6,979	8,751
41017	Edgewood	(606)	7,230	4,139
42701	Elizabethtown	(502)	15,380	11,748
41018	Elsmere	(606)	7,203	5,161
41018	Erlanger	(606)	14,433	12,676
40118	Fairdale(u)	(502)	7,315	....
40291	Fern Creek(u)	(502)	16,866	....
41139	Flatwoods	(606)	8,354	7,380
41042	Florence	(606)	15,586	11,661
42223	Fort Campbell North(u)	(502)	17,211	13,616
40121	Fort Knox(u)	(502)	31,035	37,608
41017	Fort Mitchell	(606)	7,297	6,982
41075	Fort Thomas	(606)	16,012	16,338
40601	Frankfort	(502)	25,973	21,902
42134	Franklin	(502)	7,738	6,553
40324	Georgetown	(502)	10,972	8,629
42141	Glasgow	(502)	12,958	11,301
40330	Harrodsburg	(606)	7,265	6,741
41701	Hazard	(606)	5,429	5,459
42420	Henderson	(502)	24,834	22,976
40228	Highview(u)	(502)	13,286	....
40229	Hillview	(502)	5,196	....
42240	Hopkinsville	(502)	27,318	21,395
41051	Independence	(606)	7,998	1,715
40299	Jeffersontown	(502)	15,795	9,701
40342	Lawrenceburg	(502)	5,167	3,579
40033	Lebanon	(502)	6,590	5,528
*40511	Lexington-Fayette	(606)	204,165	108,137
*40201	Louisville	(502)	298,451	361,706
42431	Madisonville	(502)	16,979	15,332
42066	Mayfield	(502)	10,705	10,724
41056	Maysville	(606)	7,983	7,411
40965	Middlesborough	(606)	12,251	11,878
42633	Monticello	(606)	5,677	3,618
40351	Morehead	(606)	7,789	7,191
40353	Mount Sterling	(606)	5,820	5,083
42071	Murray	(502)	14,248	13,537
40218	Newburg(u)	(502)	24,612	....
*41071	Newport	(606)	21,587	25,998
40356	Nicholasville	(606)	10,400	5,829
40219	Okolona(u)	(502)	20,039	17,643
42301	Owensboro	(502)	54,450	50,329
42001	Paducah	(502)	29,315	31,627
40361	Paris	(606)	7,935	7,823
40258	Pleasure Ridge Park(u)	(502)	27,332	28,566
42445	Princeton	(502)	7,073	6,292
40160	Radcliff	(502)	14,519	8,426
40475	Richmond	(606)	21,705	16,861
42276	Russellville	(502)	7,520	6,456
40207	St. Matthews	(502)	13,354	13,152
40065	Shelbyville	(502)	5,308	4,182
40216	Shively	(502)	16,819	19,139
42501	Somerset	(606)	10,649	10,436
40272	Valley Station(u)	(502)	24,474	24,471
40383	Versailles	(606)	6,427	5,679
41101	Westwood(u)	(606)	5,973	777
40769	Williamsburg	(606)	5,560	3,687
40391	Winchester	(606)	15,216	13,402

Louisiana

ZIP code	Place		1980	1970
70510	Abbeville	(318)	12,391	10,996
71301	Alexandria	(318)	51,565	41,811
70032	Arabi(u)	(504)	10,248	....
70094	Avondale(u)	(504)	6,699	....
70714	Baker	(504)	12,865	8,281
71220	Bastrop	(318)	15,527	14,713
*70821	Baton Rouge	(504)	219,486	165,921
70360	Bayou Cane(u)	(504)	15,723	9,077
70380	Bayou Vista(u)	(504)	5,805	5,121
70037	Belle Chasse(u)	(504)	5,412	....
70427	Bogalusa	(504)	16,976	18,412
71010	Bossier City	(318)	49,969	43,769
70517	Breaux Bridge	(318)	5,922	4,942
....	Broadmoor(u)	(318)	7,051	....
71291	Brownsville-Bawcomville(u)	(318)	7,252	....
71322	Bunkie	(318)	5,364	5,395
70043	Chalmette(u)	(504)	33,847	....
71291	Claiborne(u)	(318)	6,278	....
70433	Covington	(504)	7,892	7,170
70526	Crowley	(318)	16,036	16,104
70345	Cut Off(u)	(504)	5,049	....
70726	Denham Springs	(504)	8,412	6,752
70634	De Ridder	(318)	11,057	8,030
70346	Donaldsonville	(504)	7,901	7,367
70072	Estelle(u)	(504)	12,724	....
70535	Eunice	(318)	12,479	11,390
70538	Franklin	(318)	9,584	9,325
70354	Galliano(u)	(504)	5,159	....
70737	Gonzales	(504)	7,287	4,512
70053	Gretna	(504)	20,615	24,875
70401	Hammond	(504)	15,043	12,487
70123	Harahan	(504)	11,384	13,037
70058	Harvey(u)	(504)	22,709	6,347
70360	Houma	(504)	32,602	30,922
70544	Jeanerette	(318)	6,511	6,322
70121	Jefferson(u)	(504)	15,550	16,489
70546	Jennings	(318)	12,401	11,783
71251	Jonesboro	(318)	5,061	5,072
70548	Kaplan	(318)	5,016	5,540
70062	Kenner	(504)	66,382	29,858
70445	Lacombe(u)	(504)	5,146	....
70501	Lafayette	(318)	81,961	68,908
70601	Lake Charles	(318)	75,051	77,998
71254	Lake Providence	(318)	6,361	6,183
70068	Laplace(u)	(504)	16,112	5,953
70373	Larose(u)	(504)	5,234	4,267
71446	Leesville	(318)	9,054	8,928
70123	Little Farms(u)	(504)	NA	15,713
70448	Mandeville	(504)	6,076	2,571
71052	Mansfield	(318)	6,485	6,432
71351	Marksville	(318)	5,113	4,519
70072	Marrero(u)	(504)	36,548	29,015
*70004	Metairie(u)	(504)	164,160	136,477
71055	Minden	(318)	15,074	13,996
71201	Monroe	(318)	57,597	56,374
70380	Morgan City	(504)	16,114	16,586
70601	Moss Bluff(u)	(318)	7,004	....
71457	Natchitoches	(318)	16,664	15,974
70560	New Iberia	(318)	32,766	30,147
*70113	New Orleans	(504)	557,482	593,471
71463	Oakdale	(318)	7,155	7,301
70570	Opelousas	(318)	18,903	20,387
71360	Pineville	(318)	12,034	8,951
70764	Plaquemine	(504)	7,521	7,739
70454	Ponchatoula	(504)	5,469	4,545
70767	Port Allen	(504)	6,114	5,728
70085	Poydras(u)	(504)	5,722	....
70601	Prien(u)	(318)	6,224	....
70394	Raceland(u)	(504)	6,302	4,880
70578	Rayne	(318)	9,066	9,510
70084	Reserve(u)	(504)	7,288	6,381
70123	River Ridge(u)	(504)	17,146	....
71270	Ruston	(318)	20,585	17,365
70582	St. Martinville	(318)	7,965	7,153
70807	Scotlandville(u)	(504)	15,113	22,599
*71102	Shreveport	(318)	205,815	182,064
70458	Slidell	(504)	26,718	16,101
71459	South Fort Polk(u)	(318)	12,498	15,600
71075	Springhill	(318)	6,516	6,496
70663	Sulphur	(318)	19,709	14,959
71282	Tallulah	(318)	10,392	9,643
71285	Terrytown(u)	(318)	23,548	13,382
70301	Thibodaux	(504)	15,810	15,028
70053	Timberlane(u)	(504)	11,579	....
71373	Vidalia	(318)	5,936	5,538
70586	Ville Platte	(318)	9,201	9,692
70092	Violet(u)	(504)	11,678	....
70094	Waggaman(u)	(504)	9,004	....
70669	Westlake	(318)	5,246	4,082
71291	West Monroe	(318)	14,993	14,868
70094	Westwego	(504)	12,663	11,402
71483	Winnfield	(318)	7,311	7,142
71295	Winnsboro	(318)	5,921	5,349
70791	Zachary	(504)	7,297	4,964

Maine (207)

See Note Page 218

ZIP code	Place	1980	1970
04210	Auburn	23,128	24,151
04330	Augusta	21,819	21,945
04401	Bangor	31,643	33,168
04530	Bath	10,246	9,679
04915	Belfast	6,243	5,957
04005	Biddeford	19,638	19,983
04412	Brewer	9,017	9,300
04011	Brunswick Center(u)	10,990	10,867
04011	*Brunswick*	17,366	16,195
04093	*Buxton*	5,775	3,135
04107	*Cape Elizabeth*	7,838	7,873
04736	Caribou	9,916	10,419
04021	*Cumberland*	5,284	4,096
04605	Ellsworth	5,179	4,603
04937	*Fairfield*	6,113	5,684
04105	*Falmouth*	6,853	6,291
04938	*Farmington*	6,730	5,657
04032	*Freeport*	5,863	4,781
04345	Gardiner	6,485	6,685
04038	*Gorham*	10,101	7,839
04444	*Hampden*	5,250	4,693
04730	Houlton Center(u)	5,730	6,760
04730	*Houlton*	6,766	8,111
04239	*Jay*	5,080	3,954
04043	*Kennebunk*	6,621	5,646
03904	Kittery Center(u)	5,465	7,363
03904	*Kittery*	9,314	11,028
04240	Lewiston	40,481	41,779

ZIP code	Place	1980	1970
04750	*Limestone*	8,719	10,360
04457	*Lincoln*	5,066	4,759
04250	*Lisbon*	8,769	6,544
04750	Loring(u)	6,572	7,881
04756	*Madawaska*	5,282	5,585
04462	Millinocket Center(u)	7,567	7,558
04462	*Millinocket*	7,567	7,742
04062	North Windham(u)	5,492	....
04963	*Oakland*	5,162	3,535
04064	Old Orchard Beach Ctr.(u)	6,023	5,273
04064	*Old Orchard Beach*	6,291	5,404
04468	Old Town	8,422	8,741
04473	Orono Center(u)	9,891	9,146
04473	*Orono*	10,578	9,989
*04101	Portland	61,572	65,116
04769	Presque Isle	11,172	11,452
04841	Rockland	7,919	8,505
04276	Rumford Compact(u)	6,256	6,198
04276	*Rumford*	8,240	9,363
04072	Saco	12,921	11,678
04073	Sanford Center(u)	10,268	10,457
04073	*Sanford*	18,020	15,812
04074	*Scarborough*	11,347	7,845
04976	Skowhegan Center(u)	6,517	6,571
04976	*Skowhegan*	8,098	7,601
04106	South Portland	22,712	23,267
04084	*Standish*	5,946	3,122
04086	*Topsham*	6,431	5,022
04901	Waterville	17,779	18,192
04090	*Wells*	8,211	4,448
04092	Westbrook	14,976	14,444
04082	*Windham*	11,282	6,593
04901	Winslow Center(u)	5,903	5,389
04901	*Winslow*	8,057	7,299
04364	*Winthrop*	5,889	4,335
04096	*Yarmouth*	6,585	4,854
03909	*York*	8,465	5,690

Maryland (301)

ZIP code	Place	1980	1970
21001	Aberdeen	11,533	7,403
21005	Aberdeen Proving Ground(u)	5,772	7,403
20783	Adelphi(u)	12,530	....
20331	Andrews(u)	10,064	6,418
*21401	Annapolis	31,740	30,095
21227	Arbutus(u)	20,163	22,745
21012	Arnold(u)	12,285	....
20853	Aspen Hill(u)	47,455	16,887
*21233	Baltimore	786,775	905,787
21014	Bel Air	7,814	6,307
21050	Bel Air North(u)	5,043	....
21014	Bel Air South(u)	8,461	....
20705	Beltsville(u)	12,760	8,912
20014	Bethesda(u)	63,022	71,621
20710	Bladensburg	7,691	7,977
20715	Bowie	33,695	35,028
21225	Brooklyn Park(u)	11,508	....
20731	Cabin John-Brookmont(u)	5,135	....
20619	California(u)	5,770	....
21613	Cambridge	11,703	11,595
20031	Camp Springs(u)	16,118	22,776
21401	Cape St. Clair(u)	6,022	....
20027	Carmody Hills-Pepper Mill(u)	5,571	6,245
21234	Carney(u)	21,488	....
21228	Catonsville(u)	33,208	54,812
20785	Cheverly	5,751	6,808
20015	Chevy Chase(u)	12,232	16,424
20783	Chillum(u)	32,775	35,656
20735	Clinton(u)	16,438	....
20904	Cloverly(u)	5,153	....
21030	Cockeysville(u)	17,013	....
20904	Colesville(u)	14,359	9,455
20740	College Park	23,614	26,156
21043	Columbia(u)	52,518	8,815
20027	Coral Hills(u)	11,602	9,058
21114	Crofton(u)	12,009	4,478
21502	Cumberland	25,933	29,724
20028	District Heights	6,799	7,846
20785	Dodge Park(u)	5,275	....
21222	Dundalk(u)	71,293	85,377
21601	Easton	7,536	6,809
20840	East Riverdale(u)	14,117	....
21219	Edgemere(u)	9,078	10,352
21040	Edgewood	19,455	8,551
21921	Elkton	6,468	5,362
*21043	Ellicott(u)	21,784	9,435
21221	Essex(u)	39,614	38,193
20904	Fairland(u)	5,154	....
21047	Fallston(u)	5,572	....
21061	Ferndale(u)	14,314	9,929
20028	Forestville(u)	16,401	16,188
20755	Fort Meade(u)	14,083	16,699
21701	Frederick	27,557	23,641
.....	Friendly(u)	8,848	....
21532	Frostburg	7,715	7,327
20760	Gaithersburg	26,424	8,344
20767	Germantown(u)	9,721	....
.....	Glassmanor(u)	7,751	....
21061	Glen Burnie(u)	37,263	38,608
20769	Glenn Dale(u)	5,106	....
20770	Goddard(u)	6,147	....
20770	Greenbelt	16,000	18,199
21122	Green Haven(u)	6,577	....
21740	Hagerstown	34,132	35,862
21740	Halfway(u)	8,659	6,106
21204	Hampton(u)	5,220	....
21078	Havre De Grace	8,763	9,791
20903	Hillandale(u)	9,686	....
20031	Hillcrest Heights	17,021	24,037
*20780	Hyattsville	12,709	14,998
21085	Joppatowne(u)	11,348	9,092
20785	Kentland(u)	8,596	9,649
20870	Kettering(u)	6,972	....
21122	Lake Shore(u)	10,181	....
20785	Landover(u)	5,374	5,597
20787	Langley Park(u)	14,038	11,564
20801	Lanham-Seabrook(u)	15,814	13,244
21227	Lansdowne-Baltimore Highlands(u)	16,759	17,770
.....	Largo(u)	5,557	....
20810	Laurel	12,103	10,525
21502	La Vale-Narrows Park(u)	5,523	3,971
20653	Lexington Pk.(u)	10,361	9,136
21090	Linthicum(u)	7,457	9,775
21207	Lochearn(u)	26,908	....
21037	Londontowne(u)	6,052	3,864
21093	Lutherville-Timonium(u)	17,854	24,055
20031	Marlow Heights(u)	5,824	....
20810	Maryland City(u)	6,949	7,102
.....	Mays Chapel(u)	5,213	....
21220	Middle River(u)	26,756	19,935
.....	Milford Mill(u)	20,354	....
20760	Montgomery Village(u)	18,725	....
20822	Mount Rainier	7,361	8,180
21402	Naval Academy(u)	5,367	....
20784	New Carrollton	12,632	14,870
20014	North Bethesda(u)	22,671	....
20795	North Kensington(u)	9,039	....
20810	North Laurel(u)	6,093	....
21113	Odenton(u)	13,270	5,989
20832	Olney(u)	13,026	2,138
21206	Overlea(u)	12,965	13,124
21117	Owings Mills(u)	9,526	7,360
20021	Oxon Hill(u)	36,267	11,974
20785	Palmer Park(u)	7,986	8,172
21234	Parkville	35,159	33,589
21122	Pasadena(u)	7,439	....
21128	Perry Hall(u)	13,455	5,446
21208	Pikesville(u)	22,555	25,395
20854	Potomac(u)	40,402	....
21227	Pumphrey(u)	5,666	6,425
20760	Quince Orchard(u)	5,107	....
21133	Randallstown(u)	25,927	33,683
.....	Redland(u)	10,759	....
21136	Reisterstown(u)	19,385	12,568
21122	Riviera Beach(u)	8,812	7,464
*20850	Rockville	43,811	42,739
21237	Rosedale(u)	19,956	19,417
21221	Rossville(u)	8,646	....
20601	St. Charles(u)	13,921	....
21801	Salisbury	16,429	15,252
20027	Seat Pleasant	5,217	7,217
21740	Security(u)	29,453	....
21144	Severn(u)	20,147	....
21146	Severna Park	21,253	16,358
*20907	Silver Spring(u)	72,893	77,411
21061	South Gate(u)	24,185	9,356
20795	South Kensington(u)	9,344	10,289
20810	South Laurel(u)	18,034	13,345
20023	Suitland-Silver Hills(u)	32,164	30,355
20012	Takoma Park	16,231	18,507
.....	Tantallon(u)	9,945	....
20031	Temple Hills(u)	6,630	....
21204	Towson(u)	51,083	77,768
20601	Waldorf(u)	9,782	7,368
20028	Walker Mill(u)	10,651	7,103
21157	Westminster	8,808	7,207
20902	Wheaton Glenmont(u)	48,598	66,280
20903	White Oak(u)	13,700	19,769
20695	White Plains(u)	5,167	....
21207	Woodlawn(u)	5,306	....

Massachusetts

See Note on Page 218

ZIP code	Place	Area code	1980	1970
02351	*Abington*	(617)	13,517	12,334
01720	*Acton*	(617)	17,544	14,770
02743	*Acushnet*	(617)	8,704	7,767
01220	Adams Center(u)	(413)	6,857	11,256
.....	*Adams*	(413)	10,381	11,772
01001	*Agawam*	(413)	26,271	21,717
01913	Amesbury Center(u)	(617)	12,236	10,088
.....	*Amesbury*	(617)	13,971	11,388
01002	Amherst Center	(413)	17,773	17,926
.....	*Amherst*	(413)	33,229	26,331
01810	*Andover*	(617)	26,370	23,695
02174	*Arlington*	(617)	48,219	53,524
01721	*Ashland*	(617)	9,165	8,882

ZIP code	Place		1980	1970
01331	Athol Center(u)	(617)	8,708	9,723
.....	*Athol*	(617)	10,634	11,185
02703	Attleboro	(617)	34,196	32,907
01501	*Auburn*	(617)	14,845	15,347
02322	*Avon*	(617)	5,026	5,295
*01432	*Ayer*	(617)	6,993	8,325
02630	*Barnstable*	(617)	30,898	19,842
01730	*Bedford*	(617)	13,067	13,513
01007	*Belchertown*	(413)	8,339	5,936
02019	*Bellingham*	(617)	14,300	13,967
02178	*Belmont*	(617)	26,100	28,285
01915	Beverly	(617)	37,655	38,348
01821	*Billerica*	(617)	36,727	31,648
01504	*Blackstone*	(617)	6,570	6,566
*02109	Boston	(617)	562,994	641,071
02532	*Bourne*	(617)	13,874	12,636
01921	*Boxford*	(617)	5,374	4,032
02184	*Braintree*	(617)	36,337	35,050
02631	*Brewster*	(617)	5,226	1,790
02324	*Bridgewater*	(617)	17,202	12,911
*02403	Brockton	(617)	95,172	89,040
02145	*Brookline*	(617)	55,062	58,689
01803	*Burlington*	(617)	23,486	21,980
*02138	Cambridge	(617)	95,322	100,361
02021	*Canton*	(617)	18,182	17,100
02330	*Carver*	(617)	6,988	2,420
01507	*Charlton*	(617)	6,719	4,654
02633	*Chatham*	(617)	6,071	4,554
01824	*Chelmsford*	(617)	31,174	31,432
02150	Chelsea	(617)	25,431	30,625
*01021	Chicopee	(413)	55,112	66,676
01510	*Clinton*	(617)	12,771	13,383
01778	Cochituate(u)	(617)	6,126	....
02025	*Cohasset*	(617)	7,174	6,954
01742	*Concord*	(617)	16,293	16,148
01226	*Dalton*	(413)	6,797	7,505
01923	*Danvers*	(617)	24,100	26,151
02714	*Dartmouth*	(617)	23,966	18,800
02026	*Dedham*	(617)	25,298	26,938
02638	*Dennis*	(617)	12,360	6,454
02715	*Dighton*	(617)	5,352	4,667
01826	*Dracut*	(617)	21,249	18,214
01570	*Dudley*	(617)	8,717	8,087
02332	*Duxbury*	(617)	11,807	7,636
02333	*East Bridgewater*	(617)	9,945	8,347
02536	East Falmouth(u)	(617)	5,181	2,971
01027	*Easthampton*	(413)	15,580	13,012
01028	*East Longmeadow*	(413)	12,905	13,029
02334	*Easton*	(617)	16,623	12,157
01249	Everett	(617)	37,195	42,485
02719	*Fairhaven*	(617)	15,759	16,332
*02722	Fall River	(617)	92,574	96,898
*02540	Falmouth Center(u)	(617)	5,720	5,806
.....	*Falmouth*	(617)	23,640	15,942
01420	Fitchburg	(617)	39,580	43,343
01433	Fort Devens(u)	(617)	9,546	12,915
02035	*Foxborough*	(617)	14,148	14,218
01701	*Framingham*	(617)	65,113	64,048
02038	Franklin Center(u)	(617)	9,296	8,863
.....	*Franklin*	(617)	18,217	17,830
02702	*Freetown*	(617)	7,058	4,270
01440	Gardner	(617)	17,900	19,748
01833	*Georgetown*	(617)	5,687	5,290
01930	Gloucester	(617)	27,768	27,941
01519	*Grafton*	(617)	11,238	11,659
01033	*Granby*	(413)	5,380	5,473
01230	*Great Barrington*	(413)	7,405	7,537
01301	Greenfield Center(u)	(413)	14,198	14,642
.....	*Greenfield*	(413)	18,436	18,116
01450	*Groton*	(617)	6,154	5,109
01834	*Groveland*	(617)	5,040	5,382
02338	*Halifax*	(617)	5,513	3,537
01936	*Hamilton*	(617)	6,960	6,373
02339	*Hanover*	(617)	11,358	10,107
02341	*Hanson*	(617)	8,617	7,148
01451	*Harvard*	(617)	12,170	12,494
02645	*Harwich*	(617)	8,971	5,892
01830	Haverhill	(617)	46,865	46,120
02043	*Hingham*	(617)	20,339	18,845
02343	*Holbrook*	(617)	11,140	11,775
01520	*Holden*	(617)	13,336	12,564
01746	*Holliston*	(617)	12,622	12,069
01040	Holyoke	(413)	44,678	50,112
01748	*Hopkinton*	(617)	7,114	5,981
01749	Hudson Center(u)	(617)	14,156	14,283
.....	*Hudson*	(617)	16,408	16,084
02045	*Hull*	(617)	9,714	9,961
02601	Hyannis(u)	(617)	9,118	6,847
01938	Ipswich(u)	(617)	NA	5,022
.....	*Ipswich*	(617)	11,158	10,750
02364	*Kingston*	(617)	7,362	5,999
02346	*Lakeville*	(617)	5,931	4,376
01523	*Lancaster*	(617)	6,334	6,095
*01842	Lawrence	(617)	63,175	66,915
01238	*Lee*	(413)	6,247	6,426
01524	*Leicester*	(617)	9,446	9,140
01240	*Lenox*	(413)	6,523	5,804
01453	Leominster	(617)	34,508	32,939
02173	*Lexington*	(617)	29,479	31,886
01773	*Lincoln*	(617)	7,098	7,567
01460	*Littleton*	(617)	6,970	6,380
01106	*Longmeadow*	(413)	16,301	15,630
*01853	Lowell	(617)	92,418	94,239
01056	*Ludlow*	(413)	18,150	17,580
01462	*Lunenburg*	(617)	8,405	7,419
*01901	Lynn	(617)	78,471	90,294
01940	*Lynnfield*	(617)	11,267	10,826
02148	Malden	(617)	53,386	56,127
01944	*Manchester*	(617)	5,424	5,151
02048	*Mansfield*	(617)	13,453	9,939
01945	*Marblehead*	(617)	20,126	21,295
01752	Marlborough	(617)	30,617	27,936
02050	*Marshfield*	(617)	20,916	15,223
02739	*Mattapoisett*	(617)	5,597	4,500
01754	*Maynard*	(617)	9,590	9,710
02052	*Medfield*	(617)	10,220	9,821
02155	Medford	(617)	58,076	64,397
02053	*Medway*	(617)	8,447	7,938
02176	Melrose	(617)	30,055	33,180
01844	*Methuen*	(617)	36,701	35,456
02346	Middleborough Center(u)	(617)	7,012	6,259
.....	*Middleborough*	(617)	16,404	13,607
01757	Milford Center(u)	(617)	NA	13,740
.....	*Milford*	(617)	23,390	19,352
01527	*Millbury*	(617)	11,808	11,987
02054	*Millis*	(617)	6,908	5,686
02186	*Milton*	(617)	25,860	27,190
01057	*Monson*	(413)	7,315	7,355
01351	*Montague*	(413)	8,011	8,451
02554	*Nantucket*	(617)	5,087	3,774
01760	*Natick*	(617)	29,461	31,057
02192	*Needham*	(617)	27,901	29,748
*02741	New Bedford	(617)	98,478	101,777
01950	Newburyport	(617)	15,900	15,807
02158	Newton	(617)	83,622	91,263
02056	*Norfolk*	(617)	6,363	4,656
01247	North Adams	(413)	18,063	19,195
01002	North Amherst(u)	(413)	5,616	2,854
01060	Northampton	(413)	29,286	29,664
01845	*North Andover*	(617)	20,129	16,284
*02760	*North Attleborough*	(617)	21,095	18,665
01532	*Northborough*	(617)	10,568	9,218
01534	*Northbridge*	(617)	12,246	11,795
01864	*North Reading*	(617)	11,455	11,264
02060	North Scituate(u)	(617)	5,221	5,507
02766	*Norton*	(617)	12,690	9,487
02061	*Norwell*	(617)	9,182	7,796
02062	*Norwood*	(617)	29,711	30,815
01364	*Orange*	(617)	6,844	6,104
02653	*Orleans*	(617)	5,306	3,055
01253	Otis(u)	(413)	NA	5,596
01540	Oxford Center(u)	(617)	6,369	6,109
.....	*Oxford*	(617)	11,680	10,345
01069	*Palmer*	(413)	11,389	11,680
01960	Peabody	(617)	45,976	48,080
02359	*Pembroke*	(617)	13,487	11,193
01463	*Pepperell*	(617)	8,061	5,887
01866	Pinehurst(u)	(617)	6,588	....
01201	Pittsfield	(413)	51,974	57,020
02762	*Plainville*	(617)	5,857	4,953
*02360	Plymouth Center(u)	(617)	7,232	6,940
.....	*Plymouth*	(617)	35,913	18,606
02169	Quincy	(617)	84,743	87,966
02368	*Randolph*	(617)	28,218	27,035
02767	*Raynham*	(617)	9,085	6,705
01867	*Reading*	(617)	22,678	22,539
02769	*Rehoboth*	(617)	7,570	6,512
02151	Revere	(617)	42,423	43,159
02370	*Rockland*	(617)	15,695	15,674
01966	*Rockport*	(617)	6,345	5,636
01970	Salem	(617)	38,220	40,556
01950	*Salisbury*	(617)	5,973	4,179
02563	*Sandwich*	(617)	8,727	5,239
01906	*Saugus*	(617)	24,746	25,110
02066	*Scituate*	(617)	17,317	16,973
02771	*Seekonk*	(617)	12,269	11,116
02067	*Sharon*	(617)	13,601	12,367
01464	*Shirley*	(617)	5,124	4,909
01545	*Shrewsbury*	(617)	22,674	19,196
02725	*Somerset*	(617)	18,813	18,088
02143	Somerville	(617)	77,372	88,779
01772	*Southborough*	(617)	6,193	5,798
01550	Southbridge Center(u)	(617)	12,882	14,261
.....	*Southbridge*	(617)	16,665	17,057
01075	*South Hadley*	(413)	16,399	17,033
01077	*Southwick*	(413)	7,382	6,330
02664	South Yarmouth(u)	(617)	7,525	5,380
01562	Spencer Center	(617)	6,350	5,895
.....	*Spencer*	(617)	10,774	8,779
*01101	Springfield	(413)	152,319	163,905
01564	*Sterling*	(617)	5,440	4,247
02180	*Stoneham*	(617)	21,424	20,725
02072	*Stoughton*	(617)	26,710	23,459
01775	*Stow*	(617)	5,144	3,984
01566	*Sturbridge*	(617)	5,976	4,878
01776	*Sudbury*	(617)	14,027	13,506
01527	*Sutton*	(617)	5,855	4,590
01907	*Swampscott*	(617)	13,837	13,578
02777	*Swansea*	(617)	15,461	12,640
02780	Taunton	(617)	45,001	43,756

ZIP code	Place		1980	1980
01468	*Templeton*	(617)	6,070	5,863
01876	*Tewksbury*	(617)	24,635	22,755
01983	*Topsfield*	(617)	5,709	5,225
01469	*Townsend*	(617)	7,201	4,281
01376	Turners Falls(u)	(413)	NA	5,168
01879	*Tyngsborough*	(617)	5,683	4,204
01569	*Uxbridge*	(617)	8,374	8,253
01880	*Wakefield*	(617)	24,895	25,402
02081	*Walpole*	(617)	18,859	18,149
02154	Waltham	(617)	58,200	61,582
01082	Ware Center(u)	(413)	6,806	6,509
.....	*Ware*	(413)	8,953	8,187
02571	*Wareham*	(617)	18,457	11,492
02172	*Watertown*	(617)	34,384	39,307
01778	*Wayland*	(617)	12,170	13,461
01570	Webster Center(u)	(617)	11,175	12,432
.....	*Webster*	(617)	14,480	14,917
02181	*Wellesley*	(617)	27,209	28,051
01581	*Westborough*	(617)	13,619	12,594
01583	*West Boylston*	(617)	6,204	6,369
02379	*West Bridgewater*	(617)	6,359	6,070
01742	West Concord(u)	(617)	5,331	....
01085	Westfield	(413)	36,465	31,433
01886	*Westford*	(617)	13,434	10,368
01473	*Westminster*	(617)	5,139	4,273
02193	*Weston*	(617)	11,169	10,870
02790	*Westport*	(617)	13,763	9,791
01089	*West Springfield*	(413)	27,042	28,461
02090	*Westwood*	(617)	13,212	12,570
02188	*Weymouth*	(617)	55,601	54,610
01588	Whitinsville(u)	(617)	5,379	5,210
02382	*Whitman*	(617)	13,534	13,059
01095	*Wilbraham*	(413)	12,053	11,984
01267	*Williamstown*	(413)	8,741	8,454
01887	*Wilmington*	(617)	17,471	17,102
01475	*Winchendon*	(617)	7,019	6,635
01890	*Winchester*	(617)	20,701	22,269
02152	*Winthrop*	(617)	19,294	20,335
01801	Woburn	(617)	36,626	37,406
*01613	Worcester	(617)	161,799	176,572
02093	*Wrentham*	(617)	7,580	7,315
02675	*Yarmouth*	(617)	18,449	12,033

Michigan

49221	Adrian	(517)	21,186	20,382
49224	Albion	(517)	11,059	12,112
48101	Allen Park	(313)	34,196	40,747
48801	Alma	(517)	9,652	9,611
49707	Alpena	(517)	12,214	13,805
*48106	Ann Arbor	(313)	107,316	100,035
48063	Avon(u)	(313)	40,779	....
*49016	Battle Creek	(616)	35,724	38,931
48706	Bay City	(517)	41,593	49,449
48505	Beecher(u)	(313)	17,178	....
48809	Belding	(616)	5,634	5,121
49022	Benton Harbor	(616)	14,707	16,481
49022	Benton Heights(u)	(616)	6,787	....
48072	Berkley	(313)	18,637	21,879
48009	Beverly Hills	(313)	11,598	13,598
49307	Big Rapids	(616)	14,361	11,995
*48012	Birmingham	(313)	21,689	26,170
48013	Bloomfield(u)	(313)	42,876	....
49107	Buchanan	(616)	5,142	4,645
*48502	Burton	(313)	29,976	32,540
49601	Cadillac	(616)	10,199	9,990
48724	Carrollton(u)	(517)	7,482	7,300
48015	Center Line	(313)	9,293	10,379
48813	Charlotte	(517)	8,251	8,244
49721	Cheboygan	(616)	5,106	5,553
48017	Clawson	(313)	15,103	17,617
48043	Clinton(u)	(313)	72,400	1,677
49036	Coldwater	(517)	9,461	9,155
49321	Comstock Park(u)	(616)	5,506	5,766
49508	Cutlerville(u)	(616)	8,256	6,267
48423	Davison	(313)	6,087	5,259
*48120	Dearborn	(313)	90,660	104,199
48127	Dearborn Heights	(313)	67,706	80,069
*48233	Detroit	(313)	1,203,339	1,514,063
49047	Dowagiac	(616)	6,307	6,583
48021	East Detroit	(313)	38,280	45,920
49506	East Grand Rapids	(616)	10,914	12,565
48823	East Lansing	(517)	48,309	47,540
49001	Eastwood(u)	(517)	7,186	9,682
48229	Ecorse	(313)	14,447	17,515
49829	Escanaba	(906)	14,355	15,368
49022	Fair Plain(u)	(616)	8,289	3,680
48024	Farmington	(313)	11,022	10,329
48024	Farmington Hills	(313)	58,056	48,694
48430	Fenton	(313)	8,098	8,284
48220	Ferndale	(313)	26,227	30,850
48134	Flat Rock	(313)	6,853	5,643
*48502	Flint	(313)	159,611	193,317
48433	Flushing	(313)	8,624	7,190
48026	Fraser	(313)	14,560	11,868
48135	Garden City	(313)	35,640	41,864
48439	Grand Blanc	(313)	6,848	5,132
49417	Grand Haven	(616)	11,763	11,844
48837	Grand Ledge	(517)	6,920	6,032
*49501	Grand Rapids	(616)	181,843	197,649
49418	Grandville	(616)	12,412	10,764
48838	Greenville	(616)	8,019	7,493
48138	Grosse Ile(u)	(313)	9,320	8,306
48236	Grosse Pointe	(313)	5,901	6,637
48236	Grosse Pointe Farms	(313)	10,551	11,701
48236	Grosse Pointe Park	(313)	13,639	15,641
48236	Grosse Pointe Woods	(313)	18,886	21,878
48212	Hamtramck	(313)	21,300	26,783
49930	Hancock	(906)	5,122	4,820
48236	Harper Woods	(313)	16,361	20,186
48043	Harrison(u)	(313)	23,649	....
48840	Haslett(u)	(517)	7,025	....
49058	Hastings	(616)	6,418	6,501
48030	Hazel Park	(313)	20,914	23,784
48203	Highland Park	(313)	27,909	35,444
49242	Hillsdale	(517)	7,432	7,728
49423	Holland	(616)	26,281	26,479
48842	Holt(u)	(517)	10,097	6,980
49931	Houghton	(906)	7,512	6,067
48843	Howell	(517)	6,976	5,224
48070	Huntington Woods	(313)	6,937	8,536
48141	Inkster	(313)	35,190	38,595
48846	Ionia	(616)	5,920	6,361
49801	Iron Mountain	(906)	8,341	8,702
49938	Ironwood	(906)	7,741	8,711
49849	Ishpeming	(906)	7,538	8,245
*49201	Jackson	(517)	39,739	45,484
49428	Jenison(u)	(616)	16,330	11,266
*49001	Kalamazoo	(616)	79,722	85,555
49508	Kentwood	(616)	30,438	20,310
49801	Kingsford	(906)	5,290	5,276
49843	K.I. Sawyer(u)	(906)	7,345	8,224
49015	Lakeview(u)	(517)	13,345	11,391
48144	Lambertville(u)	(313)	6,341	5,711
*48924	Lansing	(517)	130,414	131,403
48446	Lapeer	(313)	6,225	6,314
48146	Lincoln Park	(313)	45,105	52,984
*48150	Livonia	(313)	104,814	110,109
49431	Ludington	(616)	8,937	9,021
48071	Madison Heights	(313)	35,375	38,599
49660	Manistee	(616)	7,566	7,723
49855	Marquette	(906)	23,288	21,967
49068	Marshall	(616)	7,201	7,253
48040	Marysville	(313)	7,345	5,610
48854	Mason	(517)	6,019	5,468
48122	Melvindale	(313)	12,322	13,862
49858	Menominee	(906)	10,099	10,748
49254	Michigan Center(u)	(517)	5,244	....
48640	Midland	(517)	37,250	35,176
48042	Milford	(313)	5,041	4,699
48161	Monroe	(313)	23,531	23,894
48043	Mount Clemens	(313)	18,806	20,476
48858	Mount Pleasant	(517)	23,746	20,524
*49440	Muskegon	(616)	40,823	44,631
49444	Muskegon Heights	(616)	14,611	17,304
49866	Negaunee	(906)	5,189	5,248
48047	New Baltimore	(313)	5,439	4,132
49120	Niles	(616)	13,115	12,988
.....	Northview(u)		11,662	....
48167	Northville	(313)	5,698	5,400
49441	Norton Shores	(616)	22,025	22,271
48050	Novi	(313)	22,525	9,668
48237	Oak Park	(313)	31,537	36,762
48864	Okemos(u)	(517)	8,882	7,770
48867	Owosso	(517)	16,455	17,179
49770	Petoskey	(616)	6,097	6,342
48170	Plymouth	(313)	9,986	11,758
*48053	Pontiac	(313)	76,715	85,279
49081	Portage	(616)	38,157	33,590
48060	Port Huron	(313)	33,981	35,794
48239	Redford(u)	(313)	58,441	....
48218	River Rouge	(313)	12,912	15,947
48192	Riverview	(313)	14,569	11,342
48063	Rochester	(313)	7,203	7,054
48174	Romulus	(313)	24,857	22,879
48066	Roseville	(313)	54,311	60,529
*48068	Royal Oak	(313)	70,893	86,238
*48605	Saginaw	(517)	77,508	91,849
*48083	St. Clair Shores	(313)	76,210	88,093
48879	St. Johns	(517)	7,376	6,672
49085	St. Joseph	(616)	9,622	11,042
48176	Saline	(313)	6,483	4,811
49793	Sault Ste. Marie	(906)	14,448	15,136
*48075	Southfield	(313)	75,568	69,285
48198	Southgate	(313)	32,058	33,909
49090	South Haven	(616)	5,943	6,471
48178	South Lyon	(313)	5,214	2,675
49015	Springfield	(616)	5,917	3,994
*48078	Sterling Heights	(313)	108,999	61,365
49091	Sturgis	(616)	9,468	9,295
48473	Swartz Creek	(313)	5,013	4,928
48180	Taylor	(313)	77,568	70,020
49286	Tecumseh	(517)	7,320	7,120
49093	Three Rivers	(616)	7,015	7,355
49684	Traverse City	(616)	15,516	18,048
48183	Trenton	(313)	22,762	24,127
48084	Troy	(313)	67,102	39,419
48087	Utica	(313)	5,282	3,504
49504	Walker	(616)	15,088	11,492

ZIP code	Place		1980	1970
*48089	Warren	(313)	161,134	179,260
48095	Waterford(u)	(313)	64,250	....
48184	Wayne	(313)	21,159	21,054
48033	West Bloomfield(u)	(313)	41,962	....
48185	Westland	(313)	84,603	86,749
49007	Westwood(u)	(616)	8,519	9,143
48019	White Lake-Seven Harbors(u)	(313)	7,557	....
48096	Wixom	(313)	6,705	2,010
48183	Woodhaven	(313)	10,902	3,566
48753	Wurtsmith(u)	(517)	5,166	6,932
*48192	Wyandotte	(313)	34,006	41,061
49509	Wyoming	(616)	59,616	56,560
48197	Ypsilanti	(313)	24,031	29,538

Minnesota

ZIP code	Place		1980	1970
56007	Albert Lea	(507)	19,190	19,418
56308	Alexandria	(612)	7,608	6,973
55303	Andover	(612)	9,387	....
55303	Anoka	(612)	15,634	13,298
55068	Apple Valley	(612)	21,818	8,502
55112	Arden Hills	(612)	8,012	5,149
55912	Austin	(507)	23,020	26,210
56601	Bemidji	(218)	10,949	11,490
55433	Blaine	(612)	28,558	20,573
55420	Bloomington	(612)	81,831	81,970
56401	Brainerd	(218)	11,489	11,667
55429	Brooklyn Center	(612)	31,230	35,173
55429	Brooklyn Park	(612)	43,332	26,230
55337	Burnsville	(612)	35,674	19,940
55316	Champlin	(612)	9,006	2,275
55317	Chanhassen	(612)	6,359	4,879
55318	Chaska	(612)	8,346	4,352
55719	Chisholm	(218)	5,930	5,913
55720	Cloquet	(218)	11,142	8,699
55421	Columbia Heights	(612)	20,029	23,997
55433	Coon Rapids	(612)	35,826	30,505
55016	Cottage Grove	(612)	18,994	13,419
56716	Crookston	(218)	8,628	8,312
55428	Crystal	(612)	25,543	30,925
56501	Detroit Lakes	(218)	7,106	5,797
*55806	Duluth	(218)	92,811	100,578
55121	Eagan	(612)	20,532	10,398
55005	East Bethel	(612)	6,626	2,586
56721	East Grand Forks	(218)	8,537	7,607
55343	Eden Prairie	(612)	16,263	6,938
55424	Edina	(612)	46,073	44,046
55330	Elk River	(612)	6,785	2,252
55734	Eveleth	(218)	5,042	4,721
56031	Fairmont	(507)	11,506	10,751
55113	Falcon Heights	(507)	5,291	5,530
55021	Faribault	(507)	16,241	16,595
56537	Fergus Falls	(218)	12,519	12,443
55421	Fridley	(612)	30,228	29,233
55427	Golden Valley	(612)	22,775	24,246
55744	Grand Rapids	(218)	7,934	7,247
55303	Ham Lake	(612)	7,832	3,327
55033	Hastings	(612)	12,827	12,195
55811	Hermantown	(218)	6,759	....
55746	Hibbing	(218)	21,193	16,104
55343	Hopkins	(612)	15,336	13,428
55350	Hutchinson	(612)	9,244	8,031
56649	International Falls	(218)	5,611	6,439
55075	Inver Grove Heights	(612)	17,171	12,148
55042	Lake Elmo	(612)	5,296	3,565
55044	Lakeville	(612)	14,790	7,556
55355	Litchfield	(612)	5,904	5,262
55110	Little Canada	(612)	7,102	3,481
56345	Little Falls	(612)	7,250	7,467
56001	Mankato	(507)	28,651	30,895
55369	Maple Grove	(612)	20,525	6,275
55109	Maplewood	(612)	26,990	25,186
56258	Marshall	(507)	11,161	9,886
55118	Mendota Heights	(612)	7,288	6,565
*55401	Minneapolis	(612)	370,951	434,400
55343	Minnetonka	(612)	38,683	35,776
56265	Montevideo	(612)	5,845	5,661
56560	Moorhead	(218)	29,998	29,687
56267	Morris	(612)	5,367	5,366
55364	Mound	(612)	9,280	7,572
55112	Mounds View	(612)	12,593	10,599
55112	New Brighton	(612)	23,269	19,507
54428	New Hope	(612)	23,087	23,180
56073	New Ulm	(507)	13,755	13,051
55057	Northfield	(507)	12,562	10,235
56001	North Mankato	(507)	9,145	7,347
55109	North St. Paul	(612)	11,921	11,950
55119	Oakdale	(612)	12,123	7,795
55323	Orono	(612)	6,845	6,787
55060	Owatonna	(507)	18,632	15,341
55427	Plymouth	(612)	31,615	18,077
55372	Prior Lake	(612)	7,284	1,114
55303	Ramsey	(612)	10,093	....
55066	Red Wing	(612)	13,736	10,441
56283	Redwood Falls	(507)	5,210	4,774
55423	Richfield	(612)	37,851	47,231
55422	Robbinsdale	(612)	14,422	16,845
55901	Rochester	(507)	57,855	53,766
55068	Rosemount	(612)	5,083	1,337
55113	Roseville	(612)	35,820	34,438
55418	St. Anthony	(612)	7,981	9,239
56301	St. Cloud	(612)	42,566	39,691
55426	St. Louis Park	(612)	42,931	48,883
*55101	St. Paul	(612)	270,230	309,866
56082	St. Peter	(507)	9,056	8,339
56379	Sauk Rapids	(612)	5,793	5,051
55379	Shakopee	(612)	9,941	6,876
55112	Shoreview	(612)	17,300	10,978
55075	South St. Paul	(612)	21,235	25,016
55432	Spring Lake Park	(612)	6,477	6,417
55082	Stillwater	(612)	12,290	10,191
56701	Thief River Falls	(218)	9,105	8,618
55110	Vadnais Heights	(612)	5,111	3,411
55792	Virginia	(218)	11,056	12,450
56093	Waseca	(507)	8,219	6,789
55118	West St. Paul	(612)	18,527	18,802
55110	White Bear Lake	(612)	22,538	23,313
56201	Willmar	(612)	15,895	12,869
55987	Winona	(507)	25,075	26,438
55119	Woodbury	(612)	10,297	6,184
56187	Worthington	(507)	10,243	9,916

Mississippi (601)

ZIP code	Place	1980	1970
39730	Aberdeen	7,184	6,507
38821	Amory	7,307	7,236
39520	Bay St. Louis	7,891	6,752
*39530	Biloxi	49,311	48,486
38829	Booneville	6,199	5,895
39042	Brandon	9,626	2,685
39601	Brookhaven	10,800	10,700
39046	Canton	11,116	10,503
38614	Clarksdale	21,137	21,673
38732	Cleveland	14,524	13,327
39056	Clinton	14,660	7,289
39429	Columbia	7,733	7,587
39701	Columbus	27,383	25,795
38834	Corinth	13,839	11,581
39532	D'Iberville(u)	13,369	7,288
39552	Escatawpa(u)	5,367	1,579
39074	Forest	5,229	4,085
39553	Gautier(u)	8,917	2,087
38701	Greenville	40,613	39,648
38930	Greenwood	20,115	22,400
38901	Grenada	12,641	9,944
39501	Gulfport	39,676	40,791
39401	Hattiesburg	40,829	38,277
38635	Holly Springs	7,285	5,728
38751	Indianola	8,221	8,947
*39205	Jackson	202,895	153,968
39090	Kosciusko	7,415	7,266
39440	Laurel	21,897	24,145
38756	Leland	6,667	6,000
39560	Long Beach	7,967	6,170
39339	Louisville	7,323	6,626
39648	McComb	12,331	11,851
39301	Meridian	46,577	45,083
39563	Moss Point	18,998	19,321
39120	Natchez	22,015	19,704
38652	New Albany	7,072	6,426
39501	North Gulfport(u)	6,660	6,996
39560	North Long Beach(u)	7,063	....
39564	Ocean Springs	14,504	19,160
39567	Orange Grove(u)	13,476	....
38655	Oxford	9,882	8,519
39567	Pascagoula	29,318	27,264
39571	Pass Christian	5,014	2,979
39208	Pearl	20,778	9,623
39465	Petal	8,476	6,986
39350	Philadelphia	6,434	6,274
39466	Picayune	10,361	9,760
39157	Ridgeland	5,461	1,650
38668	Senatobia	5,013	4,247
38671	Southaven(u)	16,071	8,931
39759	Starkville	15,169	11,369
38801	Tupelo	23,905	20,471
39180	Vicksburg	25,434	25,478
39367	Waynesboro	5,349	4,368
39773	West Point	8,811	8,714
38967	Winona	6,177	5,521
39194	Yazoo City	12,426	11,688

Missouri

ZIP code	Place		1980	1970
63123	Affton(u)	(314)	23,181	24,264
63010	Arnold	(314)	19,141	17,381
65605	Aurora	(417)	6,437	5,359
63011	Ballwin	(314)	12,750	10,656
63137	Bellefontaine Neighbors	(314)	12,082	14,084
64012	Belton	(816)	12,708	12,270
63134	Berkeley	(314)	16,146	19,743
63031	Black Jack	(314)	5,293	4,145
64015	Blue Springs	(816)	25,927	6,779
65613	Bolivar	(417)	5,919	4,769
65233	Boonville	(816)	6,959	7,514
63114	Breckenridge Hills	(816)	5,666	7,011
63144	Brentwood	(314)	8,209	11,248
63044	Bridgeton	(314)	18,445	19,992

ZIP code	Place		1980	1970
64628	Brookfield	(816)	5,555	5,491
63701	Cape Girardeau	(314)	34,361	31,282
64836	Carthage	(417)	11,104	11,035
63830	Caruthersville	(314)	7,958	7,350
63834	Charleston	(314)	5,230	5,131
64601	Chillicothe	(816)	9,089	9,519
63105	Clayton	(314)	14,219	16,100
64735	Clinton	(816)	8,366	7,504
65201	Columbia	(314)	62,061	58,812
63128	Concord(u)	(314)	20,896	21,217
63126	Crestwood	(314)	12,815	15,123
63141	Creve Coeur	(314)	12,694	8,967
63136	Dellwood	(314)	6,200	7,137
63020	De Soto	(314)	5,993	5,984
63131	Des Peres	(314)	8,254	5,333
63841	Dexter	(314)	7,043	6,024
63011	Ellisville	(314)	6,233	4,681
64024	Excelsior Springs	(816)	10,424	9,411
63640	Farmington	(314)	8,270	6,590
63135	Ferguson	(314)	24,740	28,759
63028	Festus	(314)	7,574	7,530
*63033	Florissant	(314)	55,372	65,908
65473	Fort Leonard Wood(u)	(314)	21,262	33,799
65251	Fulton	(314)	11,046	12,248
64118	Gladstone	(816)	24,990	23,422
63122	Glendale	(314)	6,035	6,981
64030	Grandview	(816)	24,502	17,456
63401	Hannibal	(314)	18,811	18,609
64701	Harrisonville	(816)	6,372	5,052
*63042	Hazelwood	(314)	12,935	14,082
*64051	Independence	(816)	111,806	111,630
63755	Jackson	(314)	7,827	5,896
65101	Jefferson City	(314)	33,619	32,407
63136	Jennings	(314)	17,026	19,379
64801	Joplin	(417)	38,893	39,256
*64108	Kansas City	(816)	448,159	507,330
63857	Kennett	(314)	10,145	10,090
63501	Kirksville	(816)	17,167	15,560
63122	Kirkwood	(314)	27,987	31,679
63124	Ladue	(314)	9,376	10,306
65536	Lebanon	(417)	9,507	8,616
64063	Lee's Summit	(816)	28,741	16,230
63125	Lemay(u)	(314)	35,424	40,529
64067	Lexington	(816)	5,063	5,388
64068	Liberty	(816)	16,251	13,704
63552	Macon	(816)	5,680	5,301
63863	Malden	(314)	6,096	5,374
63011	Manchester	(314)	6,191	5,031
63143	Maplewood	(314)	10,960	12,785
65340	Marshall	(816)	12,781	12,051
63043	Maryland Heights(u)	(314)	5,676	8,805
64468	Maryville	(816)	9,558	9,970
65265	Mexico	(314)	12,276	11,807
65270	Moberly	(816)	13,418	12,988
65708	Monett	(417)	6,148	5,937
63026	Murphy(u)	(314)	8,121	....
64850	Neosho	(417)	9,493	7,517
64772	Nevada	(417)	9,044	9,736
63121	Normandy	(314)	5,174	6,236
63121	Northwoods	(314)	5,831	4,607
63366	O'Fallon	(314)	8,654	7,018
63124	Olivette	(314)	8,039	9,156
63114	Overland	(314)	19,620	24,819
63775	Perryville	(314)	7,343	5,149
63120	Pine Lawn	(314)	6,662	5,745
63901	Poplar Bluff	(314)	17,139	16,653
64133	Raytown	(816)	31,759	33,306
64085	Richmond	(816)	5,499	4,948
63117	Richmond Heights	(314)	11,516	13,802
63124	Rock Hill	(314)	5,702	6,815
65401	Rolla	(314)	13,303	13,571
63074	St. Ann	(314)	15,523	18,215
63301	St. Charles	(314)	37,379	31,834
63114	St. John	(314)	7,854	8,960
*64501	St. Joseph	(816)	76,691	72,748
*63155	St. Louis	(314)	453,085	622,236
63376	St. Peters	(314)	15,700	486
63126	Sappington(u)	(314)	11,388	10,603
65301	Sedalia	(816)	20,927	22,847
63119	Shrewsbury	(314)	5,077	5,896
63801	Sikeston	(314)	17,431	14,699
63138	Spanish Lake(u)	(314)	20,632	15,647
*65801	Springfield	(417)	133,116	120,096
63080	Sullivan	(314)	5,461	5,111
64683	Trenton	(816)	6,811	6,063
63084	Union	(314)	5,506	5,183
63130	University City	(314)	42,738	47,527
64093	Warrensburg	(816)	13,807	13,125
63090	Washington	(314)	9,251	8,499
64870	Webb City	(417)	7,309	6,923
63119	Webster Groves	(314)	23,097	27,457
65775	West Plains	(417)	7,741	6,893

Montana (406)

59711	Anaconda-Deer Lodge County	12,518	9,771
59101	Billings	66,798	61,581
59101	Billings Heights(u)	8,480	....
59715	Bozeman	21,645	18,670
59701	Butte-Silver Bow	37,205	23,368
59330	Glendive	5,978	6,305
*59401	Great Falls	56,725	60,091
59501	Havre	10,891	10,558
59601	Helena	23,938	22,730
59901	Kalispell	10,648	10,526
59044	Laurel	5,481	4,454
59457	Lewistown	7,104	6,437
59047	Livingston	6,994	6,883
59402	Malmstrom AFB(u)	6,675	8,374
59301	Miles City	9,602	9,023
59801	Missoula	33,388	29,497
59801	Missoula South(u)	5,557	4,886
59801	Orchard Homes(u)	10,837	....
59270	Sidney	5,726	4,543

Nebraska

69301	Alliance	(308)	9,869	6,862
68310	Beatrice	(402)	12,891	12,389
68005	Bellevue	(402)	21,813	21,953
68008	Blair	(402)	6,418	6,106
69337	Chadron	(308)	5,933	5,921
68601	Columbus	(402)	17,328	15,471
68355	Falls City	(402)	5,374	5,444
68025	Fremont	(402)	23,979	22,962
69341	Gering	(308)	7,760	5,639
68801	Grand Island	(308)	33,180	32,358
68901	Hastings	(402)	23,045	23,580
68949	Holdrege	(308)	5,624	5,635
68847	Kearney	(308)	21,158	19,181
68128	La Vista	(402)	9,588	4,858
68850	Lexington	(308)	6,898	5,654
*68501	Lincoln	(402)	171,932	149,518
69001	McCook	(308)	8,404	8,285
68410	Nebraska City	(402)	7,127	7,441
68701	Norfolk	(402)	19,449	16,607
69101	North Platte	(308)	24,479	19,447
68113	Offutt AFB West(u)	(402)	8,787	8,445
69153	Ogallala	(308)	5,638	4,976
*68108	Omaha	(402)	311,681	346,929
68046	Papillion	(402)	6,399	5,606
68048	Plattsmouth	(402)	6,295	6,371
68127	Ralston	(402)	5,143	4,731
69361	Scottsbluff	(308)	14,156	14,507
68434	Seward	(402)	5,713	5,294
69162	Sidney	(308)	6,010	6,403
68776	South Sioux City	(402)	9,339	7,920
68787	Wayne	(402)	5,240	5,379
68467	York	(402)	7,723	6,778

Nevada (702)

89005	Boulder City	9,590	5,223
89701	Carson City	32,022	15,468
89112	East Las Vegas(u)	6,449	6,501
89801	Elko	8,758	7,621
89015	Henderson	24,363	16,395
89450	Incline Village-Crystal Bay(u)	6,225	....
*89114	Las Vegas	164,674	125,787
89110	Nellis AFB(u)	6,205	6,449
89030	North Las Vegas	42,739	46,067
89109	Paradise(u)	84,818	24,477
*89501	Reno	100,756	72,863
89431	Sparks	40,780	24,187
89110	Sunrise Manor(u)	44,155	9,684
89431	Sun Valley(u)	8,822	2,414
89109	Vegas Creek(u)	NA	8,970
89101	Winchester(u)	19,728	13,981

New Hampshire (603)

See note on page 218

03102	*Bedford*	9,481	5,859
03570	Berlin	13,084	15,256
03743	Claremont	14,557	14,221
03301	Concord	30,400	30,022
03038	Derry Compact(u)	12,248	6,090
.....	*Derry*	18,875	11,712
03820	Dover	22,377	20,850
03824	Durham Compact(u)	8,448	7,221
.....	*Durham*	10,652	8,869
03833	Exeter Compact(u)	8,947	6,439
.....	*Exeter*	11,024	8,892
03235	Franklin	7,901	7,292
03045	*Goffstown*	11,315	9,284
03842	Hampton Compact(u)	6,779	5,407
.....	*Hampton*	10,493	8,011
03755	Hanover Compact(u)	6,861	6,147
.....	*Hanover*	9,119	8,494
03106	*Hooksett*	7,303	5,564
03061	*Hudson*	14,022	10,638
03431	Keene	21,449	20,467
03246	Laconia	15,575	14,888

ZIP code	Place		1980	1970
03766	Lebanon		11,134	9,725
03516	*Littleton*		5,558	5,290
03053	*Londonderry*		13,598	5,346
*03101	Manchester		90,936	87,754
03054	*Merrimack*		15,406	8,595
03055	*Milford*		8,685	6,622
03060	Nashua		67,865	55,820
03773	*Newport*		6,229	5,899
03076	*Pelham*		8,090	5,408
03801	Portsmouth		26,254	25,717
03867	Rochester		21,560	17,938
03079	*Salem*		24,124	20,142
03874	*Seabrook*		5,917	3,053
03878	Somersworth		10,350	9,026

New Jersey

ZIP code	Place	Area code	1980	1970
07747	Aberdeen(u)	(201)	17,235	....
08201	Absecon	(609)	6,859	6,094
07401	Allendale	(201)	5,901	6,240
07712	Asbury Park	(201)	17,015	16,533
*08401	Atlantic City	(609)	40,199	47,859
08106	Audubon	(609)	9,533	10,802
08007	Barrington	(609)	7,418	8,409
07002	Bayonne	(201)	65,047	72,743
08722	Beachwood	(201)	7,687	4,390
07109	Belleville	(201)	35,367	37,629
08030	Bellmawr	(609)	13,721	15,618
07719	Belmar	(201)	6,771	5,782
07621	Bergenfield	(201)	25,568	29,000
07922	Berkeley Hts. Twp.	(201)	12,549	13,078
08009	Berlin	(609)	5,786	4,997
07924	Bernardsville	(201)	6,715	6,652
08012	Blackwood(u)	(609)	5,219	....
07003	Bloomfield	(201)	47,792	52,029
07403	Bloomingdale	(201)	7,867	7,797
07603	Bogota	(201)	8,344	8,960
07005	Boonton	(201)	8,620	9,261
08805	Bound Brook	(201)	9,710	10,450
08723	Brick Twp	(201)	53,629	35,057
08302	Bridgeton	(609)	18,795	20,435
08203	Brigantine	(609)	8,318	6,741
08015	Browns Mills(u)	(609)	10,568	7,144
07828	Budd Lake	(201)	6,523	....
08016	Burlington	(609)	10,246	12,010
07405	Butler	(201)	7,616	7,051
07006	Caldwell	(201)	7,624	8,677
*08101	Camden	(609)	84,910	102,551
08701	Candlewood(u)	(201)	6,750	5,629
07072	Carlstadt	(201)	6,166	6,724
08069	Carney's Point	(609)	7,574	....
07008	Carteret	(201)	20,598	23,137
07009	Cedar Grove Twp.	(201)	12,600	15,582
07928	Chatham	(201)	8,537	9,566
*08002	Cherry Hill Twp.	(609)	68,785	64,395
08077	Cinnaminson Twp.	(609)	16,072	16,962
07066	Clark Twp.	(201)	16,699	18,829
08312	Clayton	(609)	6,013	5,193
08021	Clementon	(609)	5,764	4,492
07010	Cliffside Park	(201)	21,464	18,891
07721	Cliffwood-Cliffwood Beach(u)	(201)	NA	7,056
*07015	Clifton	(201)	74,388	82,437
07624	Closter	(201)	8,164	8,604
08108	Collingswood	(609)	15,838	17,422
07016	Cranford Twp.	(201)	24,573	27,391
07626	Cresskill	(201)	7,609	8,298
.....	Crestwood Village	(201)	7,965	....
08075	Delran Twp.	(609)	14,811	10,065
07834	Denville Twp.	(201)	14,380	14,045
08096	Deptford Twp.	(609)	23,473	24,232
07801	Dover	(201)	14,681	15,039
07628	Dumont	(201)	18,334	20,155
08812	Dunellen	(201)	6,593	7,072
08816	East Brunswick Twp.	(201)	37,711	34,166
07936	East Hanover	(201)	9,319	....
*07019	East Orange	(201)	77,025	75,471
07073	East Rutherford	(201)	7,849	8,536
08520	East Windsor Twp.	(609)	21,041	11,736
07724	Eatontown	(201)	12,703	14,619
08010	Edgewater Park	(609)	9,273	....
08817	Edison Twp.	(201)	70,193	67,120
*07201	Elizabeth	(201)	106,201	112,654
07407	Elmwood Park	(201)	18,377	20,511
07630	Emerson	(201)	7,793	8,428
*07631	Englewood	(201)	23,701	24,985
07632	Englewood Cliffs	(201)	5,698	5,938
08053	Evesham Twp.	(609)	21,659	13,477
08618	Ewing Twp.	(609)	34,842	32,831
07006	Fairfield	(201)	7,987	6,731
07701	Fair Haven	(201)	5,679	6,142
07410	Fair Lawn	(201)	32,229	38,040
07022	Fairview	(201)	10,519	10,698
07023	Fanwood	(201)	7,767	8,920
08518	Florence-Roebling(u)	(609)	7,677	7,551
07932	Florham Park	(201)	9,359	9,373
08640	Fort Dix(u)	(609)	14,297	26,290
07024	Fort Lee	(201)	32,449	30,631
07417	Franklin Lakes	(201)	8,769	7,550
07728	Freehold	(201)	10,020	10,545
07026	Garfield	(201)	26,803	30,797
08753	Gilford Park	(201)	6,528	4,007
08028	Glassboro	(609)	14,574	12,938
08029	Glendora	(609)	5,632	....
07028	Glen Ridge	(201)	7,855	8,518
07452	Glen Rock	(201)	11,497	13,011
08030	Gloucester City	(609)	13,121	14,707
.....	Gordon's Corner	(201)	6,320	....
07093	Guttenberg	(201)	7,340	5,754
*07602	Hackensack	(201)	36,039	36,008
07840	Hackettstown	(201)	8,850	9,472
08108	Haddon Twp.	(609)	15,875	18,192
08033	Haddonfield	(609)	12,337	13,118
08035	Haddon Heights	(609)	8,361	9,365
07508	Haledon	(201)	6,607	6,767
08037	Hammonton	(609)	12,298	11,464
07981	Hanover Twp.	(201)	11,846	10,700
07029	Harrison	(201)	12,242	11,811
07604	Hasbrouck Heights	(201)	12,166	13,651
07506	Hawthorne	(201)	18,200	19,173
07730	Hazlet Twp.	(201)	23,013	22,239
08904	Highland Park	(201)	13,396	14,385
07732	Highlands	(201)	5,187	3,916
07642	Hillsdale	(201)	10,495	11,768
07205	Hillside Twp.	(201)	21,440	21,636
07030	Hoboken	(201)	42,460	45,380
08753	Holiday City-Berkeley	(201)	9,019	....
07843	Hopatcong	(201)	15,531	9,052
08560	Hopewell Twp. (Mercer)	(609)	10,893	10,030
07111	Irvington	(201)	61,493	59,743
08527	Jackson Twp.	(201)	25,644	18,276
*07303	Jersey City	(201)	223,532	260,350
07734	Keansburg	(201)	10,613	9,720
07032	Kearny	(201)	35,735	37,585
08824	Kendall Park(u)	(201)	7,419	7,412
07033	Kenilworth	(201)	8,221	9,165
07735	Keyport	(201)	7,413	7,205
07405	Kinnelon	(201)	7,770	7,600
07034	Lake Hiawatha(u)	(201)	NA	11,389
07871	Lake Mohawk(u)	(201)	8,498	6,262
07054	Lake Parsippany(u)	(201)	NA	7,488
08701	Lakewood(u)	(201)	22,863	17,874
08879	Laurence Harbor(u)	(201)	6,737	6,715
07605	Leonia	(201)	8,027	8,847
07035	Lincoln Park	(201)	8,806	9,034
07036	Linden	(201)	37,836	41,409
08021	Lindenwold	(609)	18,196	12,199
08221	Linwood	(609)	6,144	6,159
07424	Little Falls Twp.	(201)	11,496	11,727
07643	Little Ferry	(201)	9,399	9,064
07739	Little Silver	(201)	5,548	6,010
07039	Livingston Twp.	(201)	28,040	30,127
07644	Lodi	(201)	23,956	25,163
07740	Long Branch	(201)	29,819	31,774
07071	Lyndhurst Twp.	(201)	20,326	22,729
07940	Madison	(201)	15,357	16,710
08859	Madison Park	(201)	7,447	....
07430	Mahwah Twp.	(201)	12,127	10,800
08736	Manasquan	(201)	5,354	4,971
08835	Manville	(201)	11,278	13,029
08052	Maple Shade Twp.	(609)	20,525	16,464
07040	Maplewood Twp.	(201)	22,950	24,932
08402	Margate City	(609)	9,179	10,576
07746	Marlboro Twp.	(201)	17,560	12,273
08053	Marlton(u)	(609)	9,411	10,180
07747	Matawan	(201)	8,837	9,136
07607	Maywood	(201)	9,895	11,087
07641	McGuire AFB(u)	(609)	7,853	10,933
08619	Mercerville-Hamilton Sq.(u)	(609)	25,446	24,465
08840	Metuchen	(201)	13,762	16,031
08846	Middlesex	(201)	13,480	15,038
07748	Middletown Twp.	(201)	61,615	54,623
07432	Midland park	(201)	7,381	8,159
07041	Milburn Twp.	(201)	19,543	21,089
08850	Milltown	(201)	7,136	6,470
08332	Millville	(609)	24,815	21,366
08094	Monroe Twp. (Gloucester)	(609)	21,639	14,071
*07042	Montclair	(201)	38,321	44,043
07645	Montvale	(201)	7,318	7,327
07045	Montville Twp.	(201)	14,290	11,846
08057	Moorestown-Lenola(u)	(609)	13,695	14,179
07950	Morris Plains	(201)	5,305	5,540
07960	Morristown	(201)	16,614	17,662
07092	Mountainside	(201)	7,118	7,520
08060	Mount Holly Twp.	(609)	10,818	12,713
07753	Neptune Twp.	(201)	28,366	27,863
07753	Neptune City	(201)	5,276	5,502
*07102	Newark	(201)	329,248	381,930
*08901	New Brunswick	(201)	41,442	41,885
08511	New Hanover	(201)	14,248	27,410
07646	New Milford	(201)	16,876	19,149
07974	New Providence	(201)	12,426	13,796
07860	Newton	(201)	7,748	7,297
07032	North Arlington	(201)	16,587	18,096
07047	North Bergen Twp.	(201)	47,019	47,751
08902	North Brunswick Twp.	(201)	22,220	16,691
07006	North Caldwell	(201)	5,832	6,733
08225	Northfield	(609)	7,795	8,646
07508	North Haledon	(201)	8,177	7,614

ZIP code	Place		1980	1970
07060	North Plainfield	(201)	19,108	21,796
07647	Northvale	(201)	5,046	5,177
07110	Nutley	(201)	28,998	31,913
07755	Oakhurst(u)	(201)	NA	5,558
07436	Oakland	(201)	13,443	14,420
08226	Ocean City	(609)	13,949	10,575
07757	Oceanport	(201)	5,888	7,503
08758	Ocean Twp	(201)	23,570	....
08857	Old Bridge	(201)	21,815	25,176
08857	Old Bridge Twp	(201)	51,515	48,715
07649	Oradell	(201)	8,658	8,903
*07050	Orange	(201)	31,136	32,566
07650	Palisades Park	(201)	13,732	13,351
08065	Palmyra	(609)	7,085	6,969
07652	Paramus	(201)	26,474	28,381
07656	Park Ridge	(201)	8,515	8,709
07054	Parsippany-Troy Hills	(201)	49,868	....
*07055	Passaic	(201)	52,463	55,124
*07510	Paterson	(201)	137,970	144,824
08066	Paulsboro	(609)	6,944	8,084
08110	Pennsauken Twp	(609)	33,775	36,394
08069	Penns Grove	(609)	5,760	5,727
08070	Pennsville Center(u)	(609)	12,467	11,014
07440	Pequannock Twp	(201)	13,776	14,350
*08861	Perth Amboy	(201)	38,951	38,798
08865	Phillipsburg	(201)	16,647	17,849
08021	Pine Hill	(201)	8,684	5,132
08854	Piscataway Twp	(201)	42,223	36,418
08071	Pitman	(609)	9,744	10,257
*07061	Plainfield	(201)	45,555	46,862
08232	Pleasantville	(609)	13,435	14,007
08742	Point Pleasant	(201)	17,747	15,968
08742	Point Pleasant Beach	(201)	5,415	4,882
07442	Pompton Lakes	(201)	10,660	11,397
08540	Princeton	(609)	12,035	12,311
08540	Princeton North(u)	(609)	NA	5,488
07508	Prospect Park	(201)	5,142	5,176
*07065	Rahway	(201)	26,723	29,114
08057	Ramblewood(u)	(609)	6,475	5,556
07446	Ramsey	(201)	12,899	12,571
07970	Randolph Twp	(201)	17,828	13,296
08869	Raritan	(201)	6,128	6,691
07701	Red Bank	(201)	12,031	12,847
07657	Ridgefield	(201)	10,294	11,308
07660	Ridgefield Park	(201)	12,738	13,990
*07451	Ridgewood	(201)	25,208	27,547
07456	Ringwood	(201)	12,625	10,393
07661	River Edge	(201)	11,111	12,850
08075	Riverside Twp	(609)	7,941	8,591
07675	River Vale	(201)	9,489	....
07726	Robertsville	(201)	8,461	....
07662	Rochell Park Twp	(201)	5,603	6,380
07866	Rockaway	(201)	6,852	6,383
07068	Roseland	(201)	5,330	4,453
07203	Roselle	(201)	20,641	22,585
07204	Roselle Park	(201)	13,377	14,277
07760	Rumson	(201)	7,623	7,421
08078	Runnemede	(609)	9,461	10,475
*07070	Rutherford	(201)	19,068	20,802
07662	Saddle Brook Twp	(201)	14,084	15,910
08079	Salem	(609)	6,959	7,648
08872	Sayreville	(201)	29,969	32,508
07076	Scotch Plains Twp	(201)	20,774	22,279
07094	Secaucus	(201)	13,719	13,228
08753	Silverton	(201)	7,236	....
08083	Somerdale	(609)	5,900	6,510
08873	Somerset	(201)	21,731	....
08244	Somers Point	(609)	10,330	7,919
08876	Somerville	(201)	11,973	13,652
08879	South Amboy	(201)	8,322	9,338
07079	South Orange Vill. Twp	(201)	15,864	....
07080	South Plainfield	(201)	20,521	21,142
08882	South River	(201)	14,361	15,428
07871	Sparta Twp	(201)	13,333	10,819
08884	Spotswood	(201)	7,840	7,891
07081	Springfield Twp	(201)	13,955	15,740
07762	Spring Lake Heights	(201)	5,424	4,602
08084	Stratford	(609)	8,005	9,801
07747	Strathmore(u)	(609)	NA	7,674
07876	Succasunna-Kenvil	(201)	10,931	....
07901	Summit	(201)	21,071	23,620
07666	Teaneck Twp	(201)	39,007	42,355
07670	Tenafly	(201)	13,552	14,827
07724	Tinton Falls	(201)	7,740	8,395
08753	Toms River(u)	(201)	7,465	7,303
07512	Totowa	(201)	11,448	11,580
*08608	Trenton	(609)	92,124	104,786
08520	Twin Rivers	(609)	7,742	....
07083	Union Twp	(201)	50,184	53,077
07735	Union Beach	(201)	6,354	6,472
07087	Union City	(201)	55,593	57,305
07458	Upper Saddle River	(201)	7,958	7,949
08406	Ventnor City	(609)	11,704	10,385
07044	Verona	(201)	14,166	15,067
08251	Villas	(609)	5,909	3,155
08360	Vineland	(609)	53,753	47,399
07463	Waldwick	(201)	10,802	12,313
07057	Wallington	(201)	10,741	10,284
07465	Wanaque	(201)	10,025	8,636
07882	Washington	(201)	6,429	5,943
07675	Washington Twp. (Bergen)	(201)	9,550	10,577
07060	Watchung	(201)	5,290	4,750
07470	Wayne Twp	(201)	46,474	49,141
07087	Weehawken Twp	(201)	13,168	13,383
07006	West Caldwell	(201)	11,407	11,913
*07091	Westfield	(201)	30,447	33,720
07728	West Freehold	(201)	9,929	....
07764	West Long Branch	(201)	7,380	6,845
07480	West Milford Twp	(201)	22,750	17,304
07093	West New York	(201)	39,194	40,627
07052	West Orange	(201)	39,510	43,715
07424	West Paterson	(201)	11,293	11,692
07675	Westwood	(201)	10,714	11,105
07885	Wharton	(201)	5,485	5,535
08610	White Horse	(609)	10,098	....
07886	White Meadow Lake(u)	(201)	8,429	8,499
08094	Williamstown	(609)	5,768	4,075
08046	Willingboro Twp	(609)	39,912	43,386
08095	Winslow Twp	(609)	20,034	11,202
07095	Woodbridge Twp	(201)	90,074	98,944
08096	Woodbury	(609)	10,353	12,408
07675	Woodcliff Lake	(201)	5,644	5,506
07075	Wood-Ridge	(201)	7,929	8,311
07481	Wyckoff Twp	(201)	15,500	16,039
08620	Yardville-Groveville	(609)	9,414	....
.....	Yorketown	(201)	5,330	....

New Mexico (505)

ZIP code	Place		1980	1970
88310	Alamogordo		24,024	23,035
*87101	Albuquerque		331,767	244,501
88210	Artesia		10,385	10,315
87410	Aztec		5,512	3,354
87002	Belen		5,617	4,823
88101	Cannon(u)		NA	5,461
88220	Carlsbad		25,496	21,297
88101	Clovis		31,194	28,495
88030	Deming		9,964	8,343
87532	Espanola		6,803	4,528
87401	Farmington		30,729	21,979
87301	Gallup		18,161	14,596
87020	Grants		11,451	8,768
88240	Hobbs		28,794	26,025
88330	Holloman AFB(u)		7,245	8,001
88001	Las Cruces		45,086	37,857
87701	Las Vegas		14,322	7,528
87544	Los Alamos(u)		11,039	11,310
88260	Lovington		9,727	8,915
87107	North Valley(u)		13,006	10,366
87114	Paradise Hills		5,096	....
88130	Portales		9,940	10,554
87740	Raton		8,225	6,962
87124	Rio Rancho Estates		9,985	....
88201	Roswell		39,676	33,908
87115	Sandia(u)		5,288	6,867
87501	Santa Fe		48,899	41,167
87420	Shiprock		7,237	....
88061	Silver City		9,887	8,557
87801	Socorro		7,576	5,849
87105	South Valley(u)		38,916	29,389
87901	Truth or Consequences		5,219	4,656
88401	Tucumcari		6,765	7,189
87544	White Rock		6,560	3,861
..87327	Zuni Pueblo		5,551	3,958

New York

ZIP code	Place		1980	1970
*12207	Albany	(518)	101,727	115,781
11507	Albertson(u)	(516)	5,561	6,825
11701	Amityville	(516)	9,076	9,794
12010	Amsterdam	(518)	21,872	25,524
12603	Arlington(u)	(914)	11,305	11,203
13021	Auburn	(315)	32,548	34,599
*11702	Babylon	(516)	12,388	12,897
11510	Baldwin(u)	(516)	31,630	34,525
13027	Baldwinsville	(315)	6,446	6,298
14020	Batavia	(716)	16,703	17,338
14810	Bath	(607)	6,042	6,053
13088	Bayberry-Lynelle Meadows(u)	(315)	14,813	....
11705	Bayport(u)	(516)	9,282	8,232
11706	Bay Shore(u)	(516)	10,784	11,119
11709	Bayville	(516)	7,034	6,147
12508	Beacon	(914)	12,937	13,255
11710	Bellmore(u)	(516)	18,106	18,431
11714	Bethpage(u)	(516)	16,840	18,555
*13902	Binghamton	(607)	55,860	64,123
10913	Blauvelt(u)	(914)	NA	5,426
11716	Bohemia(u)	(516)	9,308	8,926
11717	Brentwood(u)	(516)	44,321	28,327
10510	Briarcliff Manor	(914)	7,115	6,521
14610	Brighton (u)	(716)	35,776	....
14420	Brockport	(716)	9,776	7,878
10708	Bronxville	(914)	6,267	6,674
*14240	Buffalo	(716)	357,870	462,768
14424	Canandaigua	(716)	10,419	10,488

ZIP code	Place		1980	1970
13617	Canton	(315)	7,055	6,398
11514	Carle Place(u)	(516)	5,470	6,326
11516	Cedarhurst	(516)	6,162	6,941
11720	Centereach(u)	(516)	30,136	9,427
11934	Center Moriches(u)	(516)	5,703	3,802
11721	Centerport(u)	(516)	6,576	....
11722	Central Islip(u)	(516)	19,734	36,391
14225	Cheektowaga(u)	(716)	92,145	....
12065	Clifton Knolls(u)	(518)	5,636	5,771
12043	Cobleskill	(518)	5,272	4,368
12047	Cohoes	(518)	18,144	18,653
11724	Cold Spring Harbor(u)	(516)	5,336	5,509
12205	Colonie	(518)	8,869	8,701
11725	Commack(u)	(516)	34,719	24,138
10920	Congers(u)	(914)	7,123	5,928
11726	Copiague(u)	(516)	20,132	19,632
11727	Coram(u)	(516)	24,752	....
14830	Corning	(607)	12,953	15,792
13045	Cortland	(607)	20,138	19,621
10520	Croton-on-Hudson	(914)	6,889	7,523
11729	Deer Park(u)	(516)	30,394	32,274
12054	Delmar(u)	(518)	8,423	....
14043	Depew	(716)	19,819	22,158
13214	DeWitt(u)	(315)	9,024	10,032
11746	Dix Hills(u)	(516)	26,693	10,050
10522	Dobbs Ferry	(914)	10,053	10,353
14048	Dunkirk	(716)	15,310	16,855
14052	East Aurora	(716)	6,803	7,033
10709	Eastchester(u)	(914)	20,305	23,750
11735	East Farmingdale(u)	(516)	5,522	....
12302	East Glenville(u)	(518)	6,537	5,898
11746	East Half Hollow Hills(u)	(516)	NA	9,691
11576	East Hills	(516)	7,160	8,624
11730	East Islip(u)	(516)	13,852	6,861
11758	East Massapequa(u)	(516)	13,987	15,926
11554	East Meadow(u)	(516)	39,317	46,290
11743	East Neck(u)	(516)	NA	5,221
11731	East Northport(u)	(516)	20,187	12,392
11772	East Patchogue(u)	(516)	18,139	8,092
14445	East Rochester	(716)	7,596	8,347
11518	East Rockaway	(516)	10,917	11,795
13902	East Vestal(u)	(607)	NA	10,472
*14901	Elmira	(607)	35,327	39,945
11003	Elmont(u)	(516)	27,592	29,363
11731	Elwood(u)	(516)	11,847	15,031
13760	Endicott	(607)	14,457	16,556
13760	Endwell(u)	(607)	13,745	15,999
13219	Fairmount(u)	(315)	13,415	15,317
14450	Fairport	(716)	5,970	6,474
12601	Fairview(u)	(914)	5,852	8,517
11735	Farmingdale	(516)	7,946	9,297
11738	Farmingville(u)	(516)	13,398	....
*11001	Floral Park	(516)	16,805	18,466
11768	Fort Salonga(u)	(516)	9,550	....
11010	Franklin Square(u)	(516)	29,051	32,156
14063	Fredonia	(716)	11,126	10,326
11520	Freeport	(516)	38,272	40,374
13069	Fulton	(315)	13,312	14,003
11530	Garden City	(516)	22,927	25,373
11040	Garden City Park(u)	(516)	7,712	7,488
14624	Gates-North Gates(u)	(716)	15,244	....
14454	Geneseo	(716)	6,746	5,714
14456	Geneva	(315)	15,133	16,793
11542	Glen Cove	(516)	24,618	25,770
12801	Glens Falls	(518)	15,897	17,222
12801	Glens Falls North(u)	(518)	6,956	....
12078	Gloversville	(518)	17,836	19,677
*11022	Great Neck	(516)	9,168	10,798
11020	Great Neck Plaza	(516)	5,604	6,043
14616	Greece(u)	(716)	16,177	....
11740	Greenlawn(u)	(516)	13,869	8,493
10583	Greenville(u)	(914)	8,706	....
11746	Half Hollow Hills(u)	(516)	NA	12,081
14075	Hamburg	(716)	10,582	10,215
11946	Hampton Bays(u)	(516)	7,256	1,862
14221	Harris Hill(u)	(716)	5,087	....
10528	Harrison	(914)	23,046	21,544
10530	Hartsdale(u)	(914)	10,216	12,226
10706	Hastings-on-Hudson	(914)	8,573	9,479
11787	Hauppauge(u)	(516)	20,960	13,957
10927	Haverstraw	(914)	8,800	8,198
10532	Hawthorne(u)	(914)	5,010	....
*11551	Hempstead	(516)	40,404	39,411
13350	Herkimer	(315)	8,383	8,960
11040	Herricks(u)	(516)	8,123	9,112
11557	Hewlett(u)	(516)	6,986	6,796
*11802	Hicksville(u)	(516)	43,245	49,820
10977	Hillcrest(u)	(914)	5,733	5,357
11741	Holbrook(u)	(516)	24,382	....
11742	Holtsville(u)	(516)	13,515	....
14843	Hornell	(607)	10,234	12,144
14845	Horseheads	(607)	7,348	7,989
12534	Hudson	(518)	7,986	8,940
12839	Hudson Falls	(518)	7,419	7,917
11743	Huntington(u)	(516)	19,567	12,601
11746	Huntington Station(u)	(516)	28,769	28,817
13357	Ilion	(315)	9,190	9,808
11696	Inwood(u)	(516)	8,228	8,433
14617	Irondequoit(u)	(716)	57,648	....
10533	Irvington	(914)	5,774	5,878
11751	Islip(u)	(516)	13,438	7,692
11752	Islip Terrace(u)	(516)	5,588	....
14850	Ithaca	(607)	28,732	26,226
14701	Jamestown	(716)	35,775	39,795
10535	Jefferson Valley-Yorktown(u)	(914)	13,380	9,008
11753	Jericho(u)	(516)	12,739	14,010
13790	Johnson City	(607)	17,126	18,025
12095	Johnstown	(518)	9,360	10,045
14217	Kenmore	(716)	18,474	20,980
11754	Kings Park(u)	(516)	16,131	5,555
11024	Kings Point	(516)	5,234	5,614
12401	Kingston	(914)	24,481	25,544
14218	Lackawanna	(716)	22,701	28,657
10512	Lake Carmel(u)	(914)	7,295	4,796
11755	Lake Grove	(516)	9,692	8,133
11779	Lake Ronkonkoma(u)	(516)	38,336	7,284
11552	Lakeview(u)	(516)	5,276	5,471
14086	Lancaster	(716)	13,056	13,365
10538	Larchmont	(914)	6,308	7,203
12110	Latham(u)	(914)	11,182	9,661
11559	Lawrence	(516)	6,175	6,566
11756	Levittown(u)	(516)	57,045	65,440
11757	Lindenhurst	(516)	26,919	28,359
13365	Little Falls	(315)	6,156	7,629
14094	Lockport	(716)	24,844	25,399
11791	Locust Grove(u)	(516)	9,670	11,626
11561	Long Beach	(516)	34,073	33,127
12211	Loudonville(u)	(518)	11,480	9,299
11563	Lynbrook	(516)	20,431	23,151
13208	Lyncourt(u)	(315)	5,129	....
10541	Mahopac(u)	(914)	7,681	5,265
12953	Malone	(518)	7,668	8,048
11565	Malverne	(516)	9,262	10,036
10543	Mamaroneck	(914)	17,616	18,909
11030	Manhasset(u)	(516)	8,485	8,541
13104	Manlius	(315)	5,241	4,295
11050	Manorhaven	(516)	5,384	5,488
11758	Massapequa(u)	(516)	24,454	26,821
11762	Massapequa Park	(516)	19,779	22,112
13662	Massena	(315)	12,851	14,042
11950	Mastic(u)	(516)	10,413	....
11951	Mastic Beach(u)	(516)	8,318	4,870
13211	Mattydale(u)	(315)	7,511	8,292
12118	Mechanicville	(518)	5,500	6,247
11763	Medford(u)	(516)	20,418	....
14103	Medina	(716)	6,392	6,415
11746	Melville(u)	(516)	8,139	6,641
11566	Merrick(u)	(516)	24,478	25,904
11953	Middle Island(u)	(516)	5,703	....
10940	Middletown	(914)	21,454	22,607
11764	Miller Place(u)	(516)	7,877	....
11501	Mineola	(516)	20,757	21,845
10950	Monroe	(914)	5,996	4,439
10952	Monsey(u)	(914)	12,380	8,797
12701	Monticello	(914)	6,306	5,991
10549	Mt. Kisco	(914)	8,025	8,172
11766	Mount Sinai(u)	(516)	6,591	....
*10551	Mount Vernon	(914)	66,713	72,788
12590	Myers Corner(u)	(914)	5,180	2,826
10954	Nanuet(u)	(914)	12,578	10,447
11767	Nesconset(u)	(516)	10,706	10,048
14513	Newark	(315)	10,017	11,644
12550	Newburgh	(914)	23,438	26,219
11590	New Cassel(u)	(516)	9,635	8,721
10956	New City(u)	(914)	35,859	27,344
11040	New Hyde Park	(516)	9,801	10,116
*10802	New Rochelle	(914)	70,794	75,385
*12550	New Windsor Center(u)	(914)	7,812	8,803
*10001	New York	(212)	7,071,030	7,895,563
*10451	Bronx	(212)	1,169,115	1,471,701
*11201	Brooklyn	(212)	2,230,936	2,602,102
*10001	Manhattan	(212)	1,427,533	1,539,233
*(Q)	Queens	(212)	1,891,325	1,987,174

(Q) There are 4 P.O.s for Queens: 11101 for L.I. City; 11690 Far Rockaway; 11351 Flushing; and 11431 Jamaica.

ZIP code	Place		1980	1970
*10314	Staten Island	(212)	352,121	295,443
14301	Niagara(u)	(716)	9,648	....
*14302	Niagara Falls	(716)	71,384	85,615
12309	Niskayuna(u)	(518)	5,223	6,186
11701	North Amityville(u)	(516)	13,140	11,936
11703	North Babylon(u)	(516)	19,019	39,526
11706	North Bay Shore(u)	(516)	35,020	....
11710	North Bellmore(u)	(516)	20,630	22,893
11713	North Bellport(u)	(516)	7,432	5,903
11752	North Great River(u)	(516)	11,416	12,080
11757	North Lindenhurst(u)	(516)	11,511	11,117
11758	North Massapequa(u)	(516)	21,385	23,123
11566	North Merrick(u)	(516)	12,848	13,650
11040	North New Hyde Park(u)	(516)	15,114	18,154
11772	North Patchogue(u)	(516)	7,126	5,232
11768	Northport	(516)	7,651	7,494
13212	North Syracuse	(315)	7,970	8,687
10591	North Tarrytown	(914)	7,994	8,334
14120	North Tonawanda	(716)	35,760	36,012
11580	North Valley Stream(u)	(516)	14,530	14,881
11793	North Wantagh(u)	(516)	12,677	15,053
13815	Norwich	(607)	8,082	8,843
10960	Nyack	(914)	6,428	6,659
11769	Oakdale(u)	(516)	8,090	7,334

ZIP code	Census Division		1980	1970
11572	Oceanside(u)	(516)	33,639	35,372
13669	Ogdensburg	(315)	12,375	14,554
11804	Old Bethpage(u)	(516)	6,215	7,084
14760	Olean	(716)	18,207	19,169
13421	Oneida	(315)	10,810	11,658
13820	Oneonta	(607)	14,933	16,030
12550	Orange Lake(u)	(914)	5,120	4,348
10562	Ossining	(914)	20,196	21,659
13126	Oswego	(315)	19,793	20,913
11771	Oyster Bay(u)	(516)	6,497	6,822
11772	Patchogue	(516)	11,291	11,582
10965	Pearl River(u)	(914)	15,893	17,146
10566	Peekskill	(914)	18,236	19,283
10803	Pelham	(914)	6,848	2,076
10803	Pelham Manor	(914)	6,130	6,673
14527	Penn Yan	(315)	5,242	5,293
13212	Pitcher Hill	(315)	6,063	....
11714	Plainedge(u)	(516)	9,629	10,759
11803	Plainview(u)	(516)	28,037	31,695
12901	Plattsburgh	(518)	21,057	18,715
12903	Plattsburgh AFB(u)	(518)	5,905	7,078
10570	Pleasantville	(914)	6,749	7,110
10573	Port Chester	(914)	23,565	25,803
11777	Port Jefferson	(516)	6,731	5,515
11776	Port Jefferson Station(u)	(516)	17,009	7,403
12771	Port Jervis	(914)	8,699	8,852
11050	Port Washington(u)	(516)	14,521	15,923
13676	Potsdam	(315)	10,635	10,303
*12601	Poughkeepsie	(914)	29,757	32,029
12603	Red Oaks Mill(u)	(914)	5,236	3,919
12144	Rensselaer	(518)	9,047	10,136
11961	Ridge(u)	(516)	8,977	....
11901	Riverhead(u)	(516)	6,339	7,585
11901	Riverside-Flanders(u)	(516)	5,400	....
*14603	Rochester	(716)	241,741	295,011
*11570	Rockville Centre	(516)	25,405	27,444
11778	Rocky Point(u)	(516)	7,012	....
12205	Roessleville(u)	(518)	11,685	5,476
13440	Rome	(315)	43,826	50,148
11575	Roosevelt(u)	(516)	14,109	15,008
11577	Roslyn Heights(u)	(516)	6,546	7,242
12303	Rotterdam(u)	(518)	22,933	25,214
10580	Rye	(914)	15,083	15,869
11780	St. James(u)	(516)	12,122	10,500
14779	Salamanca	(716)	6,890	7,877
12983	Saranac Lake	(518)	5,578	6,086
12866	Saratoga Springs	(518)	23,906	18,845
11782	Sayville(u)	(516)	12,013	11,680
10583	Scarsdale	(914)	17,650	19,229
*12301	Schenectady	(518)	67,972	77,958
10940	Scotchtown(u)	(914)	7,352	2,119
12302	Scotia	(518)	7,280	7,370
11579	Sea Cliff	(516)	5,364	5,890
11783	Seaford(u)	(516)	16,117	17,379
11784	Selden(u)	(516)	17,259	11,613
13148	Seneca Falls	(315)	7,466	7,794
11733	Setauket-East Setauket(u)	(516)	10,176	6,857
11967	Shirley(u)	(516)	18,072	6,280
11787	Smithtown(u)	(516)	30,906	....
13209	Solvay	(315)	7,140	8,280
11789	South Beach(u)	(516)	8,071	....
11735	South Farmingdale(u)	(516)	16,439	20,464
14850	South Hill(u)	(607)	5,276	....
11746	South Huntington(u)	(516)	14,854	9,115
14904	Southport(u)	(607)	8,329	8,685
11581	South Valley Stream(u)	(516)	5,462	6,595
11590	South Westbury(u)	(516)	9,732	10,978
10977	Spring Valley	(914)	20,537	18,112
11790	Stony Brook(u)	(516)	16,155	6,391
10980	Stony Point(u)	(914)	8,686	8,270
10901	Suffern	(914)	10,794	8,273
11791	Syosset(u)	(516)	9,818	10,084
*13201	Syracuse	(315)	170,105	197,297
10983	Tappan(u)	(914)	8,267	7,424
10591	Tarrytown	(914)	10,648	11,115
10594	Thornwood(u)	(914)	7,197	6,874
14150	Tonawanda	(716)	18,693	21,898
*12180	Troy	(518)	56,638	62,918
10707	Tuckahoe	(914)	6,076	6,236
11553	Uniondale(u)	(516)	20,016	22,077
*13503	Utica	(315)	75,632	91,373
10989	Valley Cottage(u)	(914)	8,214	6,007
*11580	Valley Stream	(516)	35,769	40,413
10901	Viola(u)	(914)	5,340	5,136
12586	Walden	(914)	5,659	5,277
11793	Wantagh(u)	(516)	19,817	21,783
12590	Wappingers Falls	(914)	5,110	5,607
13165	Waterloo	(315)	5,303	5,418
13601	Watertown	(315)	27,861	30,787
12189	Watervliet	(518)	11,354	12,404
14580	Webster	(716)	5,499	5,037
14895	Wellsville	(716)	5,769	5,815
11758	West Amityville(u)	(516)	6,623	6,424
11704	West Babylon(u)	(516)	41,699	12,893
11706	West Bay Shore(u)	(516)	5,118	....
11590	Westbury	(516)	13,871	15,362
14905	West Elmira(u)	(607)	5,485	5,901
12801	West Glens Falls(u)	(518)	5,331	3,363
10993	West Haverstraw	(914)	9,181	8,558
11552	West Hempstead(u)	(516)	18,536	20,375
11743	West Hills(u)	(516)	6,071	....
11795	West Islip(u)	(516)	29,533	17,374
12203	Westmere(u)	(518)	6,881	6,364
10994	West Nyack(u)	(914)	8,553	5,510
10996	West Point(u)	(914)	8,105	....
11796	West Sayville(u)	(516)	8,185	7,386
14224	West Seneca(u)	(716)	51,210	....
13219	Westvale(u)	(315)	6,169	7,253
*10602	White Plains	(914)	46,999	50,346
14221	Williamsville	(716)	6,017	6,878
11596	Williston Park	(516)	8,216	9,154
11797	Woodbury(u)	(516)	7,043	....
11598	Woodmere(u)	(516)	17,205	19,831
11798	Wyandach(u)	(516)	13,215	15,716
*10701	Yonkers	(914)	195,351	204,297
10598	Yorktown Heights(u)	(914)	7,696	6,805

North Carolina

28001	Albemarle	(704)	15,110	11,126
27263	Archdale	(919)	5,305	4,874
27203	Asheboro	(919)	15,252	10,797
*28801	Asheville	(704)	53,281	57,820
28303	Bonnie Doone(u)	(919)	5,950	....
28607	Boone	(704)	10,191	8,754
28712	Brevard	(704)	5,323	5,243
27215	Burlington	(919)	37,266	35,930
28542	Camp Le Jeune(u)	(919)	30,764	34,549
27510	Carrboro	(919)	7,517	5,058
27511	Cary	(919)	21,612	7,640
27514	Chapel Hill	(919)	32,421	26,199
*28202	Charlotte	(704)	314,447	241,420
27012	Clemmons(u)	(919)	7,401	....
28328	Clinton	(919)	7,552	7,157
28025	Concord	(704)	16,942	18,464
28334	Dunn	(919)	8,962	8,302
*27701	Durham	(919)	100,831	95,438
28379	East Rockingham(u)	(919)	5,190	2,858
27288	Eden	(919)	15,672	15,871
27932	Edenton	(919)	5,264	4,956
27909	Elizabeth City	(919)	13,784	14,381
28728	Enka(u)	(704)	5,567	....
*28302	Fayetteville	(919)	59,507	53,510
28043	Forest City	(704)	7,688	7,179
28307	Fort Bragg(u)	(919)	37,834	46,995
27529	Garner	(919)	9,556	4,923
28052	Gastonia	(704)	47,333	47,322
27530	Goldsboro	(919)	31,871	26,960
27253	Graham	(919)	8,415	8,172
*27420	Greensboro	(919)	155,642	144,076
27834	Greenville	(919)	35,740	29,063
28532	Havelock	(919)	17,718	3,012
27536	Henderson	(919)	13,522	13,896
28739	Hendersonville	(704)	6,862	6,443
28601	Hickory	(704)	20,757	20,569
*27260	High Point	(919)	64,107	63,229
28348	Hope Mills	(919)	5,412	1,866
28540	Jacksonville	(919)	17,056	16,289
28081	Kannapolis(u)	(704)	34,564	36,293
27284	Kernersville	(919)	6,802	4,815
27021	King(u)	(919)	8,757	1,033
.....	Kings Grant(u)	(919)	6,652	....
28086	Kings Mountain	(704)	9,080	8,465
28501	Kinston	(919)	25,234	23,020
28352	Laurinburg	(919)	11,480	8,859
28645	Lenoir	(704)	13,748	14,705
27292	Lexington	(704)	15,711	17,205
28358	Lumberton	(919)	18,340	16,961
28212	Mint Hill	(704)	9,830	....
28110	Monroe	(704)	12,639	11,282
28115	Mooresville	(704)	8,575	8,808
28655	Morganton	(704)	13,763	13,625
27030	Mount Airy	(919)	6,862	7,325
28560	New Bern	(919)	14,557	14,660
27604	New Hope (Wake)(u)	(919)	6,768	....
.....	New Hope (Wayne)(u)	(919)	6,685	....
28540	New River Station(u)	(919)	5,401	....
28658	Newton	(704)	7,624	7,857
28012	North Belmont(u)	(704)	10,762	10,672
27565	Oxford	(919)	7,580	7,178
.....	Piney Green-White Oak(u)	(919)	6,058	....
*27611	Raleigh	(919)	149,771	122,830
27320	Reidsville	(919)	12,492	13,636
27870	Roanoke Rapids	(919)	14,702	13,508
28379	Rockingham	(919)	8,300	5,852
27801	Rocky Mount	(919)	41,283	34,284
27573	Roxboro	(919)	7,532	5,370
28601	St. Stephens(u)	(704)	10,797	....
28144	Salisbury	(704)	22,677	22,515
27330	Sanford	(919)	14,773	11,716
28150	Shelby	(704)	15,310	16,328
27577	Smithfield	(919)	7,288	6,677
28387	Southern Pines	(919)	8,620	5,937
28390	Spring Lake	(919)	6,273	3,968
27045	Stanleyville(u)	(919)	5,039	2,362
28677	Statesville	(704)	18,622	20,007
28778	Swannanoa(u)	(704)	5,586	1,966
27886	Tarboro	(919)	8,634	9,425
27360	Thomasville	(919)	14,144	15,230

ZIP code	Place		1980	1970
27370	Trinity(u)	(919)	6,726	....
27889	Washington	(919)	8,418	8,961
28786	Waynesville	(704)	6,765	6,488
28025	West Concord(u)	(704)	5,859	5,347
28472	Whiteville	(919)	5,565	4,195
27892	Williamston	(919)	6,159	6,570
28401	Wilmington	(919)	44,000	46,169
27893	Wilson	(919)	34,424	29,347
*27102	Winston-Salem	(919)	131,885	133,683

North Dakota (701)

ZIP code	Place	1980	1970
58501	Bismarck	44,485	34,703
58301	Devils Lake	7,442	7,078
58601	Dickinson	15,924	12,405
58102	Fargo	61,308	53,365
58237	Grafton	5,293	5,946
58201	Grand Forks(u)	43,765	39,008
58201	Grand Forks AFB(u)	9,390	10,474
58401	Jamestown	16,280	15,385
58554	Mandan	15,513	11,093
58701	Minot	32,843	32,290
58701	Minot AFB(u)	9,880	12,077
58072	Valley City	7,774	7,843
58075	Wahpeton	9,064	7,076
58078	West Fargo	10,099	5,161
58801	Williston	13,336	11,280

Ohio

ZIP code	Place		1980	1970
45810	Ada	(419)	5,669	5,309
*44309	Akron	(216)	237,177	275,425
44601	Alliance	(216)	24,315	26,547
44001	Amherst	(216)	10,638	9,902
44805	Ashland	(419)	20,326	19,872
44004	Ashtabula	(216)	23,449	24,313
45701	Athens	(614)	19,743	24,168
44202	Aurora	(216)	8,177	6,549
44515	Austintown(u)	(216)	33,636	29,393
44011	Avon	(216)	7,241	7,214
44012	Avon Lake	(216)	13,222	12,261
44203	Barberton	(216)	29,751	33,052
44140	Bay Village	(216)	17,846	18,163
44122	Beachwood	(216)	9,983	9,631
45385	Beavercreek	(513)	31,589	...
44146	Bedford	(216)	15,056	17,552
44146	Bedford Heights	(216)	13,214	13,063
43906	Bellaire	(614)	8,241	9,655
45305	Bellbrook	(513)	5,174	1,268
43311	Bellefontaine	(513)	11,888	11,255
44811	Bellevue	(419)	8,187	8,604
45714	Belpre	(614)	7,193	7,189
44017	Berea	(216)	19,567	22,465
43209	Bexley	(614)	13,405	14,888
43004	Blacklick Estates(u)	(614)	11,223	8,351
45242	Blue Ash	(513)	9,506	8,324
44512	Boardman(u)	(216)	39,161	30,852
43402	Bowling Green	(419)	25,728	14,656
44141	Brecksville	(216)	10,132	9,137
45231	Brentwood(u)	(513)	5,508	....
45211	Bridgetown(u)	(513)	11,460	13,352
44141	Broadview Heights	(216)	10,920	11,463
44144	Brooklyn	(216)	12,342	13,142
44142	Brook Park	(216)	26,195	30,774
44212	Brunswick	(216)	27,689	15,852
43506	Bryan	(419)	7,879	7,008
44820	Bucyrus	(419)	13,433	13,111
43725	Cambridge	(614)	13,573	13,656
44405	Campbell	(216)	11,619	12,577
44406	Canfield	(216)	5,535	4,997
*44711	Canton	(216)	94,730	110,053
45822	Celina	(419)	9,137	8,072
45459	Centerville	(513)	18,886	10,333
45211	Cheviot	(513)	9,888	11,135
45601	Chillicothe	(614)	23,420	24,842
*45234	Cincinnati	(513)	385,457	453,514
43113	Circleville	(614)	11,700	11,687
*44101	Cleveland	(216)	573,822	750,879
44118	Cleveland Heights	(216)	56,438	60,767
43410	Clyde	(419)	5,489	5,503
*43216	Columbus	(614)	564,871	540,025
44030	Conneaut	(216)	13,835	14,552
44410	Cortland	(216)	5,011	2,525
43812	Coshocton	(614)	13,405	13,747
45238	Covedale(u)	(513)	5,830	6,639
44827	Crestline	(419)	5,406	5,965
*44222	Cuyahoga Falls	(216)	43,710	49,815
*45401	Dayton	(513)	203,588	243,023
45236	Deer Park	(513)	6,745	7,415
43512	Defiance	(419)	16,810	16,281
43015	Delaware	(614)	18,780	15,008
45238	Delhi Hills(u)	(513)	27,647	....
45833	Delphos	(419)	7,314	7,608
44622	Dover	(216)	11,526	11,516
44112	East Cleveland	(216)	36,957	39,600
44094	Eastlake	(216)	22,104	19,690
43920	East Liverpool	(216)	16,687	20,020
44413	East Palestine	(216)	5,306	5,604
45320	Eaton	(513)	6,839	6,020
*44035	Elyria	(216)	57,504	53,427
45322	Englewood	(513)	11,329	7,885
44117	Euclid	(216)	59,999	71,552
45324	Fairborn	(513)	29,702	32,267
45014	Fairfield	(513)	30,777	14,680
44313	Fairlawn	(216)	6,100	6,102
44126	Fairview Park	(216)	19,311	21,699
45840	Findlay	(419)	35,594	35,800
45405	Forest Park	(513)	18,675	15,139
45426	Fort McKinley(u)	(513)	10,161	11,536
44830	Fostoria	(419)	15,743	16,037
45005	Franklin	(513)	10,711	10,075
43420	Fremont	(419)	17,834	18,490
43230	Gahanna	(614)	18,001	12,400
44833	Galion	(419)	12,391	13,123
45631	Gallipolis	(614)	5,576	7,490
44125	Garfield Heights	(216)	33,380	41,417
44041	Geneva	(216)	6,655	6,449
45327	Germantown	(513)	5,015	4,088
44420	Girard	(216)	12,517	14,119
43212	Grandview Heights	(614)	7,420	8,460
45123	Greenfield	(513)	5,034	4,780
45331	Greenville	(513)	12,999	12,380
45239	Groesbeck(u)	(513)	9,594	....
43123	Grove City	(614)	16,793	13,911
*45012	Hamilton	(513)	63,189	67,865
45030	Harrison	(513)	5,855	4,408
43055	Heath	(614)	6,969	6,768
44124	Highland Heights	(216)	5,739	5,926
43026	Hilliard	(614)	8,008	8,369
45133	Hillsboro	(513)	6,356	5,584
44484	Howland(u)	(216)	7,441	....
44425	Hubbard	(216)	9,245	8,583
45424	Huber Heights(u)	(513)	31,731	18,943
43081	Huber Ridge(u)	(614)	5,835	....
44839	Huron	(419)	7,123	6,896
44131	Independence	(216)	8,165	7,034
45638	Ironton	(614)	14,290	15,030
45640	Jackson	(614)	6,675	6,843
44240	Kent	(216)	26,164	28,183
43326	Kenton	(419)	8,605	8,315
45236	Kenwood(u)	(513)	9,928	15,789
45429	Kettering	(513)	61,186	71,864
44094	Kirtland	(216)	5,969	5,530
44107	Lakewood	(216)	61,963	70,173
43130	Lancaster	(614)	34,953	32,911
45036	Lebanon	(513)	9,636	7,934
*45802	Lima	(419)	47,381	53,734
45215	Lincoln Heights	(513)	5,259	6,099
43228	Lincoln Village(u)	(614)	10,548	11,215
43138	Logan	(614)	6,557	6,269
43140	London	(614)	6,958	6,481
*44052	Lorain	(216)	75,416	78,185
44641	Louisville	(216)	7,873	6,298
45140	Loveland	(513)	9,106	7,126
44124	Lyndhurst	(216)	18,092	19,749
44056	Macedonia	(216)	6,571	6,375
45243	Madeira	(513)	9,341	6,713
*44901	Mansfield	(419)	53,927	55,047
44137	Maple Heights	(216)	29,735	34,093
45750	Marietta	(614)	16,467	16,861
43302	Marion	(614)	37,040	38,646
43935	Martins Ferry	(614)	9,331	10,757
43040	Marysville	(513)	7,414	5,744
45040	Mason	(513)	8,692	5,677
44646	Massillon	(216)	30,557	32,539
43537	Maumee	(419)	15,747	15,937
44124	Mayfield Heights	(216)	21,550	22,139
44256	Medina	(216)	15,268	10,913
44060	Mentor	(216)	42,065	36,912
44060	Mentor-on-the-Lake	(216)	7,919	6,517
45342	Miamisburg	(513)	15,304	14,797
44130	Middleburg Heights	(216)	16,218	12,367
45042	Middletown	(513)	43,719	48,767
45042	Middletown South(u)	(513)	5,260	....
45150	Milford	(513)	5,232	4,828
45239	Monfort Heights(u)	(513)	9,745	....
45242	Montgomery	(513)	10,088	5,683
45439	Moraine	(513)	5,325	4,898
45231	Mount Healthy	(513)	7,562	7,446
43050	Mount Vernon	(614)	14,380	13,373
43545	Napoleon	(419)	8,614	7,791
43055	Newark	(614)	41,200	41,836
45344	New Carlisle	(513)	6,498	6,112
43764	New Lexington	(614)	5,179	4,921
44663	New Philadelphia	(216)	16,883	15,184
44446	Niles	(216)	23,088	21,581
45239	Northbrook(u)	(513)	8,357	....
44720	North Canton	(216)	14,228	15,228
45239	North College Hill	(513)	10,990	12,363
44057	North Madison(u)	(216)	8,741	6,882
44070	North Olmsted	(216)	36,486	34,861
45502	Northridge(u) (Clark)	(513)	5,559	12
45414	Northridge(u) (Montgomery)	(513)	9,720	10,084
44039	North Ridgeville	(216)	21,522	13,152
44133	North Royalton	(216)	17,671	12,807
.....	Northview(u)	(513)	9,973	....
43619	Northwood	(419)	5,495	4,222

ZIP code	Place		1980	1970
44203	Norton	(216)	12,242	12,308
44857	Norwalk	(419)	14,358	13,386
45212	Norwood	(513)	26,342	30,420
45419	Oakwood	(513)	9,372	10,095
44074	Oberlin	(216)	8,660	8,761
44138	Olmsted Falls	(216)	5,868	2,504
43616	Oregon	(419)	18,675	16,563
44667	Orrville	(216)	7,511	7,408
45431	Overlook-Page Manor(u)	(513)	14,825	19,719
45056	Oxford	(513)	17,655	15,868
44077	Painesville	(216)	16,391	16,536
45344	Park Layne(u)	(513)	5,372	....
44129	Parma	(216)	92,548	100,216
44130	Parma Heights	(216)	23,112	27,192
44124	Pepper Pike	(216)	6,177	5,382
44646	Perry Heights(u)	(216)	9,206	....
43551	Perrysburg	(419)	10,215	7,693
45356	Piqua	(513)	20,480	20,741
45069	Pisgah(u)	(513)	15,660	....
44319	Portage Lakes(u)	(216)	11,310	....
43452	Port Clinton	(419)	7,223	7,202
45662	Portsmouth	(614)	25,943	27,633
44266	Ravenna	(216)	11,987	11,780
45215	Reading	(513)	12,879	14,617
43068	Reynoldsburg	(614)	20,661	13,921
44143	Richmond Heights	(213)	10,095	9,220
44270	Rittman	(216)	6,063	6,308
44116	Rocky River	(216)	21,084	22,958
43460	Rossford	(419)	5,978	5,302
45217	St. Bernard	(513)	5,396	6,131
43950	St. Clairsville	(614)	5,452	4,754
45885	St. Marys	(419)	8,414	7,699
44460	Salem	(216)	12,869	14,186
44870	Sandusky	(419)	31,360	32,674
44870	Sandusky South(u)	(419)	6,548	8,501
44672	Sebring	(216)	5,078	4,954
44131	Seven Hills	(216)	13,650	12,700
44120	Shaker Heights	(216)	32,487	36,306
45241	Sharonville	(513)	10,108	11,393
44054	Sheffield Lake	(216)	10,484	8,734
44875	Shelby	(419)	9,645	9,847
45415	Shiloh(u)	(419)	11,735	11,368
45365	Sidney	(513)	17,657	16,332
45236	Silverton	(513)	6,172	6,588
44139	Solon	(216)	14,341	11,147
44121	South Euclid	(216)	25,713	29,579
45246	Springdale	(216)	10,111	8,127
*45501	Springfield	(513)	72,563	81,941
43952	Steubenville	(614)	26,400	30,771
44224	Stow	(216)	25,303	20,061
44240	Streetsboro	(216)	9,055	7,966
44136	Strongsville	(216)	28,577	15,182
44471	Struthers	(216)	13,624	15,343
43560	Sylvania	(419)	15,527	12,031
44278	Tallmadge	(216)	15,269	15,274
45243	The Village of Indian Hill	(513)	5,521	5,651
44883	Tiffin	(419)	19,549	21,596
45371	Tipp City	(513)	5,595	5,090
*43601	Toledo	(419)	354,635	383,062
43964	Toronto	(614)	6,934	7,705
45067	Trenton	(513)	6,401	5,278
45426	Trotwood	(513)	7,802	6,997
45373	Troy	(513)	19,086	17,186
44087	Twinsburg	(216)	7,632	6,432
44683	Uhrichsville	(614)	6,130	5,731
45322	Union	(513)	5,219	3,654
44118	University Heights	(216)	15,401	17,055
43221	Upper Arlington	(614)	35,648	38,727
43351	Upper Sandusky	(419)	5,967	5,645
43078	Urbana	(513)	10,762	11,237
45377	Vandalia	(513)	13,161	10,796
45891	Van Wert		11,035	11,320
44089	Vermilion	(216)	11,012	9,872
44281	Wadsworth	(216)	15,166	13,142
45895	Wapakoneta	(419)	8,402	7,324
*44481	Warren	(216)	56,629	63,494
44122	Warrensville Heights	(216)	16,565	18,925
43160	Washington	(513)	12,682	12,495
43567	Wauseon	(419)	6,173	4,932
45692	Wellston	(614)	6,016	5,410
43968	Wellsville	(216)	5,095	5,891
45449	West Carrollton	(513)	13,148	10,748
43081	Westerville	(614)	23,414	12,530
44145	Westlake	(216)	19,483	15,689
43213	Whitehall	(614)	21,299	25,263
45239	White Oak(u)	(513)	9,563	....
44092	Wickliffe	(216)	16,790	20,632
44890	Willard	(419)	5,674	5,510
44094	Willoughby	(216)	19,329	18,634
44094	Willoughby Hills	(216)	8,612	5,969
44094	Willowick	(216)	17,834	21,237
45177	Wilmington	(513)	10,431	10,051
45459	Woodbourne-Hyde Park(u)	(513)	8,826	....
44691	Wooster	(216)	19,289	18,703
43085	Worthington	(614)	15,016	15,326
45215	Wyoming	(513)	8,282	9,089
45385	Xenia	(513)	24,653	25,373
*44501	Youngstown	(216)	115,436	140,909
43701	Zanesville	(614)	28,655	33,045

Oklahoma

ZIP code	Place		1980	1970
74820	Ada	(405)	15,902	14,859
73521	Altus	(405)	23,101	23,302
73717	Alva	(405)	6,416	7,440
73005	Anadarko	(405)	6,378	6,682
73401	Ardmore	(405)	23,689	20,881
74003	Bartlesville	(918)	34,568	29,683
73008	Bethany	(405)	22,130	22,694
74008	Bixby	(918)	6,969	3,973
74631	Blackwell	(405)	8,400	8,645
74012	Broken Arrow	(918)	35,761	11,018
73018	Chickasha	(405)	15,828	14,194
73020	Choctaw	(405)	7,520	4,750
74017	Claremore	(918)	12,085	9,084
73601	Clinton	(405)	8,796	8,513
74023	Cushing	(918)	7,720	7,529
73115	Del City	(405)	28,424	27,133
73533	Duncan	(405)	22,517	19,718
74701	Durant	(405)	11,972	11,118
73034	Edmond	(405)	34,637	16,633
73644	Elk City	(405)	9,579	7,323
73036	El Reno	(405)	15,486	14,510
73701	Enid	(405)	50,363	44,986
73503	Fort Sill(u)	(405)	15,924	21,217
73542	Frederick	(405)	6,153	6,132
73044	Guthrie	(405)	10,312	9,575
73942	Guymon	(405)	8,492	7,674
74437	Henryetta	(918)	6,432	6,430
74848	Holdenville	(405)	5,469	5,181
74743	Hugo	(405)	7,172	6,585
74745	Idabel	(405)	7,622	5,946
74037	Jenks	(918)	5,876	2,685
73501	Lawton	(405)	80,054	74,470
73055	Marlow	(405)	5,017	3,995
74501	McAlester	(918)	17,255	18,802
74354	Miami	(918)	14,237	13,880
73110	Midwest City	(405)	49,559	48,212
73060	Moore	(405)	35,063	18,761
74401	Muskogee	(918)	40,011	37,331
73064	Mustang	(405)	7,496	2,637
73069	Norman	(405)	68,020	52,117
*73125	Oklahoma City	(405)	403,213	368,164
74447	Okmulgee	(918)	16,263	15,180
74055	Owasso	(918)	6,149	3,491
73075	Pauls Valley	(405)	5,664	5,769
73077	Perry	(405)	5,796	5,341
74601	Ponca City	(405)	26,238	25,940
74953	Poteau	(918)	7,089	5,500
74361	Pryor Creek	(918)	8,483	7,057
74955	Sallisaw	(918)	6,403	4,888
74063	Sand Springs	(918)	13,246	10,565
74066	Sapulpa	(918)	15,853	15,159
74868	Seminole	(405)	8,590	7,878
74801	Shawnee	(405)	26,506	25,075
74074	Stillwater	(405)	38,268	31,126
73086	Sulphur	(405)	5,516	5,158
74464	Tahlequah	(918)	9,708	9,254
74873	Tecumseh	(405)	5,123	4,451
73120	The Village	(405)	11,049	13,695
*74101	Tulsa	(918)	360,919	330,350
74156	Turley(u)	(918)	6,336	....
74301	Vinita	(918)	6,740	5,847
74467	Wagoner	(918)	6,191	4,959
73132	Warr Acres	(405)	9,940	9,887
73096	Weatherford	(405)	9,640	7,959
74884	Wewoka	(405)	5,480	5,284
73801	Woodward	(405)	13,610	9,563
73099	Yukon	(405)	17,112	8,411

Oregon (503)

ZIP code	Place	1980	1970
97321	Albany	26,546	18,181
97005	Aloha(u)	28,353	....
97601	Altamont(u)	19,805	15,746
97520	Ashland	14,943	12,342
97103	Astoria	9,998	10,244
97814	Baker	9,471	9,354
97005	Beaverton	30,582	18,577
97701	Bend	17,263	13,710
97013	Canby	7,659	3,813
97225	Cedar Hills(u)	9,619	....
.....	Centennial(u)	22,118	....
97502	Central Point	6,357	4,004
97420	Coos Bay	14,424	13,466
97330	Corvallis	40,960	35,056
97424	Cottage Grove	7,148	6,004
.....	Cully(u)	10,569	....
97338	Dallas	8,530	6,361
97266	Errol Heights(u)	10,487	....
*97401	Eugene	105,624	79,028
97116	Forest Grove	11,499	8,275
97301	Four Corners(u)	11,331	5,823
97223	Garden Home-Whitford(u)	6,926	....
97027	Gladstone	9,500	6,254
97526	Grants Pass	14,997	12,455
97030	Gresham	33,005	10,030
97303	Hayesville(u)	9,213	5,518
97230	Hazelwood(u)	25,541	....
97838	Hermiston	9,408	4,893

ZIP code	Place	1980	1970
97123	Hillsboro	27,664	14,675
97303	Keizer(u)	18,592	11,405
97601	Klamath Falls	16,661	15,775
97850	La Grande	11,354	9,645
97034	Lake Oswego	22,868	14,615
97355	Lebanon	10,413	6,636
97367	Lincoln City	5,469	4,198
97128	McMinnville	14,080	10,125
97501	Medford	39,603	28,973
97223	Metzger(u)	5,544	....
97862	Milton-Freewater	5,086	4,105
97222	Milwaukie	17,931	16,444
97361	Monmouth	5,594	5,237
97132	Newberg	10,394	6,507
97365	Newport	7,519	5,188
97459	North Bend	9,779	8,553
.....	North Springfield(u)	6,140	....
97268	Oak Grove(u)	11,640	....
97914	Ontario	8,814	6,523
97045	Oregon City	14,673	9,176
97220	Parkrose(u)	21,108	....
97801	Pendleton	14,521	13,197
*97208	Portland	366,383	379,967
97236	Powellhurst(u)	20,132	....
97754	Prineville	5,276	4,101
97225	Raleigh Hills(u)	6,517	....
97756	Redmond	6,452	3,721
97404	River Road(u)	10,370	....
97470	Roseburg	16,644	14,461
97051	St. Helens	7,064	6,212
*97301	Salem	89,233	68,725
97401	Santa Clara(u)	14,288	....
97138	Seaside	5,193	4,402
97381	Silverton	5,168	4,301
97477	Springfield	41,621	26,874
97386	Sweet Home	6,921	3,799
97058	The Dalles	10,820	10,423
97223	Tigard	14,286	6,499
97060	Troutdale	5,908	1,661
97062	Tualatin	7,348	750
97068	West Linn	12,956	7,091
97225	West Slope(u)	5,364	....
97501	White City(u)	5,445	....
97233	Wilkes-Rockwood(u)	23,216	....
97071	Woodburn	11,196	7,495

Pennsylvania

ZIP code	Place	Area code	1980	1970
19001	Abington Township(u)	(215)	59,084	63,625
15001	Aliquippa	(412)	17,094	22,277
*18101	Allentown	(215)	103,758	109,871
*16603	Altoona	(814)	57,078	63,115
19002	Ambler	(215)	6,628	7,800
15003	Ambridge	(412)	9,575	11,324
18403	Archbald	(717)	6,295	6,118
19003	Ardmore(u)	(215)	NA	5,131
15068	Arnold	(412)	6,853	8,174
19014	Aston Township(u)	(215)	14,530	13,704
15202	Avalon	(412)	6,240	7,010
15005	Baden	(412)	5,318	5,536
19004	Bala-Cynwyd(u)	(215)	NA	6,483
15234	Baldwin	(412)	24,598	26,729
18013	Bangor	(215)	5,006	5,425
15009	Beaver	(412)	5,441	6,100
15010	Beaver Falls	(412)	12,525	14,635
16823	Bellefonte	(814)	6,300	6,828
15202	Bellevue	(412)	10,128	11,586
.....	Bensalem Township(u)	(215)	52,399	33,038
18603	Berwick	(717)	12,189	12,274
15102	Bethel Park	(412)	34,755	34,758
*18016	Bethlehem	(215)	70,419	72,686
18447	Blakely	(717)	7,438	6,391
17815	Bloomsburg	(717)	11,717	11,652
15104	Braddock	(412)	5,634	8,795
16701	Bradford	(814)	11,211	12,672
15227	Brentwood	(412)	11,907	13,732
15017	Bridgeville	(412)	6,154	6,717
19007	Bristol	(215)	10,867	12,085
.....	Bristol Twp(u)	(215)	58,733	67,498
19015	Brookhaven	(215)	7,912	7,370
16001	Butler	(412)	17,026	18,691
15419	California	(412)	5,703	6,635
17011	Camp Hill	(717)	8,422	9,931
15317	Canonsburg	(412)	10,459	11,439
18407	Carbondale	(717)	11,255	12,478
17013	Carlisle	(717)	18,314	18,079
15106	Carnegie	(412)	10,099	10,864
15108	Carnot-Moon(u)	(412)	11,102	13,093
15234	Castle Shannon	(412)	10,164	12,036
18032	Catasauqua	(215)	7,944	5,702
17201	Chambersburg	(717)	16,174	17,315
15022	Charleroi	(412)	5,717	6,723
19012	Cheltenham Twp(u)	(215)	35,509	40,238
*19003	Chester	(215)	45,794	56,331
.....	Chester Twp(u)	(215)	5,687	5,708
15025	Clairton	(412)	12,188	15,051
16214	Clarion	(814)	6,664	6,095
18411	Clarks Summit	(717)	5,272	5,376

ZIP code	Place	Area code	1980	1970
16830	Clearfield	(814)	7,580	8,176
19018	Clifton Heights	(215)	7,320	8,348
19320	Coatesville	(215)	10,698	12,331
19023	Collingdale	(215)	9,539	10,605
17512	Columbia	(717)	10,466	11,237
15425	Connellsville	(412)	10,319	11,643
19428	Conshohocken	(215)	8,475	10,195
15108	Coraopolis	(412)	7,308	8,435
16407	Corry	(814)	7,149	7,435
15205	Crafton	(412)	7,623	8,233
17821	Danville	(717)	5,239	6,176
19023	Darby	(215)	11,513	13,729
19036	Darby Twp(u)	(215)	12,264	....
.....	Devon-Berwyn(u)	(215)	5,246	....
18519	Dickson City	(717)	6,699	7,698
15033	Donora	(412)	7,524	8,825
15216	Dormont	(412)	11,275	12,856
19335	Downingtown	(215)	7,650	7,437
18901	Doylestown	(215)	8,717	8,270
15801	Du Bois	(814)	9,290	10,112
18512	Dunmore	(717)	16,781	18,168
15110	Duquesne	(412)	10,094	11,410
18642	Duryea	(717)	5,415	5,264
19401	East Norriton(u)	(215)	12,711	....
18042	Easton	(215)	26,027	29,450
18301	East Stroudsburg	(717)	8,039	7,894
15005	Economy	(412)	9,538	7,176
16412	Edinboro	(814)	6,324	4,871
18704	Edwardsville	(717)	5,729	5,633
17022	Elizabethtown	(717)	8,233	8,072
16117	Ellwood City	(412)	9,998	10,857
18049	Emmaus	(215)	11,001	11,511
17522	Ephrata	(717)	11,095	9,662
*16501	Erie	(814)	119,123	129,265
18643	Exeter	(717)	5,493	4,670
19054	Falls Twp(u)	(215)	36,083	35,830
16121	Farrell	(412)	8,645	11,000
19032	Folcroft	(215)	8,231	9,610
15221	Forest Hills	(412)	8,198	9,561
18704	Forty Fort	(717)	5,590	6,114
15238	Fox Chapel	(412)	5,049	4,684
17931	Frackville	(215)	5,308	5,445
16323	Franklin	(814)	8,146	8,629
15143	Franklin Park	(412)	6,135	5,310
18052	Fullerton(u)	(215)	8,055	7,908
17325	Gettysburg	(717)	7,194	7,275
15045	Glassport	(412)	6,242	7,450
19036	Glenolden	(215)	7,633	8,697
15601	Greensburg	(412)	17,558	17,077
15220	Green Tree	(412)	5,722	6,441
16125	Greenville	(412)	7,730	8,704
16127	Grove City	(412)	8,162	8,312
17331	Hanover	(717)	14,890	15,623
*17105	Harrisburg	(717)	53,264	68,061
19040	Hatboro	(215)	7,579	8,880
19083	Haverford Twp(u)	(215)	52,349	55,132
18201	Hazleton	(717)	27,318	30,426
18055	Hellertown	(215)	6,025	6,615
17033	Hershey(u)	(717)	13,249	7,407
18042	Highland Park (Northampton)(u)	(717)	5,922	5,500
16648	Hollidaysburg	(814)	5,892	6,262
16001	Homeacre-Lyndora(u)	(412)	8,333	8,415
15120	Homestead	(412)	5,092	6,309
18431	Honesdale	(717)	5,128	5,224
19044	Horsham(u)	(215)	9,900	....
17036	Hummelstown	(717)	6,159	4,723
16652	Huntingdon	(814)	7,042	6,987
15701	Indiana	(412)	16,051	16,100
15644	Jeannette	(412)	13,106	15,209
15344	Jefferson	(412)	8,643	8,512
18229	Jim Thorpe	(717)	5,263	5,456
*15901	Johnstown	(814)	35,496	42,476
15108	Kennedy Twp(u)	(412)	7,159	6,859
18704	Kingston	(717)	15,681	18,325
16201	Kittanning	(412)	5,432	6,231
*17604	Lancaster	(717)	54,725	57,690
19446	Lansdale	(215)	16,526	18,451
19050	Lansdowne	(215)	11,891	14,090
15650	Latrobe	(412)	10,799	11,749
17042	Lebanon	(717)	25,711	28,572
18235	Lehighton	(215)	5,826	6,095
17837	Lewisburg	(717)	5,407	5,718
17044	Lewistown	(717)	9,830	11,098
17543	Lititz	(717)	7,590	7,072
17745	Lock Haven	(717)	9,617	11,427
15068	Lower Burrell	(412)	13,200	13,654
19003	Lower Merion Twp(u)	(215)	59,651	63,392
19006	Lower Moreland Twp(u)	(215)	12,472	11,746
19047	Lower Southampton Twp(u)	(215)	18,305	17,578
19008	Marple Twp(u)	(215)	23,642	25,040
15237	McCandless Twp(u)	(412)	26,250	22,404
*15134	McKeesport	(412)	31,012	37,977
15136	McKees Rocks	(412)	8,742	11,901
17948	Mahanoy City	(717)	6,167	7,257
17545	Manheim	(717)	5,015	5,434
16335	Meadville	(814)	15,544	16,573
17055	Mechanicsburg	(717)	9,487	9,385
*19063	Media	(215)	6,119	6,444
17057	Middletown (Dauphin)	(717)	10,122	9,080
18017	Middletown (Northampton)(u)	(215)	5,801	....

ZIP code	Place		1980	1970
.....	Middletown Twp (Delaware)(u)	(215)	12,463	12,878
17551	Millersville	(717)	7,668	6,396
17847	Milton	(717)	6,730	7,723
17954	Minersville	(717)	5,635	6,012
15061	Monaca	(412)	7,661	7,486
15062	Monessen	(412)	11,928	15,216
15063	Monongahela	(412)	5,950	7,113
15146	Monroeville	(412)	30,977	29,011
17754	Montoursville	(717)	5,403	5,985
18507	Moosic	(717)	6,068	4,646
19067	Morrisville	(215)	9,845	11,309
17851	Mount Carmel	(717)	8,190	9,317
17552	Mount Joy	(717)	5,680	5,041
15228	Mount Lebanon(u)	(412)	....	34,414
15666	Mount Pleasant	(412)	5,354	5,895
15228	Mount Lebanon(u)	(412)	34,414	....
15120	Munhall	(412)	14,532	16,574
15668	Murrysville	(412)	16,036	12,661
18634	Nanticoke	(717)	13,044	14,638
18064	Nazareth	(215)	5,443	5,815
.....	Nether Providence Twp(u)	(215)	12,730	13,644
15066	New Brighton	(412)	7,364	7,637
16101	New Castle	(412)	33,621	38,559
17070	New Cumberland	(717)	8,051	9,803
15068	New Kensington	(412)	17,660	20,312
19401	Norristown	(215)	34,684	38,169
18067	Northampton	(215)	8,240	8,389
15104	North Braddock	(412)	8,711	10,838
15137	North Versailles(u)	(412)	13,294	....
.....	Northwest Harbor-Creek(u)	(814)	7,485	.....
19074	Norwood	(215)	6,647	7,229
15139	Oakmont	(412)	7,039	7,550
16301	Oil City	(814)	13,881	15,033
18518	Old Forge	(717)	9,304	9,522
18447	Olyphant	(717)	5,204	5,422
18071	Palmerton	(215)	5,455	5,620
17078	Palmyra	(717)	7,228	7,615
19301	Paoli(u)	(215)	6,698	5,835
17331	Parkville(u)	(717)	5,009	5,120
15235	Penn Hills(u)	(412)	57,632	....
18944	Perkasie	(215)	5,241	5,451
19104	Philadelphia	(215)	1,688,210	1,949,996
19460	Phoenixville	(215)	14,165	14,823
15219	Pittsburgh	(412)	423,938	520,089
18640	Pittston	(717)	9,930	11,113
18705	Plains(u)	(717)	5,455	6,606
15236	Pleasant Hills	(412)	9,676	10,409
15239	Plum	(412)	25,390	21,932
18651	Plymouth	(717)	7,605	9,536
19462	Plymouth Twp(u)	(215)	17,168	16,876
15133	Port Vue	(412)	5,316	5,862
19464	Pottstown	(215)	22,729	25,355
17901	Pottsville	(717)	18,195	19,715
19076	Prospect Park	(215)	6,593	7,250
15767	Punxsutawney	(814)	7,479	7,792
18951	Quakertown	(215)	8,867	7,276
19087	Radnor Twp(u)	(215)	27,676	27,459
19603	Reading	(215)	78,686	87,643
17356	Red Lion	(717)	5,824	5,645
18954	Richboro(u)	(215)	5,141	....
15853	Ridgway	(814)	5,604	6,022
19078	Ridley Park	(215)	7,889	9,025
19033	Ridley Twp(u)	(215)	33,771	39,085
15237	Ross Twp(u)	(412)	35,102	32,892
15857	St. Marys	(814)	6,417	7,470
18840	Sayre	(717)	6,951	7,473
17972	Schuylkill Haven	(717)	5,977	6,125
15683	Scottdale	(412)	5,833	5,818
15106	Scott Twp(u)	(412)	20,413	21,856
*18503	Scranton	(717)	88,117	102,696
17870	Selinsgrove	(717)	5,227	5,116
15116	Shaler Twp(u)	(412)	33,712	33,369
17872	Shamokin	(717)	10,357	11,719
16146	Sharon	(412)	19,057	22,653
19079	Sharon Hill	(215)	6,221	7,464
16150	Sharpsville	(412)	5,375	6,126
17976	Shenandoah	(717)	7,589	8,287
19607	Shillington	(215)	5,601	6,249
17404	Shiloh(u)	(717)	5,315	....
17257	Shippensburg	(717)	5,261	6,536
15501	Somerset	(814)	6,474	6,269
18964	Souderton	(215)	6,657	6,366
17701	South Williamsport		6,581	7,153
19064	Springfield(u)	(215)	25,326	....
19118	Springfield Twp(u)	(215)	20,344	22,394
16801	State College	(814)	36,130	32,833
17113	Steelton	(717)	6,484	8,556
15136	Stowe Twp(u)	(412)	9,202	10,119
18360	Stroudsburg	(717)	5,148	5,451
16323	Sugar Creek	(717)	5,954	5,944
17801	Sunbury	(717)	12,292	13,025
19081	Swarthmore	(215)	5,950	6,156
17111	Swatara Twp(u)	(717)	18,796	17,178
15218	Swissvale	(412)	11,345	13,819
18704	Swoyersville	(717)	5,795	6,786
18252	Tamaqua	(717)	8,843	9,246
15084	Tarentum	(412)	6,419	7,379
18517	Taylor	(717)	7,246	6,977
16354	Titusville	(814)	6,884	7,331
19401	Trooper(u)	(215)	7,370	....
15145	Turtle Creek	(412)	6,959	8,308
16686	Tyrone	(814)	6,346	7,072
15401	Uniontown	(814)	14,510	16,282
19061	Upper Chichester Twp(u)	(215)	14,377	11,414
19082	Upper Darby(u)	(215)	84,054	95,910
19034	Upper Dublin Twp(u)	(215)	22,348	19,449
19406	Upper Merion Twp(u)	(215)	26,138	23,699
19090	Upper Moreland Twp(u)	(215)	25,874	24,866
19063	Upper Providence Twp(u)	(215)	9,477	9,234
15241	Upper St. Clair(u)	(412)	19,023	....
19006	Upper Southampton Twp(u)	(215)	15,806	13,936
15690	Vandergrift	(412)	6,823	7,889
18974	Warminster(u)	(215)	35,543	....
16365	Warren	(814)	12,146	12,998
15301	Washington	(412)	18,363	19,827
17268	Waynesboro	(717)	9,726	10,011
.....	Weigelstown(u)	(717)	5,213	....
19380	West Chester	(215)	17,435	19,301
19380	West Goshen(u)	(215)	7,998	....
15122	West Mifflin	(412)	26,279	28,070
19401	West Norriton(u)	(215)	14,034	....
15905	Westmont	(814)	6,113	6,673
18643	West Pittston	(717)	5,980	7,074
15229	West View	(412)	7,648	8,312
18052	Whitehall	(412)	15,206	16,450
19428	Whitemarsh Twp(u)	(215)	15,101	15,886
15131	White Oak	(717)	9,480	9,304
*18701	Wilkes-Barre	(717)	51,551	58,856
15221	Wilkinsburg	(412)	23,669	26,780
15145	Wilkins Twp(u)	(412)	8,472	8,749
17701	Williamsport	(717)	33,401	37,918
15025	Wilson	(412)	7,564	8,406
15963	Windber	(814)	5,585	6,332
19610	Wyomissing	(215)	6,551	7,136
19050	Yeadon	(215)	11,727	12,136
*17405	York	(717)	44,619	50,335

Rhode Island (401)

See Note on Page 218

ZIP code	Place	1980	1970
02806	*Barrington*	16,174	17,554
02809	*Bristol*	20,128	17,860
02830	*Burrillville*	13,164	10,087
02863	Central Falls	16,995	18,716
02816	*Coventry*	27,065	22,947
02910	Cranston	71,992	74,287
02864	*Cumberland*	27,069	26,605
02864	Cumberland Hill(u)	5,421	....
02818	*East Greenwich*	10,211	9,577
02914	East Providence	50,980	48,207
02814	*Glocester*	7,550	5,160
02828	Greenville(u)	7,576	....
02833	*Hopkinton*	6,406	5,392
02919	*Johnston*	24,907	22,037
02881	Kingston(u)	5,479	5,601
02865	*Lincoln*	16,949	16,182
02840	*Middletown*	17,216	29,290
02882	*Narragansett*	12,088	7,138
02840	Newport	29,259	34,562
02843	Newport East(u)	11,030	10,285
02852	*North Kingstown*	21,938	29,793
02908	*North Providence*	29,188	24,337
02876	*North Smithfield*	9,972	9,349
*02860	Pawtucket	71,204	76,984
02871	*Portsmouth*	14,257	12,521
*02904	Providence	156,804	179,116
02857	*Scituate*	8,405	7,489
02917	*Smithfield*	16,886	13,468
02879	*South Kingstown*	20,414	16,913
02878	*Tiverton*	13,526	12,559
02864	Valley Falls(u)	10,892	....
*02880	Wakefield-Peacedale(u)	6,474	6,331
02885	*Warren*	10,640	10,523
*02887	Warwick	87,123	83,694
02891	*Westerly*	18,580	17,248
02891	Westerly Center(u)	14,093	13,654
02893	*West Warwick*	27,026	24,323
02895	Woonsocket	45,914	46,820

South Carolina (803)

ZIP code	Place	1980	1970
29620	Abbeville	5,863	5,515
29801	Aiken	14,978	13,436
29621	Anderson	27,313	27,556
29407	Avondale-Moorland(u)	5,355	5,236
29812	Barnwell	5,572	4,439
29902	Beaufort	8,634	9,434
29627	Belton	5,312	5,257
29841	Belvedere(u)	6,859	....
29512	Bennettsville	8,774	7,468
29611	Berea(u)	13,164	7,186
.....	Brookdale(u)	6,123	....
29020	Camden	7,462	8,532
29209	Capitol View(u)	9,962	....
29033	Cayce	11,701	9,967
*29401	Charleston	69,510	66,945
29404	Charleston Base(u)	NA	6,238

ZIP code	Place	1980	1970
29408	Charleston Yard(u)	NA	13,565
29520	Cheraw	5,654	5,627
29706	Chester	6,820	7,045
29631	Clemson	8,118	6,690
29325	Clinton	8,596	8,138
*29201	Columbia	99,296	113,542
29526	Conway	10,240	8,151
29532	Darlington	7,989	6,990
29204	Dentsville(u)	13,579	....
29536	Dillon	7,042	6,391
29405	Dorchester Terrace-Brentwood(u)	7,862	....
29601	Dunean(u)	5,146	1,266
29640	Easley	14,264	11,175
29501	Florence	30,062	25,997
29206	Forest Acres	6,033	6,808
29340	Gaffney	13,453	13,131
29605	Gantt(u)	13,719	11,386
29440	Georgetown	10,144	10,449
29445	Goose Creek	17,811	3,825
*29602	Greenville	58,242	61,436
29203	Greenview(u)	5,515	....
29646	Greenwood	21,613	21,069
29651	Greer	10,525	10,642
29410	Hanahan	13,224	9,118
29550	Hartsville	7,631	8,017
29928	Hilton Head Island(u)	11,344	....
29621	Homeland Park(u)	6,720	....
29412	James Island(u)	24,124	....
29456	Ladson(u)	13,246	....
29560	Lake City	5,636	6,247
29720	Lancaster	9,603	9,186
29902	Laurel Bay(u)	5,238	....
29360	Laurens	10,587	10,298
29571	Marion	7,700	7,435
29662	Mauldin	8,245	3,797
29464	Mount Pleasant	13,838	6,879
29574	Mullins	6,068	6,006
29577	Myrtle Beach	18,758	9,035
29108	Newberry	9,866	9,218
29841	North Augusta	13,593	12,883
29406	North Charleston	65,630	21,211
.....	North Trenholm(u)	10,962	....
29565	Oak Grove(u)	7,092	....
29115	Orangeburg	14,933	13,252
29905	Parris Island(u)	7,752	8,868
29483	Pinehurst-Sheppard Park(u)	6,956	1,711
29730	Rock Hill	35,344	33,846
29407	St. Andrews (Charleston)(u)	9,908	9,202
29210	St. Andrews (Richland)(u)	20,245	....
29609	Sans Souci(u)	8,393	....
29678	Seneca	7,436	6,573
.....	Seven Oaks(u)	16,604	....
29152	Shaw AFB(u)	6,939	5,819
29681	Simpsonville	9,037	3,308
.....	South Sumter(u)	7,096	....
*29301	Spartanburg	43,968	44,546
29483	Summerville	6,368	3,839
29150	Sumter	24,890	24,555
29687	Taylors(u)	15,801	6,831
29379	Union	10,523	10,775
29205	Valencia Heights(u)	5,328	....
29607	Wade-Hampton(u)	20,180	17,152
29488	Walterboro	6,036	6,257
29405	Wando Woods(u)	5,266	....
29611	Welcome(u)	6,922	....
29169	West Columbia	10,409	7,838
29206	Woodfield(u)	9,588	....
29388	Woodruff	5,171	4,690
29745	York	6,412	5,081

South Dakota (605)

ZIP code	Place	1980	1970
57401	Aberdeen	25,956	26,476
57006	Brookings	14,951	13,717
57350	Huron	13,000	14,299
57042	Madison	6,210	6,315
57301	Mitchell	13,916	13,425
57501	Pierre	11,973	9,699
57701	Rapid City	46,492	43,836
*57101	Sioux Falls	81,343	72,488
57785	Sturgis	5,184	4,536
57069	Vermillion	9,582	9,128
57201	Watertown	15,649	13,388
57078	Yankton	12,011	11,919

Tennessee

ZIP code	Place	Area code	1980	1970
37701	Alcoa	(615)	6,870	7,739
37303	Athens	(615)	12,080	11,790
38134	Bartlett	(901)	17,170	1,150
37660	Bloomingdale(u)	(615)	12,088	3,120
38008	Bolivar	(901)	6,597	6,674
37027	Brentwood	(615)	9,431	4,099
37620	Bristol	(615)	23,986	20,064
38012	Brownsville	(901)	9,307	7,011
*37401	Chattanooga	(615)	169,565	119,923
37040	Clarksville	(615)	54,777	31,7
37311	Cleveland	(615)	26,415	21,44
37716	Clinton	(615)	5,245	4,79
38017	Collierville	(901)	7,839	3,65
37663	Colonial Heights(u)	(615)	6,744	3,02
38401	Columbia	(615)	25,767	21,47
37922	Concord (Knox)(u)	(615)	8,569	..
..38501	Cookeville	(615)	20,350	14,40
38019	Covington	(901)	6,065	5,80
38555	Crossville	(615)	6,394	5,38
37321	Dayton	(615)	5,913	4,36
37055	Dickson	(615)	7,040	5,66
38024	Dyersburg	(901)	15,856	14,52
37801	Eagleton Village(u)	(615)	5,331	5,34
37412	East Ridge	(615)	21,236	21,79
37643	Elizabethton	(615)	12,431	12,26
37334	Fayetteville	(615)	7,559	7,69
37064	Franklin	(615)	12,407	9,49
37066	Gallatin	(615)	17,191	13,25
38138	Germantown	(901)	20,459	3,47
37072	Goodlettsville	(615)	8,327	6,16
37075	Greater Hendersonville(u)	(615)	25,029	11,99
37743	Greeneville	(615)	14,097	13,72
37918	Halls(u)	(615)	10,363	..
..37748	Harriman	(615)	8,303	8,73
37341	Harrison(u)	(615)	6,206	...
..37075	Hendersonville	(615)	26,561	41
38343	Humboldt	(901)	10,209	10,06
38301	Jackson	(901)	49,131	39,99
37760	Jefferson City	(615)	5,612	5,124
37601	Johnson City	(615)	39,753	33,770
*37662	Kingsport	(615)	32,027	31,938
*37901	Knoxville	(615)	183,139	174,587
37766	La Follette	(615)	8,176	6,902
37086	LaVergne	(615)	5,495	5,220
38464	Lawrenceburg	(615)	10,175	8,889
37087	Lebanon	(615)	11,872	12,492
37771	Lenoir City	(615)	5,446	5,324
37091	Lewisburg	(615)	8,760	7,207
38351	Lexington	(901)	5,934	5,024
37665	Lynn Garden(u)	(615)	7,213	....
38201	McKenzie	(901)	5,405	4,873
37110	McMinnville	(615)	10,683	10,662
37355	Manchester	(615)	7,250	6,208
38237	Martin	(901)	8,898	7,781
37801	Maryville	(615)	17,480	13,808
*38101	Memphis	(901)	646,356	623,988
37343	Middle Valley(u)	(615)	11,420	....
38358	Milan	(901)	8,083	7,313
38053	Millington	(901)	20,236	21,177
37814	Morristown	(615)	19,683	20,318
37130	Murfreesboro	(615)	32,845	26,360
*37202	Nashville-Davidson	(615)	455,651	**426,029
37821	Newport	(615)	7,580	7,328
37830	Oak Ridge	(615)	27,662	28,319
38242	Paris	(901)	10,728	9,892
37849	Powell(u)	(615)	7,220	....
38478	Pulaski	(615)	7,184	6,989
37415	Red Bank White Oak	(615)	13,297	12,715
38063	Ripley	(901)	6,366	4,794
37854	Rockwood	(615)	5,767	5,259
38372	Savannah	(901)	6,992	5,576
37160	Shelbyville	(615)	13,530	12,262
37377	Signal Mountain	(615)	5,818	4,839
37167	Smyrna	(615)	8,839	5,698
37379	Soddy-Daisy	(615)	8,388	7,569
37172	Springfield	(615)	10,814	9,720
37363	Summit (Hamilton)(u)	(615)	8,345	....
37388	Tullahoma	(615)	15,800	15,311
38261	Union City	(901)	10,436	11,925
37398	Winchester	(615)	5,821	5,256

***Comprises the Metropolitan Government of Nashville and Davidsor County.*

Texas

ZIP code	Place	Area code	1980	1970
*79604	Abilene	(915)	98,315	89,653
75001	Addison	(214)	5,553	593
78516	Alamo	(512)	5,831	4,291
78209	Alamo Heights	(512)	6,252	6,933
77039	Aldine(u)	(713)	12,623	...
78332	Alice	(512)	20,961	20,121
75002	Allen	(214)	8,314	1,940
79830	Alpine	(915)	5,465	5,971
77511	Alvin	(713)	16,515	10,671
*79105	Amarillo	(806)	149,230	127,010
79714	Andrews	(915)	11,061	8,625
77515	Angleton	(713)	13,929	9,906
78336	Aransas Pass	(512)	7,173	5,813
*76010	Arlington	(817)	160,123	90,229
75751	Athens	(214)	10,197	9,582
75551	Atlanta	(214)	6,272	5,007
*78710	Austin	(512)	345,496	253,539
76020	Azle	(817)	5,822	4,493
75149	Balch Springs	(214)	13,746	10,464
77414	Bay City	(713)	17,837	13,445
77520	Baytown	(713)	56,923	43,980
*77704	Beaumont	(713)	118,102	117,548
76021	Bedford	(817)	20,821	10,049
78102	Beeville	(512)	14,574	13,506

ZIP code	Place		1980	1970
77401	Bellaire	(713)	14,950	19,009
76704	Bellmead	(817)	7,569	7,698
76513	Belton	(817)	10,660	8,696
76126	Benbrook	(817)	13,579	8,169
79720	Big Spring	(915)	24,804	28,735
75418	Bonham	(214)	7,338	7,698
79007	Borger	(806)	15,837	14,195
76230	Bowie	(817)	5,610	5,185
76825	Brady	(915)	5,969	5,557
76024	Breckenridge	(817)	6,921	5,944
77833	Brenham	(713)	10,966	8,922
77611	Bridge City	(713)	7,667	8,164
79316	Brownfield	(806)	10,387	9,647
78520	Brownsville	(512)	84,997	52,522
76801	Brownwood	(915)	19,203	17,368
77801	Bryan	(713)	44,337	33,719
76354	Burkburnett	(817)	10,668	9,230
76028	Burleson	(817)	11,734	7,713
76520	Cameron	(817)	5,721	5,546
79015	Canyon	(806)	10,724	8,333
78834	Carrizo Springs	(512)	6,886	5,374
75006	Carrolton	(214)	40,591	13,855
75633	Carthage	(214)	6,447	5,392
75104	Cedar Hill	(214)	6,849	2,610
75935	Center	(713)	5,827	4,989
....	Champions(u)	(713)	14,692	....
77530	Channelview(u)	(713)	17,471	....
79201	Childress	(817)	5,817	5,408
76031	Cleburne	(817)	19,218	16,015
77327	Cleveland	(713)	5,977	5,627
77015	Clover Leaf(u)	(713)	17,317	....
77531	Clute	(713)	9,577	6,023
76834	Coleman	(915)	5,960	5,608
77840	College Station	(713)	37,272	17,676
76034	Colleyville	(817)	6,700	3,342
79512	Colorado City	(915)	5,405	5,227
75428	Commerce	(214)	8,136	9,534
77301	Conroe	(713)	18,034	11,969
76522	Copperas Cove	(817)	19,469	10,818
*78408	Corpus Christi	(512)	231,999	204,525
75110	Corsicana	(214)	21,712	19,972
75835	Crockett	(713)	7,405	6,616
76036	Crowley	(817)	5,852	2,662
78839	Crystal City	(512)	8,334	8,104
77954	Cuero	(512)	7,124	6,956
79022	Dalhart	(806)	6,854	5,705
*75260	Dallas	(214)	904,078	844,401
77536	Deer Park	(713)	22,648	12,773
78840	Del Rio	(512)	30,034	21,330
75020	Denison	(214)	23,884	24,923
76201	Denton	(817)	48,063	39,874
75115	De Soto	(214)	15,538	6,617
75941	Diboll	(713)	5,227	3,557
77539	Dickinson	(713)	7,505	10,776
79027	Dimmitt	(806)	5,019	4,327
78537	Donna	(512)	9,952	7,365
79029	Dumas	(806)	12,194	9,771
75116	Duncanville	(214)	27,781	14,105
78852	Eagle Pass	(512)	21,407	15,364
78539	Edinburg	(512)	24,075	17,163
77957	Edna	(512)	5,650	5,332
77437	El Campo	(713)	10,462	9,332
79910	El Paso	(915)	425,259	322,261
78543	Elsa	(512)	5,061	4,400
75119	Ennis	(214)	12,110	11,046
76039	Euless	(817)	24,002	19,316
76140	Everman	(817)	5,387	4,570
78355	Falfurrias	(512)	6,103	6,355
75234	Farmers Branch	(214)	24,863	27,492
76119	Forest Hill	(817)	11,684	8,236
79906	Fort Bliss(u)	(915)	12,687	13,288
76544	Fort Hood(u)	(817)	31,250	32,597
79735	Fort Stockton	(915)	8,688	8,283
76101	Fort Worth	(817)	385,141	393,455
78624	Fredericksburg	(512)	6,412	5,326
77541	Freeport	(713)	13,444	11,997
77546	Friendswood	(713)	10,719	5,675
76240	Gainesville	(817)	14,081	13,830
77547	Galena Park	(713)	9,879	10,479
77550	Galveston	(713)	61,902	61,809
*75040	Garland	(214)	138,857	81,437
76528	Gatesville	(817)	6,260	4,683
78626	Georgetown	(512)	9,468	6,395
75644	Gilmer	(214)	5,167	4,196
75647	Gladewater	(214)	6,548	5,574
78629	Gonzales	(512)	7,152	5,854
76046	Graham	(817)	9,055	7,477
75050	Grand Prairie	(214)	71,462	50,904
76051	Grapevine	(817)	11,801	7,049
75401	Greenville	(214)	22,161	22,043
77619	Groves	(713)	17,090	18,067
76117	Haltom City	(817)	29,014	28,127
76541	Harker Heights	(817)	7,345	4,216
78550	Harlingen	(512)	43,543	33,503
77859	Hearne	(713)	5,418	4,982
75652	Henderson	(214)	11,473	10,187
79045	Hereford	(806)	15,853	13,414
76643	Hewitt	(817)	5,247	569
75205	Highland Park	(214)	8,909	10,133
77562	Highlands	(713)	6,467	3,462
76645	Hillsboro	(817)	7,397	7,224
77563	Hitchcock	(713)	6,655	5,565
78861	Hondo	(512)	6,057	5,487
*77013	Houston	(713)	1,594,086	1,233,535
77338	Humble	(713)	6,729	3,272
77340	Huntsville	(713)	23,936	17,610
76053	Hurst	(817)	31,420	27,215
78362	Ingleside	(512)	5,436	3,763
76367	Iowa Park	(817)	6,184	5,796
*75061	Irving	(214)	109,943	97,260
77029	Jacinto City	(713)	8,953	9,563
75766	Jacksonville	(214)	12,264	9,734
75951	Jasper	(713)	6,959	6,251
77450	Katy	(713)	5,660	2,923
79745	Kermit	(915)	8,015	7,884
78028	Kerrville	(512)	15,276	12,672
75662	Kilgore	(214)	10,968	9,495
76541	Killeen	(817)	46,296	35,507
78363	Kingsville	(512)	28,808	28,915
.....	Kingwood	(713)	16,261	....
78219	Kirby	(512)	6,385	3,238
78236	Lackland AFB(u)	(512)	14,459	19,141
77566	Lake Jackson	(713)	19,102	13,376
77568	La Marque	(713)	15,372	16,131
79631	Lamesa	(806)	11,790	11,559
76550	Lampasas	(512)	6,165	5,922
75146	Lancaster	(214)	14,807	10,522
77571	La Porte	(713)	14,062	7,149
78040	Laredo	(512)	91,449	69,024
77573	League City	(713)	16,578	10,818
78238	Leon Valley	(512)	8,951	2,487
79336	Levelland	(806)	13,809	11,445
75067	Lewisville	(214)	24,273	9,264
77575	Liberty	(713)	7,945	5,591
79339	Littlefield	(806)	7,409	6,738
78233	Live Oak	(512)	8,183	2,779
78644	Lockhart	(512)	7,953	6,489
75601	Longview	(214)	62,762	45,547
*79408	Lubbock	(806)	173,979	149,101
75901	Lufkin	(713)	28,562	23,049
78648	Luling	(512)	5,039	4,719
78501	McAllen	(512)	67,042	37,636
75069	McKinney	(214)	16,249	15,193
76063	Mansfield	(817)	8,092	3,658
76661	Marlin	(817)	7,099	6,351
75670	Marshall	(214)	24,921	22,937
78368	Mathis	(512)	5,667	5,351
78570	Mercedes	(512)	11,851	9,355
75149	Mesquite	(214)	67,053	55,131
76667	Mexia	(214)	7,094	5,943
79701	Midland	(915)	70,525	59,463
76067	Mineral Wells	(817)	14,468	18,411
78572	Mission	(512)	22,589	13,043
77459	Missouri City	(713)	24,533	4,136
79756	Monahans	(915)	8,397	8,333
75455	Mount Pleasant	(214)	11,003	9,459
75961	Nacogdoches	(713)	27,149	22,544
77868	Navasota	(713)	5,971	5,111
77627	Nederland	(713)	16,855	16,810
78130	New Braunfels	(512)	22,402	17,859
76118	North Richland Hills	(817)	30,592	16,514
*79760	Odessa	(915)	90,027	78,380
77630	Orange	(713)	23,628	24,457
75801	Palestine	(214)	15,948	14,525
79065	Pampa	(806)	21,396	21,726
75460	Paris	(214)	25,498	23,441
*77501	Pasadena	(713)	112,560	89,957
77581	Pearland	(713)	13,248	6,444
78061	Pearsall	(512)	7,383	5,545
79772	Pecos	(915)	12,855	12,682
79070	Perryton	(806)	7,991	7,810
78577	Pharr	(512)	21,381	15,829
79072	Plainview	(806)	22,187	19,096
75074	Plano	(214)	72,331	17,872
78064	Pleasanton	(512)	6,346	5,407
77640	Port Arthur	(713)	61,195	57,371
78374	Portland	(512)	12,023	7,302
77979	Port Lavaca	(512)	10,911	10,491
77651	Port Neches	(713)	13,944	10,894
78580	Raymondville	(512)	9,493	7,987
75080	Richardson	(214)	72,496	48,405
76118	Richland Hills	(817)	7,977	8,865
77469	Richmond	(713)	9,692	5,777
78582	Rio Grande City(u)	(512)	8,930	5,676
77019	River Oaks	(817)	6,890	8,193
76701	Robinson	(817)	6,074	3,807
78380	Robstown	(512)	12,100	11,217
76567	Rockdale	(512)	5,611	4,655
75087	Rockwall	(214)	5,939	3,121
77471	Rosenberg	(713)	17,995	12,098
78664	Round Rock	(512)	11,812	2,811
75088	Rowlett	(214)	7,522	2,243
76179	Saginaw	(817)	5,736	2,382
76901	San Angelo	(915)	73,240	63,884
*78284	San Antonio	(512)	785,410	654,153
78586	San Benito	(512)	17,988	15,176
78384	San Diego	(512)	5,225	4,490
78589	San Juan	(512)	7,608	5,070
78666	San Marcos	(512)	23,420	18,860
77550	Santa Fe	(713)	5,413	...

ZIP code	Place		1980	1970
78154	Schertz	(512)	7,262	4,061
75159	Seagoville	(214)	7,304	4,390
78155	Seguin	(512)	17,854	15,934
79360	Seminole	(915)	6,080	5,007
75090	Sherman	(214)	30,413	29,061
77656	Silsbee	(713)	7,684	7,271
78387	Sinton	(512)	6,044	5,563
79364	Slaton	(806)	6,804	6,583
79549	Snyder	(915)	12,705	11,171
77587	South Houston	(713)	13,293	11,527
76401	Stephenville	(214)	11,881	9,277
77478	Sugar Land	(713)	8,826	3,318
75482	Sulphur Springs	(214)	12,804	10,642
79556	Sweetwater	(915)	12,242	12,020
76574	Taylor	(512)	10,619	9,616
76501	Temple	(817)	42,483	33,431
75160	Terrell	(214)	13,225	14,182
75501	Texarkana	(214)	31,271	30,497
77590	Texas City	(713)	41,403	38,908
...	The Colony	(817)	11,586	...
77380	The Woodlands	(713)	8,443	....
79088	Tulia	(806)	5,033	5,294
75701	Tyler	(214)	70,508	57,770
78148	Universal City	(512)	10,720	7,613
76308	University Park	(214)	22,254	23,498
78801	Uvalde	(512)	14,178	10,764
76384	Vernon	(817)	12,695	11,454
77901	Victoria	(512)	50,695	41,349
77662	Vidor	(713)	12,117	9,738
*76701	Waco	(817)	101,261	95,326
76148	Watauga	(817)	10,284	3,778
75165	Waxahachie	(214)	14,624	13,452
76086	Weatherford	(817)	12,049	11,750
78596	Weslaco	(512)	19,331	15,313
77005	West University Place	(713)	12,010	13,317
77488	Wharton	(713)	9,033	7,881
76108	White Settlement	(817)	13,508	13,449
*76307	Wichita Falls	(817)	94,201	96,265
78239	Windcrest	(512)	5,332	3,371
76710	Woodway	(817)	7,091	4,819
77995	Yoakum	(512)	6,148	5,755

Utah (801)

ZIP code	Place	1980	1970
84003	American Fork	12,417	7,713
84118	Bennion(u)	9,632	....
84010	Bountiful	32,877	27,751
84302	Brigham City	15,596	14,007
84720	Cedar City	10,972	8,946
84014	Centerville	8,069	3,268
84015	Clearfield	17,982	13,316
84015	Clinton	5,777	1,768
84121	Cottonwood(u)	11,554	8,431
84121	Cottonwood Heights(u)	22,665	....
84020	Draper	5,530	...
84109	East Millcreek(u)	24,150	26,579
84106	Granite Park(u)	5,554	9,573
84117	Holladay(u)	22,189	23,014
84037	Kaysville	9,811	6,192
84118	Kearns(u)	21,353	17,247
84041	Layton	22,862	13,603
84043	Lehi	6,848	4,659
84321	Logan	26,844	22,333
84044	Magna(u)	13,138	5,509
84047	Midvale	10,144	7,840
84532	Moab	5,333	4,793
84117	Mount Olympus(u)	6,068	5,909
84107	Murray	25,750	21,206
84404	North Ogden	9,309	5,257
84054	North Salt Lake	5,548	2,143
*84401	Ogden	64,407	69,478
84057	Orem	52,399	25,729
84651	Payson	8,246	4,501
84062	Pleasant Grove	10,669	5,327
84501	Price	9,086	6,218
84601	Provo	73,907	53,131
84701	Richfield	5,482	4,471
84065	Riverton	7,293	2,820
84067	Roy	19,694	14,356
84770	St. George	11,350	7,097
*84101	Salt Lake City	163,033	175,885
84070	Sandy City	51,022	6,438
84121	South Cottonwood(u)	11,117	....
84065	South Jordan	7,492	2,942
84403	South Ogden	11,366	9,991
84115	South Salt Lake	10,561	7,810
84660	Spanish Fork	9,825	7,284
84663	Springville	12,101	8,790
84015	Sunset	5,733	6,268
84107	Taylorsville(u)	17,448	....
84074	Tooele	14,335	12,539
84047	Union-East Midvale(u)	9,663	....
84010	Val Verda(u)	6,422	....
84078	Vernal	6,600	3,908
84403	Washington Terrace	8,212	7,241
84084	West Jordan	26,794	4,221
84119	West Valley(u)	72,299	....
84070	White City(u)	7,180	6,402

Vermont (802)

See Note on Page 218

ZIP code	Place	1980	1970
05641	Barre	9,824	10,209
.....	*Barre*	7,090	6,509
05201	*Bennington*	15,815	14,586
.....	Bennington(u)	9,349	7,950
05301	Brattleboro Center(u)	8,596	9,055
.....	*Brattleboro*	11,886	12,239
05401	Burlington	37,712	38,633
05446	*Colchester*	12,629	8,776
05451	*Essex*	14,392	10,951
05452	Essex Junction	7,033	6,511
05753	*Middlebury*	7,574	6,532
05602	Montpelier	8,241	8,609
05701	Rutland	18,436	19,293
05478	St. Albans	7,308	8,082
05819	*St. Johnsbury*	7,938	8,409
05401	*South Burlington*	10,679	10,032
05156	Springfield Center(u)	5,603	5,632
.....	*Springfield*	10,190	10,063
05404	Winooski	6,318	7,309

Virginia

ZIP code	Place		1980	1970
*22313	Alexandria	(703)	103,217	110,927
22003	Annandale(u)	(703)	49,524	27,405
*22210	Arlington(u)	(703)	152,599	174,284
22041	Bailey's Crossroads(u)	(703)	12,564	7,295
24523	Bedford	(703)	5,991	6,011
22307	Belle Haven(u)	(703)	6,520	....
23234	Bellwood(u)	(804)	6,439	....
23234	Bensley(u)	(804)	5,299	....
24060	Blacksburg	(703)	30,638	9,384
24605	Bluefield	(703)	5,946	5,286
23235	Bon Air(u)	(804)	16,224	10,771
24201	Bristol	(703)	19,042	14,857
24416	Buena Vista	(703)	6,717	6,425
22015	Burke(u)	(703)	33,835	....
24018	Cave Spring(u)	(703)	21,682	....
22020	Centreville(u)	(703)	7,473	....
23227	Chamberlayne(u)	(804)	5,136	....
22021	Chantilly(u)	(703)	12,259	....
*22906	Charlottesville	(804)	45,010	38,880
*23320	Chesapeake	(804)	114,226	89,580
23831	Chester(u)	(804)	11,728	5,556
24073	Christiansburg	(703)	10,345	7,857
24422	Clifton Forge	(703)	5,046	5,501
24078	Collinsville(u)	(703)	7,517	6,015
23834	Colonial Heights	(804)	16,509	15,097
24426	Covington	(703)	9,063	10,060
22701	Culpeper	(703)	6,621	6,056
22191	Dale City(u)	(703)	33,127	13,857
24541	Danville	(804)	45,642	46,391
23228	Dumbarton(u)	(804)	8,149	....
22027	Dunn Loring(u)	(703)	6,077	....
23222	East Highland Park(u)	(804)	11,797	
22030	Fairfax	(703)	19,390	22,727
*22046	Falls Church	(703)	9,515	10,772
23901	Farmville	(804)	6,067	4,331
22060	Fort Belvoir(u)	(703)	7,726	14,591
22308	Fort Hunt(u)	(703)	14,294	10,415
23801	Fort Lee(u)	(804)	9,784	12,435
22310	Franconia(u)	(703)	8,476	....
23851	Franklin	(804)	7,308	6,880
22401	Fredericksburg	(703)	15,322	14,450
22630	Front Royal	(703)	11,126	8,211
24333	Galax	(703)	6,524	6,278
23060	Glen Allen(u)	(804)	6,202	....
23062	Gloucester Point(u)	(804)	5,841	....
22306	Groveton(u)	(703)	18,860	11,761
*23360	Hampton	(804)	122,617	120,779
22801	Harrisonburg	(703)	19,671	14,605
22070	Herndon	(703)	11,449	4,301
23075	Highland Springs(u)	(804)	12,146	7,345
24019	Hollins(u)	(703)	12,187	....
23860	Hopewell	(804)	23,397	23,471
22303	Huntington(u)	(703)	5,813	5,559
22306	Hybla Valley(u)	(703)	15,533	
22043	Idylwood(u)	(703)	11,982	....
22042	Jefferson(u)	(804)	24,342	25,432
22041	Lake Barcroft(u)	(703)	8,725	11,605
22191	Lake Ridge(u)	(703)	11,072	....
23228	Lakeside(u)	(804)	12,289	11,137
23060	Laurel(u)	(804)	10,569	....
22075	Leesburg	(703)	8,357	4,821
24450	Lexington	(703)	7,292	7,597
22312	Lincolnia(u)	(703)	10,350	10,355
22079	Lorton(u)	(703)	5,813	....
*24505	Lynchburg	(804)	66,743	54,083
24572	Madison Heights(u)	(804)	14,146	....
22110	Manassas	(703)	15,438	9,164
22110	Manassas Park	(703)	6,524	6,844
22030	Mantua(u)	(703)	6,523	6,911
24354	Marion	(703)	7,029	8,158
24112	Martinsville	(703)	18,149	19,653
22101	McLean(u)	(703)	35,664	17,698
23111	Mechanicsville(u)	(804)	9,269	5,189
22116	Merrifield(u)	(703)	7,525	....

ZIP code	Place		1980	1970
23231	Montrose(u)	(804)	5,349	....
22121	Mount Vernon(u)	(703)	24,058	....
22122	Newington(u)	(703)	8,313	....
*23607	Newport News	(804)	144,903	138,177
*23501	Norfolk	(804)	266,979	307,951
22151	North Springfield(u)	(703)	9,538	8,631
22124	Oakton(u)	(703)	19,150	....
23803	Petersburg	(804)	41,055	36,103
22043	Pimmit Hills(u)	(703)	6,658	....
23662	Poquoson	(804)	8,726	5,441
*23705	Portsmouth	(804)	104,577	110,963
24301	Pulaski	(703)	10,106	10,279
22134	Quantico Station(u)	(703)	7,121	6,213
24141	Radford	(703)	13,225	11,596
22070	Reston(u)	(703)	36,407	5,723
24641	Richlands	(703)	5,796	4,843
*23232	Richmond	(804)	219,214	249,332
*24001	Roanoke	(703)	100,427	92,115
22310	Rose Hill(u)	(703)	11,926	14,492
24153	Salem	(703)	23,958	21,982
22044	Seven Corners(u)	(703)	6,058	5,590
24592	South Boston	(804)	7,093	6,889
*22150	Springfield	(703)	21,435	11,613
24401	Staunton	(703)	21,857	24,504
22170	Sterling Park(u)	(703)	16,080	8,321
23434	Suffolk	(804)	47,621	9,858
22170	Sugarland Run(u)	(703)	6,258	....
24502	Timberlake(u)	(804)	9,697	....
23229	Tuckahoe(u)	(804)	39,868	....
22101	Tysons Corner(u)	(703)	10,065	....
22180	Vienna	(703)	15,469	17,146
24179	Vinton	(703)	8,027	6,347
*23458	Virginia Beach	(804)	262,199	172,106
22980	Waynesboro	(703)	15,329	16,707
22110	West Gate(u)	(703)	7,119	....
22152	West Springfield(u)	(703)	25,012	14,143
23185	Williamsburg	(804)	9,870	9,069
22601	Winchester	(703)	20,217	14,643
24592	Wolf Trap(u)	(804)	9,875	....
22191	Woodbridge(u)	(703)	24,004	25,412
24382	Wytheville	(703)	7,135	6,069

Washington

ZIP code	Place		1980	1970
98520	Aberdeen	(206)	18,739	18,489
98036	Alderwood Manor(u)	(206)	16,524	....
98221	Anacortes	(206)	9,013	7,701
98002	Auburn	(206)	26,417	21,653
*98009	Bellevue	(206)	73,903	61,196
98225	Bellingham	(206)	45,794	39,375
98390	Bonney Lake	(206)	5,328	2,700
98011	Bothell	(206)	7,943	5,420
.....	Boulevard Park(u)	(206)	8,382	....
98310	Bremerton	(206)	36,208	35,307
98178	Bryn Mawr-Skyway(u)	(206)	11,754	....
98166	Burien(u)	(206)	23,189	....
98607	Camas	(206)	5,681	5,790
98055	Cascade-Fairwood(u)	(206)	16,939	....
98531	Centralia	(206)	10,809	10,054
98532	Chehalis	(206)	6,100	5,727
99004	Cheney	(509)	7,630	6,358
99403	Clarkston	(509)	6,903	6,312
99324	College Place	(509)	5,771	4,510
98188	Des Moines	(206)	7,378	3,951
99213	Dishman(u)	(509)	10,169	9,079
.....	Dumas Bay-Twin Lakes(u)	(206)	14,535	....
98004	Eastgate(u)	(206)	8,341	....
.....	East Renton Highlands(u)	(206)	12,033	....
98801	East Wenatchee Bench(u)	(509)	11,410	2,446
98020	Edmonds	(206)	27,526	23,684
98926	Ellensburg	(509)	11,752	13,568
98022	Enumclaw	(206)	5,427	4,703
98823	Ephrata	(509)	5,359	5,255
99210	Esperance(u)	(509)	11,120	....
*98201	Everett	(206)	54,413	53,622
99011	Fairchild AFB(u)	(509)	5,353	6,754
98201	Fairmont-Intercity(u)	(206)	6,997	....
98055	Fairwood(u)	(206)	5,337	....
98466	Fircrest	(206)	5,477	5,651
98433	Fort Lewis(u)	(206)	23,761	38,054
98930	Grandview	(509)	5,615	3,605
98660	Hazel Dell(u)	(206)	15,386	....
98550	Hoquiam	(206)	9,719	10,466
98011	Inglewood(u)	(206)	12,467	....
98027	Issaquah	(206)	5,536	4,313
98033	Juanita(u)	(206)	17,232	....
98626	Kelso	(206)	11,129	10,296
98028	Kenmore(u)	(206)	7,281	....
99336	Kennewick	(509)	34,397	15,212
98031	Kent	(206)	23,152	17,711
98033	Kingsgate(u)	(206)	12,652	....
98033	Kirkland	(206)	18,779	14,970
98503	Lacey	(206)	13,940	9,696
98155	Lake Forest North(u)	(206)	7,995	....
.....	Lakeland North(u)	(206)	11,451	....
.....	Lakeland South(u)	(206)	5,225	....

ZIP code	Place		1980	1970
.....	Lake Stickney(u)	(206)	6,135	....
98499	Lakes District(u)	(206)	54,533	48,195
98632	Longview	(206)	31,052	28,373
98036	Lynnwood	(206)	21,937	17,381
.....	Martha Lake(u)	(206)	7,022	....
98270	Marysville	(206)	5,080	4,343
98438	McChord AFB(u)	(206)	5,746	6,515
98040	Mercer Island	(206)	21,522	19,047
98837	Moses Lake	(509)	10,629	10,310
98043	Mountlake Terrace	(206)	16,534	16,600
98273	Mount Vernon	(206)	13,009	8,804
98006	Newport Hills(u)	(206)	12,245	....
98155	North City-Ridgecrest(u)	(206)	13,551	....
.....	North Hill(u)	(206)	10,170	....
98270	North Marysville(u)	(206)	15,159	....
98277	Oak Harbor	(206)	12,271	9,167
*98501	Olympia	(206)	27,447	23,296
99214	Opportunity(u)	(509)	21,241	16,604
98662	Orchards(u)	(206)	8,828	....
98444	Parkland(u)	(206)	23,355	21,012
99301	Pasco	(509)	17,944	13,920
98362	Port Angeles	(206)	17,311	16,367
98368	Port Townsend	(206)	6,067	5,241
.....	Poverty Bay(u)	(206)	8,353	....
99163	Pullman	(509)	23,579	20,509
98371	Puyallup	(206)	18,251	14,742
98052	Redmond	(206)	23,318	11,020
98055	Renton	(206)	30,612	25,878
99352	Richland	(509)	33,578	26,290
98160	Richmond Beach-Innis Arden(u)	(206)	6,700	....
98113	Richmond Highlands(u)	(206)	24,463	....
98188	Riverton(u)	(206)	14,182	....
98033	Rose Hill(u)	(206)	7,616	....
*98109	Seattle	(206)	493,846	530,831
98284	Sedro Woolley	(206)	6,110	4,598
98584	Shelton	(206)	7,629	6,515
98155	Sheridan Beach(u)	(206)	6,873	....
98201	Silver Lake-Fircrest(u)		10,299	....
98290	Snohomish	(206)	5,294	5,174
98387	Spanaway(u)	(206)	8,868	5,768
*99210	Spokane	(509)	171,300	170,516
98944	Sunnyside	(509)	9,225	6,751
*98402	Tacoma	(206)	158,501	154,407
98501	Tanglewilde-Thompson Place(u)		5,910	3,423
98948	Toppenish	(509)	6,517	5,744
99268	Town and Country(u)	(509)	5,578	6,484
98502	Tumwater	(206)	6,705	5,373
98406	University Place(u)	(206)	20,381	13,230
.....	Valley Ridge(u)	(206)	17,961	....
*98660	Vancouver	(206)	42,834	41,859
99037	Veradale(u)	(509)	7,256	....
99362	Walla Walla	(509)	25,618	23,619
98801	Wenatchee	(509)	17,257	16,912
98003	West Federal Way(u)	(206)	16,872	....
99301	West Pasco(u)	(509)	6,210	....
98166	White Center-Shorewood(u)	(206)	19,362	....
*98901	Yakima	(509)	49,826	45,588
98188	Zenith-Saltwater(u)	(206)	8,982	....

West Virginia (304)

ZIP code	Place	1980	1970
25801	Beckley	20,492	19,884
24701	Bluefield	16,060	15,921
26330	Bridgeport	6,604	4,777
26201	Buckhannon	6,820	7,261
*25301	Charleston	63,968	71,505
26301	Clarksburg	22,371	24,864
25064	Dunbar	9,285	9,151
26241	Elkins	8,536	8,287
26554	Fairmont	23,863	26,093
26354	Grafton	6,845	6,433
*25701	Huntington	63,684	74,315
26726	Keyser	6,569	6,586
25401	Martinsburg	13,063	14,626
26505	Morgantown	27,605	29,431
26041	Moundsville	12,419	13,560
26155	New Martinsville	7,109	6,528
25143	Nitro	8,074	8,019
25901	Oak Hill	7,120	4,738
26101	Parkersburg	39,967	44,208
25550	Point Pleasant	5,682	6,122
24740	Princeton	7,493	7,253
25177	St. Albans	12,402	14,356
25303	South Charleston	15,968	16,333
26105	Vienna	11,618	11,549
26062	Weirton	24,736	27,131
26452	Weston	6,250	7,323
26003	Wheeling	43,070	48,188
25661	Williamson	5,219	5,831

Wisconsin

ZIP code	Place		1980	1970
54301	Allouez(u)	(414)	14,882	13,753
54409	Antigo	(715)	8,653	9,005
59411	Appleton	(414)	59,032	56,377
54806	Ashland	(715)	9,115	9,615

ZIP code	Place		1980	1970
54304	Ashwaubenon	(414)	14,486	9,323
53913	Baraboo	(608)	8,081	7,931
53916	Beaver Dam	(414)	14,149	14,265
53511	Beloit	(608)	35,207	35,729
53511	Beloit North(u)	(608)	5,457	....
54923	Berlin	(414)	5,478	5,338
53005	Brookfield	(414)	34,035	31,761
53209	Brown Deer	(414)	12,921	12,582
53105	Burlington	(414)	8,385	7,479
53012	Cedarburg	(414)	9,005	7,697
54729	Chippewa Falls	(715)	11,845	12,351
53110	Cudahy	(414)	19,547	22,078
53115	Delavan	(414)	5,684	5,526
54115	De Pere	(414)	14,892	13,309
54701	Eau Claire	(715)	51,509	44,619
53122	Elm Grove	(414)	6,735	7,201
54935	Fond Du Lac	(414)	35,863	35,515
53538	Fort Atkinson	(414)	9,785	9,164
53217	Fox Point	(414)	7,649	7,939
53132	Franklin	(414)	16,871	12,247
53022	Germantown	(414)	10,729	6,974
53209	Glendale	(414)	13,882	13,426
53024	Grafton	(414)	8,381	5,998
*54305	Green Bay	(414)	87,899	87,809
53129	Greendale	(414)	16,928	15,089
53220	Greenfield	(414)	31,467	24,424
53130	Hales Corners	(414)	7,110	7,771
53027	Hartford	(414)	7,046	6,499
53029	Hartland	(414)	5,559	2,763
54303	Howard	(414)	8,240	4,911
54016	Hudson	(715)	5,434	5,049
53545	Janesville	(608)	51,071	46,426
53549	Jefferson	(414)	5,647	5,429
54130	Kaukauna	(414)	11,310	11,308
53140	Kenosha	(414)	77,685	78,805
54136	Kimberly	(414)	5,881	6,131
54601	La Crosse	(608)	48,347	50,286
53147	Lake Geneva	(414)	5,607	4,890
54140	Little Chute	(414)	7,907	5,522
*53701	Madison	(608)	170,616	171,809
54220	Manitowoc	(414)	32,547	33,430
54143	Marinette	(715)	11,965	12,696
54449	Marshfield	(715)	18,290	15,619
54952	Menasha	(414)	14,728	14,836
53051	Menomonee Falls	(414)	27,845	31,697
54751	Menomonie	(414)	12,769	11,112
53092	Mequon	(414)	16,193	12,150
54452	Merrill	(715)	9,578	9,502
53562	Middleton	(608)	11,779	8,246
*53203	Milwaukee	(414)	636,212	717,372
53716	Monona	(608)	8,809	10,420
53566	Monroe	(608)	10,027	8,654
53150	Muskego	(414)	15,277	11,573
54956	Neenah	(414)	23,272	22,902
53151	New Berlin	(414)	30,529	26,910
54961	New London	(414)	6,210	5,801
53154	Oak Creek	(414)	16,932	13,928
53066	Oconomowoc	(414)	9,909	8,741
54650	Onalaska	(608)	9,249	4,909
54901	Oshkosh	(414)	49,678	53,082
53818	Platteville	(608)	9,580	9,599
54467	Plover	(715)	5,310	...
53073	Plymouth	(414)	6,027	5,810
53901	Portage	(608)	7,896	7,821
53074	Port Washington	(414)	8,612	8,752
53821	Prairie du Chien	(608)	5,859	5,540
*53401	Racine	(414)	85,725	95,162
53959	Reedsburg	(608)	5,038	4,585
54501	Rhinelander	(715)	7,873	8,218
54868	Rice Lake	(715)	7,691	7,278
54971	Ripon	(414)	7,111	7,053
54022	River Falls	(715)	9,036	7,238
53207	St. Francis	(414)	10,066	10,489
54166	Shawano	(715)	7,013	6,488
53081	Sheboygan	(414)	48,085	48,484
53085	Sheboygan Falls	(414)	5,253	4,771
53211	Shorewood	(414)	14,327	15,576
53172	South Milwaukee	(414)	21,069	23,297
54656	Sparta	(608)	6,934	6,258
54481	Stevens Point	(715)	22,970	23,479
53589	Stoughton	(608)	7,589	6,096
54235	Sturgeon Bay	(414)	8,847	6,776
53590	Sun Prairie	(608)	12,931	9,935
54880	Superior	(715)	29,571	32,237
54660	Tomah	(608)	7,204	5,647
54241	Two Rivers	(414)	13,354	13,732
53094	Watertown	(414)	18,113	15,683
53186	Waukesha	(414)	50,319	39,695
53963	Waupun	(414)	8,132	7,946
54401	Wausau	(715)	32,426	32,806
54401	Wausau West Rib Mt.(u)	(715)	6,005	....
53213	Wauwatosa	(414)	51,308	58,676
53214	West Allis	(414)	63,982	71,649
53095	West Bend	(414)	21,484	16,555
54476	Weston(u)	(715)	8,775	3,375
53217	Whitefish Bay	(414)	14,930	17,402
53190	Whitewater	(414)	11,520	12,038
54494	Wisconsin Rapids	(715)	17,995	18,587

Wyoming (307)

82601	Casper	51,016	39,361
82001	Cheyenne	47,283	41,254
82414	Cody	6,790	5,161
82633	Douglas	6,030	2,677
82930	Evanston	6,421	4,462
82716	Gillette	12,134	7,194
82335	Green River	12,807	4,196
82520	Lander	9,126	7,125
82070	Laramie	24,410	23,143
82435	Powell	5,310	4,807
82301	Rawlins	11,547	7,855
82501	Riverton	9,588	7,995
82901	Rock Springs	19,458	11,657
82801	Sheridan	15,146	10,856
82240	Torrington	5,441	4,237
82201	Wheatland	5,816	2,498
82401	Worland	6,391	5,055

Census and Areas of Counties and States

Source: U.S. Bureau of the Census
With names of county seats or court houses

Population figures listed below are final counts in the 1980 census, conducted on Apr. 1, 1980, for all counties and states. Figures are subject to change pending the outcome of various lawsuits dealing with the census counts.

Alabama

(67 counties, 50,767 sq. mi. land; pop., 3,890,061)

County	Pop.	County seat or court house	Land area sq. mi.
Autauga	32,259	Prattville	597
Baldwin	78,440	Bay Minette	1,589
Barbour	24,756	Clayton	884
Bibb	15,723	Centreville	625
Blount	36,459	Oneonta	643
Bullock	10,596	Union Springs	625
Butler	21,680	Greenville	779
Calhoun	116,936	Anniston	611
Chambers	39,191	Lafayette	596
Cherokee	18,760	Centre	553
Chilton	30,612	Clanton	695
Choctaw	16,839	Butler	909
Clarke	27,702	Grove Hill	1,230
Clay	13,703	Ashland	605
Cleburne	12,595	Heflin	561
Coffee	38,533	Elba	680
Colbert	54,519	Tuscumbia	589
Conecuh	15,884	Evergreen	854
Coosa	11,377	Rockford	657
Covington	36,850	Andalusia	1,038
Crenshaw	14,110	Luverne	611
Cullman	61,642	Cullman	738
Dale	47,821	Ozark	561
Dallas	53,981	Selma	975
De Kalb	53,658	Fort Payne	778
Elmore	43,390	Wetumpka	622
Escambia	38,392	Brewton	951
Etowah	103,057	Gadsden	542
Fayette	18,809	Fayette	630
Franklin	28,350	Russellville	643
Geneva	24,253	Geneva	578
Greene	11,021	Eutaw	631
Hale	15,604	Greensboro	661
Henry	15,302	Abbeville	557
Houston	74,632	Dothan	577
Jackson	51,407	Scottsboro	1,070
Jefferson	671,197	Birmingham	1,119
Lamar	16,453	Vernon	605
Lauderdale	80,504	Florence	661
Lawrence	30,170	Moulton	693
Lee	76,283	Opelika	609
Limestone	46,005	Athens	559
Lowndes	13,253	Hayneville	714
Macon	26,829	Tuskegee	614
Madison	196,966	Huntsville	806
Marengo	25,047	Linden	982
Marion	30,041	Hamilton	743
Marshall	65,622	Guntersville	567
Mobile	364,379	Mobile	1,238
Monroe	22,651	Monroeville	1,019
Montgomery	197,038	Montgomery	793
Morgan	90,231	Decatur	575
Perry	15,012	Marion	718
Pickens	21,481	Carrollton	890
Pike	28,050	Troy	672
Randolph	20,075	Wedowee	584

County	Pop.	County Seat or court house	Land area sq. mi.
Russell	47,356	Phenix City	634
St. Clair	41,205	Ashville & Pell City	646
Shelby	66,298	Columbiana	800
Sumter	16,908	Livingston	907
Talladega	73,826	Talladega	753
Tallapoosa	38,676	Dadeville	701
Tuscaloosa	137,473	Tuscaloosa	1,336
Walker	68,660	Jasper	804
Washington	16,821	Chatom	1,081
Wilcox	14,755	Camden	883
Winston	21,953	Double Springs	613

Alaska

(23 divisions, 570,833 sq. mi. land; pop., 400,481)

Census area	Pop.	Land area sq. mi.
Aleutian Islands	7,768	10,890
Anchorage Borough	173,017	1,732

Census division	Pop.	Land area sq. mi.
Bethel	10,999	36,104
Bristol Bay Borough	1,094	531
Dillingham	4,616	46,042
Fairbanks North Star Borough	53,983	7,404
Haines Borough	1,680	2,374
Juneau Borough	19,528	2,626
Kenai Peninsula Borough	25,282	16,056
Ketchikan Gateway Borough	11,316	1,242
Kobuk	4,831	31,593
Kodiak Island Borough	9,939	4,796
Matanuska-Susitna Borough	17,766	24,502
Nome	6,537	23,871
North Slope Borough	4,199	90,955
Prince of Wales-Outer Ketchikan	3,822	7,660
Sitka Borough	7,803	2,938
Skagway-Yakutat-Angoon	3,478	13,239
Southeast Fairbanks	5,770	24,169
Valdez-Cordova	8,348	39,229
Wade Hampton	4,665	17,816
Wrangell-Petersburg	6,167	5,965
Yukon-Koyukuk	7,873	159,099

Arizona

(14 counties, 113,508 sq. mi. land; pop. 2,717,866)

Apache	52,083	Saint Johns	11,211
Cochise	86,717	Bisbee	6,218
Coconino	74,947	Flagstaff	18,608
Gila	37,080	Globe	4,752
Graham	22,862	Safford	4,630
Greenlee	11,406	Clifton	1,837
Maricopa	1,508,030	Phoenix	9,127
Mohave	55,693	Kingman	13,285
Navajo	67,709	Holbrook	9,955
Pima	531,263	Tucson	9,187
Pinal	90,918	Florence	5,343
Santa Cruz	20,459	Nogales	1,238
Yavapai	68,145	Prescott	8,123
Yuma	90,554	Yuma	9,994

Arkansas

(75 counties, 52,078 sq. mi. land; pop. 2,285,513)

Arkansas	24,175	DeWitt & Stuttgart	1,006
Ashley	26,538	Hamburg	934
Baxter	27,409	Mountain Home	546
Benton	78,115	Bentonville	843
Boone	26,067	Harrison	584
Bradley	13,803	Warren	654
Calhoun	6,079	Hampton	628
Carroll	16,203	Berryville and Eureka Sp.	634
Chicot	17,793	Lake Village	649
Clark	23,326	Arkadelphia	867
Clay	20,616	Corning; Piggott	641
Cleburne	16,909	Heber Springs	551
Cleveland	7,868	Rison	599
Columbia	26,644	Magnolia	767
Conway	19,505	Morrilton	558
Craighead	63,218	Jonesboro and Lake City	713
Crawford	36,892	Van Buren	594
Crittenden	49,097	Marion	599
Cross	20,434	Wynne	622
Dallas	10,515	Fordyce	668
Desha	19,760	Arkansas City	746
Drew	17,910	Monticello	831
Faulkner	46,192	Conway	645
Franklin	14,705	Charleston and Ozark	609
Fulton	9,975	Salem	616
Garland	69,916	Hot Spgs. Nat'l Pk.	657
Grant	13,008	Sheridan	633
Greene	30,744	Paragould	579
Hempstead	23,635	Hope	725
Hot Spring	26,819	Malvern	615
Howard	13,459	Nashville	574
Independence	30,147	Batesville	763
Izard	10,768	Melbourne	581
Jackson	21,646	Newport	633
Jefferson	90,718	Pine Bluff	882
Johnson	17,423	Clarksville	676
Lafayette	10,213	Lewisville	518
Lawrence	18,447	Walnut Ridge	589
Lee	15,539	Marianna	602
Lincoln	13,369	Star City	562
Little River	13,952	Ashdown	516
Logan	20,144	Booneville & Paris	717
Lonoke	34,518	Lonoke	783
Madison	11,373	Huntsville	837
Marion	11,334	Yellville	587
Miller	37,766	Texarkana	619
Mississippi	59,517	Blytheville and Osceola	896
Monroe	14,052	Clarendon	609
Montgomery	7,771	Mount Ida	774
Nevada	11,097	Prescott	620
Newton	7,756	Jasper	823
Ouachita	30,541	Camden	737
Perry	7,266	Perryville	550
Phillips	34,772	Helena	685
Pike	10,373	Murfreesboro	598
Poinsett	27,032	Harrisburg	762
Polk	17,007	Mena	860
Pope	39,003	Russellville	820
Prairie	10,140	Des Arc and De Valls Bluff	656
Pulaski	340,613	Little Rock	767
Randolph	16,834	Pocahontas	656
St. Francis	30,858	Forrest City	638
Saline	52,881	Benton	725
Scott	9,685	Waldron	896
Searcy	8,847	Marshall	668
Sebastian	94,930	Fort Smith; Greenwood	535
Sevier	14,060	De Queen	560
Sharp	14,607	Ash Flat	606
Stone	9,022	Mountain View	606
Union	49,988	El Dorado	1,053
Van Buren	13,357	Clinton	709
Washington	99,735	Fayetteville	951
White	50,835	Searcy	1,040
Woodruff	11,222	Augusta	592
Yell	17,026	Danville and Dardanelle	930

California

(58 counties, 156,299 sq. mi. land; pop. 23,668,562)

Alameda	1,105,379	Oakland	736
Alpine	1,097	Markleeville	738
Amador	19,314	Jackson	589
Butte	143,851	Oroville	1,646
Calaveras	20,710	San Andreas	1,021
Colusa	12,791	Colusa	1,152
Contra Costa	657,252	Martinez	730
Del Norte	18,217	Crescent City	1,007
El Dorado	85,812	Placerville	1,715
Fresno	515,013	Fresno	5,978
Glenn	21,350	Willows	1,319
Humboldt	108,024	Eureka	3,579
Imperial	92,110	El Centro	4,173
Inyo	17,895	Independence	10,223
Kern	403,089	Bakersfield	8,130
Kings	73,738	Hanford	1,392
Lake	36,366	Lakeport	1,262
Lassen	21,661	Susanville	4,553
Los Angeles	7,477,657	Los Angeles	4,070
Madera	63,116	Madera	2,145
Marin	222,952	San Rafael	523
Mariposa	11,108	Mariposa	1,456
Mendocino	66,738	Ukiah	3,512
Merced	134,560	Merced	1,944
Modoc	8,610	Alturas	4,064
Mono	8,577	Bridgeport	3,018
Monterey	290,444	Salinas	3,303
Napa	99,199	Napa	744
Nevada	51,645	Nevada City	960
Orange	1,931,570	Santa Ana	798
Placer	117,247	Auburn	1,416
Plumas	17,340	Quincy	2,573
Riverside	663,923	Riverside	7,214
Sacramento	783,381	Sacramento	971
San Benito	25,005	Hollister	1,388
San Bernardino	893,157	San Bernardino	20,064
San Diego	1,861,846	San Diego	4,212
San Francisco	678,974	San Francisco	46
San Joaquin	347,342	Stockton	1,415
San Luis Obispo	155,345	San Luis Obispo	3,308
San Mateo	588,164	Redwood City	447
Santa Barbara	298,660	Santa Barbara	2,748
Santa Clara	1,295,071	San Jose	1,293
Santa Cruz	188,141	Santa Cruz	446
Shasta	115,715	Redding	3,786
Sierra	3,073	Downieville	959
Siskiyou	39,732	Yreka	6,281
Solano	235,203	Fairfield	834
Sonoma	299,827	Santa Rosa	1,604
Stanislaus	265,902	Modesto	1,506
Sutter	52,246	Yuba City	602
Tehama	38,888	Red Bluff	2,953
Trinity	11,858	Weaverville	3,190
Tulare	245,751	Visalia	4,808
Tuolumne	33,920	Sonora	2,234
Ventura	529,899	Ventura	1,862

County	Pop.	County seat or court house	Land area sq. mi.
Yolo	113,374	Woodland	1,014
Yuba	49,733	Marysville	640

Colorado

(63 counties, 103,595 sq. mi. land; pop. 2,888,834)

County	Pop.	County seat or court house	Land area sq. mi.
Adams	245,944	Brighton	1,235
Alamosa	11,799	Alamosa	719
Arapahoe	293,621	Littleton	800
Archuleta	3,664	Pagosa Springs	1,353
Baca	5,419	Springfield	2,554
Bent	5,945	Las Animas	1,517
Boulder	189,625	Boulder	742
Chaffee	13,227	Salida	1,008
Cheyenne	2,153	Cheyenne Wells	1,783
Clear Creek	7,308	Georgetown	396
Conejos	7,794	Conejos	1,284
Costilla	3,071	San Luis	1,227
Crowley	2,988	Ordway	790
Custer	1,528	Westcliffe	740
Delta	21,225	Delta	1,141
Denver	491,396	Denver	111
Dolores	1,658	Dove Creek	1,064
Douglas	25,153	Castle Rock	841
Eagle	13,171	Eagle	1,690
Elbert	6,850	Kiowa	1,851
El Paso	309,424	Colorado Springs	2,129
Fremont	28,676	Canon City	1,538
Garfield	22,514	Glenwood Springs	2,952
Gilpin	2,441	Central City	149
Grand	7,475	Hot Sulphur Springs	1,854
Gunnison	10,689	Gunnison	3,238
Hinsdale	408	Lake City	1,115
Huerfano	6,440	Walsenburg	1,584
Jackson	1,863	Walden	1,614
Jefferson	371,741	Golden	768
Kiowa	1,936	Eads	1,758
Kit Carson	7,599	Burlington	2,160
Lake	8,830	Leadville	379
La Plata	27,424	Durango	1,692
Larimer	149,184	Fort Collins	2,604
Las Anima	14,897	Trinidad	4,771
Lincoln	4,663	Hugo	2,586
Logan	19,800	Sterling	1,818
Mesa	81,530	Grand Junction	3,309
Mineral	804	Creede	877
Moffat	13,133	Craig	4,732
Montezuma	16,510	Cortez	2,038
Montrose	24,352	Montrose	2,240
Morgan	22,513	Fort Morgan	1,276
Otero	22,567	LaJunta	1,247
Ouray	1,925	Ouray	542
Park	5,333	Fairplay	2,192
Phillips	4,542	Holyoke	688
Pitkin	10,338	Aspen	968
Prowers	13,070	Lamar	1,629
Pueblo	125,972	Pueblo	2,377
Rio Blanco	6,255	Meeker	3,222
Rio Grande	10,511	Del Norte	913
Routt	13,404	Steamboat Springs	2,367
Saguache	3,935	Saguache	3,167
San Juan	833	Silverton	388
San Miguel	3,192	Telluride	1,287
Sedgwick	3,266	Julesburg	540
Summit	8,848	Breckenridge	607
Teller	8,034	Cripple Creek	559
Washington	5,304	Akron	2,520
Weld	123,438	Greeley	3,990
Yuma	9,682	Wray	2,365

Connecticut

(8 counties, 4,872 sq. mi. land; pop. 3,107,576)

County	Pop.	County seat or court house	Land area sq. mi.
Fairfield	807,143	Bridgeport	632
Hartford	807,766	Hartford	739
Litchfield	156,769	Litchfield	921
Middlesex	129,017	Middletown	373
New Haven	761,337	New Haven	610
New London	238,409	Norwich	669
Tolland	114,823	Rockville	412
Windham	92,312	Putnam	515

Delaware

(3 counties, 1,932 sq. mi. land; pop. 595,225)

County	Pop.	County seat or court house	Land area sq. mi.
Kent	98,219	Dover	595
New Castle	399,002	Wilmington	396
Sussex	98,004	Georgetown	942

District of Columbia

(63 sq. mi. land; pop. 637,651)

Florida

(67 counties, 54,153 sq. mi. land; pop. 9,739,992)

County	Pop.	County seat or court house	Land area sq. mi.
Alachua	151,348	Gainesville	901
Baker	15,289	Macclenny	585
Bay	97,740	Panama City	758
Bradford	20,023	Starke	293
Brevard	272,959	Titusville	995
Broward	1,014,043	Fort Lauderdale	1,211
Calhoun	9,294	Blountstown	568
Charlotte	59,115	Punta Gorda	690
Citrus	54,703	Inverness	629
Clay	67,052	Green Cove Spgs	592
Collier	85,791	Naples	1,994
Columbia	35,399	Lake City	796
Dade	1,625,979	Miami	1,955
De Soto	19,039	Arcadia	636
Dixie	7,751	Cross City	701
Duval	570,981	Jacksonville	776
Escambia	233,794	Pensacola	660
Flagler	10,913	Bunnell	491
Franklin	7,661	Apalachicola	545
Gadsden	41,565	Quincy	518
Gilchrist	5,767	Trenton	354
Glades	5,992	Moore Haven	763
Gulf	10,658	Port St. Joe	559
Hamilton	8,761	Jasper	517
Hardee	19,379	Wauchula	637
Hendry	18,599	La Belle	1,163
Hernando	44,469	Brooksville	477
Highlands	47,526	Sebring	1,029
Hillsborough	646,960	Tampa	1,053
Holmes	14,723	Bonifay	488
Indian River	59,896	Vero Beach	497
Jackson	39,154	Marianna	942
Jefferson	10,703	Monticello	609
Lafayette	4,035	Mayo	545
Lake	104,870	Tavares	954
Lee	205,266	Fort Myers	803
Leon	148,655	Tallahassee	676
Levy	19,870	Bronson	1,100
Liberty	4,260	Bristol	837
Madison	14,894	Madison	710
Manatee	148,442	Bradenton	747
Marion	122,488	Ocala	1,610
Martin	64,014	Stuart	555
Monroe	63,098	Key West	1,034
Nassau	32,894	Fernandina Beach	649
Okaloosa	109,920	Crestview	936
Okeechobee	20,264	Okeechobee	770
Orange	471,660	Orlando	910
Osceola	49,287	Kissimmee	1,350
Palm Beach	573,125	West Palm Beach	1,993
Pasco	194,123	Dade City	738
Pinellas	728,409	Clearwater	280
Polk	321,652	Bartow	1,823
Putnam	50,549	Palatka	733
St. Johns	51,303	Saint Augustine	617
St. Lucie	87,182	Fort Pierce	581
Santa Rosa	55,988	Milton	1,024
Sarasota	202,251	Sarasota	573
Seminole	179,752	Sanford	298
Sumter	24,272	Bushnell	561
Suwannee	22,287	Live Oak	690
Taylor	16,532	Perry	1,058
Union	10,166	Lake Butler	246
Volusia	258,762	De Land	1,113
Wakulla	10,887	Crawfordville	601
Walton	21,300	De Funiak Springs	1,066
Washington	14,509	Chipley	590

Georgia

(159 counties, 58,056 sq. mi. land; pop. 5,464,265)

County	Pop.	County seat or court house	Land area sq. mi.
Appling	15,565	Baxley	510
Atkinson	6,141	Pearson	344
Bacon	9,379	Alma	286
Baker	3,808	Newton	347
Baldwin	34,686	Milledgeville	257
Banks	8,702	Horner	234
Barrow	21,293	Winder	163
Bartow	40,760	Cartersville	456
Ben Hill	16,000	Fitzgerald	254
Berrien	13,525	Nashville	456
Bibb	151,085	Macon	253
Bleckley	10,767	Cochran	219
Brantley	8,701	Nahunta	445
Brooks	15,255	Quitman	491
Bryan	10,175	Pembroke	441
Bulloch	35,785	Statesboro	678
Burke	19,349	Waynesboro	833
Butts	13,665	Jackson	187
Calhoun	5,717	Morgan	284
Camden	13,371	Woodbine	649
Candler	7,518	Metter	248
Carroll	56,346	Carrollton	501
Catoosa	36,991	Ringgold	162
Charlton	7,343	Folkston	780
Chatham	202,226	Savannah	443
Chattahoochee	21,732	Cusseta	250
Chattooga	21,856	Summerville	313
Cherokee	51,699	Canton	424
Clarke	74,498	Athens	122
Clay	3,553	Fort Gaines	196
Clayton	150,357	Jonesboro	148
Clinch	6,660	Homerville	821
Cobb	297,694	Marietta	343
Coffee	26,894	Douglas	602
Colquitt	35,376	Moultrie	557

County	Pop.	County seat or court house	Land area sq. mi.
Columbia	40,118	Appling	290
Cook	13,490	Adel	233
Coweta	39,268	Newnan	444
Crawford	7,684	Knoxville	328
Crisp	19,489	Cordele	275
Dade	12,318	Trenton	176
Dawson	4,774	Dawsonville	210
Decatur	25,495	Bainbridge	586
De Kalb	483,024	Decatur	270
Dodge	16,955	Eastman	504
Dooly	10,826	Vienna	397
Dougherty	100,978	Albany	330
Douglas	54,573	Douglasville	203
Early	13,158	Blakely	516
Echols	2,297	Statenville	421
Effingham	18,327	Springfield	482
Elbert	18,758	Elberton	367
Emanuel	20,795	Swainsboro	688
Evans	8,428	Claxton	186
Fannin	14,748	Blue Ridge	384
Fayette	29,043	Fayetteville	199
Floyd	79,800	Rome	519
Forsyth	27,958	Cumming	226
Franklin	15,185	Carnesville	264
Fulton	589,904	Atlanta	534
Gilmer	11,110	Ellijay	427
Glascock	2,382	Gibson	144
Glynn	54,981	Brunswick	412
Gordon	30,070	Calhoun	355
Grady	19,845	Cairo	459
Greene	11,391	Greensboro	389
Gwinnett	166,903	Lawrenceville	435
Habersham	25,020	Clarkesville	278
Hall	75,649	Gainesville	379
Hancock	9,466	Sparta	470
Haralson	18,422	Buchanan	283
Harris	15,464	Hamilton	464
Hart	18,585	Hartwell	230
Heard	6,520	Franklin	292
Henry	36,309	McDonough	321
Houston	77,605	Perry	380
Irwin	8,988	Ocilla	362
Jackson	25,343	Jefferson	342
Jasper	7,553	Monticello	371
Jeff Davis	11,473	Hazlehurst	335
Jefferson	18,403	Louisville	529
Jenkins	8,841	Millen	353
Johnson	8,660	Wrightsville	306
Jones	16,579	Gray	394
Lamar	12,215	Barnesville	186
Lanier	5,654	Lakeland	194
Laurens	36,990	Dublin	816
Lee	11,684	Leesburg	358
Liberty	37,583	Hinesville	517
Lincoln	6,949	Lincolnton	196
Long	4,524	Ludowici	402
Lowndes	67,972	Valdosta	507
Lumpkin	10,762	Dahlonega	287
McDuffie	18,546	Thomson	256
McIntosh	8,046	Darien	425
Macon	14,003	Oglethorpe	404
Madison	17,747	Danielsville	285
Marion	5,297	Buena Vista	366
Meriwether	21,229	Greenville	506
Miller	7,038	Colquitt	284
Mitchell	21,114	Camilla	512
Monroe	14,610	Forsyth	397
Montgomery	7,011	Mount Vernon	244
Morgan	11,572	Madison	349
Murray	19,685	Chatsworth	345
Muscogee	170,108	Columbus	218
Newton	34,489	Covington	277
Oconee	12,427	Watkinsville	186
Oglethorpe	8,929	Lexington	442
Paulding	26,042	Dallas	312
Peach	19,151	Fort Valley	152
Pickens	11,652	Jasper	232
Pierce	11,897	Blackshear	344
Pike	8,937	Zebulon	219
Polk	32,386	Cedartown	311
Pulaski	8,950	Hawkinsville	249
Putnam	10,295	Eatonton	344
Quitman	2,357	Georgetown	146
Rabun	10,466	Clayton	370
Randolph	9,599	Cuthbert	431
Richmond	181,629	Augusta	326
Rockdale	36,747	Conyers	132
Schley	3,433	Ellaville	169
Screven	14,043	Sylvania	655
Seminole	9,057	Donalsonville	225
Spalding	47,899	Griffin	199
Stephens	21,763	Toccoa	177
Stewart	5,896	Lumpkin	452
Sumter	29,360	Americus	489
Talbot	6,536	Talbotton	395
Taliaferro	2,032	Crawfordville	196
Tattnall	18,134	Reidsville	484
Taylor	7,902	Butler	382
Telfair	11,445	MacRae	444
Terrell	12,017	Dawson	337
Thomas	38,098	Thomasville	551
Tift	32,862	Tifton	268
Toombs	22,592	Lyons	371
Towns	5,638	Hiawassee	165
Treutlen	6,087	Soperton	202
Troup	50,003	La Grange	414
Turner	9,510	Ashburn	289
Twiggs	9,354	Jeffersonville	362
Union	9,390	Blairsville	320
Upson	25,998	Thomaston	326
Walker	56,470	La Fayette	446
Walton	31,211	Monroe	330
Ware	37,180	Waycross	907
Warren	6,583	Warrenton	286
Washington	18,842	Sandersville	684
Wayne	20,750	Jesup	647
Webster	2,341	Preston	210
Wheeler	5,155	Alamo	299
White	10,120	Cleveland	242
Whitfield	65,780	Dalton	291
Wilcox	7,682	Abbeville	382
Wilkes	10,951	Washington	470
Wilkinson	10,368	Irwinton	451
Worth	18,064	Sylvester	575

Hawaii

(4 counties, 6,425 sq. mi. land; pop. 965,000)

Hawaii	92,053	Hilo	4,034
Honolulu	762,874	Honolulu	596
Kauai	39,082	Lihue	620
Maui*	70,991	Wailuku	1,175

*Includes population of Kalawao County (146).

Idaho

(44 counties, 82,412 sq. mi. land; pop. 943,935)

Ada	173,036	Boise	1,052
Adams	3,347	Council	1,362
Bannock	65,421	Pocatello	1,112
Bear Lake	6,931	Paris	990
Benewah	8,292	Saint Maries	784
Bingham	36,489	Blackfoot	2,096
Blaine	9,841	Hailey	2,634
Boise	2,999	Idaho City	1,901
Bonner	24,163	Sandpoint	1,726
Bonneville	65,980	Idaho Falls	1,840
Boundary	7,289	Bonners Ferry	1,268
Butte	3,342	Arco	2,236
Camas	818	Fairfield	1,071
Canyon	83,756	Caldwell	584
Caribou	8,695	Soda Springs	1,763
Cassia	19,427	Burley	2,560
Clark	798	Dubois	1,763
Clearwater	10,390	Orofino	2,236
Custer	3,385	Challis	4,927
Elmore	21,565	Mountain Home	3,071
Franklin	8,895	Preston	664
Fremont	10,813	Saint Anthony	1,852
Gem	11,972	Emmett	558
Gooding	11,874	Gooding	728
Idaho	14,769	Grangeville	8,497
Jefferson	15,304	Rigby	1,093
Jerome	14,840	Jerome	601
Kootenai	59,770	Coeur d'Alene	1,240
Latah	28,749	Moscow	1,077
Lemhi	7,460	Salmon	4,564
Lewis	4,118	Nezperce	478
Lincoln	3,436	Shoshone	1,205
Madison	19,480	Rexberg	468
Minidoka	19,718	Rupert	757
Nez Perce	33,220	Lewiston	845
Oneida	3,258	Malad City	1,200
Owyhee	8,272	Murphy	7,643
Payette	15,722	Payette	405
Power	6,844	American Falls	1,403
Shoshone	19,226	Wallace	2,641
Teton	2,897	Driggs	448
Twin Falls	52,927	Twin Falls	1,944
Valley	5,604	Cascade	3,670
Washington	8,803	Weiser	1,454

Illinois

(102 counties, 55,645 sq. mi. land; pop. 11,418,461)

Adams	71,622	Quincy	852
Alexander	12,264	Cairo	236
Bond	16,224	Greenville	377
Boone	28,630	Belvidere	282
Brown	5,411	Mount Sterling	306
Bureau	39,114	Princeton	869
Calhoun	5,867	Hardin	250
Carroll	18,779	Mount Carroll	444
Cass	15,084	Virginia	374
Champaign	168,392	Urbana	998
Christian	36,446	Taylorville	710
Clark	16,913	Marshall	506
Clay	15,283	Louisville	469
Clinton	32,617	Carlyle	472
Coles	52,992	Charleston	509

County	Pop.	County seat or court house	Land area sq. mi.
Cook	5,253,190	Chicago	958
Crawford	20,818	Robinson	446
Cumberland	11,062	Toledo	346
De Kalb	74,624	Sycamore	634
De Witt	18,108	Clinton	397
Douglas	19,774	Tuscola	417
Du Page	658,177	Wheaton	337
Edgar	21,725	Paris	623
Edwards	7,961	Albion	223
Effingham	30,944	Effingham	478
Fayette	22,167	Vandalia	709
Ford	15,265	Paxton	486
Franklin	43,201	Benton	414
Fulton	43,687	Lewiston	871
Gallatin	7,590	Shawneetown	325
Greene	16,661	Carrollton	543
Grundy	30,582	Morris	423
Hamilton	9,172	McLeansboro	436
Hancock	23,877	Carthage	796
Hardin	5,383	Elizabethtown	181
Henderson	9,114	Oquawka	373
Henry	57,968	Cambridge	824
Iroquois	32,976	Watseka	1,118
Jackson	61,522	Murphysboro	590
Jasper	11,318	Newton	496
Jefferson	36,354	Mount Vernon	570
Jersey	20,538	Jerseyville	373
Jo Daviess	23,520	Galena	603
Johnson	9,624	Vienna	346
Kane	278,405	Geneva	524
Kankakee	102,926	Kankakee	679
Kendall	37,202	Yorkville	322
Knox	61,607	Galesburg	720
Lake	440,372	Waukegan	454
La Salle	109,139	Ottawa	1,139
Lawrence	17,807	Lawrenceville	374
Lee	36,328	Dixon	725
Livingston	41,381	Pontiac	1,046
Logan	31,802	Lincoln	619
McDonough	37,236	Macomb	590
McHenry	147,724	Woodstock	606
McLean	119,149	Bloomington	1,185
Macon	131,375	Decatur	581
Macoupin	49,384	Carlinville	865
Madison	247,671	Edwardsville	728
Marion	43,523	Salem	573
Marshall	14,479	Lacon	388
Mason	19,492	Havana	536
Massac	14,990	Metropolis	241
Menard	11,700	Petersburg	315
Mercer	19,286	Aledo	559
Monroe	20,117	Waterloo	388
Montgomery	31,686	Hillsboro	705
Morgan	37,502	Jacksonville	568
Moultrie	14,546	Sullivan	325
Ogle	46,338	Oregon	759
Peoria	200,466	Peoria	621
Perry	21,714	Pinckneyville	443
Piatt	16,581	Monticello	439
Pike	18,896	Pittsfield	830
Pope	4,404	Golconda	374
Pulaski	8,840	Mound City	203
Putnam	6,085	Hennepin	160
Randolph	35,566	Chester	583
Richland	17,587	Olney	360
Rock Island	165,968	Rock Island	423
St. Clair	265,469	Belleville	672
Saline	27,360	Harrisburg	385
Sangamon	176,089	Springfield	866
Schuyler	8,365	Rushville	436
Scott	6,142	Winchester	251
Shelby	23,923	Shelbyville	747
Stark	7,389	Toulon	288
Stephenson	49,536	Freeport	564
Tazewell	132,078	Pekin	650
Union	16,851	Jonesboro	414
Vermilion	95,222	Danville	900
Wabash	13,713	Mt. Carmel	224
Warren	21,943	Monmouth	543
Washington	15,472	Nashville	563
Wayne	18,059	Fairfield	715
White	17,864	Carmi	497
Whiteside	65,970	Morrison	682
Will	324,460	Joliet	844
Williamson	56,538	Marion	427
Winnebago	250,884	Rockford	516
Woodford	33,320	Eureka	527

Indiana

(92 counties, 35,932 sq. mi. land; pop. 5,490,179)

County	Pop.	County seat or court house	Land area sq. mi.
Adams	29,619	Decatur	340
Allen	294,335	Fort Wayne	659
Bartholomew	65,088	Columbus	409
Benton	10,218	Fowler	407
Blackford	15,570	Hartford City	166
Boone	36,446	Lebanon	423
Brown	12,377	Nashville	312
Carroll	19,722	Delphi	372
Cass	40,936	Logansport	414
Clark	88,838	Jeffersonville	376
Clay	24,862	Brazil	360
Clinton	31,545	Frankfort	405
Crawford	9,820	English	307
Daviess	27,836	Washington	432
Dearborn	34,291	Lawrenceburg	307
Decatur	23,841	Greensburg	373
DeKalb	33,606	Auburn	364
Delaware	128,587	Muncie	392
Dubois	34,238	Jasper	429
Elkhart	137,330	Goshen	466
Fayette	28,272	Connersville	215
Floyd	61,169	New Albany	150
Fountain	19,033	Covington	398
Franklin	19,612	Brookville	385
Fulton	19,335	Rochester	369
Gibson	33,156	Princeton	490
Grant	80,934	Marion	415
Greene	30,416	Bloomfield	546
Hamilton	82,381	Noblesville	398
Hancock	43,939	Greenfield	307
Harrison	27,276	Corydon	486
Hendricks	69,804	Danville	409
Henry	53,336	New Castle	394
Howard	86,896	Kokomo	293
Huntington	35,596	Huntington	366
Jackson	36,523	Brownstown	513
Jasper	26,138	Rensselaer	561
Jay	23,239	Portland	384
Jefferson	30,419	Madison	363
Jennings	22,854	Vernon	378
Johnson	77,240	Franklin	321
Knox	41,838	Vincennes	520
Kosciusko	59,555	Warsaw	540
Lagrange	25,550	Lagrange	380
Lake	522,965	Crown Point	501
La Porte	108,632	La Porte	600
Lawrence	42,472	Bedford	452
Madison	139,336	Anderson	453
Marion	765,233	Indianapolis	396
Marshall	39,155	Plymouth	444
Martin	11,001	Shoals	339
Miami	39,820	Peru	369
Monroe	98,387	Bloomington	385
Montgomery	35,501	Crawfordsville	505
Morgan	51,999	Martinsville	409
Newton	14,844	Kentland	401
Noble	35,443	Albion	413
Ohio	5,114	Rising Sun	87
Orange	18,677	Paoli	408
Owen	15,840	Spencer	386
Parke	16,372	Rockville	444
Perry	19,346	Cannelton	382
Pike	13,465	Petersburg	341
Porter	119,816	Valparaiso	418
Posey	26,414	Mount Vernon	409
Pulaski	13,258	Winamac	435
Putnam	29,163	Greencastle	482
Randolph	29,997	Winchester	454
Ripley	24,398	Versailles	447
Rush	19,604	Rushville	408
St. Joseph	241,617	South Bend	459
Scott	20,422	Scottsburg	191
Shelby	39,887	Shelbyville	413
Spencer	19,361	Rockport	400
Starke	21,997	Knox	309
Steuben	24,694	Angola	308
Sullivan	21,107	Sullivan	452
Switzerland	7,153	Vevay	223
Tippecanoe	121,702	Lafayette	502
Tipton	16,819	Tipton	260
Union	6,860	Liberty	162
Vanderburgh	167,515	Evansville	236
Vermillion	18,229	Newport	260
Vigo	112,385	Terre Haute	405
Wabash	36,640	Wabash	398
Warren	8,976	Williamsport	366
Warrick	41,474	Boonville	391
Washington	21,932	Salem	516
Wayne	76,058	Richmond	404
Wells	25,401	Bluffton	370
White	23,867	Monticello	506
Whitley	26,215	Columbia City	336

Iowa

(99 counties; 55,965 sq. mi. land; pop. 2,913,387)

County	Pop.	County seat or court house	Land area sq. mi.
Adair	9,509	Greenfield	570
Adams	5,731	Corning	425
Allamakee	15,108	Waukon	633
Appanoose	15,511	Centerville	498
Audubon	8,559	Audubon	444
Benton	23,649	Vinton	718
Black Hawk	137,961	Waterloo	573
Boone	26,184	Boone	573
Bremer	24,820	Waverly	439
Buchanan	22,900	Independence	572
Buena Vista	20,774	Storm Lake	575
Butler	17,668	Allison	582
Calhoun	13,542	Rockwell City	571

County	Pop.	County seat or court house	Land area sq. mi.
Carroll	22,951	Carroll	570
Cass	16,932	Atlantic	565
Cedar	18,635	Tipton	582
Cerro Gordo	48,458	Mason City	569
Cherokee	16,238	Cherokee	577
Chickasaw	15,437	New Hampton	505
Clarke	8,612	Oscea	431
Clay	19,576	Spencer	569
Clayton	21,098	Elkader	779
Clinton	57,122	Clinton	695
Crawford	18,935	Denison	714
Dallas	29,513	Adel	591
Davis	9,104	Bloomfield	504
Decatur	9,794	Leon	535
Delaware	18,933	Manchester	578
Des Moines	46,203	Burlington	414
Dickinson	15,629	Spirit Lake	381
Dubuque	93,745	Dubuque	607
Emmet	13,336	Estherville	394
Fayette	25,488	West Union	731
Floyd	19,597	Charles City	501
Franklin	13,036	Hampton	583
Fremont	9,401	Sidney	515
Greene	12,119	Jefferson	571
Grundy	14,366	Grundy Center	501
Guthrie	11,983	Guthrie Center	590
Hamilton	17,862	Webster City	576
Hancock	13,833	Garner	571
Hardin	21,776	Eldora	569
Harrison	16,348	Logan	697
Henry	18,890	Mount Pleasant	436
Howard	11,114	Cresco	473
Humboldt	12,246	Dakota City	436
Ida	8,908	Ida Grove	432
Iowa	15,429	Marengo	587
Jackson	22,503	Maquoketa	638
Jasper	36,425	Newton	731
Jefferson	16,316	Fairfield	440
Johnson	81,717	Iowa City	614
Jones	20,401	Anamosa	576
Keokuk	12,921	Sigourney	580
Kossuth	21,891	Algona	974
Lee	43,106	Fort Madison and Keokuk	522
Linn	169,775	Cedar Rapids	724
Louisa	12,055	Wapello	402
Lucas	10,313	Chariton	432
Lyon	12,896	Rock Rapids	588
Madison	12,597	Winterset	563
Mahaska	22,507	Oskaloosa	571
Marion	29,669	Knoxville	560
Marshall	41,652	Marshalltown	573
Mills	13,406	Glenwood	439
Mitchell	12,329	Osage	470
Monona	11,692	Onawa	697
Monroe	9,209	Albia	434
Montgomery	13,413	Red Oak	424
Muscatine	40,436	Muscatine	442
O'Brien	16,972	Primghar	574
Osceola	8,371	Sibley	399
Page	19,063	Clarinda	535
Palo Alto	12,721	Emmetsburg	562
Plymouth	24,743	Le Mars	864
Pocahontas	11,369	Pocahontas	577
Polk	303,170	Des Moines	582
Pottawattamie	86,500	Council Bluffs	953
Poweshiek	19,306	Montezuma	585
Ringgold	6,112	Mount Ayr	535
Sac	14,118	Sac City	576
Scott	160,022	Davenport	459
Shelby	15,043	Harlan	591
Sioux	30,813	Orange City	769
Story	72,326	Nevada	574
Tama	19,533	Toledo	721
Taylor	8,353	Bedford	537
Union	13,858	Creston	426
Van Buren	8,626	Keosauqua	484
Wapello	40,241	Ottumwa	434
Warren	34,878	Indianola	573
Washington	20,141	Washington	570
Wayne	8,199	Corydon	526
Webster	45,953	Fort Dodge	718
Winnebago	13,010	Forest City	401
Winneshiek	21,876	Decorah	690
Woodbury	100,884	Sioux City	873
Worth	9,075	Northwood	401
Wright	16,319	Clarion	579

Kansas

(105 counties, 81,778 sq. mi. land; pop. 2,363,208)

Allen	15,654	Iola	505
Anderson	8,749	Garnett	584
Atchison	18,397	Atchison	431
Barber	6,548	Medicine Lodge	1,136
Barton	31,343	Great Bend	895
Bourbon	15,969	Fort Scott	638
Brown	11,955	Hiawatha	572
Butler	44,782	El Dorado	1,443
Chase	3,309	Cottonwood Falls	777
Chautauqua	5,016	Sedan	644
Cherokee	22,304	Columbus	590
Cheyenne	3,678	Saint Francis	1,021
Clark	2,599	Ashland	975
Clay	9,802	Clay Center	632
Cloud	12,494	Concordia	718
Coffey	9,370	Burlington	615
Comanche	2,554	Coldwater	789
Cowley	36,824	Winfield	1,128
Crawford	37,916	Girard	595
Decatur	4,509	Oberlin	894
Dickinson	20,175	Abilene	852
Doniphan	9,268	Troy	388
Douglas	67,640	Lawrence	461
Edwards	4,271	Kinsley	620
Elk	3,918	Howard	650
Ellis	26,098	Hays	900
Ellsworth	6,640	Ellsworth	717
Finney	23,825	Garden City	1,302
Ford	24,315	Dodge City	1,099
Franklin	21,813	Ottawa	577
Geary	29,852	Junction City	377
Gove	3,726	Gove	1,072
Graham	3,995	Hill City	898
Grant	6,977	Ulysses	575
Gray	5,138	Cimarron	868
Greeley	1,845	Tribune	778
Greenwood	8,764	Eureka	1,135
Hamilton	2,514	Syracuse	998
Harper	7,778	Anthony	802
Harvey	30,531	Newton	540
Haskell	3,814	Sublette	578
Hodgeman	2,269	Jetmore	860
Jackson	11,644	Holton	658
Jefferson	15,207	Oskaloosa	535
Jewell	5,241	Mankato	910
Johnson	270,269	Olathe	478
Kearny	3,435	Lakin	868
Kingman	8,960	Kingman	865
Kiowa	4,046	Greensburg	723
Labette	25,682	Oswego	653
Lane	2,472	Dighton	717
Leavenworth	54,809	Leavenworth	463
Lincoln	4,145	Lincoln	720
Linn	8,234	Mound City	601
Logan	3,478	Oakley	1,073
Lyon	35,108	Emporia	844
McPherson	26,855	McPherson	900
Marion	13,522	Marion	944
Marshall	12,720	Marysville	878
Meade	4,788	Meade	979
Miami	21,618	Paola	590
Mitchell	8,117	Beloit	717
Montgomery	42,281	Independence	646
Morris	6,419	Council Grove	693
Morton	3,454	Elkhart	731
Nemaha	11,211	Seneca	719
Neosho	18,967	Erie	576
Ness	4,498	Ness City	1,074
Norton	6,689	Norton	873
Osage	15,319	Lyndon	695
Osborne	5,959	Osborne	882
Ottawa	5,971	Minneapolis	721
Pawnee	8,065	Larned	755
Phillips	7,406	Phillipsburg	887
Pottawatomie	14,782	Westmoreland	828
Pratt	10,275	Pratt	735
Rawlins	4,105	Atwood	1,069
Reno	64,983	Hutchinson	1,259
Republic	7,569	Belleville	719
Rice	11,900	Lyons	728
Riley	63,505	Manhattan	593
Rooks	7,006	Stockton	888
Rush	4,516	LaCrosse	718
Russell	8,868	Russell	869
Saline	48,905	Salina	721
Scott	5,782	Scott City	718
Sedgwick	366,531	Wichita	1,007
Seward	17,071	Liberal	640
Shawnee	154,916	Topeka	549
Sheridan	3,544	Hoxie	896
Sherman	7,759	Goodland	1,057
Smith	5,947	Smith Center	897
Stafford	5,539	Saint John	788
Stanton	2,339	Johnson	681
Stevens	4,736	Hugoton	727
Sumner	24,928	Wellington	1,183
Thomas	8,451	Colby	1,075
Trego	4,165	Wakeeney	890
Wabaunsee	6,867	Alma	797
Wallace	2,045	Sharon Springs	914
Washington	8,543	Washington	898
Wichita	3,041	Leoti	719
Wilson	12,128	Fredonia	575
Woodson	4,600	Yates Center	498
Wyandotte	172,335	Kansas City	149

Kentucky

(120 counties, 39,669 sq. mi. land; pop. 3,661,433)

Adair	15,233	Columbia	407

County	Pop.	County seat or court house	Land area sq. mi.
Allen	14,128	Scottsville	338
Anderson	12,567	Lawrenceburg	204
Ballard	8,798	Wickliffe	254
Barren	34,009	Glasgow	482
Bath	10,025	Owingsville	277
Bell	34,330	Pineville	361
Boone	45,842	Burlington	246
Bourbon	19,405	Paris	292
Boyd	55,513	Catlettsburg	160
Boyle	25,066	Danville	182
Bracken	7,738	Brooksville	203
Breathitt	17,004	Jackson	495
Breckinridge	16,861	Hardinsburg	565
Bullitt	43,346	Shepherdsville	300
Butler	11,064	Morgantown	431
Caldwell	13,473	Princeton	347
Calloway	30,031	Murray	386
Campbell	83,317	Alexandria	152
Carlisle	5,487	Bardwell	191
Carroll	9,270	Carrollton	130
Carter	25,060	Grayson	407
Casey	14,818	Liberty	445
Christian	66,878	Hopkinsville	722
Clark	28,322	Winchester	255
Clay	22,752	Manchester	471
Clinton	9,321	Albany	196
Crittenden	9,207	Marion	360
Cumberland	7,289	Burkesville	304
Daviess	85,949	Owensboro	463
Edmonson	9,962	Brownsville	302
Elliott	6,908	Sandy Hook	234
Estill	14,495	Irvine	256
Fayette	204,165	Lexington	285
Fleming	12,323	Flemingsburg	351
Floyd	48,764	Prestonsburg	393
Franklin	41,830	Frankfort	212
Fulton	8,971	Hickman	211
Gallatin	4,842	Warsaw	99
Garrard	10,853	Lancaster	232
Grant	13,308	Williamstown	259
Graves	34,049	Mayfield	557
Grayson	20,854	Leitchfield	493
Green	11,043	Greensburg	289
Greenup	39,132	Greenup	347
Hancock	7,742	Hawesville	189
Hardin	88,917	Elizabethtown	629
Harlan	41,889	Harlan	468
Harrison	15,166	Cynthiana	310
Hart	15,402	Munfordville	412
Henderson	40,849	Henderson	438
Henry	12,740	New Castle	291
Hickman	6,065	Clinton	245
Hopkins	46,174	Madisonville	552
Jackson	11,996	McKee	346
Jefferson	684,793	Louisville	386
Jessamine	26,653	Nicholasville	174
Johnson	24,432	Paintsville	264
Kenton	137,058	Independence	163
Knott	17,940	Hindman	352
Knox	30,239	Barbourville	388
Larue	11,983	Hodgenville	263
Laurel	38,982	London	434
Lawrence	14,121	Louisa	420
Lee	7,754	Beattyville	211
Leslie	14,882	Hyden	402
Letcher	30,687	Whitesburg	339
Lewis	14,545	Vanceburg	484
Lincoln	19,053	Stanford	337
Livingston	9,219	Smithland	312
Logan	24,138	Russellville	556
Lyon	6,490	Eddyville	209
McCracken	61,310	Paducah	251
McCreary	15,634	Whitley City	427
McLean	10,090	Calhoun	256
Madison	53,352	Richmond	443
Magoffin	13,515	Salyersville	310
Marion	17,910	Lebanon	347
Marshall	25,637	Benton	304
Martin	13,925	Inez	230
Mason	17,760	Maysville	241
Meade	22,854	Brandenburg	306
Menifee	5,117	Frenchburg	203
Mercer	19,011	Harrodsburg	250
Metcalfe	9,484	Edmonton	291
Monroe	12,353	Tompkinsville	331
Montgomery	20,046	Mount Sterling	199
Morgan	12,103	West Liberty	382
Muhlenberg	32,238	Greenville	478
Nelson	27,584	Bardstown	424
Nicholas	7,157	Carlisle	197
Ohio	21,765	Hartford	596
Oldham	28,094	La Grange	190
Owen	8,924	Owenton	354
Owsley	5,709	Booneville	198
Pendleton	10,989	Falmouth	281
Perry	33,763	Hazard	341
Pike	81,123	Pikeville	785
Powell	11,101	Stanton	180
Pulaski	45,803	Somerset	660
Robertson	2,270	Mount Olivet	100
Rockcastle	13,973	Mount Vernon	318
Rowan	19,049	Morehead	282
Russell	13,708	Jamestown	250
Scott	21,813	Georgetown	286
Shelby	23,328	Shelbyville	385
Simpson	14,673	Franklin	236
Spencer	5,929	Taylorsville	192
Taylor	21,178	Campbellsville	270
Todd	11,874	Elkton	377
Trigg	9,384	Cadiz	421
Trimble	6,253	Bedford	148
Union	17,821	Morganfield	341
Warren	71,828	Bowling Green	548
Washington	10,764	Springfield	301
Wayne	17,022	Monticello	446
Webster	14,832	Dixon	336
Whitley	33,396	Williamsburg	443
Wolfe	6,698	Campton	223
Woodford	17,778	Versailles	192

Louisiana

(64 parishes, 44,521 sq. mi. land; pop. 4,203,972)

Acadia	56,427	Crowley	657
Allen	21,390	Oberlin	765
Ascension	50,068	Donaldsville	296
Assumption	22,084	Napoleonville	342
Avoyelles	41,393	Marksville	846
Beauregard	29,692	De Ridder	1,163
Bienville	16,387	Arcadia	816
Bossier	80,721	Benton	845
Caddo	252,294	Shreveport	894
Calcasieu	167,048	Lake Charles	1,082
Caldwell	10,761	Columbia	541
Cameron	9,336	Cameron	1,417
Catahoula	12,287	Harrisonburg	732
Claiborne	17,095	Homer	765
Concordia	22,981	Vidalia	717
De Soto	25,664	Mansfield	880
East Baton Rouge	366,164	Baton Rouge	458
East Carroll	11,772	Lake Providence	426
East Feliciana	19,015	Clinton	455
Evangeline	33,343	Ville Platte	667
Franklin	24,141	Winnsboro	635
Grant	16,703	Colfax	653
Iberia	63,752	New Iberia	589
Iberville	32,159	Plaquemine	638
Jackson	17,321	Jonesboro	579
Jefferson	454,592	Gretna	348
Jefferson Davis	32,168	Jennings	655
Lafayette	150,017	Lafayette	270
Lafourche	82,483	Thibodaux	1,141
La Salle	17,004	Jena	638
Lincoln	39,763	Ruston	472
Livingston	58,655	Livingston	661
Madison	14,733	Tallulah	631
Morehouse	34,803	Bastrop	807
Natchitoches	39,863	Natchitoches	1,264
Orleans	557,482	New Orleans	199
Ouachita	139,241	Monroe	627
Plaquemines	26,049	Pointe a la Hache	1,035
Pointe Coupee	24,045	New Roads	566
Rapides	135,282	Alexandria	1,341
Red River	10,433	Coushatta	394
Richland	22,187	Rayville	563
Sabine	25,280	Many	855
St. Bernard	64,097	Chalmette	486
St. Charles	37,259	Hahnville	286
St. Helena	9,827	Greensburg	409
St. James	21,495	Convent	248
St. John The Baptist	31,924	Edgard	213
St. Landry	84,128	Opelousas	936
St. Martin	40,214	Saint Martinville	749
St. Mary	64,395	Franklin	613
St. Tammany	110,554	Covington	873
Tangipahoa	80,698	Amite	783
Tensas	8,525	Saint Joseph	623
Terrebonne	94,393	Houma	1,367
Union	21,167	Farmerville	884
Vermilion	48,458	Abbeville	1,205
Vernon	53,475	Leesville	1,332
Washington	44,207	Franklinton	676
Webster	43,631	Minden	602
West Baton Rouge	19,086	Port Allen	194
West Carroll	12,922	Oak Grove	360
West Feliciana	12,186	Saint Francisville	406
Winn	17,253	Winnfield	953

Maine

(16 counties, 30,995 sq. mi. land; pop. 1,124,660)

Androscoggin	99,657	Auburn	477
Aroostook	91,331	Houlton	6,721
Cumberland	215,789	Portland	876
Franklin	27,098	Farmington	1,699
Hancock	41,781	Ellsworth	1,537
Kennebec	109,889	Augusta	876
Knox	32,941	Rockland	370
Lincoln	25,691	Wiscasset	458
Oxford	48,968	South Paris	2,053

County	Pop.	County seat or court house	Land area sq. mi.
Penobscot	137,015	Bangor	3,430
Piscataquis	17,634	Dover-Foxcroft	3,986
Sagadahoc	28,795	Bath	257
Somerset	45,028	Skowhegan	3,930
Waldo	28,414	Belfast	730
Washington	34,963	Machias	2,586
York	139,666	Alfred	1,008

Maryland

(23 cos., 1 ind. city, 9,837 sq. mi. land; pop. 4,216,446)

County	Pop.	County seat or court house	Land area sq. mi.
Allegany	80,548	Cumberland	421
Anne Arundel	370,775	Annapolis	418
Baltimore	655,615	Towson	598
Calvert	34,638	Prince Frederick	213
Caroline	23,143	Denton	321
Carroll	96,356	Westminster	452
Cecil	60,430	Elkton	360
Charles	72,751	La Plata	452
Dorchester	30,623	Cambridge	593
Frederick	114,263	Frederick	663
Garrett	26,498	Oakland	657
Harford	145,930	Bel Air	448
Howard	118,572	Ellicott City	251
Kent	16,695	Chestertown	278
Montgomery	579,053	Rockville	495
Prince George's	665,071	Upper Marlboro	487
Queen Anne's	25,508	Centreville	372
St. Mary's	59,895	Leonardtown	373
Somerset	19,188	Princess Anne	338
Talbot	25,604	Easton	259
Washington	113,086	Hagerstown	455
Wicomico	64,540	Salisbury	379
Worcester	30,889	Snow Hill	475
Independent City			
Baltimore	786,775		80

Massachusetts

(14 counties; 7,824 sq. mi. land; pop. 5,737,037)

County	Pop.	County seat or court house	Land area sq. mi.
Barnstable	147,925	Barnstable	400
Berkshire	145,110	Pittsfield	929
Bristol	474,641	Taunton	557
Dukes	8,942	Edgartown	102
Essex	633,632	Salem	495
Franklin	64,317	Greenfield	702
Hampden	443,018	Springfield	618
Hampshire	138,813	Northampton	528
Middlesex	1,367,034	Cambridge	822
Nantucket	5,087	Nantucket	47
Norfolk	606,587	Dedham	400
Plymouth	405,437	Plymouth	655
Suffolk	650,142	Boston	57
Worcester	646,352	Worcester	1,513

Michigan

(83 counties; 56,954 sq. mi. land; pop. 9,258,344)

County	Pop.	County seat or court house	Land area sq. mi.
Alcona	9,740	Harrisville	679
Alger	9,225	Munising	912
Allegan	81,555	Allegan	832
Alpena	32,315	Alpena	567
Antrim	16,194	Bellaire	480
Arenac	14,706	Standish	367
Baraga	8,484	L'Anse	901
Barry	45,781	Hastings	560
Bay	119,881	Bay City	447
Benzie	11,205	Beulah	322
Berrien	171,276	Saint Joseph	576
Branch	40,188	Coldwater	508
Calhoun	141,557	Marshall	712
Cass	49,499	Cassopolis	496
Charlevoix	19,907	Charlevoix	421
Cheboygan	20,649	Cheboygan	720
Chippewa	29,029	Sault Sainte Marie	1,590
Clare	23,822	Harrison	570
Clinton	55,893	Saint Johns	573
Crawford	9,465	Grayling	559
Delta	38,947	Escanaba	1,173
Dickinson	25,341	Iron Mountain	770
Eaton	88,337	Charlotte	579
Emmet	22,992	Petoskey	468
Genesee	450,449	Flint	642
Gladwin	19,957	Gladwin	505
Gogebic	19,686	Bessemer	1,105
Grand Traverse	54,899	City	466
Gratiot	40,448	Ithaca	570
Hillsdale	42,071	Hillsdale	603
Houghton	37,872	Houghton	1,014
Huron	36,459	Bad Axe	830
Ingham	272,437	Mason	560
Ionia	51,815	Ionia	577
Iosco	28,349	Iawas City	546
Iron	13,635	Crystal Falls	1,163
Isabella	54,110	Mount Pleasant	577
Jackson	151,495	Jackson	705
Kalamazoo	212,378	Kalamazoo	562
Kalkaska	10,952	Kalkaska	563
Kent	444,506	Grand Rapids	862
Keweenaw	1,963	543 River	543
Lake	7,711	Baldwin	568
Lapeer	70,038	Lapeer	658
Leelanau	14,007	Leland	341
Lenawee	89,948	Adrian	753
Livingston	100,289	Howell	574
Luce	6,659	Newberry	904
Mackinac	10,178	Saint Ignace	1,025
Macomb	694,600	Mount Clemens	482
Manistee	23,019	Manistee	543
Marquette	74,101	Marquette	1,821
Mason	26,365	Ludington	494
Mecosta	36,961	Big Rapids	560
Menominee	26,201	Menominee	1,045
Midland	73,578	Midland	525
Missaukee	10,009	Lake City	565
Monroe	134,659	Monroe	557
Montcalm	47,555	Stanton	713
Montmorency	7,492	Atlanta	550
Muskegon	157,589	Muskegon	507
Newaygo	34,917	White Cloud	847
Oakland	1,011,793	Pontiac	875
Oceana	22,002	Hart	541
Ogemaw	16,436	West Branch	570
Ontonagon	9,861	Ontonagon	1,311
Osceola	18,928	Reed City	569
Oscoda	6,858	Mio	568
Otsego	14,993	Gaylord	516
Ottawa	157,174	Grand Haven	567
Presque Isle	14,267	Rogers City	656
Roscommon	16,374	Roscommon	528
Saginaw	228,059	Saginaw	815
St. Clair	138,802	Port Huron	734
St. Joseph	56,083	Centreville	503
Sanilac	40,789	Sandusky	964
Schoolcraft	8,575	Manistique	1,173
Shiawassee	71,140	Corunna	540
Tuscola	56,961	Caro	812
Van Buren	66,814	Paw Paw	611
Washtenaw	264,748	Ann Arbor	710
Wayne	2,337,240	Detroit	615
Wexford	25,102	Cadillac	566

Minnesota

(87 counties; 79,548 sq. mi. land; pop., 4,077,148)

County	Pop.	County seat or court house	Land area sq. mi.
Aitkin	13,404	Aitkin	1,834
Anoka	195,998	Anoka	430
Becker	29,336	Detroit Lakes	1,312
Beltrami	30,982	Bemidji	2,507
Benton	25,187	Foley	408
Big Stone	7,716	Ortonville	497
Blue Earth	52,314	Mankato	749
Brown	28,645	New Ulm	610
Carlton	29,936	Carlton	864
Carver	37,046	Chaska	351
Cass	21,050	Walker	2,033
Chippewa	14,941	Montevideo	584
Chisago	25,717	Center City	417
Clay	49,327	Moorhead	1,049
Clearwater	8,761	Bagley	999
Cook	4,092	Grand Marais	1,412
Cottonwood	14,854	Windom	640
Crow Wing	41,722	Brainerd	1,008
Dakota	194,111	Hastings	574
Dodge	14,773	Mantorville	439
Douglas	27,839	Alexandria	643
Faribault	19,714	Blue Earth	714
Fillmore	21,930	Preston	862
Freeborn	36,329	Albert Lea	705
Goodhue	38,749	Red Wind	763
Grant	7,171	Elbow Lake	547
Hennepin	941,411	Minneapolis	541
Houston	19,617	Caledonia	564
Hubbard	14,098	Park Rapids	936
Isanti	23,600	Cambridge	440
Itasca	43,006	Grand Rapids	2,661
Jackson	13,690	Jackson	699
Kanabec	12,161	Mora	527
Kandiyohi	36,763	Willmar	784
Kittson	6,672	Hallock	1,104
Koochiching	17,571	International Falls	3,108
Lac qui Parle	10,592	Madison	772
Lake	13,043	Two Harbors	2,053
Lake of the Woods	3,764	Baudette	1,296
Le Sueur	23,434	Le Center	446
Lincoln	8,207	Ivanhoe	538
Lyon	25,207	Marshall	714
McLeod	29,657	Glencoe	489
Mahnomen	5,535	Mahnomen	559
Marshall	13,027	Warren	1,760
Martin	24,687	Fairmont	706
Meeker	20,594	Litchfield	624
Mille Lacs	18,430	Milaca	578
Morrison	29,311	Falls	1,124
Mower	40,390	Austin	711
Murray	11,507	Slayton	702
Nicollet	26,929	Saint Peter	440
Nobles	21,840	Worthington	714
Norman	9,379	Ada	877
Olmsted	91,971	Rochester	655
Otter Tail	51,937	Fergus Falls	1,973

County	Pop.	County seat or court house	Land area sq. mi.
Pennington	15,258	Thief River Falls	618
Pine	19,871	Pine City	1,421
Pipestone	11,690	Pipestone	466
Polk	34,844	Crookston	1,982
Pope	11,657	Glenwood	668
Ramsey	459,784	Saint Paul	154
Red Lake	5,471	Red Lake Falls	433
Redwood	19,341	Redwood Falls	882
Renville	20,401	Olivia	984
Rice	46,087	Faribault	501
Rock	10,703	Luverne	483
Roseau	12,574	Roseau	1,677
St. Louis	222,229	Duluth	6,125
Scott	43,784	Shakopee	357
Sherburne	29,908	Elk River	435
Sibley	15,448	Gaylord	593
Stearns	108,161	Saint Cloud	1,338
Steele	30,328	Owatonna	431
Stevens	11,322	Morris	560
Swift	12,920	Benson	743
Todd	24,991	Long Prairie	941
Traverse	5,542	Wheaton	575
Wabasha	19,335	Wabasha	537
Wadena	14,192	Wadena	538
Waseca	18,448	Waseca	422
Washington	113,571	Stillwater	390
Watonwan	12,361	Saint James	435
Wilkin	8,382	Breckenridge	751
Winona	46,256	Winona	630
Wright	58,962	Buffalo	672
Yellow Medicine	13,653	Granite Falls	758

Mississippi

(82 counties, 47,233 sq. mi. land; pop. 2,520,638)

Adams	38,035	Natchez	456
Alcorn	33,036	Corinth	401
Amite	13,369	Liberty	732
Attala	19,865	Kosciusko	737
Benton	8,153	Ashland	407
Bolivar	45,965	Cleveland & Rosedale	892
Calhoun	15,664	Pittsboro	573
Carroll	9,776	Carrollton & Vaiden	634
Chickasaw	17,853	Houston & Okolona	503
Choctaw	8,996	Ackerman	420
Claiborne	12,279	Port Gibson	494
Clarke	16,945	Quitman	692
Clay	21,082	West Point	415
Coahoma	36,918	Clarksdale	559
Copiah	26,503	Hazlehurst	779
Covington	15,927	Collins	416
De Soto	53,930	Hernando	483
Forrest	66,018	Hattiesburg	469
Franklin	8,208	Meadville	566
George	15,297	Lucedale	483
Greene	9,827	Leakesville	718
Grenada	21,043	Grenada	421
Hancock	24,537	Bay Saint Louis	478
Harrison	157,665	Gulfport	581
Hinds	250,998	Jackson & Raymond	875
Holmes	22,970	Lexington	759
Humphreys	13,931	Belzoni	430
Issaquena	2,513	Mayersville	406
Itawamba	20,518	Fulton	540
Jackson	118,015	Pascagoula	731
Jasper	17,265	Bat Springs & Paulding	678
Jefferson	9,181	Fayette	523
Jefferson Davis	13,846	Prentiss	409
Jones	61,912	Ellisville & Laurel	696
Kemper	10,148	De Kalb	766
Lafayette	31,030	Oxford	669
Lamar	23,821	Purvis	499
Lauderdale	77,285	Meridian	705
Lawrence	12,518	Monticello	435
Leake	18,790	Carthage	584
Lee	57,061	Tupelo	451
Leflore	41,525	Greenwood	605
Lincoln	30,174	Brookhaven	587
Lowndes	57,304	Columbus	517
Madison	41,613	Canton	718
Marion	25,708	Columbia	548
Marshall	29,296	Holly Springs	709
Monroe	36,404	Aberdeen	772
Montgomery	13,366	Winona	408
Neshoba	23,789	Philadelphia	572
Newton	19,944	Decatur	580
Noxubee	13,212	Macon	698
Oktibbeha	36,018	Starkville	459
Panola	28,164	Batesville & Sardis	694
Pearl River	33,795	Poplarville	818
Perry	9,864	New Augusta	651
Pike	36,173	Magnolia	410
Pontotoc	20,918	Pontotoc	499
Prentiss	24,025	Booneville	418
Quitman	12,636	Marks	406
Rankin	69,427	Brandon	782
Scott	24,556	Forest	610
Sharkey	7,964	Rolling Fork	435
Simpson	23,441	Mendenhall	59
Smith	15,077	Raleigh	63
Stone	9,716	Wiggins	44
Sunflower	34,844	Indianola	70
Tallahatchie	17,157	Charleston & Sumner	65
Tate	20,119	Senatobia	40
Tippah	18,739	Ripley	45
Tishomingo	18,434	Iuka	43
Tunica	9,652	Tunica	46
Union	21,741	New Albany	41
Walthall	13,761	Tylertown	40
Warren	51,627	Vicksburg	59
Washington	72,344	Greenville	73
Wayne	19,135	Waynesboro	81
Webster	10,300	Walthall	42
Wilkinson	10,021	Woodville	67
Winston	19,474	Louisville	61
Yalobusha	13,139	Coffeeville & Water Valley	47
Yazoo	27,349	Yazoo City	93

Missouri

(114 cos., 1 ind. city, 68,945 sq. mi. land; pop. 4,917,444)

Adair	24,870	Kirksville	56
Andrew	13,980	Savannah	43
Atchison	8,605	Rockport	54
Audrain	26,458	Mexico	69
Barry	24,408	Cassville	77
Barton	11,292	Lamar	59
Bates	15,873	Butler	84
Benton	12,183	Warsaw	72
Bollinger	10,301	Marble Hill	62
Boone	100,376	Columbia	68
Buchanan	87,888	Saint Joseph	40
Butler	37,693	Poplar Buff	69
Caldwell	8,660	Kingston	43
Callaway	32,252	Fulton	84
Camden	19,963	Camdenton	64
Cape Girardeau	58,837	Jackson	57
Carroll	12,131	Carrollton	69
Carter	5,428	Van Buren	50
Cass	51,029	Harrisonville	70
Cedar	11,894	Stockton	47
Chariton	10,489	Keytesville	75
Christian	22,402	Ozark	56
Clark	8,493	Kahoka	50
Clay	136,488	Liberty	40
Clinton	15,916	Plattsburg	42
Cole	56,663	Jefferson City	39
Cooper	14,643	Boonville	56
Crawford	18,300	Steelville	74
Dade	7,383	Greenfield	49
Dallas	12,096	Buffalo	54
Daviess	8,905	Gallatin	56
De Kalb	8,222	Maysville	42
Dent	14,517	Salem	75
Douglas	11,594	Ava	81
Dunklin	36,324	Kennett	54
Franklin	71,233	Union	92
Gasconade	13,181	Hermann	52
Gentry	7,887	Albany	49
Greene	185,302	Springfield	67
Grundy	11,959	Trenton	43
Harrison	9,890	Bethany	72
Henry	19,672	Clinton	72
Hickory	6,367	Hermitage	37
Holt	6,882	Oregon	45
Howard	10,008	Fayette	46
Howell	28,807	West Plains	92
Iron	11,084	Ironton	55
Jackson	629,180	Independence	61
Jasper	86,958	Carthage	64
Jefferson	146,814	Hillsboro	66
Johnson	39,059	Warrensburg	83
Knox	5,508	Edina	50
Laclede	24,323	Lebanon	76
Lafayette	29,925	Lexington	63
Lawrence	28,973	Mount Vernon	61
Lewis	10,901	Monticello	50
Lincoln	22,193	Troy	62
Linn	15,495	Linneus	62
Livingston	15,739	Chillicothe	53
McDonald	14,917	Pineville	54
Macon	16,313	Macon	79
Madison	10,725	Fredericktown	49
Maries	7,551	Vienna	52
Marion	28,638	Palmyra	43
Mercer	4,685	Princeton	45
Miller	18,532	Tuscumbia	59
Mississippi	15,726	Charleston	41
Moniteau	12,068	California	41
Monroe	9,716	Paris	67
Montgomery	11,537	Montgomery City	54
Morgan	13,807	Versailles	59
New Madrid	22,945	New Madrid	65
Newton	40,555	Neosho	62
Nodaway	21,996	Maryville	87
Oregon	10,238	Alton	79
Osage	12,014	Linn	60
Ozark	7,961	Gainesville	73
Pemiscot	24,987	Caruthersville	51
Perry	16,784	Perryville	47

County	Pop.	County seat or court house	Land area sq. mi.
Pettis	36,378	Sedalia	686
Phelps	33,633	Rolla	674
Pike	17,568	Bowling Green	673
Platte	46,341	Platte City	421
Polk	18,822	Bolivar	636
Pulaski	42,011	Waynesville	550
Putnam	6,092	Unionville	520
Ralls	8,911	New London	482
Randolph	25,460	Huntsville	477
Ray	21,378	Richmond	568
Reynolds	7,230	Centerville	809
Ripley	12,458	Doniphan	631
St. Charles	143,455	St. Charles	558
St. Clair	8,622	Osceola	699
St. Francois	42,600	Farmington	451
St. Louis	974,815	Clayton	506
Ste. Genevieve	15,180	Ste. Genevieve	504
Saline	24,919	Marshall	755
Schuyler	4,979	Lancaster	309
Scotland	5,415	Memphis	438
Scott	39,647	Benton	423
Shannon	7,885	Eminence	1,004
Shelby	7,826	Shelbyville	501
Stoddard	29,009	Bloomfield	815
Stone	15,587	Galena	451
Sullivan	7,434	Milan	651
Taney	20,467	Forsyth	608
Texas	21,070	Houston	1,180
Vernon	19,806	Nevada	837
Warren	14,900	Warrenton	429
Washington	17,983	Potosi	762
Wayne	11,277	Greenville	762
Webster	20,414	Marshfield	594
Worth	3,008	Grant City	266
Wright	16,188	Hartville	682
Independent City			
St. Louis	453,085	.....	61

Montana

(57 counties, 145,388 sq. mi. land; pop., 786,690)

Beaverhead	8,186	Dillon	5,529
Big Horn	11,096	Hardin	4,983
Blaine	6,999	Chinook	4,257
Broadwater	3,267	Townsend	1,189
Carbon	8,099	Red Lodge	2,056
Carter	1,799	Ekalaka	3,342
Cascade	80,696	Great Falls	2,699
Chouteau	6,092	Fort Benton	3,987
Custer	13,109	Miles City	3,776
Daniels	2,835	Scobey	1,427
Dawson	11,805	Glendive	2,374
Deer Lodge	12,518	Anaconda	740
Fallon	3,763	Baker	1,623
Fergus	13,076	Lewistown	4,340
Flathead	51,966	Kalispell	5,112
Gallatin	42,865	Bozeman	2,510
Garfield	1,656	Jordan	4,491
Glacier	10,628	Cut Bank	2,994
Golden Valley	1,026	Ryegate	1,172
Granite	2,700	Philipsburg	1,729
Hill	17,985	Havre	2,897
Jefferson	7,029	Boulder	1,657
Judith Basin	2,646	Stanford	1,871
Lake	19,056	Polson	1,445
Lewis & Clark	43,039	Helena	3,461
Liberty	2,329	Chester	1,426
Lincoln	17,752	Libby	3,616
McCone	2,702	Circle	2,626
Madison	5,448	Virginia City	3,590
Meagher	2,154	White Sulphur Springs	2,392
Mineral	3,675	Superior	1,216
Missoula	76,016	Missoula	2,582
Musselshell	4,428	Roundup	1,871
Park	12,660	Livingston	2,665
Petroleum	655	Winnett	1,652
Phillips	5,367	Malta	5,130
Pondera	6,731	Conrad	1,632
Powder River	2,520	Broadus	3,288
Powell	6,958	Deer Lodge	2,329
Prairie	1,836	Terry	1,732
Ravalli	22,493	Hamilton	2,384
Richland	12,243	Sidney	2,081
Roosevelt	10,467	Wolf Point	2,357
Rosebud	9,899	Forsyth	5,019
Sanders	8,675	Thompson Falls	2,749
Sheridan	5,414	Plentywood	1,681
Silver Bow	38,092	Butte	718
Stillwater	5,598	Columbus	1,793
Sweet Grass	3,216	Big Timber	1,903
Teton	6,491	Choteau	2,275
Toole	5,559	Shelby	1,931
Treasure	981	Hysham	975
Valley	10,250	Glasgow	4,936
Wheatland	2,359	Harlowton	1,419
Wibaux	1,476	Wibaux	888
Yellowstone	108,035	Billings	2,624
Yellowstone Nat. Park	275		245

Nebraska

(93 counties, 76,644 sq. mi. land; pop., 1,570,006)

Adams	30,656	Hastings	564
Antelope	8,675	Neligh	859
Arthur	513	Arthur	711
Banner	918	Harrisburg	747
Blaine	867	Brewster	714
Boone	7,391	Albion	687
Box Butte	13,696	Alliance	1,077
Boyd	3,331	Butte	532
Brown	4,377	Ainsworth	1,214
Buffalo	34,797	Kearney	945
Burt	8,813	Tekamah	486
Butler	9,330	David City	584
Cass	20,297	Plattsmouth	557
Cedar	10,852	Hartington	740
Chase	4,758	Imperial	894
Cherry	6,758	Valentine	5,961
Cheyenne	10,057	Sidney	1,196
Clay	8,106	Clay Center	574
Colfax	9,890	Schuyler	410
Cuming	11,664	West Point	575
Custer	13,877	Broken Bow	2,571
Dakota	16,573	Dakota City	258
Dawes	9,609	Chadron	1,397
Dawson	22,162	Lexington	982
Deuel	2,462	Chappell	437
Dixon	7,137	Ponca	474
Dodge	35,847	Fremont	534
Douglas	397,884	Omaha	333
Dundy	2,861	Benkelman	920
Fillmore	7,920	Geneva	576
Franklin	4,377	Franklin	576
Frontier	3,647	Stockville	976
Furnas	6,486	Beaver City	721
Gage	24,456	Beatrice	858
Garden	2,802	Oshkosh	1,680
Garfield	2,363	Burwell	570
Gosper	2,140	Elwood	461
Grant	877	Hyannis	775
Greeley	3,462	Greeley	570
Hall	47,690	Grand Island	537
Hamilton	9,301	Aurora	543
Harlan	4,292	Alma	555
Hayes	1,356	Hayes Center	713
Hitchcock	4,079	Trenton	709
Holt	13,552	O'Neil	2,406
Hooker	990	Mullen	721
Howard	6,773	Saint Paul	564
Jefferson	9,817	Fairbury	575
Johnson	5,285	Tecumseh	377
Kearney	7,053	Minden	519
Keith	9,364	Ogallala	1,039
Keya Paha	1,301	Springview	769
Kimball	4,882	Kimball	952
Knox	11,457	Center	1,105
Lancaster	192,884	Lincoln	839
Lincoln	36,455	North Platte	2,525
Logan	983	Stapleton	571
Loup	859	Taylor	574
McPherson	593	Tryon	859
Madison	31,382	Madison	575
Merrick	8,945	Central City	478
Morrill	6,085	Bridgeport	1,405
Nance	4,740	Fullerton	439
Nemaha	8,367	Auburn	409
Nuckolls	6,726	Nelson	576
Otoe	15,183	Nebraska City	615
Pawnee	3,937	Pawnee City	433
Perkins	3,637	Grant	885
Phelps	9,769	Holdrege	540
Pierce	8,481	Pierce	575
Platte	28,852	Columbus	669
Polk	6,320	Osceola	437
Red Willow	12,615	McCook	718
Richardson	11,315	Falls City	553
Rock	2,383	Bassett	1,003
Saline	13,131	Wilber	575
Sarpy	86,015	Papillion	238
Saunders	18,716	Wahoo	753
Scotts Bluff	38,344	Gering	725
Seward	15,789	Seward	575
Sheridan	7,544	Rushville	2,453
Sherman	4,226	Loup City	564
Sioux	1,845	Harrison	2,070
Stanton	6,549	Stanton	431
Thayer	7,582	Hebron	575
Thomas	973	Thedford	713
Thurston	7,186	Pender	391
Valley	5,633	Ord	567
Washington	15,508	Blair	386
Wayne	9,858	Wayne	443
Webster	4,858	Red Cloud	575
Wheeler	1,060	Bartlett	575
York	14,798	York	576

Nevada

(16 cos., 1 ind. city, 109,894 sq. mi. land; pop., 799,184)

Churchill	13,917	Fallon	4,990
Clark	461,816	Las Vegas	7,881

County	Pop.	County seat or court house	Land area sq. mi.
Douglas	19,421	Minden	708
Elko	17,269	Elko	17,135
Esmeralda	777	Goldfield	3,587
Eureka	1,198	Eureka	4,175
Humboldt	9,434	Winnemucca	9,698
Lander	4,082	Austin	5,515
Lincoln	3,732	Pioche	10,635
Lyon	13,594	Yerington	2,007
Mineral	6,217	Hawthorne	3,744
Nye	9,048	Tonopah	18,155
Pershing	3,408	Lovelock	6,036
Storey	1,459	Virginia City	264
Washoe	193,623	Reno	6,317
White Pine	8,167	Ely	8,902
Independent City			
Carson City	32,022	Carson City	146

New Hampshire

(10 counties, 8,993 sq. mi. land; pop., 920,610)

County	Pop.	County seat or court house	Land area sq. mi.
Belknap	42,884	Laconia	404
Carroll	27,931	Ossipee	933
Cheshire	62,116	Keene	711
Coos	35,147	Lancaster	1,804
Grafton	65,806	Woodsville	1,719
Hillsborough	276,608	Nashua	876
Merrimack	98,302	Concord	936
Rockingham	190,345	Exeter	699
Strafford	85,408	Dover	370
Sullivan	36,063	Newport	540

New Jersey

(21 counties, 7,468 sq. mi. land; pop., 7,364,158)

County	Pop.	County seat or court house	Land area sq. mi.
Atlantic	194,119	Mays Landing	568
Bergen	845,385	Hackensack	237
Burlington	362,542	Mount Holly	808
Camden	471,650	Camden	223
Cape May	82,266	Cape May Court House	263
Cumberland	132,866	Bridgeton	498
Essex	850,451	Newark	127
Gloucester	199,917	Woodbury	327
Hudson	556,972	Jersey City	46
Hunterdon	87,361	Flemington	426
Mercer	307,863	Trenton	227
Middlesex	595,893	New Brunswick	316
Monmouth	503,173	Freehold	472
Morris	407,630	Morristown	470
Ocean	346,038	Toms River	641
Passaic	447,585	Paterson	187
Salem	64,676	Salem	338
Somerset	203,129	Somerville	305
Sussex	116,119	Newton	526
Union	504,094	Elizabeth	103
Warren	84,429	Belvidere	359

New Mexico

(32 counties, 121,335 sq. mi. land; pop., 1,299,968)

County	Pop.	County seat or court house	Land area sq. mi.
Bernalillo	419,700	Albuquerque	1,169
Catron	2,720	Reserve	6,929
Chaves	51,103	Roswell	6,066
Colfax	13,706	Raton	3,762
Curry	42,019	Clovis	1,408
De Baca	2,454	Fort Sumner	2,323
Dona Ana	96,340	Las Cruces	3,819
Eddy	47,855	Carlsbad	4,184
Grant	26,204	Silver City	3,969
Guadalupe	4,496	Santa Rosa	3,032
Harding	1,090	Mosquero	2,122
Hidalgo	6,049	Lordsburg	3,445
Lea	55,634	Lovington	4,389
Lincoln	10,997	Carrizozo	4,832
Los Alamos	17,599	Los Alamos	109
Luna	15,585	Deming	2,965
McKinley	54,950	Gallup	5,442
Mora	4,205	Mora	1,930
Otero	44,665	Alamogordo	6,626
Quay	10,577	Tucumcari	2,874
Rio Arriba	29,282	Tierra Amarilla	5,856
Roosevelt	15,695	Portales	2,453
Sandoval	34,799	Bernalillo	3,707
San Juan	80,833	Aztec	5,521
San Miguel	22,751	Las Vegas	4,709
Santa Fe	75,306	Santa Fe	1,905
Sierra	8,454	Truth or Consequences	4,178
Socorro	12,969	Socorro	6,625
Taos	18,862	Taos	2,204
Torrance	7,491	Estancia	3,335
Union	4,725	Clayton	3,830
Valencia	60,853	Los Lunas	5,616

New York

(62 counties, 47,377 sq. mi. land; pop., 17,557,288)

County	Pop.	County seat or court house	Land area sq. mi.
Albany	285,909	Albany	524
Allegany	51,742	Belmont	1,032
Bronx	1,169,115	Bronx	42
Broome	213,648	Binghamton	712
Cattaraugus	85,697	Little Valley	1,306
Cayuga	79,894	Auburn	695
Chautauqua	146,925	Mayville	1,064
Chemung	97,656	Elmira	411
Chenango	49,344	Norwich	897
Clinton	80,750	Plattsburgh	1,043
Columbia	59,487	Hudson	638
Cortland	48,820	Cortland	500
Delaware	46,931	Delhi	1,440
Dutchess	245,055	Poughkeepsie	804
Erie	1,015,472	Buffalo	1,046
Essex	36,176	Elizabethtown	1,806
Franklin	44,929	Malone	1,642
Fulton	55,153	Johnstown	497
Genesee	59,400	Batavia	495
Greene	40,861	Catskill	648
Hamilton	5,034	Lake Pleasant	1,721
Herkimer	66,714	Herkimer	1,416
Jefferson	88,151	Watertown	1,273
Kings	2,230,936	Brooklyn	70
Lewis	25,035	Lowville	1,283
Livingston	57,006	Geneseo	633
Madison	65,150	Wampsville	656
Monroe	702,238	Rochester	663
Montgomery	53,439	Fonda	404
Nassau	1,321,582	Mineola	287
New York	1,427,533	New York	22
Niagara	227,101	Lockport	526
Oneida	253,466	Utica	1,219
Onondaga	463,324	Syracuse	784
Ontario	88,909	Canandaigua	644
Orange	259,603	Goshen	826
Orleans	38,496	Albion	391
Oswego	113,901	Oswego	954
Otsego	59,075	Cooperstown	1,004
Putnam	77,193	Carmel	231
Queens	1,891,325	Jamaica	109
Rensselaer	151,966	Troy	655
Richmond	352,121	Saint George	59
Rockland	259,530	New City	175
St. Lawrence	114,254	Canton	2,728
Saratoga	153,759	Ballston Spa	810
Schenectady	149,946	Schenectady	206
Schoharie	29,710	Schoharie	624
Schuyler	17,686	Watkins Glen	329
Seneca	33,733	Ovid & Waterloo	327
Steuben	99,135	Bath	1,396
Suffolk	1,284,231	Riverhead	911
Sullivan	65,155	Monticello	976
Tioga	49,812	Owego	519
Tompkins	87,085	Ithaca	477
Ulster	158,158	Kingston	1,131
Warren	54,854	Lake George	882
Washington	54,795	Hudson Falls	836
Wayne	85,230	Lyons	605
Westchester	866,599	White Plains	438
Wyoming	39,895	Warsaw	595
Yates	21,459	Penn Yan	339

North Carolina

(100 counties, 48,843 sq. mi. land; pop., 5,874,429)

County	Pop.	County seat or court house	Land area sq. mi.
Alamance	99,136	Graham	433
Alexander	24,999	Taylorsville	259
Alleghany	9,587	Sparta	235
Anson	25,562	Wadesboro	533
Ashe	22,325	Jefferson	426
Avery	14,409	Newland	247
Beaufort	40,266	Washington	826
Bertie	21,024	Windsor	701
Bladen	30,448	Elizabethtown	879
Brunswick	35,767	Southport	860
Buncombe	160,934	Asheville	659
Burke	72,504	Morganton	504
Cabarrus	85,895	Concord	364
Caldwell	67,746	Lenoir	471
Camden	5,829	Camden	240
Carteret	41,092	Beaufort	526
Caswell	20,705	Yanceyville	428
Catawba	105,208	Newton	396
Chatham	33,415	Pittsboro	708
Cherokee	18,933	Murphy	452
Chowan	12,558	Edenton	182
Clay	6,619	Hayesville	214
Cleveland	83,435	Shelby	468
Columbus	51,037	Whiteville	938
Craven	71,043	New Bern	701
Cumberland	247,160	Fayetteville	657
Currituck	11,089	Currituck	256
Dare	13,377	Manteo	391
Davidson	113,162	Lexington	548
Davie	24,599	Mocksville	267
Duplin	40,952	Kenansville	819
Durham	152,785	Durham	298
Edgecombe	55,988	Tarboro	506
Forsyth	243,683	Winston-Salem	412
Franklin	30,055	Louisburg	494
Gaston	162,568	Gastonia	357
Gates	8,875	Gatesville	338
Graham	7,217	Robbinsville	289
Granville	33,995	Oxford	534
Greene	16,117	Snow Hill	266

County	Pop.	County seat or court house	Land area sq. mi.
ilford	317,154	Greensboro	651
lifax	55,286	Halifax	724
rnett	59,570	Lillington	601
ywood	46,495	Waynesville	555
nderson	58,580	Hendersonville	374
rtford	23,368	Winton	356
ke	20,383	Raeford	391
de	5,873	Swanquarter	624
dell	82,538	Statesville	574
ckson	25,811	Sylva	491
hnston	70,599	Smithfield	795
nes	9,705	Trenton	470
e	36,718	Sanford	259
noir	59,819	Kinston	402
ncoln	42,372	Lincolnton	298
Dowell	35,135	Marion	437
acon	20,178	Franklin	517
adison	16,827	Marshall	451
artin	25,948	Williamston	461
ecklenburg	404,270	Charlotte	528
tchell	14,428	Bakersville	222
ontgomery	22,469	Troy	490
oore	50,505	Carthage	701
ash	67,153	Nashville	540
ew Hanover	103,471	Wilmington	185
orthampton	22,584	Jackson	538
nslow	112,784	Jacksonville	763
ange	77,055	Hillsboro	400
amlico	10,398	Bayboro	341
asquotank	28,462	Elizabeth City	228
ender	22,215	Burgaw	875
erquimans	9,486	Hertford	246
erson	29,164	Roxboro	398
tt	83,651	Greenville	657
olk	12,984	Columbus	238
andolph	91,861	Asheboro	789
chmond	45,481	Rockingham	477
obeson	101,577	Lumberton	949
ockingham	83,426	Wentworth	569
owan	99,186	Salisbury	519
utherford	53,787	Rutherfordton	568
ampson	49,687	Clinton	947
cotland	32,273	Laurinburg	319
anly	48,517	Albemarle	396
okes	33,086	Danbury	452
urry	59,449	Dobson	539
wain	10,283	Bryson City	526
ansylvania	23,417	Brevard	378
yrrell	3,975	Columbia	407
nion	70,380	Monroe	639
ance	36,748	Henderson	249
ake	300,833	Raleigh	854
arren	16,232	Warrenton	427
ashington	14,801	Plymouth	332
atauga	31,678	Boone	314
ayne	97,054	Goldsboro	554
ilkes	58,657	Wilkesboro	752
ilson	63,132	Wilson	374
adkin	28,439	Yadkinville	336
ancey	14,934	Burnsville	314

North Dakota

(53 counties, 69,300 sq. mi. land; pop., 652,695)

County	Pop.	County seat or court house	Land area sq. mi.
dams	3,584	Hettinger	988
arnes	13,960	Valley City	1,498
enson	7,944	Minnewaukan	1,412
llings	1,138	Medora	1,152
ottineau	9,338	Bottineau	1,668
owman	4,229	Bowman	1,162
urke	3,822	Bowbells	1,118
urleigh	54,811	Bismarck	1,618
ass	88,247	Fargo	1,767
avalier	7,636	Langdon	1,507
ickey	7,207	Ellendale	1,139
ivide	3,494	Crosby	1,288
unn	4,627	Manning	1,993
ddy	3,554	New Rockford	634
mmons	5,877	Linton	1,499
oster	4,611	Carrington	640
olden Valley	2,391	Beach	1,003
rand Forks	66,100	Grand Forks	1,440
rant	4,274	Carson	1,660
riggs	3,714	Cooperstown	708
ettinger	4,275	Mott	1,133
idder	3,833	Steele	1,362
a Moure	6,473	La Moure	1,150
ogan	3,493	Napoleon	1,000
cHenry	7,858	Towner	1,887
cIntosh	4,800	Ashley	984
cKenzie	7,132	Watford City	2,754
cLean	12,288	Washburn	2,065
ercer	9,378	Stanton	1,044
orton	25,177	Mandan	1,921
ountrail	7,679	Stanley	1,837
elson	5,233	Lakota	991
liver	2,495	Center	723
embina	10,399	Cavalier	1,120
Pierce	6,166	Rugby	1,037
Ramsey	13,048	Devils Lake	1,241
Ransom	6,698	Lisbon	862
Renville	3,608	Mohall	874
Richland	19,207	Wahpeton	1,436
Rolette	12,177	Rolla	914
Sargent	5,512	Forman	857
Sheridan	2,819	McClusky	989
Sioux	3,620	Fort Yates	1,099
Slope	1,157	Amidon	1,219
Stark	23,697	Dickinson	1,338
Steele	3,106	Finley	713
Stutsman	24,154	Jamestown	2,263
Towner	4,052	Cando	1,035
Traill	9,624	Hillsboro	861
Walsh	15,371	Grafton	1,290
Ward	58,392	Minot	2,041
Wells	6,979	Fessenden	1,288
Williams	22,237	Williston	2,074

Ohio

(88 counties, 41,004 sq. mi. land; pop., 10,797,419)

County	Pop.	County seat or court house	Land area sq. mi.
Adams	24,328	West Union	586
Allen	112,241	Lima	405
Ashland	46,178	Ashland	424
Ashtabula	104,215	Jefferson	703
Athens	56,399	Athens	508
Auglaize	42,554	Wapakoneta	398
Belmont	82,569	Saint Clairsville	537
Brown	31,920	Georgetown	493
Butler	258,787	Hamilton	470
Carroll	25,598	Carrollton	393
Champaign	33,649	Urbana	429
Clark	150,236	Springfield	398
Clermont	128,483	Batavia	456
Clinton	34,603	Wilmington	410
Columbiana	113,572	Lisbon	534
Coshocton	36,024	Coshocton	566
Crawford	50,075	Bucyrus	403
Cuyahoga	1,498,295	Cleveland	459
Darke	55,096	Greenville	600
Defiance	39,987	Defiance	414
Delaware	53,840	Delaware	443
Erie	79,655	Sandusky	264
Fairfield	93,678	Lancaster	506
Fayette	27,467	Washington C. H.	405
Franklin	869,109	Columbus	543
Fulton	37,751	Wauseon	407
Gallia	30,098	Gallipolis	471
Geauga	74,474	Chardon	408
Greene	129,769	Xenia	416
Guernsey	42,024	Cambridge	522
Hamilton	873,136	Cincinnati	412
Hancock	64,581	Findlay	532
Hardin	32,719	Kenton	471
Harrison	18,152	Cadiz	400
Henry	28,383	Napoleon	415
Highland	33,477	Hillsboro	553
Hocking	24,304	Logan	423
Holmes	29,416	Millersburg	424
Huron	54,608	Norwalk	494
Jackson	30,592	Jackson	420
Jefferson	91,564	Steubenville	410
Knox	46,309	Mount Vernon	529
Lake	212,801	Painesville	231
Lawrence	63,849	Ironton	457
Licking	120,981	Newark	686
Logan	39,155	Bellefontaine	458
Lorain	274,909	Elyria	495
Lucas	471,741	Toledo	341
Madison	33,004	London	467
Mahoning	289,487	Youngstown	417
Marion	67,974	Marion	403
Medina	113,150	Medina	422
Meigs	23,641	Pomeroy	432
Mercer	38,334	Celina	457
Miami	90,381	Troy	410
Monroe	17,382	Woodsfield	457
Montgomery	571,697	Dayton	458
Morgan	14,241	McConnelsville	420
Morrow	26,480	Mount Gilead	406
Muskingum	83,340	Zanesville	654
Noble	11,310	Caldwell	399
Ottawa	40,076	Port Clinton	253
Paulding	21,302	Paulding	419
Perry	31,032	New Lexington	412
Pickaway	43,662	Circleville	503
Pike	22,802	Waverly	443
Portage	135,856	Ravenna	493
Preble	38,223	Eaton	426
Putnam	32,991	Ottawa	484
Richland	131,205	Mansfield	497
Ross	65,004	Chillicothe	692
Sandusky	63,267	Fremont	409
Scioto	84,545	Portsmouth	613
Seneca	61,901	Tiffin	553
Shelby	43,089	Sidney	409
Stark	378,823	Canton	574
Summit	524,472	Akron	412
Trumbull	241,863	Warren	612
Tuscarawas	84,614	New Philadelphia	570

County	Pop.	County seat or court house	Land area sq. mi.
Union	29,536	Marysville	437
Van Wert	30,458	Van Wert	410
Vinton	11,584	McArthur	414
Warren	99,276	Lebanon	403
Washington	64,266	Marietta	640
Wayne	97,408	Wooster	557
Williams	36,369	Bryan	422
Wood	107,372	Bowling Green	619
Wyandot	22,651	Upper Sandusky	406

Oklahoma

(77 counties, 68,655 sq. mi. land; pop., 3,025,266)

Adair	18,575	Stillwell	577
Alfalfa	7,077	Cherokee	864
Atoka	12,748	Atoka	980
Beaver	6,806	Beaver	1,808
Beckham	19,243	Sayre	904
Blaine	13,443	Watonga	920
Bryan	30,535	Durant	902
Caddo	30,905	Anadarko	1,286
Canadian	56,452	El Reno	901
Carter	43,610	Ardmore	828
Cherokee	30,684	Tahlequah	748
Choctaw	17,203	Hugo	762
Cimarron	3,648	Boise City	1,842
Cleveland	133,173	Norman	529
Coal	6,041	Coalgate	520
Comanche	112,456	Lawton	1,076
Cotton	7,338	Walters	656
Craig	15,014	Vinita	763
Creek	59,210	Sapulpa	930
Custer	25,995	Arapaho	981
Delaware	23,946	Jay	720
Dewey	5,922	Taloga	1,007
Ellis	5,596	Arnett	1,232
Garfield	62,820	Enid	1,060
Garvin	27,856	Pauls Valley	813
Grady	39,490	Chickasha	1,106
Grant	6,518	Medford	1,004
Greer	6,877	Mangum	638
Harmon	4,519	Hollis	537
Harper	4,715	Buffalo	1,039
Haskell	11,010	Stigler	570
Hughes	14,338	Holdenville	806
Jackson	30,356	Altus	817
Jefferson	8,183	Waurika	769
Johnston	10,356	Tishomingo	639
Kay	49,852	Newkirk	921
Kingfisher	14,187	Kingfisher	906
Kiowa	12,711	Hobart	1,019
Latimer	9,840	Wilburton	728
Le Flore	40,698	Poteau	1,585
Lincoln	26,601	Chandler	964
Logan	26,881	Guthrie	748
Love	7,469	Marietta	519
McClain	20,291	Purcell	582
McCurtain	36,151	Idabel	1,826
McIntosh	15,495	Eufaula	599
Major	8,772	Fairview	958
Marshall	10,550	Madill	372
Mayes	32,261	Pryor	644
Murray	12,147	Sulphur	420
Muskogee	66,939	Muskogee	815
Noble	11,573	Perry	736
Nowata	11,486	Nowata	540
Okfuskee	11,125	Okemah	628
Oklahoma	568,933	Oklahoma City	708
Okmulgee	39,169	Okmulgee	698
Osage	39,327	Pawhuska	2,265
Ottawa	32,870	Miami	465
Pawnee	15,310	Pawnee	551
Payne	62,435	Stillwater	691
Pittsburg	40,524	McAlester	1,251
Pontotoc	32,598	Ada	717
Pottawatomie	55,239	Shawnee	783
Pushmataha	11,773	Antlers	1,417
Roger Mills	4,799	Cheyenne	1,146
Rogers	46,436	Claremore	683
Seminole	27,473	Wewoka	639
Sequoyah	30,749	Sallisaw	678
Stephens	43,419	Duncan	884
Texas	17,727	Guymon	2,040
Tillman	12,398	Frederick	904
Tulsa	470,593	Tulsa	572
Wagoner	41,801	Wagoner	559
Washington	48,113	Bartlesville	423
Washita	13,798	Cordell	1,006
Woods	10,923	Alva	1,291
Woodward	21,172	Woodward	1,242

Oregon

(36 counties, 96,184 sq. mi. land; pop., 2,632,663)

Baker	16,134	Baker	3,072
Benton	68,211	Corvallis	679
Clackamas	241,919	Oregon City	1,870
Clatsop	32,489	Astoria	805
Columbia	35,646	Saint Helens	651
Coos	64,047	Coquille	1,606
Crook	13,091	Prineville	2,984
Curry	16,992	Gold Beach	1,629
Deschutes	62,142	Bend	3,02
Douglas	93,748	Roseburg	5,044
Gilliam	2,057	Condon	1,213
Grant	8,210	Canyon City	4,525
Harney	8,314	Burns	10,174
Hood River	15,835	Hood River	521
Jackson	132,456	Medford	2,787
Jefferson	11,599	Madras	1,789
Josephine	58,820	Grants Pass	1,640
Klamath	59,117	Klamath Falls	5,954
Lake	7,532	Lakeview	8,251
Lane	275,226	Eugene	4,562
Lincoln	35,264	Newport	980
Linn	89,495	Albany	2,296
Malheur	26,896	Vale	9,861
Marion	204,692	Salem	1,184
Morrow	7,519	Heppner	2,044
Multnomah	562,640	Portland	431
Polk	45,203	Dallas	741
Sherman	2,172	Moro	827
Tillamook	21,164	Tillamook	1,101
Umatilla	58,861	Pendleton	3,218
Union	23,921	La Grande	2,035
Wallowa	7,273	Enterprise	3,150
Wasco	21,732	The Dalles	2,384
Washington	245,401	Hillsboro	725
Wheeler	1,513	Fossil	1,713
Yamhill	55,332	McMinnville	715

Pennsylvania

(67 counties, 44,888 sq. mi. land; pop., 11,866,728)

Adams	68,292	Gettysburg	52
Allegheny	1,450,085	Pittsburgh	72
Armstrong	77,768	Kittanning	64
Beaver	204,441	Beaver	43
Bedford	46,784	Bedford	1,01
Berks	312,509	Reading	86
Blair	136,621	Hollidaysburg	52
Bradford	62,919	Towanda	1,15
Bucks	479,211	Doylestown	61
Butler	147,912	Butler	78
Cambria	183,263	Ebensburg	69
Cameron	6,674	Emporium	39
Carbon	53,285	Jim Thorpe	38
Centre	112,760	Bellefonte	1,10
Chester	316,660	West Chester	758
Clarion	43,362	Clarion	607
Clearfield	83,578	Clearfield	1,149
Clinton	38,971	Lock Haven	89
Columbia	61,967	Bloomsburg	486
Crawford	88,869	Meadville	1,01
Cumberland	178,037	Carlisle	547
Dauphin	232,317	Harrisburg	528
Delaware	555,007	Media	184
Elk	38,338	Ridgeway	830
Erie	279,780	Erie	804
Fayette	160,395	Uniontown	794
Forest	5,072	Tionesta	428
Franklin	113,629	Chambersburg	774
Fulton	12,842	McConnellsburg	438
Greene	40,355	Waynesburg	577
Huntingdon	42,253	Huntingdon	877
Indiana	92,281	Indiana	829
Jefferson	48,303	Brookville	657
Juniata	19,188	Mifflintown	392
Lackawanna	227,908	Scranton	461
Lancaster	362,346	Lancaster	952
Lawrence	107,150	New Castle	363
Lebanon	109,829	Lebanon	363
Lehigh	273,582	Allentown	348
Luzerne	343,079	Wilkes-Barre	891
Lycoming	118,416	Williamsport	1,237
McKean	50,635	Smethport	979
Mercer	128,299	Mercer	672
Mifflin	46,908	Lewistown	413
Monroe	69,409	Stroudsburg	609
Montgomery	643,621	Norristown	486
Montour	16,675	Danville	131
Northampton	225,418	Easton	376
Northumberland	100,381	Sunbury	461
Perry	35,718	New Bloomfield	557
Philadelphia	1,688,210	Philadelphia	136
Pike	18,271	Milford	550
Potter	17,726	Coudersport	1,081
Schuylkill	160,630	Pottsville	782
Snyder	33,584	Middleburg	329
Somerset	81,243	Somerset	1,073
Sullivan	6,349	Laporte	451
Susquehanna	37,876	Montrose	826
Tioga	40,973	Wellsboro	1,131
Union	32,870	Lewisburg	317
Venango	64,444	Franklin	679
Warren	47,449	Warren	885
Washington	217,074	Washington	958
Wayne	35,237	Honesdale	731
Westmoreland	392,294	Greensburg	1,033
Wyoming	26,433	Tunkhannock	399
York	312,963	York	906

Rhode Island

(5 counties, 1,055 sq. mi. land; pop., 947,154)

County	Pop.	County seat or court house	Land area sq. mi.
Bristol	46,942	Bristol	26
Kent	154,163	East Greenwich	172
Newport	81,383	Newport	107
Providence	571,349	Providence	416
Washington	93,317	West Kingston	333

South Carolina

(46 counties, 30,203 sq. mi. land; pop., 3,119,208)

County	Pop.	County seat or court house	Land area sq. mi.
Abbeville	22,627	Abbeville	508
Aiken	105,625	Aiken	1,092
Allendale	10,700	Allendale	413
Anderson	133,235	Anderson	718
Bamberg	18,118	Bamberg	395
Barnwell	19,868	Barnwell	558
Beaufort	65,364	Beaufort	579
Berkeley	94,727	Moncks Corner	1,108
Calhoun	12,206	Saint Matthews	380
Charleston	277,308	Charleston	938
Cherokee	40,983	Gaffney	396
Chester	30,148	Chester	580
Chesterfield	38,161	Chesterfield	802
Clarendon	27,464	Manning	602
Colleton	31,676	Walterboro	1,052
Darlington	62,717	Darlington	563
Dillon	31,083	Dillon	406
Dorchester	58,266	Saint George	575
Edgefield	17,528	Edgefield	490
Fairfield	20,700	Winnsboro	685
Florence	110,163	Florence	804
Georgetown	42,461	Georgetown	822
Greenville	287,913	Greenville	795
Greenwood	57,847	Greenwood	451
Hampton	18,159	Hampton	561
Horry	101,419	Conway	1,143
Jasper	14,504	Ridgeland	655
Kershaw	39,015	Camden	723
Lancaster	53,361	Lancaster	552
Laurens	52,214	Laurens	712
Lee	18,929	Bishopville	411
Lexington	140,353	Lexington	707
McCormick	7,797	McCormick	350
Marion	34,179	Marion	493
Marlboro	31,634	Bennettsville	483
Newberry	31,111	Newberry	634
Oconee	48,611	Walhalla	629
Orangeburg	82,276	Orangeburg	1,111
Pickens	79,292	Pickens	499
Richland	267,823	Columbia	762
Saluda	16,150	Saluda	456
Spartanburg	201,553	Spartanburg	814
Sumter	88,243	Sumter	665
Union	30,751	Union	515
Williamsburg	38,226	Kingstree	934
York	106,720	York	685

South Dakota

(67 counties, 75,952 sq. mi. land; pop., 690,178)

County	Pop.	County seat or court house	Land area sq. mi.
Aurora	3,628	Plankinton	707
Beadle	19,195	Huron	1,259
Bennett	3,236	Martin	1,182
Bon Homme	8,059	Tyndall	552
Brookings	24,332	Brookings	795
Brown	36,962	Aberdeen	1,722
Brule	5,245	Chamberlain	815
Buffalo	1,795	Gannvalley	475
Butte	8,372	Belle Fourche	2,251
Campbell	2,243	Mound City	732
Charles Mix	9,680	Lake Andes	1,090
Clark	4,894	Clark	953
Clay	13,135	Vermillion	409
Codington	20,885	Watertown	694
Corson	5,196	McIntosh	2,467
Custer	6,000	Custer	1,559
Davison	17,820	Mitchell	436
Day	8,133	Webster	1,022
Deuel	5,289	Clear Lake	631
Dewey	5,366	Timber Lake	2,310
Douglas	4,181	Armour	434
Edmunds	5,159	Ipswich	1,149
Fall River	8,439	Hot Springs	1,740
Faulk	3,327	Faulkton	1,004
Grant	9,013	Milbank	681
Gregory	6,015	Burke	1,013
Haakon	2,794	Philip	1,822
Hamlin	5,261	Hayti	512
Hand	4,948	Miller	1,437
Hanson	3,415	Alexandria	433
Harding	1,700	Buffalo	2,678
Hughes	14,220	Pierre	757
Hutchinson	9,350	Olivet	816
Hyde	2,069	Highmore	860
Jackson	3,437	Kadoka	1,872
Jerauld	2,929	Wessington Spgs	530
Jones	1,463	Murdo	971
Kingsbury	6,679	De Smet	824
Lake	10,724	Madison	560
Lawrence	18,339	Deadwood	800
Lincoln	13,942	Canton	578
Lyman	3,864	Kennebec	1,679
McCook	6,444	Salem	576
McPherson	4,027	Leola	1,148
Marshall	5,404	Britton	848
Meade	20,717	Sturgis	3,481
Mellette	2,249	White River	1,311
Miner	3,739	Howard	570
Minnehaha	109,435	Sioux Falls	810
Moody	6,692	Flandreau	520
Pennington	70,133	Rapid City	2,783
Perkins	4,700	Bison	2,884
Potter	3,674	Gettysburg	869
Roberts	10,911	Sisseton	1,102
Sanborn	3,213	Woonsocket	569
Shannon	11,323	(Attached to Fall River)	2,094
Spink	9,201	Redfield	1,505
Stanley	2,533	Fort Pierce	1,431
Sully	1,990	Onida	972
Todd	7,328	(Attached to Tripp)	1,388
Tripp	7,268	Winner	1,618
Turner	9,255	Parker	617
Union	10,938	Elk Point	453
Walworth	7,011	Selby	707
Washabaugh	—	(Attached to Jackson)	—
Yankton	18,952	Yankton	518
Ziebach	2,308	Dupree	1,969

Tennessee

(95 counties, 41,155 sq. mi. land; pop., 4,590,750)

County	Pop.	County seat or court house	Land area sq. mi.
Anderson	67,346	Clinton	339
Bedford	27,916	Shelbyville	475
Benton	14,901	Camden	392
Bledsoe	9,478	Pikeville	407
Blount	77,770	Maryville	558
Bradley	67,547	Cleveland	327
Campbell	34,841	Jacksboro	479
Cannon	10,234	Woodbury	266
Carroll	28,285	Huntingdon	600
Carter	50,205	Elizabethton	341
Cheatham	21,616	Ashland City	304
Chester	12,727	Henderson	289
Claiborne	24,595	Tazewell	432
Clay	7,676	Celina	227
Cocke	28,792	Newport	432
Coffee	38,311	Manchester	428
Crockett	14,941	Alamo	266
Cumberland	28,676	Crossville	682
Davidson	477,811	Nashville	501
Decatur	10,857	Decaturville	330
De Kalb	13,589	Smithville	291
Dickson	30,037	Charlotte	491
Dyer	34,663	Dyersburg	520
Fayette	25,305	Somerville	705
Fentress	14,826	Jamestown	498
Franklin	31,983	Winchester	543
Gibson	49,467	Trenton	602
Giles	24,625	Pulaski	610
Grainger	16,751	Rutledge	273
Greene	54,406	Greeneville	619
Grundy	13,787	Altamont	361
Hamblen	49,300	Morristown	156
Hamilton	287,740	Chattanooga	539
Hancock	6,887	Sneedville	223
Hardeman	23,873	Bolivar	670
Hardin	22,280	Savannah	578
Hawkins	43,751	Rogersville	486
Haywood	20,318	Brownsville	534
Henderson	21,390	Lexington	520
Henry	28,656	Paris	560
Hickman	15,151	Centerville	610
Houston	6,871	Erin	200
Humphreys	15,957	Waverly	528
Jackson	9,398	Gainesboro	308
Jefferson	31,284	Dandridge	265
Johnson	13,745	Mountain City	297
Knox	319,694	Knoxville	506
Lake	7,455	Tiptonville	169
Lauderdale	24,555	Ripley	474
Lawrence	34,110	Lawrenceburg	617
Lewis	9,700	Hohenwald	282
Lincoln	26,483	Fayetteville	571
Loudon	28,553	Loudon	235
McMinn	41,878	Athens	429
McNairy	22,525	Selmer	562
Macon	15,700	Lafayette	307
Madison	74,546	Jackson	558
Marion	24,416	Jasper	512
Marshall	19,698	Lewisburg	376
Maury	51,095	Columbia	616
Meigs	7,431	Decatur	189
Monroe	28,700	Madisonville	648
Montgomery	83,342	Clarksville	539
Moore	4,510	Lynchburg	129
Morgan	16,604	Wartburg	523
Obion	32,781	Union City	550
Overton	17,575	Livingston	433
Perry	6,111	Linden	412
Pickett	4,358	Byrdstown	159

County	Pop.	County seat or court house	Land area sq. mi.
Polk	13,602	Benton	438
Putnam	47,601	Cookeville	399
Rhea	24,235	Dayton	309
Roane	48,425	Kingston	357
Robertson	37,021	Springfield	476
Rutherford	84,058	Murfreesboro	606
Scott	19,259	Huntsville	528
Sequatchie	8,605	Dunlap	266
Sevier	41,418	Sevierville	590
Shelby	777,113	Memphis	772
Smith	14,935	Carthage	313
Stewart	8,665	Dover	454
Sullivan	143,968	Blountville	415
Sumner	85,790	Gallatin	529
Tipton	32,747	Covington	454
Trousdale	6,137	Hartsville	114
Unicoi	16,362	Erwin	186
Union	11,707	Maynardville	218
Van Buren	4,728	Spencer	273
Warren	32,653	McMinnville	431
Washington	88,755	Jonesboro	326
Wayne	13,946	Waynesboro	734
Weakley	32,896	Dresden	581
White	19,567	Sparta	373
Williamson	58,108	Franklin	584
Wilson	56,064	Lebanon	570

Texas

(254 counties, 262,017 sq. mi. land; pop., 14,228,383)

County	Pop.	County seat or court house	Land area sq. mi.
Anderson	38,381	Palestine	1,077
Andrews	13,323	Andrews	1,501
Angelina	64,172	Lufkin	807
Aransas	14,260	Rockport	280
Archer	7,266	Archer City	907
Armstrong	1,994	Claude	909
Atascosa	25,055	Jourdanton	1,218
Austin	17,726	Bellville	656
Bailey	8,168	Muleshoe	826
Bandera	7,084	Bandera	793
Bastrop	24,726	Bastrop	895
Baylor	4,919	Seymour	862
Bee	26,030	Beeville	880
Bell	157,889	Belton	1,055
Bexar	988,800	San Antonio	1,248
Blanco	4,681	Johnson City	714
Borden	859	Gail	900
Bosque	13,401	Meridian	989
Bowie	75,301	Boston	891
Brazoria	169,587	Angleton	1,407
Brazos	93,588	Bryan	589
Brewster	7,573	Alpine	6,169
Briscoe	2,579	Silverton	887
Brooks	8,428	Falfurrias	942
Brown	33,057	Brownwood	936
Burleson	12,313	Caldwell	669
Burnet	17,803	Burnet	994
Caldwell	23,637	Lockhart	546
Calhoun	19,574	Port Lavaca	540
Callahan	10,992	Baird	899
Cameron	209,680	Brownsville	906
Camp	9,275	Pittsburg	203
Carson	6,672	Panhandle	924
Cass	29,430	Linden	937
Castro	10,556	Dimmitt	899
Chambers	18,538	Anahuac	616
Cherokee	38,127	Rusk	1,052
Childress	6,950	Childress	707
Clay	9,582	Henrietta	1,086
Cochran	4,825	Morton	775
Coke	3,196	Robert Lee	908
Coleman	10,439	Coleman	1,277
Collin	144,490	McKinney	851
Collingsworth	4,648	Wellington	909
Colorado	18,823	Columbus	965
Comal	36,446	New Braunfels	555
Comanche	12,617	Comanche	930
Concho	2,915	Paint Rock	992
Cooke	27,656	Gainesville	893
Coryell	56,767	Gatesville	1,057
Cottle	2,947	Paducah	895
Crane	4,600	Crane	782
Crockett	4,608	4,588 Ozona	2,806
Crosby	8,859	Crosbyton	899
Culberson	3,315	Van Horn	3,815
Dallam	6,531	Dalhart	1,505
Dallas	1,556,549	Dallas	880
Dawson	16,184	Lamesa	903
Deaf Smith	21,165	Hereford	1,497
Delta	4,839	Cooper	278
Denton	143,126	Denton	911
Dewitt	18,903	Cuero	910
Dickens	3,539	Dickens	907
Dimmit	11,367	Carrizo Springs	1,307
Donley	4,075	Clarendon	929
Duval	12,517	San Diego	1,795
Eastland	19,480	Eastland	924
Ector	115,374	Odessa	903
Edwards	2,033	Rocksprings	2,121
Ellis	59,743	Waxahachie	93
El Paso	479,899	El Paso	1,01
Erath	22,560	Stephenville	1,08
Falls	17,946	Marlin	77
Fannin	24,285	Bonham	89
Fayette	18,832	La Grange	95
Fisher	5,891	Roby	89
Floyd	9,834	Floydada	99
Foard	2,158	Crowell	70
Fort Bend	130,846	Richmond	87
Franklin	6,893	Mount Vernon	29
Freestone	14,830	Fairfield	88
Frio	13,785	Pearsall	1,13
Gaines	13,150	Seminole	1,50
Galveston	195,940	Galveston	39
Garza	5,336	Post	89
Gillespie	13,532	Fredericksburg	1,06
Glasscock	1,304	Garden City	90
Goliad	5,193	Goliad	85
Gonzales	16,883	Gonzales	1,06
Gray	26,386	Pampa	92
Grayson	89,796	Sherman	93
Gregg	99,487	Longview	27
Grimes	13,580	Anderson	79
Guadalupe	46,708	Seguin	71
Hale	37,592	Plainview	1,00
Hall	5,594	Memphis	87
Hamilton	8,297	Hamilton	83
Hansford	6,209	Spearman	92
Hardeman	6,368	Quanah	68
Hardin	40,721	Kountze	89
Harris	2,409,544	Houston	1,73
Harrison	52,265	Marshall	90
Hartley	3,987	Channing	1,46
Haskell	7,725	Haskell	90
Hays	40,594	San Marcos	67
Hemphill	5,304	Canadian	90
Henderson	42,606	Athens	88
Hidalgo	283,229	Edinburg	1,56
Hill	25,024	Hillsboro	96
Hockley	23,230	Levelland	90
Hood	17,714	Granbury	42
Hopkins	25,247	Sulphur Springs	78
Houston	22,299	Crockett	1,23
Howard	33,142	Big Spring	90
Hudspeth	2,728	Sierra Blanca	4,56
Hunt	55,248	Greenville	84
Hutchinson	26,304	Stinnett	87
Irion	1,386	Mertzon	1,05
Jack	7,408	Jacksboro	92
Jackson	13,352	Edna	84
Jasper	30,781	Jasper	92
Jeff Davis	1,647	Fort Davis	2,25
Jefferson	250,938	Beaumont	93
Jim Hogg	5,168	Hebbronville	1,13
Jim Wells	36,498	Alice	86
Johnson	67,649	Cleburne	73
Jones	17,268	Anson	93
Karnes	13,593	Karnes City	75
Kaufman	39,015	Kaufman	78
Kendall	10,635	Boerne	66
Kenedy	543	Sarita	1,38
Kent	1,145	Jayton	87
Kerr	28,780	Kerrville	1,10
Kimble	4,063	Junction	1,25
King	425	Guthrie	91
Kinney	2,279	Brackettville	1,35
Kleberg	33,358	Kingsville	85
Knox	5,329	Benjamin	84
Lamar	42,156	Paris	91
Lamb	18,669	Littlefield	1,01
Lampasas	12,005	Lampasas	71
La Salle	5,514	Cotulla	1,51
Lavaca	19,004	Hallettsville	97
Lee	10,952	Giddings	63
Leon	9,594	Centerville	1,07
Liberty	47,088	Liberty	1,17
Limestone	20,224	Groesbeck	93
Lipscomb	3,766	Lipscomb	93
Live Oak	9,606	George West	1,05
Llano	10,144	Llano	93
Loving	91	Mentone	67
Lubbock	211,651	Lubbock	90
Lynn	8,605	Tahoka	88
McCulloch	8,735	Brady	1,07
McLennan	170,755	Waco	1,03
McMullen	789	Tilden	1,16
Madison	10,649	Madisonville	47
Marion	10,360	Jefferson	38
Martin	4,684	Staton	91
Mason	3,683	Mason	93
Matagorda	37,828	Bay City	1,12
Maverick	31,398	Eagle Pass	1,28
Medina	23,164	Hondo	1,33
Menard	2,346	Menard	90
Midland	82,636	Midland	90
Milam	22,732	Cameron	1,01
Mills	4,477	Goldthwaite	74
Mitchell	9,088	Colorado City	91
Montague	17,410	Montague	92
Montgomery	128,487	Conroe	1,04

County	Pop.	County seat or court house	Land area sq. mi.
Moore	16,575	Dumas	905
Morris	14,629	Daingerfield	256
Motley	1,950	Matador	959
Nacogdoches	46,786	Nacogdoches	939
Navarro	35,323	Corsicana	1,068
Newton	13,254	Newton	935
Nolan	17,359	Sweetwater	915
Nueces	268,215	Corpus Christi	847
Ochiltree	9,588	Perryton	919
Oldham	2,283	Vega	1,485
Orange	83,838	Orange	362
Palo Pinto	24,062	Palo Pinto	949
Panola	20,724	Carthage	812
Parker	44,609	Weatherford	902
Parmer	11,038	Farwell	885
Pecos	14,618	Fort Stockton	4,777
Polk	24,407	Livingston	1,061
Potter	98,637	Amarillo	902
Presidio	5,188	Marfa	3,857
Rains	4,839	Emory	243
Randall	75,062	Canyon	917
Reagan	4,135	Big Lake	1,173
Real	2,469	Leakey	697
Red River	16,101	Clarksville	1,054
Reeves	15,801	Pecos	2,626
Refugio	9,289	Refugio	771
Roberts	1,187	Miami	915
Robertson	14,653	Franklin	864
Rockwall	14,528	Rockwall	128
Runnels	11,872	Ballinger	1,056
Rusk	41,382	Henderson	932
Sabine	8,702	Hemphill	486
San Augustine	8,785	San Augustine	524
San Jacinto	11,434	Coldspring	572
San Patricio	58,013	Sinton	693
San Saba	5,693	San Saba	1,136
Schleicher	2,820	Eldorado	1,309
Scurry	18,192	Snyder	900
Shackelford	3,915	Albany	915
Shelby	23,084	Center	791
Sherman	3,174	Stratford	923
Smith	128,366	Tyler	932
Somervell	4,154	Glen Rose	188
Starr	27,266	Rio Grande City	1,226
Stephens	9,926	Breckenridge	894
Sterling	1,206	Sterling City	923
Stonewall	2,406	Aspermont	925
Sutton	5,130	5,120 Sonora	1,455
Swisher	9,723	Tulia	902
Tarrant	860,880	Fort Worth	868
Taylor	110,932	Abilene	917
Terrell	1,595	Sanderson	2,357
Terry	14,581	Brownfield	887
Throckmorton	2,053	Throckmorton	912
Titus	21,442	Mount Pleasant	412
Tom Green	84,784	San Angelo	1,515
Travis	419,335	Austin	989
Trinity	9,450	Groveton	692
Tyler	16,223	Woodville	922
Upshur	28,595	Gilmer	587
Upton	4,619	Rankin	1,243
Uvalde	22,441	Uvalde	1,564
Val Verde	35,910	Del Rio	3,150
Van Zandt	31,426	Canton	855
Victoria	68,807	Victoria	887
Walker	41,789	Huntsville	786
Waller	19,798	Hempstead	514
Ward	13,976	Monahans	836
Washington	21,998	Brenham	610
Webb	99,258	Laredo	3,362
Wharton	40,242	Wharton	1,086
Wheeler	7,137	Wheeler	904
Wichita	121,082	Wichita Falls	606
Wilbarger	15,931	Vernon	947
Willacy	17,495	Raymondville	589
Williamson	76,521	Georgetown	1,137
Wilson	16,756	Floresville	807
Winkler	9,944	Kermit	840
Wise	26,525	Decatur	902
Wood	24,697	Quitman	689
Yoakum	8,299	Plains	800
Young	19,001	Graham	919
Zapata	6,628	Zapata	999
Zavala	11,666	Crystal City	1,298

Utah

(29 counties, 82,073 sq. mi. land; pop. 1,461,037

Beaver	4,378	Beaver	2,586
Box Elder	33,222	Brigham City	5,614
Cache	57,176	Logan	1,171
Carbon	22,179	Price	1,479
Daggett	769	Manila	699
Davis	146,540	Farmington	299
Duchesne	12,565	Duchesne	3,233
Emery	11,451	Castle Dale	4,449
Garfield	3,673	Panguitch	5,148
Grand	8,241	Moab	3,689
Iron	17,349	Parowan	3,301
Juab	5,530	Nephi	3,396
Kane	4,024	Kanab	3,898
Millard	8,970	Fillmore	6,818
Morgan	4,917	Morgan	603
Piute	1,329	Junction	759
Rich	2,100	Randolph	1,034
Salt Lake	619,066	Salt Lake City	756
San Juan	12,253	Monticello	7,725
Sanpete	14,620	Manti	1,587
Sevier	14,727	Richfield	1,910
Summit	10,198	Coalville	1,865
Tooele	26,033	Tooele	6,919
Uintah	20,506	Vernal	4,479
Utah	218,106	Provo	2,018
Wasatch	8,523	Heber City	1,191
Washington	26,065	Saint George	2,422
Wayne	1,911	Loa	2,461
Weber	144,616	Ogden	566

Vermont

(14 counties, 9,273 sq. mi. land; pop. 511,456)

Addison	29,406	Middlebury	773
Bennington	33,345	Bennington	677
Caledonia	25,808	Saint Johnsbury	651
Chittenden	115,534	Burlington	540
Essex	6,313	Guildhall	666
Franklin	34,788	Saint Albans	649
Grand Isle	4,613	North Hero	89
Lamoille	16,767	Hyde Park	461
Orange	22,739	Chelsea	690
Orleans	23,440	Newport	697
Rutland	58,347	Rutland	932
Washington	52,393	Montpelier	690
Windham	36,933	Newfane	787
Windsor	51,030	Woodstock	972

Virginia

(95 cos., 41 ind. cities, 39,704 sq. mi. land; pop. 5,346,279)

Accomack	31,268	Accomac	476
Albemarle	50,689	Charlottesville	725
Alleghany	14,333	Covington	446
Amelia	8,405	Amelia, C.H.	357
Amherst	29,122	Amherst	479
Appomattox	11,971	Appomattox	336
Arlington	152,599	Arlington	26
Augusta	53,732	Staunton	989
Bath	5,860	Warm Springs	538
Bedford	34,927	Bedford	747
Bland	6,349	Bland	359
Botetourt	23,270	Fincastle	545
Brunswick	15,632	Lawrenceville	563
Buchanan	37,989	Grundy	504
Buckingham	11,751	Buckingham	583
Campbell	45,424	Rustburg	505
Caroline	17,904	Bowling Green	535
Carroll	27,270	Hillsville	478
Charles City	6,692	Charles City	181
Charlotte	12,266	Charlotte Courthouse	477
Chesterfield	141,372	Chesterfield	434
Clarke	9,965	Berryville	178
Craig	3,948	New Castle	330
Culpeper	22,620	Culpeper	382
Cumberland	7,881	Cumberland	300
Dickenson	19,806	Clintwood	331
Dinwiddie	22,602	Dinwiddie	507
Essex	8,864	Tappahannock	263
Fairfax	596,901	Fairfax	394
Fauquier	35,889	Warrenton	651
Floyd	11,563	Floyd	381
Fluvanna	10,244	Palmyra	290
Franklin	35,740	Rocky Mount	683
Frederick	34,150	Winchester	415
Giles	17,810	Pearisburg	362
Gloucester	20,107	Gloucester	225
Goochland	11,761	Goochland	281
Grayson	16,579	Independence	446
Greene	7,625	Stanardsville	157
Greensville	10,903	Emporia	300
Halifax	30,418	Halifax	816
Hanover	50,398	Hanover	467
Henrico	180,735	Richmond	238
Henry	57,654	Martinsville	382
Highland	2,937	Monterey	416
Isle of Wight	21,603	Isle of Wight	319
James City	22,763	Williamsburg	153
King and Queen	5,968	King and Queen	317
King George	10,543	King George	180
King William	9,327	King William	278
Lancaster	10,129	Lancaster	133
Lee	25,956	Jonesville	437
Loudoun	57,427	Leesburg	521
Louisa	17,825	Louisa	497
Lunenburg	12,124	Lunenburg	432
Madison	10,232	Madison	322
Mathews	7,995	Mathews	87
Mecklenburg	29,444	Boydton	616
Middlesex	7,719	Saluda	134
Montgomery	63,516	Christiansburg	390
Nelson	12,204	Lovingston	474
New Kent	8,781	New Kent	213

County	Pop.	County seat or court house	Land area sq. mi.
Northampton	14,625	Eastville	226
Northumberland	9,828	Heathsville	185
Nottoway	14,666	Nottoway	316
Orange	17,827	Orange	342
Page	19,401	Luray	313
Patrick	17,585	Stuart	481
Pittsylvania	66,147	Chatham	995
Powhatan	13,062	Powhatan	261
Prince Edward	16,456	Farmville	354
Prince George	25,733	Prince George	266
Prince William	144,703	Manassas	339
Pulaski	35,229	Pulaski	318
Rappahannock	6,093	Washington	267
Richmond	6,952	Warsaw	193
Roanoke	72,945	Salem	251
Rockbridge	17,911	Lexington	603
Rockingham	57,038	Harrisonburg	865
Russell	31,761	Lebanon	479
Scott	25,068	Gate City	535
Shenandoah	27,559	Woodstock	512
Smyth	33,366	Marion	452
Southampton	18,731	Courtland	603
Spotsylvania	34,435	Spotsylvania	404
Stafford	40,470	Stafford	271
Surry	6,046	Surry	281
Sussex	10,874	Sussex	491
Tazewell	50,511	Tazewell	520
Warren	21,200	Front Royal	217
Washington	46,487	Abingdon	562
Westmoreland	14,041	Montross	227
Wise	43,863	Wise	405
Wythe	25,522	Wytheville	465
York	35,463	Yorktown	113
Independent cities			
Alexandria	103,217		15
Bedford	5,991		7
Bristol	19,042		12
Buena Vista	6,717		3
Charlottesville	45,010		10
Chesapeake	114,226		340
Clifton Forge	5,046		3
Colonial Heights	16,509		8
Covington	9,063		4
Danville	45,642		17
Emporia	4,840		2
Fairfax	19,390		6
Falls Church	9,515		2
Franklin	7,308		4
Fredericksburg	15,322		6
Galax	6,524		8
Hampton	122,617		51
Harrisonburg	19,671		6
Hopewell	23,397		10
Lexington	7,292		2
Lynchburg	66,743		50
Manassas	15,438		8
Manassas Park	6,524		2
Martinsville	18,149		11
Newport News	144,903		65
Norfolk	266,979		53
Norton	4,757		7
Petersburg	41,055		23
Poquoson	8,726		17
Portsmouth	104,577		30
Radford	13,225		7
Richmond	219,214		60
Roanoke	100,427		43
Salem	23,958		14
South Boston	7,093		6
Staunton	21,857		9
Suffolk	47,621		409
Virginia Beach	262,199		256
Waynesboro	15,329		8
Williamsburg	9,870		5
Winchester	20,217		9

Washington

(39 counties, 66,511 sq. mi. land; pop., 4,130,163)

Adams	13,267	Ritzville	1,921
Asotin	16,823	Asotin	635
Benton	109,444	Prosser	1,715
Chelan	45,061	Wenatchee	2,916
Clallam	51,648	Port Angeles	1,753
Clark	192,227	Vancouver	627
Columbia	4,057	Dayton	865
Cowlitz	79,548	Kelso	1,140
Douglas	22,144	Waterville	1,817
Ferry	5,811	Republic	2,200
Franklin	35,025	Pasco	1,243
Garfield	2,468	Pomeroy	706
Grant	48,522	Ephrata	2,660
Grays Harbor	66,314	Montesano	1,918
Island	44,048	Coupeville	212
Jefferson	15,965	Port Townsend	1,805
King	1,269,749	Seattle	2,128
Kitsap	146,609	Port Orchard	393
Kittitas	24,877	Ellensburg	2,308
Klickitat	15,822	Goldendale	1,88
Lewis	55,279	Chehalis	2,40
Lincoln	9,604	Davenport	2,31
Mason	31,184	Shelton	96
Okanogan	30,639	Okanogan	5,281
Pacific	17,237	South Bend	90
Pend Oreille	8,580	Newport	1,40
Pierce	485,643	Tacoma	1,67
San Juan	7,838	Friday Harbor	17
Skagit	64,138	Mount Vernon	1,73
Skamania	7,919	Stevenson	1,67
Snohomish	337,016	Everett	2,09
Spokane	341,835	Spokane	1,76
Stevens	28,979	Colville	2,47
Thurston	124,264	Olympia	72
Wahkiakum	3,832	Cathlamet	261
Walla Walla	47,435	Walla Walla	1,261
Whatcom	106,701	Bellingham	2,12
Whitman	40,103	Colfax	2,151
Yakima	172,508	Yakima	4,28

West Virginia

(55 counties, 24,119 sq. mi. land; pop., 1,949,644)

Barbour	16,639	Philippi	34
Berkeley	46,775	Martinsburg	32
Boone	30,447	Madison	50
Braxton	13,894	Sutton	51
Brooke	31,117	Wellsburg	9
Cabell	106,835	Huntington	28
Calhoun	8,250	Grantsville	28
Clay	11,265	Clay	34
Doddridge	7,433	West Union	32
Fayette	57,863	Fayetteville	66
Gilmer	8,334	Glenville	34
Grant	10,210	Petersburg	48
Greenbrier	37,665	Lewisburg	1,02
Hampshire	14,867	Romney	64
Hancock	40,418	New Cumberland	8
Hardy	10,030	Moorefield	58
Harrison	77,710	Clarksburg	41
Jackson	25,794	Ripley	46
Jefferson	30,302	Charles Town	20
Kanawha	231,414	Charleston	90
Lewis	18,813	Weston	38
Lincoln	23,675	Hamlin	43
Logan	50,679	Logan	45
McDowell	49,899	Welch	53
Marion	65,789	Fairmont	31
Marshall	41,608	Moundsville	30
Mason	27,045	Point Pleasant	43
Mercer	73,942	Princeton	42
Mineral	27,234	Keyser	32
Mingo	37,336	Williamson	42
Monongalia	75,024	Morgantown	36
Monroe	12,873	Union	47
Morgan	10,711	Berkeley Springs	23
Nicholas	28,126	Summersville	65
Ohio	61,389	Wheeling	10
Pendleton	7,910	Franklin	69
Pleasants	8,236	St. Marys	13
Pocahontas	9,919	Marlinton	94
Preston	30,460	Kingwood	65
Putnam	38,181	Winfield	34
Raleigh	86,821	Beckley	60
Randolph	28,734	Elkins	1,04
Ritchie	11,442	Harrisville	45
Roane	15,952	Spencer	48
Summers	15,875	Hinton	35
Taylor	16,584	Grafton	17
Tucker	8,675	Parsons	42
Tyler	11,320	Middlebourne	25
Upshur	23,427	Buckhannon	35
Wayne	46,021	Wayne	50
Webster	12,245	Webster Springs	55
Wetzel	21,874	New Martinsville	35
Wirt	4,922	Elizabeth	23
Wood	93,648	Parkersburg	36
Wyoming	35,993	Pineville	50

Wisconsin

(72 counties, 54,426 sq. mi. land; pop., 4,705,335)

Adams	13,457	Friendship	64
Ashland	16,783	Ashland	1,04
Barron	38,730	Barron	86
Bayfield	13,822	Washburn	1,46
Brown	175,280	Green Bay	52
Buffalo	14,309	Alma	69
Burnett	12,340	Grantsburg	81
Calumet	30,867	Chilton	32
Chippewa	51,702	Chippewa Falls	1,01
Clark	32,910	Neillsville	1,21
Columbia	43,222	Portage	77
Crawford	16,556	Prairie du Chien	56
Dane	323,545	Madison	1,20
Dodge	74,747	Juneau	88
Door	25,029	Sturgeon Bay	49
Douglas	44,421	Superior	1,30
Dunn	34,314	Menomonie	85
Eau Claire	78,805	Eau Claire	63
Florence	4,172	Florence	48

County	Pop.	County seat or court house	Land area sq. mi.
Fond Du Lac	88,952	Fond du Lac	725
Forest	9,044	Crandon	1,011
Grant	51,736	Lancaster	1,144
Green	30,012	Monroe	583
Green Lake	18,370	Green Lake	357
Iowa	19,802	Dodgeville	760
Iron	6,730	Hurley	751
Jackson	16,831	Black River Falls	998
Jefferson	66,152	Jefferson	562
Juneau	21,039	Mauston	774
Kenosha	123,137	Kenosha	273
Kewaunee	19,539	Kewaunee	343
La Crosse	91,056	La Crosse	457
Lafayette	17,412	Darlington	634
Langlade	19,978	Antigo	873
Lincoln	26,311	Merrill	886
Manitowoc	82,918	Manitowoc	594
Marathon	111,270	Wausau	1,559
Marinette	39,314	Marinette	1,395
Marquette	11,672	Montello	455
Menominee	3,373	Keshena	359
Milwaukee	964,988	Milwaukee	241
Monroe	35,074	Sparta	904
Oconto	28,947	Oconto	1,002
Oneida	31,216	Rhinelander	1,130
Outagamie	128,726	Appleton	642
Ozaukee	66,981	Port Washington	235
Pepin	7,477	Durand	231
Pierce	31,149	Ellsworth	577
Polk	32,351	Balsam Lake	919
Portage	57,420	Stevens Point	810
Price	15,788	Phillips	1,256
Racine	173,132	Racine	335
Richland	17,476	Richland Center	585
Rock	139,420	Janesville	723
Rusk	15,589	Ladysmith	913
St. Croix	43,872	Hudson	723
Sauk	43,469	Baraboo	838
Sawyer	12,843	Hayward	1,255
Shawano	35,928	Shawano	897
Sheboygan	100,935	Sheboygan	515
Taylor	18,817	Medford	975
Trempealeau	26,158	Whitehall	736
Vernon	25,642	Viroqua	808
Vilas	16,535	Eagle River	867
Walworth	71,507	Elkhorn	556
Washburn	13,174	Shell Lake	815
Washington	84,848	West Bend	430
Waukesha	280,326	Waukesha	554
Waupaca	42,831	Waupaca	754
Waushara	18,526	Wautoma	628
Winnebago	131,732	Oshkosh	449
Wood	72,799	Wisconsin Rapids	801

Wyoming

(23 counties, 96,989 sq. mi. land; pop., 470,816)

County	Pop.	County seat or court house	Land area sq. mi.
Albany	29,062	Laramie	4,268
Big Horn	11,896	Basin	3,139
Campbell	24,367	Gillette	4,796
Carbon	21,896	Rawlins	7,877
Converse	14,069	Douglas	4,271
Crook	5,308	Sundance	2,855
Fremont	40,251	Lander	9,181
Goshen	12,040	Torrington	2,186
Hot Springs	5,710	Thermopolis	2,005
Johnson	6,700	Buffalo	4,166
Laramie	68,649	Cheyenne	2,684
Lincoln	12,177	Kemmerer	4,070
Natrona	71,856	Casper	5,347
Niobrara	2,924	Lusk	2,684
Park	21,639	Cody	6,936
Platte	11,975	Wheatland	2,023
Sheridan	25,048	Sheridan	2,532
Sublette	4,548	Pinedale	4,872
Sweetwater	41,723	Green River	10,352
Teton	9,355	Jackson	4,011
Uinta	13,021	Evanston	2,085
Washakie	9,496	Worland	2,243
Weston	7,106	Newcastle	2,402

Population of Outlying Areas

Source: U.S. Bureau of the Census

Population figures are final for Puerto Rico, preliminary for other areas, from the census conducted on Apr. 1, 1980.

Puerto Rico

ZIP code	Municipios	Pop.	Land area sq. mile
00601	Adjuntas	18,786	67
00602	Aguada	31,567	31
00603	Aguadilla	54,606	37
00607	Aguas Buenas	22,429	30
00609	Aibonito	22,167	31
00610	Anasco	23,274	40
00612	Arecibo	86,766	127
00615	Arroyo	17,014	15
00617	Barceloneta	18,942	24
00618	Barranquitas	21,639	34
00619	Bayamon	196,206	45
00623	Cabo Rojo	34,045	72
00625	Caguas	117,959	59
00627	Camuy	24,884	47
00629	Canovanas	31,880	33
00630	Carolina	165,954	48
00632	Catano	26,243	6
00633	Cayey	41,099	52
00635	Ceiba	14,944	27
00638	Ciales	16,211	67
00639	Cidra	28,365	36
00640	Coamo	30,822	78
00642	Comerio	18,212	29
00643	Corozal	28,221	43
00645	Culebra	1,265	13
00646	Dorado	25,511	24
00648	Fajardo	32,087	31
00650	Florida	7,232	10
00653	Guanica	18,799	37
00654	Guayama	40,183	65
00656	Guayanilla	21,050	42
00657	Guaynabo	80,742	27
00658	Gurabo	23,574	28
00659	Hatillo	28,958	42
00660	Hormigueros	14,030	11
00661	Humacao	46,134	45
00662	Isabela	37,435	56
00664	Jayuya	14,722	44
00665	Juana Diaz	43,505	61
00666	Juncos	25,397	27
00667	Lajas	21,236	60
00669	Lares	26,743	62
00670	Las Marias	8,747	46
00671	Las Piedras	22,412	34
00672	Loiza	20,867	21
00673	Luquillo	14,895	26
00701	Manati	36,562	46
00706	Maricao	6,737	37
00707	Maunabo	11,813	21
00708	Mayaguez	96,193	77
00716	Moca	29,185	50
00717	Morovis	21,142	39
00718	Naguabo	20,617	52
00719	Naranjito	23,633	28
00720	Orocovis	19,332	64
00723	Patillas	17,774	47
00724	Penuelas	19,116	45
00731	Ponce	189,046	117
00742	Quebradillas	19,728	23
00743	Rincon	11,788	14
00745	Rio Grande	34,283	62
00747	Sabana Grande	20,207	36
00751	Salinas	26,438	71
00753	San German	32,922	54
*00936	San Juan	434,849	47
00754	San Lorenzo	32,428	53
00755	San Sebastian	35,690	71
00757	Santa Isabel	19,854	35
00758	Toa Alta	31,910	28
00759	Toa Baja	78,246	24
00760	Trujillo Alto	51,389	21
00761	Utuado	34,505	115
00762	Vega Alta	28,696	28
00763	Vega Baja	47,115	48
00765	Vieques	7,662	53
00766	Villalba	20,734	37
00767	Yabucoa	31,425	55
00768	Yauco	37,742	69
Total		**3,196,520**	**3,459**

ZIP code	Area	Pop.	Land area sq. mile
	American Samoa		
96799	American Samoa	32,395	77
	Guam		
	Guam	**105,821**	**209**
96910	Agana	881	1
	Agana Hts.	3,284	1
96915	Agat	3,979	10
	Asan	2,024	6
96913	Barrigada	7,762	9
	Chalan-Pago-Ordot	3,135	6
96912	Dededo	23,646	30
96916	Inarajan	2,062	19
	Mangilao	6,810	10
96916	Merizo	1,658	6
	Mongmong-Toto-Maite	5,230	2
	Piti	1,518	7
96915	Santa Rita	10,408	17
	Sinajana	2,471	1
	Talofofo	2,016	17
96911	Tamuning	13,537	6
	Umatac	732	6
	Yigo	10,435	35
96914	Yona	4,233	20
	Virgin Islands		
	St. Croix	49,013	80
	St. John	2,360	20
	St. Thomas	44,218	32
00801	Charlotte Amalie	11,756	
00820	Christiansted	2,856	
00840	Frederiksted	1,054	
Total		**95,591**	**132**
	Trust Territory of Pacific Islands		
	Kosrae	NA	42
	Marshall Islands	NA	70
	Palau	NA	192
	Ponape	NA	176
	Truk	NA	49
	Yap	NA	46
Total		**NA**	**533**
	No. Mariana Islands	**16,758**	**184**

Women 1982: The Year That Time Ran Out

by June Foley

1982 was the year that time ran out for the proposed equal rights amendment. Eleanor Smeal, president of the National Organization for Women, the group that headed the intense, 10-year struggle for the ERA, conceded defeat on June 24. Only 24 words in all, the ERA read simply: "Equality of rights under the law shall not be denied or abridged by the United States or by any state on account of sex." Two major opinion polls had reported just weeks before the ERA's defeat that a majority of Americans continued to favor the amendment.

The effort to achieve an equal rights amendment dated from 1923, when legislation was first introduced in Congress. By 1972, the proposed amendment passed the House and Senate by wide margins. The bill stipulated a period of 5 years during which three-fourths of the state legislatures had to ratify the amendment in order for it to become part of the Constitution. Two hours after clearing Congress, the ERA was ratified by Hawaii. A year later it had been ratified by 30 states.

However, between 1973 and 1977, only 5 more states ratified, while 5 rescinded ratification. As the deadline approached, the amendment was 3 states short of the necessary 38. In the fall of 1978, Congress granted a 3-year, 3-month extension to June 30, 1982. But not one state passed the amendment after 1977. In mid-June 1982, the ERA went down to certain defeat with its rejection by the legislatures of Illinois and Florida—the 2 states in which supporters believed it had the best last chance.

NOW's Smeal said the blame for the defeat could not be placed solely on state legislators who voted against the proposed amendment. The real opposition, she said, was special corporate interests that profit from sex discrimination by paying lower wages to women and charging higher insurance rates. Smeal maintained that major corporate interests made large contributions to the ERA opposition.

Others attributed the defeat to the political expertise and media savvy of Phyllis Schlafly, the Illinois housewife who founded Stop-ERA. Schlafly had characterized ERA activists as "a bunch of anti-family radicals and lesbians." She received tremendous publicity about her insistence that the ERA meant government-financed abortions, marriage licenses for homosexuals, unisex toilets, and the invalidation of laws requiring husbands to support their dependent wives and children.

Still others believed that Schlafly's significance was magnified by the mistakes of feminists. Several major strategies were singled out as ill-conceived. For example, the 1977 NOW boycott aimed at the states of Illinois, Florida, Georgia, Louisiana, Missouri, and Nevada did not result in a single new ratification. Schlafly claimed that the boycott was unfair, because, in lobbying major organizations against holding meetings and conventions in these states, it mainly penalized such people as waitresses, bellhops, and hotel maids, and thus backfired for NOW. In addition, the 39-month extension angered a number of legislators, some of them pro-ERA. The *New York Times, Washington Post,* and *Chicago Tribune,* among other respected newspapers, referred to the extension with such words as "unfair" and "a dangerous precedent." Further, Congress's decision not to allow rescissions was unpopular. (In any case, on December 23, 1981 U.S. District Court Judge Marion J. Callister ruled that the extension was illegal and that the 5 states that had rescinded between 1973 and 1977 had the power to do so. NOW announced that it would appeal the decision to the Supreme Court, but the Court had yet to hear the case when the ERA was defeated.)

Schlafly called the failure of the ERA "the most remarkable political victory of the 20th century." She said her 50,000 member organization, Eagle Forum, would now campaign against the nuclear freeze, sex education in the schools, and feminist-influenced school textbooks.

NOW Plans Political and Legal Battles

Smeal said NOW would only pursue the ERA again after "we've made a dent in the memberships of Congress and state legislatures" by electing more women and more feminist men. On August 26, NOW celebrated the 62nd anniversary of women's winning the right to vote by launching a $3 million fund-raising drive to support candidates who favored the ERA. Smeal said that NOW planned to have more than 80 political action committees in 39 states before the elections. She said that $1 million of the money would go to local and state contests and $2 million to federal races.

Along with the political fight, NOW planned legal battles. "In the absence of a national mandate and clear policy statement," stated Phyllis N. Segal, legal director of NOW's Legal Defense and Education Fund, NOW would "apply and defend the progress that has been made and develop tools to take the profit and habit out of sexual discrimination." Segal added: "To do this case by case, law by law, is expensive and not very glamorous. But by choosing our cases carefully, we'll be involved where our impact is greatest." Potential issues, Segal said, were: obtaining equal pay for equal or comparable work; ending sexual discrimination in pension and insurance plans; increasing access to blue-collar jobs; changing laws on family and domestic relations to benefit women; and increasing educational opportunities for women.

Meanwhile, other women's rights activists were taking a close look at Title IX of the Education Amendments of 1972, which prohibits sex discrimination in schools receiving Federal aid. Laws to enforce this measure did not appear until 1975, and the courts have not yet defined its scope. The Women's Law Center in Washington had a suit pending against the Department of Education, charging the Department with failing to enforce Title IX adequately. In another case handled by the Women's Law Center, 11 women sued Temple University in Philadelphia for alleged sexual discrimination in the school's athletic department.

In another crucial legal area, the Women's Rights Project of the American Civil Liberties Union was investigating Title VII of the Civil Rights Act of 1964, which prohibits employers of more than 15 workers to discriminate on the basis of sex, race, color, religion, or national origin. The group is attempting to eliminate the experience requirements for long-distance truck drivers in Georgia, and to challenge the upper-age limits of apprenticeship programs in New York's construction industry. In state courts, women were attempting to change laws involving child custody, child support, the disposition of marital property, and credit. In some instances, these cases were being pursued under the equal rights amendments adopted by 16 states.

The Feminization of Poverty

Many of these court-tested issues can be summed up as an attempt to end a process termed "the feminization of poverty." A 1981 study by the National Advisory Council on Economic Opportunity predicted that if the present trends of limited job opportunities, rising divorce rates, and a weak economy were to continue, by the year 2001 nearly all the nation's poor would be women and children.

A recent study prepared for the Equal Employment Opportunity Commission underscored these predictions. The study found that women were concentrated in low-paying occupations, were more likely to work for low-paying concerns, and were "systematically underpaid." Estimating that "women's work" paid about $4,000 a year less than work usually performed by men, the study recommended that the concept of "comparable worth" be considered as a means of reducing, if not eradicating, sexual discrimination. The idea of comparable worth involves measuring the value of such traditional women's occupations as typist, librarian, and receptionist against such traditional men's occupations as construction worker, security guard, and machine operator.

"Comparable worth" was an issue in a Bureau of Labor Statistics study, as well. This study found that the median weekly earnings of women were much lower than those of men doing *the same work* in many occupations. For example, women held 90.6% of the bookkeeping jobs, but earned an average of $98 a week less than men who held the same job; female elementary school teachers earned an average of $68 a week less than males, even though women held 82.2% of those jobs; male administrators of elementary and secondary schools earned an average of $520 a week against $363 for women; male computer systems analysts received an average weekly salary of $546 while their female counterparts earned $420. The study concluded that employers tended to value traditional women's jobs less than those of men, even when those jobs were comparably productive. "The work women do is paid less, and the more an occupation is dominated by women, the less it pays," according to the report.

Family Planning

Many women's rights advocates were concerned about a Reagan Administration regulation that went into effect at the end of April 1982, requiring notification of parents when young women under age 18 requested contraceptive devices from federally-funded clinics. Opponents of the proposal maintained that it would deter teenagers from visiting the clinics, and would result in increased teenage pregnancy. A recent study of young patients at federally-funded family planning clinics suggested that 25% would stop applying for prescription contraceptives if their parents were notified, but only 2% said they would stop sexual activity. Most agencies said that they did in fact encourage teenagers to inform their families of clinic visits, and that a majority did so.

Family planning advocates also experienced a setback in March, when the Senate Judiciary Committee approved a Constitutional amendment that could enable Congress and individual states to adopt laws banning abortion. The measure was sponsored by Sen. Orrin G. Hatch (R, Ut.). The vote was the first time that a full Congressional committee had supported an anti-abortion amendment, and it opened the way to a full-fledged floor debate on the issue. Dr. J.C. Wilkie, president of the National Right to Life Committee, called the vote a "major victory" and a "milestone." However, opponents of abortion lost a second Senate test in August, when a proposal of Sen. Jesse Helms (R, N.C.) to restrict access to abortion was unsuccessful.

Advocates of legal abortion gathered in Washington in June to hear leaders of the National Abortion Rights League plan its most aggressive campaign to date. The pro-choice forces said they were not trying to change people's minds about abortion. They pointed out that national polls consistently showed 60 to 80% support for legalized abortions, and said they planned to mobilize this majority. League leaders specified the major legislative threat as a bill introduced by Sen. Mark O. Hatfield (R, Ore.) that would restrict all Federal funds for abortions, cut off funds for medical schools that taught techniques in abortion and for birth control clinics that made abortion referrals—unless a woman's life were endangered. In effect, the proposal would make permanent the prohibitions enacted in the last 5 years.

Significant Gains?

Were there no important gains for women over the last year? There were a few. In the courts, the Supreme Court broadened the interpretation of Title IX of the Education Amendments of 1972, which prohibits sexual discrimination in education programs or activities receiving federal financial assistance. The Court ruled that this law covered employees as well as students. Also, the Supreme Court ruled unanimously that subsidiaries of Japanese companies incorporated and doing business in the U.S. must follow American laws against discrimination in employment, under Title VII of the Civil Rights Act of 1964. Further, a Federal District judge ordered the Univ. of South Alabama to pay about $1 million in back wages to female faculty members and administrators in one of the largest sex discrimination lawsuits filed against a university.

For the most part, however, 1982 could be most optimistically summed up in the words of Pat Carbine, publisher of Ms. magazine. At a celebration of the tenth anniversary of Ms., Carbine acknowledged: "We are in a very long process for full equality."

America's 25 Most Influential Women in 1982

The following women were chosen by The World Almanac co-sponsoring newspapers. In first place as America's most influential woman is Sandra Day O'Connor, 52, the first female U.S. Supreme Court justice, who makes her first appearance on the list.

Arts

Beverly Sills, general director of the New York City Opera.

Sarah Caldwell, director of the Boston Opera Company.

Business

Katharine Graham, Washington Post. Co. board chairman.

Mary Cunningham, a vice president of Joseph E. Seagram & Sons' New York subsidiary.

Education, Scholarship, Science

Barbara Jordan, professor, University of Texas at Austin.

Rosalyn Yalow, Nobel Prize-winning physicist.

Barbara Tuchman, historian, bestselling author.

Entertainment

Katharine Hepburn, 1981 Academy Award-winner for film "On Golden Pond."

Carol Burnett, actress, comedienne, star of film "Annie."

Brooke Shields, model, actress, star of film "Endless Love."

Government

Sandra Day O'Connor, U.S. Supreme Court justice.

Jeane J. Kirkpatrick, U.N. ambassador.

Jane Byrne, mayor of Chicago.

Nancy Reagan, First Lady.

Millicent Fenwick, U.S. Representative (R, N.J.).

Media

Ann Landers, advice columnist.

Ellen Goodman, syndicated Boston-Globe columnist.

Barbara Walters, ABC-TV journalist.

Sylvia Porter, financial columnist.

Abigail Van Buren, advice columnist.

Social Activists

Eleanor Smeal, president of National Organization for Women.

Phyllis Schlafly, head of Stop-ERA.

Gloria Steinem, editor of Ms. magazine.

Sports

Billie Jean King, veteran tennis player and feminist.

Chris Evert Lloyd, tennis player.

Presidential Election Statistics

Popular and Electoral Vote, 1976 and 1980

Source: Clerk of the House of Representatives, Federal Election Commission

	1976				1980				
States	Electoral Vote Carter	Electoral Vote Ford	Democrat Carter	Republican Ford	Electoral Vote Carter	Electoral Vote Reagan	Democrat Carter	Republican Reagan	Indep. Anderson
Ala. . . .	9		659,170	504,070	0	9	636,730	654,192	16,481
Alas. . .		3	44,058	71,555	0	3	41,842	86,112	11,156
Ariz. . . .		6	295,602	418,642	0	6	246,843	529,688	76,952
Ark. . . .	6		498,604	267,903	0	6	398,041	403,164	22,468
Cal. . . .		45	3,742,284	3,882,244	0	45	3,083,652	4,524,835	739,832
Col. . . .		7	460,353	584,367	0	7	368,009	652,264	130,633
Conn. . .		8	647,895	719,261	0	8	541,732	677,210	171,807
Del. . . .	3		122,596	109,831	0	3	105,754	111,252	16,288
D.C. . . .	3		137,818	27,873	3	0	130,231	23,313	16,131
Fla. . . .	17		1,636,000	1,469,531	0	17	1,419,475	2,046,951	189,692
Ga. . . .	12		979,409	483,743	12	0	890,733	654,168	36,055
Ha. . . .	4		147,375	140,003	4	0	135,879	130,112	32,021
Ida. . . .		4	126,549	204,151	0	4	110,192	290,699	27,058
Ill.		26	2,271,295	2,364,269	0	26	1,981,413	2,358,094	346,754
Ind. . . .		13	1,014,714	1,185,958	0	13	844,197	1,255,656	111,639
Ia.		8	619,931	632,863	0	8	508,672	676,026	115,633
Kan. . .		7	430,421	502,752	0	7	326,150	566,812	68,231
Ky. . . .	9		615,717	531,852	0	9	617,417	635,274	31,127
La. . . .	10		661,365	587,446	0	10	708,453	792,853	26,345
Me. . . .		4	232,279	236,320	0	4	220,974	238,522	53,327
Md. . . .	10		759,612	672,661	10	0	726,161	680,606	119,537
Mass. . .	14		1,429,475	1,030,276	0	14	1,053,802	1,056,223	382,539
Mich. . .		21	1,696,714	1,893,742	0	21	1,661,532	1,915,225	275,223
Minn. . .	10		1,070,440	819,395	10	0	954,173	873,268	174,997
Miss. . .	7		381,309	366,846	0	7	429,281	441,089	12,036
Mo. . . .	12		999,163	928,808	0	12	931,182	1,074,181	77,920
Mon. . .		4	149,259	173,703	0	4	118,032	206,814	29,281
Neb. . .		5	233,287	359,219	0	5	166,424	419,214	44,854
Nev. . .		3	92,479	101,273	0	3	66,666	155,017	17,651
N.H.. . .		4	147,645	185,935	0	4	108,864	221,705	49,693
N.J. . . .		17	1,444,653	1,509,688	0	17	1,147,364	1,546,557	234,632
N.M. . .		4	201,148	211,419	0	4	167,826	250,779	29,459
N.Y. . . .	41		3,389,558	3,100,791	0	41	2,728,372	2,893,831	467,801
N.C. . . .	13		927,365	741,960	0	13	875,635	915,018	52,800
N.D.. . .		3	136,078	153,470	0	3	79,189	193,695	23,640
Oh. . . .	25		2,011,621	2,000,505	0	25	1,752,414	2,206,545	254,472
Okla. . .		8	532,442	545,708	0	8	402,026	695,570	38,284
Ore. . . .		6	490,407	492,120	0	6	456,890	571,044	112,389
Pa. . . .	27		2,328,677	2,205,604	0	27	1,937,540	2,261,872	292,921
R.I. . . .	4		227,636	181,249	4	0	198,342	154,793	59,819
S.C. . . .	8		450,807	346,149	0	8	428,220	439,277	13,868
S.D. . . .		4	147,068	151,505	0	4	103,855	198,343	21,431
Tenn. . .	10		825,879	633,969	0	10	783,051	787,761	35,991
Tex. . . .	26		2,082,319	1,953,300	0	26	1,881,147	2,510,705	111,613
Ut. . . .		4	182,110	337,908	0	4	124,266	439,687	30,284
Vt.		3	78,789	100,387	0	3	81,952	94,628	31,761
Va. . . .		12	813,896	836,554	0	12	752,174	989,609	95,418
Wash. .		8*	717,323	777,732	0	9	650,193	865,244	185,073
W.Va. . .	6		435,864	314,726	6	0	367,462	334,206	31,691
Wis. . . .	11		1,040,232	1,004,987	0	11	981,584	1,088,845	160,657
Wyo. . .		3	62,239	92,717	0	3	49,427	110,700	12,072
Total . .	**297**	**240**	**40,828,929**	**39,148,940**	**49**	**489**	**35,481,435**	**43,899,248**	**5,719,437**

*One elector in Washington for Reagan. In 1976, McCarthy (Independent) received 739,256 votes; McBride (Libertarian) received 171,818 votes.

Presidential Election Returns by Counties

Compiled from official state returns by The World Almanac.

Alabama

County	1976 Carter (D)	1976 Ford (R)	1980 Carter (D)	1980 Reagan (R)	1980 Anderson (I)
Autauga	4,640	4,512	4,295	6,292	125
Baldwin	9,191	13,256	8,448	18,652	414
Barbour	4,730	3,758	4,458	4,171	65
Bibb	2,850	1,591	3,097	2,491	22
Blount	6,645	4,233	5,656	6,819	75
Bullock	3,536	1,482	3,960	1,446	29
Butler	4,271	2,909	4,156	3,810	59
Calhoun	20,466	11,763	17,017	17,475	433
Chambers	6,164	5,488	6,649	4,864	122
Cherokee	4,668	1,492	3,764	2,482	63
Chilton	5,550	4,725	4,706	6,615	60
Choctaw	3,911	3,033	3,680	2,859	22
Clarke	4,737	4,126	5,249	5,059	55
Clay	2,946	1,883	2,858	2,764	34
Cleburne	2,490	1,436	2,050	2,389	34
Coffee	7,844	4,683	6,140	6,760	189
Colbert	11,996	4,471	12,550	6,619	209
Conecuh	3,086	1,812	3,102	2,948	29
Coosa	2,533	1,196	2,383	1,714	19
Covington	7,081	4,977	6,305	7,014	110
Crenshaw	3,372	1,801	2,704	2,478	39
Cullman	12,961	6,899	11,525	10,212	228
Dale	6,346	4,996	4,936	7,247	134
Dallas	8,866	7,144	9,770	7,647	131
DeKalb	9,759	6,597	8,820	9,673	107
Elmore	6,646	6,551	5,947	8,688	171
Escambia	5,957	4,934	5,148	6,513	87
Etowah	25,020	10,333	20,790	16,177	358
Fayette	4,076	2,165	3,389	3,315	47
Franklin	6,279	3,345	6,136	4,448	51
Geneva	5,983	2,663	4,703	4,747	67
Greene	2,900	903	3,474	1,034	16
Hale	3,236	2,034	3,583	2,074	56
Henry	3,144	2,052	2,973	2,813	18
Houston	8,787	10,672	7,848	14,884	184
Jackson	10,989	3,913	8,776	4,897	156
Jefferson	99,531	113,590	113,069	132,612	3,509
Lamar	3,860	1,739	3,366	2,778	16
Lauderdale	15,549	7,226	15,379	10,467	431
Lawrence	6,810	1,415	6,112	2,456	64
Lee	8,427	9,884	9,606	10,982	643
Limestone	8,803	2,997	8,180	4,574	183
Lowndes	3,732	1,621	3,577	1,524	15
Macon	5,915	1,387	7,028	1,259	36
Madison	35,497	20,959	30,469	30,604	2,246
Marengo	4,731	3,841	5,178	4,048	35
Marion	6,244	3,036	5,450	5,182	61
Marshall	13,696	6,006	10,854	8,159	283
Mobile	50,264	53,835	46,180	67,515	1,333
Monroe	3,669	3,476	4,262	4,615	43
Montgomery	24,641	29,360	28,018	35,745	985
Morgan	16,547	9,058	14,703	13,214	457
Perry	4,486	2,164	4,208	2,262	28
Pickens	3,776	2,969	4,504	3,582	61
Pike	5,387	4,363	4,417	5,220	83
Randolph	3,539	2,286	3,378	3,279	58
Russell	8,077	4,150	8,123	4,485	137
St. Clair	5,653	4,877	5,236	7,768	121
Shelby	7,197	9,035	7,396	14,957	407
Sumter	3,457	2,191	5,015	2,104	45
Talladega	10,577	6,425	10,159	9,902	140
Tallapoosa	7,614	5,237	7,260	5,958	96
Tuscaloosa	20,275	16,021	19,103	19,750	789
Walker	16,232	7,389	13,616	8,795	82
Washington	3,471	2,171	3,520	3,045	24
Wilcox	3,723	1,824	4,951	2,280	13
Winston	4,134	3,710	3,368	4,981	39
Totals	**659,170**	**504,070**	**636,730**	**654,192**	**16,481**

Alabama Vote Since 1932

1932 (Pres.), Roosevelt, Dem., 207,910; Hoover, Rep., 34,675; Foster, Com., 406; Thomas, Soc. 2,030; Upshaw, Proh., 13.

1936 (Pres.), Roosevelt, Dem., 238,195; Landon, Rep., 35,358; Colvin, Proh., 719; Browder, Com., 679; Lemke, Union, 549; Thomas, Soc., 242.

1940 (Pres.), Roosevelt, Dem., 250,726; Willkie, Rep., 42,174; Babson, Proh., 698; Browder, Com., 509; Thomas, Soc., 100.

1944 (Pres.), Roosevelt, Dem., 198,918; Dewey, Rep., 44,540; Watson, Proh., 1,095; Thomas, Soc., 190.

1948 (Pres.), Thurmond, States' Rights, 171,443; Dewey, Rep., 40,930; Wallace, Prog., 1,522; Watson, Proh., 1,085.

1952 (Pres.), Eisenhower, Rep., 149,231; Stevenson, Dem., 275,075; Hamblen, Proh., 1,814.

1956 (Pres.), Stevenson, Dem., 290,844; Eisenhower, Rep. 195,694; Independent electors, 20,323.

1960 (Pres.), Kennedy, Dem., 324,050; Nixon, Rep., 237,981; Faubus, States' Rights, 4,367; Decker, Proh., 2,106; King, Afro-Americans, 1,485; scattering, 236.

1964 (Pres.), Dem. 209,848 (electors unpledged); Goldwater, Rep., 479,085; scattering, 105.

1968 (Pres.), Nixon, Rep., 146,923; Humphrey, Dem., 196,579; Wallace, 3d party, 691,425; Munn, Proh., 4,022.

1972 (Pres.), Nixon, Rep., 728,701; McGovern, Dem., 219,108 plus 37,815 Natl. Demo. Party of Alabama; Schmitz, Conservative, 11,918; Munn., Proh., 8,551.

1976 (Pres.), Carter, Dem., 659,170; Ford, Rep., 504,070; Maddox, Am. Ind., 9,198; Bubar, Proh., 6,669; Hall, Com., 1,954; MacBride, Libertarian, 1,481.

1980 (Pres.), Reagan, Rep., 654,192; Carter, Dem., 636,730; Anderson, Libertarian, 16,481; Rarick, Amer. Ind., 15,010; Clark, Libertarian, 13,318; Bubar, Statesman, 1,743; Hall, Com., 1,629; DeBerry, Soc. Work., 1,303; McReynolds, Socialist, 1,006; Commoner, Citizens, 517.

Alaska

Election District	1976 Carter (D)	1976 Ford (R)	1980 Carter (D)	1980 Reagan (R)	1980 Anderson (I)
No. 1	1,983	2,994	1,772	3,473	440
No. 2	1,022	1,423	1,256	1,612	329
No. 3	1,152	1,710	1,354	2,019	346
No. 4	3,214	5,252	3,899	5,345	1,282
No. 5	1,307	2,071	973	2,847	288
No. 6	1,486	2,882	1,316	5,008	402
No. 7	2,935	4,105	2,620	4,311	676
No. 8	3,368	5,412	2,860	7,432	737
No. 9	1,726	2,561	1,164	2,363	342
No. 10	2,839	6,837	2,778	7,659	849
No. 11	3,568	6,588	3,308	9,741	1,016
No. 12	2,700	6,381	2,456	7,450	829
No. 13	2,099	4,057	1,806	6,170	479
No. 14	856	1,380	844	1,473	254
No. 15	538	746	710	832	213
No. 16	876	1,063	1,083	869	204
No. 17	1,149	1,074	1,623	720	280
No. 18	804	942	1,327	769	193
No. 19	1,415	1,893	1,168	2,255	267
No. 20	6,706	10,306	5,310	11,673	1,304
No. 21	1,229	749	1,022	1,010	223
No. 22	1,086	1,129	1,193	1,081	202
Totals	**44,058**	**71,555**	**41,842**	**86,112**	**11,155**

Alaska Vote Since 1960

1960 (Pres.), Kennedy, Dem., 29,809; Nixon, Rep. 30,953.

1964 (Pres.), Johnson, Dem., 44,329; Goldwater, Rep., 22,930.

1968 (Pres.), Nixon, Rep., 37,600; Humphrey, Dem., 35,411; Wallace, 3d party, 10,024.

1972 (Pres.), Nixon, Rep., 55,349; McGovern, Dem., 32,967; Schmitz, American, 6,903.

1976 (Pres.), Carter, Dem., 44,058; Ford, Rep., 71,555; MacBride, Libertarian, 6,785.

1980 (Pres.), Reagan, Rep., 86,112; Carter, Dem., 41,842; Clark, Libertarian, 18,479; Anderson, Ind., 11,155; Write-in, 857.

Arizona

County	1976 Carter (D)	1976 Ford (R)	1980 Carter (D)	1980 Reagan (R)	1980 Anderson (I)
Apache	6,583	3,447	3,917	5,991	495
Cochise	9,281	9,921	7,028	13,351	1,656
Coconino	9,450	11,036	7,832	14,613	2,815
Gila	6,440	5,136	5,068	7,405	656
Graham	3,050	3,659	2,801	4,765	268
Greenlee	2,601	1,532	2,043	1,537	150
Maricopa	144,613	258,262	119,752	316,287	38,975
Mohave	6,504	7,601	4,900	13,809	978
Navajo	7,323	6,796	5,110	10,790	710
Pima	71,214	77,264	64,418	93,055	25,294
Pinal	10,595	9,354	9,207	12,195	1,346
Santa Cruz	2,265	2,312	2,089	2,674	482
Yavapai	7,685	12,998	6,664	19,823	1,754
Yuma	7,998	9,324	6,014	13,393	1,373
Totals	**295,602**	**418,642**	**246,843**	**529,688**	**76,952**

Arizona Vote Since 1932

1932 (Pres.), Roosevelt, Dem., 79,264; Hoover, Rep., 36,104; Thomas, Soc., 2,618; Foster, Com., 256.

1936 (Pres.), Roosevelt, Dem., 86,722; Landon, Rep., 33,433; Lemke, Union, 3,307; Colvin, Proh., 384; Thomas, Soc., 317.

1940 (Pres.), Roosevelt, Dem., 95,267; Willkie, Rep., 54,030; Babson, Proh., 742.

1944 (Pres.), Roosevelt, Dem., 80,926; Dewey, Rep., 56,287; Watson, Proh., 421.

1948 (Pres.), Truman, Dem., 95,251; Dewey, Rep., 77,597; Wallace, Prog., 3,310; Watson, Proh., 786; Teichert, Soc. Labor, 121.

1952 (Pres.), Eisenhower, Rep., 152,042; Stevenson, Dem., 108,528.

1956 (Pres.), Eisenhower, Rep., 176,990; Stevenson, Dem., 112,880; Andrews, Ind. 303.

1960 (Pres.), Kennedy, Dem., 176,781; Nixon, Rep., 221,241; Hass, Soc. Labor, 469.

1964 (Pres.), Johnson, Dem., 237,753; Goldwater, Rep., 242,535; Hass, Soc. Labor, 482.

1968 (Pres.), Nixon, Rep., 266,721; Humphrey, Dem., 170,514; Wallace, 3d party, 46,573; McCarthy, New Party, 2,751; Halstead, Soc. Worker, 85; Cleaver, Peace and Freedom, 217; Blomen, Soc. Labor, 75.

1972 (Pres.), Nixon, Rep., 402,812; McGovern, Dem., 198,540; Schmitz, Amer., 21,208; Soc. Workers, 30,945. (Due to ballot peculiarities in 3 counties (particularly Pima), thousands of voters cast ballots for the Socialist Workers Party *and* one of the major candidates. Court ordered both votes counted as official.

1976 (Pres.), Carter, Dem., 295,602; Ford, Rep., 418,642; McCarthy, Ind., 19,229; MacBride, Libertarian, 7,647; Camejo, Soc. Workers, 928; Anderson, Amer., 564; Maddox, Am. Ind., 85.

1980 (Pres.), Reagan, Rep., 529,688; Carter, Dem., 246,843; Anderson, Ind., 76,952; Clark, Libertarian, 18,784; De Berry, Soc. Workers, 1,100; Commoner, Citizens, 551; Hall, Com., 25; Griswold, Workers World, 2.

Arkansas

County	1976 Carter (D)	1976 Ford (R)	1980 Carter (D)	1980 Reagan (R)	1980 Anderson (I)
Arkansas	5,640	2,480	4,303	3,409	193
Ashley	5,253	3,092	4,552	3,960	130
Baxter	5,766	5,885	4,789	9,684	494
Benton	11,289	12,670	9,231	18,830	1,018
Boone	5,388	3,959	4,576	6,778	429
Bradley	3,567	1,134	3,139	1,650	66
Calhoun	2,014	495	1,438	896	52
Carroll	3,791	2,804	2,977	4,273	298
Chicot	3,868	1,621	3,445	2,239	26
Clark	6,641	1,816	6,122	2,743	215
Clay	5,664	1,893	3,985	3,091	121
Cleburne	5,726	1,992	4,021	4,042	204
Cleveland	2,320	646	1,856	1,124	36
Columbia	4,708	4,287	4,445	5,259	107
Conway	6,443	2,177	4,698	4,145	232
Craighead	13,840	6,213	9,231	11,010	708
Crawford	5,946	4,764	3,948	8,542	245
Crittenden	8,249	5,202	7,022	6,248	185
Cross	4,198	1,909	3,471	2,895	89
Dallas	3,266	1,012	2,838	1,596	74
Desha	4,228	1,372	3,748	2,057	77
Drew	3,750	1,730	3,757	2,272	117
Faulkner	11,423	3,904	8,528	7,544	769
Franklin	3,703	1,973	2,716	3,448	197
Fulton	2,670	1,038	2,037	2,101	83
Garland	15,707	10,394	12,515	15,739	1,042
Grant	3,797	1,047	3,078	2,007	102
Greene	7,495	2,690	5,996	4,514	219
Hempstead	5,397	2,859	4,671	3,852	72
Hot Spring	7,809	2,187	6,897	3,561	244
Howard	3,207	1,575	2,564	2,386	63
Independence	7,116	2,878	5,683	5,076	276
Izard	3,328	1,394	2,750	2,266	160
Jackson	6,456	1,783	4,651	3,191	174
Jefferson	21,001	8,034	17,292	10,697	802
Johnson	5,044	2,173	3,709	3,619	187
Lafayette	2,342	1,467	1,947	1,756	47
Lawrence	5,167	1,708	3,547	3,245	117
Lee	3,463	1,574	3,103	1,711	47
Lincoln	3,045	699	2,517	1,243	56
Little River	3,142	1,431	2,631	2,272	41
Logan	5,313	2,909	4,098	4,511	166
Lonoke	7,761	2,522	5,605	5,619	246
Madison	2,926	2,502	2,434	3,180	126
Marion	2,979	2,045	2,046	3,059	160
Miller	6,821	4,737	5,996	6,770	105
Mississippi	10,292	6,009	8,908	7,170	234
Monroe	3,556	1,285	2,686	2,027	82
Montgomery	2,420	924	1,878	1,585	86
Nevada	3,101	1,163	2,631	1,697	50
Newton	1,840	1,641	1,436	2,423	100
Ouachita	8,946	2,753	7,152	4,329	248
Perry	2,310	832	1,606	1,459	73
Phillips	7,774	3,342	6,642	4,270	163
Pike	2,822	1,234	2,094	1,916	58
Poinsett	6,835	2,726	4,894	4,040	153
Polk	3,505	2,432	2,617	3,993	139
Pope	8,355	4,348	6,364	7,217	471
Prairie	2,836	813	1,928	1,855	64
Pulaski	63,541	37,690	54,839	52,125	4,657
Randolph	4,551	1,571	3,070	2,579	125
St. Francis	6,851	3,639	5,816	4,485	132
Saline	12,008	4,123	10,368	8,330	643
Scott	2,880	1,427	2,236	2,228	92
Searcy	2,067	1,767	1,536	2,459	101
Sebastian	15,698	17,665	10,141	23,403	1,023
Sevier	3,391	1,468	2,854	2,502	97
Sharp	3,532	2,151	2,774	3,420	160
Stone	2,718	1,014	1,968	1,793	133
Union	8,257	7,918	6,852	9,401	313
Van Buren	4,004	1,624	2,968	3,090	153
Washington	15,610	14,132	12,276	20,788	1,737
White	11,412	4,756	8,750	8,079	309
Woodruff	3,040	848	2,452	1,204	74
Yell	5,785	1,932	3,702	3,187	181
Totals	**498,604**	**267,903**	**398,041**	**403,164**	**22,468**

Arkansas Vote Since 1932

1932 (Pres.), Roosevelt, Dem., 189,602; Hoover, Rep., 28,467; Thomas, Soc., 1,269; Harvey, Ind., 1,049; Foster, Com., 175.

1936 (Pres.), Roosevelt, Dem. 146,765; Landon, Rep., 32,039; Thomas, Soc., 446; Browder, Com., 164; Lemke, Union, 4.

1940 (Pres.), Roosevelt, Dem., 158,622; Willkie, Rep., 42,121; Babson, Proh., 793; Thomas, Soc., 305.

1944 (Pres.), Roosevelt, Dem., 148,965; Dewey, Rep., 63,551; Thomas, Soc. 438.

1948 (Pres.), Truman, Dem., 149,659; Dewey, Rep., 50,959; Thurmond, States' Rights, 40,068; Thomas, Soc., 1,037; Wallace, Prog., 751; Watson, Proh., 1.

1952 (Pres.), Eisenhower, Rep., 177,155; Stevenson, Dem., 226,300; Hamblen, Proh., 886; MacArthur, Christian Nationalist, 458; Hass, Soc. Labor, 1.

1956 (Pres.), Stevenson, Dem., 213,277; Eisenhower, Rep., 186,287; Andrews, Ind., 7,008.

1960 (Pres.), Kennedy, Dem., 215,049; Nixon, Rep., 184,508; Nat'l. States' Rights, 28,952.

1964 (Pres.), Johnson, Dem., 314,197; Goldwater, Rep., 243,264; Kasper, Nat'l. States Rights, 2,965.

1968 (Pres.), Nixon, Rep., 189,062; Humphrey, Dem., 184,901; Wallace, 3d party, 235,627.

1972 (Pres.), Nixon, Rep., 445,751; McGovern, Dem., 198,899; Schmitz, Amer. , 3,016.

1976 (Pres.), Carter, Dem., 498,604; Ford, Rep., 267,903; McCarthy, Ind., 639; Anderson, Amer., 389.

1980 (Pres.), Reagan, Rep., 403,164; Carter, Dem., 398,041; Anderson, Ind., 22,468; Clark, Libertarian, 8,970; Commoner, Citizens, 2,345; Bubar, Statesman, 1,350; Hall, Comm., 1,244.

California

County	1976 Carter (D)	1976 Ford (R)	1980 Carter (D)	1980 Reagan (R)	1980 Anderson (I)
Alameda	235,988	155,280	201,720	158,531	40,834
Alpine	189	255	133	254	50
Amador	4,037	3,699	3,191	5,401	788
Butte	24,203	28,400	19,520	38,188	6,108
Calaveras	3,607	3,695	3,076	6,054	776
Colusa	2,340	2,733	1,605	2,897	325
Contra Costa	123,742	126,598	107,398	144,112	28,209
Del Norte	2,789	2,481	2,338	4,016	486
El Dorado	12,763	12,472	10,765	21,238	3,287
Fresno	74,958	72,533	65,254	82,515	10,727
Glenn	3,501	4,094	2,227	5,386	537
Humboldt	23,500	18,034	17,113	24,047	5,440
Imperial	10,244	10,618	7,961	12,068	1,203
Inyo	2,635	3,905	2,080	5,201	515
Kern	50,567	58,023	41,097	72,842	5,799
Kings	8,061	8,263	7,299	10,531	901
Lake	6,374	5,462	5,978	8,934	1,157
Lassen	3,801	3,007	2,941	4,464	543
Los Angeles	1,221,893	1,174,926	979,830	1,224,533	175,882

	1976 (D)	1976 (R)	1980 (D)	1980 (R)	1980 (I)
Madera	7,625	6,844	7,783	10,599	1,013
Marin	43,590	53,425	39,231	49,678	13,805
Mariposa	2,093	2,012	1,889	3,082	458
Mendocino	10,653	9,784	10,784	12,432	2,747
Merced	16,637	14,842	15,886	18,043	2,316
Modoc	1,733	1,917	1,046	2,579	293
Mono	1,025	1,600	865	2,132	302
Monterey	36,849	40,896	29,086	47,452	8,008
Napa	18,048	20,839	14,898	23,632	4,218
Nevada	7,926	8,170	7,605	15,207	2,235
Orange	232,246	408,632	176,704	529,797	55,299
Placer	21,026	18,154	17,311	28,179	4,356
Plumas	3,429	2,884	2,911	4,182	783
Riverside	96,228	97,774	76,650	145,642	16,362
Sacramento	144,203	123,110	130,031	153,721	29,655
San Benito	3,122	3,398	2,749	4,054	552
San Bernardino	109,636	113,265	91,790	172,957	19,106
San Diego	263,654	353,302	195,410	435,910	67,491
San Francisco	133,733	103,561	133,184	80,967	29,365
San Joaquin	48,733	50,277	41,551	64,718	8,416
San Luis Obispo	24,926	27,785	20,508	38,631	8,407
San Mateo	102,896	117,338	87,335	116,491	27,985
Santa Barbara	55,018	60,922	40,650	69,629	14,786
Santa Clara	208,023	219,188	166,995	229,048	65,481
Santa Cruz	37,772	31,872	32,346	37,347	10,590
Shasta	19,200	17,273	15,364	27,547	3,220
Sierra	841	680	651	855	156
Siskiyou	7,060	7,070	5,664	9,331	1,269
Solano	33,682	26,136	30,952	40,919	6,713
Sonoma	50,353	50,555	45,596	60,722	14,068
Stanislaus	38,448	32,937	33,683	41,595	7,134
Sutter	6,966	8,745	5,103	11,778	1,089
Tehama	6,990	6,110	4,832	9,140	1,014
Trinity	2,172	1,989	1,734	3,048	506
Tulare	25,551	31,864	25,155	41,317	3,244
Tuolumne	6,492	6,104	5,449	8,810	1,390
Ventura	68,529	82,670	56,311	114,930	14,887
Yolo	23,533	18,376	21,527	19,603	6,669
Yuba	6,451	5,496	4,896	7,942	878
Totals	**3,742,284**	**3,882,244**	**3,083,661**	**4,524,858**	**739,833**

California Vote Since 1932

1932 (Pres.), Roosevelt, Dem., 1,324,157; Hoover, Rep., 847,902; Thomas, Soc., 63,299; Upshaw, Proh., 20,637; Harvey, Liberty, 9,827; Foster, Com., 1,023.

1936 (Pres.), Roosevelt, Dem., 1,766,836; Landon, Rep., 836,431; Colvin, Proh., 12,917; Thomas, Soc., 11,325; Browder, Com., 10,877.

1940 (Pres.), Roosevelt, Dem., 1,877,618; Willkie, Rep., 1,351,419; Thomas, Prog., 16,506; Browder, Com., 13,586; Babson, Proh., 9,400.

1944 (Pres.), Roosevelt, Dem., 1,988,564; Dewey, Rep., 1,512,965; Watson, Proh., 14,770; Thomas, Soc., 3,923; Teichert, Soc. Labor, 327.

1948 (Pres.), Truman, Dem., 1,913,134; Dewey, Rep., 1,895,269; Wallace, Prog., 190,381; Watson, Proh., 16,926; Thomas, Soc., 3,459; Thurmond, States' Rights, 1,228; Teichert, Soc. Labor, 195; Dobbs, Soc. Workers, 133.

1952 (Pres.), Eisenhower, Rep., 2,897,310; Stevenson, Dem., 2,197,548; Hallinan, Prog., 24,106; Hamblen, Proh., 15,653; MacArthur, (Tenny Ticket), 3,326; (Kellems Ticket) 178; Hass, Soc. Labor, 273; Hoopes, Soc., 206; scattered, 3,249.

1956 (Pres.), Eisenhower, Rep., 3,027,668; Stevenson, Dem., 2,420,136; Holtwick, Proh., 11,119; Andrews, Constitution, 6,087; Hass, Soc. Labor, 300; Hoopes, Soc., 123; Dobbs, Soc. Workers, 96; Smith, Christian Nat'l., 8.

1960 (Pres.), Kennedy, Dem., 3,224,099; Nixon, Rep., 3,259,722; Decker, Proh., 21,706; Hass, Soc. Labor, 1,051.

1964 (Pres.), Johnson, Dem., 4,171,877; Goldwater, Rep., 2,879,108; Hass, Soc. Labor, 489; DeBerry, Soc. Worker, 378; Munn, Proh., 305; Hensley, Universal, 19.

1968 (Pres.), Nixon, Rep., 3,467,664; Humphrey, Dem., 3,244,318; Wallace, 3d party, 487,270; Peace and Freedom party, 27,707; McCarthy, Alternative, 20,721; Gregory, write-in, 3,230; Mitchell, Com., 260; Munn, Proh., 59; Blomen, Soc. Labor, 341; Soeters, Defense, 17.

1972 (Pres.), Nixon, Rep., 4,602,096; McGovern, Dem., 3,475,847; Schmitz, Amer., 232,554; Spock, Peace and Freedom, 55,167; Hall, Com., 373; Hospers, Libertarian, 980; Munn, Proh., 53; Fisher, Soc. Labor, 197; Jenness, Soc. Workers, 574; Green, Universal, 21.

1976 (Pres.), Carter, Dem., 3,742,284; Ford, Rep., 3,882,244; MacBride, Libertarian, 56,388; Maddox, Am. Ind., 51,098; Wright, People's, 41,731; Camejo, Soc. Workers, 17,259; Hall, Com., 12,766; write-in, McCarthy, 58,412; other write-in, 4,935.

1980 (Pres.) Reagan, Rep. 4,524,858; Carter, Dem., 3,083,661; Anderson, Ind., 739,833; Clark, Libertarian, 148,434; Commoner, Ind. 61,063; Smith, Peace & Freedom, 18,116; Rarick, Amer. Ind., 9,856.

Colorado

County	1976 Carter (D)	1976 Ford (R)	1980 Carter (D)	1980 Reagan (R)	1980 Anderson (I)
Adams	40,551	35,392	31,357	42,916	8,342
Alamosa	2,052	2,599	1,821	2,601	289
Arapahoe	33,685	63,154	30,148	79,594	15,329
Archuleta	632	768	532	1,252	83
Baca	1,164	1,303	551	1,999	106
Bent	1,268	1,156	894	1,206	164
Boulder	33,284	42,830	28,422	40,698	13,712
Chaffee	2,064	2,925	1,583	3,327	432
Cheyenne	625	610	322	816	76
Clear Creek	1,069	1,477	837	1,784	402
Conejos	1,698	1,426	1,503	1,597	90
Costilla	1,033	392	1,036	489	38
Crowley	667	834	472	926	57
Custer	259	491	231	674	59
Delta	3,232	4,980	2,348	6,179	455
Denver	112,229	105,960	85,903	88,398	28,610
Dolores	374	343	157	615	32
Douglas	2,459	5,078	2,108	8,126	1,058
Eagle	1,502	2,963	1,608	3,061	906
Elbert	1,068	1,279	698	2,107	238
El Paso	32,911	50,929	27,463	66,199	7,886
Fremont	4,886	5,647	3,952	7,162	731
Garfield	2,852	4,699	2,639	5,416	978
Gilpin	563	451	441	694	175
Grand	910	1,703	820	2,133	413
Gunnison	1,250	2,568	1,297	2,756	704
Hinsdale	83	189	76	232	13
Huerfano	1,932	1,182	1,574	1,258	146
Jackson	279	455	283	673	80
Jefferson	52,782	87,080	41,525	97,008	19,530
Kiowa	529	598	331	754	61
Kit Carson	1,647	1,888	790	2,622	185
Lake	1,549	1,575	1,213	1,375	289
La Plata	3,843	6,228	3,034	7,291	1,537
Larimer	19,005	32,169	17,072	36,240	8,887
Las Animas	4,459	2,615	4,117	2,917	278
Lincoln	1,059	1,276	602	1,535	175
Logan	3,543	4,256	2,332	5,238	588
Mesa	8,807	17,924	7,549	22,686	2,004
Mineral	167	235	125	271	41
Moffat	1,451	2,099	1,079	3,344	329
Montezuma	1,993	3,002	1,467	4,120	275
Montrose	3,164	4,838	2,232	6,685	635
Morgan	3,798	4,603	2,246	5,209	693
Otero	4,118	4,597	3,294	4,801	572
Ouray	333	645	237	813	129
Park	741	1,034	674	1,623	293
Philips	1,173	1,142	640	1,488	193
Pitkin	2,194	2,955	1,760	2,153	1,128
Prowers	2,861	2,578	1,669	3,115	340
Pueblo	25,841	18,518	21,874	20,770	3,102
Rio Blanco	627	1,439	462	1,971	143
Rio Grande	1,475	2,627	1,370	2,844	185
Routt	2,130	2,822	1,944	3,574	920
Saguache	1,059	1,094	893	1,124	71
San Juan	167	221	146	268	94
San Miguel	674	622	651	774	297
Sedgwick	773	902	438	1,151	100
Summit	1,087	1,826	1,285	2,027	845
Teller	986	1,410	802	2,457	322
Washington	1,211	1,440	568	2,007	160
Weld	16,501	21,976	11,433	23,901	4,309
Yuma	2,025	2,350	1,043	3,220	319
Total	**460,353**	**58,367**	**367,973**	**652,264**	**130,633**

Colorado Vote Since 1932

1932 (Pres.), Roosevelt, Dem., 250,877; Hoover, Rep., 189,617; Thomas, Soc., 14,018; Upshaw, Proh., 1,928

1936 (Pres.), Roosevelt, Dem., 295,081; Landon, Rep., 181,267; Lemke, Union, 9,962; Thomas, Soc., 1,593; Browder, Com., 497; Aiken, Soc. Labor, 336.

1940 (Pres.), Roosevelt, Dem., 265,554; Willkie, Rep., 279,576; Thomas, Soc., 1,899; Babson, Proh., 1,597; Browder, Com., 378.

1944 (Pres.), Roosevelt, Dem., 234,331; Dewey, Rep., 268,731; Thomas, Soc., 1,977.

1948 (Pres.), Truman, Dem., 267,288; Dewey, Rep., 239,714; Wallace, Prog., 6,115; Thomas, Soc., 1,678; Dobbs, Soc. Workers, 228; Teichert, Soc. Labor, 214.

1952 (Pres.), Eisenhower, Rep., 379,782; Stevenson, Dem., 245,504; MacArthur, Constitution, 2,181; Hallinan, Prog., 1,919; Hoopes, Soc., 365; Hass, Soc. Labor, 352.

1956 (Pres.), Eisenhower, Rep., 394,479; Stevenson, Dem., 263,997; Hass, Soc. Lab., 3,308; Andrews, Ind., 759; Hoopes, Soc., 531.

1960 (Pres.), Kennedy, Dem., 330,629; Nixon, Rep., 402,242; Hass, Soc. Labor, 2,803; Dobbs, Soc. Workers, 572.

1964 (Pres.), Johnson, Dem., 476,024; Goldwater, Rep., 296,767; Hass, Soc. Labor, 302; DeBerry, Soc. Worker, 2,537; Munn, Proh., 1,356.

1968 (Pres.), Nixon, Rep., 409,345; Humphrey, Dem., 335,174; Wallace, 3d party, 60,813; Blomen, Soc. Labor, 3,016; Gregory, New-party, 1,393; Munn, Proh., 275; Halstead, Soc. Worker, 235.

1972 (Pres.), Nixon, Rep., 597,189; McGovern, Dem., 329,980; Fisher, Soc. Labor, 4,361; Hospers, Libertarian, 1,111; Hall, Com., 432; Jenness, Soc. Workers, 555; Munn, Proh., 467; Schmitz, Amer., 17,269; Spock, Peoples, 2,403.

1976 (Pres.), Carter, Dem., 460,353; Ford, Rep., 584,367; McCarthy, Ind., 26,107; MacBride, Libertarian, 5,330; Bubar, Proh., 2,882.

1980 (Pres.), Reagan, Rep., 652,264; Carter, Dem., 367,973; Anderson, Ind., 130,633; Clark, Libertarian, 25,744; Commoner, Citizens, 5,614; Bubar, Statesman, 1,180; Pulley, Socialist, 520; Hall, Com., 487.

Connecticut

	1976		1980		
County	Carter (D)	Ford (R)	Carter (D)	Reagan (R)	Anderson (I)
Fairfield	148,353	209,458	124,074	201,997	38,363
Hartford	191,257	175,064	164,643	150,265	52,856
Litchfield	32,419	40,705	26,705	38,725	10,027
Middlesex	29,097	31,115	24,768	28,989	9,062
New Haven	157,402	174,342	130,913	169,038	34,450
New London	45,908	47,231	36,628	47,217	13,577
Tolland	23,079	23,703	18,557	22,127	8,908
Windham	20,380	17,643	15,444	18,852	4,564
Totals	**647,895**	**719,261**	**541,732**	**677,210**	**171,807**

Connecticut Vote Since 1932

1932 (Pres.), Roosevelt, Dem., 281,632; Hoover, Rep., 288,420; Thomas, Soc., 22,767.

1936 (Pres.), Roosevelt, Dem., 382,129; Landon, Rep., 278,685; Lemke, Union, 21,805; Thomas, Soc., 5,683; Browder, Com., 1,193.

1940 (Pres.), Roosevelt, Dem., 417,621; Willkie, Rep., 361,021; Browder, Com., 1,091; Aiken, Soc. Labor, 971; Willkie, Union, 798.

1944 (Pres.), Roosevelt, Dem., 435,146; Dewey, Rep., 390,527; Thomas, Soc., 5,097; Teichert, Soc. Labor, 1,220.

1948 (Pres.), Truman, Dem., 423,297; Dewey, Rep., 437,754; Wallace, Prog., 13,713; Thomas, Soc., 6,964; Teichert, Soc. Labor, 1,184; Dobbs, Soc. Workers, 606.

1952 (Pres.), Eisenhower, Rep., 611,012; Stevenson, Dem., 481,649; Hoopes, Soc., 2,244; Hallinan, Peoples, 1,466; Hass, Soc. Labor, 535; write-in, 5.

1956 (Pres.), Eisenhower, Rep., 711,837; Stevenson, Dem., 405,079; scattered, 205.

1960 (Pres.), Kennedy, Dem., 657,055; Nixon, Rep., 565,813.

1964 (Pres.), Johnson, Dem., 826,269; Goldwater, Rep., 390,996; scattered, 1,313.

1968 (Pres.), Nixon, Rep., 556,721; Humphrey, Dem., 621,561; Wallace, 3d party, 76,650; scattered, 1,300.

1972 (Pres.), Nixon, Rep., 810,763; McGovern, Dem., 555,498; Schmitz, Amer., 17,239; scattered, 777.

1976 (Pres.), Carter, Dem., 647,895; Ford, Rep., 719,261; Maddox, George Wallace Party, 7,101; LaRouche, U.S. Labor, 1,789.

1980 (Pres.), Reagan, Rep., 677,210; Carter, Dem., 541,732; Anderson, Ind., 171,807; Clark, Libertarian, 8,570; Commoner, Citizens, 6,130; scattered, 836.

Delaware

	1976		1980		
County	Carter (D)	Ford (R)	Carter (D)	Reagan (R)	Anderson (I)
Kent	16,523	12,604	12,884	14,882	1,831
New Castle	87,521	80,074	76,897	76,898	12,828
Sussex	18,552	17,153	15,973	19,472	1,629
Totals	**122,596**	**109,831**	**105,754**	**111,252**	**16,288**

Delaware Vote Since 1932

1932 (Pres.), Hoover, Rep., 57,074; Roosevelt, Dem., 54,319; Thomas, Soc., 1,376; Foster, Com., 133.

1936 (Pres.), Roosevelt, Dem., 69,702; Landon, Rep. 54,014; Lemke, Union, 442; Thomas, Soc., 179; Browder, Com., 52.

1940 (Pres.), Roosevelt, Dem., 74,559; Willkie, Rep., 61,440; Babson, Proh., 220; Thomas, Soc., 115.

1944 (Pres.), Roosevelt, Dem., 68,166; Dewey, Rep., 56,747; Watson, Proh., 294; Thomas, Soc., 154.

1948 (Pres.), Truman, Dem., 67,813; Dewey, Rep., 69,688; Wallace, Prog., 1,050; Watson, Proh., 343; Thomas, Soc., 250; Teichert, Soc. Labor, 29.

1952 (Pres.), Eisenhower, Rep., 90,059; Stevenson, Dem., 83,315; Hass, Soc. Labor, 242; Hamblen, Proh., 234; Hallinan, Prog., 155; Hoopes, Soc., 20.

1956 (Pres.), Eisenhower, Rep., 98,057; Stevenson, Dem., 79,421; Oltwick, Proh., 400; Hass, Soc. Labor, 110.

1960 (Pres.), Kennedy, Dem., 99,590; Nixon, Rep., 96,373; Faubus, States' Rights, 354; Decker, Proh., 284; Hass, Soc. Labor, 82.

1964 (Pres.), Johnson, Dem., 122,704; Goldwater, Rep., 78,078; Hass, Soc. Labor, 113; Munn, Proh., 425.

1968 (Pres.), Nixon, Rep., 96,714; Humphrey, Dem., 89,194; Wallace, 3d party, 28,459.

1972 (Pres.), Nixon, Rep., 140,357; McGovern, Dem., 92,283; Schmitz, Amer., 2,638; Munn, Proh., 238.

1976 (Pres.), Carter, Dem., 122,596; Ford, Rep., 109,831; McCarthy, non-partisan, 2,437; Anderson, Amer., 645; LaRouche, U.S. Labor, 136; Bubar, Proh., 103; Levin, Soc. Labor, 86.

1980 (Pres.), Reagan, Rep., 111,252; Carter, Dem., 105,754; Anderson, Ind., 16,288; Clark, Libertarian, 1,974; Greaves, American, 400.

District of Columbia

	1976		1980		
County	Carter (D)	Ford (R)	Carter (D)	Reagan (R)	Anderson (I)
Totals	**137,818**	**27,873**	**130,231**	**23,313**	**16,131**

District of Columbia Vote Since 1964

1964 (Pres.), Johnson, Dem., 169,796; Goldwater, Rep., 28,801.

1968 (Pres.), Nixon, Rep., 31,012; Humphrey, Dem., 139,566.

1972 (Pres.), Nixon, Rep., 35,226; McGovern, Dem., 127,627; Reed, Soc. Workers, 316; Hall, Com., 252.

1976 (Pres.), Carter, Dem., 137,818; Ford, Rep., 27,873; Camejo, Soc. Workers, 545; MacBride, Libertarian, 274; Hall, Com., 219; LaRouche, U.S. Labor, 157.

1980 (Pres.), Reagan, Rep., 23,313; Carter, Dem., 130,231; Anderson, Ind., 16,131; Commoner, Citizens, 1,826; Clark, Libertarian, 1,104; Hall, Com., 369; De Berry, Soc. Work., 173; Griswold, Workers World, 52; write-ins, 690.

Florida

	1976		1980		
County	Carter (D)	Ford (R)	Carter (D)	Reagan (R)	Anderson (I)
Alachua	27,895	15,546	26,817	19,771	4,167
Baker	2,985	1,058	2,606	2,271	56
Bay	14,858	14,208	12,338	20,815	720
Bradford	3,868	1,680	3,340	2,771	89
Brevard	46,421	44,470	38,915	69,228	5,820
Broward	176,491	161,411	146,322	229,693	31,553
Calhoun	2,487	1,153	2,295	1,504	52
Charlotte	10,300	12,703	9,750	20,433	1,204
Citrus	9,438	7,973	9,148	14,276	784
Clay	8,410	8,468	7,589	15,497	679
Collier	8,764	14,643	7,735	23,878	1,675
Columbia	6,683	3,947	5,677	5,638	246
Dade	303,047	211,148	210,683	265,550	44,723
De Soto	2,715	2,000	2,709	3,340	155
Dixie	2,169	558	2,007	1,098	45
Duval	105,912	74,997	90,330	98,389	5,153
Escambia	38,279	41,471	33,378	51,443	2,595
Flagler	2,086	1,262	2,494	2,876	153
Franklin	1,859	1,054	1,772	1,500	53

	1976		1980		
	(D)	(R)	(D)	(R)	(I)
Gadsden	6,798	3,531	8,207	3,708	201
Gilchrist	1,807	528	1,625	1,089	55
Glades	1,311	624	1,203	1,096	61
Gulf	2,641	1,584	2,680	2,116	56
Hamilton	2,053	794	1,921	1,301	40
Hardee	2,670	2,189	2,597	2,595	83
Hendry	2,337	1,843	2,540	2,696	130
Hernando	7,717	5,793	8,835	12,099	852
Highlands	7,218	8,317	6,685	11,914	531
Hillsborough	94,589	78,504	88,221	106,080	8,939
Holmes	3,256	1,850	2,767	3,208	68
Indian River	3,316	9,818	7,748	15,545	1,184
Jackson	7,687	4,795	7,549	6,331	158
Jefferson	2,310	1,361	2,366	1,621	96
Lafayette	1,126	523	1,034	795	22
Lake	14,369	19,976	13,121	26,775	1,240
Lee	30,567	38,038	28,007	60,717	4,191
Leon	28,729	23,739	28,420	24,840	3,181
Levy	4,025	1,965	4,170	3,203	175
Liberty	1,137	620	1,111	895	24
Madison	3,218	1,761	3,129	2,275	65
Manatee	24,342	29,300	21,660	40,506	2,921
Marion	16,963	16,163	15,362	23,668	1,173
Martin	8,785	11,682	8,078	20,493	1,317
Monroe	11,079	8,232	7,875	11,546	1,914
Nassau	5,896	3,136	5,051	5,414	178
Okaloosa	14,210	18,598	10,738	27,665	1,080
Okeechobee	3,184	1,598	3,226	2,778	156
Orange	58,442	70,451	48,732	87,375	5,389
Osceola	6,893	7,062	6,594	10,839	560
Palm Beach	96,705	98,236	91,932	143,491	15,178
Pasco	33,710	28,306	34,045	50,080	3,565
Pinellas	141,879	150,003	138,307	185,482	17,789
Polk	47,286	44,238	43,291	59,600	2,618
Putnam	9,597	5,040	8,898	8,258	410
St. Johns	7,412	6,660	6,879	11,179	546
St. Lucie	12,386	11,502	10,341	18,107	1,109
Santa Rosa	8,020	9,122	6,964	13,802	606
Sarasota	26,293	44,157	25,557	67,946	4,773
Seminole	19,609	26,655	17,431	39,970	2,451
Sumter	4,721	2,212	4,378	3,666	141
Suwannee	4,718	2,405	4,345	3,894	135
Taylor	3,370	1,983	2,955	2,772	78
Union	1,480	544	1,235	1,120	45
Volusia	49,161	37,523	44,476	52,598	3,296
Wakulla	2,353	1,580	2,078	2,014	111
Walton	5,196	2,927	4,323	4,651	194
Washington	3,566	2,313	3,095	3,222	92
Absentees			1,788	3,945	593
Totals	**1,636,000**	**1,469,531**	**1,419,475**	**2,046,951**	**189,692**

Florida Vote Since 1932

1932 (Pres.), Roosevelt, Dem., 206,307; Hoover, Rep., 69,170; Thomas, Soc., 775.

1936 (Pres.), Roosevelt, Dem., 249,117; Landon, Rep., 78,248.

1940 (Pres.), Roosevelt, Dem., 359,334; Willkie, Rep., 126,158.

1944 (Pres.), Roosevelt, Dem., 339,377; Dewey, Rep., 143,215.

1948 (Pres.), Truman, Dem., 281,988; Dewey, Rep., 194,280; Thurmond, States' Rights, 89,755; Wallace, Prog., 11,620.

1952 (Pres.), Eisenhower, Rep., 544,036; Stevenson, Dem., 444,950; scattered, 351.

1956 (Pres.), Eisenhower, Rep., 643,849; Stevenson, Dem., 480,371.

1960 (Pres.), Kennedy, Dem., 748,700; Nixon, Rep., 795,476.

1964 (Pres.), Johnson, Dem., 948,540; Goldwater, Rep., 905,941.

1968 (Pres.), Nixon, Rep., 886,804; Humphrey, Dem., 676,794; Wallace, 3d party, 624,207.

1972 (Pres.), Nixon, Rep., 1,857,759; McGovern, Dem., 718,117; scattered, 7,407.

1976 (Pres.), Carter, Dem., 1,636,000; Ford, Rep., 1,469,531; McCarthy, Ind., 23,643; Anderson, Amer., 21,325.

1980 (Pres.), Reagan, Rep., 2,046,951; Carter, Dem., 1,419,475; Anderson, Ind., 189,692; Clark, Libertarian, 30,524; write-ins, 285.

Georgia

	1976		1980		
County	Carter (D)	Ford (R)	Carter (D)	Reagan (R)	Anderson (I)
Appling	3,585	961	2,985	1,961	41
Atkinson	1,560	347	1,449	747	16
Bacon	2,395	594	1,622	1,427	32
Baker	1,162	305	1,035	510	11
Baldwin	4,674	3,612	4,368	3,639	230
Banks	2,387	330	2,091	746	18
Barrow	4,756	1,364	3,876	2,284	99
Bartow	8,166	1,876	7,490	3,135	135
Ben Hill	2,449	814	2,544	1,459	41
Berrien	3,394	555	2,869	1,487	24
Bibb	31,902	12,819	31,770	15,175	848
Bleckley	2,605	972	2,014	1,261	47
Brantley	2,294	358	2,066	882	17
Brooks	2,653	1,102	2,230	1,546	39
Bryan	2,045	761	1,966	1,212	51
Bulloch	5,199	3,156	4,921	3,750	160
Burke	3,014	1,565	3,047	1,871	56
Butts	2,898	819	2,574	1,210	38
Calhoun	1,394	436	1,414	652	16
Camden	2,962	995	2,924	1,439	62
Candler	1,388	646	1,358	1,030	24
Carroll	10,050	3,640	8,202	5,815	294
Catoosa	6,020	3,799	4,921	5,962	121
Charlton	1,750	452	1,469	779	26
Chatham	32,075	24,160	28,635	26,499	1,244
Chattahoochee	506	178	476	256	16
Chattooga	4,686	1,087	4,279	1,946	61
Cherokee	6,539	2,609	6,020	5,250	230
Clarke	11,342	6,610	10,519	8,094	1,060
Clay	947	295	909	316	9
Clayton	21,432	12,905	17,540	19,160	923
Clinch	1,414	383	1,325	513	18
Cobb	45,002	34,324	39,157	51,977	3,229
Coffee	4,601	1,417	4,038	2,499	58
Colquitt	6,928	2,181	5,353	3,593	80
Columbia	4,674	3,423	5,335	6,293	248
Cook	2,882	670	2,461	1,188	25
Coweta	6,195	3,044	5,697	4,480	161
Crawford	1,842	378	1,673	642	35
Crisp	3,747	1,328	3,403	1,861	54
Dade	2,263	1,388	1,735	2,114	62
Dawson	1,384	370	1,072	729	23
Decatur	3,736	2,500	3,242	2,919	54
DeKalb	86,872	67,160	82,743	74,904	7,241
Dodge	5,267	848	4,635	1,719	56
Dooly	2,441	655	2,364	1,083	31
Dougherty	11,461	9,337	13,430	12,726	326
Douglas	7,805	3,959	6,807	6,945	304
Early	2,405	1,157	2,110	1,538	23
Echols	585	111	515	259	8
Effingham	2,906	1,654	2,783	2,528	38
Elbert	4,730	961	4,014	1,967	50
Emanuel	4,603	1,493	3,971	2,199	45
Evans	1,631	746	1,456	1,090	20
Fannin	3,402	2,646	2,526	3,196	61
Fayette	3,718	2,837	3,798	6,351	272
Floyd	15,151	7,713	13,710	9,220	398
Forsyth	4,693	1,443	4,325	3,157	160
Franklin	4,192	687	3,528	1,387	30
Fulton	129,849	61,552	118,748	64,909	6,738
Gilmer	2,499	1,261	2,246	2,170	72
Glascock	704	371	614	510	7
Glynn	9,459	5,403	7,540	7,214	296
Gordon	6,052	1,698	5,199	3,107	141
Grady	3,758	1,209	3,023	2,018	56
Greene	2,534	652	2,571	961	29
Gwinnett	20,838	13,912	21,958	27,185	1,497
Habersham	5,120	1,315	4,394	2,224	100
Hall	12,804	5,093	12,124	7,760	463
Hancock	2,117	651	2,205	573	23
Haralson	4,550	1,301	3,606	2,229	71
Harris	2,861	1,544	2,807	2,001	100
Hart	4,605	860	4,539	1,577	59
Heard	1,593	433	1,348	875	35
Henry	5,717	2,622	5,635	5,326	163
Houston	13,164	5,404	10,915	9,005	536
Irwin	2,012	561	1,555	1,056	11
Jackson	5,931	1,239	4,591	2,209	107
Jasper	1,852	689	1,546	879	38
Jeff Davis	2,405	622	2,059	1,191	40
Jefferson	3,115	1,309	3,305	1,605	44
Jenkins	1,820	563	1,632	824	24
Johnson	2,210	698	1,854	1,123	29
Jones	3,471	1,317	3,239	1,828	112
Lamar	2,785	847	2,453	1,298	42
Lanier	1,269	207	1,116	470	9
Laurens	8,617	3,281	7,860	4,392	147
Lee	1,727	1,110	1,670	1,942	26
Liberty	3,328	979	3,099	1,507	49
Lincoln	1,583	576	1,617	806	10
Long	1,243	222	1,202	514	23
Lowndes	8,830	4,512	5,989	6,622	214
Lumpkin	2,301	547	1,951	1,024	83
Macon	3,013	638	3,025	894	39
Madison	3,367	1,115	2,980	2,330	59
Marion	1,314	291	1,174	567	16
McDuffie	3,024	1,694	2,667	1,928	59
McIntosh	1,978	535	2,104	876	38
Meriwether	4,830	1,450	3,876	1,838	59
Miller	1,536	476	1,127	900	19
Mitchell	4,495	1,572	3,566	2,231	40
Monroe	2,962	1,078	2,542	1,242	43
Montgomery	1,610	626	1,663	948	23

	1976 (D)	1976 (R)	1980 (D)	1980 (R)	1980 (I)
Morgan	2,274	904	2,276	1,323	57
Murray	3,511	889	3,094	1,538	42
Muscogee	24,092	13,496	23,272	15,203	811
Newton	6,294	2,137	5,611	3,206	150
Oconee	2,228	1,184	2,141	2,065	106
Oglethorpe	1,854	811	1,611	1,187	44
Paulding	5,420	1,432	4,686	2,845	97
Peach	3,989	1,163	3,415	1,642	68
Pickens	2,571	973	2,358	1,612	73
Pierce	2,628	544	1,918	1,027	21
Pike	1,903	776	1,755	1,271	45
Polk	6,115	1,944	5,421	2,949	116
Pulaski	2,318	485	1,997	1,153	54
Putnam	2,040	835	1,951	1,166	35
Quitman	677	313	589	240	2
Rabun	2,398	591	2,327	1,070	67
Randolph	2,186	747	1,861	879	1
Richmond	24,042	17,893	24,104	19,619	887
Rockdale	4,640	2,974	4,395	5,300	219
Schley	783	268	613	453	9
Screven	2,168	1,176	2,117	1,490	36
Seminole	2,074	681	1,794	1,117	16
Spalding	7,593	3,739	7,176	4,809	248
Stephens	5,560	1,340	4,529	2,045	69
Stewart	1,632	433	1,440	611	23
Sumter	5,328	2,053	4,956	2,957	103
Talbot	1,634	459	1,635	572	20
Taliaferro	748	236	670	270	8
Tattnall	3,556	1,326	2,864	2,082	37
Taylor	1,962	504	1,845	815	19
Telfair	3,534	637	2,700	1,173	41
Terrell	2,348	1,168	2,010	1,378	21
Thomas	6,147	3,263	5,695	4,294	117
Tift	5,185	2,162	4,572	3,280	99
Toombs	4,047	2,126	3,255	2,835	68
Towns	1,786	1,175	1,510	1,475	57
Treutlen	1,567	465	1,307	668	21
Troup	7,699	4,422	7,716	5,398	191
Turner	2,265	416	1,990	898	16
Twiggs	2,515	513	2,213	747	8
Union	2,795	1,154	1,700	1,546	43
Upson	4,219	2,897	4,713	2,788	77
Walker	8,007	4,807	6,809	7,088	171
Walton	5,402	1,687	4,525	2,618	112
Ware	7,719	2,661	6,307	3,715	77
Warren	1,335	720	1,517	779	20
Washington	3,865	1,657	3,452	1,822	60
Wayne	4,489	1,499	3,843	2,213	52
Webster	622	165	608	312	8
Wheeler	1,378	344	1,599	550	28
White	2,125	625	2,017	1,175	58
Whitfield	10,475	4,498	9,691	6,404	229
Wilcox	2,153	346	1,780	827	13
Wilkes	2,461	1,067	2,350	1,212	31
Wilkinson	2,652	837	2,365	1,116	31
Worth	2,790	1,156	2,567	2,076	35
Totals	**979,409**	**483,743**	**890,955**	**654,168**	**36,055**

Georgia Vote Since 1932

1932 (Pres.), Roosevelt, Dem., 234,118; Hoover, Rep., 19,863; Upshaw, Proh., 1,125; Thomas, Soc., 461; Foster, Com., 23.

1936 (Pres.), Roosevelt, Dem., 255,364; Landon, Rep., 36,942; Colvin, Proh., 660; Lemke, Union, 141; Thomas, Soc., 68.

1940 (Pres.), Roosevelt, Dem., 265,194; Willkie, Rep., 23,934; Ind. Dem., 22,428; total, 46,362; Babson, Proh., 983.

1944 (Pres.), Roosevelt, Dem., 268,187; Dewey, Rep., 56,506; Watson, Proh., 36.

1948 (Pres.), Truman, Dem., 254,646; Dewey, Rep., 76,691; Thurmond, States' Rights, 85,055; Wallace, Prog., 1,636; Watson, Proh., 732.

1952 (Pres.), Eisenhower, Rep., 198,979; Stevenson, Dem., 456,823; Liberty Party, 1.

1956 (Pres.), Stevenson, Dem., 444,388; Eisenhower, Rep., 222,778; Andrews, Ind., write-in, 1,754.

1960 (Pres.), Kennedy, Dem., 458,638; Nixon, Rep., 274,472; write-in, 239.

1964 (Pres.), Johnson, Dem., 522,557; Goldwater, Rep., 616,600.

1968 (Pres.), Nixon, Rep., 380,111; Humphrey, Dem., 334,440; Wallace, 3d party, 535,550; write-in, 162.

1972 (Pres.), Nixon, Rep., 881,496; McGovern, Dem., 289,529; Schmitz, Amer., 2,288; scattered.

1976 (Pres.), Carter, Dem., 979,409; Ford, Rep., 483,743; write-in, 4,306.

1980 (Pres.), Reagan, Rep., 654,168; Carter, Dem., 890,955; Anderson, Ind., 36,055; Clark, Libertarian, 15,627.

Hawaii

County	1976 Carter (D)	1976 Ford (R)	1980 Carter (D)	1980 Reagan (R)	1980 Anderson (I)
Hawaii	091	15,960	17,630	14,247	3,091
Oahu	111,389	108,041	96,472	99,596	25,331
Kauai	8,105	6,278	9,081	5,883	1,352
Maui	11,921	10,318	12,674	10,359	2,237
Absentees			22	27	10
Totals	**147,375**	**140,003**	**135,879**	**130,112**	**32,021**

Hawaii Vote Since 1960

1960 (Pres.), Kennedy, Dem., 92,410; Nixon, Rep., 92,295.

1964 (Pres.), Johnson, Dem., 163,249; Goldwater, Rep., 44,022.

1968 (Pres.), Nixon, Rep., 91,425; Humphrey, Dem., 141,324; Wallace, 3d party, 3,469.

1972 (Pres.), Nixon, Rep., 168,865; McGovern, Dem., 101,409.

1976 (Pres.), Carter, Dem., 147,375; Ford, Rep., 140,003; MacBride, Libertarian, 3,923.

1980 (Pres.), Reagan, Rep., 130,112; Carter, Dem., 135,879; Anderson, Ind., 32,021; Clark, Libertarian, 3,269; Commoner, Citizens, 1,548; Hall, Com., 458.

Idaho

County	1976 Carter (D)	1976 Ford (R)	1980 Carter (D)	1980 Reagan (R)	1980 Anderson (I)
Ada	21,125	41,135	21,324	55,205	7,987
Adams	639	809	590	1,189	88
Bannock	10,261	13,172	8,639	18,477	1,896
Bear Lake	960	2,094	508	2,941	63
Benewah	1,549	1,458	1,361	2,111	286
Bingham	4,347	7,327	2,933	11,781	489
Blaine	1,604	2,176	1,840	2,716	775
Boise	433	684	518	1,134	86
Bonner	4,065	4,549	4,060	6,727	880
Bonneville	7,230	15,793	5,052	24,715	1,355
Boundary	1,217	1,458	1,087	2,088	225
Butte	663	751	424	1,275	35
Camas	160	288	145	360	16
Canyon	9,460	17,263	9,172	24,375	1,798
Caribou	1,110	2,253	481	3,234	106
Cassias	1,881	4,575	1,369	6,511	212
Clark	169	334	87	379	11
Clearwater	1,752	1,469	1,699	2,178	291
Custer	516	850	398	1,398	64
Elmore	2,164	2,808	1,760	3,994	311
Franklin	1,157	2,720	511	3,669	61
Fremont	1,445	2,581	926	4,167	108
Gem	1,978	2,401	1,613	3,766	218
Gooding	1,923	2,909	1,481	3,897	218
Idaho	2,323	3,185	2,078	4,425	409
Jefferson	1,745	3,599	833	5,860	135
Jerome	1,800	3,188	1,368	4,962	178
Kootenai	7,225	10,493	7,521	17,022	1,808
Latah	5,314	6,846	5,037	6,967	2,465
Lemhi	1,159	1,685	794	2,646	167
Lewis	898	824	774	1,088	160
Lincoln	615	909	462	1,294	83
Madison	1,320	4,190	728	6,555	64
Minidoka	2,441	3,600	1,689	6,035	260
Nez Perce	6,324	6,151	6,565	7,495	1,344
Oneida	637	1,065	434	1,461	50
Owyhee	1,054	1,519	732	2,257	93
Payette	2,195	3,115	1,828	4,508	253
Power	1,286	1,374	727	2,235	119
Shoshone	3,216	3,570	3,102	3,994	407
Teton	514	904	360	1,227	67
Twin Falls	6,085	12,659	4,835	17,425	976
Valley	897	1,374	926	2,041	245
Washington	1,693	2,044	1,421	2,915	172
Totals	**126,549**	**204,151**	**110,192**	**290,699**	**27,058**

Idaho Vote Since 1932

1932 (Pres.), Roosevelt, Dem., 109,479; Hoover, Rep., 71,312; Harvey, Lib., 4,712; Thomas, Soc., 526; Foster, Com., 491.

1936 (Pres.), Roosevelt, Dem., 125,683; Landon, Rep., 66,256; Lemke, Union, 7,684.

1940 (Pres.), Roosevelt, Dem., 127,842; Willkie, Rep., 106,553; Thomas, Soc., 497; Browder, Com., 276.

1944 (Pres.), Roosevelt, Dem., 107,399; Dewey, Rep., 100,137; Watson, Proh., 503; Thomas, Soc., 282.

1948 (Pres.), Truman, Dem., 107,370; Dewey, Rep., 101,514; Wallace, Prog., 4,972; Watson, Proh., 628; Thomas, Soc., 332.

1952 (Pres.), Eisenhower, Rep., 180,707; Stevenson Dem.,

95,081; Hallinan, Prog., 443; write-in, 23.

1956 (Pres.), Eisenhower, Rep., 166,979; Stevenson, Dem., 105,868; Andrews, Ind., 126; write-in, 16.

1960 (Pres.), Kennedy, Dem., 138,853; Nixon, Rep., 161,597.

1964 (Pres.), Johnson, Dem., 148,920; Goldwater, Rep., 143,557.

1968 (Pres.), Nixon, Rep., 165,369; Humphrey, Dem., 89,273; Wallace, 3d party, 36,541.

1972 (Pres.), Nixon, Rep., 199,384; McGovern, Dem., 80,826; Schmitz, Amer., 28,869; Spock, Peoples, 903.

1976 (Pres.), Carter, Dem., 126,549; Ford, Rep., 204,151; Maddox, Amer., 5,935; MacBride, Libertarian, 3,558; LaRouche, U.S. Labor, 739.

1980 (Pres.), Reagan, Rep., 290,699; Carter, Dem., 110,192; Anderson, Ind., 27,058; Clark, Libertarian, 8,425; Rarick, Amer., 1,057.

Illinois

County	1976 Carter (D)	1976 Ford (R)	1980 Carter (D)	1980 Reagan (R)	1980 Anderson (I)
Adams	11,926	18,189	10,606	19,842	1,202
Alexander	3,246	2,349	2,925	2,650	74
Bond	3,682	3,716	2,834	4,398	244
Boone	4,458	6,470	3,175	6,697	1,578
Brown	1,533	1,519	950	1,660	59
Bureau	7,566	10,854	5,753	11,484	1,093
Calhoun	1,549	1,364	1,208	1,591	76
Carroll	3,372	5,059	2,154	5,084	705
Cass	3,589	3,524	2,543	3,965	199
Champaign	26,858	34,546	21,017	33,329	9,972
Christian	9,306	7,445	6,625	8,770	499
Clark	4,071	4,506	2,855	5,476	243
Clay	3,837	3,860	2,587	4,447	187
Clinton	6,275	7,245	4,470	8,500	528
Coles	8,639	11,021	6,743	11,994	1,726
Cook	1,180,814	987,498	1,124,584	856,574	149,712
Crawford	5,007	5,522	3,372	5,894	341
Cumberland	2,752	2,518	1,892	3,159	190
DeKalb	11,535	18,193	8,913	16,370	4,526
DeWitt	3,477	4,137	2,262	4,648	368
Douglas	3,826	4,635	2,564	5,330	344
DuPage	72,137	175,055	68,991	182,308	29,810
Edgar	5,058	5,842	3,394	6,639	400
Edwards	1,648	2,379	1,041	2,556	118
Effingham	5,952	7,194	4,229	9,104	393
Fayette	383	6,523	3,614	6,523	229
Ford	2,690	4,801	1,803	5,024	328
Franklin	12,818	7,420	9,425	9,731	558
Fulton	9,314	9,588	7,481	10,316	838
Gallatin	2,611	1,499	1,678	1,700	78
Greene	4,057	3,706	2,607	4,224	220
Grundy	5,534	7,581	3,970	8,397	701
Hamilton	3,036	2,433	1,990	3,254	171
Hancock	4,730	6,043	3,522	6,597	383
Hardin	1,602	1,393	1,314	1,721	56
Henderson	2,152	2,210	1,609	2,443	143
Henry	9,822	12,849	7,977	14,506	1,440
Iroquois	5,167	10,129	3,362	11,247	592
Jackson	12,940	10,152	10,291	10,505	2,526
Jasper	2,772	2,794	1,846	3,548	157
Jefferson	8,989	7,422	6,761	8,972	506
Jersey	4,625	4,273	3,324	5,266	314
JoDaviess	3,979	5,478	2,678	5,186	983
Johnson	2,182	2,417	1,586	3,201	84
Kane	34,057	59,275	29,015	64,106	9,179
Kankakee	18,394	23,003	14,626	23,810	1,802
Kendall	4,202	9,011	3,143	10,028	979
Knox	11,525	14,123	8,749	14,907	2,069
Lake	57,741	92,231	48,287	96,350	17,726
LaSalle	23,105	25,114	16,818	27,323	3,041
Lawrence	4,044	4,345	3,030	4,453	293
Lee	6,076	8,674	3,170	11,373	781
Livingston	5,174	10,097	4,111	11,544	980
Logan	5,686	8,623	3,916	9,681	650
Macon	28,243	24,893	22,325	28,298	2,804
Macoupin	11,910	10,242	9,116	12,131	901
Madison	56,457	44,183	43,860	51,160	4,206
Marion	9,834	8,729	6,990	10,969	567
Marshall	2,570	4,017	1,903	4,349	336
Mason	3,947	3,847	2,680	4,644	267
Massac	3,666	3,226	2,821	4,284	124
McDonough	5,464	9,683	4,093	8,995	1,230
McHenry	16,799	37,115	14,540	40,045	5,871
McLean	16,601	28,493	13,587	30,096	4,961
Menard	2,301	3,137	1,589	3,622	274
Mercer	4,090	4,816	3,361	5,144	540
Monroe	3,984	5,602	3,121	6,315	405
Montgomery	8,322	7,379	5,721	8,947	611
Morgan	7,403	8,885	5,483	10,406	900
Moultrie	3,332	2,803	2,332	3,495	280
Ogle	6,463	11,073	4,067	12,533	2,042
Peoria	34,606	46,526	28,276	47,815	6,169
Perry	5,976	5,286	4,337	5,888	319
Piatt	3,509	4,442	2,421	4,867	447
Pike	5,006	4,975	3,695	5,301	303
Pope	1,070	1,187	880	1,501	58
Pulaski	2,489	1,836	1,955	2,083	49
Putnam	1,344	1,572	1,158	1,959	235
Randolph	8,693	8,190	6,052	8,810	514
Richland	3,485	4,434	2,463	5,241	358
Rock Island	35,994	34,007	30,045	34,788	5,818
St. Clair	59,177	40,333	50,046	46,063	3,879
Saline	7,472	5,970	5,683	7,157	321
Sangamon	38,017	43,309	29,354	49,372	5,439
Schuyler	2,014	5,234	1,445	2,799	155
Scott	1,424	1,789	941	1,990	80
Shelby	61,172	2,191	3,988	6,441	381
Stark	1,146	2,191	806	2,358	147
Stephenson	7,192	11,678	6,195	10,779	3,145
Tazewell	22,821	28,951	16,924	35,481	3,206
Union	5,003	3,531	3,781	4,289	291
Vermilion	18,438	19,751	14,498	22,579	2,110
Wabash	2,781	3,388	1,975	3,571	230
Warren	3,808	5,822	2,756	5,667	489
Washington	3,222	4,485	2,158	5,354	205
Wayne	4,303	5,211	3,258	6,013	222
White	5,306	4,600	3,463	5,279	274
Whiteside	11,255	14,308	7,191	17,389	1,242
Will	51,103	61,784	41,975	69,310	7,855
Williamson	13,600	10,703	10,779	14,451	793
Winnebago	42,399	52,736	32,384	48,825	22,596
Woodford	4819	8,899	3,552	10,791	711
Totals	**2,271,295**	**2,364,269**	**1,981,413**	**2,358,049**	**346,754**

Illinois Vote Since 1932

1932 (Pres.), Roosevelt, Dem., 1,882,304; Hoover, Rep., 1,432,756; Thomas, Soc., 67,258; Foster, Com., 15,582; Upshaw, Proh., 6,388; Reynolds, Soc. Labor, 3,638.

1936 (Pres.), Roosevelt, Dem., 2,282,999; Landon, Rep., 1,570,393; Lemke, Union, 89,439; Thomas, Soc., 7,530; Colvin, Proh., 3,439; Aiken, Soc. Labor, 1,921.

1940 (Pres.), Roosevelt, Dem., 2,149,934; Willkie, Rep., 2,047,240; Thomas, Soc., 10,914; Babson, Proh., 9,190.

1944 (Pres.), Roosevelt, Dem., 2,079,479; Dewey, Rep., 1,939,314; Teichert, Soc. Labor, 9,677; Watson, Proh., 7,411; Thomas, Soc., 180.

1948 (Pres.), Truman, Dem., 1,994,715; Dewey, Rep., 1,961,103; Watson, Proh., 11,959; Thomas, Soc., 11,522; Teichert, Soc. Labor, 3,118.

1952 (Pres.), Eisenhower, Rep., 2,457,327; Stevenson, Dem., 2,013,920; Hass, Soc. Labor, 9,363; write-in, 448.

1956 (Pres.), Eisenhower, Rep., 2,623,327; Stevenson, Dem., 1,775,682; Hass, Soc. Labor, 8,342; write-in, 56.

1960 (Pres.), Kennedy, Dem., 2,377,846; Nixon, Rep., 2,368,988; Hass, Soc. Labor, 10,560; write-in, 15.

1964 (Pres.), Johnson, Dem., 2,796,833; Goldwater, Rep., 1,905,946; write-in, 62.

1968 (Pres.), Nixon, Rep., 2,174,774; Humphrey, Dem., 2,039,814; Wallace, 3d party, 390,958; Blomen, Soc. Labor, 13,878; write-in, 325.

1972 (Pres.), Nixon, Rep. 2,788,179; McGovern, Dem., 1,913,472; Fisher, Soc. Labor, 12,344; Schmitz, Amer., 2,471; Hall, Com., 4,541; others, 2,229.

1976 (Pres.), Carter, Dem., 2,271,295; Ford, Rep., 2,364,269; McCarthy, Ind., 55,939; Hall, Com., 9,250; MacBride, Libertarian, 8,057; Camejo, Soc. Workers, 3,615; Levin, Soc. Labor, 2,422; LaRouche, U.S. Labor, 2,018; write-in, 1,968.

1980 (Pres.), Reagan, Rep., 2,358,049; Carter, Dem., 1,981,413; Anderson, Ind., 346,754; Clark, Libertarian, 38,939; Commoner, Citizens, 10,692; Hall, Com., 9,711; Griswold, Workers World, 2,257; DeBerry, Socialist Workers, 1,302; write-ins, 604.

Indiana

County	1976 Carter (D)	1976 Ford (R)	1980 Carter (D)	1980 Reagan (R)	1980 Anderson (I)
Adams	4,908	6,280	4,673	6,368	767
Allen	44,744	71,321	37,765	68,524	10,368
Bartholomew	11,203	14,771	9,260	15,801	1,604
Benton	2,071	3,093	1,520	3,189	187
Blackford	3,174	2,886	2,431	3,168	258
Boone	5,686	9,214	4,535	10,484	681
Brown	2,381	2,466	2,014	2,884	237
Carroll	3,606	4,797	2,966	5,262	338
Cass	7,610	10,342	5,838	11,500	696
Clark	16,670	12,732	14,137	15,508	1,102
Clay	5,433	5,674	4,363	6,980	311
Clinton	6,662	8,199	5,258	8,158	427
Crawford	2,721	2,181	2,130	2,554	124

	1976 (D)	1976 (R)	1980 (D)	1980 (R)	1980 (I)
Daviess	4,952	6,829	4,057	7,022	345
Dearborn	6,348	6,176	5,135	7,467	464
Decatur	4,365	5,555	3,646	5,819	377
Dekalb	6,151	7,860	4,911	7,886	883
Delaware	25,151	26,417	20,923	28,342	2,743
Dubois	7,385	6,383	6,700	6,775	578
Elkhart	17,581	27,291	14,883	30,081	3,256
Fayette	5,519	5,704	4,304	6,004	293
Floyd	12,744	11,259	11,543	12,456	1,047
Fountain	4,089	4,903	2,845	5,289	280
Franklin	3,234	3,557	2,834	4,551	234
Fulton	3,488	5,083	2,788	5,458	349
Gibson	8,430	7,105	6,834	7,643	591
Grant	13,468	16,847	10,390	19,078	1,043
Greene	7,263	6,442	6,027	7,452	299
Hamilton	7,857	21,828	7,036	26,218	1,736
Hancock	6,191	10,072	5,124	12,093	746
Harrison	5,685	4,911	4,865	6,287	341
Hendricks	9,066	16,725	7,412	19,366	1,048
Henry	10,137	11,620	7,626	12,724	562
Howard	14,815	19,571	12,916	21,272	1,325
Huntington	6,515	9,182	5,415	9,497	824
Jackson	7,610	7,615	6,425	8,903	430
Jasper	3,286	5,398	2,544	6,316	283
Jay	4,124	4,606	3,256	5,351	484
Jefferson	6,139	5,573	5,496	6,831	477
Jennings	4,430	4,505	3,931	5,498	281
Johnson	10,075	16,414	8,445	20,018	1,348
Knox	9,612	9,100	7,829	10,083	617
Kosciusko	7,328	14,505	5,684	15,633	1,164
LaGrange	2,835	3,876	2,095	4,259	377
Lake	120,700	90,119	101,145	95,408	8,275
LaPorte	18,217	21,989	15,387	22,424	2,080
Lawrence	7,908	9,278	5,826	10,846	380
Madison	29,811	32,437	23,554	35,582	2,389
Marion	145,274	177,767	126,103	168,680	15,709
Marshall	6,424	9,707	5,113	10,209	836
Martin	2,827	2,702	2,479	3,082	149
Miami	6,257	8,263	4,927	8,672	508
Monroe	16,609	18,938	13,316	18,233	3,921
Montgomery	5,320	9,509	4,158	9,936	622
Morgan	7,181	10,983	5,439	13,321	498
Newton	2,236	3,204	1,649	3,850	194
Noble	5,875	6,885	4,721	7,624	749
Ohio	1,300	1,027	1,074	1,264	57
Orange	4,031	4,399	3,228	5,073	181
Owen	3,103	2,896	2,325	3,632	188
Parke	3,158	3,929	2,432	4,595	194
Perry	5,620	4,088	4,540	4,350	448
Pike	3,938	3,138	3,346	3,343	190
Porter	16,468	25,489	12,869	30,055	3,061
Posey	5,298	5,136	4,465	6,096	667
Pulaski	2,813	3,586	2,092	3,916	175
Putnam	5,116	6,063	3,996	7,090	501
Randolph	5,330	6,891	4,025	7,762	426
Ripley	4,792	5,293	4,022	5,770	303
Rush	3,052	4,723	2,388	4,829	224
St. Joseph	49,156	50,358	44,218	50,607	6,962
Scott	4,229	2,657	3,694	3,432	139
Shelby	7,098	8,918	5,861	10,496	614
Spencer	4,796	4,166	4,153	5,284	196
Starke	4,753	4,354	3,615	5,035	297
Steuben	3,323	5,079	2,606	5,670	602
Sullivan	5,198	3,747	4,335	4,465	212
Switzerland	2,150	1,329	1,704	1,584	38
Tippecanoe	17,850	29,186	14,636	27,589	5,141
Tipton	3,428	4,776	2,547	5,150	285
Union	1,160	1,631	898	1,766	92
Vanderburgh	34,911	37,975	29,930	36,248	4,150
Vermillion	4,791	3,674	3,793	4,195	269
Vigo	24,684	23,555	19,261	24,133	2,484
Wabash	5,704	8,534	4,620	8,738	797
Warren	1,906	2,377	1,287	2,665	145
Warrick	7,804	7,200	6,845	8,681	890
Washington	4,409	3,794	3,663	5,234	191
Wayne	12,306	16,697	9,599	16,981	1,174
Wells	4,250	5,596	3,760	5,864	717
White	3,963	6,287	3,247	6,999	466
Whitley	5,445	6,761	4,497	7,146	928
Totals	**1,014,714**	**1,185,958**	**844,197**	**1,255,656**	**111,639**

Indiana Vote Since 1932

1932 (Pres.), Roosevelt, Dem., 862,054; Hoover, Rep., 677,184; Thomas, Soc., 21,388; Upshaw, Proh., 10,399; Foster, Com., 2,187; Reynolds, Soc. Labor, 2,070.

1936 (Pres.), Roosevelt, Dem., 943,974; Landon, Rep., 691,570; Lemke, Union, 19,407; Thomas, Soc., 3,856; Browder, Com., 1,090.

1940 (Pres.), Roosevelt, Dem., 874,063; Willkie, Rep., 899,466; Babson, Proh., 6,437; Thomas, Soc., 2,075; Aiken, Soc. Labor, 706.

1944 (Pres.), Roosevelt, Dem., 781,403; Dewey, Rep., 875,891; Watson, Proh., 12,574; Thomas, Soc., 2,223.

1948 (Pres.), Truman, Dem., 807,833; Dewey, Rep., 821,079; Watson, Proh., 14,711; Wallace, Prog., 9,649; Thomas, Soc., 2,179; Teichert, Soc. Labor, 763.

1952 (Pres.), Eisenhower, Rep., 1,136,259; Stevenson, Dem., 801,530; Hamblen, Proh., 15,335; Hallinan, Prog., 1,222; Hass, Soc. Labor, 979.

1956 (Pres.), Eisenhower, Rep., 1,182,811; Stevenson, Dem., 783,908; Holtwick, Proh., 6,554; Hass, Soc. Labor, 1,334.

1960 (Pres.), Kennedy, Dem., 952,358; Nixon, Rep., 1,175,120; Decker, Proh., 6,746; Hass, Soc. Labor, 1,136.

1964 (Pres.), Johnson, Dem. 1,170,848; Goldwater, Rep., 911,118; Munn, Proh., 8,266; Hass, Soc. Labor, 1,374.

1968 (Pres.), Nixon, Rep., 1,067,885; Humphrey, Dem., 806,659; Wallace, 3d party, 243,108; Munn, Proh., 4,616; Halstead, Soc. Worker, 1,293; Gregory, write-in, 36.

1972 (Pres.), Nixon, Rep., 1,405,154; McGovern, Dem., 708,568; Reed, Soc. Workers, 5,575; Fisher, Soc. Labor, 1,688; Spock, Peace & Freedom, 4,544.

1976 (Pres.), Carter, Dem., 1,014,714; Ford, Rep., 1,185,958; Anderson, Amer., 14,048; Camejo, Soc. Workers, 5,695; LaRouche, U.S. Labor, 1,947.

1980 (Pres.) Reagan, Rep., 1,255,656; Carter, Dem., 844,197; Anderson, Ind., 111,639; Clark, Libertarian, 19,627; Commoner, Citizens, 4,852; Greaves, American, 4,750; Hall, Com., 702; DeBerry, Soc., 610.

Iowa

County	1976 Carter (D)	1976 Ford (R)	1980 Carter (D)	1980 Reagan (R)	1980 Anderson (I)
Adair	2,294	2,326	1,454	2,821	356
Adams	1,507	1,388	940	1,779	214
Allamakee	2,568	3,648	2,170	4,000	343
Appanoose	3,424	3,036	2,769	3,544	353
Audubon	2,104	1,978	1,546	2,523	251
Benton	5,514	5,014	4,223	5,329	948
Black Hawk	29,508	30,994	27,443	29,627	5,847
Boone	6,595	5,413	5,126	5,732	1,081
Bremer	4,203	6,252	3,527	6,706	970
Buchanan	4,258	4,794	3,605	5,041	689
Buena Vista	4,227	5,126	3,468	5,272	771
Butler	2,503	4,207	1,990	4,730	392
Calhoun	3,001	3,215	2,150	3,633	407
Carroll	5,333	4,094	3,885	5,017	736
Cass	2,866	4,589	2,176	5,391	475
Cedar	3,354	4,308	2,589	4,398	697
Cerro Gordo	11,189	10,604	9,363	11,189	2,024
Cherokee	3,358	3,993	2,719	4,087	599
Chickasaw	3,503	3,432	2,935	3,929	500
Clarke	2,333	1,737	1,614	2,417	310
Clay	3,776	4,548	3,179	4,479	991
Clayton	3,804	4,826	3,297	5,115	669
Clinton	11,746	12,401	9,698	13,025	2,140
Crawford	3,903	3,879	2,500	4,883	509
Dallas	6,722	5,308	5,310	6,296	1,200
Davis	2,426	1,631	1,689	2,003	200
Decatur	2,698	1,932	2,048	2,212	318
Delaware	3,168	4,161	2,671	4,316	727
Des Moines	11,268	9,023	9,977	9,158	1,041
Dickinson	3,074	3,795	2,620	4,028	687
Dubuque	20,548	17,459	18,689	18,649	3,708
Emmet	2,720	2,872	2,153	3,062	446
Fayette	5,220	6,618	4,377	6,374	647
Floyd	4,646	4,361	3,634	4,665	728
Franklin	2,682	3,056	1,920	3,290	406
Fremont	1,964	2,163	1,203	2,693	191
Greene	3,094	2,811	2,210	3,154	510
Grundy	2,410	4,173	1,869	4,644	440
Guthrie	2,873	2,644	1,866	3,214	384
Hamilton	3,953	3,932	2,741	4,745	679
Hancock	2,975	3,127	1,918	3,681	462
Hardin	4,479	4,682	3,757	5,329	730
Harrison	3,228	3,489	2,152	4,502	311
Henry	3,882	3,848	3,317	4,430	629
Howard	2,917	2,618	2,214	2,975	336
Humboldt	2,677	3,075	1,840	3,575	394
Ida	1,868	2,590	1,235	2,825	254
Iowa	3,367	3,926	2,606	4,153	667
Jackson	4,467	4,221	3,518	4,479	622
Jasper	8,783	7,728	7,258	8,286	1,221
Jefferson	3,377	3,746	2,577	4,099	505
Johnson	20,208	16,090	20,122	13,642	8,101
Jones	4,245	4,463	3,521	4,506	759
Keokuk	3,482	2,920	2,390	3,145	369
Kossuth	5,190	4,653	3,810	5,568	775
Lee	9,017	8,195	8,204	8,793	1,047
Linn	38,252	36,513	31,950	36,254	8,773
Louisa	2,089	2,284	1,700	2,530	291
Lucas	2,733	2,071	1,989	2,593	291
Lyon	1,870	3,558	1,431	4,349	375
Madison	3,109	2,681	2,496	3,320	505
Mahaska	4,838	5,267	3,968	5,650	603
Marion	6,226	5,429	5,490	6,665	1,232
Marshall	8,695	9,562	7,114	10,707	1,541
Mills	1,908	2,722	1,244	3,581	281

	1976 (D)	1976 (R)	1980 (D)	1980 (R)	1980 (I)
Mitchell	2,906	2,887	2,040	3,401	361
Monona	2,661	2,636	1,660	3,268	275
Monroe	2,360	1,581	1,866	2,003	216
Montgomery	2,229	3,673	1,556	4,115	301
Muscatine	6,567	7,697	5,597	7,829	1,522
O'Brien	2,732	4,643	2,210	4,937	536
Osceola	1,309	1,955	1,051	2,177	234
Page	2,865	5,343	1,772	5,618	356
Palo Alto	3,182	2,623	2,463	3,025	412
Plymouth	4,284	5,590	2,965	6,515	756
Pocahontas	3,055	2,700	1,959	3,194	397
Polk	71,917	62,316	61,984	64,156	15,819
Pottawattamie	14,754	17,264	10,709	20,222	1,870
Poweshiek	4,360	4,194	3,529	4,598	821
Ringgold	1,739	1,543	1,150	1,884	191
Sac	2,996	3,347	1,976	3,725	467
Scott	29,771	35,021	26,391	34,701	5,760
Shelby	2,851	3,301	1,892	4,147	372
Sioux	3,322	9,448	2,698	10,768	610
Story	15,717	18,394	13,529	15,829	7,252
Tama	4,580	4,379	3,049	4,840	593
Taylor	1,947	2,059	1,226	2,715	240
Union	2,955	2,873	2,182	3,372	368
Van Buren	1,807	1,804	1,311	2,142	183
Wapello	10,249	6,786	8,923	7,475	1,050
Warren	7,653	6,099	6,610	7,360	1,369
Washington	3,448	4,218	2,877	3,967	703
Wayne	2,145	1,781	1,627	2,221	218
Webster	10,543	9,068	9,001	10,438	1,386
Winnebago	2,950	3,315	2,208	3,808	417
Winneshiek	4,158	4,765	3,201	5,033	938
Woodbury	19,664	22,853	15,930	23,553	3,184
Worth	2,399	1,964	1,721	2,247	301
Wright	3,637	3,544	2,645	3,936	497
Total	**619,931**	**632,863**	**508,672**	**676,026**	**115,633**

Iowa Vote Since 1932

1932 (Pres.), Roosevelt, Dem., 598,019; Hoover, Rep., 414,433; Thomas, Soc., 20,467; Upshaw, Proh., 2,111; Coxey, Farm-Lab., 1,094; Foster, Com., 559.

1936 (Pres.), Roosevelt, Dem., 621,756; Landon, Rep., 487,977; Lemke, Union, 29,687; Thomas, Soc., 1,373; Colvin, Proh., 1,182; Browder, Com., 506; Aiken, Soc. Labor, 252.

1940 (Pres.), Roosevelt, Dem., 578,800; Willkie, Rep., 632,370; Babson, Proh., 2,284; Browder, Com., 1,524; Aiken, Soc. Labor, 452.

1944 (Pres.), Roosevelt, Dem., 499,876; Dewey, Rep., 547,267; Watson, Proh., 3,752; Thomas, Soc., 1,511; Teichert, Soc. Labor, 193.

1948 (Pres.), Truman, Dem., 522,380; Dewey, Rep., 494,018; Wallace, Prog., 12,125; Teichert, Soc. Labor, 4,274; Watson, Proh., 3,382; Thomas, Soc., 1,829; Dobbs, Soc. Workers, 26.

1952 (Pres.), Eisenhower, Rep., 808,906; Stevenson, Dem., 451,513; Hallinan, Prog., 5,085; Hamblen, Proh., 2,882; Hoopes, Soc., 219; Hass, Soc. Labor, 139; scattering 29.

1956 (Pres.), Eisenhower, Rep., 729,187; Stevenson, Dem., 501,858; Andrews (A.C.P. of Iowa), 3,202; Hoopes, Soc., 192; Hass, Soc. Labor, 125.

1960 (Pres.), Kennedy, Dem., 550,565; Nixon, Rep., 722,381; Hass, Soc. Labor, 230; write-in, 634.

1964 (Pres.), Johnson, Dem., 733,030; Goldwater, Rep., 449,148; Hass, Soc. Labor, 182; DeBerry, Soc. Worker, 159; Munn, Proh., 1,902.

1968 (Pres.), Nixon, Rep., 619,106; Humphrey, Dem., 476,699; Wallace, 3d party, 66,422; Munn, Proh., 362; Halstead, Soc. Worker, 3,377; Cleaver, Peace and Freedom, 1,332; Blomen, Soc. Labor, 241.

1972 (Pres.), Nixon, Rep., 706,207; McGovern, Dem., 496,206; Schmitz, Amer., 22,056; Jenness, Soc. Workers, 488; Fisher, Soc. Labor, 195; Hall, Com. 272; Green, Universal, 199; scattered, 321.

1976 (Pres.), Carter, Dem., 619,931; Ford, Rep., 632,863; McCarthy, Ind., 20,051; Anderson, Amer., 3,040; MacBride, Libertarian, 1,452.

1980 (Pres.), Reagan, Rep., 676,026; Carter, Dem., 508,672; Anderson, Ind., 115,633; Clark, Libertarian, 13,123; Commoner, Citizens, 2,273; McReynolds, Socialist, 534; Hall Com., 298; DeBerry, Soc. Work., 244; Greaves, American, 189; Bubar, Statesman, 150; scattering, 519.

Kansas

County	1976 Carter (D)	1976 Ford (R)	1980 Carter (D)	1980 Reagan (R)	1980 Anderson (I)
Allen	2,746	3,269	2,009	3,811	380
Anderson	1,886	1,872	1,170	2,363	184
Atchison	4,108	4,030	3,063	4,084	345
Barber	1,494	1,568	914	1,872	168
Barton	5,497	7,311	3,663	9,147	793
Bourbon	3,237	3,589	2,605	4,263	251
Brown	1,745	3,407	1,370	3,598	286
Butler	8,540	8,390	6,875	10,210	1,015
Chase	643	922	413	1,073	92
Chautauqua	866	1,159	543	1,566	57
Cherokee	5,154	3,957	3,969	5,296	282
Cheyenne	758	1,008	358	1,330	81
Clark	680	761	430	901	67
Clay	1,610	3,085	932	3,449	217
Cloud	2,976	2,954	1,793	3,581	344
Coffey	1,549	2,145	938	2,491	128
Comanche	630	719	393	877	50
Cowley	7,095	7,513	5,474	8,749	866
Crawford	9,021	7,225	7,658	8,058	847
Decatur	1,011	1,232	443	1,642	125
Dickinson	3,672	4,759	2,108	5,654	469
Doniphan	1,428	2,649	1,001	2,523	146
Douglas	11,922	14,277	9,360	14,106	4,770
Edwards	1,304	1,001	616	1,409	127
Elk	865	1,087	482	1,280	54
Ellis	6,280	4,719	3,940	5,634	923
Ellsworth	1,573	1,618	886	2,155	167
Finney	3,813	3,711	2,689	4,831	531
Ford	4,934	4,679	3,194	5,686	622
Franklin	3,607	4,760	2,726	5,525	432
Geary	2,843	3,230	2,357	3,534	332
Gove	848	860	396	1,263	91
Graham	936	1,112	473	1,450	98
Grant	1,151	1,226	683	1,711	150
Gray	1,111	837	583	1,310	123
Greeley	479	389	235	600	85
Greenwood	1,737	2,319	1,241	2,685	170
Hamilton	746	560	402	889	66
Harper	1,681	1,777	990	2,254	182
Harvey	6,003	6,624	4,173	7,045	1,356
Haskell	676	761	374	1,014	84
Hodgeman	697	576	339	831	69
Jackson	2,129	2,725	1,537	3,211	234
Jefferson	2,470	3,225	1,776	4,046	364
Jewell	1,111	1,592	578	2,074	153
Johnson	35,605	75,798	33,210	78,048	10,947
Kearny	658	674	375	924	62
Kingman	2,142	1,839	1,133	2,610	286
Kiowa	764	1,180	438	1,433	88
Labette	5,294	4,640	3,947	5,244	588
Lane	646	651	321	924	100
Leavenworth	8,022	8,407	6,354	9,157	955
Lincoln	985	1,225	528	1,685	96
Linn	1,681	1,873	1,157	2,407	103
Logan	694	957	358	1,261	66
Lyon	5,634	7,062	4,680	8,431	1,216
Marion	2,483	3,519	1,569	3,960	488
Marshall	3,004	3,226	1,555	4,127	330
McPherson	5,366	6,187	3,340	6,843	1,222
Meade	526	983	482	1,618	121
Miami	4,000	3,999	3,071	4,740	368
Mitchell	1,700	2,095	876	2,821	197
Montgomery	7,157	8,864	5,282	10,856	488
Morris	1,337	1,698	810	1,933	166
Morton	735	738	414	1,157	71
Nemaha	2,586	2,759	1,600	3,546	243
Neosho	3,842	4,038	2,923	4,613	432
Ness	1,106	1,016	616	1,657	136
Norton	1,337	2,201	666	2,625	151
Osage	2,755	2,945	2,088	3,817	330
Osborne	1,190	1,574	620	2,188	125
Ottawa	1,393	1,629	630	2,118	150
Pawnee	1,959	1,692	1,184	2,170	281
Phillips	1,264	2,317	748	2,731	143
Pottawatomie	2,316	3,483	1,724	3,895	444
Pratt	2,307	2,427	1,369	2,866	329
Rawlins	903	1,148	427	1,524	87
Reno	14,620	11,212	9,615	13,804	2,225
Republic	1,617	2,294	850	3,031	183
Rice	3,056	2,584	1,847	3,211	426
Riley	6,540	9,518	5,224	8,904	2,443
Rooks	1,412	1,664	725	2,275	144
Rush	1,359	1,170	557	1,840	144
Russell	1,453	3,165	910	3,241	229
Saline	8,476	11,218	6,382	12,758	1,706
Scott	919	1,195	456	1,829	99
Sedgwick	63,989	69,828	55,105	75,317	10,222
Seward	1,907	3,604	1,460	4,385	250
Shawnee	28,578	37,101	24,852	36,290	5,524
Sheridan	793	838	391	1,202	68
Sherman	1,573	1,671	779	2,315	215
Smith	1,333	2,009	719	2,415	183
Stafford	1,659	1,430	872	1,865	184
Stanton	489	510	231	672	62
Stevens	901	1,262	478	1,502	67
Sumner	5,385	4,645	3,761	6,038	486

	1976		1980		
	(D)	(R)	(D)	(R)	(I)
Thomas	1,802	2,246	1,045	2,789	269
Trego	1,003	1,025	523	1,340	138
Wabaunsee	1,354	1,921	853	2,255	173
Wallace	486	600	167	811	36
Washington	1,564	2,543	784	3,058	195
Wichita	614	593	303	880	60
Wilson	2,047	2,682	1,205	3,328	208
Woodson	904	1,104	646	1,435	89
Wyandotte	37,478	23,141	32,763	23,012	3,018
Totals	**430,421**	**502,752**	**326,150**	**566,812**	**68,231**

Kansas Vote Since 1932

1932 (Pres.), Roosevelt, Dem., 424,204; Hoover, Rep., 349,498; Thomas, Soc., 18,276.

1936 (Pres.), Roosevelt, Dem., 464,520; Landon, Rep., 397,727; Thomas, Soc., 2,766; Lemke, Union, 494.

1940 (Pres.), Roosevelt, Dem., 364,725; Willkie, Rep., 489,169; Babson, Proh., 4,056; Thomas, Soc., 2,347.

1944 (Pres.), Roosevelt, Dem., 287,458; Dewey, Rep., 442,096; Watson, Proh., 2,609; Thomas, Soc., 1,613.

1948 (Pres.), Truman, Dem., 351,902; Dewey, Rep., 423,039; Watson, Proh., 6,468; Wallace, Prog., 4,603; Thomas, Soc., 2,807.

1952 (Pres.), Eisenhower, Rep., 616,302; Stevenson, Dem., 273,296; Hamblen, Proh., 6,038; Hoopes, Soc., 530.

1956 (Pres.), Eisenhower, Rep., 566,878; Stevenson. Dem., 296,317; Holtwick, Proh., 3,048.

1960 (Pres.), Kennedy, Dem., 363,213; Nixon, Rep., 561,474; Decker, Proh., 4,138.

1964 (Pres.), Johnson, Dem., 464,028; Goldwater, Rep., 386,579; Munn, Proh., 5,393; Hass, Soc. Labor, 1,901.

1968 (Pres.), Nixon, Rep., 478,674; Humphrey, Dem., 302,996; Wallace, 3d, 88,921; Munn, Proh., 2,192.

1972 (Pres.), Nixon, Rep., 619,812; McGovern, Dem., 270,287; Schmitz, Cons., 21,808; Munn, Proh., 4,188.

1976 (Pres.), Carter, Dem., 430,421; Ford, Rep., 502,752; McCarthy, Ind., 13,185; Anderson, Amer., 4,724; MacBride, Libertarian, 3,242; Maddox, Cons., 2,118; Bubar, Proh., 1,403.

1980 (Pres.), Reagan, Rep., 566,812; Carter, Dem., 326,150; Anderson, Ind., 68,231; Clark, Libertarian, 14,470; Shelton, American, 1,555; Hall, Com., 967; Bubar, Statesman, 821; Rarick, Conservative, 789.

Kentucky

	1976		1980		
County	Carter (D)	Ford (R)	Carter (D)	Reagan (R)	Anderson (I)
Adair	2,366	3,201	2,285	4,051	53
Allen	2,231	2,508	2,010	3,186	54
Anderson	2,388	1,682	2,567	2,052	90
Ballard	2,794	649	2,583	1,190	23
Barren	5,878	3,797	5,285	6,405	164
Bath	2,113	938	2,174	1,463	47
Bell	5,284	5,035	6,362	5,433	150
Boone	5,602	5,602	5,374	8,263	383
Bourbon	3,504	2,260	3,641	2,475	153
Boyd	11,150	9,106	10,702	10,367	496
Boyle	4,095	3,511	4,429	3,848	254
Bracken	1,577	879	1,420	1,154	36
Breathitt	3,544	1,014	3,916	1,532	68
Breckinridge	3,347	2,698	3,163	3,629	72
Bullitt	5,623	3,639	5,884	6,364	202
Butler	1,588	2,363	1,274	3,129	28
Caldwell	3,016	1,808	2,924	2,609	66
Calloway	8,141	3,171	6,809	4,498	318
Campbell	12,423	15,798	11,059	16,743	943
Carlisle	1,985	435	1,542	975	8
Carroll	2,251	815	2,127	1,076	82
Carter	3,915	3,185	3,782	3,934	86
Casey	1,602	3,379	1,298	4,239	38
Christian	7,845	4,964	7,048	8,209	190
Clark	4,575	3,114	5,071	4,302	242
Clay	1,674	3,652	2,121	4,594	37
Clinton	987	2,354	1,000	3,539	34
Crittenden	1,715	1,596	1,508	2,219	28
Cumberland	853	1,653	821	2,216	27
Daviess	14,114	12,826	14,902	14,643	752
Edmonson	1,418	1,976	1,252	2,913	28
Elliott	1,987	455	1,668	551	15
Estill	2,034	2,250	1,965	2,818	45
Fayette	28,012	35,170	30,511	35,349	4,933
Fleming	2,317	1,647	2,051	2,189	54
Floyd	10,151	3,108	10,975	4,179	171
Franklin	10,475	5,536	11,193	6,455	610
Fulton	2,370	1,060	2,016	1,462	31
Gallatin	1,164	436	988	684	20
Garrard	1,887	2,045	1,774	2,585	62
Grant	2,336	1,212	2,272	1,779	76
Graves	8,982	3,195	6,999	6,556	135
Grayson	3,064	3,658	2,788	5,084	78
Green	2,085	2,397	1,758	2,775	39
Greenup	6,880	5,062	7,126	6,857	220
Hancock	1,562	1,124	1,530	1,367	52
Hardin	7,977	6,965	8,339	9,779	452
Harlan	7,300	4,624	8,798	5,460	131
Harrison	3,582	1,911	3,319	2,184	107
Hart	3,189	2,013	3,005	3,129	42
Henderson	7,916	4,053	8,082	5,074	354
Henry	2,985	1,192	2,999	1,723	69
Hickman	2,035	585	1,456	1,143	28
Hopkins	7,749	5,115	8,810	6,238	213
Jackson	680	2,766	702	3,379	29
Jefferson	122,731	130,262	125,844	127,254	9,686
Jessamine	2,795	3,081	3,310	4,809	278
Johnson	3,683	4,891	3,142	5,039	96
Kenton	18,833	22,087	17,907	25,965	1,583
Knott	4,762	962	5,405	1,602	25
Knox	3,642	4,931	3,543	5,539	113
Larue	2,207	1,409	2,183	2,000	43
Laurel	3,813	6,186	3,969	8,868	114
Lawrence	2,402	1,838	2,362	2,564	32
Lee	1,091	1,449	1,017	1,650	41
Leslie	1,478	3,770	1,327	3,536	40
Letcher	4,590	3,122	4,280	3,426	78
Lewis	1,929	2,383	1,543	2,802	34
Lincoln	3,198	2,694	2,991	3,034	58
Livingston	2,497	878	2,287	1,670	30
Logan	4,850	2,430	4,264	3,366	85
Lyon	1,606	585	1,496	968	26
McCracken	14,956	6,997	13,365	10,281	369
McCreary	1,827	3,272	1,377	3,786	40
McLean	2,346	1,212	2,147	1,497	44
Madison	7,299	6,581	8,208	8,437	739
Magoffin	2,451	1,793	2,986	2,265	25
Marion	3,520	1,723	3,577	2,126	87
Marshall	6,906	2,578	6,231	4,403	96
Martin	1,267	2,120	1,567	2,793	51
Mason	3,397	2,529	3,181	2,926	127
Meade	3,030	1,755	3,205	2,740	90
Menifee	1,041	304	966	547	11
Mercer	3,411	2,451	3,528	3,275	92
Metcalfe	1,877	1,356	1,628	2,013	39
Monroe	1,412	3,352	1,156	4,592	47
Montgomery	3,141	2,032	3,391	2,869	117
Morgan	2,897	973	2,698	1,450	31
Muhlenberg	7,058	4,292	6,616	4,893	148
Nelson	4,454	2,804	5,514	3,349	162
Nicholas	1,582	738	1,349	915	56
Ohio	3,508	3,764	3,486	5,272	103
Oldham	2,819	3,695	3,487	5,586	351
Owen	2,332	676	2,323	944	43
Owsley	305	1,053	437	1,250	7
Pendleton	2,147	1,230	1,992	1,757	69
Perry	5,633	4,434	6,031	4,226	72
Pike	14,320	9,178	14,878	10,550	204
Powell	1,859	1,148	2,006	1,716	33
Pulaski	5,752	9,226	6,570	12,970	257
Robertson	546	275	562	416	14
Rockcastle	1,408	2,583	1,345	3,543	37
Rowen	3,541	2,244	2,975	2,758	191
Russell	1,803	2,882	1,693	3,804	29
Scott	3,118	2,408	3,531	2,868	197
Shelby	3,841	2,916	4,429	3,423	178
Simpson	2,782	1,481	2,713	2,020	59
Spencer	1,209	742	1,216	935	27
Taylor	3,456	3,337	3,400	4,243	84
Todd	2,436	1,095	1,956	1,945	44
Trigg	2,727	991	2,619	1,913	56
Trimble	1,568	517	1,478	824	49
Union	3,540	1,716	3,479	1,847	68
Warren	9,657	9,439	9,643	12,184	602
Washington	2,376	1,765	2,147	2,008	43
Wayne	2,537	3,243	2,673	3,972	50
Webster	3,523	1,402	3,506	1,939	52
Whitley	4,212	6,100	3,889	7,007	125
Wolfe	1,777	659	1,814	951	19
Woodford	2,689	2,646	3,122	3,105	213
Totals	**615,717**	**531,852**	**616,417**	**635,274**	**31,127**

Kentucky Vote Since 1932

1932 (Pres.), Roosevelt, Dem., 580,574; Hoover, Rep., 394,716; Upshaw, Proh., 2,252; Thomas, Soc., 3,853; Reynolds, Soc. Labor, 1,396; Foster, Com., 272.

1936 (Pres.), Roosevelt, Dem., 541,944; Landon, Rep., 369,702; Lemke, Union, 12,501; Colvin, Proh., 929; Thomas, Soc., 627; Aiken, Soc. Labor, 294; Browder, Com., 204.

1940 (Pres.), Roosevelt, Dem., 557,222; Willkie, Rep., 410,384; Babson, Proh., 1,443; Thomas, Soc., 1,014.

1944 (Pres.), Roosevelt, Dem., 472,589; Dewey, Rep., 392,448; Watson, Proh., 2,023; Thomas, Soc., 535; Teichert, Soc. Labor, 326.

1948 (Pres.), Truman, Dem., 466,756; Dewey, Rep.,

341,210; Thurmond, States' Rights, 10,411; Wallace, Prog., 1,567; Thomas, Soc., 1,284; Watson, Proh., 1,245; Teichert, Soc. Labor, 185.

1952 (Pres.), Eisenhower, Rep., 495,029; Stevenson, Dem., 495,729; Hamblen, Proh., 1,161; Hass, Soc. Labor, 893; Hallinan, Proh., 336.

1956 (Pres.), Eisenhower, Rep., 572,192; Stevenson, Dem., 476,453; Byrd, States' Rights, 2,657; Holtwick, Proh., 2,145; Hass, Soc. Labor, 358.

1960 (Pres.), Kennedy, Dem., 521,855; Nixon, Rep., 602,607.

1964 (Pres.), Johnson, Dem., 669,659; Goldwater, Rep., 372,977; John Kasper, Nat'l. States Rights, 3,469.

1968 (Pres.), Nixon, Rep., 462,411; Humphrey, Dem., 397,547; Wallace, 3d p., 193,098; Halstead, Soc. Worker, 2,843.

1972 (Pres.), Nixon, Rep., 676,446; McGovern, Dem., 371,159; Schmitz, Amer., 17,627; Jenness, Soc. Workers, 685; Hall, Com., 464; Spock, Peoples, 1,118.

1976 (Pres.), Carter, Dem., 615,717; Ford, Rep., 531,852; Anderson, Amer., 8,308; McCarthy, Ind., 6,837; Maddox, Amer. Ind., 2,328; MacBride, Libertarian, 814.

1980 (Pres.), Reagan, Rep., 635,274; Carter, Dem., 616,417; Anderson, Ind., 31,127; Clark, Libertarian, 5,531; McCormack, Respect For Life, 4,233; Commoner, Citizens, 1,304; Pulley, Socialist, 393; Hall, Com., 348.

Louisiana

Parish	1976 Carter (D)	1976 Ford (R)	1980 Carter (D)	1980 Reagan (R)	1980 Anderson (I)
Acadia	10,814	6,296	9,948	11,533	416
Allen	5,373	2,080	6,057	3,328	110
Ascension	9,100	4,435	12,381	7,238	286
Assumption	4,401	3,117	4,679	4,001	153
Avoyelles	8,104	4,574	7,174	8,216	190
Beauregard	5,322	3,196	5,556	5,250	163
Bienville	3,402	2,499	4,123	3,508	51
Bossier	8,062	12,132	9,377	16,515	327
Caddo	30,593	42,627	36,422	51,202	1,128
Calcasieu	33,980	17,485	35,446	27,600	1,259
Caldwell	1,830	1,890	1,786	2,653	43
Cameron	2,432	819	2,221	1,449	82
Catahoula	2,547	2,086	2,414	2,942	38
Claiborne	2,891	3,216	3,443	3,538	53
Concordia	3,892	3,849	3,956	4,933	52
DeSoto	4,630	3,601	5,861	4,349	49
E. Baton Rouge	49,956	51,655	57,442	71,063	3,312
East Carroll	2,367	1,681	2,283	1,867	24
East Feliciana	3,485	1,668	4,033	2,650	53
Evangeline	7,578	3,715	6,722	7,412	160
Franklin	3,824	3,947	4,177	5,301	65
Grant	3,670	2,280	3,290	3,611	77
Iberia	9,984	10,392	9,681	14,273	410
Iberville	7,254	3,822	9,361	4,463	172
Jackson	3,605	3,310	3,609	3,923	56
Jefferson	53,257	71,787	50,870	99,403	3,578
Jefferson Davis	6,376	3,603	6,140	5,667	201
Lafayette	19,918	22,805	19,694	31,429	1,263
Lafourche	14,131	11,434	14,222	14,951	675
LaSalle	2,961	3,161	2,665	3,792	61
Lincoln	4,971	6,828	5,598	7,515	177
Livingston	9,875	5,555	11,319	10,666	287
Madison	4,933	2,096	3,264	2,531	16
Morehouse	4,017	5,418	4,856	7,254	65
Natchitoches	6,692	5,248	7,102	6,668	158
Orleans	93,130	70,925	106,858	74,302	4,246
Ouachita	15,738	24,082	16,306	29,799	495
Plaquemines	2,614	6,052	4,318	5,489	154
Pointe Coupee	5,147	2,567	6,395	3,667	105
Rapides	20,851	17,766	19,436	25,576	530
Red River	1,906	1,728	2,776	2,147	29
Richland	3,495	3,630	3,745	4,772	48
Sabine	4,555	3,531	5,100	4,265	74
St. Bernard	12,969	12,707	11,367	19,410	616
St. Charles	6,872	4,270	7,898	6,779	283
St. Helen	2,622	1,046	3,183	1,531	42
St. James	4,531	2,751	6,206	3,429	113
St. John	5,700	3,597	7,647	5,819	261
St. Landry	15,631	9,956	17,125	14,940	332
St. Martin	7,992	4,112	7,760	6,701	281
St. Mary	9,401	8,919	10,506	10,378	339
St. Tammany	14,691	15,822	14,161	27,214	872
Tangipahoa	14,432	9,242	15,272	15,187	491
Tensas	2,081	1,553	2,046	1,645	25
Terrebonne	10,627	12,895	10,804	16,644	559
Union	3,600	4,139	3,841	5,130	60
Vermilion	11,246	6,133	9,743	10,481	473
Vernon	6,202	3,970	7,198	5,869	167
Washington	10,000	5,677	10,413	8,681	170
Webster	7,286	7,550	8,568	8,865	118
W. Baton Rouge	3,809	1,913	4,739	2,828	117
West Carroll	2,595	2,407	2,118	3,430	38
West Feliciana	1,890	990	2,341	1,237	40
Winn	3,543	3,209	3,411	3,944	57
Totals	**661,365**	**587,446**	**708,453**	**792,853**	**26,345**

Louisiana Vote Since 1932

1932 (Pres.), Roosevelt, Dem., 249,418; Hoover, Rep., 18,863.

1936 (Pres.), Roosevelt, Dem., 292,894; Landon, Rep., 36,791.

1940 (Pres.), Roosevelt, Dem., 319,751; Willkie, Rep., 52,446.

1944 (Pres.), Roosevelt, Dem., 281,564; Dewey, Rep., 67,750.

1948 (Pres.), Thurmond, States' Rights, 204,290; Truman, Dem., 136,344; Dewey, Rep., 72,657; Wallace, Prog., 3,035.

1952 (Pres.), Eisenhower, Rep., 306,925, Stevenson, Dem., 345,027.

1956 (Pres.), Eisenhower, Rep., 329,047; Stevenson, Dem., 243,977; Andrews, States' Rights, 44,520.

1960 (Pres.), Kennedy, Dem., 407,339; Nixon, Rep., 230,890; States' Rights (unpledged) 169,572.

1964 (Pres.), Johnson, Dem., 387,068; Goldwater, Rep., 509,225.

1968 (Pres.), Nixon, Rep., 257,535; Humphrey, Dem., 309,615; Wallace, 3d party, 530,300.

1972 (Pres.), Nixon, Rep., 686,852; McGovern, Dem., 298,142; Schmitz, Amer., 52,099; Jenness, Soc. Workers, 14,398.

1976 (Pres.), Carter, Dem., 661,365; Ford, Rep., 587,446; Maddox, Amer., 10,058; Hall, Com., 7,417; McCarthy, Ind., 6,588; MacBride, Libertarian, 3,325.

1980 (Pres.), Reagan, Rep., 792,853; Carter, Dem., 708,453; Anderson, Ind., 26,345; Rarick, Amer. Ind., 10,333; Clark, Libertarian, 8,240; Commoner, Citizens, 1,584; DeBerry, Soc. Work., 783.

Maine

County	1976 Carter (D)	1976 Ford (R)	1980 Carter (D)	1980 Reagan (R)	1980 Anderson (I)
Androscoggin	26,484	16,330	22,715	18,399	4,300
Aroostook	15,484	15,550	14,492	16,343	2,528
Cumberland	47,007	48,959	47,337	45,820	12,214
Franklin	5,140	5,799	4,979	5,680	1,205
Hancock	6,725	12,,064	7,027	11,435	2,300
Kennebec	23,473	22,534	20,943	21,517	5,553
Knox	5,922	8,315	5,732	7,631	1,842
Lincoln	4,818	7,554	4,776	7,434	1,556
Oxford	10,340	10,551	9,914	11,041	2,063
Penobscot	24,672	29,016	26,519	28,869	6,287
Piscataquis	3,727	4,084	3,550	4,015	781
Sagadahoc	5,529	5,988	5,663	5,946	1,252
Somerset	9,465	8,868	8,115	9,286	1,673
Waldo	4,853	6,289	4,883	6,514	1,304
Washington	6,644	7,039	6,050	7,180	1,301
York	31,996	27,380	28,279	31,412	7,168
Totals	**232,279**	**236,320**	**220,974**	**238,522**	**53,327**

Maine Vote Since 1932

1932 (Pres.), Roosevelt, Dem., 128,907; Hoover, Rep., 166,631; Thomas, Soc., 2,439; Reynolds, Soc. Labor, 255; Foster, Com., 162.

1936 (Pres.), Landon, Rep., 168,823; Roosevelt, Dem., 126,333; Lemke, Union, 7,581; Thomas, Soc., 783; Colvin, Proh., 334; Browder, Com., 257; Aiken, Soc. Labor, 129.

1940 (Pres.), Roosevelt, Dem., 156,478; Willkie, Rep., 165,951; Browder, Com., 411.

1944 (Pres.), Roosevelt, Dem., 140,631; Dewey, Rep., 155,434; Teichert, Soc. Labor, 335.

1948 (Pres.), Truman, Dem., 111,916; Dewey, Rep., 150,234; Wallace, Prog., 1,884; Thomas, Soc., 547; Teichert, Soc. Labor, 206.

1952 (Pres.), Eisenhower, Rep., 232,353; Stevenson, Dem., 118,806; Hallinan, Prog., 332; Hass, Soc. Labor, 156; Hoopes, Soc., 138; scattered, 1.

1956 (Pres.), Eisenhower, Rep., 249,238; Stevenson, Dem., 102,468.

1960 (Pres.), Kennedy, Dem., 181,159; Nixon, Rep., 240,608.

1964 (Pres.), Johnson, Dem., 262,264; Goldwater, Rep., 118,701.

1968 (Pres.), Nixon, Rep., 169,254; Humphrey, Dem., 217,312; Wallace, 3d party, 6,370.

1972 (Pres.), Nixon, Rep., 256,458; McGovern, Dem., 160,584; scattered, 229.

1976 (Pres.), Carter, Dem., 232,279; Ford, Rep., 236,320; McCarthy, Ind., 10,874; Bubar, Proh., 3,495.

1980 (Pres.), Reagan, Rep., 238,522; Carter, Dem., 220,974; Anderson, Ind., 53,327; Clark, Libertarian, 5,119; Commoner, Citizens, 4,394; Hall, Com., 591; write-ins, 84.

Maryland

	1976		1980		
County	Carter (D)	Ford (R)	Carter (D)	Reagan (R)	Anderson (I)
Allegany	15,967	15,435	12,167	17,512	1,486
Anne Arundel	54,351	61,353	50,780	69,443	10,020
Baltimore	118,505	143,293	121,280	132,490	23,096
Calvert	4,626	3,439	4,745	5,440	590
Caroline	3,017	3,114	2,833	3,582	291
Carroll	9,940	15,661	10,393	19,859	2,243
Cecil	8,950	7,833	7,937	9,673	1,037
Charles	9,525	7,792	8,887	11,807	1,153
Dorchester	4,528	4,768	4,908	5,160	360
Frederick	14,542	17,941	13,629	22,033	2,891
Garrett	3,332	4,640	2,708	5,475	270
Harford	19,890	24,309	20,042	26,713	3,761
Howard	20,533	21,200	20,702	24,272	6,028
Kent	3,211	2,821	2,986	2,889	371
Montgomery	131,098	122,674	105,822	125,515	32,730
Prince George	111,743	81,027	98,757	78,977	14,574
Queen Anne	3,457	3,479	3,820	4,749	480
St. Mary's	7,227	5,640	6,773	8,267	892
Somerset	3,472	3,254	3,342	3,312	215
Talbot	3,715	5,848	3,995	6,044	570
Washington	15,902	20,194	14,118	22,901	1,689
Wicomico	9,412	10,537	9,431	11,229	1,092
Worcester	4,076	4,647	4,195	5,362	586
BALTIMORE CITY	178,593	81,762	191,911	57,902	13,112
Totals	**759,612**	**672,661**	**726,161**	**680,606**	**119,537**

Maryland Vote Since 1932

1932 (Pres.), Roosevelt, Dem., 314,314; Hoover, Rep., 184,184; Thomas, Soc., 10,489; Reynolds, Soc. Labor, 1,036; Foster, Com., 1,031.

1936 (Pres.), Roosevelt, Dem., 389,612; Landon, Rep., 231,435; Thomas, Soc., 1,629; Aiken, Soc. Labor, 1,305; Browder, Com., 915.

1940 (Pres.), Roosevelt, Dem., 384,546; Willkie, Rep., 269,534; Thomas, Soc., 4,093; Browder, Com., 1,274; Aiken, Soc. Labor, 657.

1944 (Pres.), Roosevelt, Dem., 315,490; Dewey, Rep., 292,949.

1948 (Pres.), Truman, Dem., 286,521; Dewey, Rep., 294,814; Wallace, Prog., 9,983; Thomas, Soc., 2,941; Thurmond, States' Rights, 2,476; Wright, write-in, 2,294.

1952 (Pres.), Eisenhower, Rep., 499,424; Stevenson, Dem., 395,337; Hallinan, Prog., 7,313.

1956 (Pres.), Eisenhower, Rep., 559,738; Stevenson, Dem., 372,613.

1960 (Pres.), Kennedy, Dem., 565,800; Nixon, Rep., 489,538.

1964 (Pres.), Johnson, Dem., 730,912; Goldwater, Rep., 385,495; write-in, 50.

1968 (Pres.), Nixon, Rep., 517,995; Humphrey, Dem., 538,310; Wallace, 3d party, 178,734.

1972 (Pres.), Nixon, Rep., 829,305; McGovern, Dem., 505,781; Schmitz, Amer., 18,726.

1976 (Pres.), Carter, Dem., 759,612; Ford, Rep., 672,661.

1980 (Pres.), Reagan, Rep., 680,606; Carter, Dem., 726,161; Anderson, Ind., 119,537; Clark, Libertarian, 14,192.

Massachusetts

	1976		1980		
County	Carter (D)	Ford (R)	Carter (D)	Reagan (R)	Anderson (I)
Barnstable	31,268	39,295	23,952	41,493	15,951
Berkshire	39,337	27,462	29,458	27,063	10,575
Bristol	116,318	69,957	83,460	77,545	25,423
Dukes	2,513	2,365	2,370	1,809	1,127
Essex	165,710	125,538	116,173	130,252	47,670
Franklin	14,985	14,837	11,830	12,528	5,162
Hampden	110,028	70,008	80,369	72,528	24,765
Hampshire	34,947	22,219	27,611	21,117	10,119
Middlesex	359,919	260,044	270,751	256,999	102,180
Nantucket	1,115	1,399	1,040	1,149	614
Norfolk	155,342	136,628	117,274	136,184	47,076
Plymouth	83,663	74,684	58,772	85,593	26,510
Suffolk	142,010	80,623	113,416	73,271	26,988
Worcester	172,320	105,217	117,326	120,100	38,379
Totals	**1,429,475**	**1,030,276**	**1,053,802**	**1,057,631**	**382,539**

Massachusetts Vote Since 1932

1932 (Pres.), Roosevelt, Dem., 800,148; Hoover, Rep. 736,959; Thomas, Soc., 34,305; Foster, Com., 4,821; Reynolds, Soc. Labor, 2,668; Upshaw, Proh., 1,142.

1936 (Pres.), Roosevelt, Dem., 942,716; Landon, Rep. 768,613; Lemke, Union, 118,639; Thomas, Soc., 5,111 Browder, Com., 2,930; Aiken, Soc. Labor, 1,305; Colvin Proh., 1,032.

1940 (Pres.), Roosevelt, Dem., 1,076,522; Willkie, Rep. 939,700; Thomas, Soc., 4,091; Browder, Com., 3,806; Aiken, Soc. Labor, 1,492; Babson, Proh., 1,370.

1944 (Pres.), Roosevelt, Dem., 1,035,296; Dewey, Rep. 921,350; Teichert, Soc. Labor, 2,780; Watson, Proh., 973.

1948 (Pres.), Truman, Dem., 1,151,788; Dewey, Rep., 909,370; Wallace, Prog., 38,157; Teichert, Soc. Labor, 5,535; Watson, Proh., 1,663.

1952 (Pres.), Eisenhower, Rep., 1,292,325; Stevenson, Dem., 1,083,525; Hallinan, Prog., 4,636; Hass, Soc. Labor, 1,957; Hamblen, Proh., 886; scattered, 69; blanks, 41,150.

1956 (Pres.), Eisenhower, Rep., 1,393,197; Stevenson, Dem., 948,190; Hass, Soc. Labor, 5,573; Holtwick, Proh., 1,205; others, 341.

1960 (Pres.), Kennedy, Dem., 1,487,174; Nixon, Rep., 976,750; Hass, Soc. Labor, 3,892; Decker, Proh., 1,633; others, 31; blank and void, 26,024.

1964 (Pres.), Johnson, Dem., 1,786,422; Goldwater, Rep., 549,727; Hass, Soc. Labor, 4,755; Munn, Proh., 3,735; scattered, 159; blank, 48,104.

1968 (Pres.), Nixon, Rep., 766,844; Humphrey, Dem., 1,469,218; Wallace, 3d party, 87,088; Blomen, Soc. Labor, 6,180; Munn, Proh., 2,369; scattered, 53; blanks, 25,394.

1972 (Pres.), Nixon, Rep., 1,112,078; McGovern, Dem., 1,332,540; Jenness, Soc. Workers, 10,600; Fisher, Soc. Labor, 129; Schmitz, Amer., 2,877; Spock, Peoples, 101; Hall, Com., 46; Hospers, Libertarian, 43; scattered, 342.

1976 (Pres.), Carter, Dem., 1,429,475; Ford, Rep., 1,030,276; McCarthy, Ind., 65,637; Camejo, Soc. Workers, 8,138; Anderson, Amer., 7,555; La Rouche, U.S. Labor, 4,922; MacBride, Libertarian, 135.

1980 (Pres.), Reagan, Rep., 1,057,631; Carter, Dem., 1,053,802; Anderson, Ind., 382,539; Clark, Libertarian, 22,038; DeBerry, Soc. Workers, 3,735; Commoner, Citizens, 2,056; McReynolds, Socialist, 62; Bubar, Statesman, 34; Griswold, Workers World, 19; scattered, 2,382.

Michigan

	1976		1980		
County	Carter (D)	Ford (R)	Carter (D)	Reagan (R)	Anderson (I)
Alcona	2,038	2,328	1,857	2,905	247
Alger	2,379	1,722	2,242	2,059	263
Allegan	9,794	19,330	9,877	20,560	1,984
Alpena	6,310	6,380	5,834	6,901	913
Antrim	3,032	4,369	2,909	4,706	602
Arenac	2,695	2,687	2,547	3,436	333
Baraga	1,778	1,788	1,609	2,046	201
Barry	6,967	11,178	6,857	12,006	1,399
Bay	25,958	23,174	24,517	25,331	3,886
Benzie	1,891	3,085	1,842	3,054	455
Berrien	25,163	40,835	22,152	41,458	3,422
Branch	6,301	8,251	4,635	10,224	1,102
Calhoun	25,229	30,390	23,022	30,912	4,468
Cass	7,843	9,893	7,058	11,206	1,156
Charlevoix	3,953	5,145	3,741	5,053	816
Cheboygan	3,880	4,894	3,938	5,221	638
Chippewa	6,022	7,025	5,268	7,059	951
Clare	4,153	4,879	4,164	5,719	663
Clinton	7,549	13,475	7,539	14,968	1,736
Crawford	1,889	2,359	1,826	2,652	390
Delta	9,027	7,809	8,475	8,146	849
Dickinson	6,134	5,922	5,694	6,614	596
Eaton	12,083	22,120	12,742	22,927	3,533
Emmet	4,013	5,910	3,724	5,930	1,134
Genesee	88,967	80,004	90,393	78,572	12,274
Gladwin	3,719	3,794	3,733	4,509	463

	1976 (D)	1976 (R)	1980 (D)	1980 (R)	1980 (I)
Gogebic	6,341	3,953	5,254	4,388	493
Grand Traverse	7,263	13,505	7,150	14,484	2,568
Gratiot	5,429	9,526	4,916	9,294	1,193
Hillsdale	5,427	9,307	4,375	10,951	882
Houghton	7,352	8,049	6,858	7,926	1,423
Huron	5,721	9,297	4,434	10,553	976
Ingham	47,890	66,729	48,278	56,777	17,139
Ionia	6,820	11,737	7,039	12,040	1,539
Iosco	4,875	5,500	4,255	6,680	739
Iron	4,401	3,224	3,742	3,507	371
Isabella	7,281	10,577	7,293	10,407	2,511
Jackson	24,726	32,873	23,685	33,749	4,165
Kalamazoo	33,411	51,462	34,528	48,669	10,833
Kalkaska	1,957	2,280	1,807	2,802	260
Kent	59,000	126,805	72,790	112,,604	17,913
Keweenaw	658	606	570	583	87
Lake	2,179	1,598	2,041	1,730	187
Lapeer	9,503	12,349	9,671	15,996	1,868
Leelanau	2,437	4,240	2,348	4,585	839
Lenawee	14,610	18,397	12,935	20,366	2,230
Livingston	12,415	19,437	12,626	25,012	3,247
Luce	1,099	1,379	992	1,659	177
Mackinac	2,452	3,107	2,262	3,021	415
Macomb	121,176	132,499	120,125	154,155	18,975
Manistee	4,479	5,532	4,164	5,662	699
Marquette	12,837	12,984	13,312	13,181	2,481
Mason	4,541	6,812	4,134	7,137	825
Mecosta	4,725	7,287	5,228	7,754	1,322
Menominee	5,596	5,633	4,962	6,170	452
Midland	11,959	17,631	12,019	17,828	3,152
Missaukee	1,688	2,943	1,563	3,221	230
Monroe	23,290	20,676	20,578	25,612	3,111
Montcalm	6,684	10,439	6,706	10,822	1,309
Montmorency	1,684	1,882	1,654	2,400	195
Muskegon	27,013	35,548	26,645	36,512	4,094
Newaygo	5,622	8,258	5,236	8,918	850
Oakland	164,266	244,271	164,869	253,211	38,273
Oceana	3,427	5,236	3,386	5,465	570
Ogemaw	3,545	3,212	3,426	4,169	425
Ontonagon	3,104	2,462	2,375	2,569	237
Osceola	2,603	4,467	2,650	4,902	466
Oscoda	1,108	1,541	1,325	1,915	183
Otsego	2,724	3,155	2,666	3,771	493
Ottawa	16,381	49,196	18,435	51,217	4,903
Presque Isle	3,334	3,545	2,952	3,486	382
Roscommon	3,691	4,608	3,763	5,280	508
Saginaw	36,280	46,765	41,650	45,233	5,677
St. Clair	22,734	26,311	20,410	31,021	3,592
St. Joseph	7,306	11,784	6,318	13,631	1,283
Sanilac	6,042	10,597	4,898	12,158	863
Schoolcraft	2,158	1,933	1,964	2,097	243
Shiawassee	12,202	15,113	11,985	15,756	2,121
Tuscola	7,932	12,059	7,632	13,306	1,266
Van Buren	10,366	13,615	9,248	14,451	1,691
Washtenaw	50,917	56,807	51,013	48,699	13,463
Wayne	548,767	348,588	522,024	315,532	43,608
Wexford	4,519	5,670	4,173	6,027	752
Totals	**1,696,714**	**1,893,742**	**1,661,532**	**1,915,225**	**275,223**

Michigan Vote Since 1932

1932 (Pres.), Roosevelt, Dem., 871,700; Hoover, Rep., 739,894; Thomas, Soc., 39,025; Foster, Com., 9,318; Upshaw, Proh., 2,893; Reynolds, Soc. Labor, 1,041; Harvey, Lib., 217.

1936 (Pres.), Roosevelt, Dem., 1,016,794; Landon, Rep., 699,733; Lemke, Union, 75,795; Thomas, Soc., 8,208; Browder, Com., 3,384; Aiken, Soc. Labor, 600; Colvin, Proh., 579.

1940 (Pres.), Roosevelt, Dem., 1,032,991; Willkie, Rep., 1,039,917; Thomas, Soc., 7,593; Browder, Com., 2,834; Babson, Proh., 1,795; Aiken, Soc. Labor, 795.

1944 (Pres.), Roosevelt, Dem., 1,106,899; Dewey, Rep., 1,084,423; Watson, Proh., 6,503; Thomas, Soc., 4,598; Smith, America First, 1,530; Teichert, Soc. Labor, 1,264.

1948 (Pres.), Truman, Dem., 1,003,448; Dewey, Rep., 1,038,595; Wallace, Prog., 46,515; Watson, Proh., 13,052; Thomas, Soc. 6,063; Teichert, Soc. Labor, 1,263; Dobbs, Soc. Workers, 672.

1952 (Pres.), Eisenhower, Rep., 1,551,529; Stevenson, Dem., 1,230,657; Hamblen, Proh., 10,331; Hallinan, Prog., 3,922; Hass, Soc. Labor, 1,495; Dobbs, Soc. Workers, 655; scattered, 3.

1956 (Pres.), Eisenhower, Rep., 1,713,647; Stevenson, Dem., 1,359,898; Holtwick, Proh., 6,923.

1960 (Pres.), Kennedy, Dem., 1,687,269; Nixon, Rep., 1,620,428; Dobbs, Soc. Workers, 4,347; Decker, Proh., 2,029; Daly, Tax Cut, 1,767; Hass, Soc. Labor, 1,718; Ind. American, 539.

1964 (Pres.), Johnson, Dem., 2,136,615; Goldwater, Rep., 1,060,152; DeBerry, Soc. Workers, 3,817; Hass, Soc. Labor, 1,704; Proh. (no candidate listed), 699, scattering, 145.

1968 (Pres.), Nixon, Rep., 1,370,665; Humphrey, Dem., 1,593,082; Wallace, 3d party, 331,968; Halstead, Soc. Worker, 4,099; Blomen, Soc. Labor, 1,762; Cleaver, New Politics, 4,585; Munn, Proh., 60; scattering, 29.

1972 (Pres.), Nixon, Rep., 1,961,721; McGovern, Dem., 1,459,435; Schmitz, Amer., 63,321; Fisher, Soc. Labor, 2,437; Jenness, Soc. Workers, 1,603; Hall, Com., 1,210.

1976 (Pres.), Carter, Dem., 1,696,714; Ford, Rep., 1,893,742; McCarthy, Ind., 47,905; MacBride, Libertarian, 5,406; Wright, People's, 3,504, Camejo, Soc. Workers, 1,804; LaRouche, U.S. Labor, 1,366; Levin, Soc. Labor, 1,148; scattering, 2,160.

1980 (Pres.), Reagan, Rep., 1,915,225; Carter, Dem., 1,661,532; Anderson, Ind., 275,223; Clark, Libertarian, 41,597; Commoner, Citizens, 11,930; Hall, Com., 3,262; Griswold, Workers World, 30; Greaves, American, 21; Bubar, Statesman, 9.

Minnesota

County	1976 Carter (D)	1976 Ford (R)	1980 Carter (D)	1980 Reagan (R)	1980 Anderson (I)
Aitkin	4,308	2,476	3,677	3,396	380
Anoka	48,173	27,863	45,532	33,100	6,828
Becker	6,597	5,611	5,221	6,848	866
Beltrami	7,540	5,214	7,432	6,481	1,254
Benton	6,235	4,099	5,272	5,513	646
Big Stone	2,581	1,332	1,814	1,950	249
Blue Earth	12,930	11,998	10,930	11,966	2,698
Brown	5,792	7,479	4,915	8,051	842
Carlton	9,247	4,371	8,822	4,760	883
Carver	7,574	8,199	6,621	9,909	1,496
Cass	5,424	4,443	4,717	6,119	434
Chippewa	4,648	3,254	3,164	4,252	532
Chisago	6,625	3,874	6,240	5,017	939
Clay	10,876	10,317	8,940	10,447	2,773
Clearwater	2,437	1,374	1,955	1,919	185
Cook	1,018	1,034	871	1,174	182
Cottonwood	3,813	3,906	2,958	4,258	535
Crow Wing	10,653	8,072	9,323	10,844	1,046
Dakota	44,253	37,542	43,433	40,708	8,588
Dodge	3,009	3,446	2,698	3,900	367
Douglas	7,097	5,910	5,530	7,778	844
Faribault	5,049	5,577	3,620	6,206	525
Fillmore	4,758	5,984	4,010	6,452	650
Freeborn	9,470	8,220	8,212	8,475	808
Goodhue	8,926	9,967	8,566	9,329	1,964
Grant	2,624	1,635	1,822	2,054	333
Hennepin	257,380	211,892	239,592	194,998	56,390
Houston	3,861	4,853	3,218	5,582	477
Hubbard	3,196	2,985	2,840	4,172	365
Isanti	6,013	3,159	5,457	4,480	641
Itasca	12,979	6,646	12,138	8,368	1,080
Jackson	4,311	2,870	3,062	3,391	463
Kanabec	3,188	1,943	2,654	2,500	269
Kandiyohi	9,992	6,664	8,038	8,480	1,244
Kittson	2,008	1,555	1,407	1,875	243
Koochiching	4,846	2,893	4,181	3,433	496
LacQuiParle	3,647	2,292	2,457	2,981	334
Lake	3,973	2,313	3,864	2,414	443
Lake O'Woods	1,105	757	763	1,052	128
Le Sueur	6,556	4,565	5,161	5,478	731
Lincoln	2,594	1,599	1,640	2,122	295
Lyon	7,122	5,036	5,626	5,852	1,129
McLeod	6,249	6,519	4,987	7,819	852
Mahnomen	1,590	905	1,175	1,275	153
Marshall	3,744	2,605	2,636	3,638	397
Martin	5,672	6,484	4,301	7,057	751
Meeker	5,295	4,097	4,238	5,032	668
Mille Lacs	5,172	3,212	4,443	3,860	550
Morrison	8,176	4,590	6,930	6,296	559
Mower	12,837	8,163	10,538	7,908	1,465
Murray	3,685	2,605	2,714	3,004	359
Nicollet	5,777	6,071	5,400	6,436	1,519
Nobles	6,034	4,503	4,703	4,706	657
Norman	2,946	1,983	2,253	2,192	369
Olmsted	14,676	24,030	13,983	22,704	3,638
Otter Tail	11,881	12,113	9,108	15,091	1,538
Pennington	3,787	3,023	3,101	3,715	472
Pine	5,442	3,057	5,121	3,899	467
Pipestone	3,272	3,018	2,392	3,207	561
Polk	9,078	6,522	7,151	9,036	1,207
Pope	3,746	2,251	2,527	3,159	354
Ramsey	133,682	86,480	124,774	78,860	23,222
Red Lake	1,748	737	1,318	1,223	116
Redwood	4,525	4,926	2,952	5,993	548
Renville	5,762	4,482	4,058	5,544	653
Rice	10,590	8,311	9,531	8,168	2,414
Rock	2,769	2,892	2,089	3,164	397
Roseau	3,215	2,382	2,616	3,358	259
St. Louis	75,040	35,331	69,403	33,407	8,719

	1976		1980		
	(D)	(R)	(D)	(R)	(I)
Scott	9,912	7,154	9,115	9,018	1,475
Sherburne	6,678	4,361	6,229	6,035	985
Sibley	3,752	3,871	2,521	4,460	509
Stearns	25,027	19,574	21,862	24,888	3,555
Steele	6,263	7,053	5,095	7,805	1,087
Stevens	3,171	2,484	2,559	3,283	524
Swift	4,428	2,190	3,245	2,943	511
Todd	6,530	4,278	4,975	6,451	451
Traverse	2,020	1,130	1,258	1,574	159
Wabasha	4,286	4,484	3,712	4,886	549
Wadena	3,164	3,048	2,635	4,089	265
Waseca	4,002	4,582	3,535	4,801	777
Washington	26,454	20,716	25,634	22,718	5,050
Watonwan	3,177	3,351	2,442	3,629	415
Wilkin	2,103	1,882	1,496	2,224	318
Winona	10,939	10,436	9,814	10,332	1,780
Wright	13,379	9,314	12,383	12,293	1,692
Yellow Med	4,337	2,946	2,833	4,004	456
Totals	**1,070,440**	**819,395**	**954,173**	**873,268**	**174,997**

Minnesota Vote Since 1932

1932 (Pres.), Roosevelt, Dem., 600,806; Hoover, Rep., 363,959; Thomas, Soc., 25,476; Foster, Com., 6,101; Coxey, Farm.-Lab., 5,731; Reynolds, Ind., 770.

1936 (Pres.), Roosevelt, Dem., 698,811; Landon, Rep., 350,461; Lemke, Union, 74,296; Thomas, Soc., 2,872; Browder, Com., 2,574; Aiken, Soc. Labor, 961.

1940 (Pres.), Roosevelt, Dem., 644,196; Willkie, Rep., 596,274; Thomas, Soc., 5,454; Browder, Com., 2,711; Aiken, Ind., 2,553.

1944 (Pres.), Roosevelt, Dem., 589,864; Dewey, Rep., 527,416; Thomas, Soc., 5,073; Teichert, Ind. Gov't., 3,176.

1948 (Pres.), Truman, Dem., 692,966; Dewey, Rep., 483,617; Wallace, Prog., 27,866; Thomas, Soc., 4,646; Teichert, Soc. Labor, 2,525; Dobbs, Soc. Workers, 606.

1952 (Pres.), Eisenhower, Rep., 763,211; Stevenson, Dem., 608,458; Hallinan, Prog., 2,666; Hass, Soc. Labor, 2,383; Hamblen, Proh., 2,147; Dobbs, Soc. Workers, 618.

1956 (Pres.), Eisenhower, Rep., 719,302; Stevenson, Dem., 617,525; Hass, Soc. Labor (Ind. Gov.), 2,080; Dobbs, Soc. Workers, 1,098.

1960 (Pres.), Kennedy, Dem., 779,933; Nixon, Rep., 757,915; Dobbs, Soc. Workers, 3,077; Industrial Gov., 962.

1964 (Pres.), Johnson, Dem., 991,117; Goldwater, Rep., 559,624; DeBerry, Soc. Workers, 1,177; Hass, Industrial Gov., 2,544.

1968 (Pres.), Nixon, Rep., 658,643; Humphrey, Dem., 857,738; Wallace, 3d party, 68,931; scattered, 2,443; Halstead, Soc. Worker, 808; Blomen, Ind. Gov't., 285; Mitchell, Com., 415; Cleaver, Peace, 935; McCarthy, write-in, 585; scattered, 170.

1972 (Pres.), Nixon, Rep., 898,269; McGovern, Dem., 802,346; Schmitz, Amer., 31,407; Spock, Peoples, 2,805; Fisher, Soc. Labor, 4,261; Jenness, Soc. Workers, 940; Hall, Com., 662; scattered, 962.

1976 (Pres.), Carter, Dem., 1,070,440; Ford, Rep., 819,395; McCarthy, Ind., 35,490; Anderson, Amer., 13,592; Camejo, Soc. Workers, 4,149; MacBride, Libertarian, 3,529; Hall, Com., 1,092.

1980 (Pres.), Reagan, Rep., 873, 268; Carter, Dem., 954,173; Anderson, Ind., 174,997; Clark, Libertarian, 31,593; Commoner, Citizens, 8,406; Hall, Com., 1,117; DeBerry, Soc. Workers, 711; Griswold, Workers World, 698; McReynolds, Socialist, 536; write-ins, 281.

Mississippi

	1976		1980		
	Carter	Ford	Carter	Reagan	Anderson
County	(D)	(R)	(D)	(R)	(I)
Adams	6,619	6,431	7,228	7,523	151
Alcorn	6,995	3,430	6,242	5,196	898
Amite	2,574	2,256	3,229	2,653	43
Attala	4,068	3,146	4,117	3,975	71
Benton	2,375	790	2,094	1,254	35
Bolivar	7,561	5,136	8,839	5,148	280
Calhoun	2,724	1,892	3,295	2,579	64
Carroll	1,566	1,561	2,037	2,153	22
Chickasaw	2,891	2,581	3,622	2,540	71
Choctaw	1,520	1,562	1,729	1,927	26
Claiborne	2,657	1,078	3,032	1,129	22
Clarke	2,816	2,935	3,303	3,303	41
Clay	3,514	3,017	4,275	3,439	124
Coahoma	6,412	4,269	7,030	4,592	256
Copiah	4,267	4,108	5,517	4,461	76
Covington	2,862	2,591	2,956	3,471	39
DeSoto	7,756	6,240	6,344	9,655	237
Forrest	7,914	10,770	8,274	12,656	275
Franklin	1,578	1,719	2,040	2,026	23
George	3,072	1,957	2,757	3,052	64
Greene	2,127	1,538	1,740	1,772	23
Grenada	3,263	3,569	4,182	3,993	59
Hancock	3,855	3,765	3,544	5,088	159
Harrison	16,569	19,207	16,318	25,175	822
Hinds	28,748	45,803	39,369	48,135	1,414
Holmes	4,616	2,438	5,463	2,693	57
Humphreys	2,172	1,445	2,970	1,841	68
Issaquena	567	325	598	349	5
Itawamba	4,480	2,153	4,852	2,906	57
Jackson	12,533	17,177	12,226	22,498	653
Jasper	3,109	2,356	3,813	2,781	34
Jefferson	2,562	782	2,871	751	41
Jefferson Davis	2,747	1,868	3,831	2,280	24
Jones	10,139	11,098	11,117	12,900	155
Kemper	2,436	1,680	2,601	1,822	12
Lafayette	4,375	3,735	4,887	4,366	243
Lamar	3,109	4,056	3,005	5,395	84
Lauderdale	9,813	14,273	9,918	14,727	784
Lawrence	2,242	2,109	2,692	2,781	49
Leake	3,415	2,952	4,033	3,624	40
Lee	8,504	7,366	10,047	8,326	321
Leflore	6,135	5,872	7,498	5,798	166
Lincoln	4,043	6,084	5,213	7,286	75
Lowndes	6,181	8,003	6,187	9,973	140
Madison	6,240	4,838	7,621	6,024	276
Marion	5,283	5,300	5,366	5,218	62
Marshall	6,769	2,242	7,153	3,455	121
Monroe	6,097	4,737	6,998	4,793	177
Montgomery	2,410	2,278	2,730	2,479	42
Neshoba	3,891	3,859	3,872	5,165	72
Newton	2,741	3,813	3,455	4,317	86
Noxubee	2,121	1,860	3,434	1,970	47
Oktibbeha	4,339	5,194	6,039	6,300	258
Panola	5,517	3,341	6,179	4,219	149
Pearl River	5,024	4,332	5,028	6,822	161
Perry	1,965	1,527	1,957	2,255	25
Pike	5,749	5,659	6,694	6,661	129
Pontotoc	4,066	2,245	4,499	3,198	58
Prentiss	4,431	2,362	4,832	3,264	40
Quitman	2,621	1,287	2,926	1,691	83
Rankin	6,937	11,507	8,047	16,650	296
Scott	3,643	3,649	4,043	4,645	72
Sharkey	1,283	1,024	1,957	996	28
Simpson	3,600	4,291	4,015	5,190	70
Smith	2,434	3,147	2,474	3,772	46
Stone	1,648	1,575	1,821	1,888	53
Sunflower	4,322	3,456	5,035	3,728	82
Tallahatchie	2,991	2,146	3,467	2,183	45
Tate	3,747	2,497	3,892	3,343	80
Tippah	4,260	1,887	3,878	3,338	116
Tishomingo	3,734	1,969	4,595	2,489	79
Tunica	1,695	951	2,198	954	24
Union	5,021	2,507	5,001	3,545	94
Walthall	2,650	2,110	2,960	2,703	34
Warren	6,299	8,699	7,489	10,151	274
Washington	9,650	7,474	10,722	8,978	186
Wayne	3,306	3,022	3,494	3,844	26
Webster	2,218	1,943	2,178	2,386	75
Wilkinson	2,514	1,273	2,981	1,442	25
Winston	3,956	3,659	4,416	3,998	65
Yalobusha	2,603	1,808	3,432	2,224	78
Yazoo	4,053	4,255	5,468	4,819	99
Totals	**381,309**	**366,846**	**429,281**	**441,089**	**12,036**

Mississippi Vote Since 1932

1932 (Pres.), Roosevelt, Dem., 140,168; Hoover, Rep., 5,180; Thomas, Soc., 686.

1936 (Pres.), Roosevelt, Dem., 157,318; Landon, Rep., Howard faction, 2,760; Rowlands faction, 1,675 total 4,435; Thomas, Soc., 329.

1940 (Pres.), Roosevelt, Dem., 168,252; Willkie, Ind. Rep., 4,550; Rep., 2,814; total, 7,364; Thomas, Soc., 103.

1944 (Pres.), Roosevelt, Dem., 158,515; Dewey, Rep., 3,742; Reg. Dem., 9,964; Ind. Rep., 7,859.

1948 (Pres.), Thurmond, States' Rights, 167,538; Truman, Dem., 19,384; Dewey, Rep., 5,043; Wallace, Prog., 225.

1952 (Pres.), Eisenhower, Ind. vote pledged to Rep. candidate, 112,966; Stevenson, Dem., 172,566.

1956 (Pres.), Stevenson, Dem., 144,498; Eisenhower, Rep., 56,372; Black and Tan Grand Old Party, 4,313; total, 60,685; Byrd, Ind., 42,966.

1960 (Pres.), Democratic unpledged electors, 116,248; Kennedy, Dem., 108,362; Nixon, Rep., 73,561. Mississippi's victorious slate of 8 unpledged Democratic electors cast their votes for Sen. Harry F. Byrd (D-Va.).

1964 (Pres.), Johnson, Dem., 52,618; Goldwater, Rep.,

356,528.

1968 (Pres.), Nixon, Rep., 88,516; Humphrey, Dem., 150,644; Wallace, 3d party, 415,349.

1972 (Pres.), Nixon, Rep., 505,125; McGovern, Dem., 126,782; Schmitz, Amer., 11,598; Jenness, Soc. Workers, 2,458.

1976 (Pres.), Carter, Dem., 381,309; Ford, Rep., 366,846; Anderson, Amer., 6,678; McCarthy, Ind., 4,074; Maddox, Ind., 4,049; Camejo, Soc. Workers, 2,805; MacBride, Libertarian, 2,609.

1980 (Pres.), Reagan, Rep., 441,089; Carter, Dem., 429,281; Anderson, Ind., 12,036; Clark, Libertarian, 5,465; Griswold, Workers World, 2,402; Pulley, Soc. Worker, 2,347.

Missouri

	1976		1980		
County	Carter (D)	Ford (R)	Carter (D)	Reagan (R)	Anderson (I)
Adair	3,684	5,249	3,507	5,513	414
Andrew	3,042	3,130	2,575	3,690	245
Atchison	1,126	1,960	1,273	2,096	151
Audrain	5,600	5,378	5,168	6,347	233
arry	5,046	5,053	4,193	7,038	150
arton	2,326	2,708	1,901	3,337	115
ates	4,288	3,350	3,297	4,061	114
enton	2,684	2,875	2,241	3,451	126
ollinger	2,740	2,113	2,160	2,863	35
oone	17,674	16,373	18,527	16,313	3,519
uchanan	17,427	16,446	16,967	16,551	1,301
utler	6,759	5,669	5,605	8,342	181
aldwell	2,113	2,094	1,541	2,551	108
allaway	4,843	5,115	5,560	6,755	420
amden	3,975	4,469	3,416	6,541	218
ape Girardeau	10,440	12,607	8,625	14,861	873
arroll	3,114	2,936	2,130	3,291	130
arter	1,154	842	1,087	1,218	37
ass	9,008	7,182	8,198	10,105	667
edar	2,192	2,752	1,703	3,469	86
hariton	3,055	2,128	2,250	2,641	63
hristian	3,830	4,553	3,502	6,487	205
lark	1,679	1,582	1,494	2,042	56
lay	26,609	24,962	24,250	28,521	2,782
linton	3,424	2,807	3,001	3,599	184
ole	7,949	14,370	9,210	16,373	691
ooper	3,087	3,694	2,687	3,996	130
rawford	3,565	3,224	2,710	4,081	170
ade	1,681	2,015	1,283	2,410	61
allas	2,453	2,430	2,011	3,297	114
aviess	2,250	1,919	1,770	2,125	61
eKalb	2,023	1,739	1,677	2,062	111
ent	2,931	2,433	2,528	3,477	86
ouglas	1,981	2,652	1,677	3,440	93
unklin	7,107	3,314	6,120	5,253	128
ranklin	11,695	12,242	10,480	15,210	863
asconade	1,702	3,925	1,550	4,481	136
entry	2,249	1,772	1,720	2,005	117
reene	33,824	37,691	30,498	43,116	3,261
rundy	2,597	2,646	2,064	2,890	110
arrison	2,304	2,478	1,732	2,734	140
enry	5,282	4,168	4,648	4,807	238
ickory	1,398	1,403	1,248	1,893	52
olt	1,529	1,777	1,119	1,993	59
oward	2,769	1,690	2,243	2,179	114
owell	5,265	4,692	4,472	7,149	211
on	2,646	1,765	2,226	2,205	94
ackson	130,120	101,401	135,805	106,156	12,260
asper	14,910	17,086	11,953	21,664	785
efferson	25,159	18,261	24,042	28,546	1,753
ohnson	5,551	5,513	5,441	6,449	571
nox	1,319	1,216	1,187	1,475	36
aclede	4,381	4,067	3,443	5,642	153
afayette	6,410	6,823	5,792	7,271	339
awrence	5,315	5,784	4,670	7,921	184
ewis	2,486	1,983	2,314	2,350	102
ncoln	4,473	3,581	4,110	4,963	182
nn	4,092	3,114	3,467	3,585	139
vingston	3,819	3,010	3,368	3,654	205
cDonald	3,111	2,949	2,485	4,114	124
acon	4,296	3,360	3,578	4,430	135
adison	2,229	1,739	2,231	2,618	70
aries	1,796	1,485	1,732	1,985	39
arion	6,124	5,501	5,890	6,036	192
ercer	1,177	1,025	821	1,266	54
iller	2,739	4,095	2,469	5,560	115
ississippi	3,366	1,733	3,040	2,459	64
oniteau	2,462	3,077	2,284	3,430	98
onroe	3,039	1,585	2,445	2,026	53
ontgomery	2,535	2,665	2,007	3,061	124
organ	2,738	2,831	2,460	3,577	114
ew Madrid	5,319	2,798	4,171	4,041	64
ewton	7,045	7,142	5,621	10,515	341
odaway	4,875	4,558	4,257	4,544	414
regon	2,564	1,122	2,326	1,523	26
sage	2,015	3,224	2,045	3,679	72
zark	1,341	1,754	1,242	2,434	63
emiscot	4,681	2,541	4,140	3,519	52
Perry	2,801	4,086	2,416	5,053	178
Pettis	7,887	7,344	6,475	8,833	435
Phelps	6,261	6,153	5,470	7,366	620
Pike	3,770	3,355	3,454	3,932	158
Platte	8,651	8,103	7,342	10,092	1,107
Polk	3,663	3,893	3,336	4,842	135
Pulaski	4,370	2,865	3,707	3,998	128
Putnam	1,097	1,444	871	1,722	44
Ralls	2,318	1,334	2,069	1,968	75
Randolph	5,839	3,594	4,884	5,141	213
Ray	5,535	2,853	4,518	4,064	215
Reynolds	2,143	879	1,919	1,271	44
Ripley	2,577	1,640	2,156	2,524	61
St. Charles	22,063	26,105	20,668	36,050	2,494
St. Clair	2,271	1,808	1,706	2,419	60
St. Francois	8,852	7,002	7,495	8,914	397
Ste. Genevieve	3,091	2,241	3,324	2,768	151
St. Louis	196,915	246,988	192,796	263,518	25,032
Saline	5,890	4,883	4,943	5,218	353
Schuyler	1,417	1,193	1,114	1,386	48
Scotland	1,449	1,286	1,200	1,592	63
Scott	8,075	5,473	6,854	8,227	203
Shannon	1,960	989	1,818	1,523	44
Shelby	2,227	1,453	1,849	2,151	60
Stoddard	6,097	3,989	5,128	6,199	132
Stone	2,358	3,457	2,210	4,780	180
Sullivan	2,313	2,141	1,824	2,412	76
Taney	3,626	4,696	3,389	6,230	195
Texas	4,638	3,338	4,261	4,879	125
Vernon	4,921	3,715	3,704	4,391	285
Warren	2,164	3,214	2,132	4,366	192
Washington	3,543	2,526	2,873	3,439	89
Wayne	2,987	1,963	2,549	2,823	44
Webster	3,759	3,510	3,409	5,121	149
Worth	969	771	760	833	47
Wright	2,781	3,397	2,182	4,451	56
ST. LOUIS CITY	118,703	58,367	113,697	50,333	5,656
Write-in Vote	1,576	1,365			
Totals	**999,163**	**928,808**	**931,182**	**1,074,181**	**77,920**

Missouri Vote Since 1932

1932 (Pres.), Roosevelt, Dem., 1,025,406; Hoover, Rep., 564,713; Thomas, Soc., 16,374; Upshaw, Proh., 2,429; Foster, Com., 568; Reynolds, Soc. Labor, 404.

1936 (Pres.), Roosevelt, Dem., 1,111,403; Landon, Rep., 697,891; Lemke, Union, 14,630; Thomas, Soc., 3,454; Colvin, Proh., 908; Browder, Com., 417; Aiken, Soc. Labor, 292.

1940 (Pres.), Roosevelt, Dem., 958,476; Willkie, Rep., 871,009; Thomas, Soc., 2,226; Babson, Proh., 1,809; Aiken, Soc. Labor, 209.

1944 (Pres.), Roosevelt, Dem., 807,357; Dewey, Rep., 761,175; Thomas, Soc., 1,750; Watson, Proh., 1,175; Teichert, Soc. Labor, 221.

1948 (Pres.), Truman, Dem., 917,315; Dewey, Rep., 655,039; Wallace, Prog., 3,998; Thomas, Soc., 2,222.

1952 (Pres.), Eisenhower, Rep., 959,429; Stevenson, Dem., 929,830; Hallinan, Prog., 987; Hamblen, Proh., 885; MacArthur, Christian Nationalist, 302; America First, 233; Hoopes, Soc., 227; Hass, Soc. Labor, 169.

1956 (Pres.), Stevenson, Dem., 918,273; Eisenhower, Rep., 914,299.

1960 (Pres.), Kennedy, Dem., 972,201; Nixon, Rep., 962,221.

1964 (Pres.), Johnson, Dem., 1,164,344; Goldwater, Rep., 653,535.

1968 (Pres.), Nixon, Rep., 811,932; Humphrey, Dem., 791,444; Wallace, 3d party, 206,126.

1972 (Pres.), Nixon, Rep., 1,154,058; McGovern, Dem., 698,531.

1976 (Pres.), Carter, Dem., 999,163; Ford, Rep., 928,808; McCarthy, Ind., 24,329.

1980 (Pres.), Reagan, Rep., 1,074,181; Carter, Dem., 931,182; Anderson, Ind., 77,920; Clark, Libertarian, 14,422; DeBerry, Soc. Workers, 1,515; Commoner, Citizens, 573; write-ins, 31.

Montana

	1976		1980		
County	Carter (D)	Ford (R)	Carter (D)	Reagan (R)	Anderson (I)
Beaverhead	1,013	2,461	842	2,955	205
Big Horn	1,962	1,615	1,644	1,730	308
Blaine	1,356	1,349	1,107	1,686	163
Broadwater	557	820	401	1,052	69
Carbon	1,853	2,121	1,468	2,471	331
Carter	344	558	237	766	37

	1976 (D)	1976 (R)	1980 (D)	1980 (R)	1980 (I)
Cascade	14,678	15,289	11,105	17,664	2,655
Chouteau	1,568	1,814	853	2,448	216
Custer	2,425	3,120	1,822	3,533	369
Daniels	797	816	483	1,086	77
Dawson	2,201	2,639	1,543	3,045	424
Deer Lodge	3,859	2,197	3,077	1,905	474
Fallon	847	934	512	1,286	94
Fergus	2,470	3,556	1,840	4,455	388
Flathead	7,827	10,494	6,349	15,102	1,621
Gallatin	6,215	11,062	5,747	12,738	2,432
Garfield	273	625	169	760	29
Glacier	1,755	1,892	1,394	2,283	297
Golden Valley	255	302	155	362	28
Granite	509	746	439	811	76
Hill	3,878	3,274	2,875	4,448	604
Jefferson	1,210	1,387	1,055	1,841	216
Judith Basin	772	809	480	1,030	93
Lake	3,253	3,809	2,615	5,083	573
Lewis & Clark	8,118	10,155	6,815	12,128	1,793
Liberty	506	638	283	872	71
Lincoln	3,146	3,017	2,422	4,202	485
Madison	870	1,688	676	2,220	174
McCone	749	730	349	1,000	86
Meagher	364	565	247	689	41
Mineral	819	679	660	800	138
Missoula	15,099	16,350	13,115	16,161	3,847
Musselshell	922	1,117	784	1,279	106
Park	2,364	3,281	1,663	3,929	459
Petroleum	110	211	90	225	15
Phillips	1,117	1,347	745	1,723	146
Pondera	1,413	1,666	897	2,270	207
Powder River	429	683	336	985	94
Powell	1,302	1,610	883	1,770	198
Prairie	415	597	283	580	57
Ravalli	3,504	4,894	3,063	7,268	743
Richland	1,961	2,189	1,252	3,348	343
Roosevelt	2,061	1,822	1,504	2,298	304
Rosebud	1,413	1,538	1,167	1,875	265
Sanders	1,725	1,738	1,395	2,194	291
Sheridan	1,560	1,114	955	1,658	247
Silver Bow	11,377	7,506	9,721	7,301	1,752
Stillwater	1,143	1,446	919	1,828	181
Sweet Grass	502	1,135	440	1,169	98
Teton	1,506	1,730	902	2,415	186
Toole	1,080	1,469	634	2,000	154
Treasure	239	315	181	321	34
Valley	2,352	2,520	1,567	3,242	264
Wheatland	535	755	381	742	88
Wibaux	352	308	219	450	45
Yellowstone	18,329	25,201	15,272	27,332	4,590
Totals	**149,259**	**173,703**	**118,032**	**206,814**	**29,281**

Montana Vote Since 1932

1932 (Pres.), Roosevelt, Dem., 127,286; Hoover, Rep., 78,078; Thomas, Soc., 7,891; Foster, Com., 1,775; Harvey, Lib., 1,449.

1936 (Pres.), Roosevelt, Dem., 159,690; Landon, Rep., 63,598; Lemke, Union, 5,549; Thomas, Soc., 1,066; Browder, Com., 385; Colvin, Proh., 224.

1940 (Pres.), Roosevelt, Dem., 145,698; Willkie, Rep., 99,579; Thomas, Soc., 1,443; Babson, Proh., 664; Browder, Com., 489.

1944 (Pres.), Roosevelt, Dem., 112,556; Dewey, Rep., 93,163; Thomas, Soc., 1,296; Watson, Proh., 340.

1948 (Pres.), Truman, Dem., 119,071; Dewey, Rep., 96,770; Wallace, Prog., 7,313; Thomas, Soc., 695; Watson, Proh., 429.

1952 (Pres.), Eisenhower, Rep., 157,394; Stevenson, Dem., 106,213; Hallinan, Prog., 723; Hamblen, Proh., 548; Hoopes, Soc., 159.

1956 (Pres.), Eisenhower, Rep., 154,933; Stevenson, Dem., 116,238.

1960 (Pres.), Kennedy, Dem., 134,891; Nixon, Rep., 141,841; Decker, Proh., 456; Dobbs, Soc. Workers, 391.

1964 (Pres.), Johnson, Dem., 164,246; Goldwater, Rep., 113,032; Kasper, Nat'l States Rights, 519; Munn, Proh., 499; DeBerry, Soc. Worker, 332.

1968 (Pres.), Nixon, Rep., 138,835; Humphrey, Dem., 114,117; Wallace, 3d party, 20,015; Halstead, Soc. Worker, 457; Munn, Proh., 510; Caton, New Reform, 470.

1972 (Pres.), Nixon, Rep., 183,976; McGovern, Dem., 120,197; Schmitz, Amer., 13,430.

1976 (Pres.), Carter, Dem., 149,259; Ford, Rep., 173,703; Anderson, Amer., 5,772.

1980 (Pres.), Reagan, Rep., 206,814; Carter, Dem., 118,032; Anderson, Ind., 29,281; Clark, Libertarian, 9,825.

Nebraska

County	1976 Carter (D)	1976 Ford (R)	1980 Carter (D)	1980 Reagan (R)	1980 Anderson (I)
Adams	4,949	7,612	3,361	8,469	879
Antelope	1,325	2,488	659	3,192	150
Arthur	64	193	55	242	9
Banner	210	281	33	481	14
Blaine	133	281	63	361	15
Boone	1,329	2,035	769	2,598	176
Box Butte	1,516	2,956	1,206	3,898	307
Boyd	792	1,004	376	1,261	62
Brown	557	1,239	341	1,614	105
Buffalo	4,296	8,083	3,162	9,764	1,028
Burt	1,373	2,507	814	2,806	232
Butler	2,336	1,808	1,112	2,596	159
Cass	3,202	3,800	2,007	5,180	487
Cedar	2,225	2,415	1,265	3,257	273
Chase	724	1,146	324	1,593	91
Cherry	906	2,197	489	2,517	105
Cheyenne	1,663	2,285	776	3,073	196
Clay	1,369	2,254	840	2,739	190
Colfax	1,666	2,363	892	3,259	230
Cuming	1,367	3,298	803	3,999	266
Custer	1,985	3,935	1,011	4,562	285
Dakota	2,290	2,629	1,928	3,165	317
Dawes	1,278	2,435	703	3,281	228
Dawson	2,393	5,411	1,462	6,687	357
Deuel	398	775	192	943	63
Dixon	1,286	1,981	822	2,328	200
Dodge	5,276	8,972	3,556	9,514	988
Douglas	61,692	92,980	51,504	96,741	13,198
Dundy	457	774	192	1,135	55
Fillmore	1,483	2,098	1,025	2,435	221
Franklin	941	1,170	441	1,672	109
Frontier	588	994	259	1,345	84
Furnas	1,126	1,884	536	2,483	113
Gage	4,506	5,199	2,258	6,072	722
Garden	445	928	202	1,297	63
Garfield	343	726	238	811	42
Gosper	332	654	181	783	47
Grant	116	313	76	373	13
Greeley	877	787	495	1,028	78
Hall	6,077	10,931	4,391	12,083	981
Hamilton	1,337	2,737	777	3,199	245
Harlan	879	1,325	486	1,690	109
Hayes	267	411	82	617	21
Hitchcock	786	898	328	1,471	115
Holt	1,751	3,389	1,016	4,488	243
Hooker	98	326	63	386	18
Howard	1,316	1,362	788	1,969	170
Jefferson	2,067	2,628	1,125	3,090	297
Johnson	1,115	1,298	623	1,716	180
Kearney	1,218	1,827	726	2,510	227
Keith	1,139	2,485	710	3,373	199
Keya Paha	245	405	130	524	27
Kimball	696	1,257	385	1,615	97
Knox	1,922	2,610	1,057	3,404	245
Lancaster	28,193	38,937	27,040	38,630	9,221
Lincoln	5,352	7,074	3,762	9,631	841
Logan	195	283	71	442	17
Loup	140	299	74	368	21
McPherson	104	221	49	285	5
Madison	3,433	7,844	1,924	9,715	552
Merrick	1,360	2,229	712	2,710	212
Morrill	971	1,351	512	1,887	96
Nance	936	1,119	561	1,439	100
Nemaha	1,404	2,092	929	2,693	221
Nuckolls	1,424	1,752	899	2,180	159
Otoe	2,436	3,715	1,471	4,611	391
Pawnee	845	990	431	1,418	122
Perkins	622	981	313	1,338	81
Phelps	1,166	3,209	734	3,465	192
Pierce	1,004	2,172	517	2,935	155
Platte	3,681	7,206	2,385	8,781	546
Polk	1,190	1,795	538	2,206	149
Red Willow	1,722	2,978	892	4,019	254
Richardson	2,415	3,117	1,350	3,634	264
Rock	255	732	145	855	39
Saline	3,205	2,330	1,908	2,934	480
Sarpy	7,384	11,912	5,678	15,523	1,685
Saunders	3,504	3,840	2,034	5,222	516
Scotts Bluff	4,297	6,885	2,851	9,485	677
Seward	2,609	3,215	1,799	3,525	533
Sheridan	810	2,003	369	2,747	121
Sherman	1,078	935	576	1,253	116
Sioux	329	532	120	759	32
Stanton	763	1,462	361	1,942	118
Thayer	1,315	1,994	925	2,514	178
Thomas	103	343	65	306	26
Thurston	1,020	1,290	724	1,454	140
Valley	1,042	1,587	654	2,100	124
Washington	2,233	3,792	1,445	4,560	356
Wayne	1,089	2,521	733	2,844	300
Webster	1,130	1,267	547	1,676	138
Wheeler	146	274	93	371	22
York	1,655	4,202	1,118	5,065	323
Totals	**233,287**	**359,219**	**166,424**	**419,214**	**44,854**

Nebraska Vote Since 1932

1932 (Pres.), Roosevelt, Dem., 359,082; Hoover, Rep., 201,177; Thomas, Soc., 9,876.
1936 (Pres.), Roosevelt, Dem., 347,454; Landon, Rep., 248,731; Lemke, Union, 12,847.
1940 (Pres.), Roosevelt, Dem., 263,677; Willkie, Rep., 352,201.
1944 (Pres.), Roosevelt, Dem., 233,246; Dewey, Rep., 329,880.
1948 (Pres.), Truman, Dem., 224,165; Dewey, Rep., 264,774.
1952 (Pres.), Eisenhower, Rep., 421,603; Stevenson Dem., 188,057.
1956 (Pres.), Eisenhower, Rep., 378,108; Stevenson, Dem., 199,029.
1960 (Pres.), Kennedy, Dem., 232,542; Nixon, Rep., 380,553.
1964 (Pres.), Johnson, Dem., 307,307; Goldwater, Rep., 276,847.
1968 (Pres.), Nixon, Rep., 321,163; Humphrey, Dem., 170,784; Wallace, 3d party, 44,904.
1972 (Pres.), Nixon, Rep., 406,298; McGovern, Dem., 169,991; scattered 817.
1976 (Pres.), Carter, Dem., 233,287; Ford, Rep., 359,219; McCarthy, Ind., 9,383; Maddox, Amer. Ind., 3,378; MacBride, Libertarian, 1,476.
1980 (Pres.), Reagan, Rep., 419,214; Carter, Dem., 166,424; Anderson, Ind., 44,854; Clark, Libertarian, 9,041.

Nevada

County	1976 Carter (D)	1976 Ford (R)	1980 Carter (D)	1980 Reagan (R)	1980 Anderson (I)
Churchill	1,800	2,358	1,055	3,841	257
Clark	51,178	48,236	38,313	76,194	8,702
Douglas	1,934	3,095	1,352	5,254	511
Elko	1,955	3,293	1,296	4,393	301
Esmeralda	214	181	110	311	29
Eureka	163	272	103	430	13
Humboldt	1,074	1,380	684	1,950	128
Lander	518	561	361	935	64
Lincoln	642	700	396	1,087	38
Lyon	1,866	2,068	1,288	3,709	271
Mineral	1,361	1,104	631	1,628	147
Nye	1,261	1,027	973	2,387	204
Pershing	633	635	311	877	60
Storey	310	274	222	460	62
Washoe	21,687	29,264	15,621	41,276	5,705
White Pine	2,009	1,543	1,181	1,896	195
CARSON CITY	3,874	5,282	2,769	8,389	964
Totals	**92,479**	**101,273**	**66,666**	**155,017**	**17,651**

Nevada Vote Since 1932

1932 (Pres.), Roosevelt, Dem., 28,756; Hoover, Rep., 12,674.
1936 (Pres.), Roosevelt, Dem., 31,925; Landon, Rep., 11,923.
1940 (Pres.), Roosevelt, Dem., 31,945; Willkie, Rep., 21,229.
1944 (Pres.), Roosevelt, Dem., 29,623; Dewey, Rep., 24,611.
1948 (Pres.), Truman, Dem., 31,291; Dewey, Rep., 29,357; Wallace, Prog., 1,469.
1952 (Pres.), Eisenhower, Rep., 50,502; Stevenson, Dem., 31,688.
1956 (Pres.), Eisenhower, Rep., 56,049; Stevenson, Dem., 40,640.
1960 (Pres.), Kennedy, Dem., 54,880; Nixon, Rep., 52,387.
1964 (Pres.), Johnson, Dem., 79,339; Goldwater, Rep., 56,094.
1968 (Pres.), Nixon, Rep., 73,188; Humphrey, Dem., 60,598; Wallace, 3d party, 20,432.
1972 (Pres.), Nixon, Rep., 115,750; McGovern, Dem. 66,016.
1976 (Pres.), Carter Dem., 92,479; Ford, Rep., 101,273; MacBride, Libertarian, 1,519; Maddox, Amer. Ind., 1,497; scattered 5,108.
1980 (Pres.), Reagan, Rep., 155,017; Carter, Dem., 66,666; Anderson, Ind., 17,651; Clark, Libertarian, 4,358.

New Hampshire

County	1976 Carter (D)	1976 Ford (R)	1980 Carter (D)	1980 Reagan (R)	1980 Anderson (I)
Belknap	6,143	9,876	4,365	12,077	1,996
Carroll	3,374	8,561	3,119	9,980	1,584
Cheshire	10,388	12,554	7,835	13,242	4,090
Coos	7,385	7,094	4,749	8,724	941
Grafton	8,996	14,430	7,282	15,273	4,279
Hillsborough	45,554	53,581	31,789	68,994	13,613
Merrimack	14,865	21,853	12,083	23,584	5,894
Rockingham	30,051	36,738	21,712	45,960	10,974
Strafford	14,566	14,569	11,041	16,399	4,700
Sullivan	6,323	6,679	4,889	7,472	1,622
Totals	**147,645**	**185,935**	**108,864**	**221,705**	**49,693**

New Hampshire Vote Since 1932

1932 (Pres.), Roosevelt, Dem., 100,680; Hoover, Rep., 103,629; Thomas, Soc., 947; Foster, Com., 264.
1936 (Pres.), Roosevelt, Dem., 108,640; Landon, Rep., 104,642; Lemke, Union, 4,819; Browder, Com., 193.
1940 (Pres.), Roosevelt, Dem., 125,292; Willkie, Rep., 110,127.
1944 (Pres.), Roosevelt, Dem., 119,663; Dewey, Rep., 109,916; Thomas, Soc., 46.
1948 (Pres.), Truman, Dem., 107,995; Dewey, Rep., 121,299; Wallace, Prog., 1,970; Thomas, Soc., 86; Teichert, Soc. Labor, 83; Thurmond, States' Rights, 7.
1952 (Pres.), Eisenhower, Rep., 166,287; Stevenson, Dem., 106,663.
1956 (Pres.), Eisenhower, Rep., 176,519; Stevenson, Dem., 90,364; Andrews, Const., 111.
1960 (Pres.), Kennedy, Dem., 137,772; Nixon, Rep., 157,989.
1964 (Pres.), Johnson, Dem., 182,065; Goldwater, Rep., 104,029.
1968 (Pres.), Nixon, Rep., 154,903; Humphrey, Dem., 130,589; Wallace, 3d party, 11,173; New Party, 421; Halstead, Soc. Worker, 104.
1972 (Pres.), Nixon, Rep., 213,724; McGovern, Dem., 116,435; Schmitz, Amer., 3,386; Jenness, Soc. Workers, 368; scattered, 142.
1976 (Pres.), Carter, Dem., 147,645; Ford, Rep., 185,935; McCarthy, Ind., 4,095; MacBride, Libertarian, 936; Reagan, write-in, 388; La Rouche, U.S. Labor, 186; Camejo, Soc. Workers, 161, Levin, Soc. Labor, 66; scattered, 215.
1980 (Pres.), Reagan, Rep., 221,705; Carter, Dem., 108,864; Anderson, Ind., 49,693; Clark, Libertarian, 2,067; Commoner, Citizens, 1,325; Hall, Com., 129; Griswold, Workers World, 76; DeBerry, Soc. Workers, 72; scattered, 68.

New Jersey

County	1976 Carter (D)	1976 Ford (R)	1980 Carter (D)	1980 Reagan (R)	1980 Anderson (I)
Atlantic	41,965	36,733	31,286	37,973	5,582
Bergen	180,738	237,331	139,474	232,043	38,242
Burlington	63,309	60,960	50,083	68,415	11,314
Camden	108,854	82,801	80,033	87,939	16,125
Cape May	16,489	19,498	12,708	22,729	2,550
Cumberland	29,165	20,535	19,356	23,242	3,253
Essex	174,434	133,911	145,281	117,222	21,271
Gloucester	38,726	34,888	29,804	40,306	7,533
Hudson	116,241	92,636	95,622	91,207	8,941
Hunterdon	12,592	19,616	10,029	21,403	3,610
Mercer	69,621	58,453	60,888	53,450	12,117
Middlesex	122,859	113,539	97,304	122,354	17,463
Monmouth	88,956	110,104	71,328	120,173	17,444
Morris	63,749	105,921	48,965	105,260	17,181
Ocean	56,413	77,875	46,923	98,433	10,073
Passaic	76,194	85,102	61,486	82,531	9,385
Salem	12,826	11,639	10,209	13,000	1,800
Somerset	36,258	51,260	29,470	52,591	8,346
Sussex	14,759	23,613	10,531	27,063	3,988
Union	106,267	118,019	86,074	112,288	15,586
Warren	14,238	15,254	10,510	16,935	2,828
Totals	**1,444,653**	**1,509,688**	**1,147,364**	**1,546,557**	**234,632**

New Jersey Vote Since 1932

1932 (Pres.), Roosevelt, Dem., 806,630; Hoover, Rep., 775,684; Thomas, Soc., 42,998; Foster, Com., 2,915; Reynolds, Soc. Labor, 1,062; Upshaw, Proh., 774.

1936 (Pres.), Roosevelt, Dem., 1,083,549; Landon, Rep., 719,421; Lemke, Union, 9,405; Thomas, Soc., 3,895; Browder, Com., 1,590; Colvin, Proh., 916; Aiken, Soc. Labor, 346.

1940 (Pres.), Roosevelt, Dem., 1,016,404; Willkie, Rep., 944,876; Browder, Com., 8,814; Thomas, Soc., 2,823; Babson, Proh., 851; Aiken, Soc. Labor, 446.

1944 (Pres.), Roosevelt, Dem., 987,874; Dewey, Rep., 961,335; Teichert, Soc. Labor, 6,939; Watson, Nat'l. Proh., 4,255; Thomas, Soc., 3,385.

1948 (Pres.), Truman, Dem., 895,455; Dewey, Rep., 981,124; Wallace, Prog., 42,683; Watson, Proh., 10,593; Thomas, Soc., 10,521; Dobbs, Soc. Workers, 5,825; Teichert, Soc. Labor, 3,354.

1952 (Pres.), Eisenhower, Rep., 1,373,613; Stevenson, Dem., 1,015,902; Hoopes, Soc., 8,593; Hass, Soc. Labor, 5,815; Hallinan, Prog., 5,589; Krajewski, Poor Man's, 4,203; Dobbs, Soc. Workers, 3,850; Hamblen, Proh., 989.

1956 (Pres.), Eisenhower, Rep., 1,606,942; Stevenson Dem., 850,337; Holtwick, Proh., 9,147; Hass, Soc. Labor, 6,736; Andrews, Conservative, 5,317; Dobbs, Soc. Workers, 4,004; Krajewski, American Third Party, 1,829.

1960 (Pres.), Kennedy, Dem., 1,385,415; Nixon, Rep., 1,363,324; Dobbs, Soc. Workers, 11,402; Lee, Conservative, 8,708; Hass, Soc. Labor, 4,262.

1964 (Pres.), Johnson, Dem., 1,867,671; Goldwater, Rep., 963,843; DeBerry, Soc. Workers, 8,181; Hass, Soc. Labor, 7,075.

1968 (Pres.), Nixon, Rep., 1,325,467; Humphrey, Dem., 1,264,206; Wallace, 3d party, 262,187; Halstead, Soc. Worker, 8,667; Gregory, Peace Freedom, 8,084; Blomen, Soc. Labor, 6,784.

1972 (Pres.), Nixon, Rep., 1,845,502; McGovern, Dem., 1,102,211; Schmitz, Amer., 34,378; Spock, Peoples, 5,355; Fisher, Soc. Labor, 4,544; Jenness, Soc. Workers, 2,233; Mahalchik, Amer. First, 1,743; Hall, Com., 1,263.

1976 (Pres.), Carter, Dem., 1,444,653; Ford, Rep., 1,509,688; McCarthy, Ind., 32,717; MacBride, Libertarian, 9,449; Maddox, Amer., 7,716; Levin, Soc. Labor, 3,686; Hall, Com., 1,662; LaRouche, U.S. Labor, 1,650; Camejo, Soc. Workers, 1,184; Wright, People's, 1,044; Bubar, Proh., 554; Zeidler, Soc., 469.

1980 (Pres.), Reagan, Rep., 1,546,557; Carter, Dem., 1,147,364; Anderson, Ind., 234,632; Clark, Libertarian, 20,652; Commoner, Citizens, 8,203; McCormack, Right to Life, 3,927; Lynen, Middle Class, 3,694; Hall, Com., 2,555; Pulley, Soc. Workers, 2,198; McReynolds, Soc., 1,973; Gahres, Down With Lawyers, 1,718; Griswold, Workers World, 1,288; Wendelken, Ind., 923.

New Mexico

County	1976 Carter (D)	1976 Ford (R)	1980 Carter (D)	1980 Reagan (R)	1980 Anderson (I)
Bernalillo	63,949	76,614	54,841	83,956	15,118
Catron	517	602	466	906	40
Chaves	7,139	10,631	5,350	12,502	543
Colfax	2,718	2,259	2,266	2,537	199
Curry	5,004	6,232	3,622	8,132	183
De Baca	597	556	484	655	14
Dona Ana	12,036	13,888	10,839	15,539	1,863
Eddy	9,073	7,698	7,028	9,817	326
Grant	5,176	4,095	4,600	4,628	349
Guadalupe	1,379	1,047	980	1,065	58
Harding	285	387	225	356	14
Hidalgo	938	891	840	1,059	59
Lea	6,533	8,773	5,006	10,727	298
Lincoln	1,415	2,320	1,127	3,009	172
Los Alamos	2,890	5,383	2,368	5,460	1,388
Luna	2,872	2,966	2,443	3,636	157
McKinley	6,856	4,617	4,869	7,329	498
Mora	1,438	904	1,274	1,037	44
Otero	5,333	5,914	4,111	7,210	478
Quay	2,095	2,059	1,422	2,499	58
Rio Arriba	7,125	3,213	6,245	3,794	379
Roosevelt	3,111	3,269	2,240	3,950	208
Sandoval	5,072	4,110	4,740	6,762	789
San Juan	8,615	10,852	6,705	15,579	741
San Miguel	5,204	3,162	4,514	3,292	416
Santa Fe	14,127	11,576	12,658	12,361	3,123
Sierra	1,564	1,665	1,169	2,222	117
Socorro	2,606	2,265	2,226	2,685	387
Taos	4,414	3,012	4,346	3,584	482
Torrance	1,526	1,462	1,261	1,907	101
Union	975	1,146	675	1,407	32
Valencia	8,566	7,851	6,886	11,177	825
Totals	201,148	211,419	167,826	250,779	29,459

New Mexico Vote Since 1932

1932 (Pres.), Roosevelt, Dem., 95,089; Hoover, Rep. 54,217; Thomas, Soc., 11,776; Harvey, Lib., 389; Foster Com., 135.

1936 (Pres.), Roosevelt, Dem., 105,838; Landon, Rep. 61,710; Lemke, Union, 942; Thomas, Soc., 343; Browder Com., 43.

1940 (Pres.), Roosevelt, Dem., 103,699; Willkie, Rep. 79,315.

1944 (Pres.), Roosevelt, Dem., 81,389; Dewey, Rep., 70,688 Watson, Proh., 148.

1948 (Pres.), Truman, Dem., 105,464; Dewey, Rep., 80,30 Wallace, Prog., 1,037; Watson, Proh., 127; Thomas, Soc 83; Teichert, Soc. Labor, 49.

1952 (Pres.), Eisenhower, Rep., 132,170; Stevenson, Dem. 105,661; Hamblen, Proh., 297; Hallinan, Ind. Prog., 225 MacArthur, Christian National, 220; Hass, Soc. Labor 35.

1956 (Pres.), Eisenhower, Rep., 146,788; Stevenson, Dem. 106,098; Holtwick, Proh., 607; Andrews, Ind., 364; Hass Soc. Labor, 69.

1960 (Pres.), Kennedy, Dem., 156,027; Nixon, Rep. 153,733; Decker, Proh., 777; Hass, Soc. Labor, 570.

1964 (Pres.), Johnson, Dem., 194,017; Goldwater, Rep 131,838; Hass, Soc. Labor, 1,217; Munn, Proh., 543.

1968 (Pres.), Nixon, Rep., 169,692; Humphrey, Dem 130,081; Wallace, 3d party, 25,737; Chavez, 1,519; Halstead, Soc. Worker, 252.

1972 (Pres.), Nixon, Rep., 235,606; McGovern, Dem 141,084; Schmitz, Amer., 8,767; Jenness, Soc. Workers 474.

1976 (Pres.), Carter, Dem., 201,148; Ford, Rep., 211,419 Camejo, Soc. Workers, 2,462; MacBride, Libertarian 1,110; Zeidler, Soc., 240; Bubar, Proh., 211.

1980 (Pres.), Reagan, Rep., 250,779; Carter, Dem., 167,826 Anderson, Ind., 29,459; Clark, Libertarian, 4,365; Commoner, Citizens, 2,202; Bubar, Statesman, 1,281; Pulley Soc. Worker, 325.

New York

County	1976 Carter (D-L*)	1976 Ford (R-C**)	1980 Carter (D)	1980 Reagan (R-C**)	1980 Anderson (L)
Albany	71,616	69,592	74,429	52,354	14,56
Allegany	6,134	11,769	5,879	10,423	97
Broome	39,827	50,340	37,013	39,275	11,38
Cattaraugus	13,768	19,469	12,917	17,222	1,84
Cayuga	13,348	19,775	11,708	17,945	2,53
Chautauqua	27,447	33,730	22,871	30,081	4,69
Chemung	17,207	20,640	14,565	19,674	2,46
Chenango	7,356	12,384	6,917	10,400	1,90
Clinton	11,555	15,433	11,498	13,120	1,90
Columbia	10,514	15,871	9,500	13,946	2,20
Cortland	6,947	11,222	6,176	9,885	1,60
Delaware	7,254	12,443	6,333	10,609	1,86
Dutchess	37,531	51,312	28,616	53,616	8,82
Erie	229,397	220,310	215,283	169,209	29,58
Essex	6,556	10,194	6,443	9,025	1,21
Franklin	7,248	8,846	7,281	7,620	1,18
Fulton	9,323	12,161	8,105	11,448	1,56
Genesee	10,803	14,567	10,677	11,650	1,65
Greene	7,740	11,370	6,488	11,286	1,33
Hamilton	1,052	2,306	925	2,038	17
Herkimer	12,875	15,362	11,497	14,105	1,83
Jefferson	13,503	20,401	13,271	16,455	2,83
Lewis	3,764	5,840	3,973	4,937	7
Livingston	9,629	14,044	9,030	11,193	1,69
Madison	8,822	15,674	7,843	13,369	2,12
Monroe	134,739	167,303	142,423	128,615	29,1
Montgomery	11,271	13,281	9,645	11,917	2,08
Niagara	43,667	46,101	40,405	38,760	6,01
Oneida	47,779	57,655	44,292	51,968	6,92
Onondaga	76,097	115,474	73,453	97,887	18,80
Ontario	14,044	21,118	14,477	17,036	3,14
Orange	40,362	49,685	30,022	51,268	7,65
Orleans	5,927	8,994	5,767	7,536	97
Oswego	16,332	23,949	15,343	22,816	3,33
Otsego	9,787	14,796	8,795	11,814	2,87
Putnam	11,963	18,523	8,691	20,193	2,34
Rensselaer	28,979	40,229	29,880	32,005	6,44

	1976		1980		
Rockland	48,673	52,087	35,277	59,068	8,709
St. Lawrence	17,503	16,173	17,006	18,437	3,544
Saratoga	23,768	38,296	23,641	34,184	6,201
Schenectady	31,838	40,789	29,932	32,003	7,146
Schoharie	5,250	7,154	4,715	6,382	940
Schuyler	2,885	4,267	2,514	3,838	476
Seneca	5,745	7,659	5,010	7,174	1,205
Steuben	14,685	23,164	12,826	22,418	2,257
Sullivan	14,189	13,709	9,553	15,089	2,095
Tioga	6,969	11,824	6,690	10,291	1,851
Tompkins	12,808	15,463	11,970	12,448	4,081
Ulster	30,190	35,353	22,179	36,709	5,995
Warren	7,264	14,548	6,971	13,264	1,766
Washington	7,262	13,946	7,144	12,835	1,501
Wayne	12,061	19,324	12,590	16,498	2,623
Wyoming	5,737	9,726	5,234	8,108	855
Yates	2,903	5,796	2,828	4,694	690
Outside N.Y. Metro Area	**1,281,893**	**1,607,517**	**1,188,511**	**1,386,140**	**244,336**
Nassau	302,869	329,176	207,602	333,567	44,758
Suffolk	208,263	248,908	149,945	256,294	34,743
Westchester	173,153	208,527	130,136	198,552	30,119
N.Y. Suburban	**648,285**	**786,611**	**487,683**	**788,413**	**109,620**
Bronx	238,786	96,842	181,090	86,843	11,286
Kings	419,382	190,728	288,893	200,306	24,341
New York	337,438	117,702	275,742	115,911	38,597
Queens	379,907	244,396	269,147	251,333	32,566
Richmond	47,867	56,995	37,306	64,885	7,055
N.Y. City	**1,423,380**	**706,663**	**1,052,178**	**719,278**	**113,845**
N.Y. Metro Area	**2,107,665**	**1,493,274**	**1,539,861**	**1,507,691**	**223,465**
D/R Total	**3,244,165**	**2,825,913**	**2,728,372**	**2,637,700**	-
2d party (Con)	**145,393**	**274,878**	-	**256,131**	-
Totals	**3,389,558**	**3,100,791**	**2,728,372**	**2,893,831**	**467,801**

*Democratic and Liberal **Republican and Conservative

New York Vote Since 1932

1932 (Pres.), Roosevelt, Dem., 2,534,959; Hoover, Rep., 1,937,963; Thomas, Soc., 177,397; Foster, Com., 27,956; Reynolds, Soc. Labor, 10,339.

1936 (Pres.), Roosevelt, Dem., 3,018,298; American Lab., 274,924; total 3,293,222; Landon, Rep., 2,180,670; Thomas, Soc., 86,879; Browder, Com., 35,609.

1940 (Pres.), Roosevelt, Dem., 2,834,500; American Lab., 417,418; total, 3,251,918; Willkie, Rep., 3,027,478; Thomas, Soc., 18,950; Babson, Proh., 3,250.

1944 (Pres.), Roosevelt, Dem., 2,478,598; American Lab., 496,405; Liberal, 329,325; total, 3,304,238; Dewey, Rep., 2,987,647; Teichert, Ind. Gov't., 14,352; Thomas, Soc., 10,553.

1948 (Pres.), Truman, Dem., 2,557,642; Liberal, 222,562; total, 2,780,204; Dewey, Rep., 2,841,163; Wallace, Amer. Lab., 509,559; Thomas, Soc., 40,879; Teichert, Ind. Gov't., 2,729; Dobbs, Soc. Workers, 2,675.

1952 (Pres.), Eisenhower, Rep., 3,952,815; Stevenson, Dem., 2,687,890, Liberal, 416,711; total, 3,104,601; Hallinan, American Lab., 64,211; Hoopes, Soc., 2,664; Dobbs, Soc. Workers, 2,212; Hass, Ind. Gov't., 1,560; scattering, 178; blank and void, 87,813.

1956 (Pres.), Eisenhower, Rep., 4,340,340; Stevenson, Dem., 2,458,212; Liberal, 292,557; total, 2,750,769; write-in votes for Andrews, 1,027; Werdel, 492; Hass, 150; Hoopes, 82; others, 476.

1960 (Pres.), Kennedy, Dem., 3,423,909; Liberal, 406,176; total, 3,830,085; Nixon, Rep., 3,446,419; Dobbs, Soc. Workers, 14,319; scattering, 256; blank and void, 88,896.

1964 (Pres.), Johnson, Dem., 4,913,156; Goldwater, Rep., 2,243,559; Hass, Soc. Labor, 6,085; DeBerry, Soc. Workers, 3,215; scattering, 188; blank and void, 151,383.

1968 (Pres.), Nixon, Rep., 3,007,932; Humphrey, Dem., 3,378,470; Wallace, 3d party, 358,864; Blomen, Soc. Labor, 8,432; Halstead, Soc. Worker, 11,851; Gregory, Freedom and Peace, 24,517; blank, void, and scattering, 171,624.

1972 (Pres.), Nixon, Rep., 3,824,642; Conservative, 368,136; McGovern, Dem., 2,767,956; Liberal, 183,128; Reed, Soc. Workers, 7,797; Fisher, Soc. Labor, 4,530; Hall, Com., 5,641; blank, void, or scattered, 161,641.

1976 (Pres.), Carter, Dem., 3,389,558; Ford, Rep., 3,100,791; MacBride, Libertarian, 12,197; Hall, Com., 10,270; Camejo, Soc. Workers, 6,996; LaRouche, U.S. Labor, 5,413; blank, void, or scattered, 143,037.

1980 (Pres.), Reagan, Rep., 2,893,831; Carter, Dem., 2,728,372; Anderson, Lib., 467,801; Clark, Libertarian, 52,648; McCormack, Right To Life, 24,159; Commoner, Citizens, 23,186; Hall, Com., 7,414; DeBerry, Soc. Workers, 2,068; Griswold, Workers World, 1,416; scattering, 1,064.

North Carolina

	1976		1980		
County	Carter (D)	Ford (R)	Carter (D)	Reagan (R)	Anderson (I)
Alamance	17,371	12,680	15,042	18,077	760
Alexander	5,287	4,661	4,546	6,376	137
Alleghany	2,550	1,532	2,198	1,995	91
Anson	4,796	1,608	4,973	1,968	111
Ashe	5,193	4,937	4,461	5,643	154
Avery	1,869	3,085	1,527	3,480	147
Beaufort	5,728	4,677	6,024	6,773	186
Bertie	4,117	1,332	3,863	1,695	45
Bladen	6,009	1,546	6,104	2,745	64
Brunswick	7,377	3,636	6,761	5,897	265
Buncombe	26,633	22,461	24,837	26,124	2,153
Burke	14,254	10,070	11,680	12,956	558
Cabarrus	12,049	12,455	9,768	15,143	562
Caldwell	11,894	9,872	8,738	12,965	440
Camden	1,231	562	1,212	813	45
Carteret	7,080	5,786	6,485	7,733	460
Caswell	3,707	1,761	3,529	2,156	66
Catawba	16,862	18,696	13,873	22,873	866
Chatham	6,397	4,279	7,144	5,414	481
Cherokee	3,571	3,210	3,114	3,849	80
Chowan	1,862	1,019	2,146	1,424	71
Clay	1,569	1,428	1,324	2,136	53
Cleveland	14,406	8,106	12,219	10,828	333
Columbus	11,148	3,184	10,212	5,522	148
Craven	7,553	5,881	7,781	8,554	356
Cumberland	24,297	14,226	22,073	21,540	1,261
Currituck	1,999	954	1,980	1,668	97
Dare	2,191	1,680	2,497	2,794	260
Davidson	17,859	18,813	14,579	22,794	679
Davie	3,635	4,772	3,289	6,302	223
Duplin	7,696	3,912	7,524	5,403	109
Durham	22,425	18,945	24,969	19,276	3,052
Edgecombe	8,001	4,850	7,945	5,916	148
Forsyth	39,561	38,886	38,870	42,389	2,897
Franklin	5,405	2,630	5,427	3,508	104
Gaston	22,878	19,727	19,016	25,139	823
Gates	2,291	722	2,435	957	61
Graham	1,791	1,621	1,608	1,961	36
Granville	5,244	2,955	5,556	3,513	133
Greene	2,740	1,356	2,835	2,221	34
Guilford	46,826	45,441	44,516	53,291	4,019
Halifax	7,892	5,257	8,364	6,033	180
Harnett	8,992	5,935	8,791	7,284	165
Haywood	10,692	5,885	9,814	7,217	349
Henderson	8,155	10,830	7,578	13,573	901
Hertford	3,986	1,517	4,102	1,854	80
Hoke	3,186	920	3,376	1,168	56
Hyde	1,084	623	1,221	807	37
Iredell	13,295	11,573	12,067	14,926	624
Jackson	5,223	3,536	4,857	4,140	246
Johnston	10,301	8,511	9,601	10,444	271
Jones	2,016	948	2,198	1,401	18
Lee	5,104	3,691	5,426	4,847	251
Lenoir	7,650	7,715	7,546	9,832	263
Lincoln	9,462	6,682	7,796	9,009	299
Macon	4,406	3,673	4,105	4,727	153
Madison	3,433	2,446	3,202	2,629	108
Martin	4,518	1,931	4,750	2,564	81
McDowell	6,246	4,450	4,703	5,680	175
Mecklenburg	63,198	61,715	66,995	68,384	6,560
Mitchell	2,031	3,728	1,765	4,322	146
Montgomery	4,308	2,872	4,129	3,587	99
Moore	7,373	7,577	8,084	10,158	563
Nash	8,937	8,477	8,184	11,043	293
New Hanover	14,504	13,687	13,670	17,243	1,114
Northampton	5,118	1,238	4,933	1,847	62
Onslow	7,954	5,953	7,371	8,861	400
Orange	15,755	9,302	15,226	9,261	3,364
Pamlico	2,113	1,068	2,224	1,504	48
Pasquotank	4,302	2,651	4,128	3,340	179
Pender	4,422	2,063	4,382	3,018	103
Perquimans	1,666	909	1,560	1,210	63
Person	3,977	3,038	4,111	3,281	104
Pitt	11,636	9,532	12,590	12,816	827
Polk	3,155	2,605	2,375	3,021	160
Randolph	12,714	14,337	10,107	19,881	563
Richmond	8,793	2,848	7,416	3,911	224
Robeson	20,695	4,907	17,618	6,982	331
Rockingham	13,413	9,362	11,708	11,205	463
Rowan	15,363	14,644	11,671	18,566	707
Rutherford	10,361	6,718	8,315	8,363	203

	1976 (D)	1976 (R)	1980 (D)	1980 (R)	1980 (I)
Sampson	8,869	6,968	9,090	8,097	308
Scotland	4,430	1,932	4,446	2,133	155
Stanly	9,262	8,845	7,784	9,734	248
Stokes	6,647	6,029	5,764	7,275	151
Surry	10,024	7,403	8,987	10,065	256
Swain	2,141	1,608	1,987	1,457	70
Transylvania	4,636	4,089	4,008	4,826	274
Tyrrell	900	403	887	466	14
Union	10,578	6,184	10,073	9,012	487
Vance	5,620	3,813	5,415	4,217	101
Wake	44,005	44,291	49,003	49,768	5,455
Warren	3,185	1,427	3,750	1,582	74
Washington	2,840	1,486	3,008	1,943	68
Watauga	5,358	5,400	5,022	6,149	645
Wayne	9,265	9,607	9,586	12,860	322
Wilkes	10,176	11,768	8,184	14,462	282
Wilson	8,209	6,795	8,042	8,329	243
Yadkin	4,497	5,916	3,850	7,530	136
Yancey	3,932	2,688	4,010	3,363	110
Totals	**927,365**	**741,960**	**875,635**	**915,018**	**52,800**

North Carolina Vote Since 1932

1932 (Pres.), Roosevelt, Dem., 497,566; Hoover, Rep., 208,344; Thomas, Soc., 5,591.

1936 (Pres.), Roosevelt, Dem., 616,141; Landon, Rep., 223,283; Thomas, Soc., 21; Browder, Com., 11; Lemke, Union 2.

1940 (Pres.), Roosevelt, Dem., 609,015; Willkie, Rep., 213,633.

1944 (Pres.), Roosevelt, Dem., 527,399; Dewey, Rep., 263,155.

1948 (Pres.), Truman, Dem., 459,070; Dewey, Rep., 258,572; Thurmond, States' Rights, 69,652; Wallace, Prog., 3,915.

1952 (Pres.), Eisenhower, Rep., 558,107; Stevenson, Dem., 652,803.

1956 (Pres.), Eisenhower, Rep., 575,062; Stevenson, Dem., 590,530.

1960 (Pres.), Kennedy, Dem., 713,136; Nixon, Rep., 655,420.

1964 (Pres.), Johnson, Dem., 800,139; Goldwater Rep., 624,844.

1968 (Pres.), Nixon, Rep., 627,192; Humphrey, Dem., 464,113; Wallace, 3d party, 496,188.

1972 (Pres.), Nixon, Rep., 1,054,889; McGovern, Dem., 438,705; Schmitz, Amer., 25,018.

1976 (Pres.), Dem., 927,365; Ford, Rep., 741,960; Anderson, Amer., 5,607; MacBride, Libertarian, 2,219; LaRouche, U.S. Labor, 755.

1980 (Pres.), Reagan, Rep., 915,018; Carter, Dem., 875,635; Anderson, Ind., 52,800; Clark, Libertarian, 9,677; Commoner, Citizens, 2,287; DeBerry, Soc. Workers, 416.

North Dakota

County	1976 Carter (D)	1976 Ford (R)	1980 Carter (D)	1980 Reagan (R)	1980 Anderson (I)
Adams	959	940	470	1,334	107
Barnes	3,321	4,011	2,128	4,392	705
Benson	1,973	1,689	1,119	2,149	262
Billings	285	351	122	524	33
Bottineau	1,987	2,638	1,090	3,394	267
Bowman	911	1,033	454	1,507	142
Burke	899	1,087	418	1,442	82
Burleigh	9,188	13,680	6,129	18,437	2,109
Cass	17,879	22,583	13,562	23,886	5,421
Cavalier	2,178	2,046	1,105	2,582	238
Dickey	1,612	2,027	917	2,455	161
Divide	1,057	881	509	1,267	109
Dunn	1,051	1,041	532	1,706	115
Eddy	1,123	890	539	1,153	145
Emmons	1,459	1,370	502	2,369	132
Foster	1,147	1,120	586	1,534	152
Golden Valley	479	663	259	1,006	62
Grand Forks	11,545	13,820	6,997	14,257	2,932
Grant	952	1,205	317	1,891	110
Griggs	1,122	1,086	636	1,342	158
Hettinger	1,095	1,135	434	1,699	104
Kidder	936	954	326	1,474	85
La Moure	1,718	1,735	850	2,136	254
Logan	809	944	283	1,474	69
McHenry	1,994	2,043	939	2,922	190
McIntosh	912	1,785	308	2,471	72
McKenzie	1,335	1,595	867	2,265	182
McLean	2,815	2,729	1,613	4,234	318
Mercer	1,298	1,982	1,209	3,224	20
Morton	5,241	4,921	2,861	7,659	74
Mountrail	2,189	1,430	1,183	2,165	18
Nelson	1,610	1,336	726	1,611	22
Oliver	529	575	270	966	5
Pembina	2,274	2,810	1,239	3,101	30
Pierce	1,434	1,396	517	2,273	16
Ramsey	3,096	3,293	1,607	4,078	51
Ransom	1,715	1,696	974	1,883	23
Renville	1,008	812	570	1,154	9
Richland	4,592	4,991	2,698	5,711	75
Rolette	2,531	1,094	1,660	1,599	26
Sargent	1,644	1,344	1,048	1,565	17
Sheridan	569	935	208	1,326	6
Sioux	697	354	383	620	7
Slope	347	355	128	462	4
Stark	4,076	4,374	2,016	6,312	51
Steele	1,066	835	617	997	22
Stutsman	4,883	5,653	2,573	6,545	96
Towner	1,216	993	568	1,375	15
Traill	2,352	2,800	1,428	3,092	51
Walsh	3,555	3,518	1,850	4,488	48
Ward	9,484	12,751	5,554	14,997	1,23
Wells	1,742	1,941	746	2,660	14
Williams	4,189	4,230	2,545	6,530	59
Totals	**136,078**	**153,470**	**79,189**	**193,695**	**23,64**

North Dakota Vote Since 1932

1932 (Pres.), Roosevelt, Dem., 178,350; Hoover, Rep. 71,772; Harvey, Lib., 1,817; Thomas, Soc., 3,521; Foster Com., 830.

1936 (Pres.), Roosevelt, Dem., 163,148; Landon, Rep. 72,751; Lemke, Union, 36,708; Thomas, Soc., 552 Browder, Com., 360; Colvin, Proh., 197.

1940 (Pres.), Roosevelt, Dem., 124,036; Willkie, Rep. 154,590; Thomas, Soc., 1,279; Knutson, Com., 545; Babson, Proh., 325.

1944 (Pres.), Roosevelt, Dem., 100,144; Dewey, Rep. 118,535; Thomas, Soc., 943, Watson, Proh., 549.

1948 (Pres.), Truman, Dem., 95,812; Dewey, Rep., 115,139 Wallace, Prog., 8,391; Thomas, Soc., 1,000, Thurmond States' Rights, 374.

1952 (Pres.), Eisenhower, Rep., 191,712; Stevenson, Dem. 76,694; MacArthur, Christian Nationalist, 1,075; Hallinan, Prog., 344; Hamblen, Proh., 302.

1956 (Pres.), Eisenhower, Rep., 156,766; Stevenson, Dem. 96,742; Andrews, Amer., 483.

1960 (Pres.), Kennedy, Dem., 123,963; Nixon, Rep 154,310; Dobbs, Soc. Workers, 158.

1964 (Pres.), Johnson, Dem., 149,784; Goldwater, Rep 108,207; DeBerry, Soc. Worker, 224; Munn, Proh., 174.

1968 (Pres.), Nixon, Rep., 138,669; Humphrey, Dem 94,769; Wallace, 3d party, 14,244; Halstead, Soc. Worker 128; Munn, Prohibition, 38; Troxell, Ind., 34.

1972 (Pres.), Nixon, Rep., 174,109; McGovern, Dem 100,384; Jenness, Soc. Workers, 288; Hall, Com., 87 Schmitz, Amer., 5,646.

1976 (Pres.), Carter, Dem., 136,078; Ford, Rep., 153,470 Anderson, Amer., 3,698; McCarthy, Ind., 2,952; Maddox Amer. Ind., 269; MacBride, Libertarian, 256; scattering 371.

1980 (Pres.), Reagan, Rep., 193,695; Carter, Dem., 79,189 Anderson, Ind., 23,640; Clark, Libertarian, 3,743; Commoner, Libertarian, 429; McLain, Nat'l People's League 296; Greaves, American, 235; Hall, Com., 93; DeBerry Soc. Workers, 89; McReynolds, Soc., 82; Bubar, Statesman, 54.

Ohio

County	1976 Carter (D)	1976 Ford (R)	1980 Carter (D)	1980 Reagan (R)	1980 Anders (I)
Adams	4,450	4,197	4,161	5,336	3
Allen	14,627	23,721	13,140	29,070	1,4
Ashland	7,205	9,761	5,142	11,691	1,1
Ashtabula	20,883	16,885	17,363	19,847	2,4
Athens	9,896	8,387	9,514	8,170	1,5
Auglaize	5,840	9,772	5,022	11,537	7
Belmont	21,162	13,550	16,653	13,601	1,4
Brown	5,432	4,549	4,706	6,065	3
Butler	35,123	49,625	31,796	61,231	4,7
Carroll	5,006	5,091	3,476	5,806	4
Champaign	4,748	6,526	4,109	7,356	5
Clark	26,135	26,745	22,630	27,237	3,4

	1976		1980		
	(D)	(R)	(D)	(R)	(I)
Clermont	14,850	19,616	13,199	26,674	1,697
Clinton	4,959	6,597	3,967	7,675	608
Columbiana	23,096	22,318	17,459	20,798	2,320
Coshocton	5,827	6,361	4,725	8,359	525
Crawford	7,553	10,801	6,058	12,424	915
Cuyahoga	349,186	255,594	307,448	254,883	40,750
Darke	9,901	11,580	7,635	12,773	1,198
Defiance	5,850	7,526	5,096	9,358	896
Delaware	7,058	12,285	6,417	14,740	1,278
Erie	13,843	14,742	12,343	15,628	1,908
Fairfield	13,361	19,098	13,144	24,096	1,689
Fayette	4,477	5,719	2,810	5,827	327
Franklin	141,624	189,645	143,932	200,948	21,269
Fulton	4,850	7,891	3,972	9,519	1,026
Gallia	4,971	5,198	4,406	6,469	401
Geauga	10,449	15,004	9,542	17,762	2,359
Greene	20,245	22,598	20,068	24,922	3,160
Guernsey	7,573	7,746	5,121	8,180	604
Hamilton	135,605	211,267	129,114	206,979	17,898
Hancock	8,548	15,983	6,843	18,264	1,467
Hardin	4,650	6,076	3,863	7,457	528
Harrison	4,070	3,509	2,848	3,639	331
Henry	4,592	7,656	3,059	7,584	691
Highland	6,327	6,853	4,363	7,359	454
Hocking	5,126	4,114	3,765	4,588	312
Holmes	2,242	2,870	2,094	3,860	329
Huron	7,742	9,386	6,537	11,173	1,110
Jackson	6,699	5,987	4,409	5,902	274
Jefferson	22,318	14,839	20,382	15,777	1,797
Knox	7,361	9,290	6,586	10,384	987
Lake	40,734	36,390	35,246	43,485	5,925
Lawrence	12,072	10,668	11,366	13,799	813
Licking	19,247	23,518	17,208	28,425	2,419
Logan	5,949	9,092	4,319	9,727	718
Lorain	52,387	39,459	40,919	51,034	7,324
Lucas	103,658	76,069	85,341	86,653	16,636
Madison	4,885	7,074	3,565	7,166	438
Mahoning	75,837	46,314	63,677	50,153	9,490
Marion	10,962	13,141	9,419	14,605	1,255
Medina	16,251	19,066	13,573	24,723	2,965
Meigs	5,262	4,942	3,827	4,911	294
Mercer	6,724	7,678	5,506	8,673	941
Miami	13,074	18,686	12,893	19,928	2,429
Monroe	4,296	2,728	3,166	2,870	266
Montgomery	106,468	100,223	105,110	101,443	13,817
Morgan	2,727	2,971	1,875	3,236	156
Morrow	4,870	5,814	3,239	6,179	383
Muskingum	14,178	15,358	12,584	17,921	1,329
Noble	2,612	3,007	1,944	3,025	208
Ottawa	9,646	8,241	6,753	8,641	1,281
Paulding	3,229	3,593	2,778	4,971	550
Perry	6,268	5,637	4,383	5,725	369
Pickaway	5,907	7,695	5,052	9,289	515
Pike	5,734	3,729	4,938	4,426	257
Portage	24,417	17,927	20,570	22,829	3,798
Preble	5,850	6,654	5,416	8,376	687
Putnam	5,035	7,332	3,742	9,752	533
Richland	23,065	24,310	18,253	29,213	2,586
Ross	10,743	11,477	9,355	13,251	812
Sandusky	11,202	13,074	8,482	13,420	1,851
Scioto	18,019	13,021	15,552	15,881	816
Seneca	10,074	11,730	7,303	14,172	1,415
Shelby	6,414	8,011	6,425	8,988	895
Stark	70,012	72,607	59,005	87,769	8,030
Summit	123,711	80,415	102,459	92,299	15,002
Trumbull	53,828	36,469	44,366	41,056	6,281
Tuscarawas	16,880	14,279	12,117	15,708	1,779
Union	4,377	7,464	3,038	7,576	421
Van Wert	5,689	8,344	4,070	7,866	741
Vinton	2,629	2,148	2,381	2,484	138
Warren	13,349	16,115	11,306	22,430	1,348
Washington	8,914	11,513	7,936	14,310	1,121
Wayne	13,087	16,976	12,129	18,962	2,313
Williams	4,920	7,596	4,015	9,146	872
Wood	16,926	19,331	14,139	23,315	4,156
Wyandot	4,043	5,661	2,757	5,786	407
Totals	**2,011,621**	**2,000,505**	**1,752,414**	**2,206,545**	**254,472**

Ohio Vote Since 1932

1932 (Pres.), Roosevelt, Dem., 1,301,695; Hoover, Rep., 1,227,679; Thomas, Soc., 64,094; Upshaw, Proh., 7,421; Foster, Com., 7,221; Reynolds, Soc. Labor, 1,968.

1936 (Pres.), Roosevelt, Dem., 1,747,122; Landon, Rep., 1,127,709; Lemke, Union, 132,212; Browder, Com., 5,251; Thomas, Soc., 117; Aiken, Soc. Labor, 14.

1940 (Pres.), Roosevelt, Dem., 1,733,139; Willkie, Rep., 1,586,773.

1944 (Pres.), Roosevelt, Dem., 1,570,763; Dewey, Rep., 1,582,293.

1948 (Pres.), Truman, Dem., 1,452,791; Dewey, Rep., 1,445,684; Wallace, Prog., 37,596.

1952 (Pres.), Eisenhower, Rep., 2,100,391; Stevenson, Dem., 1,600,367.

1956 (Pres.), Eisenhower, Rep., 2,262,610; Stevenson, Dem., 1,439,655.

1960 (Pres.), Kennedy, Dem., 1,944,248; Nixon, Rep., 2,217,611.

1964 (Pres.), Johnson, Dem., 2,498,331; Goldwater, Rep., 1,470,865.

1968 (Pres.), Nixon, Rep., 1,791,014; Humphrey, Dem., 1,700,586; Wallace, 3d party, 467,495; Gregory, 372; Munn, Proh., 19; Blomen, Soc. Labor, 120; Halstead, Soc. Worker, 69; Mitchell, Com., 23.

1972 (Pres.), Nixon, Rep., 2,441,827; McGovern, Dem., 1,558,889; Fisher, Soc. Labor, 7,107; Hall, Com., 6,437; Schmitz, Amer., 80,067; Wallace, Ind., 460.

1976 (Pres.), Carter, Dem., 2,011,621; Ford, Rep., 2,000,505; McCarthy, Ind., 58,258; Maddox, Amer. Ind., 15,529; MacBride, Libertarian, 8,961; Hall, Com., 7,817; Camejo, Soc. Workers, 4,717; LaRouche, U.S. Labor, 4,335; scattered, 130.

1980 (Pres.), Reagan, Rep., 2,206,545; Carter, Dem., 1,752,414; Anderson, Ind., 254,472; Clark, Libertarian, 49,033; Commoner, Citizens, 8,564; Hall, Com., 4,729; Congress, Ind. 4,029; Griswold, Workers World, 3,790; Bubar, Statesman, 27.

Oklahoma

	1976		1980		
County	Carter (D)	Ford (R)	Carter (D)	Reagan (R)	Anderson (I)
Adair	3,183	3,013	2,761	3,429	107
Alfalfa	1,725	2,113	899	2,628	86
Atoka	3,276	1,098	2,505	1,613	66
Beaver	1,213	1,801	696	2,430	58
Beckham	4,530	2,351	3,298	3,637	123
Blaine	2,297	2,682	1,399	3,708	103
Bryan	7,410	2,848	6,410	3,980	129
Caddo	7,382	3,854	4,695	5,945	232
Canadian	7,288	9,766	4,889	15,272	642
Carter	8,319	6,668	6,509	9,262	258
Cherokee	6,006	4,443	5,215	5,594	362
Choctaw	4,269	1,821	3,507	2,394	73
Cimarron	962	872	373	1,404	23
Cleveland	20,054	22,098	14,536	31,178	3,910
Coal	1,774	769	1,442	926	47
Comanche	12,910	13,163	9,972	16,609	1000
Cotton	1,911	1,127	1,410	1,702	63
Craig	3,577	2,540	2,801	2,956	156
Creek	8,964	8,458	7,339	11,749	460
Custer	4,597	4,847	3,008	6,469	290
Delaware	4,924	3,642	4,244	5,302	177
Dewey	1,540	1,230	826	1,943	70
Ellis	1,256	1,429	561	1,908	54
Garfield	8,969	14,202	5,718	17,989	846
Garvin	6,797	3,905	5,033	5,520	210
Grady	7,155	4,686	5,330	8,131	351
Grant	1,853	1,685	927	2,411	84
Greer	2,113	1,164	1,492	1,535	48
Harmon	1,371	666	961	676	21
Harper	978	1,303	517	1,652	40
Haskell	3,388	1,401	2,874	2,024	65
Hughes	4,185	1,715	3,211	2,170	85
Jackson	4,914	3,189	4,031	4,327	144
Jefferson	2,303	956	1,812	1,440	55
Johnston	2,765	1,127	2,066	1,701	57
Kay	9,371	12,441	6,449	15,004	665
Kingfisher	2,372	3,443	1,282	4,962	122
Kiowa	3,403	1,971	2,372	2,636	88
Latimer	2,661	1,312	2,105	1,737	71
Le Flore	8,033	4,907	6,668	6,807	174
Lincoln	4,988	4,429	3,231	6,064	204
Logan	4,594	4,382	3,246	6,311	259
Love	1,923	846	1,578	1,449	31
McClain	4,048	2,444	2,990	4,284	185
McCurtain	7,560	3,423	5,953	5,189	149
McIntosh	4,145	1,822	3,654	2,925	118
Major	1,357	2,282	584	3,059	62
Marshall	2,939	1,358	2,157	1,961	52
Mayes	6,298	5,040	5,344	6,633	256
Murray	2,932	1,563	2,384	2,494	126
Muskogee	14,678	10,287	13,341	11,,511	633
Noble	2,278	2,634	1,398	3,663	124
Nowata	2,195	2,077	1,694	2,640	75
Okfuskee	2,663	1,630	2,177	2,126	58
Oklahoma	87,185	119,120	58,765	139,538	9,190
Okmulgee	8,449	5,333	7,236	6,652	286
Osage	6,832	6,398	5,687	8,044	363
Ottawa	7,446	4,985	6,143	6,362	317
Pawnee	3,031	3,111	2,020	3,902	161
Payne	9,987	13,481	7,466	15,955	1,812
Pittsburg	10,743	4,807	8,292	7,062	339

	1976 (D)	1976 (R)	1980 (D)	1980 (R)	1980 (I)
Pontotoc	7,466	4,895	5,942	6,232	335
Pottawatomie . . .	11,255	9,090	8,526	12,466	625
Pushmataha	2,987	1,360	2,666	1,989	65
Roger Mills	1,346	873	877	1,221	50
Rogers	7,368	7,318	6,399	11,581	461
Seminole	5,874	4,237	4,726	5,067	224
Sequoyah	5,873	3,938	4,983	5,987	178
Stephens	9,795	7,099	7,191	10,199	310
Texas	2,591	3,919	1,451	5,503	93
Tillman	2,852	1,802	2,144	2,450	69
Tulsa	65,298	108,653	53,438	124,643	7,802
Wagoner	5,879	5,071	5,235	8,969	369
Washington	6,898	14,560	5,854	16,563	851
Washita	3,304	2,165	2,044	3,206	71
Woods	2,530	2,788	1,364	3,592	191
Woodward	2,807	3,782	1,703	5,318	175
Totals	**532,442**	**545,708**	**402,026**	**695,570**	**38,284**

Oklahoma Vote Since 1932

1932 (Pres.), Roosevelt, Dem., 516,468; Hoover, Rep., 188,165.

1936 (Pres.), Roosevelt, Dem., 501,069; Landon, Rep., 245,122; Thomas, Soc., 2,221; Colvin, Proh., 1,328.

1940 (Pres.), Roosevelt, Dem., 474,313; Willkie, Rep., 348,872; Babson, Proh., 3,027.

1944 (Pres.), Roosevelt, Dem., 401,549; Dewey, Rep., 319,424; Watson, Proh., 1,663.

1948 (Pres.), Truman, Dem., 452,782; Dewey, Rep., 268,817.

1952 (Pres.), Eisenhower, Rep., 518,045; Stevenson, Dem., 430,939.

1956 (Pres.), Eisenhower, Rep., 473,769; Stevenson, Dem., 385,581.

1960 (Pres.), Kennedy, Dem., 370,111; Nixon, Rep., 533,039.

1964 (Pres.), Johnson, Dem., 519,834; Goldwater, Rep. 412,665.

1968 (Pres.), Nixon, Rep., 449,697; Humphrey, Dem., 301,658; Wallace, 3d party, 191,731.

1972 (Pres.), Nixon, Rep. 759,025; McGovern, Dem., 247,147; Schmitz, Amer., 23,728.

1976 (Pres.), Carter, Dem., 532,442; Ford, Rep., 545,708; McCarthy, Ind., 14,101.

1980 (Pres.), Reagan, Rep., 695,570; Carter, Dem., 402,026; Anderson, Ind., 38,284; Clark, Libertarian, 13,828.

Oregon

County	1976 Carter (D)	1976 Ford (R)	1980 Carter (D)	1980 Reagan (R)	1980 Anderson (I)
Baker	3,306	3,340	2,515	4,747	487
Benton	11,887	15,555	13,150	14,982	4,950
Clackamas	42,504	47,671	40,462	54,111	11,386
Clatsop	6,690	6,178	6,482	6,124	1,854
Columbia	8,005	5,226	7,124	6,623	1,158
Coos	14,168	9,481	11,817	13,041	2,428
Crook	2,536	2,093	2,162	3,113	435
Curry	3,227	2,962	2,656	4,910	652
Deschutes	9,480	9,054	9,641	15,186	2,909
Douglas	14,965	16,500	12,564	23,101	2,529
Gilliam	508	612	394	622	85
Grant	1,393	1,640	1,274	2,519	273
Harney	1,567	1,652	1,110	2,313	255
Hood River	3,114	3,210	2,924	3,450	530
Jackson	23,384	24,237	19,903	32,879	4,019
Jefferson	1,769	1,810	1,654	2,523	431
Josephine	9,061	10,726	7,116	16,827	1,401
Klamath	9,659	11,649	7,371	16,060	1,427
Lake	1,381	1,575	1,147	2,234	201
Lane	56,479	46,245	52,240	54,750	12,076
Lincoln	6,685	5,755	7,009	7,637	1,637
Linn	15,776	14,128	13,516	18,943	2,823
Malheur	3,507	5,682	2,937	7,705	472
Marion	33,781	35,497	32,134	42,191	8,755
Morrow	1,162	1,091	1,077	1,728	239
Multnomah	129,060	112,400	120,487	101,606	27,572
Polk	8,141	8,528	7,833	10,006	2,026
Sherman	491	567	389	677	62
Tillamook	4,456	4,033	4,521	4,123	931
Umatilla	7,985	9,345	7,382	12,950	1,531
Union	4,280	5,111	3,677	6,514	763
Wallowa	1,310	1,693	995	2,485	216
Wasco	4,560	4,258	4,336	4,703	819
Washington	34,847	52,376	37,915	57,165	13,076
Wheeler	402	355	282	442	62
Yamhill	8,881	9,885	8,694	12,054	1,919
Totals	**490,407**	**492,120**	**456,890**	**571,044**	**112,389**

Oregon Vote Since 1932

1932 (Pres.), Roosevelt, Dem., 213,871; Hoover, Rep., 136,019; Thomas, Soc., 15,450; Reynolds, Soc. Labor, 1,730; Foster, Com., 1,681.

1936 (Pres.), Roosevelt, Dem., 266,733; Landon, Rep., 122,706; Lemke, Union, 21,831; Thomas, Soc., 2,143; Aiken, Soc. Labor, 500; Browder, Com., 104; Colvin, Proh., 4.

1940 (Pres.), Roosevelt, Dem., 258,415; Willkie, Rep., 219,555; Aiken, Soc. Labor, 2,487; Thomas, Soc., 398; Browder, Com., 191; Babson, Proh., 154.

1944 (Pres.), Roosevelt, Dem., 248,635; Dewey, Rep. 225,365; Thomas, Soc., 3,785; Watson, Proh., 2,362.

1948 (Pres.), Truman, Dem., 243,147; Dewey, Rep., 260,904; Wallace, Prog., 14,978; Thomas, Soc., 5,051.

1952 (Pres.), Eisenhower, Rep., 420,815; Stevenson, Dem. 270,579; Hallinan, Ind., 3,665.

1956 (Pres.), Eisenhower, Rep., 406,393; Stevenson, Dem. 329,204.

1960 (Pres.), Kennedy, Dem., 367,402; Nixon, Rep. 408,060.

1964 (Pres.), Johnson, Dem., 501,017; Goldwater, Rep. 282,779; write-in, 2,509.

1968 (Pres.), Nixon, Rep., 408,433; Humphrey, Dem. 358,866; Wallace, 3d party, 49,683; write-in, McCarthy 1,496; N. Rockefeller, 69; others, 1,075.

1972 (Pres.), Nixon, Rep., 486,686; McGovern, Dem. 392,760, Schmitz, Amer., 46,211; write-in, 2,289.

1976 (Pres.), Carter, Dem., 490,407; Ford, Rep., 492,12C McCarthy, Ind., 40,207; write-in, 7,142.

1980 (Pres.), Reagan, Rep., 571,044; Carter, Dem., 456,890 Anderson, Ind., 112,389; Clark, Libertarian, 25,838 Commoner, Citizens, 13,642; scattered, 1,713.

Pennsylvania

County	1976 Carter (D)	1976 Ford (R)	1980 Carter (D)	1980 Reagan (R)	1980 Anders (I)
Adams	8,771	12,133	7,266	13,760	1,13
Allegheny	328,343	303,127	297,464	271,850	38,71
Armstrong	15,179	13,378	12,718	12,955	1,15
Beaver	46,117	33,593	43,955	30,496	4,54
Bedford	6,652	9,355	4,950	10,930	41
Berks	50,994	54,452	36,449	60,576	8,86
Blair	18,397	28,290	15,014	28,931	2,01
Bradford	7,913	12,851	6,439	13,139	1,06
Bucks	79,838	85,628	59,120	100,536	18,10
Butler	22,611	26,366	19,711	28,821	3,45
Cambria	38,797	32,469	36,121	33,072	2,39
Cameron	1,319	1,616	1,112	1,795	9
Carbon	10,791	8,883	8,009	10,042	95
Centre	17,867	21,177	15,987	20,605	5,24
Chester	42,712	67,686	34,307	73,046	10,91
Clarion	6,585	8,360	5,472	8,812	67
Clearfield	13,714	13,626	11,647	15,299	94
Clinton	6,532	5,858	4,842	6,288	73
Columbia	12,051	11,508	9,449	12,426	1,19
Crawford	14,712	15,301	11,778	16,552	2,09
Cumberland	23,008	39,950	19,789	41,152	5,43
Dauphin	34,342	46,819	27,252	44,039	6,03
Delaware	117,252	148,679	88,314	143,282	20,90
Elk	6,713	6,159	5,898	7,175	47
Erie	55,385	49,641	45,946	48,918	6,34
Fayette	32,232	20,021	27,963	19,252	1,34
Forest	1,017	1,135	819	1,206	9
Franklin	14,643	20,009	12,061	22,716	1,72
Fulton	1,737	2,219	1,342	2,740	10
Greene	8,769	5,293	8,193	5,336	45
Huntingdon	5,410	7,843	5,094	8,140	56
Indiana	14,650	15,786	13,828	15,607	1,70
Jefferson	7,456	9,437	6,296	9,628	68
Juniata	3,105	3,991	2,696	4,139	28
Lackawanna	57,685	43,354	45,257	44,242	4,2
Lancaster	35,533	72,106	30,026	79,963	7,44
Lawrence	23,337	18,546	19,506	18,404	1,9
Lebanon	11,785	20,880	8,281	24,495	2,3
Lehigh	46,620	46,895	34,827	50,782	8,97
Luzerne	74,655	60,058	59,976	67,822	4,94
Lycoming	18,635	22,648	14,609	23,415	2,03
McKean	6,424	10,305	5,064	9,229	6
Mercer	25,041	22,469	19,716	22,372	3,24
Mifflin	6,210	7,698	5,226	7,541	5
Monroe	9,544	10,228	7,551	12,357	1,9

	1976 (D)	1976 (R)	1980 (D)	1980 (R)	1980 (I)
Montgomery	112,644	155,480	84,289	156,996	26,133
Montour	2,727	3,259	2,272	3,399	375
Northampton. . . .	42,514	32,926	31,920	35,787	6,823
Northumberland . .	18,939	19,283	13,750	20,608	1,515
Perry	4,605	7,454	3,681	8,026	717
Philadelphia	494,579	239,000	421,253	244,108	42,967
Pike	2,775	4,241	2,132	5,249	452
Potter	2,983	3,828	2,299	4,073	225
Schuylkill	33,905	31,944	24,968	36,273	3,079
Snyder	3,097	6,557	2,418	7,634	451
Somerset.	13,452	15,960	11,695	17,729	815
Sullivan.	1,347	1,584	1,074	1,676	130
Susquehanna . . .	6,075	8,331	4,660	8,994	786
Tioga	5,795	8,417	4,273	8,770	664
Union	3,405	6,309	2,687	6,798	628
Venango	8,653	12,270	7,800	11,547	1,015
Warren	7,412	8,508	5,560	9,165	922
Washington	49,317	32,827	45,295	32,532	3,413
Wayne	4,244	7,811	3,375	8,468	496
Westmoreland . . .	74,217	59,172	68,627	63,140	5,985
Wyoming	3,628	5,705	2,766	5,919	384
York.	41,281	56,912	33,406	61,098	5,779
Totals	**2,328,677**	**2,205,604**	**1,937,540**	**2,261,872**	**292,921**

Pennsylvania Vote Since 1932

1932 (Pres.), Roosevelt, Dem., 1,295,948; Hoover, Rep., 1,453,540; Thomas, Soc., 91,119; Upshaw, Proh., 11,319; Foster, Com., 5,658; Cox, Jobless, 725; Reynolds, Indust., 659.

1936 (Pres.), Roosevelt, Dem., 2,353,788; Landon, Rep., 1,690,300; Lemke, Royal Oak, 67,467; Thomas, Soc., 14,375; Colvin, Proh., 6,691; Browder, Com., 4,060; Aiken, Ind. Lab., 1,424.

1940 (Pres.), Roosevelt, Dem., 2,171,035; Willkie, Rep., 1,889,848; Thomas, Soc., 10,967; Browder, Com., 4,519; Aiken, Ind. Gov., 1,518.

1944 (Pres.), Roosevelt, Dem., 1,940,479; Dewey, Rep., 1,835,054; Thomas, Soc., 11,721; Watson, Proh., 5,750; Teichert, Ind. Gov., 1,789.

1948 (Pres.), Truman, Dem., 1,752,426; Dewey, Rep., 1,902,197; Wallace, Prog., 55,161; Thomas, Soc., 11,325; Watson, Proh., 10,338; Dobbs, Militant Workers, 2,133; Teichert, Ind. Gov., 1,461.

1952 (Pres.), Eisenhower, Rep., 2,415,789; Stevenson, Dem., 2,146,269; Hamblen, Proh., 8,771; Hallinan, Prog., 4,200; Hoopes, Soc., 2,684; Dobbs, Militant Workers, 1,502; Hass, Ind. Gov., 1,347; scattered, 155.

1956 (Pres.), Eisenhower, Rep., 2,585,252; Stevenson, Dem., 1,981,769; Hass, Soc. Labor, 7,447; Dobbs, Militant Workers, 2,035.

1960 (Pres.), Kennedy, Dem., 2,556,282; Nixon, Rep., 2,439,956; Hass, Soc. Labor, 7,185; Dobbs, Soc. Workers, 2,678; scattering, 440.

1964 (Pres.), Johnson, Dem., 3,130,954; Goldwater, Rep., 1,673,657; DeBerry, Soc. Workers, 10,456; Hass, Soc. Labor, 5,092; scattering, 2,531.

1968 (Pres.), Nixon, Rep., 2,090,017; Humphrey, Dem., 2,259,405; Wallace, 3d party, 378,582; Blomen, Soc. Labor, 4,977; Halstead, Soc. Workers, 4,862; Gregory, 7,821; others, 2,264.

1972 (Pres.), Nixon, Rep., 2,714,521; McGovern, Dem., 1,796,951; Schmitz, Amer., 70,593; Jenness, Soc. Workers, 4,639; Hall, Com., 2,686; others, 2,715.

1976 (Pres.), Carter, Dem., 2,328,677; Ford, Rep., 2,205,604; McCarthy, Ind., 50,584; Maddox, Constitution, 25,344; Camejo, Soc. Workers, 3,009; LaRouche, U.S. Labor, 2,744; Hall, Com., 1,891; others, 2,934.

1980 (Pres.), Reagan, Rep., 2,261,872; Carter, Dem., 1,937,540; Anderson, Ind., 292,921; Clark, Libertarian, 33,263; DeBerry, Soc. Workers, 20,291; Commoner, Consumer, 10,430; Hall, Com., 5,184.

Rhode Island

County	1976 Carter (D)	1976 Ford (R)	1980 Carter (D)	1980 Reagan (R)	1980 Anderson (I)
Bristol.	11,228	10,131	9,851	8,508	3,358
Kent.	35,855	34,131	31,350	28,331	10,793
Newport	17,768	15,155	13,904	14,555	5,575
Providence.	144,805	103,976	126,808	86,467	32,994
Washington	17,980	17,856	16,429	16,932	7,099
Totals	**227,636**	**181,249**	**198,342**	**154,793**	**59,819**

Rhode Island Vote Since 1932

1932 (Pres.), Roosevelt, Dem., 146,604; Hoover, Rep., 115,266; Thomas, Soc., 3,138; Foster, Com., 546; Reynolds, Soc. Labor, 433; Upshaw, Proh., 183.

1936 (Pres.), Roosevelt, Dem., 165,238; Landon, Rep., 125,031; Lemke, Union, 19,569; Aiken, Soc. Labor, 929; Browder, Com., 411.

1940 (Pres.), Roosevelt, Dem., 182,182; Willkie, Rep., 138,653; Browder, Com., 239; Babson, Proh., 74.

1944 (Pres.), Roosevelt, Dem., 175,356; Dewey, Rep., 123,487; Watson, Proh., 433.

1948 (Pres.), Truman, Dem., 188,736; Dewey, Rep., 135,787; Wallace, Prog., 2,619; Thomas, Soc., 429; Teichert, Soc. Labor, 131.

1952 (Pres.), Eisenhower, Rep., 210,935; Stevenson, Dem., 203,293; Hallinan, Prog., 187; Hass, Soc. Labor, 83.

1956 (Pres.), Eisenhower, Rep., 225,819; Stevenson, Dem., 161,790.

1960 (Pres.), Kennedy, Dem., 258,032; Nixon, Rep., 147,502.

1964 (Pres.), Johnson, Dem., 315,463; Goldwater, Rep., 74,615.

1968 (Pres.), Nixon, Rep., 122,359; Humphrey, Dem., 246,518; Wallace, 3d party, 15,678; Halstead, Soc. Worker, 383.

1972 (Pres.), Nixon, Rep., 220,383; McGovern, Dem., 194,645; Jenness, Soc. Workers, 729.

1976 (Pres.), Carter, Dem., 227,636; Ford, Rep., 181,249; MacBride, Libertarian, 715; Camejo, Soc. Workers, 462; Hall, Com., 334; Levin, Soc. Labor, 188.

1980 (Pres.), Reagan, Rep., 154,793; Carter, Dem., 198,342; Anderson, Ind., 59,819; Clark, Libertarian, 2,458; Hall, Com., 218; McReynolds, Socialist, 170; DeBerry, Soc. Worker, 90; Griswold, Workers World, 77.

South Carolina

County	1976 Carter (D)	1976 Ford (R)	1980 Carter (D)	1980 Reagan (R)	1980 Anderson (I)
Abbeville	4,700	1,791	4,049	2,261	111
Aiken	14,927	16,011	13,014	18,568	601
Allendale	2,634	1,064	2,775	1,181	18
Anderson.	19,002	9,496	18,796	15,666	474
Bamberg	3,330	1,849	3,294	2,098	18
Barnwell	4,083	2,569	3,399	3,228	64
Beaufort	6,049	5,935	7,415	8,620	513
Berkeley	9,741	6,981	9,850	12,790	17
Calhoun	2,055	1,382	2,043	1,767	31
Charleston	34,328	34,010	32,744	44,006	2,213
Cherokee.	7,765	3,931	6,891	5,378	86
Chester.	5,200	2,982	5,145	3,104	87
Chesterfield	7,687	2,537	6,393	3,477	65
Clarendon	5,489	3,040	5,980	4,158	28
Colleton	5,134	3,324	5,745	4,719	58
Darlington	10,165	6,678	9,009	8,289	219
Dillon	5,089	2,527	4,518	3,384	59
Dorchester	8,046	6,695	7,237	10,893	140
Edgefield	3,216	1,878	3,465	2,415	30
Fairfield.	4,155	1,817	4,153	2,098	37
Florence	16,294	13,539	16,391	17,069	348
Georgetown	7,169	4,068	6,701	5,151	148
Greenville	35,923	39,099	32,135	46,168	1,600
Greenwood.	9,976	5,974	9,283	7,287	230
Hampton	3,923	1,773	4,329	2,217	35
Horry	15,720	9,339	13,885	14,322	530
Jasper	2,903	1,221	3,316	1,617	33
Kershaw	6,211	6,126	5,103	6,652	145
Lancaster.	8,324	4,997	8,282	6,409	331
Laurens.	7,440	5,300	7,858	6,034	129
Lee	3,869	2,357	4,816	2,952	18
Lexington.	14,339	21,442	12,334	28,313	762
Marion	5,927	3,076	1,774	797	22
Marlboro	5,409	1,961	5,377	3,318	80
585	1,774	640	5,378	2,585	52
Newberry.	5,034	4,931	4,825	5,568	80
Oconee.	8,447	3,805	7,677	5,652	188
Orangeburg	13,652	8,794	16,178	11,313	141
Pickens	8,505	8,029	7,789	9,574	402
Richland	36,855	32,727	33,298	35,843	1,808
Saluda	2,715	2,085	2,649	2,451	38
Spartanburg	27,925	20,456	27,238	28,820	933
Sumter	10,471	9,332	9,205	10,655	250
Union	6,363	3,463	6,274	4,035	93

	1976		1980		
	(D)	(R)	(D)	(R)	(I)
Williamsburg	8,745	5,275	8,135	5,110	64
York	14,099	9,843	12,075	11,265	539
Totals	**450,807**	**346,149**	**428,220**	**439,277**	**13,868**

South Carolina Vote Since 1932

1932 (Pres.), Roosevelt, Dem., 102,347; Hoover, Rep., 1,978; Thomas, Soc., 82.

1936 (Pres.), Roosevelt, Dem., 113,791; Landon, Rep., Tolbert faction 953, Hambright faction 693, total, 1,646.

1940 (Pres.), Roosevelt, Dem., 95,470; Willkie, Rep., 1,727.

1944 (Pres.), Roosevelt, Dem., 90,601; Dewey, Rep., 4,547; Southern Democrats, 7,799; Watson, Proh., 365; Rep. Tolbert faction, 63.

1948 (Pres.), Thurmond, States' Rights, 102,607; Truman, Dem., 34,423; Dewey, Rep., 5,386; Wallace, Prog., 154; Thomas, Soc., 1.

1952 (Pres.), Eisenhower ran on two tickets. Under state law vote cast for two Eisenhower slates of electors could not be combined. Eisenhower, Ind., 158,289; Rep., 9,793; total, 168,082; Stevenson, Dem., 173,004; Hamblen, Proh., 1.

1956 (Pres.), Stevenson, Dem., 136,372; Byrd, Ind., 88,509; Eisenhower, Rep., 75,700; Andrews, Ind., 2.

1960 (Pres.), Kennedy, Dem., 198,129; Nixon, Rep., 188,558; write-in, 1.

1964 (Pres.), Johnson, Dem., 215,700; Goldwater, Rep., 309,048; write-ins: Nixon, 1, Wallace, 5; Powell, 1; Thurmond, 1.

1968 (Pres.), Nixon, Rep., 254,062; Humphrey, Dem., 197,486; Wallace, 3d party, 215,430.

1972 (Pres.), Nixon, Rep., 477,044; McGovern, Dem., 184,559, United Citizens, 2,265; Schmitz, Amer., 10,075; write-in, 17.

1976 (Pres.), Carter, Dem., 450,807; Ford, Rep., 346,149; Anderson, Amer., 2,996; Maddox, Amer. Ind., 1,950; write-in, 681.

1980 (Pres.), Reagan, Rep., 439,277; Carter, Dem., 428,220; Anderson, Ind., 13,868; Clark, Libertarian, 4,807; Rarick, Amer. Ind., 2,086.

South Dakota

	1976		1980		
County	Carter (D)	Ford (R)	Carter (D)	Reagan (R)	Anderson (I)
Aurora	1,269	831	709	1,251	125
Beadle	4,846	4,758	3,521	5,921	545
Bennett	481	610	350	919	42
Bon Homme	2,154	1,897	1,191	2,794	214
Brookings	4,685	5,278	3,934	5,727	1,169
Brown	8,888	7,609	6,050	10,550	1,143
Brule	1,534	1,175	925	1,674	153
Buffalo	240	194	147	272	26
Butte	1,366	2,055	843	2,850	150
Campbell	489	897	182	1,271	39
Chas. Mix	2,593	1,779	1,741	2,608	203
Clark	1,376	1,449	774	1,963	151
Clay	2,593	2,647	2,271	3,004	906
Codington	4,680	4,504	3,353	5,903	638
Corson	967	846	522	1,233	82
Custer	995	1,373	708	2,057	129
Davison	4,510	3,688	3,107	4,743	568
Day	2,610	1,617	1,720	2,507	259
Deuel	1,465	1,177	891	1,657	169
Dewey	706	820	600	1,045	109
Douglas	975	1,315	508	1,855	91
Edmunds	1,629	1,294	883	1,881	125
Fall River	1,537	2,046	982	2,831	184
Faulk	1,063	868	520	1,300	110
Grant	2,398	2,051	1,602	2,691	254
Gregory	1,658	1,475	883	2,283	121
Haakon	477	812	255	1,162	38
Hamlin	1,402	1,452	903	1,885	197
Hand	1,477	1,510	803	2,066	159
Hanson	1,005	693	598	1,015	93
Harding	459	470	205	727	28
Hughes	2,506	3,997	1,751	4,652	554
Hutchinson	2,062	2,822	1,145	3,789	228
Hyde	572	687	273	864	60
Jackson	313	532	354	929	50
Jerauld	845	821	595	1,018	103
Jones	374	515	189	689	37
Kingsbury	1,762	1,844	1,132	2,376	258
Lake	2,930	2,530	2,207	3,093	504
Lawrence	3,102	4,206	2,259	5,306	574
Lincoln	2,957	3,105	2,261	3,848	524
Lyman	831	892	486	1,256	106
Marshall	1,721	1,233	1,120	1,710	147
McCook	1,822	1,744	1,223	2,014	269
McPherson	693	1,662	287	2,056	54
Meade	2,478	3,096	1,721	5,349	342
Mellette	429	508	279	624	46
Miner	1,289	839	833	1,172	148
Minnehaha	22,068	23,286	20,008	26,256	4,658
Moody	1,942	1,475	1,364	1,807	279
Pennington	10,058	13,352	7,121	18,991	1,650
Perkins	1,262	1,298	595	1,931	93
Potter	908	1,136	436	1,633	81
Roberts	2,890	1,915	1,829	2,904	235
Sanborn	1,025	881	628	1,178	107
Shannon	756	301	1,132	438	91
Spink	2,650	2,003	1,572	2,915	294
Stanley	548	637	339	892	55
Sully	505	630	220	852	60
Todd	826	583	972	803	112
Tripp	1,822	1,980	947	2,669	130
Turner	1,906	2,694	1,369	3,343	281
Union	2,540	2,297	1,830	2,788	359
Walworth	1,516	2,187	753	2,675	139
Washabaugh	276	229			
Yankton	3,987	4,029	2,698	5,355	553
Ziebach	370	369	246	523	30
Totals	**147,068**	**151,505**	**103,855**	**198,343**	**21,431**

South Dakota Vote Since 1932

1932 (Pres.), Roosevelt, Dem., 183,515; Hoover, Rep., 99,212; Harvey, Lib., 3,333; Thomas, Soc., 1,551; Upshaw, Proh., 463; Foster, Com., 364.

1936 (Pres.), Roosevelt, Dem., 160,137; Landon, Rep., 125,977; Lemke, Union, 10,338.

1940 (Pres.), Roosevelt, Dem., 131,862; Willkie, Rep., 177,065.

1944 (Pres.), Roosevelt, Dem., 96,711; Dewey, Rep., 135,365.

1948 (Pres.), Truman, Dem., 117,653; Dewey, Rep., 129,651; Wallace, Prog., 2,801.

1952 (Pres.), Eisenhower, Rep., 203,857; Stevenson, Dem., 90,426.

1956 (Pres.), Eisenhower, Rep., 171,569; Stevenson, Dem., 122,288.

1960 (Pres.), Kennedy, Dem., 128,070; Nixon, Rep., 178,417.

1964 (Pres.), Johnson, Dem., 163,010; Goldwater, Rep., 130,108.

1968 (Pres.), Nixon, Rep., 149,841; Humphrey, Dem., 118,023; Wallace, 3d party, 13,400.

1972 (Pres.), Nixon, Rep., 166,476; McGovern, Dem., 139,945; Jenness, Soc. Workers, 994.

1976 (Pres.), Carter, Dem., 147,068; Ford, Rep., 151,505; MacBride, Libertarian, 1,619; Hall, Com., 318; Camejo, Soc. Workers, 168.

1980 (Pres.), Reagan, Rep., 198,343; Carter, Dem., 103,855; Anderson, Ind., 21,431; Clark, Libertarian, 3,824; Pulley, Soc. Workers, 250.

Tennessee

	1976		1980		
County	Carter (D)	Ford (R)	Carter (D)	Reagan (R)	Anderson (I)
Anderson	13,455	10,494	10,194	14,235	1,161
Bedford	7,228	3,023	5,987	3,377	159
Benton	4,088	1,678	3,811	2,281	71
Bledsoe	1,757	1,620	1,585	1,970	26
Blount	12,096	13,851	9,412	17,959	620
Bradley	8,776	9,136	7,638	11,869	316
Campbell	5,206	4,277	4,752	5,537	120
Cannon	2,463	908	2,351	1,403	41
Carroll	5,581	4,031	5,277	5,681	125
Carter	7,443	8,934	6,006	11,648	326
Cheatham	4,225	1,376	3,771	2,296	90
Chester	2,532	1,949	2,123	2,751	52
Claiborne	3,461	3,227	2,844	4,289	94
Clay	1,671	982	1,376	1,344	27
Cocke	3,141	5,004	2,139	6,802	139
Coffee	8,017	3,848	7,612	5,454	239
Crockett	2,963	1,694	2,422	2,117	27
Cumberland	4,543	4,119	3,775	6,354	227
Davidson	99,007	60,662	103,741	65,772	4,834
Decatur	2,432	1,637	2,139	2,095	35
De Kalb	3,222	1,443	2,948	1,841	48
Dickson	6,551	2,285	6,622	3,636	157
Dyer	5,937	4,391	5,713	5,475	158
Fayette	3,853	2,133	4,141	2,944	75
Fentress	1,953	1,767	1,543	2,493	49
Franklin	6,788	2,619	6,760	3,995	251
Gibson	10,356	5,563	9,829	6,792	227

	1976 (D)	1976 (R)	1980 (D)	1980 (R)	1980 (I)
Giles	5,225	1,952	4,653	2,757	85
Grainger	2,018	2,805	1,495	3,254	66
Greene	7,070	8,664	5,822	10,704	338
Grundy	2,850	850	2,837	1,139	33
Hamblen	7,504	6,989	5,890	9,741	336
Hamilton	45,348	47,969	41,913	57,575	2,087
Hancock	764	1,309	704	1,734	32
Hardeman	3,934	2,254	4,153	2,931	73
Hardin	3,438	3,362	3,164	4,152	76
Hawkins	5,931	6,407	5,283	7,836	310
Haywood	3,681	1,952	3,445	2,435	49
Henderson	3,366	4,152	2,702	5,108	78
Henry	7,162	2,585	6,601	4,299	200
Hickman	3,590	1,154	3,225	1,903	78
Houston	1,990	407	1,757	738	31
Humphreys	4,021	1,338	3,974	1,897	74
Jackson	2,959	591	2,480	995	27
Jefferson	3,995	5,459	3,180	6,944	201
Johnson	1,464	2,986	1,141	3,716	66
Knox	53,034	56,013	45,634	66,153	4,801
Lake	1,933	591	1,718	823	11
Lauderdale	4,747	2,105	4,318	2,818	73
Lawrence	7,140	4,967	6,082	6,532	212
Lewis	2,391	617	2,190	1,076	33
Lincoln	5,732	1,724	5,387	2,856	119
Loudon	4,683	4,458	3,699	6,382	235
McMinn	7,020	6,638	5,460	7,825	200
McNairy	4,293	3,388	3,801	4,603	76
Macon	1,951	2,063	1,947	2,925	65
Madison	12,989	11,364	12,986	13,667	363
Marion	4,615	2,965	4,623	3,902	93
Marshall	4,457	1,674	4,277	2,282	78
Maury	8,747	5,327	7,957	6,637	225
Meigs	1,254	975	999	1,278	31
Monroe	5,368	5,335	4,612	6,246	125
Montgomery	12,310	5,923	11,573	8,503	490
Moore	1,101	331	993	551	34
Morgan	2,953	1,949	2,094	2,823	70
Obion	7,204	2,986	5,766	5,397	138
Overton	3,897	1,115	3,343	1,869	38
Perry	1,660	520	1,401	783	32
Pickett	948	986	758	1,319	12
Polk	3,284	1,835	2,470	2,414	45
Putnam	8,485	4,079	8,084	6,235	342
Rhea	3,735	3,449	3,070	4,689	93
Roane	9,216	7,121	6,473	11,096	481
Robertson	7,547	2,505	7,381	3,560	127
Rutherford	14,854	7,921	15,213	11,208	703
Scott	2,260	2,432	1,724	3,014	63
Sequatchie	1,733	1,065	1,509	1,512	23
Sevier	3,993	7,608	3,450	10,576	338
Shelby	147,893	128,646	159,240	140,157	7,180
Smith	3,753	1,332	3,674	1,755	69
Stewart	2,442	510	2,274	985	42
Sullivan	23,353	22,087	22,341	25,963	1,874
Sumner	13,848	7,946	14,150	11,876	540
Tipton	5,667	3,329	4,934	4,339	109
Trousdale	1,385	332	1,674	629	30
Unicoi	2,526	3,211	1,880	3,828	97
Union	1,631	1,801	1,435	2,453	45
Van Buren	1,085	346	886	499	11
Warren	6,666	2,364	6,021	3,680	148
Washington	13,951	14,770	11,599	17,457	934
Wayne	1,891	2,597	1,633	3,418	78
Weakley	6,605	2,875	5,910	5,668	136
White	3,874	1,382	3,415	2,100	64
Williamson	8,183	7,880	8,815	11,597	551
Wilson	10,537	4,696	11,248	7,535	380
Totals	**825,879**	**633,969**	**783,051**	**787,761**	**35,991**

Tennessee Vote Since 1932

1932 (Pres.), Roosevelt, Dem., 259,817; Hoover, Rep., 126,806; Upshaw, Proh., 1,995; Thomas, Soc., 1,786; Foster, Com., 234.

1936 (Pres.), Roosevelt, Dem., 327,083; Landon, Rep., 146,516; Thomas, Soc., 685; Colvin, Proh., 632; Browder, Com., 319; Lemke, Union, 296.

1940 (Pres.), Roosevelt, Dem., 351,601; Willkie, Rep., 169,153; Babson, Proh., 1,606; Thomas, Soc., 463.

1944 (Pres.), Roosevelt, Dem., 308,707; Dewey, Rep., 200,311; Watson, Proh., 882; Thomas, Soc., 892.

1948 (Pres.), Truman, Dem., 270,402; Dewey, Rep., 202,914; Thurmond, States' Rights, 73,815; Wallace, Prog., 1,864; Thomas, Soc., 1,288.

1952 (Pres.), Eisenhower, Rep., 446,147; Stevenson, Dem., 443,710; Hamblen, Proh., 1,432; Hallinan, Prog., 885; MacArthur, Christian Nationalist, 379.

1956 (Pres.), Eisenhower, Rep., 462,288; Stevenson, Dem., 456,507; Andrews, Ind., 19,820; Holtwick, Proh., 789.

1960 (Pres.), Kennedy, Dem., 481,453; Nixon, Rep., 556,577; Faubus, States' Rights, 11,304; Decker, Proh., 2,458.

1964 (Pres.), Johnson, Dem. 635,047; Goldwater, Rep., 508,965; write-in, 34.

1968 (Pres.), Nixon, Rep., 472,592; Humphrey, Dem., 351,233; Wallace, 3d party, 424,792.

1972 (Pres.), Nixon, Rep., 813,147; McGovern, Dem., 357,293; Schmitz, Amer., 30,373; write-in, 369.

1976 (Pres.), Carter, Dem., 825,879; Ford, Rep., 633,969; Anderson, Amer., 5,769; McCarthy, Ind., 5,004; Maddox, Am. Ind., 2,303; MacBride, Libertarian, 1,375; Hall, Com., 547; LaRouche, U.S. Labor, 512; Bubar, Proh., 442; Miller, Ind., 316; write-in, 230.

1980 (Pres.), Reagan, Rep., 787,761; Carter, Dem., 783,051; Anderson, Ind., 35,991; Clark, Libertarian, 7,116; Commoner, Citizens, 1,112; Bubar, Statesman, 521; McReynolds, Socialist, 519; Hall, Com., 503; DeBerry, Soc. Worker, 490; Griswold, Workers World, 400; write-ins, 152.

Texas

County	1976 Carter (D)	1976 Ford (R)	1980 Carter (D)	1980 Reagan (R)	1980 Anderson (I)
Anderson	5,499	4,172	5,163	5,970	137
Andrews	1,777	2,127	1,155	2,800	39
Angelina	9,750	7,223	10,140	9,900	232
Aransas	2,136	1,985	1,800	3,081	134
Archer	1,577	966	1,444	1,804	30
Armstrong	513	506	333	709	9
Atascosa	4,565	2,415	3,980	4,364	93
Austin	2,313	2,686	1,893	3,734	87
Bailey	1,356	1,255	800	1,809	26
Bandera	1,183	1,554	894	2,373	64
Bastrop	4,788	2,383	4,716	3,768	205
Baylor	1,335	783	1,183	1,098	14
Bee	3,690	2,953	3,606	4,171	125
Bell	17,499	15,126	15,823	20,729	934
Bexar	146,581	121,176	137,729	159,578	9,467
Blanco	923	1,015	794	1,434	52
Borden	234	150	131	279	3
Bosque	2,954	1,912	2,431	2,908	62
Bowie	12,445	9,590	11,339	13,942	244
Brazoria	21,711	19,475	18,253	27,614	1,205
Brazos	10,628	15,685	9,856	17,798	1,453
Brewster	1,227	1,368	1,271	1,496	89
Briscoe	823	285	561	562	13
Brooks	2,782	641	2,488	780	43
Brown	5,577	4,483	4,867	6,515	102
Burleson	2,924	1,142	2,615	1,943	33
Burnet	3,818	2,777	3,711	4,033	132
Caldwell	3,647	2,235	3,155	2,879	112
Calhoun	3,642	2,377	3,034	3,312	136
Callahan	2,241	1,581	2,002	2,284	29
Cameron	25,310	16,448	23,200	22,041	801
Camp	2,146	1,133	2,052	1,531	19
Carson	1,542	1,269	1,006	1,888	26
Cass	5,134	3,712	5,578	4,993	60
Castro	2,033	1,007	1,199	1,955	44
Chambers	2,927	1,835	2,517	3,140	96
Cherokee	6,509	3,921	5,726	5,629	92
Childress	1,578	1,043	1,222	1,443	33
Clay	2,568	1,200	2,233	1,824	40
Cochran	1,031	701	513	1,064	23
Coke	844	517	838	708	10
Coleman	2,264	1,669	1,719	2,228	33
Collin	14,039	21,608	15,187	36,559	1,559
Collingsworth	1,169	629	798	1,020	18
Colorado	3,028	2,991	2,377	3,520	58
Comal	4,068	6,377	3,554	9,758	324
Comanche	3,414	1,297	2,550	1,977	40
Concho	715	474	702	700	8
Cooke	4,483	4,804	3,842	6,760	129
Coryell	4,710	4,140	4,097	5,494	228
Cottle	1,047	311	732	511	9
Crane	664	963	607	1,310	23
Crockett	804	802	595	885	10
Crosby	2,176	897	1,408	1,361	17
Culberson	407	373	423	541	7
Dallam	1,029	936	632	965	33
Dallas	196,303	263,081	190,459	306,682	14,271
Dawson	2,162	2,474	1,867	3,267	55
Deaf Smith	2,613	2,776	1,666	4,073	77
Delta	1,563	421	1,347	767	18
Denton	18,887	20,440	17,381	29,908	1,953
DeWitt	2,540	2,754	2,044	3,450	66
Dickens	1,222	343	912	554	13
Dimmit	1,721	890	2,102	1,173	25
Donley	1,095	704	751	1,106	22
Duval	4,267	661	3,706	1,012	28
Eastland	4,320	2,340	3,346	3,442	37
Ector	10,802	18,973	9,069	26,188	636
Edwards	258	412	237	575	11
Ellis	9,991	6,996	9,219	10,046	214
El Paso	45,477	42,697	40,082	53,276	5,096
Erath	4,821	2,925	4,156	3,981	92
Falls	4,277	2,261	3,328	2,606	51

	1976		1980		
	(D)	(R)	(D)	(R)	(I)
Fannin	5,845	2,102	5,284	3,196	74
Fayette	3,428	3,030	2,590	4,104	77
Fisher	1,993	573	1,564	838	23
Floyd	1,991	1,402	1,477	2,043	24
Foard	706	240	617	349	7
Fort Bend	11,264	17,354	11,583	25,366	1,005
Franklin	1,636	758	1,487	1,105	14
Freestone	2,679	1,674	2,739	2,468	33
Frio	2,598	1,280	2,849	1,753	47
Gaines	1,880	1,643	1,182	2,390	46
Galveston	37,873	25,251	30,778	29,527	1,955
Garza	957	755	677	1,188	22
Gillespie	1,260	3,541	1,170	4,736	90
Glasscock	190	218	116	416	2
Goliad	875	846	1,081	1,170	22
Gonzales	3,219	1,789	2,896	2,931	61
Gray	3,872	6,010	2,786	7,187	103
Grayson	17,015	11,981	13,807	16,811	532
Gregg	9,827	17,582	10,219	23,399	311
Grimes	2,656	1,473	2,440	2,087	42
Guadalupe	6,054	6,766	5,049	9,901	407
Hale	5,580	5,390	3,610	7,277	123
Hall	1,633	671	1,057	1,141	13
Hamilton	1,981	1,176	1,526	1,683	30
Hansford	983	1,401	518	2,046	17
Hardeman	1,403	805	1,174	1,056	28
Hardin	6,558	4,046	7,358	6,087	200
Harris	321,897	357,336	274,061	416,655	22,917
Harrison	7,796	7,787	7,746	9,328	125
Hartley	774	811	470	1,248	28
Haskell	2,512	838	1,951	1,447	22
Hays	7,005	5,714	6,013	6,517	590
Hemphill	707	858	592	1,152	21
Henderson	8,245	4,658	8,199	7,903	134
Hidalgo	35,021	19,199	34,542	25,808	1,063
Hill	5,327	2,680	4,688	4,113	73
Hockley	3,949	3,137	2,447	4,599	90
Hood	3,181	1,857	3,001	3,755	109
Hopkins	4,992	2,556	4,344	3,834	93
Houston	3,179	2,229	4,181	2,889	47
Howard	6,984	4,899	4,451	6,658	158
Hudspeth	479	395	394	471	14
Hunt	8,543	6,676	8,773	9,283	327
Hutchinson	3,691	6,137	2,935	7,439	170
Irion	297	302	239	427	2
Jack	1,814	1,049	1,349	1,482	29
Jackson	2,524	1,884	1,826	2,540	66
Jasper	5,422	3,167	5,707	4,396	98
Jeff Davis	309	288	300	409	10
Jefferson	47,581	32,451	45,642	36,763	1,664
Jim Hogg	1,645	429	1,437	535	23
Jim Wells	7,961	3,547	7,267	4,606	102
Johnson	10,864	7,194	10,542	11,411	333
Jones	3,318	2,072	3,043	2,765	45
Karnes	2,996	1,675	2,284	2,719	52
Kaufman	6,302	3,867	6,266	5,852	110
Kendall	1,190	2,543	1,075	3,890	88
Kenedy	139	65	106	76	2
Kent	474	171	351	339	0
Kerr	3,767	6,021	3,387	9,090	259
Kimble	759	846	608	1,011	22
King	100	96	55	144	5
Kinney	516	318	472	543	23
Kleberg	5,803	3,771	5,125	4,608	231
Knox	1,498	551	1,163	783	17
Lamar	8,601	4,443	7,178	6,094	148
Lamb	3,374	2,413	2,132	3,723	51
Lampasas	2,376	1,563	1,979	2,323	56
LaSalle	1,294	677	1,442	773	19
Lavaca	3,458	2,466	2,678	3,254	54
Lee	1,937	1,348	1,581	1,803	59
Leon	2,085	1,161	2,190	1,821	19
Liberty	7,086	4,552	6,810	6,470	163
Limestone	3,825	2,045	3,403	2,835	45
Lipscomb	644	911	338	1,343	28
Live Oak	1,656	1,287	1,380	2,193	32
Llano	2,361	1,947	2,130	2,866	72
Loving	35	47	22	50	0
Lubbock	24,797	38,478	18,732	46,711	1,952
Lynn	1,575	1,166	1,236	1,603	28
Madison	1,885	1,062	1,583	1,389	32
Marion	1,860	1,291	2,015	1,666	28
Martin	907	698	605	1,093	15
Mason	814	805	630	966	17
Matagorda	4,971	3,679	4,585	5,545	146
Maverick	2,840	924	2,932	1,370	39
McCulloch	1,888	1,300	1,750	1,572	24
McLennan	30,091	25,370	26,305	31,968	964
McMullen	194	217	122	271	4
Medina	3,681	3,252	3,034	4,742	84
Menard	543	441	489	548	11
Midland	7,725	19,178	6,839	25,027	586
Milam	4,871	2,404	4,230	3,251	111
Mills	1,012	684	1,028	985	24
Mitchell	1,730	1,058	1,446	1,455	12
Montague	4,087	2,182	3,233	3,143	59
Montgomery	13,718	15,739	12,593	26,237	819
Moore	2,767	2,759	1,743	3,736	67
Morris	3,071	1,843	3,105	2,133	27
Motley	522	428	341	573	7
Nacogdoches	6,697	7,315	5,981	8,626	422
Navarro	6,995	4,012	6,988	5,400	126
Newton	3,468	1,011	3,284	1,379	24
Nolan	3,094	2,431	2,796	2,781	87
Nueces	52,755	32,797	43,424	40,586	2,045
Ochiltree	1,084	2,471	594	3,032	52
Oldham	554	354	290	557	9
Orange	15,177	9,147	14,928	12,389	395
Palo Pinto	5,170	2,684	4,244	4,068	98
Panola	3,731	3,218	3,637	4,022	58
Parker	8,186	4,692	7,336	8,505	189
Parmer	1,914	1,487	707	2,640	30
Pecos	1,971	2,234	1,602	2,723	37
Polk	4,384	2,529	4,213	3,771	80
Potter	11,917	13,819	9,633	16,327	545
Presidio	1,232	687	1,039	723	22
Rains	1,339	510	1,174	813	18
Randall	9,074	17,115	7,323	23,136	677
Reagan	563	666	414	917	14
Real	510	448	603	832	14
Red River	3,670	1,852	3,501	2,225	31
Reeves	2,613	1,711	2,138	2,315	52
Refugio	2,218	1,537	2,224	1,944	57
Roberts	202	350	150	482	4
Robertson	3,741	1,244	3,572	1,661	33
Rockwall	1,828	2,087	1,985	4,036	113
Runnels	2,068	2,203	1,648	2,532	36
Rusk	6,063	6,800	5,582	8,705	116
Sabine	2,391	904	1,983	1,387	15
San Augustine	1,817	1,047	1,674	1,397	14
San Jacinto	2,406	1,094	2,376	1,726	42
San Patricio	9,469	5,853	8,627	8,326	280
San Saba	1,408	582	1,405	948	23
Schleicher	468	516	444	672	6
Scurry	2,639	2,797	2,003	3,745	53
Shackelford	764	748	606	959	9
Shelby	4,680	2,695	4,215	3,500	71
Sherman	718	679	286	1,128	28
Smith	16,856	22,238	14,838	28,236	414
Somervell	1,054	332	1,015	792	21
Starr	4,646	664	4,782	1,389	50
Stephens	1,796	1,621	1,372	2,161	34
Sterling	174	202	218	364	2
Stonewall	812	252	719	488	6
Sutton	768	831	485	1,000	13
Swisher	2,811	753	1,854	1,450	50
Tarrant	122,287	124,433	121,068	173,466	7,818
Taylor	14,453	19,822	13,245	22,961	620
Terrell	321	317	260	411	14
Terry	2,859	2,113	1,945	3,178	45
Throckmorton	658	356	455	444	7
Titus	4,205	2,603	3,872	3,747	44
Tom Green	11,064	12,316	9,892	16,555	661
Travis	78,585	71,031	75,028	73,151	9,796
Trinity	2,100	1,042	2,510	1,503	32
Tyler	3,322	1,965	3,540	2,545	70
Upshur	4,902	3,272	4,894	4,836	78
Upton	686	869	485	1,169	13
Uvalde	2,299	3,103	2,402	3,887	62
Val Verde	4,603	3,476	4,116	5,055	145
Van Zandt	6,449	3,385	5,707	5,495	78
Victoria	7,326	9,594	7,382	13,392	347
Walker	5,105	4,974	4,869	5,657	274
Waller	2,828	1,992	3,329	3,019	76
Ward	2,046	2,123	1,405	2,912	50
Washington	2,635	3,820	2,518	4,821	95
Webb	10,362	4,222	11,856	5,421	242
Wharton	5,914	4,682	5,138	6,598	160
Wheeler	1,598	1,273	1,090	1,626	16
Wichita	22,017	19,024	17,657	22,884	847
Wilbarger	3,280	2,145	2,347	3,031	53
Willacy	2,984	1,542	3,047	1,995	38
Williamson	9,355	7,481	10,408	15,035	946
Wilson	3,973	1,926	3,097	3,443	73
Winkler	1,382	1,842	1,021	2,160	35
Wise	5,133	2,856	4,674	4,350	108
Wood	4,107	3,076	4,033	4,515	74
Yoakum	1,181	1,477	715	1,937	28
Young	3,473	2,652	2,740	4,153	84
Zapata	1,216	462	1,218	874	19
Zavala	1,822	735	2,621	831	69
Totals	**2,082,319**	**1,953,300**	**1,881,147**	**2,510,705**	**111,613**

Texas Vote Since 1932

1932 (Pres.), Roosevelt, Dem., 760,348; Hoover, Rep., 97,959; Thomas, Soc., 4,450; Harvey, Lib., 324; Foster, Com., 207; Jackson Party, 104.

1936 (Pres.), Roosevelt, Dem., 734,485; Landon, Rep., 103,874; Lemke, Union, 3,281; Thomas, Soc., 1,075; Colvin, Proh., 514; Browder, Com., 253.

1940 (Pres.), Roosevelt, Dem., 840,151; Willkie, Rep., 199,152; Babson, Proh., 925; Thomas, Soc., 728; Browder, Com., 212.

1944 (Pres.), Roosevelt, Dem., 821,605; Dewey, Rep., 191,425; Texas Regulars, 135,439; Watson, Proh., 1,017; Thomas, Soc., 594; America First, 250.

1948 (Pres.), Truman, Dem., 750,700; Dewey, Rep., 282,240; Thurmond, States' Rights, 106,909; Wallace, Prog., 3,764; Watson, Proh., 2,758; Thomas, Soc., 874.

1952 (Pres.), Eisenhower, Rep., 1,102,878; Stevenson, Dem., 969,228; Hamblen, Proh., 1,983; MacArthur, Christian Nationalist, 833; MacArthur, Constitution, 730; Hallinan, Prog., 294.

1956 (Pres.), Eisenhower, Rep., 1,080,619; Stevenson, Dem., 859,958; Andrews, Ind., 14,591.

1960 (Pres.), Kennedy, Dem., 1,167,932; Nixon, Rep., 1,121,699; Sullivan, Constitution, 18,169; Decker, Proh., 3,870; write-in, 15.

1964 (Pres.), Johnson, Dem., 1,663,185; Goldwater, Rep., 958,566; Lightburn, Constitution, 5,060.

1968 (Pres.), Nixon, Rep., 1,227,844; Humphrey, Dem., 1,266,804; Wallace, 3d party, 584,269; write-in, 489.

1972 (Pres.), Nixon, Rep., 2,298,896; McGovern, Dem., 1,154,289; Schmitz, Amer., 6,039; Jenness, Soc. Workers, 8,664; others, 3,393.

1976 (Pres.), Carter, Dem., 2,082,319; Ford, Rep., 1,953,300; McCarthy, Ind., 20,118; Anderson, Amer., 11,442; Camejo, Soc. Workers, 1,723; write-in, 2,982.

1980 (Pres.), Reagan, Rep., 2,510,705; Carter, Dem., 1,881,147; Anderson, Ind., 111,613; Clark, Libertarian, 37,643; write-in, 528.

Utah

County	1976 Carter (D)	1976 Ford (R)	1980 Carter (D)	1980 Reagan (R)	1980 Anderson (I)
Beaver	963	1,088	621	1,477	43
Box Elder	3,353	9,319	2,142	12,500	306
Cache	5,430	16,636	3,639	20,251	1,494
Carbon	5,157	3,360	4,317	4,320	309
Daggett	131	217	109	290	10
Davis	14,084	31,216	9,065	45,695	2,253
Duchesne	1,110	2,619	854	3,827	87
Emery	1,771	1,717	1,315	3,076	90
Garfield	539	1,163	375	1,578	50
Grand	931	1,781	703	2,362	205
Iron	1,700	4,757	1,242	6,207	240
Juab	1,091	1,290	720	1,872	51
Kane	330	1,094	256	1,492	59
Millard	1,224	2,484	795	3,620	72
Morgan	701	1,356	373	1,985	42
Piute	265	377	157	551	3
Rich	248	541	143	762	18
Salt Lake	86,659	144,100	58,472	169,411	19,547
San Juan	1,182	1,856	763	2,774	72
Sanpete	1,925	3,683	1,260	5,143	112
Sevier	1,564	3,686	1,112	5,614	117
Summit	1,282	2,316	1,184	3,330	480
Tooele	4,371	4,657	3,132	6,024	391
Uintah	1,342	4,017	1,049	6,045	155
Utah	18,327	49,328	12,166	71,859	1,264
Wasatch	1,092	1,940	994	2,799	113
Washington	1,893	5,944	1,678	10,181	185
Wayne	334	555	226	835	15
Weber	23,111	34,811	15,404	43,807	2,501
Totals	**182,110**	**337,908**	**124,266**	**439,687**	**30,284**

Utah Vote Since 1932

1932 (Pres.), Roosevelt, Dem., 116,750; Hoover, Rep., 84,795; Thomas, Soc., 4,087; Foster, Com., 947.

1936 (Pres.), Roosevelt, Dem., 150,246; Landon, Rep., 64,555; Lemke, Union, 1,121; Thomas, Soc., 432; Browder, Com., 280; Colvin, Proh., 43.

1940 (Pres.), Roosevelt, Dem., 154,277; Willkie, Rep., 93,151; Thomas, Soc., 200; Browder, Com., 191.

1944 (Pres.), Roosevelt, Dem., 150,088; Dewey, Rep., 97,891; Thomas, Soc., 340.

1948 (Pres.), Truman, Dem., 149,151; Dewey, Rep., 124,402; Wallace, Prog., 2,679; Dobbs, Soc. Workers, 73.

1952 (Pres.), Eisenhower, Rep., 194,190; Stevenson, Dem., 135,364.

1956 (Pres.), Eisenhower, Rep., 215,631; Stevenson, Dem., 118,364.

1960 (Pres.), Kennedy, Dem., 169,248; Nixon, Rep., 205,361; Dobbs, Soc. Workers, 100.

1964 (Pres.), Johnson, Dem., 219,628; Goldwater, Rep., 181,785.

1968 (Pres.), Nixon, Rep., 238,728; Humphrey, Dem., 156,665; Wallace, 3d party, 26,906; Halstead, Soc. Worker, 89; Peace and Freedom, 180.

1972 (Pres.), Nixon, Rep., 323,643; McGovern, Dem., 126,284; Schmitz, Amer., 28,549.

1976 (Pres.), Carter, Dem., 182,110; Ford, Rep., 337,908; Anderson, Amer., 13,304; McCarthy, Ind., 3,907; MacBride, Libertarian, 2,438; Maddox, Am. Ind., 1,162; Camejo, Soc. Workers, 268; Hall, Com., 121.

1980 (Pres.), Reagan, Rep., 439,687; Carter, Dem., 124,266; Anderson, Ind., 30,284; Clark, Libertarian, 7,226; Commoner, Citizens, 1,009; Greaves, American, 965; Rarick, Amer. Ind., 522; Hall, Com., 139; DeBerry, Soc. Worker, 124.

Vermont

County	1976 Carter (D)	1976 Ford (R)	1980 Carter (D)	1980 Reagan (R)	1980 Anderson (I)
Addison	4,164	5,726	4,351	5,216	1,751
Bennington	5,443	6,712	5,361	6,091	1,978
Caledonia	3,511	5,488	3,284	5,986	1,068
Chittenden	17,992	22,013	18,967	18,310	8,409
Essex	1,002	1,161	799	1,305	148
Franklin	5,610	6,190	5,914	5,998	1,350
Grand Isle	866	1,004	999	947	260
Lamoille	2,016	3,535	2,414	3,228	1,048
Orange	3,171	4,768	3,079	4,656	1,371
Orleans	3,561	4,075	3,671	4,473	865
Rutland	7,613	9,867	9,596	11,142	3,174
Washington	8,764	10,919	9,559	9,714	3,256
Windham	6,794	7,928	5,830	7,062	3,167
Windsor	8,282	11,001	8,067	10,470	3,915
Totals	**78,789**	**100,387**	**81,891**	**94,598**	**31,760**

Vermont Vote Since 1932

1932 (Pres.), Roosevelt, Dem., 56,266; Hoover, Rep., 78,984; Thomas, Soc., 1,533; Foster, Com., 195.

1936 (Pres.), Landon, Rep., 81,023; Roosevelt, Dem., 62,124; Browder, Com., 405.

1940 (Pres.), Roosevelt, Dem., 64,269; Willkie, Rep., 78,371; Browder, Com., 411.

1944 (Pres.), Roosevelt, Dem., 53,820; Dewey, Rep., 71,527.

1948 (Pres.), Truman, Dem., 45,557; Dewey, Rep., 75,926; Wallace, Prog., 1,279; Thomas, Soc., 585.

1952 (Pres.), Eisenhower, Rep., 109,717; Stevenson, Dem., 43,355; Hallinan, Prog., 282; Hoopes, Soc., 185.

1956 (Pres.), Eisenhower, Rep., 110,390; Stevenson, Dem., 42,549; scattered, 39.

1960 (Pres.), Kennedy, Dem., 69,186; Nixon, Rep., 98,131.

1964 (Pres.), Johnson, Dem., 107,674; Goldwater, Rep., 54,868.

1968 (Pres.), Nixon, Rep., 85,142; Humphrey, Dem., 70,255; Wallace, 3d party, 5,104; Halstead, Soc. Worker, 295; Gregory, New Party, 579.

1972 (Pres.), Nixon, Rep., 117,149; McGovern, Dem., 68,174; Spock, Liberty Union, 1,010; Jenness, Soc. Workers, 296; scattered, 318.

1976 (Pres.), Carter, Dem., 77,798; Carter, Ind. Vermonter, 991; Ford, Rep., 100,387; McCarthy, Ind., 4,001; Camejo, Soc. Workers, 430; LaRouche, U.S. Labor, 196; scattered, 99.

1980 (Pres.), Reagan, Rep., 94,598; Carter, Dem., 81,891; Anderson, Ind., 31,760; Commoner, Citizens, 2,316; Clark, Libertarian, 1,900; McReynolds, Liberty Union, 136; Hall, Com. 118; DeBerry, Soc. Worker, 75; scattering, 413.

Virginia

County	1976 Carter (D)	1976 Ford (R)	1980 Carter (D)	1980 Reagan (R)	1980 Anderson (I)
Accomack	4,807	4,494	4,872	5,371	292
Albemarle	7,310	9,084	7,293	10,424	1,435
Alleghany	2,462	1,756	2,411	2,185	116
Amelia	1,715	1,634	1,643	1,969	52
Amherst	3,675	3,956	3,476	5,088	208
Appomattox	1,702	1,964	1,492	2,548	85
Arlington	32,536	30,972	26,502	30,854	8,042
Augusta	5,626	8,452	5,202	11,011	539
Bath	1,029	888	999	921	70
Bedford	4,766	4,189	4,721	6,608	336
Bland	961	1,047	1,002	1,278	35
Botetourt	4,021	3,343	3,698	4,408	329
Brunswick	3,071	2,387	3,430	2,310	70
Buchanan	5,791	3,850	5,768	4,554	95
Buckingham	2,179	1,487	1,933	1,864	77
Campbell	4,354	7,442	4,473	9,592	396
Caroline	3,064	1,648	2,924	2,071	116
Carroll	4,010	4,820	3,437	5,905	183
Charles City	1,455	439	1,564	506	39

	1976		1980		
	(D)	(R)	(D)	(R)	(I)
Charlotte	2,312	2,023	2,108	2,322	59
Chesterfield	14,126	27,812	13,060	37,908	2,182
Clarke	1,276	1,440	1,156	1,876	177
Craig	1,103	546	946	768	41
Culpeper	2,892	3,659	2,519	4,312	231
Cumberland	1,302	1,284	1,355	1,515	51
Dickenson	4,583	3,471	4,177	3,687	77
Dinwiddie	3,873	2,413	3,475	3,369	107
Essex	1,306	1,380	1,280	1,581	76
Fairfax	92,037	110,424	73,734	137,620	24,605
Fauquier	4,002	4,715	4,119	6,782	548
Floyd	1,728	2,071	1,642	2,447	131
Fluvanna	1,415	1,296	1,424	1,605	108
Franklin	6,439	3,532	5,685	4,993	304
Frederick	3,389	5,162	2,948	7,293	455
Giles	3,779	2,731	3,627	2,978	211
Gloucester	3,156	3,025	3,138	4,261	354
Goochland	2,259	2,104	2,290	2,423	113
Grayson	3,146	3,021	2,875	3,494	106
Greene	895	1,095	925	1,702	105
Greensville	2,413	1,137	2,142	1,583	39
Halifax	4,352	4,045	4,528	5,088	125
Hanover	6,069	11,559	5,383	14,262	589
Henrico	21,729	45,405	21,023	50,505	2,956
Henry	9,680	5,612	8,800	8,258	355
Highland	493	629	487	751	25
Isle of Wight	4,145	2,718	3,951	3,526	197
James City	3,000	3,186	3,068	4,289	551
King George	1,513	1,383	1,318	1,784	185
King and Queen	1,111	778	1,128	949	43
King William	1,501	1,597	1,446	2,036	80
Lancaster	1,581	2,381	1,567	2,780	106
Lee	5,415	4,679	4,758	4,417	137
Loudoun	7,995	9,192	6,694	12,076	1,312
Louisa	2,857	2,151	2,809	2,633	160
Lunenburg	1,739	1,816	1,958	2,045	59
Madison	1,466	1,710	1,351	1,959	156
Mathews	1,309	1,908	1,300	2,204	148
Mecklenburg	4,076	4,423	3,790	4,853	142
Middlesex	1,312	1,608	1,395	1,810	90
Montgomery	7,539	7,971	7,455	8,222	1,400
Nelson	2,426	1,516	2,410	1,866	143
New Kent	1,338	1,259	1,204	1,739	68
Northampton	2,459	2,043	2,363	2,165	114
Northumberland	1,814	2,167	1,551	2,598	109
Nottoway	2,556	2,486	2,593	2,813	113
Orange	2,309	2,549	2,420	3,381	241
Page	3,401	3,780	2,607	4,297	161
Patrick	2,740	2,349	2,382	3,436	105
Pittsylvania	7,929	9,173	7,653	12,022	250
Powhatan	1,528	2,010	1,484	2,933	98
Prince Edward	2,448	2,734	2,553	2,774	137
Prince George	2,630	2,254	2,310	3,389	130
Prince William	15,215	15,446	12,787	23,061	2,676
Pulaski	5,546	4,764	5,769	5,747	343
Rappahannock	1,071	881	1,055	1,179	99
Richmond	864	1,391	854	1,567	49
Roanoke	13,120	13,587	12,114	17,182	1,286
Rockbridge	2,525	2,157	2,475	2,784	296
Rockingham	5,349	9,768	5,294	11,397	771
Russell	6,014	4,287	5,764	4,778	125
Scott	4,496	4,313	4,314	4,744	153
Shenandoah	3,364	6,296	3,137	7,517	385
Smyth	5,246	5,032	5,335	6,033	224
Southampton	3,399	2,366	3,347	2,997	163
Spotsylvania	4,210	3,210	4,039	5,385	464
Stafford	4,900	4,451	4,211	7,106	623
Surry	1,829	929	1,756	962	63
Sussex	2,497	1,360	2,447	1,664	86
Tazewell	7,565	5,565	7,003	7,021	225
Warren	3,221	2,985	2,597	3,861	297
Washington	6,547	6,865	6,390	8,402	382
Westmoreland	2,355	1,909	2,271	2,510	133
Wise	7,134	5,691	6,779	5,767	258
Wythe	3,578	4,231	3,677	4,758	164
York	4,736	5,603	4,532	6,744	723
Total	**489,208**	**540,351**	**445,151**	**665,012**	**63,068**
CITIES					
Alexandria	19,858	16,880	17,134	17,865	4,546
Bedford	1,122	1,043	1,149	1,145	75
Bristol	3,343	2,943	2,889	3,432	160
Buena Vista	993	771	1,031	942	59
Charlottesville	6,846	6,673	6,866	5,907	1,377
Chesapeake	17,651	12,851	17,155	17,888	1,189
Clifton Forge	993	770	1,012	716	68
Colonial Heights	2,409	4,291	1,692	5,012	219
Covington	1,820	1,173	1,813	1,187	101
Danville	6,425	10,235	6,138	10,665	296
Emporia	899	1,055	855	988	41
Fairfax	3,464	4,174	2,614	4,475	800
Falls Church	2,202	2,323	1,703	2,485	497
Franklin	1,116	1,127	1,324	1,045	62
Fredericksburg	2,550	2,527	2,174	2,502	245
Galax	1,218	1,128	1,061	1,188	31
Hampton	19,202	15,021	18,517	17,023	1,598
Harrisonburg	1,803	3,376	1,896	3,388	403
Hopewell	3,691	3,764	3,102	4,423	178
Lexington	945	1,027	963	956	129
Lynchburg	8,227	14,564	7,783	15,245	854
Manassas	1,646	1,992	1,565	3,009	318
Manassas Park	709	444	447	729	52
Martinsville	3,491	3,147	3,337	3,433	162
Newport News	23,058	20,914	22,066	22,423	2,068
Norfolk	39,295	28,099	35,118	27,506	3,333
Norton	811	577	762	572	42
Petersburg	7,852	5,041	7,931	5,001	254
Poquoson	1,140	1,461	877	2,338	158
Portsmouth	22,837	12,872	20,900	13,660	1,124
Radford	2,240	1,844	2,225	1,964	233
Richmond	44,687	37,176	47,975	34,629	3,502
Roanoke	20,696	14,738	18,139	15,164	1,350
Salem	4,404	4,196	4,091	4,862	359
South Boston	1,001	1,389	971	1,615	51
Staunton	2,951	4,681	2,658	4,819	311
Suffolk	9,246	6,066	9,064	7,179	360
Virginia Beach	25,824	34,593	24,895	47,936	4,830
Waynesboro	2,209	3,528	1,926	3,697	255
Williamsburg	1,468	1,654	1,199	1,344	340
Winchester	2,346	4,075	2,006	4,240	320
Total	**324,688**	**296,203**	**307,023**	**324,597**	**32,350**
Aggregate	**813,896**	**836,554**	**752,174**	**989,609**	**95,418**

Virginia Vote Since 1932

1932 (Pres.), Roosevelt, Dem., 203,979; Hoover, Rep., 89,637; Thomas, Soc., 2,382; Upshaw, Proh., 1,843; Foster, Com., 86; Cox, Ind. 15.

1936 (Pres.), Roosevelt, Dem., 234,980; Landon, Rep., 98,366; Colvin, Proh., 594; Thomas, Soc., 313; Lemke, Union, 233; Browder, Com., 98.

1940 (Pres.), Roosevelt, Dem., 235,961; Willkie, Rep., 109,363; Babson, Proh., 882; Thomas, Soc., 282; Browder, Com., 71; Aiken, Soc. Labor, 48.

1944 (Pres.), Roosevelt, Dem., 242,276; Dewey, Rep., 145,243; Watson, Proh., 459; Thomas, Soc., 417; Teichert, Soc. Labor, 90.

1948 (Pres.), Truman, Dem., 200,786; Dewey, Rep., 172,070; Thurmond, States' Rights, 43,393; Wallace, Prog., 2,047; Thomas, Soc., 726; Teichert, Soc. Labor, 234.

1952 (Pres.), Eisenhower, Rep., 349,037; Stevenson, Dem., 268,677; Hass, Soc. Labor, 1,160; Hoopes, Social Dem., 504; Hallinan, Prog., 311.

1956 (Pres.), Eisenhower, Rep., 386,459; Stevenson, Dem., 267,760; Andrews, States' Rights, 42,964; Hoopes, Soc. Dem., 444; Hass, Soc. Labor, 351.

1960 (Pres.), Kennedy, Dem., 362,327; Nixon, Rep., 404,521; Coiner, Conservative, 4,204; Hass, Soc. Labor, 397.

1964 (Pres.), Johnson, Dem., 558,038; Goldwater, Rep., 481,334; Hass, Soc. Labor, 2,895.

1968 (Pres.), Nixon, Rep., 590,319; Humphrey, Dem., 442,387; Wallace, 3d party, *320,272; Blomen, Soc. Labor, 4,671; Munn, Proh., 601; Gregory, Peace and Freedom, 1,680.

*10,561 votes for Wallace were omitted in the count.

1972 (Pres.), Nixon, Rep., 988,493; McGovern, Dem., 438,887; Schmitz, Amer., 19,721; Fisher, Soc. Labor, 9,918.

1976 (Pres.), Carter, Dem., 813,896; Ford, Rep., 836,554; Camejo, Soc. Workers, 17,802; Anderson, Amer., 16,686; LaRouche, U.S. Labor, 7,508; MacBride, Libertarian, 4,648.

1980 (Pres.), Reagan, Rep., 989,609; Carter, Dem., 752,174; Anderson, Ind., 95,418; Commoner, Citizens, 14,024; Clark, Libertarian, 12,821; DeBerry, Soc. Worker, 1,986.

Washington

County	1976 Carter (D)	1976 Ford (R)	1980 Carter (D)	1980 Reagan (R)	1980 Anderson (I)
Adams	1,790	2,795	1,223	3,248	255
Asotin	2,898	2,752	2,724	3,275	539
Benton	11,306	22,135	11,561	28,728	3,301
Chelan	7,623	10,492	6,483	11,299	1,608
Clallam	8,268	9,132	8,029	11,515	2,172
Clark	31,080	27,938	30,584	33,223	6,445
Columbia	829	1,153	587	1,349	119
Cowlitz	14,958	12,531	12,560	13,154	2,336
Douglas	3,809	4,547	2,833	5,171	564
Ferry	814	776	802	1,108	127
Franklin	4,369	5,671	3,719	7,327	699
Garfield	616	892	509	875	122
Grant	7,777	9,192	5,673	11,152	1,091
Grays Harbor	13,478	9,464	11,290	10,226	3,267
Island	5,859	7,804	5,422	10,926	1,800
Jefferson	2,913	2,794	3,279	3,645	876

	1976		1980		
	(D)	(R)	(D)	(R)	(I)
King	248,743	279,382	235,046	272,567	76,119
Kitsap	25,701	23,124	20,893	29,420	8,525
Kittitas	4,858	4,765	4,075	5,359	1,066
Klickitat	2,890	2,573	2,596	3,113	423
Lewis	9,026	10,933	6,962	13,636	1,603
Lincoln	1,978	2,925	1,597	3,324	357
Mason	6,060	4,758	5,241	6,745	1,353
Okanogan	5,543	5,455	4,634	6,460	1,030
Pacific	4,278	2,781	3,727	3,132	945
Pend Oreille	1,533	1,516	1,399	2,136	221
Pierce	78,238	74,668	64,444	90,247	18,345
San Juan	1,467	1,998	1,666	2,363	728
Skagit	12,718	13,060	11,299	15,520	2,854
Skamania	1,436	1,102	1,373	1,416	218
Snohomish	55,623	55,375	52,003	66,153	14,465
Spokane	55,660	68,290	49,263	78,096	11,258
Stevens	3,824	4,719	3,584	7,094	601
Thurston	21,247	21,000	20,508	26,369	5,993
Wahkiakum	942	704	751	828	148
Walla Walla	7,012	10,883	5,825	11,223	1,591
Whatcom	19,739	20,007	18,430	21,371	4,906
Whitman	6,197	8,168	5,726	8,636	2,331
Yakima	24,223	29,478	21,873	33,815	4,672
Totals	**717,323**	**777,732**	**650,193**	**865,244**	**185,073**

Washington Vote Since 1932

1932 (Pres.), Roosevelt, Dem., 353,260; Hoover, Rep., 208,645; Harvey, Lib., 30,308; Thomas, Soc., 17,080; Foster, Com., 2,972; Upshaw, Proh., 1,540; Reynolds, Soc. Labor, 1,009.

1936 (Pres.), Roosevelt, Dem., 459,579; Landon, Rep., 206,892; Lemke, Union, 17,463; Thomas, Soc., 3,496; Browder, Com., 1,907; Pellsy, Christian, 1,598; Colvin, Proh., 1,041; Aiken, Soc. Labor, 362.

1940 (Pres.), Roosevelt, Dem., 462,145; Willkie, Rep., 322,123; Thomas, Soc., 4,586; Browder, Com., 2,626; Babson, Proh., 1,686; Aiken, Soc. Labor, 667.

1944 (Pres.), Roosevelt, Dem., 486,774; Dewey, Rep., 361,689; Thomas, Soc., 3,824; Watson, Proh., 2,396; Teichert, Soc. Labor, 1,645.

1948 (Pres.), Truman, Dem., 476,165; Dewey, Rep., 386,315; Wallace, Prog., 31,692; Watson, Proh., 6,117; Thomas, Soc., 3,534; Teichert, Soc. Labor, 1,133; Dobbs, Soc. Workers, 103.

1952 (Pres.), Eisenhower, Rep., 599,107; Stevenson, Dem., 492,845; MacArthur, Christian Nationalist, 7,290; Hallinan, Prog., 2,460; Hass, Soc. Labor, 633; Hoopes, Soc., 254; Dobbs, Soc. Workers, 119.

1956 (Pres.), Eisenhower, Rep., 620,430; Stevenson, Dem., 523,002; Hass, Soc. Labor, 7,457.

1960 (Pres.), Kennedy, Dem., 599,298; Nixon, Rep., 629,273; Hass, Soc. Labor, 10,895; Curtis, Constitution, 1,401; Dobbs, Soc. Workers, 705.

1964 (Pres.), Johnson, Dem., 779,699; Goldwater, Rep., 470,366; Hass, Soc. Labor, 7,772; DeBerry, Freedom Soc., 537.

1968 (Pres.), Nixon, Rep., 588,510; Humphrey, Dem., 616,037; Wallace, 3d party, 96,990; Blomen, Soc. Labor, 488; Cleaver, Peace and Freedom, 1,609; Halstead, Soc. Worker, 270; Mitchell, Free Ballot, 377.

1972 (Pres.), Nixon, Rep., 837,135; McGovern, Dem., 568,334; Schmitz, Amer., 58,906; Spock, Ind., 2,644; Fisher, Soc. Labor, 1,102; Jenness, Soc. Worker, 623; Hall, Com., 566; Hospers, Libertarian, 1,537.

1976 (Pres.), Carter, Dem., 717,323; Ford, Rep., 777,732; McCarthy, Ind., 36,986; Maddox, Amer. Ind., 8,585; Anderson, Amer., 5,046; MacBride, Libertarian, 5,042; Wright, People's, 1,124; Camejo, Soc. Workers, 905; LaRouche, U.S. Labor, 903; Hall, Com., 817; Levin, Soc. Labor, 713; Zeidler, Soc., 358.

1980 (Pres.), Reagan, Rep., 865,244; Carter, Dem., 650,193; Anderson, Ind., 185,073; Clark, Libertarian, 29,213; Commoner, Citizens, 9,403; DeBerry, Soc. Worker, 1,137; McReynolds, Socialist, 956; Hall, Com., 834; Griswold, Workers World, 341.

West Virginia

	1976		1980		
County	Carter (D)	Ford (R)	Carter (D)	Reagan (R)	Anderson (I)
Barbour	3,647	3,235	3,451	3,311	292
Berkeley	8,216	8,935	6,783	9,955	625
Boone	8,528	3,072	7,515	4,164	268
Braxton	4,012	1,912	3,795	2,403	173
Brooke	8,197	4,792	6,430	4,622	634
Cabell	20,811	19,644	17,732	19,482	2,146
Calhoun	2,173	1,283	1,717	1,606	92
Clay	2,662	1,282	2,185	1,452	102
Doddridge	1,245	1,804	1,043	1,888	120
Fayette	15,496	5,459	13,175	5,784	725
Gilmer	2,245	1,371	1,854	1,452	153
Grant	1,323	2,976	1,041	3,452	87
Greenbrier	8,291	5,862	7,128	6,221	546
Hampshire	3,104	2,097	2,522	2,879	157
Hancock	10,627	6,771	8,784	6,610	917
Hardy	2,993	1,858	2,050	2,329	99
Harrison	21,467	15,172	18,813	14,251	1,339
Jackson	5,334	5,360	4,120	6,041	352
Jefferson	5,166	3,864	4,679	4,454	572
Kanawha	53,602	42,213	42,829	42,604	5,838
Lewis	3,960	3,736	3,455	3,747	359
Lincoln	5,260	2,997	5,317	4,009	128
Logan	13,122	4,021	12,024	4,945	381
Marion	17,800	10,391	14,189	10,952	1,171
Marshall	8,641	6,705	7,832	7,252	725
Mason	6,769	5,205	5,683	6,040	312
McDowell	10,557	4,107	9,822	3,862	216
Mercer	14,761	10,791	11,804	12,273	563
Mineral	5,898	5,130	4,671	6,125	386
Mingo	8,655	3,010	9,328	3,716	208
Monongalia	16,163	11,827	12,883	11,972	2,745
Monroe	3,297	2,750	2,877	2,999	166
Morgan	1,929	2,369	1,594	2,833	172
Nicholas	6,235	3,462	5,265	3,885	322
Ohio	11,817	12,476	10,973	11,414	1,334
Pendleton	2,104	1,554	1,724	1,677	80
Pleasants	1,699	1,608	1,494	1,852	84
Pocahontas	2,330	1,740	2,170	2,011	150
Preston	5,595	5,719	4,317	5,828	515
Putnam	8,226	6,334	6,409	7,561	632
Raleigh	19,768	10,637	16,955	10,713	1,046
Randolph	7,265	4,822	5,937	4,374	518
Ritchie	1,941	2,874	1,450	3,081	128
Roane	3,519	3,216	2,498	3,219	184
Summers	3,943	2,254	3,114	2,456	201
Taylor	3,905	2,891	3,216	3,010	233
Tucker	2,323	1,396	1,862	1,798	153
Tyler	1,817	2,514	1,482	2,707	163
Upshur	3,513	4,789	2,867	4,751	415
Wayne	9,958	6,009	8,687	7,541	441
Webster	2,931	971	2,578	1,262	117
Wetzel	5,042	3,793	4,035	3,588	327
Wirt	1,182	1,031	1,058	1,176	44
Wood	17,025	18,348	13,622	20,080	1,536
Wyoming	7,775	4,286	6,624	4,537	299
Totals	**435,864**	**314,726**	**367,462**	**334,206**	**31,691**

West Virginia Vote Since 1932

1932 (Pres.), Roosevelt, Dem., 405,124; Hoover, Rep., 330,731; Thomas, Soc., 5,133; Upshaw, Proh., 2,342; Foster, Com., 444.

1936 (Pres.), Roosevelt, Dem., 502,582; Landon, Rep., 325,358; Colvin, Prog., 1,173; Thomas, Soc., 832.

1940 (Pres.), Roosevelt, Dem., 495,662; Willkie, Rep., 372,414.

1944 (Pres.), Roosevelt, Dem., 392,777; Dewey, Rep., 322,819.

1948 (Pres.), Truman, Dem., 429,188; Dewey, Rep., 316,251; Wallace, Prog., 3,311.

1952 (Pres.), Eisenhower, Rep., 419,970; Stevenson, Dem., 453,578.

1956 (Pres.), Eisenhower, Rep., 449,297; Stevenson, Dem., 381,534.

1960 (Pres.), Kennedy, Dem., 441,786; Nixon, Rep., 395,995.

1964 (Pres.), Johnson, Dem., 538,087; Goldwater, Rep., 253,953.

1968 (Pres.), Nixon, Rep., 307,555; Humphrey, Dem., 374,091; Wallace, 3d party, 72,560.

1972 (Pres.), Nixon, Rep., 484,964; McGovern, Dem., 277,435.

1976 (Pres.), Carter, Dem., 435,864; Ford, Rep., 314,726.

1980 (Pres.), Reagan, Rep., 334,206; Carter, Dem., 367,462; Anderson, Ind., 31,691; Clark, Libertarian, 4,356.

Wisconsin

	1976		1980		
County	Carter (D)	Ford (R)	Carter (D)	Reagan (R)	Anderson (I)
Adams	3,089	2,377	2,773	3,304	318
Ashland	4,688	3,045	4,469	3,262	685
Barron	8,678	7,393	8,654	8,791	883
Bayfield	3,885	2,624	3,705	3,278	554
Brown	33,572	36,571	29,796	47,067	4,680

	1976			1980	
	(D)	(R)	(D)	(R)	(I)
Buffalo	3,448	2,844	3,276	3,569	404
Burnett	3,720	2,573	3,200	3,027	393
Calumet	6,241	6,589	5,036	7,885	1,064
Chippewa	11,538	8,137	9,836	10,531	1,160
Clark	7,238	6,095	6,091	7,921	679
Columbia	9,457	10,075	8,715	10,478	1,373
Crawford	3,629	3,393	3,392	3,934	371
Dane	82,321	63,466	85,609	57,545	19,772
Dodge	13,643	17,335	11,966	19,435	1,709
Door	4,553	6,557	4,961	7,170	655
Douglas	13,478	6,999	11,703	7,258	1,728
Dunn	7,882	6,751	7,743	7,428	1,565
Eau Claire	18,263	16,388	17,602	17,304	3,486
Florence	965	922	943	1,187	86
Fond duLac	16,571	22,226	15,293	24,196	2,191
Forest	2,574	1,604	2,402	2,070	141
Grant	9,639	12,016	8,406	13,298	1,690
Green	5,632	7,085	5,336	7,714	947
Green Lake	3,411	5,020	2,851	5,868	368
Iowa	4,252	4,195	4,154	4,068	546
Iron	2,399	1,340	1,941	1,811	219
Jackson	3,735	3,406	3,629	4,327	413
Jefferson	12,577	15,528	11,335	16,174	1,925
Juneau	4,512	4,242	3,884	5,591	463
Kenosha	27,585	22,349	26,738	24,481	3,802
Kewaunee	4,607	4,447	3,706	5,577	318
La Crosse	16,674	24,188	17,304	23,427	3,652
La Fayette	3,839	4,131	3,598	4,421	450
Langlade	4,134	4,630	4,498	4,866	369
Lincoln	5,800	5,672	5,438	6,473	630
Manitowoc	19,819	16,039	17,330	18,591	2,014
Marathon	24,934	21,898	23,281	25,868	3,257
Marinette	8,482	8,591	7,718	10,444	683
Marquette	2,516	2,607	2,180	3,166	270
Menominee	766	324	544	302	57
Milwaukee	249,739	192,008	240,174	183,450	34,281
Monroe	6,465	7,242	6,521	8,136	780
Oconto	6,541	6,232	5,352	8,292	440
Oneida	7,216	7,347	7,008	8,602	832
Outagamie	23,079	28,363	21,284	31,500	5,735
Ozaukee	11,271	19,817	10,779	21,371	2,463
Pepin	1,955	1,312	1,673	1,541	183
Pierce	8,039	5,676	7,312	6,209	1,752
Polk	8,485	6,159	7,607	7,207	1,102
Portage	15,912	9,520	16,443	10,465	2,851
Price	4,028	3,204	3,595	4,028	394
Racine	36,740	37,088	33,565	39,683	5,167
Richland	3,634	4,466	3,413	4,601	413
Rock	28,048	28,325	24,740	30,960	4,408
Rusk	4,050	2,724	3,584	3,704	340
St. Croix	10,203	7,685	10,203	9,265	1,867
Sauk	9,204	9,577	8,456	9,992	1,405
Sawyer	3,055	2,720	3,065	3,548	323
Shawano	6,751	8,505	5,410	9,922	652
Sheboygan	24,226	22,332	20,974	23,036	3,859
Taylor	4,101	3,591	3,739	4,596	403
Trempealeau	6,218	5,341	5,390	5,992	558
Vernon	5,534	6,132	5,501	6,528	494
Vilas	3,209	4,929	3,293	6,034	421
Walworth	12,418	18,091	11,344	19,194	2,581
Washburn	3,503	2,787	3,172	3,193	355
Washington	14,422	18,798	12,944	23,213	2,654
Waukesha	47,487	70,418	46,612	81,059	9,778
Waupaca	6,857	10,849	6,401	12,568	1,072
Waushara	3,485	4,449	2,987	5,576	335
Winnebago	24,485	32,149	24,203	34,286	4,779
Wood	14,728	15,479	13,804	17,987	2,010
Totals	**1,040,232**	**1,004,987**	**981,584**	**1,088,845**	**160,657**

Wisconsin Vote Since 1932

1932 (Pres.), Roosevelt, Dem., 707,410; Hoover, Rep., 347,741; Thomas, Soc. 53,379; Foster, Com., 3,112; Upshaw Proh., 2,672; Reynolds, Soc. Labor, 494.

1936 (Pres.), Roosevelt, Dem., 802,984; Landon, Rep., 380,828; Lemke, Union, 60,297; Thomas, Soc., 10,626; Browder, Com., 2,197; Colvin, Proh., 1,071; Aiken, Soc. Labor, 557.

1940 (Pres.), Roosevelt, Dem., 704,821; Willkie, Rep., 679,260; Thomas, Soc., 15,071; Browder, Com., 2,394; Babson, Proh., 2,148; Aiken, Soc. Labor, 1,882.

1944 (Pres.), Roosevelt, Dem., 650,413; Dewey, Rep., 674,532; Thomas, Soc., 13,205; Teichert, Soc. Labor, 1,002.

1948 (Pres.), Truman, Dem., 647,310; Dewey, Rep., 590,959; Wallace, Prog., 25,282; Thomas, Soc., 12,547; Teichert, Soc. Labor, 399; Dobbs, Soc. Workers, 303.

1952 (Pres.), Eisenhower, Rep., 979,744; Stevenson, Dem., 622,175; Hallinan, Ind., 2,174; Dobbs, Ind., 1,350; Hoopes, Ind., 1,157; Hass, Ind., 770.

1956 (Pres.), Eisenhower, Rep., 954,844; Stevenson, Dem., 586,768; Andrews, Ind., 6,918; Hoopes, Soc., 754; Hass, Soc. Labor, 710; Dobbs, Soc. Workers, 564.

1960 (Pres.), Kennedy, Dem., 830,805; Nixon, Rep., 895,175; Dobbs, Soc. Workers, 1,792; Hass, Soc. Labor, 1,310.

1964 (Pres.), Johnson, Dem., 1,050,424; Goldwater, Rep., 638,495; DeBerry, Soc. Worker, 1,692; Hass, Soc. Labor, 1,204.

1968 (Pres.), Nixon, Rep., 809,997; Humphrey, Dem., 748,804; Wallace, 3d party, 127,835; Blomen, Soc. Labor, 1,338; Halstead, Soc. Worker, 1,222; scattered, 2,342.

1972 (Pres.) Nixon, Rep., 989,430; McGovern, Dem., 810,174; Schmitz, Amer., 47,525; Spock, Ind., 2,701; Fisher, Soc. Labor, 998; Hall, Com., 663; Reed, Ind., 506; scattered, 893.

1976 (Pres.), Carter, Dem., 1,040,232; Ford, Rep., 1,004,987; McCarthy, Ind., 34,943; Maddox, Amer. Ind., 8,552; Zeidler, Soc., 4,298; MacBride, Libertarian, 3,814; Camejo, Soc. Workers, 1,691; Wright, People's, 943; Hall, Com., 749; LaRouche, U.S. Lab., 738; Levin, Soc. Labor, 389; scattered, 2,839.

1980 (Pres.), Reagan, Rep., 1,088,845; Carter, Dem., 981,584; Anderson, Ind., 160,657; Clark, Libertarian, 29,135; Commoner, Citizens, 7,767; Rarick, Constitution, 1,519; McReynolds, Socialist, 808; Hall, Com., 772; Griswold, Workers World, 414; DeBerry, Soc. Workers, 383; scattering, 1,337.

Wyoming

	1976			1980	
County	Carter (D)	Ford (R)	Carter (D)	Reagan (R)	Anderson (I)
Albany	4,663	6,734	3,772	5,830	1,630
Big Horn	1,618	3,117	1,212	3,709	209
Campbell	1,620	3,306	1,400	5,613	460
Carbon	3,010	3,556	2,272	4,337	493
Converse	1,150	2,188	922	2,987	215
Crook	653	1,438	413	1,909	70
Fremont	4,423	6,584	3,307	9,077	731
Goshen	2,262	2,764	1,373	3,572	269
Hot Springs	958	1,413	745	1,602	136
Johnson	797	2,042	635	2,291	139
Laramie	12,040	14,061	9,512	15,361	2,225
Lincoln	1,555	2,464	1,063	3,412	120
Natrona	8,640	13,761	7,111	16,801	1,768
Niobrara	427	1,042	270	1,075	38
Park	2,656	5,878	1,718	6,435	496
Platte	1,593	1,844	1,555	2,642	262
Sheridan	3,206	5,382	3,034	5,649	641
Sublette	528	1,284	357	1,538	139
Sweetwater	5,575	4,937	4,728	6,265	826
Teton	1,204	2,667	1,361	3,004	664
Uinta	1,559	2,124	1,138	2,738	189
Washakie	1,168	2,361	945	2,634	230
Weston	934	1,770	584	2,219	122
Totals	**62,239**	**92,717**	**49,427**	**110,700**	**12,072**

Wyoming Vote Since 1932

1932 (Pres.), Roosevelt, Dem., 54,370; Hoover, Rep., 39,583; Thomas, Soc. 2,829; Foster, Com., 180.

1936 (Pres.), Roosevelt, Dem., 62,624; Landon, Rep., 38,739; Lemke, Union, 1,653; Thomas, Soc., 200; Browder, Com., 91; Colvin, Proh., 75.

1940 (Pres.), Roosevelt, Dem., 59,287; Willkie, Rep., 52,633; Babson, Proh., 172; Thomas, Soc., 148.

1944 (Pres.), Roosevelt, Dem., 49,419; Dewey, Rep., 51,921.

1948 (Pres.), Truman, Dem., 52,354; Dewey, Rep., 47,947; Wallace, Prog., 931; Thomas, Soc., 137; Teichert, Soc. Labor, 56.

1952 (Pres.), Eisenhower, Rep., 81,047; Stevenson, Dem., 47,934; Hamblen, Proh., 194; Hoopes, Soc., 40; Haas, Soc. Labor, 36.

1956 (Pres.), Eisenhower, Rep., 74,573; Stevenson, Dem., 49,554.

1960 (Pres.), Kennedy, Dem., 63,331; Nixon, Rep., 77,451.

1964 (Pres.), Johnson, Dem., 80,718; Goldwater, Rep., 61,998.

1968 (Pres.), Nixon, Rep., 70,927; Humphrey, Dem., 45,173; Wallace, 3d party, 11,105.

1972 (Pres.), Nixon, Rep., 100,464; McGovern, Dem., 44,358; Schmitz, Amer., 748.

1976 (Pres.), Carter, Dem., 62,239; Ford, Rep., 92,717; McCarthy, Ind., 624; Reagan, Ind., 307; Anderson, Amer., 290; MacBride, Libertarian, 89; Brown, Ind., 47; Maddox, Amer. Ind., 30.

1980 (Pres.), Reagan, Rep., 110,700; Carter, Dem., 49,427; Anderson, Ind., 12,072; Clark, Libertarian, 4,514.

Major Parties' Popular and Electoral Vote for President

(F) Federalist; (D) Democrat; (R) Republican; (DR) Democrat Republican; (NR) National Republican; (W) Whig; (P) People's; (PR) Progressive; (SR) States' Rights; (LR) Liberal Republican; Asterisk (*)—See notes.

Year	President elected	Popular	Elec.	Losing candidate	Popular	Elec.
1789	George Washington (F)	Unknown	69	No opposition		
1792	George Washington (F)	Unknown	132	No opposition		
1796	John Adams (F)	Unknown	71	Thomas Jefferson (DR)	Unknown	68
1800*	Thomas Jefferson (DR)	Unknown	73	Aaron Burr (DR)	Unknown	73
1804	Thomas Jefferson (DR)	Unknown	162	Charles Pinckney (F)	Unknown	14
1808	James Madison (DR)	Unknown	122	Charles Pinckney (F)	Unknown	47
1812	James Madison (DR)	Unknown	128	DeWitt Clinton (F)	Unknown	89
1816	James Monroe (DR)	Unknown	183	Rufus King (F)	Unknown	34
1820	James Monroe (DR)	Unknown	231	John Quincy Adams (DR)	Unknown	1
1824*	John Quincy Adams (DR)	105,321	84	Andrew Jackson (DR)	155,872	99
				Henry Clay (DR)	46,587	37
				William H. Crawford (DR)	44,282	41
1828	Andrew Jackson (D)	647,231	178	John Quincy Adams (NR)	509,097	83
1832	Andrew Jackson (D)	687,502	219	Henry Clay (NR)	530,189	49
1836	Martin Van Buren (D)	762,678	170	William H. Harrison (W)	548,007	73
1840	William H. Harrison (W)	1,275,017	234	Martin Van Buren (D)	1,128,702	60
1844	James K. Polk (D)	1,337,243	170	Henry Clay (W)	1,299,068	105
1848	Zachary Taylor (W)	1,360,101	163	Lewis Cass (D)	1,220,544	127
1852	Franklin Pierce (D)	1,601,474	254	Winfield Scott (W)	1,386,578	42
1856	James C. Buchanan (D)	1,927,995	174	John C. Fremont (R)	1,391,555	114
1860	Abraham Lincoln (R)	1,866,352	180	Stephen A. Douglas (D)	1,375,157	12
				John C. Breckinridge (D)	845,763	72
				John Bell (Const. Union)	589,581	39
1864	Abraham Lincoln (R)	2,216,067	212	George McClellan (D)	1,808,725	21
1868	Ulysses S. Grant (R)	3,015,071	214	Horatio Seymour (D)	2,709,615	80
1872*	Ulysses S. Grant (R)	3,597,070	286	Horace Greeley (D-LR)	2,834,079	...
1876*	Rutherford B. Hayes (R)	4,033,950	185	Samuel J. Tilden (D)	4,284,757	184
1880	James A. Garfield (R)	4,449,053	214	Winfield S. Hancock (D)	4,442,030	155
1884	Grover Cleveland (D)	4,911,017	219	James G. Blaine (R)	4,848,334	182
1888*	Benjamin Harrison (R)	5,444,337	233	Grover Cleveland (D)	5,540,050	168
1892	Grover Cleveland (D)	5,554,414	277	Benjamin Harrison (R)	5,190,802	145
				James Weaver (P)	1,027,329	22
1896	William McKinley (R)	7,035,638	271	William J. Bryan (D-P)	6,467,946	176
1900	William McKinley (R)	7,219,530	292	William J. Bryan (D)	6,358,071	155
1904	Theodore Roosevelt (R)	7,628,834	336	Alton B. Parker (D)	5,084,491	140
1908	William H. Taft (R)	7,679,006	321	William J. Bryan (D)	6,409,106	162
1912	Woodrow Wilson (D)	6,286,214	435	Theodore Roosevelt (PR)	4,216,020	88
				William H. Taft (R)	3,483,922	8
1916	Woodrow Wilson (D)	9,129,606	277	Charles E. Hughes (R)	8,538,221	254
1920	Warren G. Harding (R)	16,152,200	404	James M. Cox (D)	9,147,353	127
1924	Calvin Coolidge (R)	15,725,016	382	John W. Davis (D)	8,385,586	136
				Robert M. LaFollette (PR)	4,822,856	13
1928	Herbert Hoover (R)	21,392,190	444	Alfred E. Smith (D)	15,016,443	87
1932	Franklin D. Roosevelt (D)	22,821,857	472	Herbert Hoover (R)	15,761,841	59
				Norman Thomas (Socialist)	884,781	...
1936	Franklin D. Roosevelt (D)	27,751,597	523	Alfred Landon (R)	16,679,583	8
1940	Franklin D. Roosevelt (D)	27,243,466	449	Wendell Willkie (R)	22,304,755	82
1944	Franklin D. Roosevelt (D)	25,602,505	432	Thomas E. Dewey (R)	22,006,278	99
1948	Harry S. Truman (D)	24,105,812	303	Thomas E. Dewey (R)	21,970,065	189
				J. Strom Thurmond (SR)	1,169,021	39
				Henry A. Wallace (PR)	1,157,172	...
1952	Dwight D. Eisenhower (R)	33,936,252	442	Adlai E. Stevenson (D)	27,314,992	89
1956*	Dwight D. Eisenhower (R)	35,585,316	457	Adlai E. Stevenson (D)	26,031,322	73
1960*	John F. Kennedy (D)	34,227,096	303	Richard M. Nixon (R)	34,108,546	219
1964	Lyndon B. Johnson (D)	43,126,506	486	Barry M. Goldwater (R)	27,176,799	52
1968	Richard M. Nixon (R)	31,785,480	301	Hubert H. Humphrey (D)	31,275,166	191
				George C. Wallace (3d party)	9,906,473	46
1972*	Richard M. Nixon (R)	47,165,234	520	George S. McGovern (D)	29,170,774	17
1976*	Jimmy Carter (D)	40,828,929	297	Gerald R. Ford (R)	39,148,940	240
1980	Ronald Reagan (R)	43,899,248	489	Jimmy Carter (D)	35,481,435	49
				John B. Anderson (independent)	5,719,437	...

1800—Elected by House of Representatives because of tied electoral vote.

1824—Elected by House of Representatives. No candidate polled a majority. In 1824, the Democrat Republicans had become a loose coalition of competing political groups. By 1828, the supporters of Jackson were known as Democrats, and the J.Q. Adams and Henry Clay supporters as National Republicans.

1872—Greeley died Nov. 29, 1872. His electoral votes were split among 4 individuals.

1876—Fla., La., Ore., and S. C. election returns were disputed. Congress in joint session (Mar. 2, 1877) declared Hayes and Wheeler elected President and Vice-President.

1888—Cleveland had more votes than Harrison but the 233 electoral votes cast for Harrison against the 168 for Cleveland elected Harrison president.

1956—Democrats elected 74 electors but one from Alabama refused to vote for Stevenson.

1960—Sen. Harry F. Byrd (D-Va.) received 15 electoral votes.

1972—John Hospers of Cal. and Theodora Nathan of Ore. received one vote from an elector of Virginia.

1976—Ronald Reagan of Cal. received one vote from an elector of Washington.

Electoral Votes for President, 1964-80

The Constitution, Article 2, Section 1 (consult index), provides for the appointment of electors, the counting of the electoral ballots and the procedure in the event of a tie. (*see Electoral College.*)

State	1964		1968			1972		1976		1980	
	R.	D.	R.	D.	3d	R.	D.	R.	D.	R.	D.
Ala.	10	...	...	...	10	9	...	...	9	9	...
Alas.	...	3	3	...	...	3	...	3	...	3	...
Ariz.	5	...	5	...	...	6	...	6	...	6	...
Ark.	...	6	...	...	6	6	...	...	6	6	...
Cal.	...	40	40	...	...	45	...	45	...	45	...
Col.	...	6	6	...	...	7	...	7	...	7	...
Conn.	...	8	...	8	...	8	...	8	...	8	...
Del.	...	3	3	...	...	3	...	...	3	3	...
D.C.	...	3	...	3	...	...	3	...	3	...	3
Fla.	...	14	14	...	...	17	...	...	17	17	...
Ga.	12	...	...	...	12	12	...	...	12	...	12
Ha.	...	4	...	4	...	4	...	...	4	...	4
Ida.	...	4	4	...	...	4	...	4	...	4	...
Ill.	...	26	26	...	...	26	...	26	...	26	...
Ind.	...	13	13	...	...	13	...	13	...	13	...
Ia.	...	9	9	...	...	8	...	8	...	8	...
Kan.	...	7	7	...	...	7	...	7	...	7	...
Ky.	...	9	9	...	...	9	...	...	9	9	...
La.	10	...	...	...	10	10	...	...	10	10	...
Me.	...	4	...	4	...	4	...	4	...	4	...
Md.	...	10	...	10	...	10	...	...	10	...	10
Mass.	...	14	...	14	...	...	14	...	14	14	...
Mich.	...	21	...	21	...	21	...	21	...	21	...
Minn.	...	10	...	10	...	10	...	...	10	...	10
Miss.	7	...	...	...	7	7	...	...	7	7	...
Mo.	...	12	12	...	...	12	...	...	12	12	...
Mon.	...	4	4	...	...	4	...	4	...	4	...
Neb.	...	5	5	...	...	5	...	5	...	5	...
Nev.	...	3	3	...	...	3	...	3	...	3	...
N.H.	...	4	4	...	...	4	...	4	...	4	...
N.J.	...	17	17	...	...	17	...	17	...	17	...
N.M.	...	4	4	...	...	4	...	4	...	4	...
N.Y.	...	43	...	43	...	41	...	...	41	41	...
N.C.	...	13	12	...	(1)	13	...	...	13	13	...
N.D.	...	4	4	...	...	3	...	3	...	3	...
Oh.	...	26	26	...	...	25	...	...	25	25	...
Okla.	...	8	8	...	...	8	...	8	...	8	...
Ore.	...	6	6	...	...	6	...	6	...	6	...
Pa.	...	29	...	29	...	27	...	...	27	27	...
R.I.	...	4	...	4	...	4	...	...	4	...	4
S.C.	8	...	8	...	...	8	...	...	8	8	...
S.D.	...	4	4	...	...	4	...	4	...	4	...
Tenn.	...	11	11	...	...	10	...	...	10	10	...
Tex.	...	25	...	25	...	26	...	...	26	26	...
Ut.	...	4	4	...	...	4	...	4	...	4	...
Vt.	...	3	3	...	...	3	...	3	...	3	...
Va.	...	12	12	...	...	11(2)	12	...	...	12	..
Wash.	...	9	...	9	...	9	...	8(3)	...	9	...
W.Va.	...	7	...	7	...	6	...	...	6	...	6
Wis.	...	12	12	...	...	11	...	...	11	11	...
Wy.	...	3	3	...	...	3	...	3	...	3	...
Totals	**52**	**486**	**301**	**191**	**46**	**520**	**17**	**240**	**297**	**489**	**49**
Plurality	...	**434**	**110**	**(1)**	...	**503**	**(2)**	...	**(3)57**	**440**	...

(1) In 1968 in N. C. one Rep. elector cast his ballot for Wallace. (2) In 1972 one Rep. elector in Va. cast his ballot for John Hospers. (3) In 1976 one Rep. elector in Wash. cast his ballot for Reagan.

Voter Turnout in Presidential Elections

Source: Committee for the Study of the American Electorate

National average of voting age population voting: 1960—62.8; 1964—61.9; 1968—60.6; 1972—55.5; 1976—54.3; 1980—53.9. The sharp drop in 1972 reflects the expansion of eligibility with the enfranchisement of 18 to 21 year olds.

	1980		1976
	Registered voters voting	Voting age population voting	Voting age population voting
Ala.	62.9%	49.7%	47.2%
Alas.	60.7	61.3	48.3
Ariz.	78.0	49.1	48.6
Ark.	70.6	53.6	52.2
Cal.	75.6	50.6	51.3
Col.	82.6	57.8	60.4
Conn.	82.4	60.6	62.4
Del.	78.4	56.1	58.4
D.C.	60.2	36.6	33.3
Fla.	76.7	53.6	51.5
Ga.	n/a	43.6	43.3
Ha.	75.3	46.2	48.1
Ida.	75.3	69.0	61.6
Ill.	76.2	59.0	60.6
Ind.	n/a	58.2	61.6
Ia.	76.7	63.0	63.7
Kan.	75.9	55.8	58.4
Ky.	71.0	51.2	49.1
La.	76.8	55.7	49.8
Me.	68.8	66.2	65
Md.	74.6	50.7	49.9
Mass.	80.1	58.7	61.6
Mich.	68.3	59.6	58.7
Minn.	86.9	69.2	71.4
Miss.	60.2	54.1	49.5
Mo.	73.9	58.8	57.7
Mon.	73.3	65.0	63.7
Neb.	74.7	56.2	56.1
Nev.	81.7	45.7	47.5
N.H.	73.5	58.4	58.8
N.J.	79.0	55.1	58.1
N.M.	69.9	52.5	54.6
N.Y.	n/a	48.1	50.8
N.C.	66.9	45.8	44.1
N.D.	n/a	64.3	67.2
Oh.	72.8	55.6	55.4
Okla.	78.2	54.0	55.6
Ore.	75.3	61.9	62.1
Pa.	79.3	52.7	54.7
R.I.	78.4	60.5	61.5
S.C.	71.9	42.9	41.7
S.D.	73.2	67.6	63.8
Tenn.	75.3	50.5	49.6
Tex.	68.4	47.1	47.3
Ut.	77.3	67.1	69.4
Vt.	68.4	59.4	56.9
Va.	81.0	48.9	47.7
Wash.	79.8	62.3	61.1
W.Va.	71.0	54.4	58.1
Wis.	n/a	66.0	65.9
Wy.	80.5	52.8	58.1

n/a—not available.

Party Nominees for President and Vice President

Asterisk (*) denotes winning ticket

	Democratic		Republican	
Year	President	Vice President	President	Vice President
1916	Woodrow Wilson*	Thomas R. Marshall	Charles E. Hughes	Charles W. Fairbanks
1920	James M. Cox	Franklin D. Roosevelt	Warren G. Harding*	Calvin Coolidge
1924	John W. Davis	Charles W. Bryan	Calvin Coolidge*	Charles G. Dawes
1928	Alfred E. Smith	Joseph T. Robinson	Herbert Hoover*	Charles Curtis
1932	Franklin D. Roosevelt*	John N. Garner	Herbert Hoover	Charles Curtis
1936	Franklin D. Roosevelt*	John N. Garner	Alfred M. Landon	Frank Knox
1940	Franklin D. Roosevelt*	Henry A. Wallace	Wendell L. Willkie	Charles McNary
1944	Franklin D. Roosevelt*	Harry S. Truman	Thomas E. Dewey	John W. Bricker
1948	Harry S. Truman*	Alben W. Barkley	Thomas E. Dewey	Earl Warren
1952	Adlai E. Stevenson	John J. Sparkman	Dwight D. Eisenhower*	Richard M. Nixon
1956	Adlai E. Stevenson	Estes Kefauver	Dwight D. Eisenhower*	Richard M. Nixon
1960	John F. Kennedy*	Lyndon B. Johnson	Richard M. Nixon	Henry Cabot Lodge
1964	Lyndon B. Johnson*	Hubert H. Humphrey	Barry M. Goldwater	William E. Miller
1968	Hubert H. Humphrey	Edmund S. Muskie	Richard M. Nixon*	Spiro T. Agnew
1972	George S. McGovern	R. Sargent Shriver Jr.	Richard M. Nixon*	Spiro T. Agnew
1976	Jimmy Carter*	Walter F. Mondale	Gerald R. Ford	Robert J. Dole
1980	Jimmy Carter	Walter F. Mondale	Ronald Reagan*	George Bush

Presidents of the U.S.

No.	Name	Politics	Born	in	Inaug.	at age	Died	at age
1	George Washington	Fed.	1732, Feb. 22	Va.	1789	57	1799, Dec. 14	67
2	John Adams	Fed.	1735, Oct. 30	Mass.	1797	61	1826, July 4	90
3	Thomas Jefferson	Dem.-Rep.	1743, Apr. 13	Va.	1801	57	1826, July 4	83
4	James Madison	Dem.-Rep.	1751, Mar. 16	Va.	1809	57	1836, June 28	85
5	James Monroe	Dem.-Rep.	1758, Apr. 28	Va.	1817	58	1831, July 4	73
6	John Quincy Adams	Dem.-Rep.	1767, July 11	Mass.	1825	57	1848, Feb. 23	80
7	Andrew Jackson	Dem.	1767, Mar. 15	S.C.	1829	61	1845, June 8	78
8	Martin Van Buren	Dem.	1782, Dec. 5	N.Y.	1837	54	1862, July 24	79
9	William Henry Harrison	Whig	1773, Feb. 9	Va.	1841	68	1841, Apr. 4	68
10	John Tyler	Whig	1790, Mar. 29	Va.	1841	51	1862, Jan. 18	71
11	James Knox Polk	Dem.	1795, Nov. 2	N.C.	1845	49	1849, June 15	53
12	Zachary Taylor	Whig	1784, Nov. 24	Va.	1849	64	1850, July 9	65
13	Millard Fillmore	Whig	1800, Jan. 7	N.Y.	1850	50	1874, Mar. 8	74
14	Franklin Pierce	Dem.	1804, Nov. 23	N.H.	1853	48	1869, Oct. 8	64
15	James Buchanan	Dem.	1791, Apr. 23	Pa.	1857	65	1868, June 1	77
16	Abraham Lincoln	Rep.	1809, Feb. 12	Ky.	1861	52	1865, Apr. 15	56
17	Andrew Johnson	(1)	1808, Dec. 29	N.C.	1865	56	1875, July 31	66
18	Ulysses Simpson Grant	Rep.	1822, Apr. 27	Oh.	1869	46	1885, July 23	63
19	Rutherford Birchard Hayes	Rep.	1822, Oct. 4	Oh.	1877	54	1893, Jan. 17	70
20	James Abram Garfield	Rep.	1831, Nov. 19	Oh.	1881	49	1881, Sept. 19	49
21	Chester Alan Arthur	Rep.	1829, Oct. 5	Vt.	1881	50	1886, Nov. 18	57
22	Grover Cleveland	Dem.	1837, Mar. 18	N.J.	1885	47	1908, June 24	71
23	Benjamin Harrison	Rep.	1833, Aug. 20	Oh.	1889	55	1901, Mar. 13	67
24	Grover Cleveland	Dem.	1837, Mar. 18	N.J.	1893	55	1908, June 24	71
25	William McKinley	Rep.	1843, Jan. 29	Oh.	1897	54	1901, Sept. 14	58
26	Theodore Roosevelt	Rep.	1858, Oct. 27	N.Y.	1901	42	1919, Jan. 6	60
27	William Howard Taft	Rep.	1857, Sept. 15	Oh.	1909	51	1930, Mar. 8	72
28	Woodrow Wilson	Dem.	1856, Dec. 28	Va.	1913	56	1924, Feb. 3	67
29	Warren Gamaliel Harding	Rep.	1865, Nov. 2	Oh.	1921	55	1923, Aug. 2	57
30	Calvin Coolidge	Rep.	1872, July 4	Vt.	1923	51	1933, Jan. 5	60
31	Herbert Clark Hoover	Rep.	1874, Aug. 10	Ia.	1929	54	1964, Oct. 20	90
32	Franklin Delano Roosevelt	Dem.	1882, Jan. 30	N.Y.	1933	51	1945, Apr. 12	63
33	Harry S. Truman	Dem.	1884, May 8	Mo.	1945	60	1972, Dec. 26	88
34	Dwight David Eisenhower	Rep.	1890, Oct. 14	Tex.	1953	62	1969, Mar. 28	78
35	John Fitzgerald Kennedy	Dem.	1917, May 29	Mass.	1961	43	1963, Nov. 22	46
36	Lyndon Baines Johnson	Dem.	1908, Aug. 27	Tex.	1963	55	1973, Jan. 22	64
37	Richard Milhous Nixon (2)	Rep.	1913, Jan. 9	Cal.	1969	56		
38	Gerald Rudolph Ford	Rep.	1913, July 14	Neb.	1974	61		
39	Jimmy (James Earl) Carter	Dem.	1924, Oct. 1	Ga.	1977	52		
40	Ronald Reagan	Rep.	1911, Feb. 6	Ill.	1981	69		

(1) Andrew Johnson — a Democrat, nominated vice president by Republicans and elected with Lincoln on National Union ticket. (2) Resigned Aug. 9, 1974.

Presidents, Vice Presidents, Congresses

	President	Service		Vice President	Congress
1	George Washington	Apr. 30, 1789—Mar. 3, 1797	1	John Adams	1, 2, 3, 4
2	John Adams	Mar. 4, 1797—Mar. 3, 1801	2	Thomas Jefferson	5, 6
3	Thomas Jefferson	Mar. 4, 1801—Mar. 3, 1805	3	Aaron Burr	7, 8
	"	Mar. 4, 1805—Mar. 3, 1809	4	George Clinton	9, 10
4	James Madison	Mar. 4, 1809—Mar. 3, 1813		"(1)	11, 12
	"	Mar. 4, 1813—Mar. 3, 1817	5	Elbridge Gerry (2)	13, 14
5	James Monroe	Mar. 4, 1817—Mar. 3, 1825	6	Daniel D. Tompkins	15, 16, 17, 18
6	John Quincy Adams	Mar. 4, 1825—Mar. 3, 1829	7	John C. Calhoun	19, 20
7	Andrew Jackson	Mar. 4, 1829—Mar. 3, 1833		"(3)	21, 22
	"	Mar. 4, 1833—Mar. 3, 1837	8	Martin Van Buren	23, 24
8	Martin Van Buren	Mar. 4, 1837—Mar. 3, 1841	9	Richard M. Johnson	25, 26
9	William Henry Harrison (4)	Mar. 4, 1841—Apr. 4, 1841	10	John Tyler	27
10	John Tyler	Apr. 6, 1841—Mar. 3, 1845			27, 28
11	James K. Polk	Mar. 4, 1845—Mar. 3, 1849	11	George M. Dallas	29, 30
12	Zachary Taylor (4)	Mar. 5, 1849—July 9, 1850	12	Millard Fillmore	31
13	Millard Fillmore	July 10, 1850—Mar. 3, 1853			31, 32
14	Franklin Pierce	Mar. 4, 1853—Mar. 3, 1857	13	William R. King (5)	33, 34
15	James Buchanan	Mar. 4, 1857—Mar. 3, 1861	14	John C. Breckinridge	35, 36
16	Abraham Lincoln	Mar. 4, 1861—Mar. 3, 1865	15	Hannibal Hamlin	37, 38
	"(4)	Mar. 4, 1865—Apr. 15, 1865	16	Andrew Johnson	39
17	Andrew Johnson	Apr. 15, 1865—Mar. 3, 1869			39, 40
18	Ulysses S. Grant	Mar. 4, 1869—Mar. 3, 1873	17	Schuyler Colfax	41, 42
	"	Mar. 4, 1873—Mar. 3, 1877	18	Henry Wilson (6)	43, 44
19	Rutherford B. Hayes	Mar. 4, 1877—Mar. 3, 1881	19	William A. Wheeler	45, 46
20	James A. Garfield (4)	Mar. 4, 1881—Sept. 19, 1881	20	Chester A. Arthur	47
21	Chester A. Arthur	Sept. 20, 1881—Mar. 3, 1885			47, 48
22	Grover Cleveland (7)	Mar. 4, 1885—Mar. 3, 1889	21	Thomas A. Hendricks (8)	49, 50
23	Benjamin Harrison	Mar. 4, 1889—Mar. 3, 1893	22	Levi P. Morton	51, 52
24	Grover Cleveland (7)	Mar. 4, 1893—Mar. 3, 1897	23	Adlai E. Stevenson	53, 54
25	William McKinley	Mar. 4, 1897—Mar. 3, 1901	24	Garret A. Hobart (9)	55, 56
	"(4)	Mar. 4, 1901—Sept. 14, 1901	25	Theodore Roosevelt	57
26	Theodore Roosevelt	Sept. 14, 1901—Mar. 3, 1905			57, 58
	"	Mar. 4, 1905—Mar. 3, 1909	26	Charles W. Fairbanks	59, 60

	President	Service		Vice President	Congress
27	William H. Taft	Mar. 4, 1909—Mar. 3, 1913	27	James S. Sherman (10)	61, 62
28	Woodrow Wilson	Mar. 4, 1913—Mar. 3, 1921	28	Thomas R. Marshall	63, 64, 65, 66
29	Warren G. Harding (4)	Mar. 4, 1921—Aug. 2, 1923	29	Calvin Coolidge	67
30	Calvin Coolidge	Aug. 3, 1923—Mar. 3, 1925			68
	"	Mar. 4, 1925—Mar. 3, 1929	30	Charles G. Dawes	69, 70
31	Herbert C. Hoover	Mar. 4, 1929—Mar. 3, 1933	31	Charles Curtis	71, 72
32	Franklin D. Roosevelt (16)	Mar. 4, 1933—Jan. 20, 1941	32	John N. Garner	73, 74, 75, 76
	"	Jan. 20, 1941—Jan. 20, 1945	33	Henry A. Wallace	77, 78
	"(4)	Jan. 20, 1945—Apr. 12, 1945	34	Harry S. Truman	79
33	Harry S. Truman	Apr. 12, 1945—Jan. 20, 1949			79, 80
	"	Jan. 20, 1949—Jan. 20, 1953	35	Alben W. Barkley	81, 82
34	Dwight D. Eisenhower	Jan. 20, 1953—Jan. 20, 1961	36	Richard M. Nixon	83, 84, 85, 86
35	John F. Kennedy (4)	Jan. 20, 1961—Nov. 22, 1963	37	Lyndon B. Johnson	87, 88
36	Lyndon B. Johnson	Nov. 22, 1963—Jan. 20, 1965			88
	"	Jan. 20, 1965—Jan. 20, 1969	38	Hubert H. Humphrey	89, 90
37	Richard M. Nixon	Jan. 20, 1969—Jan. 20, 1973	39	Spiro T. Agnew (11)	91, 92, 93
	"(12)	Jan. 20, 1973—Aug. 9, 1974	40	Gerald R. Ford (13)	93
38	Gerald R. Ford (14)	Aug. 9, 1974—Jan. 20, 1977	41	Nelson A. Rockefeller (15)	93, 94
39	Jimmy (James Earl) Carter	Jan. 20, 1977—Jan. 20, 1981	42	Walter F. Mondale	95, 96
40	Ronald Reagan	Jan. 20, 1981—	43	George Bush	97

(1) Died Apr. 20, 1812. (2) Died Nov. 23, 1814. (3) Resigned Dec. 28, 1832, to become U.S. Senator. (4) Died in office. (5) Died Apr. 18, 1853. (6) Died Nov. 22, 1875. (7) Terms not consecutive. (8) Died Nov. 25, 1885. (9) Died Nov. 21, 1899. (10) Died Oct. 30, 1912. (11) Resigned Oct. 10, 1973. (12) Resigned Aug. 9, 1974. (13) First non-elected vice president, chosen under 25th Amendment procedure. (14) First non-elected president. (15) 2d non-elected vice president. (16) First president to be inaugurated under 20th Amendment, Jan. 20, 1937.

Vice Presidents of the U.S.

The numerals given vice presidents do not coincide with those given presidents, because some presidents had none and some had more than one.

	Name	Birthplace	Year	Home	Inaug.	Politics	Place of death	Year	Age
1	John Adams	Quincy, Mass.	1735	Mass.	1789	Fed.	Quincy, Mass.	1826	90
2	Thomas Jefferson	Shadwell, Va.	1743	Va.	1797	Dem.-Rep.	Monticello, Va.	1826	83
3	Aaron Burr	Newark, N.J.	1756	N.Y.	1801	Dem.-Rep.	Staten Island, N.Y.	1836	80
4	George Clinton	Ulster Co., N.Y.	1739	N.Y.	1805	Dem.-Rep.	Washington, D.C.	1812	73
5	Elbridge Gerry	Marblehead, Mass.	1744	Mass.	1813	Dem.-Rep.	Washington, D.C.	1814	70
6	Daniel D. Tompkins	Scarsdale, N.Y.	1774	N.Y.	1817	Dem.-Rep.	Staten Island, N.Y.	1825	51
7	John C. Calhoun (1)	Abbeville, S.C.	1782	S.C.	1825	Dem.-Rep.	Washington, D.C.	1850	68
8	Martin Van Buren	Kinderhook, N.Y.	1782	N.Y.	1833	Dem.	Kinderhook, N.Y.	1862	79
9	Richard M. Johnson	Louisville, Ky.	1780	Ky.	1837	Dem.	Frankfort, Ky.	1850	70
10	John Tyler	Greenway, Va.	1790	Va.	1841	Whig	Richmond, Va.	1862	71
11	George M. Dallas	Philadelphia, Pa.	1792	Pa.	1845	Dem.	Philadelphia, Pa.	1864	72
12	Millard Fillmore	Summerhill, N.Y.	1800	N.Y.	1849	Whig	Buffalo, N.Y.	1874	74
13	William R. King	Sampson Co., N.C.	1786	Ala.	1853	Dem.	Dallas Co., Ala.	1853	67
14	John C. Breckinridge	Lexington, Ky.	1821	Ky.	1857	Dem.	Lexington, Ky.	1875	54
15	Hannibal Hamlin	Paris, Me.	1809	Me.	1861	Rep.	Bangor, Me.	1891	81
16	Andrew Johnson	Raleigh, N.C.	1808	Tenn.	1865	(2)	Carter Co., Tenn.	1875	66
17	Schuyler Colfax	New York, N.Y.	1823	Ind.	1869	Rep.	Mankato, Minn.	1885	62
18	Henry Wilson	Farmington, N.H.	1812	Mass.	1873	Rep.	Washington, D.C.	1875	63
19	William A. Wheeler	Malone, N.Y.	1819	N.Y.	1877	Rep.	Malone, N.Y.	1887	68
20	Chester A. Arthur	Fairfield, Vt.	1829	N.Y.	1881	Rep.	New York, N.Y.	1886	57
21	Thomas A. Hendricks	Muskingum Co., Oh.	1819	Ind.	1885	Dem.	Indianapolis, Ind.	1885	66
22	Levi P. Morton	Shoreham, Vt.	1824	N.Y.	1889	Rep.	Rhinebeck, N.Y.	1920	96
23	Adlai E. Stevenson (3)	Christian Co., Ky.	1835	Ill.	1893	Dem.	Chicago, Ill.	1914	78
24	Garret A. Hobart	Long Branch, N.J.	1844	N.J.	1897	Rep.	Paterson, N.J.	1899	55
25	Theodore Roosevelt	New York, N.Y.	1858	N.Y.	1901	Rep.	Oyster Bay, N.Y.	1919	60
26	Charles W. Fairbanks	Unionville Centre, Oh.	1852	Ind.	1905	Rep.	Indianapolis, Ind.	1918	66
27	James S. Sherman	Utica, N.Y.	1855	N.Y.	1909	Rep.	Utica, N.Y.	1912	57
28	Thomas R. Marshall	N. Manchester, Ind.	1854	Ind.	1913	Dem.	Washington, D.C.	1925	71
29	Calvin Coolidge	Plymouth, Vt.	1872	Mass.	1921	Rep.	Northampton, Mass.	1933	60
30	Charles G. Dawes	Marietta, Oh.	1865	Ill.	1925	Rep.	Evanston, Ill.	1951	85
31	Charles Curtis	Topeka, Kan.	1860	Kan.	1929	Rep.	Washington, D.C.	1936	76
32	John Nance Garner	Red River Co., Tex.	1868	Tex.	1933	Dem.	Uvalde, Tex.	1967	98
33	Henry Agard Wallace	Adair County, Ia.	1888	Iowa	1941	Dem.	Danbury, Conn.	1965	77
34	Harry S. Truman	Lamar, Mo.	1884	Mo.	1945	Dem.	Kansas City, Mo.	1972	88
35	Alben W. Barkley	Graves County, Ky.	1877	Ky.	1949	Dem.	Lexington, Va.	1956	78
36	Richard M. Nixon	Yorba Linda, Cal.	1913	Cal.	1953	Rep.			
37	Lyndon B. Johnson	Johnson City, Tex.	1908	Tex.	1961	Dem.	San Antonio, Tex.	1973	64
38	Hubert H. Humphrey	Wallace, S.D.	1911	Minn.	1965	Dem.	Waverly, Minn.	1978	66
39	Spiro T. Agnew	Baltimore, Md.	1918	Md.	1969	Rep.			
40	Gerald R. Ford	Omaha, Neb.	1913	Mich.	1973	Rep.			
41	Nelson A. Rockefeller	Bar Harbor, Me.	1908	N.Y.	1974	Rep.	New York, N.Y.	1979	70
42	Walter F. Mondale	Ceylon, Minn.	1928	Minn.	1977	Dem.			
43	George Bush	Milton, Mass.	1924	Tex.	1981	Rep.			

(1) John C. Calhoun resigned Dec. 28, 1832, having been elected to the Senate to fill a vacancy. (2) Andrew Johnson — a Democrat nominated by Republicans and elected with Lincoln on the National Union Ticket. (3) Adlai E. Stevenson, 23d vice president, was grandfather of Democratic candidate for president, 1952 and 1956.

The Continental Congress: Meetings, Presidents

Meeting places	Dates of meetings	Congress presidents	Date elected
Philadelphia	Sept. 5 to Oct. 26, 1774	Peyton Randolph, Va. (1)	Sept. 5, 1774
"	"	Henry Middleton, S.C.	Oct. 22, 1774
Philadelphia	May 10, 1775 to Dec. 12, 1776	Peyton Randolph, Va.	May 10, 1775
"	"	John Hancock, Mass.	May 24, 1775
Baltimore	Dec. 20, 1776 to Mar. 4, 1777	"	
Philadelphia	Mar. 5 to Sept. 18, 1777	"	
Lancaster, Pa.	Sept. 27, 1777 (one day)	"	
York, Pa.	Sept. 30, 1777 to June 27, 1778	Henry Laurens, S.C.	Nov. 1, 1777(4)
Philadelphia	July 2, 1778 to June 21, 1783	John Jay, N.Y.	Dec. 10, 1778
"	"	Samuel Huntington, Conn.	Sept. 28, 1779
"	"	Thomas McKean, Del.	July 10, 1781
"	"	John Hanson, Md. (2)	Nov. 5, 1781
"	"	Elias Boudinot, N.J.	Nov. 4, 1782
Princeton, N.J.	June 30 to Nov. 4, 1783	Thomas Mifflin, Pa.	Nov. 3, 1783
Annapolis, Md.	Nov. 26, 1783 to June 3, 1784	"	
Trenton, N.J.	Nov. 1 to Dec. 24, 1784	Richard Henry Lee, Va.	Nov. 30, 1784
New York City	Jan. 11 to Nov. 4, 1785	"	
"	Nov. 7, 1785 to Nov. 3, 1786	John Hancock, Mass. (3)	Nov. 23, 1785
"	"	Nathaniel Gorham, Mass.	June 6, 1786
"	Nov. 6, 1786 to Oct. 30, 1787	Arthur St. Clair, Pa.	Feb. 2, 1787
"	Nov. 5, 1787 to Oct. 21, 1788	Cyrus Griffin, Va.	Jan. 22, 1788
"	Nov. 3, 1788 to Mar. 2, 1789	"	

(1) Resigned Oct. 22, 1774. (2) Titled "President of the United States in Congress Assembled," John Hanson is considered by some to be the first U.S. President as he was the first to serve under the Articles of Confederation. He was, however, little more than presiding officer of the Congress, which retained full executive power. He could be considered the head of government, but not head of state. (3) Resigned May 29, 1786, without serving, because of illness. (4) Articles of Confederation agreed upon, Nov. 15, 1777; last ratification from Maryland, Mar. 1, 1781.

Cabinets of the U. S.

Secretaries of State

The Department of Foreign Affairs was created by act of Congress July 27, 1789, and the name changed to Department of State on Sept. 15.

President	Secretary	Home	Apptd.
Washington	Thomas Jefferson	Va.	1789
"	Edmund Randolph	"	1794
"	Timothy Pickering	Pa.	1795
Adams, J.	"	"	1797
"	John Marshall	Va.	1800
Jefferson	James Madison	"	1801
Madison	Robert Smith	Md.	1809
"	James Monroe	Va.	1811
Monroe	John Quincy Adams	Mass.	1817
Adams, J.Q.	Henry Clay	Ky.	1825
Jackson	Martin Van Buren	N.Y.	1829
"	Edward Livingston	La.	1831
"	Louis McLane	Del.	1833
"	John Forsyth	Ga.	1834
Van Buren	"	"	1837
Harrison, W.H.	Daniel Webster	Mass.	1841
Tyler	"	"	1841
"	Abel P. Upshur	Va.	1843
"	John C. Calhoun	S.C.	1844
Polk	"	"	1845
"	James Buchanan	Pa.	1845
Taylor	"	"	1849
"	John M. Clayton	Del.	1849
Fillmore	"	"	1850
"	Daniel Webster	Mass.	1850
"	Edward Everett	"	1852
Pierce	William L. Marcy	N.Y.	1853
Buchanan	"	"	1857
"	Lewis Cass	Mich.	1857
"	Jeremiah S. Black	Pa.	1860
Lincoln	"	"	1861
"	William H. Seward	N.Y.	1861
Johnson, A.	"	"	1865
Grant	Elihu B. Washburne	Ill.	1869
"	Hamilton Fish	N.Y.	1869
Hayes	"	"	1877
"	William M. Evarts	"	1877
Garfield	"	"	1881
"	James G. Blaine	Me.	1881
Arthur	"	"	1881
"	F.T. Frelinghuysen	N.J.	1881
Cleveland	"	"	1885
"	Thomas F. Bayard	Del.	1885
Harrison, B.	"	"	1889
"	James G. Blaine	Me.	1889
"	John W. Foster	Ind.	1892
Cleveland	Walter Q. Gresham	Ill.	1893
"	Richard Olney	Mass.	1895
McKinley	"	"	1897
"	John Sherman	Oh.	1897
"	William R. Day	"	1898
"	John Hay	D.C.	1898
Roosevelt, T.	"	"	1901
"	Elihu Root	N.Y.	1905
"	Robert Bacon	"	1909
Taft	"	"	1909
"	Philander C. Knox	Pa.	1909
Wilson	"	"	1913
"	William J. Bryan	Neb.	1913
"	Robert Lansing	N.Y.	1915
"	Bainbridge Colby	"	1920
Harding	Charles E. Hughes	"	1921
Coolidge	"	"	1923
"	Frank B. Kellogg	Minn.	1925
Hoover	"	"	1929
"	Henry L. Stimson	N.Y.	1929
Roosevelt, F.D.	Cordell Hull	Tenn.	1933
"	E.R. Stettinius Jr.	Va.	1944
Truman	"	"	1945
"	James F. Byrnes	S.C.	1945
"	George C. Marshall	Pa.	1947
"	Dean G. Acheson	Conn.	1949
Eisenhower	John Foster Dulles	N.Y.	1953
"	Christian A. Herter	Mass.	1959
Kennedy	Dean Rusk	N.Y.	1961
Johnson, L.B.	"	"	1963
Nixon	William P. Rogers	N.Y.	1969
"	Henry A. Kissinger	D.C.	1973
Ford	"	"	1974
Carter	Cyrus R. Vance	N.Y.	1977
"	Edmund S. Muskie	Me.	1980
Reagan	Alexander M. Haig Jr.	Conn.	1981
"	George P. Shultz	Cal.	1982

Secretaries of the Treasury

The Treasury Department was organized by act of Congress Sept. 2, 1789.

President	Secretary	Home	Apptd.
Washington	Alexander Hamilton	N.Y.	1789
"	Oliver Wolcott	Conn.	1795
Adams, J.	"	"	1797
"	Samuel Dexter	Mass.	1801
Jefferson	"	"	1801
"	Albert Gallatin	Pa.	1801
Madison	"	Pa	1809
"	George W. Campbell	Tenn.	1814
"	Alexander J. Dallas	Pa.	1814
"	William H. Crawford	Ga.	1816
Monroe	"	"	1817
Adams, J.Q.	Richard Rush	Pa.	1825
Jackson	Samuel D. Ingham	"	1829
"	Louis McLane	Del.	1831
"	William J. Duane	Pa.	1833
"	Roger B. Taney	Md.	1833
"	Levi Woodbury	N.H.	1834
Van Buren	"	"	1837
Harrison, W.H.	Thomas Ewing	Oh.	1841
Tyler	"	"	1841
"	Walter Forward	Pa.	1841
"	John C. Spencer	N.Y.	1843
Tyler	George M. Bibb	Ky.	1844
Polk	Robert J. Walker	Miss.	1845
Taylor	William M. Meredith	Pa.	1849
Fillmore	Thomas Corwin	Oh.	1850
Pierce	James Guthrie	Ky.	1853
Buchanan	Howell Cobb	Ga.	1857
"	Phillip F. Thomas	Md.	1860
"	John A. Dix	N.Y.	1861
Lincoln	Salmon P. Chase	Oh.	1861
"	William P. Fessenden	Me.	1864
"	Hugh McCulloch	Ind.	1865
Johnson, A.	"	"	1865
Grant	George S. Boutwell	Mass.	1869
"	William A. Richardson	Mass.	1873
"	Benjamin H. Bristow	Ky.	1874
"	Lot M. Morrill	Me.	1876
Hayes	John Sherman	Oh.	1877
Garfield	William Windom	Minn.	1881
Arthur	Charles J. Folger	N.Y.	1881
"	Walter Q. Gresham	Ind.	1884
"	Hugh McCulloch	"	1884
Cleveland	Daniel Manning	N.Y.	1885
Cleveland	Charles S. Fairchild	"	1887
Harrison, B.	William Windom	Minn.	1889
"	Charles Foster	Oh.	1891
Cleveland	John G. Carlisle	Ky.	1893
McKinley	Lyman J. Gage	Ill.	1897
Roosevelt, T.	"	"	1901
"	Leslie M. Shaw	Ia.	1902
"	George B. Cortelyou	N.Y.	1907
Taft	Franklin MacVeagh	Ill.	1909
Wilson	William G. McAdoo	N.Y.	1913
"	Carter Glass	Va.	1918
"	David F. Houston	Mo.	1920
Harding	Andrew W. Mellon	Pa.	1921
Coolidge	"	"	1923
Hoover	"	"	1929
"	Ogden L. Mills	N.Y.	1932
Roosevelt, F.D.	William H. Woodin	"	1933
"	Henry Morgenthau, Jr.	"	1934
Truman	Fred M. Vinson	Ky.	1945
"	John W. Snyder	Mo.	1946
Eisenhower	George M. Humphrey	Oh.	1953
"	Robert B. Anderson	Conn.	1957
Kennedy	C. Douglas Dillon	N.J.	1961
Johnson, L.B.	"	"	1963
"	Henry H. Fowler	Va.	1965
"	Joseph W. Barr	Ind.	1968
Nixon	David M. Kennedy	Ill.	1969
"	John B. Connally	Tex.	1971
"	George P. Shultz	Ill.	1972
"	William E. Simon	N.J.	1974
Ford	"	"	1974
Carter	W. Michael Blumenthal	Mich.	1977
"	G. William Miller	R.I.	1979
Reagan	Donald T. Regan	N.Y.	1981

Secretaries of Defense

The Department of Defense, originally designated the National Military Establishment, was created Sept. 18, 1947. It is headed by the secretary of defense, who is a member of the president's cabinet.

The departments of the army, of the navy, and of the air force function within the Department of Defense, and their respective secretaries are no longer members of the president's cabinet.

President	Secretary	Home	Apptd.
Truman	James V. Forrestal	N.Y.	1947
"	Louis A. Johnson	W.Va.	1949
"	George C. Marshall	Pa.	1950
"	Robert A. Lovett	N.Y.	1951
Eisenhower	Charles E. Wilson	Mich.	1953
"	Neil H. McElroy	Oh.	1957
"	Thomas S. Gates Jr.	Pa.	1959
Kennedy	Robert S. McNamara	Mich.	1961
Johnson, L.B.	Robert S. McNamara	Mich.	1963
"	Clark M. Clifford	Md.	1968
Nixon	Melvin R. Laird	Wis.	1969
"	Elliot L. Richardson	Mass.	1973
"	James R. Schlesinger	Va.	1973
Ford	"	"	1974
"	Donald H. Rumsfeld	Ill.	1975
Carter	Harold Brown	Cal.	1977
Reagan	Caspar W. Weinberger	Cal.	1981

Secretaries of the Armed Services

Not members of the president's Cabinet

The Department of Defense; created Sept. 18, 1947, consolidated the navy, army, air force into a single department.

Secretary of the Air Force	Appointed
W. Stuart Symington	1947
Thomas K. Finletter	1950
Harold E. Talbot	1953
Donald A. Quarles	1955
James H. Douglas	1957
Dudley C. Sharpe	1959
Eugene M. Zuckert	1961
Dr. Harold Brown	1965
Robert C. Seamans Jr.	1969
John L. McLucas	1973
Thomas C. Reed	1976
John C. Stetson	1977
Hans M. Mark	1979
Verne Orr	1981

Secretary of the Army	Appointed
Kenneth C. Royall	1947
Gordon Gray*	1949
Frank Pace Jr.	1950
Earl D. Johnson (acting)	1953
Robert T. Stevens	1953
Wilber M. Brucker	1955
Elvis J. Stahr Jr.	1961
Cyrus R. Vance	1962
Stephen Ailes	1964
Stanley R. Resor	1965
Robert F. Froehlke	1971
Howard H. Callaway	1973
Norman R. Augustine (acting)	1975
Martin R. Hoffman	1975
Clifford L. Alexander Jr.	1977
John O. Marsh Jr.	1981

*In addition, Gordon Gray was acting secretary of the army from Apr. 28, 1949, and under secretary from May 25, 1949, until June 20, 1949.

Secretary of the Navy	Appointed
John L. Sullivan	1947
Francis P. Matthews	1949
Dan A. Kimball	1951
Robert B. Anderson	1953
Charles S. Thomas	1954
Thomas S. Gates Jr.	1957
William B. Franke	1958
John B. Connally Jr.	1961
Fred Korth	1961
Paul H. Nitze	1963
John T. McNaughton	1967
Paul R. Ignatius	1967

John H. Chafee	1969
John W. Warner	1972
J. William Middendorf 2d	1974
W. Graham Claytor Jr.	1977
Edward Hidalgo	1979
John F. Lehman Jr.	1981

Secretaries of War

The War (and Navy) Department was created by act of Congress Aug. 7, 1789, and Gen. Henry Knox was commissioned secretary of war under that act Sept. 12, 1789.

President	Secretary	Home	Apptd.
Washington	Henry Knox	Mass.	1789
"	Timothy Pickering	Pa.	1795
"	James McHenry	Md.	1796
Adams, J.	"	"	1797
"	Samuel Dexter	Mass.	1800
Jefferson	Henry Dearborn	"	1801
Madison	William Eustis	Mass.	1809
"	John Armstrong	N.Y.	1813
Madison	James Monroe	Va.	1814
"	William H. Crawford	Ga.	1815
Monroe	John C. Calhoun	S.C.	1817
Adams, J.Q.	James Barbour	Va.	1825
"	Peter B. Porter	N.Y.	1828
Jackson	John H. Eaton	Tenn.	1829
"	Lewis Cass	Oh.	1831
"	Benjamin F. Butler	N.Y.	1837
Van Buren	Joel R. Poinsett	S.C.	1837
Harrison, W.H.	John Bell	Tenn.	1841
Tyler	"	"	1841
Tyler	John C. Spencer	N.Y.	1841
"	James M. Porter	Pa.	1843
"	William Wilkins		1844
Polk	William L. Marcy	N.Y.	1845
Taylor	George W. Crawford	Ga.	1849
Fillmore	Charles M. Conrad	La.	1850
Pierce	Jefferson Davis	Miss.	1853
Buchanan	John B. Floyd	Va.	1857
"	Joseph Holt	Ky.	1861
Lincoln	Simon Cameron	Pa.	1861
"	Edwin M. Stanton	Pa.	1862
Johnson, A.	"	"	1865
"	John M. Schofield	Ill.	1868
Grant	John A. Rawlins	Ill.	1869
"	William T. Sherman	Oh.	1869
"	William W. Belknap	Ia.	1869
"	Alphonso Taft	Oh.	1876
Grant	James D. Cameron	Pa.	1876
Hayes	George W. McCrary	Ia.	1877
"	Alexander Ramsey	Minn.	1879
Garfield	Robert T. Lincoln	Ill.	1881
Arthur	"	"	1881
Cleveland	William C. Endicott	Mass.	1885
Harrison, B.	Redfield Proctor	Vt.	1889
"	Stephen B. Elkins	W.Va.	1891
Cleveland	Daniel S. Lamont	N.Y.	1893
McKinley	Russel A. Alger	Mich.	1897
"	Elihu Root	N.Y.	1899
Roosevelt, T.	"	"	1901
"	William H. Taft	Oh.	1904
"	Luke E. Wright	Tenn.	1908
Taft	Jacob M. Dickinson	"	1909
"	Henry L. Stimson	N.Y.	1911
Wilson	Lindley M. Garrison	N.J.	1913
"	Newton D. Baker	Oh.	1916
Harding	John W. Weeks	Mass.	1921
Coolidge	"	"	1923
"	Dwight F. Davis	Mo.	1925
Hoover	James W. Good	Ill.	1929
Hoover	Patrick J. Hurley	Okla.	1929
Roosevelt, F.D.	George H. Dern	Ut.	1933
"	Harry H. Woodring	Kan.	1937
Roosevelt, F.D.	Henry L. Stimson	N.Y.	1940
Truman	Robert P. Patterson	N.Y.	1945
"	*Kenneth C. Royall	N.C.	1947

Secretaries of the Navy

The Navy Department was created by act of Congress Apr. 30, 1798.

President	Secretary	Home	Apptd.
Adams, J.	Benjamin Stoddert	Md.	1798
Jefferson	"	"	1801
"	Robert Smith	"	1801
Madison	Paul Hamilton	S.C.	1809
"	William Jones	Pa.	1813
"	Benjamin Williams Crowninshield	Mass.	1814
Monroe	"	"	1817
"	Smith Thompson	N.Y.	1818
"	Samuel L. Southard	N.J.	1823
Adams, J.Q.	"	"	1825
Jackson	John Branch	N.C.	1829
"	Levi Woodbury	N.H.	1831
"	Mahlon Dickerson	N.J.	1834
Van Buren	"	"	1837
"	James K. Paulding	N.Y.	1838
Harrison, W.H.	George E. Badger	N.C.	1841
Tyler	"	"	1841
"	Abel P. Upshur	Va.	1841
"	David Henshaw	Mass.	1843
"	Thomas W. Gilmer	Va.	1844
"	John Y. Mason	"	1844
Polk	George Bancroft	Mass.	1845
"	John Y. Mason	Va.	1846
Taylor	William B. Preston	"	1849
Fillmore	William A. Graham	N.C.	1850
"	John P. Kennedy	Md.	1852
Pierce	James C. Dobbin	N.C.	1853
Buchanan	Isaac Toucey	Conn.	1857
Lincoln	Gideon Welles	Conn.	1861
Johnson, A.	"	"	1865
Grant	Adolph E. Borie	Pa.	1869
"	George M. Robeson	N.J.	1869
Hayes	Richard W. Thompson	Ind.	1877
"	Nathan Goff Jr.	W.Va.	1881
Garfield	William H. Hunt	La.	1881
Arthur	William E. Chandler	N.H.	1882
Cleveland	William C. Whitney	N.Y.	1885
Harrison, B.	Benjamin F. Tracy	N.Y.	1889
Cleveland	Hilary A. Herbert	Ala.	1893
McKinley	John D. Long	Mass.	1897
Roosevelt, T.	"	"	1901
"	William H. Moody	"	1902
"	Paul Morton	Ill.	1904
"	Charles J. Bonaparte	Md.	1905
"	Victor H. Metcalf	Cal.	1906
"	Truman H. Newberry	Mich.	1908
Taft	George von L. Meyer	Mass.	1909
Wilson	Josephus Daniels	N.C.	1913
Harding	Edwin Denby	Mich.	1921
Coolidge	"	"	1923
"	Curtis D. Wilbur	Cal.	1924
Hoover	Charles Francis Adams	Mass.	1929
Roosevelt, F.D.	Claude A. Swanson	Va.	1933
"	Charles Edison	N.J.	1940
"	Frank Knox	Ill.	1940
"	*James V. Forrestal	N.Y.	1944
Truman	"	"	1945

*Last members of Cabinet. The War Department became the Department of the Army and it and the Navy Department became branches of the Department of Defense, created Sept. 18, 1947.

Attorneys General

The office of attorney general was organized by act of Congress Sept. 24, 1789. The Department of Justice was created June 22, 1870.

President	Attorney General	Home	Apptd.
Washington	Edmund Randolph	Va.	1789
"	William Bradford	Pa.	1794
"	Charles Lee	Va.	1795
Adams, J.	"	"	1797
Jefferson	Levi Lincoln	Mass.	1801
"	John Breckenridge	Ky.	1805
Jefferson	Caesar A. Rodney	Del.	1807
Madison	"	"	1809
"	William Pinkney	Md.	1811
"	Richard Rush	Pa.	1814
Monroe	"	"	1817
"	William Wirt	Va.	1817

President	Attorney General	Home	Apptd.
Adams, J.Q.	"	"	1825
Jackson	John M. Berrien	Ga.	1829
"	Roger B. Taney	Md.	1831
"	Benjamin F. Butler	N.Y.	1833
Van Buren	"	"	1837
"	Felix Grundy	Tenn.	1838
"	Henry D. Gilpin	Pa.	1840
Harrison, W.H.	John J. Crittenden	Ky.	1841
Tyler	"	"	1841
"	Hugh S. Legare	S.C.	1841
"	John Nelson	Md.	1843
Polk	John Y. Mason	Va.	1845
"	Nathan Clifford	Me.	1846
"	Isaac Toucey	Conn.	1848
Taylor	Reverdy Johnson	Md.	1849
Fillmore	John J. Crittenden	Ky.	1850
Pierce	Caleb Cushing	Mass.	1853
Buchanan	Jeremiah S. Black	Pa.	1857
"	Edwin M. Stanton	Pa.	1860
Lincoln	Edward Bates	Mo.	1861
"	James Speed	Ky.	1864
Johnson, A.	"	"	1865
"	Henry Stanbery	Oh.	1866
"	William M. Evarts	N.Y.	1868
Grant	Ebenezer R. Hoar	Mass.	1869
"	Amos T. Akerman	Ga.	1870
"	George H. Williams	Ore.	1871
"	Edwards Pierrepont	N.Y.	1875
"	Alphonso Taft	Oh.	1876
Hayes	Charles Devens	Mass.	1877
Garfield	Wayne MacVeagh	Pa.	1881
Arthur	Benjamin H. Brewster	"	1881
Cleveland	Augustus Garland	Ark.	1885
Harrison, B.	William H. H. Miller	Ind.	1889
Cleveland	Richard Olney	Mass.	1893
"	Judson Harmon	Oh.	1895
McKinley	Joseph McKenna	Cal.	1897
"	John W. Griggs	N.J.	1898
"	Philander C. Knox	Pa.	1901
Roosevelt, T.	"	"	1901
"	William H. Moody	Mass.	1904
"	Charles J. Bonaparte	Md.	1906
Taft	George W. Wickersham	N.Y.	1909
Wilson	J.C. McReynolds	Tenn.	1913
"	Thomas W. Gregory	Tex.	1914
"	A. Mitchell Palmer	Pa.	1919
Harding	Harry M. Daugherty	Oh.	1921
Coolidge	"	"	1923
"	Harlan F. Stone	N.Y.	1924
"	John G. Sargent	Vt.	1925
Hoover	William D. Mitchell	Minn.	1929
Roosevelt, F.D.	Homer S. Cummings	Conn.	1933
"	Frank Murphy	Mich.	1939
"	Robert H. Jackson	N.Y.	1940
"	Francis Biddle	Pa.	1941
Truman	Thomas C. Clark	Tex.	1945
"	J. Howard McGrath	R.I.	1949
"	J.P. McGranery	Pa.	1952
Eisenhower	Herbert Brownell Jr.	N.Y.	1953
"	William P. Rogers	Md.	1957
Kennedy	Robert F. Kennedy	Mass.	1961
Johnson, L.B.	"	"	1963
"	N. de B. Katzenbach	Ill.	1964
"	Ramsey Clark	Tex.	1967
Nixon	John N. Mitchell	N.Y.	1969
"	Richard G. Kleindienst	Ariz.	1972
"	Elliot L. Richardson	Mass.	1973
"	William B. Saxbe	Oh.	1974
Ford	"	"	1974
"	Edward H. Levi	Ill.	1975
Carter	Griffin B. Bell	Ga.	1977
"	Benjamin R. Civiletti	Md.	1979
Reagan	William French Smith	Cal.	1981

Secretaries of the Interior

The Department of Interior was created by act of Congress Mar. 3, 1849

President	Secretary	Home	Apptd.
Taylor	Thomas Ewing	Oh.	1849
Fillmore	Thomas M. T. McKennan	Pa.	1850
Fillmore	Alex H. H. Stuart	Va.	1850
Pierce	Robert McClelland	Mich.	1853
Buchanan	Jacob Thompson	Miss.	1857
Lincoln	Caleb B. Smith	Ind.	1861
"	John P. Usher	"	1863
Johnson, A.	"	"	1865
"	James Harlan	Ia.	1865
"	Orville H. Browning	Ill.	1866
Grant	Jacob D. Cox	Oh.	1869
"	Columbus Delano	"	1870
"	Zachariah Chandler	Mich.	1875
Hayes	Carl Schurz	Mo.	1877
Garfield	Samuel J. Kirkwood	Ia.	1881
Arthur	Henry M. Teller	Col.	1882
Cleveland	Lucius Q.C. Lamar	Miss.	1885
"	William F. Vilas	Wis.	1888
Harrison, B.	John W. Noble	Mo.	1889
Cleveland	Hoke Smith	Ga.	1893
"	David R. Francis	Mo.	1896
McKinley	Cornelius N. Bliss	N.Y.	1897
"	Ethan A. Hitchcock	Mo.	1898
Roosevelt, T.	"	"	1901
"	James R. Garfield	Oh.	1907
Taft	Richard A. Ballinger	Wash.	1909
"	Walter L. Fisher	Ill.	1911
Wilson	Franklin K. Lane	Cal.	1913
"	John B. Payne	Ill.	1920
Harding	Albert B. Fall	N.M.	1921
"	Hubert Work	Col.	1923
Coolidge	"	"	1923
"	Roy O. West	Ill.	1929
Hoover	Ray Lyman Wilbur	Cal.	1929
Roosevelt, F.D.	Harold L. Ickes	Ill.	1933
Truman	"	"	1945
"	Julius A. Krug	Wis.	1946
"	Oscar L. Chapman	Col.	1949
Eisenhower	Douglas McKay	Ore.	1953
"	Fred A Seaton	Neb.	1956
Kennedy	Stewart L. Udall	Ariz.	1961
Johnson, L.B.	"	"	1963
Nixon	Walter J. Hickel	Alas.	1969
"	Rogers C.B. Morton	Md.	1971
Ford	"	"	1974
"	Stanley K. Hathaway	Wyo.	1975
"	Thomas S. Kleppe	N.D.	1975
Carter	Cecil D. Andrus	Ida.	1977
Reagan	James G. Watt	Cal.	1981

Secretaries of Agriculture

The Department of Agriculture was created by act of Congress May 15, 1862. On Feb. 8, 1889, its commissioner was renamed secretary of agriculture and became a member of the cabinet.

President	Secretary	Home	Apptd.
Cleveland	Norman J. Colman	Mo.	1889
Harrison, B.	Jeremiah M. Rusk	Wis.	1889
Cleveland	J. Sterling Morton	Neb.	1893
McKinley	James Wilson	Ia.	1897
Roosevelt, T.	"	"	1901
Taft	"	"	1909
Wilson	David F. Houston	Mo.	1913
"	Edwin T. Meredith	Ia.	1920
Harding	Henry C. Wallace	Ia.	1921
Coolidge	"	"	1923
"	Howard M. Gore	W.Va.	1924
"	William M. Jardine	Kan.	1925
Hoover	Arthur M. Hyde	Mo.	1929
Roosevelt, F.D.	Henry A. Wallace	Ia.	1933
"	Claude R. Wickard	Ind.	1940
Truman	Clinton P. Anderson	N.M.	1945
"	Charles F. Brannan	Col.	1948
Eisenhower	Ezra Taft Benson	Ut.	1953
Kennedy	Orville L. Freeman	Minn.	1961
Johnson, L.B.	"	"	1963
Nixon	Clifford M. Hardin	Ind.	1969
"	Earl L. Butz	Ind.	1971
Ford	"	"	1974
"	John A. Knebel	Va.	1976
Carter	Bob Bergland	Minn.	1977
Reagan	John R. Block	Ill.	1981

Secretaries of Commerce and Labor

The Department of Commerce and Labor, created by Congress Feb. 14, 1903, was divided by Congress Mar. 4, 1913, into separate departments of Commerce and Labor. The secretary of each was made a cabinet member.

President	Secretary	Home	Apptd.
	Secretaries of Commerce and Labor		
Roosevelt, T.	George B. Cortelyou	N.Y.	1903
"	Victor H. Metcalf	Cal.	1904
"	Oscar S. Straus	N.Y.	1906
Taft	Charles Nagel	Mo.	1909
	Secretaries of Labor		
Wilson	William B. Wilson	Pa.	1913
Harding	James J. Davis	Pa.	1921
Coolidge	"	"	1923
Hoover	"	"	1929
"	William N. Doak	Va.	1930
Roosevelt, F.D.	Frances Perkins	N.Y.	1933
Truman	L.B. Schwellenbach	Wash.	1945
"	Maurice J. Tobin	Mass.	1949
Eisenhower	Martin P. Durkin	Ill.	1953
"	James P. Mitchell	N.J.	1953
Kennedy	Arthur J. Goldberg	Ill.	1961
"	W. Willard Wirtz	Ill.	1962
Johnson, L.B.	"	Ill.	1963
Nixon	George P. Shultz	Ill.	1969
"	James D. Hodgson	Cal.	1970
	Peter J. Brennan	N.Y.	1973
Ford	"	"	1974
"	John T. Dunlop	Cal.	1975
"	W.J. Usery Jr.	Ga.	1976
Carter	F. Ray Marshall	Tex.	1977
Reagan	Raymond J. Donovan	N.J.	1981
	Secretaries of Commerce		
Wilson	William C. Redfield	N.Y.	1913
"	Joshua W. Alexander	Mo.	1919

President	Secretary	Home	Apptd.
Harding	Herbert C. Hoover	Cal.	1921
Coolidge	"	"	1923
"	William F. Whiting	Mass.	1928
Hoover	Robert P. Lamont	Ill.	1929
"	Roy D. Chapin	Mich.	1932
Roosevelt, F.D.	Daniel C. Roper	S.C.	1933
"	Harry L. Hopkins	N.Y.	1939
"	Jesse Jones	Tex.	1940
"	Henry A. Wallace	Ia.	1945
Truman	"	"	1945
"	W. Averell Harriman	N.Y.	1947
"	Charles Sawyer	Oh.	1948
Eisenhower	Sinclair Weeks	Mass.	1953
"	Lewis L. Strauss	N.Y.	1958
"	Frederick H. Mueller	Mich.	1959
Kennedy	Luther H. Hodges	N.C.	1961
Johnson, L.B.	"	"	1963
"	John T. Connor	N.J.	1965
"	Alex B. Trowbridge	N.J.	1967
"	Cyrus R. Smith	N.Y.	1968
Nixon	Maurice H. Stans	Minn.	1969
"	Peter G. Peterson	Ill.	1972
"	Frederick B. Dent	S.C.	1973
Ford	"	"	1974
"	Rogers C.B. Morton	Md.	1975
"	Elliot L. Richardson	Mass.	1975
Carter	Juanita M. Kreps	N.C.	1977
"	Philip M. Klutznick	Ill.	1979
Reagan	Malcolm Baldrige	Conn.	1981

Secretaries of Education, and Health and Human Services

The Department of Health, Education and Welfare, created by Congress Apr. 11, 1953, was divided by Congress Sept. 27, 1979, into separate departments of Education, and Health and Human Services. The secretary of each is a cabinet member.

President	Secretary	Home	Apptd.
	Secretaries of Health, Education, and Welfare		
Eisenhower	Oveta Culp Hobby	Tex.	1953
"	Marion B. Folsom	N.Y.	1955
"	Arthur S. Flemming	Oh.	1958
Kennedy	Abraham A. Ribicoff	Conn.	1961
"	Anthony J. Celebrezze	Oh.	1962
Johnson, L.B.	"	"	1963
"	John W. Gardner	N.Y.	1965
Johnson, L.B.	Wilbur J. Cohen	Mich.	1968
Nixon	Robert H. Finch	Cal.	1969
"	Elliot L. Richardson	Mass.	1970

President	Secretary	Home	Apptd.
"	Caspar W. Weinberger	Cal.	1973
Ford	"	"	1974
"	Forrest D. Mathews	Ala.	1975
Carter	Joseph A. Califano, Jr.	D.C.	1977
"	Patricia Roberts Harris	D.C.	1979
	Secretaries of Health and Human Services		
Carter	Patricia Roberts Harris	D.C.	1979
Reagan	Richard S. Schweiker	Pa.	1981
	Secretaries of Education		
Carter	Shirley Hufstedler	Cal.	1979
Reagan	Terrel Bell	Ut.	1981

Secretaries of Housing and Urban Development

The Department of Housing and Urban Development was created by act of Congress Sept. 9, 1965.

President	Secretary	Home	Apptd.
Johnson, L.B.	Robert C. Weaver	Wash.	1966
"	Robert C. Wood	Mass.	1969
Nixon	George W. Romney	Mich.	1969
"	James T. Lynn	Oh.	1973
Ford	"	"	1974

President	Secretary	Home	Apptd.
"	Carla Anderson Hills	Cal.	1975
Carter	Patricia Roberts Harris	D.C.	1977
"	Moon Landrieu	La.	1979
Reagan	Samuel R. Pierce Jr.	N.Y.	1981

Secretaries of Transportation

The Department of Transportation was created by act of Congress Oct. 15, 1966.

President	Secretary	Home	Apptd.
Johnson, L.B.	Alan S. Boyd	Fla.	1966
Nixon	John A. Volpe	Mass.	1969
"	Claude S. Brinegar	Cal.	1973
Ford	Claude S. Brinegar	Cal.	1974
"	William T. Coleman Jr.	Pa.	1975

President	Secretary	Home	Apptd.
Carter	Brock Adams	Wash.	1977
"	Neil E. Goldschmidt	Ore.	1979
Reagan	Andrew L. Lewis Jr.	Pa.	1981

Secretaries of Energy

The Department of Energy was created by federal law Aug. 4, 1977.

President	Secretary	Home	Apptd.
Carter	James R. Schlesinger	Va.	1977

President	Secretary	Home	Apptd.
"	Robert W. Duncan Jr.	Wyo.	1979
Reagan	James B. Edwards	S.C.	1981

Postmasters General

Congress established the Post Office Department as a branch of the Treasury Sept. 22, 1789. The postmaster general was made a member of the Cabinet Mar. 9, 1829. The Postal Reorganization Act of 1970 replaced the department with the U.S. Postal Service, an independent federal agency. Its head, the postmaster general, is not a member of the Cabinet.

President	Postmaster General	Home	Apptd.
Washington	Samuel Osgood	Mass.	1789
"	Timothy Pickering	Pa.	1791
"	Joseph Habersham	Ga.	1795
Adams, J.	"	"	1797
Jefferson	"	"	1801
"	Gideon Granger	Conn.	1801
Madison	"	"	1809
"	Return J. Meigs Jr.	Ohio	1814
Monroe	"	"	1817
"	John McLean	"	1823
Adams, J.Q.	"	"	1825
Jackson	William T. Barry	Ky.	1829
"	Amos Kendall	"	1835
Van Buren	"	"	1837
"	John M. Niles	Conn.	1840
Harrison, W.H.	Francis Granger	N.Y.	1841
Tyler	"	N.Y.	1841
"	Charles A. Wickliffe	Ky.	1841
Polk	Cave Johnson	Tenn.	1845
Taylor	Jacob Collamer	Vt.	1849
Fillmore	Nathan K. Hall	N.Y.	1850
"	Samuel D. Hubbard	Conn.	1852
Pierce	James Campbell	Pa.	1853
Buchanan	Aaron V. Brown	Tenn.	1857
"	Joseph Holt	Ky.	1859
"	Horatio King	Me.	1861
Lincoln	Montgomery Blair	D.C.	1861
"	William Dennison	Oh.	1864
Johnson, A.	"	"	1865
"	Alex W. Randall	Wis.	1866
Grant	John A.J. Creswell	Md.	1869
"	James W. Marshall	Va.	1874
"	Marshall Jewell	Conn.	1874
"	James N. Tyner	Ind.	1876
Hayes	David McK. Key	Tenn.	1877
"	Horace Maynard	Tenn.	1880
Garfield	Thomas L. James	N.Y.	1881
Arthur	Timothy O. Howe	Wis.	1881
"	Walter Q. Gresham	Ind.	1883
"	Frank Hatton	Ia.	1884
Cleveland	William F. Vilas	Wis.	1885
"	Don M. Dickinson	Mich.	1888
Harrison, B.	John Wanamaker	Pa.	1889
Cleveland	Wilson S. Bissel	N.Y.	1893
"	William L. Wilson	W.Va.	1895
McKinley	James A. Gary	Md.	1897
"	Charles E. Smith	Pa.	1898
Roosevelt, T.	"	"	1901
"	Henry C. Payne	Wis.	1902
"	Robert J. Wynne	Pa.	1904
"	George B. Cortelyou	N.Y.	1905
"	George von L. Meyer	Mass.	1907
Taft	Frank H. Hitchcock	"	1909
Wilson	Albert S. Burleson	Tex.	1913
Harding	Will H. Hays	Ind.	1921
"	Hubert Work	Col.	1922
"	Harry S. New	Ind.	1923
Coolidge	"	"	1923
Hoover	Walter F. Brown	Oh.	1929
Roosevelt, F.D.	James A. Farley	N.Y.	1933
"	Frank C. Walker	Pa.	1940
Truman	Robert E. Hannegan	Mo.	1945
"	Jesse M. Donaldson	Mo.	1947
Eisenhower	A.E. Summerfield	Mich.	1953
Kennedy	J. Edward Day	Cal.	1961
"	John A. Gronouski	Wis.	1963
Johnson, L.B.	"	"	1963
"	Lawrence F. O'Brien	Mass.	1965
"	W. Marvin Watson	Tex.	1968
Nixon	Winton M. Blount	Ala.	1969

Law on Succession to the Presidency

If by reason of death, resignation, removal from office, inability, or failure to qualify there is neither a president nor vice president to discharge the powers and duties of the office of president, then the speaker of the House of Representatives shall upon his resignation as speaker and as representative, act as president. The same rule shall apply in the case of the death, resignation, removal from office, or inability of an individual acting as president.

If at the time when a speaker is to begin the discharge of the powers and duties of the office of president there is no speaker, or the speaker fails to qualify as acting president, then the president pro tempore of the Senate, upon his resignation as president pro tempore and as senator, shall act as president.

An individual acting as president shall continue to act until the expiration of the then current presidential term, except that (1) if his discharge of the powers and duties of the office is founded in whole or in part in the failure of both the president-elect and the vice president-elect to qualify, then he shall act only until a president or vice president qualifies, and (2) if his discharge of the powers and duties of the office is founded in whole or in part on the inability of the president or vice president, then he shall act only until the removal of the disability of one of such individuals.

If, by reason of death, resignation, removal from office, or failure to qualify, there is no president pro tempore to act as president, then the officer of the United States who is highest on the following list, and who is not under disability to discharge the powers and duties of president, shall act as president; the secretaries of state, treasury, defense, attorney general; secretaries of interior, agriculture, commerce, labor, health and human services, housing and urban development, transportation, energy, education.

(Legislation approved July 18, 1947; amended Sept. 9, 1965, Oct. 15, 1966, Aug. 4, 1977, and Sept. 27, 1979. (See also Constitutional Amendment XXV.)

Burial Places of the Presidents

Washington	Mt. Vernon, Va.
J. Adams	Quincy, Mass.
Jefferson	Charlottesville, Va.
Madison	Montpelier Station, Va.
Monroe	Richmond, Va.
J.Q. Adams	Quincy, Mass.
Jackson	Nashville, Tenn.
Van Buren	Kinderhook, N.Y.
W.H. Harrison	North Bend, Oh.
Tyler	Richmond, Va.
Polk	Nashville, Tenn.
Taylor	Louisville, Ky.
Fillmore	Buffalo, N.Y.
Pierce	Concord, N.H.
Buchanan	Lancaster, Pa.
Lincoln	Springfield, Ill.
A. Johnson	Greeneville, Tenn.
Grant	New York City
Hayes	Fremont, Oh.
Garfield	Cleveland, Oh.
Arthur	Albany, N.Y.
Cleveland	Princeton, N.J.
B. Harrison	Indianapolis, Ind.
McKinley	Canton, Oh.
T. Roosevelt	Oyster Bay, N.Y.
Taft	Arlington Nat'l. Cem'y.
Wilson	Washington Cathedral
Harding	Marion, Oh.
Coolidge	Plymouth, Vt.
Hoover	West Branch, Ia.
F.D. Roosevelt	Hyde Park, N.Y.
Truman	Independence, Mo.
Eisenhower	Abilene, Kan.
Kennedy	Arlington Nat'l. Cem'y.
L.B. Johnson	Stonewall, Tex.

BIOGRAPHIES OF U.S. PRESIDENTS

George Washington

George Washington, first president, was born Feb. 22, 1732 (Feb. 11, 1731, old style), the son of Augustine Washington and Mary Ball, at Wakefield on Pope's Creek, Westmoreland Co., Va. His early childhood was spent on the Ferry farm, near Fredericksburg. His father died when George was 11. He studied mathematics and surveying and when 16 went to live with his half brother Lawrence, who built and named Mount Vernon. George surveyed the lands of William Fairfax in the Shenandoah Valley, keeping a diary. He accompanied Lawrence to Barbados, West Indies, contracted small pox, and was deeply scarred. Lawrence died in 1752 and George acquired his property by inheritance. He valued land and when he died owned 70,000 acres in Virginia and 40,000 acres in what is now West Virginia.

Washington's military service began in 1753 when Gov. Dinwiddie of Virginia sent him on missions deep into Ohio country. He clashed with the French and had to surrender Fort Necessity July 3, 1754. He was an aide to Braddock and at his side when the army was ambushed and defeated on a march to Ft. Duquesne, July 9, 1755. He helped take Fort Duquesne from the French in 1758.

After his marriage to Martha Dandridge Custis, a widow, in 1759, Washington managed his family estate at Mount Vernon. Although not at first for independence, he opposed British exactions and took charge of the Virginia troops before war broke out. He was made commander-in-chief by the Continental Congress June 15, 1775.

The successful issue of a war filled with hardships was due to his leadership. He was resourceful, a stern disciplinarian, and the one strong, dependable force for unity. He favored a federal government and became chairman of the Constitutional Convention of 1787. He helped get the Constitution ratified and was unanimously elected president by the electoral college and inaugurated, Apr. 30, 1789, on the balcony of New York's Federal Hall.

He was reelected 1792, but refused to consider a 3d term and retired to Mount Vernon. He suffered acute laryngitis after a ride in snow and rain around his estate, was bled profusely, and died Dec. 14, 1799.

John Adams

John Adams, 2d president, Federalist, was born in Braintree (Quincy), Mass., Oct. 30, 1735 (Oct. 19, o. s.), the son of John Adams, a farmer, and Susanna Boylston. He was a great-grandson of Henry Adams who came from England in 1636. He was graduated from Harvard, 1755, taught school, studied law. In 1765 he argued against taxation without representation before the royal governor. In 1770 he defended the British soldiers who fired on civilians in the "Boston Massacre." He was a delegate to the first Continental Congress, and signed the Declaration of Independence. He was a commissioner to France, 1778, with Benjamin Franklin and Arthur Lee; won recognition of the U.S. by The Hague, 1782; was first American minister to England, 1785-1788, and was elected vice president, 1788 and 1792.

In 1796 Adams was chosen president by the electors. Intense antagonism to America by France caused agitation for war, led by Alexander Hamilton. Adams, breaking with Hamilton, opposed war.

To fight alien influence and muzzle criticism Adams supported the Alien and Sedition laws of 1798, which led to his defeat for reelection. He died July 4, 1826, on the same day as Jefferson (the 50th anniversary of the Declaration of Independence).

Thomas Jefferson

Thomas Jefferson, 3d president, was born Apr. 13, 1743 (Apr. 2, o. s.), at Shadwell, Va., the son of Peter Jefferson, a civil engineer of Welsh descent who raised tobacco, and Jane Randolph. His father died when he was 14, leaving him 2,750 acres and his slaves. Jefferson attended the College of William and Mary, 1760-1762, read classics in Greek and Latin and played the violin. In 1769 he was elected to the House of Burgesses. In 1770 he began building Monticello, near Charlottesville. He was a member of the Virginia Committee of Correspondence and the Continental Congress. Named a member of the committee to draw up a Declaration of Independence, he wrote the basic draft. He was a member of the Virginia House of Delegates, 1776-79, elected governor to succeed Patrick Henry, 1779, reelected 1780, resigned June 1781, amid charges of ineffectual military preparation. During his term he wrote the statute on religious freedom. In the Continental Congress, 1783, he drew up an ordinance for the Northwest Territory, forbidding slavery after 1800; its terms were put into the Ordinance of 1787. He was sent to Paris with Benjamin Franklin and John Adams to negotiate commercial treaties, 1784; made minister to France, 1785.

Washington appointed him secretary of state, 1789. Jefferson's strong faith in the consent of the governed, as opposed to executive control favored by Hamilton, secretary of the treasury, often led to conflict: Dec. 31, 1793, he resigned. He was the Republican candidate for president in 1796; beaten by John Adams, he became vice president. In 1800, Jefferson and Aaron Burr received equal electoral college votes for president. The House of Representatives elected Jefferson. Major events of his administration were the Louisiana Purchase, 1803, and the Lewis and Clark Expedition. He established the Univ. of Virginia and designed its buildings. He died July 4, 1826, on the same day as John Adams.

James Madison

James Madison, 4th president, Republican, was born Mar. 16, 1751 (Mar. 5, 1750, o. s.) at Port Conway, King George Co., Va., eldest son of James Madison and Eleanor Rose Conway. Madison was graduated from Princeton, 1771; studied theology, 1772; sat in the Virginia Constitutional Convention, 1776. He was a member of the Continental Congress. He was chief recorder at the Constitutional Convention in 1787, and supported ratification in the Federalist Papers, written with Alexander Hamilton and John Jay. He was elected to the House of Representatives in 1789, helped frame the Bill of Rights and fought the Alien and Sedition Acts. He became Jefferson's secretary of state, 1801.

Elected president in 1808, Madison was a "strict constructionist," opposed to the free interpretation of the Constitution by the Federalists. He was reelected in 1812 by the votes of the agrarian South and recently admitted western states. Caught between British and French maritime restrictions, the U.S. drifted into war, declared June 18, 1812. The war ended in a stalemate. He retired in 1817 to his estate at Montpelier. There he edited his famous papers on the Constitutional Convention. He became rector of the Univ. of Virginia, 1826. He died June 28, 1836.

James Monroe

James Monroe, 5th president, Republican, was born Apr. 28, 1758, in Westmoreland Co., Va., the son of Spence Monroe and Eliza Jones, who were of Scottish and Welsh descent, respectively. He attended the College of William and Mary, fought in the 3d Virginia Regiment at White Plains, Brandywine, Monmouth, and was wounded at Trenton. He studied law with Thomas Jefferson, 1780, was a member of the Virginia House of Delegates and of Congress, 1783-86. He opposed ratification of the Constitution because it lacked a bill of rights; was U.S. senator, 1790; minister to France, 1794-96; governor of Virginia, 1799-1802, and 1811. Jefferson sent him to France as minister, 1803. He helped R. Livingston negotiate the Louisiana Purchase, 1803. He ran against Madison for president in 1808. He was elected to the Virginia Assembly, 1810-1811; was secretary of state under Madison, 1811-1817.

In 1816 Monroe was elected president; in 1820 reelected

with all but one electoral college vote. Monroe's administration became the "Era of Good Feeling." He obtained Florida from Spain; settled boundaries with Canada, and eliminated border forts. He supported the anti-slavery position that led to the Missouri Compromise. His most significant contribution was the "Monroe Doctrine," which became a cornerstone of U.S. foreign policy. Monroe retired to Oak Hill, Va. Financial problems forced him to sell his property. He moved to New York City to live with a daughter. He died there July 4, 1831.

John Quincy Adams

John Quincy Adams, 6th president, independent Federalist, was born July 11, 1767, at Braintree (Quincy), Mass., the son of John and Abigail Adams. His father was the 2d president. He was educated in Paris, Leyden, and Harvard, graduating in 1787. He served as American minister in various European capitals, and helped draft the War of 1812 peace treaty. He was U.S. Senator, 1803-08. President Monroe made him secretary of state, 1817, and he negotiated the cession of the Floridas from Spain, supported exclusion of slavery in the Missouri Compromise, and helped formulate the Monroe Doctrine. In 1824 he was elected president by the House after he failed to win an electoral college majority. His expansion of executive powers was strongly opposed and he was beaten in 1828 by Jackson. In 1831 he entered Congress and served 17 years with distinction. He opposed slavery, the annexation of Texas, and the Mexican War. He helped establish the Smithsonian Institution. He had a stroke in the House and died in the Speaker's Room, Feb. 23, 1848.

Andrew Jackson

Andrew Jackson, 7th president, was a Jeffersonian-Republican, later a Democrat. He was born in the Waxhaws district, New Lancaster Co., S.C., Mar. 15, 1767, the posthumous son of Andrew Jackson and Elizabeth Hutchinson, who were Irish immigrants. At 13, he joined the militia in the Revolution and was captured.

He read law in Salisbury, N.C., moved to Nashville, Tenn., speculated in land, married, and practiced law. In 1796 he helped draft the constitution of Tennessee and for a year occupied its one seat in Congress. He was in the Senate in 1797, and again in 1823. He defeated the Creek Indians at Horseshoe Bend, Ala., 1814. With 6,000 backwoods fighters he defeated Packenham's 12,000 British troops at the Chalmette, outside New Orleans, Jan. 8, 1815. In 1818 he briefly invaded Spanish Florida to quell Seminoles and outlaws who harassed frontier settlements. In 1824 he ran for president against John Quincy Adams and had the most popular and electoral votes but not a majority; the election was decided by the House, which chose Adams. In 1828 he defeated Adams, carrying the West and South. He was a noisy debater and a duelist and introduced rotation in office called the "spoils system." Suspicious of privilege, he ruined the Bank of the United States by depositing federal funds with state banks. Though "Let the people rule" was his slogan, he at times supported strict constructionist policies against the expansionist West. He killed the Congressional caucus for nominating presidential candidates and substituted the national convention, 1832. When South Carolina refused to collect imports under his protective tariff he ordered army and naval forces to Charleston. Jackson recognized the Republic of Texas, 1836. He died at the Hermitage, June 8, 1845.

Martin Van Buren

Martin Van Buren, 8th president, Democrat, was born Dec. 5, 1782, at Kinderhook, N.Y., the son of Abraham Van Buren, a Dutch farmer, and Mary Hoes. He was surrogate of Columbia County, N.Y., state senator and attorney general. He was U.S. senator 1821, reelected, 1827, elected governor of New York, 1828. He helped swing eastern support to Jackson in 1828 and was his secretary of state 1829-31. In 1832 he was elected vice president. He was a consummate politician, known as "the little magician," and influenced Jackson's policies. In 1836 he defeated William Henry Harrison for president and took office as the Panic of 1837 initiated a 5-year nationwide depression. He inaugurated the independent treasury system. His refusal to spend land revenues led to his defeat by Harrison in 1840. He lost the Democratic nomination of 1844 to Polk. In 1848 he ran for president on the Free Soil ticket and lost. He died July 24, 1862, at Kinderhook.

William Henry Harrison

William Henry Harrison, 9th president, Whig, who served only 31 days, was born in Berkeley, Charles City Co., Va., Feb. 9, 1773, the 3d son of Benjamin Harrison, signer of the Declaration of Independence. He attended Hampden Sydney College. He was secretary of the Northwest Territory, 1798; its delegate in Congress, 1799; first governor of Indiana Territory, 1800; and superintendent of Indian affairs. With 900 men he routed Tecumseh's Indians at Tippecanoe, Nov. 7, 1811. A major general, he defeated British and Indians at Battle of the Thames, Oct. 5, 1813. He served in Congress, 1816-19; Senate, 1825-28. In 1840, when 68, he was elected president with a "log cabin and hard cider" slogan. He caught pneumonia during the inauguration and died Apr. 4, 1841.

John Tyler

John Tyler, 10th president, independent Whig, was born Mar. 29, 1790, in Greenway, Charles City Co., Va., son of John Tyler and Mary Armistead. His father was governor of Virginia, 1808-11. Tyler was graduated from William and Mary, 1807; member of the House of Delegates, 1811; in congress, 1816-21; in Virginia legislature, 1823-25; governor of Virginia, 1825-26; U.S. senator, 1827-36. In 1840 he was elected vice president and, on Harrison's death, succeeded him. He favored pre-emption, allowing settlers to get government land; rejected a national bank bill and thus alienated most Whig supporters; refused to honor the spoils system. He signed the resolution annexing Texas, Mar. 1, 1845. He accepted renomination, 1844, but withdrew before election. In 1861, he chaired an unsuccessful Washington conference called to avert civil war. After its failure he supported secession, sat in the provisional Confederate Congress, became a member of the Confederate House, but died, Jan. 18, 1862, before it met.

James Knox Polk

James Knox Polk, 11th president, Democrat, was born in Mecklenburg Co., N.C., Nov. 2, 1795, the son of Samuel Polk, farmer and surveyor of Scotch-Irish descent, and Jane Knox. He graduated from the Univ. of North Carolina, 1818; member of the Tennessee state legislature, 1823-25. He served in Congress 1825-39 and as speaker 1835-39. He was governor of Tennessee 1839-41, but was defeated 1841 and 1843. In 1844, when both Clay and Van Buren announced opposition to annexing Texas, the Democrats made Polk the first dark horse nominee because he demanded control of all Oregon and annexation of Texas. Polk reestablished the independent treasury system originated by Van Buren. His expansionist policy was opposed by Clay, Webster, Calhoun; he sent troops under Zachary Taylor to the Mexican border and, when Mexicans attacked, declared war existed. The Mexican war ended with the annexation of California and much of the Southwest as part of America's "manifest destiny." He compromised on the Oregon boundary ("54-40 or fight!") by accepting the 49th parallel and giving Vancouver to the British. Polk died in Nashville, June 15, 1849.

Zachary Taylor

Zachary Taylor, 12th president, Whig, who served only 16 months, was born Nov. 24, 1784, in Orange Co., Va., the son of Richard Taylor, later collector of the port of Louisville, Ky., and Sarah Strother. Taylor was commissioned first lieutenant, 1808; fought in the War of 1812; the Black

Hawk War, 1832; and the second Seminole War, 1837. He was called Old Rough and Ready. He settled on a plantation near Baton Rouge, La. In 1845 Polk sent him with an army to the Rio Grande. When the Mexicans attacked him, Polk declared war. Taylor was successful at Palo Alto and Resaca de la Palma, 1846; occupied Monterey. Polk made him major general but sent many of his troops to Gen. Winfield Scott. Outnumbered 4-1, he defeated Santa Anna at Buena Vista, 1847. A national hero, he received the Whig nomination in 1848, and was elected president. He resumed the spoils system and though once a slave-holder worked to have California admitted as a free state. He died in office July 9, 1850.

Millard Fillmore

Millard Fillmore, 13th president, Whig, was born Jan. 7, 1800, in Cayuga Co., N.Y., the son of Nathaniel Fillmore and Phoebe Miller. He taught school and studied law; admitted to the bar, 1823. He was a member of the state assembly, 1829-32; in Congress, 1833-35 and again 1837-43. He opposed the entrance of Texas as slave territory and voted for a protective tariff. In 1844 he was defeated for governor of New York. In 1848 he was elected vice president and succeeded as president July 10, 1850, after Taylor's death. Fillmore favored the Compromise of 1850 and signed the Fugitive Slave Law. His policies pleased neither expansionists nor slave-holders and he was not renominated in 1852. In 1856 he was nominated by the American (Know-Nothing) party and accepted by the Whigs, but defeated by Buchanan. He died in Buffalo, Mar. 8, 1874.

Franklin Pierce

Franklin Pierce, 14th president, Democrat, was born in Hillsboro, N. H., Nov. 23, 1804, the son of Benjamin Pierce, veteran of the Revolution and governor of New Hampshire, 1827. He graduated from Bowdoin, 1824. A lawyer, he served in the state legislature 1829-33; in Congress, supporting Jackson, 1833-37; U.S. senator, 1837-42. He enlisted in the Mexican War, became brigadier general under Gen. Winfield Scott. In 1852 Pierce was nominated on the 49th ballot over Lewis Cass, Stephen A. Douglas, and James Buchanan, and defeated Gen. Scott, Whig. Though against slavery, Pierce was influenced by Southern pro-slavery men. He ignored the Ostend Manifesto that the U.S. either buy or take Cuba. He approved the Kansas-Nebraska Act, leaving slavery to popular vote ("squatter sovereignty"), 1854, He signed a reciprocity treaty with Canada and approved the Gadsden Purchase from Mexico, 1853. Denied renomination by the Democrats, he spent most of his remaining years in Concord, N.H., where he died Oct. 8, 1869.

James Buchanan

James Buchanan, 15th president, Federalist, later Democrat, was born of Scottish descent near Mercersburg, Pa., Apr. 23, 1791. He graduated from Dickinson, 1809; was a volunteer in the War of 1812; member, Pennsylvania legislature, 1814-16, Congress, 1820-31; Jackson's minister to Russia, 1831-33; U.S. senator 1834-45. As Polk's secretary of state, 1845-49, he ended the Oregon dispute with Britain, supported the Mexican War and annexation of Texas. As minister to Britain, 1853, he signed the Ostend Manifesto. Nominated by Democrats, he was elected, 1856, over John C. Fremont (Republican) and Millard Fillmore (American Know-Nothing and Whig tickets). On slavery he favored popular sovereignty and choice by state constitutions; he accepted the pro-slavery Dred Scott decision as binding. He denied the right of states to secede. A strict constructionist, he desired to keep peace and found no authority for using force. He died at Wheatland, near Lancaster, Pa., June 1, 1868.

Abraham Lincoln

Abraham Lincoln, 16th president, Republican, was born Feb. 12, 1809, in a log cabin on a farm then in Hardin Co., Ky., now in Larue. He was the son of Thomas Lincoln, a carpenter, and Nancy Hanks.

The Lincolns moved to Spencer Co., Ind., near Gentryville, when Abe was 7. Nancy died 1818, and his father married Mrs. Sarah Bush Johnston, 1819; she had a favorable influence on Abe. In 1830 the family moved to Macon Co., Ill. Lincoln lost election to the Illinois General Assembly, 1832, but later won 4 times, beginning in 1834. He enlisted in the militia for the Black Hawk War, 1832. In New Salem he ran a store, surveyed land, and was postmaster.

In 1837 Lincoln was admitted to the bar and became partner in a Springfield, Ill., law office. He was elected to Congress, 1847-49. He opposed the Mexican War. He supported Zachary Taylor, 1848. He opposed the Kansas-Nebraska Act and extension of slavery, 1854. He failed, in his bid for the Senate, 1855. He supported John C. Fremont, 1856.

In 1858 Lincoln had Republican support in the Illinois legislature for the Senate but was defeated by Stephen A. Douglas, Dem., who had sponsored the Kansas-Nebraska Act.

Lincoln was nominated for president by the Republican party on an anti-slavery platform, 1860. He ran against Douglas, a northern Democrat; John C. Breckinridge, southern pro-slavery Democrat; John Bell, Constitutional Union party. When he won the election, South Carolina seceded from the Union Dec. 20, 1860, followed in 1861 by 10 Southern states.

The Civil War erupted when Fort Sumter was attacked Apr. 12, 1861. On Sept. 22, 1862, 5 days after the battle of Antietam, he announced that slaves in territory then in rebellion would be free Jan. 1, 1863, date of the Emancipation Proclamation, His speeches, including his Gettysburg and Inaugural addresses, are remembered for their eloquence.

Lincoln was reelected, 1864, over Gen. George B. McClellan, Democrat. Lee surrendered Apr. 9, 1865. On Apr. 14, Lincoln was shot by actor John Wilkes Booth in Ford's Theatre, Washington. He died the next day.

Andrew Johnson

Andrew Johnson, 17th president, Democrat, was born in Raleigh, N.C., Dec. 29, 1808, the son of Jacob Johnson, porter at an inn and church sexton, and Mary McDonough. He was apprenticed to a tailor but ran away and eventually settled in Greeneville, Tenn. He became an alderman, 1828; mayor, 1830; state representative and senator, 1835-43; member of Congress, 1843-53; governor of Tennessee, 1853-57; U.S. senator, 1857-62. He supported John C. Breckinridge against Lincoln in 1860. He had held slaves, but opposed secession and tried to prevent his home state, Tennessee, from seceding. In Mar. 1862, Lincoln appointed him military governor of occupied Tennessee. In 1864 he was nominated for vice president with Lincoln on the National Union ticket to win Democratic support. He succeeded Lincoln as president April 15, 1865. In a controversy with Congress over the president's power over the South, he proclaimed, May 26, 1865, an amnesty to all Confederates except certain leaders if they would ratify the 13th Amendment abolishing slavery. States doing so added anti-Negro provisions that enraged Congress, which restored military control over the South. When Johnson removed Edwin M. Stanton, secretary of war, without notifying the Senate, thus repudiating the Tenure of Office Act, the House impeached him for this and other reasons. He was tried by the Senate, and acquitted by only one vote, May 26, 1868. He returned to the Senate in 1875. Johnson died July 31, 1875.

Ulysses Simpson Grant

Ulysses S. Grant, 18th president, Republican, was born at Point Pleasant, Oh., Apr. 27, 1822, son of Jesse R. Grant, a tanner, and Hannah Simpson. The next year the family moved to Georgetown, Oh. Grant was named Hiram Ulysses, but on entering West Point, 1839, his name was entered as Ulysses Simpson and he adopted it. he was graduated in 1843; served under Gens. Taylor and Scott in the Mexican War; resigned, 1854; worked in St. Louis until 1860, then went to Galena, Ill. With the start of the Civil War, he was named colonel of the 21st Illinois Vols., 1861, then brigadier general; took Forts Henry and Donelson; fought at Shiloh, took Vicksburg. After his victory at Chattanooga, Lincoln placed him in command of the Union Armies. He accepted Lee's surrender at Appomattox, Apr., 1865. President Johnson appointed Grant secretary of war when he suspended Stanton, but Grant was not confirmed. He was nominated for president by the Republicans and elected over Horatio Seymour, Democrat. The 15th Amendment, amnesty bill, and civil service reform were events of his administration. The Liberal Republicans and Democrats opposed him with Horace Greeley, 1872, but he was reelected. An attempt by the Stalwarts (Old Guard) to nominate him in 1880 failed. In 1884 the collapse of Grant & Ward, investment house, left him penniless. He wrote his personal memoirs while ill with cancer and completed them 4 days before his death at Mt. McGregor, N.Y., July 23, 1885. The book realized over $450,000.

Rutherford Birchard Hayes

Rutherford B. Hayes, 19th president, Republican, was born in Delaware, Oh., Oct. 4, 1822, the posthumous son of Rutherford Hayes, a farmer, and Sophia Birchard. He was raised by his uncle Sardis Birchard. He graduated from Kenyon College, 1842, and Harvard Law School, 1845. He practiced law in Lower Sandusky, Oh., now Fremont; was city solicitor of Cincinnati, 1858-61. In the Civil War, he was major of the 23d Ohio Vols., was wounded several times, and rose to the rank of brevet major general, 1864. He served in Congress 1864-67, supporting Reconstruction and Johnson's impeachment. He was elected governor of Ohio, 1867 and 1869; beaten in the race for Congress, 1872; reelected governor, 1875. In 1876 he was nominated for president and believed he had lost the election to Samuel J. Tilden, Democrat. But a few Southern states submitted 2 different sets of electoral votes and the result was in dispute. An electoral commission, appointed by Congress, 8 Republicans and 7 Democrats, awarded all disputed votes to Hayes allowing him to become president by one electoral vote. Hayes, keeping a promise to southerners, withdrew troops from areas still occupied in the South, ending the era of Reconstruction. He proceeded to reform the civil service, alienating political spoilsmen. He advocated repeal of the Tenure of Office Act. He supported sound money and specie payments. Hayes died in Fremont, Oh., Jan. 17, 1893.

James Abram Garfield

James A. Garfield, 20th president, Republican, was born Nov. 19, 1831, in Orange, Cuyahoga Co., Oh., the son of Abram Garfield and Eliza Ballou. His father died in 1833. He worked as a canal bargeman, farmer, and carpenter; attended Western Reserve Eclectic, later Hiram College, and was graduated from Williams in 1856. He taught at Hiram, and later became principal. He was in the Ohio senate in 1859. Anti-slavery and anti-secession, he volunteered for the war, became colonel of the 42d Ohio Infantry and brigadier in 1862. He fought at Shiloh, was chief of staff for Rosecrans and was made major general for gallantry at Chickamauga. He entered Congress as a radical Republican in 1863; supported specie payment as against paper money (greenbacks). On the electoral commission in 1876 he voted for Hayes against Tilden on strict party lines. He was senator-elect in 1880 when he became the Republican nominee for president. He was chosen as a compromise over Gen. Grant, James G. Blaine, and John Sherman. This alienated the Grant following but Garfield was elected. On July 2, 1881, Garfield was shot by mentally disturbed office-seeker, Charles J. Guiteau, while entering a railroad station in Washington. He died Sept. 19, 1881, at Elberon, N.J.

Chester Alan Arthur

Chester A. Arthur, 21st president, Republican, was born at Fairfield, Vt., Oct. 5, 1829, the son of the Rev. William Arthur, from County Antrim, Ireland, and Malvina Stone. He graduated from Union College, 1848, taught school at Pownall, Vt., studied law in New York. In 1853 he argued in a fugitive slave case that slaves transported through N.Y. State were thereby freed; in 1885 he obtained a ruling that Negroes were to be treated the same as whites on street cars. He was made collector of the Port of New York, 1871. President Hayes, reforming the civil service, forced Arthur to resign, 1879. This made the New York machine stalwarts enemies of Hayes. Arthur and the stalwarts tried to nominate Grant for a 3d term in 1880. When Garfield was nominated, Arthur received 2d place in the interests of harmony. When Garfield died, Arthur became president. He supported civil service reform and the tariff of 1883. He was defeated for renomination by James G. Blaine. He died in New York City Nov. 18, 1886.

Grover Cleveland

(According to a ruling of the State Dept., Grover Cleveland is both the 22d and the 24th president, because his 2 terms were not consecutive. By individuals, he is only the 22d.)

Grover Cleveland, 22d and 24th president, Democrat, was born in Caldwell, N.J. Mar. 18, 1837, the son of Richard F. Cleveland, a Presbyterian minister, and Ann Neale. He was named Stephen Grover, but dropped the Stephen. He clerked in Clinton and Buffalo, N.Y., taught at the N.Y. City Institution for the Blind; was admitted to the bar in Buffalo, 1859; became assistant district attorney, 1863; sheriff, 1871; mayor, 1881; governor of New York, 1882. He was an independent, honest administrator who hated corruption. He was nominated for president over Tammany Hall opposition, 1884, and defeated Republican James G. Blaine. He enlarged the civil service, vetoed many pension raids on the Treasury. In 1888 he was defeated by Benjamin Harrison, although his popular vote was larger. Reelected over Harrison in 1892, he faced a money crisis brought about by lowering of the gold reserve, circulation of paper and exorbitant silver purchases under the Sherman Act; obtained a repeal of the latter and a reduced tariff. A severe depression and labor troubles racked his administration but he refused to interfere in business matters and rejected Jacob Coxey's demand for unemployment relief. He broke the Pullman strike, 1894. In 1896, the Democrats repudiated his administration and chose silverite William Jennings Bryan as their candidate. Cleveland died in Princeton, N.J., June 24, 1908.

Benjamin Harrison

Benjamin Harrison, 23d president, Republican, was born at North Bend, Oh., Aug. 20, 1833. His great-grandfather, Benjamin Harrison, was a signer of the Declaration of Independence; his grandfather, William Henry Harrison, was 9th President; his father, John Scott Harrison, was a member of Congress. His mother was Elizabeth F. Irwin. He attended school on his father's farm; graduated from Miami Univ. at Oxford, Oh., 1852; admitted to the bar, 1853, and practiced in Indianapolis. In the Civil War, he rose to the rank of brevet brigadier general, fought at Kennesaw Mountain, Peachtree Creek, Nashville, and in the Atlanta campaign. He failed to be elected governor of Indiana, 1876; but became senator, 1881, and worked for the G. A. R. pensions vetoed by Cleveland. In 1888 he defeated Cleveland for president despite having fewer popular votes. He expanded the pension list; signed the McKinley high tariff bill and the Sherman Silver Purchase Act. During his administration, 6 states were admitted to the union. He was defeated for reelection, 1892. He represented Venezuela in a boundary arbitration with Great Britain in Paris, 1899. He died at Indianapolis, Mar. 13, 1901.

William McKinley

William McKinley, 25th president, Republican, was born in Niles, Oh., Jan. 29, 1843, the son of William McKinley, an ironmaker, and Nancy Allison. McKinley attended school in Poland, Oh., and Allegheny College, Meadville, Pa., and enlisted for the Civil War at 18 in the 23d Ohio, in which Rutherford B. Hayes was a major. He rose to captain and in 1865 was made brevet major. He studied law in the Albany, N.Y., law school; opened an office in Canton, Oh., in 1867, and campaigned for Grant and Hayes. He served in the House of Representatives, 1877-83, 1885-91, and led the fight for passage of the McKinley Tarriff, 1890. Defeated for reelection on the issue in 1890, he was governor of Ohio, 1892-96. He had support for president in the convention that nominated Benjamin Harrison in 1892. In 1896 he was elected president on a protective tariff, sound money (gold standard) platform over William Jennings Bryan, Democratic proponent of free silver. McKinley was reluctant to intervene in Cuba but the loss of the battleship Maine at Havana crystallized opinion. He demanded Spain's withdrawal from Cuba; Spain made some concessions but Congress announced state of war as of Apr. 21. He was reelected in the 1900 campaign, defeating Bryan's anti-imperialist arguments with the promise of a "full dinner pail." McKinley was respected for his conciliatory nature, but conservative on business issues. On Sept. 6, 1901, while welcoming citizens at the Pan-American Exposition, Buffalo, N.Y., he was shot by Leon Czolgosz, an anarchist. He died Sept. 14.

Theodore Roosevelt

Theodore Roosevelt, 26th president, Republican, was born in N.Y. City, Oct. 27, 1858, the son of Theodore Roosevelt, a glass importer, and Martha Bulloch. He was a 5th cousin of Franklin D. Roosevelt and an uncle of Mrs. Eleanor Roosevelt. Roosevelt graduated from Harvard, 1880; attended Columbia Law School briefly; sat in the N.Y. State Assembly, 1882-84; ranched in North Dakota, 1884-86; failed election as mayor of N.Y. City, 1886; member of U.S. Civil Service Commission, 1889; president, N.Y. Police Board, 1895, supporting the merit system; assistant secretary of the Navy under McKinley, 1897-98. In the war with Spain, he organized the 1st U.S. Volunteer Cavalry (Rough Riders) as lieutenant colonel; led the charge up Kettle Hill at San Juan. Elected New York governor, 1898-1900, he fought the spoils system and achieved taxation of corporation franchises. Nominated for vice president, 1900, he became nation's youngest president when McKinley died. As president he fought corruption of politics by big business; dissolved Northern Securities Co. and others for violating anti-trust laws; intervened in coal strike on behalf of the public, 1902; obtained Elkins Law forbidding rebates to favored corporations, 1903; Hepburn Law regulating railroad rates, 1906; Pure Food and Drugs Act, 1906, Reclamation Act and employers' liability laws. He organized conservation, mediated the peace between Japan and Russia, 1905; won the Nobel Peace Prize. He was the first to use the Hague Court of International Arbitration. By recognizing the new Republic of Panama he made Panama Canal possible. He was reelected in 1904.

In 1908 he obtained the nomination of William H. Taft, who was elected. Feeling that Taft had abandoned his policies, Roosevelt unsuccessfully sought the nomination in 1912. He bolted the party and ran on the Progressive "Bull Moose", ticket against Taft and Woodrow Wilson, splitting the Republicans and insuring Wilson's election. He was shot during the campaign but recovered. In 1916 he supported Charles E. Hughes, Republican. A strong friend of Britain, he fought American isolation in World War I. He wrote some 40 books on many topics; his *Winning of the West* is best known. He died Jan. 6, 1919, at Sagamore Hill, Oyster Bay, N.Y.

William Howard Taft

William Howard Taft, 27th president, Republican, was born in Cincinnati, Oh., Sept. 15, 1857, the son of Alphonso Taft and Louisa Maria Torrey. His father was secretary of war and attorney general in Grant's cabinet; minister to Austria and Russia under Arthur. Taft was graduated from Yale, 1878; Cincinnati Law School, 1880; became law reporter for Cincinnati newspapers; was assistant prosecuting attorney, 1881-83; assistant county solicitor, 1885; judge, superior court, 1887; U.S. solicitor-general, 1890; federal circuit judge, 1892. In 1900 he became head of the U.S. Philippines Commission and was first civil governor of the Philippines, 1901-04; secretary of war, 1904; provisional governor of Cuba, 1906. He was groomed for president by Roosevelt and elected over Bryan, 1908. His administration dissolved Standard Oil and tobacco trusts; instituted Dept. of Labor; drafted direct election of senators and income tax amendments. His tariff and conservation policies angered progressives; though renominated he was opposed by Roosevelt; the result was Democract Woodrow Wilson's election. Taft, with some reservations, supported the League of Nations. He was professor of constitutional law, Yale, 1913-21; chief justice of the U.S., 1921-30; illness forced him to resign. He died in Washington, Mar. 8, 1930.

Woodrow Wilson

Woodrow Wilson, 28th president, Democrat, was born at Staunton, Va., Dec. 28, 1856, as Thomas Woodrow Wilson, son of a Presbyterian minister, the Rev. Joseph Ruggles Wilson and Janet (Jessie) Woodrow. In his youth Wilson lived in Augusta, Ga., Columbia, S.C., and Wilmington, N.C. He attended Davidson College, 1873-74; was graduated from Princeton, A.B., 1879; A.M., 1882; read law at the Univ. of Virginia, 1881; practiced law, Atlanta, 1882-83; Ph.D., Johns Hopkins, 1886. He taught at Bryn Mawr, 1885-88; at Wesleyan, 1888-90; was professor of jurisprudence and political economy at Princeton, 1890-1910; president of Princeton, 1902-1910; governor of New Jersey, 1911-13. In 1912 he was nominated for president with the aid of William Jennings Bryan, who sought to block James "Champ" Clark and Tammany Hall. Wilson won the election because the Republican vote for Taft was split by the Progressives under Roosevelt.

Wilson protected American interests in revolutionary Mexico and fought for American rights on the high seas. His sharp warnings to Germany led to the resignation of his secretary of state, Bryan, a pacifist. In 1916 he was reelected by a slim margin with the slogan, "He kept us out of war." Wilson's attempts to mediate in the war failed. After 4 American ships had been sunk by the Germans, he secured a declaration of war against Germany on Apr. 6, 1917.

Wilson proposed peace Jan. 8, 1918, on the basis of his "Fourteen Points," a state paper with worldwide influence. His doctrine of self-determination continues to play a major role in territorial disputes. The Germans accepted his terms and an armistice, Nov. 11.

Wilson went to Paris to help negotiate the peace treaty, the crux of which he considered the League of Nations. The Senate demanded reservations that would not make the U.S. subordinate to the votes of other nations in case of war. Wilson refused to consider any reservations and toured the country to get support. He suffered a stroke, Oct., 1919. An invalid for months, he clung to his executive powers while his wife and doctor sought to shield him from affairs which would tire him.

He was awarded the 1919 Nobel Peace Prize, but the treaty embodying the League of Nations was rejected by the Senate, 1920. He died Feb. 3, 1924.

Warren Gamaliel Harding

Warren Gamaliel Harding, 29th president, Republican, was born near Corsica, now Blooming Grove, Oh., Nov. 2, 1865, the son of Dr. George Tyron Harding, a physician, and Phoebe Elizabeth Dickerson. He attended Ohio Central College. He was state senator, 1900-04; lieutenant governor, 1904-06; defeated for governor, 1910; chosen U.S. senator, 1915. He supported Taft, opposed federal control of food and fuel; voted for anti-strike legislation, woman's suffrage, and the Volstead prohibition enforcement act over President Wilson's veto; and opposed the League of Nations. In 1920 he was nominated for president and defeated James M. Cox in the election. The Republicans capitalized on war weariness and fear that Wilson's League of Nations would curtail U.S. sovereignty. Harding stressed a return to "normalcy"; worked for tariff revision and repeal of excess profits law and high income taxes. Two Harding appointees, Albert B. Fall (interior) and Harry Daugherty (attorney general), became involved in the Teapot Dome scandal that embittered Harding's last days. He called the International Conference on Limitation of Armaments, 1921-22. Returning from a trip to Alaska he became ill and died in San Francisco, Aug. 2, 1923.

Calvin Coolidge

Calvin Coolidge, 30th president, Republican, was born in Plymouth, Vt., July 4, 1872, the son of John Calvin Coolidge, a storekeeper, and Victoria J. Moor, and named John

Calvin Coolidge. Coolidge graduated from Amherst in 1895. He entered Republican state politics and served as mayor of Northampton, Mass., state senator, lieutenant governor, and, in 1919, governor. In Sept., 1919, Coolidge attained national prominence by calling out the state guard in the Boston police strike. He declared: "There is no right to strike against the public safety by anybody, anywhere, anytime." This brought his name before the Republican convention of 1920, where he was nominated for vice president. He succeeded to the presidency on Harding's death. He opposed the League of Nations; approved the World Court; vetoed the soldiers' bonus bill, which was passed over his veto. In 1924 he was elected by a huge majority. He reduced the national debt by $2 billion in 3 years. He twice provided relief to financially hard-pressed farmers. With Republicans eager to renominate him he announced, Aug. 2, 1927: "I do not choose to run for president in 1928." He died in Northampton, Jan. 5, 1933.

Herbert Hoover

Herbert C. Hoover, 31st president, Republican, was born at West Branch, Ia., Aug. 10, 1874, son of Jesse Clark Hoover, a blacksmith, and Hulda Randall Minthorn. Hoover grew up in Indian Territory (now Oklahoma) and Oregon; won his A.B. in engineering at Stanford, 1891. He worked briefly with U.S. Geological Survey and western mines; then was a mining engineer in Australia, Asia, Europe, Africa, America. While chief engineer, imperial mines, China, he directed food relief for victims of Boxer Rebellion, 1900. He directed American Relief Committee, London, 1914-15; U.S. Comm. for Relief in Belgium, 1915-1919; was U.S. Food Administrator, 1917-1919; American Relief Administrator, 1918-1923, feeding children in defeated nations; Russian Relief, 1918-1923. He was secy. of commerce, 1921-28. He was elected president over Alfred E. Smith, 1928. In 1929 the stock market crashed and the economy collapsed. During the depression, Hoover opposed federal aid to the unemployed. He was defeated in the 1932 election by Franklin D. Roosevelt. President Truman made him coordinator of European Food Program, 1947, chairman of the Commission for Reorganization of the Executive Branch, 1947-49. He founded the Hoover Institution on War, Revolution, and Peace at Stanford Univ. He died in N.Y. City, Oct. 20, 1964.

Franklin Delano Roosevelt

Franklin D. Roosevelt, 32d president, Democrat, was born near Hyde Park, N.Y., Jan. 30, 1882, the son of James Roosevelt and Sara Delano. He graduated from Harvard, 1904; attended Columbia Law School; was admitted to the bar. He went to the N.Y. Senate, 1910 and 1913. In 1913 President Wilson made him assistant secretary of the navy.

Roosevelt ran for vice president, 1920, with James Cox and was defeated. From 1920 to 1928 he was a N.Y. lawyer and vice president of Fidelity & Deposit Co. In Aug., 1921, polio paralyzed his legs. He learned to walk with leg braces and a cane.

Roosevelt was elected governor of New York, 1928 and 1930. In 1932, W. G. McAdoo, pledged to John N. Garner, threw his votes to Roosevelt, who was nominated. The depression and the promise to repeal prohibition insured his election. He asked emergency powers, proclaimed the New Deal, and put into effect a vast number of administrative changes. Foremost was the use of public funds for relief and public works, resulting in deficit financing. He greatly expanded the controls of the central government over business, and by an excess profits tax and progressive income taxes produced a redistribution of earnings on an unprecedented scale. The Wagner Act gave labor many advantages in organizing and collective bargaining. He was the last president inaugurated on Mar. 4 (1933) and the first inaugurated on Jan. 20 (1937).

Roosevelt was the first president to use radio for "fireside chats." When the Supreme Court nullified some New Deal laws, he sought power to "pack" the court with additional justices, but Congress refused to give him the authority. He was the first president to break the "no 3d term" tradition (1940) and was elected to a 4th term, 1944, despite failing health. He was openly hostile to fascist governments before World War II and launched a lend-lease program on behalf of the Allies. He wrote the principles of fair dealing into the Atlantic Charter, Aug. 14, 1941 (with Winston Churchill), and urged the Four Freedoms (freedom of speech, of worship, from want, from fear) Jan. 6, 1941. When Japan attacked Pearl Harbor, Dec. 7, 1941, the U.S. entered the war. He conferred with allied heads of state at Casablanca, Jan., 1943; Quebec, Aug., 1943; Teheran, Nov.-Dec., 1943; Cairo, Dec., 1943; Yalta, Feb., 1945. He died at Warm Springs, Ga., Apr. 12, 1945.

Harry S. Truman

Harry S. Truman, 33d president, Democrat, was born at Lamar, Mo., May 8, 1884, the son of John Anderson Truman and Martha Ellen Young. A family disagreement on whether his middle name was Shippe or Solomon, after names of 2 grandfathers, resulted in his using only the middle initial S. He attended public schools in Independence, Mo., worked for the Kansas City Star, 1901, and as railroad timekeeper, and helper in Kansas City banks up to 1905. He ran his family's farm, 1906-17. He was commissioned a first lieutenant and took part in the Vosges, Meuse-Argonne, and St. Mihiel actions in World War I. After the war he ran a haberdashery, became judge of Jackson Co. Court, 1922-24; attended Kansas City School of Law, 1923-25.

Truman was elected U.S. senator in 1934; reelected 1940. In 1944 with Roosevelt's backing he was nominated for vice president and elected. On Roosevelt's death Truman became president. In 1948 he was elected president.

Truman authorized the first uses of the atomic bomb (Hiroshima and Nagasaki, Aug. 6 and 9, 1945), bringing World War II to a rapid end. He was responsible for creating NATO, the Marshall Plan, and what came to be called the Truman Doctrine (to aid nations such as Greece and Turkey, threatened by Russian or other communist takeover). He broke a Russian blockade of West Berlin with a massive airlift, 1948-49. When communist North Korea invaded South Korea, June, 1950, he won UN approval for a "police action" and sent in forces under Gen. Douglas MacArthur. When MacArthur sought to pursue North Koreans into China, Truman removed him from command.

On the domestic front, Truman was responsible for higher minimum-wage, increased social-security, and aid-for-housing laws. Truman died Dec. 26, 1972, in Independence, Mo.

Dwight David Eisenhower

Dwight D. Eisenhower, 34th president, Republican, was born Oct. 14, 1890, at Denison, Tex., the son of David Jacob Eisenhower and Ida Elizabeth Stover. The next year, the family moved to Abilene, Kan. He graduated from West Point, 1915. He was on the American military mission to the Philippines, 1935-39 and during 4 of those years on the staff of Gen. Douglas MacArthur. He was made commander of Allied forces landing in North Africa, 1942, full general, 1943. He became supreme Allied commander in Europe, 1943, and as such led the Normandy invasion June 6, 1944. He was given the rank of general of the army Dec. 20, 1944, made permanent in 1946. On May 7, 1945, he received the surrender of the Germans at Rheims. He returned to the U.S. to serve as chief of staff, 1945-1948. In 1948, Eisenhower published *Crusade in Europe*, his war memoirs, which quickly became a best seller. From 1948 to 1953, he was president of Columbia Univ., but took leave of absence in 1950, to command NATO forces.

Eisenhower resigned from the army and was nominated for president by the Republicans, 1952. He defeated Adlai E. Stevenson in the election. He again defeated Stevenson, 1956. He called himself a moderate, favored "free market system" vs. government price and wage controls; kept goverment out of labor disputes; reorganized defense establishment; promoted missile programs. He continued foreign aid; sped end of Korean fighting; endorsed Taiwan and SE Asia defense treaties; backed UN in condemning Anglo-French raid on Egypt; advocated "open skies" policy of mutual inspection to USSR. He sent U.S. troops into Little Rock, Ark., Sept., 1957, during the segregation crisis and ordered Marines into Lebanon July-Aug., 1958.

During his retirement at his farm near Gettysburg, Pa., Eisenhower took up the role of elder statesman, counseling his 3 successors in the White House. He died Mar. 28, 1969, in Washington.

John Fitzgerald Kennedy

John F. Kennedy, 35th president, Democrat, was born May 29, 1917, in Brookline, Mass., the son of Joseph P. Kennedy, financier, who later became ambassador to Great Britain, and Rose Fitzgerald. He entered Harvard, attended the London School of Economics briefly in 1935, received a B.S., from Harvard, 1940. He served in the Navy, 1941-1945, commanded a PT boat in the Solomons and won the Navy and Marine Corps Medal. He wrote *Profiles in Courage*, which won a Pulitzer prize. He served as representative in Congress, 1947-1953; was elected to the Senate in 1952, reelected 1958. He nearly won the vice presidential nomination in 1956.

In 1960, Kennedy won the Democratic nomination for president and defeated Richard M. Nixon, Republican. He was the first Roman Catholic president.

Kennedy's most important act was his successful demand Oct. 22, 1962, that the Soviet Union dismantle its missile bases in Cuba. He established a quarantine of arms shipments to Cuba and continued surveillance by air. He defied Soviet attempts to force the Allies out of Berlin. He made the steel industry rescind a price rise. He backed civil rights, a mental health program, arbitration of railroad disputes, and expanded medical care for the aged. Astronaut flights and satellite orbiting were greatly developed during his administration.

On Nov. 22, 1963, Kennedy was assassinated in Dallas, Tex.

Lyndon Baines Johnson

Lyndon B. Johnson, 36th president, Democrat, was born near Stonewall, Tex., Aug. 27, 1908, son of Sam Ealy Johnson and Rebekah Baines. He received a B.S. degree at Southwest Texas State Teachers College, 1930, attended Georgetown Univ. Law School, Washington, 1935. He taught public speaking in Houston, 1930-32; served as secretary to Rep. R. M. Kleberg, 1932-35. In 1937 Johnson won a contest to fill the vacancy caused by the death of a representative and in 1938 was elected to the full term, after which he returned for 4 terms. He was elected U.S. senator in 1948 and reelected in 1954. He became Democratic leader, 1953. Johnson was Texas' favorite son for the Democratic presidential nomination in 1956 and had strong support in the 1960 convention, where the nominee, John F. Kennedy, asked him to run for vice president. His campaigning helped overcome religious bias against Kennedy in the South.

Johnson became president on the death of Kennedy. Johnson worked hard for welfare legislation, signed civil rights, anti-proverty, and tax reduction laws, and averted strikes on railroads. He was elected to a full term, 1964. The war in Vietnam overshadowed other developments, 1965-68.

In face of increasing division in the nation and his own party over his handling of the war, Johnson announced that he would not seek another term, Mar. 31, 1968.

Retiring to his ranch near Johnson City, Tex., Johnson wrote his memoirs and oversaw the construction of the Lyndon Baines Johnson Library on the campus of the Univ. of Texas in Austin. He died Jan. 22, 1973.

Richard Milhous Nixon

Richard M. Nixon, 37th president, Republican, was the only president to resign without completing an elected term. He was born in Yorba Linda, Cal., Jan. 9, 1913, the son of Francis Anthony Nixon and Hannah Milhous. Nixon graduated from Whittier College, 1934; Duke Univ. Law School, 1937. After practicing law in Whittier and serving briefly in the Office of Price Administration in 1942, he entered the navy, serving in the South Pacific, and was discharged as a lieutenant commander.

Nixon was elected to the House of Representatives in 1946 and 1948. He achieved prominence as the House Un-American Activities Committee member who forced the showdown that resulted in the Alger Hiss perjury conviction. In 1950 Nixon moved to the Senate.

He was elected vice president in the Eisenhower landslides of 1952 and 1956. With Eisenhower's endorsement, Nixon won the Republican nomination in 1960. He was defeated by Democrat John F. Kennedy, returned to Cal. and was defeated in his race for governor, 1962.

In 1968, he won the presidential nomination and went on to defeat Democrat Hubert H. Humphrey.

Nixon became the first U.S. president to visit China and Russia (1972). He and his foreign affairs advisor, Henry A. Kissinger, achieved a detente with China. Nixon appointed 4 new Supreme Court justices, including the chief justice, thus altering the court's balance in favor of a more conservative view.

Reelected 1972, Nixon secured a cease-fire agreement in Vietnam and completed the withdrawal of U.S. troops.

Nixon's 2d term was cut short by a series of scandals beginning with the burglary of Democratic party national headquarters in the Watergate office complex on June 17, 1972. Nixon denied any White House involvement in the Watergate break-in. On July 16, 1973, a White House aide, under questioning by a Senate committee, revealed that most of Nixon's office conversations and phone calls had been recorded. Nixon claimed executive privilege to keep the tapes secret and the courts and Congress sought the tapes for criminal proceedings against former White House aides and for a House inquiry into possible impeachment.

On Oct. 10, 1973, Nixon fired the Watergate special prosecutor and the attorney general resigned in protest. The public outcry which followed caused Nixon to appoint a new special prosecutor and to turn over to the courts a number of subpoenaed tape recordings. Public reaction also brought the initiation of a formal inquiry into impeachment.

On July 24, 1974, the Supreme Court ruled that Nixon's claim of executive privilege must fall before the special prosecutor's subpoenas of tapes relevant to criminal trial proceedings. That same day, the House Judiciary Committee opened debate on impeachment. On July 30, the committee recommended House adoption of 3 articles of impeachment charging Nixon with obstruction of justice, abuse of power, and contempt of Congress.

On Aug. 5, Nixon released transcripts of conversations held 6 days after the Watergate break-in showing that Nixon had known of, approved, and directed Watergate cover-up activities. Nixon resigned from office Aug. 9.

Gerald Rudolph Ford

Gerald R. Ford, 38th president, Republican, was born July 14, 1913, in Omaha, Neb., son of Leslie King and Dorothy Gardner, and was named Leslie Jr. When he was 2, his parents were divorced and his mother moved with the boy to Grand Rapids, Mich. There she met and married Gerald R. Ford, who formally adopted the boy and gave him his own name.

He graduated from the Univ. of Michigan, 1935 and Yale Law School, 1941.

He began practicing law in Grand Rapids, but in 1942 joined the navy and served in the Pacific, leaving the service in 1946 as a lieutenant commander.

He entered congress in 1948 and continued to win elections, spending 25 years in the House, 8 of them as Republican leader.

On Oct. 12, 1973, after Vice President Spiro T. Agnew resigned, Ford was nominated by President Nixon to replace him. It was the first use of the procedures set out in the 25th Amendment.

When Nixon resigned Aug. 9, 1974, Ford became president, the first to serve without being chosen in a national election. On Sept. 8 he pardoned Nixon for any federal crimes he might have committed as president. Ford veoted 48 bills in his first 21 months in office, saying most would prove too costly. He visited China. In 1976, he was defeated in the election by Democrat Jimmy Carter.

Jimmy (James Earl) Carter

Jimmy (James Earl) Carter, 39th president, Democrat, was the first president from the Deep South since before the Civil War. He was born Oct. 1, 1924, at Plains, Ga., where his parents, James and Lillian Gordy Carter, had a farm and several businesses.

After studying at Georgia Tech, he entered the Naval Academy at Annapolis. On graduating, he entered the Navy's nuclear submarine program as an aide to Adm. Hyman Rickover, and also studied nuclear physics at Union College, Schenectady.

His father died in 1953 and Carter left the Navy to take over the family businesses — peanut-raising, warehousing, and cotton-ginning. He became a Baptist Church deacon, a Sunday school teacher, and public school board member, was elected to the Georgia state senate, was defeated for governor, 1966, but elected in 1970.

Carter won the Democratic nomination and defeated President Gerald R. Ford in the election of 1976.

In 1979, Carter played a major role in the peace negotiations between Israel and Egypt. In Nov., Iranian student militants attacked the U.S. embassy in Teheran and held members of the embassy staff hostage.

During 1980, Carter was widely criticized for the poor state of the economy and high inflation. He was also viewed as weak in his handling of foreign policy. He reacted to the Soviet invasion of Afghanistan by imposing a grain embargo and boycotting the Moscow Olympic games. His failure to obtain the release of the remaining 52 hostages held in Iran, whose first anniversary of capture fell on Election Day, plagued Carter to the end of his term. He was defeated by Ronald Reagan in the election. Carter finally succeeded in obtaining the release of the hostages on Inauguration Day, as the new president was taking the oath of office.

Ronald Wilson Reagan

Ronald Wilson Reagan, 40th president, Republican, was born Feb. 6, 1911, in Tampico, Ill., the son of John Edward Reagan and Nellie Wilson. Reagan graduated from Eureka (Ill.) College in 1932. Following his graduation, he worked for 5 years as a sports announcer in Des Moines, Ia.

Reagan began a successful career as a film actor in 1937, and starred in numerous movies, and later television, until the 1960s. He was a captain in the Army Air Force during World War II.

He served as president of the Screen Actors Guild from 1947 to 1952, and in 1959.

Once a liberal Democrat, Reagan became active in Republican politics during the 1964 presidential campaign of Barry Goldwater. He was elected governor of California in 1966, and reelected in 1970.

Following his retirement as governor, Reagan became the leading spokesman for the conservative wing of the Republican Party, and made a strong bid for the party's 1976 presidential nomination.

In 1980, he gained the Republican nomination and won a landslide victory over Jimmy Carter.

As president, he successfully forged a bipartisan coalition in Congress which led to enactment of his economic program which included the largest budget and tax cuts in U.S. history. In his 1982 State of the Union message, Reagan proposed a "new federalism," a sweeping transfer of social programs to the states.

During 1982, Reagan was plagued by a severe recession which caused high unemployment, and high interest rates which threatened to delay an economic recovery. There was a negative reaction in Congress to the massive deficit in his proposed fiscal 1983 budget.

Wives and Children of the Presidents

Listed in order of presidential administrations.

Name	State	Born	Married	Died	Sons	Daughters
Martha Dandridge Custis Washington	Va.	1732	1759	1802	...	...
Abigail Smith Adams	Mass.	1744	1764	1818	3	2
Martha Wayles Skelton Jefferson	Va.	1748	1772	1782	1	5
Dorothea "Dolley" Payne Todd Madison	N.C.	1768	1794	1849	...	...
Elizabeth Kortright Monroe	N.Y.	1768	1786	1830	... (1)	2
Louise Catherine Johnson Adams	Md. (2)	1775	1797	1852	3	1
Rachel Donelson Robards Jackson	Va.	1767	1791	1828	...	...
Hannah Hoes Van Buren	N.Y.	1783	1807	1819	4	...
Anna Symmes Harrison	N.J.	1775	1795	1864	6	4
Letitia Christian Tyler	Va.	1790	1813	1842	3	4
Julia Gardiner Tyler	N.Y.	1820	1844	1889	5	2
Sarah Childress Polk	Tenn.	1803	1824	1891	...	...
Margaret Smith Taylor	Md.	1788	1810	1852	1	5
Abigail Powers Fillmore	N.Y.	1798	1826	1853	1	1
Caroline Carmichael McIntosh Fillmore	N.J.	1813	1858	1881	...	...
Jane Means Appleton Pierce	N.H.	1806	1834	1863	3	...
Mary Todd Lincoln	Ky.	1818	1842	1882	4	...
Eliza McCardle Johnson	Tenn.	1810	1827	1876	3	2
Julia Dent Grant	Mo.	1826	1848	1902	3	1
Lucy Ware Webb Hayes	Oh.	1831	1852	1889	7	1
Lucretia Rudolph Garfield	Oh.	1832	1858	1918	4	1
Ellen Lewis Herndon Arthur	Va.	1837	1859	1880	2	1
Frances Folsom Cleveland	N.Y.	1864	1886	1947	2	3
Caroline Lavinia Scott Harrison	Oh.	1832	1853	1892	1	1
Mary Scott Lord Dimmick Harrison	Pa.	1858	1896	1948	...	1
Ida Saxton McKinley	Oh.	1847	1871	1907	...	2
Alice Hathaway Lee Roosevelt	Mass.	1861	1880	1884	...	1
Edith Kermit Carow Roosevelt	Conn.	1861	1886	1948	4	1
Helen Herron Taft	Oh.	1861	1886	1943	2	1
Ellen Louise Axson Wilson	Ga.	1860	1885	1914	...	3
Edith Bolling Galt Wilson	Va.	1872	1915	1961	...	...
Florence Kling De Wolfe Harding	Oh.	1860	1891	1924	...	...
Grace Anna Goodhue Coolidge	Vt.	1879	1905	1957	2	...
Lou Henry Hoover	Ia.	1875	1899	1944	2	...
Anna Eleanor Roosevelt Roosevelt	N.Y.	1884	1905	1962	4 (1)	1
Bess Wallace Truman	Mo.	1885	1919	...	...	1
Mamie Geneva Doud Eisenhower	Ia.	1896	1916	1979	1 (1)	...
Jacqueline Lee Bouvier Kennedy	N.Y.	1929	1953	...	1 (1)	1
Claudia "Lady Bird" Alta Taylor Johnson	Tex.	1912	1934	...	...	2
Thelma Catherine Patricia Ryan Nixon	Nev.	1912	1940	...	...	2
Elizabeth Bloomer Warren Ford	Ill.	1918	1948	...	3	1
Rosalynn Smith Carter	Ga.	1927	1946	...	3	1
Anne Frances "Nancy" Robbins Davis Reagan	N.Y.	1923	1952	...	1 (3)	1(3)

James Buchanan, 15th president, was unmarried. (1) plus one infant, deceased. (2) Born London, father a Md. citizen. (3) President Reagan has a son and daughter from a former marriage.

Presidents Pro Tempore of the Senate

Until 1890, presidents "pro tem" were named "for the occasion only." Beginning with that year, they have served "until the Senate otherwise ordered." Sen. John J. Ingalls, chosen under the old rule in 1887, was again elected, under the new rule, in 1890. Party designations are D, Democrat; R, Republican.

Name	Party	State	Elected
John J. Ingalls	R	Kan.	Apr. 3, 1890
Charles F. Manderson	R	Neb.	Mar. 2, 1891
Isham G. Harris	D	Tenn.	Mar. 22, 1893
Matt W. Ransom	D	N.C.	Jan. 7, 1895
Isham G. Harris	D	Tenn.	Jan. 10, 1895
William P. Frye	R	Me.	Feb. 7, 1896
Charles Curtis	R	Kan.	Dec. 4, 1911
Augustus O. Bacon	D	Ga.	Jan. 15, 1912
Jacob H. Gallinger	R	N.H.	Feb. 12, 1912
Henry Cabot Lodge	R	Mass.	Mar. 25, 1912
Frank R. Brandegee	R	Conn.	May 25, 1912
James P. Clarke	D	Ark.	Mar. 23, 1915
Willard Saulsbury	D	Del.	Dec. 14, 1916
Albert B. Cummins	R	Ia.	May 19, 1919
George H. Moses	R	N.H.	Mar. 6, 1925
Key Pittman	D	Nev.	Mar. 9, 1933
William H. King	D	Ut.	Nov. 19, 1940
Pat Harrison	D	Miss.	Jan. 6, 1941
Carter Glass	D	Va.	July 10, 1941
Kenneth McKellar	D	Tenn.	Jan. 6, 1945
Arthur H. Vandenberg	R	Mich.	Jan. 4, 1947
Kenneth McKellar	D	Tenn.	Jan. 3, 1949
Styles Bridges	R	N.H.	Jan. 3, 1953
Walter F. George	D	Ga.	Jan. 5, 1955
Carl Hayden	D	Ariz.	Jan. 3, 1957
Richard B. Russell	D	Ga.	Jan. 3, 1969
Allen J. Ellender	D	La.	Jan. 22, 1971
James O. Eastland	D	Miss.	July 28, 1972
Warren G. Magnuson	D	Wash.	Jan. 23, 1979
Strom Thurmond	R	S.C.	Jan. 5, 1981

Speakers of the House of Representatives

Party designations: A, American; D, Democratic; DR, Democratic Republican; F, Federalist; R, Republican; W, Whig. *Served only one day.

Name	Party	State	Tenure
Frederick Muhlenberg	F	Pa.	1789-1791
Jonathan Trumbull	F	Conn.	1791-1793
Frederick Muhlenberg	F	Pa.	1793-1795
Jonathan Dayton	F	N.J.	1795-1799
Theodore Sedgwick	F	Mass.	1799-1801
Nathaniel Macon	DR	N.C.	1801-1807
Joseph B. Varnum	DR	Mass.	1807-1811
Henry Clay	DR	Ky.	1811-1814
Langdon Cheves	DR	S.C.	1814-1815
Henry Clay	DR	Ky.	1815-1820
John W. Taylor	DR	N.Y.	1820-1821
Philip P. Barbour	DR	Va.	1821-1823
Henry Clay	DR	Ky.	1823-1825
John W. Taylor	D	N.Y.	1825-1827
Andrew Stevenson	D	Va.	1827-1834
John Bell	D	Tenn.	1834-1835
James K. Polk	D	Tenn.	1835-1839
Robert M. T. Hunter	D	Va.	1839-1841
John White	W	Ky.	1841-1843
John W. Jones	D	Va.	1843-1845
John W. Davis	D	Ind.	1845-1847
Robert C. Winthrop	W	Mass.	1847-1849
Howell Cobb	D	Ga.	1849-1851
Linn Boyd	D	Ky.	1851-1855
Nathaniel P. Banks	A	Mass.	1856-1857
James L. Orr	D	S.C.	1857-1859
William Pennington	R	N.J.	1860-1861
Galusha A. Grow	R	Pa.	1861-1863
Schuyler Colfax	R	Ind.	1863-1869
*Theodore M. Pomeroy	R	N.Y.	1869-1869
James G. Blaine	R	Me.	1869-1875
Michael C. Kerr	D	Ind.	1875-1876
Samuel J. Randall	D	Pa.	1876-1881
Joseph W. Keifer	R	Oh.	1881-1883
John G. Carlisle	D	Ky.	1883-1889
Thomas B. Reed	R	Me.	1889-1891
Charles F. Crisp	D	Ga.	1891-1895
Thomas B. Reed	R	Me.	1895-1899
David B. Henderson	R	Ia.	1899-1903
Joseph G. Cannon	R	Ill.	1903-1911
Champ Clark	D	Mo.	1911-1919
Frederick H. Gillett	R	Mass.	1919-1925
Nicholas Longworth	R	Oh.	1925-1931
John N. Garner	D	Tex.	1931-1933
Henry T. Rainey	D	Ill.	1933-1935
Joseph W. Byrns	D	Tenn.	1935-1936
William B. Bankhead	D	Ala.	1936-1940
Sam Rayburn	D	Tex.	1940-1947
Joseph W. Martin Jr.	R	Mass.	1947-1949
Sam Rayburn	D	Tex.	1949-1953
Joseph W. Martin Jr.	R	Mass.	1953-1955
Sam Rayburn	D	Tex.	1955-1961
John W. McCormack	D	Mass.	1962-1971
Carl Albert	D	Okla.	1971-1977
Thomas P. O'Neill Jr.	D	Mass.	1977-

National Political Parties

As of Mid-1982

Republican Party

National Headquarters—310 First St., SE, Washington, DC 20003.
Chairman—Richard Richards
Co-Chairman—Betty Heitman.
Deputy Chairmen—Richard Bond, Fred Biebel.
Vice Chairmen—Ranny Riecker, Clarke Reed, Bernard M. Shanley, Paula F. Hawkins, Shelia Roberge, Dennis Dunn, Edith Holm.
Secretary—Jean G. Birch.
Treasurer—Wm. J. McManus.
General Counsel—Roger Allan Moore.

Democratic Party

National Headquarters—1625 Massachusetts Ave., NW, Washington, DC 20036.
Chairman—Charles T. Manatt.
Vice Chairpersons—Richard Hatcher, Polly Baca Barragan, Lynn Culter.
Secretary—Dorothy V. Bush.
Treasurer—Charles Curry.
Finance Chairman—Peter G. Kelly.

Other Major Political Organizations

American Independent Party

(P.O. Box 3737, Simi Valley, CA 93063)
National Chairman—Tom Goodloe.
Secretary—Patricia Manning.
Treasurer—Lon L. Laymon.

American Party of the United States

(3600 Market St., Salt Lake City, UT 84119)
National Chairman—Earl Jeppson.
Secretary—Doris Feimer.
Treasurer—Dr. R. L. Youngblood.

Americans For Democratic Action

(1411 K St. NW, Washington, DC 20005)
President—Father Robert Drinan.
National Director—Leon Shull.
Chairperson Exec. Comm.—Winn Newman.

Comm. on Political Education, AFL-CIO

(AFL-CIO Building, 815 16th St., Wash., DC 20006)
Chairman—Lane Kirkland.
Secretary-Treasurer—Thomas R. Donahue.

Communist Party U.S.A.

(235 W. 23d St., New York, NY 10011)
National Chairman—Henry Winston.
General Secretary—Gus Hall.

Conservative Party of the State of N.Y.

(45 E. 29th St., New York, NY 10016)
Chairman—J. Daniel Mahoney.
Executive Director—Serphin R. Maltese.
Secretary—Wilson G. Price.
Treasurer—James E. O'Doherty.

Liberal Party of New York State

(1560 Broadway, New York, NY 10036)
Chairman—Donald S. Harrington.
First Vice Chairman—Nicholas Gyory.
Treasurer—Bernice Benedick.
Secretary & Executive Director—James F. Notaro.

Libertarian National Committee

(2300 Wisconsin Ave. NW, Washington, DC 20007)
Chair—Alicia G. Clark.
Vice-Chair—Sheldon Richman.
Secretary—Frances Eddy.
Treasurer—Vivian Baures.
National Director—Eric O'Keefe.

National States' Rights Party

(P.O. Box 1211, Marietta, GA 30061)
Chairman—J.B. Stoner.
Secretary—Edward R. Fields.
Treasurer—Peter Xavier.

Prohibition National Committee

(P.O. Box 2635, Denver, CO 80201)
National Chairman—Earl F. Dodge.
National Secretary—Rayford G. Feather.

Socialist Labor Party

In Minnesota: Industrial Gov't. Party
(914 Industrial Ave., Palo Alto, CA 94303)
National Secretary—Robert Bills.
Financial Secretary—Nathan Karp.

Socialist Workers Party

(14 Charles Lane, New York, NY 10014)
National Secretary—Jack Barnes.
National Co-Chairpersons—Malik Miah, Barry Sheppard, Mary-Alice Waters.

America's Third Parties

Since 1860, there have been only 4 presidential elections in which all third parties together polled more than 10% of the vote: the Populists (James Baird Weaver) in 1892, the National Progressives (Theodore Roosevelt) in 1912, the La Follette Progressives in 1924, and George Wallace's American Party in 1968. In 1948, the combined third parties (Henry Wallace's Progessives, Strom Thurmond's States' Rights party or Dixiecrats, Prohibition, Socialists, and others) received only 5.75% of the vote. In most elections since 1860, fewer than one vote in 20 has been cast for a third party. The only successful third party in American history was the Republican Party in the election of Abraham Lincoln in 1860.

Notable Third Parties

Party	Presidential nominee	Election	Issues	Strength in
Anti-Masonic	William Wirt	1832	Against secret societies and oaths	Pa., Vt.
Liberty	James G. Birney	1844	Anti-slavery	North
Free Soil	Martin Van Buren	1848	Anti-slavery	New York, Ohio
American (Know Nothing)	Millard Fillmore	1856	Anti-immigrant	Northeast, South
Greenback	Peter Cooper	1876	For "cheap money,"	
Greenback	James B. Weaver	1880	labor rights	National
Prohibition	John P. St. John	1884	Anti-liquor	National
Populist	James B. Weaver	1892	For "cheap money," end of national banks	South, West
Socialist	Eugene V. Debs	1900-20	For public ownership	National
Progressive (Bull Moose)	Theodore Roosevelt	1912	Against high tariffs	Midwest, West
Progressive	Robert M. LaFollette	1924	Farmer & labor rights	Midwest, West
Socialist	Norman Thomas	1928-48	Liberal reforms	National
Union	William Lemke	1936	Anti "New Deal"	National
States' Rights	Strom Thurmond	1948	For segregation	South
Progressive	Henry Wallace	1948	Anti-cold war	New York, California
American Independent	George Wallace	1968	For states' rights	South
American	John G. Schmitz	1972	For "law and order"	Far West, Oh., La.
None (Independent)	John B. Anderson	1980	A 3d choice	National

The Electoral College

The president and the vice president of the United States are the only elective federal officials not elected by direct vote of the people. They are elected by the members of the Electoral College, an institution that has survived since the founding of the nation despite repeated attempts in Congress to alter or abolish it. In the elections of 1824, 1876 and 1888 the presidential candidate receiving the largest popular vote failed to win a majority of the electoral votes.

On presidential election day, the first Tuesday after the first Monday in November of every 4th year, each state chooses as many electors as it has senators and representatives in Congress. In 1964, for the first time, as provided by the 23d Amendment to the Constitution, the District of Columbia voted for 3 electors. Thus, with 100 senators and 435 representatives, there are 538 members of the Electoral College, with a majority of 270 electoral votes needed to elect the president and vice president.

Political parties customarily nominate their lists of electors at their respective state conventions. An elector cannot be a member of Congress or any person holding federal office.

Some states print the names of the candidates for president and vice president at the top of the November ballot while others list only the names of the electors. In either case, the electors of the party receiving the highest vote are elected. The electors meet on the first Monday after the 2d Wednesday in December in their respective state capitals or in some other place prescribed by state legislatures. By long-established custom they vote for their party nominees, although the Constitution does not require them to do so. All of the state's electoral votes are then awarded to the winners. The only Constitutional requirement is that at least one of the persons each elector votes for shall not be an inhabitant of that elector's home state.

Certified and sealed lists of the votes of the electors in each state are mailed to the president of the U.S. Senate. He opens them in the presence of the members of the Senate and House of Representatives in a joint session held on Jan. 6 (the next day if that falls on a Sunday), and the electoral votes of all the states are then counted. If no candidate for president has a majority, the House of Representatives chooses a president from among the 3 highest candidates, with all representatives from each state combining to cast one vote for that state. If no candidate for vice president has a majority, the Senate chooses from the top 2, with the senators voting as individuals.

Political Divisions of the U.S. Senate and House of Representatives From 1857 (35th Cong.) to 1981-1983 (97th Cong.)

Source: Clerk of the House of Representatives

All figures reflect immediate result of elections.

		Senate					House of Representatives				
Congress	Years	Number of Senators	Democrats	Republicans	Other parties	Vacant	Number of Representatives	Democrats	Republicans	Other parties	Vacant
35th. . . .	1857-59	64	39	20	5		237	131	92	14	
36th. . . .	1859-61	66	38	26	2		237	101	113	23	
37th. . . .	1861-63	50	11	31	7	1	178	42	106	28	2
38th. . . .	1863-65	51	12	39			183	80	103		
39th. . . .	1865-67	52	10	42			191	46	145		
40th. . . .	1867-69	53	11	42			193	49	143		1
41st. . . .	1869-71	74	11	61		2	243	73	170		
42d	1871-73	74	17	57			243	104	139		
43d	1873-75	74	19	54		1	293	88	203		2
44th. . . .	1875-77	76	29	46		1	293	181	107	3	2
45th. . . .	1877-79	76	36	39	1		293	156	137		
46th. . . .	1879-81	76	43	33			293	150	128	14	1
47th. . . .	1881-83	76	37	37	2		293	130	152	11	
48th. . . .	1883-85	76	36	40			325	200	119	6	
49th. . . .	1885-87	76	34	41		1	325	182	140	2	1
50th. . . .	1887-89	76	37	39			325	170	151	4	
51st. . . .	1889-91	84	37	47			330	156	173	1	
52d	1891-93	88	39	47	2		333	231	88	14	
53d	1893-95	88	44	38	3	3	356	220	126	10	
54th. . . .	1895-97	88	39	44	5		357	104	246	7	
55th. . . .	1897-99	90	34	46	10		357	134	206	16	1
56th. . . .	1899-1901	90	26	53	11		357	163	185	9	
57th. . . .	1901-03	90	29	56	3	2	357	153	198	5	1
58th. . . .	1903-05	90	32	58			386	178	207		1
59th. . . .	1905-07	90	32	58			386	136	250		
60th. . . .	1907-09	92	29	61		2	386	164	222		
61st. . . .	1909-11	92	32	59		1	391	172	219		
62d	1911-13	92	42	49		1	391	228	162	1	
63d	1913-15	96	51	44	1		435	290	127	18	
64th. . . .	1915-17	96	56	39	1		435	231	193	8	3
65th. . . .	1917-19	96	53	42	1		435	[1]210	216	9	
66th. . . .	1919-21	96	47	48	1		435	191	237	7	
67th. . . .	1921-23	96	37	59			435	132	300	1	2
68th. . . .	1923-25	96	43	51	2		435	207	225	3	
69th. . . .	1925-27	96	40	54	1	1	435	183	247	5	
70th. . . .	1927-29	96	47	48	1		435	195	237	3	
71st. . . .	1929-31	96	39	56	1		435	163	267	1	4
72d	1931-33	96	47	48	1		435	[2]216	218	1	
73d	1933-35	96	59	36	1		435	313	117	5	
74th. . . .	1935-37	96	69	25	2		435	322	103	10	
75th. . . .	1937-39	96	75	17	4		435	333	89	13	
76th. . . .	1939-41	96	69	23	4		435	262	169	4	
77th. . . .	1941-43	96	66	28	2		435	267	162	6	
78th. . . .	1943-45	96	57	38	1		435	222	209	4	
79th. . . .	1945-47	96	57	38	1		435	243	190	2	
80th. . . .	1947-49	96	45	51			435	188	246	1	
81st. . . .	1949-51	96	54	42			435	263	171	1	
82d	1951-53	96	48	47	1		435	234	199	2	
83d	1953-55	96	46	48	2		435	213	221	1	
84th. . . .	1955-57	96	48	47	1		435	232	203		
85th. . . .	1957-59	96	49	47			435	234	201		
86th. . . .	1959-61	98	64	34			[3]436	283	153		
87th. . . .	1961-63	100	64	36			[4]437	262	175		
88th. . . .	1963-65	100	67	33			435	258	176		1
89th. . . .	1965-67	100	68	32			435	295	140		
90th. . . .	1967-69	100	64	36			435	248	187		
91st. . . .	1969-71	100	58	42			435	243	192		
92d	1971-73	100	54	44	2		435	255	180		
93d	1973-75	100	56	42	2		435	242	192	1	
94th. . . .	1975-77	100	61	37	2		435	291	144		
95th. . . .	1977-79	100	61	38	1		435	292	143		
96th. . . .	1979-81	100	58	41	1		435	277	158		
97th. . . .	1981-83	100	46	53	1		435	242	190		3

(1) Democrats organized House with help of other parties. (2) Democrats organized House due to Republican deaths. (3) Proclamation declaring Alaska a State issued Jan. 3, 1959. (4) Proclamation declaring Hawaii a State issued Aug. 21, 1959.

UNITED STATES GOVERNMENT

The Reagan Administration

As of mid-1982

Terms of office of the president and vice president, from Jan. 20, 1981 to Jan. 20, 1985. No person may be elected president of the United States for more than two 4-year terms.

President — Ronald Reagan of California receives salary of $200,000 a year taxable; in addition an expense allowance of $50,000 to assist in defraying expenses resulting from his official duties. Also there may be expended not exceeding $100,000, nontaxable, a year for travel expenses and $15,000 for official entertainment available for allocation within the Executive Office of the President. Congress has provided lifetime pensions of $69,630 a year, free mailing privileges, free office space, and up to $96,000 a year for office help for former Presidents except for the first 30 month period during which a former President is entitled to staff assistance for which an amount up to $150,000 a year may be paid, and $20,000 annually for their widows.

Vice President — George Bush of Texas receives salary of $79,125 a year and $10,000 for expenses, all of which is taxable.

For succession to presidency, see Succession in Index.

The Cabinet

(Salary: $69,630 per annum)

Secretary of State — George P. Shultz, Cal.
Secretary of Treasury — Donald T. Regan, N.Y.
Secretary of Defense — Caspar W. Weinberger, Cal.
Attorney General — William French Smith, Cal.
Secretary of Interior — James G. Watt, Col.
Secretary of Agriculture — John R. Block, Ill.
Secretary of Commerce — Malcoln Baldridge, Conn.
Secretary of Labor — Raymond J. Donovan, N.J.
Secretary of Health and Human Services — Richard S. Schweiker, Pa.
Secretary of Housing and Urban Development — Samuel R. Pierce Jr., N.Y.
Secretary of Transportation — Andrew L. Lewis Jr., Pa.
Secretary of Energy — James B. Edwards, S.C.
Secretary of Education — Terrel H. Bell, Ut.

The White House Staff

1600 Pennsylvania Ave. NW 20500

Counsellor to the President — Edwin Meese 3d.
Chief of Staff — James A. Baker 3d.
Deputy Chief of Staff — Michael K. Deaver.
Press Secretary to the President — James S. Brady.
Counsel to the President — Fred F. Fielding.
Presidential Assistants — Elizabeth Hanford-Dole (Public Liaison); Kenneth M. Duberstein (Legislative Affairs); David R. Gergen (Communications); E. Pendleton James (Presidential Personnel); Edward J. Rollins (Political Affairs); Richard Salisbury Williamson (Intergovernmental Affairs); Craig L. Fuller (Cabinet Affairs); Edward V. Hickey Jr. (Special Support Services).

Executive Agencies

National Security Council — Assistant to the President for Natl. Security Affairs — William P. Clark.
Council of Economic Advisers — Murray L. Weidenbaum, chmn.
Central Intelligence Agency — William J. Casey, dir.
Office of Management and Budget — David A. Stockman, dir.
U.S. Trade Representative — William E. Brock.
Office of Administration — John F. W. Rogers, dir.
Office of Policy Development — Asst. to the President for Policy Development — Edwin L. Harper.
Office of Science and Technology Policy — George A. Keyworth 2d, dir.
Council on Environmental Quality — A. Alan Hill, chmn.

Department of State

2201 C St. NW 20520

Secretary of State — George P. Shultz.
Deputy Secretary — Walter J. Stoessel.
Under Sec. for Political Affairs — Lawrence Eagleburger.
Under Sec. for Security Assistance, Science and Technology — vacant.
Under Sec. for Economic Affairs — vacant.
Under Secretary for Management — Richard T. Kennedy.
Counselor — James L. Buckley.
Legal Advisor — Davis Robinson.
Assistant Secretaries for:
- **Administration** — Thomas M. Tracy.
- **African Affairs** — Chester Crocker.
- **Congressional Relations** — Richard Fairbanks.
- **Economic Affairs** — Robert D. Hormats.
- **European Affairs** — Richard Burt.
- **Human Rights & Humanitarian Affairs** — Elliott Abrams.
- **Inter-American Affairs** — Thomas Enders.
- **International Organization Affairs** — Nicholas Platt, act.
- **Near-Eastern & S. Asian Affairs** — Nicholas Veliotes.
- **Public Affairs** — Dean Fischer.
- **Oceans & International Environmental & Scientific Affairs** — James L. Malone.

Consular Affairs — Diego Asencio.
Chief of Protocol — Selwa Roosevelt.
Dir. General, Foreign Service & Dir. of Personnel — Joan M. Clark.
Dir. of Intelligence & Research — Hugh Montgomery.
Dir. of Politico-Military Affairs — Richard Burt.
Office of Inspector General — Robert Lyle Brown.
Policy Planning Staff — Paul Wolfowitz.
Agency for International Development — M. Peter McPherson.
U.S. Rep. to the UN — Jeane Kirkpatrick.

Treasury Department

1500 Pennsylvania Ave. NW 20220

Secretary of the Treasury — Donald T. Regan.
Deputy Sec. of the Treasury — R. Tim McNamar.
Under Sec. for Monetary Affairs — Dr. Beryl Sprinkel.
Under Sec. for Tax and Economic Affairs — Dr. Norman Ture.
General Counsel — Peter J. Wallison.
Assistant Secretaries: — Marc Leland, John Walker, W. Dennis Thomas, Roger Mehle, John F. Kelly, Craig Roberts, John Chapoton, Ann Dore McLaughlin, Cora Beebe.
Bureaus:
- **Comptroller of the Currency** — Charles E. Lord, act.
- **Customs** — William T. Archey, act.
- **Engraving & Printing** — Harry R. Clements, dir.
- **Government Financial Operations** — William E. Douglas, comm.
- **Internal Revenue Service** — Roscoe Egger, comm.
- **Mint** — Donna Pope, dir.
- **Public Debt** — H. J. Hintgen, comm.
- **Treasurer of the U.S.** — Angela M. Buchanan.
- **U.S. Secret Service** — H. Stuart Knight, dir.

Department of Defense

The Pentagon 20301

Secretary of Defense — Caspar Weinberger.
Deputy Secretary — Frank C. Carlucci.
Executive Secretariat — Col. John H. Stanford.

Asst. Secretaries of Defense:
- **Policy** — Fred C. Ikle.
- **International Security Affairs** — Francis J. West Jr.
- **International Security Policy** — Richard N. Perle.
- **Research and Engineering** — Richard DeLauer.
- **Atomic Energy** — Richard Wagner.
- **Comptroller** — Jack Borsting.
- **Health Affairs** — Robert N. Smith.
- **Manpower, Reserve Affairs and Logistics** — Lawrence J. Korb.
- **Program Analysis and Evaluation** — David S. C. Chu.
- **Public Affairs** — Henry Catto Jr.
- **Legislative Affairs** — Russell A. Rourke.

Inspector General for Defense Intelligence — Werner E. Michel.
Chairman, Joint Chiefs of Staff — Gen. John W. Vessey Jr.
NATO Affairs: — Gen. Richard H. Groves.
General Counsel — William Howard Taft IV.

Department of the Army

The Pentagon 20301

Secretary of the Army — John O. Marsh Jr.
Under Secretary — James R. Ambrose.
Assistant Secretaries for:
- **Civil Works** — William R. Gianelli.
- **Installations, Logistics and Financial Management** — Joel E. Bonner Jr.
- **Research, Development and Acquisition** — Jay R. Sculley.
- **Manpower & Reserve Affairs** — Harry Walters.

Chief of Public Affairs — Brig. Gen. Lyle J. Barker Jr.
Chief of Staff — Gen. Edward C. Meyer.
General Counsel — Delbert Spurlock Jr.
Comptroller of the Army — Lt. Gen. Ernest Peixotto.
Surgeon General — Lt. Gen. Bernhard T. Mittemeyer.
Adjutant General — Gen. Robert M. Joyce.
Inspector General — Lt. Gen. Richard G. Trefry.
Judge Advocate General — Maj. Gen. Hugh Clausen.
Deputy Chiefs of Staff:
- **Logistics** — Lt. Gen. Richard H. Thompson.
- **Operations & Plans** — Lt. Gen. William R. Richardson.
- **Research, Development, Acquisition** — Lt. Gen. James H. Merryman.
- **Personnel** — Lt. Gen. Maxwell R. Thurman.

Ass't. Chief of Staff, Intelligence — Maj. Gen. William E. Odom.
Commanders:
- **U.S. Army Material Development and Readiness Command** — Gen. Donald R. Keith.
- **U.S. Army Forces Command** — Gen. Richard E. Cavazos.
- **U.S. Army Training and Doctrine Command** — Gen. Glenn T. Otis.
- **First U.S. Army** — Lt. Gen. Donald E. Rosenblum.
- **Fifth U.S. Army** — Lt. Gen. John R. McGiffert 2d.
- **Sixth U.S. Army** — Lt. Gen. Donald E. Grange Jr.
- **Military Dist. of Washington** — Maj. Gen. Jerry Curry.

Department of the Navy

The Pentagon 20350

Secretary of the Navy — John Lehman.
Under Secretary — James F. Goodrich
Assistant Secretaries for:
- **Financial Management** — Robert Conn, act.
- **Manpower, Reserve Affairs** — John S. Herrington.
- **Research & Engineering** — Melvin Paisley.
- **Shipbuilding & Logistics** — George A. Sawyer.

Judge Advocate General — RADM John S. Jenkins.
Chief of Naval Operations — Adm. Thomas B. Hayward.
Chief of Naval Material — Adm. John G. Williams Jr.
Chief of Information — COMO Jack J. Garrow.
Surgeon General/Chief, Bureau of Medicine & Surgery — VADM J. William Cox.
Naval Military Personnel Command — RADM Robert F. Dunn.
Military Sealift Command — VADM K. J. Carroll.
Chief of Naval Personnel — VADM Lando W. Zech Jr.
Commandants, Naval Bases:
- **Philadelphia** — RADM Clarence A. E. Johnson Jr.
- **Norfolk** — RADM Joseph F. Frick.
- **Charleston** — RADM Robert B. McClinton.
- **San Diego and San Francisco** — RADM Paul T. Gillcrist.
- **Seattle** — RADM James D. Williams.
- **Pearl Harbor** — RADM Stanley J. Anderson.
- **Commandant, Naval District Washington** — RADM Lowell R. Myers.

U.S. Marine Corps: (zip code: 20380)

Commandant — Gen. Robert H. Barrow.
- **Asst. Commandant/Chief of Staff** — Gen. Paul X. Kelley.

Department of the Air Force

The Pentagon 20330

Secretary of the Air Force — Verne Orr.
Under Secretary — Edward C. Aldridge Jr.
Assistant Secretaries for:
- **Financial Management** — Russell D. Hale.
- **Research, Development & Logistics** — Alton G. Keel Jr.
- **Manpower, Reserve Affairs & Installations** — Tidal W. McCoy.

General Counsel — David E. Place.
Public Affairs — Richard Abel.
Director of Space Systems — Jimmie D. Hill.
Chief of Staff — Gen. Lew Allen Jr.
Surgeon General — Lt. Gen. Paul W. Myers.
Judge Advocate — Maj. Gen. Thomas B. Bruton.
Inspector General — Maj. Gen. Howard W. Leaf.
Deputy Chiefs of Staff:
- **Logistics & Engineering** — Lt. Gen. Billy M. Minter.
- **Programs & Resources** — Lt. Gen. Charles C. Blanton.
- **Manpower & Personnel** — Lt. Gen. Andrew P. Iosue.
- **Research, Development & Acquisition** — Lt. Gen. Kelly H. Burke.
- **Plans & Operations** — Lt. Gen. Jerome F. O'Malley.

Major Air Commands:
- **AF Logistics Command** — Gen. James P. Mullins.
- **AF Systems Command** — Gen. Robert T. Marsh.
- **Air Training Command** — Gen. Thomas M. Ryan Jr.
- **Military Airlift Command** — Gen. James R. Allen.
- **Strategic Air Command** — Gen. Bennie L. Davis.
- **Tactical Air Command** — Gen. Wilbur L. Creech.
- **Alaskan Air Command** — Lt. Gen. Lynwood E. Clark.
- **Pacific Air Forces** — Lt. Gen. Arnold W. Braswell.
- **USAF Europe** — Gen. Charles A. Gabriel.
- **Electronic Security Command** — Maj. Gen. Doyle E. Larson.
- **AF Communications Command** — Maj. Gen. Robert F. McCarthy.

Department of Justice

Constitution Ave. & 10th St. NW 20530

Attorney General — William French Smith.
Deputy Attorney General — Edward C. Schmults.
Legal Policy — Jonathan C. Rose.
Legal Counsel — Theodore B. Olsen.
Intelligence Policy & Review — Richard C. Willard.
Professional Responsibility —Michael E. Shaheen Jr.
Solicitor General — Rex E. Lee.
Associate Attorney General — Rudolph W. Giuliani.
- **Antitrust Division** — William F. Baxter.
- **Civil Division** — J. Paul McGrath.
- **Civil Rights Division** — Bradford Reynolds.
- **Criminal Division** — D. Lowell Jensen.
- **Drug Enforcement Admin.** — Francis Mullen.
- **Justice Management Division** — Kevin D. Rooney.
- **Land & Natural Resources Division** — Carol E. Dinkins.
- **Office of Legislative Affairs** — Robert A. McConnel.
- **Tax Division** — Glenn L. Archer Jr.

Fed. Bureau of Investigation — William H. Webster, dir.
Board of Immigr. Appeals — David L. Milhollan, chmn.

Bureau of Prisons — Norman A. Carlson, dir.
Office of Public Affairs — Thomas P. DeCair.
Immigration and Naturalization Service — Doris Meissner, act. comm.
Pardon Attorney — D. C. Stephenson, act.
U.S. Parole Commission — Benjamin Baer, chmn.
U.S. Marshalls Service — William E. Hall.

Department of the Interior

C St. between 18th & 19th Sts. NW 20240

Secretary of the Interior — James G. Watt.
Under Secretary — Donald P. Hodel.
Assistant Secretaries for:
- **Fish, Wildlife and Parks** — G. Ray Arnett.
- **Energy & Minerals** — Daniel L. Miller Jr.
- **Land and Water Resources** — Garrey Carruthers.
- **Policy, Budget, and Administration** — J. Robinson West.
- **Indian Affairs** — Kenneth L. Smith.

Bureau of Land Management — Bob Burford, dir.
Bureau of Mines — Robert C. Horton, Dir.
Bureau of Reclamation — Robert Broadbent, comm.
Fish & Wildlife Service — Robert A. Jantzen, Dir.
Geological Survey — Dallas L. Peck, dir.
National Park Service — Russell Dickenson, dir.
Public Affairs — Douglas Baldwin.
Office of Water Research and Technology — Gary D. Cobb.
Office of Congressional and Legislative Affairs — Stanley W. Hulett.
Solicitor — William H. Coldiron.

Department of Agriculture

The Mall, 12th & 14th Sts. 20250

Secretary of Agriculture — John R. Block.
Deputy Secretary — Raymond E. Lyng.
Executive Assistant — Ray Lett.
Administration — John E. Schrote.
Internat. Affairs & Commodity Programs — Seely Lodwick.
Food & Consumer Services — Mary C. Jarratt.
Marketing Services & Transportation — C. W. McMillan.
Small Community Rural Development — Frank Naylor.
Economics, Policy Analysis and Budget — William Gene Lesher.
Governmental & Public Affairs — Claude Gifford, act.
Natural Resources & Environment — John B. Crowell.
General Counsel — A. James Barnes.
Science & Education Admin. — Anson R. Bertrand, dir.

Department of Commerce

14th St. between Constitution & E St. NW 20230

Secretary of Commerce — Malcolm Baldridge.
Deputy Secretary — Guy W. Fiske.
Congressional Affairs — Paul A. Vander Myde.
Inspector General — Sherman M. Funk.
General Counsel — Sherman E. Unger.
Off. of Productivity, Technology & Innovation — Egils Milbergs, dir.
Administration — Arlene Triplett.
Bureau of the Census — Bruce K. Chapman, dir.
Bureau of Economic Analysis — George Jaszi, Dir.
Under Secy. for International Trade — Lionel H. Olmer
Asst. Secy. for Econ. Affairs — Robert Dederick.
Natl. Oceanic & Atmospheric Admin. — John V. Byrne.
Natl. Technical Info. Service — Melvin Day, dir.
Economic Develop. Admin. — Carlos Campbell.
Natl. Bureau of Standards — Ernest Ambler, dir.
Minority Business Development Agency — Victor M. Rivera, dir.
Office of Product Standards — Howard I. Forman.
Natl. Telecomm. & Information Admin. — Bernard J. Wunder Jr.
Travel & Tourism Adm. — Peter McCoy.
Bureau of Industrial Economics — Beatrice N. Vaccaro, dir.
Public Affairs — Mary A. Nimmo.

Department of Labor

200 Constitution Ave. NW 20210

Secretary of Labor — Raymond J. Donovan.
Under Secretary — Malcolm Lovell.
Executive Assistant-Counselor — Donald Rosenthal.
Assistant Secretaries for:
- **Administration and Management** — Alfred M. Zuck.
- **Employment and Training** — Albert Angrisani.
- **Mine Safety & Health** — Ford B. Ford.
- **Occupational Safety & Health** — Thorne G. Auchter.
- **Policy, Evaluation and Research** — John F. Cogan.
- **Labor Management Relations** — Donald Dotson.
- **Veterans Employment** — William Plowden.

Solicitor of Labor — T. Timothy Ryan.
Comm. of Labor Statistics — Janet Norwood.
Dep. Under Secy. for Employment Standards — Robert B. Collyer.
Dep. Under Secy. for Internatl. Affairs — vacant.
Dep. Under Secy. for Legislation & Intergovernmental Relations — Robert W. Searby.
Office of Information & Public Affairs — Earl G. Cox.
Dir. of Women's Bureau — Lenora Cole-Alexander.

Department of Health and Human Services

200 Independence Ave. SW 20201

Secretary of HHS — Richard S. Schweiker.
Under Secretary — David Swoap.
Assistant Secretaries for:
- **Management and Budget** — Dale W. Sopper.
- **Public Affairs** — Pamila Bailey.
- **Health** — Edward Brandt, M.D.
- **Planning and Evaluation** — Robert J. Rubin, M.D.
- **Human Development Services** — Dorcas Hardy.
- **Legislation** — Thomas Donnelly.
- **Personnel Administration** — Thomas McFee.

General Counsel — Juan Del Real.
Inspector General — Richard P. Kusserow.
Civil Rights — Betty Lou Dotson.
Health Care Financing Admin. — Carolyn Davis, adm.
Social Security Adm. — John Svahn, comm.

Department of Housing and Urban Development

451 7th St. SW 20410

Secretary of Housing & Urban Development — Samuel R. Pierce Jr.
Under Secretary — Donald I. Hovde.
Assistant Secretaries for:
- **Administration** — Judith L. Tardy.
- **Community Planning & Development** — Stephen Bollinger.
- **Fair Housing & Equal Opportunity** — Antonio Monroig.
- **Housing & Federal Housing Commissioner** — Philip Winn.
- **Legislation & Intergovernmental Relations** — Steve May.
- **Policy Development & Research** — E. S. Savas.

President, Govt. Natl. Mortgage Assn. — Robert W. Karpe.
Public Affairs — Leonard Burchman.
International Affairs — Theodore Britton Jr., act.
Labor Relations — B.A. Smith.
General Counsel — John J. Knapp.
Inspector General — Charles L. Dempsey.

Department of Transportation

400 7th St. SW 20590

Secretary of Transportation — Andrew L. Lewis.
Deputy Secretary — Darrell T. Trent.
Assistant Secretaries — Judith T. Connor (Policy and International Affairs); Donald Derman (Budget and Programs); Robert Fairman, act. (Administration); Lee L. Verstandig (Governmental Affairs).
General Counsel — John M. Fowler.
National Highway Traffic Safety Admin. — Raymond A. Peck Jr.
U. S. Coast Guard Commandant — John B. Hayes.

Federal Aviation Admin. — J. Lynn Helms.
Federal Highway Admin. — Ray Barnhart.
Federal Railroad Admin. — Robert W. Blanchette.
Urban Mass Transportation Admin. — Arthur E. Teele Jr.
Research & Special Programs Admin. — Howard Duqoff.
Saint Lawrence Seaway Development Corp. Admin. — David W. Oberlin.

Department of Energy

1000 Independence Ave. SW 20585

Secretary of Energy — James B. Edwards.
Deputy Secy. — W. Kenneth Davis.
Assistant Secretaries — William S. Heffelfinger (Management & Administration); Robert C. Odle Jr. (Congressional, Intergovernmental & Public Affairs); Henry Thomas (International Affairs); Shelby Brewer (Nuclear Energy); Jan W. Mares (Fossil Energy); Herman Roser (Defense Programs); William A. Vaughn (Environmental Protection Safety & Emergency Preparedness); Joseph Tribble (Conservation & Renewable Energy).
Federal Energy Regulatory Comm. — Charles M. Butler 3d, chmn.
Off. of Policy Planning & Analysis — Jay Hunter Chiles.
Inspector General — James R. Richards.
Economic Regulatory Admin. — Rayburn Hanzlik.
Energy Information Adm. — J. Erich Evered.
Office of Energy Research — Alvin Trivelpiece, dir.

Department of Education

Wash., D.C. 20202

Secretary of Education — Terrel H. Bell.
Under Secretary — William C. Clohan Jr.
Deputy Under Secretaries — Gary Jones, Kent Lloyd, John Rodriguez.
General Counsel — Dan Oliver.
Assistant Secretaries:
- **Legislation & Public Affairs** — Anne Graham.
- **Elementary and Secondary Education** — Vincent Reed.
- **Postsecondary Education** — Thomas P. Melady.
- **Educational Research and Improvement** — Donald J. Senese.
- **Vocational & Adult Education** — Robert Worthington.
- **Special Education and Rehabilitative Services** — Jean Tufts.
- **Civil Rights** — Clarence Thomas.

Judiciary of the U.S.

Data as of mid 1982

Justices of the United States Supreme Court

The Supreme Court comprises the chief justice of the United States and 8 associate justices, all appointed by the president with advice and consent of the Senate. Salaries: chief justice $96,800 annually, associate justice $93,000.

Name; apptd from *Chief Justices in italics*	Service Term	Yrs.	Born	Died
John Jay, N. Y.	1789-1795	5	1745	1829
John Rutledge, S. C.	1789-1791	1	1739	1800
William Cushing, Mass.	1789-1810	20	1732	1810
James Wilson, Pa.	1789-1798	8	1742	1798
John Blair, Va.	1789-1796	6	1732	1800
James Iredell, N. C.	1790-1799	9	1751	1799
Thomas Johnson, Md.	1791-1793	1	1732	1819
William Paterson, N. J.	1793-1806	13	1745	1806
John Rutledge, S.C.	1795(a)	—	1739	1800
Samuel Chase, Md.	1796-1811	15	1741	1811
Oliver Ellsworth, Conn.	1796-1800	4	1745	1807
Bushrod Washington, Va.	1798-1829	31	1762	1829
Alfred Moore, N. C.	1799-1804	4	1755	1810
John Marshall, Va.	1801-1835	34	1755	1835
William Johnson, S. C.	1804-1834	30	1771	1834
Henry B. Livingston, N. Y.	1806-1823	16	1757	1823
Thomas Todd, Ky.	1807-1826	18	1765	1826
Joseph Story, Mass.	1811-1845	33	1779	1845
Gabriel Duval, Md.	1811-1835	22	1752	1844
Smith Thompson, N. Y.	1823-1843	20	1768	1843
Robert Trimble, Ky.	1826-1828	2	1777	1828
John McLean, Oh.	1829-1861	32	1785	1861
Henry Baldwin, Pa.	1830-1844	14	1780	1844
James M. Wayne, Ga.	1835-1867	32	1790	1867
Roger B. Taney, Md.	1836-1864	28	1777	1864
Philip P. Barbour, Va.	1836-1841	4	1783	1841
John Catron, Tenn.	1837-1865	28	1786	1865
John McKinley, Ala.	1837-1852	15	1780	1852
Peter V. Daniel, Va.	1841-1860	19	1784	1860
Samuel Nelson, N. Y.	1845-1872	27	1792	1873
Levi Woodbury, N. H.	1845-1851	5	1789	1851
Robert C. Grier, Pa.	1846-1870	23	1794	1870
Benjamin R. Curtis, Mass.	1851-1857	6	1809	1874
John A. Campbell, Ala.	1853-1861	8	1811	1889
Nathan Clifford, Me.	1858-1881	23	1803	1881
Noah H. Swayne, Oh.	1862-1881	18	1804	1884
Samuel F. Miller, Ia.	1862-1890	28	1816	1890
David Davis, Ill.	1862-1877	14	1815	1886
Stephen J. Field, Cal.	1863-1897	34	1816	1899
Salmon P. Chase, Oh.	1864-1873	8	1808	1873
William Strong, Pa.	1870-1880	10	1808	1895
Joseph P. Bradley, N. J.	1870-1892	21	1813	1892
Ward Hunt, N. Y.	1872-1882	9	1810	1886
Morrison R. Waite, Oh.	1874-1888	14	1816	1888
John M. Harlan, Ky.	1877-1911	34	1833	1911
William B. Woods, Ga.	1880-1887	6	1824	1887
Stanley Matthews, Oh.	1881-1889	7	1824	1889
Horace Gray, Mass.	1881-1902	20	1828	1902
Samuel Blatchford, N. Y.	1882-1893	11	1820	1893
Lucius Q. C. Lamar, Miss.	1888-1893	5	1825	1893
Melville W. Fuller, Ill.	1888-1910	21	1833	1910
David J. Brewer, Kan.	1889-1910	20	1837	1910
Henry B. Brown, Mich.	1890-1906	15	1836	1913
George Shiras Jr., Pa.	1892-1903	10	1832	1924
Howell E. Jackson, Tenn.	1893-1895	2	1832	1895
Edward D. White, La.	1894-1910	16	1845	1921
Rufus W. Peckham, N. Y.	1895-1909	13	1838	1909
Joseph McKenna, Cal.	1898-1925	26	1843	1926
Oliver W. Holmes, Mass.	1902-1932	29	1841	1935
William R. Day, Oh.	1903-1922	19	1849	1923
William H. Moody, Mass.	1906-1910	3	1853	1917
Horace H. Lurton, Tenn.	1909-1914	4	1844	1914
Charles E. Hughes, N. Y.	1910-1916	5	1862	1948
Willis Van Devanter, Wy.	1910-1937	26	1859	1941
Joseph R. Lamar, Ga.	1910-1916	5	1857	1916
Edward D. White, La.	1910-1921	10	1845	1921
Mahlon Pitney, N. J.	1912-1922	10	1858	1924
James C. McReynolds, Tenn.	1914-1941	26	1862	1946
Louis D. Brandeis, Mass.	1916-1939	22	1856	1941
John H. Clarke, Oh.	1916-1922	5	1857	1945
William H. Taft, Conn.	1921-1930	8	1857	1930
George Sutherland, Ut.	1922-1938	15	1862	1942
Pierce Butler, Minn.	1922-1939	16	1866	1939
Edward T. Sanford, Tenn.	1923-1930	7	1865	1930
Harlan F. Stone, N. Y.	1925-1941	16	1872	1946
Charles E. Hughes, N. Y.	1930-1941	11	1862	1948
Owen J. Roberts, Pa.	1930-1945	15	1875	1955
Benjamin N. Cardozo, N.Y.	1932-1938	6	1870	1938
Hugo L. Black, Ala.	1937-1971	34	1886	1971
Stanley F. Reed, Ky.	1938-1957	19	1884	1980
Felix Frankfurter, Mass.	1939-1962	23	1882	1965
William O. Douglas, Conn.	1939-1975	36	1898	1980
Frank Murphy, Mich.	1940-1949	9	1890	1949
Harlan F. Stone, N. Y.	1941-1946	5	1872	1946
James F. Byrnes, S. C.	1941-1942	1	1879	1972
Robert H. Jackson, N. Y.	1941-1954	12	1892	1954
Wiley B. Rutledge, Ia.	1943-1949	6	1894	1949
Harold H. Burton, Oh.	1945-1958	13	1888	1964
Fred M. Vinson, Ky.	1946-1953	7	1890	1953
Tom C. Clark, Tex.	1949-1967	18	1899	1977
Sherman Minton, Ind.	1949-1956	7	1890	1965
Earl Warren, Cal.	1953-1969	16	1891	1974

Name; apptd from	Service Term	Yrs.	Born	Died
John Marshall Harlan, N. Y.	1955-1971	16	1899	1971
William J. Brennan Jr., N. J.	1956	—	1906	—
Charles E. Whittaker, Mo.	1957-1962	5	1901	1973
Potter Stewart, Oh.	1958-1981	23	1915	—
Byron R. White, Col.	1962	—	1917	—
Arthur J. Goldberg, Ill.	1962-1965	3	1908	—
Abe Fortas, Tenn.	1965-1969	4	1910	1982
Thurgood Marshall, N.Y.	1967	—	1908	—
Warren E. Burger, Va.	1969	—	1907	—
Harry A. Blackmun, Minn.	1970	—	1908	—
Lewis F. Powell Jr., Va.	1972	—	1907	—
William H. Rehnquist, Ariz.	1972	—	1924	—
John Paul Stevens, Ill.	1975	—	1920	—
Sandra Day O'Connor, Ariz.	1981	—	1930	

(a) Rejected Dec. 15, 1795.

U.S. Court of Customs and Patent Appeals

Washington, DC 20439 (Salaries, $74,300)

Chief Judge — Howard T. Markey.

Associate Judges — Giles S. Rich, Phillip B. Baldwin, Jack R. Miller, Helen W. Niles.

U.S. Court of International Trade

New York, NY 10007 (Salaries, $70,300)

Chief Judge — Edward D. Re.

Judges — Paul P. Rao, Morgan Ford, Scovel Richardson, Frederick Landis, James L. Watson, Herbert N. Maletz, Bernard Newman, Nils A. Boe.

U.S. Court of Claims

Washington, DC 20005 (Salaries, $74,300)

Chief Judge — Daniel M. Friedman

Associate Judges — Oscar H. Davis, Shiro Kashiwa, Robert L. Kunzig, Marion T. Bennett, Philip Nichols Jr., Edward S. Smith.

U.S. Tax Court

Washington DC 20217 (Salaries, $70,300)

Chief Judge — Theodore Tannenwald Jr.

Judges — Irene F. Scott, William M. Fay, Howard A. Dawson Jr., Charles R. Simpson, Leo H. Irwin, Samuel B. Sterrett, William A. Goffe, Darrell D. Wiles, Richard C. Wilbur, Herbert L. Chabot, Arthur L. Nims 3d, Edna G. Parker, C. Moxley Featherston, Jules J. Korner 3d, Meade Whitaker.

U.S. Courts of Appeals

(Salaries, $74,300. CJ means Chief Judge)

District of Columbia — Spottswood W. Robinson 3d, CJ; J. Skelly Wright, Edward Allen Tamm, Roger Robb, George E. MacKinnon, Malcolm Richard Wilkey, Patricia M. Wald, Abner J. Mikva, Harry T. Edwards, Ruth Bader Ginsburg; Clerk's Office, Washington, DC 20001.

First Circuit (Me., Mass., N.H., R.I., Puerto Rico) — Frank M. Coffin, CJ; Levin H. Campbell, Hugh H. Bownes, Stephen Breyer; Clerk's Office, Boston, MA 02109.

Second Circuit (Conn., N.Y., Vt.) — Wilfred Feinberg, CJ; Irving R. Kaufman, James L. Oakes, Ellsworth Van Graafeiland, Thomas J. Meskill, Jon O. Newman, Amalya Lyle Kearse, Richard J. Cardamone, Lawrence W. Pierce, Ralph K. Winter Jr.; Clerk's Office, New York, NY 10007.

Third Circuit (Del., N.J., Pa., Virgin Is.) — Collins J. Seitz, CJ; Ruggero J. Aldisert, Arlin M. Adams, John J. Gibbons, James Hunter 3d, Joseph F. Weis Jr., Leonard I. Garth, A. Leon Higginbotham Jr., Dolores K. Sloviter; Clerk's Office, Philadelphia, PA 19106.

Fourth Circuit (Md., N.C., S.C., Va., W.Va.) — Harrison L. Winter, CJ; Kenneth K. Hall, John D. Butzner Jr., Donald Stuart Russell, H. Emory Widener Jr., James D. Phillips Jr., Francis D. Murnaghan Jr., James M. Sprouse, Sam J. Ervin 3d, Robert F. Chapman; Clerk's Office, Richmond, VA 23219.

Fifth Circuit (La., Miss., Tex., Canal Zone) — Charles Clark, CJ; John R. Brown, Thomas G. Gee, Alvin B. Rubin, Reynaldo G. Garza, Thomas M. Reavley, Henry A. Politz, Carolyn D. Randall, Samuel D. Johnson, Albert Tate Jr., Jerre S. Williams, William L. Garwood; Clerk's Office, New Orleans, LA 70130.

Sixth Circuit (Ky., Mich., Ohio, Tenn.) — George Clifton Edwards Jr., CJ; Albert J. Engel, Pierce Lively, Gilbert S. Merritt, Damon J. Keith, Bailey Brown, Cornelia G. Kennedy, Boyce F. Martin Jr., Nathaniel R. Jones; Clerk's Office, Cincinnati, OH 45202.

Seventh Circuit (Ill., Ind., Wis.) — Walter J. Cummings, CJ; Wilbur F. Pell Jr., Robert A. Sprecher, Harlington Wood Jr., William J. Bauer, Richard D. Cudahy, Richard A. Posner, Jesse E. Eschbach; Clerk's Office, Chicago, IL 60604.

Eighth Circuit (Ark., Ia., Minn., Mo., Neb., N.D., S.D.) — Donald P. Lay, CJ; Gerald W. Heaney, Myron H. Bright, Donald R. Ross, Roy L. Stephenson, J. Smith Henley, Theodore McMillian, Richard S. Arnold; Clerk's Office, St. Louis, MO 63101.

Ninth Circuit (Ariz., Cal., Ida., Mont., Nev., Ore., Wash., Alaska, Ha., Guam, N. Mariana Islands) — James R. Browning, CJ; Eugene A. Wright, Herbert Y. C. Choy, J. Clifford Wallace, Alfred T. Goodwin, Anthony M. Kennedy, J. Blaine Anderson, Procter Hug Jr., Thomas Tang, Joseph T. Sneed, Jerome Farris, Betty B. Fletcher, Mary M. Schroeder, Otto R. Skopil Jr., Harry Pregerson, Arthur L. Alarcon, Cecil F. Poole, Warren J. Ferguson, Dorothy W. Nelson, William C. Canby Jr., Robert Boochever, William A. Norris, Stephen Reinhardt; Clerk's Office, San Francisco, CA 94101.

Tenth Circuit (Col., Kan., N.M., Okla., Ut., Wy.) — Oliver Seth, CJ; William J. Holloway Jr., Robert H. McWilliams, James E. Barrett, William E. Doyle, Monroe G. McKay, James K. Logan, Stephanie K. Seymour; Clerk's Office, Denver, CO 80294.

Eleventh Circuit (Ala. Fla., Ga.)— John C. Godbold, CJ; Paul H. Roney, Gerald B. Tjoflat, James C. Hill, Peter T. Fay, Robert S. Vance, Phyllis A. Kravitch, Frank M. Johnson Jr., Albert J. Henderson, Joseph W. Hatchett, R. Lanier Anderson 3d, Thomas C. Clark; Clerk's Office, Atlanta GA 30303.

Temporary Emergency Court of Appeals — Edward Allen Tamm, CJ; Clerk's Office, Washington, DC 20001.

U.S. District Courts

(Salaries, $70,300. CJ means Chief Judge)

Alabama — Northern: Sam C. Pointer Jr., CJ; James Hughes Hancock, J. Foy Guin Jr., Robert B. Probst, E. B. Haltom Jr., U. W. Clemon; Clerk's Office, Birmingham 35203. **Middle:** Robert E. Varner, CJ; Truman M. Hobbs, Myron H. Thompson; Clerk's Office, Montgomery 36101. **Southern:** William Brevard Hand, CJ; Emmett R. Cox; Clerk's Office, Mobile 36601.

Alaska — James A. von der Heydt, CJ; James M. Fitzgerald; Clerk's Office, Anchorage 99513.

Arizona — C. A. Muecke, CJ; William P. Copple, Mary Ann Richey, Vlademar A. Cordova, Richard M. Bilby, Charles L. Hardy, Alfredo C. Marquez, Earl H. Carroll; Clerk's Office, Phoenix 85025.

Arkansas — Eastern: Garnett Thomas Eisele, CJ; Elsijane Trimble Roy, William Ray Overton, Henry Woods, George Howard Jr.; Clerk's Office, Little Rock 72203. **Western:** H. Franklin Waters, CJ; Elsijane Trimble Roy, George Howard Jr.; Clerk's Office, Fort Smith 72902.

California — Northern: Robert F. Peckham, CJ; Lloyd H. Burke, Stanley A. Weigel, Robert H. Schnacke, Samuel Conti, Spencer M. Williams, William H. Orrick Jr., William W. Schwarzer, William A. Ingram, Robert P. Aguilar, Thelton E. Henderson, Marilyn H. Patel, George B. Harris, William T. Sweigert, Alfonso Zirpoli; Clerk's Office, San Francisco 94102. **Eastern:** Philip C. Wilkins, CJ; Lawrence K. Karlton, Milton L. Schwartz, Edward Dean Price, Raul A. Ramirez; Clerk's Office, Sacramento 95814. **Central:** A. Andrew Hauk, CJ; William P. Gray, Manuel L. Real, Robert J. Kelleher, Wm. Matthew Byrne Jr., Lawrence T. Lydick, Malcolm M. Lucas, Robert M. Takasugi, Laughlin E. Waters, Mariana R. Pfaelzer, Terry J. Hatter Jr., A. Wallace Tashima, Consuelo Bland Marshall, David V. Kenyon, Cynthia H. Hall; Clerk's Office, Los Angeles 90012. **Southern:** Edward J. Schwartz, CJ; Howard B. Turrentine, Gordon Thompson Jr., Leland C. Nielsen, William B. Enright, Judith N. Keep, Earl B. Gilliam; Clerk's Office, San Diego 92189.

Colorado — Fred M. Winner, CJ; Sherman G. Finesilver, Richard P. Matsch, John L. Kane, Jim R. Carrigan, Zita L. Weinshienk; Clerk's Office, Denver 80294.

Connecticut — T. Emmet Clarie, CJ; T. F. Gilroy Daly, Ellen B. Burns, Warren W. Eginton, Jose A. Cabranes; Clerk's Office, New Haven 06505.

Delaware — James L. Latchum, CJ; Walter K. Stapleton, Murray M. Schwartz; Clerk's Office, Wilmington 19801.

District of Columbia — John Lewis Smith Jr., CJ; Aubrey E. Robinson Jr., Gerhard A. Gesell, John H. Pratt, June L. Green, Barrington D. Parker, Charles R. Richey, Thomas A. Flannery, Louis F. Oberdorfer, Harold H. Greene, John Garrett Penn, Joyce

Hens Green, Norma H. Johnson; Clerk's Office, Washington DC 20001.

Florida — Northern: William H. Stafford Jr. CJ; Lynn C. Higby; Clerk's Office, Tallahassee 32301. **Middle:** Ben Krentzman, CJ; Howell W. Melton, William Terrell Hodges, John A. Reed Jr., George C. Carr, Susan H. Black, William J. Castagna; John H. Moore 2d; Clerk's Office, Jacksonville 32201. **Southern:** C. Clyde Atkins, CJ; Joe Eaton, James Lawrence King, Norman C. Roettger Jr.; Sidney M. Aronovitz, William H. Hoeveler, Jose A. Gonzalez, James W. Kehoe, Eugene P. Spellman, Edward B. Davis, James C. Paine, Alcee L. Hastings; Clerk's Office, Miami 33101.

Georgia — Northern: Charles A.Moye Jr., CJ; William C.O'Kelley, Richard C. Freeman, Harold L. Murphy, Marvin H. Shoob, G. Ernest Tidwell, Orinda Dale Evans, Robert L. Vining Jr., Robert H. Hall, Harold T. Ward, J. Owen Forrester; Clerk's Office, Atlanta 30335. **Middle:** Wilbur D. Owens Jr., CJ; J. Robert Elliott; Clerk's Office, Macon 31202. **Southern:** Anthony A. Alaimo, CJ; B. Avant Edenfield, Dudley H. Bowen Jr.; Clerk's Office, Savannah 31412.

Hawaii — Samuel P. King, CJ; Clerk's Office, Honolulu 96850.

Idaho — Marion J. Callister, CJ; Harold L. Ryan; Clerk's Office; Boise, 83724.

Illinois — Northern: Frank J. McGarr, CJ; Thomas R. McMillen, Prentice H. Marshall, Joel M. Flaum, John F. Grady, George N. Leighton, Nicholas J. Bua, Stanley J. Roszkowski, James B. Moran, Marvin E. Aspen, Milton I. Shadur, Charles P. Kocoras, Susan Getzendanner; Clerk's Office, Chicago 60604. **Central** Robert D. Morgan, CJ; J. Waldo Ackerman, Harold A. Baker; Clerk's Office, Peoria 61602. **Southern:** James L. Foreman, CJ; William L. Beatty; Clerk's Office, E. St. Louis 62202.

Indiana — Northern: Allen Sharp, CJ; William C. Lee; Clerk's Office, South Bend 46601. **Southern:** William E. Steckler, CJ; Cale J. Holder, S. Hugh Dillin, James E. Noland, Gene E. Brooke; Clerk's Office, Indianapolis 46204.

Iowa — Northern: Edward J. McManus, CJ; Donald E. O'-Brien; Clerk's Office, Cedar Rapids 52407. **Southern:** William C. Stuart, CJ; Donald E. O'Brien, Harold D. Vietor; Clerk's Office, Des Moines 50309.

Kansas — Earl E. O'Connor, CJ; Richard Dean Rogers, Dale E. Saffels, Patrick F. Kelly, Sam A. Crow; Clerk's Office, Wichita 67201.

Kentucky — Eastern: Bernard T. Moynahan Jr., CJ; Eugene E. Siler Jr., Scott Reed, William Bertelsman, G. Wix Unthank, Henry R. Wilhoit Jr.; Clerk's Office, Lexington 40501. **Western:** Charles M. Allen, CJ; Eugene E. Siler Jr., Edward H. Johnstone, Thomas A. Ballantine; Clerk's Office, Louisville 40202.

Louisiana — Eastern: Frederick J. R. Heebe, CJ; Fred J. Cassibry, Jack M. Gordon, Morey L. Sear, Charles Schwartz Jr., Adrian A. Duplantier, Robert F. Collins, George Arceneaux Jr., Veronica D. Wicker, Patrick E. Carr, Peter Hill Beer; Clerk's Office, New Orleans 70130. **Middle:** John V. Parker, CJ; Frank J. Polozola; Clerk's Office, Baton Rouge 70801. **Western:** Nauman S. Scott, CJ; Tom Stagg, W. Eugene Davis, Earl Ernest Veron, John M. Shaw; Clerk's Office, Shreveport 71101.

Maine — Edward Thaxter Gignoux, CJ; Conrad K. Cyr; Clerk's Office, Portland 04112.

Maryland — Frank A. Kaufman, CJ; Alexander Harvey 2d, James R. Miller Jr., Joseph H. Young, Herbert F. Murray, Shirley B. Jones, Joseph C. Howard, Norman P. Ramsey; Clerk's Office, Baltimore 21201.

Massachusetts — Andrew A. Caffrey, CJ; W. Arthur Garrity Jr., Frank H. Freedman, Joseph L. Tauro, Walter Jay Skinner, A. David Mazzone, Robert E. Keeton, John J. McNaught, Rya W. Zobel, David S. Nelson; Clerk's Office, Boston 02109:

Michigan — Eastern: John Feikens, CJ; Philip Pratt, Robert E. DeMascio, Charles W. Joiner, James Harvey, James P. Churchill, Ralph B. Guy Jr., Julian A. Cook, Patricia J. Boyle, Stewart A. Newblatt, Avern Cohn, Anna Diggs Taylor, Horace W. Gilmore; Clerk's Office, Detroit 48226. **Western:** Wendell A. Miles, CJ; Douglas W. Hillman, Benjamin F. Gibson, Richard A. Enslen; Clerk's Office, Grand Rapids 49503.

Minnesota — Miles W. Lord, CJ; Donald D. Alsop, Harry H. MacLaughlin, Robert G. Renner, Diana E. Murphy, Paul A. Magnuson; Clerk's Office, St. Paul 55101.

Mississippi — Northern: William C. Keady, CJ; L. T. Senter Jr.; Clerk's Office, Oxford 38655. **Southern:** Dan M. Russell Jr., CJ; William Harold Cox, Walter L. Nixon Jr.; Clerk's Office, Jackson 39205.

Missouri — Eastern: H. Kenneth Wangelin, CJ; John F. Nangle, Edward D. Filippine, William L. Hungate, Clyde S. Cahill Jr.; Clerk's Office, St. Louis 63101. **Western:** Russell G. Clark, CJ; Harold Sachs, Scott O. Wright, John R. Gibson, James E. Stephens Jr., D. Brook Bartlett; Clerk's Office, Kansas City 64106.

Montana — James F. Battin, CJ; Paul G. Hatfield; Clerk's Office, Billings 59101.

Nebraska — Warren K. Urbom, CJ; Clarence A. Beam, Albert G. Schatz; Clerk's Office, Omaha 68101.

Nevada — Harry E. Claiborne, CJ; Roger D. Foley, Edward C. Reed Jr.; Clerk's Office, Las Vegas 89101.

New Hampshire — Shane Devine, CJ; Martin J. Loughlin; Clerk's Office, Concord 03301.

New Jersey — Clarkson S. Fisher, CJ; Frederick B. Lacey, Vincent P. Biunno, Herbert J. Stern, H. Curtis Meanor, John F. Gerry, Stanley S. Brotman, Anne E. Thompson, D. R. Debevoise, H. Lee Sarokin, Harold Ackerman; Clerk's Office, Trenton 08605.

New Mexico — Howard C. Bratton, CJ; Edwin L. Mechem, Santiago E. Campos, Juan G. Burciaga; Clerk's Office, Albuquerque 87103.

New York — Northern: Howard G. Munson, CJ; Neal P. McCurn, Roger J. Miner; Clerk's Office, Albany 12201. **Eastern:** Jack B. Weinstein, CJ; Mark A. Costantino, Edward R. Neaher, Thomas C. Platt Jr., Henry Bramwell, George C. Pratt, Charles P. Sifton, Eugene H. Nickerson, Joseph M. McLaughlin, Israel Leo Glasser; Clerk's Office, Brooklyn 11201. **Southern:** Lloyd F. MacMahon, CJ; David N. Edelstein, Edward Weinfeld, Constance Baker Motley, Milton Pollack, Morris E. Lasker, Lee P. Gagliardi, Charles L. Brieant, Whitman Knapp, Charles E. Stewart Jr., Thomas P. Griesa, Robert L. Carter, Robert J. Ward, Kevin Thomas Duffy, William C. Conner, Richard Owen, Leonard B. Sand, Mary Johnson Lowe, Henry F. Werker, Gerard L. Goettel, Charles S. Haight Jr., Vincent L. Broderick, Pierre N. Leval, Robert W. Sweet, Abraham D. Sofaer, John E. Sprizzo; Clerk's Office N. Y. City 10007. **Western:** John T. Curtin, CJ; John T. Elfvin; Clerk's Office, Buffalo 14202.

North Carolina — Eastern: Franklin T. Dupree Jr., CJ; W. Earl Britt; Clerk's Office, Raleigh 27611. **Middle:** Eugene A. Gordon, CJ; Hiram H. Ward, Richard C. Erwin; Clerk's Office, Greensboro 27402. **Western:** Woodrow Wilson Jones, CJ; James B. McMillan, Robert D. Potter; Clerk's Office Asheville 28802.

North Dakota — Paul Benson, CJ; Bruce M. Van Sickle; Clerk's Office, Bismarck 58501.

Ohio — Northern: Frank J. Battisti, CJ; Thomas D. Lambros, Robert B. Krupansky, Nicholas J. Walinski, Leroy J. Contie Jr., John M. Manos, George W. White, Ann Aldrich, Alvin I. Krenzler; Clerk's Office, Cleveland 44114. **Southern:** Carl B. Rubin, CJ; Joseph P. Kinneary, Robert M. Duncan, John D. Holschuh, Walter H. Rice, S. Arthur Spiegel; Clerk's Office, Columbus 43215.

Oklahoma — Northern: H. Dale Cook, CJ; James O. Ellison, Thomas R. Brett, David L. Russell; Clerk's Office, Tulsa 74103. **Eastern:** Frank H. Shey, CJ; H. Dale Cook, David L. Russell; Clerk's Office, Muskogee 74401. **Western:** Luther B. Eubanks, CJ; H. Dale Cook, Ralph G. Thompson, Lee R. West, David L. Russell; Clerk's Office, Oklahoma City

Oregon — James M. Burns, CJ; Robert C. Belloni, Owen M. Panner, James A. Redden, Helen J. Frye; Clerk's Office, Portland 97205.

Pennsylvania — Eastern: Joseph S. Lord 3d, CJ; Alfred L. Luongo, John P. Fullam, Charles R. Weiner, E. Mac Troutman, John B. Hannum, Daniel H. Huyett 3d, Donald W. VanArtsdalen, J. William Ditter Jr., Edward R. Becker, Raymond J. Broderick, Clarence C. Newcomer, Clifford Scott Green, Louis Charles Bechtle, Joseph L. McGlynn Jr., Edward N. Cahn, Louis H. Pollak, Norma L. Shapiro, James T. Giles; Clerk's Office, Philadelphia 19106. **Middle:** William J. Nealon Jr., CJ; Malcolm Muir, Richard P. Conaboy, Sylvia H. Rambo; Clerk's Office, Scranton 18501. **Western:** Gerald J. Weber, CJ; Hubert I. Teitelbaum, Barron P. McCune, Maurice B. Cohill Jr., Paul A. Simmons, Gustave Diamond, Donald E. Zeigler, Alan N. Bloch; Clerk's Office, Pittsburgh 15230.

Rhode Island — Raymond J. Pettine, CJ; Francis J. Boyle; Clerk's Office, Providence 02903

South Carolina — Charles E. Simons Jr., CJ; Solomon Blatt Jr., C. Weston Houck, Falcon B. Hawkins, Matthew J. Perry Jr., George R. Anderson Jr., William W. Wilkins Jr., Clyde H. Hamilton; Clerk's Office, Columbia 29202.

South Dakota — Andrew A. Bogue, CJ; Donald J. Porter, John Bailey Jones; Clerk's Office, Sioux Falls 57102.

Tennessee — Eastern: Frank W. Wilson, CJ; Robert L. Taylor, C. G. Neese; Clerk's Office, Knoxville 37901. **Middle:** L. Clure Morton, CJ, Thomas A. Wiseman Jr, Jon T. Nixon; Clerk's Office, Nashville 37203. **Western:** Robert M. McRae Jr., CJ; Harry W. Wellford, Odell Horton; Clerk's Office, Memphis 38103.

Texas — Northern: Halbert O. Woodward, CJ; Eldon B. Mahon, Robert M. Hill, Robert W. Porter, Patrick E. Higginbotham, Mary Lou Robinson, Barefoot Sanders, David O. Belew Jr., Jerry Buchmeyer; Clerks's Office, Dallas 75242. **Southern:** John V. Singleton Jr., CJ; Woodrow B. Seals, Carl O. Bue Jr., Robert O'Connor Jr., Ross N. Sterling, Norman W. Black, James De Anda, George E. Cire, Gabrielle K. McDonald, George P. Kazen, Hugh Gibson, Filemon B. Vela, Hayden W. Head Jr.; Clerk's Office, Houston 77208. **Eastern:** William Wayne Justice, CJ; Joe J. Fisher, William M. Steger, Robert M. Parker; Clerk's Office, Beaumont 77701. **Western:** William S. Sessions, CJ; Lucius D. Bunton 3d, Harry Lee Hudspeth, Fred Shannon, Hipolito F. Garcia, James R. Nowlin; Clerk's Office, San Antonio 78206.

Utah — Aldon J. Anderson, CJ; Bruce S. Jenkins, David K. Winder; Clerk's Office, Salt Lake City 84110.

Vermont — James S. Holden, CJ; Albert W. Coffrin; Clerk's Office, Burlington 05402.

Virginia — Eastern: John A. MacKenzie, CJ; Robert R. Merhige Jr., Albert V. Bryan Jr., D. Dortch Warriner, J. Calvitt Clarke, Richard L. Williams, James C. Cacheris, Robert G. Doumar; Clerk's Office, Norfolk 23501. **Western:** James C. Turk, CJ; Glen M. Williams, James H. Michael Jr., Jackson L. Kiser; Clerk's Office, Roanoke 24006.

Washington — Eastern: Robert J. McNichols, CJ; Justin L. Quackenbush; Clerk's Office, Spokane 99210. **Western:** Walter T. McGovern, CJ; Donald S. Voorhees, Jack E. Tanner, Barbara J. Rothstein, John C. Coughenour; Clerk's Office, Seattle 98104.

West Virginia — Northern: Robert Earl Maxwell, CJ; Charles H. Haden 2d; Clerk's Office, Elkins 26241. **Southern:** Dennis Raymond Knapp, CJ; John T. Copenhaver Jr., Charles H. Haden 2d, Robert J. Staker, William M. Kidd; Clerk's Office Charleston 25329.

Wisconsin — Eastern: John W. Reynolds, CJ; Myron L. Gordon, Robert W. Warren, Terence T. Evans; Clerk's Office, Milwaukee 53202. **Western:** Barbara B. Crabb, CJ; Clerk's Office, Madison 53701.

Wyoming — Clarence A. Brimmer; Clerk's Office, Cheyenne 82001.

U.S. Territorial District Courts

Canal Zone — Morey L. Sear; Clerk's Office, Balboa Heights.
Guam — Cristobal C. Duenas; Clerk's Office, P.O. Box DC, Agana 96910.
Puerto Rico — Hernan G. Pesquera, CJ; Juan R. Torruella, Juan M. Perez-Gimenez, Gilberto Gierbolini-Ortiz, Carman Consuelo Cerezo; Clerk's Office, San Juan 00904.
Virgin Islands — Almeric L. Christian, CJ; David V. O'Brien; Clerk's Office, Charlotte Amalie, St. Thomas 00801.

State Officials, Salaries, Party Membership

Compiled from data supplied by state officials, mid-1982

Alabama

Governor — Forrest "Fob" James, D., $50,000.
Lt. Gov. — George McMillan Jr. D., $67 per legislative day, plus annual salary of $400 per month.
Sec. of State — Don Siegelman, D., $25,800.
Atty. Gen. — Charles Graddick, D., $49,000.
Treasurer — Mrs. Annie Laurie Gunter, D., $25,800.
Legislature: meets annually the first Tuesday in Apr. (first year of term of office, first Tuesday in Feb. (2d and 3d years), 2d Tuesday in Jan. (4th year) at Montgomery. Members receive $400 per month, plus $67 per day during legislative sessions, and mileage of 10c per mile.
Senate — Dem., 35; Rep., 0. Total, 35.
House — Dem., 101; Rep., 4. Total, 105.

Alaska

Governor — Jay S. Hammond, R., $74,196.
Lt. Gov. — Terry Miller, R., $69,240.
Atty. General — Wilson Condon, D., $66,700.
Legislature: meets annually in January at Juneau, for as long as may be necessary. First session in odd years. Members receive $18,768 per year plus $67 per day while in session (Juneau legislators receive $50 per day). Also $4,000 for postage, personal stationery, and other expenses.
Senate — Dem., 10; Rep., 10. Total, 20.
House — Dem., 22; Rep., 16; Libertarian 2. Total, 40.

Arizona

Governor — Bruce Babbitt, D., $50,000.
Sec. of State — Rose Mofford, D., $28,000.
Atty. Gen. — Bob Corbin, R., $45,000.
Treasurer — Clark Dierks, R., $30,000.
Legislature: meets annually in January at Phoenix. Each member receives an annual salary of $15,000.
Senate — Dem., 14; Rep., 16. Total, 30.
House — Dem., 17; Rep., 43. Total, 60.

Arkansas

Governor — Frank White, R., $35,000.
Lt. Gov. — Winston Bryant, D., $14,000.
Sec. of State — Paul Riviere, D., $22,500.
Atty. Gen. — Steve Clark, D., $26,500.
Treasurer — Jimmie Lou Fisher, D., $22,500.
General Assembly: meets odd years in January at Little Rock. Members receive $7,500 per year, $45 a day while in regular session, plus 13c a mile travel expense.
Senate — Dem., 33; Rep., 1; 1 vacancy. Total, 35.
House — Dem., 92; Rep., 7; 1 vacancy. Total, 100.

California

Governor — Edmund G. Brown Jr., D., $49,100.
Lt. Gov. — Mike Curb, R., $42,500.
Sec. of State — March Fong Eu, D., $42,500.
Controller — Kenneth Cory, D., $42,500.
Atty. Gen. — George Deukmejian, R., $47,500.
Treasurer — Jesse M. Unruh, D., $42,500.
Legislature: meets at Sacramento; regular sessions commence on the first Monday in Dec. of every even-numbered year; each session lasts 2 years. Members receive $28,110 per year plus mileage and $50 per diem.
Senate — Dem., 23; Rep., 17. Total, 40.
Assembly — Dem., 49; Rep., 31. Total, 80.

Colorado

Governor — Richard D. Lamm, D., $50,000.
Lt. Gov. — Nancy Dick, D., $25,000.
Secy. of State — Mary Estill Buchanan, R., $27,500.
Atty. Gen. — J.D. MacFarlane, D., $35,000.
Treasurer — Roy Romer, D., $27,500.
General Assembly: meets annually in January at Denver. Members receive $14,000 annually, except holdover senators who receive $12,000.
Senate — Dem., 13; Rep., 22. Total, 35.
House — Dem., 25; Rep., 40. Total, 65.

Connecticut

Governor — William A. O'Neill, D., $42,000.
Lt. Gov. — Joseph J. Fauliso, D., $25,000.
Sec. of State — Maura L. Melley, D., $25,000.
Treasurer — Henry E. Parker, D., $25,000.
Comptroller — J. Edward Caldwell, D., $25,000.
Atty. Gen. — Carl R. Ajello, D., $38,500.
General Assembly: meets annually odd years in January and even years in February at Hartford. Salary $17,000 per 2-year term plus $2,000 per year for expenses, plus travel allowance.
Senate — Dem., 23; Rep., 13. Total, 36.
House — Dem., 82, Rep., 69. Total, 151.

Delaware

Governor — Pierre S. du Pont 4th, R., $35,000.
Lt. Gov. — Michael N. Castle, R., $15,500.
Sec. of State — Glenn C. Kenton, R., $41,900.
Atty. Gen. — Richard S. Gebelein, R., $37,000.
Treasurer — Thomas R. Carper, D., $24,000.
General Assembly: meets annually at Dover from the 2d Tuesday in January to midnight June 30. Members receive $11,400 base salary.
Senate — Dem., 12; Rep., 9. Total, 21.
House — Dem., 16; Rep., 25. Total, 41.

Florida

Governor — Robert Graham, D., $60,498.
Lt. Gov. — Wayne Mixon, D., $55,500.
Sec. of State — George Firestone, D., $55,500.
Comptroller — Gerald Lewis, D., $55,500.
Atty. Gen. — Jim Smith, D., $55,500.
Treasurer — Bill Gunter, D., $55,500.
Legislature: meets annually in April at Tallahassee. Members receive $12,000 per year plus expense allowance while on official business.
Senate — Dem., 27; Rep., 13. Total, 40.
House — Dem., 80; Rep., 40. Total, 120.

Georgia

Governor — George Busbee, D., $65,934.
Lt. Gov. — Zell Miller, D., $31,698.
Sec. of State — David B. Poythress, D., $44,518.
Comptroller General — Johnnie L. Caldwell, D., $44,518.
Atty. Gen. — Michael J. Bowers, $53,329.
General Assembly: meets annually at Atlanta. Members receive $7,200 per year. During session $44 per day for expenses.
Senate — Dem., 51; Rep., 5. Total, 56.
House — Dem., 155; Rep., 25. Total, 180.

Hawaii

Governor — George R. Ariyoshi, D., $50,000.
Lt. Gov. — Jean King, D., $45,000.
Dir., Budg. & Finance — Eileen Anderson, D., $42,500.
Atty. Gen. — Tany Hong, D., $42,500.
Comptroller — Hideo Murakami, D., $42,500.
Dir. of Finance & Budget — Jensen S. L. Hee, D., $42,500.
Legislature: meets annually on 3d Wednesday in January at Honolulu. Members receive $12,000 per year plus expenses.
Senate — Dem., 17. Rep., 8. Total, 25.
House — Dem., 39. Rep., 12. Total, 51.

Idaho

Governor — John V. Evans, D., $40,000.
Lt. Gov. — Philip E. Batt, R., $12,000.
Sec. of State — Pete T. Cenarrusa, R., $28,000.
Treasurer — Marjorie Ruth Moon, D., $28,000.
Atty. Gen. — David Leroy, R., $35,000.
Legislature: meets annually on the Monday after the first day in January at Boise. Members receive $4,200 per year, plus $25 per day when authorized, plus travel allowances.
Senate — Dem., 12; Rep., 23. Total, 35.
House — Dem., 14; Rep., 56. Total, 70.

Illinois

Governor — James R. Thompson, R., $58,000.
Lt. Gov. — vacant, $45,500.
Sec. of State — Jim Edgar, R., $50,500.
Comptroller — Roland W. Burris, D., $48,000.
Atty. Gen. — Tyrone C. Fahner, R., $50,500.
Treasurer — Jerome A. Cosentimo, D., $48,000.
General Assembly: meets annually in January at Springfield. Members receive $28,000 per annum.
Senate — Dem., 30; Rep., 29. Total, 59.
House — Dem., 85; Rep., 91; 1 3d party. Total, 177.

Indiana

Governor — Robert D. Orr, R., $48,000 plus discretionary expenses.
Lt. Gov. — John M. Mutz, R., $34,000 plus discretionary expenses.
Sec. of State — Edwin J. Simcox, R., $34,000.
Atty. Gen. — Linley E. Pearson, R., $39,000.
Treasurer — Julian Ridlen, R., $34,000.
General Assembly: meets annually in January. Members receive $9,600 per year plus $50 per day while in session, $12.50 per day while not in session.
Senate — Dem., 15; Rep., 35. Total, 50.
House — Dem., 37; Rep., 63. Total, 100.

Iowa

Governor — Robert D. Ray, R., $60,000 plus $5,724 expenses.
Lt. Gov. — Terry Branstad, R., $20,500 plus personal expenses and travel allowances at same rate as for a senator.
Sec. of State — Mary Jane Odell, R., $35,600.
Atty. Gen. — Tom Miller, D., $47,000.
Treasurer — Maurice E. Baringer, R., $35,600.
General Assembly: meets annually in January at Des Moines. Members receive $13,700 annually plus maximum expense allowance of $30 per day for first 120 days of first session, and first 100 days of 2d session; mileage expenses at 20c a mile.
Senate — Dem., 21; Rep., 29. Total, 50.
House — Dem., 44; Rep., 55; 1 vacancy. Total, 100.

Kansas

Governor — John Carlin, D., $45,000.
Lt. Gov. — Paul V. Dugan, D., $13,500 plus expenses.
Sec. of State — Jack H. Brier, R., $27,500.
Atty. Gen. — Robert T. Stephan, R., $40,000.
Treasurer — Joan Finney, D., $27,500.
Legislature: meets annually in January at Topeka. Members receive $42 a day plus $50 a day expenses while in session, plus $400 per month while not in session.
Senate — Dem., 16; Rep., 24. Total, 40.
House — Dem., 53; Rep., 72. Total, 125.

Kentucky

Governor — John Y. Brown Jr., D., $50,000.
Lt. Gov. — Martha L. Collins, D., $47,311.
Sec. of State — Francis Jones Mills, D., $47,311.
Atty. Gen. — Steve Beshear, D., $47,311.
Treasurer — Drexel Davis, D., $47,311.
General Assembly: meets even years in January at Frankfort. Members receive $50 per day and $75 per day during session and $750 per month for expenses for interim.
Senate — Dem., 29; Rep., 9. Total, 38.
House — Dem., 76; Rep., 24. Total, 100.

Louisiana

Governor — David C. Treen, R., $73,440.
Lt. Gov. — Robert L. Freeman, D., $63,367.
Sec. of State — James H. Brown, D., $60,169.
Atty. Gen. — William J. Guste Jr., D., $60,169.
Treasurer — Mary Evelyn Parker, D., $60,169.
Legislature: meets annually for 60 legislative days commencing on 3d Monday in April. Members receive $75 per day and mileage at 21c a mile for 8 round trips, plus $1,400 per month expense allowance.
Senate — Dem., 39; Rep., 0. Total, 39.
House — Dem., 95; Rep., 10. Total, 105.

Maine

Governor — Joseph E. Brennan, D., $35,000.
Sec. of State — Rodney Quinn, D., $25,000.
Atty. Gen. — James Tierney, D., $38,468.
Treasurer — Samuel Shapiro, D., $25,000.
Legislature: meets biennially in January at Augusta. Members receive $4,500 for regular sessions, $2,500 for special session plus expenses; presiding officers receive 50% more.
Senate — Dem., 16; Rep., 17. Total, 33.
House — Dem., 82; Rep., 69. Total, 151.

Maryland

Governor — Harry Hughes, D., $60,000.
Lt. Gov. — Samuel Bogley, D., $52,500.
Comptroller — Louis L. Goldstein, D., $50,000.
Atty. Gen. — Stephen H. Sachs, D., $50,000.
Sec. of State — Fred L. Wineland, D., $36,000.
Treasurer — William S. James, D., $50,000.
General Assembly: meets 90 days annually on the 2d Wednesday in January at Annapolis. Members receive $17,600 per year.
Senate — Dem., 40; Rep., 7. Total, 47.
House — Dem., 125; Rep., 16. Total, 141.

Massachusetts

Governor — Edward J. King, D., $40,000.
Lt. Gov. — Thomas P. O'Neill 3d, D., $30,000.
Sec. of the Commonwealth — Michael Joseph Connolly, D., $30,000.
Atty. Gen. — Francis X. Bellotti, D., $37,500.
Treasurer — Robert Q. Crane, D., $30,000.
Auditor — John J. Finnegan, D., $30,000.
General Court (Legislature): meets each January in Boston. Salaries $19,766 per annum.
Senate — Dem., 32; Rep., 8. Total, 40.
House — Dem., 126; Rep., 31; 1 vacancy; 2 Ind. Total, 160.

Michigan

Governor — William G. Milliken, R., $70,000.
Lt. Gov. — James H. Brickley, R., $50,000.
Sec. of State — Richard H. Austin, D., $60,000.
Atty. Gen. — Frank J. Kelley, D., $60,000.
Treasurer — Loren Monroe, non-part., $58,400.
Legislature: meets annually in January at Lansing. Members receive $31,000 per year, plus $6,200 expense allowance.
Senate — Dem., 24; Rep., 14. Total, 38.
House — Dem., 64; Rep., 46. Total, 110.

Minnesota

Governor — Albert H. Quie, IR, $66,500.
Lt. Gov. — Lou Wangberg, IR, $38,000.
Sec. of State — Joan Anderson Growe, DFL., $36,000.
Atty. Gen. — Warren Spannaus, DFL., $56,000.
Treasurer — Jim Lord, DFL., $36,000.
Auditor — Arne H. Carlson, IR, $36,000.
Legislature: meets for a total of 120 days within every 2 years at St. Paul. Members receive $18,500 per year, plus expense allowance during session.
Senate — DFL., 45; IR, 22. Total, 67.
House — DFL., 70; IR, 64. Total, 134.
(DFL means Democratic-Farmer-Labor. IR means Independent Republican.)

Mississippi

Governor — William Winter, D., $53,000.
Lt. Gov. — Brad Dye, D., $34,000 per regular legislative session, plus expense allowance.
Sec. of State — Edwin Lloyd Pittman, D., $34,000.
Atty. Gen. — William A. Allain, D., $41,000.
Treasurer — William J. Cole 3d, D., $34,000.
Legislature: meets annually in January at Jackson. Members receive $8,100 per regular session plus travel allowance, and $210 per month while not in session.
Senate — Dem., 48; Rep., 4. Total, 52.
House — Dem., 116; Rep., 4; Ind., 2. Total, 122.

Missouri

Governor — Christopher S. Bond, R., $55,000.
Lt. Gov. — Kenneth J. Rothman, D., $30,000.
Sec. of State — James C. Kirkpatrick, D., $42,500.
Atty. Gen. — John Ashcroft, R., $45,000.
Treasurer — Mel Carnahan, D., $42,500.
General Assembly: meets annually in Jefferson City on the first Wednesday after first Monday in January; adjournment in odd-numbered years by June 30, in even-numbered years by May 15. Members receive $15,000 annually.
Senate — Dem., 23; Rep., 11. Total, 34.
House — Dem., 111; Rep., 52. Total, 163.

Montana

Governor — Ted Schwinden, D., $43,360.
Lt. Gov. — George Turman, D., $31,077.
Sec. of State — Jim Waltermire, R., $28,685.
Atty. Gen. — Mike Greely, D., $39,555.
Legislative Assembly: meets odd years in January at Helena. Members receive $39.50 per legislative day plus $45 per day for expenses while in session.
Senate — Dem., 21; Rep., 29. Total, 50.
House — Dem., 43; Rep., 57. Total, 100.

Nebraska

Governor — Charles Thone, R., $40,000.
Lt. Gov. — Roland Luedtke, R., $32,000.
Sec. of State — Allen J. Beermann, R., $32,000.
Atty. Gen. — Paul Douglas, R., $39,500.
Treasurer — Kay Orr, R., $32,000.
Legislature: meets annually in January at Lincoln. Members receive salary of $4,800 annually plus travelling expenses for one round trip to and from session.
Unicameral body composed of 49 members who are elected on a nonpartisan ballot and are classed as senators.

Nevada

Governor — Robert List, R., $50,000.
Lt. Gov. — Myron E. Leavitt, D., $8,000 plus $60 per day when acting as governor and president of the Senate during legislative sessions.
Sec. of State — William D. Swackhamer, D., $32,500.
Comptroller — Wilson McGowen, R., $32,500.
Atty. Gen. — Richard H. Bryan, D., $40,500.
Treasurer — Stanton B. Colton, D., $31,500.
Legislature: meets odd years in January at Carson City. Members receive $80 per day for 60 days (20 days for special sessions), plus per diem of $40 per day for entire length of session. Travel allowance of 17c per mile.
Senate — Dem., 15; Rep., 5. Total, 20.
Assembly — Dem., 26; Rep., 14. Total, 40.

New Hampshire

Governor — Hugh J. Gallen, D., $44,520.
Sec. of State — William M. Gardner, D., $31,270.
Atty. Gen. — Gregory H. Smith, $38,690.
Comptroller — Arthur H. Fowler.
Treasurer — Robert W. Flanders, R., $31,270.
General Court (Legislature): meets odd years in January at Concord. Members receive $200; presiding officers $250.
Senate — Dem., 10; Rep., 13; 1 vacancy. Total, 24.
House — Rep., 234; Dem., 158; 8 vacancies. Total, 400.

New Jersey

Governor — Thomas H. Kean, R., $85,000.
Sec. of State — Jane Burgio, R., $60,000.
Atty. Gen. — Irwin I. Kimmelman, R., $70,000.
Treasurer — Kenneth R. Biederman, D., $70,000.
Legislature: meets throughout the year at Trenton. Members receive $18,000 per year, except president of Senate and speaker of Assembly who receive 1/3 more.
Senate — Dem., 22; Rep., 18. Total, 40.
Assembly — Dem., 43; Rep. 37. Total, 80.

New Mexico

Governor — Bruce King, D., $60,000.
Lt. Gov. — Roberto Mondragon, D., $38,500. Acting governor, $150 per day.
Sec. of State — Shirley Hooper, D., $38,500.
Atty. Gen. — Jeff Bingaman, D., $44,000.
Treasurer — Jan Alan Hartke, D., $38,500.
Legislature: meets in January at Sante Fe; odd years for 60 days, even years for 30 days. Members receive $40 per day while in session.
Senate — Dem., 22; Rep., 20. Total, 42.
House — Dem., 41; Rep., 29. Total, 70.

New York

Governor — Hugh L. Carey, D., $85,000.
Lt. Gov. — Mario M. Cuomo, D., $60,000.
Sec. of State — Basil A. Paterson, D., $69,000.
Comptroller — Edward V. Regan, R., $60,000.
Atty. Gen. — Robert Abrams, D., $60,000.
Legislature: meets annually in January at Albany. Members receive $30,804 per year.
Senate — Dem., 25; Rep., 33; 2 vacancies. Total, 60.
Assembly — Dem., 84; Rep., 62; 1 Lib.; 3 vacancies. Total, 150.

North Carolina

Governor — James B. Hunt, D., $57,864 plus $11,500 per year expenses.
Lt. Gov. — James C. Green, D., $47,928 per year, plus $11,500 per year expense allowance.
Sec. of State — Thad Eure, D., $47,928
Atty. Gen. — Rufus L. Edmisten, D., $53,976.
Treasurer — Harlan E. Boyles, D., $47,928.
General Assembly: meets odd years in January at Raleigh. Members receive $6,936 annual salary and $2,064 annual expense allowance, plus $50 per diem subsistence and travel allowance while in session.
Senate — Dem., 40; Rep., 10. Total, 50.
House — Dem., 96; Rep., 24. Total, 120.

North Dakota

Governor — Allen I. Olson, R., $47,000 plus $13,862 expenses.
Lt. Gov. — Ernest Sands, R., $33,500.
Sec. of State — Ben Meier, R., $33,500 plus $9,880 expenses.
Atty. Gen. — Bob Wefald, R., $38,000 plus $11,206 expenses.
Treasurer — John Lesmeister, R., $33,500 plus $9,880 expenses.
Legislative Assembly: meets odd years in January at Bismarck. Members receive $85 per day plus expenses during session and $180 per month when not in session.
Senate — Dem., 10; Rep., 40. Total, 50.
House — Dem., 27; Rep., 73. Total, 100.

Ohio

Governor — James A. Rhodes, R., $50,000.
Lt. Gov. — vacancy.
Sec. of State — Anthony J. Celebrezze Jr., D., $50,000.
Atty. Gen. — William J. Brown, D., $50,000.
Treasurer — Gertrude W. Donahey, D., $50,000.
Auditor — Thomas E. Ferguson, D., $50,000.
General Assembly: meets odd years at Columbus on first Monday in January for the 1st session, and no later than Mar. 15th of the following year for the 2d session. Members receive $22,500 per annum.
Senate — Dem., 15; Rep., 18. Total, 33.
House — Dem., 56; Rep., 43. Total, 99.

Oklahoma

Governor — George Nigh, D., $48,000.
Lt. Gov. — Spencer T. Bernard, D., $27,500.
Sec. of State — Jeannette B. Edmondson, D., $24,000.
Atty. Gen. — Jan Cartwright, D., $35,000.
Treasurer — Leo Winters, D., $30,000.
Legislature: meets annually in January at Oklahoma City. Members receive $18,000 annually.
Senate — Dem., 37; Rep., 11. Total, 48.
House — Dem., 73; Rep., 28. Total, 101.

Oregon

Governor — Victor Atiyeh, R., $55,423, plus $1,000 monthly expenses.
Sec. of State — Norma Paulus, R., $45,619.
Atty. Gen. — David B. Frohnmayer, R., $53,308.
Treasurer — Clay Myers, R., $45,619.
Legislative Assembly: meets odd years in January at Salem. Members receive $700 monthly and $44 expenses per day while in session; $300 per month while not in session.
Senate — Dem., 22; Rep., 8. Total, 30.
House — Dem., 33; Rep., 27. Total, 60.

Pennsylvania

Governor — Richard Thornburgh, R., $66,000.
Lt. Gov. — William W. Scranton 3d, R., $49,500.
Sec. of the Commonwealth — William R. Davis, R., $38,500.
Atty. Gen. — LeRoy S. Zimmerman, R., $55,000.
Treasurer — R. Budd Dwyer, R., $48,000.
General Assembly — convenes annually in January at Harrisburg. Members receive $25,000 per year plus $7,500 for expenses.
Senate — Dem., 24; Rep., 26. Total, 50.
House — Dem., 98; Rep., 102; 3 vacancies. Total, 203.

Rhode Island

Governor — J. Joseph Garrahy, D., $49,500.
Lt. Gov. — Thomas R. DiLuglio, D., $35,500.
Sec. of State — Robert F. Burns, D., $35,500.
Atty. Gen. — Dennis J. Roberts 2d, D., $41,875.
Treasurer — Anthony J. Solomon, D., $35,500.
General Assembly: meets annually in January at Providence. Members receive $5 per day for 60 days, and travel allowance of 8c per mile.
Senate — Dem., 43; Rep., 7. Total, 50.
House — Dem., 82; Rep., 18. Total, 100.

South Carolina

Governor — Richard W. Riley, D., $60,000.
Lt. Gov. — Nancy Stevenson, D., $30,000.
Sec. of State — John T. Campbell, D., $45,000.
Comptroller Gen. — Earle E. Morris Jr., D., $45,000.
Atty. Gen. — Daniel R. McLeod, D., $45,000.
Treasurer — G.L. Patterson Jr., D., $45,000.
General Assembly: meets annually in January at Columbia. Members receive $10,000 per year and expense allowance of $50 per day, plus travel and postage allowance.
Senate — Dem., 41; Rep., 5. Total, 46.
House — Dem. 106; Rep., 18. Total, 124.

South Dakota

Governor — William J. Janklow, R., $46,750.
Lt. Gov. — Lowell C. Hansen 2d, R., $6,500 plus $50 per day during legislative session.
Sec. of State — Alice Kundert, R., $31,750.
Treasurer — David Volk, R., $31,750.
Atty. Gen. — Mark Meierhenry, R., $39,750.
Auditor — Vernon Larson, $31,750.
Legislature: meets annually in January at Pierre. Members receive $3,200 for 40-day session in odd-numbered years, and $2,800 for 35-day session in even-numbered years, plus $50 per legislative day.
Senate — Dem., 10; Rep., 25. Total, 35.
House — Dem., 21; Rep., 49. Total, 70.

Tennessee

Governor — Lamar Alexander, R., $68,226.
Lt. Gov. — John S. Wilder, D., $8,308.
Sec. of State — Gentry Crowell, D., $51,510.
Comptroller — William Snodgrass, D., $51,510.
Atty. Gen. — William M. Leech, D., $64,494.
General Assembly: meets annually in January at Nashville. Members receive $8,308 yearly plus $66.47 expenses for each day in session, plus mileage and expense allowances.
Senate — Dem., 21; Rep., 11; Ind., 1. Total, 33.
House — Dem., 58; Rep., 39; Ind., 2. Total, 99.

Texas

Governor — William P. Clements Jr., R., $71,400.
Lt. Gov. — Bill Hobby, D., $7,200, plus living quarters. Governor's salary when acting as governor.
Sec. of State — David A. Dean, R., $42,700.
Comptroller — Bob Bullock, D., $43,700.
Atty. Gen. — Mark White, D., $45,200.
Treasurer — Warren G. Harding, D., $45,200.
Legislature: meets odd years in January at Austin. Members receive annual salary not exceeding $7,200, per diem while in session, and travel allowance.
Senate — Dem., 24; Rep., 7. Total, 31.
House — Dem., 115; Rep., 35. Total, 150.

Utah

Governor — Scott M. Matheson, D., $48,000.
Sec. of State/Lt. Gov. — David S. Monson, R., $33,500.
Atty. Gen. — David L. Wilkinson, R., $36,500.
Treasurer — Edward T. Alter, D., $33,500.
Legislature: convenes for 60 days on 2d Monday in January in odd-numbered years; for 20 days in even-numbered years; members receive $25 per day, $15 daily expenses, and mileage.
Senate — Dem., 7; Rep., 22. Total, 29.
House — Dem., 17; Rep., 58. Total, 75.

Vermont

Governor — Richard A. Snelling, R., $44,850.
Lt. Gov. — Madeleine M. Kunin, D., $19,200.
Sec. of State — James H. Douglas, R., $24,380.
Atty. Gen. — John J. Easton Jr., R., $31,400.
Treasurer — Emory Hebard, R., $24,380.
Auditor of Accounts — Alexander V. Acebo, R., $24,380.
General Assembly: meets odd years in January at Montpelier. Members receive $250 weekly while in session, with a limit of $7,500 for a regular session and $50 per day for special session, plus specified expenses.
Senate — Dem., 14; Rep., 16. Total, 30.
House — Dem., 64; Rep., 83; 2 Ind.; 1 vacancy. Total, 150.

Virginia

Governor — Charles S. Robb, D., $75,000.
Lt. Gov. — Richard J. Davis, D., $20,000.
Atty. Gen. — Gerald L. Baliles, D., $56,000.
Sec. of the Commonwealth — Laurie Naismith, D., $29,200.
Treasurer — C. J. Boehm, $53,000.
General Assembly: meets annually in January at Richmond. Members receive $5,475 annually plus expense and mileage allowances.
Senate — Dem., 31; Rep., 9. Total, 40.
House — Dem., 66; Rep., 33; Ind., 1. Total, 100.

Washington

Governor — John Spellman, R., $63,000.
Lt. Gov. — John A. Cherberg, D., $28,600.
Sec. of State — Ralph Munro, R., $31,000.
Atty. Gen. — Ken Eikenberry, R., $47,100.
Treasurer — Robert S. O'Brien, D., $37,200.
Legislature: meets annually in January at Olympia. Half the Senate members receive $12,000 annually, the other half $9,800. All House members receive $12,000 annually, plus per diem of $4 per day and 10¢ per mile while in session; 18 1/2¢ per mile when not in session.
Senate — Dem., 24; Rep., 25. Total, 49.
House — Dem., 42; Rep., 56. Total, 98.

West Virginia

Governor — Jay Rockefeller, D., $60,000
Sec. of State — A. James Manchin, D., $36,000.
Atty. Gen. — Chauncey Browning, D., $42,000.
Treasurer — Larrie Bailey, D., $42,000.
Comm. of Agric. — Gus R. Douglass, D., $39,000.
Auditor — Glen B. Gainer Jr., D., $39,000.
Legislature: meets annually in January at Charleston. Members receive $5,136.
Senate — Dem., 27; Rep., 7. Total, 34.
House — Dem., 78; Rep., 22. Total, 100.

Wisconsin

Governor — Lee Dreyfus, R., $65,801.
Lt. Gov. — Russell A. Olson, R., $36,151.
Sec. of State — Vel R. Phillips, D., $32,608.
Treasurer — Charles P. Smith, D., $32,608.
Atty. Gen. — Bronson C. La Follette, D., $50,780.
Superintendent of Public Instruction — Herbert J. Grover, $58,139.
Legislature: meets in January at Madison. Members receive $22,638 annually plus $30 per day expenses.
Senate — Dem., 19; Rep., 14. Total, 33.
Assembly — Dem., 58; Rep., 39; 2 vacancies. Total, 99.

Wyoming

Governor — Ed Herschler, D., $55,000.
Sec. of State — Thyra Thomson, R., $37,500.
Atty. Gen. — Steven F. Freudental.
Treasurer — Shirley Wittler, R., $37,500.
Legislature: meets odd years in January, even years in February, at Cheyenne. Members receive $30 per day while in session, plus $44 per day for expenses.
Senate — Dem., 11; Rep., 19. Total, 30.
House — Dem., 23; Rep. 39. Total, 62.

Puerto Rico

Governor — Carlos Romero-Barcelo.
Secretary of State — Carlos S. Quirós.
Secy. of Justice — Hector Reichard.
These officials belong to the New Progressive Party.
Legislative Assembly: composed of a Senate of 27 members and a House of Representatives of 51 members. Majority of both Houses belongs to the Popular Democratic Party. Meets annually, in January at San Juan.

U.S. Government Independent Agencies

Source: General Services Administration
Address: Washington, DC. Location and ZIP codes of agencies in parentheses; as of May, 1982.

ACTION — Thomas Pauken, dir. (806 Connecticut Ave., NW, 20525).

Administrative Conference of the United States — Loren A. Smith, chmn. (2120 L St., NW, 20037).

American Battle Monuments Commission — Mark W. Clark, chmn. (5127 Pulaski Bldg., 20314).

Appalachian Regional Commission — Albert P. Smith Jr., federal co-chmn.; Gov. Lamar Alexander of Tenn., states co-chmn. (1666 Connecticut Ave. NW, 20235).

Arms Control & Disarmament Agency — James Malone, act. dir. (Department of State Bldg. 20451).

Board for International Broadcasting — Charles D. Ablard, act. chmn. (1130 15th St., 20005).

Central Intelligence Agency — William J. Casey, dir. (Wash., DC 20505).

Civil Aeronautics Board — Marvin S. Cohen, chmn. (1825 Connecticut Ave. NW, 20428).

Commission on Civil Rights — Arthur S. Fleming, chmn. (1121 Vermont Ave. NW, 20425).

Commission of Fine Arts — J. Carter Brown, chmn. (708 Jackson Pl. NW, 20006).

Commodity Futures Trading Commission — Philip F. Johnson, chmn. (2033 K St. NW, 20581).

Consumer Product Safety Commission — Stuart M. Statler, chmn. (1111 18th St. NW, 20036).

Environmental Protection Agency — Ann McGill Gorsuch, adm. (401 M St., SW, 20460).

Equal Employment Opportunity Commission — vacancy, chmn. (2401 E St., NW, 20506).

Export-Import Bank of the United States — Margaret W. Kahliff, pres. and chmn. (811 Vermont Ave. NW, 20571).

Farm Credit Administration — William Dale Nix, chmn. (490 L'Enfant Plaza East SW, 20578).

Federal Communications Commission — Charles D. Ferris, chmn. (1919 M St. NW, 20554).

Federal Deposit Insurance Corporation — Irvine H. Sprague, chmn. (550 17th St. NW, 20429).

Federal Election Commission — John Warren McGarry, chmn. (1325 K St. NW, 20463).

Federal Emergency Management Agency — Louis O. Giuffrida, dir. (1725 I St., 20472).

Federal Home Loan Bank Board — Richard T. Pratt, chmn. (1700 G St. NW, 20552).

Federal Labor Relations Authority — Ronald W. Haughton, chmn. (1900 E St. NW, 20424).

Federal Maritime Commission — Leslie L. Kanuk, chmn. (1100 L St. NW, 20573).

Federal Mediation and Conciliation Service — vacancy, dir. (2100 K St. NW, 20427).

Federal Reserve System — Chairman, board of governors: Paul A. Volcker. (20th St. & Constitution Ave. NW, 20551).

Federal Trade Commission — Commissioners: David A. Clanton, act. chmn., Paul Rand Dixon, Robert Pitofsky, Patricia P. Bailey, Michael Pertschuk. (Pennsylvania Ave. at 6th St. NW, 20580).

General Accounting Office — Comptroller general of the U.S.; Milton J. Socolar, act. (441 G St. NW, 20548).

General Services Administration — Gerald P. Carmen, adm. (18th & F Sts. NW, 20405).

Government Printing Office — Public printer: Danford L. Sawyer. (North Capitol and H Sts. NW, 20401).

Inter-American Foundation — Peter T. Jones, chmn. (1515 Wilson Blvd., Rosslyn, VA 22209).

International Communication Agency — John W. Shirley, dir. (1750 Pennsylvania Ave. NW, 20547).

Interstate Commerce Commission — Marcus Alexis, act. chmn. (12th St. and Constitution Ave. NW, 20423).

Library of Congress — Daniel J. Boorstin, librarian (10 First St. SE, 20540).

Merit Systems Protection Board — vacancy, chmn. (1717 H St. NW, 20419).

National Aeronautics and Space Administration — Alan M. Lovelace, adm. (400 Maryland Ave., SW 20546).

National Capital Planning Commission — Helen M. Scharf, chmn. (1325 G St., 20576).

National Credit Union Administration — Lawrence Connell, chmn. (1776 G St. NW, 20456).

National Foundation on the Arts and Humanities — Francis S. M. Hodsoll, chmn. (arts). Joseph D. Duffey, chmn. (arts: 2401 E St. NW, 20506; humanities: 806 15th St. NW, 20506).

National Labor Relations Board — John H. Fanning, chmn. (1717 Pennsylvania Ave. NW, 20570).

National Mediation Board — George S. Ives, chmn. (1425 K St. NW, 20572).

National Science Foundation — Lewis M. Branscomb, chmn. (1800 G St. NW, 20550).

National Transportation Safety Board — James B. King, chmn. (800 Independence Ave. SW, 20594).

Nuclear Regulatory Commission — Joseph M. Hendrie, chmn. (1717 H St. NW, 20555).

Occupational Safety and Health Review Commission — Timothy F. Cleary, chmn. (1825 K St. NW, 20006).

Office of Personnel Management — Donald J. Devine, dir., (1900 E St. NW, 20415).

Overseas Private Investment Corporation — Gerald T. West, pres. (1129 20th St. NW, 20527).

Panama Canal Commission — Dennis P. McAuliffe, adm. (in Panama); Michael Rhode Jr., secy. (in Washington).

Pennsylvania Avenue Development Corporation — Max N. Berry, chmn., board of directors (425 13th St. NW, 20004).

Pension Benefit Guaranty Corporation — Robert E. Nagle, exec. dir. (2020 K St. NW, 20006).

Postal Rate Commission — A. Lee Fritschler, chmn. (2000 L St. NW, 20268).

Railroad Retirement Board — William P. Adams, chmn. (Rm. 444, 425 13th St. NW, 20004), Main Office (844 Rush St., Chicago, IL 60611).

Securities and Exchange Commission — Commissioners: Harold M. Williams, chmn.; Philip Loomis Jr., John R. Evans, Stephen J. Friedman, Barbara Thomas (500 N. Capitol St., 20549).

Selective Service System — Bernard D. Rostker, dir. (600 E St. NW, 20435).

Small Business Administration — Michael Cardenas, adm. (1441 L St. NW, 20416).

Smithsonian Institution — S. Dillon Ripley, secy. (1000 Jefferson Dr. SW, 20560).

Tennessee Valley Authority — Chairman, board of directors: S. David Freeman. (400 Commerce Ave., Knoxville, TN 37902 and Woodward Bldg. 15th and H Sts. NW, Washington, D.C. 20444).

United States International Development Cooperation Agency — M. Peter McPherson, act. dir. (320 21st St., 20523).

United States International Trade Commission — Bill Alberger, chmn. (701 E St. NW, 20436).

United States Metric Board — Louis F. Polk, chmn. (1815 N. Lynn St. Arlington, Va. 22209).

United States Postal Service — William F. Bolger, postmaster general (475 L'Enfant Plaza West SW, 20260).

Veterans Administration — Donald H. Curtis, M.D., act. adm. (810 Vermont Ave. NW, 20420).

NATIONAL DEFENSE

Data as of July, 1982

Chairman, Joint Chiefs of Staff
John W. Vessey Jr. (USA)

The Joint Chiefs of Staff consists of the Chairman of the Joint Chiefs of Staff; the Chief of Staff, U.S. Army; the Chief of Naval Operations; the Chief of Staff, U.S. Air Force; and the Commandant of the Marine Corps.

Army

Chief of Staff—Edward C. Meyer

Generals

	Date of Rank
Cavazos, Richard G.	Feb. 15, 1982
Keith, Donald R.	Sept. 1, 1981
Kroesen, Frederick J.	Oct. 1, 1976
Meyer, Edward C.	June 22, 1979
Otis, Glenn K.	Aug. 1, 1981
Rogers, Bernard W.	Nov. 7, 1974
Sennewald, Robert W.	May 24, 1982
Starry, Donn A.	Jul. 1, 1977
Vessey Jr., John W.	Nov. 1, 1976
Wickham, John A.	July 10, 1979

Air Force

Chief of Staff—Charles A. Gabriel

Generals

Allen, James R.	Aug. 1, 1977
Creech, Wilbur L.	May 1, 1978
Davis, Bennie L.	Apr. 1, 1979
Gabriel, Charles A.	Aug. 1, 1980
Hartinger, James V.	Oct. 1, 1981
Lawson, Richard L.	July 1, 1980
Marsh, Robert T.	Feb. 1, 1981
Minter, Billy M.	July 1, 1982
O'Malley, Jerome F.	June 1, 1982
Ryan Jr., Thomas M.	July 31, 1981
Smith, William Y.	July 1, 1979

Navy

Chief of Naval Operations
Admiral James D. Watkins (submariner)

Admirals

Crowe, William J., Jr. (submariner)	May 30, 1980
Foley, Sylvester R., Jr. (aviator)	May 28, 1982
Inman, Bobby R.	Feb. 12, 1981
Kinnear, George E. R., II (aviator)	July 31, 1981
Long, Robert L.J. (submariner)	July 5, 1977
Small, William N. (aviator)	July 1, 1981
Train, Harry D. II (surface warfare)	Oct. 1, 1978
Watkins, James D. (submariner)	Sept. 18, 1979
Williams, John G., Jr. (submariner)	July 1, 1981

Marine Corps

Corps Commandant, with rank of General

Robert H. Barrow . . . . July 1, 1978

Asst. Commandant and Chief of Staff, with rank of General

Paul X. Kelley . . . . July 1, 1981

Coast Guard

Commandant, with rank of Admiral

James S. Gracey. . . . . May 27, 1982

Vice Commandant, with rank of Vice Admiral

Benedict Stabile . . . . May 21, 1982

United States Unified and Specified Commands

Atlantic Command—Admiral Harry D. Train II, USN

HQ Aerospace Defense Command—Lt. Gen. James V. Hartinger, USAF

U.S. European Command—General Bernard W. Rogers, USA

Pacific Command—Admiral Robert L. Long, USN

U.S. Southern Command—Lt. Gen. Wallace H. Nutting, USA

Strategic Air Command—General Bennie L. Davis, USAF

U.S. Readiness Command—General Donn A. Starry, USA

Military Air Lift Command—General James R. Allen, USAF

Military Sea Lift Command—Rear Admiral Bruce Keener III, USN

North Atlantic Treaty Organization International Commands

Supr. Allied Commander, Europe (SACEUR)—Gen. Bernard W. Rogers, USA

Deputy SACEUR—Air Ch. Marshal Sir Peter Terry (UK), Adm. G. Luther (Germany)

C-in-C Allied Forces, Northern Europe—Gen. Sir Anthony Farrar-Hockley (UK)

C-in-C Allied Forces, Central Europe—Gen. Dr. F. von Senger und Etterlin (Germany)

C-In-C Allied Forces, Southern Europe—Adm. W.J. Crowe, USN

Supr. Allied Commander Atlantic (SACLANT)—Adm. Harry D. Train II, USN

Deputy SACLANT—V. Adm. Sir Cameron Rusby (UK)

Commander Strike Force South—V. Adm. W.N. Small, USN

Allied Commander in Chief, Channel—Adm. Sir Edward Ashmore (UK)

Principal U.S. Military Training Centers

Army

Name, P.O. address	Zip	Nearest city
Aberdeen Proving Ground, MD	21005	Aberdeen
Carlisle Barracks, PA	17013	Carlisle
Fort Belvoir, VA	22060	Alexandria
Fort Benning, GA	31905	Columbus
Fort Bliss, TX	79916	El Paso
Fort Bragg, NC	28307	Fayetteville
Fort Devens, MA	01433	Ayer
Fort Dix, NJ	08640	Trenton
Fort Eustis, VA	23604	Newport News
Fort Gordon, GA	30905	Augusta
Fort Benjamin Harrison, IN	46216	Indianapolis
Fort Sam Houston, TX	78234	San Antonio
Fort Huachuca, AZ	85613	Sierra Vista
Fort Jackson, SC	29207	Columbia
Fort Knox, KY	40121	Louisville
Fort Leavenworth, KS	66027	Leavenworth
Fort Lee, VA	23801	Petersburg
Fort McClellan, AL	36205	Anniston
Fort Monmouth, NJ	07703	Red Bank
Fort Rucker, AL	36362	Dothan
Fort Sill, OK	73503	Lawton
Fort Leonard Wood, MO	65473	Rolla
National Training Center	92311	Ft. Irwin
Redstone Arsenal, AL	35809	Huntsville
The Judge Advocate General School, VA	22901	Charlottesville

Navy Recruit Training Centers

Great Lakes, IL	60088	North Chicago
San Diego, CA	92133	San Diego
Orlando, FL	32813	Orlando

Major Marine Corps Facilities

Name, P.O. address	Zip	Nearest city
MCB Camp Lejeune, NC	28542	Jacksonville
MCB Camp Pendleton, CA	92055	Oceanside
MCB Camp Butler, Okinawa	FPO Seattle 98773	Futenma, Okinawa
MCAGCC Twentynine Palms, CA	92278	Palm Springs
MCDEC Quantico, VA	22134	Quantico
MCRD Parris Island, SC	29905	Beaufort
MCRD San Diego, CA	92140	San Diego
MCAS Cherry Point, NC	28533	Cherry Point
MCAS El Toro (Santa Ana), CA	92709	Santa Ana
MCAS (Helo) Tustin, CA	92780	Santa Ana
MCAS (Helo) New River, NC	28540	Jacksonville
MCAS Iwakuni, Japan	FPO Seattle 98764	Iwakuni
MCAS Kaneohe Bay, Oahu, HI	FPO San Francisco 96615	Kailua
MCAS (Helo) Futenma, Okinawa	FPO Seattle 98764	Futenma
MCAS Beaufort, SC	29902	Beaufort
MCAS Yuma, AZ	85364	Yuma
MCMWTC Bridgeport, CA	93517	Bridgeport

MCB = Marine Corps Base. MCDEC = Marine Corps Development & Education Command. MCAS = Marine Corps Air Station. Helo = Helicopter. MCAGCC = Marine Corps Air-Ground Combat Center. MCMWTC = Marine Corps Mountain Warfare Training Center.

Air Force

Chanute AFB, IL	61868	Rantoul
Columbus AFB, MS	36701	Columbus
Fairchild AFB, WA	99011	Spokane
Goodfellow AFB, TX	76903	San Angelo
Keesler AFB, MS	39534	Biloxi
Lackland AFB, TX	78236	San Antonio
Laughlin AFB, TX	78840	Del Rio
Lowry AFB, CO	80230	Denver
Mather AFB, CA	95655	Sacramento
Maxwell AFB, AL	36112	Montgomery
Randolph AFB, TX	78148	San Antonio
Reese AFB, TX	79489	Lubbock
Sheppard AFB, TX	76311	Wichita Falls
Vance AFB, OK	73701	Enid
Williams AFB, AZ	85224	Chandler

Personal Salutes and Honors

The United States national salute, 21 guns, is also the salute to a national flag. The independence of the United States is commemorated by the salute to the union — one gun for each state — fired at noon on July 4 at all military posts provided with suitable artillery.

A-21-gun salute on arrival and departure, with 4 ruffles and flourishes, is rendered to the President of the United States, to an ex-President and to a President-elect. The national anthem or *Hail to the Chief*, as appropriate, is played for the President, and the national anthem for the others. A 21-gun salute on arrival and departure with 4 ruffles and flourishes, also is rendered to the sovereign or chief of state of a foreign country or a member of a reigning royal family; the national anthem of his or her country is played. The music is considered an inseparable part of the salute and will immediately follow the ruffles and flourishes without pause.

Rank	Salute—guns Arrive	Leave	Ruffles, flourishes	Music
Vice President of United States	19		4	Hail Columbia
Speaker of the House	19		4	March
American or foreign ambassador	19		4	Nat. anthem of official
Premier or prime minister	19		4	Nat. anthem of official
Secretary of Defense, Army, Navy or Air Force	19	19	4	March
Other Cabinet members, Senate President pro tempore, Governor, or Chief Justice of U.S.	19		4	March
Chairman, Joint Chiefs of Staff	19	19	4	
Army Chief of Staff, Chief of Naval Operations, Air Force Chief of Staff, Marine Commandant	19	19	4	General's or Admiral's March
General of the Army, General of the Air Force, Fleet Admiral	19	19	4	
Generals, Admirals	17	17	4	
Assistant Secretaries of Defense, Army, Navy or Air Force	17	17	4	March
Chairman of a Committee of Congress	17		4	March

Other salutes (on arrival only) include 15 guns for American envoys or ministers and foreign envoys or ministers accredited to the United States; 15 guns for a lieutenant general or vice admiral; 13 guns for a major general or rear admiral (upper half); 13 guns for American ministers resident and ministers resident accredited to the U.S.; 11 guns for a brigadier general or rear admiral (lower half); 11 guns for American charges d'affaires and like officials accredited to U.S.; and 11 guns for consuls general accredited to U.S.

Military Units, U.S. Army and Air Force

Army units. Squad. In infantry usually ten men under a staff sergeant. **Platoon.** In infantry 4 squads under a lieutenant. **Company.** Headquarters section and 4 platoons under a captain. (Company in the artillery is a battery; in the cavalry, a troop.) **Battalion.** Hdqts. and 4 or more companies under a lieutenant colonel. (Battalion size unit in the cavalry is a squadron.) **Brigade.** Hdqts. and 3 or more battalions under a colonel. **Division.** Hdqts. and 3 brigades with artillery, combat support, and combat service support units under a major general. **Army Corps.** Two or more divisions with corps troops under a lieutenant general. **Field Army.** Hdqts. and two or more corps with field Army troops under a general.

Air Force Units. Flight. Numerically designated flights are the lowest level unit in the Air Force. They are used primarily where there is a need for small mission elements to be incorporated into an organized unit. **Squadron.** A squadron is the basic unit in the Air Force. It is used to designate the mission units in operational commands. **Group.** The group is a flexible unit composed of two or more squadrons whose functions may be either tactical, support or administrative in nature. **Wing.** An operational wing normally has two or more assigned mission squadrons in an area such as combat, flying training or airlift. **Air Division.** The organization of the air division may be similar to that of the numbered air force, though on a much smaller scale. Functions are usually limited to operations and logistics. **Numbered Air Forces.** Normally an operationally oriented agency, the numbered air force is designed for the control of two or more air divisions or units of comparable strength. It is a flexible organization and may be of any size. Its wings may be assigned to air divisions or directly under the numbered air force. **Major Command.** A major subdivision of the Air Force that is assigned a major segment of the USAF mission.

U.S. Army Insignia and Chevrons

Source: Department of the Army

Grade **Insignia**

General of the Armies

General John J. Pershing, the only person to have held this rank, was authorized to prescribe his own insignia, but never wore in excess of four stars. The rank originally was established by Congress for George Washington in 1799, and he was promoted to the rank by joint resolution of Congress, approved by Pres. Ford Oct. 19, 1976.

General of Army... Five silver stars fastened together in a circle and the coat of arms of the United States in gold color metal with shield and crest enameled.

Grade	Insignia
General	Four silver stars
Lieutenant General	Three silver stars
Major General	Two silver stars
Brigadier General	One silver star
Colonel	Silver eagle
Lieutenant Colonel	Silver oak leaf
Major	Gold oak leaf
Captain	Two silver bars
First Lieutenant	One silver bar
Second Lieutenant	One gold bar

Warrant officers

Grade Four—Silver bar with 4 enamel black bands.
Grade Three—Silver bar with 3 enamel black bands.
Grade Two—Silver bar with 2 enamel black bands.
Grade One—Silver bar with 1 enamel black band.

Non-commissioned Officers

Sergeant Major of the Army (E-9). Same as Command Sergeant Major (below) but with 2 stars. Also wears distinctive red and white shield on lapel.

Command Sergeant Major (E-9). Three chevrons above three arcs with a 5-pointed star with a wreath around the star between the chevrons and arcs.

Sergeant Major (E-9). Three chevrons above three arcs with a five-pointed star between the chevrons and arcs.

First Sergeant (E-8). Three chevrons above three arcs with a lozenge between the chevrons and arcs.

Master Sergeant (E-8). Three chevrons above three arcs.

Platoon Sergeant or Sergeant First Class (E-7). Three chevrons above two arcs.

Staff Sergeant (E-6). Three chevrons above one arc.

Sergeant (E-5). Three chevrons.

Corporal (E-4). Two chevrons.

Specialists

Specialist Seven (E-7). Three arcs above the eagle device.

Specialist Six (E-6). Two arcs above the eagle device.

Specialist Five (E-5). One arc above the eagle device.

Specialist Four (E-4). Eagle device only.

Other enlisted

Private First Class (E-3). One chevron above one arc.

Private (E-2). One chevron.

Private (E-1). None.

U.S. Army

Source: Department of the Army

Army Military Personnel on Active Duty[1]

June 30[2]	Total strength	Commissioned officers			Warrant officers		Enlisted personnel		
		Total	Male	Female[3]	Male[4]	Female	Total	Male	Female
1940	267,767	17,563	16,624	939	763	—	249,441	249,441	—
1942	3,074,184	203,137	190,662	12,475	3,285	—	2,867,762	2,867,762	—
1943	6,993,102	557,657	521,435	36,222	21,919	0	6,413,526	6,358,200	55,325
1944	7,992,868	740,077	692,351	47,726	36,893	10	7,215,888	7,144,601	71,287
1945	8,266,373	835,403	772,511	62,892	56,216	44	7,374,710	7,283,930	90,780
1946	1,889,690	257,300	240,643	16,657	9,826	18	1,622,546	1,605,847	16,699
1950	591,487	67,784	63,375	4,409	4,760	22	518,921	512,370	6,551
1955	1,107,606	111,347	106,173	5,174	10,552	48	985,659	977,943	7,716
1960	871,348	91,056	86,832	4,224	10,141	39	770,112	761,833	8,279
1965	967,049	101,812	98,029	3,783	10,285	23	854,929	846,409	8,520
1969	1,509,637	148,836	143,699	5,137	23,734	20	1,337,047	1,316,326	10,721
1970	1,319,735	143,704	138,469	5,235	23,005	13	1,153,013	1,141,537	11,476
1975	781,316	89,756	85,184	4,572	13,214	22	678,324	640,621	37,703
1977 (Mar. 31)	774,664	84,984	79,599	5,385	13,005	36	676,639	631,410	45,229
1978 (May 31)	772,202	96,553	90,749	5,804	13,160	57	662,432	614,961	47,471
1979 (May 31)	757,822	87,420	80,922	6,498	13,181	78	657,143	606,872	50,271
1980 (Mar. 31)	762,739	83,117	76,237	6,880	13,093	103	666,426	608,223	58,203
1981 (Jan.) . .	769,673	85,017	77,179	7,374	13,563	120	671,057	608,293	62,764
1982 (Mar.) . .	788,026	87,874	79,379	8,495	14,058	143	685,951	618,783	67,168

(1) Represents strength of the active Army, including Philippine Scouts, retired Regular Army personnel on extended active duty, and National Guard and Reserve personnel on extended active duty; excludes U.S. Military Academy cadets, contract surgeons, and National Guard and Reserve personnel not on extended active duty.
(2) Data for 1940 to 1947 include personnel in the Army Air Forces and its predecessors (Air Service and Air Corps).
(3) Includes: women doctors, dentists, and Medical Service Corps officers for 1946 and subsequent years, women in the Army Nurse Corps for all years, and the Women's Army Corps and Women's Medical Specialists Corps (dieticians, physical therapists, and occupational specialists) for 1943 and subsequent years.
(4) Act of Congress approved April 27, 1926, directed the appointment as warrant officers of field clerks still in active service. Includes flight officers as follows: 1943, 5,700; 1944, 13,615; 1945, 31,117; 1946, 2,580.

The Federal Service Academies

U.S. Military Academy, West Point, N.Y. Founded 1802. Awards B.S. degree and Army commission for a 5-year service obligation. For admissions information, write Admissions Office, USMA, West Point, NY 10996.

U.S. Naval Academy, Annapolis, Md. Founded 1845. Awards B.S. degree and Navy or Marine Corps commission for a 5-year service obligation. For admissions information, write Dean of Admissions, Naval Academy, Annapolis, MD 21402.

U.S. Air Force Academy, Colorado Springs, Colo. Founded 1954. Awards B.S. degree and Air Force commission for a 5-year service obligation. For admissions information, write Registrar, U.S. Air Force Academy, CO 80840.

U.S. Coast Guard Academy, New London, Conn. Founded 1876. Awards B.S. degree and Coast Guard commission for a 5-year service obligation. For admissions information, write Director of Admissions, Coast Guard Academy, New London, CT 06320.

U.S. Merchant Marine Academy, Kings Point, N.Y. Founded 1943. Awards B.S. degree, a license as a deck, engineer, or dual officer, and a U.S. Naval Reserve commission. Service obligations vary according to options taken by the graduate. For admissions information, write Admission Office, U.S. Merchant Marine Academy, Kings Point, NY 11024.

U.S. Navy Insignia

Source: Department of the Navy

Navy

Stripes and corps device are of gold embroidery.

	Stripes
Fleet Admiral	1 two inch with 4 one-half inch.
Admiral	1 two inch with 3 one-half inch.
Vice Admiral	1 two inch with 2 one-half inch.
Rear Admiral	1 two inch with 1 one-half inch.
Commodore Admiral	1 two inch.
Captain	4 one-half inch.
Commander	3 one-half inch.
Lieut. Commander	2 one-half inch, with 1 one-quarter inch between.
Lieutenant	2 one-half inch.
Lieutenant (j.g.)	1 one-half inch with one-quarter inch above.
Ensign	1 one-half inch.

Warrant Officers—One 1/2" broken with 1/2" intervals of blue as follows:

Warrant Officer W-4—1 break
Warrant Officer W-3—2 breaks, 2" apart
Warrant Officer W-2—3 breaks, 2" apart

The breaks are symmetrically centered on outer face of the sleeve.

Enlisted personnel (non-Commissioned petty officers). . .A rating badge worn on the upper left arm, consisting of a spread eagle, appropriate number of chevrons, and centered specialty mark.

Marine Corps

Marine Corps and Army officer insignia are similar. Marine Corps and Army enlisted insignia, although basically similar, differ in color, design, and fewer Marine Corps subdivisions. The Marine Corps' distinctive cap and collar ornament is a combination of the American eagle, globe, and anchor.

Coast Guard

Coast Guard insignia follow Navy custom, with certain minor changes such as the officer cap insignia. The Coast Guard shield is worn on both sleeves of officers and on the right sleeve of all enlisted men.

U.S. Navy Personnel on Active Duty

June 30	Officers[1]	Nurses	Enlisted[2]	Off. Cand.	Total
1940	13,162	442	144,824	2,569	160,997
1945	320,293	11,086	2,988,207	61,231	3,380,817
1950	42,687	1,964	331,860	5,037	381,538
1960	67,456	2,103	544,040	4,385	617,984
1970	78,488	2,273	605,899	6,000	692,660
1975	65,900	—	483,500	—	549,400
1980	63,100	—	464,100	—	527,200
1982 (est)	67,200	—	485,800	—	553,000

(1) Nurses are included after 1973. (2) Officer candidates are included after 1973.

Marine Corps Personnel On Active Duty

Yr.	Officers	Enl.	Total	Yr.	Officers	Enl.	Total	Yr.	Officers	Enl.	Total
1955	18,417	186,753	205,170	1965	17,258	172,955	190,213	1980	18,198	170,271	188,469
1960	16,203	154,418	170,621	1970	24,941	234,796	259,737	1981	18,363	172,257	190,620

Armed Services Senior Enlisted Adviser

The U.S. Army, Navy and Air Force in 1966-67 each created a new position of senior enlisted adviser whose primary job is to represent the point of view of his services' enlisted men and women on matters of welfare, morale, and any problems concerning enlisted personnel. The senior adviser will have direct access to the military chief of his branch of service and policy-making bodies.

The senior enlisted adviser for each Dept. is:

Army-Sgt. Major of the Army William A. Connelly.

Navy-Master Chief Petty Officer of the Navy Thomas S. Crow.

Air Force-Chief Master Sgt. of the AF James M. McCoy.

Marines-Sgt. Major of the Marine Corps Leland D. Crawford.

Veteran Population

Source: Veterans Administration

	March 1982
Veterans in civil life, end of month — Total	**30,006,000**
War Veterans — Total	**25,625,000**
Vietnam Era — Total (a)(b)	9,110,000
And service in Korean Conflict	548,000
No service in Korean Conflict	8,562,000
Korean Conflict — Total (includes line 4)	5,754,000
And service in WW II	1,137,000
No service in WW II	4,617,000
World War II (includes line 7)	12,030,000
World War I	416,000
Spanish-American War	72
Post-Vietnam Era (b)	1,347,000
Service between Korean Conflict (January 31, 1955) and Vietnam (August 5, 1964) only (b)	3,034,000

(a) Service between Aug. 4, 1964 and May 8, 1975; (b) excludes those who served on active duty for training only.

Pension Cases and Compensation Payments

Fiscal year	Living veteran cases No.	Deceased veteran cases No.	Total cases No.	Total disbursement Dollars	Fiscal year	Living veteran cases No.	Deceased veteran cases No.	Total cases No.	Total disbursement Dollars
1890	415,654	122,290	537,944	106,093,850	1965	3,204,275	1,277,009	4,481,284	3,901,598,01
1900	752,510	241,019	993,529	138,462,130	1970	3,127,338	1,487,176	4,614,514	5,113,649,49
1910	602,622	318,461	921,083	159,974,056	1975	3,226,701	1,628,146	4,854,847	7,600,000,00
1920	419,627	349,916	769,543	316,418,029	1976	3,235,778	1,630,830	4,866,608	8,074,488,00
1930	542,610	298,223	840,833	418,432,808	1977	3,272,821	1,628,488	4,901,309	8,874,720,00
1940	610,122	239,176	849,298	429,138,465	1978	3,283,120	1,622,269	4,905,389	9,371,704,00
1950	2,368,238	658,123	3,026,361	2,009,462,298	1979	3,240,283	1,529,206	4,769,489	10,324,258,00
1955	2,668,786	808,303	3,477,089	2,634,292,537	1980	3,195,395	1,450,785	4,646,180	11,045,412,00
1960	3,008,935	950,802	3,959,737	3,314,761,383	1981	3,154,030	1,381,280	4,535,310	12,225,027,341

U.S. Air Force

Source: Department of the Air Force

The Army Air forces were started Aug. 1, 1907, as the Aeronau-ical Division of the Signal Corps, U.S. Army. The division con-isted of one officer and two enlisted men, and it was more than a ear before it carried out its first mission in an airplane of its own. When the U.S. entered World War I (April 6, 1917), the Aviation ervice, as it was called then, had 55 planes and 65 officers, only 35 f whom were fliers. On the day the Japanese struck at Pearl Har-or (Dec. 7, 1941), the Army Air Forces, as they had been re-named 6 months previously, had 10,329 planes, of which only 2,846 were suited for combat service. But when the Army's air arm reached its peak during World War II (in July, 1944), it had 79,908 of all types of aircraft and (in May 1945) 43,248 combat aircraft and (in March, 1944) 2,411,294 officers and enlisted men. The Air Force was established under the Armed Services Unification Act of July 26, 1947.

USAF Personnel at Home and Overseas — Officers and Enlisted

June 30	Continental U.S.	Overseas	Total	June 30	Continental U.S.	Overseas	Total
940	40,229	10,936	51,165	1970	531,386	255,819	787,205
945	1,153,373	1,128,886	2,282,259	1975	457,484	150,853	608,337
950	317,816	93,461	411,277	1979	417,196	140,660	557,856
955	689,635	270,311	959,946	1980	434,646	118,604	553,250
957[1]	651,674	268,161	919,835	1981	424,504	137,880	562,384
960[2]	607,383	207,369	814,752	1982	437,184	142,638	578,822
965	635,430	189,232	824,662				

(1) Since 1957 continental U.S. includes Air Force Academy Cadets as follows: (1957) 504; (1960) 1,949; (1963) 2,660; (1964) ,838; (1965) 2,907; (1966) 3,152; (1967) 3,361; (1968) 3,652; (1969) 3,941; (1970) 4,144; (1971) 2,997; (1972) 2,885; (1973) 4,356; 974) 4,412; (1975) 4,414; (1976) 4,415; (1977) 4,680; (1978) 4,524; (1979) 4,578; (1980) 4,000; (1981) 4,178; (1982) 4,688.
(2) Since 1960 Overseas includes Alaska and Hawaii. All figures include Mobilized Personnel.

USAF Military Personnel

June 30	Officers & Enlisted	Male commissioned officers: USAF	USAFR	ANG	AFUS & AUS	Warrant officers
955	959,946	23,463	105,587	984	2	3,961
960	814,752	49,584	72,115	248	3	4,069
965	824,662	62,076	62,537	280	54	2,532
970	787,205	63,678	65,852	168	105	639
975	608,337	57,854	42,131	128	28	39
979	557,856	55,815	39,688	142	15	2
980	553,250	54,621	35,454	115	6	1
981	562,384	55,317	35,762	295	—	0
982	578,822	58,052	34,251	297	—	0

Female Commissioned Officers, and Enlisted Personnel

June 30	Female commissioned officers: Total	USAF	Nurses	WMSC	Female WO	Enlisted personnel: Total	Male	Female
960	3,858	679	3,020	159	5	685,063	679,412	5,651
965	4,099	708	3,185	206	1	690,177	685,436	4,741
970	4,667	1,072	3,407	188	0	657,402	648,415	8,987
975	4,981	1,542	3,236	203	0	503,176	477,944	25,232
980	8,060	4,291	3,200	569	0	454,994	404,480	50,514
981	9,045	5,016	3,317	712	0	462,212	408,460	53,752
982	9,796	5,646	3,414	736	0	476,723	422,240	54,483

Women in the Armed Forces

The Army, Navy, Air Force, Marines, and Coast Guard re all fully integrated. Expansion of military women's pro-rams began in the Department of Defense in fiscal year 973. The planned end strength for fiscal year 1983 is ap-roximately 199,000, which is 11.1% of the planned strength f the active forces.

Although women are prohibited by law and directives ased on law from serving in combat positions, policy hanges in the department have resulted in making possible he assignment of women to almost all other career fields. areer progression for women is now comparable to that for ale personnel. Women are routinely assigned to overseas ocations formerly closed to female personnel. Women are in ommand of activities and units that have missions other han administration of women.

Admission of women to the service academies began in he fall of 1976 and will further the goal of increased num-ers of women officers. The academies will provide single rack education, allowing only for minor variations in the adet program based on physiological differences between en and women.

Army — Information: Chief, Office of Public Affairs, Dept. of Army, Wash., DC 20310; 8,638 women officers, cluding Army Nurse Corps, and 67,168 enlisted women; omen excluded only from direct combat roles in infantry and armor.

Army Nurse Corps — Brig. Gen. Hazel Johnson, Chief Army Nurse Corps, Office of the Surgeon General, Dept. of Army, Wash., DC 20310; includes 29% men.

Navy — Information: Chief of Information, Dept. of Navy, Wash., DC 20350; 5,345 women officers; 34,244 en-listed women.

Navy Nurse Corps — Rear Adm. Frances T. Shea, Direc-tor, Navy Nurse Corps, Bureau of Medicine and Surgery, Dept. of Navy, Wash., DC 20372; 1,982 women officers; in-cludes 712 men.

Air Force — Information: Office of Public Affairs, Dept. of the Air Force, Wash., DC 20330; 9,666 women officers; 54,564 enlisted women.

Air Force Nurse Corps — Brig. Gen. Sarah P. Wells, Chief, Air Force Nurse Corps, Office of the Surgeon Gen., USAF, Bolling AFB, Wash., DC 20332; 4,354 officers; in-cludes 3,412 women, 942 men.

Marine Corps — Information: Commandant of the Ma-rine Corps (Code PA), Headquarters, Marine Corps, Wash., DC 20380; 546 women officers; 7,645 enlisted women.

Coast Guard — Information: Commandant (G-BPA), U.S. Coast Guard, 2100 Second St., SW, Wash., DC 20593; 127 women officers; 1,600 enlisted women.

Monthly Pay Scale o

Fisca

Commissioned Officers

Pay grade	Army rank	Navy rank	Under 2	Over 2	Over 3	Over 4	Over 6	Over 8
	Rank or pay grade		Cumulative years of service					
0-10[1]	General*	Admiral	$4,506.60	$4,665.30	$4,665.30	$4,665.30	$4,665.30	$4,844.1
0-9	Lieutenant General	Vice Admiral	3,994.20	4,090.90	4,186.20	4,186.20	4,186.20	4,292.7
0-8	Major General	Rear Admiral (up. half)	3,617.70	3,726.00	3,814.50	3,814.50	3,814.50	4,090.9
0-7	Brigadier General	Rear Admiral (low half)	3,006.00	3,210.60	3,210.60	3,210.60	3,354.30	3,354.3
0-6	Colonel	Captain	2,228.10	2,448.30	2,608.20	2,608.20	2,608.20	2,608.2
0-5	Lieutenant Colonel	Commander	1,782.00	2,092.80	2,237.10	2,237.10	2,237.10	2,237.1
0-4	Major	Lieutenant Comdr.	1,502.10	1,828.80	1,951.20	1,951.20	1,986.90	2,075.1
0-3	Captain	Lieutenant	1,395.90	1,560.60	1,668.30	1,845.90	1,934.10	2,004.0
0-2	First Lieutenant	Lieutenant (J.G.)	1,217.10	1,329.30	1,596.90	1,650.60	1,685.10	1,685.1
0-1	Second Lieutenant	Ensign	1,056.60	1,099.80	1,329.30	1,329.30	1,329.30	1,329.3
Commissioned officers with over 4 years service as enlisted member or warrant officer								
0-3	Capitain	Lieutenant	0.00	0.00	0.00	1,845.90	1,934.10	2,004.0
0-2	First Lieutenant	Lieutenant (J.G.)	0.00	0.00	0.00	1,650.60	1,685.10	1,738.5
0-1	Second Lieutenant	Ensign	0.00	0.00	0.00	1,329.30	1,419.90	1,472.4

Warrant Officers

Pay grade	Army rank	Navy rank	Under 2	Over 2	Over 3	Over 4	Over 6	Over 8
W-4	Chief Warrant	Comm. Warrant	1,422.00	1,525.50	1,525.50	1,560.60	1,631.40	1,703.4
W-3	Chief Warrant	Comm. Warrant	1,292.70	1,402.20	1,402.20	1,419.90	1,436.70	1,541.7
W-2	Chief Warrant	Comm. Warrant	1,132.20	1,224.60	1,224.60	1,260.30	1,329.30	1,402.2
W-1	Warrant Officer	Warrant Officer	943.20	1,081.50	1,081.50	1,171.90	1,224.60	1,277.4

Enlisted Personnel[2]

Pay grade	Army rank	Navy rank	Under 2	Over 2	Over 3	Over 4	Over 6	Over 8
E-9[3]	Sergeant Major**	Master C.P.O.	0.00	0.00	0.00	0.00	0.00	0.0
E-8[3]	Master Sergeant	Senior C.P.O.	0.00	0.00	0.00	0.00	0.00	1,387.5
E-7	Sgt. 1st Class	Chief Petty Officer	968.70	1,045.50	1,084.50	1,122.00	1,160.70	1,197.3
E-6	Staff Sergeant	Petty Officer 1st Class	833.10	908.40	946.50	986.40	1,023.00	1,060.5
E-5	Sergeant	Petty Officer 2nd Cl.	731.40	796.20	834.60	870.90	927.90	965.7
E-4	Corporal	Petty Officer 3rd Cl.	682.20	720.30	762.30	821.70	854.40	854.4
E-3	Private 1st Class	Seaman	642.60	673.70	705.00	732.90	732.90	732.9
E-2	Private	Seaman Apprentice	618.30	618.30	618.30	618.30	618.30	618.3
E-1	Private	Seaman Recruit	551.40	551.40	551.40	551.40	551.40	551.4

The pay scale also applies to: Coast Guard and Marine Corps, National Oceanic and Atmospheric Administration, Public Health Ser vice, National Guard, and the Organized Reserves.

*Basic pay is limited to $4,791.60 by Level V of the Executive Schedule and further limited by Sec. 101C, P.L. 96-86 to $4,176.00 max Four star General or Admiral—personal money allowances of $2,200 per annum, or $4,000 if Chief of Staff of the Army, Chief of Staff c the Air Force, Chief of Naval Operations, Commandant of the Marine Corps, or Commandant of the Coast Guard. Three star General o Admiral—personal money allowance of $500 per annum.

**A new title of Chief Master Sergeant created in 1965 rates E-9 classification.

(1) While serving as Chairman of Joint Chiefs of Staff, Chief of Staff of the Army, Chief of Naval Operations, Chief of Staff of the Ai Forces, or Commandant of the Marine Corps, basic pay for this grade is $6,988.50 regardless of years of service.

(2) Air Force enlisted personnel pay grades, E-9, Chief Master Sergeant; E-8, Sr. Master Sergeant; E-7, Master Sergeant; E-6, Technica Sergeant; E-5, Staff Sergeant; E-4, Sergeant; E-3, Airman 1st Class; E-2, Airman; E-1, Basic Airman.

Marine Corps enlisted ranks are as follows: E-9, Sergeant Major and Master Gunnery Sergeant; E-8, First Sergeant and Master Sergeant E-7, Gunnery Sergeant; E-6, Staff Sergeant; E-5, Sergeant; E-4, Corporal; E-3, Lance Corporal; E-2, Private, First Class Marine; E-1, Pri vate.

Marine Corps and Air Force officer ranks are same as Army.

(3) While serving as Sergeant Major of the Army, Master Chief Petty Officer of the Navy, Chief Master Sergeant of the Air Force, o Sergeant Major of the Marine Corps, basic pay for this grade is $2,589.90 regardless of years of service.

American Military Actions, 1900-1973

1900—Occupation of Puerto Rico (ceded to U.S., 1899).

1900—500 Marines, 1,500 Army troops help relieve Peking in Boxer Rebellion.

1900-1902—Occupation of Cuba.

1900-1902—Guerrilla war in Philippines.

1903—Sailors and Marines from U.S.S. Nashville stop Colombian Army at Panama.

1904—Brief intervention in Dominican Republic.

1906-1909—Intervention in Cuba.

1909—Brief intervention in Honduras.

1910, 1912-1913—Intervention in Nicaragua.

1911—Intervention (to collect customs) in Honduras, Nicaragua, Dominican Republic.

1912-1917—Intervention in Cuba.

1914—Intervention in Dominican Republic.

1914—April 21 to Nov. 23. Marines in Veracruz.

1914—Navy and Marines enter Haiti, stay until 1934.

1916—Gen. John J. Pershing and 10,000 into Northern Mexico to stop raids by Pancho Villa, Mar. 15-Nov. 24.

1916-1924—Marines in Dominican Republic.

1917—Apr. 6 to Nov. 11, 1918. War with Germany, Austria-Hungary.

1918-1920—Expeditions into North Russia, Siberia.

1918-1923—Occupation of Germany.

1922-1924—Marines in Nicaragua.

1926-1933—Marines in Nicaragua.

1927—1,000 Marines in China.

1941-1945—War with Japan, Germany, Italy and allies.

1950-1953—U.S. and other UN countries aid the Republi of Korea to repel North Korean invaders; U.S. Navy protects Taiwan.

1956—U.S. Fleet evacuates U.S. nationals during Suez cri sis.

1957—U.S. Fleet to Near East during Jordan crisis.

1958—Navy, Marines and Army units support Lebanon.

1960—Navy patrol in Caribbean to protect Guatemala an Nicaragua.

1961—Army units to Vietnam.

1962—Units of Navy on Cuban quarantine duty. Marines i Thailand.

1962-1965—U.S. Military Assistance Command, Vietnam units of Army, Navy, Air Force, Marine Corps, Coas

·he Uniformed Services
/ear 1981

Commissioned Officers

Cumulative years of service Over 10	Over 12	Over 14	Over 16	Over 18	Over 20	Over 22	Over 26	Basic allowances for quarters Without dependents	With dependents
$4,844.10	$5,215.20	$5,215.20	$5,588.10	$5,588.10	$5,961.90	$5,961.90	$6,333.90	$489.00	$611.70
4,292.70	4,471.20	4,471.20	4,844.10	4,844.10	5,215.20	5,215.20	5,588.10	489.00	611.70
4,090.90	4,292.70	4,292.70	4,471.20	4,665.30	4,844.10	5,038.20	5,038.20	489.00	611.70
3,549.00	3,549.00	3,726.00	4,090.90	4,380.60	4,380.60	4,380.60	4,380.60	489.00	611.70
2,608.20	2,608.20	2,696.70	3,123.60	3,283.20	3,354.30	3,540.90	3,849.00	438.90	535.50
2,305.20	2,428.80	2,591.40	2,785.50	2,945.40	3,034.20	3,140.40	3,140.40	404.70	487.20
2,216.40	2,341.20	2,448.30	2,555.40	2,626.20	2,626.20	2,626.20	2,626.20	360.30	434.70
2,111.70	2,216.40	2,271.00	2,271.00	2,271.00	2,271.00	2,271.00	2,271.00	316.80	390.90
1,685.10	1,685.10	1,685.10	1,685.10	1,685.10	1,685.10	1,685.10	1,685.10	275.10	348.00
1,329.30	1,329.30	1,329.30	1,329.30	1,329.30	1,329.30	1,329.30	1,329.30	214.80	279.60
2,111.70	2,216.40	2,305.20	2,305.20	2,305.20	2,305.20	2,305.20	2,305.20	316.80	390.90
1,828.80	1,899.00	1,951.20	1,951.20	1,951.20	1,951.20	1,951.20	1,951.20	275.10	348.00
1,525.50	1,578.60	1,650.60	1,650.60	1,650.60	1,650.60	1,650.60	1,650.60	214.80	279.60

Warrant Officers

1,774.80	1,899.00	1,986.90	2,057.10	2,111.70	2,180.40	2,253.60	2,428.80	347.10	419.10
1,631.40	1,685.10	1,738.50	1,790.70	1,845.90	1,917.30	1,986.90	2,057.10	309.60	381.60
1,455.00	1,508.40	1,560.60	1,615.20	1,668.30	1,721.10	1,790.70	1,790.70	269.10	342.60
1,329.30	1,384.20	1,436.70	1,489.50	1,541.70	1,596.90	1,596.90	1,596.90	243.00	314.70

Enlisted Personnel

1,653.90	1,691.40	1,729.80	1,760.70	1,809.00	1,844.10	1,941.30	2,130.00	261.90	368.70
1,426.60	1,464.30	1,502.70	1,542.00	1,577.70	1,616.40	1,711.50	1,902.30	241.50	340.50
1,236.00	1,274.10	1,331.70	1,369.50	1,400.10	1,426.50	1,522.20	1,711.50	205.50	316.80
1,099.20	1,155.90	1,192.20	1,230.60	1,249.20	1,249.20	1,249.20	1,249.20	186.60	291.60
1,004.40	1,041.30	1,060.50	1,060.50	1,060.50	1,060.50	1,060.50	1,060.50	179.40	267.90
854.40	854.40	854.40	854.40	854.40	854.40	854.40	854.40	158.10	235.50
732.90	732.90	732.90	732.90	732.90	732.90	732.90	732.90	141.30	205.50
618.30	618.30	618.30	618.30	618.30	618.30	618.30	618.30	124.80	205.50
551.40	551.40	551.40	551.40	551.40	551.40	551.40	551.40	117.90	205.50

Basic Allowance for Subsistence

This allowance, the quarters allowance, and any other allowance are not subject to income tax.

·fficers — Subsistence (food) is paid to all officers regardless of rank. . . . . $94.39 per month

·nlisted members: When on leave or authorized to mess separately. . . . . $4.50 per day

When rations in kind are not available. . . . . $5.09 per day

When assigned to duty under emergency conditions where no government messing facilities are available . . . . $6.73 per day (maximum rate)

Family Separation Allowance

Under certain conditions of family separation of more than 30 days, a member in Pay Grades E-4 (with over 4 years' service) and above ·ill be allowed $30 a month in addition to any other allowances to which he is entitled. When separated from family and required to main- ·ain a home for his family and one for himself, the member is entitled to an additional monthly basic allowance for quarters at the "without ·ependents" rate for his grade.

Guard.

·965—Navy, Marines, Army units to Dominican Republic.

·965—American commanders in Vietnam authorized to send U.S. Armed Force into combat.

·969—President Nixon announces, June 8, first phase of withdrawal of U.S. troops from Vietnam.

1970—Army units participate in Cambodian sanctuary operations, Apr. 29-June 30.

1973—Last U.S. troops leave Vietnam, U.S. Military Assistance Command deactivated, March 29.

1973—End of all U.S. bombing operations over Indochina, Aug. 15.

The Medal of Honor

The Medal of Honor is the highest military award for ·ravery that can be given to any individual in the United ·tates. The first Army Medals were awarded on March 25, ·863, and the first Navy Medals went to sailors and Marines ·n April 3, 1863.

The Medal of Honor, established by Joint Resolution of ·ongress, 12 July 1862 (amended by Act of 9 July 1918 and ·ct of 25 July 1963) is awarded in the name of Congress to ·person who, while a member of the Armed Forces, distin- ·uishes himself conspicuously by gallantry and intrepidity at ·e risk of his life above and beyond the call of duty while ·ngaged in an action against any enemy of the United ·tates; while engaged in military operations involving con- ·ict with an opposing foreign force; or while serving with ·iendly foreign forces engaged in an armed conflict against ·n opposing armed force in which the United States is not a ·elligerent party. The deed performed must have been one of personal bravery or self-sacrifice so conspicuous as to clearly distinguish the individual above his comrades and must have involved risk of life. Incontestable proof of the performance of service is exacted and each recommendation for award of this decoration is considered on the standard of extraordinary merit.

Prior to World War I, the 2,625 Army Medal of Honor awards up to that time were reviewed to determine which past awards met new stringent criteria. The Army removed 911 names from the list, most of them former members of a volunteer infantry group during the Civil War who had been induced to extend their enlistments when they were promised the Medal.

Since that review Medals of Honor have been awarded in the following numbers:

World War I . . . . . . 124 Korean War. 131
World War II . . . . . . 434 Vietnam (to date) 239

Major New U.S. Weapons Systems

Source: DMS, Inc., U.S. Defense Department

(As of April 1, 1982)

Item	Description	Estimated total cost (millions)	Estimated production	Major contractors	Comment
F-14 Tomcat	Swing-wing jet fighter	$35,836.4	845	Grumman	In production
F-15 Eagle	Tactical jet fighter	40,553.9	1,107	McDonnell Douglas	In production
F-16 Fighting Falcon	Supersonic, day-time fighter	42,289.6	2,333	General Dynamics	In production
F-18 Hornet	All-weather fighter and attack plane	39,725.0	1,377 for U.S.	McDonnell Douglas; Northrop	Advanced development
AH-64	Attack helicopter	7,380.8	446	Hughes	In production
Trident	Nuclear-powered submarine carries 24 missiles	28,426.0	15 boats; 969 missiles	Gen. Dyn. Lockheed	Boats in production, missiles in development
CG-47 Aegis	Missile cruiser	27,583.4	21	Litton Ind.	In production
SSN-688 Los Angeles	Nuclear-powered attack submarines	24,266.1	56	Newport News; Gen. Dynamics	In production
FFG-7	Guided-missile frigate	14,245.7	58	Bath; Todd	In production
DDG-5	Guided-missile destroyer	N.A.	61 (by 1987)	N.A.	In design
M-1 Abrams	Main battle tank Army	19,574.2	7,058	Gen. Dyn.	In production
IFV/CFV	Infantry or Cavalry fighting vehicle	13,398.0	6,882	FMC Corp., Chrysler	In production
Copperhead	Cannon-launched, laser-guided projectile	1,609.1	30,000	Martin Marietta	In production
Hellfire	Missile for AH-64; may be laser-guided	2,047.6	30,600	Rockwell	In development
Patriot (SAM-D)	Surface-to-air missile	11,312.2	103 batteries[1]	M. Marietta; Raytheon	In engineering development
MX	Advanced ICBM to replace Minuteman	15,000.0	226	Martin Marietta	In development
GLCM	Ground-launched, cruise missile	3,415.2	560	General Dynamics	In development
ALCM	Air-launched, air-to-ground	8,314.2	3,418	Boeing	In development
Tomahawk SLCM	Sea-launched	11,778.8	2,500	Gen. Dyn.	Near production
B-1B	Strategic bomber	29,537.6	100	Rockwell	In development

(1) Batteries consist of 5 launch vehicles and 2 fire control centers.

Some comparable costs: Total moon program, $30 billion, Bay Area Rapid Transit system, $1.6 billion; World Trade Center, land acquisition and construction, $1 billion; one manned moon shot, $400 million.

Strategic Nuclear Armaments: U.S. and USSR

Source: International Institute for Strategic Services, London

United States

		Range[2] (km)	Estimated warhead yield[3]	Deployed (July 1981)
Land-based missiles[1]				
ICBM	Titan 2	15,000	9 MT	52
	Minuteman 2	11,300	1-2 MT	450
	Minuteman 3	13,000	3x165 KT	550
Sea-based missiles				
SLBM (nuclear subs)	Polaris A3	4,600	3x200 KT	180
	Poseidon C3	4,600	10x50 KT	432
	Trident C4	7,400	8x100 KT	64

		Range[9] (km)	Weapons load (lb)	Deployed (July 1981)
Aircraft[8]				
Long-range	B-52D	9,900	60,000	75
	B-52G-H	14,000	70,000	90
Medium range	FB-111A	4,700	37,500	60
Strike aircraft; land-based	F-4C-E	2,250	16,000	204[10]
	F-111E/F	4,700	25,000	156
Strike aircraft: carrier-based	A-6E	3,200	18,000	(60)[10]
	A-7E	2,800	15,000	(144)[10]
	F-4J/N	2,250	16,000	(144)[10]

Soviet Union

		Range[2] (km)	Estimated warhead yield[3]	Deploye (July 1981)
Land-based missiles[1]				
ICBM	SS-11 Sego	10,500	1-2 MT[4]	580
	SS-13 Savage	10,000	1 MT	60
	SS-17	10,000	4x KT[5]	150
	SS-18	9,933	25 MT[6]	308
	SS-19	5,750	6x550 KT	300
Sea-based missiles				
SLBM (nuclear subs)	SS-N-6-Sawfly	1,750	MT[7]	453
	SS-N-8	4,800	MT	329
	SS-NX-17	5,000	MT	12
	SS-N-18	8,000	MT	176

	Range[9] (km)	Weapons load (lb)	Deploye (July 1981)
Aircraft[8]			
Tu-95 Bear	12,800	40,000	105
Mya-4 Bison	11,200	20,000	45
Tu-16 Badger	6,400	20,000	580
Backfire B	8,000	20,000	135
Su-7 Fitter A	1,400	4,500	165
Tu-22 Blinder	2,250	12,000	165
MiG-21 Fishbed J/K/L/N	1,100	2,000	(750)[10]
MiG-27 Flogger D	1,400	2,800	500
Su-17/20 Fitter C/D	1,800	5,000	740
Su-19A Fencer	1,600	8,000	480

(1) ICBM = intercontinental ballistic missille. IRBM = intermediate-range ballistic missile. MRBM = medium-range missile. SLBM = submarine-launched ballistic missile. SLCM = sub-launched cruise missile. (2) Operation range depends upon the payload carrie use of maximum payload may reduce missile range by up to 25%. (3) MT = megaton range = 1,000,000 tons of TNT equivalent over; KT = kiloton range = 1,000 tons of TNT equivalent or more, but less than 1 MT. (4) Some SS-11 missiles carry 3x100-200K warheads. (5) Some SS-17 carry 1x5MT warheads. (6) Four SS-18 warhead variants: 1x18-25 MT, 8x2 MT, 1 yield unknown, 1x10-5 MT. (7) SS-N-6, 1x1-2 MT or 2x3KT warheads. (8) All aircraft listed are dual-capable and many, especially in the categories of strik

aircraft, would be more likely to carry conventional than nuclear weapons. (9) Theoretical maximum range, with internal fuel only, at optimum altitude and speed. Ranges for strike aircraft assume no weapons load. Especially in the case of strike aircraft, therefore, range falls sharply for flights at lower altitude, at higher speed, or with full weapons load. (10) Figures in parentheses are estimates of Europe-based systems only.

Casualties in Principal Wars of the U.S.

Data on Revolutionary War casualties is from **The Toll of Independence,** Howard H. Peckham, ed., U. of Chicago Press, 1974.

Data prior to World War I are based on incomplete records in many cases. Casualty data are confined to dead and wounded personnel and therefore exclude personnel captured or missing in action who were subsequently returned to military control. Dash (—) indicates information is not available.

			Casualties			
Wars	**Branch of service**	**Number serving**	**Battle deaths**	**Other deaths**	**Wounds not mortal[8]**	**Total**
Revolutionary War	**Total**	—	**6,824**	**18,500**	**8,445**	**33,769**
1775-1783	Army	184,000	5,992	—	7,988	13,980
	Navy &	to	—	—	—	—
	Marines	250,000	832	—	457	1,289
War of 1812	**Total**	**[9]286,730**	**2,260**	—	**4,505**	**6,765**
1812-1815	Army	—	1,950	—	4,000	5,950
	Navy	—	265	—	439	704
	Marines	—	45	—	66	111
Mexican War	**Total**	**[9]78,718**	**1,733**	**11,550**	**4,152**	**17,435**
1846-1848	Army	—	1,721	11,500	4,102	17,373
	Navy	—	1	—	3	4
	Marines	—	11	—	47	58
Civil War	**Total**	**[9]2,213,363**	**140,414**	**224,097**	**281,881**	**646,392**
(Union forces only)	Army	2,128,948	138,154	221,374	280,040	639,568
1861-1865	Navy	—	2,112	2,411	1,710	6,233
	Marines	84,415	148	312	131	591
Confederate forces	**Total**	—	**74,524**	**59,297**	—	**133,821**
(estimate)[1]	Army	600,000	—	—	—	—
1863-1866	Navy	to	—	—	—	—
	Marines	1,500,000	—	—	—	—
Spanish-American War	**Total**	**306,760**	**385**	**2,061**	**1,662**	**4,108**
1898	Army[4]	280,564	369	2,061	1,594	4,024
	Navy	22,875	10	0	47	57
	Marines	3,321	6	0	21	27
World War I	**Total**	**4,743,826**	**53,513**	**63,195**	**204,002**	**320,710**
April 6, 1917-	Army[5]	4,057,101	50,510	55,868	193,663	300,041
Nov. 11, 1918	Navy	599,051	431	6,856	819	8,106
	Marines	78,839	2,461	390	9,520	12,371
	Coast Gd.	8,835	111	81	—	192
World War II	**Total**	**16,353,659**	**292,131**	**115,185**	**670,846**	**1,078,162**
Dec. 7, 1941-	Army[6]	11,260,000	234,874	83,400	565,861	884,135
Dec. 31, 1946[2]	Navy[7]	4,183,466	36,950	25,664	37,778	100,392
	Marines	669,100	19,733	4,778	67,207	91,718
	Coast Gd.	241,093	574	1,343	—	1,917
Korean War	**Total**	**5,764,143**	**33,629**	**20,617**	**103,284**	**157,530**
June 25, 1950-	Army	2,834,000	27,704	9,429	77,596	114,729
July 27, 1953[3]	Navy	1,177,000	458	4,043	1,576	6,077
	Marines	424,000	4,267	1,261	23,744	29,272
	Air Force	1,285,000	1,200	5,884	368	7,452
	Coast Gd.	44,143	—	—	—	—
Vietnam (preliminary)[10]	**Total**	**8,744,000**	**47,752**	**10,903**	**155,419**	**214,074**
Aug. 4, 1964-	Army	4,368,000	30,839	7,242	96,811	134,892
Jan. 27, 1973	Navy	1,842,000	1,592	907	4,180	6,679
	Marines	794,000	13,053	1,682	51,399	66,134
	Air Force	1,740,000	1,708	1,072	3,029	5,809

(1) Authoritative statistics for the Confederate Forces are not available. An estimated 26,000-31,000 Confederate personnel died in Union prisons.

(2) Data are for the period Dec. 1, 1941 through Dec. 31, 1946 when hostilities were officially terminated by Presidential Proclamation, but few battle deaths or wounds not mortal were incurred after the Japanese acceptance of Allied peace terms on Aug. 14, 1945. Numbers serving from Dec. 1, 1941-Aug. 31, 1945 were: Total—14,903,213; Army—10,420,000; Navy—3,883,520; and Marine Corps—599,693.

(3) Tentative final data based upon information available as of Sept. 30, 1954, at which time 24 persons were still carried as missing in action.

(4) Number serving covers the period April 21-Aug. 13, 1898, while dead and wounded data are for the period May 1-Aug. 31, 1898. Active hostilities ceased on Aug. 13, 1898, but ratifications of the treaty of peace were not exchanged between the United States and Spain until April 11, 1899.

(5) Includes Air Service Battle deaths and wounds not mortal include casualties suffered by American forces in Northern Russia to Aug. 25, 1919 and in Siberia to April 1, 1920. Other deaths covered the period April 1, 1917-Dec. 31, 1918.

(6) Includes Army Air Forces.

(7) Battle deaths and wounds not mortal include casualties incurred in Oct. 1941 due to hostile action.

(8) Marine Corps data for World War II, the Spanish-American War and prior wars represent the number of individuals wounded, whereas all other data in this column represent the total number (incidence) of wounds.

(9) As reported by the Commissioner of Pensions in his Annual Report for Fiscal Year 1903.

(10) Number serving covers the period Aug. 4 1964-Jan. 27, 1973 (date of ceasefire). Number of casualties incurred in connection with the conflict in Vietnam from Jan. 1, 1961-Sept. 30, 1977. Includes casualties incurred in Mayaguez Incident. Wounds not mortal exclude 150,375 persons not requiring hospital care.

ASSOCIATIONS AND SOCIETIES

Source: World Almanac questionnaire

Arranged according to **key words** in titles. Founding year of organization in parentheses; last figure after ZIP code indicates membership.

Aaron Burr Assn. (1946), R.D. #1, Route 33, Box 429, Hightstown-Freehold, Hightstown, NJ 08520; 500.

Abortion Federation, Natl. (1977), 110 E. 59th St., Suite 1011, N.Y., NY 10022; 375.

Abortion Rights Action League, Natl. (1968), 1424 K St. NW, Wash., DC 20005; 90,000.

Accountants, Amer. Institute of Certified Public (1887), 1211 Ave. of the Americas, N.Y., NY 10036; 168,424.

Accountants, Natl. Assn. of (1919), 919 Third Ave., N.Y., NY 10022; 96,500.

Accountants, Natl. Soc. of for Cooperatives (1943), 6320 Augusta Dr., Springfield, VA 22150; 2,100.

Accountants, Natl. Society of Public (1945), 1717 Pennsylvania Ave., NW, Wash., DC 20006; 17,000.

Acoustical Society of America (1929), 335 E. 45 St., N.Y., NY 10017; 5,600.

Actors' Equity Assn. (1913), 165 W. 46 St., N.Y., NY 10036; 28,000.

Actors' Fund of America (1882), 1501 Broadway, N.Y., NY 10036; 4,000.

Actuaries, American Academy of (1965), 1835 K St. NW, Wash., DC 20006; 6,400.

Actuaries, Society of (1949), 208 S. La Salle St., Chicago, Il. 60604; 6,700.

Adirondack Mountain Club (1922), 172 Ridge St., Glens Falls, NY 12801; 9,000.

Adult Education Assn. of the U.S.A. (1951), 810 18th St. NW, Wash., DC 20006; 3,000.

Advertisers, Assn. of Natl. (1910), 155 E. 44th St., N.Y., NY 10017; 500+cos.

Advertising Agencies, Amer. Assn. of (1917), 666 Third Ave., N.Y., NY 10017; 520 agencies.

Aeronautic Assn., Natl. (1922), 821 15th St. NW, Wash., DC 20005; 3,000.

Aeronautics and Astronautics, Amer. Institute of (1932), 1290 Ave. of the Americas, N.Y., NY 10104; 30,000.

Aerospace Industries Assn. of America (1919), 1725 De Sales St. NW, Wash., DC 20036; 59 cos.

Aerospace Medical Assn. (1929), Washington Natl. Airport, Wash., DC 20001; 3,400.

Afro-American Life and History, Assn. for the Study of (1915), 1401 14th St. NW, Wash., DC 20005; 16,289.

Aging Assn., Amer. (1970), Univ. of Nebraska Medical Center, 42d & Dewey Ave., Omaha, NE 68105; 500.

Agricultural Chemicals Assn., Natl. (1933), 1155 15th St. NW, Wash., DC 20005; 125 cos.

Agricultural Economics Assn., Amer. (1910), Iowa State Univ., Ames, IA 50011; 4,332.

Agricultural Engineers, Amer. Society of (1907), 2950 Niles Rd., St. Joseph, MI 49085; 11,300.

Agricultural History Society (1919), Room 140, 500-12th St., SW, Wash., DC 20250; 1,400.

Agronomy, Amer. Society of (1907), 677 S. Segoe Rd., Madison, WI 53711; 11,744.

Aircraft Assn., Experimental (1953), 11311 W. Forest Home Ave., Franklin, WI 53132; 70,000.

Aircraft Owners and Pilots Assn. (1939), 7315 Wisconsin Ave., Wash., DC 20014; 260,000.

Air Force Assn. (1946), 1750 Pennsylvania Ave. NW, Wash., DC 20006; 157,000.

Air Force Sergeants Assn. (1961), 4235 28th Ave., Marlow Heights, MD 20031; 128,000.

Air Line Employees Assn. (1952), 5600 S. Central Ave., Chicago, IL 60638; 10,000.

Air Line Pilots Assn. (1931), 1625 Massachusetts Ave. NW, Wash., DC 20036; 32,000.

Air Pollution Control Assn. (1907), P.O. Box 2861, Pittsburgh, PA 15230; 8,020.

Airport Operators Council Intl. (1948), 1700 K St. NW, Wash., DC 20006; 187.

Air Transport Assn., Intl. (1945), 2000 Peel St., Montreal, Quebec, Canada H3A 2R4; 116 airlines.

Air Transport Assn. of America (1936), 1709 New York Ave. NW, Wash., DC 20006; 31 airlines.

Alcohol Problems, Amer. Council on (1895), 119 Constitution Ave. NE, Wash., DC 20002; 4,000.

Alcoholics Anonymous (1935), P.O. Box 459, Grand Central Station, N.Y., NY 10163; over 1,000,000.

Alcoholism, Natl. Council on (1944), 733 Third Ave., N.Y., NY 10017; 220 affiliates.

Allergy, Amer. Academy of (1943), 611 E. Wells St., Milwaukee, WI 53202; 2,906.

Alpine Club, Amer. (1902), 113 E. 90th St., N.Y., NY 10028; 1,500.

Altrusa Intl. (1917), 8 S. Michigan Ave., Chicago, IL 60603; 19,800.

American Federation of Labor & Congress of Industrial Organizations (AFL-CIO) (1955, by merging **American Federation of Labor** estab. 1881 and **Congress of Industrial Organizations** estab. 1935), 815 16th St. NW, Wash., DC 20006; 15,000,000.

Amer. Field Service (1947), 313 E. 43d St., N.Y., NY 10017; 100,000.

Amer. Indian Affairs, Assn. on (1923), 432 Park Ave. So., N.Y., NY, 10016; 50,000.

American Legion, The (1919), 700 N. Pennsylvania St., Indianapolis, IN 46204; 2,650,000. **American Legion Auxiliary** (1921), 777 N. Meridian St., Indianapolis, IN 46204; 1,000,000.

Amer. States, Organization of (1948), General Secretariat, Wash., DC 20006; 28 countries.

Amer. Veterans of World War II, Korea & Vietnam (AMVETS), (1944), 4647 Forbes Blvd., Lanham, MD 20706; 200,000. **AMVETS Auxiliary** (1947), Saco Rd., Old Orchard Beach, ME 04064; 60,000.

Amnesty Intl. (1961), 304 W. 58th St., N.Y., NY 10019; 13,000.

Amputation Foundation, Natl. (1919), 12-45 150th St., Whitestone, NY 11357; 2,000.

Animal Protection Institute of America (1968), P.O. Box 22505, Sacramento, CA 95822; 100,000.

Animal Welfare Institute (1951), P.O. Box 3650, Wash., DC 20007; 4,000.

Animals, Amer. Society for Prevention of Cruelty to (ASPCA) (1866), 441 E. 92d St., N.Y., NY 10028.

Animals, Friends of (1957), 11 W. 60th St., N.Y., NY 10023; 100,000.

Animals, The Fund for (1967), 140 W. 57th St., N.Y., NY 10019; 172,000.

Anthropological Assn., Amer. (1902), 1703 New Hampshire Ave. NW, Wash., DC 20009; 10,000.

Antiquarian Society, Amer. (1812), 185 Salisbury St., Worcester, MA 01609; 386.

Anti-Vivisection Society, Amer. (1883), Suite 204, Noble Plaza, 801 Old York Rd., Jenkintown, PA 19046; 10,500.

Appalachian Mountain Club (1876), 5 Joy St., Boston, MA 02108; 25,000.

Appalachian Trail Conference (1937), Box 236, Harpers Ferry, WV 25425; 15,000.

Appraisers, Amer. Society of (1936), Dulles Intl Airport, Box 17265, Wash., DC 20041; 5,000.

Arab Americans, Natl. Assn. of (1972), Suite 211, 1825 Connecticut Ave. NW, Wash., DC 20009; 3,000.

Arbitration Assn., Amer. (1926), 140 W. 51st St., N.Y., NY 10020; 4,500.

Arboriculture, Intl. Society of (1924), P.O. Box 71, 5 Lincoln Sq., Urbana, IL 61801; 4,000.

Archaeological Institute of America (1879), 53 Park Place, N.Y., NY 10007; 9,500.

Archaeology, Institute of Nautical (1974), Texas A & M University, Drawer AU, College Station, TX 77840; 430.

Archery, Assn., Natl. (1879), 1750 E. Boulder St., Colorado Springs, CO 80909; 10,000.

Architects, Amer. Institute of (1857), 1735 New York Ave. NW, Wash., DC 20006; 38,758.

Architectural Historians, Society of (1940), 1700 Walnut St., Phila., PA 19103; 4,500.

Archivists, Society of Amer. (1936), 330 S. Wells St., Suite 810, Chicago, IL 60606; 4,000.

Armed Forces Communications and Electronics Assn. (1946), 5205 Leesburg Pike, Falls Church, VA 22041; 22,000.

Army, Assn. of the United States (1950), 2425 Wilson Blvd., Arlington, VA 22201; 145,500.

Art, Natl. Assn. of Schools of (1944), 11250 Roger Bacon Dr. 5, Reston, VA 22090; 104 institutions.

Arts, Amer. Council for the (1960), 570 7th Ave., N.Y., NY 10018; 1,200.

Arts, Amer. Federation of (1909), 41 E. 65th St., N.Y., NY 10021; 1,600.

Arts, Associated Councils of the (1969), 570 Seventh Ave., N.Y., NY 10018; 2,000.

Arts, Natl. Endowment for the (1965), 2401 E. St. NW, Wash., DC 20506.

Arts and Letters, Amer. Academy and Institute of (1898), 633 W. 155th St., N.Y., NY 10032; 250.

Arts and Letters, Natl. Society of (1944), 9915 Litzsinger Rd., St. Louis, MO 63124; 1,600.

Arts & Psychology, Assn. for the (1976), P.O. Box 160371, Sacramento, CA 95816.

Arts & Sciences, Amer. Academy of (1780), Norton's Woods, 136 Irving St., Cambridge, MA 02138; 2,700.

Assistance League, Natl. (1935), 5627 Fernwood Ave., Los Angeles, CA 90028; 14,735.

Astrologers, Amer. Federation of (1938), P.O. Box 22040, Tempe, AZ 85282; 4,000+.

Astronautical Society, Amer. (1953), 6060 Duke St., Alexandria, VA 22304; 800.

Astronomical Society, Amer. (1899), 1816 Jefferson Pl. NW, Wash., DC 20036; 3,850.

Atheist Assn. (1925), 3024 5th Ave., San Diego, CA 92103; 400.

Atheists, Amer. (1963), 2210 Hancock Dr., Austin, TX 78756; 30,000 families.

Athletic Associations, Natl. Federation of State High School (1920), 11724 Plaza Circle, Box 20626, Kansas City, MO 64195; 51.

Athletic Union of the U.S., Amateur (1888), 3400 W. 86th St., Indianapolis, IN 46268; 500,000.

Athletics Congress/USA, The (1979), P.O. Box 120, 155 W. Washington St., Suite 220, Indianapolis, IN 46206; 250,000.

Audubon Society, Natl. (1905), 950 Third Ave., N.Y., NY 10022; 400,000.

Authors and Composers, Amer. Guild of (1931), 40 W. 57th St., N.Y., NY 10019; 3,500.

Authors League of America (1912), 234 W. 44th St., N.Y., NY 10036; 11,000.

Autistic Children, Natl. Society for, 1234 Massachusetts Ave. NW, Wash., DC 20005; 5,600.

Automobile Assn., Amer. (1902), 8111 Gatehouse Rd., Falls Church, VA 22047; 22.3 million.

Automobile Club, Natl. (1924), One Market Plaza, San Francisco, CA 94105; 385,000.

Automobile Club of America, Antique (1935), 501 W. Governor Rd., Hershey, PA 17033; 47,000.

Automobile Dealers Assn., Natl. (1917), 8400 Westpark Dr., McLean, VA 22102; 19,000.

Automobile License Plate Collectors' Assn. (1954), P.O. Box 712, Weston, W. VA 26452; 1,600.

Automotive Booster Clubs Intl. (1921), 5105 Tollview Dr., Rolling Meadows, IL 60008; 3,100.

Automotive Hall of Fame (1939), P.O. Box 1742, Midland, MI 48640; 3,000.

Automotive Organization Team (1939), P.O. Box 1742, Midland, MI 48640; 3,000.

Aviation Historical Society, Amer. (1956), P.O. Box 99, Garden Grove, CA 92642; 4,200.

B-24 Liberator Club, Intl. (1968), P.O. Box 841, San Diego, CA 92112; 6,000.

Backpackers' Assn., Intl. (1973), P.O. Box 85, Lincoln Center, ME 04458; 22,861.

Badminton Assn., U.S. (1937), P.O. Box 237, Swartz Creek, MI 48473; 2,500.

Bald-Headed Men of America (1976), 901 Arendell St., Morehead City, N.C. 28557; 7,200.

Ballplayers of Amer., Assn. of Professional (1924), 12062 Valley View St., #211, Garden Grove, CA 92745.

Bankers Assn., Amer. (1875), 1120 Connecticut Ave. NW, Wash., DC 20036; 13,200 banks.

Bankers Assn. of America, Independent (1930), 1168 S. Main St., Sauk Centre, MN 56378; 7,400 banks.

Banks, Natl. Assn. of Mutual Savings (1920), 200 Park Ave., N.Y., NY 10166; 435 banks.

Bar Assn., Amer. (1878), 1155 E. 60th St., Chicago, IL 60637; 290,000.

Bar Assn., Federal (1920), 1815 H St. NW, Wash., DC 20006; 15,000.

Barbershop Quartet Singing in America, Society for the Preservation & Encouragement of (1939), 6315 Third Ave., Kenosha, WI 53141; 37,530.

Baseball Congress, Amer. Amateur (1935), 212 Plaza Bldg., 2855 W. Market St., P.O. Box 5332, Akron, OH 44313; 6,905 teams.

Baseball Congress, Natl. (1931), 338 S. Sycamore, Wichita, KS 67213; 15,150.

Baseball Players of America, Assn. of Professional (1924), 12062 Valley View St., Suite 211, Garden Grove, CA 92645; 10,200.

Basketball Assn., Natl. (1946), 645 5th Ave., N.Y., NY 10022; 22 teams.

Baton Twirling Assn. of America & Abroad, Intl. (1967), Box 234, Waldwick, NJ 07463; 1,500.

Battleship Assn., Amer. (1964), P.O. Box 11247, San Diego, CA 92111; 3,075.

Beer Can Collectors of America (1970), 747 Merus Ct., Fenton, MO 63026; 6,800.

Beta Gamma Sigma (1913), 11500 Olive Blvd., Suite 142, St. Louis, MO 63033; 165,000.

Beta Sigma Phi (1931), 1800 W. 91st Pl., Kansas City, MO 64114; 250,000.

Biblical Literature, Society of (1880), 2201 S. University Blvd., Denver, CO 80210; 5,000.

Bibliographical Society of America (1904), P.O. Box 397, Grand Central Sta., N.Y., NY 10163; 1,300.

Bide-A-Wee Home Assn. (1903), 410 E. 38th St., N.Y., NY 10016; 8,600.

Big Brothers/Big Sisters of America (1903), 117 S. 17th St., Suite 1200, Phila., PA 19103; 80,000.

Biological Chemists, Amer. Society of (1906), 9650 Rockville Pike, Bethesda, MD 20814; 5,290.

Biological Sciences, Amer. Institute of (1947), 1401 Wilson Blvd., Arlington, VA 22209; 8,500.

Birding Assn., Amer. (1969), Box 4335, Austin, TX 78765; 4,000.

Blind, Amer. Council of the (1961) 1211 Connecticut Ave. NW, Suite 506, Wash., DC 20036.

Blind, Amer. Foundation for the (1921), 15 W. 16th St., N.Y., NY 10011.

Blind, Natl. Federation of the (1940), 1629 K St., NW, Wash., DC 20006; 50,000.

Blind & Visually Handicapped, Natl. Accreditation Council for Agencies Serving the (1967), 79 Madison Ave., N.Y., NY 10016; 119 agencies and schools.

Blindness, Natl. Society to Prevent (1908), 79 Madison Ave., N.Y., NY 10010.

Blindness, Research to Prevent (1960), 598 Madison Ave., N.Y., NY 10022; 2,000.

Blizzard Club, January 12th, 1888, (1940), c/o Historian, 4827 Hillside Ave., Lincoln, NE 68506; 52.

Blood Banks, Amer. Assn. of (1947), 1117 N. 19th St., Suite 600, Arlington, VA 22209; 2,300.

Blue Cross Assn. (1948), 676 St. Clair, Chicago, IL 60611; 69 plans.

Blue Shield Plans, Natl. Assn. of (1946), 676 St. Clair, Chicago, IL 60611; 69 plans.

Blueberry Council, No. Amer. (1965), P.O. Box 166, Marmora, NJ 08223; 35 organizations.

Bluebird Society, No. Amer. (1978), 2 Countryside Ct., Silver Spring, MD 20904; 3,000+.

B'nai B'rith Intl. (1843), 1640 Rhode Island Ave. NW, Wash., DC 20036; 500,000.

Boat Owners Assn. of the U.S. (1966), 880 S. Pickett St., Alexandria, VA 22304; 92,000.

Booksellers Assn., Amer. (1900), 122 E. 42d St., N.Y., NY 10168; 5,000+.

Botanical Gardens & Arboreta, Amer. Assn. of (1940), Dept. of Biology, 124 Botany Bldg., Univ. of Cal., Los Angeles, CA 90024; 1,250.

Bottle Clubs, Federation of Historical (1969), 5001 Queen Ave. N., Minneapolis, MN 55430; 125 clubs.

Bowling Congress, Amer. (1895), 5301 S. 76th St., Greendale, WI 53129.

Boys' Brigades of America, United (1893), P.O. Box 8406, Baltimore, MD 21234; 200.

Boys' Clubs of America (1906), 771 First Ave., N.Y., NY 10017; 1,000,000+.

Boy Scouts of America (1910), 1325 Walnut Hill Lane, Irving, TX 75062; 4,355,723.

Brand Names Foundation (1943), 477 Madison Ave., N.Y., NY 10022; 400.

Bread for the World (1974), 32 Union Sq. E., N.Y., NY 10003; 31,000.

Brick Institute of America (1934), 1750 Old Meadow Rd., McLean, VA 22102; 100 cos.

Bridge, Tunnel and Turnpike Assn., Intl. (1932), 2120 L St., Suite 305, Wash., DC 20036; 70.

Brith Sholom (1905), 3939 Conshohocken Ave., Philadelphia, PA 19131; 6,000.

Broadcasters, Natl. Assn. of (1927), 1771 N St. NW, Wash., DC 20036; 5,000+.

Burroughs Bibliophiles, The (1960), 454 Elaine Dr., Pittsburgh, PA 15236; 245.

Bus Assn., Amer. (1926), 1025 Connecticut Ave. NW, Wash., DC 20036; 700.

Business Bureaus, Council of Better (1970), 1150 17th St. NW, Wash., DC 20036; 146.

Business Clubs, Natl. Assn. of Amer. (1922), 3315 No. Main St., High Point, NC 27262; 5,678.

Business Communication Assn., Amer. (1935), Univ. of Illinois, English Bldg., 608 S. Wright St., Urbana, IL 61801; 1,550.

Business Communicators, Intl. Assn. of (1970), 870 Market St., Suite 928, San Francisco, CA 94102; 7,000+.
Business Education Assn., Natl. (1946), 1906 Association Dr., Reston, VA 22091; 18,000.
Business Law Assn., Amer. (1924), Dept. of Legal Studies, Univ. of Georgia, Athens, GA 30602; 875.
Business-Professional Advertising Assn. (1922), 205 E. 42d St., N.Y., NY 10017; 3,700.
Button Society, Natl. (1938), 2733 Juno Pl., Akron, OH 44313; 1,680.
Byron Society, The (1971 England, 1973 in U.S.), 259 New Jersey Ave., Collingswood, NJ 08108; 300.

CARE (Cooperative For American Relief Everywhere) (1945), 660 First Ave., N.Y., NY 10016.
CORE (Congress of Racial Equality) (1942), 1916-38 Park Ave., N.Y., NY 10037; 75,000.
Campers & Hikers Assn., Natl. (1954), 7172 Transit Rd., Buffalo, NY 14221; 40,000 families.
Camp Fire (1910), 4601 Madison Ave., Kansas City, MO 64112; 500,000.
Camping Assn., Amer. (1910), Bradford Woods, Martinsville, IN 46151; 5,500.
Cancer Council, United (1963), 1803 N. Meridian St., Indianapolis, IN 46202.
Cancer Society, Amer. (1913), 777 Third Ave., N.Y., NY 10017; 247.
Canoe Assn., U.S. (1968), 617 South 94, Milwaukee, WI 53214; 1,700.
Carillonneurs in North America, Guild of (1936), 3718 Settle Rd., Cincinnati, OH 45227; 470.
Carnegie Hero Fund Commission (1904), 606 Oliver Bldg., Pittsburgh, PA 15222.
Cartoonists Society, Natl. (1946), 9 Ebony Ct., Brooklyn, NY 11229; 450.
Catholic Bishops, Natl. Conference of/U.S. Catholic Conference (1966), 1312 Massachusetts Ave. NW, Wash., DC 20015; 350.
Catholic Charities, Natl. Conference of (1910), 1346 Connecticut Ave. NW, Wash., DC 20036; 3,000.
Catholic Church Extension Society of the U.S.A. (1905), 35 E. Wacker Dr., Chicago, IL 60601; 60,000.
Catholic Daughters of America (1903), 10 W. 71st St., N.Y., NY 10023; 167,000.
Catholic Educational Assn., Natl. (1904), One Dupont Circle NW, Wash., DC 20036; 14,000.
Catholic Extension Society (1905), 35 E. Wacker Dr., Chicago, IL 60601; 60,000.
Catholic Library Assn. (1929), 461 W. Lancaster Ave., Haverford, PA 19041; 3,061.
Catholic Press Assn. (1912), 119 N. Park Ave., Rockville Centre, NY 11570; 500.
Catholic Rural Life Conference, Natl. (1923), 4625 NW Beaver Dr., Des Moines, IA 50322; 3,500.
Catholic War Veterans of the U.S.A. (1935), 2 Massachusetts Ave. NW, Wash., DC 20001; 35,000.
Cemetery Assn., Amer. (1887), 5201 Leesburg Pike, Falls Church, VA 22041; 2,504.
Ceramic Society, Amer. (1899), 65 Ceramic Dr., Columbus, OH 43214; 7,500.
Cerebral Palsy Assns., United (1949), 66 E. 34th St., N.Y., NY 10016; 241 affiliates.
Chamber of Commerce of the U.S.A. (1912), 1615 H St. NW, Wash., DC 20062; 100,000+.
Chamber Music Players, Amateur (1947), P.O. Box 547, Vienna, VA 22180; 4,000.
Chaplain's Assn., Intl. (1962), U.S. Box 4266, Norton Air Force Base, CA 92409; 230.
Chaplain's Assn., Natl. (1900), Gatlinburg, TN 37738; 3,150.
Chaplains Assn. of the U.S.A., Military (1925), 7758 Wisconsin Ave., Bethesda, MD 20814; 1,984.
Chartered Life Underwriters, Amer. Society of (1927), 270 Bryn Mawr Ave., Bryn Mawr, PA 19010; 28,000.
Chemical Manufacturers Assn. (1872), 2501 M St. NW, Wash., DC 20037; 200 cos.
Chemical Society, Amer. (1876), 1155 16th St. NW, Wash., DC 20036; 125,000.
Chemistry, Amer. Assn. for Clinical (1948), 1725 K St. NW, Wash., DC 20006; 5,512.
Chemists, Amer. Institute of (1923), 7315 Wisconsin Ave., Wash., DC 20814; 5,000.
Chemists and Chemical Engineers, Assn. of Consulting (1928), 50 E. 41st St., N.Y. NY 10017; 120.
Chemists Assn., Manufacturing (1872), 1825 Connecticut Ave. NW, Wash., DC 20009; 200 cos.
Chess Federation, U.S. (1939), 186 Rte. 9W, New Windsor, NY 12550; 54,000.
Chess League of Amer., Correspondence (1897), Box 363, Decatur, IL 62525; 1,500.
Child Welfare League of America (1920), 67 Irving Pl., N.Y., NY 10003; 387 agencies.
Childbirth Without Pain Education Assn. (1960), 20134 Snowden, Detroit, MI 48235; 2,000.
Childhood Education Intl., Assn. for (1892), 3615 Wisconsin Ave. NW, Wash., DC 20016; 15,000.
Children of the Amer. Revolution, Natl. Society (1895), 1776 D St. NW, Wash., DC 20006; 12,000.
Children's Aid Society (1853), 105 E. 22d St., N.Y., NY 10010.
Children's Book Council (1945), 67 Irving Pl., N.Y., NY 10003; 75 publishing houses.
Chiropractic Assn., Amer. (1963), 1916 Wilson Blvd., Arlington, VA 22201; 18,103.
Chiropractors Assn., Intl. (1926), 1901 L St. NW, Wash., DC 20036; 6,000.
Christian Culture Society (1974), P.O. Box 325, Kokomo, IN 46901; 16,124.
Christian Endeavor, Intl. Society of (1881), 1221 E. Broad St., P.O. Box 1110, Columbus, OH 43216.
Christian Laity Counseling Board (1970), 5901 Plainfield Dr., Charlotte, NC 28215; 38,000,000.
Christians and Jews, Natl. Conference of (1928), 43 W. 57th St., N.Y., NY 10019.
Church Business Administrators, Natl. Assn. of (1956), Suite 324, 7001 Grapevine Hwy., Ft. Worth, TX 76118; 761.
Churches, U.S. Conference for the World Council of (1948), 475 Riverside Dr., Room 1062, N.Y., NY 10115; 27 churches.
Church Women United in the U.S.A. (1941), 475 Riverside Dr., N.Y., NY 10027; 2,000,000.
Cincinnati, Society of the (1783), 2118 Massachusetts Ave. NW, Wash., DC 20008; 2,800.
Circulation Managers Assn., Intl. (1898), 11600 Sunrise Valley Dr., Reston, VA 22091; 1,390.
Circus Fans Assn. of America (1926), 4 Center Dr., Camp Hill, PA 17011; 2,500.
Cities, Natl. League of (1924), 1301 Pennsylvania Ave. NW, Wash., DC 20004; 900 cities.
Citizens Band Radio Patrol (1972), 1100 NE 125th St., N. Miami, FL 33161; 32,000.
City Management Assn., Intl. (1914), 1140 Connecticut Ave. NW, Wash., DC 20036; 7,000.
Civil Air Patrol, (1941), Maxwell Air Force Base, AL 36112; 60,000.
Civil Engineers, Amer. Society of (1852), 345 E. 47th St., N.Y., NY 10017; 80,000.
Civil Liberties Union, Amer. (1920), 132 W. 43rd St., N.Y. NY 10036; 200,000.
Civil War Round Table of New York (1951), 820 Carleton Rd., Westfield, NJ 07090; 135.
Civitan Internatl. (1920), P.O. Box 2102, Birmingham, AL 35201; 31,000.
Classical League, Amer. (1918), Miami Univ., Oxford, OH 45056; 3,000.
Clergy, Academy of Parish (1968), 12604 Britton Dr., Cleveland, OH 44120, 550.
Clinical Pastoral Education, Assn. for (1967), 475 Riverside Dr., N.Y., NY 10115; 3,500.
Clinical Pathologists, Amer. Society of (1922), 2100 W. Harrison St., Chicago, IL 60612; 34,000.
Clowns of America (1968), P.O. Box 3906, Baltimore, MD 21222; 11,000.
Coal Association, Natl. (1917), 1130 17th St. NW, Wash., DC 20036; 200+ companies.
Collectors Assn., Amer. (1939), 4040 W. 70th St., Minneapolis, MN 55435; 2,700.
College Athletic Assn., Natl. Junior (1938), 12 E. 2d, Box 1586, Hutchinson, KS 67501; 995.
College Athletic Conference, Eastern (1938), 1311 Craigville Beach Rd., P.O. Box 3, Centerville, MA 02632; 229.
College Board, The (1900), 888 Seventh Ave., N.Y., NY 10106; 2,600 institutions.
College Physical Education Assn. for Men, Natl. (1897), 108 Cooke Hall, Univ. of Minnesota, Minneapolis, MN 55455; 1,200.
College Music Society (1958), Regent Box 44, Univ. of Colorado, Boulder, CO 80309; 5,000.
College Placement Council (1956), 62 Highland Ave., Bethlehem, PA 18018; 2,400.
Colleges, Amer. Assn. of Community and Jr. (1920), One Dupont Circle, Wash., DC 20036; 910 institutions.
Colleges, Assn. of Amer. (1915), 1818 R St. NW, Wash., DC 20009; 653 institutions.
Collegiate Athletic Assn., Natl. (1906), P.O. Box 1906, Shawnee Mission, KS 66222; 880.

Collegiate Schools of Business, Amer. Assembly of (1916), 11500 Olive Blvd., St. Louis, MO 63141; 650 schools.
Colonial Dames of America (1890), 421 E. 61 St., N.Y., NY 10021; 2,000.
Colonial Dames XVII Century, Natl. Society (1915), 1300 New Hampshire Ave. NW, Wash., DC 20036; 12,000.
Colonial Wars, Society of (1893), 840 Woodbine Ave., Glendale, OH 45246; 4,350.
Commercial Law League of America (1895), 222 W. Adams St., Chicago, IL 60606; 6,000+.
Commercial Travelers of America, Order of United (1888), 632 N. Park St., Columbus, OH 43215; 193,882.
Common Cause (1970), 2030 M St. NW, Wash., DC 20036; 215,000.
Community Cultural Center Assoc., Amer. (1978), 19 Foothills Dr., Pompton Plains, NJ 07444.
Composers/USA, Natl. Assn. of (1929), P.O. Box 49652, Barrington Sta., Los Angeles, CA 90049; 500.
Composers, Authors & Publishers, Amer. Society of (ASCAP) (1914), One Lincoln Plaza, N.Y., NY 10023; 24,000.
Computing Machinery, Assn. for (1947), 11 W. 42nd St., N.Y., NY 10036; 55,000.
Concrete Institute, Amer. (1904), 22400 W. Seven Mile Rd., Detroit, MI 48219; 15,937.
Conference Board, The (1916), 845 Third Ave., N.Y., NY 10022; 4,000.
Consairway (1942), P.O. Box 1642, La Mesa, CA 92041; 500.
Conscientious Objection, Central Committee for (1948), 2208 South St., Phila., PA 19146.
Conservation Engineers, Assn. of (1961), Missouri Dept. of Conservation, P.O. Box 180, Jefferson City, MO 65101; 161.
Conservation Foundation (1948), 1717 Massachusetts Ave. NW, Wash., DC 20036.
Construction Industry Manufacturers Assn. (1903), 111 E. Wisconsin Ave., Milwaukee, WI 53202; 200 companies.
Construction Specifications Institute (1948), 1150 17th St. NW, Wash., DC 20036; 11,500.
Consumer Credit Assn., Intl. (1912), 243 N. Lindbergh, St. Louis, MO 63141; 22,000.
Consumer Federation of America (1968), 1314 14th St. NW, Wash., DC 20005; 240 organizations.
Consumer Interests, Amer. Council on (1953), 162 Stanley Hall, Univ. of Missouri, Columbia, MO 65211; 2,700.
Consumer Protection Institute (1970), 5901 Plainfield Dr., Charlotte, NC 28215.
Consumers League, Natl. (1899), 1522 K St. NW, Suite 406, Wash., DC 20005; 120,000.
Consumers Union of the U.S. (1936), 256 Washington St., Mount Vernon, NY 10550; 250,000.
Consumers Unions, Intl. Organization of (1960), 9 Emmastraat, The Hague, Netherlands; 115 organizations.
Contract Bridge League, Amer. (1927), 2200 Democrat Rd., Memphis, TN 38116; 187,447.
Contract Management Assn., Natl. (1959), 6728 Old McLean Village Dr., McLean, VA 22101; 10,000.
Contractors of Amer., General (1918), 1957 E St. NW, Wash., DC 20036; 30,000.
Cooperative League of the U.S.A. (1916), 1828 L St. NW, Wash., DC 20036; 176 co-ops.
Correctional Assn., Amer. (1870), 4321 Hartwick Rd., Suite L-208, College Park, MD 20740; 10,000.
Correctional Officers, Amer. Assn. of (1980), 1474 Willow Ave., Des Plaines, IL 60016; 3,200.
Cosmopolitan Intl. (1914), 7341 W. 108 Pl., Overland Park, KS 66204; 4,000.
Cotton Council of America, Natl. (1938), 1918 North Parkway, Memphis, TN 38112; 290.
Country Music Assn. (1958), P.O. Box 22299, Nashville, TN 37202; 6,300.
Creative Children and Adults, Natl. Assn. for (1974), 8080 Springvalley Dr., Cincinnati, OH 45236; 1,000.
Credit Management, Nat. Assn. of (1896), 475 Park Ave. So., N.Y., NY 10016; 44,492.
Crime and Delinquency, Natl. Council on (1907), 411 Hackensack Ave., Hackensack, NJ 07601; 10,000.
Criminology, Amer. Assn. of (1953), P.O. Box 1115, North Marshfield, MA 02339; 2,500.
Criminology, Amer. Society of (1940), 1314 Kinnear Rd., Columbus, OH 43212; 1,850.
Crop Science Society of America (1955), 677 S. Segoe Rd., Madison, WI 53711; 4,035.
Cross-Examination Debate Assn. (1971), Speech Dept., Cal. State Univ., Long Beach, CA 90840; 241 institutions.
Cryptogram Assn., Amer. (1932) 39 Roslyn Ave., Hudson, OH 44236; 1,000.
Cyprus, Sovereign Order of (1192, 1964 in U.S.), 853 Seventh Ave., N.Y., NY 10019; 457.

Dairy Council, Natl. (1915), 6300 N. River Rd., Rosemont, IL 60018; 600.
Dairy and Food Industries Supply Assn. (1919), 6245 Executive Blvd., Rockville, MD 20852; 540 organizations.
Dairylea Cooperative (1919), One Blue Hill Plaza, Pearl River, NY 10965; 4,200.
Daughters of the American Revolution, Natl. Society, (1890), 1776 D St. NW, Wash., DC 20006; 208,248.
Daughters of the Confederacy, United (1894), 328 N. Blvd., Richmond, VA 23220; 26,000.
Daughters of 1812, Natl. Society, U.S. (1892), 1461 Rhode Island Ave. NW, Wash., DC 20005; 4,300.
Daughters of Union Veterans of the Civil War (1885), 503 S. Walnut St., Springfield, IL 62704; 6,500.
Deaf, Alexander Graham Bell Assn. for the (1890), 3417 Volta Pl. NW, Wash., DC 20007; 5,643.
Deaf, Natl. Assn. of the (1880), 814 Thayer Ave., Silver Spring, MD 20910; 19,700.
Defense Preparedness Assn., Amer. (1919), 1700 N. Moore St., Arlington, VA 22209; 35,000.
Delta Kappa Gamma Society Intl. (1929), P.O. Box 1589, Austin, TX 78767; 154,000+.
Deltiologists of America (1960), 10 Felton Ave., Ridley Park, PA 19078; 1,450.
Democratic Natl. Committee (1848), 1625 Massachusetts Ave. NW, Wash., DC 20036; 374
Democratic Socialists of Amer. (1982), 853 Broadway, Suite 801, New York, NY 10003.
DeMolay, Intl. Council, Order of (1919), 201 E. Armour Blvd., Kansas City, MO 64111; 100,000.
Dental Assn., Amer. (1859), 211 E. Chicago Ave., Chicago, IL 60611; 140,495.
Descendants of the Colonial Clergy, Society of the (1933), 30 Leewood Rd., Wellesley, MA 02181; 1,400.
Descendants of the Signers of the Declaration of Independence (1907), 1300 Locust St., Phila., PA 19107; 937.
Descendants of Washington's Army at Valley Forge, Society of (1976), Valley Forge, PA 19481; 400.
Desert Protective Council (1959), Box 4294, Palm Springs, CA 92263; 400+.
Diabetes Assn., Amer. (1940), 2 Park Ave., N.Y., NY 10016; 3,500.
Dialect Society, Amer. (1890), MacMurray College, Jacksonville, IL 62650; 750.
Dietetic Assn., Amer. (1917), 430 N. Michigan Ave., Chicago, IL 60611; 42,405.
Ding-A-Ling Club, Natl. (1972), Box 2188, Glen Ellyn, IL 60137; 2,050.
Direct Mail/Marketing Assn. (1916), 6 E. 43d St., N.Y., NY 10017; 4,730 companies.
Directors Guild of America (1936), 7950 Sunset Blvd., Los Angeles, CA 90046; 6,300.
Disability Examiners, Natl. Assn. of (1968), P.O. Box 44237, Indianapolis, IN 46244; 1,600.
Disabled Amer. Veterans (1920), 3725 Alexandria Pike, Cold Spring, KY 41076; 685,000.
Disabled Officers Assn. (1919), 927 S. Walter Reed Dr. #6, Arlington, VA 22204; 5,000.
Divorce Reform, U.S. (1961), P.O. Box 243, Kenwood, CA 95452; 6,000.
Dowsers, Amer. Society of (1961), P.O. Box 24, Danville, VT 05828; 2,400.
Dozenal Soc. of America (1944), Math Dept., Nassau Community College, Garden City, L.I. 11530; 108.
Dracula Society, Count (1962), 334 W. 54th St., Los Angeles, CA 90037; 500.
Dragon, Imperial Order of the (1900), P.O. Box 1707, San Francisco, CA 94101.
Drug, Chemical and Allied Trades Assn. (1891), 42-40 Bell Blvd., Suite 604, Bayside, NY 11361; 500 cos.
Drum Corps Internatl. (1971), 719 S. Main St., Lombard, IL 60148; 26.
Ducks Unlimited (1937), One Waterfowl Way, Lake Zurich, IL 60047; 420,000.
Dulcimer Assn., Southern Appalachian (1974), Rte. 1, Box 473, Helena, AL 35080; 114.
Dutch Settlers Soc. of Albany (1924), Box 163, R.D. 2, Troy, NY 12182; 277.

Earth, Friends of the (1969), 1045 Sansome St., San Francisco, CA 94111; 27,000.
Easter Seal Society, Natl. (1919), 2023 W. Ogden Ave., Chicago, IL 60612.
Eastern Star, Order of the (1876), 1618 New Hampshire Ave. NW, Wash., DC 20009; 2,500,000.
Economic Assn., Amer. (1885), 1313 21st Ave. So., Nashville, TN 37212; 26,000.

Economic Development, Committee for (1942), 477 Madison Ave., N.Y., NY 10022.
Edison Electric Institute (1933), 1111 19th St. NW, Wash., DC 20036; 189 cos.
Education, Amer. Council on (1918), One Dupont Circle NW, Wash., DC 20036; 1,400 schools.
Education, Council for Advancement & Support of (1974), 11 Dupont Circle NW, Wash., DC 20036; 2,200 schools.
Education, Council for Basic (1956), 725 15th St. NW, Wash., DC 20005; 8,400.
Education, Natl. Committee for Citizens in (1973), 410 Wilde Lake Village Green, Columbia, MD 21044; 352.
Education, Natl. Society for the Study of (1902), 5835 Kimbark Ave., Chicago, IL 60637; 4,500.
Education, Society for the Advancement of (1939), 1860 Broadway, N.Y., NY 10023; 3,000.
Education, Institute of Intl. (1919), 809 United Nations Plaza, N.Y., NY 10017; 500 colleges and universities.
Education Assn., Natl. (1857), 1201 16th St. NW, Wash., DC 20036; 1,600,000.
Education Society, Comparative and Intl. (1956), Univ. of S. California, Univ. Park, Los Angeles, CA 90007; 2,300.
Education of Young Children, Natl. Assn. for the (1926), 1834 Connecticut Ave. NW, Wash., DC 20009; 35,000.
Educational Broadcasters, Natl. Assn. of (1925), 1346 Connecticut Ave. NW, Wash., DC 20036; 2,500.
Educational Exchange, Council on Intl. (1947), 205 E. 42d St., N.Y., NY 10017; 162 organizations.
Educational Research Assn., Amer. (1915), 1230 17th St. NW, Wash., DC 20036; 14,000.
Electric Railroaders Assn. (1934), Grand Central Terminal, 89 E. 42d St., N.Y., NY 10017; 1,500.
Electrical and Electronics Engineers, Institute of (1884), 345 E. 47th St., N.Y., NY 10017; 202,000.
Electrical Manufacturers Assn., Natl. (1926), 2101 L St. NW, Wash., DC 20037; 560 companies.
Electrochemical Society (1902), 10 S. Main St., Pennington, NJ 08534; 5,000.
Electronic Industries Assn. (1924), 2001 Eye St. NW, Wash., DC 20006; 350 firms.
Electronic Service Dealers Assn., Natl. (1963), 2708 W. Berry, Ft. Worth, TX 76109; 1,500.
Electronics Technicians, Intl. Society of Certified (1970), 2708 W. Berry, Ft. Worth, TX 76109; 750.
Electroplaters' Society, Amer. (1909), 1201 Louisiana Ave., Winter Park, FL 32789; 8,400.
Elks of the U.S.A., Benevolent and Protective Order of (1868), 2750 N. Lake View Ave., Chicago, IL 60614; 1,640,000.
Energy, Intl. Assn. for Hydrogen (1974), P.O. Box 24866, Coral Gables, FL 33124; 1,500.
Engine and Boat Manufacturers, Natl. Assn. of (1904), 666 Third Ave., N.Y., NY 10017; 435 firms.
Engineering, Natl. Academy of (1964), 2101 Constitution Ave. NW, Wash., DC 20418; 1,107.
Engineering, Soc. for the Advancement of Material & Process (1944), 668 S. Azusa Ave., Azusa, CA 91702; 3,000.
Engineering Societies, Amer. Assn. of (1979), 345 E. 47th St., N.Y., NY 10017; 38 societies.
Engineering Society of N. America, Illuminating (1907), 345 E. 47th St., N.Y., NY 10017; 8,800.
Engineering Technicians, Amer. Society of Certified (1964), 4550 W. 109th, Suite 220, Overland Park, KS 66211; 6,500.
Engineering Trustees, United (1904), 345 E. 47th St., N.Y., NY 10017.
Engineers, Amer. Society of Lubrication (1944), 838 Busse Hwy., Park Ridge, IL 60068; 3,200.
Engineers, Amer. Soc. of Plumbing (1964), 15233 Ventura Blvd., #811, Sherman Oaks, CA 91403; 4,500.
Engineers, Assn. of Energy (1977), 4025 Pleasantdale Rd., Suite 340, Atlanta, GA 30340; 4,500.
Engineers, Natl. Society of Professional (1934), 2029 K St. NW, Wash., DC 20006; 80,000.
Engineers, Institute of Transportation (1930), 525 School St. SW, Suite 410, Wash., DC 20024; 6,500.
Engineers, Soc. of American Military (1920), 607 Prince St., Alexandria, VA 22313; 23,000.
Engineers, Soc. of Manufacturing (1932), P.O. Box 930, Dearborn, MI 48128; 63,694.
English Assn., College (1939), Univ. of Houston, Downtown, 1 Main St., Houston, TX 77002.
English-Speaking Union of the U.S. (1920), 16 E. 69th St., N.Y., NY 10021; 30,000.
Entomological Society of America (1889), 4603 Calvert Rd., P.O. Box AJ, College Park, MD 20740; 8,500.
Epigraphic Society, Inc., The (1974), 6625 Bamburgh Dr., San Diego, CA 92117; 1,050.
Esperanto League for North America (1952), P.O. Box 1129, El Cerrito, CA 94530; 750.
Euthanasia Foundation, Amer. (1972), 95 N. Birch Rd., Ft. Lauderdale, FL 33304; 40,000.
Evangelicals, Natl. Assn. of (1942), Box 28, Wheaton, IL 60187.
Evangelism Crusades, Intl. (1959), 7970 Woodman Ave., Van Nuys, CA 91402; 15,000.
Exchange Club, Natl. (1917), 3050 Central Ave., Toledo, OH 43606; 46,000.
Experiment in Internatl. Living (1932), Kipling Rd., Brattleboro, VT 05301; 64,000.

Fairs & Expositions, Intl. Assn. of (1885), P.O. Box 985, Springfield, MO 65801; 1,000.
Family Life, Natl. Alliance for, Inc. (1973), Ste. 4, 225 Jericho Tpk., Floral Park, NY 11001; 510.
Family Service Assn. of America (1911), 44 E. 23d St., N.Y., NY 10010; 260 agencies.
Farm Bureau Federation, Amer. (1919), 225 Touhy Ave., Park Ridge, IL 60068; 3,500,000 families.
Farmer Cooperatives, Natl. Council of (1929), 1800 Massachusetts Ave. NW, Wash., DC 20036; 121 co-ops.
Farmers of America, Future (1928), Box 15160, Alexandria, VA 22309; 483,000.
Farmers Educational and Co-Operative Union of America (1902), Box 117, Bailey, CO 80421; 300,000 families.
Fat Americans, Natl. Assn. to Aid (NAAFA) (1969), P.O. Box 43, Bellerose, NY 11426; 2,000.
Federal Employees, Natl. Federation of (1917), 1016 16th St. NW, Wash., DC 20036; 135,000.
Federal Employees Veterans Assn. (1954), P.O. Box 183 Merion Sta., PA 19066; 635.
Feline Society, Amer. (1938), 41 Union Sq. W., N.Y., NY 10003; 450.
Feminists for Life of America (1972), 1503 N. 47, Milwaukee, WI 53208; 1,000.
Fencers League of America, Amateur (1893), 601 Curtis St., Albany, CA 94706; 8,000.
Fiddlers Assn., Amer. Old Time (1965), 6141 Morrill Ave., Lincoln, NE 68507; 5,000.
Film Library Assn., Educational (1943), 43 W. 61st St., N.Y., NY 10023; 1,500.
Financial Analysts Federation (1947), 1633 Broadway, N.Y., NY 10019; 14,900.
Financial Executives Institute (1931), 633 Third Ave., N.Y., NY 10017; 12,100.
Financiers, Intl. Soc. of (1979), 399 Laurel St., Suite 6, San Carlos, CA 94070; 100+.
Finishing Processes of SME, Assn. for (1975), One SME Dr., P.O. Box 930, Dearborn, MI 48128; 1,925.
Fire Chiefs, Intl. Assn. of (1873), 1329 18th St. NW, Wash. DC 20036; 8,000.
Fire Marshals Assn. of No. America (1906), Capital Gallery Suite 220, 600 Maryland Ave. SW, Wash., DC 20024; 1,000.
Fire Protection Assn., Natl. (1896), Batterymarch Park Quincy MA 02269; 31,500.
Fire Protection Engineers, Society of (1950), 60 Batterymarch St., Boston, MA 02110; 3,150.
Fish Assn., Intl. Game (1939), 3000 E. Las Olas Blvd., Ft Lauderdale, FL 33316; 20,000.
Fishes, Soc. for the Protection of old (1967), College of Fisheries, Univ. of Washington, Seattle, WA 98195; 200.
Fishing Institute, Sport (1949), 608 13th St. NW, Wash., DC 20005; 107.
Fishing Tackle Manufacturers Assn., Amer. (1933), 2625 Clearbrook Dr., Arlington Heights, IL 60005; 400 organizations.
Flag Assn., Amer. (1888), P.O. Box 1121, Denver, CO 80201.
Flag Institute, The Amer. (1976), 205 E. 78th St., N.Y., NY 10021; 557.
Fluid Power Society (1957), 909 N. Mayfair Rd., Milwaukee WI 53226; 3,000.
Food Processing Machinery and Supplies Assn. (1885) 1828 L St. NW, Wash., DC 20036; 475 organizations.
Food Processors Assn., Natl. (1907), 1133 20th St. NW Wash., DC 20036.
Football Assn., U.S. Touch and Flag (1976), 2705 Normandy Dr., Youngstown, OH 44511; 20,000.
Footwear Industries Assn., Amer. (1869), 1611 N. Kent St. Arlington, VA 22209; 260.
Foreign Policy Assn. (1918), 205 Lexington Ave., N.Y., NY 10016.
Foreign Relations, Council on (1921), 58 E. 68th St., N.Y. NY 10021; 2,031.
Foreign Student Affairs, Natl. Assn. for (1948), 1860 19th St. NW, Wash., DC 20009; 4,000.
Foreign Study, Amer. Institute for (1964), 102 Greenwich Ave., Greenwich, CT 06830; 250,000.

Foreign Trade Council, Inc., Natl. (1914), 10 Rockefeller Center, N.Y., NY 10020; 650 companies.
Forensic Sciences, Amer. Academy of (1954), 225 S. Academy Blvd., Colorado Springs, CO 80910; 2,250.
Forest Institute, Amer. (1932), 1619 Massachusetts Ave. NW, Wash., DC 20036; 60 companies.
Forest Products Assn., Natl. (1902), 1619 Massachusetts Ave. NW, Wash., DC 20036; 41.
Forest Products Research Society (1947), 2801 Marshall Ct., Madison, WI 53705; 4,500.
Foresters, Society of Amer. (1900), 5400 Grosvenor La., Wash., DC 20814; 20,903.
Forestry Assn., Amer. (1875), 1319 18th St. NW, Wash., DC 20036; 80,000.
Fortean Organization, Intl. (1965), P.O. Box 367, Arlington, VA 22210; 700.
Foundrymen's Society, Amer. (1896), Golf & Wolf Rds., Des Plaines, IL 60016; 17,000.
4-H Clubs (1901-1905), Extension Service, U.S. Dept of Agriculture, Wash., DC 20250; 5.8 million.
Franklin D. Roosevelt Philatelic Society (1963), 154 Laguna Ct., St. Augustine Shores, FL 32084; 384.
Freedom, Young Americans for (1960), Woodland Rd., Sterling, VA 22170; 80,000.
Freedoms Foundation at Valley Forge (1949), Valley Forge, PA 19481; 9,000.
Freidreich's Ataxia Group in Amer. (1969), P.O. Box 11116, Oakland, CA 94611; 2,100.
French Institute (1911), 22 E. 60th St., N.Y., NY 10022; 20,000.
Friends Service Committee, Amer. (1917), 1501 Cherry St., Phila., PA 19102; 157,000.
Frisbee Assn., Intl. (1967), 900 E. El Monte, San Gabriel, CA 91776; 110,000.
Funeral and Memorial Societies, Continental Assn. of (1963), 1828 L St. NW, Wash., DC 20036; 900,000.

GASP (Group Against Smokers' Pollution) (1971), P.O. Box 632, College Park, MD 20740; 200 chapters.
Gamblers Anonymous (1957), 2703A W. 8th St., Los Angeles, CA 90005; 6,000.
Garden Club of America (1913), 598 Madison Ave., N.Y., NY 10022; 14,000.
Garden Clubs, Natl. Council of State (1929), 4401 Magnolia Ave., St. Louis, MO 63110; 350,524.
Garden Clubs of America, Men's (1932), 5560 Merle Hay Rd., Des Moines, IA 50323; 10,000.
Gas Appliance Manufacturers Assn. (1935), 1901 N. Ft. Myer Dr., Arlington, VA 22209; 240 companies.
Gas Assn., Amer. (1918), 1515 Wilson Blvd., Arlington, VA 22209; 300 cos.
Gay Academic Union (1974), P.O. Box 927, Los Angeles, CA 90028; 650.
Gay Task Force, Natl. (1973), 80 Fifth Ave., Suite 1601, N.Y., NY 10011; 10,000.
Genealogical Society, Natl. (1903), 1921 Sunderland Pl. NW, Wash., DC 20036; 5,400.
Genetic Assn., Amer. (1913), 818 18th St. NW, Wash., DC 20006; 1,600.
Geographers, Assn. of Amer. (1904), 1710 16th St. NW, Wash., DC 20009; 5,000.
Geographic Education, Natl. Council for (1914), 115 N. Marion St., Oak Park, IL 60301; 5,000.
Geographic Society, Natl. (1888), 1145 17th St. NW, Wash., DC 20036, 10,700,000.
Geographical Society, Amer. (1851), 25 W. 39th St., N.Y., NY 10018; 4,000.
Geolinguistics, Amer. Society of (1964), Bronx Community College, 120 E. 181st St., Bronx, NY 10453; 100.
Geological Institute, Amer. (1948), 5205 Leesburg Pike, Falls Church, VA 22041; 17 societies.
Geological Society of America (1888), 3300 Penrose Pl., Boulder, CO 80301; 12,000.
Geologists, Assn. of Engineering (1957), 8310 San Fernando Way, Dallas, TX 75218; 2,700.
Geophysicists, Society of Exploration (1930), 3707 E. 51st St., Tulsa, OK 74135; 15,000.
George S. Patton, Jr. Historical Society (1970), 11307 Vela Dr., San Diego, CA 92126.
Geriatrics Society, Amer. (1942), 10 Columbus Circle, N.Y., NY 10019; 6,000.
Gideons Intl. (1899), 2900 Lebanon Rd., Nashville, TN 37214; 72,000.
Gifted Children, Amer. Assn. for (1946), 15 Gramercy Park, N.Y., NY 10003.
Gifted Children, Natl. Assn. for (1952), 2070 Country Rd. H, St. Paul, MN 55112; 5,000.

Girls Clubs of America (1945), 205 Lexington Ave., N.Y., NY 10016; 220,000.
Girl Scouts of the U.S.A. (1912), 830 Third Ave., N.Y., NY 10022; 2,784,000.
Gladiolus Council, No. Amer. (1945), 21 S. Drive, E. Brunswick, NJ 08316; 1,500.
Goat Assn., American Dairy (1904), 209 W. Main St., Spindale, NC 28160; 17,700.
Gold Star Mothers, Amer. (1928), 2128 Leroy Pl. NW, Wash., DC 20008; 6,600.
Golf Association, U.S. (1894), Golf House, Far Hills, NJ 07931; 4,987 clubs.
Goose Island Bird & Girl Watching Society (1960), 301 Arthur Ave., Park Ridge, IL 60068; 941.
Gospel Music Assn. (1964), P.O. Box 23201, Nashville, TN 37202; 3,000.
Governmental Research Assn. (1914), 4302 Airport Blvd., Austin, TX 78722; 400.
Graduate Schools in the U.S., Council of (1961), One Dupont Circle NW, Wash., DC 20036; 365 institutions.
Grandmother Clubs of America, Natl. Federation of (1938), 203 N. Wabash Ave., Chicago, IL 60601; 15,000.
Grange, Natl. (1867), 1616 H St. NW, Wash., DC 20006; 450,000.
Graphic Artists, Society of Amer. (1915), 32 Union Sq., 1214, N.Y., NY 10003; 232.
Graphic Arts, Amer. Institute of (1914), 1059 Third Ave., N.Y., NY 10021; 2,000.
Gray Panthers (1970), 3635 Chestnut, Phila., PA 19103; 61,000.
Greek-Amer. War Veterans in America, Natl. Legion (1938), 739 W. 186th St., N.Y., NY 10033; 41.
Green Mountain Club, The (1910), 43 State St., Box 889, Montpelier, VT 05602; 4,000.
Grocers, Natl. Assn. of Retail (1893), 11800 Sunrise Valley Dr., Reston, VA 22091; 40,000.
Grocery Manufacturers of America (1908), 1010 Wisconsin Ave., Wash., DC 20006; 130 cos.
Guide Dog Foundation for the Blind (1946), 109-19 72d Ave., Forest Hills, NY 11375; 35,000.
Gyro Intl. (1912), 1096 Mentor Ave., Painesville, OH 44077; 5,473.

HIAS (Hebrew Immigrant Aid Society) (1884), 200 Park Ave. S, N.Y., NY 10003; 14,000.
Hadassah, the Women's Zionist Organization of America (1912), 50 W. 58th St., N.Y., NY 10019; 370,000+.
Hairdressers and Cosmetologists Assn., Natl. (1921), 3510 Olive St., St. Louis, MO 63103; 58,000.
Handball Assn., U.S. (1951), 4101 Dempster St., Skokie, IL 60076; 15,000.
Handicapped, Federation of the (1935), 211 W. 14th St., N.Y., NY 10011; 650.
Handicapped, Natl. Assn. of the Physically (1958), 2 Meetinghouse Rd., Merrimack, N.H. 03054; 700.
Hang Gliding Assn., U.S. (1971), 11312 1/2 Venice Blvd., Los Angeles, CA 90066; 8,000.
Health Council, Natl. (1920), 70 W. 40th St., N.Y., NY 10018; 77 agencies.
Health Insurance Assn. of America (1956), 1750 K St. NW, Wash., DC 20006; 306 companies.
Health Insurance Institute (1956), 1850 K St. NW, Wash., DC; 325 companies.
Health, Physical Education, Recreation and Dance, Amer. Alliance for (1885), 1900 Association Dr., Reston, VA 22091; 40,000.
Hearing Aid Society, Natl. (1951), 20361 Middlebelt Rd., Livonia, MI 48152; 3,600.
Hearing and Speech Action, Natl. Assn. for (1919), 814 Thayer Ave., Silver Spring, MD 20910; 12,000.
Heart Assn., Amer. (1924), 7320 Greenville Ave., Dallas TX 75231; 144,000.
Hearts, Mended (1955), 7320 Greenville Ave., Dallas TX 75231; 15,000.
Heating, Refrigerating & Air Conditioning Engineers, Amer. Society of (1894), 1791 Tullie Circle, NE, Atlanta GA 30329; 45,000.
Helicopter Assn. Intl. (1948), 1110 Vermont Ave. NW, Wash., DC 20005; 840 companies.
Helicopter Society, Amer. (1943), 1325 18th St. NW, Wash., DC 20036; 4,500.
Hemispheric Affairs, Council on (1975), 1201 16th St. NW, Wash., DC 20036.
High School Assns., Natl. Federation of State (1920), 11724 Plaza Circle, Kansas City, MO 64195; 50.
High Twelve Internatl. (1921), 3681 Lindell Blvd., St. Louis, MO 63108; 26,000.

Historians, Organization of Amer. (1907), 112 N. Bryan St., Bloomington, IN 47401; 8,229.
Historical Assn., Amer. (1884), 400 A St. SE, Wash., DC 20003.
Historic Preservation, Natl. Trust for (1949), 1785 Massachusetts Ave. NW, Wash., DC 20036; 160,000.
Hockey Assn. of the U.S., Amateur (1937), 2997 Broadmoor Valley Rd., Colorado Springs, CO 80906; 10,490 teams.
Holiday Institute of Yonkers (1969), Box 414, Yonkers, NY 10710.
Holy Cross of Jerusalem, Order of (1965), 853 Seventh Ave., N.Y., NY 10019; 2,014.
Home Builders, Natl. Assn. of (1942), 15th & M Sts. NW, Wash., DC 20005; 114,000+ firms.
Home Economics Assn., Amer. (1909), 2010 Massachusetts Ave. NW, Wash., DC 20036; 33,000.
Home Improvement Council, Natl. (1956), 11 E. 44th St., N.Y., NY 10017; 3,300.
Homemakers of America, Future (1945), 2010 Massachusetts Ave. NW, Wash., DC 20036; 400,000.
Homemakers Council, Natl. Extension (1936), Route 2, Box 3070, Vale, OR 97918; 500,000.
Horatio Alger Society (1961), 4907 Allison Dr., Lansing, MI 48910; 250.
Horse Protection Assn., Amer. (1966), 1312 18th St. NW, Wash., DC 20036; 15,000.
Horse Show Assn. of America Ltd., Natl. (1883), One Penn Plaza, Rm. 4501, N.Y., NY 10001.
Horse Shows Assn., Amer. (1917), 598 Madison Ave., N.Y., NY 10022; 25,000.
Hospital Associaton, Amer. (1898), 840 N. Lake Shore Dr., Chicago, IL 60611; 6,000 institutions.
Hospital Public Relations, Amer. Society for (1965), 840 N. Lake Shore Dr., Chicago, IL 60611; 2,000.
Hotel & Motel Assn., Amer. (1910), 888 Seventh Ave., N.Y., NY 10019; 8,200 hotels & motels.
Hot Rod Assn., Natl. (1951), 10639 Riverside Dr., N. Hollywood, CA 91602; 37,500.
Human Relations, Centers for (1980), 23820 Arlington #15, Torrance, CA 90501; 40 centers.
Humane Legislation, Committee for (1976), 11 W. 60th St., N.Y., NY 10023; 100,000.
Humane Society of the U.S. (1954), 2100 L St. NW, Wash., DC 20037; 170,000.
Humanics Foundation, Amer. (1948), 912 Baltimore Ave., Kansas City, MO 64105; 2,000.
Humanities, Natl. Endowment for the (1965), 806 15th St. NW, Wash., DC 20506.
Human Rights and Social Justice, Americans for (1977), 109 Bentbridge Rd., Greenville, SC 29611; 1,400.
Hydrogen Energy, Intl. Assn. for (1975), P.O. Box 248266, Coral Gables, FL 33124; 2,455.

Iceland Veterans (1948), 2101 Walnut St., Phila., PA 19103; 1,600+.
Identification, Intl. Assn. for (1915), P.O. Box 139, Utica, NY 13503; 2,500.
Illustrators, Society of (1901), 128 E. 63d St., N.Y., NY 10021; 800.
Indian Rights Assn. (1882), 1505 Race St., Phila., PA 19102; 1,300.
Industrial Democracy, League for (1905), 275 Seventh Ave., N.Y., NY 10001; 1,500.
Industrial Designers Society of America, 1717 N St. NW, Wash., DC 20036; 1,500.
Industrial Engineers, Amer. Institute of (1948), 25 Technology Park, Norcross, GA 30092; 35,000.
Industrial Health Foundation (1935), 5231 Centre Ave., Pittsburgh, PA 15232; 150 companies.
Industrial Management Society (1936), 570 Northwest Hwy., Des Plaines, IL 60016; 1,200.
Industrial Security, Amer. Soc. for (1955), 2000 K St. NW, Wash., DC 20006; 17,000.
Infant Death Syndrome (SIDS) Foundation, Natl. Sudden (1962), 310 S. Michigan Ave., Chicago, IL 60604; 69 chapters.
Information, Freedom of, Center (1958), P.O. Box 858, Columbia, MO 65205; 900.
Information Managers, Associated (1978), 316 Pennsylvania Ave. SE, Suite 502, Wash., DC 20003; 850.
Information Industry Assn. (1968), 316 Pennsylvania Ave. SE, Suite 502, Wash., DC 20003; 150 companies.
Insurance Assn., Amer. (1866), 85 John St., N.Y., NY 10038; 150 companies.
Insurance Seminars, Intl. (1964), P.O. Box J, University, AL 35486; 5,000.
Intelligence Officers, Assn. of Former (1975), 6723 Whittier Ave., Suite 303A, McLean, VA 22101; 3,000.
Intercollegiate Athletics, Natl. Assn. of (1940), 1221 Baltimore Ave., Kansas City, MO 64105; 520 schools.
Interior Designers, Amer. Society of (1975), 730 Fifth Ave. N.Y., NY 10019; 17,000.
Inventors, Amer. Assn. of (1975), 6562 E. Curtis Rd. Bridgeport, MI 48722; 5,600.
Investment Clubs, Natl. Assn. of (1951), 1515 E. Eleven Mile Rd., Royal Oak, MI 48067; 57,264.
Iron Castings Society (1975), 20611 Center Ridge Rd. Rocky River, OH 44116; 250 firms.
Iron and Steel Engineers, Assn. of (1907), Three Gateway Center, Suite 2350, Pittsburgh, PA 15222; 12,375.
Iron and Steel Institute, Amer. (1908), 1000 16th St. NW Wash., DC 20036; 2,500.
Italian Historical Society of America (1949), 111 Columbia Heights, Bklyn., NY 11201; 2,477.
Italy-America Chamber of Commerce (1887), 350 Fifth Ave., N.Y., NY 10118; 750.
Izaak Walton League of America, The (1922), 1800 N. Kent St., Arlington, VA 22209; 48,000.

Jamestowne Society (1936), P.O. Box 14523, Richmond VA 23221; 2,000.
Japanese Amer. Citizens League (1930), 1765 Sutter St. San Francisco, CA 94115; 30,000.
Japos Study Group (1974), 154 Laguna Ct., St. Augustine Shores, FL 32084; 120.
Jaycees, U.S. (1915), 4 W. 21st St., Tulsa, OK 74115 280,000.
Jewish Appeal, United (1939), 1290 Ave. of the Americas N.Y., NY 10019.
Jewish Center Workers, Assn. of (1918), 15 E. 26th St N.Y., NY 10010; 1,015.
Jewish Committee, Amer. (1906), 165 E. 56th St., N.Y., NY 10022; 40,000.
Jewish Congress, Amer. (1918), 15 E. 84th St., N.Y., NY 10028; 50,000.
Jewish Federations, Council of (1932), 575 Lexington Ave N.Y., NY 10022; 200 agencies.
Jewish Historical Society, Amer. (1892), 2 Thornton Rd Waltham, MA 02154; 3,750.
Jewish War Veterans of the U.S.A. (1896), 1712 New Hampshire Ave. NW, Wash., DC 20009; 73,000.
Jewish Welfare Board, Natl. (1917), 15 E. 26th St., N.Y., NY 10010.
Jewish Women, Natl. Council of (1893), 15 E. 26th St., N.Y. NY 10010; 100,000.
Job's Daughters, Internatl. Order of (1921), 119 S. 19th St Rm. 402, Omaha, NE 68102; 65,000.
Jockey Club (1894), 380 Madison Ave., N.Y., NY 10017; 91.
Jogging Assn., Natl. (1968), 2420 K St. NW, Wash., DC 20037; 35,000.
John Birch Society (1958), 395 Concord Ave., Belmont, MA 02178; 50,000 to 100,000.
Joseph's Diseases Foundation, Intl. (1977), 1832 Holme St., Build. E, Livermore, CA 94550; 3,500.
Journalists, Society of Professional; (Sigma Delta Chi) (1909), 840 N. Lake Shore Dr., Suite 801, Chicago, IL 60611 28,000.
Journalists and Authors, Amer. Society of (1948), 150 Broadway, Suite 1907, N.Y., NY 10036; 650.
Judaism, Amer. Council for (1943), 307 Fifth Ave., N.Y., NY 10016; 20,000.
Judicature Society, Amer. (1913), 200 W. Monroe, Suite 1606, Chicago, IL 60606; 30,000.
Juggler's Assn., Intl. (1947), P.O. Box 29, Kenmore, NY 14217; 1,300.
Junior Achievement (1919), 550 Summer St., Stamford, CT 06901; 300,000.
Junior Colleges, Amer. Assn. of Community and (1920) One Dupont Circle NW, Wash., DC 20036; 900.
Junior Leagues, Assn. of (1921), 825 Third Ave., N.Y., NY 10022; 140,000+.

Kennel Club, Amer. (1884), 51 Madison Ave., N.Y., NY 10010; 413 clubs.
Key Club Intl. (1925), 101 E. Erie St., Chicago, IL 6061 100,000.
Kitefliers Assn., Intl. (1955), 321 E. 48th St., N.Y., NY 1001 30,000.
Kiwanis Intl. (1915), 101 E. Erie St., Chicago, IL 6061 300,000.
Knights of Columbus (1882), One Columbus Plaza, New Haven, CT 06507; 1,359,000.

Knights Templar U.S.A., Grand Encampment (1816), 14 E. Jackson Blvd., Suite 1700, Chicago, IL 60604; 340,000.
Krishna Consciousness, Intl. Soc. for (1966), 3764 Watseka Ave., Los Angeles, CA 90034; 5,000.

La Leche League Intl. (1956), 9616 Minneapolis, Franklin Park, IL 60131; 150,000.
Lambs, The (1876), 3 W. 51st St., N.Y., NY 10019; 250.
Landscape Architects, Amer. Society of (1899), 1900 M St. NW, Wash., DC 20036; 4,700.
Law, Amer. Society of Intl. (1906), 2223 Massachusetts Ave. NW, Wash., DC 20008; 5,500.
Law Enforcement Officers Assn., Amer. (1966), 1000 Connecticut Ave. NW, Suite 9, Wash., DC 20036; 50,000.
Law Libraries, Amer. Assn. of (1906), 53 W. Jackson Blvd., Chicago, IL 60604; 3,100.
Law and Social Policy, Center for (1969), 1751 N St. NW, Wash., DC 20036; 500.
Learned Societies, Amer. Council of (1919), 800 Third Ave., N.Y., NY 10022; 43 societies.
Lefthanders, League of (1975), P.O. Box 89, New Milford, NJ 07646; 400.
Lefthanders Intl. (1975), 3601 SW 29th St., Topeka, KS 66614; 8,000.
Legal Administrators, Assn. of (1971), 1800 Pickwick Ave., Glenview, IL 60025; 3,000.
Legal Secretaries, Natl. Assn. of (1950), 3005 E. Skelly Dr., Tulsa, OK 74105; 25,000+.
Legion of Valor of the U.S.A. (1890), 548 Bellemeade, Gretna, LA 70053; 750.
Leprosy Missions, Amer. (1906), 1262 Broad St., Bloomfield, NJ 07003.
Lesbian & Gay Academic Union (1979), P.O. Box 82123, San Diego, CA 92138; 3,500.
Leukemia Society of America (1949), 800 Second Ave., N.Y., NY 10017; 55 chapters.
Lewis Carroll Society of N. America (1974), 617 Rockford Rd., Silver Spring, MD 20902; 300.
Liberty Lobby (1955), 300 Independence Ave. SE, Wash., DC 20003; 33,000.
Libraries Assn., Special (1909), 235 Park Ave. So., N.Y., NY 10003; 12,000.
Library Assn., Amer. (1876), 50 E. Huron St., Chicago, IL 60611; 37,954.
Library Assn., Medical (1898), 919 N. Michigan Ave., Chicago, IL 60611; 5,000.
Life, Americans United for (1971), 230 N. Michigan Ave., Suite 915, Chicago, IL 60601, 12,000.
Life Office Management Assn. (1924), 100 Colony Sq., Atlanta, GA 30361; 630 companies.
Life Underwriters, Natl. Assn. of (1890), 1922 F St. NW, Wash., DC 20006; 132,000.
Lighter-Than-Air Society (1952), 1800 Triplett Blvd., Akron, OH 44306; 1,000.
Lions Clubs, Intl. Assn. of (1917), 300 22d St., Oak Brook, IL 60570; 1,332,000.
Literacy Volunteers of America (1962), 404 Oak St., Syracuse, NY 13203.
Little League Baseball (1939), P.O. Box 3485, Williamsport, PA 17701; 14,720 leagues.
Little People of America (1957), Box 633, San Bruno, CA 94066; 3,000.
London Club (1975), P.O. Box 4527, Topeka, KS 66604; 1,000+.
Lung Assn., Amer. (1904), 1740 Broadway, N.Y., NY 10019.
Lutheran Education Assn. (1942), 7400 Augusta St., River Forest, IL 60305; 3,000.
Lutheran World Ministries, 360 Park Ave. S., N.Y., NY 10010.

Macaroni Manufacturers Assn., Natl. (1904), 19 S. Bothwell, Box 336, Palatine, IL 60067; 93 firms.
Magazine Publishers Assn. (1919), 575 Lexington Ave., N.Y., NY 10022; 190 publishers.
Magicians, Intl. Brotherhood of (1926), 28 N. Main St., Kenton, OH 43326; 11,000.
Magicians, Society of Amer. (1902), 325 Maple St., Lynn, MA 01904; 5,800.
Magicians Guild of America (1946), 20 W. 40th St., N.Y., NY 10018; 187.
Male Nurse Assn., Natl. (1971), Rush Univ., 1725 W. Harrison St., Chicago, IL 60612; 1,400.
Management Assns., Amer. (1923), 135 W. 50th St., N.Y., NY 10020; 92,000.
Management Consultants, Institute of (1968), 19 W. 44th St., N.Y., NY 10036; 1,500.
Management Engineers, Assn. of Consulting (1929), 230 Park Ave., N.Y., NY 10169; 59 firms.
Manufacturers, Natl. Assn. of (1895), 1776 F St. NW, Wash., DC 20006; 12,000 companies.
Manufacturers' Agents Natl. Assn. (1947), 2021 Business Center Dr., Irvine, CA 92713; 6,000.
Man Watchers (1974), 2865 State St., San Diego, CA 92103; 4,000.
March of Dimes Birth Defects Foundation (1938), 1275 Mamaroneck Ave., White Plains, NY 10605; 760 chapters.
Marijuana Laws, Natl. Organization for the Reform of (NORML) (1970), 530 8th St. SE, Wash., DC 20003; 25,000.
Marine Corps League (1923), 933 N. Kenmore St., Arlington, VA 22201; 26,000.
Marine Manufacturers Assn., Natl. (1904), 401 N. Michigan Ave., Chicago, IL 60611; 800 companies.
Marine Surveyors, Natl. Assn. of (1960), 86 Windsor Gate Dr., N. Hills, NY 11040; 400.
Marine Technology Society (1963), 1730 M St. NW, Wash., DC 20036; 3,500.
Marketing Assn., Amer. (1937), 250 S. Wacker Dr., Chicago, IL 60606; 40,105.
Masonic Relief Assn. of U.S. and Canada (1885), 32613 Seidel Dr., Burlington, WS 53105; 14,700.
Masonic Service Assn. of the U.S. (1919), 8120 Fenton St., Silver Spring, MD 20910; 43 Grand Lodges.
Masons, Ancient and Accepted Scottish Rite, Southern Jurisdiction, Supreme Council (1801), 1733 16th St. NW, Wash., DC 20009; 656,000.
Masons, Supreme Council 33°, Ancient and Accepted Scottish Rite, Northern Masonic Jurisdiction (1813), 33 Marrett Rd., Lexington, MA 02173; 496,824.
Masons, Royal Arch, General Grand Chapter (1797), P.O. Box 5320, Lexington, KY 40505; 325,000.
Mathematical Assn. of America (1915), 1225 Connecticut Ave. NW, Wash., DC 20036; 18,500.
Mathematical Society, Amer. (1894), Box 6248, Providence, RI 02940; 19,000.
Mathematical Statistics, Institute of (1935), 3401 Investment Blvd., 6, Hayward, CA 94545; 3,000.
Mathematics, Society for Industrial and Applied (1952), 117 S. 17th St., Phila., PA 19103; 5,500.
Mayflower Descendants, General Society of (1897), 4 Winslow St., Plymouth, MA 02360; 20,000.
Mayors, U.S. Conference of (1932), 1620 Eye St. NW, Wash., DC 20006; 840 cities.
Mechanical Engineers, Amer. Society of (1880), 345 E. 47th St., N.Y., NY 10017; 75,000.
Mechanics, Amer. Academy of (1969), Dept. of Civil Engineering, Northwestern Univ., Evanston, IL 60201; 990.
Mechanics, Assn. of Chairmen of Departments of (1969), Dept. of Theoretical and Applied Mechanics, Univ. of Ill. at Urbana-Champaign, Urbana, IL 61801; 96.
Mediaeval Academy of America (1925), 1430 Massachusetts Ave., Cambridge, MA 02138; 3,900.
Medical Assn., Amer. (1847), 535 N. Dearborn St., Chicago, IL 60610.
Medical Assn., Natl. (1895), 1301 Pennsylvania Ave. NW, Wash., DC 20004; 10,500.
Medical Record Assn., Amer. (1928), 875 N. Michigan Ave., Chicago, IL 60611; 26,000.
Medical Technicians, Natl. Assn. of Emergency (1975), P.O. Box 334, Newton Highlands, MA 02161; 20,000.
Medical Technologists, Amer. College of (1942), 5608 Lane, Raytown, MO 64133; 368.
Memorabilia Americana (1973), 1211 Ave. Eye, Brooklyn, NY 11230; 2,000.
Mensa, Amer. (1960), 1701 W. 3d St., Brooklyn, NY 11223; 50,000.
Mental Health, Natl. Assn. for (1950), 1800 N. Kent St., Arlington, VA 22209; 1,000,000+.
Mental Health Program Directors, Natl. Assn. of State (1963), 1001 3d St. SW, Wash., DC 20024, 54.
Merchant Marine Library Assn., Amer. (1921), One World Trade Center, Suite 2601, N.Y., NY 10048; 1,100.
Merchants Assn., Natl. Retail (1911), 100 W. 31st St., N.Y., NY 10001; 35,000 stores.
Metal Finishers, Natl. Assn. of (1955), 111 E. Wacker Dr., Chicago, IL 60601; 1,216.
Metallurgy Institute, Amer. Powder (1959), 105 College Rd. East, Princeton, NJ 08540; 2,300.
Metal Powder Industries Federation, (1946), 105 College Rd. East, Princeton, NJ 08540; 260 cos.
Metals, Amer. Society for (1913), Metals Park, OH 44073; 51,000.
Meteorological Society, Amer. (1919), 45 Beacon St., Boston, MA 02108; 9,850.

Metric Assn., U.S. (1916), 10245 Andasol Ave., Northridge, CA 91325; 3,500.
Microbiology, Amer. Society for (1899), 1913 Eye St. NW, Wash. DC 20006; 31,829.
Micrographics Assn., Natl. (1942), 8719 Colesville Rd., Silver Spring, MD 20910; 9,000.
Mideast Educational and Training Services, America-, formerly **Amer. Friends of the Middle East** (1951), 1717 Massachusetts Ave. NW, Wash., DC 20036; 390.
Military Order of the Loyal Legion of the U.S.A. (1865), 1805 Pine St., Phila., PA 19103; 1,200.
Military Order of the Purple Heart (1782, by Gen. George Washington; reactivated Feb. 22, 1932, by President Herbert Hoover and Chief of Staff Douglas MacArthur), 1022 Wilson Blvd., Arlington, VA 22209; 10,000.
Military Order of the USA (1932), 5413-B Backlick Rd., Springfield, VA 22151; 10,000.
Military Order of the World Wars (1920), 1100 17th St. NW, Wash., DC 20036; 14,500.
Mining, Metallurgical and Petroleum Engineers, Amer. Institute of (1871), 345 E. 47th St., N.Y., NY 10017; 86,279.
Mining and Metallurgical Society of America (1908), 230 Park Ave., N.Y., NY 10017; 310.
Ministerial Assn., Amer. (1929), 2210 Wilshire Blvd., Suite 582, Santa Monica, CA 90403; 1,800.
Ministerial Training, Amer. Commission on (1950), 23820 Arlington, Suite 15, Torrance, CA 90501; 45.

Model Railroad Assn., Natl. (1935), 7061 Twin Oaks Dr., Indianapolis, IN 46226; 27,000.
Modern Language Assn. of America (1883), 62 Fifth Ave., N.Y., NY 10011; 28,000.
Modern Language Teachers Assns., Natl. Federation of (1916), Paul W. Peterson, Gannon Univ., Erie, PA 16541; 7,000.
Moose, Loyal Order of (1888), Mooseheart, IL 60539; 1,746,733.
Mothers Committee, Amer. (1933), Waldorf Astoria Hotel, 301 Park Ave., N.Y., NY 10022; 5,000.
Mothers-in-Law Club Intl. (1970), 420 Adelberg Ln., Cedarhurst, NY 11516; 5,000.
Mothers of Twins Clubs, Natl. Organization of (1960), 5402 Amberwood Ln., Rockville, MD 20853; 8,103.
Motion Picture Arts & Sciences, Academy of (1927), 8949 Wilshire Blvd., Beverly Hills, CA 90211; 4,226.
Motion Pictures, Natl. Board of Review of (1909), P.O. Box 589, Lenox Hill Sta., N.Y., NY 10021; 7,000.
Motion Picture & Television Engineers, Society of (1916), 862 Scarsdale Ave., Scarsdale, NY 10583; 9,442.
Motor Vehicle Administrators, Amer. Assn. of (1933), 1201 Connecticut Ave. NW, Wash., DC 20036; 2,000.
Motor Vehicle Manufacturers Assn. (1913), 300 New Center Building, Detroit, MI 48202; 9 companies.
Motorcyclist Assn., Amer. (1924), 33 Collegeview, Westerville, OH 43081; 130,000.

Multiple Sclerosis Society, Natl. (1946), 205 E. 42d St., N.Y., NY 10017; 567,822.
Municipal Finance Officers Assn. (1971), 180 N. Michigan Ave., Suite 800, Chicago, IL 60601; 9,218.
Municipal League, Natl. (1894), 47 E. 68th St., N.Y., NY 10021; 6,500.
Murray Hill Assn., (1914), 237 Madison Ave., N.Y., NY 10016; 100.
Muscular Dystrophy Assn. (1950), 810 Seventh Ave., N.Y., NY 10019, 1,800,000.
Museums, Amer. Assn. of (1906), 1055 Thomas Jefferson St. NW, Wash., DC 20007; 6,166.
Music, Natl. Assn. of Schools of (1924), 11250 Roger Bacon Dr. #5, Reston, VA 22090; 520 institutions.
Music Center, Amer. (1940), 250 W. 54th St., N.Y., NY 10019; 1,200.
Music Conference, Amer. (1947), 1000 Skokie Blvd., Wilmette, IL 60091; 400.
Music Council, Natl. (1940), 250 W. 54th St., N.Y., NY 10019; 60 organizations.
Music Educators Natl. Conference (1907), 1902 Association Dr., Reston, VA 22091; 55,000.
Musicians, Amer. Federation of (1896), 1500 Broadway, N.Y., NY 10036; 330,000.
Musicological Society, Amer. (1934), 201 S. 34th St., Phila., PA 19104, 3,500.
Music Publishers' Assn., Natl. (1917), 110 E. 59th St., N.Y., NY 10022; 275.
Music Scholarship Assn., Amer. (1957), 1826 Carew Tower, Cincinnati, OH 45202; 4,500.
Music Teachers Natl. Assn. (1876), 2113 Carew Tower, Cincinnati, OH 45202; 19,167.
Muzzle Loading Rifle Assn., Natl. (1933), P.O. Box 67, Friendship, IN 47021; 25,000.
Mystic Seaport Museum (1929), 30 Greenmanville Ave., Mystic, CT 06355; 16,291.

NAACP (Natl. Assn. for the Advancement of Colored People (1909), 1790 Broadway, N.Y., NY 10019, 500,000.
Name Society, Amer. (1951), N. Country Community College, Saranac Lake, NY 12983; 950.
Narcolepsy and Cataplexy Foundation of Amer. (1975), 1410 York Ave., Suite 2D, N.Y. NY 10021; 3,605.
Narcolepsy Assoc., Amer. (1975), P.O. Box 5846, Stanford, CA 94305; 2,500.
National Guard Assn. of the U.S. (1878), One Massachusetts Ave. NW, Wash., DC 20001; 54,000.
Nationalities Service, Amer. Council for (1918), 20 W. 40th St., N.Y., NY 10018; 31 agencies.

Naturalists, Assn. of Interpretive (1961), 6700 Needwood Rd., Derwood, MD 20855; 1,300.
Natural Science for Youth Foundation (1961), 763 Silvermine Rd., New Canaan, CT 06840; 400.
Nature Conservancy (1951), 1800 N. Kent St., Arlington, VA 22209; 125,000.
Nature & Natural Resources, Intl. Union for Conservation of (1948), Avenue du Mont Blanc, 1196 Gland, Switzerland; 471.
Nature Study Society, Amer. (1908), 790 Ewing Ave., Franklin Lakes, NJ 07417; 1,000.
Navajo Code Talkers Assn. (1971), Red Rock State Park, P.O. Box 328, Church Rock, NM 87311; 90.
Naval Architects & Marine Engineers, Society of (1893), One World Trade Center, Suite 1369, N.Y., NY 10048; 13,000.
Naval Engineers, Amer. Society of (1888), 1012 14th St. NW, Wash., DC 20005; 5,800.
Naval Institute, U.S. (1873), U.S. Naval Academy, Annapolis, MD 21402; 82,000.
Naval Reserve Assn. (1954), 910 17th St. NW, Wash., DC 20006; 21,500.
Navigation, Institute of (1945), 815 15th St. NW, Suite 832, Wash., DC 20005; 2,600.
Navy Club of the U.S.A. Auxiliary (1940), 418 W. Pontiac St., Ft. Wayne, IN 46807; 1,000.
Navy League of the U.S. (1902); 818 18th St. NW, Wash., DC 20006; 40,000.

Needlework Guild of America (1885), 1342 E. Lincoln Hwy., Langhorne, PA 19047.
Negro College Fund, United (1944), 500 E. 62d St., N.Y. NY 10021; 41 institutions.
Newspaper Editors, Amer. Society of (1922), 1350 Sullivan Trail, Easton, PA 18042; 885.
Newspaper Promotion Assn., Intl. (1930), 11600 Sunrise Valley Dr., Reston, VA 22091; 1,300.
Newspaper Publishers Assn., Amer. (1887), 11600 Sunrise Valley Dr., Reston, VA 22091; 1,420 newspapers.
Ninety-Nines (Intl. Organization of Women Pilots) (1929), P.O. Box 59965; Will Rogers World Airport, Oklahoma City, OK 73159, 6,000.

Non-Commissioned Officers Assn. (1960), 10635 IH 35 No., San Antonio, TX 78233; 200,000+.
Non-Parents, Natl. Organization for (1972), 3 N. Liberty Baltimore, MD 21201; 1,500.
Notaries, Amer. Society of (1965), 810 18th St. NW, Wash. DC 20006; 11,260.

Nuclear Society, Amer. (1954), 555 N. Kensington Ave., La Grange Park, IL 60525; 13,000.
Numismatic Assn., Amer. (1891), 818 N. Cascade Ave., Colorado Springs, CO 80903; 43,000.
Numismatic Society, Amer. (1858), Broadway at 155th St. N.Y., NY 10032; 2,181.
Nurse Education and Service, Natl. Assn. for Practical (1941), 254 W. 31st St., N.Y., NY 10001; 25,000.
Nurses, Natl. Federation of Licensed Practical (1949), 888 7th Ave., N.Y., NY 10019; 18,000.
Nurses' Assn., Amer. (1897), 2420 Pershing Rd., Kansas City, MO 64108; 165,000.
Nursing, Natl. League for (1952), 10 Columbus Circle, N.Y. NY 10019; 16,500.
Nutrition, Amer. Institute of (1928), 9650 Rockville Pike Bethesda, MD 20814; 2,100.

ORT Federation, Amer. (Org. for Rehabilitation through Training) (1925), 817 Broadway, N.Y., NY 10003, 18,000.
OTC Companies, Natl. Assn. of (1973), P.O. Box 60, Oreland, PA 19075; 169.
Odd Fellows, Sovereign Grand Lodge Independent Order of (1819), 422 Trade St., Winston Salem, NC 27101; 637,653.
Old Crows, Assn. of (1964), 2300 9th St. S., Arlington, VA 22204; 10,000.
Olympic Committee, U.S. (1920), 1750 E. Boulder St., Colorado Springs, CO 80909.
Optical Society of America (1916), 1816 Jefferson Pl. NW Wash., DC 20036; 8,600.

Optimist Intl. (1919), 4494 Lindell Blvd., St. Louis, MO 63108; 38,000.
Optometric Assn., Amer. (1898), 243 N. Lindbergh Blvd., St. Louis, MO 63141; 21,845.
Oral and Maxillofacial Surgeons, Amer. Assn. of (1918), 211 E. Chicago Ave., Chicago, IL 60611; 4,053.
Organists, Amer. Guild of (1896), 815 Second Ave., Suite 318, N.Y., NY 10017; 19,000.
Oriental Society, Amer. (1842), 329 Sterling Memorial Library, Yale Sta., New Haven, CT 06520; 1,650.
Ornithologists' Union, Amer. (1883), c/o National Museum of Natural History, Smithsonian Institution, Wash., DC 20560; ,000.
Osteopathic Assn., Amer. (1897), 212 E. Ohio St., Chicago, IL 60611; 14,419.
Ostomy Assn., United (1962), 2001 W. Beverly Blvd., Los Angeles, CA 90057; 45,000.
Outlaw and Lawman History, Natl. Assn. for (1974), Western Research Center, Univ. of Wyoming, Box 3334, Laramie, WY 82071; 500.
Overeaters Anonymous (1960), 2190 190th St., Torrance, CA 90504; 80,000.
Over-the-Counter Cos., Natl. Assn. of (1973), Box 60, Oreland, PA 19075; 225

PTA (Parent-Teacher Assn.), Natl. (1897), 700 N. Rush St., Chicago, IL 60611; 5,000,000+.
Paleontological Research Institution (1932), 1259 Trumansburg Rd., Ithaca, NY 14850, 600.
Paper Converters Assn. (1934), 1000 Vermont Ave. NW, Wash., DC 20005; 45 companies.
Paper Institute, Amer. (1966), 260 Madison Ave., N.Y., NY 10016; 175 companies.
Parasitologists, Amer. Society of (1924), 1041 New Hampshire St., Box 368, Lawrence, KS 66044; 1,500.
Parenthood, Natl. Alliance for Optional (1972), 2010 Massachusetts Ave. NW, Wash., DC 20036; 1,000+.
Parents Without Partners (1957), 7910 Woodmont Ave. NW, Wash., DC 20854; 205,000.
Parking Assn., Natl. (1951), 1101 17th St. NW, Wash., DC 20036; 1,000 companies.
Parkinson's Disease Foundation (1957), Columbia Univ. Medical Center, 650 W. 168th St., N.Y., NY 10032.
Parliamentarians, Amer. Institute of (1958), 229 Army Post Rd., Suite B, Des Moines, IA 50315; 1,200.
Pastoral Counseling, Amer. Board of Examiners in (1977), 916 Sepulveda Blvd., Suite 111, Torrance, CA 90505; 175.
Pathologists, Amer. Assn. of (1976), 9650 Rockville Pike, Bethesda, MD 20014; 2,100.
Patriotism, Natl. Committee for Responsible (1967), P.O. Box 665, Grand Central Sta., N.Y., NY 10163; 150.
Patriotism, Natl. Council for the Encouragement of (1968), Box 3271, Munster, IN 46321; 1,500.
Pearl Harbor Survivors Assn. (1958), P.O. Box 205, Sperryville, VA 22740; 9,300.
Pedestrian Tolls, Committee for (1979), P.O. Box 283, Philipsburg, NJ 08865; 416.
P.E.N. Amer. Center (1921), 47 Fifth Ave., N.Y., NY 10003; ,800.
Pen Women, Natl. League of Amer. (1897), 1300 17th St. NW, Wash., DC 20036; 6,200.
Pennsylvania Society (1899), Suite 1850, Waldorf Astoria Hotel, 301 Park Ave., N.Y., NY 10022; 2,200.
Pension Actuaries, Amer. Society of (1966), 1700 K St. NW, Ste. 404, Wash., DC 20006; 1,800.
P.E.O (Philanthropic Educational Organization) Sisterhood (1869), 3700 Grand Ave., Des Moines, IA 50312; 215,000.
Personnel Administration, Amer. Society for (1948), 30 Park Dr., Berea, OH 44017; 30,000.
Petroleum Geologists, Amer. Assn. of (1917), Box 979, 1444 S. Boulder, Tulsa, OK 74101; 33,000.
Petroleum Institute, Amer. (1919), 2101 L St. NW, Wash., DC 20037; 7,500.
Petroleum Landmen, Amer. Assn. of (1955), 2408 Continental Life Bldg., Fort Worth, TX 76102; 6,200.
Pharmaceutical Assn., Amer. (1852), 2215 Constitution Ave. NW, Wash., DC 20037; 55,000.
Philatelic Americans, Society of (1894), 58 W. Salisbury Dr., Wilmington, DE 19809; 8,550.
Philatelic Society, Amer. (1886), P.O. Box 800, 336 S. Fraser St., State College, PA 16801; 53,541.
Philaticians, Society of (1972), 154 Laguna Ct., St. Augustine Shores, FL 32084; 300.
Philological Assn., Amer. (1869), 617 Hamilton Hall, Columbia Univ., N.Y., NY 10027; 2,500.
Philosophical Assn., Amer. (1900), Univ. of Delaware, Newark, DE 19711; 6,500.
Philosophical Enquiry, Intl. Society for (1974), P.O. Box 3282, Kingsport, TN 37664; 254.
Philosophical Society, Amer. (1743), 104 S. 5th St., Phila., PA 19106; 625.
Photographers of America, Professional (1880), 1090 Executive Way, Des Plaines, IL 60018; 1,500.
Photographic Society of Amer. (1934), 2005 Walnut St., Phila. PA 19103; 1,700.
Physical Therapy Assn., Amer. (1921), 1156 15th St. NW. Wash., DC 20005; 27,835.
Physicians, Amer. Academy of Family (1947), 1740 W. 92nd St., Kansas City, MO 64114; 50,000.
Physics, Amer. Institute of (1931), 335 E. 45th St., N.Y., NY 10017; 59,474.
Physiological Society, Amer. (1887), 9650 Rockville Pike, Bethesda, MD 20814; 6,000.
Pilgrim Society (1820), 75 Court St., Plymouth, MA 02360; 700.
Pilgrims of the U.S. (1903), 74 Trinity Pl., N.Y., NY 10006; 1,000.
Pilot Club Intl. (1921), 244 College St., Macon, GA 31213; 20,000+.
Pioneer Women, The Women's Labor Zionist Organization of America (1925), 200 Madison Ave., N.Y., NY 10016; 50,000.
Planned Parenthood Federation of America (1916), 810 Seventh Ave., N.Y., NY 10019; 189 affiliates.
Planning Assn., Amer. (1917), 1976 Massachusetts Ave. NW, Wash., DC 20036; 21,500.
Plastic Modelers Society, Intl. (1962), P.O. Box 480, Denver, CO 80201; 5,200.
Plastics Engineers, Society of (1942), 14 Fairfield Dr., Brookfield Cntr., CT 06805; 23,500.
Plastics Industry, Society of (1937), 355 Lexington Ave., N.Y., NY 10017; 1,400 companies.
Platform Assn., Intl. (1831), 2564 Berkshire Rd., Cleveland Heights, OH 44106; 5,000+.
Podiatry Assn., Amer. (1912), 20 Chevy Chase Circle NW, Wash., DC 20015; 8,054.
Poetry Day Committee, Natl. (1947), 1110 N. Venetian Dr., Miami, FL 33139; 17,000.
Poetry Society of America (1910), 15 Gramercy Park, N.Y., NY 10003; 1,050.
Poets, Academy of Amer. (1934), 177 E. 87th St., N.Y., NY 10028; 3,500.
Polar Society, Amer. (1934), c/o Secretary, 98-20 62d Dr., Apt. 7H, Rego Park, NY 11374; 2,175.
Police Hall of Fame and Museum, Amer. (1960), 14600 S. Tamiami Trail US 41, N. Port, FL 33596.
Police, Internatl. Assn. of Chiefs of (1893), 13 Firstfield Rd., Gaithersburg, MD 20878; 13,300.
Police Reserve Officers Assn., Natl. (1967), 609 W. Main St., Louisville, KY 40202; 11,000.
Polish Army Veterans Assn. of America (1921), 19 Irving Pl., N.Y., NY 10003; 9,762.
Polish Cultural Society of America (1940), 43 John St., N.Y., NY 10038; 70,331.
Polish Legion of American Veterans (1921), 3024 N. Laramie Ave., Chicago, IL 60641; 15,000.
Political Items Collectors, Amer. (1945), 1054 Sharpsburg Dr., Huntsville, AL 35803; 2,300.
Political Science, Academy of (1880), 2852 Broadway, N.Y., NY 10025; 10,500.
Political Science Assn., Amer. (1903), 1527 New Hampshire Ave. NW, Wash., DC 20036; 12,000.
Political & Social Science, Amer. Academy of (1889), 3937 Chestnut St., Phila., PA 19104; 7,000.
Pollution Control, Internatl. Assn. for (1970), 1625 Eye St. NW, Wash. DC 20006; 500.
Polo Assn., U.S. (1890), 1301 W. 22d St., Oak Brook, IL 60521; 2,000.
Population Assn. of America (1931), 806 15th St. NW, Wash., DC 20005; 2,600.
Portuguese Continental Union of the U.S.A. (1925), 899 Boylston St., Boston, MA 02115; 8,688.
Postmasters of the U.S., Natl. Assn. of (1898), 1616 N. Ft. Myer Dr., Arlington, VA 22209; 34,000.
Postmasters of the U.S., Natl. League of (1904), 1023 N. Royal St., Alexandria, VA 22314; 22,000.
Poultry Science Assn. (1926), 309 W. Clark, Champaign, IL 61820; 1,676.
Power Boat Assn., Amer. (1903), 17640 E. Nine Mile Rd., E. Detroit, MI 48021; 5,500.
Precancel Collectors, Natl. Assn. of (1950), 5121 Park Blvd., Wildwood, NJ 08260; 7,500.
Press, Associated (1848), 50 Rockefeller Plaza, N.Y., NY 10020; 1,365 newspapers & 3,600 broadcast stations.
Press Club, Natl. (1908), 529 14th St. NW, Wash., DC 20045; 4,500.
Press Intl., United (1907), 220 E. 42d St., N.Y., NY 10017.

Press and Radio Club (1948), P.O. Box 7023, Montgomery, AL 36107; 718.
Press Women, Natl. Federation of (1937), 1105 Main St., Blue Springs, MD 64015; 5,000.
Printing Industries of America. (1887), 1730 N. Lynn St., Arlington, VA 22209; 10,000 companies.
Procrastinators' Club of America (1956), 1111 Broad–Locust Bldg., Phila., PA 19102; 4,200.
Propeller Club of the U.S. (1927), 1730 M St. NW, Suite 413, Wash., DC 20036; 16,000+.
Psychiatric Assn., Amer. (1844), 1700 18th St. NW, Wash., DC 20009; 26,777.
Psychical Research, Amer. Society for (1907), 5 W. 73d St., N.Y., NY 10023; 2,100.
Psychoanalytic Assn., Amer. (1911), One E. 57th St., N.Y., NY 10022; 2,697.
Psychological Assn., Amer. (1892), 1200 17th St. NW, Wash., DC 20036; 50,000.
Psychological Assn. for Psychoanalysis, Natl. (1948), 150 W. 13th St., N.Y., NY 10011; 246.
Psychological Minorities, Society for the Aid of (1963), 42-25 Hampton St., Elmhurst, NY 11373; 500.
Psychotherapy Assn., Amer. Group (1942), 1995 Broadway, N.Y., NY 10023; 3,000.
Public Health Assn., Amer. (1872), 1015 15th St. NW, Wash., DC 20005; 30,000.
Public Relations Society of America (1947), 845 Third Ave., N.Y., NY 10022; 10,000.
Publishers, Assn. of Amer. (1970), One Park Ave., N.Y., NY 10016; 450 publishing houses.
Puppeteers of Amer. (1936), 5 Cricklewood Path, Pasadena, CA 91107; 2,500.

Quality Control, Amer. Society for (1946), 230 W. Wells St., Milwaukee, WI 53203; 37,000.

Rabbinical Alliance of America (1944), 156 5th Ave., N.Y., NY 10010; 502.
Rabbinical Assembly (1900), 3080 Broadway, N.Y., NY 10027; 1,400.
Rabbis, Central Conference of Amer. (1889), 21 E. 40th St., N.Y., NY 10016; 1,300.
Racquetball Assn., U.S. (1973), 4101 Dempster St., Skokie, IL 60076; 45,000.
Radio Clubs, Assn. of N. American (1964), 557 N. Madison Ave., Pasadena, CA 91101.
Radio Union, Intl. Amateur (1925), P.O. Box AAA, Newington, CT 06111; 113 societies.
Radio and Television Society, Intl. (1939), 420 Lexington Ave., N.Y., NY 10017; 1,680.
Radio Relay League, Amer. (1914), 225 Main St., Newington, CT 06111; 150,000+.
Railroad Passengers, Natl. Assn. of (1967), 417 New Jersey Ave. SE, Wash., DC 20003; 11,500.
Railroads, Assn. of Amer. (1934), 1920 L St. NW, Wash., DC 20036; 65.
Railway Historical Society, Natl. (1935), P.O. Box 2051, Phila., PA 19103; 10,500.
Railway Progress Institute (1908), 700 N. Fairfax St., Alexandria, VA 22314; 150 companies.
Range Management, Society for (1948), 2760 W. 5th Ave., Denver, CO 80204; 5,000.
Real Estate Appraisers, Natl. Assn. of (1967), 853 Broadway, N.Y., NY 10003; 1,000.
Real Estate Investment Trusts, Natl. Assn. of (1960), 1101 17th St. NW, Wash., DC 20036; 141 trusts, 223 associates.
Rebekah Assemblies, Intl. Assn. of (1914), P.O. Box 153, Minneapolis, KS 67467; 338,050.
Reconciliation, Fellowship of (1914), 523 N. Broadway, Nyack, NY 10960; 29,000.
Recording Industry Assn. of America (1951), 1370 Ave. of Amer., N.Y., NY 10019; 68.
Records Managers & Administrators, Assn. of (1975), 4200 Somerset Dr., Suite 215, Prairie Village, KS 66208; 7,000.
Recreation and Park Assn., Natl. (1965), 1601 N. Kent St., Arlington, VA 22209; 16,000.
Red Cross, Amer. Natl. (1881), 17th & D Sts. NW, Wash., DC 20006; 3,108 chapters.
Red Men, Improved Order of (1765), 1525 West Ave., P.O. Box 683, Waco, TX 76703; 45,000.
Redwoods League, Save-the- (1918), 114 Sansome St., San Francisco, CA 94104; 45,000.
Regional Plan Assn. (1929), 1040 Ave. of the Americas, N.Y., NY 10018; 3,000.
Rehabilitation Assn., Natl. (1925), 1522 K St. NW, Wash., DC 20005; 25,000.
Religion, Amer. Academy of (1909), Dept. of Religious Studies, Cal. State Univ., Chico, CA 95929; 4,200.

Renaissance Society of America (1954), 1161 Amsterdan Ave., N.Y., NY 10027; 2,900.
Reserve Officers Assn. of the U.S. (1922), One Constitutio Ave., NE, Wash., DC 20002; 123,000.
Restaurant Assn., Natl. (1919), 311 First St. NW, Wash., DC 20001; 11,580.
Retarded Citizens, Natl. Assn. for (1950), 2501 Ave. J, Arlington, TX 76011; 250,000.
Retired Federal Employees, Natl. Assn. of (1921), 153 New Hampshire Ave. NW, Wash., DC 20036; 300,000.
Retired Officers Assn. (1929), 201 N. Washington St., Alexandria, VA 22314; 308,000.
Retired Persons, Amer. Assn. of (1958), 1909 K St. NW Wash., DC 20049; 13,000,000+.
Retired Teachers Assn., Natl. (1947), 1909 K St. NW Wash., DC 20049; 540,000.
Retreads (of World War I & II) (1947), 40-07 154th St Flushing, NY 11354; 1,000.
Revolver Assn., U.S. (1900), 59 Alvin St., Springfield, M 01104; 1,250.
Reye's Syndrome Foundation, Natl. (1974), P.O. Box 829 Bryan, OH 43506; 10,000.
Richard III Society (1924), P.O. Box 217, Sea Cliff, N 11579; 500.
Rifle Assn., Natl. (1871), 1600 Rhode Island Ave. NW, Wash DC 20036; 1,600,000.
Road & Transportation Builders' Assn., Amer. (1902), 52 School St. SW, Wash., DC 20024; 5,800.
Rodeo Cowboys Assn., Professional (1936), 101 Pro Rodeo Dr., Colorado Springs, CO 80919; 5,434.
Roller Skating, U.S. Amateur Confederation of (1971), P.C Box 83067, Lincoln, NE 68501; 40,000.
Roller Skating Rink Operators Assn. (1937), 7700 A St Lincoln, NE 68501; 2,300.
Rose Society, Amer. (1899), P.O. Box 30,000, Shrevepor LA 71130; 25,800.
Rosicrucian Fraternity (1614, Germany, 1861 in U.S.), R.D No. 3, Box 220, Quakertown, PA 18951.
Rosicrucian Order, AMORC (1915), Rosicrucian Park, Sa Jose, CA 95191.
Rosicrucians, Society of (1909), 321 W. 101st St., N.Y., N 10025.
Rotary Intl. (1905), 1600 Ridge Ave., Evanston, IL 6020 19,500 clubs.
Running and Fitness Assn., Amer. (1968), 2420 K St. NW Wash, DC 20037.
Ruritan Natl. (1928), Ruritan Natl. Rd., Dublin, VA 2408 38,790.
Russian Americans, Congress of (1973), P.O. Box 502 Long Island City, NY 11105.

Safety and Fairness Everywhere, Natl. Assn. Tauntin (1980), PoB 5743A, Montecito, CA 93108; 366.
Safety Council, Natl. (1913), 444 N. Michigan Ave., Chicag IL 60611; 13,000.
Safety Engineers, Amer. Society of (1911), 850 Buss Hwy., Park Ridge, IL 60068; 18,000.
Sailors, Tin Can (1976), Battleship Cove, Fall River, M 02721; 2,000.
St. Dennis of Zante, Sovereign Greek Order of (109 1953 in U.S.), 739 W. 186th St., N.Y., NY 10033; 1,200.
St. Luke the Physician, Order of (1880), 2210 Wilshire Blvd Suite 582, Santa Monica, CA 90403; 120.
St. Paul, Natl. Guild of (1937), 601 Hill 'n Dale, Lexington, K 40503; 13,652.
Salesmen, Natl. Assn. of Professional (1970), 266 Trar Rd., Columbia, SC 29210; 20,000.
Salt Institute (1914), 206 N. Washington St., Alexandria, V 22314; 25 cos.
Samuel Butler Society (1978), Chaplain Library, William College, P.O. Box 426, Williamstown, MA 01267; 100.
Sane World, A Citizen's Organization for a (1957), 514 St. NE, Wash., DC 20002; 24,000.
Savings & Loan League, Natl. (1943), 1101 15th St. NW Wash., DC 20005; 300 associations.
School Administrators, Amer. Assn. of (1865), 1801 N Moore St., Arlington, VA 22209; 18,000.
School Boards Assn., Natl. (1940), 1055 Thomas Jefferso St. NW, Wash., DC 20007; 52 boards.
School Counselor Assn., Amer. (1952), 2 Skyline Pl., Suit 400, 5203 Leesburg Pk., Falls Church, VA 22041; 10,000+.
Schools of Art and Design, Natl. Assn. of (1944), 1125 Roger Bacon Dr. #5, Reston, VA 22090; 120.
Schools & Colleges, Amer. Council on (1927), 4009 Pacif Coast Hwy., Suite 462, Torrance, CA 90505; 35 institutions.
Science, Amer. Assn. for the Advancement of (1848 1515 Massachusetts Ave. NW, Wash., DC 20005; 128,308.
Science Club of Amer., Jr. (1978), 2505 Prestwick, Richmond, VA 23229; 116.

Science Fiction, Fantasy and Horror Films, Academy of (1962), 334 W. 54th St., Los Angeles, CA 90037; 3,000.

Sciences, Natl. Academy of (1863), 2101 Constitution Ave. NW, Wash., DC 20418; 1,300.

Science Service (1921), 1719 N St. NW, Wash., DC 20036.

Science Teachers Assn., Natl. (1944), 1742 Connecticut Ave. NW, Wash., DC 20009; 19,272.

Science Writers, Natl. Assn. of (1934), P.O. Box 294, Greenlawn, NY 11740; 1,100.

Scientists, Federation of Amer. (1946), 307 Massachusetts Ave. NE, Wash., DC 20002; 7,000.

Screen Actors Guild (1933), 7750 Sunset Blvd., Hollywood, CA 90046; 53,000.

Sculpture Society, Natl. (1893), 15 E. 26th St., N.Y., NY 10010; 300.

Seamen's Service, United (1942), One World Trade Ctr., Suite 2601, N.Y., NY 10048.

2d Air Division Assn. (1947), 1 Jeffrey's Neck Rd., Ipswich, MA 01938; 4,186.

Secondary School Principals, Natl. Assn. of (1916), 1904 Association Dr., Reston, VA 22091; 35,000.

Secretaries, Natl. Assn. of Legal (1950), 3005 E. Skelly Dr., Tulsa, OK 74105; 23,000.

Secularists of America, United (1947), 377 Vernon St., Oakland, CA 94610.

Securities Industry Assn. (1972), 20 Broad St., N.Y., NY 10005; 500+ firms.

Seeing Eye, The (1929), Box 375, Morristown, NJ 07960; 4,300.

Semantics, Institute of General (1938), R.R. 1; Box 215, Lakeville, CT 06039; 500.

Separation of Church & State, Americans United for (1947), 8120 Fenton St., Silver Spring, MD 20910; 55,000.

Sertoma Internatl. (1912), 1912 E. Meyer Blvd., Kansas City, MO 64132; 36,000.

Sex Information & Education Council of the U.S. (SIECUS) (1964), 84 5th Ave., N.Y., NY 10011; 1,000.

Shakespeare Assn. of America (1972), Box 6328, Vanderbilt Sta., Nashville, TN 37235; 650.

Sheriff's Assn., Natl. (1940), 1250 Connecticut Ave. NW, Wash., DC 195,000. 52,000+.

Shipbuilders Council of America (1921), 1110 Vermont Ave. NW, Wash., DC 20037; 44 companies.

Ship Society, World (1946), 3319 Sweet Dr., Lafayette, CA 94549; 4,200.

Shoe Retailers Assn., Natl. (1912), 200 Madison Ave., N.Y., NY 10016; 4,000.

Shore & Beach Preservation Assn., Amer. (1926), 412 O'Brien Hall, Univ. of California, Berkeley, CA 94720; 1,500.

Shrine, Ancient Arabic Order of the Nobles of the Mystic (1872), 2900 Rocky Pt. Dr., Tampa, FL 33607; 1,000,000.

Shut-Ins, Natl. Society for (1970), P.O. Box 1392, Reading, PA 19603.

Sierra Club (1892), 530 Bush St., San Francisco, CA 94108; 290,000.

Signalmen, Society of (1981), P.O. Box 11247, San Diego, CA 92111; 125.

Silurians, Society of the (1924), 45 John St., N.Y., NY 10010; 740.

Skating Union of the U.S., Amateur (1928), 4423 W. Deming Pl., Chicago, IL 60639; 2,000.

Skeet Shooting Assn., Natl. (1946), P.O. Box 28188, San Antonio, TX 78228; 16,602.

Ski Assn., U.S. (1904), 1726 Champa St., Denver, CO 80202; 110,000.

Small Business, Amer. Federation of (1963), 407 S. Dearborn St., Chicago, IL 60605; 5,000.

Small Business Assn., Natl. (1937), 1604 K St. NW, Wash., DC 20006; 50,000.

Smoking & Health, Natl. Clearinghouse for (1965), Center for Disease Control, 1600 Clifton Road NE, Atlanta, GA 30333.

Soaring Society of America (1932), 3200 Airport Ave., Rm. 25, Santa Monica, CA 90405; 17,370.

Soccer Federation, U.S. (1913), 350 Fifth Ave., N.Y., NY 10001; 700,000.

Social Biology, Society for the Study of (1926), Medical Dept., Brookhaven Natl. Laboratory, Upton, NY 11973; 415.

Social Science Research Council (1923), 605 Third Ave., N.Y., NY 10016.

Social Sciences, Natl. Institute of (1899), 16 E. 73rd St., Suite 5R, N.Y., NY 10021; 803.

Social Service, Intl., Amer. Branch (1925), 291 Broadway, N.Y., NY 10007.

Social Work Education, Council on (1952), 111 8th Ave., N.Y., NY 10017; 4,500.

Social Workers, Natl. Assn. of (1955), 1425 H St. NW, Wash., DC 20005; 90,000.

Sociological Assn., Amer. (1905), 1722 N St. NW, Wash., DC 20036; 14,000.

Softball Assn. of America, Amateur (1933), 2801 N.E. 50th St., Oklahoma City, OK 73111; 2,000,000+.

Softball League, Cinderella (1958), P.O. Box 1411, Corning, NY 14830.

Soft Drink Assn., Natl. (1919), 1101 16th St. NW, Wash., DC 20036; 1,500.

Soil Conservation Society of America (1945), 7515 N.E. Ankeny Rd., Ankeny, IA 50021; 15,000.

Soil Science Society of America (1936), 677 S. Segoe Rd., Madison, WI 53711; 4,595.

Sojourners, Natl. (1921), 8301 E. Boulevard Dr., Alexandria, VA 22308; 9,000.

Soldier's, Sailor's and Airmen's Club (1919), 283 Lexington Ave., N.Y., NY 10016.

Sons of the Amer. Legion (1932), 700 N. Pennsylvania, Indianapolis, IN 46204; 57,927.

Sons of the American Revolution, Natl. Society of (1876), 1000 S. 4th, Louisville, KY 40203; 22,500.

Sons of Confederate Veterans (1896), Southern Sta., P.O. Box 5164, Hattiesburg, MS 39401; 6,000.

Sons of the Desert (1966), P.O. Box 8341, Universal City, CA 91608; 1,500.

Sons of Norway (1895), 1455 W. Lake St., Minneapolis, MN 55408; 105,429.

Sons of Poland, Assn. of the (1903), 591 Summit Ave., Jersey City, NJ 07306; 10,000.

Sons of St. Patrick, Society of the Friendly (1784), 80 Wall St., N.Y., NY 10005; 1,000.

Sons of Sherman's March to the Sea (1966), 1725 Farmers Ave., Tempe, AZ 85281; 484.

Sons of Union Veterans of the Civil War (1881), P.O. Box 24, Gettysburg, PA 17325; 3,100.

Soroptimist Intl. of the Americas (1921), 1616 Walnut St., Phila., PA 19103; 32,000.

Southern Christian Leadership Conference (1957), 334 Auburn Ave. NE, Atlanta, GA 30303; 1,000,000.

Southern Regional Council (1944), 75 Marietta St. NW, Atlanta, GA 30303; 120.

Space Education Assoc., U.S. (1973), 746 Turnpike Rd., Elizabethtown, PA 17022; 9 countries.

Spanish War Veterans, United (1904), 810 Vermont Ave. NW, Room B-35, Wash., DC 20420; 36.

Speech Communication Assn. (1914), 5105 Backlick Rd., Annandale, VA 22003; 5,000.

Speech-Language-Hearing Assn., Amer. (1925), 10801 Rockville Pike, Rockville, MD 20852; 36,000.

Speleological Society, Natl. (1941), Cave Ave., Huntsville, AL 35810; 5,800.

Sports Car Club of America (1944), 6750 S. Emporia, Englewood, CO 80112; 24,000.

Sports Club, Indoor (1930), 1145 Highland St., Napoleon, OH 43545; 1,600.

Standards Institute, Amer. Natl. (1918), 1430 Broadway, N.Y., NY 10018; 1,000.

State Communities Aid Assn. (1872), 105 E. 22d St., N.Y., NY 10010; 170.

State Governments, Council of (1933), P.O. Box 11910, Iron Works Pike, Lexington, KY 40578; 50 states.

State & Local History, Amer. Assn. for (1940), 708 Berry Rd., Nashville, TN 37204; 7,556.

Statistical Assn., Amer. (1839), 806 15th St. NW, Wash., DC 20005; 14,000.

Steamship Historical Society of America (1935), 414 Pelton Ave., Staten Island, NY 10310; 3,237.

Steel Construction, Amer. Institute of (1921), 400 N. Michigan Ave., Chicago, IL 60611; 350.

Sterilization, Assn. for Voluntary (1943), 122 E. 42nd St., N.Y., NY 10168; 3,000.

Stock Car Auto Racing, Natl. Assn. for (NASCAR) (1948), 1801 Speedway Blvd., Daytona Beach, FL 32015; 17,000.

Stock Exchange, Amer. (1971), 86 Trinity Pl., N.Y., NY 10006; 611.

Stock Exchange, New York (1792), 11 Wall St., N.Y., NY 10005; 1,366.

Stock Exchange, Philadelphia (1790), 1900 Market St., Phila., PA 19103; 505.

Structural Stability Research Council (1944), Fritz Engineering Laboratory No. 13, Lehigh Univ., Bethlehem, PA 18015; 200.

Student Assn., U.S. (1947), 1220 G St. SE, Wash., DC 20024; 3,400,000.

Student Councils, Natl. Assn. of (1931), 1904 Association Dr., Reston, VA 22091; 10,000 secondary schools.

Student Consumer Protection Council, Natl. (1972), Villanova Univ., Villanova, PA 19085; 50.

Stuttering Project, Natl. (1977), 1269 7th Ave., San Francisco, CA 94122; 200.

Sugar Brokers Assn., Natl. (1893), 1 World Trade Center N.Y., NY 10047; 120.

Sunbathing Assn., Amer. (1931), 810 N. Mills Ave., Orlando, FL 32803; 25,000.

Sunday League (1933), 279 Highland Ave., Newark, NJ 07104; 25,000.
Surfing Assn., American (1966), Box 2622, Newport Beach, CA 92663; 12,000.
Surfing Assn., Amer. Pro. (1940), Box 1315, Beverly Hills, CA 90213; 2,300.
Surfing, Intl. Council for the Advancement of (1974), 2131 Kalakaua Ave., Honolulu, HI 96815; 273,000.
Surgeons, Amer. College of (1913), 55 E. Erie St., Chicago IL 60611; 44,847.
Surgeons, Intl. College of (1935), 1516 N. Lake Shore Dr., Chicago IL 60610; 13,000.
Surgeons of the U.S., Assn. of Military (1891), 10605 Concord St., Kensington, MD 20795; 14,000.
Surveying & Mapping, Amer. Congress on (1941), 210 Little Falls, Falls Church, VA 22046; 11,130.
Symphony Orchestra League, Amer. (1942), P.O. Box 669, Vienna, VA 22180; 4,324.
Systems Management, Assn. for (1947), 24587 Bagley Rd., Cleveland, OH 44138; 10,000.

Table Tennis Assn., U.S. (1933), Olympic House, 1750 E. Boulder, Colorado Springs, CO 80909; 5,800.
Tall Buildings and Urban Habitat, Council on (1969), Fritz Engineering Laboratory, Lehigh Univ., Bethlehem, PA 18015; 1,200.
Tattoo Club of America (1970), 36 Mill Hill Rd., Woodstock, NY 12498; 10,000.
Tax Accountants, Natl. Assn. of Enrolled Federal (1960), 6108 N. Harding Ave., Chicago, IL 60659; 500.
Tax Administrators, Federation of (1937), 444 N. Capitol St. NW, Wash., DC 20001; 50 revenue departments.
Tax Assn.-Natl. Tax Institute of America (1907), 21 E. State St., Columbus, OH 43215; 2,100.
Tax Foundation (1937), 1875 Connecticut Ave. NW, Wash., DC 20009; 1,400.
Tea Assn. of the U.S.A. (1899), 230 Park Ave., N.Y., NY 10169; 275.
Teachers of English, Natl. Council of (1911), 1111 Kenyon Rd., Urbana, IL 61801; 80,000.
Teachers of English to Speakers of Other Languages (1966), 202 DC Transit Bldg., Georgetown Univ., Wash., DC 20057; 9,500.
Teachers of French, Amer. Assn. of (1927), 57 E. Armory Ave., Champaign, IL 61820; 9,400.
Teachers of German, Amer. Assn. of (1928), 523 Bldg., Suite 201, Route 38, Cherry Hill, NJ 08034; 7,000+.
Teachers of Mathematics, Natl. Council of (1920), 1906 Association Dr., Reston, VA 22091; 40,000.
Teachers of Singing, Natl. Assn. of (1944), 250 W. 57th St., N.Y., NY 10107; 3,750.
Teachers of Spanish & Portuguese, Amer. Assn. of (1917), Holy Cross Coll., Worcester, MA 01610; 13,000.
Teaching of Foreign Languages, Amer. Council on the (1967), 2 Park Ave., N.Y., NY 10016; 10,000.
Technical Communication, Society for (1958), 815 15th St. NW, Wash., DC 20005; 5,000.
Telephone Pioneers of Amer. (1911), 195 Broadway, N.Y., NY 10007; 577,000.
Television Arts & Sciences, Natl. Academy of (1947), 291 S. La Cienega Blvd., Beverly Hills, CA 90211; 11,000.
Television Bureau of Advertising (1954), 1345 Ave. of the Americas, N.Y., NY 10019; 560 stations.
Television & Radio Artists, Amer. Federation of (1937), 1350 Ave. of the Americas, N.Y., NY 10019; 55,000.
Telluride Assn. (1910), 217 West Ave., Ithaca, NY 14850; 84.
Tennis Assn., U.S. (1881), 51 E. 42d St., N.Y., NY 10017; 195,000.
Terrain Vehicle Owners Assn., Natl., All- (1972), P.O. Box 574, Feasterville, PA 19047; 1,352.
Testing & Materials, Amer. Society for (1898), 1916 Race St., Phila., PA 19103; 28,500.
Textile Assn., Northern (1854), 211 Congress St., Boston, MA 02110; 150.
Textile Manufacturers Institute, Amer. (1949), 2124 Wachovia Ctr., Charlotte, NC 28285; 250 companies.
Theatre & Academy, Amer. Natl. (1935), 245 W. 52d St., N.Y., NY 10019; 1,500.
Theatre Assn., Amer. (1936), 1000 Vermont Ave. NW, Wash., DC 20005; 7,500.
Theatre Organ Society, Amer. (1955), 1930-301 Encinitas Rd., San Marcos, CA 92069; 4,405.
Theodore Roosevelt Assn. (1919), P.O. Box 720, Oyster Bay, NY 11771; 700.
Theological Library Assn., Amer. (1947), 5600 S. Woodlawn Ave., Chicago, IL 60637; 600.
Theological Schools in the U.S. and Canada, Assn. of (1918), 42 E. Natl. Rd., P.O. Box 130, Vandalia, OH 45377; 197 schools.
Theological Seminary, Intl. (1979), 7970 Woodman Ave., Suite A, Van Nuys, CA 91402; 300.
Theosophical Society (1875), P.O. Box 270, 1926 N. Main St., Wheaton, IL 60187; 6,000.
Thoreau Society (1941), SUNY-Geneseo, Geneseo, NY 14454; 1,300.
Thoroughbred Racing Assn. of North America (1942), 3000 Marcus Ave., Lake Success, NY 11042; 54 racetracks.
Titanic Historical Society (1963), P.O. Box 53, Indian Orchard, MA 01151; 2,500.
Toastmasters Intl. (1932), 2200 N. Grand Ave., Santa Ana,, CA 92711; 100,000.
Toastmistress Clubs, Intl. (1938), 2519 Woodland Dr., Anaheim, CA 92801; 25,000.
Topical Assn., Amer. (1949), 3306 N. 50th St., Milwaukee, WI 53216; 10,000.
Torch Clubs, Internatl. Assn. of (1924), P.O. Box 30578, Lincoln, NE 68503; 4,300.
Toy Manufacturers of America (1916), 200 Fifth Ave., N.Y., NY 10010; 235.
Trade Relations Council of the U.S. (1885), 1001 Connecticut Ave. NW, Wash., DC 20036; 50 companies.
Traffic and Transportation, Amer. Society of (1946), P.O. Box 33095, Louisville, KY 40232; 2,600.
Trail Association, North Country (1981), P.O. Box 311, White Cloud, MI 49349; 100.
Training Corps, Amer. (1960), 107-12 Jamaica Ave., Richmond Hill, NY 11418; 60.
Training & Development, Amer. Society for (1944), P.O. Box 5307, Madison, WI 53705; 15,000.
Transit Assn., Amer. Public (1974), 1225 Connecticut Ave. NW, Wash., DC 20036; 700.
Translators Assn., Amer. (1959), 109 Croton Ave., Ossining, NY 10562; 2,000.
Transportation Assn. of America (1935), 1100 17th St. NW, Wash., DC 20036; 400 companies.
Trapshooting Assn., Amateur (1924), 601 W. National Rd. Vandalia, OH 45377; 83,485.
Travel Agents, Amer. Society of (1931), 711 Fifth Ave., N.Y., NY 10022; 18,000.
Travel Industry Assn. of America (1965), 1899 L St. NW, Wash., DC 20036; 1,600.
Travel Organizations, Discover America (1939), 1899 L St NW, Wash., DC 20036; 1,200.
Travelers Protective Assn. of America (1890), 3755 Lindell Blvd., St. Louis, MO 63108; 220,000.
Trilateral Commission (1973), 345 E. 46th, N.Y., NY 10017; 300.
Trucking Assn., Amer. (1933), 1616 P St. NW, Wash., DC 20036; 51 assns.
True Sisters, United Order (1846), 212 Fifth Ave., N.Y., NY 10001; 12,000.
Tuberous Sclerosis Assn. of Amer. (1970), 225A Union St., Rockland, MA 02370; 1,800.

UFOs (Unidentified Flying Objects), Natl. Investigations Commitee on (1957), 7970 Woodman Ave.; Van Nuys, CA 91402; 1,500.
UNICEF, U.S. Committee for (1947), 331 E. 38th St., N.Y., NY 10016.
Uniformed Services, Natl. Assn. for (1968), 5535 Hempstead Way, Springfield, VA 22151; 25,000.
UNIMA (l'Union Internationale de la Marionnette)–USA (1966), 117 E. 69th St., N.Y., NY 10021; 600.
United Nations Assn. of the U.S.A. (1923, as League of Nations Assn.) 300 E. 42d St., N.Y., NY 10017; 25,000.
United Service Organizations (USO) (1941), 237 E. 52d St., N.Y., NY 10022.
U.S., Amer. Assn. for Study of in World Affairs (1948), 3813 Annandale Rd., Annandale, VA 22003; 1,000.
United Way of America (1918), 801 N. Fairfax St., Alexandria, VA 22309; 1,200.
Universities, Assn. of Amer. (1900), One Dupont Circle NW, Wash., DC 20036; 50 institutions.
Universities & Colleges, Assn. of Governing Boards of (1921), One Dupont Circle NW, Wash., DC 20036; 24,000.
University Extension Assn., Natl. (1915), One Dupont Circle, Suite 360, NW, Wash., DC 20036; 1,200.
University Foundation, Intl. (1973), 1301 S. Noland Rd., Independence, MO 64055; 7,000+.
University Professors, Amer. Assn. of (1915), One Dupont Circle, Suite 500, NW, Wash., DC 20036; 70,000.
University Professors for Academic Order (1970), 635 SW 4th St., Corvallis, OR 97333.
University Women, Amer. Assn. of (1881), 2401 Virginia Ave. NW, Wash., DC 20037; 190,000.
Urban Coalition, Natl. (1968), 1201 Connecticut Ave. NW, Wash., DC 20024.
Urban League, Natl. (1910), 500 E. 62d St., N.Y., NY 10021.

Utility Commissioners, Natl. Assn. of Regulatory (1889), 1101 ICC Bldg., P.O. Box 684, Wash., DC 20044; 332.

Valley Forge, Society of the Descendants of Washington's Army at (1976), 7740 Palmyra Dr., Fair Oaks, CA 95628.
Variety Clubs Intl. (1928), 58 W. 58th St., N.Y., NY 10019; 11,000.
VASA Order of America (1896), 3720 Daryl Dr., Landisville, PA 17538; 35,000.
Veterans Assn., Blinded (1945), 1735 DeSales St. NW, Wash., DC 20036; 3,300.
Veterans Assn., China-Burma-India (1947), 750 N. Lincoln Memorial Dr., Milwaukee, WI 53201; 3,221+.
Veterans Committee, Amer. (1944), 1346 Connecticut Ave. NW, Wash., DC 20036; 25,000.
Veterans of Foreign Wars of the U.S. (1899) **& Ladies Auxiliary** (1914), 406 W. 34th St., Kansas City, MO 64111; 1,920,000 & 658,000.
Veterans of World War I (1958), 916 Prince St., Alexandria, VA 22314; 432,000.
Veterinary Medical Assn., Amer. (1863), 930 N. Meacham Rd., Schaumburg, IL 60196; 34,734.
Victorian Society in America (1966), The Athenaeum, East Washington Sq., Phila., PA 19106; 5,500.
Vocational Assn., Amer. (1925), 2020 N. 14th St., Arlington, VA 22201; 56,000.
Volleyball Assn., U.S. (1928), 1750 E. Boulder, Colorado Springs, CO 80909.

Walking Assn. (1976), 4113 Lee Hwy., Arlington, VA 22207; 281.
Walking Society, Amer. (1980), P.O. Box 2622, Newport Beach, CA 92663; 72,000.
War of 1812, General Society of the (1814), 1307 New Hampshire Ave. NW, Wash., DC 20036; 1,100.
War Mothers, Amer. (1917), 2615 Woodley Pl. NW, Wash., DC 20008; 11,000.
Warrant and Warrant Officers' Assn., Chief, U.S. Coast Guard (1929), 492 L'Enfant Plaza E., SW, Wash., DC 20024; 3,438.
Watch & Clock Collectors, Natl. Assn. of (1943), 514 Poplar St., Columbia, PA 17512; 33,400.
Watercolor Society, Amer. (1866), 14 E. 90th St., N.Y., NY 10028; 600.
Water Pollution Control Federation (1928), 2626 Pennsylvania Ave. NW, Wash., DC 20037; 30,000.
Water Resources Assn., Amer. (1964), St. Anthony Falls Hydraulic Lab, Mississippi River at 3d Ave. SE, Minneapolis, MN 55414; 3,500.
Water Ski Assn., Amer. (1939), 799 Overlook Dr., P.O. Box 191, Winter Haven, FL 33880; 15,000.
Water Well Assn., Natl. (1948), 500 W. Wilson Bridge Rd., Worthington, OH 43085; 8,400.
Water Works Assn., Amer. (1881), 6666 W. Quincy Ave., Denver, CO 80235; 31,000.
Watts Family Assn. (1969), 12401 Burton St., N. Hollywood, CA 91605; 12 branches.
Weather Modification Assn. (1969), P.O. Box 8116, Fresno, CA 93727; 250.
Welding Society, Amer. (1919), 550 N.W. Le Jeune Rd., Miami, FL 33126; 35,000+.
Wheelchair Athletic Assn., Natl. (1958), Nassau Community College, Garden City, NY 11530; 2,000+.
Wilderness Society (1935), 1901 Pennsylvania Ave. NW, Wash., DC 20006; 45,000.
Wild Horse Organized Assistance (WHOA!) (1971), 140 Greenstone Dr., Reno, NV 89512; 10,000.
Wildlife, Defenders of (1925), 1244 19th St. NW, Wash., DC 20036; 70,000.
Wildlife Federation, Natl. (1936), 1412 16th St. NW, Wash., DC 20036; 4,600,000.
Wildlife Foundation, No. Amer. (1911), 1000 Vermont Ave. NW, Wash., DC 20005.
Wildlife Fund, World (1961), 1601 Connecticut Ave. NW, Wash., DC 20009; 85,000.
Wildlife Management Institute (1911), 1000 Vermont Ave. NW, Wash., DC 20005.
William Penn Assn. (1886), 429 Forbes Ave., Pittsburgh, PA 15219; 75,000.
Wireless Pioneers, Society of (1968), 3366—15 Mendocino Ave., Santa Rosa, CA 95401; 4,352.
Wizard of Oz Club, Intl. (1957), Box 95, Kinderhook, IL 62345; 1,700.
Woman's Assn., Amer. (1914), 1270 Ave. of the Americas, N.Y., NY 10020; 250.
Woman's Christian Temperance Union, Natl. (1874), 1730 Chicago Ave., Evanston, IL 60201; 250,000.
Women, Natl. Assn. of Bank (1921), 500 No. Michigan Ave., Chicago, IL 60611; 26,500.
Women, Natl. Organization for (NOW) (1966), 425 13th St. NW, Wash., DC 20004; 120,000.
Women Artists, Natl. Assn. (1889), 41 Union Sq., N.Y., NY 10003; 650.
Women, Rural American (1977), 1522 K St. NW, Wash., DC 20005; 35,000.
Women Engineers, Society of (1950), 345 E. 47th St., N.Y., NY 10017; 10,000+.
Women in Communications (1909), P.O. Box 9561, Austin, TX 78766; 9,000.
Women Geographers, Society of (1925), 1619 New Hampshire Ave. NW, Wash., DC 20009; 500.
Women Marines Assn. (1960), 2545 E. Reno Ave., Las Vegas, NV 89120; 2,300.
Women Strike for Peace (1961), 145 S. 13th St., Phila., PA 19107.
Women's Army Corps Veterans Assn. (1946), 1409 E. Euclid Ave., Arlington Heights, IL 60004; 2,400.
Women's Clubs, General Federation of (1889), 1734 N St. NW, Wash., DC 20036; 600,000.
Women's Clubs, Natl. Federation of Business & Professional (1919), 2012 Massachusetts Ave. NW, Wash., DC 20036; 160,800.
Women's Educational & Industrial Union (1877), 356 Boylston St., Boston, MA 02116; 3,200.
Women's Intl. League for Peace & Freedom (1915), 1213 Race St., Phila., PA 19107; 9,000.
Women's Overseas Service League (1921), P.O. Box 39058, Friendship Sta., Wash., DC 20016; 1,466.
Women of the U.S., Natl. Council of (1888), 777 U.N. Plaza, N.Y., NY 10017; 27 organizations.
Women Voters of the U.S., League of (1920), 1730 M St. NW, Wash., DC 20036; 122,000.
Women World War Veterans (1919), 237 Madison Ave., N.Y., NY 10016; 84,000.
Woodmen of America, Modern (1883), 1701 First Ave., Rock Island, IL 61201; 500,000.
Woodmen of the World (1890), 1450 Speer Blvd., Denver, CO 80204; 28,954.
Woodmen of the World Life Ins. Soc. (1890), 1700 Farnam St., Omaha, NE 68102; 908,000.
Wool Growers Assn., Natl. (1865), 425 13th St., Rm. 548, Wash., DC 20004; 24 state assns.
Workmen's Circle (1900), 45 E. 33d St., N.Y., NY 10016; 57,204.
World Future Society (1966), 4916 St. Elmo Ave., Wash., DC 20814; 35,000.
World Health, Amer. Assn. for (1951), 2121 Virginia Ave. NW, Wash., DC 20037; 400.
World Health, U.S. Committee for (1951), 777 United Nations Plaza, N.Y., NY 10017; 2,017.
Writers of America, Western (1950), News Service, Univ. of Texas at El Paso, El Paso, TX 79968; 400.
Writers Assn. of America, Outdoor (1927), 4141 W. Bradley Rd., Milwaukee, WI 53209; 1,500.
Writers Guild of America, West (1954), 8955 Beverly Blvd., Los Angeles, CA 90048; 6,000.

Yeoman F. Natl. (1936), 223 El Camino Real, Vallejo, CA 94590; 800.
Young Americans for Freedom (1960), Woodland Rd., Sterling, VA 22170; 55,000.
Young Men's Christian Assns. of the U.S.A., Natl. Council of (1851), 101 N. Wacker Dr., Chicago, IL 60606; 10,662,904.
YM-YWHAs of Greater New York, Associated (1957), 130 E. 59th St., N.Y., NY 10022; 70,000.
Young Women's Christian Assn. of the U.S.A. (1858), 600 Lexington Ave., N.Y., NY 10022; 2,500,000.
Young Scientists of Amer. Foundation (1959), P.O. Box 9066, Phoenix, AZ 85068; 2,850.
Youth, Allied (1936), 1556 Wisconsin Ave., Wash., DC 20007; 10,000.
Youth Hostels, Amer. (1934), Natl. Campus, Delaplane, VA 22025; 80,000.

Zero Population Growth (1968), 1346 Connecticut Ave. NW, Wash., DC 20036; 10,000.
Ziegfeld Club (1936), 3 W. 51st St., N.Y., NY 10019; 399.
Zionist Organization of America (1897), 4 E. 34th St., N.Y., NY 10016; 130,000.
Zonta Intl. (1919), 35 E. Wacker Dr., Rm. 2040, Chicago, IL 60605; 30,000.
Zoological Parks & Aquariums, Amer. Assn. of (1924), Oglebay Park, Wheeling, WV 26003; 3,400.
Zoologists, Amer. Society of (1913), Box 2739, California Lutheran College, Thousand Oaks, CA 91360; 4,500.

RELIGIOUS INFORMATION

Census of Religious Groups in the U.S.

Source: World Almanac questionnaire and 1982 Yearbook of American and Canadian Churches

Membership figures in the following table are the latest available. Some denominations submitted carefully compiled data while others approached the task more casually. The number of churches is given in parentheses. Asterisk (*) indicates church declines to publish membership figures.

Group	Members
Adventist churches:	
Advent Christian Ch. (365)	30,000
Primitive Advent Christian Ch. (10)	547
Seventh-day Adventists (3,730)	571,141
American Rescue Workers (15)	**2,140**
Anglican Orthodox Church (7)	**1,325**
2,630	
Baha'i Faith (7,000)	*
Baptist churches:	
Amer. Baptist Assn. (2,000)	1,350,000
Amer. Baptist Chs. in U.S.A. (5,777)	1,593,534
Baptist General Conference (715)	127,662
Baptist Missionary Assn. of America (1,415)	102,006
Conservative Baptist Assn. of America (1,126)	225,000
Duck River (and Kindred) Assn. of Baptists (85)	8,632
Free Will Baptists (2,479)	216,848
Gen. Assn. of General Baptists (870)	75,028
Gen. Assn. of Regular Baptist Chs. (1,585)	243,141
Natl. Baptist Convention of America (11,398)	2,668,799
Natl. Baptist Convention, U.S.A. (30,000)	6,300,000
Natl. Primitive Baptist Convention (606)	250,000
No. Amer. Baptist Conference (260)	43,146
Seventh Day Baptist General Conference (60)	5,181
Southern Baptist Convention (36,079)	13,789,580
United American Free Will Baptists (250)	55,000
Brethren (German Baptists):	
Brethren Ch. (Ashland, Ohio) (126)	15,000
Christian Congregation (La Follette, IN) (1,426)	100,245
Ch. of the Brethren (1,063)	170,839
Old German Baptist Brethren (50)	4,898
Brethren, River:	
Brethren in Christ Ch. (171)	14,971
Buddhist Churches of America (60)	**250,000**
Calvary Grace Christian Churches of Faith (360)	*
Calvary Grace Church of Faith, Inc. (150)	**15,000**
Christadelphians (100)	*
The Christian and Missionary Alliance (1,436)	**195,042**
Christian Catholic Church (6)	**2,500**
Christian Church (Disciples of Christ) (4,295)	**1,177,984**
Christian Churches and Churches of Christ (5,605)	**1,063,254**
Christian Nation Church U.S.A. (18)	**2,000**
Christian Union (104)	**4,590**
Churches of Christ (17,000)	**2,500,000**
Churches of Christ in Christian Union (250)	**11,000**
Churches of God:	
Chs. of God, General Conference (345)	34,773
Church of God (2,035)	75,890
Ch. of God (Anderson, Ind.) (2,275)	178,581
Ch. of God (Seventh Day), Denver, Col. (120)	3,200
Church of Christ, Scientist (3,000)	*
The Church of God by Faith (105)	**4,500**
Church of the Nazarene (4,888)	**492,203**
National Council of Community Churches (200)	**190,000**
Natl. Assn. of Congregational Christian Churches (409)	**101,899**
Conservative Congregational Christian Conference (132)	**24,410**
Eastern Orthodox churches:	
Albanian Orth. Diocese of America (10)	40,000
American Carpatho-Russian Orth. Greek Catholic Ch. (70)	100,000
Antiochian Orth. Christian Archdiocese of No. Amer. (125)	250,000
Diocese of the Armenian Ch. of America (52)	150,000
Bulgarian Eastern Orth. Ch. (13)	86,000
Coptic Orthodox Ch. (25)	100,000
Greek Orth. Archdiocese of N. and S. America (550)	3,000,000
Orthodox Ch. in America (440)	1,000,000
Patriarchal Parishes of the Russian Orth. Ch. in the U.S.A. (41)	51,500
Romanian Orth. Episcopate of America (34)	40,000
Serbian Eastern Orth. Ch. (52)	65,000
Syrian Orth. Ch. of Antioch (Archdiocese of the U.S.A. and Canada) (13)	30,000
Ukrainian Orth. Ch. of America (Ecumenical Patriarchate) (30)	30,000
The Episcopal Church in the U.S.A. (7,215)	**2,786,004**
American Ethical Union (Ethical Culture Movement) (21)	**4,000**
Evangelical Christian Churches (137)	**54,000**
Evangelical Christian Churches, California Synod (166)	**82,799**
Evangelical Church of North America (143)	**13,088**
Evangelical Congregational Church (161)	**28,459**
The Evangelical Covenant Church (546)	**79,634**
Evangelical Free Church of America (621)	**100,000**
Evangelical associations:	
Apostolic Christian Chs. of America (80)	11,556
Apostolic Christian Ch. (Nazarean) (42)	4,804
Christian Congregation (1,266)	89,379
Friends:	
Evangelical Friends Alliance (247)	26,912
Friends General Conference (350)	33,000
Friends United Meeting (513)	56,447
Religious Society of Friends (Conservative) (27)	1,728
Religious Society of Friends (Unaffiliated Meetings) (112)	6,386
Independent Fundamental Churches of America (1,019)	**120,446**
Grace Gospel Fellowship (52)	**4,000**
Jehovah's Witnesses (7,515)	**565,309**
Jewish congregations:	
Agudath Israel of America (Orthodox) (40)	100,000
Union of Amer. Hebrew Congregations (Reformed) (750)	1,200,000
Natl. Council of Young Israel (Orthodox) (167)	250,000+
Union of Orthodox Jewish Congregations of America (1,700)	1,000,000
United Synagogue of America (Conservative) (815)	221,000
Latter-day Saints:	
Ch. of Jesus Christ (Bickertonites) (60)	2,551
Ch. of Jesus Christ of Latter-day Saints (Mormon) (7,379)	2,811,000
Reorganized Ch. of Jesus Christ of Latter Day Saints (1,061)	160,800
Lutheran churches:	
American Lutheran Ch. (4,861)	2,345,434
Ch. of the Lutheran Brethren (106)	10,153
Ch. of the Lutheran Confession (70)	6,739
Assn. of Evangelical Lutheran Chs. (273)	109,000
Evangelical Lutheran Synod (108)	19,795
Assn. of Free Lutheran Congregations (140)	15,430
Latvian Evangelical Lutheran Church in America (62)	14,274
Lutheran Ch. in America (5,801)	2,921,829
Lutheran Ch.-Missouri Synod (5,636)	2,635,055
Protestant Conference (Lutheran) (7)	1,325
Wisconsin Evangelical Lutheran Synod (1,139)	407,987
Mennonite churches:	
Beachy Amish Mennonite Chs. (79)	5,350
Evangelical Mennonite Ch. (22)	3,762
General Conference of Mennonite Brethren Chs. (127)	17,813

Group	Members
The General Conference Mennonite Ch. (201)	36,508
Hutterian Brethren (35)	3,684
Mennonite Ch. (1,151)	99,651
Old Order Amish Ch. (535)	80,250
Old Order (Wisler) Mennonite Ch. (60)	8,400
Methodist churches:	
African Methodist Episcopal Ch. (6,000)	2,050,000
African Methodist Episcopal Zion Ch. (6,020)	1,134,176
Evangelical Methodist Ch. (132)	9,730
Free Methodist Ch. of North America (1,050)	72,000
Fundamental Methodist Ch. (14)	700
Primitive Methodist Ch., U.S.A. (87)	10,138
Reformed Methodist Union Episcopal Ch. (20)	45,000
Southern Methodist Ch. (169)	11,000
United Methodist Ch. (38,417)	10,854,522
Moravian churches:	
Moravian Ch. (Unitas Fratrum), Northern Province (97)	26,824
Moravian Ch. in America (Unitas Fratrum), Southern Province (53)	17,423
Unity of the Brethren (26)	*
Muslims	**2,000,000+**
New Apostolic Church of North America (384)	**27,986**
North American Old Roman Catholic Church (134)	**61,263**
Old Catholic churches:	
American Catholic Ch. (Syro-Antiochean) (3)	501
Christ Catholic Ch. (7)	1,453
Mariavite Old Cath. Ch. Province of North America (158)	358,066
No. Amer. Old Roman Cath. Ch. (Schweikert) (121)	60,124
Pentecostal churches:	
Apostolic Faith (45)	4,100
Assemblies of God (9,930)	1,103,134
Bible Church of Christ (5)	3,095
Bible Way Church of Our Lord Jesus Christ World Wide (350)	30,000
Church of God (Cleveland, Tenn.) (5,018)	411,385
Church of God of Prophecy (1,977)	72,977
Congregational Holiness Ch. (175)	5,925
Gen. Conference, Christian Ch. of No. Amer. (102)	15,000
Intl. Ch. of the Foursquare Gospel (1,000)	154,645

Group	Members
Open Bible Standard Chs. (292)	36,000
Pentecostal Assemblies of the World (150)	15,000
Pentecostal Church of God (1,147)	113,000
United Pentecostal Ch. (3,500)	300,000+
Pentecostal Free-Will Baptist Ch. (126)	13,000
Plymouth Brethren (1,100)	**98,000**
Polish Natl. Catholic Church (162)	**282,411**
Presbyterian churches:	
Associate Reformed Presbyterian Ch. (Gen. Synod) (156)	31,518
Cumberland Presbyterian Ch. (833)	91,665
Orthodox Presbyterian Ch. (150)	16,590
Presbyterian Ch. in America (487)	81,111
Presbyterian Ch. in the U.S. (4,159)	838,485
Reformed Presbyterian Ch., Evangelical Synod (195)	29,489
Reformed Presbyterian Ch. of No. Amer. (68)	4,878
United Presbyterian Ch. in the U.S.A. (8,933)	2,387,882
Reformed churches:	
Christian Reformed Ch. in N. America (634)	136,781
Hungarian Reformed Ch. in America (29)	10,500
Protestant Reformed Chs. in America (21)	4,544
Reformed Ch. in America (902)	345,532
Reformed Ch. in the U.S. (29)	3,660
The Roman Catholic Church (19,000)	**52,000,000**
The Salvation Army (1,099)	**414,999**
The Schwenkfelder Church (5)	**2,763**
Social Brethren (30)	**1,784**
Natl. Spiritualist Assn. of Churches (164)	**5,168**
Gen. Convention, The Swedenborgian Church (47)	**2,842**
Unitarian Universalist Assn. (946)	**170,352**
United Brethren:	
Ch. of the United Brethren in Christ (268)	28,048
United Christian Ch. (11)	430
United Church of Christ (6,443)	**1,726,535**
Universal Fellowship of Metropolitan Community Chs. (155)	**23,000**
Vedanta Society (13)	**1,000**
Volunteers of America (602)	**36,380**
The Wesleyan Church (1,789)	**108,904**

Religious Population of the World

Source: The 1982 Encyclopaedia Britannica Book of the Year

Religion	N. America[1]	S. America	Europe[2]	Asia[3]	Africa	Oceania[4]	Totals
Total Christian	238,028,500	174,112,000	340,780,400	95,787,240	130,917,000	18,158,000	997,783,140
Roman Catholic	133,889,000	161,489,000	177,187,300	55,027,000	48,024,500	4,445,000	580,061,800
Eastern Orthodox	4,782,000	514,000	53,035,600	2,328,000	13,106,000[5]	409,000	74,174,600
Protestant[5]	99,357,500	12,109,000	110,557,500	38,432,240	69,786,500[7]	13,304,000	343,546,740
Jewish	6,295,340	585,800	4,057,120	3,492,880	176,900	76,500	14,684,520
Muslim[6]	386,200	254,000	15,945,000	429,766,000	145,714,700	92,000	592,157,900
Zoroastrian	2,750	2,600	12,000	257,000	700	1,000	276,050
Shinto	60,000	90,000	—	58,003,000	1,200	—	58,154,200
Taoist	16,000	10,000	—	30,260,000	—	—	30,286,000
Confucian	97,100	70,000	—	153,887,500	1,500	24,000	154,080,100
Buddhist	197,250	194,450	194,500	255,741,000	25,000	35,000	256,387,200
Hindu	96,500	852,000	425,000	478,073,000	1,379,800	415,000	481,241,300
Totals	245,179,640	176,170,850	361,414,020	1,505,267,800	278,216,800	18,801,500	2,585,050,410
Population[7]	376,000,000	251,000,000	754,000,000	2,607,000,000	483,000,000	23,000,000	4,495,000,000

(1) Includes Central America and West Indies. (2) Includes communist countries where it is difficult to determine religious affiliation. (3) Includes areas in which persons have traditionally enrolled in several religions, as well as China, with an official communist establishment. (4) Includes Australia, New Zealand, and islands of the South Pacific. (5) Protestant figures outside Europe usually include "full members" (adults) rather than all baptized persons and are not comparable to those of ethnic religions or churches counting all adherents. (6) According to the Islamic Center, Wash., D.C., there are 1 billion Muslims worldwide. (7) United Nations data, midyear 1981.

National Council of Churches

The National Council of the Churches of Christ in the U.S.A. is a cooperative federation of 32 Protestant and Orthodox churches which seeks to advance programs and policies of mutual interest to its members. The NCC was formed in 1950 by the merger of 12 inter-denominational agencies. The Council's member churches now have an aggregate membership totaling approximately 40 million. The NCC is not a governing body and has no control over the policies or operations of any church belonging to it. The work of the Council is divided into 3 divisions — Church and Society; Education and Ministry; Overseas Ministries — and 5 commissions — Faith and Order; Regional and Local Ecumenism; Communication; Stewardship; and Justice, Liberation, and Human Fulfillment. The chief administrative officer of the NCC is Dr. Claire Randall, 475 Riverside Drive, N.Y., NY 10115.

Headquarters, Leaders of U.S. Religious Groups

See Associations and Societies section for religious organizations. (year organized in parentheses)

Adventist churches:

Advent Christian Church (1854) — Pres., Glennon Balser; exec. v.p., Rev. Adrian B. Shepard, Box 23152, Charlotte, NC 28212.

Primitive Advent Christian Church — Pres., Elza Moss; sec., Hugh W. Good, 395 Frame Rd., Elkview, WV 25071.

Seventh-day Adventists (1863) — Pres., Neal C. Wilson; sec., G. Ralph Thompson, 6840 Eastern Ave. NW, Wash., DC 20012.

Baha'i Faith — Chpsn., Judge James E. Nelson; sec., Glenford E. Mitchell, 536 Sheridan Rd., Wilmette, IL 60091.

Baptist churches:

American Baptist Assn. (1905) — Pres., Dr. W. A. Dillard; rec. clk., W E. Norris, 4605 N. State Line, Texarkana, TX 75504.

American Baptist Churches in the U.S.A. (1907) — Pres., John F. Mandt; gen. sec., Rev. Dr. Robert C. Campbell, Valley Forge, PA 19481.

Baptist General Conference (1879) — Gen. sec., Dr. Warren Magnuson, 2002 S. Arlington Heights Rd., Arlington Heights, IL 60005.

Baptist Missionary Assn. of America (formerly **North American Baptist Assn.**) (1950) — Pres., Rev. Gordon Renshaw, rec. sec., Rev. Ralph Cottrell, Box 2866, Texarkana, AR 75501.

Conservative Baptist Assn. of America (1947) — Gen. Dir., Dr. Russell A. Shive, Box 66, Wheaton, IL 60187.

Free Will Baptists (1727) — Mod., Rev. Bobby Jackson; exec. sec., Dr. Melvin Worthington, Box 1088, Nashville, TN 37202.

General Assn. of General Baptists (1823) — Exec. sec., Rev. Glen Spence, 100 Stinson Dr., Poplar Bluff, MO 63901.

General Assn. of Regular Baptist Churches (1932) — Chpsn., Dr. Mark Jackson; natl. rep., Dr. Paul N. Tassell, 1300 N. Meacham Rd., Schaumburg, IL 60195.

Natl. Baptist Convention, U.S.A. (1880) — Pres., Dr. J.H. Jackson, 405 E. 31st St., Chicago, IL 60616.

North American Baptist Conference (1865) — Mod., Dr. Peter Fehr; exec. dir., Dr. John Binder, 1 S. 210 Summit Ave., Oakbrook Terrace, IL 60181.

Southern Baptist Convention (1945) — Pres., James T. Draper; exec. sec., exec. comm., Dr. Harold C. Bennett, 460 James Robertson Pkwy., Nashville, TN 37219.

United America Free Will Baptist Church (1870) — Gen. Bishop, W.L. Jones; gen. fin. sec., Bishop J.E. Reddick, 1101 University St., Kinston, NC 28501.

Brethren in Christ Church (1798) — Mod., Bishop Harvey R. Sider, sec., Dr. Arthur M. Climenhaga, 1125 W. Arrow Highway, Upland, CA 91786.

Brethren (German Baptists):

Brethren Church (Ashland, Oh.) (1708) — Adm., Charles Beekley, 524 College Ave., Ashland, OH 44805.

Church of the Brethren (1719) — Mod., Earle W. Fike, Jr.; gen. sec., Robert Neff, 1451 Dundee Ave., Elgin, IL 60120.

Buddhist Churches of America (1899) — Bishop, Rt. Rev. Seigen H. Yamaoka, 1710 Octavia St., San Francisco, CA 94109.

Calvary Grace Christian Church of Faith (1898) — Intl. gen. supt., Col. Herman Keck Jr., U.S. Box 4266, Norton AFB, San Bernardino, CA 92409.

Calvary Grace Church of Faith (1874) — Intl. gen. supt., Rev. A.C. Spern, Box 333, Rillton, PA 15678.

The Christian and Missionary Alliance (1887) — Pres., Dr. Louis L. King; sec., Dr. Elwood N. Nielsen, 350 N. Highland Ave., Nyack, NY 10960.

Christian Church (Disciples of Christ) (1809) — Gen. minister and pres., Dr. Kenneth L. Teegarden, 222 S. Downey Ave., Box 1986, Indianapolis, IN 46206.

The Christian Congregation (1887) — Gen. supt., Rev. Ora Wilbert Eads, 804 W. Hemlock St., LaFollette, TN 37766.

Churches of Christ in Christian Union (1909) — Gen. supt., Rev. Robert Kline; gen. sec., Rev. Paul Dorsey, Box 30, Circleville, OH 43113.

Churches of God:

Churches of God, General Conference (1825) — Admin., Dr. Richard E. Wilkin, Box 926, Findlay, OH 45840.

Church of God (Anderson, Ind.) (1880) — Chpsn., Paul L. Hart; exec. sec., Paul A. Tanner, Box 2420, Anderson, IN 46011.

Church of Christ, Scientist (1879) — Pres., Dorothy E. Klein; clerk, Ruth Elizabeth Jenks, Christian Science Center, Boston, MA 02115.

Church of the Nazarene (1908) — Gen. sec., B. Edgar Johnson, 6401 The Paseo, Kansas City, MO 64131.

National Association of Congregational Christian Churches (1955) — Mod., Richard Bower; exec. sec., A. Ray Appelquist, Box 1620, Oak Creek, WI 53154.

Eastern Orthodox churches:

Antiochian Orthodox Christian Archdiocese of North America (formerly **Syrian Antiochian Orthodox Church**) (1894) — Primate, Metropolitan Archbishop Philip (Saliba); aux., Archbishop Michael Shaheen, 358 Mountain Rd., Englewood, NJ 07631.

Diocese of the Armenian Church of America (1889) — Primate, His Eminence Archbishop Torkom Manoogian; sec., V. Rev. Houssig Bagdasian, 630 2d Ave., N.Y., NY 10016.

Coptic Orthodox Ch. — Correspnt., Archpriest Fr. Gabriel Abdelsayed, 427 West Side Ave., Jersey City, NJ 07304.

Greek Orthodox Archdiocese of North and South America (1864) — Primate, Archbishop Iakovos; sec., Peter Kourides, 8-10 E. 79th St., N.Y., NY 10021.

Orthodox Church in America (formerly **Russian Orthodox Greek Catholic Church of North America**) (1792) — Primate, Metropolitan Theodosius; sec., Serge Troubetzkoy, P.O. Box 675, Syosset, NY 11791.

Romanian Orthodox Episcopate of America (1929) — Archbishop, Valerian (D. Trifa); sec., Most Rev. Laurence C. Lazar, 2522 Grey Tower Rd., Jackson, MI 49201.

Serbian Eastern Orthodox Church for the U.S.A. and Canada — Bishops, Rt. Rev. Bishop Firmilian, Rt. Rev. Bishop Gregory; Bishop Christophor; St. Sava Monastery, Libertyville, IL 60048.

Syrian Orthodox Church of Antioch, Archdiocese of the U.S.A. and Canada (1957) — Primate, Archbishop MarAthanasius Y. Samuel; gen. sec., Rev. Fr. John Meno, 45 Fairmount Ave., Hackensack, NJ 07601.

Ukrainian Orthodox Church in America (Ecumenical Patriarchate) (1928) — Primate, Most. Rev. Bishop Andrei Kuschak, 90-34 139th St., Jamaica, NY 11435.

Ukrainian Orthodox Church in the U.S.A. (1919) — Metropolitan, Most Rev. Mstyslav S. Skrypnyk, Box 495, South Bound Brook, NJ 08880.

The Episcopal Church (1789) — Presiding bishop, Rt. Rev. John M. Allin; exec. off., Rev. James R. Gundrum, 815 2d Ave., N.Y., NY 10017.

Evangelical Christian Churches (1966) — Pres., Rev. John Wahnert, 336 E. Olney Ave., Phila., PA 19120.

Evangelical Christian Churches, California Synod (1966) — Pres.-Treas., Dr. Richard W. Hart Sr., P.O. Box 1478, San Bernardino, CA 92402.

The Evangelical Covenant Church (1885) — Pres., Dr. Milton B. Engebretson; sec., Rev. Clifford Bjorklund, 5101 N. Francisco Ave., Chicago, IL 60625.

Friends:

Evangelical Friends Alliance (1965) — Pres., Maurice A. Roberts, 2018 Maple, Wichita, KS 67213.

Friends General Conference (1900) — Clk., George N. Webb; gen. sec., Lloyd Lee Wilson, 1520B Race St., Phila., PA 19102.

Friends United Meeting (formerly **Five Years Meeting of Friends**) (1902) — Presiding clerk, Walter E. Schutt, 101 Quaker Hill Dr., Richmond, IN 47374.

Independent Fundamental Churches of America (1930) — Pres., Rev. Calvin H.C. Probasco, 5640 Vega Ct., Carmichael, CA 95608.

Federation of Islamic Assns. in U.S. and Canada — 300 E. 44th St., N.Y., NY 10017.

Jehovah's Witnesses (1879) — Watch Tower Pres., Frederick W. Franz, 124 Columbia Heights, Brooklyn, NY 11201.

Jewish congregations:

Union of American Hebrew Congregations (Reform) —

Pres., Rabbi Alexander M. Schindler, 838 5th Ave., N.Y., NY 10021.
National Council of Young Israel (Orthodox) (1912) — Pres., Dr. Harold M. Jacobs; exec. v.p., Rabbi Ephraim H. Sturm, 3 W. 16th St., N.Y., NY 10011.
Union of Orthodox Jewish Congregations of America — Pres., Julius Berman, 116 E. 27th St., N.Y., NY 10016.
United Synagogue of America (Conservative) — Pres., Simon Schwartz, exec. v.p., Rabbi Benjamin Z. Kreitman, 155 5th Ave., N.Y., NY 10010.

Latter-day Saints:
The Church of Jesus Christ of Latter-day Saints (Mormon) (1830) — Pres., Spencer W. Kimball, 50 E. North Temple St., Salt Lake City, UT 84150.
Reorganized Church of Jesus Christ of Latter Day Saints (1830) — Pres., Wallace B. Smith, The Auditorium, Independence, MO 64051.

Lutheran churches:
The American Lutheran Church (1961) — Pres., Dr. David W. Preus; gen. sec., Dr. A.R. Mickelson, 422 S. 5th St., Minneapolis, MN 55415.
Church of the Lutheran Brethren (1900) — Pres., Rev. Everald H. Strom; sec., Rev. George Aase, 1007 Westside Dr., Box 655, Fergus Falls, MN 56537.
Church of the Lutheran Confession (1960) — Pres., Rev. Egbert Albrecht, Rt. 2, Markesan, WI 53946; sec., Rev. Paul Nolting.
Assn. of Evangelical Lutheran Churches (1976) — Pres., Dr. William H. Kohn; exec. sec., Elwyn Ewald, 12015 Manchester Rd., St. Louis, MO 63131.
Evangelical Lutheran Synod (1853) — Pres., Rev. George Orvick; sec., Rev. Alf Merseth, 106 13th St. S., Northwood, IA 50459.
Assn. of Free Lutheran Congregations (1962) — Pres., Richard Snipstead; sec., Rev. Hubert DeBoer, 3110 E. Medicine Lake Blvd., Minneapolis, MN 55441.
Lutheran Church in America (1962) — Bishop, Rev. Dr. James R. Crumley Jr.; sec., Rev. Dr. Reuben T. Swanson, 231 Madison Ave., N.Y. NY 10016.
Lutheran Church — Missouri Synod (1847) — Pres., Dr. Ralph Bohlmann; sec., Rev. Herbert A. Mueller, 500 N. Broadway, St. Louis, MO 63102.
Wisconsin Evangelical Lutheran Synod (1850) — Pres., Rev. Carl H. Mischke; 3512 W. North Ave., Milwaukee, WI 53208; sec., David Worgull, 4055 Lancer Circle, Manitowac, WI 54220.

Mennonite churches:
The General Conference Mennonite Church (1860) — Pres. Jacob Tilitzky; gen. sec., Vern Preheim, 722 Main, Box 347, Newton, KS 67114.
Mennonite Church (1690) — Mod., Ross T. Bender, sec., Ivan J. Kauffmann, 528 E. Madison St., Lombard, IL 60148.

Methodist churches:
African Methodist Episcopal Zion Church (1796) — Sr. Bishop, William M. Smith; sec., Bish. Charles H. Foggie, 1200 Windermere Dr., Pittsburgh, PA 15218.
Evangelical Methodist Church (1946) — Gen. supt., John F. Kunkle; gen. sec., Rev. R.D. Driggers, 3000 W. Kellogg Dr., Wichita, KS 67213.
Free Methodist Church of North America (1860) — Bishops R. Andrews, D. Bastian, W. Cryderman, E. Parsons, C. Van Valin, gen. conf. sec., C.T. Denbo, 901 College Ave., Winona Lake, IN 46590.
The United Methodist Church (1968) — Sec. Counc. of Bishops, Bishop James M. Ault, 223 Fourth Ave., Pittsburgh, PA 15222; sec., gen. conf., Dr. J.B. Holt, Perkins School of Theology, Dallas, TX 75275.

Universal Fellowship of Metropolitan Community Churches —Mod., Rev. Troy Perry; 5300 Santa Monica Blvd., Suite 304, Los Angeles, CA 90029.

Moravian Church (Unitas Fratum) (1740) **Northern Province** — Pres., Dr. J.S. Groenfeldt, 69 W. Church St., Box 1245, Bethlehem, PA 18018. **Southern Province** — Pres., Dr. Richard E. Amos, 459 S. Church St., Winston-Salem, NC 27101.

Old Catholic churches:
Mariavite Old Catholic Church-Province of North America (1932) — Prime bishop, Most Rev. Robert R.J.M. Zaborowski O.M., D.D., 2803 10th St., Wyandotte, MI 48192.
North American Old Roman Catholic Church (1915) — Archbishop, Most Rev. J.E. Schweikert, 4200 N. Kedvale Ave., Chicago, IL 60641.

Pentecostal churches:
Assemblies of God (1914) — Gen. supt., Thomas F. Zimmerman; gen. sec., Joseph R. Flower, 1445 Boonville Ave., Springfield, MO 65802.
Bible Way Church of Our Lord Jesus Christ World Wide (1927) — Presiding bishop, Dr. Smallwood E. Williams, 1100 New Jersey Ave. NW, Wash., DC 20001.
Gen. Council, Christian Church of No. America (1948) — Gen. overseer; Rev. Dr. Carmine Saginario; gen. sec., Rev. Richard Tedesco, Box 141-A, RD #15, Rt. 18 & Rutledge Rd., Transfer, PA 16154.
The Church of God (1903) — Gen. overseer, Bishop Voy M. Bullen, 2504 Arrow Wood Dr. SE, Huntsville, AL 35803.
Church of God (Cleveland, Tenn.) (1886) — Gen. overseer, Dr. Ray H. Hughes; gen. sec.-treas., Dr. E. C. Thomas, Keith at 25th St. NW, Cleveland, TN 37311.
International Church of the Foursquare Gospel (1927) — Pres., Dr. Rolf K. McPherson; sec., Dr. Leland E. Edwards, 1100 Glendale Blvd., Los Angeles, CA 90026.
National Gay Pentecostal Alliance (1980) — Pres., Rev. Wm. H. Carey, P.O. Box 55194, Omaha, NE 68155.
Open Bible Standard Churches (1919) — Gen. supt., Ray E. Smith; sec.-treas., Patrick L. Bowlin, 2020 Bell Ave., Des Moines, IA 50315.
Pentecostal Church of God (1919) — Gen. supt., Rev. Roy M. Chappell; sec.-treas., Rev. Ronald R. Minor, 211 Main St., Joplin, MO 64801.
United Pentecostal Church International (1945) — Gen. supt., Nathaniel A. Urshan; gen. sec., Cleveland Becton 8855 Dunn Rd., Hazelwood, MO 63042.
Pentecostal Free Will Baptist Church (1959) — Gen. supt., Rev. Herbert Carter; gen. sec., Rev. Don Sauls, Box 1568, Dunn, NC 28334.

Presbyterian churches:
Cumberland Presbyterian Church (1810) — Mod., W.A. Rawlins; stated clerk, T.V. Warnick, 1978 Union Ave., Memphis, TN 38104.
The Orthodox Presbyterian Church (1936) — Mod. Glenn T. Black, stated clerk, Richard A. Barker, 7401 Old York Rd., Phila., PA 19126.
Presbyterian Church in America (1973) — Mod., Rev. Kenneth L. Ryskamp; stated clerk, Rev. Morton H. Smith, Box 312, Brevard, NC 28712.
Presbyterian Church in the U.S. (1865) — Mod., Dorothy Barnard; stated clerk, James E. Andrews, 341 Ponce de Leon Ave. NE, Atlanta, GA 30365.
Reformed Presbyterian Church, Evangelical Synod (1965) — Mod., Rev. Roger B. Lambert; stated clerk, Dr. Paul R. Gilchrist, 107 Hardy Rd., Lookout Mountain, TN 37350.
United Presbyterian Church in the U.S.A. (1958) — Mod., Rev. James H. Costen; stated clerk, William P. Thompson, 475 Riverside Dr., N.Y., NY 10115.

Reformed Episcopal Church (1873) — Pres., Rev. Theophilos J. Herter; sec., Rev. Dale H. Crouthamel, 14 Culberson Rd., Basking Ridge, NJ 07920.

Reformed churches:
Christian Reformed Church in North America (1857) — Stated clerk, Rev. William P. Brink, 2850 Kalamazoo Ave., SE, Grand Rapids, MI 49560.
Reformed Church in America (1628) — Pres., Rev. Jack Hascup; gen. sec., Rev. Dr. Arie R. Brouwer, 475 Riverside Dr., N.Y., NY 10115.

Roman Catholic Church — National Conference of Catholic Bishops. Pres., Archbishop John R. Roach; sec., Msgr. Daniel Hoye, 1312 Massachusetts Ave. NW, Wash., DC 20005.

The Salvation Army (1880) — Natl. cmdr., John E. Needham; natl. chief sec., Col. G. Ernest Murray, 799 Bloomfield Ave., Verona, NJ 07044.

Sikh (1972) — Chief adm., Siri Singh Sahib, Harbhajan Singh Khalsa Yogiji; sec. gen., Mukhia Sardarni Sahiba, Sardarni Premka Kaur Khalsa, 1649 S. Robertson Blvd., Los Angeles, CA 90035.

Unitarian Universalist Assn. (1961) — Pres., Rev. Dr. Eugene Pickett; sec., Lori Pederson, 25 Beacon St., Boston, MA 02108.

United Brethren in Christ (1789) — Chpsn., Bishop C. Ray Miller; 302 Lake St., Huntington, IN 46750.

United Church of Christ (1957) — Pres., Rev. Avery D. Post; sec., Rev. Joseph H. Evans, 105 Madison Ave., N.Y., NY 10016.
Volunteers of America (1896) — Cmdr.-in-chief, Gen. Ray C. Tremont; natl. field sec., Maj. John A. Hood, 3939 N. Causeway Blvd., Metairie, LA 70002.

The Wesleyan Church (1968) — Gen. supts., Drs. J Abbott, O.D. Emery, R. McIntyre, V. Mitchell; sec., D. Wayne Brown, Box 2000, Marion, IN 46952.

Headquarters of Religious Groups in Canada

(year organized in parentheses)

Anglican Church of Canada (creation of General Synod 1893) - Primate, Most Rev. E.W. Scott; 600 Jarvis St., Toronto, Ont. M4Y 2J6.

Apostolic Church in Canada - H.O. 27 Castlefield Ave., Toronto, Ont. M4R 1G3; Pres., Rev. D.S. Morris, 685 Park St. South, Peterborough, Ont. K9J 3S9.

Baha'is of Canada, The National Spiritual Assembly of the (1949) - Gen. Sec. Ed Muttart, 7200 Leslie St., Thornhill, Ont. L3T 2A1.

Baptist Federation of Canada - Pres., Jerry Zeman; Gen. Sec.-Treasurer, Rev. Michael Steeves, 219 St. George St., Toronto, Ont. M5R 2M2.

Bible Holiness Movement, The (1949) - Pres., Evangelist Wesley H. Wakefield, Box 223, Stn. A, Vancouver, B.C. V6C 2M3.

Buddhist Churches of Canada (1945) - Administrative H.O., 220 Jackson Ave., Vancouver, B.C. V6A 3B3.

Canadian Council of Churches, The (1938) - Gen. Sec., Rev. Donald W. Anderson, 40 St. Clair Ave. E., Suite 201, Toronto, Ont. M4T 1M9.

Christian and Missionary Alliance in Canada, The (1889) - Pres., Rev. M.P. Sylvester, Box 7900, Stn. B, Willowdale, Ont. M2K 2R3.

Christian Church (Disciples of Christ) (All Canada Committee formed 1922) - 39 Arkell Rd., R.R. 2, Guelph, Ont. N1H 6H8.

Christian Science in Canada - Mr. J. Don Fulton, 339 Bloor St. W., Ste. 214, Toronto, Ont. M5S 1W7.

Church of Jesus Christ of Latter-Day Saints (Mormons) (1830) - Pres. Calgary Stake, R.H. Walker, 930 Prospect Ave. S.W., Calgary Alta. T2T 0W5; Pres. Edmonton Stake, Warren Wilde, 5108-112 St., Edmonton, Alta. T6H 3J2; Pres. Toronto Stake, James L. Kirschbaum, 5 Edenbrook Hill, Islington, Ont. M9A 3Z5; Pres. Vancouver Stake, R.W. Komm, 1348 Chartwell Dr., West Vancouver, B.C. V7S 2R5.

Church of the Nazarene (1902) - Dist. Superintendent of Canada Central District, Rev. Lorne MacMillan, 38 Riverhead Dr., Rexdale, Ont. M9W 4G6; Chairman of Exec. Board, Rev. Alexander Ardrey, 2236 Capitol Hill Cres. N.W., Calgary, Alta. T2M 4B9.

Fellowship of Evangelical Baptist Churches in Canada (1953) - Gen. Sec. Dr. Roy W. Lawson, 74 Sheppard Ave. W., Willowdale, Ont. M2N 1M3.

Free Methodist Church in Canada (1880) - Pres., Bishop D.N. Bastian, 96 Elmbrook Cres., Etobicoke, Ont. M9C 5E2; Exec. Sec., Rev. C.A. Horton, 833-D Upper James St., Hamilton, Ont. L9C 3A3.

Greek Orthodox Church in Canada - His Grace Bishop Sotirios, 27 Teddington Park Ave., Toronto, Ont. M4N 2C4.

Jehovah's Witnesses (Branch Office estab. in Winnipeg 1918) - Branch Coordinator, Mr. Kenneth A. Little, Box 4100, Georgetown, Ont. L7J 4Y4.

Jewish Congress, Canadian (1919) - Exec. Vice-Pres., Alan Rose, 1590 Avenue Docteur Penfield, Montreal, Que. H3G 1C5.

Lutheran Council in Canada (a joint body of **The Evangelical Lutheran Church of Canada, Lutheran Church-Canada,** and **Lutheran Church in America - Canada Section**) - Pres., Rev. Val Hennig; Exec. Dir. W.A. Schultz, 500-365 Hargrave St., Winnipeg, Man. R3B 2K3.

Mennonite Brethren Churches of North America, Canadian Conference (inc. 1945) - Mod. David Redekop, 101 Lamont Blvd., Winnipeg, Man. R3P 0E7.

Mennonites in Canada, Conference of (1903) - Chairman, Jake Fransen, Smithville, Ont. L0R 2A0.

Pentecostal Assemblies of Canada, The (inc. 1919) - Gen. Supt., Rev. Robert W. Taitinger, 10 Overlea Blvd., Toronto, Ont. M4H 1A5.

Presbyterian Church in Canada, The (1875) - Mod., Dr. Wayne A. Smith, 50 Wynford Dr., Don Mills, Ont. M3C 1J7.

Religious Society of Friends (Quakers), (Canadian Yearly Meeting of the Religious Society of Friends formed 1955) - Presiding Clerk, Joan Benz, 60 Lowther Ave., Toronto, Ont. M5R 1C7.

Reorganized Church of Jesus Christ of Latter-Day Saints (Canada) (1830) - Ont. Region Pres., Donald H. Comer; Bishop of Canada and Ont. Region, Kenneth G. Fisher, 390 Speedvale Ave. E., Guelph, Ont. N1E 1N5.

Roman Catholic Church in Canada - Canadian Conference of Catholic Bishops, 90 Parent Ave., Ottawa, Ont. K1N 7B1.

Salvation Army, The (1882) - Commissioner John D. Waldron, P.O. Box 4021, Postal Station A, Toronto, Ont. M5W 2B1.

Seventh-day Adventist Church in Canada - Pres., J.W. Wilson; Sec., P.F. Lemon; 1148 King St. E., Oshawa, Ont. L1H 1H8.

Ukrainian Greek Orthodox Church in Canada - Primate, Metropolitan of Winnipeg and of all Canada, His Beatitude Metropolitan Andrew (Metiuk), 9 St. Johns Ave., Winnipeg, Man. R2W 0T9.

Union of Spiritual Communities of Christ (Orthodox Doukhobors in Canada) (1938) - Honorary Chmn. of the Exec. Comm., John J. Verigin, Box 760, Grand Forks, B.C. V0H 1H0.

Unitarian Council, Canadian (1961) - Pres., Brian Reid; Admin. Sec. Mrs. Thelma Peters, 175 St. Clair Ave. W., Toronto, Ont. M4V 1P7.

United Church of Canada, The (1925) - Mod. Rt. Rev. Lois Wilson; Sec. of General Council, Rev. Donald Ray, 85 St. Clair Ave. E., Toronto, Ont. M4T 1M8.

Episcopal Church Calendar and Liturgical Colors

White—from Christmas Day through the First Sunday after Epiphany; Maundy Thursday (as an alternative to crimson at the Eucharist); from the Vigil of Easter to the Day of Pentecost (Whitsunday); Trinity Sunday; Feasts of the Lord (except Holy Cross Day); the Confession of St. Peter; the Conversion of St. Paul; St. Joseph; St. Mary Magdalene; St. Mary the Virgin; St. Michael and All Angels; All Saint's Day; St. John the Evangelist; memorials of other saints who were not martyred; Independence Day and Thanksgiving Day; weddings and funerals. **Red.**—the Day of Pentecost; Holy Cross Day; feasts of apostles and evangelists (except those listed above); feasts and memorials of martyrs (including Holy Innocents' Day). **Violet**—Advent and Lent. **Crimson** (dark red)—Holy Week. **Green**—the seasons after Epiphany and after Pentecost. **Black**—optional alternative for funerals. Alternative colors used in some churches: **Blue**—Advent; **Lenten White**—Ash Wednesday to Palm Sunday.

Days, etc.	1982	1983	1984	1985	1986	1987
Golden Number	7	8	9	10	11	12
Sunday Letter	C	B	AG	F	E	D
Sundays after Epiphany	7	6	9	6	5	8
Ash Wednesday	Feb. 24	Feb. 16	Mar. 7	Feb. 20	Feb. 12	Mar. 4
First Sunday in Lent	Feb. 28	Feb. 20	Mar. 11	Feb. 24	Feb. 16	Mar. 8
Passion/Palm Sunday	Apr. 4	Mar. 27	Apr. 15	Mar. 31	Mar. 23	Apr. 12
Good Friday	Apr. 9	Apr. 1	Apr. 20	Apr. 5	Mar. 28	Apr. 17
Easter Day	Apr. 11	Apr. 3	Apr. 22	Apr. 7	Mar. 30	Apr. 19
Ascension Day	May 20	May 12	May 31	May 16	May 8	May 28
The Day of Pentecost	May 30	May 22	June 10	May 26	May 18	June 7
Trinity Sunday	June 6	May 29	June 17	June 2	May 25	June 14
Numbered Proper of 2 Pentecost	#6	#5	#7	#5	#4	#7
First Sunday of Advent	Nov. 28	Nov. 27	Dec. 2	Dec. 1	Nov. 30	Nov. 29

In the Episcopal Church the days of fasting are Ash Wednesday and Good Friday. Other days of special devotion (abstinence) are the 40 days of Lent and all Fridays of the year, except those in Christmas and Easter seasons and any Feasts of the Lord which occur on a Friday or during Lent. Ember Days (optional) are days of prayer for the Church's ministry. They fall on the Wednesday, Friday, and Saturday after the first Sunday in Lent, the Day of Pentecost, Holy Cross Day, and the Third Sunday of Advent. Rogation Days (also optional) are the three days before Ascension Day, and are days of prayer for God's blessing on the crops, on commerce and industry, and for the conservation of the earth's resources.

Ash Wednesday and Easter Sunday

Year	Ash Wed.	Easter Sunday	Year	Ash Wed.	Easter Sunday	Year	Ash Wed.	Easter Sunday	Year	Ash Wed.	Easter Sunday
1901	Feb. 20	Apr. 7	1951	Feb. 7	Mar. 25	2001	Feb. 28	Apr. 15	2051	Feb. 15	Apr. 2
1902	Feb. 12	Mar. 30	1952	Feb. 27	Apr. 13	2002	Feb. 13	Mar. 31	2052	Mar. 6	Apr. 21
1903	Feb. 25	Apr. 12	1953	Feb. 18	Apr. 5	2003	Mar. 5	Apr. 20	2053	Feb. 19	Apr. 6
1904	Feb. 17	Apr. 3	1954	Mar. 3	Apr. 18	2004	Feb. 25	Apr. 11	2054	Feb. 11	Mar. 29
1905	Mar. 8	Apr. 23	1955	Feb. 23	Apr. 10	2005	Feb. 9	Mar. 27	2055	Mar. 3	Apr. 18
1906	Feb. 28	Apr. 15	1956	Feb. 15	Apr. 1	2006	Mar. 1	Apr. 16	2056	Feb. 16	Apr. 2
1907	Feb. 13	Mar. 31	1957	Mar. 6	Apr. 21	2007	Feb. 21	Apr. 8	2057	Mar. 7	Apr. 22
1908	Mar. 4	Apr. 19	1958	Feb. 19	Apr. 6	2008	Feb. 6	Mar. 23	2058	Feb. 27	Apr. 14
1909	Feb. 24	Apr. 11	1959	Feb. 11	Mar. 29	2009	Feb. 25	Apr. 12	2059	Feb. 12	Mar. 30
1910	Feb. 9	Mar. 27	1960	Mar. 2	Apr. 17	2010	Feb. 17	Apr. 4	2060	Mar. 3	Apr. 18
1911	Mar. 1	Apr. 16	1961	Feb. 15	Apr. 2	2011	Mar. 9	Apr. 24	2061	Feb. 23	Apr. 10
1912	Feb. 21	Apr. 7	1962	Mar. 7	Apr. 22	2012	Feb. 22	Apr. 8	2062	Feb. 8	Mar. 26
1913	Feb. 5	Mar. 23	1963	Feb. 27	Apr. 14	2013	Feb. 13	Mar. 31	2063	Feb. 28	Apr. 15
1914	Feb. 25	Apr. 12	1964	Feb. 12	Mar. 29	2014	Mar. 5	Apr. 20	2064	Feb. 20	Apr. 6
1915	Feb. 17	Apr. 4	1965	Mar. 3	Apr. 18	2015	Feb. 18	Apr. 5	2065	Feb. 11	Mar. 29
1916	Mar. 8	Apr. 23	1966	Feb. 23	Apr. 10	2016	Feb. 10	Mar. 27	2066	Feb. 24	Apr. 11
1917	Feb. 21	Apr. 8	1967	Feb. 8	Mar. 26	2017	Mar. 1	Apr. 16	2067	Feb. 16	Apr. 3
1918	Feb. 13	Mar. 31	1968	Feb. 28	Apr. 14	2018	Feb. 14	Apr. 1	2068	Mar. 7	Apr. 22
1919	Mar. 5	Apr. 20	1969	Feb. 19	Apr. 6	2019	Mar. 6	Apr. 21	2069	Feb. 27	Apr. 14
1920	Feb. 18	Apr. 4	1970	Feb. 11	Mar. 29	2020	Feb. 26	Apr. 12	2070	Feb. 12	Mar. 30
1921	Feb. 9	Mar. 27	1971	Feb. 24	Apr. 11	2021	Feb. 17	Apr. 4	2071	Mar. 4	Apr. 19
1922	Mar. 1	Apr. 16	1972	Feb. 16	Apr. 2	2022	Mar. 2	Apr. 17	2072	Feb. 24	Apr. 10
1923	Feb. 14	Apr. 1	1973	Mar. 7	Apr. 22	2023	Feb. 22	Apr. 9	2073	Feb. 8	Mar. 26
1924	Mar. 5	Apr. 20	1974	Feb. 27	Apr. 14	2024	Feb. 14	Mar. 31	2074	Feb. 28	Apr. 15
1925	Feb. 25	Apr. 12	1975	Feb. 12	Mar. 30	2025	Mar. 5	Apr. 20	2075	Feb. 20	Apr. 7
1926	Feb. 17	Apr. 4	1976	Mar. 3	Apr. 18	2026	Feb. 18	Apr. 5	2076	Mar. 4	Apr. 19
1927	Mar. 2	Apr. 17	1977	Feb. 23	Apr. 10	2027	Feb. 10	Mar. 28	2077	Feb. 24	Apr. 11
1928	Feb. 22	Apr. 8	1978	Feb. 8	Mar. 26	2028	Mar. 1	Apr. 16	2078	Feb. 16	Apr. 3
1929	Feb. 13	Mar. 31	1979	Feb. 28	Apr. 15	2029	Feb. 14	Apr. 1	2079	Mar. 8	Apr. 23
1930	Mar. 5	Apr. 20	1980	Feb. 20	Apr. 6	2030	Mar. 6	Apr. 21	2080	Feb. 21	Apr. 7
1931	Feb. 18	Apr. 5	1981	Mar. 4	Apr. 19	2031	Feb. 26	Apr. 13	2081	Feb. 12	Mar. 30
1932	Feb. 10	Mar. 27	1982	Feb. 24	Apr. 11	2032	Feb. 11	Mar. 28	2082	Mar. 4	Apr. 19
1933	Mar. 1	Apr. 16	1983	Feb. 16	Apr. 3	2033	Mar. 2	Apr. 17	2083	Feb. 17	Apr. 4
1934	Feb. 14	Apr. 1	1984	Mar. 7	Apr. 22	2034	Feb. 22	Apr. 9	2084	Feb. 9	Mar. 26
1935	Mar. 6	Apr. 21	1985	Feb. 20	Apr. 7	2035	Feb. 7	Mar. 25	2085	Feb. 28	Apr. 15
1936	Feb. 26	Apr. 12	1986	Feb. 12	Mar. 30	2036	Feb. 27	Apr. 13	2086	Feb. 13	Mar. 31
1937	Feb. 10	Mar. 28	1987	Mar. 4	Apr. 19	2037	Feb. 18	Apr. 5	2087	Mar. 5	Apr. 20
1938	Mar. 2	Apr. 17	1988	Feb. 17	Apr. 3	2038	Mar. 10	Apr. 25	2088	Feb. 25	Apr. 11
1939	Feb. 22	Apr. 9	1989	Feb. 8	Mar. 26	2039	Feb. 23	Apr. 10	2089	Feb. 16	Apr. 3
1940	Feb. 7	Mar. 24	1990	Feb. 28	Apr. 15	2040	Feb. 15	Apr. 1	2090	Mar. 1	Apr. 16
1941	Feb. 26	Apr. 13	1991	Feb. 13	Mar. 31	2041	Mar. 6	Apr. 21	2091	Feb. 21	Apr. 8
1942	Feb. 18	Apr. 5	1992	Mar. 4	Apr. 19	2042	Feb. 19	Apr. 6	2092	Feb. 13	Mar. 30
1943	Mar. 10	Apr. 25	1993	Feb. 24	Apr. 11	2043	Feb. 11	Mar. 29	2093	Feb. 25	Apr. 12
1944	Feb. 23	Apr. 9	1994	Feb. 16	Apr. 3	2044	Mar. 2	Apr. 17	2094	Feb. 17	Apr. 4
1945	Feb. 14	Apr. 1	1995	Mar. 1	Apr. 16	2045	Feb. 22	Apr. 9	2095	Mar. 9	Apr. 24
1946	Mar. 6	Apr. 21	1996	Feb. 21	Apr. 7	2046	Feb. 7	Mar. 25	2096	Feb. 29	Apr. 15
1947	Feb. 19	Apr. 6	1997	Feb. 12	Mar. 30	2047	Feb. 27	Apr. 14	2097	Feb. 13	Mar. 31
1948	Feb. 11	Mar. 28	1998	Feb. 25	Apr. 12	2048	Feb. 19	Apr. 5	2098	Mar. 5	Apr. 20
1949	Mar. 2	Apr. 17	1999	Feb. 17	Apr. 4	2049	Mar. 3	Apr. 18	2099	Feb. 25	Apr. 12
1950	Feb. 22	Apr. 9	2000	Mar. 8	Apr. 23	2050	Feb. 23	Apr. 10	2100	Feb. 10	Mar. 28

A lengthy dispute over the date for the celebration of Easter was settled by the first Council of the Christian Churches at Nicaea, in Asia Minor, in 325 A.D. The Council ruled that Easter would be observed on the first Sunday following the 14th day of the Paschal Moon, referred to as the Paschal Full Moon. The Paschal Moon is the first moon whose 14th day comes on or after March 21. Dates of the Paschal Full Moon, which are not necessarily the same as those of the real or astronomical full moon, are listed in the table below with an explanation of how to compute the date of Easter.

If the Paschal Full Moon falls on a Sunday, then Easter is the following Sunday. The earliest date on which Easter can fall is March 22; it fell on that date in 1761 and 1818 but will not do so in the 20th or 21st century. The latest possible date for Easter is April 25; it fell on that date in 1943 and will again in 2038.

For western churches Lent begins on Ash Wednesday, which comes 40 days before Easter Sunday, not counting Sundays. Originally it was a period of but 40 hours. Later it comprised 30 days of fasting, omitting all the Sundays and also all the Saturdays except one. Pope Gregory (590-604) added Ash Wednesday to the fast, together with the remainder of that week.

The last seven days of Lent constitute Holy Week, beginning with Palm Sunday. The last Thursday — Maundy Thursday — commemorates the institution of the Eucharist. The following day, Good Friday, commemorates the day of the Crucifixion.

Easter is the chief festival of the Christian year, commemorating the Resurrection of Christ. It occurs about the same time as the ancient Roman celebration of the Vernal Equinox, the arrival of spring. In the second century, A.D., Easter Day among Christians in Asia Minor was the 14th Nisan, the seventh month of the Jewish calendar. The Christians in Europe observed the nearest Sunday.

Date of Paschal Full Moon, 1900-2199

The Golden Number, used in determining the date of Easter, is greater by unity (one) than the remainder obtained upon dividing the given year by 19. For example, when dividing 1983 by 19, one obtains a remainder of 7. Adding 1 gives 8 as the Golden Number for the year 1983. From the table then the date of the Paschal Full Moon is Mar. 28, 1983. Since this is a Monday, Easter is celebrated on the next Sunday, Apr. 3.

Golden Number	Date	Golden Number	Date	Golden Number	Date	Golden Number	Date
1	Apr. 14	6	Apr. 18	11	Mar. 25	16	Mar. 30
2	Apr. 3	7	Apr. 8	12	Apr. 13	17	Apr. 17
3	Mar. 23	8	Mar. 28	13	Apr. 2	18	Apr. 7
4	Apr. 11	9	Apr. 16	14	Mar. 22	19	Mar. 27
5	Mar. 31	10	Apr. 5	15	Apr. 10		

Jewish Holy Days, Festivals, and Fasts

Source: Synagogue Council of America

Festivals and fasts	Hebrew date		5743 (1982-1983)	5744 (1983-1984)	5745 (1984-1985)	5746 (1985-1986)
Rosh Hashana (New Year)[1]	Tishri	1	Sept. 18 Sa	Sept. 8 Th	Sept. 27 Th	Sept. 16 Mo
Fast of Gedalia	Tishri	3	Sept. 20 Mo	....	....	Sept. 18 We
Fast of Gedalia	Tishri	4	....	Sept. 11 Su	Sept. 30 Su	....
Yom Kippur (Day of Atonement)	Tishri	10	Sept. 27 Mo	Sept. 17 Sa	Oct. 6 Sa	Sept. 25 We
Sukkoth (Feast of Tabernacles), 1st Day[1]	Tishri	15	Oct. 2 Sa	Sept. 22 Th	Oct. 11 Th	Sept. 30 Mo
Sukkoth, 8th Day of Assembly (Shemini Atzereth)	Tishri	22	Oct. 9 Sa	Sept. 29 Th	Oct. 18 Th	Oct. 7 Mo
Simchat Torah (Rejoicing of the Law)	Tishri	23	Oct. 10 Su	Sept. 30 Fr	Oct. 19 Fr	Oct. 8 Tu
Chanukah (Feast of Lights)	Kislev	25	Dec. 11 Sa	Dec. 1 Th	Dec. 19 We	Dec. 8 Su
Fast of Tebet[2]	Tebet	10	Dec. 26 Su	Dec. 16 Fr	Jan. 3 Th	Dec. 22 Su
Fast of Esther[2]	Adar	13	Feb. 24 Th	....	Mar. 6 We	....
Fast of Esther[2]	Adar II	13	....	Mar. 15 Th	....	Mar. 24 Mo
Purim (Feast of Lots)	Adar	14	Feb. 27 Su	....	Mar. 7 Th	....
Purim	Adar II	14	....	Mar. 18 Su	....	Mar. 25 Tu
Pesach (Passover), 1st Day[1]	Nisan	15	Mar. 29 Tu	Apr. 17 Tu	Apr. 6 Sa	Apr. 24 Th
Pesach, 7th Day[1]	Nisan	21	Apr. 4 Mo	Apr. 23 Mo	Apr. 12 Fr	Apr. 30 We
Lag B'Omer	Iyar	18	May 1 Su	May 20 Su	May 9 Th	May 27 Tu
Shavuoth (Feast of Weeks)[1]	Sivan	6	May 18 We	June 6 We	May 26 Su	June 13 Fr
Fast of Tammuz[2]	Tammuz	17	June 28 Tu	July 17 Tu	July 7 Su	July 24 Th
Tisha B'Av (Fast of Av)[2]	Av	9	July 19 Tu	Aug. 7 Tu	July 28 Su	Aug. 14 Th

The months of the Jewish year are: 1) Tishri; 2) Cheshvan (also Marcheshvan); 3) Kislev; 4) Tebet (also Tebeth); 5) Shebat (also Shebhat); 6) Adar; 6a) Adar Sheni (II) added in leap years; 7) Nisan; 8) Iyar; 9) Sivan; 10) Tammuz; 11) Av (also Abh); 12) Elul. All Jewish holy days, etc., begin at sunset on the day previous. (1) Also observed the following day. (2) Hebrew date varies to avoid conflict with Sabbath.

Greek Orthodox Church Calendar, 1983

Date		Holy Days
Jan.	1	Circumcision of Jesus Christ; feast day of St. Basil
Jan.	6	Epiphany: Baptism of Jesus Christ - Sanctification of the Waters
Jan.	7	Feast day of St. John the Baptist
Jan.	30	Feast day of the Three Hierarchs: St. Basil the Great, St. Gregory the Theologian, and St. John Chrysostom
Feb.	2	Presentation of Jesus Christ in the Temple
*Mar.	21	Easter Lent begins
Mar.	25	Annunciation of the Virgin Mary
*Mar.	27	Sunday of Orthodoxy (1st. Sunday of Lent)
*May	1	Palm Sunday
*May	2-7	Holy Week
*May	6	Holy (Good) Friday: Burial of Jesus Christ
*May	8	Easter Sunday: Resurrection of Jesus Christ
*May	9	Feast of St. George
May	21	Feast day of Sts. Constantine and Helen
*June	16	Ascension of Jesus Christ
*June	26	Sunday of Pentecost
June	29	Feast day of Sts. Peter and Paul
June	30	Feast day of the Twelve Apostles of Jesus Christ
Aug.	6	Transfiguration of Jesus Christ
Aug.	15	Dormition of the Virgin Mary
Aug.	29	Beheading of St. John the Baptist
Sept.	1	Beginning of the Church Year
Sept.	14	Adoration of the Holy Cross
Oct.	23	Feast day of St. James
Oct.	26	Feast day of St. Demetrios the Martyr
Nov.	15	Christmas Lent begins
Nov.	21	Presentation of the Virgin Mary
Nov.	30	Feast day of St. Andrew the Apostle
Dec.	6	Feast day of St. Nicholas, Bishop of Myra
Dec.	25	Christmas Day; Nativity of Jesus Christ

*Movable holy days dependent upon the date of Easter. (The feast day of St. George is normally celebrated Apr. 23. If this day arrives during Lent, it is then celebrated the day after Easter.) The Greek Orthodox Church celebrates holy days in accordance with the Gregorian Calendar. Some Eastern Orthodox Churches still adhere to the Julian Calendar and observe the holy days (with the exception of the Easter cycle) 13 days later.

Islamic (Moslem) Calendar 1982-1983

The Islamic Calendar, often referred to as Mohammedan, is a lunar reckoning from the year of the *hegira*, 622 A.D., when Muhammed moved from Medina to Mecca. It runs in cycles of 30 years, of which the 2d, 5th, 7th, 10th, 13th, 16th, 18th, 21st, 24th, 26th, and 29th are leap years; 1403 and 1404 are the 23rd and 24th years, respectively, of the cycle. Common years have 354 days, leap years 355, the extra day being added to the last month, Zu'lhijjah. Except for this case, the 12 months beginning with Muharram have alternately 30 and 29 days.

Year	Name of month	Month begins	Year	Name of Month	Month begins
1403	Muharram (New Year)	Oct. 8, 1982	1404	Muharram (New Year)	Oct. 8, 1983
1403	Safar	Nov. 7, 1982	1404	Safar	Nov. 7, 1983
1403	Rabia I	Dec. 6, 1982	1404	Rabia I	Dec. 6, 1983
1403	Rabia II	Jan. 5, 1983	1404	Rabia II	Jan. 5, 1984
1403	Jumada I	Feb. 3, 1983	1404	Jumada I	Feb. 3, 1984
1403	Jumada II	Mar. 5, 1983	1404	Jumada II	Mar. 4, 1984
1403	Rajab	Apr. 3, 1983	1404	Rajab	Apr. 2, 1984
1403	Shaban	May 3, 1983	1404	Shaban	May 2, 1984
1403	Ramadan*	June 12, 1983	1404	Ramadan*	May 31, 1984
1403	Shawwai	July 12, 1983	1404	Shawwai	June 30, 1984
1403	Zu'lkadah	Aug. 10, 1983	1404	Zu'lkadah	July 29, 1984
1403	Zu'lhijjah	Sept. 9, 1983	1404	Zu'lhijjah	Aug. 28, 1984

* The date on which Ramadan begins may vary from the calendar date. It actually starts only after the new moon is sighted from the Naval Observatory in Cairo.

The Major World Religions

Buddhism

Founded: About 525 BC, reportedly near Benares, India.
Founder: Gautama Siddhartha (ca. 563-480), the Buddha, who achieved enlightenment through intense meditation.
Sacred Texts: The *Tripitaka*, a collection of the Buddha's teachings, rules of monastic life, and philosophical commentaries on the teachings; also a vast body of Buddhist teachings and commentaries, many of which are called *sutras*.
Organization: The basic institution is the *sangha* or monastic order through which the traditions are passed to each generation. Monastic life tends to be democratic and anti-authoritarian. Large lay organizations have developed in some sects.
Practice: Varies widely according to the sect and ranges from austere meditation to magical chanting and elaborate temple rites. Many practices, such as exorcism of devils, reflect pre-Buddhist beliefs.
Divisions: A wide variety of sects grouped into 3 primary branches: Therevada (sole survivor of the ancient Hinayana schools) which emphasizes the importance of pure thought and deed; Mahayana, which includes Zen and Soka-gakkai, ranges from philosophical schools to belief in the saving grace of higher beings or ritual practices, and to practical meditative disciplines; and Tantrism, an unusual combination of belief in ritual magic and sophisticated philosophy.
Location: Throughout Asia, from Ceylon to Japan. Zen and Soka-gakkai have several thousand adherents in the U.S.
Beliefs: Life is misery and decay, and there is no ultimate reality in it or behind it. The cycle of endless birth and rebirth continues because of desire and attachment to the unreal "self". Right meditation and deeds will end the cycle and achieve Nirvana, the Void, nothingness.

Hinduism

Founded: Ca. 1500 BC by Aryan invaders of India where their Vedic religion intermixed with the practices and beliefs of the natives.
Sacred texts: The *Veda*, including the *Upanishads*, a collection of rituals and mythological and philosophical commentaries; a vast number of epic stories about gods, heroes and saints, including the *Bhagavadgita*, a part of the *Mahabharata*, and the *Ramayana;* and a great variety of other literature.
Organization: None, strictly speaking. Generally, rituals should be performed or assisted by Brahmins, the priestly caste, but in practice simpler rituals can be performed by anyone. Brahmins are the final judges of ritual purity, the vital element in Hindu life. Temples and religious organizations are usually presided over by Brahmins.
Practice: A variety of private rituals, primarily passage rites (eg. initiation, marriage, death, etc.) and daily devotions, and a similar variety of public rites in temples. Of the latter, the *puja*, a ceremonial dinner for a god, is the most common.
Divisions: There is no concept of orthodoxy in Hinduism, which presents a bewildering variety of sects, most of them devoted to the worship of one of the many gods. The 3 major living traditions are those devoted to the gods Vishnu and Shiva and to the goddess Shakti; each of them divided into further sub-sects. Numerous folk beliefs and practices, often in amalgamation with the above groups, exist side-by-side with sophisticated philosophical schools and exotic cults.
Location: Confined to India, except for the missionary work of Vedanta, the Krishna Consciousness society, and individual *gurus* (teachers) in the West.
Beliefs: There is only one divine principle; the many gods are only aspects of that unity. Life in all its forms is an aspect of the divine, but it appears as a separation from the divine, a meaningless cycle of birth and rebirth (*samsara*) determined by the purity or impurity of past deeds (*karma*). To improve one's *karma* or escape *samsara* by pure acts, thought, and/or devotion is the aim of every Hindu.

Islam (submission)

Founded: 622 AD in Medina, Arabian peninsula.
Founder: Mohammed (ca. 570-632), the Prophet, as a result of visions.
Sacred texts: *Koran*, the words of God, delivered to Mohammed by the angel Gabriel; *Hadith*, collections of the sayings of the Prophet.
Organization: Theoretically the state and religious community are one, administered by a caliph. In practice, Islam is a loose collection of congregations united by a very conservative tradition. Islam is basically egalitarian and non-authoritarian.
Practice: Every Moslem is supposed to make the profession of faith ("There is no god but Allah . . ."), pray 5 times a day, give a regular portion of his goods to charity, fast during the day in the month of Ramadan, and make at least one pilgrimage to Mecca if possible. Additionally saints' days are celebrated and pilgrimages made to shrines.
Divisions: The 2 major sects of Islam are the Sunni (orthodox) and the Shi'ah. The Shi'ah believe in 12 *imams*, perfect teachers, who still guide the faithful from Paradise. Shi'ah practice tends toward the ecstatic, while the Sunni is staid and simple. The Shi'ah sect affirms man's free will; the Sunni is deterministic. The mystic tradition in Islam is Sufism. A Sufi adept believes he has acquired a special inner knowledge direct from Allah.
Location: From the west coast of Africa to the Philipines across a broad band that includes Tanzania, southern USSR and western China, India, Malaysia and Indonesia. Islam has perhaps 100,000 adherents among American blacks.
Beliefs: Strictly monotheistic. God is creator of the universe, omnipotent, just, and merciful. Man is God's highest creation, but limited and sinful. He is misled by Satan, a prideful angel. God gave the *Koran* to Mohammed to guide men to the truth. Those who repent and sincerely submit to God return to a state of sinlessness. In the end, the sinless go to Paradise, a place of physical and spiritual pleasure, and the wicked burn in Hell.

Judaism

Founded: About 1300 BC, reportedly at Mt. Sinai.
Founder: Moses, probably an historical person.
Sacred Texts: Torah, or divine teaching, found particularly in the first 5 books of the Bible; Talmud and Midrash, commentaries on Torah.
Organization: Originally theocratic, Judaism has evolved a congregational polity. The basic institution is the local synagogue, operated by the congregation and led by a rabbi of their choice. Chief Rabbis in France and Great Britain have authority only over those who accept it; in Israel, the 2 Chief Rabbis have civil authority in family law.
Practice: Among the very conservative, prayers accompany almost every action of daily life. Synagogue services center around the Torah reading. The chief annual observances are Passover, celebrating the liberation of the Israelites from Egypt and marked by the ritual Seder meal in the home, and the 10 days from Rosh Hashana (New Year) to Yom Kippur (Day of Atonement), a period of fasting and penitence.
Divisions: Judaism is an unbroken spectrum from ultra-conservative to ultra-liberal. Distinctions depend primarily on the care taken to observe the many prescribed duties and prohibitions in daily life, particularly the dietary and Sabbath regulations, and whether these are seen as binding or optional. The amount of Hebrew used in services distinguishes groups on the liberal end of the spectrum. Hasidism is a pietistic movement which emphasizes joyful devotion and the charismatic power of individual Hasidic leaders.
Location: Almost world-wide, with concentrations in Israel and the U.S.
Beliefs: Strictly monotheistic. God is the creator and absolute ruler of the universe. Men are free to choose to rebel against God's rule. God established a particular relationship with the Hebrew people: by obeying the divine law God gave them they would be a special witness to God's mercy and justice. The emphasis in Judaism is on ethical behavior (and, among the conservative, careful ritual obedience) as the true worship of God.

Major Christian Denominations:

Italics indicate that area which, generally speaking, most

Denomination	Origins	Organization	Authority	Special rites
Baptists	In radical Reformation objections to infant baptism, demands for church-state separation; John Smyth, English Separatist in 1609; Roger Williams, 1638, Providence, R.I.	Congregational, *i.e.*, each local church is autonomous.	Scripture; some Baptists, particularly in the South, interpret the Bible literally.	Baptism, after about age 12, by total immersion; Lord's Supper.
Church of Christ (Disciples)	Among evangelical Presbyterians in Ky. (1804) and Penn. (1809), in distress over Protestant factionalism and decline of fervor. Organized 1832.	Congregational.	*"Where the Scriptures speak, we speak; where the Scriptures are silent, we are silent."*	Adult baptism, Lord's Supper (weekly).
Episcopalians	Henry VIII separated English Catholic Church from Rome, 1534, for political reasons. Protestant Episcopal Church in U.S. founded 1789.	*Bishops, in apostolic succession, are elected by diocesan representatives; part of Anglican Communion, symbolically headed by Archbishop of Canterbury.*	Scripture as interpreted by tradition, esp. *39 Articles* (1563); not dogmatic. Tri-annual convention of bishops, priests, and laymen.	Infant baptism, Holy Communion, others. Sacrament is symbolic, but has real spiritual effect.
Lutherans	Martin Luther in Wittenberg, Germany, 1517, objected to Catholic doctrine of salvation by merit and sale of indulgences; break complete by 1519.	Varies from congregational to episcopal; in U.S. a combination of regional synods and congregational polities is most common.	*Scripture, and tradition as spelled out in Augsburg Confession (1530) and other creeds. These confessions of faith are binding although interpretations vary.*	Infant baptism, Lord's Supper. Christ's true body and blood present "in, with, and under the bread and wine."
Methodists	Rev. John Wesley began movement, 1738, to infuse pietist enthusiasm into Church of England formalism. First U.S. conference, 1773.	*Bishops (not a priestly order, only an office) are elected for life, appoint district superintendants and local ministers.*	Scripture as interpreted by tradition, reason, and personal insight.	Infant baptism, Lord's Supper.
Mormons	In visions of the Angel Moroni by Joseph Smith, 1827, in New York, in which he received a new revelation on golden tablets: *The Book of Mormon.*	Theocratic; all male adults are in priesthood which culminates in Council of 12 Apostles and 1st Presidency (1st President, 2 counselors).	*The Bible, Book of Mormon and other revelations to Smith, and certain pronouncements of the 1st Presidency.*	Adult baptism, laying on of hands (which grants gifts of the Spirit), Lord's Supper. Temple rites: baptism for the dead, marriage for eternity, others.
Orthodox	Original Christian proselytizing in 1st century; broke with Rome, 1054, after centuries of doctrinal disputes and diverging traditions.	Synods of bishops in autonomous, usually national, churches elect a patriarch, archbishop or metropolitan. These men, as a group, are the heads of the church.	Scripture, tradition, and the first 7 church councils up to Nicaea II in 787. Bishops in council have authority in doctrine and policy.	Seven sacraments: infant baptism and anointing, Eucharist (both bread and wine), ordination, penance, anointing of the sick, marriage.
Pentecostal	In Topeka, Kansas (1901), and Los Angeles (1906) in reaction to loss of evangelical fervor among Methodists and other denominations.	Originally a movement, not a formal organization, Pentecostalism now has a variety of organized forms and continues also as a movement.	Scripture, individual charismatic leaders, the teachings of the Holy Spirit.	*Spirit baptism, esp. as shown in "speaking in tongues"; healing and sometimes exorcism; adult baptism, Lord's Supper.*
Presbyterians	In Calvinist Reformation in 1500s; differed with Lutherans over sacraments, church government. John Knox founded Scotch Presbyterian church about 1560.	*Highly structured representational system of ministers and laypersons (presbyters) in local, regional and national bodies. (synods).*	Scripture.	Infant baptism, Lord's Supper; bread and wine symbolize Christ's spiritual presence.
Roman Catholics	Traditionally, by Jesus who named St. Peter the 1st Vicar; historically, in early Christian proselytizing and the conversion of imperial Rome in the 4th century.	Hierarchy with supreme power vested in Pope elected by cardinals. Councils of Bishops advise on matters of doctrine and policy.	*The Pope, when speaking for the whole church in matters of faith and morals, and tradition, which is partly recorded in scripture and expressed in church councils.*	Seven sacraments: baptism, contrition and penance, confirmation, Eucharist, marriage, ordination, and anointing of the sick (unction).
United Church of Christ	*By ecumenical union, 1957, of Congregationalists and Evangelical & Reformed, representing both Calvinist and Lutheran traditions.*	Congregational; a General Synod, representative of all congregations, sets general policy.	Scripture.	Infant baptism, Lord's Supper.

How Do They Differ?

distinguishes that denomination from any other.

Practice	Ethics	Doctrine	Other	Denomination
Worship style varies from staid to evangelistic. Extensive missionary activity.	Usually opposed to alcohol and tobacco; sometimes tends toward a perfectionist ethical standard.	*No creed; true church is of believers only, who are all equal.*	Since no authority can stand between the believer and God, the Baptists are strong supporters of church-state separation.	**Baptists**
Tries to avoid any rite or doctrine not explicitly part of the 1st century church. Some congregations may reject instrumental music.	Some tendency toward perfectionism; increasing interest in social action programs.	Simple New Testament faith; avoids any elaboration not firmly based on Scripture.	Highly tolerant in doctrinal and religious matters; strongly supportive of scholarly education.	**Church of Christ (Disciples)**
Formal, based on *Book of Common Prayer* (1549); services range from austerely simple to highly elaborate.	Tolerant; sometimes permissive; some social action programs.	*Apostles' Creed* is basic; otherwise, considerable variation ranges from rationalist and liberal to acceptance of most Roman Catholic dogma.	Strongly ecumenical, holding talks with all other branches of Christendom.	**Episcopalians**
Relatively simple formal liturgy with emphasis on the sermon.	Generally, conservative in personal and social ethics; doctrine of "2 kingdoms" (worldly and holy) supports conservatism in secular affairs.	Salvation by faith alone through grace. Lutheranism has made major contributions to Protestant theology.	Though still somewhat divided along ethnic lines (German, Swede, etc.), main divisions are between funamentalists and liberals.	**Lutherans**
Worship style varies; usually staid, sometimes evangelistic.	Originally pietist and perfectionist with a tendency to withdraw from secular affairs; now with strong social activist elements.	No distinctive theological development; *25 Articles,* abridged from Church of England's 39, not binding.	In 1968, the United Methodist Church was formed by the union of the major Methodist church and the 1946 union of Evangelical and United Brethren churches.	**Methodists**
Staid service with hymns, sermon. Secret temple ceremonies may be more elaborate. Strong missionary activity.	Temperance; strict tithing. Combine a strong work ethic with communal self-reliance.	God is a material being; he created the universe out of pre-existing matter; all persons can be saved and many will become divine. Most other beliefs are traditionally Christian.	Mormons regard mainline churches as apostate, corrupt. Reorganized Church (founded 1852) rejects most Mormon doctrine and practice except Book of Mormon.	**Mormons**
Elaborate liturgy, usually in the vernacular, though extremely traditional. The liturgy is the essence of Orthodoxy. Veneration of icons.	Tolerant; very little social action; divorce, remarriage permitted in some cases. Priests need not be celibate; bishops are.	Emphasis on Christ's resurrection, rather than crucifixion; the Holy Spirit proceeds from God the Father only.	Orthodox Church in America, orginally under Patriarch of Moscow, was granted autonomy in 1970. Greek Orthodox do not recognize this autonomy.	**Orthodox**
Loosely structured service with rousing hymns and sermons, culminating in spirit baptism.	Usually, emphasis on perfectionism with varying degrees of tolerance.	Simple traditional beliefs, usually Protestant, with emphasis on the immediate presence of God in the Holy Spirit	Once confined to lower-class "holy rollers," Pentecostalism now appears in mainline churches and has established middle-class congregations.	**Pentecostal**
A simple, sober service in which the sermon is central.	Traditionally, a tendency toward strictness with firm church- and self-discipline; otherwise tolerant.	Emphasizes the sovereignty and justice of God; no longer doctrinaire.	While traces of belief in predestination (that God has foreordinated salvation for the "elect") remain, this idea is no longer a central element in Presbyterianism.	**Presbyterians**
Relatively elaborate ritual; wide variety of public and private rites, eg., rosary recitation, processions, novenas.	Theoretically very strict; tolerant in practice on most issues. Divorce and remarriage not accepted. Celibate clergy, except in Eastern rite.	Highly elaborated. Salvation by merit gained through faith. Unusual development of doctrines surrounding Mary. Dogmatic.	Roman Catholicism is presently in a period of relatively rapid change as a result of Vatican Councils I and II.	**Roman Catholics**
Usually simple services with emphasis on the sermon.	Tolerant; some social action emphasis.	Standard Protestant; *Statement of Faith* (1959) is not binding.	The 2 main churches in the 1957 union represented earlier unions with small groups of almost every Protestant denomination.	**United Church of Christ**

Roman Catholic Hierarchy

Source: Apostolic Delegation, Washington, D.C.

Supreme Pontiff

At the head of the Roman Catholic Church is the Supreme Pontiff, Pope John Paul II, Karol Wojtyla, born at Wadowice (Krakow), Poland, May 18, 1920; ordained priest Nov. 1, 1946; promoted to Archbishop of Krakow Jan. 13, 1964; proclaimed Cardinal June 26, 1967; elected pope as successor of Pope John Paul I Oct. 16, 1978; solemn commencement as pope Oct. 22, 1978.

College of Cardinals

Members of the Sacred College of Cardinals are chosen by the Pope to be his chief assistants and advisors in the administration of the church. Among their duties is the election of the Pope when the Holy See becomes vacant. The title of cardinal is a high honor, but it does not represent any increase in the powers of holy orders.

In its present form, the College of Cardinals dates from the 12th century. The first cardinals, from about the 6th century, were deacons and priests of the leading churches of Rome, and bishops of neighboring diocese. The title of cardinal was limited to members of the college in 1567. The number of cardinals was set at 70 in 1586 by Pope Sixtus V. From 1959 Pope John XXIII began to increase the number. The greatest membership of the college was 145 under Pope Paul VI in 1973. However, the number of cardinals eligible to participate in papal elections was limited to 120. There were lay cardinals until 1918, when the Code of Canon Law specified that all cardinals must be priests. Pope John XXIII in 1962 established that all cardinals must be bishops. The first age limits were set in 1971 by Pope Paul VI, who decreed that at age 80 cardinals must retire from curial departments and offices and from participation in papal elections. They continue as members of the college, with all other rights and privileges.

Name	Office	Nationality	Born	Named
Alfrink, Bernard		Dutch	1900	1960
Antonelli, Ferdinando		Italian	1896	1973
Aponte Martinez, Luis	Archbishop of San Juan in Puerto Rico	American	1922	1973
Aramburu, Juan	Archbishop of Buenos Aires	Argentinian	1912	1976
Arns, Paulo	Archbishop of Sao Paulo	Brazilian	1921	1973
Bafile, Corrado		Italian	1903	1976
Baggio, Sebastiano	Prefect of the Sacred Congregation for the Bishops	Italian	1913	1969
Ballestrero, Anastasio A.	Archbishop of Turin	Italian	1913	1979
Baum, William	Prefect of the Sacred Congregation for Catholic Education	American	1926	1976
Benelli, Giovanni	Archbishop of Florence	Italian	1921	1977
Bertoli, Paolo	Chamberlain of the Holy Roman Church	Italian	1908	1969
Brandao Vilela, Avelar	Archbishop of Sao Salvador da Bahia	Brazilian	1912	1973
Caprio, Giuseppe	President of Administration of Patrimony of the Holy See	Italian	1914	1979
Carberry, John		American	1904	1969
Carpino, Francesco		Italian	1905	1967
Carter, Gerald E.	Archbishop of Toronto	Canadian	1912	1979
Casariego, Mario	Archbishop of Guatemala	Guatemalan	1909	1969
Casaroli, Agostino	Secretary of State of His Holiness	Italian	1914	1979
Cè, Marco	Patriarch of Venice	Italian	1925	1979
Ciappi, O.P., Mario Luigi	Pro-Theologian of Pontifical Household	Italian	1909	1977
Civardi, Ernesto		Italian	1906	1979
Colombo, Giovanni		Italian	1902	1965
Confalonieri, Carlo	Dean of the Sacred College	Italian	1893	1958
Cooke, Terence	Archbishop of New York	American	1921	1969
Cooray, Thomas B.		Ceylonese	1901	1965
Cordeiro, Joseph	Archbishop of Karachi	Pakistanian	1918	1973
Corripio Ahumada, Ernesto	Archbishop of Mexico City	Mexican	1919	1979
Darmojuwono, Justinus	Archbishop of Semarang	Indonesian	1914	1967
de Araujo Sales, Eugenio	Archbishop of St. Sebastian of Rio de Janeiro	Brazilian	1920	1969
Dearden, John		American	1907	1969
de Furstenberg, Maximilian		Belgian	1904	1967
Duval, Leon-Etienne	Archbishop of Algiers	Algerian	1903	1965
Ekandem, Dominic	Bishop of Ikot Ekpene	Nigerian	1917	1976
Enrique y Tarancon, Vicente	Archbishop of Madrid	Spanish	1907	1969
Etchegaray, Roger	Archbishop of Marseilles	French	1922	1979
Florit, Ermenegildo		Italian	1901	1965
Freeman, James	Archbishop of Sydney	Australian	1907	1973
Gantin, Bernardin	President, Pontifical Commission "Justitia et Pax"	Benin	1922	1977
Garrone, Gabriel-Marie		French	1901	1967
Gonzalez Martin, Marcelo	Archbishop of Toledo	Spanish	1918	1973
Gouyon, Paul	Archbishop of Rennes	French	1910	1969
Gray, Gordon	Archbishop of St. Andrews and Edinburgh	Scottish	1910	1969
Guyot, Jean		French	1905	1973
Hoffner, Joseph	Archbishop of Cologne	German	1906	1969
Hume, George Basil	Archbishop of Westminster	English	1923	1976
Jubany Arnau, Narciso	Archbishop of Barcelona	Spanish	1913	1973
Kim, Stephan Sou Hwan	Archbishop of Seoul	Korean	1922	1969
Knox, James	President, Pontifical Council for the Family	Australian	1914	1973
König, Franz	Archbishop of Vienna	Austrian	1905	1958
Krol, John	Archbishop of Philadelphia	American	1910	1967

Name	Office	Nationality	Born	Named
Landazuri, Ricketts Juan	Archbishop of Lima	Peruvian	1913	1962
Léger, Paul		Canadian	1904	1953
Lékai, Laszlo	Archbishop of Esztergom	Hungarian	1910	1976
Lorscheider, Aloisio	Archbishop of Fortaleza	Brazilian	1924	1976
Macharski, Franciszek	Archbishop of Cracow	Polish	1927	1979
Malula, Joseph	Archbishop of Kinshasa	Congolese	1917	1969
Manning, Timothy	Archbishop of Los Angeles	American	1909	1973
Marella, Paolo		Italian	1895	1959
Marty, Francois		French	1904	1969
Maurer, Jose	Archbishop of Sucre	Bolivian	1900	1967
McCann, Owen	Archbishop of Cape Town	S. African	1907	1965
Medeiros, Humberto	Archbishop of Boston	American	1915	1973
Miranda y Gomez, Miguel		Mexican	1895	1969
Motta, Carlos Carmelo de Vasconcellos	Archbishop of Aparecida	Brazilian	1890	1946
Mozzoni, Umberto		Italian	1904	1973
Munoz Duque, Anibal	Archbishop of Bogota	Colombian	1908	1973
Munoz Vega, Paolo	Archbishop of Quito	Ecuadorian	1903	1969
Nasalli Rocca di Corneliano, Mario		Italian	1903	1969
Nsubuga, Emmanuel	Archbishop of Kampala	Ugandan	1914	1976
O'Boyle, Patrick		American	1896	1967
Oddi, Silvio	Prefect of Sacred Congregation for the Clergy	Italian	1910	1969
O'Fiaich, Tomás	Archbishop of Armagh, Primate of all Ireland	Irish	1923	1979
Otunga, Maurice	Archbishop of Nairobi	Kenyan	1923	1973
Palazzini, Pietro	Prefect of the Sacred Congregation for the Causes of Saints	Italian	1912	1973
Pappalardo, Salvatore	Archbishop of Palermo	Italian	1918	1973
Parecattil, Joseph	Archbishop of Ernakulam	Indian	1912	1969
Parente, Pietro		Italian	1891	1967
Paupini, Giuseppe	Grand Penitentiary	Italian	1907	1969
Pellegrino, Michele		Italian	1903	1967
Philippe, Paul		French	1905	1973
Picachy, Lawrence	Archbishop of Calcutta	Indian	1916	1976
Pironio, Eduardo	Prefect of the Sacred Congregation for Religious and for Secular Institutes	Argentinian	1920	1976
Poletti, Ugo	Vicar General of His Holiness for the City of Rome	Italian	1914	1973
Poma, Antonio	Archbishop of Bologna	Italian	1910	1969
Primatesta, Raul Francisco	Archbishop of Cordoba	Argentinian	1919	1973
Quintero, Jose	Archbishop of Caracas	Venezuelan	1902	1961
Ratzinger, Joseph	Prefect of Sacred Congregation for the Doctrine of the Faith	German	1927	1977
Razafimahatratra, Victor	Archbishop of Tananarive	Madagascan	1921	1976
Ribeiro, Antonio	Patriarch of Lisbon	Portugese	1928	1973
Righi-Lambertini, Egano		Italian	1906	1979
Rosales, Julio	Archbishop of Cebu	Filipino	1906	1969
Rossi, Agnelo	Prefect of the Sacred Congregation for the Evangelization of Peoples	Brazilian	1913	1965
Rossi, Opilio	President of the Council for the Laity and the Committee for the Family	Italian	1910	1976
Rubin, Wladyslaw	Prefect of the Sacred Congregation for the Oriental Churches	Polish	1917	1979
Rugambwa, Laurean	Archbishop of Dar-es-Salaam	Tanzanian	1912	1960
Salazar Lopez, Jose	Archbishop of Guadalajara	Mexican	1910	1973
Samore, Antonio	Librarian and Archivist of the Holy Roman Church	Italian	1905	1967
Satowaki, Joseph A.	Archbishop of Nagasaki	Japanese	1904	1979
Schroeffer, Joseph		German	1903	1976
Sensi, Giuseppe		Italian	1907	1976
Shehan, Lawrence		American	1898	1965
Sidarouss, Stephanos	Coptic Patriarch of Alexandria	Egyptian	1904	1965
Silva Henriquez, Raul	Archbishop of Santiago	Chilean	1907	1962
Sin, Jaime	Archbishop of Manila	Filipino	1928	1976
Siri, Giuseppe	Archbishop of Genoa	Italian	1906	1953
Slipyj, Josyf	Ukrainian Archbishop of Lwow	Ukrainian	1892	1965
Suenens, Leo		Belgian	1904	1962
Taofinu'u, Pio	Bishop of Samoa and Tokelau	Samoan	1923	1973
Thiandoum, Hyacinthe	Archbishop of Dakar	Senegalese	1921	1976
Tomasek, Frantisek	Archbishop of Prague	Czechoslovakian	1899	1977
Trinh Van Can, Joseph-Marie	Archbishop of Hanoi	Vietnamese	1921	1979
Ursi, Corrado	Archbishop of Naples	Italian	1908	1967
Vilela, Avelar	Archbishop of Sao Salvador	Brazilian	1912	1973
Volk, Hermann	Bishop of Mainz	German	1903	1973
Willebrands, John	President of Secretariat for the Union of Christians Archbishop of Utrecht	Dutch	1909	1969
Zoungrana, Paul	Archbishop of Ouagadougou	Upper Voltan	1917	1965

NOTED PERSONALITIES

Widely Known Americans of the Present

Statesmen, authors, military men, and other prominent persons not listed in other categories.

Name (Birthplace)	Birthdate
Abel, I. W. (Magnolia, Oh.)	8/11/08
Abernathy, Ralph (Linden, Ala.)	3/11/26
Abzug, Bella (New York, N.Y.)	7/24/20
Agnew, Spiro (Baltimore, Md.)	11/9/18
Albert, Carl (McAlester, Okla.)	5/10/08
Aldrin, Edwin E. Jr. "Buzz" (Glen Ridge, N.J.)	1/20/30
Alsop, Joseph W. Jr. (Avon, Conn.)	10/11/10
Anderson, Jack (Long Beach, Cal.)	10/19/22
Armstrong, Neil (Wapakoneta, Oh.)	8/5/30
Bailey, F. Lee (Waltham, Mass.)	6/10/33
Baker, Howard (Huntsville, Tenn.)	11/15/25
Baker, James A. (Houston, Tex.)	4/28/30
Baker, Russell (Loudoun Co., Va.)	8/14/25
Ball, George (Des Moines, Ia.)	12/21/09
Bellamy, Carol (Plainfield, N.J.)	1942
Belli, Melvin (Sonora, Cal.)	7/29/07
Bentsen, Lloyd (Mission, Tex.)	2/11/21
Blackmun, Harry (Nashville, Ill.)	11/12/08
Bok, Derek (Ardmore, Pa.)	3/22/30
Bombeck, Erma (Dauton, Oh.)	2/21/27
Bond, Julian (Nashville, Tenn.)	1/14/40
Borman, Frank (Gary, Ind.)	3/14/28
Bradley, Bill (Crystal City, Mo.)	7/28/43
Bradley, Ed (Philadelphia, Pa.)	6/22/41
Bradley, Thomas (Calvert, Tex.)	12/29/17
Brady, James (Centralia, Ill.)	8/29/40
Brennan, William J. (Newark, N.J.)	4/25/06
Breslin, Jimmy (Jamaica, N.Y.)	10/17/30
Brewster, Kingman (Longmeadow, Mass.)	6/17/19
Brinkley, David (Wilmington, N.C.)	7/10/20
Brock, William (Chattanooga, Tenn.)	11/23/30
Brokaw, Tom (Webster, S. Dak.)	2/6/40
Brown, Edmund G. Jr. (San Francisco, Cal.)	4/7/38
Brown, Harold (New York, N.Y.)	9/19/27
Brown, Helen Gurley (Green Forest, Ark.)	2/18/22
Brzezinski, Zbigniew (Warsaw, Poland)	3/28/28
Buchwald, Art (Mt. Vernon, N.Y.)	10/20/25
Buckley, William F. (New York, N.Y.)	11/24/25
Burger, Warren (St. Paul, Minn.)	9/17/07
Burns, Arthur F. (Stanislau, Aust.)	4/27/04
Burton, Phillip (Cincinnati, Oh.)	6/1/26
Bush, George (Milton, Mass.)	6/12/24
Byrd, Robert (N. Wilkesboro, N.C.)	11/20/17
Byrne, Jane M. (Chicago, Ill.)	5/24/34
Carey, Hugh (Brooklyn, N.Y.)	4/11/19
Carter, Jimmy (Plains, Ga.)	10/1/24
Carter, Lillian (Richland, Ga.)	8/15/98
Carter, Rosalynn (Plains, Ga.)	8/18/27
Chancellor, John (Chicago, Ill.)	7/14/27
Chavez, Cesar (Yuma, Ariz.)	3/31/27
Child, Julia (Pasadena, Cal.)	8/15/12
Chisholm, Shirley (Brooklyn, N.Y.)	11/30/24
Claiborne, Craig (Sunflower, Miss.)	9/4/20
Commager, Henry Steele (Pittsburgh, Pa.)	10/25/02
Commoner, Barry (Brooklyn, N.Y.)	5/28/17
Connally, John B. (Floresville, Tex.)	2/28/17
Cooke, Terence Cardinal (New York, N.Y.)	3/1/21
Cooney, Joan Ganz (Phoenix, Ariz.)	10/30/29
Cosell, Howard (Winston-Salem, N.C.)	1920
Cousins, Norman (Union Hill, N.J.)	6/24/12
Cox, Archibald (Plainfield, N.J.)	5/17/12
Cranston, Alan (Palo Alto, Cal.)	6/19/14
Crippen, Robert L. (Beaumont, Tex.)	9/11/37
Cronkite, Walter (St. Joseph, Mo.)	11/4/16
Curtis, Charlotte (Chicago, Ill.)	1929
Davis, Angela (Birmingham, Ala.)	1/26/44
Deaver, Michael K. (Bakersfield, Cal.)	4/11/38
Dole, Elizabeth (Salisbury, N.C.)	7/29/36
Dole, Robert (Russell, Kan.)	7/22/23
Donaldson, Sam (El Paso, Tex.)	3/11/34
Doolittle, James H. (Alameda, Cal.)	12/14/96
Eagleton, Thomas (St. Louis, Mo.)	9/4/29
Eastland, James O. (Doddsville, Miss.)	11/28/04
Ehrlichman, John (Tacoma, Wash.)	3/20/25
Eisenhower, Milton S. (Abilene, Kan.)	9/15/99
Ervin, Sam (Morganton, N.C.)	9/27/96
Falwell, Jerry (Lynchburg, Va.)	8/11/33
Farmer, James (Marshall, Tex.)	1/12/20
Fenwick, Millicent (New York, N.Y.)	2/25/10
Fitzsimmons, Frank (Jeannette, Pa.)	4/7/08
Flynt, Larry (Salyersville, Ky.)	11/1/42
Foley, Thomas S. (Spokane, Wash.)	3/6/29
Fong, Hiram (Honolulu, Ha.)	10/1/07
Ford, Elizabeth (Mrs. Gerald) (Chicago, Ill.)	4/8/18
Ford, Gerald R. (Omaha, Neb.)	7/14/13
Fraser, Douglas A. (Glasgow, Scotland)	12/18/16
Friedan, Betty (Peoria, Ill.)	2/4/21
Friedman, Milton (Brooklyn, N.Y.)	7/31/12
Fulbright, J. William (Sumner, Mo.)	4/9/05
Furness, Betty (New York, N.Y.)	1/3/16
Galbraith, John Kenneth (Ontario, Can.)	10/15/08
Gardner, John (Los Angeles, Cal.)	10/8/12
Gifford, Frank (Santa Monica, Cal.)	8/16/30
Ginsberg, Allen (Paterson, N.J.)	6/3/21
Glenn, John (Cambridge, Oh.)	7/18/21
Goheen, Robert F. (Vengurla, India)	8/15/19
Goldberg, Arthur J. (Chicago, Ill.)	8/8/08
Goldwater, Barry M. (Phoenix, Ariz.)	1/1/09
Graham, Billy (Charlotte, N.C.)	11/7/18
Graham, Katharine (New York, N.Y.)	6/16/17
Greenspan, Alan (New York, N.Y.)	3/6/26
Gumble, Bryant (New Orleans, La.)	9/29/48
Haig, Alexander (Philadelphia, Pa.)	12/2/24
Harriman, W. Averell (New York, N.Y.)	11/15/91
Harris, Patricia Roberts (Mattoon, Ill.)	5/31/24
Hart, Gary (Ottawa, Kan.)	11/28/37
Hartman, David (Pawtucket, R.I.)	5/19/35
Hatfield, Mark O. (Dallas, Ore.)	7/12/22
Hefner, Hugh (Chicago, Ill.)	4/9/26
Heller, Walter (Buffalo, N.Y.)	8/27/15
Hershey, Lenore (New York, N.Y.)	3/20/20
Hesburgh, Theodore (Syracuse, N.Y.)	5/25/17
Hiss, Alger (Baltimore, Md.)	11/11/04
Hollings, Ernest (Charleston, S.C.)	1/1/22
Iacocca, Lee A. (Allentown, Pa.)	10/15/24
Inouye, Daniel (Honolulu, Ha.)	9/7/24
Jackson, Henry (Everett, Wash.)	5/31/12
Jackson, Jesse (Greenville, N.C.)	10/8/41
Javits, Jacob K. (New York, N.Y.)	5/18/04
Jennings, Peter (Toronto, Ont.)	8/29/38
Johnson, Lady Bird (Mrs. Lyndon) (Karnack, Tex.)	12/22/12
Jordan, Barbara (Houston, Tex.)	2/21/36
Jordan, Vernon (Atlanta, Ga.)	8/15/35
Kahn, Alfred E. (Paterson, N.J.)	10/17/17
Kemp, Jack (Los Angeles, Cal.)	7/13/35
Kennedy, Edward M. (Brookline, Mass.)	2/22/32
Kennedy, Rose (Mrs. Joseph P.) (Boston, Mass.)	7/22/90
Kerr, Walter (Evanston, Ill.)	7/8/13
King, Coretta (Mrs. Martin L.) (Marion, Ala.)	4/27/27
Kirkland, Lane (Camden, S.C.)	3/12/22
Kissinger, Henry (Fuerth, Germany)	5/27/23
Koch, Edward I. (New York, N.Y.)	12/12/24
Koppel, Ted (Lancashire, Eng.)	2/8/40
Landers, Ann (Sioux City, Ia.)	7/4/18
Landon, Alfred (West Middlesex, Pa.)	9/9/87
Laxalt, Paul (Reno, Nev.)	8/2/22
LeMay, Curtis (Ohio)	11/15/06
Lemnitzer, Lyman L. (Honesdale, Pa.)	8/29/99
Lindbergh, Anne Morrow (Englewood, N.J.)	1906
Lipshutz, Robert J. (Atlanta, Ga.)	12/27/21
Lodge, Henry Cabot (Nahant, Mass.)	7/5/02
Long, Russell B. (Shreveport, La.)	11/3/18
Luce, Clare Boothe (New York, N.Y.)	4/10/03
Maddox, Lester (Atlanta, Ga.)	9/30/15
Mansfield, Mike (New York, N.Y.)	3/16/03
Marshall, Thurgood (Baltimore, Md.)	7/2/08
Mayer, Martin (New York, N.Y.)	1/14/28
McCarthy, Eugene (Watkins, Minn.)	3/29/16
McCloskey, Paul (San Bernardino, Cal.)	9/29/27
McGovern, George (Avon, S.D.)	7/19/22
McNamara, Robert S. (San Francisco, Cal.)	6/9/16
Meese, Edwin (Oakland, Cal.)	12/2/31
Meredith, Don (Mt. Vernon, Tex.)	4/10/38

Name, (Birthplace)	Birthdate
Miller, G. William (Sapulpa, Okla.)	3/9/25
Milliken, William (Traverse City, Mich.)	3/26/22
Mitchell, John (Detroit, Mich.)	9/15/13
Mondale, Walter (Ceylon, Minn.)	1/5/28
Morgan, Marabel (Crestline, Oh.)	6/25/37
Moynihan, Daniel P. (Tulsa, Okla.)	3/16/27
Mudd, Roger (Washington, D.C.)	2/9/28
Muskie, Edmund (Rumford, Me.)	3/28/14
Nader, Ralph (Winsted, Conn.)	2/27/34
Nixon, Julie (Mrs. David Eisenhower) (Wash., D.C.)	7/5/48
Nixon, Pat (Mrs. Richard) (Ely, Nev.)	3/16/12
Nixon, Richard (Yorba Linda, Cal.)	1/9/13
Nixon, Tricia (Mrs. Edward Cox) (Cal.)	2/21/46
Nizer, Louis (London, England)	2/6/02
Norton, Eleanor Holmes (Washington, D.C.)	6/13/37
Nunn, Sam (Perry, Ga.)	9/8/38
O'Brien, Lawrence F. (Springfield, Mass.)	7/7/17
O'Connor, Sandra Day (nr. Duncan, Ariz.)	3/26/30
Onassis, Jacqueline (Southampton, N.Y.)	7/28/29
O'Neill, Thomas P. (Cambridge, Mass.)	12/9/12
Paley, William S. (Chicago, Ill.)	9/28/01
Pauley, Jane (Indianapolis, Ind.)	10/31/50
Pauling, Linus (Portland, Ore.)	2/28/01
Peale, Norman Vincent (Bowersville, Oh.)	5/31/98
Percy, Charles H. (Pensacola, Fla.)	9/27/19
Pierce, Samuel R. (Glen Cove, N.Y.)	9/8/22
Porter, Sylvia (Patchogue, N.Y.)	6/18/13
Powell, Lewis F. (Suffolk, Va.)	9/19/07
Proxmire, William (Lake Forest, Ill.)	1/11/15
Rather, Dan (Wharton, Tex.)	10/31/31
Reagan, Nancy (New York, N.Y.)	7/6/23
Reagan, Ronald (Tampico, Ill.)	2/6/11
Reasoner, Harry (Dakota City, Ia.)	4/17/23
Regan, Donald T. (Cambridge, Mass.)	12/21/18
Rehnquist, William (Milwaukee, Wis.)	10/1/24
Reston, James (Clydebank, Scotland)	11/3/09
Reynolds, Frank (East Chicago, Ind.)	11/29/23
Rhodes, John (Council Grove, Kan.)	9/18/16
Ribicoff, Abe (New Britain, Conn.)	4/9/10
Richardson, Elliot L. (Boston, Mass.)	7/20/20
Rickover, Hyman (Makowa, Poland)	1/27/00
Roberts, Oral (nr. Ada, Okla.)	1/24/18
Robinson, Max (Richmond, Va.)	5/1/39
Rockefeller, David (New York, N.Y.)	6/12/15
Rockefeller, John D. 4th "Jay" (New York, N.Y.)	6/18/37
Rockefeller, Laurance S. (New York, N.Y.)	5/26/10
Rodino, Peter (Newark, N.J.)	6/7/09
Romney, George W. (Chihuahua, Mexico)	7/8/07
Rooney, Andy (Albany, N.Y.)	1/14/19
Roosevelt, Elliot (New York, N.Y.)	9/23/10
Roosevelt, Franklin D. Jr. (Canada)	8/17/14
Rusk, Dean (Cherokee Co., Ga.)	2/9/09
Safer, Morley (Toronto, Ontario)	11/8/31
Safire, William (New York, N.Y.)	12/17/29
Sagan, Carl (New York, N.Y.)	11/9/34
Salk, Lee (New York, N.Y.)	12/27/26
Salk, Jonas (New York, N.Y.)	10/28/14
Samuelson, Paul A. (Gary, Ind.)	5/15/15
Savitch, Jessica (Kennett Sq., Pa.)	2/1/48
Sawyer, Diane (Glasgow, Ky.)	12/22/45
Schlafly, Phyllis (St. Louis, Mo.)	8/15/24
Schlesinger, Arthur Jr. (Columbus, Oh.)	10/15/17
Schlesinger, James R. (New York, N.Y.)	2/15/29
Schultze, Charles (Alexandria, Va.)	12/22/24
Schweiker, Richard S. (Norristown, Pa.)	1/1/26

Name (Birthplace)	Birthdate
Seaborg, Glenn T. (Ishpeming, Mich.)	4/19/12
Sevareid, Eric (Velva, N.D.)	11/26/12
Shanker, Albert (New York, N.Y.)	9/14/28
Sheehy, Gail (Mamaroneck, N.Y.)	11/27/37
Shirer, William L. (Chicago, Ill.)	2/23/04
Shriver, R. Sargent (Westminster, Md.)	11/9/15
Silverstein, Shel (Chicago, Ill.)	1932
Simon, William (Paterson, N.J.)	1927
Sirica, John J. (Waterbury, Conn.)	3/19/04
Smeal, Eleanor (Ashtabula, Oh.)	7/30/39
Smith, Howard K. (Ferriday, La.)	5/12/14
Smith, Margaret Chase (Skowhegan, Me.)	12/14/97
Smith, William French (Wilton, N.H.)	8/26/17
Snyder, Tom (Milwaukee, Wisc.)	5/12/36
Spock, Benjamin (New Haven, Conn.)	5/2/03
Stahl, Leslie (Lynn, Mass.)	12/16/41
Stassen, Harold (West St. Paul, Minn.)	4/13/07
Steinbrenner, George (Rocky River, Oh.)	7/4/30
Steinem, Gloria (Toledo, Oh.)	3/25/34
Stennis, John (Kamper City, Miss.)	8/3/01
Stevens, John Paul (Chicago, Ill.)	4/20/20
Stockman, David (Ft. Hood, Tex.)	11/10/46
Strauss, Robert S. (Lockhart, Tex.)	10/19/18
Sulzberger, Arthur Ochs (New York, N.Y.)	2/5/26
Symington, Stuart (Amherst, Mass.)	6/26/01
Taft, Robert Jr. (Cincinnati, Oh.)	2/26/17
Taylor, Maxwell D. (Keytesville, Mo.)	8/26/01
Thomas, Helen (Winchester, Ky.)	8/4/20
Thompson, James R. (Chicago, Ill.)	5/8/36
Thurmond, J. Strom (Edgefield, S.C.)	12/5/02
Tower, John (Houston, Tex.)	9/29/25
Truman, Mrs. Harry (Independence, Mo.)	2/13/85
Truman, Margaret (Mrs. Clifton Daniel) (Independence, Mo.)	2/17/24
Tuchman, Barbara (New York, N.Y.)	1/30/12
Turner, Ted (Cincinnati, Oh.)	1938
Udall, Morris K. (St. Johns, Ariz.)	6/15/22
Ullman, Al (Great Falls, Mont.)	3/9/14
Van Buren, Abigail (Sioux City, Ia.)	7/4/18
Vance, Cyrus R. (Clarksburg, W. Va.)	3/27/17
Vanderbilt, Alfred G. (London, England)	9/22/12
Veeck, Bill (Chicago, Ill.)	2/9/14
Volcker, Paul A. (Cape May, N.J.)	9/5/27
Wallace, George (Clio, Ala.)	8/25/19
Wallace, Mike (Brookline, Mass.)	5/9/18
Walters, Barbara (Boston, Mass.)	9/25/31
Washington, Walter E. (Dawson, Ga.)	4/15/15
Watt, James G. (Lusk., Wyo.)	1/31/38
Webster, William H. (St. Louis, Mo.)	3/6/24
Weicker, Lowell (Paris, France)	5/16/31
Weidenbaum, Murray (Bronx, N.Y.)	2/10/27
Weinberger, Caspar (San Francisco, Cal.)	8/18/17
Westmoreland, William (Spartanburg, S.C.)	3/26/14
White, Byron R. (Ft. Collins, Col.)	6/8/17
White, E.B. (Mt. Vernon, N.Y.)	7/11/99
White, Theodore (Boston, Mass.)	5/6/15
Wicker, Tom (Hamlet, N.C.)	6/18/26
Williams, Edward Bennett (Hartford, Conn.)	5/31/20
Wolfe, Tom (Richmond, Va.)	3/2/31
Woodcock, Leonard (Providence, R.I.)	2/15/11
Woodruff, Judy (Tulsa, Okla.)	11/20/46
Wright, James C. Jr. (Ft. Worth, Tex.)	12/22/22
Young, Andrew (New Orleans, La.)	3/12/32
Young, Coleman (Tuscaloosa, Ala.)	5/24/18
Young, John W. (San Francisco, Cal.)	9/24/30
Zumwalt, Elmo (San Francisco, Cal.)	11/29/20

Noted Black Americans

Names of black athletes and entertainers are not included here as they are listed elsewhere in The World Almanac.

The Rev. Dr. Ralph David Abernathy, b. 1926, organizer, 1957, and president, 1968, of the Southern Christian Leadership Conference.

Crispus Attucks, c. 1723-1770, agitator led group that precipitated the "Boston Massacre," Mar. 5, 1770.

James Baldwin, b. 1924, author, playwright; *The Fire Next Time, Blues for Mister Charlie, Just Above My Head.*

Benjamin Banneker, 1731-1806, inventor, astronomer, mathematician, and gazeteer; served on commission that surveyed and laid out Washington, D. C.

Imamu Amiri Baraka, b. LeRoi Jones, 1934, poet, playwright.

James P. Beckwourth, 1798-c. 1867, western fur-trader, scout, after whom Beckwourth Pass in northern California is named.

Dr. Mary McCleod Bethune, 1875-1955, adviser to presidents F. D. Roosevelt and Truman; division administrator, National Youth Administration, 1935; founder, president of Bethune-Cookman College.

Henry Blair, 19th century, obtained patents (believed the first issued to a black) for a corn-planter, 1834, and for a cotton-planter, 1836.

Julian Bond, b. 1940, civil rights leader first elected to the Georgia state legislature, 1965; helped found Student Nonviolent Coordinating Committee.

Edward Bouchet, 1852-1918, first black to earn a Ph.D., Yale, 1876, at a U. S. university; first black elected to Phi Beta Kappa.

Thomas Bradley, b. 1917, elected mayor of Los Angeles, 1973.
Andrew F. Brimmer, b. 1926, first black member, 1966, Federal Reserve Board.
Edward W. Brooke, b. 1919, attorney general, 1962, of Massachusetts; first black elected to U. S. Senate, 1967, since 19th century Reconstruction.
Gwendolyn Brooks, b. 1917, poet, novelist; first black to win a Pulitzer Prize, 1950, for *Annie Allen.*
William Wells Brown, 1815-1884, novelist, dramatist; first American black to publish a novel.
Dr. Ralph Bunche, 1904-1971, first black to win the Nobel Peace Prize, 1950; undersecretary of the UN, 1950.
George E. Carruthers, b. 1940, physicist developed the Apollo 16 lunar surface ultraviolet camera/spectograph.
George Washington Carver, 1861-1943, botanist, chemurgist, and educator; his extensive experiments in soil building and plant diseases revolutionized the economy of the South.
Charles Waddell Chestnutt, 1858-1932, author known primarily for his short stories, including *The Conjure Woman.*
Shirley Chisholm, b. 1924, first black woman elected to House of Representatives, Brooklyn, N. Y., 1968.
Countee Cullen, 1903-1946, poet; won many literary prizes.
Lt. Gen. Benjamin O. Davis Jr. b. 1912, West Point, 1936, first black Air Force general, 1954.
Brig. Gen. Benjamin O. Davis Sr., 1877-1970, first black general, 1940, in U. S. Army.
William L. Dawson, 1886-1970, Illinois congressman, first black chairman of a major House of Representatives committee.
Isaiah Dorman, 19th century, U. S. Army interpreter, killed with Custer, 1876, at Battle of the Little Big Horn.
Aaron Douglas, 1900-1979, painter; called father of black American art.
Frederick Douglass, 1817-1895, author, editor, orator, diplomat; edited the abolitionist weekly, The North Star, in Rochester, N. Y.; U.S. minister and counsul general to Haiti.
Dr. Charles Richard Drew, 1904-1950, pioneer in development of blood banks; director of American Red Cross blood donor project in World War II.
William Edward Burghardt Du Bois, 1868-1963, historian, sociologist; a founder of the National Association for the Advancement of Colored People (NAACP), 1909, and founder of its magazine The Crisis; author, *The Souls of Black Folk.*
Paul Laurence Dunbar, 1872-1906, poet, novelist; won fame with *Lyrics of Lowly Life,* 1896.
Jean Baptiste Point du Sable, c. 1750-1818, pioneer trader and first settler of Chicago, 1779.
Ralph Ellison, b. 1914, novelist, winner of 1952 National Book Award, for *Invisible Man.*
Estevanico, explorer led Spanish expedition of 1538 into the American Southwest.
James Farmer, b. 1920, a founder of the Congress of Racial Equality, 1942; asst. secretary, Dept. of HEW, 1969.
Henry O. Flipper, 1856-1940, first black to graduate, 1877, from West Point.
Charles Fuller, b. 1939, Pulitzer Prize-winning playwright; *A Soldier's Play.*
Marcus Garvey, 1887-1940, founded Universal Negro Improvement Assn., 1911.
Kenneth Gibson, b. 1932, elected Newark, N.J., mayor, 1970.
Charles Gordone, b. 1925, won 1970 Pulitzer Prize in Drama, with *No Place to Be Somebody.*
Vice Adm. Samuel L. Gravely Jr. b. 1922, first black admiral, 1971, served in World War II, Korea, and Vietnam; commander, Third Fleet.
Alex Haley, b. 1921, Pulitzer Prize-winning author; *Roots, The Autobiography of Malcolm X.*
Jupiter Hammon, c. 1720-1800, poet; the first black American to have his works published, 1761.
Lorraine Hansberry, 1930-1965, playwright; won N. Y. Drama Critics Circle Award, 1959, with *Raisin in the Sun.*
Patricia Roberts Harris, b. 1924, U. S. ambassador to Luxembourg, 1965-67, secretary; Dept. of HUD, 1977-1979, Dept. of H.H.S., 1979-1981.
William H. Hastie, 1904-1976 first black federal judge, appointed 1937; governor of Virgin Islands, 1946-49; judge, U.S. Circuit Court of Appeals, 1949.
Matthew A. Henson, 1866-1955, member of Peary's 1909 expedition to the North Pole; placed U.S. flag at the Pole.
Dr. William A. Hinton, 1883-1959, developed the Hinton and Davies-Hinton tests for detection of syphilis; first black professor, 1949, at Harvard Medical School.
Benjamin L. Hooks, b. 1925, first black member, 1972-1979, Federal Communications Comm.; exec. dir., 1977, NAACP.
Langston Hughes, 1902-1967, poet; story, song lyric author.
The Rev. Jesse Jackson, b. 1941, national director, Operation Bread Basket, and major community leader in Chicago.
Maynard Jackson, b. 1938, elected mayor of Atlanta, 1973.
Gen. Daniel James Jr. 1920-1978, first black 4-star general, 1975; Commander, North American Air Defense Command.
Pvt. Henry Johnson, 1897-1929, the first American decorated by France in World War I with the Croix de Guerre.
James Weldon Johnson, 1871-1938, poet, lyricist, novelist; first black admitted to Florida bar; U.S. consul in Venezuela and Nicaragua.
Barbara Jordan, b. 1936, former congresswoman from Texas; member, House Judiciary Committee.
Vernon E. Jordan, b. 1935, exec. dir. Natl. Urban League, 1972.
Ernest E. Just, 1883-1941, marine biologist, studied egg development; author, *Biology of Cell Surfaces,* 1941.
The Rev. Dr. Martin Luther King Jr., 1929-1968, led 382-day, Montgomery, Ala., boycott which brought 1956 U.S. Supreme Court decision holding segregation on buses unconstitutional; founder, president of the Southern Christian Leadership Conference, 1957; won Nobel Peace Prize, 1964.
Lewis H. Latimer, 1848-1928, associate of Edison; supervised installation of first electric street lighting in N.Y.C.
Malcolm X, 1925-1965, leading spokesman for black pride, founded, 1963, Organization of Afro-American Unity.
Thurgood Marshall, b. 1908, first black U.S. solicitor general 1965; first black justice of the U. S. Supreme Court, 1967; as a lawyer led the legal battery that won the historic decision from the Supreme Court declaring racial segregation of public schools unconstitutional, 1954.
Jan Matzeliger, 1852-1889, invented lasting machine, patented 1883, which revolutionized the shoe industry.
Wade H. McCree Jr., b. 1920, solicitor general of the U.S.
Donald E. McHenry, b. 1936, U.S. ambassador to the United Nations, 1979-1981.
Dorie Miller, 1919-1943, Navy hero of Pearl Harbor attack; awarded the Navy Cross.
Ernest N. Morial, b. 1929, elected first black mayor of New Orleans, 1977.
Willard Motley, 1912-1965, novelist; *Knock on Any Door.*
Elijah Muhammad, 1897-1975, founded Black Muslims, 1931.
Pedro Alonzo Nino, navigator of the Nina, one of Columbus' 3 ships on his first voyage of discovery to the New World, 1492.
Adam Clayton Powell, 1908-1972, early civil rights leader, congressman, 1945-1969; chairman, House Committee on Education and Labor, 1960-1967.
Joseph H. Rainey, 1832-1887, first black elected to House of Representatives, 1869, from South Carolina.
A. Philip Randolph, 1889-1979, organized the Brotherhood of Sleeping Car Porters, 1925; organizer of 1941 and 1963 March on Washington movements; vice president, AFL-CIO.
Charles Rangel, b. 1930, congressman from N.Y.C., 1970; chairman, Congressional Black Caucus.
Hiram R. Revels, 1822-1901, first black U.S. senator, elected in Mississippi, served 1870-1871.
Wilson C. Riles, b. 1917, elected, 1970, California State Superintendent of Public Instruction.
Norbert Rillieux, 1806-1894; invented a vacuum pan evaporator, 1846, revolutionizing the sugar-refining industry.
Carl T. Rowan, b. 1925, prize-winning journalist; director of the U.S. Information Agency, 1964, the first black to sit on the National Security Council; U. S. ambassador to Finland, 1963.
John B. Russwurm, 1799-1851, with **Samuel E. Cornish,** 1793-1858, founded, 1827, the nation's first black newspaper, Freedom's Journal, in N.Y.C.
Bayard Rustin, b. 1910, organizer of the 1963 March on Washington; executive director, A. Philip Randolph Institute.
Peter Salem, at the Battle of Bunker Hill, June 17, 1775, shot and killed British commander Maj. John Pitcairn.
Ntozake Shange, b. Paulette Williams, 1948, playwright, *For Colored Girls Who Have Considered Suicide/When the Rainbow is Enuf.*
Bishop Stephen Spottswood, 1897-1974, board chairman of NAACP from 1966.
Willard Townsend, 1895-1957, organized the United Transport Service Employees, 1935 (redcaps, etc.); vice pres. AFL-CIO.
Sojourner Truth, 1797-1883, born Isabella Baumfree; preacher, abolitonist; raised funds for Union in Civil War; worked for black educational opportunities.
Harriet Tubman, 1823-1913, Underground Railroad conductor served as nurse and spy for Union Army in the Civil War.
Nat Turner, 1800-1831, leader of the most significant of over 200 slave revolts in U.S. history, in Southampton, Va.; he and 16 others were hanged.
Booker T. Washington, 1856-1915, founder, 1881, and first president of Tuskegee Institute; author, *Up From Slavery.*
Dr. Robert C. Weaver, b. 1907, first black member of the U.S. Cabinet, secretary, Dept. of HUD, 1966.
Phillis Wheatley, c. 1753-1784, poet; 2d American woman and first black woman to have her works published, 1770.
Walter White, 1893-1955, exec. secretary, NAACP, 1931-1955.
Roy Wilkins, 1901-1981, exec. director, NAACP, 1955-1977.
Dr. Daniel Hale Williams, 1858-1931, performed one of first 2 open-heart operations, 1893; founded Provident, Chicago's

first Negro hospital; first black elected a fellow of the American College of Surgeons.

Granville T. Woods, 1856-1910, invented the third-rail system now used in subways, a complex railway telegraph device that helped reduce train accidents, and an automatic air brake.

Dr. Carter G. Woodson, 1875-1950, historian; founded Assn. for the Study of Negro Life and History, 1915, and Journal of Negro History, 1916.

Richard Wright, 1908-1960, novelist; *Native Son, Black Boy.*

Frank Yerby, b. 1916, most successful of American black novelists; *The Foxes of Harrow, Vixen.*

Andrew Young, b. 1932, civil rights leader, congressman from Georgia, U.S. ambassador to the United Nations, 1977-79.

Whitney M. Young Jr., 1921-1971, exec. director, 1961, National Urban League; author, lecturer, newspaper columnist.

About 5,000 blacks served in the Continental Army during the **American Revolution,** mostly in integrated units, some in all-black combat units. Some 200,000 blacks served in the Union Army during the **Civil War;** 38,000 gave their lives; 22 won the Medal of Honor, the nation's highest award. Of 367,000 blacks in the armed forces during **World War I,** 100,000 served in France. More than 1,000,000 blacks served in the armed forces during **World War II;** all-black fighter and bomber AAF units and infantry divisions gave distinguished service. In 1954 the policy of all-black units was finally abolished. Of 274,937 blacks who served in the armed forces during the **Vietnam War** (1965-1974), 5,681 were killed in combat.

As of July, 1981, there were 204 black mayors, 2,384 members of municipal governing bodies, 449 county officers, 341 state legislators, and 18 U.S. representatives. There are now 5,038 blacks holding elected office in the U.S. and Virgin Islands, an increase of 2.6% over the previous year, according to a survey by the Joint Center for Political Studies, Washington, D.C.

Notable American Fiction Writers and Playwrights

Name (Birthplace)	Birthdate
Abbott, George (Forestville, N.Y.)	6/25/87
Albee, Edward (Washington, D.C.)	3/12/28
Algren, Nelson (Detroit, Mich.)	3/28/09
Anderson, Robert (New York, N.Y.)	4/28/17
Asimov, Isaac (Petrovichi, Russia)	1/2/20
Auchincloss, Louis (Lawrence, N.Y.)	9/27/17
Baldwin, James (New York, N.Y.)	8/2/24
Barth, John (Cambridge, Md.)	5/27/30
Barthelme, Donald (Philadelphia, Pa.)	1931
Bellow, Saul (Quebec, Canada)	7/10/15
Benchley, Peter (New York, N.Y.)	5/8/40
Bishop, Jim (Jersey City, N.J.)	11/21/07
Blume, Judy (Elizabeth, N.J.)	2/12/38
Bradbury, Ray (Waukegan, Ill.)	8/22/20
Brooks, Gwendolyn (Topeka, Kan.)	6/7/17
Burrows, Abe (New York, N.Y.)	12/18/10
Caldwell, Erskine (Coweta Co., Ga.)	12/17/03
Caldwell, Taylor (London, England)	1900
Calisher, Hortense (New York, N.Y.)	12/20/11
Capote, Truman (New Orleans, La.)	9/30/24
Clavell, James (England)	10/10/24
Crews, Harry (Alma, Ga.)	6/6/35
Crichton, Michael (Chicago, Ill.)	10/23/42
De Vries, Peter (Chicago, Ill.)	2/27/10
Dickey, James (Atlanta, Ga.)	2/2/23
Didion, Joan (Sacramento, Cal.)	12/5/34
Doctorow, E. L. (New York, N.Y.)	1/6/31
Drury, Allen (Houston, Tex.)	9/2/18
Elkin, Stanley (New York, N.Y.)	5/11/30
Ellison, Ralph (Oklahoma City, Okla.)	3/1/14
Fast, Howard (New York, N.Y.)	11/11/14
Geisel, Theodore ("Dr. Seuss," Springfield, Mass.)	3/2/04
Gibson, William (New York, N.Y.)	11/13/14
Gilroy, Frank (New York, N.Y.)	10/13/25
Godwin, Gail (Birmingham, Ala.)	6/18/37
Goldman, William (Chicago, Ill.)	8/12/31
Grau, Shirley Ann (New Orleans, La.)	7/8/29
Hailey, Arthur (Luton, England)	4/5/20
Haley, Alex (Ithaca, N.Y.)	8/11/21
Hawkes, John (Stamford, Conn.)	8/17/25
Heinlein, Robert (Butler, Mon.)	7/7/07
Heller, Joseph (Brooklyn, N.Y.)	5/1/23
Hellman, Lillian (New Orleans, La.)	6/20/07
Hersey, John (Tientsin, China)	6/17/14
Himes, Chester (Jefferson City, Mo.)	7/29/09
Irving, John (Exeter, N.H.)	3/2/42
Jaffe, Rona (New York, N.Y.)	6/12/32
Jong, Erica (New York, N.Y.)	3/26/42
Kazan, Elia (Constantinople, Turkey)	9/7/09
Kerr, Jean (Scranton, Pa.)	7/?/23
Kesey, Ken (La Junta, Col.)	9/17/35
King, Stephen (Portland, Me.)	9/21/47
Kingsley, Sidney (New York, N.Y.)	10/22/06
Knowles, John (Fairmont, W. Va.)	9/16/26
Kosinski, Jerzy (Lódz, Poland)	6/14/33
L'Amour, Louis (Jamestown, N.D.)	———
Lee, Harper (Alabama)	1926
LeGuin, Ursula (Berkeley, Cal.)	10/21/29
Levin, Ira (New York, N.Y.)	8/27/29
Ludlum, Robert (New York, N.Y.)	5/25/27
MacDonald, John D. (Sharon, Pa.)	7/24/16
MacDonald, Ross (Los Gatos, Cal.)	12/13/15
MacInnes, Helen (Glasgow, Scotland)	10/7/07
Mailer, Norman (Long Branch, N.J.)	1/31/23
Malamud, Bernard (Brooklyn, N.Y.)	4/26/14
Mamet, David (Chicago, Ill.)	11/30/47
McCarthy, Mary (Seattle, Wash.)	6/21/12
McMurtry, Larry (Wichita Falls, Tex.)	6/3/36
Michener, James A. (New York, N.Y.)	2/3/07
Miller, Arthur (New York, N.Y.)	10/17/15
Oates, Joyce Carol (Lockport, N.Y.)	6/16/38
Percy, Walker (Birmingham, Ala.)	5/28/16
Potok, Chaim (New York, N.Y.)	2/17/29
Puzo, Mario (New York, N.Y.)	10/15/20
Pynchon, Thomas (Glen Cove, N.Y.)	5/8/37
Reed, Ishmael (Chattanooga, Tenn.)	2/22/38
Robbins, Harold (New York, N.Y.)	5/21/12
Rogers, Rosemary (Panadora, Ceylon)	12/7/32
Roth, Henry (Austria-Hungary)	2/8/06
Roth, Philip (Newark, N.J.)	3/19/33
Salinger, J. D. (New York, N.Y.)	1/1/19
Sanders, Lawrence (New York, N.Y.)	1920
Scarry, Richard (Boston, Mass.)	6/5/19
Schisgal, Murray (New York, N.Y.)	11/25/26
Schulberg, Budd (New York, N.Y.)	3/27/14
Segal, Erich (Brooklyn, N.Y.)	6/16/37
Sendak, Maurice (New York, N.Y.)	6/10/28
Shaw, Irwin (New York, N.Y.)	2/27/13
Shepard, Sam (Ft. Sheridan, Fla.)	11/5/42
Simon, Neil (New York, N.Y.)	7/4/27
Singer, Isaac Bashevis (Radzymin, Poland)	7/14/04
Slaughter, Frank (Washington, D.C.)	2/25/08
Spillane, Mickey (Brooklyn, N.Y.)	3/9/18
Stegner, Wallace (Lake Mills, Ia.)	2/18/09
Stone, Irving (San Francisco, Cal.)	7/14/03
Styron, William (Newport News, Va.)	6/11/25
Theroux, Paul (Medford, Mass.)	4/10/41
Tryon, Thomas (Hartford, Conn.)	1/14/26
Updike, John (Shillington, Pa.)	3/18/32
Uris, Leon (Baltimore, Md.)	8/3/24
Vidal, Gore (West Point, N.Y.)	10/3/25
Vonnegut, Kurt Jr. (Indianapolis, Ind.)	11/11/22
Wallace, Irving (Chicago, Ill.)	3/18/16
Wambaugh, Joseph (East Pittsburgh, Pa.)	1/22/37
Warren, Robert Penn (Guthrie, Ky.)	4/24/05
Welty, Eudora (Jackson, Miss.)	4/13/09
Williams, Tennessee (Columbus, Miss.)	3/26/11
Wilson, Lanford (Lebanon, Mo.)	4/13/37
Willingham, Calder (Atlanta, Ga.)	12/23/22
Wouk, Herman (New York, N.Y.)	5/27/15
Yerby, Frank (Augusta, Ga.)	9/5/16
Zindel, Paul (New York, N.Y.)	5/15/36

American Architects and Some of Their Achievements

Max Abramovitz, b. 1908, Avery Fisher Hall, Lincoln Center, N.Y.C.
Henry Bacon, 1866-1924, Lincoln Memorial.
Pietro Belluschi, b. 1899, Juilliard School of Music, Lincoln Center, N.Y.C.
Marcel Breuer, 1902-1981, Whitney Museum of American Art, N.Y.C. (with Hamilton Smith).
Charles Bulfinch, 1763-1844, State House, Boston; Capitol, Wash. D.C., (part).
Daniel H. Burnham, 1846-1912, Union Station, Wash. D.C.; Flatiron, N.Y.C.
Ralph Adams Cram, 1863-1942, Cathedral of St. John the Divine, N.Y.C.; U.S. Military Academy (part).
R. Buckminster Fuller, b. 1895, U.S. Pavilion, Expo 67, Montreal (geodesic domes).
Cass Gilbert, 1859-1934, Custom House, Woolworth Bldg., N.Y.C.; Supreme Court bldg., Wash., D.C.
Bertram G. Goodhue, 1869-1924, Capitol, Lincoln, Neb.; St. Thomas, St. Bartholomew, N.Y.C.
Walter Gropius, 1883-1969, Pan Am Building, N.Y.C. (with Pietro Belluschi).
Peter Harrison, 1716-1775, Touro Synagogue, Redwood Library, Newport, R.I.
Wallace K. Harrison, b. 1895, Metropolitan Opera House, Lincoln Center, N.Y.C.
Thomas Hastings, 1860-1929, Public Library, Frick Mansion, N.Y.C.
James Hoban, 1762-1831, The White House.
William Holabird, 1854-1923, Crerar Library, City Hall, Chicago.
Raymond Hood, 1881-1934, Rockefeller Center, N.Y.C. (part); Daily News, N.Y.C.; Tribune, Chicago.
Richard M. Hunt, 1827-1895, Metropolitan Museum, N.Y.C. (part); Natl. Observatory, Wash., D.C.
William Le Baron Jenney, 1832-1907, Home Insurance, Chicago (demolished 1931).
Philip C. Johnson, b. 1906, N.Y. State Theater, Lincoln Center, N.Y.C.
Albert Kahn, 1869-1942, Athletic Club Bldg., General Motors Bldg., Detroit.
Louis Kahn, 1901-1974, Salk Laboratory, La Jolla, Cal.; Yale Art Gallery.
Christopher Grant LaFarge, 1862-1938, Roman Catholic Chapel, West Point.
Benjamin H. Latrobe, 1764-1820, U.S. Capitol (part).
William Lescaze, 1896-1969, Philadelphia Savings Fund Society; Borg-Warner Bldg., Chicago.
Charles F. McKim, 1847-1909, Public Library, Boston, Columbia Univ., N.Y.C. (part).
Charles M. McKim, b. 1920, KUHT-TV Transmitter Building, Houston; Lutheran Church of the Redeemer, Houston.
Ludwig Mies van der Rohe, 1886-1969, Seagram Building, N.Y.C. (with Philip C. Johnson); National Gallery, Berlin.
Robert Mills, 1781-1855, Washington Monument.
Richard J. Neutra, 1892-1970, Mathematics Park, Princeton; Orange Co. Courthouse, Santa Ana, Cal.
Gyo Obata, b. 1923, Natl. Air & Space Mus., Smithsonian Institution; Dallas-Ft. Worth Airport.
Frederick L. Olmsted, 1822-1903, Central Park, N.Y.C.; Fairmount Park, Philadelphia.
Ieoh Ming Pei, b. 1917, National Center for Atmospheric Research, Boulder, Col.
William Pereira, b. 1909, Cape Canaveral; Transamerica Bldg., San Francisco.
John Russell Pope, 1874-1937, National Gallery.
John Portman, b. 1924, Peachtree Center, Atlanta.
James Renwick Jr., 1818-1895, Grace Church, St. Patrick's Cathedral, N.Y.C.; Smithsonian, Corcoran Galleries, Wash., D.C.
Henry H. Richardson, 1838-1886, Trinity Church, Boston.
Kevin Roche, b. 1922, Oakland Cal. Museum; Fine Arts Center, U. of Mass.
James Gamble Rogers, 1867-1947, Columbia-Presbyterian Medical Center, N.Y.C.; Northwestern Univ., Chicago.
John Wellborn Root, 1887-1963, Palmolive Building, Chicago; Hotel Statler, Washington; Hotel Tamanaco, Caracas.
Paul Rudolph, b. 1918, Jewitt Art Center, Wellesley College; Art & Architecture Bldg., Yale.
Eero Saarinen, 1910-1961, Gateway to the West Arch, St. Louis; Trans World Flight Center, N.Y.C.
Louis Skidmore, 1897-1962, AEC town site, Oak Ridge, Tenn.; Terrace Plaza Hotel, Cincinnati.
Clarence S. Stein, 1882-1975, Temple Emanu-El, N.Y.C.
Edward Durell Stone, 1902-1978, U.S. Embassy, New Delhi, India; (H. Hartford) Gallery of Modern Art, N.Y.C.
Louis H. Sullivan, 1856-1924, Auditorium, Chicago.
Richard Upjohn, 1802-1878, Trinity Church, N.Y.C.
Ralph T. Walker, 1889-1973, N.Y. Telephone Hdqrs., N.Y.C.; IBM Research Lab., Poughkeepsie, N.Y.
Roland A. Wank, 1898-1970, Cincinnati Union Terminal; head architect TVA, 1933-44.
Stanford White, 1853-1906, Washington Arch; first Madison Square Garden, N.Y.C.
Frank Lloyd Wright, 1867 or 1869-1959, Imperial Hotel, Tokyo; Guggenheim Museum, N.Y.C.
William Wurster, 1895-1973, Ghirardelli Sq., San Francisco; Cowell College, U. Cal., Berkeley.
Minoru Yamasaki, b. 1912, World Trade Center, N.Y.C.

Noted American Cartoonists

Charles Addams, b. 1912, noted for macabre cartoons.
Peter Arno, 1904-1968, noted for urban characterizations.
George Baker, 1915-1975, The Sad Sack.
C. C. Beck, b. 1910, Captain Marvel.
Herb Block (Herblock), b. 1909, leading political cartoonist.
Clare Briggs, 1875-1930, Mr. & Mrs.
Dik Browne, b. 1917, Hi & Lois, Hagar the Horrible.
Ernie Bushmiller, b. 1905, Nancy.
Milton Caniff, b. 1907, Terry & the Pirates; Steve Canyon.
Al Capp, 1909-1979, Li'l Abner.
Roy Crane, 1901-1977, Captain Easy; Buz Sawyer.
Robert Crumb, b. 1943, "Underground" cartoonist.
Jay N. Darling (Ding), 1876-1962, political cartoonist.
Jim Davis, b. 1945, Garfield.
Billy DeBeck, 1890-1942, Barney Google.
Rudolph Dirks, 1877-1968, The Katzenjammer Kids.
Walt Disney, 1901-1966, producer of animated cartoons created Mickey Mouse & Donald Duck.
Jules Feiffer, b. 1929, satirical *Village Voice* cartoonist.
Bud Fisher, 1884-1954, Mutt & Jeff.
Ham Fisher, 1900-1955, Joe Palooka.
James Montgomery Flagg, 1877-1960, illustrator created the famous Uncle Sam recruiting poster during WWI.
Hal Foster, 1892-1982, Tarzan; Prince Valiant.
Fontaine Fox, 1884-1964, Toonerville Folks.
Rube Goldberg, 1883-1970, Boob McNutt.
Chester Gould, b. 1900, Dick Tracy.
Harold Gray, 1894-1968, Little Orphan Annie.
Johnny Hart, b. 1931, BC, Wizard of Id.
Jimmy Hatlo, 1898-1963, Little Iodine.
John Held Jr., 1889-1958, "Jazz Age" cartoonist.
George Herriman, 1881-1944, Krazy Kat.
Harry Hershfield, 1885-1974, Abie the Agent.
Burne Hogarth, b. 1911, Tarzan.
Helen Hokinson, 1900-1949, satirical drawings of clubwomen.
Walt Kelly, 1913-1973, Pogo.
Hank Ketcham, b. 1920, Dennis the Menace.
Ted Key, b. 1912 Hazel.
Frank King, 1883-1969, Gasoline Alley.
Jack Kirby, b. 1917, Captain America.
Rollin Kirby, 1875-1952, political cartoonist.
Bill Mauldin, b. 1921, depicted squalid life of the G.I. in WWII.
Winsor McCay, 1872-1934, Little Nemo.
John T. McCutcheon, 1870-1949, midwestern rural life.
George McManus, 1884-1954, Bringing Up Father (Maggie & Jiggs).
Dale Messick, b. 1906, Brenda Starr.
Bob Montana, 1920-1975, Archie.
Willard Mullin, 1902-1978, sports cartoonist created the Dodgers "Bum" and the Mets "Kid".
Thomas Nast, 1840-1902, political cartoonist instrumental in breaking the corrupt Boss Tweed ring in N.Y. Created the Democratic donkey and Republican elephant.
Frederick Burr Opper, 1857-1937, Happy Hooligan.
Richard Outcault, 1863-1928, Yellow Kid; Buster Brown.
Alex Raymond, 1909-1956, Flash Gordon; Jungle Jim.
Charles Schulz, b. 1922, Peanuts.
Elzie C. Segar, 1894-1938, Popeye.
Sydney Smith, 1887-1935, The Gumps.
Otto Soglow, 1900-1975, Little King; Canyon Kiddies.
James Swinnerton, 1875-1974, Little Jimmy.
James Thurber, 1894-1961, *New Yorker* cartoonist of the smugly childish line coupled with the sophisticated caption.
Garry Trudeau, b. 1948, Doonesbury.
Mort Walker, b. 1923, Beetle Bailey.
Russ Westover, 1887-1966, Tillie the Toiler.
Frank Willard, 1893-1958, Moon Mullins.
J. R. Williams, 1888-1957, The Willets Family; Out Our Way.
Gahan Wilson, b. 1930, cartoonist of the macabre.
Art Young, 1866-1943, political radical and satirist.
Chic Young, 1901-1973, Blondie.

Business Hall of Fame

Established and supported by Junior Achievement Inc. Laureates selected by *Fortune* board of editors.

William M. Allen
William Milfred Batten
Stephen D. Bechtel Sr.
William Blackie
Andrew Carnegie
Willis Haviland Carrier
Frederick Coolidge Crawford
Harry B. Cunningham
Arthur Vining Davis
Walter E. Disney
Georges Frederic Doriot
Donald W. Douglas
Pierre S. du Pont
George Eastman
Thomas A. Edison
Henry Ford
Benjamin Franklin
Roswell Garst
Amadeo P. Giannini
Florence Nightingale Graham
Walter Abraham Haas
Joyce Clyde Hall
H.J. Heinz
James J. Hill
Conrad N. Hilton
Edward C. Johnson II
J. Erik Jonsson
Henry John Kaiser
Charles F. Kettering
Robert Justus Kleberg Sr.
Edwin Herbert Land
Albert D. Lasker
Royal Little
Francis Cabot Lowell
Henry R. Luce
Ian Kinloch MacGregor
John J. McCloy
Cyrus H. McCormick
Malcolm P. McLean
Andrew W. Mellon
Charles E. Merrill
J. Irwin Miller
George S. Moore
J. Pierpont Morgan
Howard J. Morgens
Adolph S. Ochs
David MacKenzie Ogilvy
John Henry Patterson
William Allan Patterson
James Cash Penney
William C. Procter
M.J. Rathbone
Donald T. Regan
John D. Rockefeller
James Wilson Rouse
David Sarnoff
Jacob H. Schiff
Charles M. Schwab
Alfred P. Sloan Jr.
Cyrus R. Smith
Charles Clinton Spaulding
Alexander T. Stewart
J. Edgar Thomson
Theodore N. Vail
Cornelius Vanderbilt
De Witt Wallace
Lila Acheson Wallace
George Washington
Thomas J. Watson Jr.
George Westinghouse
Frederick W. Weyerhaeuser
Eli Whitney
Charles K. Wilson
Joseph C. Wilson
Robert Elkington Wood
Robert W. Woodruff
Owen D. Young

Noted Political Leaders of the Past

(U.S. presidents and most vice presidents, Supreme Court justices, signers of Declaration of Independence, listed elsewhere.)

Abu Bakr, 573-634, Mohammedan leader, first caliph, chosen successor to Mohammed.

Dean Acheson, 1893-1971, (U.S.) secretary of state, chief architect of cold war foreign policy.

Samuel Adams, 1722-1803, (U.S.) patriot, Boston Tea Party firebrand.

Konrad Adenauer, 1876-1967, (G.) West German chancellor.

Emilio Aguinaldo, 1869-1964, (Philip.) revolutionary, fought against Spain and the U.S.

Akbar, 1542-1605, greatest Mogul emperor of India.

Salvador Allende Gossens, 1908-1973, (Chil.) president, advocate of democratic socialism.

Herbert H. Asquith, 1852-1928, (Br.) Liberal prime minister, instituted an advanced program of social reform.

Atahualpa, ?-1533, Inca (ruling chief) of Peru, executed by Pizarro.

Kemal Atatürk, 1881-1938, (Turk.) founded modern Turkey.

Clement Attlee, 1883-1967, (Br.) Labour party leader, prime minister, enacted national health, nationalized many industries.

Stephen F. Austin, 1793-1836, (U.S.) led Texas colonization.

Mikhail Bakunin, 1814-1876, (R.) revolutionary, leading exponent of anarchism.

Arthur J. Balfour, 1848-1930, (Br.) as foreign secretary under Lloyd George issued Balfour Declaration expressing official British approval of Zionism.

Bernard M. Baruch, 1870-1965, (U.S.) financier, gvt. adviser.

Fulgencio Batista y Zaldívar, 1901-1973, (Cub.) dictator overthrown by Castro.

Lord Beaverbrook, 1879-1964, (Br.) financier, statesman, newspaper owner.

Eduard Benes, 1884-1948, (Czech.) president during interwar and post-WW II eras.

David Ben-Gurion, 1886-1973, (Isr.) first premier of Israel.

Thomas Hart Benton, 1782-1858, (U.S.) Missouri senator, championed agrarian interests and westward expansion.

Lavrenti Beria, 1899-1953, (USSR) Communist leader prominent in political purges under Stalin.

Aneurin Bevan, 1897-1960, (Br.) Labour party leader, developed socialized medicine system.

Ernest Bevin, 1881-1951, (Br.) Labour party leader, foreign minister, helped lay foundation for NATO.

Otto von Bismarck, 1815-1898, (G.) statesman known as the Iron Chancellor, uniter of Germany, 1870.

James G. Blaine, 1830-1893, (U.S.) Republican politician, diplomat, influential in launching Pan-American movement.

Léon Blum, 1872-1950, (F.) socialist leader, writer, headed first Popular Front government.

Simón Bolívar, 1783-1830, (Venez.) South American revolutionary who liberated much of the continent from Spanish rule.

William E. Borah, 1865-1940, (U.S.) isolationist senator, instrumental in blocking U.S. membership in League of Nations and the World Court.

Cesare Borgia, 1476-1507, (It.) soldier, politician, an outstanding figure of the Italian Renaissance.

Aristide Briand, 1862-1932, (F.) foreign minister, chief architect of Locarno Pact and anti-war Kellogg-Briand Pact.

William Jennings Bryan, 1860-1925, (U.S.) Democratic, populist leader, orator, 3 times lost race for presidency.

Nikolai Bukharin, 1888-1938, (USSR) communist leader.

William C. Bullitt, 1891-1967, (U.S.) diplomat, first ambassador to USSR, ambassador to France.

Ralph Bunche, 1904-1971, (U.S.) a founder and key diplomat of United Nations for more than 20 years.

John C. Calhoun, 1782-1850, (U.S.) political leader, champion of states' rights and a symbol of the Old South.

Robert Castlereagh, 1769-1822, (Br.) foreign secretary, guided Grand Alliance against Napoleon, major figure at the Congress of Vienna, 1814-15.

Camillo Benso Cavour, 1810-1861, (It.) statesman, largely responsible for uniting Italy under the House of Savoy.

Austen Chamberlain, 1863-1937, (Br.) Conservative party leader, largely responsible for Locarno Pact of 1925.

Neville Chamberlain, 1869-1940, (Br.) Conservative prime minister whose appeasement of Hitler led to Munich Pact.

Salmon P. Chase, 1808-1873, (U.S.) public official, abolitionist, jurist, 6th Supreme Court chief justice.

Chiang Kai-shek, 1887-1975, (Chin.) Nationalist Chinese president whose govt. was driven from mainland to Taiwan.

Chou En-lai, 1898-1976, (Chin.) diplomat, prime minister, a leading figure of the Chinese Communist party.

Winston Churchill, 1874-1965, (Br.) prime minister, soldier, author, guided Britain through WW II.

Galeazzo Ciano, 1903-1944, (It.) fascist foreign minister, helped create Rome-Berlin Axis, executed by Mussolini.

Henry Clay, 1777-1852, (U.S.) "The Great Compromiser," one of most influential pre-Civil War political leaders.

Georges Clemenceau, 1841-1929, (F.) twice premier, Wilson's chief antagonist at Paris Peace Conference after WW I.

DeWitt Clinton, 1769-1828, (U.S.) political leader, responsible for promoting idea of the Erie Canal.

Robert Clive, 1725-1774, (Br.) first administrator of Bengal, laid foundation for British Empire in India.

Jean Baptiste Colbert, 1619-1683, (F.) statesman, influential under Louis XIV, created the French navy.

Oliver Cromwell, 1599-1658, (Br.) Lord Protector of England, led parliamentary forces during Civil War.

Curzon of Kedleston, 1859-1925, (Br.) viceroy of India, foreign secretary, major force in dealing with post-WW I problems in Europe and Far East.

Édouard Daladier, 1884-1970, (F.) radical socialist politician, arrested by Vichy, interned by Germans until liberation in 1945.

Georges Danton, 1759-1794, (F.) a leading figure in the French Revolution.

Jefferson Davis, 1808-1889, (U.S.) president of the Confederate States of America.

Charles G. Dawes, 1865-1951, (U.S.) statesman, banker, advanced Dawes Plan to stabilize post-WW I German finances.

Alcide De Gasperi, 1881-1954, (It.) premier, founder of the Christian Democratic party.

Charles DeGaulle, 1890-1970, (F.) general, statesman, and first president of the Fifth Republic.

Eamon De Valera, 1882-1975, (Ir.-U.S.) statesman, led fight for Irish independence.

Thomas E. Dewey, 1902-1971, (U.S.) New York governor, twice loser in try for presidency.

Ngo Dinh Diem, 1901-1963, (Viet.) South Vietnamese president, assassinated in government take-over.

Everett M. Dirksen, 1896-1969, (U.S.) Senate Republican

minority leader, orator.

Benjamin Disraeli, 1804-1881, (Br.) prime minister, considered founder of modern Conservative party.

Engelbert Dollfuss, 1892-1934, (Aus.) chancellor, assassinated by Austrian Nazis.

Andrea Doria, 1466-1560, (It.) Genoese admiral, statesman, called "Father of Peace" and "Liberator of Genoa."

Stephen A. Douglas, 1813-1861, (U.S.) Democratic leader, orator, opposed Lincoln for the presidency.

John Foster Dulles, 1888-1959, (U.S.) secretary of state under Eisenhower, cold war policy maker.

Friedrich Ebert, 1871-1925, (G.) Social Democratic movement leader, instrumental in bringing about Weimar constitution.

Sir Anthony Eden, 1897-1977, (Br.) foreign secretary, prime minister during Suez invasion of 1956.

Ludwig Erhard, 1897-1977, (G.) economist, West German chancellor, led nation's economic rise after WW II.

Hamilton Fish, 1808-1893, (U.S.) secretary of state, successfully mediated disputes with Great Britain, Latin America.

James V. Forrestal, 1892-1949, (U.S.) secretary of navy, first secretary of defense.

Francisco Franco, 1892-1975, (Sp.) leader of rebel forces during Spanish Civil War and dictator of Spain.

Benjamin Franklin, 1706-1790, (U.S.) printer, publisher, author, inventor, scientist, diplomat.

Louis de Frontenac, 1620-1698, (F.) governor of New France (Canada) where he encouraged explorations and fought Iroquois.

Hugh Gaitskell, 1906-1963, (Br.) Labour party leader, major force in reversing its stand for unilateral disarmament.

Albert Gallatin, 1761-1849, (U.S.) second secretary of treasury, instrumental in negotiating end of War of 1812.

Léon Gambetta, 1838-1882, (F.) statesman, politician, one of the founders of the Third Republic.

Mohandas K. Gandhi, 1869-1948, (Ind.) political leader, ascetic, led nationalist movement against British rule.

Giuseppe Garibaldi, 1807-1882, (It.) patriot, soldier, a leading figure in the Risorgimento, the Italian unification movement.

Genghis Khan, c. 1167-1227, brilliant Mongol conqueror, ruler of vast Asian empire.

William E. Gladstone, 1809-1898, (Br.) prime minister 4 times, dominant force of Liberal party from 1868 to 1894.

Paul Joseph Goebbels, 1897-1945, (G.) Nazi propagandist, master of mass psychology.

Klement Gottwald, 1896-1953, (Czech.) communist leader ushered communism into his country.

Che (Ernesto) Guevara, 1928-1967, (Arg.) guerilla leader, prominent in Cuban revolution, killed in Bolivia.

Haile Selassie, 1891-1975, (Eth.) emperor, maintained traditional monarchy in face of foreign invasion, occupation, and internal resistance.

Alexander Hamilton, 1755-1804, (U.S.) first treasury secretary, champion of strong central government.

Dag Hammarskjold, 1905-1961, (Swed.) statesman, UN secretary general.

John Hancock, 1737-1793, (U.S.) revolutionary leader, first signer of Declaration of Independence.

John Hay, 1838-1905, (U.S.) secretary of state, primarily associated with Open Door Policy toward China.

Patrick Henry, 1736-1799, (U.S.) major revolutionary figure, remarkable orator.

Édouard Herriot, 1872-1957, (F.) Radical Socialist leader, twice premier, president of National Assembly.

Theodor Herzl, 1860-1904, (Aus.) founder of modern Zionism.

Heinrich Himmler, 1900-1945, (G.) chief of Nazi SS and Gestapo, primarily responsible for the Holocaust.

Paul von Hindenburg, 1847-1934, (G.) field marshal, president.

Adolf Hitler, 1889-1945, (G.) dictator, founder of National Socialism.

Ho Chi Minh, 1890-1969, (Viet.) North Vietnamese president, Vietnamese Communist leader, national hero.

Harry L. Hopkins, 1890-1946, (U.S.) New Deal administrator, closest adviser to FDR during WW II.

Edward M. House, 1858-1938, (U.S.) diplomat, confidential adviser to Woodrow Wilson.

Samuel Houston, 1793-1863, (U.S.) leader of struggle to win control of Texas from Mexico.

Cordell Hull, 1871-1955, (U.S.) secretary of state, initiated reciprocal trade to lower tariffs, helped organize UN.

Hubert H. Humphrey, 1911-1978, (U.S.) Minnesota Democrat, senator, vice president, spent 32 years in public service.

Ibn Saud, c. 1888-1953, (S. Arab.) founder of Saudi Arabia and its first king.

Benito Juarez, 1806-1872, (Mex.) national hero, rallied countrymen against foreign threats, sought to create democratic, federal republic.

Frank B. Kellogg, 1856-1937, (U.S.) secretary of state, negotiated Kellogg-Briand Pact to outlaw war.

Robert F. Kennedy, 1925-1968, (U.S.) attorney general, senator, assassinated while seeking presidential nomination.

Aleksandr Kerensky, 1881-1970, (R.) revolutionary, served as premier after Feb. 1917 revolution until Bolshevik overthrow.

Nikita Khrushchev, 1894-1971, (USSR) communist leader, premier, first secretary of Communist party, initiated de-Stalinization.

Lajos Kossuth, 1802-1894, (Hung.) principal figure in 1848 Hungarian revolution.

Pyotr Kropotkin, 1842-1921, (R.) anarchist, championed the peasants but opposed Bolshevism.

Kublai Khan, c. 1215-1294, Mongol emperor, founder of Yüan dynasty in China.

Béla Kun, 1886-c.1939, (Hung.) communist dictator, member of 3d International, tried to foment worldwide revolution.

Robert M. LaFollette, 1855-1925, (U.S.) Wisconsin public official, leader of progressive movement.

Pierre Laval, 1883-1945, (F.) politician, Vichy foreign minister, executed for treason.

Andrew Bonar Law, 1858-1923, (Br.) Conservative party politician, led opposition to Irish home rule.

Vladimir Ilyich Lenin (Ulyanov), 1870-1924, (USSR) revolutionary, founder of Bolshevism, Soviet leader 1917-1924.

Ferdinand de Lesseps, 1805-1894, (F.) diplomat, engineer, conceived idea of Suez Canal.

Liu Shao-ch'i, c.1898-1974, (Chin.) communist leader, fell from grace during "cultural revolution."

Maxim Litvinov, 1876-1951, (USSR), revolutionary, commissar of foreign affairs, proponent of cooperation with western powers.

David Lloyd George, 1863-1945, (Br.) Liberal party prime minister, laid foundations for the modern welfare state.

Henry Cabot Lodge, 1850-1924, (U.S.) Republican senator, led opposition to participation in League of Nations.

Huey P. Long, 1893-1935, (U.S.) Louisiana political demagogue, governor, assassinated.

Rosa Luxemburg, 1871-1919, (G.) revolutionary, leader of the German Social Democratic party and Spartacus party.

J. Ramsay MacDonald, 1866-1937, (Br.) first Labour party prime minister of Great Britain.

Joseph R. McCarthy, 1908-1957, (U.S.) senator notorious for his witch hunt for communists in the government.

Makarios III, 1913-1977, (Cypr.) Greek Orthodox archbishop, first president of Cyprus.

Malcolm X (Malcolm Little), 1925-1965, (U.S.) black separatist leader, assassinated.

Mao Tse-tung, 1893-1976, (Chin.) chief Chinese Marxist theorist, soldier, lead Chinese revolution establishing his nation as an important communist state.

Jean Paul Marat, 1743-1793, (F.) revolutionary politician, identified with radical Jacobins, assassinated by Charlotte Corday.

José Martí, 1853-1895, (Cub.) patriot, poet, leader of Cuban struggle for independence.

Jan Masaryk, 1886-1948, (Czech.) foreign minister, died by mysterious suicide following communist coup.

Thomas G. Masaryk, 1850-1937, (Czech.) statesman, philosopher, first president of Czechoslovak Republic.

Jules Mazarin, 1602-1661, (F.) cardinal, statesman, prime minister under Louis XIII and queen regent Anne of Austria.

Tom Mboya, 1930-1969, (Kenyan) political leader, instrumental in securing independence for his country.

Cosimo I de' Medici, 1519-1574 (It.) Duke of Florence, grand duke of Tuscany.

Lorenzo de' Medici, the Magnificent, 1449-1492, (It.) merchant prince, a towering figure in Italian Renaissance.

Catherine de Medicis, 1519-1589, (F.) queen consort of Henry II, regent of France, influential in Catholic-Huguenot wars.

Golda Meir, 1898-1978, (Isr.) prime minister, 1969-74.

Klemens W.N.L. Metternich, 1773-1859, (Aus.) statesman, arbiter of post-Napoleonic Europe.

Anastas Mikoyan, 1895-1978, (USSR) prominent Soviet leader from 1917; president, 1964-65.

Guy Mollet, 1905-1975, (F.) socialist politician, resistance leader.

Henry Morgenthau Jr., 1891-1967, (U.S.) secretary of treasury, raised funds to finance New Deal and U.S. WW II activities.

Gouverneur Morris, 1752-1816, (U.S.) statesman, diplomat, financial expert who helped plan decimal coinage system.

Wayne Morse, 1900-1974, (U.S.) senator, long-time critic of Vietnam War.

Muhammad Ali, 1769?-1849, (Egypt), pasha, founder of dynasty that encouraged emergence of modern Egyptian state.

Benito Mussolini, 1883-1945, (It.) dictator and leader of the Italian fascist movement.

Imre Nagy, c. 1895-1958, (Hung.) communist premier, assassinated after Soviets crushed 1956 uprising.

Gamel Abdel Nasser, 1918-1970, (Egypt.) leader of Arab unification, second Egyptian president.

Jawaharlal Nehru, 1889-1964, (Ind.) prime minister, guided

India through its early years of independence.

Kwame Nkrumah, 1909-1972, (Ghan.) dictatorial prime minister, deposed in 1966.

Frederick North, 1732-1792, (Br.) prime minister, his inept policies led to loss of American colonies.

Daniel O'Connell, 1775-1847, (Ir.) political leader, known as The Liberator.

Omar, c.581-644, Mohammedan leader, 2d caliph, led Islam to become an imperial power.

Ignace Paderewski, 1860-1941, (Pol.) statesman, pianist, composer, briefly prime minister, an ardent patriot.

Viscount Palmerston, 1784-1865, (Br.) Whig-Liberal prime minister, foreign minister, embodied British nationalism.

George Papandreou, 1888-1968, (Gk.) Republican politician, served three times as prime minister.

Franz von Papen, 1879-1969, (G.) politician, played major role in overthrow of Weimar Republic and rise of Hitler.

Charles Stewart Parnell, 1846-1891, (Ir.) nationalist leader, "uncrowned king of Ireland."

Lester Pearson, 1897-1972, (Can.) diplomat, Liberal party leader, prime minister.

Robert Peel, 1788-1850, (Br.) reformist prime minister, founder of the Conservative party.

Juan Perón, 1895-1974, (Arg.) president, dictator.

Joseph Pilsudski, 1867-1935, (Pol.) statesman, instrumental in re-establishing Polish state in the 20th century.

Charles Pinckney, 1757-1824, (U.S.) founding father, his Pinckney plan was largely incorporated into constitution.

William Pitt, the Elder, 1708-1778, (Br.) statesman, called the "Great Commoner," transformed Britain into imperial power.

William Pitt, the Younger, 1759-1806, (Br.) prime minister during the French Revolutionary wars.

Georgi Plekhanov, 1857-1918, (R.) revolutionary, social philosopher, called "father of Russian Marxism."

Raymond Poincaré, 1860-1934, (F.) 9th president of the Republic, advocated harsh punishment of Germany after WW I.

Georges Pompidou, 1911-1974, (F.) Gaullist political leader, president from 1969 to 1974.

Grigori Potemkin, 1739-1791, (R.) field marshal, favorite of Catherine II.

Edmund Randolph, 1753-1813, (U.S.) attorney, prominent in drafting, ratification of constitution.

John Randolph, 1773-1833, (U.S.) southern planter, strong advocate of states' rights.

Jeanette Rankin, 1880-1973, (U.S.) pacifist, first woman member of U.S. Congress.

Walter Rathenau, 1867-1922, (G.) industrialist, social theorist, statesman.

Sam Rayburn, 1882-1961, (U.S.) Democratic leader, representative for 47 years, House speaker for 17.

Paul Reynaud, 1878-1966, (F.) statesman, premier in 1940 at the time of France's defeat by Germany.

Syngman Rhee, 1875-1965, (Kor.) first president of the Republic of Korea.

Cecil Rhodes, 1853-1902, (Br.) imperialist, industrial magnate, established Rhodes scholarships in his will.

Cardinal de Richelieu, 1585-1642, (F.) statesman, known as "red eminence," chief minister to Louis XIII.

Maximilien Robespierre, 1758-1794, (F.) leading figure of French Revolution, responsible for much of Reign of Terror.

Nelson Rockefeller, 1908-1979, (U.S.) Republican gov. of N.Y., 1958-73; U.S. vice president, 1974-77.

Eleanor Roosevelt, 1884-1962, (U.S.) humanitarian, United Nations diplomat.

Elihu Root, 1845-1937, (U.S.) lawyer, statesman, diplomat, leading Republican supporter of the League of Nations.

John Russell, 1792-1878, (Br.) Liberal prime minister during the Irish potato famine.

Anwar el-Sadat, 1918-1981, (Egypt) president, 1970-1981, promoted peace with Israel.

António de O. Salazar, 1899-1970, (Port.) statesman, longtime dictator.

José de San Martin, 1778-1850, South American revolutionary, protector of Peru.

Eisaku Sato, 1901-1975, (Jap.) prime minister, presided over Japan's post-WW II emergence as major world power.

Philipp Scheidemann, 1865-1939, (G.) Social Democratic leader, first chancellor of the German republic.

Robert Schuman, 1886-1963, (F.) statesman, founded European Coal and Steel Community.

Carl Schurz, 1829-1906, (U.S.) German-American political leader, journalist, orator, dedicated reformer.

Kurt Schuschnigg, 1897-1977, (Aus.) chancellor, unsuccessful in stopping his country's annexation by Germany.

William H. Seward, 1801-1872, (U.S.) anti-slavery activist, as Lincoln's secretary of state purchased Alaska.

Carlo Sforza, 1872-1952, (It.) foreign minister, prominent Italian anti-fascist.

Alfred E. Smith, 1873-1944, (U.S.) New York Democratic governor, first Roman Catholic to run for presidency.

Jan C. Smuts, 1870-1950, (S.Af.) statesman, philosopher, soldier, prime minister.

Paul Henri Spaak, 1899-1972, (Belg.) statesman, socialist leader.

Joseph Stalin, 1879-1953, (USSR) Soviet dictator from 1924 to 1953.

Edwin M. Stanton, 1814-1869, (U.S.) Lincoln's secretary of war during the Civil War.

Edward R. Stettinius Jr., 1900-1949, (U.S.) industrialist, secretary of state who coordinated aid to WW II allies.

Adlai E. Stevenson, 1900-1965, (U.S.) Democratic leader, diplomat, Illinois governor, presidential candidate.

Henry L. Stimson, 1867-1950, (U.S.) statesman, served in 5 administrations, influenced foreign policy in 1930s and 1940s.

Gustav Stresemann, 1878-1929, (G.) chancellor, foreign minister, dedicated to regaining friendship for post-WW I Germany.

Sukarno, 1901-1970, (Indon.) dictatorial first president of the Indonesian republic.

Sun Yat-sen, 1866-1925, (Chin.) revolutionary, leader of Kuomintang, regarded as the father of modern China.

Robert A. Taft, 1889-1953, (U.S.) conservative Senate leader, called "Mr. Republican."

Charles de Talleyrand, 1754-1838, (F.) statesman, diplomat, the major force of the Congress of Vienna of 1814-15.

U Thant, 1909-1974, (Bur.) statesman, UN secretary-general.

Norman M. Thomas, 1884-1968, (U.S.) social reformer, 6 times unsuccessful Socialist party presidential candidate.

Josip Broz Tito, 1892-1980, (Yug.) president of Yugoslavia from 1953, World War II guerrilla chief, postwar rival of Stalin, leader of 3d world movement.

Palmiro Togliatti, 1893-1964, (It.) major leader of Italian Communist party.

Hideki Tojo, 1885-1948, (Jap.) statesman, soldier, prime minister during most of WW II.

François Toussaint L'Ouverture, c. 1744-1803, (Hait.) patriot, martyr, thwarted French colonial aims.

Leon Trotsky, 1879-1940, (USSR) revolutionary, communist leader, founded Red Army, expelled from party in conflict with Stalin.

Rafael L. Trujillo Molina, 1891-1961, (Dom.) absolute dictator, assassinated.

Moise K. Tshombe, 1919-1969, (Cong.) politician, president of secessionist Katanga, premier of Repubic of Congo (Zaire).

William M. Tweed, 1823-1878, (U.S.) politician, absolute leader of Tammany Hall, NYC's Democratic political machine.

Walter Ulbricht, 1893-1973, (G.) communist leader of German Democratic Republic.

Arthur H. Vandenberg, 1884-1951, (U.S.) senator, proponent of anti-communist bipartisan foreign policy after WW II.

Eleutherios Venizelos, 1864-1936, (Gk.) most prominent Greek statesman in early 20th century, considerably expanded Greek territory through his diplomacy.

Hendrik F. Verwoerd, 1901-1966, (S.Af.) prime minister, rigorously applied apartheid policy despite protest.

Robert Walpole, 1676-1745, (Br.) statesman, generally considered Britain's first prime minister.

Daniel Webster, 1782-1852, (U.S.) orator, politician, enthusiastic nationalist, advocate of business interests during Jacksonian agrarianism.

Chaim Weizmann, 1874-1952, Zionist leader, scientist, first Israeli president.

Wendell L. Willkie, 1892-1944, (U.S.) Republican who tried to unseat FDR when he ran for his 3d term.

Emiliano Zapata, c. 1879-1919, (Mex.) revolutionary, major influence on modern Mexico.

Notable Military and Naval Leaders of the Past

Creighton Abrams, 1914-1974, (U.S.) commanded forces in Vietnam, 1968-72.

Harold Alexander, 1891-1969, (Br.) led Allied invasion of Italy, 1943.

Ethan Allen, 1738-1789, (U.S.) headed Green Mountain Boys; captured Ft. Ticonderoga, 1775.

Edmund Allenby, 1861-1936, (Br.) in Boer War, WW1; led Egyptian expeditionary force, 1917-18.

Benedict Arnold, 1741-1801, (U.S.) victorious at Saratoga; tried to betray West Point to British.

Henry "Hap" Arnold, 1886-1950, (U.S.) commanded Army Air Force in WW2.

Petr Bagration, 1765-1812, (R.) hero of Napoleonic wars.

John Barry, 1745-1803, (U.S.) won numerous sea battles during revolution.

Pierre Beauregard, 1818-1893, (U.S.) Confederate general ordered bombardment of Ft. Sumter that began the Civil War.

Gebhard v. Blücher, 1742-1819, (G.) helped defeat Napoleon at Waterloo.

Napoleon Bonaparte, 1769-1821, (F.) defeated Russia and Austria at Austerlitz, 1805; invaded Russia, 1812; defeated at Waterloo, 1815.

Edward Braddock, 1695-1755, (Br.) commanded forces in French and Indian War.

Omar N. Bradley, 1893-1981, (U.S.) headed U.S. ground troops in Normandy invasion, 1944.

John Burgoyne, 1722-1792, (Br.) defeated at Saratoga.

Claire Chennault, 1890-1958, (U.S.) headed Flying Tigers in WW2.

Karl v. Clausewitz, 1780-1831, (G.) wrote books on military theory.

Henry Clinton, 1738-1795, (Br.) commander of forces in America, 1778-81.

Lucius D. Clay, 1897-1978, (U.S.) led Berlin airlift, 1948-49.

Charles Cornwallis, 1738-1805, (Br.) victorious at Brandywine, 1777; surrendered at Yorktown.

Crazy Horse, 1849-1877, (U.S.) Sioux war chief victorious at Little Big Horn.

George A. Custer, 1839-1876, (U.S.) defeated and killed at Little Big Horn.

Moshe Dayan, 1915-1981, (Isr.) directed campaigns in the 1967, 1973 wars.

Stephen Decatur, 1779-1820, (U.S.) naval hero of Barbary wars, War of 1812.

Anton Denikin, 1872-1947, (R.) led White forces in Russian civil war.

George Dewey, 1837-1917, (U.S.) destroyed Spanish fleet at Manila, 1898.

Hugh C. Dowding, 1883-1970, (Br.) headed RAF, 1936-40.

Jubal Early, 1816-1894, (U.S.) Confederate general led raid on Washington, 1864.

Dwight D. Eisenhower, 1890-1969, (U.S.) commanded Allied forces in Europe, WW2.

David Farragut, 1801-1870, (U.S.) Union admiral captured New Orleans, Mobile Bay.

Ferdinand Foch, 1851-1929, (F.) headed victorious Allied armies, 1918.

Nathan Bedford Forrest, 1821-1877, (U.S.) Confederate general led cavalry raids against Union supply lines.

Frederick the Great, 1712-1786, (G.) led Prussia in The Seven Years War.

Nathanael Greene, 1742-1786, (U.S.) defeated British in Southern campaign, 1780-81.

Charles G. Gordon, 1833-1885, (Br.) led forces in China; killed at Khartoum.

Horatio Gates, 1728-1806, (U.S.) commanded army at Saratoga.

Ulysses S. Grant, 1822-1885, (U.S.) headed Union army, 1864-65; forced Lee's surrender, 1865.

Heinz Guderian, 1888-1953, (G.) tank theorist led panzer forces in Poland, France, Russia.

Douglas Haig, 1861-1928, (Br.) led British armies in France, 1915-18.

William F. Halsey, 1882-1959, (U.S.) defeated Japanese fleet at Leyte Gulf, 1944.

Richard Howe, 1726-1799, (Br.) commanded navy in America, 1776-78; first of June victory against French, 1794.

William Howe, 1729-1814, (Br.) commanded forces in America, 1776-78.

Isaac Hull, 1773-1843, (U.S.) sunk British frigate Guerriere, 1812.

Thomas (Stonewall) Jackson, 1824-1863, (U.S.) Confederate general led forces in the Shenandoah Valley campaign.

Joseph Joffre, 1852-1931, (F.) headed Allied armies, won Battle of the Marne, 1914.

John Paul Jones, 1747-1792, (U.S.) raided British coast; commanded Bonhomme Richard in victory over Serapis, 1779.

Stephen Kearny, 1794-1848, (U.S.) headed Army of the West in Mexican War.

Ernest J. King, 1878-1956, (U.S.) chief naval strategist in WW2.

Horatio H. Kitchener, 1850-1916, (Br.) led forces in Boer War; victorious at Khartoum; organized army in WW1.

Lavrenti Kornilov, 1870-1918, (R.) Commander-in-Chief, 1917; led counter-revolutionary march on Petrograd.

Thaddeus Kosciusko, 1746-1817, (P.) aided American cause in revolution.

Mikhail Kutuzov, 1745-1813, (R.) fought French at Borodino, 1812; abandoned Moscow; forced French retreat.

Marquis de Lafayette, 1757-1834, (F.) aided American cause in the revolution.

Thomas E. Lawrence (of Arabia), 1888-1935, (Br.) organized revolt of Arabs against Turks in WW1.

Henry (Light-Horse Harry) Lee, 1756-1818, (U.S.) cavalry officer in revolution.

Robert E. Lee, 1807-1870, (U.S.) Confederate general defeated at Gettysburg; surrendered to Grant, 1865.

James Longstreet, 1821-1904, (U.S.) aided Lee at Gettysburg.

Douglas MacArthur, 1880-1964, (U.S.) commanded forces in SW Pacific in WW2; headed occupation forces in Japan, 1945-50; UN commander in Korean War.

Francis Marion, 1733-1795, (U.S.) led guerrilla actions in S.C. during revolution.

Duke of Marlborough, 1650-1722, (Br.) led forces against Louis XIV in War of the Spanish Sucession.

George C. Marshall, 1880-1959, (U.S.) chief of staff in WW2; authored Marshall Plan.

George B. McClellan, 1826-1885, (U.S.) Union general commanded Army of the Potomac, 1861-62.

George Meade, 1815-1872; (U.S.) commanded Union forces at Gettysburg.

Billy Mitchell, 1879-1936, (U.S.) air-power advocate; court-martialed for insubordination, later vindicated.

Helmuth v. Moltke, 1800-1891; (G.) victorious in Austro-Prussian, Franco-Prussian wars.

Louis de Montcalm, 1712-1759, (F.) headed troops in Canada; defeated at Quebec, 1759.

Bernard Law Montgomery, 1887-1976, (Br.) stopped German offensive at Alamein, 1942; helped plan Normandy invasion.

Daniel Morgan, 1736-1802, (U.S.) victorious at Cowpens, 1781.

Louis Mountbatten, 1900-1979, (Br.) Supreme Allied Commander of SE Asia, 1943-46.

Joachim Murat, 1767-1815, (F.) leader of cavalry at Marengo, 1800; Austerlitz, 1805; and Jena, 1806.

Horatio Nelson, 1758-1805, (Br.) naval commander destroyed French fleet at Trafalgar.

Michel Ney, 1769-1815, (F.) commanded forces in Switzerland, Austria, Russia; defeated at Waterloo.

Chester Nimitz, 1885-1966, (U.S.) commander of naval forces in Pacific in WW2.

George S. Patton, 1885-1945, (U.S.) led assault on Sicily, 1943; headed 3d Army invasion of German-occupied Europe.

Oliver Perry, 1785-1819, (U.S.) won Battle of Lake Erie in War of 1812.

John Pershing, 1860-1948, (U.S.) commanded Mexican border campaign, 1916; American expeditionary forces in WW1.

Henri Philippe Pétain, 1856-1951, (F.) defended Verdun, 1916; headed Vichy government in WW2.

George E. Pickett, 1825-1875, (U.S.) Confederate general famed for "charge" at Gettysburg.

Erwin Rommel, 1891-1944, (G.) headed Afrika Korps.

Karl v. Rundstedt, 1875-1953, (G.) supreme commander in West, 1943-45.

Aleksandr Samsonov, 1859-1914, (R.) led invasion of E. Prussia, defeated at Tannenberg, 1914.

Winfield Scott, 1786-1866, (U.S.) hero of War of 1812; headed forces in Mexican war, took Mexico City.

Philip Sheridan, 1831-1888, (U.S.) Union cavalry officer headed Army of the Shenandoah, 1864-65.

William T. Sherman, 1820-1891, (U.S.) Union general sacked Atlanta during "march to the sea," 1864.

Carl Spaatz, 1891-1974, (U.S.) directed strategic bombing against Germany, later Japan, in WW2.

Raymond Spruance, 1886-1969, (U.S.) victorious at Midway Island, 1942.

Joseph W. Stilwell, 1883-1946, (U.S.) headed forces in the China, Burma, India theater in WW2.

J.E.B. Stuart, 1833-1864, (U.S.) Confederate cavalry commander.

George H. Thomas, 1816-1870, (U.S.) saved Union army at Chattanooga, 1863; victorious at Nashville, 1864.

Semyon Timoshenko, 1895-1970, (USSR) defended Moscow, Stalingrad; led winter offensive, 1942-43.

Alfred v. Tirpitz, 1849-1930, (G.) responsible for submarine blockade in WW1.

Jonathan M. Wainwright, 1883-1953, (U.S.) forced to surrender on Corregidor, 1942.

George Washington, 1732-1799, (U.S.) led Continental army, 1775-83.

Archibald Wavell, 1883-1950, (Br.) commanded forces in N. and E. Africa, and SE Asia in WW2.

Anthony Wayne, 1745-1796, (U.S.) captured Stony Point, 1779; defeated Indians at Fallen Timbers, 1794.

Duke of Wellington, 1769-1852, (Br.) defeated Napoleon at Waterloo.

James Wolfe, 1727-1759, (Br.) captured Quebec from French, 1759.

Georgi Zhukov, 1895-1974, (USSR) defended Moscow, 1941; led assault on Berlin.

Noted Writers of the Past

Henry Adams, 1838-1918, (U.S.) historian, philosopher. *The Education of Henry Adams.*

George Ade, 1866-1944, (U.S.) humorist. *Fables in Slang.*

Conrad Aiken, 1889-1973, (U.S.) poet, critic.

Louisa May Alcott, 1832-1888, (U.S.) novelist. *Little Women.*

Sholom Aleichem, 1859-1916. (R.) Yiddish writer. *Tevye's Daughter, The Great Fair.*

Horatio Alger, 1832-1899, (U.S.) author of "rags-to-riches" boys' books.

Hans Christian Anderson, 1805-1875, (Den.) author of fairy tales. *The Princess and the Pea, The Ugly Duckling.*

Maxwell Anderson, 1888-1959, (U.S.) playwright. *What Price Glory?, High Tor, Winterset, Key Largo.*

Sherwood Anderson, 1876-1941, (U.S.) author. *Winesburg, Ohio.*

Matthew Arnold, 1822-1888, (Br.) poet, critic. "Thrysis," "Dover Beach."

Jane Austen, 1775-1817, (Br.) novelist. *Pride and Prejudice, Sense and Sensibility, Emma, Mansfield Park.*

Isaac Babel, 1894-1941, (R.) short-story writer, playwright. *Odessa Tales, Red Cavalry.*

Enid Bagnold, 1890-1981, (Br.) playwright, novelist. *National Velvet.*

James M. Barrie, 1860-1937, (Br.) playwright, novelist. *Peter Pan, Dear Brutus, What Every Woman Knows.*

Honoré de Balzac, 1799-1850, (Fr.) novelist. *Le Père Goriot, Cousine Bette, Eugénie Grandet, The Human Comedy.*

Charles Baudelaire, 1821-1867, (Fr.) symbolist poet. *Les Fleurs du Mal.*

L. Frank Baum, 1856-1919, (U.S.) children's author. Wizard of Oz series.

Brendan Behan, 1923-1964, (Ir.) playwright. *The Quare Fellow, The Hostage, Borstal Boy.*

Robert Benchley, 1889-1945, (U.S.) humorist. *From Bed to Worse, My Ten Years in a Quandary.*

Stephen Vincent Benét, 1898-1943, (U.S.) poet, novelist. *John Brown's Body.*

John Berryman, 1914-1972, (U.S.) poet. *Homage to Mistress Bradstreet.*

Ambrose Bierce, 1842-1914, (U.S.) short-story writer, journalist. *In the Midst of Life, The Devil's Dictionary.*

William Blake, 1757-1827, (Br.) poet, mystic, artist. *Songs of Innocence, Songs of Experience.*

Giovanni Boccaccio, 1313-1375, (It.) poet, storyteller. *Decameron, Filostrato.*

James Boswell, 1740-1795, (Sc.) author. *The Life of Samuel Johnson.*

Anne Bradstreet, c. 1612-1672, (U.S.) poet. *The Tenth Muse Lately Sprung Up in America.*

Bertolt Brecht, 1898-1956, (G.) dramatist, poet. *The Threepenny Opera, Mother Courage and Her Children.*

Charlotte Brontë, 1816-1855, (Br.) novelist. *Jane Eyre.*

Emily Brontë, 1818-1848, (Br.) novelist. *Wuthering Heights.*

Elizabeth Barrett Browning, 1806-1861, (Br.) poet. *Sonnets from the Portuguese.*

Robert Browning, 1812-1889, (Br.) poet. "My Last Duchess," "Soliloquy of the Spanish Cloister."

Pearl Buck, 1892-1973, (U.S.) novelist. *The Good Earth.*

Mikhail Bulgakov, 1891-1940, (R.) novelist, playwright. *The Heart of a Dog, The Master and Margarita.*

John Bunyan, 1628-1688, (Br.) writer. *Pilgrim's Progress.*

Robert Burns, 1759-1796, (Sc.) poet. "Flow Gently, Sweet Afton," "My Heart's in the Highlands," "Auld Lang Syne."

Edgar Rice Burroughs, 1875-1950, (U.S.) novelist. *Tarzan of the Apes.*

George Gordon Lord Byron, 1788-1824, (Br.) poet. *Don Juan, Childe Harold.*

Albert Camus, 1913-1960, (F.) novelist. *The Plague, The Stranger, Caligula, The Fall.*

Lewis Carroll, 1832-1898, (Br.) writer, mathematician. *Alice's Adventures in Wonderland, Through the Looking Glass.*

Karel Capek, 1890-1938, (Czech.) playwright, novelist, essayist. *R.U.R. (Rossum's Universal Robots).*

Giacomo Casanova, 1725-1798, (It.) Venetian adventurer, author, world famous for his memoirs.

Willa Cather, 1876-1947, (U.S.) novelist, essayist. *O Pioneers!, My Antonia.*

Miguel de Cervantes Saavedra, 1547-1616, (Sp.) novelist, dramatist, poet. *Don Quixote de la Mancha.*

Raymond Chandler, 1888-1959, (U.S.) writer of detective fiction. Philip Marlowe series.

Geoffrey Chaucer, c. 1340-1400, (Br.) poet. *The Canterbury Tales.*

Anton Chekhov, 1860-1904, (R.) short-story writer, dramatist. *Uncle Vanya, The Cherry Orchard, The Three Sisters.*

G.K. Chesterton, 1874-1936, (Br.) author, Fr. Brown series.

Agatha Christie, 1891-1976, (Br.) mystery writer. *And Then There Were None, Murder on the Orient Express.*

Jean Cocteau, 1889-1963, (F.) writer, visual artist, filmmaker. *The Beauty and the Beast, Enfants Terribles.*

Samuel Taylor Coleridge, 1772-1834, (Br.) poet, man of letters. "Kubla Khan," "The Rime of the Ancient Mariner."

Sidonie Colette, 1873-1954, (F.) novelist. *Claudine, Gigi.*

Joseph Conrad, 1857-1924, (Br.) novelist. *Lord Jim, Heart of Darkness, The Nigger of the Narcissus.*

James Fenimore Cooper, 1789-1851, (U.S.) novelist. *Leather-Stocking Tales.*

Pierre Corneille, 1606-1684, (F.) Dramatist. *Medeé, Le Cid, Horace, Cinna, Polyeucte.*

Hart Crane, 1899-1932, (U.S.) poet. "The Bridge."

Stephen Crane, 1871-1900, (U.S.) novelist. *The Red Badge of Courage.*

e.e. cummings, 1894-1962, (U.S.) poet. *Tulips and Chimneys.*

Gabriele D'Annunzio, 1863-1938, (It.) poet, novelist, dramatist. *The Child of Pleasure, The Intruder, The Victim.*

Dante Alighieri, 1265-1321, (It.) poet. *The Divine Comedy.*

Daniel Defoe, 1660-1731, (Br.) writer. *Robinson Crusoe, Moll Flanders, Journal of the Plague Year.*

Charles Dickens, 1812-1870, (Br.) novelist. *David Copperfield, Oliver Twist, Great Expectations, The Pickwick Papers.*

Emily Dickinson, 1830-1886, (U.S.) poet.

Isak Dinesen (Karen Blixen), 1885-1962, (Dan.) author. *Out of Africa, Seven Gothic Tales, Winter's Tales.*

John Donne, 1573-1631, (Br.) poet. *Songs and Sonnets, Holy Sonnets,* "Death Be Not Proud."

John Dos Passos, 1896-1970, (U.S.) author. *U.S.A.*

Fyodor Dostoyevsky, 1821-1881, (R.) author. *Crime and Punishment, The Brothers Karamazov, The Possessed.*

Arthur Conan Doyle, 1859-1930, (Br.) author, created Sherlock Holmes.

Theodore Dreiser, 1871-1945, (U.S.) novelist. *An American Tragedy, Sister Carrie.*

John Dryden, 1631-1700, (Br.) poet, dramatist, critic. *Fables, Ancient and Modern.*

Alexandre Dumas, 1802-1870, (F.) novelist, dramatist. *The Three Musketeers, The Count of Monte Cristo.*

Alexandre Dumas (fils), 1824-1895, (F.) dramatist, novelist. *La Dame aux camélias, Le Demi-Monde.*

Ilya G. Ehrenburg, 1891-1967, (R.) novelist, journalist. *The Thaw.*

George Eliot, 1819-1880, (Br.) novelist. *Adam Bede, Silas Marner, The Mill on the Floss.*

T.S. Eliot, 1888-1965, (Br.) poet, critic. *The Waste Land,* "The Love Song of J. Alfred Prufrock," *Murder in the Cathedral.*

Ralph Waldo Emerson, 1803-1882, (U.S.) poet, essayist. "The Concord Hymn," "Brahma," "The Rhodora."

James T. Farrell, 1904-1979, (U.S.) novelist. Studs Lonigan trilogy.

William Faulkner, 1897-1962, (U.S.) novelist. *Sanctuary, Light in August, The Sound and the Fury, Absalom, Absalom!*

Edna Ferber, 1885-1968, (U.S.) novelist, dramatist. *Show Boat, Saratoga Trunk, Giant, Dinner at Eight.*

Henry Fielding, 1707-1754, (Br.) novelist. *Tom Jones.*

F. Scott Fitzgerald, 1896-1940, (U.S.) short-story writer, novelist. *The Great Gatsby, Tender is the Night.*

Gustave Flaubert, 1821-1880, (F.) novelist. *Madame Bovary.*

C.S. Forester, 1899-1966, (Br.) novelist. Horatio Hornblower series.

E.M. Forster, 1879-1970, (Br.) novelist. *A Passage to India, Where Angels Fear to Tread, Maurice.*

Anatole France, 1844-1924. (F.) writer. *Penguin Island, My Friend's Book, Le Crime de Sylvestre Bonnard.*

Robert Frost, 1874-1963, (U.S.) poet. "Birches," "Fire and Ice," "Stopping by Woods on a Snowy Evening."

John Galsworthy, 1867-1923, (Br.) novelist, dramatist. *The Forsyte Saga, A Modern Comedy.*

Erle Stanley Gardner, 1889-1970, (U.S.) author, lawyer. Perry Mason series.

André Gide, 1869-1951, (F.) writer, *The Immoralist, The Pastoral Symphony, Strait is the Gate.*

Jean Giraudoux, 1882-1944, (F.) novelist, dramatist. *Electra, The Madwoman of Chaillot, Ondine, Tiger at the Gate.*

Johann W. von Goethe, 1749-1832, (G.) poet, dramatist, novelist. *Faust.*

Nikolai Gogol, 1809-1852, (R.) short-story writer, dramatist, novelist. *Dead Souls, The Inspector General.*

Oliver Goldsmith, 1730?-1774, (Br.-Ir.) writer. *The Vicar of Wakefield, She Stoops to Conquer.*

Maxim Gorky, 1868-1936, (R.) writer, founder of Soviet realism. *Mother, The Lower Depths.*

Thomas Gray, 1716-1771, (Br.) poet. "Elegy Written in a Country Churchyard."

Zane Grey, 1875-1939, (U.S.) writer of western stories.

Jakob Grimm, 1785-1863, (G.) philologist, folklorist. *German Methodology, Grimm's Fairy Tales.*

Wilhelm Grimm, 1786-1859, (G.) philologist, folklorist.

Grimm's Fairy Tales.

Edgar A. Guest, 1881-1959, (U.S.) poet. *A Heap of Livin!*

Dashiell Hammett, 1894-1961, (U.S.) writer of detective fiction, created Sam Spade.

Thomas Hardy, 1840-1928, (Br.) novelist, poet. *The Return of the Native, Tess of the D'Urbervilles, Jude the Obscure.*

Joel Chandler Harris, 1848-1908, (U.S.) short-story writer. Uncle Remus series.

Moss Hart, 1904-1961, (U.S.) playwright. *Once in a Lifetime, You Can't Take It With You.*

Bret Harte, 1836-1902, (U.S.) short-story writer, poet. *The Luck of Roaring Camp.*

Jaroslav Hasek, 1883-1923, (Czech.) writer. *The Good Soldier Schweik.*

Nathaniel Hawthorne, 1804-1864, (U.S.) novelist, short story writer. *The Scarlet Letter, The House of the Seven Gables.*

Heinrich Heine, 1797-1856, (G.) poet. *Book of Songs.*

Ernest Hemingway, 1899-1961, (U.S.) novelist, short-story writer. *A Farewell to Arms, For Whom the Bell Tolls.*

O. Henry (W.S. Porter), 1862-1910, (U.S.) short-story writer. "The Gift of the Magi."

Hermann Hesse, 1877-1962, (G.) novelist, poet. *Death and the Lover, Steppenwolf, Siddhartha.*

Oliver Wendell Holmes, 1809-1894, (U.S.) poet, novelist. *The Autocrat of the Breakfast-Table.*

Alfred E. Housman, 1859-1936, (Br.) poet. *A Shropshire Lad.*

William Dean Howells, 1837-1920, (U.S.) novelist, critic, dean of late 19th century American letters.

Langston Hughes, 1902-1967, (U.S.) poet, playwright. *The Weary Blues, One-Way Ticket, Shakespeare in Harlem.*

Victor Hugo, 1802-1885, (F.) poet, dramatist, novelist. *Notre Dame de Paris, Les Misérables.*

Aldous Huxley 1894-1963, (Br.) author. *Point Counter Point, Brave New World.*

Henrik Ibsen, 1828-1906, (Nor.) dramatist, poet. *A Doll's House, Ghosts, The Wild Duck, Hedda Gabler.*

William Inge, 1913-1973, (U.S.) playwright. *Come Back Little Sheba, Bus Stop, The Dark at the Top of the Stairs, Picnic.*

Washington Irving, 1783-1859, (U.S.) essayist, author. "Rip Van Winkle," "The Legend of Sleepy Hollow."

Shirley Jackson, 1919-1965, (U.S.) writer. *The Lottery.*

Henry James, 1843-1916, (U.S.) novelist, critic. *Washington Square, Portrait of a Lady, The American.*

Robinson Jeffers, 1887-1962, (U.S.) poet, dramatist. *Tamar and Other Poems, Medea.*

Samuel Johnson, 1709-1784, (Br.) author, scholar, critic. *Dictionary of the English Language.*

Ben Jonson, 1572-1637, (Br.) dramatist, poet. *Volpone.*

James Joyce, 1882-1941, (Ir.) novelist. *Ulysses, A Portrait of the Artist as a Young Man, Finnegans Wake.*

Franz Kafka, 1883-1924, (G.) novelist, short-story writer. *The Trial, Amerika, The Castle.*

George S. Kaufman, 1889-1961, (U.S.) playwright. *The Man Who Came to Dinner, You Can't Take It With You, Stage Door.*

Nikos Kazantzakis, 1883?-1957, (Gk.) novelist. *Zorba the Greek, A Greek Passion.*

John Keats, 1795-1821, (Br.) poet. *On a Grecian Urn, La Belle Dame Sans Merci.*

Joyce Kilmer, 1886-1918, (U.S.) poet, "Trees."

Rudyard Kipling, 1865-1936, (Br.) author, poet. "The White Man's Burden," "Gunga Din," *The Jungle Book.*

Jean de la Fontaine, 1621-1695, (F.) poet. *Fables choisies.*

Pär Lagerkvist, 1891-1974, (Swed.) poet, dramatist, novelist. *Barabbas, The Sybil.*

Selma Lagerlöf, 1858-1940, (Swed.) novelist. *Jerusalem, The Ring of the Lowenskolds.*

Alphonse de Lamartine, 1790-1869, (F.) poet, novelist, statesman. *Méditations poétiques.*

Charles Lamb, 1775-1834, (Br.) essayist. *Specimens of English Dramatic Poets, Essays of Elia.*

Giuseppe di Lampedusa, 1896-1957, (It.) novelist. *The Leopard.*

Ring Lardner, 1885-1933, (U.S.) short story writer, humorist. *You Know Me, Al.*

D. H. Lawrence, 1885-1930, (Br.) novelist. *Women in Love, Lady Chatterley's Lover, Sons and Lovers.*

Mikhail Lermontov, 1814-1841, (R.) novelist, poet. "Demon," *Hero of Our Time.*

Alain-René Lesage, 1668-1747, (F.) novelist. *Gil Blas de Santillane.*

Gotthold Lessing, 1729-1781, (G.) dramatist, philosopher, critic. *Miss Sara Sampson, Minna von Barnhelm.*

Sinclair Lewis, 1885-1951, (U.S.) novelist, playwright. *Babbitt, Arrowsmith, Dodsworth, Main Street.*

Vachel Lindsay, 1879-1931, (U.S.) poet. *General William Booth Enters into Heaven, The Congo.*

Hugh Lofting, 1886-1947, (Br.) children's author. Dr. Doolittle series.

Jack London, 1876-1916, (U.S.) novelist, journalist. *Call of the Wild, The Sea-Wolf.*

Henry Wadsworth Longfellow, 1807-1882, (U.S.) poet. *Evangeline, The Song of Hiawatha.*

Amy Lowell, 1874-1925, (U.S.) poet, critic. *A Dome of Many-Colored Glass,* "Patterns," "Lilacs."

James Russell Lowell, 1819-1891, (U.S.) poet, editor. *Poems, The Bigelow Papers.*

Robert Lowell, 1917-1977, (U.S.) poet. "Lord Weary's Castle," "For the Union Dead."

Emil Ludwig, 1881-1948, (G.) biographer. *Goethe, Beethoven, Napoleon, Bismarck.*

Niccolò Machiavelli, 1469-1527, (It.) author, statesman. *The Prince, Discourses on Livy.*

Stéphane Mallarmé, 1842-1898, (F.) poet. *The Afternoon of a Faun.*

Thomas Malory, ?-1471, (Br.) writer. *Morte d'Arthur.*

Andre Malraux, 1901-1976, (F.) novelist. *Man's Fate, The Voices of Silence.*

Osip Mandelstam, 1891-1938, (R.) Acmeist poet.

Thomas Mann, 1875-1955, (G.) novelist, essayist. *Buddenbrooks, Death in Venice, The Magic Mountain.*

Katherine Mansfield, 1888-1923, (Br.) short story writer. *Bliss, The Garden Party.*

Christopher Marlowe, 1564-1593, (Br.) dramatist, poet. *Tamburlaine the Great, Dr. Faustus, The Jew of Malta.*

John Masefield, 1878-1967, (Br.) poet. "Sea Fever," "Cargoes," *Salt Water Ballads.*

Edgar Lee Masters, 1869-1950, (U.S.) poet, biographer. *Spoon River Anthology.*

W. Somerset Maugham, 1874-1965, (Br.) author. *Of Human Bondage, The Razor's Edge, The Moon and Sixpence.*

Guy de Maupassant, 1850-1893, (F.) novelist, short-story writer. *A Life, Bel-Ami,* "The Necklace."

François Mauriac, 1885-1970, (F.) novelist, dramatist. *Viper's Tangle, The Kiss to the Leper.*

Vladimir Mayakovsky, 1893-1930, (R.) poet, dramatist. *The Cloud in Trousers.*

Carson McCullers, 1917-1967, (U.S.) novelist. *The Heart is a Lonely Hunter, Member of the Wedding.*

Herman Melville, 1819-1891, (U.S.) novelist, poet. *Moby Dick, Typee, Billy Budd, Omoo.*

H.L. Mencken, 1880-1956, (U.S.) author, critic, editor. *Prejudices, The American Language.*

George Meredith, 1828-1909, (Br.) novelist, poet. *The Ordeal of Richard Feverel, The Egoist.*

Prosper Mérimée, 1803-1870, (F.) author. *Carmen.*

Edna St. Vincent Millay, 1892-1950, (U.S.) poet. *The Harp Weaver and Other Poems, A Few Figs from Thistles.*

A.A. Milne, 1882-1956, (Br.) author. *When We Were Very Young, Winnie-the-Pooh, The House at Pooh Corner.*

John Milton, 1608-1674, (Br.) poet. *Paradise Lost, Samson Agonistes.*

Gabriela Mistral, 1889-1957, (Chil.) poet. *Sonnets of Death, Desolación, Tala, Lagar.*

Margaret Mitchell, 1900-1949, (U.S.) novelist. *Gone With the Wind.*

Jean Baptiste Molière, 1622-1673, (F.) dramatist. *Le Tartuffe, Le Misanthrope, Le Bourgeois Gentilhomme.*

Ferenc Molnár, 1878-1952, (Hung.) dramatist, novelist. *Liliom, The Guardsman, The Swan.*

Michel de Montaigne, 1533-1592, (F.) essayist. *Essais.*

Eugenio Montale, 1896-1981, (It.) poet.

Clement C. Moore, 1779-1863, (U.S.) poet, educator. "A Visit from Saint Nicholas."

Marianne Moore, 1887-1972, (U.S.) poet. *O to Be a Dragon.*

Thomas More, 1478-1535, (Br.) author. *Utopia.*

H.H. Munro (Saki), 1870-1916, (Br.) author. *Reginald, The Chronicles of Clovis, Beasts and Super-Beasts.*

Alfred de Musset, 1810-1857, (F.) poet, dramatist. *Confession d'un enfant du siècle.*

Vladimir Nabokov, 1899-1977, (U.S.) author. *Lolita, Ada.*

Ogden Nash, 1902-1971, (U.S.) poet. *Hard Lines, I'm a Stranger Here Myself, The Private Dining Room.*

Pablo Neruda, 1904-1973, (Chil.) poet. *Twenty Love Poems and One Song of Despair, Toward the Splendid City.*

Sean O'Casey, 1884-1964, (Ir.) dramatist. *Juno and the Paycock, The Plough and the Stars.*

Flannery O'Connor, 1925-1964, (U.S.) novelist, short story writer. *Wise Blood,* "A Good Man Is Hard to Find."

Clifford Odets, 1906-1963, (U.S.) playwright. *Waiting for Lefty, Awake and Sing, Golden Boy, The Country Girl.*

John O'Hara, 1905-1970, (U.S.) novelist. *Butterfield 8, From the Terrace, Appointment in Samarra.*

Omar Khayyam, c. 1028-1122, (Per.) poet. *Rubaiyat.*

Eugene O'Neill, 1888-1953, (U.S.) playwright. *Emperor Jones, Anna Christie, Long Day's Journey into Night, Desire Under the Elms, Mourning Becomes Electra.*

George Orwell, 1903-1950, (Br.) novelist, essayist. *Animal Farm, Nineteen Eighty-Four.*

Thomas (Tom) Paine, 1737-1809, (U.S.) author, political theorist. *Common Sense.*

Dorothy Parker, 1893-1967, (U.S.) poet, short-story writer. *Enough Rope, Laments for the Living.*

Boris Pasternak, 1890-1960, (R.) poet, novelist. *Doctor Zhivago, My Sister, Life.*

Samuel Pepys, 1633-1703, (Br.) public official, author of the greatest diary in the English language.

S. J. Perelman, 1904-1979, (U.S.) humorist. *The Road to Miltown, Under the Spreading Atrophy.*

Francesco Petrarca, 1304-1374, (It.) poet, humanist. *Africa, Trionfi, Canzoniere, On Solitude.*

Luigi Pirandello, 1867-1936, (It.) novelist, dramatist. *Six Characters in Search of an Author.*

Edgar Allan Poe, 1809-1849, (U.S.) poet, short-story writer, critic. "Annabel Lee," "The Raven," "The Purloined Letter."

Alexander Pope, 1688-1744, (Br.) poet. *The Rape of the Lock, An Essay on Man.*

Katherine Anne Porter, 1890-1980, (U.S.) novelist, short story writer. *Ship of Fools.*

Ezra Pound, 1885-1972, (U.S.) poet. *Cantos.*

Marcel Proust, 1871-1922, (F.) novelist. *A la recherche du temps perdu (Remembrance of Things Past).*

Aleksandr Pushkin, 1799-1837, (R.) poet, prose writer. *Boris Godunov, Eugene Onegin, The Bronze Horseman.*

François Rabelais, 1495-1553, (F.) writer, physician. Gargantua, Pantagruel.

Jean Racine, 1639-1699, (F.) dramatist. *Andromaque, Phèdre, Bérénice, Britannicus.*

Erich Maria Remarque, 1898-1970, (Ger.-U.S.) novelist. *All Quiet on the Western Front.*

Samuel Richardson, 1689-1761, (Br.) novelist. *Clarissa Harlowe, Pamela; or, Virtue Rewarded.*

James Whitcomb Riley, 1849-1916, (U.S.) poet. "When the Frost is on the Pumpkin," "Little Orphant Annie."

Rainer Maria Rilke, 1875-1926, (G.) poet. *Life and Songs, Divine Elegies, Sonnets to Orpheus.*

Arthur Rimbaud, 1854-1891, (F.) *A Season in Hell,* "Le Bateau ivre."

Edwin Arlington Robinson, 1869-1935, (U.S.) poet. "Richard Cory," "Miniver Cheevy."

Theodore Roethke, 1908-1963, (U.S.) poet. *Open House, The Waking, The Far Field.*

Romain Rolland, 1866-1944, (F.) novelist, biographer. *Jean-Christophe.*

Pierre de Ronsard, 1524-1585, (F.) poet. *Sonnets pour Hélène.*

Edmond Rostand, 1868-1918, (F.) poet, dramatist. *Cyrano de Bergerac.*

Damon Runyon, 1884-1946, (U.S.) short-story writer, journalist. *Guys and Dolls, Blue Plate Special.*

John Ruskin, 1819-1900, (Br.) critic, social theorist. *Modern Painters, The Seven Lamps of Architecture.*

Antoine de Saint-Exupery, 1900-1944, (F.) writer, aviator. *Wind, Sand and Stars, Le Petit Prince.*

George Sand, 1804-1876, (F.) novelist. *Consuelo, The Haunted Pool, Les Maitres sonneurs.*

Carl Sandburg, 1878-1967, (U.S.) poet. *Chicago Poems, Smoke and Steel, Harvest Poems.*

George Santayana, 1863-1952, (U.S.) poet, essayist, philosopher. *The Sense of Beauty, The Realms of Being.*

William Saroyan, 1908-1981, (U.S.) playwright, novelist. *The Time of Your Life, The Human Comedy.*

Friedrich von Schiller, 1759-1805, (G.) dramatist, poet, historian. *Don Carlos, Maria Stuart, Wilhelm Tell.*

Sir Walter Scott, 1771-1832, (Sc.) novelist, poet. Ivanhoe, Rob Roy, The Bride of Lammermoor.

William Shakespeare, 1564-1616, (Br.) dramatist, poet. *Romeo and Juliet, Hamlet, King Lear, The Merchant of Venice.*

George Bernard Shaw, 1856-1950, (Ir.) playwright, critic. *St. Joan, Pygmalion, Major Barbara, Man and Superman.*

Mary Wollstonecraft Shelley, 1797-1851, (Br.) author. *Frankenstein.*

Percy Bysshe Shelley, 1792-1822, (Br.) poet. *Prometheus Unbound, Adonais,* "Ode to the West Wind," "To a Skylark."

Richard B. Sheridan, 1751-1816, (Br.) dramatist. *The Rivals, School for Scandal.*

Robert Sherwood, 1896-1955, (U.S.) playwright. *The Petrified Forest, Abe Lincoln in Illinois, Reunion in Vienna.*

Upton Sinclair, 1878-1968, (U.S.) novelist. *The Jungle.*

Edmund Spenser, 1552-1599, (Br.) poet. *The Faerie Queen.*

Richard Steele, 1672-1729, (Br.) essayist, playwright, began the Tatler and Spectator. *The Conscious Lovers.*

Lincoln Steffens, 1866-1936, (U.S.) editor, author. *The Shame of the Cities.*

Gertrude Stein, 1874-1946, (U.S.) author. *Three Lives.*

John Steinbeck, 1902-1968, (U.S.) novelist. *Grapes of Wrath, Of Mice and Men, Winter of Our Discontent.*

Stendhal (Marie Henri Beyle), 1783-1842, (F.) poet, novelist. *The Red and the Black, The Charterhouse of Parma.*

Laurence Sterne, 1713-1768, (Br.) novelist. *Tristram Shandy.*

Wallace Stevens, 1879-1955, (U.S.) poet. *Harmonium, The Man With the Blue Guitar, Transport to Summer.*

Robert Louis Stevenson, 1850-1894, (Br.) novelist, poet, essayist. *Treasure Island, A Child's Garden of Verses.*

Rex Stout, 1886-1975, (U.S.) novelist, created Nero Wolfe.

Harriet Beecher Stowe, 1811-1896, (U.S.) novelist. *Uncle Tom's Cabin.*

Lytton Strachey, 1880-1932, (Br.) biographer, critic. *Eminent Victorians, Queen Victoria, Elizabeth and Essex.*

August Strindberg, 1849-1912, (Swed.) dramatist, novelist. *The Father, Miss Julie, The Creditors.*

Jonathan Swift, 1667-1745, (Br.) author. *Gulliver's Travels.*

Algernon C. Swinburne, 1837-1909, (Br.) poet, critic. *Songs Before Sunrise.*

John M. Synge, 1871-1909, (Ir.) poet, dramatist. *Riders to the Sea, The Playboy of the Western World.*

Rabindranath Tagore, 1861-1941, (Ind.), author, poet. *Sadhana, The Realization of Life, Gitanjali.*

Booth Tarkington, 1869-1946, (U.S.) novelist. *Seventeen, Alice Adams, Penrod.*

Sara Teasdale, 1884-1933, (U.S.) poet. *Helen of Troy and Other Poems, Rivers to the Sea, Flame and Shadow.*

Alfred Lord Tennyson, 1809-1892, (Br.) poet. *Idylls of the King, In Memoriam,* "The Charge of the Light Brigade."

William Makepeace Thackeray, 1811-1863, (Br.) novelist. *Vanity Fair.*

Dylan Thomas, 1914-1953, (Welsh) poet. *Under Milk Wood, A Child's Christmas in Wales.*

James Thurber, 1894-1961, (U.S.) humorist, artist. *The New Yorker, The Owl in the Attic, Thurber Carnival.*

J.R.R. Tolkien, 1892-1973, (Br.) author. *The Hobbit, Lord of the Rings.*

Lev Tolstoy, 1828-1910, (R.) novelist. *War and Peace, Anna Karenina.*

Anthony Trollope, 1815-1882, (Br.) novelist. *The Warden, Barchester Towers,* The Palliser novels.

Ivan Turgenev, 1818-1883, (R.) novelist, short-story writer. *Fathers and Sons, First Love, A Month in the Country.*

Mark Twain (Samuel Clemens), 1835-1910, (U.S.) novelist, humorist. *The Adventures of Huckleberry Finn, Tom Sawyer.*

Sigrid Undset, 1881-1949, (Nor.) novelist, poet. *Kristin Lavransdatter.*

Paul Valéry, 1871-1945, (F.) poet, critic. *La Jeune Parque, The Graveyard by the Sea.*

Jules Verne, 1828-1905, (F.) novelist, originator of modern science fiction. *Twenty Thousand Leagues Under the Sea.*

François Villon, 1431-1463?, (F.) poet. *Le petit et le Grand, Testament.*

Evelyn Waugh, 1903-1966, (Br.) satirist. *The Loved One.*

H.G. Wells, 1866-1946, (Br.) author. *The Time Machine, The Invisible Man, The War of the Worlds.*

Edith Wharton, 1862-1937, (U.S.) novelist. *The Age of Innocence, The House of Mirth.*

T.H. White, 1906-1964, (Br.) author. *The Once and Future King.*

Walt Whitman, 1819-1892, (U.S.) poet. *Leaves of Grass.*

John Greenleaf Whittier, 1807-1892, (U.S.) poet, journalist. *Snow-bound.*

Oscar Wilde, 1854-1900, (Ir.) author, wit. *The Picture of Dorian Gray, The Importance of Being Earnest.*

Thornton Wilder, 1897-1975, (U.S.) playwright. *Our Town, The Skin of Our Teeth, The Matchmaker.*

William Carlos Williams, 1883-1963, (U.S.) poet, physician. *Tempers, Al Que Quiere!, Paterson.*

Edmund Wilson, 1895-1972, (U.S.) author, literary and social critic. *Axel's Castle, To the Finland Station.*

P.G. Wodehouse, 1881-1975, (U.S.) poet, dramatist. The "Jeeves" novels, *Anything Goes.*

Thomas Wolfe, 1900-1938, (U.S.) novelist. *Look Homeward, Angel, You Can't Go Home Again, Of Time and the River.*

Virginia Woolf, 1882-1941, (Br.) novelist, essayist. *Mrs. Dalloway, To the Lighthouse, The Waves.*

William Wordsworth, 1770-1850, (Br.) poet. "Tintern Abbey," "Ode: Intimations of Immortality."

William Butler Yeats, 1865-1939, (Ir.) poet, playwright. *The Wild Swans at Coole, The Tower, Last Poems.*

Émile Zola, 1840-1902, (F.) novelist. *Nana, The Dram Shop.*

Poets Laureate of England

There is no authentic record of the origin of the office of Poet Laureate of England. According to Warton, there was a Versificator Regis, or King's Poet, in the reign of Henry III (1216-1272), and he was paid 100 shillings a year. Geoffrey Chaucer (1340-1400) assumed the title of Poet Laureate, and in 1389 got a royal grant of a yearly allowance of wine.

In the reign of Edward IV (1461-1483), John Kay held the post. Under Henry VII (1485-1509), Andrew Bernard was the Poet Laureate, and was succeeded under Henry VIII (1509-1547) by John Skelton. Next came Edmund Spenser, who died in 1599; then Samuel Daniel, appointed 1599, and then Ben Jonson, 1619. Sir William D'Avenant was appointed in 1637. He was a godson of William Shakespeare.

Others were John Dryden, 1670; Thomas Shadwell, 1688; Nahum Tate, 1692; Nicholas Rowe, 1715; the Rev. Laurence Eusden, 1718; Colley Cibber, 1730; William Whitehead, 1757, on the refusal of Gray; Rev. Thomas Warton, 1785, on the refusal of Mason; Henry J. Pye, 1790; Robert Southey, 1813, on the refusal of Sir Walter Scott; William Wordsworth, 1843; Alfred, Lord Tennyson, 1850; Alfred Austin, 1896; Robert Bridges, 1913; John Masefield, 1930; Cecil Day Lewis, 1967; Sir John Betjeman, 1972.

Noted Artists and Sculptors of the Past

Artists are painters unless otherwise indicated.

Washington Allston, 1779-1843, landscapist. Belshazzar's Feast.

Albrecht Altdorfer, 1480-1538, landscapist. Battle of Alexander.

Andrea del Sarto, 1486-1530, frescoes. Madonna of the Harpies.

Fra Angelico, c. 1400-1455, Renaissance muralist. Madonna of the Linen Drapers' Guild.

Alexsandr Archipenko, 1887-1964, sculptor. Boxing Match, Medranos.

John James Audubon, 1785-1851, Birds of America.

Hans Baldung Grien, 1484-1545, Todentanz.

Ernst Barlach, 1870-1938, Expressionist sculptor. Man Drawing a Sword.

Frederic-Auguste Bartholdi, 1834-1904, Liberty Enlightening the World, Lion of Belfort.

Fra Bartolommeo, 1472-1517, Vision of St. Bernard.

Aubrey Beardsley, 1872-1898, illustrator. Salome, Lysistrata.

Max Beckmann, 1884-1950, Expressionist. The Descent from the Cross.

Gentile Bellini, 1426-1507, Renaissance. Procession in St. Mark's Square.

Giovanni Bellini, 1428-1516, St. Francis in Ecstasy.

Jacopo Bellini, 1400-1470, Crucifixion.

George Wesley Bellows, 1882-1925, sports artist. Stag at Sharkey's.

Thomas Hart Benton, 1889-1975, American regionalist. Threshing Wheat, Arts of the West.

Gianlorenzo Bernini, 1598-1680, Baroque sculpture. The Assumption.

Albert Bierstadt, 1830-1902, landscapist. The Rocky Mountains, Mount Corcoran.

George Caleb Bingham, 1811-1879, Fur Traders Descending the Missouri.

William Blake, 1752-1827, engraver. Book of Job, Songs of Innocence, Songs of Experience.

Rosa Bonheur, 1822-1899, The Horse Fair.

Pierre Bonnard, 1867-1947, Intimist. The Breakfast Room.

Paul-Emile Borduas, 1905-1960, Abstractionist. Leeward of the Island, Enchanted Shields.

Gutzon Borglum, 1871-1941, sculptor. Mt. Rushmore Memorial.

Hieronymus Bosch, 1450-1516, religious allegories. The Crowning with Thorns.

Sandro Botticelli, 1444-1510, Renaissance. Birth of Venus.

Constantin Brancusi, 1876-1957, Nonobjective sculptor. Flying Turtle, The Kiss.

Georges Braque, 1882-1963, Cubist. Violin and Palette.

Pieter Bruegel the Elder, c. 1525-1569, The Peasant Dance.

Pieter Bruegel the Younger, 1564-1638, Village Fair, The Crucifixion.

Edward Burne-Jones, 1833-1898, Pre-Raphaelite artist-craftsman. The Mirror of Venus.

Alexander Calder, 1898-1976, sculptor. Lobster Trap and Fish Tail.

Michelangelo Merisi da Caravaggio, 1573-1610, Baroque. The Supper at Emmaus.

Emily Carr, 1871-1945, landscapist. Blunden Harbour, Big Raven.

Carlo Carra, 1881-1966, Metaphysical school. Lot's Daughters.

Mary Cassatt, 1845-1926, Impressionist. Woman Bathing.

George Catlin, 1796-1872, American Indian life. Gallery of Indians.

Benvenuto Cellini, 1500-1571, Mannerist sculptor, goldsmith. Perseus.

Paul Cezanne, 1839-1906, Card Players, Mont-Sainte-Victoire with Large Pine Trees.

Jean Simeon Chardin, 1699-1779, still lifes. The Kiss, The Grace.

Frederic Church, 1826-1900, Hudson River school. Niagara, Andes of Ecuador.

Cimabue, 1240-1302, Byzantine mosaicist. Madonna Enthroned with St. Francis.

Claude Lorrain, 1600-1682, ideal-landscapist. The Enchanted Castle.

Thomas Cole, 1801-1848, Hudson River school. The Ox-Bow.

John Constable, 1776-1837, landscapist. Salisbury Cathedral from the Bishop's Grounds.

John Singleton Copley, 1738-1815, portraitist. Samuel Adams, Watson and the Shark.

Lovis Corinth, 1858-1925, Expressionist. Apocalypse.

Jean-Baptiste-Camille Corot, 1796-1875, landscapist. Souvenir de Mortefontaine, Pastorale.

Correggio, 1494-1534, Renaissance muralist. Mystic Marriages of St. Catherine.

Gustave Courbet, 1819-1877, Realist. The Artist's Studio.

Lucas Cranach the Elder, 1472-1553, Protestant Reformation portraitist. Luther.

Nathaniel Currier, 1813-1888, and **James M. Ives,** 1824-1895, lithographers. A Midnight Race on the Mississippi.

Honore Daumier, 1808-1879, caricaturist. The Third-Class Carriage.

Jacques-Louis David, 1748-1825, Neoclassicist. The Oath of the Horatii.

Arthur Davies, 1862-1928, Romantic landscapist. Unicorns.

Edgar Degas, 1834-1917, The Ballet Class.

Eugene Delacroix, Co. 1400-1455, Romantic. Massacre at Chios.

Paul Delaroche, 1797-1856, historical themes. Children of Edward IV.

Luca Della Robbia, 1400-1482, Renaissance terracotta artist. Cantoria (singing gallery), Florence cathedral.

Donatello, 1386-1466, Renaissance sculptor. David, Gattamelata.

Raoul Dufy, 1877-1953, Fauvist. Chateau and Horses.

Asher Brown Durand, 1796-1886, Hudson River school. Kindred Spirits.

Albrecht Durer, 1471-1528, Renaissance engraver, woodcuts. St. Jerome in His Study, Melancholia I, Apocalypse.

Anthony van Dyck, 1599-1641, Baroque portraitist. Portrait of Charles I Hunting.

Thomas Eakins, 1844-1916, Realist. The Gross Clinic.

Jacob Epstein, 1880-1959, religious and allegorical sculptor. Genesis, Ecce Homo.

Jan van Eyck, 1380-1441, naturalistic panels. Adoration of the Lamb.

Anselm Feuerbach, 1829-1880, Romantic Classicism. Judgement of Paris, Iphigenia.

John Bernard Flannagan, 1895-1942, animal sculptor. Triumph of the Egg.

Jean-Honore Fragonard, 1732-1806, Rococo. The Swing.

Daniel Chester French, 1850-1931, The Minute Man of Concord; seated Lincoln, Lincoln Memorial, Washington, D.C.

Caspar David Friedrich, 1774-1840, Romantic landscapes. Man and Woman Gazing at the Moon.

Thomas Gainsborough, 1727-1788, portraitist. The Blue Boy.

Paul Gauguin, 1848-1903, Post-impressionist. The Tahitians.

Lorenzo Ghiberti, 1378-1455, Renaissance sculptor. Gates of Paradise baptistry doors, Florence.

Alberto Giacometti, 1901-1966, attenuated sculptures of solitary figures. Man Pointing.

Giorgione, c. 1477-1510, Renaissance. The Tempest.

Giotto di Bondone, 1267-1337, Renaissance. Presentation of Christ in the Temple.

Francois Girardon, 1628-1715, Baroque sculptor of classical themes. Apollo Tended by the Nymphs.

Vincent van Gogh, 1853-1890, The Starry Night, L'Arlesienne.

Arshile Gorky, 1905-1948, Surrealist. The Liver Is the Cock's Comb.

Francisco de Goya y Lucientes, 1746-1828, The Naked Maja, The Disasters of War (etchings).

El Greco, 1541-1614, View of Toledo, Burial of the Count of Orgaz.

Horatio Greenough, 1805-1852, Neo-classical sculptor. George Washington.

Matthias Grünewald, 1480-1528, mystical religious themes.

The Resurrection.

Frans Hals, c. 1580-1666, portraitist. Laughing Cavalier, Gypsy Girl.

Childe Hassam, 1859-1935, Impressionist. Southwest Wind.

Edward Hicks, 1780-1849, folk painter. The Peaceable Kingdom.

Hans Hofmann, 1880-1966, early Abstract Expressionist. Spring. The Gate.

William Hogarth, 1697-1764, caricaturist. The Rake's Progress.

Katsushika Hokusai, 1760-1849, printmaker. Crabs.

Hans Holbein the Elder, 1460-1524, late Gothic. Presentation of Christ in the Temple.

Hans Holbein the Younger, 1497-1543, portraitist. Henry VIII.

Winslow Homer, 1836-1910, marine themes. Marine Coast, High Cliff.

Edward Hopper, 1882-1967, realistic urban scenes. Sunlight in a Cafeteria.

Jean-Auguste-Dominique Ingres, 1780-1867, Classicist. Valpincon Bather.

George Inness, 1825-1894, luminous landscapist. Delaware Water Gap.

Vasily Kandinsky, 1866-1944, Abstractionist. Capricious Forms.

Paul Klee, 1879-1940, Abstractionist. Twittering Machine.

Kathe Kollwitz, 1867-1945, printmaker, social justice themes. The Peasant War.

Gaston Lachaise, 1882-1935, figurative sculptor. Standing Woman.

John La Farge, 1835-1910, muralist. Red and White Peonies.

Fernand Leger, 1881-1955, machine art. The Cyclists, Adam and Eve.

Leonardo da Vinci, 1452-1519, Mona Lisa, Last Supper, The Annunciation.

Emanuel Leutze, 1816-1868, historical themes. Washington Crossing the Delaware.

Jacques Lipchitz, 1891-1973, Cubist sculptor. Harpist.

Filippino Lippi, 1457-1504, Renaissance. The Vision of St. Bernard.

Fra Filippo Lippi, 1406-1469, Renaissance. Coronation of the Virgin.

Morris Louis, 1912-1962, abstract expressionist. Signa, Stripes.

Aristide Maillol, 1861-1944, sculptor. Night, The Mediterranean.

Edouard Manet, 1832-1883, forerunner of Impressionism. Luncheon on the Grass, Olympia.

Andrea Mantegna, 1431-1506, Renaissance frescoes. Triumph of Caesar.

Franz Marc, 1880-1916, Expressionist. Blue Horses.

John Marin, 1870-1953, expressionist seascapes. Maine Island.

Reginald Marsh, 1898-1954, satirical artist. Tattoo and Haircut.

Masaccio, 1401-1428, Renaissance. The Tribute Money.

Henri Matisse, 1869-1954, Fauvist. Woman with the Hat.

Michelangelo Buonarroti, 1475-1564, Pieta, David, Moses, The Last Judgment, Sistine Ceiling.

Carl Milles, 1875-1955, expressive rhythmic sculptor. Playing Bears.

Jean-Francois Millet, 1814-1875, painter of peasant subjects. The Gleaners, The Man with a Hoe.

David Milne, 1882-1953, landscapist. Boston Corner, Berkshire Hills.

Amedeo Modigliani, 1884-1920, Reclining Nude.

Piet Mondrian, 1872-1944, Abstractionist. Composition.

Claude Monet, 1840-1926, Impressionist. The Bridge at Argenteuil, Haystacks.

Gustave Moreau, 1826-1898, Symbolist. The Apparition, Dance of Salome.

James Wilson Morrice, 1865-1924, landscapist. The Ferry, Quebec, Venice, Looking Over the Lagoon.

Grandma Moses, 1860-1961, folk painter. Out for the Christmas Trees.

Edvard Munch, 1863-1944, Expressionist death themes. The Cry.

Bartolome Murillo, 1618-1682, Baroque religious artist. Vision of St. Anthony. The Two Trinities.

Barnett Newman, 1905-1970, Abstract Expressionist. Stations of the Cross.

Jose Clemente Orozco, 1883-1949, frescoes. House of Tears.

Charles Willson Peale, 1741-1827, American Revolutionary portraitist. Washington, Franklin, Jefferson, John Adams.

Rembrandt Peale, 1778-1860, portraitist. Thomas Jefferson.

Pietro Perugino, 1446-1523, Renaissance. Delivery of the Keys to St. Peter.

Pablo Picasso, 1881-1973, Guernica, Dove, Head of a Woman.

Piero della Francesca, c. 1415-1492, Renaissance. Duke of Urbino, Flagellation of Christ.

Camille Pissarro, 1830-1903, Impressionist. Morning Sunlight.

Jackson Pollock, 1912-1956, Abstract Expressionist. Autumn Rhythm.

Nicolas Poussin, 1594-1665, Baroque pictorial classicism. St. John on Patmos.

Maurice B. Prendergast, c. 1860-1924, Post-impressionist water colorist. Umbrellas in the Rain.

Pierre-Paul Prud'hon, 1758-1823, Romanticist. Crime pursued by Vengeance and Justice.

Pierre Cecile Puvis de Chavannes, 1824-1898, muralist. The Poor Fisherman.

Raphael Sanzio, 1483-1520, Renaissance. Disputa, School of Athens, Sistine Madonna.

Man Ray, 1890-1976, Dadaist. Observing Time, The Lovers.

Odilon Redon, 1840-1916, Symbolist lithographer. In the Dream.

Rembrandt van Rijn, 1606-1669, The Bridal Couple, The Night Watch.

Frederic Remington, 1861-1909, painter, sculptor, portrayer of the American West. Bronco Buster, Cavalry Charge on the Southern Plains.

Pierre-Auguste Renoir, 1841-1919, Impressionist. The Luncheon of the Boating Party.

Ilya Repin, 1844-1918, historical canvases. Zaporozhye Cossacks.

Joshua Reynolds, 1723-1792, portraitist. Mrs. Siddons as the Tragic Muse.

Diego Rivera, 1886-1957, frescoes. The Fecund Earth.

Auguste Rodin, 1840-1917, sculptor. The Thinker, The Burghers of Calais.

Mark Rothko, 1903-1970, Abstract Expressionist. Light, Earth and Blue.

Georges Rouault, 1871-1958, Expressionist. The Old King.

Henri Rousseau, 1844-1910, primitive exotic themes. The Snake Charmer.

Theodore Rousseau, 1812-1867, landscapist. Under the Birches, Evening.

Peter Paul Rubens, 1577-1640, Baroque. Mystic Marriage of St. Catherine.

Andrey Rublyov, 1370-1430, icon painter. Old Testament Trinity.

Jacob van Ruisdael, c. 1628-1682, landscapist. Jewish Cemetery.

Salomon van Ruysdael, c. 1600-1670, landscapist. River with Ferry-Boat.

Albert Pinkham Ryder, 1847-1917, seascapes and allegories. Toilers of the Sea.

Augustus Saint-Gaudens, 1848-1907, memorial statues. Farragut, Mrs. Henry Adams (Grief).

Andrea Sansovino, 1460-1529, Renaissance sculptor. Baptism of Christ.

Jacopo Sansovino, 1486-1570, Renaissance sculptor. St. John the Baptist.

John Singer Sargent, 1856-1925, Edwardian society portraitist. The Wyndham Sisters, Madam X.

Johann Gottfried Schadow, 1764-1850, monumental sculptor. Quadriga, Brandenburg Gate.

Georges Seurat, 1859-1891, Pointillist. Sunday Afternoon on the Island of Grande Jatte.

Gino Severini, 1883-1891, Futurist and Cubist. Dynamic Hieroglyph of the Bal Tabarin.

Ben Shahn, 1898-1969, social and political themes. Sacco and Vanzetti series, Seurat's Lunch, Handball.

Charles Sheeler, 1883-1965, Abstractionist. Upper Deck, Rolling Power.

David Alfaro Siqueiros, 1896-1974, political muralist. March of Humanity.

John F. Sloan, 1871-1951, depictions of New York City. Wake of the Ferry.

David Smith, 1906-1965, welded metal sculpture. Hudson River Landscape, Zig, Cubi series.

Gilbert Stuart, 1755-1828, portraitist. George Washington.

Thomas Sully, 1783-1872, portraitist. Col. Thomas Handasyd Perkins, The Passage of the Delaware.

Yves Tanguy, 1900-1955, Surrealist. Rose of the Four Winds.

Thomas J. Thomson, 1877-1918, landscapist. Spring Ice.

Giovanni Battista Tiepolo, 1696-1770, Rococo frescoes. The Crucifixion.

Jacopo Tintoretto, 1518-1594, Mannerist. The Last Supper.

Titian, c. 1485-1576, Renaissance. Venus and the Lute Player, The Bacchanal.

Henri de Toulouse-Lautrec, 1864-1901, At the Moulin Rouge.

John Trumbull, 1756-1843, historical themes. The Declaration of Independence.

Joseph Mallord William Turner, 1775-1851, Romantic landscapist. Snow Storm.

Paolo Uccello, 1397-1475, Gothic-Renaissance. The Rout of San Romano.

Maurice Utrillo, 1883-1955, Impressionist. Sacre-Coeur de Montmartre.

John Vanderlyn, 1775-1852, Neo-classicist. Ariadne Asleep on the Island of Naxos.

Diego Velazquez, 1599-1660, Baroque. Las Meninas, Portrait of Juan de Pareja.

Jan Vermeer, 1632-1675, interior genre subjects. Young Woman with a Water Jug.

Paolo Veronese, 1528-1588, devotional themes, vastly peopled canvases. The Temptation of St. Anthony.

Andrea del Verrocchio, 1435-1488, Florentine sculptor. Colleoni.

Maurice de Vlaminck, 1876-1958, Fauvist landscapist. The Storm.

Antoine Watteau, 1684-1721, Rococo painter of "scenes of gallantry". The Embarkation for Cythera.

George Frederic Watts, 1817-1904, painter and sculptor of grandiose allegorical themes. Hope, Physical Energy.

Benjamin West, 1738-1820, realistic historical themes. Death of General Wolfe.

James Abbott McNeill Whistler, 1834-1903, Arrangement in Grey and Black, No. 1: The Artist's Mother.

Archibald M. Willard, 1836-1918, The Spirit of '76.

Grant Wood, 1891-1942, Midwestern regionalist. American Gothic, Daughters of Revolution.

Ossip Zadkine, 1890-1967, School of Paris sculptor. The Destroyed City, Musicians, Christ.

Noted Philosophers and Religionists of the Past

Lyman Abbott, 1835-1922, (U.S.) clergyman, reformer; advocate of Christian Socialism.

Pierre Abelard, 1079-1142, (F.) philosopher, theologian, and teacher, used dialectic method to support Christian dogma.

Felix Adler, 1851-1933, (U.S.) German-born founder of the Ethical Culture Society.

St. Augustine, 354-430, Latin bishop considered the founder of formalized Christian theology.

Averroes, 1126-1198, (Sp.) Islamic philosopher.

Roger Bacon, c.1214-1294, (Br.) philosopher and scientist.

Karl Barth, 1886-1968, (Sw.) theologian, a leading force in 20th-century Protestantism.

St. Benedict, c.480-547, (It.) founded the Benedictines.

Jeremy Bentham, 1748-1832, (Br.) philosopher, reformer, founder of Utilitarianism.

Henri Bergson, 1859-1941, (F.) philosopher of evolution.

George Berkeley, 1685-1753, (Ir.) philosopher, churchman.

John Biddle, 1615-1662, (Br.) founder of English Unitarianism.

Jakob Boehme, 1575-1624, (G.) theosophist and mystic.

William Brewster, 1567-1644, (Br.) headed Pilgrims, signed Mayflower Compact.

Emil Brunner, 1889-1966, (Sw.) theologian.

Giordano Bruno, 1548-1600, (It.) philosopher.

Martin Buber, 1878-1965, (G.) Jewish philosopher, theologian, wrote *I and Thou.*

Buddha (Siddhartha Gautama), c.563-c.483 BC, (Ind.) philosopher, founded Buddhism.

John Calvin, 1509-1564, (F.) theologian, a key figure in the Protestant Reformation.

Rudolph Carnap, 1891-1970, (U.S.) German-born philosopher, a founder of logical positivism.

William Ellery Channing, 1780-1842, (U.S.) clergyman, early spokesman for Unitarianism.

Auguste Comte, 1798-1857, (F.) philosopher, the founder of positivism.

Confucius, 551-479 BC, (Chin.) founder of Confucianism.

John Cotton, 1584-1652, (Br.) Puritan theologian.

Thomas Cranmer, 1489-1556, (Br.) churchman, wrote much of the first *Book of Common Prayer;* promoter of the English Reformation.

René Descartes, 1596-1650, (F.) philosopher, mathematician.

John Dewey, 1859-1952, (U.S.) philosopher, educator; helped inaugurate the progressive education movement.

Denis Diderot, 1713-1784, (F.) philosopher, creator of first modern encyclopedia.

Mary Baker Eddy, 1821-1910, (U.S.) founder of Christian Science.

Jonathan Edwards, 1703-1758, (U.S.) preacher, theologian.

(Desiderius) Erasmus, c.1466-1536, (Du.) Renaissance humanist.

Johann Fichte, 1762-1814, (G.) philosopher, the first of the Transcendental Idealists.

George Fox, 1624-1691, (Br.) founder of Society of Friends.

St. Francis of Assisi, 1182-1226, (It.) founded the Franciscans.

al Ghazali, 1058-1111, Islamic philosopher.

Georg W. Hegel, 1770-1831, (G.) Idealist philosopher.

Martin Heidegger, 1889-1976, (G.) existentialist philosopher, affected fields ranging from physics to literary criticism.

Johann G. Herder, 1744-1803, (G.) philosopher, cultural historian; a founder of German Romanticism.

David Hume, 1711-1776, (Sc.) philosopher, historian.

Jan Hus, 1369-1415, (Czech.) religious reformer.

Edmund Husserl, 1859-1938, (G.) philosopher, founded the Phenomenological movement.

Thomas Huxley, 1825-1895, (Br.) agnostic philosopher, educator.

Ignatius of Loyola, 1491-1556, (Sp.) founder of the Jesuits.

William Inge, 1860-1954, (Br.) theologian, explored the mystic aspects of Christianity.

William James, 1842-1910, (U.S.) philosopher, psychologist; advanced theory of the pragmatic nature of truth.

Karl Jaspers, 1883-1969, (G.) existentialist philosopher.

Immanuel Kant, 1724-1804, (G.) metaphysician, preeminent founder of modern critical philosophy.

Soren Kierkegaard, 1813-1855, (Den.) philosopher, considered the father of Existentialism.

John Knox, 1505-1572, (Sc.) leader of the Protestant Reformation in Scotland.

Lao-Tzu, 604-531 BC, (Chin.) philosopher, considered the founder of the Taoist religion.

Gottfried von Leibniz, 1646-1716, (G.) philosopher, mathematician.

Martin Luther, 1483-1546, (G.) leader of the Protestant Reformation, founded Lutheran church.

Maimonides, 1135-1204, (Sp.) Jewish physician and philosopher.

Jacques Maritain, 1882-1973, (F.) Neo-Thomist philosopher.

Cotton Mather, 1663-1728, (U.S.) defender of orthodox Puritanism; founded Yale, 1703.

Aimee Semple McPherson, 1890-1944, (U.S.) evangelist.

Philipp Melanchthon, 1497-1560, (G.) theologian, humanist; an important voice in the Reformation.

Mohammed, c.570-632, Arab prophet of the religion of Islam.

Dwight Moody, 1837-1899, (U.S.) evangelist.

George E. Moore, 1873-1958, (Br.) ethical theorist.

Elijah Muhammad, 1897-1975, (U.S.) leader of the Black Muslim sect.

Heinrich Muhlenberg, 1711-1787, (G.) organized the Lutheran Church in America.

John H. Newman, 1801-1890, (Br.) Roman Catholic cardinal, led Oxford Movement.

Reinhold Niebuhr, 1892-1971, (U.S.) Protestant theologian, social and political critic.

Friedrich Nietzsche, 1844-1900, (G.) moral philosopher.

Blaise Pascal, 1623-1662, (F.) philosopher and mathematician.

St. Patrick, c.389-c.461, brought Christianity to Ireland.

St. Paul, ?-c.67, a founder of the Christian religion.

Charles S. Peirce, 1839-1914, (U.S.) philosopher, logician; originated concept of Pragmatism, 1878.

Josiah Royce 1855-1916, (U.S.) Idealist philosopher.

Charles T. Russell, 1852-1916, (U.S.) founder of Jehovah's Witnesses.

Fredrich von Schelling, 1775-1854, (G.) philosopher.

Friedrich Schleiermacher, 1768-1834, (G.) theologian, a founder of modern Protestant theology.

Arthur Schopenhauer, 1788-1860, (G.) philosopher.

Joseph Smith, 1805-1844, (U.S.) founded Latter Day Saints (Mormon) movement, 1830.

Herbert Spencer, 1820-1903, (Br.) philosopher of evolution.

Baruch Spinoza, 1632-1677, (Du.) rationalist philosopher.

Billy Sunday, 1862-1935, (U.S.) evangelist.

Daisetz Teitaro Suzuki, 1870-1966, (Jap.) Buddhist scholar.

Emanuel Swedenborg, 1688-1722, (Swed.) philosopher, mystic.

Thomas à Becket, 1118-1170, (Br.) archbishop of Canterbury, opposed Henry II.

Thomas à Kempis, c.1380-1471, (G.) theologian probably wrote *Imitation of Christ.*

Thomas Aquinas, 1225-1274, (It.) theologian and philosopher.

Paul Tillich, 1886-1965, (U.S.) German-born philosopher and theologian.

John Wesley, 1703-1791, (Br.) theologian, evangelist; founded Methodism.

Alfred North Whitehead, 1861-1947, (Br.) philosopher, mathematician.

William of Occam, c.1285-c.1349 (Br.) philosopher.

Roger Williams, c.1603-1683, (U.S.) clergyman, championed

religious freedom and separation of church and state.
Ludwig Wittgenstein, 1889-1951, (Aus.) philosopher.
John Wycliffe, 1320-1384, (Br.) theologian, reformer.
Brigham Young, 1801-1877, (U.S.) Mormon leader, colonized Utah.
Huldrych Zwingli, 1484-1531, (Sw.) theologian, led Swiss Protestant Reformation.

Noted Social Reformers and Educators of the Past

Jane Addams, 1860-1935, (U.S.) co-founder of Hull House; won Nobel Peace Prize, 1931.
Susan B. Anthony, 1820-1906, (U.S.) a leader in temperance, anti-slavery, and women's suffrage movements.
Henry Barnard, 1811-1900, (U.S.) public school reformer.
Thomas Barnardo, 1845-1905, (Br.) social reformer, pioneered in the care of destitute children.
Clara Barton, 1821-1912, (U.S.) organizer of the American Red Cross.
Henry Ward Beecher, 1813-1887, (U.S.) clergyman, abolitionist.
Amelia Bloomer, 1818-1894, (U.S.) social reformer, women's rights advocate.
William Booth, 1829-1912, (Br.) founded the Salvation Army.
Nicholas Murray Butler, 1862-1947, (U.S.) educator headed Columbia Univ., 1902-45; won Nobel Peace Prize, 1931.
Frances X. (Mother) Cabrini, 1850-1917, (U.S.) Italian-born nun founded numerous charitable institutions; first American to be canonized.
Carrie Chapman Catt, 1859-1947, (U.S.) suffragette, helped win passage of the 19th amendment.
Dorothy Day, 1897-1980, (U.S.) founder of Catholic Worker Movement.
Eugene V. Debs, 1855-1926, (U.S.) labor leader, led Pullman strike, 1894; 4-time Socialist presidential candidate.
Melvil Dewey, 1851-1931, (U.S.) devised decimal system of library-book classification.
Dorothea Dix, 1802-1887, (U.S.) crusader for humane care of mentally ill.
Frederick Douglass, 1817-1895, (U.S.) abolitionist.
W.E.B. DuBois, 1868-1963, (U.S.) Negro-rights leader, educator, and writer.
William Lloyd Garrison, 1805-1879, (U.S.) abolitionist, reformer.
Giovanni Gentile, 1875-1944, (It.) philosopher, educator; reformed Italian educational system.
Samuel Gompers, 1850-1924, (U.S.) labor leader; a founder and president of AFL.
William Green, 1873-1952, (U.S.) president of AFL, 1924-52.
Sidney Hillman, 1887-1946, (U.S.) labor leader, helped organize CIO.
Samuel G. Howe, 1801-1876, (U.S.) social reformer, changed public attitudes toward the handicapped.
Helen Keller, 1880-1968, (U.S.) crusader for better treatment for the handicapped.
Martin Luther King Jr., 1929-1968, (U.S.) civil rights leader; won Nobel Peace Prize, 1964.
John L. Lewis, 1880-1969, (U.S.) labor leader, headed United Mine Workers, 1920-60.
Horace Mann, 1796-1859, (U.S.) pioneered modern public school system.
William H. McGuffey, 1800-1873, (U.S.) author of *Reader,* the mainstay of 19th century U.S. public education.
Alexander Meiklejohn, 1872-1964, (U.S.) British-born educator, championed academic freedom and experimental curricula.
Lucretia Mott, 1793-1880, (U.S.) reformer, pioneer feminist.
Philip Murray, 1886-1952, (U.S.) Scotch-born labor leader.
Florence Nightingale, 1820-1910, (Br.) founder of modern nursing.
Emmeline Pankhurst, 1858-1928, (Br.) woman suffragist.
Elizabeth P. Peabody, 1804-1894, (U.S.) education pioneer, founded 1st kindergarten in U.S., 1860.
Walter Reuther, 1907-1970, (U.S.) labor leader, headed UAW.
Jacob Riis, 1849-1914, (U.S.) crusader for urban reforms.
Margaret Sanger, 1883-1966, (U.S.) social reformer, pioneered the birth control movement.
Elizabeth Seton, 1774-1821, (U.S.) established parochial school education in U.S.
Earl of Shaftesbury (A.A. Cooper), 1801-1885, (Br.) social reformer.
Elizabeth Cady Stanton, 1815-1902, (U.S.) women's suffrage pioneer.
Lucy Stone, 1818-1893, (U.S.) feminist, abolitionist.
Harriet Tubman, c.1820-1913, (U.S.) abolitionist, ran Underground Railroad.
Booker T. Washington, 1856-1915, (U.S.) educator, reformer; championed vocational training for blacks.
Walter F. White, 1893-1955, (U.S.) headed NAACP, 1931-55.
William Wilberforce, 1759-1833, (Br.) social reformer, prominent in struggle to abolish the slave trade.
Emma Hart Willard, 1787-1870, (U.S.) pioneered higher education for women.
Frances E. Willard, 1839-1898, (U.S.) temperance, woman's rights leader.
Whitney M. Young Jr., 1921-1971, (U.S.) civil rights leader, headed National Urban League, 1961-71.

Noted Historians, Economists, and Social Scientists of the Past

Brooks Adams, 1848-1927, (U.S.) historian, political theoretician.
Francis Bacon, 1561-1626, (Br.) philosopher, essayist, and statesman.
George Bancroft, 1800-1891, (U.S.) historian, wrote 10-volume *History of the United States.*
Charles A. Beard, 1874-1948, (U.S.) historian, attacked motives of the Founding Fathers.
Bede (the Venerable), c.673-735, (Br.) scholar, historian.
Ruth Benedict, 1887-1948, (U.S.) anthropologist, studied Indian tribes of the Southwest.
Louis Blanc, 1811-1882, (F.) Socialist leader and historian whose ideas were a link between utopian and Marxist socialism.
Franz Boas, 1858-1942, (U.S.) German-born anthropologist, studied American Indians.
Van Wyck Brooks, 1886-1963, (U.S.) cultural historian, critic.
Edmund Burke, 1729-1797, (Ir.) British parliamentarian and political philosopher; influenced many Federalists.
Thomas Carlyle, 1795-1881, (Sc.) philosopher, historian, and critic.
Edward Channing, 1856-1931, (U.S.) historian wrote 6-volume *A History of the United States.*
John R. Commons, 1862-1945, (U.S.) economist, labor historian.
Benedetto Croce, 1866-1952, (It.) philosopher, statesman, and historian.
Bernard A. De Voto, 1897-1955, (U.S.) historian, won Pulitzer prize in 1948 for *Across the Wide Missouri.*
Ariel Durant, 1898-1981, (U.S.) historian, collaborated with husband on 11-volume *The Story of Civilization.*
Will Durant, 1885-1981, (U.S.) historian. *The Story of Civilization, The Story of Philosophy.*
Emile Durkheim, 1858-1917, (F.) a founder of modern sociology.
Friedrich Engels, 1820-1895, (G.) political writer, with Marx wrote the *Communist Manifesto.*
Irving Fisher, 1867-1947, (U.S.) economist, contributed to the development of modern monetary theory.
John Fiske, 1842-1901, (U.S.) historian and lecturer, popularized Darwinian theory of evolution.
Charles Fourier, 1772-1837, (F.) utopian socialist.
Henry George, 1839-1897, (U.S.) economist, reformer, led single-tax movement.
Edward Gibbon, 1737-1794, (Br.) historian, wrote *The History of the Decline and Fall of the Roman Empire.*
Francesco Guicciardini, 1483-1540, (It.) historian, wrote *Storia d'Italia,* principal historical work of the 16th-century.
Alvin Hansen, 1887-1975, (U.S.) economist.
Thomas Hobbes, 1588-1679, (Br.) social philosopher.
Richard Hofstadter, 1916-1970, (U.S.) historian, wrote *The Age of Reform.*
John Maynard Keynes, 1883-1946, (Br.) economist, principal advocate of deficit spending.
Alfred L. Kroeber, 1876-1960, (U.S.) cultural anthropologist, studied Indians of North and South America.
James L. Laughlin, 1850-1933, (U.S.) economist, helped establish Federal Reserve System.
Lucien Lévy-Bruhl, 1857-1939, (F.) philosopher, studied the psychology of primitive societies.
Kurt Lewin, 1890-1947, (U.S.) German-born psychologist, studied human motivation and group dynamics.
John Locke, 1632-1704, (Br.) political philosopher.
Thomas B. Macauley, 1800-1859, (Br.) historian, statesman.
Bronislaw Malinowski, 1884-1942, (Pol.) anthropologist, considered the father of social anthropology.
Thomas R. Malthus, 1766-1834, (Br.) economist, famed for *Essay on the Principle of Population.*
Karl Mannheim, 1893-1947, (Hung.) sociologist, historian.

Karl Marx, 1818-1883, (G.) political philosopher, proponent of modern communism.
Giuseppe Mazzini, 1805-1872, (It.) political philosopher.
George H. Mead, 1863-1931, (U.S.) philosopher and social psychologist.
Margaret Mead, 1901-1978, (U.S.) cultural anthropologist, popularized field.
James Mill, 1773-1836, (Sc.) philosopher, historian, and economist; a proponent of Utilitarianism.
John Stuart Mill, 1806-1873, (Br.) philosopher, political economist.
Perry G. Miller, 1905-1963, (U.S.) historian, interpreted 17th-century New England.
Theodor Mommsen, 1817-1903, (G.) historian, wrote *The History of Rome.*
Charles-Louis Montesquieu, 1689-1755, (F.) social philosopher.
Samuel Eliot Morison, 1887-1976, (U.S.) historian, chronicled voyages of early explorers.
Allan Nevins, 1890-1971, (U.S.) historian, biographer; twice won Pulitzer prize.
Jose Ortega y Gasset, 1883-1955, (Sp.) philosopher and humanist; advocated control by an elite.
Robert Owen, 1771-1858, (Br.) political philosopher, reformer.
Vilfredo Pareto, 1848-1923, (It.) economist, sociologist.
Francis Parkman, 1823-1893, (U.S.) historian, wrote 8-volume *France and England in North America, 1851-92.*
Marco Polo, c.1254-1324, (It.) narrated an account of his travels to China.
William Prescott, 1796-1859, (U.S.) early American historian.
Pierre Joseph Proudhon, 1809-1865, (F.) social theorist, regarded as the father of anarchism.
Francois Quesnay, 1694-1774, (F.) economic theorist, demonstrated the circular flow of economic activity throughout society.
David Ricardo, 1772-1823, (Br.) economic theorist, advocated free international trade.
James H. Robinson, 1863-1936, (U.S.) historian, educator.
Jean-Jacques Rousseau, 1712-1778, (F.) social philosopher, author.
Hjalmar Schacht, 1877-1970, (G.) economist.
Joseph Schumpeter, 1883-1950, (U.S.) Czech.-born economist, championed big business, capitalism.
Albert Schweitzer, 1875-1965, (Alsatian) social philosopher, theologian, and humanitarian.
George Simmel, 1858-1918, (G.) sociologist, philosopher.
Adam Smith, 1723-1790, (Br.) economist, advocated laissez-faire economy and free trade.
Jared Sparks, 1789-1866, (U.S.) historian, among first to do research from original documents.
Oswald Spengler, 1880-1936, (G.) philosopher and historian, wrote *The Decline of the West.*
William G. Sumner, 1840-1910, (U.S.) social scientist, economist; championed laissez-faire economy, Social Darwinism.
Hippolyte Taine, 1828-1893, (F.) historian.
Frank W. Taussig, 1859-1940, (U.S.) economist, educator.
Alexis de Tocqueville, 1805-1859, (F.) political scientist, historian.
Francis E. Townsend, 1897-1960, (U.S.) author of old-age pension plan.
Arnold Toynbee, 1889-1975, (Br.) historian, wrote 10-volume *A Study of History.*
Heinrich von Treitschke, 1834-1896, (G.) historian, political writer.
George Trevelyan, 1838-1928, (Br.) historian, statesman.
Frederick J. Turner, 1861-1932, (U.S.) historian, educator.
Thorstein B. Veblen, 1857-1929, (U.S.) economist, social philosopher.
Giovanni Vico, 1668-1744, (It.) historian, philosopher.
Voltaire (F.M. Arouet), 1694-1778, (F.) philosopher, historian, and poet.
Izaak Walton, 1593-1683, (Br.) author, wrote first biographical works in English literature.
Sidney J., 1859-1947, and wife **Beatrice,** 1858-1943, **Webb** (Br.) leading figures in Fabian Society and British Labour Party.
Walter P. Webb, 1888-1963, (U.S.) historian of the West.
Max Weber, 1864-1920, (G.) sociologist.

Noted Scientists of the Past

Howard H. Aiken, 1900-1973, (U.S.) mathematician, designed world's first large-scale digital computer (Mark I) for IBM.
Albertus Magnus, 1193-1280, (G.) theologian, philosopher, scientist, established medieval Christian study of natural science.
Andre-Marie Ampère, 1775-1836, (F.) scientist known for contributions to electrodynamics.
Amedeo Avogadro, 1776-1856, (It.) chemist, physicist, advanced important theories on properties of gases.
A.C. Becquerel, 1788-1878, (F.) physicist, pioneer in electrochemical science.
A.H. Becquerel, 1852-1908, (F.) physicist, discovered radioactivity in uranium.
Alexander Graham Bell, 1847-1922, (U.S.) inventor, first to patent and commercially exploit the telephone, 1876.
Daniel Bernoulli, 1700-1782, (Swiss) mathematician, advanced kinetic theory of gases and fluids.
Jöns Jakob Berzelius, 1779-1848, (Swed.) chemist, developed modern chemical symbols and formulas.
Henry Bessemer, 1813-1898, (Br.) engineer, invented Bessemer steel-making process.
Louis Blériot, 1872-1936, (F.) engineer, pioneer aviator, invented and constructed monoplanes.
Niels Bohr, 1885-1962, (Dan.) physicist, leading figure in the development of quantum theory.
Max Born, 1882-1970, (G.) physicist known for research in quantum mechanics.
Robert Bunsen, 1811-1899, (G.) chemist, invented Bunsen burner.
Luther Burbank, 1849-1926, (U.S.) plant breeder whose work developed plant breeding into a modern science.
Vannevar Bush, 1890-1974, (U.S.) electrical engineer, developed differential analyzer, first electronic analogue computer.
Alexis Carrel, 1873-1944, (F.) surgeon, biologist, developed methods of suturing blood vessels and transplanting organs.
George Washington Carver, 1860?-1943, (U.S.) agricultural chemist, experimenter, benefactor of South, a black hero.
Henry Cavendish, 1731-1810, (Br.) chemist, physicist, discovered hydrogen.
James Chadwick, 1891-1974, (Br.) physicist, discovered the neutron.
Jean M. Charcot, 1825-1893, (F.) neurologist known for work on hysteria, hypnotism, sclerosis.
John D. Cockcroft, 1897-1967, (Br.) nuclear physicist, constructed first atomic particle accelerator with E.T.S. Walton.
William Crookes, 1832-1919, (Br.) physicist, chemist, discovered thallium, invented a cathode-ray tube, radiometer.
Marie Curie, 1867-1934, (Pol.-F.) physical chemist known for work on radium and its compounds.
Pierre Curie, 1859-1906, (F.) physical chemist known for work with his wife on radioactivity.
Gottlieb Daimler, 1834-1900, (G.) engineer, inventor, pioneer automobile manufacturer.
John Dalton, 1766-1844, (Br.) chemist, physicist, formulated atomic theory, made first table of atomic weights.
Charles Darwin, 1809-1882, (Br.) naturalist, established theory of organic evolution.
Humphry Davy, 1778-1829, (Br.) chemist, research in electrochemistry led to isolation of potassium, sodium, calcium, barium, boron, magnesium, and strontium.
Lee De Forest, 1873-1961, (U.S.) inventor, pioneer in development of wireless telegraphy, sound pictures, television.
Max Delbruck, 1907-1981, (U.S.) pioneer in modern molecular genetics.
Rudolf Diesel, 1858-1913, (G.) mechanical engineer, patented Diesel engine.
Thomas Dooley, 1927-1961, (U.S.) "jungle doctor," noted for efforts to supply medical aid to underdeveloped countries.
Christian Doppler, 1803-1853, (Aus.) physicist, demonstrated Doppler effect (change in energy wavelengths caused by motion).
Thomas A. Edison, 1847-1931, (U.S.) inventor, held over 1,000 patents, including incandescent electric lamp, phonograph.
Paul Ehrlich, 1854-1915, (G.) bacteriologist, pioneer in modern immunology and bacteriology.
Albert Einstein, 1879-1955, (U.S.) theoretical physicist, known for formulation of relativity theory.
Leonhard Euler, 1707-1783, (Swiss), mathematician, physicist, authored first calculus book.
Gabriel Fahrenheit, 1686-1736, (G.) physicist, introduced Fahrenheit scale for thermometers.
Michael Faraday, 1791-1867, (Br.) chemist, physicist, known for work in field of electricity.
Pierre de Fermat, 1601-1665, (F.) mathematician, discovered analytic geometry, founded modern theory of numbers and calculus of probabilities.
Enrico Fermi, 1901-1954, (It.) physicist, one of chief architects of the nuclear age.
Galileo Ferraris, 1847-1897, (It.) physicist, electrical engineer, discovered principle of rotary magnetic field.
Camille Flammarion, 1842-1925, (F.) astronomer, popularized study of astronomy.
Alexander Fleming, 1881-1955, (Br.) bacteriologist, discovered penicillin.
Jean B.J. Fourier, 1768-1830, (F.) mathematician, discovered

theorem governing periodic oscillation.

James Franck, 1882-1964, (G.) physicist, proved value of quantum theory.

Sigmund Freud, 1856-1939, (Aus.) psychiatrist, founder of psychoanalysis.

Galileo Galilei, 1564-1642, (It.) astronomer, physicist, a founder of the experimental method.

Luigi Galvani, 1737-1798, (It.) physician, physicist, known as founder of galvanism.

Carl Friedrich Gauss, 1777-1855, (G.) mathematician, astronomer, physicist, made important contributions to almost every field of physical science, founded a number of entirely new fields.

Joseph Gay-Lussac, 1778-1850, (F.) chemist, physicist, investigated behavior of gases, discovered law of combining volumes.

Josiah W. Gibbs, 1839-1903, (U.S.) theoretical physicist, chemist, founded chemical thermodynamics.

George W. Goethals, 1858-1928, (U.S.) army engineer, built the Panama Canal.

William C. Gorgas, 1854-1920, (U.S.) sanitarian, U.S. army surgeon-general, his work to prevent yellow fever, malaria helped insure construction of Panama Canal.

Ernest Haeckel, 1834-1919, (G.) zoologist, evolutionist, a strong proponent of Darwin.

Otto Hahn, 1879-1968, (G.) chemist, worked on atomic fission.

J.B.S. Haldane, 1892-1964, (Sc.) scientist, known for work as geneticist and application of mathematics to science.

James Hall, 1761-1832, (Br.) geologist, chemist, founded experimental geology, geochemistry.

Edmund Halley, 1656-1742, (Br.) astronomer, calculated the orbits of many planets.

William Harvey, 1578-1657, (Br.) physician, anatomist, discovered circulation of the blood.

Hermann v. Helmholtz, 1821-1894, (G.) physicist, anatomist, physiologist, made fundamental contributions to physiology, optics, electrodynamics, mathematics, meteorology,

William Herschel, 1738-1822, (Br.) astronomer, discovered Uranus.

Heinrich Hertz, 1857-1894, (G.) physicist, his discoveries led to wireless telegraphy.

David Hilbert, 1862-1943, (G.) mathematician, formulated first satisfactory set of axioms for modern Euclidean geometry.

Edwin P. Hubble, 1889-1953, (U.S.) astronomer, produced first observational evidence of expanding universe.

Alexander v. Humboldt, 1769-1859, (G.) explorer, naturalist, propagator of earth sciences, originated ecology, geophysics.

Julian Huxley, 1887-1975, (Br.) biologist, a gifted exponent and philosopher of science.

Edward Jenner, 1749-1823, (Br.) physician, discovered vaccination.

William Jenner, 1815-1898, (Br.) physician, pathological anatomist.

Frederic Joliot-Curie, 1900-1958, (F.) physicist, with his wife continued work of Curies on radioactivity.

Irene Joliot-Curie, 1897-1956, (F.) physicist, continued work of Curies in radioactivity.

James P. Joule, 1818-1889, (Br.) physicist, determined relationship between heat and mechanical energy (conservation of energy).

Carl Jung, 1875-1961, (Sw.) psychiatrist, founder of analytical psychology.

Wm. Thomas Kelvin, 1824-1907, (Br.) mathematician, physicist, known for work on heat and electricity.

Sister Elizabeth Kenny, 1886-1952, (Austral.) nurse, developed method of treatment for polio.

Johannes Kepler, 1571-1630, (G.) astronomer, discovered important laws of planetary motion.

Joseph Lagrange, 1736-1813, (F.) geometer, astronomer, worked in all fields of analysis, and number theory, and analytical and celestial mechanics.

Jean B. Lamarck, 1744-1829, (F.) naturalist, forerunner of Darwin in evolutionary theory.

Irving Langmuir, 1881-1957, (U.S.) physical chemist, his studies of molecular films on solid and liquid surfaces opened new fields in colloid research and biochemistry.

Pierre S. Laplace, 1749-1827, (F.) astronomer, physicist, put forth nebular hypothesis of origin of solar system.

Antoine Lavoisier, 1743-1794, (F.) chemist, founder of modern chemistry.

Ernest O. Lawrence, 1901-1958, (U.S.) physicist, invented the cyclotron.

Louis Leakey, 1903-1972, (Br.) anthropologist, discovered important fossils, remains of early hominids.

Anton van Leeuwenhoek, 1632-1723, (Du.) microscopist, father of microbiology.

Gottfried Wilhelm Leibniz, 1646-1716, (G.) mathematician, developed theories of differential and integral calculus.

Justus von Liebig, 1803-1873, (G.) chemist, established quantitative organic chemical analysis.

Joseph Lister, 1827-1912, (Br.) pioneer of antiseptic surgery.

Percival Lowell, 1855-1916, (U.S.) astronomer, predicted the existence of Pluto.

Guglielmo Marconi, 1874-1937, (It.) physicist, known for his development of wireless telegraphy.

James Clerk Maxwell, 1831-1879, (Sc.) physicist, known especially for his work in electricity and magnetism.

Maria Goeppert Mayer, 1906-1972, (G.-U.S.) physicist, independently developed theory of structure of atomic nuclei.

Lise Meitner, 1878-1968, (Aus.) physicist whose work contributed to the development of the atomic bomb.

Gregor J. Mendel, 1822-1884, (Aus.) botanist, known for his experimental work on heredity.

Franz Mesmer, 1734-1815, (G.) physician, developed theory of animal magnetism.

Albert A. Michelson, 1852-1931, (U.S.) physicist, established speed of light as a fundamental constant.

Robert A. Millikan, 1868-1953, (U.S.) physicist, noted for study of elementary electronic charge and photoelectric effect.

Thomas Hunt Morgan, 1866-1945, (U.S.) geneticist, embryologist, established chromosome theory of heredity.

Isaac Newton, 1642-1727, (Br.) natural philosopher, mathematician, discovered law of gravitation, laws of motion.

J. Robert Oppenheimer, 1904-1967, (U.S.) physicist, director of Los Alamos during development of the atomic bomb.

Wilhelm Ostwald, 1853-1932, (G.) physical chemist, philosopher, chief founder of physical chemistry.

Louis Pasteur, 1822-1895, (F.) chemist, originated process of pasteurization.

Max Planck, 1858-1947, (G.) physicist, originated and developed quantum theory.

Henri Poincaré, 1854-1912, (F.) mathematician, physicist, influenced cosmology, relativity, and topology.

Joseph Priestley, 1733-1804, (Br.) chemist, one of the discoverers of oxygen.

Walter S. Reed, 1851-1902, (U.S.) army pathologist, bacteriologist, proved mosquitos transmit yellow fever.

Bernhard Riemann, 1826-1866, (G.) mathematician, contributed to development of calculus, complex variable theory, and mathematical physics.

Wilhelm Roentgen, 1845-1923, (G.) physicist, discovered X-rays.

Bertrand Russell, 1872-1970, (Br.) logician, philosopher, one of the founders of modern logic, wrote *Principia Mathematica.*

Ernest Rutherford, 1871-1937, (Br.) physicist, discovered the atomic nucleus.

Giovanni Schiaparelli, 1835-1910, (It.) astronomer, hypothesized canals on the surface of Mars.

Angelo Secchi, 1818-1878, (It.) astronomer, pioneer in classifying stars by their spectra.

Harlow Shapley, 1885-1972, (U.S.) astronomer, noted for his studies of the galaxy.

Charles P. Steinmetz, 1865-1923, (U.S.) electrical engineer, developed fundamental ideas on alternating current systems.

Leo Szilard, 1898-1964, (U.S.) physicist, helped create first sustained nuclear reaction.

Rudolf Virchow, 1821-1902, (G.) pathologist, a founder of cellular pathology.

Alessandro Volta, 1745-1827, (It.) physicist, pioneer in electricity.

Alfred Russell Wallace, 1823-1913, (Br.) naturalist, proposed concept of evolution similar to Darwin.

August v. Wasserman, 1866-1925, (G.) bacteriologist, discovered reaction used as test for syphilis.

James E. Watt, 1736-1819, (Sc.) mechanical engineer, inventor, invented modern steam condensing engine.

Alfred L. Wegener, 1880-1930, (G.) meteorologist, geophysicist, postulated theory of continental drift.

Norbert Wiener, 1894-1964, (U.S.) mathematician, founder of the science of cybernetics.

Ferdinand v. Zeppelin, 1838-1917 (G.) soldier, aeronaut, airship designer.

Noted Business Leaders, Industrialists, and Philanthropists of the Past

Elizabeth Arden (F.N. Graham), 1884-1966, (U.S.) Canadian-born businesswoman founded and headed cosmetics empire.

Philip D. Armour, 1832-1901, (U.S.) industrialist, streamlined meat packing.

John Jacob Astor, 1763-1848, (U.S.) German-born fur trader, banker, real estate magnate; at death, richest in U.S.

Francis W. Ayer, 1848-1923, (U.S.) ad industry pioneer.

August Belmont, 1816-1890, (U.S.) German-born financier.

James B. (Diamond Jim) Brady, 1856-1917, (U.S.) financier, philanthropist, legendary bon vivant.

Adolphus Busch, 1839-1913, (U.S.) German-born businessman, established brewery empire.
Asa Candler, 1851-1929, (U.S.) founded Coca-Cola Co.
Andrew Carnegie, 1835-1919, (U.S.) Scots-born industrialist, founded U.S. Steel; financed over 2,800 libraries.
William Colgate, 1783-1857, (U.S.) British-born businessman, philanthropist; founded soap-making empire.
Jay Cooke, 1821-1905, (U.S.) financier, sold $1 billion in Union bonds during Civil War.
Peter Cooper, 1791-1883, (U.S.) industrialist, inventor, philanthropist.
Ezra Cornell, 1807-1874, (U.S.) businessman, philanthropist; headed Western Union, established univ.
Erastus Corning, 1794-1872, (U.S.) financier, headed N.Y. Central.
Charles Crocker, 1822-1888, (U.S.) railroad builder, financier.
Samuel Cunard, 1787-1865, (Can.) pioneered trans-Atlantic steam navigation.
Marcus Daly, 1841-1900, (U.S.) Irish-born copper magnate.
Walt Disney, 1901-1966, (U.S.) pioneer in cinema animation, built entertainment empire.
Herbert H. Dow, 1866-1930, (U.S.) Canadian-born founder of chemical co.
James Duke, 1856-1925, (U.S.) founded American Tobacco, Duke Univ.
Eleuthere I. du Pont, 1771-1834, (U.S.) French-born gunpowder manufacturer; founded one of world's largest business empires.
Thomas C. Durant, 1820-1885, (U.S.) railroad official, financier.
William C. Durant, 1861-1947, (U.S.) industrialist, formed General Motors.
George Eastman, 1854-1932, (U.S.) inventor, manufacturer of photographic equipment.
Marshall Field, 1834-1906, (U.S.) merchant, founded Chicago's largest department store.
Harvey Firestone, 1868-1938, (U.S.) industrialist, founded tire co.
Henry M. Flagler, 1830-1913, (U.S.) financier, helped form Standard Oil; developed Florida as resort state.
Henry Ford, 1863-1947, (U.S.) auto maker, developed first popular low-priced car.
Henry C. Frick, 1849-1919, (U.S.) industrialist, helped organize U.S. Steel.
Jakob Fugger (Jakob the Rich), 1459-1525, (G.) headed leading banking house, trading concern, in 16th-century Europe.
Alfred C. Fuller, 1885-1973, (U.S.) Canadian-born businessman, founded brush co.
Elbert H. Gary, 1846-1927, (U.S.) U.S. Steel head, 1903-27.
Amadeo P. Giannini, 1870-1949, (U.S.) founded Bank of America.
Stephen Girard, 1750-1831, (U.S.) French-born financier, philanthropist; richest man in U.S. at his death.
Jean Paul Getty, 1892-1976, (U.S.) founded oil empire.
Jay Gould, 1836-1892, (U.S.) railroad magnate, financier, speculator.
Hetty Green, 1834-1916, (U.S.) financier, the "witch of Wall St."; richest woman in U.S in her day.
William Gregg, 1800-1867, (U.S.) launched textile industry in the South.
Meyer Guggenheim, 1828-1905, (U.S.) Swiss-born merchant, philanthropist; built merchandising, mining empires.
Edward H. Harriman, 1848-1909, (U.S.) railroad financier, administrator; headed Union Pacific.
William Randolph Hearst, 1863-1951, (U.S.) a dominant figure in American journalism; built vast publishing empire.
Henry J. Heinz, 1844-1919, (U.S.) founded food empire.
James J. Hill, 1838-1916, (U.S.) Canadian-born railroad magnate, financier; founded Great Northern Railway.
Conrad N. Hilton, 1888-1979, (U.S.) intl. hotel chain founder.
Howard Hughes, 1905-1976, (U.S.) industrialist, financier, movie maker.
H.L. Hunt, 1889-1974, (U.S.) oil magnate.
Collis P. Huntington, 1821-1900, (U.S.) railroad magnate.
Henry E. Huntington, 1850-1927, (U.S.) railroad builder, philanthropist.
Howard Johnson, 1896-1972, (U.S.) founded restaurant chain.
Henry J. Kaiser, 1882-1967, (U.S.) industrialist, built empire in steel, aluminum.
Minor C. Keith, 1848-1929, (U.S.) railroad magnate; founded United Fruit Co.
Will K. Kellogg, 1860-1951, (U.S.) businessman, philanthropist, founded breakfast food co.
Richard King, 1825-1885, (U.S.) cattleman, founded half-million acre King Ranch in Texas.
William S. Knudsen, 1879-1948, (U.S.) Danish-born auto industry executive.
Samuel H. Kress, 1863-1955, (U.S.) businessman, art collector, philanthropist; founded "dime store" chain.
Alfred Krupp, 1812-1887, (G.) armaments magnate.
Albert Lasker, 1880-1952, (U.S.) businessman, philanthropist.
Thomas Lipton, 1850-1931, (Ir.) merchant, built tea empire.
James McGill, 1744-1813, (Can.) Scots-born fur trader, founded univ.
Andrew W. Mellon, 1855-1937, (U.S.) financier, industrialist; benefactor of National Gallery of Art.
Charles E. Merrill, 1885-1956, (U.S.) financier, developed firm of Merrill Lynch.
John Pierpont Morgan, 1837-1913, (U.S.) most powerful figure in finance and industry at the turn-of-the-century.
Malcolm Muir, 1885-1979, (U.S.) created *Business Week* magazine; headed *Newsweek*, 1937-61.
Samuel Newhouse, 1895-1979, (U.S.) publishing and broadcasting magnate, built communications empire.
Aristotle Onassis, 1900-1975, (Gr.) shipping magnate.
George Peabody, 1795-1869, (U.S.) merchant, financier, philanthropist.
James C. Penney, 1875-1971, (U.S.) businessman, developed department store chain.
William C. Procter, 1862-1934, (U.S.) headed soap co.
John D. Rockefeller, 1839-1937, (U.S.) industrialist, established Standard Oil; became world's wealthiest person.
John D. Rockefeller Jr., 1874-1960, (U.S.) philanthropist, established foundation; provided land for United Nations.
Meyer A. Rothschild, 1743-1812, (G.) founded international banking house.
Thomas Fortune Ryan, 1851-1928, (U.S.) financier, dominated N.Y. City public transportation; helped found American Tobacco.
Russell Sage, 1816-1906, (U.S.) financier.
David Sarnoff, 1891-1971, (U.S.) broadcasting pioneer, established first radio network, NBC.
Richard W. Sears, 1863-1914, (U.S.) founded mail-order co.
(Ernst) Werner von Siemens, 1816-1892, (G.) industrialist, inventor.
Alfred P. Sloan, 1875-1966, (U.S.) industrialist, philanthropist; headed General Motors.
A. Leland Stanford, 1824-1893, (U.S.) railroad official, philanthropist; founded univ.
Nathan Strauss, 1848-1931, (U.S.) German-born merchant, philanthropist; headed Macy's.
Levi Strauss, c.1829-1902, (U.S.) pants manufacturer.
Clement Studebaker, 1831-1901, (U.S.) wagon, carriage manufacturer.
Gustavus Swift, 1839-1903, (U.S.) pioneer meat-packer; promoted refrigerated railroad cars.
Gerard Swope, 1872-1957, (U.S.) industrialist, economist; headed General Electric.
James Walter Thompson, 1847-1928, (U.S.) ad executive.
Theodore N. Vail, 1845-1920, (U.S.) organized Bell Telephone system, headed ATT.
Cornelius Vanderbilt, 1794-1877, (U.S.) financier, established steamship, railroad empires.
Henry Villard, 1835-1900, (U.S.) German-born railroad executive, financier.
Charles R. Walgreen, 1873-1939, (U.S.) founded drugstore chain.
DeWitt Wallace, 1890-1981, (U.S.) founder of *Reader's Digest* magazine.
John Wanamaker, 1838-1922, (U.S.) pioneered department-store merchandising.
Aaron Montgomery Ward, 1843-1913, (U.S.) established first mail-order firm.
Thomas J. Watson, 1874-1956, (U.S.) headed IBM, 1924-49.
John Hay Whitney, 1905-1982, (U.S.) publisher, sportsman, philanthropist.
Charles E. Wilson, 1890-1961, (U.S.) auto industry executive; public official.
Frank W. Woolworth, 1852-1919, (U.S.) created 5 & 10 chain.
William Wrigley Jr., 1861-1932, (U.S.) founded chewing gum co.

Composers of the Western World

Carl Philipp Emanuel Bach, 1714-1788, (G.) Prussian and Wurtembergian Sonatas.
Johann Christian Bach, 1735-1782, (G.) Concertos; sonatas.
Johann Sebastian Bach, 1685-1750, (G.) St. Matthew Passion, The Well-Tempered Clavichord.
Samuel Barber, b. 1910, (U.S.) Adagio for Strings, Vanessa.
Bela Bartok, 1881-1945, (Hung.) Concerto for Orchestra, The Miraculous Mandarin.
Ludwig Van Beethoven, 1770-1827, (G.) Concertos (Emperor); sonatas (Moonlight, Pastorale, Pathetique); symphonies

(Eroica).

Vincenzo Bellini, 1801-1835, (It.) La Sonnambula, Norma, I Puritani.

Alban Berg, 1885-1935, (Aus.) Wozzeck, Lulu.

Hector Berlioz, 1803-1869, (F.) Damnation of Faust, Symphonie Fantastique, Requiem.

Leonard Bernstein, b. 1918, (U.S.) Jeremiah, West Side Story.

Georges Bizet, 1838-1875, (F.) Carmen, Pearl Fishers.

Ernest Bloch, 1880-1959, (Swiss) Schelomo, Voice in the Wilderness, Sacred Service.

Luigi Boccherini, 1743-1805, (It.) Cello Concerto in B Flat, Symphony in C.

Alexander Borodin, 1834-1887, (R.) Prince Igor, In the Steppes of Central Asia.

Johannes Brahms, 1833-1897, (G.) Liebeslieder Waltzes, Rhapsody in E Flat Major, Opus 119 for Piano, Academic Festival Overture; symphonies; quartets.

Benjamin Britten, 1913-1976, (Br.) Peter Grimes, Turn of the Screw, Ceremony of Carols, War Requiem.

Anton Bruckner, 1824-1896, (Aus.) Symphonies (Romantic), Intermezzo for String Quintet.

Ferruccio Busoni, 1866-1924, (It.) Doctor Faust, Comedy Overture.

Dietrich Buxtehude, 1637-1707, (D.) Cantatas, trio sonatas.

William Byrd, 1543-1623, (Br.) Masses, sacred songs.

Alexis Emmanuel Chabrier, 1841-1894, (Fr.) Le Roi Malgre Lui, Espana.

Gustave Charpentier, 1860-1956, (F.) Louise.

Frederic Chopin, 1810-1849, (P.) Concertos, Polonaise No. 6 in A Flat Major (Heroic); sonatas.

Aaron Copland, b. 1900, (U.S.) Appalachian Spring.

Claude Achille Debussy, 1862-1918, (F.) Pelleas et Melisande, La Mer, Prelude to the Afternoon of a Faun.

C.P. Leo Delibes, 1836-1891, (F.) Lakme, Coppelia, Sylvia.

Norman Dello Joio, b. 1913, (U.S.), Triumph of St. Joan, Psalm of David.

Gaetano Donizetti, 1797-1848, (It.) Elixir of Love, Lucia Di Lammermoor, Daughter of the Regiment.

Paul Dukas, 1865-1935, (Fr.) Sorcerer's Apprentice.

Antonin Dvorak, 1841-1904, (C.) Symphony in E Minor (From the New World).

Edward Elgar, 1857-1934, (Br.) Pomp and Circumstance.

Manuel de Falla, 1876-1946, (Sp.) La Vide Breve, El Amor Brujo.

Gabriel Faure, 1845-1924, (Fr.) Requiem, Ballade.

Friedrich von Flotow, 1812-1883, (G.) Martha.

Cesar Franck, 1822-1890, (Belg.) D Minor Symphony.

George Gershwin, 1898-1937, (U.S.) Rhapsody in Blue, American in Paris, Porgy and Bess.

Umberto Giordano, 1867-1948, (It.) Andrea Chenier.

Alex K. Glazunoff, 1865-1936, (R.) Symphonies, Stenka Razin.

Mikhail Glinka, 1804-1857, (R.) Ruslan and Ludmilla.

Christoph W. Gluck, 1714-1787, (G.) Alceste, Iphigenie en Tauride.

Charles Gounod, 1818-1893, (F.) Faust, Romeo and Juliet.

Edvard Grieg, 1843-1907, (Nor.) Peer Gynt Suite, Concerto in A Minor.

George Frederick Handel, 1685-1759, (G., Br.) Messiah, Xerxes, Berenice.

Howard Hanson, 1896-1981, (U.S.) Symphonies No. 1 (Nordic) and 2 (Romantic).

Roy Harris, 1898-1979, (U.S.) Symphonies, Amer. Portraits.

Joseph Haydn, 1732-1809, (Aus.) Symphonies (Clock); oratorios; chamber music.

Paul Hindemith, 1895-1963, (U.S.) Mathis Der Maler.

Gustav Holst, 1874-1934, (Br.) The Planets.

Arthur Honegger, 1892-1955, (Swiss) Judith, Le Roi David, Pacific 231.

Alan Hovhaness, b. 1911, (U.S.) Symphonies, Magnificat.

Engelbert Humperdinck, 1854-1921, (G.) Hansel and Gretel.

Charles Ives, 1874-1954, (U.S.) Third Symphony.

Aram Khachaturian, 1903-1978, (R.) Gayane (ballet), symphonies.

Zoltan Kodaly, 1882-1967, (Hung.) Hary Janos, Psalmus Hungaricus.

Fritz Kreisler, 1875-1962, (Aus.) Caprice Viennois, Tambourin Chinois.

Rodolphe Kreutzer, 1766-1831, (F.) 40 etudes for violin.

Edouard V.A. Lalo, 1823-1892, (F.) Symphonie Espagnole.

Ruggiero Leoncavallo, 1858-1919, (It.) I Pagliacci.

Franz Liszt, 1811-1886, (Hung.) 20 Hungarian rhapsodies; symphonic poems.

Edward MacDowell, 1861-1908, (U.S.) To a Wild Rose.

Gustav Mahler, 1860-1911, (Aus.) Lied von der Erde.

Pietro Mascagni, 1863-1945, (It.) Cavalleria Rusticana.

Jules Massenet, 1842-1912, (F.) Manon, Le Cid, Thais.

Mendelssohn-Bartholdy, 1809-1847, (G.) Midsummer Night's Dream, Songs Without Words.

Gian-Carlo Menotti, b. 1911, (It.-U.S.) The Medium, The Consul, Amahl and the Night Visitors.

Giacomo Meyerbeer, 1791-1864, (G.) Robert le Diable, Les Huguenots.

Claudio Monteverdi, 1567-1643, (It.) Opera; masses; madrigals.

Wolfgang Amadeus Mozart, 1756-1791, (Aus.) Magic Flute, Marriage of Figaro; concertos; symphonies, etc.

Modest Moussorgsky, 1835-1881, (R.) Boris Godunov, Pictures at an Exhibition.

Jacques Offenbach, 1819-1880, (F.) Tales of Hoffman.

Karl Orff, 1895-1982, (G.) Carmina Burana.

Ignace Paderewski, 1860-1941, (P.) Minuet in G.

Giovanni P. da Palestrina, 1524-1594, (It.) Masses; madrigals.

Amilcare Ponchielli, 1834-1886, (It.) La Gioconda.

Francis Poulenc, 1899-1963, (F.) Dialogues des Carmelites.

Serge Prokofiev, 1891-1953, (R.) Love for Three Oranges, Lt. Kije, Peter and the Wolf.

Giacomo Puccini, 1858-1924, (It.) La Boheme, Manon Lescaut, Tosca, Madame Butterfly.

Sergei Rachmaninov, 1873-1943, (R.) Prelude in C Sharp Minor.

Maurice Ravel, 1875-1937, (Fr.) Bolero, Daphnis et Chloe, Rapsodie Espagnole.

Nikolai Rimsky-Korsakov, 1844-1908, (R.) Golden Cockerel, Capriccio Espagnol, Scheherazade, Russian Easter Overture.

Gioacchino Rossini, 1792-1868, (It.) Barber of Seville, Semiramide, William Tell.

Chas. Camille Saint-Saens, 1835-1921, (F.) Samson and Delilah, Danse Macabre.

Alessandro Scarlatti, 1659-1725, (It.) Cantatas; concertos.

Domenico Scarlatti, 1685-1757, (It.) Harpsichord sonatas.

Arnold Schoenberg, 1874-1951, (Aus.) Pelleas and Melisande, Transfigured Night, De Profundis.

Franz Schubert, 1797-1828, (A.) Lieder; symphonies (Unfinished); overtures (Rosamunde).

William Schuman, b. 1910, (U.S.) Credendum, New England Triptych.

Robert Schumann, 1810-1856, (G.) Symphonies, songs.

Aleksandr Scriabin, 1872-1915, (R.) Prometheus.

Dimitri Shostakovich, 1906-1975, (R.) Symphonies, Lady Macbeth of Minsk, The Nose.

Jean Sibelius, 1865-1957, (Finn.) Finlandia, Karelia.

Bedrich Smetana, 1824-1884, (Cz.). The Bartered Bride.

Karlheinz Stockhausen, b. 1928, (G.) Kontrapunkte, Kontakte.

Richard Strauss, 1864-1949, (G.) Salome, Elektra, Der Rosenkavalier, Thus Spake Zarathustra.

Igor F. Stravinsky, 1882-1971, (R.-U.S.) Oedipus Rex, Le Sacre du Printemps, Petrushka.

Peter I. Tchaikovsky, 1840-1893, (R.) Nutcracker Suite, Swan Lake, Eugene Onegin.

Ambroise Thomas, 1811-1896, (F.) Mignon.

Virgil Thomson, b. 1896, (U.S.) Opera, ballet; Four Saints in Three Acts.

Ralph Vaughan Williams, 1872-1958, (Br.) Job, London Symphony, Symphony No. 7 (Antarctica).

Giuseppe Verdi, 1813-1901, (It.) Aida, Rigoletto, Don Carlo, Il Trovatore, La Traviata, Falstaff, Macbeth.

Heitor Villa-Lobos, 1887-1959, (Brazil) Choros.

Antonio Vivaldi, 1678-1741, (It.) Concerti, The Four Seasons.

Richard Wagner, 1813-1883, (G.) Rienzi, Tannhauser, Lohengrin, Tristan und Isolde.

Karl Maria von Weber, 1786-1826, (G.) Der Freischutz.

Composers of Operettas, Musicals, and Popular Music

Richard Adler, b. 1921, (U.S.) *Pajama Game; Damn Yankees.*

Milton Ager, 1893-1979, (U.S.) I Wonder What's Become of Sally; Hard Hearted Hannah; Ain't She Sweet?

Leroy Anderson, 1908-1975, (U.S.) Syncopated Clock; Blue Tango; Sleigh Ride.

Harold Arlen, b. 1905, (U.S.) Stormy Weather; Over the Rainbow; Blues in the Night; That Old Black Magic.

Burt Bacharach, b. 1928, (U.S.) Raindrops Keep Fallin' on My Head; Walk on By; What the World Needs Now is Love.

Ernest Ball, 1878-1927, (U.S.) Mother Machree; When Irish Eyes Are Smiling.

Irving Berlin, b. 1888, (U.S.) *This is the Army; Annie Get Your Gun; Call Me Madam;* God Bless America; White Christmas.

Eubie Blake, b. 1883, (U.S.) *Shuffle Along;* I'm Just Wild about Harry.

Jerry Bock, b. 1928, (U.S.) *Mr. Wonderful; Fiorello; Fiddler on the Roof; The Rothschilds.*

Carrie Jacobs Bond, 1862-1946, (U.S.) I Love You Truly.

Nacio Herb Brown, 1896-1964, (U.S.) Singing in the Rain; You Were Meant for Me; All I Do Is Dream of You.

Hoagy Carmichael, 1899-1981, (U.S.) Stardust; Georgia on My Mind; Old Buttermilk Sky.

George M. Cohan, 1878-1942, (U.S.) Give My Regards to Broadway; You're A Grand Old Flag; Over There.

Noel Coward, 1899-1973 (Br.) *Bitter Sweet;* Mad Dogs and Englishmen; Mad About the Boy.

Walter Donaldson, 1893-1947, (U.S.) My Buddy; Carolina in the Morning; You're Driving Me Crazy; Makin' Whoopee.

Vernon Duke, 1903-1969, (U.S.) April in Paris.

Gus Edwards, 1879-1945, (U.S.) School Days; By the Light of the Silvery Moon; In My Merry Oldsmobile.

Sherman Edwards, b. 1919, (U.S.) See You in September; Wonderful! Wonderful!

Sammy Fain, b. 1902, Wedding Bells Are Breaking Up That Old Gang of Mine; Let a Smile Be Your Umbrella.

Fred Fisher, 1875-1942, (U.S.) Peg O' My Heart; Chicago; Dardanella.

Stephen Collins Foster, 1826-1864, (U.S.) My Old Kentucky Home; Old Folks At Home.

Rudolf Friml, 1879-1972, (naturalized U.S.) *The Firefly; Rose Marie; Vagabond King; Bird of Paradise.*

John Gay, 1685-1732, (Br.) *The Beggar's Opera.*

Edwin F. Goldman, 1878-1956, (U.S.) marches.

Percy Grainger, 1882-1961, (Br.) Country Gardens.

John Green, b. 1908, (U.S.) Body and Soul; Out of Nowhere; I Cover the Waterfront.

Ferde Grofe, 1892-1972, (U.S.) Grand Canyon Suite.

W. C. Handy, 1873-1958, (U.S.) St. Louis Blues.

Ray Henderson, 1896-1970, (U.S.) *George White's Scandals;* That Old Gang of Mine; Five Foot Two, Eyes of Blue.

Victor Herbert, 1859-1924, (Ir.-U.S.) *Mlle. Modiste; Babes in Toyland; The Red Mill; Naughty Marietta; Sweethearts.*

Jerry Herman, b. 1932, (U.S.) *Milk and Honey; Hello Dolly; Mame; Dear World.*

Al Hoffman, 1902-1960, (U.S.) Heartaches, Mairzy Doats.

Scott Joplin, 1868-1917, (U.S.) *Treemonisha.*

John Kander, b. 1927, (U.S.) *Cabaret; Chicago; Funny Lady.*

Jerome Kern, 1885-1945, (U.S.) *Sally; Sunny; Show Boat; Cat and the Fiddle; Music in the Air; Roberta.*

Burton Lane, b. 1912, (U.S.) *Three's a Crowd; Finian's Rainbow; On A Clear Day You Can See Forever.*

Franz Lehar, 1870-1948, (Hung.) *Merry Widow.*

Mitch Leigh, b. 1928, (U.S.) *Man of La Mancha.*

John Lennon, 1940-1980, (Br.) Hard Day's Night, Yesterday, I Want to Hold Your Hand.

Frank Loesser, 1910-1969, (U.S.) *Guys and Dolls; Where's Charley?; The Most Happy Fella; How to Succeed . . . .*

Frederick Loewe, b. 1901, (Aust.-U.S.) *The Day Before Spring; Brigadoon; Paint Your Wagon; My Fair Lady; Camelot.*

Henry Mancini, b. 1924, (U.S.) Moon River; Days of Wine and Roses; Pink Panther Theme.

Paul McCartney, b. 1942, (Br.) Michelle, Hey Jude, And I Love Her.

Jimmy McHugh, 1894-1969, (U.S.) I Can't Give You Anything But Love; I Feel a Song Coming On.

Joseph Meyer, b. 1894, (U.S.) If You Knew Susie; California, Here I Come; Crazy Rhythm.

Chauncey Olcott, 1860-1932, (U.S.) Mother Machree; My Wild Irish Rose.

Cole Porter, 1893-1964, (U.S.) *Anything Goes; Jubilee; DuBarry Was a Lady; Panama Hattie; Mexican Hayride; Kiss Me Kate; Can Can; Silk Stockings.*

Andre Previn, b. 1929, (U.S.) *Coco.*

Richard Rodgers, 1902-1979, (U.S.) *Garrick Gaieties; Connecticut Yankee; America's Sweetheart; On Your Toes; Babes in Arms; The Boys from Syracuse; Oklahoma!; Carousel; South Pacific; The King and I; Flower Drum Song; The Sound of Music.*

Sigmund Romberg, 1887-1951, (Hung.) *Maytime; The Student Prince; Desert Song; Blossom Time.*

Harold Rome, b. 1908, (U.S.) *Pins and Needles; Call Me Mister; Wish You Were Here; Fanny; Destry Rides Again.*

Vincent Rose, b. 1880-1944, (U.S.) Avalon; Whispering; Blueberry Hill.

Harry Ruby, 1895-1974, (U.S.) Three Little Words; Who's Sorry Now?

Arthur Schwartz, b. 1900, (U.S.) *The Band Wagon; Inside U.S.A.; A Tree Grows in Brooklyn.*

Stephen Sondheim, b. 1930, (U.S.) *A Little Night Music; Company.*

John Philip Sousa. 1854-1932, (U.S.) *El Capitan;* Stars and Stripes Forever.

Oskar Straus, 1870-1954, (Aus.) *Chocolate Soldier.*

Johann Strauss, 1825-1899, (Aus.) *Gypsy Baron; Die Fledermaus;* waltzes: Blue Danube, Artist's Life.

Charles Strouse, b. 1928, (U.S.) *Bye Bye, Birdie; All American; Golden Boy; Applause; Annie.*

Jule Styne, b. 1905, (b. London-U.S.) *Gentlemen Prefer Blondes; Bells Are Ringing; Gypsy; Funny Girl.*

Arthur S. Sullivan, 1842-1900, (Br.) *H.M.S. Pinafore, Pirates of Penzance; The Mikado.*

Deems Taylor, 1885-1966, (U.S.) *Peter Ibbetson.*

Egbert van Alstyne, 1882-1951, (U.S.) In the Shade of the Old Apple Tree; Memories; Pretty Baby.

James Van Heusen, b. 1913, (U.S.) Moonlight Becomes You; Swinging on a Star.

Albert von Tilzer, 1878-1956, (U.S.) I'll Be With You in Apple Blossom Time; Take Me Out to the Ball Game.

Harry von Tilzer, 1872-1946, (U.S.) Only a Bird in a Gilded Cage; On a Sunday Afternoon.

Harry Warren, 1893-1981, (U.S.) You're My Everything; We're in the Money; I Only Have Eyes for You; September in the Rain.

Kurt Weill, 1900-1950, (G.-U.S.) *Threepenny Opera; Lady in the Dark; Knickerbocker Holiday; One Touch of Venus.*

Percy Wenrich, 1887-1952, (U.S.) When You Wore a Tulip; Moonlight Bay; Put On Your Old Gray Bonnet.

Richard A. Whiting, 1891-1938, (U.S.) Till We Meet Again; Sleepytime Gal; Beyond the Blue Horizon.

Meredith Willson, b. 1902, (U.S.) *The Music Man.*

Vincent Youmans, 1898-1946, (U.S.) *Two Little Girls in Blue; Wildflower; No, No, Nanette; Hit the Deck; Rainbow; Smiles.*

Lyricists

Sammy Cahn, b. 1913, (U.S.) High Hopes; Love and Marriage; The Second Time Around.

Betty Comden, b. 1919 (U.S.) and **Adolph Green,** b. 1915 (U.S.) The Party's Over; Just in Time; New York, New York.

Buddy De Sylva, 1895-1950, (U.S.) When Day is Done; Look for the Silver Lining; April Showers.

Hal David, b. 1921 (U.S.) What the World Needs Now Is Love.

Howard Dietz, b. 1896, (U.S.) Dancing in the Dark; You and the Night and the Music.

Al Dubin, 1891-1945, (U.S.) Tiptoe Through the Tulips; Anniversary Waltz; Lullaby of Broadway.

Dorothy Fields, 1905-1974, (U.S.) On the Sunny Side of the Street; Don't Blame Me; The Way You Look Tonight.

Ira Gershwin, b. 1896, (U.S.) The Man I Love; Fascinating Rhythm; S'Wonderful; Embraceable You.

Wm. S. Gilbert, 1836-1911, (Br.) *The Mikado; H.M.S. Pinafore.*

Oscar Hammerstein II, 1895-1960, (U.S.) Ol' Man River; *Oklahoma; Carousel.*

E. Y. (Yip) Harburg, 1898-1981, (U.S.) Brother, Can You Spare a Dime; April in Paris; Over the Rainbow.

Lorenz Hart, 1895-1943, (U.S.) Isn't It Romantic; Blue Moon; Lover; Manhattan; My Funny Valentine.

DuBose Heyward, 1885-1940, (U.S.) Summertime; A Woman Is A Sometime Thing.

Gus Kahn, 1886-1941, (U.S.) Memories; Ain't We Got Fun.

Johnny Mercer, 1909-1976, (U.S.) Blues in the Night; Come Rain or Come Shine; Laura; That Old Black Magic.

Jack Norworth, 1879-1959, (U.S.) Take Me Out to the Ball Game; Shine On Harvest Moon.

Jack Yellen, b. 1892, (U.S.) Down by the O-Hi-O; Ain't She Sweet; Happy Days Are Here Again.

Noted Jazz Artists

Jazz has been called America's only completely unique contribution to Western culture. The following individuals have made major contributions in this field:

Julian "Cannonball" Adderley, 1928-1975: alto sax.

Henry "Red" Allen, 1908-1967: trumpet.

Albert Ammons, 1907-1949: boogie-woogie pianist.

Louis "Satchmo" Armstrong, 1900-1971: trumpet, singer; originated the "scat" vocal.

Mildred Bailey, 1907-1951: blues singer.

Count Basie, b. 1904: orchestra leader, piano.

Sidney Bechet, 1897-1950: early innovator, soprano sax.

Bix Beiderbecke, 1903-1931: cornet, piano, composer.

Bunny Berrigan, 1909-1942: trumpet, singer.

Barney Bigard, b. 1906: clarinet.

Art Blakey, b. 1919: drums, leader.

Jimmy Blanton, 1921-1942: bass.

Charles "Buddy" Bolden, 1868-1931: cornet; formed the first jazz band in the 1890s.

Big Bill Broonzy, 1893-1958: blues singer, guitar.

Dave Brubeck, b. 1920: piano, combo leader.

Harry Carney, 1910-1974: baritone sax.

Benny Carter, b. 1907: alto sax, trumpet, clarinet.
Sidney Catlett, 1910-1951: drums.
Charlie Christian, 1919-1942: guitar; often given credit for the rm "bebop".
Kenny Clarke, b. 1914: pioneer of modern drums; founder-ember Modern Jazz Quartet, 1952.
Buck Clayton, b. 1911: trumpet, arranger.
Al Cohn, b. 1925: tenor sax, composer.
Cozy Cole, 1909-1981: drums.
Ornette Coleman, b. 1930: saxophone; unorthodox style.
John Coltrane, 1926-1967: tenor sax innovator.
Eddie Condon, 1904-1973: guitar, band leader; promoter of ixieland.
Chick Corea, b. 1941: pianist, composer.
Miles Davis, b. 1926: trumpet; pioneer of cool jazz.
Tadd Dameron, 1917-1965: piano, composer.
Wild Bill Davison, b. 1906: cornet, leader; prominent in early hicago jazz.
Buddy De Franco, b. 1933: clarinet.
Paul Desmond, 1924-1977: alto sax.
Vic Dickenson, b. 1906: trombone, composer.
Warren "Baby" Dodds, 1898-1959: Dixieland drummer.
Johnny Dodds, 1892-1940: clarinet.
Jimmy Dorsey, 1904-1957: clarinet, alto sax; band leader.
Tommy Dorsey, 1905-1956: trombone; band leader.
Roy Eldridge, b. 1911: trumpet, drums, singer.
Duke Ellington, 1899-1974: piano, orchestra leader, com-oser.
Bill Evans, 1929-1980: piano.
Gil Evans, b. 1912: composer, piano.
Ella Fitzgerald, b. 1918: singer.
Erroll Garner, 1921-1977: piano, composer, "Misty."
Stan Getz, b. 1927: tenor sax.
Dizzy Gillespie, b. 1917: trumpet, composer; bop developer.
Benny Goodman, b. 1909: clarinet, band and combo leader.
Dexter Gordon, b. 1923: tenor sax; bop-derived style.
Stephane Grappelli, b. 1908: violin.
Bobby Hackett, 1915-1976: trumpet, cornet.
Lionel Hampton, b. 1913: vibes, drums, piano, combo leader.
W. C. Handy, 1873-1958: composer, "St. Louis Blues."
Coleman Hawkins, 1904-1969: tenor sax; 1939 recording of Body and Soul", a classic.
Roy Haynes, b. 1926: drums.
Fletcher Henderson, 1898-1952: orchestra leader, arranger; ioneered jazz and dance bands of the 30s.
Woody Herman, b. 1913: clarinet, alto sax, band leader.
Jay C. Higginbotham, 1906-1973: trombone.
Earl "Fatha" Hines, b. 1905: piano, songwriter.
Johnny Hodges, 1906-1971: alto sax.
Billie Holiday, 1915-1959: blues singer, "Strange Fruit."
Sam "Lightnin' " Hopkins, 1912-1982: blues singer, guitar.
Mahalia Jackson, 1911-1972: gospel singer.
Milt Jackson, b. 1923: vibes, piano, guitar.
Illinois Jacquet, b. 1922: tenor sax.
Keith Jarrett, b. 1945: technically phenomenal pianist.
Blind Lemon Jefferson, 1897-1930: blues singer, guitar.
Bunk Johnson, 1879-1949: cornet, trumpet.
James P. Johnson, 1891-1955: piano, composer.
J. J. Johnson, b. 1924: trombone, composer.
Jo Jones, b. 1911: drums.
Philly Joe Jones, 1923: drums.
Quincy Jones, b. 1933: arranger.
Thad Jones, b. 1923: trumpet, cornet.
Scott Joplin, 1868-1917: composer; "Maple Leaf Rag."
Stan Kenton, 1912-1979: orchestra leader, composer, piano.
John Kirby, 1908-1952: major combo leader of the 30s.
Lee Konitz, b. 1927: alto sax.
Gene Krupa, 1909-1973: drums, band and combo leader.
Tommy Ladnier, 1900-1939: trumpet.
Scott LaFaro, 1936-1961: bass.
Eddie Lang, 1904-1933: guitar.
Huddie Ledbetter (Leadbelly), 1888-1949: blues singer, gui-ar.
John Lewis, b. 1920: composer, piano, combo leader.
Jimmie Lunceford, 1902-1947: band leader, sax.
Jimmy McPartland, b. 1907: trumpet.
Glenn Miller, 1904-1944: trombone, dance band leader.
Charles Mingus, 1922-1979: bass, composer, combo leader.
Thelonious Monk, 1920-1982: piano, composer, combo leader; a developer of bop.
Wes Montgomery, 1925-1971: guitar.
"Jelly Roll" Morton, 1885-1941: composer, piano, singer.
Bennie Moten, 1894-1935: piano; an early organizer of large jazz orchestras.
Gerry Mulligan, b. 1927: baritone sax, arranger, leader.
Turk Murphy, b. 1915: trombone, band leader.
Theodore "Fats" Navarro, 1923-1950: trumpet.
Red Nichols, 1905-1965: cornet, combo leader.
Jimmie Noone, 1895-1944: clarinet, leader.
Red Norvo, b. 1908: vibes, band leader.
Anita O'Day, b. 1919: singer.
King Oliver, 1885-1938: cornet, band leader; teacher of Louis Armstrong.
Kid Ory, 1886-1973: trombone, composer, "Muskrat Ramble".
Charlie "Bird" Parker, 1920-1955: alto sax, composer; rated by many as the greatest jazz improviser.
Oscar Peterson, b. 1925: piano, composer, combo leader.
Oscar Pettiford, 1922-1960: a leading bassist in the bop era.
Bud Powell, 1924-1966: piano, composer; modern jazz pioneer.
Gertrude "Ma" Rainey, 1886-1939: blues singer.
Don Redman, 1900-1964: composer, arranger; pioneer in the evolution of the large orchestra.
Django Reinhardt, 1910-1953: guitar; Belgian gypsy, first European to influence American jazz.
Buddy Rich, b. 1917: drums, band leader.
Max Roach, b. 1925: drums.
Shorty Rogers, b. 1924: composer, trumpet, band leader.
Sonny Rollins, b. 1929: tenor sax.
Pete Rugolo, b. 1915: composer, orchestra leader.
Jimmy Rushing, 1903-1972: blues singer.
George Russell, b. 1923: composer, piano.
Pee Wee Russell, 1906-1969: clarinet.
Artie Shaw, b. 1910: clarinet, combo leader.
George Shearing, b. 1919: piano, composer, "Lullaby of Birdland."
Horace Silver, b. 1928: piano, combo leader.
Zoot Sims, b 1925: tenor, alto sax; clarinet.
Zutty Singleton, 1898-1975: Dixieland drummer.
Bessie Smith, 1894-1937: blues singer.
Clarence "Pinetop" Smith, 1904-1929: piano, singer; pioneer of boogie woogie.
Joe Smith, 1902-1937: trumpet.
Willie "The Lion" Smith, 1897-1973: stride style pianist.
Muggsy Spanier, 1906-1967: cornet, band leader.
Billy Strayhorn, 1915-67: composer, piano.
Sonny Stitt, b. 1924: alto, tenor sax.
Art Tatum, 1910-1956: piano; technical virtuoso.
Cecil Taylor, b. 1933: avant-garde pianist, composer.
Jack Teagarden, 1905-1964: trombone, singer.
Dave Tough, 1908-1948: drums.
Lennie Tristano, 1919-1978: piano, composer.
Joe Turner, b. 1911: blues singer.
Joe Turner, b. 1907: stride piano.
McCoy Tyner, b. 1938: piano, composer.
Sarah Vaughan, b. 1924: singer.
Joe Venuti, 1904-1978: first great jazz violinist.
Thomas "Fats" Waller, 1904-1943: piano, singer, composer, "Ain't Misbehavin' ".
Dinah Washington, 1924-1963: singer.
Chick Webb, 1902-1939: band leader, drums; generally credited with laying the foundations for jazz percussion.
Paul Whiteman, 1890-1967: orchestra leader; a major figure in the introduction of jazz to a large audience.
Charles "Cootie" Williams, b. 1908: trumpet, band leader.
Mary Lou Williams, 1914-1981: pianist, composer.
Teddy Wilson, b. 1912: piano, composer.
Kai Winding, b. 1922: trombone, composer.
Jimmy Yancey, 1894-1951: piano.
Lester "Pres" Young, 1909-1959: tenor sax, composer: a bop pioneer.

Popular American Songs

(m-music; w-words)

After You've Gone: Turner Layton(m); Henry Creamer(w); 918; popularized by Al Jolson, Sophie Tucker.
Ain't She Sweet: Milton Ager(m); Jack Yellen(w); 1927; introuced by Paul Ash orch., Oriental Theater, Chicago.
Alexander's Ragtime Band: Irving Berlin(m,w); 1911.
Always (I'll Be Loving You): Irving Berlin(m,w); 1925.
April In Paris: Vernon Duke(m); E. Y. Harburg(w); 1932.
April Showers: Louis Silvers(m); Buddy De Sylva(w); 1921; troduced by Al Jolson in musical *Bombo.*
As Time Goes By: Herman Hupfeld(m,w); 1931, in musical *Everbody's Welcome,* also movie *Casablanca,* in 1942.
Baby Face: Harry Akst(m); Benny Davis(w); 1926; introduced by Jan Garber on RCA Victor record.
The Band Played On: C. B. Ward(m); J. E. Palmer(w); 1895; song owned and promoted by newspaper, New York *World.*
Beer Barrel Polka: J. Vejvoda and Lew Brown(w); 1934; music was a Czech popular song.
The Best Things in Life Are Free: Ray Henderson(m);

Buddy De Sylva and Lew Brown(w); 1927; in musical *Good News.*

Beyond the Blue Horizon: R. A. Whiting(m); Leo Robin(w); 1930; introduced by Jeanette MacDonald in movie *Monte Carlo.*

Blowin' in the Wind: Bob Dylan(m,w); 1963.

Blue Skies: Irving Berlin(m,w); 1926.

Body and Soul: John Green(m); E. Heyton, R. Sour, F. Eyton(w); 1930; introduced by Gertrude Lawrence on BBC.

Bye, Bye Blackbird: R. Henderson(m); Mort Dixon(w); 1926; popularized by Eddie Cantor.

By the Beautiful Sea: Harry Carroll(m); Harold Atteridge(w); 1914; vaudeville.

By the Light of the Silvery Moon: Gus Edwards(m); Edward Madden(w); 1909; in revue *School Boys and Girls.*

Chicago: Fred Fisher(m,w); 1922; vaudeville.

California, Here I Come: Joseph Meyer(m); Al Jolson, Buddy De Sylva(w); 1923; by Al Jolson in road tour of *Bombo.*

Daisy Bell (Bicycle Built for Two): Harry Dacre(m,w); circa 1892; London tune popularized in U.S. by Tony Pastor.

Dancing in the Dark: Arthur Schwartz(m); Howard Dietz(w); 1931; in revue *The Band Wagon.*

Down by the Old Mill Stream: Tell Taylor(m,w); 1910.

Easter Parade: Irving Berlin(m,w); 1933; introduced by Clifton Webb and Marilyn Miller in musical *As Thousands Cheer.*

Feelings: Paul Evans(m); Paul Parnes(w); 1969.

For Me and My Gal: G. W. Meyer(m); Edgar Leslie, E. R. Goetz(w); 1917; sung by Jolson, Cantor, Sophie Tucker, others.

Give My Regards to Broadway: George M. Cohan(m,w); 1904; in musical *Little Johnny Jones.*

Good Night Irene: Huddie Ledbetter(m,w); 1936; found by John Lomax in Louisiana State Prison, Angola, La.

Hail, Hail, the Gang's All Here: Arthur S. Sullivan(m); T. A. Morse(w), under pseudonym. D. A. Esrom; 1917.

Happy Days Are Here Again: Milton Ager(m); Jack Yellen(w); 1929; introduced on Black Thursday (10-24-29).

Heartaches: Al Hoffman(m); John Klenner(w); 1931; popularized by Ted Weems.

Hello, Dolly: Jerry Herman(m,w); 1964; by Carol Channing in musical of same name.

Home on the Range: Daniel E. Kelly?(m); Brewster (Bruce) Higley (w,m); 1904, called Arizona Home(w) 1873; composer and author uncertain.

Hot Time in the Old Town Tonight: T. M. Metz(m); Joe Hayden(w); 1896; minstrel show.

I Can't Give You Anything But Love: Jimmy McHugh(m); Dorothy Fields(w); 1928; in revue *Delmar's Revels.*

I Could Have Danced All Night: F. Loewe(m); A. J. Lerner(w); 1956; by Julie Andrews in *My Fair Lady.*

I Don't Know Why I Love You Like I Do: F. E. Ahlert(m); Roy Turk(w); 1931.

If You Knew Susie: Bud De Sylva and Joseph Meyer(w,m); 1925; by Al Jolson in *Big Boy.*

I Got Plenty o'Nothin': G. Gershwin(m); I. Gershwin, DuBose Heyward(w); 1935; in *Porgy and Bess.*

I'll Be Seeing You: Sammy Fain(m); Irving Kahal(w); 1938; popularized by Sinatra, Hildegarde, in 1943.

I'll See You in My Dreams: Isham Jones(m); Gus Kahn(w); 1924.

I Love You Truly: Carrie Jacobs Bond(m,w); 1901; originally an art song, later picked up by vaudeville.

I'm in the Mood for Love: J. McHugh(m); Dorothy Fields(w); 1935; by Alice Faye in movie *Every Night at Eight.*

The Impossible Dream: Mitch Leigh(m); Joe Darion(w); 1966; in musical *Man of La Mancha.*

I'm Sitting on Top of the World: Ray Henderson(m); Sam M. Lewis, Joe Young(w); 1925; popularized by Jolson in 1929 movie *The Singing Fool.*

In the Good Old Summertime: George Evans(m); Ren Shields(w); 1902.

I Only Have Eyes for You: Harry Warren(m); Al Dubin(w); 1934; by Dick Powell in movie *Dames.*

It Had To Be You: Isham Jones(m); Gus Kahn(w); 1924.

It's Been a Long, Long Time: Julie Styne(m); Sammy Cahn(w); 1945.

It Was a Very Good Year: Ervin Drake(m,w); 1965; introduced by Kingston Trio on record; popularized by Sinatra.

I've Got You Under My Skin: Cole Porter(m,w); 1936.

I Want a Girl Just Like the Girl: Harry von Tilzer(m); William Dillon(w); 1911.

I Wish You Love: Charles Trenet (French w,m); Albert A. Beach (Eng. w); 1946.

I Wonder Who's Kissing Her Now: J. E. Howard, H. Orlob(m); Wm. M. Hough, F. R. Adams(w); 1909.

Jeannie With the Light Brown Hair: Stephen Foster(m,w); 1854.

June is Busting Out All Over: R. Rodgers(m); O. Hammerstein II(w); 1945; in *Carousel.*

Lazy River: S. Arodin, Hoagy Carmichael(m,w); 1931; on record by Carmichael with band including both Dorseys, Teagarden, Krupa, Goodman, Venuti, and Beiderbecke.

Let Me Call You Sweetheart: Leo Friedman(m); Beth Slat Whitson(w); 1910.

Lover: R. Rodgers(m); Lorenz Hart(w); 1933; by Jeanet MacDonald in movie *Love Me Tonight.*

Lullaby of Broadway: Harry Warren(m); Al Dubin(w); 193 in movie *Gold Diggers of 1935.*

Memories: Egbert van Alstyne(m); Gus Kahn(w); 1915.

Misty: Erroll Garner(m); Johnny Burke(w); 1955.

Moon River: Henry Mancini(m); Johnny Mercer(w); 1961; Andy Williams under title for movie *Breakfast at Tiffany's.*

Moonlight Bay: Percy Wenrich(m); Edward Madden(w 1912; vaudeville.

My Blue Heaven: Walter Donaldson(m); George Whiting(w 1927; Tommy Lyman radio theme song.

Melancholy Baby; Ernie Burnett(m); George A. Norton(w 1912; vaudeville.

My Wild Irish Rose: Chauncey Olcott(m,w); 1899; in music *A Romance of Athlone.*

Night and Day: Cole Porter(m,w); 1932; by Fred Astaire ar Claire Luce in musical *Gay Divorce;* title of Porter film biograph

Oh, What a Beautiful Mornin': R. Rodgers(m); O. Hamme stein II(w); 1943; by Alfred Drake in *Oklahoma!*

Oh! You Beautiful Doll: Nat D. Ayer(m); A. Seymo Brown(w); 1911; vaudeville.

Old Folks at Home (Swanee River): Stephen Foster(m,w 1851; minstrel show.

Ol' Man River: Jerome Kern(m); O. Hammerstein II(w); 192 by Jules Bledsoe in *Show Boat.*

On the Sunny Side of the Street: J. McHugh(m); Doroth Fields(w); 1930; in *International Revue* with Gertrude Lawrence

Over The Rainbow: Harold Arlen(m); E. Y. Harburg(w); 193 by seventeen-year-old Judy Garland in *Wizard of Oz.*

Peg O'My Heart: Fred Fisher(m); Alfred Bryan(w); in *Ziegfe Follies of 1913.*

Pennies From Heaven: Arthur Johnston(m); Johnny Burke(w); 1936; by Bing Crosby in movie of same name.

People: Jule Styne(m); Bob Merrill(w); 1964; by Barbra Stre sand in musical *Funny Girl.*

Pretty Baby: E. van Alstyne, Tony Jackson(m); Gus Kahn(w 1916; by Dolly Hackett in musical *The Passing Show.*

A Pretty Girl Is Like a Melody: Irving Berlin(m,w); in *Ziegfe Follies of 1919;* became Follies theme song.

Put On Your Old Gray Bonnet: Percy Wenrich(m); Stanle Murphy(w); 1909.

Put Your Arms Around Me, Honey: Albert von Tilzer(m Junie McCree(w); 1910; vaudeville.

Raindrops Keep Falling on My Head: Burt Bacharach(m Hal David(w); 1969, in film *Butch Cassidy and the Sundance K.*

Rudolph, the Red-Nosed Reindeer: Johnny Marks(m,w 1949; by Gene Autry on Columbia record.

School Days: Gus Edwards(m); Will D. Cobb(w); 190 vaudeville.

September Song: Kurt Weill(m); Maxwell Anderson(w); 193 by Walter Huston in play *Knickerbocker Holiday.*

The Shadow of Your Smile: Johnny Mandel(m); Paul Franc Webster(w); 1965; in film *The Sandpiper.*

Shine On Harvest Moon: Nora Bayes, Jack Norworth(m Norworth(w); introduced by Nora Bayes in *Ziegfeld Follies 1908.*

Sidewalks of New York: J. W. Blake, C. B. Lawlor(m,w 1894; by Lottie Gilson at Old London Theatre on the Bowery.

Singing in the Rain: Nacio Herb Brown(m); Arthur Freed(w 1929; by Cliff Edwards in movie *Hollywood Revue of 1929.*

Smoke Gets in Your Eyes: Jerome Kern(m); Otto Ha bach(w); 1933; by Tamara in musical *Roberta.*

Somebody Loves Me: G. Gershwin(m); B. DeSylva, B. Ma Donald(w); 1924; *George White's Scandals of 1924.*

Some Enchanted Evening: R. Rodgers(m); O. Hammerste II(w); 1949; by Ezio Pinza in *South Pacific.*

Stardust: Hoagy Carmichael(m); Mitchell Parish(w); 1929.

Stormy Weather: Harold Arlen(m); Ted Koehler(w); 193 popularized by Ethel Waters.

Strike Up the Band: George Gershwin(m); Ira Gershwin(w 1930; in musical of the same name.

Summertime: George Gershwin(m); DuBose Heyward(w 1935; by Abbie Mitchell opening *Porgy and Bess.*

Sweet Georgia Brown: Ben Bernie, M. Pinkard, K. Casey(m,w); 1925.

Sweethearts: Victor Herbert(m); R. B. Smith(w); 1913; in musical of the same name.

Take Me Out to the Ball Game: Albert von Tilzer(m); Jac Norworth(w); 1908; vaudeville.

Tea for Two: Vincent Youmans(m); Irving Caesar(w); 192 by Louise Groody, John Barker, in *No, No, Nanette.*

Tennessee Waltz: Redd Stewart, Pee Wee King(m,w); 194 popularized by Patti Page.

That Old Black Magic: Harold Arlen(m); Johnny Mercer(w 1942; in movie *Star Spangled Rhythm.*

Three Little Words: Harry Ruby(m); Bert Kalmar(w); 1930; Bing Crosby in Amos & Andy movie *Check and Double Check.*

Toot, Toot, Tootsie, Goodbye: Dan Russo(m); Gus Kahn, nie Erdman(w); 1922; by Jolson in *Bombo;* later in first talkie *he Jazz Singer.*

When Irish Eyes Are Smiling: Ernest R. Ball(m); C. Olcott, Graft(w); 1912; by Olcott in musical *Isle of Dreams.*

When Johnny Comes Marching Home: Louis Lamert(m,w); 1863; Lambert thought pen-name for Patrick S. Gilore.

When You're Smiling: M. Fisher, J. Goodwin, L. Shay(m,w); 928.

When You Wish Upon A Star: Leigh Harline(m); Ned Waington(w); 1940; by Cliff Edwards in animated *Pinocchio.*

When You Wore a Tulip: Percy Wenrich(m); Jack Mahoey(w); 1914; vaudeville.

Whispering: John Schonberger, Vincent Rose(m); Richard Coburn(w); 1920; introduced by Paul Whiteman.

White Christmas: Irving Berlin(m,w); 1942; by Bing Crosby in movie *Holiday Inn.*

With a Song in My Heart: R. Rodgers(m); Lorenz Hart(w); 1929; in musical *Spring Is Here.*

Without a Song: Vincent Youmans(m); Billy Rose, E. Eliscu(w); 1929; in musical *Great Day.*

Yellow Rose of Texas: nothing is known of the songwriter but initials "J. K."; 1853; minstrel show.

Yes, Sir, That's My Baby: Walter Donaldson(m); Gus Kahn(w); 1925; popularized by Eddie Cantor.

You and the Night and the Music: Arthur Schwartz(m); Howard Dietz(w); 1934; in musical play *Revenge With Music.*

You Are My Sunshine: Jimmie Davis(m); C. Mitchell(w); 1940; in Tex Ritter movie *Take Me Back to Oklahoma.* Davis governor of Louisiana, 1944-48.

You Made Me Love You: J. V. Monaco(m); Joe McCarthy(w); 1913; by Al Jolson in musical *Honeymoon Express.*

Original Names of Selected Entertainers

Edie Adams: Elizabeth Edith Enke
Anouk Aimee: Francoise Sorya
Eddie Albert: Edward Albert Heimberger
Alan Alda: Alphonso D'Abruzzo
Fred Allen: John Sullivan
Woody Allen: Allen Konigsberg
Julie Andrews: Julia Wells
Eve Arden: Eunice Quedens
Beatrice Arthur: Bernice Frankel
Jean Arthur: Gladys Greene
Fred Astaire: Frederick Austerlitz
Lauren Bacall: Betty Joan Perske
Anne Bancroft: Anna Maria Italiano
Brigitte Bardot: Camille Javal
Tony Bennett: Anthony Benedetto
Busby Berkeley: William Berkeley Enos
Jack Benny: Benjamin Kubelsky
Robert Blake: Michael Gubitosi
Dirk Bogarde: Derek Van der Bogaerd
Fanny Brice: Fanny Borach
Charles Bronson: Charles Buchinski
Mel Brooks: Melvin Kaminsky
George Burns: Nathan Birnbaum
Ellen Burstyn: Edna Gilhooley
Richard Burton: Richard Jenkins
Red Buttons: Aaron Chwatt
Michael Caine: Maurice Micklewhite
Maria Callas: Maria Kalogeropoulos
Diahann Carroll: Carol Diahann Johnson
Cyd Charisse: Tula Finklea
Chubby Checker: Ernest Evans
Cher: Cherilyn Sarkisian
Claudette Colbert: Lily Chauchoin
Michael Connors: Kreker Ohanian
Robert Conrad: Conrad Robert Falk
Howard Cosell: Howard Cohen
Alice Cooper: Vincent Furnier
Elvis Costello: Declan Patrick McManus
Joan Crawford: Lucille Le Sueur
Tony Curtis: Bernard Schwartz
Kim Darby: Deborah Zenby
Bobby Darin: Walden Waldo Cassotto
Doris Day: Doris von Kappelhoff
Yvonne De Carlo: Peggy Middleton
Ruby Dee: Ruby Ann Wallace
Sandra Dee: Alexandra Zuck
John Denver: Henry John Deutschendorf Jr.
John Derek: Derek Harris
Angie Dickinson: Angeline Brown
Marlene Dietrich: Maria von Losch
Diana Dors: Diana Fluck
Melvyn Douglas: Melvyn Hesselberg
Bob Dylan: Robert Zimmerman
Barbara Eden: Barbara Huffman
Ron Ely: Ronald Pierce
Chad Everett: Raymond Cramton
Douglas Fairbanks: Douglas Ullman
Alice Faye: Ann Leppert
W.C. Fields: William Claude Dukenfield
Peter Finch: William Mitchell
Joan Fontaine: Joan de Havilland
John Forsythe: John Freund
Redd Foxx : John Sanford
Anthony Franciosa: Anthony Papaleo
Arlene Francis: Arlene Kazanjian
Connie Francis: Concetta Franconero
Greta Garbo: Greta Gustafsson
Ava Gardner: Lucy Johnson
Judy Garland: Frances Gumm
James Garner: James Baumgardner
Bobbie Gentry: Roberta Streeter
Stewart Granger: James Stewart
Cary Grant: Archibald Leach
Joel Grey: Joe Katz
Buddy Hackett: Leonard Hacker
Jon Hall: Charles Locher
Jean Harlow: Harlean Carpentier
Helen Hayes: Helen Brown
Rita Hayworth: Margarita Cansino
William Holden: William Beedle
Judy Holliday: Judith Tuvim
Harry Houdini: Ehrich Weiss
Leslie Howard: Leslie Stainer
Rock Hudson: Roy Scherer Jr.
Engelbert Humperdinck: Arnold Dorsey
Kim Hunter: Janet Cole
Betty Hutton: Betty Thornberg
David Janssen: David Meyer
Elton John: Reginald Dwight
Jennifer Jones: Phyllis Isley
Tom Jones: Thomas Woodward
Louis Jourdan: Louis Gendre
Boris Karloff: William Henry Platt
Carole King: Carole Klein
Ted Knight: Tadeus Wladyslaw Konopka
Cheryl Ladd: Cheryl Stoppelmoor
Veronica Lake: Constance Ockleman
Michael Landon: Eugene Orowitz
Robert Lansing: Robert Broom
Mario Lanza: Alfredo Cocozza
Stan Laurel: Arthur Jefferson
Steve Lawrence: Sidney Leibowitz
Gypsy Rose Lee: Rose Louise Hovick
Peggy Lee: Norma Egstrom
Janet Leigh: Jeanette Morrison
Vivian Leigh: Vivien Hartley
Jerry Lewis: Joseph Levitch
Hal Linden: Harold Lipshitz
Jack Lord: John Joseph Ryan
Sophia Loren: Sophia Scicoloni
Peter Lorre: Laszio Lowenstein
Myrna Loy: Myrna Williams
Shirley MacLaine: Shirley Beaty
Karl Malden: Malden Sekulovich
Jayne Mansfield: Vera Jane Palmer
Fredric March: Frederick Bickel
Dean Martin: Dino Crocetti
Ross Martin: Martin Rosenblatt
Tony Martin: Alvin Morris
Elaine May: Elaine Berlin
Ethel Merman: Ethel Zimmerman
Ray Milland: Reginald Truscott-Jones
Ann Miller: Lucille Collier
Marilyn Monroe: Norma Jean Mortenson, (later) Baker
Yves Montand: Ivo Levi
Garry Moore: Thomas Garrison Morfit
Harry Morgan: Harry Bratsburg
Gene Nelson: Gene Berg
Mike Nichols: Michael Igor Peschowsky
Sheree North: Dawn Bethel
Hugh O'Brian: Hugh Krampke
Maureen O'Hara: Maureen Fitzsimmons
Jack Palance: Walter Palanuik
Lilli Palmer: Lilli Peiser
Bert Parks: Bert Jacobson
Minnie Pearl: Sarah Ophelia Cannon

Bernadette Peters: Bernadette Lazzaro
Mary Pickford: Gladys Smith
Robert Preston: Robert Preston Meservey
Martha Raye: Margaret Reed
Della Reese: Delloreese Patricia Early
Ginger Rogers: Virginia McMath
Roy Rogers: Leonard Slye
Mickey Rooney: Joe Yule Jr.
Lillian Russell: Helen Leonard
Susan St. James: Susan Miller
Randolph Scott: Randolph Crance
Omar Sharif: Michael Shalhoub
Martin Sheen: Ramon Estevez
Beverly Sills: Belle Silverman
Suzanne Somers: Suzanne Mahoney
Elke Sommer: Elke Schletz
Ann Sothern: Harriette Lake
Kim Stanley: Patricia Reid
Barbara Stanwyck: Ruby Stevens
Jean Stapleton: Jeanne Murray
Ringo Starr: Richard Starkey
Connie Stevens: Concetta Ingolia
Donna Summers: LaDonna Gaines
Robert Taylor: Spangler Arlington Brugh
Danny Thomas: Amos Jacobs
Sophie Tucker: Sophia Kalish
Conway Twitty: Harold Lloyd Jenkins
Rudolph Valentino: Rudolpho D'Antonguolla
Frankie Valli: Frank Castelluccio
Nancy Walker: Myrtle Swoyer
David Wayne: Wayne McMeekan
John Wayne: Marion Morrison
Raquel Welch: Raquel Tejada
Gene Wilder: Jerome Silberman
Shelly Winters: Shirley Schrift
Stevie Wonder: Stevland Morris
Natalie Wood: Natasha Gurdin
Jane Wyman: Sarah Jane Fulks
Gig Young: Byron Barr

Entertainment Personalities — Where and When Born

Actors, Actresses, Dancers, Musicians, Producers, Radio-TV Performers, Singers

Name	Birthplace	Born
Abbott, George	Forestville, N.Y.	6/25/87
Abel, Walter	St. Paul, Minn.	6/6/98
Ackermann, Bettye	Cottageville, S.C.	2/28/28
Acuff, Roy	Maynardville, Tenn.	9/15/03
Adams, Don	New York, N.Y.	4/19/27
Adams, Edie	Kingston, Pa.	4/16/29
Adams, Joey	New York, N.Y.	1/6/11
Adams, Julie	Waterloo, Ia.	10/17/28
Adams, Mason	New York, N.Y.	2/26/-
Adler, Larry	Baltimore, Md.	2/10/14
Adler, Luther	New York, N.Y.	5/4/03
Agar, John	Chicago, Ill.	1/31/21
Aherne, Brian	Worcestershire, England.	5/2/02
Ailey, Alvin	Rogers, Tex.	1/5/31
Aimee, Anouk	Paris, France	4/27/32
Akins, Claude	Nelson, Ga.	5/25/18
Albanese, Licia	Bari, Italy	7/22/13
Alberghetti, Anna Maria	Pesaro, Italy	5/15/36
Albert, Eddie	Rock Island, Ill.	4/22/08
Albert, Edward	Los Angeles, Cal.	2/20/51
Albright, Lola	Akron, Oh.	7/20/24
Alda, Alan	New York, N.Y.	1/28/36
Alda, Robert	New York, N.Y.	2/26/14
Alexander, Jane	Boston, Mass.	10/28/39
Allan, Elizabeth	England	1910
Allen, Mel	Birmingham, Ala.	2/14/13
Allen, Steve	New York, N.Y.	12/26/21
Allen, Woody	Brooklyn, N.Y.	12/1/35
Allison, Fran	LaPorte City, Ia.	—
Allman, Gregg	Nashville, Tenn.	12/7/47
Allyson, June	Lucerne, N.Y.	10/7/23
Alpert, Herb	Los Angeles, Cal.	3/31/35
Altman, Robert	Kansas City, Mo.	2/20/25
Ameche, Don	Kenosha, Wis.	5/31/08
Ames, Ed	Boston, Mass.	1929
Ames, Leon	Portland, Ind.	1/20/03
Amos, John	Newark, N.J.	—
Amsterdam, Morey	Chicago, Ill.	12/14/14
Anderson, Ian	Dunfermline, Scotland	8/10/47
Anderson, Judith	Adelaide, Australia	2/10/98
Anderson, Loni	St. Paul, Minn.	8/5/-
Anderson, Lynn	Grand Forks, N.D.	9/26/47
Anderson, Marian	Philadelphia, Pa.	2/17/02
Anderson, Mary	Birmingham, Ala.	1922
Anderson, Melissa Sue	Berkeley, Cal.	9/26/62
Anderson, Michael Jr.	London, England	1943
Anderson, Richard	Long Branch, N.J.	8/8/26
Andersson, Bibi	Stockholm, Sweden	11/11/35
Andress, Ursula	Switzerland	3/19/36
Andrews, Dana	Collins, Miss.	1/1/12
Andrews, Edward	Griffin, Ga.	10/9/15
Andrews, Julie	Walton, England	10/1/35
Andrews, Maxene	Minneapolis, Minn.	1/3/18
Andrews, Patty	Minneapolis, Minn.	2/16/20
Angel, Heather	Oxford, England	2/9/09
Anka, Paul	Ottawa, Ont.	7/30/41
Ann-Margret	Stockholm, Sweden	4/28/41
Ansara, Michael	Lowell, Mass.	4/15/27
Arden, Eve	Mill Valley, Cal.	4/30/12
Arkin, Alan	New York, N.Y.	3/26/34
Arnaz, Desi	Santiago, Cuba	3/2/17
Arnaz, Desi Jr.	Los Angeles, Cal.	1/19/53
Arnaz, Lucie	Hollywood, Cal.	7/17/51
Arness, James	Minneapolis, Minn.	5/26/
Arnold, Eddy	Henderson, Tenn.	5/15/
Arrau, Claudio	Chillau, Chile	2/6/
Arroyo, Martina	New York, N.Y.	19
Arthur, Beatrice	New York, N.Y.	5/13/
Arthur, Jean	New York, N.Y.	10/17/
Ashley, Elizabeth	Ocala, Fla.	8/30/
Asner, Edward	Kansas City, Mo.	11/15/
Astaire, Fred	Omaha, Neb.	5/10/
Astin, John	Baltimore, Md.	3/30/
Astor, Mary	Quincy, Ill.	5/3/
Atkins, Chet	Luttrell, Tenn.	6/20/
Attenborough, Richard	Cambridge, England	8/29/
Auberjonois, Rene	New York, N.Y.	6/1/
Aumont, Jean-Pierre	Paris, France	1/5/
Autry, Gene	Tioga, Tex.	9/29/
Avalon, Frankie	Philadelphia, Pa.	9/8/
Aykroyd, Dan	Ottawa, Ont.	7/1/
Ayres, Lew	Minneapolis, Minn.	12/28/
Aznavour, Charles	Paris, France	5/22/
Bacall, Lauren	New York, N.Y.	9/16/
Bach, Catherine	Warren, Oh.	3/1
Backus, Jim	Cleveland, Oh.	2/25/
Baddeley, Hermione	Shropshire, England	11/13/
Baer, Max Jr.	Oakland, Cal.	12/4/
Baez, Joan	Staten Island, N.Y.	1/9/
Bailey, Pearl	Newport News, Va.	3/29/
Bain, Barbara	Chicago, Ill.	19
Bain, Conrad	Lethbridge, Alta.	2/4/
Baio, Scott	Brooklyn, N.Y.	9/22/
Baird, Bil	Grand Island, Neb.	8/15/
Baker, Carroll	Johnstown, Pa.	5/28/
Baker, Diane	Hollywood, Cal.	19
Baker, Joe Don	Groesbeck, Tex.	2/12/
Baker, Kenny	Monrovia, Cal.	9/30/
Bakewell, William	Hollywood, Cal.	19
Balanchine, George	St. Petersburg, Russia	1/9/
Ball, Lucille	Jamestown, N.Y.	8/6/
Ballard, Kaye	Cleveland, Oh.	11/20/
Balsam, Martin	New York, N.Y.	11/4/
Bancroft, Anne	New York, N.Y.	9/17/
Barber, Red	Columbus, Miss.	2/17/
Bardot, Brigitte	Paris, France	9/28/
Bari, Lynn	Roanoke, Va.	19
Barker, Bob	Darrington, Wash.	12/12
Barnes, Priscilla	Ft. Dix, N.J.	12/7
Barrault, Jean-Louis	Le Vesinet, France	19
Barrie, Barbara	Chicago, Ill.	5/23/
Barrie, Mona	London, England	12/18/
Barris, Chuck	Philadelphia, Pa.	6/2/
Barry, Gene	New York, N.Y.	6/4/
Barry, Jack	Lindenhurst, N.Y.	3/20/
Bartholomew, Freddie	London, England	3/28/
Bartok, Eva	Budapest, Hungary	19
Baryshnikov, Mikhail	Riga, Latvia	1/28/
Basehart, Richard	Zanesville, Oh.	8/31/
Basie, Count (Wm.)	Red Bank, N.J.	8/21/
Bassey, Shirley	Cardiff, Wales	19
Bates, Alan	Allestree, England	2/17/
Baxter, Anne	Michigan City, Ind.	5/7/
Baxter-Birney, Meredith	Los Angeles, Cal.	6/21
Beal, John	Joplin, Mo.	8/13/
Bean, Orson	Burlington, Vt.	7/22/

Name	Birthplace	Born
Beatty, Ned	Louisville, Ky.	7/6/37
Beatty, Robert	Hamilton, Ont.	10/19/09
Beatty, Warren	Richmond, Va.	3/30/38
Bedelia, Bonnie	New York, N.Y.	3/25/48
Bee Gees		
Gibb, Barry	Manchester, England.	9/1/46
Gibb, Robin	" "	12/22/49
Gibb, Maurice	" "	12/22/49
Beery, Noah Jr.	New York, N.Y.	8/10/16
Belafonte, Harry	New York, N.Y.	3/1/27
Bel Geddes, Barbara	New York, N.Y.	10/31/22
Bellamy, Ralph	Chicago, Ill.	6/17/04
Belmondo, Jean-Paul	Neuilly-sur-Seine, France	4/9/33
Benjamin, Richard	New York, N.Y.	5/22/38
Bennett, Joan	Palisades, N.J.	2/27/10
Bennett, Michael	Buffalo, N.Y.	4/8/43
Bennett, Tony	Astoria, N.Y.	8/3/26
Benson, George	Pittsburgh, Pa.	3/2/43
Benson, Robby	Dallas, Tex.	1957
Bentley, John	Warwickshire, England.	12/2/16
Bergen, Candice	Beverly Hills, Cal.	5/9/46
Bergen, Polly	Knoxville, Tenn.	7/14/30
Bergerac, Jacques	Biarritz, France	5/26/27
Bergman, Ingmar	Uppsala, Sweden.	7/14/18
Bergman, Ingrid	Stockholm, Sweden	8/29/15
Bergner, Elisabeth	Vienna, Austria	8/22/00
Berle, Milton	New York, N.Y.	7/12/08
Berlinger, Warren	Brooklyn, N.Y.	8/31/37
Berman, Shelley	Chicago, Ill.	2/3/26
Bernardi, Herschel	New York, N.Y.	1923
Bernstein, Elmer	New York, N.Y.	4/4/22
Bernstein, Leonard	Lawrence, Mass.	8/25/18
Berry, Chuck	San Jose, Cal.	1/15/26
Berry, Ken	Moline, Ill.	—
Bertinelli, Valerie	Wilmington, Del.	4/23/60
Bikel, Theodore	Vienna, Austria	5/2/24
Birney, David	Washington, D.C.	4/23/40
Bishop, Joey	Bronx, N.Y.	2/3/18
Bisoglio, Val	New York, N.Y.	5/7/26
Bisset, Jacqueline	Weybridge, England	9/13/46
Bixby, Bill	San Francisco, Cal.	1/22/34
Black, Karen	Park Ridge, Ill.	7/1/42
Blaine, Vivian	Newark, N.J.	11/21/23
Blair, Linda	St. Louis, Mo.	1/22/59
Blake, Amanda	Buffalo, N.Y.	2/20/31
Blake, Robert	Nutley, N.J.	9/18/38
Blakeley, Ronee	Idaho	1946
Blakely, Susan	Germany	—
Blanc, Mel	San Francisco, Cal.	5/30/08
Bloom, Claire	London, England	2/15/31
Blyth, Ann	Mt. Kisco, N.Y.	8/16/28
Bogarde, Dirk	London, England	3/28/21
Bogdanovich, Peter	Kingston, N.Y.	7/30/39
Bolger, Ray	Dorchester, Mass.	1/10/04
Bono, Sonny	Detroit, Mich.	2/16/40
Boone, Debby	Hackensack, N.J.	9/22/56
Boone, Pat	Jacksonville, Fla.	6/1/34
Booth, Shirley	New York, N.Y.	8/30/09
Borge, Victor	Copenhagen, Denmark	1/3/09
Borgnine, Ernest	Hamden, Conn.	1/24/17
Bosley, Tom	Chicago, Ill.	10/1/27
Bottoms, Joseph	Santa Barbara, Cal.	4/22/54
Bottoms, Timothy	Santa Barbara, Cal.	8/30/51
Bowie, David	London, England	1/8/47
Boyle, Peter	Philadelphia, Pa.	1933
Bracken, Eddie	New York, N.Y.	2/7/20
Brand, Neville	Kewanee, Ill.	8/13/21
Brando, Marlon	Omaha, Neb.	4/3/24
Brazzi, Rossano	Bologna, Italy	9/18/16
Brennan, Eileen	Los Angeles, Cal.	9/3/35
Brenner, David	Philadelphia, Pa.	1945
Brewer, Teresa	Toledo, Oh.	5/7/31
Brian, David	New York, N.Y.	8/5/14
Bridges, Beau	Hollywood, Cal.	12/9/41
Bridges, Jeff	Los Angeles, Cal.	12/4/49
Bridges, Lloyd	San Leandro, Cal.	1/15/13
Bridges, Todd	San Francisco, Cal.	5/27/65
Brisebois, Danielle	New York, N.Y.	6/28/69
Broderick, James	Charlestown, N.H.	3/7/27
Brolin, James	Los Angeles, Cal.	7/10/42
Bronson, Charles	Scooptown, Pa.	11/3/22
Brooks, Louise	Cherryvale, Kan.	1906
Brooks, Mel	New York, N.Y.	1926
Brooks, Stephen	Columbus, Oh.	1942
Brown, James	Pulaski, Tenn.	6/17/28
Brown, Jimmy	St. Simons Island, Ga.	2/17/36
Brown, Les	Reinerton, Pa.	3/14/12
Brown, Ray	Pittsburgh, Pa.	10/13/26
Brown, Tom	New York, N.Y.	1/6/13
Browne, Roscoe Lee	Woodbury, N.J.	1925
Bruce, Carol	Great Neck, N.Y.	11/15/19
Bryant, Anita	Barnsdall, Okla.	3/25/40
Brynner, Yul	Sakhalin, Japan.	7/11/20
Buchholz, Horst	Berlin, Germany	12/4/33
Bujold, Genevieve	Montreal, Que.	7/1/42
Bumbry, Grace	St. Louis, Mo.	1/4/37
Burghoff, Gary	Bristol, Conn.	5/24/-
Burke, Paul	New Orleans, La.	7/21/26
Burnett, Carol	San Antonio, Tex.	4/26/36
Burns, George	New York, N.Y.	1/20/96
Burr, Raymond	New Westminster, B.C.	5/21/17
Burstyn, Ellen	Detroit, Mich.	12/7/32
Burton, Richard	South Wales	11/10/25
Bushell, Anthony	Kent, England	1904
Buttons, Red	New York, N.Y.	2/5/19
Buzzi, Ruth	Westerly, R.I.	7/24/36
Caan, James	New York, N.Y.	3/26/39
Caballe, Montserrat	Barcelona, Spain	4/12/33
Caesar, Sid	Yonkers, N.Y.	9/8/22
Cagney, James	New York, N.Y.	7/17/99
Caine, Michael	London, England	3/14/33
Caldwell, Sarah	Maryville, Mo.	1929
Caldwell, Zoe	Melbourne, Australia	9/14/33
Calhoun, Rory	Los Angeles, Cal.	8/8/22
Callan, Michael	Philadelphia, Pa.	1935
Callas, Charlie	Brooklyn, N.Y.	12/20/-
Calloway, Cab	Rochester, N.Y.	12/25/07
Calvert, Phyllis	London, England	2/18/15
Calvet, Corinne	Paris, France	4/30/26
Cameron, Rod	Calgary, Canada	12/7/12
Campbell, Glen	Billstown, Ark.	4/22/36
Cannon, Dyan	Tacoma, Wash.	1/4/37
Canova, Judy	Starke, Fla.	11/20/16
Cantrell, Lana	Sydney, Australia	8/7/43
Capra, Frank	Palermo, Italy	5/18/97
Cardinale, Claudia	Tunisia	1939
Carey, Macdonald	Sioux City, Ia.	3/15/13
Carey, Phil	Hackensack, N.J.	7/15/25
Carey, Ron	Newark, N.J.	12/11/35
Carle, Frankie	Providence, R.I.	1903
Carlin, George	New York, N.Y.	5/12/37
Carlisle, Kitty	New Orleans, La	9/3/15
Carman, Eric	Cleveland, Oh.	8/11/49
Carmichael, Ian	Hull, England	6/18/20
Carne, Judy	Northampton, England	1939
Carney, Art	Mt. Vernon, N.Y.	11/4/18
Carnovsky, Morris	St. Louis, Mo.	9/5/97
Caron, Leslie	Boulogne, France	7/1/31
Carpenter, Karen	New Haven, Conn.	3/2/50
Carpenter, Richard	New Haven, Conn.	10/15/46
Carr, Vikki	El Paso, Tex.	7/19/42
Carradine, David	Hollywood, Cal.	12/8/36
Carradine, John	New York, N.Y.	2/5/06
Carradine, Keith	San Mateo, Cal.	8/8/49
Carreras, Jose	Barcelona, Spain	12/5/47
Carroll, Diahann	Bronx, N.Y.	7/17/35
Carroll, Madeleine	W. Bromwich, England	2/26/06
Carroll, Pat	Shreveport, La.	5/5/27
Carson, Johnny	Corning, Ia.	10/23/25
Carter, Jack	New York, N.Y.	6/24/23
Carter, June	Maces Spring, Va.	6/23/29
Carter, Lynda	Phoenix, Ariz.	7/24/-
Casadesus, Gaby	Marseilles, France	1902
Cash, Johnny	Kingsland, Ark.	2/26/32
Cass, Peggy	Boston, Mass.	5/21/24
Cassavetes, John	New York, N.Y.	12/9/29
Cassidy, David	New York, N.Y.	4/12/50
Cassidy, Shaun	Los Angeles, Cal.	9/27/59
Castellano, Richard	New York, N.Y.	9/4/33
Caulfield, Joan	West Orange, N.J.	6/1/22
Cavallaro, Carmen	New York, N.Y.	1913
Cavett, Dick	Gibbon, Neb.	11/19/36
Chamberlain, Richard	Beverly Hills, Cal.	3/31/35
Champion, Marge	Los Angeles, Cal.	9/2/23
Channing, Carol	Seattle, Wash.	1/31/23
Channing, Stockard	New York, N.Y.	—
Chaplin, Geraldine	Santa Monica, Cal.	7/31/44
Chaplin, Sydney	Beverly Hills, Cal.	3/31/26
Charisse, Cyd	Amarillo, Tex.	3/8/23
Charles, Ray	Albany, Ga.	9/23/30
Chase, Chevy	New York, N.Y.	10/8/43
Checker, Chubby	Philadelphia, Pa.	10/3/41
Cher	El Centro, Cal.	5/20/46
Chong, Thomas	Edmonton, Alta.	5/24/38
Christian, Linda	Tampico, Mexico	11/13/24
Christie, Julie	Chukur, India	4/14/41
Christopher, Jordon	Youngstown, Oh.	1941
Christy, June	Springfield, Ill.	1925

Name	Birthplace	Born
Cilento, Diane	Queensland, Australia	10/5/33
Cimino, Michael	New York, N.Y.	1943
Claire, Ina	Washington, D.C.	1892
Clapton, Eric	Surrey, England	3/30/45
Clark, Dane	New York, N.Y.	2/18/15
Clark, Dick	Mt. Vernon, N.Y.	11/30/29
Clark, Petula	Ewell, Surrey, England	11/15/32
Clark, Roy	Meherrin, Va.	4/15/33
Clark, Susan	Sarnia, Ont.	3/8/44
Clayburgh, Jill	New York, N.Y.	4/30/44
Clayton, Jan	Tularosa, N.M.	—
Cliburn, Van	Shreveport, La.	7/12/34
Clooney, Rosemary	Maysville, Ky.	5/23/28
Coburn, James	Laurel, Neb.	8/31/28
Coca, Imogene	Philadelphia, Pa.	11/18/08
Coco, James	New York, N.Y.	3/21/30
Cohen, Myron	Grodno, Poland	1902
Colbert, Claudette	Paris, France	9/18/05
Cole, Michael	Madison, Wis.	1945
Cole, Natalie	Los Angeles, Cal.	2/6/50
Coleman, Gary	Zion, Ill.	2/8/68
Collins, Dorothy	Windsor, Ont.	11/18/26
Collins, Joan	London, England	5/23/36
Collins, Judy	Seattle, Wash.	5/1/39
Colonna, Jerry	Boston, Mass.	1903
Comden, Betty	Brooklyn, N.Y.	5/3/19
Como, Perry	Canonsburg, Pa.	5/18/12
Conaway, Jeff	New York, N.Y.	10/5/50
Conner, Nadine	Compton, Cal.	1913
Connery, Sean	Edinburgh, Scotland	8/25/30
Conniff, Ray	Attleboro, Mass.	11/6/16
Connors, Chuck	Brooklyn, N.Y.	4/10/21
Connors, Michael	Fresno, Cal.	8/15/25
Conrad, Michael	New York, N.Y.	10/16/-
Conrad, Robert	Chicago, Ill.	3/1/35
Conrad, William	Louisville, Ky.	9/27/20
Constantine, Michael	Reading, Pa.	5/22/27
Convy, Bert	St. Louis, Mo.	6/23/39
Conway, Gary	Boston, Mass.	1938
Conway, Tim	Willoughby, Oh.	12/15/33
Coogan, Jackie	Los Angeles, Cal.	10/26/14
Cook, Barbara	Atlanta, Ga.	10/25/27
Cook, Peter	Torquay, England	11/17/37
Cooke, Alistair	England	11/20/08
Coolidge, Rita	Nashville, Tenn.	5/1/45
Cooper, Alice	Detroit, Mich.	2/4/48
Cooper, Jackie	Los Angeles, Cal.	9/15/22
Coppola, Francis Ford	Detroit, Mich.	4/7/39
Corby, Ellen	Racine, Wis.	1913
Corelli, Franco	Ancona, Italy	4/8/23
Corey, Jeff	New York, N.Y.	8/10/14
Cosby, Bill	Philadelphia, Pa.	7/12/37
Costello, Elvis	London, England	1954
Cotten, Joseph	Petersburg, Va.	5/15/05
Courtenay, Tom	Hull, England	2/25/37
Crabbe, Buster	Oakland, Cal.	2/07/08
Craddock, Crash	Greensboro, N.C.	6/16/40
Crain, Jeanne	Barstow, Cal.	5/25/25
Crawford, Broderick	Philadelphia, Pa.	12/9/11
Crawford, Michael	Salisbury, England	1942
Crenna, Richard	Los Angeles, Cal.	11/30/27
Cronyn, Hume	London, Ont.	7/18/11
Crosby, Bob	Spokane, Wash.	8/23/13
Crosby, Cathy Lee	Los Angeles, Cal.	12/2/-
Crosby, David	Los Angeles, Cal.	8/14/41
Crosby, Kathryn	Houston, Tex.	11/25/33
Crosby, Mary	Los Angeles, Cal.	9/14/-
Crosby, Norm	Boston, Mass.	1/15/-
Crothers, Scatman	Terre Haute, Ind.	5/23/32
Crowley, Pat	Scranton, Pa.	1929
Crystal, Billy	Long Beach, N.Y.	3/14/47
Cugat, Xavier	Barcelona, Spain	1/1/00
Cullen, Bill	Pittsburgh, Pa.	2/18/20
Cullum, John	Knoxville, Tenn.	3/2/30
Culp, Robert	Oakland, Cal.	8/16/30
Cummings, Constance	Seattle, Wash.	5/15/10
Cummings, Robert	Joplin, Mo.	6/9/10
Curtin, Phyllis	Clarksburg, W.Va.	12/3/30
Curtis, Keene	Salt Lake City, Ut.	2/15/23
Curtis, Ken	Lamar, Col.	7/2/16
Curtis, Tony	New York, N.Y.	6/3/25
Cusack, Cyril	Durban, S. Africa	11/26/10
Cushing, Peter	Surrey, England	5/26/13
Dagmar (Egnor)	Huntington, W.Va.	1926
Dahl, Arlene	Minneapolis, Minn.	8/11/28
Dale, Jim	Rothwell, England	8/15/35
Dalrymple, Jean	Morristown, N.J.	9/2/10
Dalton, Abby	Las Vegas, Nev.	1935
Daly, John	Johannesburg, S. Africa	2/20/14
Damone, Vic	Brooklyn, N.Y.	6/12/28
Dangerfield, Rodney	Babylon, N.Y.	1921
Daniels, William	Brooklyn, N.Y.	3/31/27
Danilova, Alexandra	Peterhof, Russia	1907
Danner, Blythe	Philadelphia, Pa.	—
Danton, Ray	New York, N.Y.	9/19/31
Darby, Kim	Hollywood, Cal.	7/8/48
Darcel, Denise	Paris, France	9/8/25
Darren, James	Philadelphia, Pa.	6/8/36
Darrieux, Danielle	Bordeaux, France	5/1/17
Darrow, Henry	New York, N.Y.	1933
Da Silva, Howard	Cleveland, Oh.	5/4/09
Dassin, Jules	Middletown, Conn.	12/18/11
Davidson, John	Pittsburgh, Pa.	12/13/41
Davis, Ann B.	Schenectady, N.Y.	5/5/26
Davis, Bette	Lowell, Mass.	4/5/08
Davis, Clifton	Chicago, Ill.	1945
Davis, Mac	Lubbock, Tex.	1/21/42
Davis, Ossie	Cogdell, Ga.	12/18/17
Davis, Sammy Jr.	New York, N.Y.	12/8/25
Davis, Skeeter	Dry Ridge, Ky.	12/30/31
Dawber, Pam	Detroit, Mich.	10/18/-
Dawn, Hazel	Ogden, Ut.	1898
Dawson, Richard	Hampshire, England	11/20/-
Day, Dennis	New York, N.Y.	5/21/17
Day, Doris	Cincinnati, Oh.	4/3/24
Day, Laraine	Roosevelt, Ut.	10/13/20
Dean, Jimmy	Plainview, Tex.	8/10/28
De Camp, Rosemary	Prescott, Ariz.	1913
DeCarlo, Yvonne	Vancouver, B.C.	9/4/22
Dee, Frances	Los Angeles, Cal.	1907
Dee, Joey	Passaic, N.J.	1940
Dee, Ruby	Cleveland, Oh.	10/27/23
Dee, Sandra	Bayonne, N.J.	4/23/42
Defore, Don	Cedar Rapids, Ia.	8/25/17
DeHaven, Gloria	Los Angeles, Cal.	7/23/25
de Havilland, Olivia	Tokyo, Japan	7/1/16
De Niro, Robert	New York, N.Y.	8/17/45
Del Rio, Dolores	Durango, Mexico	8/3/08
Dell, Gabriel	Brooklyn, N.Y.	1921
Della Chiesa, Vivienne	Chicago, Ill.	1920
Delon, Alain	Sceaux, France	11/8/35
DeLuise, Dom	Brooklyn, N.Y.	8/1/33
Demarest, William	St. Paul, Minn.	2/27/92
De Mille, Agnes	New York, N.Y.	1905
Dempster, Carol	Duluth, Minn.	1901
Deneuve, Catherine	Paris, France	10/22/43
Denning, Richard	Poughkeepsie, N.Y.	3/27/14
Dennis, Sandy	Hastings, Neb.	4/27/37
Denver, Bob	New Rochelle, N.Y.	1935
Denver, John	Roswell, N.M.	12/31/43
DePalma, Brian	Newark, N.J.	9/11/40
Derek, Bo	Long Beach, Cal.	1956
Derek, John	Hollywood, Cal.	1926
Dern, Bruce	Chicago, Ill.	6/4/36
Desmond, Johnny	Detroit, Mich.	11/14/21
Devane, William	Albany, N.Y.	9/5/37
DeVito, Danny	Neptune, N.J.	11/17/-
Dewhurst, Colleen	Montreal, Que.	6/3/26
DeWitt, Joyce	Wheeling, W.Va.	4/23/49
Dey, Susan	Pekin, Ill.	12/10/52
Diamond, Neil	Brooklyn, N.Y.	1/24/41
Dickinson, Angie	Kulm, N.D.	9/30/31
Dierkop, Charles	La Crosse, Wis.	9/11/36
Dietrich, Marlene	Berlin, Germany	1901
Diller, Phyllis	Lima, Oh.	7/17/17
Dillman, Bradford	San Francisco, Cal.	4/14/30
Dixon, Ivan	New York, N.Y.	4/6/31
Domingo, Placido	Madrid, Spain	1/21/41
Domino, Fats	New Orleans, La.	2/26/28
Donahue, Phil	Cleveland, Oh.	12/21/35
Donahue, Troy	New York, N.Y.	1/27/36
Donald, James	Aberdeen, Scotland	5/18/17
Donnelly, Ruth	Trenton, N.J.	1896
Donovan	Glasgow, Scotland	5/10/46
Dors, Diana	Swindon, England	10/23/31
d'Orsay, Fifi	Montreal, Que.	1908
Douglas, Kirk	Amsterdam, N.Y.	12/9/18
Douglas, Michael	New Brunswick, N.J.	9/25/45
Douglas, Mike	Chicago, Ill.	8/11/25
Down, Leslie-Ann	London, England	3/17/54
Downey, Morton	Wallingford, Conn.	11/14/01
Downs, Hugh	Akron, Oh.	2/14/21
Doyle, David	Lincoln, Neb.	12/1/29
Dragon, Daryl	Los Angeles Cal.	8/27/42
Drake, Alfred	Bronx, N.Y.	10/7/14
Drew, Ellen	Kansas City, Mo.	11/23/15
Dreyfuss, Richard	Brooklyn, N.Y.	10/29/47
Dru, Joanne	Logan, W.Va.	1/31/23

Name	Birthplace	Born
Drury, James	New York, N.Y.	1934
Duchin, Peter	New York, N.Y.	7/28/37
Duff, Howard	Bremerton, Wash.	11/24/17
Duffy, Patrick	Townsend, Mont.	3/17/49
Dufour, Val	New Orleans, La.	2/5/27
Duke, Patty	New York, N.Y.	12/14/46
Dullea, Keir	Cleveland, Oh.	5/30/36
Dunaway, Faye	Bascom, Fla.	1/14/41
Duncan, Sandy	Henderson, Tex.	2/20/46
Duncan, Todd	Danville, Ky.	1900
Duncan, Vivian	Los Angeles, Cal.	1902
Dunham, Katherine	Chicago, Ill.	6/22/10
Dunne, Irene	Louisville, Ky.	12/20/04
Dunnock, Mildred	Baltimore, Md.	1/25/06
Durbin, Deanna	Winnipeg, Man.	12/4/22
Dussault, Nancy	Pensacola, Fla.	6/30/36
Duvall, Robert	San Diego, Cal.	1931
Duvall, Shelley	Houston, Tex.	1949
Dylan, Bob	Duluth, Minn.	5/24/41
Eastwood, Clint	San Francisco, Cal.	5/31/30
Ebsen, Buddy	Belleville, Ill.	4/2/08
Eckstine, Billy	Pittsburgh, Pa.	7/8/14
Edelman, Herb.	Brooklyn, N.Y.	11/5/33
Eden, Barbara	Tucson, Ariz.	1934
Edwards, Ralph	Merino, Col.	1913
Edwards, Vincent	Brooklyn, N.Y.	7/7/28
Egan, Richard	San Francisco, Cal.	7/29/23
Eggar, Samantha	London, England	3/5/39
Ekberg, Anita	Malmo, Sweden	9/29/31
Ekland, Britt	Stockholm, Sweden	1942
Elam, Jack	Miami, Ariz.	11/13/16
Eldridge, Florence	Brooklyn, N.Y.	9/5/01
Elgart, Larry	New London, Conn.	3/20/22
Elgart, Les	New Haven, Conn.	1918
Elliott, Bob	Boston, Mass.	1923
Emerson, Faye	Elizabeth, La.	7/8/17
Erickson, Leif.	Alameda, Cal.	10/27/11
Esmond, Jill	London, England	1908
Estrada, Erik	New York, N.Y.	3/16/49
Evans, Dale	Uvalde, Tex.	10/31/12
Evans, Gene	Holbrook, Ariz.	7/11/24
Evans, Maurice	Dorchester, England	6/3/01
Evans, Robert	New York, N.Y.	6/29/30
Everett, Chad	South Bend, Ind.	6/11/37
Everly, Don.	Brownie, Ky.	2/1/37
Everly, Phil	Brownie, Ky.	1/19/38
Ewell, Tom	Owensboro, Ky.	4/29/09
Fabares, Shelley	Santa Monica, Cal.	1/19/42
Fabian (Forte)	Philadelphia, Pa.	2/6/43
Fabray, Nanette	San Diego, Cal.	10/27/20
Fadiman, Clifton	Brooklyn, N.Y.	5/15/04
Fairbanks, Douglas Jr.	New York, N.Y.	12/9/09
Fairchild, Morgan	Dallas, Tex.	2/3/-
Falana, Lola	Philadelphia, Pa.	1947
Falk, Peter	New York, N.Y.	9/16/27
Falkenberg, Jinx	Barcelona, Spain	1/21/19
Farber, Barry	Baltimore, Md.	1930
Farentino, James	Brooklyn, N.Y.	2/24/38
Fargo, Donna	Mt. Airy, N.C.	11/10/49
Farr, Jamie	Toledo, Oh.	7/1/36
Farrell, Charles	Onset Bay, Mass.	8/6/06
Farrell, Eileen	Willimantic, Conn.	2/13/20
Farrell, Mike	St. Paul, Minn.	2/6/42
Farrow, Mia	Los Angeles, Cal.	2/9/45
Fawcett, Farrah	Corpus Christi, Tex.	2/2/47
Faye, Alice	New York, N.Y.	5/5/15
Feld, Fritz.	Berlin, Germany	10/15/00
Feldman, Marty	England	1933
Feldon, Barbara	Pittsburgh, Pa.	3/12/41
Feldshun, Tovah	New York, N.Y.	12/27/52
Feliciano, Jose	Puerto Rico	9/10/45
Fell, Norman	Philadelphia, Pa.	3/24/25
Fellini, Federico	Rimini, Italy	1/20/20
Fellows, Edith	Boston, Mass.	1923
Ferrer, Jose	Santurce, P.R.	1/8/12
Ferrer, Mel	Elberon, N.J.	8/25/17
Ferrigno, Lou.	Brooklyn, N.Y.	11/9/52
Ferris, Barbara	London, England	1942
Fetchit, Stepin	Key West, Fla.	1902
Field, Sally	Pasadena, Cal.	11/6/46
Finney, Albert	Salford, England	5/9/36
Firkusny, Rudolf	Napajedla, Czechoslovakia	2/11/12
Firth, Peter	Yorkshire, England	10/27/53
Fischer-Dieskau, Dietrich	Berlin, Germany	5/28/25
Fisher, Carrie	Beverly Hills, Cal.	10/21/56
Fisher, Eddie	Philadelphia, Pa.	8/10/28
Fitzgerald, Ella	Newport News, Va.	4/25/18
Fitzgerald, Geraldine	Dublin, Ireland	11/24/13
Fitzgerald, Pegeen	Norcatur, Kan.	1910
Fix, Paul	Dobbs Ferry, N.Y.	3/13/02
Flack, Roberta	Black Mountain, N.C.	2/10/39
Fleming, Rhonda	Hollywood, Cal.	8/10/23
Flanders, Ed	Minneapolis, Minn.	12/29/34
Fletcher, Louise	Birmingham, Ala.	1936
Foch, Nina	Leyden, Netherlands	4/20/24
Fonda, Henry	Grand Island, Neb.	5/16/05
Fonda, Jane	New York, N.Y.	12/21/37
Fonda, Peter	New York, N.Y.	2/23/40
Fontaine, Joan	Tokyo, Japan	10/22/17
Fontanne, Lynn	London, England	12/6/87
Fonteyn, Margot	Reigate, England	5/18/19
Forbes, Bryan	London, England	7/22/26
Ford (Tenn.), Ernie	Bristol, Tenn.	2/13/19
Ford, Glenn	Quebec, Canada	5/1/16
Ford, Harrison	Chicago, Ill.	7/13/42
Ford, Ruth	Hazelhurst, Miss.	1920
Forrest, Steve	Huntsville, Tex.	9/29/25
Forsythe, John	Penns Grove, N.J.	1/29/18
Fosse, Bob	Chicago, Ill.	6/23/27
Foster, Jodie	Los Angeles, Cal.	11/19/62
Foster, Phil	Brooklyn, N.Y.	3/29/14
Fox, James	London, England	1939
Foxx, Redd	St. Louis, Mo.	12/9/22
Foy, Eddie Jr.	New Rochelle, N.Y.	2/4/05
Frampton, Peter	Kent, England	4/22/50
Francescatti, Zino	Marseilles, France	8/9/05
Franciosa, Anthony	New York, N.Y.	10/25/28
Francis, Anne	Ossining, N.Y.	9/16/32
Francis, Arlene	Boston, Mass.	10/20/08
Francis, Connie	Newark, N.J.	12/12/38
Franciscus, James	Clayton, Mo.	1/31/34
Frankenheimer, John	Malba, N.Y.	2/19/30
Franklin, Aretha	Memphis, Tenn.	3/25/42
Franklin, Bonnie	Santa Monica, Cal.	1/6/44
Franklin, Joe	New York, N.Y.	1929
Franz, Arthur	Perth Amboy, N.J.	2/29/20
Freberg, Stan	Pasadena, Cal.	8/7/26
Freed, Bert	New York, N.Y.	11/3/19
Freeman Jr., Al	San Antonio, Tex.	3/21/34
Freeman, Mona	Baltimore, Md.	1926
Frick, Mr. (G. Werner)	Basel, Switzerland	4/21/15
Friedkin, William	Chicago, Ill.	8/29/39
Frost, David	Tenterden, England	4/7/39
Frye, David	Brooklyn, N.Y.	1934
Funicello, Annette	Utica, N.Y.	10/22/42
Funt, Allen	New York, N.Y.	9/16/14
Furness, Betty	New York, N.Y.	1/3/16
Gabel, Martin	Philadelphia, Pa.	6/19/12
Gabor, Eva	Hungary	1921
Gabor, Zsa Zsa	Hungary	—
Gail, Max	Detroit, Mich.	4/5/43
Galloway, Don	Brooksville, Ky.	7/27/37
Galway, James	Galway, Ireland	12/8/39
Gam, Rita	Pittsburgh, Pa.	1929
Gambling, John	New York, N.Y.	1930
Garagiola, Joe	St. Louis, Mo.	2/12/26
Garbo, Greta	Stockholm, Sweden	9/18/05
Gardenia, Vincent	Naples, Italy	1/7/22
Gardner, Ava	Smithfield, N.C.	12/24/22
Garfunkel, Art	New York, N.Y.	10/13/41
Garland, Beverly	Santa Cruz, Cal.	10/17/29
Garner, James	Norman, Okla.	4/7/28
Garner, Peggy Ann	Canton, Oh.	2/3/32
Garrett, Betty	St. Joseph, Mo.	5/23/19
Garson, Greer	Co. Down, N. Ireland	9/29/08
Gary, John	Watertown, N.Y.	11/29/32
Gavin, John	Los Angeles, Cal.	4/8/32
Gaye, Marvin	Washington, D.C.	4/2/39
Gayle, Crystal	Paintsville, Ky.	1951
Gaynor, Janet	Philadelphia, Pa.	10/6/06
Gaynor, Mitzi	Chicago, Ill.	9/4/30
Gazzara, Ben	New York, N.Y.	8/28/30
Geary, Anthony	Coalville, Ut.	5/29/-
Gedda, Nicolai	Stockholm, Sweden	7/11/25
Gennaro, Peter	Metairie, La.	1924
Gentry, Bobbie	Chickasaw Co., Miss.	7/27/44
Gerard, Gil	Little Rock, Ark.	1/23/43
Gere, Richard	Philadelphia, Pa.	1950
Ghostley, Alice	Eve, Mo.	8/14/26
Giannini, Giancarlo	Spezia, Italy	8/1/42
Gibb, Andy	Manchester, England	3/5/58
Gibson, Henry	Germantown, Pa.	9/21/35
Gielgud, John	London, England	4/14/04
Gilbert, Melissa	Los Angeles, Cal.	5/8/64
Gilford, Jack	New York, N.Y.	7/25/07
Gillette, Anita	Baltimore, Md.	8/16/36

Name	Birthplace	Born
Gingold, Hermione	London, England	12/9/97
Ginty, Robert	New York, N.Y.	11/14/48
Gish, Lillian	Springfield, Oh.	10/14/96
Givot, George	Omaha, Neb.	1903
Glaser, Paul Michael	Cambridge, Mass.	3/25/-
Glass, Ron	Evansville, Ind.	7/1/-
Gleason, Jackie	Brooklyn, N.Y.	2/26/16
Gobel, George	Chicago, Ill.	5/20/19
Godard, Jean Luc	Paris, France	12/3/30
Goddard, Paulette	Great Neck, N.Y.	6/3/15
Godfrey, Arthur	New York, N.Y.	8/31/03
Goldsboro, Bobby	Marianna, Fla.	1/11/41
Goodman, Benny	Chicago, Ill.	5/30/09
Goodman, Dody	Columbus, Oh.	10/28/29
Gordon, Gale	New York, N.Y.	2/2/06
Gordon, Ruth	Wollaston, Mass.	10/30/96
Gorin, Igor	Ukraine, Russia	1909
Gorman, Cliff	New York, N.Y.	10/13/36
Gorme, Eydie	Bronx, N.Y.	8/16/32
Gorshin, Frank	Pittsburgh, Pa.	4/5/34
Gortner, Marjoe	Long Beach, Cal.	1/14/45
Gosden, Freeman (Amos)	Richmond, Va.	5/5/99
Gossett, Louis	Brooklyn, N.Y.	5/27/36
Gould, Elliott	Brooklyn, N.Y.	8/29/38
Gould, Morton	Richmond Hill, N.Y.	12/10/13
Goulding, Ray	Lowell, Mass.	3/20/22
Goulet, Robert	Lawrence, Mass.	11/26/33
Gowdy, Curt	Green River, Wyo.	1919
Graham, Martha	Pittsburgh, Pa.	5/11/94
Graham, Virginia	Chicago, Ill.	7/4/12
Granger, Farley	San Jose, Cal.	7/1/25
Granger, Stewart	London, England	5/6/13
Granville, Bonita	New York, N.Y.	1923
Grant, Cary	Bristol, England	1/18/04
Grant, Lee	New York, N.Y.	10/31/31
Graves, Peter	Minneapolis, Minn.	3/18/26
Gray, Coleen	Staplehurst, Neb.	10/23/22
Gray, Linda	Santa Monica, Cal.	9/12/-
Grayson, Kathryn	Winston-Salem, N.C.	2/9/23
Graziano, Rocky	New York, N.Y.	6/7/22
Greco, Buddy	Philadelphia, Pa.	8/14/26
Greco, Jose	Abruzzi, Italy	12/23/18
Green, Adolph	New York, N.Y.	12/2/15
Green, Al	Forest City, Ark.	4/13/46
Greene, Lorne	Ottawa, Ont.	2/12/15
Greene, Richard	England	1918
Greenwood, Joan	London, England	3/4/21
Greer, Jane	Washington, D.C.	9/9/24
Gregory, Dick	St. Louis, Mo.	10/12/32
Gregory, James	Bronx, N.Y.	12/23/11
Grey, Joel	Cleveland, Oh.	4/11/32
Griffin, Merv	San Mateo, Cal.	7/6/25
Griffith, Andy	Mount Airy, N.C.	6/1/26
Grimes, Gary	San Francisco, Cal.	1955
Grimes, Tammy	Lynn, Mass.	1/30/34
Grizzard, George	Roanoke Rapids, N.C.	4/1/28
Grodin, Charles	Pittsburgh, Pa.	4/21/35
Guardino, Harry	New York, N.Y.	12/23/25
Guillaume, Robert	St. Louis, Mo.	11/30/-
Guinness, Alec	London, England	4/2/14
Gunn, Moses	St. Louis, Mo.	10/2/29
Guthrie, Arlo	New York, N.Y.	7/10/47
Hackett, Buddy	Brooklyn, N.Y.	8/31/24
Hackett, Joan	New York, N.Y.	3/1/-
Hackman, Gene	San Bernardino, Cal.	1/30/30
Hagen, Uta	Gottingen, Germany	6/12/19
Haggard, Merle	Bakersfield, Cal.	4/6/37
Haggerty, Dan	Hollywood, Cal.	11/19/41
Hagman, Larry	Ft. Worth, Tex.	9/21/31
Hale, Barbara	DeKalb, Ill.	1922
Hall, Huntz	New York, N.Y.	1920
Hall, Monty	Winnipeg, Man.	1925
Hall, Tom T.	Olive Hill, Ky.	5/25/36
Hamel, Veronica	Philadelphia, Pa.	11/20/-
Hamill, Mark	Oakland, Cal.	9/25/52
Hamilton, George	Memphis, Tenn.	8/12/39
Hamilton, Margaret	Cleveland, Oh.	9/12/02
Hamilton, Neil	Lynn, Mass	1899
Hampshire, Susan	London, England	5/12/42
Hampton, Lionel	Birmingham, Ala.	4/12/13
Harmon, Mark	Burbank, Cal.	9/2/-
Harper, David W.	Abilene, Tex.	10/4/61
Harper, Valerie	Suffern, N.Y.	8/22/40
Harrington, Pat Jr.	New York, N.Y.	8/13/29
Harris, Barbara	Evanston, Ill.	1935
Harris, Emmylou	Birmingham, Ala.	4/2/49
Harris, Julie	Grosse Pte. Park, Mich.	12/2/25
Harris, Phil	Linton, Ind.	6/24/06
Harris, Richard	Co. Limerick, Ireland	10/1/33
Harris, Rosemary	Ashby, England	9/19/30
Harrison, George	Liverpool, England	2/25/43
Harrison, Gregory	Avalon, Cal.	5/31/50
Harrison, Rex	Huyton, England	3/5/08
Harry, Deborah	New Jersey	1944
Hartley, Mariette	New York, N.Y.	6/21/40
Hartman, David	Pawtucket, R.I.	5/19/35
Hasso, Signe	Stockholm, Sweden	8/15/18
Haver, June	Rock Island, Ill.	6/10/26
Havoc, June	Vancouver, B.C.	11/8/16
Hawn, Goldie	Washington, D.C.	11/21/45
Hayden, Melissa	Toronto, Ont.	4/25/23
Hayden, Sterling	Montclair, N.J.	3/26/16
Hayes, Helen	Washington, D.C.	10/10/00
Hayes, Isaac	Covington, Tenn.	8/20/42
Hayes, Peter Lind	San Francisco, Cal.	6/25/15
Hayward, Louis	Johannesburg, S. Africa	1909
Hayworth, Rita	New York, N.Y.	10/17/18
Healy, Mary	New Orleans, La.	4/14/18
Heatherton, Joey	Rockville Centre, N.Y.	9/14/44
Heckart, Eileen	Columbus, Oh.	3/29/19
Hefner, Hugh	Chicago, Ill.	4/9/26
Heifetz, Jascha	Vilna, Lithuania	2/2/01
Helpmann, Robert	Mt. Gambier, Australia	4/9/09
Hemingway, Margaux	Portland, Ore.	1955
Hemmings, David	Guilford, England	11/2/41
Hemsley, Sherman	Philadelphia, Pa.	2/1/-
Henderson, Florence	Dale, Ind.	2/14/34
Henderson, Skitch	Halstad, Minn.	1/27/18
Henner, Marilu	Chicago, Ill.	4/6/-
Henning, Doug	Ft. Garry, Man., Canada	1947
Henreid, Paul	Trieste, Austria	1/10/08
Henson, Jim	Greenville, Miss.	9/24/36
Hepburn, Audrey	Brussels, Belgium	5/4/29
Hepburn, Katharine	Hartford, Conn.	11/8/09
Herbert, Evelyn	Philadelphia, Pa.	1898
Herrmann, Edward	Washington, D.C.	7/21/43
Hesseman, Howard	Lebanon, Ore.	2/27/40
Heston, Charlton	Evanston, Ill.	10/4/24
Heywood, Anne	Birmingham, England	1937
Hickman, Darryl	Los Angeles, Cal.	1931
Hickman, Dwayne	Los Angeles, Cal.	1934
Hildegarde	Adell, Wis.	2/1/06
Hill, Arthur	Melfort, Sask.	8/1/22
Hill, Benny	Southampton, England	1/21/25
Hill, George Roy	Minneapolis, Minn.	12/20/22
Hiller, Wendy	Stockport, England	8/15/12
Hines, Earl (Fatha)	Duquesne, Pa.	12/28/05
Hines, Jerome	Hollywood, Cal.	11/8/21
Hines, Mimi	Vancouver, B.C.	1933
Hingle, Pat	Denver, Col.	7/19/24
Hirsch, Judd	Bronx, N.Y.	3/15/35
Hirt, Al	New Orleans, La.	11/7/22
Ho, Don	Kakaako, Oahu, Ha.	1930
Hoffman, Dustin	Los Angeles, Cal.	8/8/37
Holbrook, Hal	Cleveland, Oh.	2/17/25
Holder, Geoffrey	Trinidad	8/1/30
Holliday, Polly	Jasper, Ala.	7/2/37
Holliman, Earl	Delhi, La.	9/11/28
Holloway, Sterling	Cedartown, Ga.	1905
Holm, Celeste	New York, N.Y.	4/29/19
Hooks, Robert	Washington, D.C.	4/18/37
Hope, Bob	London, England	5/29/03
Hopkins, Anthony	Wales	12/31/37
Hopper, Dennis	Dodge City, Kan.	5/17/36
Horne, Lena	Brooklyn, N.Y.	6/30/17
Horne, Marilyn	Bradford, Pa.	1/16/34
Horowitz, Vladimir	Kiev, Russia	10/1/04
Horton, Robert	Los Angeles, Cal.	7/29/24
Houseman, John	Bucharest, Romania	9/22/02
Howard, Ken	El Centro, Cal.	3/28/44
Howard, Ron	Duncan, Okla.	3/1/54
Howard, Trevor	Kent, England	9/29/16
Howes, Sally Ann	London, England	7/20/34
Hudson, Rock	Winnetka, Ill.	11/17/25
Hughes, Barnard	Bedford Hills, N.Y.	7/16/15
Humperdinck, Engelbert	Madras, India	5/3/36
Hunt, Lois	York, Pa.	11/26/25
Hunt, Marsha	Chicago, Ill.	10/17/17
Hunter, Kim	Detroit, Mich.	11/12/22
Hunter, Ross	Cleveland, Oh.	5/6/26
Hunter, Tab	New York, N.Y.	7/11/31
Hurt, John	Chesterfield, England	1/22/40
Hussey, Olivia	Buenos Aires, Argentina	1952
Hussey, Ruth	Providence, R.I.	10/30/17
Huston, John	Nevada, Mo.	8/5/06
Hutchinson, Josephine	Seattle, Wash.	1916
Hutton, Betty	Battle Creek, Mich.	2/26/21

ame	Birthplace	Born
utton, Ina Ray	Chicago, Ill.	1918
utton, Lauren	Charleston, S.C.	1944
yde-White, Wilfrid	Gloucester, England	5/12/03
n, Janis	New York, N.Y.	5/7/51
eland, Jill	London, England	4/24/41
eland, John	Vancouver, B.C.	1/30/15
es, Burl	Hunt, Ill.	6/14/09
ackson, Anne	Allegheny, Pa.	9/3/26
ackson, Glenda	Cheshire, England	5/9/36
ackson, Kate	Birmingham, Ala.	10/29/48
ackson, Michael	Gary, Ind.	8/29/58
acobi, Derek	London, England	10/22/38
aeckel, Richard	Long Beach, Cal.	10/10/26
affe, Sam	New York, N.Y.	3/10/91
agger, Dean	Columbus Grove, Oh.	11/7/05
agger, Mick	Dartford, England	7/26/43
ames, Dennis	Jersey City, N.J.	8/24/17
ames, Harry	Albany, Ga.	3/15/16
anis, Conrad	New York, N.Y.	2/11/28
eanmaire, Renee	Paris, France	4/29/24
effreys, Anne	Goldsboro, N.C.	1/26/23
effries, Fran	San Jose, Cal.	1939
effries, Lionel	England	1926
enner, Bruce	Mt. Kisco, N.Y.	10/28/49
ennings, Waylon	Littlefield, Tex.	6/15/37
ens, Salome	Milwaukee, Wis.	5/8/35
epson, Helen	Titusville, Pa.	1907
illian, Ann	Cambridge, Mass.	—
oel, Billy	Bronx, N.Y.	5/9/49
ohn, Elton	Middlesex, England	3/25/47
ohns, Glynis	Durban, S. Africa	10/5/23
ohnson, Arte	Benton Harbor, Mich.	1/20/34
ohnson, Ben	Foraker, Okla.	1918
ohnson, Van	Newport, R.I.	8/25/16
ones, Allan	Scranton, Pa.	1907
ones, Carolyn	Amarillo, Tex.	4/28/33
ones, Chris	Jackson, Tenn.	1941
ones, Dean	Morgan City, Ala.	1/25/35
ones, George	Saratoga, Tex.	9/12/31
ones, Grandpa	Niagara, Ky.	10/20/13
ones, Henry	Philadelphia, Pa.	8/1/12
ones, Jack	Hollywood, Cal.	1938
ones, James Earl	Tate Co., Miss.	1/17/31
ones, Jennifer	Tulsa, Okla.	3/2/19
ones, Shirley	Smithton, Pa.	3/31/34
ones, Tom	Pontypridd, Wales	6/7/40
ourdan, Louis	Marseilles, France	6/19/21
urado, Katy	Guadalajara, Mexico	1927
ahn, Madeline	Boston, Mass.	9/29/42
analy, Steve	Burbank, Cal.	3/14/-
ane, Carol	Cleveland, Oh.	1952
aplan, Gabe	Brooklyn, N.Y.	3/31/45
aufman, Andy	New York, N.Y.	1/17/49
avner, Judy	Los Angeles, Cal.	9/7/51
aye, Danny	Brooklyn, N.Y.	1/18/13
aye, Sammy	Lakewood, Oh.	3/13/13
azan, Elia	Constantinople, Turkey	9/7/09
azan, Lainie	New York, N.Y.	5/15/42
each, Stacy	Savannah, Ga.	6/2/41
eaton, Diane	Santa Ana, Cal.	1/5/46
eel, Howard	Gillespie, Ill.	4/13/17
eeler, Ruby	Halifax, N.S.	8/25/10
eeshan, Bob	Lynbrook, N.Y.	6/27/27
eitel, Harvey	Brooklyn, N.Y.	1947
eith, Brian	Bayonne, N.J.	11/14/21
eller, Marthe	Basel, Switzerland	1945
ellerman, Sally	Long Beach, Cal.	6/2/37
elley, DeForrest	Atlanta, Ga.	1/20/20
elly, Gene	Pittsburgh, Pa.	8/23/12
elly, Grace	Philadelphia, Pa.	11/12/29
elly, Jack	Astoria, N.Y.	1927
elly, Nancy	Lowell, Mass.	3/25/21
elsey, Linda	Minneapolis, Minn.	7/28/-
ennedy, Arthur	Worcester, Mass.	2/17/14
ennedy, George	New York, N.Y.	2/18/26
ennedy, Mimi	Rochester, N.Y.	9/25/49
ent, Allegra	Los Angeles, Cal.	8/11/37
err, Deborah	Helensburgh, Scotland	9/30/21
err, John	New York, N.Y.	11/15/31
ert, Larry	Los Angeles, Cal.	12/5/30
eyes, Evelyn	Port Arthur, Tex.	1925
idd, Michael	New York, N.Y.	8/12/25
idder, Margot	Yellow Knife, B.C., Canada	10/17/48
iley, Richard	Chicago, Ill.	3/31/22
ing, Alan	Brooklyn, N.Y.	12/26/27
ing, B. B.	Itta Bena, Miss.	9/16/25
ing, Carole	Brooklyn, N.Y.	2/9/42
ing, Walter Woolf	San Francisco, Cal.	1899

Name	Birthplace	Born
King, Wayne	Savannah, Ill.	1901
Kirby, Durward	Covington, Ky.	8/24/12
Kirk, Phyllis	Plainfield, N.J.	9/18/30
Kirkland, Gelsey	Bethlehem, Pa.	12/29/52
Kirsten, Dorothy	Montclair, N.J.	7/6/19
Kitt, Eartha	North, S.C.	1/26/28
Klemperer, Werner	Cologne, Germany	3/22/20
Klein, Robert	New York, N.Y.	2/8/42
Klugman, Jack	Philadelphia, Pa.	4/27/22
Knight, Gladys	Atlanta, Ga.	5/28/44
Knight, Ted	Terryville, Conn.	12/7/23
Knotts, Don	Morgantown, W. Va.	7/21/24
Knox, Alexander	Strathroy, Canada	1/16/07
Kopell, Bernard	New York, N.Y.	6/21/33
Korman, Harvey	Chicago, Ill.	2/15/27
Kramer, Stanley	New York, N.Y.	9/29/13
Kristofferson, Kris	Brownsville, Tex.	6/22/36
Kruger, Hardy	Berlin, Germany	4/12/28
Kubelik, Rafael	Bychori, Czechoslovakia	6/29/14
Kubrick, Stanley	Bronx, N.Y.	7/26/28
Kulp, Nancy	Harrisburg, Pa.	8/28/21
Kyser, Kay	Rocky Mount, N.C.	6/18/05
Ladd, Cheryl	Huron, S.D.	7/12/51
Laine, Frankie	Chicago, Ill.	3/30/13
Lamarr, Hedy	Vienna, Austria	9/11/15
Lamas, Fernando	Buenos Aires, Argentina	1/9/25
Lamas, Lorenzo	Los Angeles, Cal.	1/20/-
Lamb, Gil	Minneapolis, Minn.	6/14/06
Lamour, Dorothy	New Orleans, La.	12/10/14
Lancaster, Burt	New York, N.Y.	11/2/13
Lanchester, Elsa	London, England	10/28/02
Landau, Martin	Brooklyn, N.Y.	1934
Landon, Michael	Forest Hills, N.Y.	—
Lane, Abbe	Brooklyn, N.Y.	1932
Lane, Priscilla	Indianola, Ia.	1917
Lange, Hope	Redding Ridge, Conn.	11/28/31
Langella, Frank	Bayonne, N.J.	1/1/46
Langford, Frances	Lakeland, Fla.	4/4/13
Lansbury, Angela	London, England	10/16/25
Lansing, Robert	San Diego, Cal.	6/5/29
La Rue, Jack	New York, N.Y.	—
Lasser, Louise	New York N.Y.	1941
Laughlin, Tom	Minneapolis, Minn.	1938
Laurie, Piper	Detroit, Mich.	1/22/32
Lavin, Linda	Portland, Me.	10/15/37
Lawford, Peter	London, England	9/7/23
Lawrence, Carol	Melrose Park, Ill.	9/5/34
Lawrence, Steve	Brooklyn, N.Y.	7/8/35
Lawrence, Vicki	Inglewood, Cal.	3/26/49
Leachman, Cloris	Des Moines, Ia.	4/4/26
Lean, David	Croydon, England	3/25/08
Lear, Norman	New Haven, Conn.	7/27/22
Learned, Michael	Washington, D.C.	4/9/39
Lederer, Francis	Prague, Czechoslovakia	11/6/06
Lee, Brenda	Atlanta, Ga.	12/11/44
Lee, Christopher	London, England	5/27/22
Lee, Michele	Los Angeles, Cal.	1942
Lee, Peggy	Jamestown, N.D.	5/26/20
Lee, Pinky	St. Paul, Minn.	—
Le Gallienne, Eva	London, England	1/11/99
Legrand, Michel	Paris, France	1932
Leibman, Ron	New York, N.Y.	10/11/37
Leigh, Janet	Merced, Cal.	7/6/27
Leinsdorf, Erich	Vienna, Austria	2/4/12
Lemmon, Jack	Boston, Mass.	2/8/25
Lennon, Dianne	Los Angeles, Cal.	1939
Lennon, Janet	Culver City, Cal.	1946
Lennon, Kathy	Santa Monica, Cal.	1944
Lennon, Peggy	Los Angeles, Cal.	1941
Leonard, Sheldon	New York, N.Y.	2/22/07
Leontovich, Eugenie	Moscow, Russia	3/21/00
LeRoy, Mervyn	San Francisco, Cal.	10/15/00
Leslie, Joan	Detroit, Mich.	1/26/25
Lester, Jerry	Chicago, Ill.	1911
Levine, James	Cincinnati, Oh.	6/23/43
Lewis, Jerry	Newark, N.J.	3/16/26
Lewis, Jerry Lee	Ferriday, La.	9/29/35
Lewis, Shari	New York, N.Y.	1/17/34
Liberace	West Allis, Wis.	5/16/19
Lightfoot, Gordon	Orillia, Ont.	11/17/38
Lillie, Beatrice	Toronto, Ont.	5/29/94
Linden, Hal	New York, N.Y.	3/20/31
Lindfors, Viveca	Uppsala, Sweden	12/29/20
Lindsey, Mort	Newark, N.J.	1923
Linkletter, Art	Saskatchewan, Canada	7/17/12
Little, Cleavon	Chickasha, Okla.	6/1/39
Little, Rich	Ottawa, Ont.	11/26/38
Little Richard	Macon, Ga.	1935
Livingstone, Mary	Seattle, Wash.	1909

Name	Birthplace	Born
Lloyd, Christopher	Stamford, Conn.	10/22/-
Lockhart, June	New York, N.Y.	6/25/25
Lockwood, Margaret	Karachi, India	9/15/16
Loder, John	London, England	1898
Logan, Joshua	Texarkana, Tex.	10/5/08
Loggins, Kenny	Everett, Wash.	1/7/48
Lollobrigida, Gina	Subiaco, Italy	7/4/28
Lom, Herbert	Prague, Czechoslovakia	1917
London, Julie	Santa Rosa, Cal.	9/26/26
Longet, Claudine	Paris, France	1/29/42
Lopez, Trini	Dallas, Tex.	5/15/37
Lord, Jack	New York, N.Y.	—
Loren, Sophia	Rome, Italy	9/20/34
Loudon, Dorothy	Boston, Mass.	9/17/33
Louise, Tina	New York, N.Y.	1934
Love, Bessie	Midland, Tex.	9/10/98
Loy, Myrna	Helena, Mon.	8/2/05
Lucas, George	Modesto, Cal.	5/14/44
Luckinbill, Laurence	Ft. Smith, Ark.	11/21/34
Ludwig, Christa	Berlin, Germany	1928
Luke, Keye	Canton, China	1904
Lumet, Sidney	Philadelphia, Pa.	6/25/24
Lund, John	Rochester, N.Y.	1913
Lupino, Ida	London, England	2/4/18
Lynley, Carol	New York, N.Y.	2/13/42
Lynn, Jeffrey	Auburn, Mass.	1909
Lynn, Loretta	Butcher Hollow, Ky.	4/14/35
Lyon, Sue	Davenport, Ia.	7/10/46
Maazel, Lorin	Paris, France	3/6/30
MacArthur, James	Los Angeles, Cal.	12/8/37
MacGraw, Ali	Pound Ridge, N.Y.	4/1/39
MacKenzie, Gisele	Winnipeg, Man.	1/10/27
MacLaine, Shirley	Richmond, Va.	4/24/34
MacMurray, Fred	Kankakee, Ill.	8/30/08
MacNeil, Cornell	Minneapolis, Minn.	9/24/22
MacRae, Gordon	East Orange, N.J.	3/12/21
MacRae, Sheila	London, England	9/24/24
Macy, Bill	Revere, Mass.	5/18/22
Madden, John	Austin, Minn.	4/10/36
Madison, Guy	Bakersfield, Cal.	1/19/22
Majors, Lee	Wyandotte, Mich.	4/23/40
Makarova, Natalia	Leningrad, USSR	11/21/40
Malbin, Elaine	New York, N.Y.	1932
Malden, Karl	Chicago, Ill.	3/22/13
Malle, Louis	Thumeries, France	1932
Malone, Dorothy	Chicago, Ill.	1/30/25
Manchester, Melissa	Bronx, N.Y.	2/15/51
Mancini, Henry	Cleveland, Oh.	4/16/24
Mandrell, Barbara	Houston, Tex.	12/25/48
Mangione, Chuck	Rochester, N.Y.	11/29/40
Manilow, Barry	New York, N.Y.	6/17/46
Mann, Herbie	New York, N.Y.	4/16/30
Marceau, Marcel	France	3/22/23
Marchand, Nancy	Buffalo, N.Y.	6/19/28
Margo	Mexico City, Mexico	5/10/18
Margolin, Janet	New York, N.Y.	1943
Marin, Cheech	Los Angeles, Cal.	7/13/46
Markova, Alicia	London, England	12/1/10
Marriner, Neville	Lincoln, England	4/15/25
Marsh, Jean	London, England	7/1/34
Marshall, E. G.	Awatonna, Minn.	6/18/10
Marshall, Penny	New York, N.Y.	10/15/45
Marshall, Peter	Huntington, W.Va.	3/30/-
Martin, Dean	Steubenville, Oh.	6/17/17
Martin, Dick	Detroit, Mich.	1/30/23
Martin, Mary	Weatherford, Tex.	12/1/13
Martin, Steve	Waco, Tex.	1945
Martin, Tony	San Francisco, Cal.	12/25/13
Martino, Al	Philadelphia, Pa.	10/7/27
Marvin, Lee	New York, N.Y.	2/19/24
Mason, Jackie	Sheboygan, Wis.	1931
Mason, James	Huddersfield, England	5/15/09
Mason, Marsha	St. Louis, Mo.	4/3/42
Mason, Pamela	London, England	3/10/22
Massey, Raymond	Toronto, Ont.	8/30/96
Mastroianni, Marcello	Rome, Italy	9/28/24
Matheson, Tim	Glendale, Cal.	12/31/47
Mathieu, Mireille	Avignon, France	1946
Mathis, Johnny	San Francisco, Cal.	9/30/35
Matthau, Walter	New York, N.Y.	10/1/20
Mature, Victor	Louisville, Ky.	1/29/16
May, Elaine	Philadelphia, Pa.	4/21/32
Mayehoff, Eddie	Baltimore, Md.	7/7/14
Mayo, Virginia	St. Louis, Mo.	11/30/20
Mazurki, Mike	Austria	12/25/09
Mazursky, Paul	Brooklyn, N.Y.	4/25/30
McArdle, Andrea	Philadelphia, Pa.	11/4/63
McBride, Patricia	Teaneck, N.J.	8/23/42
McCallum, David	Glasgow, Scotland	9/19/33
McCambridge, Mercedes	Joliet, Ill.	3/17/1
McCarthy, Kevin	Seattle, Wash.	2/15/1
McCartney, Paul	Liverpool, England	6/18/4
McClure, Doug	Glendale, Cal.	5/11/3
McCord, Kent	Los Angeles, Cal.	194
McCrary, Tex (John)	Calvert, Tex.	10/13/1
McCrea, Joel	Los Angeles, Cal.	11/5/0
McDonough, Mary	Los Angeles, Cal.	5/4/6
McDowall, Roddy	London, England	9/17/2
McDowell, Malcolm	Leeds, England	6/19/4
McEachin, James	Pennert, N.C.	193
McFarland, George (Spanky)	Dallas, Tex.	192
McGavin, Darren	San Joaquin, Cal.	5/7/2
McGee, Fibber	Peoria, Ill.	11/6/9
McGoohan, Patrick	New York, N.Y.	3/19/2
McGuire, Dorothy	Omaha, Neb.	6/14/1
McGuire Sisters:		
Christine	Middletown, Oh.	192
Dorothy	Middletown, Oh.	193
Phyllis	Middletown, Oh.	193
McIntire, John	Spokane, Wash.	6/27/0
McKechnie, Donna	Pontiac, Mich.	11/16/4
McKenna, Siobhan	Belfast, Ireland	5/24/2
McLean, Don	New Rochelle, N.Y.	10/2/4
McLerie, Allyn	Grand Mere, Que.	12/1/2
McLeod, Gavin	Mt. Kisco, N.Y.	2/28/
McMahon, Ed	Detroit, Mich.	3/6/2
McNair, Barbara	Racine, Wis.	3/4/3
McNichol, Jimmy	Los Angeles, Cal.	7/2/6
McNichol, Kristy	Los Angeles, Cal.	9/11/6
McQueen, Butterfly	Tampa, Fla.	1/7/1
Meadows, Audrey	Wu Chang, China	192
Meadows, Jayne	Wu Chang, China	9/27/2
Meara, Anne	New York, N.Y.	192
Meeker, Ralph	Minneapolis, Minn.	11/21/2
Mehta, Zubin	Bombay, India	4/29/3
Melanie	New York, N.Y.	1/3/4
Menuhin, Yehudi	New York, N.Y.	4/22/1
Mercouri, Melina	Athens, Greece	10/18/2
Meredith, Burgess	Cleveland, Oh.	11/16/0
Merkel, Una	Covington, Ky.	12/10/0
Merman, Ethel	Astoria, N.Y.	1/16/0
Merrick, David	Hong Kong	11/27/1
Merrill, Dina	New York, N.Y.	12/9/2
Merrill, Gary	Hartford, Conn.	8/2/1
Merrill, Robert	Brooklyn, N.Y.	6/4/1
Messina, Jim	Maywood, Cal.	12/5/4
Midler, Bette	Paterson, N.J.	12/1/4
Milanov, Zinka	Zagreb, Yugoslavia	5/17/0
Miles, Sarah	Ingatestone, England	12/31/4
Miles, Vera	near Boise City, Okla.	8/23/3
Milland, Ray	Neath, Wales	1/3/0
Miller, Ann	Houston, Tex.	4/12/2
Miller, Jason	Scranton, Pa.	4/22/3
Miller, Mitch	Rochester, N.Y.	7/4/1
Miller, Roger	Ft. Worth, Tex.	1/2/3
Mills, Donna	Chicago, Ill.	12/11/
Mills, Hayley	London, England	4/18/4
Mills, John	Suffolk, England	2/22/0
Mills, Juliet	London, England	11/21/4
Mills Brothers:		
Mills, Herbert	Piqua, Oh.	4/12/1
Mills, Harry	Piqua, Oh.	8/19/1
Mills, Donald	Piqua, Oh.	4/29/1
Milner, Martin	Detroit, Mich.	12/28/3
Milnes, Sherrill	Downers Grove, Ill.	1/10/3
Milsap, Ronnie	Robinsville, N.C.	1/16/
Milstein, Nathan	Odessa, Russia	12/31/0
Mimieux, Yvette	Hollywood, Cal.	1/8/4
Minnelli, Liza	Los Angeles, Cal.	3/12/4
Mitchell, Cameron	Dallastown, Pa.	11/4/1
Mitchell, Guy	Detroit, Mich.	2/22/2
Mitchell, Joni	McLeod, Alta.	11/7/4
Mitchum, Robert	Bridgeport, Conn.	8/6/1
Moffo, Anna	Wayne, Pa.	6/27/3
Molinaro, Al	Kenosha, Wis.	6/24/
Montalban, Ricardo	Mexico City, Mexico	11/25/2
Montand, Yves	Monsummano, Italy	10/13/2
Montgomery, Elizabeth	Hollywood, Cal.	4/15/3
Montgomery, George	Brady, Mon.	8/29/1
Moody, Ron	London, England	1/8/2
Moore, Clayton	Chicago, Ill.	9/14/1
Moore, Constance	Sioux City, Ia.	1/18/2
Moore, Dudley	London, England	4/19/3
Moore, Garry	Baltimore, Md.	1/31/1
Moore, Mary Tyler	Brooklyn, N.Y.	12/29/3
Moore, Melba	New York, N.Y.	10/29/4

Name	Birthplace	Born
Moore, Roger	London, England	10/14/27
Moore, Terry	Los Angeles, Cal.	1/1/32
Moran, Erin	Los Angeles, Cal.	10/18/61
Moreau, Jeanne	Paris, France	1/23/28
Moreno, Rita	Humacao, P.R.	12/11/31
Morgan, Dennis	Prentice, Wis.	1910
Morgan, Harry	Detroit, Mich.	4/10/15
Morgan, Henry	New York, N.Y.	3/31/15
Morgan, Jane	Boston, Mass.	1920
Morgan, Jaye P.	Mancos, Col.	12/3/31
Morgana, Nina	Buffalo, N.Y.	1895
Moriarty, Michael	Detroit, Mich.	4/5/41
Morini, Erika	Vienna, Austria	1/5/10
Morley, Robert	Wiltshire, England	5/26/08
Morris, Greg	Cleveland, Oh.	9/27/34
Morris, Howard	New York, N.Y.	9/4/25
Morse, Robert	Newton, Mass.	5/18/31
Moss, Arnold	Brooklyn, N.Y.	1/28/10
Mulhare, Edward	Ireland	1923
Mull, Martin	Chicago, Ill.	1943
Mulligan, Richard	New York, N.Y.	11/13/32
Munsel, Patrice	Spokane, Wash.	5/14/25
Murphy, George	New Haven, Conn.	7/4/02
Murphy, Michael	Los Angeles, Cal.	5/5/38
Murray, Anne	Springhill, Nova Scotia	6/20/45
Murray, Arthur	New York, N.Y.	4/4/95
Murray, Don	Hollywood, Cal.	7/31/29
Murray, Jan	New York, N.Y.	1917
Murray, Kathryn	Jersey City, N.J.	9/15/06
Murray, Ken	New York, N.Y.	7/14/03
Musante, Tony	Bridgeport, Conn.	6/30/-
Musburger, Brent	Portland, Ore.	5/26/39
Nabors, Jim	Sylacauga, Ala.	6/12/33
Natwick, Mildred	Baltimore, Md.	6/19/08
Neal, Patricia	Packard, Ky.	1/20/26
Neff, Hildegarde	Ulm, Germany	12/28/25
Negri, Pola	Lipno, Poland	1899
Nelson, Barry	San Francisco, Cal.	1920
Nelson, David	New York, N.Y.	10/24/36
Nelson, Ed	New Orleans, La.	12/21/28
Nelson, Gene	Seattle, Wash.	3/24/20
Nelson, Harriet (Hilliard)	Des Moines, Ia.	7/18/14
Nelson, Rick	Teaneck, N.J.	5/8/40
Nelson, Willie	Waco, Tex.	4/30/33
Nero, Peter	New York, N.Y.	5/22/34
Nesbitt, Cathleen	Cheshire, England	11/24/89
Newhart, Bob	Oak Park, Ill.	9/5/29
Newley, Anthony	Hackney, England	9/24/31
Newman, Barry	Boston, Mass.	11/7/38
Newman, Paul	Cleveland, Oh.	1/26/25
Newman, Phyllis	Jersey City, N.J.	3/19/35
Newman, Randy	Los Angeles, Cal.	11/28/43
Newton, Wayne	Roanoke, Va.	4/3/42
Newton-John, Olivia	Cambridge, England	9/26/48
Nichols, Mike	Berlin, Germany	11/6/31
Nicholson, Jack	Neptune, N.J.	4/28/37
Nielsen, Leslie	Regina, Sask	2/11/26
Nilsson, Birgit	Karup, Sweden	5/17/18
Nimoy, Leonard	Boston, Mass.	3/26/31
Niven, David	Kirriemuir, Scotland	3/1/10
Noble, James	Dallas, Tex.	3/5/22
Nolan, Jeannette	Los Angeles, Cal.	1911
Nolan, Kathy	St. Louis, Mo.	9/27/33
Nolan, Lloyd	San Francisco, Cal.	8/11/02
Nolte, Nick	Omaha, Neb.	1940
Norman, Jessye	Augusta, Ga.	9/15/45
North, Sheree	Los Angeles, Cal.	1/17/33
Norton-Taylor, Judy	Santa Monica, Cal.	1/29/58
Novak, Kim	Chicago, Ill.	2/18/33
Nureyev, Rudolf	Russia	3/17/38
Oakes, Randi	Randalia, Ia.	8/19/-
Oakland, Simon	New York, N.Y.	1922
O'Brian, Hugh	Rochester, N.Y.	4/19/30
O'Brien, Edmond	New York, N.Y.	9/10/15
O'Brien, Margaret	San Diego, Cal.	1/15/37
O'Brien, Pat	Milwaukee, Wis.	11/11/99
O'Connell, Helen	Lima, Oh.	1920
O'Connor, Carroll	New York, N.Y.	8/2/24
O'Connor, Donald	Chicago, Ill.	8/28/25
Odetta	Birmingham, Ala.	12/31/30
O'Hara, Maureen	Dublin, Ireland	8/17/21
O'Herlihy, Dan	Wexford, Ireland	5/1/19
O'Keefe, Walter	Hartford, Conn.	1907
Olivier, Laurence	Dorking, England	5/22/07
Olsen, Merlin	Logan, Ut.	9/15/40
O'Malley, J. Pat	Burnley, England	1901
O'Neal, Patrick	Ocala, Fla.	9/26/27
O'Neal, Ryan	Los Angeles, Cal.	4/20/41
O'Neal, Tatum	Los Angeles, Cal.	11/5/63
O'Neill, Jennifer	Brazil	2/20/49
Opatoshu, David	New York, N.Y.	1/30/18
Orbach, Jerry	New York, N.Y.	10/20/35
Orlando, Tony	New York, N.Y.	4/3/44
Ormandy, Eugene	Budapest, Hungary	11/18/99
Osmond, Donny	Ogden, Ut.	12/9/57
Osmond, Marie	Ogden, Ut.	10/13/59
O'Sullivan, Maureen	Boyle, Ireland	5/17/11
O'Toole, Peter	Connemara, Ireland	8/2/32
Owens, Buck	Sherman, Tex.	8/12/29
Owens, Gary	Mitchell, S.D.	5/10/36
Ozawa, Seiji	Shenyang, China	9/1/35
Paar, Jack	Canton, Oh.	5/1/18
Pacino, Al	New York, N.Y.	4/25/40
Page, Geraldine	Kirksville, Mo.	11/22/24
Page, LaWanda	Cleveland, Oh.	10/19/20
Page, Patti	Claremore, Okla.	11/8/27
Paige, Janis	Tacoma, Wash.	9/16/22
Palance, Jack	Lattimer, Pa.	2/18/20
Palmer, Betsy	East Chicago, Ind.	11/1/29
Palmer, Lilli	Posen, Germany	5/24/14
Papas, Irene	Greece	1926
Papp, Joseph	Brooklyn, N.Y.	6/22/21
Parker, Eleanor	Cedarville, Oh.	6/26/22
Parker, Fess	Ft. Worth, Tex.	8/16/25
Parker, Frank	New York, N.Y.	1906
Parker, Jean	Deer Lodge, Mon.	1916
Parker, Suzy	San Antonio, Tex.	10/28/33
Parkins, Barbara	Vancouver, B.C.	1942
Parks, Bert	Atlanta, Ga.	12/30/14
Parsons, Estelle	Lynn, Mass.	11/20/27
Parton, Dolly	Sevierville, Tenn.	1/19/46
Pasternak, Joseph	Hungary	9/19/01
Patane, Giuseppe	Napoli, Italy	1/1/32
Patterson, Lorna	Whittier, Cal.	7/1/56
Paulsen, Pat	South Bend, Wash.	—
Pavan, Marisa	Cagliari, Sardinia	6/19/32
Pavarotti, Luciano	Modena, Italy	10/12/35
Payne, John	Roanoke, Va.	1912
Pearl, Minnie	Centerville, Tenn.	10/25/12
Peck, Gregory	La Jolla, Cal.	4/5/16
Peckinpah, Sam	Fresno, Cal.	2/21/25
Peerce, Jan	New York, N.Y.	1904
Pendergrass, Teddy	Philadelphia, Pa.	3/26/50
Penn, Arthur	Philadelphia, Pa.	9/27/22
Peppard, George	Detroit, Mich.	10/1/28
Perkins, Anthony	New York, N.Y.	4/4/32
Perlman, Itzhak	Tel Aviv, Israel	10/31/45
Perrine, Valerie	Galveston, Tex.	9/3/43
Persoff, Nehemiah	Jerusalem, Palestine	8/14/20
Peters, Bernadette	New York, N.Y.	2/28/48
Peters, Brock	New York, N.Y.	7/2/27
Peters, Jean	Canton, Oh.	10/15/26
Peters, Roberta	New York, N.Y.	5/4/30
Petit, Pascale	France	1937
Phillips, MacKenzie	Alexandria, Va.	11/10/59
Phillips, Michelle	Long Beach, Cal.	4/6/44
Piazza, Marguerite	New Orleans, La.	5/6/26
Pickens, Slim	Kingsberg, Cal.	6/29/19
Picon, Molly	New York, N.Y.	6/1/98
Pidgeon, Walter	E. St. John, N.B.	9/23/97
Plato, Dana	Maywood, Cal.	11/7/64
Pleasance, Donald	Worksop, England	10/5/21
Pleshette, Suzanne	New York, N.Y.	1/31/37
Plowright, Joan	Brigg, England	10/28/29
Plummer, Christopher	Toronto, Ont.	12/13/29
Poitier, Sidney	Miami, Fla.	2/20/27
Polanski, Roman	Paris, France	8/18/33
Ponti, Carlo	Milan, Italy	12/11/13
Poston, Tom	Columbus, Oh.	10/17/21
Powell, Jane	Portland, Ore.	4/1/29
Powell, William	Pittsburgh, Pa.	7/29/92
Powers, Mala	San Francisco, Cal.	1931
Powers, Stefanie	Hollywood, Cal.	11/12/42
Preminger, Otto	Vienna, Austria	12/5/06
Prentiss, Paula	San Antonio, Tex.	3/4/39
Preston, Robert	Newton, Mass.	6/8/18
Previn, Andre	Berlin, Germany	4/6/29
Price, Leontyne	Laurel, Miss.	2/10/27
Price, Ray	Perryville, Tex.	1/12/26
Price, Vincent	St. Louis, Mo.	5/27/11
Pride, Charlie	Sledge, Miss.	3/18/39
Prince, William	Nichols, N.Y.	1/26/13
Principal, Victoria	Fukuoka, Japan	1/3/-
Provine, Dorothy	Deadwood, S.D.	1/20/37
Prowse, Juliet	Bombay, India	9/25/37
Pryor, Richard	Peoria, Ill.	12/1/40
Pyle, Denver	Bethune, Col.	5/11/20

Name	Birthplace	Born
Qualen, John	Vancouver, B.C.	1899
Quayle, Anthony	Lancashire, England	9/7/13
Quillan, Eddie	Philadelphia, Pa.	3/31/07
Quinn, Anthony	Chihuahua, Mexico	4/21/15
Rabb, Ellis	Memphis, Tenn.	6/20/30
Rabbitt, Eddie	Brooklyn, N.Y.	11/27/41
Radner, Gilda	Detroit, Mich.	6/28/46
Rae, Charlotte	Milwaukee, Wis.	4/22/26
Raffin, Deborah	Los Angeles, Cal.	1953
Rainer, Luise	Vienna, Austria	1912
Raines, Ella	Snoqualmie Falls, Wash.	8/6/21
Raitt, John	Santa Ana, Cal.	1/19/17
Ralston, Esther	Bar Harbor, Me.	9/19/02
Ralston, Vera Hruba	Prague, Czechoslovakia	1921
Randall, Tony	Tulsa, Okla.	2/26/20
Rawls, Lou	Chicago, Ill.	12/1/35
Ray, Aldo	Pen Argyl, Pa.	9/25/26
Ray, Johnnie	Dallas, Ore.	1927
Rayburn, Gene	Christopher, Ill.	12/22/17
Raye, Martha	Butte, Mon.	8/27/16
Raymond, Gene	New York, N.Y.	8/13/08
Reddy, Helen	Melbourne, Australia	10/25/41
Redford, Robert	Santa Monica, Cal.	8/18/37
Redgrave, Lynn	London, England	3/8/43
Redgrave, Michael	Bristol, England	3/20/08
Redgrave, Vanessa	London, England	1/30/37
Reed, Donna	Denison, Ia.	1/27/21
Reed, Jerry	Atlanta, Ga.	3/20/37
Reed, Oliver	London, England	2/13/38
Reed, Rex	Ft. Worth, Tex.	10/2/38
Reed, Robert	Highland Park, Ill.	1932
Reese, Della	Detroit, Mich.	7/6/31
Reeves, Dell	Sparta, N.C.	7/14/33
Regan, Phil	Brooklyn, N.Y.	5/28/06
Reid, Kate	London, England	11/4/30
Reilly, Charles Nelson	New York, N.Y.	1/13/31
Reiner, Carl	Bronx, N.Y.	3/20/22
Reiner, Rob	Bronx, N.Y.	3/6/45
Remick, Lee	Boston, Mass.	12/14/35
Resnik, Regina	New York, N.Y.	8/30/24
Rey, Alejandro	Buenos Aires, Argentina	2/8/30
Reynolds, Burt	Waycross, Ga.	2/11/36
Reynolds, Debbie	El Paso, Tex.	4/1/32
Reynolds, Marjorie	Buhl, Ida.	8/12/21
Rich, Charlie	Forest City, Ark.	12/14/32
Rich, Irene	Buffalo, N.Y.	10/13/97
Richardson, Ralph	Cheltenham, England	12/19/02
Richardson, Tony	Shipley, England	6/5/28
Rickles, Don	New York, N.Y.	5/8/26
Riddle, Nelson	Hackensack, N.J.	6/1/21
Rigg, Diana	Doncaster, England	7/20/38
Ritter, John	Burbank, Cal.	9/17/48
Ritz, Harry	Newark, N.J.	1908
Ritz, Jimmy	Newark, N.J.	1905
Rivera, Chita	Washington, D.C.	1/23/33
Rivers, Joan	Brooklyn, N.Y.	1937
Robards, Jason Jr.	Chicago, Ill.	7/26/22
Robbins, Jerome	New York, N.Y.	10/11/18
Robbins, Marty	Glendale, Ariz.	9/26/25
Roberts, Doris	St. Louis, Mo.	11/4/30
Roberts, Pernell	Waycross, Ga.	5/18/-
Robertson, Cliff	La Jolla, Cal.	9/9/25
Robertson, Dale	Oklahoma City, Okla.	7/14/23
Robinson, Smokey	Detroit, Mich.	2/19/40
Robson, Flora	South Shields, England	3/28/02
Rodgers, Jimmie	Camas, Wash.	1933
Rodriquez, Johnny	Sabinal, Tex.	12/10/51
Rogers, Chas. (Buddy)	Olathe, Kan.	8/13/04
Rogers, Ginger	Independence, Mo.	7/16/11
Rogers, Kenny	Houston, Tex.	8/21/38
Rogers, Roy	Cincinnati, Oh.	11/5/12
Roland, Gilbert	Juarez, Mexico	12/11/05
Rolle, Esther	Pompano Beach, Fla.	11/8/-
Roman, Ruth	Boston, Mass.	12/23/24
Romero, Cesar	New York, N.Y.	2/15/07
Ronstadt, Linda	Tucson, Ariz.	7/15/46
Rooney, Mickey	Brooklyn, N.Y.	9/23/20
Rose, George	Bicester, England	2/19/20
Rose Marie	New York, N.Y.	—
Ross, Diana	Detroit, Mich.	3/26/44
Ross, Katharine	Hollywood, Cal.	1/29/43
Ross, Lanny	Seattle, Wash.	1/19/06
Rostropovich, Mstislav	Baku, USSR.	3/27/27
Roundtree, Richard	New Rochelle, N.Y.	7/9/42
Rowan, Dan	Beggs, Okla.	7/2/22
Rowlands, Gena	Cambria, Wis.	6/19/36
Rubin, Benny	Boston, Mass.	1899
Rubinoff, David	Grodno, Russia	1897
Rubinstein, Artur	Lodz, Poland	1/28/87
Rudolf, Max	Frankfurt, Germany	6/15/02
Rule, Janice	Norwood, Oh.	8/15/31
Rush, Barbara	Denver, Col.	1/4/30
Russell, Jane	Bemidji, Minn.	6/21/21
Russell, Ken	Southampton, England	7/3/27
Russell, Kurt	Springfield, Mass.	3/17/51
Russell, Nipsey	Atlanta, Ga.	1924
Rutherford, Ann	Toronto, Ont.	1924
Ryan, Peggy	Long Beach, Cal.	8/28/24
Rydell, Bobby	Philadelphia, Pa.	1942
Sahl, Mort	Montreal, Que.	5/11/27
Saint, Eva Marie	Newark, N.J.	7/4/24
St. James, Susan	Los Angeles, Cal.	8/14/46
St. John, Jill	Los Angeles, Cal.	8/19/40
Sainte-Marie, Buffy	Maine	2/20/41
Saks, Gene	New York, N.Y.	11/8/21
Sales, Soupy	Franklinton, N.C.	1926
Sand, Paul	Los Angeles, Cal.	3/5/35
Sanford, Isabel	New York, N.Y.	8/29/-
Santana, Carlos	Mexico	7/20/47
Sarnoff, Dorothy	New York, N.Y.	1919
Sarrazin, Michael	Quebec City, Que.	5/22/40
Savalas, Telly	Garden City, N.Y.	1/21/24
Saxon, John	Brooklyn, N.Y.	8/5/35
Sayao, Bidu	Rio de Janeiro, Brazil	5/11/02
Sayer, Leo	Sussex, England	5/21/48
Scaggs, Boz	Dallas, Tex.	6/8/44
Schallert, William	Los Angeles, Cal.	7/6/22
Scheider, Roy	Orange, N.J.	11/10/35
Schell, Maria	Vienna, Austria	1/15/26
Schell, Maximilian	Vienna, Austria	12/8/30
Schenkel, Chris	Bippus, Ind.	1924
Schnabel, Stefan	Berlin, Germany	2/2/12
Schneider, Alexander	Vilna, Poland	10/21/08
Schneider, John	Mt. Kisco, N.Y.	4/8/-
Schreiber, Avery	Chicago, Ill.	1935
Schwarzkopf, Elisabeth	Jarotschin, Poland	12/9/15
Scofield, Paul	Hurst, Pierpont, England	1/21/22
Scorsese, Martin	New York, N.Y.	11/17/42
Scott, George C.	Wise, Va.	10/18/27
Scott, Lizabeth	Scranton, Pa.	1923
Scott, Martha	Jamesport, Mo.	9/22/14
Scott, Randolph	Orange Co., Va.	1/23/03
Scotto, Renata	Savona, Italy	2/24/34
Scully, Vin	New York, N.Y.	11/29/27
Scourby, Alexander	New York, N.Y.	11/13/13
Sebastian, John	New York N.Y.	3/17/44
Sedaka, Neil	New York, N.Y.	3/13/39
Seeger, Pete	New York, N.Y.	5/3/19
Segal, George	Great Neck, N.Y.	2/13/34
Segal, Vivienne	Philadelphia, Pa.	4/19/97
Segovia, Andres	Linares, Spain	2/21/93
Selleck, Tom	Detroit, Mich.	1/29/-
Serkin, Rudolf	Eger, Austria	3/28/03
Severinsen, Doc	Arlington, Ore.	7/7/27
Seymour, Jane	England	2/15/51
Shankar, Ravi	India	4/7/20
Sharif, Omar	Alexandria, Egypt	4/10/32
Shatner, William	Montreal, Que.	3/22/31
Shaw, Robert	Red Bluff, Cal.	4/30/16
Shawn, Dick	Buffalo, N.Y.	12/1/29
Shearer, Moira	Scotland	1/17/26
Shearer, Norma	Montreal Que.	1904
Sheen, Martin	Dayton, Oh.	8/3/40
Sheldon, Jack	Jacksonville, Fla.	1931
Shelley, Carole	London, England	8/16/39
Shepherd, Cybill	Memphis, Tenn.	2/18/50
Shepherd, Jean	Chicago, Ill.	7/26/29
Shera, Mark	Bayonne, N.J.	7/10/49
Sherwood, Roberta	St. Louis, Mo.	1913
Shields, Brooke	New York, N.Y.	5/31/65
Shire, Talia	New York, N.Y.	4/25/46
Shirley, Ann	New York, N.Y.	1918
Shore, Dinah	Winchester, Tenn.	3/1/17
Short, Bobby	Danville, Ill.	9/15/24
Sidney, Sylvia	New York, N.Y.	8/8/10
Siepi, Cesare	Milan, Italy	2/10/23
Signoret, Simone	Wiesbaden, Germany	3/25/21
Sills, Beverly	Brooklyn, N.Y.	5/25/29
Silvers, Phil	Brooklyn, N.Y.	5/11/12
Simmons, Jean	London, England	1/31/29
Simon, Carly	New York, N.Y.	6/25/45
Simon, Paul	Newark, N.J.	11/5/41
Simon, Simone	Marseilles, France	4/23/14
Simone, Nina	Tyron, N.C.	2/21/33
Sinatra, Frank	Hoboken, N.J.	12/12/15
Sinatra, Nancy	Jersey City, N.J.	6/8/40
Skelton, Red (Richard)	Vincennes, Ind.	7/18/13
Slezak, Walter	Vienna, Austria	5/3/02

Name	Birthplace	Born
Slick, Grace	Chicago, Ill.	10/30/39
Smith, Alexis	Penticton, B.C.	6/8/21
Smith, Bob	Buffalo, N.Y.	1917
Smith, Connie	Elkhart, Ind.	1941
Smith, Ethel	Pittsburgh, Pa.	1921
Smith, Jaclyn	Houston, Tex.	10/26/48
Smith, Kate	Greenville, Va.	5/1/07
Smith, Keeley	Norfolk, Va.	3/9/35
Smith, Maggie	Ilford, England	12/28/34
Smith, Patti	Chicago, Ill.	1946
Smith, Roger	South Gate, Cal.	12/18/32
Smothers, Dick	New York, N.Y.	11/20/39
Smothers, Tom	New York, N.Y.	2/2/37
Snodgress, Carrie	Park Ridge, Ill.	10/27/45
Snow, Hank	Nova Scotia, Canada	5/9/14
Snyder, Jimmy "Greek"	Steubenville, Oh.	9/9/19
Snyder, Tom	Milwaukee, Wis.	5/12/36
Solti, Georg	Budapest, Hungary	10/21/12
Somes, Michael	nr. Stroud, England	1917
Somers, Suzanne	San Bruno, Cal.	10/16/46
Sommer, Elke	Berlin, Germany	11/5/41
Sorvino, Paul	Brooklyn, N.Y.	1939
Sothern, Ann	Valley City, N.D.	1/22/12
Soul, David	Chicago, Ill.	8/28/-
Spacek, Sissy	Quitman, Tex.	12/25/49
Spewack, Bella	Hungary	1899
Speilberg, Stephen	Cincinnati, Oh.	12/18/47
Spivak, Lawrence	Brooklyn, N.Y.	6/11/00
Springfield, Dusty	London, England	4/16/39
Springfield, Rick	Australia	—
Springsteen, Bruce	Freehold, N.J.	9/23/49
Stack, Robert	Los Angeles, Cal.	1/13/19
Stafford, Jo	Coalinga, Cal.	1918
Stallone, Sylvester	New York, N.Y.	7/6/46
Stamp, Terence	London, England	1940
Stang, Arnold	Chelsea, Mass.	1925
Stanley, Kim	Tularosa, N.M.	2/11/25
Stanwyck, Barbara	Brooklyn, N.Y.	7/16/07
Stapleton, Jean	New York, N.Y.	1/19/23
Stapleton, Maureen	Troy, N.Y.	6/21/25
Starr, Kay	Dougherty, Okla.	7/21/22
Starr, Ringo	Liverpool, England	7/7/40
Steber, Eleanor	Wheeling, W. Va.	7/17/16
Steele, Tommy	London, England	12/17/36
Steiger, Rod	W. Hampton, N.Y.	4/14/25
Steinberg, David	Winnipeg, Man.	8/9/42
Stephens, James	Mt. Kisco, N.Y.	5/18/51
Sterling, Jan	New York, N.Y.	4/3/23
Sterling, Robert	New Castle, Pa.	11/13/17
Stern, Isaac	Kreminiecz, Russia	7/21/20
Sternhagen, Frances	Washington, D.C.	1/13/30
Stevens, Andrew	Memphis, Tenn.	1956
Stevens, Cat	London, England	7/21/48
Stevens, Connie	Brooklyn, N.Y.	8/8/38
Stevens, Mark	Cleveland, Oh.	12/13/22
Stevens, Rise	New York, N.Y.	6/11/13
Stevens, Stella	Yazoo City, Miss.	10/1/36
Stevens, Warren	Clark's Summit, Pa.	11/2/19
Stevenson, McLean	Normal, Ill.	11/14/29
Stevenson, Parker	Philadelphia, Pa.	6/4/53
Stewart, Don	New York, N.Y.	11/14/35
Stewart, James	Indiana, Pa.	5/20/08
Stewart, Rod	London, England	1/10/45
Stickney, Dorothy	Dickinson, N.D.	6/21/00
Stiers, David Ogden	Peoria, Ill.	10/31/42
Stills, Stephen	Dallas, Tex.	1/3/45
Stockwell, Dean	Hollywood, Cal.	3/5/36
Stone, Ezra	New Bedford, Mass.	12/2/17
Storch, Larry	New York, N.Y.	1/8/25
Storm, Gale	Bloomington, Tex.	4/5/22
Storrs, Suzanne	Salt Lake City, Ut.	1934
Straight, Beatrice	Old Westbury, N.Y.	8/2/18
Strasberg, Susan	New York, N.Y.	5/22/38
Stratas, Teresa	Toronto, Ont.	5/26/39
Strauss, Peter	New York, N.Y.	1947
Streep, Meryl	Summit, N.J.	1949
Streisand, Barbra	Brooklyn, N.Y.	4/24/42
Stritch, Elaine	Detroit, Mich.	2/2/26
Strode, Woody	Los Angeles, Cal.	1914
Struthers, Sally	Portland, Ore.	7/28/48
Sullivan, Barry	New York, N.Y.	8/29/12
Sumac, Yma	Ichocan, Peru	9/10/27
Summer, Donna	Boston, Mass.	12/31/48
Susskind, David	New York, N.Y.	12/19/20
Sutherland, Donald	St. John, New Brunswick	7/17/34
Sutherland, Joan	Sydney, Australia	11/7/26
Suzuki, Pat	Cressey, Cal	1931
Swanson, Gloria	Chicago, Ill.	3/27/99
Sweet, Blanche	Chicago, Ill.	6/18/95
Swenson, Inga	Omaha, Neb.	12/29/34
Swit, Loretta	Passaic, N.J.	11/4/-
Talbot, Lyle	Pittsburgh, Pa.	1902
Talbot, Nita	New York, N.Y.	1930
Tallchief, Maria	Fairfax, Okla.	1/24/25
Tamblyn, Russ	Los Angeles, Cal.	12/30/35
Tandy, Jessica	London, England	6/7/09
Tarkenton, Fran	Richmond, Va.	2/30/40
Tayback, Vic	New York, N.Y.	1/6/-
Taylor, Elizabeth	London, England	2/27/32
Taylor, James	Boston, Mass.	3/12/48
Taylor, Kent	Nashua, Ia.	5/11/07
Taylor, Rod	Sydney, Australia	1/11/30
Tebaldi, Renata	Pesaro, Italy	2/1/22
Temple, Shirley	Santa Monica, Cal.	4/23/28
Tennille, Toni	Montgomery, Ala.	5/8/43
Terris, Norma	Columbus, Kan.	1904
Terry-Thomas	London, England	7/14/11
Tewes, Lauren	Braddock, Pa.	10/26/-
Thaxter, Phyllis	Portland, Me.	11/20/21
Thinnes, Roy	Chicago, Ill.	4/6/38
Thomas, B.J.	Houston, Tex.	8/7/42
Thomas, Betty	St. Louis, Mo.	7/27/-
Thomas, Danny	Deerfield, Mich.	1/6/14
Thomas, Marlo	Detroit, Mich.	11/21/43
Thomas, Richard	New York, N.Y.	6/13/51
Thompson, Marshall	Peoria, Ill.	11/27/26
Thompson, Sada	Des Moines, Ia.	9/27/29
Thulin, Ingrid	Sweden	1/27/29
Tiegs, Cheryl	Alhambra, Cal.	1947
Tierney, Gene	Brooklyn, N.Y.	11/20/20
Tierney, Lawrence	Brooklyn, N.Y.	3/15/19
Tillis, Mel	Tampa, Fla.	8/8/32
Tillstrom, Burr	Chicago, Ill.	10/13/17
Tilton, Charlene	San Diego, Cal.	12/1/-
Tiny Tim	New York, N.Y.	—
Todd, Richard	Dublin, Ireland	6/11/19
Tomlin, Lily	Detroit, Mich.	9/1/39
Tomlinson, David	Scotland	5/7/17
Toomey, Regis	Pittsburgh, Pa.	8/13/02
Torme, Mel	Chicago, Ill.	9/13/25
Torn, Rip	Temple, Tex.	2/6/31
Tracy, Arthur	Kamenetz, Podolsk, Russia	6/25/03
Travanti, Daniel J.	Kenosha, Wis.	—
Travers, Mary	Louisville, Ky.	11/9/36
Travolta, John	Englewood, N.J.	2/18/54
Trevor, Claire	New York, N.Y.	3/8/09
Truffaut, Francois	Paris, France	2/6/32
Tucker, Forrest	Plainfield, Ind.	2/12/19
Tucker, Tanya	Seminole, Tex.	10/10/58
Tune, Tommy	Wichita Falls, Tex.	2/28/39
Turner, Ike	Clarksdale, Miss.	11/5/31
Turner, Lana	Wallace, Ida.	2/8/20
Turner, Tina	Brownsville, Tex.	11/25/41
Tushingham, Rita	Liverpool, England	3/14/42
Twiggy (Leslie Hornby)	London, England	9/19/49
Twitty, Conway	Friar's Point, Miss.	9/1/33
Tyrell, Susan	New Canaan, Conn.	1946
Tyson, Cicely	New York, N.Y.	12/19/33
Uggams, Leslie	New York, N.Y.	5/25/43
Ullmann, Liv	Tokyo, Japan	12/16/39
Umeki, Miyoshi	Hokkaido, Japan	1929
Ustinov, Peter	London, England	4/16/21
Vaccaro, Brenda	Brooklyn, N.Y.	11/18/39
Vale, Jerry	New York, N.Y.	1931
Valente, Caterina	Paris, France	1/14/32
Valentine, Karen	Santa Rosa, Cal.	1947
Vallee, Rudy	Island Pond, Vt.	7/28/01
Valli, Alida	Pola, Italy	5/31/21
Valli, Frankie	Newark, N.J.	5/3/37
Van Cleef, Lee	Somerville, N.J.	1/9/25
Van Devere, Trish	Tenafly, N.J.	1945
Van Doren, Mamie	Rowena, S.D.	2/6/33
Van Dyke, Dick	West Plains, Mo.	12/13/25
Van Dyke, Jerry	Danville, Ill.	1932
Van Fleet, Jo	Oakland, Cal.	1922
Van Pallandt, Nina	Copenhagen, Denmark	7/15/32
Van Patten, Dick	New York, N.Y.	12/9/28
Van Vooren, Monique	Brussels, Belgium	4/17/33
Vaughan, Sarah	Newark, N.J.	3/27/24
Vaughn, Robert	New York, N.Y.	11/22/32
Venuta, Benay	San Francisco, Cal.	1/27/11
Verdon, Gwen	Los Angeles, Cal.	1/13/25
Vereen, Ben	Miami, Fla.	10/10/46
Vernon, Jackie	New York, N.Y.	1929
Verrett, Shirley	New Orleans, La.	5/31/31
Vickers, Jon	Prince Albert, Sask.	10/26/26
Vidor, King Wallis	Galveston, Tex.	2/8/95

Name	Birthplace	Born
Vigoda, Abe	New York, N.Y.	2/24/21
Villechaize, Herve	Paris, France	4/23/43
Villella, Edward	Long Island, N.Y.	10/1/36
Vincent, Jan-Michael	Ventura, Cal.	7/15/44
Vinson, Helen	Beaumont, Tex.	1907
Vinton, Bobby	Canonsburg, Pa.	4/16/35
Voight, Jon	Yonkers, N.Y.	12/29/38
Von Furstenberg, Betsy	Neihem Heusen, Germany	8/16/32
Von Sydow, Max	Lund, Sweden	4/10/29
Voorhees, Donald	Allentown, Pa.	7/26/03
Waggoner, Lyle	Kansas City, Kan.	4/13/35
Wagner, Lindsay	Los Angeles, Cal.	6/22/49
Wagner, Robert	Detroit, Mich.	2/10/30
Wagoner, Porter	West Plains, Mo.	8/12/27
Wain, Bea	Bronx, N.Y.	1917
Waite, Ralph	White Plains, N.Y.	6/22/29
Waldon, Robert	New York, N.Y.	9/25/43
Walken, Christopher	New York, N.Y.	3/31/43
Walker, Clint	Hartford, Ill.	5/30/27
Walker, Jimmy	New York, N.Y.	—
Walker, Nancy	Philadelphia, Pa.	5/10/21
Wallach, Eli	Brooklyn, N.Y.	12/7/15
Wallenstein, Alfred	Chicago, Ill.	10/7/98
Wallis, Hal	Chicago, Ill.	9/14/99
Walston, Ray	Laurel, Miss.	12/2/14
Wanamaker, Sam	Chicago, Ill.	6/14/19
Ward, Simon	London, England	10/19/41
Warden, Jack	Newark, N.J.	9/18/20
Warfield, William	W. Helena, Ark.	1/22/20
Warhol, Andy	Pittsburgh, Pa.	8/6/27
Waring, Fred	Tyrone, Pa.	6/9/00
Warwick, Dionne	E. Orange, N.J.	12/12/41
Waters, Muddy	Rolling Fork, Miss.	4/4/15
Watson, Mills	Oakland, Cal.	7/10/40
Watts, Andre	Nuremberg, Germany	6/20/46
Wayne, David	Traverse City, Mich.	1/30/14
Wayne, Patrick	Los Angeles, Cal.	7/15/39
Weaver, Dennis	Joplin, Mo.	6/4/24
Weaver, Fritz	Pittsburgh, Pa.	1/19/26
Webb, Jack	Santa Monica, Cal.	4/2/20
Weissmuller, Johnny	Windber, Pa.	6/2/03
Welch, Raquel	Chicago, Ill.	9/5/42
Weld, Tuesday	New York, N.Y.	8/27/43
Welk, Lawrence	nr. Strasburg, N.D.	3/11/03
Welles, Orson	Kenosha, Wis.	5/6/15
Wells, Kitty	Nashville, Tenn.	8/30/19
Werner, Oskar	Vienna, Austria	11/13/22
White, Barry	Galveston, Tex.	9/12/44
White, Betty	Oak Park, Ill.	1/17/-
White, Jesse	Buffalo, N.Y.	1/3/19
Whiting, Margaret	Detroit, Mich.	7/22/24
Whitman, Stuart	San Francisco, Cal.	2/1/26
Whitmore, James	White Plains, N.Y.	10/1/21
Widmark, Richard	Sunrise, Minn.	12/26/14
Wilcox, Larry	San Diego, Cal.	8/8/47
Wilcoxon, Henry	British West Indies	1905
Wilde, Cornel	New York, N.Y.	10/13/18
Wilder, Billy	Vienna, Austria	6/22/06

Name	Birthplace	Born
Wilder, Gene	Milwaukee, Wis.	6/11/3
Williams, Andy	Wall Lake, Ia.	12/3/3
Williams, Billy Dee	New York, N.Y.	4/6/3
Williams, Cindy	Van Nuys, Cal.	8/22/4
Williams, Clarence	New York, N.Y.	8/21/3
Williams, Emlyn	Mostyn, Wales	11/26/0
Williams, Esther	Los Angeles, Cal.	8/8/2
Williams Jr., Hank	Shreveport, La.	5/26/4
Williams, Joe	Cordele, Ga.	191
Williams, Paul	Omaha, Neb.	9/19/4
Williams, Robin	Chicago, Ill.	7/21/5
Williams, Roger	Omaha, Neb.	192
Williams, Treat	Rowayton, Conn.	-
Williamson, Nicol	Hamilton, Scotland	9/14/3
Wilson, Demond	Valdosta, Ga.	-
Wilson, Dolores	Philadelphia, Pa.	192
Wilson, Flip	Jersey City, N.J.	12/8/3
Wilson, Nancy	Chillicothe, Oh.	2/20/3
Winchell, Paul	New York, N.Y.	12/21/2
Windom, William	New York, N.Y.	9/28/2
Winfield, Paul	Los Angeles, Cal.	5/22/4
Winkler, Henry	New York, N.Y.	10/30/4
Winters, Jonathan	Dayton, Oh.	11/11/2
Winters, Shelley	St. Louis, Mo.	8/18/2
Winwood, Estelle	Lee, England	1/24/8
Wiseman, Joseph	Montreal, Que.	5/15/1
Withers, Jane	Atlanta, Ga.	192
Wonder, Stevie	Saginaw, Mich.	5/13/5
Woodward, Joanne	Thomasville, Ga.	2/27/3
Wopat, Tom	Lodi, Wis.	9/9
Worley, Jo Anne	Lowell, Ind.	9/6/3
Worth, Irene	Nebraska	6/23/1
Wray, Fay	Alberta, Canada	9/10/0
Wright, Martha	Seattle, Wash.	192
Wright, Teresa	New York, N.Y.	10/27/1
Wrightson, Earl	Baltimore, Md.	191
Wyatt, Jane	Campgaw, N.J.	8/12/1
Wyman, Jane	St. Joseph, Mo.	1/4/1
Wynette, Tammy	Red Bay, Ala.	5/5/4
Wynn, Keenan	New York, N.Y.	7/27/1
Wynter, Dana	London, England	6/8/3
Yarborough, Glenn	Milwaukee, Wis.	193
Yarrow, Peter	New York, N.Y.	5/31/3
York, Dick	Ft. Wayne, Ind.	9/4/2
York, Michael	Fulmer, England	3/27/
York, Susannah	London, England	1/9/
Young, Alan	Northumberland, England	11/19/
Young, Burt	New York, N.Y.	4/30/
Young, Loretta	Salt Lake City, Ut.	1/6/
Young, Neil	Toronto, Ont.	11/12/
Young, Robert	Chicago, Ill.	2/22/
Youngman, Henny	Liverpool, England	19
Zappa, Frank	Baltimore, Md.	12/21/4
Zeffirelli, Franco	Florence, Italy	2/12/2
Zimbalist, Efrem	Rostov, Russia	4/9/8
Zimbalist, Efrem Jr.	New York, N.Y.	11/30/
Zimmer, Norma	Larsen, Ida	
Zorina, Vera	Berlin, Germany	1/2/
Zukerman, Pinchas	Tel Aviv, Israel	7/16/4

Entertainment Personalities of the Past

Born	Died	Name
1896	1974	Abbott, Bud
1872	1953	Adams, Maude
1855	1926	Adler, Jacob P.
1898	1933	Adoree, Renee
1909	1964	Albertson, Frank
1910	1981	Albertson, Jack
1885	1952	Alda, Frances
1894	1956	Allen, Fred
1906	1964	Allen, Gracie
1883	1950	Allgood, Sara
1882	1971	Anderson, Gilbert (Bronco Billy)
1886	1954	Anderson, John Murray
1915	1967	Andrews, Laverne
1933	1971	Angeli, Pier
1876	1958	Anglin, Margaret
1887	1933	Arbuckle, Fatty (Roscoe)
1900	1976	Arlen, Richard
1868	1946	Arliss, George
1900	1971	Armstrong, Louis
1890	1956	Arnold, Edward
1905	1974	Arquette, Cliff (Charlie Weaver)
1885	1946	Atwill, Lionel
1845	1930	Auer, Leopold
1905	1967	Auer, Mischa
1900	1972	Austin, Gene
1898	1940	Ayres, Agnes
1864	1922	Bacon, Frank
1891	1968	Bainter, Fay
1895	1957	Baker, Belle
1906	1975	Baker, Josephine
1898	1963	Baker, Phil
1882	1956	Bancroft, George
1903	1968	Bankhead, Tallulah
1890	1952	Banks, Leslie
1890	1955	Bara, Theda
1810	1891	Barnum, Phineas T.
1912	1978	Barrie, Wendy
1879	1959	Barrymore, Ethel
1882	1942	Barrymore, John
1878	1954	Barrymore, Lionel
1848	1905	Barrymore, Maurice
1897	1963	Barthelmess, Richard
1890	1962	Barton, James
1873	1951	Bauer, Harold
1893	1951	Baxter, Warner
1880	1928	Bayes, Nora
1904	1965	Beatty, Clyde
1904	1962	Beavers, Louise
1884	1946	Beery, Noah
1889	1949	Beery, Wallace
1901	1970	Begley, Ed
1854	1931	Belasco, David
1949	1982	Belushi, John
1906	1968	Benaderet, Bea
1906	1964	Bendix, William
1904	1965	Bennett, Constance
1873	1944	Bennett, Richard
1894	1974	Benny, Jack

Born	Died	Name
1924	1970	Benzell, Mimi
1899	1966	Berg, Gertrude
1903	1978	Bergen, Edgar
1895	1976	Berkeley, Busby
1863	1927	Bernard, Sam
1844	1923	Bernhardt, Sarah
1893	1943	Bernie, Ben
1889	1967	Bickford, Charles
1911	1960	Bjoerling, Jussi
1898	1973	Blackmer, Sidney
1882	1951	Blaney, Charles E.
1900	1943	Bledsoe, Jules
1928	1972	Blocker, Dan
1909	1979	Blondell, Joan
1888	1959	Blore, Eric
1901	1975	Blue, Ben
1899	1957	Bogart, Humphrey
1880	1965	Boland, Mary
1897	1969	Boles, John
1903	1960	Bond, Ward
1892	1981	Bondi, Beulah
1917	1981	Boone, Richard
1833	1893	Booth, Edwin
1796	1852	Booth, Junius Brutus
1894	1953	Bordoni, Irene
1888	1960	Bori, Lucrezia
1905	1965	Bow, Clara
1874	1946	Bowes, Maj. Edward
1928	1977	Boyd, Stephen
1898	1972	Boyd, William
1899	1978	Boyer, Charles
1893	1939	Brady, Alice
1871	1936	Breese, Edmund
1898	1964	Brendel, El
1894	1974	Brennan, Walter
1904	1979	Brent, George
1875	1948	Brian, Donald
1891	1951	Brice, Fanny
1891	1959	Broderick, Helen
1904	1951	Bromberg, J. Edward
1892	1973	Brown, Joe E.
1926	1966	Bruce, Lenny
1895	1953	Bruce, Nigel
1910	1982	Bruce, Virginia
1903	1979	Buchanan, Edgar
1891	1957	Buchanan, Jack
1885	1957	Buck, Gene
1938	1982	Buono, Victor
1885	1970	Burke, Billie
1912	1967	Burnette, Smiley
1896	1956	Burns, Bob
1902	1971	Burns, David
1882	1941	Burr, Henry
1897	1946	Busch, Mae
1883	1966	Bushman, Francis X.
1896	1946	Butterworth, Charles
1893	1971	Byington, Spring
1905	1972	Cabot, Bruce
1918	1977	Cabot, Sebastian
1895	1956	Calhern, Louis
1923	1977	Callas, Maria
1853	1942	Calve, Emma
1933	1976	Cambridge, Godfrey
1865	1940	Campbell, Mrs. Patrick
1892	1964	Cantor, Eddie
1878	1947	Carey, Harry
1880	1961	Carrillo, Leo
1892	1972	Carroll, Leo G.
1905	1965	Carroll, Nancy
1910	1963	Carson, Jack
1862	1937	Carter, Mrs. Leslie
1873	1921	Caruso, Enrico
1876	1973	Casals, Pablo
1927	1976	Cassidy, Jack
1893	1969	Castle, Irene
1887	1918	Castle, Vernon
1889	1960	Catlett, Walter
1887	1950	Cavanaugh, Hobart
1873	1938	Chaliapin, Feodor
1921	1980	Champion, Gower
1918	1961	Chandler, Jeff
1883	1930	Chaney, Lon
1906	1973	Chaney Jr., Lon
1889	1977	Chaplin, Charles
1893	1940	Chase, Charlie
1893	1961	Chatterton, Ruth
1888	1972	Chevalier, Maurice
1888	1960	Clark, Bobby

Born	Died	Name
1914	1968	Clark, Fred
1887	1950	Clayton, Lou
1920	1966	Clift, Montgomery
1932	1963	Cline, Patsy
1900	1937	Clive, Colin
1892	1967	Clyde, Andy
1911	1976	Cobb, Lee J.
1877	1961	Coburn, Charles
1887	1934	Cody, Lew
1878	1942	Cohan, George M.
1919	1965	Cole, Nat (King)
1878	1955	Collier, Constance
1890	1965	Collins, Ray
1891	1958	Colman, Ronald
1908	1934	Columbo, Russ
1907	1944	Compton, Betty
1887	1940	Connolly, Walter
1915	1982	Conried, Hans
1855	1909	Conried, Henrich
1918	1975	Conte, Richard
1901	1961	Cooper, Gary
1891	1971	Cooper, Gladys
1896	1973	Cooper, Melville
1914	1968	Corey, Wendell
1893	1974	Cornell, Katherine
1890	1972	Correll, Charles (Andy)
1905	1979	Costello, Dolores
1904	1957	Costello, Helene
1906	1959	Costello, Lou
1877	1950	Costello, Maurice
1899	1973	Coward, Noel
1890	1950	Cowl, Jane
1924	1973	Cox, Wally
1847	1924	Crabtree, Lotta
1928	1978	Crane, Bob
1875	1945	Craven, Frank
1903	1977	Crawford, Joan
1916	1944	Cregar, Laird
1880	1942	Crews, Laura Hope
1880	1974	Crisp, Donald
1942	1973	Croce, Jim
1910	1960	Cromwell, Richard
1903	1977	Crosby, Bing
1897	1975	Cross, Milton
1878	1968	Currie, Finlay
1816	1876	Cushman, Charlotte
1917	1978	Dailey, Dan
1899	1981	Chief Dan George
1923	1965	Dandridge, Dorothy
1869	1941	Danforth, William
1894	1963	Daniell, Henry
1901	1971	Daniels, Bebe
1860	1935	Daniels, Frank
1936	1973	Darin, Bobby
1921	1965	Darnell, Linda
1879	1967	Darwell, Jane
1866	1949	Davenport, Harry
1897	1961	Davies, Marion
1907	1961	Davis, Joan
1931	1955	Dean, James
1881	1950	DeCordoba, Pedro
1905	1968	Dekker, Albert
1898	1965	Demarco, Tony
1881	1959	DeMille, Cecil B.
1891	1967	Denny, Reginald
1901	1974	DeSica, Vittorio
1905	1977	Devine, Andy
1942	1972	De Wilde, Brandon
1907	1974	De Wolfe, Billy
1865	1950	De Wolfe, Elsie
1879	1947	Digges, Dudley
1901	1966	Disney, Walt
1894	1949	Dix, Richard
1856	1924	Dockstader, Lew
1892	1941	Dolly, Jennie
1892	1970	Dolly, Rosie
1905	1958	Donat, Robert
1903	1972	Donlevy, Brian
1901	1981	Douglas, Melvyn
1907	1959	Douglas, Paul
—	1980	Dragonette, Jessica
1889	1956	Draper, Ruth
1881	1965	Dresser, Louise
1869	1934	Dressler, Marie
1820	1897	Drew, Mrs. John
1853	1927	Drew, John (son)
1909	1951	Duchin, Eddy
1890	1965	Dumont, Margaret
1878	1927	Duncan, Isadora

Born	Died	Name
1905	1967	Dunn, James
1893	1980	Durante, Jimmy
1907	1968	Duryea, Dan
1858	1924	Duse, Eleanora
1894	1929	Eagels, Jeanne
1896	1930	Eames, Clare
1865	1952	Eames, Emma
1901	1967	Eddy, Nelson
1897	1971	Edwards, Cliff
1879	1945	Edwards, Gus
1899	1974	Ellington, Duke
1941	1974	Elliot, Cass
1871	1940	Elliott, Maxine
1891	1967	Elman, Mischa
1881	1951	Errol, Leon
1903	1967	Erwin, Stuart
1888	1976	Evans, Edith
1913	1967	Evelyn, Judith
1883	1939	Fairbanks, Douglas
1915	1970	Farmer, Frances
1870	1929	Farnum, Dustin
1876	1953	Farnum, William
1882	1967	Farrar, Geraldine
1904	1971	Farrell, Glenda
1868	1940	Faversham, William
1861	1939	Fawcett, George
1897	1960	Fay, Frank
1895	1962	Fazenda, Louise
1894	1979	Fiedler, Arthur
1918	1973	Field, Betty
1898	1979	Fields, Gracie
1867	1941	Fields, Lew
1879	1946	Fields, W.C.
1931	1978	Fields, Totie
1916	1977	Finch, Peter
1865	1932	Fiske, Minnie Maddern
1888	1961	Fitzgerald, Barry
1895	1962	Flagstad, Kirsten
1900	1971	Flippen, Jay C.
1909	1959	Flynn, Errol
1925	1974	Flynn, Joe
1880	1942	Fokine, Michel
1910	1968	Foley, Red
1920	1978	Fontaine, Frank
1853	1937	Forbes-Robertson, J.
1887	1970	Ford, Ed (Senator)
1895	1973	Ford, John
1901	1976	Ford, Paul
1899	1966	Ford, Wallace
1806	1872	Forrest, Edwin
1904	1970	Foster, Preston
1857	1928	Foy, Eddie
1905	1968	Francis, Kay
1893	1966	Frawley, William
1885	1938	Frederick, Pauline
1870	1955	Friganza, Trixie
1890	1958	Frisco, Joe
1860	1915	Frohman, Charles
1851	1940	Frohman, Daniel
1885	1947	Fyffe, Will
1901	1960	Gable, Clark
1889	1963	Galli-Curci, Amelita
1877	1967	Garden, Mary
1913	1952	Garfield, John
1922	1969	Garland, Judy
1893	1963	Gaxton, William
1902	1978	Geer, Will
1904	1954	George, Gladys
1892	1962	Gibson, Hoot
1890	1957	Gigli, Beniamino
1894	1971	Gilbert, Billy
1897	1936	Gilbert, John
1855	1937	Gillette, William
1867	1943	Gillmore, Frank
1879	1939	Gilpin, Charles
1898	1968	Gish, Dorothy
1886	1959	Gleason, James
1884	1938	Gluck, Alma
1874	1955	Golden, John
1884	1974	Goldwyn, Samuel
1917	1969	Gorcey, Leo
1884	1940	Gordon, C. Henry
1869	1944	Gottschalk, Ferdinand
1829	1869	Gottschalk, Louis
1916	1973	Grable, Betty
1929	1981	Grahame, Gloria
1901	1959	Gray, Gilda
1879	1954	Greenstreet, Sydney

Born	Died	Name
1874	1948	Griffith, David Wark
1885	1957	Guitry, Sacha
1912	1967	Guthrie, Woody
1875	1959	Gwenn, Edmund
1888	1942	Hackett, Charles
1902	1958	Hackett, Raymond
1870	1943	Haines, Robert T.
1892	1950	Hale, Alan
1927	1981	Haley, Bill
1899	1979	Haley, Jack
1847	1919	Hammerstein, Oscar
1879	1955	Hampden, Walter
1924	1964	Haney, Carol
1893	1964	Hardwicke, Sir Cedric
1892	1957	Hardy, Oliver
1883	1939	Hare, T.E. (Ernie)
1911	1937	Harlow, Jean
1872	1946	Harned, Virginia
1844	1911	Harrigan, Edward
1870	1946	Hart, William S.
1907	1955	Hartman, Grace
1928	1973	Harvey, Laurence
1910	1973	Hawkins, Jack
1890	1973	Hayakawa, Sessue
1885	1969	Hayes, Gabby
1918	1980	Haymes, Dick
1902	1971	Hayward, Leland
1917	1975	Hayward, Susan
1896	1937	Healy, Ted
1910	1971	Heflin, Van
1879	1936	Heggie, O.P.
1873	1918	Held, Anna
1942	1970	Hendrix, Jimi
1913	1969	Henie, Sonja
1879	1942	Herbert, Henry
1887	1951	Herbert, Hugh
1886	1956	Hersholt, Jean
1895	1942	Hibbard, Edna
1899	1980	Hitchcock, Alfred
1914	1955	Hodiak, John
1894	1973	Holden, Fay
1918	1981	Holden, William
1922	1965	Holliday, Judy
1936	1959	Holly, Buddy
1888	1951	Holt, Jack
1918	1973	Holt, Tim
1871	1947	Homer, Louise
1898	1978	Homolka, Oscar
1902	1972	Hopkins, Miriam
1858	1935	Hopper, DeWolf
1874	1959	Hopper, Edna Wallace
1890	1966	Hopper, Hedda
1888	1970	Horton, Edward Everett
1874	1926	Houdini, Harry
1881	1965	Howard, Eugene
1867	1961	Howard, Joe
1893	1943	Howard, Leslie
1885	1955	Howard, Tom
1885	1949	Howard, Willie
1914	1972	Hudson, Rochelle
1890	1977	Hull, Henry
1886	1957	Hull, Josephine
1895	1958	Humphrey, Doris
1895	1945	Hunter, Glenn
1925	1969	Hunter, Jeffrey
1901	1962	Husing, Ted
1884	1950	Huston, Walter
1892	1950	Ingram, Rex
1895	1969	Ingram, Rex
1895	1980	Iturbi, Jose
1838	1905	Irving, Henry
1871	1944	Irving, Isabel
1872	1914	Irving, Laurence
1862	1938	Irvin, May
1875	1942	Jackson, Joe
1911	1972	Jackson, Mahalia
1889	1956	Janis, Elsie
1886	1950	Jannings, Emil
1930	1980	Janssen, David
1829	1905	Jefferson, Joseph
1859	1923	Jefferson, Thomas
1900	1974	Jenkins, Allen
1898	1981	Jessel, George
1862	1930	Jewett, Henry
1892	1962	Johnson, Chic
1878	1952	Johnson, Edward
1886	1950	Jolson, Al
1889	1942	Jones, Buck
1911	1965	Jones, Spike
1943	1970	Joplin, Janis
1897	1961	Jordan, Marian (Molly McGee)
1905	1981	Joslyn, Allyn
1890	1955	Joyce, Alice
1910	1966	Kane, Helen
1887	1969	Karloff, Boris
1893	1970	Karns, Roscoe
1811	1868	Kean, Charles
1806	1880	Kean, Mrs. Charles
1787	1833	Kean, Edmund
1895	1966	Keaton, Buster
1858	1929	Keenan, Frank
1830	1873	Keene, Laura
1841	1893	Keene, Thomas W.
1899	1960	Keith, Ian
1894	1973	Kellaway, Cecil
1898	1979	Kelly, Emmett
1910	1981	Kelly, Patsy
1899	1956	Kelly, Paul
1873	1939	Kelly, Walter C.
1909	1968	Kelton, Pert
1823	1895	Kemble, Agnes
1775	1854	Kemble, Charles
1809	1893	Kemble, Fannie
1848	1935	Kendal, Dame Madge
1843	1917	Kendal, William H.
1926	1959	Kendall, Kay
1890	1948	Kennedy, Edgar
1886	1945	Kent, William
1880	1947	Kerrigan, J. Warren
1886	1956	Kibbee, Guy
1902	1966	Kiepura, Jan
1888	1964	Kilbride, Percy
1863	1933	Kilgour, Joseph
1897	1971	King, Dennis
1901	1980	Kostelanetz, Andre
1919	1962	Kovacs, Ernie
1885	1974	Kruger, Otto
1913	1964	Ladd, Alan
1895	1967	Lahr, Bert
1919	1973	Lake, Veronica
1919	1948	Landis, Carole
1904	1972	Landis, Jessie Royce
1884	1944	Langdon, Harry
1853	1929	Langtry, Lillie
1921	1959	Lanza, Mario
1881	1958	Lasky, Jesse L.
1870	1950	Lauder, Harry
1899	1962	Laughton, Charles
1890	1965	Laurel, Stan
1892	1954	Laurie Jr., Joe
1898	1952	Lawrence, Gertrude
1890	1929	Lawrence, Margaret
1940	1973	Lee, Bruce
1907	1952	Lee, Canada
1914	1970	Lee, Gypsy Rose
1848	1929	Lehmann, Lilli
1888	1976	Lehmann, Lotte
1896	1950	Lehr, Lew
1913	1967	Leigh, Vivien
1852	1908	Leighton, Margaret
1922	1976	Leighton, Margaret
1894	1931	Leitzel, Lillian
1940	1980	Lennon, John
1900	1981	Lenya, Lotte
1870	1941	Leonard, Eddie
1911	1973	Leonard, Jack E.
1906	1972	Levant, Oscar
1905	1980	Levene, Sam
1911	1980	Levenson, Sam
1881	1955	Levy, Ethel
1902	1971	Lewis, Joe E.
1892	1971	Lewis, Ted
1874	1944	Lhevinne, Josef
1889	1952	Lincoln, Elmo
1820	1887	Lind, Jenny
1889	1968	Lindsay, Howard
1869	1952	Lipman, Clara
1893	1971	Lloyd, Harold
1870	1922	Lloyd, Marie
1891	1957	Lockhart, Gene
1913	1969	Logan, Ella
1909	1942	Lombard, Carole
1902	1977	Lombardo, Guy
1927	1974	Long, Richard
1895	1975	Lopez, Vincent
1888	1968	Lorne, Marion
1904	1964	Lorre, Peter
1917	1970	Louise, Anita
1914	1962	Lovejoy, Frank
1892	1971	Lowe, Edmund
1892	1947	Lubitsch, Ernst
1884	1956	Lugosi, Bela
1895	1971	Lukas, Paul
1892	1977	Lunt, Alfred
1853	1932	Lupino, George
1893	1942	Lupino, Stanley
1897	1957	Lyman, Abe
1926	1982	Lynde, Paul
1926	1971	Lynn, Diana
1885	1954	Lytell, Bert
1867	1936	Lytton, Henry
1907	1965	MacDonald, Jeanette
1902	1969	MacLane, Barton
1909	1973	Macready, George
1861	1946	Macy, George Carleton
1908	1973	Magnani, Anna
1896	1967	Mahoney, Will
1890	1975	Main, Marjorie
1933	1967	Mansfield, Jayne
1854	1907	Mansfield, Richard
1905	1980	Mantovani, Annunzio
1897	1975	March, Fredric
1920	1970	March, Hal
1865	1950	Marlowe, Julia
1890	1966	Marshall, Herbert
1864	1943	Marshall, Tully
1920	1981	Martin, Ross
1885	1969	Martinelli, Giovanni
1888	1964	Marx, Arthur (Harpo)
1890	1977	Marx, Julius (Groucho)
1887	1961	Marx, Leonard (Chico)
1862	1951	Maude, Cyril
1922	1972	Maxwell, Marilyn
1879	1948	May, Edna
1885	1957	Mayer, Louis B.
1895	1973	Maynard, Ken
1884	1945	McCormack, John
1907	1962	McCormick, Myron
1888	1931	McCoy, Bessie
1883	1936	McCullough, Paul
1895	1952	McDaniel, Hattie
1924	1965	McDonald, Marie
1913	1975	McGiver, John
1899	1981	McHugh, Frank
1879	1949	McIntyre, Frank J.
1857	1937	McIntyre, James
1879	1937	McKinley, Mabel
1883	1959	McLaglen, Victor
1907	1971	McMahon, Horace
1930	1980	McQueen, Steve
1920	1980	Medford, Kay
1880	1946	Meek, Donald
1879	1936	Meighan, Thomas
1861	1931	Melba, Nellie
1890	1973	Melchior, Lauritz
1904	1961	Melton, James
1890	1963	Menjou, Adolphe
1902	1966	Menken, Helen
1904	1944	Miller, Glenn
1860	1926	Miller, Henry
1898	1936	Miller, Marilyn
1895	1927	Mills, Florence
1939	1976	Mineo, Sal
1903	1955	Minnevitch, Borrah
1913	1955	Miranda, Carmen
1892	1962	Mitchell, Thomas
1880	1940	Mix, Tom
1845	1909	Modjeska, Helena
1926	1962	Monroe, Marilyn
1911	1973	Monroe, Vaughn
1875	1964	Monteux, Pierre
1919	1951	Montez, Maria
1904	1981	Montgomery, Robert
1901	1947	Moore, Grace
1885	1955	Moore, Tom
1876	1962	Moore, Victor
1906	1974	Moorehead, Agnes
1882	1949	Moran, George
1884	1952	Moran, Polly
1890	1949	Morgan, Frank
1900	1941	Morgan, Helen
1888	1956	Morgan, Ralph
1901	1970	Morris, Chester

Born	Died	Name
1849	1925	Morris, Clara
1914	1959	Morris, Wayne
1943	1971	Morrison, Jim
1915	1977	Mostel, Zero
1897	1969	Mowbray, Alan
1895	1967	Muni, Paul
1894	1953	Munn, Frank
1924	1971	Murphy, Audie
1885	1965	Murray, Mae
1896	1970	Nagel, Conrad
1900	1973	Naish, J. Carroll
1898	1961	Naldi, Nita
1888	1950	Nash, Florence
1865	1945	Nash, George
1879	1945	Nazimova, Alla
1846	1905	Neilson, Ada
1848	1880	Neilson, Adelaide
1868	1957	Neilson-Terry, Julia
1907	1975	Nelson, Ozzie
1885	1967	Nesbit, Evelyn
1870	1951	Nethersole, Olga
1905	1956	Newton, Robert
1874	1948	Niblo, Fred
1890	1950	Nijinsky, Vaslav
1893	1974	Nilsson, Anna Q.
1898	1930	Normand, Mabel
1879	1959	Norworth, Jack
1905	1968	Novarro, Ramon
1893	1951	Novello, Ivor
1903	1978	Oakie, Jack
1860	1926	Oakley, Annie
1911	1979	Oberon, Merle
1908	1981	O'Connell, Arthur
1898	1943	O'Connell, Hugh
1883	1959	O'Connor, Una
1878	1945	O'Hara, Fiske
1908	1968	O'Keefe, Dennis
1880	1938	Oland, Warner
1860	1932	Olcott, Chauncey
1883	1942	Oliver, Edna May
1892	1963	Olsen, Ole
1849	1920	O'Neill, James
1876	1949	Ouspenskaya, Maria
1887	1972	Owen, Reginald
1860	1941	Paderewski, Ignace
1889	1954	Pallette, Eugene
1894	1958	Pangborn, Franklin
1914	1975	Parks, Larry
1881	1972	Parsons, Louella
1881	1940	Pasternack, Josef A.
1837	1908	Pastor, Tony
1843	1919	Patti, Adelina
1840	1889	Patti, Carlotta
1885	1931	Pavlova, Anna
1900	1973	Paxinou, Katina
1917	1966	Pearce, Alice
1885	1950	Pemberton, Brock
1899	1967	Pendleton, Nat
1905	1941	Penner, Joe
1892	1937	Perkins, Osgood
1893	1956	Peters, Brandon
1915	1963	Piaf, Edith
1893	1979	Pickford, Mary
1892	1957	Pinza, Ezio
1900	1963	Pitts, Zasu
1904	1976	Pons, Lili
1897	1981	Ponselle, Rosa
1903	1969	Portman, Eric
1904	1963	Powell, Dick
1912	1982	Powell, Eleanor
1913	1958	Power, Tyrone
1872	1935	Powers, Eugene
1935	1977	Presley, Elvis
1900	1964	Price, George E.
1856	1919	Primrose, George
1954	1977	Prinze, Freddie
1879	1956	Prouty, Jed
1871	1942	Pryor, Arthur
1895	1980	Raft, George
1890	1967	Rains, Claude
1889	1970	Rambeau, Marjorie
1900	1947	Rankin, Arthur
1892	1967	Rathbone, Basil
1897	1960	Ratoff, Gregory
1883	1953	Rawlinson, Herbert
1891	1943	Ray, Charles
1941	1967	Redding, Otis
1914	1959	Reeves, George
1860	1916	Rehan, Ada
1892	1923	Reid, Wallace
1873	1943	Reinhardt, Max
1909	1971	Rennie, Michael
1870	1940	Richman, Charles
1895	1972	Richman, Harry
1872	1961	Ring, Blanche
1898	1977	Ritchard, Cyril
1907	1974	Ritter, Tex
1905	1969	Ritter, Thelma
1903	1966	Ritz, Al
1898	1976	Robeson, Paul
1878	1949	Robinson, Bill
1893	1973	Robinson, Edward G.
1865	1942	Robson, May
1905	1977	Rochester (E. Anderson)
1897	1933	Rodgers, Jimmy
1894	1958	Rodzinsky, Artur
1879	1935	Rogers, Will
1897	1937	Roland, Ruth
1880	1962	Rooney, Pat
1899	1966	Rose, Billy
1910	1980	Roth, Lillian
1882	1936	Rothafel, S. L. (Roxy)
1878	1953	Ruffo, Titta
1892	1970	Ruggles, Charles
1864	1936	Russell, Annie
1924	1961	Russell, Gail
1861	1922	Russell, Lillian
1911	1976	Russell, Rosalind
1892	1972	Rutherford, Margaret
1902	1973	Ryan, Irene
1909	1973	Ryan, Robert
1924	1963	Sabu (Dastagir)
1877	1968	St. Denis, Ruth
1884	1955	Sakall, S.Z.
1885	1936	Sale (Chic), Charles
1906	1972	Sanders, George
1934	1973	Sands, Diana
1896	1960	Savo, Jimmy
1879	1954	Scheff, Fritzi
1892	1930	Schenck, Joe
1895	1964	Schildkraut, Joseph
1865	1930	Schildkraut, Rudolph
1889	1965	Schipa, Tito
1882	1951	Schnabel, Artur
1938	1982	Schneider, Romy
1910	1949	Schumann, Henrietta
1861	1936	Schumann-Heink, E.
1866	1945	Scott, Cyril
1914	1965	Scott, Zachary
1843	1896	Scott-Siddons, Mrs.
1938	1979	Seberg, Jean
1892	1974	Seeley, Blossom
1902	1965	Selznick, David O.
1858	1935	Sembrich, Marcella
1880	1960	Sennett, Mack
1881	1951	Shattuck, Arthur
1860	1929	Shaw, Mary
1927	1978	Shaw, Robert
1891	1972	Shawn, Ted
1868	1949	Shean, Al
1915	1967	Sheridan, Ann
1924	1973	Sherman, Allan
1885	1934	Sherman, Lowell
1918	1970	Shriner, Herb
1875	1953	Shubert, Lee
1755	1831	Siddons, Mrs. Sarah
1882	1930	Sills, Milton
1914	1970	Silvera, Frank
1900	1976	Sim, Alastair
1878	1946	Sis Hopkins (Melville)
1891	1934	Skelly, Hal
1858	1942	Skinner, Otis
1870	1952	Skipworth, Alison
1863	1948	Smith, C. Aubrey
1917	1979	Soo, Jack
1826	1881	Sothern, Edward A.
1859	1933	Sothern, Edward H.
1884	1957	Sothern, Harry
1854	1932	Sousa, John Philip
1884	1957	Sparks, Ned
1876	1948	Speaks, Oley
1890	1970	Spitalny, Phil
1873	1937	Standing, Guy
1900	1941	Stephenson, James
1883	1939	Sterling, Ford
1882	1928	Stevens, Emily A.
1934	1970	Stevens, Inger
1896	1961	Stewart, Anita
1882	1977	Stokowski, Leopold
1873	1959	Stone, Fred
1879	1953	Stone, Lewis
1904	1980	Stone, Milburn
1898	1959	Sturges, Preston
1911	1960	Sullavan, Margaret
1902	1974	Sullivan, Ed
1903	1956	Sullivan, Francis L.
1892	1946	Summerville, Slim
1904	1969	Swarthout, Gladys
1893	1957	Talmadge, Norma
1900	1972	Tamiroff, Akim
1878	1947	Tanguay, Eva
1899	1934	Tashman, Lilyan
1885	1966	Taylor, Deems
1899	1958	Taylor, Estelle
1887	1946	Taylor, Laurette
1911	1969	Taylor, Robert
1878	1938	Tearle, Conway
1884	1953	Tearle, Godfrey
1892	1937	Tell, Alma
1864	1942	Tempest, Marie
1910	1963	Templeton, Alec
1847	1928	Terry, Ellen
1871	1940	Tetrazzini, Luisa
1899	1936	Thalberg, Irving
1857	1914	Thomas, Brandon
1892	1960	Thomas, John Charles
1882	1976	Thorndike, Sybil
		(Three Stooges)
1902	1975	Fine, Larry
1906	1952	Howard, Curly
1897	1975	Howard, Moe
1869	1936	Thurston, Howard
1896	1960	Tibbett, Lawrence
1887	1940	Tinney, Frank
1909	1958	Todd, Michael
1906	1935	Todd, Thelma
1874	1947	Toler, Sidney
1905	1968	Tone, Franchot
1867	1957	Toscanini, Arturo
1898	1968	Tracy, Lee
1900	1967	Tracy, Spencer
1903	1972	Traubel, Helen
1894	1975	Treacher, Arthur
1853	1917	Tree, Herbert Beerbohm
1889	1973	Truex, Ernest
1915	1975	Tucker, Richard
1884	1966	Tucker, Sophie
1911	1970	Tufts, Sonny
1874	1940	Turpin, Ben
1908	1959	Twelvetrees, Helen
1894	1970	Ulric, Lenore
1933	1975	Ure, Mary
1895	1926	Valentino, Rudolph
1870	1950	Van, Billy B.
1912	1979	Vance, Vivian
1893	1943	Veidt, Conrad
1926	1981	Vera-Ellen
1885	1957	Von Stroheim, Erich
1906	1981	Von Zell, Harry
1887	1969	Walburn, Raymond
1874	1946	Waldron, Charles D.
1904	1966	Walker, June
1914	1951	Walker, Robert
1887	1980	Walsh, Raoul
1876	1962	Walter, Bruno
1878	1936	Walthall, Henry B.
1872	1952	Ward, Fannie
1866	1951	Warfield, David
1876	1958	Warner, H. B.
1878	1964	Warwick, Robert
1924	1963	Washington, Dinah
1900	1977	Waters, Ethel
1867	1945	Watson, Billy
1879	1962	Watson, Lucille
1890	1965	Watson, Minor
1907	1979	Wayne, John
1896	1966	Webb, Clifton
1867	1942	Weber, Joe
1905	1973	Webster, Margaret
1896	1975	Wellman, William
1883	1953	Werrenrath, Reinald
1892	1980	West, Mae
1879	1942	Westley, Helen
1895	1968	Wheeler, Bert

Born	Died	Name
1889	1938	White, Pearl
1891	1967	Whiteman, Paul
1865	1948	Whitty, Dame May
1906	1966	Whorf, Richard
1912	1979	Wilding, Michael
1895	1948	William, Warren
1877	1922	Williams, Bert
1867	1918	Williams, Evan
1923	1953	Williams, Hank
1902	1978	Wills, Chill
1900	1982	Wilson, Don
1917	1972	Wilson, Marie
1884	1969	Winninger, Charles
1904	1959	Withers, Grant
1881	1931	Wolheim, Louis
1907	1961	Wong, Anna May
1938	1981	Wood, Natalie
1892	1978	Wood, Peggy
1888	1963	Woolley, Monty
1889	1938	Woolsey, Robert
1881	1956	Wycherly, Margaret
1902	1981	Wyler, William
1886	1966	Wynn, Ed
1906	1964	Wynyard, Diana
1890	1960	Young, Clara Kimball
1917	1978	Young, Gig
1887	1953	Young, Roland
1902	1979	Zanuck, Darryl F.
1869	1932	Ziegfeld, Florenz
1873	1976	Zukor, Adolph

Ancient Greeks and Latins

Greeks

Aeschines, orator, 389-314BC.
Aeschylus, dramatist, 525-456BC.
Aesop, fableist, c620-c560BC.
Anacreon, poet, c582-c485BC.
Anaxagoras, philosopher, c500-428BC.
Archimedes, math. c287-212BC.
Aristophanes, dramatist, c448-380BC.
Aristotle, philosopher, 384-322BC.
Athenaeus, scholar, fl.c200.
Callicrates, architect, fl.5th cent.BC.
Callimachus, poet, c305-240BC.
Democritus, philosopher, c460-370BC.
Demosthenes, orator, 384-322BC.
Diodorus, historian, fl.20BC.
Diogenes, philosopher, c372-c287BC.
Dionysius, historian, d.c7BC.
Empedocles, philosopher, c490-430BC.
Epictetus, philosopher, c55-c135.
Epicurus, philosopher, 341-270BC.
Euclid, mathematician, fl.c300BC.
Euripides, dramatist, c484-406BC.
Heraclitus, philosopher, c535-c475BC.
Herodotus, historian, c484-420BC.
Hesiod, poet, 8th cent. BC.
Hippocrates, physician, c460-377BC.
Homer, poet, believed lived c850BC.
Menander, dramatist, 342-292BC.
Pindar, poet, c518-c438BC.
Plato, philosopher, c428-c347BC.
Plutarch, biographer, c46-120.
Polybius, historian, c200-c118BC.
Pythagoras, phil., math., c580-c500BC.
Sappho, poet, c610-c580BC.
Simonides, poet, 556-c468BC.
Socrates, philosopher, c470-399BC.
Sophocles, dramatist, C496-406BC.
Strabo, geographer, c63BC-AD24.
Thales, philosopher, c634-c546BC.
Themistocles, politician, c524-c460BC.
Theocritus, poet, c310-250BC.
Theophrastus, phil. c372-c287BC.
Thucydides, historian, fl.5th cent.BC.
Timon, philosopher, c320-c230BC.
Xenophon, historian, c434-c355BC.
Zeno, philosopher, c495-c430BC.

Latins

Ammianus, historian, c330-395.
Apuleius, satirist, c124-c170.
Boethius, scholar, c480-524
Caesar, Julius, general, 100-44BC.
Cato (Elder), statesman, 234-149BC.
Catullus, poet, c84-54BC.
Cicero, orator, 106-43BC.
Claudian, poet, c370-c404.
Gellius, author, c130-c165.
Horace, poet, 65-8BC.
Juvenal, satirist, c60-c127.
Livy, historian, 59BC-AD17.
Lucan, poet, 39-65.
Lucilius, poet, c180-c102BC.
Lucretius, poet, c99-c55BC.
Martial, epigrammatist, c38-c103.
Nepos, historian, c100-c25BC.
Ovid, poet, 43BC-AD17.
Persius, satirist, 34-62.
Plautus, dramatist, c254-c184BC.
Pliny, scholar, 23-79.
Pliny (Younger), author, 62-113.
Quintilian, rhetorician, c35-c97.
Sallust, historian, 86-34BC.
Seneca, philosopher, 4BC-AD65.
Silius, poet, c25-101.
Statius, poet, c45-c96.
Suetonius, biographer, c69-c122.
Tacitus, historian, c56-c120.
Terence, dramatist, 185-c159BC.
Tibullus, poet, c55-c19BC.
Virgil, poet, 70-19BC.
Vitruvius, architect, fl.1st cent.BC.

Rulers of England and Great Britain

England

Name		Began	Died	Age	Rgd
Saxons and Danes					
Egbert	King of Wessex, won allegiance of all English	829	839	—	10
Ethelwulf	Son, King of Wessex, Sussex, Kent, Essex	839	858	—	19
Ethelbald	Son of Ethelwulf, displaced father in Wessex	858	860	—	2
Ethelbert	2d son of Ethelwulf, united Kent and Wessex	860	866	—	6
Ethelred I	3d son, King of Wessex, fought Danes	866	871	—	5
Alfred	The Great, 4th son, defeated Danes, fortified London	871	899	52	28
Edward	The Elder, Alfred's son, united English, claimed Scotland	899	924	55	25
Athelstan	The Glorious, Edward's son, King of Mercia, Wessex	924	940	45	16
Edmund I	3d son of Edward, King of Wessex, Mercia	940	946	25	6
Edred	4th son of Edward	946	955	32	9
Edwy	The Fair, eldest son of Edmund, King of Wessex	955	959	18	3
Edgar	The Peaceful, 2d son of Edmund, ruled all English	959	975	32	17
Edward	The Martyr, eldest son of Edgar, murdered by stepmother	975	978	17	4
Ethelred II	The Unready, 2d son of Edgar, married Emma of Normandy	978	1016	48	37
Edmund II	Ironside, son of Ethelred II, King of London	1016	1016	27	0
Canute	The Dane, gave Wessex to Edmund, married Emma	1016	1035	40	19
Harold I	Harefoot, natural son of Canute	1035	1040	—	5
Hardecanute	Son of Canute by Emma, Danish King	1040	1042	24	2
Edward	The Confessor, son of Ethelred II (Canonized 1161)	1042	1066	62	24
Harold II	Edward's brother-in-law, last Saxon King	1066	1066	44	0
House of Normandy					
William I	The Conqueror, defeated Harold at Hastings	1066	1087	60	21
William II	Rufus, 3d son of William I, killed by arrow	1087	1100	43	13
Henry I	Beauclerc, youngest son of William I	1100	1135	67	35
House of Blois					
Stephen	Son of Adela, daughter of William I, and Count of Blois	1135	1154	50	19
House of Plantagenet					
Henry II	Son of Geoffrey Plantagenet (Angevin) by Matilda, dau. of Henry I	1154	1189	56	35
Richard I	Coeur de Lion, son of Henry II, crusader	1189	1199	42	10
John	Lackland, son of Henry II, signed Magna Carta, 1215	1199	1216	50	17
Henry III	Son of John, acceded at 9, under regency until 1227	1216	1272	65	56
Edward I	Longshanks, son of Henry III	1272	1307	68	35
Edward II	Son of Edward I, deposed by Parliament, 1327	1307	1327	43	20
Edward III	Of Windsor, son of Edward II	1327	1377	65	50
Richard II	Grandson of Edw. III, minor until 1389, deposed 1399	1377	1400	34	22
House of Lancaster					
Henry IV	Son of John of Gaunt, Duke of Lancaster, son of Edw. III	1399	1413	47	13
Henry V	Son of Henry IV, victor of Agincourt	1413	1422	34	9
Henry VI	Son of Henry V, deposed 1461, died in Tower	1422	1471	49	39

House of York

Edward IV	Great-great-grandson of Edward III, son of Duke of York	**1461**	**1483**	41	22
Edward V	Son of Edward IV, murdered in Tower of London	**1483**	**1483**	13	0
Richard III	Crookback, bro. of Edward IV, fell at Bosworth Field	**1483**	**1485**	35	2

House of Tudor

Henry VII	Son of Edmund Tudor, Earl of Richmond, whose father had married the widow of Henry V; descended from Edward III through his mother, Margaret Beaufort via John of Gaunt. By marriage with dau. of Edward IV he united Lancaster and York	**1485**	**1509**	53	24
Henry VIII	Son of Henry VII by Elizabeth, dau. of Edward IV.	**1509**	**1547**	56	38
Edward VI	Son of Henry VIII, by Jane Seymour, his 3d queen. Ruled under regents. Was forced to name Lady Jane Grey his successor. Council of State proclaimed her queen July 10, 1553. Mary Tudor won Council, was proclaimed queen July 19, 1553. Mary had Lady Jane Grey beheaded for treason, Feb., 1554	**1547**	**1553**	16	6
Mary I	Daughter of Henry VIII, by Catherine of Aragon	**1553**	**1558**	43	5
Elizabeth I	Daughter of Henry VIII, by Anne Boleyn	**1558**	**1603**	69	44

Great Britain

House of Stuart

James I	James VI of Scotland, son of Mary, Queen of Scots. *First to call himself King of Great Britain. This became official with the Act of Union, 1707*	**1603**	**1625**	59	22
Charles I	Only surviving son of James I; beheaded Jan. 30, 1649	**1625**	**1649**	48	24

Commonwealth, 1649-1660

Council of State, 1649; Protectorate, 1653

The Cromwells	Oliver Cromwell, Lord Protector	**1653**	**1658**	59	—
	Richard Cromwell, son, Lord Protector, resigned May 25, 1659	**1658**	**1712**	86	—

House of Stuart (Restored)

Charles II	Eldest son of Charles I, died without issue	**1660**	**1685**	55	25
James II	2d son of Charles I. Deposed 1688. Interregnum Dec. 11, 1688, to Feb. 13, 1689	**1685**	**1701**	68	3
William III	Son of William, Prince of Orange, by Mary, dau. of Charles I	**1689**	**1702**	51	13
and Mary II	Eldest daughter of James II and wife of William III		**1694**	33	6
Anne	2d daughter of James II	**1702**	**1714**	49	12

House of Hanover

George I	Son of Elector of Hanover, by Sophia, grand-dau. of James I	**1714**	**1727**	67	13
George II	Only son of George I, married Caroline of Brandenburg	**1727**	**1760**	77	33
George III	Grandson of George II, married Charlotte of Mecklenburg	**1760**	**1820**	81	59
George IV	Eldest son of George III, Prince Regent, from Feb., 1811	**1820**	**1830**	67	10
William IV	3d son of George III, married Adelaide of Saxe-Meiningen	**1830**	**1837**	71	7
Victoria	Dau. of Edward, 4th son of George III; married (1840) Prince Albert of Saxe-Coburg and Gotha, who became Prince Consort	**1837**	**1901**	81	63

House of Saxe-Coburg and Gotha

Edward VII	Eldest son of Victoria, married Alexandra, Princess of Denmark	**1901**	**1910**	68	9

House of Windsor

Name Adopted July 17, 1917

George V	2d son of Edward VII, married Princess Mary of Teck	**1910**	**1936**	70	25
Edward VIII	Eldest son of George V; acceded Jan. 20, 1936, abdicated Dec. 11	**1936**	**1972**	77	1
George VI	2d son of George V; married Lady Elizabeth Bowes-Lyon	**1936**	**1952**	56	15
Elizabeth II	Elder daughter of George VI, acceded Feb. 6, 1952	**1952**	—	—	—

Rulers of Scotland

Kenneth I MacAlpin was the first Scot to rule both Scots and Picts, 846 AD.

Duncan I was the first general ruler, 1034. Macbeth seized the kingdom 1040, was slain by Duncan's son, Malcolm III MacDuncan (Canmore), 1057.

Malcolm married Margaret, Saxon princess who had fled from the Normans. Queen Margaret introduced English language and English monastic customs. She was canonized, 1250. Her son Edgar, 1097, moved the court to Edinburgh. His brothers Alexander I and David I succeeded. Malcolm IV, the Maiden, 1153, grandson of David I, was followed by his brother, William the Lion, 1165, whose son was Alexander II, 1214. The latter's son, Alexander III, 1249, defeated the Norse and regained the Hebrides. When he died, 1286, his granddaughter, Margaret, child of Eric of Norway and grandniece of Edward I of England, known as the Maid of Norway, was chosen ruler, but died 1290, aged 8.

John Baliol, 1292-1296. (Interregnum, 10 years).

Robert Bruce (The Bruce), 1306-1329, victor at Bannockburn, 1314.

David II, only son of Robert Bruce, ruled 1329-1371.

Robert II, 1371-1390, grandson of Robert Bruce, son of Walter, the Steward of Scotland, was called The Steward, first of the so-called Stuart line.

Robert III, son of Robert II, 1390-1406.

James I, son of Robert III, 1406-1437.

James II, son of James I, 1437-1460.

James III, eldest son of James II, 1460-1488.

James IV, eldest son of James III, 1488-1513.

James V, eldest son of James IV, 1513-1542.

Mary, daughter of James V, born 1542, became queen when one week old; was crowned 1543. Married, 1558, Francis, son of Henry II of France, who became king 1559, died 1560. Mary ruled Scots 1561 until abdication, 1567. She also married (2) Henry Stewart, Lord Darnley, and (3) James, Earl of Bothwell. Imprisoned by Elizabeth I, Mary was beheaded 1587.

James VI, 1566-1625, son of Mary and Lord Darnley, became King of England on death of Elizabeth in 1603. Although the thrones were thus united, the legislative union of Scotland and England was not effected until the Act of Union, May 1, 1707.

Rulers of France: Kings, Queens, Presidents

Caesar to Charlemagne

Julius Caesar subdued the Gauls, native tribes of Gaul (France) 57 to 52 BC. The Romans ruled 500 years. The Franks, a Teutonic tribe, reached the Somme from the East ca. 250 AD. By the 5th century the Merovingian Franks ousted the Romans. In 451 AD, with the help of Visigoths, Burgundians and others, they defeated Attila and the Huns at Chalons-sur-Marne.

Childeric I became leader of the Merovingians 458 AD. His son Clovis I (Chlodwig, Ludwig, Louis), crowned 481, founded the dynasty. After defeating the Alemanni (Germans) 496, he was baptized a Christian and made Paris his capital. His line ruled until Childeric III was deposed, 751.

The West Merovingians were called Neustrians, the eastern

Austrasians. Pepin of Herstal (687-714) major domus, or head of the palace, of Austrasia, took over Neustria as dux (leader) of the Franks. Pepin's son, Charles, called Martel (the Hammer) defeated the Saracens at Tours-Poitiers, 732; was succeeded by his son, Pepin the Short, 741, who deposed Childeric III and ruled as king until 768.

His son, Charlemagne, or Charles the Great (742-814) became king of the Franks, 768, with his brother Carloman, who died 771. He ruled France, Germany, parts of Italy, Spain, Austria, and enforced Christianity. Crowned Emperor of the Romans by Pope Leo III in St. Peter's, Rome, Dec. 25, 800 AD. Succeeded by son, Louis I the Pious, 814. At death, 840, Louis left empire to sons, Lothair (Roman emperor); Pepin I (king of Aquitaine); Louis II (of Germany); Charles the Bald (France). They quarreled and by the peace of Verdun, 843, divided the empire.

AD Name, year of accession

The Carolingians

843 Charles I (the Bald), Roman Emperor, 875
877 Louis II (the Stammerer), son
879 Louis III (died 882) and Carloman, brothers
885 Charles II (the Fat), Roman Emperor, 881
888 Eudes (Odo) elected by nobles
898 Charles III (the Simple), son of Louis II, defeated by
922 Robert, brother of Eudes, killed in war
923 Rudolph (Raoul) Duke of Burgundy
936 Louis IV, son of Charles III
954 Lothair, son, aged 13, defeated by Capet
986 Louis V (the Sluggard), left no heirs

The Capets

987 Hugh Capet, son of Hugh the Great
996 Robert II (the Wise), his son
1031 Henry I, his son, last Norman
1060 Philip I (the Fair), son
1108 Louis VI (the Fat), son
1137 Louis VII (the Younger), son
1180 Philip II (Augustus), son, crowned at Reims
1223 Louis VIII (the Lion), son
1226 Louis IX, son, crusader; Louis IX (1214-1270) reigned 44 years, arbitrated disputes with English King Henry III; led crusades, 1248 (captured in Egypt 1250) and 1270, when he died of plague in Tunis. Canonized 1297 as St. Louis.
1270 Philip III (the Hardy), son
1285 Philip IV (the Fair), son, king at 17
1314 Louis X (the Headstrong), son. His posthumous son, John I, lived only 7 days
1316 Philip V (the Tall), brother of Louis X
1322 Charles IV (the Fair), brother of Louis X

House of Valois

1328 Philip VI (of Valois), grandson of Philip III
1350 John II (the Good), his son, retired to England
1364 Charles V (the Wise), son
1380 Charles VI (the Beloved), son
1422 Charles VII (the Victorious), son. In 1429 Joan of Arc (Jeanne d'Arc) promised Charles to oust the English, who occupied northern France. Joan won at Orleans and Patay and had Charles crowned at Reims July 17, 1429. Joan was captured May 24, 1430, and executed May 30, 1431, at Rouen for heresy. Charles ordered her rehabilitation, effected 1455.
1461 Louis XI (the Cruel), son, civil reformer
1483 Charles VIII (the Affable), son
1498 Louis XII, great-grandson of Charles V
1515 Francis I, of Angouleme, nephew, son-in-law. Francis I (1494-1547) reigned 32 years, fought 4 big wars, was patron of the arts, aided Cellini, del Sarto, Leonardo da Vinci, Rabelais, embellished Fontainebleau.
1547 Henry II, son, killed at a joust in a tournament. He was the husband of Catherine de Medicis (1519-1589) and the lover of Diane de Poitiers (1499-1566). Catherine was born in Florence, daughter of Lorenzo de Medicis. By her marriage to Henry II she became the mother of Francis II, Charles IX, Henry III and Queen Margaret (Reine Margot) wife of Henry IV. She persuaded Charles IX to order the massacre of Huguenots on the Feast of St. Bartholomew, Aug. 24, 1572, the day her daughter was married to Henry of Navarre.
1559 Francis II, son. In 1548, Mary, Queen of Scots since infancy, was betrothed when 6 to Francis, aged 4. They were married 1558. Francis died 1560, aged 16; Mary ruled Scotland, abdicated 1567.
1560 Charles IX, brother
1574 Henry III, brother, assassinated

House of Bourbon

1589 Henry IV, of Navarre, assassinated. Henry IV made enemies when he gave tolerance to Protestants by Edict of Nantes, 1598. He was grandson of Queen Margaret of Navarre, literary patron. He married Margaret of Valois, daughter of Henry II and Catherine de Medicis; was divorced; in 1600 married Marie de Medicis, who became Regent of France, 1610-17 for her son, Louis XIII, but was exiled by Richelieu, 1631.
1610 Louis XIII (the Just), son. Louis XIII (1601-1643) married Anne of Austria. His ministers were Cardinals Richelieu and Mazarin.
1643 Louis XIV (The Grand Monarch), son. Louis XIV was king 72 years. He exhausted a prosperous country in wars for thrones and territory. By revoking the Edict of Nantes (1685) he caused the emigration of the Huguenots. He said: "I am the state."
1715 Louis XV, great-grandson. Louis XV married a Polish princess; lost Canada to the English. His favorites, Mme. Pompadour and Mme. Du Barry, influenced policies. Noted for saying "After me, the deluge".
1774 Louis XVI, grandson; married Marie Antoinette, daughter of Empress Maria Therese of Austria. King and queen beheaded by Revolution, 1793. Their son, called Louis XVII, died in prison, never ruled.

First Republic

1792 National Convention of the French Revolution
1795 Directory, under Barras and others
1799 Consulate, Napoleon Bonaparte, first consul. Elected consul for life, 1802.

First Empire

1804 Napoleon I, emperor. Josephine (de Beauharnais) empress, 1804-09; Marie Louise, empress, 1810-1814. Her son, Francois (1811-1832), titular King of Rome, later Duke de Reichstadt and "Napoleon II," never ruled. Napoleon abdicated 1814, died 1821.

Bourbons Restored

1814 Louis XVIII king; brother of Louis XVI.
1824 Charles X, brother; reactionary; deposed by the July Revolution, 1830.

House of Orleans

1830 Louis-Philippe, the "citizen king."

Second Republic

1848 Louis Napoleon Bonaparte, president, nephew of Napoleon I. He became:

Second Empire

1852 Napoleon III, emperor; Eugenie (de Montijo) empress. Lost Franco-Prussian war, deposed 1870. Son, Prince Imperial (1856-79), died in Zulu War. Eugenie died 1920.

Third Republic—Presidents

1871 Thiers, Louis Adolphe (1797-1877)
1873 MacMahon, Marshal Patrice M. de (1808-1893)
1879 Grevy, Paul J. (1807-1891)
1887 Sadi-Carnot, M. (1837-1894), assassinated
1894 Casimir-Perier, Jean P. P. (1847-1907)
1895 Faure, Francois Felix (1841-1899)
1899 Loubet, Emile (1838-1929)
1906 Fallieres, C. Armand (1841-1931)
1913 Poincare, Raymond (1860-1934)
1920 Deschanel, Paul (1856-1922)
1920 Millerand, Alexandre (1859-1943)
1924 Doumergue, Gaston (1863-1937)
1931 Doumer, Paul (1857-1932), assassinated
1932 Lebrun, Albert (1871-1950), resigned 1940
1940 **Vichy govt.** under German armistice: Henri Philippe Petain (1856-1951) Chief of State, 1940-1944.
Provisional govt. after liberation: Charles de Gaulle (1890-1970) Oct. 1944-Jan. 21, 1946; Felix Gouin (1884-1977) Jan. 23, 1946; Georges Bidault (1899-) June 24, 1946.

Fourth Republic—Presidents

1947 Auriol, Vincent (1884-1966)
1954 Coty, Rene (1882-1962)

Fifth Republic—Presidents

1959 de Gaulle, Charles Andre J. M. (1890-1970)
1969 Pompidou, Georges (1911-1974)
1974 Giscard d'Estaing, Valery (1926-)
1981 Mitterrand, Francois (1916-)

Rulers of Middle Europe; Rise and Fall of Dynasties

Carolingian Dynasty

Charles the Great, or Charlemagne, ruled France, Italy, and Middle Europe; established Ostmark (later Austria); crowned Roman emperor by pope in Rome, 800 AD; died 814.

Louis I (Ludwig) the Pious, son; crowned by Charlemagne 814,

d. 840.

Louis II, the German, son; succeeded to East Francia (Germany) 843-876.

Charles the Fat, son; inherited East Francia and West Francia (France) 876, reunited empire, crowned emperor by pope, 881, deposed 887.

Arnulf, nephew, 887-899. Partition of empire.

Louis the Child, 899-911, last direct descendant of Charlemagne.

Conrad I, duke of Franconia, first elected German king, 911-918, founded House of Franconia.

Saxon Dynasty; First Reich

Henry I, the Fowler, duke of Saxony, 919-936.

Otto I, the Great, 936-973, son; crowned Holy Roman Emperor by pope, 962.

Otto II, 973-983, son; failed to oust Greeks and Arabs from Sicily.

Otto III, 983-1002, son; crowned emperor at 16.

Henry II, the Saint, duke of Bavaria, 1002-1024, great-grandson of Otto the Great.

House of Franconia

Conrad II, 1024-1039, elected king of Germany.

Henry III, the Black, 1039-1056, son; deposed 3 popes; annexed Burgundy.

Henry IV, 1056-1106, son; regency by his mother, Agnes of Poitou. Banned by Pope Gregory VII, he did penance at Canossa.

Henry V, 1106-1125, son; last of Salic House.

Lothair, duke of Saxony, 1125-1137. Crowned emperor in Rome, 1134.

House of Hohenstaufen

Conrad III, duke of Swabia, 1138-1152. In 2d Crusade.

Frederick I, Barbarossa, 1152-1190; Conrad's nephew.

Henry VI, 1190-1196, took lower Italy from Normans. Son became king of Sicily.

Philip of Swabia, 1197-1208, brother.

Otto IV, of House of Welf, 1198-1215; deposed.

Frederick II, 1215-1250, son of Henry VI; king of Sicily; crowned king of Jerusalem; in 5th Crusade.

Conrad IV, 1250-1254, son; lost lower Italy to Charles of Anjou.

Conradin (1252-1268) son, king of Jerusalem and Sicily, beheaded. Last Hohenstaufen.

Interregnum, 1254-1273, Rise of the Electors.

Transition

Rudolph I of Hapsburg, 1273-1291, defeated King Ottocar II of Bohemia. Bequeathed duchy of Austria to eldest son, Albert.

Adolph of Nassau, 1292-1298, killed in war with Albert of Austria.

Albert I, king of Germany, 1298-1308, son of Rudolph.

Henry VII, of Luxemburg, 1308-1313, crowned emperor in Rome. Seized Bohemia, 1310.

Louis IV of Bavaria (Wittelsbach), 1314-1347. Also elected was Frederick of Austria, 1314-1330 (Hapsburg). Abolition of papal sanction for election of Holy Roman Emperor.

Charles IV, of Luxemburg, 1347-1378, grandson of Henry VII, German emperor and king of Bohemia, Lombardy, Burgundy; took Mark of Brandenburg.

Wenceslaus, 1378-1400, deposed.

Rupert, Duke of Palatine, 1400-1410.

Hungary

Stephen I, house of Arpad, 997-1038. Crowned king 1000; converted Magyars; canonized 1083. After several centuries of feuds Charles Robert of Anjou became Charles I, 1308-1342.

Louis I, the Great, son, 1342-1382; joint ruler of Poland with Casimir III, 1370. Defeated Turks.

Mary, daughter, 1382-1395, ruled with husband. Sigismund of Luxemburg, 1387-1437, also king of Bohemia. As bro. of Wenceslaus he succeeded Rupert as Holy Roman Emperor, 1410.

Albert II, 1438-1439, son-in-law of Sigismund; also Roman emperor. *(see under Hapsburg.)*

Ulaszlo I of Poland, 1440-1444.

Ladislaus V, posthumous son of Albert II, 1444-1457. John Hunyadi (Hunyadi Janos) governor (1446-1452), fought Turks, Czechs; died 1456.

Matthias I (Corvinus) son of Hunyadi, 1458-1490. Shared rule of Bohemia, captured Vienna, 1485, annexed Austria, Styria, Carinthia.

Ladislas II (king of Bohemia), 1490-1516.

Louis II, son, aged 10, 1516-1526. Wars with Suleiman, Turk. In 1527 Hungary was split between Ferdinand I, Archduke of Austria, bro.-in-law of Louis II, and John Zapolya of Transylvania. After Turkish invasion, 1547, Hungary was split between Ferdinand, Prince John Sigismund (Transylvania) and the Turks.

House of Hapsburg

Albert V of Austria, Hapsburg, crowned king of Hungary, Jan. 1438, Roman emperor, March, 1438, as Albert II; died 1439.

Frederick III, cousin, 1440-1493. Fought Turks.

Maximilian I, son, 1493-1519. Assumed title of Holy Roman Emperor (German), 1493.

Charles V, grandson, 1519-1556. King of Spain with mother co-regent; crowned Roman emperor at Aix, 1520. Confronted Luther at Worms; attempted church reform and religious conciliation; abdicated 1556.

Ferdinand I, king of Bohemia, 1526, of Hungary, 1527; disputed. German king, 1531. Crowned Roman emperor on abdication of brother Charles V, 1556.

Maximilian II, son, 1564-1576.

Rudolph II, son, 1576-1612.

Matthias, brother, 1612-1619, king of Bohemia and Hungary.

Ferdinand II of Styria, king of Bohemia, 1617, of Hungary, 1618, Roman emperor, 1619. Bohemian Protestants deposed him, elected Frederick V of Palatine, starting Thirty Years War.

Ferdinand III, son, king of Hungary, 1625, Bohemia, 1627, Roman emperor, 1637. Peace of Westphalia, 1648, ended war. Leopold I, 1658-1705; Joseph I, 1705-1711; Charles VI, 1711-1740.

Maria Theresa, daughter, 1740-1780, Archduchess of Austria, queen of Hungary; ousted pretender, Charles VII, crowned 1742; in 1745 obtained election of her husband Francis I as Roman emperor and co-regent (d. 1765). Fought Seven Years' War with Frederick II (the Great) of Prussia. Mother of Marie Antoinette, Queen of France.

Joseph II, son 1765-1790, Roman emperor, reformer; powers restricted by Empress Maria Theresa until her death, 1780. First partition of Poland. Leopold II, 1790-1792.

Francis II, son, 1792-1835. Fought Napoleon. Proclaimed first hereditary emperor of Austria, 1804. Forced to abdicate as Roman emperor, 1806; last use of title. Ferdinand I, son, 1835-1848, abdicated during revolution.

Austro-Hungarian Monarchy

Francis Joseph I, nephew, 1848-1916, emperor of Austria, king of Hungary. Dual monarchy of Austria-Hungary formed, 1867. After assassination of heir, Archduke Francis Ferdinand, June 28, 1914, Austrian diplomacy precipitated World War I.

Charles I, grand-nephew, 1916-1918, last emperor of Austria and king of Hungary. Abdicated Nov. 11-13, 1918, died 1922.

Rulers of Prussia

Nucleus of Prussia was the Mark of Brandenburg. First margrave was Albert the Bear (Albrecht), 1134-1170. First Hohenzollern margrave was Frederick, burgrave of Nuremberg, 1417-1440.

Frederick William, 1640-1688, the Great Elector. Son, Frederick III, 1688-1713, was crowned King Frederick of Prussia, 1701.

Frederick William I, son, 1713-1740.

Frederick II, the Great, son, 1740-1786, annexed Silesia part of Austria.

Frederick William II, nephew, 1786-1797.

Frederick William III, son, 1797-1840. Napoleonic wars.

Frederick William IV, son, 1840-1861. Uprising of 1848 and first parliament and constitution.

Second and Third Reich

William I, 1861-1888, brother. Annexation of Schleswig and Hanover; Franco-Prussian war, 1870-71, proclamation of German Reich, Jan. 18, 1871, at Versailles; William, German emperor (Deutscher Kaiser), Bismarck, chancellor.

Frederick III, son, 1888.

William II, son, 1888-1918. Led Germany in World War I, abdicated as German emperor and king of Prussia, Nov. 9, 1918. Died in exile in Netherlands June 4, 1941. Minor rulers of Bavaria, Saxony, Wurttemberg also abdicated.

Germany proclaimed a republic at Weimar, July 1, 1919. Presidents: Frederick Ebert, 1919-1925, Paul von Hindenburg-Beneckendorff, 1925, reelected 1932, d. Aug. 2, 1934. Adolf Hitler, chancellor, chosen successor as Leader-Chancellor (Fuehrer & Reichskanzler) of Third Reich. Annexed Austria, March, 1938. Precipitated World War II, 1939-1945. Committed suicide April 30, 1945.

Rulers of Poland

House of Piasts

Miesko I, 962?-992; Poland Christianized 966. Expansion under 3 Boleslavs: I, 992-1025, son, crowned king 1024; II, 1058-1079, great-grandson, exiled after killing bishop Stanislav who became chief patron saint of Poland: III, 1106-1138, nephew, divided Poland among 4 sons eldest suzerain.

1138-1306, feudal division. 1226 founding in Prussia of military order Teutonic Knights. 1226 invasion by Tartars/Mongols.

Vladislav I, 1306-1333, reunited most Polish territories, crowned king 1320. Casimir III the Great, 1333-1370, son, developed economic, cultural life, foreign policy.

House of Anjou

Louis I, 1370-1382, nephew/identical with Louis I of Hungary.

Jadwiga, 1384-1399, daughter, married 1386 Jagiello, Grand Duke of Lituania.

House of Jagelloneans

Vladislav II, 1386-1434, Christianized Lituania, founded personal union between Poland & Lituania. Defeated 1410 Teutonic Knights at Grunwald.

Vladislav III, 1434-1444, son, simultaneously king of Hungary. Fought Turks, killed 1444 in battle of Varna.

Casimir IV, 1446-1492, brother, competed with Hapsburgs, put son Vladislav on throne of Bohemia, later also of Hungary.

Sigismund I, 1506-1548, brother, patronized science & arts, his & son's reign "Golden Age."

Sigismund II, 1548-1572, son, established 1569 real union of Poland and Lituania (lasted until 1795).

Elective kings

Polish nobles proclaimed 1572 Poland a Republic headed by king to be elected by whole nobility.

Stephen Batory, 1576-1586, duke of Transylvania, married Ann, sister of Sigismund II August. Fought Russians.

Sigismund III Vasa, 1587-1632, nephew of Sigismund II. 1592-1598 also king of Sweden. His generals fought Russians, Turks.

Vladislav II Vasa, 1632-1648, son. Fought Russians.

John II Casimir Vasa, 1648-1668, brother. Fought Cossacks, Swedes, Russians, Turks, Tartars (the "Deluge"). Abdicated 1668.

John III Sobieski, 1674-1696. Won Vienna from Turks, 1683.

Stanislav II, 1764-1795, last king. Encouraged reforms; 1791 1st modern Constitution in Europe. 1772, 1793, 1795 Poland partitioned among Russia, Prussia, Austria. Unsuccessful insurrection against foreign invasion 1794 under Kosciuszko, Amer-Polish gen.

1795-1918 Poland under foreign rule

1807-1815 Grand Duchy of Warsaw created by Napoleon I, Frederick August of Saxony grand duke.

1815 Congress of Vienna proclaimed part of Poland "Kingdom" in personal union with Russia.

Polish uprisings: 1830 against Russia, 1846, 1848 against Austria, 1863 against Russia—all repressed.

1918-1939 Second Republic

1918-1922 Head of State Jozef Pilsudski. Presidents: Gabriel Narutowicz 1933, assassinated. Stanislav Wojsiechowski 1922-1926, had to abdicate after Pilsudski's coup d'état. Ignacy Moscieckі, 1926-1939, ruled with Pilsudski as (until 1935) virtual dictator.

1939-1945 Poland under foreign occupation

Nazi aggression Sept. 1939. Polish govt.-in-exile, first in France, then in England. Vladislav Raczkiewicz pres., Gen. Vladislav Sikorski, then Stanislav Mikolajczyk, prime ministers. Polish Committee of Natl. Liberation proclaimed at Lublin July 1944, transformed into govt. Jan. 1, 1945.

Rulers of Denmark, Sweden, Norway

Denmark

Earliest rulers invaded Britain; King Canute, who ruled in London 1016-1035, was most famous. The Valdemars furnished kings until the 15th century. In 1282 the Danes won the first national assembly, Danehof, from King Erik V.

Most redoubtable medieval character was Margaret, daughter of Valdemar IV, born 1353, married at 10 to King Haakon VI of Norway. In 1376 she had her first infant son Olaf made king of Denmark. After his death, 1387, she was regent of Denmark and Norway. In 1388 Sweden accepted her as sovereign. In 1389 she made her grand-nephew, Duke Erik of Pomerania, titular king of Denmark, Sweden, and Norway, with herself as regent. In 1397 she effected the Union of Kalmar of the three kingdoms and had Erik VII crowned. In 1439 the three kingdoms deposed him and elected, 1440, Christopher of Bavaria king (Christopher III). On his death, 1448, the union broke up.

Succeeding rulers were unable to enforce their claims as rulers of Sweden until 1520, when Christian II conquered Sweden. He was thrown out 1522, and in 1523 Gustavus Vasa united Sweden. Denmark continued to dominate Norway until the Napoleonic wars, when Frederick VI, 1808-1839, joined the Napoleonic cause after Britain had destroyed the Danish fleet, 1807. In 1814 he was forced to cede Norway to Sweden and Helgoland to Britain, receiving Lauenburg. Successors Christian VIII, 1839; Frederick VII, 1848; Christian IX, 1863; Frederick VIII, 1906; Christian X, 1912; Frederick IX, 1947; Margrethe II, 1972.

Sweden

Early kings ruled at Uppsala, but did not dominate the country. Sverker, c1130-c1156, united the Swedes and Goths. In 1435 Sweden obtained the Riksdag, or parliament. After the Union of Kalmar, 1397, the Danes either ruled or harried the country until Christian II of Denmark conquered it anew, 1520. This led to a rising under Gustavus Vasa, who ruled Sweden 1523-1560, and established an independent kingdom. Charles IX, 1599-1611, crowned 1604, conquered Moscow. Gustavus II Adolphus, 1611-1632, was called the Lion of the North. Later rulers: Christina, 1632; Charles X, Gustavus 1654; Charles XI, 1660; Charles XII (invader of Russia and Poland, defeated at Poltava, June 28, 1709), 1697; Ulrika Eleanora, sister, elected queen 1718; Frederick I (of Hesse), her husband, 1720; Adolphus Frederick, 1751; Gustavus III, 1771; Gustavus IV Adolphus, 1792; Charles XIII, 1809. (Union with Norway began 1814.) Charles XIV John, 1818. He was Jean Bernadotte, Napoleon's Prince of Ponte Corvo, elected 1810 to succeed Charles XIII. He founded the present dynasty: Oscar I, 1844, Charles XV, 1859; Oscar II, 1872; Gustavus V, 1907; Gustav VI Adolf, 1950; Carl XVI Gustaf, 1973.

Norway

Overcoming many rivals, Harald Haarfager, 872-930, conquered Norway, Orkneys, and Shetlands; Olaf I, great-grandson, 995-1000, brought Christianity into Norway, Iceland, and Greenland. In 1035 Magnus the Good also became king of Denmark. Haakon V, 1299-1319, had married his daughter to Erik of Sweden. Their son, Magnus, became ruler of Norway and Sweden at 6. His son, Haakon VI, married Margaret of Denmark; their son Olaf IV became king of Norway and Denmark, followed by Margaret's regency and the Union of Kalmar, 1397.

In 1450 Norway became subservient to Denmark. Christian IV, 1588-1648, founded Christiania, now Oslo. After Napoleonic wars, when Denmark ceded Norway to Sweden, a strong nationalist movement forced recognition of Norway as an independent kingdom united with Sweden under the Swedish kings, 1814-1905. In 1905 the union was dissolved and Prince Carl of Denmark became Haakon VII. He died Sept. 21, 1957, aged 85; succeeded by son, Olav V, b. July 2, 1903.

Rulers of the Netherlands and Belgium

The Netherlands (Holland)

William Frederick, Prince of Orange, led a revolt against French rule, 1813, and was crowned King of the Netherlands, 1815. Belgium seceded Oct. 4, 1830, after a revolt, and formed a separate government. The change was ratified by the two kingdoms by treaty Apr. 19, 1839.

Succession: William II, son, 1840; William III, son, 1849; Wilhelmina, daughter of William III and his 2d wife Princess Emma of Waldeck, 1890; Wilhelmina abdicated, Sept. 4, 1948, in favor of daughter, Juliana. Juliana abdicated Apr. 30, 1980, in favor of daughter, Beatrix.

Belgium

A national congress elected Prince Leopold of Saxe-Coburg King; he took the throne July 21, 1831, as Leopold I. Succession: Leopold II, son 1865; Albert I, nephew of Leopold II, 1909; Leopold III, son of Albert, 1934; Prince Charles, Regent 1944; Leopold returned 1950, yielded powers to son Baudouin, Prince Royal, Aug. 6, 1950, abdicated July 16, 1951. Baudouin I took throne July 17, 1951.

For political history prior to 1830 see articles on the Netherlands and Belgium.

Roman Rulers

From Romulus to the end of the Empire in the West. Rulers of the Roman Empire in the East sat in Constantinople and for a brief period in Nicaea, until the capture of Constantinople by the Turks in 1453, when Byzantium was succeeded by the Ottoman Empire.

BC	Name
	The Kingdom
753	Romulus (Quirinus)
716	Numa Pompilius
673	Tullus Hostilius
640	Ancus Marcius
616	L. Tarquinius Priscus
578	Servius Tullius
534	L. Tarquinius Superbus
	The Republic
509	Consulate established
509	Quaestorship instituted
498	Dictatorship introduced
494	Plebeian Tribunate created
494	Plebeian Aedileship created
444	Consular Tribunate organized
435	Censorship instituted
366	Praetorship established
366	Curule Aedileship created
362	Military Tribunate elected
326	Proconsulate introduced
311	Naval Duumvirate elected
217	Dictatorship of Fabius Maximus
133	Tribunate of Tiberius Gracchus

123 Tribunate of Gaius Gracchus
82 Dictatorship of Sulla
60 First Triumvirate formed (Caesar, Pompeius, Crassus)
46 Dictatorship of Caesar
43 Second Triumvirate formed (Octavianus, Antonius, Lepidus)

The Empire

27 Augustus (Gaius Julius Caesar Octavianus)

AD

14 Tiberius I
37 Gaius Caesar (Caligula)
41 Claudius I
54 Nero
68 Galba
69 Galba; Otho, Vitellius
69 Vespasianus
79 Titus
81 Domitianus
96 Nerva
98 Trajanus
117 Hadrianus
138 Antoninus Pius
161 Marcus Aurelius and Lucius Verus
169 Marcus Aurelius (alone)
180 Commodus
193 Pertinax; Julianus I
193 Septimius Severus
211 Caracalla and Geta
212 Caracalla (alone)
217 Macrinus
218 Elagabalus (Heliogabalus)
222 Alexander Severus
235 Maximinus I (the Thracian)
238 Gordianus I and Gordianus II; Pupienus and Balbinus
238 Gordianus III
244 Philippus (the Arabian)
249 Decius
251 Gallus and Volusianus
253 Aemilianus
253 Valerianus and Gallienus
258 Gallienus (alone)
268 Claudius II (the Goth)
270 Quintillus
270 Aurelianus
275 Tacitus
276 Florianus
276 Probus
282 Carus
283 Carinus and Numerianus
284 Diocletianus
286 Diocletianus and Maximianus
305 Galerius and Constantius I
306 Galerius, Maximinus II, Severus I
307 Galerius, Maximinus II, Constantinus I, Licinius, Maxentius
311 Maximinus II, Constantinus I, Licinius, Maxentius
314 Maximinus II, Constantinus I, Licinius
314 Constantinus I and Licinius
324 Constantinus I (the Great)
337 Constantinus II, Constans I, Constantius II
340 Constantius II and Constans I
350 Constantius II
361 Julianus II (the Apostate)
363 Jovianus

West (Rome) and East (Constantinople)

364 Valentinianus I (West) and Valens (East)
367 Valentinianus I with Gratianus (West) and Valens (East)
375 Gratianus with Valentinianus II (West) and Valens (East)
378 Gratianus with Valentinianus II (West) Theodosius I (East)
383 Valentinianus II (West) and Theodosius I (East)
394 Theodosius I (the Great)
395 Honorius (West) and Arcadius (East)
408 Honorius (West) and Theodosius II (East)
423 Valentinianus III (West) and Theodosius II (East)
450 Valentinianus III (West) and Marcianus (East)
455 Maximus (West), Avitus (West); Marcianus (East)
456 Avitus (West), Marcianus (East)
457 Majorianus (West), Leo I (East)
461 Severus II (West), Leo I (East)
467 Anthemius (West), Leo I (East)
472 Olybrius (West), Leo I (East)
473 Glycerius (West), Leo I (East)
474 Julius Nepos (West), Leo II (East)
475 Romulus Augustulus (West) and Zeno (East)
476 End of Empire in West; Odovacar, King, drops title of Emperor; murdered by King Theodoric of Ostrogoths 493 AD

Rulers of Modern Italy

After the fall of Napoleon in 1814, the Congress of Vienna, 1815, restored Italy as a political patchwork, comprising the Kingdom of Naples and Sicily, the Papal States, and smaller units. Piedmont and Genoa were awarded to Sardinia, ruled by King Victor Emmanuel I of Savoy.

United Italy emerged under the leadership of Camillo, Count di Cavour (1810-1861), Sardinian prime minister. Agitation was led by Giuseppe Mazzini (1805-1872) and Giuseppe Garibaldi (1807-1882), soldier, Victor Emmanuel I abdicated 1821. After a brief regency for a brother, Charles Albert was King 1831-1849, abdicating when defeated by the Austrians at Novara. Succeeded by Victor Emmanuel II, 1849-1861.

In 1859 France forced Austria to cede Lombardy to Sardinia, which gave rights to Savoy and Nice to France. In 1860 Garibaldi led 1,000 volunteers in a spectacular campaign, took Sicily and expelled the King of Naples. In 1860 the House of Savoy annexed Tuscany, Parma, Modena, Romagna, the Two Sicilies, the Marches, and Umbria. Victor Emmanuel assumed the title of King of Italy at Turin Mar. 17, 1861. In 1866 he allied with Prussia in the Austro-Prussian War, with Prussia's victory received Venetia. On Sept. 20, 1870, his troops under Gen. Raffaele Cardorna entered Rome and took over the Papal States, ending the temporal power of the Roman Catholic Church.

Succession: Umberto I; 1878, assassinated 1900; Victor Emmanuel III, 1900, abdicated 1946, died 1947; Umberto II, 1946, ruled a month. In 1921 Benito Mussolini (1883-1945) formed the Fascist party and became prime minister Oct. 31, 1922. He made the King Emperor of Ethiopia, 1937; entered World War II as ally of Hitler. He was deposed July 25, 1943.

At a plebiscite June 2, 1946, Italy voted for a republic; Premier Alcide de Gasperi became chief of state June 13, 1946. On June 28, 1946, the Constituent Assembly elected Enrico de Nicola, Liberal, provisional president. Successive presidents: Luigi Einaudi, elected May 11, 1948, Giovanni Gronchi, Apr. 29, 1955; Antonio Segni, May 6, 1962; Giuseppe Saragat, Dec. 28, 1964; Giovanni Leone, Dec. 29, 1971; Alessandro Pertini, July 9, 1978.

Rulers of Spain

From 8th to 11th centuries Spain was dominated by the Moors (Arabs and Berbers). The Christian reconquest established small competing kingdoms of the Asturias, Aragon, Castile, Catalonia, Leon, Navarre, and Valencia. In 1474 Isabella (Isabel), b. 1451, became Queen of Castile & Leon. Her husband, Ferdinand, b. 1452, inherited Aragon 1479, with Catalonia, Valencia, and the Balearic Islands, became Ferdinand V of Castile. By Isabella's request Pope Sixtus IV established the Inquisition, 1478. Last Moorish kingdom, Granada, fell 1492. Columbus opened New World of colonies, 1492. Isabella died 1504, succeeded by her daughter, Juana "the Mad," but Ferdinand ruled until his death 1516.

Charles I, b. 1500, son of Juana and grandson of Ferdinand and Isabella, and of Maximilian I of Hapsburg; succeeded later as Holy Roman Emperor, Charles V, 1520; abdicated 1556. Philip II, son, 1556-1598, inherited only Spanish throne; conquered Portugal, fought Turks, persecuted non-Catholics, sent Armada against England. Was briefly married to Mary I of England, 1554-1558. Succession: Philip III, 1598-1621; Philip IV, 1621-1665; Charles II, 1665-1700, left Spain to Philip of Anjou, grandson of Louis XIV, who as Philip V, 1700-1746, founded Bourbon dynasty. Ferdinand VI, 1746-1759; Charles III, 1759-1788; Charles IV, 1788-1808, abdicated.

Napoleon now dominated politics and made his brother Joseph King of Spain 1808, but the Spanish ousted him finally in 1813. Ferdinand VII, 1808, 1814-1833, lost American colonies; succeeded by daughter Isabella II, aged 3, with wife Maria Christina of Naples regent until 1843. Isabella deposed by revolution 1868. Elected king by the Cortes, Amadeo of Savoy, 1870; abdicated 1873. First republic, 1873-1874. Alphonso XII, son of Isabella, 1875-1885. His posthumous son was Alphonso XIII, with his mother, Queen Maria Christina regent; Spanish-American war, Spain lost Cuba, gave up Puerto Rico, Philippines, Sulu Is., Marianas. Alphonso took throne 1902, aged 16, married British Princess Victoria Eugenia of Battenberg. The dictatorship of Primo de Rivera, 1923-30, precipitated the revolution of 1931. Alphonso agreed to leave without formal abdication. The monarchy was abolished and the second republic established, with strong socialist backing. Presidents were Niceto Alcala Zamora, to 1936, when Manuel Azaña was chosen.

In July, 1936, the army in Morocco revolted against the government and General Francisco Franco led the troops into Spain. The revolution succeeded by Feb., 1939, when Azaña resigned. Franco became chief of state, with provisions that if he was incapacitated the Regency Council by two-thirds vote may propose a king to the Cortes, which must have a two-thirds majority to elect him.

Alphonso XIII died in Rome Feb. 28, 1941, aged 54. His property and citizenship had been restored.

A succession law restoring the monarchy was approved in a 1947 referendum. Prince Juan Carlos, son of the pretender to the throne, was designated by Franco and the Cortes in 1969 as the future king and chief of state. Upon Franco's death, Nov. 20, 1975, Juan Carlos was proclaimed king, Nov. 22, 1975.

Leaders in the South American Wars of Liberation

Simon Bolivar (1783-1830), Jose Francisco de San Martin (1778-1850), and Francisco Antonio Gabriel Miranda (1750-1816), are among the heroes of the early 19th century struggles of South American nations to free themselves from Spain. All three, and their contemporaries, operated in periods of intense factional strife, during which soldiers and civilians suffered.

Miranda, a Venezuelan, who had served with the French in the American Revolution and commanded parts of the French Revolutionary armies in the Netherlands, attempted to start a revolt in Venezuela in 1806 and failed. In 1810, with British and American backing, he returned and was briefly a dictator, until the British withdrew their support. In 1812 he was overcome by the royalists in Venezuela and taken prisoner, dying in a Spanish prison in 1816.

San Martin was born in Argentina and during 1789-1811 served in campaigns of the Spanish armies in Europe and Africa. He first joined the independence movement in Argentina in 1812 and then in 1817 invaded Chile with 4,000 men over the high mountain passes. Here he and General Bernardo O'Higgins (1778-1842) defeated the Spaniards at Chacabuco, 1817, and O'Higgins was named Liberator and became first director of Chile, 1817-1823. In 1821 San Martin occupied Lima and Callao, Peru, and became protector of Peru.

Bolivar, the greatest leader of South American liberation from Spain, was born in Venezuela, the son of an aristocratic family. His organizing and administrative abilities were superior and he foresaw many of the political difficulties of the future. He first served under Miranda in 1812 and in 1813 captured Caracas, where he was named Liberator. Forced out next year by civil strife, he led a campaign that captured Bogota in 1814. In 1817 he was again in control of Venezuela and was named dictator. He organized Nueva Granada with the help of General Francisco de Paula Santander (1792-1840). By joining Nueva Granada, Venezuela, and the present terrain of Panama and Ecuador, the republic of Colombia was formed with Bolivar president. After numerous setbacks he decisively defeated the Spaniards in the second battle of Carabobo, Venezuela, June 24, 1821.

In May, 1822, Gen. Antonio Jose de Sucre, Bolivar's trusted lieutenant, took Quito. Bolivar went to Guayaquil to confer with San Martin, who resigned as protector of Peru and withdrew from politics. With a new army of Colombians and Peruvians Bolivar defeated the Spaniards in a saber battle at Junín in 1824 and cleared Peru.

De Sucre organized Charcas (Upper Peru) as Republica Bolivar (now Bolivia) and acted as president in place of Bolivar, who wrote its constitution. De Sucre defeated the Spanish faction of Peru at Ayacucho, Dec. 19, 1824.

Continued civil strife finally caused the Colombian federation to break apart. Santander turned against Bolivar, but the latter defeated him and banished him. In 1828 Bolivar gave up the presidency he had held precariously for 14 years. He became ill from tuberculosis and died Dec. 17, 1830. He was honored as the great liberator and is buried in the national pantheon in Caracas.

Rulers of Russia; Premiers of the USSR

First ruler to consolidate Slavic tribes was Rurik, leader of the Russians who established himself at Novgorod, 862 A.D. He and his immediate successors had Scandinavian affiliations. They moved to Kiev after 972 AD and ruled as Dukes of Kiev. In 988 Vladimir was converted and adopted the Byzantine Greek Orthodox service, later modified by Slav influences. Important as organizer and lawgiver was Yaroslav, 1019-1054, whose daughters married kings of Norway, Hungary, and France. His grandson, Vladimir II (Monomakh), 1113-1125, was progenitor of several rulers, but in 1169 Andrew Bogolubski overthrew Kiev and began the line known as Grand Dukes of Vladimir.

Of the Grand Dukes of Vladimir, Alexander Nevsky, 1246-1263, had a son, Daniel, first to be called Duke of Muscovy (Moscow) who ruled 1294-1303. His successors became Grand Dukes of Muscovy. After Dmitri III Donskoi defeated the Tartars in 1380, they also became Grand Dukes of all Russia. Independence of the Tartars and considerable territorial expansion were achieved under Ivan III, 1462-1505.

Tsars of Muscovy—Ivan III was referred to in church ritual as Tsar. He married Sofia, niece of the last Byzantine emperor. His successor, Basil III, died in 1533 when Basil's son Ivan was only 3. He became Ivan IV, "the Terrible"; crowned 1547 as Tsar of all the Russias, ruled till 1584. Under the weak rule of his son, Feodor I, 1584-1598, Boris Godunov had control. The dynasty died, and after years of tribal strife and intervention by Polish and Swedish armies, the Russians united under 17-year-old Michael Romanov, distantly related to the first wife of Ivan IV. He ruled 1613-1645 and established the Romanov line. Fourth ruler after Michael was Peter I.

Tsars, or Emperors of Russia (Romanovs)—Peter I, 1682-1725, known as Peter the Great, took title of Emperor in 1721. His successors and dates of accession were: Catherine, his widow, 1725, Peter II, his grandson, 1727-1730; Anne, Duchess of Courland, 1730, daughter of Peter the Great's brother, Tsar Ivan V; Ivan VI, 1740-1741, great-grandson of Ivan V, child, kept in prison and murdered 1764; Elizabeth, daughter of Peter I, 1741; Peter III, grandson of Peter I, 1761, deposed 1762 for his consort, Catherine II, former princess of Anhalt Zerbst (Germany) who is known as Catherine the Great, 1762-1796; Paul I, her son, 1796, killed 1801; Alexander I, son of Paul, 1801-1825, defeated Napoleon; Nicholas I, his brother, 1825; Alexander II, son of Nicholas, 1855, assassinated 1881 by terrorists; Alexander III, son, 1881-1894.

Nicholas II, son, 1894-1917, last Tsar of Russia, was forced to abdicate by the Revolution that followed losses to Germany in WWI. The Tsar, the Empress, the Tsesarevich (Crown Prince) and the Tsar's 4 daughters were murdered by the Bolsheviks in Ekaterinburg, July 16, 1918.

Provisional Government—Prince Georgi Lvov and Alexander Kerensky, premiers, 1917.

Union of Soviet Socialist Republics

Bolshevik Revolution, Nov. 7, 1917, displaced Kerensky; council of People's Commissars formed, Lenin (Vladimir Ilyich Ulyanov), premier. Lenin died Jan. 21, 1924. Aleksei Rykov (executed 1938) and V. M. Molotov held the office, but actual ruler was Joseph Stalin (Joseph Vissarionovich Djugashvili), general secretary of the Central Committee of the Communist Party. Stalin became president of the Council of Ministers (premier) May 7, 1941, died Mar. 5, 1953. Succeeded by Georgi M. Malenkov, as head of the Council and premier and Nikita S. Khrushchev, first secretary of the Central Committee. Malenkov resigned Feb. 8, 1955, became deputy premier, was dropped July 3, 1957. Marshal Nikolai A. Bulganin became premier Feb. 8, 1955; was demoted and Khrushchev became premier Mar. 27 1958. Khrushchev was ousted Oct. 14-15, 1964, replaced by Leonid I. Brezhnev as first secretary of the party and by Aleksei N. Kosygin as premier. On June 16, 1977, Brezhnev took office as president.

Governments of China

(Until 221 BC and frequently thereafter, China was not a unified state. Where dynastic dates overlap, the rulers or events referred to appeared in different areas of China.)

Hsia	c1994BC	-	c1523BC
Shang	c1523	-	c1028
Western Chou	c1027	-	770
Eastern Chou	770	-	256
Warring States	403	-	222
Ch'in (first unified empire)	221	-	206
Han	202BC	-	220AD
Western Han (expanded Chinese state beyond the Yellow and Yangtze River valleys)	202BC	-	9AD
Hsin (Wang Mang, usurper)	9AD	-	23AD
Eastern Han (expanded Chinese state into Indo-China and Turkestan)	25	-	220
Three Kingdoms (Wei, Shu, Wu)	220	-	265
Chin (western)	265	-	317
(eastern)	317	-	420
Northern Dynasties (followed several short-lived governments by Turks, Mongols, etc.)	386	-	581
Southern Dynasties (capital: Nanking)	420	-	589
Sui (reunified China)	581	-	618
Tang (a golden age of Chinese culture; capital: Sian)	618	-	906
Five Dynasties (Yellow River basin)	902	-	960
Ten Kingdoms (southern China)	907	-	979
Liao (Khitan Mongols; capital: Peking)	947	-	1125
Sung	960	-	1279
Northern Sung (reunified central and southern China)	960	-	1126
Western Hsai (non-Chinese rulers in northwest)	990	-	1227
Chin (Tartars; drove Sung out of central China)	1115	-	1234
Yuan (Mongols; Kublai Khan made Peking his capital in 1267)	1271	-	1368
Ming (China reunified under Chinese rule; capital: Nanking, then Peking in 1420)	1368	-	1644
Ch'ing (Manchus, descendents of Tartars)	1644	-	1911
Republic (disunity; provincial rulers, warlords)	1912	-	1949
People's Republic of China (Nationalist China established on Taiwan)	1949	-	—

Chronological List of Popes

Source: Annuario Pontificio. Table lists year of accession of each Pope.

The Roman Catholic Church names the Apostle Peter as founder of the Church in Rome. He arrived there c. 42, was martyred there c. 67, and raised to sainthood.

The Pope's temporal title is: Sovereign of the State of Vatican City.

The Pope's spiritual titles are: Bishop of Rome, Vicar of Jesus Christ, Successor of St. Peter, Prince of the Apostles, Supreme Pontiff of the Universal Church, Patriarch of the West, Primate of Italy, Archbishop and Metropolitan of the Roman Province.

Anti-Popes are in *Italics*. Anti-Popes were illegitimate claimants of or pretenders to the papal throne.

Year	Name of Pope
See above.	St. Peter
67	St. Linus
76	St. Anacletus or Cletus
88	St. Clement I
97	St. Evaristus
105	St. Alexander I
115	St. Sixtus I
125	St. Telesphorus
136	St. Hyginus
140	St. Pius I
155	St. Anicetus
166	St. Soter
175	St. Eleutherius
189	St. Victor I
199	St. Zephyrinus
217	St. Callistus I
217	*St. Hippolytus*
222	St. Urban I
230	St. Pontian
235	St. Anterus
236	St. Fabian
251	St. Cornelius
251	*Novatian*
253	St. Lucius I
254	St. Stephen I
257	St. Sixtus II
259	St. Dionysius
269	St. Felix I
275	St. Eutychian
283	St. Caius
296	St. Marcellinus
308	St. Marcellus I
309	St. Eusebius
311	St. Melchiades
314	St. Sylvester I
336	St. Marcus
337	St. Julius I
352	Liberius
355	*Felix II*
366	St. Damasus I
366	*Ursinus*
384	St. Siricius
399	St. Anastasius I
401	St. Innocent I
417	St. Zosimus
418	St. Boniface I
418	*Eulalius*
422	St. Celestine I
432	St. Sixtus III
440	St. Leo I
461	St. Hilary
468	St. Simplicius
483	St. Felix III (II)
492	St. Gelasius I
496	Anastasius II
498	St. Symmachus
498	*Lawrence (501-505)*
514	St. Hormisdas
523	St. John I, Martyr
526	St. Felix IV (III)
530	Boniface II
530	*Dioscorus*
533	John II
535	St. Agapitus I
536	St. Silverius, Martyr
537	Vigilius
556	Pelagius I
561	John III
575	Benedict I
579	Pelagius II
590	St. Gregory I
604	Sabinian
607	Boniface III
608	St. Boniface IV
615	St. Deusdedit or Adeodatus
619	Boniface V
625	Honorius I
640	Severinus
640	John IV
642	Theodore I
649	St. Martin I, Martyr
654	St. Eugene I
657	St. Vitalian
672	Adeodatus II
676	Donus
678	St. Agatho
682	St. Leo II
684	St. Benedict II
685	John V
686	Conon
687	*Theodore*
687	*Paschal*
687	St. Sergius I
701	John VI
705	John VII
708	Sisinnius
708	Constantine
715	St. Gregory II
731	St. Gregory III
741	St. Zachary
752	Stephen II (III)
757	St. Paul I
767	*Constantine*
768	*Philip*
768	Stephen III (IV)
772	Adrian I
795	St. Leo III
816	Stephen IV (V)
817	St. Paschal I
824	Eugene II
827	Valentine
827	Gregory IV
844	*John*
844	Sergius II
847	St. Leo IV
855	Benedict III
855	*Anastasius*
858	St. Nicholas I
867	Adrian II
872	John VIII
882	Marinus I
884	St. Adrian III
885	Stephen V (VI)
891	Formosus
896	Boniface VI
896	Stephen VI (VII)
897	Romanus
897	Theodore II
898	John IX
900	Benedict IV
903	Leo V
903	*Christopher*
904	Sergius III
911	Anastasius III
913	Landus
914	John X
928	Leo VI
928	Stephen VII (VIII)
931	John XI
936	Leo VII
939	Stephen VIII (IX)
942	Marinus II
946	Agapitus II
955	John XII
963	Leo VIII
964	Benedict V
965	John XIII
973	Benedict VI
974	*Boniface VII*
974	Benedict VII
983	John XIV
985	John XV
996	Gregory V
997	*John XVI*
999	Sylvester II
1003	John XVII
1004	John XVIII
1009	Sergius IV
1012	Benedict VIII
1012	*Gregory*
1024	John XIX
1032	Benedict IX
1045	Sylvester III
1045	Benedict IX
1045	Gregory VI
1046	Clement II
1047	Benedict IX
1048	Damasus II
1049	St. Leo IX
1055	Victor II
1057	Stephen IX (X)
1058	*Benedict X*
1059	Nicholas II
1061	Alexander II
1061	*Honorius II*
1073	St. Gregory VII
1080	*Clement III*
1086	Bl. Victor III
1088	Bl. Urban II
1099	Paschal II
1100	*Theodoric*
1102	*Albert*
1105	*Sylvester IV*
1118	Gelasius II
1118	*Gregory VIII*
1119	Callistus II
1124	Honorius II
1124	*Celestine II*
1130	Innocent II
1130	*Anacletus II*
1138	*Victor IV*
1143	Celestine II
1144	Lucius II
1145	Bl. Eugene III
1153	Anastasius IV
1154	Adrian IV
1159	Alexander III
1159	*Victor IV*
1164	*Paschal III*
1168	*Callistus III*
1179	*Innocent III*
1181	Lucius III
1185	Urban III
1187	Gregory VIII
1187	Clement III
1191	Celestine III
1198	Innocent III
1216	Honorius III
1227	Gregory IX
1241	Celestine IV
1243	Innocent IV
1254	Alexander IV
1261	Urban IV
1265	Clement IV
1271	Bl. Gregory X
1276	Bl. Innocent V
1276	Adrian V
1276	John XXI
1277	Nicholas III
1281	Martin IV
1285	Honorius IV
1288	Nicholas IV
1294	St. Celestine V
1294	Boniface VIII
1303	Bl. Benedict XI
1305	Clement V
1316	John XXII
1328	*Nicholas V*
1334	Benedict XII
1342	Clement VI
1352	Innocent VI
1362	Bl. Urban V
1370	Gregory XI
1378	Urban VI
1378	*Clement VII*
1389	Boniface IX
1394	*Benedict XIII*
1404	Innocent VII
1406	Gregory XII
1409	*Alexander V*
1410	*John XXIII*
1417	Martin V
1431	Eugene IV
1439	*Felix V*
1447	Nicholas V
1455	Callistus III
1458	Pius II
1464	Paul II
1471	Sixtus IV
1484	Innocent VIII
1492	Alexander VI
1503	Pius III
1503	Julius II
1513	Leo X
1522	Adrian VI
1523	Clement VII
1534	Paul III
1550	Julius III
1555	Marcellus II
1555	Paul IV
1559	Pius IV
1566	St. Pius V
1572	Gregory XIII
1585	Sixtus V
1590	Urban VII
1590	Gregory XIV
1591	Innocent IX
1592	Clement VIII
1605	Leo XI
1605	Paul V
1621	Gregory XV
1623	Urban VIII
1644	Innocent X
1655	Alexander VII
1667	Clement IX
1670	Clement X
1676	Bl. Innocent XI
1689	Alexander VIII
1691	Innocent XII
1700	Clement XI
1721	Innocent XIII
1724	Benedict XIII
1730	Clement XII
1740	Benedict XIV
1758	Clement XIII
1769	Clement XIV
1775	Pius VI
1800	Pius VII
1823	Leo XII
1829	Pius VIII
1831	Gregory XVI
1846	Pius IX
1878	Leo XIII
1903	St. Pius X
1914	Benedict XV
1922	Pius XI
1939	Pius XII
1958	John XXIII
1963	Paul VI
1978	John Paul I
1978	John Paul II

AWARDS — MEDALS — PRIZES

The Alfred B. Nobel Prize Winners

Alfred B. Nobel, inventor of dynamite, bequeathed $9,000,000, the interest to be distributed yearly to those who had most benefited mankind in physics, chemistry, medicine-physiology, literature, and peace. The first Nobel Memorial Prize in Economics was awarded in 1969. No awards given for years omitted. In 1981, each prize was worth approximately $180,000.

Physics

1981 Nicolaas Boembergen, Arthur Schlawlow, both U.S.; Kai M. Siegbahn, Swedish
1980 James W. Cronin, Val L. Fitch, both U.S.
1979 Steven Weinberg, Sheldon L. Glashow, both U.S.; Abdus Salam, Pakistani
1978 Pyotr Kapitsa, USSR; Arno Penzias, Robert Wilson, both U.S.
1977 John H. Van Vleck, Philip W. Anderson, both U.S.; Nevill F. Mott, British
1976 Burton Richter, U.S.
Samuel C.C. Ting, U.S.
1975 James Rainwater, U.S.
Ben Mottelson, U.S.-Danish,
Aage Bohr, Danish
1974 Martin Ryle, British
Antony Hewish, British
1973 Ivar Giaever, U.S.
Leo Esaki, Japan
Brian D. Josephson, British
1972 John Bardeen, U.S.
Leon N. Cooper, U.S.
John R. Schrieffer, U.S.
1971 Dennis Gabor, British
1970 Louis Neel, French
Hannes Alfven, Swedish
1969 Murray Gell-Mann, U.S.
1968 Luis W. Alvarez, U.S.
1967 Hans A. Bethe, U.S.
1966 Alfred Kastler, French
1965 Richard P. Feynman, U.S.
Julian S. Schwinger, U.S.
Shinichiro Tomonaga, Japanese
1964 Nikolai G. Basov, USSR
Aleksander M. Prochorov, USSR
Charles H. Townes, U.S.
1963 Maria Goeppert-Mayer, U.S.
J. Hans D. Jensen, German
Eugene P. Wigner, U.S.
1962 Lev. D. Landau, USSR
1961 Robert Hofstadter, U.S.
Rudolf L. Mossbauer, German
1960 Donald A. Glaser, U.S.
1959 Owen Chamberlain, U.S.
Emilio G. Segre, U.S.
1958 Pavel Cherenkov, Ilya Frank, Igor Y. Tamm, all USSR
1957 Tsung-dao Lee, Chen Ning Yang, both U.S.
1956 John Bardeen, U.S.
Walter H. Brattain, U.S.
William Shockley, U.S.
1955 Polykarp Kusch, U.S.
Willis E. Lamb, U.S.
1954 Max Born, British
Walter Bothe, German
1953 Frits Zernike, Dutch
1952 Felix Bloch, U.S.
Edward M. Purcell, U.S.
1951 Sir John D. Cockroft, British
Ernest T. S. Walton, Irish
1950 Cecil F. Powell, British
1949 Hideki Yukawa, Japanese
1948 Patrick M. S. Blackett, British
1947 Sir Edward V. Appleton, British
1946 Percy Williams Bridgman, U.S.
1945 Wolfgang Pauli, U.S.
1944 Isidor Isaac Rabi, U.S.
1943 Otto Stern, U.S.
1939 Ernest O. Lawrence, U.S.
1938 Enrico Fermi, U.S.
1937 Clinton J. Davisson, U.S.
Sir George P. Thomson, British
1936 Carl D. Anderson, U.S.
Victor F. Hess, Austrian
1935 Sir James Chadwick, British
1933 Paul A. M. Dirac, British
Erwin Schrodinger, Austrian
1932 Werner Heisenberg, German
1930 Sir Chandrasekhara V. Raman, Indian
1929 Prince Louis-Victor de Broglie, French
1928 Owen W. Richardson, British
1927 Arthur H. Compton, U.S.
Charles T. R. Wilson, British
1926 Jean B. Perrin, French
1925 James Franck, Gustav Hertz, both German
1924 Karl M. G. Siegbahn, Swedish
1923 Robert A. Millikan, U.S.
1922 Niels Bohr, Danish
1921 Albert Einstein, Ger.-U.S.
1920 Charles E. Guillaume, French
1919 Johannes Stark, German
1918 Max K. E. L. Planck, German
1917 Charles G. Barkla, British
1915 Sir William H. Bragg, British
Sir William L. Bragg, British
1914 Max von Laue, German
1913 Heike Kamerlingh-Onnes, Dutch
1912 Nils G. Dalen, Swedish
1911 Wilhelm Wien, German
1910 Johannes D. van der Waals, Dutch
1909 Carl F. Braun, German
Guglielmo Marconi, Italian
1908 Gabriel Lippmann, French
1907 Albert A. Michelson, U.S.
1906 Sir Joseph J. Thomson, British
1905 Philipp E. A. von Lenard, Ger.
1904 John W. Strutt, Lord Rayleigh, British
1903 Antoine Henri Becquerel, French
Marie Curie, Polish-French
Pierre Curie, French
1902 Hendrik A. Lorentz, Pieter Zeeman, both Dutch
1901 Wilhelm C. Roentgen, German

Chemistry

1981 Kenichi Fukui, Japan,
Roald Hoffmann, U.S.
1980 Paul Berg., U.S.;
Walter Gilbert, U.S.,
Frederick Sanger, U.K.
1979 Herbert C. Brown, U.S.
George Wittig, German
1978 Peter Mitchell, British
1977 Ilya Prigogine, Belgian
1976 William N. Lipscomb, U.S.
1975 John Cornforth, Austral.-Brit.,
Vladimir Prelog, Yugo.-Switz.
1974 Paul J. Flory, U.S.
1973 Ernst Otto Fischer, W. German
Geoffrey Wilkinson, British
1972 Christian B. Anfinsen, U.S.
Stanford Moore, U.S.
William H. Stein, U.S.
1971 Gerhard Herzberg, Canadian
1970 Luis F. Leloir, Arg.
1969 Derek H. R. Barton, British
Odd Hassel, Norwegian
1968 Lars Onsager, U.S.
1967 Manfred Eigen, German
Ronald G. W. Norrish, British
George Porter, British
1966 Robert S. Mulliken, U.S.
1965 Robert B. Woodward, U.S.
1964 Dorothy C. Hodgkin, British
1963 Giulio Natta, Italian
Karl Ziegler, German
1962 John C. Kendrew, British
Max F. Perutz, British
1961 Melvin Calvin, U.S.
1960 Willard F. Libby, U.S.
1959 Jaroslav Heyrovsky, Czech
1958 Frederick Sanger, British
1957 Sir Alexander R. Todd, British
1956 Sir Cyril N. Hinshelwood, British
Nikolai N. Semenov, USSR
1955 Vincent du Vigneaud, U.S.
1954 Linus C. Pauling, U.S.
1953 Hermann Staudinger, German
1952 Archer J. P. Martin, British
Richard L. M. Synge, British
1951 Edwin M. McMillan, U.S.
Glenn T. Seaborg, U.S.
1950 Kurt Alder, German
Otto P. H. Diels, German
1949 William F. Giauque, U.S.
1948 Arne W. K. Tiselius, Swedish
1947 Sir Robert Robinson, British
1946 James B. Sumner, John H. Northrop, Wendell M. Stanley, all U.S.
1945 Artturi I. Virtanen, Finnish
1944 Otto Hahn, German
1943 Georg de Hevesy, Hungarian
1939 Adolf F. J. Butenandt, German
Leopold Ruzicka, Swiss
1938 Richard Kuhn, German
1937 Walter N. Haworth, British
Paul Karrer, Swiss
1936 Peter J. W. Debye, Dutch
1935 Frederic Joliot-Curie, French
Irene Joliot-Curie, French
1934 Harold C. Urey, U.S.
1932 Irving Langmuir, U.S.
1931 Friedrich Bergius, German
Karl Bosch, German
1930 Hans Fischer, German
1929 Sir Arthur Harden, British
Hans von Euler-Chelpin, Swed.
1928 Adolf O. R. Windaus, German
1927 Heinrich O. Wieland, German
1926 Theodor Svedberg, Swedish
1925 Richard A. Zsigmondy, German
1923 Fritz Pregl, Austrian
1922 Francis W. Aston, British
1921 Frederick Soddy, British
1920 Walther H. Nernst, German
1918 Fritz Haber, German
1915 Richard M. Willstatter, German
1914 Theodore W. Richards, U.S.
1913 Alfred Werner, Swiss
1912 Victor Grignard, French
Paul Sabatier, French
1911 Marie Curie, Polish-French
1910 Otto Wallach, German
1909 Wilhelm Ostwald, German
1908 Ernest Rutherford, British
1907 Eduard Buchner, German
1906 Henri Moissan, French
1905 Adolf von Baeyer, German
1904 Sir William Ramsay, British
1903 Svante A. Arrhenius, Swedish
1902 Emil Fischer, German
1901 Jacobus H. van't Hoff, Dutch

Physiology or Medicine

1981 Roger W. Sperry, David H. Hubel, Tosten N. Wiesel, all U.S.

1980 Baruj Benacerraf, George Snell, both U.S.; Jean Dausset, France

1979 Alian M. Cormack, U.S. Geoffrey N. Hounsfield, British

1978 Daniel Nathans, Hamilton O. Smith, both U.S.; Werner Arber, Swiss

1977 Rosalyn S. Yalow, Roger C.L. Guillemin, Andrew V. Schally, all U.S.

1976 Baruch S. Blumberg, U.S. Daniel Carleton Gajdusek, U.S.

1975 David Baltimore, Howard Temin, both U.S.; Renato Dulbecco, Ital.-U.S.

1974 Albert Claude, Lux.-U.S.; George Emil Palade, Rom.-U.S.; Christian Rene de Duve, Belg.

1973 Karl von Frisch, Ger.; Konrad Lorenz, Ger.-Austrian; Nikolaas Tinbergen, Brit.

1972 Gerald M. Edelman, U.S. Rodney R. Porter, British

1971 Earl W. Sutherland Jr., U.S.

1970 Julius Axelrod, U.S. Sir Bernard Katz, British Ulf von Euler, Swedish

1969 Max Delbruck, Alfred D. Hershey, Salvador Luria, all U.S.

1968 Robert W. Holley, H. Gobind Khorana, Marshall W. Nirenberg, all U.S.

1967 Ragnar Granit, Swedish Haldan Keffer Hartline, U.S. George Wald, U.S.

1966 Charles B. Huggins, Francis Peyton Rous, both U.S.

1965 Francois Jacob, Andre Lwoff, Jacques Monod, all French

1964 Konrad E. Bloch, U.S. Feodor Lynen, German

1963 Sir John C. Eccles, Australian Alan L. Hodgkin, British Andrew F. Huxley, British

1962 Francis H. C. Crick, British James D. Watson, U.S. Maurice H. F. Wilkins, British

1961 Georg von Bekesy, U.S.

1960 Sir F. MacFarlane Burnet, Australian Peter B. Medawar, British

1959 Arthur Kornberg, U.S. Severo Ochoa, U.S.

1958 George W. Beadle, U.S. Edward L. Tatum, U.S. Joshua Lederberg, U.S.

1957 Daniel Bovet, Italian

1956 Andre F. Cournand, U.S. Werner Forssmann, German Dickinson W. Richards, Jr., U.S.

1955 Alex H. T. Theorell, Swedish

1954 John F. Enders, Frederick C. Robbins, Thomas H. Weller, all U.S.

1953 Hans A. Krebs, British Fritz A. Lipmann, U.S.

1952 Selman A. Waksman, U.S.

1951 Max Theiler, U.S.

1950 Philip S. Hench, Edward C. Kendall, both U.S. Tadeus Reichstein, Swiss

1949 Walter R. Hess, Swiss Antonio Moniz, Portuguese

1948 Paul H. Müller, Swiss

1947 Carl F. Cori, Gerty T. Cori, both U.S. Bernardo A. Houssay, Arg.

1946 Hermann J. Muller, U.S.

1945 Ernst B. Chain, British Sir Alexander Fleming, British Sir Howard W. Florey, British

1944 Joseph Erlanger, U.S. Herbert S. Gasser, U.S.

1943 Henrik C. P. Dam, Danish Edward A. Doisy, U.S.

1939 Gerhard Domagk, German

1938 Corneille J. F. Heymans, Belg.

1937 Albert Szent-Gyorgyi, U.S.

1936 Sir Henry H. Dale, British Otto Loewi, U.S.

1935 Hans Spemann, German

1934 George R. Minot, Wm. P. Murphy, G. H. Whipple, all U.S.

1933 Thomas H. Morgan, U.S.

1932 Edgar D. Adrian, British Sir Charles S. Sherrington, Brit.

1931 Otto H. Warburg, German

1930 Karl Landsteiner, U.S.

1929 Christiaan Eijkman, Dutch Sir Frederick G. Hopkins, British

1928 Charles J. H. Nicolle, French

1927 Julius Wagner-Jauregg, Aus.

1926 Johannes A. G. Fibiger, Danish

1924 Willem Einthoven, Dutch

1923 Frederick G. Banting, Canadian John J. R. Macleod, Scottish

1922 Archibald V. Hill, British Otto F. Meyerhof, German

1920 Schack A. S. Krogh, Danish

1919 Jules Bordet, Belgian

1914 Robert Barany, Austrian

1913 Charles R. Richet, French

1912 Alexis Carrel, French

1911 Allvar Gullstrand, Swedish

1910 Albrecht Kossel, German

1909 Emil T. Kocher, Swiss

1908 Paul Ehrlich, German Elie Metchnikoff, French

1907 Charles L. A. Laveran, French

1906 Camillo Golgi, Italian Santiago Ramon y Cajal, Sp.

1905 Robert Koch, German

1904 Ivan P. Pavlov, Russian

1903 Niels R. Finsen, Danish

1902 Sir Ronald Ross, British

1901 Emil A. von Behring, German

Literature

1981 Elias Cenetti, Bulgarian-British

1980 Czeslaw Milosz, Polish-U.S.

1979 Odysseus Elytis, Greek

1978 Isaac Bashevis Singer, U.S. (Yiddish)

1977 Vicente Aleixandre, Spanish

1976 Saul Bellow, U.S.

1975 Eugenio Montale, Ital.

1974 Eyvind Johnson, Harry Edmund Martinson, both Swedish

1973 Patrick White, Australian

1972 Heinrich Boll, W. German

1971 Pablo Neruda, Chilean

1970 Aleksandr I. Solzhenitsyn, Russ.

1969 Samuel Beckett, Irish

1968 Yasunari Kawabata, Japanese

1967 Miguel Angel Asturias, Guate.

1966 Samuel Joseph Agnon, Israeli Nelly Sachs, Swedish

1965 Mikhail Sholokhov, Russian

1964 Jean Paul Sartre, French (Prize declined)

1963 Giorgos Seferis, Greek

1962 John Steinbeck, U.S.

1961 Ivo Andric, Yugoslavian

1960 Saint-John Perse, French

1959 Salvatore Quasimodo, Italian

1958 Boris L. Pasternak, Russian (Prize declined)

1957 Albert Camus, French

1956 Juan Ramon Jimenez, Puerto Rican-Span.

1955 Halldor K. Laxness, Icelandic

1954 Ernest Hemingway, U.S.

1953 Sir Winston Churchill, British

1952 Francois Mauriac, French

1951 Par F. Lagerkvist, Swedish

1950 Bertrand Russell, British

1949 William Faulkner, U.S.

1948 T.S. Eliot, British

1947 Andre Gide, French

1946 Hermann Hesse, Swiss

1945 Gabriela Mistral, Chilean

1944 Johannes V. Jensen, Danish

1939 Frans E. Sillanpaa, Finnish

1938 Pearl S. Buck, U.S.

1937 Roger Martin du Gard, French

1936 Eugene O'Neill, U.S.

1934 Luigi Pirandello, Italian

1933 Ivan A. Bunin, French

1932 John Galsworthy, British

1931 Erik A. Karlfeldt, Swedish

1930 Sinclair Lewis, U.S.

1929 Thomas Mann, German

1928 Sigrid Undset, Norwegian

1927 Henri Bergson, French

1926 Grazia Deledda, Italian

1925 George Bernard Shaw, British

1924 Wladyslaw S. Reymont, Polish

1923 William Butler Yeats, Irish

1922 Jacinto Benavente, Spanish

1921 Anatole France, French

1920 Knut Hamsun, Norwegian

1919 Carl F. G. Spitteler, Swiss

1917 Karl A. Gjellerup, Danish Henrik Pontoppidan, Danish

1916 Verner von Heidenstam, Swed.

1915 Romain Rolland, French

1913 Rabindranath Tagore, Indian

1912 Gerhart Hauptmann, German

1911 Maurice Maeterlinck, Belgian

1910 Paul J. L. Heyse, German

1909 Selma Lagerlof, Swedish

1908 Rudolf C. Eucken, German

1907 Rudyard Kipling, British

1906 Giosue Carducci, Italian

1905 Henryk Sienkiewicz, Polish

1904 Frederic Mistral, French Jose Echegaray, Spanish

1903 Bjornsterne Bjornson, Norw.

1902 Theodor Mommsen, German

1901 Rene F. A Sully Prudhomme, French

Peace

1981 Office of U.N. High Commissioner for Refugees

1980 Adolfo Perez Esquivel, Argentine

1979 Mother Theresa of Calcutta, Albanian-Indian

1978 Anwar Sadat, Egyptian Menachem Begin, Israeli

1977 Amnesty International

1976 Mairead Corrigan, Betty Williams, N. Irish

1975 Andrei Sakharov, USSR

1974 Eisaku Sato, Japanese, Sean MacBride, Irish

1973 Henry Kissinger, U.S. Le Duc Tho, N. Vietnamese (Tho declined)

1971 Willy Brandt, W. German

1970 Norman E. Borlaug, U.S.

1969 Intl. Labor Organization

1968 Rene Cassin, French

1965 U.N. Children's Fund (UNICEF)

1964 Martin Luther King Jr., U.S.

1963 International Red Cross, League of Red Cross Societies

1962 Linus C. Pauling, U.S.

1961 Dag Hammarskjold, Swedish

1960 Albert J. Luthuli, South African

1959 Philip J. Noel-Baker, British

1958 Georges Pire, Belgian

1957 Lester B. Pearson, Canadian

1954 Office of the UN High Commissioner for Refugees

1953 George C. Marshall, U.S.

1952 Albert Schweitzer, French

1951 Leon Jouhaux, French

1950 Ralph J. Bunche, U.S.

1949 Lord John Boyd Orr of Brechin Mearns, British

1947 Friends Service Council, Brit.

Amer. Friends Service Com.
1946 Emily G. Balch,
John R. Mott, both U.S.
1945 Cordell Hull, U.S.
1944 International Red Cross
1938 Nansen International Office
for Refugees
1937 Viscount Cecil of Chelwood, Brit.
1936 Carlos de Saavedra Lamas, Arg.
1935 Carl von Ossietzky, German
1934 Arthur Henderson, British
1933 Sir Norman Angell, British
1931 Jane Addams, U.S.
Nicholas Murray Butler, U.S.
1930 Nathan Soderblom, Swedish
1929 Frank B. Kellogg, U.S.
1927 Ferdinand E. Buisson, French
Ludwig Quidde, German
1926 Aristide Briand, French
Gustav Stresemann, German
1925 Sir J. Austen Chamberlain, Brit.
Charles G. Dawes, U.S.
1922 Fridtjof Nansen, Norwegian
1921 Karl H. Branting, Swedish
Christian L. Lange, Norwegian
1920 Leon V.A. Bourgeois, French
1919 Woodrow Wilson, U.S.
1917 International Red Cross
1913 Henri La Fontaine, Belgian
1912 Elihu Root, U.S.
1911 Tobias M.C. Asser, Dutch
Alfred H. Fried, Austrian
1910 Permanent International Peace
Bureau
1909 Auguste M. F. Beernaert, Belg.
Paul H. B. B. d'Estournelles de
Constant, French
1908 Klas P. Arnoldson, Swedish
Fredrik Bajer, Danish
1907 Ernesto T. Moneta, Italian
Louis Renault, French
1906 Theodore Roosevelt, U.S.
1905 Baroness Bertha von Suttner,
Austrian
1904 Institute of International Law
1903 Sir William R. Cremer, British
1902 Elie Ducommun,
Charles A. Gobat, both Swiss
1901 Jean H. Dunant, Swiss
Frederic Passy, French

Nobel Memorial Prize in Economics

1981 James Tobin, U.S.
1980 Lawrence R. Klein, U.S.
1979 Theodore W. Schultz, U.S.,
Sir Arthur Lewis, British
1978 Herbert A. Simon, U.S.
1977 Bertil Ohlin, Swedish
James E. Meade, British
1976 Milton Friedman, U.S.
1975 Tjalling Koopmans, Dutch-U.S.,
Leonid Kantorovich, USSR
1974 Gunnar Myrdal, Swed.,
Friedrich A. von Hayek, Austrian
1973 Wassily Leontief, U.S.
1972 Kenneth J. Arrow, U.S.
John R. Hicks, British
1971 Simon Kuznets, U.S.
1970 Paul A. Samuelson, U.S.
1969 Ragnar Frisch, Norwegian
Jan Tinbergen, Dutch

Pulitzer Prizes in Journalism, Letters, and Music

The Pulitzer Prizes were endowed by Joseph Pulitzer (1847-1911), publisher of The World, New York, N.Y., in a beques to Columbia University, New York, N.Y., and are awarded annually by the president of the university on recommendation o the Pulitzer Prize Board for work done during the preceding year. The administrator is Prof. Richard T. Baker of Columbi Univ. All prizes are $1,000 (originally $500) in each category, except Meritorious Public Service for which a gold medal i given.

Journalism

Meritorious Public Service

For distinguished and meritorious public service by a United States newspaper.
1918—New York Times. Also special award to Minna Lewinson and Henry Beetle Hough.
1919—Milwaukee Journal.
1921—Boston Post.
1922—New York World.
1923—Memphis (Tenn.) Commercial Appeal.
1924—New York World.
1926—Enquirer-Sun, Columbus, Ga.
1927—Canton (Oh.) Daily News.
1928—Indianapolis Times.
1929—Evening World, New York.
1931—Atlanta (Ga.) Constitution
1932—Indianapolis (Ind.) News.
1933—New York World-Telegram.
1934—Medford (Ore.) Mail-Tribune.
1935—Sacramento (Cal.) Bee.
1936—Cedar Rapids (Ia.) Gazette.
1937—St. Louis Post-Dispatch.
1938—Bismarck (N.D.) Tribune.
1939—Miami (Fla.) Daily News.
1940—Waterbury (Conn.) Republican and American.
1941—St. Louis Post-Dispatch.
1942—Los Angeles Times.
1943—Omaha World Herald.
1944—New York Times.
1945—Detroit Free Press.
1946—Scranton (Pa.) Times.
1947—Baltimore Sun.
1948—St. Louis Post-Dispatch.
1949—Nebraska State Journal.
1950—Chicago Daily News; St. Louis Post-Dispatch.
1951—Miami (Fla.) Herald and Brooklyn Eagle.
1952—St. Louis Post-Dispatch.
1953—Whiteville (N.C.) News Reporter; Tabor City (N.C.) Tribune.
1954—Newsday (Long Island, N.Y.)
1955—Columbus (Ga.) Ledger and Sunday Ledger-Enquirer.
1956—Watsonville (Cal.) Register-Pajaronian.
1957—Chicago Daily News.
1958—Arkansas Gazette, Little Rock.
1959—Utica (N.Y.) Observer-Dispatch and Utica Daily Press.
1960—Los Angeles Times.
1961—Amarillo (Tex.) Globe-Times.
1962—Panama City (Fla.) News-Herald.
1963—Chicago Daily News.
1964—St. Petersburg (Fla.) Times.
1965—Hutchinson (Kan.) News.
1966—Boston Globe.
1967—The Louisville Courier-Journal; The Milwaukee Journal.
1968—Riverside (Cal.) Press-Enterprise.
1969—Los Angeles Times.
1970—Newsday (Long Island, N.Y.).
1971—Winston Salem (N.C.) Journal & Sentinel.
1972—New York Times.
1973—Washington Post.
1974—Newsday (Long Island, N.Y.).
1975—Boston Globe.
1976—Anchorage Daily News.
1977—Lufkin (Tex.) News.
1978—Philadelphia Inquirer.
1979—Point Reyes (Cal.) Light.
1980—Gannett News Service.
1981—Charlotte (N.C.) Observer.
1982—Detroit News.

Reporting

This category originally embraced all fields, local, national, and inte national. Later separate categories were created for the different field of reporting.
1917—Herbert Bayard Swope, New York World.
1918—Harold A. Littledale, New York Evening Post.
1920—John J. Leary, Jr., New York World.
1921—Louis Seibold, New York World.
1922—Kirke L. Simpson, Associated Press.
1923—Alva Johnston, New York Times.
1924—Magner White, San Diego Sun.
1925—James W. Mulroy and Alvin H. Goldstein, Chicago Daily News.
1926—William Burke Miller, Louisville Courier-Journal.
1927—John T. Rogers, St. Louis Post-Dispatch.
1929—Paul Y. Anderson, St. Louis Post-Dispatch.
1930—Russell D. Owens, New York Times. Also $500 to W.O. Dapping Auburn (N.Y.) Citizen.
1931—A.B. MacDonald, Kansas City (Mo.) Star.
1932—W.C. Richards, D.D. Martin, J.S. Pooler, F.D. Webb, J.N.V Sloan, Detroit Free Press.
1933—Francis A. Jamieson, Associated Press.
1934—Royce Brier, San Francisco Chronicle.
1935—William H. Taylor, New York Herald Tribune.
1936—Lauren D. Lyman, New York Times.
1937—John J. O'Neill, N. Y. Herald Tribune; William L. Laurence, N. Times; Howard W. Blakeslee, A. P.; Gobind Behan Lal, University Se vice; and David Dietz, Scripps-Howard Newspapers.
1938—Raymond Sprigle, Pittsburgh Post-Gazette.
1939—Thomas L. Stokes, Scripps-Howard Newspaper Alliance.
1940—S. Burton Heath, New York World-Telegram.
1941—Westbrook Pegler, New York World-Telegram.
1942—Stanton Delaplane, San Francisco Chronicle.
1943—George Weller, Chicago Daily News.
1944—Paul Schoenstein, N.Y. Journal-American.
1945—Jack S. McDowell, San Francisco Call-Bulletin.
1946—William L. Laurence, New York Times.
1947—Frederick Woltman, N.Y. World-Telegram.
1948—George E. Goodwin, Atlanta Journal.
1949—Malcolm Johnson, New York Sun.
1950—Meyer Berger, New York Times.
1951—Edward S. Montgomery, San Francisco Examiner.
1952—Geo. de Carvalho, San Francisco Chronicle.

(1) General or Spot; (2) Special or Investigative

1953—(1) Providence (R.I.) Journal and Evening Bulletin; (2) Edward Mowery, N.Y. World-Telegram & Sun.

1954—(1) Vicksburg (Miss.) Sunday Post-Herald; (2) Alvin Scott McCoy, Kansas City (Mo.) Star.
1955—(1) Mrs. Caro Brown, Alice (Tex.) Daily Echo; (2) Roland K. Towery, Cuero (Tex.) Record.
1956—(1) Lee Hills, Detroit Free Press; (2) Arthur Daley, New York Times.
1957—(1) Salt Lake Tribune, Salt Lake City, Ut.; (2) Wallace Turner and William Lambert, Portland Oregonian.
1958—(1) Fargo, (N.D.) Forum; (2) George Beveridge, Evening Star, Washington, D.C.
1959—(1) Mary Lou Werner, Washington Evening Star; (2) John Harold Brislin, Scranton (Pa.) Tribune, and The Scrantonian.
1960—(1) Jack Nelson, Atlanta Constitution; (2) Miriam Ottenberg, Washington Evening Star.
1961—(1) Sanche de Gramont, N.Y. Herald Tribune; (2) Edgar May, Buffalo Evening News.
1962—(1) Robert D. Mullins, Deseret News, Salt Lake City; (2) George Bliss, Chicago Tribune.
1963—(1) Shared by Sylvan Fox, William Longgood, and Anthony Shannon, N.Y. World-Telegram & Sun; (2) Oscar Griffin, Jr., Pecos (Tex.) Independent and Enterprise.
(1) General Reporting; (2) Special Reporting.
1964—(1) Norman C. Miller, Wall Street Journal; (2) Shared by James V. Magee, Albert V. Gaudiosi, and Frederick A. Meyer, Philadelphia Bulletin.
1965—(1) Melvin H. Ruder, Hungry Horse News (Columbia Falls, Mon.); (2) Gene Goltz, Houston Post.
1966—(1) Los Angeles Times Staff; (2) John A. Frasca, Tampa (Fla.) Tribune.
1967—(1) Robert V. Cox, Chambersburg (Pa.) Public Opinion; (2) Gene Miller, Miami Herald.
1968—Detroit Free Press Staff; (2) J. Anthony Lukas, N.Y. Times.
1969—(1) John Fetterman, Louisville Courier-Journal and Times; (2) Albert L. Delugach, St. Louis Globe Democrat, and Denny Walsh, Life.
1970—(1) Thomas Fitzpatrick, Chicago Sun-Times; (2) Harold Eugene Martin, Montgomery Advertiser & Alabama Journal.
1971—(1) Akron Beacon Journal Staff, (2) William Hugh Jones, Chicago Tribune.
1972—(1) Richard Cooper and John Machacek, Rochester Times-Union; (2) Timothy Leland, Gerard M. O'Neill, Stephen Kurkjian and Anne De Santis, Boston Globe.
1973—(1) Chicago Tribune; (2) Sun Newspapers of Omaha.
1974—(1) Hugh F. Hough, Arthur M. Petacque, Chicago Sun-Times; (2) William Sherman, N.Y. Daily News.
1975—(1) Xenia (Oh.) Daily Gazette; (2) Indianapolis Star.
1976—(1) Gene Miller, Miami Herald; (2) Chicago Tribune.
1977—(1) Margo Huston, Milwaukee Journal; (2) Acel Moore, Wendell Rawls Jr., Philadelphia Inquirer.
1978—(1) Richard Whitt, Louisville Courier-Journal; (2) Anthony R. Dolan, Stamford (Conn.) Advocate.
1979—(1) San Diego (Cal.) Evening Tribune; (2) Gilbert M. Gaul, Elliot G. Jaspin, Pottsville (Pa.) Republican.
1980—(1) Philadelphia Inquirer; (2) Stephen A. Korkjian, Alexander B. Hawes Jr., Nils Bruzelius, Joan Vennochi, Boston Globe.
1981—(1) Longview (Wash.) Daily News staff; (2) Clark Hallas and Robert B. Lowe, Arizona Daily Star.
1982—(1) Kansas City Star, Kansas City Times; (2) Paul Henderson, Seattle Times.

Criticism or Commentary

(1) Criticism; (2) Commentary

1970—(1) Ada Louise Huxtable, N.Y. Times; (2) Marquis W. Childs, St. Louis Post-Dispatch.
1971—(1) Harold C. Schonberg, N.Y. Times; (2) William A. Caldwell, The Record, Hackensack, N.J.
1972—(1) Frank Peters Jr., St. Louis Post-Dispatch; (2) Mike Royko, Chicago Daily News.
1973—(1) Ronald Powers, Chicago Sun-Times; (2) David S. Broder, Washington Post.
1974—(1) Emily Genauer, Newsday, (N.Y.); (2) Edwin A. Roberts, Jr., National Observer.
1975—(1) Roger Ebert, Chicago Sun Times; (2) Mary McGrory, Washington Star.
1976—(1) Alan M. Kriegsman, Washington Post; (2) Walter W. (Red) Smith, N.Y. Times.
1977—(1) William McPherson, Washington Post; (2) George F. Will, Wash. Post Writers Group.
1978—(1) Walter Kerr, New York Times; (2) William Safire, New York Times.
1979—(1) Paul Gapp, Chicago Tribune; (2) Russell Baker, New York Times.
1980—(1) William A. Henry III, Boston Globe; (2) Ellen Goodman, Boston Globe.
1981—(1) Jonathan Yardley, Washington Star; (2) Dave Anderson, New York Times.
1982—(1) Martin Bernheimer, Los Angeles Times; (2) Art Buchwald, Los Angeles Times Syndicate.

National Reporting

1942—Louis Stark, New York Times.
1944—Dewey L. Fleming, Baltimore Sun.
1945—James B. Reston, New York Times.
1946—Edward A. Harris, St. Louis Post-Dispatch.
1947—Edward T. Folliard, Washington Post.
1948—Bert Andrews, New York Herald Tribune; Nat S. Finney, Minneapolis Tribune.
1949—Charles P. Trussell, New York Times.
1950—Edwin O. Guthman, Seattle Times.
1952—Anthony Leviero, New York Times.
1953—Don Whitehead, Associated Press.
1954—Richard Wilson, Cowles Newspapers.
1955—Anthony Lewis, Washington Daily News.
1956—Charles L. Bartlett, Chattanooga Times.
1957—James Reston, New York Times.
1958—Relman Morin, AP; Clark Mollenhoff, Des Moines Register & Tribune.
1959—Howard Van Smith, Miami (Fla.) News.
1960—Vance Trimble, Scripps-Howard, Washington, D.C.
1961—Edward R. Cony, Wall Street Journal.
1962—Nathan G. Caldwell and Gene S. Graham, Nashville Tennessean.
1963—Anthony Lewis, New York Times.
1964—Merriman Smith, UPI.
1965—Louis M. Kohlmeier, Wall Street Journal.
1966—Haynes Johnson, Washington Evening Star.
1967—Monroe Karmin and Stanley Penn, Wall Street Journal.
1968—Howard James, Christian Science Monitor; Nathan K. Kotz, Des Moines Register.
1969—Robert Cahn, Christian Science Monitor.
1970—William J. Eaton, Chicago Daily News.
1971—Lucinda Franks & Thomas Powers, UPI.
1972—Jack Anderson, United Features.
1973—Robert Boyd and Clark Hoyt, Knight Newspapers.
1974—James R. Polk, Washington Star-News; Jack White, Providence Journal-Bulletin.
1975—Donald L. Barlett and James B. Steele, Philadelphia Inquirer.
1976—James Risser, Des Moines Register.
1977—Walter Mears, Associated Press.
1978—Gaylord D. Shaw, Los Angeles Times.
1979—James Risser, Des Moines Register.
1980—Charles Stafford, Bette Swenson Orsini, St. Petersburg (Fla.) Times.
1981—John M. Crewdson, New York Times.
1982—Rick Atkinson, Kansas City Times.

International Reporting

1942—Laurence Edmund Allen, Associated Press.
1943—Ira Wolfert, No. Am. Newspaper Alliance.
1944—Daniel DeLuce, Associated Press.
1945—Mark S. Watson, Baltimore Sun.
1946—Homer W. Bigart, New York Herald Tribune.
1947—Eddy Gilmore, Associated Press.
1948—Paul W. Ward, Baltimore Sun.
1949—Price Day, Baltimore Sun.
1950—Edmund Stevens, Christian Science Monitor.
1951—Keyes Beech and Fred Sparks, Chicago Daily News; Homer Bigart and Marguerite Higgins, New York Herald Tribune; Relman Morin and Don Whitehead, AP.
1952—John M. Hightower, Associated Press.
1953—Austin C. Wehrwein, Milwaukee Journal.
1954—Jim G. Lucas, Scripps-Howard Newspapers.
1955—Harrison Salisbury, New York Times.
1956—William Randolph Hearst, Jr., Frank Conniff, Hearst Newspapers; Kingsbury Smith, INS.
1957—Russell Jones, United Press.
1958—New York Times.
1959—Joseph Martin and Philip Santora, N.Y. News.
1960—A.M. Rosenthal, New York Times.
1961—Lynn Heinzerling, Associated Press.
1962—Walter Lippmann, N.Y. Herald Tribune Synd.
1963—Hal Hendrix, Miami (Fla.) News.
1964—Malcolm W. Browne, AP; David Halberstam, N.Y. Times.
1965—J.A. Livingston, Philadelphia Bulletin.
1966—Peter Arnett, AP.
1967—R. John Hughes, Christian Science Monitor.
1968—Alfred Friendly, Washington Post.
1969—William Tuohy, L.A. Times.
1970—Seymour M. Hersh, Dispatch News Service.
1971—Jimmie Lee Hoagland, Washington Post.
1972—Peter R. Kann, Wall Street Journal.
1973—Max Frankel, N.Y. Times.
1974—Hedrick Smith, N.Y. Times.
1975—William Mullen and Ovie Carter, Chicago Tribune.
1976—Sydney H. Schanberg, N.Y. Times.
1978—Henry Kamm, N.Y. Times.
1979—Richard Ben Cramer, Philadelphia Inquirer.
1980—Joel Brinkley, Jay Mather, Louisville (Ky.) Courier-Journal.
1981—Shirley Christian, Miami Herald.
1982—John Darnton, New York Times.

Correspondence

For Washington or foreign correspondence. Category was merged with those in national and international reporting in 1948.
1929—Paul Scott Mowrer, Chicago Daily News.
1930—Leland Stowe, New York Herald Tribune.
1931—H.R. Knickerbocker, Philadelphia Public Ledger and New York Evening Post.
1932—Walter Duranty, New York Times, and Charles G. Ross, St. Louis Post-Dispatch.
1933—Edgar Ansel Mowrer, Chicago Daily News.
1934—Frederick T. Birchall, New York Times.
1935—Arthur Krock, New York Times.
1936—Wilfred C. Barber, Chicago Tribune.
1937—Anne O'Hare McCormick, New York Times.
1938—Arthur Krock, New York Times.
1939—Louis P. Lochner, Associated Press.
1940—Otto D. Tolischus, New York Times.
1941—Bronze plaque to commemorate work of American correspondents on war fronts.
1942—Carlos P. Romulo, Philippines Herald.
1943—Hanson W. Baldwin, New York Times.

1944—Ernest Taylor Pyle, Scripps-Howard Newspaper Alliance.
1945—Harold V. (Hal) Boyle, Associated Press.
1946—Arnaldo Cortesi, New York Times.
1947—Brooks Atkinson, New York Times.

Editorial Writing

1917—New York Tribune.
1918—Louisville (Ky.) Courier-Journal.
1920—Harvey E. Newbranch, Omaha Evening World-Herald.
1922—Frank M. O'Brien, New York Herald.
1923—William Allen White, Emporia Gazette.
1924—Frank Buxton, Boston Herald, Special Prize. Frank I. Cobb, New York World.
1925—Robert Lathan, Charleston (S.C.) News and Courier.
1926—Edward M. Kingsbury, N. Y. Times.
1927—F. Lauriston Bullard, Boston Herald.
1928—Grover C. Hall, Montgomery Advertiser.
1929—Louis Isaac Jaffe, Norfolk Virginian-Pilot.
1931—Chas. Ryckman, Fremont (Neb.) Tribune.
1933—Kansas City (Mo.) Star
1934—E. P. Chase, Atlantic (Ia.) News Telegraph.
1936—Felix Morley, Washington Post. George B. Parker, Scripps-Howard Newspapers.
1937—John W. Owens, Baltimore Sun.
1938—W.W. Waymack. Des Moines (Ia.) Register and Tribune.
1939—Ronald G. Callvert, Portland Oregonian.
1940—Bart Howard, St. Louis Post-Dispatch.
1941—Reuben Maury, Daily News, N.Y.
1942—Geoffrey Parsons, New York Herald Tribune.
1943—Forrest W. Seymour, Des Moines (Ia.) Register and Tribune.
1944—Henry J. Haskell, Kansas City (Mo.) Star.
1945—George W. Potter, Providence (R.I.) Journal-Bulletin.
1946—Hodding Carter, Greenville (Miss.) Delta Democrat-Times.
1947—William H. Grimes, Wall Street Journal.
1948—Virginius Dabney, Richmond (Va.) Times-Dispatch.
1949—John H. Crider, Boston (Mass.) Herald, Herbert Elliston, Washington Post.
1950—Carl M. Saunders, Jackson (Mich.) Citizen-Patriot.
1951—William H. Fitzpatrick, New Orleans States.
1952—Louis LaCoss, St. Louis Globe Democrat.
1953—Vermont C. Royster, Wall Street Journal.
1954—Don Murray, Boston Herald.
1955—Royce Howes, Detroit Free Press.
1956—Lauren K. Soth, Des Moines (Ia.) Register and Tribune.
1957—Buford Boone, Tuscaloosa (Ala.) News.
1958—Harry S. Ashmore, Arkansas Gazette.
1959—Ralph McGill, Atlanta Constitution.
1960—Lenoir Chambers, Norfolk Virginian-Pilot.
1961—William J. Dorvillier, San Juan (Puerto Rico) Star.
1962—Thomas M. Storke, Santa Barbara (Cal.) News-Press.
1963—Ira B. Harkey, Jr., Pascagoula (Miss.) Chronicle.
1964—Hazel Brannon Smith, Lexington (Miss.) Advertiser.
1965—John R. Harrison, The Gainesville (Fla.) Sun.
1966—Robert Lasch, St. Louis Post-Dispatch.
1967—Eugene C. Patterson, Atlanta Constitution.
1968—John S. Knight, Knight Newspapers.
1969—Paul Greenberg, Pine Bluff (Ark.) Commercial.
1970—Philip L. Geyelin, Washington Post.
1971—Horance G. Davis, Jr., Gainesville (Fla.) Sun.
1972—John Strohmeyer, Bethlehem (Pa.) Globe-Times.
1973—Roger B. Linscott, Berkshire Eagle, Pittsfield, Mass.
1974—F. Gilman Spencer, Trenton (N.J.) Trentonian.
1975—John D. Maurice, Charleston (W. Va.) Daily Mail.
1976—Philip Kerby, Los Angeles Times.
1977—Warren L. Lerude, Foster Church, and Norman F. Cardoza, Reno (Nev.) Evening Gazette and Nevada State Journal.
1978—Meg Greenfield, Washington Post.
1979—Edwin M. Yoder, Washington Star.
1980—Robert L. Bartley, Wall Street Journal.
1982—Jack Rosenthal, New York Times.

Editorial Cartooning

1922—Rollin Kirby, New York World.
1924—Jay N. Darling, New York Herald Tribune.
1925—Rollin Kirby, New York World.
1926—D. R. Fitzpatrick, St. Louis Post-Dispatch.
1927—Nelson Harding, Brooklyn Eagle.
1928—Nelson Harding, Brooklyn Eagle.
1929—Rollin Kirby, New York World.
1930—Charles Macauley, Brooklyn Eagle.
1931—Edmund Duffy, Baltimore Sun.
1932—John T. McCutcheon, Chicago Tribune.
1933—H. M. Talburt, Washington Daily News.
1934—Edmund Duffy, Baltimore Sun.
1935—Ross A. Lewis, Milwaukee Journal.
1937—C. D. Batchelor, New York Daily News.
1938—Vaughn Shoemaker, Chicago Daily News.
1939—Charles G. Werner, Daily Oklahoman.
1940—Edmund Duffy, Baltimore Sun.
1941—Jacob Burck, Chicago Times.
1942—Herbert L. Block, Newspaper Enterprise Assn.
1943—Jay N. Darling, New York Herald Tribune.
1944—Clifford K. Berryman, Washington Star.
1945—Bill Mauldin, United Feature Syndicate.
1946—Bruce Alexander Russell, Los Angeles Times.
1947—Vaughn Shoemaker, Chicago Daily News.
1948—Reuben L. (Rube) Goldberg, N. Y. Sun.
1949—Lute Pease, Newark (N.J.) Evening News.
1950—James T. Berryman, Washington Star.
1951—Reginald W. Manning, Arizona Republic.
1952—Fred L. Packer, New York Mirror.
1953—Edward D. Kuekes, Cleveland Plain Dealer.
1954—Herbert L. Block, Washington Post & Times-Herald.
1955—Daniel R. Fitzpatrick, St. Louis Post-Dispatch.
1956—Robert York, Louisville (Ky.) Times.
1957—Tom Little, Nashville Tennessean.
1958—Bruce M. Shanks, Buffalo Evening News.
1959—Bill Mauldin, St. Louis Post-Dispatch.
1961—Carey Orr, Chicago Tribune.
1962—Edmund S. Valtman, Hartford Times.
1963—Frank Miller, Des Moines Register.
1964—Paul Conrad, Denver Post.
1966—Don Wright, Miami News.
1967—Patrick B. Oliphant, Denver Post.
1968—Eugene Gray Payne, Charlotte Observer.
1969—John Fischetti, Chicago Daily News.
1970—Thomas F. Darcy, Newsday.
1971—Paul Conrad, L. A. Times.
1972—Jeffrey K. MacNelly, Richmond News-Leader.
1974—Paul Szep, Boston Globe.
1975—Garry Trudeau, Universal Press Syndicate.
1976—Tony Auth, Philadelphia Inquirer.
1977—Paul Szep, Boston Globe.
1978—Jeffrey K. MacNelly, Richmond News Leader.
1979—Herbert L. Block, Washington Post.
1980—Don Wright, Miami (Fla.) News.
1981—Mike Peters, Dayton (Oh.) Daily News.
1982—Ben Sargent, Austin American-Statesman.

Spot News Photography

1942—Milton Brooks, Detroit News.
1943—Frank Noel, Associated Press.
1944—Frank Filan, AP; Earl L. Bunker, Omaha World-Herald.
1945—Joe Rosenthal, Associated Press, for photograph of planting American flag on Iwo Jima.
1947—Arnold Hardy, amateur, Atlanta, Ga.
1948—Frank Cushing, Boston Traveler.
1949—Nathaniel Fein, New York Herald Tribune.
1950—Bill Crouch, Oakland (Cal.) Tribune.
1951—Max Desfor, Associated Press.
1952—John Robinson and Don Ultang, Des Moines Register and Tribune.
1953—William M. Gallagher, Flint (Mich.) Journal.
1954—Mrs. Walter M. Schau, amateur.
1955—John L. Gaunt, Jr., Los Angeles Times.
1956—New York Daily News.
1957—Harry A. Trask, Boston Traveler.
1958—William C. Beall, Washington Daily News.
1959—William Seaman, Minneapolis Star.
1960—Andrew Lopez, UPI.
1961—Yasushi Nagao, Mainichi Newspapers, Tokyo.
1962—Paul Vathis, Associated Press.
1963—Hector Rondon, La Republica, Caracas, Venezuela.
1964—Robert H. Jackson, Dallas Times-Herald.
1965—Horst Faas, Associated Press.
1966—Kyoichi Sawada, UPI.
1967—Jack R. Thornell, Associated Press.
1968—Rocco Morabito, Jacksonville Journal.
1969—Edward Adams, AP.
1970—Steve Starr, AP.
1971—John Paul Filo, Valley Daily News & Daily Dispatch of Tarentum & New Kensington, Pa.
1972—Horst Faas and Michel Laurent, AP.
1973—Huynh Cong Ut, AP.
1974—Anthony K. Roberts, AP.
1975—Gerald H. Gay, Seattle Times.
1976—Stanley Forman, Boston Herald American.
1977—Neal Ulevich, Associated Press; Stanley Forman, Boston Herald American.
1978—Jim Schweiker, UPI.
1979—Thomas J. Kelly III, Pottstown (Pa.) Mercury.
1980—UPI.
1981—Larry C. Price, Ft. Worth (Tex.) Star-Telegram.
1982—Ron Edmonds, Associated Press.

Feature Photography

1968—Toshio Sakai, UPI.
1969—Moneta Sleet Jr., Ebony.
1970—Dallas Kinney, Palm Beach Post.
1971—Jack Dykinga, Chicago Sun-Times.
1972—Dave Kennerly, UPI.
1973—Brian Lanker, Topeka Capitol-Journal.
1974—Slava Veder, AP.
1975—Matthew Lewis, Washington Post.
1976—Louisville Courier-Journal and Louisville Times.
1977—Robin Hood, Chattanooga News-Free Press.
1978—J. Ross Baughman, AP.
1979—Staff Photographers, Boston Herald American.
1980—Erwin H. Hagler, Dallas Times-Herald.
1981—Taro M. Yamasaki, Detroit Free Press.
1982—John H. White, Chicago Sun-Times.

Special Citation

1938—Edmonton (Alberta) Journal, bronze plaque.
1941—New York Times.
1944—Byron Price and Mrs. William Allen White. Also to Richard Rodgers and Oscar Hammerstein 2d, for musical, Oklahoma!
1945—Press cartographers for war maps.
1947—(Pulitzer centennial year.) Columbia Univ. and the Graduate School of Journalism, and St. Louis Post-Dispatch.
1948—Dr. Frank Diehl Fackenthal.
1951—Cyrus L. Sulzberger, New York Times.

1952—Max Kase, New York Journal-American.
1953—The New York Times; Lester Markel.
1957—Kenneth Roberts, for his historical novels.
1958—Walter Lippmann, New York Herald Tribune.
1960—Garrett Mattingly, for The Armada.
1961—American Heritage Picture History of the Civil War.
1964—The Gannett Newspapers.
1973—James T. Flexner, for "George Washington," a four-volume biography.
1976—John Hohenberg, for services to American journalism.
1977—Alex Haley, for Roots, $1,000.
1978—Richard Lee Strout, Christian Science Monitor and New Republic. —E.B. White, for his work.

Feature Writing

Category was inaugurated in 1979.
1979—Jon D. Franklin, Baltimore Evening Sun.
1980—Madeleine Blais, Miami Herald Tropic Magazine.
1981—Teresa Carpenter, Village Voice, New York City.
1982—Saul Pett, Associated Press.

Letters

Fiction

For fiction in book form by an American author, preferably dealing with American life.
1918—Ernest Poole, His Family.
1919—Booth Tarkington, The Magnificent Ambersons.
1921—Edith Wharton, The Age of Innocence.
1922—Booth Tarkington, Alice Adams.
1923—Willa Cather, One of Ours.
1924—Margaret Wilson, The Able McLaughlins.
1925—Edna Ferber, So Big.
1926—Sinclair Lewis, Arrowsmith. (Refused prize.)
1927—Louis Bromfield, Early Autumn.
1928—Thornton Wilder, Bridge of San Luis Rey.
1929—Julia M. Peterkin, Scarlet Sister Mary.
1930—Oliver LaFarge, Laughing Boy.
1931—Margaret Ayer Barnes, Years of Grace.
1932—Pearl S. Buck, The Good Earth.
1933—T. S. Stribling, The Store.
1934—Caroline Miller, Lamb in His Bosom.
1935—Josephine W. Johnson, Now in November.
1936—Harold L. Davis, Honey in the Horn.
1937—Margaret Mitchell, Gone with the Wind.
1938—John P. Marquand, The Late George Apley.
1939—Marjorie Kinnan Rawlings, The Yearling.
1940—John Steinbeck, The Grapes of Wrath.
1942—Ellen Glasgow, In This Our Life.
1943—Upton Sinclair, Dragon's Teeth.
1944—Martin Flavin, Journey in the Dark.
1945—John Hersey, A Bell for Adano.
1947—Robert Penn Warren, All the King's Men.
1948—James A Michener, Tales of the South Pacific.
1949—James Gould Cozzens, Guard of Honor.
1950—A. B. Guthrie Jr., The Way West.
1951—Conrad Richter, The Town.
1952—Herman Wouk, The Caine Mutiny.
1953—Ernest Hemingway, The Old Man and the Sea.
1955—William Faulkner, A Fable.
1956—MacKinlay Kantor, Andersonville.
1958—James Agee, A Death in the Family.
1959—Robert Lewis Taylor, The Travels of Jaimie McPheeters.
1960—Allen Drury, Advise and Consent.
1961—Harper Lee, To Kill a Mockingbird.
1962—Edwin O'Connor, The Edge of Sadness.
1963—William Faulkner, The Reivers.
1965—Shirley Ann Grau, The Keepers of the House.
1966—Katherine Anne Porter, Collected Stories of Katherine Anne Porter.
1967—Bernard Malamud, The Fixer.
1968—William Styron, The Confessions of Nat Turner.
1969—N. Scott Momaday, House Made of Dawn.
1970—Jean Stafford, Collected Stories.
1972—Wallace Stegner, Angle of Repose.
1973—Eudora Welty, The Optimist's Daughter.
1975—Michael Shaara, The Killer Angels.
1976—Saul Bellow, Humboldt's Gift.
1978—James Alan McPherson, Elbow Room.
1979—John Cheever, The Stories of John Cheever.
1980—Norman Mailer, The Executioner's Song.
1981—John Kennedy Toole, A Confederacy of Dunces.
1982—John Updike, Rabbit is Rich.

Drama

For an American play, preferably original and dealing with American life.
1918—Jesse Lynch Williams, Why Marry?
1920—Eugene O'Neill, Beyond the Horizon.
1921—Zona Gale, Miss Lulu Bett.
1922—Eugene O'Neill, Anna Christie.
1923—Owen Davis, Icebound.
1924—Hatcher Hughes, Hell-Bent for Heaven.
1925—Sidney Howard, They Knew What They Wanted.
1926—George Kelly, Craig's Wife.
1927—Paul Green, In Abraham's Bosom.
1928—Eugene O'Neill, Strange Interlude.
1929—Elmer Rice, Street Scene.
1930—Marc Connelly, The Green Pastures.
1931—Susan Glaspell, Alison's House.
1932—George S. Kaufman, Morrie Ryskind and Ira Gershwin, Of Thee I Sing.
1933—Maxwell Anderson, Both Your Houses.
1934—Sidney Kingsley, Men in White.
1935—Zoe Akins, The Old Maid.
1936—Robert E. Sherwood, Idiot's Delight.
1937—George S. Kaufman and Moss Hart, You Can't Take It With You.
1938—Thornton Wilder, Our Town.
1939—Robert E. Sherwood, Abe Lincoln in Illinois.
1940—William Saroyan, The Time of Your Life.
1941—Robert E. Sherwood, There Shall Be No Night.
1943—Thornton Wilder, The Skin of Our Teeth.
1945—Mary Chase, Harvey.
1946—Russel Crouse and Howard Lindsay, State of the Union.
1948—Tennessee Williams, A Streetcar Named Desire.
1949—Arthur Miller, Death of a Salesman.
1950—Richard Rodgers, Oscar Hammerstein 2d, and Joshua Logan, South Pacific.
1952—Joseph Kramm, The Shrike.
1953—William Inge, Picnic.
1954—John Patrick, Teahouse of the August Moon.
1955—Tennessee Williams, Cat on a Hot Tin Roof.
1956—Frances Goodrich and Albert Hackett, The Diary of Anne Frank.
1957—Eugene O'Neill, Long Day's Journey Into Night.
1958—Ketti Frings, Look Homeward, Angel.
1959—Archibald MacLeish, J. B.
1960—George Abbott, Jerome Weidman, Sheldon Harnick and Jerry Bock, Fiorello.
1961—Tad Mosel, All the Way Home.
1962—Frank Loesser and Abe Burrows, How To Succeed In Business Without Really Trying.
1965—Frank D. Gilroy, The Subject Was Roses.
1967—Edward Albee, A Delicate Balance.
1969—Howard Sackler, The Great White Hope.
1970—Charles Gordone, No Place to Be Somebody.
1971—Paul Zindel, The Effect of Gamma Rays on Man-in-the-Moon Marigolds.
1973—Jason Miller, That Championship Season.
1975—Edward Albee, Seascape.
1976—Michael Bennett, James Kirkwood, Nicholas Dante, Marvin Hamlisch, Edward Kleban, A Chorus Line.
1977—Michael Cristofer, The Shadow Box.
1978—Donald L. Coburn, The Gin Game.
1979—Sam Shepard, Buried Child.
1980—Lanford Wilson, Talley's Folly.
1981—Beth Henley, Crimes of the Heart.
1982—Charles Fuller, A Soldier's Play.

History

For a book on the history of the United States.
1917—J. J. Jusserand, With Americans of Past and Present Days.
1918—James Ford Rhodes, History of the Civil War.
1920—Justin H. Smith, The War with Mexico.
1921—William Sowden Sims, The Victory at Sea.
1922—James Truslow Adams, The Founding of New England.
1923—Charles Warren, The Supreme Court in United States History.
1924—Charles Howard McIlwain, The American Revolution: A Constitutional Interpretation.
1925—Frederick L. Paxton, A History of the American Frontier.
1926—Edward Channing, A History of the U.S.
1927—Samuel Flagg Bemis, Pinckney's Treaty.
1928—Vernon Louis Parrington, Main Currents in American Thought.
1929—Fred A. Shannon, The Organization and Administration of the Union Army, 1861-65.
1930—Claude H. Van Tyne, The War of Independence.
1931—Bernadotte E. Schmitt, The Coming of the War, 1914.
1932—Gen. John J. Pershing, My Experiences in the World War.
1933—Frederick J. Turner, The Significance of Sections in American History.
1934—Herbert Agar, The People's Choice.
1935—Charles McLean Andrews, The Colonial Period of American History.
1936—Andrew C. McLaughlin, The Constitutional History of the United States.
1937—Van Wyck Brooks, The Flowering of New England.
1938—Paul Herman Buck, The Road to Reunion, 1865-1900.
1939—Frank Luther Mott, A History of American Magazines.
1940—Carl Sandburg, Abraham Lincoln: The War Years.
1941—Marcus Lee Hansen, The Atlantic Migration, 1607-1860.
1942—Margaret Leech, Reveille in Washington.
1943—Esther Forbes, Paul Revere and the World He Lived In.
1944—Merle Curti, The Growth of American Thought.
1945—Stephen Bonsal, Unfinished Business.
1946—Arthur M. Schlesinger Jr., The Age of Jackson.
1947—James Phinney Baxter 3d, Scientists Against Time.
1948—Bernard De Voto, Across the Wide Missouri.
1949—Roy F. Nichols, The Disruption of American Democracy.
1950—O. W. Larkin, Art and Life in America.
1951—R. Carlyle Buley, The Old Northwest: Pioneer Period 1815-1840.
1952—Oscar Handlin, The Uprooted.
1953—George Dangerfield, The Era of Good Feelings.
1954—Bruce Catton, A Stillness at Appomattox.
1955—Paul Horgan, Great River: The Rio Grande in North American History.

1956—Richard Hofstadter, The Age of Reform.
1957—George F. Kennan, Russia Leaves the War.
1958—Bray Hammond, Banks and Politics in America—From the Revolution to the Civil War.
1959—Leonard D. White and Jean Schneider, The Republican Era; 1869-1901.
1960—Margaret Leech, In the Days of McKinley.
1961—Herbert Feis, Between War and Peace: The Potsdam Conference.
1962—Lawrence H. Gibson, The Triumphant Empire: Thunderclouds Gather in the West.
1963—Constance McLaughlin Green, Washington: Village and Capital, 1800-1878.
1964—Sumner Chilton Powell, Puritan Village: The Formation of A New England Town.
1965—Irwin Unger, The Greenback Era.
1966—Perry Miller, Life of the Mind in America.
1967—William H. Goetzmann, Exploration and Empire: the Explorer and Scientist in the Winning of the American West.
1968—Bernard Bailyn, The Ideological Origins of the American Revolution.
1969—Leonard W. Levy, Origin of the Fifth Amendment.
1970—Dean Acheson, Present at the Creation: My Years in the State Department.
1971—James McGregor Burns, Roosevelt: The Soldier of Freedom.
1972—Carl N. Degler, Neither Black Nor White.
1973—Michael Kammen, People of Paradox: An Inquiry Concerning the Origins of American Civilization.
1974—Daniel J. Boorstin, The Americans: The Democratic Experience.
1975—Dumas Malone, Jefferson and His Time.
1976—Paul Horgan, Lamy of Santa Fe.
1977—David M. Potter, The Impending Crisis.
1978—Alfred D. Chandler, Jr., The Visible Hand: The Managerial Revolution in American Business.
1979—Don E. Fehrenbacher, The Dred Scott Case: Its Significance in American Law and Politics.
1980—Leon F. Litwack, Been in the Storm So Long.
1981—Lawrence A. Cremin, American Education: The National Experience, 1783-1876.
1982—C. Vann Woodward, ed., Mary Chestnut's Civil War.

Biography or Autobiography

For a distinguished biography or autobiography by an American author, preferably on an American subject.
1917—Laura E. Richards and Maude Howe Elliott, assisted by Florence Howe Hall, Julia Ward Howe.
1918—William Cabell Bruce, Benjamin Franklin, Self-Revealed.
1919—Henry Adams, The Education of Henry Adams.
1920—Albert J. Beveridge, The Life of John Marshall.
1921—Edward Bok, The Americanization of Edward Bok.
1922—Hamlin Garland, A Daughter of the Middle Border.
1923—Burton J. Hendrick, The Life and Letters of Walter H. Page.
1924—Michael Pupin, From Immigrant to Inventor.
1925—M. A. DeWolfe Howe, Barrett Wendell and His Letters.
1926—Harvey Cushing, Life of Sir William Osler.
1927—Emory Holloway, Whitman: An Interpretation in Narrative.
1928—Charles Edward Russell, The American Orchestra and Theodore Thomas.
1929—Burton J. Hendrick, The Training of an American: The Earlier Life and Letters of Walter H. Page.
1930—Marquis James, The Raven (Sam Houston).
1931—Henry James, Charles W. Eliot.
1932—Henry F. Pringle, Theodore Roosevelt.
1933—Allan Nevins, Grover Cleveland.
1934—Tyler Dennett, John Hay.
1935—Douglas Southall Freeman, R. E. Lee
1936—Ralph Barton Perry, The Thought and Character of William James.
1937—Allan Nevins, Hamilton Fish: The Inner History of the Grant Administration.
1938—Divided between Odell Shepard, Pedlar's Progress; Marquis James, Andrew Jackson.
1939—Carl Van Doren, Benjamin Franklin.
1940—Ray Stannard Baker, Woodrow Wilson, Life and Letters.
1941—Ola Elizabeth Winslow, Jonathan Edwards.
1942—Forrest Wilson, Crusader in Crinoline.
1943—Samuel Eliot Morison, Admiral of the Ocean Sea (Columbus).
1944—Carleton Mabee, The American Leonardo: The Life of Samuel F. B. Morse.
1945—Russell Blaine Nye, George Bancroft; Brahmin Rebel.
1946—Linny Marsh Wolfe, Son of the Wilderness.
1947—William Allen White, The Autobiography of William Allen White.
1948—Margaret Clapp, Forgotten First Citizen: John Bigelow.
1949—Robert E. Sherwood, Roosevelt and Hopkins.
1950—Samuel Flag Bemis, John Quincy Adams and the Foundations of American Foreign Policy.
1951—Margaret Louise Coit, John C. Calhoun: American Portrait.
1952—Merlo J. Pusey, Charles Evans Hughes.
1953—David J. Mays, Edmund Pendleton, 1721-1803.
1954—Charles A. Lindbergh, The Spirit of St. Louis.
1955—William S. White, The Taft Story.
1956—Talbot F. Hamlin, Benjamin Henry Latrobe.
1957—John F. Kennedy, Profiles in Courage.
1958—Douglas Southall Freeman (decd. 1953), George Washington, Vols. I-VI: John Alexander Carroll and Mary Wells Ashworth, Vol. VII.
1959—Arthur Walworth, Woodrow Wilson: American Prophet.
1960—Samuel Eliot Morison, John Paul Jones.
1961—David Donald, Charles Sumner and The Coming of the Civil War.
1963—Leon Edel, Henry James: Vol. II. The Conquest of London, 1870-1881; Vol. III, The Middle Years, 1881-1895.
1964—Walter Jackson Bate, John Keats.
1965—Ernest Samuels, Henry Adams.
1966—Arthur M. Schlesinger Jr., A Thousand Days.
1967—Justin Kaplan, Mr. Clemens and Mark Twain.
1968—George F. Kennan, Memoirs (1925-1950).
1969—B. L. Reid, The Man from New York: John Quinn and his Friends.
1970—T. Harry Williams, Huey Long.
1971—Lawrence Thompson, Robert Frost: The Years of Triumph, 1915-1938.
1972—Joseph P. Lash, Eleanor and Franklin.
1973—W. A. Swanberg, Luce and His Empire.
1974—Louis Sheaffer, O'Neill, Son and Artist.
1975—Robert A. Caro, The Power Broker: Robert Moses and the Fall of New York.
1976—R.W.B. Lewis, Edith Wharton: A Biography.
1977—John E. Mack, A Prince of Our Disorder, The Life of T.E. Lawrence.
1978—Walter Jackson Bate, Samuel Johnson.
1979—Leonard Baker, Days of Sorrow and Pain: Leo Baeck and the Berlin Jews.
1980—Edmund Morris, The Rise of Theodore Roosevelt.
1981—Robert K. Massie, Peter the Great: His Life and World.
1982—William S. McFeely, Grant: A Biography.

American Poetry

Before this prize was established in 1922, awards were made from gifts provided by the Poetry Society: **1918**—Love Songs, by Sara Teasdale. **1919**—Old Road to Paradise, by Margaret Widemer; Corn Huskers, by Carl Sandburg.
1922—Edwin Arlington Robinson, Collected Poems.
1923—Edna St. Vincent Millay, The Ballad of the Harp-Weaver; A Few Figs from Thistles; Eight Sonnets in American Poetry, 1922; A Miscellany.
1924—Robert Frost, New Hampshire: A Poem with Notes and Grace Notes.
1925—Edwin Arlington Robinson, The Man Who Died Twice.
1926—Amy Lowell, What's O'Clock.
1927—Leonora Speyer, Fiddler's Farewell.
1928—Edwin Arlington Robinson, Tristram.
1929—Stephen Vincent Benet, John Brown's Body.
1930—Conrad Aiken, Selected Poems.
1931—Robert Frost, Collected Poems.
1932—George Dillon, The Flowering Stone.
1933—Archibald MacLeish, Conquistador.
1934—Robert Hillyer, Collected Verse.
1935—Audrey Wurdemann, Bright Ambush.
1936—Robert P. Tristram Coffin, Strange Holiness.
1937—Robert Frost, A Further Range.
1938—Marya Zaturenska, Cold Morning Sky.
1939—John Gould Fletcher, Selected Poems.
1940—Mark Van Doren, Collected Poems.
1941—Leonard Bacon, Sunderland Capture.
1942—William Rose Benet, The Dust Which Is God.
1943—Robert Frost, A Witness Tree.
1944—Stephen Vincent Benet, Western Star.
1945—Karl Shapiro, V-Letter and Other Poems.
1947—Robert Lowell, Lord Weary's Castle.
1948—W. H. Auden, The Age of Anxiety.
1949—Peter Viereck, Terror and Decorum.
1950—Gwendolyn Brooks, Annie Allen.
1951—Carl Sandburg, Complete Poems.
1952—Marianne Moore, Collected Poems.
1953—Archibald MacLeish, Collected Poems.
1954—Theodore Roethke, The Waking.
1955—Wallace Stevens, Collected Poems.
1956—Elizabeth Bishop, Poems, North and South.
1957—Richard Wilbur, Things of This World.
1958—Robert Penn Warren, Promises: Poems 1954-1956.
1959—Stanley Kunitz, Selected Poems 1928-1958.
1960—W. D. Snodgrass, Heart's Needle.
1961—Phyllis McGinley, Times Three: Selected Verse from Three Decades.
1962—Alan Dugan, Poems.
1963—William Carlos Williams, Pictures From Breughel.
1964—Louis Simpson, At the End of the Open Road.
1965—John Berryman, 77 Dream Songs.
1966—Richard Eberhart, Selected Poems.
1967—Anne Sexton, Live or Die.
1968—Anthony Hecht, The Hard Hours.
1969—George Oppen, Of Being Numerous.
1970—Richard Howard, Untitled Subjects.
1971—William S. Merwin, The Carrier of Ladders.
1972—James Wright, Collected Poems.
1973—Maxine Winokur Kumin, Up Country.
1975—Gary Snyder, Turtle Island.
1976—John Ashbery, Self-Portrait in a Convex Mirror.
1977—James Merrill, Divine Comedies.
1978—Howard Nemerov, Collected Poems.
1979—Robert Penn Warren, Now and Then: Poems 1976-1978.
1980—Donald Justice, Selected Poems.
1981—James Schuyler, The Morning of the Poem.
1982—Sylvia Plath, The Collected Poems.

General Non-Fiction

For best book by an American, not eligible in any other category.
1962—Theodore H. White, The Making of the President 1960.
1963—Barbara W. Tuchman, The Guns of August.
1964—Richard Hofstadter, Anti-Intellectualism in American Life.
1965—Howard Mumford Jones, O Strange New World.
1966—Edwin Way Teale, Wandering Through Winter.

1967—David Brion Davis, The Problem of Slavery in Western Culture.
1968—Will and Ariel Durant, Rousseau and Revolution.
1969—Norman Mailer, The Armies of the Night; and Rene Jules Dubos, So Human an Animal: How We Are Shaped by Surroundings and Events.
1970—Eric H. Erikson, Gandhi's Truth.
1971—John Toland, The Rising Sun.
1972—Barbara W. Tuchman, Stilwell and the American Experience in China, 1911-1945.
1973—Frances FitzGerald, Fire in the Lake: The Vietnamese and the Americans in Vietnam; and Robert Coles, Children of Crisis, Volumes II and III.
1974—Ernest Becker, The Denial of Death.
1975—Annie Dillard, Pilgrim at Tinker Creek.
1976—Robert N. Butler, Why Survive? Being Old in America.
1977—William W. Warner, Beautiful Swimmers.
1978—Carl Sagan, The Dragons of Eden.
1979—Edward O. Wilson, On Human Nature.
1980—Douglas R. Hofstadter, Gödel, Escher, Bach: An Eternal Golden Braid.
1981—Carl E. Schorske, Fin-de-Siecle Vienna: Politics and Culture.
1982—Tracy Kidder, The Soul of a New Machine.

Music

For composition by an American (before 1977, by a composer resident in the U.S.), in the larger forms of chamber, orchestra or choral music or for an operatic work including ballet. A special posthumous award was granted in 1976 to Scott Joplin.

1943—William Schuman, Secular Cantata No. 2, A Free Song.
1944—Howard Hanson, Symphony No. 4, Op. 34.
1945—Aaron Copland, Appalachian Spring.
1946—Leo Sowerby, The Canticle of the Sun.
1947—Charles E. Ives, Symphony No. 3.
1948—Walter Piston, Symphony No. 3.
1949—Virgil Thomson, Louisiana Story.
1950—Gian-Carlo Menotti, The Consul.
1951—Douglas Moore, Giants in the Earth.
1952—Gail Kubik, Symphony Concertante.
1954—Quincy Porter, Concerto for Two Pianos and Orchestra.
1955—Gian-Carlo Menotti, The Saint of Bleecker Street.
1956—Ernest Toch, Symphony No. 3.
1957—Norman Dello Joio, Meditations on Ecclesiastes.
1958—Samuel Barber, Vanessa.
1959—John La Montaine, Concerto for Piano and Orchestra.
1960—Elliott Carter, Second String Quartet.
1961—Walter Piston, Symphony No. 7.
1962—Robert Ward, The Crucible.
1963—Samuel Barber, Piano Concerto No. 1.
1966—Leslie Bassett, Variations for Orchestra.
1967—Leon Kirchner, Quartet No. 3.
1968—George Crumb, Echoes of Time and The River.
1969—Karel Husa, String Quartet No. 3.
1970—Charles W. Wuorinen, Time's Encomium.
1971—Mario Davidovsky, Synchronisms No. 6.
1972—Jacob Druckman, Windows.
1973—Elliott Carter, String Quartet No. 3.
1974—Donald Martino, Notturno. (Special citation) Roger Sessions.
1975—Dominick Argento, From the Diary of Virginia Woolf.
1976—Ned Rorem, Air Music.
1977—Richard Wernick, Visions of Terror and Wonder.
1978—Michael Colgrass, Deja Vu for Percussion and Orchestra.
1979—Joseph Schwantner, Aftertones of Infinity.
1980—David Del Tredici, In Memory of a Summer Day.
1982—Roger Sessions, Concerto For Orchestra. (Special Citation) Milton Babbitt.

Special Awards

Awarded in 1982 unless otherwise designated

Books, Allied Arts

Academy of American Poets Fellowship, for distinguished achievement, $10,000: John Frederick Nims.

Nelson Algren Award, by *Chicago* magazine, $5,000: Louise Erdrich, "The World's Greatest Fisherman."

American Academy and Institute of Arts and Letters Awards, $5,000 each: David H. Bradley, Frederich Buechner, Mac Donald Harris, Daryl Hine, Josephine Jacobsen, Donald Keene, Berton Roueche, Robert Stone.

American Book Awards, by Assn. of American Publishers: National Medal for Literature, $15,000: John Cheever; fiction: John Updike, *Rabbit Is Rich;* paperback: William Maxwell, *So Long, See You Tomorrow;* biography: David McCullough, *Mornings on Horseback;* paperback: Ronald Steel, *Walter Lippman and the American Century;* first novel: Robb Forman Dew, *Dale Loves Sophie to Death;* general nonfiction: Tracy Kidder, *The Soul of a New Machine;* paperback: Victor S. Navasky, *Naming Names;* history: Father Peter John Powell, *People of the Sacred Mountain;* paperback: Robert Wohl, *The Generation of 1914;* poetry: William Bronk, *Life Supports;* science: Donald C. Johanson, Maitland A. Edey, *Lucy;* paperback: Fred Alan Wolf, *Taking the Quantum Leap;* translation: Robert Lyons Danly, *In the Shade of Spring Leaves;* Ian Hideo Levy, *The Ten Thousand Leaves;* children's fiction: Lloyd Alexander, *Westmark;* paperback: Ouida Sebestyen, *Words by Heart;* non-fiction: Susan Bonner, *A Penguin Year;* picture: Maurice Sendak: *Outside Over There;* paperback: Peter Spier: *Noah's Ark.*

Bancroft Prizes: by Columbia Univ., for American history, $4,000 each: Edward Countryman, *A People in Revolution;* Mary P. Ryan, *Cradle of the Middle Class.*

Irma Simonton Black Award, by Bank Street College, for children's literature (1981): William Steig, *Gorky Rises.*

Boston Globe-Horn Book Awards, for children's literature (1981): fiction: Lynn Hall, *The Leaving;* Kathryn Lasky: *The Weaver's Gift;* illustration: Maurice Sendak; *Outside Over There.*

Randolph Caldecott Medal, by American Library Assn., for children's book illustration: Chris Van Allsburg, *Jumanji.*

Canada Council Children's Literature Prizes (1981), $5,000 each: Monica Hughes, *The Guardian of Isis;* Suzanne Martel, *Nos amis robots;* illustrations: Heather Woodall, *Ytek and the Arctic Orchid;* Joanne Ouellet, *Les Papinachois.*

Christopher Awards, for affirmation of human spirit: Donald Woods, *Asking for Trouble;* Karen Burton Mains, *The Fragile Curtain;* Joanna L. Stratton, *Pioneer Women;* Barry Neil Kaufman, *A Miracle to Believe In;* Mark Ya. Azbel, *Refusenik;* John Bierman, *Righteous Gentile;* Eugenia Ginsburg, *Within the Whirlwind;* children: Caroline Feller Bauer, *My Mom Travels a Lot,* illustrations, Nancy Winslow Parker; Barbara Shook Haven, *Even If I Did Something Awful;* Malcolm MacCloud, *A Gift of Mirrorvax;* John Rowe Townsend, *The Islanders.*

Golden Kite Awards (1981), by Society of Children's Book Writers: fiction: M.E. Kerr, *Little, Little;* non-fiction: Elizabeth Helfman, *Blissymbolics.*

Ernest Hemingway Award, $7,500: Marilynne Robinson, *Housekeeping.*

University of Iowa School of Letters Award, for Short Fiction, $1,000: Dianne Benedict, *Shiny Objects.*

Lamont Poetry Selection, by Academy of American Poets: Carolyn Forche, *The Country Between Us.*

Lenore Marshall Poetry Prize, by *Saturday Review* and New Hope Foundation: Sterling A. Brown, *The Collected Poems of Sterling A. Brown.*

Mystery Writers of America Edgar Allan Poe awards: Grand Master: Julian Symons: novel: William Bayer, *Peregrine;* first novel: Stuart Woods, *Chiefs;* fact crime: Robert W. Greene, *The Sting Man;* critical-biographical: Jon L. Breen, *What About Murder;* paperback: L.A. Morse, *The Old Dick;* juvenile: Norma Fox Mazer, *Taking Terri Mueller;* short story: Jack Richie, "The Absence of Emily"; special: William Vivian, *The Young Detective's Handbook;* Jerome Chodorov, Norman Panama, "A Talent for Murder."

National Arts Club Gold Medal of Honor for Literature: Leon Edel.

National Book Critics Circle Awards (1981): fiction: John Updike, *Rabbit Is Rich;* general nonfiction: Stephen Jay Gould, *The Mismeasure of Man;* poetry: A.R. Ammons, *A Coast of Trees;* criticism: Virgil Thomson: *A Virgil Thomson Reader.*

National Jewish Book Awards, by Jewish Book Council, $500 each: fiction: Mark Helprin, *Ellis Island and Other Stories;* children's literature: Kathryn Lasky, *The Night Journey;* Jewish thought: Robert Alter, *The Art of Biblical Narrative;* Jewish history: David Ruderman, *The World of a Renaissance Jew;* holocaust: Michael Marrus, Robert O. Paxton, *Vichy France and the Jews;* Israel: Howard M. Sacher, *Egypt and Israel,* visual arts: Jannet Blatter, Sybil Milton, *Art of the Holocaust;* Yiddish literature: Joshua A. Fishman, *Never Say Die!*

John Newbery Medal, by American Library Assn., for

children's book: Nancy Willard, *A Visit to William Blake's Inn.*

New York Times Best Illustrated Children's Books: Suekichi Akaba, *The Crane Wife;* Stephen Gammel, *Where the Buffaloes Begin;* Warwick Hutton, *The Nose Tree;* Anita Lobel, *On Market Street;* Nancy Winslow Parker, *My Mom Travels a Lot;* Robert Andrew Parker, *Flight;* Marcia Sewall, *The Story of Old Mrs. Brubeck;* Maurice Sendak, *Outside Over There;* Chris Van Allsburg, *Jumanji;* Paul O. Zelinsky, *The Maid and the Mouse and the Odd-Shaped House.*

PEN Writing Awards for Prisoners: Malcolm Braly Prize for fiction: Tony Menninger; nonfiction: William Williams; Richard C. Stanin; Muriel Rukeyser Prize in poetry: D.L. Adamson.

Poetry Society of America: Melville Cane Award: Paul H. Fry, *The Poet's Calling in the English Ode;* Alice Fay diCastagnola Award: Carolyn Forche, *The Country Between Us;* Shelley Memorial Award: Robert Creeley; William Carlos Williams Award: Brewster Ghiselin: *Windrose.*

Phi Beta Kappa Awards: Ralph Waldo Emerson Award: George Frederickson, *White Supremacy;* Christian Gauss Award: Robert Bernard Martin: *Tennyson;* science Award: Eric Chaisson, *Cosmic Dawn.*

Regina Medal, by Catholic Library Association: Theodor ("Dr. Seuss") Geisel.

Delmore Schwartz Memorial Poetry Award: Constance Urdang.

Science Fiction Writers of America Nebula Awards (1981): novel: Gene Wolfe, *The Claw of the Conciliator;* novella: Poul Anderson, *The Saturn Game;* novelette: Michael Bishop, *The Quickening;* short story: Lisa Tuttle, "The Bone Flute."

National Council of Teachers of English Award, for excellence in poetry for children (1981): Eve Merriam.

Western Writers of America Spur Awards: novel: Jeanne Williams, *The Valiant Woman;* Stan Hoig, *The Peace Chiefs of the Cheyennes.*

Walt Whitman Award, Academy of American Poets, $1,000: Anthony Petrosky, Jurgis Petraskas.

Yale Series of Younger Poets, by Yale University: David Wojahn, *Icehouse Lights.*

Journalism Awards

Worth Bingham Prizes, for political reporting or commentary, $1,000: Ralph Soda, Gannett News Service, Jonathan Neumann, Ted Gup, *Washington Post.*

Heywood Broun Awards, for concern for the underdog (1981), $1,000: Barb Brucker, Jim Underwood, *Mansfield* (Oh.) *News.*

Raymond Clapper Award, for reporting on national government (1981), $1,500: Nicholas Lemann, *Washington Post;* John Fialka, *Washington Star;* Jerry Landauer, *Wall Street Journal.*

John L. Dougherty Memorial Award, for young Associated Press writer, by AP managing editors (1981), $1,000: James Litke.

John Hancock Awards, John Hancock Mutual Life Ins. Co., for writing on business and financial subjects, $6,000: Ralph Soda, Gannett News Service; Thomas N. Bethell, Gregg Easterbrook, *Washington Monthly;* William Wolman and team, *Business Week;* A. Kent MacDougall, *Los Angeles Times;* Philip Moeller, *Louisville Courier-Journal;* Charlotte Wittwer, *Pensacola* (Fla.) *News-Journal.*

Sidney Hillman Foundation Prizes, for humanitarian causes (1981), $750: *Miami Herald* team.

Robert F. Kennedy Journalism Awards, for problems of disadvantaged (1981), $6,000: Len Lahman, *Escondido* (Calif.) *Times Advocate;* Mary Ellen Mark, *Life; Charlotte Observer* staff.

H.L. Mencken Prize, for newspaper writing in Mencken spirit, $2,500: Mike Royko, *Chicago Sun-Times.*

Roland Michener Award, for public service journalism in Canada: Wendy Koenig, *Edmonton Journal;* Frank Jones, *Toronto Star;* Mary Kate Ronan, James Jefferson, *Toronto Globe and Mail.*

National Magazine Awards, by American Society of Magazine Editors: general excellence: *Newsweek, Science '81, Rocky Mountain, Camera Arts;* public service: *Atlantic;* fiction: *New Yorker;* reporting: John Pekkanen, *Washingtonian;* essays and criticism: *Atlantic;* service to individual: Carol Saline, *Philadelphia;* single-topic: Peter Goldman, *Newsweek;* design: *Nautical Quarterly.*

Penney-Missouri Awards, Univ. of Missouri School of Journalism, $12,850: single story: David Hacker, *Kansas City* (Mo.) *Times;* series: Madeleine Blais, *Miami Herald;* consumer affairs: Ben Z. Hershberg, Loni White, *Courier-Journal,* Louisville, Ky.; fashion: Tracy Brobston, *Dallas Morning News;* sections: Tom Shantz, ed., *Concord* (N.H.) *Monitor;* Janet J. Woods, ed., *Evening Independent,* St. Petersburg, Fla.; Richard Curtis, ed., *News-American,* Baltimore; Ande Zellman, ed., *Boston Phoenix;* Carroll Stoner, ed., *Chicago Sun-Times.*

Penney-Missouri Magazine Awards, for lifestyle journalism, $6,000: Ron Javers, *Philadelphia;* John Underwood, *Sports Illustrated;* John Pekkanen, *Washingtonian;* Noriko Sawads, *Ms.;* D. Susan Barron, *Boston;* Lee Walburn, *Atlanta.*

Pictures of the Year, by Nikon, National Press Photographers Assn., and University of Missouri: newspaper photographer of the year: George Wedding, *San Jose Mercury-News;* magazine photographer of the year: Jim Brandenburg, *National Geographic;* world understanding: Bryce Flynn, *Providence Journal;* newspaper picture editor: Rick Perry, *Seattle Times;* newspaper-magazine picture editor: J. Bruce Baumann, *San Jose Mercury-News;* magazine picture editor: Elisabeth Biondi, *GEO.*

George Polk Awards, by Long Island Univ., for reporting: foreign: John Darnton, *New York Times;* national: Seymour M. Hersh, Jeff Gerth, Philip Taubman, *New York Times;* regional: Stephanie Saul, W. Stevens Ricks, *Jackson* (Miss.) *Clarion-Ledger;* local: Orlando (Fla.) *Sentinel Star;* consumer: Phil Norman, *Louisville* (Ky.) *Courier-Journal;* magazine: William Greider, *Atlantic;* science: *Science* magazine's "News and Comment" section; special: George Seldes, for entire career.

Reuben Awards, cartoons, by Nat. Cartoonists Society: Charles Saxon, *The New Yorker;* John Cullen Murphy, "Prince Valiant"; Bill Hoest, "The Lockhorns"; Dick Moores, "Gasoline Alley"; Karl Hubenthal, *Los Angeles Herald-Examiner;* Sam Norkin, *New York Daily News;* Brant Parker, "The Wizard of Id"; Larry Wright, *Detroit News.*

Scripps-Howard Foundation Awards, $25,500: Walker Stone Award, for editorial writing: Jay Ambrose, *Rocky Mountain News;* Edward Willis Scripps Award, for First Amendment reporting: *Des Moines* (Ia.) *Register;* Edward J. Meeman Awards, for conservation reporting: *Newsday,* Long Island, N.Y., *Arizona Daily Star;* Ernie Pyle Memorial Award, for human interest writing: Mike Royko, *Chicago Sun-Times;* Charles M. Schulz Award, for promising cartoonist: Paul Kolsti, *Dallas Morning News;* Roy M. Howard Award, for public service: *Seattle Times.*

Sigma Delta Chi Awards, by Society of Professional Journalists (1981): general reporting: David L. Ashenfelter, Sydney P. Freedberg, *Detroit News;* news photography: Ron Edmonds, Associated Press; editorial writing: Jon T. Sendering, *Dallas Times-Herald;* Washington correspondence: Jerome Watson, *Chicago Sun-Times;* foreign correspondence: Richard Ben Cramer, *Philadelphia Inquirer;* editorial cartoon: Paul Conrad, *Los Angeles Times;* magazine reporting: Seymour Hersh, *New York Times Magazine;* public service: *National Geographic.*

Merriman Smith Award, for presidential news coverage on deadline, $750: Ed Walsh, *Washington Post.*

Edward Weintal Prize, for U.S. foreign policy reporting and analysis (1981), $5,000: Geoffrey Godsell, *Christian Science Monitor.*

Broadcasting and Theater Awards

Christopher Awards: special: James Cagney, *Today,* NBC; *Bill,* CBS; *Bitter Harvest,* NBC; *Close Harmony,* WNET/PBS; *The Color of Friendship,* ABC; *Crisis at Central High,* CBS; *Family Renunion,* NBC; *That Yankee Doodle Dandy,* PBS; *A Long Way Home,* ABC; *The Marva Collins Story,* CBS; *Miracle on Ice,* ABC; *The Patricia Neal*

Story, CBS; *Pride of Jesse Hallam*, CBS.

DuPont-Columbia Awards, for broadcast journalism, $20,000: Peter Karl, Pam Zekman, WLS-TV, Chicago, with *Chicago Sun-Times;* Carol Mon Pere, Sandra Nichols, KTEH-TV, San Jose, Calif; Walter Jacobson, WBBM-TV, Chicago; Mary Feldhous-Weber, WGBY-TV, Springfield, Mass.; Perry Miller, WNET/13, New York City; Julius Cain, Robert Squier, Mississippi ETV; Dave Bryan, Tony Lame, Doug Macomber, Group W; Barbara Cohen, Christopher Koch, Frank Fitzmaurice, NPR; William Lord, ABC-TV; Ed Bradley, CBS-TV; Roger Mudd, CBS-TV; Reuven Frank, NBC-TV.

Emmy Awards, by Academy of Television Arts and Sciences, for nighttime programs, 1980-81: dramatic series: *Hill Street Blues;* actor: Daniel J. Travanti, *Hill Street Blues;* actress: Barbara Babcock, *Hill Street Blues;* supporting actor: Michael Conrad: *Hill Street Blues;* supporting actress: Nancy Marchand, *Lou Grant;* director: Robert Butler, *Hill Street Blues;* writer: Michael Kozoll, Steven Bochco, *Hill Street Blues;* comedy series: *Taxi;* actor: Judd Hirsch, *Taxi;* actress: Isabel Sanford, *The Jeffersons;* supporting actor: Danny De Vito, *Taxi;* supporting actress: Eileen Brennan, *Private Benjamin;* director: James Burrows, *Taxi;* writer: Michael Leeson, *Taxi;* special: drama: *Playing for Time;* actor: Anthony Hopkins, *The Bunker;* actress: Vanessa Redgrave, *Playing for Time;* director: James Goldstone, *Kent State;* writer: Arthur Miller, *Playing for Time;* supporting actor: David Warner, *Masada;* supporting actress: Jane Alexander, *Playing for Time;* limited series: *Shogun;* variety, music, or comedy: Lily, Sold-Out; director: Don Mischer, *The Kennedy Center Honors;* writer: Jerry Juhl, David Odell, Chris Langham, Jim Henson, Don Hinkley, *The Muppet Show* with Carol Burnett; lighting: Ralph Holmes, *Nureyev and the Joffrey Ballet;* hairstyling, Shirley Padgett, *Madame X.*

George Jean Nathan Award, for drama criticism, $5,000: Sylvianne Gold and Carolyn Clay, *The Boston Phoenix.*

New York Film Critics Circle: film: *Reds;* actor: Burt Lancaster, *Atlantic City;* actress: Glenda Jackson, *Stevie;* supporting actor: John Gielgud, *Arthur;* supporting actress: Mona Washbourne, *Stevie;* director: Sidney Lumet, *Prince of the City;* screenwriter: John Guare, *Atlantic City;* cinematography: *Chariots of Fire;* foreign: Pixote: special awards: Kryzsztof Zanussi, Andrej Wajda; Abdel Gance's *Napoleon.*

Obie Awards, for Off- or Off-Off Broadway theater: play: Tadeusz Kantor, *Wielopole, Wielopole;* American play: Squat, *Mr. Dead and Mrs. Free,* Martha Clarke, Linda Hunt, David Rounds, Jeff Wanshel, Noa Ain, Penny Stegenga, *A Metamorphosis in Miniature;* sustained achievement: Maria Irene Fornes; playwriting: Caryl Churchill, *Cloud 9;* Robert Auletta, *Virgins* and *Stops;* performance: Kevin Bacon, *Forty Deuce* and *Poor Little Lambs;* James Barbarosa, *Soon Jack November;* Ray Dooley, *Peer Gynt;* Christine Estabrook, *Pastorale;* Michael Gross, *No End of Blame;* E. Katherine Kerr, *Cloud 9;* Kenneth McMillan, *Weekends Like Other People;* Kevin O'Connor, *Chucky's Hunch, Birdbath, Crossing the Crab Nebula;* Carole Shelley, *Twelve Dreams;* Josef Sommer, *Lydie Breeze;* Irene Worth, *The Chalk Garden;* ensemble performance: Adolph Caesar, Larry Riley, Denzel Washington, *A Soldier's Play;* Lisa Banes, Brenda Currin, Beverly May, Elizabeth McGovern, *My Sister In This House;* set design: Jim Clayburgh; lighting design: Arden Fingerhut.

George Foster Peabody Broadcasting Awards, by Univ. of Georgia School of Journalism: *She's Nobody's Baby,* HBO; *An Evening with Danny Kaye and the New York Philharmonic,* PBS; *Skokie,* CBS; WJR radio, Detroit; *The Odyssey of Homer,* National Radio Theatre, Chicago; *Carl Sandburg at Connemara,* Canadian Broadcasting Corp.; *The Todds' Teddy Bears Picnic,* Timothy and Susan Todd; WQDR-FM, Raleigh, N.C.; *Eyewitness News,* WLS-TV, Chicago; Bill Leonard, CBS News, New York; John Goldsmith, WDVM-TV, Washington; *Hill Street Blues,* NBC and M.T.M. Enterprises; Nebraska Educational Television; *General Electric Theater,* CBS-TV, Alan Landsburg Productions.

Antoinette Perry Awards (Tonys), for Broadway theater: play: *The Life and Adventures of Nicholas Nickleby,* David Edgar; actor: Roger Rees, *The Life and Adventures of Nicholas Nickleby;* actress: Zoe Caldwell, *Medea;* featured actor: Zakes Mokae, *Master Harold...and the Boys;* featured actress: Amanda Plummer, *Agnes of God;* director: Trevor Nunn, John Caird, *The Life and Adventures of Nicholas Nickleby;* musical: *Dreamgirls,* Tom Eyen, Harvey Krieger; actor: Adam Harney, *Dreamgirls;* actress: Jennifer Holiday, *Dreamgirls;* featured actor: Cleavon Derrick, *Dreamgirls;* director: Tommy Tune, *9;* choreographer, Michael Bennett, Michael Peters, *Dreamgirls;* score: Maury Yeston, *9;* scenic design: John Napier, Dermit Hayes, *The Life and Adventures of Nicholas Nickleby;* costume design: William Ivey Long, *9;* lighting design: Tharon Musser, *Dreamgirls.*

Richard Rodgers Production Award, by American Academy and Institute of Arts and Letters: Damien Leake, *Child of the Sun.*

Theater Hall of Fame, by American Theater Critics Assn.: Gower Champion, George Kelly, Angela Lansbury, Burgess Meredith, Harold Prince, Stephen Sondheim, Lee Strasberg.

Miscellaneous Awards

Brandeis University Creative Arts Awards, $2,500: C. Vann Woodward, historian; Stephen Sondheim, composer; Trisha Brown, dancer, choreographer; Jennifer Tipton, lighting designer; Peter Voulkos, sculptor.

Crafoord Mathematics Prize, by Sweden's Royal Academy, $30,000: Louis Nirenberg, New York Univ. Courant Institute of Math. Sciences; V.I. Arnold, Soviet Union.

General Motors Cancer Research Awards, $1,000 each: Dr. Denis Parsons Burkitt, senior research fellow, St. Thomas Hospital, London; Dr. Howard Earle Skipper, Southern Research Institute, Birmingham, Ala.; Dr. Stanley Cohen, Vanderbilt Univ. School of Medicine.

John D. and Catherine MacArthur Prize, $24,000-$60,000 each: Conlon Nancarrow, composer; Fouad Ajami, Middle East Affairs specialist; Charles Bigelow, graphic designer trained in anthropological linguistics; Peter Brown, social historian; Robert Darnton, historian; Persi Diaconis, specialist in mathematical statistics; William Gaddis, novelist; Ved Mehta, nonfiction writer; Robert Moses, graduate student in education; Richard Muller, physicist; Alfonso Ortiz, anthropologist; Francesca Rochberg-Halton, historian; Charles Sabel, social theorist; Ralph Shapey, composer; Michael Silverstein, anthropoligist; Randolph Whitfield, ophthalmologist; Frank Wilczek, physicist; Frederick Wiseman, documentary filmmaker; Edward Witten, physicist.

Edward MacDowell Medal, for lifelong contribution to the arts: sculptor Isamu Noguchi.

Samuel H. Scripps-American Dance Festival Award: choreographer Merce Cunningham.

Motion Picture Academy Awards (Oscars)

1927-28

Actor: Emil Jannings, *The Way of All Flesh.*
Actress: Janet Gaynor, *Seventh Heaven.*
Picture: *Wings,* Paramount.

1928-29

Actor: Warner Baxter, *In Old Arizona.*
Actress: Mary Pickford, *Coquette.*
Picture: *Broadway Melody,* MGM.

1929-30

Actor: George Arliss, *Disraeli.*
Actress: Norma Shearer, *The Divorcee.*
Picture: *All Quiet on the Western Front,* Univ.

1930-31

Actor: Lionel Barrymore, *Free Soul.*
Actress: Marie Dressler, *Min and Bill.*
Picture: *Cimarron,* RKO.

1931-32

Actor: Fredric March, *Dr. Jekyll and Mr. Hyde;* Wallace Beery, *The Champ* (tie).
Actress: Helen Hayes, *Sin of Madelon Claudet.*

Picture: *Grand Hotel,* MGM.
Special: Walt Disney, *Mickey Mouse.*

1932-33

Actor: Charles Laughton, *Private Life of Henry VIII.*
Actress: Katharine Hepburn, *Morning Glory.*
Picture: *Cavalcade,* Fox.

1934

Actor: Clark Gable, *It Happened One Night.*
Actress: Claudette Colbert, same.
Picture: *It Happened One Night,* Columbia.

1935

Actor: Victor McLaglen, *The Informer.*
Actress: Bette Davis, *Dangerous.*
Picture: *Mutiny on the Bounty,* MGM.

1936

Actor: Paul Muni, *Story of Louis Pasteur.*
Actress: Luise Rainer, *The Great Ziegfeld.*
Picture: *The Great Ziegfeld,* MGM.

1937

Actor: Spencer Tracy, *Captains Courageous.*
Actress: Luise Rainer, *The Good Earth.*
Picture: *Life of Emile Zola,* Warner.

1938

Actor: Spencer Tracy, *Boys Town.*
Actress: Bette Davis, *Jezebel.*
Picture: *You Can't Take It With You,* Columbia.

1939

Actor: Robert Donat, *Goodbye Mr. Chips.*
Actress: Vivien Leigh, *Gone With the Wind.*
Picture: *Gone With the Wind,* Selznick International.

1940

Actor: James Stewart, *The Philadelphia Story.*
Actress: Ginger Rogers, *Kitty Foyle.*
Picture: *Rebecca,* Selznick International.

1941

Actor: Gary Cooper, *Sergeant York.*
Actress: Joan Fontaine, *Suspicion.*
Picture: *How Green Was My Valley,* 20th Cent.-Fox.

1942

Actor: James Cagney, *Yankee Doodle Dandy.*
Actress: Greer Garson, *Mrs. Miniver.*
Picture: *Mrs. Miniver,* MGM.

1943

Actor: Paul Lukas, *Watch on the Rhine.*
Actress: Jennifer Jones, *The Song of Bernadette.*
Picture: *Casablanca,* Warner.

1944

Actor: Bing Crosby, *Going My Way.*
Actress: Ingrid Bergman, *Gaslight.*
Picture: *Going My Way,* Paramount.

1945

Actor: Ray Milland, *The Lost Weekend.*
Actress: Joan Crawford, *Mildred Pierce.*
Picture: *The Lost Weekend,* Paramount.

1946

Actor: Fredric March, *Best Years of Our Lives.*
Actress: Olivia de Havilland, *To Each His Own.*
Picture: *The Best Years of Our Lives,* Goldwyn, RKO.

1947

Actor: Ronald Colman, *A Double Life.*
Actress: Loretta Young, *The Farmer's Daughter.*
Picture: *Gentleman's Agreement,* 20th Cent.-Fox.

1948

Actor: Laurence Olivier, *Hamlet.*
Actress: Jane Wyman, *Johnny Belinda.*
Picture: *Hamlet,* Two Cities Film, Universal International.

1949

Actor: Broderick Crawford. *All the King's Men.*
Actress: Olivia de Havilland, *The Heiress.*
Picture: *All the King's Men,* Columbia.

1950

Actor: Jose Ferrer, *Cyrano de Bergerac.*
Actress: Judy Holliday, *Born Yesterday.*
Picture: *All About Eve,* 20th Century-Fox.

1951

Actor: Humphrey Bogart, *The African Queen.*
Actress: Vivien Leigh, *A Streetcar Named Desire.*
Picture: *An American in Paris,* MGM.

1952

Actor: Gary Cooper, *High Noon.*
Actress: Shirley Booth, *Come Back, Little Sheba.*
Picture: *Greatest Show on Earth,* C.B. DeMille, Paramount.

1953

Actor: William Holden, *Stalag 17.*
Actress: Audrey Hepburn, *Roman Holiday.*
Picture: *From Here to Eternity,* Columbia.

1954

Actor: Marlon Brando, *On the Waterfront.*
Actress: Grace Kelly, *The Country Girl.*
Picture: *On the Waterfront,* Horizon-American, Colum.

1955

Actor: Ernest Borgnine, *Marty.*
Actress: Anna Magnani, *The Rose Tattoo.*
Picture: *Marty,* Hecht and Lancaster's Steven Prods., U.A.

1956

Actor: Yul Brynner, *The King and I.*
Actress: Ingrid Bergman, *Anastasia.*
Picture: *Around the World in 80 Days,* Michael Todd, U.A.

1957

Actor: Alec Guinness, *The Bridge on the River Kwai.*
Actress: Joanne Woodward, *The Three Faces of Eve.*
Picture: *The Bridge on the River Kwai,* Columbia.

1958

Actor: David Niven, *Separate Tables.*
Actress: Susan Hayward, *I Want to Live.*
Picture: *Gigi,* Arthur Freed Production, MGM.

1959

Actor: Charlton Heston, *Ben-Hur.*
Actress: Simone Signoret, *Room at the Top.*
Picture: *Ben-Hur,* MGM.

1960

Actor: Burt Lancaster, *Elmer Gantry.*
Actress: Elizabeth Taylor, *Butterfield 8.*
Picture: *The Apartment,* Mirisch Co., U.A.

1961

Actor: Maximilian Schell, *Judgment at Nuremberg.*
Actress: Sophia Loren, *Two Women.*
Picture: *West Side Story,* United Artists.

1962

Actor: Gregory Peck, *To Kill a Mockingbird.*
Actress: Anne Bancroft, *The Miracle Worker.*
Picture: *Lawrence of Arabia,* Columbia.

1963

Actor: Sidney Poitier, *Lilies of the Field.*
Actress: Patricia Neal, *Hud.*
Picture: *Tom Jones,* Woodfall Prod., UA-Lopert Pictures.

1964

Actor: Rex Harrison, *My Fair Lady.*
Actress: Julie Andrews, *Mary Poppins.*
Picture: *My Fair Lady,* Warner Bros.

1965

Actor: Lee Marvin, *Cat Ballou.*
Actress: Julie Christie, *Darling.*
Picture: *The Sound of Music,* 20th Century-Fox.

1966

Actor: Paul Scofield, *A Man for All Seasons.*
Actress: Elizabeth Taylor, *Who's Afraid of Virginia Woolf?*
Picture: *A Man for All Seasons,* Columbia.

1967

Actor: Rod Steiger, *In the Heat of the Night.*
Actress: Katharine Hepburn, *Guess Who's Coming to Dinner.*
Picture: *In the Heat of the Night.*

1968

Actor: Cliff Robertson, *Charly.*
Actress: Katharine Hepburn, *The Lion in Winter;* Barbra Streisand, *Funny Girl* (tie).
Picture: *Oliver.*

1969

Actor: John Wayne, *True Grit.*
Actress: Maggie Smith, *The Prime of Miss Jean Brodie.*
Picture: *Midnight Cowboy.*

1970

Actor: George C. Scott, *Patton* (refused).
Actress: Glenda Jackson, *Women in Love.*
Picture: *Patton.*

1971

Actor: Gene Hackman, *The French Connection.*
Actress: Jane Fonda, *Klute.*
Picture: *The French Connection.*

1972

Actor: Marlon Brando, *The Godfather* (refused).
Actress: Liza Minnelli, *Cabaret.*
Picture: *The Godfather.*

1973

Actor: Jack Lemmon, *Save the Tiger.*
Actress: Glenda Jackson, *A Touch of Class.*
Picture: *The Sting.*

1974

Actor: Art Carney, *Harry and Tonto.*
Actress: Ellen Burstyn, *Alice Doesn't Live Here Anymore.*
Picture: *The Godfather, Part II.*

1975
Actor: Jack Nicholson, *One Flew Over the Cuckoo's Nest.*
Actress: Louise Fletcher, same.
Picture: *One Flew Over the Cuckoo's Nest.*

1976
Actor: Peter Finch, *Network.*
Actress: Faye Dunaway, same.
Picture: *Rocky.*

1977
Actor: Richard Dreyfuss, *The Goodbye Girl.*
Actress: Diane Keaton, *Annie Hall.*
Picture: *Annie Hall.*

1978
Actor: Jon Voight, *Coming Home.*
Actress: Jane Fonda, *Coming Home.*
Picture: *The Deer Hunter.*

1979
Actor: Dustin Hoffman, *Kramer vs. Kramer.*
Actress: Sally Field, *Norma Rae.*
Picture: *Kramer vs. Kramer.*

1980
Actor: Robert De Niro, *Raging Bull.*
Actress: Sissy Spacek, *Coal Miner's Daughter.*
Picture: *Ordinary People.*

1981
Actor: Henry Fonda, *On Golden Pond.*
Actress: Katharine Hepburn, *On Golden Pond.*
Picture: *Chariots of Fire.*
Director: Warren Beatty, *Reds.*
Foreign Film: *Mephisto.*
Supporting Actor: John Gielgud, *Arthur.*
Supporting Actress: Maureen Stapleton, *Reds.*
Screenplay (original): Colin Welland, *Chariots of Fire.*
(adapted): Ernest Thompson, *On Golden Pond.*
Editing: Michael Kahn, *Raiders of the Lost Ark.*
Cinematography: Vittorio Storaro, *Reds.*
Score (original): Vangelis, *Chariots of Fire.*
Song: "Arthur's Theme," *Arthur.*
Art Direction: Norman Reynolds, Leslie Dilley, Michael Ford, *Raiders of the Lost Ark.*
Costumes: Milena Canonero, *Chariots of Fire.*
Sound: Bill Varney, Steve Maslow, Gregg Landaker, Roy Charman, *Raiders of the Lost Ark.*
Visual Effects: Richard Edlund, Kit West, Bruce Nicholson, Joe Johnston, *Raiders of the Lost Ark.*

Genie (Canadian Film) Awards

Source: Academy of Canadian Cinema

(To qualify, films must be Canadian-made; actors and actresses must be Canadian citizens or landed immigrants starring in a Canadian film. Awards apply to films released the previous year.)

1976
Actor: Andre Melancon, Partis pur la gloire
Actress: Marilyn Lightstone, Lies My Father Told Me
Picture: Lies My Father Told Me

1977
Actor: Len Cariou, One Man
Actress: Monique Mercure, J.A. Martin: Photographe
Picture: J.A. Martin: Photographe

1978
Actor: Richard Gabourie, Three Card Monte
Actress: Helen Shaver, In Praise of Older Women
Picture: The Silent Partner

1979
No awards

1980
Actor: Christopher Plummer, Murder By Decree
Actress: Kate Lynch, Meatballs
Picture: The Changeling

1981
Actor: Thomas Peacocke, The Hounds of Notre Dame
Actress: Marie Tifo, Les Bons Debarras
Picture: Les Bons Debarras

1982
Actor: Nick Mancuso, Ticket to Heaven
Actress: Margot Kidder, Heartaches
Picture: Ticket to Heaven

The Spingarn Medal

The Spingarn Medal has been awarded annually since 1914 by the National Association for the Advancement of Colored People for the highest achievement by a black American.

1946 Dr. Percy L. Julian
1947 Channing H. Tobias
1948 Ralph J. Bunche
1949 Charles Hamilton Houston
1950 Mabel Keaton Staupers
1951 Harry T. Moore
1952 Paul R. Williams
1953 Theodore K. Lawless
1954 Carl Murphy
1955 Jack Roosevelt Robinson
1956 Martin Luther King Jr.
1957 Mrs. Daisy Bates and the Little Rock Nine
1958 Edward Kennedy (Duke) Ellington
1959 Langston Hughes
1960 Kenneth B. Clark
1961 Robert C. Weaver
1962 Medgar Wiley Evers
1963 Roy Wilkins
1964 Leontyne Price
1965 John H. Johnson
1966 Edward W. Brooke
1967 Sammy Davis Jr.
1968 Clarence M. Mitchell Jr.
1969 Jacob Lawrence
1970 Leon Howard Sullivan
1971 Gordon Parks
1972 Wilson C. Riles
1973 Damon Keith
1974 Henry (Hank) Aaron
1975 Alvin Ailey
1976 Alex Haley
1977 Andrew Young
1978 Mrs. Rosa L. Parks
1979 Dr. Rayford W. Logan
1980 Coleman Young
1981 Dr. Benjamin Elijah Mays

The Governor General's Literary Awards

Canada's most prestigious literary awards, instituted in 1937 by the Canadian Authors Association with the agreement of then Governor General John Buchan (Lord Tweedsmuir), a novelist. The awards, now administered by the Canada Council, include a $5,000 cash prize.

	English	French
1979		
Fiction:	The Resurrection of Joseph Bourne, Jack Hodkins	Le Sourd dans la ville, Marie- Claire Blais
Non-fiction:	Emily Carr: A Biography, Maria Tippett	Le fait anglais au Quebec, Dominique Clift and Sheila McLeod Arnopoulos
Poetry or Drama:	There's a Trick with a Knife I'm Learning to Do, Michael Ondaatje	Peinture aveugle, Robert Melancon
1980		
Fiction:	Burning Water, George Bowering	La première personne, Pierre Turgeon
Non-fiction:	Discipline of Power: The Conservative Interlude and the Liberal Restoration, Jeffrey Simpson	La famille et l'homme à délivrer du pouvoir, Maurice Champagne-Gilbert
Poetry or Drama:	McAlmon's Chinese Opera, Stephen Scobie	
1981		
Fiction:	Home Truths, Mavis Gallant	La Province Lunaire, Denys Chabot
Non-fiction:	Caribou and the Barren Lands, George Calef	L'Echappee des Discours de L'Oeil, Madelaine Ouellette-Michalska
Poetry:	Collected Poems, R.F. Scott	Visages, Michele Beaulieu
Drama:	Blood Relations and Other Plays, Sharon Pollock	C'Etait Avant A Guerre A L'anse A Gilles, Marie Laberge

ARTS AND MEDIA

Notable New York Theater Openings, 1981-82 Season

A Soldier's Play, drama by Charles Fuller; directed by Douglas Turner Ward; winner of the 1982 Pulitzer Prize.

A Talent for Murder, mystery/comedy by Jerome Chodorov and Norman Panama; with Claudette Colbert and Jean-Pierre Aumont.

Agnes of God, play by John Pielmeier; with Geraldine Page, Elizabeth Ashley, and Amanda Plummer.

American Buffalo, revival of the David Mamet play; with Al Pacino.

Blues in the Night, musical revue; with Leslie Uggams, Debbie Shapiro, and Jean Du Shon.

Camelot, revival of the 1961 Lerner and Loewe musical; with Richard Harris, Meg Bussert, and Richard Muenz.

Candida, revival of the George Bernard Shaw comedy; with Joanne Woodward.

Cloud 9, comedy by Caryl Churchill; directed by Tommy Tune.

Come Back to the 5 & Dime Jimmy Dean, Jimmy Dean, play by Ed Craczyk; directed by Robert Altman; with Sandy Dennis, Karen Black, and Cher.

Crimes of the Heart, play by Beth Henley; winner of the 1981 Pulitzer Prize; with Mary Beth Hurt, Mia Dillon, and Lizabeth Mackay.

Dreamgirls, musical by Henry Krieger and Tom Eyen about the rise of a black female singing group in the 1960s; directed and choreographed by Michael Bennett; with Jennifer Holliday.

Duet for One, play by Tom Kempinski; with Anne Bancroft and Max von Sydow.

Joseph and the Amazing Technicolor Dreamcoat, musical by Andrew Lloyd Webber and Tim Rice; directed by Tony Tanner.

Little Johnny Jones, revival of the 1904 George M. Cohan musical; with Donny Osmond.

Little Me, revival of the Neil Simon, Cy Coleman, Carolyn Leigh musical; with James Coco and Victor Garber.

Macbeth, revival of the Shakespearean tragedy; directed by Nicol Williamson; with Nicol Williamson.

Marlowe, contemporary rock musical by Jimmy Horowitz based on the life of Christopher Marlowe; with Lisa Mordente and Patrick Jude.

Mass Appeal, comedy by Bill C. Davis; with Milo O'Shea and Michael O'Keefe.

Master Harold...and the Boys, drama set in South Africa by Athol Fugard; with Zakes Mokae, Danny Glover, and Lonny Price.

Merrily We Roll Along, musical by Stephen Sondheim; with Lonny Price, Ann Morrison, and Jim Walton.

My Fair Lady, revival of the Lerner and Loewe musical classic; with Rex Harrison, Nancy Ringham, and Milo O'-Shea.

Nine, musical by Maury Yeston based on Fellini's *8 1/2;* directed and choreographed by Tommy Tune; with Raul Julia, Anita Morris, Karen Akers, and Liliane Montevecchi.

Othello, revival of the Shakespearean tragedy; with James Earl Jones and Christopher Plummer, and Dianne Wiest.

Pump Boys and Dinettes, musical entertainment of bluegrass, rockabilly, and blues.

Sister Mary Ignatius Explains It All for You, and **The Actor's Nightmare,** 2 comedies by Christopher Durang; with Elizabeth Franz and Jeff Brooks.

Special Occasions, comedy by Bernard Slade; with Suzanne Pleshette and Richard Mulligan.

The Curse of an Aching Heart, drama by William Alfred; with Faye Dunaway.

The Dresser, drama by Ronald Harwood about an aging British Shakespearean actor and his loyal assistant; with Tom Courtenay and Paul Rogers.

The First, musical about the early years of baseball's Jackie Robinson by Bob Brush and Martin Charnin; with David Alan Grier.

The Life and Adventures of Nicholas Nickleby, 2-part, 8 1/2-hour play adapted by David Edgar from the Dickens novel; with Roger Rees and Emily Richard.

The Supporting Cast, comedy by George Furth; with Hope Lange, Betty Garrett, Sandy Dennis, and Jack Gilford.

The West Side Waltz, play by Ernest Thompson; with Katharine Hepburn and Dorothy Loudon.

Torch Song Trilogy, 3 plays by Harvey Fierstein.

Record Long Run Broadway Plays *Still Running June 23, 1982

Grease	3,388
Fiddler on the Roof	3,242
Life With Father	3,224
Tobacco Road	3,182
Hello Dolly	2,844
*Chorus Line	2,842
My Fair Lady	2,717
*Oh, Calcutta (revival)	2,419
Man of La Mancha	2,329
Abie's Irish Rose	2,327
Oklahoma!	2,212
*Annie	2,152
Pippin	1,900
Magic Show	1,859
Deathtrap	1,793
Harvey	1,775
*Dancin'	1,760
Hair	1,742
Gemini	1,740
South Pacific	1,694
The Wiz	1,666
Born Yesterday	1,643
Best Little Whorehouse in Texas	1,584
*Ain't Misbehavin'	1,575
Mary, Mary	1,572
Voice of the Turtle	1,557
Barefoot in the Park	1,532
Mame	1,508
Arsenic and Old Lace	1,444
Same Time, Next Year	1,444
The Sound of Music	1,443
How To Succeed in Business Without Really Trying	1,417
Hellzapoppin	1,404
The Music Man	1,375
Funny Girl	1,348
Oh! Calcutta!	1,316
Angel Street	1.295
Lightnin'	1,291
Promises, Promises	1,281
The King and I	1,246
Cactus Flower	1,234
Sleuth	1,222
"1776"	1,217
Equus	1,207
Guys and Dolls	1,200
Cabaret	1,166
Mister Roberts	1,157
Annie Get Your Gun	1,147
*Evita	1,143
*Sugar Babies	1,128
Butterflies Are Free	1,128
Pins and Needles	1,108
Plaza Suite	1,097
Kiss Me Kate	1,070

Plays in London *Still running June 22, 1982

*The Mousetrap	12,296
Black and White Minstrels	4,354
*No Sex Please, We're British	4,620
Oh! Calcutta!	3,863
Jesus Christ Superstar	3,401
Oliver	2,618
There's a Girl in my Soup	2,547
Pyjama Tops	2,498
Sound of Music	2,386
Sleuth	2,359
Salad Days	2,283
My Fair Lady	2,281
Chu Chin Chow	2,238
Charley Girl	2,202
The Boy Friend	2,084
Canterbury Tales	2,082
Boeing Boeing	2,035

Symphony Orchestras of the U.S. and Canada

Source: American Symphony Orchestra League
(as of June 29, 1982)

Classifications are based on annual incomes or budgets of orchestras.

	Major Symphony Orchestras	Conductor
Atlanta Symphony	1280 Peachtree St., NE, Atlanta, GA 30309	Robert Shaw
Baltimore Symphony	1313 St. Paul St., Baltimore, MD 21210	Sergiu Comissiona
Boston Symphony	Symphony Hall, Boston, MA 02115	Seiji Ozawa
Buffalo Philharmonic	26 Richmond Ave., Buffalo, NY 14222	Julius Rudel
Chicago Symphony	220 S. Michigan Ave., Chicago, IL 60604	Sir Georg Solti
Cincinnati Symphony	1241 Elm St., Cincinnati, OH 45210	Michael Gielen
Cleveland Orchestra	11001 Euclid Ave., Cleveland, OH 44106	Christoph von Dohnanyi
Dallas Symphony	P.O. Box 26207, Dallas, TX 75226	Eduardo Mata
Denver Symphony	1245 Champa St., Denver, CO 80204	Gaetano Delogu
Detroit Symphony	20 Auditorium Dr., Detroit, MI 48226	Gary Bertini
Houston Symphony	615 Louisiana, Houston, TX 77002	Sergiu Comissiona
Indianapolis Symphony	P.O. Box 88207, Indianapolis, IN 46208	John Nelson
Kansas City Philharmonic	200 W. 14th Street, Kansas City, MO 64105	Thomas Michalak
Los Angeles Philharmonic	135 North Grand, Los Angeles, CA 90012	Carlo Giulini
Milwaukee Symphony	929 N. Water St., Milwaukee, WI 53202	Lukas Foss
Minnesota Orchestra	1111 Nicollet Mall, Minneapolis, MN 55403	Neville Marriner
Montreal Symphony	200 de Maisonneuve W., Montreal, Que. H2X 1Y9	Charles Dutoit
National Symphony	JFK Center for the Performing Arts, Wash., DC 20566	Mstislav Rostropovich
New Orleans Philharmonic-Symphony	203 Carondelet St., New Orleans, LA 70130	Philippe Entremont
New York Philharmonic	Avery Fisher Hall, New York, NY 10023	Zubin Mehta
Oregon Symphony	813 SW Alder St., Portland, OR 97205	James DePreist
Philadelphia Orchestra	1420 Locust St., Philadelphia, PA 19102	Ricardo Muti
Pittsburgh Symphony	600 Penn Ave., Pittsburgh, PA 15222	Andre Previn
Rochester Philharmonic	20 Grove Pl., Rochester, NY 14605	David Zinman
St. Louis Symphony	718 N. Grand Blvd., St. Louis, MO 63103	Leonard Slatkin
St. Paul Chamber Orchestra	315 Landmark Ctr., St. Paul, MN 55102	Pinchas Zukerman
San Antonio Symphony	109 Lexington Ave., San Antonio, TX 78205	Lawrence Smith
San Diego Symphony	P.O. Box 3175, San Diego, CA 92103	David Atherton
San Francisco Symphony	Davies Symphony Hall, San Fran., CA 94102	Edo de Waart
Seattle Symphony	305 Harrison St., Seattle, WA 98108	Rainer Miedel
Syracuse Symphony	411 Montgomery St., Syracuse, NY 13202	Christopher Keene
Toronto Symphony	60 Simcoe St., Suite C-116, Toronto, ON M5J 2H5	Andrew Davis
Utah Symphony	123 W. South Temple, Salt Lake City, UT 84101	Varujan Kojian
Vancouver Symphony	873 Beatty St., Vancouver, B.C. V6B 2M6	Kazuyoshi Akiyama

	Regional Orchestras	
Alabama Symphony	P.O. Box 2125, N., Birmingham, AL 35201	Amerigo Marino
American Symphony	119 W. 57th St., New York, NY 10019	Moshe Atmon Guiseppe Patane
Calgary Philharmonic	200-505 Fifth St. SW, Calgary, Alta. T2P 3J2	Mario Bernardi
Charlotte Symphony	110 E. 7th Street, Charlotte, NC 28202	Leo Driehuys
Columbus Symphony	101 E. Town St., Columbus. OH 43215	Evan Whallon
Edmonton Symphony Society	11712 87 Avenue, Edmonton, Alta. T6G 0Y3	Uri Mayer
Flint Symphony	1025 E. Kearsley St., Flint, MI 48503	Isaiah Jackson
Florida Gulf Coast Symphony	3430 W. Kennedy Blvd., Tampa, FL 33609	Irwin Hoffman
Florida Philharmonic	265 Sevilla Ave., Coral Gables, FL 33134	Ranier Meidel
Florida Symphony	P.O. Box 782, Orlando, FL 32802	Sidney Rothstein
Fort Worth Symphony	4401 Trail Lake Dr., Fort Worth, TX 76109	John Giordano
Grand Rapids Symphony	Exhibitors Bldg., Grand Rapids, MI 49503	Semyon Bychkov
Hamilton Philharmonic	P.O. Box 2080, Sta. A, Hamilton, Ont. L8N 3Y7	Boris Brott
Hartford Symphony	609 Farmington, Hartford, CT 06105	Arthur Winograd
Honolulu Symphony	1000 Bishop St., Honolulu, HI 96813	Donald Johanos
Jacksonville Symphony	580 W. 8th St., Suite 9009, Jacksonville, FL 32209	Willis Page
Long Beach Symphony	121 Linden Ave., Long Beach, CA 90802	Murry Sidlin
Los Angeles Chamber Orchestra	285 W. Green St., Pasadena, CA 91105	Gerard Schwarz
Louisville Orchestra	609 W. Main St., Louisville, KY 40202	Akira Endo
Memphis Symphony	3100 Walnut Grove Rd., Memphis, TN 38111	Vincent de Frank
Nashville Symphony	1805 West End Ave., Nashville, TN 37203	Kenneth Schermerhorn
New Jersey Symphony	213 Washington St., Newark, NJ 07101	Thomas Michalak
Oakland Symphony	Paramount Theatre, 2025 Broadway, Oakland, CA 94612	Calvin Simmons
Oklahoma Symphony	512 Civic Center Music Hall, Oklahoma City, OK 73102	Luis Herrera de la Fuente
Omaha Symphony	310 Aquila Ct., Omaha, NE 68102	Thomas Briccetti
Phoenix Symphony	6328 N. 7th St., Phoenix, AZ 85014	Theo Alcantara
Puerto Rico Symphony	Apto 41227, Minillas Sta., Santurce, PR 00940	John Barnett
Quebec Symphony	350 E. St.-Cyrille Blvd., Quebec G1R 2B4	James DePreist
Richmond Symphony	211 W. Franklin St., Richmond, VA 23220	Jacques Houtmann
Sacramento Symphony	Suite 11, 451 Parkfair Dr., Sacramento, CA 95825	Carter Nice
San Jose Symphony	170 Park Center Plaza, San Jose, CA 95113	George Cleve
Spokane Symphony	West 621 Mallon, Spokane, WA 99201	Donald Thulean
Springfield Symphony	56 Dwight St., Springfield, MA 01103	Robert Gutter
Toledo Symphony	1 Stranahan Sq., Toledo, OH 43604	Yuval Zaliouk
Tulsa Philharmonic	2210 South Main, Tulsa, OK 74114	Joel Lazar
Victoria Symphony	631 Superior St., Victoria, B.C. V8V 1V1	Paul Freeman
Virginia Orchestra Group	P.O. Box 26, Norfolk, VA 23501	Richard D. Williams
Wichita Symphony	225 W. Douglas, Wichita, KS 67202	Michael Palmer
Winnipeg Symphony	555 Main St., Winnipeg, Man. R3B 1C3	Vacant

Metropolitan Orchestras

Akron Symphony	Thomas Hall, Hill & Center Sts., Akron, OH 44325	Louis Lane
Albany Symphony	19 Clinton Ave., Albany, NY 12207	Julius Hegyi
Amarillo Symphony	P.O. Box 2552, Amarillo, TX 79105	Thomas Conlin
Arkansas Symphony	P.O. Box 3295, Little Rock, AR 72203	Robert Henderson
Atlantic Symphony	5639 Spring Garden Rd., Halifax, Nova Scot. B3J 1G9	Victor Yampolsky
Austin Symphony	1101 Red River St., Austin, TX 78701	Sung Kwak
B.C. Pops Orchestra	233 Main St., Vestal City, NY 13850	David L. Agard
Bakersfield Symphony	400 Truxton Ave., Suite 201, Bakersfield, CA 93301	John Farrer
Baton Rouge Symphony	P.O. Box 103, Baton Rouge, LA 70821	James Paul
Battle Creek Symphony	P.O. Box 1319, Battle Creek, MI 49016	William Stein
Boise Philharmonic	P.O. Box 2205, Boise, IA 83701	Daniel Stern
(Greater) Bridgeport Symphony	Univ. of Bridgeport, Bridgeport, CT 06602	Gustav Meier
Brooklyn Philharmonia	30 Lafayette Ave., Brooklyn, NY 11217	Lukas Foss
Cabrillo Music Festival	6500 Soquel Dr., Aptos, CA 95003	Dennis Davies
California Chamber Symphony	6380 Wilshire Blvd., Los Angeles, CA 90048	Henri Temianka
Canton Symphony	1001 Market Ave. N., Canton, OH 44702	Gerhardt Zimmerman
Cedar Rapids Symphony	201 Second St. SE, Cedar Rapids, IA 52401	Christian Tiemeyer
Charleston Symphony	3 Chisholm St., Charleston, SC 29401	Lucien DeGroote
Charleston Symphony	P.O. Box 2292, Charleston, WV 25328	Vacant
Chattanooga Symphony	615 Lindsay St., Chattanooga, TN 37402	Richard Cormier
Chautauqua Symphony	Chautauqua Institute, Chautauqua, NY 14722	Varujan Kojian
Clarion Music Society	1860 Broadway, New York, NY 10023	Newell Jenkins
Colorado Music Festival	1245 Pearl, No. 210, Boulder, CO 80302	Giora Bernstein
Colorado Springs Symphony	P.O. Box 1692, Colorado Springs, CO 80901	Charles Ansbacher
Concerto Soloists of Philadelphia	1732 Spruce St., Philadelphia, PA 19103	Marc Mostovoy
Corpus Christi Symphony	P.O. Box 495, Corpus Christi, TX 78403	Cornelius Eberhardt
County Symphony of Westchester	58 W. 58th St., New York, NY 10019	Stephen Simon
Dayton Philharmonic	125 E. First St., Dayton, OH 45402	C. Wendelken-Wilson
Delaware Symphony	P.O. Box 1870, Wilmington, DE 19899	Stephen Gunzenhauser
Des Moines Symphony	411 Shops Bldg., Des Moines, IA 50309	Yuri Krasnapolsky
Duluth-Superior Symphony	506 W. Michigan St., Duluth, MN 55802	Taavo Virkhaus
Eastern Philharmonic	200 N. Davie St., Greensboro, NC 27401	Sheldon Morgenstern
Elkhart Symphony	P.O. Box 144, Elkhart, IN 46514	Michael J. Esselstrom
El Paso Symphony	P.O. Box 180, El Paso, TX 79942	Abraham Chavez Jr.
Erie Philharmonic	409 G. Daniel Baldwin Bldg., Erie, PA 16501	Walter Hendl
Eugene Symphony	1231 Olive St., Eugene, OR 97401	William McGlaughlin
Evansville Philharmonic	P.O. Box 84, Evansville, IN 47701	Stewart Kershaw
Florida Chamber Orchestra	120 E. Oakland Park Blvd., Ft. Lauderdale, FL 33334	James A. Brooks
Florida West Coast Symphony	709 N. Tamiami Trail, Sarasota, FL 33577	Paul Wolfe
Fort Lauderdale Symphony	1430 N. Federal Hwy., Fort Lauderdale, FL 33304	Emerson Buckley
Fort Wayne Philharmonic	1107 S. Harrison, Fort Wayne, IN 46802	Ronald Ondrejka
Fresno Philharmonic	1382 N. Fresno St., Fresno, CA 93703	Guy Taylor
Glendale Symphony	401 N. Brand Blvd., Glendale, CA 91203	Carmen Dragon
Grant Park Symphony	425 E. McFetridge Dr., Chicago, IL 60605	Vacant
Greensboro Symphony	200 N. Davie St., Greensboro, NC 27401	Peter Paul Fuchs
Harrisburg Symphony	22 S. Third St., Harrisburg, PA 17101	Larry Newland
Hartford Chamber Orchestra	15 Lewis St., Hartford, CT 06103	Daniel Parker
Hudson Valley Philharmonic	P.O. Box 191, Poughkeepsie, NY 12602	Imre Pallo
Jackson Symphony	P.O. Box 4584, Jackson, MS 39216	Lewis Dalvit
Johnstown Symphony	230 Walnut St., Johnstown, PA 15901	Donald Barra
Kalamazoo Symphony	426 S. Park St., Kalamazoo, MI 49007	Yoshimi Takeda
Kingston Symphony	86 Lakeshore Blvd., Kingston, Ont. K7L 5C8	Vacant
Kitchener-Waterloo Symphony	101 Queen St. N., Kitchener, Ont., N2H 6P7	Raffi Armenian
Knoxville Symphony	618 Gay St., Knoxville, TN 37902	Zoltan Rozsnyai
Lansing Symphony	230 N. Washington Sq., Lansing, MI 48933	Gustav Meier
Lexington Philharmonic	412 Rose St., Lexington, KY 40508	George Zack
Lincoln Symphony	1315 Sharp Bldg., Lincoln, NE 68508	Robert Emile
Orchestra London Canada	520 Wellington St., London, Ont. N6A 3P9	Alexis Hauser
Long Island Philharmonic	100 Baylis Rd., Huntington, NY 11743	Christopher Keene
Lubbock Symphony	1721 Broadway, Lubbock, TX 79401	William A. Harrod
Madison Symphony	211 N. Carroll St., Madison, WI 53703	Roland Johnson
Marin Symphony	4172 Redwood Hwy., San Rafael, CA 94903	Sandor Salgo
Miami Beach Symphony	420 Lincoln Rd. Mall, Miami Beach, FL 33139	Barnett Breeskin
Midland Symphony	1801 W. St. Andrews, Midland, MI 48640	Adrian Gnam
Midland-Odessa Symphony	P.O. Box 6266, Midland, TX 79701	Thomas Hohstadt
Monterey County Symphony	P.O. Box 3965, Carmel, CA 93921	Haymo Taeuber
National Arts Centre Orchestra	P.O. Box 1534, Sta. B, Ott., Ont. K1P 5W1	Mario Bernardi
New Haven Symphony	33 Whitney Ave., New Haven, CT 06511	Murry Sidlin
New Mexico Symphony	P.O. Box 769, Albuquerque, NM 87103	Yoshima Takeda
Niagara Symphony	P.O. Box 401, St. Catherines, Ont. L2R 6V9	Uri Mayer
Northeastern Pennsylvania Philharmonic	P.O. Box 71, Avoca, PA 18641	Hugh H. Wolff
Northwest Chamber Orchestra	1205 E. Pike, Seattle, WA 98122	Alun Francis
Ohio Chamber Orchestra	11125 Magnolia Dr., Cleveland, OH 44106	Dwight Oltman
Opera Orchestra of N.Y.	211 W. 56th St., N.Y., NY 10019	Eve Queler
Orchestra da Camera	129 East Dr., N. Massapequa, NY 11758	James Conlon James Levine
(Greater) Palm Beach Symphony	P.O. Box 2232, Palm Beach, FL 33480	John Iuele
Pasadena Symphony	300 E. Green St., Pasadena, CA 91101	Daniel Lewis
Peoria Symphony	416 Hamilton, Peoria, IL 61602	William Wilsen
Portland Symphony	30 Myrtle St., Portland, ME 04101	Bruce Hangen
Queens Symphony	99-11 Queens Blvd., Rego Park, NY 11374	David Katz
Regina Symphony	200 Lakeshore Dr., Regina, Sask. S4S 0B3	Simon Streatfeild
Rhode Island Philharmonic	334 Westminster Mall, Providence, RI 02903	Alvaro Cassuto
Rockford Symphony	415 N. Church St., Rockford, IL 61103	Crawford Gates
Saginaw Symphony	P.O. Box 415, Saginaw, MI 48606	Leo Najar
San Francisco Orchestra	840 Battery St., San Francisco, CA 94111	Edgar J. Braun
Santa Barbara Symphony	3 W. Carrillo, Santa Barbara, CA 93101	Frank Collura

Santa Rosa Symphony	P.O. Box 1081, Santa Rosa, CA 95402	Corrick L. Brown
Saskatoon Symphony	P.O. Box 1361, Saskatoon, SK S7K 3N9	Ruben Gurevich
Savannah Symphony	P.O. Box 9505, Savannah, GA 31412	Christian Badea
Shreveport Symphony	P.O. Box 4057, Shreveport, LA 71104	John Shenaut
Sioux City Symphony	P.O. Box 754, Sioux City, IA 51102	Thomas Lewis
South Bend Symphony	215 W. North Shore Drive, South Bend, IN 46617	Herbert Butler
South Dakota Symphony	707 E. 41st St., Sioux Falls, SD 57105	Emanuel Vardi
Springfield Symphony	Box 1374, Springfield, OH 45501	John E. Ferritto
Stockton Symphony	Box 4273, Stockton, CA 95204	Kyung-Soo Won
Tacoma Symphony	P.O. Box 19, Tacoma, WA 98401	Edward Seferian
Tri-City Symphony	P.O. Box 67, Davenport, IA 52805	James Dixon
Tucson Symphony	443 So. Stone Ave., Tucson, AZ 85701	William McGlaughlin
Vermont Symphony	77 College St., Burlington VT 05401	Efrain Guigui
Warren Symphony	4504 E. Nine Mile Rd., Warren, MI 48091	David Daniels
Wheeling Symphony	Hawley Bldg., Wheeling, WV 26003	Jeff Holland Cook
White Plains Symphony	P.O. Box 35, Gedney Sta., White Plains, NY 10605	Paul Dunkel
Windsor Symphony	586 Ouellette Ave., 307, Windsor, ON N9A 1B7	Laszlo Gati
Winston-Salem Symphony	610 Coliseum Dr., Winston-Salem, NC 27106	Peter Perret
Youngstown Symphony	260 Federal Plaza West, Youngstown, OH 44503	J. Peter Leonard

U.S. and Canadian Opera Companies with Budgets of $500,000 or More

Source: Central Opera Service, New York, N.Y.

Anchorage Civic Opera; Michael More, adm. dir.
Arizona Opera Co. (Tucson); Suzanne Clark, bus. mgr.
Hidden Valley Opera (Carmel, Calif.); Peter Meckel, gen. dir.
Los Angeles Opera Theatre; Johanna Dordick, art. dir.
San Diego Opera Assn.; Tito Capobianco, gen. dir.
San Francisco Opera; Terence McEwen, gen. dir.
Western Opera Theater (San Francisco); Terence McEwen, gen. dir.
Central City Opera House Assn. (Denver); vacant.
Opera Colorado (Denver); Nathaniel Merrill, art. dir.
Connecticut Opera (Hartford); George Osborne, gen. dir.
Washington Opera (D.C.); Martin Feinstein, gen. dir.
Greater Miami Opera Assn.; Robert Herman, gen. mgr.
Orlando Opera (Florida); Dwight Bowes, gen. mgr.
Chicago Opera Theatre; Alan Stone, art. dir.
Lyric Opera of Chicago; Ardis Krainik, gen. mgr.
Kentucky Opera Assn. (Louisville); Thomson Smillie, gen. dir.
New Orleans Opera Assn.; Arthur Cosenza, gen. dir.
Baltimore Opera Co.; Jay Holbrook, gen. mgr.
Opera Company of Boston; Sarah Caldwell, art. dir.
Michigan Opera Theatre (Detroit); David DiChiera, gen. dir.
Minnesota Opera Co. (St. Paul); Dolores Johnson, gen. mgr.
Lyric Opera of Kansas City (Missouri); Russell Patterson, gen. dir. & art. dir.
Opera Theatre of St. Louis (Missouri); Richard Gaddes, gen. dir.
New Jersey State Opera (Newark); Alfredo Silipigni, art. dir.
Santa Fe Opera (Calif.); John Crosby, gen. dir.
Opera Theatre of Syracuse (New York); Robert Driver, art, dir.
Artpark/Natural Heritage Trust (Lewiston, N.Y.); Joanne Allison, exec. dir.
Metropolitan Opera Assn. (New York City); Anthony A. Bliss, gen. mgr.
New York City Opera; Beverly Sills, gen. dir.
Opera Orchestra of New York (New York City); Eve Queler, dir.
Charlotte (No. Carolina) Opera Assn.; Bruce Chalmers, gen. dir.
Cincinnati Opera Assn.; James deBlasis, gen. mgr.
Cleveland Opera Company; David Bamberger, gen. mgr. & art. dir.
Tulsa Opera (Oklahoma); Edward Purrington, gen. dir.
Portland Opera Assn. (Oregon); Robert Bailey, exec. dir.
Opera Company of Philadelphia; Margaret Anne Everitt, mgr.
Pittsburgh Opera Co.; Vincent Artz, gen. mgr.
Spoleto Festival USA (Charleston, So. Carolina); James Kearney, gen. mgr.
Opera Memphis, Anne Atherton Randolph, exec. dir.
Dallas Opera; Plato Karayanis, gen. dir.
Fort Worth Opera Assn.; Rudolf Kruger, gen. mgr. & mus. dir.
Houston Grand Opera Assn.; David Gockley, gen. dir.
Texas Opera Theater (Houston); M. Jane Weaver, mng. dir.
Utah Opera Company (Salt Lake City); Glade Peterson, gen. dir.
Virginia Opera Assn. (Norfolk); Peter Mark, gen. dir.
Seattle Opera Assn.; Glynn Ross, gen. dir.
Florentine Opera of Milwaukee; John Gage, gen. mgr.
Southern Alberta Opera Assn. (Calgary); Brian Hanson, gen. mgr.
Edmonton Opera Assn.; Lorin J. Moore, adm. dir.
Vancouver Opera; Hamilton McClymont, gen. mgr.
Manitoba Opera Assn.; Irving Guttman, art. dir.
Festival Ottawa Opera Plus; Andree Gingras, adm.
Canadian Opera Co. (Toronto); Lotfi Mansouri, gen. dir.
L'Opera de Montreal; Jean-Paul Jeannotte, art. dir.

Recordings

The Recording Industry Association of America, Inc. confers Gold Record Awards on single records that sell one million units, Platinum Awards to those selling two million, Gold Awards to albums and their tape equivalents that sell 500,000 units, Platinum Awards to those selling one million. Platinum Album Awards, Platinum and Gold Single Awards in 1981-82 follow:

Artists and Recording Titles

Albums, Platinum

AC/DC; *For Those About to Rock We Salute You.*
Air Supply; *The One That You Love.*
Alabama; *Feel So Right.*
Alabama; *My Home's in Alabama.*
Alabama; *Mountain Music.*
Annie Soundtrack.

Asia; *Asia.*
Buckner & Garcia; *Chanesonebowie.*
Kim Carnes; *Mistaken Identity.*
The Cars; *Shake It Up.*
Commodores; *In the Pocket.*
Neil Diamond; *On the Way to the Sky.*
The Doors; *Greatest Hits.*
Earth, Wind & Fire; *Raise.*
Fame Soundtrack.
Dan Fogelberg; *The Innocent Age.*
Foreigner; *4.*
Crystal Gayle; *When I Dream.*
The J. Geils Band; *On the Way to the Sky.*
Genesis; *Abacab.*
The Go-Go's; *Beauty and the Beat.*
Hall & Oates; *Voices.*
Hall & Oates; *Private Eyes.*
Rick James; *Street Songs.*
Joan Jett; *I Love Rock 'n' Roll.*
Billy Joel; *Songs in the Attic.*
Quincy Jones; *The Dude.*
Journey; *Escape.*
Journey; *Captured.*
Kool & the Gang; *Something Special.*
Loggins and Messina; *Best of Friends.*
Loverboy; *Loverboy.*
Paul McCartney; *Tug of War.*
Ronnie Milsap; *Greatest Hits.*
The Moody Blues; *Long Distance Voyager.*
Willie Nelson; *Somewhere Over the Rainbow.*
Willie Nelson; *Always on My Mind.*
Willie Nelson; *Willie Nelson's Greatest Hits (& Some That Will Be).*
Juice Newton; *Juice.*
Olivia Newton-John; *Physical.*
Stevie Nicks; *Bella Donna.*
The Oak Ridge Boys; *Fancy Free.*
The Oak Ridge Boys; *The Oak Ridge Boys' Greatest Hits.*
Ozzy Osbourne; *Blizzard of Ozz.*
Ozzy Osbourne; *Diary of a Madman.*
Alan Parson's Project; *The Turn of a Friendly Card.*
Tom Petty & the Heartbreakers; *Hard Promises.*
The Police; *Ghost in the Machine.*
Quarterflash; *Quarterflash.*
Queen; *Greatest Hits.*
Kenny Rogers; *Christmas.*
Kenny Rogers; *Share Your Love.*
The Rolling Stones; *Tattoo You.*
Diana Ross; *Why Do Fools Fall in Love?*
The Royal Philharmonic Orchestra; *Hooked on Classics.*
Bob Seger; *Wine Tonight.*
Richard Simmons; *Reach.*
Rick Springfield; *Working Class Dog.*
Rick Springfield; *Success Hasn't Spoiled Me Yet.*
Billy Squier; *Don't Say No.*
Rod Stewart; *Tonight I'm Yours.*

Singles, Platinum

Olivia Newton-John; *Physical.*
Oak Ridge Boys; *Elvira.*
Diana Ross & Lionel Richie; *Endless Love.*

Singles, Gold

A Taste of Honey; *Sukiyaki.*
Air Supply: *The One That You Love.*
The Beach Boys; *I Get Around.*
Buckner & Garcia; *Pac-Man Fever.*
Carl Carlton; *She's a Bad Mama Jama.*
Christopher Cross; *Arthur's Theme.*
Earth, Wind & Fire; *Let's Groove.*
Sheena Easton; *Morning Train.*
The Empire Strikes Back Soundtrack.
The J. Geils Band; *Freeze Frame.*
The J. Geils Band; *Centerfold.*
The Go-Go's; *We Got the Beat.*
Hall & Oates; *I Can Go for That.*
Hall & Oates; *Private Eyes.*
Human League; *Don't You Want Me?*
Joan Jett; *I Love Rock 'n' Roll.*
Foreigner; *Waiting for a Girl Like You.*
Juice Newton; *Angel of the Morning.*
Juice Newton; *Queen of Hearts.*
Pointer Sisters; *Slowhand.*
Smokey Robinson; *Being with You.*
Diana Ross; *Upside Down.*
Diana Ross & Lionel Richie; *Endless Love.*
Joey Scarbury; *Theme from Greatest American Hero.*
Frankie Smith; *Double Dutch Bus* "7"
Rick Springfield; *Jessie's Girl.*
Stars On; *Stars On 45.*
Star Wars Soundtrack.
Survivor; *Eye of the Tiger.*
Stevie Wonder & Paul McCartney; *Ebony & Ivory.*

Grammy Awards

Source: National Academy of Recording Arts & Sciences

1958
Record: Domenico Modugno, *Nel Blu Dipinto Di Blu (Volare).*
Album: Henry Mancini, *The Music from Peter Gunn.*
Male vocalist: Perry Como, *Catch a Falling Star.*
Female vocalist: Ella Fitzgerald, *The Irving Berlin Song Book* (album).
Group: Louis Prima & Keely Smith, *That Old Black Magic.*

1959
Record: Bobby Darin, *Mack the Knife.*
Album: Frank Sinatra, *Come Dance With Me.*
Male vocalist: Frank Sinatra, *Come Dance With Me* (album).
Female vocalist: Ella Fitzgerald, *But Not For Me.*
Group: Mormon Tabernacle Choir, *Battle Hymn of the Republic.*

1960
Record: Percy Faith, *Theme From A Summer Place.*
Album: Bob Newhart, *Button Down Mind.*
Male vocalist (single): Ray Charles, *Georgia On My Mind.*
Female vocalist (single): Ella Fitzgerald, *Mack the Knife.*
Group: Steve Lawrence & Eydie Gorme, *We Got Us.*

1961
Record: Henry Mancini, *Moon River.*
Album: Judy Garland, *Judy At Carnegie Hall.*
Male vocalist: Jack Jones, *Lollipops and Roses.*
Female vocalist: Judy Garland, *Judy at Carnegie Hall* (album).
Group: Lambert, Hendricks and Ross, *High Flying.*

1962
Record: Tony Bennett, *I Left My Heart in San Francisco.*
Album: Vaughn Meader, *The First Family.*
Male vocalist: Tony Bennett, *I Left My Heart in San Francisco.*
Female vocalist: Ella Fitzgerald, *Ella Swings Brightly with Nelson Riddle* (album).
Group: Peter, Paul and Mary, *If I Had a Hammer.*

1963
Record: Henry Mancini, *The Days of Wine and Roses.*
Album: *The Barbra Streisand Album.*
Male vocalist: Jack Jones, *Wives and Lovers.*
Female vocalist: *The Barbra Streisand Album.*
Group: Peter, Paul and Mary, *Blowin' in the Wind.*

1964
Record: Stan Getz and Astrud Gilberto, *The Girl From Ipanema.*
Album: *Getz/Gilberto.*
Male vocalist: Louis Armstrong, *Hello, Dolly!*
Female vocalist: Barbra Streisand, *People.*
Group: The Beatles, *A Hard Day's Night.*

1965
Record: Herb Alpert, *A Taste Of Honey.*
Album: Frank Sinatra, *September of My Years.*

Male vocalist: Frank Sinatra, *It Was a Very Good Year.*
Female vocalist: Barbra Streisand, *My Name is Barbra* (album).
Group: Anita Kerr Singers, *We Dig Mancini* (album).

1966

Record: Frank Sinatra, *Strangers in the Night.*
Album: Frank Sinatra, *A Man and His Music.*
Male vocalist: Frank Sinatra, *Strangers in the Night.*
Female vocalist: Eydie Gorme, *If He Walked into My Life.*
Group: Anita Kerr Singers, *A Man and A Woman.*

1967

Record: 5th Dimension, *Up, Up and Away.*
Album: The Beatles, *Sgt. Pepper's Lonely Hearts Club Band.*
Male vocalist: Glen Campbell, *By the Time I Get to Phoenix.*
Female vocalist: Bobbie Gentry, *Ode to Billie Joe.*
Group: 5th Dimension, *Up, Up and Away.*

1968

Record: Simon & Garfunkel, *Mrs. Robinson.*
Album: Glen Campbell, *By the Time I Get to Phoenix.*
Male pop vocalist: Jose Feliciano, *Light My Fire.*
Female pop vocalist: Dionne Warwick, *Do You Know the Way to San Jose.*
Pop group: Simon & Garfunkel, *Mrs. Robinson.*

1969

Record: 5th Dimension, *Aquarius/Let the Sunshine In.*
Album: *Blood, Sweat and Tears.*
Male pop vocalist: Harry Nilsson, *Everybody's Talkin'.*
Female pop vocalist: Peggy Lee, *Is That All There Is.*
Pop group: 5th Dimension, *Aquarius/Let the Sunshine In.*

1970

Record: Simon & Garfunkel, *Bridge Over Troubled Waters.*
Album: *Bridge Over Troubled Waters.*
Male pop vocalist: Ray Stevens, *Everything is Beautiful.*
Female pop vocalist: Dionne Warwick, *I'll Never Fall in Love Again.*
Pop group: The Carpenters, *Close to You.*

1971

Record: Carole King, *It's Too Late.*
Album: Carole King, *Tapestry.*
Male pop vocalist: James Taylor, *You've Got a Friend.*
Female pop vocalist: Carole King, *Tapestry (album).*
Pop group: *The Carpenters (album).*

1972

Record: Roberta Flack, *The First Time Ever I Saw Your Face.*
Album: *The Concert For Bangla Desh.*
Male pop vocalist: Harry Nilsson, *Without You.*
Female pop vocalist: Helen Reddy, *I Am Woman.*
Pop group: Roberta Flack, Donny Hathaway, *Where is the Love.*

1973

Record: Roberta Flack, *Killing Me Softly with His Song.*
Album: Stevie Wonder, *Innervisions.*
Male pop vocalist: Stevie Wonder, *You Are the Sunshine of My Life.*
Female pop vocalist: Roberta Flack, *Killing Me Softly with His Song.*
Pop group: Gladys Knight & The Pips, *Neither One of Us (Wants to Be the First to Say Goodbye).*

1974

Record: Olivia Newton-John, *I Honestly Love You.*
Album: Stevie Wonder, *Fulfullingness' First Finale.*
Male pop vocalist: Stevie Wonder, *Fulfillingness' First Finale* (album).
Female pop vocalist: Olivia Newton-John, *I Honestly Love You.*
Pop group: Paul McCartney & Wings, *Band on the Run.*

1975

Record: Captain & Tennille, *Love Will Keep Us Together.*
Album: Paul Simon, *Still Crazy After All These Years.*
Male pop vocalist: Paul Simon, *Still Crazy After All These Years* (album).
Female pop vocalist: Janis Ian, *At Seventeen.*
Pop group: Eagles, *Lyin' Eyes.*

1976

Record: George Benson, *This Masquerade.*
Album: Stevie Wonder, *Songs in the Key of Life.*
Male pop vocalist: Stevie Wonder, *Songs in the Key of Life* (album).
Female pop vocalist: Linda Ronstadt, *Hasten Down the Wind* (album).
Pop group: Chicago, *If You Leave Me Now.*

1977

Record: Eagles, *Hotel California.*
Album: Fleetwood Mac, *Rumours.*
Male pop vocalist: James Taylor, *Handy Man.*
Female pop vocalist: Barbra Streisand, *Evergreen.*
Pop group: Bee Gees, *How Deep is Your Love.*

1978

Record: Billy Joel, *Just the Way You Are.*
Album: Bee Gees, *Saturday Night Fever.*
Male pop vocalist: Barry Manilow, *Copacabana.*
Female pop vocalist: Anne Murray, *You Needed Me.*
Pop group: Bee Gees, *Saturday Night Fever* (album).

1979

Record: The Doobie Brothers, *What a Fool Believes.*
Album: Billy Joel, *52nd Street.*
Male pop vocalist: Billy Joel, *52nd Street* (album).
Female pop vocalist: Dionne Warwick, *I'll Never Love This Way Again.*
Pop group: The Doobie Brothers, *Minute by Minute* (album).

1980

Record: Christopher Cross, *Sailing.*
Album: Christopher Cross, *Christopher Cross.*
Male pop vocalist: Kenny Loggins, *This Is It.*
Female pop vocalist: Bette Midler, *The Rose.*
Pop group: Barbra Streisand & Barry Gibb, *Guilty* (album).

1981

Record: Kim Carnes, *Bette Davis Eyes.*
Album: John Lennon, Yoko Ono, *Double Fantasy.*
Male pop vocalist: Al Jarreau, *Breaking Away* (album).
Female pop vocalist: Lena Horne, *Lena Horne: The Lady and Her Music,* Live on Broadway (album).
Pop group: Manhattan Transfer, *Boy from New York City.*

Miss America Winners

1921	Margaret Gorman, Washington, D.C.
1922-23	Mary Campbell, Columbus, Ohio
1924	Ruth Malcolmson, Philadelphia, Pennsylvania
1925	Fay Lamphier, Oakland, California
1926	Norma Smallwood, Tulsa, Oklahoma
1927	Lois Delaner, Joliet, Illinois
1933	Marion Bergeron, West Haven, Connecticut
1935	Henrietta Leaver, Pittsburgh, Pennsylvania
1936	Rose Coyle, Philadelphia, Pennsylvania
1937	Bette Cooper, Bertrand Island, New Jersey
1938	Marilyn Meseke, Marion, Ohio
1939	Patricia Donnelly, Detroit, Michigan
1940	Frances Marie Burke, Philadelphia, Pennsylvania
1941	Rosemary LaPlanche, Los Angeles, California
1942	Jo-Caroll Dennison, Tyler, Texas
1943	Jean Bartel, Los Angeles, California
1944	Venus Ramey, Washington, D.C.
1945	Bess Myerson, New York City, N.Y.
1946	Marilyn Buferd, Los Angeles, California
1947	Barbara Walker, Memphis, Tennessee
1948	BeBe Shopp, Hopkins, Minnesota
1949	Jacque Mercer, Litchfield, Arizona
1951	Yolande Betbeze, Mobile, Alabama
1952	Coleen Kay Hutchins, Salt Lake City, Utah
1953	Neva Jane Langley, Macon, Georgia
1954	Evelyn Margaret Ay, Ephrata, Pennsylvania
1955	Lee Meriwether, San Francisco, California
1956	Sharon Ritchie, Denver, Colorado
1957	Marian McKnight, Manning, South Carolina
1958	Marilyn Van Derbur, Denver, Colorado
1959	Mary Ann Mobley, Brandon, Mississippi
1960	Lynda Lee Mead, Natchez, Mississippi
1961	Nancy Fleming, Montague, Michigan
1962	Maria Fletcher, Asheville, North Carolina
1963	Jacquelyn Mayer, Sandusky, Ohio
1964	Donna Axum, El Dorado, Arkansas
1965	Vonda Kay Van Dyke, Phoenix, Arizona
1966	Deborah Irene Bryant, Overland Park, Kansas
1967	Jane Anne Jayroe, Laverne, Oklahoma
1968	Debra Dene Barnes, Moran, Kansas
1969	Judith Anne Ford, Belvidere, Illinois
1970	Pamela Anne Eldred, Birmingham, Michigan
1971	Phyllis Ann George, Denton, Texas
1972	Laurie Lea Schaefer, Columbus, Ohio
1973	Terry Anne Meeuwsen, DePere, Wisconsin
1974	Rebecca Ann King, Denver, Colorado
1975	Shirley Cothran, Fort Worth, Texas
1976	Tawney Elaine Godin, Yonkers, N.Y.
1977	Dorothy Kathleen Benham, Edina, Minnesota
1978	Susan Perkins, Columbus, Ohio
1979	Kylene Baker, Galax, Virginia
1980	Cheryl Prewitt, Ackerman, Mississippi
1981	Susan Powell, Elk City, Oklahoma
1982	Elizabeth Ward, Russellville, Arkansas

Best-Selling Books of 1981-82

Listed according to frequency of citation on best seller reports from Aug. 1981 through July 1982.
Numbers in parentheses show rank on top ten list for calendar year 1981, according to Publishers Weekly.

Hardcover Fiction

1. The Hotel New Hampshire, John Irving (2)
2. An Indecent Obsession, Colleen McCullough (4)
3. Noble House, James Clavell (1)
4. Cujo, Stephen King (3)
5. The Parsifal Mosaic, Robert Ludlum
6. North and South, John Jakes
7. Spring Moon, Bette Bao Lord
8. Gorky Park, Martin Cruz Smith (5)
9. The Third Deadly Sin, Lawrence Sanders (8)
10. The Man from St. Petersburg, Ken Follett
11. The One Tree, Stephen R. Donaldson
12. Marco Polo, If You Can, William F. Buckley Jr.
13. No Time for Tears, Cynthia Freeman (10)
14. Celebrity, Thomas Thompson
15. A Green Desire, Anton Myrer
16. The Dean's December, Saul Bellow
    (tie) The Prodigal Daughter, Jeffery Archer
17. The Glitter Dome, Joseph Wambaugh (9)
18. Twice Shy, Dick Francis
19. The Legacy, Howard Fast (12)
20. Rabbit Is Rich, John Updike
21. Goodbye, Janette, Harold Robbins (7)
22. Thy Brother's Wife, Andrew M. Greeley
23. Remembrance, Danielle Steel
    (tie) Eden Burning, Belva Plain
24. The Last Days of America, Paul Erdman (14)
25. The Clowns of God, Morris West
    (tie) For Special Services, John Gardner

Hardcover Nonfiction

1. A Light in the Attic, Shel Silverstein (4)
2. Jane Fonda's Workout Book, Jane Fonda
3. The Lord God Made Them All, James Herriot (3)
4. A Few Minutes with Andy Rooney, Andrew A. Rooney (10)
5. Richard Simmons Never-Say-Diet Book, Richard Simmons (3)
6. The Beverly Hills Diet, Judy Mazel (1)
7. When Bad Things Happen to Good People, Harold S. Kushner
8. No Bad Dogs: The Woodhouse Way, Barbara Woodhouse
9. Living, Loving & Learning, Leo Buscaglia
10. Cosmos, Carl Sagan (5)
11. How to Make Love to a Man, Alexandra Penney (12)
12. Pathfinders, Gail Sheehy (11)
13. Miss Piggy's Guide to Life, Henry Beard (7)
14. The Cinderella Complex, Colette Dowling
15. At Dawn We Slept, Gordon W. Prange
16. The Fate of the Earth, Jonathan Schell
17. The Walk West, Peter and Barbara Jenkins (13)
18. The I Love New York Diet, Bess Myerson and Bill Adler
19. America in Search of Itself: The Making of the President, 1956-80, Theodore H. White
20. From Bauhaus to Our House, Tom Wolfe
    (tie) Witness to Power, John Ehrlichman
21. Weight Watchers' 365-Day Menu Cookbook (8)
    (tie) The Never-Say-Diet Cookbook, Richard Simmons
22. Living Alone and Liking It!, Lynn Shahan
    (tie) Jane Brody's Nutrition Book, Jane Brody
23. Theory Z, William G. Ouchi
24. Years of Upheaval, Henry Kissinger
25. Keep It Simple, Marian Burros
    (tie) Laid Back in Washington, Art Buchwald

Mass Market Paperback

1. The Simple Solution to Rubik's Cube, James G. Nourse
2. The Cardinal Sins, Andrew M. Greeley
3. Gorky Park, Martin Cruz Smith
4. The Key to Rebecca, Ken Follett
5. Answer As a Man, Taylor Caldwell
6. Shadowland, Peter Straub
7. Firestarter, Stephen King
8. Goodbye, Janette, Harold Robbins
9. The Road to Gandolfo, Robert Ludlum
10. Noble House, James Clavell
11. A Perfect Stranger, Danielle Steel
12. Come Pour the Wine, Cynthia Freeman
13. The Covenant, James A. Michener
14. No Love Lost, Helen Van Slyke
15. The Lord God Made Them All, James Herriot
16. The Ring, Danielle Steel
17. The Sins of the Fathers, Susan Howatch
18. Aztec, Gary Jennings
    (tie) The White Hotel, D.M. Thomas
19. The Second Lady, Irving Wallace
20. Free Fall in Crimson, John D. MacDonald
21. Congo, Michael Crichton
22. The Glitter Dome, Joseph Wambaugh
23. The Midwife, Gay Courter
    (tie) Rage of Angels, Sidney Sheldon
24. The Last Mafioso, Ovid Demaris
25. Athabasca, Alistair MacLean

Trade Paperback

1. Color Me Beautiful, Carole Jackson
2. 101 Uses for a Dead Cat, Simon Bond
3. Mastering Rubik's Cube, Don Taylor
4. Garfield Bigger Than Life, Jim Davis
5. Garfield Gains Weight, Jim Davis
6. Never-Say-Diet Book, Richard Simmons
7. Garfield Weighs In, Jim Davis
8. You Can Do the Cube, Patrick Bossert
9. Once in a Lifetime, Danielle Steel
10. Brideshead Revisited, Evelyn Waugh
11. A Confederacy of Dunces, John Kennedy Toole
12. Garfield at Large, Jim Davis
13. What Color Is Your Parachute?, Richard Nelson Bolles
14. Real Men Don't Eat Quiche, Bruce Feirstein
    (tie) Love Play, Rosemary Rogers
15. This Calder Sky, Janet Dailey
16. The Official Preppy Handbook, ed. Lisa Birnbach
17. This Calder Range, Janet Dailey
18. Pills That Don't Work, Sidney M. Wolfe, M.D. & Christopher M. Coley
19. Thin Thighs in 30 Days, Wendy Stehling
20. Personhood, Leo F. Buscaglia
21. The Prophecies of Nostradamus, ed. Erika Cheetham
22. God Emperor of Dune, Frank Herbert
23. Chocolate: The Consuming Passion, Sandra Boynton
24. Solving the Cube, Cyril Ostrop
25. The Cat's Revenge, Philip Lief

Selected U.S. Daily Newspaper Circulation

Source: Audit Bureau of Circulations' FAS-FAX Report. Average paid circulation for 6 months to Mar. 31, 1982. †3 months. For the 6 months up to Feb. 1, 1982, 1,730 English language dailies in the U.S. (408 morning, 1,352 evening, 30 all day) had an average audited circulation of 61,430,745. Sunday papers included 755 with audited average circulation of 55,180,004. (m) morning; (e) evening; *Mon.-Fri. average.

Newspaper	Daily	Sunday
Akron Beacon Journal (e)	163,409	225,667
Albuquerque Journal (m)	†90,204	†131,745
Albuquerque Tribune (e)	†44,735	
Allentown Call (m)	*123,396	160,496
Asbury Park Press (e)	112,912	158,638
Atlanta Constitution (m)	208,289	
Atlanta Journal (e)	184,237	499,084
Austin American-Statesman (m&e)	136,685	162,238
Baltimore News-American (e)	*141,449	196,438
Baltimore Sun (m&e)	*344,832	382,953
Bergen Co. (N.J.) Record (e)	†148,387	†214,713
Birmingham News (e)	*168,565	216,012
Birmingham Post-Herald (m)	*66,800	
Boston Globe (m&e)	*502,868	751,289
Boston Herald American (m)	*211,930	231,106
Bristol Herald-Courier (m)	*31,782	40,006
Bristol Virginia-Tennessean (e)	*8,858	
Buffalo Courier-Express (m)	127,124	265,449
Buffalo News (e)	*264,272	268,928
Camden (N.J.) Courier-Post (e)	†128,503	†118,362
Charlotte News (e)	44,810	
Charlotte Observer (m)	169,291	241,903
Chicago Sun-Times (m)	*663,410	700,769
Chicago Tribune (m&e)	*790,475	1,107,574
Christian Science Monitor (m)	*153,676	
Cincinnati Enquirer (m)	193,090	298,257
Cincinnati Post (e)	147,560	
Cleveland Plain Dealer (m)	405,842	448,219
Columbia, S.C. State (m)	108,620	136,195
Columbia, S.C. Record (e)	31,750	
Columbus, Ga. Enquirer (m)	*30,972	63,274
Columbus, Ga. Ledger (e)	*24,948	
Columbus, O. Citizen-Journal (m)	117,178	
Columbus, O. Dispatch (e)	202,720	340,484
Dallas News (m)	308,649	380,981
Dallas Times Herald (e)	267,579	352,372
Dayton Journal-Herald (m)	103,452	
Dayton News (e)	131,511	221,799
Denver Post (e)	258,376	356,372
Denver: Rocky Mountain News (m)	312,873	335,665
Des Moines Register (m)	205,640	143,851
Des Moines Tribune (e)	67,596	
Detroit Free Press (m)	*627,640	758,706
Detroit News (e)	*629,392	825,384
Flint Journal (e)	†108,533	111,438
Ft. Myers News-Press (m)	78,173	
Ft. Worth Star-Telegram (m&e)	230,654	260,710
Fresno Bee (m)	137,699	156,376
Grand Rapids Press (e)	†128,099	155,930
Hartford Courant (m)	208,845	290,254
Honolulu Advertiser (m)	85,848	
Honolulu Star-Bulletin (e)	112,716	199,245
Houston Chronicle (m&e)	*393,730	481,319
Houston Post (m)	*376,879	440,135
Indianapolis News (e)	†136,034	
Indianapolis Star (m)	†220,947	†361,571
Jacksonville Journal (e)	43,649	
Jacksonville: Fla. Times Union (m)	160,905	207,724
Kansas City Star (e)	*240,529	391,626
Kansas City Times (m)	287,441	
Knoxville News-Sentinel (e)	100,910	160,163
Little Rock: Ark. Gazette (m)	131,929	158,202
Long Island, N.Y.: Newsday (e)	*513,728	582,261
Los Angeles Herald-Examiner (e)	*285,656	303,724
Los Angeles Times (m)	*1,062,707	1,317,817
Louisville Courier-Journal (m)	182,843	324,624
Louisville Times (e)	143,121	
Madison, Wis. State Journal	75,423	126,251
Memphis Commercial Appeal (m)	202,272	284,377
Memphis Press Scimitar (e)	90,581	
Miami Herald (m)	435,071	521,091
Milwaukee Journal (e)	308,764	516,858
Milwaukee Sentinel (m)	176,680	
Minneapolis Star (e)	*169,184	
Minneapolis Tribune (m)	*239,332	576,994
Nashville Banner (e)	74,235	
Nashville Tennessean (m)	127,296	246,081
Newark Star-Ledger (m)	*†415,406	†606,044
New Haven Register (e)	92,423	137,044
New Haven Journal-Courier (m)	*36,417	

Newspaper	Daily	Sunday
New Orleans Times-Picayune/ States-Item (m&e)	*†280,655	†332,410
New York News (m)	*1,540,218	2,042,830
New York Post (m&e)	*904,476	
New York Times (m)	*947,682	1,524,830
Norfolk Ledger-Star (e)	†93,922	
Norfolk Virginian-Pilot (m)	†133,237	†218,929
Oakland Tribune (e)	*120,011	172,549
Oklahoma City Oklahoman (m)	*195,180	300,358
Oklahoma City Times (e)	*85,004	
Omaha World-Herald (m&e)	224,380	276,431
Orange Co. (Cal.) Register (m&e)	*251,647	286,096
Orlando Sentinel-Star (m&e)	*215,015	249,974
Peoria Journal Star (m&e)	101,717	118,798
Philadelphia Inquirer (m)	*547,547	1,029,410
Philadelphia News (e)	*299,380	
Phoenix Gazette (e)	†119,116	
Phoenix Republic (m)	†286,984	†432,397
Pittsburgh Post Gazette (m)	*181,397	
Pittsburgh Press (e)	*266,307	616,373
Portland, Me. Press-Herald (m)	57,329	
Portland, Me. Express (e) & Maine Sunday Telegram	30,046	124,257
Portland Oregonian (m)	237,141	409,641
Portland: Oregon Journal (e)	*100,039	
Providence Bulletin (e)	*137,258	
Providence Journal (m)	*82,182	238,908
Raleigh News & Observer (m)	†129,240	†170,137
Raleigh Times (e)	†33,338	
Richmond News Leader (e)	113,404	
Richmond Times Dispatch (m)	135,240	218,929
Rochester Democrat-Chronicle (m)	*127,283	241,545
Rochester Times-Union (e)	*113,104	
Sacramento Bee (m)	219,216	244,841
Sacramento Union (m)	112,022	103,701
St. Louis Globe-Democrat (m)	*261,329	248,668
St. Louis Post-Dispatch (e)	*238,099	443,422
St. Paul Dispatch (e)	*112,783	
St. Paul Pioneer Press (m)	*105,301	245,622
St. Petersburg Independent (e)	37,985	
St. Petersburg Times (m)	259,715	321,935
Salt Lake City Tribune (m)	114,800	183,580
San Antonio Express (m)	*84,879	193,635
San Antonio News (e)	*75,512	
San Antonio Light (e)	*112,319	187,976
San Diego Union (m)	†216,252	†339,992
San Diego Tribune (e)	†126,308	
San Francisco Examiner (e)	*155,298	
San Francisco Chronicle (m)	*530,672	673,029
San Jose Mercury (m)	*163,285	276,293
San Jose News (e)	*63,544	
Seattle Post-Intelligencer (m)	*191,158	209,061
Seattle Times (m&e)	*256,888	339,921
South Bend Tribune (e)	104,858	124,484
Spokane Chronicle (e)	58,028	
Spokane Spokesman-Review (m)	77,627	129,149
Springfield, Ill. State Journal-Register (m&e)	*70,333	71,367
Springfield, Mass. Union (m)	70,840	
Springfield, Mass. News (e) & Sunday Republican	73,645	146,723
Syracuse Herald-Journal (e)	107,668	234,258
Syracuse Post-Standard (m)	78,760	
Tacoma News Tribune (e)	107,383	113,123
Tampa Tribune (m)	202,363	256,463
Toledo Blade (e)	165,034	208,527
Tucson Daily Star (m)	78,039	142,265
Tulsa Tribune (e)	†75,769	
Tulsa World (m)	†138,268	†219,100
Wall St. Journal (m) (total)	*2,002,727	
Washington, D.C. Post (m)	*760,950	986,024
West Palm Beach Post (m)	100,952	155,614
West Palm Beach Times (e)	27,651	
Wichita Eagle (m)	124,171	183,080
Winston-Salem Journal (m)	71,681	97,511
Winston-Salem Sentinel (e)	34,478	
Worcester Telegram (m)	†55,568	†115,327
Worcester Gazette (e)	†87,329	
Youngstown Vindicator (e)	†100,222	†150,222

Circulation of Leading U.S. Magazines

Source: Audit Bureau of Circulations' FAS-FAX Report

General magazines, exclusive of groups and comics. Based on total average paid circulation during the 6 months prior to Dec. 31, 1981.

Magazine	Circulation	Magazine	Circulation	Magazine	Circulation
Reader's Digest	17,926,542	Hustler	1,238,955	Soap Opera Digest	668,602
TV Guide	17,670,543	Vogue	1,217,453	National Examiner	657,548
National Geographic Magazine	10,861,186	Psychology Today	1,188,083	Esquire Magazine	656,269
Better Homes & Gardens	8,059,717	Mademoiselle	1,186,416	Modern Photography	654,769
Family Circle	7,427,979	The American Rifleman	1,185,236	Road & Track	650,978
Modern Maturity	7,309,035	Teen	1,122,562	Essence	650,426
Woman's Day	7,004,367	Nation's Business	1,113,573	Grit	645,679
McCall's	6,266,090	House & Garden	1,111,539	Signature	644,522
Ladies' Home Journal	5,527,071	US	1,107,819	Country Living	642,614
Good Housekeeping	5,425,790	1001 Home Ideas	1,105,003	Gourmet	641,752
Playboy	5,013,941	Family Handyman	1,078,569	Catholic Digest	603,027
National Inquirer	4,602,524	Mother Earth News	1,072,797	Discover	602,833
Redbook	4,368,523	Discovery	1,055,675	Saturday Evening Review	601,918
Time	4,337,988	Self	1,029,315	Flower & Garden	592,165
Penthouse	4,051,696	Golf Digest	1,025,088	Architectural Digest	570,002
The Star	3,515,530	Sport	998,821	Colonial Homes	566,355
Newsweek	2,848,399	Money	959,023	HomeOwners "How To"	549,777
Cosmopolitan	2,848,399	Travel & Leisure	932,865	Weekly World News	545,199
American Legion	2,587,751	Scouting	909,438	Club	534,739
People Weekly	2,551,642	The American Hunter	872,404	Stereo Review	534,071
Prevention	2,462,023	Popular Photography	870,917	National Lampoon	532,208
Senior Scholastic	2,299,709	House Beautiful	858,455	Science Digest	530,083
Sports Illustrated	2,284,800	Yankee	854,980	Sports Afield	526,546
U.S. News & World Report	2,063,366	Health	853,295	Girl Scout Leader	526,506
Glamour	2,052,115	Hot Rod	849,888	Young Miss	515,083
Field & Stream	2,023,785	Junior Scholastic	826,416	Guns and Ammo	509,673
Southern Living	1,973,219	Michigan Living	818,533	The New Yorker	505,107
Smithsonian	1,936,726	Co-ed	802,345	New Shelter	495,464
Globe	1,912,684	Omni	785,395	Tennis	488,972
V.F.W. Magazine	1,867,201	Business Week	777,523	The Rotarian	482,135
Popular Science	1,803,309	Motor Trend	763,002	Westways	472,154
Today's Education	1,649,494	Oui	752,616	Book Digest	469,692
The Elks Magazine	1,645,905	Discover	750,545	GQ-Gentlemen's Quarterly	469,423
Mechanix Illustrated	1,602,777	Golf	735,383	Saturday Review	468,598
Parents	1,568,221	Weight Watchers Magazine	733,240	Ms. Magazine	466,634
The Workbasket	1,565,992	Car & Driver	729,916	Cheri	464,917
Outdoor Life	1,535,929	Decorating & Craft Ideas	729,034	Natural History	462,069
True Story	1,525,089	Rolling Stone	724,431	Working Woman	454,925
Seventeen	1,480,236	Workbench	720,239	Country Music	454,141
Life	1,461,964	Metropolitan Home	711,176	Easyriders	452,811
Boy's Life	1,450,841	Playgirl	701,830	NRTA Journal	441,494
Changing Times	1,421,176	Forbes	700,127	The Sporting News	438,565
Sunset	1,417,333	Science 81	699,633	NRTA News Bulletin	433,892
Bon Appetit	1,340,653	Jet	696,218	Skiing Magazine	430,016
Motorland	1,314,538	Eagle	694,316	Cycle	429,019
Organic Gardening	1,314,536	Harper's Bazaar	684,000	High Society	423,325
Ebony	1,306,549	Fortune	674,100	Ski	411,073
New Woman	1,306,387	Games	674,085	Car Craft	409,473
				New York Magazine	408,873

Selected Canadian Daily Newspaper Circulation

Source: Audit Bureau of Circulations' FAS-FAX Report of average paid circulation for 6 months ending Mar. 31, 1982.

For the 6 months up to Mar. 31, 1982. 121 daily newspapers in Canada (28 morning: 95 evening), had an average audited circulation of 5,407,499; 37 Saturday-Sunday-weekend newspapers had an average circulation of 4,861,809.

Newspaper	Daily	Saturday	Newspaper	Daily	Saturday
Calgary Sun. (m)	65,187		Regina Leader Post (e)	69,670	
Calgary Herald (e)	*148,197	183,260	St. Catharines Standard (e)	†43,059	
Edmonton Journal (e)	*185,162	**178,028	St. John's Telegram (e)	*34,242	46,434
Halifax Chronicle-Herald (m)	71,901		Saint John Telegraph-Journal (m)	*30,405	68,516
Halifax Mail-Star (e)	59,229		Saint John Times Globe (e)	*31,776	
Hamilton Spectator (e)	†151,314		Saskatoon Star-Phoenix (e)	56,851	
Kingston Whig-Standard (e)	†34,688		Sudbury Star (e)	30,213	
Kitchener-Waterloo Record (e)	†72,960		Sydney: Cape Breton Post (e)	31,145	
London Free Press (m & e)	126,313		Toronto Globe and Mail (m)	353,859	
Montreal Gazette (m)	*204,134	283,128	Toronto Star (e)	*484,856	801,492
Montreal: La Presse (m)	*201,217	296,721	Toronto Sun (m)	*231,570	**416,309
Montreal: Le Devoir (m)	*41,349	43,473	Trois Rivieres Nouvelliste (e)	52,211	
Montreal: Le Journal de Montreal (m)	*317,841	**294,185	Vancouver Province (m)	*133,242	**159,444
Ottawa Citizen (e)	*175,368	215,958	Vancouver Sun (e)	*230,154	278,813
Ottawa: Le Droit (e)	*46,398	51,279	Windsor Star (e)	90,777	
Quebec: Le Journal de Quebec (m)	*103,299	97,163	Winnipeg Free Press (e)	*180,174	238,320
Quebec: Le Soleil (e)	*129,070	143,287			

(m) Morning; (e) Evening; * Based on Monday to Friday average; **Sunday. (†) Indicates 3 month circulation average.

Circulation of Leading Canadian Magazines

Source: Audit Bureau of Circulations' FAS-FAX Report.

General magazines, exclusive of groups and comics. Statistics based on average paid circulation during the 6 months prior to June 30, 1982.

Magazine	Circulation	Magazine	Circulation	Magazine	Circulation
Reader's Digest (Eng.-Fr.)	1,601,935	MacLean's Magazine	641,541	T.V. Hebdo	273,913
Chatelaine (English-French)	1,357,204	Leisure Ways	361,276	L'Actualite	238,912
Reader's Digest (English)	1,288,404	Canadian Living	349,897	Flare	196,780
Chatelaine (English)	1,065,972	Time Canada	319,044	Harrowsmith Magazine	156,568
TV Guide (English-French)	937,017	Selection du Reader's Digest	313,531	Almanach Moderne 1981	133,215
National Examiner	657,548	Chatelaine (French)	291,232	Saturday Night	128,782

America's Favorite Television Programs

Source: A.C. Nielsen

(Percent of TV households and persons in TV households)

Network Programs (Oct. to Dec. 1981)

(Nielsen average audience estimates)

	TV House-holds	Women	Men	Teens	Chil-dren
60 Minutes	28.1	21.3	23.2		
Dallas	27.7	24.5	16.4		
Three's Company	24.0	17.7	14.6	20.5	
M*A*S*H	23.4	18.3	14.6	13.5	
Too Close For Comfort	22.7	17.3	13.8	18.0	
One Day At A Time	22.4	18.4	14.3		
ABC Sunday Night Movie	21.9	17.2	17.4	15.7	
NFL Monday Night Football	21.8		21.4		
Archie Bunker's Place	21.7		15.0		
Dukes of Hazzard	21.3				28.2
Magnum P.I.	21.2	17.3		12.4	
Alice	21.0	17.9			
Facts of Life	20.9	16.2		14.8	
Happy Days	20.9			19.3	19.6
Love Boat	20.9	16.9		13.6	
NBC Monday Night Movies		17.4			
Little House on the Prairie		16.5			
Hart To Hart		16.5			
Jeffersons		16.2			
CBS NFL Football Gm 2			18.7		
CBS NFL Football Game 1			18.4		
NFL Football Gm. 2-NBC			16.2		
Fall Guy			15.4		
That's Incredible			14.2		
NBC Sunday Night Movie			13.9		
NFL Football Game 1-NBC			13.8		
Laverne & Shirley				20.1	21.7
Greatest American Hero				16.7	24.7
Private Benjamin				14.6	
Chips				13.4	18.6
Mork & Mindy				12.9	22.1
NBC Friday Night Movie				12.4	
Diff'rent Strokes				12.3	
Walt Disney					24.4
Smurfs II					23.0
Incredible Hulk					22.9
Here's Boomer					20.1
Smurfs I					18.1

Syndicated Programs (Nov. 1981)

(Average ratings for total U.S.)

	TV house-holds	Women	Men	Teens	Chil-dren
M*A*S*H	13.9	9.7	9.4	9.8	
Family Feud PM	13.2	11.2	8.0	6.2	
PM Magazine	12.7	10.0	8.5		
Hee Haw	9.7	7.6	7.3		
Happy Days Again	8.8			12.1	11.8
Barney Miller	8.7	5.9	5.6		
Tic Tac Dough	8.7	7.4	5.0		
Laverne & Shirley	8.4			10.8	11.4
You Asked For It	8.4	6.3	5.7		
Dance Fever	8.1	6.3	4.8	6.5	
Entertainment Tonight	8.1	6.3	4.9		
Lawrence Welk Show	8.1	7.3	4.9		
Muppet Show	7.8				
Little House On The Prairie	7.7	5.8		7.4	8.9
Jefferson	7.5	5.5		7.1	

Total TV Households — 81.5 million, 18 + women — 84.72 million; 18 + men — 76.14 million; teens 12–17 — 22.03 million; children 2–11 — 32.76 million.

Average Television Viewing Time

Source: A.C. Nielsen estimates, Nov. 1981 (hours: minutes, per week)

		Total	Mon.-Fri. 10am-4:30pm	Mon.-Fri. 4:30pm-7:30pm	Mon.-Sun. 8-11pm	Sat. 8am-1pm	Mon.-Fri. 11:30pm-1am
Avg. all persons		29:32	4:08	4:34	9:02	:44	1:04
Women	Total 18+	33:41	6:19	4:57	10:20	:28	1:18
	18-24	28:58	5:47	3:52	8:14	:45	1:08
	55+	39:20	7:54	6:30	11:33	:23	1:16
Men	Total 18+	29:16	2:34	4:10	9:29	:29	1:21
	18-24	23:14	2:25	3:02	6:35	:33	1:18
	55+	35:43	4:14	6:09	11:16	:29	1:10
Teens	Female	18:19	2:48	3:14	5:48	:42	:32
	Male	22:28	1:53	3:34	7:28	:56	:40
Children	2-5	27:04	4:50	5:38	5:05	2:04	:07
	6-11	24:48	2:30	5:04	5:56	1:53	:10

All-time Top Television Programs

Source: A.C. Nielsen estimates

Program	Date	Network	Households
Dallas	11/21/80	CBS	41,470,000
Super Bowl XVI	1/24/82	CBS	40,020,000
Roots	1/30/77	ABC	36,380,000
Super Bowl XIV	1/20/80	CBS	35,330,000
Super Bowl XIII	1/21/79	NBC	35,090,000
CBS NFC Championship Game	1/10/82	CBS	34,960,000
Super Bowl XV	1/25/81	NBC	34,540,000
Super Bowl XII	1/15/78	CBS	34,410,000
Gone With The Wind, Pt. 1	11/7/76	NBC	33,960,000
Gone With The Wind, Pt. 2	11/8/76	NBC	33,750,000
Roots	1/28/77	ABC	32,680,000
Roots	1/27/77	ABC	32,540,000
Roots	1/25/77	ABC	31,900,000
Super Bowl XI	1/9/77	NBC	31,610,000
Roots	1/24/77	ABC	31,400,000
Roots	1/26/77	ABC	31,190,000
World Series Game 6	10/21/80	NBC	31,120,000
Dallas	11/9/80	CBS	31,120,000
World Series Game 6	10/28/81	ABC	30,320,000
Roots	1/29/77	ABC	30,120,000
Jaws	11/4/79	ABC	29,830,000
Dallas	11/7/80	CBS	29,720,000
Super Bowl X	1/18/76	CBS	29,440,000
Super Bowl IX	1/12/75	NBC	29,040,000
Dallas	12/5/80	CBS	29,020,000
Roots	1/23/77	ABC	28,840,000
Shogun, Pt. 3	9/17/80	NBC	28,710,000

U.S. Television Sets and Stations Received

Set Ownership
(Nielsen est. as of Jan. 1, 1982)

Total TV homes	81,500,000	100%
(98% of U.S. homes own at least one TV set)		
Homes with:		
Color TV sets	71,400,000	88%
B&W only	9,780,000	12
2 or more sets	43,300,000	53
One set	38,305,000	47
CATV (Feb. 1982)	23,726,220	29.0

Number of Stations
(FCC, May 31, 1982)

Commercial	**789**
Educational	**265**
Total	**1,054**

Stations Receivable
(Nielsen, Jan. 1982)
% of TV homes receiving:

1-4 stations	8%
5	8
6	9
7	10
8	9
9	13
10	11
11+	32%

35 Top U.S. Advertisers: Expenditures by Type of Media

Source: Advertising Age, Sept. 10, 1981; copyright © Crain Communications Inc., 1981.

			% of Total Dollars							
Rank	Company	Total (000)	Newspapers	Genl. mags.	Farm pub.	Spot TV	Net TV	Spot Radio	Net Radio	Outdoor
1	Proctor & Gamble	$545,723.2	1.4	6.8	—	24.8	66.1	0.8	—	0.1
2	General Foods Corp.	338,717.0	2.9	10.1	—	24.6	59.5	1.6	1.2	0.1
3	Philip Morris Inc.	319,594.7	24.2	24.8	—	7.1	30.5	3.5	—	9.9
4	General Motors Corp.	295,968.4	17.6	18.7	0.7	6.4	41.7	10.9	1.3	2.7
5	R.J. Reynolds Industries	294,124.1	38.5	40.3	—	2.8	3.7	0.2	—	14.5
6	Ford Motor Co.	247,310.5	9.9	14.5	1.0	12.8	50.8	7.9	2.3	0.8
7	American Telephone & Telegraph Co.	180,665.6	10.6	19.1	—	28.1	31.8	6.7	3.3	0.4
8	American Home Products Corp.	180,288.2	0.8	5.2	0.3	20.2	68.7	2.9	1.9	—
9	Chrysler Corp.	165,451.4	12.8	9.9	0.6	7.1	39.5	29.8	0.2	0.1
10	General Mills	161,142.7	2.1	9.3	—	40.6	47.0	0.7	0.2	0.1
11	PepsiCo Inc.	160,869.9	1.1	1.8	—	36.0	55.2	5.4	—	0.5
12	Bristol-Myers Co.	150,996.3	1.7	12.2	—	13.9	70.2	1.8	—	0.2
13	Sears, Roebuck & Co.	143,265.9	—	22.4	—	10.9	60.7	1.8	3.7	0.5
14	McDonald's Corp.	130,862.1	—	1.8	—	54.0	41.0	0.7	0.1	2.4
15	Coca-Cola Inc.	129,481.7	4.2	3.1	—	36.9	44.7	7.7	1.1	2.3
16	Unilever U.S.	129,329.1	1.3	11.2	—	29.8	57.3	0.2	—	0.2
17	Anheuser-Busch	127,661.6	1.3	4.0	—	19.0	51.2	21.5	2.0	1.0
18	Dart & Kraft Inc.	122,841.5	5.4	22.4	—	27.1	39.2	4.5	0.9	0.5
19	Johnson & Johnson	120,409.1	4.2	15.3	0.2	4.1	75.1	0.5	0.6	—
20	Seagram Co.	117,339.9	15.4	60.2	—	4.6	9.6	0.3	—	9.9
21	Ralston Purina Co.	114,887.7	1.9	11.8	0.6	17.5	63.8	4.3	—	0.1
22	Loews Corp.	112,785.2	40.8	34.2	—	1.4	3.9	0.3	—	19.4
23	Warner-Lambert Co.	98,202.0	2.9	5.8	—	21.7	64.3	0.1	5.0	0.2
24	Pillsbury Co.	96,895.1	3.2	5.3	—	32.9	55.0	2.9	0.3	0.4
25	Kellogg Co.	90,486.2	4.6	4.9	—	21.0	66.1	2.8	0.6	—
26	Time Inc.	86,773.5	12.6	41.0	—	35.0	10.1	0.4	0.8	0.1
27	Gillette Co.	85,981.7	1.4	14.0	—	15.3	69.2	—	—	0.1
28	Sterling Drug	83,517.4	0.5	13.9	0.2	6.5	68.8	2.0	8.0	0.1
29	Heublein Inc.	82,959.3	6.1	19.8	—	21.6	36.5	7.7	—	8.3
30	Consolidated Foods Co.	82,571.0	2.1	15.3	—	26.4	52.4	2.2	1.3	0.3
31	B.A.T. Industries Ltd.	79,457.0	17.2	41.3	—	8.5	—	0.1	—	32.9
32	Colgate-Palmolive Co.	79,336.1	2.6	9.0	0.2	29.8	50.5	7.8	—	0.1
33	RCA Corp.	77,297.3	32.5	31.4	—	8.0	25.7	0.2	1.8	0.4
34	Toyota Motor Sales	75,128.0	9.3	9.3	—	44.0	30.5	4.8	—	2.1
35	General Electric Co.	74,296.3	16.3	22.1	—	11.3	44.4	1.9	3.7	0.3

Network TV Program Ratings

Source: A. C. Nielson, November, 1981

Program or type	TV Households: Rating %	TV Households: No. (000)	Audience Composition (thousands): Men (18+)	Women (18+)	Teens 12-17	Children 2-11
Today (7:30-8:00)	4.9	3,990	1,820	2,990	170	360
Morning (7:15-8:00)	2.4	1,960	760	1,270	80	230
Good Morning Amer. (7:30-8:00)	5.3	4,320	1,650	3,400	240	400
Daytime						
Drama (Soaps)	7.0	5,690	1,350	5,180	460	430
Quiz & Aud. Participation	4.6	3,750	1,270	3,100	160	370
All 10am-4:30pm	6.1	4,960	1,280	4,350	380	450
Evening						
Informational	13.4	10,920	6,930	8,180	610	980
General Drama	17.6	14,330	7,670	12,500	1,390	2,360
Susp. & Mystery	16.0	13,080	8,420	10,650	1,790	2,130
Sit. Comedy	18.5	15,080	8,620	11,780	2,510	4,280
Feature Film	17.5	14,280	9,550	11,510	2,220	2,270
All 7-11pm regular	17.9	14,550	9,220	11,440	1,940	2,950

Television Network Addresses

American Broadcasting Company (ABC)
1330 Avenue of Americas
New York, NY 10019

Columbia Broadcasting System (CBS)
51 W. 52nd St.
New York, NY 10019

National Broadcasting Company (NBC)
30 Rockefeller Plaza
New York, NY 10020

Westinghouse Broadcasting (Group W)
90 Park Ave.
New York, NY 10016

Metromedia
485 Lexington Ave.
New York, NY 10017

Public Broadcasting Service (PBS)
609 Fifth Ave.
New York, NY 10017

Canadian Broadcasting Corp. (CBC)
1500 Bronson Ave.
Ottawa, Ontario, Canada K1G 3J5

50 Leading U.S. Advertisers, 1980

Source: Advertising Age, Sept. 10, 1981; copyright © Crain Communications Inc. 1981.

Rank	Company	Ad Costs (000)	Sales (000)	Ads as % sales
	Appliances, TV, radio			
27	RCA Corp.	$164,328	$ 8,011,300	2.1
29	General Electric	156,196	24,959,000	0.6
	Automobiles			
6	General Motors Corp.	316,000	57,728,508	0.5
8	Ford Motor Corp.	280,000	37,085,500	0.8
32	Chrysler Corp.	150,000	9,225,300	1.6
	Chemicals			
43	American Cyanamid Co.	125,000	3,453,934	3.6
49	Dupont	98,300	13,652,000	0.7
	Communications			
37	Time Inc.	141,851	2,881,783	4.9
40	CBS Inc.	132,372	4,062,052	3.3
	Drugs			
38	Richardson-Vicks	134,000	1,211,151	11.1
47	Schering-Plough Corp.	100,000	1,740,000	5.7
	Food			
3	General Foods Corp.	410,000	6,601,300	6.2
14	McDonald's Corp.	206,962	6,226,000	3.3
15	Ralston Purina Co.	206,795	4,885,000	4.2
19	Esmark Inc.	189,907	2,956,422	6.4
23	Beatrice Foods	175,000	8,772,804	2.0
25	General Mills	171,115	4,852,400	3.5
33	Nabisco Inc.	150,000	2,568,700	5.8
34	Consolidated Foods Corp.	149,221	5,600,000	2.7
35	Norton Simon Inc.	149,000	3,012,772	4.9
41	Dart & Kraft	128,283	9,411,000	1.4
44	Pillsbury Co.	124,026	3,301,700	3.8
48	Quaker Oats Co.	99,667	2,405,200	4.1
	Retail Chains			
2	Sears, Roebuck & Co.	599,600	25,195,000	2.4
5	K mart	319,311	14,200,000	2.2
45	J.C. Penney Co.	108,000	11,353,000	0.9
	Soaps, cleansers			
1	Procter & Gamble	649,624	11,416,000	5.7
13	Colgate-Palmolive Co.	225,000	5,130,464	9.4
28	Unilever U.S. Inc.	74,554	637,433	11.7
	Soft drinks			
12	PepsiCo Inc.	233,400	5,975,220	3.9
20	Coca-Cola Co.	184,185	5,912,600	3.1
	Telephones			
9	American T & T	259,170	50,791,200	0.5
36	International T & T	143,000	18,529,655	0.7
	Tobacco			
4	Philip Morris	364,595	9,822,300	3.7
7	R.J. Reynolds Industries	298,524	10,354,100	2.9
50	B.A.T. Industries	95,757	1,475,000	6.5
	Toiletries, cosmetics			
10	Warner-Lambert Co.	235,202	3,479,207	6.8
16	American Home Products	197,000	4,074,095	4.8
17	Bristol-Myers Co.	196,286	3,158,300	6.2
31	Gillette Co.	150,982	2,315,294	6.5
41	Chesebrough-Pond's	128,316	1,377,484	9.3
	Wine, beer, liquor			
21	Anheuser-Busch	181,279	3,822,400	4.7
26	Heublein Inc.	170,000	1,921,879	8.8
30	Seagram Co.	152,000	2,534,952	6.0
	Miscellaneous			
11	Gulf & Western Industries	233,800	6,885,000	3.4
18	Mobil Corp.	194,817	63,726,000	0.3
22	Johnson & Johnson	177,000	2,633,600	6.7
24	U.S. Government	172,965	—	—
39	Loews Corp.	132,785	4,530,000	2.9

Major Movies of the Year (Sept. 1, 1981 to Aug. 1, 1982)

Movie	Stars	Director
A Midsummer Night's Sex Comedy	Woody Allen, Mia Farrow, Jose Ferrer, Mary Sternburgen	Woody Allen
Absence of Malice	Paul Newman, Sally Field	Sidney Pollack
All the Marbles	Peter Falk, Vicki Frederick, Laurene Landon	Robert Aldrich
An American Werewolf in London	David Naughton, Griffin Dunne, Jenny Agutter	John Landis
An Officer and a Gentleman	Richard Gere, Debra Winger, Louis Gossett Jr.	Taylor Hackford
Annie	Aileen Quinn, Albert Finney, Carol Burnett, Bernadette Peters	John Huston
Author!Author!	Al Pacino, Tuesday Weld, Dyan Cannon, Alan King	Arthur Hiller
Barbarosa	Willie Nelson, Gary Busey, Gilbert Roland	Fred Schepisi
Blade Runner	Harrison Ford, Joanna Cassidy, Sean Young	Ridley Scott
Body Heat	William Hurt, Kathleen Turner	Lawrence Kasdan
Buddy Buddy	Walter Matthau, Jack Lemmon, Paula Prentiss	Billy Wilder
Butterfly	Stacy Keach, Pia Zadora, Orson Welles	Matt Cimber
Cannery Row	Nick Nolte, Debra Winger	David S. Ward
Carbon Coby	George Segal, Susan St. James, Jack Warden	Michael Schultz
Chariots of Fire	Ben Cross, Ian Charleson	Hugh Hudson
Conan the Barbarian	Arnold Schwarzenegger, James Earl Jones	John Milius
Continental Divide	John Belushi, Blair Brown	Michael Apted
Das Boot	Jurgen Prochnow	Wolfgang Peterson
Dead Men Don't Wear Plaid	Steve Martin, Rachel Ward, Carl Reiner	Carl Reiner
Death Wish II	Charles Bronson, Jill Ireland	Michael Winner
Deathtrap	Michael Caine, Christopher Reeve, Dyan Cannon	Sidney Lumet
Diner	Steve Guttenberg, Michey Rourke, Timothy Daly	Jerry Weintraub
E.T. The Extra-Terrestrial	Henry Thomas, Dee Wallace	Steven Spielberg
Evil Under the Sun	Peter Ustinov, Maggie Smith, James Mason	Guy Hamilton
Firefox	Clint Eastwood	Clint Eastwood
First Monday in October	Walter Matthau, Jill Clayburgh	Ronald Neame
Gallipoli	Mark Lee, Mel Gibson	Peter Weir
Ghost Story	Melvin Douglas, Fred Astaire, John Houseman, Douglas Fairbanks Jr.	John Irvin
Grease II	Maxwell Caulfield, Michelle Pfeiffer, Eve Arden	Patricia Birch
Gregory's Girl	Gordon John Sinclair, Dee Hepburn	Bill Forsyth
Halloween II	Jamie Lee Curtis, Donald Pleasence	Rick Rosenthal
Hanky Panky	Gene Wilder, Gilda Radner, Richard Widmark	Sidney Poitier
I'm Dancing As Fast As I Can	Jill Clayburgh, Nicol Williamson	Jack Hofsiss
Making Love	Kate Jackson, Michael Ontkean, Harry Hamlin	Arthur Hiller
Missing	Jack Lemmon, Sissy Spacek	Costa-Gavras
Mommie Dearest	Faye Dunaway, Mara Hobel, Steve Forrest	Frank Perry
My Dinner with Andre	Wallace Shawn, Andre Gregory	Louis Malle
Neighbors	John Belushi, Dan Aykroyd, Cathy Moriarty	John G. Avildsen
Night Crossing	John Hurt, Jane Alexander	Delbert Mann
Night Shift	Henry Winkler, Michael Keaton, Shelly Long	Ron Howard
On Golden Pond	Henry Fonda, Katherine Hepburn, Jane Fonda	Mark Rydell
One From the Heart	Frederick Forrest, Teri Garr, Raul Julia	Francis Ford Coppola
Only When I Laugh	Marsha Mason, Kristy McNichol, James Coco	Glenn Jordan
Partners	Ryan O'Neal, John Hurt	James Burrows
Paternity	Burt Reynolds, Beverly D'Angelo, Elizabeth Ashley	David Steinberg
Pennies From Heaven	Steve Martin, Bernadette Peters, Christopher Walken	Herbert Ross
Personal Best	Mariel Hemingway, Patrice Donnelly, Kenny Moore	Robert Towne
Poltergeist	Craig T. Nelson, Jobeth Williams, Beatrice Straight	Tobe Hooper
Prince of the City	Treat Williams	Sidney Lumet
Private Lessons	Howard Hesseman, Sylvia Kristel	Alan Myerson
Quartet	Maggie Smith, Alan Bates, Isabelle Adjani	James Ivory
Quest for Fire	Everett McGill, Ron Perlman, Rae Dawn Chong	Jean-Jacques Annaud
Raggedy Man	Sissy Spacek	Jack Fisk
Ragtime	James Cagney, Elizabeth McGovern, Howard E. Rollins	Milos Forman
Reds	Warren Beatty, Diane Keaton, Jack Nicholson, Maureen Stapleton	Warren Beatty
Rich and Famous	Jacqueline Bisset, Candice Bergen	George Cukor
Richard Pryor Live on Sunset Strip	Richard Pryor	Joe Layton
Right Is Wrong	Sean Connery, George Grizzard, Katherine Ross	Richard Brooks
Rocky III	Sylvester Stallone, Talia Shire, Burgess Meredith	Sylvester Stallone
Rollover	Jane Fonda, Kris Kristofferson	Alan J. Pakula
Sharky's Machine	Burt Reynolds, Rachel Ward, Brian Keith	Burt Reynolds
Shoot the Moon	Albert Finney, Diane Keaton	Allan Parker
Southern Comfort	Les Lannom, Keith Carradine, Powers Boothe	Walter Hill
Star Trek II: The Wrath of Khan	William Shatner, Leonard Nimoy, Ricardo Montalban	Nicolas Meyer
Taps	George C. Scott, Timothy Hutton	Harold Becker
Tarzan, the Ape Man	Bo Derek	John Derek
Tattoo	Bruce Dern, Maude Adams	Bob Brooks
The Best Little Whorehouse in Texas	Burt Reynolds, Dolly Parton, Dom DeLuise	Colin Higgins
The Border	Jack Nicholson, Valerie Perrine	Tony Richardson
The Chosen	Rod Steiger, Maximilian Schell, Robby Benson	Jeremy Paul Kagan
The French Lieutenant's Woman	Meryl Streep, Jeremy Irons	Karl Reisz
The Night the Lights Went Out in Georgia	Kristy McNichol, Dennis Quaid	Ronald F. Maxwell
The Pursuit of D.B. Cooper	Robert Duvall, Treat Williams	Roger Spottiswoode
The Thing	Kurt Russell, T.K. Carter, Richard Masur	John Carpenter
The Woman Next Door	Gerard DePardieu, Fanny Ardant	Francois Truffaut
The World According to Garp	Robin Williams, Mary Beth Hurt, Glenn Close	George Roy Hill
They All Laughed	Audrey Hepburn, Ben Gazzara	Peter Bogdanovich
Time Bandits	Sean Connery, Shelley Duvall, Craig Warnock, Ian Holm	Terry Gilliam
Tron	Jeff Bridges, Bruce Boxleitner, Barnard Hughes	Steven Lisberger
True Confessions	Robert De Niro, Robert Duvall, Burgess Meredith	Ulu Grosberd
Under the Rainbow	Chevy Chase, Carrie Fisher	Steve Rash
Victor/Victoria	Julie Andrews, James Garner, Robert Preston	Blake Edwards
Whose Life Is It Anyway?	Richard Dreyfuss, John Cassavetes	John Badham
Young Doctors in Love	Dabney Coleman, Michael Keaton, Sean Young	Garry Marshall

Superlative U.S. Statistics

Source: National Geographic Society, Washington, D.C.

Area for 50 states	Total	3,623,420 sq. mi.
	Land 3,543,883 sq. mi.—Water 79,537 sq. mi.	
Largest state	Alaska	591,004 sq. mi.
Smallest state	Rhode Island	1,212 sq. mi.
Largest county	San Bernardino County, California	20,102 sq. mi.
Smallest county	New York, New York	22 sq. mi.
Northernmost city	Barrow, Alaska	71°17′N.
Northernmost point	Point Barrow, Alaska	71°23′N.
Southernmost city	Hilo, Island of Hawaii	19°43′N.
Southernmost town	Naalehu, Island of Hawaii	19°03′N.
Southernmost point	Ka Lae (South Cape), Island of Hawaii	18°56′N. (155°41′W.)
Easternmost city	Eastport, Maine	66°59′02″W.
Easternmost town	Lubec, Maine	66°58′49″W.
Easternmost point	West Quoddy Head, Maine	66°57′W.
Westernmost city	Lihue, Island of Kauai, Hawaii	159°22′W.
Westernmost town	Adak, Aleutians, Alaska	176°45′W.
Westernmost point	Cape Wrangell, Attu Island, Aleutians, Alaska	172°27′E.
Highest city	Leadville, Colorado	10,200 ft.
Lowest town	Calipatria, California	−184 ft.
Highest point on Atlantic coast	Cadillac Mountain, Mount Desert Is., Maine	1,530 ft.
Largest and oldest national park	Yellowstone National Park (1872), Wyoming, Montana, Idaho	3,468 sq. mi.
Largest national monument	Wrangell-St. Elias, Alaska	18,630 sq. mi.
Highest waterfall	Yosemite Falls—Total in three sections	2,425 ft.
	Upper Yosemite Fall	1,430 ft.
	Cascades in middle section	675 ft.
	Lower Yosemite Fall	320 ft.
Longest river	Mississippi-Missouri	3,710 mi.
Highest mountain	Mount McKinley, Alaska	20,320 ft.
Lowest point	Death Valley, California	−282 ft.
Deepest lake	Crater Lake, Oregon	1,932 ft.
Rainiest spot	Mt. Waialeale, Hawaii	Annual aver. rainfall 460 inches
Largest gorge	Grand Canyon, Colorado River, Arizona	277 miles long, 600 ft. to 18 miles wide, 1 mile deep
Deepest gorge	Hell's Canyon, Snake River, Idaho-Oregon	7,900 ft.
Strongest surface wind	Mount Washington, New Hampshire recorded 1934	231 mph
Biggest dam	New Cornelia Tailings, Ten Mile Wash, Arizona	274,026,000 cu. yds. material used
Tallest building	Sears Tower, Chicago, Illinois	1,454 ft.
Largest building	Boeing 747 Manufacturing Plant, Everett, Washington	205,600,000 cu. ft.; covers 47 acres.
Tallest structure	TV tower, Blanchard, North Dakota	2,063 ft.
Longest bridge span	Verrazano-Narrows, New York	4,260 ft.
Highest bridge	Royal Gorge, Colorado	1,053 ft. above water
Deepest well	Gas well, Washita County, Oklahoma	31,441 ft.

The 49 States, Including Alaska

Area for 49 states	Total	3,616,949 sq. mi.
	Land 3,537,458 sq. mi.—Water 79,491 sq. mi.	

The 48 Contiguous States

Area for 48 states	Total	3,025,945 sq. mi.
	Land 2,966,625 sq. mi.—Water 59,320 sq. mi.	
Largest state	Texas	267,338 sq. mi
Northernmost town	Angle Inlet, Minnesota	49°22′N.
Northernmost point	Northwest Angle, Minnesota	49°23′N.
Southernmost city	Key West, Florida	24°33′N.
Southernmost mainland city	Florida City, Florida	25°27′N.
Southernmost point	Key West, Florida	24°33′N.
Westernmost town	La Push, Washington	124°38′W.
Westernmost point	Cape Alava, Washington	124°44′W.
Highest mountain	Mount Whitney, California	14,494 ft.

Note to users: The distinction between cities and towns varies from state to state. In this table the U.S. Bureau of the Census usage was followed.

Geodetic Datum Point of North America

The geodetic datum point of the U.S. is the National Ocean Survey's triangulation station Meades Ranch in Osborne County, Kansas, at latitude 39° 13′26″. 686 N and longitude 98° 32′30″. 506 W. This geodetic datum point is a fundamental point from which all latitude and longitude computations originate for North America and Central America.

Statistical Information about the U.S.

In the *Statistical Abstract of the United States* the Bureau of the Census, U.S. Dept. of Commerce, annually publishes a summary of social, political, and economic information. A book of more than 1,000 pages, it presents in 34 sections comprehensive data on population, housing, health, education, employment, income, prices, business, banking, energy, science, defense, trade, government finance, foreign country comparison, and other subjects. Special features include an appendix on statistical methodology and reliability and Standard Metropolitan Statistical Areas. The book is prepared under the direction of Glenn W. King, Chief, Statistical Compendia Staff, Bureau of the Census. Supplements to the *Statistical Abstract* are *Pocket Data Book USA, 1979; County and City Data Book, 1977; Historical Statistics of the United States, Colonial Times to 1970;* and *State and Metropolitan Area Data Book, 1982* (in production). Information concerning these and other publications may be obtained from the Supt. of Documents, Government Printing Office, Wash., D.C. 20402, or from the U.S. Bureau of the Census, Data User Services Division, Wash., D.C. 20233.

Highest and Lowest Altitudes in the U.S. and Territories

Source: Geological Survey, U.S. Interior Department. (Minus sign means below sea level; elevations are in feet.)

State	Highest Point Name	Highest Point County	Elev.	Lowest Point Name	Lowest Point County	Elev.
Alabama	Cheaha Mountain	Cleburne	2,407	Gulf of Mexico		Sea level
Alaska	Mount McKinley		20,320	Pacific Ocean		Sea level
Arizona	Humphreys Peak	Coconino	12,633	Colorado R.	Yuma	70
Arkansas	Magazine Mountain	Logan	2,753	Ouachita R.	Ashley Union	55
California	Mount Whitney	Inyo-Tulare	14,494	Death Valley	Inyo	−282
Colorado	Mount Elbert	Lake	14,433	Arkansas R.	Prowers	3,350
Connecticut	Mount Frissell	Litchfield	2,380	L.I. Sound		Sea level
Delaware	On Ebright Road	New Castle	442	Atlantic Ocean		Sea level
Dist. of Col.	Tenleytown	N. W. part	410	Potomac R.		1
Florida	Sec. 30, T 6N, R 20W	Walton	345	Atlantic Ocean		Sea level
Georgia	Brasstown Bald	Towns-Union	4,784	Atlantic Ocean		Sea level
Guam	Mount Lamlam	Agat District	1,329	Pacific Ocean		Sea level
Hawaii	Mauna Kea	Hawaii	13,796	Pacific Ocean		Sea level
Idaho	Borah Peak	Custer	12,662	Snake R.	Nez Perce	710
Illinois	Charles Mound	Jo Daviess	1,235	Mississippi R.	Alexander	279
Indiana	Franklin Township	Wayne	1,257	Ohio R.	Posey	320
Iowa	Sec. 29, T 100N, R 41W	Osceola	1,670	Mississippi R.	Lee	480
Kansas	Mount Sunflower	Wallace	4,039	Verdigris R.	Montgomery	680
Kentucky	Black Mountain	Harlan	4,145	Mississippi R.	Fulton	257
Louisiana	Driskill Mountain	Bienville	535	New Orleans	Orleans	−5
Maine	Mount Katahdin	Piscataquis	5,268	Atlantic Ocean		Sea level
Maryland	Backbone Mountain	Garrett	3,360	Atlantic Ocean		Sea level
Massachusetts	Mount Greylock	Berkshire	3,491	Atlantic Ocean		Sea level
Michigan	Mount Curwood	Baraga	1,980	Lake Erie		572
Minnesota	Eagle Mountain	Cook	2,301	Lake Superior		602
Mississippi	Woodall Mountain	Tishomingo	806	Gulf of Mexico		Sea level
Missouri	Taum Sauk Mt.	Iron	1,772	St. Francis R.	Dunklin	230
Montana	Granite Peak	Park	12,799	Kootenai R.	Lincoln	1,800
Nebraska	Johnson Township	Kimball	5,426	S.E. cor. State	Richardson	840
Nevada	Boundary Peak	Esmeralda	13,143	Colorado R.	Clark	470
New Hamp.	Mt. Washington	Coos	6,288	Atlantic Ocean		Sea level
New Jersey	High Point	Sussex	1,803	Atlantic Ocean		Sea level
New Mexico	Wheeler Peak	Taos	13,161	Red Bluff Res.	Eddy	2,817
New York	Mount Marcy	Essex	5,344	Atlantic Ocean		Sea level
North Carolina	Mount Mitchell	Yancey	6,684	Atlantic Ocean		Sea level
North Dakota	White Butte	Slope	3,506	Red R.	Pembina	750
Ohio	Campbell Hill	Logan	1,550	Ohio R.	Hamilton	433
Oklahoma	Black Mesa	Cimarron	4,973	Little R.	McCurtain	287
Oregon	Mount Hood	Clackamas-Hood R.	11,239	Pacific Ocean		Sea level
Pennsylvania	Mt. Davis	Somerset	3,213	Delaware R.	Delaware	Sea level
Puerto Rico	Cerro de Punta	Ponce District	4,389	Atlantic Ocean		Sea level
Rhode Island	Jerimoth Hill	Providence	812	Atlantic Ocean		Sea level
Samoa	Lata Mountain	Tau Island	3,160	Pacific Ocean		Sea level
South Carolina	Sassafras Mountain	Pickens	3,560	Atlantic Ocean		Sea level
South Dakota	Harney Peak	Pennington	7,242	Big Stone Lake	Roberts	962
Tennessee	Clingmans Dome	Sevier	6,643	Mississippi R.	Shelby	182
Texas	Guadalupe Peak	Culberson	8,749	Gulf of Mexico		Sea level
Utah	Kings Peak	Duchesne	13,528	Beaverdam Cr.	Washington	2,000
Vermont	Mount Mansfield	Lamoille	4,393	Lake Champlain	Franklin	95
Virginia	Mount Rogers	Grayson-Smyth	5,729	Atlantic Ocean		Sea level
Virgin Islands	Crown Mountain	St. Thomas Island	1,556	Atlantic Ocean		Sea level
Washington	Mount Rainier	Pierce	14,410	Pacific Ocean		Sea level
West Virginia	Spruce Knob	Pendleton	4,863	Potomac R.	Jefferson	240
Wisconsin	Timms Hill	Price	1,951	Lake Michigan		581
Wyoming	Gannett Peak	Fremont	13,804	B. Fourche R.	Crook	3,100

U.S. Coastline by States

Source: NOAA, U.S. Commerce Department
(statute miles)

State	Coastline[1]	Shoreline[2]
Atlantic coast	**2,069**	**28,673**
Connecticut	0	618
Delaware	28	381
Florida	580	3,331
Georgia	100	2,344
Maine	228	3,478
Maryland	31	3,190
Massachusetts	192	1,519
New Hampshire	13	131
New Jersey	130	1,792
New York	127	1,850
North Carolina	301	3,375
Pennsylvania	0	89
Rhode Island	40	384
South Carolina	187	2,876
Virginia	112	3,315
Gulf coast	**1,631**	**17,141**
Alabama	53	607
Florida	770	5,095
Louisiana	397	7,721
Mississippi	44	359
Texas	367	3,359
Pacific coast	**7,623**	**40,298**
Alaska	5,580	31,383
California	840	3,427
Hawaii	750	1,052
Oregon	296	1,410
Washington	157	3,026
Arctic coast, Alaska	**1,060**	**2,521**
United States	**12,383**	**88,633**

(1) Figures are lengths of general outline of seacoast. Measurements were made with a unit measure of 30 minutes of latitude on charts as near the scale of 1:1,200,000 as possible. Coastline of sounds and bays is included to a point where they narrow to width of unit measure, and includes the distance across at such point. (2) Figures obtained in 1939-40 with a recording instrument on the largest-scale charts and maps then available. Shoreline of outer coast, offshore islands, sounds, bays, rivers, and creeks is included to the head of tidewater or to a point where tidal waters narrow to a width of 100 feet.

States: Settled, Capitals, Entry into Union, Area, Rank

The original 13 states—The 13 colonies that seceded from Great Britain and fought the War of Independence (American Revolution) became the 13 original states. They were: Delaware, Pennsylvania, New Jersey, Georgia, Connecticut, Massachusetts, Maryland, South Carolina, New Hampshire, Virginia, New York, North Carolina, and Rhode Island. The order for the original 13 states is the order in which they ratified the Constitution.

State	Settled*	Capital	Entered Union Date	Entered Union Order	Extent in miles Long (approx.)	Extent in miles Wide (mean)	Area in square miles Land	Area in square miles Inland water	Area in square miles Total	Rank in area
Ala.	1702	Montgomery	Dec. 14, 1819	22	330	190	50,708	901	51,609	29
Alas.	1784	Juneau	Jan. 3, 1959	49	(a)1,480	810	569,600	20,157	589,757	1
Ariz.	1776	Phoenix	Feb. 14, 1912	48	400	310	113,417	492	113,909	6
Ark.	1686	Little Rock	June 15, 1836	25	260	240	51,945	1,159	53,104	27
Cal.	1769	Sacramento	Sept. 9, 1850	31	770	250	156,361	2,332	158,693	3
Col.	1858	Denver	Aug. 1, 1876	38	380	280	103,766	481	104,247	8
Conn.	1634	Hartford	Jan. 9, 1788	5	110	70	4,862	147	5,009	48
Del.	1638	Dover	Dec. 7, 1787	1	100	30	1,982	75	2,057	49
D.C.	. . .	Washington			...	...	61	6	67	51
Fla.	1565	Tallahassee	Mar. 3, 1845	27	500	160	54,090	4,470	58,560	22
Ga.	1733	Atlanta	Jan. 2, 1788	4	300	230	58,073	803	58,876	21
Ha.	1820	Honolulu	Aug. 21, 1959	50	...	...	6,425	25	6,450	47
Ida.	1842	Boise	July 3, 1890	43	570	300	82,677	880	83,557	13
Ill.	1720	Springfield	Dec. 3, 1818	21	390	210	55,748	652	56,400	24
Ind.	1733	Indianapolis	Dec. 11, 1816	19	270	140	36,097	194	36,291	38
Ia.	1788	Des Moines	Dec. 28, 1846	29	310	200	55,941	349	56,290	25
Kan.	1727	Topeka	Jan. 29, 1861	34	400	210	81,787	477	82,264	14
Ky.	1774	Frankfort	June 1, 1792	15	380	140	39,650	745	40,395	37
La.	1699	Baton Rouge	Apr. 30, 1812	18	380	130	44,930	3,593	48,523	31
Me.	1624	Augusta	Mar. 15, 1820	23	320	190	30,920	2,295	33,215	39
Md.	1634	Annapolis	Apr. 28, 1788	7	250	90	9,891	686	10,577	42
Mass.	1620	Boston	Feb. 6, 1788	6	190	50	7,826	431	8,257	45
Mich.	1668	Lansing	Jan. 26, 1837	26	490	240	56,817	1,399	58,216	23
Minn.	1805	St. Paul	May 11, 1858	32	400	250	79,289	4,779	84,068	12
Miss.	1699	Jackson	Dec. 10, 1817	20	340	170	47,296	420	47,716	32
Mo.	1735	Jefferson City	Aug. 10, 1821	24	300	240	68,995	691	69,686	19
Mon.	1809	Helena	Nov. 8, 1889	41	630	280	145,587	1,551	147,138	4
Neb.	1823	Lincoln	Mar. 1, 1867	37	430	210	76,483	744	77,227	15
Nev.	1849	Carson City	Oct. 31, 1864	36	490	320	109,889	651	110,540	7
N.H.	1623	Concord	June 21, 1788	9	190	70	9,027	277	9,304	44
N.J.	1664	Trenton	Dec. 18, 1787	3	150	70	7,521	315	7,836	46
N.M.	1610	Santa Fe	Jan. 6, 1912	47	370	343	121,412	254	121,666	5
N.Y.	1614	Albany	July 26, 1788	11	330	283	47,831	1,745	49,576	30
N.C.	1660	Raleigh	Nov. 21, 1789	12	500	150	48,798	3,788	52,586	28
N.D.	1812	Bismarck	Nov. 2, 1889	39	340	211	69,273	1,392	70,665	17
Oh.	1788	Columbus	Mar. 1, 1803	17	220	220	40,975	247	41,222	35
Okla.	1889	Oklahoma City	Nov. 16, 1907	46	400	220	68,782	1,137	69,919	18
Ore.	1811	Salem	Feb. 14, 1859	33	360	261	96,184	797	96,981	10
Pa.	1682	Harrisburg	Dec. 12, 1787	2	283	160	44,966	367	45,333	33
R.I.	1636	Providence	May 29, 1790	13	40	30	1,049	165	1,214	50
S.C.	1670	Columbia	May 23, 1788	8	260	200	30,225	830	31,055	40
S.D.	1859	Pierre	Nov. 2, 1889	40	380	210	75,955	1,092	77,047	16
Tenn.	1769	Nashville	June 1, 1796	16	440	120	41,328	916	42,244	34
Tex.	1692	Austin	Dec. 29, 1845	28	790	660	262,134	5,204	267,338	2
Ut.	1847	Salt Lake City	Jan. 4, 1896	45	350	270	82,096	2,820	84,916	11
Vt.	1724	Montpelier	Mar. 4, 1791	14	160	80	9,267	342	9,609	43
Va.	1607	Richmond	June 25, 1788	10	430	200	39,780	1,037	40,817	36
Wash.	1811	Olympia	Nov. 11, 1889	42	360	240	66,570	1,622	68,192	20
W.Va.	1727	Charleston	June 20, 1863	35	240	130	24,070	111	24,181	41
Wis.	1766	Madison	May 29, 1848	30	310	260	54,464	1,690	56,154	26
Wy.	1834	Cheyenne	July 10, 1890	44	360	280	97,203	711	97,914	9

*First European permanent settlement. (a) Aleutian Islands and Alexander Archipelago are not considered in these lengths.

The Continental Divide

Source: Geological Survey, U.S. Interior Department

The Continental Divide: watershed, created by mountain ranges or table-lands of the Rocky Mountains, from which the drainage is easterly or westerly; the easterly flowing waters reaching the Atlantic Ocean chiefly through the Gulf of Mexico, and the westerly flowing waters reaching the Pacific Ocean through the Columbia River, or through the Colorado River, which flows into the Gulf of California.

The location and route of the Continental Divide across the United States may briefly be described as follows:

Beginning at point of crossing the United States-Mexican boundary, near long. 108°45'W., the Divide, in a northerly direction, crosses New Mexico along the western edge of the Rio Grande drainage basin, entering Colorado near long. 106°41'W.

Thence by a very irregular route northerly across Colorado along the western summits of the Rio Grande and of the Arkansas, the South Platte, and the North Platte River basins, and across Rocky Mountain National Park, entering Wyoming near long. 106°52'W.

Thence in a northwesterly direction, forming the western rims of the North Platte, Big Horn, and Yellowstone River basins, crossing the southwestern portion of Yellowstone National Park.

Thence in a westerly and then a northerly direction forming the common boundary of Idaho and Montana, to a point on said boundary near long. 114°00'W.

Thence northeasterly and northwesterly through Montana and the Glacier National Park, entering Canada near long. 114°04'W.

Chronological List of Territories

Source: National Archives and Records Service

Name of territory	Date of Organic Act	Organic Act effective	Admission as state	Yrs. terr.
Northwest Territory(a)	July 13, 1787	No fixed date	Mar. 1, 1803(b)	16
Territory southwest of River Ohio	May 26, 1790	No fixed date	June 1, 1796(c)	6
Mississippi	Apr. 7, 1798	When president acted	Dec. 10, 1817	19
Indiana	May 7, 1800	July 4, 1800	Dec. 11, 1816	16
Orleans	Mar. 26, 1804	Oct. 1, 1804	Apr. 30, 1812(d)	7
Michigan	Jan. 11, 1805	June 30, 1805	Jan. 26, 1837	31
Louisiana-Missouri(e)	Mar. 3, 1805	July 4, 1805	Aug. 10, 1821	16
Illinois	Feb. 3, 1809	Mar. 1, 1809	Dec. 3, 1818	9
Alabama	Mar. 3, 1817	When Miss. became a state	Dec. 14, 1819	2
Arkansas	Mar. 2, 1819	July 4, 1819	June 15, 1836	17
Florida	Mar. 30, 1822	No fixed date	Mar. 3, 1845	23
Wisconsin	Apr. 20, 1836	July 3, 1836	May 29, 1848	12
Iowa	June 12, 1838	July 3, 1838	Dec. 28, 1846	7
Oregon	Aug. 14, 1848	Date of act	Feb. 14, 1859	10
Minnesota	Mar. 3, 1849	Date of act	May 11, 1858	9
New Mexico	Sept. 9, 1850	On president's proclamation	Jan. 6, 1912	61
Utah	Sept. 9, 1850	Date of act	Jan. 4, 1896	44
Washington	Mar. 2, 1853	Date of act	Nov. 11, 1889	36
Nebraska	May 30, 1854	Date of act	Mar. 1, 1867	12
Kansas	May 30, 1854	Date of act	Jan. 29, 1861	6
Colorado	Feb. 28, 1861	Date of act	Aug. 1, 1876	15
Nevada	Mar. 2, 1861	Date of act	Oct. 31, 1864	3
Dakota	Mar. 2, 1861	Date of act	Nov. 2, 1889	28
Arizona	Feb. 24, 1863	Date of act	Feb. 14, 1912	49
Idaho	Mar. 3, 1863	Date of act	July 3, 1890	27
Montana	May 26, 1864	Date of act	Nov. 8, 1889	25
Wyoming	July 25, 1868	When officers were qualified	July 10, 1890	22
Alaska(f)	May 17, 1884	No fixed date	Jan. 3, 1959	75
Oklahoma	May 2, 1890	Date of act	Nov. 16, 1907	17
Hawaii	Apr. 30, 1900	June 14, 1900	Aug. 21, 1959	59

(a) Included Ohio, Indiana, Illinois, Michigan, Wisconsin, eastern Minnesota; (b) as the state of Ohio; (c) as the state of Tennessee; (d) as the state of Louisiana; (e) organic act for Missouri Territory of June 4, 1812, became effective Dec. 7, 1812; (f) Although the May 17, 1884 act actually constituted Alaska as a district, it was often referred to as a territory, and unofficially administered as such. The Territory of Alaska was legally and formally organized by an act of Aug. 24, 1912.

Geographic Centers, U.S. and Each State

Source: Geological Survey, U.S. Interior Department

United States, including Alaska and Hawaii — South Dakota; Butte County, W of Castle Rock, Approx. lat. 44°58′N. long. 103°46′W.

Contiguous U. S. (48 states) — Near Lebanon, Smith Co., Kansas, lat. 39°50′N. long. 98°35′W.

North American continent — The geographic center is in Pierce County, North Dakota, 6 miles W of Balta, latitude 48°10′, longitude 100°10′W.

State—county, locality

Alabama—Chilton, 12 miles SW of Clanton.
Alaska—lat. 63°50′N. long. 152°W. Approx. 60 mi. NW of Mt. McKinley.
Arizona—Yavapai, 55 miles ESE of Prescott.
Arkansas—Pulaski, 12 miles NW of Little Rock.
California—Madera, 38 miles E of Madera.
Colorado—Park, 30 miles NW of Pikes Peak.
Connecticut—Hartford, at East Berlin.
Delaware—Kent, 11 miles S of Dover.
District of Columbia—Near 4th and L Sts., NW.
Florida—Hernando, 12 miles NNW of Brooksville.
Georgia—Twiggs, 18 miles SE of Macon.
Hawaii—Hawaii, 20°15′N, 156°20′W, off Maui Island.
Idaho—Custer, at Custer, SW of Challis.
Illinois—Logan, 28 miles NE of Springfield.
Indiana—Boone, 14 miles NNW of Indianapolis.
Iowa—Story, 5 miles NE of Ames.
Kansas—Barton, 15 miles NE of Great Bend.
Kentucky—Marion, 3 miles NNW of Lebanon.
Louisiana—Avoyelles, 3 miles SE of Marksville.
Maine—Piscataquis, 18 miles north of Dover.
Maryland—Prince Georges, 4.5 miles NW of Davidsonville.
Massachusetts—Worcester, north part of city.
Michigan—Wexford, 5 miles NNW of Cadillac.
Minnesota—Crow Wing, 10 miles SW of Brainerd.
Mississippi—Leake, 9 miles WNW of Carthage.
Missouri—Miller, 20 miles SW of Jefferson City.
Montana—Fergus, 12 miles west of Lewistown.
Nebraska—Custer, 10 miles NW of Broken Bow.
Nevada—Lander, 26 miles SE of Austin.
New Hampshire—Belknap, 3 miles E of Ashland.
New Jersey—Mercer, 5 miles SE of Trenton.
New Mexico—Torrance, 12 miles SSW of Willard.
New York—Madison, 12 miles S of Oneida and 26 miles SW of Utica.
North Carolina—Chatham, 10 miles NW of Sanford.
North Dakota—Sheridan, 5 miles SW of McClusky.
Ohio—Delaware, 25 miles NNE of Columbus.
Oklahoma—Oklahoma, 8 miles N of Oklahoma City.
Oregon—Crook, 25 miles SSE of Prineville.
Pennsylvania—Centre, 2.5 miles SW of Bellefonte.
Rhode Island—Kent, 1 mile SSW of Crompton.
South Carolina—Richland, 13 miles SE of Columbia.
South Dakota—Hughes, 8 miles NE of Pierre.
Tennessee—Rutherford, 5 mi. NE of Murfreesboro.
Texas—McCulloch, 15 miles NE of Brady.
Utah—Sanpete, 3 miles N of Manti.
Vermont—Washington, 3 miles E of Roxbury.
Virginia—Buckingham, 5 miles SW of Buckingham.
Washington—Chelan, 10 mi. WSW of Wenatchee.
West Virginia—Braxton, 4 miles E of Sutton.
Wisconsin—Wood, 9 miles SE of Marshfield.
Wyoming—Fremont, 58 miles ENE of Lander.

There is no generally accepted definition of geographic center, and no satisfactory method for determining it. The geographic center of an area may be defined as the center of gravity of the surface, or that point on which the surface of the area would balance if it were a plane of uniform thickness.

No marked or monumented point has been established by any government agency as the geographic center of either the 50 states, the contiguous United States, or the North American continent. A monument was erected in Lebanon, Kan., contiguous U.S. center, by a group of citizens.

International Boundary Lines of the U.S.

The length of the northern boundary of the contiguous U.S. — the U.S.-Canadian border, excluding Alaska — is 3,987 miles according to the U.S. Geological Survey, Dept. of the Interior. The length of the Alaskan-Canadian border is 1,538 miles. The length of the U.S.-Mexican border, from the Gulf of Mexico to the Pacific Ocean, is approximately 1,933 miles (1963 boundary agreement).

Origin of the Names of U.S. States

Source: State officials, the Smithsonian Institution, and the Topographic Division, U.S. Geological Survey.

Alabama—Indian for tribal town, later a tribe (Alabamas or Alibamons) of the Creek confederacy.

Alaska—Russian version of Aleutian (Eskimo) word, alakshak, for "peninsula," "great lands," or "land that is not an island."

Arizona—Spanish version of Pima Indian word for "little spring place," or Aztec arizuma, meaning "silver-bearing."

Arkansas—French variant of Kansas, a Sioux Indian name for "south wind people."

California—Bestowed by the Spanish conquistadors (possibly by Cortez). It was the name of an imaginary island, an earthly paradise, in "Las Serges de Esplandian," a Spanish romance written by Montalvo in 1510. Baja California (Lower California, in Mexico) was first visited by Spanish in 1533. The present U.S. state was called Alta (Upper) California.

Colorado—Spanish, red, first applied to Colorado River.

Connecticut—From Mohican and other Algonquin words meaning "long river place."

Delaware—Named for Lord De La Warr, early governor of Virginia; first applied to river, then to Indian tribe (Lenni-Lenape), and the state.

District of Columbia—For Columbus, 1791.

Florida—Named by Ponce de Leon on Pascua Florida, "Flowery Easter," on Easter Sunday, 1513.

Georgia—For King George II of England by James Oglethorpe, colonial administrator, 1732.

Hawaii—Possibly derived from native world for homeland, Hawaiki or Owhyhee.

Idaho—A coined name with an invented Indian meaning: "gem of the mountains;" originally suggested for the Pike's Peak mining territory (Colorado), then applied to the new mining territory of the Pacific Northwest. Another theory suggests Idaho may be a Kiowa Apache term for the Comanche.

Illinois—French for Illini or land of Illini, Algonquin word meaning men or warriors.

Indiana—Means "land of the Indians."

Iowa—Indian word variously translated as "one who puts to sleep" or "beautiful land."

Kansas—Sioux word for "south wind people."

Kentucky—Indian word variously translated as "dark and bloody ground," "meadow land" and "land of tomorrow."

Louisiana—Part of territory called Louisiana by Sieur de La Salle for French King Louis XIV.

Maine—From Maine, ancient French province. Also: descriptive, referring to the mainland as distinct from the many coastal islands.

Maryland—For Queen Henrietta Maria, wife of Charles I of England.

Massachusetts—From Indian tribe named after "large hill place" identified by Capt. John Smith as being near Milton, Mass.

Michigan—From Chippewa words mici gama meaning "great water," after the lake of the same name.

Minnesota—From Dakota Sioux word meaning "cloudy water" or "sky-tinted water" of the Minnesota River.

Mississippi—Probably Chippewa; mici zibi, "great river" or "gathering-in of all the waters." Also: Algonquin word, "Messipi."

Missouri—Algonquin Indian tribe named after Missouri River, meaning "muddy water."

Montana—Latin or Spanish for "mountainous."

Nebraska—From Omaha or Otos Indian word meaning "broad water" or "flat river," describing the Platte River.

Nevada—Spanish, meaning snow-clad.

New Hampshire—Named 1629 by Capt. John Mason of Plymouth Council for his home county in England.

New Jersey—The Duke of York, 1664, gave a patent to John Berkeley and Sir George Carteret to be called Nova Caesaria, or New Jersey, after England's Isle of Jersey.

New Mexico—Spaniards in Mexico applied term to land north and west of Rio Grande in the 16th century.

New York—For Duke of York and Albany who received patent to New Netherland from his brother Charles II and sent an expedition to capture it, 1664.

North Carolina—In 1619 Charles I gave a large patent to Sir Robert Heath to be called Province of Carolana, from Carolus, Latin name for Charles. A new patent was granted by Charles II to Earl of Clarendon and others. Divided into North and South Carolina, 1710.

North Dakota—Dakota is Sioux for friend or ally.

Ohio—Iroquois word for "fine or good river."

Oklahoma—Choctaw coined word meaning red man, proposed by Rev. Allen Wright, Choctaw-speaking Indian.

Oregon—Origin unknown. One theory holds that the name may have been derived from that of the Wisconsin River shown on a 1715 French map as "Ouaricon-sint."

Pennsylvania—William Penn, the Quaker, who was made full proprietor by King Charles II in 1681, suggested Sylvania, or woodland, for his tract. The king's government owed Penn's father, Admiral William Penn, £16,000, and the land was granted as partial settlement. Charles II added the Penn to Sylvania, against the desires of the modest proprietor, in honor of the admiral.

Puerto Rico—Spanish for Rich Port.

Rhode Island—Exact origin is unknown. One theory notes that Giovanni de Verrazano recorded an island about the size of Rhodes in the Mediterranean in 1524, but others believe the state was named Roode Eylandt by Adriaen Block, Dutch explorer, because of its red clay.

South Carolina—See North Carolina.

South Dakota—See North Dakota.

Tennessee—Tanasi was the name of Cherokee villages on the Little Tennessee River. From 1784 to 1788 this was the State of Franklin, or Frankland.

Texas—Variant of word used by Caddo and other Indians meaning friends or allies, and applied to them by the Spanish in eastern Texas. Also written texias, tejas, teysas.

Utah—From a Navajo word meaning upper, or higher up, as applied to a Shoshone tribe called Ute. Spanish form is Yutta, English Uta or Utah. Proposed name Deseret, "land of honeybees," from Book of Mormon, was rejected by Congress.

Vermont—From French words vert (green) and mont (mountain). The Green Mountains were said to have been named by Samuel de Champlain. The Green Mountain Boys were Gen. Stark's men in the Revolution. When the state was formed, 1777, Dr. Thomas Young suggested combining vert and mont into Vermont.

Virginia—Named by Sir Walter Raleigh, who fitted out the expedition of 1584, in honor of Queen Elizabeth, the Virgin Queen of England.

Washington—Named after George Washington. When the bill creating the Territory of Columbia was introduced in the 32d Congress, the name was changed to Washington because of the existence of the District of Columbia.

West Virginia—So named when western counties of Virginia refused to secede from the United States, 1863.

Wisconsin—An Indian name, spelled Ouisconsin and Mesconsing by early chroniclers. Believed to mean "grassy place" in Chippewa. Congress made it Wisconsin.

Wyoming—The word was taken from Wyoming Valley, Pa., which was the site of an Indian massacre and became widely known by Campbell's poem, "Gertrude of Wyoming." In Algonquin it means "large prairie place."

Accession of Territory by the U.S.

Source: Statistical Abstract of the United States

Division	Year	Sq. mi.[1]	Division	Year	Sq. mi.[1]	Division	Year	Sq. mi.[1]
Total U.S.	**1970**	**3,630,854**	Oregon	**1846**	285,580	American Samoa	**1900**	76
50 states & D.C.		3,618,467	Mexican Cession	**1848**	529,017	Corn Islands[4]	**1914**	4
Territory in 1790[2]		888,685	Gadsden Purchase	**1853**	29,640	Virgin Islands, U.S.	**1917**	133
Louisiana Purchase	**1803**	827,192	Alaska	**1867**	589,757	Trust Territory of		
By treaty with Spain:			Hawaii	**1898**	6,450	the Pacific Is.	**1947**	8,489
Florida	**1819**	58,560	The Philippines[3]	**1898**	115,600	All other[5]		42
Other areas	**1819**	13,443	Puerto Rico	**1899**	3,435			
Texas	**1845**	390,143	Guam	**1899**	212			

(1) Gross area (land and water). (2) Includes drainage basin of Red River on the north, south of 49th parallel, sometimes considered a part of the Louisiana Purchase. (3) Area not included in total; became Republic of the Philippines July 4, 1946. (4) Leased from Nicaragua for 99 years but returned Apr. 25, 1971; area not included in total. (5) See index for Outlying Areas, U.S.

Public Lands of the U. S.

Source: Bureau of Land Management, U.S. Interior Department

Acquisition of the Public Domain 1781-1867

Acquisition	Area* (acres) Land	Water	Total	Cost[1]
State Cessions (1781-1802)	233,415,680	3,409,920	236,825,600	[2]$6,200,000
Louisiana Purchase (1803)[3]	523,446,400	6,465,280	529,911,680	23,213,568
Red River Basin[4]	29,066,880	535,040	29,601,920	
Cession from Spain (1819)	43,342,720	2,801,920	46,144,640	6,674,057
Oregon Compromise (1846)	180,644,480	2,741,760	183,386,240	
Mexican Cession (1848)	334,479,360	4,201,600	338,680,960	16,295,149
Purchase from Texas (1850)	78,842,880	83,840	78,926,720	15,496,448
Gadsden Purchase (1853)	18,961,920	26,880	18,988,800	10,000,000
Alaska Purchase (1867)	362,516,480	12,787,200	375,303,680	7,200,000
Total	**1,804,716,800**	**33,053,440**	**1,837,770,240**	**$85,079,222**

*All areas except Alaska were computed in 1912, and have not been adjusted for the recomputation of the area of the United States which was made for the 1950 Decennial Census. (1) Cost data for all except "State Cessions" obtained from U.S. Geological Survey. (2) Paid by federal government for Georgia cession, 1802 (56,689,920 acres). (3) Excludes areas eliminated by Treaty of 1819 with Spain. (4) Basin of the Red River of the North, south of the 49th parallel.

Disposition of Public Lands 1781 to 1970

Disposition by methods not elsewhere classified[1]	Acres
Disposition by methods not elsewhere classified[1]	303,500,000
Granted or sold to homesteaders	287,500,000
Granted to railroad corporations	94,300,000
Granted to veterans as military bounties	61,100,000
Confirmed as private land claims[2]	34,000,000
Sold under timber and stone law[3]	13,900,000
Granted or sold under timber culture law[4]	10,900,000
Sold under desert land law[5]	10,700,000

Granted to states for:	Acres
Support of common schools	77,600,000
Reclamation of swampland	64,900,000
Construction of railroads	37,100,000
Support of misc. institutions[6]	21,700,000
Purposes not elsewhere classified[7]	117,600,000
Canals and rivers	6,100,000
Construction of wagon roads	3,400,000
Total granted to states	**328,300,000**

(1) Chiefly public, private, and preemption sales, but includes mineral entries, script locations, sales of townsites and townlots. (2) The Government has confirmed title to lands claimed under valid grants made by foreign governments prior to the acquisition of the public domain by the United States. (3) The law provided for the sale of lands valuable for timber or stone and unfit for cultivation. (4) The law provided for the granting of public lands to settlers on condition that they plant and cultivate trees on the lands granted. (5) The law provided for the sale of arid agricultural public lands to settlers who irrigate them and bring them under cultivation. (6) Universities, hospitals, asylums, etc. (7) For construction of various public improvements (individual items not specified in the granting act) reclamation of desert lands, construction of water reservoirs, etc.

Public Lands Administered by Federal Agencies

Agency (Acres, June 30, 1979)	Public domain	Acquired	Total
Bureau of Land Management	395,155,546	2,367,290	397,522,836
Forest Service	160,002,140	27,506,087	187,508,227
Fish and Wildlife Service	38,686,170	4,364,420	43,050,590
National Park Service	61,547,223	6,716,663	68,263,886
U.S. Army	6,616,134	4,041,741	10,657,875
U.S. Air Force	6,923,551	1,352,686	8,276,237
Corps of Engineers	658,984	7,575,499	8,234,483
U.S. Navy	1,976,128	1,182,494	3,158,622
Water and Power Resources Services	4,684,992	1,930,826	6,615,818
Energy Research and Development Admin.	627,182	701,727	1,328,909
Others	980,196	2,057,536	3,037,732
Total	**677,858,246**	**59,796,969**	**737,655,215**
	Grand Total		**1,144,300,000**

National Parks, Other Areas Administered by Nat'l Park Service

Figures given are date area was set aside by Congress or proclaimed by president, and gross area in acres Dec. 31, 1981.

National Parks

Acadia, Me. (1916) 39,056. Includes Mount Desert Island, half of Isle au Haut, Schoodic Point on mainland. Highest elevation on Eastern seaboard.

Arches, Ut. (1929) 73,379. Contains giant red sandstone arches and other products of erosion.

Badlands, S.D. (1929) 243,302; eroded prairie, bison, bighorn and antelope. Renamed national park in 1978.

Big Bend, Tex. (1935) 741,118. Rio Grande, Chisos Mts.

Biscayne, Fla. (1968) 180,128. Nat'l monument redesignated acquatic nat'l park by 1980 act.

Bryce Canyon, Ut. (1923) 35,835. Spectacularly colorful and unusual display of erosion effects.

Canyonlands, Ut. (1964) 337,570. At junction of Colorado and Green rivers, extensive evidence of prehistoric Indians.

Capitol Reef, Ut. (1937) 241,904. A 70-mile uplift of sandstone cliffs dissected by high-walled gorges.

Carlsbad Caverns, N.M. (1923) 46,755. Largest known caverns; not yet fully explored.

Channel Islands, Cal. (1938) 249,354. Park absorbed national monument in 1980 park act.

Crater Lake, Ore. (1902) 160,290. Extraordinary blue lake in crater of extinct volcano encircled by lava walls 500 to 2,000 feet high.

Denali, Alas. (1917) 4,698,583. Name changed from Mt. McKinley NP Dec. 2, 1980. Contains highest mountain in U.S., wildlife.

Everglades, Fla. (1934) 1,398,800. Largest remaining subtropical wilderness in Continental U.S.

Gates of the Arctic, Alas. (1978) 7,498,066. Vast wilderness in north central region. Park status: Dec. 2, 1980.

Glacier, Mon. (1910) 3,020,396. Superb Rocky Mountain scenery, numerous glaciers and glacial lakes. Part of Waterton-Glacier International Peace Park established by U.S. and Canada in 1932.

Glacier Bay, Alas. (1925) 3,020,396. Nat'l monument popular for its glaciers became nat'l park Dec. 2, 1980.

Grand Canyon, Ariz. (1908) 1,218,375. Most spectacular part of Colorado River's greatest canyon.

Grand Teton, Wy. (1929) 310,516. Most impressive part of the Teton Mountains, winter feeding ground of largest American elk herd.

Great Smoky Mountains, N.C.-Tenn. (1926) 520,269. Largest eastern mountain range, magnificent forests.

Guadalupe Mountains, Tex. (1966) 76,293. Extensive Permian limestone fossil reef; tremendous earth fault.

Haleakala, Ha. (1960) 28,655. 10,023 foot dormant volcano on Maui.

Hawaii Volcanoes, Ha. (1916) 229,177. Contains Kilauea and Mauna Loa, active volcanoes.

Hot Springs, Ark. (1832) 5,826. Government supervised bath houses use waters of 45 of the 47 natural hot springs.

Isle Royale, Mich. (1931) 571,796. Largest island in Lake Superior, noted for its wilderness area and wildlife.

Katmai, Alas. (1918) 3,678,929. Nat'l monument famous for brown bear and salmon upgraded to park Dec. 2, 1980.

Kenai Fjords, Alas. (1978) 676,667. Abundant mountain goats, marine mammals, birdlife. Park status Dec. 2, 1980.

Kings Canyon, Cal. (1890) 460,136. Mountain wilderness, dominated by Kings River Canyons and High Sierra; contains giant sequoias.

Kobuk Valley, Alas. (1978) 1,749,037. Broad river is core of native culture. Park status Dec. 2, 1980.

Lake Clark, Alas. (1978) 2,633,933. Across Cook Inlet from Anchorage. A scenic wilderness rich in fish and wildlife. Park status Dec. 2, 1980.

Lassen Volcanic, Cal. (1907) 106,372. Contains Lassen Peak, recently active volcano, and other volcanic phenomena.

Mammoth Cave, Ky. (1926) 52,370. 144 miles of surveyed underground passages, beautiful natural formations, river 360 feet below surface.

Mesa Verde, Col. (1906) 52,085. Most notable and best preserved prehistoric cliff dwellings in the United States.

Mount Rainier, Wash. (1899) 235,404. Greatest single-peak glacial system in the lower 48 states.

North Cascades, Wash. (1968) 504,781. Spectacular mountainous region with many glaciers, lakes.

Olympic, Wash. (1909) 915,426. Mountain wilderness containing finest remnant of Pacific Northwest rain forest, active glaciers, Pacific shoreline, rare elk.

Petrified Forest, Ariz. (1906) 93,493. Extensive petrified wood and Indian artifacts. Contains part of Painted Desert.

Redwood, Cal. (1968) 109,256. Forty miles of Pacific coastline, groves of ancient redwoods and world's tallest trees.

Rocky Mountain, Col. (1915) 266,943 On the continental divide, includes 107 named peaks over 11,000 feet.

Sequoia, Cal. (1890) 402,488. Groves of giant sequoias, highest mountain in contiguous United States — Mount Whitney (14,494 feet). World's largest tree.

Shenandoah, Va. (1926) 195,057. Portion of the Blue Ridge Mountains; overlooks Shenandoah Valley; Skyline Drive.

Theodore Roosevelt, N.D. (1947) 70,416; contains part of T.R.'s ranch and scenic badlands. National park in 1978.

Virgin Islands, V.I. (1956) 14,695. Covers 75% of St. John Island, lush growth, lovely beaches, Indian relics, evidence of colonial Danes.

Voyageurs, Minn. (1971) 219,128. Abundant lakes, forests, wildlife, canoeing, boating.

Wind Cave, S.D. (1903) 28,292. Limestone Caverns in Black Hills. Extensive wildlife includes a herd of bison.

Wrangell-St. Elias, Alas. (1978) 8,331,406. Largest area in parks system, most peaks over 16,000 feet, abundant wildlife; day's drive east of Anchorage.

Yellowstone, Ida., Mon., Wy., (1872) 2,219,823. Oldest national park. World's greatest geyser area has about 3,000 geysers and hot springs; spectacular falls and impressive canyons of the Yellowstone River; grizzly bear, moose, bison, other wildlife are major attractions.

Yosemite, Cal. (1890) 760,917. Yosemite Valley, the nation's highest waterfall, 3 groves of sequoias, and mountainous.

Zion, Ut. (1909) 146,551. Unusual shapes and landscapes have resulted from erosion and faulting; Zion Canyon, with sheer walls ranging up to 2,500 feet, is readily accessible.

National Historical Parks

Appomattox Court House, Va. (1930) 1,319. Where Lee surrendered to Grant.

Boston, Mass. (1974) 41. Includes Faneuil Hall, Old North Church, Bunker Hill, Paul Revere House.

Chaco Culture, N.M. (1907) 33,969. Enlarged and redesignated in 1980 from nat'l monument status.

Chesapeake and Ohio Canal, Md.-W.Va.-D.C. (1961) 20,781. 185 mile historic canal; D.C. to Cumberland, Md.

Colonial, Va. (1930) 9,316. Includes most of Jamestown Island, site of first successful English colony; Yorktown, site of Cornwallis' surrender to George Washington; and the Colonial Parkway.

Cumberland Gap, Ky.-Tenn.-Va. (1940) 20,351. Mountain pass of the Wilderness Road which carried the first great migration of pioneers into America's interior.

George Rogers Clark, Vincennes, Ind. (1966) 24. Commemorates American defeat of British in west during Revolution.

Harpers Ferry, Md., W. Va. (1944) 2,239. At the confluence of the Shenandoah and Potomac rivers, the site of John Brown's 1859 raid on the Army arsenal. Scene of several Civil War maneuvers.

Independence, Pa. (1948) 45. Contains several properties in Philadelphia associated with the Revolutionary War and the founding of the U.S.

Jean Laffite (and preserve), La. (1978) 20,000. Includes Chalmette, site of 1814 Battle of New Orleans; French Quarter.

Kalaupapa, Ha. (1980) 10,902. Molokai's former leper colony site and other historic areas.

Kaloko-Honokohau, Ha. (1978) 1,250. Culture center has 234 historic features and grave of first king, Kamehameha.

Klondike Gold Rush, Alas.-Wash. (1976) 13,270. Skagway, Alaskan Trails in 1898 Gold Rush. Museum in Seattle.

Lowell, Mass. (1978) 137. Seven mills, canal, 19th C. structures, park to show planned city of Industrial Revolution.

Lyndon B. Johnson, Tex. (1969) 1,478. Redesignated from nat'l historic site in 1980. President's birthplace, boyhood home, ranch.

Minute Man, Mass. (1959) 752. Where the colonial Minute Men battled the British, April 19, 1775. Also contains Nathaniel Hawthorne's home.

Morristown, N.J. (1933) 1,678. Sites of important military encampments during the Revolutionary War; Washington's headquarters 1777, 1779-80.

Nez Perce, Ida. (1965) 2,109. Illustrates the history and culture of the Nez Perce Indian country. 22 separate sites.

Pu'uhonua o Honaunau, Ha. (1955) 182. Until 1819, a sanctuary for Hawaiians vanquished in battle, and those guilty of crimes or breaking taboos.

San Antonio Missions, Tex. (1978) 483. Four of finest Spanish missions in U.S., 18th C. irrigation system.

San Juan Island, Wash. (1966) 1,752. Commemorates peaceful relations of the U.S., Canada and Great Britain since the 1872 boundary disputes.

Saratoga, N.Y. (1938) 2,605. Scene of a major battle which became a turning point in the War of Independence.

Sitka, Alas. (1910) 108. Scene of last major resistance of the Tlingit Indians to the Russians, 1804.

Valley Forge, Pa. (1976) 3,470. Continental Army campsite in 1777-78 winter.

War in the Pacific, Guam (1978) 1,920. Scenic park memorial for WWII combatants in Pacific.

Women's Rights, N.Y. (1980) 2.45. Seneca Falls site where Susan B. Anthony, Elizabeth Cady Stanton began rights movement in 1848.

National Battlefields

Antietam, Md. (1890) 3,246. Battle ended first Confederate invasion of North, Sept. 17, 1862.

Big Hole, Mon. (1910) 656. Site of major battle with Nez Perce Indians.

Cowpens, S.C. (1929) 841. Revolutionary War battlefield.

Fort Necessity, Pa. (1931) 903. First battle of French and Indian War.

Monocacy, Md. (1976) 1,647. Civil War battle in defense of Wash., D.C., July 9, 1864.

Moores Creek, N.C. (1926) 87. Pre-Revolutionary War battle.

Petersburg, Va. (1926) 1,536. Scene of 10-month Union campaign 1864-65.

Stones River, Tenn. (1927) 331. Civil War battle leading to Sherman's "March to the Sea."

Tupelo, Miss. (1929) 1. Crucial battle over Sherman's supply line.

Wilson's Creek, Mo. (1960) 1,750. Civil War battle for control of Missouri.

National Battlefield Parks

Kennesaw Mountain, Ga. (1917) 2,884. Two major battles of Atlanta campaign in Civil War.

Manassas, Va. (1940) 4,513. 7c Two 103. Civil War battles. 8

Richmond, Va. (1936) 769. Site of battles defending Confederate capital.

National Battlefield Site

Brices Cross Roads, Miss. (1929) 1. Civil War battlefield.

National Military Parks

Chickamauga and Chattanooga, Ga.-Tenn. (1890) 8,103. Four Civil War battlefields.

Fort Donelson, Tenn. (1928) 536. Site of first major Union victory.

Fredericksburg and Spotsylvania County, Va. (1927) 5,909. Sites of several major Civil War battles and campaigns.

Gettysburg, Pa. (1895) 3,863. Site of decisive Confederate defeat in North. Gettysburg Address.

Guilford Courthouse, N.C. (1917) 220. Revolutionary War battle site.

Horseshoe Bend, Ala. (1956) 2,040. On Tallapoosa River, where Gen. Andrew Jackson broke the power of the Creek Indian Confederacy.

Kings Mountain, S.C. (1931) 3,945. Revolutionary War battle.

Pea Ridge, Ark. (1956) 4,300. Civil War battle.

Shiloh, Tenn. (1894) 3,838. Major Civil War battle; site includes some well-preserved Indian burial mounds.

Vicksburg, Miss. (1899) 1,741. Union victory gave North control of the Mississippi and split the Confederacy in two.

National Memorials

Arkansas Post, Ark. (1960) 389. First permanent French settlement in the lower Mississippi River valley.

Arlington House, the Robert E. Lee Memorial, Va. (1925) 28.

Lee's home overlooking the Potomac.

Chamizal, El Paso, Tex. (1966) 55. Commemorates 1963 settlement of 99-year border dispute with Mexico.

Coronado, Ariz. (1952) 4,977. Commemorates first European exploration of the Southwest.

DeSoto, Fla. (1948) 27. Commemorates 16th-century Spanish explorations.

Federal Hall, N.Y. (1939) 0.45. First seat of U.S. government under the Constitution.

Fort Caroline, Fla. (1950) 139. On St. Johns River, overlooks site of second attempt by French Huguenots to colonize North America.

Fort Clatsop, Ore. (1958) 125. Lewis and Clark encampment 1805-06.

General Grant, N.Y. (1958) 0.76. Tombs of Pres. and wife.

Hamilton Grange, N.Y. (1962) 0.71. Home of Alexander Hamilton.

John F. Kennedy Center for the Performing Arts, D.C. (1972) 18.

Johnstown Flood, Pa. (1964) 163. Commemorates tragic flood of 1889.

Lincoln Boyhood, Ind. (1962) 198. Lincoln grew up here.

Lincoln Memorial, D.C. (1911) 164.

Lyndon B. Johnson Grove on the Potomac, D.C. (1973) 17.

Mount Rushmore, S.D. (1925) 1,278. World famous sculpture of 4 presidents.

Roger Williams, R.I. (1965) 5. Memorial to founder of Rhode Island.

Thaddeus Kosciuszko, Pa. (1972) 0.02. Memorial to Polish hero of American Revolution.

Theodore Roosevelt Island, D.C. (1947) 89.

Thomas Jefferson Memorial, D.C. (1943) 18.

USS Arizona, Ha. (1980) 14. Memorializes American losses at Pearl Harbor.

Washington Monument, D.C. (1848) 106.

Wright Brothers, N.C. (1927) 431. Site of first powered flight.

National Historic Sites

Abraham Lincoln Birthplace, Hodgenville, Ky. (1916) 117.

Adams, Quincy, Mass. (1946) 9. Home of Presidents John Adams, John Quincy Adams, and celebrated descendants.

Allegheny Portage Railroad, Pa. (1964) 1,135. Part of the Pennsylvania Canal system.

Andersonville, Andersonville, Ga. (1970) 476. Noted Civil War prison.

Andrew Johnson, Greeneville, Tenn. (1935) 17. Home of the President.

Bent's Old Fort, Col. (1960) 800. Old West fur-trading post.

Carl Sandburg Home, N.C. (1968) 264. Poet's farm home.

Christiansted, St. Croix; V.I. (1952) 27. Commemorates Danish colony.

Clara Barton, Md. (1974) 9. Home of founder of American Red Cross.

Edgar Allan Poe, Pa. (1978) 0.52. Poet's home.

Edison, West Orange, N.J. (1955) 21. Home and laboratory.

Eisenhower, Gettysburg, Pa. (1967) 690. Home of 34th president. Not open to public.

Eleanor Roosevelt, Hyde Park, N.Y. (1977) 180.

Eugene O'Neill, Danville, Cal. (1980) 14. Playwright's home.

Ford's Theatre, Washington, D.C. (1866) 0.29. Includes theater, now restored, where Lincoln was assassinated, house where he died, and Lincoln Museum.

Fort Bowie, Ariz. (1964) 1,000. Focal point of operations against Geronimo and the Apaches.

Fort Davis, Tex. (1961) 460. Frontier outpost battled Comanches and Apaches.

Fort Laramie, Wy. (1938) 832. Military post on Oregon Trail.

Fort Larned, Kan. (1964) 718. Military post on Sante Fe Trail.

Fort Point, San Francisco, Cal. (1970) 29. Largest West Coast fortification.

Fort Raleigh, N.C. (1941) 157. First English settlement.

Fort Scott, Kan. (1978) 17. Commemorates events of Civil War period.

Fort Smith, Ark. (1961) 63. Active post from 1817 to 1890.

Fort Union Trading Post, Mon., N.D. (1966) 436. Principal fur-trading post on upper Missouri, 1828-1867.

Fort Vancouver, Wash. (1948) 209. Hdqts. for Hudson's Bay Company in 1825. Early military and political seat.

Frederick Law Olmsted, Mass. (1979) 1.75. Home of famous park planner (1822-1903).

Friendship Hill, Pa. (1978) 675. Home of Albert Gallatin, Jefferson's Sec'y of Treasury.

Georgia O'Keeffe, Abiquiu, N.M. (1980) 4. Artist's home, studio.

Golden Spike, Utah (1957) 2,203. Commemorates completion of first transcontinental railroad in 1869.

Grant-Kohrs Ranch, Mon. (1972) 1,502. Ranch house and part of 19th century ranch.

Hampton, Md. (1948) 59. 18th-century Georgian mansion.

Herbert Hoover, West Branch, Ia. (1965) 187. Birthplace and boyhood home of 31st president.

Home of Franklin D. Roosevelt, Hyde Park, N.Y. (1944) 264. Birthplace, home and "Summer White House".

Hopewell Village, Pa. (1938) 848. 19th-century iron making village.

Hubbell Trading Post, Ariz. (1965) 160. Indian trading post.

James A. Garfield, Mentor, Oh. (1980) 7.6. President's home.

Jefferson National Expansion Memorial, St. Louis, Mo. (1935) 91. Commemorates westward expansion with park and memorial arch.

John Fitzgerald Kennedy, Brookline, Mass. (1967) 0.09. Birthplace and childhood home of the President.

John Muir, Martinez, Cal. (1964) 9. Home of early conservationist and writer.

Knife River Indian Villages, N.D. (1974) 1,293. Remnants of 5 Hidatsa villages.

Lincoln Home, Springfield, Ill. (1971) 12. Lincoln's residence when he was elected President, 1860.

Longfellow, Cambridge, Mass. (1972) 2. Longfellow's home, 1837-82, and Washington's hq. during Boston Siege, 1775-76. **No federal facilities.**

Maggie L. Walker, Va. (1978) 1.29. Richmond home of black leader and 1903 founder of bank.

Martin Luther King, Jr., Atlanta, Ga. (1980) 23. Birthplace, grave.

Martin Van Buren, N.Y. (1974) 40. Lindenwald, home of 8th president, near Kinderhook.

Ninety Six, S.C. (1976) 1,115. Colonial trading village.

Palo Alto Battlefield, Tex. (1978) 50. One of 2 Mexican War battles fought in U.S.

Puukohola Heiau, Ha. (1972) 77. Ruins of temple built by King Kamehameha.

Sagamore Hill, Oyster Bay, N.Y. (1962) 78. Home of President Theodore Roosevelt from 1885 until his death in 1919.

Saint-Gaudens, Cornish, N.H. (1964) 148. Home, studio and gardens of American sculptor Augustus Saint-Gaudens.

Salem Maritime, Mass. (1938) 9. Only port never seized from the patriots by the British. Major fishing and whaling port.

San Juan, P.R. (1949) 53. 16th-century Spanish fortifications.

Saugus Iron Works, Mass. (1968) 9. Reconstructed 17th-century colonial ironworks.

Sewall-Belmont House, D.C. (1974) 0.35. National Women's Party headquarters 1929-74.

Springfield Armory, Mass. (1974) 55. Small arms manufacturing center for nearly 200 years.

Theodore Roosevelt Birthplace, N.Y., N.Y. (1962) 0.11.

Theodore Roosevelt Inaugural, Buffalo, N.Y. (1966) 1. Wilcox House where he took oath of office, 1901.

Thomas Stone, Md. (1978) 328. Home of signer of Declaration, built in 1771.

Tuskegee Institute, Ala. (1974) 74. College founded by Booker T. Washington in 1881 for blacks, includes student-made brick buildings.

Vanderbilt Mansion, Hyde Park, N.Y. (1940) 212. Mansion of 19th-century financier.

Whitman Mission, Wash. (1936) 98. Site where Dr. and Mrs. Marcus Whitman ministered to the Indians until slain by them in 1847.

William Howard Taft, Cincinnati, Oh. (1969) 4. Birthplace and early home of the 27th president.

National Capital Parks

District of Columbia — Maryland — Virginia (1790) 6,468. Comprises 346 units.

White House

Washington, D.C. (1792) 18. Presidential residence since November 1800.

National Monuments

Name	State	Year	Acreage
Agate Fossil Beds	Neb.	1965	3,055
Alibates Flint Quarries	N.M.-Tex.	1965	1,371
Aniakchak	Alas.	1978	136,955
Aztec Ruins	N.M.	1923	27
Bandelier	N.M.	1916	36,971
Black Canyon of the Gunnison	Col.	1933	13,672
Booker T. Washington	Va.	1956	224
Buck Island Reef	V.I.	1961	880
Cabrillo	Cal.	1913	144
Canyon de Chelly	Ariz.	1931	83,840
Cape Krusenstern	Alas.	1978	656,685
Capulin Mountain	N.M.	1916	775
Casa Grande Ruins	Ariz.	1892	473
Castillo de San Marcos	Fla.	1924	20
Castle Clinton	N.Y.	1946	1
Cedar Breaks	Ut.	1933	6,155
Chiricahua	Ariz.	1924	11,088
Colorado	Col.	1911	20,454
Congaree Swamp	S.C.	1976	15,138
Craters of the Moon	Ida.	1924	53,545
Custer Battlefield	Mon.	1879	765

Name	State	Year	Acreage
Death Valley	Cal.-Nev.	1933	2,067,628
Devils Postpile	Cal.	1911	798
Devils Tower	Wy.	1906	1,347
Dinosaur	Col.-Ut.	1915	211,058
Effigy Mounds	Ia.	1949	1,475
El Morro	N.M.	1906	1,279
Florissant Fossil Beds**	Col.	1969	5,998
Fort Frederica	Ga.	1936	214
Fort Jefferson	Fla.	1935	47,125
Fort Matanzas	Fla.	1924	299
Fort McHenry National Monument and Historic Shrine	Md.	1925	43
Fort Pulaski	Ga.	1924	5,616
Fort Stanwix	N.Y.	1935	16
Fort Sumter	S.C.	1948	67
Fort Union	N.M.	1954	721
Fossil Butte	Wy.	1972	8,198
G. Washington Birthplace	Va.	1930	538
George Washington Carver	Mo.	1943	210
Gila Cliff Dwellings	N.M.	1907	533
Grand Portage	Minn.	1951	710
Great Sand Dunes	Col.	1932	38,952
Hohokam Pima*	Ariz.	1972	1,690
Homestead Nat'l. Monument of America	Neb.	1936	195
Hovenweep	Col.-Ut.	1923	785
Jewel Cave	S.D.	1908	1,275
John Day Fossil Beds	Ore.	1974	14,012
Joshua Tree	Cal.	1936	559,960
Lava Beds	Cal.	1925	46,560
Lehman Caves	Nev.	1922	640
Montezuma Castle	Ariz.	1906	858
Mound City Group	Oh.	1923	68
Muir Woods	Cal.	1908	554
Natural Bridges	Ut.	1908	7,779
Navajo	Ariz.	1909	360
Ocmulgee	Ga.	1934	683
Oregon Caves	Ore.	1909	488
Organ Pipe Cactus	Ariz.	1937	330,689
Pecos	N.M.	1965	365
Pinnacles	Cal.	1908	16,222
Pipe Spring	Ariz.	1923	40
Pipestone	Minn.	1937	282
Rainbow Bridge	Ut.	1910	160
Russell Cave	Ala.	1961	310
Saguaro	Ariz.	1933	83,576
Saint Croix Island**	Me.	1949	35
Salinas	N.M.	1900	1,080
Scotts Bluff	Neb.	1919	2,997
Statue of Liberty	N.J.-N.Y.	1924	58
Sunset Crater	Ariz.	1930	3,040
Timpanogos Cave	Ut.	1922	250
Tonto	Ariz.	1907	1,120
Tumacacori	Ariz.	1908	17
Tuzigoot	Ariz.	1939	809
Walnut Canyon	Ariz.	1915	2,249
White Sands	N.M.	1933	144,458
Wupatki	Ariz.	1924	35,253
Yucca House*	Col.	1919	10

National Preserves

Name	State	Year	Acreage
Aniakchak	Alas.	1978	466,238
Bering Land Bridge	Alas.	1978	2,774,182
Big Cypress	Fla.	1974	570,000
Big Thicket	Tex.	1974	85,846
Denali	Alas.	1978	1,335,380
Gates of the Arctic	Alas.	1978	943,327
Glacier Bay	Alas.	1978	54,948
Katmai	Alas.	1978	410,473
Lake Clark	Alas.	1978	1,405,847
Noatak	Alas.	1978	6,557,204
Wrangell-St. Elias	Alas.	1978	4,872,953
Yukon-Charley Rivers	Alas.	1978	2,516,821

National Seashores

Name	State	Year	Acreage
Assateague Island	Md.-Va.	1965	39,631
Canaveral	Fla.	1975	57,627
Cape Cod	Mass.	1961	44,596
Cape Hatteras	N.C.	1937	30,319
Cape Lookout**	N.C.	1966	28,415
Cumberland Island	Ga.	1972	36,978
Fire Island	N.Y.	1964	19,579
Gulf Islands	Fla.-Miss.	1971	139,775
Padre Island	Tex.	1962	130,697
Point Reyes	Cal.	1962	71,000

National Parkways

Name	State	Year	Acreage
Blue Ridge	Va.-N.C.	1936	82,329
George Washington Memorial	Va.-Md.	1930	7,142
John D. Rockefeller Jr. Mem.	Wy.	1972	23,777
Natchez Trace	Ala.-Miss.-Tenn.	1938	50,197

National Lakeshores

Name	State	Year	Acreage
Apostle Islands	Wis.	1970	67,885
Indiana Dunes	Ind.	1966	12,535
Pictured Rocks	Mich.	1966	72,259
Sleeping Bear Dunes	Mich.	1970	79,452

National Rivers

Name	State	Year	Acreage
Big South Fork	Ky.-Tenn.	1976	122,960
Buffalo	Ark.	1972	94,146
New River Gorge	W.Va.	1978	62,024

National Scenic Rivers and Riverways

Name	State	Year	Acreage
Delaware	N.Y.-N.J.-Pa.	1978	1,973
Lower Saint Croix	Minn.-Wis.	1972	9,411
Obed Wild	Tenn.	1976	5,250
Ozark	Mo.	1964	81,218
Rio Grande	Tex.	1978	9,600
Saint Croix	Minn.-Wis.	1968	64,166
Upper Delaware	N.Y.-N.J.	1978	75,000

Parks (no other classification)

Name	State	Year	Acreage
Catoctin Mountain	Md.	1954	5,769
Fort Benton	Mon.	1976	...
Fort Washington	Md.	1930	341
Frederick Douglass Home	D.C.	1962	8
Greenbelt	Md.	1933	1,176
Perry's Victory	Oh.	1936	25
Piscataway	Md.	1961	4,251
Prince William Forest	Va.	1948	18,572
Rock Creek	D.C.	1890	1,754
Wolf Trap Farm Park for the Performing Arts	Va.	1966	130

National Recreation Areas

Name	State	Year	Acreage
Amistad	Tex.	1965	62,452
Bighorn Canyon	Mon.-Wy.	1964	120,278
Chattahoochee R.	Ga.	1978	7,274
Chickasaw	Okla.	1976	9,500
Coulee Dam	Wash.	1946	100,059
Curecanti	Col.	1965	42,114
Cuyahoga Valley	Oh.	1974	32,460
Delaware Water Gap	N.J.-Pa.	1965	69,629
Gateway	N.Y.-N.J.	1972	26,172
Glen Canyon	Ariz.-Ut.	1958	1,236,880
Golden Gate	Cal.	1972	38,677
Lake Chelan	Wash.	1968	61,890
Lake Mead	Ariz.-Nev.	1936	1,496,601
Lake Meredith	Tex.	1965	44,978
Ross Lake	Wash.	1968	117,574
Santa Monica Mts.	Cal.	1978	150,000
Whiskeytown	Cal.	1962	42,503

National Mall

Name	State	Year	Acreage
National Mall	D.C.	1933	146

National Scenic Trail

Name	State	Year	Acreage
Appalachian	Me. to Ga.	1968	52,034

*Not open to the public **No federal facilities

National Recreation Areas Administered by Forest Service

Name	State	Year	Acreage
Arapaho	Col.	1978	35,697
Flaming Gorge	Ut.-Wyo.	1968	201,114
Hell's Canyon	Ida.-Ore.	1975	525,608
Mount Rogers	Va.	1966	154,770
Oregon Dunes	Ore.	1972	32,348
Rattlesnake	Mon.	1980	61,000
Sawtooth	Ida.	1972	754,999
Whiskeytown Shasta-Trinity	Cal.	1965	203,587
Spruce Knob-Seneca Rocks	W. Va.	1965	100,000

The Homestead Act; Sale of Public Land

On October 21, 1976 Congress repealed the Homestead Act of 1862 for all states except Alaska. The Homestead Act is scheduled to expire in Alaska in 1986.

The Homestead Act was repealed because there was no longer any land in the public domain suitable for cultivation. The law had been in effect for 114 years. During that time it had exerted a profound influence on the settlement of the west. Under the authority of the Homestead Act more than 1.6 million settlers claimed more than 270 million acres of public lands. The influx of settlers into the west made such states as Oklahoma, Kansas, Nebraska, and North and South Dakota a reality and brought substantial numbers of settlers into many other western states.

Federal Indian Reservations[1]

Source: Bureau of Indian Affairs, U.S. Interior Department (data as of 1979)

State	No. of reser.	Tribally-owned acreage[2]	Allotted acreage[2]	No. of tribes[3]	No. of persons[4]	Avg. (%) unemp. rate[5]	Major tribes and/or natives
Alaska	1[6]	86,741	299,400	6	72,664	51	Aleut, Eskimo, Athapascan[7], Haida, Tlingit, Tsimpshian
Arizona	20	19,554,391	252,972	13	145,258	21	Navajo, Apache, Papago, Hopi, Yavapai, Pima
California	78	500,036	73,014	—[8]	11,608	35	Hoopa, Paiute, Yurok, Karok, Mission Bands
Colorado	2	752,017	3,878	1	2,285	57	Ute
Florida	3	79,015	—	1	1,567	31	Seminole, Miccosukee[9]
Idaho	4	459,756	334,475		5,847	30	Shoshone, Bannock, Nez Perce
Iowa	1	4,164	0		649	34	Sac and Fox[10]
Kansas	4	5,504	22,522		2,225	17	Potawatomi, Kickapoo, Iowa
Louisiana	2	374	—		554	7	Chitimacha, Coushatta
Maine	3	71,568	—		1,247	20	Passamaquoddy, Penobscot, Maliseet
Michigan	5	12,039	9,247		3,354	50	Chippewa, Potawatomi, Ottawa
Minnesota	14	712,125	50,750		16,476	50	Chippewa, Sioux
Mississippi	1	17,478	18		4,490	18	Choctaw
Montana	7	2,170,265	3,051,321		16,483	27	Blackfeet, Crow, Sioux, Assiniboine, Cheyenne
Nebraska	3	22,275	42,531		3,318	42	Omaha, Winnebago, Santee Sioux
Nevada	23	1,067,674	78,388		6,281	30	Paiute, Shoshone, Washoe
New Mexico	24	6,462,826	677,845		104,153	20	Zuni, Apache, Navajo
New York	6	—	—		8,753	23	Seneca, Mohawk, Onondaga, Oneida[11]
North Carolina	1	56,460	—		5,925	17	Cherokee
North Dakota	5	200,683	650,481		18,386	31	Sioux, Chippewa, Mandan, Arikara, Hidatsa
Oklahoma	—[12]	85,566	1,145,871		126,213	15	Cherokee, Creek, Choctaw, Chickasaw, Osage, Cheyenne, Arapahoe, Kiowa, Comanche
Oregon	5	615,692	11,293		3,873	20	Warm Springs, Wasco, Paiute, Umatilla, Siletz
S. Dakota	9	2,572,817	2,516,505		42,439	34	Sioux
Utah	6	2,249,068	34,525		8,755	20	Ute, Goshute, Southern Paiute
Washington	26	1,996,018	497,219		34,940	35	Yakima, Lummi, Quinault
Wisconsin	15	328,437	80,886		16,544	34	Chippewa, Oneida, Winnebago
Wyoming	1	1,791,808	94,927		6,926	37	Shoshone, Arapahoe

(1) As of 1979 the federal government recognized and acknowledged that it had a special relationship with, and a trust responsibility for, 496 Federally recognized Indian entities in the U.S., including Alaska. The term "Indian entities" encompasses Indian tribes, bands, villages, groups, pueblos, Eskimos, and Aleuts, eligible for federal services and classified in the following 3 categories: (a) Officially approved Indian organizations pursuant to federal statutory authority (Indian Reorganization Act; Oklahoma Indian Welfare Act and Alaska Native Act.) (b) Officially approved Indian organizations outside of specified federal statutory authority. (c) Traditional Indian organizations recognized without formal federal approval of organizational structure.

(2) The acreages refer only to Indian lands which are either owned by the tribes or individual Indians, and held in trust by the U.S. government.

(3) "Tribe" among the North American Indians originally meant a body of persons bound together by blood ties who were socially, politically, and religiously organized, and who lived together, occupying a definite territory and having a common language or dialect. With the relegation of Indians to reservations, the word "tribe" developed a number of different meanings. Today, it can be a distinct group within an Indian village or community, the entire community, a large number of communities, several different groups or villages speaking different languages but sharing a common government, or a widely scattered number of villages with a common language but no common government.

(4) Number of Indians living on or adjacent to federally recognized reservations comprising the BIA service population.

(5) Unemployment rate of Indian work force consisting of all those 16 years old and over who are able and actively seeking work.

(6) Alaskan Indian Affairs are carried out under the Alaska Native Claims Settlement Act (Dec. 18, 1971). The Act provided for the establishment of regional and village corporations to conduct business for profit and non-profit purposes. There are 13 such regional corporations, each one with organized village corporations. The Metlakatla Reservation remains the only federally recognized reservation in Alaska in the sense of specific reservation boundaries, trust lands, etc.

(7) Aleuts and Eskimos are racially and linguistically related. Athapascans are related to the Navaho and Apache Indians.

(8) Some 62 distinct tribes are known to have lived in or wandered through what is now California at some time in the past. Many of these were village groups and are historically associated with bands which settled near Spanish missions where much of the traditional culture was destroyed. Many of these bands, however, still retain some of their Indian language and customs. Excluding the 30 mission bands, who are primarily of the Cahuilla, Diegueno, or Luiseno, there are some 22 tribes represented on the California reservations.

(9) "Seminole" means "runaways" and these Indians from various tribes were originally refugees from whites in the Carolinas and Georgia. Later joined by runaway slaves, the Seminole were united by their hostility to the United States. Formal peace with the Seminoles in Florida was not achieved until 1934. The Miccosukee are a branch of the Seminole; they retain their Indian religion and have not made formal peace with the United States.

(10) Once two tribes, the Sac and Fox formed a political alliance in 1734.

(11) These 4 tribes along with the Cayuga and Tuscarora made up the Iroquois League, which ruled large portions of New York, New England and Pennsylvania and ranged into the Midwest and South. The Onondaga, who traditionally provide the president of the league, maintain that they are a foreign nation within New York and the United States.

(12) Indian land status in Oklahoma is unique and there are no reservations in the sense that the term is used elsewhere in the U.S. Likewise, many of the Oklahoma tribes are unique in their high degree of assimilation to the white culture.

Declaration of Independence

The Declaration of Independence was adopted by the Continental Congress in Philadelphia, on July 4, 1776. John Hancock was president of the Congress and Charles Thomson was secretary. A copy of the Declaration, engrossed on parchment, was signed by members of Congress on and after Aug. 2, 1776. On Jan. 18, 1777, Congress ordered that "an authenticated copy, with the names of the members of Congress subscribing the same, be sent to each of the United States, and that they be desired to have the same put upon record." Authenticated copies were printed in broadside form in Baltimore, where the Continental Congress was then in session. The following text is that of the original printed by John Dunlap at Philadelphia for the Continental Congress.

IN CONGRESS, July 4, 1776.

A DECLARATION

By the REPRESENTATIVES of the

UNITED STATES OF AMERICA,

In GENERAL CONGRESS assembled

When in the Course of human Events, it becomes necessary for one People to dissolve the Political Bands which have connected them with another, and to assume among the Powers of the Earth, the separate and equal Station to which the Laws of Nature and of Nature's God entitle them, a decent Respect to the Opinions of Mankind requires that they should declare the causes which impel them to the Separation.

We hold these Truths to be self-evident, that all Men are created equal, that they are endowed by their Creator with certain unalienable Rights, that among these are Life, Liberty, and the Pursuit of Happiness—That to secure these Rights, Governments are instituted among Men, deriving their just Powers from the Consent of the Governed, that whenever any Form of Government becomes destructive of these Ends, it is the Right of the People to alter or to abolish it, and to institute new Government, laying its Foundation on such Principles, and organizing its Powers in such Form, as to them shall seem most likely to effect their Safety and Happiness. Prudence, indeed, will dictate that Governments long established should not be changed for light and transient Causes; and accordingly all Experience hath shewn, that Mankind are more disposed to suffer, while Evils are sufferable, than to right themselves by abolishing the Forms to which they are accustomed. But when a long Train of Abuses and Usurpations, pursuing invariably the same Object, evinces a Design to reduce them under absolute Despotism, it is their Right, it is their Duty, to throw off such Government, and to provide new Guards for their future Security. Such has been the patient Sufferance of these Colonies; and such is now the Necessity which constrains them to alter their former Systems of Government. The History of the present King of Great-Britain is a History of repeated Injuries and Usurpations, all having in direct Object the Establishment of an absolute Tyranny over these States. To prove this, let Facts be submitted to a candid World.

He has refused his Assent to Laws, the most wholesome and necessary for the public Good.

He has forbidden his Governors to pass Laws of immediate and pressing Importance, unless suspended in their Operation till his Assent should be obtained; and when so suspended, he has utterly neglected to attend to them.

He has refused to pass other Laws for the Accommodation of large Districts of People, unless those People would relinquish the Right of Representation in the Legislature, a Right inestimable to them, and formidable to Tyrants only.

He has called together Legislative Bodies at Places unusual, uncomfortable, and distant from the Depository of their Public Records, for the sole Purpose of fatiguing them into Compliance with his Measures.

He has dissolved Representative Houses repeatedly, for opposing with manly Firmness his Invasions on the Rights of the People.

He has refused for a long Time, after such Dissolutions, to cause others to be elected; whereby the Legislative Powers, incapable of Annihilation, have returned to the People at large for their exercise; the State remaining in the mean time exposed to all the Dangers of Invasion from without, and Convulsions within.

He has endeavoured to prevent the Population of these States; for that Purpose obstructing the Laws for Naturalization of Foreigners; refusing to pass others to encourage their Migrations hither, and raising the Conditions of new Appropriations of Lands.

He has obstructed the Administration of Justice, by refusing his Assent to Laws for establishing Judiciary Powers.

He has made Judges dependent on his Will alone, for the Tenure of their Offices, and the Amount and payment of their Salaries.

He has erected a Multitude of new Offices, and sent hither Swarms of Officers to harrass our People, and eat out their Substance.

He has kept among us, in Times of Peace, Standing Armies, without the consent of our Legislatures.

He has affected to render the Military independent of, and superior to the Civil Power.

He has combined with others to subject us to a Jurisdiction foreign to our Constitution, and unacknowledged by our Laws; giving his Assent to their Acts of pretended Legislation:

For quartering large Bodies of Armed Troops among us:

For protecting them, by a mock Trial, from Punishment for any Murders which they should commit on the Inhabitants of these States:

For cutting off our Trade with all Parts of the World:

For imposing Taxes on us without our Consent:

For depriving us, in many Cases, of the Benefits of Trial by Jury:

For transporting us beyond Seas to be tried for pretended Offences:

For abolishing the free System of English Laws in a neighbouring Province, establishing therein an arbitrary Government, and enlarging its Boundaries, so as to render it at once an Example and fit Instrument for introducing the same absolute Rule into these Colonies:

For taking away our Charters, abolishing our most valuable Laws, and altering fundamentally the Forms of our Governments:

For suspending our own Legislatures, and declaring themselves invested with Power to legislate for us in all Cases whatsoever.

He has abdicated Government here, by declaring us out of his Protection and waging War against us.

He has plundered our Seas, ravaged our Coasts, burnt our towns, and destroyed the Lives of our People.

He is, at this Time, transporting large Armies of foreign Mercenaries to compleat the works of Death, Desolation, and Tyranny, already begun with circumstances of Cruelty and Perfidy, scarcely paralleled in the most barbarous Ages, and totally unworthy the Head of a civilized Nation.

He has constrained our fellow Citizens taken Captive on the high Seas to bear Arms against their Country, to become the Executioners of their Friends and Brethren, or to fall themselves by their Hands.

He has excited domestic Insurrections amongst us, and has endeavoured to bring on the Inhabitants of our Frontiers, the merciless Indian Savages, whose known Rule of Warfare, is an undistinguished Destruction, of all Ages, Sexes and Conditions.

In every stage of these Oppressions we have Petitioned for Redress in the most humble Terms: Our repeated Petitions have been answered only by repeated Injury. A Prince, whose Character is thus marked by every act which may define a Tyrant, is unfit to be the Ruler of a free People.

Nor have we been wanting in Attentions to our British Brethren. We have warned them from Time to Time of Attempts by their Legislature to extend an unwarrantable Jurisdiction over us. We have reminded them of the Circumstances of our Emigration and Settlement here. We have appealed to their native Justice and Magnanimity, and we have conjured them by the Ties of our common Kindred to disavow these Usurpations, which, would inevitably interrupt our Connections and Correspondence. They too have been deaf to the Voice of Justice and of Consanguinity. We must, therefore, acquiesce in the Necessity, which denounces our Separation, and hold them, as we hold the rest of Mankind, Enemies in War, in Peace, Friends.

We, therefore, the Representatives of the UNITED STATES OF AMERICA, in General Congress, Assembled, appealing to the Supreme Judge of the World for the Rectitude of our Intentions, do, in the Name, and by Authority of the good People of these Colonies, solemnly Publish and Declare, That these United Colonies are, and of Right ought to be, Free and Independent States; that they are absolved from all Allegiance to the British Crown, and that all political Connection between them and the State of Great-Britain, is and ought to be totally dissolved; and that as Free and Independent States, they have full Power to levy War, conclude Peace, contract Alliances, establish Commerce, and to do all other Acts and Things which Independent States may of right do. And for the support of this declaration, with a firm Reliance on the Protection of divine Providence, we mutually pledge to each other our lives, our Fortunes, and our sacred Honor.

JOHN HANCOCK, President

Attest.
CHARLES THOMSON, Secretary.

Signers of the Declaration of Independence

Delegate and state	Vocation	Birthplace	Born	Died
Adams, John (Mass.)	Lawyer	Braintree (Quincy), Mass.	Oct. 30, 1735	July 4, 1826
Adams, Samuel (Mass.)	Political leader	Boston, Mass.	Sept. 27, 1722	Oct. 2, 1803
Bartlett, Josiah (N.H.)	Physician, judge	Amesbury, Mass.	Nov. 21, 1729	May 19, 1795
Braxton, Carter (Va.)	Farmer	Newington Plantation, Va.	Sept. 10, 1736	Oct. 10, 1797
Carroll, Chas. of Carrollton (Md.)	Lawyer	Annapolis, Md.	Sept. 19, 1737	Nov. 14, 1832
Chase, Samuel (Md.)	Judge	Princess Anne, Md.	Apr. 17, 1741	June 19, 1811
Clark, Abraham (N.J.)	Surveyor	Roselle, N.J.	Feb. 15, 1726	Sept. 15, 1794
Clymer, George (Pa.)	Merchant	Philadelphia, Pa.	Mar. 16, 1739	Jan. 23, 1813
Ellery, William (R.I.)	Lawyer	Newport, R.I.	Dec. 22, 1727	Feb. 15, 1820
Floyd, William (N.Y.)	Soldier	Brookhaven, N.Y.	Dec. 17, 1734	Aug. 4, 1821
Franklin, Benjamin (Pa.)	Printer, publisher.	Boston, Mass.	Jan. 17, 1706	Apr. 17, 1790
Gerry, Elbridge (Mass.)	Merchant	Marblehead, Mass.	July 17, 1744	Nov. 23, 1814
Gwinnett, Button (Ga.)	Merchant	Down Hatherly, England	c. 1735	May 19, 1777
Hall, Lyman (Ga.)	Physician	Wallingford, Conn.	Apr. 12, 1724	Oct. 19, 1790
Hancock, John (Mass.)	Merchant	Braintree (Quincy), Mass.	Jan. 12, 1737	Oct. 8, 1793
Harrison, Benjamin (Va.)	Farmer	Berkeley, Va.	Apr. 5, 1726	Apr. 24, 1791
Hart, John (N.J.)	Farmer	Stonington, Conn.	c. 1711	May 11, 1779
Hewes, Joseph (N.C.)	Merchant	Princeton, N.J.	Jan. 23, 1730	Nov. 10, 1779
Heyward, Thos. Jr. (S.C.)	Lawyer, farmer	St. Luke's Parish, S.C.	July 28, 1746	Mar. 6, 1809
Hooper, William (N.C.)	Lawyer	Boston, Mass.	June 28, 1742	Oct. 14, 1790
Hopkins, Stephen (R.I.)	Judge, educator	Providence, R.I.	Mar. 7, 1707	July 13, 1785
Hopkinson, Francis (N.J.)	Judge, author	Philadelphia, Pa.	Sept. 21, 1737	May 9, 1791
Huntington, Samuel (Conn.)	Judge	Windham County, Conn.	July 3, 1731	Jan. 5, 1796
Jefferson, Thomas (Va.)	Lawyer	Shadwell, Va.	Apr. 13, 1743	July 4, 1826
Lee, Francis Lightfoot (Va.)	Farmer	Westmoreland County, Va.	Oct. 14, 1734	Jan. 11, 1797
Lee, Richard Henry (Va.)	Farmer	Westmoreland County, Va.	Jan. 20, 1732	June 19, 1794
Lewis, Francis (N.Y.)	Merchant	Llandaff, Wales	Mar., 1713	Dec. 31, 1802
Livingston, Philip (N.Y.)	Merchant	Albany, N.Y.	Jan. 15, 1716	June 12, 1778
Lynch, Thomas Jr. (S.C.)	Farmer	Winyah, S.C.	Aug. 5, 1749	(at sea) 1779
McKean, Thomas (Del.)	Lawyer	New London, Pa.	Mar. 19, 1734	June 24, 1817
Middleton, Arthur (S.C.)	Farmer	Charleston, S.C.	June 26, 1742	Jan. 1, 1787
Morris, Lewis (N.Y.)	Farmer	Morrisania (Bronx County), N.Y.	Apr. 8, 1726	Jan. 22, 1798
Morris, Robert (Pa.)	Merchant	Liverpool, England	Jan. 20, 1734	May 9, 1806
Morton, John (Pa.)	Judge	Ridley, Pa.	1724	Apr., 1777
Nelson, Thos. Jr. (Va.)	Farmer	Yorktown, Va.	Dec. 26, 1738	Jan. 4, 1789
Paca, William (Md.)	Judge	Abingdon, Md.	Oct. 31, 1740	Oct. 23, 1799
Paine, Robert Treat (Mass.)	Judge	Boston, Mass.	Mar. 11, 1731	May 12, 1814
Penn, John (N.C.)	Lawyer	Near Port Royal, Va.	May 17, 1741	Sept. 14, 1788
Read, George (Del.)	Judge	Near North East, Md.	Sept. 18, 1733	Sept. 21, 1798
Rodney, Caesar (Del.)	Judge	Dover, Del.	Oct. 7, 1728	June 29, 1784
Ross, George (Pa.)	Judge	New Castle, Del.	May 10, 1730	July 14, 1779
Rush, Benjamin (Pa.)	Physician	Byberry, Pa. (Philadelphia)	Dec. 24, 1745	Apr. 19, 1813
Rutledge, Edward (S.C.)	Lawyer	Charleston, S.C.	Nov. 23, 1749	Jan. 23, 1800
Sherman, Roger (Conn.)	Lawyer	Newton, Mass.	Apr. 19, 1721	July 23, 1793
Smith, James (Pa.)	Lawyer	Dublin, Ireland	c. 1719	July 11, 1806
Stockton, Richard (N.J.)	Lawyer	Near Princeton, N.J.	Oct. 1, 1730	Feb. 28, 1781
Stone, Thomas (Md.)	Lawyer	Charles County, Md.	1743	Oct. 5, 1787
Taylor, George (Pa.)	Ironmaster	Ireland	1716	Feb. 23, 1781
Thornton, Matthew (N.H.)	Physician	Ireland	1714	June 24, 1803
Walton, George (Ga.)	Judge	Prince Edward County, Va.	1741	Feb. 2, 1804
Whipple, William (N.H.)	Merchant, judge	Kittery, Me.	Jan. 14, 1730	Nov. 28, 1785
Williams, William (Conn.)	Merchant	Lebanon, Conn.	Apr. 23, 1731	Aug. 2, 1811
Wilson, James (Pa.)	Judge	Carskerdo, Scotland	Sept. 14, 1742	Aug. 28, 1798
Witherspoon, John (N.J.)	Educator	Gifford, Scotland	Feb. 5, 1723	Nov. 15, 1794
Wolcott, Oliver (Conn.)	Judge	Windsor, Conn.	Dec. 1, 1726	Dec. 1, 1797
Wythe, George (Va.)	Lawyer	Elizabeth City Co. (Hampton), Va.	1726	June 8, 1806

Constitution of the United States

The Original 7 Articles

PREAMBLE

We, the people of the United States, in order to form a more perfect Union, establish justice, insure domestic tranquility, provide for the common defense, promote the general welfare, and secure the blessings of liberty to ourselves and our posterity do ordain and establish this Constitution for the United States of America.

ARTICLE I.

Section 1—Legislative powers; in whom vested:

All legislative powers herein granted shall be vested in a Congress of the United States, which shall consist of a Senate and House of Representatives.

Section 2—House of Representatives, how and by whom chosen. Qualifications of a Representative. Representatives and direct taxes, how apportioned. Enumeration. Vacancies to be filled. Power of choosing officers, and of impeachment.

1. The House of Representatives shall be composed of members chosen every second year by the people of the several States, and the electors in each State shall have the qualifications requisite for electors of the most numerous branch of the State Legislature.

2. No person shall be a Representative who shall not have attained to the age of twenty-five years, and been seven years a citizen of the United States, and who shall not, when elected, be an inhabitant of that State in which he shall be chosen.

3. *(Representatives and direct taxes shall be apportioned among the several States which may be included within this Union, according to their respective numbers, which shall be determined by adding to the whole number of free persons, including those bound to service for a term of years, and excluding Indians not taxed, three-fifths of all other persons.) (The previous sentence was superseded by Amendment XIV, section 2.)* The actual enumeration shall be made within three years after the first meeting of the Congress of the United States, and within every subsequent term of ten years, in such manner as they shall by law direct. The number of Representatives shall not exceed one for every thirty thousand, but each State shall have at least one Representative; and until such enumeration shall be made, the State of New Hampshire shall be entitled to choose three, Massachusetts eight, Rhode Island and Providence Plantations one, Connecticut five, New York six, New Jersey four, Pennsylvania eight, Delaware one, Maryland six, Virginia ten, North Carolina five, South Carolina five, and Georgia three.

4. When vacancies happen in the representation from any State, the Executive Authority thereof shall issue writs of election to fill such vacancies.

5. The House of Representatives shall choose their Speaker and other officers; and shall have the sole power of impeachment.

Section 3—Senators, how and by whom chosen. How classified. Qualifications of a Senator. President of the Senate, his right to vote. President pro tem., and other officers of the Senate, how chosen. Power to try impeachments. When President is tried, Chief Justice to preside. Sentence.

1. The Senate of the United States shall be composed of two Senators from each State, *(chosen by the Legislature thereof), (The preceding five words were superseded by Amendment XVII, section 1.)* for six years; and each Senator shall have one vote.

2. Immediately after they shall be assembled in consequence of the first election, they shall be divided as equally as may be into three classes. The seats of the Senators of the first class shall be vacated at the expiration of the second year, of the second class at the expiration of the fourth year, and of the third class at the expiration of the sixth year, so that one-third may be chosen every second year; *(and if vacancies happen by resignation, or otherwise, during the recess of the Legislature of any State, the Executive thereof may make temporary appointments until the next meeting of the Legislature, which shall then fill such vacancies.) (The words in parentheses were superseded by Amendment XVII, section 2.)*

3. No person shall be a Senator who shall not have attained to the age of thirty years, and been nine years a citizen of the United States, and who shall not, when elected, be an inhabitant of that State for which he shall be chosen.

4. The Vice President of the United States shall be President of the Senate, but shall have no vote, unless they be equally divided.

5. The Senate shall choose their other officers, and also a President pro tempore, in the absence of the Vice President, or when he shall exercise the office of President of the United States.

6. The Senate shall have the sole power to try all impeachments. When sitting for that purpose, they shall be on oath or affirmation. When the President of the United States is tried, the Chief Justice shall preside: and no person shall be convicted without the concurrence of two-thirds of the members present.

7. Judgment in cases of impeachment shall not extend further than to removal from office, and disqualification to hold and enjoy any office of honor, trust or profit under the United States: but the party convicted shall nevertheless be liable and subject to indictment, trial, judgment and punishment, according to law.

Section 4—Times, etc., of holding elections, how prescribed. One session each year.

1. The times, places and manner of holding elections for Senators and Representatives, shall be prescribed in each State by the Legislature thereof; but the Congress may at any time by law make or alter such regulations, except as to the places of choosing Senators.

2. The Congress shall assemble at least once in every year, and such meeting shall *(be on the first Monday in December,) (The words in parentheses were superseded by Amendment XX, section 2).* unless they shall by law appoint a different day.

Section 5—Membership, quorum, adjournments, rules. Power to punish or expel. Journal. Time of adjournments, how limited, etc.

1. Each House shall be the judge of the elections, returns and qualifications of its own members, and a majority of each shall constitute a quorum to do business; but a smaller number may adjourn from day to day, and may be authorized to compel the attendance of absent members, in such manner, and under such penalties as each House may provide.

2. Each House may determine the rules of its proceedings, punish its members for disorderly behavior, and, with the concurrence of two-thirds, expel a member.

3. Each House shall keep a journal of its proceedings, and from time to time publish the same, excepting such parts as may in their judgment require secrecy; and the yeas and nays of the members of either House on any question shall, at the desire of one-fifth of those present, be entered on the journal.

4. Neither House, during the session of Congress, shall, without the consent of the other, adjourn for more than three days, nor to any other place than that in which the two Houses shall be sitting.

Section 6—Compensation, privileges, disqualifications in certain cases.

1. The Senators and Representatives shall receive a compensation for their services, to be ascertained by law, and paid out of the Treasury of the United States. They shall in all cases, except treason, felony and breach of the peace, be privileged from arrest during their attendance at the session of their respective Houses, and in going to and returning from the same; and for any speech or debate in either House, they shall not be questioned in any other place.

2. No Senator or Representative shall, during the time for which he was elected, be appointed to any civil office under the authority of the United States, which shall have been created, or the emoluments whereof shall have been increased during such time; and no person holding any office under the United States, shall be a member of either House

during his continuance in office.

Section 7—House to originate all revenue bills. Veto. Bill may be passed by two-thirds of each House, notwithstanding, etc. Bill, not returned in ten days, to become a law. Provisions as to orders, concurrent resolutions, etc.

1. All bills for raising revenue shall originate in the House of Representatives; but the Senate may propose or concur with amendments as on other bills.

2. Every bill which shall have passed the House of Representatives and the Senate, shall, before it becomes a law, be presented to the President of the United States; if he approves he shall sign it, but if not he shall return it, with his objections to that House in which it shall have originated, who shall enter the objections at large on their journal, and proceed to reconsider it. If after such reconsideration two-thirds of that House shall agree to pass the bill, it shall be sent, together with the objections, to the other House, by which it shall likewise be reconsidered, and if approved by two-thirds of that House, it shall become a law. But in all such cases the votes of both Houses shall be determined by yeas and nays, and the names of the persons voting for and against the bill shall be entered on the journal of each House respectively. If any bill shall not be returned by the President within ten days (Sundays excepted) after it shall have been presented to him, the same shall be a law, in like manner as if he had signed it, unless the Congress by their adjournment prevent its return, in which case it shall not be a law.

3. Every order, resolution, or vote to which the concurrence of the Senate and House of Representatives may be necessary (except on a question of adjournment) shall be presented to the President of the United States; and before the same shall take effect, shall be approved by him, or being disapproved by him, shall be repassed by two-thirds of the Senate and House of Representatives, according to the rules and limitations prescribed in the case of a bill.

Section 8—Powers of Congress.

The Congress shall have power

1. To lay and collect taxes, duties, imposts and excises, to pay the debts and provide for the common defense and general welfare of the United States; but all duties, imposts and excises shall be uniform throughout the United States;

2. To borrow money on the credit of the United States;

3. To regulate commerce with foreign nations, and among the several States, and with the Indian tribes;

4. To establish a uniform rule of naturalization, and uniform laws on the subject of bankruptcies throughout the United States;

5. To coin money, regulate the value thereof, and of foreign coin, and fix the standard of weights and measures;

6. To provide for the punishment of counterfeiting the securities and current coin of the United States;

7. To establish post-offices and post-roads;

8. To promote the progress of science and useful arts, by securing for limited times to authors and inventors the exclusive right to their respective writings and discoveries;

9. To constitute tribunals inferior to the Supreme Court;

10. To define and punish piracies and felonies committed on the high seas, and offenses against the law of nations;

11. To declare war, grant letters of marque and reprisal, and make rules concerning captures on land and water;

12. To raise and support armies, but no appropriation of money to that use shall be for a longer term than two years;

13. To provide and maintain a navy;

14. To make rules for the government and regulation of the land and naval forces;

15. To provide for calling forth the militia to execute the laws of the Union, suppress insurrections and repel invasions;

16. To provide for organizing, arming, and disciplining the militia, and for governing such part of them as may be employed in the service of the United States, reserving to the States respectively, the appointment of the officers, and the authority of training and militia according to the discipline prescribed by Congress;

17. To exercise exclusive legislation in all cases whatsoever, over such district (not exceeding ten miles square) as may, by cession of particular States, and the acceptance of Congress, become the seat of the Government of the United States, and to exercise like authority over all places purchased by the consent of the Legislature of the State in which the same shall be, for the erection of forts, magazines, arsenals, dockyards, and other needful buildings;—And

18. To make all laws which shall be necessary and proper for carrying into execution the foregoing powers, and all other powers vested by this Constitution in the Government of the United States, or in any department or officer thereof.

Section 9—Provision as to migration or importation of certain persons. Habeas corpus, bills of attainder, etc. Taxes, how apportioned. No export duty. No commercial preference. Money, how drawn from Treasury, etc. No titular nobility. Officers not to receive presents, etc.

1. The migration or importation of such persons as any of the States now existing shall think proper to admit, shall not be prohibited by the Congress prior to the year one thousand eight hundred and eight, but a tax or duty may be imposed on such importation, not exceeding ten dollars for each person.

2. The privilege of the writ of habeas corpus shall not be suspended, unless when in cases of rebellion or invasion the public safety may require it.

3. No bill of attainder or ex post facto law shall be passed.

4. No capitation, or other direct, tax shall be laid, unless in proportion to the census or enumeration herein before directed to be taken. *(Modified by Amendment XVI.)*

5. No tax or duty shall be laid on articles exported from any State.

6. No preference shall be given by any regulation of commerce or revenue to the ports of one State over those of another: nor shall vessels bound to, or from, one State, be obliged to enter, clear, or pay duties in another.

7. No money shall be drawn from the Treasury, but in consequence of appropriations made by law; and a regular statement and account of the receipts and expenditures of all public money shall be published from time to time.

8. No title of nobility shall be granted by the United States: and no person holding any office of profit or trust under them, shall, without the consent of the Congress, accept of any present, emolument, office, or title, of any kind whatever, from any king, prince, or foreign state.

Section 10—States prohibited from the exercise of certain powers.

1. No State shall enter into any treaty, alliance, or confederation; grant letters of marque and reprisal; coin money; emit bills of credit; make anything but gold and silver coin a tender in payment of debts; pass any bill of attainder, ex post facto law, or law impairing the obligation of contracts, or grant any title of nobility.

2. No State shall, without the consent of the Congress, lay any imposts or duties on imports or exports, except what may be absolutely necessary for executing its inspection laws: and the net produce of all duties and imposts, laid by any State on imports or exports, shall be for the use of the Treasury of the United States; and all such laws shall be subject to the revision and control of the Congress.

3. No State shall, without the consent of Congress, lay any duty of tonnage, keep troops, or ships of war in time of peace, enter into any agreement or compact with another State, or with a foreign power, or engage in war, unless actually invaded, or in such imminent danger as will not admit of delay.

ARTICLE II.

Section 1—President: his term of office. Electors of President; number and how appointed. Electors to vote on same day. Qualification of President. On whom his duties devolve in case of his removal, death, etc. President's compensation. His oath of office.

1. The Executive power shall be vested in a President of the United States of America. He shall hold his office during the term of four years, and together with the Vice President, chosen for the same term, be elected as follows

2. Each State shall appoint, in such manner as the Legis-

lature thereof may direct, a number of electors, equal to the whole number of Senators and Representatives to which the State may be entitled in the Congress: but no Senator or Representative, or person holding an office of trust or profit under the United States, shall be appointed an elector.

(The electors shall meet in their respective States, and vote by ballot for two persons, of whom one at least shall not be an inhabitant of the same State with themselves. And they shall make a list of all the persons voted for, and of the number of votes for each; which list they shall sign and certify, and transmit sealed to the seat of the Government of the United States, directed to the President of the Senate. The President of the Senate shall, in the presence of the Senate and House of Representatives, open all the certificates, and the votes shall then be counted. The person having the greatest number of votes shall be the President, if such number be a majority of the whole number of electors appointed; and if there be more than one who have such majority, and have an equal number of votes, then the House of Representatives shall immediately choose by ballot one of them for President; and if no person have a majority, then from the five highest on the list the said House shall in like manner choose the President. But in choosing the President, the votes shall be taken by States, the representation from each State having one vote; a quorum for this purpose shall consist of a member or members from two-thirds of the States, and a majority of all the States shall be necessary to a choice. In every case, after the choice of the President, the person having the greatest number of votes of the electors shall be the Vice President. But if there should remain two or more who have equal votes, the Senate shall choose from them by ballot the Vice President.)

(This clause was superseded by Amendment XII.)

3. The Congress may determine the time of choosing the electors, and the day on which they shall give their votes; which day shall be the same throughout the United States.

4. No person except a natural born citizen, or a citizen of the United States, at the time of the adoption of this Constitution, shall be eligible to the office of President; neither shall any person be eligible to that office who shall not have attained to the age of thirty-five years, and been fourteen years a resident within the United States.

(For qualification of the Vice President, see Amendment XII.)

5. In case of the removal of the President from office, or of his death, resignation, or inability to discharge the powers and duties of the said office, the same shall devolve on the Vice President, and the Congress may by law provide for the case of removal, death, resignation or inability, both of the President and Vice President, declaring what officer shall then act as President, and such officer shall act accordingly, until the disability be removed, or a President shall be elected.

(This clause has been modified by Amendments XX and XXV.)

6. The President shall, at stated times, receive for his services, a compensation, which shall neither be increased nor diminished during the period for which he shall have been elected, and he shall not receive within that period any other emolument from the United States, or any of them.

7. Before he enter on the execution of his office, he shall take the following oath or affirmation:

"I do solemnly swear (or affirm) that I will faithfully execute the office of President of the United States, and will to the best of my ability, preserve, protect and defend the Constitution of the United States."

Section 2—President to be Commander-in-Chief. He may require opinions of cabinet officers, etc., may pardon. Treaty-making power. Nomination of certain officers. When President may fill vacancies.

1. The President shall be Commander-in-Chief of the Army and Navy of the United States, and of the militia of the several States, when called into the actual service of the United States; he may require the opinion, in writing, of the principal officer in each of the executive departments, upon any subject relating to the duties of their respective offices, and he shall have power to grant reprieves and pardons for offenses against the United States, except in cases of impeachment.

2. He shall have power, by and with the advice and consent of the Senate, to make treaties, provided two-thirds of the Senators present concur; and he shall nominate, and by and with the advice and consent of the Senate, shall appoint ambassadors, other public ministers and consuls, judges of the Supreme Court, and all other officers of the United States, whose appointments are not herein otherwise provided for, and which shall be established by law: but the Congress may by law vest the appointment of such inferior officers, as they think proper, in the President alone, in the courts of law, or in the heads of departments.

3. The President shall have power to fill up all vacancies that may happen during the recess of the Senate, by granting commissions, which shall expire at the end of their next session.

Section 3—President shall communicate to Congress. He may convene and adjourn Congress, in case of disagreement, etc. Shall receive ambassadors, execute laws, and commission officers.

He shall from time to time give to the Congress information of the state of the Union, and recommend to their consideration such measures as he shall judge necessary and expedient; he may, on extraordinary occasions, convene both Houses, or either of them, and in case of disagreement between them, with respect to the time of adjournment, he may adjourn them to such time as he shall think proper; he shall receive ambassadors and other public ministers; he shall take care that the laws be faithfully executed, and shall commission all the officers of the United States.

Section 4—All civil offices forfeited for certain crimes.

The President, Vice President, and all civil officers of the United States, shall be removed from office on impeachment for, and conviction of, treason, bribery, or other high crimes and misdemeanors.

ARTICLE III.

Section 1—Judicial powers, Tenure. Compensation.

The judicial power of the United States, shall be vested in one Supreme Court, and in such inferior courts as the Congress may from time to time ordain and establish. The judges, both of the Supreme and inferior courts, shall hold their offices during good behavior, and shall at stated times, receive for their services, a compensation, which shall not be diminished during their continuance in office.

Section 2—Judicial power; to what cases it extends. Original jurisdiction of Supreme Court; appellate jurisdiction. Trial by jury, etc. Trial, where.

1. The judicial power shall extend to all cases, in law and equity, arising under this Constitution, the laws of the United States, and treaties made, or which shall be made, under their authority; to all cases affecting ambassadors, other public ministers and consuls; to all cases of admiralty and maritime jurisdiction; to controversies to which the United States shall be a party; to controversies between two or more States; between a State and citizens of another State; between citizens of different States, between citizens of the same State claiming lands under grants of different States, and between a State, or the citizens thereof, and foreign states, citizens or subjects.

(This section is modified by Amendment XI.)

2. In all cases affecting ambassadors, other public ministers and consuls, and those in which a State shall be party, the Supreme Court shall have original jurisdiction. In all the other cases before mentioned, the Supreme Court shall have appellate jurisdiction, both as to law and fact, with such exceptions, and under such regulations as the Congress shall make.

3. The trial of all crimes, except in cases of impeachment, shall be by jury; and such trial shall be held in the State where the said crimes shall have been committed; but when not committed within any State, the trial shall be at such place or places as the Congress may by law have directed.

Section 3—Treason Defined, Proof of, Punishment of.

1. Treason against the United States, shall consist only in levying war against them, or in adhering to their enemies,

giving them aid and comfort. No person shall be convicted of treason unless on the testimony of two witnesses to the same overt act, or on confession in open court.

2. The Congress shall have power to declare the punishment of treason, but no attainder of treason shall work corruption of blood, or forfeiture except during the life of the person attainted.

ARTICLE IV.

Section 1—Each State to give credit to the public acts, etc., of every other State.

Full faith and credit shall be given in each State to the public acts, records, and judicial proceedings of every other State. And the Congress may by general laws prescribe the manner in which such acts, records and proceedings shall be proved, and the effect thereof.

Section 2—Privileges of citizens of each State. Fugitives from justice to be delivered up. Persons held to service having escaped, to be delivered up.

1. The citizens of each State shall be entitled to all privileges and immunities of citizens in the several States.

2. A person charged in any State with treason, felony, or other crime, who shall flee from justice, and be found in another State, shall on demand of the Executive authority of the State from which he fled, be delivered up, to be removed to the State having jurisdiction of the crime.

(3. No person held to service or labor in one State, under the laws thereof, escaping into another, shall in consequence of any law or regulation therein, be discharged from such service or labor, but shall be delivered up on claim of the party to whom such service or labor may be due.) (This clause was superseded by Amendment XIII.)

Section 3—Admission of new States. Power of Congress over territory and other property.

1. New States may be admitted by the Congress into this Union; but no new State shall be formed or erected within the jurisdiction of any other State; nor any State be formed by the junction of two or more States, or parts of States, without the consent of the Legislatures of the States concerned as well as of the Congress.

2. The Congress shall have power to dispose of and make all needful rules and regulations respecting the territory or other property belonging to the United States; and nothing in this Constitution shall be so construed as to prejudice any claims of the United States, or of any particular State.

Section 4—Republican form of government guaranteed. Each state to be protected.

The United States shall guarantee to every State in this Union a Republican form of government, and shall protect each of them against invasion; and on application of the Legislature, or of the Executive (when the Legislature cannot be convened) against domestic violence.

ARTICLE V.

Constitution: how amended; proviso.

The Congress, whenever two-thirds of both Houses shall deem it necessary, shall propose amendments to this Constitution, or, on the application of the Legislatures of two-thirds of the several States, shall call a convention for proposing amendments, which, in either case, shall be valid to all intents and purposes, as part of this Constitution, when ratified by the Legislatures of three-fourths of the several States, or by conventions in three-fourths thereof, as the one or the other mode of ratification may be proposed by the Congress; provided that no amendment which may be made prior to the year one thousand eight hundred and eight shall in any manner affect the first and fourth clauses in the Ninth Section of the First Article; and that no State, without its consent, shall be deprived of its equal suffrage in the Senate.

ARTICLE VI.

Certain debts, etc., declared valid. Supremacy of Constitution, treaties, and laws of the United States. Oath to support Constitution, by whom taken. No religious test.

1. All debts contracted and engagements entered into, before the adoption of this Constitution, shall be as valid against the United States under this Constitution, as under the Confederation.

2. This Constitution, and the laws of the United States which shall be made in pursuance thereof; and all treaties made, or which shall be made, under the authority of the United States, shall be the supreme law of the land; and the judges in every State shall be bound thereby, any thing in the Constitution or laws of any State to the contrary notwithstanding.

3. The Senators and Representatives before mentioned, and the members of the several State Legislatures, and all executive and judicial officers, both of the United States and of the several States, shall be bound by oath or affirmation, to support this Constitution; but no religious test shall ever be required as a qualification to any office or public trust under the United States.

ARTICLE VII.

What ratification shall establish Constitution.

The ratification of the Conventions of nine States, shall be sufficient for the establishment of this Constitution between the States so ratifying the same.

Done in convention by the unanimous consent of the States present the Seventeenth day of September in the year of our Lord one thousand seven hundred and eighty seven, and of the independence of the United States of America the Twelfth. In witness whereof we have hereunto subscribed our names.

George Washington, President and deputy from Virginia.

New Hampshire—John Langdon, Nicholas Gilman.

Massachusetts—Nathaniel Gorham, Rufus King.

Connecticut—Wm. Saml. Johnson, Roger Sherman.

New York—Alexander Hamilton.

New Jersey—Wil: Livingston, David Brearley, Wm. Paterson, Jona: Dayton.

Pennsylvania—B. Franklin, Thomas Mifflin, Robt. Morris, Geo. Clymer, Thos. FitzSimons, Jared Ingersoll, James Wilson, Gouv. Morris.

Delaware—Geo: Read, Gunning Bedford Jun., John Dickinson, Richard Bassett, Jaco: Broom.

Maryland—James McHenry, Daniel of Saint Thomas' Jenifer, Danl. Carroll.

Virginia—John Blair, James Madison Jr.

North Carolina—Wm. Blount, Rich'd. Dobbs Spaight, Hugh Williamson.

South Carolina—J. Rutledge, Charles Cotesworth Pinckney, Charles Pinckney, Pierce Butler.

Georgia—William Few, Abr. Baldwin.

Attest: William Jackson, Secretary.

Ten Original Amendments: The Bill of Rights

In force Dec. 15, 1791

(The First Congress, at its first session in the City of New York, Sept. 25, 1789, submitted to the states 12 amendments to clarify certain individual and state rights not named in the Constitution. They are generally called the Bill of Rights.

(Influential in framing these amendments was the Declaration of Rights of Virginia, written by George Mason (1725-1792) in 1776. Mason, a Virginia delegate to the Constitutional Convention, did not sign the Constitution and opposed its ratification on the ground that it did not sufficiently oppose slavery or safeguard individual rights.

(In the preamble to the resolution offering the proposed amendments, Congress said: "The conventions of a number of the States having at the time of their adopting the Constitution, expressed a desire, in order to prevent misconstruction or abuse of its powers, that further declaratory and restrictive clauses should be added, and as extending the ground of public confidence in the government will best insure the beneficent ends of its institution, be it resolved," etc.

(Ten of these amendments now commonly known as one to 10 inclusive, but originally 3 to 12 inclusive, were ratified by the states as follows: New Jersey, Nov. 20, 1789; Maryland, Dec. 19, 1789; North Carolina, Dec. 22, 1789; South Carolina, Jan. 19, 1790; New Hampshire, Jan 25, 1790; Delaware, Jan 28, 1790; New York, Feb. 24, 1790; Pennsylvania, Mar. 10, 1790; Rhode

Island, June 7, 1790; Vermont, Nov 3, 1791; Virginia, Dec. 15, 1791; Massachusetts, Mar. 2, 1939; Georgia, Mar. 18, 1939; Connecticut, Apr. 19, 1939. These original 10 ratified amendments follow as Amendments I to X inclusive.

(Of the two original proposed amendments which were not ratified by the necessary number of states, the first related to apportionment of Representatives; the second, to compensation of members.)

AMENDMENT I.

Religious establishment prohibited. Freedom of speech, of the press, and right to petition.

Congress shall make no law respecting an establishment of religion, or prohibiting the free exercise thereof; or abridging the freedom of speech, or of the press; or the right of the people peaceably to assemble, and to petition the Government for a redress of grievances.

AMENDMENT II.

Right to keep and bear arms.

A well-regulated militia, being necessary to the security of a free State, the right of the people to keep and bear arms, shall not be infringed.

AMENDMENT III.

Conditions for quarters for soldiers.

No soldier shall, in time of peace be quartered in any house, without the consent of the owner, nor in time of war, but in a manner to be prescribed by law.

AMENDMENT IV.

Right of search and seizure regulated.

The right of the people to be secure in their persons, houses, papers, and effects, against unreasonable searches and seizures, shall not be violated, and no warrants shall issue, but upon probable cause, supported by oath or affirmation, and particularly describing the place to be searched, and the persons or things to be seized.

AMENDMENT V.

Provisions concerning prosecution. Trial and punishment—private property not to be taken for public use without compensation.

No person shall be held to answer for a capital, or otherwise infamous crime, unless on a presentment or indictment of a Grand Jury, except in cases arising in the land or naval forces, or in the militia, when in actual service in time of war or public danger; nor shall any person be subject for the same offense to be twice put in jeopardy of life or limb; nor shall be compelled in any criminal case to be a witness against himself, nor be deprived of life, liberty, or property, without due process of law; nor shall private property be taken for public use without just compensation.

AMENDMENT VI.

Right to speedy trial, witnesses, etc.

In all criminal prosecutions, the accused shall enjoy the right to a speedy and public trial, by an impartial jury of the State and district wherein the crime shall have been committed, which district shall have been previously ascertained by law, and to be informed of the nature and cause of the accusation; to be confronted with the witnesses against him; to have compulsory process for obtaining witnesses in his favor, and to have the assistance of counsel for his defense.

AMENDMENT VII.

Right of trial by jury.

In suits at common law, where the value in controversy shall exceed twenty dollars, the right of trial by jury shall be preserved, and no fact tried by a jury shall be otherwise reexamined in any court of the United States, than according to the rules of the common law.

AMENDMENT VIII.

Excessive bail or fines and cruel punishment prohibited.

Excessive bail shall not be required, nor excessive fines imposed, nor cruel and unusual punishments inflicted.

AMENDMENT IX.

Rule of construction of Constitution.

The enumeration in the Constitution, of certain rights, shall not be construed to deny or disparage others retained by the people.

AMENDMENT X.

Rights of States under Constitution.

The powers not delegated to the United States by the Constitution, nor prohibited by it to the States, are reserved to the States respectively, or to the people.

Amendments Since the Bill of Rights

AMENDMENT XI.

Judicial powers construed.

The judicial power of the United States shall not be construed to extend to any suit in law or equity, commenced or prosecuted against one of the United States by citizens of another State, or by citizens or subjects of any foreign state.

(This amendment was proposed to the Legislatures of the several States by the Third Congress on March 4, 1794, and was declared to have been ratified in a message from the President to Congress, dated Jan. 8, 1798.

(It was on Jan 5, 1798, that Secretary of State Pickering received from 12 of the States authenticated ratifications, and informed President John Adams of that fact.

(As a result of later research in the Department of State, it is now established that Amendment XI became part of the Constitution on Feb. 7, 1795, for on that date it had been ratified by 12 States as follows:

(1. New York, Mar. 27, 1794. 2. Rhode Island, Mar. 31, 1794. 3. Connecticut, May 8, 1794. 4. New Hampshire, June 16, 1794. 5. Massachusetts, June 26, 1794. 6. Vermont, between Oct 9, 1794, and Nov. 9, 1794. 7. Virginia, Nov. 18, 1794. 8. Georgia, Nov. 29, 1794. 9. Kentucky, Dec. 7, 1794. 10. Maryland, Dec. 26, 1794. 11. Delaware, Jan 23, 1795. 12. North Carolina, Feb. 7, 1795.

(On June 1, 1796, more than a year after Amendment XI had become a part of the Constitution (but before anyone was officially aware of this), Tennessee had been admitted as a State; but not until Oct. 16, 1797, was a certified copy of the resolution of Congress proposing the amendment sent to the Governor of Tennessee (John Sevier) by Secretary of State Pickering, whose office was then at Trenton, New Jersey, because of the epidemic of yellow fever at Philadelphia; it seems, however, that the Legislature of Tennessee took no action on Amendment XI, owing doubtless to the fact that public announcement of its adoption was made soon thereafter.

(Besides the necessary 12 States, one other, South Carolina, ratified Amendment XI, but this action was not taken until Dec. 4, 1797; the two remaining States, New Jersey and Pennsylvania, failed to ratify.)

AMENDMENT XII.

Manner of choosing President and Vice-President.

(Proposed by Congress Dec. 9, 1803; ratification completed June 15, 1804.)

The Electors shall meet in their respective States and vote by ballot for President and Vice-President, one of whom, at least, shall not be an inhabitant of the same State with themselves; they shall name in their ballots the person voted for as President, and in distinct ballots the person voted for as Vice-President, and they shall make distinct lists of all persons voted for as President, and of all persons voted for as Vice-President, and of the number of votes for each, which lists they shall sign and certify, and transmit sealed to the seat of the Government of the United States, directed to the President of the Senate; the President of the Senate shall, in the presence of the Senate and House of Representatives, open all the certificates and the votes shall then be counted;—The person having the greatest number of votes for President, shall be the President, if such number be a majority of the whole number of Electors appointed; and if no person have such majority, then from the persons having the highest numbers not exceeding three on the list of those voted for as President, the House of Representatives shall choose immediately, by ballot, the President. But in choosing the President, the votes shall be taken by States, the representation from each State having one vote; a quorum for this purpose shall consist of a member or members from two-thirds of the States, and a majority of all the States shall be necessary to a choice. *(And if the House of Representatives shall not choose a President whenever the right of choice shall devolve upon them, before the fourth day of March next following, then the Vice-President shall act as President, as in the case of the death or other constitutional disability of the President.) (The words in parentheses were superseded by Amendment XX, section 3.)* The person having the greatest number of votes as Vice-President, shall be the Vice-President, if such number be a majority of the whole number of Electors appointed, and if no person have a majority, then from the two highest numbers on the list, the Senate shall choose the Vice-President; a quorum for the purpose shall consist of two-thirds of the whole number of Senators, and a majority of the whole number shall be necessary to a choice. But no person constitutionally ineligible to the office of President shall be eligible to that of Vice-President of the United States.

THE RECONSTRUCTION AMENDMENTS

(Amendments XIII, XIV, and XV are commonly known as the Reconstruction Amendments, inasmuch as they followed the Civil War, and were drafted by Republicans who were bent on imposing their own policy of reconstruction on the South. Post-bellum legislatures there—Mississippi, South Carolina, Georgia, for example—had set up laws which, it was charged, were contrived to perpetuate Negro slavery under other names.)

AMENDMENT XIII.

Slavery abolished.

(Proposed by Congress Jan. 31, 1865; ratification completed Dec. 18, 1865. The amendment, when first proposed by a resolution in Congress, was passed by the Senate, 38 to 6, on Apr. 8, 1864, but was defeated in the House, 95 to 66 on June 15, 1864. On reconsideration by the House, on Jan. 31, 1865, the resolution passed, 119 to 56. It was approved by President Lincoln on Feb. 1, 1865, although the Supreme Court had decided in 1798 that the President has nothing to do with the proposing of amendments to the Constitution, or their adoption.)

1. Neither slavery nor involuntary servitude, except as a punishment for crime whereof the party shall have been duly convicted, shall exist within the United States or any place subject to their jurisdiction.

2. Congress shall have power to enforce this article by appropriate legislation.

AMENDMENT XIV.

Citizenship rights not to be abridged.

(The following amendment was proposed to the Legislatures of the several states by the 39th Congress, June 13, 1866, and was declared to have been ratified in a proclamation by the Secretary of State, July 28, 1868.

(The 14th amendment was adopted only by virtue of ratification subsequent to earlier rejections. Newly constituted legislatures in both North Carolina and South Carolina (respectively July 4 and 9, 1868), ratified the proposed amendment, although earlier legislatures had rejected the proposal. The Secretary of State issued a proclamation, which, though doubtful as to the effect of attempted withdrawals by Ohio and New Jersey, entertained no doubt as to the validity of the ratification by North and South Carolina. The following day (July 21, 1868), Congress passed a resolution which declared the 14th Amendment to be a part of the Constitution and directed the Secretary of State so to promulgate it. The Secretary waited, however, until the newly constituted Legislature of Georgia had ratified the amendment, subsequent to an earlier rejection, before the promulgation of the ratification of the new amendment.)

1. All persons born or naturalized in the United States, and subject to the jurisdiction thereof, are citizens of the United States and of the State wherein they reside. No State shall make or enforce any law which shall abridge the privileges or immunities of citizens of the United States; nor shall any State deprive any person of life, liberty, or property, without due process of law; nor deny to any person within its jurisdiction the equal protection of the laws.

2. Representatives shall be apportioned among the several States according to their respective numbers, counting the whole number of persons in each State, excluding Indians not taxed. But when the right to vote at any election for the choice of Electors for President and Vice-President of the United States, Representatives in Congress, the executive and judicial officers of a State, or the members of the Legislature thereof, is denied to any of the male inhabitants of such State, being twenty-one years of age, and, citizens of the United States, or in any way abridged, except for participation in rebellion, or other crime, the basis of representation therein shall be reduced in the proportion which the number of such male citizens shall bear to the whole number of male citizens twenty-one years of age in such State.

3. No person shall be a Senator or Representative in Congress, or Elector of President and Vice-President, or hold any office, civil or military, under the United States, or under any State, who, having previously taken an oath, as a member of Congress, or as an officer of the United States, or as a member of any State Legislature, or as an executive or judicial officer of any State, to support the Constitution of the United States, shall have engaged in insurrection or rebellion against the same, or given aid or comfort to the enemies thereof. But Congress may by a vote of two-thirds of each House, remove such disability.

4. The validity of the public debt of the United States, authorized by law, including debts incurred for payment of pensions and bounties for services in suppressing insurrection or rebellion, shall not be questioned. But neither the United States nor any State shall assume or pay any debt or obligation incurred in aid of insurrection or rebellion against the United States, or any claim for the loss or emancipation of any slave; but all such debts, obligations and claims, shall be held illegal and void.

5. The Congress shall have power to enforce, by appropriate legislation, the provisions of this article.

AMENDMENT XV.

Race no bar to voting rights.

(The following amendment was proposed to the legislatures of the several States by the 40th Congress, Feb. 26, 1869, and was declared to have been ratified in a proclamation by the Secretary of State, Mar. 30, 1870.)

1. The right of citizens of the United States to vote shall not be denied or abridged by the United States or by any State on account of race, color, or previous condition of servitude.

2. The Congress shall have power to enforce this article by appropriate legislation.

AMENDMENT XVI.

Income taxes authorized.

(Proposed by Congress July 12, 1909; ratification declared by the Secretary of State Feb. 25, 1913.)

The Congress shall have power to lay and collect taxes on incomes, from whatever source derived, without apportionment among the several States, and without regard to any census or enumeration.

AMENDMENT XVII.

United States Senators to be elected by direct popular vote.

(Proposed by Congress May 13, 1912; ratification declared by the Secretary of State May 31, 1913.)

1. The Senate of the United States shall be composed of two Senators from each State, elected by the people thereof, for six years; and each Senator shall have one vote. The electors in each State shall have the qualifications requisite for electors of the most numerous branch of the State Legislatures.

2. When vacancies happen in the representation of any State in the Senate, the executive authority of such State shall issue writs of election to fill such vacancies: Provided, That the Legislature of any State may empower the Executive thereof to make temporarv appointments until the peo-

ple fill the vacancies by election as the Legislature may direct.

3. This amendment shall not be so construed as to affect the election or term of any Senator chosen before it becomes valid as part of the Constitution.

AMENDMENT XVIII.

Liquor prohibition amendment.

(Proposed by Congress Dec. 18, 1917; ratification completed Jan. 16, 1919. Repealed by Amendment XXI, effective Dec. 5, 1933.)

(1. After one year from the ratification of this article the manufacture, sale, or transportation of intoxicating liquors within, the importation thereof into, or the exportation thereof from the United States and all territory subject to the jurisdiction thereof for beverage purposes is hereby prohibited.

(2. The Congress and the several States shall have concurrent power to enforce this article by appropriate legislation.

(3. This article shall be inoperative unless it shall have been ratified as an amendment to the Constitution by the Legislatures of the several States, as provided in the Constitution, within seven years from the date of the submission hereof to the States by the Congress.)

(The total vote in the Senates of the various States was 1,310 for, 237 against—84.6% dry. In the lower houses of the States the vote was 3,782 for, 1,035 against—78.5% dry.

(The amendment ultimately was adopted by all the States except Connecticut and Rhode Island.)

AMENDMENT XIX.

Giving nationwide suffrage to women.

(Proposed by Congress June 4, 1919; ratification certified by Secretary of State Aug. 26, 1920.)

1. The right of citizens of the United States to vote shall not be denied or abridged by the United States or by any State on account of sex.

2. Congress shall have power to enforce this Article by appropriate legislation.

AMENDMENT XX.

Terms of President and Vice President to begin on Jan. 20; those of Senators, Representatives, Jan. 3.

(Proposed by Congress Mar. 2, 1932; ratification completed Jan. 23, 1933.)

1. The terms of the President and Vice President shall end at noon on the 20th day of January, and the terms of Senators and Representatives at noon on the 3rd day of January, of the years in which such terms would have ended if this article had not been ratified; and the terms of their successors shall then begin.

2. The Congress shall assemble at least once in every year, and such meeting shall begin at noon on the 3rd day of January, unless they shall by law appoint a different day.

3. If, at the time fixed for the beginning of the term of the President, the President elect shall have died, the Vice President elect shall become President. If a President shall not have been chosen before the time fixed for the beginning of his term, or if the President elect shall have failed to qualify, then the Vice President elect shall act as President until a President shall have qualified; and the Congress may by law provide for the case wherein neither a President elect nor a Vice President elect shall have qualified, declaring who shall then act as President, or the manner in which one who is to act shall be selected, and such person shall act accordingly until a President or Vice President shall have qualified.

4. The Congress may by law provide for the case of the death of any of the persons from whom the House of Representatives may choose a President whenever the right of choice shall have devolved upon them, and for the case of the death of any of the persons from whom the Senate may choose a Vice President whenever the right of choice shall have devolved upon them.

5. Sections 1 and 2 shall take effect on the 15th day of October following the ratification of this article (Oct., 1933).

6. This article shall be inoperative unless it shall have been ratified as an amendment to the Constitution by the Legislatures of three-fourths of the several States within seven years from the date of its submission.

AMENDMENT XXI.

Repeal of Amendment XVIII.

(Proposed by Congress Feb. 20, 1933; ratification completed Dec. 5, 1933.)

1. The eighteenth article of amendment to the Constitution of the United States is hereby repealed.

2. The transportation or importation into any State, Territory, or Possession of the United States for delivery or use therein of intoxicating liquors, in violation of the laws thereof, is hereby prohibited.

3. This article shall be inoperative unless it shall have been ratified as an amendment to the Constitution by conventions in the several States, as provided in the Constitution, within seven years from the date of the submission hereof to the States by the Congress.

AMENDMENT XXII.

Limiting Presidential terms of office.

(Proposed by Congress Mar. 24, 1947; ratification completed Feb. 27, 1951.)

1. No person shall be elected to the office of the President more than twice, and no person who has held the office of President, or acted as President, for more than two years of a term to which some other person was elected President shall be elected to the office of the President more than once. But this Article shall not apply to any person holding the office of President when this Article was proposed by the Congress, and shall not prevent any person who may be holding the office of President, or acting as President, during the term within which this Article becomes operative from holding the office of President or acting as President during the remainder of such term.

2. This article shall be inoperative unless it shall have been ratified as an amendment to the Constitution by the Legislatures of three-fourths of the several States within seven years from the date of its submission to the States by the Congress.

AMENDMENT XXIII.

Presidential vote for District of Columbia.

(Proposed by Congress June 16, 1960; ratification completed Mar. 29, 1961.)

1. The District constituting the seat of Government of the United States shall appoint in such manner as the Congress may direct:

A number of electors of President and Vice President equal to the whole number of Senators and Representatives in Congress to which the District would be entitled if it were a State, but in no event more than the least populous State; they shall be in addition to those appointed by the States, but they shall be considered, for the purposes of the election of President and Vice President, to be electors appointed by a State; and they shall meet in the District and perform such duties as provided by the twelfth article of amendment.

2. The Congress shall have power to enforce this article by appropriate legislation.

AMENDMENT XXIV.

Barring poll tax in federal elections.

(Proposed by Congress Aug. 27, 1962; ratification completed Jan. 23, 1964.)

1. The right of citizens of the United States to vote in any primary or other election for President or Vice President, for electors for President or Vice President, or for Senator or Representative in Congress, shall not be denied or abridged by the United States or any State by reason of failure to pay any poll tax or other tax.

2. The Congress shall have power to enforce this article by appropriate legislation.

AMENDMENT XXV.

Presidential disability and succession.

(Proposed by Congress July 6, 1965; ratification completed Feb. 10, 1967.)

1. In case of the removal of the President from office or of

his death or resignation, the Vice President shall become President.

2. Whenever there is a vacancy in the office of the Vice President, the President shall nominate a Vice President who shall take office upon confirmation by a majority vote of both houses of Congress.

3. Whenever the President transmits to the President pro tempore of the Senate and the Speaker of the House of Representatives his written declaration that he is unable to discharge the powers and duties of his office, and until he transmits to them a written declaration to the contrary, such powers and duties shall be discharged by the Vice President as Acting President.

4. Whenever the Vice President and a majority of either the principal officers of the executive departments or of such other body as Congress may by law provide, transmit to the President pro tempore of the Senate and the Speaker of the House of Representatives their written declaration that the President is unable to discharge the powers and duties of his office, the Vice President shall immediately assume the powers and duties of the office as Acting President.

Thereafter, when the President transmits to the President pro tempore of the Senate and the Speaker of the House of Representatives his written declaration that no inability exists, he shall resume the powers and duties of his office unless the Vice President and a majority of either the principal officers of the executive department or of such other body as Congress may by law provide, transmit within four days to the President pro tempore of the Senate and the Speaker of the House of Representatives their written declaration that the President is unable to discharge the powers and duties of his office. Thereupon Congress shall decide the issue, assembling within forty-eight hours for that purpose if not in session. If the Congress, within twenty-one days after receipt of the latter written declaration, or, if Congress is not in session, within twenty-one days after Congress is required to assemble, determines by two-thirds vote of both houses that the President is unable to discharge the powers and duties of his office, the Vice President shall continue to discharge the same as Acting President; otherwise, the President shall resume the powers and duties of his office.

AMENDMENT XXVI.

Lowering voting age to 18 years.

(Proposed by Congress Mar. 8, 1971; ratification completed July 1, 1971.)

1. The right of citizens of the United States, who are 18 years of age or older, to vote shall not be denied or abridged by the United States or any state on account of age.

2. The Congress shall have the power to enforce this article by appropriate legislation.

PROPOSED EQUAL RIGHTS AMENDMENT

(Proposed by Congress Mar. 22, 1972; ratified, as of mid-1982, by 35 states: 5 voted later to rescind their approval. Total of 38 needed for approval before deadline, originally Mar. 22, 1979; extended to June 30, 1982, by Senate action Oct. 6, 1978.)

1. Equality of rights under the law shall not be denied or abridged by the United States or by any State on account of sex.

2. The Congress shall have the power to enforce, by appropriate legislation, the provisions of this article.

3. This amendment shall take effect two years after the date of ratification.

PROPOSED D.C. REPRESENTATION AMENDMENT

(Proposed by Congress Aug. 22, 1978; ratified, as of mid-1982, by 8 states.)

1. For purposes of representation in the Congress, election of the President and Vice President, and article V of this Constitution, the District constituting the seat of government of the United States shall be treated as though it were a State.

2. The exercise of the rights and powers conferred under this article shall be by the people of the District constituting the seat of government, and as shall be provided by the Congress.

3. The twenty-third article of amendment to the Constitution of the United States is hereby repealed.

4. This article shall be inoperative, unless it shall have been ratified as an amendment to the Constitution by the legislatures of three-fourths of the several States within seven years from the date of its submission.

Origin of the Constitution

The War of Independence was conducted by delegates from the original 13 states, called the Congress of the United States of America and generally known as the Continental Congress. In 1777 the Congress submitted to the legislatures of the states the Articles of Confederation and Perpetual Union, which were ratified by New Hampshire, Massachusetts, Rhode Island, Connecticut, New York, New Jersey, Pennsylvania, Delaware, Virginia, North Carolina, South Carolina, and Georgia, and finally, in 1781, by Maryland.

The first article of the instrument read: "The stile of this confederacy shall be the United States of America." This did not signify a sovereign nation, because the states delegated only those powers they could not handle individually, such as power to wage war, establish a uniform currency, make treaties with foreign nations and contract debts for general expenses (such as paying the army). Taxes for the payment of such debts were levied by the individual states. The president under the Articles signed himself "President of the United States in Congress assembled," but here the United States were considered in the plural, a cooperating group. Canada was invited to join the union on equal terms but did not act.

When the war was won it became evident that a stronger federal union was needed to protect the mutual interests of the states. The Congress left the initiative to the legislatures. Virginia in Jan. 1786 appointed commissioners to meet with representatives of other states, with the result that delegates from Virginia, Delaware, New York, New Jersey, and Pennsylvania met at Annapolis. Alexander Hamilton prepared for their call by asking delegates from all states to meet in Philadelphia in May 1787 "to render the Constitution of the Federal government adequate to the exigencies of the union." Congress endorsed the plan Feb. 21, 1787. Delegates were appointed by all states except Rhode Island.

The convention met May 14, 1787. George Washington was chosen president (presiding officer). The states certified 65 delegates, but 10 did not attend. The work was done by 55, not all of whom were present at all sessions. Of the 55 attending delegates, 16 failed to sign, and 39 actually signed Sept. 17, 1787, some with reservations. Some historians have said 74 delegates (9 more than the 65 actually certified) were named and 19 failed to attend. These 9 additional persons refused the appointment, were never delegates and never counted as absentees. Washington sent the Constitution to Congress with a covering letter and that body, Sept. 28, 1787, ordered it sent to the legislatures, "in order to be submitted to a convention of delegates chosen in each state by the people thereof."

The Constitution was ratified by votes of state conventions as follows: Delaware, Dec. 7, 1787, unanimous; Pennsylvania, Dec. 12, 1787, 43 to 23; New Jersey, Dec. 18, 1787, unanimous; Georgia, Jan 2, 1788, unanimous; Connecticut, Jan. 9, 1788, 128 to 40; Massachusetts, Feb. 6, 1788, 187 to 168; Maryland, Apr. 28, 1788, 63 to 11; South Carolina, May 23, 1788, 149 to 73; New Hampshire, June 21, 1788, 57 to 46; Virginia, June 26, 1788, 89 to 79; New York, July 26, 1788, 30 to 27. Nine states were needed to establish the operation of the Constitution "between the states so ratifying the same" and New Hampshire was the 9th state. The government did not declare the Constitution in effect until the first Wednesday in Mar. 1789 which was Mar. 4. After that North Carolina ratified it Nov. 21, 1789, 194 to 77; and Rhode Island, May 29, 1790, 34 to 32. Vermont in convention ratified it Jan. 10, 1791, and by act of Congress approved Feb. 18, 1791, was admitted into the Union as the 14th state, Mar. 4, 1791.

How the Declaration of Independence Was Adopted

On June 7, 1776, Richard Henry Lee, who had issued the first call for a congress of the colonies, introduced in the Continental Congress at Philadelphia a resolution declaring "that these United Colonies are, and of right ought to be, free and independent states, that they are absolved from all allegiance to the British Crown, and that all political connection between them and the state of Great Britain is, and ought to be, totally dissolved."

The resolution, seconded by John Adams on behalf of the Massachusetts delegation, came up again June 10 when a committee of 5, headed by Thomas Jefferson, was appointed to express the purpose of the resolution in a declaration of independence. The others on the committee were John Adams, Benjamin Franklin, Robert R. Livingston, and Roger Sherman.

Drafting the Declaration was assigned to Jefferson, who worked on a portable desk of his own construction in a room at Market and 7th Sts. The committee reported the result June 28, 1776. The members of the Congress suggested a number of changes, which Jefferson called "deplorable." They didn't approve Jefferson's arraignment of the British people and King George III for encouraging and fostering the slave trade, which Jefferson called "an execrable commerce." They made 86 changes, eliminating 480 words and leaving 1,337. In the final form capitalization was erratic. Jefferson had written that men were endowed with "inalienable" rights; in the final copy it came out as "unalienable" and has been thus ever since.

The Lee-Adams resolution of independence was adopted by 12 yeas July 2 — the actual date of the act of independence. The Declaration, which explains the act, was adopted July 4, in the evening.

After the Declaration was adopted, July 4, 1776, it was turned over to John Dunlap, printer, to be printed on broadsides. The original copy was lost and one of his broadsides was attached to a page in the journal of the Congress. It was read aloud July 8 in Philadelphia, Easton, Pa., and Trenton, N.J. On July 9 at 6 p.m. it was read by order of Gen. George Washington to the troops assembled on the Common in New York City (City Hall Park).

The Continental Congress of July 19, 1776, adopted the following resolution:

"Resolved, That the Declaration passed on the 4th, be fairly engrossed on parchment with the title and stile of 'The Unanimous Declaration of the thirteen United States of America' and that the same, when engrossed, be signed by every member of Congress."

Not all delegates who signed the engrossed Declaration were present on July 4. Robert Morris (Pa.), William Williams (Conn.) and Samuel Chase (Md.) signed on Aug. 2, Oliver Wolcott (Conn.), George Wythe (Va.), Richard Henry Lee (Va.) and Elbridge Gerry (Mass.) signed in August and September, Matthew Thornton (N. H.) joined the Congress Nov. 4 and signed later. Thomas McKean (Del.) rejoined Washington's Army before signing and said later that he signed in 1781.

Charles Carroll of Carrollton was appointed a delegate by Maryland on July 4, 1776, presented his credentials July 18, and signed the engrossed Declaration Aug. 2. Born Sept. 19, 1737, he was 95 years old and the last surviving signer when he died Nov. 14, 1832.

Two Pennsylvania delegates who did not support the Declaration on July 4 were replaced.

The 4 New York delegates did not have authority from their state to vote on July 4. On July 9 the New York state convention authorized its delegates to approve the Declaration and the Congress was so notified on July 15, 1776. The 4 signed the Declaration on Aug. 2.

The original engrossed Declaration is preserved in the National Archives Building in Washington.

The Liberty Bell: Its History and Significance

The Liberty Bell, in Independence Hall, Philadelphia, is an object of great reverence to Americans because of its association with the historic events of the War of Independence.

The original Province bell, ordered to commemorate the 50th anniversary of the Commonwealth of Pennsylvania, was cast by Thomas Lister, Whitechapel, London, and reached Philadelphia in Aug. 1752. It bore an inscription from Leviticus XXV, 10: "Proclaim liberty throughout all the land unto all the inhabitants thereof."

The bell was cracked by a stroke of its clapper in Sept. 1752 while it hung on a truss in the State House yard for testing. Pass & Stow, Philadelphia founders, recast the bell, adding 1 1/2 ounces of copper to a pound of the original metal to reduce brittleness. It was found that the bell contained too much copper, injuring its tone, so Pass & Stow recast it again, this time successfully.

In June 1753 the bell was hung in the wooden steeple of the State House, erected on top of the brick tower. In use while the Continental Congress was in session in the State House, it rang out in defiance of British tax and trade restrictions, and proclaimed the Boston Tea Party and the first public reading of the Declaration of Independence.

On Sept. 18, 1777, when the British Army was about to occupy Philadelphia, the bell was moved in a baggage train of the American Army to Allentown, Pa. where it was hidden in the Zion Reformed Church until June 27, 1778. It was moved back to Philadelphia after the British left.

In July 1781 the wooden steeple became insecure and had to be taken down. The bell was lowered into the brick section of the tower. Here it was hanging in July, 1835, when it cracked while tolling for the funeral of John Marshall, chief justice of the United States. Because of its association with the War of Independence it was not recast but remained mute in this location until 1846, the year of the Mexican War, when it was placed on exhibition in the Declaration Chamber of Independence Hall.

In 1876, when many thousands of Americans visited Philadelphia for the Centennial Exposition, it was placed in its old walnut frame in the tower hallway. In 1877 it was hung from the ceiling of the tower by a chain of 13 links. It was returned again to the Declaration Chamber and in 1896 taken back to the tower hall, where it occupied a glass case. In 1915 the case was removed so that the public might touch it. On Jan. 1, 1976, just after midnight to mark the opening of the Bicentennial Year, the bell was moved to a new glass and steel pavilion behind Independence Hall for easier viewing by the larger number of visitors expected during the year.

The measurements of the bell follow: circumference around the lip, 12 ft.; circumference around the crown, 7 ft. 6 in.; lip to the crown, 3 ft.; height over the crown, 2 ft. 3 in.; thickness at lip, 3 in.; thickness at crown, 1 1/4 in.; weight, 2080 lbs.; length of clapper, 3 ft. 2 in.; cost, £60 14s 5d.

Confederate States and Secession

The American Civil War, 1861-65, grew out of sectional disputes over the continued existence of slavery in the South and the contention of Southern legislators that the states retained many sovereign rights, including the right to secede from the Union.

The war was not fought by state against state but by one federal regime against another, the Confederate government in Richmond assuming control over the economic, political, and military life of the South, under protest from Georgia and South Carolina.

South Carolina voted an ordinance of secession from the Union, repealing its 1788 ratification of the U.S. Constitution on Dec. 20, 1860, to take effect Dec. 24. Other states seceded in 1861. Their votes in conventions were:

Mississippi, Jan. 9, 84-15; Florida, Jan. 10, 62-7; Alabama, Jan. 11, 61-39; Georgia, Jan. 19, 208-89; Louisiana, Jan. 26, 113-17; Texas, Feb. 1, 166-7, ratified by popular vote Feb. 23 (for 34,794, against 11,325); Virginia, Apr. 17, 88-55, ratified by popular vote May 23 (for 128,884; against 32,134); Arkansas, May 6, 69-1; Tennessee, May 7, ratified by popular vote June 8 (for 104,019, against 47,238); North Carolina, May 21.

Missouri Unionists stopped secession in conventions Feb. 28 and Mar. 9. The legislature condemned secession Mar. 7. Under the protection of Confederate troops, secessionist members of the legislature adopted a resolution of secession at Neosho, Oct. 31. The Confederate Congress seated the secessionists' representatives.

Kentucky did not secede and its government remained Unionist. In a part occupied by Confederate troops, Kentuckians approved secession and the Confederate Congress admitted their representatives.

The Maryland legislature voted against secession Apr. 27, 53-13. Delaware did not secede. Western Virginia held conventions at Wheeling, named a pro-Union governor June 11, 1861; admitted to Union as West Virginia June 30, 1863; its constitution provided for gradual abolition of slavery.

Confederate Government

Forty-two delegates from South Carolina, Georgia, Alabama, Mississippi, Louisiana, and Florida met in convention at Montgomery, Ala., Feb. 4, 1861. They adopted a provisional constitution of the Confederate States of America, and elected Jefferson Davis (Miss.) provisional president, and Alexander H. Stephens (Ga.) provisional vice president.

A permanent constitution was adopted Mar. 11; it abolished the African slave trade. The Congress moved to Richmond, Va. July 20. Davis was elected president in October, and was inaugurated Feb. 22, 1862.

The Congress adopted a flag, consisting of a red field with a white stripe, and a blue jack with a circle of white stars. Later the more popular flag was the red field with blue diagonal cross bars that held 13 white stars. The stars represented the 11 states actually in the Confederacy plus Kentucky and Missouri.

(*See also Civil War, U.S., in Index*)

Lincoln's Address at Gettysburg, 1863

Fourscore and seven years ago our fathers brought forth on this continent a new nation, conceived in liberty and dedicated to the proposition that all men are created equal.

Now we are engaged in a great civil war, testing whether that nation or any nation so conceived and so dedicated can long endure. We are met on a great battle field of that war. We have come to dedicate a portion of that field, as a final resting-place for those who here gave their lives that that nation might live. It is altogether fitting and proper that we should do this.

But, in a larger sense, we can not dedicate — we can not consecrate — we can not hallow — this ground. The brave men, living and dead, who struggled here, have consecrated it, far above our poor power to add or detract. The world will little note, nor long remember, what we say here, but it can never forget what they did here. It is for us the living, rather, to be dedicated here to the unfinished work which they who fought here have thus far so nobly advanced. It is rather for us to be here dedicated to the great task remaining before us — that from these honored dead we take increased devotion to that cause for which they gave the last full measure of devotion — that we here highly resolve that these dead shall not have died in vain — that this nation, under God, shall have a new birth of freedom — and that government of the people, by the people, for the people, shall not perish from the earth.

History of the Address

President Lincoln delivered his address at the dedication of the military cemetery at Gettysburg, Pa., Nov. 19, 1863. The battle had been fought July 1-3, 1863. He was preceded by Edward Everett, former president of Harvard, secretary of state and senator from Massachusetts, then 69 and one of the nation's great orators. Everett gave a full resume of the battle, Lincoln's speech was so short that the photographer did not get his camera adjusted in time. The report that newspapers ignored Lincoln's address is not entirely accurate; Everett's address swamped their columns, but the greatness of Lincoln's speech was immediately recognized. Everett wrote him: "I should be glad if I could flatter myself that I came as near the central idea of the occasion in 2 hours as you did in 2 minutes."

Five copies of the Gettysburg address in Lincoln's hand are extant. The first and 2d drafts, prepared in Washington and Gettysburg just before delivery, are in the Library of Congress. The 3d draft, written at the request of Everett to be sold at a fair in New York for the benefit of soldiers, was given the Illinois State Historical Library by popular subscription.

The 4th copy was written out by Lincoln for George Bancroft, the historian, and remained in custody of the Bancroft family until 1929, when it was acquired by Mrs. Nicholas H. Noyes, of Indianapolis, Ind. In 1949 Mrs. Noyes presented this copy to the Cornell University Library, Ithaca, N.Y. The 5th copy, usually described as the clearest and best, was also written by Lincoln for George Bancroft. It is in the Lincoln Room of the White House, where it was placed in Mar. 1959. Lincoln's spelling of battle field and can not as separated words in that version is reproduced above.

The National Anthem — The Star-Spangled Banner

The Star-Spangled Banner was ordered played by the military and naval services by President Woodrow Wilson in 1916. It was designated the National Anthem by Act of Congress, Mar. 3, 1931. It was written by Francis Scott Key, of Georgetown, D. C., during the bombardment of Fort McHenry, Baltimore, Md., Sept. 13-14, 1814. Key was a lawyer, a graduate of St. John's College, Annapolis, and a volunteer in a light artillery company. When a friend, Dr. Beanes, a physician of Upper Marlborough, Md., was taken aboard Admiral Cockburn's British squadron for interfering with ground troops, Key and J. S. Skinner, carrying a note from President Madison, went to the fleet under a flag of truce on a cartel ship to ask Beanes' release. Admiral Cockburn consented, but as the fleet was about to sail up the Patapsco to bombard Fort McHenry he detained them, first on H. M. S. Surprise, and then on a supply ship.

Key witnessed the bombardment from his own vessel. It began at 7 a.m., Sept. 13, 1814, and lasted, with intermissions, for 25 hours. The British fired over 1,500 shells, each weighing as much as 220 lbs. They were unable to approach closely because the Americans had sunk 22 vessels in the channel. Only four Americans were killed and 24 wounded. A British bomb-ship was disabled.

During the bombardment Key wrote a stanza on the back of an envelope. Next day at Indian Queen Inn, Baltimore, he wrote out the poem and gave it to his brother-in-law, Judge J. H. Nicholson. Nicholson suggested the tune, Anacreon in Heaven, and had the poem printed on broadsides, of which two survive. On Sept. 20 it appeared in the "Baltimore American." Later Key made 3 copies; one is in the Library of Congress and one in the Pennsylvania Historical Society.

The copy that Key wrote in his hotel Sept. 14, 1814, remained in the Nicholson family for 93 years. In 1907 it was sold to Henry Walters of Baltimore. In 1934 it was bought at auction in New York from the Walters estate by the Walters Art Gallery, Baltimore, for $26,400. The Walters Gallery in 1953 sold the manuscript to the Maryland Historical Society for the same price.

The flag that Key saw during the bombardment is preserved in the Smithsonian Institution, Washington. It is 30 by 42 ft., and has 15 alternate red and white stripes and 15 stars, for the original 13 states plus Kentucky and Vermont.

It was made by Mary Young Pickersgill. The Baltimore Flag House, a museum, occupies her premises, which were restored in 1953.

The Star-Spangled Banner

I

Oh, say can you see by the dawn's early light
What so proudly we hailed at the twilight's last gleaming?
Whose broad stripes and bright stars thru the perilous fight,
O'er the ramparts we watched were so gallantly streaming?
And the rocket's red glare, the bomb bursting in air,
Gave proof through the night that our flag was still there.
Oh, say does that star-spangled banner yet wave
O'er the land of the free and the home of the brave?

II

On the shore, dimly seen through the mists of the deep,
Where the foe's haughty host in dread silence reposes,
What is that which the breeze, o'er the towering steep,
As it fitfully blows, half conceals, half discloses?
Now it catches the gleam of the morning's first beam,
In full glory reflected now shines in the stream:
'Tis the star-spangled banner! Oh long may it wave
O'er the land of the free and the home of the brave!

III

And where is that band who so vauntingly swore
That the havoc of war and the battle's confusion,
A home and a country should leave us no more!
Their blood has washed out their foul footsteps' pollution.
No refuge could save the hireling and slave
From the terror of flight, or the gloom of the grave:
And the star-spangled banner in triumph doth wave
O'er the land of the free and the home of the brave!

IV

Oh! thus be it ever, when freemen shall stand
Between their loved home and the war's desolation!
Blest with victory and peace, may the heav'n rescued land
Praise the Power that hath made and preserved us a nation.
Then conquer we must, when our cause it is just,
And this be our motto: "In God is our trust."
And the star-spangled banner in triumph shall wave
O'er the land of the free and the home of the brave!

Statue of Liberty National Monument

Since 1886, the Statue of Liberty Enlightening the World has stood as a symbol cf freedom in New York harbor. It also commemorates French-American friendship for it was given by the people of France, designed by Frederic Auguste Bartholdi (1834-1904). A $2.5 million building housing the American Museum of Immigration was opened by Pres. Nixon Sept. 26, 1972, at the base of the statue. It houses a permanent exhibition of photos, posters, and artifacts tracing the history of American immigration. In addition, there is a small immigration library. The Monument is administered by the National Park Service.

Nearby Ellis Island, gateway to America for more than 12 million immigrants between 1892 and 1954, was proclaimed part of the National Monument in 1965 by Pres. Johnson. It can be visited between May and October.

Edouard de Laboulaye, French historian and admirer of American political institutions, suggested that the French present a monument to the United States, the latter to provide pedestal and site. Bartholdi visualized a colossal statue at the entrance of New York harbor, welcoming the peoples of the world with the torch of liberty.

The French approved the idea and formed the Franco-American Union to raise funds, which eventually reached $250,000. Bartholdi began work about 1874 in Paris.

On Washington's birthday, Feb. 22, 1877, Congress approved the use of a site on Bedloe's Island suggested by Bartholdi. This island of 12 acres had been owned in the 17th century by a Walloon named Isaac Bedloe. It was called Bedloe's until Aug. 3, 1956, when Pres. Eisenhower approved a resolution of Congress changing the name to Liberty Island.

The statue was finished May 21, 1884, and formally presented to U.S. Minister Morton July 4, 1884, by Ferdinand de Lesseps, head of the Franco-American Union, promoter of the Panama Canal, and builder of the Suez Canal.

On Aug. 5, 1884, the Americans laid the cornerstone for the pedestal. This was to be built on the foundations of Fort Wood, which had been erected by the Government in 1811. The American committee had raised $125,000, but this was found to be inadequate. Joseph Pulitzer, owner of the New York World, appealed on Mar. 16, 1885, for general donations. By Aug. 11, 1885, he had raised $100,000.

The statue arrived dismantled, in 214 packing cases, from Rouen, France, in June, 1885. The last rivet of the statue was driven Oct. 28, 1886, when Pres. Grover Cleveland dedicated the monument.

The statue weighs 450,000 lbs. or 225 tons. The copper sheeting weighs 200,000 lbs. There are 167 steps from the land level to the top of the pedestal, 168 steps inside the statue to the head, and 54 rungs on the ladder leading to the arm that holds the torch.

Dimensions of the Statue	Ft.	In.
Height from base to torch (45.3 meters)	151	1
Foundation of pedestal to torch (91.5 meters)	305	1
Heel to top of head	111	1
Length of hand	16	5
Index finger	8	0
Circumference at second joint	3	6
Size of finger nail	13x10 in.	
Head from chin to cranium	17	3
Head thickness from ear to ear	10	0
Distance across the eye	2	6
Length of nose	4	6
Right arm, length	42	0
Right arm, greatest thickness	12	0
Thickness of waist	35	0
Width of mouth	3	0
Tablet, length	23	7
Tablet, width	13	7
Tablet, thickness	2	0

Emma Lazarus' Famous Poem

A poem by Emma Lazarus is graven on a tablet within the pedestal on which the statue stands.

The New Colossus

Not like the brazen giant of Greek fame,
With conquering limbs astride from land to land;
Here at our sea-washed, sunset gates shall stand
A mighty woman with a torch, whose flame
Is the imprisoned lightning, and her name
Mother of Exiles. From her beacon-hand
Glows world-wide welcome; her mild eyes command
The air-bridged harbor that twin cities frame.
"Keep ancient lands, your storied pomp!" cries she
With silent lips. "Give me your tired, your poor,
Your huddled masses yearning to breathe free,
The wretched refuse of your teeming shore.
Send these, the homeless, tempest-tost to me,
I lift my lamp beside the golden door!"

Forms of Address for Persons of Rank and Public Office

In these examples John Smith is used as a representative American name. The salutation Dear Sir or Dear Madam is always permissible when addressing a person not known to the writer.

President of the United States

Address: The President, The White House, Washington, DC 20500. Also, The President and Mrs. ____.

Salutation: Dear Sir or Mr. President or Dear Mr. President. More intimately: My dear Mr. President. Also: Dear Mr. President and Mrs. ____

The vice president takes the same forms.

Cabinet Officers

Address: Mr. John Smith, Secretary of State, Washington, D.C. or The Hon. John Smith. Similar addresses for other members of the cabinet. Also: Secretary and Mrs. John Smith.

Salutation: Dear Sir, or Dear Mr. Secretary. Also: Dear Mr. and Mrs. Smith.

The Bench

Address: The Hon. John Smith, Chief Justice of the United States. The Hon. John Smith, Associate Justice of the Supreme Court of the United States. The Hon. John Smith, Associate Judge, U.S. District Court.

Salutation: Dear Sir, or Dear Mr. Chief Justice. Dear Mr. Justice. Dear Judge Smith.

Members of Congress

Address: The Hon. John Smith, United States Senate, Washington, DC 20510, or Sen. John Smith, etc. Also The Hon. John Smith, House of Representatives, Washington, DC 20515, or Rep. John Smith, etc.

Salutation: Dear Mr. Senator or Dear Mr. Smith; for Representative, Dear Mr. Smith.

Officers of Armed Forces

Address: Careful attention should be given to the precise rank, thus: General of the Army John Smith, Fleet Admiral John Smith. The rules for Air Force are same as Army.

Salutation: Dear Sir, or Dear General. All general officers, whatever rank, are entitled to be addressed as generals. Likewise a lieutenant colonel is addressed as colonel and first and second lieutenants are addressed as lieutenant.

Warrant officers and flight officers are addressed as Mister. Chaplains are addressed as Chaplain. A Catholic chaplain may be addressed as Father. Cadets of the United States Military Academy and Air Force Academy are addressed as Cadet. Noncommissioned officers are addressed by their titles. In the U. S. Navy all men from midshipman at Annapolis up to and including lieutenant commander are addressed as Mister.

Ambassador, Governor, Mayor

Address: The Hon. John Smith, followed by his or her title. They can be addressed either at their embassy, or at the Department of State, Washington, D.C. An ambassador from a foreign nation may be addressed as His or Her Excellency. An American is not to be so addressed.

Salutation: Dear Mr. or Madam Ambassador. An ambassador from a foreign nation may be called Your Excellency.

Governors and mayors are often addressed as The Hon. Jane Smith, Governor of ______, or The Hon. John Smith, Mayor of ______; also Governor John Smith, State House, Albany, N.Y., or Mayor Jane Smith, City Hall, Erie, Pa.

The Clergy

Address: His Holiness, the Pope, or His Holiness Pope (name), State of Vatican City, Italy.

Salutation: Your Holiness or Most Holy Father.

Also: His Eminence, John, Cardinal Smith; salutation: Your Eminence. An archbishop or a bishop is addressed The Most Reverend, and the salutation is Your Excellency. A monsignor who is a papal chamberlain is The Very Reverend Monsignor and the salutation is Dear Sir or Very Reverend Monsignor; a monsignor who is a domestic prelate is The Right Reverend Monsignor and salutation is Right Reverend Monsignor. A priest is addressed Reverend John Smith. A brother of an order is addressed Brother —. A sister takes the same form.

A bishop of the Protestant Episcopal Church is The Right Reverend John Smith; salutation is Right Reverend Sir, or Dear Bishop Smith. If a clergyman is a doctor of divinity, he is addressed: The Reverend John Smith, D.D., and the salutation is Reverend Sir, or Dear Dr. Smith. When a clergyman does not have the degree the salutation is Dear Mr. Smith.

A bishop of the Methodist Church is addressed Bishop John Smith with titles following.

Royalty and Nobility

An emperor is to be addressed in a letter as Sir, or Your Imperial Majesty.

A king or queen is addressed as His Majesty (Name), King of (Name), or Her Majesty (Name), Queen of (Name), Salutation: Sir, or Madam, or May it please Your Majesty.

Princes and princesses and other persons of royal blood are addressed as His (or Her) Royal Highness, and saluted with May it please Your Royal Highness.

A duke or marquis is My Lord Duke (or Marquis), a duke is His (or Your) Grace.

Code of Etiquette for Display and Use of the U.S. Flag

Although the Stars and Stripes originated in 1777, it was not until 146 years later that there was a serious attempt to establish a uniform code of etiquette for the U.S. flag. The War Department issued Feb. 15, 1923, a circular on the rules of flag usage. These were adopted almost in their entirety June 14, 1923, by a conference of 68 patriotic organizations in Washington. Finally, on June 22, 1942, a joint resolution of Congress, amended by Public Law 94-344 July 7, 1976, codified "existing rules and customs pertaining to the display and use of the flag. . ."

When to Display the Flag—The flag should be displayed on all days, especially on legal holidays and other special occasions, on official buildings when in use, in or near polling places on election days, and in or near schools when in session. A citizen may fly the flag at any time he wishes. It is customary to display the flag only from sunrise to sunset on buildings and on stationary flagstaffs in the open. However, it may be displayed at night on special occasions, preferably lighted. In Washington, the flag now flies over the White House both day and night. It flies over the Senate wing of the Capitol when the Senate is in session and over the House wing when that body is in session. It flies day and night over the east and west fronts of the Capitol, without floodlights at night but receiving light from the illuminated Capitol Dome. It flies 24 hours a day at several other places, including the Fort McHenry Nat'l Monument in Baltimore, where it inspired Francis Scott Key to write The Star Spangled Banner.

How to Fly the Flag—The flag should be hoisted briskly and lowered ceremoniously, and should never be allowed to touch the ground or the floor. When hung over a sidewalk from a rope extending from a building to a pole, the union should be away from the building. When hung over the center of a street it should have the union to the north in an east-west street and to the east in a north-south street. No other flag may be flown above or, if on the same level, to the right of the U.S. flag, except that at the United Nations Headquarters the UN flag may be placed above flags of all member nations and other national flags may be flown with equal prominence or honor with the flag of the U.S. At services by Navy chaplains at sea, the church pennant may be flown above the flag.

When two flags are placed against a wall with crossed staffs, the U.S. flag should be at right—its own right, and its staff should be in front of the staff of the other flag; when a number of flags are grouped and displayed from staffs, it should be at the center and highest point of the group.

Church and Platform Use—In an auditorium, the flag may be displayed flat, above and behind the speaker. When displayed from a staff in a church or public auditorium, the flag should hold the position of superior prominence, in advance of the audience, and in the position of honor at the clergyman's or speaker's right as he faces the audience. Any other flag so displayed should be placed on the left of the clergyman or speaker or to the right of the audience.

When the flag is displayed horizontally or vertically against a wall, the stars should be uppermost and at the observer's left.

When to Salute the Flag—All persons present should face the flag, stand at attention and salute on the following occasions: (1) When the flag is passing in a parade or in a review, (2) During the ceremony of hoisting or lowering, (3) When the National Anthem is played, and (4) During the Pledge of Allegiance. Those present in uniform should render the military salute. When not in uniform, men should remove the hat with the right hand holding it at the left shoulder, the hand being over the heart. Men without hats should salute in the same manner. Aliens should stand at attention. Women should salute by placing the right hand over the heart.

On Memorial Day, the flag should fly at half-staff until noon, then be raised to the peak.

As provided by Presidential proclamation the flag should fly at half-staff for 30 days from the day of death of a president or former president; for 10 days from the day of death of a vice president, chief justice or retired chief justice of the U.S., or speaker of the House of Representatives; from day of death until burial of an associate justice of the Supreme Court, cabinet member, former vice president, or Senate president pro tempore, majority or minority Senate leader, or majority or minority House leader; for a U.S. senator, representative, territorial delegate, or the resident commissioner of Puerto Rico, on day of death and the following day within the metropolitan area of the District of Columbia and from day of death until burial within the decedent's state, congressional district, territory or commonwealth; and for the death of the governor of a state, territory, or possession of the U.S., from day of death until burial within that state, territory, or possession.

When used to cover a casket, the flag should be placed so that the union is at the head and over the left shoulder. It should not be lowered into the grave nor touch the ground.

Prohibited Uses of the Flag—The flag should not be dipped to any person or thing. (An exception—customarily, ships salute by dipping their colors.) It should never be displayed with the union down save as a distress signal. It should never be carried flat or horizontally, but always aloft and free.

It should not be displayed on a float, motor car or boat except from a staff.

It should never be used as a covering for a ceiling, nor have placed upon it any word, design, or drawing. It should never be used as a receptacle for carrying anything. It should not be used to cover a statue or a monument.

The flag should never be used for advertising purposes, nor be embroidered on such articles as cushions or hankerchiefs, printed or otherwise impressed on boxes or used as a costume or athletic uniform. Advertising signs should not be fastened to its staff or halyard.

The flag should never be used as drapery of any sort, never festooned, drawn back, nor up, in folds, but always allowed to fall free. Bunting of blue, white and red always arranged with the blue above and the white in the middle, should be used for covering a speaker's desk, draping the front of a platform, and for decoration in general.

An Act of Congress approved Feb. 8, 1917, provided certain penalties for the desecration, mutilation or improper use of the flag within the District of Columbia. A 1968 federal law provided penalties of up to a year's imprisonment or a $1,000 fine or both, for publicly burning or otherwise desecrating any flag of the United States. In addition, many states have laws against flag desecration.

How to Dispose of Worn Flags—The flag, when it is in such condition that it is no longer a fitting emblem for display, should be destroyed in a dignified way, preferably by burning in private.

Pledge of Allegiance to the Flag

I pledge allegiance to the flag of the United States of America and to the republic for which it stands, one nation under God, indivisible, with liberty and justice for all.

This, the current official version of the Pledge of Allegiance, has developed from the original pledge, which was first published in the Sept. 8, 1892, issue of the Youth's Companion, a weekly magazine then published in Boston. The original pledge contained the phrase "my flag," which was changed more than 30 years later to "flag of the United States of America." An act of Congress in 1954 added the words "under God."

The authorship of the pledge had been in dispute for many years. The Youth's Companion stated in 1917 that the original draft was written by James B. Upham, an executive of the magazine who died in 1910. A leaflet circulated by the magazine later named Upham as the originator of the draft "afterwards condensed and perfected by him and his associates of the Companion force."

Francis Bellamy, a former member of the Youth's Companion editorial staff, publicly claimed authorship of the pledge in 1923. The United States Flag Assn., acting on the advice of a committee named to study the controversy, upheld in 1939 the claim of Bellamy, who had died 8 years earlier. The Library of Congress issued in 1957 a report attributing the authorship to Bellamy.

The Flag of the U.S.—The Stars and Stripes

The 50-star flag of the United States was raised for the first time officially at 12:01 a.m. on July 4, 1960, at Fort McHenry National Monument in Baltimore, Md. The 50th star had been added for Hawaii; a year earlier the 49th, for Alaska. Before that, no star had been added since 1912, when N.M. and Ariz. were admitted to the Union.

History of the Flag

The true history of the Stars and Stripes has become so cluttered by a volume of myth and tradition that the facts are difficult, and in some cases impossible, to establish. For example, it is not certain who designed the Stars and Stripes, who made the first such flag, or even whether it ever flew in any sea fight or land battle of the American Revolution.

One thing all agree on is that the Stars and Stripes originated as the result of a resolution offered by the Marine Committee of the Second Continental Congress at Philadelphia and adopted June 14, 1777. It read:

Resolved: that the flag of the United States be thirteen stripes, alternate red and white; that the union be thirteen stars, white in a blue field, representing a new constellation.

Congress gave no hint as to the designer of the flag, no instructions as to the arrangement of the stars, and no information on its appropriate uses. Historians have been unable to find the original flag law.

The resolution establishing the flag was not even published until Sept. 2, 1777. Despite repeated requests, Washington did not get the flags until 1783, after the Revolutionary War was over. And there is no certainty that they were the Stars and Stripes.

Early Flags

Although it was never officially adopted by the Continental Congress, many historians consider the first flag of the United States to have been the Grand Union (sometimes called Great Union) flag. This was a modification of the British Meteor flag, which had the red cross of St. George and the white cross of St. Andrew combined in the blue canton. For the Grand Union flag, 6 horizontal stripes were imposed on the red field, dividing it into 13 alternate red and white stripes. On Jan. 1, 1776, when the Continental Army came into formal existence, this flag was unfurled on Prospect Hill, Somerville, Mass. Washington wrote that "we hoisted the Union Flag in compliment to the United Colonies."

One of several flags about which controversy has raged for years is at Easton, Pa. Containing the devices of the national flag in reversed order, this has been in the public library at Easton for over 150 years. Some contend that this flag was actually the first Stars and Stripes, first displayed on July 8, 1776. This flag has 13 red and white stripes in the canton, 13 white stars centered in a blue field.

A flag was hastily improvised from garments by the defenders of Fort Schuyler at Rome, N.Y., Aug. 3-22, 1777. Historians believe it was the Grand Union Flag.

The Sons of Liberty had a flag of 9 red and white stripes, to signify 9 colonies, when they met in New York in 1765 to oppose the Stamp Tax. By 1775, the flag had grown to 13 red and white stripes, with a rattlesnake on it.

At Concord, Apr. 19, 1775, the minute men from Bedford, Mass., are said to have carried a flag having a silver arm with sword on a red field.

At Cambridge, Mass., the Sons of Liberty used a plain red flag with a green pine tree on it.

In June 1775, Washington went from Philadelphia to Boston to take command of the army, escorted to New York by the Philadelphia Light Horse Troop. It carried a yellow flag which had an elaborate coat of arms — the shield charged with 13 knots, the motto "For These We Strive" — and a canton of 13 blue and silver stripes.

In Feb., 1776, Col. Christopher Gadsden, member of the Continental Congress, gave the South Carolina Provincial Congress a flag "such as is to be used by the commander-in-chief of the American Navy." It had a yellow field, with a rattlesnake about to strike and the words "Don't Tread on Me."

At the battle of Bennington, Aug. 16, 1777, patriots used a flag of 7 white and 6 red stripes with a blue canton extending down 9 stripes and showing an arch of 11 white stars over the figure 76and a star in each of the upper corners. The stars are seven-pointed. This flag is preserved in the Historical Museum at Bennington, Vt.

At the Battle of Cowpens, Jan. 17, 1781, the 3d Maryland Regt. is said to have carried a flag of 13 red and white stripes, with a blue canton containing 12 stars in a circle around one star.

Legends about the Flag

Who Designed the Flag? No one knows for a certainty. Francis Hopkinson, designer of a naval flag, declared he also had designed the flag and in 1781 asked Congress to reimburse him for his services. Congress did not do so. Dumas Malone of Columbia Univ. wrote: "This talented man . . . designed the American flag."

Who Called the Flag Old Glory? — The flag is said to have been named Old Glory by William Driver, a sea captain of Salem, Mass. One legend has it that when he raised the flag on his brig, the Charles Doggett, in 1824, he said: "I name thee Old Glory." But his daughter, who presented the flag to the Smithsonian Institution, said he named it at his 21st birthday celebration Mar. 17, 1824, when his mother presented the homemade flag to him.

The Betsy Ross Legend — The widely publicized legend that Mrs. Betsy Ross made the first Stars and Stripes in June 1776, at the request of a committee composed of George Washington, Robert Morris, and George Ross, an uncle, was first made public in 1870, by a grandson of Mrs. Ross. Historians have been unable to find a historical record of such a meeting or committee.

Adding New Stars

The flag of 1777 was used until 1795. Then, on the admission of Vermont and Kentucky to the Union, Congress passed and Pres. Washington signed an act that after May 1, 1795, the flag should have 15 stripes, alternate red and white, and 15 white stars on a blue field in the union.

When new states were admitted it became evident that the flag would become burdened with stripes. Congress thereupon ordered that after July 4, 1818, the flag should have 13 stripes, symbolizing the 13 original states; that the union have 20 stars, and that whenever a new state was admitted a new star should be added on the July 4 following admission. No law designates the permanent arrangement of the stars. However, since 1912 when a new state has been admitted, the new design has been announced by executive order. No star is specifically identified with any state.

CANADA

See Index for Calgary, Edmonton, Halifax, Hamilton, Kitchener-Waterloo, Lethbridge, Montreal, Ottawa, Quebec, Regina, Saskatoon, Toronto, Vancouver, Windsor, Winnipeg.

Capital: Ottawa. Area: 3,849,670 sq. mi. Population (1981 Census): 24,343,181. Monetary unit: Canadian dollar.

The Land

The world's second largest country in land size, Canada stretches 3,223 miles from east to west and extends southward from the North Pole to the U.S. border. Its seacoast includes 36,356 miles of mainland and 115,133 miles of islands, including the Arctic islands almost from Greenland to near the Alaskan border.

Canada's continental climate, while generally temperate, varies from freezing winter cold to blistering summer heat - a range beyond 100 degrees Fahrenheit.

Major cities, industrial centres, agricultural regions, and the vast majority of the population are situated along a thin, southern fringe bordering the United States. To the north lie vast expanses of varied, virgin land. The remote north, due to extreme cold, is virtually uninhabitable.

Fragmented by history, geography, and economic factors, the country is as diverse as it is large. Regionally, Canada's 10 provinces can be put into 5 groups: the industrially-poor Atlantic Provinces of New Brunswick, Newfoundland, Nova Scotia, and Prince Edward Island; predominantly French-speaking Quebec; Ontario, financial and governmental heartland of the nation; the Prairies, including Manitoba, Saskatchewan, and oil-rich Alberta; and British Columbia, separated from the rest of the country by the Rocky Mountains.

Despite continuing problems of regional disparity in political, economic, and cultural outlook, Canada has survived as a nation by accepting the need to recognize and tolerate differences. Unlike the U.S., Canada has never been a melting pot, nor has it strived to become one.

History

French explorer Jacques Cartier, who discovered the Gulf of St. Lawrence in 1534, is generally regarded as the founder of Canada. But English seaman John Cabot sighted Newfoundland 37 years earlier, in 1497, and Vikings are believed to have reached the Atlantic coast centuries before either explorer.

Canadian settlement was pioneered by the French who established Quebec City (1608) and Montreal (1642) and declared New France a colony in 1663.

Britain, as part of its American expansion, acquired Acadia (later Nova Scotia) in 1717 and, through military victory over French forces in Canada (an extension of a European conflict between the 2 powers), captured Quebec (1759) and obtained control of the rest of New France in 1763. The French, through the Quebec Act of 1774, retained the rights to their own language, religion, and civil law.

The British presence in Canada increased during the American Revolution when many colonials, proudly calling themselves United Empire Loyalists, moved north to Canada.

Fur traders and explorers led Canadians westward across the continent. Sir Alexander Mackenzie reached the Pacific in 1793 and scrawled on a rock by the ocean, "from Canada by land."

In Upper and Lower Canada (later called Ontario and Quebec) and in the Maritimes, legislative assemblies appeared in the 18th century and reformers called for responsible government. But the War of 1812 intervened. The war, a conflict between Great Britain and the United States fought mainly in Upper Canada, ended in a stalemate in 1814.

In 1837 political agitation for more democratic government culminated in rebellions in Upper and Lower Canada. Britain sent Lord Durham to investigate and, in a famous report (1839), he recommended union of the 2 parts into one colony called Canada. The union lasted until Confederation, July 1, 1867, when proclamation of the British North America (BNA) Act launched the Dominion of Canada, consisting of Ontario, Quebec, and the former colonies of Nova Scotia and New Brunswick.

Since 1840 the Canadian colonies had held the right to internal self-government. The BNA act, which became the country's written constitution, established a federal system of government on the model of a British parliament and cabinet structure under the crown. Canada was proclaimed a self-governing Dominion within the British Empire in 1931. Empire has given way to Commonwealth, of which Canada is an independent member.

The Government

Canada is a constitutional monarchy with a parliamentary system of government. It is also a federal state. Official head of state remains England's Queen Elizabeth, represented by a resident governor-general. But in practice the nation is governed by the Prime Minister, leader of the party able to command the support of a majority of members of the House of Commons, dominant chamber of Canada's bicameral Parliament.

The Commons' 282 members are elected at least every 5 years - sooner if the Prime Minister so chooses or if the government is defeated in Parliament. This can occur either through passage of a motion of nonconfidence in the government or by defeat of a major piece of government legislation.

The upper house of Canada's Parliament is the Senate, comprised of 104 members traditionally appointed by party patronage and serving to age 75.

Legislation becomes law by receiving 3 "readings" in the Commons, passing in the Senate and obtaining assent from the governor-general. The latter 2 steps are, in practice, mere formality.

The Prime Minister heads the executive branch of government composed of the cabinet and governor-general. The cabinet is chosen by the Prime Minister, almost always from among members of his party holding seats in the House of Commons.

Provincial governments follow a modified version of the Ottawa pattern, with a unicameral legislature and an executive head usually referred to as the Premier.

Politics

A new Canadian constitution, including a Charter of Rights guaranteeing basic rights and freedoms, was proclaimed Apr. 17, 1982, by Queen Elizabeth, thereby severing Canada's last formal legislative link with Britain. The document (known as the Constitution Act, 1982) includes a formula allowing the federal Parliament to amend its existing constitution (the British North America Act, now known as the Constitution Act, 1867) with the support of 7 provinces representing at least 50% of the Canadian population. But, in a major concession safeguarding provincial autonomy, provinces are given the right to "opt out" of any constitutional changes they may disagree with. The compromise constitutional agreement reached in November 1981, between Prime Minister Pierre Trudeau and 9 of the 10 provincial premiers (Quebec's Rene Levesque being the sole dissenter) ended months of heated debate between the federal and provincial governments.

While the constitutional agreement and the earlier resolution of an oil-pricing conflict between Ottawa and Alberta eased some causes of federal-provincial tension, many more remain.

The constitutional accord further isolated Quebec's separatist Parti Quebecois (PQ) government which viewed it as a challenge to the province's legislative autonomy, particularly regarding minority language rights—an area in which the New Charter of Rights is in conflict with Quebec's own language legislation. The PQ, returned to power by a wide margin in an April 1981 election in which Quebec separation from Canada was not a major issue, has said it will base its next campaign on separatism. The PQ can call an election any time up to April of 1986.

Newfoundland and Ottawa continue to squabble over control of offshore oil and gas resources. Provincial Premier Brian Peckford won a landslide victory in an April 1982 election in which he asked for a mandate to press for a large share of the resource revenue. Ottawa has sent the dispute to the Supreme Court of Canada.

In Alberta, the Western Canada Concept (a political party whose goal is to separate Western Canada from the rest of the nation) elected a member to the provincial legislature in a February 1982 by-election.

The increased political fragmentation of Canada was reflected in the most recent federal election held in 1980 in which voting was split along regional and linguistic lines. The Liberal Party, with Trudeau as leader, formed a majority government by capturing 74 of 75 seats in predominantly French-speaking Quebec but won only 2 of 80 seats west of Ontario. The Progressive Conservative Party, led by Joe Clark, won only one seat in Quebec but 51 in western Canada—an area of increasing political importance because of the westward shift of economic power, especially to oil-rich Alberta. The election results and voting pattern increased the alienation that some western Canadians feel towards the central government.

The Economy

Canada's troubled economic situation continued to worsen through the first half of 1982 as the unemployment rate hit a post-Depression high, inflation remained well above 10 percent, real economic growth declined, and the Canadian dollar fell to an all-time low compared to U.S. currency.

Unemployment reached 10.9% of the labor force in June 1982, the highest since the 1930s. Inflation, as measured by the Consumer Price Index, averaged 12.5% in 1981, the highest since 1948, and was at 11.3% in April 1982.

The Canadian economy entered a recession at the end of 1981 as real growth in the Gross Domestic Product (a measure of all goods and services produced in the country and considered the best barometer of economic activity) declined 1.5% during the last half of the year and began 1982 with a 2% decline in real GNP during the first 3 months.

Despite efforts by the Bank of Canada to prop up the Canadian dollar, it dropped to an all-time low near .77 U.S. in June 1982, reflecting both the strength of American currency and investors' lack of confidence in Canada's economy.

On June 28, 1982, Finance Minister Allan MacEachen unveiled a new budget aimed at reducing inflation to 6%. It included a mandatory 1983 6% salary increase ceiling for federal civil servants and employees of Crown corporations (including those with contracts calling for higher raises); public salaries would rise by only 5% in 1984 under the plan, and strikes by federal employees would be illegal during this time.

Principal Canadian industries are motor vehicle manufacturing, petroleum refining, pulp and paper production, slaughtering and meat processing, iron and steel production, the manufacture of miscellaneous machinery and equipment, saw and planing mill industries, and smelting and refining.

In Canada, an historical tradition of state aid necessitated by a harsh climate and sparse population has fostered development of a mixed economic system in which publicly-owned corporations exist alongside—and sometimes compete with—private enterprise. Most hydroelectric and many transportation and communication enterprises are government-owned. Air Canada and the Canadian National Railways, both large federal Crown corporations, compete with the privately-owned Canadian Pacific Ltd, whose 1981 operating revenue was the largest of any company in Canada.

Foreign Policy

Canada's major foreign ally and trading partner remains the United States with whom she shares a broad range of mutually beneficial ties. But relations between the two nations have been strained in recent years by disagreement over such issues as foreign investment policies, pollution, and fishing rights.

Through its National Energy Program and its Foreign Investment Review Agency, Canada aims to reduce foreign domination of its economy, especially its energy industry; U.S. officials have said these policies discriminate against American firms in Canada. Lengthy U.S.—Canadian negotiations to reduce "acid rain" pollution of both nations' lakes by industrial emmissions on either side of the border were unsuccessful as of the summer of 1982 when Canadian Environment Minister John Roberts accused the U.S. of "dragging its feet" in the negotiations. Prolonged U.S.-Canadian disputes over maritime boundaries and fish catch quotas still had not been settled by mid 1982.

In addition, Canada has opposed high U.S. interest rates (which lead to higher rates in Canada) and, at the June 1982 meeting of Western leaders, asked the Reagan administration to reconsider this policy.

Also in June 1982, Prime Minister Pierre Trudeau publicly disagreed with the U.S. policy of linking arms reduction negotiations with the Soviet Union to other issues in East-West relations. Trudeau called for a global freeze on the nuclear arsenals of both the U.S. and the Soviet Union and for negotiations between the two powers to reduce their existing weaponry.

A major recent Canadian foreign policy thrust calls for promotion of a North-South dialogue to reduce the economic gap between the developed nations of the northern hemisphere and the under-developed ones below the Equator. In a foreign policy speech to the House of Commons in July 1981, Trudeau called for "a major assault on world poverty" in the interests of justice and world security. The promotion of North-South relations is also seen by the Canadian government as a means of extending economic links and improving trade with such nations as Venezuela and Mexico—major suppliers of imported oil—as well as Brazil, Algeria, Saudi Arabia, Nigeria, and several Asian nations including China.

In support of Britain in its Falkland Islands dispute with Argentina, Canada in April 1982, recalled its ambassador in Argentina, banned shipments of military material to Argentina, and banned imports from that country.

Canada's Native Peoples

Canada's native population consists of 3 groups, the Indian, Inuit (Eskimo), and Métis. The Indian and Inuit are thought to have crossed from Asia via the Bering Sea several thousand years before the arrival of Europeans in North America. Metis are of mixed native Indian and non-Indian ancestry.

There are approximately 316,700 "status" Indians - those registered under the federal Indian Act - most of whom belong to one of 576 Indian bands. About 70% live on one of the 2,250 federal reserves or on other government lands set aside for their use. Only Newfoundland had no registered Indians. The majority (82%) live in Ontario and the 4 western provinces. In addition, there are an estimated one million non-registered Indians and Metis.

The number of Inuit (meaning "the people" in their language, Inuktitut; Eskimo is an Indian word adopted by European settlers) in Canada is approximately 23,000. More than 75% live in the Northwest Territories, the remainder in Arctic Quebec and northern Labrador.

Due to the remoteness of their settlements close to the northern coasts where sea mammals provided the chief source of food, fuel and clothing, the Inuit lifestyle was affected later and less directly than that of the Indian by the encroachment of western civilization. Many Inuit still live by their traditional skills of hunting, trapping and fishing as well as through the production and sale of artwork. But increasing numbers now find work outside their communities, particularly since the search for oil, gas and minerals has brought more jobs to the north.

Both Inuit and status Indians are entitled to a broad range of government benefits administered through the federal Dept. of Indian and Northern Affairs as well as through provincial and territorial governments. Indian people living on reserves are eligible for direct federal assistance in such areas as education, housing, social services, and community development.

In addition, approximately half the registered Indians in Canada (mainly those living in Ontario and the 3 Prairie provinces) are entitled to payments as a result of treaties between their ancestors and the federal government during the early 19th and early 20th centuries. In remote northern areas, however, no such legal settlements were made, and recently Indian and Inuit groups have pressed claims to aboriginal rights to vast areas of land in northern British Columbia, the Yukon and Northwest Territories, and northern Quebec and Labrador.

The federal government has re-affirmed a 1973 commitment to settle both comprehensive (based on aboriginal rights) and specific (treaty) claims. A 1975 agreement settled the claims of the Inuit and Cree of northern Quebec; in 1978 this settlement was extended to include the Naskapis of Schefferville. In October 1978, the government reached an agreement-in-principal with the Inuit of the western Arctic (the Inuvialiut).

Inuit cultural and legal interests are represented by district Inuit associations and nationally by the Inuit Tapirisat, founded in 1971. The interests of status Indians are represented by provincial Indian associations and, at the national level, by the National Indian Brotherhood, incorporated in 1970. The Métis and non-status Indians are represented by the Native Council of Canada.

Provinces of Canada

Alberta

People. Population (Jan. 1982: 2,212,300; **rank:** 4. **Pop. density:** 9 per sq. mi. **Urban** (1981) 77%. **Ethnic distrib.** (1981): English 81%; German 4.1%; Ukrainian 3%; French 2.8%. **Net migration** (1980-81) +38,128.

Geography: Total area: 255,290 sq. mi.; **rank:** 4. **Land area:** 248,800 sq. mi. **Forested land:** 131,660 sq. mi. **Location:** Canada's 2d most westerly province, bounded to the W by British Columbia, to the E by Saskatchewan, to the N by the Northwest Territories, and to the S by Montana. **Climate:** great variance in temperatures between regions and seasons; summer highs can range between 16°C and 32°C; winter temperatures can drop as low as −45°C; mean Jan. temperature in Edmonton is −14°C. **Topography:** ranges from the Rocky Mountains in the SW to flat prairie in the SE; the far north is a wilderness of forest and muskeg.

Economy. Principal industries: mining, oil production, agriculture, manufacturing, construction. **Principal manufactured goods:** foods and beverages, wood products, fabricated metal, transportation equipment, refined petroleum. **Value added by manufacture** (1979): $3 billion. **Gross Domestic Product** (1980): $40 billion. **Agriculture: Chief crops:** wheat, barley, rapeseed, sugar beets, flaxseed. **Livestock** (1981): 3,695,000 cattle; 1,280,000 pigs; 114,000 sheep. **Forestry production** (1979): $36 million. **Mineral production** (1980): total value, $16.4 billion; fuels, $15.7 billion (87% of national production of petroleum, 93% of natural gas); structural materials, $175 million. **Commercial fishing** (1979): $800,000. **Value of construction** (1979): $5.5 billion. **Employment distribution** (1981): 28% services; 17% trade; 11% construction; 9% manufacturing; 7.7% agriculture; 7% public administration. **Per capita income** (1980): $11,067. **Unemployment** (1981): 3.8%.

Finance: No. banks: 811; **No. credit unions, caisses populaires:** 154.

International airports: Edmonton, Calgary.

Federal government: No. federal employees (Dec. 1981). 11,538; **Federal payroll** (1981): $295 million.

Energy. Electricity production, by mwh, (1980): mineral, 20,558,979; hydroelectric, 2,035,397.

Education. No schools: 1,383 elementary; 168 secondary; 23 higher education. **Avg. salary, public school teachers** (1980-81): $24,819.

Provincial data. Motto: none. **Flower:** The Wild Rose. **Bird:** Great horned owl. **Date entered Confederation:** 1905. **Capital:** Edmonton.

Politics. Premier: Peter Lougheed (Progressive Conservative). **Leaders, opposition parties:** Ray Speaker (Social Credit), Grant Notley (New Democratic). **Composition of legislature** (May, 1982): PC 73; SC 3; NDP 1; Western Canada Concept 1; 1 independent. **Date of last general election:** Mar. 14, 1979.

Tourist attractions: Banff, Jasper, and Waterton Lakes national parks; resorts at Banff, Jasper and Lake Louise; spectacular skiing, hiking, trail riding and camping in the Canadian Rockies; the Badlands near Drumheller; Elk Island National Park.

British Columbia

People. Population (Jan. 1982): 2,737,700; **rank:** 3. **Pop. density:** 7.6 per sq. mi. **Urban** (1981) 78%. **Ethnic distrib.** (1981): English 82%; German 3.4%; Chinese 2.8%; French 1.7%. **Net migration** (1980-81): +37,949.

Geography. Total area: 365,950 sq. mi.; **rank:** 3. **Land area:** 358,970 sq. mi. **Forested land:** 201,158 sq. mi. **Location:** bounded to the N by the Yukon and Northwest Territories, to the NW by the Alaskan panhandle, to the W by the Pacific Ocean, to the E by Alberta, and to the S by Washington, Idaho and Montana. **Climate:** maritime with mild termperatures and abundant rainfall in the coastal areas; continental climate with temperature extremes in the interior and northeast. **Topography:** mostly mountainous except for the NE corner which is an extension of the

Great Plains.

Economy. Principal industries: forestry, mining, tourism, agriculture, fishing, manufacturing. **Principal manufactured goods:** wood products, paper and allied products, food and beverages, petroleum and coal products, primary metals, transportation equipment. **Value added by manufacture** (1979): $6.5 billion. **Gross Domestic Product** (1980): $36.5 billion (including GDP for Yukon and NWT). **Agriculture: Chief crops:** fruits and vegetables, barley, oats. **Livestock** (1981): 654,000 cattle; 245,000 pigs; 34,000 sheep. **Forestry production** (1979): $1.2 billion. **Mineral production** (1980): $2.8 billion; fuels, $968 million; metals, $1.4 billion; structural materials, $247 million. **Commercial fishing** (1979): $333 million. **Value of construction** (1979): $2.8 billion. **Employment distribution** (1981): 30% services; 18% trade; 14% manufacturing; 7.6% construction; 6% public administration; 2% agriculture. **Per capita income** (1980): $11,027. **Unemployment** (1981): 6.7%.

Finance: No. banks: 862; **No. credit unions, caisses populaires:** 150.

International airports: Vancouver, Victoria.

Federal government: No. federal employees (Dec. 1981). 8,033. **Federal payroll** (1981): $209 million.

Energy. Electricity production, by mwh, (1981): mineral, 23,759, hydroelectric, 38,616,114.

Education. No schools: 1,560 elementary; 332 secondary; 27 higher education. **Avg. salary, public school teachers** (1980-81): $25,206.

Provincial data. Motto: Splendor Sine Occasu (Spendor Without Diminishment). **Flower:** Dogwood. **Bird:** None. **Date entered Confederation:** 1871. **Capital:** Victoria.

Politics. Premier: William R. Bennett (Social Credit). **Leaders, opposition parties:** Dave Barrett (New Democratic), Shirley McLoughlin (Liberal), Brian Westwood (Progressive Conservative). **Composition of legislature** (May 1982): SC 31; NDP 26. **Date of last general election:** May 10, 1979.

Tourist attractions. Victoria: Butchart Gardens, Crystal Garden, Provincial Museum; Vancouver: Stanley Park Zoo, Capilano Canyon, Gastown, Public Aquarium, Grouse Mountain, Planetarium; also Pacific Rim National Park, the Gulf Islands, Okanagan Valley, Yellowhead Highway, Totem Triangle Tour.

Manitoba

People. Population (Jan. 1982): 1,034,400; **rank:** 5. **Pop. density:** 4.8 per sq. mi. **Urban** (1981) 71.2%. **Ethnic distrib.** (1981): English 71.7%; German 7.3%; Ukrainian 5.7%; French 5.1%; Native Indians 2.5%. **Net migration** (1980-81): −11,276.

Geography. Total area: 250,950 sq. mi.; **rank:** 6. **Land area:** 211,720 sq. mi. **Forested land:** 99,227 sq. mi. **Location:** bounded to the N by the Northwest Territories, to the S by Minnesota and North Dakota, to the E by Ontario and Hudson Bay, to the W by Saskatchewan. **Climate:** continental, with seasonal extremes: Winnipeg avg. Jan. low −23°C, avg. July high 26°C. **Topography:** the land rises gradually S and W from Hudson Bay; most of the province is between 500 and 1,000 feet above sea level.

Economy. Principal industries: manufacturing, agriculture, slaughtering and meat processing, mining. **Principal manufactured goods:** agricultural implements, processed food, machinery, transportation equipment, clothing. **Value added by manufacture** (1979): $1.66 billion. **Gross Domestic Product** (1980): $11.1 billion. **Agriculture: Chief crops:** cereal grains, mustard seed, sunflower seeds, rape, flax. **Livestock** (1981): 1,060,000 cattle; 826,300 pigs; 13,400 sheep; **Forestry production** (1979): $13.8 million. **Mineral production** (1980): total value, $803 million; metals, $665 million; structural materials, $72 million; petroleum, $55 million. **Commercial fishing:** (1979): $10.8 million. **Value of construction** (1979): $660 million. **Employment distribution** (1981): 29% services; 17% trade; 15% manufacturing; 9% agriculture; 7% public administration; 5% construction. **Per capita income** (1980): $8,876. **Unemployment** (1981): 6.0%.

Finance: No. banks: 360; **No. credit unions, caisses populaires:** 143.

International airports: Winnipeg.

Federal Government: No. federal employees (Dec. 1981): 12,881. **Federal payroll** (1981): $320 million.

Energy. Electricity production, by mwh, (1981): mineral, 364,051; hydroelectric, 17,899,048.

Education. No. schools: 706 elementary; 113 secondary; 15 higher education. **Avg. salary, public school teachers** (1980-81): $23,010.

Provincial data. Motto: None. **Flower:** Prairie crocus. **Bird:** none. **Date entered Confederation:** July 15, 1870. **Capital:** Winnipeg.

Politics. Premier: Howard Pawley (New Democratic). **Leaders, opposition parties:** Sterling Lyon (Progressive Conservative). **Composition of legislature:** (May, 1982): NDP 34; PC 23. **Date of last general election:** Nov. 17, 1981.

Tourist attractions. Museum of Man and Nature (Winnipeg), Lower Fort Garry (near Lockport), Red River cruises, Riding Mountain National Park, canoeing, fishing and camping on northern lakes.

New Brunswick

People. Population (Jan. 1982): 712,500; **rank:** 8. **Pop. density:** 24.8 per sq. mi. **Urban** (1981) 51.1%. **Ethnic distrib.** (1981): English 65%; French 33.6%. **Net migration** (1980-81): −2,422.

Geography. Total area: 28,360 sq. mi.; **rank:** 8. **Land area:** 27,840 sq. mi. **Forested land:** 25,482 sq. mi. **Location:** bounded by Quebec to the N, Nova Scotia and the Bay of Fundy to the S, the Gulf of St. Lawrence and Northumberland Strait to the E, and Maine to the W. **Climate:** humid continental climate except along the shores where there is a marked maritime effect; avg. Jan. low in Fredericton is −14°C, avg. July high 22°C. **Topography:** upland, lowland and plateau regions throughout the province.

Economy. Principal industries: manufacturing, mining, forestry, pulp and paper. **Principal manufactured goods:** paper and allied products, wood products, fish products, semi-processed mineral products. **Value added by manufacture** (1979): $950.6 million. **Gross Domestic Product** (1980): $5.2 billion. **Agriculture: Chief crops:** potatoes, apples, blueberries, oats. **Livestock** (1981): 103,000 cattle; 61,000 pigs; 8,700 sheep. **Forestry production** (1979): $108.5 million. **Mineral production** (1980): total value, $372 million; metals, $303 million; structural materials, $41 million; coal, $17 million. **Commercial fishing** (1979): $54 million. **Value of construction** (1979): $570 million. **Employment distribution** (1981): 28% services; 19% trade; 15% manufacturing; 8% public administration; 7% construction; 2.7% agriculture. **Per capita income** (1980): $7,085. **Unemployment** (1981): 11.7%.

Finance: No. banks: 181; **No. credit unions, caisses populaires:** 130.

International airports: none.

Federal Government: No. federal employees (Dec. 1981): 6,697. **Federal payroll** (1981): $163.4 million.

Energy. Electricity production, by mwh, (1980): mineral, 4,470,515; hydroelectric, 3,752,335.

Education. No. schools: 425 elementary; 65 secondary; 13 higher education. **Avg. salary, public school teachers** (1980-81): $21,225.

Provincial Data. Motto: Spem Reduxit (Hope Restored). **Flower:** Purple violet. **Bird:** none. **Date entered Confederation:** 1867. **Capital:** Fredericton.

Politics. Premier: Richard Hatfield (Progressive Conservative). **Leaders, opposition parties:** Doug Young (Liberal). **Composition of legislature** (May, 1982): P.C. 31; Lib. 27. **Date of last general election:** Oct. 23, 1978.

Tourist attractions: Roosevelt-Campobello International Memorial Park; the tidal bore at Chignacto Bay (Moncton); Magnetic Hill (Moncton); sport salmon fishing in the Miramichi River; 108 covered bridges including the world's longest at Hartland.

Newfoundland

People. Population (Jan. 1982): 588,300; **rank:** 9. **Pop. density:** 4 per sq. mi. **Urban** (1981) 58.6%. **Ethnic distrib.** (1981): English 98.7%. **Net migration** (1980-81): −1,385.

Geography. Total area: 156,650 sq. mi.; **rank:** 7. **Land area:** 143,510 sq. mi. **Forested land:** 130,501 sq. mi. **Location:** 2 parts: a 43,010 sq. mi. Atlantic island and 100,500 sq. mi. mainland Labrador, bordered to the E by northern Quebec and to the W by the Atlantic Ocean. **Climate:** ranges from subarctic in Labrador and northern tip of island to humid continental with cool summers and heavy precipitation. **Topography:** highlands of the Long Range (max. elev. 2,673 ft.) along the western coast; central plateau contains uplands descending to lowlands towards the northeast; interior barren and rocky with many lakes and bogs; Labrador is part of the Canadian Shield.

Economy. Principal industries: mining, manufacturing, fishing, pulp and paper, electricity production. **Principal manufactured goods:** fish products, paper products. **Value added by manufacture** (1979): $497.9 million. **Gross Domestic Product** (1980): $3.7 billion. **Agriculture: Forestry production** (1979): $39.3 million. **Mineral production** (1980): total value, $1 billion; metals, $969 million; asbestos, $45 million; structural materials, $16 million. **Commercial fishing:** (1979) $162 million. **Value of construction** (1979): $447 million. **Employment distribution** (1981): 26% services; 18% trade; 14.7% manufacturing; 8.7% public administration; 7.8% construction. **Per capita income** (1980): $6,343. **Unemployment** (1981): 14.1%.

Finance: No. banks: 154; **no. credit unions, caisses populaires:** 14.

International airports: Gander.

Federal Government: No. federal employees (Dec. 1981): 4,548. **Federal payroll** (1981): $101.5 million.

Energy. Electricity production, by mwh, (1981): mineral, 411,775; hydroelectric, 43,691,882.

Education. No. schools: 530 elementary; 136 secondary; 7 higher education. **Avg. salary, public school teachers** (1980-81): $21,749.

Provincial data. Motto: Quaerite prime regnum Dei (Seek ye first the kingdom of God). **Flower:** Pitcher plant. **Bird:** none. **Date entered Confederation:** 1949. **Capital:** St. John's.

Politics. Premier: Brian Peckford (Progressive Conservative). **Leaders, opposition parties:** Len Stirling, (Liberal) Peter Fenwick, (New Democratic). **Composition of legislature** (May, 1982): PC 44; Lib. 8. **Date of last general election:** April 6, 1982.

Tourist attractions: numerous picturesque "outport" fishing villages; Signal Hill National Historical Park (St. John's); the Aviation Museum at Gander International Airport; Witless Bay Island Seabird Sanctuary.

Nova Scotia

People. Population (Jan. 1982): 859,400; **rank:** 7. **Pop. density:** 42 per sq. mi. **Urban** (1981) 55.19. **Ethnic distrib.** (1981): English 93.6%; French 4.3%. **Net migration** (1980-81): −1,197.

Geography. Total area: 21,420 sq. mi.; **rank:** 9. **Land area:** 20,400 sq. mi. **Forested land:** 15,830 sq. mi. **Location:** connected to New Brunswick by a 17-mi. isthmus, otherwise surrounded by water - the Gulf of St. Lawrence, Atlantic Ocean and Bay of Fundy. **Climate:** humid continental, with some moderating effects due to the province's maritime location; avg. July temperature high in Halifax is 23°C, avg. Jan. low −10°C. **Topography:** the Atlantic Uplands in the southern half of the province descend to lowlands in the northern portion; 6,479 mi. of coastline, 3,000 lakes, hundreds of rivers.

Economy. Principal industries: manufacturing, fishing, mining, tourism, agriculture, petroleum refining. **Principal manufactured goods:** paper and allied products, petroleum and coal products, fish products. **Value added by manufacture** (1979): $1.1 billion. **Gross Domestic Product** (1980); $6.4 billion. **Agriculture: Chief crops:** apples, blueberrries, strawberries, oats, potatoes. **Livestock** (1981): 127,000 cattle; 110,000 pigs; 28,000 sheep. **Forestry production** (1979): $28.6 million. **Mineral production** (1980): total value, $247 million; coal, $133 million; structural materials, $56 million; salt, $27 million. **Commercial fishing** (1979): $226.3 million. **Value of construction** (1979): $542.9 million. **Employment distribution** (1981): 30% services; 19% trade; 14% manufacturing; 9% public administration; 7% construction; 2.2% agriculture. **Per capita income** (1980): $7,845. **Unemployment** (1981): 10.2%.

Finance: No. banks: 250; **No. credit unions, caisses populaires:** 116.

International airports: Halifax.

Federal Government: No. federal employees (Dec. 1981): 4,405. **Federal payroll** (1981): $102 million.

Energy. Electricity production, by mwh, (1981): mineral, 5,009,826; hydroelectric, 1,126,873.

Education. No. schools: 536 elementary; 79 secondary; 24 higher education. **Avg. salary, public school teachers** (1980-81): $23,775.

Provincial Data. Motto: Munit Haec et Altera Vincit (One Defends and the Other Conquers). **Flower:** Trailing arbutus. **Bird:** None. **Date entered Confederation:** 1867. **Capital:** Halifax.

Politics. Premier: John M. Buchanan (Progressive conservative). **Leaders, opposition parties:** A.M. "Sandy" Cameron (Liberal); Alexa McDonough (New Democratic). **Composition of legislature** (May, 1982): P.C. 37; Lib. 13; NDP 1; 1 independent. **Date of last general election:** Sept. 19, 1978.

Tourist attractions: Cabot Trail around Cape Breton Island; Fortress Louisbourg; Peggy's Cove; Alexander Graham Bell Museum (Baddeck); the Miners' Museum (Glace Bay); Nova Scotia Museum (Halifax); Citadel Hill (Halifax).

Ontario

People. Population (Jan. 1982); 8,664,600; **rank:** 1. **Pop. density:** 25 per sq. mi. **Urban** (1981) 81.7% **Ethnic distrib.** (1981): English 77.4%; French 5.5%; Italian 3.9%; German 2%; Portuguese 1.3%. **Net migration** (1980-81) −33,248.

Geography. Total area: 412,580 sq. mi.; **rank:** 2. **Land area:** 344,090 sq. mi. **Forested land:** 220,077 sq. mi. **Location:** Canada's most centrally-situated province, with Quebec on the E and Manitoba to the W; extends N to shores of James and Hudson Bays; southern boundary with New York, Michigan, Minnesota, and 4 Great Lakes. **Climate:** ranges from humid continental in southern regions to subarctic in the far north, westerly winds bring winter storms; the Great Lakes moderate winter temperatures. **Topography:** 2/3 of province is Precambrian rock of the Canadian Shield; lowland areas lie along the shores of Hudson Bay, the St. Lawrence River and the southern Great Lakes region.

Economy. Principal industries: manufacturing, construction, tourism, agriculture, mining, forestry, fisheries and wildlife. **Principal manufactured goods:** motor vehicles, iron and steel, motor vehicle parts and accessories, foods and beverages, paper and allied products. **Value added by manufacture** (1979): $32.7 billion. **Gross Domestic Product** (1980): $111.7 billion. **Agriculture: Chief crops:** corn, wheat, oats, barley, soybeans, tobacco, tree fruits. **Livestock** (1981): 3,030,000 cattle; 3,155,000 pigs; 162,000 sheep. **Forestry production** (1979): $279 million. **Mineral production** (1980): total value, $4.6 billion; metals, $3.9 billion; structural materials, $606 million. **Commercial fishing** (1979): $26 million. **Value of construction** (1979): $5.8 billion. **Employment distribution** (1981): 29% services; 25% manufacturing; 16% trade; 6% public administration; 5.5% construction; 3.4% agriculture. **Per capita income:** (1980): $10,614. **Unemployment** (1981): 6.6%

Finance: No. banks: 2,849; **No credit unions, caisses populaires:** 969

International airports: Toronto, Ottawa.

Federal Government: No. federal employees (Dec. 1981): 40,748. **Federal payroll** (1981): $993 million.

Energy. Electricity production, by mwh, (1980): mineral, 32,260,527; hydroelectric, 36,478,704; nuclear, 36,891,505.

Education. No. schools: 4,555 elementary; 830 secondary; 51 higher education. **Avg. salary, public school teachers** (1980-81): $26,045.

Provincial data. Motto: Ut Incepit Fidelis Sic Permanet (Loyal she began, loyal she remains). **Flower:** White trillium. **Bird:** none. **Date entered Confederation:** 1867. **Capital:** Toronto.

Politics. Premier: William (Bill) Davis (Progressive Conservative), **Leaders, opposition parties:** David Peterson (Liberal); Bob Rae (New Democratic). **Composition of legislature** (May, 1982): PC 70; Lib. 34; NDP 21. **Date of last general election:** March 19, 1981.

Tourist attractions. Toronto C.N. Tower, Ontario Science Centre, Ontario Place, Metro Toronto Zoo, McLaughlin Planetarium, Black Creek Pioneer Village, Canadian Nation Exhibition (mid Aug. to Labor Day); Ottawa's Parliament buildings; Niagara Falls; Polar Bear Express and Agawa Canyon train rides into northern Ontario.

Prince Edward Island

People. Population (Jan. 1982): 124,900; **rank:** 10. **Pop. density:** 56.2 per sq. mi. **Urban** (1981) 36.3% **Ethnic distrib.** (1981): English 93.9%; French 5%. **Net migration** (1980-81): −938.

Geography. Total area: 2,180 sq. mi.; **rank:** 10. **Land area:** 2,180 sq. mi. **Forested land:** 1,158 sq. mi. **Location:** an island 140 mi. long, between 40 and 140 mi. wide, situated in the Gulf of St. Lawrence approx. 10 mi. from the coasts of Nova Scotia and New Brunswick. **Climate:** humid continental with temperatures moderated by maritime location; avg. Jan. low in Charlottetown is −11°C, avg. July high 23°C. **Topography:** gently rolling hills; sharply indented coastline; many streams but only small rivers and lakes.

Economy. Principal industries: agriculture, tourism, fisheries, light manufacturing. **Principal manufactured goods:** paint, farm vehicles, metal products, electronic equipment. **Value added by manufacture** (1979): $85 million. **Gross Domestic Product** (1980): $787 million. **Agriculture: Chief crops:** potatoes, mixed grains, oats, barley. **Livestock** (1981): 99,000 cattle; 101,500 pigs; 5,000 sheep. **Mineral production** (1980): total value, $2.3 million, all from sand and gravel. **Commercial fishing:** (1979): $29.4 million. **Value of construction** (1979): $84 million. **Employment distribution** (1981): 30% services; 17% trade; 13% agriculture; 9% manufacturing; 9% public administration; 7% construction. **Per capita income** (1980): $7,048. **Unemployment** (1981): 11.4%.

Finance: No. banks: 33; **No. credit unions, caisses populaires:** 11.

International airports: none.

Federal Government: No. federal employees (Dec. 1981): 820. **Federal payroll:** (1981): $17.9 million.

Energy. Electricity production, by mwh, (1981): mineral, 29,901.

Education. No. schools: 60 elementary; 13 secondary; 3 higher education. **Avg. salary, public school teachers** (1980-81): $22,359.

Provincial Data. Motto: Parva Sub Ingenti (The small under the protection of the large). **Flower:** Lady's slipper. **Bird:** Blue jay. **Date entered Confederation:** 1873. **Capital:** Charlottetown.

Politics. Premier: James M. Lee (Progressive Conservative). **Leaders, opposition parties:** Joe Ghiz (Liberal), Douglas Murray (New Democratic). **Composition of legislature** (May, 1982): P.C. 21; Lib. 10; 1 vacant. **Date of last general election:** Apr. 23, 1979.

Tourist attractions: P.E.I. National Park; beaches all along the coastline; 9 golf courses; 70 campgrounds; Summerside Lobster Carnival, 3d wk. in July; Charlottetown Old Home Week, 3d wk. in Aug.; Charlottetown Confederation Centre; Woodleigh Replicas (Burlington).

Quebec

People. Population (Jan. 1982): 6,358,200; **rank:** 2. **Pop. density:** 12.3 per sq. mi. **Urban** (1981) 77.6%. **Ethnic distrib.** (1981): French 82.4%; English 11%; Italian 2%. **Net migration** (1980-81): −23,631. **Geography. Total area:** 594,860 sq. mi.; **rank:** 1. **Land area:** 523,860 sq. mi. **Forested land:** 237,065 sq. mi. **Location:** borders Ontario on the W and Labrador and New Brunswick on the E; extends N to Hudson Strait and NW to James and Hudson Bays; the southern border touches New York, Vermont, New Hampshire and Maine. **Climate:** varies from subarctic in the northern half of the province to continental in the southern populated regions; avg. Jan. low in Montreal is −14°C, avg. Jan. High 26°C. **Topography:** half a million sq. mi. of Quebec consists of the Laurentian Uplands, part of the Canadian Shield; Appalachian Highlands are in southeastern Quebec; lowlands form a small area along the shore of the St. Lawrence River.

Economy. Principal industries: manufacturing, agriculture, electrical production, mining, meat processing, petroleum refining. **Principal manufactured goods:** foods and beverages, clothing, textiles, paper and paper products, furniture. **Value added by manufacture** (1979): $17.11 billion. **Gross Domestic Product** (1980): $67.8 billion. **Agriculture: Chief crops:** oats, corn grains, potatoes, mixed grains, tame hay, apples. **Livestock** (1981): 1,605,000 cattle; 3,150,000 pigs; 58,000 sheep. **Forestry production** (1979): $356 million. **Mineral production** (1980): total value, $2.5 billion; metals, $1.4 billion; asbestos, $496 million; structural materials, $402 million. **Commercial fishing** (1979): $41.6 million. **Value of construction** (1979): $4.3 billion. **Employment distribution** (1981): 30% services; 22% manufacturing; 16% trade; 7% public administration; 5% construction; 2.8% agriculture. **Per capita income** (1980): $9,370. **Unemployment** (1981): 10.4%.

Finance: No. banks: 1,455; **no. credit unions, caisses populaires:** 1,554.

International airports: Dorval, Mirabel (both near Montreal).

Federal Government: No. federal employees (Dec. 1981): 44,474. **Federal payroll** (1981): $1.1 billion.

Energy. Electricity production, by mwh, (1981): hydroelectric, 84,678,213.

Education. No. schools: 1,955 elementary; 673 secondary; 91 higher education. **Avg. salary, public school teachers** (1980-81): $n.a.

Provincial Data. Motto Je me souviens (I remember). **Flower:** Fleur de Lys. **Birds:** Alouette (lark). **Date entered Confederation:** 1867. **Capital:** Quebec City.

Politics. Premier: Rene Levesque (Parti Quebecois). **Leaders, opposition parties:** Claude Ryan (Liberal); **Composition of legislature** (May, 1982): PQ 79; Lib. 43. **Date of last general election:** April 13, 1981.

Tourist attractions: Quebec City, often described as North America's "most European city", and sophisticated Montreal each offer numerous attractions; the north shore of the St. Lawrence River and the Gaspé Peninsula are picturesque.

Saskatchewan

People. Population (Jan. 1982): 988,400; **rank:** 6. **Pop. density:** 4.4 per sq. mi. **Urban** (1981) 58.2% **Ethnic distrib.** (1981): English 79.6%; German 5.2%; Ukrainian 4.6%; French 2.6%; Native Indian 2.4%. **Net migration** (1980-81): −1,348.

Geography. Total area: 251,870 sq. mi.; **rank:** 5. **Land area:** 220,350 sq. mi. **Forested land:** 54,054 sq. mi. **Location:** borders on the Northwest Territories to the N, Manitoba to the E, Alberta to the W, and Montana and North Dakota to the S. **Climate:** continental, with cold winters (Jan. avg. low in Regina is −23°C) and hot summers (July avg. high in Regina is 26°C). **Topography:** southern 2/3ds of province is plains and grassland; northern 3d is Canadian Shield.

Economy. Principal industries: agriculture, mining of

potash, meat processing, electricity production, petroleum refining. **Principal manufactured goods:** foods and beverages, agricultural implements, fabricated metals, nonmetallic mineral products. **Value added by manufacture** (1979): $693 million. **Gross domestic product** (1980): $13 billion. **Agriculture: Chief crops:** wheat (57% of national total), barley, oats, mustard seed, rapeseed, flax. **Livestock** (1981): 2,095,000 cattle; 625,000 pigs; 65,000 sheep. **Forestry production** (1979): $24 million. **Mineral production** (1980): total value, $2.3 billion; potash, $1 billion; petroleum, $864 million; structural materials, $52 million. **Commercial fishing** (1979): $2.7 million. **Value of construction** (1979): $1 billion. **Employment distribution** (1981): 27% services; 20% agriculture; 17% trade; 7% public administration; 7% construction; 6% manufacturing. **Per capita income** (1980): $9,028. **Unemployment** (1981): 4.6%.

Finance: No. banks: 394; **No. credit unions, caisses populaires:** 225.

International airports: none.

Federal Government: No. Federal employees (Dec. 1981): 4,232. **Federal payroll** (1981): $114.9 million.

Energy. Electricity production, by mwh, (1981): mineral, 6,221,932; hydroelectric, 3,014,975.

Education. No. schools: 909 elementary; 143 secondary; 6 higher education. **Avg. salary, public school teachers** (1980-81): $23,025.

Provincial Data. Motto: none. **Flower:** Red prairie lily. **Bird:** Prairie sharp-tailed grouse. **Date entered Confederation:** 1905. **Capital:** Regina.

Politics. Premier: Grant Devine (Progressive Conservative). **Leader, opposition party:** Allan Blakeney (New Democratic). **Composition of legislature** (May, 1982): PC 57; NDP 7. **Date of last general election:** Apr. 26, 1982.

Tourist attractions. Regina: RCMP Museum, Museum of Natural History, Wascana Centre; Western Development Museums located at Saskatoon, Yorkton, North Battleford, Moose Jaw.

Territories of Canada

In addition to its 10 provinces, Canada contains the Yukon and Northwest Territories making up more than a third of the nation's land area but less than .3% of its population. A resident commissioner in each territory is appointed by the federal government which retains control over natural resources excluding wildlife. An elected legislative assembly in each territory exercises jurisdiction over such matters as education, housing, social services and renewable resources. The Commissioner of the Northwest Territories serves as chairman of and acts on the advice of a 9-member executive committee, 7 of them appointed from a 22-member elected assembly. The Yukon commissioner acts on the advice of a 5-member executive council, all of whom are appointed on the recommendation of the leader of the majority party in the assembly.

The NWT elects 2 members to the federal parliament, the Yukon one member. Each territory has one Senate representative. There is strong support in both territories for increased autonomy or provincial status.

The Yukon

*Data applies to both Territories.

People. Population (Jan. 1982): 22,600; **Pop. density:** 0.1 per sq. mi. **Urban** (1981) 64%. **Ethnic distrib. by mother tongue** (1981): English 87.4%; Native Indian 3.6%; French 2.5%; German 2.1%. (Using other criteria Native Indians make up 19% of the population). **Net migration** (1980-81): +144.

Geography. Total area: 186,660 sq. mi. **Land area:** 184,930 sq. mi. **Forested land:** 84,556 sq. mi. **Location:** extreme northwestern area of mainland Canada; bounded on the N by the Beaufort Sea, on the S by British Columbia, on the E by the Mackenzie District of the Northwest Territories, and on the W by Alaska. **Climate:** great variance in temperatures; warm summers, very cold winters; low precipitation. **Topography:** main feature is the Yukon plateau with 21 peaks exceeding 10,000 ft.; open tundra in the far north.

Economy. Principal industries: mining, tourism. **Principal manufactured goods:** small amounts of cement, explosives, forest products, and outdoor recreation equipment. **Value added by manufacture** (1979) $10.5 million*. **Gross domestic product** (1980): $923 million*. **Agriculture:** hay, oats, vegetable gardens for local use. **Mineral production** (1980): total value, $361 million—all from metals. **Commercial fishing:** (1979) $2 million*. **Value of construction** (1979): $274 million*. **Per capita income** (1980): $10,231.* **No. of banks:** 13.

Federal Government: No. federal employees (Dec. 1981): 484. **Federal payroll** (1981): $11.6 million.

Energy. Electricity production, by mwh, (1981): hydroelectric, 290,045.

Education. No. schools: 22 elementary; 1 secondary; 0 higher education. **Avg. salary, public school teachers** (1980-81): $27,445.

Territorial Data. Flower: Fireweed. **Date established:** June 13, 1898. **Capital:** Whitehorse. **Commissioner:** Doug Bell. **Party leaders:** Chris Pearson (Progressive Conservative), Ron Veale (Liberal), Tony Penikett (New Democratic). **Composition of assembly** (June 1982): P.C. 9; NDP 6; 1 independent. **Date of last general election:** June 7, 1982.

Tourist attractions: Historic sites from the Gold Rush period in Whitehorse and Dawson City; Miles Canyon; Kluane National Park.

The Northwest Territories

People. Population (Jan. 1982): 44,100; **Pop. density:** 0.04 per sq. mi. **Urban** (1981) 48% **Ethnic distrib. by mother tongue** (1981): English 54.1%; Inuit 28.9%; Native Indian 10.7%; French 2.7%. (Using other criteria the Inuit make up 34% of the population, Native Indians 18%.) **Net migration** (1980-81): −776.

Geography. Total area: 1,322,900 sq. mi. **Land area:** 1,271,440 sq. mi. **Forested land:** 18,532 sq. mi. **Location:** all land north of the 60th parallel between the Yukon Territory and Hudson Bay and all northern islands east to Greenland; land area bounded by the Yukon Territory to the W, Hudson Bay to the E, the Beaufort Sea to the N and B.C, Alta., Sask. and Man. to S. **Climate:** extreme temperatures and low precipitation; Arctic and sub-Arctic. **Topography:** mostly tundra plains formed on the rocks of the Canadian Shield; the Mackenzie Lowland is a continuation of the Great Plains; the Mackenzie River Valley is forested.

Economy. Principal industries: mining, mineral and hydrocarbon exploration; oil refining. **Value added by manufacture** (1979): see Yukon. **Gross domestic product** (1980): see Yukon. **Agriculture:** scattered market gardening in the southern Mackenzie district only. **Mineral production** (1980): total value, $425 million; metals, $367 million; fuels, $57 million. **Commercial fishing:** (1979): see Yukon. **Value of construction** (1979): see Yukon. **Per capita income** (1980): see Yukon. **No. of banks** 16.

Federal Government: No. federal employees (Dec. 1981): 463. **Federal payroll** (1981); $16.5 million.

Energy. Electricity production, by mwh, (1981): hydroelectric, 230,584.

Education. No. schools: 64 elementary; 7 secondary; 0 higher education. **Avg. salary, public school teachers** (1980-81): $29,448.

Territorial Data. Flower: Mountain avens. **Date Established:** June 22, 1869. **Capital:** Yellowknife. **Commissioner:** John H. Parker. **Council:** 22 independent elected representatives.

Tourist attractions: Wood Buffalo, Auyuittuq, and Nahanni National Parks; Mackenzie River and Delta; annual Midnight Golf Tournament in Yellowknife July 21.

Head of State and Cabinet

Canada's official head of state, Queen Elizabeth of England, who succeeded to the throne in 1952, is represented by Governor-General Rt. Hon. Edward Schreyer, appointed in 1979. Titles: Minister unless otherwise stated or *Minister of State.

(in order of precedence, April 1982)

Prime Minister — Pierre Elliott Trudeau
Deputy Prime Minister and Minister of Finance — Allan J. MacEachen
Transport — Jean-Luc Pepin
Justice, Attorney General of Canada, *Social Development — Jean Chrétien
Indian Affairs and Northern Development — John C. Munro
***Economic and Regional Development** — H.A. (Bud) Olson
Industry, Trade, and Commerce; Regional Economic Expansion — Herb Gray
Agriculture — Eugene F. Whelan
Consumer and Corporate Affairs and Minister responsible for Canada Post Corporation — André Ouellet
Energy, Mines and Resources — Marc Lalonde
Leader of the Government in the Senate — Raymond J. Perrault
Fisheries and Oceans — Roméo A. LeBlanc
Environment, *Science and Technology — John Roberts
National Health and Welfare — Monique Bégin
Supply and Services — Jean-Jacques Blais
Communications — Francis Fox
National Defence — Gilles Lamontagne
***External Relations** — Pierre De Bane
***Canadian Wheat Board** — Hazen R. Argue
Secretary of State of Canada and Minister responsible for Fitness and Amateur Sports — Gerald A. Regan
***External Affairs** — Mark MacGuigan
Solicitor General of Canada — Robert P. Kaplan
***Multiculturalism** — James S. Fleming
National Revenue — William Rompkey
***Finance** — Pierre Bussieres
***Small Businesses and Tourism** — Charles Lapointe
***International Trade** — Edward Lumley
President of the Queen's Privy Council for Canada — Yvon Pinard
President of the Treasury Board — Donald Johnston
Employment and Immigration — Lloyd Axworthy
Public Works — Paul Cosgrove
***Mines** — Judy Erola
Minister of State — Jack Austin
Labour — Charles L. Caccia
Minister of State — Serge Joyal
Veterans Affairs — W. Bennett Campbell

Governors-General of Canada Since Confederation, 1867

Name	Term
The Viscount Monck of Ballytrammon	1867-1868
The Baron Lisgar of Lisgar and Bailieborough	1869-1872
The Earl of Dufferin	1872-1878
The Marquis of Lorne	1878-1883
The Marquis of Lansdowne	1883-1888
The Baron Stanley of Preston	1888-1893
The Earl of Aberdeen	1893-1898
The Earl of Minto	1898-1904
The Earl Grey	1904-1911
Field Marshall H.R.H. The Duke of Connaught	1911-1916
The Duke of Devonshire	1916-1921
General The Baron Byng of Vimy	1921-1926
The Viscount Willingdon of Ratton	1926-1931
The Earl of Bessborough	1931-1935
The Baron Tweedsmuir of Elsfield	1935-1940
Major General The Earl of Athlone	1940-1946
Field Marshall The Viscount Alexander of Tunis	1946-1952
The Right Hon. Vincent Massey	1952-1959
General The Right Hon. Georges P. Vanier	1959-1967
The Right Hon. Roland Michener	1967-1974
The Right Hon. Jules Leger	1974-1979
The Right Hon. Edward Schreyer	1979-

Fathers of Confederation

Union of the British North American colonies into the Dominion of Canada was discussed and its terms negotiated at 3 confederation conferences held at Charlottetown (C), Sept. 1, 1864; Quebec (Q), Oct. 10, 1864; and London (L), Dec. 4, 1866. The names of delegates are followed by the provinces they represented. Canada refers to what are now the provinces of Ontario and Quebec.

Adams G. Archibald, N.S.	(C,Q,L)
George Brown, Canada	(C,Q)
Alexander Campbell, Canada	(C,Q)
Frederick B.T. Carter, Nfld.	(Q)
George-Etienne Cartier, Canada	(C,Q,L)
Edward B. Chandler, N.B.	(C,Q)
Jean-Charles Chapais, Canada	(Q)
James Cockburn, Canada	(Q)
George H. Coles, P.E.I.	(C,Q)
Robert B. Dickey, N.S.	(Q)
Charles Fisher, N.B.	(Q,L)
Alexander T. Galt, Canada	(C,Q,L)
John Hamilton Gray, N.B.	(C,Q)
John Hamilton Gray, P.E.I.	(C,Q)
Thomas Heath Haviland, P.E.I.	(Q)
William A. Henry, N.S.	(C,Q,L)
William P. Howland, Canada	(L)
John M. Johnson, N.B.	(C,Q,L)
Hector L. Langevin, Canada	(C,Q,L)
Jonathan McCully, N.S.	(C,Q,L)
A.A. Macdonald, P.E.I.	(C,Q)
John A. Macdonald, Canada	(C,Q,L)
William McDougall, Canada	(C,Q,L)
Thomas D'Arcy McGee, Canada	(C,Q)
Peter Mitchell, N.B.	(Q,L)
Oliver Mowat, Canada	(Q)
Edward Palmer, P.E.I.	(C,Q)
William H. Pope, P.E.I.	(C,Q)
John W. Ritchie, N.S.	(L)
J. Ambrose Shea, Nfld.	(Q)
William H. Steeves, N.B.	(C,Q)
Sir Etienne-Paschal Tache, Canada	(Q)
Samuel Leonard Tilley, N.B.	(C,Q,L)
Charles Tupper, N.S.	(C,Q,L)
Edward Whelan, P.E.I.	(Q)
R.D. Wilmot, N.B.	(L)

The Political Parties

Canadian parties, from whatever point in the political spectrum they begin, gravitate towards the middle of the road where most of the votes lie. Despite variations in outlook and policy, all 3 official parties tend to adopt a practical rather than dogmatic line on most issues.

Progressive Conservatives — Canada's oldest party and theoretically the furthest to the right, the Conservatives have nevertheless endorsed an extension of social welfare. Though their support is based in western Canada, the Conservatives were the only party to elect at least one representative from each province in the 1980 election. The party has held office only briefly since 1962, and then only with minority governments, mainly due to a failure to gain support in Quebec. **Leader: Joe Clark.**

Liberals — Though politically situated between the Conservatives to the right and the New Democrats on the left, the Liberals are flexible enough to lean in either direction depending on specific issues and political situations. In 1975 they belatedly adopted a Conservative proposal for wage and price controls; in 1979 they sided with the NDP to oppose Conservative plans to return some government-owned corporations to the private sector. Most of their traditional electoral support comes from middle and upper class urban residents, from ethnic voters, and among French-speaking Canadians. **Leader:** Pierre Trudeau.

New Democratic Party — Successor to the Cooperative Commonwealth Federation, which combined the agrarian protest movement in western Canada with a democratic socialism of the British Labor Party variety, the NDP was founded in 1961. It now attempts to attract the vote of middle-class Canadians and fuse it with the party's labor support. **Leader:** Ed Broadbent.

Political power in Canada has been dominated by the Conservative and Liberal parties. Of 32 federal elections since Confederation, the Conservatives have won 13, holding power for 47 years; the Liberals have gained office 19 times, governing for 68 years. As a measure of Liberal strength, all of the party's 20th century leaders have been elected Prime Minister—though not always on the first attempt.

Despite the dominance of the Liberals and Conservatives, third parties have played an important role under Canada's parliamentary system in which a governing party holding less than half the seats in the House of Commons can remain in office and pass legislation only with the support of a minor party. A minority Conservative Government lost power in 1979 when none of the opposition parties supported its proposed budget.

The NDP has been the most influential of the third parties, consistently winning between 15% and 20% of the popular vote—though its proportion of elected members is always less. NDP pressure from the left has influenced policy decisions by both major parties. The Social Credit Party, once a strong political force with federal support in Quebec and the western provinces, has declined in stature over the past 2 decades and in 1980 failed to elect any members to Parliament.

Prime Ministers of Canada

Name	Party	Term
Sir John A. MacDonald	Conservative	1867-1873 1878-1891
Alexander Mackenzie	Liberal	1873-1878
Sir John J. C. Abbott	Conservative	1891-1892
Sir John S. D. Thompson	Conservative	1892-1894
Sir Mackenzie Bowell	Conservative	1894-1896
Sir Charles Tupper	Conservative	1896
Sir Wilfrid Laurier	Liberal	1896-1911
Sir Robert L. Borden	Conservative Unionist	1911-1920
Arthur Meighen	Cons. Union.	1920-1921
W.L. Mackenzie King	Liberal	1921-1926[1] 1926-1930 1935-1948
R. B. Bennett	Conservative	1930-1935
Louis St. Laurent	Liberal	1948-1957
John G. Diefenbaker	Prog. Cons.	1957-1963
Lester B. Pearson	Liberal	1963-1968
Pierre Elliott Trudeau	Liberal	1968-1979
Joe Clark	Prog. Cons.	1979-1980
Pierre Elliott Trudeau	Liberal	1980-

(1) King's term was interrupted from June 26-Sept. 25, 1926, when Arthur Meighen again served as prime minister.

Election Results by Province and Party, May 22, 1980

Province	Total Valid Votes	Liberal	Conservative	New Dem.	Soc. Cred.	Other
Alberta	794,946	176,565	515,639	81,732	8,162	12,848
British Columbia	1,209,453	268,069	501,921	426,857	1,709	10,897
Manitoba	476,001	133,353	179,607	159,432	—	3,609
New Brunswick	335,702	168,316	109,053	54,481	—	3,852
Newfoundland	203,045	95,354	72,999	33,943	—	749
Nova Scotia	422,281	168,303	163,436	88,115	—	2,427
Ontario	4,000,162	1,675,164	1,420,263	874,092	804	29,839
Prince Edward Island	66,174	31,055	30,576	4,335	—	208
Quebec	2,957,120	2,017,067	373,233	268,677	174,282	123,861
Saskatchewan	455,709	110,501	177,338	165,294	178	2,398
N.W. Territories	16,195	5,801	4,000	6,214	—	180
Yukon	9,669	3,825	3,926	1,918	—	—
TOTAL	**10,946,457**	**4,853,373**	**3,551,991**	**2,165,090**	**185,135**	**190,868**
Percent	100	44.34	32.45	19.78	1.69	1.71
Seats	282	147	103	32	0	0

Party Representation by Regions, 1949-1980

Canada	1949	1953	1957	1958	1962	1963	1965	1968	1972	1974	1979	1980
Liberal	193	171	105	48	100	129	131	155	109	141	114	147
Conservative	41	51	112	208	116	95	97	72	107	95	136	103
New Democratic[1]	13	23	25	8	19	17	21	22	31	16	26	32
Social Credit	10	15	19	—	30	24	14	14	15	11	6	0
Other	5	5	4	1	—	—	2	1	2	1	0	0
Ontario												
Liberal	56	51	21	14	44	52	51	64	36	55	32	52
Conservative	25	33	61	67	35	27	25	17	40	25	57	38
New Democratic[1]	1	1	3	3	6	6	9	6	11	8	6	5
Quebec												
Liberal	68	66	62	25	35	47	56	56	56	60	67	74
Conservative	2	4	9	50	14	8	8	4	2	3	2	1
Social Credit	—	—	—	—	26	20	9	14	15	11	6	—
Atlantic												
Liberal	26	27	12	8	14	20	15	7	10	13	12	19
Conservative	7	5	21	25	18	13	18	25	22	17	18	13
New Democratic[1]	1	1	—	—	1	—	—	—	—	1	2	—
Western[2]												
Liberal	43	27	10	1	7	10	9	28	7	13	3	2
Conservative	7	9	21	66	49	47	46	26	43	50	59	51
New Democratic[1]	11	21	22	5	12	11	12	16	20	7	18	27
Social Credit	10	15	19	—	4	4	5	—	—	—	—	—

(1) Prior to 1962 election was known as the Cooperative Commonwealth Federation.
(2) Includes the Yukon and Northwest Territories.

Canadian Armed Forces

Canada has an all-volunteer Armed Forces which, since 1968, has been a single body composed of what had been a separate army, navy, and air force. Canada's defense budget for 1981-82 (ending Mar. 31) was $5,906,620,000. The projected 1982-83 budget is $7,041,275,000.

Chief of the Defense Staff: Gen. R.M. Withers
Vice Chief of the Defense Staff: Lieut. Gen. G.C.E. Theriault

Maritime Command — Vice Admiral J.A. Fulton
Mobile Command — Lieut. Gen. C. H. Belzile
Air Command — Lieut. Gen. K.E. Lewis
Communications Command — Brig. Gen. D. P. Harrison
Canadian Forces Europe — Maj. Gen. Francois Richard

Regular Forces Strength

(as of March 31)

Year	Navy	Army	Air Force	Total
1945	92,529	494,258	174,254	761,041
1955	19,207	49,409	49,461	118,077
1965	19,756	46,264	48,144	114,164

Year	Total	Year	Total	Year	Total
1970	91,433	1977	78,091	1980	78,909
1975	78,448	1978	79,656	1981	79,549
1976	78,394	1979	78,974	1982	82,858

Canadian Military Participation in Major Conflicts

Northwest Rebellion (1885)[1]
Participants—3,323
Killed—38
Last veteran died at the age of 104 in 1971.
South African War (1899-1902)
Participants—7,368[2]
Killed—89
Living Veterans—less than 20
First World War (1914-1918)
Participants—626,636[3]
Killed—61,332[4]
Living Veterans—31,275[5]
Second World War (1939-1945)
Participants—1,086,343 (inc. 45,423 women)
Killed—32,714 (inc. 8 women)
Living Veterans—712,047[5 6]
Korean War (1950-1953)
Participants—25,583
Killed—314

(1) First battle in history to be fought entirely by Canadian troops. (2) Includes Canadians in the South African constabulary and 8 nursing sisters. (3) Includes 2,854 nursing sisters. (4) Includes 21 nursing sisters and 1,563 airmen serving with the British air forces. (5) 1980 est. based on mortality rates applied to 1971 census data. (6) Includes Korean War veterans.

Canadian Peacekeeping Operations

Canada has played a major role in the United Nations' efforts to preserve peace and promote international security, participating in almost all UN peacekeeping operations to date - in Egypt, Israel, Syria, Lebanon, Cyprus, Korea, India, Pakistan, West New Guinea, the Congo, Yemen and Nigeria.

Nearly 900 Canadian soldiers served in the Gaza Strip following the Israeli-Egyptian crisis of 1956 until the peacekeeping force there was disbanded in 1967. Another 850 Canadians served with the United Nations Emergency Force in the Middle East from 1973 until it was disbanded in Nov., 1979.

In the Congo, a 300-man signals unit provided communications for the UN force from 1960 to 1964.

Canadian participation in the International Commission for Control and Supervision in Vietnam and Laos began in 1954, and, at its height following U.S. military withdrawal from Vietnam in 1973, involved 245 Canadian Forces personnel. The Canadian Vietnam supervisory contingent was withdrawn in July 1973, the Laos mission in 1974.

Canadian peacekeeping operations in 1982:

—some 515 Canadians in the UN Peacekeeping Force in Cyprus where Canadian participation began in 1964 and was augmented in 1974.

—250 Canadians, mostly logistics troops, with the UN Disengagement Observer Force in the Middle East.

—20 Canadian combat arms officers with the UN Truce Supervisory Organization, Israel.

Area of Canada by Provinces

Source: Energy, Mines, and Resources Canada

		Area in square miles			Area in square kilometers		
Province, territory	Capital	Land	Fresh water	Total	Land	Fresh water	Total
Newfoundland	St. John's	143,510	13,140	156,650	371,690	34,030	405,720
Prince Edward Island	Charlottetown	2,180	...	2,180	5,660	...	5,660
Nova Scotia	Halifax	20,400	1,020	21,420	52,840	2,650	55,490
New Brunswick	Fredericton	27,840	520	28,360	72,090	1,350	73,440
Quebec	Quebec	523,860	71,000	594,860	1,356,790	183,890	1,540,680
Ontario	Toronto	344,090	68,490	412,580	891,190	177,390	1,068,580
Manitoba	Winnipeg	211,720	39,230	250,950	548,360	101,590	649,950
Saskatchewan	Regina	220,350	31,520	251,870	570,700	81,630	652,330
Alberta	Edmonton	248,800	6,490	255,290	644,390	16,800	661,190
British Columbia	Victoria	358,970	6,980	365,950	929,730	18,070	947,800
Yukon Territory	Whitehorse	184,930	1,730	186,660	478,970	4,480	483,450
Northwest Territories	Yellowknife	1,271,440	51,460	1,322,900	3,293,020	133,300	3,426,320
Total		**3,558,090**	**291,580**	**3,849,670**	**9,215,430**	**755,180**	**9,970,610**

Population of Canada by Province, 1871 - 1981

Source: Statistics Canada

Province, territory	1871 census	1901 census	1941 census	1951 census	1961 census	1971 census	1976 census	1981 census
Newfoundland	—	—	—	361,416	457,853	522,104	557,725	567,681
Prince Edward Island	94,021	103,259	95,047	98,429	104,629	111,641	118,229	122,506
Nova Scotia	387,800	459,574	577,942	642,584	737,007	788,960	828,571	847,442
New Brunswick	285,594	331,120	457,401	515,697	597,936	634,557	677,250	691,403
Quebec	1,191,516	1,648,898	3,331,882	4,055,681	5,259,211	6,027,764	6,234,445	6,438,403
Ontario	1,620,851	2,182,947	3,787,655	4,597,542	6,236,092	7,703,106	8,264,465	8,625,107
Manitoba	25,228	255,211	729,744	776,541	921,686	988,247	1,021,506	1,026,241
Saskatchewan	—	91,279	895,992	831,728	925,181	926,242	921,323	968,313
Alberta	—	73,022	796,169	939,501	1,331,944	1,627,874	1,838,037	2,237,724
British Columbia	36,247	178,657	817,861	1,165,210	1,629,082	2,184,621	2,466,608	2,744,467
Yukon	—	27,219	4,914	9,096	14,628	18,388	21,836	23,153
Northwest Territories	48,000	20,129	12,028	16,004	22,998	34,807	42,609	45,741
Total	**3,689,257**	**5,371,315**	**11,506,655**	**14,009,429**	**18,238,247**	**21,568,311**	**22,992,604**	**24,343,181**

Population of Major Canadian Cities and Metropolitan Areas

Source: Statistics Canada, from 1981 Census.

	City	Metro Area[1]
Montreal, Quebec	980,354	2,828,349
Toronto, Ontario	599,217	2,998,947[2]
Calgary, Alberta	592,743	592,743
Winnipeg, Manitoba	564,473	584,842
North York, Ontario	559,521	—
Edmonton, Alberta	532,246	657,057
Vancouver, British Columbia	414,281	1,268,183
Mississauga, Ontario	315,056	—
Hamilton, Ontario	306,434	542,095
Ottawa, Ontario	295,163	717,578[3]
Laval, Quebec	268,335	—
London, Ontario	254,280	283,668
Windsor, Ontario	192,083	246,110
Quebec, Quebec	166,474	576,075
Regina, Saskatchewan	162,613	164,313
Saskatoon, Saskatchewan	154,210	154,210
Brampton, Ontario	149,030	—
Kitchener, Ontario	139,734	287,801
Longueuil, Quebec	124,320	—
St. Catharines, Ontario	124,018	304,353
Oshawa, Ontario	117,519	154,217
Burlington, Ontario	114,853	—
Halifax, Nova Scotia	114,594	277,727
Thunder Bay, Ontario	112,486	121,379
Sudbury, Ontario	91,829	149,923
St. John's, Newfoundland	83,770	154,820
Saint John, New Brunswick	80,521	112,974
Victoria, British Columbia	64,379	233,481

(1) Figures are for Census Metro Areas which, in some cases, include municipalities outside the metro political boundaries. (2) Includes the city of Mississauga. (3) Includes the city of Hull, Que.

Immigration to Canada, by Province of Intended Destination

Source: Canadian Statistical Review, April 1982

Year	Canada	Nfld.	P.E.I.	N.S.	N.B.	Que.	Ont.	Man.	Sask.	Alta.	B.C.	N.W.T. Yukon
1975	187,881	1,106	235	2,124	2,093	28,042	98,471	7,134	2,837	16,277	29,272	290
1976	149,429	725	235	1,942	1,752	29,282	72,031	5,509	2,323	14,896	20,484	250
1977	114,914	583	192	1,587	1,158	19,248	56,594	5,058	2,231	12,694	15,395	174
1978	86,313	374	145	980	661	14,290	42,397	3,574	1,564	9,826	12,331	171
1979	112,096	553	289	1,338	1,145	19,534	51,979	4,906	2,762	12,786	16,596	208
1980	143,117	541	190	1,615	1,207	22,541	62,264	7,684	3,604	18,841	24,440	189
1981	128,421	480	120	1,401	992	21,064	55,032	5,383	2,391	19,289	22,067	202

Superlative Canadian Statistics

Source: Statistics Canada; Dept. of Energy, Mines and Resources

Area	Total: Land 3,558,090 sq. mi.; Water 291,580 sq. mi.	3,849,670 sq. mi.
Largest city in area	Timmins, Ont.	1,230 sq. mi.
Smallest city in area (east)	Vanier, Ont.	1.1 sq. mi.
Smallest city in area (west)	Chilliwack, B.C.	1.6 sq. mi.
Northernmost point	Cape Columbia, Ellesmere Island, N.W.T.	83°07'30"N.
Northernmost settlement	Alert, Ellesmere Island, N.W.T.	82°30'N.
Southernmost point	Middle Island (Lake Erie), Ont.	41°41'N.
Southernmost settlement	Pelee Island South, Essex Co., Ont.	41°45'N.
Easternmost point	Cape Spear, Nfld.	52°37'28"W.
Easternmost settlement	Blackhead, St. John's, Nfld.	52°39'W.
Westernmost point	Mount St. Elias, Yukon (at Alaskan border)	141°W.
Westernmost settlement	Beaver Creek, Yukon	140°52'W.
Highest city	Rossland, B.C. at R.R. Stn. (49°05'N,117°47'W)	3,465 ft.
Highest town	Lake Louise, Alta.	5,051 ft.
Highest waterfall	Takakkaw Falls (Daly Glacier), B.C. (51°30'N,116°29'W)	1,650 ft.
Longest river	Mackenzie (from head of Finlay R.)	2,635 mi.
Highest mountain	Mt. Logan (Yukon)	19,524 ft.
Rainiest spot	Henderson Lake, Vancouver Is. yrly. avg. rainfall	262 inches
Highest lake	Chilco Lake (51°20'N,124°05'W) 75.1 sq. mi.	3,842 ft

Immigration to Canada by Country of Last Permanent Residence

Source: Canadian Statistical Review, April 1982

Year	Total	UK and Ireland	France	Germany	Netherlands	Greece	Italy
1977	114,914	18,568	2,757	2,254	1,247	1,960	3,411
1978	86,313	12,270	1,754	1,471	1,237	1,474	2,976
1979	112,096	13,406	1,900	1,323	1,479	1,247	1,996
1980	143,117	18,924	1,900	1,643	1,866	1,093	1,740
1981	128,421	21,872	2,079	2,185	1,788	952	2,036

Year	Portugal	Other Europe	Asia	Australasia	United States	West Indies	All Other
1977	3,579	6,972	31,368	1,545	12,888	12,022	16,343
1978	1,898	6,995	24,007	1,233	9,945	8,231	12,822
1979	3,723	7,784	50,540	1,395	9,617	6,262	11,424
1980	4,228	9,774	71,602	1,555	9,926	7,254	11,612
1981	3,259	11,920	48,483	1,315	10,471	8,504	13,557

Canadian Population by Mother Tongue, 1981

Source: Statistics Canada: 1981 Census

Province	English	French	Italian	German	Ukrainian	Indian, Inuit	Chinese	Portuguese	Other
Newfoundland	560,460	2,655	90	445	50	1,600	725	205	1,450
Prince Edward Island	115,045	6,080	20	175	35	90	115	20	925
Nova Scotia	793,165	36,030	1,055	1,865	640	3,055	1,305	235	1,440
New Brunswick	453,310	234,030	525	1,220	195	2,115	730	165	4,115
Quebec.	706,115	5,307,010	133,710	24,060	10,765	28,080	15,270	25,495	187,895
Ontario	6,678,770	475,605	338,980	174,545	81,595	22,255	89,355	114,275	649,725
Manitoba	735,920	52,560	6,170	75,180	58,855	27,185	6,075	6,840	57,455
Saskatchewan.	770,815	25,535	1,280	59,625	44,660	24,265	5,000	335	36,795
Alberta	1,810,545	62,145	16,175	91,480	68,130	27,565	28,910	5,560	127,215
British Columbia	2,249,310	45,615	30,595	93,380	26,950	11,445	76,270	12,340	198,560
Yukon.	20,245	580	45	495	170	835	125	5	655
Northwest Territories	24,755	1,240	130	385	210	18,090	145	25	765
Total.	**14,918,445**	**6,249,095**	**528,775**	**522,855**	**292,265**	**166,575**	**224,030**	**165,510**	**1,275,630**

Population by Religious Denomination

Source: Statistics Canada

Denomination	1961	1971	Denomination	1961	1971
Adventist	25,999	28,590	Lutheran	662,744	715,740
Anglican	2,409,068	2,543,180	Mennonite(2)	152,452	168,150
Baptist	593,553	667,245	Mormon	50,016	66,635
Buddhist	11,611	16,175	Orthodox(3)	239,766	316,605
Chr. & Miss'nary Alliance	18,006	23,630	Pentecostal	143,877	220,390
Christian Reformed	62,257	83,390	Presbyterian	818,588	872,335
Ch. of Christ, Disciples	19,512	16,405	Roman Catholic	8,342,826	9,974,895
Confucian	5,089	2,165	Salvation Army	92,054	119,665
Doukhobor	13,234	9,107	Ukrainian Catholic(4)	189,653	227,730
Free Methodist	14,245	19,125	Unitarian	15,062	20,995
Hutterite	(1)	13,650	United Church	3,664,008	3,768,800
Jehovah's Witnesses	68,018	174,810	Other	277,508	293,240
Jewish	254,368	276,025	No religion	94,763	929,575

(1) Included with Mennonite. (2) Includes Hutterites in 1961. (3) Those churches which observe the Eastern Orthodox rite, including Greek, Russian, Ukrainian, and Syrian Orthodox. (4) Includes other "Greek Catholic."

Births and Deaths in Canada by Province

Source: Statistics Canada

Province	Births 1980	Births 1981	Deaths 1980	Deaths 1981	Province	Births 1980	Births 1981	Deaths 1980	Deaths 1981
Newfoundland	10,332	11,310	3,345	3,070	Saskatchewan	17,057	16,920	7,651	7,160
Prince Edward Island	1,958	1,970	1,035	970	Alberta	39,749	39,810	12,710	12,260
Nova Scotia	12,369	12,000	7,004	6,440	British Columbia . . .	40,104	39,700	19,371	19,680
New Brunswick. . . .	10,636	10,910	5,297	5,320	Yukon.	476	520	128	140
Quebec.	97,421	95,790	43,512	43,440	Northwest Territories	1,302	1,060	238	170
Ontario	123,316	123,240	62,746	63,390	**Total . . . .**	**370,709**	**370,150**	**171,473**	**170,910**
Manitoba	15,989	16,920	8,436	8,870					

Marriages, Divorces in Canada

Source: Statistics Canada
(Rates per 1,000 population)

Year	Marriages No.	Marriages Rate	Divorces No.	Divorces Rate	Year	Marriages No.	Marriages Rate	Divorces No.	Divorces Rate
1940.	125,709	10.8	2,416	0.21	1975.	197,585	8.7	50,611	2.22
1950.	125,083	9.1	5,386	0.39	1978.	185,523	7.9	57,155	2.43
1960.	130,338	7.3	6,980	0.39	1979.	187,811	7.9	59,474	2.51
1970.	188,428	8.8	29,775	1.39	1980.	191,069	8.0	62,019	2.59

Canadian Legal or Public Holidays, 1983

Legal public holidays in all provinces are: New Year's Day, Good Friday, Easter Monday, Victoria Day, Canada Day, Labor Day, Remembrance Day and Christmas Day. Additional holidays may be proclaimed provincially by the Lieutenant-Governor or in the municipalities by an order of the local council. For some holidays, government and business closing practices vary. In most provinces the provincial Ministry or Department of Labor can provide details of holiday closings.

Chief Legal or Public Holidays

Jan. 1 (Saturday) - New Year's Day. All provinces.

Apr. 1 - Good Friday. All provinces.

Apr. 4 - Easter Monday. Que. (businesses remain open in other provinces)

May 23 (the Monday preceding May 25) - Victoria Day. All provinces.

July 1 (Friday) - Canada Day. All provinces.

Aug. 1 (1st Monday in Aug.) - Civic Holiday. Alb. B.C. Man. N.B. NWT Ont. Sask.

Sept. 5 (1st Monday in Sept.) - Labor Day. All provinces.

Oct. 10 (2d Monday in Oct.) - Thanksgiving. All provinces.

Nov. 11 (Friday) - Remembrance Day. Observed in all provinces but most businesses remain open.

Dec. 25 (Sunday) - Christmas Day. All provinces.

Dec. 26 (Monday) - Boxing Day. All provinces except Que.

Other Legal or Public Holidays

Jan. 11 (Tuesday) - Sir John A. MacDonald's Birthday. Schools closed in some provinces.

March 14 (Monday) - St. Patrick's Day. Nfld.

April 25 (Monday) - St. George's Day. Nfld.

June 20 (Monday) - Discovery Day. Nfld.

June 24 (Friday) - St. John the Baptist's Day. Que.

July 11 (Monday) - Orangemen's Day. Nfld.

Aug. 15 (3d Monday in Aug.) - Discovery Day. Yukon.

Widely Known Canadians of the Present

Statesmen, authors, performers, artists, industrialists, and other prominent persons. (Canadians widely known in the North American entertainment industry are found on pages 388-398; some sports personalities can be found in sports section).

Barbara Amiel, b. Watford, Eng., 12/4/40, columnist, author.

Doris Anderson, b. Calgary, Alta., 11/20/25, former president Canadian Advisory Council on Status of Women, journalist and author.

Margaret Atwood, b. Ottawa, Ont., 11/18/39, poet and author; *Lady Oracle* (1976), *Bodily Harm* (1981).

Harold Ballard, b. Toronto, Ont., 7/30/03, majority owner of Toronto Maple Leafs, Hamilton Tiger-Cats, Maple Leaf Gardens.

William Bennett, b. Kelowna, B.C., 4/14/32, leader of British Columbia Social Credit Party since 1973, B.C. premier (1975-).

Pierre Berton, b. Whitehorse, Yukon, 7/12/20, author; *The National Dream* (1970), *The Last Spike* (1971), *Flames Across the Border* (1981).

Conrad Black, b. Montreal, Que., 8/25/44, businessman, including chairman of the board of Argus Corp. Ltd.

Peter Blaikie, b. Shawinigan, Que., 5/10/37, national president of Progressive Conservative Party.

Gerald Bouey, b. Axford, Sask., 4/2/20, governor of the Bank of Canada (1973-).

Ed Broadbent, b. Oshawa, Ont., 3/21/36, national leader of New Democratic Party (1975-).

Charles Bronfman, b. Montreal, Que., 6/27/31, deputy chairman of the Seagram Co. Ltd.; Chairman of the Montreal Expos.

John M. Buchanan, b. Sydney, N.S., 4/22/31, leader of Nova Scotia Progressive Conservative Party since 1971; Nova Scotia premier (1978-).

Jean Chrétien, b. Shawinigan, Que., 1/11/34, justice minister (1980-).

Joe Clark, b. High River, Alta., 6/5/39, leader of Progressive Conservative Party since 1976; prime minister from May 1979 election victory until defeat February 1980.

Leonard Cohen, b. Montreal, Que., 9/21/34, poet, novelist, songwriter.

Alex Colville, b. Toronto, Ont., 8/24/20, artist.

John Crosbie, b. St. John's, Nfld., 1/30/31, former finance minister in Progressive Conservative government.

Ken Danby, b. Sault Ste. Marie, Ont., 3/16/40, artist.

Robertson Davies, b. Thamesville, Ont., 8/28/13, educator, author of *The Rebel Angels* (1981).

Bill Davis, b. Brampton, Ont., 7/30/29, Ontario premier (1971-).

Paul Desmarais, b. Sudbury, Ont., 1/4/27, industrial executive, including chairman of Power Corp. of Canada.

Grant Devine, b. Regina, Sask., 7/5/44, leader Manitoba Progressive Party since 1979, Manitoba premier (1982-).

Jean Drapeau, b. Montreal, Que., 2/18/16, mayor of Montreal (1954-57 and 1960-).

Alan Eagleson, b. St. Catharines, Ont., 4/24/33, executive director of National Hockey League Players' Assn.; arranges international hockey competition.

Maureen Forrester, b. Montreal, Que., 7/25/30, contralto.

Barbara Frum, b. Niagara Falls, Ont., 9/8/38, broadcaster.

Northrop Frye, b. Sherbrooke, Que., 7/14/12, educator, literary critic and author *The Great Code* (1982).

Glenn Gould, b. Toronto, Ont., 9/25/32, classical pianist and composer.

Peter Gzowski, b. Toronto, Ont., 7/13/34, radio host and author of *The Game of Our Lives* (1981).

Don Harron, b. Toronto, Ont., 9/19/24, comedian and actor, best known for alter-ego Charlie Farquharson.

Richard Hatfield, b. Hartland, N.B., 4/9/31, New Brunswick premier (1970-).

Mel Hurtig, b. Edmonton, Alta., 6/24/32, book publisher, proponent of Canadian nationalism.

Karen Kain, b. Hamilton, Ont., 3/28/51, principal dancer of the National Ballet of Canada.

Yousuf Karsh, b. Armenia-in-Turkey, 12/23/08, portrait photographer.

Marc Lalonde, b. Ile Perrot, Que., 7/26/29, minister of energy, mines and resources (1980-).

Bora Laskin, b. Fort William, Ont., 10/5/12, chief justice, Supreme Court of Canada (1973-).

Margaret Laurence, b. Neapawa, Man., 7/18/26, novelist; *The Stone Angel* (1964), *The Diviners* (1974).

Irving Layton, b. Neamtz, Romania, 3/12/12, poet.

René Lévesque, b. New Carlisle, Que., 8/24/22, leader of Quebec separatist Parti Quebecois since 1968, Quebec premier (1976-).

James Lee, b. Charlottetown, P.E.I., 3/26/37, leader P.E.I. Progressive Conservative Party and premier (1981-).

Gordon Lightfoot, b. Orillia, Ont., 11/17/38, singer, songwriter.

Peter Lougheed, b. Calgary, Alta., 7/26/28, Alberta Progressive Conservative leader since 1965, Alberta prenier (1971-).

Donald MacDonald, b. Ottawa, Ont., 3/1/32, lawyer; former Liberal cabinet minister; considered possible successor to Pierre Trudeau as national Liberal leader.

Flora Macdonald, b. North Sydney, N.S., 6/3/26, secretary of state for external affairs in 1979; candidate for Progressive Conservative Party leadership in 1976.

Allan MacEachen, b. Inverness, N.S., 7/6/21, deputy prime minister, finance minister (1980-).

Mark MacGuigan, b. Charlottetown, P.E.I., 2/17/31, secretary of state for external affairs (1980-).

Dennis McDermott, b. Portsmouth, Eng., 11/3/22, president of Canadian Labour Congress (1978-).

W.O. Mitchell, b. Weyburn, Sask., 3/13/14, author; *Who Has Seen the Wind* (1947), *How I Spent My Summer Holidays* (1981).

Farlay Mowat, b. Belleville, Ont., 5/12/21, author, known for books on the North.

Brian Mulroney, b. Baie Comeau, Que., 3/20/39, president of Iron Ore Co. of Canada; unsuccessful candidate for Progressive Conservative leadership in 1976, possible successor to current leader Joe Clark.

Knowlton Nash, b. Toronto, Ont., 11/18/27, broadcaster, announcer for CBC national news.

Peter C. Newman, b. Vienna, Austria, 5/10/29, author, editor of Maclean's magazine (1971-82); *The Canadian Establishment* (1975), *Bronfman Dynasty* (1978), *The Acquisitors* (1981).

Howard Pawley, b. Brampton, Ont., 11/21/34, leader of Manitoba New Democratic Party since 1979, Manitoba premier (1981-).

Brian Peckford, b. Whitehorse, Nfld., 8/27/42, leader of Newfoundland Progressive Conservative Party and premier since 1979.

Peter Pocklington, b. Regina, Sask., 11/18/41, entrepreneur, owner of Edmonton Oilers and other sports franchises.

Steve Podborski, b. Toronto, Ont., 7/25/57, 1981 men's downhill World Cup skiing champion.

Christopher Pratt, b. St. John's, Nfld., 12/9/35, artist, has developed style known as "conceptual realism".

Mordecai Richler, b. Montreal, Que., 1/27/31, author; *The Apprenticeship of Duddy Kravitz* (1959), *Joshua Then and Now* (1980).

Gabrielle Roy, b. St. Boniface, Man., 3/22/09, novelist.

Claude Ryan, b. Montreal, Que., 1/26/25, leader of Quebec Liberal Party (1978-).

Edward Schreyer, b. Beausejour, Man., 12/21/35, premier of Manitoba (1969-77); governor-general of Canada, (1979-).

Gordon Sinclair, b. Toronto, Ont., 6/3/00, broadcaster, journalist, panelist on TV's "Front Page Challenge."

Nelson Skalbania, b. Regina, Sask., 2/12/38, real estate and sports franchise entrepreneur.

Joey Smallwood, b. Gambo, Nfld., 12/24/00, led Newfoundland into Canada and served as province's first premier (1949-72).

David Suzuki, b. Vancouver, B.C., 3/24/36, scientist, educator, television personality.

E.P. (Edward Plunket) **Taylor,** b. Ottawa, Ont., 1/29/01, industrialist, financier; now lives in the Bahamas.

Ken Taylor, b. Calgary, Alta., 10/5/34, diplomat, engineered escape of 6 U.S. embassy staff members from Iran (1980); Canadian counsul general in New York (1981-).

Charles Templeton, b. Toronto, Ont., 10/7/15, broadcaster, author.

Ken Thomson, b. Toronto, Ont., 9/1/23, chairman of the board of Thomson Newspapers Ltd.

Margaret Trudeau, b. Vancouver, B.C., 9/10/48, author of autobiographies *Beyond Reason* and *Consequences*; television host.

Pierre Elliott Trudeau, b. Montreal, Que., 10/18/19, Canadian prime minister (1968-79) and (1980-); leader federal Liberal Party (1968-); member of parliament since 1965; associate professor of law, Univ. of Montreal (1961-65).

John Turner, b. Richmond, Eng., 6/7/29, lawyer, cabinet minister in Liberal government (1965-75); possible future leader of national Liberal Party.

Galen Weston, b. England, 10/26/40, chairman and president of George Weston Ltd.

Noted Canadians of the Past

William Aberhart, 1878-1943, b. Hibbard twp., Ont., spellbinding orator, founded Social Credit Party in Canada, premier of Alberta (1935-43).

Frederick G. Banting, 1891-1941, b. Alliston, Ont., codiscoverer of insulin, demonstrated its beneficial effects on diabetes (1922), awarded Nobel prize (1923).

William M. Aitken (Baron Beaverbrook), 1879-1964, b. Maple, Ont., best known in Canada as publisher and philanthropist, held several positions in British Cabinet up to 1945.

Charles H. Best, 1899-1978, b. West Pembroke, Me., co-discoverer of insulin.

Norman Bethune, 1890-1939, b. Gravenhurst, Ont., died in northern China as a surgeon with the Chinese revolutionary army.

Billy Bishop, 1894-1956, b. Owen Sound, Ont., WWI flying ace, shot down 72 enemy aircraft, including 25 in a 10-day period in 1918.

Samuel Bronfman, 1891-1971, b. Brandon, Man., industrialist, established Distiller's Corporation—Seagram's Limited.

Emily Carr, 1871-1945, b. Victoria, B.C., painter, best known for sketches of Indian life.

George Etienne Cartier, 1814-1873, b. St. Antoine, Upper Canada; leading French-Canadian Father of Confederation, joint premier of United Canada (1857-62).

John Diefenbaker, 1895-1979, b. Grey Co., Ont., leader of Progressive Conservative Party (1956-67) and prime minister of Canada (1957-63).

Terry Fox, 1958-1981, b. Winnipeg, Man., in 1980, with an artificial leg, began "Marathon of Hope" run across Canada to raise funds for cancer research; run halted by recurring cancer but succeeded in raising more than $20 million.

Joseph Howe, 1804-1873, b. Halifax, N.S., politician, orator and writer, at first fought Nova Scotia entry into Canadian union but later accepted post in federal cabinet.

A.Y. Jackson, 1882-1974, b. Montreal Que., best known of "Group of Seven" Canadian painters.

Pauline Johnson, 1862-1913, b. Six Nations Indian Reserve, Ont., poet.

Cornelius Krieghoff, 1815-1872, b. Amsterdam, Holland, painter, did finest work after moving to Canada in 1846.

W.L. Mackenzie King, 1874-1950, b. Kitchener, Ont., prime minister of Canada a record 22 years (1921-26, 1926-30, 1935-48).

Wilfrid Laurier, 1841-1919, b. Saint Lin, Lower Canada, leader of Canadian Liberal Party (1887-1919) and prime minister (1896-1911).

Stephen Leacock, 1869-1944, b. Swanmoor, Hants, Eng., humorist, author, *Sunshine Sketches of a Little Town.*

John A. Macdonald, 1815-1891, b. Glasgow, Scotland, chief architect of Confederation and Canada's first prime minister (1867-1873 and 1878-1891).

William Lyon Mackenzie, 1795-1861, b. Scotland; politician and rebel, chief organizer of 1837 rebellion for political reform in Upper Canada, first mayor of Toronto (1835).

Vincent Massey, 1887-1967, b. Toronto, Ont., first native-born governor-general of Canada (1952-1959).

John (Bud) McDougald, 1908-1938, b. Toronto, Ont., financier and industrialist.

Thomas D'Arcy McGee, 1825-1868, b. Carlingford, Ireland, eloquent advocate of confederation; assassinated Apr. 7, 1868.

Marshall McLuhan, 1911-1980, b. Edmonton, Alta., author and educator best known for theories on communication. *The Medium is the Message* (1967).

Nellie McClung, 1873-1951, b. Chatsworth, Ont., author and feminist.

John McCrae, 1872-1918, b. Guelph, Ont., poet, best known for *In Flanders Fields.*

Lucy Maud Montgomery, 1874-1942, b. Clifton, P.E.I., author, *Anne of Green Gables* (1908).

Susanna Moodie, 1803-1885, b. Suffolk, Eng., author, best known for *Roughing It In the Bush* (1852).

William Osler, 1849-1919, b. Bond Head, Upper Canada, physician and author.

Louis Joseph Papineau, 1786-1871, b. Montreal, Lower Canada, led movement for political reform in Lower Canada.

Lester B. Pearson, 1897-1972, b. Toronto, Ont., Canadian prime minister (1963-68); awarded Nobel peace prize (1957).

Edwin J. Pratt, 1883-1964, b. Western Bay, Nfld., poet.

Louis Riel, 1844-1885, b. St. Boniface, Man., led Meti of Western Canada in North West rebellions of 1870 an 1885, hung for treason in Regina.

Mazo de la Roche, 1879-1961, b. Toronto, Ont., nove ist, best known for Jalna series.

Robert W. Service, 1874-1958, b. Preston, Eng., poe *Songs of a Sourdough* (1907).

Roy Thomson (Lord Thomson of Fleet), 1894-1976, b Toronto, Ont., newspaper publisher.

Tom Thomson, 1877-1917, b. Claremont, Ont painter, influenced "Group of Seven" Canadian artists.

W. Garfield Weston, 1898-1978, b. Toronto, Ont., in dustrialist.

James S. Woodsworth, 1874-1942, b. Etobicoke Ont., a founder of the Co-operative Commonwealth Fed eration, forerunner of the New Democratic Party.

Canadian Government Budget

Source: Canadian Statistical Review
(millions of Canadian dollars)

Expenditures

Fiscal Year	National defense	Health and welfare	Agriculture	Post Office	Public works	Transport	Veterans affairs	Payments to provinces	Total expendi tures
1975-76. .	2,973	9,731	651	913	624	1,185	684	2,460	33,97
1976-77. .	3,365	10,952	631	1,104	684	1,314	754	3,356	38,95
1977-78. .	3,771	11,635	959	1,237	1,431	1,478	841	3,003	42,90
1978-79. .	4,108	13,024	768	1,275	1,657	1,725	890	3,028	46,92
1979-80. .	4,389	14,038	782	1,412	1,615	1,726	933	3,522	52,29
1980-81. .	5,078	15,792	881	1,597	1,883	2,640	1,006	3,788	58,81

Revenues[1]

Fiscal year	Personal income tax	Corporation income tax	Sales tax	Other excise tax[2]	Excise duties	Customs duties	Estate taxes	Post Office	Total budgetary revenues
1975-76. .	12,708	5,748	3,939	1,501	817	1,887	12	443	29,95
1976-77. .	14,620	5,377	4,529	1,146	865	2,097	70	615	32,65
1977-78. .	13,439	5,828	5,026	904	882	2,312	66	773	32,86
1978-79. .	14,048	6,262	5,245	827	878	2,747	77	903	35,21
1979-80. .	16,327	7,537	5,119	1,252	895	3,000	96	1,118	40,15
1980-81. .	19,837	8,133	5,882	1,602	1,042	3,188	99	1,109	46,73

(1) This statement includes only receipts relating to revenue. Excluded are non-budgetary revenues such as Old Age Security Fun taxes, Prairie Farm Assistance Act levies, employer and employee contributions to government-held funds. (2) Beginning in Dec 1973, this category includes oil export tax.

Canadian Income Tax Rates

Source: Revenue Canada

1982 Rates of Federal Income Tax

Taxable income		Tax	
$ 1,111 or less		—	
1,112	$ 67	16% on next	$ 1,112
2,224	245	17% on next	2,224
4,448	623	18% on next	2,224
6,672	1,023	19% on next	4,448
11,120	1,868	20% on next	4,448
15,568	2,758	23% on next	4,448
20,016	3,781	25% on next	11,120
31,136	6,561	30% on next	22,240
53,376	13,233	34% on remainder	

1982 Rates of Provincial Income Tax[1]

Taxable income	Tax
Newfoundland	58%
Prince Edward Island	52.5%
Nova Scotia	52.5%
New Brunswick	55.5%
Ontario	48%
Manitoba	54%
Saskatchewan	51%[2]
Alberta	38.5%
British Columbia	44%[3]
N.W.T. and Yukon	43%

(1) Rates are applied to basic federal tax payable. (2) Plus surtax of 12% of basic provincial tax over $4,000. (3) Plus surtax of 10% of basi provincial tax over $3,500.

Canada: Taxable Returns by Income, 1979

Source: Revenue Canada Taxation Statistics

Total income in dollars	Number of tax returns	Percent of tax returns	Total income (millions)	Percent of total income	Taxed income (millions)	Federal tax (millions)	Percent of Fed. tax	Fed. Tax rate on total income
$1-2,500	1,662,094	11.32	2,196.4	1.24	7.2	—	—	–
2,500-5,000	1,743,330	11.88	6,536.6	3.68	858.0	1.6	.01	.0
5,000-7,500	1,596,927	10.87	9,945.8	5.60	3,432.2	153.2	.91	1.5
7,500-10,000	1,514,370	10.32	13,225.0	7.45	6,347.5	577.7	3.40	4.3
10,000-15,000	2,602,489	17.72	32,157.3	18.11	18,881.1	2,397.0	14.09	7.4
15,000-20,000	1,917,774	13.07	33,303.1	18.75	21,693.6	3,270.9	19.22	9.8
20,000-25,000	1,210,498	8.24	26,970.9	15.19	18,508.0	3,025.2	17.77	11.2
25,000-30,000	631,569	4.30	17,187.9	9.68	12,202.0	2,110.3	12.41	12.2
30,000-40,000	474,724	3.24	16,101.1	9.06	11,741.2	2,153.6	12.65	13.3
40,000-50,000	143,694	.97	6,358.2	3.58	4,799.6	920.3	5.41	14.4
50,000-100,000	134,150	.92	8,768.6	4.94	6,862.9	1,449.6	8.52	16.5
100,000-200,000	23,278	.16	3,017.4	1.70	2,387.0	591.0	3.47	19.5
200,000 and over	4,995	.03	1,808.1	1.02	1,276.3	367.6	2.16	20.3

Average Canadian Income and Taxes by Occupation, 1979

Source: Revenue Canada Taxation Statistics

Occupation	Number[1]	Average income[2]	Average federal tax
Self-employed doctors and surgeons	27,943	$57,553	$11,145
Self-employed dentists	7,185	51,815	10,005
Self-employed lawyers and notaries	15,474	44,660	7,906
Self-employed accountants	9,398	35,976	5,757
Self-employed engineers and architects	3,645	34,469	5,377
Teachers and professors	320,841	21,988	2,555
Federal government employees	378,313	17,587	1,901
Armed Forces employees	81,009	16,993	1,769
Other self-employed professionals	34,746	16,571	1,995
Provincial government employees	515,030	16,547	1,750
Municipal government employees	531,068	14,696	1,438
Investors	881,830	14,156	1,097
Business employees	7,002,055	13,691	1,394
Property owners	107,028	13,470	1,384
Self-employed salesmen	37,253	13,251	1,347
Fishermen	37,445	12,625	1,236
Farmers	279,288	12,598	771
Employees of institutions	791,852	12,112	1,031
Business proprietors	496,150	11,423	1,009
Self-employed entertainers and artists	17,867	8,284	623
Unclassified employees	287,418	7,663	518
Pensioners	1,125,507	6,336	207
Unclassified	1,693,810	1,892	75
Total	**14,682,155**	**12,079**	**1,159**

(1) Based on number of tax returns (2) Average total income after business expense deductions but before personal deductions.

Average Income in Selected Canadian Cities, 1979

Source: Revenue Canada Taxation Statistics

City	Average income[1]	Rank	No. of tax returns
Markham, Ont.	16,461	1	33,919
Oakville, Ont.	15,718	2	32,535
Calgary, Alta.	15,030	3	264,394
Burlington, Ont.	14,751	4	48,429
Edmonton, Alta.	14,192	5	292,175
Mississauga, Ont.	14,080	6	133,641
Vancouver, B.C.	14,009	7	509,977
Ottawa, Ont.	13,887	8	230,594
Prince George, B.C.	13,658	9	31,117
Brossard, Que.	13,653	10	19,122
Milton, Ont.	13,563	11	11,836
Red Deer, Alta.	13,443	12	19,488
Pickering, Ont.	13,424	13	17,026
Sept-Iles, Que.	13,322	14	11,978
Richmond Hill, Ont.	13,301	15	16,333
Victoria, B.C.	13,214	16	94,450
Whitby, Ont.	13,133	17	15,077
Regina, Sask.	13,119	18	71,679
Sarnia, Ont.	13,032	19	27,930
Nanaimo, B.C.	13,032	20	18,277
Waterloo, Ont.	12,994	21	22,103
Kamloops, B.C.	12,977	22	25,895
Brampton, Ont.	12,923	23	62,316
Lethbridge, Alta.	12,903	24	23,454
Langley, B.C.	12,866	25	22,307
Toronto, Ont.	12,866	26	1,017,368
Montreal, Que.	12,458	32	818,431
Windsor, Ont.	12,258	38	84,032
Halifax, N.S.	12,193	40	70,485
Quebec, Que.	12,176	41	162,252
London, Ont.	12,029	44	112,013
Hull, Que.	11,674	51	56,831
Kitchener, Ont.	11,522	55	62,587
Fredericton, N.B.	11,302	60	26,416
Hamilton, Ont.	11,287	61	130,438
Winnipeg, Man.	11,111	65	247,580
St. John's, Nfld.	11,091	66	51,602
Sydney, N.S.	9,431	100	44,510

(1) Average total income after business deductions but before personal deductions.

Canadian Labor Force

Source: Statistics Canada; 1981 annual averages (thousands of persons)

	Can.	Nfld.	P.E.I.	N.S.	N.B.	Que.	Ont.	Man.	Sask.	Alta.	B.C.
Labor force	11,830	218	54	367	296	2,996	4,481	492	453	1,136	1,337
Employed	10,933	187	48	330	262	2,685	4,186	462	432	1,093	1,247
Unemployed	898	31	6	37	35	311	295	29	21	43	90
Percent unemployed	7.6	14.1	11.4	10.2	11.7	10.4	6.6	6.0	4.6	3.8	6.7

Canadian Labor Force Characteristics

Source: Statistics Canada (thousands of workers)

Year	Labor force	Employed	Unemployed	Agriculture	Private sector	Govt. business	Govt. non-business	Employers
1975	9,974	9,284	690	483	6,554	457	1,364	234
1976	10,206	9,476	727	437	6,704	479	1,372	228
1977	10,498	9,754	850	468	6,832	485	1,459	257
1978	10,882	9,972	911	473	7,004	500	1,432	260
1979	11,207	10,369	838	483	7,447	463	1,388	262
1980	11,522	10,655	867	477	7,714	480	1,411	250
1981	11,830	10,933	898	484	7,937	494	1,436	259

Average Weekly Canadian Wages and Salaries, by Province

Source: Statistics Canada (Canadian dollars)

Year & month	Canada[1]	Nfld.	P.E.I.	N.S.	N.B.	Que.	Ont.	Man.	Sask.	Alta.	B.C.
1970	126.82	117.70	83.82	104.21	104.01	122.38	131.52	115.88	114.87	128.15	137.97
1975	203.34	196.50	149.84	172.40	182.40	199.22	204.86	186.01	188.31	207.39	229.97
1978	265.37	248.36	196.72	223.72	232.89	262.82	264.04	239.71	250.44	276.32	301.26
1979	288.32	271.64	209.77	245.23	261.98	284.18	285.57	259.00	275.79	306.79	327.14
1980	317.39	288.90	230.03	265.95	284.36	315.36	311.45	283.20	303.71	341.93	363.51
1981	355.12	328.08	250.13	296.35	313.37	351.57	347.92	314.42	336.78	390.43	407.03
1982 (Jan.)	377.74	353.84	270.50	320.55	335.32	374.27	370.02	329.64	352.92	412.99	431.31

(1) Includes Yukon and Northwest Territories.

Canadian Unemployment Insurance Commission

Source: Canadian Statistical Review, March 1982
(Canadian dollars)

	Claims data				Benefits paid				
Year	Beneficiaries[1] [2] (000)	Claims received (000)	Weeks paid	Total paid (thousands of dollars)	Regular	Sickness	Maternity	Retirement	Fishing
1977	750	2,807	38,701	3,909,045	3,485,080	155,828	172,228	13,543	48,400
1978	803	2,809	41,355	4,536,910	4,006,868	157,405	195,297	14,831	63,434
1979	713	2,602	36,896	4,008,002	3,431,216	145,183	207,649	15,055	70,897
1980	703	2,762	36,333	4,393,307	3,748,551	154,671	234,746	15,950	82,570
1981	718	2,895	37,013	4,828,273	4,115,888	164,262	273,054	17,582	92,444

(1) Refer to the number of persons receiving $1.00 or more in unemployment insurance benefits during a specific week each month. (2) Annual figures are average of 12 months.

Canadian Provincial Unemployment Rates

Source: Statistics Canada

Year	Can.	Nfld.	P.E.I.	N.S.	N.B.	Que.	Ont.	Man.	Sask.	Alta.	B.C.
1977	8.1	15.9	10.0	10.7	13.4	10.3	7.0	5.9	4.5	4.4	8.5
1978	8.4	16.4	9.9	10.6	12.6	10.9	7.2	6.5	4.9	4.7	8.3
1979	7.5	15.4	11.3	10.2	11.1	9.6	6.5	5.4	4.2	3.9	7.7
1980	7.5	13.5	10.8	9.8	11.1	9.9	6.9	5.5	4.4	3.7	6.8
1981	7.6	14.1	11.4	10.2	11.7	10.4	6.6	6.0	4.6	3.8	6.7

Canadian Economic Indicators

Source: Statistics Canada

Year	Per capita personal income	Unemploy-ment rate	Inflation rate(1)	Federal budget surplus or deficit(2) (millions of $)	Per capita national debt(3)	Gross national product(4) (millions of $)	GNP real growth(5)
1950	$ 1,040	3.6%	2.9%		$ 849.2	33,762	7.6%
1955	1,355	4.4%	.1%	−151.9	717.5	43,891	9.4%
1960	1,656	7.0%	1.4%	−413.1	676.5	53,231	2.9%
1965	2,091	3.9%	2.4%	−37.9	789.3	69,981	6.7%
1970	3,129	5.7%	3.3%	+392.5	795.6	88,390	2.5%
1975	6,001	6.9%	10.8%	−1,146.1	849.3	113,005	1.2%
1977	7,356	8.1%	8.0%	−6,290	1,270.3	121,762	2.1%
1978	8,091	8.4%	9.0%	−10,036	1,687.4	126,191	3.6%
1979	8,956	7.5%	9.1%	−16,185	2,363.9	129,850	2.9%
1980	9,972	7.5%	10.1%	−12,788	2,865.7	130,467	.5%
1981	11,520	7.6%	12.5%	−12,668	3,359.4	134,540	3.1%

(1) Rate of inflation as measured by % change in the Consumer Price Index from previous year. (2) Difference between federal government revenues and expenditures. (3) Per capita federal government debt measured by accumulated budgetary deficits since 1967. (4) Gross National Product is a measure of all goods and services produced in the country; in constant dollars. (5) Real (after inflation) change in Gross National Product over the previous year.

Canadian Consumer Price Index

Source: Statistics Canada
(All items: 1971 = 100)

Year	Avg.	Year	Avg.	Year	Avg.	Year	Avg.
1965	80.5	1970	97.2	1974	125.0	1978	175.2
1967	86.5	1971	100.0	1975	138.5	1979	191.2
1968	90.0	1972	104.8	1976	148.9	1980	210.6
1969	94.1	1973	112.7	1977	160.8	1981	236.9

Price Indexes By Item

Source: Canadian Statistical Review, March 1982 (1971 = 100)

Year and month	All items	Food	Shelter	Clothing	Trans-portation	Health, personal	Recreation, education	Tobacco, alcohol	Total services
976	148.9	166.2	145.7	132.0	143.3	144.3	136.2	134.3	149.6
977	160.8	180.1	159.3	141.0	153.3	155.0	142.7	143.8	163.2
978	175.2	208.0	170.8	146.4	162.2	166.2	148.2	155.5	174.3
979	191.2	235.4	180.5	159.9	178.0	181.2	158.4	166.7	186.5
980	210.6	260.6	192.4	178.7	200.7	199.3	173.5	185.3	201.8
981	236.9	290.4	213.2	191.4	237.6	221.0	191.0	209.2	225.0
982 (Jan.). .	249.7	295.4	228.8	193.2	258.8	230.6	198.0	227.4	241.7

Personal Expenditure on Consumer Goods and Services in Current Dollars

Source: Statistics Canada (millions of dollars)

	1973	1974	1975	1976	1977	1978	1979	1980
Food, beverages and tobacco.	15,395	17,762	20,757	22,679	24,756	27,655	30,782	34,381
Clothing and footwear	5,120	6,412	7,155	8,132	8,773	9,508	10,621	11,600
Gross rent, fuel and power.	12,506	14,271	16,445	19,146	21,850	24,374	27,235	31,046
Furniture, furnishings household equipment and operation. . .	7,304	8,652	9,884	11,117	12,016	12,976	14,281	15,508
Medical care and health services	2,054	2,466	2,896	3,465	3,829	4,272	4,755	5,266
Transportation and communication	10,551	12,161	14,292	16,390	17,957	19,606	22,395	24,843
Recreation, entertainment, education and cultural services	7,265	8,655	9,972	11,554	12,691	13,854	15,383	17,055
Personal goods and services	10,912	12,870	15,062	17,463	19,308	21,636	24,390	27,569
Total	**71,278**	**83,388**	**96,995**	**110,886**	**122,530**	**135,271**	**150,617**	**168,146**
Durable goods.	11,481	13,139	15,320	17,021	18,335	19,998	22,593	24,154
Semi-durable goods	9,059	11,184	12,428	14,176	15,374	16,710	18,709	20,554
Non-durable goods	22,302	26,218	30,422	33,967	37,383	41,689	46,451	52,422
Services	28,436	32,847	38,825	45,722	51,438	56,874	62,864	71,016

Canada's Largest Corporations

Source: The Financial Post 500; Toronto, Canada; June, 1982

Industrials Company (Home office)	Sales or operating revenue C$000	Assets	Foreign ownership %	Major shareholders
Canadian Pacific Ltd. (Montreal, Que.)	12,336,266	16,330,185	28	Power Corp. of Canada 11%
General Motors of Canada Ltd. (Oshawa, Ont.)	10,416,050	3,479,547	100	General Motors Corp., Detroit
Imperial Oil Ltd. (Toronto, Ont.)	8,185,000	7,096,000	76	Exxon Corp., New York 70%
George Weston Ltd. (Toronto, Ont.)	7,428,609	1,898,090	1	Weston family 54%
Bell Canada (Montreal, Que.)	7,389,900	12,452,000	4	Wide distribution
Ford Motor Co. of Canada (Oakville, Ont.)	7,206,600	2,172,600	92	Ford Motor Co., Dearborn, Mich.
Alcan Aluminium Ltd. (Montreal, Que.)	5,968,622(1)	7,517,420	52	Wide distribution
Shell Canada Ltd. (Toronto, Ont.)	4,751,000	3,778,000	79	Shell Investments Ltd., Neth./Brit.
Gulf Canada Ltd. (Toronto, Ont.)	4,583,000	4,468,000	60	Gulf Oil Corp., Pittsburgh
Texaco Canada Inc. (Toronto, Ont.)	4,375,332	2,879,063	90	Texaco Inc. 68%; Texaco International; New York
Canadian National Railway (Montreal, Que.)	4,285,821	6,140,167		Canadian govt. 100%
Hudson's Bay Co. (Winnipeg, Man.)	4,172,442	3,895,185		Woodbridge Co. (Thomson family) 73%
TransCanada Pipelines Ltd. (Calgary, Alta.)	3,404,897	4,586,300	1	Dome Petroleum Ltd. 46%
Provigo Inc. (Montreal, Que.)	3,293,960	624,525		Sobey Stores Ltd. 13%; Caisse de depot 30%
Massey-Ferguson Ltd. (Toronto, Ont.)	3,175,031(1)	3,011,841	67	Comp. pension funds 16%
Ontario Hydro (Toronto, Ont.)	3,161,508	17,829,621		Ontario govt. 100%
Canada Development Corp. (Vancouver, B.C.)	3,136,351	7,093,162		Canadian govt. 49%
Simpsons-Sears Ltd. (Toronto, Ont.)	3,129,625	1,741,258	40	Sears Roebuck & Co., Chicago; Hudson's Bay Co. 36%
Noranda Mines Ltd. (Toronto, Ont.)	3,030,394	5,248,644	4	Brascade Resources 37%
Canada Safeway Ltd. (Winnipeg, Man.)	3,006,302	830,832	96	Safeway Stores Inc., Oakland, Ca.

(1) Converted from U.S. $.

Foreign Ownership and Control of Major Canadian Industries, 1976

Source: Statistics Canada

Industry	Percent foreign ownership	Percent foreign control
Manufacturing: Total	**50**	**55**
Beverages.	31	29
Rubber.	73	98
Textiles	27	32
Pulp and paper	53	42
Agricultural machinery(1) . .	52	50
Automobiles and parts. . . .	92	96
Transportation equipment . .	45	54
Iron and steel mills	11	2
Aluminum	54	n.a.
Electrical apparatus	66	73
Chemicals.	66	74
Other manufacturing.	49	62
Petroleum and Natural Gas .	**51**	**68**
Mining and Smelting	**57**	**55**
Total	**52**	**59**

(1) Includes enterprises also engaged in the manufacture of other heavy equipment which tends to overstate foreign-owned and controlled proportion of capital actually engaged in the manufacture of agricultural implements only.

Canadian Imports and Exports of Leading Commodities

Source: Statistics Canada

(millions of dollars)

Commodity	Imports 1979	Imports 1980	Imports 1981	Exports 1979	Exports 1980	Exports 19
Total	**$62,871**	**$69,128**	**$78,665**	**$64,317**	**$74,259**	**$80,8**
Live Animals	75	113	202	245	254	2
Meat and fish	668	662	689	1,720	1,766	2,1
Cereals	255	348	396	3,076	4,794	5,3
Wheat	...	...	...	2,180	3,796	3,7
Fruits and vegetables	1,462	1,498	1,802	221	295	3
Crude materials, inedible, except fuels	1,086	1,051	1,162	1,492	1,347	1,4
Metal ores, concentrates, and scrap	1,130	2,125	1,865	2,402	2,862	2,5
Crude petroleum	4,497	6,919	7,854	2,405	2,899	2,5
Natural gas	...	...	...	2,889	3,984	4,3
Coal(1)	865	811	837	835	934	1,1
Wood and paper	975	918	1,174	11,621	12,458	12,6
Textiles	1,391	1,275	1,424	178	234	2
Chemicals	3,240	3,354	3,811	3,322	4,055	4,6
Iron and steel	1,669	1,415	2,263	1,599	2,039	2,3
Non-ferrous metals	1,924	2,579	2,194	3,652	6,070	5,4
General and industrial machinery	5,691	6,751	7,288	1,949	2,176	2,7
Agricultural machinery	2,115	2,092	2,394	848	876	8
Transportation equipment	17,512	16,284	19,084	13,876	13,255	15,5
Cars and chassis	4,381	4,417	5,058	4,322	4,611	5,2
Trucks, tractors, chassis	1,778	1,135	1,397	2,734	2,416	2,8
Motor vehicle parts, except engines	6,984	6,031	7,071	3,662	3,011	3,6
Other equipment and tools	6,998	8,078	9,923	1,747	1,975	2,3

(1) Coal exports include other crude bitumen substances.

Canadian Foreign Trade with Leading Countries

Source: Statistics Canada

(millions of dollars)

Exports from Canada to the following areas and countries and imports into Canada from those areas and countries:	Imports 1979	Imports 1980	Imports 1981	Exports 1979	Exports 1980	Exports 1981
Total	**$62,871**	**$69,128**	**$78,665**	**$64,317**	**$74,259**	**$80,89**
United States	**45,571**	**48,473**	**54,131**	**43,521**	**46,829**	**53,66**
Western Europe	**6,809**	**7,006**	**7,817**	**8,295**	**11,069**	**10,01**
United Kingdom	1,928	1,974	2,234	2,589	3,187	3,32
West Germany	1,559	1,455	1,603	1,368	1,640	1,27
France	779	772	847	620	995	96
Italy	636	610	696	729	983	90
Netherlands	252	264	294	1,083	1,434	1,14
Belgium and Luxembourg	241	251	296	668	989	80
Asia	**4,287**	**5,030**	**6,880**	**6,142**	**7,453**	**7,42**
Japan	2,159	2,796	4,040	4,083	4,364	4,48
Taiwan	522	558	729	104	252	23
Hong Kong	427	574	673	138	193	18
South Korea	463	414	608	365	504	44
China, People's Republic of	167	155	220	604	870	99
India	93	94	107	226	353	34
South America	**2,226**	**3,013**	**3,240**	**1,695**	**2,253**	**1,89**
Venezuela	1,505	2,217	2,385	671	656	55
Brazil	313	348	429	422	893	67
Middle East	**1,926**	**3,027**	**2,721**	**816**	**1,120**	**1,49**
Saudi Arabia	1,242	2,452	2,266	252	310	45
Central America and Antilles	**693**	**1,035**	**1,820**	**1,153**	**1,530**	**1,86**
Mexico	208	345	971	236	483	71
Cuba	107	163	197	257	417	45
Africa	**418**	**538**	**1,049**	**790**	**1,060**	**1,22**
Oceania	**613**	**696**	**656**	**657**	**791**	**93**
Australia	462	517	496	558	664	77
Eastern Europe	**327**	**307**	**349**	**1,225**	**2,125**	**2,33**
USSR	64	59	78	773	1,535	1,86

Canadian Sea Fish Catch and Exports

Source: Fisheries and Oceans Canada

Year	Total Value	Landings of Sea Fish (in metric tons): Total	Nfld.	P.E.I.	N.S.	N.B.	Que.	B.C.	Exports to[1] (in millions of pounds): Total	U.S.	Other	Exports[1]: Salmon	Lobst
1974	$259,108,000	834,165	234,510	16,329	283,045	160,120	53,524	132,904	551.4	394.6	155.0	78.5	18.2
1975	225,423,000	688,591	86,637	13,608	263,993	121,564	48,988	114,306	558.9	397.8	191.1	51.3	19.5
1976	364,754,000	1,063,071	340,241	17,123	368,456	117,937	41,948	177,366	652.9	427.2	225.7	30.6	19.3
1977	456,130,000	1,211,408	394,148	19,801	407,368	131,937	54,292	203,862	830.6	450.7	379.9	66.6	20.0
1978	668,191,000	1,352,027	463,959	25,660	444,869	151,393	67,350	198,796	931.2	494.0	436.9	78.2	21.9
1979	840,267,000	1,393,295	569,107	31,059	421,154	137,217	79,165	155,593	938.6	514.6	424.0	69.7	28.2
1980	692,356,000	1,286,014	499,199	33,463	436,822	105,356	81,248	129,926	950.0	486.1	463.2	64.9	28.6

(1) Exports include sea and freshwater fish and shellfish products but exclude bait, meal, oils, offal, livers, fish roe, and fishery foods a feeds.

Marketed Value of Canadian Fish Catches

Source: Fisheries and Oceans Canada (thousands of Canadian dollars)

Province	1979[1]	1980[1]	Province	1979[1]	1980[1]
Newfoundland	411,212	404,655	Manitoba	21,940	27,687
Prince Edward Island	71,935	54,046	Saskatchewan	7,255	8,480
Nova Scotia	418,311	438,796	Alberta	1,749	1,956
New Brunswick	223,066	220,641	British Columbia	565,630	403,941
Quebec	72,833	81,950	Yukon & NWT	3,222	3,190
Ontario	51,746	47,288	**Total**[2]	**1,804,689**	**1,651,439**

(1) Value after processing, both sea and freshwater fisheries; includes marine plants, aquatic mammals etc. (2) The sum of the provincial totals differs from the Canada total due to removal of inter-provincial shipments.

Canadian Farm Cash Receipts

Source: Statistics Canada
(millions of Canadian Dollars)
Cash receipts from farming operations excluding supplementary payments. Excludes Newfoundland

		Crops											
Year	Total cash receipts	Total crops	Wheat	Barley	C.W.B. advance payments[1]	Deferred grain receipts	Other grains[2]	Potatoes	Fruits	Vegetables	Floriculture and nursery	Tobacco	Other crops[3]
1977	10,190.3	4,435.2	1,650.3	319.8	252.9	112.2	834.9	173.8	164.3	238.5	184.4	182.1	322.0
1978	12,016.6	5,046.6	1,674.7	398.2	349.6	83.8	1,100.4	151.8	207.2	281.8	201.2	267.5	330.4
1979	14,258.4	6,128.7	1,908.4	493.8	711.2	−55.3	1,354.4	160.1	219.7	313.4	237.8	289.7	495.5
1980	15,619.9	6,882.1	2,744.3	542.8	459.4	−242.7	1,544.0	203.5	226.5	345.8	256.6	213.8	588.1
1981	18,403.5	8,849.0	3,211.6	790.3	1,392.0	−153.1	1,370.3	308.8	224.8	384.0	279.5	380.5	660.3

		Livestock and Products									
Year	Total	Cattle and calves	Hogs	Dairy products	Poultry	Eggs	Other products[4]	Forest and maple products	Provincial income stabilization payments	Dairy Supplementary payments	Deficiency[5] payments
1977	5,755.1	2,101.5	837.9	1,413.8	484.5	299.1	125.4	55.3	119.5	269.4	48.7
1978	6,970.0	2,868.8	1,155.8	1,559.6	536.7	303.5	154.8	63.5	31.6	253.1	42.6
1979	8,129.6	3,512.0	1,302.6	1,753.9	653.5	339.6	171.7	84.0	9.7	246.1	56.6
1980	8,737.8	3,600.1	1,402.5	2,061.3	663.0	395.0	195.8	81.5	46.9	255.1	36.6
1981	9,554.5	3,545.1	1,637.0	2,372.9	783.8	452.3	199.8	87.7	62.9	281.1	131.9

(1) Represents participation payments made by the Canadian Wheat Board direct to producers, net cash advances and Western Grain Stabilization payments. (2) Includes oats, rye, flaxseed, rapeseed, soybeans and corn. (3) Includes sugar beets, clover and grass seed, hay, clover, mustard seed, sunflower seed, dry beans and dry peas, net non-grain cash advances, crop insurance payments and miscellaneous products. (4) Including sheep and lambs. (5) Payments to farmers from the Agricultural Stabilization Board, made when prices for farm products are less than the previous 5-year average.

Canadian Farm Cash Receipts by Province

Source: Statistics Canada
(thousands of Canadian dollars)

Province	1976	1977	1978	1979	1980	1981
Prince Edward Island	104,005	91,039	101,066	121,439	142,992	190,004
Nova Scotia	126,508	133,373	156,609	174,571	203,967	216,697
New Brunswick	113,145	109,814	123,104	136,713	154,806	194,862
Quebec	1,371,590	1,422,497	1,716,886	1,975,910	2,252,464	2,638,908
Ontario	2,791,900	2,865,736	3,417,018	4,032,472	4,322,541	4,926,541
Manitoba	895,017	899,282	1,132,132	1,308,352	1,445,554	1,600,195
Saskatchewan	2,326,301	2,163,204	2,500,168	3,033,132	3,218,562	3,908,310
Alberta	1,858,629	1,989,243	2,286,876	2,823,508	3,132,923	3,851,972
British Columbia	481,076	516,157	582,788	652,263	746,117	876,094
Total	**10,068,171**	**10,190,345**	**12,016,647**	**14,258,360**	**15,619,926**	**18,403,583**

Harvested Acreage of Principal Canadian Crops

Source: Statistics Canada (thousands of acres)

Province	1978	1979	1980	1981	Province	1978	1979	1980	1981
Prince Edward Island	376	382	386	396	Manitoba	10,036	9,959	9,745	10,779
Nova Scotia	228	233	233	237	Saskatchewan	27,350	27,298	26,560	28,262
New Brunswick	311	308	306	307	Alberta	18,581	18,972	19,262	20,227
Quebec	4,003	4,073	4,141	4,188	British Columbia	1,186	1,251	1,296	1,308
Ontario	8,296	8,433	8,482	8,479	**Total**	**70,667**[1]	**70,909**[1]	**70,411**[1]	**74,184**[1]

Crops included are winter wheat, spring wheat, oats, barley, fall rye, flaxseed, mixed grains, corn for grain, buckwheat, peas, dry beans, soybeans, rapeseed, potatoes, mustard seed, sunflower seed, tame hay, fodder corn, and sugar beets. (1) Totals include Newfoundland potatoes (1978) 1,120 acres, (1979) 940 acres, (1980) 880 acres, (1981) 840 acres.

Production of Principal Field Crops in Canada

Source: Statistics Canada

1981	Wheats 1,000 bushels	Oats 1,000 bushels	Barley 1,000 bushels	Ryes 1,000 bushels	Flaxseed 1,000 bushels
Canada(1)	**900,955**	**231,509**	**614,708**	**37,923**	**18,800**
Prince Edward Island	205	3,306	3,224	—	—
Nova Scotia	308	1,155	400	—	—
New Brunswick	369	2,322	799	—	—
Quebec	5,743	23,726	8,125	248	—
Ontario	26,730	18,900	27,560	2,830	—
Manitoba	123,000	33,000	107,000	8,870	10,600
Saskatchewan	518,000	55,000	155,000	13,000	6,000
Alberta	222,000	91,000	303,000	12,700	2,200
British Columbia	4,600	3,100	9,600	275	—

	Mixed grains 1,000 bushels	Corn grains 1,000 bushels	Soybeans 1,000 bushels	Rapeseed 1,000 bushels	Potatoes 1,000 c.w.t.
Canada(1)	**76,399**	**244,648**	**23,200**	**79,150**	**56,325**
Prince Edward Island	4,176	—	—	—	15,180
Nova Scotia	364	—	—	—	780
New Brunswick	459	—	—	—	12,720
Quebec	6,340	24,408	—	—	8,320
Ontario	45,000	200,000	23,200	—	6,933
Manitoba	5,700	19,500	—	15,000	6,888
Saskatchewan	3,700	—	—	30,000	264
Alberta	10,500	740	—	33,000	3,710
British Columbia	160	—	—	1,150	1,425

	Mustard seed 1,000 pounds	Sunflower seed 1,000 pounds	Tame hay 1,000 tons	Fodder corn 1,000 tons	Sugar beets 1,000 tons
Canada(1)	**182,000**	**384,400**	**29,204**	**15,396**	**1,335**
Prince Edward Island	—	—	273	136	—
Nova Scotia	—	—	432	135	—
New Brunswick	—	—	357	90	—
Quebec	—	—	6,022	4,085	180
Ontario	—	—	8,020	9,520	—
Manitoba	38,000	376,000	2,600	470	367
Saskatchewan	102,000	8,400	2,500	—	—
Alberta	42,000	—	7,100	450	788
British Columbia	—	—	1,900	510	—

(1) Excluding Newfoundland.

Canadian Balance of International Payments

Source: Statistics Canada (millions of Canadian dollars)

Year	Total current receipts	Total current payments	Current account balance	Goods and Services: Receipts	Payments	Balance	Merchandise trade: Exports	Imports	Balance	Service transactions: Receipts	Payments	Balance
1930	1,297	1,634	−337	1,272	1,579	−307	880	973	−93	392	606	−214
1935	1,152	1,027	+125	1,129	1,000	+129	732	526	+206	397	474	−77
1940	1,799	1,648	+151	1,749	1,606	+143	1,202	1006	+196	547	600	−53
1945	4,486	3,797	+689	4,402	2,889	1,513	3,474	1,442	2,032	928	1,447	−519
1950	4,284	4,603	−319	4,158	4,492	−334	3,139	3,132	+7	1,019	1,360	−341
1955	5,926	6,613	−687	5,737	6,390	−653	4,332	4,543	−211	1,405	1,847	−442
1960	7,215	8,448	−1,233	6,982	8,089	−1,107	5,392	5,540	−148	1,590	2,549	−959
1965	11,648	12,778	−1,130	11,182	12,341	−1,159	8,745	8,627	+118	2,437	3,714	−1,277
1970	21,932	20,826	1,106	21,167	20,214	+953	16,921	13,869	+3,052	4,246	6,345	−2,099
1975	41,840	46,597	−4,757	40,452	45,589	−5,137	33,511	33,962	−451	6,941	11,627	−4,686
1977	54,103	58,404	−4,301	52,548	57,262	−4,714	44,253	41,523	+2,730	8,295	15,739	−7,444
1978	64,577	69,512	−4,935	62,985	67,970	−4,985	53,054	49,047	+4,007	9,931	18,923	−8,992
1979	79,088	83,982	−4,894	77,087	82,671	−5,584	65,275	61,125	+4,150	11,812	21,546	−9,734
1980	92,921	94,825	−1,904	90,258	93,443	−3,185	76,170	68,360	+7,810	14,088	25,083	−10,995
1981	102,057	108,633	−6,576	98,999	107,177	−8,178	84,140	77,504	+6,636	14,859	29,673	−14,814

Canadian General and Allied Special Hospitals

Source: Health and Welfare Canada

1980-81[1]	Hospitals: Public	Private	Fed.	Public	Beds: Private	Fed.	Public	Admissions: Private	Fed.	Expenses ($1,000) Public
Newfoundland	47	—	—	3,321	—	—	92,949	—	—	191,058
Prince Edward Is.	10	—	1	757	—	14	25,715	—	n.a.	30,489
Nova Scotia	48	—	3	5,503	—	162	143,863	—	2,277	300,732
New Brunswick	33	—	1	4,237	—	10	115,792	—	n.a.	221,244
Quebec	196	41	11	49,225	2,842	1,262	763,326	11,959	566	2,743,706
Ontario	230	17	17	48,442	555	612	1,272,407	11,077	8,877	2,867,437
Manitoba	79	—	24	6,278	—	553	154,388	—	4,592	331,061
Saskatchewan	139	—	3	7,804	—	71	205,029	—	1,198	331,326
Alberta	146	—	7	16,245	—	123	369,244	—	1,675	795,183
British Columbia	118	1	15	18,785	7	80	422,458	205	—	1,007,433
Yukon	—	—	6	—	—	161	—		3,772	—
N.W.T.	3	—	43	147	—	281	3,336		3,197	7,968
Canada	**1,049**	**59**	**131**	**160,744**	**3,404**	**3,329**	**3,568,507**	**23,241**	**26,154**	**8,827,637**

(1) Preliminary data.

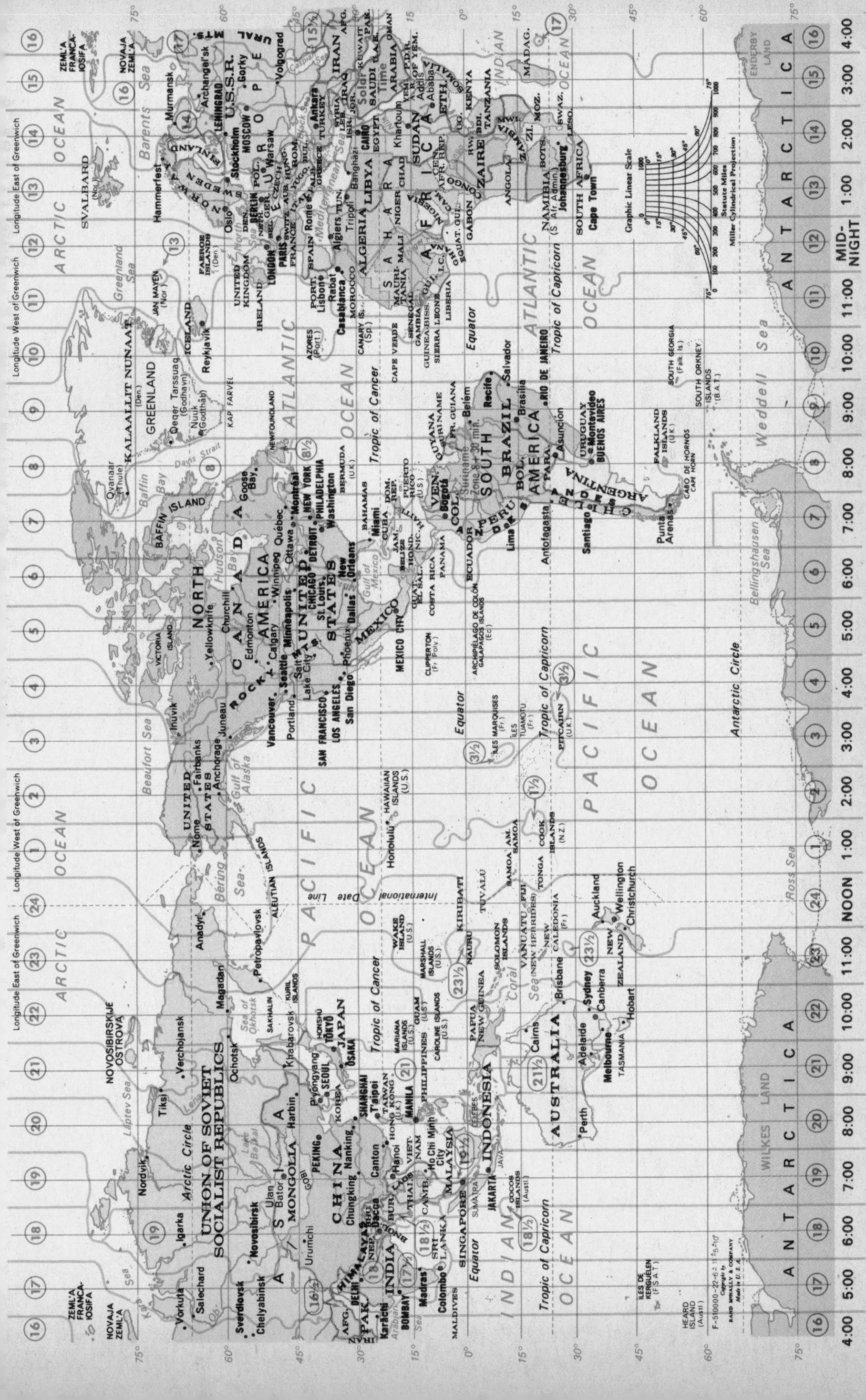
Longitude East of Greenwich
Longitude West of Greenwich
4:00
5:00
6:00
7:00
8:00
9:00
10:00
11:00
NOON
1:00
2:00
3:00
4:00
5:00
6:00
7:00
8:00
9:00
10:00
11:00
MID-NIGHT
1:00
2:00
3:00
4:00
ARCTIC OCEAN
PACIFIC OCEAN
ATLANTIC OCEAN
INDIAN OCEAN
Tropic of Cancer
Tropic of Capricorn
Equator
Arctic Circle
Antarctic Circle
International Date Line
UNION OF SOVIET SOCIALIST REPUBLICS
CHINA
MONGOLIA
INDIA
JAPAN
INDONESIA
AUSTRALIA
CANADA
NORTH AMERICA
UNITED STATES
MEXICO
SOUTH AMERICA
BRAZIL
ARGENTINA
GREENLAND
KALAALLIT NUNAAT
AFRICA
EUROPE
ANTARCTICA
WILKES LAND
ENDERBY LAND
Weddell Sea
Ross Sea
Bellingshausen Sea
Beaufort Sea
Barents Sea
Greenland Sea
Baffin Bay
Hudson Bay
Davis Strait
Bering Sea
Gulf of Alaska
Gulf of Mexico
Coral Sea
Mediterranean Sea
Laptev Sea
Sea of Okhotsk
NEW ZEALAND
TASMANIA
PAPUA NEW GUINEA
PHILIPPINES
HAWAIIAN ISLANDS (U.S.)
Honolulu
Vancouver
Seattle
Portland
SAN FRANCISCO
LOS ANGELES
San Diego
Phoenix
Dallas
Chicago
DETROIT
NEW YORK
PHILADELPHIA
Washington
Montreal
Ottawa
Winnipeg
Quebec
Miami
New Orleans
Mexico City
Bogotá
Lima
Santiago
BUENOS AIRES
Montevideo
RIO DE JANEIRO
Brasília
Recife
Salvador
LONDON
PARIS
Rome
Madrid
Lisbon
BERLIN
Warsaw
Stockholm
Oslo
MOSCOW
LENINGRAD
CAIRO
Algiers
Casablanca
Johannesburg
Cape Town
Addis Ababa
Khartoum
Ankara
PEKING
SHANGHAI
TOKYO
OSAKA
SEOUL
MANILA
SINGAPORE
JAKARTA
BOMBAY
Madras
Karachi
DELHI
Sydney
Melbourne
Perth
Adelaide
Brisbane
Canberra
Auckland
Wellington
Christchurch
Graphic Linear Scale
Statute Miles
Miller Cylindrical Projection
F-510000-22-6
Copyright by RAND McNALLY & COMPANY
Made in U.S.A.

INDEX

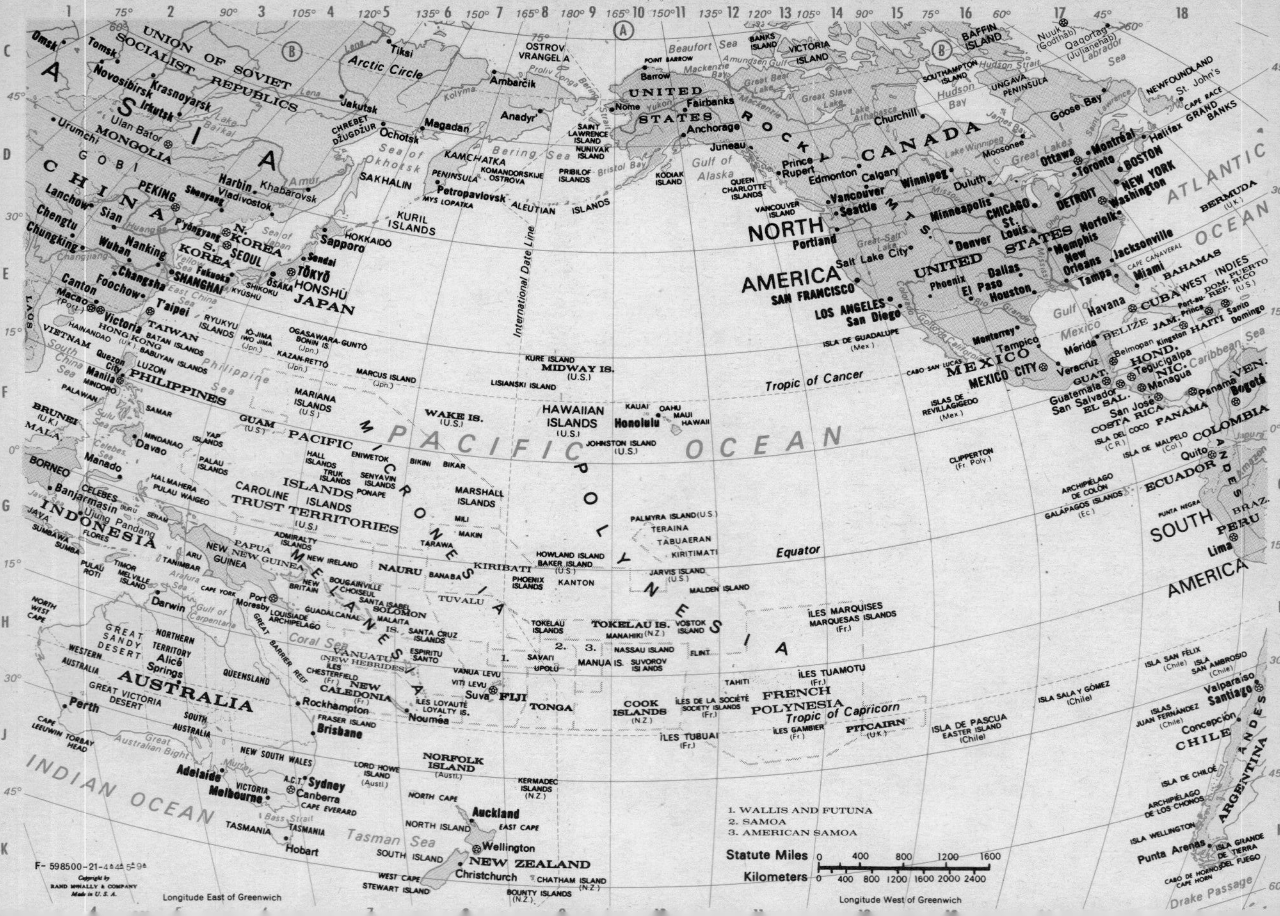

PACIFIC OCEAN
INDIAN OCEAN
ATLANTIC OCEAN
ASIA
UNION OF SOVIET SOCIALIST REPUBLICS
CHINA
MONGOLIA
JAPAN
INDONESIA
PHILIPPINES
AUSTRALIA
NEW ZEALAND
NORTH AMERICA
SOUTH AMERICA
CANADA
UNITED STATES
MEXICO
MICRONESIA
MELANESIA
POLYNESIA
International Date Line
Tropic of Cancer
Equator
Tropic of Capricorn
Arctic Circle
HAWAIIAN ISLANDS (U.S.)
Honolulu
MIDWAY IS. (U.S.)
WAKE IS. (U.S.)
GUAM (U.S.)
FIJI
TONGA
COOK ISLANDS (N.Z.)
FRENCH POLYNESIA
PITCAIRN (U.K.)
NORFOLK ISLAND (Austl.)
1. WALLIS AND FUTUNA
2. SAMOA
3. AMERICAN SAMOA
Statute Miles 0 400 800 1200 1600
Kilometers 0 400 800 1200 1600 2000 2400
Longitude East of Greenwich
Longitude West of Greenwich
F- 598500-21-4-4-4-5-9-8
Copyright by RAND McNALLY & COMPANY Made in U.S.A.

INDEX

PROVINCES OF CHINA

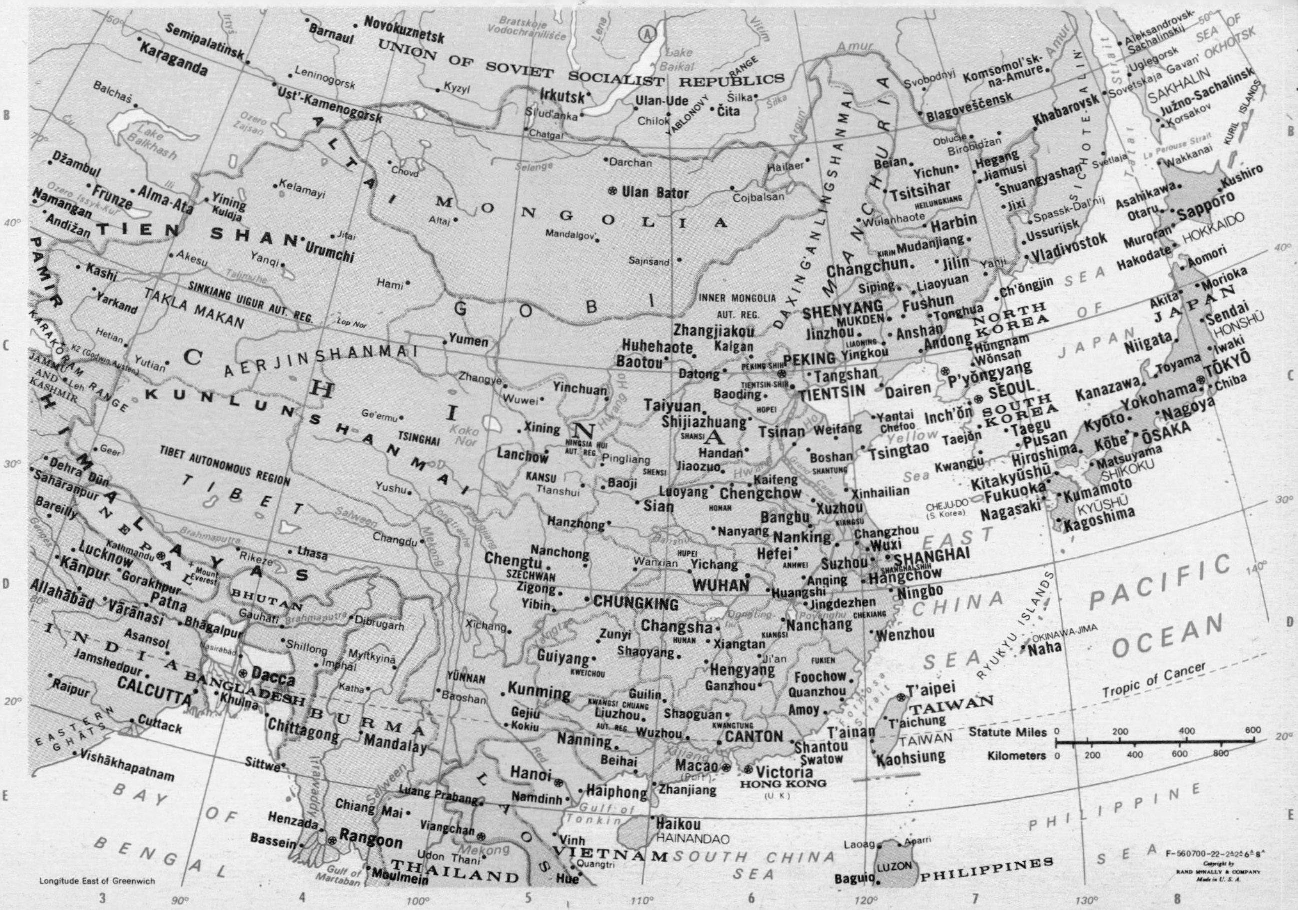

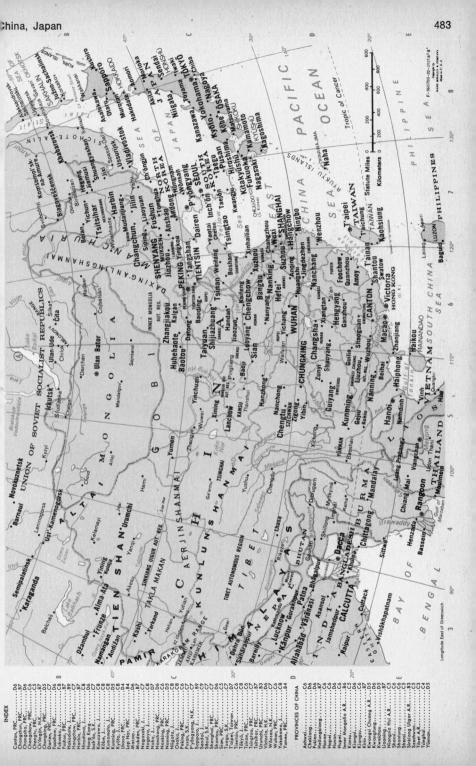

INDEX

MISCELLANEOUS

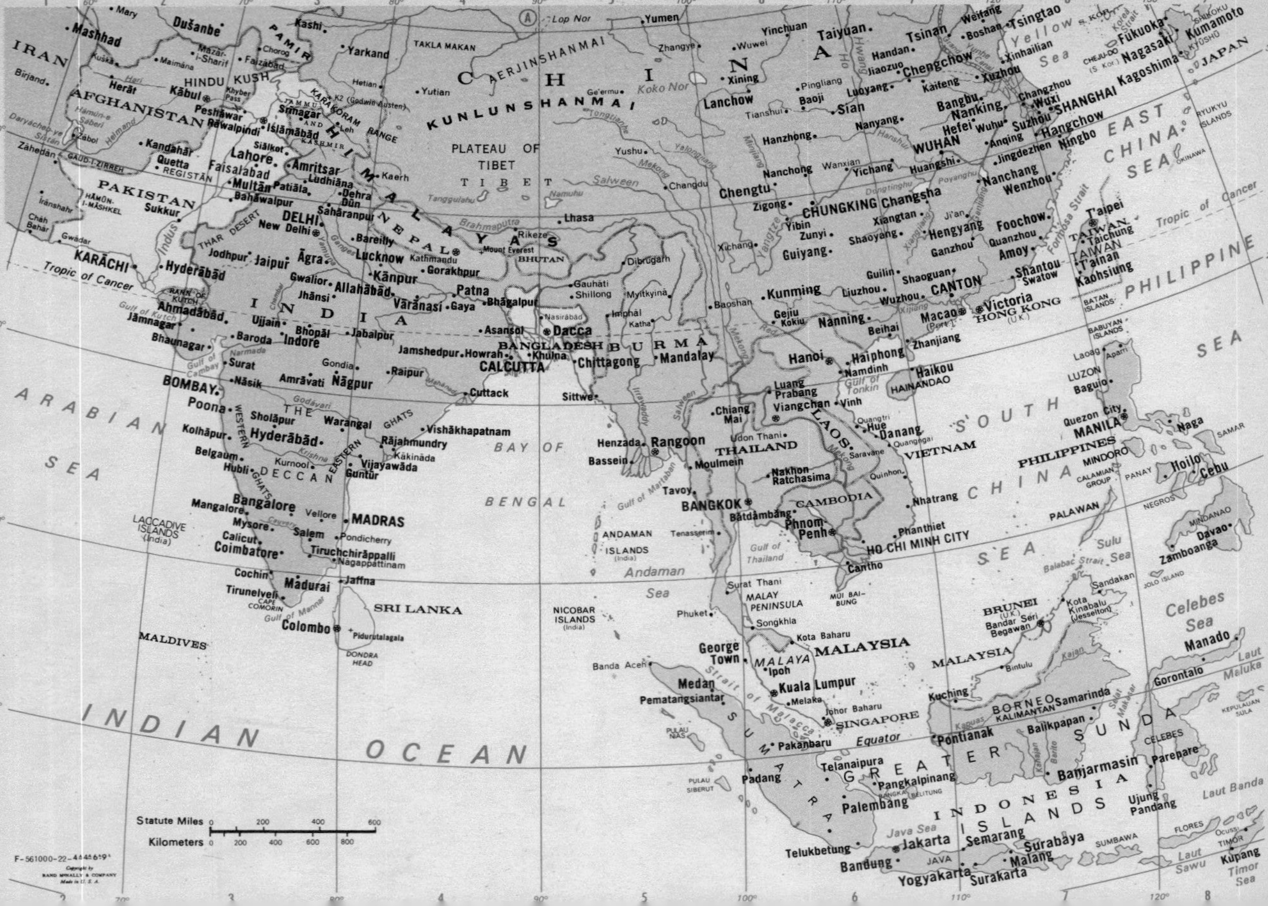

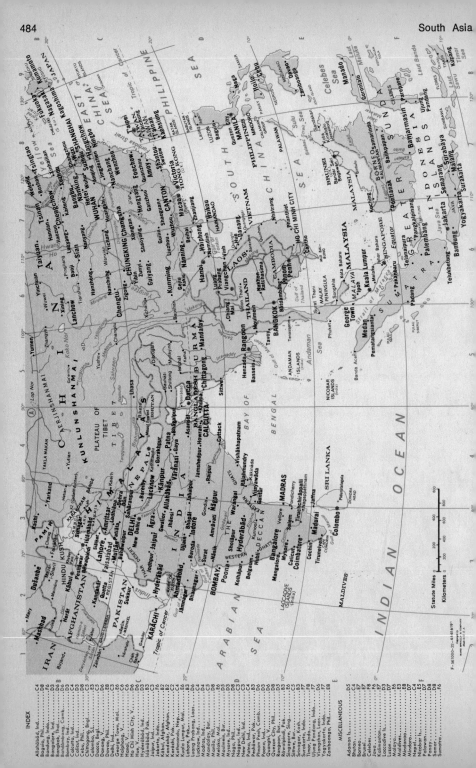

INDEX

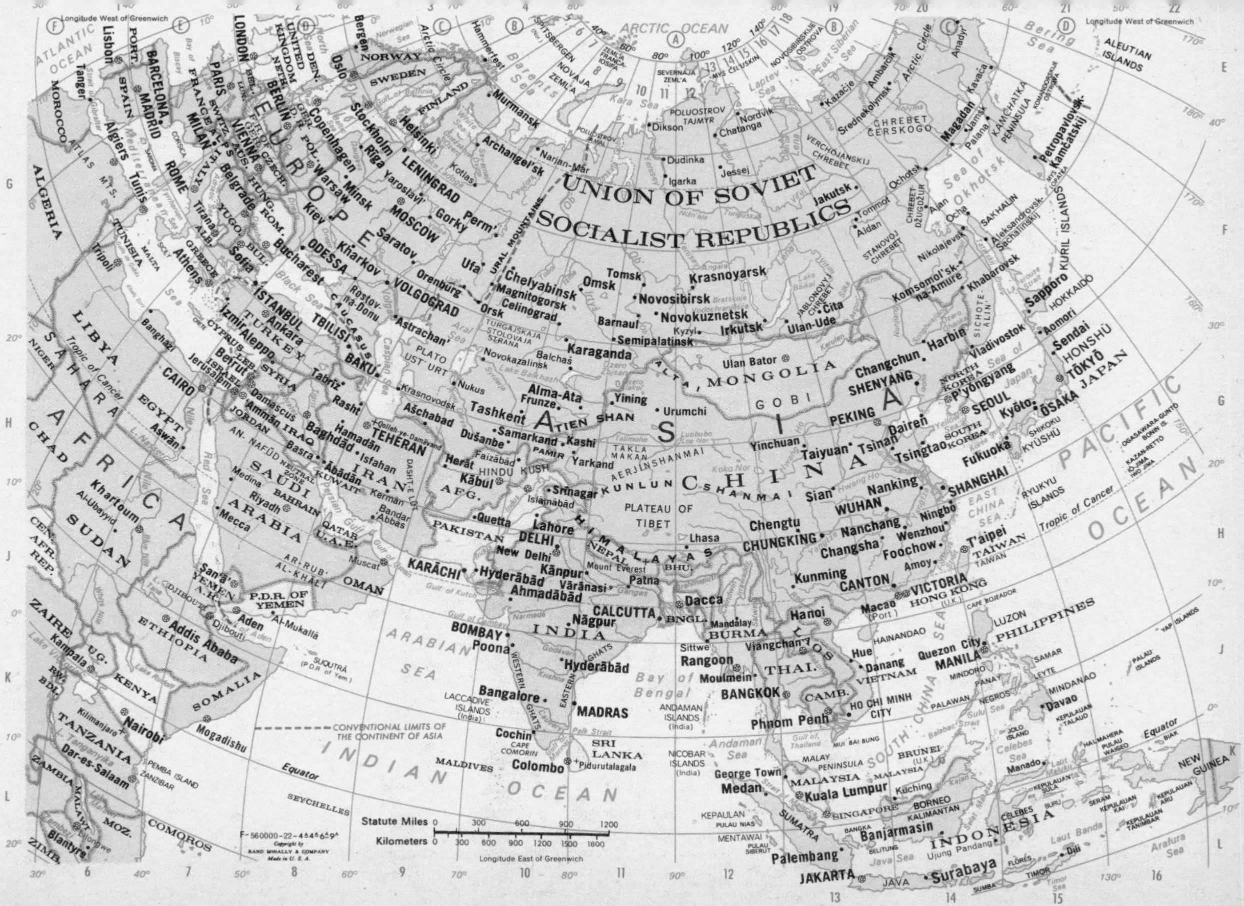

ARCTIC OCEAN
UNION OF SOVIET SOCIALIST REPUBLICS
EUROPE
ASIA
CHINA
MONGOLIA
GOBI
AFRICA
INDIA
PACIFIC OCEAN
INDIAN OCEAN
ARABIAN SEA
Bay of Bengal
SOUTH CHINA SEA
EAST CHINA SEA
Sea of Okhotsk
Bering Sea
Barents Sea
Kara Sea
Laptev Sea
East Siberian Sea
Black Sea
Caspian Sea
Red Sea
Aral Sea
Arctic Circle
Tropic of Cancer
Equator
URAL MOUNTAINS
CAUCASUS
HIMALAYAS
TIEN SHAN
KUNLUN SHAN
HINDU KUSH
PLATEAU OF TIBET
Mount Everest
JAPAN
PHILIPPINES
INDONESIA
MALAYSIA
BORNEO
SUMATRA
JAVA
SRI LANKA
SAUDI ARABIA
IRAN
TURKEY
EGYPT
LIBYA
SUDAN
ETHIOPIA
SOMALIA
KENYA
TANZANIA
MOSCOW
LENINGRAD
PEKING
SHANGHAI
TŌKYŌ
CALCUTTA
BOMBAY
DELHI
KARĀCHI
TEHERAN
ISTANBUL
CAIRO
LONDON
PARIS
Statute Miles 0 300 600 900 1200
Kilometers 0 300 600 900 1200 1500 1800
Longitude East of Greenwich
Longitude West of Greenwich
CONVENTIONAL LIMITS OF THE CONTINENT OF ASIA
F-560000-22-4-4-4-6-9-A
Copyright by RAND McNALLY & COMPANY
Made in U. S. A.

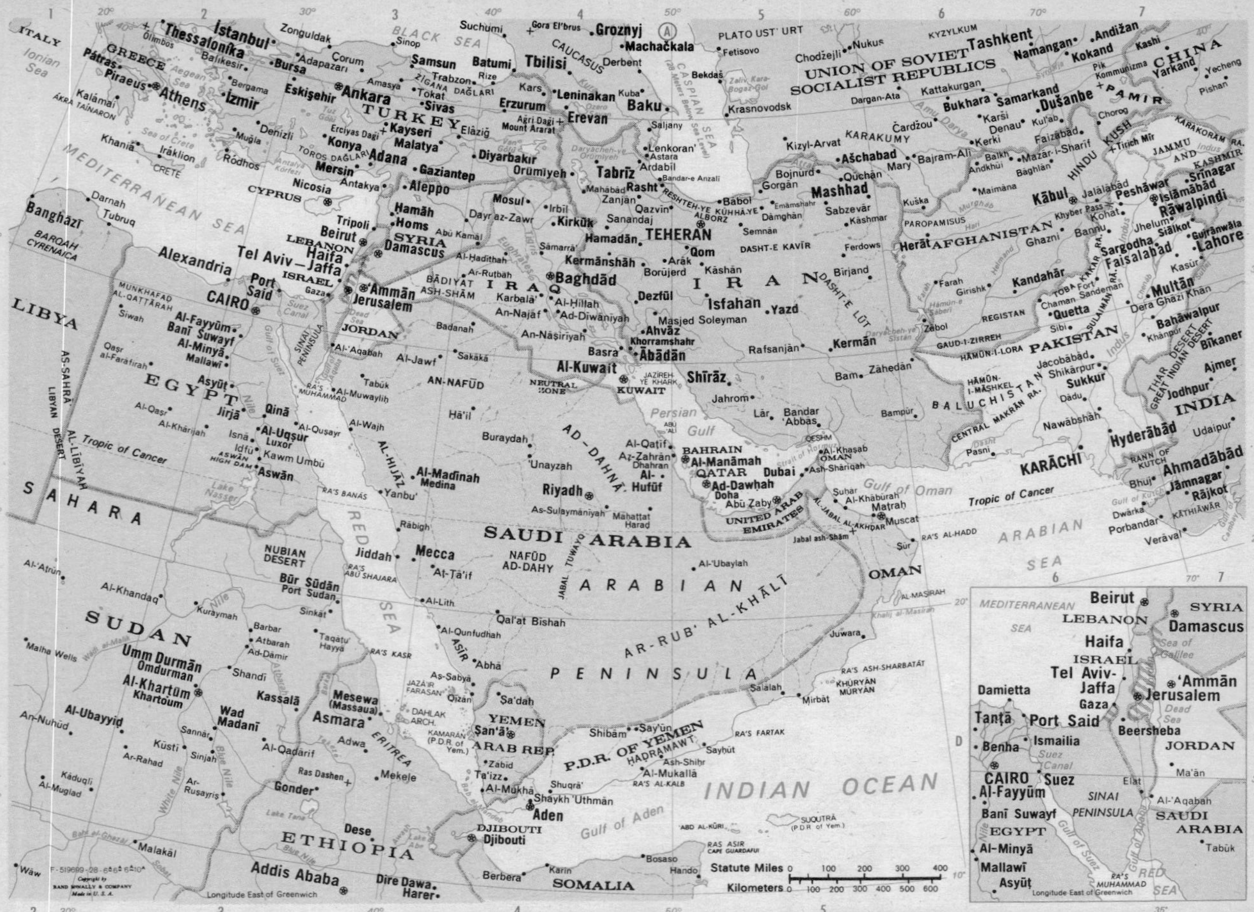
UNION OF SOVIET SOCIALIST REPUBLICS
TURKEY
SYRIA
IRAQ
IRAN
AFGHANISTAN
PAKISTAN
INDIA
CHINA
SAUDI ARABIA
KUWAIT
BAHRAIN
QATAR
UNITED ARAB EMIRATES
OMAN
YEMEN ARAB REP.
P.D.R. OF YEMEN
JORDAN
LEBANON
ISRAEL
EGYPT
LIBYA
SUDAN
ETHIOPIA
DJIBOUTI
SOMALIA
CYPRUS
GREECE
ITALY
BLACK SEA
CASPIAN SEA
MEDITERRANEAN SEA
RED SEA
ARABIAN SEA
INDIAN OCEAN
Persian Gulf
Gulf of Oman
Gulf of Aden
ARABIAN PENINSULA
AR-RUB' AL-KHĀLĪ
SAHARA
Tropic of Cancer
İstanbul
Ankara
Baku
Tbilisi
Erevan
Tashkent
Samarkand
Aščhabad
Mashhad
TEHERAN
Baghdād
Damascus
Beirut
Tel Aviv–Jaffa
Jerusalem
'Ammān
CAIRO
Alexandria
Riyadh
Mecca
Jiddah
Medina
Kābul
Karāchi
Lahore
Al-Kuwait
Muscat
Aden
Ṣan'ā'
Al-Kharṭūm
Addis Ababa
Statute Miles 0 100 200 300 400
Kilometers 0 100 200 300 400 500 600
Longitude East of Greenwich
Copyright by RAND McNALLY & COMPANY Made in U.S.A.

INDEX

INDEX

COUNTRIES

INDEX

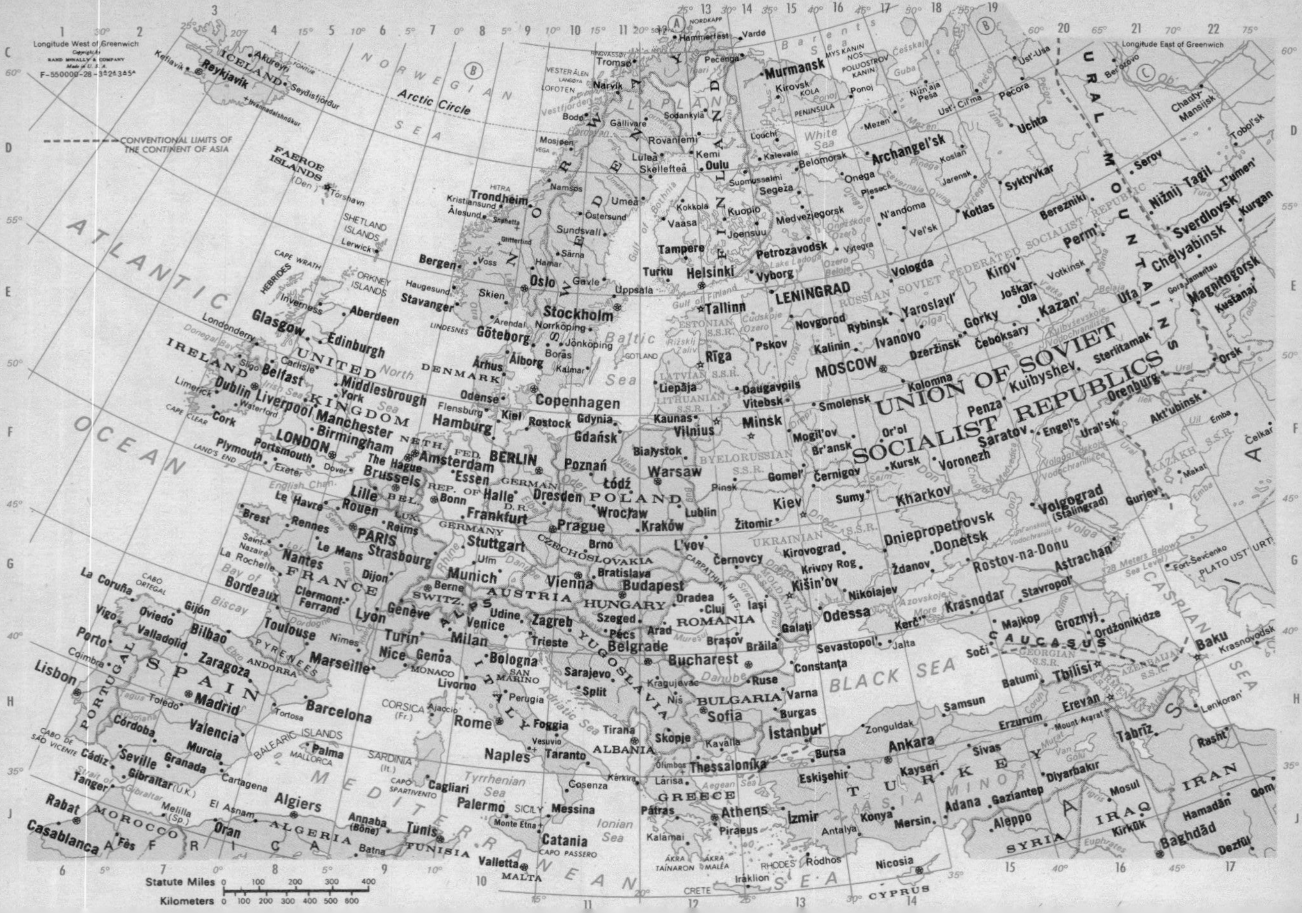

Longitude West of Greenwich
F-550000-28-3-2-3-4-5-A
CONVENTIONAL LIMITS OF THE CONTINENT OF ASIA
Longitude East of Greenwich
NORWEGIAN SEA
Arctic Circle
ATLANTIC OCEAN
ICELAND
Reykjavík
FAEROE ISLANDS (Den.)
SHETLAND ISLANDS
ORKNEY ISLANDS
HEBRIDES
IRELAND
UNITED KINGDOM
LONDON
North Sea
NORWAY
SWEDEN
FINLAND
LAPLAND
DENMARK
Baltic Sea
Barents Sea
White Sea
URAL MOUNTAINS
UNION OF SOVIET SOCIALIST REPUBLICS
RUSSIAN SOVIET FEDERATED SOCIALIST REPUBLIC
MOSCOW
LENINGRAD
BERLIN
POLAND
CZECHOSLOVAKIA
AUSTRIA
HUNGARY
ROMANIA
YUGOSLAVIA
BULGARIA
ALBANIA
GREECE
ITALY
FRANCE
PARIS
SPAIN
PORTUGAL
MOROCCO
ALGERIA
AFRICA
TUNISIA
MEDITERRANEAN SEA
BLACK SEA
CASPIAN SEA
CAUCASUS
TURKEY
ASIA MINOR
SYRIA
IRAQ
IRAN
CYPRUS
Statute Miles
Kilometers

Tropic of Cancer
CARIBBEAN SEA
PANAMA
Colón
Chepo
Panamá
Balboa Heights
La Chorrera
Penonomé
Bay of Panama
U.S.A.
Miami
BAHAMAS
Nassau
SAN SALVADOR
Havana
CUBA
WEST INDIES
Santiago de Cuba
CAYMAN IS. (U.K.)
Kingston
JAMAICA
GREATER ANTILLES
HAITI
Port-au-Prince
DOM. REP.
Santo Domingo
San Juan
PUERTO RICO (U.S.)
VIRGIN IS. (U.K. and U.S.)
BARBUDA
ANTIGUA
GUADELOUPE (Fr.)
DOMINICA
MARTINIQUE (Fr.)
Fort-de-France
LESSER ANTILLES
WINDWARD IS.
Bridgetown
BARBADOS
GRENADA
Port of Spain
TRINIDAD AND TOBAGO
NETHERLANDS ANTILLES
ISLA DE MARGARITA
Mérida
BELIZE
Belmopan
Gulf of Honduras
Guatemala
HONDURAS
Tegucigalpa
San Salvador
EL SALV.
NICARAGUA
Managua
Lago de Nicaragua
Bluefields
COSTA RICA
San José
David
PANAMA
Gulf of Panama
CARIBBEAN SEA
Barranquilla
Santa Marta
Cartagena
Maracaibo
CARACAS
Barcelona
Barquisimeto
Cúcuta
San Cristóbal
Ciudad Bolívar
Ciudad Guayana
VENEZUELA
Bucaramanga
Medellín
Manizales
BOGOTÁ
Nevado del Tolima
Buenaventura
Cali
COLOMBIA
Puerto Ayacucho
Mt. Roraima
San Fernando de Atabapo
Georgetown
GUYANA
Paramaribo
SURINAME
Cayenne
FR. GUIANA
ISLA DE MARACÁ
Amapá
Macapá
ILHA DE MARAJÓ
Boa Vista
ISLA DEL COCO (C.R.)
ISLA DE MALPELO (Col.)
Tumaco
CABO DE SAN FRANCISCO
Esmeraldas
ARCHIPIÉLAGO DE COLÓN
GALAPAGOS ISLANDS (Ec.)
ISLA ISABELA
Quito
ECUADOR
Chimborazo
Guayaquil
Cuenca
Golfo de Guayaquil
Mitú
Iquitos
Loja
Piura
Chiclayo
Cajamarca
Trujillo
Chimbote
Nevado Huascarán
Huaraz
Cerro de Pasco
LIMA
Callao
Huancayo
Pucallpa
Cuzco
Ica
Lago Titicaca
Puno
Volcán Misti
Arequipa
Mollendo
Arica
Iquique
PERU
ANDES
Leticia
Fonte Boa
SELVAS
Manaus
Óbidos
Santarém
Amazon
Belém
Porto de Moz
São Luís
Parnaíba
ILHA FERNANDO DE NORONHA (Braz.)
Fortaleza
Teresina
CABO DE SÃO ROQUE
Natal
João Pessoa
Campina Grande
Paulistana
Caruaru
Recife
Juàzeiro
Maceió
Penedo
Aracaju
Marabá
Carolina
Porto Velho
Rio Branco
BRAZIL
Guajará Mirim
Riberalta
SERRA DOS PARECIS
Cobija
Puerto Maldonado
Porto Nacional
Barra
Salvador
PLANALTO DO MATO GROSSO
Trinidad
Mato Grosso
Cuiabá
Brasília
Ilhéus
Itabuna
Belmonte
Goiânia
Montes Claros
SERRA DO ESPINHAÇO
Governador Valadares
Belo Horizonte
Vitória
Nevado Illampu
La Paz
BOLIVIA
Oruro
Santa Cruz
Sucre
Potosí
Corumbá
Campo Grande
CHACO
Tarija
PARAGUAY
DESIERTO DE ATACAMA
Antofagasta
San Salvador de Jujuy
Tropic of Capricorn
Concepción
Campinas
Londrina
SÃO PAULO
Santos
RIO DE JANEIRO
CABO DE SÃO TOMÉ
Campos
CABO FRIO
Ponta Grossa
Curitiba
SERRA DO MAR
Florianópolis
Salta
San Miguel de Tucumán
Asunción
Corrientes
Posadas
Cerro Ojos del Salado
Santiago del Estero
ISLA SAN FÉLIX
ISLA SAN AMBROSIO (Chile)
PUNTA MORRO
Coquimbo
Santa Maria
Porto Alegre
Pelotas
Rio Grande
Salto
Paysandú
URUGUAY
Montevideo
Rocha
San Juan
Córdoba
Santa Fe
Rosario
Viña del Mar
Valparaíso
Cerro Aconcagua
Mendoza
SANTIAGO
Talca
BUENOS AIRES
La Plata
Río de la Plata
Talcahuano
Concepción
Mar del Plata
CABO SAN ANTONIO
GRAN CHACO
ARGENTINA
PAMPA
CHILE
ISLAS JUAN FERNÁNDEZ (Chile)
ISLA ALEJANDRO SELKIRK
ISLA RÓBINSON CRUSOE
Temuco
Neuquén
Valdivia
Bahía Blanca
Osorno
Viedma
Golfo San Matías
Puerto Montt
ISLA DE CHILOÉ
Rawson
CABO DOS BAHÍAS
Comodoro Rivadavia
Golfo San Jorge
PATAGONIA
Monte San Valentín
ISLA WELLINGTON
PACIFIC OCEAN
ATLANTIC OCEAN
Equator
Puerto Natales
Río Gallegos
FALKLAND ISLANDS (U.K.)
Stanley
Punta Arenas
Strait of Magellan
TIERRA DEL FUEGO
Ushuaia
CABO DE HORNOS
CAPE HORN
SOUTH GEORGIA (Falk. Is.)
Longitude West of Greenwich
Statute Miles 0 200 400 600 800
Kilometers 0 200 400 600 800 1000 1200
Copyright by RAND McNALLY & COMPANY Made in U. S. A.

INDEX

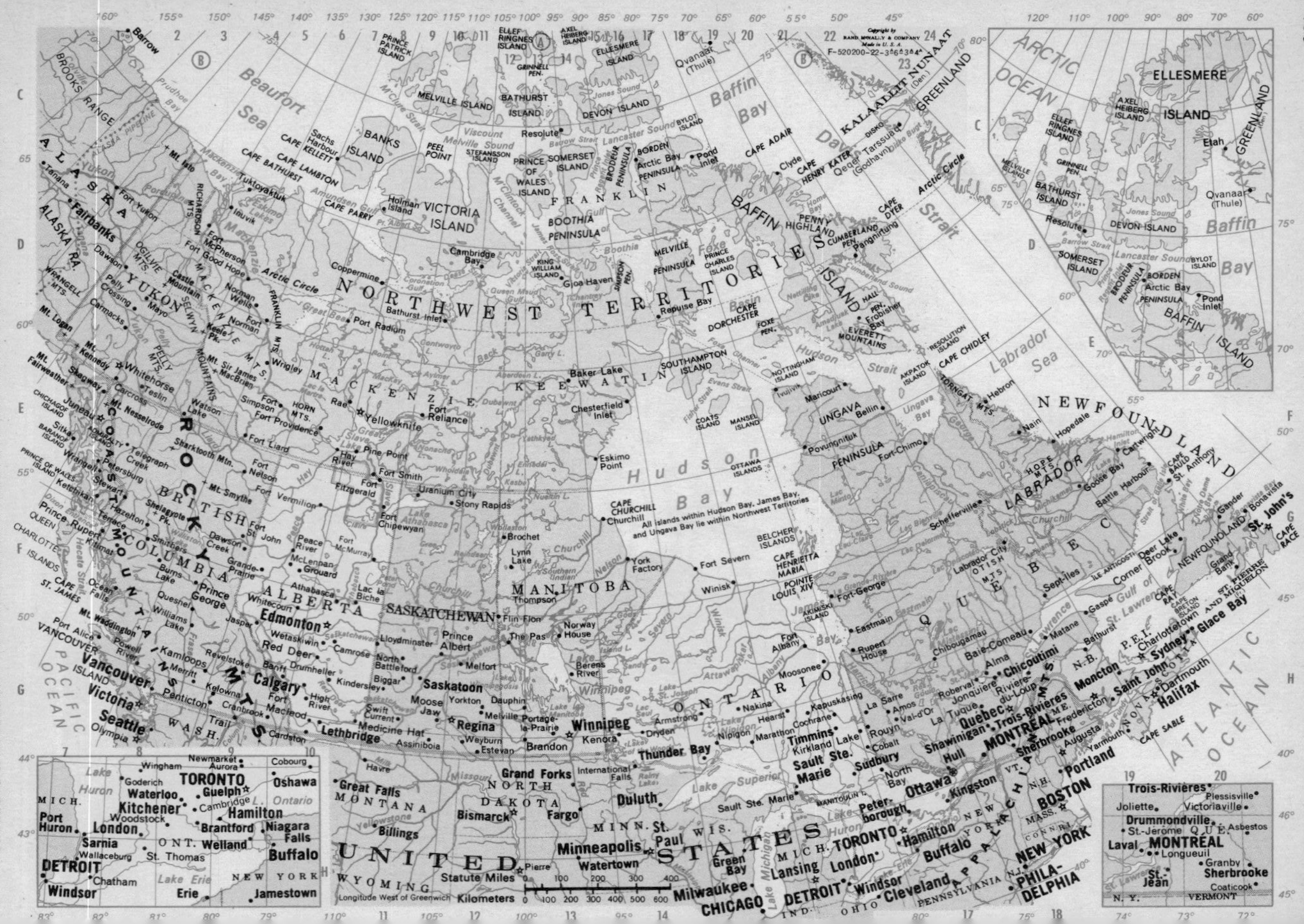
NORTHWEST TERRITORIES
FRANKLIN
KEEWATIN
MACKENZIE
YUKON
BRITISH COLUMBIA
ALBERTA
SASKATCHEWAN
MANITOBA
ONTARIO
QUEBEC
LABRADOR
NEWFOUNDLAND
ALASKA
UNITED STATES
ROCKY MOUNTAINS
Hudson Bay
Beaufort Sea
Baffin Bay
Labrador Sea
PACIFIC OCEAN
ATLANTIC OCEAN
ARCTIC OCEAN
GREENLAND
KALAALLIT NUNAAT
BAFFIN ISLAND
VICTORIA ISLAND
BANKS ISLAND
ELLESMERE ISLAND
DEVON ISLAND
SOUTHAMPTON ISLAND
All islands within Hudson Bay, James Bay, and Ungava Bay lie within Northwest Territories
Statute Miles
Kilometers
Longitude West of Greenwich
Copyright by RAND McNALLY & COMPANY Made in U.S.A.

INDEX

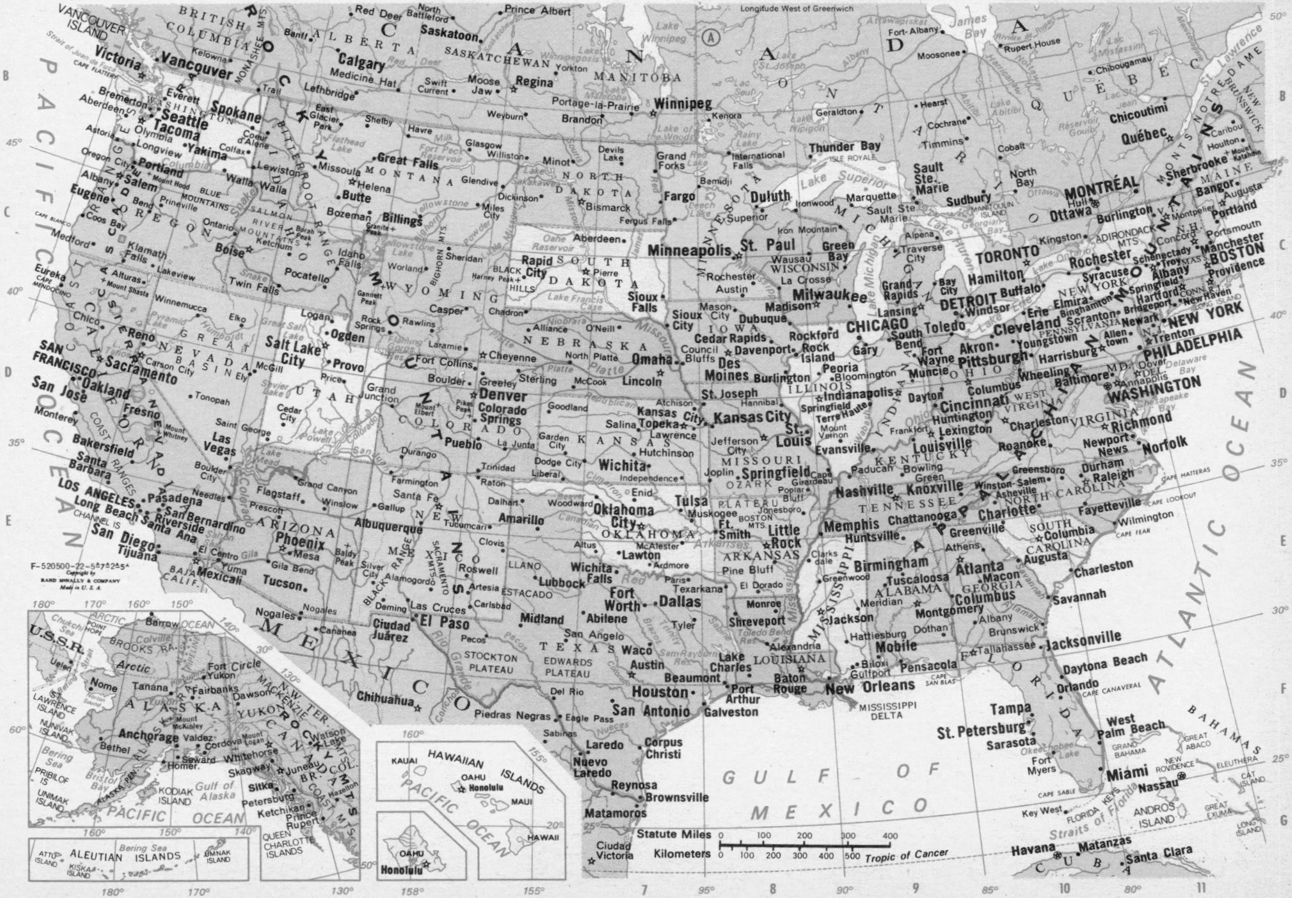
PACIFIC OCEAN
ATLANTIC OCEAN
GULF OF MEXICO
CANADA
MEXICO
ROCKY MOUNTAINS
APPALACHIAN MOUNTAINS
Longitude West of Greenwich
Seattle
Portland
San Francisco
Los Angeles
San Diego
Salt Lake City
Denver
Minneapolis
St. Paul
Chicago
Detroit
Toronto
Montréal
Boston
New York
Philadelphia
Washington
Houston
Dallas
New Orleans
Miami
Statute Miles
Kilometers
Tropic of Cancer
HAWAIIAN ISLANDS
ALEUTIAN ISLANDS
F-520500-22-5-7-2-5-4
RAND McNALLY & COMPANY
Made in U.S.A.

WORLD FLAGS AND MAPS

AFGHANISTAN

ALBANIA

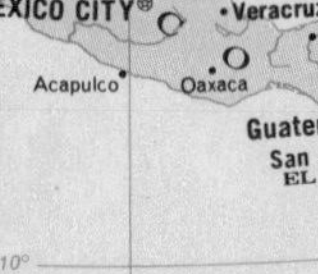
ALGERIA

ANDORRA

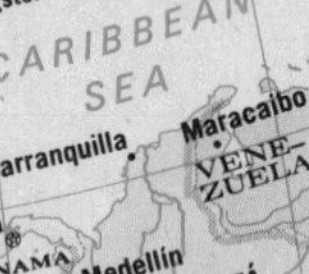
ANGOLA

Flags shown are *national* flags in common use and vary slightly from official *state* flags, most particularly by omitting coats of arms in some cases.

ARGENTINA

AUSTRALIA

AUSTRIA

BAHAMAS

BAHRAIN

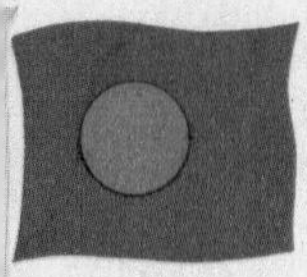
BANGLADESH

BARBADOS

BELGIUM

BENIN

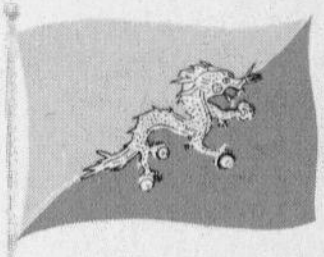
BHUTAN

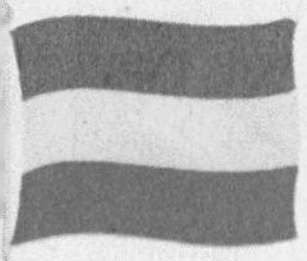
BOLIVIA

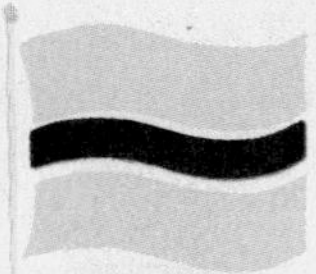
BOTSWANA

BRAZIL

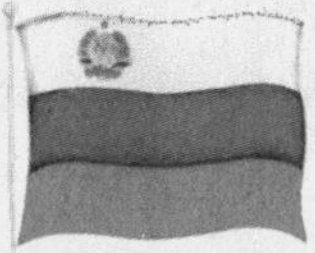
BULGARIA

BURMA

BURUNDI

CAMBODIA

CAMEROON

CANADA

CAPE VERDE

CENTRAL AFRICAN REPUBLIC

CHAD

CHILE

CHINA (MAINLAND)

CHINA (TAIWAN)

COLOMBIA

COMOROS

CONGO

COSTA RICA

CUBA

CYPRUS

CZECHOSLOVAKIA

DENMARK

DJIBOUTI

DOMINICA

DOMINICAN REPUBLIC

ECUADOR

EGYPT

EL SALVADOR

EQUATORIAL GUINEA

ETHIOPIA

FIJI

FINLAND

FRANCE

GABON

GAMBIA

GERMAN DEM. REP.

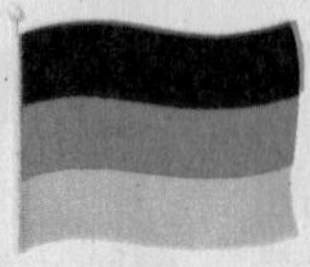
GERMANY, FED. REP. OF

GHANA

GREECE

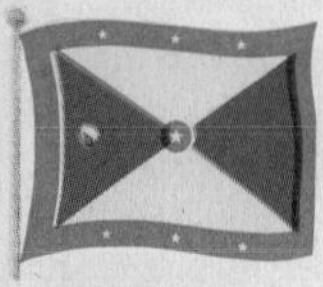
GRENADA

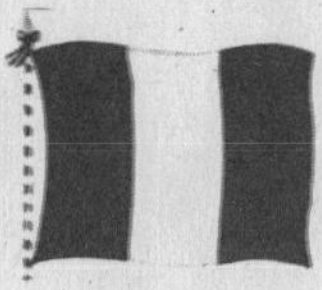
GUATEMALA

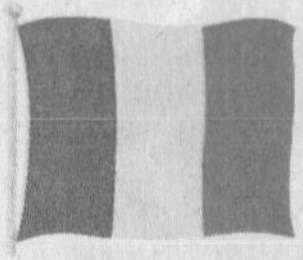
GUINEA

GUINEA-BISSAU

GUYANA

HAITI

HONDURAS

HUNGARY

ICELAND

INDIA

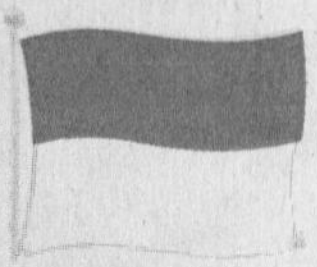
INDONESIA

IRAN

IRAQ

IRELAND

ISRAEL

ITALY

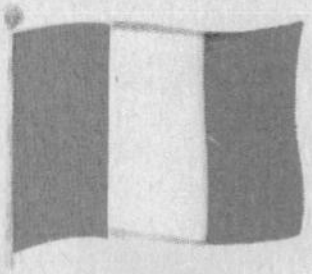
IVORY COAST

JAMAICA

JAPAN

JORDAN

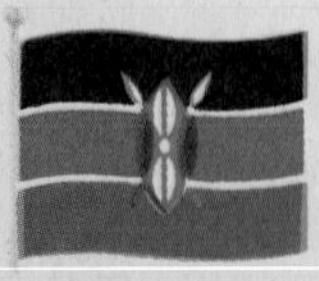
KENYA

KIRIBATI

KOREA, NORTH

KOREA, SOUTH

KUWAIT

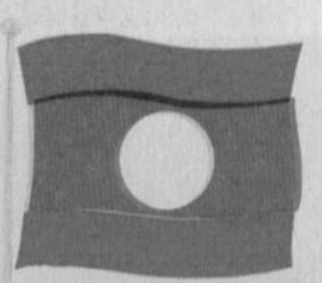
LAOS

LEBANON

LESOTHO

LIBERIA

LIBYA

LIECHTENSTEIN

LUXEMBOURG

MADAGASCAR

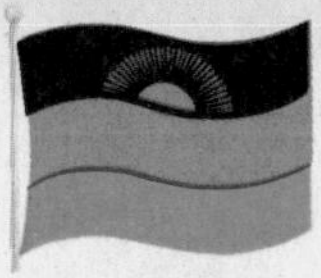
MALAWI

MALAYSIA

MALDIVES

MALI

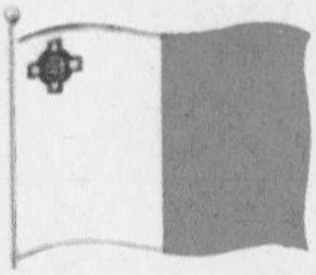
MALTA

MAURITANIA

MAURITIUS

MEXICO

MONACO

MONGOLIA

MOROCCO

MOZAMBIQUE

NAURU

NEPAL

NETHERLANDS

NEW ZEALAND

NICARAGUA

NIGER

NIGERIA

NORWAY

OMAN

PAKISTAN

PANAMA

PAPUA NEW GUINEA

PARAGUAY

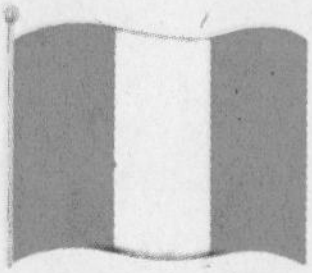
PERU

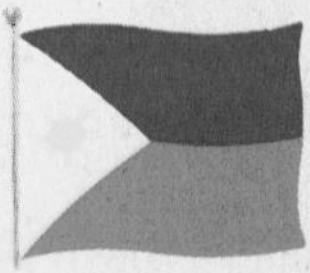
PHILIPPINES

POLAND

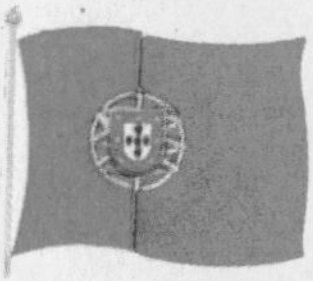
PORTUGAL

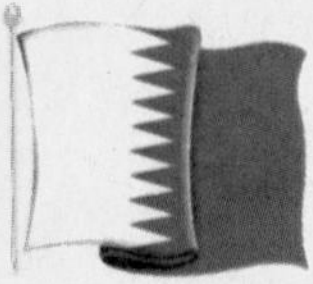
QATAR

ROMANIA

RWANDA

SAINT LUCIA

ST. VINCENT/
GRENADINES

SAMOA

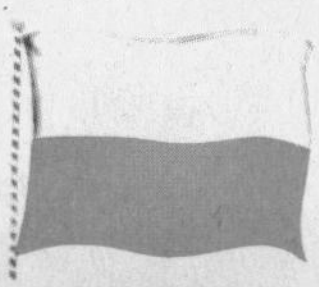
SAN MARINO

SAO TOME &
PRINCIPE

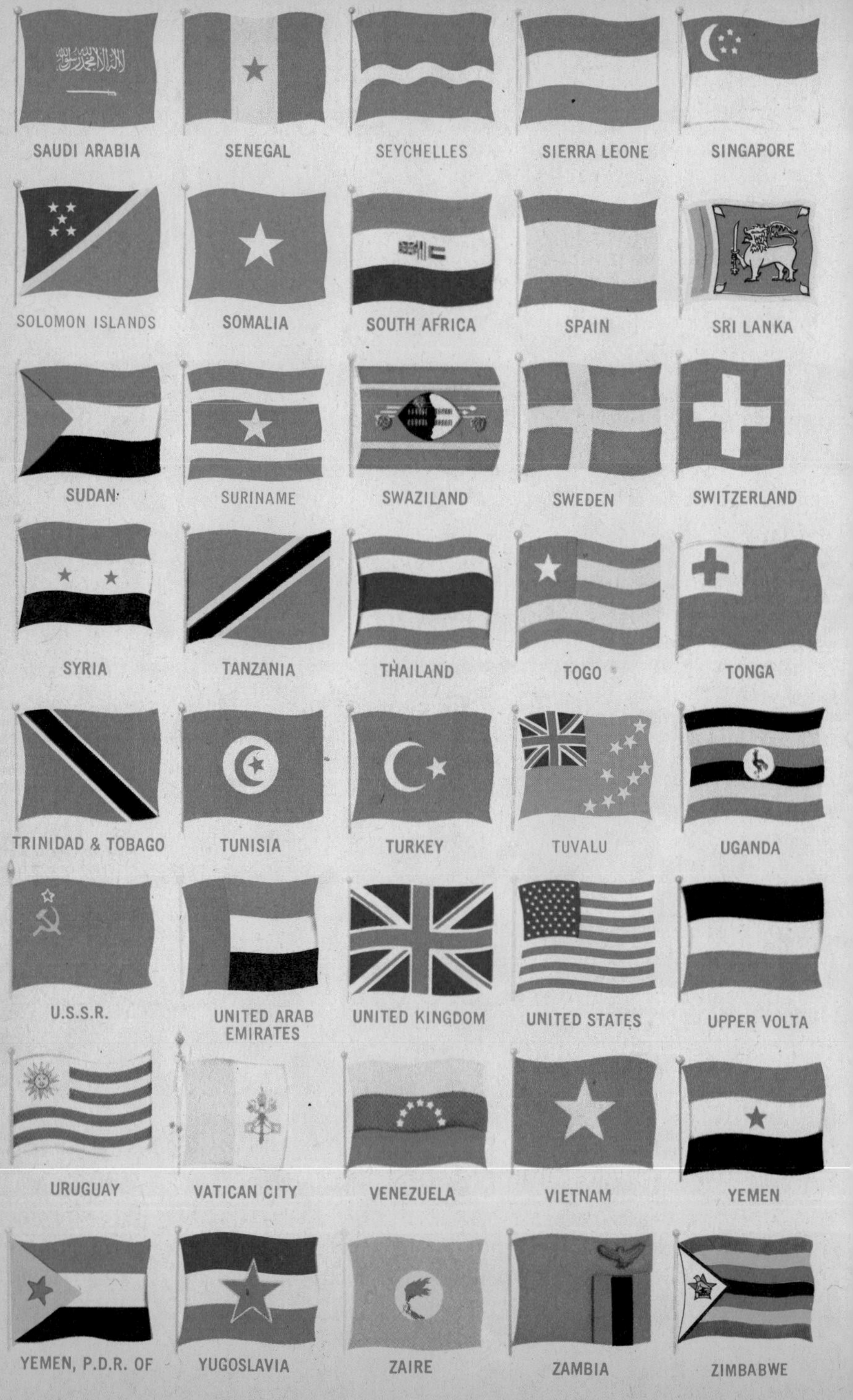
SAUDI ARABIA
SENEGAL
SEYCHELLES
SIERRA LEONE
SINGAPORE
SOLOMON ISLANDS
SOMALIA
SOUTH AFRICA
SPAIN
SRI LANKA
SUDAN
SURINAME
SWAZILAND
SWEDEN
SWITZERLAND
SYRIA
TANZANIA
THAILAND
TOGO
TONGA
TRINIDAD & TOBAGO
TUNISIA
TURKEY
TUVALU
UGANDA
U.S.S.R.
UNITED ARAB EMIRATES
UNITED KINGDOM
UNITED STATES
UPPER VOLTA
URUGUAY
VATICAN CITY
VENEZUELA
VIETNAM
YEMEN
YEMEN, P.D.R. OF
YUGOSLAVIA
ZAIRE
ZAMBIA
ZIMBABWE

NATIONS OF THE WORLD

The nations of the world are listed in alphabetical order. Initials in the following articles include UN (United Nations), OAS (Org. of American States), NATO (North Atlantic Treaty Org.), EC (European Communities or Common Market), OAU (Org. of African Unity). **Sources:** Population figures: International Demographic Data Center, U.S. Bureau of the Census; areas: U.S. State Department; crude steel production statistics: International Iron and Steel Institute, Brussels. Health and education statistics as reported in *World Military and Social Expenditures 1981*, Ruth Leger Sivard; copyright © 1981, by World Priorities Inc., Box 1003, Leesburg, VA 22075.

See special color section for maps and flags of all nations.

Afghanistan

Democratic Republic of Afghanistan

People: Population (1981 est.): 15,400,000. **Pop. density:** 56 per sq. mi. **Ethnic groups:** Pashtoon 50%; Tajiks 25%; Uzbek 9%; Hazara 9%. **Languages:** Pashta (Iranian), Dari Persian (spoken by Tajiks, Hazaras), Uzbek (Turkic). **Religions:** Sunni Muslim (80%), Shi'a Muslim (20%).

Geography: Area: 251,773 sq. mi., slightly smaller than Texas. **Location:** Between Soviet Central Asia and the Indian subcontinent. **Neighbors:** Pakistan on E, S, Iran on W, USSR on N; the NE tip touches China. **Topography:** The country is landlocked and mountainous, much of it over 4,000 ft. above sea level. The Hindu Kush Mts. tower 16,000 ft. above Kabul and reach a height of 25,000 ft. to the E. Trade with Pakistan flows through the 35-mile long Khyber Pass. The climate is dry, with extreme temperatures, and large desert regions, though mountain rivers produce intermittent fertile valleys. **Capital:** Kabul. **Cities** (1979 est.): Kabul 891,750; Kandahar 230,000; Herat 150,000; Baghlan 110,874; Kundus 108,000; Mazir-i-Sharif 100,000.

Government: Head of state, head of government, and secy. gen., People's Democratic Party: Pres. Babrak Karmal; b. 1929; in office: Dec. 27, 1979. **Local divisions:** 24 provinces, each under a governor. **Armed forces:** regulars 90,000; reserves 150,000.

Economy: Industries: Textiles, carpets, cement, sheepskin coats. **Chief crops:** Cotton, oilseeds, fruits. **Minerals:** Copper, lead, gas, coal, zinc, iron, silver, asbestos. **Crude oil reserves** (1978): 284 mln. bbls. **Other resources:** Wool, hides, karacul pelts. **Per capita arable land:** 1.3 acres. **Meat prod.** (1980): beef: 67,000 metric tons; lamb: 125,000 metric tons. **Electricity prod.** (1980): 908.00 mln. kwh. **Labor force:** 53% agric., 7% commerce, 16% services.

Finance: Currency: Afghani (Jan. 1982: 50.60 = $1 US). **Gross domestic product** (1978 est.): $3.76 bln. **Per capita income** (1978): $168. **Imports** (1980): $438 mln.; partners (1978): USSR 22%, Jap. 21%, Iran 13%. **Exports** (1980): $670 mln.; partners (1978): USSR 37%, Pak. 12%, UK 12%. **Tourists** (1977): 117,100; receipts: $38 mln. **International reserves less gold** (Dec. 1981): $274.2 mln. **Gold:** 965,000 oz t. **Consumer prices** (change in 1976): 0.04%

Transport: Motor vehicles: in use (1978): 34,506 passenger cars, 22,100 comm. vehicles. **Civil aviation:** 163 mln. passenger-km (1980); 21 mln. net ton-km.

Communications: Radios: 115,000 in use (1976). **Telephones in use** (1978): 31,200. **Daily newspaper circ.** (1980): 11 per 1,000 pop.

Health: Life expectancy at birth (1975): 39.9 male; 40.7 female. **Births** (per 1,000 pop. 1979): 52. **Deaths** (per 1,000 pop. 1979): 30. **Natural increase** (1979): 2.2%. **Hospital beds** (per 100,000 pop. 1977): 21. **Physicians** (per 100,000 pop. 1978): 27.

Education (1978): **Literacy:** 12% **Pop. 5-19:** in school: 13%, teachers per 1,000: 4.

Afghanistan, occupying a favored invasion route since antiquity, has been variously known as Ariana or Bactria (in ancient times) and Khorasan (in the Middle Ages). Foreign empires alternated rule with local emirs and kings until the 18th century, when a unified kingdom was established. In 1973, a military coup ushered in a republic.

Pro-Soviet leftists took power in a bloody 1978 coup, and concluded a 20-year economic and military treaty with the USSR.

Late in Dec. 1979, the USSR began a massive military airlift into Kabul. The three-month old regime of Hafizullah Amin ended with a Soviet backed coup, Dec. 27th. He was replaced by Babrak Karmal, considered a more pro-Soviet leader. Soviet troops, estimated at between 60,000-100,000, fanned out over Afghanistan, fighting rebels. Fighting continued during 1982 as the Soviets found themselves engaged in a long, protracted guerilla war.

Albania

People's Socialist Republic of Albania

People: Population (1981 est.): 2,730,000. **Pop. density:** 245.95 per sq. mi. **Urban** (1980): 33%. **Ethnic groups:** Albanians (Gegs in N, Tosks in S) 95%, Greeks 2.5%. **Languages:** Albanian (Tosk is official dialect), Greek. **Religions:** (officially) atheist; (historically) Moslems, Orthodox, Roman Catholic. All public worship and religious institutions were outlawed in 1967.

Geography: Area: 11,100 sq. mi., slightly larger than Maryland. **Location:** On SE coast of Adriatic Sea. **Neighbors:** Greece on S, Yugoslavia on N, E. **Topography:** Apart from a narrow coastal plain, Albania consists of hills and mountains covered with scrub forest, cut by small E-W rivers. **Capital:** Tirana. **Cities** (1980 est.): Tirana 198,000; Durres 80,000; Vlore 58,400.

Government: Head of state: Pres. Haxhi Leshi; b. 1913; in office: Aug. 1, 1953. **Head of government:** Prime Min. Adil Carcani; in office: Jan. 15, 1982. **Head of Communist Party:** Enver Hoxha; b. Oct. 16, 1908; in office: Nov. 8, 1941. **Local divisions:** 29 administrative districts and one independent city. **Armed forces:** regulars 41,000 (1980).

Economy: Industries: Chem. fertilizers, textiles, electric cables. **Chief crops:** Grain, corn, sugar beets, cotton, potatoes, tobacco, fruits. **Minerals:** Chromium, coal, copper, bitumen, iron, oil. **Other resources:** Forests. **Per capita arable land:** 0.5 acres. **Meat prod.** (1980): beef: 20,000 metric tons; pork: 12,000 metric tons; lamb: 24,000 metric tons. **Electricity prod.** (1978): 2.35 bln. kwh. **Labor force:** 61% agric; 40% industry and commerce.

Finance: Currency: Lek (Mar. 1980: 7.00 = $1 US). **Gross domestic product** (1976 est.) $1.3 bln. **Per capita income** (1976): $490. **Imports** (1976): $250 mln.; partners (1979): Czech., Yugoslavia, China. **Exports** (1976): $200 mln.; partners (1979): Czech., Yugoslavia, China, Italy.

Transport: Motor vehicles: in use (1971): 3,500 passenger cars, 11,200 comm. vehicles. **Chief ports:** Durres, Vlone.

Communications: Television sets: 4,500 in use (1977). **Radios:** 200,000 in use (1977). **Daily newspaper circ.** (1980): 54 per 1,000 pop.

Health: Life expectancy at birth (1979): 69 male; 69 female. **Births** (per 1,000 pop. 1975): 29.4. **Deaths** (per 1,000 pop. 1975): 6.7. **Natural increase** 22.6%. **Hospital beds** (per 100,000 pop. 1977): 649. **Physicians** (per 100,000 pop. 1977): 104. **Infant mortality** (per 1,000 live births 1971): 86.8.

Education (1978): **Literacy:** 75%. **Pop. 5-19:** in school: 64%, teachers per 1,000: 29.

Ancient Illyria was conquered by Romans, Slavs, and Turks (15th century); the latter Islamized the population. Independent Albania was proclaimed in 1912, republic was formed in 1920. Self-styled King Zog I ruled 1925-39, until Italy invaded.

Communist partisans took over in 1944, allied Albania with USSR, then broke with USSR in 1960 over de-Stalinization. Strong political alliance with China followed, leading to several billion dollars in aid, which was curtailed after 1974. China cut off aid in 1978 when Albania attacked its policies after the 1977 death of Chinese ruler Mao Tse-tung.

In 1971, after years of mistrust, Albania resumed relations with Greece and Yugoslavia, but ties with U.S. and USSR are still rejected.

Industrialization, pressed in 1960s, slowed in 1970s. Large-scale purges of officials occurred 1973-76.

Algeria

Democratic and Popular Republic of Algeria

People: Population (1981 est.); 19,300,000. **Age distrib.** (%): 0–14: 47.9; 15–59: 46.3; 60+: 5.7. **Pop. density:** 21.45 per sq. mi. **Urban** (1977): 40.6%. **Ethnic groups:** Arabs 75%, Berbers 25%. **Languages:** Arab, Berber (indigenous language), French. **Religions:** Sunni Moslem (state religion).

Geography: Area: 919,595 sq. mi., more than 3 times the size of Texas. **Location:** In NW Africa, from Mediterranean Sea into Sahara Desert. **Neighbors:** Morocco on W, Mauritania, Mali, Niger on S, Libya, Tunisia on E. **Topography:** The Tell, located on the coast, comprises fertile plains 50-100 miles wide, with a moderate climate and adequate rain. Two major chains of the Atlas Mts., running roughly E-W, and reaching 7,000 ft., enclose a dry plateau region. Below lies the Sahara, mostly desert with major mineral resources. **Capital:** Algiers. **Cities** (1980 est.): Algiers 2,200,000; Oran 633,000; Constantine 384,000; Annaba 284,000.

Government: Head of state: Pres. Chadli Bendjedid; b. Apr. 14, 1929; in office: Feb. 9, 1979. **Head of government:** Mohammed Ben Ahmed Abdelghani; in office: Mar. 8, 1979. **Local divisions:** 31 wilayas (states); governors are responsible to the center. **Armed forces:** regulars 101,000 (1980).

Economy: Industries: Oil, iron, steel, textiles, fertilizer, plastics. **Chief crops:** Grains, corn, wine-grapes, potatoes, dates, tomatoes, onions, oranges. **Minerals:** Mercury, oil, iron, zinc, lead, coal, copper, natural gas, phosphates. **Crude oil reserves** (1980): 8.44 bln. bbls. **Other resources:** Cork trees. **Per capital arable land:** .9 acres. **Meat prod.** (1980): beef: 33,000 metric tons; lamb: 67,000 metric tons. **Fish catch** (1978): 34,100 metric tons. **Electricity prod.** (1980): 5.5 bln. kwh. **Crude steel prod.** (1981): 550,000 metric tons. **Labor force:** 50% agric.; 20% ind. and commerce; 10% government; 10% services.

Finance: Currency: Dinar (Mar. 1982: 4.54 = $1 US). **Gross domestic product** (1979): $29 bln. **Per capita income** (1979): $1,600. **Imports** (1980): $10.56 bln.; partners (1978); France 18%, W. Ger. 18%, It. 11%, Japan 9%. **Exports** (1981): $11.8 bln.; partners (1978): U.S. 51%, W. Ger. 14%, France 11%, It. 7%. **Tourists** (1977): 241,700; receipts: $56 mln. **National budget** (1980): $11.2 bln. revenues; $11.2 bln. expenditures. **International reserves less gold** (Jan. 1982): $3.59 bln. **Gold:** 5.56 mln. oz t. **Consumer prices** (change in 1980): 9.7%

Transport: Railway traffic (1978): 1.4 bln. passenger-km; 2.01 bln. net ton-km. **Motor vehicles:** in use (1978): 396,800 passenger cars, 206,500 comm. vehicles; assembled (1977): 6,360 comm. vehicles. **Chief ports:** Algiers, Oran.

Communications: Television sets: 560,000 in use (1977). **Radios:** 3 mln. in use (1976). **Telephones in use** (1979): 346,400. **Daily newspaper circ.** (1980): 26 per 1,000 pop.

Health: Life expectancy at birth (1975): 52.9 male; 55.0 female. **Births** (per 1,000 pop. 1979): 46. **Deaths** (per 1,000 pop. 1979): 14. **Natural increase** (1979); 3.2%. **Hospital beds,** (per 100,000 pop. 1977): 263. **Physicians** (per 100,000 pop. 1977): 19. **Infant mortality** (per 1,000 live births 1977): 110.

Education (1978): **Literacy:** 37%. **Pop. 5-19:** in school: 55%, teachers per 1,000: 16.

Earliest known inhabitants were ancestors of Berbers, followed by Phoenicians, Romans, Vandals, and, finally, Arabs; but 25% still speak Berber dialects. Turkey ruled 1518 to 1830, when France took control.

Large-scale European immigration and French cultural inroads did not prevent an Arab nationalist movement from launching guerilla war. Peace, and French withdrawal, was negotiated with French Pres. Charles de Gaulle. One million Europeans left.

Ahmed Ben Bella was the victor of infighting, and ruled 1962-65, when an army coup installed Col. Houari Boumedienne as leader. Ben Bella remained under house arrest until 1979.

In 1967, Algeria declared war with Israel, broke with U.S., and moved toward eventual military and political ties with the USSR. French oil interests were partly seized in 1971, but relations with the West have since improved, based on oil and gas exports; U.S. ties were resumed 1974.

Algeria, strongly backing Saharan guerillas' demands for a cease fire and self-determination, encouraged Mauritania to come to terms with the Polisario Front, 1979.

The one-party Socialist regime faces endemic mass unemployment and poverty, despite land reform and industrialization attempts.

Andorra

Principality of Andorra

People: Population (1981 est.): 36,000. **Age distrib.** (%): 0–14: 29.2; 14–59: 61.7; 60+: 9.1. **Pop. density:** 180.85 per sq. mi. **Ethnic groups:** Spanish over 60%, Andorran 30%, French 6%. **Languages:** Catalan (official), Spanish, French. **Religion:** Roman Catholic.

Geography: Area: 188 sq. mi., half the size of New York City. **Location:** In Pyrenees Mtns. **Neighbors:** Spain on S, France on N. **Topography:** High mountains and narrow valleys over the country. **Capital:** Andorra la Vella.

Government: Head of state: Co-princes are the president of France (François Mitterrand; in office: May 21, 1981) and the Roman Catholic bishop of Urgel in Spain. **Head of govt.:** Syndic Estanislau Sangra Font, in office: Jan 1, 1979. **Local divisions:** 7 parishes.

Economy: Industries: Tourism, sheep raising. **Labor force:** 20% agric.; 80% ind. and commerce; services; government.

Finance: Currency: French franc, Spanish peseta.

Communications: Television sets: 3,000 in use (1977). **Radios:** 7,000 in use (1977). **Telephones in use** (1978): 11,700.

Health: Births (per 1,000 pop. 1976): 16.5. **Deaths** (per 1,000 pop. 1976): 5.0. **Natural increase** (1976): 1.2%.

Education (1981): **Literacy:** 100%. School compulsory to age 16.

The present political status, with joint sovereignty by France and the bishop of Urgel, dates from 1278.

Tourism, especially skiing, is the economic mainstay. A free port, allowing for an active trading center, draws more than 7 million tourists annually. The ensuing economic prosperity accompanied by Andorra's virtual law-free status, has given rise to calls for reform.

Angola

People's Republic of Angola

People: Population (1981 est.): 6,700,000. **Pop. density:** 14.70 per sq. mi. **Ethnic groups:** Ovimbundu 38%, Kimbundu 23%; Bakongo 13%, European 1%; Mesticos 2%. **Languages:** Portuguese (official), various Bantu languages. **Religions:** Traditional beliefs 45%, Roman Catholic 43%, Protestant 12%.

Geography: Area: 481,353 sq. mi., larger than Texas and California combined. **Location:** In SW Africa on Atlantic coast. **Neighbors:** Namibia (SW Africa) on S, Zambia on E, Zaire on N; Cabinda, an enclave separated from rest of country by short Atlantic coast of Zaire, borders Congo Republic. **Topography:** Most of Angola consists of a plateau elevated 3,000 to 5,000 feet above sea level, rising from a narrow coastal strip. There is also a temperate highland area in the west-central region, a desert in the S, and a tropical rain forest covering Cabinda. **Capital:** Luanda 475,300 (1979 est.).

Government: Head of state: Pres. Jose Eduardo dos Santos b. Aug. 28, 1942; in office: Sept. 20, 1979. **Local divisions:** 18 provinces. **Armed forces:** regulars 31,500 (1980).

Economy: Industries: Alcohol, cotton goods, fishmeal, paper, palm oil, footwear. **Chief crops:** Coffee, corn, sweet potatoes, dry beans, bananas, citrus fruit, palm oil, cotton. **Minerals:** Iron, diamonds (over 2 mln. carats a year), copper, manganese, sulphur, phosphates, oil. **Crude oil reserves** (1980): 1.2 bln. bbls. **Per capita arable land:** 0.5 acres. **Meat prod.** (1980): beef: 51,000 metric tons; pork: 13,000 metric tons. **Fish catch** (1979): 106,000 metric tons. **Electricity prod.** (1978): 1.36 bln. kwh. **Labor force:** 75% agric., industry, commerce, service.

Finance: Currency: Kwanza (Mar. 1982: 27.6 = $1 US). **Gross domestic product** (1980): $1.82 bln. **Per capita income** (1976): $500. **Imports** 1979): $830 mln.; partners: So. Afr. 12%, Port. 12%, W. Ger. 9%, U.S. 9%. **Exports** (1979): $1.4 bln.; partners: Bahamas 45%, U.S. 20%, Virgin Islands 8%.

Transport: Railway traffic (1974): 418 mln. passenger-km; 5.46 bln. net ton-km. **Motor vehicles:** in use (1978): 143,100 passenger cars, 42,000 comm. vehicles. **Chief ports:** Lobito, Luanda.

Communications: Radios: 118,000 in use (1977). **Telephones in use** (1979): 29,400. **Daily newspaper circ.** (1980): 85 per 1,000 pop.

Health: Life expectancy at birth (1975): 37.0 male; 40.1 female. **Births** (per 1,000 pop. 1979): 47.0. **Deaths** (per 1,000 pop. 1979): 23. **Natural increase** (1979): 1.3%. **Hospital beds** (per 100,000 pop. 1977): 306. **Physicians** (per 100,000 pop 1977): 6. **Infant mortality** (per 1,000 live births 1979): 182.

Education (1978): **Literacy:** 12%. **Pop. 5-19:** in school: 28%, teachers per 1,000: 9.

From the early centuries AD to 1500, Bantu tribes penetrated most of the region. Portuguese came in 1583, allied with the Bakongo kingdom in the north, and developed the slave trade. Large-scale colonization did not begin until the 20th century, when 400,000 Portuguese immigrated.

A guerrilla war begun in 1961 lasted until 1974, when Portugal offered independence. Violence between the National Front, based in Zaire, the Soviet-backed Popular Movement, and the National Union, aided by the U.S. and S. Africa, killed thousands of blacks, drove most whites to emigrate, and completed economic ruin. Some 15,000 Cuban troops and massive Soviet aid helped the Popular Movement win most of the country after independence Nov. 11, 1975.

S. African troops crossed the southern Angolan border June 7, 1981, killing more than 300 civilians and occupying several towns. The S. Africans withdrew in Sept.

Russian influence, backed by 25,000 Cubans, East Germans, and Portuguese Communists, is strong in the Marxist regime.

In 1982, there were several border clashes between S. African troops and the South West Africa People's Organization (SWAPO), a guerrilla group supporting the independence of Namibia.

Antigua and Barbuda

People: Population (1981 est.) 76,000. **Language:** English. **Religion:** Predominantly Church of England.

Geography: Area: 171 sq. mi. **Location:** Eastern Caribbean. **Neighbors:** approx. 30 mi. north of Guadeloupe. **Capital:** St. John's.

Government: Head of Government: Prime Min. Vere Cornwall Bird; b. Dec. 7, 1910; in office Nov. 1, 1981.

Economy: Industries: manufacturing, tourism.

Finance: Currency: East Caribbean dollar (Sept. 1981): 2.70 = $1 U.S. **Consumer prices** (change in 1980): 16%.

Antigua was discovered by Columbus in 1493. The British colonized it in 1632.

The British associated state of Antigua achieved independence as Antigua and Barbuda on Nov. 1, 1981. The government maintains close relations with the U.S.. United Kingdom, and Venezuela.

Argentina

Argentine Republic

People: Population (1980 cen.): 27,900,000. **Age distrib.** (%): 0–14: 28.5; 15–59: 59.6; 60+: 11.9. **Pop. density:** 25.46 per sq. mi. **Urban** (1977): 72%. **Ethnic groups:** Europeans 97% (Spanish, Italian), Indians, Mestizos, Arabs. **Languages:** Spanish (official), English, Italian, German, French. **Religions:** Roman Catholic 92%.

Geography: Area: 1,065,189 sq. mi., 4 times the size of Texas, second largest in S. America. **Location:** Occupies most of southern S. America. **Neighbors:** Chile on W, Bolivia, Paraguay on N, Brazil, Uruguay on NE. **Topography:** The mountains in W: the Andean, Central, Misiones, and Southern. Aconcagua is the highest peak in the Western hemisphere, alt. 22,834 ft. E of the Andes are heavily wooded plains, called the Gran Chaco in the N, and the fertile, treeless Pampas in the central region. Patagonia, in the S, is bleak and arid. Rio de la Plata, 170 by 140 mi., is mostly fresh water, from 2,500-mi. Paranak and 1,000-mi. Uruguay rivers. **Capital:** Buenos Aires. **Cities** (1978 est.): Buenos Aires 2,982,000; Cordoba 781,565; Rosario 750,455; La Plata 391,247; San Miguel de Tucuman 321,567.

Government: Head of state: Pres. Reynaldo Benito Antonio Bignone; b. Jan. 21, 1928; in office: July 1, 1982. **Local divisions:** 22 provinces, 1 natl. terr. and 1 federal dist., under military governors. **Armed forces:** regulars 136,000; reserves 250,000.

Economy: Industries: Meat processing, flour milling, chemicals, textiles, machinery, autos. **Chief crops:** Grains, corn, grapes, linseed, sugar, tobacco, rice, soybeans, citrus fruits. **Minerals:** Oil, coal, lead, zinc, iron, sulphur, silver, copper, gold. **Crude oil reserves** (1980): 2.40 bln. bbls. **Per capita arable land:** 2.3 acres. **Meat prod.** (1980): beef: 2.92 mln. metric tons; pork: 246,000 metric tons; lamb: 117,000 metric tons. **Fish catch** (1979): 566,000 metric tons. **Electricity prod.** (1980): 35.7 bln. kwh. **Crude steel prod.** (1981): 2.5 mln. metric tons. **Labor force:** 19% agric.; 36% ind. and man.; 20% services.

Finance: Currency: Peso (Mar. 1982: 11,575.0 = $1 US). **Gross domestic product** (1978 est.): $61.5 bln. **Per capita income** (1978 est.): $2,331. **Imports** (1980): $10.5 bln.; partners (1979): U.S. 21%, W. Ger. 10%, Braz. 10%, Jap. 5%. **Exports** (1980): $8.0 bln.; partners (1977): Braz. 11%, Neth. 10%, It. 8%, U.S. 7%. **Tourists** (1977): 1,350,000; receipts: $213 mln. **National budget** (1980): $4.9 bln. revenues; $5.7 bln. expenditures. **International reserves less gold** (Nov. 1981): $3.32 bln. **Gold:** 4.37 mln. oz t. **Consumer prices** (change in 1981): 104.5%.

Transport: Railway traffic (1979): 11.05 bln. passenger-km; 10.94 bln. net ton-km. **Motor vehicles:** in use (1978): 2.8 mln. passenger cars, 1.2 mln. comm. vehicles. **Civil aviation:** 7,935 mln. passenger-km (1978); 199 mln. freight ton-km (1978). **Chief ports:** Buenos Aires, Bahia Blanca, La Plata.

Communications: Television sets: 5.5 mln. in use (1979), 219,000 manuf. (1978). **Radios:** 10 mln. in use (1977). **Telephones in use** (1979): 2.6 mln. **Daily newspaper circ.** (1976): 2,682,000.

Health: Life expectancy at birth (1975): 65.16 male; 71.38 female. **Births** (per 1,000 pop. 1979): 26. **Deaths** (per 1,000 pop. 1979): 9. **Natural increase** (1979): 1.6%. **Hospital beds** (per 100,000 pop. 1977): 524. **Physicians** (per 100,000 pop. 1977): 192. **Infant mortality** (per 1,000 live births 1970): 59.0.

Education (1978): Literacy: 94%. **Pop. 5-19:** in school: 58%, teachers per 1,000: 37.

Nomadic Indians roamed the Pampas when Spaniards arrived, 1515-1516, led by Juan Diaz de Solis. Nearly all the Indians were killed by the late 19th century. The colonists won independence, 1810-1819, and a long period of disorders ended in a strong centralized government.

Large-scale Italian, German, and Spanish immigration in the decades after 1880 spurred modernization, making Argentina the most prosperous, educated, and industrialized of the major Latin American nations. Social reforms were enacted in the 1920s, but military coups prevailed 1930-46, until the election of Gen. Juan Peron as president.

Peron, with his wife Eva Duarte effected labor reforms, but also suppressed speech and press freedoms, closed religious schools, and ran the country into debt. A 1955 coup exiled Peron, who was followed by a series of military and civilian regimes. Peron returned in 1973, and was once more elected president. He died 10 months later, succeeded by his wife, Isabel, who had been elected vice president, and who became the first woman head of state in the Western hemisphere.

A military junta ousted Mrs. Peron in 1976 amid charges of corruption. Under a continuing state of siege, the army battled guerrillas and leftists, killed 5,000 people, and jailed and tortured others. The government rejected a report of the Inter-American Human Rights Commission, 1980, which charged widespread killing, torture, and arbitrary detention.

A severe worsening in economic conditions placed extreme pressure on the military government. In 1981, unemployment doubled, inflation was into triple figures and the peso was devalued by more than 200 percent.

Several thousand Argentine troops seized control of the British, held Falkland Islands on Apr. 2, 1982. Both countries have claimed sovereignty over the islands, located 250 miles off the Argentine coast, since 1833. The British government dispatched a task force and declared a total air and sea blockade around the Falklands as of Apr. 30. Despite intense mediation efforts by the U.S., fighting began May 1. Several hundred lost their lives as the result of the destruction of a British destroyer and the sinking of an Argentine cruiser. British troops landed in force on East Falkland Island May 21. By June 2, the British had surrounded Stanley, the capital city and Argentine stronghold. The Argentine troops surrendered, June 14; Argentine President Leopoldo Galtieri resigned June 17. (*See Chronology*).

Australia

Commonwealth of Australia

People: Population (1981 cen.): 14,926,800. **Age distrib.** (%): 0–14: 27.2; 15–59: 59.5; 60+: 13. **Pop. density:** 4.93 per sq. mi. **Urban** (1976): 86%. **Ethnic groups:** British 95%, other European 3%, aborigines (including mixed) 1.5%. **Languages:** English, aboriginal languages. **Religions:** Anglican 27.7%, other Protestant 25%, Roman Catholic 25%.

Geography: Area: 2,966,200 sq. mi., almost as large as the 48 contiguous U.S. states. **Location:** SE of Asia, Indian O. is W and S, Pacific O. (Coral, Tasman seas) is E; they meet N of Australia in Timor and Arafura seas: Tasmania lies 150 mi. S of Victoria state, across Bass Strait. **Neighbors:** Nearest are Indonesia, Papua New Guinea on N, Solomons, Fiji, and New Zealand on E. **Topography:** An island continent. The Great Dividing Range along the E coast has Mt. Kosciusko, 7,310 ft. The W plateau rises to 2,000 ft., with arid areas in the Great Sandy and Great Victoria deserts. The NW part of Western Australia and Northern Terr. are arid and hot. The NE has heavy rainfall and Cape York Peninsula has jungles. The Murray R. rises in New South Wales and flows 1,600 mi. to the Indian O. **Capital:** Canberra. **Cities** (1980 est.): Sydney 3,231,700; Melbourne 2,994,600; Brisbane 1,101,700; Adelaide 1,035,000; Perth 925,750.

Government: Head of state: Queen Elizabeth II, represented by Gov.-Gen. Ninian Martin Stephens; in office: July, 1982. **Head of government:** Prime Min. John Malcolm Fraser; b. May 21, 1930; in office: Nov. 11, 1975. **Local divisions:** 6 states, with elected governments and substantial powers; 2 territories. **Armed forces:** regulars 71,360 (1980).

Economy: Industries: Iron, steel, textiles, electrical equip., chemicals, autos, aircraft, ships, machinery. **Chief crops:** Wheat (a leading export), barley, oats, corn, sugar, wine, fruit, vegetables. **Minerals:** Bauxite, antimony, coal, cobalt, copper, gold, iron, lead, manganese, nickel, silver, tin, tungsten, uranium, zinc. **Crude oil reserves** (1980): 2.13 bln. bbls. **Other resources:** Wool (30% of world output). **Per capita arable land:** 7.8 acres. **Meat prod.** (1980): beef: 1.55 mln. metric tons; pork: 217,000 metric tons; lamb: 539,000 metric tons. **Fish catch** (1978): 122,900 metric tons. **Electricity prod.** (1980): 98 bln. kwh. **Crude steel prod.** (1981): 7.6 mln. metric tons. **Labor force:** 14% agric.; 47% ind. and commerce; 37% service.

Finance: Currency: Dollar (Mar. 1982: 1.05 = $1 US). **Gross domestic product** (1980): $121.2 bln. **Per capita income** (1978): $7,720. **Imports** (1981): $26.1 bln; partners (1980): U.S. 22%, Jap. 17%, UK 9%, W. Ger. 6%. **Exports** (1981): $21.80 bln.; partners (1980): Jap. 27%, U.S. 12%, NZ 5%, USSR 5%. **Tourists** (1979): 793,345. **National budget** (1980): $38.80 bln. revenues; $36.15 bln. expenditures. **International reserves less gold** (Jan. 1982): $1.2 bln. **Gold:** 7.93 mln. oz t. **Consumer prices** (change in 1980): 10.2%.

Transport: Railway traffic (1977): 32.03 bln. net ton-km. **Motor vehicles:** in use (1979): 5.7 mln. passenger cars, 1.4 mln. comm. vehicles; manuf. (1978): 315,600 passenger cars; 69,600 comm. vehicles. **Civil aviation:** 25,506 mln. passenger-km. (1980); 515.6 mln. freight ton-km. (1980). **Chief ports:** Sydney, Melbourne, Newcastle, Port Kembla, Fremantle, Geelong.

Communications: Television sets: 5 mln. licensed (1977), 325,000 manuf. (1978). **Radios:** 14.6 mln. licensed (1977), 68,000 manuf. (1977). **Telephones in use** (1979): 6.6 mln. **Daily newspaper circ.** (1980): 370 per 1,000 pop.

Health: Life expectancy at birth (1977): 69.9 male; 76.8 female. **Births** (per 1,000 pop. 1980): 15.4. **Deaths** (per 1,000 pop. 1980): 7.4. **Natural increase** (1979): 1.2%. **Hospital beds** (per 100,000 pop. 1977): 1,244. **Physicians** (per 100,000 pop. 1977): 154. **Infant mortality** (per 1,000 live births 1978): 12.5.

Education (1978): **Literacy:** 99%. **Pop. 5-19:** in school: 73%, teachers per 1,000: 44.

Capt. James Cook explored the E coast in 1770, when the continent was inhabited by a variety of different tribes. Within decades, Britain had claimed the entire continent, which became a penal colony until immigration increased in the 1850s. The commonwealth was proclaimed Jan. 1, 1901. Northern Terr. was granted limited self-rule July 1, 1978. Their capitals and 1980 pop.:

	Area (sq. mi.)	**Population**
New South Wales, Sydney	309,418	5,078,500
Victoria, Melbourne	87,854	3,853,500
Queensland, Brisbane	666,699	2,197,400
South Aust., Adelaide	379,824	1,293,800
Western Aust., Perth	974,843	1,242,800
Tasmania, Hobart	26,178	417,700
Aust. Capital Terr., Canberra	926	222,300
Northern Terr., Darwin	519,633	115,900

Australia's racially discriminatory immigration policies were abandoned in 1973, after 3 million Europeans (half British) had entered since 1945. The 50,000 aborigines and 150,000 part-aborigines are mostly detribalized, but there are several preserves in the Northern Territory. They remain economically disadvantaged.

Australia's agricultural success makes it among the top exporters of beef, lamb, wool, and wheat. Major mineral deposits have been developed as well, largely for exports. Industrialization has been completed.

Australia harbors many plant and animal species not found elsewhere, including the kangaroo, koala bear, platypus, dingo (wild dog), Tasmanian devil (racoon-like marsupial), wombat (bear-like marsupial), and barking and frilled lizards.

Australian External Territories

Norfolk Is., area 13½ sq. mi., pop. (1978) 1,900, was taken over, 1914. The soil is very fertile, suitable for citrus fruits, bananas, and coffee. Many of the inhabitants are descendants of the Bounty mutineers, moved to Norfolk 1856 from Pitcairn Is. Australia offered the island limited home rule, 1978.

Coral Sea Is. Territory, 1 sq. mi., is administered from Norfolk Is.

Territory of Ashmore and Cartier Is., area 2 sq. mi., in the Indian O. came under Australian authority 1934 and are administered as part of Northern Territory. **Heard** and **McDonald Is.** are administered by the Dept. of Science.

Cocos (Keeling) Is., 27 small coral islands in the Indian O. 1,750 mi. NW of Australia. Pop. (1980) 487, area: 5½ sq. mi.

Christmas Is., 52 sq. mi., pop. 3,094 (1978), 230 mi. S of Java, was transferred by Britain in 1958. It has phosphate deposits.

Australian Antarctic Territory was claimed by Australia in 1933, including 2,472,000 sq. mi. of territory S of 60th parallel S Lat. and between 160th-45th meridians E Long.

Austria

Republic of Austria

People: Population (1981 est.): 7,546,200. **Age distrib.** (%): 0–14: 22.8; 15–59: 57.0; 60+: 20.2. **Pop. density:** 231.97 per sq. mi. **Urban** (1971): 51.9%. **Ethnic groups:** German 99%, Slovene, Croatian. **Languages:** German 95%, Slovene. **Religions:** Roman Catholic 90%, Protestant 6%, none 4.5%.

Geography: Area: 32,374 sq. mi., slightly smaller than Maine. **Location:** In S Central Europe. **Neighbors:** Switzerland, Liechtenstein on W, W. Germany, Czechoslovakia on N, Hungary on E, Yugoslavia, Italy on S. **Topography:** Austria is primarily mountainous, with the Alps and foothills covering the western and southern provinces. The eastern provinces and Vienna are located in the Danube River Basin. **Capital:** Vienna. **Cities** (1981 cen.): Vienna 1,504,200.

Government: Head of state: Pres. Rudolf Kirchschlaeger; b. Mar. 20, 1915; in office: July 8, 1974. **Head of government:** Chancellor Bruno Kreisky; b. Jan. 22, 1911; in office: Apr. 21, 1970. **Local divisions:** 9 lander (states), each with a legislature. **Armed forces:** regulars 50,300 (1980).

Economy: Industries: Steel, machinery, autos, electrical and optical equip., glassware, sport goods, paper, textiles, chemicals, cement. **Chief crops:** Grains, potatoes, beets, grapes. **Minerals:** Iron ore, oil, magnesite, aluminum, coal, lignite, copper. **Crude oil reserves** (1980): 140 mln. bbls. **Other resources:** Forests, hydro power. **Per capita arable land:** 0.5 acres. **Meat prod.** (1980): beef: 196,000 metric tons; pork: 330,000 metric tons. **Electricity prod.** (1980): 41.9 bln. kwh. **Crude steel prod.** (1980): 4.6 mln. metric tons. **Labor force:** 13.8% agric.; 60% manuf.; 25.5% service.

Finance: Currency: Schilling (Mar. 1982: 16.97 = $1 US). **Gross domestic product** (1980): $76.34 bln. **Per capita in-**

come (1979): $9,114. **Imports** (1981): $21.05 bln.; partners (1980): W. Ger. 41%, It. 9%, Switz. 5%. **Exports** (1981): $15.83 bln.; partners (1980): W. Ger. 31%, It. 11%, Switz. 8%. **Tourists** (1979): 12.8 mln. receipts: $5.5 bln. **National budget** (1979): $14.19 bln. revenues; $16.55 bln. expenditures. **International reserves less gold** (Jan. 1982): $5.03 bln. **Gold:** 21.11 mln. oz t. **Consumer prices** (change in 1981): 6.8%.

Transport: Railway traffic (1980): 7.4 bln. passenger-km; 11 bln. net ton-km. **Motor vehicles:** in use (1979): 2.1 mln. passenger cars, 172,500 comm. **Civil aviation** (1980): 1.2 bln. passenger-km; 14.6 mln. freight ton-km.

Communications: Television sets: 2.1 mln. licensed (1978), 375,000 manuf. (1978). **Radios:** 2.2 mln. licensed (1978). **Telephones in use** (1978): 2.6 mln. **Daily newspaper circ.** (1980): 412 per 1,000 pop.

Health: Life expectancy at birth (1976): 68.1 male; 75.1 female. **Births** (per 1,000 pop. 1980): 12.0. **Deaths** (per 1,000 pop. 1980): 12.2. **Natural increase** (1978): −.1%. **Hospital beds** (per 100,000 pop. 1977): 1,128. **Physicians** (per 100,000 pop. 1977): 233. **Infant mortality** (per 1,000 live births 1978): 16.

Education (1978): Literacy: 99%. **Pop. 5-19:** in school: 58%, teachers per 1,000: 38.

Rome conquered Austrian lands from Celtic tribes around 15 BC. In 788 the territory was incorporated into Charlemagne's empire. By 1300, the House of Hapsburg had gained control; they added vast territories in all parts of Europe to their realm in the next few hundred years.

Austrian dominance of Germany was undermined in the 18th century and ended by Prussia by 1866. But the Congress of Vienna, 1815, confirmed Austrian control of a large empire in southeast Europe consisting of Germans, Hungarians, Slavs, Italians, and others.

The dual Austro-Hungarian monarchy was established in 1867, giving autonomy to Hungary and almost 50 years of peace.

World War I, started after the June 28, 1914 assassination of Archduke Franz Ferdinand, the Hapsburg heir, by a Serbian nationalist, destroyed the empire. By 1918 Austria was reduced to a small republic, with the borders it has today.

Nazi Germany invaded Austria Mar. 13, 1938. The republic was reestablished in 1945, under Allied occupation. Full independence and neutrality were guaranteed by a 1955 treaty with the major powers.

Austria produces 85% of its food, as well as an array of industrial products. A large part of Austria's economy is controlled by state enterprises. Socialists have shared or alternated power with the conservative People's Party.

Economic agreements with the Common Market give Austria access to a free-trade area encompassing most of West Europe.

Bahamas

Commonwealth of the Bahamas

People: Population (1981 est.): 260,000. **Age distrib.** (%): 0–14: 43.6; 15–59: 50.9; 60+: 5.5. **Pop. density:** 44.61 per sq. mi. **Urban** (1970): 57.9%. **Ethnic groups:** Negro 85%, Caucasian (British, Canadian, U.S.). **Languages:** English. **Religions:** Baptist 29%, Anglican 23%, Roman Catholic 22%.

Geography: Area: 5,353 sq. mi., slightly smaller than Connecticut. **Location:** In Atlantic O., E of Florida. **Neighbors:** Nearest are U.S. on W, Cuba on S. **Topography:** Nearly 700 islands (30 inhabited) and over 2,000 islets in the western Atlantic extend 760 mi. NW to SE. **Capital:** Nassau. **Cities:** (1979 est.) Nassau 138,500; Freeport 16,000.

Government: Head of state: Queen Elizabeth II, represented by Gov.-Gen. Gerald C. Cash; b. May 28, 1917, in office: Sept. 29, 1979. **Head of government:** Prime Min. Lynden Oscar Pindling; b. Mar. 22, 1930; in office: Jan. 16, 1967. **Local divisions:** 18 districts.

Economy: Industries: Tourism (66% of employment), intl. banking, rum, drugs. **Chief crops:** Fruits, vegetables. **Minerals:** Salt. **Other resources:** Lobsters. **Per capita arable land:** 0.02 acres. **Electricity prod.** (1977): 650.00 mln. kwh. **Labor force:** 9% agric.; 91% ind., tourism, commerce.

Finance: Currency: Dollar (Apr. 1982: 1 = $1 US). **Gross domestic product** (1975 est.): $500 mln. **Per capita income** (1975 est): $3,310. **Imports** (1980): $5.48 bln.; partners (1977): U.S. 35%, S. Arab. 24%, Iran 10%, Nigeria 9%. **Exports** (1980): $4.84 bln.; partners (1977): U.S. 81%, S. Arab. 10%. **Tourists** (1978): 1.1 mln.; receipts: $495 mln. **National budget** (1980): $245 mln. revenues; $245 mln. expenditures. **International reserves less gold** (Jan. 1982): $98.1 mln. **Consumer prices** (change in 1980): 12.1%.

Transport: Motor vehicles: in use (1976): 36,500 passenger cars, 5,300 comm. vehicles. **Chief ports:** Nassau, Freeport.

Communications: Radios: 97,000 in use (1977). **Television sets** (1977): 30,000. **Telephones in use** (1979): 66,200. **Daily newspaper circ.** (1980): 140 per 1,000 pop.

Health: Life expectancy at birth (1971): 64.0 male; 67.3 female. **Births** (per 1,000 pop. 1979): 25. **Deaths** (per 1,000 pop. 1978): 5. **Natural increase** (1979): 3.6%. **Infant mortality** (per 1,000 live births 1976): 24.7.

Christopher Columbus first set foot in the New World on San Salvador (Watling I.) in 1492, when Arawak Indians inhabited the islands. British settlement began in 1647; the islands became a British colony in 1783. Internal self-government was granted in 1964; full independence within the Commonwealth was attained July 10, 1973.

International banking and investment management has become a major industry alongside tourism, despite controversy over financial irregularities.

Bahrain

State of Bahrain

People: Population (1981 cen.): 360,000. **Age distrib.** (%): 0–14: 44.3; 15–59: 51.1; 60+: 4.6. **Pop. density:** 1,471.86 per sq. mi. **Urban** (1971): 78.1%. **Ethnic groups:** Arabs 80%, Iranians 12%, Indians, Pakistanis 5%. **Languages:** Arabic (official), Persian. **Religions:** Sunni Moslem 40%, Shi'ah Moslem 50%.

Geography: Area: 258 sq. mi., smaller than New York City. **Location:** In Persian Gulf. **Neighbors:** Nearest are Saudi Arabia on W. Qatar on E. **Topography:** Bahrain Island, and several adjacent, smaller islands, are flat, hot and humid, with little rain. **Capital:** Manama. **Cities** (1980 est.): Manama 150,000.

Government: Head of state: Amir Isa bin Sulman al-Khalifa; b. July 3, 1933; in office: Nov. 2, 1961. **Head of government:** Prime Min. Kahlifa ibn Sulman al-Khalifa; b. 1935; in office: Jan. 19, 1970. **Local divisions:** 6 towns and cities. **Armed forces:** regulars 2,300 (1980).

Economy: Industries: Oil products, aluminum smelting, shipping. **Chief crops:** Fruits, vegetables. **Minerals:** Oil, gas. **Crude oil reserves** (1980): 240 mln. bbls. **Per capita arable land:** 0.007 acres. **Electricity prod.** (1979): 12.2 mln. kwh. **Labor force:** 5% agric.; 90% ind. and commerce; 5% services; 3% gov.

Finance: Currency: Dinar (Apr. 1982: 0.38 = $1 US). **Gross domestic product** (1980 est.): $3.4 bln. **Per capita income** (1979 est.): $4,967. **Imports** (1979): $2.48 bln.; partners (1979): Sau. Ar. 51%, UK 9%, U.S. 8%. **Exports** (1981): $4.22 bln.; partners (1979): UAE 19%, Jap. 12%, Sing. 8%, Sau. Ar. 6%. **National Budget** (1980): $622 mln. revenues; $407 mln. expenditures. **International reserves less gold** (Jan. 1982): $1 bln. **Gold:** 150,000 oz t. **Consumer prices** (change in 1980): 3.9%.

Transport: Motor vehicles: in use (1977): 35,500 passenger cars, 13,200 comm. vehicles. **Chief ports:** Sitra.

Communications: Television sets: 31,000 in use (1976). **Radios:** 100,000 in use (1975). **Telephones in use** (1978): 38,284.

Health: Births (per 1,000 pop. 1975): 30.0. **Hospital beds** (per 100,000 pop. 1977): 303. **Physicians** (per 100,000 pop. 1977): 62.

Education (1978): **Literacy:** 40%. **Pop. 5–19:** in school: 58%, teachers per 1,000: 36.

Long ruled by the Khalifa family, Bahrain was a British protectorate from 1861 to 1971, when it regained independence.

Pearls, shrimp, fruits, and vegetables were the mainstays of the economy until oil was discovered in 1932. By the 1970s, oil reserves were depleted; international banking thrived.

Bahrain took part in the 1973-74 Arab oil embargo against the U.S. and other nations. The government bought controlling interest in the oil industry in 1975.

Saudi Arabia announced, Dec., 1979, that it will build a 15-mile, $1 billion causeway linking Bahrain with the Arab mainland.

Bangladesh

People's Republic of Bangladesh

People: Population (1981 est.): 93,100,000. **Age distrib.** (%): 0-14: 43.2; 15-59: 52.4; 60+: 4.4. **Pop. density:** 1,608.32 per sq. mi. **Urban** (1979): 10.1%. **Ethnic groups:** Bengali 98%, Bihari, tribesmen. **Languages:** Bengali (official), English. **Religions:** Moslems 83%, Hindu 16%, Christian, Buddhist.

Geography: Area: 55,598 sq. mi. slightly smaller than Wisconsin. **Location:** In S Asia, on N bend of Bay of Bengal. **Neighbors:** India nearly surrounds country on W, N, E; Burma on SE. **Topography:** The country is mostly a low plain cut by the Ganges and Brahmaputra rivers and their delta. The land is alluvial and marshy along the coast, with hills only in the extreme SE and NE. A tropical monsoon climate prevails, among the rainiest in the world. **Capital:** Dacca. **Cities** (1976 est.): Dacca (met.) 2 mln.; Chittagong (met.) 889,760; Khulna (met.) 437,304.

Government: Head of state: A.F.M. Ahsanuddin Choudhury; in office. Mar. 27, 1982. **Head of government:** Prime Minister Shah Mohammad Azizur Rahman, b. 1925, in office: Mar. 16, 1979. **Local divisions:** 19 districts. **Armed forces:** regulars 76,500; para-military 66,000.

Economy: Industries: Cement, jute, fertilizers, petroleum products. **Chief crops:** Jute (most of world output), rice. **Minerals:** Natural gas, offshore oil. **Per capita arable land:** 0.3 acres. **Meat prod.** (1980): beef: 187,000 metric tons; lamb: 46,000 metric tons. **Fish catch** (1979): 640,000 metric tons. **Electricity prod.** (1979): 2.6 bln. kwh. **Labor force:** 74% agric.

Finance: Currency: Taka (Apr. 1982: 21.54 = $1 US). **Gross domestic product** (1980): $10.50 bln. **Per capita income** (1980) $105. **Imports** (1980): $2.42 bln.; partners (1979): U.S. 13%, Jap. 13%, UK 7%, W. Ger. 6%. **Exports** (1980): $758 mln.; partners (1979): U.S. 14%, UK 8%. **Tourists** (1977): 45,300; receipts: $3 mln. **International reserves less gold** (Jan. 1982): $84.1 mln. **Gold:** 54,000 oz t. **Consumer prices** (change in 1981): 13.2%.

Transport: Railway traffic (1978): 5.1 bln. passenger-km; 722 mln. net ton-km. **Motor vehicles:** in use (1978): 24,600 passenger cars, 10,000 comm. vehicles. **Chief ports:** Chittagong, Chalna.

Communications: Telephones in use (1979): 102,300. **Daily newspaper circ.** (1980) 6 per 1,000 pop.

Health: Life expectancy at birth (1974): 45.8 male; 46.6 female. **Births** (per 1,000 pop. 1979): 46. **Deaths** (per 1,000 pop. 1979): 19. **Natural increase** (1979): 2.8%. **Hospital beds** (per 100,000 pop. 1977): 22. **Physicians** (per 100,000 pop. 1977): 8.

Education (1978): **Literacy:** 29%. **Pop. 5–19:** in school: 32%, teachers per 1,000: 9.

Moslem invaders conquered the formerly Hindu area in the 12th century. British rule lasted from the 18th century to 1947, when East Bengal became part of Pakistan.

Charging West Pakistani domination, the Awami League, based in the East, won National Assembly control in 1971. Assembly sessions were postponed; riots broke out. Pakistani troops attacked Mar. 25; Bangladesh independence was proclaimed the next day. In the ensuing civil war, one million died amid charges of Pakistani atrocities. Ten million fled to India.

War between India and Pakistan broke out Dec. 3, 1971. Pakistan surrendered in the East Dec. 15. Sheik Mujibur Rahman became prime minister. The country moved into the Indian and Soviet orbits, in response to U.S. support of Pakistan, and much of the economy was nationalized.

In 1974, the government took emergency powers to curb widespread violence; Mujibur was assassinated and a series of coups followed.

Chronic destitution among the densely crowded population has been worsened by the decline of jute as a major world commodity.

A Ganges waterpact with India, signed 1977, was recommitted by the 2 nations, 1979. Martial law, in force since 1975, was lifted on Apr. 6, 1979, prior to the opening of the new parliament.

On May 30, 1981, Pres. Ziaur Rahman was shot and killed in an unsuccessful coup attempt by army rivals. Vice President Abdus Sattar assumed the duties of acting president. Sattar was ousted in a coup led by army chief of staff Gen. H.M. Ershad, Mar. 1982. Ershad announced that he would govern under martial law for the next 2 years.

Barbados

People: Population (1981 est.): 290,000 **Age distrib.** (%): 0–14: 29.9%; 15–59: 48.6; 60+: 13.8. **Pop. density:** 1,506.02 per sq. mi. **Urban** (1970): 3.7%. **Ethnic groups:** African 80%, mixed 16%, Caucasian 4%. **Languages:** English. **Religions:** Anglican 53%, Methodist 9%, Roman Catholic 4%.

Geography: Area: 166 sq. mi. **Location:** In Atlantic, farthest E of W. Indies. **Neighbors:** Nearest are Trinidad, Grenada on SW. **Topography:** The island lies alone in the Atlantic almost completely surrounded by coral reefs. Highest point is Mt. Hillaby, 1,115 ft. **Capital:** Bridgetown. **Cities** (1980 est.): Bridgetown 7,600.

Government: Head of state: Queen Elizabeth II, represented by Gov.-Gen. Deighton L. Ward; b. May 16, 1909; in office: Nov. 17, 1976. **Head of government:** Prime Min. John M.G. Adams; b. Sept. 24, 1931; in office: Sept. 2, 1976. **Local divisions:** 11 parishes, one city.

Economy: Industries: Rum, molasses, tourism. **Chief crops:** Sugar, corn. **Minerals:** Lime. **Crude oil reserves** (1980): 1.5 mln. bbls. **Other resources:** Fish. **Per capita arable land:** 0.3 acres. **Electricity prod.** (1978): 264.00 mln. kwh. **Labor force:** 9.8% agric.; 24.6% ind. and commerce; 65.6% services and government.

Finance: Currency: Dollar (Apr. 1982: 2.01 = $1 US). **Gross domestic product** (1979): $636.90 mln. **Per capita income** (1978): $3,040. **Imports** (1980): $524 mln.; partners (1979): U.S. 32%, UK 16%, Trin./Tob. 10%, Can. 8%. **Exports** (1980): $226 mln.; partners (1979): U.S. 36%, UK 13%, Trin./Tob. 12%. **Tourists** (1979): 371,000; receipts: $184 million. **National budget** (1980): $188 mln. revenues; $198 mln. expenditures. **International reserves less gold** (Jan. 1982): $100.29 mln. **Consumer prices** (change in 1980): 18.7%.

Transport: Motor vehicles: in use (1976): 24,700 passenger cars; 4,000 comm. vehicles. **Chief ports:** Bridgetown.

Communications: Television sets: 48,000 in use (1976). **Radios:** 130,000 in use (1976). **Telephones in use** (1978): 47,266. **Daily newspaper circ.** (1980): 130 per 1,000 pop.

Health: Life expectancy at birth (1981): 70.8. **Births** (per 1,000 pop. 1979): 16. **Deaths** (per 1,000 pop. 1979): 7. **Natural increase** (1976): 2.3%. **Hospital beds** (per 100,000 pop. 1977): 833. **Physicians** (per 100,000 pop. 1977): 76. **Infant mortality** (per 1,000 live births 1981): 28.3.

Education (1978): **Literacy:** 97%. **Pop. 5-19:** in school: 71%, teachers per 1,000: 36.

Barbados was probably named by Portuguese sailors in reference to bearded fig trees. An English ship visited in 1605, and British settlers arrived on the uninhabited island in 1627. Slaves worked the sugar plantations, but were freed in 1834.

Self-rule came gradually, with full independence proclaimed Nov. 30, 1966. British traditions have remained. Pres. Ronald Reagan became the first U.S. president to visit the island, Apr. 1982.

Belgium

Kingdom of Belgium

People: Population (1981 est.): 9,800,000. **Age distrib.** (%): 0–14: 21.8; 15–59: 59.3; 60+: 18.9 **Pop. density:** 842.18 per sq. mi. **Urban** (1976): 94.6%. **Ethnic groups:** Flemings 58%, Walloons 41%. **Languages:** Flemish (Dutch) 56%, French 32%, legally bilingual 11%, German 1%. **Religions:** Roman Catholic 75%, Protestant.

Geography: Area: 11,779 sq. mi., slightly larger than Maryland. **Location:** In NW Europe, on N. Sea. **Neighbors:** France on W, S, Luxembourg on SE, W. Germany on E, Netherlands on N. **Topography:** Mostly flat, the country is trisected by the Scheldt and Meuse, major commercial rivers. The land becomes hilly and forested in the SE (Ardennes) region. **Capital:** Brussels. **Cities** (1980 est.): Antwerp 194,000; Ghent 241,000; Liege 220,000; Brugge 118,023; Brussels 1,008,715.

Government: Head of state: King Baudouin; b. Sept. 7, 1930; in office: July 17, 1951. **Head of government:** Prime Min. Wilfried Martens; b. Apr. 19, 1936; in office: Dec. 17, 1981. **Lo-**

cal divisions: 9 provinces. **Armed forces:** regulars 87,600 (1980).

Economy: Industries: Steel, glassware, diamond cutting, textiles, chemicals. **Chief crops:** Grains, potatoes, sugar beets. **Minerals:** Coal. **Other resources:** Forests. **Per capita arable land** (incl. Lux.): 0.2 acres. **Meat prod.** (1980): beef: 300,000 metric tons; pork: 690,000 metric tons. **Fish catch** (1979): 47,000 metric tons. **Electricity prod.** (1980): 53.6 bln. kwh. **Crude steel prod.** (1981): 12.2 mln. metric tons. **Labor force:** 3.4% agric.; 37% manuf.

Finance: Currency: Franc (Mar. 1982: 45.56 = $1 US). **Gross domestic product** (1979): $110.9 bln. **Per capita income** (1979): $10,800. *Note:* the following trade and tourist data includes Luxembourg. **Imports** (1981): $61.5 bln.; partners (1980): W. Ger. 20%, Neth. 16%, France 14%, UK 8%, U.S. 8%. **Exports** (1981): $55.57 bln.; partners (1980): W. Ger. 21%, France 19%, Neth. 15%, UK 8%. **Tourists** (1977): 7,623,300; receipts: $993 mln. **National budget** (1980): $34.62 bln. revenues; $44.90 bln. expenditures. **International reserves less gold** (Jan. 1982): $4.43 bln. **Gold:** 34.18 mln. oz t. **Consumer prices** (change in 1981): 7.6%.

Transport: Railway traffic (1979): 6.9 bln. passenger-km; 7.99 bln. net ton-km. **Motor vehicles:** in use (1979): 3.07 mln. passenger cars, 258,000 comm. vehicles; assembled (1978): 1.01 mln. passenger cars; 37,090 comm. vehicles. **Civil aviation:** 4,852 mln. passenger-km (1980): 405.8 mln. freight ton-km (1980). **Chief ports:** Antwerp, Zeebrugge, Ghent.

Communications: Television sets: 2.9 mln. licensed (1979), 650,000 manuf. (1978). **Radios:** 4.5 mln. licensed (1979), 1.31 mln. manuf. (1978). **Telephones in use** (1979): 3.2 mln. **Daily newspaper circ.** (1980): 418 per 1,000 pop.

Health: Life expectancy at birth (1976): 68.6 male; 75.1 female. **Births** (per 1,000 pop. 1980): 12.7. **Deaths** (per 1,000 pop. 1980): 11.6. **Natural increase** (1978) .07%. **Hospital beds** (per 100,000 pop. 1977): 894. **Physicians** (per 100,000 pop. 1977): 211. **Infant mortality** (per 1,000 live births 1978): 11.9.

Education (1980): Literacy: 99%. **Pop. 5-19:** in school: 58%, teachers per 1,000: 40.

Belgium derives its name from the Belgae, the first recorded inhabitants, probably Celts. The land was conquered by Julius Caesar, and was ruled for 1800 years by conquerors, including Rome, the Franks, Burgundy, Spain, Austria, and France. After 1815, Belgium was made a part of the Netherlands, but it became an independent constitutional monarchy in 1830.

Belgian neutrality was violated by Germany in both world wars. King Leopold III surrendered to Germany, May 28, 1940. After the war, he was forced by political pressure to abdicate in favor of his son, King Baudouin.

The Flemings of northern Belgium speak Dutch while French is the language of the Walloons in the south. The language difference has been a perennial source of controversy. Tension between the 2 groups erupted repeatedly in 1981.

Belgium lives by its foreign trade; about 50% of its entire production is sold abroad. The poor economy deteriorated public finances and weakened balance of payments in 1981.

The economy continued to falter in 1982. The government's austere economic policies brought about widespread strikes and scattered violence in February.

Belize

People: Population (1981 est.): 146,000. **Languages:** English, Spanish, native Creole dialects. **Religions:** Roman Catholic, Methodist, Anglican.

Geography: Area: 8,867 sq. mi. **Location:** eastern coast of Central America. **Neighbors:** Mexico on N., Guatemala on W. and S. **Capital:** Belmopan. **Cities:** (1980 est.): Belize City 42,200.

Head of Government: Prime Min. George Cadle Price; b. Jan. 15, 1919; in office: Sept. 21, 1981.

Economy: Sugar is the main export, citrus fruits, fish.

Finance: Currency: Belize dollar (Sept. 1981) 2 = $1 U.S. **Imports** (1978) $110 mln.; partners (1977): U.S. 42%, UK 15%. **Exports:** partners (1977): U.S. 47%, UK 44%. **National Budget** (1979): $31.3 mln. revenues; $26.2 mln. expenditures.

Education: approximately 40,000 pupils attend primary schools.

Belize (formerly called British Honduras), Great Britain's last colony on the American mainland, achieved independence on Sept. 21, 1981. Guatemala claims territorial sovereignty over the country and has refused to recognize Belize's independence. There are 1,600 British troops in Belize to guarantee security.

Benin

People's Republic of Benin

People: Population (1981 est.): 3,600,000. **Age distrib.** (%): 0–14: 46.1; 15–59: 48.3; 60+: 5.6. **Pop. density:** 82.10 per sq. mi. **Urban** (1979): 13.9%. **Ethnic groups:** Fons, Adjas, Baribas, Yorubas. **Languages:** French, local dialects. **Religions:** Mainly animist with Christian, Muslim minorities.

Geography: Area: 43,475 sq. mi., slightly smaller than Pennsylvania. **Location:** In W Africa on Gulf of Guinea. **Neighbors:** Togo on W, Upper Volta, Niger on N, Nigeria on E. **Topography:** most of Benin is flat and covered with dense vegetation. The coast is hot, humid, and rainy. **Capital:** Porto–Novo. **Cities** (1980 est.): Cotonou 215,000; Porto-Novo 123,000.

Government: Head of state: Pres. Ahmed Kerekou; b. Sept. 2, 1933; in office: Oct. 27, 1972. **Local divisions:** 6 departments. **Armed forces:** regulars 2,600; para-military 1,000 (1980).

Economy: Chief crops: Palm products, peanuts, cotton, kapok, coffee, tobacco. **Minerals:** Oil. **Per capita arable land:** 2.1 acres. **Fish catch** (1978): 25,500 metric tons. **Electricity prod.** (1977): 5.00 mln. kwh. **Labor force:** 90% agric.

Finance: Currency: CFA franc (Mar. 1982: 312.10 = $1 US). **Gross domestic product** (1978): $734 mln. **Per capita income** (1975): $162. **Imports** (1979): $320 mln.; partners (1977): Fr. 23%, UK 13%, W. Ger. 8%, Neth. 6%. **Exports** (1979): $26 mln.; partners (1977): Neth. 28%, Jap. 27%, Fr. 24%. **Tourists** (1977): 23,000; receipts b.b. $3 mln. **International reserves less gold** (Jan. 1982): $50.4 mln. **Gold:** 11,000 oz t.

Transport: Railway traffic (1978): 133.2 mln. passenger-km; 152 mln. net ton-km. **Motor vehicles:** in use (1976): 17,000 passenger cars, 9,500 comm. vehicles. **Chief ports:** Cotonou.

Communications: Radios: 150,000 in use (1976). **Daily newspaper circ.** (1980): 3 per 1,000 pop.

Health: Life expectancy at birth (1975): 44.8 male; 45.0 female. **Births** (per 1,000 pop. 1978): 52. **Deaths** (per 1,000 pop. 1978): 25. **Natural increase** (1978): 2.7%. **Hospital beds** (per 100,000 pop. 1977): 137. **Physicians** (per 100,000 pop. 1977): 3. **Infant mortality** (per 1,000 live births 1975): 109.6.

Education (1978): **Literacy:** 20%. **Pop. 5-19:** in school: 34%, teachers per 1,000: 7.

The Kingdom of Abomey, rising to power in wars with neighboring kingdoms in the 17th century, came under French domination in the late 19th century, and was incorporated into French West Africa by 1904.

Under the name Dahomey, the country became independent Aug. 1, 1960. The name was changed to Benin in 1975. In the fifth coup since independence Col. Ahmed Kerekou took power in 1972; two years later he declared a socialist state with a "Marxist-Leninist" philosophy. The economy relies on the development of agriculturally-based industries.

Bhutan

Kingdom of Bhutan

People: Population (1981 est.): 1,400,000. **Pop. density:** 67.34 per sq. mi. **Ethnic groups:** Bhotia (Tibetan) 60%. Nepalese 25%, Lepcha (indigenous), Indians. **Languages:** Dzongkha (official), Nepali. **Religions:** Buddhist 75%, Hindu 25%.

Geography: Area: 17,800 sq. mi., the size of Vermont and New Hampshire combined. **Location:** In eastern Himalayan Mts. **Neighbors:** India on W (Sikkim) and S, China on N. **Topography:** Bhutan is comprised of very high mountains in the N, fertile valleys in the center, and thick forests in the Duar Plain in the S. **Capital:** Thimphu. **City** (1980 est.): Thimphu 10,000.

Government: Head of state: King Jigme Singye Wangchuk; b. Nov. 11, 1955; in office: July 21, 1972. **Local divisions:** 4 regions comprised of 17 districts.

Economy: Industries: Cloth. **Chief crops:** Rice, corn, wheat, oranges, cardamon, yak butter, lac, wax. **Other resources:** Elephants, timber. **Per capita arable land:** 0.5 acres. **Labor force:** 95% agric.

Finance: Currency: Ngultrum (Oct. 1981: 9.02 = 1 US)

(Indian Rupee also used). **Gross domestic product** (1976 est.): $90 mln. **Per capita income** (1976): $70. **Imports** (1980): $2 mln.; partners India 99%. **Exports** (1980): $1.5 mln.; partners India 99%.

Communications: Radios: 10,000 licensed (1976). **Telephones in use** (1978): 1,355.

Health: Life expectancy at birth (1975): 42.0 male; 40.5 female. **Births** (per 1,000 pop. 1978): 43. **Deaths** (per 1,000 pop. 1978): 20. **Natural increase** (1978): 2.3%. **Pop. per hospital bed** (1975): 1,616. **Pop. per physician** (1975): 4,264.

The region came under Tibetan rule in the 16th century. British influence grew in the 19th century. A monarchy, set up in 1907, became a British protectorate by a 1910 treaty. The country became independent in 1949, with India guiding foreign relations and supplying aid.

Links to India have been strengthened by airline service and a road network. Most of the population engages in subsistence agriculture.

Bolivia

Republic of Bolivia

People: Population (1981 est.): 5,500,000. **Age distrib.** (%): 0–14: 41.9; 15–59: 52.0; 60+: 6.4. **Pop. density:** 13.20 per sq. mi. **Ethnic groups:** Quechua 30%, Aymara 25%, Mestizo (cholo) 25-30%, European 5-15%. **Languages:** Spanish (official) 55%, Quechua, Aymara. **Religions:** Roman Catholic 93%.

Geography: Area: 424,165 sq. mi., the size of Texas and California combined. **Location:** In central Andes Mtns. **Neighbors:** Peru, Chile on W, Argentina, Paraguay on S, Brazil on E and N. **Topography:** The great central plateau, at an altitude of 12,000 ft., over 500 mi. long, lies between two great cordilleras having 3 of the highest peaks in S. America. Lake Titicaca, on Peruvian border, is highest lake in world on which steamboats ply (12,506 ft.). The E central region has semitropical forests; the llanos, or Amazon-Chaco lowlands are in E. **Capitals:** Sucre, (legal), La Paz (de facto). **Cities** (1981 est.): La Paz 689,000; Santa Cruz 300,000; Cochabamba 216,000.

Government: Head of state: Pres. Celso Torrelio Villa; in office: Sept. 4, 1981. **Local divisions:** 9 departments headed by prefects, 94 provinces. **Armed forces:** regulars 21,500 (1980).

Economy: Chief crops: Potatoes, sugar, coffee, barley, cocoa, rice, corn, bananas, citrus. **Minerals:** Antimony, tin, tungsten, silver, copper, lead, zinc, oil, gas, gold, iron, cadmium, borate of lime. **Crude oil reserves** (1980): 150 mln. bbls. **Other resources:** rubber, cinchona bark. **Per capita arable land:** 1.5 acres. **Meat prod.** (1980): beef: 84,000 metric tons; pork: 31,000 metric tons; lamb: 26,000 metric tons. **Electricity prod.** (1978): 1.35 bln. kwh. **Labor force:** 51% agric. 24% ind. & comm.

Finance: Currency: Peso (Mar. 1982: 43.18 = $1 US). **Gross domestic product** (1980): $6.10 bln. **Per capita income** (1979): $510. **Imports** (1980): $814 mln.; partners (1978): U.S. 28%, Arg. 11%, Braz. 9%. **Exports** (1980): $942.1 mln.; partners (1978): U.S. 31%, Arg. 17%, UK 12%, W. Ger. 5%. **National budget** (1980): $3.8 bln. revenues; $4.7 bln. expenditures. **International reserves less gold** (Jan. 1982): $100.8 mln. **Gold:** 829,000 oz t. **Consumer prices** (change in 1980): 47.2%

Transport: Railway traffic (1979): 395 mln. passenger-km; 579 mln. net ton-miles. **Motor vehicles:** in use (1979): 35,900 passenger cars, 50,000 comm. vehicles. **Civil aviation:** 1.342 bln. passenger-km. (1979); 38.4 mln. freight ton-km. (1979).

Communications: Television sets: 49,000 (1977). **Radios:** 440,000 in use (1977). **Telephones in use** (1979): 125,800. **Daily newspaper circ.** (1980): 46 per 1,000 pop.

Health: Life expectancy at birth (1975): 46.5 male; 51.1 female. **Births** (per 1,000 pop. 1978): 44. **Deaths** (per 1,000 pop. 1978): 19. **Natural increase** (1978): 2.4%. **Hospital beds** (per 100,000 pop. 1977): 228. **Physicians** (per 100,000 pop. 1977): 38. **Infant mortality** (per 1,000 live births 1975): 77.3.

Education (1978): **Literacy:** 63%. **Pop. 5-19:** in school: 58%, teachers per 1,000: 25.

The Incas conquered the region from earlier Indian inhabitants in the 13th century. Spanish rule began in the 1530s, and lasted until Aug. 6, 1825. The country is named after Simon Bolivar, independence fighter.

In a series of wars, Bolivia lost its Pacific coast to Chile, the oilbearing Chaco to Paraguay, and rubber-growing areas to Brazil, 1879-1935.

Economic unrest, especially among the militant mine workers, has contributed to continuing political instability. A reformist government under Victor Paz Estenssoro, 1951-64, nationalized tin mines and attempted to improve conditions for the Indian majority, but was overthrown by a military junta. A series of coups and countercoups continued through 1981, until the military junta elected Gen. Villa as president. Villa promised to restore democratic rule in 1983.

Bolivia has a host of economic problems and its foreign exchange reserves were nearly exhausted by the end of 1981.

Botswana

Republic of Botswana

People: Population (1981 est.): 810,000. **Age distrib.** (%): 0–14: 46.1; 15–59: 43.1; 60+: 7.4. **Pop. density:** 3.73 per sq. mi. **Urban** (1974): 12.3%. **Ethnic groups:** Bantus (8 main tribes), Bushmen. **Languages:** English (official), Setswana (national). **Religions:** Christian 60%, animist.

Geography: Area: 224,600 sq. mi., slightly smaller than Texas. **Location:** In southern Africa. **Neighbors:** Namibia (S.W. Africa) on N and W, S. Africa on S, Zimbabwe on NE; Botswana claims border with Zambia on N. **Topography:** The Kalahari Desert, supporting nomadic Bushmen and wildlife, spreads over SW; there are swamplands and farming areas in N, and rolling plains in E where livestock are grazed. **Capital:** Gaborone. **Cities** (1981 est.): Gaborone 59,000; Francistown 33,000.

Government: Head of state: Pres. Quett Masire; in office: July 13, 1980. **Local divisions:** 9 districts and 4 independent towns, all with local councils. **Armed forces:** regulars 2,000; para-military 1,260 (1980).

Economy: Industries: Tourism. **Chief crops:** Corn, sorghum, peanuts. **Minerals:** Copper, coal, nickel, diamonds. **Other resources:** Big game. **Per capita arable land:** 4.6 acres. **Meat prod.** (1980): beef: 48,000 metric tons; lamb: 5,000 metric tons **Electricity prod.** (1980): 471 mln. kwh. **Labor force:** 68% agric.

Finance: Currency: Pula (Apr. 1982: 0.96 = $1 US). **Gross domestic product** (1978): $401 mln. **Per capita income** (1978): $544. **Imports** (1980): $672 mln.; partners (1980): S. Africa 88%. **Exports** (1980): $504 mln.; partners (1980): Europe 67%, U.S. 17%, S. Africa 7%. **National budget** (1980): $221 mln. revenues; $215.0 mln. expenditures. **International reserves less gold** (Jan. 1982): $241.8 mln. **Consumer prices** (change in 1979): 11.7%

Transport: Railway traffic (1978): 1.04 bln. net ton km. **Motor vehicles:** in use (1977): 3,400 passenger cars, 10,800 comm. vehicles.

Communications: Radios: 60,000 in use (1976). **Daily newspaper circ.** (1980): 23 per 1,000 pop.

Health: Life expectancy at birth (1975): 44.3 male; 47.5 female. **Births** (annual per 1,000 pop. 1978): 40 **Deaths** (per 1,000 pop. 1978): 13. **Natural increase** (1978): 2.8%. **Hospital beds** (per 100,000 pop. 1977): 303. **Physicians** (per 100,000 pop. 1977): 14.

Education (1978): **Literacy:** 30%. **Pop. 5-19:** in school: 55% teachers per 1,000: 16.

First inhabited by bushmen, then by Bantus, the region became the British protectorate of Bechuanaland in 1886, halting encroachment by Boers and Germans from the south and southwest. The country became fully independent Sept. 30, 1966 changing its name to Botswana.

Cattle-raising and mining (diamonds, copper, nickel) have contributed to the country's rapid economic growth. Many workers are migrants in S. Africa, and much of Botswana's exports go to that country.

Brazil

Federative Republic of Brazil

People: Population (1981 est.): 124,700,000. **Age distrib.** (%): 0–14: 41.1; 15–59: 53.7; 60+: 5.2. **Pop. density:** 36 per sq. mi. **Urban** (1979): 62.7%. **Ethnic groups:** Portuguese, Afr cans, and mulattoes make up the vast majority; Italians, Germans, Japanese, Indians, Jews, Arabs. **Languages:** Portuguese. **Religions:** Roman Catholic 90%.

Geography: Area: 3,286,470 sq. mi., larger than contiguous 48 U.S. states; largest country in S. America. **Location:** Occupies eastern half of S. America. **Neighbors:** French Guiana, Suriname, Guyana, Venezuela on N, Colombia, Peru, Bolivia, Paraguay, Argentina on W, Uruguay on S. **Topography:** Brazil's Atlantic coastline stretches 4,603 miles. In N is the heavily-wooded Amazon basin covering half the country. Its network of rivers navigable for 15,814 mi. The Amazon itself flows 2,093 miles in Brazil, all navigable. The NE region is semiarid scrubland, heavily settled and poor. The S central region, favored by climate and resources, has 45% of the population, produces 75% of farm goods and 80% of industrial output. The narrow coastal belt includes most of the major cities. Almost the entire country has a tropical or semitropical climate. **Capital:** Brasilia. **Cities** (1979 est.): Sao Paulo 8.4 mln.; Rio de Janeiro 5.3 mln.; Belo Horizonte 1.8 mln.; Recife 1.3 mln.; Salvador 1.4 mln.; Fortaleza 1.2 mln.; Porto Alegre 1.1 mln.; Nova Iguacu 1.1 mln.

Government: Head of state: Pres. Joao Baptista de Oliveira Figueiredo; b. Jan. 15, 1918; in office: Mar. 15, 1979. **Local divisions:** 22 states, with individual constitutions and elected governments; 4 territories, federal district. **Armed forces:** regulars 269,000; para-military 200,000 (1980).

Economy: Industries: Steel, autos, chemicals, ships, appliances, shoes, paper, petrochemicals, machinery. **Chief crops:** Coffee (largest grower), cotton, soybeans, sugar, cocoa, rice, corn, fruits. **Minerals:** Chromium, iron, manganese, tin, quartz crystals, beryl, sheet mica, columbium, titanium, diamonds, thorium, gold, nickel, gem stones, coal, tin, tungsten, bauxite, oil. **Crude oil reserves** (1980): 1.22 bln. bbls. **Per capita arable land:** 0.7 acres. **Meat prod.** (1980): beef: 2.20 mln. metric tons; pork: 1.05 mln. metric tons; lamb: 52,000 metric tons. **Fish catch** (1979): 843,000 metric tons. **Electricity prod.** (1979): 124.6 bln. kwh. **Crude steel prod.** (1981): 13.2 mln. metric tons. **Labor force:** 41% service, 36% agric.; 23% ind.

Finance: Currency: Cruzeiro (Apr. 1982: 148.21 = $1 US). **Gross domestic product** (1980): $237 bln. **Per capita income** (1978): $1,523. **Imports** (1981): $24.0 bln.; partners (1979): U.S. 18%, Iraq 14%, Sau. Ar. 10%, W. Ger. 7%, Jap. 6%. **Exports** (1981): $23.29 bln.; partners (1979): U.S. 19%, W. Ger. 7%, Neth. 7%, Japan 6%. **Tourists** (1977): 634,600; receipts: $55 mln. **National budget** (1979): $18.91 bln. revenues; $18.83 bln. expenditures. **International reserves less gold** (Dec. 1981): $6.60 bln. **Gold:** 2.20 mln. oz t. **Consumer prices** (change in 1981): 120%.

Transport: Railway traffic (1979): 11.95 bln. passenger-km; 63 bln. net ton-km. **Motor vehicles:** in use (1979): 8.2 mln. passenger cars, 926,300 mln. comm. vehicles; manuf. (1979): 553,000 passenger cars; 575,000 comm. vehicles. **Civil aviation:** 15 bln. passenger-km (1980): 610 mln. freight ton-km (1980): **Chief ports:** Santos, Rio de Janeiro, Vitoria, Salvador, Rio Grande, Recife.

Communications: Television sets: 11 mln. in use (1977): 2.07 mln. manuf. (1978). **Radios:** 16.98 mln. in use (1975), 759,000 manuf. (1976). **Telephones in use** (1978): 5.7 mln. **Daily newspaper circ.** (1976): 4,895,000; 45 per 1,000 pop.

Health: Life expectancy at birth (1970): 57.61 male; 61.10 female. **Births** (per 1,000 pop. 1978): 32. **Deaths** (per 1,000 pop. 1978): 9. **Natural increase** (1978): 2.3%. **Hospital beds** (per 100,000 pop. 1977): 327. **Physicians** (per 100,000 pop. 1977): 59.

Education (1978): **Literacy:** 75%. **Pop. 5-19:** in school: 52%, teachers per 1,000: 25.

Pedro Alvares Cabral, a Portuguese navigator, is generally credited as the first European to reach Brazil, in 1500. The country was thinly settled by various Indian tribes. Only a few have survived to the present, mostly in the Amazon basin.

In the next centuries, Portuguese colonists gradually pushed inland, bringing along large numbers of African slaves. Slavery was not abolished until 1888.

The King of Portugal, fleeing before Napoleon's army, moved the seat of government to Brazil in 1808. Brazil thereupon became a kingdom under Dom Joao VI. After his return to Portugal, his son Pedro proclaimed the independence of Brazil, Sept. 7, 1822, and was acclaimed emperor. The second emperor, Dom Pedro II, was deposed in 1889, and a republic proclaimed, called the United States of Brazil. In 1967 the country was renamed the Federative Republic of Brazil.

A military junta took control in 1930; dictatorial power was assumed by Getúlio Vargas, who alternated with military coups until finally forced out by the military in 1954. A democratic regime prevailed 1956-64, during which time the capital was moved from Rio de Janeiro to Brasilia in the interior.

The next 5 presidents were all military leaders. Censorship was imposed, and much of the opposition was suppressed amid charges of torture. In 1974 elections, the official opposition party made gains in the chamber of deputies; some relaxation of censorship occurred, though church liberals, labor leaders, and intellectuals continued to report cases of arrest and torture.

Since 1930, successive governments have pursued industrial and agricultural growth and the development of interior areas. Exploiting vast mineral resources, fertile soil in several regions, and a huge labor force, Brazil became the leading industrial power of Latin America by the 1970s, while agricultural output soared. The 1979 government declared an amnesty and enacted democratic reforms.

However, income maldistribution, a return of inflation (120% in 1981), and government land policies have all come under attack. Huge oil imports increased the foreign debt to $60 bln. in 1981.

Bulgaria

People's Republic of Bulgaria

People: Population (1981 est.): 8,800,000. **Age distrib.** (%): 0–14: 22.3; 15–59: 61.7; 60+: 16.0. **Pop. density:** 206.87 per sq. mi. **Urban** (1978): 60.5%. **Ethnic groups:** Bulgarians 85%, Turks 9%, Gypsies 2%. **Languages:** Bulgarian, Turkish, Greek. **Religions:** Orthodox 85%, Moslem 13%.

Geography: Area: 42,823 sq. mi., slightly larger than Tennessee. **Location:** In eastern Balkan Peninsula on Black Sea. **Neighbors:** Romania on N, Yugoslavia on W, Greece, Turkey on S. **Topography:** The Stara Planina (Balkan) Mts. stretch E-W across the center of the country, with the Danubian plain on N, the Rhodope Mts. on SW, and Thracian Plain on SE. **Capital:** Sofia. **Cities** (1979 est.): Sofia 1,031,600; Plovdiv 307,414; Varna 257,731.

Government: Head of state: Pres. Todor Zhivkov; b. Sept. 7, 1911; in office: July 7, 1971. **Head of government:** Premier Grisha Filipov; in office: June 16, 1981. **Head of Communist Party:** First Sec. Todor Zhivkov; in office: Jan. 1954. **Local divisions:** 28 provinces. **Armed forces:** regulars 150,000; reserves 240,000 (1980).

Economy: Industries: Chemicals, machinery, metals, textiles, fur, leather goods, vehicles, wine, processed food. **Chief crops:** Grains, fruit, corn, potatoes, tobacco. **Minerals:** Lead, molybdenum, coal, oil, zinc. **Per capita arable land:** 1.1 acres. **Meat prod.** (1980): beef: 129,000 metric tons; pork: 256,000 metric tons; lamb: 65,000 metric tons. **Fish catch** (1978): 140,000 metric tons. **Electricity prod.** (1980): 34.3 bln. kwh. **Crude steel prod.** (1981): 2.6 mln. metric tons. **Labor force:** 24% agric.; 32% manuf.

Finance: Currency: Lev (Sept. 1981: .95 = $1 US). **Net material product** (1978): $14.4 bln. **Per capita income** (1976): $2,100. **Imports** (1980): $7.86 bln.; partners: USSR 57%, E. Ger. 7%, W. Ger. 5%. **Exports** (1980): $8.45 bln.; partners: USSR 50%, E. Ger. 5%. **Tourists** (1979): 5.1 mln.

Transport: Railway traffic (1979): 6.9 bln. passenger-km; 17.68 bln. net ton-km. **Motor vehicles:** in use (1978) 480,000 passenger cars, 110,000 commercial; manuf. (1977): 15,000 passenger cars, 6,900 comm. vehicles. **Chief ports:** Burgas, Varna.

Communications: Television sets: 1.6 mln. licensed (1979), 70,000 manuf. (1978). **Radios:** 2.1 mln. licensed (1979), 86,000 manuf. (1978). **Telephones in use** (1979): 1.032 mln. **Daily newspaper circ.** (1980): 214 per 1,000 pop.

Health: Life expectancy at birth (1976): 68.68 male; 73.91 female. **Births** (per 1,000 pop. 1978): 15.5. **Deaths** (per 1,000 pop. 1978): 10.5. **Natural increase** (1978): .2%. **Hospital beds** (per 100,000 pop. 1977): 872. **Physicians** (per 100,000 pop. 1977): 226. **Infant mortality** (per 1,000 live births 1978): 21.8

Education (1978): **Literacy:** 95%. **Pop. 5-19:** in school: 56%, teachers per 1,000: 30.

Bulgaria was settled by Slavs in the 6th century. Turkic Bulgars arrived in the 7th century, merged with the Slavs, became Christians by the 9th century, and set up powerful empires in the 10th and 12th centuries. The Ottomans prevailed in 1396 and remained for 500 years.

A revolt in 1876 led to an independent kingdom in 1908. Bulgaria expanded after the first Balkan War but lost its Aegean coastline in World War I, when it sided with Germany. Bulgaria joined the Axis in World War II, but withdrew in 1944. Communists took power with Soviet aid; the monarchy was abolished Sept. 8, 1946.

Burma

Socialist Republic of the Union of Burma

People: Population (1981 est.): 35,200,000. **Age distrib.** (%): 0–14: 40.5; 15–59: 53.5; 60+: 6.0. **Pop. density:** 123.04 per sq. mi. **Ethnic groups:** Burmans (related to Tibetans) 72%; Karen 7%, Shan 6%, Kachin 2%, Chinese 2%, Indians 3%, others. **Languages:** Burmese (official). **Religions:** Buddhist 80%; Hinduism, Islam, Christians.

Geography: Area: 261,288 sq. mi., nearly as large as Texas. **Location:** Between S. and S.E. Asia, on Bay of Bengal. **Neighbors:** Bangladesh, India on W, China, Laos, Thailand on E. **Topography:** Mountains surround Burma on W, N, and E, and dense forests cover much of the nation. N-S rivers provide habitable valleys and communications, especially the Irrawaddy, navigable for 900 miles. The country has a tropical monsoon climate. **Capital:** Rangoon. **Cities** (1980 est.): Rangoon 2,186,000; Mandalay 458,000; Karbe ('73 cen.): 253,600; Moulmein 188,000.

Government: Head of state: Pres. U San Yu in office: Nov. 9, 1981. **Head of government:** Prime Min. U. Maung Maung Kha; b. Nov. 2, 1917; in office: Mar. 29, 1977. **Local divisions:** 7 states and 7 divisions. **Armed forces:** regulars 176,500; para-military 73,000 (1980).

Economy: Chief crops: Rice, sugarcane, peanuts, beans. **Minerals:** Oil, lead, silver, tin, tungsten, zinc, rubies, sapphires, jade. **Crude oil reserves** (1980): 25 mln. bbls. **Other resources:** Rubber, teakwood. **Per capita arable land:** 0.7 acres. **Meat prod.** (1980): beef: 94,000 metric tons; pork: 81,000 metric tons; lamb: 4,000 metric tons. **Fish catch** (1979): 565,300 metric tons. **Electricity prod.** (1978): 960.00 mln. kwh. **Labor force:** 67% agric.

Finance: Currency: Kyat (Apr. 1982: 7.71 = $1 US). **Gross domestic product** (1979): $5.16 bln. **Per capita income** (1981): $174. **Imports** (1980): $354 mln.; partners (1978): Jap. 31%, U.S. 12%, UK 9%, W. Ger. 6%. **Exports** (1980): $472 mln.; partners (1978): Bang. 14%, Switz. 12%, Sing. 10%. **Tourists** (1976): 18,280; receipts (1975): $3 mln. **National budget** (1980): $3.9 bln. revenues; $4.2 bln. expenditures. **International reserves less gold** (Feb. 1982): $196.8 mln. **Gold:** 251,000 oz t. **Consumer prices** (change in 1981): 0.3%.

Transport: Railway traffic (1979): 3.7 bln. passenger-km; 600 mln. net ton-km. **Motor vehicles:** in use (1978): 33,000 passenger cars, 41,500 comm. vehicles. **Civil aviation:** 218 mln. passenger-km. (1980); 1.6 mln. net ton-km. (1980). **Chief ports:** Rangoon, Sittwe, Bassein, Moulmein, Tavoy.

Communications: Radios: 693,000 licensed (1977), 12,000 manuf. (1977). **Telephones in use** (1978): 32,600. **Daily newspaper circ.** (1980): 24 per 1,000 pop.

Health: Life expectancy at birth (1975): 48.6 male; 51.5 female. **Births** (per 1,000 pop. 1978): 39. **Deaths** (per 1,000 pop. 1978): 14. **Natural increase** (1978): 2.4%. **Hospital beds** (per 100,000 pop. 1977): 89. **Physicians** (per 100,000 pop. 1977): 19. **Infant mortality** (per 1,000 live births 1975): 195-300.

Education (1978): **Literacy:** 68%. **Pop. 5-19:** in school: 40%, teachers per 1,000: 8.

The Burmese arrived from Tibet before the 9th century, displacing earlier cultures, and a Buddhist monarchy was established by the 11th. Burma was conquered by the Mongol dynasty of China in 1272, then ruled by Shans as a Chinese tributary, until the 16th century.

Britain subjugated Burma in 3 wars, 1824-84, and ruled the country as part of India until 1937, when it became self-governing. Independence outside the Commonwealth was achieved Jan. 4, 1948.

Gen. Ne Win dominated politics during the 1960s and 1970s. He led a Revolutionary Council set up in 1962, which drove Indians from the civil service and Chinese from commerce. Socialization of the economy was advanced, isolation from foreign countries enforced. Lagging production and export have begun to turn around, due to government incentives in the agriculture and petroleum sectors and receptivity to foreign investment in the economy.

Burundi

Republic of Burundi

People: Population (1981 est.): 4,400,000. **Age distrib.** (%): 0–14: 44.1; 15–59: 51.9; 60+: 4.1. **Pop. density:** 419.96 per sq. mi. **Urban** (1970): 2.2%. **Ethnic groups:** Hutu 85%, Tutsi 14%, Twa (pygmy) 1%. **Languages:** French, Rundi. **Religions:** Roman Catholic 60%, animist 30%.

Geography: Area: 10,759 sq. mi., the size of Maryland. **Location:** In central Africa. **Neighbors:** Rwanda on N, Zaire on W, Tanzania on E. **Topography:** Much of the country is grassy highland, with mountains reaching 8,900 ft. The southernmost source of the White Nile is located in Burundi. Lake Tanganyika is the second deepest lake in the world. **Capital:** Bujumbura. **Cities** (1979 est.): Bujumbura 151,000.

Government: Head of state and head of government: Pres. Jean Baptiste Bagaza; b. Aug. 29, 1946; in office: Nov. 9, 1976 (govt: Oct. 1978). **Local divisions:** 8 provinces and capital city. **Armed forces:** regulars 6,000; para-military 1,500 (1981).

Economy: Chief crops: Coffee (89% of exports), cotton, tea. **Minerals:** Nickel. **Per capita arable land:** 0.6 acres. **Fish catch** (1978): 15,700 metric tons. **Electricity prod.** (1977): 27.00 mln. kwh. **Labor force:** 85% agric.

Finance: Currency: Franc (Apr. 1982: 90 = $1 US). **Gross domestic product** (1979 est.): $700 mln. **Per capita income** (1979 est.) $171. **Imports** (1980): $168 mln.; partners (1979): Belg.-Lux. 11%, Jap. 6%. **Exports** (1980): $65.1 mln.; partners (1979): U.S. 33%, Belg. 16%. **Tourists** (1977): 32,000; receipts (1975): $1 mln. **National budget** (1980): $127 mln. revenues; $145 mln. expenditures. **International reserves less gold** (Feb. 1982): $65.37 mln. **Gold:** 17,000 oz t. **Consumer prices** (change in 1980): 2.3%.

Transport: Motor vehicles: in use (1976): 5,100 passenger cars, 2,200 comm. vehicles.

Communications: Radios: 105,000 in use (1976). **Telephones in use** (1978): 4,995. **Daily newspaper circ.** (1970): 300; 0.1 per 1,000 pop.

Health: Life expectancy at birth (1980): 43.3 male; 45.3 female. **Births** (per 1,000 pop. 1978): 42. **Deaths** (per 1,000 pop. 1978): 17. **Natural increase** (1978): 2.5%. **Hospital beds** (per 100,000 pop. 1977): 118. **Physicians** (per 100,000 pop. 1977): 3. **Infant mortality** (per 1,000 live births 1971): 150.

Education (1978): **Literacy:** 25%. **Pop. 5-19:** in school: 10%, teachers per 1,000: 3.

The pygmy Twa were the first inhabitants, followed by Bantu Hutus, who were conquered in the 16th century by the tall Tutsi (Watusi), probably from Ethiopia. Under German control in 1899, the area fell to Belgium in 1916, which exercised successively a League of Nations mandate and UN trusteeship over Ruanda-Urundi (now 2 countries).

Independence came in 1962, and the monarchy was overthrown in 1966. An unsuccessful Hutu rebellion in 1972-73 left 10,000 Tutsi and 150,000 Hutu dead. Over 100,000 Hutu fled to Tanzania and Zaire. The present regime is pledged to ethnic reconciliation, but Burundi remains one of the poorest and most densely populated countries in Africa.

Cambodia (Kampuchea)

Cambodian People's Republic

People: Population (1981 est.): 5,400,000. **Pop. density:** 126.89 per sq. mi. **Ethnic groups:** Khmers 93%, Vietnamese 4%, Chinese 3%. **Languages:** Khmer (official), French. **Religions:** Theravada Buddhism, animism, atheism.

Geography: Area: 69,900 sq. mi., the size of Missouri. **Location:** In Indochina Peninsula. **Neighbors:** Thailand on W, N, Laos on NE, Vietnam on E. **Topography:** The central area, formed by the Mekong R. basin and Tonle Sap lake, is level. Hills and mountains are in SE, a long escarpment separates the country from Thailand on NW. 75% of the area is forested. **Capital:** Phnom Penh. **Cities** (1981 est.): Phnom Penh 500,000.

Government: Head of government: Pres., People's Revolutionary Council Heng Samrin; in office: Jan. 7, 1979. **Local divisions:** 5 regions and a special capital region.

Economy: Industries: Textiles, paper, plywood, oil products. **Chief crops:** Rice, corn, pepper, tobacco, cotton, oil seeds, beans, palm sugar. **Minerals:** Iron, copper, manganese, gold. **Other resources:** Forests, rubber, kapok. **Per capita arable**

land: 0.8 acres. **Meat prod.** (1980): beef: 17,000 metric tons; pork: 26,000 metric tons. **Fish catch** (1978): 84,700 metric tons. **Electricity prod.** (1977): 150.00 mln. kwh.

Finance: Currency: Riel (Dec. 1980: 4 = $1 US). **Per capita income** (1976): $90. **Imports** (1979): $150 mln. **Exports** (1979): $2 mln.

Transport: Railway traffic (1973): 33.53 mln. passenger-miles; 6.21 mln. net ton-miles. **Motor vehicles:** in use (1972): 27,200 passenger cars, (1973) 10,100 comm. vehicles. **Chief ports:** Kompong Som.

Communications: Television sets: 35,000 in use (1977). **Radios:** 110,000 in use (1975). **Telephones in use** (1977): 71,000.

Health: Life expectancy at birth (1975): 44.0 male; 46.9 female. **Births** (per 1,000 pop. 1975): 45.9. **Deaths** (per 1,000 pop. 1975): 16.9. **Natural increase** (1975): 2.9%. **Hospital beds** (per 100,000 pop. 1977): 106. **Physicians** (per 100,000 pop. 1977): 7.

Education (1978): **Literacy:** 48%. **Pop. 5-19:** (1975): in school: 40%, per teacher: 124.

Early kingdoms dating from that of Funan in the 1st century AD culminated in the great Khmer empire which flourished from the 9th century to the 13th, encompassing present-day Thailand, Cambodia, Laos, and southern Vietnam. The peripheral areas were lost to invading Siamese and Vietnamese, and France established a protectorate in 1863. Independence came in 1953.

Prince Norodom Sihanouk, king 1941-1955 and head of state from 1960, tried to maintain neutrality. Relations with the U.S. were broken in 1965, after South Vietnam planes attacked Vietcong forces within Cambodia. Relations were restored in 1969, after Sihanouk charged Viet communists with arming Cambodian insurgents.

In 1970, pro-U.S. premier Lon Nol seized power, demanding removal of 40,000 North Viet troops; the monarchy was abolished. Sihanouk formed a government-in-exile in Peking, and open war began between the government and Khmer Rouge. The U.S. provided heavy military and economic aid. U.S. troops fought Vietcong forces within Cambodia for 2 months in 1970.

Khmer Rouge forces captured Phnom Penh April 17, 1975. Over 100,000 people had died in 5 years of fighting. The new government evacuated all cities and towns, and shuffled the rural population, sending virtually the entire population to clear jungle, forest, and scrub, which covered half the country.

The government guarded its international isolation, but repeated reports from refugees in Thailand and Vietnam indicated that over one million people were killed in executions and enforced hardships.

Severe border fighting broke out with Vietnam in 1978; developed into a full-fledged Vietnamese invasion. The Vietnamese-backed Kampuchean National United Front for National Salvation, a Cambodian rebel movement, announced, Jan. 8, 1979, the formation of a government one day after the Vietnamese capture of Phnom Pehn. Civil war continued into 1980; thousands of refugees flowed into Thailand. Widespread starvation was reported; by Sept., when the UN confirmed diplomatic recognition to the ousted Pol Pot government, international food assistance was allowed to aid the famine-stricken country. In July 1981, renewed efforts to bring about a Vietnamese troop withdrawal and institute supervised elections were pursued in a UN conference on Cambodia. But prospects for a diplomatic settlement were dimmed when Vietnam and the Soviet Union boycotted the proceedings.

Cameroon

United Republic of Cameroon

People: Population (1981 est.): 8,700,000. **Age distrib.** (%): 0–14: 43.4; 15–59: 50.8; 60+: 5.8. **Pop. density:** 45.76 per sq. mi. **Urban** (1970): 20.3%. **Ethnic groups:** Some 200 tribes; largest are Bamileke 30%, Fulani 7%. **Languages:** English, French (both official), Bantu, Sudanic. **Religions:** animist, Roman Catholic, Protestant, Islam (mostly in N).

Geography: Area: 179,558 sq. mi., somewhat larger than California. **Location:** Between W and central Africa. **Neighbors:** Nigeria on NW, Chad, Central African Republic on E, Congo, Gabon, Equatorial Guinea on S. **Topography:** A low coastal plain with rain forests is in S; plateaus in center lead to forested mountains in W, including Mt. Cameroon, 13,000 ft.; grasslands in N lead to marshes around Lake Chad. **Capital:** Yaounde. **Cities** (1976 est.): Douala 458,400; Yaounde 313,700.

Government: Head of state: Pres. Ahmadou Ahidjo; b. Aug. 5, 1924; in office: Jan. 1, 1960. **Head of government:** Prime Minister Paul Biya; b. Feb. 13, 1933; in office: June 30, 1975. **Local divisions:** 7 provinces with appointed governors. **Armed forces:** regulars 8,500 (1980).

Economy: Industries: Aluminum processing, palm products. **Chief crops:** Cocoa, coffee, peanuts, tea, bananas, cotton, tobacco. **Crude oil reserves** (1980): 140 mln. bbls. **Other resources:** Timber, rubber. **Per capita arable land:** 2.1 acres. **Meat prod.** (1978): beef: 47,000 metric tons; pork: 19,000 metric tons; lamb: 17,000 metric tons. **Fish catch** (1977): 71,600 metric tons. **Electricity prod.** (1978): 1.34 bln. kwh. **Labor force:** 75-80% agric., 10-15% ind. and commerce.

Finance: Currency: CFA franc (Mar. 1982: 312.10 = $1 US). **Gross domestic product** (1979): $5.2 bln. **Per capita income** (1979): $628. **Imports** (1980): 1.60 bln.; partners (1979): Fr. 44%, W. Ger. 8%, U.S. 6%, Italy 5%. **Exports** (1980): $1.38 bln.; partners (1979): Fr. 25%, Neth. 21%, U.S. 21%, It. 7%. **Tourists** (1974): 96,100; receipts (1977): $21 mln. **National budget** (1980): $928 mln. revenues; $928 mln. expenditures. **International reserves less gold** (Oct. 1981): $117.92 mln. **Gold:** 11,000 oz t. **Consumer prices** (change in 1980): 9.3%.

Transport: Railway traffic (1980): 230 mln. passenger-km; 513.6 mln. net ton-km. **Motor vehicles:** in use (1978): 58,600 passenger cars, 37,600 comm. vehicles. **Chief ports:** Douala.

Communications: Radios: 240,000 in use (1977), 80,000 manuf. (1977). **Telephones in use** (1978): 14,321. **Daily newspaper circ.** (1980): 6 per 1,000 pop.

Health: Life expectancy at birth (1975): 41.9 male; 45.1 female. **Births** (per 1,000 pop. 1978): 46. **Deaths** (per 1,000 pop. 1978): 20. **Natural increase** (1978): 2.6%. **Hospital beds** (per 100,000 pop. 1977): 269. **Physicians** (per 100,000 pop. 1977): 6.

Education (1978): **Literacy:** 34%. **Pop. 5-19:** in school: 52%, teachers per 1,000: 10.

Portuguese sailors were the first Europeans to reach Cameroon, in the 15th century. The European and American slave trade was very active in the area. German control lasted from 1884 to 1916, when France and Britain divided the territory, later receiving League of Nations mandates and UN trusteeships. French Cameroon became independent Jan. 1, 1960; one part of British Cameroon joined Nigeria in 1961, the other part joined Cameroon. Stability has allowed for development of roads, railways, agriculture, and petroleum production.

Canada

See also Canada in Index.

People: Population (1981 est.): 24,100,000. **Age distrib.** (%): 0–14: 24.9; 15–59: 62.2; 60+: 12.8. **Pop. density:** 6.10 per sq. mi. **Urban** (1976): 75.5%. **Cities** (met. 1981 est.): Montreal 2,800,000; Toronto 2,800,000; Vancouver 1,100,000; Ottawa 695,000; Winnipeg 570,000; Edmonton 529,000.

Government: Head of state: Queen Elizabeth II, represented by Gov.-Gen. Edward R. Schreyer; b. Dec. 21, 1935; in office: Jan. 22, 1979. **Head of government:** Prime Min. Pierre Elliott Trudeau; b. Oct. 18, 1919; in office: Mar. 3, 1980. **Local divisions:** 10 provinces, 2 territories. **Armed forces:** regulars 80,000; reserves 19,100.

Economy: Minerals: Nickel, zinc, antimony, cobalt, copper, gold, iron, lead, molybdenum, potash, silver, tungsten, uranium. **Crude oil reserves** (1980): 6.8 bln. bbls. **Per capita arable land:** 4.6 acres. **Meat prod.** (1980): beef: 950,000 metric tons; pork 890,000 metric tons. **Fish catch** (1979): 1.3 mln. metric tons. **Electricity prod.** (1978): 335.71 bln. kwh. **Crude steel prod.** (1981): 14.8 mln. metric tons. **Labor force:** 5% agric.; 43.5% ind. & comm., 38% service.

Finance: Currency: Dollar (Mar. 1982: 1.23 = $1 US). **Gross domestic product** (1980): $245.8 bln. **Per capita income** (1980 est.) $10,296. **Imports** (1981): $69.6 bln.; partners (1980): U.S. 70%, Jap. 4%. **Exports** (1981): $72.62 bln.; partners (1980): U.S. 63%, Jap. 6%. **Tourists** (1979): 12.2 mln.; receipts: $2 bln. **National budget** (1980-81): 50.3 bln. revenues; $56.4 bln. expenditures. **International reserves less gold** (Feb. 1982): $2.69 bln. **Gold:** 20.40 mln. oz t. **Consumer prices** (change in 1981): 12.4%.

Transport: Railway traffic (1979): 2.7 bln. passenger-km;

221.9 bln. net ton-km. **Motor vehicles:** in use (1978): 9.7 mln. passenger cars, 2.7 mln. comm. vehicles; manuf. (1980): 847,000 passenger cars; 527,000 comm. vehicles. **Civil aviation:** 36,169 mln. passenger-km (1980): 762.2 mln. net ton-km (1980).

Communications: Television sets: 10 mln. in use (1977), 606,000 manuf. (1977). **Radios:** 24.3 mln. in use (1977), 837,000 manuf. (1976). **Telephones in use** (1978): 15 mln. **Daily newspaper circ.** (1980): 218 per 1,000 pop.

Health: Life expectancy at birth (1981): 69 male; 76 female. **Births** (per 1,000 pop. 1979): 15.5. **Deaths** (per 1,000 pop. 1979): 7.1. **Natural increase** (1977): .8%. **Hospital beds** (per 100,000 pop. 1977): 875. **Physicians** (per 100,000 pop. 1977): 178. **Infant mortality** (per 1,000 live births 1977): 12.4.

Education (1978): **Literacy:** 98%. **Pop. 5-19:** in school: 75%, teachers per 1,000: 40.

Cape Verde

Republic of Cape Verde

People: Population (1981 est.): 340,000. **Age distrib.** (%): 0–14: 46.9; 15–59: 44.9; 60+: 7.9. **Pop. density:** 199.10 per sq. mi. **Urban** (1970): 19.7%. **Ethnic groups:** Creole (mulatto) 70%, African 28%, European 1%. **Languages:** Portuguese (official), Crioulo. **Religions:** 91% Roman Catholic.

Geography: Area: 1,557 sq. mi., a bit larger than Rhode Island. **Location:** In Atlantic O., off western tip of Africa. **Neighbors:** Nearest are Mauritania, Senegal. **Topography:** Cape Verde Islands are 15 in number, volcanic in origin (active crater on Fogo). The landscape is eroded and stark, with vegetation mostly in interior valleys. **Capital:** Praia. **Cities** (1980 est.): Mindelo 40,000; Praia 36,600.

Government: Head of state: Pres. Aristide Pereira; b. Nov. 17, 1923; in office: July 5, 1975. **Head of government:** Prime Min. Pedro Pires, b. Apr. 29, 1934; in office: July 5, 1975. **Local divisions:** 24 electoral districts.

Economy: Chief crops: Bananas, coffee, sugarcane, corn. **Minerals:** Salt. **Other resources:** Fish. **Per capita arable land:** 0.3 acres. **Electricity prod.** (1977): 7.00 mln. kwh.

Finance: Currency: Escudo (June 1981: 50 = $1 US). **Gross domestic product** (1979 est.): $57 mln. **Per capita income** (1979): $200. **Imports** (1979): $40 mln.; partners: Port. 58%, Neth. 5%. **Exports** (1979): $4 mln.; partners: Port. 63%, Ang. 14%, UK 5%, Zaire 5%. **Consumer prices** (change in 1977): 4.8%.

Transport: Motor vehicles: in use (1977): 3,100 passenger cars, 900 comm. vehicles. **Chief ports:** Mindelo, Praia.

Communications: Radios: 36,000 licensed (1976). **Telephones in use** (1978): 1,717.

Health: Life expectancy at birth (1975): 56.3 male; 60.0 female. **Births** (per 1,000 pop. 1978): 29. **Deaths** (per 1,000 pop. 1978): 8. **Natural increase** (1978): 2.1%. **Pop. per hospital bed** (1977): 516. **Pop. per physician** (1977): 7,750. **Infant mortality** (per 1,000 live births 1975): 104.9.

The uninhabited Cape Verdes were discovered by the Portuguese in 1456 or 1460. The first Portuguese colonists landed in 1462; African slaves were brought soon after, and most Cape Verdeans descend from both groups. Cape Verde independence came July 5, 1975. The islands have suffered from repeated extreme droughts and famines, especially 1978. Emphasis is placed on the development of agriculture and on fishing, which accounts for 70% of export earnings.

Central African Republic

People: Population (1981 est.): 2,400,000. **Pop. density:** 10.82 per sq. mi. **Ethnic groups:** Banda 47%, Baya 27%, 80 other groups. **Languages:** French (official), local dialects. **Religions:** animist 60%, Christian 35%, Moslem 5%.

Geography: Area: 240,324 sq. mi., slightly smaller than Texas. **Location:** In central Africa. **Neighbors:** Chad on N, Cameroon on W, Congo, Zaire on S, Sudan on E. **Topography:** Mostly rolling plateau, average altitude 2,000 ft., with rivers draining S to the Congo and N to Lake Chad. Open, well-watered savanna covers most of the area, with an arid area in NE, and tropical rainforest in SW. **Capital:** Bangui. **Cities** (1979 est.): Bangui (met.) 362,700.

Government: Head of state: Gen. Andre Kolingba; in office: Sept. 1, 1981. **Local divisions:** 14 prefectures. **Armed forces:** regulars 1,650.

Economy: Industries: Textiles, light manuf. **Chief crops:** Cotton, coffee, peanuts, corn, sorghum. **Minerals:** Diamonds (chief export), uranium, iron, copper. **Other resources:** Timber. **Per capita arable land:** 5.5 acres. **Meat prod.** (1980): beef: 22,000 metric tons. **Fish catch** (1978): 13,000 metric tons. **Electricity prod.** (1978): 60.00 mln. kwh. **Labor force:** 87% agric.

Finance: Currency: CFA franc (Mar. 1982: 312.10 = $1 US). **Gross domestic product** (1979): $592 mln. **Per capita income** (1979): $257. **Imports** (1979): $70 mln.; partners (1979): Fr. 63%, U.S. 5%. **Exports** (1979): $79.6 mln.; partners (1979): Fr. 46%, Bel.-Lux. 21%. **International reserves less gold** (Oct. 1981): $69.89 mln. **Gold:** 11,000 oz t. **Consumer prices** (change in 1978): 11.9%.

Transport: Motor vehicles: in use (1974): 9,100 passenger cars, 3,900 comm. vehicles.

Communications: Radios: 75,000 in use (1976), 11,000 manuf. (1977).

Health: Life expectancy at birth (1960): 33 male; 36 female. **Births** (per 1,000 pop. 1978): 47. **Deaths** (per 1,000 pop. 1978): 20%. **Natural increase** (1978): 2.7%. **Hospital beds** (per 100,000 pop. 1977): 138. **Physicians** (per 100,000 pop. 1977): 5. **Infant mortality** (per 1,000 live births 1975): 190.

Education (1978): **Literacy:** 16%. **Pop. 5-19:** in school: 37%, teachers per 1,000: 7.

Various Bantu tribes migrated through the region for centuries before French control was asserted in the late 19th century, when the region was named Ubangi-Shari. Complete independence was attained Aug. 13, 1960.

All political parties were dissolved in 1960, and the country became a center for Chinese political influence in Africa. Relations with China were severed after 1965. Elizabeth Domitien, premier 1975-76, was the first woman to hold that post in an African country. Pres. Jean-Bedel Bokassa, who seized power in a 1965 military coup, proclaimed himself constitutional emperor of the renamed Central African Empire Dec. 1976.

Emp. Bokassa's rule was characterized by virtually unchecked ruthless and cruel authority, and human rights violations. Bokassa was ousted in a bloodless coup aided by the French government, Sept. 20, 1979, and replaced by his cousin David Dacko, former president from 1960 to 1965. In 1981, the political situation deteriorated amid strikes and economic crisis. Gen. Kolingba replaced Dacko as head of state in a bloodless coup.

Chad

Republic of Chad

People: Population (1981 est.): 4,700,000. **Age distrib.** (%): 0–14: 40.7; 15–59: 54.9; 60+: 4.4. **Pop. density:** 8.69 per sq. mi. **Urban** (1978): 18.4%. **Ethnic groups:** Sudanese Arab 30%, Sudanic tribes 25%, Nilotic, Saharan tribes. **Languages:** French (official), Arabic, others. **Religions:** Moslems 45%, animist 45%, Christian 10%.

Geography: Area: 495,755 sq. mi., four-fifths the size of Alaska. **Location:** In central N. Africa. **Neighbors:** Libya on N, Niger, Nigeria, Cameroon on W, Central African Republic on S, Sudan on E. **Topography:** Southern wooded savanna, steppe, and desert, part of the Sahara, in the N. Southern rivers flow N to Lake Chad, surrounded by marshland. **Capital:** N'Djamena. **Cities** (1979 est.): N'Djamena (met.) 303,000.

Government: Head of state: Hissen Habre; in office: June 7, 1982. **Local divisions:** 14 prefectures with appointed governors. **Armed forces:** regulars 20,000.

Economy: Chief crops: Cotton. **Minerals:** Uranium. **Per capita arable land:** 4.0 acres. **Meat prod.** (1980): beef: 28,000 metric tons; lamb: 16,000 metric tons. **Fish catch** (1978): 115,000 metric tons. **Electricity prod.** (1978): 62.40 mln. kwh. **Labor force:** 90% agric.

Finance: Currency: CFA franc (Mar. 1982: 312.10 = $1 US). **Gross domestic product** (1976 est.): $540 mln. **Per capita income** (1976): $73. **Imports** (1979): $140 mln.; partners (1976): Fr. 47%, Nigeria 22%. **Exports** (1979): $58 mln.; partners (1976): Nigeria 19%, Fr. 13%, Jap. 13%. **Tourist receipts** (1977): $7 mln. **National budget** (1978): $64 mln. revenues; $64 mln. expenditures. **International reserves less gold** (Oct.

1981): $6.63 mln. **Gold:** 11,000 oz t. **Consumer prices** (change in 1977): 9.3%.

Transport: Motor vehicles: in use (1973): 5,800 passenger cars, 6,300 comm. vehicles.

Communications: Radios: 80,000 in use (1978). **Telephones in use** (1978): 3,850.

Health: Life expectancy at birth (1964): 29 male; 35 female. **Births** (per 1,000 pop. 1978): 50. **Deaths** (per 1,000 pop. 1978): 26. **Natural increase** (1978): 2.4%. **Hospital beds** (per 100,000 pop. 1977): 82. **Physicians** (per 100,000 pop. 1977): 2. **Infant mortality** (per 1,000 live births 1975): 160.

Education (1978): **Literacy:** 15%. **Pop. 5-19:** in school: 18%, teachers per 1,000: 2.

Chad was the site of paleolithic and neolithic cultures before the Sahara Desert formed. A succession of kingdoms and Arab slave traders dominated Chad until France took control around 1900. Independence came Aug. 11, 1960.

Northern Moslem rebels, have fought animist and Christian southern government and French troops from 1966, despite numerous cease-fires and peace pacts.

Libyan troops entered the country at the request of the Chad government, December 1980. On Jan. 6, 1981 Libya and Chad announced their intention to unite. France together with several African nations condemned the agreement as a menace to African security. The Libyan troops were withdrawn from Chad in November 1981.

Rebel forces, led by Hissen Habre, captured the capital and forced Pres. Oueddei to flee the country in June 1982.

Chile

Republic of Chile

People: Population (1981 est.): 11,100,000. **Age distrib.** (%): 0–14: 34.4; 15–59: 57.7; 60+: 7.9. **Pop. density:** 38.76 per sq. mi. **Urban** (1978): 79.8%. **Ethnic groups:** Mestizo 66%, Spanish 25%, Indian 5%. **Languages:** Spanish. **Religions:** Predominantly Roman Catholic.

Geography: Area: 292,135 sq. mi., larger than Texas. **Location:** Occupies western coast of southern S. America. **Neighbors:** Peru on N, Bolivia on NE, Argentina on E. **Topography:** Andes Mtns. are on E border including some of the world's highest peaks; on W is 2,650-mile Pacific Coast. Width varies between 100 and 250 miles. In N is Atacama Desert, in center are agricultural regions, in S are forests and grazing lands. **Capital:** Santiago. **Cities** (1978 est.) Santiago 3,448,700; Vina del Mar 262,100; Valparaiso 248,200; Concepción 209,986.

Government: Head of state: Pres. Augusto Pinochet Ugarte; b. Nov. 25, 1915; in office: Sept. 11, 1973. **Local divisions:** 12 regions and Santiago region, comprised of 25 provinces. **Armed forces:** regulars 85,000; reserves 160,000.

Economy: Industries: Steel, textiles, wood products. **Chief crops:** Grain, rice, beans, potatoes, peas, fruits, grapes. **Minerals:** Copper (10% world output), molybdenum, silver, nitrates, iodine (half world output), iron, coal, oil, gas, gold, cobalt, zinc, manganese, borate, mica, mercury, salt, sulphur, marble, onyx. **Crude oil reserves** (1980): 400 mln. bbls. **Other resources:** Water, forests. **Per capita arable land:** 1.3 acres. **Meat prod.** (1980): beef: 180,000 metric tons; pork: 53,000 metric tons; lamb: 23,000 metric tons. **Fish catch** (1979): 2.6 mln. metric tons. **Electricity prod.** (1978): 10.16 bln. kwh. **Crude steel prod.** (1981): 657,000 metric tons. **Labor force:** 19% agric.; 30% manuf.; 6.5% government.

Finance: Currency: Peso (Mar. 1982: 39.0 = $1 US). **Gross domestic product** (1979): $19.8 bln. **Per capita income** (1979): $1,950. **Imports** (1981): $6.37 bln.; partners (1979): U.S. 23%, Braz. 9%, Jap. 8% Iran 8%. **Exports** (1981): $3.93 bln.; partners (1979): W. Ger. 16%, Braz. 11%, Jap. 11%, U.S. 11%. **Tourists** (1977): 296,900; receipts: $97 mln. **National budget** (1979): $6.57 bln. revenues; $5.79 bln. expenditures. **International reserves less gold** (Feb. 1982): $2.9 bln. **Gold:** 1.70 mln. oz. t. **Consumer prices** (change in 1981): 19.7%.

Transport: Railway traffic (1980): 1.3 bln. passenger-km; 1.5 bln. net ton-km. **Motor vehicles:** in use (1979): 379,200 passenger cars, 180,700 comm. vehicles; assembled (1977): 9,000 passenger cars; 3,200 comm. vehicles. **Civil aviation:** 1.8 bln. passenger-km (1980); 103.9 mln. net ton-km (1980). **Chief ports:** Valparaiso, Arica, Antofagasta.

Communications: Television sets: 710,000 in use (1976), 70,000 manuf. (1978). **Radios:** 2 mln. in use (1977). 29,000 manuf. (1978). **Telephones in use** (1979): 531,100.

Health: Life expectancy at birth (1975): 59.5 male; 65.7 female. **Births** (per 1,000 pop. 1978): 22. **Deaths** (per 1,000 pop. 1978): 7. **Natural increase** (1978): 1.5%. **Hospital beds** (per 100,000 pop. 1977): 359. **Physicians** (per 100,000 pop. 1977): 62. **Infant mortality** (per 1,000 live births 1978): 39.7.

Education (1978): **Literacy:** 90%. **Pop. 5–19:** in school: 71%, teachers per 1,000: 25.

Northern Chile was under Inca rule before the Spanish conquest, 1536-40. The southern Araucanian Indians resisted until the late 19th century. Independence was gained 1810-18, under Jose de San Martin and Bernardo O'Higgins; the latter, as supreme director 1817-23, sought social and economic reforms until deposed. Chile defeated Peru and Bolivia in 1836-39 and 1879-84, gaining mineral-rich northern land.

Eduardo Frei Montalva came into office in 1964, instituting social programs and gradual nationalization of foreign-owned mining companies. In 1970, Salvador Allende Gossens, a Marxist, became president with a third of the national vote.

The Allende government furthered nationalizations, and improved conditions for the poor. But illegal and violent actions by extremist supporters of the government, the regime's failure to attain majority support, and poorly planned socialist economic programs led to political and financial chaos.

A military junta seized power Sept. 11, 1973, and said Allende killed himself. The junta named a mostly military cabinet, and announced plans to "exterminate Marxism."

Repression continued during 1981. In July, an Amnesty International report produced evidence of physical and psychological torture. The UN passed a resolution expressing concern at the deterioration of the human rights situation.

Tierra del Fuego is the largest (17,800 sq. mi.) island in the archipelago of the same name at the southern tip of South America, an area of majestic mountains, tortuous channels, and high winds. It was discovered 1520 by Magellan and named the Land of Fire because of its many Indian bonfires. Part of the island is in Chile, part in Argentina. Punta Arenas, on a mainland peninsula, is a center of sheep-raising and the world's southernmost city (pop. 67,600); Puerto Williams, pop. 949, is the southernmost settlement.

China

People's Republic of China

People: Population (1981 est.): 1,004,000,000. **Pop. density:** 278.24 per sq. mi. **Ethnic groups:** Han Chinese 94%, Mongol, Korean, Turkic groups, Manchu, others. **Languages:** Mandarin Chinese (official), Shanghai, Canton, Fukien, Hakka dialects; Tibetan, Vigus (Turkic). **Religions:** Confucianism, Buddhism, Taoism, are traditional; Moslems 5%.

Geography: Area: 3,691,521 sq. mi., slightly larger than the U.S. **Location:** Occupies most of the habitable mainland of E. Asia. **Neighbors:** Mongolia on N, USSR on NE and NW, Afghanistan, Pakistan on W, India, Nepal, Bhutan, Burma, Laos, Vietnam on S, N. Korea on NW. **Topography:** Two-thirds of the vast territory is mountainous or desert, and only one-tenth is cultivated. Rolling topography rises to high elevations in the N in the Daxinganlingshanmai separating Manchuria and Mongolia; the Tienshan in Xinjiang; the Himalayan and Kunlunshanmai in the SW and in Tibet. Length is 1,860 mi. from N to S, width E to W is more than 2,000 mi. The eastern half of China is one of the best-watered lands in the world. Three great river systems, the Changjiang, the Huanghe, and the Xijiang provide water for vast farmlands. **Capital:** Peking. **Cities** (1981 est.): Shanghai 12,000,000; Peking 8,500,000; Tianjin 7,200,000; Canton 5,200,000; Shenyang 4,800,000; Wuhan 4,400,000; Chendu 4,000,000.

Government: Chmn. Natl. People's Congress Ye Jianying; b. 1899; in office: Mar. 5, 1978. **Head of government:** Party Chairman Hu Yaobang, b. 1915; in office: June 29, 1981. **Effective head of government:** Premier Zhao Ziyang; b. 1919; in office: Sept. 1980. **Local divisions:** 21 provinces, 5 ethnic autonomous regions, and 3 cities. **Armed forces:** regulars 4,390,000; civil militia 7,000,000.

Economy: Industries: Iron and steel, plastics, agriculture implements, trucks. **Chief crops:** Grain, rice, cotton. **Minerals:** Tungsten, antimony, coal, iron, lead, manganese, mercury, molybdenum, phosphates, potash, tin. **Crude oil reserves** (1980): 20 bln. bbls. **Other resources:** Silk. **Per capita arable land:** 0.3 acres. **Meat prod.** (1980): beef: 2.33 mln. metric tons; pork: 16.4 mln. metric tons; lamb: 747,000 metric tons. **Fish catch** (1979): 4.0 mln. metric tons. **Electricity prod.** (1978): 256 bln. kwh. **Crude steel prod.** (1981 est). 35.6 mln. metric tons. **Labor force:** 85% agric.; 15% man.

Finance: Currency: Yuan (Mar. 1982): 1.86 = $1 US). **Gross domestic product** (1980): $540 bln. **Per capita income** (1980): $566. **Imports** (1980): $20.1 bln.; partners (1980): Jap. 26%, U.S. 21%, W. Ger. 6%. **Exports** (1980): $19.3 bln.; partners (1980): Hong Kong 22%, Jap. 24%, U.S. 6%. **Foreign currency reserves** (1978): $3 bln.

Transport: Railway traffic (1980): 517 bln. net ton-km. **Motor vehicles:** in use (1978): 50,000 passenger cars, 710,000 comm. vehicles. **Chief ports:** Shanghai, Tianjin, Luda.

Communications: Television sets: over 1.2 mln. in use (1978). **Radios:** 150 mln. in use (1978).

Health: Life expectancy at birth (1980): 68.0 male; 68.0 female. **Births** (per 1,000 pop. 1978): 24. **Deaths** (per 1,000 pop. 1978): 8. **Natural increase** (1978): 1.6%. **Hospital beds** (per 100,000 pop. 1977): 185. **Physicians** (per 100,000 pop. 1977): 33.

Education (1978): **Literacy:** 70%. **Pop. 5-19:** in school: 62%, teachers per 1,000: 18. **PQLI:** 71.

History. Remains of various man-like creatures who lived as early as several hundred thousand years ago have been found in many parts of China. Neolithic agricultural settlements dotted the Huanghe basin from about 5,000 BC. Their language, religion, and art were the sources of later Chinese civilization.

Bronze metallurgy reached a peak and Chinese pictographic writing, similar to today's, was in use in the more developed culture of the Shang Dynasty (c. 1500 BC-c. 1000 BC) which ruled much of North China.

A succession of dynasties and interdynastic warring kingdoms ruled China for the next 3,000 years. They expanded Chinese political and cultural domination to the south and west, and developed a brilliant technologically and culturally advanced society. Rule by foreigners (Mongols in the Yuan Dynasty, 1271-1368, and Manchus in the Ch'ing Dynasty, 1644-1911) did not alter the underlying culture.

A period of relative stagnation left China vulnerable to internal and external pressures in the 19th century. Rebellions left tens of millions dead, and Russia, Japan, Britain, and other powers exercised political and economic control in large parts of the country. China became a republic Jan. 1, 1912, following the Wuchang Uprising inspired by Dr. Sun Yat-sen.

For a period of 50 years, 1894-1945, China was involved in conflicts with Japan. In 1895, China ceded Korea, Taiwan, and other areas. On Sept. 18, 1931, Japan seized the Northeastern Provinces (Manchuria) and set up a puppet state called Manchukuo. The border province of Jehol was cut off as a buffer state in 1933. Japan invaded China proper July 7, 1937. After its defeat in World War II, Japan gave up all seized land.

After the war with Japan ended, Aug. 15, 1945, internal disturbances arose involving the Kuomintang, communists, and other factions. China proper came under domination of communist armies, 1949-1950. The Kuomintang government moved to Taiwan (Formosa), 90 mi. off the mainland, Dec. 8, 1949.

The People's Republic of China was proclaimed in Peking Sept. 21, 1949, by the Chinese People's Political Consultative Conference under Mao Tse-tung, communist leader.

The communist regime and the USSR signed a 30-year treaty of "friendship, alliance and mutual assistance," Feb. 15, 1950, repudiating the 1945 treaty between the Soviet Union and the Kuomintang government authorized by the Yalta Agreement. Great Britain recognized the People's Republic in 1950 and France did so in 1964. By 1975, over 100 nations had recognized the regime.

The U.S. refused recognition, and after its consular officers met with abuse, withdrew them. On Nov. 26, 1950, the People's Republic sent armies into Korea against U.S. troops and forced a stalemate.

By the 1960s, relations with the USSR deteriorated, with disagreements on borders, idealogy and leadership of world communism. The USSR cancelled aid accords, and China, with Albania, launched anti-Soviet propaganda drives.

China sought to promote revolutionary movements in Africa, Asia and South America.

On Oct. 25, 1971, the UN General Assembly ousted the Taiwan government from the UN and seated Communist China in its place. The U.S. had supported the mainland's admission but opposed Taiwan's expulsion.

U.S. Pres. Nixon visited China Feb. 21-28, 1972, on invitation from Premier Chou En-lai, ending years of antipathy between the 2 nations. China and the U.S. opened liaison offices in each other's capitals, May-June 1973. The U.S., Dec. 15, 1978, formally recognized the People's Republic of China as the sole legal government of China; diplomatic relations between the 2 nations were established, Jan. 1, 1979. Trade between the two countries neared $1 billion in 1974, largely U.S. grain exports, declined in subsequent years, but was revitalized with U.S. recognition, 1979.

In a continuing "reassessment" of the policies of Mao Zedong, Mao's widow, Jiang Quing, and other Gang of Four members were convicted of "committing crimes during the 'Cultural Revolution,'" Jan. 25, 1981. The ouster of Hua Guofeng, Jun. 29, 1981, the handpicked successor of Mao, was seen as another step in China's attempt to redefine Maoist policies.

Internal developments. After an initial period of consolidation, 1949-52, industry, agriculture, and social and economic institutions were forcibly molded according to Maoist ideals. However, frequent drastic changes in policy and violent factionalism have interfered with economic development.

In 1957, Mao Tse-tung admitted an estimated 800,000 people had been executed 1949-54; opponents claimed much higher figures. Some 110,000 political prisoners seized in 1957 were released in 1978.

The Great Leap Forward, 1958-60, tried to force the pace of economic development through intensive labor on huge new rural communes, and through emphasis on ideological purity and enthusiasm. The program caused resistance and was largely abandoned. Serious food shortages developed, and the government was forced to buy grain from the West.

The Great Proletarian Cultural Revolution, 1965, was an attempt to oppose pragmatism and bureaucratic power and instruct a new generation in revolutionary principles. Massive purges took place. A program of forcibly relocating millions of urban teenagers into the countryside was launched.

By 1968 the movement had run its course; many purged officials returned to office in subsequent years, and reforms in education and industry that had placed ideology above expertise were gradually weakened.

In the mid-1970s, factional and ideological fighting increased, and emerged into the open after the 1976 deaths of Mao and Premier Chou En-lai. Chiang Ching, Mao's widow and 3 other leading leftists were purged and placed under arrest, after reportedly trying to seize power. Their opponents said the "gang of four" had used severe repression and mass torture, had sparked local fighting and had disrupted production. The new ruling group modified Maoist policies in education, culture, and industry, and sought better ties with non-communist countries.

Sweeping reforms of the central bureaucracy were announced March 1982.

Relations with Vietnam deteriorated in 1978 as China charged persecution of ethnic Chinese. In retaliation for Vietnam's invasion of Cambodia, China attacked 4 Vietnamese border provinces Feb. 17, 1979; heavy border fighting ensued. Peace talks between the 2 countries continued through the year.

About 800,000 people were killed in 1976 when an earthquake leveled the northern industrial city of Tangshan. Drought and transport disruptions reportedly caused food shortages.

Increased army influence was reflected by a series of nuclear test explosions in 1976. The first Chinese atomic bomb was exploded in 1964; the first hydrogen bomb in 1967. There is a growing stockpile of nuclear weapons and intermediate range missiles. Long range missiles have been tested. The Chinese navy has been built into one of the world's largest. The first orbiting space satellite was launched in 1970.

Manchuria. Home of the Manchus, rulers of China 1644-1911, Manchuria has accommodated millions of Chinese settlers in the 20th century. Under Japanese rule 1931-45, the area became industrialized. China no longer uses the name Manchuria for the region, which is divided into the 3 NE provinces of Heilongjiang, Jilin, and Liaoning.

Guandong is the southernmost part of Manchuria. Russia in 1898 forced China to lease it Guandong, and built Port Arthur (Lushun) and the port of Dairen (Luda). Japan seized Port Arthur in 1905. It was turned over to the USSR by the 1945 Yalta agreement, but finally returned to China in 1950.

Inner Mongolia was organized by the People's Republic in

1947. Its boundaries have undergone frequent changes, reaching its greatest extent (and restored in 1979) in 1956, with an area of 460,000 sq. mi., allegedly in order to dilute the minority Mongol population. Chinese settlers outnumber the Mongols more than 10 to 1. Total pop., 8.5 million. Capital: Hohhot.

Xinjiang Uygur Autonomous Region, in Central Asia, is 633,802 sq. mi., pop. 11 million (75% Uygurs, a Turkic Moslem group, with a heavy Chinese increase in recent years). Capital: Urumqi. It is China's richest region in strategic minerals. Some Uygurs have fled to the USSR, claiming national oppression.

Tibet, 470,000 sq. mi., is a thinly populated region of high plateaus and massive mountains, the Himalayas on the S, the Kunluns on the N. High passes connect with India and Nepal; roads lead into China proper. Capital: Lhasa. Average altitude is 15,000 ft. Jiachan, 15,870 ft., is believed to be the highest inhabited town on earth. Agriculture is primitive. Pop. 1.7 million (of whom 500,000 are Chinese). Another 4 million Tibetans form the majority of the population of vast adjacent areas that have long been incorporated into China.

China ruled all of Tibet from the 18th century, but independence came in 1911. China reasserted control in 1951, and a communist government was installed in 1953, revising the theocratic Lamaist Buddhist rule. Serfdom was abolished, but all land remained collectivized.

A Tibetan uprising within China in 1956 spread to Tibet in 1959. The rebellion was crushed with Chinese troops, and Buddhism was almost totally suppressed. The Dalai Lama and 100,000 Tibetans fled to India.

China (Taiwan)

Republic of China

People: Population (1981 est.): 18,200,000. **Pop. density:** 1,181 per sq. mi. **Ethnic groups:** Han Chinese 98% (18% from mainland), aborigines (of Indonesian origin) 2%. **Languages:** Mandarin Chinese (official), Taiwan, Hakka dialects, Japanese, English. **Religions:** Buddhism, Taoism, Confucianism prevail, Christians 2.5%.

Geography: Area: 13,814 sq. mi., the size of Maryland and Delaware combined. **Location:** Off SE coast of China, between E. and S. China Seas. **Neighbors:** Nearest is China. **Topography:** A mountain range forms the backbone of the island; the eastern half is very steep and craggy, the western slope is flat, fertile, and well-cultivated. **Capital:** Taipei. **Cities** (1981 est.): Taipei (met.) 2,252,700; (1978) Kaohsiung 1,062,999; Taichung 578,935; Tainan 557,075.

Government: Head of state: Chiang Ching-kuo; b. Mar. 18, 1910; in office: May 20, 1978. **Head of government:** Prime Min. Sun Yun-suan; b. Nov. 11, 1913; in office: May 30, 1978. **Local divisions:** Taiwan province, Taipei Municipality. **Armed forces:** regulars 539,000; reserves 1,170,000.

Economy: Industries: Textiles, clothing, electrical and electronic equip., processed foods, chemicals, glass, machinery. **Chief crops:** Rice, bananas, pineapples, sugarcane, sweet potatoes, peanuts. **Minerals:** Coal, limestone, marble. **Crude oil reserves** (1980): 10.2 mln. bbls. **Per capita arable land:** 0.2 acres. **Meat prod.** (1977): beef: 15,798 metric tons; pork: 574,656 metric tons. **Fish catch** (1977): 854,900 metric tons. **Crude steel prod.** (1981): 3.1 mln. metric tons. **Labor force:** 34% agric.; 37.8% manuf.; 29% transportation and service.

Finance: Currency: New Taiwan dollar (Sept. 1981: 36 = $1 US). **Gross domestic product** (1980): $40.2 bln. **Per capita income** (1978): $1,300. **Imports** (1980): $19.7 bln.; partners (1980): U.S. 24%, Jap. 13%, Kuw. 11%, Saudi Ar. 7%. **Exports** (1980): $19.7 bln.; partners (1980): U.S. 34%, Jap. 11%, Hong Kong 8%. **Tourists** (1978): 1,270,977; receipts (1978): $608 mln. **National budget** (1980): $10.1 bln. revenues; $9.6 bln. expenditures. **International reserves less gold** (Mar. 1980): $1.51 bln. **Gold:** 2.49 mln. oz t. **Consumer prices** (change in 1979): 9.7%.

Transport: Motor vehicles: in use (1980): 425,400 passenger cars, 236,700 comm. vehicles; assembled (1975): 23,000 passenger cars, 6,500 comm. vehicles. **Chief ports:** Kaohsiung, Keelung, Hualien, Taichung.

Communications: Television sets: 3.2 mln. in use (1979). **Radios:** 1.4 mln. in use (1976). **Telephones in use** (1980): 2.3 mln. **Daily newspaper circ.** (1980): 171 per 1,000 pop.

Health: Life expectancy at birth (1979): 69.4 male; 74.5 female. **Births** (per 1,000 pop. 1978): 24.1. **Deaths** (per 1,000 pop. 1978): 4.7. **Natural increase** (1978): 1.90%. **Hospital beds** (per 100,000 pop. 1977): 143. **Physicians** (per 100,000 pop. 1977): 33. **Infant mortality** (per 1,000 live births 1978): 14.

Education (1978): **Literacy:** 82%. **Pop. 5-19:** in school: 65%, teachers per 1,000: 17.

Large-scale Chinese immigration began in the 17th century. The island came under mainland control after an interval of Dutch rule, 1620-62. Taiwan (also called Formosa) was ruled by Japan 1895-1945. Two million Kuomintang supporters fled to Taiwan in 1949. Both the Taipei and Peking governments consider Taiwan an integral part of China. In 1981, Peking made several proposals for reunification, and invited government officials to visit the mainland. Taiwan rejected the proposals.

The U.S. upon its recognition of the People's Republic of China, Dec. 15, 1978, severed diplomatic ties with Taiwan. It maintains the unofficial American Institute in Taiwan, while Taiwan has established the Coordination Council for North American Affairs in Washington, D.C.

Land reform, government planning, U.S. aid and investment, and free universal education have brought huge advances in industry, agriculture, and mass living standards.

The Penghu (Pescadores), 50 sq. mi., pop. 120,000, lie between Taiwan and the mainland. **Quemoy** and **Matsu,** pop. (1979) 63,800 lie just off the mainland.

Colombia

Republic of Colombia

People: Population (1981 est.): 27,030,000. **Age distrib.** (%): 0–14: 44.6; 15–59: 50.7; 60+: 4.7. **Pop. density:** 60.44 per sq. mi. **Urban** (1973): 59.5%. **Ethnic groups:** Mestizo 58%, Caucasian 20%, Mulatto 14%, Negro 4%, Indian 1%. **Languages:** Spanish. **Religions:** Roman Catholic 96%.

Geography: Area: 440,831 sq. mi., larger than Texas and California combined. **Location:** At the NW corner of S. America. **Neighbors:** Panama on NW, Ecuador, Peru on S, Brazil, Venezuela on E. **Topography:** Three ranges of Andes, the Western, Central, and Eastern Cordilleras, run through the country from N to S. The eastern range consists mostly of high table lands, densely populated. The Magdalena R. rises in Andes, flows N to Carribean, through a rich alluvial plain. Sparsely-settled plains in E are drained by Orinoco and Amazon systems. **Capital:** Bogota. **Cities** (1981 est.): Bogota 4,486,200; (1973 cen.); Medellin 1,112,390; Cali 967,908; Barranquilla 690,471.

Government: Head of state: Pres. Belisario Betancur Cuartas; in office: May 31, 1982. **Local divisions:** 23 departments, 8 national territories, and federal district of Bogota. **Armed forces:** regulars 67,500; reserves 500,000.

Economy: Industries: Textiles, processed goods, hides, steel, cement, chemicals. **Chief crops:** Coffee (2d in exports), rice, tobacco, cotton, sugar, bananas. **Minerals:** Oil, gas, emeralds (90% world output), gold, copper, lead, coal, iron, nickel, salt. **Crude oil reserves** (1981): 3.2 bln. bbls. **Other resources:** Rubber, balsam, dye-woods, copaiba, hydro power. **Per capita arable land:** 0.4 acres. **Meat prod.** (1980): beef: 608,000 metric tons; pork: 126,000 metric tons; last 11,000 metric tons. **Fish catch** (1978): 64,000 metric tons. **Electricity prod.** (1979): 18.0 bln. kwh. **Crude steel prod.** (1980-81 est.): 391,000 metric tons. **Labor force:** 27% agric.; 21% man.; 18% services.

Finance: Currency: Peso (Mar. 1982: 61.40 = $1 US). **Gross domestic product** (1980): $30.6 bln. **Per capita income** (1981): $1,112. **Imports** (1980): $4.74 bln.; partners (1978): U.S. 35%, W. Ger. 7%, Jap. 10%. **Exports** (1980): $3.92 bln.; partners (1978): U.S. 29%, W. Ger. 21%, Venez. 8%. **Tourists** (1978): 826,000; receipts: $329 mln. **National budget** (1979): $2.69 bln. revenues; $2.60 bln. expenditures. **International reserves less gold** (Feb. 1982): $4.56 bln. **Gold** 3.41 mln. oz t. **Consumer prices** (change in 1981): 27.5%.

Transport: Railway traffic (1978): 322 mln. passenger-km; 1.1 bln. net ton-km. **Motor vehicles:** in use (1979): 509,000 passenger cars, 94,800 comm. vehicles; assembled (1976): 26,900 passenger cars; 9,500 comm. vehicles. **Civil aviation:** 4.1 bln. passengers-km (1980); 155 mln. net ton-km (1980). **Chief ports:** Buena Ventura, Santa Marta, Barranquilla, Cartagena.

Communications: Television sets: 1.8 in use (1977), 76,000 manuf. (1974). **Radios:** 2.9 in use (1977). **Telephones in use** (1979): 1.4 mln. **Daily newspaper circ.** (1976): 1,330,000.

Health: Life expectancy at birth (1979): 65 male; 70 female.

Births (per 1,000 pop. 1978): 31. **Deaths** (per 1,000 pop. 1978): 8. **Natural increase** (1978): 2.1%. **Hospital beds** (per 100,000 pop. 1977): 161. **Physicians** (per 100,000 pop. 1977): 51. **Infant mortality** (per 1,000 live births 1978): 65%.

Education (1978): **Literacy:** 82%. **Pop. 5-19:** in school: 54%, teachers per 1,000: 19.

Spain subdued the local Indian kingdoms (Funza, Tunja) by the 1530s, and ruled Colombia and neighboring areas as New Granada for 300 years. Independence was won by 1819. Venezuela and Ecuador broke away in 1829-30, and Panama withdrew in 1903.

One of the few functioning Latin American democracies, Colombia is nevertheless plagued by rural and urban violence, though scaled down from "La Violencia" of 1948-58, which claimed 200,000 lives. Attempts at land and social reform, and progress in industrialization have not yet succeeded in reducing massive social problems aggravated by a very high birth rate.

Comoros

Federal and Islamic Republic of the Comoros

People: Population (1981 est.): 380,000. **Age distrib.** (%): 0–14: 43.0; 15–59: 47.0; 60+: 8.0. **Pop. density:** 461.76 per sq. mi. **Ethnic groups:** Arabs, Africans, East Indians. **Languages:** Comorian, Arabic, French. **Religions:** Islam (official).

Geography: Area: 693 sq. mi., half the size of Rhode Island. **Location:** 3 islands (Grande Comore, Anjouan, and Moheli) in the Mozambique Channel between NW Madagascar and SE Africa. **Neighbors:** Nearest are Mozambique on W, Madagascar on E. **Topography:** The islands are of volcanic origin, with an active volcano on Grand Comoro. **Capital:** Moroni. **Cities** (1980 est.): Moroni (met.) 20,000.

Government: Head of state: Pres. Ahmed Abdallah; in office: May 23, 1978. **Head of govt.:** Prime Min. Salim Ben Ali; in office: Dec. 22, 1978. **Local divisions:** each of the 3 main islands is a prefecture.

Economy: Industries: Perfume. **Chief crops:** Vanilla, copra, perfume plants, fruits. **Per capita arable land:** 0.6 acres. **Electricity prod.** (1977): 3.0 mln. kwh. **Labor force:** 87% agric.

Finance: Currency: CFA franc (Sept. 1981: 265 = $1 US). **Gross domestic product** (1976 est.): $51 mln. **Per capita income** (1976): $153. **Imports** (1979): $24 mln.; partners: Fr. 41%, Madag. 20%, Pak. 8%, Ken. 5%. **Exports** (1979): $15 mln.; partners: Fr. 65%, U.S. 21%, Mad. 5%.

Transport: Chief ports: Dzaoudzi.

Communications: Radios: 36,000 in use (1976). **Telephones in use** (1977): 1,035.

Health: Life expectancy at birth (1975): 43.4 male; 46.6 female. **Births** (per 1,000 pop. 1978): 43. **Deaths** (per 1,000 pop. 1978): 18. **Natural increase** (1978): 2.5%. **Infant mortality** (per 1,000 live births 1975): 51.7.

The islands were controlled by Moslem sultans until the French acquired them 1841-1909. A 1974 referendum favored independence, with only the Christian island of Mayotte preferring association with France. The French National Assembly decided to allow each of the islands to decide its own fate. The Comoro Chamber of Deputies declared independence July 6, 1975. In a referendum in 1976, Mayotte voted to remain French. A leftist regime that seized power in 1975 was deposed in a pro-French 1978 coup.

Congo

People's Republic of the Congo

People: Population (1981 est.): 1,600,000. **Pop. density:** 11.66 per sq. mi. **Ethnic groups:** Bakongo 45%, Bateke 20%, others. **Languages:** French (official), Bantu dialects. **Religions:** Christians 50% (two-thirds Roman Catholic), animists 47%, Muslim 2%.

Geography: Area: 132,046 sq. mi., slightly smaller than Montana. **Location:** In western central Africa. **Neighbors:** Gabon, Cameroon on W, Central African Republic on N, Zaire on E, Angola (Cabinda) on SW. **Topography:** Much of the Congo is covered by thick forests. A coastal plain leads to the fertile Niari Valley. The center is a plateau; the Congo R. basin consists of flood plains in the lower and savanna in the upper portion. **Capital:** Brazzaville. **Cities** (1980 est.): Brazzaville (met.) 200,000; Pointe-Noire 135,000; Loubomo 34,000.

Government: Head of state: Pres. Denis Sassou-Nguesso; b. 1943; in office: Feb. 8, 1979. **Head of government:** Prime Min. Louis Sylvain Ngoma; in office: Dec. 18, 1975. **Local divisions:** 9 regions and capital district. **Armed forces:** regulars 7,000; para-military 3,900.

Economy: Chief crops: Palm oil and kernels, cocoa, coffee, tobacco. **Minerals:** Oil, potash, natural gas. **Crude oil reserves** (1980): 400 mln. bbls. **Per capita arable land:** 1.1 acres. **Fish catch** (1978): 17,300 metric tons. **Electricity prod.** (1980): 126 mln. kwh. **Labor force:** 90% agric.

Finance: Currency: CFA franc (Mar. 1982: 312.10 = $1 US). **Gross domestic product** (1978 est.): $89 mln. **Per capita income** (1978): $500. **Imports** (1978): $261 mln.; partners (1978): Fr. 50%, W. Ger. 5%. **Exports** (1977): $185 mln.; partners (1978): Ital. 31%, Fr. 24%, Sp. 8%. **Tourist receipts** (1977): $4 mln. **International reserves less gold** (Oct. 1981): $129.81 mln. **Gold:** 11,000 oz t. **Consumer prices** (change in 1980): 7.2%.

Transport: Railway traffic (1979): 286 mln. passenger-km; 470 mln. net ton-km. **Motor vehicles:** in use (1977): 13,250 passenger cars, 3,700 comm. vehicles. **Chief ports:** Pointe-Noire, Brazzaville.

Communications: Television sets: 3,500 in use (1977). Radios: 88,000 in use (1977). **Telephones in use** (1978): 12,000.

Health: Life expectancy at birth (1980): 46.9 male; 50.2 female. **Births** (per 1,000 pop. 1978): 45. **Deaths** (per 1,000 pop. 1978): 18. **Natural increase** (1978): 2.7%. **Hospital beds** (per 100,000 pop. 1977): 499. **Physicians** (per 100,000 pop. 1977): 14. **Infant mortality** (per 1,000 live births 1978): 200.

Education (1978): **Literacy:** 50%. **Pop. 5-19:** in school: 75%, teachers per 1,000: 20.

The Loango Kingdom flourished in the 15th century, as did the Anzico Kingdom of the Batekes; by the late 17th century they had become weakened. France established control by 1885. Independence came Aug. 15, 1960.

After a 1963 coup sparked by trade unions, the country adopted a Marxist-Leninist stance, with the USSR and China vying for influence. Tribal divisions remain strong. France remains a dominant trade partner and source of technical assistance, and French-owned private enterprise retained a major economic role. However, the government of Pres. Sassou-Nguesso favored a strengthening of relations with the USSR, a socialist constitution was adopted, 1979, and on May 13, 1981 a treaty of friendship and cooperation was signed with the Soviets.

Costa Rica

Republic of Costa Rica

People: Population (1981 est.): 2,300,000. **Age distrib.** (%): 0–14: 44.0; 15–59: 50.4; 60+: 5.6. **Pop. density:** 112.45 per sq. mi. **Urban** (1973): 40.6%. **Ethnic groups:** Spanish (with Mestizo minority); Indians 0.4%, Jamaican Negroes 2%. **Language:** Spanish (official). **Religions:** Roman Catholicism prevails.

Geography: Area: 19,653 sq. mi., smaller than W. Virginia. **Location:** In central America. **Neighbors:** Nicaragua on N, Panama on S. **Topography:** Lowlands by the Caribbean are tropical. The interior plateau, with an altitude of about 4,000 ft., is temperate. **Capital:** San Jose. **Cities** (1981 est.): San Jose 843,800; Alajuela (1979 est.) 40,000; Cartago (1979 est.) 40,000.

Government: Head of state: Pres. Luis Alberto Monge; b. Dec. 29, 1925; in office May 8, 1982. **Local divisions:** 7 provinces and 80 cantons. **Armed forces:** para-military 5,000.

Economy: Industries: Fiberglass, aluminum, textiles, fertilizers, roofing, cement. **Chief crops:** Coffee (chief export), bananas, sugar, cocoa, cotton, hemp. **Minerals:** Gold, salt, sulphur, iron. **Other resources:** Fish, forests. **Per capita arable land:** 0.3 acres. **Meat prod.** (1980): beef: 81,000 metric tons; pork: 10,000 metric tons. **Fish catch** (1978): 14,500 metric tons. **Electricity prod.** (1979): 1.9 bln. kwh. **Labor force:** 34.1% agric.; 36.4% manuf.; 25% service and government.

Finance: Currency: Colone (Dec. 1982: 36.09 = $1 US). **Gross domestic product** (1980): $1.9 bln. **Per capita income** (1978): $1,512. **Imports** (1980): $1.46 bln.; partners (1979): U.S. 30%, Jap. 12%, Neth. Ant. 9%, Guat. 6%, W. Ger. 5%. **Exports**

(1980): $1.0 bln.; partners (1979): U.S. 37%, W. Ger. 12%, Guat. 7%. **Tourists** (1978): 340,000; receipts: $71 mln. **National budget** (1979): $217 mln. revenues; $332 mln. expenditures. **International reserves less gold** (Feb. 1982): $141.58 mln. **Gold:** 39,000 oz t. **Consumer prices** (change in 1981): 37.0%.

Transport: Railway traffic (1979): 81 mln. passenger-km; 14 mln. net ton-km. **Motor vehicles:** in use (1978): 62,000 passenger cars, 65,900 comm. vehicles. **Civil aviation:** 495 mln. passenger-km (1980); 23 mln. net ton-km (1980). **Chief ports:** Limon, Puntarenas.

Communications: Television sets: 160,000 in use (1977). **Radios:** 400,000 in use (1977). **Telephones in use** (1979): 175,400. **Daily newspaper circ.** (1980): 109 per 1,000 pop.

Health: Life expectancy at birth (1974): 66.26 male; 70.49 female. **Births** (per 1,000 pop. 1978): 31. **Deaths** (per 1,000 pop. 1978): 5. **Natural increase** (1978): 2.6%. **Hospital beds** (per 100,000 pop 1977): 345. **Physicians** (per 100,000 pop. 1977): 72. **Infant mortality** (per 1,000 live births 1977): 27.8.

Education (1978): **Literacy:** 90%. **Pop. 5-19:** in school: 54%, teachers per 1,000: 21.

Guaymi Indians inhabited the area when Spaniards arrived, 1502. Independence came in 1821. Costa Rica seceded from the Central American Federation in 1838. Since the civil war of 1948-49, there has been little violent social conflict, and free political institutions have been preserved.

Costa Rica, though still a largely agricultural country, has achieved a relatively high standard of living and social services, and land ownership is widespread. There were severe economic problems in 1981 as the inflation rate approached 40%.

Cuba

Republic of Cuba

People: Population (1981 est.): 10,000,000. **Age distrib.** (%): 0–14: 36.9; 15–59: 53.5; 60+: 9.6. **Pop. density:** 225.70 per sq. mi. **Urban** (1970): 60.3%. **Ethnic groups:** Spanish, Negro, and mixtures. **Languages:** Spanish. **Religions:** Roman Catholicism prevailed in past.

Geography: Area: 42,827 sq. mi., nearly as large as Pennsylvania. **Location:** Westernmost of West Indies. **Neighbors:** Bahamas, U.S., on N, Mexico on W, Jamaica on S, Haiti on E. **Topography:** The coastline is about 2,500 miles. The N coast is steep and rocky, the S coast low and marshy. Low hills and fertile valleys cover more than half the country. Sierra Maestra, in the E is the highest of 3 mountain ranges. **Capital:** Havana. **Cities** (1978 est.): Havana 1,008,500; Santiago de Cuba 315,801; Camaguey 221,826.

Government: Head of state: Pres. Fidel Castro Ruz; b. Aug. 13, 1926; in office: Dec. 3, 1976 (formerly Prime Min. since Feb. 16, 1959). **Local divisions:** 14 provinces, 169 municipal assemblies. **Armed forces:** regulars 189,000; reserves 90,000.

Economy: Industries: Texiles, wood products, cement, chemicals, cigars. **Chief crops:** Sugar cane (80% of exports), tobacco, coffee, pineapples, bananas, citrus fruit, coconuts. **Minerals:** Cobalt, nickel, iron, copper, manganese, salt. **Other resources:** Forests. **Per capita arable land:** 0.6 acres. **Meat prod.** (1980); beef: 147,000 metric tons; pork: 61,000 metric tons. **Fish catch** (1978): 213,200 metric tons. **Electricity prod.** (1977): 7.70 bln. kwh. **Crude steel prod.** (1981 est.): 300,000 metric tons. **Labor force:** 34% agric.

Finance: Currency: Peso (Mar. 1980: .72 = $1 US). **Gross national product** (1979): $13.9 bln. **Per capita income** (1977): $840. **Imports** (1979): $5.1 bln.; partners (1977): USSR 54%, Jap. 8%, Canada 6%. **Exports** (1979): $5.3 bln.; partners (1977): USSR 71%.

Transport: Railway traffic (1979): 1.6 bln. passenger-km; 1.89 bln. net ton-km. **Motor vehicles:** in use (1976): 80,000 passenger cars, 40,000 comm. vehicles. **Chief ports:** Havana, Matanzas, Cienfuegos, Santiago de Cuba.

Communications: Television sets: 805,000 in use (1978). **Radios:** 2.1 mln. in use (1978), 121,000 manuf. (1978). **Telephones in use** (1978): 321,054.

Health: Life expectancy at birth: (1970): 68.5 male; 71.8 female. **Births** (per 1,000 pop. 1978): 18. **Deaths** (per 1,000 pop. 1978): 6. **Natural increase** (1978): 1.2%. **Hospital beds** (per 100,000 pop. 1977): 413. **Physicians** (per 100,000 pop. 1977): 94. **Infant mortality** (per 1,000 live births 1977): 24.8.

Education (1978): **Literacy:** 96%. **Pop. 5-19:** in school: 76% teachers per 1,000: 43.

Some 50,000 Indians lived in Cuba when it was discovered by Columbus in 1492. Its name derives from the Indian Cubanacan. Except for British occupation of Havana, 1762-63, Cuba remained Spanish until 1898. A slave-based sugar plantation economy developed from the 18th century, aided by early mechanization of milling. Sugar remains the chief product and chief export despite government attempts to diversify.

A ten-year uprising ended in 1878 with guarantees of rights by Spain, which Spain failed to carry out. A full-scale movement under Jose Marti began Feb. 24, 1895.

The U.S. declared war on Spain in April, 1898, after the sinking of the U.S.S. Maine in Havana harbor, and defeated it in the short Spanish-American War. Spain gave up all claims to Cuba. U.S. troops withdrew in 1902, but under 1903 and 1934 agreements, the U.S. leases a site at Guantanamo Bay in the SE as a naval base. U.S. and other foreign investments acquired a dominant role in the economy.

In 1952, former president Fulgencio Batista seized control and established a dictatorship, which grew increasingly harsh and corrupt. Former student leader Fidel Castro assembled a rebel band in 1956; guerrilla fighting intensified in 1958. Batista fled Jan. 1, 1959, and in the resulting political vacuum Castro took power, becoming premier Feb. 16.

The government, quickly dominated by extreme leftists, began a program of sweeping economic and social changes, without restoring promised liberties. Opponents were imprisoned and some were executed. Some 700,000 Cubans emigrated in the years after the Castro takeover, mostly to the U.S.

Cattle and tobacco lands were nationalized, while a system of cooperatives was instituted. By the end of 1960 all banks and industrial companies had been nationalized, including over $1 billion worth of U.S.-owned properties, mostly without compensation.

Poor sugar crops resulted in collectivization of farms, stringent labor controls, and rationing, despite continued aid from the USSR and other Communist countries.

The U.S. cut back Cuba's sugar quota in 1960, and imposed a partial export embargo, which became total in 1962, severely damaging the economy. In 1961, some 1,400 Cubans, trained and backed by the U.S. Central Intelligence Agency, unsuccessfully tried to invade and overthrow the regime. It was revealed in 1975 that CIA agents had plotted to kill Castro in 1959 or 1960.

In the fall of 1962, the U.S. learned that the USSR had brought nuclear missiles to Cuba. After an Oct. 22 warning from Pres. Kennedy, the missiles were removed.

In 1973, Cuba and the U.S. signed an agreement providing for extradition or punishment of hijackers of planes or vessels, and for each nation to bar activity from its territory against the other. In 1977, the 2 countries signed agreements to exchange diplomats, without restoring full ties, and to regulate offshore fishing. In 1978, and again in 1980, the U.S. agreed to accept political prisoners released by Cuba.

But relations were, and continue to be strained by ongoing Cuban military involvement abroad. In 1975-78, Cuba sent over 20,000 troops to aid one faction in the Angola Civil War. Some 35,000 Cuban troops or advisers are stationed in Africa, mainly in Angola and Ethiopia. This presence, along with Cuba's growing involvement in Central America and the Caribbean has contributed to worsening relations with the U.S.

Cyprus

Republic of Cyprus

People: Population (1981 est.): 630,000. **Age distrib.** (%): 0–14: 25.0; 15–59: 61.0; 60+: 14.0. **Pop. density:** 176.37 per sq. mi. **Urban** (1974): 42.2%. **Ethnic groups:** Greeks 77.1%, Turks 18.2%, Armenians, Maronites. **Languages:** Greek, Turkish. **Religions:** Orthodox 77%, Moslems 18%.

Geography: Area: 3,572 sq. mi., smaller than Connecticut. **Location:** In eastern Mediterranean Sea, off Turkish coast. **Neighbors:** Nearest are Turkey on N, Syria, Lebanon on E. **Topography:** Two mountain ranges run E-W, separated by a wide, fertile plain. **Capital:** Nicosia. **Cities** (1980 est.): Nicosia (met. 1980 est.) 161,000.

Government: Head of state: Pres. Spyros Kyprianou; b. Oct. 28, 1932; in office: Aug. 3, 1977. **Local divisions:** 6 districts. **Armed forces:** Greek: regulars 9,000; Turkish: 4,500 (1980).

Economy: Industries: Wine, clothing, construction. **Chief crops:** Grains, grapes, carobs, citrus fruits, potatoes, olives. **Minerals:** Copper, iron, asbetos, gypsum, umber. **Per capita arable land:** 1.5 acres. **Meat prod.** (1980): pork: 15,000 metric tons; lamb: 10,000 metric tons. **Electricity prod.** (1980): 1.035 mln. kwh. **Labor force:** 20% agric.; 40% manuf., 16.3% service.

Finance: Currency: Pound (Mar. 1982: 0.45 = $1 US). **Gross domestic product** (1980): $2.12 bln. **Per capita income** (1981): $2,940. **Imports** (1980): $1.21 bln.; partners (1980): UK 15%, It. 11%, Iraq 10%, W. Ger. 8%. **Exports** (1980): $536 mln.; partners (1980): UK 21%, Leb. 10%, Sau. Ar. 8%, Syria 7%. **Tourists** (1979): 400,000; receipts: $141 mln. **National budget** (1980): $331 mln. revenues; $304 mln. expenditures. **International reserves less gold** (Feb. 1982): $417.2 mln. **Gold** (Feb. 1982): 459,000 oz. t. **Consumer prices** (change in 1980): 13.6%.

Transport: Motor vehicles: in use (1979): 86,200 passenger cars, 19,800 comm. vehicles. **Civil aviation:** 798 mln. passenger-km (1980); 19.8 mln. net ton-km (1980). **Chief ports:** Famagusta, Limassol.

Communications: Television sets: 68,000 licensed (1977). **Radios:** 212,000 licensed (1977). **Telephones in use** (1979): 92,600. **Daily newspaper circ.** (1980): 96 per 1,000 pop.

Health: Life expectancy at birth (1981): 69.5 male; 73.4 female. **Births** (per 1,000 pop. 1978): 19. **Deaths** (per 1,000 pop. 1978): 8. **Natural increase** (1978): .7%. **Hospital beds** (per 100,000 pop. 1977): 538. **Physicians** (per 100,000 pop. 1977): 82. **Infant mortality** (per 1,000 live births 1975): 17.5.

Education (1978): **Literacy:** 86%. **Pop. 5-19:** in school: 56%, teachers per 1,000: 22. **PQLI:** 85.

Agitation for enosis (union) with Greece increased after World War II, with the Turkish minority opposed, and broke into violence in 1955-56. In 1959, Britain, Greece, Turkey, and Cypriot leaders approved a plan for an independent republic, with constitutional guarantees for the Turkish minority and permanent division of offices on an ethnic basis. Greek and Turkish Communal Chambers dealt with religion, education, and other matters.

Archbishop Makarios, formerly the leader of the enosis movement, was elected president, and full independence became final Aug. 16, 1960. Makarios was re-elected in 1968 and 1973.

Further communal strife led the United Nations to send a peace-keeping force in 1964; its mandate has been repeatedly renewed.

The Cypriot National Guard, led by officers from the army of Greece, seized the government July 15, 1974, and named Nikos Sampson, an advocate of union with Greece, president. Makarios fled the country. On July 20, Turkey invaded the island; Greece mobilized its forces but did not intervene. A cease-fire was arranged July 22. On the 23d, Sampson turned over the presidency to Glafkos Clerides (on the same day, Greece's military junta resigned). A peace conference collapsed Aug. 14; fighting resumed. By Aug. 16 Turkish forces had occupied the NE 40% of the island, despite the presence of UN peace forces. Makarios resumed the presidency in Dec., until his death, 1977.

Turkish Cypriots voted overwhelmingly, June 8, 1975, to form a separate Turkish Cypriot federated state. A president and assembly were elected in 1976. Some 200,000 Greeks have been expelled from the Turkish-controlled area, replaced by thousands of Turks, some from the mainland.

Czechoslovakia

Czechoslovak Socialist Republic

People: Population (1981 est.): 15,400,000. **Age distrib.** (%): 0–14: 23.4; 15–59: 52.5; 60+: 17.4. **Pop. density:** 310.30 per sq. mi. **Urban** (1974): 66.7%. **Ethnic groups:** Czechs 65%, Slovaks 30%, Hungarians 4%, Germans, Poles, Ukrainians. **Languages:** Czech, Slovak (both official). **Religions:** Roman Catholics were majority, Lutherans, Orthodox.

Geography: Area: 49,365 sq. mi., the size of New York. **Location:** In E central Europe. **Neighbors:** Poland, E. Germany on N, W. Germany on W. Austria, Hungary on S, USSR on E. **Topography:** Bohemia, in W, is a plateau surrounded by mountains; Moravia is hilly, Slovakia, in E, has mountains (Carpathians) in N, fertile Danube plain in S. Vltava (Moldau) and Labe (Elbe) rivers flow N from Bohemia to G. **Capital:** Prague. **Cities** (1979 est.): Prague 1.1 mln.; Brno 369,000; Bratislava 368,000; Ostrava 322,000.

Government: Head of state: Pres. Gustav Husak; b. Jan 10, 1913; in office: May 29, 1975; **Head of government:** Prime Min. Lubomir Strougal; b. Oct. 19, 1924; in office: Jan. 28, 1970. **Head of Communist Party:** First Sec. Gustav Husak; in office: Apr. 17, 1969. **Local divisions:** Czech and Slovak republics each have an assembly. **Armed forces:** regulars 194,000; reserves 350,000 (1980).

Economy: Industries: Machinery, oil products, iron and steel, glass, chemicals, motor vehicles, cement. **Chief crops:** Wheat, sugar beets, potatoes, rye, corn, barley. **Minerals:** Mercury, coal, iron. Jáchymor has Europe's greatest pitchblende (for uranium and radium) deposits. **Per capita arable land:** 0.8 acres. **Meat prod.** (1980): beef: 390,000 metric tons; pork: 805,000 metric tons; lamb 6,000 metric tons. **Fish catch** (1978): 17,200 metric tons. **Electricity prod.** (1980): 1.035 bln. kwh. **Crude steel prod.** (1981): 15.2 mln. metric tons. **Labor force:** 12% agric.; 66% ind., comm.; 18% service, govt.

Finance: Currency: Koruna (Dec. 1980: 9.75 = $1 US). **Net material product** (1979): $77 bln. **Per capita income** (1976): $3,985. **Imports** (1979): $14.3 bln.; partners (1980): USSR 36%, E. Ger. 10%, Pol. 8%, W. Ger. 5%. **Exports** (1980): $13.2 bln.; partners (1980): USSR 36%, E. Ger. 9%, Pol. 8%, Hung. 5%. **Tourists** (1978): 14.4 mln. **Consumer prices** (change in 1979): 3.7%.

Transport: Railway traffic (1979): 18.1 bln. passenger-km; 72.6 bln. net ton-km. **Motor vehicles:** in use (1979): 1.9 mln. passenger cars, 324,800 comm. vehicles; manuf. (1980): 184,000 passenger cars; (1980): 88,000 comm. vehicles. **Civil aviation:** 1,540 mln. passenger-km (1980); 14.6 mln. net ton-km (1980).

Communications: Television sets: 4 mln. licensed (1979), 482,000 manuf. (1978). **Radios:** 3.7 mln. licensed (1979), 241,000 manuf. (1978). **Telephones in use** (1979): 3.076 mln. **Daily newspaper circ.** (1980): 286 per 1,000 pop.

Health: Life expectancy at birth (1977): 67.0 male; 74.1 female. **Births** (per 1,000 pop. 1980): 16.4 **Deaths** (per 1,000 pop. 1980): 12.1. **Natural increase** (1978): .7%. **Hospital beds** (per 100,000 pop. 1977): 1,229. **Physicians** (per 100,000 pop. 1977): 254. **Infant mortality** (per 1,000 live births 1978): 18.7.

Education (1981): **Literacy:** 99%. **Pop. 5–19:** in school: 60%, teachers per 1,000: 30.

Bohemia, Moravia and Slovakia were part of the Great Moravian Empire in the 9th century. Later, Slovakia was overrun by Magyars, while Bohemia and Moravia became part of the Holy Roman Empire. Under the kings of Bohemia, Prague in the 14th century was the cultural center of Central Europe. Bohemia and Hungary became part of Austria-Hungary.

In 1914-1918 Thomas G. Masaryk and Eduard Benes formed a provisional government with the support of Slovak leaders including Milan Stefanik. They proclaimed the Republic of Czechoslovakia Oct. 30, 1918.

By 1938 Nazi Germany had worked up disaffection among German-speaking citizens in Sudetenland and demanded its cession. Prime Min. Neville Chamberlain of Britain, with the acquiescense of France, signed with Hitler at Munich, Sept. 30, 1938, an agreement to the cession, with a guarantee of peace by Hitler and Mussolini. Germany occupied Sudetenland Oct. 1-2.

Hitler on Mar. 15, 1939, dissolved Czechoslovakia, made protectorates of Bohemia and Moravia, and supported the autonomy of Slovakia, which was proclaimed independent Mar. 14, 1939, with Josef Tiso president.

Soviet troops with some Czechoslovak contingents entered eastern Czechoslovakia in 1944 and reached Prague in May 1945; Benes returned as president. In May 1946 elections, the Communist Party won 38% of the votes, and Benes accepted Klement Gottwald, a Communist, as prime minister. Tiso was executed in 1947.

In February, 1948, the Communists seized power in advance of scheduled elections. In May 1948 a new constitution was approved. Benes refused to sign it. On May 30 the voters were offered a one-slate ballot and the Communists won full control. Benes resigned June 7. Gottwald became president and Benes died Sept. 3. A harsh Stalinist period followed, with complete and violent suppression of all opposition.

In Jan. 1968 a liberalization movement spread explosively through Czechoslovakia. Antonin Novotny, long the Stalinist boss of the nation, was deposed as party leader and succeeded by Alexander Dubcek, a Slovak, who declared he intended to make communism democratic. On Mar. 22 Novotny resigned as president and was succeeded by Gen. Ludvik Svoboda. On Apr. 6, Premier Joseph Lenart resigned and was succeeded by Oldrich Cernik, whose new cabinet was pledged to carry out democratization and economic reforms.

In July 1968 the USSR and 4 hard-core Warsaw Pact nations demanded an end to liberalization. On Aug. 20, the Russian, Polish, East German, Hungarian, and Bulgarian armies invaded Czechoslovakia.

Despite demonstrations and riots by students and workers, press censorship was imposed, liberal leaders were ousted from office and promises of loyalty to Soviet policies were made by some old-line Communist Party leaders.

On Apr. 17, 1969, Dubcek resigned as leader of the Communist Party and was succeeded by Gustav Husak. In Jan. 1970, Premier Cernik was ousted. Censorship was tightened and the Communist Party expelled a third of its members. In 1972, more than 40 liberals were jailed on subversion charges. In 1973, amnesty was offered to some of the 40,000 who fled the country after the 1968 invasion, but repressive policies continue to remain in force.

More than 700 leading Czechoslovak intellectuals and former party leaders signed a human rights manifesto in 1977, called Charter 77, prompting a renewed crackdown by the regime.

Czechoslovakia has long been an industrial and technological leader of the eastern European countries, though its relative standing has declined in recent years.

Denmark

Kingdom of Denmark

People: Population (1981 est.): 5,100,000. **Age distrib.** (%): 0–14: 22.4 15–59: 58.7; 60+: 18.9. **Pop. density:** 308 per sq. mi. **Urban** (1970): 66.9%. **Ethnic groups:** Almost all Scandinavian. **Languages:** Danish. **Religions:** Predominantly Lutherans.

Geography: Area: 16,633 sq. mi., the size of Massachusetts and New Hampshire combined. **Location:** In northern Europe, separating the North and Baltic seas. **Neighbors:** W. Germany on S., Norway on NW, Sweden on NE. **Topography:** Denmark consists of the Jutland Peninsula and about 500 islands, 100 inhabited. The land is flat or gently rolling, and is almost all in productive use. **Capital:** Copenhagen. **Cities** (1980): Copenhagen 654,437; Arhus 244,839.

Government: Head of state: Queen Margrethe II; b. Apr. 16, 1940; in office: Jan. 14, 1972. **Head of government:** Prime Min. Anker Joergensen; b. July 13, 1922; in office: Feb. 13, 1975. **Local divisions:** 14 counties and one city (Copenhagen). **Armed forces:** regulars 34,650; reserves 154,260 (1980).

Economy: Industries: Machinery, textiles, furniture, electronics. **Chief crops:** Dairy products. **Crude oil reserves** (1980): 375 mln. bbls. **Per capita arable land:** 1.2 acres. **Meat prod.** (1980): beef: 245,000 metric tons; pork: 953,000 metric tons. **Fish catch** (1979): 1.7 mln. metric tons. **Electricity prod.** (1980): 25.1 bln. kwh. **Crude steel prod.** (1981): 612,000 metric tons. **Labor force:** 8.2% agric.; 45% manuf.

Finance: Currency: Krone (Mar. 1982: 8.23 = $1 US). **Gross domestic product** (1980): $66.40 bln. **Per capita income** (1980): $12,956. **Imports** (1981): $17.03 bln.; partners (1980): W. Ger. 18%, Swed. 13%, UK 12%, Neth. 7%. **Exports** (1981): $16.13 bln.; partners (1980): W. Ger. 19%, UK 14%, Swed. 13%, Nor. 6%. **Tourists** (1976): 16,231,900; receipts: (1979) 1.3 bln. **National budget** (1980): $15.4 bln. revenues; $16.9 bln. expenditures. **International reserves less gold** (Feb. 1982): $2.28 bln. **Gold:** 1.62 mln. oz t. **Consumer prices** (change in 1981): 11.7%.

Transport: Railway traffic (1979): 1.9 bln. passenger-km; 1.79 bln. net ton-km. **Motor vehicles:** in use (1979): 1.4 mln. passenger cars, 264,000 comm. vehicles; assembled (1975): 1,000 passenger cars; (1977): 900 comm. vehicles. **Civil aviation:** 3,043 mln. passenger-km (1980); 128.5 mln. net ton-km (1980). **Chief ports:** Copenhagen, Alborg, Arhus, Odense.

Communications: Television sets: 1.8 mln. licensed (1979), 86,000 manuf. (1978). **Radios:** 1.9 mln. licensed (1979), 66,000 manuf. (1978). **Telephones in use** (1979): 2.9 mln. **Daily newspaper circ.** (1980): 367 per 1,000 pop.

Health: Life expectancy at birth (1981): 71.3 male; 77.4 female. **Births** (per 1,000 pop. 1980): 11.2. **Deaths** (per 1,000 pop. 1980): 10.9. **Natural increase** (1978): .2%. **Hospital beds** (per 100,000 pop. 1977): 853. **Physicians** (per 100,000 pop. 1977): 204. **Infant mortality** (per 1,000 live births 1981): 8.5.

Education (1981): **Literacy:** 99%. **Pop. 5–19:** in school: 70%, teachers per 1,000; 51.

The origin of Copenhagen dates back to ancient times, when the fishing and trading place named Havn (port) grew up on a cluster of islets, but Bishop Absalon (1128-1201) is regarded as the actual founder of the city.

Danes formed a large component of the Viking raiders in the early Middle Ages. The Danish kingdom was a major north European power until the 17th century, when it lost its land in southern Sweden. Norway was separated in 1815, and Schleswig-Holstein in 1864. Northern Schleswig was returned in 1920.

The **Faeroe Islands** in the N. Atlantic, about 300 mi. NE of the Shetlands, and 850 mi. from Denmark proper, 18 inhabited, have an area of 540 sq. mi. and pop. (1980) of 43,300. They are self-governing in most matters.

Greenland

(Kalaallit Nunaat)

Greenland, a huge island between the N. Atlantic and the Polar Sea, is separated from the North American continent by Davis Strait and Baffin Bay. Its total area is 840,000 sq. mi., 705,234 of which are ice-capped. Most of the island is a lofty plateau 9,000 to 10,000 ft. in altitude. The average thickness of the cap is 1,000 ft. The population (1980 est.) is 49,800. Under the 1953 Danish constitution the colony became an integral part of the realm with representatives in the Folketing. The Danish parliament, 1978, approved home rule for Greenland, effective May 1, 1979. Accepting home rule the islanders elected a socialist-dominated legislature, Apr. 4th. With home rule, Greenlandic place names came into official use. The technically-correct name for Greenland is now Kalaallit Nunaat; its capital is Nuuk, rather than Gothab. Fish and fur are exported.

Djibouti

Republic of Djibouti

People: Population (1981 est.): 460,000. **Pop. density:** 12.23 per sq. mi. **Ethnic groups:** Issa (Somali) 47%; Afar 37%; European 8%; Arab 6%. **Languages:** Somali, Saho-Afar, French, Arabic. **Religions:** Most are Moslems.

Geography: Area: 8,996 sq. mi., about the size of Massachusetts. **Location:** On E coast of Africa, separated from Arabian Peninsula by the strategically vital strait of Bab el-Mandeb. **Neighbors:** Ethiopia on N (Eritrea) and W, Somalia on S. **Topography:** The territory, divided into a low coastal plain, mountains behind, and an interior plateau, is arid, sandy, and desolate. The climate is generally hot and dry. **Capital:** Djibouti. **Cities** (1980 est): Djibouti (met.) 200,000.

Government: Head of state: Pres. Hassan Gouled Aptidon b. 1916; in office: June 24, 1977; **Head of government:** Prem. Barkat Gourat Hamadou; in office: Sept. 30, 1978. **Local divisions:** 5 cercles (districts). **Armed forces:** regulars 3,000; paramilitary 10,000.

Economy: Minerals: Salt. **Electricity prod.** (1977): 62 mln. kwh.

Finance: Currency Franc (Sept. 1981: 178=$1 US). **Per capita income** (1976): $1,000. **Imports** (1979): $140 mln.; partners (1977): Fr. 55%, Jap. 6%, UK 6%. **Exports** (1979): $20 mln.; partners (1977): Fr. 74%.

Transport: Motor vehicles: in use (1977): 11,800 passenger cars, 3,300 commercial vehicles. **Chief ports:** Djibouti.

Communications: Television sets: 3,500 in use (1976). **Radios:** 15,000 in use (1976). **Telephones in use** (1978): 3,675.

Health: Births (per 1,000 pop. 1978): 49. **Deaths** (per 1,000 pop. 1978): 23. **Natural increase** (1978): 9.2%.

France gained control of the territory in stages between 1862 and 1900.

Ethiopia and Somalia have renounced their claims to the area, but each has accused the other of trying to gain control. There were clashes between Afars (ethnically related to Ethiopians) and Issas (related to Somalis) in 1976. Immigrants from both countries continued to enter the country up to independence, which came June 27, 1977.

Unemployment is about 80%. There are few natural resources; trade is the main contributor to domestic product. French aid is the mainstay of the economy and 7,000 French troops are present.

Dominica

Commonwealth of Dominica

People: Population (1981 est.): 80,000. **Pop. density:** 275.86 per sq. mi. **Ethnic groups:** nearly all African or mulatto, Caribs. **Languages:** English, French patois. **Religions:** mainly Roman Catholic.

Geography: Area: 290 sq. mi., about one-fourth the size of Rhode Island. **Location:** In Eastern Caribbean, most northerly Windward Is. **Neighbors:** Guadeloupe to N, Martinique to S. **Topography:** Mountainous, a central ridge running from N to S, terminating in cliffs; volcanic in origin, with numerous thermal springs; rich deep topsoil on leeward side, red tropical clay on windward coast. **Capital** (1971 est.) Roseau 20,000.

Government: Head of state: Pres. Aurelius Marie; in office: 1980. **Head of government:** Prime Min. Mary Eugenia Charles; elected to office: July 21, 1980. **Local divisions:** 25 village councils and 2 town councils.

Economy: Industries: Agriculture, tourism. **Chief crops:** Bananas, citrus fruits, coconuts. **Minerals:** Pumice. **Other resources:** Forests. **Per capita arable land:** 0.2 acres. **Electricity prod.** (1977): 16 mln. kwh.

Finance: Currency: East Caribbean dollar (Sept. 1981: 2.70 = $1 US). **Gross domestic product** (1977): $33.48 mln. **Per capita income** (1976): $460. **Imports** (1978): $28.4 mln.; partners (1978): UK 27%, U.S. 15%, Can. 5%. **Exports** (1978): $15.8 mln.; partners (1978): UK 67%. **Tourists** (1977): 31,000; receipts: $3 mln. **National budget** (1976): $6.29 mln. revenues; $7.51 mln. expenditures. **Consumer prices** (change in 1978): 7.7%.

Transport: Chief ports: Roseau.

Communications: Telephones in use (1978): 4,036.

Health: Life expectancy at birth (1962): 56.97 male; 59.18 female. **Births** (per 1,000 pop. 1978): 21.4. **Deaths** (per 1,000 pop. 1978): 5.3. **Natural increase** (1978): 1.6%. **Pop. per hospital bed** (1973): 234. **Pop. per physician** (1971): 5,385. **Infant mortality** (per 1,000 live births 1978): 19.6.

Education: Pop. 5–19: in school (1975): 24,113.

A British colony since 1805, Dominica was granted self government in 1967. Independence was achieved Nov. 3, 1978. Tourism is a small sector of the economy. France was expected to increase aid to the island.

Hurricane David struck, Aug. 30, 1979, devastating the island and destroying the banana plantations, Dominica's economic mainstay. Coups were attempted in 1980 and 1981. U.S. authorities arrested 10 people, some linked to the Ku Klux Klan, in an attempted invasion of Dominica from Louisiana in Apr. 1981.

Dominican Republic

People: Population (1981 est.): 5,900,000. **Age distrib.** (%): 0–14: 47.5; 15–59: 47.5; 60+: 4.9. **Pop. density:** 273.74 per sq. mi. **Urban** (1979): 50.2%. **Ethnic groups:** Caucasian 16%, mulatto 73%, Negro 11%. **Languages:** Spanish. **Religions:** Roman Catholic 95%.

Geography: Area: 18,704 sq. mi., the size of Vermont and New Hampshire combined. **Location:** In West Indies, sharing I. of Hispaniola with Haiti. **Neighbors:** Haiti on W. **Topography:** The Cordillera Central range crosses the center of the country, rising to over 10,000 ft., highest in the Caribbean. The Cibao valley to the N is major agricultural area. **Capital:** Santo Domingo. **Cities** (1980 est.): Santo Domingo 1.3 mln.; Santiago de Los Caballeros 326,000.

Government: Head of state: Pres. Salvador Jorge Blanco; b. July 5, 1926; in office: May 16, 1982. **Local divisions:** 26 provinces and a national district. **Armed forces:** regulars 18,500 (1980).

Economy: Industries: Sugar refining, cement, textiles, pharmaceuticals. **Chief crops:** sugar, cocoa, coffee, tobacco, rice. **Minerals:** Nickel, gold, silver, bauxite. **Other resources:** Timber. **Per capita arable land:** 0.4 acres. **Meat prod.** (1980): beef: 43,000 metric tons; pork: 12,000 metric tons. **Electricity prod.** (1979): 2.8 bln. kwh. **Labor force:** 47% agric.; 23% manuf.

Finance: Currency: Peso (Mar. 1982: 1.11 = $1 US). **Gross domestic product** (1980): $6.7 bln. **Per capita income** (1980): $1,221. **Imports** (1980): $1.65 bln.; partners (1979): U.S. 42%, Venez. 18%, Jap. 7%. **Exports** (1980): $961.9 mln.; partners (1979): U.S. 53% Swit. 15%, Venez. 6%, Neth. 5%. **Tourists** (1977): 265,000; receipts: $93 mln. **National budget** (1979): $745.6 mln. revenues; $973.9 mln. expenditures. **International reserves less gold** (Feb. 1982): $169.6 mln. **Gold:** 131,000 oz t. **Consumer prices** (change in 1980): 16.8%

Transport: Motor vehicles: in use (1980): 115,300 passenger cars, 77,221 comm. vehicles. **Chief ports:** Santo Domingo, San Pedro de Macoris, Puerto Plata.

Communications: Television sets: 385,000 in use (1978). **Radios:** 210,000 in use (1977). **Telephones in use** (1980): 155,400. **Daily newspaper circ.** (1980): 45 per 1,000 pop.

Health: Life expectancy at birth (1961): 57.15 male; 58.59 female. **Births** (per 1,000 pop. 1978): 36. **Deaths** (per 1,000 pop. 1978): 9. **Natural increase** (1978): 2.5%. **Hospital beds** (per 100,000 pop. 1977): 233. **Physicians** (per 100,000 pop. 1977): 53. **Infant mortality** (per 1,000 live births 1981): 96.

Education (1981): **Literacy:** 62%. **Pop. 5–19:** in school: 51%, teachers per 1,000: 12.

Carib and Arawak Indians inhabited the island of Hispaniola when Columbus landed in 1492. The city of Santo Domingo, founded 1496, is the oldest settlement by Europeans in the hemisphere and has the supposed ashes of Columbus in an elaborate tomb in its ancient cathedral.

The western third of the island was ceded to France in 1697. Santo Domingo itself was ceded to France in 1795. Haitian leader Toussaint L'Ouverture seized it, 1801. Spain returned intermittently 1803-21, as several native republics came and went. Haiti ruled again, 1822-44, and Spanish occupation occurred 1861-63.

The country was occupied by U.S. Marines from 1916 to 1924, when a constitutionally elected government was installed.

In 1930, Gen. Rafael Leonidas Trujillo Molina was elected president. Trujillo ruled brutally until his assassination in 1961. Pres. Joaquin Balaguer, appointed by Trujillo in 1960, resigned under pressure in 1962. Juan Bosch, elected president in the first free elections in 38 years, was overthrown in 1963.

On April 24, 1965, a revolt was launched by followers of Bosch and others, including a few communists. Four days later U.S. Marines intervened against the pro-Bosch forces. Token units were later sent by 5 So. American countries as a peacekeeping force.

A provisional government supervised a June 1966 election, in which Balaguer defeated Bosch by a 3-2 margin; there were some charges of election fraud.

The Inter-American Peace Force completed its departure Sept. 20, 1966. Balaguer was reelected, 1970 and 1974, the latter time without real opposition.

In 1971, scores of leftists were reported killed by terrorists. Renewed violence occurred in 1975.

Continued depressed world prices affected the main export commodity, sugar. In 1981, several strikes and demonstrations were met with violence by security forces.

Ecuador

Republic of Ecuador

People: Population (1981 est.): 8,350,000. **Age distrib.** (%): 0–14: 44.5; 15–59: 49.6; 60+: 6.0. **Pop. density:** 79.00 per sq. mi. **Urban** (1978): 42.8% **Ethnic groups:** Indians 25%, Mestizos 55%, Caucasians 10%, Negroes 10%. **Languages:** Spanish (official), Quechuan, Jivaroan. **Religions:** Predominantly Roman Catholic.

Geography: Area: 113,424 sq. mi., the size of Colorado. **Location:** In NW S. America, on Pacific coast, astride Equator. **Neighbors:** Colombia to N, Peru to E and S. **Topography:** Two ranges of Andes run N and S, splitting the country into 3 zones: hot, humid lowlands on the coast; temperate highlands between the ranges, and rainy, tropical lowlands to the E. **Capital:** Quito. **Cities** (1980 est.): Guayaquil 1,116,300; Quito 807,700.

Government: Head of state: Pres. Osvaldo Hurtado Larrea; in office: May 24, 1981. **Local divisions:** 20 provinces. **Armed forces:** regulars 38,600 (1980).

Economy: Industries: Food processing, wood prods. **Chief crops:** Bananas (largest exporter), coffee, rice, grains, fruits, cocoa, kapok. **Minerals:** Oil, copper, iron, lead, coal, sulphur. **Crude oil reserves** (1980): 1.1 bln. bbls. **Other resources:** Rubber, bark. **Per capita arable land:** 1.3 acres. **Meat prod.** (1980): beef: 92,000 metric tons; pork: 63,000 metric tons; lamb: 10,000 metric tons. **Fish catch** (1979): 644,300 metric tons.

Electricity prod. (1978): 2.34 bln. kwh. **Labor force:** 50% agric., 20% ind., 15% services.

Finance: Currency: Sucre (Apr. 1982: 25.00 = $1 US). **Gross domestic product** (1980): $11.3 bln. **Per capita income** (1980): $1,050. **Imports** (1980): $2.24 bln.; partners (1979): U.S. 35%, Jap. 13%, W. Ger. 8%. **Exports** (1980): $2.30 bln.; partners (1979): U.S. 36%, Pan. 9%, Chile 7%. **Tourists** (1977): 240,000. **National budget** (1980): $1.5 bln. revenues; $1.6 bln. expenditures. **International reserves less gold** (Feb. 1982): $622.8 mln. **Gold:** 414,000 oz t. **Consumer prices** (change in 1981): 16.4%.

Transport: Railway traffic (1978) 65 mln. passenger-km; 34 mln. net ton-km. **Motor vehicles:** in use (1978): 66,100 passenger cars, 137,400 comm. vehicles. **Chief ports:** Guayaquil, Manta, Esmeraldas.

Communications: Television sets: 550,000 in use (1979), 5,000 manuf. (1975). **Radios:** 1.7 mln. in use (1971). **Telephones in use** (1980): 260,000. **Daily newspaper circ.** (1980): 49 per 1,000 pop.

Health: Life expectancy at birth (1974): 54.89 male; 58.07 female. **Births** (per 1,000 pop. 1978): 42. **Deaths** (per 1,000 pop. 1978): 10. **Natural increase** (1978): 3.1%. **Hospital beds** (per 100,000 pop.1977): 204. **Physicians** (per 100,000 pop. 1977): 64. **Infant mortality** (per 1,000 live births 1978): 66.

Education (1978): Literacy: 74%. **Pop. 5–19:** in school: 61%, teachers per 1,000: 20.

Spain conquered the region, which was the northern Inca empire, in 1633. Liberation forces defeated the Spanish May 24, 1822, near Quito. Ecuador became part of the Great Colombia Republic but seceded, May 13, 1830.

Ecuador had been ruled by civilian and military dictatorships since 1968. A peaceful transfer of power from the military junta to the democratic civilian government took place, 1979.

Since 1972, the economy has revolved around its petroleum exports. Despite this, Ecuador remains an underdeveloped country.

Ecuador and Peru have long disputed their Amazon Valley boundary.

President Jaime Roldós Aguilera was killed, May 24, 1981, in a plane crash. Vice President Larrea assumed the presidency and will serve out the remaining three years of Mr. Roldós term.

The **Galapagos Islands,** 600 mi. to the W, are the home of hugh tortoises and other unusual animals.

Egypt

Arab Republic of Egypt

People: Population (1981 est.): 43,200,000. **Pop. density:** 115.60 per sq. mi. **Urban** (1977): 44.1%. **Ethnic groups:** Egyptians, Bedouins, Nubians. **Languages:** Arabic. **Religions:** Mostly Sunni Moslems (state religion).

Geography: Area: 385,201 sq. mi, the size of Texas and Oregon combined. **Location:** NE corner of Africa. **Neighbors:** Libya on W, Sudan on S, Israel on E. **Topography:** Almost entirely desolate and barren, with hills and mountains in E and along Nile. The Nile Valley, where most of the people live, stretches 550 miles. **Capital:** Cairo. **Cities** (1976 cen.): Cairo 5,084,463; Alexandria 2,318,655; Giza 1,246,713; Subra-El Khema 393,700; El-Mahalla El-Kubra 292,853.

Government: Head of state: Pres. Hosni Mubarak; b. 1929; in office: Oct. 14, 1981. **Head of Government:** Ahmed Fuad Mohieddin; in office: Jan. 2, 1982. **Local divisions:** 25 governorates. **Armed forces:** regulars 367,000 (1980).

Economy: Industries: Textiles, chemicals, steel, cement, fertilizers, motion pictures. **Chief crops:** Cotton (one of largest producers), grains, vegetables, sugar cane, fruits. **Minerals:** Oil, phosphates, salt, iron, manganese, cement, gold, gypsum, kaolin, titanium. **Crude oil reserves** (1980): 3.1 bln. bbls. **Per capita arable land:** 0.2 acres. **Meat prod.** (1980): beef: 243,000 metric tons; lamb: 45,000 metric tons. **Fish catch** (1978): 99,900 metric tons. **Electricity prod.** (1978): 14.5 bln. kwh. **Crude steel prod.** (1981 est.): 900,000 metric tons. **Labor force:** 50% agric.

Finance: Currency: Pound (Mar. 1982: 0.78 = $1 US). **Gross domestic product** (1979): $18.9 bln. **Per capita income** (1977): $448. **Imports** (1980): $4.8 bln.; partners (1979): U.S. 18%, W. Ger. 11%, It. 8%, France 8%. **Exports** (1980): $3.04 bln.; partners (1979): It. 27%, Neth. 8%. **Tourists** (1977): 1,003,900; receipts: $658 mln. **International reserves less gold** (Dec. 1981): $1.18 bln. **Gold:** 2.43 mln. oz t. **Consumer prices** (change in 1980): 20.6%.

Transport: Railway traffic (1978): 9.2 bln. passenger-km; 2.30 bln. net ton-km. **Motor vehicles:** in use (1980): 325,500 passenger cars, 114,700 comm. vehicles; assembled (1978): 15,024 passenger cars; 4,080 comm. vehicles. **Civil aviation:** 2,040 mln. passenger-km (1977); 25 mln. freight ton-km (1977). **Chief ports:** Alexandria, Port Said, Suez.

Communications: Television sets: one mln. in use (1977), 184,000 manuf. (1978). **Radios:** 5.27 mln. in use (1977), 348,000 manuf. (1978). **Telephones in use** (1977): 503,947. **Daily newspaper circ.** (1980): 102 per 1,000 pop.

Health: Life expectancy at birth (1980): 53.6 male; 56.1 female. **Births** (per 1,000 pop. 1978): 37.6. **Deaths** (per 1,000 pop. 1978): 10.5. **Natural increase** (1978): 2.7%. **Hospital beds** (per 100,000 pop. 1977): 209. **Physicians** (per 100,000 pop. 1977): 92. **Infant mortality** (per 1,000 live births 1978): 89.2.

Education (1978): **Literacy:** 44%. **Pop. 5-19:** in school: 45%, teachers per 1,000: 13. **PQLI:** 52.

Archeological records of ancient Egyptian civilization date back to 4000 BC. A unified kingdom arose around 3200 BC, and extended its way south into Nubia and north as far as Syria. A high culture of rulers and priests was built on an economic base of serfdom, fertile soil, and annual flooding of the Nile banks.

Imperial decline facilitated conquest by Asian invaders (Hyksos, Assyrians). The last native dynasty fell in 341 BC to the Persians, who were in turn replaced by Greeks (Alexander and the Ptolemies), Romans, Byzantines, and Arabs, who introduced Islam and the Arabic language. The ancient Egyptian language is preserved only in the liturgy of the Coptic Christians.

Egypt was ruled as part of larger Islamic empires for several centuries. The Mamluks, a military caste of Caucasian origin, ruled Egypt from 1250 until defeat by the Ottoman Turks in 1517. Under Turkish sultans the khedive as hereditary viceroy had wide authority. Britain intervened in 1882 and took control of administration, though nominal allegiance to the Ottoman Empire continued until 1914.

The country was a British protectorate from 1914 to 1922. A 1936 treaty strengthened Egyptian autonomy, but Britain retained bases in Egypt and a condominium over the Sudan. Britain fought German and Italian armies from Egypt, 1940-42, but Egypt did not declare war against Germany until 1945. In 1951 Egypt abrogated the 1936 treaty. The Sudan became independent in 1956.

The uprising of July 23, 1952, led by the Society of Free Officers, named Maj. Gen. Mohammed Naguib commander in chief and forced King Farouk to abdicate. When the republic was proclaimed June 18, 1953, Naguib became its first president and premier. Lt. Col. Gamal Abdel Nasser removed Naguib and became premier in 1954. In 1956, he was voted president. Nasser died in 1970 and was replaced by Vice Pres. Anwar Sadat.

A series of decrees in July, 1961, nationalized about 90% of industry. Economic liberalization was begun, 1974, with more emphasis on private domestic and foreign investment.

In July, 1956, the U. S. and UK withdrew support for loans to start the Aswan High Dam. Nasser obtained credits and technicians from the USSR to build the dam. The billion-dollar Aswan High Dam project, begun 1960, completed 1971, provided irrigation for more than a million acres of land and a potential of 10 billion kwh of electricity per year. Artesian wells, drilled in the Western Desert, reclaimed 43,000 acres, 1960-66.

When the state of Israel was proclaimed in 1948, Egypt joined other Arab nations invading Israel and was defeated.

After terrorist raids across its border, Israel invaded Egypt's Sinai Peninsula, Oct. 29, 1956. Egypt rejected a cease-fire demand by Britain and France; on Oct. 31 the 2 nations dropped bombs and on Nov. 5-6 landed forces. Egypt and Israel accepted a UN cease-fire; fighting ended Nov. 7.

A UN Emergency Force guarded the 117-mile long border between Egypt and Israel until May 19, 1967, when it was withdrawn at Nasser's demand. Egyptian troops entered the Gaza Strip and the heights of Sharm el Sheikh and 3 days later closed the Strait of Tiran to all Israeli shipping. Full-scale war broke out June 5 and before it ended under a UN cease-fire June 10, Israel had captured Gaza and the Sinai Peninsula, controlled the east bank of the Suez Canal and reopened the gulf.

Sporadic fighting with Israel broke out late in 1968 and continued almost daily, 1969-70. Military and economic aid was received from the USSR; it was est. in 1971 there were 19,000 or more Soviet military personnel in Egypt. Israel and Egypt agreed, Aug. 7, 1970, to a cease-fire and peace negotiations proposed by the U.S. Negotiations failed to achieve results, but the cease-fire continued into 1973.

In July 1972 Sadat ordered most of the 20,000 Soviet military advisers and personnel to leave Egypt.

In a surprise attack Oct. 6, 1973, Egyptian forces crossed the Suez Canal into the Sinai. (At the same time, Syrian forces attacked Israelis on the Golan Heights.) Egypt was supplied by a USSR military airlift; the U.S. responded with an airlift to Israel. Israel counter-attacked, crossed the canal, surrounded Suez City. A UN cease-fire took effect Oct. 24.

A disengagement agreement was signed Jan. 18, 1974. Under it, Israeli forces withdrew from the canal's W bank; limited numbers of Egyptian forces occupied a strip along the E bank. A second accord was signed in 1975, with Israel yielding Sinai oil fields. Pres. Sadat's surprise visit to Jerusalem, Nov. 1977, opened the prospect of peace with Israel, but worsened relations with Libya (border clashes, July 1977). On Mar. 26, 1979, Egypt and Israel signed a formal peace treaty, ending 30 years of war, and establishing diplomatic relations. Israel returned control of the Sinai to Egypt in April 1982.

Tension between Muslim fundamentalists and Christians in 1981 caused street riots and culminated in a nationwide security crackdown in September. Pres Sadat was assassinated on Oct. 6.

The **Suez Canal,** 103 mi. long, links the Mediterranean and Red seas. It was built by a French corporation 1859-69, but Britain obtained controlling interest in 1875. The last British troops were removed June 13, 1956. On July 26, Egypt nationalized the canal. French and British stockholders eventually received some compensation.

Egypt had barred Israeli ships and cargoes destined for Israel since 1948, and closed the canal to all shipping after the 1967 Arab-Israeli War. The canal was reopened in 1975; Egypt agreed to allow passage to Israeli cargo in third party ships. By 1979, annual tolls, at $700 million, had once more become a major source of government revenue. A $1.3 billion expansion project will enable the canal to accomodate larger tankers.

El Salvador

Republic of El Salvador

People: Population (1981 est.): 5,000,000. **Age distrib.** (%): 0–14; 46.2; 15–59: 48.4; 60+: 5.4. **Pop. density:** 570 per sq. mi. **Urban** (1978): 40.1%. **Ethnic groups:** Mestizos 89%, Indians 10%, Caucasians 1%. **Languages:** Spanish, Nahuatl (among some Indians). **Religions:** Roman Catholicism prevails.

Geography: Area: 8,124 sq. mi., the size of Massachusetts. **Location:** In Central America. **Neighbors:** Guatemala on W, Honduras on N. **Topography:** A hot Pacific coastal plain in the south rises to a cooler plateau and valley region, densely populated. The N is mountainous, including many volcanoes. **Capital:** San Salvador. **Cities** (1981 est.): San Salvador 400,000.

Government: Pres., Alvaro Alfredo Magana; b. Oct. 8, 1925; in office: Apr. 25, 1982. **Local divisions:** 14 departments; pres. appoints governors. **Armed forces:** regulars 6,930; para-military 3,000.

Economy: Industries: Food and beverages, textiles, petroleum products. **Chief crops:** Coffee, cotton, corn, sugar. **Other resources:** Rubber, forests. **Per capita arable land:** 0.3 acres. **Meat prod.** (1980): beef: 28,000 metric tons; pork: 16,000 metric tons. **Electricity prod.** (1979): 1.5 bln. kwh. **Labor force:** 47% agric.; 8% man.; 14% services.

Finance: Currency: Colon (Mar. 1982: 2.78 = $1 US). **Gross domestic product** (1980): $3.77 bln. **Per capita income** (1978): $639. **Imports** (1980): $971 mln.; partners (1979): U.S. 29%, Guat. 18%, Jap. 8%, Venez. 8%. **Exports** (1980): $967 mln.; partners (1979): U.S. 27%, W. Ger. 20%, Guat. 16%, Neth. 9%. **Tourists** (1976): 277,900; receipts (1977): $23 mln. **National budget** (1980): $412 mln. revenues; $569 mln. expenditures. **International reserves less gold** (Jan. 1982): $73.8 mln. **Gold:** 516,000 oz t. **Consumer prices** (change in 1981): 14.8%.

Transport: Motor vehicles: in use (1977): 70,000 passenger cars, 35,500 comm. vehicles. **Chief ports:** La Union, Acajutla.

Communications: Television sets: 148,000 in use (1977). **Radios:** 1.4 mln. in use (1977). **Telephones in use** (1978): 70,400. **Daily newspaper circ.** (1976): 331,000.

Health: Life expectancy at birth (1980): 56.7 male; 59.7 female. **Births** (per 1,000 pop. 1980): 34.7. **Deaths** (per 1,000 pop. 1980): 7.9. **Natural increase** (1977): 3.4%. **Hospital beds** (per 100,000 pop. 1977): 161. **Physicians** (per 100,000 pop. 1977): 27. **Infant mortality** (per 1,000 live births 1979): 60.0.

Education (1978): **Literacy:** 63%. **Pop. 5–19:** in school: 50%, teachers per 1,000: 11.

El Salvador became independent of Spain in 1821, and of the Central American Federation in 1839.

A fight with Honduras in 1969 over the presence of 300,000 Salvadorean workers left 2,000 dead. Clashes were renewed 1970 and 1974.

A military coup overthrew the Romero government, 1979, but the ruling military-civilian junta failed to quell the extremist violence and unrest that contines to undermine the economy. In 1982, the Reagan administration attempted to increase economic and military aid to El Salvador but was rebuffed by the U.S. Senate which sought certification that the Salvadoran government was making progress on land reform and human rights.

Voters turned out in large numbers in the March elections despite the absence of candidates representing antigovernment rebels and the rebels' call for an election boycott. Five right-wing parties, after much political infighting, formed a new government April 29.

Equatorial Guinea

Republic of Equatorial Guinea

People: Population (1981 est.): 250,000. **Age distrib.** (%): 0–14: 35.2; 15–59: 57.1; 60+: 7.7. **Pop. density:** 33.23 per sq. mi. **Ethnic groups:** Fangs 75%, several other groups. **Languages:** Spanish (official), Fang, English. **Religions:** Roman Catholics 60%, Protestants, others.

Geography: Area: 10,832 sq. mi., the size of Maryland. **Location:** Bioko Is. off W. Africa coast in Gulf of Guinea, and Rio Muni, mainland enclave. **Neighbors:** Gabon on S, Cameroon on E, N. **Topography:** Bioko Is. consists of 2 volcanic mountains and a connecting valley. Rio Muni, with over 90% of the area, has a coastal plain and low hills beyond. **Capital:** Malabo. **Cities** (1974 est.): Malabo 25,000.

Government: Head of state: Pres., Supreme Military Council Teodoro Obiang Nguema Mbasogo; b. June 5, 1942; in office: Oct. 10, 1979. **Local divisions:** 2 provinces.

Economy: Chief crops: Cocoa, coffee, bananas, palm oil. **Other resources:** Timber. **Per capita arable land:** 0.9 acres. **Electricity prod.** (1977): 23 mln. kwh. **Labor force:** 95% agric.

Finance: Currency: Ekuele (Sept. 1981: 184 = $1 US). **Gross domestic product** (1976 est.): $112 mln. **Per capita income** (1975): $342. **Imports** (1980): $54 mln.; partners (1980): Spain 70%, China 13%. **Exports** (1980): $16 mln.; partners (1980): Neth. 46%, W. Ger. 17%, Sen. 16%, Spain 10%.

Transport: Chief ports: Malabo, Bata.

Communications: Radios: 80,000 in use (1976).

Health: Life expectancy at birth (1975): 41.9 male; 45.1 female. **Births** (per 1,000 pop. 1978): 42. **Deaths** (per 1,000 pop. 1978): 19. **Natural increase** (1978): 2.3% **Hospital beds** (per 100,000 pop. 1977): 704. **Physicians** (per 100,000 pop. 1977): 2. **Infant mortality** (per 1,000 live births 1975): 53.2.

Education (1978): **Literacy:** 20%. **Pop. 5–19:** in school: 45%, teachers per 1,000: 9.

Fernando Po (now Bioko) Island was discovered by Portugal in the late 15th century and ceded to Spain in 1778. Independence came Oct. 12, 1968. Riots occurred in 1969 over disputes between the island and the more backward Rio Muni province on the mainland. Masie Nguema Biyogo, himself from the mainland, became president for life in 1972.

Masie's 11-year reign was described as one of the most brutal in Africa, resulting in a bankrupted nation. Most of the nation's 7,000 Europeans emigrated. In 1976, 45,000 Nigerian workers were evacuated amid charges of a reign of terror. According to reports, slavery had been revived and as many as 50,000 people were murdered by government forces. Masie was ousted in a military coup, Aug., 1979.

Ethiopia

Socialist Ethiopia

People: Population (1981 est.): 33,300,000. **Age distrib.** (%): 0–14: 43.1; 15–59: 52.5; 60+: 4.4. **Pop. density:** 71.31 per sq. mi. **Urban** (1979): 13.5%. **Ethnic groups:** Oromo 40%, Amhara 25%, Tigre 12%, Somali, Afar, Sidama. **Languages:** Amharic, Tigre (Semitic languages); Galla (Hamitic), Arabic, others. **Religions:** Orthodox Christian 40%, Moslem 40%.

Geography: Area: 472,400 sq. mi., four-fifths the size of Alaska. **Location:** In E. Africa. **Neighbors:** Sudan on W, Kenya on S. Somalia, Djibouti on E. **Topography:** A high central plateau, between 6,000 and 10,000 ft. high, rises to higher mountains near the Great Rift Valley, cutting in from the SW. The Blue Nile and other rivers cross the plateau, which descends to plains on both W and SE. **Capital:** Addis Ababa. **Cities** (1981 est.): Addis Ababa 1,200,000; Asmara 240,000.

Government: Head of state and head of gov't.: Chmn. of Provisional Military Administrative Council Mengistu Haile Mariam; b. 1937; in office: Feb. 11, 1977. **Local divisions:** 14 administrative regions. **Armed forces:** 250,000.

Economy: Industries: Food processing, cement, textiles. **Chief crops:** Coffee (64% export earnings), grains. **Minerals:** Coal, platinum, gold, copper, asbestos, potash. **Other resources:** Hydro power potential. **Per capita arable land:** 1.1 acres. **Meat prod.** (1980): beef: 214,000 metric tons; lamb: 132,000 metric tons. **Fish catch** (1978): 26,800 metric tons. **Electricity prod.** (1978): 690 mln. kwh. **Labor force:** 86% agric.

Finance: Currency: Birr (Apr. 1982: 2.07 = $1 US). **Gross domestic product** (1980): $4.07 bln. **Per capita income** (1980): $117. **Imports** (1980): $722 mln.; partners (1979): Ku. 15%, U.S. 12%, Jap. 10%, W.Ger. 10%. **Exports** (1980): $425 mln.; partners (1979): U.S. 29%, Italy 11%, Saud. Ar. 8%. **Tourists** (1976): 36,900; receipts (1977): $3 mln. **National budget** (1980): $985 mln. revenues; $1.8 bln. expenditures. **International reserves less gold** (Feb. 1982): $230.0 mln. **Gold:** 260,000 oz t. **Consumer prices** (change in 1980): 4.5%.

Transport: Railway traffic (1979): 171 mln. passenger-km; 148 mln. net ton-km. **Motor vehicles:** in use (1980): 38,600 passenger cars, 11,700 comm. vehicles. **Civil aviation:** 647 mln. passenger-km (1980); 26 mln. net ton-km (1980). **Chief ports:** Masewa, Aseb.

Communications: Television sets: 30,000 in use (1978), **Radios:** 215,000 in use (1977). **Telephones in use** (1980): 83,800. **Daily newspaper circ.** (1980): 2 per 1,000 pop.

Health: Life expectancy at birth (1975): 37.0 male; 40.1 female. **Births** (per 1,000 pop. 1978): 48. **Deaths** (per 1,000 pop. 1978): 23. **Natural increase** (1978): 2.4%. **Hospital beds** (per 100,000 pop. 1977): 29. **Physicians** (per 100,000 pop. 1977): 1. **Infant mortality** (per 1,000 live births 1981): 155.

Education (1981): **Literacy:** 8%. **Pop 5-19:** in school: 12%, teachers per 1,000: 3.

Ethiopian culture was influenced by Egypt and Greece. The ancient monarchy was invaded by Italy in 1880, but maintained its independence until another Italian invasion in 1936. British forces freed the country in 1941.

The last emperor, Haile Selassie I, established a parliament and judiciary system in 1931, but barred all political parties.

A series of droughts since 1972 have killed hundreds of thousands. An army mutiny, strikes, and student demonstrations led to the dethronement of Selassie in 1974. The ruling junta pledged to form a one-party socialist state, and instituted a successful land reform; opposition was violently suppressed. The influence of the Coptic Church, embraced in 330 AD, was curbed, and the monarchy was abolished in 1975.

The regime, torn by bloody coups, faced uprisings by tribal and political groups in part aided by Sudan and Somalia. Ties with the U.S., once a major arms and aid source, deteriorated, while cooperation accords were signed with the USSR in 1977. In 1978, Soviet advisors and 20,000 Cuban troops helped defeat Somali rebels & Somalia forces.

Eritrea, an Italian colony since 1890, reverted to Ethiopia in 1952 in accordance with a UN General Assembly vote.

Fiji

Dominion of Fiji

People: Population (1981 est.): 640,000. **Age distrib.** (%): 0–14: 41.1; 15–59: 54.7; 60+: 4.0. **Pop. density:** 87.87 per sq. mi. **Urban** (1976): 37.2%. **Ethnic groups:** Indian 50%, Fijian (Melanesian-Polynesian) 44%, Europeans 2%. **Languages:** English (official), Fijian, Hindi. **Religions:** Christian, Hindu.

Geography: Area: 7,056 sq. mi., the size of New Jersey. **Location:** In western S. Pacific O. **Neighbors:** Nearest are Solomons on NW, Tonga on E. **Topography:** 840 islands (106 inhabited), many mountainous, with tropical forests and large fertile areas. Viti Levu, the largest island, has over half the total land area. **Capital:** Suva. **Cities** (1978): Suva 64,000.

Government: Head of state: Queen Elizabeth II, represented by Gov. Gen. George Cakobau; b. Nov. 6, 1912; in office: Jan. 13, 1973. **Head of government:** Prime Min. Kamisese Mara; b. May 13, 1920; in office: Oct. 10, 1970. **Local divisions:** 13 provinces. **Armed forces:** regulars 1,900 (1980).

Economy: Industries: Cement, shipyards, light industry, molasses, tourism. **Chief crops:** Sugar, coconut products, ginger. **Minerals:** Gold. **Other resources:** Timber. **Per capita arable land:** 0.6 acres. **Electricity prod.** (1979): 209 mln. kwh. **Labor force:** 44% agric.

Finance: Currency: Dollar (Apr. 1982: 0.82 = $1 US). **Gross domestic product** (1978): $937 mln. **Per capita income** (1978): $1,440. **Imports** (1980): $561 mln.; partners (1980): Austral. 30%, Jap. 15%, N.Z. 15%. **Exports** (1980): $362 mln.; partners (1980): UK 25%, U.S. 10%, N.Z. 10%. **Tourists** (1979): 188,740; receipts $102 mln. **National budget** (1980): $249 mln. revenues; $253 mln. expenditures. **International reserves less gold** (Feb. 1982): $145.33 mln. **Gold:** 11,000 oz t. **Consumer prices** (change in 1980): 14.5%.

Transport: Motor vehicles: in use (1978): 19,400 passenger cars, 11,980 comm. vehicles. **Civil aviation** (1980): 241 mln. passenger-km; 3.3 mln. net ton-km. **Chief ports:** Suva, Lautoka.

Communications: Radios: 308,000 in use (1977). **Telephones in use** (1980): 37,500. **Daily newspaper circ.** (1980): 108 per 1,000 pop.

Health: Life expectancy at birth (1975): 68.5 male; 71.7 female. **Births** (per 1,000 pop. 1978): 27 **Deaths** (per 1,000 pop. 1978): 4. **Natural increase** (1978): 1.8%. **Hospital beds** (per 100,000 pop. 1977): 264. **Physicians** (per 100,000 pop. 1977): 50. **Infant mortality** (per 1,000 live births 1975): 14.5.

Education (1978): **Literacy:** 75%. **Pop. 5-19:** in school: 73%, teachers per 1,000 27.

A British colony since 1874, Fiji became an independent parliamentary democracy Oct. 10, 1970.

Cultural differences between the majority Indian community, descendants of contract laborers brought to the islands in the 19th century, and the less modernized native Fijians, who by law own 83% of the land in communal villages, have led to political polarization.

The discovery of copper on Viti Levu, and favorable off-shore oil prospects, along with an expected all-time high in sugar production bode well for the economy.

Finland

Republic of Finland

People: Population (1981 est.): 4,800,000. **Age distrib.** (%): 0–14: 21.7; 15–59: 62.6; 60+: 15.7. **Pop. density:** 36.74 per sq. mi. **Urban** (1980): 59.9%. **Ethnic groups:** Finns, Swedes. **Languages:** Finnish 93.5%, Swedish 6.5% (both official). **Religions:** Lutheran 92%, Russian Orthodox 1.3%.

Geography: Area: 130,119 sq. mi., slightly smaller than Montana. **Location:** In northern Baltic region of Europe. **Neighbors:** Norway on N, Sweden on W, USSR on E. **Topography:** South and central Finland are mostly flat areas with low hills and many lakes. The N has mountainous areas, 3,000-4,000 ft. **Capital:** Helsinki. **Cities** (1979). Helsinki 483,743; Tampere 165,883.

Government: Head of state: Pres. Mauno Koivisto; b. Nov. 25, 1923; in office: Jan. 27, 1982. **Head of government:** Prime Min. Kaleva Sorsa; in office: Jan. 27, 1982. **Local divisions:** 12 laanit (provinces). **Armed forces:** regulars and equipped reserves 700,000 (1980).

Economy: Industries: Machinery, metal, shipbuilding, textiles, leather, chemicals, tourism. **Chief crops:** Grains, potatoes. **Minerals:** Chromium, cobalt, mercury, copper, iron, zinc, lead. **Other resources:** Forests (40% of exports). **Per capita arable land:** 1.3 acres. **Meat prod.** (1980): beef: 115,000 metric tons; pork: 176,000 metric tons. **Fish catch** (1977): 117,000 metric tons. **Electricity prod.** (1980): 38.5 bln. kwh. **Crude steel prod.** (1981): 2.4 mln. metric tons. **Labor force:** 6% agric.; 38% manuf.

Finance: Currency: Markkaa (Mar. 1982: 4.62 = $1 US). **Gross domestic product** (1979): $41.28 bln. **Per capita income** (1978): $6,090. **Imports** (1981): $14.1 bln.; partners (1980): USSR 21%, Swed. 13%, W. Ger. 13%, UK 9%. **Exports** (1981): $14.00 bln.; partners (1980): USSR 18%, Swed. 17%, UK 11%, W. Ger. 11%. **Tourists** (1977): 259,000. **National budget** (1980): $11.67 bln. revenues; $12.03 bln. expenditures. **International reserves less gold** (Feb. 1982): $1.33 bln. **Gold** 1.2 mln. oz t. **Consumer prices** (change in 1981): 12.0%.

Transport: Railway traffic (1979): 3.2 bln. passenger-km; 8.3 bln. net ton-km. **Motor vehicles:** in use (1980): 1.2 mln. passenger cars, 149,150 comm. vehicles; manuf. (1976): 27,300 passenger cars. **Civil aviation:** 2.1 bln. passenger-km (1980); 52.8 mln. freight ton-km (1980). **Chief ports:** Helsinki, Turku.

Communications: Television sets: 2.01 mln. licensed (1977), 275,000 manuf. (1976). **Radios:** 2.5 licensed (1978), 185,000 manuf. (1976). **Telephones in use** (1980): 2.2 mln. **Daily newspaper circ.** (1980): 517 per 1,000 pop.

Health: Life expectancy at birth (1978): 68.5 male; 77.1 female. **Births** (per 1,000 pop. 1980): 13.1. **Deaths** (per 1,000 pop. 1980): 9.4. **Natural increase** (1978): .4%. **Hospital beds** (per 100,000 pop. 1977): 1,531. **Physicians** (per 100,000 pop. 1977): 160. **Infant mortality** (per 1,000 live births 1978): 12.0.

Education (1978): **Literacy:** 99%. **Pop. 5–19:** in school: 68%, teachers per 1,000: 41.

The early Finns probably migrated from the Ural area at about the beginning of the Christian era. Swedish settlers brought the country into Sweden, 1154 to 1809, when Finland became an autonomous grand duchy of the Russian Empire. Russian exactions created a strong national spirit; on Dec. 6, 1917, Finland declared its independence and in 1919 became a republic. On Nov. 30, 1939, the Soviet Union invaded, and the Finns were forced to cede 16,173 sq. mi., including the Karelian Isthmus, Viipuri, and an area on Lake Ladoga. After World War II, in which Finland tried to recover its lost territory, further cessions were exacted. In 1948, Finland signed a treaty of mutual assistance with the USSR. In 1956 Russia returned Porkkala, which had been ceded as a military base.

Finland is an integral member of the Nordic group of five countries and maintains good relations with the Soviet Union. The governing coalition usually includes the Communist Party.

Aland, constituting an autonomous department, is a group of small islands, 572 sq. mi., in the Gulf of Bothnia, 25 mi. from Sweden, 15 mi. from Finland. Mariehamn is the principal port.

France

French Republic

People: Population (1981 est.): 53,900,000. **Age distrib.** (%): 0–14: 23.1; 15–59: 59.4; 60+: 17.5. **Pop. density:** 252.19 per sq. mi. **Urban** (1975): 73.0%. **Ethnic groups:** A mixture of various European and Mediterranean groups. **Languages:** French; minorities speak Breton, Alsatian German, Flemish, Italian, Basque, Catalan. **Religions:** Mostly Roman Catholic.

Geography: Area: 210,040 sq. mi., four-fifths the size of Texas. **Location:** In western Europe, between Atlantic O. and Mediterranean Sea. **Neighbors:** Spain on S, Italy, Switzerland, W. Germany on E, Luxembourg, Belgium on N. **Topography:** A wide plain covers more than half of the country, in N and W, drained to W by Seine, Loire, Garonne rivers. The Massif Central is a mountainous plateau in center. In E are Alps (Mt. Blanc is tallest in W. Europe, 15,771 ft.), the lower Jura range, and the forested Vosges. The Rhone flows from Lake Geneva to Mediterranean. Pyrenees are in SW, on border with Spain. **Capital:** Paris. **Cities** (1975 cen.): Paris 2,296,945; Marseille 912,130; Lyon 457,410; Toulouse 371,835; Nice 344,040; Nantes 255,700; Strasbourg 253,355; Bordeaux 223,845.

Government: Head of state: Pres. François Mitterrand; b. Oct. 26, 1916; in office: May 21, 1981. **Head of government:** Prime Min. Pierre Mauroy; in office: May 21, 1981. **Local divisions:** 95 departments. **Armed forces:** regulars 472,266 (1980).

Economy: Industries: Steel, chemicals, autos, textiles, wine, perfume, aircraft, ships, electronic equipment. **Chief crops:** Grains, corn, rice, fruits, vegetables. France is largest food producer, exporter, in W. Eur. **Minerals:** Bauxite, iron, coal. **Crude oil reserves** (1980): 50 mln. bbls. **Other resources:** Forests. **Per capita arable land:** 0.8 acres. **Meat prod.** (1980): beef: 1.82 mln. metric tons; pork: 1.86 mln. metric tons; lamb: 171,000 metric tons. **Fish catch** (1979): 732,100 metric tons. **Electricity prod.** (1980): 243.2 bln. kwh. **Crude steel prod.** (1981): 21.1 mln. metric tons. **Labor force:** 9% agric.; 35% manuf.; 48% services.

Finance: Currency: Franc (Mar. 1982: 6.24 = $1 US). **Gross domestic product** (1980). $585 bln. **Per capita income** (1980): $8,980. **Imports** (1981): $120.9 bln.; partners (1980): W. Ger. 16%, It. 9%, Belg. 8%, U.S. 8%. **Exports** (1981): $106.4 bln.; partners (1980): W. Ger. 15%, It. 12%, Belg. 9%, UK 7%. **Tourists** (1979) 28 mln.; receipts: $6.8 bln. **National budget** (1980): $113.5 bln. revenues; $113.6 bln. expenditures. **International reserves less gold** (Feb. 1982): $20.56 bln. **Gold:** 81.85 mln. oz t. **Consumer prices** (change in 1981): 13.3%.

Transport: Railway traffic (1979): 54.5 bln. passenger-km; 69.4 bln. net ton-km. **Motor vehicles:** in use (1980): 19.1 mln. passenger cars, 2.4 mln. comm. vehicles; manuf. (1980): 3.48 mln. passenger cars; 515,000 comm. vehicles. **Civil aviation:** 34,130 bln. passenger-km (1980); 2,092 bln net ton-km (1980). **Chief ports:** Marseille, LeHavre, Nantes, Bordeaux, Rouen.

Communications: Television sets: 14.9 mln. licensed (1977), 1.91 mln. manuf. (1978). **Radios:** 17.4 mln. licensed (1976), 3.01 mln. manuf. (1978). **Telephones in use** (1980): 22.2 mln. **Daily newspaper circ.** (1980): 214 per 1,000 pop.

Health: Life expectancy at birth (1978): 69.9 male; 78.0 female. **Births** (per 1,000 pop. 1980): 14.8. **Deaths** (per 1,000 pop. 1980): 10.1. **Natural increase** (1977): .4%. **Hospital beds** (per 100,000 pop. 1977): 1,125. **Physicians** (per 100,000 pop. 1977): 164. **Infant mortality** (per 1,000 live births 1981): 10.

Education (1978): **Literacy:** 99%. **Pop. 5-19:** in school: 68%, teachers per 1,000: 41.

Celtic Gaul was conquered by Julius Caesar 58-51 BC; Romans ruled for 500 years. Under Charlemagne, Frankish rule extended over much of Europe. After his death France emerged as one of the successor kingdoms.

The monarchy was overthrown by the French Revolution (1789-93) and succeeded by the First Republic; followed by the First Empire under Napoleon (1804-15), a monarchy (1814-48), the Second Republic (1848-52), the Second Empire (1852-70), the Third Republic (1871-1946), the Fourth Republic (1946-58), and the Fifth Republic (1958 to present).

France suffered severe losses in manpower and wealth in the first World War, 1914-18, when it was invaded by Germany. By the Treaty of Versailles, France exacted return of Alsace and Lorraine, French provinces seized by Germany in 1871. Germany invaded France again in May, 1940, and signed an armistice with a government based in Vichy. After France was liberated by the Allies Sept. 1944, Gen. Charles de Gaulle became head of the provisional government, serving until 1946.

De Gaulle again became premier in 1958, during a crisis over Algeria, and obtained voter approval for a new constitution, ushering in the Fifth Republic. Using strong executive powers, he promoted French economic and technological advances in the context of the European Economic Community, and guarded French foreign policy independence.

France had withdrawn from Indochina in 1954, and from Morocco and Tunisia in 1956. Most of its remaining African territories were freed 1958-62, but France retained strong economic and political ties.

France tested atomic bombs in the Sahara beginning in 1960. Land-based and submarine launched strategic missiles were also developed. In 1966, France withdrew all its troops from the integrated military command of NATO, though 60,000 remained stationed in Germany. France continued to attend political meetings of NATO.

In May 1968 rebellious students in Paris and other centers rioted, battled police, and were joined by workers who launched nationwide strikes. The government awarded pay increases to the strikers May 26. In elections to the Assembly in June, de Gaulle's backers won a landslide victory. Nevertheless, he resigned from office in April, 1969, after losing a nationwide referendum on constitutional reform. De Gaulle's policies were largely continued after his death in 1970.

On May 10, 1981, France elected François Mitterand, a Socialist candidate, president in a stunning victory over Valéry Giscard d'Estaing. In September, the government nationalized 5 major industries and most private banks.

The island of **Corsica,** in the Mediterranean W of Italy and N of Sardinia, is an official region of France comprising 2 departments. Area: 3,369 sq. mi.; pop. (1975 cen.): 289,842. The capital is Ajaccio, birthplace of Napoleon. A militant separatist movement led to violence after 1975.

Overseas Departments

French Guiana is on the NE coast of South America with Suriname on the W and Brazil on the E and S. Its area is 35,135 sq. mi.; pop. (1981 est.): 66,600. Guiana sends one senator and one deputy to the French Parliament. Guiana is administered by a prefect and has a Council General of 16 elected members; capital is Cayenne.

The famous penal colony, Devil's Island, was phased out between 1938 and 1951.

Immense forests of rich timber cover 90% of the land. Placer gold mining is the most important industry. Exports are shrimp, timber, and machinery.

Guadeloupe, in the West Indies' Leeward Islands, consists of 2 large islands, Basse-Terre and Grande-Terre, separated by the Salt River, plus Marie Galante and the Saintes group to the S and, to the N, Desirade, St. Barthelemy, and over half of St. Martin (the Netherlands portion is St. Maarten). A French possession since 1635, the department is represented in the French Parliament by 2 senators and 3 deputies; administration consists of a prefect (governor) and an elected General Council.

Area of the islands is 686 sq. mi.; pop. (1979 est.) 319,000, mainly descendants of slaves; capital is Basse-Terre on Basse-Terre Is. The land is fertile; sugar, rum, and bananas are exported; tourism is an important industry.

Martinique, one of the Windward Islands, in the West Indies, has been a possession since 1635, and a department since March, 1946. It is represented in the French Parliament by 2 senators and 3 deputies. The island was the birthplace of Napoleon's Empress Josephine.

It has an area of 431 sq. mi.; pop. (1979 est.) 310,000, mostly descendants of slaves. The capital is Fort-de-France. It is a popular tourist stop. The chief exports are rum, bananas, and petroleum products.

Mayotte, formerly part of Comoros, voted in 1976 to become an overseas department of France. An island NW of Madagascar, area is 144 sq. mi., pop. (1980 est.) 50,400.

Reunion is a volcanic island in the Indian O. about 420 mi. E of Madagascar, and has belonged to France since 1665. Area, 970 sq. mi.; pop. (1981 est.) 535,400, 30% of French extraction. Capital: Saint-Denis. The chief export is sugar. It elects 3 deputies, 2 senators to the French Parliament.

St. Pierre and Miquelon, formerly an Overseas Territory, made the transition to department status in 1976. It consists of 2 groups of rocky islands near the SW coast of Newfoundland, inhabited by fishermen. The exports are chiefly fish products. The St. Pierre group has an area of 10 sq. mi.; Miquelon, 83 sq. mi. Total pop. (1980 est.), 6,300. The capital is St. Pierre. A deputy and a senator are elected to the French Parliament.

Overseas Territories

French Polynesia Overseas Territory, comprises 130 islands widely scattered among 5 archipelagos in the South Pacific; administered by a governor. Territorial Assembly and a Council with headquarters at Papeete, Tahiti, one of the **Society Islands** (which include the **Windward** and **Leeward** islands). A deputy and a senator are elected to the French Parliament.

Other groups are the **Marquesas Islands,** the **Tuamotu Archipelago,** including the **Gambier Islands,** and the **Austral Islands.**

Total area of the islands administered from Tahiti is 1,544 sq. mi.; pop. (1981 est.), 160,000, more than half on Tahiti. Tahiti is picturesque and mountainous with a productive coastline bearing coconut, banana and orange trees, sugar cane and vanilla.

Tahiti was visited by Capt. James Cook in 1769 and by Capt. Bligh in the Bounty, 1788-89. Its beauty impressed Herman Melville, Paul Gauguin, and Charles Darwin.

French Southern and Antarctic Lands Overseas Territory, comprises **Adelie Land,** on Antarctica, and 4 island groups in the Indian O. Adelie, discovered 1840, has a research station, a coastline of 185 mi. and tapers 1,240 mi. inland to the South Pole. The U.S. does not recognize national claims in Antarctica. There are 2 huge glaciers, Ninnis, 22 mi. wide, 99 mi. long, and Mentz, 11 mi. wide, 140 mi. long. The Indian O. groups are:

Kerguelen Archipelago, discovered 1772, one large and 300 small islands. The chief is 87 mi. long, 74 mi. wide, and has Mt. Ross, 6,429 ft. tall. Principal research station is Port-aux-Francais. Seals often weigh 2 tons; there are blue whales, coal, peat, semi-precious stones. **Crozet Archipelago,** discovered 1772, covers 195 sq. mi. Eastern Island rises to 6,560 ft. **Saint Paul,** in southern Indian O., has warm springs with earth at places heating to 120° to 390° F. **Amsterdam** is nearby; both produce cod and rock lobster.

New Caledonia and its dependencies, an overseas territory, are a group of islands in the Pacific O. about 1,115 mi. E of Australia and approx. the same distance NW of New Zealand. Dependencies are the **Loyalty Islands,** the **Isle of Pines, Huon Islands** and the **Chesterfield Islands.**

New Caledonia, the largest, has 6,530 sq. mi. Total area of the territory is 8,548 sq. mi.; population (1980 est.) 139,600. The group was acquired by France in 1853.

The territory is administered by a governor and government council. There is a popularly elected Territorial Assembly. A deputy and a senator are elected to the French Parliament. Capital: Noumea.

Mining is the chief industry. New Caledonia is one of the world's largest nickel producers. Other minerals found are chrome, iron, cobalt, manganese, silver, gold, lead, and copper. Agricultural products include coffee, copra, cotton, manioc (cassava), corn, tobacco, bananas and pineapples.

Wallis and Futuna Islands, 2 archipelagos raised to status of overseas territory July 29, 1961, are in the SW Pacific S of the Equator between Fiji and Samoa. The islands have a total area of 106 sq. mi. and population (1981 est.) of 9,000. **Alofi,** attached to Futuna, is uninhabited. Capital: Mata-Utu. Chief products are copra, yams, taro roots, bananas. A senator and a deputy are elected to the French Parliament.

Gabon

Gabonese Republic

People: Population (1981 est.): 660,000. **Pop. density:** 5.72 per sq. mi. **Urban** (1970): 32.0%. **Ethnic groups:** Fangs 25%, Bapounon 10%, others. **Languages:** French (official), Bantu dialects. **Religions:** Tribal beliefs, Christian minority.

Geography: Area: 103,347 sq. mi., the size of Colorado. **Location:** On Atlantic coast of central Africa. **Neighbors:** Equatorial Guinea, Cameroon on N, Congo on E, S. **Topography:** Heavily forested, the country consists of coastal lowlands plateaus in N, E, and S, mountains in N, SE, and center. The Ogooue R. system covers most of Gabon. **Capital:** Libreville. **Cities** (1974 est.): Libreville 251,400; Port-Gentil 77,111.

Government: Head of state: Pres. Omar Bongo; b. Dec. 30, 1935; in office: Dec. 2, 1967. **Head of government:** Prime Min. Leon Mebiame, b. Sept. 1, 1934; in office: Apr. 16, 1975. **Local divisions:** 9 provinces. **Armed forces:** regulars 1,300; paramilitary 1,600.

Economy: Industries: Oil products. **Chief crops:** Cocoa, coffee, rice, peanuts, palm products, cassava, bananas. **Minerals:** Manganese, uranium, oil, iron, gas. **Crude oil reserves** (1980): 500 mln. bbls. **Other resources:** Timber. **Per capita arable land:** 1.2 acres. **Electricity prod.** (1978): 513.0 mln. kwh. **Labor force:** 65% agric.; 30% man.; 2.5% services.

Finance: Currency: CFA franc (Apr. 1982: 312.10 = $1 US). **Gross domestic product** (1979) $2.9 bln. **Per capita income** (1979): $4,487. **Imports** (1980): $835 mln.; partners (1978): Fr. 55%, U.S. 6%. **Exports** (1980): $2.17 bln.; partners (1978): Fr. 25%, U.S. 20%, Arg. 11%. **Tourists receipts** (1977): $17 mln. **National budget** (1981): $1.3 bln. revenues; $1.1 bln. expenditures. **International reserves less gold** (Oct. 1981): $237.6 mln. **Gold:** 13,000 oz t. **Consumer prices** (change in 1980): 12.3%.

Transport: Motor vehicles: in use (1976): 17,400 passenger cars, 12,700 comm. vehicles. **Civil aviation** (1980): 374 mln. passenger-km. **Chief ports** Libreville, Port-Gentil.

Communications: Television sets: 9,000 licensed (1977). **Radios:** 95,000 licensed (1978). **Telephones in use** (1980): 11,600.

Health: Life expectancy at birth (1961): 25 male; 45 female. **Births** (per 1,000 pop. 1978): 34. **Deaths** (per 1,000 pop. 1978): 22. **Natural increase** (1978): 1.2%. **Hospital beds** (per

100,000 pop. 1977): 736. **Physicians** (per 100,000 pop. 1977): 32. **Infant mortality** (per 1,000 live births 1979): 178.

Education (1978): **Literacy:** 40%. **Pop. 5-19:** in school: 74%, teachers per 1,000: 26.

France established control over the region in the second half of the 19th century. Gabon became independent Aug. 17, 1960. It is one of the most prosperous black African countries, thanks to abundant natural resources, foreign private investment, and government development programs.

The Gambia

Republic of The Gambia

People: Population (1981 est.): 620,000. **Age distrib.** (%): 0–14: 45.9; 15–59: 54.4; 60+: 3.8. **Pop. density:** 149.89 per sq. mi. **Urban** (1973): 15.9%. **Ethnic groups:** Mandinka 37.7%, Fula 16.2%, Wolof 14%, others. **Languages:** English (official), Mandinka, Wolof. **Religions:** Moslems 85%, Christian 14%.

Geography: Area: 4,127 sq. mi., smaller than Connecticut. **Location:** On Atlantic coast near western tip of Africa. **Neighbors:** Surrounded on 3 sides by Senegal. **Topography:** A narrow strip of land on each side of the lower Gambia. **Capital:** Banjul. **Cities** (1980 est.): Banjul 47,700.

Government: Head of state: Pres. Dawda Kairaba Jawara; b. May 16, 1924; in office: Apr. 24, 1970 (prime min. from June 12, 1962). **Local divisions:** 5 divisions and Banjul.

Economy: Industries: Tourism. **Chief crops:** Peanuts (main export), rice. **Per capita arable land:** 1.1 acres. **Fish catch** (1978): 10,800 metric tons. **Electricity prod.** (1978): 31.40 mln. kwh. **Labor force:** 78% agric.; 15.2% man.

Finance: Currency: Dalasi (Mar. 1982: 2.37 = $1 US). **Gross domestic product** (1979): $161 mln. **Per capita income** (1979): $275. **Imports** (1980): $164 mln.; partners (1979): UK 25%, China 13%, Fr. 9%, W. Ger. 8%. **Exports** (1980): $31.9 mln.; partners (1979): Neth. 22%, UK 14%, Swit. 13%. **Tourist receipts** (1977): $8 mln. **National budget** (1980): $35.1 mln. revenues; $33.3 mln. expenditures. **International reserves less gold** (Feb. 1982): $7.37 mln. **Consumer prices** (change in 1980): 6.7%.

Transport: Motor vehicles: in use (1973): 3,000 passenger cars, (1972): 2,500 comm. vehicles. **Chief ports:** Banjul.

Communications: Radios: 61,000 in use (1976). **Telephones in use** (1978): 2,779.

Health: Life expectancy at birth (1980): 32 male; 34 female. **Births** (per 1,000 pop. 1978): 49. **Deaths** (per 1,000 pop. 1978): 28. **Natural increase** (1978): 2.8%. **Hospital beds** (per 100,000 pop. 1977): 123. **Physicians** (per 100,000 pop. 1977): 8. **Infant mortality** (per 100,000 live births 1979): 217.

Education (1978): **Literacy:** 12%. **Pop. 5-19:** in school: 19%, teachers per 1,000: 10.

The tribes of Gambia were at one time associated with the West African empires of Ghana, Mali, and Songhay. The area became Britain's first African possession in 1588.

Independence came Feb. 18, 1965; republic status within the Commonwealth was achieved in 1970. Gambia is one of the only functioning democracies in Africa. The country suffered from severe famine in 1977-78.

An unsuccessful coup was launched July 30, 1981, while Pres. Jawara was in the UK for the royal wedding. In December, Gambia signed a treaty with Senegal to form a confederation of the 2 countries under the name of Senegambia. However, each country was to retain its sovereignty.

Germany

Now comprises 2 nations: Federal Republic of Germany (West Germany), German Democratic Republic (East Germany).

Germany, prior to World War II, was a central European nation composed of numerous states which had a common language and traditions and which had been united in one country since 1871; since World War II it has been split in 2 parts.

History and government. Germanic tribes were defeated by Julius Caesar, 55 and 53 BC, but Roman expansion N of the Rhine was stopped in 9 AD. Charlemagne, ruler of the Franks, consolidated Saxon, Bavarian, Rhenish, Frankish, and other lands; after him the eastern part became the German Empire. The Thirty Years' War, 1618-1648, split Germany into small principalities and kingdoms. After Napoleon, Austria contended with Prussia for dominance, but lost the Seven Weeks' War to Prussia, 1866. Otto von Bismarck, Prussian chancellor, formed the North German Confederation, 1867.

In 1870 Bismarck maneuvered Napoleon III into declaring war. After the quick defeat of France, Bismarck formed the **German Empire** and on Jan. 18, 1871, in Versailles, proclaimed King Wilhelm I of Prussia German emperor (Deutscher kaiser).

The German Empire reached its peak before World War I in 1914, with 208,780 sq. mi., plus a colonial empire. After that war Germany ceded Alsace-Lorraine to France; West Prussia and Posen (Poznan) province to Poland; part of Schleswig to Denmark; lost all of its colonies and the ports of Memel and Danzig.

Republic of Germany, 1919-1933, adopted the Weimar constitution; met reparation payments and elected Friedrich Ebert and Gen. Paul von Hindenburg presidents.

Third Reich, 1933-1945, Adolf Hitler led the National Socialist German Workers' (Nazi) party after World War I. In 1923 he attempted to unseat the Bavarian government and was imprisoned. Pres. von Hindenburg named Hitler chancellor Jan. 30, 1933; on Aug. 3, 1934, the day after Hindenburg's death, the cabinet joined the offices of president and chancellor and made Hitler fuehrer (leader). Hitler abolished freedom of speech and assembly, and began a long series of persecutions climaxed by the murder of millions of Jews and opponents.

Hitler repudiated the Versailles treaty and reparations agreements. He remilitarized the Rhineland 1936 and annexed Austria (Anschluss, 1938). At Munich he made an agreement with Neville Chamberlain, British prime minister, which permitted Hitler to annex part of Czechoslovakia. He signed a non-aggression treaty with the USSR, 1939. He declared war on Poland Sept. 1, 1939, precipitating World War II.

With total defeat near, Hitler committed suicide in Berlin Apr. 1945. The victorious Allies voided all acts and annexations of Hitler's Reich.

Postwar changes. The zones of occupation administered by the Allied Powers and later relinquished gave the USSR Saxony, Saxony-Anhalt, Thuringia, and Mecklenburg, and the former Prussian provinces of Saxony and Brandenburg.

The territory E of the Oder-Neisse line within 1937 boundaries comprising the provinces of Silesia, Pomerania, and the southern part of East Prussia, totaling about 41,220 sq. mi., was taken by Poland. Northern East Prussia was taken by the USSR.

The Western Allies ended the state of war with Germany in 1951. The USSR did so in 1955.

There was also created the area of Greater Berlin, within but not part of the Soviet zone, administered by the 4 occupying powers under the Allied Command. In 1948 the USSR withdrew, established its single command in East Berlin, and cut off supplies. The Allies utilized a gigantic airlift to bring food to West Berlin, 1948-1949. In Aug. 1961 the East Germans built a wall dividing Berlin, after over 3 million E. Germans had emigrated.

East Germany

German Democratic Republic

People: Population (1981 est.): 16,800,000. **Age distrib.** (%): 0–14: 20.6; 15–59: 58.7; 60+: 20.7. **Pop. density:** 413.32 per sq. mi. **Urban** (1976): 75.5%. **Ethnic groups:** Germans, Wends (0.7%). **Languages:** German. **Religions:** traditionally 80% Protestant.

Geography: Area: 41,825 sq. mi., the size of Virginia. **Location:** In E. Central Europe. **Neighbors:** W. Germany on W, Czechoslovakia on S, Poland on E. **Topography:** E. Germany lies mostly on the North German plains, with lakes in N, Harz Mtns., Elbe Valley, and sandy soil of Bradenburg in center, and highlands in S. **Capital:** East Berlin. **Cities** (1979 est.): East Berlin 1,133,854; Leipzig 563,912; Dresden 515,387.

Government: Head of state: Chmn. Erich Honecker; b. Aug. 25, 1912; in office: Oct. 29, 1976. **Head of government:** Prime Min. Willi Stoph; b. July 9, 1914; in office: Oct. 29, 1976. **Head of Communist Party:** Sec.-Gen. Erich Honecker; in office: May 3, 1971. **Local divisions:** 15 administrative districts. **Armed forces:** regulars 163,800 (1980).

Economy: Industries: Steel, chemicals, electrical prods., textiles, machinery. **Chief crops:** Grains, potatoes, sugar beets.

Minerals: Potash, lignite, uranium, coal. **Per capita arable land:** 0.7 acres. **Meat prod.** (1980): beef: 385,000 metric tons; pork: 1.15 mln. metric tons; lamb: 16,000 metric tons. **Fish catch** (1979): 224,400 metric tons. **Electricity prod.** (1978): 95.95 bln. kwh. **Crude steel prod.** (1981): 7.5 mln metric tons. **Labor force:** 10% agric.; 42.5% manuf.

Finance: Currency: Mark (July 1981: 2.40 = $1 US). **Gross national product** (1979): $89.1 bln. **Per capita income** (1979): $5,340. **Imports:** (1979): $16.21 bln.; partners (1979): USSR 36%, Czech. 7%, Pol. 7%, W. Ger. 6%. **Exports** (1979): $15.06 bln.; partners (1979): USSR 36%, Czech. 9%, Pol. 9%. **Tourists** (1977): 1,100,000.

Transport: Railway traffic (1979): 23.1 bln. passenger-km; 56.4 bln. net ton-km. **Motor vehicles:** in use (1979): 2.53 mln. passenger cars, 231,228 comm. vehicles; manuf. (1978): 177,000 passenger cars; 37,000 comm. vehicles. **Civil aviation** (1979): 1.8 bln. passenger-km; 67.3 mln. freight ton-km. **Chief ports:** Rostack, Wismar, Stralsund.

Communications: Television sets: 5.6 mln. licensed (1979), 489,000 manuf. (1978). **Radios:** 6.2 mln. licensed (1978), 1.10 mln. manuf. (1978). **Telephones in use** (1980): 3.071 mln. **Daily newspaper circ.** (1980): 517 per 1,000 pop.

Health: Life expectancy at birth (1981): 68.8 male; 74.7 female. **Births** (per 1,000 pop. 1980): 14.6. **Deaths** (per 1,000 pop. 1980): 14.2. **Natural increase** (1978): 0.0%. **Hospital beds** (per 100,000 pop. 1977): 1,065. **Physicians** (per 100,000 pop. 1977): 190. **Infant mortality** (per 1,000 live births 1981): 13.1.

Education (1981): **Literacy:** 99%. **Pop. 5-19:** in school: 66%, teachers per 1,000: 43.

The German Democratic Republic was proclaimed in the Soviet sector of Berlin Oct. 7, 1949. It was proclaimed fully sovereign in 1954, but 400,000 Soviet troops remain on grounds of security and the 4-power Potsdam agreement.

Coincident with the entrance of W. Germany into the European Defense community in 1952, the East German government decreed a prohibited zone 3 miles deep along its 600-mile border with W. Germany and cut Berlin's telephone system in two. Berlin was further divided by erection of a fortified wall in 1961, but the exodus of refugees to the West continued, though on a smaller scale.

E. Germany suffered severe economic problems until the mid-1960s. A "new economic system" was introduced, easing the former central planning controls and allowing factories to make profits provided they were reinvested in operations or redistributed to workers as bonuses. By the early 1970s, the economy was highly industrialized. In May 1972 the few remaining private firms were ordered sold to the government. The nation was credited with the highest standard of living among communist countries. But growth slowed in the late 1970s, due to shortages of natural resources and labor, and a huge debt to lenders in the West.

West Germany

Federal Republic of Germany

People: Population (1981 est.): 61,200,000. **Age distrib.** (%): 0–14: 20.3; 15–59: 58.4; 60+: 19.7. **Pop. density:** 642.49 per sq. mi. **Ethnic groups:** Germans, immigrant workers from Spain, Italy, Yugoslavia, Turkey. **Languages:** German. **Religions:** Protestant 49%, Roman Catholic 44%.

Geography: Area: 96,011 sq. mi., the size of Oregon. **Location:** In central Europe. **Neighbors:** Denmark on N, Netherlands, Belgium, Luxembourg, France on W, Switzerland, Austria on S, Czechoslovakia, E. Germany on E. **Topography:** West Germany is flat in N, hilly in center and W, and mountainous in Bavaria. Chief rivers are Elbe, Weser, Ems, Rhine, and Main, all flowing toward North Sea, and Danube, flowing toward Black Sea. **Capital:** Bonn. **Cities** (1979 est.): Berlin 1.9 mln.; Hamburg 1.6 mln.; Munich 1.2 mln.; Cologne 976,136; Essen 652,501; Frankfurt 628,203; Dortmund 609,954; Dusseldorf 594,770; Stuttgart 581,989.

Government: Head of state: Pres. Karl Carstens; b. Dec. 14, 1914; in office: July 1, 1979. **Head of government:** Chan. Helmut Schmidt; b. Dec. 23, 1918; in office: May 16, 1974. **Local divisions:** West Berlin and 10 laender (states) with substantial powers: Schleswig-Holstein, Hamburg, Lower Saxony, Bremen, North Rhine-Westphalia, Hessen, Rhineland-Palatinate, Baden-Wurttemberg, Bavaria, Saarland. **Armed forces:** regulars 495,000; reserves 1,250,000.

Economy: Industries: Steel, ships, oil products, autos, machinery, textiles, electrical and electronic equip., wine. **Chief crops:** Grains, potatoes, sugar beets, fruits, tobacco, nuts. **Minerals:** Coal, mercury, potash, lignite, iron, zinc, lead, copper, salt, oil. **Crude oil reserves** (1980): 480 mln. bbls. **Per capita arable land:** 0.3 acres. **Meat prod.** (1980): beef: 1.52 mln. metric tons; pork: 2.7 mln. metric tons; lamb: 28,000 metric tons. **Fish catch** (1979): 356,200 metric tons. **Electricity prod.** (1978): 353.41 bln. kwh. **Crude steel prod.** (1981): 41.6 mln. metric tons. **Labor force:** 6% agric.; 48% manuf.; 25% service.

Finance: Currency: Mark (Mar. 1982: 2.41 = $1 US). **Gross domestic product** (1980): $824.61 bln. **Per capita income** (1978): 9,278. **Imports** (1981): $163.9 bln.; partners (1980): Neth. 11%, Fr. 11%, It. 8%, Belg. 7%. **Exports** (1981): $176.09 bln.; partners (1980): Fr. 13%, Neth. 10%, Belg. 8%, It. 8%. **Tourists** (1979): 8.9 mln.; receipts $5.7 bln. **National budget** (1980): $109.7 bln. revenues; $125.6 bln. expenditures. **International reserves less gold** (Feb. 1982): $41.09 bln. **Gold:** 95.18 mln. oz t. **Consumer prices** (change in 1981): 5.3%.

Transport: Railway traffic (1979): 41 bln. passenger-km; 65 bln. net ton-km. **Motor vehicles:** in use (1980): 23.2 mln. passenger cars, 1.2 mln. comm. vehicles; manuf. (1980): 3.5 mln. passenger cars; 381,000 comm. vehicles. **Civil aviation:** 21 bln. passenger-km (1980); 1.5 bln. freight ton-km (1980). **Chief ports:** Hamburg, Bremen, Lubeck.

Communications: Television sets: 19.4 mln. licensed (1979), 4.2 mln. manuf. (1978). **Radios:** 21.1 mln. licensed (1979), 4.6 mln. manuf. (1978). **Telephones in use** (1980): 22.6 mln. **Daily newspaper circ.** (1980): 404 per 1,000 pop.

Health: Life expectancy at birth (1978): 69.0 male; 75.6 female. **Births** (per 1,000 pop. 1980): 10.0. **Deaths** (per 1,000 pop. 1980): 11.5. **Natural increase** (1978): –.3%. **Hospital beds** (per 100,000 pop. 1977): 1,178. **Physicians** (per 100,000 pop. 1977): 204. **Infant mortality** (per 1,000 live births 1978): 15.5.

Education (1978): **Literacy:** 99%. **Pop. 5-19:** in school: 67%, teachers per 1,000: 35.

The Federal Republic of Germany was proclaimed May 23, 1949, in Bonn, after a constitution had been drawn up by a consultative assembly formed by representatives of the 11 laender (states) in the French, British, and American zones. Later reorganized into 9 units, the laender numbered 10 with the addition of the Saar, 1957. Berlin also was granted land (state) status, but the 1945 occupation agreements placed restrictions on it.

The occupying powers, the U.S., Britain, and France, restored the civil status, Sept. 21, 1949. The U. S. resumed diplomatic relations July 2, 1951. The powers lifted controls and the republic became fully independent May 5, 1955.

Dr. Konrad Adenauer, Christian Democrat, was made chancellor Sept. 15, 1949, re-elected 1953, 1957, 1961. Willy Brandt, heading a coalition of Social Democrats and Free Democrats, became chancellor Oct. 21, 1969.

In 1970 Brandt signed friendship treaties with the USSR and Poland. In 1971, the U.S., Britain, France, and the USSR signed an agreement on Western access to West Berlin. In 1972 the Bundestag approved the USSR and Polish treaties and East and West Germany signed their first formal treaty, implementing the agreement easing access to West Berlin. In 1973 a West Germany-Czechoslovakia pact normalized relations and nullified the 1938 "Munich Agreement."

In May 1974 Brandt resigned, saying he took full responsibility for "negligence" for allowing an East German spy to become a member of his staff. Helmut Schmidt, Brandt's finance minister, succeeded him.

West Germany has experienced tremendous economic growth since the 1950s. The country leads Europe in provisions for worker participation in the management of industry.

The international economic recession began to affect W. Ger. in 1981, and unemployment rose sharply by year's end. The NATO decision to deploy medium-range nuclear missiles in Western Europe sparked a demonstration by some 300,000 protesters in Bonn in October.

Helgoland, an island of 130 acres in the North Sea, was taken from Denmark by a British Naval Force in 1807 and later ceded to Germany to become a part of Schleswig-Holstein province in return for rights in East Africa. The heavily fortified island was surrendered to UK, May 23, 1945, demilitarized in 1947, and returned to W. Germany, Mar 1, 1952. It is a free port.

Ghana

Republic of Ghana

People: Population (1981 est.): 12,500,000. **Age distrib.** (%): 0–14: 46.9; 15-59: 47.7; 60+: 5.3. **Pop. density:** 123 per sq. mi. **Urban** (1974): 31.4%. **Ethnic groups:** Akan 44%, Moshi-Dagomba 16%, Ewe 13%, Ga 8%, others. **Languages:** English (official), local Sudanic dialects. **Religions:** Christian 43%, Moslem 16%, animists 38%.

Geography: Area: 92,098 sq. mi., slightly smaller than Oregon. **Location:** On southern coast of W. Africa. **Neighbors:** Ivory Coast on W, Upper Volta on N, Togo on E. **Topography:** Most of Ghana consists of low fertile plains and scrubland, cut by rivers and by the artificial Lake Volta. **Capital:** Accra. **Cities** (1970 cen.): Accra 564,194; Kumasi 260,286.

Government: Head of government: Pres. Jerry Rawlings; in office: Dec. 31, 1981. **Local divisions:** 9 regions. **Armed forces:** regulars 20,000; para-military 3,000.

Economy: Industries: Aluminum, light industry. **Chief crops:** Cocoa (70% of exports), coffee, palm products, corn, rice, cassava, plantain, peanuts, yams, tobacco. **Minerals:** Gold, manganese, industrial diamonds, bauxite. **Crude oil reserves:** (1980): 7 mln. bbls. **Other resources:** Timber, rare woods, rubber. **Per capita arable land:** 0.2 acres. **Meat prod.** (1980): beef: 13,000 metric tons; pork: 9,000 metric tons; lamb: 11,000 metric tons. **Fish catch** (1979): 230,000 metric tons. **Electricity prod.** (1979): 4.70 bln. kwh. **Labor force:** 60% agric.; 10% man.

Finance: Currency: Cedi (Apr. 1982: 2.78 = $1 US). **Gross domestic product** (1979): $10.1 bln. **Per capita income** (1979): $380. **Imports** (1978): $937 mln.; partners (1978): UK 18%, W. Ger. 12%, Nigeria 12%. **Exports** (1978): $1.09 bln.; partners (1978): UK 16%, U.S. 16%, Neth. 9%, W. Ger. 9%. **Tourists** (1977): 58,900; receipts $6 mln. **National budget** (1979): $1.2 bln. revenues; $1.0 bln. expenditures. **International reserves less gold** (Jan. 1982): $164.4 mln. **Gold:** 314,000 oz t. **Consumer prices** (change in 1980): 50.1%.

Transport: Railway traffic (1980): 521 mln. passenger-km; 312 mln. net ton-km. **Motor vehicles:** in use (1978): 33,000 passenger cars, 27,000 comm. vehicles. **Civil aviation:** 324 mln. passenger-km (1980); 2.8 mln. freight ton-km (1980). **Chief ports:** Tema, Sekondi-Takoradi.

Communications: Television sets: 55,000 in use (1979). **Radios:** 1.09 mln. in use (1977), 90,000 manuf. (1975). **Telephones in use** (1980): 68,850. **Daily newspaper circ.** (1980): 35 per 1,000 pop.

Health: Life expectancy at birth (1975): 41.9 male; 45.1 female. **Births** (per 1,000 pop. 1978): 46. **Deaths** (per 1,000 pop. 1978): 14. **Natural increase** (1978): 3.3%. **Hospital beds** (per 100,000 pop. 1977): 146. **Physicians** (per 100,000 pop. 1977): 10. **Infant mortality** (per 1,000 live births 1975): 156.

Education (1978): **Literacy:** 30%. **Pop. 5–19:** in school: 45%, teachers per 1,000: 18.

Named for an African empire along the Niger River, 400-1240 AD, Ghana was ruled by Britain for 113 years as the Gold Coast. The UN in 1956 approved merger with the British Togoland trust territory. Independence came March 6, 1957. Republic status within the Commonwealth was attained in 1960.

Pres. Kwame Nkrumah built hospitals and schools, promoted development projects like the Volta R. hydroelectric and aluminum plants, but ran the country into debt, jailed opponents, and was accused of corruption. A 1964 referendum gave Nkrumah dictatorial powers and set up a one-party socialist state.

Nkrumah was overthrown in 1966 by a police-army coup, which expelled Chinese and East German teachers and technicians. Elections were held in 1969, but 4 further coups occurred in 1972, 1978, 1979, and 1981. The 1979 and 1981 coups were led by Flight Lieut. Jerry Rawlings. The stagnant economy has continued to deteriorate.

Greece

Hellenic Republic

People: Population (1981 est.): 9,600,000. **Age distrib.** (%): 0–14: 23.7; 15-59: 58.9; 60+: 17.5. **Pop. density:** 190.47 per sq. mi. **Urban** (1971): 64.8%. **Ethnic groups:** Greeks 98.5%, Turks 0.9%, Pomaks 0.3%, Armenians 0.2%. **Languages:** Greek, others. **Religions:** Greek Orthodox 97%.

Geography: Area: 50,962 sq. mi., the size of New York State. **Location:** Occupies southern end of Balkan Peninsula in SE Europe. **Neighbors:** Albania, Yugoslavia, Bulgaria on N, Turkey on E. **Topography:** About 75% of Greece is non-arable, with mountains in all areas. Pindus Mts. run through the country N to S. The heavily indented coastline is 9,385 mi. long. Of over 2,000 islands, only 169 are inhabited, among them Crete, Rhodes, Milos, Kerkira (Corfu), Chios, Lesbos, Samos, Euboea, Delos, Mykonos. **Capital:** Athens. **Cities** (1980 est.): Athens (met.) 3,300,000; Thessaloniki (met.) 800,000; Patras 120,000.

Government: Head of state: Pres. Constantine Karamanlis; b. Feb. 23, 1907; in office: May 15, 1980. **Head of government:** Prime Min. Andreas Papandreou; b. Feb. 5, 1919, in office: Oct. 21, 1981. **Local divisions:** 51 prefectures. **Armed forces:** regulars 184,600; reserves 290,000.

Economy: Industries: Textiles, chemicals, metals, wine, food processng, cement. **Chief crops:** Grains, corn, rice, cotton, tobacco, olives, citrus fruits, raisins, figs. **Minerals:** Bauxite, lignite, oil, manganese. **Crude oil reserves** (1980): 150 mln. bbls. **Per capita arable land:** 0.8 acres. **Meat prod.** (1980): beef: 98,000 metric tons; pork: 142,000 metric tons; lamb: 119,000 metric tons. **Fish catch** (1978): 106,000 metric tons. **Electricity prod.** (1979): 20.4 bln. kwh. **Crude steel prod.** (1981 est.): 901,000 metric tons. **Labor force:** 29% agric.; 30% manuf. 41% service.

Finance: Currency: Drachma (Mar. 1982: 63.02 = $1 US). **Gross domestic product** (1980): $43.8 bln. **Per capita income** (1980): $4,590. **Imports** (1980): $10.5 bln.; partners (1980): W. Ger. 14%, Jap. 11%, It. 8%, Fr. 6%. **Exports** (1980): $5.21 bln.; partners (1980): W. Ger. 18%, It. 10%, Fr. 7%, Saudi Ar. 5%. **Tourists** (1979): 5.2 mln.; receipts $1.66 bln. **National budget** (1980): $6.7 bln. revenues; $6.9 bln. expenditures. **International reserves less gold** (Jan. 1982): $633.3 mln. **Gold:** 3.85 mln. oz t. **Consumer prices** (change in 1981): 24.5%.

Transport: Railway traffic (1979): 1.53 bln. passenger-km; 841 mln. net ton-km. **Motor vehicles:** in use (1980): 877,900 passenger cars, 401,970 comm. vehicles. **Civil aviation:** 5.062 bln. passenger-km (1980); 68 mln. freight ton-km (1980). **Chief ports:** Piraeus, Thessaloniki, Patrai.

Communications: Television sets: 1.5 mln. in use (1978), 203,000 manuf. (1978). **Radios:** 3.3 mln. in use (1978). **Telephones in use** (1980): 2.6 mln. **Daily newspaper circ.** (1981): 69 per 1,000 pop.

Health: Life expectancy at birth (1978): 72 male; 75 female. **Births** (per 1,000 pop. 1979): 15.9. **Deaths** (per 1,000 pop. 1979): 8.7. **Natural increase** (1977): .7%. **Hospital beds** (per 100,000 pop. 1977): 638. **Physicians** (per 100,000 pop. 1977): 221. **Infant mortality** (per 1,000 live births 1978): 17.

Education (1978): Literacy: 95%. **Pop. 5–19:** in school: 70%, teachers per 1,000: 25.

The achievements of ancient Greece in art, architecture, science, mathematics, philosophy, drama, literature, and democracy became legacies for succeeding ages. Greece reached the height of its glory and power, particularly in the Athenian city-state, in the 5th century BC.

Greece fell under Roman rule in the 2d and 1st centuries BC. In the 4th century AD it became part of the Byzantine Empire and, after the fall of Constantinople to the Turks in 1453, part of the Ottoman Empire.

Greece won its war of independence from Turkey 1821-1829, and became a kingdom. A republic was established 1924; the monarchy was restored, 1935, and George II, King of the Hellenes, resumed the throne. In Oct., 1940, Greece rejected an ultimatum from Italy. Nazi support resulted in its defeat and occupation by Germans, Italians, and Bulgarians. By the end of 1944 the invaders withdrew. Communist resistance forces were defeated by Royalist and British troops. A plebiscite recalled King George II. He died Apr. 1, 1947, was succeeded by his brother, Paul I.

Communists waged guerrilla war 1947-49 against the government but were defeated with the aid of the U.S.

A period of reconstruction and rapid development followed, mainly with conservative governments under Premier Constantine Karamanlis. The Center Union led by George Papandreou won elections in 1963 and 1964. King Constantine, who acceded in 1964, forced Papandreou to resign. A period of political maneuvers ended in the military takeover of April 21, 1967, by Col. George Papadopoulos. King Constantine tried to reverse the consolidation of the harsh dictatorship Dec. 13, 1967, but failed and fled to Italy. Papadopoulos was ousted Nov. 25, 1973, in a coup led by rightist Brig. Demetrius Ioannides.

Greek army officers serving in the National Guard of Cyprus staged a coup on the island July 15, 1974. Turkey invaded Cyprus a week later, precipitating the collapse of the Greek junta, which was implicated in the Cyprus coup.

The military turned the government over to Karamanlis, who named a civilian cabinet, freed political prisoners, and sought to solve the Cyprus crisis. In Nov. 1974 elections his party won a large parliamentary majority, reduced by socialist gains in 1977. A Dec. 1974 referendum resulted in the proclamation of a republic.

Greece was reintegrated into the military wing of NATO in October 1980, and it became the 10th full member of the European Community on Jan. 1, 1981.

The 1981 victory of the Panhellenic Socialist Movement (Pasok) of Andreas Papandreou was expected to bring about substantial changes in the internal and external policies that Greece has pursued for the past 5 decades.

Grenada

State of Grenada

People: Population (1980 est.): 108,000. **Pop. density:** 812.03 per sq. mi. **Ethnic groups:** Negro 84%, mixed 11%. **Languages:** English, French-African patois. **Religions:** Catholic 64%, Anglican 22%.

Geography: Area: 133 sq. mi., twice the size of Washington, D.C. **Location:** Southernmost of West Indies, 90 mi. N. of Venezuela. **Topography:** Main island is mountainous; country includes Carriacon and Petit Martinique islands. **Capital:** St. George's. **Cities** (1978 est.): St. George's 30,813.

Government: Head of state: Queen Elizabeth II, represented by Gov.-Gen. Paul Scoon, b. July 4, 1935; in office: Sept. 30, 1978. **Head of government:** Prime Min. Maurice Bishop, b. May 29, 1944; in office: Mar. 13, 1979. **Local divisions:** 6 parishes and one dependency.

Economy: Industries: Rum. **Chief crops:** Nutmegs, bananas, cocoa, sugar, mace. **Per capita arable land:** 0.05 acres. **Electricity prod.** (1977): 28.00 mln. kwh. **Labor force:** 31% agric.; 6% man.; 62.8% service.

Finance: Currency: East Caribbean dollar (Apr. 1982: 2.70 = $1 US). **Gross domestic product** (1977 est.): $54 mln. **Per capita income** (1977): $500. **Imports** (1979): $45 mln.; partners (1979): UK 21%, Trin./Tob. 20%. **Exports** (1979): $22 mln.; partners (1979): UK 40%, W. Ger. 17%, Belg.-Lux 16%. **Tourists** (1978): 32,300; receipts $10 mln. **National budget** (1980): $38.1 mln. revenues; $38.1 mln. expenditures. **International reserves less gold** (Sept. 1981): $13.95 mln.

Transport: Motor vehicles: in use (1971): 3,800 passenger cars, 100 comm. vehicles. **Chief ports:** Saint George's.

Communications: Radios: 22,000 in use (1976). **Telephones in use** (1978): 5,217. **Daily newspaper circ.** (1970): 2,600.

Health: Life expectancy at birth (1961): 60.14 male; 65.60 female. **Births** (per 1,000 pop. 1975): 27.4. **Deaths** (per 1,000 pop. 1975): 5.9. **Natural increase** (1975): 2.2%. **Infant mortality** (per 1,000 live births 1979): 23.5.

Columbus sighted the island 1498. First European settlers were French, 1650. The island was held alternately by France and England until final British occupation, 1784. Grenada became fully independent Feb. 7, 1974 during a general strike. It is the smallest independent nation in the Western Hemisphere. In 1982, the U.S. criticized the government for following Soviet and Cuban policies.

Guatemala

Republic of Guatemala

People: Population (1981 est.): 7,200,000. **Age distrib.** (%): 0–14: 45.1; 15–59: 50.6; 60+: 4.4. **Pop. density:** 172.68 per sq. mi. **Urban** (1975): 35.6%. **Ethnic groups:** Indians 54%, Mestizos 42%, whites 4%. **Languages:** Spanish, Indian dialects. **Religions:** Roman Catholics over 88%; Mayan religion practiced.

Geography: Area: 42,042 sq. mi., the size of Tennessee. **Location:** In Central America. **Neighbors:** Mexico N, W; El Salvador on S, Honduras, Belize on E. **Topography:** The central highland and mountain areas are bordered by the narrow Pacific coast and the lowlands and fertile river valleys on the Caribbean. There are numerous volcanoes in S, more than half a dozen over 11,000 ft. **Capital:** Guatemala City. **Cities** (1981 est.): Guatemala City 1,307,300.

Government: Head of state: Pres. Efrain Rios Monet; in office: Mar. 23, 1982. **Local divisions:** Guatemala City and 22 departments. **Armed forces:** regulars 17,960; para-military 3,000.

Economy: Industries: Prepared foods, tires, textiles. **Chief crops:** Coffee (one third of exports), sugar, bananas, cotton. **Minerals:** Oil, nickel. **Crude oil reserves** (1980): 16 mln. bbls. **Other resources:** Rare woods, fish, chicle. **Per capita arable land:** 0.5 acres. **Meat prod.** (1980): beef: 79,000 metric tons; pork: 16,000 metric tons. **Electricity prod.** (1979): 1.49 bln. kwh. **Labor force:** 53% agric.; 17.2% manuf., 23.3% services.

Finance: Currency: Quetzal (Apr. 1982: 1.00 = $1 US). **Gross domestic product** (1980): $7.8 bln. **Per capita income** (1980): $1,083. **Imports** (1980): $1.70 bln.; partners (1979): U.S. 32%, El Salv. 11%, Jap. 8%, W. Ger. 7%, Venez. 7%. **Exports** (1980): $1.55 bln.; partners (1979): U.S. 29%, W. Ger. 9%, El Salv. 12%, Jap. 8%. **Tourists** (1977): 444,800; receipts: $105 mln. **National budget** (1980): $407 mln. revenues; $603 mln. expenditures. **International reserves less gold** (Feb. 1982): $82.2 mln. **Gold:** 522,000 oz t. **Consumer prices** (change in 1981): 11.4%.

Transport: Railway traffic (1976): 117 mln. net ton-km. **Motor vehicles:** in use (1979): 147,500 passenger cars, 73,100 comm. vehicles. **Civil aviation:** 159 mln. passenger-km (1980); 6.4 mln. freight ton-km (1980). **Chief ports:** Puerto Barrios, San Jose.

Communications: Television sets: 150,000 in use (1977). **Radios:** 280,000 in use (1978). **Telephones in use** (1980): 81,600. **Daily newspaper circ.** (1980): 25 per 1,000 pop.

Health: Life expectancy at birth (1965): 48.29 male; 49.74 female. **Births** (per 1,000 pop. 1978): 42. **Deaths** (per 1,000 pop. 1978): 11. **Natural increase** (1978): 3.1% **Hospital beds** (per 100,000 pop. 1977): 187. **Physicians** (per 100,000 pop. 1977): 40. **Infant mortality** (per 1,000 live births 1981): 77.

Education (1981): **Literacy:** 47%. **Pop. 5-19:** in school: 31%, teachers per 1,000: 11.

The old Mayan Indian empire flourished in what is today Guatemala for over 1,000 years before the Spanish.

Guatemala was a Spanish colony 1524-1821; briefly a part of Mexico and then of the U.S. of Central America, the republic was established in 1839.

Since 1945 when a liberal government was elected to replace the long-term dictatorship of Jorge Ubico, the country has seen a swing toward socialism, an armed revolt, renewed attempts at social reform and a military coup. Assassinations and political violence from left and right plagued the country. The Guerrilla Army of the Poor, an insurgent group founded 1975, has stepped up their military offensive by attacking army posts and has succeeded in incorporating segments of the large Indian population in its struggle against the government.

Dissident army officers seized power, Mar. 23, 1982, denouncing the Mar. 7 Presidential election as fraudulent and pledging to restore "authentic democracy" to the nation. Political violence has caused some 200,000 Guatemalans to seek refuge in Mexico.

Guinea

People's Revolutionary Republic of Guinea

People: Population (1981 est.): 5,600,000. **Pop. density:** 55.83 per sq. mi. **Ethnic groups:** Foulah 40%, Malinké 25%, Soussous 10%, 15 other tribes. **Languages:** French (official), tribal languages. **Religions:** Mostly Muslims.

Geography: Area: 94,925 sq. mi., slightly smaller than Oregon. **Location:** On Atlantic coast of W. Africa. **Neighbors:** Guinea-Bissau, Senegal, Mali on N, Ivory Coast on E, Liberia on S. **Topography:** A narrow coastal belt leads to the mountainous middle region, the source of the Gambia, Senegal, and Niger rivers. Upper Guinea, farther inland, is a cooler upland. The SE is forested. **Capital:** Conakry. **Cities** (1980 est.): Conakry 575,000; Labe 419,000; N'Zerekore 291,000; Kankan 265,000.

Government: Head of state: Pres. Ahmed Sékou Touré; b.

Jan. 9, 1922; in office: Oct. 2, 1958. **Head of government:** Prime Min. Louis Lansana Beavogui; b. 1923; in office: Apr. 26, 1972. **Local divisions:** 33 districts. **Armed forces:** regulars 8,650; para-military 8,000.

Economy: Chief crops: Bananas, pineapples, rice, corn, palm nuts, coffee, honey. **Minerals:** Bauxite, iron, diamonds. **Per capita arable land:** 2.2 acres. **Meat prod.** (1980): beef 18,000 metric tons. **Electricity prod.** (1977) 500.00 mln. kwh. **Labor force:** 84% agric.; 9% man.

Finance: Currency: Syli (Mar. 1979: 19.2 = $1 US). **Gross domestic product** (1978 est.): $1.2 bln. **Per capita income** (1978): $140. **Imports** (1978): $276 mln.; partners (1977): Fr. 20% USSR 11%, U.S. 6% It. 6%. **Exports** (1978): $342 mln.; partners (1977): U.S. 18%, Fr. 13%, W. Ger. 12%, USSR 12%.

Transport: Motor vehicles: in use (1972): 10,200 passenger cars, 10,800 comm. vehicles. **Chief ports:** Conakry.

Communications: Radios: 120,000 in use (1976). **Daily newspaper circ.** (1980): 2 per 1,000 pop.

Health: Life expectancy at birth (1975): 39.4 male; 42.6 female. **Births** (per 1,000 pop. 1978): 47. **Deaths** (per 1,000 pop. 1978): 26. **Natural increase** (1978): 2.6%. **Hospital beds** (per 100,000 pop. 1977): 158. **Physicians** (per 100,000 pop. 1977): 6. **Infant mortality** (per 1,000 live births 1980): 172.

Education (1978): **Literacy:** 15%. **Pop. 5-19:** in school: 18%, teachers per 1,000: 8.

Part of the ancient West African empires, Guinea fell under French control 1849-98. Under Sekou Toure, it opted for full independence in 1958, and France withdrew all aid.

Toure turned to communist nations for support, and set up a militant one-party state. France and Guinea restored ties in 1975, after a 10-year break. Western firms, as well as the Soviet government, have invested in Guinea's vast bauxite mines.

According to reports, thousands of opponents were jailed in the 1970s, in the aftermath of an unsuccessful Portuguese invasion. Many were tortured and killed.

Guinea-Bissau

Republic of Guinea-Bissau

People: Population (1981 est.): 660,000. **Pop. density:** 39.43 per sq. mi. **Ethnic groups:** Balanta 30%, Fula 20%, Mandyako 14%, other tribes. **Languages:** Portuguese (official), Crioulo, tribal languages. **Religions:** Moslems 30%, Christians 1%, others.

Geography: Area: 13,948 sq. mi. **Location:** On Atlantic coast of W. Africa. **Neighbors:** Senegal on N, Guinea on E, S. **Topography:** A swampy coastal plain covers most of the country; to the east is a low savanna region. **Capital:** Bissau. **Cities** (1979): Bissau 109,500.

Government: Head of government: Gen. Joao Bernardo Vieira. **Local divisions:** 8 regions. **Armed forces:** regulars 6,100; para-military 2,000.

Economy: Chief crops: Peanuts, (60% of exports). **Minerals:** Bauxite, oil. **Per capita arable land:** 1.1 acres. **Electricity prod.** (1977): 24.00 mln. kwh. **Labor force:** 86% agric.

Finance: Currency: Peso (Sept. 1981: 37.93 = $1 US). **Gross domestic product** (1976 est.): $200 mln. **Per capita income** (1976): $330. **Imports** (1979): $50 mln.; partners: Port. 27%, Swed. 10%, USSR 9%, Fr. 9%. **Exports** (1979): $14 mln.; partners: Port. 38%, Ang. 23%, Sp. 21%.

Communications: Radios: 11,000 licensed (1976). **Daily newspaper circ.** (1980): 2 per 1,000 pop.

Health: Life expectancy at birth (1975): 37.0 male; 40.1 female. **Births** (per 1,000 pop. 1978): 40. **Deaths** (per 1,000 pop. 1978): 23. **Natural increase** (1978): 1.7%. **Infant mortality** (per 1,000 live births 1969): 47.1.

Portuguese mariners explored the area in the mid-15th century; the slave trade flourished in the 17th and 18th centuries, and colonization began in the 19th.

Beginning in the 1960s, an independence movement waged a guerrilla war and formed a government in the interior that achieved international support. Full independence came Sept. 10, 1974, after the Portuguese regime was overthrown.

The November 1980 coup gave Joao Bernardo Vieira absolute power.

Guyana

Cooperative Republic of Guyana

People: Population (1981 est.): 850,000. **Age distrib.** (%): 0–14: 43.7; 5–59: 50.7; 60+: 5.6. **Pop. density:** 9.88 per sq. mi. **Urban** (1971): 29.6%. **Ethnic groups:** East Indians 50%, African 30%, mixed 10%. **Languages:** English (official), Hindi, Portuguese, Chinese, Negro patois. **Religions:** Christians 45%, Hindus 37%, Moslems 9%, others.

Geography: Area: 83,000 sq. mi., the size of Idaho. **Location:** On N coast of S. America. **Neighbors:** Venezuela on W, Brazil on S, Suriname on E. **Topography:** Dense tropical forests cover much of the land, although a flat coastal area up to 40 mi. wide, where 90% of the population lives, provides rich alluvial soil for agriculture. A grassy savanna divides the 2 zones. **Capital:** Georgetown. **Cities** (1979 est.): Georgetown 195,000.

Government: Head of state and Head of government: Prime Min. and President Linden Forbes Burnham; b. Feb. 20, 1923; in office: Dec. 14, 1964. **Local divisions:** 6 regions. **Armed forces:** regulars 5,000; para-military 10,000.

Economy: Industries: Cigarettes, rum, clothing, furniture, drugs. **Chief crops:** Sugar, rice, citrus and other fruits. **Minerals:** Bauxite, diamonds. **Other resources:** Timber, shrimp. **Per capita arable land:** 1.1 acres. **Fish catch** (1978): 17,700 metric tons. **Electricity prod.** (1978): 405 bln. kwh. **Labor force:** 30% agric.

Finance: Currency: Dollar (Mar. 1982: 3.00 = $1 US). **Gross domestic product** (1977): $437 mln. **Per capita income** (1977): $437. **Imports** (1979): $317 mln.; partners (1978): U.S. 23%, Trin-Tob. 27%, UK 22%. **Exports** (1980): $386 mln.; partners (1978): UK 30%, U.S. 20%, Trin-Tob. 7%. **Tourist receipts** (1979): $3 mln. **National budget** (1979): $205 mln. revenues; $262 mln. expenditures. **International reserves less gold** (Feb. 1982): $2.30 mln. **Consumer prices** (change in 1980): 14.1%.

Transport: Railway traffic (1974): 6 mln. passenger-km. **Motor vehicles:** in use (1977): 28,400 passenger cars, 14,700 comm. vehicles. **Chief ports:** Georgetown.

Communications: Radios: 275,000 in use (1976). **Telephones in use** (1978): 27,064. **Daily newspaper circ.** (1980): 2 per 1,000 pop.

Health: Life expectancy at birth (1961): 59.03 male; 63.01 female. **Births** (per 1,000 pop. 1978): 28.3. **Deaths** (per 1,000 pop. 1978): 7.3. **Natural increase** (1978): 2.1% **Hospital beds** (per 100,000 pop. 1977): 485. **Physicians** (per 100,000 pop. 1977): 25. **Infant mortality** (per 1,000 live births 1972): 50.5.

Education (1978): **Literacy:** 85%. **Pop. 5-19:** in school: 62%, teachers per 1,000: 24.

Guyana became a Dutch possession in the 17th century, but sovereignty passed to Britain in 1815. Indentured servants from India soon outnumbered African slaves. Ethnic tension has affected political life.

Guyana became independent May 26, 1966. A Venezuelan claim to the western half of Guyana was suspended in 1970 until June 1982. Venezuela has indicated that it intends to pursue its long-standing claim. The Suriname border is also disputed. The government has nationalized most of the economy which has remained severely depressed.

The Port Kaituma ambush of U.S. Rep. Leo J. Ryan and others investigating mistreatment of American followers of the Rev. Jim Jones' People's Temple cult, triggered a mass suicide-execution of 911 cultists in the Guyana jungle, Nov. 18, 1979.

Haiti

Republic of Haiti

People: Population (1981 est.): 6,000,000. **Age distrib.** (%): 4–14: 41.2; 15–59: 52.9; 60+: 5.9. **Pop. density:** 535.75 per sq. mi. **Urban** (1979): 24.9%. **Ethnic groups:** African descent 95%. **Languages:** French (official), Creole (majority). **Religions:** Roman Catholics 80%, Protestants 10%; Voodoo widely practiced.

Geography: Area: 10,714 sq. mi., the size of Maryland. **Location:** In West Indies, occupies western third of I. of Hispaniola. **Neighbors:** Dominican Republic on E, Cuba on W. **Topography:** About two-thirds of Haiti is mountainous. Much of the rest is semiarid. Coastal areas are warm and moist. **Capital:** Port-au-

Prince. **Cities** (1978 est.): Port-au-Prince 745,700; Cap-Haitien 50,000.

Government: Head of state: Pres. Jean-Claude Duvalier; b. July 3, 1951; in office: Apr. 22, 1971. **Local divisions:** 9 departments. **Armed forces:** regulars 6,550; para-military 14,900.

Economy: Industries: Rum, molasses, tourism. **Chief crops:** Coffee, sisal, cotton, sugar, bananas, cocoa, tobacco, rice. **Minerals:** Bauxite, copper, gold, silver, metric tons. **Other resources:** Timber. **Per capita arable land:** 0.3 acres. **Meat prod.** (1980): beef: 24,000 metric tons; pork: 33,000 metric tons; lamb: 6,000 metric tons. **Electricity prod.** (1980): 350 mln. kwh. **Labor force:** 79% agric.; 7% man.; 14% services.

Finance: Currency: Gourde (Apr. 1982: 5.00 = $1 US). **Gross domestic product** (1978): $1.34 bln. **Per capita income** (1980): $260. **Imports** (1978): $221 mln.; partners: U.S. 45%, Neth. Ant. 10%, Jap. 9%. Can. 8%. **Exports** (1980): $185 mln.; partners (1978): U.S. 59%, Fr. 13%, It. 7%, Belg. 6%. **Tourists** (1977): 96,000; receipts $37 mln. **National budget** (1979): $94 mln. revenues; $94 mln. expenditures. **International reserves less gold** (Aug. 1981): $8.0 mln. **Gold:** 18,000 oz t. **Consumer prices** (change in 1980): 17.9%.

Transport: Motor vehicles: in use (1979): 23,900 passenger cars, 8,500 comm. vehicles. **Chief ports:** Port-au-Prince, Les Cayes.

Communications: Television sets: 15,000 in use (1978). **Radios:** 100,000 in use (1978). **Telephones in use** (1980): 34,900 **Daily newspaper circ.** (1980): 30 per 1,000 pop.

Health: Life expectancy at birth (1975): 47.1 male; 50.0 female. **Births** (per 1,000 pop. 1978): 42. **Deaths** (per 1,000 pop. 1978): 16. **Natural increase** (1978): 2.4%. **Hospital beds** (per 100,000 pop. 1977): 72. **Physicians** (per 100,000 pop. 1977): 7.

Education (1978): **Literacy:** 23% **Pop. 5-19:** in school: 33%, teachers per 1,000: 9.

Haiti, visited by Columbus, 1492, and a French colony from 1677, attained its independence, 1804, following the rebellion led by former slave Toussaint L'Ouverture. Following a period of political violence, the U.S. occupied the country 1915-34.

Dr. Francois Duvalier was voted president in 1957; in 1964 he was named president for life. Upon his death in 1971, he was succeeded by his son, Jean-Claude. Drought in 1975-77 brought famine, and Hurricane Allen in 1980 destroyed most of the rice, bean, and coffee crops.

Honduras

Republic of Honduras

People: Population (1981 est.): 3,900,000. **Age distrib.** (%): 0–14: 48.1; 15–59: 47.5; 60+: 4.5. **Pop. density:** 85.26 per sq. mi. **Urban** (1974): 31.4%. **Ethnic groups:** Mestizo 90%, Caucasian, Negroes, Indians. **Languages:** Spanish, Indian dialects. **Religions:** Roman Catholics, small Protestant minority.

Geography: Area: 43,277 sq. mi., slightly larger than Tennessee. **Location:** In Central America. **Neighbors:** Guatemala on W, El Salvador, Nicaragua on S. **Topography:** The Caribbean coast is 500 mi. long. Pacific coast, on Gulf of Fonseca, is 40 mi. long. Honduras is mountainous, with wide fertile valleys and rich forests. **Capital:** Tegucigalpa. **Cities** (1980 est.) Tegucigalpa 444,700; San Pedro Sula 150,991.

Government: Head of State: Pres. Roberto Suazo Cordova; in office: Jan. 27, 1982. **Local divisions:** 18 departments. **Armed forces:** regulars 11,300; para-military 3,000.

Economy: Industries: Clothing, textiles, cement, chemicals. **Chief crops:** Bananas (chief export), coffee, cotton, sugar, timber, tobacco. **Minerals:** Gold, silver, copper, lead, zinc, iron, antimony, coal. **Other resources:** Timber. **Per capita arable land:** 0.5 acres. **Meat prod.** (1980): beef: 56,000 metric tons; pork: 9,000 metric tons. **Electricity prod.** (1978): 755 mln. kwh. **Labor force:** 56% agric.; 19% man.; 11% service.

Finance: Currency: Lempira (Apr. 1982): 2.00 = $1 US). **Gross domestic product** (1980): $2.55 bln. **Per capita income** (1978): $528. **Imports** (1980): $1.02 bln.; partners (1979): U.S. 44%, Venez. 8%, Jap. 7%, Guat. 6%. **Exports** (1980): $806 mln.; partners (1979): U.S. 54%, W. Ger. 10%, Jap. 5%, Neth. 8%. **Tourist receipts** (1977): $14 mln. **National budget** (1980): $378 mln. revenues; $448 mln. expenditures. **International reserves less gold** (Dec. 1981): $101.00 mln. **Gold:** 16,000 oz t. **Consumer prices** (change in 1979): 9.0%.

Transport: Motor vehicles: in use (1979) 19,800 passenger cars, 42,400 comm. vehicles. **Civil aviation:** 394 mln. passenger-km (1980); 3.5 mln. freight ton-km (1980). **Chief ports:** Puerto Cortes, La Ceiba.

Communications: Television sets: 48,000 in use (1977). **Radios:** 163,000 in use (1977). **Telephones in use** (1980): 27,400. **Daily newspaper circ.** (1980): 67 per 1,000 pop.

Health: Life expectancy at birth (1975): 52.4 male; 55.9 female. **Births** (per 1,000 pop. 1978): 47. **Deaths** (per 1,000 pop. 1978): 12. **Natural increase** (1978): 3.5%. **Hospital beds** (per 100,000 pop. 1977): 32. **Physicians** (per 100,000 pop. 1977): 137. **Infant mortality** (per 1,000 live births 1975): 31.4.

Education (1978): **Literacy:** 58%. **Pop. 5-19:** in school: 42%, teachers per 1,000: 14.

Mayan civilization flourished in Honduras in the 1st millenium AD. Columbus arrived in 1502. Honduras became independent after freeing itself from Spain, 1821 and from the Fed. of Central America, 1838.

Gen. Oswaldo Lopez Arellano, president for most of the period 1963-75 by virtue of one election and 2 coups, was ousted by the Army in 1975 over charges of pervasive bribery by United Brands Co. of the U.S.

The government has resumed land distribution, raised minimum wages, and started a literacy campaign. An elected civilian government took power in 1982, the country's first in 10 years.

There were several border clashes with Nicaragua during 1982. The U.S. has provided military aid and advisors to help withstand pressures from Nicaragua and help block arms shipments from Nicaragua to rebel forces in El Salvador.

Hungary

Hungarian People's Republic

People: Population (1981 est.): 10,800,000. **Age distrib.** (%): 0–14: 21.0; 15–59: 61.5; 60+: 17.5. **Pop. density:** 297.61 per sq. mi. **Urban** (1977): 51.8%. **Ethnic groups:** Magyar 98%, German 0.5%, Slovak 0.3%, Gypsy 0.3%, Croatian 0.3%. **Languages:** Hungarian (Magyar). **Religions:** Roman Catholics 61%.

Geography: Area: 35,919 sq. mi., slightly smaller than Indiana. **Location:** In East Central Europe. **Neighbors:** Czechoslovakia on N, Austria on W, Yugoslavia on S, Romania, USSR on E. **Topography:** The Danube R. forms the Czech border in the NW, then swings S to bisect the country. The eastern half of Hungary is mainly a great fertile plain, the Alfold; the W and N are hilly. **Capital:** Budapest. **Cities** (1978 est.): Budapest 2,085,615; Miskolc 205,610; Debrecen 193,958.

Government: Head of state: Pres. Pal Losonczi; b. Sept. 18, 1919; in office: Apr. 14, 1967. **Head of government:** Prem. Gyorgy Lazar; b. Sept. 15, 1924; in office: May 15, 1975. **Head of Communist Party:** Janos Kadar; b. May 26, 1912; in office: Oct. 25, 1956. **Local divisions:** 19 counties, 5 cities with county status. **Armed forces:** regulars 93,500 (1981).

Economy: Industries: Iron and steel, machinery, chemicals, vehicles, communications equip., milling, distilling. **Chief crops:** Grains, vegetables, fruits, grapes. **Minerals:** Bauxite, natural gas. **Per capita arable land:** 1.2 acres. **Meat prod.** (1980): beef: 135,000 metric tons; pork: 900,000 metric tons. **Fish catch** (1978): 32,600 metric tons. **Electricity prod.** (1978): 25.42 bln. kwh. **Crude steel prod.** (1981 est.): 3.6 mln. metric tons. **Labor force:** 23% agric.; 36% manuf.

Finance: Currency: Forint (Oct. 1981: 33.56 = $1 US). **Net material product** (1979): $16.9 bln. **Per capita income** (1980): $3,000. **Imports** (1980): $8.67 bln.; partners (1980): USSR 28%, W. Ger. 12%, E. Ger. 7%, Czech. 5%. **Exports** (1979): $7.94 bln.; partners 1980): USSR 29%, E. Ger. 7%, W. Ger. 10%, Czech. 6%. **Tourists** (1977): 7,194,000; receipts $320 mln. **Consumer prices** (change in 1979): 8.8%.

Transport: Railway traffic (1979): 12.3 bln. passenger-km; 23.8 bln. net ton-km. **Motor vehicles:** in use (1980): 1,021,330 passenger cars, 124,540 comm. vehicles; manuf. (1980): 14,000 comm. vehicles. **Civil aviation** (1980): 998 mln. Passenger-km; 19 mln. net freight-km.

Communications: Television sets: 2.7 mln. licensed (1979), 425,000 manuf. (1978). **Radios:** 2.60 mln. licensed (1979), 264,000 manuf. (1978). **Telephones in use** (1980): 1.1 mln. **Daily newspaper circ.** (1980): 275 per 1,000 pop.

Health: Life expectancy at birth (1979): 66.7 male; 73.6 female. **Births** (per 1,000 pop. 1980): 13.9 **Deaths** (per 1,000 pop. 1980): 13.6. **Natural increase** (1978): .3%. **Hospital beds** (per 100,000 pop. 1977): 690. **Physicians** (per 100,000 pop. 1977): 230. **Infant mortality** (per 1,000 live births 1979): 24.

Education (1978): **Literacy:** 98%. **Pop. 5-19:** in school: 56%, teachers per 1,000: 27.

Earliest settlers, chiefly Slav and Germanic, were overrun by Huns and Magyars from the east. Stephen I (997-1038) was made king by Pope Sylvester II in 1000 AD. The country suffered repeated Turkish invasions in the 15th-17th centuries. After the defeats of the Turks, 1686-1697, Austria dominated, but Hungary obtained concessions until it regained internal independence in 1867, with the emperor of Austria as king of Hungary in a dual monarchy with a single diplomatic service. Defeated with the Central Powers in 1918, Hungary lost Transylvania to Romania, Croatia and Bacska to Yugoslavia, Slovakia and Carpatho-Ruthenia to Czechoslovakia, all of which had large Hungarian minorities. A republic under Michael Karolyi and a bolshevist revolt under Bela Kun were followed by a vote for a monarchy in 1920 with Admiral Nicholas Horthy as regent.

Hungary joined Germany in World War II, and was allowed to annex most of its lost territories. Russian troops captured the country, 1944-1945. By terms of an armistice with the Allied powers Hungary agreed to give up territory acquired by the 1938 dismemberment of Czechoslovakia and to return to its borders of 1937.

A republic was declared Feb. 1, 1946; Zoltan Tildy was elected president. In 1947 the communists forced Tildy out. Premier Imre Nagy, in office since mid-1953, was ousted for his moderate policy of favoring agriculture and consumer production, April 18, 1955.

In 1956, popular demands for the ousting of Erno Gero, Communist party secretary, and for formation of a government by Nagy, resulted in the latter's appointment Oct. 23; demonstrations against communist rule developed into open revolt. Gero called in Soviet forces. On Nov. 4 Soviet forces launched a massive attack against Budapest with 200,000 troops, 2,500 tanks and armored cars.

Estimates varied from 6,500 to 32,000 dead, and thousands deported. About 200,000 persons fled the country. The U.S. received 38,248 under a refugee emergency program. In the spring of 1963 the regime freed many anti-communists and captives from the revolution in a sweeping amnesty. Nagy was executed by the Russians.

Some 40,000 Soviet troops are stationed in Hungary. Hungarian troops participated in the 1968 Warsaw Pact invasion of Czechoslovakia.

Major economic reforms were launched early in 1968, switching from a central planning system to one in which market forces and profit control much of production. Productivity and living standards have improved. Hungary leads the communist states in comparative tolerance for cultural freedoms and small private enterprise which accounted for about 5% of sales during 1982.

Iceland

Republic of Iceland

People: Population (1981 est.): 230,000. **Age distrib.** (%): 0–14: 29.0; 15–59: 58.0; 60+: 13.1. **Pop. density:** 5.79 per sq. mi. **Urban** (1977): 87.4% **Ethnic groups:** Homogeneous, descendants of Norwegians, Celts. **Language:** Icelandic. **Religon:** Lutherans 97%.

Geography: Area: 39,769 sq. mi., the size of Virginia. **Location:** At N end of Atlantic O. **Neighbors:** Nearest is Greenland. **Topography:** Iceland is of recent volcanic origin. Three-quarters of the surface is wasteland: glaciers, lakes, a lava desert. There are geysers and hot springs, and the climate is moderated by the Gulf Stream. **Capital:** Reykjavik. **Cities** (1980 est.): Reykjavik 83,500.

Government: Head of state: Pres. Vigdis Finnbogadottir; b. Apr. 15, 1930; in office: Aug. 1, 1980. **Head of government:** Prime Min. Gunnar Thoroddsen, b. Dec. 29, 1910; in office: Feb. 8, 1980. **Local divisions:** 7 districts.

Economy: Industries: Fish products (75% of exports), aluminum. **Chief crops:** Potatoes, turnips, hay. **Per capita arable land:** 0.09 acres. **Meat prod.** (1980): lamb: 16,000 metric tons. **Fish catch** (1979): 1.6 mln. metric tons. **Electricity prod.** (1980): 3.14 bln. kwh. **Labor force:** 19% agric.; 43% manuf.; 14% fishing.

Finance: Currency: New Krona (Mar. 1982: 10.21 = $1 US). **Gross domestic product** (1980): $1.7 bln. **Per capita income** (1979): $9,000. **Imports** (1980): $1.00 bln.; partners (1980): USSR 10%, W. Ger. 10%, UK 9%, Den. 8%. **Exports** (1980): $929 mln.; partners (1980): U.S. 22%, UK 16%, W. Ger. 10%. **Tourists** (1977): 72,700; receipts: $15 mln. **National budget** (1980): $455 mln. revenues; $451 mln. expenditures. **International reserves less gold** (Feb. 1982): $217.6 mln. **Gold:** 49,000 oz t. **Consumer prices** (change in 1980): 54.6%.

Transport: Motor vehicles: in use (1979): 81,025 passenger cars, 7,873 comm. vehicles. **Civil aviation:** 1.2 bln. passenger-km (1980); 23.6 mln. freight ton-km (1980). **Chief ports:** Reykjavik.

Communications: Television sets: 59,800 in use (1979). **Radios:** 66,500 licensed (1979). **Telephones in use** (1980): 103,800. **Daily newspaper circ.** (1980): 567 per 1,000 pop.

Health: Life expectancy at birth (1978): 73.4 male; 79.3 female. **Births** (per 1,000 pop. 1978): 18.6. **Deaths** (per 1,000 pop. 1978): 6.5. **Natural increase** (1978): 1.2%. **Hospital beds** (per 100,000 pop. 1977): 1,700. **Physicians** (per 100,000 pop. 1977): 180. **Infant mortality** per (1,000 live births 1981): 19.6.

Education (1981): **Literacy:** 99.9%. **Pop. 5-19:** in school: 70%, teachers per 1,000: 46.

Iceland was an independent republic from 930 to 1262, when it joined with Norway. Its language has maintained its purity for 1,000 years. Danish rule lasted from 1380-1918; the last ties with the Danish crown were severed in 1941. The Althing, or assembly, is the world's oldest surviving parliament.

A four-year dispute with Britain ended in 1976 when the latter accepted Iceland's 200-mile territorial waters claim.

A conservative coalition won power in 1974 and stopped plans to oust U.S. NATO air and naval personnel.

India

Republic of India

People: Population (1981 est.): 700,000,000. **Age distrib.** (%): 0–14: 40.8; 15–59: 53.9; 60+: 5.3. **Pop. density:** 519.13 per sq. mi. **Urban** (1979): 21.7%. **Ethnic groups:** Indo-Aryan groups 72%, Dravidians 25%, Mongoloids 3%. **Languages:** 15 languages, including Hindi (official) and English (associate official). **Religions:** Hindus 83%, Moslems 11%, Christians 3%, Sikhs 2%.

Geography: Area: 1,269,420 sq. mi., one third the size of the U.S. **Location:** Occupies most of the Indian subcontinent in S. Asia. **Neighbors:** Pakistan on W, China, Nepal, Bhutan on N, Burma, Bangladesh on E. **Topography:** The Himalaya Mts., highest in world, stretch across India's northern borders. Below, the Ganges Plain is wide, fertile, and among the most densely populated regions of the world. The area below includes the Deccan Peninsula. Close to one quarter the area is forested. The climate varies from tropical heat in S to near-Arctic cold in N. Rajasthan Desert is in NW; NE Assam Hills get 400 in. of rain a year. **Capital:** New Delhi. **Cities** (1980 cen.): Calcutta 9.1 mln.; Bombay (met.) 8.2 mln.; Delhi 5.2 mln.; Madras 4.3 mln.; Bangalore 2.9 mln.; Hyderabad 1.5 mln.; Ahmedabad 2.5 mln.; Kanpur 1.7 mln.; Pune 1.7 mln.; Nagpur 1.3 mln.

Government: Head of state: Pres. Zail Singh; in office: July 12, 1982. **Head of government:** Prime Min. Indira Gandhi, b. Nov. 19, 1917; in office: Jan. 14, 1980. **Local divisions:** 22 states, 9 union territories. **Armed forces:** regulars 1,096,000; reserves 200,000.

Economy: Industries: Textiles, steel, processed foods, cement, machinery, chemicals, fertilizers, consumer appliances, autos. **Chief crops:** Rice, grains, coffee, sugar cane, spices, tea, cashews, cotton, copra, coir, juta, linseed. **Minerals:** Chromium, coal, iron, manganese, mica salt, bauxite, gypsum, oil. **Crude oil reserves** (1980): 2.60 bln. bbls. **Other resources:** Rubber, timber. **Per capita arable land:** 0.6 acres. **Meat prod.** (1980): beef: 197,000 metric tons; pork: 70,000 metric tons; lamb: 402,000 metric tons. **Fish catch** (1979): 2.3 mln. metric tons. **Electricity prod.** (1980): 107 bln. kwh. **Crude steel prod.** (1981): 10.7 mln. metric tons. **Labor force:** 74% agric.

Finance: Currency: Rupee (Mar. 1982: 8.34 = $1 US). **Gross domestic product** (1979): $106.6 bln. **Per capita income** (1977): $150. **Imports** (1980): $12.6 bln.; partners (1980): U.S. 10%, USSR 9%, W. Ger. 7%, UK 8%. **Exports** (1980):

$8.24 bln.; partners (1980): U.S. 13%, USSR 10%, UK 8%, Jap. 10%. **Tourists** (1977): 640,400; receipts: $350 mln. **National budget** (1980): $13.4 bln. revenues; $14.7 bln. expenditures. **International reserves less gold** (Nov. 1981): $5.06 bln. **Gold:** 8.59 mln. oz. t. **Consumer prices** (change in 1980): 11.5%.

Transport: Railway traffic (1979): 192 bln. passenger-km; (1979) 154 bln. net ton-km. **Motor vehicles:** in use (1979): 1.03 mln. passenger cars, 440,200 comm. vehicles; manuf. (1980): 48,000 passenger cars, 65,000 comm. vehicles. **Civil aviation:** 10.7 bln. passenger-km (1980); 401 mln. freight ton-km (1980). **Chief ports:** Calcutta, Bombay, Madras, Cochin, Vishakhapatnam.

Communications: Television sets: 1.1 mln. licensed (1979). **Radios:** 19.6 mln. licensed (1978), 1.91 mln. manuf. (1978). **Telephones in use** (1980): 2.6 mln. **Daily newspaper circ.** (1977): 10,672,000.

Health: Life expectancy at birth (1970): 47.1 male; 45.6 female. **Births** (per 1,000 pop. 1978): 34. **Deaths** (per 1,000 pop. 1978): 15. **Natural increase** (1978): 1.9%. **Hospital beds** (per 100,000 pop. 1977): 75. **Physicians** (per 100,000 pop. 1977): 26. **Infant mortality** (per 1,000 live births 1976): 122.

Education (1978): **Literacy:** 36%. **Pop. 5-19:** in school: 42%, teachers per 1,000: 13.

India has one of the oldest civilizations in the world. Excavations trace the Indus Valley civilization back for at least 5,000 years. Paintings in the mountain caves of Ajanta, richly carved temples, the Taj Mahal in Agra, and the Kutab Minar in Delhi are among relics of the past.

Aryan tribes, speaking Sanskrit, invaded from the NW around 1500 BC, and merged with the earlier inhabitants to create classical Indian civilization.

Asoka ruled most of the Indian subcontinent in the 3d century BC, and established Buddhism. But Hinduism revived and eventually predominated. During the Gupta kingdom, 4th-6th century AD, science, literature, and the arts enjoyed a "golden age."

Arab invaders established a Moslem foothold in the W in the 8th century, and Turkish Moslems gained control of North India by 1200. The Mogul emperors ruled 1526-1707.

Vasco de Gama established Portuguese trading posts 1498-1503. The Dutch followed. The British East India Co. sent Capt. William Hawkins, 1609, to get concessions from the Mogul emperor for spices and textiles. Operating as the East India Co. the British gained control of most of India. The British parliament assumed political direction; under Lord Bentinck, 1828-35, rule by rajahs was curbed. After the Sepoy troops mutinied, 1857-58, the British supported the native rulers.

Nationalism grew rapidly after World War I. The Indian National Congress and the Moslem League demanded constitutional reform. A leader emerged in Mohandas K. Gandhi (called Mahatma, or Great Soul), born Oct. 2, 1869, assassinated Jan. 30, 1948. He began advocating self-rule, non-violence, removal of untouchability in 1919. In 1930 he launched "civil disobedience," including boycott of British goods and rejection of taxes without representation.

In 1935 Britain gave India a constitution providing a bicameral federal congress. Mohammed Ali Jinnah, head of the Moslem League, sought creation of a Moslem nation, Pakistan.

The British government partitioned British India into the dominions of India and Pakistan. Aug. 15, 1947, was designated Indian Independence Day. India became a self-governing member of the Commonwealth and a member of the UN. It became a democratic republic, Jan. 26, 1950.

More than 12 million Hindu & Moslem refugees crossed the India-Pakistan borders in a mass transferral of some of the 2 peoples during 1947; about 200,000 were killed in communal fighting.

After Pakistan troops began attacks on Bengali separatists in East Pakistan, Mar. 25, 1971, some 10 million refugees fled into India. On Aug. 9, India and the USSR signed a 20-year friendship pact while U.S.-India relations soured. India and Pakistan went to war Dec. 3, 1971, on both the East and West fronts. Pakistan troops in the East surrendered Dec. 16; Pakistan agreed to a cease-fire in the West Dec. 17.

India and Pakistan signed a pact agreeing to withdraw troops from their borders and seek peaceful solutions, July 3, 1972. In Aug. 1973 India agreed to release 93,000 Pakistanis held prisoner since 1971; the return was completed in Apr. 1974. The 2 countries resumed full relations in 1976.

In 2 days of carnage, the Bengali population of the village of Mandai, Tripura State, 700 people, were massacred in a raid by indigenous tribal residents of the area, June 8-9, 1980. A similar year-long campaign against Bengali immigrants had been going on in Assam State.

Prime Min. Mrs. Indira Gandhi, named Jan. 19, 1966, was the 2d successor to Jawaharlal Nehru, India's prime minister from 1947 to his death, May 27, 1964.

Long the dominant power in India's politics, the Congress party lost some of its near monopoly by 1967. The party split into New and Old Congress parties in 1969. Mrs. Gandhi's New Congress party won control of the House.

Threatened with adverse court rulings in a voting law case, an opposition protest campaign and strikes, Gandhi invoked emergency provisions of the constitution June, 1975. Thousands of opponents were arrested and press censorship imposed. Measures to control prices, protect small farmers, and improve productivity were adopted.

The emergency, especially enforcement of coercive birth control measures in some areas, and the prominent extra-constitutional role of Indira Gandhi's son Sanjay, was widely resented. Opposition parties, united in the Janata coalition, scored massive victories in federal and state parliamentary elections in 1977, turning the New Congress Party from power.

Amid growing political tensions within the majority Janata party, and facing a censure vote in Parliament, Prime Min. Morarji R. Desai resigned, July 15, 1979. He was succeeded by the coalition government of Charan Singh, which only lasted 24 days before the prime minister's resignation in the face of opposition from Indira Gandhi's New Congress Party.

With 350 candidates of her party winning seats to Parliament, Indira Gandhi became prime minister for the second time, Jan. 14, 1980.

India's 1st nuclear power plant, built with U.S. help, was dedicated in 1970 near Bombay; Canada helped India build 2 reactors. In May, 1974, India exploded a nuclear device underground, assertedly for peaceful development.

The economy improved in 1981, with both agricultural and industrial output rising.

Sikkim, bordered by Tibet, Bhutan, Nepal and India, formerly British protected, became a protectorate of India in 1950. Area, 2,818 sq. mi.; pop. 1977 est. 250,000; capital, Gangtok. In Sept. 1974 India's Parliament voted to make Sikkim an associate Indian state, absorbing it into India. The monarchy was abolished in an April, 1975, referendum.

Kashmir, a predominantly Moslem region in the northwest, has been in dispute between India and Pakistan since 1947. A cease-fire was negotiated by the UN Jan. 1, 1949; it gave Pakistan control of one-third of the area, in the west and northwest, and India the remaining two-thirds, the Indian state of Jammu and Kashmir, which enjoys internal autonomy. Repeated clashes broke out along the line.

There were also clashes in April 1965 along the Assam-East Pakistan border and in the **Rann** (swamp) **of Kutch** area along the West Pakistan-Gujarat border near the Arabian Sea. An international arbitration commission on Feb. 19, 1968, awarded 90% of the Rann to India, 10% to Pakistan.

France, 1952-54, peacefully yielded to India its 5 colonies, former French India, comprising Pondicherry, Karikal, Mahe, Yanaon (which became Pondicherry Union Territory, area 185 sq. mi., pop. 1971 471,707) and Chandernagor (which was incorporated into the state of West Bengal).

Goa, 1,429 sq. mi., pop., 1971, 795,120, which had been ruled by Portugal since 1505 AD, was taken by India by military action Dec. 18, 1961, together with 2 other Portuguese enclaves, Daman and Diu, located near Bombay.

Indonesia

Republic of Indonesia

People: Population (1981 est.): 154,000,000. **Age distrib.** (%): 0–14: 44.0; 15–59: 51.5; 60+: 4.5. **Pop. density:** 206.65 per sq. mi. **Urban** (1974): 18.2%. **Ethnic groups:** Javanese 45%, Sundanese 13.6%, Chinese 2.3%, others. **Languages:** Bahasa Indonesian (Malay) (official), Javanese, other Austronesian languages. **Religions:** Mostly Muslims, Christian, Hindu.

Geography: Area: 741,101 sq. mi. **Location:** Archipelago SE of Asia along the Equator. **Neighbors:** Malaysia on N, Papua New Guinea on E. **Topography:** Indonesia comprises 13,500 islands, including Java (one of the most densely populated areas in the world with 1,500 persons to the sq. mi.), Sumatra, Kalimantan (most of Borneo), Sulawesi (Celebes), and West Irian (Irian Jaya, the W. half of New Guinea). Also: Bangka, Billiton, Madura, Bali, Timor. The mountains and plateaus on the major islands have a cooler climate than the tropical lowlands. **Capital:** Jakarta. **Cities** (1981 est.): Jakarta 5,500,000; Surabaja 2,000,000; Bandung 1,400,000; Medan 1,000,000.

Government: Head of state: Pres. Suharto; b. June 8, 1921; in office: Mar. 6, 1967. **Local divisions:** 27 provinces with elected legislatures, appointed governors. **Armed forces:** regulars 239,000; para-military 112,000.

Economy: Industries: Food processing, textiles, light industry. **Chief crops:** Rice, coffee, sugar. **Minerals:** Nickel, tin, oil, bauxite, copper, natural gas. **Crude oil reserves** (1980): 9.6 bln. bbls. **Other resources:** Rubber, cinchona. **Per capita arable land:** 0.3 acres. **Meat prod.** (1980): beef: 168,000 metric tons; pork: 86,000 metric tons, lamb: 60,000 metric tons. **Fish catch** (1979): 1.7 mln. metric tons. **Electricity prod.** (1978): 6.2 bln. kwh. **Crude steel prod.** (1981): 375,000 metric tons. **Labor force:** 66% agric.; 23% ind. & comm.

Finance: Currency: Rupiah (Mar. 1982: 651 = $1 US). **Gross domestic product** (1980): $66.81 bln. **Per capita income** (1981): $415. **Imports** (1980): $10.8 bln.; partners (1980): Jap. 32%, U.S. 13%, Sing. 9%. **Exports** (1980): $21.9 bln.; partners (1980): Jap. 49%, U.S. 20%, Sing. 11%. **Tourists** (1977): 457,000; receipts: $39 mln. **National budget** (1980): $14.4 bln. revenues; $16.8 bln. expenditures. **International reserves less gold** (Feb. 1982): $5.35 bln. **Gold:** 3.10 mln. oz t. **Consumer prices** (change in 1980): 18.5%.

Transport: Railway traffic (1980): 5.9 bln. passenger-km; 1.016 bln. net ton-km. **Motor vehicles:** in use (1979): 577,300 passenger cars, 383,600 comm. vehicles; assembled (1977): 20,000 passenger cars, 69,400 comm. vehicles. **Civil aviation:** 5.9 bln. passenger-km (1980); 129 mln. freight ton-km (1980). **Chief ports:** Jakarta, Surabaja, Medan, Palembang, Semarang.

Communications: Television sets: 1.5 mln. in use (1979), 482,000 manuf. (1977). **Radios:** 5.2 mln. licensed (1977), 1.0 mln. manuf. (1977). **Telephones in use** (1980): 392,600. **Daily newspaper circ.** (1976): 2,358,000.

Health: Life expectancy at birth (1960): 47.5 male; 47.5 female. **Births** (per 1,000 pop. 1978): 35. **Deaths** (per 1,000 pop. 1978): 15. **Natural increase** (1978) 2.1%. **Hospital beds** (per 100,000 pop. 1977): 60. **Physicians** (per 100,000 pop. 1977): 7. **Infant mortality** (per 1,000 live births 1980): 100.

Education (1981): **Literacy:** 64%. **Pop. 5-19:** in school: 39%, teachers per 1,000: 14.

Hindu and Buddhist civilization from India reached the peoples of Indonesia nearly 2,000 years ago, taking root especially in Java. Islam spread along the maritime trade routes in the 15th century, and became predominant by the 16th century. The Dutch replaced the Portuguese as the most important European trade power in the area in the 17th century. They secured territorial control over Java by 1750. The outer islands were not finally subdued until the early 20th century, when the full area of present-day Indonesia was united under one rule for the first time in history.

Following Japanese occupation, 1942-45, nationalists led by Sukarno and Hatta proclaimed a republic. The Netherlands ceded sovereignty Dec. 27, 1949, after 4 years of fighting. West Irian, on New Guinea, remained under Dutch control.

After the Dutch in 1957 rejected proposals for new negotiations over West Irian, Indonesia stepped up the seizure of Dutch property. A U.S. mediator's plan was adopted in 1962. In 1963 the UN turned the area over to Indonesia, which promised a plebiscite. In 1969, voting by tribal chiefs favored staying with Indonesia, despite an uprising and widespread opposition.

Sukarno suspended Parliament in 1960, and was named president for life in 1963. Russian-armed Indonesian troops staged raids in 1964 and 1965 into Malaysia, whose formation Sukarno had opposed.

Indonesia's popular, pro-Peking Communist party tried to seize control in 1965; the army smashed the coup, later intimated that Sukarno had played a role in it. In parts of Java, Communists seized several districts before being defeated; over 300,000 Communists were executed.

Gen. Suharto, head of the army, was named president for 5 years in 1968, reelected 1973 and 1978. A coalition of his supporters won a strong majority in House elections in 1971, the first national vote in 16 years. Moslem opposition parties made gains in 1977 elections but lost ground in the 1982 elections. The military retains a predominant political role.

In 1966 Indonesia and Malaysia signed an agreement ending hostility. After ties with Peking were cut in 1967, there were riots against the economically important ethnic Chinese minority. Riots against Chinese and Japanese also occurred in 1974.

The former Portuguese Timor became Indonesia's 27th province in 1976 during a local civil war. The UN has not recognized the annexation of the province.

Oil export earnings, and political stability have made Indonesia's economy one of the fastest growing in the world.

Iran

Islamic Republic of Iran

People: Population (1981 est.): 39,500,000. **Age distrib.** (%): 0–14: 44.4; 15–59: 50.3; 60+: 5.2. **Pop. density:** 59.84 per sq. mi. **Urban** (1978): 48.8%. **Ethnic groups:** Iranian groups 66%, Turkish groups 25%, Kurds 5%, Arabs 4%. **Languages:** Farsi, Turk, Kurdish, Arabic, English, French. **Religions:** Moslems 99%.

Geography: Area: 636,363 sq. mi. **Location:** Between the Middle East and S. Asia. **Neighbors:** Turkey, Iraq on W, USSR of N (Armenia, Azerbaijan, Turkmenistan), Afghanistan, Pakistan on E. **Topography:** Interior highlands and plains are surrounded by high mountains, up to 18,000 ft. Large salt deserts cover much of the area, but there are many oases and forest areas. Most of the population inhabits the N and NW. **Capital:** Teheran. **Cities** (1976 cen.): Teheran 4,496,159; Isfahan 671,825; Mashhad 670,180; Tabriz 598,576.

Government: Religious head (Faghi): Ayatollah Ruhollah Khomeini, b. 1901. **Head of state:** Prime Minister Mir Hossein Moussavi; in office: Oct. 29, 1981. **Local divisions:** 21 provinces, 2 governorates. **Armed forces:** regulars 415,000; reserves 300,000.

Economy: Industries: Steel, petrochemicals, cement, auto assembly, sugar refining, carpets. **Chief crops:** Grains, rice, fruits, sugar beets, cotton, grapes. **Minerals:** Chromium, oil, gas, copper, iron, lead, manganese, zinc, barite, sulphur, coal, emeralds, turquoise. **Crude oil reserves** (1980): 58.00 bln. bbls. **Other resources:** Gums, wool, silk, caviar. **Per capita arable land:** 1.1 acres. **Meat prod.** (1980): beef: 172,000 metric tons; lamb: 277,000 metric tons. **Electricity prod.** (1979): 18.50 bln. kwh. **Crude steel prod.** (1981 est.) 1.2 mln. metric tons. **Labor force:** 37% agric.; 27% manuf.

Finance: Currency: Rial (Mar. 1982: 82.89 = $1 US). **Gross domestic product** (1977): $76.37 bln. **Per capita income** (1976): $1,986. **Imports** (1980): $10.55 bln.; partners (1980 est.): W. Ger. 14%, Jap. 14%, UK 8%. **Exports** (1981): $9.34 bln.; partners (1980): Jap. 27%, W. Ger. 12%. **National budget** (1980): $34.9 bln. revenues; $27.1 bln. expenditures. **International reserves less gold** (Jun. 1980): $15.48 bln. **Gold:** 4.34 mln. oz t. **Consumer prices** (change in 1981): 24.2%.

Transport: Railway traffic (1976): 3.51 bln. passenger-km; 4.63 bln. net ton-km. **Motor vehicles:** in use (1979): 1,028,400 passenger cars, 396,300 comm. vehicles; assembled (1977): 103,000 passenger cars; 65,000 comm. vehicles. **Chief ports:** Khorramshahr, Bushehr, Bandar-e Shahpur, Bendar Abbas.

Communications: Television sets: 2.1 mln. in use (1979). **Radios:** 2.1 mln. in use (1977). **Telephones in use** (1980): 730,000. **Daily newspaper circ.** (1980): 25 per 1,000 pop.

Health: Life expectancy at birth (1976): 57.63 male; 57.44 female. **Births** (per 1,000 pop. 1978): 41. **Deaths** (per 1,000 pop. 1978): 11. **Natural increase** (1978): 2.8%. **Hospital beds** (per 100,000 pop. 1977): 148. **Physicians** (per 100,000 pop. 1977): 39. **Infant mortality** (per 1,000 live births 1975): 108.1.

Education (1978): **Literacy:** 50% **Pop. 5-19:** in school: 52%, teachers per 100,000: 20.

Iran is the official name of the country long known as Persia. The Iranians, who supplanted an earlier agricultural civilization, came from the E during the 2d millenium BC; they were an Indo-European group related to the Aryans of India.

In 549 BC Cyrus the Great united the Medes and Persians in the Persian Empire, conquered Babylonia in 538 BC, restored Jerusalem to the Jews. Alexander the Great conquered Persia in 333 BC, but Persians regained their independence in the next century under the Parthians, themselves succeeded by Sassanian Persians in 226 AD. Arabs brought Islam to Persia in the 7th century, replacing the indigenous Zoroastrian faith. After Persian political and cultural autonomy was reasserted in the 9th century, the arts and sciences flourished for several centuries.

Turks and Mongols ruled Persia in turn from the 11th century to 1502, when a native dynasty reasserted full independence. The British and Russian empires vied for influence in the 19th century, and Afghanistan was severed from Iran by Britain in 1857.

The previous dynasty was founded by Reza Khan, a military leader, in 1925. He abdicated as shah in 1941, and was succeeded by his son, Mohammad Reza Pahlavi.

British and Russian forces entered Iran Aug. 25, 1941, withdrawing later. Britain and the USSR signed an agreement Jan. 29, 1942, to respect Iranian integrity and give economic aid. In 1946 a Soviet attempt to take over the Azerbaijan region in the NW was defeated when a puppet regime was ousted by force.

Parliament, under Premier Mohammed Mossadegh, nationalized the oil industry in 1951, leading to a British blockade. Mossadegh was overthrown in 1953; the shah assumed control. Under his rule, Iran underwent economic and social change. However, political opposition was not tolerated. Thousands were arrested in the 1970s, while hundreds of purported terrorists were executed.

Conservative Moslem protests led to 1978 violence. Martial law in 12 cities was declared Sept. 8. A military government was appointed Nov. 6 to deal with striking oil workers. Continued clashes with demonstrators led to greater violence; oil production fell to a 27-year low, Dec. 27. In a 3d change of government in 5 months, Prime Min. Shahpur Bakhtiar was designated by the shah to head a regency council in his absence. The shah left Iran Jan. 16, 1979.

Violence continued throughout January. Exiled religious leader Ayatollah Ruhollah Khomeini named a provisional government council in preparation for his return to Iran, Jan. 31. Clashes between Khomeini's supporters and government troops culminated in a rout of Iran's elite Imperial Guard Feb. 11, leading to the fall of Bakhtiar's government. Ayatollah Khomeini's choice for prime minister, Mehdi Bazargan, headed an interim government pledged to establish an Islamic republic, but resigned Nov. 6, 1979, conceding power to the Islamic authority of Ayatollah Khomeini.

The Iranian revolution was marked by revolts among the ethnic minorities and by a continuing struggle between the clerical forces and westernized intellectuals and liberals. The Islamic Constitution, drafted under the domination of the clergy, established final authority to be vested in a Faghi, the Ayatollah Khomeini.

Iranian militants seized the U.S. embassy, Nov. 4, 1979, and took 90 hostages including some 65 Americans. The militants vowed to stay in the embassy until the deposed shah was returned to Iran. Despite international condemnations and U.S. efforts, including an abortive Apr., 1980, rescue attempt, the crisis continued. The U.S. broke diplomatic relations with Iran, Apr. 7th. The shah died in Egypt, July 27th.

The hostage drama finally ended Jan. 21, 1981 when an accord, involving the release of frozen Iranian assets, was reached. Minutes after Ronald Reagan was sworn in as 40th president, the 52 Americans flew to freedom.

Turmoil continued in Teheran however. The ruling Islamic Party, increasingly dissatisfied with President Abolhassan Bani-Sadr, declared him unfit for office. In the weeks following Bani-Sadr's dismissal, June 22, 1981, a new wave of executions began. Over 2,000 people, reportedly members of the Majahedeen-i-Khalq and smaller Marxist-Leninist/Maoist factions, had died before revolutionary firing squads by the of end of 1981.

A dispute over the Shatt al-Arab waterway that divides the two countries brought Iran and Iraq, Sept. 22, 1980, into open warfare. Iraqi planes attacked Iranian air fields including Teheran airport. Iranian planes bombed Iraqi bases. Iraqi troops occupied Iranian territory including the port city of Khorramshahr in October. Iranian troops recaptured the city and drove Iraqi troops back across the border, May 1982.

On June 28, 1981, a bomb destroyed the Teheran headquarters of Iran's ruling Islamic Party, killing the party's leader, and 71 other persons.

In 1982, political upheavals had brought Iran to virtual civil war and almost total isolation from other countries.

Iraq

Republic of Iraq

People: Population (1981 est.): 13,800,000. **Age distrib.** (%): 0–14: 48.3; 15–59: 46.5; 60+: 5.3. **Pop. density:** 76.04 per sq. mi. **Urban** (1977): 65.9%. **Ethnic groups:** Arabs, Kurds, Turks. **Languages:** Arabic (official), Kurdish, others. **Religions:** Moslems 95% (Shiites two-thirds, Sunnis one-third), Christians 3%.

Geography: Area: 168,928 sq. mi., larger than California. **Location:** In the Middle East, occupying most of historic Mesopotamia. **Neighbors:** Jordan, Syria on W, Turkey on N, Iran on E, Kuwait, Saudi Arabia on S. **Topography:** Mostly an alluvial plain, including the Tigris and Euphrates rivers, descending from mountains in N to desert in SW. Persian Gulf region is marshland. **Capital:** Baghdad. **Cities** (1975 est.): Baghdad (met.) 3,205,645.

Government: Head of state: Pres. Saddam Hussein At-Takriti, b. 1935 in office: July 16, 1979. **Local divisions:** 18 governorates. **Armed forces:** regulars 222,000; reserves 250,000.

Economy: Industries: Textiles, food processing, cigarettes, oil refining, cement. **Chief crops:** Grains, rice, dates, cotton, tobacco. **Minerals:** Oil, gas. **Crude oil reserves** (1980): 31.00 bln. bbls. **Other resources:** Wool, hides. **Per capita arable land:** 1.0 acres. **Meat prod.** (1980): beef: 56,000 metric tons; lamb: 50,000 metric tons. **Fish catch** (1978): 26,100 metric tons. **Electricity prod.** (1978): 6.9 bln. kwh. **Labor force:** 50% agric.

Finance: Currency: Dinar (Mar. 1982: 0.34 = $1 US). **Gross domestic product** (1977 est.): $19 bln. **Per capita income** (1978): $1,561. **Imports** (1980): $12.94 bln.; partners (1980): W. Ger. 15%, Jap. 18%, Fr. 9%. **Exports** (1981): $10.59 bln.; partners (1980): Fr. 18%, It. 16%, Braz. 15%, Jap. 14%. **International reserves less gold** (Dec. 1977): $6.82 bln. **Gold:** 4.14 mln. oz t. **Consumer prices** (change in 1978): 4.6%.

Transport: Railway traffic (1977): 797 mln. passenger-km; 2.25 bln. net ton-km. **Motor vehicles:** in use (1979): 120,600 passenger cars, 129,400 comm. vehicles. **Civil aviation:** 1.1 bln. passenger-km (1980); 52.7 mln. freight ton-km (1980). **Chief ports:** Basra.

Communications: Television sets: 475,000 in use (1977), 25,000 manuf. (1975). **Radios:** 2 mln. in use (1977). **Telephones in use** (1978): 319,600. **Daily newspaper circ.** (1980): 21 per 1,000 pop.

Health: Life expectancy at birth (1975): 51.2 male; 54.3 female. **Births** (per 1,000 pop. 1978): 47. **Deaths** (per 1,000 pop. 1978): 13. **Natural increase** (1978): 3.4%. **Hospital beds** (per 100,000 pop. 1977): 199. **Physicians** (per 100,000 pop. 1977): 44. **Infant mortality** (per 1,000 live births 1977): 28.

Education (1978): **Literacy:** 30%. **Pop. 5-19:** in school: 68%, teachers per 1,000: 22.

The Tigris-Euphrates valley, formerly called Mesopotamia, was the site of one of the earliest civilizations in the world. The Sumerian city-states of 3,000 BC originated the culture later developed by the Semitic Akkadians, Babylonians, and Assyrians.

Mesopotamia ceased to be a separate entity after the conquests of the Persians, Greeks, and Arabs. The latter founded Baghdad, from where the caliph ruled a vast empire in the 8th and 9th centuries. Mongol and Turkish conquests led to a decline in population, the economy, cultural life, and the irrigation system.

Britain secured a League of Nations mandate over Iraq after World War I. Independence under a king came in 1932. A leftist, pan-Arab revolution established a republic in 1958, which oriented foreign policy toward the USSR. Most industry has been nationalized, and large land holdings broken up.

A local faction of the international Baath Arab Socialist party has ruled by decree since 1968. Russia and Iraq signed an aid pact in 1972, and arms were sent along with several thousand advisers. The 1978 execution of 21 Communists and a shift of trade to the West signalled a more neutral policy, straining relations with the USSR. In the 1973 Arab-Israeli war Iraq sent forces to aid Syria. Relations with Syria were improving steadily to negotiations of uniting the 2 nations as a single political entity, but were halted by the Hussein government, July, 1979. Within a month of assuming power, Saddam Hussein instituted a bloody purge in the wake of a reported coup attempt against the new regime.

Years of battling with the Kurdish minority resulted in total defeat for the Kurds in 1975, when Iran withdrew support. Kurdish rebels continued their war, 1979; fighting led to Iraqi bombing of Kurdish villages in Iran, causing relations with Iran to deteriorate.

After skirmishing intermittently for 10 months over the sovereignty of the disputed Shatt al-Arab waterway that divides the two countries, Iraq and Iran, Sept. 22, 1980, entered into open warfare when Iraqi fighter-bombers attacked 10 Iranian airfields, including Teheran airport, and Iranian planes retaliated with strikes on 2 Iraqi bases. In the following days, there was heavy ground fighting around Abadan and the adjacent port of Khurramshahr as Iraq pressed its attack on Iran's oil-rich province of Khuzistan. In May 1982, Iraqi troops were driven back across the border.

Israeli airplanes destroyed a nuclear reactor near Baghdad on June 7, 1981, claiming that it could be used to produce nuclear weapons.

Ireland

Irish Republic

People: Population (1981 est.): 3,500,000. **Age distrib. (%):** 0–14: 31.2; 15–59: 53.5; 60+:15.3. **Pop. density:** 121.8 per sq. mi. **Urban** (1971): 52.2%. **Ethnic groups:** Irish, Anglo-Irish minority. **Languages:** English predominates, Irish (Gaelic) spoken by minority. **Religions:** Roman Catholics 94%, Anglican 5%.

Geography: Area: 27,137 sq. mi. **Location:** In the Atlantic O. just W of Great Britain. **Neighbors:** United Kingdom (Northern Ireland). **Topography:** Ireland consists of a central plateau surrounded by isolated groups of hills and mountains. The coastline is heavily indented by the Atlantic O. **Capital:** Dublin. **Cities** (1981 est.): Dublin 525,360; Cork (met.) 136,269.

Government: Head of State: Pres. Patrick J. Hillery; b. May 2, 1923; in office: Dec. 3, 1976. **Head of government:** Prime Min. Charles J. Haughey; b. Sept. 16, 1925; in office: Mar. 9, 1982. **Local divisions:** 26 counties. **Armed forces:** regulars 15,000 (1980).

Economy: Industries: Food processing, auto assembly, metals, textiles, chemicals, brewing, electrical and non-electrical machinery, tourism. **Chief crops:** Potatoes, grain, sugar beets, fruits, vegetables. **Minerals:** Zinc, lead, silver, gas. **Per capita arable land:** 0.8 acres. **Meat prod.** (1980): beef: 410,000 metric tons; pork: 145,000 metric tons; lamb: 43,000 metric tons. **Fish catch** (1978): 108,400 metric tons. **Electricity prod.** (1978): 9.97 bln. kwh. **Crude steel prod.** (1981): 32,000 metric tons. **Labor force:** 26% agric.; 19% manuf.; 15% comm.

Finance: Currency: Pound (Mar. 1982: 0.69 = $1 US). **Gross domestic product** (1980): $17.2 bln. **Per capita income** (1980): $5,000. **Imports** (1981): $10.6 bln.; partners (1980): UK 51%, U.S. 9%, W. Ger. 7%, Fr. 5%. **Exports** (1981): $7.78 bln.; partners (1980): UK 43%, Fr. 8%, W. Ger. 10%, U.S. 6%. **Tourists** (1979); 1.6 mln; receipts: $384 mln. **National budget** (1980): $6.70 bln. revenues; $9.35 bln. expenditures. **International reserves less gold** (Feb. 1982): $2.50 bln. **Gold:** 359,000 oz. t. **Consumer prices** (change in 1981): 20.4%.

Transport: Railway traffic (1979): 1.007 bln. passenger-km; 580 mln. net ton-km. **Motor vehicles:** in use (1980): 734,400 passenger cars, 65,100 comm. vehicles; assembled (1978): 45,492 passenger cars; 2,376 comm. vehicles. **Civil aviation:** (1980): 2.0 bln. passenger-km; 91.9 mln. freight ton-km. **Chief ports:** Dublin, Cork.

Communications: Television sets: 592,700 licensed (1979), 33,000 manuf. (1978). **Radios:** 949,000 licensed (1976), 72,000 manuf. (1973). **Telephones in use** (1980): 586,000. **Daily newspaper circ.** (1980): 246 per 1,000 pop.

Health: Life expectancy at birth (1972): 68.77 male; 73.52 female. **Births** (per 1,000 pop. 1979): 21.5. **Deaths** (per 1,000 pop. 1979): 9.7. **Natural increase** (1977): 1.1%. **Hospital beds** (per 100,000 pop. 1977): 1,051. **Physicians** (per 100,000 pop. 1977): 116. **Infant mortality** (per 1,000 live births 1981): 12.4

Education (1978): **Literacy:** 98%. **Pop. 5-19:** in school: 70%, teachers per 1,000: 30.

Celtic tribes invaded the islands about the 4th century BC; their Gaelic culture and literature flourished and spread to Scotland and elsewhere in the 5th century AD, the same century in which St. Patrick converted the Irish to Christianity. Invasions by Norsemen began in the 8th century, ended with defeat of the Danes by the Irish King Brian Boru in 1014. English invasions started in the 12th century; for over 700 years the Anglo-Irish struggle continued with bitter rebellions and savage repressions.

The Easter Monday Rebellion (1916) failed but was followed by guerrilla warfare and harsh reprisals by British troops, the "Black and Tans." The Dail Eireann, or Irish parliament, reaffirmed independence in Jan. 1919. The British offered dominion status to Ulster (6 counties) and southern Ireland (26 counties), Dec. 1921. The constitution of the Irish Free State, a British dominion, was adopted Dec. 11, 1922. Northern Ireland remained part of the United Kingdom.

A new constitution adopted by plebiscite came into operation Dec. 29, 1937. It declared the name of the state Eire in the Irish language (Ireland in the English) and declared it a sovereign democratic state.

On Dec. 21, 1948, an Irish law declared the country a republic rather than a dominion and withdrew it from the Commonwealth. The British Parliament recognized both actions, 1949, but reasserted its claim to incorporate the 6 northeastern counties in the United Kingdom. This claim has not been recognized by Ireland. *(See United Kingdom — Northern Ireland.)*

First president was William T. Cosgrave, 1922-32. Eamon de Valera, hero of the rebellion, was president 1932-37, 1959-66, 1966-73; prime minister 1937-48, 1951-54, 1957-59.

Irish governments have favored peaceful unification of all Ireland. Ireland cooperated with England against terrorist groups.

Israel

State of Israel

People: Population (1981 est.): 4,000,000. **Age distrib.** (%): 0–14: 33.2; 15–59: 63.0; 60+: 11.7. **Pop. density:** 448.96 per sq. mi. **Urban** (1977): 87.2%. **Ethnic groups:** Jews (half Ashkenazi, half Sephardi), Arabs, Druzes, Christians. **Languages:** Hebrew and Arabic (official), Yiddish, various European and West Asian languages. **Religions:** Jews 84%, Moslems, Christians, others.

Geography: Area: 8,219 sq. mi. (the size of Massachusetts), the "Green Line" border before the 1967 war; 2,986 sq. mi. occupied territory, excluding Sinai Peninsula, 23,622 sq. mi. **Location:** On eastern end of Mediterranean Sea. **Neighbors:** Lebanon on N, Syria, Jordan on E, Egypt on W. **Topography:** The Mediterranean coastal plain is fertile and well-watered. In the center is the Judean Plateau. A triangular-shaped semi-desert region, the Negev, extends from south of Beersheba to an apex at the head of the Gulf of Aqaba. The eastern border drops sharply into the Jordan Rift Valley, including Lake Tiberias (Sea of Galilee) and the Dead Sea, which is 1,296 ft. below sea level, lowest point on the earth's surface. **Capital:** Jerusalem. **Cities** (1978 est.): Jerusalem 376,000; Tel Aviv-Yafo 343,300; Haifa 227,800.

Government: Head of state: Pres. Yitzhak Navon; b. Apr 19, 1921; in office: May 29, 1978. **Head of government:** Prime Min. Menachem Begin; b. Aug. 16, 1913; in office: June 21, 1977. **Local divisions:** 6 administrative districts. **Armed forces:** regulars 165,600; reserves 460,000.

Economy: Industries: Diamond cutting, textiles, electronics, machinery, plastics, tires, drugs, aircraft, munitions, wine. **Chief crops:** Citrus fruit, grains, olives, fruits, grapes, figs, cotton, vegetables. **Minerals:** Potash, limestone, gypsum, copper, iron, phosphates, magnesium, manganese, salt, sulphur. **Crude oil reserves** (1980): 1.0 mln. bbls. **Per capita arable land:** 0.2 acres. **Meat prod.** (1980): beef: 21,000 metric tons; pork: 13,000 metric tons. **Fish catch** (1978): 25,900 metric tons. **Electricity prod.** (1979): 12.4 bln. kwh. **Crude steel prod.** (1981 est.): 114,000 metric tons. **Labor force:** 6.5% agric.; 25.3% manuf.

Finance: Currency: Shekel (Mar. 1982: 18.08 = $1 US). **Gross domestic product** (1980): $19.91 bln. **Per capita income** (1978): $3,332. **Imports** (1980): $9.76 bln.; partners: U.S. 19%, Switz. 8%. W. Ger. 10%, UK 8%. **Exports** (1980): $5.53 bln.; partners: U.S. 16%, W. Ger. 10%, UK 8%. **Tourists** (1979): 1.1 mln.; receipts $795 mln. **National budget** (1980): $20.8 bln. revenues; $26.6 bln. expenditures. **International reserves less gold** (Jan. 1982): $3.52 bln. **Gold:** 1.19 mln. oz t. **Consumer prices** (change in 1980): 131.0%.

Transport: Railway traffic (1979): 222 mln. passenger-km, 768 mln. net ton-km. **Motor vehicles:** in use (1980): 423,000 passenger cars, 191,000 comm. vehicles; assembled (1978): 2,604 passenger cars, 4,140 comm. vehicles. **Civil aviation** (1980): 4.7 bln. passenger-km; 299 mln. freight ton-km. **Chief ports:** Haifa, Ashdod, Eilat.

Communications: Television sets: 475,000 in use (1976), 41,000 manuf. (1978). **Radios:** 750,000 in use (1977), 10,000 manuf. (1976). **Telephones in use** (1980): 1.08 mln. **Daily newspaper circ.** (1980): 156 per 1,000 pop.

Health: Life expectancy at birth (1978) Jewish pop. only 71.9 male; 75.6 female. **Births** (per 1,000 pop. 1980): 24.1. **Deaths** (per 1,000 pop. 1980): 6.7%. **Natural increase** (1977): 2.0%. **Hospital beds** (per 100,000 pop. 1977): 556. **Physicians** (per 100,000 pop. 1977): 277. **Infant mortality** (per 1,000 live births 1977): 17.8.

Education (1978): **Literacy:** 88%. **Pop. 5-19:** in school: 62%, teachers per 1,000: 50.

Occupying the SW corner of the ancient Fertile Crescent, Israel contains some of the oldest known evidence of agriculture and of primitive town life. A more advanced civilization emerged in the 3d millenium BC. The Hebrews probably arrived early in the 2d millenium BC. Under King David and his successors (c.1000 BC-597 BC), Judaism was developed and secured. After conquest by Babylonians, Persians, and Greeks, an independent Jewish kingdom was revived, 168 BC, but Rome took effective control in the next century, suppressed Jewish revolts in 70 AD and 135 AD, and renamed Judea Palestine, after the earlier coastal inhabitants, the Philistines.

Arab invaders conquered Palestine in 636. The Arabic language and Islam prevailed within a few centuries, but a Jewish minority remained. The land was ruled from the 11th century as a part of non-Arab empires by Seljuks, Mamluks, and Ottomans (with a crusader interval, 1098-1291).

After 4 centuries of Ottoman rule, during which the population declined to a low of 350,000 (1785), the land was taken in 1917 by Britain, which in the Balfour Declaration that year pledged to support a Jewish national homeland there, as foreseen by the Zionists. In 1920 a British Palestine Mandate was recognized; in 1922 the land east of the Jordan was detached.

Jewish immigration, begun in the late 19th century, swelled in the 1930s with refugees from the Nazis; heavy Arab immigration from Syria and Lebanon also occurred. Arab opposition to Jewish immigration turned violent in 1920, 1921, 1929, and 1936. The UN General Assembly voted in 1947 to partition Palestine into an Arab and a Jewish state. Britain withdrew in May 1948.

Israel was declared an independent state May 14, 1948; the Arabs rejected partition. Egypt, Jordan, Syria, Lebanon, Iraq, and Saudi Arabia invaded, but failed to destroy the Jewish state, which gained territory. Separate armistices with the Arab nations were signed in 1949; Jordan occupied the West Bank, Egypt occupied Gaza, but neither granted Palestinian autonomy. No peace settlement was obtained, and the Arab nations continued policies of economic boycott, blockade in the Suez Canal, and support of guerrillas. Several hundred thousand Arabs left the area of Jewish control; an equal number of Jews left the Arab countries for Israel 1949-53.

After persistent terrorist raids, Israel invaded Egypt's Sinai, Oct. 29, 1956, aided briefly by British and French forces. A UN cease-fire was arranged Nov. 6.

An uneasy truce between Israel and the Arab countries, supervised by a UN Emergency Force, prevailed until May 19, 1967, when the UN force withdrew at the demand of Egypt's Pres. Nasser. Egyptian forces reoccupied the Gaza Strip and closed the Gulf of Aqaba to Israeli shipping. In a 6-day war that started June 5, the Israelis took the Gaza Strip, occupied the Sinai Peninsula to the Suez Canal, and captured Old Jerusalem, Syria's Golan Heights, and Jordan's West Bank. The fighting was halted June 10 by UN-arranged cease-fire agreements.

Egypt and Syria attacked Israel, Oct. 6, 1973 (Yom Kippur, most solemn day on the Jewish calendar). Egypt and Syria were supplied by massive USSR military airlifts; the U.S. responded with an airlift to Israel. Israel counter-attacked, driving the Syrians back, and crossed the Suez Canal.

A cease fire took effect Oct. 24; a UN peace-keeping force went to the area. A disengagement agreement was signed Jan. 18, 1974, following negotiations by U.S. Secretary of State Henry Kissinger. Israel withdrew from the canal's W bank. A second withdrawal was completed in 1976; Israel returned the Sinai to Egypt in 1982.

Israel and Syria agreed to disengage June 1; Israel completed withdrawing from its salient (and a small part of the land taken in the 1967 war) June 25.

In the wake of the war, Golda Meir, long Israel's premier, resigned; severe inflation gripped the nation. Palestinian guerrillas staged massacres, killing scores of civilians 1974-75. Israel conducted preventive attacks in Lebanon through 1975. Israel aided Christian forces in the 1975-76 Lebanese civil war.

Israeli forces raided Entebbe, Uganda, July 3, 1976, and rescued 103 hostages seized by Arab and German terrorists.

In 1977, the conservative opposition, led by Menachem Begin, was voted into office for the first time. Egypt's Pres. Sadat visited Jerusalem Nov. 1977 and on Mar. 26, 1979. Egypt and Israel signed a formal peace treaty, ending 30 years of war, and establishing diplomatic relations.

A massive Israeli invasion of S. Lebanon, March 1978, following a Lebanon-based terrorist attack in Israel, left over 1,000 Lebanese and Palestinians dead. Israel withdrew in favor of a 6,000-man UN force, but continued to aid Christian militiamen.

A 5-day occupation of Israeli forces in southern Lebanon took place April 1980, in retaliation to the Palestinian raid on a kibbutz earlier that month. Violence on the Israeli-occupied West Bank rose in 1982 when Israel announced plans to build new Jewish settlements.

Israel affirmed the entire city of Jerusalem as its capital, July, 1980, encompassing the annexed Arab East Jerusalem.

Israel shot down, Apr. 28, 1981, two Syrian helicopters Israel claimed were attacking Lebanese Christian militia forces in the Beirut-Zahle area of Lebanon. Syria responded by installing Soviet-built surface-to-air missiles in Lebanon. Both the U.S. and Israel were unable to persuade Syria to withdraw the missles, and Israel threatened to destroy them.

On June 7, 1981, Israeli jets destroyed an Iraqi atomic reactor near Baghdad that, Israel claimed, would have enabled Iraq to manufacture nuclear weapons. The attack came as a complete surprise to Israeli friends and foes alike, and brought widespread condemnation.

In a close election, June 30, 1981, Prime Min. Menachem Begin was able to assemble a narrow coalition, he survived a no confidence motion in the Knesset by one vote, May 1982.

The Arab world was angered when an Israeli soldier armed with an automatic rifle ran amok killing two Arabs in the Dome of the Rock moslem shrine in Jerusalem, April 1982.

Israeli jets bombed Palestine Liberation Orgaization (PLO) strongholds in Lebanon April, May 1982. In reaction to the wounding of the Israeli ambassador to Great Britain, Israeli forces in a coordinated land, sea, and air attack invaded Lebanon, June 6, to destroy PLO strongholds in that country. Israeli and Syrian forces engaged in the Bekka Valley, June 9, but quickly agreed to a truce. Israeli forces reached the outskirts of Beirut June 10. (*See Chronology*)

Italy

Italian Republic

People: Population (1981 est.): 57,400,000. **Age distrib.** (%): 0–14: 23.7; 15–59: 58.8; 60+: 17.5. **Pop. density:** 490.44 per sq. mi. **Ethnic groups:** Italians, small minorities of Germans, Slovenes, Albanians, French, Ladins, Greeks. **Languages:** Italian. **Religions:** Predominantly Roman Catholic.

Geography: Area: 116,303 sq. mi., slightly larger than Arizona. **Location:** In S Europe, jutting into Mediterranean S. **Neighbors:** France on W, Switzerland, Austria on N, Yugoslavia on E. **Topography:** Occupies a long boot-shaped peninsula, extending SE from the Alps into the Mediterranean, with the islands of Sicily and Sardinia offshore. The alluvial Po Valley drains most of N. The rest of the country is rugged and mountainous, except for intermittent coastal plains, like the Campajna, S of Rome. Appenine Mts. run down through center of peninsula. **Capital:** Rome. **Cities** (1979 est.): Rome 2.9 mln.; Milan 1.6 mln.; Naples 1.2 mln.; Turin 1.1 mln.

Government: Head of state: Pres. Alessandro Pertini; b. Sept. 25, 1896; in office: July 9, 1978; **Head of government:** Prime Min. Giovanni Spadolini; b. June 21, 1925; in office: June 28, 1981. **Local divisions:** 20 regions with some autonomy, 94 provinces. **Armed forces:** regulars 363,900 (1981).

Economy: Industries: Steel, machinery, autos, textiles, shoes, machine tools, chemicals. **Chief crops:** Grapes, olives, citrus fruits, vegetables, wheat, rice. **Minerals:** Mercury, potash, gas, marble, sulphur, coal. **Crude oil reserves** (1980): 645 mln. bbls. **Per capita arable land:** 0.4 acres. **Meat prod.** (1980): beef: 1.13 mln. metric tons; pork: 1.06 mln. metric tons; lamb: 69,000 metric tons. **Fish catch** (1979): 427,000 metric tons. **Electricity prod.** (1980): 188.5 bln. kwh. **Crude steel prod.**

(1981): 24.5 mln. metric tons. **Labor force:** 15% agric.; 38% ind. and commerce; 46% services.

Finance: Currency: Lira (Mar. 1982: 1,322.00 = $1 US). **Gross domestic product** (1980): $394.0 bln. **Per capita income** (1980): $6,914. **Imports** (1981): $91.1 bln.; partners (1980): W. Ger. 17%, Fr. 14%, U.S. 7%. **Exports** (1981): $75.27 bln.; partners (1980): W. Ger. 18%, Fr. 15%, U.S. 5%, UK 6%. **Tourists** (1979): 21 mln.; receipts $4.76 bln. **National budget** (1980): $108.12 bln. revenues; $141.90 bln. expenditures. **International reserves less gold** (Feb. 1982): $17.98 bln. **Gold:** 66.67 mln. oz t. **Consumer prices** (change in 1981): 17.8%.

Transport: Railway traffic (1980): 38.9 bln. passenger-km; 18.2 bln. net ton-km. **Motor vehicles:** in use (1980): 17.6 mln. passenger cars, 1.3 mln. comm. vehicles; manuf. (1980): 1.4 mln. passenger cars, 167,400 comm. vehicles. **Civil aviation** (1980): 14.096 bln. passenger-km; 542.1 mln. freight ton-km. **Chief ports:** Genoa, Venice, Trieste, Taranto, Naples, La Spezia.

Communications: Television sets: 12.86 mln. licensed (1978), 1.8 mln. manuf. (1976). **Radios:** 13.4 mln. licensed (1978), 1.54 mln. manuf. (1976). **Telephones in use** (1980): 18,085,000. **Daily newspaper circ.** (1980): 123 per 1,000 pop.

Health: Life expectancy at birth (1978): 67.0 male; 73.1 female. **Births** (per 1,000 pop. 1980): 11.2. **Deaths** (per 1,000 pop. 1980): 9.7. **Natural increase** (1977): .4%. **Hospital beds** (per 100,000 pop. 1977): 1,036. **Physicians** (per 100,000 pop. 1977): 208. **Infant mortality** (per 1,000 live births 1981): 18.

Education (1978): **Literacy:** 95%. **Pop. 5-19:** in school: 61%, teachers per 1,000: 42.

Rome emerged as the major power in Italy after 500 BC, dominating the more civilized Etruscans to the N and Greeks to the S. Under the Empire, which lasted until the 5th century AD, Rome ruled most of Western Europe, the Balkans, the Near East, and North Africa.

After the Germanic invasions, lasting several centuries, a high civilization arose in the city-states of the N, culminating in the Renaissance. But German, French, Spanish, and Austrian intervention prevented the unification of the country. In 1859 Lombardy came under the crown of King Victor Emmanuel II of Sardinia. By plebiscite in 1860, Parma, Modena, Romagna, and Tuscany joined, followed by Sicily and Naples, and by the Marches and Umbria. The first Italian parliament declared Victor Emmanuel king of Italy Mar. 17, 1861. Mantua and Venetia were added in 1866 as an outcome of the Austro-Prussian war. The Papal States were taken by Italian troops Sept. 20, 1870, on the withdrawal of the French garrison. The states were annexed to the kingdom by plebiscite. Italy recognized the State of Vatican City as independent Feb. 11, 1929.

Fascism appeared in Italy Mar. 23, 1919, led by Benito Mussolini, who took over the government at the invitation of the king Oct. 28, 1922. Mussolini acquired dictatorial powers. He made war on Ethiopia and proclaimed Victor Emmanuel III emperor, defied the sanctions of the League of Nations, joined the Berlin-Tokyo axis, sent troops to fight for Franco against the Republic of Spain and joined Germany in World War II.

After Fascism was overthrown in 1943, Italy declared war on Germany and Japan and contributed to the Allied victory. It surrendered conquered lands and lost its colonies. Mussolini was killed by partisans Apr. 28, 1945.

Victor Emmanuel III abdicated May 9, 1946; his son Humbert II was king until June 10, when Italy became a republic after a referendum, June 2-3.

Reorganization of the Fascist party is forbidden. The cabinet normally represents a coalition of the Christian Democrats, largest of Italy's many parties, and one or 2 other parties.

The Vatican agreed in 1976 to revise its 1929 concordat with the state, depriving Roman Catholicism of its status as state religion. In 1974 Italians voted by a 3-to-2 margin to retain a 3-year-old law permitting divorce, which was opposed by the church.

Italy has enjoyed an extraordinary growth in industry and living standards since World War II, in part due to membership in the Common Market. Italy joined the European Monetary System, 1980. But in 1973-74, a fourfold increase in international oil prices helped disrupt the economy. Taxes were boosted in 1974. Western aid helped ease the crisis in 1975, but inflation and decline in confidence continued through 1982. A wave of left-wing political violence worsened in 1977 with kidnappings and assassinations and continued through 1982. Christian Dem. leader and former Prime Min. Moro was murdered May 1978 by Red Brigade terrorists.

There were 5 political kidnappings by terrorists in 1981 including U.S. Brig. Gen. James Dozier, a senior NATO officer, who was later rescued by Italian police.

The Cabinet of Prime Min. Arnaldo Forlani resigned, May 26, 1981, in the wake of revelations that numerous high-ranking officials were members of an illegally secret Masonic lodge. He was replaced by Giovanni Spadolini, leader of the Republican Party and the first non-Christian Democrat to head a coalition in the history of the Republic.

Sicily, 9,822 sq. mi., pop. (1980) 5,000,000, is an island 180 by 120 mi., seat of a region that embraces the island of **Pantelleria,** 32 sq. mi., and the **Lipari** group, 44 sq. mi., 63 14,000, including 2 active volcanoes: **Vulcano,** 1,637 ft. and **Stromboli,** 3,038 ft. From prehistoric times Sicily has been settled by various peoples; a Greek state had its capital at Syracuse. Rome took Sicily from Carthage 215 BC. **Mt. Etna,** 10,705 ft. active volcano, is tallest peak.

Sardinia, 9,262 sq. mi., pop. (1976) 1,600,000, lies in the Mediterranean, 115 mi. W of Italy and 7-1/2 mi. S of Corsica. It is 160 mi. long, 68 mi. wide, and mountainous, with mining of coal, zinc, lead, copper. In 1720 Sardinia was added to the possessions of the Dukes of Savoy in Piedmont and Savoy to form the Kingdom of Sardinia. Giuseppe Garibaldi is buried on the nearby isle of Caprera. **Elba,** 86 sq. mi., lies 6 mi. W of Tuscany. Napoleon I lived in exile on Elba 1814-1815.

Trieste. An agreement, signed Oct. 5, 1954, by Italy and Yugoslavia, confirmed, Nov. 10, 1975, gave Italy provisional administration over the northern section and the seaport of Trieste, and Yugoslavia the part of Istrian peninsula it has occupied.

Ivory Coast

Republic of Ivory Coast

People: Population (1981 est.): 8,300,000. **Age distrib.** (%): 0–14: 44.6; 15–59: 52.0; 60+: 3.4. **Pop. density:** 64.01 per sq. mi. **Urban** (1975): 32.4%. **Ethnic groups:** Baule 23%, Bete 18%, Senufo 15%, Malinke 11%, over 60 tribes. **Languages:** French (official), tribal languages. **Religions:** Moslems 23%, Christians 12%, animists 65%.

Geography: Area: 124,503 sq. mi., slightly larger than New Mexico. **Location:** On S. coast of W. Africa. **Neighbors:** Liberia, Guinea on W, Mali, Upper Volta on N, Ghana on E. **Topography:** Forests cover the W half of the country, and range from a coastal strip to halfway to the N on the E. A sparse inland plain leads to low mountains in NW. **Capital:** Abidjan. **Cities** (1976 est.): Abidjan 1,388,320; Bouaké (1977 cen.) 805,356.

Government: Head of state: Pres. Felix Houphouet-Boigny; b. Oct. 18, 1905; in office: Aug. 7, 1960. **Local divisions:** 26 departments. **Armed forces:** regulars 6,050 (1980).

Economy: Chief crops: Coffee, cocoa, bananas, cotton, pineapples, rice, oil palms. **Minerals:** Diamonds, manganese. **Other resources:** Tropical woods, rubber. **Per capita arable land:** 2.6 acres. **Meat prod.** (1980): beef: 41,000 metric tons; pork: 13,000 metric tons; lamb: 13,000 metric tons. **Fish catch** (1978): 79,000 metric tons. **Electricity prod.** (1980): 1.83 bln. kwh. **Labor force:** 75% agric.; 25% ind. and commerce.

Finance: Currency: CFA franc (Mar. 1982: 312.10 = $1 US). **Gross domestic product** (1980 est.): $10.6 bln. **Per capita income** (1980): $1,293. **Imports** (1979): $2.49 bln.; partners: Fr. 37%, W. Ger. 5%, Jap. 6%, U.S. 7%. **Exports** (1979): $2.51 bln.; partners: Fr. 24%, Neth. 17%, U.S. 10%, It. 8%. **Tourists** (1976): 122,200; receipts: $26 mln. **International reserves less gold** (Jan. 1982): $17.8 mln. **Gold:** 45,000 oz t. **Consumer prices** (changed in 1980): 14.6%.

Transport: Railway traffic (1978): 1.27 bln. passenger-km; 532.8 mln. net ton-km. **Motor vehicles:** in use (1976): 84,900 passenger cars, 43,500 comm. vehicles; assembled (1976): 7,000 passenger cars. **Chief ports:** Abidjan, Sassandra.

Communications: Television sets: 257,000 in use (1976). **Radios:** 600,000 in use (1976), 80,000 manuf. (1975). **Telephones in use** (1978): 58,558. **Daily newspaper circ.** (1980): 4 per 1,000 pop.

Health: Life expectancy at birth (1980): 44.4 male; 47.6 female. **Births** (per 1,000 pop. 1978): 47. **Deaths** (per 1,000 pop. 1978): 18. **Natural increase** (1978): 3.4%. **Hospital beds** (per 100,000 pop. 1977): 124. **Physicians** (per 100,000 pop. 1977): 4. **Infant mortality** (per 1,000 live births 1975): 138.

Education (1978): **Literacy:** 22%. **Pop. 5-19:** in school: 37%, teachers per 1,000: 9.

A French protectorate from 1842, Ivory Coast became independent in 1960. It is the most prosperous of tropical African nations, due to diversification of agriculture for export, close ties to France, and encouragement of foreign investment. About 20% of the population are workers from neighboring countries. Ivory Coast is a leader of the pro-Western bloc in Africa.

Jamaica

People: Population (1981 est.): 2,300,000. **Age distrib.** (%): 0–14: 45.9; 15–59: 45.7; 60+: 8.5. **Pop. density:** 501.89 per sq. mi. **Urban** (1970): 37.1%. **Ethnic groups:** Negroes 85%, mixed 10%, Chinese, Caucasians, East Indians. **Languages:** English, Jamaican Creole. **Religions:** Anglicans and Baptists in majority.

Geography: Area: 4,244 sq. mi., slightly smaller than Connecticut. **Location:** In West Indies. **Neighbors:** Nearest are Cuba on N, Haiti on E. **Topography:** The country is four-fifths covered by mountains. **Capital:** Kingston. **Cities** (1980 est.): Kingston 671,000 (met.).

Government: Head of state: Queen Elizabeth II, represented by Gov.-Gen. Florizel A. Glasspole; b. Sept. 25, 1909; in office: Mar. 2, 1973. **Head of government:** Prime Min. Edward Seaga; b. May 28, 1930; in office: Oct., 1980. **Local divisions:** 12 parishes; Kingston and St. Andrew corporate area. **Armed forces:** regulars 4,000 (1980).

Economy: Industries: Rum, molasses, cement, paper, tourism. **Chief crops:** Sugar cane, coffee, bananas, coconuts, ginger, cocoa, pimento, fruits. **Minerals:** Bauxite, limestone, gypsum. **Per capita arable land:** 0.2 acres. **Meat prod.** (1980): beef: 13,000 metric tons; pork: 9,000 metric tons. **Fish catch** (1978): 9,600 metric tons. **Electricity prod.** (1978): 2.1 bln. kwh. **Labor force:** 36.4% agric.; 32.7% services.

Finance: Currency: Dollar (Apr. 1982: 1.78 = $1 US). **Gross domestic product** (1981): $3.0 bln. **Per capita income** (1981): $1,340. **Imports** (1981): $1.4 bln.; partners (1979): U.S. 32%, Venez. 18%, Neth. Ant. 12%, UK 10%. **Exports** (1981): $994 mln.; partners (1979): U.S. 45%, UK 19%, Nor. 5%, Can. 6%. **Tourists** (1978): 382,000; receipts: $148 mln. **National budget** (1979): $446 mln. revenues; $625 mln. expenditures. **International reserves less gold** (Feb. 1982): $122.0 mln. **Consumer prices** (change in 1981): 12.8%.

Transport: Railway traffic (1977): 83 mln. passenger-km; 186 mln. net ton-km. **Chief ports:** Kingston, Montego Bay.

Communications: Television sets: 111,000 in use (1976). **Radios:** 555,000 in use (1976). **Telephones in use** (1978): 111,192. **Daily newspaper circ.** (1980): 53 per 1,000 pop.

Health: Life expectancy at birth (1961): 62.65 male; 66.63 female. **Births** (per 1,000 pop. 1978): 27. **Deaths** (per 1,000 pop. 1978): 6. **Natural increase** (1978): 1.2%. **Hospital beds** (per 100,000 pop. 1977): 369. **Physicians** (per 100,000 pop. 1977): 28. **Infant mortality** (per 1,000 live births 1981): 26.3.

Education (1978): **Literacy:** 86%. **Pop. 5-19:** in school: 66%, teachers per 1,000: 23.

Jamaica was visited by Columbus, 1494, and ruled by Spain (under whom Arawak Indians died out) until seized by Britain, 1655. Jamaica won independence Aug. 6, 1962.

In 1974 Jamaica sought an increase in taxes paid by U.S. and Canadian companies which mine bauxite on the island. The socialist government acquired 50% ownership of the companies' Jamaican interests in 1976, and was reelected that year. Rudimentary welfare state measures have been passed, but unemployment has increased. Relations with the U.S. improved greatly in 1981; Prime Minister Seaga was the first official visitor to Washington after Pres. Ronald Reagan's inauguration. Jamaica broke diplomatic relations with Cuba in December.

In 1982, Reagan became the first U.S. President to visit Jamaica and voiced strong support for the free-enterprise policies of the Seaga government.

Japan

People: Population (1981 est.): 118,000,000. **Age distrib.** (%): 0–14: 24.2; 15–59: 63.6; 60+: 12.2. **Pop. density:** 810.97 per sq. mi. **Urban** (1975): 75.9%. **Language:** Japanese. **Ethnic groups:** Japanese 99.4%, Korean 0.5%. **Religions:** Buddhism, Shintoism shared by large majority, Christians 0.8%.

Geography: Area: 145,824 sq. mi., slightly smaller than Montana. **Location:** Archipelago off E. coast of Asia. **Neighbors:** USSR on N, S. Korea on W. **Topography:** Japan consists of 4 main islands: Honshu ("mainland"), 87,805 sq. mi.; Hokkaido, 30,144 sq. mi.; Kyushu, 14,114 sq. mi.; and Shikoku, 7,049 sq. mi. The coast, deeply indented, measures 16,654 mi. The northern islands are a continuation of the Sakhalin Mts. The Kunlun range of China continues into southern islands, the ranges meeting in the Japanese Alps. In a vast transverse fissure crossing Honshu E-W rises a group of volcanoes, mostly extinct or inactive, including 12,388 ft. Fuji-San (Fujiyama) near Tokyo. **Capital:** Tokyo. **Cities** (1978 cen.): Tokyo 8.2 mln.; Osaka 2.6 mln.; Yokohama 2.7 mln.; Nagoya 2 mln.; Kyoto 1.4 mln.; Kobe 1.3 mln.; Sapporo 1.3 mln.; Kitakyushu 1 mln.; Kawasaki 1 mln.

Government: Head of state: Emp. Hirohito; b. Apr. 29, 1901; in office: Dec. 25, 1926. **Head of government:** Prime Min. Zenko Suzuki; b. Jan. 11, 1911; in office: July 17, 1980. **Local divisions:** 43 prefectures and 4 major municipal units. **Armed forces:** regulars 242,000; reserves 44,000 (1980).

Economy: Industries: Steel, vehicles, machinery, ships, electronics, precision instruments, chemicals, textiles, ceramics, wood products. **Chief crops:** Rice, grains, potatoes, tobacco, tea, beans, fruits. **Minerals:** Gold, molybdenum, silver, zinc, copper, lead, chromite, coal, sulphur, salt, oil. **Crude oil reserves** (1980): 55 mln. bbls. **Per capita arable land:** 0.09 acres. **Meat prod.** (1980): beef: 418,000 metric tons; pork: 1.47 mln. metric tons. **Fish catch** (1979): 9.6 mln. metric tons. **Electricity prod.** (1978): 495.18 bln. kwh. **Crude steel prod.** (1981): 101.6 mln. metric tons. **Labor force:** 12% agric.; 25% manuf.

Finance: Currency: Yen (Mar. 1982: 246.50 = $1 US). **Gross domestic product** (1980): $990 bln. **Per capita income** (1980): $8,460. **Imports** (1981): $142.8 bln.; partners (1980): U.S. 17%, Saudi Ar. 14%, Austral. 5%, Indon. 9%. **Exports** (1981): $151.50 bln.; partners (1980): U.S. 25%. **Tourists** (1977): 890,700; receipts: $425 mln. **National budget** (1980): $190.1 bln. revenues; $190.1 bln. expenditures. **International reserves less gold** (Apr. 1982): $27.93 bln. **Gold:** 24.23 mln. **Consumer prices** (change in 1980): 8.0%.

Transport: Railway traffic (1979): 315.3 bln. passenger-km; 39.5 bln. net ton-km. **Motor vehicles:** in use (1980): 23.6 mln. passenger cars, 13.9 mln. comm. vehicles; manuf. (1979): 7.03 mln. passenger cars; 4.004 mln. comm. vehicles. **Civil aviation** (1980): 51.2 bln. passenger-km; 2.002 bln. freight ton-km. **Chief ports:** Yokohama, Tokyo, Kobe, Osaka, Nagoya, Chiba, Kawasaki, Hakodate.

Communications: Television sets: 28.3 mln. in use (1978), 13.5 mln. manuf. (1979). **Radios:** 64.9 mln. in use (1977), 15.3 mln. manuf. (1980). **Telephones in use** (1980): 55.4 mln. **Daily newspaper circ.** (1980): 396 per 1,000 pop.

Health: Life expectancy at birth (1979): 73.4 male; 78.9 female. **Births** (per 1,000 pop. 1980): 13.7. **Deaths** (per 1,000 pop. 1980): 6.2. **Natural increase** (1977): 1.0%. **Hospital beds** (per 100,000 pop. 1977): 1,060. **Physicians** (per. 100,000 pop. 1977): 119. **Infant mortality** (per 1,000 live births 1977): 8.9.

Education (1978): **Literacy:** 99%. **Pop. 5–19:** in school: 72%, teachers per 1,000: 25.

According to Japanese legend, the empire was founded by Emperor Jimmu, 660 BC, but earliest records of a unified Japan date from 1,000 years later. Chinese influence was strong in the formation of Japanese civilization. Buddhism was introduced before the 6th century.

A feudal system, with locally powerful noble families and their samurai warrior retainers, dominated from 1192. Central power was held by successive families of shoguns (military dictators), 1192-1867, until recovered by the Emperor Meiji, 1868. The Portuguese and Dutch had minor trade with Japan in the 16th and 17th centuries; U.S. Commodore Matthew C. Perry opened it to U.S. trade in a treaty ratified 1854. Japan fought China, 1894-95, gaining Taiwan. After war with Russia, 1904-05, Russia ceded S half of Sakhalin and gave concessions in China. Japan annexed Korea 1910. In World War I Japan ousted Germany from Shantung, took over German Pacific islands. Japan took Manchuria 1931, started war with China 1932. Japan launched war against the U.S. by attack on Pearl Harbor Dec. 7, 1941. Japan surrendered Aug. 14, 1945.

In a new constitution adopted May 3, 1947, Japan renounced the right to wage war; the emperor gave up claims to divinity; the Diet became the sole law-making authority.

The U.S. and 48 other non-communist nations signed a peace

treaty and the U.S. a bilateral defense agreement with Japan, in San Francisco Sept. 8, 1951, restoring Japan's sovereignty as of April 28, 1952. Japan signed separate treaties with Nationalist China, 1952; India, 1952; a declaration with USSR ending a technical state of war, 1956. In Dec. 1965 Japan and South Korea agreed to resume diplomatic relations.

On June 26, 1968, the U.S. returned to Japanese control the Bonin Is., the Volcano Is. (including Iwo Jima) and Marcus Is. On May 15, 1972, Okinawa, the other Ryukyu Is. and the Daito Is. were returned to Japan by the U.S.; it was agreed the U.S. would continue to maintain military bases on Okinawa. Japan and the USSR have failed to resolve disputed claims of sovereignty over 4 of the Kurile Is. and over offshore fishing rights.

On Sept. 29, 1972, Japan and mainland China agreed to resume diplomatic relations; Japan and Taiwan severed diplomatic relations. A Japan-China friendship treaty was signed 1978.

Industrialization was begun in the late 19th century. After World War II, Japan emerged as one of the most powerful economies in the world, and as a leader in technology.

In 1982, the U.S. and EC member nations criticized Japan for its restrictive policy on imports which has given Japan a substantial trade surplus.

The Liberal Democratic (conservative) party controlled almost every post-war government, but by declining margins.

Jordan

Hashemite Kingdom of Jordan

Population (1981 est.): 3,500,000. **Age distrib.** (%): 0–14: 51.6; 15–59: 44.4; 60+: 4.0. **Pop. density:** 85.53 per sq. mi. **Urban** (1974): 42.0%. **Ethnic groups:** Arabs, small minorities of Circassians, Armenians, Kurds. **Languages:** Arabic. **Religions:** Sunni Moslems 93.6%, Christians 5%.

Geography: Area: 37,297 sq. mi., slightly larger than Indiana. **Location:** In W Asia. **Neighbors:** Israel on W, Saudi Arabia on S, Iraq on E, Syria on N. **Topography:** About 88% of Jordan is arid. Fertile areas are in W. Only port is on short Aqaba Gulf coast. Country shares Dead Sea (1,296 ft. below sea level) with Israel. **Capital:** Amman. **Cities** (1979 est.): Amman 684,600; Zarka 263,400; Irbid 136,770.

Government: Head of state: King Hussein I; b. Nov. 14, 1935; in office: Aug. 11, 1952. **Head of government:** Prime Min. Mudar Badran, b. 1934; in office: Aug. 28, 1980. **Local divisions:** 8 governorates. **Armed forces:** regulars 67,300 (1980).

Economy: Industries: Textiles, cement, food processing. **Chief crops:** Grains, olives, vegetables, fruits. **Minerals:** Phosphate, potash. **Per capita arable land:** 1.0 acres. **Electricity prod.** (1979): 901 mln. kwh. **Labor force:** 30% agric.

Finance: Currency: Dinar (Apr. 1982: 0.27 = $1 US). **Gross domestic product** (1980): $3.2 bln. **Per capita income** (1976): $552. **Imports** (1980): $2.3 bln.; partners (1979): Saudi Ar. 13%, W. Ger. 12%, UK 8%. **Exports** (1980): $573 mln.; partners (1979): Saudi Ar. 23%, Syria 15%, Iraq. 15%. **Tourists** (1978): 1.1 mln.; receipts: $340 mln. **National budget** (1980): $751.59 mln. revenues; $1.68 bln. expenditures. **International reserves less gold** (Feb. 1982): $1.02 bln. **Gold:** 1.07 mln. oz t. **Consumer prices** (change in 1980): 11.0%.

Transport: Motor vehicles: in use (1980): 90,400 passenger cars, 27,400 comm. vehicles. **Civil aviation** (1980): 2.6 bln. passenger-km; 81.2 mln. freight ton-km. **Chief ports:** Aqaba.

Communications: Television sets: 165,000 licensed (1977). **Radios:** 532,000 in use (1977). **Telephones in use** (1979): 52,400. **Daily newspaper circ.** (1980): 58 per 1,000 pop.

Health: Life expectancy at birth (1963): 52.6 male; 52.0 female. **Births** (per 1,000 pop. 1978): 49. **Deaths** (per 1,000 pop. 1978): 11. **Natural increase** (1978): 3.9%. **Hospital beds** (per 100,000 pop. 1977): 86. **Physicians** (per 100,000 pop. 1977): 37. **Infant mortality** (per 1,000 live births 1976): 88.

Education (1978): **Literacy:** 58%. **Pop. 5-19:** in school: 56%, teachers per 1,000: 20.

From ancient times to 1922 the lands to the E of the Jordan were culturally and politically united with the lands to the W. Arabs conquered the area in the 7th century; the Ottomans took control in the 16th. Britain's 1920 Palestine Mandate covered both sides of the Jordan. In 1921, Abdullah, son of the ruler of Hejaz in Arabia, was installed by Britain as emir of an autonomous Transjordan, covering two-thirds of Palestine. An independent kingdom was proclaimed, 1946.

During the 1948 Arab-Israeli war the West Bank and old city of Jerusalem were added to the kingdom, which changed its name to Jordan. All these territories were lost to Israel in the 1967 war, which swelled the number of Arab refugees on the East Bank. A 1974 Arab summit conference designated the Palestine Liberation Organization as the sole representative of Arabs on the West Bank. Jordan accepted the move, and was granted an annual subsidy by Arab oil states. The U.S. has also provided substantial economic and military support.

King Hussein actively promoted rejection of the Egyptian-Israeli peace treaty; Jordan was the first Arab country to sever diplomatic relations with Egypt, Mar. 1979.

Kenya

Republic of Kenya

People: Population (1981 est.): 17,100,000. **Age distrib.** (%): 0–14: 48.4; 15–59: 46.3; 60+: 5.4. **Pop. density:** 72.90 per sq. mi. **Urban** (1969): 9.9%. **Ethnic groups:** Kikuyu 20%, Luo 15%, Luhya 14%, Balhya 13%, Kamba 11%, others, including 280,000 Asians, Arabs, Europeans. **Languages:** Swahili (official), English. **Religions:** Protestants 32.6%, Roman Catholics 17.4%, Moslems 24%, others.

Geography: Area: 224,081 sq. mi., slightly smaller than Texas. **Location:** On Indian O. coast of E. Africa. **Neighbors:** Uganda on W, Tanzania on S, Somalia on E, Ethopia, Sudan on N. **Topography:** The northern three-fifths of Kenya is arid. To the S, a low coastal area and a plateau varying from 3,000 to 10,000 ft. The Great Rift Valley enters the country N-S, flanked by high mountains. **Capital:** Nairobi. **Cities** (1978 est.): Nairobi (met.) 818,000; Mombasa (met.) 391,000.

Government: Head of state: Pres. Daniel arap Moi, b. Sept., 1924; in office: Aug. 22, 1978. **Local divisions:** Nairobi and 7 provinces. **Armed forces:** regulars 14,450 (1980).

Economy: Industries: Tourism, light industry. **Chief crops:** Coffee, tea, cereals, cotton, sisal. **Minerals:** Gold, limestone, diatomite, salt, barytes, magnesite, felspar, sapphires, fluospar, garnets. **Other resources:** Timber, hides. **Per capita arable land:** 0.3 acres. **Meat prod.** (1980): beef: 193,000 metric tons; pork: 4,000 metric tons; lamb: 38,000 metric tons. **Fish catch** (1978): 42,800 metric tons. **Electricity prod.** (1979): 1.5 bln. kwh. **Labor force:** 21% agric.; 23% ind. and commerce; 13% services.

Finance: Currency: Shilling (Mar. 1982: 10.57 = $1 US). **Gross domestic product** (1979): $6.04 bln. **Per capita income** (1978): $337. **Imports** (1980): $2.30 bln.; partners: (1979): UK 23%, W. Ger. 11%, Jap. 8%, Saudi Ar. 8%. **Exports** (1980): $1.30 bln.; partners (1979): W. Ger. 15%, UK 14%, Ugan. 9%. **Tourists** (1978): 360,620; receipts: $158 mln. **National budget** (1980): $1.69 bln. revenues; $1.87 bln. expenditures. **International reserves less gold** (Feb. 1982): $203.1 mln. **Gold:** 80,000 oz t. **Consumer prices** (change in 1981): 11.8%.

Transport: Motor vehicles: in use (1979): 118,035 passenger cars, 111,048 comm. vehicles. **Chief ports:** Mombasa.

Communications: Television sets: 60,000 in use (1977). **Radios:** 525,000 in use (1977). **Telephones in use** (1980): 168,200. **Daily newspaper circ.** (1980): 12 per 1,000 pop.

Health: Life expectancy at birth (1979): 47.0 male; 51.0 female. **Births** (per 1,000 pop. 1978): 54. **Deaths** (per 1,000 pop. 1978): 14. **Natural increase** (1978): 4.0%. **Hospital beds** (per 100,000 pop. 1977): 128. **Physicians** (per 100,000 pop. 1977): 8. **Infant mortality** (per 1,000 live births 1979): 83.

Education (1978): **Literacy:** 40%. **Pop. 5-19:** in school: 62%, teachers per 1,000: 18.

Arab colonies exported spices and slaves from the Kenya coast as early as the 8th century. Britain obtained control in the 19th century. Kenya won independence Dec. 12, 1963, 4 years after the end of the violent Mau Mau uprising.

Kenya has shown steady growth in industry and agriculture under a modified private enterprise system, and has had a relatively free political life. But stability was shaken in 1974-5, with opposition charges of corruption and oppression.

In 1968 ties with Somalia were restored after 4 years of skirmishes. Tanzania closed its Kenya border in 1977 in a dispute over the collapse of the East African Community. Kenya welcomed the overthrow of Idi Amin.

The U.S. agreed in 1976 to sell several jet fighters to Kenya. A military and economic aid accord giving the U.S. access to air and naval bases was concluded, Apr. 1980.

Kiribati

Republic of Kiribati

People: Population (1980 est.): 60,000. **Pop. density:** 227.27 per sq. mi. **Ethnic groups:** nearly all Micronesian, some Polynesians. **Languages:** Gilbertese and English (official). **Religions:** evenly divided between Protestant and Roman Catholic.

Geography: Area: 266 sq. mi., slightly smaller than New York City. **Location:** 33 Micronesian islands (the Gilbert, Line, and Phoenix groups) in the mid-Pacific scattered in a 2-mln. sq. mi. chain around the point where the International Date Line cuts the Equator. **Neighbors:** Nearest are Nauru to SW, Tuvalu and Tokelau Is. to S. **Topography:** except Banaba (Ocean) I., all are low-lying, with soil of coral sand and rock fragments, subject to erratic rainfall. **Capital** (1980): Tarawa 22,148.

Government: Head of state and of government: Pres. Ieremia Tabai, b. Dec. 16, 1950; in office: July 12, 1979.

Economy: Industries: Copra. **Chief crops:** Coconuts, breadfruit, pandanus, bananas, paw paw. **Other resources:** Fish. **Electricity prod.** (1978): 5 mln. kwh.

Finance: Currency: Australian dollar. **Imports** (1979): $15.0 mln.; partners (1978): Austral. 58%, NZ 8%, UK 8%, Jap. 7%. **Exports** (1979): $20 mln.; partners (1977): Austral. 57%, NZ 29%, UK 13%. **National budget** (1978): $16.3 mln. revenues; $14 mln. expenditures.

Transport: Chief port: Tarawa.

Communications: Radios: 8,200 in use (1976). **Telephones in use** (1978): 1,386.

Health: Pop. per hospital bed (1977): 200.

Education: Pop. 5–19: in school (1977): 13,679.

A British protectorate since 1892, the Gilbert and Ellice Islands colony was completed with the inclusion of the Phoenix Islands, 1937. Self-rule was granted 1971; the Ellice Islands separated from the colony 1975 and became independent Tuvalu, 1978. Kiribati (pronounced *Kiribass)* independence was attained July 12, 1979. Under a Treaty of Friendship, pending ratification by the U.S. Senate, the U.S. relinquishes its claims to several of the Line and Phoenix islands, including Christmas, Canton, and Enderbury.

Tarawa Atoll was the scene of some of the bloodiest fighting in the Pacific during WW II.

North Korea

Democratic People's Republic of Korea

People: Population (Jan. 1981 est.): 19,900,000. **Pop. density:** 406.26 per sq. mi. **Ethnic groups:** Korean. **Languages:** Korean. **Religions:** Buddhism, Confucianism, Chondokyo.

Geography: Area: 47,077 sq. mi., slightly smaller than Mississippi. **Location:** In northern E. Asia. **Neighbors:** China, USSR on N, S. Korea on S. **Topography:** Mountains and hills cover nearly all the country, with narrow valleys and small plains in between. The N and the E coast are the most rugged areas. **Capital:** Pyongyang. **Cities** (1973 est.): Pyongyang 957,000; Hamhung 484,000; Chongjin 306,000.

Government: Head of state: Pres. Kim Il-Sung; b. Apr. 15, 1912; in office: Dec. 28, 1972. **Head of government:** Premier Li Jong Ok; in office: Dec. 15, 1977. **Head of Communist Party:** Gen. Sec. Kim Il-Sung; in office: 1945. **Local divisions:** 9 provinces, 4 municipalities, one urban district. **Armed forces:** regulars 630,000 (1980).

Economy: Industries: Textiles, fertilizers, cement. **Chief crops:** Grain, rice. **Minerals:** Coal, lead tungsten, zinc, graphite, magnesite, iron, copper, gold, phosphate, salt, fluorspar. **Per capita arable land:** 0.3 acres. **Meat prod.** (1980): beef: 31,000 metric tons; pork: 115,000 metric tons. **Fish catch** (1979): 1.3 mln. metric tons. **Crude steel prod.** (1981 est.) 5.5 mln. metric tons. **Labor force:** 48% agric.

Finance: Currency: Won (Sept. 1981): .95 = $1 US). **Gross domestic product** (1978 est.): $10.4 bln. **Per capita income** (1978, in 1975 U.S. dollars): $570. **Imports** (1980): $2.1 bln.; partners (1980): China 32%, USSR 20%, Jap. 17%. **Exports** (1980): $1.9 bln.; partners (1980): USSR 22% China 35%, Saudi Ar. 12%, Jap. 9%.

Transport: Chief ports: Chonglin, Hamhung, Nampo.

Health: Life expectancy at birth (1975): 58.8 male; 62.5 female. **Births** (per 1,000 pop. 1978): 43. **Deaths** (per 1,000 pop. 1978): 11. **Natural increase** (1978): 3.2%. **Hospital beds** (per 100,000 pop. 1977): 59. **Physicians** (per 100,000 pop. 1977): 40.

Education (1978): **Literacy:** 85%. **Pop. 5-19:** in school: 61%, teachers per 1,000: 13.

The Democratic People's Republic of Korea was founded May 1, 1948, in the zone occupied by Russian troops after World War II. Its armies tried to conquer the south, 1950. After 3 years of fighting with Chinese and U.S. intervention, a cease-fire was proclaimed. N. Korea has maintained ties with both China and Russia. The U.S. has no diplomatic ties.

Industry, begun by the Japanese during their 1910-45 occupation, and nationalized in the 1940s, had grown substantially, using N. Korea's abundant mineral and hydroelectric resources.

South Korea

Republic of Korea

People: Population (1981 est.): 40,000,000. **Age distrib.** (%): 0–14: 38.1; 15–59: 56.3; 60+: 5.6. **Pop. density:** 973.42 per sq. mi. **Urban** (1975): 48.4%. **Ethnic groups:** Korean. **Languages:** Korean. **Religions:** Buddhism, Confucianism, Christian, Chondokyo.

Geography: Area: 38,211 sq. mi., slightly larger than Indiana. **Location:** In Northern E. Asia. **Neighbors:** N. Korea on N. **Topography:** The country is mountainous, with a rugged east coast. The western and southern coasts are deeply indented, with many islands and harbors. **Capital:** Seoul. **Cities** (1980 est.): Seoul 8,000,000; Pusan 3,000,000; Taegu 1,309,131.

Government: Head of state: Pres. Chun Doo Hwan; b. Jan. 18, 1931; in office: Dec. 1979. **Head of government:** Prime Min. Yoo Chang Soon; in office: Jan. 3, 1982. **Local divisions:** 9 provinces, 2 special cities. **Armed forces:** regulars 592,000 (1980).

Economy: Industries: Electronics, ships, textiles, clothing, motor vehicles. **Chief crops:** Rice, barley, vegetables. **Minerals:** Tungsten, coal, graphite. **Per capita arable land:** 0.1 acres. **Meat prod.** (1980): beef: 97,000 metric tons; pork: 231,000 metric tons. **Fish catch:** (1979): 2.1 mln. metric tons. **Electricity prod.** (1980): 37.2 bln. kwh. **Crude steel prod.** (1981): 10.7 mln. metric tons. **Labor force:** 36% agric.; 24% manuf., 40% services.

Finance: Currency: Won (Mar. 1982: 718.30 = $1 US). **Gross domestic product** (1980): $59.17 bln. **Per capita income** (1978): $1,187. **Imports** (1981): $26.1 bln.; partners (1980): Jap. 26%, U.S. 22%, Saudi Ar. 15%, Kuw. 8%. **Exports** (1981): $21.25 bln.; partners (1980): U.S. 26%, Jap. 17%, Saudi Ar. 5%, W. Ger. 5%. **Tourists** (1978): 1.079 mln.; receipts: $408 mln. **National budget** (1981): $9.8 bln. revenues; $9.0 bln. expenditures. **International reserves less gold** (Mar. 1982): $2.82 bln. **Gold:** 303,000 oz t. **Consumer prices** (change in 1981): 23.3%.

Transport: Railway traffic (1980): 20.7 bln. passenger-km; 10.5 bln. net ton-km. **Motor vehicles:** in use (1980): 249,100 passenger cars, 226,900 comm. vehicles; assembled (1978): 92,328 passenger cars; 65,616 comm. vehicles. **Civil aviation** (1980): 10.8 bln. passenger-km; 850.3 mln. freight ton-km. **Chief ports:** Pusan, Inchon.

Communications: Television sets: 5.1 mln. in use (1978), 5.8 mln. manuf. (1979). **Radios:** 14.5 mln. in use (1977), 4.7 mln. manuf. (1979). **Telephones in use** (1980): 2.8 mln. **Daily newspaper circ.** (1980): 133 per 1,000 pop.

Health: Life expectancy at birth (1970): 63 male; 67 female. **Births** (per 1,000 pop. 1978): 23. Deaths (per 1,000 pop. 1978): 6. **Natural increase** (1978): 1.6%. **Hospital beds** (per 100,000 pop. 1977): 68. **Physicians** (per 100,000 pop. 1977): 49.

Education (1978): **Literacy:** 92%. **Pop. 5-19:** in school: 63%, teachers per 1,000: 14.

Korea, once called the Hermit Kingdom, has a recorded history since the 1st century BC. It was united in a kingdom under the Silla Dynasty, 668 AD. It was at times associated with the

Chinese empire; the treaty that concluded the Sino-Japanese war of 1894-95 recognized Korea's complete independence. In 1910 Japan forcibly annexed Korea as Chosun.

At the Potsdam conference, July, 1945, the 38th parallel was designated as the line dividing the Soviet and the American occupation. Russian troops entered Korea Aug. 10, 1945, U.S. troops entered Sept. 8, 1945. The Soviet military organized socialists and communists and blocked efforts to let the Koreans unite their country. *(See Index for Korean War.)*

The South Koreans formed the Republic of Korea in May 1948 with Seoul as the capital. Dr. Syngman Rhee was chosen president but a movement spearheaded by college students forced his resignation Apr. 26, 1960.

In an army coup May 16, 1961, Gen. Park Chung Hee became chairman of the ruling junta. He was elected president, 1963; a 1972 referendum provided more presidential powers and allowed him to be reelected for 6 year terms unlimited times. Park was assassinated by the chief of the Korean CIA, Oct. 26, 1979. The calm of the new government was halted by the rise of Gen. Chon Too Hwan, head of the military intelligence, who reinstated martial law, and reverted South Korea to the police state it was under Park.

North Korean raids across the border tapered off in 1971, but incidents occurred in 1973 and 1974. In July 1972 South and North Korea agreed on a common goal of reunifying the 2 nations by peaceful means.

Korean agents were charged in 1976-77 with giving questionable gifts to U.S. politicians to promote foreign aid.

Kuwait

State of Kuwait

People: Population (1981 est.): 1,500,000. **Age distrib.** (%): 0–14: 44.4; 15–59: 53.1; 60+: 2.6. **Pop. density:** 176.09 per sq. mi. **Ethnic groups:** Arabs 85%, Iranians, Indians, Pakistanis 13%. **Languages:** Arabic, others. **Religions:** Moslems (most Sunni) predominate.

Geography: Area: 6,532 sq. mi., the size of Massachusetts. **Location:** In Middle East, at N end of Persian Gulf. **Neighbors:** Iraq on N, Saudi Arabia on S. **Topography:** The country is flat, very dry, and extremely hot. **Capital:** Kuwait. **Cities** (1970 cen.): Hawalli 106,542; Kuwait City 80,405.

Government: Head of state: Emir Shaikh Jabir al-Ahmad al-Jabir as-Sabah; b. 1928; in office: Jan. 1, 1978. **Head of government:** Prime Min. Shaikh Saad Abdulla as-Salim as-Sabah; in office: Feb. 8, 1978. **Local divisions:** 4 governorates. **Armed forces:** regulars 11,900.

Economy: Industries: Oil products. **Minerals:** Oil, gas. **Crude oil reserves** (1980): 65.4 bln. bbls. **Per capita arable land:** 0.002 acres. **Electricity prod.** (1979): 7.2 bln. kwh. **Labor force:** 2% agric.; 8%. manuf.

Finance: Currency: Dinar (Apr. 1982: 0.26 = $1 US). **Gross domestic product** (1979): $23.17 bln. **Per capita income** (1975): $11,431. **Imports** (1980): $7.29 bln.; partners (1979): Jap. 18%, U.S. 14%, UK 10%, W. Ger. 8%. **Exports** (1980): $19.97 bln.; partners (1979): Jap. 24%, UK 6%, Neth. 11%, It. 9%. **National budget** (1980): $24.7 bln. revenues; $7.6 bln. expenditures. **International reserves less gold** (Feb. 1982): $3.72 bln. **Gold:** 2.53 mln. oz t. **Consumer prices** (change in (1980): 7.7%.

Transport: Motor vehicles: in use (1979): 363,300 passenger cars, 125,400 comm. vehicles. **Civil aviation** (1980): 2.1 bln. passenger-km; 74.7 mln. freight ton-km. **Chief ports:** Mina al-Ahmadi.

Communications: Television sets: 182,000 in use (1975). **Radios:** 506,000 in use (1976). **Telephones in use** (1978): 152,517. **Daily newspaper circ.** (1980): 322 per 1,000 pop.

Health: Life expectancy at birth (1980): 67.3 male; 71.6 female. **Births** (per 1,000 pop. 1978): 41. **Deaths** (per 1,000 pop. 1978): 5. **Natural increase** (1978): 5.9%. **Hospital beds** (per 100,000 pop. 1977): 388. **Physicians** (per. 100,000 pop. 1977): 124. **Infant mortality** (per 1,000 live births 1977): 39.1.

Education (1978): **Literacy:** 60%. **Pop. 5-19:** in school: 64%, teachers per 1,000: 49.

Kuwait is ruled by the Al-Sabah dynasty, founded 1759. Britain ran foreign relations and defense from 1899 until independence in 1961. The majority of the population is non-Kuwaiti, with many Palestinians, and cannot vote.

Iraqi troops crossed the Kuwait border in 1973 but soon withdrew. Kuwait has ordered weapons from France and the U.S.

Oil, first exported in 1946, is the fiscal mainstay, providing 92% of Kuwait's income. Oil pays for free medical care, education, and social security. There are no taxes, except customs duties.

The oil glut caused a 45% drop in oil revenues forcing a 40% cut in government spending in the 1982-83 budget.

Laos

Lao People's Democratic Republic

People: Population (1981 est.): 3,500,000. **Pop. density:** 40.69 per sq. mi. **Urban** (1973): 14.7%. **Ethnic groups:** Lao 50%, Thai 20%, Meo and Yao 15%, others. **Languages:** Lao (official), French, English. **Religions:** Buddhists 90%, tribal.

Geography: Area: 91,428 sq. mi., slightly larger than Utah. **Location:** In Indochina Peninsula in SE Asia. **Neighbors:** Burma, China on N, Vietnam on E, Cambodia on S, Thailand on W. **Topography:** Landlocked, dominated by jungle. High mountains along the eastern border are the source of the E-W rivers slicing across the country to the Mekong R., which defines most of the western border. **Capital:** Vientiane. **Cities** (1978 est.); Vientiane 200,000.

Government: Head of state: Pres. Souphanouvong; b. July 13, 1909; in office: Dec. 2, 1975. **Head of government:** Prime Min. Kaysone Phomvihan; b. Dec. 13, 1920; in office: Dec. 2, 1975. **Local divisions:** 13 provinces. **Armed forces:** regulars 54,550 (1980).

Economy: Industries: Wood products. **Chief crops:** Rice, corn, tobacco, cotton, opium, citrus fruits, coffee. **Minerals:** Tin. **Other resources:** Forests. **Per capita arable land:** 0.7 acres. **Meat prod.** (1980): beef: 12,000 metric tons; pork: 30,000 metric tons. **Fish catch** (1978): 20,000 metric tons. **Electricity prod.** (1979): 840 mln. kwh. **Labor force:** 76% agric.

Finance: Currency: New kip (Nov. 1981): 10 = $1 US). **Gross domestic product** (1978 est.): $220 mln. **Per capita income** (1976 est.): $85. **Imports** (1980): $130.1 mln.; partners (1974): Thai. 49%, Jap. 19%, Fr. 7%, W. Ger. 7%. **Exports** (1980): $30.5 mln.; partners (1974): Thai. 73%, Malaysia 11%, HK 10%. **Consumer prices** (change in 1975): 84.3%.

Transport: Motor vehicles: in use (1974): 14,100 passenger cars, 2,500 comm. vehicles. **Civil Aviation** (1980): 7 mln. passenger km; 100,000 net ton-km.

Communications: Radios: 200,000 licensed (1977).

Health: Life expectancy at birth (1975): 39.1 male; 41.8 female. **Births** (per 1,000 pop. 1978): 44. **Deaths** (per 1,000 pop. 1978): 21. **Natural increase** (1978): 0.9%. **Hospital beds** (per 100,000 pop. 1977): 98. **Physicians** (per 100,000 pop. 1977): 6.

Education: (1978): **Literacy:** 28%. **Pop. 5-19:** in school: 40%, teachers per 1,000: 14.

Laos became a French protectorate in 1893, but regained independence as a constitutional monarchy July 19, 1949.

Conflicts among neutralist, communist and conservative factions created a chaotic political situation. Armed conflict increased after 1960.

The 3 factions formed a coalition government in June 1962, with neutralist Prince Souvanna Phouma as premier. A 14-nation conference in Geneva signed agreements, 1962, guaranteeing neutrality and independence. By 1964 the Pathet Lao had withdrawn from the coalition, and, with aid from N. Vietnamese troops, renewed sporadic attacks. U.S. planes bombed the Ho Chi Minh trail, supply line from N. Vietnam to communist forces in Laos and S. Vietnam. An estimated 2.75 million tons of bombs were dropped on Laos during the fighting.

In 1970 the U.S. stepped up air support and military aid. There were an est. 67,000 N. Vietnamese troops in Laos, and some 15,000 Thais financed by the U.S.

After Pathet Lao military gains, Souvanna Phouma in May 1975 ordered government troops to cease fighting; the Pathet Lao took control. A Lao People's Democratic Republic was proclaimed Dec. 3, 1975; it is strongly influenced by Vietnam.

There were border incidents with Thailand and China in 1981.

Lebanon

Republic of Lebanon

People: Population (1981 est.): 3,000,000. **Age distrib.** (%): 0–14: 42.6; 15–59: 49.6; 60+: 7.7. **Pop. density:** 787.05 per sq. mi. **Urban** (1970): 60.1%. **Ethnic groups:** Arabs 93%, Armenians 6%. **Languages:** Arabic, French, Armenian. **Religions:** Predominately Moslems and Christians; Druze minority.

Geography: Area: 3,950 sq. mi., smaller than Connecticut. **Location:** On Eastern end of Mediterranean Sea. **Neighbors:** Syria on E. Israel on S. **Topography:** There is a narrow coastal strip, and 2 mountain ranges running N-S enclosing the fertile Beqaa Valley. The Litani R. runs S through the valley, turning W to empty into the Mediterranean. **Capital:** Beirut. **Cities** (1978 est.): Beirut 702,000; Tripoli 175,000.

Government: Head of state: Pres. Elias Sarkis; b. July 20, 1924; in office: Sept. 23, 1976; **Head of government:** Prime Min. Shafig al-Wazzan; in office: Oct. 26, 1980. **Local divisions:** 5 provinces. **Armed forces:** regulars 23,150 (1980).

Economy: Industries: Trade, food products, textiles, cement, oil products. **Chief crops:** Fruits, olives, tobacco, grapes, vegetables, grains. **Minerals:** Iron. **Per capita arable land:** 0.2 acres. **Meat prod.** (1980): beef: 13,000 metric tons; lamb: 13,000 metric tons. **Electricity prod.** (1978): 1.70 bln. kwh. **Labor force:** 18% agric.; 17% manuf.

Finance: Currency: Pound (Mar. 1982: 4.94 = $1 US). **Gross domestic product** (1973 est.): $3.0 bln. **Per capita income** (1975): $1,142. **Imports** (1980): $3.46 bln.; partners (1980): It. 12%, Fr. 9%, U.S. 8%, Saudi Ar. 9%. **Exports** (1979): $705 mln.; partners (1980): Saudi Ar. 32%, Syria 9%, Jor. 5%, Kuw. 7%. **International reserves less gold** (Feb. 1982): $1.29 bln. **Gold:** 9.22 mln. oz t.

Transport: Railway traffic (1974): 2 mln. passenger-km; 42 mln. net ton-km. **Motor vehicles:** in use (1978): 282,400 passenger cars, 28,600 comm. vehicles. **Civil aviation** (1980): 1,571 mln. passenger-km; 540 mln. freight ton-km. **Chief ports:** Beirut, Tripoli, Sidon.

Communications: Television sets: 450,000 in use (1977). **Radios:** 1.6 mln. in use (1976). **Telephones:** in use (1978): 231,000. **Daily newspaper circ.** (1980): 177 per 1,000 pop.

Health: Life expectancy at birth (1975): 61.4 male; 65.1 female. **Births** (per 1,000 pop. 1978): 36. **Deaths** (per 1,000 pop. 1978): 11. **Natural increase** (1978): 2.5%. **Hospital beds** (per 100,000 pop. 1977): 384. **Physicians** (per 100,000 pop. 1977): 75. **Infant mortality** (per 1,000 live births 1975): 13.6.

Education: (1978): **Literacy:** 76%. **Pop. 5-19:** in school: 57%, teachers per 1,000: 40.

Formed from 5 former Turkish Empire districts, Lebanon became an independent state Sept. 1, 1920, administered under French mandate 1920-41. French troops withdrew in 1946.

Under the 1943 National Covenant, all public positions were divided among the various religious communities, with Christians in the majority. By the 1970s, Moslems became the majority, and demanded a larger political and economic role.

U.S. Marines intervened, May-Oct. 1958, during a Syrian-aided revolt. Lebanon's efforts to restrain Palestinian commandos caused armed clashes in 1969. Continued raids against Israeli civilians, 1970-75, brought Israeli attacks against guerrilla camps and villages. Israeli troops occupied S. Lebanon, March 1978, but were replaced by a UN force, and again in Apr. 1980.

An estimated 60,000 were killed and billions of dollars in damage inflicted in a 1975-76 civil war. Palestinian units and leftist Moslems fought against the Maronite militia, the Phalange, and other Christians. Several Arab countries provided political and arms support to the various factions, while Israel aided Christian forces. Up to 15,000 Syrian troops intervened in 1976, and fought Palestinian groups. Arab League troops from several nations tried to impose a cease-fire.

Clashes between Syrian troops and Christian forces erupted, Apr. 1, 1981, near Zahle, Lebanon, bringing to an end the cease-fire that had been in place. By Apr. 22, fighting had broken out not only between Syrians and Christians, but also between two Moslem factions. Israeli commandos attacked Palestinian positions at Tyre and Tulin. In July, Israeli air raids on Beirut killed or wounded some 800 persons. A cease-fire between Israel and the Palestinians was concluded July 24, but hostilities continued.

Israeli forces invaded Lebanon June 6, 1982, in a coordinated land, sea, and air attack aimed at crushing strongholds of the Palestine Liberation Organization (PLO). Israeli and Syrian forces engaged in the Bekka Valley. By June 10, Israeli troops had reached the outskirts of Beirut. (*See Chronology*).

Lesotho

Kingdom of Lesotho

People: Population (1981 est.): 1,400,000. **Age distrib.** (%): 0–14: 39.5; 15–59: 53.9; 60+: 6.6. **Pop. density:** 114.37 per sq. mi. **Ethnic groups:** Sotho 85%, Nguni 15%. **Languages:** English, Southern Sotho (official). **Religions:** Christians 70%, others.

Geography: Area: 11,716 sq. mi., slightly larger than Maryland. **Location:** In Southern Africa. **Neighbors:** Completely surrounded by Republic of South Africa. **Topography:** Landlocked and mountainous, with altitudes ranging from 5,000 to 11,000 ft. **Capital:** Maseru. **Cities** (1981 est.): Maseru 75,000.

Government: Head of state: King Moshoeshoe II, b. May 2, 1938; in office: Mar. 12, 1960. **Head of government:** Prime Min. Leabua Jonathan; b. Oct. 31, 1914; in office: Oct. 4, 1966. **Local divisions:** 10 districts.

Economy: Industries: Diamond polishing, food processing. **Chief crops:** Corn, grains, peas, beans. **Other resources:** Wool, mohair. **Per capita arable land:** 0.7 acres. **Electricity prod.** (1967): 5.00 mln. kwh. **Labor force:** 87% agric.; 3% ind. and commerce.

Finance: Currency: Maloti (Mar. 1982: .95 = $1 US). **Gross domestic product** (1979 est.): $540 mln. **Per capita income** (1979): $355. **Imports** (1979): $170 mln.; partners: Mostly So. Afr. **Exports** (1979): $40 mln.; partners: Mostly So. Afr. **National budget** (1981): $204 mln. revenues; $265 mln. expenditures. **Consumer prices** (change in 1979): 19%.

Transport: Motor vehicles: in use (1975): 4,600 passenger cars, 3,200 comm. vehicles.

Communications: Radios: 23,000 licensed (1976). **Daily newspaper circ.** (1980): 24 per 1,000 pop.

Health: Life expectancy at birth (1975): 46.7 male; 48.9 female. **Births** (per 1,000 pop. 1978): 37. **Deaths** (per 1,000 pop. 1978): 14. **Natural increase** (1978): 2.3%. **Hospital beds** (per 100,000 pop. 1977): 205. **Physicians** (per 100,000 pop. 1977): 8. **Infant mortality** (per 1,000 live births 1981): 111.

Education (1978): **Literacy:** 55%. **Pop. 5-19:** in school: 58%, teachers per 1,000: 12.

Lesotho (once called Basutoland) became a British protectorate in 1868 when Chief Moshesh sought protection against the Boers. Independence came Oct. 4, 1966. Elections were suspended in 1970. Over 50% of males work abroad in So. Africa. Livestock raising is the chief industry; wool and mohair are the chief exports.

Liberia

Republic of Liberia

People: Population (1981 est.): 1,900,000. **Age distrib.** (%): 0–14: 40.9; 15–59: 53.1; 60+: 5.9. **Pop. density:** 43.26 per sq. mi. **Urban** (1971): 27.6%. **Ethnic groups:** Americo-Liberians 5%, 16 tribes 95% **Languages:** English (official), tribal dialects. **Religions:** Moslems 15%, Christians 10%, traditional 75%.

Geography: Area: 37,757 sq. mi., slightly smaller than Pennsylvania. **Location:** On SW coast of W. Africa. **Neighbors:** Sierra Leone on W, Guinea on N, Ivory Coast on E. **Topography:** Marshy Atlantic coastline rises to low mountains and plateaus in the forested interior; 6 major rivers flow in parallel courses to the ocean. **Capital:** Monrovia. **Cities** (1981 est.): Monrovia 306,000.

Government: Head of state: Pres. Samuel K. Doe; in office: Apr. 12, 1980. **Local divisions:** 9 counties and Monrovia. **Armed forces:** regulars 5,250; para-military 7,600.

Economy: Industries: Food processing and other light industry. **Chief crops:** Rice, cassava, coffee, cocoa, sugar. **Minerals:** Iron, diamonds, gold. **Other resources:** Rubber, timber. **Per capita arable land:** 0.2 acres. **Fish catch** (1978): 18,800 metric tons. **Electricity prod.** (1978): 890.0 mln. kwh. **Labor force:** 70.5% agric.

Finance: Currency: Dollar (Apr. 1982: 1.11 = $1 US). **Gross domestic product** (1979): $864.2 mln. **Per capita income** (1976): $453. **Imports** (1980): $535 mln.; partners (1979): U.S. 24%, W. Ger. 11%, Saudi Ar. 10%, Jap. 7%, Neth. 7%. **Ex-**

ports (1980): $601 mln.; partners (1979): W. Ger. 26%, U.S. 20%, It. 10%, Fr. 11%. **National budget** (1980): $202.3 mln. revenues; $281 mln. expenditures. **International reserves less gold** (Feb. 1982): $11.63 mln. **Consumer prices** (change in 1980): 13.8%.

Transport: Motor vehicles: in use (1979): 13,070 passenger cars, 8,999 comm. vehicles. **Chief ports:** Monrovia, Buchanan.

Communications: Television sets: 10,000 in use (1977). **Radios:** 274,000 in use (1977): **Telephones in use** (1980): 7,740. **Daily newspaper circ.** (1980): 6 per 1,000 pop.

Health: Life expectancy at birth (1971): 45.8 male; 44.0 female. **Births** (per 1,000 pop. 1978): 50. **Deaths** (per 1,000 pop. 1978): 20. **Natural increase** (1978): 3.1%. **Hospital beds** (per 100,000 pop. 1977): 161. **Physicians** (per 100,000 pop. 1977): 12. **Infant mortality** (per 1,000 live births 1981): 148.

Education (1978): **Literacy:** 18%. **Pop. 5-19:** in school: 36%, teachers per 1,000: 9.

Liberia was founded in 1822 by U.S. black freedmen who settled at Monrovia with the aid of colonization societies. It became a republic July 26, 1847, with a constitution modeled on that of the U.S. Descendants of freedmen dominated politics.

Charging rampant corruption, an Army Redemption Council of enlisted men staged a bloody predawn coup, April 12, 1980, in which Pres. Tolbert was killed and replaced as head of state by Sgt. Samuel Doe. Doe promised a return to civilian rule in 1985.

Libya

Socialist People's Libyan Arab Jamahiriya

People: Population: (1981 est.): 3,100,000. **Age distrib.** (%): 0–14: 51.4; 15–59: 42.6; 60+: 5.9. **Pop. density:** 4.39 per sq. mi. **Urban** (1974): 29.8%. **Ethnic groups:** Arab-Berber 97%, Italian 1.4%, others. **Languages:** Arabic. **Religions:** Predominantly Sunni Moslems.

Geography: Area: 679,536 sq. mi., larger than Alaska. **Location:** On Mediterranean coast of N. Africa. **Neighbors:** Tunisia, Algeria on W, Niger, Chad on S, Sudan, Egypt on E. **Topography:** Desert and semidesert regions cover 92% of the land, with low mountains in N, higher mountains in S, and a narrow coastal zone. **Capital:** Tripoli. **Cities** (1973 cen.): Tripoli 551,477; Benghazi 282,192.

Government: Head of state: Col. Muammar al-Qaddafi; b. Sept. 1942; in office: Sept. 1969. **Head of government:** Secy. Gen. Muhammad Az-Zaruq Rajib. **Local divisions:** 10 regions. **Armed forces:** regulars 49,000 (1980).

Economy: Industries: Carpets, textiles, shoes. **Chief crops:** Dates, olives, citrus and other fruits, grapes, tobacco. **Minerals:** Oil, gas. **Crude oil reserves** (1980): 23.5 bln. bbls. **Per capita arable land:** 2.2 acres. **Meat prod.** (1980): beef: 33,000 metric tons; lamb: 53,000 metric tons. **Labor force:** 20% agric.

Finance: Currency: Dinar (Apr. 1982: 0.33 = $1 US). **Gross domestic product** (1978): $19.97 bln. **Per capita income** (1978): $6,335. **Imports** (1980): $9.78 bln.; partners (1978): It. 24%, W. Ger. 13%, Fr. 8%, Jap. 7%. **Exports** (1981): $15.65 bln.; partners (1978): U.S. 41%, It. 22%, W. Ger. 11%, Sp. 6%. **International reserves less gold** (Feb. 1982): $7.92 bln. **Gold:** 3.57 mln. oz t. **Consumer prices** (change in 1978): 29.3%.

Transport: Motor vehicles: in use (1978): 360,000 passenger cars, 237,000 comm. vehicles. **Chief ports:** Tripoli, Benghazi.

Communications: Television sets: 160,000 licensed (1979). **Radios:** 131,000 (1979). **Daily newspaper circ.** (1980): 22 per 1,000 pop.

Health: Life expectancy at birth (1975): 51.4 male; 54.5 female. **Births** (per 1,000 pop. 1978): 48. **Deaths** (per 1,000 pop. 1978): 13. **Natural increase** (1978): 3.5%. **Hospital beds** (per 100,000 pop. 1977): 476. **Physicians** (per 100,000 pop. 1977): 106.

Education (1978): Literacy: 40%. **Pop. 5-19:** in school: 76%, teachers per 1,000: 40.

First settled by Berbers, Libya was ruled by Carthage, Rome, and Vandals, the Ottomans, Italy from 1912, and Britain and France after WW II. It became an independent constitutional monarchy Jan. 2, 1952. In 1969 a junta lead by Col. Muammar al-Qaddafi seized power, instituting socialist policies.

In the mid-1970s, it was widely reported that Libya had armed violent revolutionary groups in Egypt and Sudan, and had aided terrorists of various nationalities including Moslem rebels in the Philippines. The USSR sold several billion dollars worth of advanced arms after 1975, and established close political ties.

Libya and Egypt fought several air and land battles along their border in July, 1977. Chad charged Libya with military occupation of its uranium-rich northern region in 1977. Libya's 1979 offensive into the Aouzou Strip was repulsed by Chadian forces. Libyan forces withdrew from Chad, Nov. 1981.

Despite a new system of government of elected people's congresses, Qaddafi remained the nation's leader. Widespread nationalization, arrests, imposition of currency regulations and wholesale conscription of civil servants into the army, from Jan. 1980, paralysed the economy.

On May 6, 1981, the U.S., citing "a wide range of Libyan provocations and misconduct," closed the Libyan mission in Wash. In August, 2 Libyan jets were shot down by U.S. Navy planes taking part in naval exercises in the Gulf of Sidra. In December, the U.S. announced that it had information that Libyan-trained assassins were in North America on a mission to kill Pres. Ronald Reagan.

Liechtenstein

Principality of Liechtenstein

People: Population (1980 est.): 30,000. **Age distrib.** (%): 0–14: 27.9; 15–59: 60.2; 60+: 11.9. **Pop. density:** 491.8 per sq. mi. **Ethnic groups:** Alemannic. **Languages:** German (official), Alemannic dialects. **Religions:** Roman Catholics 88%, Protestants 7%.

Geography: Area: 62 sq. mi., the size of Washington, D.C. **Location:** In the Alps. **Neighbors:** Switzerland on W, Austria on E. **Topography:** The Rhine Valley occupies one-third of the country, the Alps cover the rest. **Capital:** Vaduz. **Cities** (1977 cen.): Vaduz 4,704.

Government: Head of state: Prince Franz Josef II; b. Aug. 16, 1906; in office: Mar. 30, 1938. **Head of government:** Hans Brunhart; b. Mar. 28, 1945; in office: Apr. 26, 1978. **Local divisions:** 11 communes.

Economy: Industries: Machines, instruments, chemicals, furniture, ceramics. **Per capita arable land:** 0.3 acres. **Labor force:** 54.6% industry, trade and building; 41.5% services; 3.9% agric., fishing, forestry.

Finance: Currency: Swiss Franc (Mar. 1982): 1.93 = $1. **Tourists** (1979): 73,657.

Communications: Radios: 8,000 licensed (1976). **Telephones in use** (1978): 17,163. **Daily newspaper circ.** (1980): 533 per 1,000 pop.

Health: Births (per 1,000 pop. 1977): 12.5. **Deaths** (per 1,000 pop. 1977): 6.0. **Natural increase** (1977): .7%. **Infant mortality** (per 1,000 live births 1980): 5.8.

Education: Literacy: 100%. **Pop. 5-19:** in school: 100%.

Liechtenstein became sovereign in 1866. Austria administered Liechtenstein's ports up to 1920; Switzerland has administered its postal services since 1921. Liechtenstein is united with Switzerland by a customs and monetary union. Taxes are low; many international corporations have headquarters there. Foreign workers comprise a third of the population.

Luxembourg

Grand Duchy of Luxembourg

People: Population: (1981 est.): 360,000. **Age distrib.** (%): 0–14: 20.2; 15–59: 61.4; 60+: 18.2. **Pop. density:** 360.36 per sq. mi. **Urban** (1974): 67.9%. **Ethnic groups:** Mixture of French and Germans predominate, Italians 7%. **Languages:** French, German, Luxembourgian. **Religions:** Roman Catholics 97%.

Geography: Area: 999 sq. mi., smaller than Rhode Island. **Location:** In W. Europe. **Neighbors:** Belgium on W, France on S, W. Germany on E. **Topography:** Heavy forests (Ardennes) cover N, S is a low, open plateau. **Capital:** Luxembourg. **Cities** (1978 est.): Luxembourg 78,400.

Government: Head of state: Grand Duke Jean; b. Jan. 5, 1921; in office: Nov. 12, 1964. **Head of government:** Prime Min. Pierre Werner, b. Dec. 29, 1913; in office: July 16, 1979. **Local divisions:** 3 districts, 12 cantons. **Armed forces:** regulars 660; para-military 430.

Economy: Industries: Steel (90% of exports), chemicals, beer, tires, tobacco, metal products, cement. **Chief crops:** Grain, potatoes, roses. **Minerals:** Iron. **Per capita arable land:** (see Belgium). **Electricity prod.** (1980): 1.1 bln. kwh. **Crude steel prod.** (1981): 3.7 mln. metric tons. **Labor force:** 6% agric.; 46% manuf.; 48% services and gov.

Finance: Currency: Franc (Mar. 1982: 45.56 = $1 US). **Gross domestic product** (1979 est.): $3.9 bln. **Per capita income** (1978): $10,040. **Note:** trade and tourist data included in Belgian statistics. **Consumer prices** (change in 1979): 4.2%.

Transport: Railway traffic (1979): 299 mln. passenger-km; 662 mln. net ton-km. **Motor vehicles:** in use (1979): 162,800 passenger cars, 10,800 comm. vehicles. **Civil aviation:** (1980): 55 mln. passenger-miles; 200,000 freight ton-miles.

Communications: Television sets: 105,000 in use (1979). **Radios:** 182,000 in use (1979). **Telephones in use** (1980): 198,900. **Daily newspaper circ.** (1980): 321 per 1,000 pop.

Health: Life expectancy at birth (1973): 67.0 male; 73.9 female. **Births** (per 1,000 pop. 1980): 11.4. **Deaths** (per 1,000 pop. 1980): 11.3. **Natural increase** (1978): –.04%. **Hospital beds** (per 100,000 pop. 1977): 978. **Physicians** (per 100,000 pop. 1977): 112. **Infant mortality** (per 1,000 live births 1978): 10.6.

Education (1977): **Literacy:** 98%. **Pop. 5–19:** in school: 59%, teachers per 1,000: 40.

Luxembourg, founded about 963, was ruled by Burgundy, Spain, Austria, and France from 1448 to 1815. It left the Germanic Confederation in 1866. Overrun by Germany in 2 world wars, Luxembourg ended its neutrality in 1948, when a customs union with Belgium and Netherlands was adopted.

Madagascar

Democratic Republic of Madagascar

People: Population (1981 est.): 8,700,000. **Pop. density:** 38.56 per sq. mi. **Urban** (1970): 14.1%. **Ethnic groups:** 18 Malayan-Indonesian tribes (Merina 26%), with Arab and African presence. **Languages:** Malagasy (national), French (official). **Religions:** animists 54%, Christian 39%, Muslim 7%.

Geography: Area: 226,658 sq. mi., slightly smaller than Texas. **Location:** In the Indian O., off the SE coast of Africa. **Neighbors:** Comoro Is., Mozambique (across Mozambique Channel). **Topography:** Humid coastal strip in the E, fertile valleys in the mountainous center plateau region, and a wider coastal strip on the W. **Capital:** Antananarivo. **Cities** (1980 est.): Antananarivo 547,100.

Government: Head of state: Pres. Didier Ratsiraka; b. Nov. 4, 1936; in office: June 15, 1975. **Head of government:** Prime Min. Desire Rakotoarijaona, b. June 19, 1934; in office: Aug. 4, 1977. **Local divisions:** 6 provinces. **Armed forces:** regulars 20,000 (1982).

Economy: Industries: Light industry. **Chief crops:** Coffee, cloves, vanilla (80% world supply), rice, sugar, sisal, tobacco, peanuts. **Minerals:** Chromium, graphite. **Per capita arable land:** 0.7 acres. **Meat prod.** (1980): beef: 119,000 metric tons; pork: 24,000 metric tons; lamb: 6,000 metric tons. **Fish catch** (1978): 54,400 metric tons. **Electricity prod.** (1978): 300.00 mln. kwh. **Labor force:** 88% agric.; 1.5% ind. and commerce.

Finance: Currency: Franc (Mar. 1982: 312.10 = $1 US). **Gross domestic product** (1980): $3.3 bln. **Per capita income** (1980): $350. **Imports** (1980): $603 mln.; partners (1979): Fr. 32%, U.S. 11%, W. Ger. 9%. **Exports** (1980): $339 mln.; partners (1979): Fr. 26%, U.S. 15%. **National budget** (1980): $890 mln. revenues; $1.04 bln. expenditures. **International reserves less gold** (Mar. 1980): $1.9 mln. **Consumer prices** (change in 1980): 18.3%.

Transport: Railway traffic (1978): 300 mln. passenger-km; 210 mln. net ton-km. **Motor vehicles:** in use (1979): 57,000 passenger cars, 50,000 comm. vehicles. **Civil aviation:** (1980): 310 mln. passenger-km; 20 mln. freight ton-km. **Chief ports:** Tamatave, Diego-Suarez, Majunga, Tulear.

Communications: Television sets: 12,000 in use (1978). **Radios:** 1.020 mln. in use (1977). **Telephones in use** (1978): 28,686.

Health: Life expectancy at birth (1982): 46 years. **Births** (per 1,000 pop. 1978): 48. **Deaths** (per 1,000 pop. 1978): 22. **Natural increase** (1978): 2.6%. **Hospital beds** (per 100,000 pop. 1977): 245. **Physicians** (per 100,000 pop. 1977): 10. **Infant mortality** (per 1,000 live births 1982): 177.

Education (1981): **Literacy:** 53%. **Pop. 5-19:** in school: 50%, teachers per 1,000: 9.

Madagascar was settled 2,000 years ago by Malayan-Indonesian people, whose descendants still predominate. A unified kingdom ruled the 18th and 19th centuries. The island became a French protectorate, 1885, and a colony 1896. Independence came June 26, 1960.

Discontent with inflation and French domination led to a coup in 1972. The new regime nationalized French-owned financial interests, closed French bases and a U.S. space tracking station, and obtained Chinese aid. The government conducted a program of arrests, expulsion of foreigners, and repression of strikes, 1979.

Malawi

Republic of Malawi

People: Population (1981 est.): 6,200,000. **Age distrib.** (%): 0–14: 43.9; 15–59: 50.4; 60+: 5.6. **Pop. density:** 130.50 per sq. mi. **Urban** (1972): 10.1%. **Ethnic groups:** Chewa, Nyanja, Lomwe, other Bantu tribes. **Languages:** English (official), Chichewa (national). **Religions:** Christians 33%, traditional beliefs.

Geography: Area: 45,747 sq. mi., the size of Pennsylvania. **Location:** In SE Africa. **Neighbors:** Zambia on W, Mozambique on SE, Tanzania on N. **Topography:** Malawi stretches 560 mi. N-S along Lake Malawi (Lake Nyasa), most of which belongs to Malawi. High plateaus and mountains line the Rift Valley the length of the nation. **Capital:** Lilongwe. **Cities** (1978 est.): Blantyre-Limbe (met.) 219,000; Lilongwe (met.) 75,000.

Government: Head of state: Pres. Hastings Kamuzu Banda, b. May 14, 1906; in office: July 6, 1966. **Local divisions:** 3 regions, 24 districts, 3 subdistricts. **Armed forces:** regulars 5,000; para-military 460.

Economy: Industries: Textiles, sugar, farm implements. **Chief crops:** Tea, tobacco, peanuts, cotton, sugar, soybeans, coffee. **Other resources:** Rubber. **Per capita arable land:** 1.0 acres. **Fish catch** (1978): 67.7 metric tons. **Electricity prod.** (1978): 276.00 mln. kwh. **Labor force:** 90% agric.; 10% ind. and commerce.

Finance: Currency: Kwacha (Mar. 1982: 0.94 = $1 US). **Gross domestic product** (1980): $1.53 bln. **Per capita income** (1979): $220. **Imports** (1980): $437 mln.; partners (1979): So. Afr. 42%, UK 19%, Jap. 9%. **Exports** (1980): $293 mln.; partners (1979): UK 41%, Neth. 9%. W. Ger. 10%. **Tourists** (1975): 40,500; receipts (1976): $3 mln. **National budget** (1980): $245 mln. revenues; $372 mln. expenditures. **International reserves less gold** (Feb. 1982): $28.16 mln. **Gold:** 13,000 oz t. **Consumer prices** (change in 1980): 18.9%.

Transport: Railway traffic (1980): 80 mln. passenger-km; 241 mln. net ton-km. **Motor vehicles:** in use (1980): 11,800 passenger cars, 13,300 comm. vehicles. **Civil aviation** (1980): 68 mln. passenger-km; one mln. freight ton-km.

Communications: Radios: 130,000 60%. use (1976). **Telephones in use** 61%, 28,800. **Daily newspaper circ.** (1980): 6 per 1,000 pop.

Health: Life expectancy at birth (1972): 40.9 male; 44.2 female. **Births** (per 1,000 pop. 1978): 53. **Deaths** (per 1,000 pop. 1978): 26. **Natural increase** (1978): 2.8%. **Hospital beds** (per 100,000 pop. 1977): 174. **Physicians** (per 100,000 pop. 1977): 2. **Infant mortality** (per 1,000 live births 1972): 142.1.

Education (1978): **Literacy:** 25%. **Pop. 5-19:** in school: 32%, teachers per 1,000: 6.

Bantus came in the 16th century, Arab slavers in the 19th. The area became the British protectorate Nyasaland, in 1891. It became independent July 6, 1964, and a republic in 1966. It has a pro-West foreign policy and cooperates economically with Zimbabwe and S. Africa.

Malaysia

People: Population (1981 est.): 14,400,000. **Age distrib.** (%): 0–14: 41.5; 15–59: 53.0; 60+: 5.4. **Pop. density:** 100.99 per sq. mi. **Urban** (1970): 20.6%. **Ethnic groups:** Malays 47%, Chinese 32%, Indians 9%, others. **Languages:** Malay (official),

English, Chinese, Indian languages. **Religions:** Moslem, Hindu, Buddhist, Confucian, Taoist, local religions.

Geography: Area: 127,316 sq. mi., slightly larger than New Mexico. **Location:** On the SE tip of Asia, plus the N. coast of the island of Borneo. **Neighbors:** Thailand on N, Indonesia on S. **Topography:** Most of W. Malaysia is covered by tropical jungle, including the central mountain range that runs N-S through the peninsula. The western coast is marshy, the eastern, sandy. E. Malaysia has a wide, swampy coastal plain, with interior jungles and mountains. **Capital:** Kuala Lumpur. **Cities** (1980 est.): Kuala Lumpur 1,081,000 (met.).

Government: Head of state: Paramount Ruler Ahmad Shah ibni Sultan Abu Bakar; b. Oct. 24, 1930; in office: Mar. 29, 1979. **Head of government:** Prime Min. Datuk Seri Mahathir bin Mohamad; b. Dec. 20, 1925; in office: July 16, 1981. **Local divisions:** 11 states, each with legislature, chief minister, and titular ruler. **Armed forces:** regulars 64,500; reserves 27,000.

Economy: Industries: Rubber goods, pottery, fertilizers. **Chief crops:** Palm oil, copra, rice, tapioca, sugar, pepper. **Minerals:** Tin (35% world output), iron. **Crude oil reserves** (1980): 2.80 bln. bbls. **Other resources:** Rubber (35% world output). **Per capita arable land:** 0.6 acres. **Meat prod.** (1980): beef: 17,000 metric tons; pork: 71,000 metric tons. **Fish catch** (1979): 698,000 metric tons. **Electricity prod.** (1979): 8.9 bln. kwh. **Crude steel prod.** (1981 est.): 210,000 metric tons. **Labor force:** 48% agric.; 32% ind. and commerce; 12% service.

Finance: Currency: Ringgit (Apr. 1982: 2.33 = $1 US). **Gross domestic product** (1980): $21.3 bln. **Per capita income** (1975): $714. **Imports** (1980): $10.82 bln.; partners (1980): Jap. 23%, U.S. 15%, Sing. 12%. **Exports** (1980): $12.93 bln.; partners (1980): Jap. 23%, U.S. 16% Sing. 19%, Neth. 6%. **Tourists** (1977): 1,289,000; receipts: $38 mln. **National budget** (1980): $5.8 bln. revenues; $8.1 bln. expenditures. **International reserves less gold** (Jan. 1982): $4.09 bln. **Gold:** 2.33 mln. oz t. **Consumer prices** (change in 1981): 9.6%

Transport: Railway traffic (incl. Singapore) (1980): 1.5 bln. passenger-km; 1.1 bln. net ton-km. **Motor vehicles:** in use (1979): 690,000 passenger cars, 154,000 comm. vehicles; assembled (1978): 61,200 passenger cars; 11,724 comm. vehicles. **Civil aviation:** (1980): 4.076 bln. passenger-km; 116.7 mln. freight ton-km. **Chief ports:** George Town, Kelang, Melaka, Kuching.

Communications: Television sets: 819,000 in use (1979), 150,000 manuf. (1978). **Radios:** 1.5 mln. in use (1977). **Telephones in use** (1979): 439,000. **Daily newspaper circ.** (1980): 139 per 1,000 pop.

Health: Life expectancy at birth (1976): 66.2 male; 71.4 female. **Births** (per 1,000 pop. 1978): 32. **Deaths** (per 1,000 pop. 1978): 8. **Natural increase** (1978): 2.5%. **Hospital beds** (per 100,000 pop. 1977): 308. **Physicians** (per 100,000 pop. 1977): 12. **Infant mortality** (per 1,000 live births 1977): 31.8.

Education (1978): **Literacy:** 60%. **Pop. 5-19:** in school: 61%, teachers per 1,000: 20.

European traders appeared in the 16th century; Britain established control in 1867. Malaysia was created Sept. 16, 1963. It included Malaya (which had become independent in 1957 after the suppression of Communist rebels), plus the formerly-British Singapore, Sabah (N Borneo), and Sarawak (NW Borneo). Singapore was separated in 1965, in order to end tensions between Chinese, the majority in Singapore, and Malays in control of the Malaysian government. Chinese have charged economical and political discrimination.

A monarch is elected by a council of hereditary rulers of the Malayan states every 5 years.

Abundant natural resources have assured prosperity, and foreign investment has aided industrialization.

The influx of thousands of Vietnamese refugees reached crisis proportions, June 1979.

Maldives

Republic of Maldives

People: Population (1980 est.): 150,000. **Age distrib.** (%): 0–14: 44.9; 15–59: 51.3; 60+: 3.8. **Pop. density:** 1,100 per sq. mi. **Urban** (1967): 11.3%. **Ethnic groups:** Sinhalese, Dravidian, Arab mixture. **Languages:** Divehi (Sinhalese dialect). **Religions:** Sunni Moslems.

Geography: Area: 115 sq. mi., twice the size of Washington, D.C. **Location:** In the Indian O. SW of India. **Neighbors:** Nearest is India on N. **Topography:** 19 atolls with 1,087 islands, 203 inhabited. None of the islands are over 5 sq. mi. in area, and all are nearly flat. **Capital:** Male. **Cities** (1980 est.): Male 32,000.

Government: Head of state: Pres. Maumoon Abdul Gayyoom; b. Dec. 29, 1939; in office: Nov. 11, 1978. **Local divisions:** 19 atolls, each with an elected committee and a government-appointed chief.

Economy: Industries: Fish processing, tourism. **Chief crops:** Coconuts, fruit, millet. **Other resources:** Shells. **Fish catch** 1978): 25,800 metric tons. **Electricity prod.** (1977): 2.00 mln. kwh. **Labor force:** 80% fishing.

Finance: Currency: Rupee (June 1981: 3.93 = $1 US). **Gross domestic product** (1978 IMF est.): $22 mln. **Per capita income** (1978 IMF est.): $150. **Imports** (1979): $24 mln.; partners: (1979): Ind. 25%, Jap. 14%, Sri Lan 11%. **Exports** (1979): $5.8 mln.; partners: (1979) Jap. 44%, Sri Lan. 14%, Thai. **Tourists** (1980): 42,000.

Transport: Chief ports: Male Atoll.

Communications: Radios: 3,500 licensed (1976). **Telephones in use** (1978): 556.

Health: Births (per 1,000 pop. 1977): 40.5. **Deaths** (per 1,000 pop. 1977): 11.8. **Natural increase** (1977): 2.9%. **Pop. per hospital bed** (1977): 3,500. **Pop. per physician** (1977): 15,555. **Infant morality** (per 1,000 live births 1977): 118.8.

Education (1975): **Literacy:** 36%. **Pop. 5-19:** in school: 40%, per teacher: 80.

The islands had been a British protectorate since 1887. The country became independent July 26, 1965. Long a sultanate, the Maldives became a republic in 1968. Natural resources and tourism are being developed; however, it remains one of the world's poorest countries.

Mali

Republic of Mali

People: Population (1981 est.): 6,900,000. **Age distrib.** (%): 0–14: 47.9; 15–59: 49.1; 60+: 3.0. **Pop. density:** 14.86 per sq. mi. **Urban** (1976): 16.6%. **Ethnic groups:** Mande (Bambara, Malinke, Sarakolle) 50%, Peul 17%, Voltaic 12%, Songhai, Tuareg, Moors. **Languages:** French (official), Hamito-Semitic, tribal dialects. **Religions:** Moslems 65%, animists 30%, Christians 5%, others.

Geography: Area: 464,873 sq. mi., larger than Texas and California combined. **Location:** In the interior of W. Africa. **Neighbors:** Mauritania, Senegal on W, Guinea, Ivory Coast, Upper Volta on S, Niger on E, Algeria on N. **Topography:** A landlocked grassy plain in the upper basins of the Senegal and Niger rivers, extending N into the Sahara. **Capital:** Bamako. **Cities** (1981 est.): Bamako (met.) 620,000.

Government: Head of state and head of govt.: Pres. Moussa Traore; b. Sept. 25, 1936; in office: Dec. 6, 1968 (state); Sept. 19, 1969 (govt.) **Local divisions:** 7 regions. **Armed forces:** regulars 4,450; para-military 5,700.

Economy: Chief crops: Millet, rice, peanuts, cotton. **Other resources:** Bauxite, iron, copper, gold. **Per capita arable land:** 3.8 acres. **Meat prod.** (1980): beef: 35,000 metric tons; lamb: 39,000 metric tons. **Fish catch** (1978): 100,000 metric tons. **Electricity prod.** (1977): 98 mln. kwh. **Labor force:** 80% agric.; 9% services.

Finance: Currency: Franc (Mar. 1982: 624.20 = $1 US). **Gross domestic product** (1980): $839 mln. **Per capita income** (1981): $140. **Imports** (1980): $417 mln.; partners (1977): Fr. 38% Ivory Coast 19%, Sen. 19%. **Exports** (1980): $176 mln.; partners (1977): Fr. 29%, Ivory Coast 14%, China 12%. **Tourists** (1977): 19,500; receipts: $8 mln. **International reserves less gold** (Feb. 1982): $19.0 mln. **Gold:** 19,000 oz t. **Consumer prices** (change in 1976): 8%.

Transport: Railway traffic (1977): 129 mln. passenger-km; 148 mln. net ton-km. **Motor vehicles:** in use (1974): 11,900 passenger cars, 7,600 comm. vehicles. **Civil aviation:** 97 mln. passenger-km (1977); 612,000 freight ton-km (1977).

Communications: Radios: 82,000 in use (1976).

Health: Life expectancy at birth (1975): 39.4 male; 42.5 female. **Births** (per 1,000 pop. 1978): 52. **Deaths** (per 1,000 pop. 1978): 24. **Natural increase** (1978): 2.9%. **Hospital beds** (per 100,000 pop. 1977): 56. **Physicians** (per 100,000 pop. 1977): 5. **Infant mortality** (per 1,000 live births 1981): 200.

Education (1977): Literacy: 10%. **Pop. 5—15:** in school: 20%, teachers per 1,000: 4.

Until the 15th century the area was part of the great Mali Empire. Timbuktu was a center of Islamic study. French rule was secured, 1898. The Sudanese Rep. and Senegal became independent as the Mali Federation June 20, 1960, but Senegal withdrew, and the Sudanese Rep. was renamed Mali.

Mali signed economic agreements with France and, in 1963, with Senegal. In 1968, a coup ended the socialist regime. Famine struck in 1973-74, killing as many as 100,000 people. Drought conditions returned 1977-78. There was unrest in 1980 and 1981, with several attempted coups.

Malta

People: Population (1981 est.): 350,000. **Age distrib.** (%): 0–14: 24.6; 15–59: 63.2; 60+: 12.2. **Pop. density:** 2,950.81 per sq. mi. **Ethnic groups:** Italian, Arab, English, and Phoenician mixture. **Languages:** Maltese, English both official. **Religions:** Mainly Roman Catholics.

Geography: Area: 124 sq. mi., twice the size of Washington, D.C. **Location:** In center of Mediterranean Sea. **Neighbors:** Nearest is Italy on N. **Topography:** Island of Malta is 95 sq. mi.; other islands in the group: Gozo, 26 sq. mi., Comino, 1 sq. mi. The coastline is heavily indented. Low hills cover the interior. **Capital:** Valletta. **Cities** (1979 est.): Valletta 15,000; Sliema 22,000.

Government: Head of state: Pres. Anton Buttigieg; b. Feb. 19, 1912; in office: Dec. 27, 1976. **Head of government:** Prime Min. Dominic Mintoff; b. Aug. 6, 1916; in office: June 17, 1971. **Armed forces:** regulars 1,000; para-military 1,400.

Economy: Industries: Textiles, tourism. **Chief crops:** Potatoes, onions, beans. **Per capita arable land:** 0.1 acres. **Electricity prod.** (1978): 456.00 mln. kwh. **Labor force:** 27.8% manuf.; 31.4% market services; 21.5% gov.

Finance: Currency: Pound (Mar. 1982: 0.39 = $1 US). **Gross domestic product** (1979): $979 mln. **Per capita income** (1978): $2,036. **Imports** (1979): $759 mln.; partners (1980): UK 22%, It. 24%, W. Ger. 14%, U.S. 6%. **Exports** (1979): $425 mln.; partners (1980): W. Ger. 31%, UK 20%, Libya 7%. **Tourists** (1979): 618,300; receipts: $213 mln. **National budget** (1981): $561 mln. revenues; $562 mln. expenditures. **International reserves less gold** (Mar. 1982): $974.4 mln. **Gold:** 456,000 oz t. **Consumer prices** (change in 1980): 25.1%.

Transport: Motor vehicles: in use (1979): 66,200 passenger cars, 13,800 comm. vehicles. **Civil aviation** (1980): 602 mln. passenger-km; 4.5 mln. freight ton-km. **Chief ports:** Valletta.

Communications: Television sets: 71,000 licensed (1979). **Radios:** 85,000 in use (1977). **Telephones in use** (1979): 77,300.

Health: Life expectancy at birth (1976): 68.27 male; 73.10 female. **Births** (per 1,000 pop. 1980: 15.4. **Deaths** (per 1,000 pop. 1980): 9.1. **Natural increase** (1978): .7%. **Hospital beds** (per 100,000 pop. 1977): 1,040. **Physicians** (per 100,000 pop. 1977): 127. **Infant mortality** (per 1,000 live births 1980): 15.

Education (1977): **Literacy:** 85%. **Pop. 5–19:** in school: 69% teachers per 1,000: 36.

Malta was ruled by Phoenicians, Romans, Arabs, Normans, the Knights of Malta, France, and Britain (since 1814). It became independent Sept. 21, 1964, with Britain retaining a naval base. Malta became a republic in 1974. The withdrawal of the last of its sailors, Apr. 1, 1979, ended 179 years of British military presence on the island.

Maltese is a Semitic language, with Italian influences, written in the Latin alphabet. Malta is democratic but nonaligned.

Mauritania

Islamic Republic of Mauritania

People: Population (1981 est.): 1,630,000. **Age distrib.** (%): 0–14: 42.2; 15–59: 49.8; 60+: 13.4. **Pop. density:** 3.89 per sq. mi. **Urban** (1977): 22.8%. **Ethnic groups:** Arab-Berber 80%, Negroes 20%. **Languages:** French (official), Hassanya Arabic (national), Niger-Congo languages. **Religions:** Predominately Moslems.

Geography: Area: 398,000 sq. mi., the size of Texas and California combined. **Location:** In W. Africa. **Neighbors:** Morocco on N, Algeria, Mali on E, Senegal on S. **Topography:** The fertile Senegal R. valley in the S gives way to a wide central region of sandy plains and scrub trees. The N is arid and extends into the Sahara. **Capital:** Nouakchott. **Cities** (1981 est.): Nouakchott 250,000; Nouadhibou 22,000; Kaedi 21,000.

Government: Head of state.: Pres. Mohamed Khouna Ould Haidalla, b. 1940: in office: May 31, 1979. **Head of Government:** Premier Maaouya Ould Sidi Ahmed Taya; in office: Apr. 25, 1981. **Local divisions:** 8 regions, one district. **Armed forces:** regulars 9,450; para-military 6,000.

Economy: Chief crops: Dates, grain. **Minerals:** Iron, ore, gypsum. **Per capita arable land:** 0.3 acres. **Meat prod.** (1980): beef: 17,000 metric tons; lamb: 12,000 metric tons. **Fish catch** (1978): 34,200 metric tons. **Electricity prod.** (1978): 96.00 mln. kwh. **Labor force:** 47% agric., 14% ind. & comm., 29% services.

Finance: Currency: Ouguiya (Mar. 1982: 51.29 = $1 US). **Gross domestic product** (1979): $618 mln. **Per capita income** (1979): $400. **Imports** (1979): $259 mln.; partners (1980): Fr. 34%, Bel. 8%, Sp. 9%. **Exports** (1980): $194 mln.; partners (1980): Fr. 29%, It. 19%, Jap. 19%, UK 9%. **Tourists** (1975): 20,700; receipts (1976): $7 mln. **International reserves less gold** (Feb. 1982): $143.9 mln. **Gold:** 11,000 oz t. **Consumer prices** (change in 1980): 9.9%.

Transport: Railway traffic (1974): 7.81 bln. net ton-km. **Motor vehicles:** in use (1972): 4,400 passenger cars, 5,000 comm. vehicles. **Chief ports:** Nouakchott, Nouadhibou.

Communications: Radios: 95,000 in use (1976).

Health: Life expectancy at birth (1975): 39.4 male; 42.5 female. **Births** (per 1,000 pop. 1978): 45. **Deaths** (per 1,000 pop. 1978): 27. **Natural increase** (1978): 1.9%. **Hospital beds** (per 100,000 pop. 1977): 38. **Physicians** (per 100,000 pop. 1977): 7. **Infant mortality** (per 1,000 live births 1981): 169.

Education (1981): **Literacy:** 17%. **Pop. 5-19:** in school: 15%, teachers per 1,000: 4.

Mauritania became independent Nov. 28, 1960. It annexed the south of former Spanish Sahara in 1976. Saharan guerrillas stepped up attacks in 1977; 8,000 Moroccan troops and French bomber raids aided the government. Mauritania signed a peace treaty with the Polsario Front, 1980, resumed diplomatic relations with Algeria while breaking a defense treaty with Morocco, and renounced sovereignty over its share of former Spanish Sahara. Morocco annexed the territory.

Famine struck in 1973-74 and again in 1977-78. France, China, and the U.S. have sent aid.

Mauritius

People: Population (1981 est.): 970,000. **Age distrib.** (%): 0–14: 36.3; 15–59: 57.2; 60+: 6.4. **Pop. density:** 1,219.82 per sq. mi. **Urban** (1976): 43.6%. **Ethnic groups:** Indian 69%, Creoles 28%, others. **Languages:** English (official), French, Creole. **Religions:** Hindu 51%, Christian 30%, Moslems 16%.

Geography: Area: 787 sq. mi., smaller than Rhode Island. **Location:** In the Indian O., 500 mi. E of Madagascar. **Neighbors:** Nearest is Madagascar on W. **Topography:** A volcanic island nearly surrounded by coral reefs. A central plateau is encircled by mountain peaks. **Capital:** Port Louis. **Cities** (1978 est.): Port Louis 141,022.

Government: Head of state: Queen Elizabeth II, represented by Gov.-Gen. Dayendranath Burrenchobay; b. Mar. 24, 1919; in office: Mar. 23, 1978. **Head of government:** Prime Min. Aneerood Jugnauth; in office: June 12, 1982. **Local divisions:** 9 administrative divisions.

Economy: Industries: Tourism. **Chief crops:** Sugar cane, tea. **Per capita arable land:** 0.3 acres. **Electricity prod.** (1978): 336.00 mln. kwh. **Labor force:** 28.9% agric.; 28% ind. and commerce.

Finance: Currency: Rupee (Mar. 1982: 10.77 = $1 US). **Gross domestic product** (1979): $1.03 bln. **Per capita income** (1978 est.): $738. **Imports** (1980): $570 mln.; partners (1979): UK 14%, Fr. 9%, So. Afr. 14%. **Exports** (1980): $429 mln.; partners (1979): UK 64%, Fr. 11%, U.S. 12%. **Tourists** (1979): 128,400; receipts: $47 mln. **National budget** (1980): $258 mln. revenues; $258 mln. expenditures. **International reserves less gold** (Feb. 1982): $28.3 mln. **Gold:** 38,000 oz t.

Consumer prices (change in 1980): 42.7%.
Transport: Motor vehicles: in use (1977): 24,300 passenger cars, 13,000 comm. vehicles. **Chief ports:** Port Louis.
Communications: Television sets: 41,000 licensed (1976). **Radios:** 200,000 licensed (1976). **Telephones in use** (1978): 29,145. **Daily newspaper circ.** (1980): 94 per 1,000 pop.
Health: Life expectancy at birth (1973): 60.68 male; 65.31 female. **Births** (per 1,000 pop. 1980): 27.0. **Deaths** (per 1,000 pop. 1980): 7.2. **Natural increase** (1978): 2.0%. **Hospital beds** (per 100,000 pop. 1977): 354. **Physicians** (per 100,000 pop. 1977): 44. **Infant mortality** (per 1,000 live births 1978): 33.8.
Education (1978): **Literacy:** 80%. **Pop. 5-19:** in school: 65%, teachers per 1,000: 24.

Mauritius was uninhabited when settled in 1638 by the Dutch, who introduced sugar cane. France took over in 1721, bringing African slaves. Britain ruled from 1810 to Mar. 12, 1968, bringing Indian workers for the sugar plantations. Mauritius has a free political life and high literacy and life expectancy. The 1970s brought declining birth rates and some economic growth.

The economy suffered in 1981 because of low world sugar prices and the effects of Cyclone Claudette, which destroyed 30% of the 1980 crop.

Mexico

United Mexican States

People: Population (1981 est.): 69,400,000. **Age distrib.** (%): 0–14: 46.2; 15–59: 50.0; 60+: 4.8. **Pop. density:** 94.49 per sq. mi. **Urban** (1978): 65.2%. **Ethnic groups:** Mestizo 55%, American Indian 29%, Caucasian 10%. **Languages:** Spanish. **Religions:** Roman Catholics 89%, Protestants 3.6%.
Geography: Area: 761,604 sq. mi., three times the size of Texas. **Location:** In southern N. America. **Neighbors:** U.S. on N, Guatemala, Belize on S. **Topography:** The Sierra Madre Occidental Mts. run NW-SE near the west coast; the Sierra Madre Oriental Mts., run near the Gulf of Mexico. They join S of Mexico City. Between the 2 ranges lies the dry central plateau, 5,000 to 8,000 ft. alt., rising toward the S, with temperate vegetation. Coastal lowlands are tropical. About 45% of land is arid. **Capital:** Mexico City. **Cities** (1978 est.): Mexico City (metro) 13.9 mln.; Guadalajara (metro) 2.1 mln.; Monterrey (metro) 1.1 mln.
Government: Head of state: Pres. Jose Lopez Portillo; b. June 16, 1920; in office: Dec. 1, 1976. **Local divisions:** Federal district and 31 states. **Armed forces:** regulars 107,000 (1980).
Economy: Industries: Steel, chemicals, electric goods, textiles, rubber, petroleum handicrafts, tourism. **Chief crops:** Cotton, coffee, sugar cane, vegetables, corn. **Minerals:** Silver, lead, zinc, gold, oil, natural gas. **Crude oil reserves** (1980): 31.25 bln. bbls. **Per capita arable land:** 0.8 acres. **Meat prod.** (1980): beef: 594,000 metric tons; pork: 490,000 metric tons; lamb: 36,000 metric tons. **Fish catch** (1979): 874,000 metric tons. **Electricity prod.** (1978): 59.4 bln. kwh. **Crude steel prod.** (1981): 7.6 mln. metric tons. **Labor force:** 41% agric.; 18% manuf.
Finance: Currency: Peso (Mar. 1982: 45.50 = $1 US). **Gross domestic product** (1980): $128 bln. **Per capita income** (1980): $1,800. **Imports** (1981): $24.06 bln.; partners (1980): U.S. 66%, Jap. 5%, W. Ger. 5%. **Exports** (1980): $15.35 bln.; partners (1980): U.S. 63% Spa. 7%. **Tourists** (1977): 3,338,000; receipts: $781 mln. **National budget** (1981): $93.3 bln. revenues; $93.3 bln. expenditures. **International reserves less gold** (Mar. 1981): $3.17 bln. **Gold:** 2.16 mln. oz t. **Consumer prices** (change in 1980): 26.4%.
Transport: Railway traffic (1979): 5.4 bln. passenger-km; 36.7 bln. net ton-km. **Motor vehicles:** in use (1980): 4 mln. passenger cars, 1.5 mln. comm. vehicles; manuf. (1980): 312,000 passenger cars, 132,000 comm. vehicles. **Civil aviation** (1980): 13.8 bln. passenger-km; 136 mln. freight ton-km. **Chief ports:** Veracruz, Tampico, Mazatlan, Coatzacoalcos.
Communications: Television sets: 5.4 mln. in use (1977), 767,000 manuf. (1978). **Radios:** 17.5 mln. in use (1978), 1.1 mln. manuf. (1978). **Telephones in use** (1980): 4.5 mln. **Daily newspaper circ.** (1976): 3,994,000.
Health: Life expectancy at birth (1975): 62.76 male; 66.57 female. **Births** (per 1,000 pop. 1978): 34.0. **Deaths** (per 1,000 pop. 1978): 6.0. **Natural increase** (1975): 3.3%. **Hospital beds** (per 100,000 pop. 1977): 115. **Physicians** (per 100,000 pop. 1977): 57. **Infant mortality** (per 1,000 live births 1975): 49.
Education (1981): **Literacy:** 74%. **Pop. 5-19:** in school: 64%, teachers per 1,000: 19.

Mexico was the site of advanced Indian civilizations. The Mayas, an agricultural people, moved up from Yucatan, built immense stone pyramids, invented a calendar. The Toltecs were overcome by the Aztecs, who founded Tenochtitlan 1325 AD, now Mexico City. Hernando Cortes, Spanish conquistador, destroyed the Aztec empire, 1519-1521.

After 3 centuries of Spanish rule the people rose, under Fr. Miguel Hidalgo y Costilla, 1810, Fr. Morelos y Payon, 1812, and Gen. Agustin Iturbide, who made independence effective Sept. 27, 1821, but made himself emperor as Agustin I. A republic was declared in 1823.

Mexican territory extended into the present American Southwest and California until Texas revolted and established a republic in 1836; the Mexican legislature refused recognition but was unable to enforce its authority there. After numerous clashes, the U.S.-Mexican War, 1846-48, resulted in the loss by Mexico of the lands north of the Rio Grande.

French arms supported an Austrian archduke on the throne of Mexico as Maximilian I, 1864-67, but pressure from the U.S. forced France to withdraw. A dictatorial rule by Porfirio Diaz, president 1877-80, 1884-1911, led to fighting by rival forces until the new constitution of Feb. 5, 1917 provided social reform. Since then Mexico has developed large-scale programs of social security, labor protection, and school improvement. A constitutional provision requires management to share profits with labor.

The Institutional Revolutionary Party has been dominant in politics since 1929. Radical opposition, including some guerrilla activity, has been contained by strong measures.

The presidency of Luis Echeverria, 1970-76, was marked by a more leftist foreign policy and domestic rhetoric. Some land redistribution begun in 1976 was reversed under the succeeding administration.

Some gains in agriculture, industry, and social services have been achieved. The land is rich, but the rugged topography and lack of sufficient rainfall are major obstacles. Crops and farm prices are controlled, as are export and import. Economic prospects brightened with the discovery of vast oil reserves, perhaps the world's greatest. But half the work force is jobless or underemployed.

Monaco

Principality of Monaco

People: Population (1980 est.): 30,000. **Age distrib.** (%): 0–14: 12.7; 15–59: 56.3 60+: 30.7. **Ethnic groups:** French 58%, Italian 17%, Monegasque 15%. **Languages:** French (official). **Religions:** Predominately Roman Catholics.
Geography: Area: 0.73 sq. mi. **Location:** On the NW Mediterranean coast. **Neighbors:** France to W, N, E. **Topography:** Monaco-Ville sits atop a high promontory, the rest of the principality rises from the port up the hillside. **Capital:** Monaco-Ville (1979 est.): 1,700.
Government: Head of state: Prince Rainier III; b. May 31, 1923; in office: May 9, 1949. **Head of government:** Min. of State Jean Herly; in office: July, 1981.
Economy: Industries: Tourism, gambling, chemicals, precision instruments, plastics.
Finance: Currency: French franc or Monégasque franc. **Tourists** (1979): 218,000.
Transport: Chief ports: La Condamine.
Communications: Television sets: 16,000 in use (1976). **Radios:** 7,500 in use (1976). **Telephones in use** (1978): 32,000. **Daily newspaper circ.** (1977): 11,000; 420 per 1,000 pop.
Health: Births (per 1,000 pop. 1977): 7.5. **Deaths** (per 1,000 pop. 1977): 10.6. **Natural increase** (1977): −.3%. **Infant mortality** (per 1,000 live births 1970): 9.3.

An independent principality for over 300 years, Monaco has belonged to the House of Grimaldi since 1297 except during the French Revolution. It was placed under the protectorate of Sardinia in 1815, and under that of France, 1861. The Prince of Monaco was an absolute ruler until a 1911 constitution.

Monaco's fame as a tourist resort is widespread. It is noted for its mild climate and magnificent scenery. The area has been extended by land reclamation.

Mongolia

Mongolian People's Republic

People: Population (1981 est.): 1,700,000. **Pop. density:** 2.76 per sq. mi. **Urban** (1973): 46.4%. **Ethnic groups:** Khalkha Mongols 76%, other Mongols 8%, Kazakhs 5%, other Turks, Russians, Chinese. **Languages:** Khalkha Mongolian (official, written in Cyrillic letters since 1941), Turkic 7%, Russian, Chinese. **Religions:** Lama Buddhism prevailed, has been curbed.

Geography: Area: 604,247 sq. mi., more than twice the size of Texas. **Location:** In E Central Asia. **Neighbors:** USSR on N, China on S. **Topography:** Mostly a high plateau with mountains, salt lakes, and vast grasslands. Arid lands in the S are part of the Gobi Desert. **Capital:** Ulaanbaatar. **Cities** (1981 est.): Ulaanbaatar 435,400, Darhan.

Government: Head of state: Chmn. Yumzhagiyen Tsedenbal; b. Sept. 17, 1916; in office: June 11, 1974. **Head of government:** Premier Zhambyn Batmunkh; b. Mar. 10, 1926; in office: June 11, 1974. **Local divisions:** 18 provinces, 2 autonomous municipalities. **Armed forces:** regulars 30,000; reserves 30,000.

Economy: Industries: Food processing, textiles, chemicals, cement. **Chief crops:** Grain. **Minerals:** Coal, tungsten, copper, molybdenum, gold, tin. **Per capita arable land:** 1.7 acres. **Meat prod.** (1980): beef: 70,000 metric tons; lamb: 106,000 metric tons. **Electricity prod.** (1980): 1.5 bln. kwh. **Labor force:** 52% agric.; 10% manuf.

Finance: Currency: Tugrik (Sept. 1981: 3.17 = $1 US). **Gross domestic product** (1976 est.): $1.20 bln. **Per capita income** (1976 est.): $750. **Imports** (1980): $1.1 bln.; partners (1980): USSR 93%. **Exports** (1980): $390 mln.; partners (1980): USSR 82%, Czech. 5%.

Transport: Railway traffic (1980): 295 mln. passenger-km; 3.3 bln. net ton-km.

Communications: Television sets: 46,400 in use (1979). **Radios:** 150,000 in use (1979). **Telephones in use** (1979): 37,700. **Daily newspaper circ.** (1980): 101 per 1,000 pop.

Health: Life expectancy at birth (1975): 59.1 male; 62.3 female. **Births** (per 1,000 pop. 1978): 38. **Deaths** (per 1,000 pop. 1978): 9. **Natural increase** (1978): 2.6%. **Hospital beds** (per 100,000 pop. 1977): 1,067. **Physicians** (per 100,000 pop. 1977): 209.

Education (1978): **Literacy:** 95%. **Pop. 5-19:** in school: 56%, teachers per 1,000: 21.

One of the world's oldest countries, Mongolia reached the zenith of its power in the 13th century when Genghis Khan and his successors conquered all of China and extended their influence as far W as Hungary and Poland. In later centuries, the empire dissolved and Mongolia came under the suzerainty of China.

With the advent of the 1911 Chinese revolution, Mongolia, with Russian backing, declared its independence. A Mongolian Communist regime was established July 11, 1921.

In the early 1970s Mongolia was changing from a nomadic culture to one of settled agriculture and growing industries with aid from the USSR and East European nations.

Mongolia has sided with the Russians in the Sino-Soviet dispute. A Mongolian-Soviet mutual assistance pact was signed Jan. 15, 1966, and thousands of Soviet troops are based in the country.

Morocco

Kingdom of Morocco

People: Population (1981 est.): 21,600,000. **Age distrib.** (%): 0–14: 46.4; 15–59: 49.2; 60+: 4.2. **Pop. density:** 109.97 per sq. mi. **Urban** (1978): 40.6%. **Ethnic groups:** Arabs 65%, Berbers 33%, Europeans 1%. **Languages:** Arabic (official), with Berber, French, Spanish minorities. **Religions:** Sunni Moslems 99%.

Geography: Area: 171,117 sq. mi., larger than California. **Location:** on NW coast of Africa. **Neighbors:** W. Sahara on S, Algeria on E. **Topography:** Consists of 5 natural regions: mountain ranges (Riff in the N, Middle Atlas, Upper Atlas, and Anti-Atlas); rich plains in the W; alluvial plains in SW; well-cultivated plateaus in the center; a pre-Sahara arid zone extending from SE. **Capital:** Rabat. **Cities** (1978 est.): Casablanca 1,371,330; Rabat-Sale 435,510; Marrakech 330,400, Tangier.

Government: Head of state: King Hassan II; b. July 9, 1929; in office: Mar. 3, 1961. **Head of government:** Prime Min. Maati Bouabid; b. Nov. 11, 1927; in office: Mar. 23, 1979. **Local divisions:** 6 prefectures, 35 provinces. **Armed forces:** regulars 98,000; para-military 30,000.

Economy: Industries: Carpets, clothing, leather goods, tourism. **Chief crops:** Grain, fruits, dates, grapes. **Minerals:** Antimony, cobalt, manganese, phosphates, lead, oil, coal. **Crude oil reserves** (1980): 100 mln. bbls. **Per capita arable land:** 1.0 acres. **Meat prod.** (1980): beef: 77,000 metric tons; lamb: 58,000 metric tons. **Fish catch** (1979): 279,900 metric tons. **Electricity prod.** (1980): 4.6 bln. kwh. **Labor force:** 50% agric., 26% services.

Finance: Currency: Dirham (Mar. 1982: 5.90 = $1 US). **Gross domestic product** (1981): $16 bln. **Per capita income** (1981): $800. **Imports** (1980): $4.26 bln.; partners (1980): Fr. 25%, Iraq 9%, Sp. 8%, Saudi Ar. 8%. **Exports** (1981): $2.54 bln.; partners (1980): Fr. 25%, W. Ger. 8%, Sp. 6%, It. 6%. **Tourists** (1979): 1.5 mln.; receipts $375 mln. **National budget** (1981): $6 bln. revenues; $6.6 bln. expenditures. **International reserves less gold** (Jan. 1982): $89 mln. **Gold:** 704,000 oz t. **Consumer prices** (change in 1980): 9.4%.

Transport: Railway traffic (1979): 803 mln. passenger-km; 3.8 bln. net ton-km. **Motor vehicles:** in use (1979): 413,700 passenger cars, 157,500 comm. vehicles; assembled (1976): 25,000 passenger cars; 6,000 comm. vehicles. **Civil aviation** (1980): 1.8 bln. passenger-km; 26.5 mln. freight ton-km. **Chief ports:** Tangier, Casablanca, Kenitra.

Communications: Television sets: 597,000 licensed (1977). **Radios:** 1.6 mln. licensed (1977), 157,000 manuf. (1975). **Telephones in use** (1980): 227,000. **Daily newspaper circ.** (1980): 13 per 1,000 pop.

Health: Life expectancy at birth (1975): 51.4 male; 54.5 female. **Births** (per 1,000 pop. 1978): 43. **Deaths** (per 1,000 pop. 1978): 14. **Natural increase** (1978): 2.9%. **Hospital beds** (per 100,000 pop. 1977): 123. **Physicians** (per 100,000 pop. 1977): 9. **Infant mortality** (per 1,000 live births 1975): 149.

Education (1978): **Literacy:** 24%. **Pop. 5-19:** in school: 34%, teachers per 1,000: 9.

Berbers were the original inhabitants, followed by Carthaginians and Romans. Arabs conquered in 683. In the 11th and 12th centuries, a Berber empire ruled all NW Africa and most of Spain from Morocco.

Part of Morocco came under Spanish rule in the 19th century; France controlled the rest in the early 20th. Tribal uprisings lasted from 1911 to 1933. The country became independent Mar. 2, 1956. Tangier, an internationalized seaport, was turned over to Morocco, 1956. Ifni, a Spanish enclave, was ceded in 1969.

Morocco annexed over 70,000 sq. mi. of phosphate-rich land Apr. 14, 1976, two-thirds of former Spanish Sahara, with the remainder annexed by Mauritania. Spain had withdrawn in February. Polisario, a guerrilla movement, proclaimed the region independent Feb. 27, and launched attacks with Algerian support. Morocco accepted U.S. military and economic aid. When Mauritania signed a treaty with the Polisario Front, and gave up its portion of the former Spanish Sahara, Morocco occupied the area, 1980. Morocco accused Algeria of instigating Polisario attacks.

After years of bitter fighting, Morocco controls the main urban areas, but the Polisario Front's guerrillas move freely in the vast, sparsely populated deserts.

Mozambique

People's Republic of Mozambique

People: Population (1981 est.): 10,600,000. **Age distrib.** (%): 0–14: 45.3; 15–59: 50.6; 60+: 4.1. **Pop. density:** 34.55 per sq. mi. **Ethnic groups:** Bantu tribes. **Languages:** Portuguese (official), Bantu languages predominate. **Religions:** Traditional beliefs 65%, Christians 21%, Moslems 10%, Hindu, Buddhist, Jewish minorities.

Geography: Area: 308,642 sq. mi., larger than Texas. **Location:** On SE coast of Africa. **Neighbors:** Tanzania on N, Malawi, Zambia, Zimbabwe on W, South Africa, Swaziland on S. **Topography:** Coastal lowlands comprise nearly half the country with plateaus rising in steps to the mountains along the western border. **Capital:** Maputo. **Cities:** (1970 cen.): Maputo 383,775.

Government: Head of state: Pres. Samora Machel; b. Sept. 29, 1933; in office: June 25, 1975. **Local divisions:** 10 provinces. **Armed forces:** regulars 24,000.

Economy: Industries: Cement, alcohol, textiles. **Chief crops:** Cashews, cotton, sugar, copra, tea. **Minerals:** Coal, bauxite. **Per capita arable land:** 0.7 acres. **Meat prod.** (1980): beef: 36,000 metric tons; pork: 8,000 metric tons. **Fish catch** (1978): 23,000 metric tons. **Electricity prod.** (1979): 7.8 bln. kwh. **Labor force:** 74% agric., 16% man., 10% services.

Finance: Currency: Metical (Sept. 1981: 29.41 = $1 US). **Gross domestic product** (1978): $2 bln. **Per capita income** (1978 est.): $170. **Imports** (1979): $280 mln.; partners (1977): So. Afr. 20%, W. Ger. 15%, Port. 10%. **Exports** (1979): $100 mln.; partners (1977): U.S. 27%, Port. 16%, UK 7%, So. Afr. 7%. **National budget** (1980): $460 mln. revenues; $460 mln. expenditures. **Consumer prices** (change in 1976): 4.5%.

Transport: Railway traffic (1979): 210 mln. passenger-km; 2.1 bln. net ton-km. **Motor vehicles:** in use (1979): 102,400 passenger cars, 24,600 comm. vehicles. **Chief ports:** Maputo, Beira, Nacala.

Communications: Television sets: 1,200 in use (1977). **Radios:** 230,000 licensed (1977), 24,000 manuf. (1974). **Telephones in use** (1980): 51,600. **Daily newspaper circ.** (1980): 4 per 1,000 pop.

Health: Life expectancy at birth (1975): 41.9 male; 45.1 female. **Births** (per 1,000 pop. 1978): 44. **Deaths** (per 1,000 pop. 1978): 19. **Natural increase** (1978): 3.1%. **Hospital beds** (per 100,000 pop. 1977): 129. **Physicians** (per 100,000 pop. 1977): 6. **Infant mortality** (per 1,000 live births 1975): 19.1

Education (1978): **Literacy:** 20%. **Pop. 5-19:** in school: 20%, teachers per 1,000: 4.

The first Portuguese post on the Mozambique coast was established in 1505, on the trade route to the East. Mozambique became independent June 25, 1975, after a ten-year war against Portuguese colonial domination. The 1974 revolution in Portugal paved the way for the orderly transfer of power to Frelimo (Front for the Liberation of Mozambique). Frelimo took over local administration Sept. 20, 1974, over the opposition, in part violent, of some blacks and whites. The new government, led by Maoist Pres. Samora Machel, promised a gradual transition to a communist system, beginning with indoctrination to combat "individualism" and capitalist or traditionalist values. All private schools were closed. Rural collective farms were called for in a July 27, 1975, directive. All private homes were nationalized in 1976. Economic problems included the emigration of most of the country's 160,000 whites, a politically untenable economic dependence on white-ruled South Africa, and a large external debt.

Mozambique closed its border with Rhodesia in March 1976. Border clashes intensified, with Rhodesian troops attacking black Rhodesian guerrillas within Mozambique. Soviet arms were sent following a 1977 friendship treaty. But most aid comes from the West, with which most trade is conducted.

Early in 1979 the government announced that the country was in a state of war as a result of increased guerrilla activities. Incidents and reprisals continued.

Nauru

Republic of Nauru

People: Population (1981): 8,000. **Pop density:** 906.75 per sq. mi. **Ethnic groups:** Nauruans 57%, Pacific Islanders 26%, Chinese 19%, European 8%. **Languages:** Nauruan, English. **Religions:** Predominately Christian.

Geography: Area: 8 sq. mi. **Location:** In Western Pacific O. just S of Equator. **Neighbors:** Nearest are Solomon Is. **Topography:** Mostly a plateau bearing high grade phosphate deposits, surrounded by a coral cliff and a sandy shore in concentric rings. **Capital:** Yaren.

Government: Head of state: Pres. Hammer DeRoburt, b. Sept. 25, 1922; in office: May 11, 1978. **Local divisions:** 14 districts.

Economy: Phosphate mining. **Electricity prod.** (1978): 26.00 mln. kwh.

Finance: Currency: Australian dollar. **Gross domestic product** (1981 est.): $155 mln. **Per capita income** (1981): $21,400. **Imports** (1979): $11 mln. **Exports** (1979): $75 mln. **National budget** (1979): $46 mln. revenues; $38 mln. expenditures.

Communications: Radios: 3,600 in use (1976). **Telephones in use** (1978): 1,500.

Health: Births (per 1,000 pop. 1976): 19.8. **Deaths** (per 1,000 pop. 1976): 4.5. **Natural increase** (1976): 1.5%. **Infant mortality** (per 1,000 live births 1976): 19.0.

Education: Literacy 99%.

The island was discovered in 1798 by the British but was formally annexed to the German Empire in 1886. After World War I, Nauru became a League of Nations mandate administered by Australia. During World War II the Japanese occupied the island and shipped 1,200 Nauruans to the fortress island of Truk as slave laborers.

In 1947 Nauru was made a UN trust territory, administered by Australia. Nauru became an independent republic Jan. 31, 1968.

Phosphate exports provide one of the world's highest per capita revenues for the Nauru people. The deposits are expected to be nearly exhausted by 1990.

Nepal

Kingdom of Nepal

People: Population (1981 est.): 15,300,000. **Age distrib.** (%): 0–14: 40.5; 15–59: 53.9; 60+: 5.6. **Pop. density:** 246.86 per sq. mi. **Urban** (1971): 4.0%. **Ethnic groups:** The many tribes are descendants of Indian, Tibetan, and Central Asian migrants. **Languages:** Nepali (official) (an Indic language), Bihari, others. **Religions:** Hindus 90%, Buddhists 7%.

Geography: Area: 56,136 sq. mi., the size of North Carolina. **Location:** Astride the Himalaya Mts. **Neighbors:** China on N, India on S. **Topography:** The Himalayas stretch across the N, the hill country with its fertile valleys extends across the center, while the southern border region is part of the flat, subtropical Ganges Plain. **Capital:** Kathmandu. **Cities** (1976 cen.): Kathmandu 171,400, Pokhara, Biratnagar, Birganj.

Government: Head of state: King Birendra Bir Bikram Shah Dev; b. Dec. 28, 1945; in office: Jan. 31, 1972. **Head of government:** Prime Min. Surya Bahadur Thapa; in office: June 1, 1979. **Local divisions:** 14 zones; 75 districts. **Armed forces:** regulars 20,000; para-military 12,000.

Economy: Industries: Hides, drugs, tourism. **Chief crops:** Jute, rice, grain. **Minerals:** Quartz. **Other resources:** Forests. **Per capita arable land:** 0.4 acres. **Meat prod.** (1980): beef: 23,000 metric tons; pork: 5,000 metric tons; lamb: 18,000 metric tons. **Electricity prod.** (1977): 180 mln. kwh. **Labor force:** 94% agric.; 1% manuf.

Finance: Currency: Rupee (Mar. 1982: 13.20 = $1 US). **Gross domestic product** (1980): $1.99 bln. **Per capita income** (1975): $114. **Imports** (1980): $342 mln.; partners (1980): India 51%, Jap. 12%. **Exports** (1980): $80 mln.; partners (1980): India 42%, Jap. 7%, W. Ger. 8%. **Tourists** (1978): 156,000; receipts: $28 mln. **National budget** (1980): $144 mln. revenues; $295 mln. expenditures. **International reserves less gold** (Oct. 1981): $186.9 mln. **Gold:** 151,000 oz t. **Consumer prices** (change in 1980): 16.4%.

Communications: Radios: 150,000 in use (1976). **Telephones in use** (1978): 9,425. **Daily newspaper circ.** (1976): 96,000.

Health: Life expectancy at birth (1975): 42.2 male; 45.0 female. **Births** (per 1,000 pop. 1978): 45. **Deaths** (per 1,000 pop. 1978): 20. **Natural increase** (1978): 2.5%. **Hospital beds** (per 100,000 pop. 1977): 15. **Physicians** (per 100,000 pop. 1977): 3.

Education (1978): **Literacy:** 19%. **Pop. 5-19:** in school: 23%, teachers per 1,000: 7.

Nepal was originally a group of petty principalities, the inhabitants of one of which, the Gurkhas, became dominant about 1769. In 1951 King Tribhubana Bir Bikram, member of the Shah family, ended the system of rule by hereditary premiers of the Ranas family, who had kept the kings virtual prisoners, and established a cabinet system of government.

Virtually closed to the outside world for centuries, Nepal is now linked to India and Pakistan by roads and air service and to Tibet by road. Polygamy, child marriage, and the caste system were officially abolished in 1963.

India, the largest aid donor, is the chief trade partner, but Nepal has cultivated good relations with China as well.

Students and political opponents were arrested in 1974 following violent protests. A new wave of protests, 1979, led to more arrests and executions, but a change in premiers.

The promised referendum on Nepalese government was held May 2, 1980, backing the retention of the partyless form of government. A general election was held in 1981.

Netherlands

Kingdom of the Netherlands

People: Population (1981 est.) 14,200,000. **Age distrib.** (%): 0–14: 24.2; 15–59: 60.5; 60+: 15.4. **Pop. density:** 1,002.62 per sq. mi. **Urban** (1976): 88.4%. **Ethnic groups:** Dutch. **Languages:** Dutch. **Religions:** Roman Catholics 40%, Dutch Reformed 23.5%.

Geography: Area: 15,892 sq. mi., the size of Mass., Conn., and R.I. combined. **Location:** In NW Europe on North Sea. **Topography:** The land is flat, an average alt. of 37 ft. above sea level, with much land below sea level reclaimed and protected by 1,500 miles of dikes. Since 1927 the government has been draining the IJsselmeer, formerly the Zuider Zee. By 1972, 410,000 of a planned 550,000 acres had been drained and reclaimed. **Capital:** Amsterdam. **Cities** (1980): Amsterdam 716,919; Rotterdam 579,194; Hague 456,886.

Government: Head of state: Queen Beatrix; b. Jan. 31, 1938; in office: Apr. 30, 1980. **Head of government:** Prime Min. Andreas van Agt, b. Feb. 2, 1931; in office: Dec. 19, 1977. **Seat of govt.:** The Hague. **Local divisions:** 11 provinces. **Armed forces:** regulars 107,900 (1980).

Economy: Industries: Metals, machinery, chemicals, textiles, oil refinery, diamond cutting, pottery, electronics, tourism. **Chief crops:** Grains, potatoes, sugar beets, vegetables, fruits, flowers. **Minerals:** Natural gas, oil. **Crude oil reserves** (1980): 60 mln. bbls. **Per capita arable land:** 0.1 acres. **Meat prod.** (1980): beef: 412,000 metric tons; pork: 1.11 mln. metric tons; lamb: 21,000 metric tons. **Fish catch** (1979): 323,700 metric tons. **Electricity prod.** (1980): 64.8 bln. kwh. **Crude steel prod.** (1981): 5.4 mln. metric tons. **Labor force:** 6% agric.; 30% ind. and commerce, 20% services, 15% gov.

Finance: Currency: Guilder (Mar. 1982: 2.67 = $1 US). **Gross domestic product** (1981): $139 bln. **Per capita income** (1981): $9,749. **Imports** (1981): $65.8 bln.; partners (1980): W. Ger. 22%, Belg. 12%, U.S. 8%, U.K. 8%. **Exports** (1981): $68.3 bln.; partners (1980): W. Ger. 30%, Belg. 15%, Fr. 11%, UK 8%. **Tourists** (1979): 2.7 mln.; receipts: $1.3 bln. **National budget** (1980): $58.02 bln. revenues; $63.33 bln. expenditures. **International reserves less gold** (Feb. 1982): $8.69 bln. **Gold:** 43.94 mln. oz t. **Consumer prices** (change in 1981): 6.6%.

Transport: Railway traffic (1979): 8.9 bln. passenger-km; 3.4 bln. net ton-km. **Motor vehicles:** in use (1979): 4.1 mln. passenger cars, 327,000 comm. vehicles; manuf. (1978): 62,400 passenger cars; 11,520 comm. vehicles. **Civil aviation** (1980): 14.6 bln. passenger-km; 995 mln. freight ton-km. **Chief ports:** Rotterdam, Amsterdam, IJmuiden.

Communications: Television sets: 4.5 mln. licensed (1977). **Radios:** 8.5 mln. licensed (1977). **Telephones in use** (1980): 6.8 mln. **Daily newspaper circ.** (1980): 315 per 1,000 pop.

Health: Life expectancy at birth (1978): 71.9 male; 78.5 female. **Births** (per 1,000 pop. 1979): 12.5. **Deaths** (per 1,000 pop. 1979): 8.0. **Natural increase** (1978): .4%. **Hospital beds** (per 100,000 pop. 1977): 1,009. **Physicians** (per 100,000 pop. 1977): 172. **Infant mortality** (per 1,000 live births 1982): 9.

Education (1978): **Literacy:** 99%. **Pop. 5-19:** school: 63%, teachers per 1,000: 29.

Julius Caesar conquered the region in 55 BC, when it was inhabited by Celtic and Germanic tribes.

After the empire of Charlemagne fell apart, the Netherlands (Holland, Belgium, Flanders) split among counts, dukes and bishops, passed to Burgundy and thence to Charles V of Spain. His son, Philip II, tried to check the Dutch drive toward political freedom and Protestantism (1568-1573). William the Silent, prince of Orange, led a confederation of the northern provinces, called Estates, in the Union of Utrecht, 1579. The Estates retained individual sovereignty, but were represented jointly in the States-General, a body that had control of foreign affairs and defense. In 1581 they repudiated allegiance to Spain. The rise of the Dutch republic to naval, economic, and artistic eminence came in the 17th century.

The United Dutch Republic ended 1795 when the French formed the Batavian Republic. Napoleon made his brother Louis king of Holland, 1806; Louis abdicated 1810 when Napoleon annexed Holland. In 1813 the French were expelled. In 1815 the Congress of Vienna formed a kingdom of the Netherlands, including Belgium, under William I. In 1830, the Belgians seceded and formed a separate kingdom.

The constitution, promulgated 1814, and subsequently revised, assures a hereditary constitutional monarchy.

The Netherlands maintained its neutrality in World War I, but was invaded and brutally occupied by Germany from 1940 to 1945. After the war, neutrality was abandoned, and the country joined NATO, the Western European Union, the Benelux Union, and, in 1957, became a charter member of the Common Market.

In 1949, after several years of fighting, the Netherlands granted independence to Indonesia, where it had ruled since the 17th century. In 1963, West New Guinea was turned over to Indonesia, after five years of controversy and seizure of Dutch property in Indonesia.

Some 200,000 Indonesians emigrated to the Netherlands. Of them, 35,000 were from the South Moluccan islands. Terrorists demanding independence for South Molucca from Indonesia staged train hijackings and other incidents in the Netherlands in 1975 and 1977.

The independence of Suriname, 1975, instigated mass emigrations to the Netherlands, adding to problems of unemployment.

Though the Netherlands has been heavily industrialized, its productive small farms export large quantities of pork and dairy foods.

Rotterdam, located along the principal mouth of the Rhine, handles the most cargo of any ocean port in the world. Canals, of which there are 3,478 miles, are important in transportation.

In Nov., 1981, 400,000 people demonstrated in Amsterdam against the deployment of new nuclear weapons in Europe.

Netherlands Antilles

The **Netherlands Antilles,** constitutionally on a level of equality with the Netherlands homeland within the kingdom, consist of 2 groups of islands in the West Indies. **Curacao, Aruba,** and **Bonaire** are near the South American coast; **St. Eustatius, Saba,** and the southern part of **St. Maarten** are SE of Puerto Rico. Northern two-thirds of St. Maarten belong to French Guadeloupe; the French call the island St. Martin. Total area of the 2 groups is 385 sq. mi., including: Aruba 74, Bonaire 111, Curacao 171, St. Eustatius 11, Saba 5, St. Maarten (Dutch part) 13.

Total pop. (est. 1979) was 246,500. Willemstad, on Curacao, is the capital. Chief products are corn, pulse, salt and phosphate; principal industry is the refining of crude oil from Venezuela. Tourism is an important industry, as are electronics and shipbuilding.

New Zealand

People: Population: (1981 est.): 3,100,000. **Age distrib.** (%): 0–14: 29.0; 15–59: 57.9; 60+: 13.1. **Pop. density:** 30.80 per sq. mi. **Urban** (1976): 83.0%. **Ethnic groups:** European (mostly British) 84%, Polynesian (mostly Maori) 8.5%. **Languages:** English (official), Maori. **Religions:** Anglican 35%, Presbyterian 22%, Roman Catholics 16%, others.

Geography: Area: 103,883 sq. mi., the size of Colorado. **Location:** In SW Pacific O. **Neighbors:** Nearest are Australia on W, Fiji, Tonga on N. **Topography:** Each of the 2 main islands (North and South Is.) is mainly hilly and mountainous. The east coasts consist of fertile plains, especially the broad Canterbury Plains on South Is. A volcanic plateau is in center of North Is. South Is. has glaciers and 15 peaks over 10,000 ft. **Capital:** Wellington. **Cities** (1981 cen.): Christchurch 321,000; Auckland 818,000; Wellington 342,000.

Government: Head of state: Queen Elizabeth II, represented by Gov.-Gen. David Stuart Beattie; in office: Nov. 6, 1980. **Head of government:** Prime Min. Robert David Muldoon; b. Sept. 21, 1921; in office: Dec. 12, 1975. **Local divisions:** 96 counties, 132 boroughs, 3 towns, 4 districts. **Armed forces:** regulars 12,696 (1980).

Economy: Industries: Food processing, textiles, paper, steel, aluminum, oil products. **Chief crops:** Grain. **Minerals:** Oil, gas, iron, coal. **Crude oil reserves** (1980): 110 mln. bbls. **Other resources:** Wool, timber. **Per capita arable land:** 0.3 acres. **Meat prod.** (1980): beef: 470,000 metric tons; pork: 39,000 metric tons; lamb: 559,000 metric tons. **Fish catch** (1978): 82,600 metric tons. **Electricity prod.** (1980): 22 bln. kwh. **Crude steel prod.** (1981 est.): 221,000 metric tons. **Labor force:** 10.3% agric.; 34% ind. and commerce, 55% services and gov.

Finance: Currency: Dollar (Mar. 1982: 1.30 = $1 US). **Gross domestic product** (1981): $23.4 bln. **Per capita income** (1981): $7,363. **Imports** (1981): $5.72 bln.; partners (1980): Austral. 19%, UK 12%, U.S. 14%, Jap. 14%. **Exports** (1981): $5.61 bln.; partners (1980): UK 14%, U.S. 14%, Jap.

13%, Austral. 13%. **Tourists** (1979): 432,400; receipts $191 mln. **National budget** (1980): $5.6 bln. revenues; $6.5 bln. expenditures. **International reserves less gold** (Feb. 1982): $347 mln. **Gold:** 22,000 oz t. **Consumer prices** (change in 1981): 16%.

Transport: Railway traffic (1979): 414 mln. passenger-km; 3.1 bln. net ton-km. **Motor vehicles:** in use (1980): 1.3 mln. passenger cars; 247,000 comm. vehicles; assembled (1978): 51,828 passenger cars; 11,088 comm. vehicles. **Civil aviation:** (1980): 5.7 bln. passenger-km, 193 mln. freight ton-km. **Chief ports:** Auckland, Wellington, Lyttleton, Tauranga.

Communications: Television sets: 891,081 mln. licensed (1980): 90,000 manuf. (1978). **Radios:** 2.7 mln. in use (1980): 143,000 manuf. (1978). **Telephones in use** (1980): 1.7 mln. **Daily newspaper circ.** (1980): 240 per 1,000 pop.

Health: Life expectancy at birth (1982): 69 male; 75.55 female. **Births** (per 1,000 pop. 1979): 16.7. **Deaths** (per 1,000 pop. 1979): 8.2. **Natural increase** (1977): .9%. **Hospital beds** (per 100,000 pop. 1977): 1,022. **Physicians** (per 100,000 pop. 1977): 135. **Infant mortality** (per 1,000 live births 1982): 14.2

Education (1978): **Literacy:** 99%. **Pop. 5-19:** in school: 81%, teachers per 1,000: 35.

The Maoris, a Polynesian group from the eastern Pacific, reached New Zealand before and during the 14th century. The first European to sight New Zealand was Dutch navigator Abel Janszoon Tasman, but Maoris refused to allow him to land. British Capt. James Cook explored the coasts, 1769-1770.

British sovereignty was proclaimed in 1840, with organized settlement beginning in the same year. Representative institutions were granted in 1853. Maori Wars ended in 1870 with British victory. The colony became a dominion in 1907, and is an independent member of the Commonwealth.

New Zealand fought on the side of the Allies in both world wars, and signed the ANZUS Treaty of Mutual Security with the U.S. and Australia in 1951. New Zealand joined with Australia and Britain in a pact to defend Singapore and Malaysia; New Zealand units are stationed in those 2 countries.

A labor tradition in politics dates back to the 19th century. Private ownership is basic to the economy, but state ownership or regulation affects many industries. Transportation, broadcasting, mining, and forestry are largely state-owned.

The native Maoris numbered an estimated 200,000 in the early 19th century; violence and European diseases cut them to 40,000 by the end of the century. They totaled over 250,000 in 1976. Four of 92 members of the House of Representatives are elected directly by the Maori people.

A 1981 South African rugby team tour deeply divided the country.

New Zealand comprises **North Island,** 44,204 sq. mi.; **South Island,** 58,304 sq. mi.; **Stewart Island,** 674 sq. mi.; **Chatham Islands,** 372 sq. mi.

In 1965, the **Cook Islands** (pop. 1980 cen., 19,200; area 93 sq. mi.) became self-governing although New Zealand retains responsibility for defense and foreign affairs. **Niue** attained the same status in 1974; it lies 400 mi. to W (pop. 1981 est., 3,400; area 100 sq. mi.). **Tokelau Is.,** (pop. 1980 est., 1,600; area 4 sq. mi.) are 300 mi. N of Samoa.

Ross Dependency, administered by New Zealand since 1923, comprises 160,000 sq. mi. of Antarctic territory.

Nicaragua

Republic of Nicaragua

People: Population (1981 est.): 2,400,000. **Age distrib.** (%): 0–14: 48.1; 15–59: 47.2; 60+: 4.7. **Pop. density:** 47.95 per sq. mi. **Urban** (1972): 48.6%. **Ethnic groups:** Mestizo 70%, Caucasian 17%, Negro 9%, Indian 4%. **Languages:** Spanish, English (on Caribbean coast). **Religions:** Predominantly Roman Catholics.

Geography: Area: 79,759 sq. mi., slightly larger than Wisconsin. **Location:** In Central America. **Neighbors:** Honduras on N, Costa Rica on S. **Topography:** Both Atlantic and Pacific coasts are over 200 mi. long. The Cordillera Mtns., with many volcanic peaks, runs NW-SE through the middle of the country. Between this and a volcanic range to the E lie Lakes Managua and Nicaragua. **Capital:** Managua. **Cities** (1971 cen.): Managua 398,514.

Government: 3-member junta; as of Mar. 5, 1981. **Local divisions:** 16 departments; one national district. **Armed forces:** regulars 8,300; para-military 4,000.

Economy: Industries: Oil refining, chemicals, textiles. **Chief crops:** Bananas, cotton, fruit, yucca, coffee, sugar, corn, beans, cocoa, rice, sesame, tobacco, wheat. **Minerals:** Gold, silver, copper, tungsten. **Other resources:** Forests, shrimp. **Per capita arable land:** 1.4 acres. **Meat prod.** (1980): beef: 69,000 metric tons; pork: 11,000 metric tons. **Fish catch:** (1978): 22,200 metric tons. **Electricity prod.** (1978): 1.1 bln. kwh. **Labor force:** 65% agric.

Finance: Currency: Cordoba (Apr. 1982: 10.05 = $1 US). **Gross domestic product** (1979): $1.45 bln. **Per capita income** (1978): $825. **Imports** (1979): $350 mln.; partners (1979): U.S. 25%, Venez. 18%, Costa Rica 11%, Guat. 10%. **Exports** (1979): $700 mln.; partners (1979): U.S. 32%, W. Ger. 10%, China 11%, Costa Rica 7%. **National budget** (1979): $175 mln. revenues; $292 mln. expenditures. **International reserves less gold** (Nov. 1979): $85.36 mln. **Gold:** 18,000 oz t. **Consumer prices** (change in 1980): 35.3%.

Transport: Railway traffic (1977): 19 mln. passenger-miles; 11 mln. net ton-miles. **Motor vehicles:** in use (1979): 37,700 passenger cars, 30,100 comm. vehicles. **Chief ports:** Corinto, Puerto Somoza, San Juan del Sur.

Communications: Television sets: 170,000 in use (1979). **Radios:** 600,000 in use (1979). **Telephones in use** (1980): 57,900 **Daily newspaper circ.** (1980): 89 per 1,000 pop.

Health: Life expectancy at birth (1975): 51.2 male; 54.6 female. **Births** (per 1,000 pop. 1978): 46. **Deaths** (per 1,000 pop. 1978): 16. **Natural increase** (1978): 0.7%. **Hospital beds** (per 100,000 pop. 1977): 207. **Physicians** (per 100,000 pop. 1977): 60. **Infant mortality** (per 1,000 live births 1975): 37.0.

Education (1978): **Literacy:** 58%. **Pop. 5-19:** in school: 48%, teachers per 1,000: 13.

Nicaragua, inhabited by various Indian tribes, was conquered by Spain in 1552. After gaining independence from Spain, 1821, Nicaragua was united for a short period with Mexico, then with the United Provinces of Central America, finally becoming an independent republic, 1838.

U.S. Marines occupied the country at times in the early 20th century, the last time from 1926 to 1933.

Gen. Anastasio Somoza-Debayle was elected president 1967. He resigned 1972, but was elected president again Sept. 1, 1974. Martial law was imposed in Dec. 1974, after officials were kidnapped by the Marxist Sandinista guerrillas. The country's Roman Catholic bishops charged in 1977 that the government had tortured, raped, and executed civilians in its anti-guerrilla campaign. The Inter-American Commission on Human Rights made a similar report to the OAS, 1978. Violent opposition spread to nearly all classes, 1978; a nationwide strike called against the government Aug. 25 touched off a state of civil war at Matagalpa.

Months of simmering civil war erupted when Sandinist guerrillas invaded Nicaragua May 29, 1979, touching off a 7-week-offensive that culminated in the resignation and exile of Somoza, July 17. Repeated border clashes with Honduras caused the government to declare a state of siege, March 1982.

Relations with the U.S. were strained in 1982 due to Nicaragua's military aid to leftist guerrillas in El Salvador. Nicaragua accused the U.S. of backing anti-Sandinist rebels.

Niger

Republic of Niger

People: Population (1981 est.): 5,600,000. **Age distrib.** (%): 0–14: 43.0; 15–59: 52.2; 60+: 4.8. **Pop. density:** 10.2 per sq. mi. **Ethnic groups:** Hausa 53%, Zerma and Songhai 23%, Fulani 10%, Beriberi-Manga 9%. **Languages:** French (official), Sudanic dialects. **Religions:** Muslims 85%, animists 14%.

Geography: Area: 459,100 sq. mi., almost twice the size of Texas. **Location:** In the interior of N. Africa. **Neighbors:** Libya, Algeria on N, Mali, Upper Volta on W, Benin, Nigeria on S, Chad on E. **Topography:** Mostly arid desert and mountains. A narrow savanna in the S and the Niger R. basin in the SW contain most of the population. **Capital:** Niamey. **Cities** (1978 est.): Niamey 225,300, (fluctuates with nomad migration in dry season).

Government: Head of state: Pres. Seyni Kountche; b. 1931; in office: Apr. 15, 1974. **Local divisions:** 7 departments. **Armed forces:** regulars 2,150; para-military 1,800.

Economy: Chief crops: Peanuts, cotton. **Minerals:** Uranium. **Per capita arable land:** 7.4 acres. **Meat prod.** (1980): beef: 37,000 metric tons; lamb: 33,000 metric tons. **Electricity prod.**

(1979): 45 mln. kwh. **Labor force:** 90% agric.

Finance: Currency: CFA franc (Mar. 1982: 312.10 = $1 US). **Gross domestic product** (1978 est.): $1.3 bln. **Per capita income** (1978 est.): $250. **Imports** (1977): $196 mln.; partners (1980): Fr. 45%, W. Ger. 8%. **Exports** (1977): $160 mln.; partners (1980): Fr. 74%, W. Ger. 16%. **National budget** (1979): $144 mln. revenues; 144 mln. expenditures. **International reserves less gold** (Jan. 1982): $105.3 mln. **Gold:** 11,000 oz t. **Consumer prices** (change in 1980): 10.3%.

Transport: Motor vehicles: in use (1980): 25,800 passenger cars, 4,400 comm. vehicles.

Communications: Radios: 150,000 in use (1971). **Telephones in use** (1977): 8,100. **Daily newspaper cir.** (1980): 1 per 1,000 pop.

Health: Life expectancy at birth (1975): 39.4 male; 42.5 female. **Births** (per 1,000 pop. 1978): 51. **Deaths** (per 1,000 pop. 1978): 23. **Natural increase** (1978): 2.9%. **Hospital beds** (per 100,000 pop 1977): 69. **Physicians** (per 100,000 pop. 1977): 2. **Infant mortality** (per 1,000 live births 1978): 162.

Education (1978): **Literacy:** 8%. **Pop. 5-19:** in school: 11%, Teachers per 1,000: 3.

Niger was part of ancient and medieval African empires. European explorers reached the area in the late 18th century. The French colony of Niger was established 1900-22, after the defeat of Tuareg fighters, who had invaded the area from the N a century before. The country became independent Aug. 3, 1960. The next year it signed a bilateral agreement with France retaining close economic and cultural ties, which have continued. Hamani Diori, Niger's first president, was ousted in a 1974 coup. Drought and famine struck in 1973-74, and again in 1975, and half the country's livestock died.

Nigeria

Federal Republic of Nigeria

People: Population (1981 est.): 88,600,000. **Pop. density:** 216.09 per sq. mi. **Ethnic groups:** Hausa 21%, Yoruba 20%, Ibo 17%, Fulani 9%, others. **Languages:** English (official), Hausa, Yoruba, Ibo. **Religions:** Moslems 47% (in N), Christians 34% (in S), others.

Geography: Area: 356,700 sq. mi., more than twice the size of California. **Location:** On the S coast of W. Africa. **Neighbors:** Benin on W, Niger on N, Chad, Cameroon on E. **Topography:** 4 E-W regions divide Nigeria: a coastal mangrove swamp 10-60 mi. wide, a tropical rain forest 50-100 mi. wide, a plateau of savanna and open woodland, and semidesert in the N. **Capital:** Lagos. **Cities:** (1978 est.): Lagos 1,060,848; Ibadan 847,000; Ogbomosho 432,000; Kano 399,000.

Government: Head of state: Pres. Alhaji Shehu Shagari; b. Apr. 25, 1925; in office: Oct. 1, 1979. **Local divisions:** 19 states, Federal Capital Territory. **Armed forces:** regulars 173,000; reserves 2,000.

Economy: Industries: Crude oil (95% of export), food processing, assembly of vehicles and other equipment. **Chief crops:** Cocoa (main export crop), tobacco, palm products, peanuts, cotton, soybeans. **Minerals:** Oil, gas, coal, iron, limestone, columbium, tin. **Crude oil reserves** (1980): 17.4 bln. bbls. **Other resources:** Timber, rubber, hides. **Per capita arable land:** 0.8 acres. **Meat prod.** (1980): beef: 251,000 metric tons; pork: 42,000 metric tons; lamb: 163,000 metric tons. **Fish catch** (1979): 535,400 metric tons. **Electricity prod.** (1979): 5.2 bln. kwh. **Labor force:** 75% agric., 10% ind., commerce and services.

Finance: Currency: Naira (Feb. 1982: .66 = $1 US). **Gross domestic product** (1978): $43 bln. **Per capita income** (1978): $523. **Imports** (1980): $15,79 bln.; partners (1980): UK 19%, W. Ger. 12%, U.S. 8%, Jap. 10%. **Exports** (1981): $20.18 bln.; partners (1980): U.S. 43%, W. Ger. 12%, Neth. 11%. **Tourist receipts** (1977): $60 mln. **National budget** (1980): $13.3 bln. revenues; $14.4 bln. expenditures. **International reserves less gold** (Mar. 1982): $2.62 bln. **Gold:** 687,000 oz t. **Consumer prices** (change in 1980): 11.4%.

Transport: Railway traffic (1975): 785 mln. passenger-km; 972 mln. net ton-km. **Motor vehicles:** in use (1980): 215,000 passenger cars, 33,100 comm. vehicles. **Civil aviation** (1980): 1.8 bln., 852 mln. passenger-km; 11.1 mln. freight ton-km. **Chief ports:** Port Harcourt, Bonny, Lagos.

Communications: Television sets: 450,000 licensed (1977), 26,000 manuf. (1978). **Radios:** 5.2 mln. licensed (1977), 92,000 manuf. (1978). **Telephones in use** (1980): 154,200. **Daily newspaper circ.** (1980): 8 per 1,000 pop.

Health: Life expectancy at birth (1980): 45.9 male; 49.2 female. **Births** (per 1,000 pop. 1978): 50. **Deaths** (per 1,000 pop. 1978): 19. **Natural increase** (1978): 3.2%. **Hospital beds** (per 100,000 pop. 1977): 80. **Physicians** (per 100,000 pop. 1977): 7.

Education (1978): **Literacy:** 25%. **Pop. 5-19:** in school: 37%, teachers per 1,000: 7.

Early cultures in Nigeria date back to at least 700 BC. From the 12th to the 14th centuries, more advanced cultures developed in the Yoruba area, at Ife, and in the north, where Moslem influence prevailed.

Portuguese and British slavers appeared from the 15th-16th centuries. Britain seized Lagos, 1861, during an anti-slave trade campaign, and gradually extended control inland until 1900. Nigeria became independent Oct. 1, 1960, and a republic Oct. 1, 1963.

On May 30, 1967, the Eastern Region seceded, proclaiming itself the Republic of Biafra, plunging the country into civil war. Casualties in the war were est. at over 1 million, including many "Biafrans" (mostly Ibos) who died of starvation despite international efforts to provide relief. The secessionists, after steadily losing ground, capitulated Jan. 12, 1970. Within a few years, the Ibos were reintegrated into national life, but mistrust among the regions persists.

Oil revenues have made possible a massive economic development program, largely using private enterprise, but agriculture has lagged. Nigeria nationalized British Petroleum's facilities, July, 1979. Slumping oil revenues forced Nigeria to impose temporary import restrictions in 1982.

Nigeria led in the formation of the Economic Community of West African States, 1975, linking 15 countries.

After 13 years of military rule, the nation experienced a peaceful return to civilian government, Oct., 1979.

Norway

Kingdom of Norway

People: Population (1981 est.): 4,100,000. **Age distrib.** (%): 0–14: 23.5; 15–59: 57.2; 60+: 19.6. **Pop. density:** 34 per sq. mi. **Urban** (1977): 44.2%. **Ethnic groups:** Germanic (Nordic, Alpine, Baltic), minority Lapps. **Languages:** Norwegian (official), Lapp. **Religions:** Lutherans 94%.

Geography: Area: 125,057 sq. mi., slightly larger than New Mexico. **Location:** Occupies the W part of Scandinavian peninsula in NW Europe (extends farther north than any European land). **Neighbors:** Sweden, Finland, USSR on E. **Topography:** A highly indented coast is lined with tens of thousands of islands. Mountains and plateaus cover most of the country, which is only 25% forested. **Capital:** Oslo. **Cities** (1980): Oslo 454,872; Bergen 208,910.

Government: Head of state: King Olav V, b. July 2, 1903; in office: Sept. 21, 1957. **Head of government:** Prime Min. Kare Isaachsen Willoch, b. Oct. 3, 1928; in office: Oct. 14, 1981. **Local divisions:** Oslo, Svalbard and 18 fylker (counties). **Armed forces:** regulars 37,000 (1980).

Economy: Industries: Paper, shipbuilding, engineering, metals, chemicals, food processing oil, gas. **Chief crops:** Grains, potatoes, fruits. **Minerals:** Oil, copper, pyrites, nickel, iron, zinc, lead. **Crude oil reserves** (1980): 5.75 bln. bbls. **Other resources:** Timber. **Per capita arable land:** 0.5 acres. **Meat prod.** (1980): beef: 74,000 metric tons; pork: 83,000 metric tons; lamb: 19,000 metric tons. **Fish catch** (1979): 2.6 mln. metric tons. **Electricity prod.** (1980): 83.9 bln. kwh. **Crude steel prod.** (1981): 848,000 metric tons. **Labor force:** 7.4% agric.; 20.5% ind., 32% services, 29% govt.

Finance: Currency: Krone (Mar. 1982: 6.12 = $1 US). **Gross domestic product** (1980): $57.32 bln. **Per capita income** (1980): $12,432. **Imports** (1981): $15.6 bln.; partners (1980): Swed. 17%, W. Ger. 14%, UK 14%, U.S. 8%. **Exports** (1981): $17.98 bln.; partners (1980): UK 41%, W. Ger. 17%, Swed. 9%. **Tourists** (1977): 447,800; receipts: $478 mln. **National budget** (1981): $16.6 bln. revenues; $17.3 bln. expenditures. **International reserves less gold** (Feb. 1982): $5.80 bln. **Gold:** 1.18 mln. oz t. **Consumer prices** (change in 1981): 13.7%.

Transport: Railway traffic (1979): 2.73 bln. passenger-km;

3.08 bln. net ton-km. **Motor vehicles:** in use (1980): 1.2 mln. passenger cars, 152,500 comm. vehicles. **Civil aviation:** (1980): 4.06 bln. passenger-km; 136 mln. freight ton-km. **Chief ports:** Bergen, Stavanger, Oslo, Tonsberg.

Communications: Television sets: 1.1 mln. licensed (1980), 108,000 manuf. (1975). **Radios:** 1.3 mln. licensed (1980), 111,000 manuf. (1973). **Telephones in use** (1979): 1.7 mln. **Daily newspaper circ.** (1980): 440 per 1,000 pop.

Health: Life expectancy at birth (1979): 72.3 male; 78.7 female. **Births** (per 1,000 pop. 1980): 12.5. **Deaths** (per 1,000 pop. 1980): 10.0. **Natural increase** (1978): .3%. **Hospital beds** (per 100,000 pop. 1977): 1,481. **Physicians** (per 100,000 pop. 1977): 186. **Infant mortality** (per 1,000 live births 1981): 8.5.

Education (1978): **Literacy:** 99%. **Pop. 5-19:** in school: 70%, teachers per 1,000: 46.

The first supreme ruler of Norway was Harald the Fairhaired who came to power in 872 AD. Between 800 and 1000, Norway's Vikings raided and occupied widely dispersed parts of Europe.

The country was united with Denmark 1381-1814, and with Sweden, 1814-1905. In 1905, the country became independent with Prince Charles of Denmark as king.

Norway remained neutral during World War I. Germany attacked Norway Apr. 9, 1940, and held it until liberation May 8, 1945. The country abandoned its neutrality after the war, and joined the NATO alliance. Norway, a member of the European Free Trade Assoc., rejected membership in the Common Market in a 1972 referendum.

Abundant hydroelectric resources provided the base for Norway's industrialization, producing one of the highest living standards in the world.

Despite an almost total lack of unemployment and an increasing labor shortage, Norway has refused to admit more than a small number of foreign workers.

Norway's merchant marine is one of the world's largest.

Norway and the Soviet Union have disputed their territorial waters boundary in the Barents Sea, north of the 2 countries' common border.

Petroleum output from oil and mineral deposits under the continental shelf raised state revenues; new refinery facilities opened in 1979, and new offshore fields were discovered.

Svalbard is a group of mountainous islands in the Arctic O., c. 23,957 sq. mi., pop. varying seasonally from 1,500 to 3,600. The largest, Spitsbergen (formerly called West Spitsbergen), 15,060 sq. mi., seat of governor, is about 370 mi. N of Norway. By a treaty signed in Paris, 1920, major European powers recognized the sovereignty of Norway, which incorporated it in 1925. Both Norway and the USSR mine rich coal deposits. Mt. Newton (Spitsbergen) is 5,633 ft. tall.

Oman

Sultanate of Oman

People: Population (1981 est.): 910,000. **Pop. density:** 10.85 per sq. mi. **Ethnic groups:** Arab 88%, Baluchi 4%, Persian 3%, Indian 2%, African 2%. **Languages:** Arabic (official), Persian, Urdu, others. **Religions:** Ibadi Moslems 75%, Sunni Moslems 25%.

Geography: Area: 120,000 sq. mi., the size of Kansas. **Location:** On SE coast of Arabian peninsula. **Neighbors:** United Arab Emirates, Saudi Arabia, South Yemen on W. **Topography:** Oman has a narrow coastal plain up to 10 mi. wide, a range of barren mountains reaching 9,900 ft., and a wide, stony, mostly waterless plateau, avg. alt. 1,000 ft. Also the tip of the Ruus-al-Jebal peninsula controls access to the Persian Gulf. **Capital:** Muscat. **Cities** (1975 est.): Matrah 20,000; Muscat 7,000.

Government: Head of state: Sultan Qabus ibn Said; b. Nov. 18, 1942; in office: July 23, 1970. **Local divisions:** 1 province, numerous districts. **Armed forces:** regulars 19,200; paramilitary 3,300.

Economy: Chief crops: Dates, fruits vegetables, wheat, bananas. **Minerals:** Oil (99% of exports). **Crude oil reserves** (1980): 2.40 bln. bbls. **Per capita arable land:** 0.05 acres. **Fish catch** (1979): 198,000 metric tons. **Electricity prod.** (1978): 550.00 mln. kwh. **Labor force:** 66% agric.

Finance: Currency: Rial Omani (Apr. 1982: .34 = $1 US). **Gross domestic product** (1980): $3.4 bln. **Per capita income** (1976): $2,400. **Imports** (1979): $1.25 bln.; partners (1980): Jap. 20%, UAE 17%, UK 16%. **Exports** (1980): $3.29 bln.; partners (1980): Jap. 50%, Sing. 11%, Neth. 11%. **National budget** (1980): $2.8 bln. revenues; $2.7 bln. expenditures. **International reserves less gold** (Jan. 1982): $1.07 bln. **Gold:** 276,000 oz t.

Transport: Chief ports: Matrah, Muscat.

Communications: Telephones in use (1978): 13,068.

Health: Hospital beds (per 100,000 pop. 1977): 173. **Physicians** (per 100,000 pop. 1977): 49.

Education (1978): **Literacy:** 50%. **Pop. 5-19:** in school: 28%, teachers per 1,000: 13.

A long history of rule by other lands, including Portugal in the 16th century, ended with the ouster of the Persians in 1744. By the early 19th century, Muscat and Oman was one of the most important countries in the region, controlling much of the Persian and Pakistan coasts, and ruling far-away Zanzibar, which was separated in 1861 under British mediation.

British influence was confirmed in a 1951 treaty, and Britain helped suppress an uprising by traditionally rebellious interior tribes against control by Muscat in the 1950s. Enclaves on the Pakistan coast were sold to that country in 1958.

On July 23, 1970, Sultan Said bin Taimur was overthrown by his son. The new sultan changed the nation's name to Sultanate of Oman. He launched a domestic development program, and battled leftist rebels in the southern Dhofar area to their defeat, Dec. 1975. Warfare was resumed, 1979.

Oil, discovered in 1964, has been the major source of income for the sultanate.

Economic and military aid accords with the U.S. gave U.S. forces access to air and naval bases around the Indian O., 1980.

Pakistan

Islamic Republic of Pakistan

People: Population (1981 est.): 89,000,000. **Pop. density:** 262 per sq. mi. **Urban** (1972): 25.5%. **Ethnic groups:** Punjabi 66%, Sindhi 13%, Pushtun (Iranian) 8.5%, Urdu 7.6%, Baluchi 2.5%, others. **Languages:** Urdu, English are both official. **Religions:** Muslim 97%, Christians 1.4%, Hindus 1.5%.

Geography: Area: 307,374 sq. mi., larger than Texas. **Location:** In W part of South Asia. **Neighbors:** Iran on W, Afghanistan, China on N, India on E. **Topography:** The Indus R. rises in the Hindu Kush and Himalaya mtns. in the N (highest is K2, or Godwin Austen, 28,250 ft., 2d highest in world), then flows over 1,000 mi. through fertile valley and empties into Arabian Sea. Thar Desert, Eastern Plains flank Indus Valley. **Capital:** Islamabad. **Cities** (1972 cen.): Karachi 3,498,634; Lahore 2,165,372; Lyallpur 822,263; Hyderabad 628,310; Rawalpindi 615,392.

Government: Head of state and head of government: Pres. Mohammad Zia ul-Haq; b. 1924; in office: Sept. 16, 1978 (state), July 5, 1977 (govt.). **Local divisions:** Federal capital and 4 provinces with elected legislatures. **Armed forces:** regulars 436,600 (1980).

Economy: Industries: Textiles, food processing, chemicals, tobacco, **Chief crops:** Rice, wheat. **Minerals:** Natural gas, iron ore. **Crude oil reserves** (1980): 200 mln. bbls. **Other resources:** Wool. **Per capita arable land:** 0.6 acres. **Meat prod.** (1980): beef: 344,000 metric tons; lamb: 313,000 metric tons. **Fish catch** (1979): 300,400 metric tons. **Electricity prod.** (1977): 11.05 bln. kwh. **Labor force:** 60% agric.; 16% ind.

Finance: Currency: Rupee (Mar. 1982: 11.46 = $1 US). **Gross domestic product** (1980): $23.22 bln. **Per capita income** (1980): $280. **Imports** (1980): $5.35 bln.; partners (1980): Jap. 12%, U.S. 11%, Kuwait 10%. **Exports** (1981): $2.88 bln.; partners (1980): Jap. 8%, HK 8%. **Tourists** (1977): 220,400; receipts: $61 mln. **National budget** (1981): $3.71 bln. revenues; $3.71 bln. expenditures. **International reserves less gold** (Feb. 1982): $707 mln. **Gold:** 1.84 mln. oz t. **Consumer prices** (change in 1981): 13.8%.

Transport: Railway traffic (1980): 16.5 bln. passenger-km; 9.3 bln. net ton-km. **Motor vehicles:** in use (1980): 135,700 passenger cars, 36,100 comm. vehicles. **Civil aviation** (1980): 5.6 bln. passenger-km; 241.3 mln. freight ton-km. **Chief ports:** Karachi.

Communications: Television sets: 625,000 in use (1977). **Radios:** 5 mln. in use (1977). **Telephones in use** (1980): 314,000. **Daily newspaper circ.** (1976): 965,000.

Health: Life expectancy at birth (1980): 51.9 male; 51.7 female. **Births** (per 1,000 pop. 1978): 45. **Deaths** (per 1,000 pop.

1978): 17. **Natural increase** 1978): 2.9%. **Hospital beds** (per 100,000 pop. 1977): 50. **Physicians** (per 100,000 pop. 1977): 25. **Infant mortality** (per 1,000 live births 1979): 142.

Education (1978): **Literacy:** 23%. **Pop. 5-19:** in school: 28%, teachers per 1,000: 9.

Present-day Pakistan shares the 5,000-year history of the India-Pakistan sub-continent. At present day Harappa and Mohenjo Daro, the Indus Valley Civilization, with large cities and elaborate irrigation systems, flourished c. 4,000-2,500 BC.

Aryan invaders from the NW conquered the region around 1,500 BC, forging a Hindu civilization that dominated Pakistan as well as India for 2,000 years.

Beginning with the Persians in the 6th century BC, and continuing with Alexander the Great and with the Sassanians, successive nations to the west ruled or influenced Pakistan, eventually separating the area from the Indian cultural sphere.

The first Arab invasion, 712 AD, introduced Islam. Under the Mogul empire (1526-1867), Moslems ruled most of India, yielding to British encroachment and resurgent Hindus.

After World War I the Moslems of British India began agitation for minority rights in elections. Mohammad Ali Jinnah (1876-1948) was the principal architect of Pakistan. A leader of the Moslem League from 1916, he worked for dominion status for India; from 1940 he advocated a separate Moslem state.

When the British withdrew Aug. 14, 1947, the Islamic majority areas of India acquired self-government as Pakistan, with dominion status in the Commonwealth. Pakistan was divided into 2 sections, West Pakistan and East Pakistan. The 2 areas were nearly 1,000 mi. apart on opposite sides of India.

Pakistan became a republic in 1956. Pakistan had a National Assembly (legislature) with equal membership from East and West Pakistan, and 2 Provincial Assemblies. In Oct. 1958, Gen. Mohammad Ayub Khan took power in a coup. He was elected president in 1960, reelected in 1965.

As a member of the Central Treaty Organization, Pakistan had been aligned with the West. Following clashes between India and China in 1962, Pakistan made commercial and aid agreements with China. U.S. aid to both Pakistan and India was suspended during the 1966 war over Kashmir but both economic aid and "nonlethal" military aid were resumed in 1966. The embargo was lifted in 1975.

Ayub resigned Mar. 25, 1969, after several months of violent rioting and unrest, most of it in East Pakistan, which demanded autonomy. The government was turned over to Gen. Agha Mohammad Yahya Khan and martial law was declared.

The Awami League, which sought regional autonomy for East Pakistan, won a majority in Dec. 1970 elections to a National Assembly which was to write a new constitution. In March, 1971 Yahya postponed the Assembly. Rioting and strikes broke out in the East.

On Mar. 25, 1971, government troops launched attacks in the East. The Easterners, aided by India, proclaimed the independent nation of Bangladesh. In months of widespread fighting, countless thousands were killed. Some 10 million Easterners fled into India.

Full scale war between India and Pakistan had spread to both the East and West fronts by December 3. Pakistan troops in the East surrendered Dec. 16; Pakistan agreed to a cease-fire in the West Dec. 17. On July 3, 1972, Pakistan and India signed a pact agreeing to withdraw troops from their borders and seek peaceful solutions to all problems. Diplomatic relations were resumed in 1976.

Zulfikar Ali Bhutto, leader of the Pakistan People's party, which had won the most West Pakistan votes in the Dec. 1970 elections, became president Dec. 20. In 1972 he announced new land reforms and said the government would control management of major industries.

A new constitution adopted Apr. 10, 1973, made Pakistan a federal Islamic republic. Bhutto became prime minister Aug. 14.

Bhutto was overthrown in a military coup July, 1977. Convicted of complicity in a 1974 political murder, Bhutto was executed Apr.4, 1979.

Relations with the U.S. were strained, 1979, when the U.S. embassy in Islamabad was stormed and burned and 2 Americans were killed, Nov. 21, along with attacks on other U.S. installations. But by June 1981, the U.S., pressured by the Soviet threat in Afghanistan, agreed to a six-year economic and military aid program with Pakistan. There are some 2 million Afghan refugees now in Pakistan.

Panama

Republic of Panama

People: Population (1981 est.): 2,000,000. **Age distrib.** (%): 0–14: 43.4; 15–59: 51.0; 60+: 5.7. **Pop. density:** 66.20 per sq. mi. **Urban** (1979): 51.2%. **Ethnic groups:** Mestizo 70%, West Indian 14%, Caucasian 10%, Indian 6%. **Languages:** Spanish (official), English. **Religions:** Roman Catholics 87%, Protestants.

Geography: Area: 29,762 sq. mi., slightly larger than West Virginia. **Location:** In Central America. **Neighbors:** Costa Rica on W., Colombia on E. **Topography:** 2 mountain ranges run the length of the isthmus. Tropical rain forests cover the Caribbean coast and eastern Panama. **Capital:** Panama. **Cities** (1981 est.): Panama 655,000; Colon 117,000.

Government: Head of state and head of government: Pres. Ricardo de la Espriella; in office: July 30, 1982. **Local divisions:** 9 provinces, 1 territory. **Armed forces:** para-military 11,000.

Economy: Industries: Oil refining, international banking. **Chief crops:** Bananas, pineapples, cocoa, corn, coconuts, sugar. **Minerals:** Copper. **Other resources:** Forests (mahogany), shrimp. **Per capita arable land:** 0.6 acres. **Meat prod.** (1980): beef: 52,000 metric tons; pork: 7,000 metric tons. **Fish catch** (1978): 113,800 metric tons. **Electricity prod.** (1979): 2.2 bln. kwh. **Labor force:** 29% agric., 29.4% ind. and commerce.

Finance: Currency: Balboa (Apr. 1982: 1.00 = $1 US). **Gross domestic product** (1980): $3.2 bln. **Per capita income** (1978): $1,116. **Imports** (1979): $1.19 bln.; partners (1979): U.S. 33%, Ecuador 14%, Saudi Ar. 8%. **Exports** (1980): $337 mln.; partners (1979): U.S. 46%, W. Ger. 8%. **Tourists** (1977): 361,900; receipts: $145 mln. **National budget** (1980): $695 mln. revenues; $818 mln. expenditures. **International reserves less gold** (Jan. 1982): $104.2 mln. **Consumer prices** (change in 1981): 5.6%.

Transport: Motor vehicles: in use (1979): 97,300 passenger cars, 25,800 comm. vehicles. **Civil aviation** (1980): 414 mln. passenger-km; 3.7 mln. net ton-km. **Chief ports:** Balboa, Cristobal, Puerto Armuelles.

Communications: Television sets: 206,000 in use (1977). **Radios:** 275,000 in use (1977). **Telephones in use** (1980): 175,000. **Daily newspaper circ.** (1980): 75 per 1,000 pop.

Health: Life expectancy at birth (1970): 64.26 male; 67.50 female. **Births** (per 1,000 pop. 1980): 26.8. **Deaths** (per 1,000 pop. 1975): 6.9. **Natural increase** (1975): 2.8%. **Hospital beds** (per 100,000 pop. 1977): 386. **Physicians** (per 100,000 pop. 1977): 78. **Infant mortality** (per 1,000 live births 1979): 27.8.

Education (1978): **Literacy:** 82%. **Pop. 5-19:** in school: 69%, teachers per 1,000: 24.

The coast of Panama was sighted by Rodrigo de Bastidas, sailing with Columbus for Spain in 1501, and was visited by Columbus in 1502. Vasco Nunez de Balboa crossed the isthmus and "discovered" the Pacific O. Sept. 13, 1513. Spanish colonies were ravaged by Francis Drake, 1572-95, and Henry Morgan, 1668-71. Morgan destroyed the old city of Panama which had been founded in 1519. Freed from Spain, Panama joined Colombia in 1821.

Panama declared its independence from Colombia Nov. 3, 1903, with U.S. recognition. U.S. naval forces deterred action by Colombia. On Nov. 18, 1903, Panama granted use, occupation and control of the Canal Zone to the U.S. by treaty, ratified Feb. 26, 1904. *(See also Panama Canal.)*

Rioting began Jan. 9, 1964, in a dispute over the flying of the U.S. and Panamanian flags and terms of the 1903 treaty. At least 21 Panamanians and 3 U.S. soldiers died in the rioting.

In 1967 new treaties were proposed, but Panama rejected them in 1970. In Feb. 1974 the U.S. and Panama agreed to negotiate a new treaty which would give the U.S. the right to operate and protect the canal for a certain period, with Panama sharing in the revenues, and would also set a date for final transfer of jurisdiction to Panama. Opposition by U.S. senators stalled the talks.

The U.S. and Panama initialed two treaties in 1977 that would provide for a gradual takeover by Panama of the canal, and withdrawal of U.S. troops, to be completed by 1999. U.S. payments would be substantially increased in the interim. The permanent neutrality of the canal would also be guaranteed. The treaties were ratified by the U.S. Senate in 1978.

After ruling single-handedly for a decade, Gen. Omar Torrijos Herrera abruptly handed over the government to former Education Minister Aristides Royo, Oct. 1978.

Due to easy Panama ship regulations and strictures in the U.S., merchant tonnage registered in Panama since World War II ranks high in size. Similarly easy financial regulations have made Panama a center for international banking.

Japan and Panama agreed, Mar. 1980, on a feasibility study for a second Panama Canal, large enough to accomodate fully-loaded 300,000-ton tankers.

Papua New Guinea

People: Population (1981 est.): 3,300,000. **Age distrib.** (%): 0–14: 43.8; 15–59: 50.3; 60+: 11.4. **Pop. density:** 17.28 per sq. mi. **Urban** (1979): 12.6%. **Ethnic groups:** Papuans (in S and interior), Melanesian (N,E), pygmies, minorities of Chinese, Australians, Polynesians. **Languages:** Melanesian Pidgin, Police Motu, English, numerous local languages. **Religions:** Lutheran 27%, Roman Catholic 31%, local religions.

Geography: Area: 178,704 sq. mi., slightly larger than California. **Location:** Occupies eastern half of island of New Guinea. **Neighbors:** Indonesia (West Irian) on W, Australia on S. **Topography:** Thickly forested mtns. cover much of the center of the country, with lowlands along the coasts. Included are some of the nearby islands of Bismarck and Solomon groups, including Admiralty Is., New Ireland, New Britain, and Bougainville. **Capital:** Port Moresby. **Cities** (1980 est.): Port Moresby 116,900.

Government: Head of state: Queen Elizabeth II, represented by Gov. Gen. Tore Lokoloko, b. Sept. 21, 1930; in office: Mar. 1, 1977. **Head of government:** Prime Min. Julius Chan; b. Aug. 29, 1939; in office: Mar. 13, 1980. **Local divisions:** National capital and 19 provinces with elected legislatures. **Armed forces:** regulars 3,500.

Economy: Chief crops: Coffee, coconuts, cocoa. **Minerals:** Gold, copper, silver, gas. **Per capita arable land:** 0.01 acres. **Meat prod.** (1980): pork: 22,000 metric tons. **Fish catch** (1978): 74,200 metric tons. **Electricity prod.** (1979): 1.2 bln. kwh. **Labor force:** 53% agric., 17% ind. and commerce, 10% services.

Finance: Currency: Kina (Mar. 1982: .71 = $1 US). **Gross domestic product** (1979): $2.27 bln. **Per capita income** (1978): $480. **Imports** (1979): $939 mln.; partners (1979): Austral. 49%, Jap. 16%, Sing. 13%. **Exports** (1980): $1.07 bln.; partners (1979): Jap. 34%, W. Ger. 25%, Austral. 8%, U.S. 6%. **National budget** (1980): $917 mln. revenues; $916 mln. expenditures **International reserves less gold** (Mar. 1982): $399.3 mln. **Gold:** 62,000 oz t. **Consumer prices** (change in 1980): 12.0%.

Transport: Motor vehicles: in use (1979): 21,600 passenger cars, 27,800 comm. vehicles. **Chief ports:** Port Moresby, Lae.

Communications: Telephones in use (1978): 37,848. **Daily newspaper circ.** (1980) 8 per 1,000 pop.

Health: Life expectancy at birth (1975): 47.5 male; 47.0 female. **Births** (per 1,000 pop. 1978): 45. **Deaths** (per 1,000 pop. 1978): 15. **Natural increase** (1978): 2.7%. **Hospital beds** (per 100,000 pop. 1977): 469. **Physicians** (per 100,000 pop. 1977): 7.

Education (1978): **Literacy:** 32%. **Pop. 5-19:** in school: 29%, teachers per 1,000: 10.

Human remains have been found in the interior of New Guinea dating back at least 10,000 years and possibly much earlier. Successive waves of peoples probably entered the country from Asia through Indonesia. Europeans visited in the 15th century, but land claims did not begin until the 19th century, when the Dutch took control of the western half of the island.

The southern half of eastern New Guinea was first claimed by Britain in 1884, and transferred to Australia in 1905. The northern half was claimed by Germany in 1884, but captured in World War I by Australia, which was granted a League of Nations mandate and then a UN trusteeship over the area. The 2 territories were administered jointly after 1949, given self-government Dec. 1, 1973, and became independent Sept. 16, 1975. Australia promised $1 billion in aid for the 5 years starting 1976-77, and pledged assistance in defense and foreign affairs.

The indigenous population consists of a huge number of tribes, many living in almost complete isolation with mutually unintelligible languages.

A secession movement in copper-rich Bougainville led to violence in 1973 and 1976. Indonesian border incursions were reported in 1978.

A series of strikes besieged the country, 1979. Tribal warfare in the western highlands took an est. 400 lives.

Paraguay

Republic of Paraguay

People: Population (1981 est.): 3,300,000. **Age distrib.** (%): 0–14: 45.1; 15–59: 49.7; 60+: 5.2. **Pop. density:** 18.4 per sq. mi. **Urban** (1975): 39.6%. **Ethnic groups:** Mestizos 95%, small Caucasian, Indian, Negro minorities. **Languages:** Spanish (official), Guarani (used by 90%). **Religions:** Roman Catholic (official).

Geography: Area: 157,047 sq. mi., the size of California. **Location:** One of the 2 landlocked countries of S. America. **Neighbors:** Bolivia on N, Argentina on S, Brazil on E. **Topography:** Paraguay R. bisects the country. To E are fertile plains, wooded slopes, grasslands. To W is the Chaco plain, with marshes and scrub trees. Extreme W is arid. **Capital:** Asunción. **Cities** (1978 est.): Asunción 434,928, Encarnación.

Government: Head of state: Pres. Alfredo Stroessner; b. Nov. 3, 1912; in office: Aug. 15, 1954. **Local divisions:** 16 departments. **Armed forces:** regulars 15,500; para-military 4,000.

Economy: Industries: Food processing, wood products. **Chief crops:** Corn, wheat, cotton, beans, peanuts, tobacco, citrus fruits, yerba mate. **Minerals:** Iron, manganese, limestone. **Other resources:** Forests. **Per capita arable land:** 0.8 acres. **Meat prod.** (1980): beef: 110,000 metric tons; pork: 79,000 metric tons. **Electricity prod.** (1979): 772 mln. kwh. **Labor force:** 49% agric., 28% ind. and commerce, 19% service.

Finance: Currency: Guarani (Mar. 1982 126.00 = $1 US). **Gross domestic product** (1979): $3.42 bln. **Per capita income** 1979 est.): $1,038. **Imports** (1980): $615 mln.; partners (1980): Braz. 24%, Arg. 22%, U.S. 10%. **Exports** (1980): $310 mln.; partners (1980): Arg. 24%, W. Ger. 12%, Braz. 12%. **Tourist receipts** (1977): $35 mln. **National budget** (1980): $432 mln. revenues; $424 mln. expenditures. **International reserves less gold** (Feb. 1982): $761.3 mln. **Gold:** 35,000 oz t. **Consumer prices** (change in 1980): 22.3%.

Transport: Railway traffic (1978): 23 mln. passenger-km; 17 mln. net ton-km. **Motor vehicles:** in use (1979): 32,100 passenger cars, 23,100 comm. vehicles. **Civil aviation** (1980): 262 mln. passenger-km; 2.8 mln. net ton-km. **Chief ports:** Asuncion.

Communications: Television sets: 55,000 in use (1977). **Radios:** 187,000 in use (1977). **Telephones in use** (1980): 41,600. **Daily newspaper circ.** (1980): 40 per 100,000 pop.

Health: Life expectancy at birth (1975): 60.3 male; 63.6 female. **Births** (per 1,000 pop. 1978): 34. **Deaths** (per 1,000 pop. 1978): 7. **Natural increase** (1978): 2.5%. **Hospital beds** (per 100,000 pop. 1977): 135. **Physicians** (per 100,000 pop. 1977): 77. **Infant mortality** (per 1,000 live births 1979): 84.2.

Education (1978): **Literacy:** 82%. **Pop. 5-19:** in school: 52%, teachers per 1,000: 24.

The Guarani Indians were settled farmers speaking a common language before the arrival of Europeans.

Visited by Sebastian Cabot in 1527 and settled as a Spanish possession in 1535, Paraguay gained its independence from Spain in 1811. It lost much of its territory to Brazil, Uruguay, and Argentina in the War of the Triple Alliance, 1865-1870. Large areas were won from Bolivia in the Chaco War, 1932-35.

Gen. Alfredo Stroessner has ruled since 1954. Suppression of the opposition and decimation of small Indian groups has been charged by international rights groups. Allegations of government corruption and inefficiency continued in 1981.

The first stages of a large hydroelectric project were completed in 1968-70. In 1973 Brazil and Paraguay agreed to build a 10-million kilowatt hydroelectric plant, largest in the world, at Itaipu of the Parana R. Income from the project fueled an economic boom in 1977-78.

Peru

Republic of Peru

People: Population (1981 est.): 18,100,000. **Age distrib.** (%): 0–14: 44.2; 15–59: 50.6; 60+: 5.2. **Pop. density:** 35.83 per sq. mi. **Urban** (1975): 62.5%. **Ethnic groups:** Indians 45%, Mestizos 37%, Caucasians 15%, blacks, Asians. **Languages:** Spanish, Quechua both official, Aymara; 30% speak no Spanish. **Religions:** Roman Catholics over 90%.

Geography: Area: 496,222 sq. mi., five-sixths the size of Alaska. **Location:** On the Pacific coast of S. America. **Neighbors:** Ecuador, Colombia on N, Brazil, Bolivia on E, Chile on S.

Topography: An arid coastal strip, 10 to 100 mi. wide, supports much of the population thanks to widespread irrigation. The Andes cover 27% of land area. The uplands are well-watered, as are the eastern slopes reaching the Amazon basin, which covers half the country with its forests and jungles. **Capital:** Lima. **Cities** (1979 cen.): Lima 3.1 mln.

Government: Head of state: Pres. Fernando Belaunde Terry; b. Oct. 7, 1912; in office: July 28, 1980. **Head of government:** Prime Min. Manuel Ulloa Elias; in office: July 28, 1980. **Local divisions:** 23 departments, 1 province. **Armed forces** (1980): regulars 105,500; para-military 25,000.

Economy: Industries: Fish meal, steel. **Chief crops:** Cotton, sugar, coffee, rice, potatoes, beans, corn, barley, tobacco. **Minerals:** Copper, lead, molybdenum, silver, zinc, iron, oil. **Crude oil reserves** (1980): 655 mln. bbls. **Other resources:** Wool, sardines. **Per capita arable land:** 0.5 acres. **Meat prod.** (1980): beef: 81,000 metric tons; pork: 71,000 metric tons; lamb: 32,000 metric tons. **Fish catch** (1979): 3.6 mln. metric tons. **Electricity prod.** (1978): 8.8 bln. kwh. **Crude steel prod.** (1981 est.): 359,000 metric tons. **Labor force:** 43% agric.; 21% ind. and mining; 36% gov.

Finance: Currency: Sol (Mar. 1982: 575.28 = $1 US). **Gross domestic product** (1980): $6.1 bln. **Per capita income** (1979): $655. **Imports** (1980): $2.49 bln.; partners (1979): U.S. 34%, It. 16%, W. Ger. 8%. **Exports** (1980): $3.89 bln.; partners (1979): U.S. 32%, Jap. 13%. **Tourists** (1976): 264,000; receipts (1977): $113 mln. **National budget** (1981): $2.05 bln. revenues; $2.22 bln. expenditures. **International reserves less gold** (Dec. 1981): $1.20 bln. **Gold:** 1.39 mln. oz t. **Consumer prices** (change in 1980): 59.2%.

Transport: Railway traffic (1978): 528 mln. passenger-km; 612 mln. net ton-km. **Motor vehicles:** in use (1979): 312,000 passenger cars, 160,700 comm. vehicles; assembled (1975): 21,200 passenger cars; 12,900 comm. vehicles. **Civil aviation** (1980): 1.9 bln. passenger-km; 40.7 mln. net ton-km. **Chief ports:** Callao, Chimbate, Mollendo.

Communications: Television sets: 825,000 in use (1977), 100,000 manuf. (1975). **Radios:** 2.2 mln. in use (1977). **Telephones in use** (1980): 402,500. **Daily newspaper circ.** (1980): 66 per 1,000 pop.

Health: Life expectancy at birth (1980): 55.1 male; 58.0 female. **Births** (per 1,000 pop. 1978): 38. **Deaths** (per 1,000 pop. 1978): 12. **Natural increase** (1978): 2.6%. **Hospital beds** (per 100,000 pop. 1977): 184. **Physicians** (per 100,000 pop. 1977): 64. **Infant mortality** (per 1,000 live births 1979): 80.

Education (1978): **Literacy:** 72%. **Pop. 5-19:** in school: 64%, teachers per 1,000: 17.

The powerful Inca empire had its seat at Cuzco in the Andes covering most of Peru, Bolivia, and Ecuador, as well as parts of Colombia, Chile, and Argentina. Building on the achievements of 800 years of Andean civilization, the Incas had a high level of skill in architecture, engineering, textiles, and social organization.

A civil war had weakened the empire when Francisco Pizarro, Spanish conquistador, began raiding Peru for its wealth, 1532. In 1533 he had the seized ruling Inca, Atahualpa, fill a room with gold as a ransom, then executed him and enslaved the natives.

Lima was the seat of Spanish viceroys until the Argentine liberator, Jose de San Martin, captured it in 1821; Spain was defeated by Simon Bolivar and Antonio J. de Sucre; recognized Peruvian independence, 1824. Chile defeated Peru and Bolivia, 1879-84, and took Tarapaca, Tacna, and Arica; returned Tacna, 1929.

On Oct. 3, 1968, a military coup ousted Pres. Fernando Belaunde Terry. In 1968-74, the military government put through sweeping agrarian changes, and nationalized oil, mining, fishmeal, and banking industries.

Food shortages, escalating foreign debt, and strikes led to another coup, Aug. 29, 1976, and to a slowdown of socialist programs.

After 12 years of military rule, Peru returned to democratic leadership under former Pres. Fernando Belaunde Terry, July 1980. The new government planned to encourage the return of private enterprise to stimulate the inflation-ridden economy.

Fighting again erupted, Jan. 28, 1981, in the ongoing border dispute between Peru and Ecuador. The border was reopened in April. There was a wave of terrorist bombings during 1981, including the U.S. embassy in August.

Philippines

Republic of the Philippines

People: Population (1981 est.): 50,000,000. **Age distrib.** (%): 0–14: 42.9; 15–59: 52.5; 60+: 4.6. **Pop. density:** 417.85 per sq. mi. **Urban** (1970): 31.8%. **Ethnic groups:** Malays the large majority, Chinese, Americans, Spanish are minorities. **Languages:** Filipino (based on Tagalog), English both official; numerous others spoken. **Religions:** Roman Catholics 85%, Moslems 4.3%.

Geography: Area: 115,831 sq. mi., slightly larger than Nevada. **Location:** An archipelago off the SE coast of Asia. **Neighbors:** Nearest are Malaysia, Indonesia on S, Taiwan on N. **Topography:** The country consists of some 7,100 islands stretching 1,100 mi. N-S. About 95% of area and population are on 11 largest islands, which are mountainous, except for the heavily indented coastlines and for the central plain on Luzon. **Capital:** Quezon City (Manila is de facto capital). **Cities** (1980 est.): Manila 1.6 mln.; Quezon City 1.1 mln.; Davao 611,311.

Government: Head of state: Pres. Ferdinand E. Marcos; b. Sept. 11, 1917; in office: Dec. 30, 1965 (pres.), Jan. 17, 1973 (premier). **Head of govt:** Prime Min. Cesar Virata; b. Dec. 12, 1930; in office: Apr. 8, 1981. **Local divisions:** 13 regions, 73 provinces, 60 cities. **Armed forces:** regulars 101,400 (1980).

Economy: Industries: Food processing, clothing, drugs, wood prods., appliances. **Chief crops:** Sugar, rice, corn, pineapple, coconut. **Minerals:** Cobalt, copper, gold, nickel, silver, iron, petroleum. **Crude oil reserves** (1980): 25 mln. bbls. **Other resources:** Forests (42% of area). **Per capita arable land:** 0.3 acres. **Meat prod.** (1980): beef: 127,000 metric tons; pork: 408,000 metric tons; lamb: 6,000 metric tons. **Fish catch** (1979): 1.4 mln. metric tons. **Electricity prod.** (1980): 21 bln. kwh. **Crude steel prod.** (1981 est.): 350,000 metric tons. **Labor force:** 47% agric., 20% ind. and comm., 20% services.

Finance: Currency: Peso (Mar. 1982: 8.35 = $1 US). **Gross domestic product** (1980): $35.7 bln. **Per capita income** (1980): $779. **Imports** (1980): $8.15 bln.; partners (1980): U.S. 24%, Jap. 20%, Saudi Ar. 10%. **Exports** (1980): $5.74 bln.; partners (1980): U.S. 28%, Jap. 26%, Neth. 6%. **Tourists** (1977): 730,100; receipts: $311 mln. **National budget** (1980): $4.93 bln. revenues; $5.37 bln. expenditures. **International reserves less gold** (Feb. 1982): $1.98 bln. **Gold:** 1.70 mln. oz t. **Consumer prices** (change in 1981): 11.8%.

Transport: Railway traffic (1979): 417 mln. passenger-km; 36 mln. net ton-km. **Motor vehicles:** in use (1979): 468,600 passenger cars, 370,200 comm. vehicles; assembled (1977): 34,300 passenger cars; 24,400 comm. vehicles. **Civil aviation** (1980): 5.9 bln. passenger-km; 155.1 mln. freight ton-km. **Chief ports:** Cebu, Manila, Iloilo, Davao.

Communications: Television sets: 850,000 in use (1977), 157,000 manuf. (1978). **Radios:** 1.9 mln. in use (1977), 124,000 manuf. (1976). **Telephones in use** (1980): 519,600. **Daily newspaper circ.** (1980): 25 per 1,000 pop.

Health: Life expectancy at birth (1975): 56.9 male; 60.0 female. **Births** (per 1,000 pop. 1978): 35. **Deaths** (per 1,000 pop. 1978): 10. **Natural increase** (1978): 2.4%. **Hospital beds** (per 100,000 pop. 1977): 146. **Physicians** (per 100,000 pop. 1977): 36. **Infant mortality** (per 1,000 live births 1976): 58.9.

Education (1978): **Literacy:** 88%. **Pop. 5-19:** in school: 55%, teachers per 1,000: 17.

The Malay peoples of the Philippine islands, whose ancestors probably migrated from Southeast Asia, were mostly hunters, fishers, and unsettled cultivators when first visited by Europeans.

The archipelago was visited by Magellan, 1521. The Spanish founded Manila, 1571. The islands, named for King Philip II of Spain, were ceded by Spain to the U.S. for $20 million, 1898, following the Spanish-American War. U.S. troops suppressed a guerrilla uprising in a brutal 6-year war, 1899-1905.

Japan attacked the Philippines Dec. 8, 1941 (Far Eastern time). Japan conquered the islands in May, 1942. It was ousted by Sept. 1945.

On July 4, 1946, independence was proclaimed in accordance with an act passed by the U.S. Congress in 1934. A republic was established.

A rebellion by Communist-led Huk guerrillas was put down by 1954. But urban and rural political violence periodically reappears.

The Philippines and the U.S. have treaties for U.S. military and naval bases and a 1951 Mutual Defense Treaty. President Ferdinand E. Marcos in 1966 concluded a pact reducing U.S. base leases from 99 to 25 years. Riots by radical youth groups and terrorism by leftist guerrillas and outlaws, increased from 1970. On Sept. 21, 1972, Marcos declared martial law. Ruling by decree, he ordered some land reform and stabilized prices. But opposition was suppressed, and a high population growth rate aggravated poverty and unemployment. Political corruption was believed to be widespread. On Jan. 17, 1973, Marcos proclaimed a new constitution with himself as president. His wife received wide powers in 1978 to supervise planning and development.

Martial law was lifted Jan. 17, 1981. Marcos turned over legislative power to the National Assembly, released political prisoners, and said he would no longer rule by decree. He was elected to a new 6-year term as president, June, with 88% of the vote.

Government troops battled Moslem (Moro) secessionists, 1973-76, in southern Mindanao. Fighting resumed, 1977, after a Libyan-mediated agreement on autonomy was rejected by the region's mainly Christian voters. Casualties have been estimated at 50,000, half civilians (10,000 civilians dead). Clashes continued through 1981.

The archipelago has a coastline of 10,850 mi. Manila Bay, with an area of 770 sq. mi., and a circumference of 120 mi., is the finest harbor in the Far East.

All natural resources of the Philippines belong to the state; their exploitation is limited to citizens of the Philippines or corporations of which 60% of the capital is owned by citizens.

Poland

Polish People's Republic

People: Population (1981 est.): 35,800,000. **Age distrib.** (%): 0–14: 23.9; 15–59: 62.7; 60+: 13.5. **Pop. density:** 295.61 per sq. mi. **Urban** (1977): 57.0%. **Ethnic groups:** Polish 98%, Germans, Ukrainians, Byelorussians. **Language:** Polish. **Religions:** Predominantly Roman Catholics.

Geography: Area: 120,727 sq. mi. **Location:** On the Baltic Sea in E Central Europe. **Neighbors:** E. Germany on W, Czechoslovakia on S, USSR (Lithuania, Byelorussia, Ukraine) on E. **Topography:** Mostly lowlands forming part of the Northern European Plain. The Carpathian Mts. along the southern border rise to 8,200 ft. **Capital:** Warsaw. **Cities** (1979): Warsaw 1.5 mln., Lodz 832,000 Cracow 705,000; Wroclaw 608,000, Poznan 544,000.

Government: Head of state: Chairman, council of state: Henryk Jablonski, b. Dec. 27, 1909; in office: Mar. 28, 1972. **Head of government:** Premier Wojciech Jaruzelski; in office: Oct. 18, 1981. **Local divisions:** 49 provinces. **Armed forces:** regulars 317,500 (1980).

Economy: Industries: Shipbuilding, textiles, chemicals, wood products, metals, autos, aircraft, machinery, cement, aluminum, oil products. **Chief crops:** Grains, potatoes, sugar beets, tobacco, flax. **Minerals:** Coal, copper, silver, zinc, sulphur, salt, cadmium, iron. **Per capita arable land:** 1.0 acres. **Meat prod.** (1980): beef: 700,000 metric tons; pork: 1.70 mln. metric tons; lamb: 21,000 metric tons. **Fish catch** (1979): 601,100 metric tons. **Electricity prod.** (1980): 121 bln. kwh. **Crude steel prod.** (1981 est.): 15.6 mln. metric tons. **Labor force:** 28% agric.; 24% manuf.

Finance: Currency: Zloty (Sept. 1981: 35.30 = $1 US). **Net material product** (1979): $55.2 bln. **Per capita income** (1976 est.): $2,500. **Imports** (1979): $17.49 bln.; partners (1980): USSR 33%, E. Ger. 7% W. Ger. 7% Czech. 6%. **Exports** (1979): $16.23 bln.; partners (1980): USSR 31%, E. Ger. 7%, Czech. 7%, W. Ger. 7%. **Tourists** (1977): 10,544,500; receipts (1976): $157 mln. **Consumer prices** (change in 1978): 68%.

Transport: Railway traffic (1980): 46.3 bln. passenger-km; 135.4 bln. net ton-km. **Motor vehicles:** in use (1980): 2.8 mln. passenger cars, 617,800 comm. vehicles; manuf. (1980): 351,000 passenger cars; 60,000 comm. vehicles. **Civil aviation** (1980): 2.2 bln. passenger-km; 18 mln. freight ton-km. **Chief ports:** Gdansk, Gdynia, Szczecin.

Communications: Television sets: 7.7 mln. licensed (1979), 972,000 manuf. (1978). **Radios:** 8.5 mln. licensed (1979), 2.5 mln. manuf. (1978). **Telephones in use** (1979): 3.2 mln. **Daily newspaper circ.** (1980): 351 per 1,000 pop.

Health: Life expectancy at birth (1976): 66.92 male; 74.55 female. **Births** (per 1,000 pop. 1980): 19.4. **Deaths** (per 1,000 pop. 1980): 9.7. **Natural increase** (1978): 1.0%. **Hospital beds** (per 100,000 pop. 1977): 767. **Physicians** (per 100,000 pop. 1977): 166. **Infant mortality** (per 1,000 live births 1978): 22.4.

Education (1978): **Literacy:** 98%. **Pop. 5-19:** in school: 54%, teachers per 1,000: 27.

Slavic tribes in the area were converted to Latin Christianity in the 10th century. Poland was a great power from the 14th to the 17th centuries. In 3 partitions (1772, 1793, 1795) it was apportioned among Prussia, Russia, and Austria. Overrun by the Austro-German armies in World War I, its independence, self-declared on Nov.11, 1918, was recognized by the Treaty of Versailles, June 28, 1919. Large territories to the east were taken in a war with Russia, 1921.

Nazi Germany and the USSR invaded Poland Sept. 1-27, 1939, and divided the country. During the war, some 6 million Polish citizens were killed by the Nazis, half of them Jews. With Germany's defeat, a Polish government-in-exile in London was recognized by the U.S., but the USSR pressed the claims of a rival group. The election of 1947 was completely dominated by the Communists.

In compensation for 69,860 sq. mi. ceded to the USSR, 1945, Poland received approx. 40,000 sq. mi. of German territory E of the Oder-Neisse line comprising Silesia, Pomerania, West Prussia, and part of East Prussia.

In 12 years of rule by Stalinists, large estates were abolished, industries nationalized, schools secularized, and Roman Catholic prelates jailed. Farm production fell off. Harsh working conditions caused a riot in Poznan June 28-29, 1956.

A new Politburo, committed to development of a more independent Polish Communism, was named Oct. 1956, with Wladyslaw Gomulka as first secretary of the Communist Party. Collectivization of farms was ended and many collectives were abolished.

In Dec. 1970 workers in port cities rioted because of price rises and new incentive wage rules. On Dec. 20 Gomulka resigned as party leader; he was succeeded by Edward Gierek; the incentive rules were dropped, price rises were revoked.

Poland was the first Communist state to get most-favored nation trade terms from the U.S.

A law promulgated Feb. 13, 1953, required government consent to high Roman Catholic church appointments. In 1956 Gomulka agreed to permit religious liberty and religious publications, provided the church kept out of politics. In 1961 religious studies in public schools were halted. Government relations with the Church improved in the 1970s. The number of priests and churches was greater in 1971 than in 1939.

After 2 months of labor turmoil had crippled the country, the Polish government, Aug. 30, 1980, met the demands of striking workers at the Lenin Shipyard, Gdansk. Among the 21 concessions granted were the right to form independent trade unions and the right to strike — unprecedented political developments in the Soviet bloc. By 1981, 9.5 mln. workers had joined the independent trade union (Solidarity). Farmers won official recognition for their independent trade union in May. Solidarity leaders proposed, Dec. 12, a nationwide referendum on establishing a non-Communist government if the government failed to agree to a series of demands which included access to the mass media and free and democratic elections to local councils in the provinces.

Spurred by the fear of Soviet intervention, the government, Dec. 13, imposed martial law. Public gatherings, demonstrations, and strikes were banned and an internal and external blackout was imposed. Solidarity leaders called for a nationwide strike, but there were only scattered work stoppages. Lech Walesa and other Solidarity leaders were arrested. The U.S. imposed economic sanctions on Poland until martial law was lifted.

Portugal

Republic of Portugal

People: Population (1981 est.): 9,930,000. **Age distrib.** (%): 0–14: 27.9; 15–59: 57.9; 60+: 14.3. **Pop. density:** 280.98 per sq. mi. **Ethnic groups:** Homogeneous, with small African minority. **Languages:** Portuguese. **Religions:** Roman Catholics 98%.

Geography: Area: 35,516 sq. mi., slightly smaller than Indiana. **Location:** At SW extreme of Europe. **Neighbors:** Spain on N, E. **Topography:** Portugal N of Tajus R, which bisects the country NE-SW, is mountainous, cool and rainy. To the S there are drier, rolling plains, and a warm climate. **Capital:** Lisbon. **Cities** (1978 est.): Lisbon 829,900; Porto 335,700.

Government: Head of state: Pres. Antonio dos Santos

Ramalho Eanes; b. Jan. 25, 1935; in office: July 14, 1976. **Head of government:** Prime Min. Francisco Pinto Balsemao b. 1937; in office: Jan. 9, 1981. **Local divisions:** 18 provinces, 2 autonomous districts. **Armed forces:** regulars 62,500 (1980).

Economy: Industries: Textiles, pottery, shipbuilding, oil products, paper, glassware, tourism. **Chief crops:** Grains, corn, rice, grapes, olives, fruits. **Minerals:** Tungsten, uranium, coal, copper, tin, kaolin, gold, iron, manganese. **Other resources:** Forests (world leader in cork production). **Per capita arable land:** 0.8 acres. **Meat prod.** (1980): beef: 92,000 metric tons; pork: 173,000 metric tons; lamb: 26,000 metric tons. **Fish catch** (1979): 241,900 metric tons. **Electricity prod.** (1980): 14.2 bln. kwh. **Crude steel prod.** (1981): 551,000 metric tons. **Labor force:** 31% agric.; 35% ind. and commerce, 34% services.

Finance: Currency: Escudo (Mar. 1982: 71.26 = $1 US). **Gross domestic product** (1979): $20.1 bln. **Per capita income** (1979): $2,000. **Imports** (1980): $9.3 bln.; partners (1980): W. Ger. 12%, U.S. 11%, UK 9%, Fr. 7%. **Exports** (1980): $4.64 bln.; partners (1980): UK 15%, W. Ger. 14%, Fr. 10%, U.S. 6%. **Tourists** (1979): 2.2 min.; receipts: $940 mln. **National budget** (1979): $4.13 bln. expenditures. **International reserves less gold** (Jan. 1982): $544 mln. **Gold:** 22.14 mln. oz t. **Consumer prices** (change in 1980): 16.6%.

Transport: Railway traffic (1979): 6.0 bln. passenger-km; 999 mln. net ton-km. **Motor vehicles:** in use (1979): 995,400 passenger cars, 63,400 comm. vehicles; assembled (1978): 20,172 passenger cars; 57,324 comm. vehicles. **Civil aviation** (1980): 3.4 bln. passenger-km; 111 mln. freight ton-km. **Chief ports:** Lisbon, Setubal, Leixoes.

Communications: Television sets: 1.1 mln. licensed (1978), 483,000 manuf. (1978). **Radios:** 1.6 licensed (1977), 763,000 manuf. (1978). **Telephones in use** (1980): 1.3 mln. **Daily newspaper circ.** (1980): 62 per 1,000 pop.

Health: Life expectancy at birth (1974): 65.29 male; 72.03 female. **Births** (per 1,000 pop. 1978): 17.1. **Deaths** (per 1,000 pop. 1978): 9.8. **Natural increase** (1977): .9%. **Hospital beds** (per 100,000 pop. 1977): 528. **Physicians** (per 100,000 pop. 1977): 142. **Infant mortality** (per 1,000 live births 1980): 39.

Education (1978): **Literacy:** 72%, **Pop. 5-19:** in school: 62%, teachers per 1,000: 30.

Portugal, an independent state since the 12th century, was a kingdom until a revolution in 1910 drove out King Manoel II and a republic was proclaimed.

From 1932 a strong, repressive government was headed by Premier Antonio de Oliveira Salazar. Illness forced his retirement in Sept. 1968; he was succeeded by Marcello Caetano.

On Apr. 25, 1974, the government was seized by a military junta led by Gen. Antonio de Spinola, who was named president.

The new government reached agreements providing independence for Guinea-Bissau, Mozambique, Cape Verde Islands, Angola, and Sao Tome and Principe. Spinola resigned Sept. 30, 1974, in face of increasing pressure from leftist officers. Despite a 64% victory for democratic parties in April 1975, the Soviet-supported Communist party increased its influence. Banks, insurance companies, and other industries were nationalized. A countercoup in November halted this trend. After years of turmoil the economy and political life were in disarray, despite aid from the U.S. and West European countries.

Azores Islands, in the Atlantic, 740 mi. W. of Portugal, have an area of 904 sq. mi. and a pop. (1975) of 292,000. A 1951 agreement gave the U.S. rights to use defense facilities in the Azores. The **Madeira Islands,** 360 mi. off the NW coast of Africa, have an area of 307 sq. mi. and a pop. (1976) of 270,000. Both groups were offered partial autonomy in 1976.

Macao, area of 6 sq. mi., is an enclave, a peninsula and 2 small islands, at the mouth of the Canton R. in China. Portugal granted broad autonomy in 1976. Pop. (1981 est.): 276,700.

Qatar

State of Qatar

People: Population (1980 est.): 220,000. **Pop. density:** 55.0 per sq. mi. **Ethnic groups:** Arabs 56%, Iranians 23%, Pakistani 7%, others. **Languages:** Arabic (official), Farsi (Persian), English. **Religions:** Moslems 98%.

Geography: Area: 4,400 sq. mi., smaller than Connecticut. **Location:** Occupies peninsula on W coast of Persian Gulf. **Neighbors:** Saudi Arabia on W, United Arab Emirates on S. **Topography:** Mostly a flat desert, with some limestone ridges, vegetation of any kind is scarce. **Capital:** Doha. **Cities** (1978 est.): Doha 130,000, Umm Said, Ruwais.

Government: Head of state and head of government: Khalifah ibn Hamad ath-Thani; b. 1932; in office: Feb. 22, 1972 (amir), 1970 (prime min.) **Armed forces:** regulars 4,300 (1980).

Economy: Crude oil reserves (1980): 3.76 bln. bbls. **Per capita arable land:** 0.02 acres. **Electricity prod.** (1978): 905 mln. kwh. **Crude steel prod.** (1981 est.): 469,000 metric tons. **Labor force:** 10% agric., 70% ind., services and commerce.

Finance: Currency: Riyal (Apr. 1982: 3.64 = $1 US). **Gross domestic product** (1979 est.): $4.5 bln. **Per capita income** (1979): $18,000. **Imports** (1979): $1.43 bln.; partners (1980): Jap. 18%, UK 18%, U.S. 11%. **Exports** (1980): $5.65 bln.; partners (1980): Neth. 12%, Jap. 11%, Fr. 11%, Thai. 8%. **National budget** (1980): $5.2 bln. revenues; $3.0 bln. expenditures. **International reserves less gold** (Sept. 1981): $347.2 mln. **Gold:** 674,000 oz t.

Transport: Chief ports: Doha, Musayid.

Communications: Radios: 40,000 in use (1976). **Telephones in use** (1978): 29,703.

Health: Hospital beds (per 100,000 pop. 1977): 389. **Physicians** (per 100,000 pop. 1977): 105.

Education (1978): **Literacy:** 20%. **Pop. 5-19:** in school: 61%, teachers per 1,000: 48.

Qatar was under Bahrain's control until the Ottoman Turks took power, 1872 to 1915. In a treaty signed 1916, Qatar gave Great Britain responsibility for its defense and foreign relations. After Britain announced it would remove its military forces from the Persian Gulf area by the end of 1971, Qatar sought a federation with other British protected States in the area; this failed and Qatar declared itself independent, Sept. 1 1971.

Oil revenues give Qatar a per capita income among the highest in the world, but lack of skilled labor hampers development plans.

Romania

Socialist Republic of Romania

People: Population (1981 est.): 22,500,000. **Age distrib.** (%): 0–14: 25.4; 15–59; 60.5; 60+: 14.2. **Pop. density:** 242.86 per sq. mi. **Urban** (1977): 48.7%. **Ethnic groups:** Romanians 88.1%, Hungarians 7.9%, Germans 1.6%. **Languages:** Romanian, Hungarian, German. **Religions:** Orthodox 80%, Roman Catholics 9%, Calvinists, Jewish, Lutherans.

Geography: Area: 91,699 sq. mi., slightly smaller than Oregon. **Location:** In SE Europe on the Black Sea. **Neighbors:** USSR on E (Moldavia) and N (Ukraine), Hungary, Yugoslavia on W, Bulgaria on S. **Topography:** The Carpathian Mts. encase the north-central Transylvanian plateau. There are wide plains S and E of the mountains, through which flow the lower reaches of the rivers of the Danube system. **Capital:** Bucharest. **Cities** (1980 est.): Bucharest 1,861,007, Brasov 299,172, Timisoara 281,320, Constanta 279,308.

Government: Head of state: Pres. Nicolae Ceausescu; b. Jan. 26, 1918; in office; Dec. 9, 1967. **Head of government:** Prime Min. Constantin Dascalescu; in office; May 21, 1982. **Head of Communist Party:** Pres. Nicolae Ceausescu; in office: Mar. 23, 1965. **Local divisions:** Bucharest and 40 districts. **Armed forces:** regulars 184,000 (1980).

Economy: Industries: Steel, metals, machinery, oil products, chemicals, textiles, shoes, tourism. **Chief crops:** Corn, wheat, sugar beets, grapes, fruits. **Minerals:** Oil, gas, coal, salt, bauxite, manganese, lead, zinc, gold, silver. **Other resources:** Timber. **Per capita arable land:** 1.1 acres. **Meat prod.** (1980): beef: 323,000 metric tons; pork: 930,000 metric tons; lamb: 78,000 metric tons. **Fish catch** (1978): 137,700 metric tons. **Electricity prod.** (1980): 67.5 bln. kwh. **Crude steel prod. (1981 est):** 13.5 mln. metric tons. **Labor force:** 40% agric.; 25% ind. and commerce.

Finance: Currency: Leu (Dec. 1981: 4.47 = $1 US). **Gross domestic product** (1978 est.): $67.5 bln. **Per capita income** (1978): $3,100. **Imports** (1980): $13.8 bln.; partners (1980): USSR 16%, W. Ger. 6%, U.S. 7%, Iraq 7%. **Exports** (1980): $11.20 bln.; partners (1980): USSR 18%, W. Ger. 8%, E. Ger. 6%. **Tourists** (1977): 3,684,800; receipts (1976): $112 min. **National budget** (1979): $76 mln. revenues; $75 mln. expenditures. **International reserves less gold** (Oct. 1981): $501 mln. **Gold:** 3.66 mln. oz t.

Transport: Railway traffic (1978): 22.7 bln. passenger-km;

76 bln. net ton-km. **Motor vehicles:** in use (1979): 235,000 passenger cars; 125,000 comm. vehicles; manuf. (1978): 81,360 passenger cars; 50,520 comm. vehicles. **Civil aviation** (1980): 1.2 bln. passenger-km; 12.3 mln. freight ton-km. **Chief ports:** Constanta, Galati, Braila.

Communications: Television sets: 3.5 mln. licensed (1979), 516,000 manuf. (1978). **Radios:** 3.10 mln. licensed (1979), 664,000 manuf. (1978). **Telephones in use** (1979): 1.4 mln. **Daily newspaper circ.** (1980): 145 per 1,000 pop.

Health: Life expectancy at birth (1978): 67.4 male; 72.1 female. **Births** (per 1,000 pop. 1979): 18.6. **Deaths** (per 1,000 pop. 1979): 9.9. **Natural increase** (1979): 8.7%. **Hospital beds** (per 100,000 pop. 1977): 919. **Physicians** (per 100,000 pop. 1977): 135. **Infant mortality** (per 1,000 live births 1979): 31.

Education (1978): **Literacy:** 98%. **Pop. 5-19:** in school: 67%, teachers per 1,000: 30.

Romania's earliest known people merged with invading Proto-Thracians, preceding by centuries the Dacians. The Dacian kingdom was occupied by Rome, 106 AD-271 AD; people and language were Romanized. The principalities of Wallachia and Moldavia, dominated by Turkey, were united in 1859, became Romania in 1861. In 1877 Romania proclaimed independence from Turkey, became an independent state by the Treaty of Berlin, 1878, a kingdom, 1881, under Carol I. In 1886 Romania became a constitutional monarchy with a bicameral legislature.

Romania helped Russia in its war with Turkey, 1877-78. After World War I it acquired Bessarabia, Bukovina, Transylvania, and Banat. In 1940 it ceded Bessarabia and Northern Bukovina to the USSR and part of Southern Dobrudja to Bulgaria.

Marshal Ion Antonescu, leader of a militarist movement, forced Romania to join Germany against the USSR in World War II in 1941. In 1944 Antonescu was overthrown by King Michael with Soviet help and Romania joined the Allies.

With occupation by Soviet troops the Communist-headed National Democratic Front displaced the National Peasant party. A People's Republic was proclaimed, Dec. 30, 1947; Michael was forced to abdicate. Land owners were dispossessed; most banks, factories and transportation units were nationalized.

On Aug. 22, 1965, a new constitution proclaimed Romania a Socialist, rather than a People's Republic. Since 1966, Romania has adopted an independent attitude toward the USSR, witnessed by the visit of U.S. Pres. Nixon in Aug. 1969 and Chinese Communist party chief Hua Guofeng in 1978. Romanian Pres. Nicolae Ceausescu visited the U.S. in 1970 and 1973. The U.S. granted most-favored-nation tariff treatment in 1975, and a 10-year U.S. trade pact was signed in 1976. Since 1959, USSR troops have not been permitted to enter Romania.

Internal policies remain oppressive. Ethnic Hungarians have protested cultural and job discrimination.

Romania has become industrialized, but lags in consumer goods and in personal freedoms. All industry is state owned, and state farms and cooperatives own over 90% of arable land. Romania was one of the few countries in Europe self-sufficient in oil, but by 1981, it was importing about 30% of its needs.

A major earthquake struck Bucharest in March, 1977, killing over 1,300 people and causing extensive damage to housing and industry. Severe economic conditions caused a series of anti-government incidents in 1981.

In 1982, Romania asked Western creditors for a rescheduling of debt repayments which totaled some $3 billion. Faced with increasing food supply problems, the government increased the cost of basic food stuffs an average of 35%.

Rwanda

Republic of Rwanda

People: Population (1981 est.): 5,300,000. **Age distrib.** (%): 0–14: 50.8; 15–59: 46.2; 60+: 3.0. **Pop. density:** 496.61 per sq. mi. **Urban** (1974): 3.5%. **Ethnic groups:** Hutu 89%, Tutsi 10%, Twa (pygmies) 1%. **Languages:** French, Kinyarwandu (both official), Swahili. **Religions:** Roman Catholics 45%, Protestants 10%, Moslems 1%.

Geography: Area: 10,169 sq. mi., the size of Maryland. **Location:** In E central Africa. **Neighbors:** Uganda on N, Zaire on W, Burundi on S, Tanzania on E. **Topography:** Grassy uplands and hills cover most of the country, with a chain of volcanoes in the NW. The source of the Nile R. has been located in the headwaters of the Kagera (Akagera) R., SW of Kigali. **Capital:** Kigali. **Cities** (1978 est.): Kigali 118,000.

Government: Head of state: Pres. Juvenal Habyarimana; b. Mar. 8, 1937; in office: July 5, 1973. **Local divisions:** 10 prefectures. **Armed forces:** regulars 3,650 (1980).

Economy: Chief crops: Coffee, tea. **Minerals:** Tin, gold, wolframite. **Per capita arable land:** 0.4 acres. **Electricity prod.** (1977): 149 mln. kwh. **Labor force:** 95% agric.

Finance: Currency: Franc (Apr. 1982: 92.84 = $1 US). **Gross domestic product** (1978): $890 mln. **Per capita income** (1978): $178. **Imports** (1979): $192 mln.; partners (1979): Belg. 17%, Jap. 10%, W. Ger. 10%. **Exports** (1980): $72 mln.; partners (1979): U.S. 28%, W. Ger. 22%, Spa. 8%. **National budget** (1980): $82.3 mln. revenues; $58.8 mln. expenditures. **International reserves less gold** (Feb. 1982): $157.2 mln. **Consumer prices** (change in 1980): 7.2%.

Transport: Motor vehicles: in use (1975): 6,500 passenger cars, 4,800 comm. vehicles.

Communications: Radios: 70,000 in use (1976), 10,000 manuf. (1978). **Telephones in use** (1978): 4,543. **Daily newspaper circ.** (1977): 200; 0.1 per 1,000 pop.

Health: Life expectancy at birth (1975): 41.8 male; 45.0 female. **Births** (per 1,000 pop. 1978): 50. **Deaths** (per 1,000 pop. 1978): 20. **Natural increase** (1978): 3.0%. **Hospital beds** (per 100,000 pop. 1977): 154. **Physicians** (per 100,000 pop. 1977): 13. **Infant mortality** (per 1,000 live births 1970): 127.

Education (1978): **Literacy:** 25%. **Pop. 5-19:** in school: 27%, teachers per 1,000: 6.

For centuries, the Tutsi (an extremely tall people) dominated the Hutus (90% of the population). A civil war broke out in 1959 and Tutsi power was ended. A referendum in 1961 abolished the monarchic system.

Rwanda, which had been part of the Belgian UN trusteeship of Rwanda-Urundi, became independent July 1, 1962. The government was overthrown in a 1973 military coup. Rwanda is one of the most densely populated countries in Africa. All available arable land is being used, and is being subject to erosion. The government has carried out economic and social improvement programs, using foreign aid and volunteer labor on public works projects.

Saint Lucia

People: Population (1981 est.): 124,000. **Age distrib.** (%): 0–20: 49.6; 21–64: 42.7; 65+: 7.7. **Pop. density:** 462.18 per sq. mi. **Ethnic groups:** Predominantly African descent. **Languages:** English (official), French patois. **Religions:** Mainly Roman Catholic.

Geography: Area: 238 sq. mi., about one-fifth the size of Rhode Island. **Location:** In Eastern Caribbean, 2d largest of the Windward Is. **Neighbors:** Martinique to N, St. Vincent to SW. **Topography:** Mountainous, volcanic in origin; Soufriere, a volcanic crater, in the S. Wooded mountains run N-S to Mt. Gimie, 3,145 ft., with streams through fertile valleys. **Capital:** Castries. **City:** Castries (1981 est.): 45,000.

Government: Head of state: Queen Elizabeth II, represented by Gov.-Gen. Boswell Williams; in office: June 19, 1980. **Head of government:** Prime Min. Winston Cenac; in office: May 4, 1981. **Local divisions:** 16 parishes and Castries.

Economy: Industries: Agriculture, tourism, manufacturing. **Chief crops:** Bananas, coconuts, cocoa, citrus fruits. **Other resources:** Forests. **Per capita arable land:** 0.1 acres. **Electricity prod.** (1977): 50.00 mln. kwh. **Labor force:** 43.4% agric., 17.7% ind. & commerce, 38.9% services.

Finance: Currency: East Caribbean dollar (Nov. 1981: 2.70 = $1 US). **Gross domestic product** (1979): $99.2 mln. **Per capita income** (1978): $698. **Imports** (1979): $72 mln.; partners: U.S. 36%, UK 19%, Trin./Tob. 10%. **Exports** (1979): $35 mln.; partners: UK 49%, Barb. 9%. **Tourists** (1978): 107,000. **National budget** (1977-78 est.): $18.4 mln. revenues; $17.2 mln. expenditures. **Consumer prices** (change in 1978): 11%.

Transport: Motor vehicles: in use (1976): 3,700 passenger cars, 1,800 comm. vehicles. **Chief ports:** Castries, Vieux Fort.

Communications: Television sets: 1,700 in use (1975). **Radios:** 82,000 in use (1976). **Telephones in use** (1978): 7,157. **Daily newspaper circ.** (1976): 4,000; 36 per 1,000 pop.

Health: Life expectancy at birth (1981): 65.3 male; 70.6 female. **Births** (per 1,000 pop. 1975): 35.0. **Deaths** (per 1,000 pop. 1975): 7.3. **Natural increase** (1975): 2.8%. **Pop. per hospital bed** (1975): 202. **Pop. per physician** (1975): 4,231. **Infant mortality** (per 1,000 live births 1979): 21.8.

Education: Literacy (1981) 78%; **Pop. 5–15:** in school (1981): 80%.

St. Lucia was ceded to Britain by France at the Treaty of Paris, 1814. Self government was granted with the West Indies Act, 1967. Independence was attained Feb. 22, 1979.

Primarily an agricultural economy, St. Lucia is undertaking an ambitious development program, including an oil transshipment terminal and free-port zone being built by a U.S. oil company. Aid has come from the Caribbean Community and Venezuela.

Saint Vincent and the Grenadines

People: Population (1980 est.): 120,000. **Pop. density:** 800 per sq. mi. **Ethnic groups:** Mainly of African descent. **Languages:** English. **Religions:** Methodists, Anglicans, Roman Catholics.

Geography: Area: 150 sq. mi., about twice the size of Washington, D.C. **Location:** In the eastern Caribbean, St. Vincent (133 sq. mi.) and the northern islets of the Grenadines form a part of the Windward chain. **Neighbors:** St. Lucia to N, Barbados to E, Grenada to S. **Topography:** St. Vincent is volcanic, with a ridge of thickly-wooded mountains running its length; Soufriere, rising in the N, erupted in Apr. 1979. **Capital:** Kingstown. **Cities** (1978): Kingstown 25,000.

Government: Head of state: Queen Elizabeth II, represented by Gov.-Gen. Sir Sydney Douglas Gun-Munro; b. Nov. 29, 1916; in office: Jan. 1, 1977. **Head of government:** Robert Milton Cato; b. June 3, 1915; in office: Dec. 11, 1974.

Economy: Industries: Agriculture, tourism. **Chief crops:** Bananas (62% of exports), arrowroot, coconuts. **Per capita arable land:** 0.3 acres. **Electricity prod.** (1977): 20 mln. kwh. **Labor force:** 30% agric.

Finance: Currency: East Caribbean dollar (Nov. 1981: 2.70 = $1 US). **Per capita income** (1979): $250. **Imports** (1979): $36 mln.; partners (1976): UK 30%, Trin./Tob. 20%, Can. 9%, U.S. 9%. **Exports** (1979): $15 mln.; partners (1976): UK 75%, Trin./Tob. 13%. **Tourists** (1977): 42,000; receipts (1977): $5.44 mln. **National budget** (1981): $17 mln. revenues; $20.3 mln. expenditures.

Transport: Motor vehicles: in use (1976): 3,500 passenger cars, 800 comm. vehicles. **Chief ports:** Kingstown.

Communications: Telephones in use (1978): 5,302.

Health: Life expectancy at birth (1961): 58.46 male; 59.67 female. **Births** (per 1,000 pop. 1977): 31. **Deaths** (per 1,000 pop. 1973): 10.0. **Natural increase** (1973): 2.2%. **Pop. per hospital bed** (1972): 170. **Infant mortality** (per 1,000 pop. under 1 yr. 1977): 55.

Education (1979): **Literacy:** 95%. **Pop. 5–19:** in school (1975): 26,938; per teacher: 18.5.

Columbus landed on St. Vincent on Jan. 22, 1498 (St. Vincent's Day). Britain and France both laid claim to the island in the 17th and 18th centuries; the Treaty of Versailles, 1783, finally ceded it to Britain. Associated State status was granted 1969; independence was attained Oct. 27, 1979.

The entire economic life of St. Vincent, dependent upon few crops and tourism, was devastated by the eruption of Mt. Soufriere, Apr. 13, 1979.

In Sept. 1980, St. Vincent was admitted as the 153rd member of the United Nations.

Western Samoa

People: Population (1980 est.): 160,000. **Age distrib.** (%): 0–14: 50.4; 15–59: 45.4; 60+: 4.3. **Pop. density:** 141.22 per sq. mi. **Urban** (1979): 21.5%. **Ethnic groups:** Samoans (Polynesians) 88%, Euronesians (mixed) 10%, Europeans, other Pacific Islanders. **Languages:** Samoan, English both official. **Religions:** Protestants 75%, Roman Catholics 20%.

Geography: Area: 1,133 sq. mi., the size of Rhode Island. **Location:** In the S. Pacific O. **Neighbors:** Nearest are Fiji on W, Tonga on S. **Topography:** Main islands, Savai'i (660 sq. mi.) and Upolu (430 sq. mi.), both ruggedly mountainous, and small islands Manono and Apolima. **Capital:** Apia. **Cities** (1980 est.): Apia 33,400.

Government: Head of state: King Malietoa Tanumafili II; b. Jan. 4, 1913; in office: Jan. 1, 1962. **Head of government:** Prime Min. Tupuola Efi; b. Mar. 1, 1938; in office: Mar. 24, 1976. **Local divisions:** 24 districts.

Economy: Chief crops: Cocoa, coconuts, bananas, taro, coffee, bark cloth. **Other resources:** Hardwoods, fish. **Per capita arable land:** 0.9 acres. **Electricity prod.** (1977): 25.00 mln. kwh. **Labor force:** 67% agric.

Finance: Currency: Tala (Jan. 1981: .94 = $1 US). **Gross domestic product** (1976 est.): $50 mln. **Per capita income** (1976): $320. **Imports** (1979): $74 mln.; partners (1979): NZ 25% W. Ger. 20%, Austral. 17%, Jap. 11%, U.S. 9%. **Exports** (1979): $18 mln.; partners (1979): NZ 24%, W. Ger. 27%, Neth. 22%. **Tourists** (1977): 22,000; receipts (1976): $3 mln. **International reserves less gold** (Mar. 1980): $1.63 mln. **Consumer prices** (change in 1979): 10.8%.

Transport: Motor vehicles: in use (1976): 1,300 passenger cars, 1,900 comm. vehicles. **Chief ports:** Apia, Asau.

Communications: Radios: 50,000 in use (1975). **Telephones in use** (1978): 3,810.

Health: Life expectancy at birth (1966): 60.8 male; 65.2 female. **Births** (per 1,000 pop. 1978): 20.0. **Deaths** (per 1,000 pop. 1978): 2.8. **Natural increase** (1978): 1.7%. **Pop. per hospital bed** (1977): 214. **Pop. per physician** (1977): 2,884. **Infant mortality** (per 1,000 live births 1978): 10.4.

Western Samoa was a German colony, 1899 to 1914, when New Zealand landed troops and took over. It became a New Zealand mandate under the League of Nations and, in 1945, a New Zealand UN Trusteeship.

An elected local government took office in Oct. 1959 and the country became fully independent Jan. 1, 1962. New Zealand has continued economic aid and educational assistance.

San Marino

Most Serene Republic of San Marino

People: Population (1980 est.): 21,537. **Age distrib.** (%): 0–14: 23.9; 15–59: 61.3; 60+: 14.8. **Pop. density:** 833.33 per sq. mi. **Urban** (1970): 92.4%. **Ethnic groups:** Sanmarinese. **Languages:** Italian. **Religions:** Roman Catholics predominate.

Geography: Area: 24 sq. mi. **Location:** In N central Italy near Adriatic coast. **Neighbors:** Completely surrounded by Italy. **Topography:** The country lies on the slopes of Mt. Titano. **Capital:** San Marino. **City** (1981 est.): San Marino 3,000.

Government: Head of state: Two co-regents appt. every 6 months. **Local divisions:** 9 sectors. **Armed forces:** 180-man ceremonial army.

Economy: Industries: Postage stamps, tourism, woolen goods, paper, cement, ceramics. **Per capita arable land:** 0.1 acres.

Finance: Currency: Lira. **Tourists** (1978): 2.9 mln.

Communications: Television sets: 4,000 licensed (1976). **Radios:** 6,000 licensed (1976). **Telephones in use** (1978): 6,276. **Daily newspaper circ.** (1976): 1,300; 65 per 1,000 pop.

Births (per 1,000 pop. 1977): 14.2. **Deaths** (per 1,000 pop. 1977): 6.9. **Natural increase** (1977): .8%. **Infant mortality** (per 1,000 live births 1981): 10.8.

San Marino claims to be the oldest state in Europe and to have been founded in the 4th century. A communist-led coalition ruled 1947-57; a similar coalition took power in 1978. It has had a treaty of friendship with Italy since 1862.

Sao Tome and Principe

Democratic Republic of Sao Tome and Principe

People: Population (1981 est.): 90,000. **Pop. density:** 241.94 per sq. mi. **Ethnic groups:** Portuguese-African mixture, African minority (Angola, Mozambique immigrants). **Languages:** Portuguese. **Religions:** Mainly Roman Catholic.

Geography: Area: 372 sq. mi., slightly larger than New York City. **Location:** In the Gulf of Guinea about 125 miles off W Central Africa. **Neighbors:** Gabon, Equatorial Guinea on E. **Topography:** Sao Tome and Principe islands, part of an extinct volcano chain, are both covered by lush forests and croplands. **Capital:** Sao Tome. **Cities** (1976 est.): Sao Tome 20,000.

Government: Head of state and head of government: Pres. Manuel Pinto da Costa, b. 1910; in office: July 12, 1975. **Local divisions:** 2 provinces, 12 counties.

Economy: Chief crops: Cocoa (82% of exports), coconut products, cinchona. **Per capita arable land:** 0.03 acres. **Electricity prod.** (1977): 8.00 mln. kwh.

Finance: Currency: Dobra (Sept. 1981): 39.33 = $1 US). **Gross domestic product** (1976 est.): $40 mln. **Per capita income** (1976): $270. **Imports** (1979): $22 mln.; partners (1975): Port. 61%, Angola 13%. **Exports** (1979): $27 mln.; partners (1975): Neth. 52%, Port. 33%, W. Ger. 8%.

Transport: Motor vehicles: in use (1973): 1,600 passenger cars, 400 comm. vehicles. **Chief ports:** Sao Tome, Santo Antonio.

Communications: Radios: 20,000 in use (1976).

Health: Births (per 1,000 pop. 1972): 45.0. **Deaths** (per 1,000 pop. 1972): 11.2. **Natural increase** (1972): 3.4%. **Pop. per hospital bed** (1976): 160. **Pop. per physician** (1973): 6,666. **Infant mortality** (per 1,000 live births 1972): 64.3.

The islands were uninhabited when discovered in 1471 by the Portuguese, who brought the first settlers — convicts and exiled Jews. Sugar planting was replaced by the slave trade as the chief economic activity until coffee and cocoa were introduced in the 19th century.

Portugal agreed, 1974, to turn the colony over to the Gabon-based Movement for the Liberation of Sao Tome and Principe, which proclaimed as first president its East German-trained leader Manuel Pinto da Costa. Independence came July 12, 1975.

Agriculture and fishing are the mainstays of the economy.

Saudi Arabia

Kingdom of Saudi Arabia

People: Population (1981 est.): 10,400,000. **Pop. density:** 9.01 per sq. mi. **Ethnic groups:** Arab tribes, immigrants from other Arab and Muslim countries. **Languages:** Arabic. **Religions:** Muslims 99%.

Geography: Area: 927,000 sq. mi., one-fourth the size of the U.S. **Location:** Occupies most of Arabian Peninsula in Middle East. **Neighbors:** Kuwait, Iraq, Jordan on N, Yemen, South Yemen, Oman on S, United Arab Emirates, Qatar on E. **Topography:** The highlands on W, up to 9,000 ft., slope as an arid, barren desert to the Persian Gulf. **Capital:** Riyadh. **Cities** (1974 cen.): Riyadh 666,840; Jidda 561,104; Mecca 366,801.

Government: Head of state and head of government: King Fahd; in office: June 13, 1982. **Effective head of government:** Dep. Prime Min. Fahd ibn Abdul Aziz Al Saud, b. 1922; in office: Mar. 28, 1975. **Local divisions:** 6 major and 12 minor provinces. **Armed forces:** regulars 41,600 (1980).

Economy: Industries: Oil products. **Chief crops:** Dates, wheat, barley, fruit. **Minerals:** Oil, gas, gold, silver, iron. **Crude oil reserves** (1980): 163.35 bln. bbls. **Per capita arable land:** 0.3 acres. **Meat prod.** (1980): beef: 19,000 metric tons, lamb: 29,000 metric tons. **Fish catch** (1978): 18,400 metric tons. **Electricity prod.** (1978): 3.5 bln. kwh. **Labor force:** 40% agric.; 11% ind. and commerce; 12% serv.; 12% govt.

Finance: Currency: Riyal (Mar. 1982: 3.41 = $1 US). **Gross domestic product** (1980): $116.16 bln. **Per capita income** (1979): $11,500. **Imports** (1980): $33.06 bln.; partners (1980): US 20%, Jap. 18%, W. Ger. 9%. **Exports** (1981): $113.32 bln.; partners (1980): US 15%, Jap., 17%, Fr. 9%. **Tourist receipts** (1977): $823 mln. **International reserves less gold** (Feb. 1982): $33.26 bln. **Gold:** 4.56 mln. oz t. **Consumer prices** (change in 1981): 2.9%.

Transport: Railway traffic (1979): 94 mln. passenger-km; 125 mln. net ton-km. **Motor vehicles:** in use (1980): 630,800 passenger cars, 522,200 comm. vehicles. **Civil aviation** (1980): 9.9 bln. passenger-km. 174 mln. net ton-km. **Chief ports:** Jidda, Ad-Dammam, Ras Tannurah.

Communications: Television sets: 300,000 in use (1977). **Radios:** 275,000 in use (1977). **Telephones in use** (1980): 280,500. **Daily newspaper circ.** (1980): 28 per 1,000 pop.

Health: Life expectancy at birth (1975): 44.2 male; 46.5 female. **Births** (per 1,000 pop. 1978): 49. **Deaths** (per 1,000 pop. 1978): 18. **Natural increase** (1978): 5.6%. **Hospital beds** (per 100,000 pop. 1977): 155. **Physicians** (per 100,000 pop. 1977): 60.

Education (1978): **Literacy:** 15%. **Pop. 5-19:** in school: 36%, teachers per 1,000: 22.

Arabia was united for the first time by Mohammed, in the early 7th century. His successors conquered the entire Near East and North Africa, bringing Islam and the Arabic language. But Arabia itself soon returned to its former status as political and cultural backwater.

Nejd, long an independent state and center of the Wahhabi sect, fell under Turkish rule in the 18th century, but in 1913 Ibn Saud, founder of the Saudi dynasty, overthrew the Turks and captured the Turkish province of Hasa; took the Hejaz in 1925 and by 1926, most of Asir. The discovery of oil by a U.S. oil company in the 1930s transformed the new country.

Crown Prince Khalid was proclaimed king on Mar. 25, 1975, after the assassination of King Faisal. Fahd became king on June 13, 1982 following Khalid's death. There is no constitution and no parliament. The king exercises authority together with a Council of Ministers. The Islamic religious code is the law of the land. Alcohol and public entertainments are restricted, and women have an inferior legal status.

Saudi units fought against Israel in the 1948 and 1973 Arab-Israeli wars. Many billions of dollars of advanced arms have been purchased from Britain, France, and the U.S., including jet fighters, missiles, and, in 1981, 5 airborne warning and control system (AWACS) aircraft from the U.S., despite strong opposition from Israel. Beginning with the 1967 Arab-Israeli war, Saudi Arabia provided large annual financial gifts to Egypt; aid was later extended to Syria, Jordan, and Palestinian guerrilla groups, as well as to other Moslem countries. The country has aided anti-radical forces in Yemen and Oman.

Faisal played a leading role in the 1973-74 Arab oil embargo against the U.S. and other nations in an attempt to force them to adopt an anti-Israel policy. Saudi Arabia joined most other Arab states, 1979, in condemning Egypt's peace treaty with Israel.

Between 1973 and 1976, Saudi Arabia acquired full ownership of Aramco (Arabian American Oil Co.). In 1981, Saudi Arabia's moderate position on crude oil prices has prevailed at OPEC meetings. Saudi Arabia announced, 1979, it will build a $1 billion causeway linking the island state Bahrain to the Arab mainland. A third 5-year $250 billion development plan was approved in 1980.

The Hejaz contains the holy cities of Islam — Medina where the Mosque of the Prophet enshrines the tomb of Mohammed, who died in the city June 7, 632, and Mecca, his birthplace. More than 600,000 Moslems from 60 nations pilgrimage to Mecca annually. The regime faced its first serious opposition when Moslem fundamentalists seized the Grand Mosque in Mecca, Nov. 20, 1979.

Senegal

Republic of Senegal

People: Population (1981 est.): 5,800,000. **Age distrib.** (%): 0–14: 44.2; 15–59: 50.5; 60+: 5.3. **Pop. density:** 74.35 per sq. mi. **Urban** (1981): 30%. **Ethnic groups:** Wolof 36%, Fulani 17.5%, Sere 16.5%, Toucouleur 9%, Diola 9%, Mandigo 6.5%. Languages: French (official), tribal languages. **Religions:** Muslims 86%, Christians 5%.

Geography: Area: 75,995 sq. mi., the size of South Dakota. **Location:** At western extreme of Africa. **Neighbors:** Mauritania on N, Mali on E, Guinea, Guinea-Bissau on S, Gambia surrounded on three sides. **Topography:** Low rolling plains cover most of Senegal, rising somewhat in the SE. Swamp and jungles are in SW. **Capital:** Dakar. **Cities** (1979): Dakar 978,553; Thies 126,889; Kaolack 115,679.

Government: Head of state: Pres. Abdou Diouf; b. Sept. 7, 1935; in office: Jan. 1, 1981. **Head of government:** Prime Min. Habib Thiam; in office: Jan. 1, 1981. **Local divisions:** 8 regions. **Armed forces:** regulars 9,010 (1980).

Economy: Industries: Food processing, fishing. **Chief crops:** Peanuts are chief export; millet, rice. **Minerals:** Phosphates. **Per capita arable land:** 1.1 acres. **Meat prod.** (1980): beef: 40,000 metric tons; pork: 8,000 metric tons; lamb: 11,000 metric tons. **Fish catch** (1979): 308,200 metric tons. **Electricity prod.** (1978): 456.00 mln. kwh. **Labor force:** 70% agric.

Finance: Currency: CFA franc (Mar. 1982: 312.10 = $1 US). **Gross domestic product** (1980): $2.2 bln. **Per capita income** (1975): $342. **Imports** (1979): $713 mln.; partners Fr. 39%, U.S. 8%. **Exports** (1979): $426 mln.; partners Fr. 37%, UK 6%. **Tourists** (1977): 168,300; receipts $11 mln. **International reserves less gold** (Jan. 1982): $8.7 mln. **Gold:** 29,000 oz t. **Consumer prices** (change in 1980): 8.8%.

Transport: Railway traffic (1976): 180 mln. passenger-km; 164 mln. net ton-km. **Motor vehicles:** in use (1974): 44,800 passenger cars, 25,000 comm. vehicles. **Chief ports:** Dakar, Saint-

Louis.

Communications: Television sets: 2,000 in use (1976). **Radios:** 290,000 in use (1976). **Telephones in use** (1978): 42,105. **Daily newspaper circ.** (1980): 6 per 1,000 pop.

Health: Life expectancy at birth (1975): 39.4 male; 42.5 female. **Births** (per 1,000 pop. 1978): 47. **Deaths** (per 1,000 pop. 1978): 20. **Natural increase** (1978): 2.7%. **Hospital beds** (per 100,000 pop. 1977): 111. **Physicians** (per 100,000 pop. 1977): 2. **Infant mortality** (per 1,000 live births 1981): 158.

Education (1981): **Literacy:** 10%. **Pop. 5-19:** in school: 22%, teachers per 1,000: 4.

Portuguese settlers arrived in the 15th century, but French control grew from the 17th century. The last independent Moslem state was subdued in 1893. Dakar became the capital of French West Africa.

Independence as part, along with the Sudanese Rep., of the Mali Federation, came June 20, 1960. Senegal withdrew Aug. 20 that year. French political and economic influence is strong.

A long drought brought famine, 1972-73, and again in 1978.

Senegal is recognized as the most democratic of the French-speaking West African nations. Opposition parties were allowed to form in 1976, 1979, and 1981.

Senegal, Dec. 17, 1981, signed an agreement with The Gambia for confederation of the 2 countries under the name of Senegambia.

Seychelles

Republic of Seychelles

People: Population (1980 est.): 70,000. **Age distrib.** (%): 0–14: 41.5; 15–59: 49.7; 60+: 8.8. **Pop. density:** 409.36 per sq. mi. **Urban** (1971): 26.1% **Ethnic groups:** Creoles (mixture of Asians, Africans, and French) predominate. **Languages:** English and French (both official), Creole 94%. **Religions:** Roman Catholics 90%, Protestants 8%, Hindus, Moslems.

Geography: Area: 171 sq. mi. **Location:** In the Indian O. 700 miles NE of Madagascar. **Neighbors:** Nearest are Madagascar on SW, Somalia on NW. **Topography:** A group of 86 islands, about half of them composed of coral, the other half granite, the latter predominantly mountainous. **Capital:** Victoria. **Cities** (1980): Port Victoria 23,000.

Government: Head of state: Pres. France-Albert Rene, b. Nov. 16, 1935; in office: June 5, 1977.

Economy: Industries: Food processing. **Chief crops:** Coconut products, cinnamon, vanilla, patchouli. **Other resources:** Guano, shark fins, tortoise shells, fish. **Electricity prod.** (1977): 36.00 mln. kwh. **Labor force:** 18.5% agric.; 19.4% mining, construction; 13.5% public admin., soc. serv.; 11.1% restaurants, hotels.

Finance: Currency: Rupee (Mar. 1982: 6.49 = $1 US). **Gross domestic product** (1979 est.): $86 mln. **Per capita income** (1979): $1,030. **Imports** (1979): $89 mln.; partners: UK 21%, Fr. 11%, So. Afr. 10%, N. Yem. 9%. **Exports** (1979): $18 mln.; partners: Pak. 17%. **National Budget** (1980): $5.9 bln. revenues; $5.9 bln. expenditures. **Tourists** (1979): 79,000; receipts: $39 mln. **International reserves less gold** (Feb. 1982): $13.46 mln. **Consumer prices** (change in 1980): 13.5%.

Transport: Motor vehicles: in use (1977): 3,000 passenger cars, 900 comm. vehicles. **Port:** Victoria.

Communications: Radios: 17,000 in use (1976). **Telephones in use** (1978): 4,560. **Daily newspaper circ.** (1980): 79 per 1,000 pop.

Health: Life expectancy at birth (1972): 61.9 male; 68.0 female. **Births** (per 1,000 pop. 1977): 25.9. **Deaths** (per 1,000 pop. 1977): 7.7. **Natural increase** (1977): 1.8%. **Pop. per hospital bed** (1975): 200. **Pop. per physician** (1975): 2,857. **Infant mortality** (per 1,000 live births 1980): 26.

The islands were occupied by France in 1768, and seized by Britain in 1794. Ruled as part of Mauritius from 1814, the Seychelles became a separate colony in 1903. The ruling party had opposed independence as impractical, but pressure from the OAU and the UN became irresistible, and independence was declared June 29, 1976. The first president was ousted in a coup a year later by a socialist leader.

A new Constitution announced Mar. 1979, turned the country into a one-party state. The government accused So. Africa of involvement in an abortive coup, Nov. 1981.

Sierra Leone

Republic of Sierra Leone

People: Population (1981 est.): 3,470,000. **Age distrib.** (%): 0–14: 40.6; 15–59: 51.5; 60+: 7.8. **Pop. density:** 124.26 per sq. mi. **Ethnic groups:** Temne 30%, Mende 30%, others. **Languages:** English (official), tribal languages. **Religions:** animist 54%, Muslims 40%, Christians 6%.

Geography: Area: 27,699 sq. mi., slightly smaller than North Carolina. **Location:** On W coast of W. Africa. **Neighbors:** Guinea on N, E, Liberia on S. **Topography:** The heavily-indented, 210-mi. coastline has mangrove swamps. Behind are wooded hills, rising to a plateau and mountains in the E. **Capital:** Freetown. **Cities** (1980 est.): Freetown 500,000; Bo, Kenema, Makeni.

Government: Head of state and head of government: Pres. Siaka P. Stevens; b. Aug. 24, 1905; in office: Apr. 21, 1971 (state), June 14, 1978 (gov't.). **Local divisions:** 3 provinces and one region including Freetown. **Armed forces:** regulars 3,000 (1980).

Economy: Industries: Wood products. **Chief crops:** Cocoa, coffee, palm kernels, rice, ginger. **Minerals:** Diamonds, iron ore, bauxite. **Per capita arable land:** 3.0 acres. **Fish catch** (1978): 50,100 metric tons. **Electricity prod.** (1978): 210 mln. kwh. **Labor force:** 75% agric.; 15% industry, serv.

Finance: Currency: Leone (Mar. 1982: 1.24 = $1 US). **Gross domestic product** (1979): $926 mln. **Per capita income** (1980): $176. **Imports** (1979): $316 mln.; partners (1979): UK 24%, Nig. 11%, W. Ger. 8%. **Exports** (1980): $190 mln.; partners (1979): UK 62%, Neth. 7%, **Tourists** (1977): 24,100; receipts: $4 mln. **National budget** (1981): $185 mln. revenues; $161 mln. expenditures. **International reserves less gold** (Feb. 1982): $16.5 mln. **Consumer prices** (change in 1979): 21.2%.

Transport: Motor Vehicles: in use (1976): 18,900 passenger cars, 6,300 comm. vehicles. **Chief ports:** Freetown, Bonthe.

Communications: Television sets: 8,500 in use (1976). **Radios:** 62,000 in use (1975). **Telephones in use** (1977): 15,060. **Daily newspaper circ.** (1970): 45,000; 18 per 1,000 pop.

Health: Life expectancy at birth (1975): 41.8 male; 45.0 female. **Births** (per 1,000 pop. 1978): 45. **Deaths** (per 1,000 pop. 1978): 27. **Natural increase** (1978): 1.9%. **Hospital beds** (per 100,000 pop. 1977): 99. **Physicians** (per 100,000 pop. 1977): 6.

Education (1977): **Literacy:** 15%. **Pop. 5-19:** in school: 24%, teachers per 1,000: 9.

Freetown was founded in 1787 by the British government as a haven for freed slaves. Their descendants, known as Creoles, number more than 60,000.

Successive steps toward independence followed the 1951 constitution. Full independence arrived Apr. 27, 1961. Sierra Leone became a republic Apr. 19, 1971. A one-party state approved by referendum 1978, brought political stability, but the economy has been plagued by inflation, corruption, and dependence upon the International Monetary Fund and creditors.

Singapore

Republic of Singapore

People: Population (1981 est.): 2,500,000. **Age distrib.** (%): 0–14: 29.6; 15–59: 63.4; 60+: 7.0. **Pop. density:** 10,575.22 per sq. mi. **Ethnic groups:** Chinese 76%, Malays 14%, Indians 6%. **Languages:** Chinese, Malay, Tamil, English all official. **Religions:** Buddhism, Taoism, Islam, Hinduism, Christianity.

Geography: Area: 239 sq. mi., smaller than New York City. **Location:** Off tip of Malayan Peninsula in S.E. Asia. **Neighbors:** Nearest are Malaysia on N, Indonesia on S. **Topography:** Singapore is a flat, formerly swampy island. The nation includes 40 nearby islets. **Capital:** Singapore. **Cities** (1978 est.): Singapore 2,334,400.

Government: Head of state: Pres. Chengara Veetil Devan Nair; in office: Oct. 21, 1981. **Head of government:** Prime Min. Lee Kuan Yew; b. Sept. 16, 1923; in office: June 5, 1959. **Armed forces:** regulars 42,000 (1980).

Economy: Industries: Shipbuilding, oil refining, electronics, banking, textiles, food, rubber, lumber processing, tourism. **Per capita arable land:** 0.002 acres. **Meat prod.** (1980): pork: 43,000 metric tons. **Fish catch** (1978): 16,100 metric tons. **Elec-**

tricity prod. (1978): 5.89 bln. kwh. **Crude steel prod.** (1981 est.): 350,000 metric tons. **Labor force:** 2% agric.; 52% ind. & comm.

Finance: Currency: Dollar (Mar. 1982: 2.13 = $1 US). **Gross domestic product** (1980): $9.01 bln. **Per capita income** (1980): $4,100. **Imports** (1981): $27.5 bln.; partners (1980): Jap. 18%, Malay. 14%, U.S. 14%. **Exports** (1981): $20.96 bln., partners (1980): U.S. 13%, Malay. 15%, Jap. 8%, HK 8%. **Tourists** (1979): 2.2 mln.; receipts $515 mln. **National budget** (1980): $2.80 bln. revenues; $2.31 bln. expenditures. **International reserves** (Nov. 1981): $7.47 bln. **Consumer prices** (change in 1981): 8.2%.

Transport: Motor vehicles: in use (1980): 164,500 passenger cars, 78,000 comm. vehicles. **Civil aviation:** (1980) 14.7 bln. passenger-km; 634 mln. freight ton-km.

Communications: Television sets: 396,800 licensed (1980). **Radios:** 459,000 licensed (1980). **Telephones in use** (1980): 702,000. **Daily newspaper circ.** (1980): 356 per 1,000 pop.

Health: Life expectancy at birth (1970): 65.1 male; 70.0 female. **Births** (per 1,000 pop. (1980): 17.3. **Deaths** (per 1,000 pop. 1980): 5.2. **Natural increase** (1978): 1.2%. **Hospital beds** (per 100,000 pop. 1977): 371. **Physicians** (per 100,000 pop. 1977): 78. **Infant mortality** (per 1,000 live births 1982): 11.7.

Education (1978): **Literacy:** 76%. **Pop. 5–19:** in school: 59%, teachers per 1,000: 21.

Founded in 1819 by Sir Thomas Stamford Raffles, Singapore was a British colony until 1959 when it became autonomous within the Commonwealth. On Sept. 16, 1963, it joined with Malaya, Sarawak and Sabah to form the Federation of Malaysia.

Tensions between Malayans, dominant in the federation, and ethnic Chinese, dominant in Singapore, led to an agreement under which Singapore became a separate nation, Aug. 9, 1965.

Singapore is the world's 4th largest port. Manufacturing has surpassed shipping, pushing per capita income to second place in Asia, following Japan. Standards in health, education, and housing are high. International banking has grown.

Solomon Islands

People: Population (1981 est.): 240,000. **Age distrib.** (%): 0–14: 48.4; 15–59: 46.5; 60+: 5.1. **Pop. density:** 18.26 per sq. mi. **Urban** (1976): 9.1%. **Ethnic groups:** A variety of Melanesian groups and mixtures, some Polynesians. **Languages:** English (official), Pidgin, local languages. **Religions:** Anglican 34%, Roman Catholic 19%, Evangelical 17%, traditional religions.

Geography: Area: 10,640 sq. mi., slightly larger than Maryland. **Location:** Melanesian archipelago in the western Pacific O. **Neighbors:** Nearest is Papua New Guinea on W. **Topography:** 10 large volcanic and rugged islands and 4 groups of smaller ones. **Capital:** Honiara. **Cities:** (1981): Honiara 19,200.

Government: Head of state: Queen Elizabeth II, represented by Gov.-Gen. Baddeley Devesi; b. Oct. 16, 1941; in office: July 7, 1978. **Head of government:** Prime Min. Solomon Mamaloni; in office: Aug. 31, 1981. **Local divisions:** 7 provinces and Honiara.

Economy: Industries: Fish canning. **Chief crops:** Coconuts, rice, bananas, yams. **Other resources:** Forests, marine shell. **Per capita arable land:** 0.6 acres. **Fish catch** (1978): 20,700 metric tons. **Electricity prod.** (1977): 18.00 mln. kwh.

Finance: Currency: Dollar (Mar. 1981: 1.05 = $1 US). **Gross domestic product** (1978): $93.9 mln. **Per capita income** (1978): $440. **Imports** (1979): $57 mln.; partners (1978): Austral. 33%, Jap. 13%, UK 10%, Sing. 10%. **Exports** (1979): $67 mln.; partners (1978): Jap. 24%, UK 20%, Neth. 10%, Sing. 10%. **Consumer prices** (change in 1980): 16%.

Communications: Radios: 11,000 in use (1976). **Telephones in use** (1978): 1,984.

Health: Births (per 1,000 pop. 1978): 44. **Deaths** (per 1,000 pop. 1978): 9. **Natural increase** (1978): 3.5%. **Infant mortality** (per 1,000 live births 1981): 52.

The Solomon Islands were sighted in 1568 by an expedition from Peru. Britain established a protectorate in the 1890s over most of the group, inhabited by Melanesians. The islands saw major World War II battles. Self-government came Jan. 2, 1976, and independence was formally attained July 7, 1978.

Somalia

Somali Democratic Republic

People: Population (1981 est.): 3,700,000. **Pop. density:** 14.83 per sq. mi. **Ethnic groups:** mainly Hamitic, others. **Languages:** Somali, Arabic (both official). **Religions:** Sunni Muslims 99%.

Geography: Area: 246,300 sq. mi., slightly smaller than Texas. **Location:** Occupies the eastern horn of Africa. **Neighbors:** Djibouti, Ethiopia, Kenya on W. **Topography:** The coastline extends for 1,700 mi. Hills cover the N; the center and S are flat. **Capital:** Mogadishu. **Cities** (1980 est.): Mogadishu 377,000.

Government: Head of state: Pres. Mohammed Siad Barre; b. 1919; in office: Oct. 21, 1969. **Local divisions:** 15 regions. **Armed forces:** regulars 61,000 (1980).

Economy: Chief crops: Incense, sugar, bananas, sorghum, corn, kapole, gum. **Minerals:** Iron, tin, gypsum, sandstone, bauxite, meerschaum, titanium, uranium. **Per capita arable land:** 0.8 acres. **Meat prod.** (1980): beef: 45,000 metric tons; lamb: 66,000 metric tons. **Fish catch** (1978): 32,600 metric tons. **Electricity prod.** (1977): 45.00 mln. kwh. **Labor force:** 60% agric.

Finance: Currency: Shilling (Feb. 1982: 7.09 = $1 US). **Gross domestic product** (1978 est.): $407 mln. **Per capita income** (1976): $105. **Imports** (1979): $287 mln.; partners (1978): It. 30%, UK 10%, W. Ger. 10%. **Exports** (1979): $111 mln.; partners (1978): Saudi Ar. 86%, It. 8%. **Tourist receipts** (1977): $4 mln. **International reserves less gold** (Feb. 1982): $15.8 mln. **Gold:** 19,000 oz t. **Consumer prices** (change in 1980): 58.8%.

Transport: Motor vehicles: in use (1977): 4,200 passenger cars, 5,700 comm. vehicles. **Chief ports:** Mogadishu, Berbera.

Communications: Radios: 75,000 in use (1977). **Daily newspaper circ.** (1970): 4,500; 2 per 1,000 pop.

Health: Life expectancy at birth (1975): 39.4 male; 42.6 female. **Births** (per 1,000 pop. 1978): 48. **Deaths** (per 1,000 pop. 1978): 22. **Natural increase** (1978): 2.6%. **Hospital beds** (per 100,000 pop. 1977): 179. **Physicians** (per 100,000 pop. 1977): 3.

Education (1978): Literacy: 5%. **Pop. 5-19:** in school: 19%, teachers per 1,000: 7.

Arab trading posts developed into sultanates. The Italian Protectorate of Somalia, acquired from 1885 to 1927, extended along the Indian O. from the Gulf of Aden to the Juba R. The UN in 1949 approved eventual creation of Somalia as a sovereign state and in 1950 Italy took over the trusteeship held by Great Britain since World War II.

British Somaliland was formed in the 19th century in the NW. Britain gave it independence June 26, 1960; on July 1 it joined with the former Italian part to create the independent Somali Republic.

On Oct. 21, 1969, a Supreme Revolutionary Council seized power in a bloodless army and police coup, named a Council of Secretaries of State, to aid it, and abolished the Assembly. In May, 1970, several foreign companies were nationalized.

A severe drought in 1975 killed tens of thousands, and spurred efforts to resettle nomads on collective farms. The U.S. charged in 1975 that Soviet naval facilities at Berbera included a missile storage site.

Somalia has laid claim to Ogaden, the huge eastern region of Ethiopia, peopled mostly by Somalis. Ethiopia battled Somali rebels and accused Somalia of sending troops and heavy arms in 1977. Russian forces were expelled in 1977 in retaliation for Soviet support of Ethiopia. Some 11,000 Cuban troops with Soviet arms defeated Somali army troops and ethnic Somali rebels in Ethiopia, 1978. As many as 1.5 mln. refugees entered Somalia. Guerrilla fighting in Ogaden has continued, although the Somali government no longer officially supports the Ogaden secessionists.

South Africa

Republic of South Africa

People: Population (1981 est.): 29,000,000. **Age distrib.** (%): 0–14: 41.5; 15–59: 54.5; 60+: 3.8. **Pop. density:** 62.08 per sq. mi. **Urban** (1972): 47.9%. **Ethnic groups:** Afrikaner, English, Zulu, Asian, Xhosa. **Religions:** Mainly Christian. **Languages:** Afrikaans, English (both official), Bantu languages predominate.

Geography: Area: 435,868 sq. mi., four-fifths the size of Alaska. **Location:** At the southern extreme of Africa. **Neighbors:** Namibia (SW Africa), Botswana, Zimbabwe on N, Mozambique, Swaziland on E; surrounds Lesotho. **Topography:** The large interior plateau reaches close to the country's 2,700-mi. coastline. There are few major rivers or lakes; rainfall is sparse in W, more plentiful in E. **Capitals:** Cape Town (legislative). Pretoria (administrative), and Bloemfontein (judicial). **Cities** (1979): Durban 851,000; Cape Town 1,108,000; Johannesburg 1,441,000; Pretoria 563,000.

Government: Head of state: Pres. Marais Viljoen, b. Dec. 2, 1915, in office: June 19, 1979. **Head of government:** Prime Min. Pieter Willem Botha; b. Jan. 12, 1916; in office: Sept. 28, 1978. **Local divisions:** 4 provinces. **Armed forces:** regulars 81,300 (1980).

Economy: Industries: Steel, tires, motors, textiles, plastics. **Chief crops:** Corn, wool, dairy products, grain, tobacco, sugar, fruit, peanuts, grapes. **Minerals:** Largest world production of gold, chromium, antimony, coal, iron, manganese, nickel, phosphates, tin, uranium, gem diamonds, platinum, copper, vanadium. **Other resources:** Wool. **Per capita arable land:** 1.3 acres. **Meat prod.** (1980): beef: 585,000 metric tons; pork: 86,000 metric tons; lamb: 161,000 metric tons. **Fish catch** (1979): 658,700 metric tons. **Electricity prod.** (1980): 92.4 bln. kwh. **Crude steel prod.** (1981): 8.9 mln. metric tons. **Labor force:** 30% agric.; 18% ind. and commerce; 35% serv.; 8% mining.

Finance: Currency: Rand (Mar. 1982: 1.05 = $1 US). **Gross domestic product** (1980): $80.21 bln. **Per capita income** (1978): $1,296. **Imports** (1981): $22.61 bln.; partners (1980): W. Ger. 13%, U.S. 13%, UK 12%, Jap. 10%. **Exports** (1981): $20.85 bln.; partners (1980): U.S. 18%, UK 17%, Jap. 16%. **Tourist receipts** (1977): $321 mln. **National budget** (1980): $16.06 bln. revenues; $17.64 bln. expenditures. **International reserves less gold** (Feb. 1982): $862 mln. **Gold:** 9.08 mln. oz t. **Consumer prices** (change in 1981): 15.2%.

Transport: Railway traffic (1980): 96.7 bln. net ton-km. **Motor vehicles:** in use (1980): 2.4 mln. passenger cars, 911,000 comm. vehicles; assembled (1977): 131,800 passenger cars; 57,900 comm. vehicles. **Civil aviation:** (1980): 8.9 bln. passenger-km: 272.3 mln. freight ton-km. **Chief ports:** Durban, Cape Town, East London, Port Elizabeth.

Communications: Television sets (1978): 1.2 mln.; **Radios:** 2.5 mln. in use (1977), 385,000 manuf. (1977). **Telephones in use** (1980): 2.6 mln. **Daily newspaper circ.** (1980): 60 per 1,000 pop.

Health: Life expectancy at birth (1975): 56.6 male; 59.4 female. **Births** (per 1,000 pop. 1978): 36. **Deaths** (per 1,000 pop. 1978): 13. **Natural increase** (1978): 2.1%. **Hospital beds** (per 100,000 pop. 1977): 614. **Physicians** (per 100,000 pop. 1977): 6. **Infant mortality** (per 1,000 live births 1979): Africans 94, Indians 37, whites 19.

Education (1978): **Literacy:** 55%. **Pop. 5-19:** in school: 61%, teachers per 1,000: 13.

Bushmen and Hottentots were the original inhabitants. Bantus, including Zulu, Xhosa, Swazi, and Sotho, had occupied the area from Transvaal to south of Transkei before the 17th century.

The Cape of Good Hope area was settled by Dutch, beginning in the 17th century. Britain seized the Cape in 1806. Many Dutch trekked north and founded 2 republics, the Transvaal and the Orange Free State. Diamonds were discovered, 1867, and gold, 1886. The Dutch (Boers) resented encroachments by the British and others; the Anglo-Boer War followed, 1899-1902. Britain won and, effective May 31, 1910, created the Union of South Africa, incorporating the British colonies of the Cape and Natal, the Transvaal and the Orange Free State. After a referendum, the Union became the Republic of South Africa, May 31, 1961, and withdrew from the Commonwealth.

With the election victory of Daniel Malan's National party in 1948, the policy of separate development of the races, or apartheid, already existing unofficially, became official. This called for separate development, separate residential areas, and ultimate political independence for the whites, Bantus, Asians, and Coloreds. In 1959 the government passed acts providing the eventual creation of several Bantu nations or Bantustans on 13% of the country's land area, though most black leaders have opposed the plan.

Under apartheid, blacks are severely restricted to certain occupations, and are paid far lower wages than are whites for similar work. Only whites may vote or run for public office, and militant white opposition has been curbed. There is an advisory Indian Council, partly elected, partly appointed. In 1969, a Colored People's Representative Council was created. Minor liberalization measures were allowed in the 1970s.

At least 600 persons, mostly Bantus, were killed in 1976 riots protesting apartheid. Black protests continued through 1982 partly fueled by rising unemployment.

In 1963, the Transkei, an area in the SE, became the first of these partially self-governing territories or "Homelands." Transkei became independent on Oct. 26, 1976, Bophuthatswana on Dec. 6, 1977, and Venda on Sept. 13, 1979; none received international recognition.

In 1981, So. Africa launched military operations in Angola and Mozambique to combat terrorists groups; So. African troops attacked the South West African People's Organization (SWAPO) guerrillas in Angola, March, 1982.

Bophuthatswana: Population (1981 est.): 1,328,600. **Area:** 15,571 sq. mi., 6 discontinuous geographic units. **Capital:** Mmabatho. **Cities:** (1977 est.): Ga-Rankawa, Mabopane (comb. metro area): 153,000. **Head of state:** Pres. Kgosi Lucas Manyane Mangope, b. Dec. 27, 1923; in office: Dec. 6, 1977.

Ciskei: Population (1981 est.): 1,250,000. **Area:** 3,200 sq. mi. **Capitol:** Bisho. **Head of State:** Pres. Lennox Sebe.

Transkei: Population (1981 est.): 2,800,000. **Area:** 15,831 sq. mi., 3 discontinuous geographic units. **Capital:** Umtata (1978 est.): 30,000. **Head of state:** Pres. Kaiser Matanzima; in office: Feb. 20, 1979. **Head of government:** Prime Min. George Matanzima; in office: Feb. 20, 1979.

Venda: Population (1979 est.): 449,000. **Area:** 2,448 sq. mi., 2 discontinuous geographic units. **Capital:** Thohoyandou. **City:** Makearela (1976 est.): 1,972. **Head of state:** Patrick Mphephu; in office: Sept. 13, 1979.

Namibia (South-West Africa)

South-West Africa is a sparsely populated land twice the size of California. Made a German protectorate in 1884, it was surrendered to South Africa in 1915 and was administered by that country under a League of Nations mandate. S. Africa refused to accept UN authority under the trusteeship system.

Other African nations charged S. Africa imposed apartheid, built military bases, and exploited S-W Africa. The UN General Assembly, May 1968, created an 11-nation council to take over administration of S-W Africa and lead it to independence. The council charged that S. Africa had blocked its efforts to visit S-W Africa.

In 1968 the UN General Assembly gave the area the name Namibia. In Jan. 1970 the UN Security Council condemned S. Africa for "illegal" control of the area. In an advisory opinion, June 1971, the International Court of Justice declared S. Africa was occupying the area illegally.

In a 1977 referendum, white voters backed a plan for a multiracial interim government to lead to independence. The Marxist South-West Africa People's Organization (SWAPO) rejected the plan, and launched a guerrilla war. Both S. Africa and Namibian rebels agreed to a UN plan for independence by the end of 1978. S. Africa rejected the plan, Sept. 20, 1978, and held elections, without UN supervision, for Namibia's constituent assembly, Dec., that were ignored by the major black opposition parties.

The UN peace plan, proposed 1980, called for a cease-fire and a demilitarized zone 31 miles deep on each side of S-W Africa's borders with Angola and Zambia that would be patrolled by UN peacekeeping forces against guerrilla actions. Impartial elections would follow. Clashes between So. African troops and SWAPO guerrillas intensified in 1982.

Most of Namibia is a plateau, 3,600 ft. high, with plains in the N, Kalahari Desert to the E, Orange R. on the S, Atlantic O. on the W. Area is 318,827 sq. mi.; pop. (1981 est.) 1,038,000; capital, Windhoek.

Products include cattle, sheep, diamonds, copper, lead, zinc, fish. People include Namas (Hottentots), Ovambos (Bantus), Bushmen, and others.

Walvis Bay, the only deepwater port in the country, was turned over to South African administration in 1922. S. Africa said in 1978 it would discuss sovereignty only after Namibian independence.

Spain

Spanish State

People: Population (1981 est.): 37,900,000 **Age distrib.** (%): 0–14: 27.6; 15–59: 58.0; 60+: 14.4. **Pop. density:** 192.06 per sq. mi. **Ethnic groups:** Spanish (Castilian, Valencian, Andalusian, Asturian) 72.8%, Catalan 16.4%, Galician 8.2%, Basque 2.3%. **Languages:** Spanish (official), Catalan, Galician (Portuguese dialect), Valencian (Spanish dialect), Basque all legally recognized. **Religions:** Roman Catholic.

Geography: Area: 194,885 sq. mi., the size of Colorado and Wyoming combined. **Location:** In SW Europe. **Neighbors:** Portugal on W. France on N. **Topography:** The interior is a high, arid plateau broken by mountain ranges and river valleys. The NW is heavily watered, the south has lowlands and a Mediterranean climate. **Capital:** Madrid. **Cities** (1978 est.): Madrid 3,520,320; Barcelona 1,809,722; Valencia 713,026; Seville 588,784; Zaragoza 547,317; Bilbao 457,655; Malaga 402,978.

Government: Head of state: King Juan Carlos I de Borbon y Borbon, b. Jan. 5, 1938; in office: Nov. 22, 1975. **Head of government:** Prime Min. Leopoldo Calvo Sotelo y Bustelo; in office: Feb. 25, 1981. **Local divisions:** 50 provinces with appointed governors. **Armed forces:** regulars 333,400 (1980).

Economy: Industries: Machinery, textiles, shoes, paper, autos, ships, cement, tourism. **Chief crops:** Grains, olives, grapes, citrus fruits, onions, almonds, esparto, flax, hemp, pulse, tobacco, cotton, rice. **Minerals:** Mercury, potash, uranium, lead, iron, copper, zinc, coal, cobalt, silver, sulphur, phosphates, oil. **Crude oil reserves** (1980): 150 mln. bbls. **Other resources:** Forests (cork). **Per capita arable land:** 1.1 acres. **Meat prod.** (1980): beef: 410,000 metric tons; pork: 975,000 metric tons; lamb: 138,000 metric tons. **Fish catch** (1979): 1.2 mln. tons. **Electricity prod.** (1980): 110.1 bln. kwh. **Crude steel prod.** (1981): 12.9 mln. metric tons. **Labor force:** 19% agric.; 37% ind. and commerce; 41% serv.

Finance: Currency: Peseta (Mar. 1982: 106.80 = $1 US). **Gross domestic product** (1979): $201 bln. **Per capita income** (1979): $5,500. **Imports** (1981): $32.15 bln.; partners (1980): U.S. 13%, W. Ger. 9%, Saudi Ar. 9%. **Exports** (1981): $20.33 bln.; partners (1980): Fr. 17%, W. Ger. 10%, U.S. 6%, UK 7%. **Tourists** (1979): 38.9 mln.; receipts: $6.4 bln. **National budget** (1980): $31.99 bln. revenues; $33.84 bln. expenditures. **International reserves less gold** (Jan. 1982): $10.68 bln. **Gold:** 14.61 mln. oz t. **Consumer prices** (change in 1981): 14.5%.

Transport: Railway traffic (1979): 17.1 bln. passenger-km; 10.9 bln. net ton-km. **Motor vehicles:** in use (1980): 7.5 mln. passenger cars, 1.3 mln. comm. vehicles; manuf. (1980): 1.02 mln. passenger cars; 151,000 comm. vehicles. **Civil aviation:** (1980): 15.5 bln. passenger-km; 417 mln. freight ton-km. **Chief ports:** Barcelona, Bilbao, Valencia, Cartagena, Gijon.

Communications: Television sets: 7.4 mln. in use (1978), 631,000 manuf. (1976). **Radios:** 9.3 mln. in use (1976), 363,000 manuf. (1976). **Telephones in use** (1979): 11.1 mln. **Daily newspaper circ.** (1980): 116 per 1,000 pop.

Health: Life expectancy at birth (1975): 70.4 male; 76.2 female. **Births** (per 1,000 pop. 1979): 16.1. **Deaths** (per 1,000 pop. 1979): 7.8. **Natural increase** (1977): 1.0%. **Hospital beds** (per 100,000 pop. 1977): 543. **Physicians** (per 100,000 pop. 1977): 176. **Infant mortality** (per 1,000 live births 1977): 15.6.

Education (1978): Literacy: 93%. **Pop. 5-19:** in school: 67%, teachers per 1,000: 28.

Spain was settled by Iberians, Basques, and Celts, partly overrun by Carthaginians, conquered by Rome c.200 BC. The Visigoths, in power by the 5th century AD, adopted Christianity but by 711 AD lost to the Islamic invasion from Africa. Christian reconquest from the N led to a Spanish nationalism. In 1469 the kingdoms of Aragon and Castile were united by the marriage of Ferdinand II and Isabella I, and the last Moorish power was broken by the fall of the kingdom of Granada, 1492. Spain became a bulwark of Roman Catholicism.

Spain obtained a colonial empire with the discovery of America by Columbus, 1492, the conquest of Mexico by Cortes, and Peru by Pizarro. It also controlled the Netherlands and parts of Italy and Germany. Spain lost its American colonies in the early 19th century. It lost Cuba, the Philippines, and Puerto Rico during the Spanish-American War, 1898.

Primo de Rivera became dictator in 1923. King Alfonso XIII revoked the dictatorship, 1930, but was forced to leave the country 1931. A republic was proclaimed which disestablished the church, curtailed its privileges, and secularized education. A conservative reaction occurred 1933 but was followed by a Popular Front (1936-1939) composed of socialists, communists, republicans, and anarchists.

Army officers under Francisco Franco revolted against the government, 1936. In a destructive 3-year war, in which some one million died, Franco received massive help and troops from Italy and Germany, while the USSR, France, and Mexico supported the republic. War ended Mar. 28, 1939. Franco was named caudillo, leader of the nation. Spain was neutral in World War II but its relations with fascist countries caused its exclusion from the UN until 1955.

In July 1969, Franco and the Cortes designated Prince Juan Carlos as the future king and chief of state. After Franco's death, Nov. 20, 1975, Juan Carlos was sworn in as king. He presided over the formal dissolution of the institutions of the Franco regime. In free elections June 1976, moderates and democratic socialists emerged as the largest parties.

In an unsuccessful attempt at a military coup, Feb. 23, 1981, rightist Civil Guards seized the lower house of Parliament and took most of the country's leaders hostage. The plot collapsed the next day when the army remained loyal to King Juan Carlos.

Catalonia and the Basque country were granted autonomy, Jan. 1980, following overwhelming approval in home-rule referendums. Basque extremists, however, continued their violent campaign for independence with numerous terrorist attacks and bombings in 1982.

The **Balearic Islands** in the western Mediterranean, 1,935 sq. mi., are a province of Spain; they include **Majorca** (Mallorca), with the capital, Palma; **Minorca, Cabrera, Ibiza** and **Formentera.** The **Canary Islands,** 2,807 sq. mi., in the Atlantic W of Morocco, form 2 provinces, including the islands of **Tenerife, Palma, Gomera, Hierro, Grand Canary, Fuerteventura,** and **Lanzarote** with Las Palmas and Santa Cruz thriving ports. **Ceuta** and **Melilla,** small enclaves on Morocco's Mediterranean coast, are part of Metropolitan Spain.

Spain has sought the return of Gibraltar, in British hands since 1704.

Sri Lanka

Democratic Socialist Republic of Sri Lanka

People: Population (1981 est.): 15,100,000. **Age distrib.** (%): 0–14: 39.0; 15–59: 54.7; 60+: 6.4. **Pop. density:** 581.87 per sq. mi. **Urban** (1971): 22.4%. **Ethnic groups:** Sinhalese 72%, Tamils 19%, Moors 7%. **Languages:** Sinhala (official), Tamil, English. **Religions:** Buddhists 67%, Hindus 18%, Christians 8%, Muslims 7%.

Geography: Area: 25,332 sq. mi. **Location:** In Indian O. off SE coast of India. **Neighbors:** India on NW. **Topography:** The coastal area and the northern half are flat; the S-central area is hilly and mountainous. **Capital:** Colombo. **Cities** (1979): Colombo 991,000; Jaffna 118,000; Kandy 103,000; Galle 79,000.

Government: Head of state: Pres. Junius Richard Jayawardene; b. Sept. 17, 1906; in office: Feb. 4, 1978. **Head of government:** Ranasinghe Premadasa, b. June 23, 1924, in office: Feb. 6, 1978. **Local divisions:** 22 districts. **Armed forces:** regulars 13,700; reserves 10,700.

Economy: Industries: Plywood, paper, glassware, ceramics, cement, chemicals, textiles. **Chief crops:** Tea, coconuts, rice, cacao, cinnamon, citronella, tobacco. **Minerals:** Graphite, limestone, iron, ilmenite, monazite, zircon, quartz, precious and semi-precious stones. **Other resources:** Forests, rubber. **Per capita arable land:** 0.2 acres. **Meat prod.** (1980): beef: 18,000 metric tons. **Fish catch** (1978): 156,600 metric tons. **Electricity prod.** (1980): 1.6 bln. kwh. **Labor force:** 53.4% agric.; 27% ind. and commerce; 19.4% serv.

Finance: Currency: Rupee (Mar. 1982: 20.70 = $1 US). **Gross domestic product** (1980): $3.4 bln. **Per capita income** (1978): $168. **Imports** (1980): $2.02 bln.; partners (1980): Jap. 13%, Saudi Ar. 10%, UK 9%. **Exports** (1980): $1.08 bln.; partners (1980): U.S. 11%, UK 7%, W. Ger. 5%. **Tourists** (1977): 153,700; receipts: $40 mln. **National budget** (1980): $703 mln. revenues; $1.44 bln. expenditures. **International reserves less gold** (Feb. 1982): $380 mln. **Gold:** 63,000 oz t. **Consumer prices** (change in 1981): 17.9%

Transport: Railway traffic (1980): 3.6 bln. passenger-km; 165 mln. net ton-km. **Motor vehicles:** in use (1979): 114,500 passenger cars, 51,700 comm. vehicles. **Civil aviation** (1980):

691 mln. passenger-km; 9.8 mln. freight ton-km. **Chief ports:** Colombo, Trincomalee, Galle.

Communications: Radios: 1 mln. in use (1977), 59,000 manuf. (1978). **Telephones in use** (1978): 74,166.

Health: Life expectancy at birth (1967): 64.8 male; 66.9 female. **Births** (per 1,000 pop. 1978): 28. **Deaths** (per 1,000 pop. 1978): 7. **Natural increase** (1978): 1.7%. **Hospital beds** (per 100,000 pop. 1977): 296. **Physicians** (per 100,000 pop. 1977): 16. **Infant mortality** (per 1,000 live births 1979): 43.

Education (1978): **Literacy:** 81%. **Pop. 5-19:** in school: 64%, teachers per 1,000: 22.

The island was known to the ancient world as Taprobane (Greek for copper-colored) and later as Serendip (from Arabic). Colonists from northern India subdued the indigenous Veddahs about 543 BC; their descendants, the Buddhist Sinhalese, still form most of the population. Hindu descendants of Tamil immigrants from southern India account for one-fifth of the population; separatism has grown. Parts were occupied by the Portuguese in 1505 and by the Dutch in 1658. The British seized the island in 1796. As Ceylon it became an independent member of the Commonwealth in 1948. On May 22, 1972, Ceylon became the Republic of Sri Lanka.

Prime Min. W. R. D. Bandaranaike was assassinated Sept. 25, 1959. In new elections, the Freedom Party was victorious under Mrs. Sirimavo Bandaranaike, widow of the former prime minister. In Apr., 1962, the government expropriated British and U.S. oil companies. In Mar. 1965 elections, the conservative United National Party won; the new government agreed to pay compensation for the seized oil companies.

After May 1970 elections, Mrs. Bandaranaike became prime minister again. In 1971 the nation suffered economic problems and terrorist activities by ultra-leftists, thousands of whom were executed. Unemployment and food shortages plagued the nation from 1973 to 1976. Massive land reform and nationalization of foreign-owned plantations was undertaken in the mid-1970s. Mrs. Bandaranaike was ousted in 1977 elections by the United Nationals. A presidential form of government was installed in 1978 to restore stability.

Racial tension between the Sinhalese and Tamil communities erupted into violence in 1981.

Sudan

Democratic Republic of the Sudan

People: Population (1981 est.): 19,600,000. **Pop. density:** 19.32 per sq. mi. **Urban** (1976): 20.4%. **Ethnic groups:** North: Arabs, Nubians; South; Nilotic; Sudanic, Negro tribes. **Languages:** Arabic (official), various tribal languages. **Religions:** Muslims 66%, animist 29%, Christians 5%.

Geography: Area: 966,757 sq. mi., the largest country in Africa, over one-fourth the size of the U.S. **Location:** At the E end of Sahara desert zone. **Neighbors:** Egypt on N, Libya, Chad, Central African Republic on W, Zaire, Uganda, Kenya on S, Ethiopia on E. **Topography:** The N consists of the Libyan Desert in the W, and the mountainous Nubia desert in E, with narrow Nile valley between. The center contains large, fertile, rainy areas with fields, pasture, and forest. The S has rich soil, heavy rain. **Capital:** Khartoum. **Cities** (1973 cen.): Khartoum 333,921; Omdurman 299,401; North Khartoum 150,991; Port Sudan 132,631.

Government: Head of state and head of government: Pres., Prime Min. Gaafar Mohammed Nimeiri; b. Jan. 1, 1930; in office: May 25, 1969 (P.M.: Sept. 10, 1977). **Local divisions:** 15 provinces; the southern 3 have a regional government. **Armed forces:** regulars 66,100 (1980).

Economy: Industries: Textiles, food processing. **Chief crops:** Gum arabic (principal world source), durra (sorghum), cotton (main export), sesame, peanuts, rice, coffee, sugar cane, tobacco, wheat, dates. **Minerals:** Chrome, gold, copper, white mica, vermiculite, asbestos. **Other resources:** Mahogany. **Per capita arable land:** 1.1 acres. **Meat prod.** (1980): beef: 208,000 metric tons; lamb: 126,000 metric tons; **Fish catch** (1978): 24,700 metric tons. **Electricity prod.** (1978): 911 mln. kwh. **Labor force:** 86% agric.; 14% ind., commerce, serv.

Finance: Currency: Pound (Mar. 1982: .90 = $1 US). **Gross domestic product** (1978 est.): $5.6 bln. **Per capita income** (1978 est.): $320. **Imports** (1981): $1.57 bln.; partners (1979): UK 16%, W. Ger. 14%, U.S. 8%. **Exports** (1981): $658 mln.; partners (1979): China 16%, It. 11%, Saudi Ar. 11%. **Tourists** (1977): 36,700; receipts: $11 mln. **National Budget** (1981): $2.01 bln. revenues; $2.69 bln. expenditures. **International reserves less gold** (Feb. 1982): $23.8 mln. **Consumer prices** (change in 1980): 25.4%.

Transport: Railway traffic (1974): 2.3 bln. net ton-km. **Motor vehicles:** in use (1979): 35,000 passenger cars, 37,000 comm. vehicles. **Civil aviation:** (1980): 710 mln. passenger-km; 12.5 mln. freight ton-km. **Chief ports:** Port Sudan.

Communications: Television sets: 100,000 in use (1977). **Radios:** 1.4 mln. licensed (1977). **Telephones in use** (1980): 63,400. **Daily newspaper circ.** (1980): 7 per 1,000 pop.

Health: Life expectancy at birth (1975): 43.0 male; 45.0 female. **Births** (per 1,000 pop. 1978): 49. **Deaths** (per 1,000 pop. 1978): 18 **Natural increase** (1978): 3.7%. **Hospital beds** (per 100,000 pop. 1977): 100. **Physicians** (per 100,000 pop. 1977): 50. **Infant mortality** (per 1,000 live births 1979): 141.

Education (1978): **Literacy:** 20%. **Pop. 5-19:** in school: 26%, teachers per 1,000: 8.

Northern Sudan, ancient Nubia, was settled by Egyptians in antiquity, and was converted to Coptic Christianity in the 6th century. Arab conquests brought Islam in the 15th century.

In the 1820s Egypt took over the Sudan, defeating the last of earlier empires, including the Fung. In the 1880s a revolution was led by Mohammed Ahmed who called himself the Mahdi (leader of the faithful) and his followers, the dervishes.

In 1898 an Anglo-Egyptian force crushed the Mahdi's successors. In 1951 the Egyptian Parliament abrogated its 1899 and 1936 treaties with Great Britain, and amended its constitution, to provide for a separate Sudanese constitution.

Sudan voted for complete independence as a parliamentary government effective Jan. 1, 1956. Gen. Ibrahim Abboud took power 1958, but resigned under pressure, 1964.

In 1969, in a second military coup, a Revolutionary Council took power, but a civilian premier and cabinet were appointed; the government announced it would create a socialist state. The northern 12 provinces are predominantly Arab-Moslem and have been dominant in the central government. The 3 southern provinces are Negro and predominantly pagan. A 1972 peace agreement gave the South regional autonomy.

The government nationalized a number of businesses in May 1970. An attempted communist coup in July 1971 failed, leading to a temporary diplomatic break with the USSR. Soviet arms shipments were announced in 1975, but relations later deteriorated and U.S. ties improved.

On Mar. 2, 1973, the U.S. ambassador and the charge d'affaires and a Belgian diplomat were slain in Khartoum by 8 Palestinian terrorists. The 8 were freed and turned over to a Palestinian liberation group in Egypt.

Sudan charged Libya with aiding an unsuccessful coup in Sudan in 1976. Sudan claimed that Libyan planes bombed several border towns, September 1981.

Economic problems plagued the nation, 1981, and were aggravated by a hugh influx of refugees from Chad.

Suriname

People: Population (1981 est.): 420,000. **Pop. density:** 5.85 per sq. mi. **Ethnic groups** Hindustanis 37%, Creole 30%, Indonesians 15%, Bush Negro 10%, Amerindians, 2.6%. **Languages:** Dutch (official), Sranan (Creole), English, others. **Religions:** Muslim, Hindu, Christian.

Geography: Area: 70,060 sq. mi., slightly larger than Georgia. **Location:** On N shore of S. America. **Neighbors:** Guyana on W, Brazil on S, French Guiana on E. **Topography:** A flat Atlantic coast, where dikes permit agriculture. Inland is a forest belt; to the S, largely unexplored hills cover 75% of the country. **Capital:** Paramaribo. **Cities** (1979): Paramaribo 150,000; Nickerie, Paranam, Moengo.

Government: Head of Military Council: Col. Deysi Bouterse; in office: Feb. 5, 1982. **Local divisions:** 9 districts.

Economy: Industries: Aluminum. **Chief crops:** Rice, sugar, fruits. **Minerals:** Bauxite. **Other resources:** Forests, shrimp. **Per capita arable land:** 0.2 acres. **Electricity prod.** (1979): 1.5 bln. kwh. **Labor force:** 29% agric.; 15% ind. and commerce.

Finance: Currency: Guilder (Mar. 1982: 1.78 = $1 US). **Gross domestic product** (1977): $529 mln. **Per capita income** (1977): $1,240. **Imports** (1979): $411 mln.; partners

(1977): U.S. 31%, Neth. 21%, Trin./Tob. 14%, Jap. 7%. **Exports** (1979): $444 mln.; partners (1977): U.S. 41%, Neth. 24%, UK 7%. **Tourists** (1976): 54,700; receipts: $10 mln. **National budget** (1978): $356 mln. revenues; $382 mln. expenditures.

International reserves less gold (Feb. 1982): $223.32 mln. **Gold:** 54,000 oz t. **Consumer prices** (change in 1979): 14.9%.

Transport: Motor vehicles: in use (1979): 22,800 passenger cars, 8,900 comm. vehicles. **Chief ports:** Paramaribo, Nieuw-Nickerie.

Communications: Television sets: 39,000 in use (1977). **Radios:** 182,000 in use (1977). **Telephones in use** (1980): 21,300. **Daily newspaper circ.** (1977): 33,000; 74 per 1,000 pop.

Health: Life expectancy at birth (1980): 64.8 male; 69.8 female. **Births** (per 1,000 pop. 1978): 29. **Deaths** (per 1,000 pop. 1978): 7. **Natural increase** (1978): 2.8%. **Pop. per hospital bed** (1975): 184. **Pop. per physician** (1974): 2,030. **Infant mortality** (per 1,000 live births 1966): 30.4.

The Netherlands acquired Suriname in 1667 from Britain, in exchange for New Netherlands (New York). The 1954 Dutch constitution raised the colony to a level of equality with the Netherlands and the Netherlands Antilles. In the 1970s the Dutch government pressured for Suriname independence, which came Nov. 25, 1975, despite objections from East Indians and some Bush Negroes. Some 40% of the population (mostly East Indians) emigrated to the Netherlands in the months before independence. The Netherlands promised $1.5 billion in aid for the first decade of independence.

The National Military Council took over control of the government, Feb. 1982.

Swaziland

Kingdom of Swaziland

People: Population (1981 est.): 570,000. **Age distrib.** (%): 0–14: 48.3; 15–59: 47.4; 60+: 4.3. **Pop. density:** 82.03 per sq. mi. **Urban** (1973): 7.9%. **Ethnic groups:** Swazi 90%, Zulu 2.3%, European 2.1%, other African, non-African groups. **Languages:** siSwati, English, (both official). **Religions:** Christians 60%, animist 40%.

Geography: Area: 6,704 sq. mi., slightly smaller than New Jersey. **Location:** In southern Africa, near Indian O. coast. **Neighbors:** South Africa on N, W, S, Mozambique on E. **Topography:** The country descends from W-E in broad belts, becoming more arid in the lowveld region, then rising to a plateau in the E. **Capital:** Mbabane. **Cities** (1980): Mbabane 25,000; Manzini 25,000.

Government: Head of state: King Sobhuza II; b. July 22, 1899; in office: 1921. **Head of government:** Prime Min. Prince Mabandla Dlamini; in office: Mar. 31, 1976. **Local divisions:** 4 districts, 2 municipalities.

Economy: Industries: Wood pulp. **Chief crops:** Corn, cotton, rice, pineapples, sugar, citrus fruits. **Minerals:** Asbestos, iron, coal. **Other resources:** Forests. **Per capita arable land:** 0.7 acres. **Meat prod.** (1980): beef: 14,000 metric tons. **Electricity prod.** (1978): 281 mln. kwh. **Labor force:** 60% agric.; 8% ind. and commerce; 9% serv.

Finance: Currency: Lilangeni (Mar. 1982: 1.05 = $1 US). **Gross domestic product** (1977): $313 mln. **Per capita income** (1977 est.): $530. **Imports** (1979): $355 mln.; partners (1977): So. Afr., 96%. **Exports** (1979): $219 mln.; partners (1977): UK 33%, So. Afr. 20%. **National budget** (1981): $145 mln. revenues; $85 mln. expenditures. **International reserves less gold** (Feb. 1982): $99.15 mln. **Consumer prices** (change in 1980): 17.7%.

Transport: Motor vehicles: in use (1976): 7,900 passenger cars, 7,100 comm. vehicles.

Communications: Radios: 60,000 in use (1976). **Telephones in use** (1978): 9,190. **Daily newspaper circ.** (1976): 5,000; 10 per 1,000 pop.

Health: Life expectancy at birth (1980): 44.3 male; 47.5 female. **Births** (per 1,000 pop. 1978): 47. **Deaths** (per 1,000 pop. 1978): 19. **Natural increase** (1978): 2.7%. **Hospital beds** (per 100,000 pop. 1977): 345. **Physicians** (per 100,000 pop. 1977): 11. **Infant mortality rate** (per 1,000 live births 1980): 156.

Education (1978): **Literacy:** 36%. **Pop. 5-19:** in school: 63%, teachers per 1,000: 21.

The royal house of Swaziland traces back 400 years, and is one of Africa's last ruling dynasties. The Swazis, a Bantu people, were driven to Swaziland from lands to the N by the Zulus in 1820. Their autonomy was later guaranteed by Britain and Transvaal, with Britain assuming control after 1903. Independence came Sept. 6, 1968. In 1973 the king repealed the constitution and assumed full powers.

A new Parliament was opened, 1979. Under the new constitution political parties were forbidden; Parliament's role in government was limited to debate and advice.

Fertile lands and mineral resources have aided development. The population is homogeneous, except for 6,000 whites who dominate the economy.

Sweden

Kingdom of Sweden

People: Population (1981 est.): 8,310,000. **Age distrib.** (%): 0–14: 20.6; 15–59: 58.2; 60+: 21.2. **Pop. density:** 47.85 per sq. mi. **Urban** (1975): 82.7%. **Ethnic groups:** Swedish 93%, Finnish 3%, Lapps, European immigrants. **Languages:** Swedish, Finnish. **Religions:** Lutherans (official) 95%, other Protestants 5%.

Geography: Area: 173,732 sq. mi., larger than California. **Location:** On Scandinavian Peninsula in N. Europe. **Neighbors:** Norway on W, Denmark on S (across Kattegat), Finland on E. **Topography:** Mountains along NW border cover 25% of Sweden, flat or rolling terrain covers the central and southern areas, which includes several large lakes. **Capital:** Stockholm. **Cities** (1978 est.): Stockholm 661,258; Goteborg 442,410; Malmo 240,220.

Government: Head of state: King Carl XVI Gustaf; b. Apr. 30, 1946; in office: Sept. 19, 1973. **Head of government:** Prime Min. Thorbjorn Falldin; b. Apr. 24, 1926; in office: Oct. 11, 1979. **Local divisions:** 24 lan (counties). **Armed forces:** regulars 69,200 (1980).

Economy: Industries: Steel, machinery, instruments, autos, shipbuilding, shipping, paper. **Chief crops:** Grains, potatoes, sugar beets. **Minerals:** Zinc, iron, lead, copper, gold, silver. **Other resources:** Forests (half the country); yield one fourth exports. **Per capita arable land:** 0.9 acres. **Meat prod.** (1980): beef: 154,000 metric tons; pork: 317,000 metric tons; lamb: 5,000 metric tons. **Fish catch** (1979): 205,600 metric tons. **Electricity prod.** (1978): 90.18 bln. kwh. **Crude steel prod.** (1981): 3.7 mln. metric tons. **Labor force:** 5% agric.; 45% ind. and commerce, 40% serv.

Finance: Currency: Krona (Mar. 1982: 5.95 = $1 US). **Gross domestic product** (1979): $101.49 bln. **Per capita income** (1978): $9,274. **Imports** (1981): $28.7 bln.; partners (1980): W. Ger. 17%, UK 12%, U.S. 7%, Fin. 7%. **Exports** (1981): $28.41 bln.; partners (1980): UK 10%, W. Ger. 12%, Nor. 10%, Den. 8%. **National budget** (1981): $28.4 bln. revenues; $38.4 bln. expenditures. **International reserves less gold** (Feb. 1982): $3.47 bln. **Gold:** 6.06 mln. oz t. **Consumer prices** (change in 1981): 12.1%.

Transport: Railway traffic (1979): 6.8 bln. passenger-km; 15.6 bln. net ton-km. **Motor vehicles:** in use (1980): 2.88 mln. passenger cars, 181,750 comm. vehicles; manuf. (1978): 258,000 passenger cars; (1975): 49,200 comm. vehicles. **Civil aviation** (1980): 5.3 bln. passenger-km: 190.9 mln. freight ton-km. **Chief ports:** Goteborg, Stockholm, Malmo.

Communications: Television sets: 3.1 mln. licensed (1979), 390,000 manuf. (1978). **Radios:** 8.3 mln. (1977), 159,000 manuf. (1976). **Telephones in use** (1979): 6.4 mln. **Daily newspaper circ.** (1980): 584 per 1,000 pop.

Health: Life expectancy at birth (1979): 72.5 male; 78.7 female. **Births** (per 1,000 pop. 1980): 11.7. **Deaths** (per 1,000 pop. 1980): 11.0. **Natural increase** (1978): 0.4%. **Hospital beds** (per 100,000 pop. 1977): 1,496. **Physicians** (per 100,000 pop. 1977): 178. **Infant mortality** (per 1,000 live births (1978): 7.7.

Education (1978): **Literacy:** 99%. **Pop. 5-19:** in school: 74%, teachers per 1,000: 46.

The Swedes have lived in present-day Sweden for at least 5,000 years, longer than nearly any other European people.

Gothic tribes from Sweden played a major role in the disintegration of the Roman Empire. Other Swedes helped create the first Russian state in the 9th century.

The Swedes were Christianized from the 11th century, and a strong centralized monarchy developed. A parliament, the Riksdag, was first called in 1435, the earliest parliament on the European continent, with all classes of society represented.

Swedish independence from rule by Danish kings (dating from 1397) was secured by Gustavus I in a revolt, 1521-23; he built up the government and military and established the Lutheran Church. In the 17th century Sweden was a major European power, gaining most of the Baltic seacoast, but its international position subsequently declined.

The Napoleonic wars, in which Sweden acquired Norway (it became independent 1905), were the last in which Sweden participated. Armed neutrality was maintained in both world wars.

Over 4 decades of Social Democratic rule was ended in 1976 parliamentary elections. Although 90% of the economy is in private hands, the government holds a large interest in water power production and the railroads are operated by a public agency.

Consumer cooperatives are in extensive operation and also are important in agriculture and housing. Per capita GNP is among the highest in the world.

Swedish voters in a national referendum, Mar. 1980, voted to support limited expansion of nuclear energy.

A labor crisis of strikes locking out more than 800,000 workers, May 1980, brought the country to an industrial standstill and shattered its image of labor tranquillity.

A Soviet submarine went aground inside Swedish territorial waters near the Karlskrona Naval Base, Oct. 27, 1981. Sweden claimed the submarine was armed with nuclear weapons and the incident a "flagrant violation" of Swedish neutrality. The submarine was towed back to international waters Nov. 6.

Switzerland

Swiss Confederation

People: Population (1981 est.): 6,343,000. **Age distrib.** (%): 0–14: 21.0; 15–59: 61.1; 60+: 17.9. **Pop. density:** 397.72 per sq. mi. **Urban** (1970): 54.6%. **Ethnic groups:** Defined by mother tongue. **Languages:** German 65%, French 18%, Italian 12%, Romansh 1%. (all official). **Religions:** Roman Catholic 49.4%, Protestant 47.8%.

Geography: Area: 15,941 sq. mi., as large as Mass., Conn., and R.I., combined. **Location:** In the Alps Mts. in Central Europe. **Neighbors:** France on W, Italy on S, Austria on E, W. Germany on N. **Topography:** The Alps cover 60% of the land area, the Jura, near France, 10%. Running between, from NE to SW, are midlands, 30%. **Capital:** Bern. **Cities** (1980 est.): Zurich 377,300; Basel 183,200; Geneva 152,400; Bern 142,000.

Government: Head of government: Pres. Fritz Honegger; in office: Dec. 9, 1981. **Local divisions:** 20 full cantons, 3 half cantons. **Armed forces:** (1980): 580,000; reserves 661,500.

Economy: Industries: Machinery, machine tools, steel, instruments, watches, textiles, foodstuffs (cheese, chocolate), chemicals, drugs, banking, tourism. **Chief crops:** Grains, potatoes, sugar beets, vegetables, tobacco. **Minerals:** Salt. **Other resources:** Hydro power potential. **Per capita arable land:** 0.1 acres. **Meat prod.** (1980): beef: 173,000 metric tons; pork: 288,000 metric tons. **Electricity prod.** (1980): 42.6 bln. kwh. **Crude steel Prod.** (1981): 900,000 metric tons. **Labor force:** 44% ind. and commerce, 8% agric., 52.5% serv.; 4.3% gvt.

Finance: Currency: Franc (Mar. 1982: 1.93 = $1 US). **Gross domestic product** (1979): $97.4 bln. **Per capita income** (1979): $15,455. **Imports** (1981): $30.6 bln.; partners (1980): W. Ger. 28%, Fr. 12%, It. 10%, U.K. 8%. **Exports** (1981): $27.04 bln.; partners (1980): W. Ger. 20%, Fr. 9%, It. 8%, U.S. 7%. **Tourists** (1979): 7.6 mln.; receipts: $2.5 bln. **National budget** (1980): $8.2 bln. revenues; $8.2 bln. expenditures. **International reserves less gold** (Feb. 1982): $10.93 bln. **Gold:** 83.28 mln. oz t. **Consumer prices** (change in 1981): 6.5%.

Transport: Railway traffic (1980): 8.4 bln. passenger-km; 7.4 bln. net ton-km. **Motor vehicles:** in use (1980): 2.2 mln. passenger cars, 169,400 comm. vehicles. **Civil aviation:** (1980): 10.8 bln. passenger-km; 453 mln. freight ton-km.

Communications: Television sets: 1.9 mln. licensed (1979). **Radios:** 2.2 mln. licensed (1979). **Telephones in use** (1979): 4.4 mln. **Daily newspaper circ.** (1980): 4.4 mln.; 233 per 1,000 pop.

Health: Life expectancy at birth (1977): 71.8 male; 76.22 female. **Births** (per 1,000 pop. 1980): 11.9. **Deaths** (per 1,000 pop. 1980): 9.2. **Natural increase** (1978): .2%. **Hospital beds** (per 100,000 pop. 1977): 1,141. **Physicians** (per 100,000 pop. 1977): 201. **Infant mortality** (per 1,000 live births 1977): 9.8.

Education (1978): **Literacy:** 99%. **Pop. 5–19:** in school: 65%, teachers per 1,000: 45.

Switzerland, the Roman province of Helvetia, is a federation of 23 cantons (20 full cantons and 6 half cantons), 3 of which in 1291 created a defensive league and later were joined by other districts. Voters in the French-speaking part of Canton Bern voted for self-government, 1978; Canton Jura was created Jan. 1, 1979.

In 1648 the Swiss Confederation obtained its independence from the Holy Roman Empire. The cantons were joined under a federal constitution in 1848, with large powers of local control retained by each canton.

Switzerland has maintained an armed neutrality since 1815, and has not been involved in a foreign war since 1515. It is not a member of NATO or the UN. However, the Cabinet took steps, Mar. 28, 1979, to recommend Swiss membership in the UN. Switzerland is a member of several UN agencies and of the European Free Trade Assoc. and has ties with the EC. It is also the seat of many UN and other international agencies.

Switzerland is a leading world banking center; stability of the currency brings funds from many quarters. Some 20% of all workers are foreign residents.

Syria

Syrian Arab Republic

People: Population (1981 est.): 9,100,000. **Age distrib.** (%): 0–14: 48.9; 15–59: 44.9; 60+: 6.2. **Pop. density:** 125.60 per sq. mi. **Urban** (1979): 47.4%. **Ethnic groups:** Arabs, Kurds 6.3%, Armenians 2.8%, Turks, Circassians, Assyrians. **Languages:** Arabic (official), Kurdish, Armenian, Circassian, Syriac. **Religions:** Predominately Muslim (Sunni, Alawi, Druze).

Geography: Area: 71,772 sq. mi., the size of North Dakota. **Location:** At eastern end of Mediterranean Sea. **Neighbors:** Lebanon, Israel on W, Jordan on S, Iraq on E, Turkey on N. **Topography:** Syria has a short Mediterranean coastline, then stretches E and S with fertile lowlands and plains, alternating with mountains and large desert areas. **Capital:** Damascus. **Cities** (1978 est.): Damascus 1,142,000; Aleppo 878,000; Homs 306,000.

Government: Head of state: Pres. Hafez al-Assad; b. Mar. 1930; in office: Feb. 22, 1971. **Head of government:** Prime Min. Abdul Rauf al-Kasm; in office: Jan. 16, 1980. **Local divisions:** Damascus and 13 provinces. **Armed forces:** regulars 247,000 (1980).

Economy: Industries: Oil products, textiles, cement, tobacco, glassware, sugar, brassware. **Chief crops:** Cotton, grain, olives, fruits, vegetables. **Minerals:** Oil, phosphate, gypsum. **Crude oil reserves** (1980): 2.00 bln. bbls. **Other resources:** Wool. **Per capita arable land:** 1.6 acres. **Meat prod.** (1980): beef: 26,000 metric tons; lamb: 65,000 metric tons. **Electricity prod.** (1979): 3.4 bln. kwh. **Labor force:** 51% agric.; 15% manuf.

Finance: Currency: Pound (Mar. 1982: 3.92 = $1 US). **Gross domestic product** (1979): $9.14 bln. **Per capita income** (1975): $702. **Imports** (1980): $4.12 bln.; partners (1979): Iraq 15%, It. 13%, W. Ger. 9%, Fr. 6%. **Exports** (1980): $2.10 bln.; partners (1979): It. 26%, Fr. 18%, U.S. 10%. **Tourists** (1977): 681,100; receipts: $110 mln. **International reserves less gold** (Mar. 1981): $264 mln. **Gold** (Feb. 1982): 833,000 oz t. **Consumer prices** (change in 1980): 19.0%.

Transport: Railway traffic (1979): 410 mln. passenger-km; 450 mln. net ton-km. **Motor vehicles:** in use (1978): 65,400 passenger cars, 81,400 comm. vehicles **Civil aviation** (1980): 948 mln. passenger-km; 16.2 mln. net ton-km. **Chief ports:** Latakia, Tartus.

Communications: Television sets: 454,000 in use (1978), 51,000 manuf. (1978). **Radios:** 1.7 mln. in use (1978). **Telephones in use** (1980): 236,000. **Daily newspaper circ.** (1980): 8 per 1,000 pop.

Health: Life expectancy at birth (1970): 54.49 male; 58.73

female. **Births** (per 1,000 pop. 1978): 43. **Deaths** (per 1,000 1978): 9. **Natural increase** (1978): 3.4%. **Hospital beds** (per 100,000 pop. 1977): 104. **Physicians** (per 100,000 pop. 1977): 39. **Infant mortality** (per 1,000 live births 1976): 15.3.

Education (1978): **Literacy:** 50%. **Pop. 5-19:** in school: 59%, teachers per 1,000: 20.

Syria contains some of the most ancient remains of civilization. It was the center of the Seleucid empire, but later became absorbed in the Roman and Arab empires. Ottoman rule prevailed for 4 centuries, until the end of World War I.

The state of Syria was formed from former Turkish districts, made a separate entity by the Treaty of Sevres 1920 and divided into the states of Syria and Greater Lebanon. Both were administered under a French League of Nations mandate 1920-1941.

Syria was proclaimed a republic by the occupying French Sept. 16, 1941, and exercised full independence effective Jan. 1, 1944. French troops left in 1946. Syria joined in the Arab invasion of Israel in 1948.

Syria joined with Egypt in Feb. 1958 in the United Arab Republic but seceded Sept. 30, 1961. The Socialist Baath party and military leaders seized power in Mar. 1963. The Baath, a pan-Arab organization, became the only legal party. The government has been dominated by members of the minority Alawite sect.

In the Arab-Israeli war of June 1967, Israel seized and occupied the Golan Heights area inside Syria, from which Israeli settlements had for years been shelled by Syria.

Syria aided Palestinian guerrillas fighting Jordanian forces in Sept. 1970 and, after a renewal of that fighting in July 1971, broke off relations with Jordan. But by 1975 the 2 countries had entered a military coordination pact.

Syria received large shipments of arms from the USSR in 1972-73 and on Oct. 6, 1973, Syria joined Egypt in an attack on Israel. Arab oil states agreed in 1974 to give Syria $1 billion a year to aid anti-Israel moves. Military supplies used or lost in the 1973 war were replaced by the USSR in 1974. Some 30,000 Syrian troops entered Lebanon in 1976 to mediate in a civil war, and fought Palestinian guerrillas and, later, fought Christian militiamen. Syrian troops again battled Christian forces in Lebanon, Apr. 1981, ending a ceasefire that had been in place.

Following the June 6, 1982 Israeli invasion of Lebanon, Israeli planes destroyed 17 Syrian antiaircraft missile batteries in the Bekka Valley, June 9. Some 25 Syrian planes were downed during the engagement. Syrian and Israeli troops exchanged fire in central Lebanon. Israel and Syria agreed to a cease fire June 11. (*See Chronology.*)

Tanzania

United Republic of Tanzania

People: Population (1981 est.) 18,400,000. **Pop. density:** 47.96 per sq. mi. **Urban** (1978): 13.3%. **Ethnic groups:** African. **Languages:** Swahili, English are official. **Religions:** Moslems 30%, Christians 30%, traditional beliefs 34%.

Geography: Area: 364,886 sq. mi., more than twice the size of California. **Location:** On coast of E. Africa. **Neighbors:** Kenya, Uganda on N, Rwanda, Burundi, Zaire on W, Zambia, Malawi, Mozambique on S. **Topography:** Hot, arid central plateau, surrounded by the lake region in the W, temperate highlands in N and S, the coastal plains. Mt. Kilimanjaro, 19,340 ft., is highest in Africa. **Capital:** Dar-es-Salaam. **Cities** (1981 est.): Dar-es-Salaam 700,000.

Government: Head of state: Pres. Julius Kambarage Nyerere; b. Mar. 1922; in office: Apr. 26, 1964. **Head of government:** Cleopa David Msuya; in office: Nov. 7, 1980. **Local divisions:** 21 regions (4 on Zanzibar), Dar-es-Salaam. **Armed forces:** regulars 51,000 (1980).

Economy: Industries: Food processing, clothing. **Chief crops:** Sisal, cotton, coffee, tea, tobacco. **Minerals:** Diamonds, gold, salt, tin, mica. **Other resources:** Hides. **Per capita arable land:** 0.6 acres. **Meat prod.** (1980): beef: 139,000 metric tons; lamb: 34,000 metric tons. **Fish catch** (1977): 250,000 metric tons. **Electricity prod.** (1979): 734 mln. kwh. **Labor force:** 90% agric.

Finance: Currency: Shilling (Feb. 1982: 8.35 = $1 US). **Gross domestic product** (1979): $4.56 bln. **Per capita income** (1978): $253. **Imports** (1980): $1.2 bln.; partners (1978): UK 19%, Jap. 11%, W. Ger. 11%. **Exports** (1980): $508 mln.; partners (1978): W. Ger. 15%, UK 21%, U.S. 11%. **Tourists** (1977): 93,000; receipts: $9 mln. **National budget** (1980): $973 mln. revenues; $933 mln. expenditures. **International reserves less gold** (Feb. 1982): $15.7 mln. **Consumer prices** (change in 1980): 30.2%.

Transport: Motor vehicles: in use (1979): 42,200 passenger cars, 51,100 comm. vehicles. **Chief ports:** Dar-es-Salaam, Tanga.

Communications: Radios: 310,000 in use (1977), 177,000 manuf. (1975). **Telephones in use** (1977): 310,000. **Daily newspaper circ.** (1980): 9 per 1,000 pop.

Health: Life expectancy at birth (1967): 40 male; 41 female. **Births** (per 1,000 pop. 1978): 47. **Deaths** (per 1,000 pop. 1978): 17. **Natural increase** (1978): 2.9%. **Hospital beds** (per 100,000 pop. 1977): 206. **Physicians** (per 100,000 pop. 1977): 20. **Infant mortality** (per 1,000 live births 1981): 125.

Education (1978): **Literacy:** 60%. **Pop. 5–19:** in school: 36%, teachers per 1,000: 7.

The Republic of Tanganyika in E. Africa and the island Republic of Zanzibar, off the coast of Tanganyika, joined into a single nation, the United Republic of Tanzania, Apr. 26, 1964. Zanzibar retains internal self-government.

Tanganyika. Arab colonization and slaving began in the 8th century AD; Portuguese sailors explored the coast by about 1500. Other Europeans followed.

In 1885 Germany established German East Africa of which Tanganyika formed the bulk. It became a League of Nations mandate and, after 1946, a UN trust territory, both under Britain. It became independent Dec. 9, 1961, and a republic within the Commonwealth a year later.

In 1967 the government set on a socialist course; it nationalized all banks and many industries. The government also ordered that Swahili, not English, be used in all official business. Nine million people have been moved into cooperative villages.

Tanzania exchanged invasion attacks with Uganda, 1978-79. Tanzanian forces drove Idi Amin from Uganda, Mar., 1979.

Zanzibar, the Isle of Cloves, lies 23 mi. off the coast of Tanganyika; its area is 640 sq. mi. The island of **Pemba,** 25 mi. to the NE, area 380 sq. mi., is included in the administration. The total population (1978 cen.) is 475,655.

Chief industry is the production of cloves and clove oil of which Zanzibar and Pemba produce the bulk of the world's supply.

Zanzibar was for centuries the center for Arab slave-traders. Portugal ruled for 2 centuries until ousted by Arabs around 1700. Zanzibar became a British Protectorate in 1890; independence came Dec. 10, 1963. Revolutionary forces overthrew the Sultan Jan. 12, 1964. The new government ousted American and British diplomats and newsmen, slaughtered thousands of Arabs, and nationalized farms. Union with Tanganyika followed, 1964. The ruling parties of Tanganyika and Zanzibar were united in 1977, as political tension eased; but a movement for greater autonomy began, 1979.

Thailand

Kingdom of Thailand

People: Population (1981 est.): 48,900,000. **Age distrib.** (%): 0–14: 42.8; 15–59: 52.3; 60+: 4.9. **Pop. density:** 227.26 per sq. mi. **Urban** (1970): 13.2%. **Ethnic groups:** Thais 75%, Chinese 14%, Malays 3%, Khmers, Soais, Karens, Indians. **Languages:** Thai, Chinese. **Religions:** Buddhists 94%, Moslems 4%.

Geography: Area: 209,411 sq. mi., three-fourths the size of Texas. **Location:** On Indochinese and Malayan Peninsulas in S.E. Asia. **Neighbors:** Burma on W. Laos on N, Cambodia on E, Malaysia on S. **Topography:** A plateau dominates the NE third of Thailand, dropping to the fertile alluvial valley of the Chao Phraya R. in the center. Forested mountains are in N, with narrow fertile valleys. The southern peninsula region is covered by rain forests. **Capital:** Bangkok. **Cities** (1979 est.): Bangkok (met.): 4.8 mln.

Government: Head of state: King Bhumibol Adulyadej; b. Dec. 5, 1927; in office: June 9, 1946. **Head of government:** Prime Min. Prem Tinsulanond; in office: Mar. 3, 1980. **Local divi-**

sions: 72 provinces. **Armed forces:** regulars 207,000 (1980).

Economy: Industries: Auto assembly, drugs, textiles, electrical goods. **Chief crops:** Rice (a major export), corn tapioca, jute, sugar, coconuts, tobacco, pepper, peanuts, beans, cotton. **Minerals:** Antimony, tin (5th largest producer), tungsten, iron, manganese, gas. **Crude oil reserves** (1979): 200 bbls. **Other resources:** Forests (teak is exported), rubber. **Per capita arable land:** 0.9 acres. **Meat prod.** (1980): beef: 214,000 metric tons; pork: 240,000 metric tons. **Fish catch** (1979): 1.7 mln. metric tons. **Electricity prod.** (1979): 14.06 bln. kwh. **Crude steel prod.** (1981 est.): 450,000 metric tons. **Labor force:** 76% agric.; 7% manuf.

Finance: Currency: Baht (Mar. 1982: 23.00 = $1 US). **Gross domestic product** (1980): $21.84 bln. **Per capita income** (1978): $444. **Imports** (1981): $9.94 bln.; partners (1979): Jap. 26%, U.S. 16%, Saudi Ar. 6%, W. Ger. 5%. **Exports** (1981): $7.03 bln.; partners (1979): Jap. 21%, Neth. 11%, U.S. 11%, Sing. 9%. **Tourists** (1979): 1.5 mln. receipts: $550 mln. **National budget** (1980): $4.14 bln. revenues; $5.26 bln. expenditures. **International reserves less gold** (Feb. 1982): $1.40 bln. **Gold:** 2.48 mln. oz t. **Consumer prices** (change in 1981): 12.7%.

Transport: Railway traffic (1980): 7 bln. passenger-km; 2.7 bln. net ton-km. **Motor vehicles:** in use (1980): 397,900 passenger cars, 451,900 comm. vehicles; assembled (1976): 15,000 passenger cars; (1974): 8,600 comm. vehicles. **Civil aviation** (1980): 6.2 bln. passenger-km; 247 mln. freight ton-km. **Chief ports:** Bangkok, Sattahip.

Communication: Television sets: 1 mln. in use (1979), 90,000 manuf. (1976). **Radios:** 5.9 mln. in use (1979). **Telephones in use** (1979): 451,400. **Daily newspaper circ.** (1980): 50 per 1,000 pop.

Health: Life expectancy at birth (1980): 57.6 male; 63.0 female. **Births** (per 1,000 pop. 1978): 31. **Deaths** (per 1,000 pop. 1978): 8. **Natural increase** (1978): 2.3%. **Hospital beds** (per 100,000 pop. 1977): 121. **Physicians** (per 100,000 pop. 1977): 12. **Infant mortality** (per 1,000 live births 1976): 25.5.

Education (1978): **Literacy:** 84%. **Pop. 5-19:** in school: 48%, teachers per 1,000: 16.

Thais began migrating from southern China in the 11th century. Thailand is the only country in SE Asia never taken over by a European power, thanks to King Mongkut and his son King Chulalongkorn who ruled from 1851 to 1910, modernized the country, and signed trade treaties with both Britain and France. A bloodless revolution in 1932 limited the monarchy.

Japan occupied the country in 1941. After the war, Thailand followed a pro-West foreign policy. Some 11,000 Thai troops fought in S. Vietnam, but were withdrawn by 1972.

The military took over the government in a bloody 1976 coup. Kriangsak Chomanan, prime minister since a 1977 military coup, resigned, Feb. 1980, under opposition over soaring inflation, oil price increases, labor unrest and growing crime.

The fertile land yields a rice surplus. Foreign investment has been encouraged.

Togo

Republic of Togo

People: Population (1981 est.): 2,600,000. **Age distrib.** (%): 0-14: 49.8; 15-59: 44.6; 60+:5.6. **Pop. density:** 93 per sq. mi. **Urban** (1974): 15.2%. **Ethnic groups:** Ewe 20%, Mina 6%, Kabye 14%. **Languages:** French (official), others. **Religions:** Animist 60%, Roman Catholics 18%, Protestants 6.5%, Muslims 7.5%.

Geography: Area: 21,853 sq. mi., slightly smaller than West Virginia. **Location:** On S coast of W. Africa. **Neighbors:** Ghana on W, Upper Volta on N, Benin on E. **Topography:** A range of hills running SW-NE splits Togo into 2 savanna plains regions. **Capital:** Lomé. **Cities** (1980 est.): Lomé 283,000.

Government: Head of state: Pres. Gnassingbe Eyadema; b. Dec. 26, 1937; in office: Apr. 14, 1967. **Local divisions:** 22 circumscriptions. **Armed forces:** regulars 3,000 (1980).

Economy: Industries: Textiles, shoes. **Chief crops:** Coffee, cocoa, yams, manioc, millet, rice. **Minerals:** Phosphates. **Per capita arable land:** 2.3 acres. **Electricity prod.** (1978): 67.20 mln. kwh. **Labor force:** 78% agric.; 22% industry.

Finance: Currency: CFA franc (Mar. 1982: 312.10 = $1 US). **Gross domestic product** (1978): $765.5 mln. **Per capita income** (1978): $319. **Imports** (1979): $518 mln.; partners (1978): Fr. 34%, Switz. 10%, U.K 10%, W. Ger. 9%. **Exports** (1979): $219 mln.; partners (1978): Neth. 31%, Fr. 14%, W. Ger. 8%, U.S. 8%. **International reserves less gold** (Jan. 1982): $151.5 mln. **Gold:** 13,000 oz t. **Consumer prices** (change in 1979): 7.5%.

Transport: Railway traffic (1976): 91.2 mln. passenger-km; 37.7 mln. net ton-km. **Motor vehicles:** in use (1974): 13,000 passenger cars, 7,000 comm. vehicles. **Chief ports:** Lome.

Communications: Radios: 52,000 in use (1976). **Telephones in use** (1978): 4,749. **Daily newspaper circ.** (1980): 4 per 1,000 pop.

Health: Life expectancy at birth (1961): 31.6 male; 38.5 female. **Births** (per 1,000 pop. 1978): 45. **Deaths** (per 1,000 pop. 1978): 17. **Natural increase** (1978): 2.9%. **Hospital beds** (per 100,000 pop. 1977): 143. **Physicians** (per 100,000 pop. 1977): 6. **Infant mortality** (per 1,000 live births 1975): 127.

Education (1978): **Literacy:** 18%. **Pop. 5-19:** in school: 55%, teachers per 1,000: 10.

The Ewe arrived in southern Togo several centuries ago. The country later became a major source of slaves. Germany took control from 1884 on. France and Britain administered Togoland as UN trusteeships. The French sector became the republic of Togo Apr. 27, 1960.

The population is divided between Bantus in the S and Hamitic tribes in the N. Togo has actively promoted regional integration, as a means of stimulating the backward economy.

Tonga

Kingdom of Tonga

People: Population (1980 est.): 100,000. **Age distrib.** (%): 0–14: 44.4; 15–59: 50.5; 60+:5.1. **Pop. density:** 370.37 per sq. mi. **Ethnic groups:** Tongans 98%, other Polynesian, European. **Languages:** Tongan, English. **Religions:** Free Wesleyan 47%, Roman Catholics 14%, Free Church of Tonga 14%, Mormons 9%, Church of Tonga 9%.

Geography: Area: 290 sq. mi., smaller than New York City. **Location:** In western S. Pacific O. **Neighbors:** Nearest is Fiji, on W, New Zealand, on S. **Topography:** Tonga comprises 169 volcanic and coral islands, 45 inhabited. **Capital:** Nuku'alofa. **Cities** (1976 cen.): Nuku'alofa (met.) 18,312.

Government: Head of state: King Taufa'ahau Tupou IV; b. July 4, 1918; in office: Dec. 16, 1965. **Head of government:** Prime Min. Fatafehi Tu'ipelehake; b. Jan. 7, 1922; in office: Dec. 16, 1965. **Local divisions:** 3 island districts.

Economy: Industries: Tourism. **Chief crops:** Coconut products, bananas are exported. **Other resources:** Fish. **Per capita arable land:** 0.4 acres. **Electricity prod.** (1977): 7.00 mln. kwh. **Labor force:** 75% agric.

Finance: Currency: Pa'anga (Sept. 1981: .86 = $1 US). **Gross domestic product** (1976 est.): $40 mln. **Per capita income** (1976): $430. **Imports** (1979): $29 mln.; partners (1980): N Z 38%, Austral. 31%, Jap. 6%, Fiji 5%. **Exports** (1979): $7 mln.; partners (1980): Aust. 36%, N Z 34%, U.S. 14%. **Tourists** (1975): 70,000; receipts: $3 mln. **Consumer prices** (change in 1976): 7.1%.

Transport: Motor vehicles: in use (1974): 1,000 passenger cars, 400 comm. vehicles. **Chief ports:** Nuku'alofa.

Communications: Radios: 15,000 in use (1976). **Telephones in use** (1978): 1,285.

Health: Births (per 1,000 pop. 1976): 13.0. **Deaths** (per 1,000 pop. 1976): 1.9. **Natural increase** (1976): 1.1%. **Pop. per hospital bed** (1976): 300. **Pop. per physician** (1976): 3,000. **Infant mortality** (per 1,000 live births 1976): 20.5.

The islands were first visited by the Dutch in the early 17th century. A series of civil wars ended in 1845 with establishment of the Tupou dynasty. In 1900 Tonga became a British protectorate. On June 4, 1970, Tonga became completely independent and a member of the Commonwealth.

Cyclone Isaac caused extensive damage, Mar. 1982.

Trinidad and Tobago

Republic of Trinidad and Tobago

People: Population (1981 est.): 1,200,000. **Age distrib.** (%): 0–14: 38.0; 15–59: 55.4; 60+: 6.6. **Pop. density:** 570.71 per sq. mi. **Urban** (1970): 49.4%. **Ethnic groups:** Negroes 43%, East Indians 40%, mixed 14%. **Languages:** English (official), Hindi, French, Spanish. **Religions:** Roman Catholics 36%, Protestants 30%, Hindus 23%, Muslims 6%.

Geography: Area: 1,980 sq. mi., the size of Delaware. **Location:** Off eastern coast of Venezuela. **Neighbors:** Nearest is Venezuela on SW. **Topography:** Three low mountain ranges cross Trinidad E-W, with a well-watered plain between N and Central Ranges. Parts of E and W coasts are swamps. Tobago, 116 sq. mi., lies 20 mi. NE. **Capital:** Port-of-Spain. **Cities** (1981 est.): Port-of-Spain (met.) 250,000; San Fernando 50,000.

Government: Head of state: Pres. Ellis E. I. Clarke; b. Dec. 28, 1917; in office: July 31, 1976. **Head of government:** Prime Min. George Chambers; b. Oct. 4, 1928; in office: Mar. 30, 1981. **Local divisions:** 8 counties, Tobago, 4 cities.

Economy: Industries: Oil products, rum, cement, tourism. **Chief crops:** Sugar, cocoa, coffee, citrus fruits, bananas. **Minerals:** Asphalt, oil, **Crude oil reserves** (1980): 700 mln. bbls. **Per capita arable land:** 0.1 acres. **Electricity prod.** (1979): 1.8 bln. kwh. **Labor force:** 10% agric., 66% construction, mining, commerce.

Finance: Currency: Dollar (Apr. 1982: 2.40 = $1 US). **Gross domestic product** (1980): $5.03 bln. **Per capita income** (1980): $4,800. **Imports** (1980): $3.16 bln.; partners (1980): Saudi Ar. 31%, U.S. 26%, UK 10%. **Exports** (1980): $3.98 bln.; partners (1980): U.S. 57%, Neth. 6%. **Tourists** (1976): 158,700; receipts: $87 mln. **National budget** (1980): $2.5 bln. revenues; $2.6 bln. expenditures. **International reserves less gold** (Feb. 1982): $3.17 bln. **Gold:** 54,000 oz t. **Consumer prices** (change in 1980): 17.5%.

Transport: Motor vehicles: in use (1979): 131,300 passenger cars, 33,100 comm. vehicles; assembled (1978): 13,752 passenger cars; 2,412 comm. vehicles. **Civil aviation:** (1980): 1.5 bln. passenger-km; 18.3 mln. freight ton-km. **Chief ports:** Port-of-Spain.

Communications: Television sets: 125,000 in use (1977), 12,000 manuf. (1978). **Radios:** 275,000 licensed (1977), 10,000 manuf. (1978). **Telephones in use** (1978): 74,908. **Daily newspaper circ.** (1980): 175 per 1,000 pop.

Health: Life expectancy at birth (1978): 64 male; 68 female. **Births** (per 1,000 pop. 1978): 25.3. **Deaths** (per 1,000 pop. 1978): 6.6. **Natural increase** (1978): 1.9%. **Hospital beds** (per 100,000 pop. 1977): 445. **Physicians** (per 100,000 pop 1977): 54. **Infant mortality** (per 1,000 pop. 1978): 286.

Education (1978): **Literacy:** 92%. **Pop. 5-19:** in school: 48%, teachers per 1,000: 22.

Columbus sighted Trinidad in 1498. A British possession since 1802, Trinidad and Tobago won independence Aug. 31, 1962. It became a republic in 1976. The People's National Movement party has held control of the government since 1956.

The nation is one of the most prosperous in the Caribbean, but unemployment usually averages 13%. Oil production has increased with offshore finds. Middle Eastern oil is refined and exported, mostly to the U.S.

Tunisia

Republic of Tunisia

People: Population (1981 est.): 6,600,000. **Age distrib.** (%) 0–14: 43.3 15–59: 50.9; 60+: 5.8. **Pop. density:** 100.35 per sq. mi. **Ethnic groups:** Arabs, small Berber and European minority. **Languages:** Arabic (official), French. **Religions:** Mainly Muslim, Christian and Jewish minorities.

Geography: Area: 63,378 sq. mi., slightly larger than Florida. **Location:** On N coast of Africa. **Neighbors:** Algeria on W, Libya on E. **Topography:** The N is wooded and fertile. The central coastal plains are given to grazing and orchards. The S is arid, approaching Sahara Desert. **Capital:** Tunis. **Cities** (1982 est.) Tunis 1,000,000, Sfax 475,000.

Government: Head of state: Pres. Habib Bourguiba; b. Aug. 3, 1903; in office: July 25, 1957. **Head of government:** Prime Min. Mohammed Mzali; b. Dec. 23, 1925; in office: Apr. 23, 1980. **Local divisions:** 21 governorates. **Armed forces:** regulars 28,600 (1980).

Economy: Industries: Food processing, textiles, oil products, construction materials, tourism. **Chief crops:** Grains, dates, olives, citrus fruits, figs, vegetables, grapes. **Minerals:** Phosphates, iron, oil, lead, zinc. **Crude oil reserves** (1980): 2.25 bln. bbls. **Per capita arable land:** 1.3 acres. **Meat prod.** (1980): beef: 26,000 metric tons; lamb: 27,000 metric tons. **Fish catch** (1978): 54,600 metric tons. **Electricity prod.** (1980): 2.4 bln. kwh. **Crude steel prod.** (1981 est.): 180,000 metric tons. **Labor force:** 35% agric.; 22% industry; 11% serv.

Finance: Currency: Dinar (Mar. 1982: 1.70 = $1 US). **Gross domestic product** (1980): $6.8 bln. **Per capita income** (1981) $1,200. **Imports** (1981): $3.99 bln.; partners (1979): Fr. 26%, W. Ger. 10%, It. 13%. **Exports** (1980): $2.20 bln.; partners (1979): It. 20%, Fr. 19%, W. Ger. 10%, Gr. 16%. **Tourists** (1979): 1.3 mln.; receipts: $525 mln. **National budget** (1980): $1.54 bln. revenues; $1.50 bln. expenditures. **International reserves less gold** (Feb. 1982): $570.3 mln. **Gold:** 187,000 oz t. **Consumer prices** (change in 1981): 8.9%.

Transport: Railway traffic (1980): 862 mln. passenger-km; 1.7 bln. net ton-km. **Motor vehicles:** in use (1979): 120,000 passenger cars, 97,000 comm. vehicles; assembled (1978): 2,124 passenger cars; 4,848 comm. vehicles. **Civil aviation:** (1980): 1.2 bln. passenger-km; 12.5 mln. freight ton-km. **Chief ports:** Tunis, Sfax, Bizerte.

Communications: Television sets: 255,000 in use (1979), 69,000 manuf. (1978). Radios: 1 mln. in use (1979), 59,000 manuf. (1978). **Telephones in use** (1980): 175,000. **Daily newspaper circ.** (1980): 22 per 1,000 pop.

Health: Life expectancy at birth (1975): 54.0 male; 56.0 female. **Births** (per 1,000 pop. 1978): 34.1. **Deaths** (per 1,000 pop. 1975): 12.5. **Natural increase** (1975): 2.4%. **Hospital beds** (per 100,000 pop. 1977): 229. **Physicians** (per 100,000 pop. 1977): 4. **Infant mortality** (per 1,000 pop. under 1 yr. 1982): 90.

Education (1978): **Literacy:** 45%. **Pop. 5-19:** in school: 50%, teachers per 1,000: 16.

Site of ancient Carthage, and a former Barbary state under the suzerainty of Turkey, Tunisia became a protectorate of France under a treaty signed May 12, 1881. The nation became independent Mar. 20, 1956, and ended the monarchy the following year. Habib Bourguiba has headed the country since independence.

Although Tunisia is a member of the Arab League, Bourguiba in the 1960s urged negotiations to end Arab-Israeli disputes and was denounced by other members. In 1966 he broke relations with Egypt but resumed them after the 1967 Arab-Israeli war. He again urged negotiations with Israel in June 1973.

Dozens were killed in rioting and labor violence in 1978, protesting wage curbs.

Tunisia survived a Libyan-engineered raid against the southern mining center of Gafsa, Jan. 1980. A liberal-minded government undertook steps to ease the blocked political situation.

Turkey

Republic of Turkey

People: Population (1981 est.): 46,800,000. **Age distrib.** (%): 0–14: 40.0; 15–59: 52.6; 60+: 7.2. **Pop. density:** 150.50 per sq. mi. **Urban** (1977): 44.6%. **Ethnic groups:** Turks 90%, Kurds 7%, Arabs 1.2%, Circassians, Greeks, Armenians, Georgians, Jews. **Languages:** Turkish (official), Kurdish, Arabic. **Religions:** Muslims 98%, Christians, Jews.

Geography: Area: 300,948 sq. mi., twice the size of California. **Location:** Occupies Asia Minor, between Mediterranean and Black Seas. **Neighbors:** Bulgaria, Greece on W, USSR (Georgia, Armenia) on N, Iran on E, Iraq, Syria on S. **Topography:** Central Turkey has wide plateaus, with hot, dry summers and cold winters. High mountains ring the interior on all but W, with more than 20 peaks over 10,000 ft. Rolling plains are in W; mild, fertile coastal plains are in S, W. **Capital:** Ankara. **Cities** (1979 est.): Istanbul 3,900,000; Ankara 2,600,000; Izmir 1,700,000; Adana 1,000,000.

Government: Head of state: Pres. Kenan Evren; in office: Oct. 27, 1980. **Head of government:** Prime Min. Bulent Ulusu;

in office: Sept. 20, 1980. **Local divisions:** 67 provinces, with appointed governors. **Armed forces:** regulars 567,000 (1980).

Economy: Industries: Silk, textiles, steel, shoes, furniture, cement, paper, glassware, appliances. **Chief crops:** Tobacco (6th largest producer), cereals, cotton, olives, figs, nuts, sugar, opium gums. **Minerals:** Antimony, chromium, mercury, borate, copper, molybdenum, magnesite, asbestos. **Crude oil reserves** (1980): 125 mln. bbls. **Other resources:** Wool, silk, forests. **Per capita arable land:** 1.4 acres. **Meat prod.** (1980): beef: 286,000 metric tons; lamb: 405,000 metric tons. **Fish catch** (1978): 155,300 metric tons. **Electricity prod.** (1980): 23.2 bln. kwh. **Crude steel prod.** (1981): 2.4 mln. metric tons. **Labor force:** 55.8% agric.; 17.2% ind. and commerce; 17% serv.; 10% govt.

Finance: Currency: Lira (Mar. 1982: 148.01 = $1 US). **Gross domestic product** (1980): $50.63 bln. **Per capita income** (1978 est.): $1,140 **Imports** (1981): $8.9 bln.; partners (1980): Iraq 14%, W. Ger. 16%, Libya 7%, Fr. 5%, U.S. 6%, **Exports** (1981): $4.69 bln.; partners (1980): W. Ger. 21%, It. 8%, Fr. 6%. **Tourists** (1979): 1.5 mln.; receipts: $281 mln. **National budget** (1981): $5.88 bln. revenues; $6.30 bln. expenditures. **International reserves less gold** (Jan. 1982): $1.28 bln. **Gold:** 3.77 mln. oz t. **Consumer prices** (change in 1981): 36.6%.

Transport: Railway traffic (1980): 6.01 bln. passenger-km; 5.03 bln. net ton-km. **Motor vehicles:** in use (1979): 658,700 passenger cars, 309,800 comm. vehicles; assembled (1978): 54,120 passenger cars; 35,784 comm. vehicles. **Civil aviation** (1980): 1.1 bln. passenger-km; 13.7 mln. freight ton-km. **Chief ports:** Istanbul, Izmir, Mersin, Samsun.

Communications: Television sets: 3.1 mln. in use (1979), 684,000 manuf. (1977). **Radios:** 4.2 mln. licensed (1979), 324,000 manuf. (1977). **Telephones in use** (1979): 1.08 mln.

Health: Life expectancy at birth (1966): 53.7 male; 53.7 female. **Births** (per 1,000 pop. 1978): 35. **Deaths** (per 1,000 pop. 1978): 12. **Natural increase** (1978): 2.4%. **Hospital beds** (per 100,000 pop.1977): 195. **Physicians** (per 100,000 pop. 1977): 56. **Infant mortality** (per 1,000 pop. under 1 yr. 1967): 153.

Education (1978): **Literacy:** 60%. **Pop. 5-19:** in school: 48%, teachers per 1,000: 15.

Ancient inhabitants of Turkey were among the worlds first agriculturalists. Such civilizations as the Hittite, Phrygian, and Lydian flourished in Asiatic Turkey (Asia Minor), as did much of Greek civilization. After the fall of Rome in the 5th century, Constantinople was the capital of the Byzantine Empire for 1,000 years. It fell in 1453 to Ottoman Turks, who ruled a vast empire for over 400 years.

Just before World War I, Turkey, or the Ottoman Empire, ruled what is now Syria, Lebanon, Iraq, Jordan, Israel, Saudi Arabia, Yemen, and islands in the Aegean Sea.

Turkey joined Germany and Austria in World War I and its defeat resulted in loss of much territory and fall of the sultanate. A republic was declared Oct. 29, 1923. The Caliphate (spiritual leadership of Islam) was renounced 1924.

Long embroiled with Greece over Cyprus, off Turkey's south coast, Turkey invaded the island July 20, 1974, after Greek officers seized the Cypriot government as a step toward unification with Greece. Turkey sought a new government for Cyprus, with Greek Cypriot and Turkish Cypriot zones. In reaction to Turkey's moves, the U.S. Congress cut off military aid in 1975. Turkey, in turn, suspended the use of most U.S. bases. A new base accord was tentatively reached in March, 1976 and aid was restored in 1978. Turkey and the USSR signed a nonaggression pact in 1978.

In June, 1971, Turkey agreed to stop all opium poppy production, in return for $37.5 million in economic aid from the U.S. In 1974 it announced it would resume opium production, with U.S. and U.N. controls, for medical use only.

Religious and ethnic tensions and active left and right extremists have caused endemic violence. Martial law was in effect from 1979, in approx. one-third of the nation's provinces and over 100,000 people have been arrested. General elections are scheduled to be held in 1984.

Tuvalu

People: Population (1979 est.): 7,400. **Pop. density:** 700 per sq. mi. **Ethnic group:** Polynesian. **Languages:** Tuvaluan, English. **Religions:** mainly Protestant.

Geography: Area: 10 sq. mi., less than one-half the size of Manhattan. **Location:** 9 islands forming a NW-SE chain 360 mi. long in the SW Pacific O. **Neighbors:** Nearest are Samoa on SE, Fiji on S. **Topography:** The islands are all low-lying atolls, nowhere rising more than 15 ft. above sea level, composed of coral reefs. **Capital:** Funafuti (pop. 1979): 2,200.

Government: Head of state: Queen Elizabeth II, represented by Gov.-Gen. Penitala Fiatau Teo, b. July 23, 1911; in office: Oct. 1, 1978. **Head of government:** Prime Min. Tomasi Puapua; in office: Sept. 8, 1981. **Local divisions:** 8 island councils on the permanently inhabited islands.

Economy: Industries: Copra. **Chief crops:** Coconuts. **Labor force:** Approx. 1,500 Tuvaluans work overseas in the Gilberts' phosphate industry, or as overseas seamen.

Finance: Currency: Australian dollar. **Imports** (1979): $1.83 mln. **Exports** (1979): $276,047; partners: UK.

Transport: Chief port: Funafuti.

Health: (including former Gilbert Is.) **Life expectancy at birth** (1962): 56.9 male; 59.0 female. **Births** (per 1,000 pop. 1971): 22.3. **Deaths** (per 1,000 pop. 1971): 6.5. **Natural increase** (1971): 1.6%. **Infant mortality** (per 1,000 pop. under 1 yr. 1971) : 48.9.

Education: Pop. 5–19: in school (1976): 1,794.

The Ellice Islands separated from the British Gilbert and Ellice Islands colony, 1975, and became independent Tuvalu Oct. 1, 1978. Under a Treaty of Friendship, pending ratification by the U.S. Senate, the U.S. relinquishes its claims to Funafuti, Nukufetau, Nukulailai (Nukulaelae), and Nurakita (Niulakita).

The only cash crop, copra, was devastated by hurricane damage, 1972. Britain is committed to providing extensive economic aid. Australian funding has provided for a marine training school and a deep-sea wharf.

Uganda

Republic of Uganda

People: Population (1981 est.): 14,100,000. **Age distrib.** (%): 0–14: 46.1; 15–59: 47.9; 60+: 5.8. **Pop. density:** 140.23 per sq. mi. **Urban** (1972): 7.1%. **Ethnic groups:** Bantu, Nilotic, Nilo-Hamitic, Sudanic tribes. **Languages:** English (official), Bantu, Nilotic, Nilo-Hamitic. **Religions:** Christians 63%, Moslems 6%, traditional beliefs.

Geography: Area: 91,104 sq. mi., slightly smaller than Oregon. **Location:** In E. Central Africa. **Neighbors:** Sudan on N, Zaire on W, Rwanda, Tanzania on S, Kenya on E. **Topography:** Most of Uganda is a high plateau 3,000-6,000 ft. high, with high Ruwenzori range in W (Mt. Margherita 16,750 ft.), volcanoes in SW, NE is arid, W and SW rainy. Lakes Victoria, Edward, Albert form much of borders. **Capital:** Kampala. **Cities** (1975): Kampala (met.) 332,000.

Government: Head of state: Pres. Milton Obote; assumed full control Sept. 17, 1980; elections held Dec. 1980. **Head of government:** Prime Min. Erifasi Otema Allimadi; in office: Dec. 1980. **Local divisions:** 10 provinces, 34 districts. **Armed forces:** regulars 21,000 (1980).

Economy: Chief Crops: Coffee, cotton, tea, corn, peanuts, bananas, sugar. **Minerals:** Copper, cobalt. **Per capita arable land:** 0.7 acres. **Meat prod.** (1980): beef: 92,000 metric tons; lamb: 13,000 metric tons. **Fish catch** (1979): 223,800 metric tons. **Electricity prod.** (1979): 630 mln. kwh. **Labor force:** 90% agric.

Finance: Currency: Shilling (Mar. 1982: 85.75 = $1 US). **Gross domestic product** (1978): $8.36 bln. **Per capita income** (1976): $240. **Imports** (1978): $255 mln.; partners: (1979): Kenya 28%, UK 17%, W. Ger. 13%, Jap. 8%, It. 7%. **Exports** (1979): $426 mln.; partners (1978): U.S. 21%, UK 16%, Fr. 10%, Jap. 9%. **Tourists** (1974): 10,300; receipts (1977): $1 mln. **National budget** (1981): $641 mln. revenues; $871 mln. expenditures. **International reserves less gold** (Apr. 1981): $45.3 mln. **Consumer prices** (change in 1978): 36.5%.

Transport: Motor vehicles: in use (1979): 26,000 passenger cars, 5,400 comm. vehicles.

Communications: Television sets: 81,000 in use (1977). **Radios:** 250,000 in use (1977). **Telephones in use** (1980): 46,400. **Daily newspaper circ.** (1980): 2 per 1,000 pop.

Health: Life expectancy at birth (1975): 48.3 male; 51.7 female. **Births** (per 1,000 pop. 1978): 48. **Deaths** (per 1,000 pop. 1978): 17. **Natural increase** (1978): 3.2%. **Hospital beds** (per 100,000 pop. 1977): 157. **Physicians** (per 100,000 pop. 1977):

20. **Infant mortality** (per 1,000 live births (1981): 120.

Education (1978): **Literacy:** 25%. **Pop. 5-19:** in school: 27%, teachers per 1,000: 8.

Britain obtained a protectorate over Uganda in 1894. The country became independent Oct. 9, 1962, and a republic within the Commonwealth a year later. In 1967, the traditional kingdoms, including the powerful Buganda state, were abolished and the central government strengthened.

Gen. Idi Amin seized power from Prime Min. Milton Obote in 1971. As many as 300,000 of his opponents were reported killed in subsequent years. Amin was named president for life in 1976.

In 1972 Amin expelled nearly all of Uganda's 45,000 Asians. In 1973 the U.S., Canada, and Norway ended economic aid programs; the U.S. withdrew all diplomatic personnel.

A June 1977 Commonwealth conference condemned the Amin government for its "disregard for the sanctity of human life."

Amid worsening economic and domestic crises, Uganda's troops exchanged invasion attacks with long-standing foe Tanzania, 1978 to 1979. Tanzanian forces, coupled with Ugandan exiles and rebels, ended the dictatorial rule of Amin, Apr. 11, 1979.

The U.S. reopened its embassy, reinstated economic aid, and ended its trade embargo in 1979.

Four governments have been in power since Amin fled. The country remains in utter economic and social chaos, and signs of repression, reminiscent of the Amin regime, have begun to reappear.

Union of Soviet Socialist Republics

People: Population (1982 est.): 268,800,000. **Age distrib.** (%): 0–19: 36.7; 20-59: 50.5; 60+: 12.7. **Pop. density:** 31 per sq. mi. **Urban** (1979): 62%. **Ethnic groups:** Russians 52% Ukrainians 16%, Uzbeks 5%, Byelorussians 4%, many others. **Languages:** Slavic (Russian, Ukrainian, Byelorussian, Polish), Altaic (Turkish, etc.), other Indo-European, Uralian, Caucasian. **Religions:** Russian Orthodox 18%, Moslems 9%, other Orthodox, Protestants, Jews, Buddhists.

Geography: Area: 8,649,490 sq. mi., the largest country in the world, nearly 2½ times the size of the U.S. **Location:** Stretches from E. Europe across N Asia to the Pacific O. **Neighbors:** Finland, Poland, Czechoslovakia, Hungary, Romania on W, Turkey, Iran, Afghanistan, China, Mongolia, N. Korea on S. **Topography:** Covering one-sixth of the earth's land area, the USSR contains every type of climate except the distinctly tropical, and has a varied topography.

The European portion is a low plain, grassy in S, wooded in N with Ural Mtns. on the E. Caucasus Mts. on the S. Urals stretch N-S for 2,500 mi. The Asiatic portion is also a vast plain, with mountains on the S and in the E; tundra covers extreme N, with forest belt below; plains, marshes are in W, desert in SW. **Capital:** Moscow. **Cities** (1980): Moscow 8 mln.; Leningrad 4.6 mln.; Kiev 2.1 mln.; Tashkent 1.8 mln.; Kharkov 1.4 mln.; Gorky 1.3 mln.; Novosibirsk 1.3 mln.; Minsk 1.2 mln.; Kuibyshev 1.2 mln.; Sverdlovsk 1.2 mln.

Government: Head of state: Pres. Leonid I. Brezhnev; b. Dec. 19, 1906; in office: June 16, 1977. **Head of government:** Premier Nikolai A. Tikhonov; b. May 1, 1905; in office: Oct. 23, 1980. **Head of Communist Party:** Gen. Sec. Leonid Brezhnev; in office: Oct. 14, 1964. **Local divisions:** 15 union republics, within which are 20 autonomous republics, 6 krays (territories), 120 oblasts (regions), 8 autonomous oblasts, 10 national areas. **Armed forces:** regulars 2.7 mln. (1980).

Economy: Industries: Steel, machinery, machine tools, vehicles, chemicals, cement, textiles, appliances, paper. **Chief crops:** Grain, cotton, sugar beets, potatoes, vegetables, sunflowers. **Minerals:** Iron (41% of world reserves), manganese (88%), mercury, potash, antimony, bauxite, cobalt, chromium, copper, coal (58%), gold, lead, molybdenum, nickel, phosphates (30%), silver, tin, tungsten, zinc, oil (59%), potassium salts (54%). **Crude oil reserves** (1980): 67.00 bln. bbls. **Other resources:** Forests (25% of world reserves). **Per capita arable land:** 2.1 acres. **Meat prod.** (1980): beef: 6.7 mln. metric tons; pork; 5.0 mln. metric tons; lamb: 853,000 metric tons. **Fish catch** (1979): 9.1 mln. metric tons. **Electricity prod.** (1980): 1,295 bln. kwh. **Crude steel prod.** (1981 est.): 149.0 mln. metric tons. **Labor force:** 20% agric.; 29% industry, 21% services.

Finance: Currency: Ruble (Sept. 1981: .71 = $1 US). **Gross national product** (1980): $1.5 tln. **Per capita income** (1976): $2,600. **Imports** (1980): $59.19 bln.; partners (1980): E. Ger. 10%, Pol. 8%, Czech. 8%, Bulg. 8%. **Exports** (1980): $66.29 bln.; partners (1980): E. Ger. 10%, Pol. 9%, Bulg. 8%, Czech. 7%. **National budget** (1981 est).: $381 bln. revenues; $381 bln. expenditures. **Tourists** (1977): 4,399,800. **Consumer prices** (change in 1979): 0.7%.

Transport: Railway traffic (1979): 335.3 bln. passenger-km; 3,349 bln. net ton-km. **Motor vehicles:** in use (1979): 8.2 mln. passenger cars, 7.2 mln. comm. vehicles; manuf. (1980): 1.3 mln. passenger cars; 780,000 comm. vehicles. **Civil aviation** (1980): 160 bln. passenger-km; 3.083 mln. freight ton-km. **Chief ports:** Leningrad, Odessa, Murmansk, Kaliningrad, Archangelsk, Riga, Vladivostock.

Communications: Television sets: 60 mln. in use (1979), 7.6 mln. manuf. (1978). **Radios:** 122.5 mln. in use (1975), 8.7 mln. manuf. (1978). **Telephones in use** (1980): 22.4 mln. **Daily newspaper circ.** (1980): 396 per 1,000 pop.

Health: Life expectancy at birth (1972): 64 male; 74 female. **Births** (per 1,000 pop. 1977): 18.1. **Deaths** (per 1,000 pop. 1976): 9.6. **Natural increase** (1976): .9%. **Hospital beds** (per 100,000 pop. 1977): 1,213. **Physicians** (per 100,000 pop. 1977): 346. **Infant mortality** (per 1,000 live births 1981): 44.

Education (1981): **Literacy:** 99%. **5-19:** in school: 90%, teachers per 1,000: 37.

The USSR is nominally a federation consisting of 15 union republics, the largest being the Russian Soviet Federated Socialist Republic. Important positions in the republics are filled by centrally chosen appointees, often ethnic Russians.

Beginning in 1939 the USSR by means of military action and negotiation overran contiguous territory and independent republics, including all or part of Lithuania, Latvia, Estonia, Poland, Czechoslovakia, Romania, Germany, Tannu Tuva, and Japan. The union republics are:

Republic	Area sq. mi.	Pop. (cen. 1979)
Russian SFSR	6,593,391	137,552,000
Ukrainian SSR	232,046	49,757,000
Uzbek SSR	158,069	15,391,000
Kazakh SSR	1,064,092	14,685,000
Byelorussian SSR	80,154	9,559,000
Azerbaijan SSR	33,436	6,028,000
Georgian SSR	26,911	5,016,000
Moldavian SSR	13,012	3,948,000
Tadzhik SSR	54,019	3,801,000
Kirghiz SSR	76,642	3,529,000
Lithuanian SSR	26,173	3,399,000
Armenian SSR	11,306	3,031,000
Turkmen SSR	188,417	2,759,000
Latvian SSR	24,695	2,521,000
Estonian SSR	17,413	1,466,000

The **Russian Soviet Federated Socialist Republic** contains over 50% of the population of the USSR and includes 76% of its territory. It extends from the old Estonian, Latvian, and Finnish borders and the Byelorussian and Ukrainian lines on the W, to the shores of the Pacific, and from the Arctic on the N to the Black and Caspian seas and the borders of Kazakh SSR, Mongolia, and Manchuria on the S. Siberia encompasses a large part of the RSFSR area. Capital: Moscow.

Parts of eastern and western Siberia have been transformed by steel mills, huge dams, oil and gas industries, electric railroads, and highways.

The **Ukraine,** the most densely populated of the republics, borders on the Black Sea, with Poland, Czechoslovakia, Hungary, and Romania on the W and SW. Capital: Kiev.

The Ukraine contains the arable black soil belt, the chief wheat-producing section of the Soviet Union. Sugar beets, potatoes, and livestock are important.

The Donets Basin has large deposits of coal, iron and other metals. There are chemical and machine industries and salt mines.

Byelorussia (White Russia). Capital: Minsk. Chief industries include machinery, tools, appliances, tractors, clocks, cameras, steel, cement, textiles, paper, leather, glass. Main crops are grain, flax, potatoes, sugar beets.

Azerbaijan boasts near Baku, the capital, important oil fields. Its natural wealth includes deposits of iron ore, cobalt, etc. A high-yield winter wheat is grown, as are fruits. It produces iron, steel, cement, fertilizers, synthetic rubber, electrical and chemical equipment. It borders on Iran and Turkey.

Georgia, in the western part of Transcaucasia, contains the largest manganese mines in the world. There are rich timber resources and coal mines. Basic industries are food, textiles, iron, steel. Grain, tea, tobacco, fruits, grapes are grown. Capital: Tbilisi (Tiflis). Despite massive party and government purges since 1972, illegal private enterprise and Georgian nationalist feelings persist; attempts to repress them have led to violence.

Armenia is mountainous, sub-tropical, extensively irrigated. Copper, zinc, aluminum, molybdenum, and marble are mined. Instrument making is important. Capital: Erevan.

Uzbekistan, most important economically of the Central Asia republics, produces 67% of USSR cotton, 50% of rice, 33% of silk, 34% of astrakhan, 85% of hemp. Industries include iron, steel, cars, tractors, TV and radio sets, textiles, food. Mineral wealth includes coal, sulphur, copper, and oil. Capital: Tashkent.

Turkmenistan in Central Asia, produces cotton, maize, carpets, chemicals. Minerals: oil, coal, sulphur, barite, lime, salt, gypsum. The Kara Kum desert occupies 80% of the area. Capital: Ashkhabad.

Tadzhikistan borders on China and Afghanistan. Over half the population are Tadzhiks, mostly Moslems, speaking an Iranian dialect. Chief occupations are farming and cattle breeding. Cotton, grain, rice, and a variety of fruits are grown. Heavy industry, based on rich mineral deposits, coal and hydroelectric power, has replaced handicrafts. Capital: Dushanbe.

Kazakhstan extends from the lower reaches of the Volga in Europe to the Altai Mtns. on the Chinese border. It has vast deposits of coal, oil, iron, tin, copper, lead, zinc, etc. Fish for its canning industry are caught in Lake Balkhash and the Caspian and Aral seas. The capital is Alma-Ata. About 50% of the population is Russian or Ukrainian, working in the virgin-grain lands opened up after 1954, and in the growing industries. Capital: Alma-Ata.

Kirghizia is the eastern part of Soviet Central Asia, on the frontier of Xinjiang, China. The people breed cattle and horses and grow tobacco, cotton, rice, sugar beets. Industries include machine and instrument making, chemicals. Capital: Frunze.

Moldavia, in the SW part of the USSR, is a fertile black earth plain bordering Romania and includes Bessarabia. It is an agricultural region that grows grains, fruits, vegetables, and tobacco. Textiles, wine, food and electrical equipment industries have been developed. Capital: Kishinev. The region was taken from Romania in 1940; the people speak Romanian.

Lithuania, on the Baltic, produces cattle, hogs, electric motors, and appliances. The capital is Vilnius (Vilna). **Latvia** on the Baltic and the Gulf of Riga, has timber and peat resources est. at 3 bln. tons. In addition to agricultural products it produces rubber goods, dyes, fertilizers, glassware, telephone apparatus, TV and radio sets, railroad cars. Capital: Riga.

Estonia, also on the Baltic, has textiles, shipbuilding, timber, roadmaking and mining equipment industries and a shale oil refining industry. Capital: Tallinn. The 3 Baltic states were provinces of imperial Russia before World War I, were independent nations between World Wars I and II, but were conquered by Russia in 1940. The U.S. has never formally recognized the takeover.

Economy. Almost all legal economic enterprises are state-owned. There were 29,600 collective farms in 1976, along with 18,064 larger state farms. A huge illegal black market plays an important role in distribution; illegal private production and service firms are periodically exposed.

The USSR is incalculably rich in natural resources; distant Siberian reserves are being exploited with Japanese assistance. Its heavy industry is 2d only to the U.S. It leads the world in oil and steel production. Consumer industries have lagged comparatively. Agricultural output has expanded, but in poor crop years the USSR has been forced to make huge grain purchases from the West. Shortages and rationing of basic food products periodically occur.

Exports include petroleum and its products, iron and steel, rolled non-ferrous metals, industrial plant equipment, arms, lumber, cotton, asbestos, gold, manganese, and others. 55% of its trade is with Communist nations, 33% with the West, which supplies advanced technology.

Industrial growth has dropped, due to short falls in oil, coal, and steel industries, as well as poor grain harvests since 1979.

History. Slavic tribes began migrating into Russia from the W in the 5th century AD. The first Russian state, founded by Scandinavian chieftains, was established in the 9th century, centering in Novgorod and Kiev.

In the 13th century the Mongols overran the country. It recovered under the grand dukes and princes of Muscovy, or Moscow, and by 1480 freed itself from the Mongols. Ivan the Terrible was the first to be formally proclaimed Tsar (1547). Peter the Great (1682-1725), extended the domain and in 1721, founded the Russian Empire.

Western ideas and the beginnings of modernization spread through the huge Russian empire in the 19th and early 20th centuries. But political evolution failed to keep pace.

Military reverses in the 1905 war with Japan and in World War I led to the breakdown of the Tsarist regime. The 1917 Revolution began in March with a series of sporadic strikes for higher wages by factory workers. A provisional democratic government under Prince Georgi Lvov was established but was quickly followed in May by the second provisional government, led by Alexander Kerensky. The Kerensky government and the freely-elected Constituent Assembly were overthrown in a Communist coup led by Vladimir Ilyich Lenin Nov. 7.

Lenin's death Jan. 21, 1924, resulted in an internal power struggle from which Joseph Stalin eventually emerged the absolute ruler of Russia. Stalin secured his position at first by exiling opponents, but from the 1930s to 1953, he resorted to a series of "purge" trials, mass executions, and mass exiles to work camps. These measures resulted in millions of deaths, according to most estimates.

Germany and the USSR signed a non-aggression pact Aug. 1939; Nazi forces launched a massive invasion of the Soviet Union, June 1941. Notable heroic episode was the "900 days" siege of Leningrad, lasting to Jan. 1944, and causing 1,000,000 deaths; the city was never taken. Russian winter counterthrusts, 1941 to '42 and 1942 to '43, stopped the German advance. Turning point was the failure of German troops to take and hold Stalingrad, Sept. 1942 to Feb. 1943. With British and U.S. Lend-Lease aid and sustaining great casualties, the Russians drove the Axis from eastern Europe and the Balkans in the next 2 years.

After Stalin died, Mar. 5, 1953, Nikita Khrushchev was elected first secretary of the Central Committee. In 1956 he condemned Stalin. "De-Stalinization" of the country on all levels was effected after Stalin's body was removed from the Lenin-Stalin tomb in Moscow.

Under Khrushchev the open antagonism of Poles and Hungarians toward domination by Moscow was brutally suppressed in 1956. He advocated peaceful co-existence with the capitalist countries, but continued arming the USSR with nuclear weapons. He aided the Cuban revolution under Fidel Castro but withdrew Soviet missiles from Cuba during confrontation by U.S. Pres. Kennedy, Sept.-Oct. 1962.

The USSR, the U.S., and Great Britain initialed a joint treaty July 25, 1963, banning above-ground nuclear tests.

Khrushchev was suddenly deposed, Oct. 1964, and replaced as party first secretary by Leonid I. Brezhnev, and as premier by Aleksei N. Kosygin.

In Aug. 1968 Russian, Polish, East German, Hungarian, and Bulgarian military forces invaded Czechoslovakia to put a curb on liberalization policies of the Czech government. The USSR declared it had a duty to intervene in nations where socialism was "imperiled" according to the "Brezhnev Doctrine."

The USSR in 1971 continued heavy arms shipments to Egypt. In July 1972 Egypt ordered most of the 20,000 Soviet military personnel in that country to leave. When Egypt and Syria attacked Israel in Oct. 1973, the USSR launched huge arms airlifts to the 2 Arab nations. In 1974, the Soviet replenished the arms used or lost by the Syrians in the 1973 war, and continued some shipments to Egypt.

Massive Soviet military aid to North Vietnam in the late 1960s and early 1970s helped assure Communist victories throughout Indo-China. Soviet arms aid and advisers were sent to several African countries in the 1970s, including Algeria, Angola, Somalia, and Ethiopia.

In 1972, the U.S. and USSR reached temporary agreements to freeze intercontinental missiles at their current levels, to limit defensive missiles to 200 each and to cooperate on health, environment, space, trade, and science.

Meanwhile, under Brezhnev, dissident intellectuals were repressed and purge-type trials resumed.

A limitation on grain sales, imposed by Pres. Carter, Jan. 4, 1980, in response to the Soviet invasion of Afghanistan, was lifted, Apr. 24, 1981, by the Reagan administration. The Afghan invasion continued to go badly in 1981 and 1982, with mounting Soviet casualties.

More than 130,000 Jews and over 40,000 ethnic Germans were allowed to emigrate from the USSR in the 1970s, following pressure from the West. Many leading figures in the arts also left the country.

The U.S. accused the Soviet Union of responsibility for the repression in Poland and imposed sanctions, December 1981. The Soviets were embarrassed when one of their submarines ran aground in Swedish territorial waters in October.

Government. The Communist Party leadership dominates all areas of national life. A Politburo of 14 full members and 8 candidate members makes all major political, economic, and foreign policy decisions. Party membership in 1978 was reported to be over 16,000,000.

United Arab Emirates

People: Population (1981 est.): 980,000. **Pop. density:** 28.13 per sq. mi. **Ethnic groups:** Arabs 42%, Iranians, Pakistanis and Indians 50%. **Languages:** Arabic (official), Persian, English, Hindi, Urdu. **Religions:** Moslems 96.7%, Christians 1.3%.

Geography: Area: 30,000 sq. mi., the size of Maine. **Location:** On the S shore of the Persian Gulf. **Neighbors:** Qatar on N, Saudi Ar. on W, S, Oman on E. **Topography:** A barren, flat coastal plain gives way to uninhabited sand dunes on the S. Hajar Mtns. are on E. **Capital:** Abu Dhabi. **Cities** (1979 est.): Abu Dhabi 300,000.

Government: Head of state: Pres. Zaid ibn Sultan an-Nahayan b. 1923; in office: Dec. 2, 1971. **Head of government:** Prime Min. Rashid ibn Said al-Maktum; in office: June 25, 1979. **Local divisions:** 7 autonomous emirates: Abu Dhabi, Ajman, Dubai, Fujaira, Ras al-Khaimah, Sharjah, Umm al-Qaiwain. **Armed forces:** regulars 25,000 (1980).

Economy: Chief crops: Vegetables, dates, limes. **Minerals:** Oil. **Crude oil reserves** (1980): 29.4 bln. bbls. **Per capita arable land:** 0.02 acres. **Fish catch** (1978): 64,400 metric tons. **Labor force:** 5% agric. 85% ind. and commerce; 5% serv.; 5% gvt.

Finance: Currency: Dirham (Apr. 1982: 3.67 = $1 US). **Gross domestic product** (1979): $9.43 bln. **Per capita income** (1979 est.) $16,000. **Imports** (1980): $16 bln.; partners (1979): Jap. 17%, UK 16%, U.S. 13%, W. Ger. 8%. **Exports** (1980): $20.69 bln.; partners (1979): Jap. 24%, U.S. 14%, Fr. 8%. **International reserves less gold** (Feb. 1982): $3.11 bln. **Gold:** 817,000 oz t.

Transport: Chief ports: Dubai, Abu Dhabi.

Communications: Radios: 55,000 in use (1975). **Telephones in use** (1978): 96,847. **Daily newspaper circ.,** (1977): 2,000, 8 per 1,000 pop.

Health: Hospital beds (per 100,000 pop. 1977): 228. **Physicians** (per 100,000 pop. 1977): 130.

Education (1978): **Literacy:** 21%. **Pop. 5-19:** in school: 36%, teachers per 1,000: 24.

The 7 "Trucial Sheikdoms" gave Britain control of defense and foreign relations in the 19th century. They merged to become an independent state Dec. 2, 1971.

The Abu Dhabi Petroleum Co. was fully nationalized in 1975. Oil revenues have given the UAE one of the highest per capita GNPs in the world. International banking has grown in recent years.

United Kingdom of Great Britain and Northern Ireland

People: Population (1981 est.): 55,901,000. **Age distrib.** (%): 0–4: 22.9; 15–59: 57.4; 60+: 19.7. **Pop. density:** 592.48 per sq. mi. **Urban** (1973): Eng. & Wales: 77.7%, N. Ire.: 54.7%, Scot. (1974): 70.0%. **Ethnic groups:** English 81.5%, Scottish 9.6%, Irish 2.4, Welsh 1.9%, Ulster 1.8%; West Indian, Indian, Pakistani over 2%; others. **Languages:** English, Welsh spoken in western Wales; Gaelic. **Religions:** Mainly Church of England with Roman Catholic, Muslim, and Jewish minorities.

Geography: Area: 94,222 sq. mi., slightly smaller than Oregon. **Location:** Off the NW coast of Europe, across English Channel, Strait of Dover, and North Sea. **Neighbors:** Ireland to W, France to SE. **Topography:** England is mostly rolling land, rising to Uplands of southern Scotland; Lowlands are in center of Scotland, granite Highlands are in N. Coast is heavily indented, especially on W. British Isles have milder climate than N Europe, due to the Gulf Stream, and ample rainfall. Severn, 220 mi., and Thames, 215 mi., are longest rivers. **Capital:** London. **Cities** (1978 est.): London 7,028,200; Birmingham 1,058,800; Glasgow 832,097; Leeds 744,500; Sheffield 588,000; Liverpool 539,700; Manchester 490,000; Edinburgh 463,923; Bradford 458,900; Bristol 416,300; Belfast 357,600.

Government: Head of state: Queen Elizabeth II; b. Apr. 21, 1926; in office: Feb. 6, 1952. **Head of government:** Prime Min. Margaret Thatcher; b. Oct. 13, 1925; in office: May 4, 1979. **Local divisions:** England and Wales: 47 non-metro counties, 6 metro counties, Greater London; Scotland: 9 regions, 3 island areas; N. Ireland: 26 districts. **Armed forces:** regulars 327,100 (1980).

Economy: Industries: Steel, metals, vehicles, shipbuilding, shipping, banking, insurance, appliances, textiles, chemicals, electronics, aircraft, machinery, scientific instruments, distilling. **Chief crops:** Grains, sugar beets, fruits, vegetables. **Minerals:** Coal, tin, oil, gas, limestone, iron, salt, clay, chalk, gypsum, lead, silica. **Crude oil reserves** (1980): 15.4 bln. bbls. **Per capita arable land:** 0.3 acres. **Meat prod.** (1980): beef: 1.09 mln. metric tons; pork: 880,000 metric tons; lamb: 270,000 metric tons. **Fish catch** (1979): 1 mln. metric tons. **Electricity prod.** (1980): 285 bln. kwh. **Crude steel prod.** (1981): 15.5 mln. metric tons. **Labor force:** 1.5% agric.; 54.4% ind. and commerce; 29.9% serv.; 6.6% govt.

Finance: Currency: Pound (Mar. 1982: .68 = $1 US). **Gross domestic product** (1980): $445.9 bln. **Per capita income** (1979): $7,216. **Imports** (1980): $119.91 bln.; partners (1980): W. Ger. 11%, U.S. 12%, Fr. 8%, Neth. 7%. **Exports** (1980): $115.18 bln.; partners (1980): U.S. 9%, W. Ger. 10%, Fr. 7%, Neth. 8%. **Tourists** (1979): 12.4 mln.; receipts $5.9 bln. **National budget** (1981): $139.8 bln. revenues; $154.9 bln. expenditures. **International reserves less gold** (Feb. 1982): $14.78 bln. **Gold:** 18.97 mln. oz t. **Consumer prices** (change in 1981): 11.9%.

Transport: Railway traffic (1979): 31.7 bln. passenger-km; 17.6 bln. net ton-km. **Motor vehicles:** in use (1980): 15.4 mln. passenger cars, 1.8 mln. comm. vehicles; manuf. (1980): 924,000 passenger cars; 389,000 comm. vehicles. **Civil aviation** (1980): 50 bln. passenger-km: 1.3 bln. freight ton-km. **Chief ports:** London, Liverpool, Glasgow, Southampton, Cardiff, Belfast.

Communications: Television sets: 18.5 mln. licensed (Dec. 1980), 2.1 mln. manuf. (1979). **Radios:** 40.0 mln. licensed (Dec. 1977), 891,000 manuf. (1977). **Telephones in use** (1980): 26.5 mln. **Daily newspaper circ.** (1980): 251 per 1,000 pop.

Health: Life expectancy at birth: (1978): 69.8 male; 75.9 female. **Births:** (per 1,000 pop. 1980): 13.5. **Deaths:** (per 1,000 pop. 1980): 12.0. **Natural increase:** (1977): .01%. **Hospital beds** (per 100,000 pop. 1977): 894. **Physicians** (per 100,000 pop. 1977): 153. **Infant mortality:** (per 1,000 live births 1981): 13.3.

Education (1981): **Literacy:** 99%. **Pop. 5-19:** in school: 99%, teachers per 1,000: 45.

The United Kingdom of Great Britain and Northern Ireland comprises England, Wales, Scotland, and Northern Ireland.

Queen and Royal Family. The ruling sovereign is Elizabeth II of the House of Windsor, born Apr. 21, 1926, elder daughter of King George VI. She succeeded to the throne Feb. 6, 1952, and was crowned June 2, 1953. She was married Nov. 20, 1947, to Lt. Philip Mountbatten, born June 10, 1921, former Prince of Greece. He was created Duke of Edinburgh, Earl of Merioneth, and Baron Greenwich, and given the style H.R.H., Nov. 19, 1947; he was given the title Prince of the United Kingdom and Northern Ireland Feb. 22, 1957. Prince Charles Philip Arthur George, born Nov. 14, 1948, is the Prince of Wales and heir apparent. His son, William Philip Arthur Louis, born June 21, 1982, is second in line to the throne.

Parliament is the legislative governing body for the United Kingdom, with certain powers over dependent units. It consists of 2 houses: The **House of Lords** includes 763 hereditary and 314 life peers and peeresses, certain judges, 2 archbishops and 24 bishops of the Church of England. Total membership is over 1,000. The **House of Commons** has 635 members, who are elected by direct ballot and divided as follows: England 516;

Wales 36; Scotland 71; Northern Ireland 12.

Resources and Industries. Great Britain's major occupations are manufacturing and trade. Metals and metal-using industries contribute more than 50% of the exports. Of about 60 million acres of land in England, Wales and Scotland, 46 million are farmed, of which 17 million are arable, the rest pastures.

Large oil and gas fields have been found in the North Sea. Commercial oil production began in 1975; self-sufficiency is expected by the early 1980s. There are large deposits of coal.

The railroads, nationalized since 1948, have been reduced in total length, with a basic network, Dec. 1978, of 11,123 mi. The merchant marine totaled 49,700,000 gross registered tons in July 1978, comprising nearly 7.5% of active world shipping.

The world's first power station using atomic energy to create electricity for civilian use began operation Oct. 17, 1956, at Calder Hall in Cumbria.

Britain imports all of its cotton, rubber, sulphur, 80% of its wool, half of its food and iron ore, also certain amounts of paper, tobacco, chemicals. Manufactured goods made from these basic materials have been exported since the industrial age began. Main exports are machinery, chemicals, woolen and synthetic textiles, clothing, autos and trucks, iron and steel, locomotives, ships, jet aircraft, farm machinery, drugs, radio, TV, radar and navigation equipment, scientific instruments, arms, whisky.

Religion and Education. The Church of England is Protestant Episcopal. The queen is its temporal head, with rights of appointments to archbishoprics, bishoprics, and other offices. There are 2 provinces, Canterbury and York, each headed by an archbishop. About 48% of the population is baptized into the Church, less than 10% is confirmed. Most famous church is Westminster Abbey (1050-1760), site of coronations, tombs of Elizabeth I, Mary of Scots, kings, poets, and of the Unknown Warrior.

Education is free and compulsory from 5 to 16. The most celebrated British universities are Oxford and Cambridge, each dating to the 13th century. There are 40 other universities.

History. Britain was part of the continent of Europe until about 6,000 BC, but migration of peoples across the English Channel continued long afterward. Celts arrived 2,500 to 3,000 years ago. Their language survives in Welsh, Cornish, and Gaelic enclaves.

England was added to the Roman Empire in 43 AD. After the withdrawal of Roman legions in 410, waves of Jutes, Angles, and Saxons arrived from German lands. They contended with Danish raiders for control from the 8th through 11th centuries.

The last successful invasion was by French-speaking Normans in 1066, who united the country with their dominions in France.

Opposition by nobles to royal authority forced King John to sign the Magna Carta in 1215, a guarantee of rights and the rule of law. In the ensuing decades, the foundations of the parliamentary system were laid.

English dynastic claims to large parts of France led to the Hundred Years War, 1338-1453, and the defeat of England. A long civil war, the War of the Roses, lasted 1455-85, and ended with the establishment of the powerful Tudor monarchy. A distinct English civilization flourished. The economy prospered over long periods of domestic peace unmatched in continental Europe. Religious independence was secured when the Church of England was separated from the authority of the Pope in 1534.

Under Queen Elizabeth I, Britain became a major naval power, leading to the founding of colonies in the new world and the expansion of trade with Europe and the Orient. Scotland was united with England when James VI of Scotland was crowned James I of England in 1603.

A struggle between Parliament and the Stuart kings led to a bloody civil war, 1642-49, and the establishment of a republic under the Puritan Oliver Cromwell. The monarchy was restored in 1660, but the "Glorious Revolution" of 1688 confirmed the sovereignty of Parliament: a Bill of Rights was granted 1689.

In the 18th century, parliamentary rule was strengthened. Technological and entrepreneurial innovations led to the Industrial Revolution. The 13 North American colonies were lost, but replaced by growing empires in Canada and India. Britain's role in the defeat of Napoleon, 1815, strengthened its position as the leading world power.

The extension of the franchise in 1832 and 1867, the formation of trade unions, and the development of universal public education were among the drastic social changes which accompanied the spread of industrialization and urbanization in the 19th century. Large parts of Africa and Asia were added to the empire during the reign of Queen Victoria, 1837-1901.

Though victorious in World War I, Britain suffered huge casualties and economic dislocation. Ireland became independent in 1921, and independence movements became active in India and other colonies.

The country suffered major bombing damage in World War II, but held out against Germany singlehandedly for a year after the fall of France in 1940.

Industrial growth continued in the postwar period, but Britain lost its leadership position to other powers. Labor governments passed socialist programs nationalizing some basic industries and expanding social security. Nearly all of the empire was given independence. Britain joined the NATO alliance and, in 1973, the European Communities (Common Market).

Wales

The Principality of Wales in western Britain has an area of 8,016 sq. mi. and a population (est. 1977) of 2,768,200. Cardiff is the capital, pop. (1979 est.) 282,000.

England and Wales are administered as a unit. Less than 20% of the population of Wales speak both English and Welsh; about 32,000 speak Welsh solely. Welsh nationalism is advocated by a segment. A 1979 referendum rejected, 4-1, the creation of an elected Welsh Assembly.

Early Anglo-Saxon invaders drove Celtic peoples into the mountains of Wales, terming them Waelise (Welsh, or foreign). There they developed a distinct nationality. Members of the ruling house of Gwynedd in the 13th century fought England but were crushed, 1283. Edward of Caernarvon, son of Edward I of England, was created Prince of Wales, 1301.

Scotland

Scotland, a kingdom now united with England and Wales in Great Britain, occupies the northern 37% of the main British island, and the Hebrides, Orkney, Shetland and smaller islands. Length, 275 mi., breadth approx. 150 mi., area, 30,405 sq. mi., population (est. 1977) 5,195,600.

The Lowlands, a belt of land approximately 60 mi. wide from the Firth of Clyde to the Firth of Forth, divide the farming region of the Southern Uplands from the granite Highlands of the North, contain 75% of the population and most of the industry. The Highlands, famous for hunting and fishing, have been opened to industry by many hydroelectric power stations.

Edinburgh, pop. (1979 est.) 453,348, is the capital. Glasgow, pop. (1979 est.) 792,616, is Britain's greatest industrial center. It is a shipbuilding complex on the Clyde and an ocean port. Aberdeen, pop. (1979 est.) 208,539, NE of Edinburgh, is a major port, center of granite industry, fish processing, and North Sea oil exploitation. Dundee, pop. (1979 est.) 190,596, NE of Edinburgh, is an industrial and fish processing center. About 90,000 persons speak Gaelic as well as English.

History. Scotland was called Caledonia by the Romans who battled early Pict and Celtic tribes and occupied southern areas from the 1st to the 4th centuries. Missionaries from Britain introduced Christianity in the 4th century; St. Columba, an Irish monk, converted most of Scotland in the 6th century.

The Kingdom of Scotland was founded in 1018. William Wallace and Robert Bruce both defeated English armies 1297 and 1314, respectively.

In 1603 James VI of Scotland, son of Mary, Queen of Scots, succeeded to the throne of England as James I, and effected the Union of the Crowns. In 1707 Scotland received representation in the British Parliament, resulting from the union of former separate Parliaments. Its executive in the British cabinet is the Secretary of State for Scotland. The growing Scottish National Party urges independence. A 1979 referendum on the creation of an elected Scotland Assembly was defeated.

There are 8 universities. Memorials of Robert Burns, Sir Walter Scott, John Knox, Mary, Queen of Scots draw many tourists, as do the beauties of the Trossachs, Loch Katrine, Loch Lomond and abbey ruins.

Industries. Engineering products are the most important industry, with growing emphasis on office machinery, autos, electronics and other consumer goods. Oil has been discovered offshore in the North Sea, stimulating on-shore support industries.

Scotland produces fine woolens, worsteds, tweeds, silks, fine linens and jute. It is known for its special breeds of cattle and sheep. Fisheries have large hauls of herring, cod, whiting. Whisky is the biggest export.

The Hebrides are a group of c. 500 islands, 100 inhabited, off the W coast. The Inner Hebrides include **Skye, Mull,** and **Iona,** the last famous for the arrival of St. Columba, 563 AD. The

Outer Hebrides include **Lewis** and **Harris.** Industries include sheep raising and weaving. The **Orkney Islands,** c. 90, are to the NE. The capital is Kirkwall, on Pomona Is. Fish curing, sheep raising and weaving are occupations. NE of the Orkneys are the 200 **Shetland Islands,** 24 inhabited, home of Shetland pony. The Orkneys and Shetlands have become centers for the North Sea oil industry.

Northern Ireland

Six of the 9 counties of Ulster, the NE corner of Ireland, constitute Northern Ireland, with the parliamentary boroughs of Belfast and Londonderry. Area 5,463 sq. mi., 1978 est. pop. 1,540,000, capital and chief industrial center, Belfast, (1978 est.) 357,600.

Industries. Shipbuilding, including large tankers, has long been an important industry, centered in Belfast, the largest port. Linen manufacture is also important, along with apparel, rope, and twine. Growing diversification has added engineering products, synthetic fibers, and electronics. They are large numbers of cattle, hogs, and sheep, potatoes, poultry, and dairy foods are also produced.

Government. An act of the British Parliament, 1920, divided Northern from Southern Ireland, each with a parliament and government. When Ireland became a dominion, 1921, and later a republic, Northern Ireland chose to remain a part of the United Kingdom. It elects 12 members to the British House of Commons.

During 1968-69, large demonstrations were conducted by Roman Catholics who charged they were discriminated against in voting rights, housing, and employment. The Catholics, a minority comprising about a third of the population, demanded abolition of property qualifications for voting in local elections. Violence and terrorism intensified, involving branches of the Irish Republican Army (outlawed in the Irish Republic), Protestant groups, police, and up to 15,000 British troops.

A succession of Northern Ireland prime ministers pressed reform programs but failed to satisfy extremists on both sides. Over 2,000 were killed in over 12 years of bombings and shootings through Mar. 1982, some in England itself. Britain suspended the Northern Ireland parliament Mar. 30, 1972, and imposed direct British rule. A coalition government was formed in 1973 when moderates won election to a new one-house Assembly. But a Protestant general strike overthrew the government in 1974. Direct rule continued in 1978, after the failure of a constitutional convention to achieve a settlement.

The turmoil and agony of Northern Ireland was dramatized in 1981 by the deaths of imprisoned Irish nationalist hunger strikers in Maze Prison near Belfast. On May 5, Robert Sands, elected a Member of Parliament, April 10, died on his 66th day without food. When the protest ended in Oct., 9 additional inmates had starved themselves to death in an attempt to achieve status as political prisoners, but the British government refused to yield to their demands.

Education and Religion. Northern Ireland is 2/3 Protestant, 1/3 Roman Catholic. Education is compulsory through age 15. There are 2 universities and 24 technical colleges.

Channel Islands

The Channel Islands, area 75 sq. mi., cen. pop. 1980 130,000, off the NW coast of France, the only parts of the one-time Dukedom of Normandy belonging to England, are **Jersey, Guernsey** and the dependencies of Guernsey — **Alderney, Brechou, Great Sark, Little Sark, Herm, Jethou and Lihou.** Jersey and Guernsey have separate legal existences and lieutenant governors named by the Crown. The islands were the only British soil occupied by German troops in World War II.

Isle of Man

The Isle of Man, area 227 sq. mi., 1980 est. pop. 64,000, is in the Irish Sea, 20 mi. from Scotland, 30 mi. from Cumberland. It is rich in lead and iron. The island has its own laws and a lieutenant governor appointed by the Crown. The Tynwald (legislature) consists of the Legislative Council, partly elected, and House of Keys, elected. Capital: Douglas. Farming, tourism, fishing (kippers, scallops) are chief occupations. Man is famous for the Manx tailless cat.

Gibraltar

Gibraltar, a dependency on the southern coast of Spain, guards the entrance to the Mediterranean. The Rock has been in British possession since 1704. The Rock is 2.75 mi. long, 3/4 of a mi. wide and 1,396 ft. in height; a narrow isthmus connects it with the mainland. Est. pop. 1980, 29,000.

In 1966 Spain called on Britain to give "substantial sovereignty" of Gibraltar to Spain and imposed a partial blockade. In 1967, residents voted 12,138 for remaining under Britain, 44 for returning to Spain. A new constitution, May 30, 1969, gave an elected House of Assembly more control in domestic affairs. A UN General Assembly resolution requested Britain to end Gibraltar's colonial status by Oct. 1, 1969. No settlement has been reached.

British West Indies

Swinging in a vast arc from the coast of Venezuela NE, then N and NW toward Puerto Rico are the Leeward Islands, forming a coral and volcanic barrier sheltering the Caribbean from the open Atlantic. Many of the islands are self-governing British possessions. Universal suffrage was instituted 1951-54; ministerial systems were set up 1956-1960.

The **Leeward Islands,** are **Montserrat** (1980 pop. 11,600, area 32 sq. mi., capital Plymouth), and **St. Kitts (St. Christopher)-Nevis-Anguilla,** 3 islands (1979 pop. 57,000, area 136 sq. mi., capital Basseterre on St. Kitts). Nearby are the small **British Virgin Islands.**

Britain granted self-government to 5 of these islands (exception, Montserrat) and island groups in 1967-1969; each became an Associated State, with Britain controlling foreign affairs and defense.

Anguilla declared its independence from St. Kitts June 16, 1967. A 1976 constitution provides for an autonomous elected government. Area 35 sq. mi., pop. 6,500.

The three **Cayman Islands,** a dependency, lie S of Cuba, NW of Jamaica. Pop. is 17,000 (1980), most of it on Grand Cayman. It is a free port; in the 1970s Grand Cayman became a tax-free refuge for foreign funds and branches of many Western banks were opened there. Total area 93 sq. mi., capital Georgetown.

The **Turks and Caicos Islands,** at the SE end of the Bahama Islands, are a separate possession. There are about 30 islands, only 6 inhabited, 1980 pop. est. 7,000, area 166 sq. mi., capital Grand Turk. Salt, crayfish and conch shells are the main exports.

Bermuda

Bermuda is a British dependency governed by a royal governor and an Assembly, dating from 1620, the oldest legislative body among British dependencies. Capital is Hamilton.

It is a group of 360 small islands of coral formation, 20 inhabited, comprising 21 sq. mi. in the western Atlantic, 580 mi. E of North Carolina. Pop., 1980 cen., was 54,893 (about 61% of African descent). Density is high.

The U.S. has air and naval bases under long-term lease, and a NASA tracking station.

Bermuda boasts many resort hotels, serving over 600,000 visitors a year. The government raises most revenue from import duties. Exports: petroleum products, drugs.

South Atlantic

Falkland Islands and Dependencies, a British dependency, lies 300 mi. E of the Strait of Magellan at the southern end of South America.

The Falklands or Islas Malvinas include about 200 islands, area 4,700 sq. mi., pop. (1980 est.) 1,800. Sheep-grazing is the main industry; wool is the principal export. There are indications of large oil and gas deposits. The islands are also claimed by Argentina though 97% of inhabitants are of British origin. Argentina invaded the islands in 1982, (*see Chronology*). **South Georgia,** area 1,450 sq. mi., and the uninhabited **South Sandwich Is.** are dependencies of the Falklands.

British Antarctic Territory, south of 60° S lat., was made a separate colony in 1962 and comprises mainly the **South Shetland Islands,** the **South Orkneys** and **Graham's Land.** A chain of meteorological stations is maintained.

St. Helena, an island 1,200 mi. off the W coast of Africa and 1,800 E of South America, has 47 sq. mi. and est. pop., 1980 of 5,200. Flax, lace and rope making are the chief industries. After Napoleon Bonaparte was defeated at Waterloo the Allies exiled him to St. Helena, where he lived from Oct. 16, 1815, to his death, May 5, 1821. Capital is Jamestown.

Tristan da Cunha is the principal of a group of islands of volcanic origin, total area 40 sq. mi., half way between the Cape of

Good Hope and South America. A volcanic peak 6,760 ft. high erupted in 1961. The 262 inhabitants were removed to England, but most returned in 1963. The islands are dependencies of St. Helena.

Ascension is an island of volcanic origin, 34 sq. mi. in area, 700 mi. NW of St. Helena, through which it is administered. It is a communications relay center for Britain, and has a U.S. satellite tracking center. Est. pop., 1976, was 1,179, half of them communications workers. The island is noted for sea turtles.

Asia and Indian Ocean

Brunei was between 1888 and 1971 a protected sultanate. It is on the N side of the Island of Borneo, between the Malaysian states of Sarawak and Sabah. Its area is 2,226 sq. mi., the size of Delaware, with population (1980 est.) 213,000, two-thirds Malay and indigenous races, one-third of Chinese descent.

A 1959 constitution was amended, 1965, to provide for general elections to the Legislative Council. There is a sultan and a British high commissioner. A 1971 agreement gave Brunei full self-government, with Britain responsible for foreign affairs. Independence was set for 1983.

Brunei's rich Seria oifield provides tax revenues well in excess of expenditures. Rubber is also exported.

Hong Kong is a Crown Colony at the mouth of the Canton R. in China, 90 mi. S of Canton. Its nucleus is Hong Kong Is., 35½ sq. mi., acquired from China 1841, on which is located Victoria, the capital. Opposite is Kowloon Peninsula, 3 sq. mi. and Stonecutters Is., ¼ sq. mi., added, 1860. An additional 355 sq. mi. known as the New Territories, a mainland area and islands, were leased from China, 1898, for 99 years. Total area of the colony is 398 sq. mi., with a population, 1981 est., of 5,108,000 including fewer than 20,000 British. From 1949 to 1962 Hong Kong absorbed more than a million refugees from the mainland.

Hong Kong harbor was long an important British naval station and one of the world's great trans-shipment ports. Britain announced in 1975 a reduction of its garrison to 6,400 men.

Principal industries are textiles and apparel (39% of exports); also tourism, shipbuilding, iron and steel, fishing, cement, and small manufactures.

Spinning mills, among the best in the world, and low wages compete with textiles elsewhere and have resulted in the protective measures in some countries. Hong Kong also has a booming electronics industry.

British Indian Ocean Territory was formed Nov. 1965, embracing islands formerly dependencies of Mauritius or Seychelles: the Chagos Archipelago (including Diego Garcia), Aldabra, Farquhar and Des Roches. The latter 3 were transferred to Seychelles, which became independent in 1976. Area 22 sq mi.; pop. 1977 est. 2,000. In 1973 the U. S. Navy established a communications station on Diego Garcia and in 1975 began constructing a naval base.

Pacific Ocean

Pitcairn Island is in the Pacific, halfway between South America and Australia. The island was discovered in 1767 by Carteret but was not inhabited until 23 years later when the mutineers of the Bounty landed there. The area is 18 sq. mi. and pop. 1980, was 63. It is a British colony and is administered by a British Representative in New Zealand and a local Council. The uninhabited islands of **Henderson, Ducie** and **Oeno** are in the Pitcairn group.

United States of America

People: Population (1980 cen.): 226,504,825. **Age distrib.**(%): 0–14: 23.9; 15–59: 61.0; 60+: 15.2. **Pop. density:** 64.0 per sq. mi. **Urban** (1980): 79.2%. **Cities** (1980 cen.): New York 7,071,030; Chicago 3,005,072; Los Angeles 2,966,763; Philadelphia 1,688,210; Houston 1,594,086; Detroit 1,203,339.

Armed forces: regulars 2,022,000; reserves 797,000.

Economy: Minerals: Coal, copper, lead, molybdenum, phosphates, uranium, bauxite, gold, iron, mercury, nickel, potash, silver, tungsten, zinc. **Crude oil reserves** (1980): 26.50 bln. bbls. **Per capita arable land:** 2.1 acres. **Meat prod.** (1980): beef: 10 mln. metric tons; pork: 7.5 mln. metric tons; lamb: 146,000 metric tons. **Fish catch** (1979): 3.5 mln. metric tons. **Electricity prod.** (1980): 2,370 bln. kwh. **Crude steel prod.** (1981): 108.8 mln. metric tons.

Finance: Gross domestic product (1981): $2,626.1 bln. **Per capita income** (1978): $8,612. **Imports** (1980): $252.99 bln.; partners (1980); Can. 17%, Jap. 13%, W. Ger. 5%, Mex. 5%. **Exports** (1981): $233.73 bln.; partners (1980): Can. 16%, Jap. 9%, Mex. 7%, W. Ger. 5%, UK 6%. **Tourists** (1979): 20 mln.; receipts $10 bln. **National budget** (1981): $650.3 bln. revenues; $695.3 bln. expenditures and lending. **International reserves less gold** (Feb. 1982): $18.92 bln. **Gold:** 264.0 mln. oz t. **Consumer prices** (change in 1981): 10.4%.

Transport: Railway traffic (1979): 18.1 bln. passenger-km; 1.4 bln. net ton-km. **Motor vehicles:** in use (1979): 120 mln. passenger cars, 33 mln. comm. vehicles; manuf. (1980): 6.4 mln. passenger cars; 1.6 mln. comm. vehicles. **Civil aviation** (1980): 409 bln. passenger-km; 10.5 bln. freight ton-km.

Communications: Television sets: 150 mln. in use (1978), 9.6 mln. manuf. (1980). **Radios:** 450 mln. in use (1978), 10.3 mln. manuf. (1978). **Telephones in use** (1980): 182 mln. **Daily newspaper circ.** (1980): 282 per 1,000 pop.

Health: Life expectancy at birth (1980): 69.8 male; 77.5 female. **Births** (per 1,000 pop. 1980): 16.2. **Deaths** (per 1,000 pop. 1980): 8.9. **Natural increase** (1977): .7%. **Hospital beds** (per 100,000 pop. 1977): 630. **Physicians** (per 100,000 pop. 1977): 176. **Infant mortality** (per 1,000 live births 1977): 14.0.

Education (1980): **Literacy:** 99%. **Pop. 5-19:** in school: 85%, teachers per 1,000: 43.

Upper Volta

Republic of Upper Volta

People: Population (1981 est.): 7,000,000. **Pop. density:** 65.27 per sq. mi. **Ethnic groups:** Voltaic groups (Mossi, Bobo), Mande. **Languages:** French (official), More, Sudanic tribal languages. **Religions:** animist 50%, Moslems 16%, Roman Catholics 8%, others.

Geography: Area: 105,869 sq. mi., the size of Colorado. **Location:** In W. Africa, S of the Sahara. **Neighbors:** Mali on NW, Niger on NE, Benin, Togo, Ghana, Ivory Coast on S. **Topography:** Landlocked Upper Volta is in the savannah region of W. Africa. The N is arid, hot, and thinly populated. **Capital:** Ouagadougou. **Cities** (1981 est.): Ouagadougou 200,000; Bobo-Dioulasso 150,000.

Government: Head of state: Pres. Saye Zerbo; b. Aug., 1932; in office: Nov. 25, 1980. **Local divisions:** 10 departments. **Armed forces:** regulars 3,775 (1980).

Economy: Chief crops: Millet, sorghum, rice, peanuts, grain. **Minerals:** Manganese, gold, diamonds. **Per capita arable land:** 2.1 acres. **Meat prod.** (1980): beef: 29,000 metric tons; lamb: 8,000 metric tons. **Electricity prod.** (1977): 70.00 mln. kwh. **Labor force:** 83% agric.; 12% industry.

Finance: Currency: CFA franc (Mar. 1982: 312.10 = $1 US). **Gross domestic product** (1979 est.): $969 mln. **Per capita income** (1978): $160. **Imports** (1979): $300 mln.; partners (1978): Fr. 40%, Ivory Coast 11%, U.S. 12% Belg. 5%. **Exports** (1979): $76 mln.; partners (1978): Ivory Coast 43%, Fr. 16%. **Tourists** (1977): 23,000; receipts: (1975): $2 mln. **International reserves less gold** (Jan. 1982): $70.8 mln. **Gold:** 11,000 oz t. **Consumer prices** (change in 1980): 12.2%.

Transport: Motor vehicles: in use (1975): 9,500 passenger cars, 10,100 comm. vehicles.

Communications: Television sets: 6,000 in use (1975). **Radios:** 105,000 in use (1976). **Telephones in use** (1978): 3,564. **Daily newspaper circ.** (1976): 1,500; 0.2 per 1,000 pop.

Health: Life expectancy at birth (1961): 32.1 male; 31.1 female. **Births** (per 1,000 pop. 1978): 50. **Deaths** (per 1,000 pop. 1978): 27. **Natural increase** (1978): 2.3%. **Hospital beds** (per 100,000 pop. 1977): 57. **Physicians** (per 100,000 pop. 1977): 3. **Infant mortality** (per 1,000 live births 1981): 260.

Education (1980): **Literacy:** 7%. **Pop. 5-19:** in school: 7%, teachers per 1,000: 2.

The Mossi tribe entered the area in the 11th to 13th centuries. Their kingdoms ruled until defeated by the Mali and Songhai empires.

French control came by 1896, but Upper Volta was not finally established as a separate territory until 1947. Full independence came Aug. 5, 1960, and a pro-French government was elected. A 1980 coup established the current regime.

Several hundred thousand farm workers migrate each year to Ivory Coast and Ghana. A long drought brought famine in 1973-74; renewed drought occurred in 1977-78. Upper Volta is heavily dependent on foreign aid.

Uruguay

Oriental Republic of Uruguay

People: Population (1981 est.): 2,910,000. **Age distrib.** (%): 0–14: 27.0; 15–59: 58.7; 60+: 14.3. **Pop. density:** 41.72 per sq. mi. **Urban** (1975): 83.0%. **Ethnic groups:** Caucasians (Iberians, Italians) 89%, mestizos 10%, mulatto and Negro. **Languages:** Spanish. **Religions:** Mainly Roman Catholics.

Geography: Area: 68,037 sq. mi., the size of Washington State. **Location:** In southern S. America, on the Atlantic O. **Neighbors:** Argentina on W, Brazil on N. **Topography:** Uruguay is composed of rolling, grassy plains and hills, well-watered by rivers flowing W to Uruguay R. **Capital:** Montevideo. **Cities** (1979 est.): Montevideo 1,500,000.

Government: Head of state: Pres. Gregorio Conrado Alvarez Armelino; b. Nov. 26, 1925; in office: Sept. 1, 1981. **Local divisions:** 19 departments. **Armed forces:** regulars 28,500 (1980).

Economy: Industries: Meat-packing, metals, textiles, wine, cement, oil products. **Chief crops:** Corn, wheat, citrus fruits, rice, oats, linseed. **Per capita arable land:** 1.6 acres. **Meat prod.** (1980): beef: 330,000 metric tons; pork: 15,000 metric tons; lamb: 34,000 metric tons. **Fish catch** (1978): 74,300 metric tons. **Electricity prod.** (1979): 2.7 bln. kwh. **Crude steel prod.** (1981): 14,000 metric tons. **Labor force** 8% agric.; 34% ind. and commerce; 10% serv.; 25% gvt.

Finance: Currency: New Peso (Mar. 1982: 12.00 = $1 US). **Gross domestic product** (1980): $1.7 bln. **Per capita income** (1978): $1,710. **Imports** (1980): $164 bln.; partners (1979): Braz. 15%, Arg. 17%, U.S. 10, Iraq 8%. **Exports** (1980): $1.06 bln.; partners (1979): Braz. 23%, U.S. 11%, W. Ger. 16%, Arg. 12%. **Tourists** (1976): 491,700; receipts (1977): $180 mln. **National budget** (1979): $1.30 bln. revenues; $1.24 bln. expeditures. **International reserves less gold** (June 1981): $401 mln. **Gold:** 3.39 mln. oz t. **Consumer prices** (change in 1980): 63.5%.

Transport: Railway traffic (1978): 494 mln. passenger-km; 303 mln. net ton-km. **Motor vehicles:** in use (1979): 168,100 passenger cars, 92,000 comm. vehicles. **Civil aviation** (1980): 178 mln. passenger-km; 1 mln. freight ton-km. **Chief ports:** Montevideo.

Communications: Television sets: 360,000 in use (1977). **Radios:** 1.6 mln. in use (1977). **Telephones in use** (1978): 268,026. **Daily newspaper circ.** (1980): 39 per 1,000 pop.

Health: Life expectancy at birth (1980): 66.3 male; 72.8 female. **0.6%.** (per 1,000 pop. 1978): 20. **Deaths** (per 1,000 pop. 1978): 10. **Natural increase** (1978): 0.6%. **Hospital beds** (per 100,000 pop. 1977): 418. **Physicians:** (per 100,000 pop. 1977): 139. **Infant mortality** (per 1,000 live births 1976): 45.9.

Education (1978): **Literacy:** 94%. **Pop. 5-19:** in school: 60%, teachers per 1,000: 34.

Spanish settlers did not begin replacing the indigenous Charrua Indians until 1624. Portuguese from Brazil arrived later, but Uruguay was attached to the Spanish Viceroyalty of Rio de la Plata in the 18th century. Rebels fought against Spain beginning in 1810. An independent republic was declared Aug. 25, 1825.

Liberal governments adopted socialist measures as far back as 1911. More than a third of the workers are employed by the state, which owns the power, telephone, railroad, cement, oil-refining and other industries. Social welfare programs are among the most advanced in the world.

Uruguay's standard of living was one of the highest in South America, and political and labor conditions among the freest. Economic stagnation, inflation, plus floods, drought in 1967 and a general strike in 1968 brought attempts by the government to strengthen the economy through a series of devaluations of the peso and wage and price controls. But inflation continued and the country was experiencing a severe recession in 1981 and 1982.

Tupamaros, leftist guerrillas drawn from the upper classes, increased terrorist actions in 1970; a U.S. police adviser was slain in Aug. In 1971 the guerrillas kidnaped and, after 8 months, freed the British ambassador. Violence continued and in Feb. 1973 Pres. Juan Maria Bordaberry agreed to military control of his administration. In June he abolished Congress and set up a Council of State in its place. By 1974 the military had apparently defeated the Tupamaros, using severe repressive measures. Bordaberry was removed by the military in a 1976 coup. Elections were promised for 1984.

Vanuatu

Republic of Vanuatu

People: Population (Jan. 1979): 112,600. **Population density:** 19.58 per sq. mi. **Ethnic groups:** Mainly Melanesian, some European, Polynesian, Micronesian. **Languages:** Bislama (national), French and English both official. **Religions:** Presbyterian 40%, Anglican 14%, Roman Catholic 16%, animist 15%.

Geography: Area: 4,707 sq. mi. **Location:** SW Pacific, 1,200 mi NE of Brisbane, Australia. **Topography:** dense forest with narrow coastal strips of cultivated land. **Capital:** Vila. **Cities:** Vila (1979): 15,100.

Government: Head of state: Pres. George Sokomanu; in office: July 30, 1980. **Head of gov't:** Prime Min. Rev. Walter Lini; in office: July 30, 1980.

Economy: Industries: Fish-freezing, meat canneries, tourism. **Chief crops:** Copra (43% of export), cocoa, coffee. **Minerals:** Manganese. **Other resources:** Forests, cattle.

Finance: Currency: Australian dollar and Vanuatu franc (Sept. 1981: VFr 81 = $1 US). **Imports** (1980): $53 mln.; partners (1978): Aus. 39%, Fr. 12%, Japan 11%. **Exports** (1980): $24 mln.; partners (1978): Fr. 33%, U.S. 34%, Sing. 11%.

Education: Education not compulsory, but 85-90% of children of primary school age attend primary schools.

The Anglo-French condominium of the New Hebrides, administered jointly by France and Great Britain since 1906, became the independent Republic of Vanuatu on July 30, 1980.

Vatican

State of Vatican City

People: Population (1979 est.): 1,000. **Ethnic groups:** Italians, Swiss. **Languages:** Italian, Latin. **Religion:** Roman Catholicism.

Geography: Area: 108.7 acres. **Location:** In Rome, Italy. **Neighbors:** Completely surrounded by Italy.

Currency: Lira.

The popes for many centuries, with brief interruptions, held temporal sovereignty over mid-Italy (the so-called Papal States), comprising an area of some 16,000 sq. mi., with a population in the 19th century of more than 3 million. This territory was incorporated in the new Kingdom of Italy, the sovereignty of the pope being confined to the palaces of the Vatican and the Lateran in Rome and the villa of Castel Gandolfo, by an Italian law, May 13, 1871. This law also guaranteed to the pope and his successors a yearly indemnity of over $620,000. The allowance, however, remained unclaimed.

A Treaty of Conciliation, a concordat and a financial convention were signed Feb. 11, 1929, by Cardinal Gasparri and Premier Mussolini. The documents established the independent state of Vatican City, and gave the Catholic religion special status in Italy. The treaty (Lateran Agreement) was made part of the Constitution of Italy (Article 7) in 1947. Italy and the Vatican reached preliminary agreement in 1976 on revisions of the concordat, that would eliminate Roman Catholicism as the state religion and end required religious education in Italian schools.

Vatican City includes St. Peter's, the Vatican Palace and Museum covering over 13 acres, the Vatican gardens, and neighboring buildings between Viale Vaticano and the Church. Thirteen buildings in Rome, outside the boundaries, enjoy extraterritorial rights; these buildings house congregations or officers necessary for the administration of the Holy See.

The legal system is based on the code of canon law, the apostolic constitutions and the laws especially promulgated for the Vatican City by the pope. The Secretariat of State represents the Holy See in its diplomatic relations. By the Treaty of Conciliation the pope is pledged to a perpetual neutrality unless his mediation is specifically requested. This, however, does not prevent the defense of the Church whenever it is persecuted. A total of 84 nations maintain diplomatic representatives in Vatican City. The U.S. does not have an official ambassador.

The present sovereign of the State of Vatican City is the Supreme Pontiff John Paul II, Karol Wojtyla, born in Wadowice, Poland, May 18, 1920, elected Oct. 16, 1978 (the first non-Italian to be elected Pope in 456 years).

Venezuela

Republic of Venezuela

People: Population (1981 est.): 15,500,000. **Age distrib.** (%): 0–14: 42.8; 15–59: 52.4; 60+: 4.8. **Pop. density:** 37.26 per sq. mi. **Urban** (1977): 75.1%. **Ethnic groups:** Mestizo 69%, white (Spanish, Portuguese, Italian) 20%, Negro 9%, Indian 2%. **Languages:** Spanish (official), Indian languages 2%. **Religions:** Predominantly Roman Catholic.

Geography: Area: 352,143 sq. mi., more than twice the size of California. **Location:** On the Caribbean coast of S. America. **Neighbors:** Colombia on W, Brazil on S, Guyana on E. **Topography:** Flat coastal plain and Orinoco Delta are bordered by Andes Mtns. and hills. Plains, called llanos, extend between mountains and Orinoco. Guyana Highlands and plains are S of Orinoco, which stretches 1,700 mi. and drains 80% of Venezuela. **Capital:** Caracas. **Cities** (1981 est.): Caracas 2,700,000; Maracaibo 845,000; Barquisimeto 459,000; Valencia 471,000.

Government: Head of state: Pres. Luis Herrera Campins; b. May 4, 1925; in office: Mar. 12, 1979. **Local divisions:** 20 states, 2 federal territories, federal district, federal dependency. **Armed forces:** regulars 29,000 (1980).

Economy: Industries: Steel, oil products, textiles, containers, paper, shoes. **Chief crops:** Coffee, rice, fruits, sugar. **Minerals:** Oil (5th largest producer), iron (extensive reserves and production), gold. **Crude oil reserves** (1980): 17.87 bln. bbls. **Per capita arable land:** 0.9 acres. **Meat prod.** (1980): beef: 337,000 metric tons; pork: 89,000 metric tons; lamb: 12,000 metric tons. **Fish catch** (1978): 174,200 metric tons. **Electricity prod.** (1978): 25.6 bln. kwh. **Crude steel prod.** (1981): 2.0 mln. metric tons. **Labor force:** 15% agric.; 42% ind. and commerce; 41% services.

Finance: Currency: Bolivar (Apr. 1982: 4.29 = $1 US). **Gross domestic product** (1980): $59.9 bln. **Per capita income** (1980): $3,639. **Imports** (1980): $11.39 bln.; partners (1979): U.S. 46%, W. Ger. 7%, Jap. 8%. **Exports** (1980): $18.77 bln.; partners (1979): U.S. 37%, Neth Ant. 22%, Can. 10%. **Tourists** (1977): 652,400; receipts: $261 mln. **National budget** (1980): $16.6 bln. revenues; $17.0 bln. expenditures. **International reserves less gold** (Feb. 1982): $7.35 bln. **Gold:** 11.46 mln. oz t. **Consumer prices** (change in 1981): 16.1%.

Transport: Railway traffic (1971): 42 mln. passenger-km; 15 mln. net ton-km. **Motor vehicles:** in use (1979): 1.3 mln. passenger cars, 639,000 comm. vehicles; assembled (1976): 97,000 passenger cars; 66,000 comm. vehicles. **Civil aviation** (1980): 4.3 bln. passenger-km; 152.7 mln. freight ton-km. **Chief ports:** Maracaibo, La Guaira, Puerto Cabello.

Communications: Television sets: 1.7 mln. in use (1978). **Radios:** 5.2 mln. in use (1977). **Telephones in use** (1980): 1.1 mln. **Daily newspaper circ.** (1980): 178 per 1,000 pop.

Health: Life expectancy at birth (1975): 65.0 male; 69.7 female. **Births** (per 1,000 pop. 1978): 36. **Deaths** (per 1,000 pop. 1978): 6. **Natural increase** (1978): 3.3%. **Hospital beds** (per 100,000 pop. 1977): 292. **Physicians** (per 100,000 pop. 1977): 107. **Infant mortality** (per 1,000 live births 1981): 31.

Education (1981): **Literacy:** 85.6%. **Pop. 5-19:** in school: 58%, teachers per 1,000: 19.

Columbus first set foot on the South American continent on the peninsula of Paria, Aug. 1498. Alonso de Ojeda, 1499, found Lake Maracaibo, called the land Venezuela, or Little Venice, because natives had houses on stilts. Venezuela was under Spanish domination until 1821. The republic was formed after secession from the Colombian Federation in 1830.

Military strongmen ruled Venezuela for most of the 20th century. They promoted the oil industry; some social reforms were implemented. Since 1959, the country has enjoyed progressive, democratically-elected governments.

Venezuela helped found the Organization of Petroleum Exporting States (OPEC). The government, Jan. 1, 1976, nationalized the oil industry with compensation. Development has begun of the Orinoco tar belt, believed to contain the world's largest oil reserves. Oil accounts for 95% of total export earnings.

Oil profits help finance a new $150 billion national development plan for 1981-85. The funds are to be spent for housing, education, and industrial expansion.

Vietnam

Socialist Republic of Vietnam

People: Population (1981 est.): 54,700,000. **Pop. density:** 413.65 per sq. mi. **Ethnic groups:** Vietnamese 85–90%, Chinese 2%, remainder Muong, Thai, Meo, Khmer, Man, Cham. **Languages:** Vietnamese (official), French, English. **Religions:** Buddhists, Confucians, and Taoists most numerous, Roman Catholics, animists, Muslims, Protestants.

Geography: Area: 127,207 sq. mi., the size of New Mexico. **Location:** On the E coast of the Indochinese Peninsula in SE Asia. **Neighbors:** China on N, Laos, Cambodia on W. **Topography:** Vietnam is long and narrow, with a 1,400-mi. coast. About 24% of country is readily arable, including the densely settled Red R. valley in the N, narrow coastal plains in center, and the wide, often marshy Mekong R. Delta in the S. The rest consists of semi-arid plateaus and barren mountains, with some stretches of tropical rain forest. **Capital:** Hanoi. **Cities** (1981): Ho Chi Minh City 3.5 mln.; Hanoi 2 mln.

Government: Head of state: Pres. Truong Chinh; in office: July 4, 1981. **Head of government:** Prime Min. Pham Van Dong; b. 1906; in office: Sept. 20, 1955. **Head of Communist Party:** First Sec. Le Duan; b. 1907; in office: Sept. 10, 1960. **Local divisions:** 39 provinces. **Armed forces:** regulars 1,023,000 (1980).

Economy: Industries: Food processing, textiles, machine building, mining, cement, chemical fertilizers, glass, tires. **Chief crops:** Rice, rubber, fruits and vegetables, corn, manioc, sugarcane, fish. **Minerals:** Phosphates, coal, iron, manganese, bauxite, apatite, chromate. **Other resources:** Forests. **Per capita arable land:** 0.2 acres. **Meat prod.** (1980): beef: 91,000 metric tons; pork: 415,000 metric tons. **Fish catch** (1979): 1 mln. metric tons. **Electricity prod.** (1978): 3.4 bln. kwh. **Labor force:** 70% agric.; 8% ind. and commerce.

Finance: Currency: Dong (Feb. 1981: 2.18 = $1 US). **Gross domestic product** (1978): $7.6 mln. **Per capita income** (1978): $150. **Imports** (1980 est.): $509 mln.; partners (1980): USSR 18%, Rom. 11%, Jap. 9%. **Exports** (1978 est.): $416 mln.; partners (1980): USSR 65%, Pol. 5%, Rom. 5%.

Transport: Motor vehicles: in use (1976): 100,000 passenger cars, 200,000 comm. vehicles. **Chief ports:** Ho Chi Minh City, Haiphong, Da Nang, Cam Ranh.

Communications: Television sets (1978) 2 mln. **Radios:** 5 mln. in use (1978). **Daily newspaper circ.** (1980): 11 per 1,000 pop.

Health: Life expectancy at birth (1975): 43.2 male; 46.0 female. **Births** (per 1,000 pop. 1978): 41. **Deaths** (per 1,000 pop. 1978): 20. **Natural increase** 1978): 2.2%. **Hospital beds** (per 100,000 pop. 1977): 343. **Physicians** (per 100,000 pop. 1977): 18.

Education (1978): **Literacy:** 78%. **Pop. 5-19:** in school: 63%, teachers per 1,000: 24.

Vietnam's recorded history began in Tonkin before the Christian era. Settled by Viets from central China, Vietnam was held by China, 111 BC-939 AD, and was a vassal state during subsequent periods. Vietnam defeated the armies of Kublai Khan, 1288. Conquest by France began in 1858 and ended in 1884 with the protectorates of Tonkin and Annam in the N. and the colony of Cochin-China in the S.

In 1940 Vietnam was occupied by Japan; nationalist aims gathered force. A number of groups formed the Vietminh (Independence) League, headed by Ho Chi Minh, communist guerrilla leader. In Aug. 1945 the Vietminh forced out Bao Dai, former emperor of Annam, head of a Japan-sponsored regime. France, seeking to reestablish colonial control, battled communist and nationalist forces, 1946-1954, and was finally defeated at Dienbienphu, May 8, 1954. Meanwhile, on July 1, 1949, Bao Dai had formed a State of Vietnam, with himself as chief of state, with French approval. Communist China backed Ho Chi Minh.

A cease-fire accord signed in Geneva July 21, 1954, divided Vietnam along the Ben Hai R. It provided for a buffer zone, withdrawal of French troops from the North and elections to determine the country's future. Under the agreement the communists gained control of territory north of the 17th parallel, 22 provinces with area of 62,000 sq. mi. and 13 million pop., with its capital at Hanoi and Ho Chi Minh as president. South Vietnam came to comprise the 39 southern provinces with approx. area of 65,000 sq. mi. and pop. of 12 million. Some 900,000 North Vietnamese fled to South Vietnam. Neither South Vietnam nor the U.S.

signed the agreement.

On Oct. 26, 1955, Ngo Dinh Diem, premier of the interim government of South Vietnam, proclaimed the Republic of Vietnam and became its first president.

The Democratic Republic of Vietnam, established in the North, adopted a constitution Dec. 31, 1959, based on communist principles and calling for reunification of all Vietnam. Pres. Ho Chi Minh, re-elected July 15, 1960, by unanimous vote of the National Assembly, had held office since 1945. He died Sept. 3, 1969.

North Vietnam sought to take over South Vietnam beginning in 1954. Fighting persisted from 1956, with the communist Vietcong, aided by North Vietnam, pressing war in the South and South Vietnam receiving U.S. aid. Northern aid to Vietcong guerrillas was intensified in 1959, and large-scale troop infiltration began in 1964, with Russian and Chinese arms assistance. Large Northern forces were stationed in border areas of Laos and Cambodia.

A serious political conflict arose in the South in 1963 when Buddhists denounced authoritarianism and brutality. This paved the way for a military coup Nov. 1-2, 1963, which overthrew Diem. Several military coups followed. In elections Sept. 3, 1967, Chief of State Nguyen Van Thieu was chosen president.

In 1964, the U.S. began air strikes against North Vietnam. Beginning in 1965, the raids were stepped up and U.S. troops became combatants. U.S. troop strength in Vietnam, which reached a high of 543,400 in Apr. 1969, was ordered reduced by U.S. President Nixon in a series of withdrawals, beginning in June 1969. U.S. bombings were resumed in 1972-73.

A ceasefire agreement was signed in Paris Jan. 27, 1973 (EST), by the U.S., North and South Vietnam, and the Vietcong. It was never implemented. U.S. aid was curbed in 1974 by the U.S. Congress. Heavy fighting continued for two years throughout Indochina.

Massive numbers of North Vietnamese troops, aided by tanks, launched attacks against remaining government outposts in the Central Highlands in the first months of 1975. Government retreats turned into a rout, and the Saigon regime surrendered April 30. Conquest of the country was effectively completed within days.

A Provisional Revolutionary Government assumed control, aided by officials and technicians from Hanoi, and first steps were taken to transform society along communist lines. All businesses and farms were to be collectivized by 1979.

The U.S. accepted over 165,000 Vietnamese fleeing the new regime, while scores of thousands more sought refuge in other countries.

The war's toll included — Combat deaths: U.S. 46,079; South Vietnam over 200,000; other allied forces 5,225. Civilian casualties were over a million. Displaced war refugees in South Vietnam totaled over 6.5 million.

After the fighting ended, 8 Northern divisions remained stationed in the South, while Southern forces of over 900,000 were demobilized, adding to severe economic problems. Over 1 million urban residents and 260,000 Montagnards were resettled in the countryside by 1978, the first of 10 million scheduled for forced resettlement. An unknown number were sent to long-term re-education camps, including thousands of adherents of the Hoa Hao sect. A 1977 crop failure caused food shortages; the south remained more prosperous than the north.

The first National Assembly of both parts of the country met June 24, 1976. The country was officially reunited July 2, 1976. The Northern capital, flag, anthem, emblem, and currency were applied to the new state. Nearly all major government posts went to officials of the former Northern government, and thousands of Northern officials were sent south.

Heavy fighting with Cambodia took place, 1977-80, amid mutual charges of aggression and atrocities against civilians. Increasing numbers of Vietnamese civilians, ethnic Chinese, escaped the country, via the sea, or the overland route across Cambodia.

Relations with China soured as 140,000 ethnic Chinese left Vietnam charging discrimination; China cut off economic aid. Reacting to Vietnam's invasion of Cambodia, China attacked 4 Vietnamese border provinces, Feb., 1979, instigating heavy fighting.

North Yemen

Yemen Arab Republic

People: Population (1981 est.): 5,300,000. **Pop. density:** 78.76 per sq. mi. **Ethnic groups:** Arabs, some Negroids. **Languages:** Arabic. **Religions:** Sunni Moslems 50%, Shiite Moslems 50%.

Geography: Area: 77,200 sq. mi., slightly smaller than South Dakota. **Location:** On the southern Red Sea coast of the Arabian Peninsula. **Neighbors:** Saudi Arabia on NE, South Yemen on S. **Topography:** A sandy coastal strip leads to well-watered fertile mountains in interior. **Capital:** Sanaa. **Cities** (1980 est.): Sanaa 210,000.

Government: Head of state: Pres. Ali Abdullah Saleh, b. 1942; in office: July 17, 1978. **Head of government:** Prime Min. Abdul Karim Al-Iriani; in office: Oct. 15, 1980. **Local divisions:** 11 governorates. **Armed forces:** regulars 31,800 (1980).

Economy: Industries: Textiles, cement. **Chief crops:** Wheat, sorghum, gat, fruits, coffee, cotton. **Minerals:** Salt. **Crude oil reserves** (1978): 370 mln. bbls. **Per capita arable land:** 0.7 acres. **Meat prod.** (1980): beef: 14,000 metric tons; lamb: 54,000 metric tons. **Fish catch** (1978): 19,300 metric tons. **Electricity prod.** (1977): 65.00 mln. kwh. **Labor force:** 55% agric.; 4% ind. and commerce; 16% serv.

Finance: Currency: Rial (Apr. 1982: 4.56 = $1 US). **Gross domestic product** (1977-78): $2.7 bln. **Per capita income** (1977-78): $475. **Imports** (1979): $1.49 bln.; partners (1979): Saudi Ar. 19%, Fr. 10%, Jap. 10%, Austral. 7%. **Exports** (1979): $14 mln.; partners (1979): S. Yemen 49%, Saudi Ar. 23%. **International reserves less gold** (Feb. 1982): $999.3 mln. **Gold:** 7,000 oz t. **Consumer prices** (change in 1978): 12.3%.

Transport: Chief ports: Al-Hudaydah, Al-Mukha.

Communications: Radios: 90,000 in use (1976). **Daily newspaper circ.** (1970): 56,000; 10 per 1,000 pop.

Health: Life expectancy at birth (1975): 37.3 male; 38.7 female. **Births** (per 1,000 pop. 1978): 48. **Deaths** (per 1,000 pop. 1978): 25. **Natural increase** (1978): 2.3%. **Hospital beds** (per 100,000 pop. 1977): 58. **Physicians** (per 100,000 pop. 1977): 8.

Education (1978): **Literacy:** 12%. **Pop. 5-19:** in school: 15%, teachers per 1,000: 4. **PQLI:** 27.

Yemen's territory once was part of the ancient kindgom of Sheba, or Saba, a prosperous link in trade between Africa and India. A Biblical reference speaks of its gold, spices and precious stones as gifts borne by the Queen of Sheba to King Solomon.

Yemen became independent in 1918, after years of Ottoman Turkish rule, but remained politically and economically backward. Imam Ahmed ruled 1948-1962. The king was reported assassinated Sept. 26, 1962, and a revolutionary group headed by Brig. Gen. Abdullah al-Salal declared the country to be the Yemen Arab Republic.

The Imam Ahmed's heir, the Imam Mohamad al-Badr, fled to the mountains where tribesmen joined royalist forces; internal warfare between them and the republican forces continued. Egypt sent troops and Saudi Arabia military aid to the royalists. About 150,000 people died in the fighting.

After its defeat in the June 1967 Arab-Israeli war, Egypt announced it would withdraw its troops from Yemen.

There was a bloodless coup Nov. 5, 1967.

In April 1970 hostilities ended with an agreement between Yemen and Saudi Arabia and appointment of several royalists to the Yemen government. There were border skirmishes with forces of the People's Democratic Republic of Yemen in 1972-73.

On June 13, 1974, an Army group, led by Col. Ibrahim al-Hamidi, seized the government. Hamidi pursued close Saudi and U.S. ties; he was assassinated in 1977.

The People's Democratic Republic of Yemen went to war with Yemen on Feb. 24, 1979. Swift Arab mediation led to a ceasefire and a mutual withdrawal of forces, Mar. 19. An Arab League-sponsored agreement between North and South Yemen on unification of the 2 countries was signed Mar. 29th.

Per capita GNP is among the lowest in the world. A prolonged drought has forced imports of food. The remittances from 400,000 Yemenis living in Arab oil countries provide most of foreign earnings.

South Yemen

People's Democratic Republic of Yemen

People: Population (1981 est.): 2,000,000. **Age distrib.** (%): 0–14: 49.4; 15–59: 45.5; 60+: 5.5. **Pop. density:** 16.67 per sq. mi. **Urban** (1973): 33.3%. **Ethnic groups:** Arabs, 75%, Indians 11%, Somalis 8%, others. **Languages:** Arabic. **Religions:** Muslims (Sunni) 91%, Christians 4%, Hindus 3.5%.

Geography: Area: 130,541 sq. mi., the size of Nevada. **Location:** On the southern coast of the Arabian Peninsula. **Neighbors:** Yemen on W, Saudi Arabia on N, Oman on E. **Topography:** The entire country is very hot and very dry. A sandy coast rises to mountains which give way to desert sands. **Capital:** Aden. **Cities** (1978 est.): Aden 271,590.

Government: Head of state: Pres. Ali Nasir Muhammad Husani; in office: Apr. 21, 1980. **Head of Communist Party:** Sec. Gen. Ali Nasir Muhammad Husani; in office: April 21, 1980. **Local divisions:** 6 governorates. **Armed forces:** regulars 23,750 (1980).

Economy: Industries: Transshipment. **Chief crops:** Cotton (main export), grains. **Per capita arable land:** 0.3 acres. **Meat prod.** (1980) lamb: 11,000 metric tons. **Fish catch** (1978): 133,100 metric tons. **Electricity prod.** (1978) 242 mln. kwh. **Labor force:** 43.8% agric.; 28% ind. and commerce; 28% serv.

Finance: Currency: Dinar (Apr. 1982: .35 = $1 US). **Gross domestic product** (1977 est.): $550 mln. **Per capita income** (1977): $310. **Imports** (1979) $480 mln.; partners (1979): Kuw. 16%, Jap. 8%, Qatar 5%, UK 6%. **Exports** (1979): $250 mln.; partners (1979): It. 22%, Jap. 16%. **Tourists** (1976): 18,000; receipts (1974): $4 mln. **National budget** (1977): $101 mln. revenues; $137 mln. expenditures. **International reserves less gold** (Jan. 1982): $254.5 mln. **Gold:** 42,000 oz t. **Consumer prices** (change in 1978): 7.1%.

Transport: Motor vehicles: in use (1979): 12,500 passenger cars, 10,500 comm. vehicles. **Chief ports:** Aden.

Communications: Television sets: 32,000 in use (1976). **Radios:** 100,000 in use (1976). **Daily newspaper circ.** (1976): 4,000; 12 per 1,000 pop.

Health: Life expectancy at birth (1975): 40.6 male; 42.4 female. **Births** (per 1,000 pop. 1978): 47. **Deaths** (per 1,000 pop. 1978): 21. **Natural increase** (1978): 1.8%. **Hospital beds** (per 100,000 pop. 1977): 154. **Physicians** (per 100,000 pop. 1977): 11. **Infant mortality rate** (per 1,000 live births in 1980): 114.

Education (1978): **Literacy:** 25%. **Pop. 5-19:** in school: 40%, teachers per 1,000: 16.

Aden, mentioned in the Bible, has been a port for trade in incense, spice and silk between the East and West for 2,000 years. British rule began in 1839. Aden provided Britain with a controlling position at the southern entrance to the Red Sea.

A war for independence began in 1963. The National Liberation Front (NLF) and the Egypt-supported Front for the Liberation of Occupied South Yemen, waged a guerrilla war against the British and local dynastic rulers. The 2 groups vied with each other for control. The NLF won out. Independence came Nov. 30, 1967. In 1969, the left wing of the NLF seized power and inaugurated a thorough nationalization of the economy and regimentation of daily life.

The new government broke off relations with the U.S. and nationalized some foreign firms. Aid has been furnished by the USSR and China, with the USSR supplying most military aid.

In 1972-73 there were border skirmishes with forces of the Yemen Arab Republic. South Yemen aided leftist guerrillas in neighboring Oman. Relations with Saudi Arabia later improved. S. Yemen troops fought in Ethiopia against Eritrean rebels in 1978; 500 Cuban troops and some Soviet facilities were reported in Yemen.

Pres. Salem Robaye Ali, who had tried to improve relations with Yemen, Saudi Arabia, Oman, and the U.S., was executed after a bloody coup June 1978. The new ruling faction was accused by N. Yemen of the murder of N. Yemen's president 2 days earlier. N. Yemen, Egypt, and Saudi Arabia froze ties with S. Yemen in July.

The People's Democratic Republic of Yemen went to war with Yemen on Feb. 24, 1979. Swift Arab mediation led to a cease-fire and a mutual withdrawal of forces, Mar. 19th. An Arab League-sponsored agreement between North and South Yemen on unification of the 2 countries was signed Mar. 29th.

The Port of Aden is the country's most valuable resource, but with the closing of the Suez Canal after the Arab-Israeli War in June 1967, the port lost much of its business. The canal was reopened in 1975.

Socotra, the largest island in the Arabian Sea, Kamaran, an island in the Red Sea near the coast of North Yemen, and Perim, an island in the strait between the Gulf of Aden and the Red Sea, are controlled by South Yemen.

Yugoslavia

Socialist Federal Republic of Yugoslavia

People: Population (1981 est.): 22,600,000. **Age distrib.** (%): 0–14: 25.6; 15-59: 61.6; 60+: 12.7. **Pop. density:** 226.19 per sq. mi. **Urban** (1971): 38.6%. **Ethnic groups:** Serbs 40%, Croats 22%, Slovenes 8%, Macedonians 6%, Bosnian Moslems 6%, Albanians 2%, Montenegrin Serbs 2%, Hungarians 2%, Turks 1%. **Languages:** Serbo-Croatian, Macedonian, Slovenian (all official), Albanian, Hungarian. **Religions:** Orthodox 50%, Roman Catholics 30%, Moslems 10%, Protestants 1%.

Geography: Area: 98,766 sq. mi., the size of Wyoming. **Location:** On the Adriatic coast of the Balkan Peninsula in SE Europe. **Neighbors:** Italy on W, Austria, Hungary on N, Romania, Bulgaria on E, Greece, Albania on S. **Topography:** The Dinaric Alps run parallel to the Adriatic coast, which is lined by offshore islands. Plains stretch across N and E river basins. S and NW are mountainous. **Capital:** Belgrade. **Cities** (1980 est.): Belgrade 1,300,000; Zagreb 700,000; Skopje 440,000; Sarajevo 400,000; Ljubljana 300,000.

Government: Head of state: Pres. Petar Stambolic; in office: May 16, 1982. **Head of government:** Prime Min. Milka Planinc; b. 1924; in office: May 16, 1982; **Head of Communist Party:** H. E. Cvijetin Mijatovic; in office: May 15, 1980. **Local divisions:** 6 republics: Serbia, Croatia, Slovenia, Bosnia-Herzegovina, Macedonia, Montenegro; 2 autonomous provinces: Vojvodina, Kosovo. **Armed forces:** regulars 244,000 (1980).

Economy: Industries: Steel, chemicals, wood products, cement, textiles, tourism. **Chief crops:** Corn, grains, tobacco, sugar beets. **Minerals:** Antimony, bauxite, lead, mercury, coal, iron, copper, chrome, manganese, zinc, salt. **Crude oil reserves** (1980): 275 mln. bbls. **Per capita arable land:** 0.8 acres. **Meat prod.** (1980): beef: 347,000 metric tons; pork: 710,000 metric tons; lamb: 62,000 metric tons. **Fish catch:** (1978): 63,000 metric tons. **Electricity prod.** (1980): 59.3 bln. kwh. **Crude steel prod.** (1981): 3.9 mln. metric tons. **Labor force:** 48% agric.; 52% ind. and commerce. manuf.

Finance: Currency: Dinar (Mar. 1982: 46.12 = $1 US). **Gross domestic product** (1979): $69 bln. **Per capita income:** $3,109. **Imports** (1981): $15.8 bln.; partners (1980): W. Ger. 17%, USSR 18%, It. 7%, U.S. 7%. **Exports** (1981): $10.94 bln.; partners (1980): USSR 28%, It. 9%, W. Ger. 9%, Czech. 5%. **Tourists** (1979): 5.9 mln.; receipts: 1 bln. **National budget** (1980): $3.5 bln. revenues; $3.5 bln. expenditures. **International reserves less gold** (Feb. 1982): $1.11 bln. **Gold:** 1.85 mln. oz t. **Consumer prices** change in 1981): 39.7%.

Transport: Railway traffic (1980): 10.2 bln. passenger-km; 24.9 bln. net ton-km. **Motor vehicles:** in use (1979): 1.8 mln. passenger cars, 129,400 comm. vehicles; manuf. (1980): 187,000 passenger cars; 64,000 comm. vehicles. **Civil aviation** (1980): 2.8 bln. passenger-km; 41.7 mln. freight ton-km. **Chief ports:** Rijeka, Split, Dubrovnik.

Communications: Television sets: 4.1 mln. licensed (1979), 599,000 manuf. (1979). **Radios:** 4.6 mln. licensed (1979), 172,000 manuf. (1978). **Telephones in use** (1979): 1.9 mln. **Daily newspaper circ.** (1980): 101 per 1,000 pop.

Health: Life expectancy at birth (1977): 67.6 male; 72.6 female. **Births** (per 1,000 pop. 1980): 17.0. **Deaths** (per 1,000 pop. 1980): 9.0. **Natural increase** (1978): .9%. **Hospital beds** (per 100,000 pop. 1977): 603. **Physicians** (per 100,000 pop. 1977): 131. **Infant mortality** (per 1,000 live births 1978): 33.6

Education (1978): **Literacy:** 85%. **Pop. 5–19:** in school: 60%, teachers per 1,000: 26.

Serbia, which had since 1389 been a vassal principality of Turkey, was established as an independent kingdom by the Treaty of Berlin, 1878. Montenegro, independent since 1389, also obtained international recognition in 1878. After the Balkan wars Serbia's boundaries were enlarged by the annexation of Old Serbia and Macedonia, 1913.

When the Austro-Hungarian empire collapsed after World War I, the Kingdom of the Serbs, Croats, and Slovenes was formed from the former provinces of Croatia, Dalmatia, Bosnia, Herzegovina, Slovenia, Voyvodina and the independent state of Montenegro. The name was later changed to Yugoslavia.

Nazi Germany invaded in 1941. Many Yugoslav partisan troops continued to operate. Among these were the Chetniks led by Draja Mikhailovich, who fought other partisans led by Josip Broz, known as Marshal Tito. Tito, backed by the USSR and Britain from 1943, was in control by the time the Germans had been driven from Yugoslavia in 1945. Mikhailovich was executed July 17, 1946, by the Tito regime.

A constituent assembly proclaimed Yugoslavia a republic Nov. 29, 1945. It became a federated republic Jan. 31, 1946, and Marshal Tito, a communist, became head of the government.

The Stalin policy of dictating to all communist nations was rejected by Tito. He accepted economic aid and military equipment from the U.S. and received aid in foreign trade also from France and Great Britain. Tito also supported the liberal government of Czechoslovakia in 1968 before the Russian invasion, but he paid a friendship visit to Moscow in 1972.

A separatist movement among Croatians, 2d to the Serbs in numbers, brought arrests and a change of leaders in the Croatian Republic in Jan. 1972. Violence by extreme Croatian nationalists and fears of Soviet political intervention have led to restrictions on political and intellectual dissent, which had previously been freer than in other East European countries. Serbians, Montenegrins, and Macedonians use Cyrillic, Croatians and Slovenians use Latin letters. Croatia and Slovenia have been the most prosperous republics.

Most industry is socialized and private enterprise is restricted to small-scale production. Since 1952 workers are guaranteed a basic wage and a share in cooperative profits. Management of industrial enterprises is handled by workers' councils. Farmland is 85% privately owned but farms are restricted to 25 acres.

Beginning in 1965, reforms designed to decentralize the administration of economic development and to force industries to produce more efficiently in competition with foreign producers were introduced.

Yugoslavia has developed considerable trade with Western Europe as well as with Eastern Europe. Money earned by Yugoslavs working temporarily in Western Europe helps pay for imports.

Pres. Tito died May 4, 1980; with his death, the post as head of the Collective Presidency and also that as head of the League of Communists became a rotating system of succession among the members representing each republic and autonomous province.

Zaire

Republic of Zaire

People: Population (1981 est.): 30,100,000. **Pop. density:** 30 per sq. mi. **Urban** (1981): 30.3%. **Ethnic groups:** Mostly Bantus: Luba 18%, Mongo 17%, Kongo 12%, Ruanda 10%, others. **Languages:** French (official), Bantu dialects. **Religions:** animist 50%, Christian 43%.

Geography: Area: 905,063 sq. mi., one-fourth the size of the U.S. **Location:** In central Africa. **Neighbors:** Congo on W, Central African Republic, Sudan on N, Uganda, Rwanda, Burundi, Tanzania on E, Zambia, Angola on S. **Topography:** Zaire includes the bulk of the Zaire (Congo) R. Basin. The vast central region is a low-lying plateau covered by rain forest. Mountainous terraces in the W, savannas in the S and SE, grasslands toward the N, and the high Ruwenzori Mtns. on the E surround the central region. A short strip of territory borders the Atlantic O. The Zaire R. is 2,718 mi. long. **Capital:** Kinshasa. **Cities** (1981 est.): Kinshasa 3,000,000; Kananga 601,239.

Government: Head of state: Pres. Mobutu Sese Seko; b. Oct. 14, 1930; in office: Nov. 25, 1965. **Head of government:** N'singa Udjuu; in office: Apr. 23, 1981. **Local divisions:** 8 regions, Kinshasa. **Armed forces:** regulars 21,000 (1980).

Economy: Chief crops: Coffee, cotton, rice, sugar cane, bananas, plantains, coconuts, manioc, mangoes, tea, cacao, palm oil. **Minerals:** Cobalt (two-thirds of world output), copper, cadmium, gold, silver, tin, germanium, zinc, iron, tungsten, manganese, uranium, radium. **Crude oil reserves** (1980): 135 mln. bbls. **Other resources:** Forests, rubber, ivory. **Per capita arable land:** 0.5 acres. Meat prod. (1980): beef: 22,000 metric tons; pork: 29,000 metric tons; lamb: 9,000 metric tons. **Fish catch** (1978): 101,000 metric tons. **Electricity prod.** (1978): 3.9 bln. kwh. **Labor force:** 75% agric.

Finance: Currency: Zaire (Mar. 1982: 5.62 = $1 US). **Gross domestic product** (1979): $6.16 bln. **Per capita income** (1975): $127. **Imports** (1980): $835 mln.; partners (1980): Belg. 16%, U.S. 10%, W. Ger. 10%, So. Afr. 9%. **Exports** (1980): $1.63 bln.; partners (1980): Ang. 22%, U.S. 13%, Moz. 10%. **Tourists** (1977): 24,500; receipts (1976): $11 mln. **National budget** (1978): $886 mln. revenues; $1.8 bln. expenditures. **International reserves less gold** (Feb. 1982): $153.4 mln. **Gold:** 361,000 oz t. **Consumer prices** (change in 1980): 42.1%.

Transport: Railway traffic (1976): 467 mln. passenger-km; 2.20 bln. net ton-km. **Motor vehicles:** in use (1979): 94,000 passenger cars, 85,500 comm. vehicles; assembled (1975): 2.1 mln. comm. vehicles. **Civil aviation** (1980): 834 mln. passenger-km. 34.9 mln. freight ton-km. **Chief ports:** Matadi, Boma.

Communications: Television sets: 8,000 in use (1977). **Radios:** 125,000 mln. in use (1977). **Telephones in use** (1980): 30,300. **Daily newspaper circ.** (1980): 2 per 1,000 pop.

Health: Life expectancy at birth (1981): 44 male; 48 female. **Births** (per 1,000 pop. 1978): 46. **Deaths** (per 1,000 pop. 1978): 18. **Natural increase** (1978): 3.5%. **Hospital beds** (per 100,000 pop. 1977): 291. **Physicians** (per 100,000 pop. 1977): 2. **Infant mortality** (per 1,000 live births 1981): 160.

Education (1978): **Literacy:** 40%. **Pop. 5-19:** in school: 43%, teachers per 1,000: 11.

The earliest inhabitants of Zaire may have been the pygmies, followed by Bantus from the E and Nilotic tribes from the N. The large Bantu Bakongo kingdom ruled much of Zaire and Angola when Portuguese explorers visited in the 15th century.

Leopold II, king of the Belgians, formed an international group to exploit the Congo in 1876. In 1877 Henry M. Stanley explored the Congo and in 1878 the king's group sent him back to organize the region and win over the native chiefs. The Conference of Berlin, 1884-85, organized the Congo Free State with Leopold as king and chief owner. Exploitation of native laborers on the rubber plantations caused international criticism and led to granting of a colonial charter, 1908.

Belgian and Congolese leaders agreed Jan. 27, 1960, that the Congo would become independent June 30. In the first general elections, May 31, the National Congolese movement of Patrice Lumumba won 35 of 137 seats in the National Assembly. He was appointed premier June 21, and formed a coalition cabinet.

Widespread violence caused Europeans and others to flee. Katanga, rich in minerals, seceded from the republic July 11, but ended the secession in 1963. The UN Security Council Aug. 9, 1960, called on Belgium to withdraw its troops and sent a UN contingent. President Kasavubu removed Lumumba as premier. Lumumba fought for control backed by Ghana, Guinea and India; he was murdered in 1961.

The last UN troops left the Congo June 30, 1964, and Moise Tshombe became president.

On Sept. 7, 1964, leftist rebels set up a "People's Republic" in Stanleyville. Tshombe hired foreign mercenaries and sought to rebuild the Congolese Army. In Nov. and Dec. 1964 rebels slew scores of white hostages and thousands of Congolese; Belgian paratroops, dropped from U.S. transport planes, rescued hundreds. By July 1965 the rebels had lost their effectiveness.

In 1965 Gen. Joseph D. Mobutu was named president. He later changed his name to Mobutu Sese Seko. On July 1 he renamed Leopoldville, Kinshasa; Stanleyville, Kisangani; and Elisabethville, Lubumbashi.

The country changed its name to Republic of Zaire on Oct. 27, 1971; in 1972 Zairians with Christian names were ordered to change them to African names.

In 1969-74, political stability under Mobutu was reflected in improved economic conditions. In 1974 most foreign-owned businesses were ordered sold to Zaire citizens, but in 1977 the government asked the original owners to return. A fall in copper prices in 1975 brought a surge in foreign debt and economic difficulties, causing political unrest.

In 1977, a force of Zairians, apparently trained by Cubans, invaded Shaba province (Katanga) from Angola. Zaire repelled the attack, with the aid of Egyptian pilots and 1,500 Moroccan troops flown in by France. The U.S. sent "nonlethal" supplies. But many Belgian and other European mining experts failed to return after a second unsuccessful invasion from Angola in May 1978.

Zambia

Republic of Zambia

People: Population (1981 est.): 6,000,000. **Age distrib.** (%): 0–14: 46.5; 15–59: 49.3; 60+: 4.1. **Pop. density:** 18.82 per sq. mi. **Urban** (1979): 40.4%. **Ethnic groups:** Africans 99%, mostly Bantu tribes, Europeans and Asians 1%. **Languages:** English (official), Bantu dialects. **Religions:** Predominantly animists, Roman Catholics 21%, Protestant, Hindu, Muslim minorities.

Geography: Area: 290,586 sq. mi., larger than Texas. **Location:** In southern central Africa. **Neighbors:** Zaire on N, Tanzania, Malawi, Mozambique on E, Zimbabwe, Namibia on S, Angola on W. **Topography:** Zambia is mostly high plateau country covered with thick forests, and drained by several important rivers, including the Zambezi. **Capital:** Lusaka. **Cities** (1978 est.): Lusaka 559,000; Kitwe 310,000; Ndola 291,000.

Government: Head of state: Pres. Kenneth David Kaunda; b. Apr. 28, 1924; in office: Oct. 24, 1964. **Head of government:** Prime Min. Nalumino Mundia; in office: Feb. 18, 1981. **Local divisions:** 9 provinces. **Armed forces:** regulars 14,300; 1980.

Economy: Chief crops: Corn, tobacco, peanuts, cotton, sugar. **Minerals:** Cobalt, copper, zinc, gold, lead, vanadium, manganese, coal. **Other resources:** Rubber, ivory. **Per capita arable land:** 2.3 acres. **Meat prod.** (1980): beef: 24,000 metric tons; pork: 7,000 metric tons. **Fish catch** (1978): 47,600 metric tons. **Electricity prod.** (1979): 8.7 bln. kwh. **Labor force:** 57% agric.; 43% ind. and commerce.

Finance: Currency: Kwacha (Jan. 1982: .80 = $1 US). **Gross domestic product** (1979): $3.24 bln. **Per capita income** (1978): $414. **Imports** (1980): $1.2 bln.; partners (1979): UK 26%, Saudi Ar. 18%, W. Ger. 18%, U.S. 9%. **Exports** (1980): $1.40 bln.; partners (1979): Jap. 19%, Fr. 15%, UK 13%, U.S. 10%, W. Ger. 9%. **Tourists** (1976): 56,200; receipts (1977): $12 mln. **National budget** (1979): $753 mln. revenues; $973 mln. expenditures. **International reserves less gold** (Jan. 1982): $49.8 mln. **Gold:** 220,000 oz t. **Consumer prices** (change in 1980): 11.7%.

Transport: Motor vehicles: in use (1979): 103,500 passenger cars, 65,500 comm. vehicles. **Civil aviation** (1980): 467 mln. passenger-km; 47.5 mln. freight ton-km.

Communications: Television sets: 60,000 in use (1978). **Radios:** 125,000 in use (1978), 28,000 manuf. (1977). **Telephones in use** (1980): 60,500. **Daily newspaper circ.** (1980): 43 per 1,000 pop.

Health: Life expectancy at birth (1975): 44.3 male; 47.5 female. **Births** (per 1,000 pop. 1978): 49. **Deaths** (per 1,000 pop. 1978): 17. **Natural increase** (1978): 3.2%. **Hospital beds** (per 100,000 pop. 1977): 366. **Physicians** (per 100,000 pop. 1977): 5. **Infant mortality** (per 1,000 live births 1978): 160.

Education (1978): **Literacy:** 50%. **Pop. 5-19:** in school: 50%, teachers per 1,000: 12.

As Northern Rhodesia, the country was under the administration of the South Africa Company, 1889 until 1924, when the office of governor was established, and, subsequently, a legislature. The country became an independent republic within the Commonwealth Oct. 24, 1964.

After the white government of Rhodesia declared its independence from Britain Nov. 11, 1965, relations between Zambia and Rhodesia became strained and use of their jointly owned railroad was disputed.

Britain gave Zambia an extra $12 million aid in 1966 after imposing an oil embargo on Rhodesia, and Zambia set up a temporary airlift to carry copper out from its mines and gasoline in. In Aug. 1968 a 1,058-mi. pipeline was completed, bringing oil from Tanzania. In 1973 a truck road to carry copper to Tanzania's port of Dar es Salaam was completed with U.S. aid. A railroad, built with Chinese aid across Tanzania, reached the Zambian border in 1974.

As part of a program of government participation in major industries, a government corporation in 1970 took over 51% of the ownership of 2 foreign-owned copper mining companies, paying with bonds. Privately-held land and other enterprises were nationalized in 1975, as were all newspapers. Decline in copper prices and strikes by copper miners hurt the economy in 1981.

Zimbabwe

People: Population (1981 est.): 7,600,000. **Age distrib.** (%): 0–14: 49.2; 15–59: 47.8; 60+: 3.0. **Pop. density:** 48.96 per sq. mi. **Urban** (1979): 19.6%. **Ethnic groups:** Shona 77%, Ndebele 19%, white 3%, Coloreds and Asians. **Languages:** English (official), Shona, Ndebele. **Religions:** Predominantly traditional tribal beliefs, Christian minority.

Geography: Area: 150,873 sq. mi., nearly as large as California. **Location:** In southern Africa. **Neighbors:** Zambia on N, Botswana on W, S. Africa on S, Mozambique on E. **Topography:** Rhodesia is high plateau country, rising to mountains on eastern border, sloping down on the other borders. **Capital:** Harare. **Cities** (1979 est.): Harare (met.) 627,000; Bulawayo (met.) 363,000.

Government: Head of state: Pres. Rev. Cannan Banana, b. Mar. 5, 1936; in office: Apr. 18, 1980. **Head of government:** Prime Min. Robert G. Mugabe; b. Apr. 14, 1928; in office: Apr. 18, 1980. **Local divisions:** 8 provinces. **Armed forces:** regulars 21,500; para-military 52,500.

Economy: Industries: Clothing, chemicals, light industries. **Chief crops:** Tobacco, sugar, cotton, corn, wheat. **Minerals:** Chromium, gold, nickel, asbestos, copper, iron, coal. **Per capita arable land:** 0.9 acres. **Meat prod.** (1980): beef: 125,000 metric tons; pork: 9,000 metric tons; lamb: 7,000 metric tons. **Electricity prod.** (1980): 4.5 bln. kwh. **Crude steel prod.** (1981): 691,000 metric tons. **Labor force:** 35% agric.; 30% ind. and commerce; 20% serv.; 15% gvt.

Finance: Currency: Dollar (Sept. 1981: .71 = $1 US). **Gross domestic product** (1979 est.): $3.4 bln. **Per capita income** (1979 est.): White $8,000, African $240-$500. **Imports** (1980): $1.1 bln.; partners (1965): UK 30%, So. Afr. 23%, U.S. 7%, Jap. 6%. **Exports** (1979): $1.15 bln.; partners (1965): Zamb. 25%, UK 22%, So. Afr. 10%, W. Ger. 9%. **Consumer prices** (change in 1977): 11.9%.

Transport: Railway traffic (1979): 5.8 bln. net ton-km. **Motor vehicles:** in use (1979): 175,000 passenger cars, 70,000 comm. vehicles.

Communications: Television sets: 74,000 in use (1980). **Radios:** 214,000 in use (1980). **Telephones in use** (1980): 214,400. **Daily newspaper circ.** (1980): 16 per 1,000 pop.

Health: Life expectancy at birth (1975): 49.8 male; 53.3 female. **Births** (per 1,000 pop. 1978): 49. **Deaths** (per 1,000 pop. 1978): 16. **Natural increase** (1978): 2.2%. **Hospital beds** (per 100,000 pop. 1977): 258. **Physicians** (per 100,000 pop. 1977): 9. **Infant mortality** (per 1,000 live births 1975): 122.

Education (1978): **Literacy:** 30%. **Pop. 5-19:** in school: 37%, teachers per 1,000: 11.

Britain took over the area as Southern Rhodesia in 1923 from the British South Africa Co. (which, under Cecil Rhodes, had conquered the area by 1897) and granted internal self-government. Under a 1961 constitution, voting was restricted to maintain whites in power. On Nov. 11, 1965, Prime Min. Ian D. Smith announced his country's unilateral declaration of independence. Britain termed the act illegal, and demanded Rhodesia broaden voting rights to provide for eventual rule by the majority Africans.

Urged by Britain, the UN imposed sanctions, including embargoes on oil shipments to Rhodesia. Some oil and gasoline reached Rhodesia, however, from South Africa and Mozambique, before the latter became independent in 1975. In May 1968, the UN Security Council ordered a trade embargo.

A new constitution came into effect, Mar. 2, 1970, providing for a republic with a president and prime minister. The election law effectively prevented full black representation through income tax requirements.

A proposed British-Rhodesian settlement was dropped in May 1972 when a British commission reported most Rhodesian blacks opposed it. Intermittent negotiations between the government and various black nationalist groups failed to prevent increasing skirmishes. By mid-1978, over 6,000 soldiers and civilians had been killed. Rhodesian troops battled guerrillas within Mozambique and Zambia. An "internal settlement" signed Mar.

1978 in which Smith and 3 popular black leaders share control until transfer of power to the black majority was rejected by guerrilla leaders.

In the country's first universal-franchise election, Apr. 21, 1979, Bishop Abel Muzorewa's United African National Council gained a bare majority control of the black-dominated parliament. Britain's Thatcher government, 1979, began efforts to normalize its relationship with Zimbabwe. A British cease-fire was accepted by all parties, Dec. 5th; elections were held in 1980. Independence was finally achieved Apr. 18, 1980.

Zimbabwe was admitted as the 154th member of the United Nations, Sept. 20, 1980.

United Nations

The 37th regular session of the United Nations General Assembly was scheduled to open in September, 1982. *See Chronology for developments at UN sessions during 1982.*

UN headquarters are in New York, N.Y., between First Ave. and Roosevelt Drive and E. 42d St. and E. 48th St. The General Assembly Bldg., Secretariat, Conference and Library bldgs. are interconnected. A new UN office building-hotel was opened in New York in 1976.

A European office at Geneva includes Secretariat and agency staff members. Other offices of UN bodies and related organizations are scattered throughout the world.

The UN has a post office originating its own stamps.

Proposals to establish an organization of nations for maintenance of world peace led to the United Nations Conference on International Organization at San Francisco, Apr. 25-June 26, 1945, where the charter of the United Nations was drawn up. It was signed June 26 by 50 nations, and by Poland, one of the original 51, on Oct. 15, 1945. The charter came into effect Oct. 24, 1945, upon ratification by the permanent members of the Security Council and a majority of other signatories.

Roster of the United Nations

(As of mid-1982)

The 157 members of the United Nations, with the years in which they became members.

Member	Year	Member	Year	Member	Year	Member	Year
Afghanistan	1946	Ecuador	1945	Lesotho	1966	Samoa (Western)	1976
Albania	1955	Egypt[2]	1945	Liberia	1945	Sao Tome e Principe	1975
Algeria	1962	El Salvador	1945	Libya	1955	Saudi Arabia	1945
Angola	1976	Equatorial Guinea	1968	Luxembourg	1945	Senegal	1960
Antigua and Barbuda	1981	Ethiopia	1945	Madagascar (Malagasy)	1960	Seychelles	1976
Argentina	1945	Fiji	1970	Malawi	1964	Sierra Leone	1961
Australia	1945	Finland	1955	Malaysia[1]	1957	Singapore[1]	1965
Austria	1955	France	1945	Maldives	1965	Solomon Islands	1978
Bahamas	1973	Gabon	1960	Mali	1960	Somalia	1960
Bahrain	1971	Gambia	1965	Malta	1964	South Africa[5]	1945
Bangladesh	1974	Germany, East	1973	Mauritania	1961	Spain	1955
Barbados	1966	Germany, West	1973	Mauritius	1968	Sri Lanka	1955
Belgium	1945	Ghana	1957	Mexico	1945	Sudan	1956
Belize	1981	Greece	1945	Mongolia	1961	Suriname	1975
Benin	1960	Grenada	1974	Morocco	1956	Swaziland	1968
Bhutan	1971	Guatemala	1945	Mozambique	1975	Sweden	1946
Bolivia	1945	Guinea	1958	Nepal	1955	Syria[2]	1945
Botswana	1966	Guinea-Bissau	1974	Netherlands	1945	Tanzania[3]	1961
Brazil	1945	Guyana	1966	New Zealand	1945	Thailand	1946
Bulgaria	1955	Haiti	1945	Nicaragua	1945	Togo	1960
Burma	1948	Honduras	1945	Niger	1960	Trinidad & Tobago	1962
Burundi	1962	Hungary	1955	Nigeria	1960	Tunisia	1956
Byelorussia	1945	Iceland	1946	Norway	1945	Turkey	1945
Cambodia (Kampuchea)	1955	India	1945	Oman	1971	Uganda	1962
Cameroon	1960	Indonesia[6]	1950	Pakistan	1947	Ukraine	1945
Canada	1945	Iran	1945	Panama	1945	USSR	1945
Cape Verde	1975	Iraq	1945	Papua New Guinea	1975	United Arab Emirates	1971
Central Afr. Rep.	1960	Ireland	1955	Paraguay	1945	United Kingdom	1945
Chad	1960	Israel	1949	Peru	1945	United States	1945
Chile	1945	Italy	1955	Philippines	1945	Upper Volta	1960
China[4]	1945	Ivory Coast	1960	Poland	1945	Uruguay	1945
Colombia	1945	Jamaica	1962	Portugal	1955	Vanuatu	1981
Comoros	1975	Japan	1956	Qatar	1971	Venezuela	1945
Congo	1960	Jordan	1955	Romania	1955	Vietnam	1977
Costa Rica	1945	Kenya	1963	Rwanda	1962	Yemen	1947
Cuba	1945	Kuwait	1963	Saint Lucia	1979	Yemen, South	1967
Cyprus	1960	Laos	1955	Saint Vincent and the Grenadines	1980	Yugoslavia	1945
Czechoslovakia	1945	Lebanon	1945			Zaire	1960
Denmark	1945					Zambia	1964
Djibouti	1977					Zimbabwe	1980
Dominica	1978						
Dominican Rep.	1945						

(1) Malaya joined the UN in 1957. In 1963, its name was changed to Malaysia following the accession of Singapore, Sabah, and Sarawak. Singapore became an independent UN member in 1965. (2) Egypt and Syria were original members of the UN. In 1958, the United Arab Republic was established by a union of Egypt and Syria and continued as a single member of the UN. In 1961, Syria resumed its separate membership. (3) Tanganyika was a member of

the United Nations from 1961 and Zanzibar was a member from 1963. Following the ratification in 1964 of Articles of Union between Tanganyika and Zanzibar, the United Republic of Tanganyika and Zanzibar continued as a single member of the United Nations, later changing its name to United Republic of Tanzania. (4) The General Assembly voted in 1971 to expel the Chinese government on Taiwan and admit the Peking government in its place. (5) The General Assembly rejected the credentials of the South African delegates in 1974, and suspended the country from the Assembly. (6) Indonesia withdrew from the UN in 1965 and rejoined in 1966.

Organization

The text of the UN Charter, and further information, may be obtained from the Office of Public Information, United Nations, N.Y.

General Assembly. The General Assembly is composed of representatives of all the member nations. Each nation is entitled to one vote.

The General Assembly meets in regular annual sessions and in special session when necessary. Special sessions are convoked by the Secretary General at the request of the Security Council or of a majority of the members of the UN.

On important questions a two-thirds majority of members present and voting is required; on other questions a simple majority is sufficient.

The General Assembly must approve the budget and apportion expenses among members. A member in arrears will have no vote if the amount of arrears equals or exceeds the amount of the contributions due for the preceeding two full years.

Security Council. The Security Council consists of 15 members, 5 with permanent seats. The remaining 10 are elected for 2-year terms by the General Assembly; they are not eligible for immediate reelection.

Permanent members of the Council: China, France, USSR, United Kingdom, United States.

Non-permanent members are Ireland, Japan, Panama, Spain and Uganda (until Dec. 31, 1982); Ghana, Jordan, Poland, Togo, and Zaire (until Dec. 31, 1983).

The Security Council has the primary responsiblity within the UN for maintaining international peace and security. The Council may investigate any dispute that threatens international peace and security.

Any member of the UN at UN headquarters may participate in its discussions and a nation not a member of UN may appear if it is a party to a dispute.

Decisions on procedural questions are made by an affirmative vote of 9 members. On all other matters the affirmative vote of 9 members must include the concurring votes of all permanent members; it is this clause which gives rise to the so-called "veto." A party to a dispute must refrain from voting.

The Security Council directs the various truce supervisory forces deployed in the Middle East, India-Pakistan, and Cyprus.

Economic and Social Council. The Economic and Social Council consists of 54 members elected by the General Assembly for 3-year terms of office. The council is responsible under the General Assembly for carrying out the functions of the United Nations with regard to international economic, social, cultural, educational, health and related matters. The council meets usually twice a year.

Trusteeship Council. The administration of trust territories is under UN supervision. The only remaining trust territory is the Pacific Islands, administered by the U.S.

Secretariat. The Secretary General is the chief administrative officer of the UN. He may bring to the attention of the Security Council any matter that threatens international peace. He reports to the General Assembly.

Javier Perez de Cuellar (Peru), secretary general, was elected to a 5-year term beginning Jan. 1, 1982.

The 1982-83 proposed program budget was $1.53 billion, exclusive of trust funds, special contributions, and expenses for the Specialized or the Related Organizations.

The US contributes 25% of the regular budget, the Soviet Union 11.33%, Japan 8.66%, W. Germany 7.74%, and France, China, and Britain about 5% each.

International Court of Justice. The International Court of Justice is the principal judicial organ of the United Nations. All members are *ipso facto* parties to the statute of the Court, as are three nonmembers — Liechtenstein, San Marino, and Switzerland. Other states may become parties to the Court's statute.

The jurisdiction of the Court comprises cases which the parties submit to it and matters especially provided for in the charter or in treaties. The Court gives advisory opinions and renders judgments. Its decisions are only binding between the parties concerned and in respect to a particular dispute. If any party to a case fails to heed a judgment, the other party may have recourse to the Security Council.

The 15 judges are elected for 9-year terms by the General Assembly and the Security Council. Retiring judges are eligible for re-election. The Court remains permanently in session, except during vacations. All questions are decided by majority. The Court sits in The Hague, Netherlands.

Judges: 9-year term in office ending 1988: Robert Ago, Italy. Stephen M. Schwebel, U.S. Abdullah Ali, Egypt. Platon D. Morozov, USSR. Jose Sette Camara, Brazil. **9-year term in office ending 1985:** Taslim Olawala Elias, Nigeria. Hermann Mosier, W. Germany. Shigeru Oda, Japan. Abdullah Fikri Al-Khani, Syria. Manfred Lachs, Poland. **9-year term in office ending 1982:** Isaac Forster, Senegal. Andre Gros, France. Jose Maria Ruda, Argentina. Nagendra Singh, India.

Specialized and Related Agencies

These agencies are autonomous, with their own memberships and organs which have a functional relationship or working agreement with the UN. (Headquarters, number of member nations.)

International Labor Org. (ILO) aims to promote social justice, employment, and sound industrial relations; improve labor conditions and living standards. (Geneva, 145)

Food & Agriculture Org. (FAO) aims to increase production from farms, forests, and fisheries; improve distribution, marketing, and nutrition; better conditions for rural people. (Rome, 147)

United Nations Educational, Scientific, & Cultural Org. (UNESCO) aims to promote collaboration among nations in the fields of education, science, and culture and communication. (Paris, 156)

World Health Org. (WHO) aims to aid the attainment of the highest possible level of health. (Geneva, 157)

International Monetary Fund (IMF) aims to promote international monetary co-operation and currency stabilization. (Washington, D.C., 141)

International Civil Aviation Org. (ICAO) promotes international civil aviation standards and regulations. (Montreal, 148)

Universal Postal Union (UPU) aims to perfect postal services and promote international collaboration. (Berne, 162)

International Telecommunication Union (ITU) sets up international regulations of radio, telegraph, telephone and space radio-communications. Allocates radio frequencies. (Geneva, 155)

World Meteorological Org. (WMO) aims to co-ordinate and improve world meteorological work, and promotes operational hydrology. (Geneva, 154)

Intergovernmental Maritime Consultative Org. (IMCO) aims to promote co-operation on technical matters affecting international shipping. (London, 121)

World Intellectual Property Organization (WIPO) seeks to protect, through international cooperation, literary, industrial, scientific, and artistic works, i.e. "intellectual property." (Geneva, 95)

International Atomic Energy Agency (IAEA) aims to promote the safe, peaceful uses of atomic energy. (Vienna, 110)

General Agreement on Tariffs and Trade (GATT) is the only treaty setting rules for world trade. Provides a forum for settling trade disputes and negotiating trade liberalization. (Geneva, 85)

International Bank for Reconstruction and Development (World Bank) provides loans and technical assistance for economic development projects in developing member countries; encourages cofinancing for projects from other public and private sources, both bilateral and multilateral (Washington, D.C., 139). **International Development Association (IDA),** an affiliate of the Bank, provides funds for development projects on concessionary terms to the poorer developing member countries. (Washington, D.C., 125)

International Finance Corporation (IFC) promotes the growth of the private sector in developing member countries; encourages the development of local capital markets; stimulates the international flow of private capital. (Washington, D.C., 118)

The World's Refugees in 1982

Source: United States Committee for Refugees

Country of Asylum	From	Number
Africa		
Algeria	Western Sahara, various	65,000
Angola	Namibia, South Africa	73,000
Botswana	Angola, Namibia, South Africa	1,500
Burundi	Rwanda	55,000
Cameroon	Chad	20,000
Central African Rep.	Chad	5,000
Djibouti	Ethiopia	30,000
Egypt	various	5,500
Ethiopia	Sudan	11,000
Kenya	Ethiopia, Rwanda, Uganda, various	3,900
Lesotho	South Africa, various	11,000
Nigeria	Chad	40,000
Rwanda	Burundi, Uganda	10,000
Senegal	various	4,000
Somalia	Ethiopia	700,000
Sudan	Ethiopia, Uganda, Chad, Zaire	500,000
Swaziland	South Africa	5,700
Tanzania	Burundi, Zaire	156,000
Uganda	Rwanda, Zaire	113,000
Zaire	Angola, Uganda, Zambia	370,000
Zambia	Angola, Namibia, various	42,000
Others		30,000
Total Africa		**2,251,600**
Asia		
Australia	various	304,000
Bhutan	Tibet	1,500
China	Indo-China	265,000
Hong Kong	Vietnam	14,000
India	Afghanistan, various	3,300
Indonesia	Vietnam	6,000
Japan	Vietnam	1,800
Laos	Cambodia	3,800
Macao	Vietnam	1,200
Malaysia	Philippines, Vietnam, Cambodia	99,000
Nepal	Tibet	11,000
New Zealand	various	10,000
Papua New Guinea	Indonesia	1,000
Philippines	Vietnam	6,600
Singapore	Vietnam	500
Thailand	Vietnam, Laos, Cambodia	193,000
Vietnam	Cambodia	33,000
Total Asia		**954,700**
Europe		
Austria	Eastern Europe	43,000
Belgium	various	33,000
Denmark	various	1,800
France	various	150,000
W. Germany	various	94,000
Greece	various	3,800
Italy	various	14,000
Netherlands	various	12,000
Norway	various	6,000
Portugal	Africa, Latin America	7,600
Romania	Chile	1,000
Spain	Latin America, Asia	40,000
Sweden	various	20,000
Switzerland	various	37,000
United Kingdom	various	148,000
Yugoslavia	various	2,000
Total Europe		**613,200**
Latin America		
Argentina	Europe, Latin America, Southeast Asia	26,000
Belize	El Salvador	7,000
Bolivia	Europe, Latin America	500
Brazil	Europe, Latin America	24,000
Chile	Europe	1,500
Colombia	Latin America	2,000
Costa Rica	El Salvador, Latin America	13,000
Cuba	Latin America	3,000
Dominican Rep.	Haiti	3,800
Ecuador	various	700
Guatemala	El Salvador	50-100,000
Honduras	El Salvador, Guatemala, others	25,000
Mexico	El Salvador	70-140,000
Nicaragua	El Salvador	20,000
Panama	El Salvador	1,000
Peru	Europe, Latin America	1,500
Uruguay	Europe, Latin America	1,700
Venezuela	Europe, Latin America	18,000
Total Latin America		**268,700-388,700**
North America		
Canada	various	338,000
United States	various	849,000
Total North America		**1,187,000**
Middle East		
Iran	Afghanistan, Kurds, Iraq	110,000
Lebanon	Ethiopia, various	3,200
Pakistan	Afghanistan	2,600,000
Others		40,000
Palestinians		
Gaza Strip		370,000
Jordan		733,000
Lebanon		232,000
Syria		215,000
West Bank		334,000
Total Middle East		**4,637,200**
Total Refugees		**10,032,000**

Ambassadors and Envoys

As of May 1982.

The address of foreign embassies to the United States is Washington, D.C. The address of U.S. embassies abroad is simply the appropriate foreign capital. The following countries are not listed due to suspension of diplomatic relations with the U.S.: Albania[1], Angola[2], Cambodia[3], Republic of China (Taiwan)[4], Cuba[5], Iran[6], Iraq,[7] Libya[10], Vietnam[3], South Yemen[3].

Countries	Envoys from United States	Envoys to United States
Afghanistan	*Vacant*	Salem M. Spartak, Chargé
Algeria	Michael H. Newlin, Amb.	Redha Malek, Amb.
Antigua & Barbuda	Milan D. Bush, Amb.	*Vacant*
Argentina	Harry W. Shlaudeman, Amb.	Estaban A. Takacs, Amb.
Australia	Robert D. Nesen, Amb.	Robert Cotton, Amb.
Austria	Theodore E. Cummings, Amb.	Thomas Klestil, Amb.
Bahamas	*Vacant*	Reginald L. Wood, Amb.
Bahrain	Peter A. Sutherland, Amb.	Abdulaziz Abdulrahman Buali, Amb.
Bangladesh	Jane A. Coon, Amb.	Tabarak Husain, Amb.
Barbados	Milan D. Bush, Amb.	Charles A. T. Skeete, Amb.
Belgium	Charles H. Price, Amb.	J. Raoul Schoumaker, Amb.
Belize	Malcolm R. Barnebey, Chargé	Robert A. Leslie, Chargé
Benin	*Vacant*	Thomas S. Boya, Amb.
Bolivia	Edwin G. Corr, Amb.	Julio Sanjines-Goitia, Amb.
Botswana	Horace G. Dawson Jr., Amb.	Moteane J. Melamu, Amb.
Brazil	Langhorne A. Motley, Amb.	Antonio F.A. da Silveira, Amb.
Bulgaria	Robert L. Barry, Amb.	Stoyan I. Zhulev, Amb.
Burma	Patricia M. Byrne, Amb.	U Kyaw Khaing, Amb.
Burundi	Frances D. Cook, Amb.	Simon Sabimbona, Amb.
Cameroon	Hume A. Horan, Amb.	Paul Pondi, Amb.
Canada	Paul H. Robinson Jr., Amb.	Allan Gotlieb, Amb.
Cape Verde	Peter Jon de Vos, Amb.	Jose Luis Fernandes Lopes, Amb.
Central African Rep.	Arthur H. Woodruff, Amb.	Jacques Topande Makombo, Amb.
Chad[9]	Donald R. Norland, Amb.	Youssouf Abaker, Chargé
Chile	*Vacant*	Enrique Valenzuela, Amb.
China, People's Rep.	Arthur W. Hummel Jr., Amb.	Chai Zemin, Amb.
Colombia	Thomas D. Boyatt, Amb.	Fernando Gaviria, Amb.
Comoros	Fernando E. Rondon, Amb.	*Vacant*
Congo	*Vacant*	Nicolas Mondjo, Amb.
Costa Rica	Francis J. McNeil, Amb.	Jose Rafael Echeverria, Amb.
Cyprus	Raymond C. Ewing, Amb.	Andrew J. Jacovides, Amb.
Czechoslovakia	Jack F. Matlock Jr., Amb.	Jaromir Johanes, Amb.
Denmark	John L. Loeb Jr., Amb	Otto R. Borch, Amb.
Djibouti	Jerrold M. North, Amb.	Salah Hadji Farah Dirir, Amb.
Dominica	Milan D. Bush, Amb.	*Vacant*
Dominican Republic	Robert L. Yost, Amb.	Rafael Molina Morillo, Amb.
Ecuador	Raymond E. González, Amb.	Ricardo Crespo-Zaldumbide, Amb.
Egypt	Alfred L. Atherton Jr., Amb.	Ashraf A. Ghorbal, Amb.
El Salvador	Dean R. Hinton, Amb.	Ernesto Rivas-Gallont, Amb.
Equatorial Guinea	Alan M. Harry, Amb.	Don Carmelo Nvono-Nca M. Oluy, Amb.
Estonia[8]		Ernst Jaakson, Consul General
Ethiopia	*Vacant*	Tesfaye Demeke, Chargé
Fiji	William Bodde Jr., Amb.	Filipe N. Bole, Amb.
Finland	Keith F. Nyborg, Amb.	Jaakko Iloniemi, Amb.
France	Evan G. Galbraith, Amb.	Bernard Vernier-Palliez, Amb.
Gabon	Francis T. McNamara, Amb.	Hubert Ondias Souna, Amb.
Gambia, The	Larry G. Piper, Amb.	Ousman A. Sallah, Amb.
Germany, East	Herbert S. Okun, Amb.	Horst Grunert, Amb.
Germany, West	Arthur F. Burns, Amb.	Peter Hermes, Amb.
Ghana	Thomas W. Smith, Amb.	Ebenezer A. Akuete, Amb.
Greece	Monteagle Sterns, Amb.	Nicholas Karandreas, Amb.
Grenada	Milan D. Bush	Bernard K. Radix, Amb.
Guatemala	Frederic L. Chapin, Amb.	Felipe D. Monterroso, Amb.
Guinea	Allen C. Davis, Amb.	Mamady Lamine Conde, Amb.
Guinea-Bissau	Peter Jon de Vos, Amb.	Inacio Semedo Jr., Amb.
Guyana	Gerald E. Thomas, Amb.	Cedric H. Grant, Amb.
Haiti	Ernest H. Preeg, Amb.	Georges Leger, Amb.
Honduras	John D. Negroponte, Amb.	Federico A. Poujol, Amb.
Hungary	Harry E. Bergold Jr., Amb.	Janos Petran, Amb.
Iceland	Marshall Brement, Amb.	Hans G. Andersen, Amb.
India	Harry G. Barnes, Amb.	K. R. Narayanan, Amb.
Indonesia	*Vacant*	D. Ashari, Amb.
Ireland	*Vacant*	Tadhg F. O'Sullivan, Amb.
Israel	Samuel W. Lewis, Amb.	Ephraim Evron, Amb.
Italy	Maxwell M. Raab, Amb.	Rinaldo Petrignani, Amb.
Ivory Coast	Nancy V. Rawls, Amb.	Timothee N'Guetta Ahoua, Amb.
Jamaica	Loren E. Lawrence, Amb.	Keith Johnson, Amb.
Japan	Michael J. Mansfield, Amb.	Yoshio Okawara, Amb.
Jordan	Richard N. Viets, Amb.	Abdul Hadi Majali, Amb.
Kenya	William C. Harrop, Amb.	John P. Mbogua, Amb.
Kiribati	William Bodde Jr., Min.	Atanradi Baiteke, Amb.
Korea, South	Richard L. Walker, Amb.	Byong H. Lew, Amb.
Kuwait	Francois M. Dickman, Amb.	Shaikh S. N. Al-Sabah, Amb.
Laos	*Vacant*	Khamtan Ratanavong, Chargé
Latvia[8]		Anatol Dinbergs, Chargé
Lebanon	Robert S. Dillon, Amb.	Khalil Itani, Amb.
Lesotho	*Vacant*	'M'alineo N. Tau, Amb.
Liberia	William Swing, Amb.	Joseph Saye Guannu, Amb.
Lithuania[8]		Stasys A. Backis, Chargé
Luxembourg	John E. Dolibois, Amb.	Adrien Meisch, Amb.
Madagascar	Fernando E. Rondon, Amb.	Henri Jux Ratsimbazafy, Chargé

Countries	Envoys from United States	Envoys to United States
Malawi	John A. Burroughs Jr., Amb.	Nelson T. Mizere, Amb.
Malaysia	Ronald D. Palmer, Amb.	Zain Azraai, Amb.
Maldives	John H. Reed, Amb.	*Vacant*
Mali	Parker W. Borg, Amb.	Maki K. A. Tall, Amb.
Malta	*Vacant*	Leslie Agius, Amb.
Mauritania	*Vacant*	Abdellah Ould Daddah, Amb.
Mauritius	Robert C. Gordon, Amb.	Chitmansing Jesseramsing, Amb.
Mexico	John A. Gavin, Amb.	Hugo B. Margain, Amb.
Morocco	Joseph V. Reed, Amb.	Ali Bengelloun, Amb.
Mozambique	*Vacant*	*Vacant*
Nauru	Robert D. Nesen, Amb.	T.W. Star, Amb.
Nepal	Carleton S. Coon, Amb.	Bhekh B. Thapa, Amb.
Netherlands	William J. Dyess, Amb.	Jan Hendrik Lubbers, Amb.
New Zealand	H. Monroe Browne, Amb.	Thomas Francis Gill, Amb.
Nicaragua	*Vacant*	Carlos Chamorro, Chargé
Niger	*Vacant*	Andre Wright, Amb.
Nigeria	Thomas R. Pickering, Amb.	Abudu Y. Eke, Amb.
Norway	Mark E. Austad, Amb.	Knut Hedemann, Amb.
Oman	John R. Countryman, Amb.	Sadek J. Sulaiman, Amb.
Pakistan	Ronald I. Spiers, Amb.	Ejaz Amim, Amb.
Panama	Ambler H. Moss Jr., Amb.	Juan Jose Amado, Amb.
Papua New Guinea	M. Virginia Schafer, Amb.	Kubulan Los, Amb.
Paraguay	Lyle F. Lane, Amb.	Mario Lopez Escobar, Amb.
Peru	Frank V. Ortiz Jr., Amb.	Fernando Schwalb, Amb.
Philippines	*Vacant*	Eduardo Z. Romualdez, Amb.
Poland	Francis J. Meehan, Amb.	Zdzislaw Ludwiczak, Chargé
Portugal	Richard J. Bloomfield, Amb.	Vasco Futschur Pereira, Amb.
Qatar	Charles E. Marthinsen, Amb.	Abdelkader B. Al-Ameri, Amb.
Romania	David B. Funderburk, Amb.	Nicolae Ionescu, Amb.
Rwanda	Harry R. Melone, Amb.	Bonaventure Ubalijoro, Amb.
St. Lucia	Milan D. Bush, Amb.	Barry B.L. Auguste, Amb.
St. Vincent and The Grenadines	Milan D. Bush, Amb.	Hudson K. Tannis, Amb.
Samoa	Anne C. Martindell, Amb.	Maiava I. Toma, Amb.
Sao Tome and Principe	Francis T. McNamera, Amb.	*Vacant*
Saudi Arabia	Richard W. Murphy, Amb.	Faisal Alhegelan, Amb.
Senegal	Charles W. Bray, Amb.	Andre Coulbary, Amb.
Seychelles	William C. Harrop, Amb.	*Vacant*
Sierra Leone	Theresa Ann Healy, Amb.	Dauda S. Kamara, Amb.
Singapore	Harry E. T. Thayer, Amb.	Punch Coomaraswamy, Amb.
Solomon Islands	M. Virginia Schafer, Amb.	Francis Bugotu, Amb.
Somalia	Donald K. Petterson, Amb.	Mohamud Haji Nur, Amb.
South Africa	William B. Edmondson, Amb.	Donald B. Sole, Amb.
Spain	Terence A. Todman, Amb.	José Llado, Amb.
Sri Lanka	John H. Reed, Amb.	Ernest Corea, Amb.
Sudan	C. William Kontos, Amb.	Omer Salih Eissa, Amb.
Suriname	John J. Crowley Jr., Amb.	Henricus A. F. Heidweiller, Amb.
Swaziland	Richard C. Matherson, Amb.	Lawrence M. Mncina, Amb.
Sweden	Franklin S. Forsberg, Amb.	Wilhelm Wachtmeister, Amb.
Switzerland	Faith R. Whittlesey, Amb.	Anton Hegner, Amb.
Syria	Robert P. Paganelli, Amb.	Rafic Jouejati, Amb.
Tanzania	David C. Miller, Amb.	Paul Bomani, Amb.
Thailand	John G. Dean, Amb.	Prok Amaranand, Amb.
Togo	*Vacant*	Yao Grunitzky, Amb.
Tonga	William Bodde Jr., Amb.	'Inoke F. Faletau, Amb.
Trinidad and Tobago	Melvin H. Evans, Amb.	Victor C. McIntyre, Amb.
Tunisia	Walter L. Cutler, Amb.	Habib B. Yahia, Amb.
Turkey	Robert Strausz-Hope Amb.	Sukru Elekdag, Amb.
Tuvalu	William Bodde Jr., Amb.	Ionatana Ionatana, Amb.
Uganda	Gordon R. Beyer, Amb.	John Wycliffe Lwamafa, Amb.
USSR	Arthur A. Hartman, Amb.	Anatoliy F. Dobrynin, Amb.
United Arab Emirates	*Vacant*	A.S. Al-Mokarrab, Amb.
United Kingdom	John J. Louis Jr., Amb.	Nicholas Henderson, Amb.
Upper Volta	Julius W. Walker Jr., Amb.	T.M. Garango, Amb.
Uruguay	Thomas Aranda Jr., Amb.	Jorge Pacheco Areco, Amb.
Venezuela	William H. Luers, Amb.	Marcial Perez-Chiriboga, Amb.
Yemen Arab Rep.	David E. Zweifel, Amb.	Mohammad Al-Eryani, Amb.
Yugoslavia	David Anderson, Amb.	Budimir Loncar, Amb.
Zaire	Robert B. Oakley, Amb.	Kasongo Mutuale, Amb.
Zambia	Frank G. Wisner II, Amb.	Putteho M. Ngonda, Amb.
Zimbabwe	Robert V. Keeley, Amb.	Elleck K. Mashingaidze, Amb.

Ambassadors at Large: Vernon Walters, Daniel J. Terra.

Special Missions

U.S. Mission to North Atlantic Treaty Organization, Brussels—W. Tapley Bennett Jr.
U.S. Mission to the European Communities, Brussels—George S. Vest
U.S. Mission to the International Atomic Energy Agency, Vienna—Richard T. Kennedy
U.S. Mission to the United Nations, New York—Jeane J. Kirkpatrick
U.S. Mission to the European Office of the UN, Geneva—vacant
U.S. Mission to the Organization for Economic Cooperation and Development, Paris—Abraham Katz
U.S. Mission to the Organization of American States, Washington—J. William Middendorf, Amb.
United Nations Educational, Scientific, and Cultural Organization, Paris—Jean B. Gerard
Council of the International Civic Aviation Organization, Montreal—John E. Downs

(1) Relations severed in 1939. (2) Post closed in 1975. (3) U.S. embassy closed in 1975. (4) U.S. severed relations in 1978; unofficial relations are maintained. (5) Relations severed in 1961; limited ties restored in 1977. (6) U.S. severed relations on Apr. 7, 1980. (7) Relations severed in 1967, limited staff returned in 1972; Belgium protects U.S. interest. (8) U.S. does not officially recognize 1940 annexation by USSR. (9) Embassy closed, Mar. 24, 1980. (10) Embassy closed, May 2, 1980. U.S. closed the Libyan mission in Wash., DC, May 6, 1981.

Major International Organizations

Association of Southeast Asian Nations (ASEAN), was formed in 1967 to promote political and economic cooperation among the non-communist states of the region. Members are Indonesia, Malaysia, Philippines, Singapore, Thailand. Annual ministerial meetings set policy; a central Secretariat in Jakarta and 11 permanent committees work in trade, transportation, communications, agriculture, science, finance, and culture.

Commonwealth of Nations originally called the British Commonwealth of Nations, is an association of nations and dependencies loosely joined by a common interest based on having been parts of the old British Empire. The British monarch is the symbolic head of the Commonwealth.

There are 44 self-governing independent nations in the Commonwealth, plus various colonies and protectorates. As of June 1981, the members were the United Kingdom of Great Britain and Northern Ireland and 14 other nations recognizing the British monarch, represented by a governor-general, as their head of state: Australia, Bahamas, Barbados, Canada, Fiji, Grenada, Jamaica, Mauritius, New Zealand, Papua New Guinea, St. Lucia, St. Vincent and the Grenadines (a special member), Solomon Islands, and Tuvalu (a special member); and 28 countries with their own heads of state: Bangladesh, Botswana, Cyprus, Dominica, The Gambia, Ghana, Guyana, India, Kenya, Kiribati, Lesotho, Malawi, Malaysia, Malta, Nauru (a special member), Nigeria, Samoa, Seychelles, Sierra Leone, Singapore, Sri Lanka, Swaziland, Tanzania, Tonga, Trinidad and Tobago, Uganda, Vanuatu, Zambia, and Zimbabwe. In addition various Caribbean dependencies take part in certain Commonwealth activities.

The Commonwealth facilitates consultation among member states through meetings of prime ministers and finance ministers, and through a permanent Secretariat. Members consult on economic, scientific, educational, financial, legal, and military matters, and try to coordinate policies.

European Communities (EC, the Common Market) is the collective designation of three organizations with common membership: the European Economic Community (Common Market), the European Coal and Steel Community, and the European Atomic Energy Community. The 10 full members are: Belgium, Denmark, France, West Germany, Greece, Ireland, Italy, Luxembourg, Netherlands, United Kingdom. Some 60 nations in Africa, the Caribbean, and the Pacific are affiliated under the Lomé Convention.

A merger of the 3 communities executives went into effect July 1, 1967, though the component organizations date back to 1951 and 1958. A Council of Ministers, a Commission, a European Parliament, and a Court of Justice comprise the permanent structure. The communities aim to integrate their economies, coordinate social developments, and ultimately, bring about political union of the democratic states of Europe.

European Free Trade Association (EFTA), consisting of Austria, Iceland, Norway, Portugal, Sweden, Switzerland and associated member Finland, was created Jan. 4, 1960, to gradually reduce customs duties and quantitative restrictions between members on industrial products. By Dec. 31, 1966, all tariffs and quotas had been eliminated. The United Kingdom and Denmark withdrew to become members of EC Jan. 1, 1973 at which time EFTA members entered into free trade agreements with the EC. All industrial customs barriers between the two blocs were removed July 1, 1976.

League of Arab States (The Arab League) was created Mar. 22, 1945, by Egypt, Iraq, Jordan, Lebanon, Saudi Arabia, Syria, and Yemen. Joining later were Algeria, Bahrain, Djibouti, Kuwait, Libya, Mauritania, Morocco, Oman, Qatar, Somalia, Sudan, Tunisia, United Arab Emirates and South Yemen. The Palestine Liberation Org. has been admitted as a full member. The League fosters cultural, economic, and communication ties and mediates disputes among the Arab states; it represents Arab states in certain international negotiations, and coordinates a military, economic, and diplomatic offensive against Israel. As a result of Egypt signing a peace treaty with Israel, the League, Mar. 1979, suspended Egypt's membership and transferred the League's headquarters from Cairo to Tunis.

North Atlantic Treaty Org. (NATO) was created by treaty (signed Apr. 4, 1949; in effect Aug. 24, 1949) among Belgium, Canada, Denmark, France, Iceland, Italy, Luxembourg, Netherlands, Norway, Portugal, the United Kingdom, and the U.S. Greece, Turkey, West Germany, and Spain have joined since. The members agreed to settle disputes by peaceful means; to develop their individual and collective capacity to resist armed attack; to regard an attack on one as an attack on all, and to take necessary action to repel an attack under Article 51 of the United Nations Charter.

The NATO structure consists of a Council and a Military Committee of 3 commands (Allied Command Europe, Allied Command Atlantic, Allied Command Channel) and the Canada-U.S. Regional Planning Group.

Following announcement in 1966 of nearly total French withdrawal from the military affairs of NATO, organization hq. moved, 1967, from Paris to Brussels. In August, 1974, Greece announced a total withdrawal of armed forces from NATO, in response to Turkish intervention in Cyprus. Greece rejoined NATO's military wing, Oct. 20, 1980.

Organization of African Unity (OAU), formed May 25, 1963, by 30 African countries (50 by 1980) to coördinate cultural, political, scientific and economic policies; to end colonialism in Africa; and to promote a common defense of members' independence. It holds annual conferences of heads of state, has a council of foreign ministers meeting at least twice a year, a secretary-general and a mediation-arbitration commission. Hq. is in Addis Ababa, Ethiopia.

Organization of American States (OAS) was formed in Bogota, Colombia, in 1948. Hq. is in Washington, D.C. It has a Permanent Council, Inter-American Economic and Social Council, and Inter-American Council for Education, Science and Culture, a Juridical Committee and a Commission on Human Rights. The Permanent Council can call meetings of foreign ministers to deal with urgent security matters. A General Assembly meets annually. A secretary general and assistant are elected for 5-year terms. There are 28 members, each with one vote in the various organizations: Argentina, Barbados, Bolivia, Brazil, Chile, Colombia, Costa Rica, Cuba, Dominica, Dominican Republic, Ecuador, El Salvador, Grenada, Guatemala, Haiti, Honduras, Jamaica, Mexico, Nicaragua, Panama, Paraguay, Peru, St. Lucia, Suriname, Trinidad & Tobago, U.S., Uruguay, Venezuela. In 1962, the OAS excluded Cuba from OAS activities but not from membership.

Organization for Economic Cooperation and Development (OECD) was established Sept. 30, 1961 to promote economic and social welfare in member countries, and to stimulate and harmonize efforts on behalf of developing nations. Nearly all the industrialized "free market" countries belong, with Yugoslavia as an associate member. OECD collects and disseminates economic and environmental information. Members in 1982 were: Australia, Austria, Belgium, Canada, Denmark, Finland, France, West Germany, Greece, Iceland, Ireland, Italy, Japan, Luxembourg, Netherlands, New Zealand, Norway, Portugal, Spain, Sweden, Switzerland, Turkey, United Kingdom, United States. Hq. is in Paris.

Organization of Petroleum Exporting Countries (OPEC) was created Nov. 14, 1960 at Venezuelan initiative. The group has been successful in determining world oil prices, and in advancing members' interests in trade and development dealings with industrialized oil-consuming nations. Members in 1982 were Algeria, Ecuador, Gabon, Indonesia, Iran, Iraq, Kuwait, Libya, Nigeria, Qatar, Saudi Arabia, United Arab Emirates, Venezuela.

Warsaw Treaty Organization (Warsaw Pact) was created May 14, 1955, as a mutual defense alliance. Members in 1982 were Bulgaria, Czechoslovakia, East Germany, Hungary, Poland, Romania, and the USSR. Hq. is in Moscow. It provides for a unified military command; if one member is attacked, the others will aid it with all necessary steps including armed force; joint maneuvers are held; there is a Political Consultative Committee and a Committee of Defense Ministers.

U.S. Aid to Foreign Nations

Source: Bureau of Economic Analysis, U.S. Commerce Department

Figures are for calendar year 1981, and are in millions of dollars. (*Less than $500,000.) Data shown by country exclude the military supplies and services furnished under the Foreign Assistance Act and direct Defense Department appropriations. Data shown include credits which have been extended to private entities in the country specified.

Grants are largely outright gifts for which no payment is expected or which at most involve an obligation on the part of the receiver to extend aid to the U.S. or other countries to achieve a common objective. Net grants and credits take into account all known returns to the U.S. government, including reverse grants, returns of grants, and payments of principal. A minus sign (—) indicates that the total of these returns to the U.S. is greater than the total of grants or credits.

Other assistance represents the transfer of U.S. farm products in exchange for foreign currencies, less the government's disbursements of the currencies as grants, credits, or for purchases.

Amounts do not include investments in international financial institutions in 1981 as follows: Asian Development Bank, $49 million; Inter-American Development Bank, $294 million; International Development Assn., $655 million; International Bank for Reconstruction and Development, $132 million; International Finance Corp., $11 million.

	Total	Net grants	Net credits	Net other
TOTAL	**9,271**	**5,106**	**4,179**	**−12**
Military grants	**919**	**919**	**—**	**—**
Other grants, credits, ass't.	**8,352**	**4,187**	**4,178**	**−12**
Western Europe	**−64**	**56**	**−123**	**3**
Austria	12	—	12	(*)
Belgium-Luxembourg	−11	—	−11	—
Denmark	3	—	3	—
Finland	16	—	16	(*)
France	35	—	35	—
Germany, West	−12	—	−12	—
Iceland	−1	—	−1	1
Ireland	44	—	44	—
Italy	123	19	104	—
Netherlands	−33	—	−33	—
Norway	−36	—	−36	—
Portugal	−111	23	−134	(*)
Spain	48	11	37	(*)
Sweden	−1	—	−1	—
Switzerland	−14	—	−14	—
United Kingdom	−125	—	−125	—
Yugoslavia	12	3	8	1
Atomic EC	−6	—	−6	—
Other & unspecified	−7	1	−8	—
Eastern Europe	**173**	**1**	**127**	**45**
Hungary	3	—	3	—
Poland	235	1	190	45
Romania	−49	—	−49	—
Soviet Union	−17	—	−17	—
Near East & South Asia	**4,480**	**1,703**	**2,837**	**−60**
Bangladesh	129	65	64	(*)
Cyprus	−1	2	−3	(*)
Egypt	1,400	293	1,149	−42
Greece	−66	(*)	−66	(*)
India	241	220	22	(*)
Israel	1,798	807	990	(*)
Jordan	247	9	238	(*)
Lebanon	32	6	26	—
Nepal	20	22	(*)	−3
Oman	30	1	29	—
Pakistan	94	60	48	−15
Saudi Arabia	6	—	6	—
Sri Lanka (Ceylon)	33	11	22	—
Syria	17	7	10	(*)
Turkey	379	100	279	(*)
Yemen (Sana)	25	22	3	—
Other & unspecified	98	77	21	(*)
East Asia & Pacific	**809**	**283**	**525**	**1**
Australia	81	—	81	—
Burma	(*)	1	−3	1
China-Taiwan	195	2	191	1
Fiji	8	3	5	—
Hong Kong	32	(*)	32	—
Indonesia	14	45	−29	−1
Japan	68	—	68	(*)
Kampuchea	25	25	(*)	—
Korea (So.)	205	1	204	(*)
Malaysia	−19	1	−20	—
Nauru	4	—	4	—
New Zealand	−18	—	−18	—
Philippines	45	40	5	(*)
Singapore	−14	(*)	−14	—
Thailand	31	14	17	—
Trust Terr. Pacific	133	133	—	—
Other & unspecified	18	18	(*)	—
Africa	**1,261**	**704**	**558**	**(*)**
Algeria	172	(*)	172	—
Angola	46	6	40	—
Benin	4	4	(*)	—
Botswana	21	21	(*)	—
Burundi	9	9	—	—
Cameroon	52	13	39	—
Cape Verde	9	9	—	—
Cen. African Rep.	2	2	—	—
Chad	2	2	—	—
Djibouti	3	3	—	—
Ethiopia	4	7	−3	(*)
Gabon	−5	1	−6	—
Gambia	7	7	—	—
Ghana	19	18	2	−1
Guinea	17	8	5	4
Guinea-Bissau	9	9	—	—
Ivory Coast	9	1	9	(*)
Kenya	87	52	35	(*)
Lesotho	33	33	—	—
Liberia	74	49	25	—
Madagascar	11	6	5	—
Malawi	5	3	2	—
Mali	18	18	(*)	(*)
Mauritania	22	20	1	—
Mauritius	5	2	3	—
Morocco	50	33	19	−1
Mozambique	21	12	8	—
Niger	12	11	1	—
Nigeria	7	(*)	7	—
Rwanda	12	11	(*)	—
Senegal	38	34	4	(*)
Sierra Leone	6	6	(*)	(*)
Somalia	70	53	17	(*)
Sudan	105	35	70	(*)
Swaziland	7	7	(*)	—
Tanzania	31	26	5	(*)
Togo	7	6	1	—
Tunisia	25	13	15	−2
Uganda	10	11	(*)	—
Upper Volta	41	41	(*)	—
Zaire	73	12	61	(*)
Zambia	29	6	23	—
Zimbabwe	28	26	1	—
Other & unspecified	54	57	−2	—
Western Hemisphere	**585**	**326**	**260**	**−1**
Argentina	−25	(*)	−25	—
Bahamas	2	—	2	—
Barbados	1	(*)	1	—
Bolivia	20	24	−4	(*)
Brazil	−80	2	−82	(*)
Canada	47	—	47	—
Cayman Islands	3	—	3	—
Chile	−87	10	−95	−1
Colombia	−5	3	−8	(*)
Costa Rica	12	5	7	—
Dominican Republic	24	15	9	—
Ecuador	2	6	−4	—
El Salvador	112	21	91	—
Guatemala	20	14	6	—
Guyana	6	3	3	—
Haiti	43	33	9	—
Honduras	45	14	31	—
Jamaica	58	5	53	—
Mexico	159	13	146	—
Nicaragua	15	8	7	—
Panama	4	7	−2	—
Paraguay	(*)	4	−3	(*)
Peru	−8	41	−49	(*)
Suriname	−1	—	−1	—
Trinidad-Tobago	51	—	51	—
Uruguay	−4	(*)	−4	(*)
Venezuela	39	(*)	39	—
Other & unspecified	129	98	31	—
Intl. orgs. & unspecified	**1,109**	**1,114**	**−5**	**—**

Military Expenditures and Social Conditions

Source: World Military and Social Expenditures 1981 by Ruth Leger Sivard; copyright © 1981 by World Priorities Inc., Box 1003, Leesburg, VA 22075.

1978

Country	Military public expenditures per capita Rank	per capita U.S. $	per soldier[1] Rank	per soldier[1] U.S. $	Economic-social standing[2] Avg. Rank[3]
Afghanistan	114	5	113	636	134
Albania	52	60	105	5,310	60
Algeria	66	36	65	7,937	72
Angola	—	—	—	—	106
Argentina	56	55	46	11,000	37
Australia	22	207	11	42,100	12
Austria	36	93	31	18,919	18
Bahrain	29	141	23	25,000	46
Bangladesh	134	1	125	1,595	135
Barbados	121	4	130	1,000	34
Belgium	13	322	18	36,448	13
Benin	127	3	85	5,000	119
Bolivia	79	18	103	3,919	81
Botswana	77	22	34	16,000	79
Brazil	79	18	68	7,536	54
Brunei	6	642	10	43,000	27
Bulgaria	44	77	91	4,527	27
Burma	114	5	129	1,018	116
Burundi	114	5	96	4,200	133
Cambodia	—	—	—	—	119
Cameroon	111	7	56	9,167	102
Canada	24	174	6	51,112	14
Central African Rep.	121	4	48	10,000	129
Chad	108	8	69	7,400	138
Chile	47	73	55	9,188	44
China	73	26	81	6,012	88
China, Taiwan	31	106	104	3,816	55
Colombia	111	7	120	2,211	69
Congo	76	23	87	4,857	90
Costa Rica	91	11	90	4,600	50
Cuba	58	49	113	2,962	36
Cyprus	65	39	116	2,400	46
Czechoslovakia	28	143	43	11,651	20
Denmark	19	259	13	38,824	2
Dominican Rep.	83	17	88	4,789	70
Ecuador	77	22	77	6,560	64
Egypt	38	91	57	9,157	83
El Salvador	85	13	61	8,429	84
Equatorial Guinea	74	25	128	1,200	111
Ethiopia	114	5	123	1,691	141
Fiji	87	12	71	7,000	51
Finland	34	102	39	12,125	10
France	11	350	16	37,091	8
Gabon	43	78	24	24,500	60
Gambia	—	—	—	—	131
East Germany	21	218	25	23,255	19
West Germany	11	350	9	43,808	5
Ghana	114	5	111	3,333	93
Greece	20	220	47	10,816	30
Guatemala	103	9	92	4,500	85
Guinea	121	4	115	2,556	126
Guyana	98	10	97	4,000	65
Haiti	129	2	121	1,857	122
Honduras	91	11	114	2,714	91
Hungary	42	79	70	7,368	32
Iceland	—	—	—	—	4
India	114	5	112	3,192	115
Indonesia	91	11	76	6,648	103
Iran	18	261	26	23,036	68
Iraq	25	159	52	9,373	65
Ireland	53	59	38	13,067	22
Israel	4	839	32	18,902	25
Italy	30	112	33	17,572	20
Ivory Coast	91	11	36	15,800	96
Jamaica	103	9	48	10,000	49
Japan	40	80	15	38,379	11
Jordan	39	87	102	3,926	87
Kenya	87	12	28	21,000	98
No. Korea	51	63	119	2,227	78
So. Korea	46	75	93	4,480	67
Kuwait	7	613	3	61,500	23
Laos	98	10	134	714	132
Lebanon	54	58	29	20,750	51
Lesotho	—	—	—	—	98
Liberia	114	5	122	1,800	105
Libya	26	156	42	11,865	39
Luxembourg	33	103	17	37,000	15
Madagascar	113	6	94	4,273	104
Malawi	121	4	44	11,500	128
Malaysia	59	45	53	9,338	62
Mali	121	4	71	7,000	138
Malta	75	24	63	8,000	35
Mauritania	69	30	107	3,667	129
Mauritius	129	2	—	—	55
Mexico	108	8	86	4,979	59
Mongolia	45	76	97	4,000	57
Morocco	62	42	54	9,281	98
Mozambique	103	9	100	3,952	117
Nepal	134	1	132	800	137
Netherlands	15	304	14	38,500	9
New Zealand	36	93	27	22,308	17
Nicaragua	71	28	51	9,714	74
Niger	129	2	97	4,000	136
Nigeria	71	28	59	8,793	101
Norway	13	322	19	33,564	3
Oman	3	914	12	40,368	72
Pakistan	87	12	118	2,308	122
Panama	103	9	126	1,545	48
Papua New Guinea	103	9	58	9,000	107
Paraguay	85	13	117	2,353	74
Peru	67	33	80	6,236	77
Philippines	91	11	84	5,172	82
Poland	35	99	45	11,287	30
Portugal	49	64	50	9,828	41
Qatar	1	1,194	4	60,000	33
Romania	55	56	75	6,757	29
Rwanda	127	3	108	3,500	126
Saudi Arabia	2	1,004	1	149,458	62
Senegal	98	10	63	8,000	124
Sierra Leone	129	2	108	3,500	118
Singapore	23	186	40	12,056	40
Somalia	87	12	133	769	124
South Africa	40	80	20	33,106	58
Spain	48	67	66	7,848	26
Sri Lanka	134	1	124	1,615	86
Sudan	84	14	89	4,731	114
Swaziland	129	2	130	1,000	89
Sweden	10	365	8	45,833	1
Switzerland	16	280	2	93,368	6
Syria	27	147	83	5,285	80
Tanzania	98	10	78	6,370	112
Thailand	79	18	101	3,943	92
Togo	108	8	79	6,333	113
Trinidad & Tobago	91	11	41	12,000	45
Tunisia	69	30	62	8,409	77
Turkey	49	64	82	5,736	70
Uganda	91	11	73	6,952	110
USSR	9	394	21	28,312	23
United Arab Emirates	5	836	22	26,462	53
UK	17	262	7	46,716	16
U.S.	8	499	5	52,802	7
Upper Volta	121	14	110	3,375	140
Uruguay	64	40	95	4,259	42
Venezuela	60	44	37	14,159	43
Vietnam	79	18	127	1,463	95
Yemen	97	52	74	6,789	119
So. Yemen	61	43	106	3,714	108
Yugoslavia	32	105	60	8,633	37
Zaire	98	10	67	7,735	109
Zambia	63	41	35	15,929	94
Zimbabwe	68	31	30	20,091	96

(1) "Soldier" represents all members of the armed forces. (2) Represents average of ranks for Gross National Product per capita, education (encompassing public expenditures per capita, school-age population per teacher, percent school-age population in school, percent women in total high school enrollment, literacy rate), and health (encompassing public expenditures per capita, population per physician, population per hospital bed, infant mortality rate, life expectancy). (3) Rank shows the standing of the country among those in the table. The rank order is repeated if more than one country has the same figure.

Population of World's Largest Urban Areas

The ranking below represents one attempt at comparing the world's largest urban areas, taking into account, where necessary and within the limits of available data, urban development extending outward from the principal city named in the table. City proper is a large locality with legally fixed boundaries and an administratively recognized urban status which is usually characterized by some form of local government. Urban agglomeration has been defined as comprising the city proper and also the suburban fringe or thickly settled territory living outside of, but adjacent to, the city boundaries. U-Urban agglomeration; C-City proper.

New York, N.Y. (est. 1977)	U 16,478,769
Mexico City, Mexico (est. 1978)	U 13,993,866
Tokyo, Japan (est. 1978)	U 11,696,373
Los Angeles-Long Beach Cal. (est. 1977)	U 10,606,665
Shanghai, China (est. 1978)	U 10,000,000
Buenos Aires, Argentina (est. 1979)	U 9,910,000
Paris, France (census, 1975)	U 8,547,625
Sao Paulo, Brazil (est. 1979)	C 8,407,500
Moscow, USSR (census, 1979)	U 8,011,000
Peking, China (est. 1978)	U 8,000,000
Chicago, Ill. (est. 1977)	U 7,664,371
Calcutta, India (census, 1971)	U 7,031,382
London, England (est. 1977)	C 6,970,100
Seoul, S. Korea (census, 1975)	C 6,879,464
Chongqing, China (est. 1977)	C 6,000,000
Bombay, India (census, 1971)	C 5,970,575
Philadelphia, Pa. (est. 1977)	U 5,625,271
Rio de Janeiro, Brazil (est. 1979)	C 5,394,900
Cairo, Egypt (census, 1976)	C 5,084,463
Canton, China (est. 1977)	C 5,000,000
San Francisco-Oakland, Cal. (est. 1977)	U 4,688,155
Detroit, Mich. (est. 1977)	U 4,620,000
Hong Kong (est. 1978)	C 4,610,000
Leningrad, USSR (census, 1979)	U 4,588,000
Jakarta, Indonesia (census, 1971)	C 4,576,009
Manila, Philippines (est. 1975)	U 4,500,000
Teheran, Iran (census, 1966)	C 4,496,159
Shenyang, China (est. 1977)	C 4,400,000
Tianjin, China (est. 1970)	U 4,280,000
Luta, China (est. 1977)	C 4,200,000
Bangkok, Thailand (est. 1975)	C 4,178,000
Boston, Mass. (est. 1977)	U 3,521,936
Istanbul, Turkey (est. 1975)	U 3,864,493
Santiago, Chile (est. 1978)	U 3,691,548
Delhi-New Delhi, India (census, 1971)	U 3,647,023
Wuhan, China (est. 1977)	C 3,500,000
Karachi, Pakistan (census, 1972)	C 3,498,634
Lima, Peru (census, 1972)	U 3,302,523
Madrid, Spain (est. 1978)	C 3,200,000
Madras, India (census, 1971)	U 3,169,930
Berlin, E. and W. (both est. 1977)	C 3,038,224
Sydney, Australia (census, 1976)	U 3,021,982
Washington, D.C.-Md.-Va. (est. 1977)	U 3,021,375
Nanking, China (est. 1977)	C 3,000,000
Rome, Italy (est. 1977)	C 2,897,505
Cleveland, Oh. (est. 1977)	U 2,872,225
Bogota, Colombia (census, 1973)	C 2,855,065
Toronto, Ontario, Canada (census, 1976)	U 2,803,101
Montreal, Quebec, Canada (census, 1976)	U 2,802,485
Yokohama, Japan (est. 1978)	C 2,729,433
Osaka, Japan (est. 1978)	C 2,700,303
Houston, Tex. (est. 1977)	U 2,696,807
Manchester, England (est. 1977)	U 2,674,800
Dallas-Ft. Worth, Tex. (est. 1977)	U 2,659,550
Melbourne, Australia (census, 1976)	U 2,604,035
Caracas, Venezuela (est. 1976)	U 2,576,000
Ankara, Turkey (est. 1975)	U 2,572,562
Pusan, S. Korea (census, 1975)	C 2,450,125
St. Louis, Mo. (est. 1977)	U 2,386,522
Guadalajara, Mexico (est. 1978)	U 2,343,034
Singapore (est. 1978)	U 2,334,400
Alexandria, Egypt (census, 1976)	C 2,317,705

U.S. Passport, Visa, and Health Requirements

Source: Passport Services, U.S. State Department and U.S. Public Health Service as of Mar. 1982

Passports are issued by the United States Department of State to citizens and nationals of the United States for the purpose of documenting them for foreign travel and identifying them as Americans.

How to Obtain a Passport

An applicant for a passport who has never been previously issued a passport in his own name, must execute an application in person before (1) a passport agent; (2) a clerk of any federal court or state court of record or a judge or clerk of any probate court, accepting applications; (3) a postal employee designated by the postmaster at a Post Office which has been selected to accept passport applications; or (4) a diplomatic or consular officer of the U.S. abroad. It is no longer possible to include family members of any age in a U.S. passport. All persons are required to obtain individual passports in their own name.

A passport previously issued to the applicant, or one in which he was included, will be accepted as proof of citizenship in lieu of the following documents. A person born in the United States shall present his birth certificate. To be acceptable, the certificate must show the given name and surname, the date and place of birth and that the birth record was filed shortly after birth. A delayed birth certificate (a record filed more than one year after the date of birth) is acceptable provided that it shows that the report of birth was supported by acceptable secondary evidence of birth.

If such primary evidence is not obtainable, a notice from the registrar shall be submitted stating that no birth record exists. The notice shall be accompanied by the best obtainable secondary evidence such as a baptismal certificate, a certificate of circumcision, or a hospital birth record.

A person who has been issued a passport in his own name within the last eight years may obtain a new passport by filling out, signing and mailing a passport by mail application together with his previous passport, two recent identical signed photographs and the established fee to the nearest Passport Agency or to the Passport Services in Wash., D.C. If, however, an applicant is applying for a passport for the first time, or his prior passport was issued before his 18th birthday, he must execute a passport application in person.

A naturalized citizen should present his naturalization certificate. A person born abroad claiming citizenship through either a native-born or naturalized citizen must submit a certificate of citizenship issued by the Immigration and Naturalization Service; or a Consular Report of Birth or Certification of Birth issued by the Dept. of State. If one of the above documents has not been obtained, he must submit evidence of citizenship of the parent(s) through whom citizenship is claimed and evidence which would establish the parent/child relationship. Additionally, if through birth to citizen parent(s), parents' marriage certificate plus an affidavit from parent(s) showing periods and places of residence or physical presence in the U.S. and abroad, specifying periods spent abroad in the employment of the U.S. government, including the armed forces, or with certain international organizations; if through naturalization of parents, evidence of admission to the U.S. for permanent residence.

Under certain conditions, married women must present evidence of marriage. Special laws govern women married prior to Mar. 3, 1931 and should be investigated.

Aliens — An alien leaving the U.S. must request passport facilities from his home government. He must have a permit from his local Collector of Internal Revenue, and if he wishes to return he should request a re-entry permit from the Immigration and Naturalization Service if it is required.

Contract Employees — Persons traveling because of a contract with the Government must submit with their applications letters from their employer stating position, destination and purpose of travel, armed forces contract number, and expiration date of contract when pertinent.

Photographs and Fees

Photographs — Two identical photographs which are sufficiently recent (normally not more than 6 months old) to be a good likeness of and satisfactorily identify the applicant. Photographs should be 2 × 2 inches in size. The image size measured from the bottom of the chin to the top of the head (including hair) should be not less than one inch nor more than 1 3/8 inches. Photographs must be signed in the center on the reverse. Photographs should be portrait-type prints.

They must be clear, front view, full face, with a plain light (white or off-white) background. Photographs which depict the applicant as relaxed and smiling are encouraged.

Fees — The passport fee is $10. A fee of $5 shall be charged for execution of the application. No execution fee is payable when using the mail-in application. All applicants must pay the passport fee and, where applicable, the execution fee unless specifically exempted by law.

The loss or theft of a valid passport is a serious matter and should be reported in writing immediately to Passport Services, Dept. of State, Wash., D.C. 20524, or to the nearest passport agency, or to the nearest consular office of the U.S. when abroad.

Foreign Regulations

A visa, usually rubber stamped in a passport by a representative of the country to be visited, certifies that the bearer of the passport is permitted to enter that country for a certain purpose and length of time. Visa information can be obtained by writing directly to foreign consular officials.

Health Information

Smallpox — Some countries require an International Certificate of Vaccination against smallpox. Vaccination is not required for direct travel from the U.S. to most other countries.

Yellow Fever — A few African countries require vaccination of all travelers. A number of countries require vaccination if travelers arrive from infected or endemic areas. Vaccination is recommended for travel to infected areas and for travel outside the urban areas of countries in the endemic zones.

Cholera — A few countries require vaccination if travelers arrive from infected areas. Mozambique and Niger require vaccination of all travelers.

Plague — Vaccination is not indicated for most travelers to countries reporting cases of plague, particularly if their travel is limited to urban areas with modern hotels.

Malaria — There is a risk in the Caribbean, Central and South America, Africa, the Middle and Far East, and the Indian subcontinent. Travelers are strongly advised to seek information from health department or private physician.

Return to the United States — No vaccinations are required to return to the United States from any country.

Vaccination Information — Yellow fever vaccine must be obtained at an officially designated Center, and the Certificate, valid for 10 years, must be stamped by the Center. The location of Centers is available from local health departments. Other vaccinations—see licensed physicians.

Travelers are advised to contact their local health department, physician, or agency that advises international travelers 2 weeks prior to departure to obtain the most current information.

Passports Issued and Renewed

Source: Bureau of Consular Affairs, U.S. State Department

Passports are actual count; other data based on sample.

Item	1960	1970[5]	1975	1976	1977	1978	1979	1980
New and renewed passports	853,087	2,219,159	2,334,359	2,816,683	3,107,122	3,234,471	3,169,999	3,020,468
Object of Travel[1]								
Government	115,910	146,169	131,739	134,883	153,992	142,901	146,879	135,868
Nongovernment	737,177	2,072,990	2,123,960	2,529,290	2,388,540	2,641,690	2,404,090	2,331,630
Personal reasons[2]	321,590	1,791,330	376,400	602,980	1,005,630	1,567,880	1,540,690	1,246,130
Pleasure[3]	350,897	216,700	1,315,600	1,511,060	1,102,250	821,070	552,580	829,680
Business[4]	24,540	39,940	273,110	272,600	190,890	163,770	202,450	161,520
Education	31,240	20,230	132,490	125,590	78,550	75,440	92,980	79,550
Religion	6,780	3,350	22,450	13,690	9,160	11,090	13,590	10,970
Health	1,460	640	1,510	1,500	1,090	980	610	990
Other	670	800	2,400	1,870	970	1,460	1,190	2,790
Not stated	NA	NA	78,660	152,510	564,590	449,880	619,030	552,970
First area designation:								
Africa	8,440	18,790	32,930	35,390	33,980	24,020	22,430	28,538
Australia and Oceania	35,220	51,210	96,300	106,540	108,280	95,670	107,180	126,420
Europe	669,662	1,910,169	1,611,410	1,990,993	2,291,942	2,535,381	2,392,029	2,192,858
Far East	55,960	116,730	154,660	180,090	187,130	170,010	187,820	198,868
North, Central, and South America	58,935	72,410	317,980	347,020	316,590	263,240	317,610	333,220
Middle-East	24,670	48,890	121,010	156,530	169,060	145,870	142,830	140,010
World Tour	200	960	60	120	140	280	100	570
Sex of passport recipients:								
Male	419,615	1,123,620	1,128,050	1,353,610	1,496,250	1,555,200	1,543,490	1,497,200
Female	433,472	1,095,539	1,206,309	1,463,073	1,610,872	1,679,271	1,626,509	1,523,268
Citizenship of passport recipients:								
Native	710,172	2,072,560	2,039,690	2,458,050	2,853,290	2,916,840	2,799,810	2,797,780
Naturalized	142,915	146,599	294,669	358,633	253,832	317,631	370,189	222,688

(1) Data not entirely comparable because of changes in classifications in 1961. (2) Includes "Personal business," "Join husband." "Accompany husband," "Business and pleasure," "Visit family." (3) Includes "Sightsee," "Vacation," "Visit," and "Tourist." (4) Includes applications formerly listed under "Employment" and "Commercial business." (5) Legislation effective Aug. 26, 1968 eliminated passport renewals.

Customs Exemptions and Advice to Travelers

United States residents returning after a stay abroad of at least 48 hours are, generally speaking, granted customs exemptions of $300 each. The duty-free articles must accompany the traveler at the time of his return, must be for his personal or household use, must have been acquired as an incident of his trip, and must be properly declared to Customs. Not more than one liter of alcoholic beverages may be included in the $300 exemption.

If a U.S. resident arrives directly or indirectly from American Samoa, Guam, or the Virgin Islands of the United States, his purchase may be valued up to $600 fair retail value, but not more than $300 of the exemption may be applied to the value of articles acquired elsewhere than in such insular possessions, and 4 liters of alcoholic beverages may be included in his exemption, but not more than 1 liter of such beverages may have been acquired elsewhere than in the designated islands.

In either case, the exemption for alcoholic beverages is accorded only when the returning resident has attained 21 years of age at the time of his arrival. One hundred cigars and 200 cigarettes may be included (except Cuban products) in either exemption. Cuban cigars may be included if obtained in Cuba and all articles acquired there do not exceed $100 in retail value.

The $300 or $600 exemption may be granted only if the exemption, or any part of it, has not been used within the preceding 30-day period and your stay abroad was for at least 48 hours. The 48-hour absence requirement does not apply if you return from Mexico or the Virgin Islands of the United States.

Bona fide gifts costing no more than $25 fair retail value or $40 from American Samoa, Guam, or Virgin Islands, may be mailed to friends at home duty-free; addressee cannot receive in a single day gifts exceeding the $25 limit.

U.S. Immigration Law

Source: Immigration and Naturalization Service, U.S. Justice Department

The Immigration and Nationality Act, as amended, provides for the numerical limitation of most immigration. Not subject to any numerical limitations are immigrants classified as immediate relatives who are spouses or children of U.S. citizens, or parents of citizens who are 21 years of age or older; returning residents; certain former U.S. citizens; ministers of religion; and certain long-term U.S. government employees.

The Refugee Act of 1980 (P.L. 96-212) became effective on April 1, 1980. Congress stated that the objectives of the Refugee Act are to provide a permanent and systematic procedure for the admission of refugees who are of special humanitarian concern to the United States, and to provide uniform provisions for the effective settlement and absorption of those refugees. Beginning in 1983, the number of refugees who may be admitted will be determined by the President, after consultation with the Committees on the Judiciary of the Senate and of the House of Representatives.

Numerical Limitation of Immigrants

Immigration to the U.S. is numerically limited to 270,000 per year. Within this quota there is an annual limitation of 20,000 for each country. The colonies and dependencies of foreign states are limited to 600 per year, chargeable to the country limitation of the mother country.

Visa Categories

Applicants for immigration are classified as either preference or nonpreference. The preference visa categories are based on certain relationships to persons in the U.S., i.e., unmarried sons and daughters over 21 of U.S. citizens, spouses and unmarried sons and daughters of resident aliens, married sons and daughters of U.S. citizens, brothers and sisters of U.S. citizens 21 or over (first, 2d, 4th, and 5th preference, respectively); members of the professions or persons of exceptional ability in the sciences and arts whose services are sought by U.S. employers (3d preference); and skilled and unskilled workers in short supply (6th preference); refugees (7th preference). Spouses and children of preference applicants are entitled to the same preference if accompanying or following to join such persons.

Except for refugee status, preference status is based upon approved petitions, filed with the Immigration and Naturalization Service, by the appropriate relative or employer (or in the 3d preference by the alien himself).

Other immigrants not within one of the above-mentioned preference groups may qualify as nonpreference applicants and receive only those visa numbers not needed by preference applicants.

Labor Certification

The Act of October 3, 1965, established new controls to protect the American labor market from an influx of skilled and unskilled foreign labor. Prior to the issuance of a visa, the would-be 3d, 6th, and nonpreference immigrant must obtain the Secretary of Labor's certification, establishing that there are not sufficient workers in the U.S. at the alien's destination who are able, willing, and qualified to perform the job; and that the employment of the alien will not adversely affect the wages and working conditions of workers in the U.S. similarly employed; or that there is satisfactory evidence that the provisions of that section do not apply to the alien's case.

Extension of Adjustment of Status

The Act of October 3, 1965, excluded Western Hemisphere natives from adjusting their status to permanent residence under Section 245 of the Immigration and Nationality Act which allows a nonimmigrant alien to adjust to permanent resident without leaving the U.S. to secure a visa. In 1976 amendments restored the adjustment of status provision to Western Hemisphere natives, and declared ineligible for adjustment of status aliens who are not defined as immediate relatives and who accept unauthorized employment prior to filing their adjustment application.

Immigrants Admitted from All Countries

Fiscal Year Ends June 30 through 1976, Sept. 30 thereafter

Year	Number	Year	Number	Year	Number	Year	Number
1820	8,385	1881-1890	5,246,613	1951-1960	2,515,479	1976	398,613
1821-1830	143,439	1891-1900	3,687,564	1961-1970	3,321,777	1976 July-Sept.	103,676
1831-1840	599,125	1901-1910	8,795,386	1971	370,478	1977	462,315
1841-1850	1,713,251	1911-1920	5,735,811	1972	384,685	1978	601,442
1851-1860	2,598,214	1921-1930	4,107,209	1973	400,063	1979	460,348
1861-1870	2,314,824	1931-1940	528,431	1974	394,861	**1820-1979**	**49,125,413**
1871-1880	2,812,191	1941-1950	1,035,039	1975	386,194		

Naturalization: How to Become an American Citizen

Source: The Federal Statutes

A person who desires to be naturalized as a citizen of the United States may obtain the necessary application form as well as detailed information from the nearest office of the Immigration and Naturalization Service or from the clerk of a court handling naturalization cases.

An applicant must be at least 18 years old. He must have been a lawful resident of the United States continuously for 5 years. For husbands and wives of U.S. citizens the period is 3 years in most instances. Special provisions apply to certain veterans of the Armed Forces.

An applicant must have been physically present in this country for at least half of the required 5 years' residence.

Every applicant for naturalization must:

(1) demonstrate an understanding of the English language, including an ability to read, write, and speak words in ordinary usage in the English language (persons physically unable to do so, and persons who, on the date of their examinations, are over 50 years of age and have been lawful permanent residents of the United States for 20 years or more are exempt).

(2) have been a person of good moral character, attached to the principles of the Constitution, and well disposed to the good order and happiness of the United States for five years just before filing the petition or for whatever other period of residence is required in his case and continue to be such a person until admitted to citizenship; and

(3) demonstrate a knowledge and understanding of the fundamentals of the history, and the principles and form of government, of the U.S.

The petitioner also is obliged to have two credible citizen witnesses. These witnesses must have personal knowledge of the applicant.

When the applicant files his petition he pays the court clerk $25. At the preliminary hearing he may be represented by a lawyer or social service agency. There is a 30-day wait. If action is favorable, there is a final hearing before a judge, who administers the following oath of allegiance:

I hereby declare, on oath, that I absolutely and entirely renounce and abjure all allegiance and fidelity to any foreign prince, potentate, state or sovereignty, to whom or which I have heretofore been a subject or citizen; that I will support and defend the Constitution and laws of the United States of America against all enemies, foreign and domestic; that I will bear true faith and allegiance to the same; that I will bear arms on behalf of the United States when required by the law; that I will perform noncombatant service in the armed forces of the United States when required by the law; that I will perform work of national importance under civilian direction when required by the law; and that I take this obligation freely without any mental reservation or purpose of evasion; so help me God.

WORLD FACTS

Early Explorers of the Western Hemisphere

The first men to discover the New World or Western Hemisphere are believed to have walked across a "land bridge" from Siberia to Alaska, an isthmus since broken by the Bering Strait. From Alaska, these ancestors of the Indians spread through North, Central, and South America. Anthropologists have placed these crossings at between 18,000 and 14,000 B.C.; but evidence found in 1967 near Puebla, Mex., indicates mankind reached there as early as 35,000-40,000 years ago.

At first, these people were hunters using flint weapons and tools. In Mexico, about 7000-6000 B.C., they founded farming cultures, developing corn, squash, etc. Eventually, they created complex civilizations — Olmec, Toltec, Aztec, and Maya and, in South America, Inca. Carbon-14 tests show men lived about 8000 B.C. near what are now Front Royal, Va., Kanawha, W. Va., and Dutchess Quarry, N.Y. The Hopewell Culture, based on farming, flourished about 1000 B.C.; remains of it are seen today in large mounds in Ohio and other states.

Norsemen (Norwegian Vikings sailing out of Iceland and Greenland) are credited by most scholars with being the first Europeans to discover America, with at least 5 voyages around 1000 A.D. to areas they called Helluland, Markland, Vinland—possibly Labrador, Nova Scotia or Newfoundland, and New England.

Christopher Columbus, most famous of the explorers, was born at Genoa, Italy, but made his discoveries sailing for the Spanish rulers Ferdinand and Isabella. Dates of his voyages, places he discovered, and other information follow:

1492—First voyage. Left Palos, Spain, Aug. 3 with 88 men (est.). Discovered San Salvador (Guanahani or Watling Is., Bahamas) Oct. 12. Also Cuba, Hispaniola (Haiti-Dominican Republic); built Fort La Navidad on latter.

1493—Second voyage, first part, Sept. 25, with 17 ships, 1,500 men. Dominica (Lesser Antilles) Nov. 3; Guadeloupe, Montserrat, Antigua, San Martin, Santa Cruz, Puerto Rico, Virgin Islands. Settled Isabela on Hispaniola. **Second part** (Columbus having remained in Western Hemisphere), Jamaica, Isle of Pines, La Mona Is.

1498—Third voyage. Left Spain May 30, 1498, 6 ships. Discovered Trinidad. Saw South American continent Aug. 1, 1498, but called it Isla Sancta (Holy Island). Entered Gulf of Paria and landed, first time on continental soil. At mouth of Orinoco Aug. 14 he decided this was the mainland.

1502—Fourth voyage, 4 caravels, 150 men. St. Lucia, Guanaja off Honduras; Cape Gracias a Dios, Honduras; San Juan River, Costa Rica; Almirante, Portobelo, and Laguna de Chiriqui, Panama.

Year	Explorer	Nationality and employer	Discovery or exploration
1497	John Cabot	Italian-English	Newfoundland or Nova Scotia
1498	John and Sebastian Cabot	Italian-English	Labrador to Hatteras
1499	Alonso de Ojeda	Spanish	South American coast, Venezuela
1500, Feb.	Vicente y Pinzon	Spanish	South American coast, Amazon River
1500, Apr.	Pedro Alvarez Cabral	Portuguese	Brazil (for Portugal)
1500-02	Gaspar Corte-Real	Portuguese	Labrador
1501	Rodrigo de Bastidas	Spanish	Central America
1513	Vasco Nunez de Balboa	Spanish	Pacific Ocean
1513	Juan Ponce de Leon	Spanish	Florida
1515	Juan de Solis	Spanish	Rio de la Plata
1519	Alonso de Pineda	Spanish	Mouth of Mississippi River
1519	Hernando Cortes	Spanish	Mexico
1520	Ferdinand Magellan	Portuguese-Spanish	Straits of Magellan, Tierra del Fuego
1524	Giovanni da Verrazano	Italian-French	Atlantic Coast-New York harbor
1532	Francisco Pizarro	Spanish	Peru
1534	Jacques Cartier	French	Canada, Gulf of St. Lawrence
1536	Pedro de Mendoza	Spanish	Buenos Aires
1536	A.N. Cabeza de Vaca	Spanish	Texas coast and interior
1539	Francisco de Ulloa	Spanish	California coast
1539-41	Hernando de Soto	Spanish	Mississippi River near Memphis
1539	Marcos de Niza	Italian-Spanish	Southwest (now U.S.)
1540	Francisco V. de Coronado	Spanish	Southwest (now U.S.)
1540	Hernando Alarcon	Spanish	Colorado River
1540	Garcia de L. Cardenas	Spanish	Grand Canyon of the Colorado
1541	Francisco de Orellana	Spanish	Amazon River
1542	Juan Rodriquez Cabrillo	Portuguese-Spanish	San Diego harbor
1565	Pedro Menendez	Spanish	St. Augustine
1576	Martin Frobisher	Engish	Frobisher's Bay, Canada
1577-80	Francis Drake	English	California Coast
1582	Antonio de Espejo	Spanish	Southwest (named New Mexico)
1584	Amadas & Barlow (for Raleigh)	English	Virginia
1585-87	Sir Walter Raleigh's men	English	Roanoke Is., N.C.
1595	Sir Walter Raleigh	English	Orinoco River
1603-09	Samuel de Champlain	French	Canadian interior, Lake Champlain
1607	Capt. John Smith	English	Atlantic coast
1609-10	Henry Hudson	English-Dutch	Hudson River, Hudson Bay
1634	Jean Nicolet	French	Lake Michigan; Wisconsin
1673	Jacques Marquette, Louis Jolliet	French	Mississippi S to Arkansas
1682	Sieur de La Salle	French	Mississippi S to Gulf of Mexico
1789	Alexander Mackenzie	Canadian	Canadian Northwest

Arctic Exploration

Early Explorers

1587 — John Davis (England). Davis Strait to Sanderson's Hope, 72° 12′ N.

1596 — Willem Barents and Jacob van Heemskerck (Holland). Discovered Bear Island, touched northwest tip of Spitsbergen, 79° 49′ N, rounded Novaya Zemlya, wintered at Ice Haven.

1607 — Henry Hudson (England). North along Greenland's east coast to Cape Hold-with-Hope, 73° 30′, then north of Spitsbergen to 80° 23′. Returning he discovered Hudson's Touches (Jan Mayen).

1616 — William Baffin and Robert Bylot (England). Baffin Bay to Smith Sound.

1728 — Vitus Bering (Russia). Proved Asia and America were separated by sailing through strait.

1733-40 — Great Northern Expedition (Russia). Surveyed Siberian Arctic coast.

1741 — Vitus Bering (Russia). Sighted Alaska from sea, named Mount St. Elias. His lieutenant, Chirikof, discovered coast.

1771 — Samuel Hearne (Hudson's Bay Co.). Overland from Prince of Wales Fort (Churchill) on Hudson Bay to mouth of Coppermine River.

1778 — James Cook (Britain). Through Bering Strait to Icy Cape, Alaska, and North Cape, Siberia.

1789 — Alexander Mackenzie (North West Co., Britain). Montreal to mouth of Mackenzie River.

1806 — William Scoresby (Britain). North of Spitsbergen to 81° 30′.

1820-3 — Ferdinand von Wrangel (Russia). Completed a survey of Siberian Arctic coast. His exploration joined that of James Cook at North Cape, confirming separation of the continents.

1845 — Sir John Franklin (Britain) was one of many to seek the Northwest Passage—an ocean route connecting the Atlantic and Pacific via the Arctic. His 2 ships (the Erebus and Terror) were last seen entering Lancaster Sound July 26.

1888 — Fridtjof Nansen (Norway) crossed Greenland's icecap, 1893-96 — Nansen in Fram drifted from New Siberian Is. to Spitsbergen; tried polar dash in 1895, reached Franz Josef Land.

1896 — Salomon A. Andree (Sweden) and companion, in June, made first attempt to reach North Pole by balloon; failed and returned in August. On July 11, 1897, Andree and 2 others started in balloon from Danes, Is., Spitsbergen, to drift across pole to America, and disappeared. Over 33 years later, Aug. 6, 1930, Dr. Gunnar Horn (Norway) found their frozen bodies on White Is., 82° 57′ N 29° 52′ E.

1903-06 — Roald Amundsen (Norway) first sailed Northwest Passage.

Discovery of North Pole

Robert E. Peary began exploring in 1886 on Greenland, when he was 30. With his hq. at McCormick Bay he explored Greenland's coast 1891-92, tried for North Pole 1893, returned with large meteorites. In 1900 he reached northern limit of Greenland and 83° 50′ N; in 1902 he reached 84° 06′ N; in 1906 he went from Ellesmere Is. to 87° 06′ N. He sailed in the Roosevelt, July, 1908, to winter off Cape Sheridan, Grant Land. The dash for the North Pole began Mar. 1 from Cape Columbia, Ellesmere Land. Peary reached the pole, 90° N, Apr. 6, 1909.

Peary had several supporting groups carrying supplies until the last group, under Capt. Robt. A. Bartlett, turned back at 87° 47′ N. Peary, Matthew Henson, and 4 eskimos proceeded with dog teams and sleds. They crossed the pole several times, finally built an igloo at 90°, remained 36 hours. Started south Apr. 7 at 4 p.m. for Cape Columbia. Eskimos were Coqueeh, Ootah, Eginwah, and Seegloo. Adm. Peary died Feb. 20, 1920. Henson, a Negro, born Aug. 8, 1866, died Mar. 9, 1955, aged 88. Ootah, the last survivor, died May, 1955, aged 80.

1914 — Donald Macmillan (U.S.). Northwest, 200 miles, from Axel Hieberg Island to seek Peary's Crocker Land.

1915-17 — Vihjalmur Stefansson (Canada) discovered Borden, Brock, Meighen, and Lougheed Islands.

1918-20 — Amundsen sailed Northeast Passage.

1925 — Roald Amundsen and Lincoln Ellsworth (U.S.) reached 87° 44′ N in attempt to fly to North Pole from Spitsbergen.

1926 — Richard E. Byrd and Floyd Bennett (U.S.) first over North Pole by air, May 9.

1926 — Amundsen, Ellsworth, and Umberto Nobile (Italy) flew from Spitsbergen over North Pole May 12, to Teller, Alaska, in dirigible Norge.

1928 — Nobile crossed North Pole in airship Italia May 24, crashed May 25. Amundsen lost while trying to effect rescue by plane.

1928 — Sir Hubert Wilkins and Eielson flew from Point Barrow to Spitsbergen, 84° N.

North Pole Exploration Records

On Aug. 3, 1958, the Nautilus, under Comdr. William R. Anderson, became the first ship to cross the North Pole beneath the Arctic ice.

The nuclear-powered U.S. submarine Seadragon, Comdr. George P. Steele 2d, made the first east-west underwater transit through the Northwest Passage during August, 1960. It sailed from Portsmouth N.H., headed between Greenland and Labrador through Baffin Bay, then west through Lancaster Sound and McClure Strait to the Beaufort Sea. Traveling submerged for the most part, the submarine made 850 miles from Baffin Bay to the Beaufort Sea in 6 days.

On Aug. 16, 1977, the Soviet nuclear icebreaker Arktika reached the North Pole and became the first surface ship to break through the Arctic ice pack to the top of the world.

On April 30, 1978, Naomi Uemura, a Japanese explorer, became the first man to reach the North Pole alone by dog sled. During the 54-day, 600-mile trek over the frozen Arctic, Uemura survived attacks by a marauding polar bear.

In April, 1982, Sir Ranulph Fiennes and Charles Burton, British explorers, reached the North Pole and became the first to circle the earth from pole to pole. They had reached the South Pole 16 months earlier. The 52,000-mile trek took 3 years, involved 23 people, and cost an estimated $18 million. The expedition was also the first to travel down the Scott Glacier and the first to journey up the Yukon and through the Northwest Passage in a single season.

Antarctic Exploration

Early History

Antarctica has been approached since 1773-75, when Capt. Jas. Cook (Britain) reached 71° 10′ S. Many sea and landmarks bear names of early explorers. Bellingshausen (Russia) discovered Peter I and Alexander I Islands, 1819-21. Nathaniel Palmer (U.S.) discovered Palmer Peninsula, 60° W, 1820, without realizing that this was a continent. Jas. Weddell (Britain) found Weddell Sea, 74° 15′ S, 1823.

First to announce existence of the continent of Antarctica was Charles Wilkes (U.S.), who followed the coast for 1,500 mi., 1840. Adelie Coast, 140° E, was found by Dumont d'Urville (France), 1840. Ross Ice Shelf was found by Jas. Clark Ross (Britain), 1841-42.

1895 — Leonard Kristensen, Norwegian whaling captain, landed a party on the coast of Victoria Land in Jan. 1895. They were the first ashore on the main continental mass. C.E. Borchgrevink, a member of that party, returned in 1899 with a British expedition, first to winter on Antarctica.

1902-04 — Robert F. Scott (Britain) discovered Edward VII Peninsula. In 1902 he reached 82° 17′ S, 146° 33′ E from McMurdo Sound.

1908-09 — Ernest Shackleton, in 1908, introduced the use of Manchurian ponies in Antarctic sledging. In 1909 he reached 88° 23′ S, discovering a route on to the plateau by way of the Beardmore Glacier and pioneering the way to the pole.

Discovery of South Pole

1911 — Roald Amundsen (Norway) with 4 men and dog teams reached the pole Dec. 14, 1911.

1912 — Capt. Scott reached the pole from Ross Island Jan. 18, 1912, with 4 companions, where they found Amundsen's tent. None of Scott's party survived. They were found Nov. 12, 1912.

1928 — First man to use an airplane over Antarctica was Hubert Wilkins (Britain).

1929 — Richard E. Byrd (U.S.) established Little America on Bay of Whales. On 1600-mi. airplane flight begun Nov. 28 he crossed South Pole Nov. 29 with his pilot, a radio operator, and a photographer. Dropped U.S. flag over pole, temp. 16° below zero.

1934-35 — Richard E. Byrd (U.S.) led 2d expedition to Little America, which explored 450,000 sq. mi. Byrd wintered alone at an advance weather station in 80° 08′ S.

1934-37 — John Rymill led British Graham Land expedition of 1934-37; discovered that Palmer Peninsula is part of Antarctic mainland.

1935 — Lincoln Ellsworth (U.S.) flew south along Palmer Peninsula's east coast, then crossed continent to Little America, making 4 landings on unprepared terrain in bad weather, a new feat.

1939-41 — U.S. Antarctic Service built West Base on Ross Ice Shelf under Paul Siple, and East Base on Palmer Peninsula under Richard Black. U.S. Navy plane flights discovered about 150,000 sq. miles of new land.

1940 — Richard E. Byrd (U.S.) charted most of coast between Ross Sea and Palmer Peninsula.

1946-47 — U.S. Navy undertook Operation High-jump under Rear Admiral Byrd. Expedition included 13 ships and 4,000 men. Airplanes photomapped coastline and penetrated beyond pole.

1946-48 — Ronne Antarctic Research Expedition, Comdr. Finn Ronne, USNR, determined the Antarctic to be only one continent with no strait between Weddell Sea and Ross Sea; discovered 250,000 sq. miles of land by flights to 79° S Lat., and made 14,000 aerial photographs over 450,000 sq. miles of land. Mrs. Ronne and Mrs. H. Darlington, who accompanied their husbands, were the first women to winter on Antarctica.

1955-57 — U.S. Navy's Operation Deep Freeze led by Adm. Richard E. Byrd. Supporting U.S. scientific efforts for the International Geophysical Year, the operation was commanded by Rear Adm. George Dufek. It established 5 coastal stations fronting the Indian, Pacific, and Atlantic Oceans and also 3 interior stations; explored more than 1,000,000 sq. miles in Wilkes Land. Seven Navy men under Adm. Dufek landed by plane at the Pole Oct. 31, 1956, and landed radar reflectors.

1957-58 — During the International Geophysical year, July, 1957, through Dec. 1958, scientists from 12 countries conducted ambitious programs of Antarctic research. A network of some 60 stations on the continent and sub-Arctic islands studied oceanography, glaciology, meteorology, seismology, geomagnetism, the ionosphere, cosmic rays, aurora, and airglow. A party from Ellsworth IGY station (U.S.) south of Weddell Sea under the direction of Captain Finn Ronne explored beyond 1947 flight and delineated Berkner Island imbedded in the Filchner Ice Shelf.

Dr. V.E. Fuchs led a 12-man Trans-Antarctic Expedition on the first land crossing of Antarctica. Starting from the Weddell Sea, they reached Scott Station Mar. 2, 1958, after traveling 2,158 miles in 98 days.

1958 — A group of 5 U.S. scientists led by Edward C. Thiel, seismologist, moving by tractor from Ellsworth Station on Weddell Sea, identified a huge mountain range, 5,000 ft. above the ice sheet and 9,000 ft. above sea level. The range, originally seen by a Navy plane, was named the Dufek Massif, for Rear Adm. George Dufek.

1959 — Twelve nations — Argentina, Australia, Belgium, Chile, France, Japan, New Zealand, Norway, South Africa, the Soviet Union, the United Kingdom, and the U.S. — signed a treaty suspending any territorial claims for 30 years and reserving the continent for research.

1961-62 — Scientists discovered a trough, the Bentley Trench, running from Ross Ice Shelf, Pacific, into Marie Byrd Land, around the end of the Ellsworth Mtns., toward the Weddell Sea, which may be the long-suspected link between the Atlantic and Pacific Oceans.

1962 — First nuclear power plant began operation at McMurdo Sound.

1963 — On Feb. 22 a U.S. plane made the longest nonstop flight ever made in the S. Pole area, covering 3,600 miles in 10 hours. The flight was from McMurdo Station south past the geographical S. Pole to Shackleton Mtns., southeast to the "Area of Inaccessibility" and back to McMurdo Station.

1963 — Three turbine-powered helicopters made the first copter landings on the S. Pole.

1964 — A British survey team was landed by helicopter on Cook Island, the first recorded visit since its discovery in 1775.

1964 — New Zealanders completed one of the last and most important surveys when they mapped the mountain area from Cape Adare west some 400 miles to Pennell Glacier.

1966-67 — Fifteen Antarctic areas set aside as Specially Protected Areas for the conservation of flora and fauna.

Notable Volcanoes of the World

Year of last eruption in parentheses.

More than 75 per cent of the world's 850 active volcanoes lie within the "Ring of Fire," a zone running along the west coast of the Americas from Chile to Alaska and down the east coast of Asia from Siberia to New Zealand. Twenty per cent of these volcanoes are located in Indonesia. Other prominent groupings are located in Japan, the Aleutian Islands, and Central America. Almost all active regions are found at the boundaries of the large moving plates which comprise the earth's surface. The "Ring of Fire" marks the boundary between the plates underlying the Pacific Ocean and those underlying the surrounding continents. Other active regions, such as the Mediterranean Sea and Iceland, are located on plate boundaries.

Major Historical Eruptions

Approximately 7,000 years ago, Mazama, a 9,900-feet-high volcano in southern Oregon, erupted violently, ejecting ash and lava. The ash spread over the entire northwestern United States and as far away as Saskatchewan, Canada. During the eruption, the top of the mountain collapsed, leaving a caldera 6 miles across and about a half mile deep, which filled with rain water to form what is now called Crater Lake.

In 79 A.D., Vesuvio, or Vesuvius, a 4,190 feet volcano overlooking Naples Bay became active after several centuries of quiescence. On Aug. 24 of that year, a heated mud and ash flow swept down the mountain engulfing the cities of Pompeii, Herculaneum, and Stabiae with debris over 60 feet deep. About 10 percent of the population of the 3 towns was killed.

The largest eruptions in recent centuries have been in Indonesia. In 1883, an eruption similar to the Mazama eruption occurred on the island of Krakatau. On August 27, the 2,640-feet-high peak of the volcano collapsed to 1,000 feet below sea level, leaving only a small portion of the island standing above the sea. Ash from the eruption colored sunsets around the world for 2 years. A tsunami ("tidal wave") generated by the collapse killed 36,000 people in nearby Java and Sumatra and eventually reached England. A similar, but even more powerful, eruption had taken place 68 years earlier at Tambora volcano on the Indonesian island of Sumbawa.

Events in 1981-82

There were only 41 volcanic eruptions in the world during 1981, the lowest reported since 1970, and well below the average over the past decade of 60 eruptions a year. Only 14 of the 41 eruptions in 1981 were of the explosive type.

The most notable eruptions in 1981 were in the western Pacific. The Alaid volcano in the Kurile Islands erupted on April 27 and spread ash over an area of about 58,000 square miles in the eastern USSR. On May 15, the North Pagan volcano in the Mariana Islands emitted a plume of ash that reached a height of about 12 miles.

There were no major eruptions in the United States during 1981. United States Geological Survey scientists were able to provide from several hours to several days of advance warning for the mostly non-explosive, dome-building eruptions at Mount St. Helens. The USGS has established a new observatory to monitor Mount St. Helens and other Cascade volcanoes.

It is estimated that, in addition to about 15 volcanic centers in the Cascade Range and vicinity, there are some 60 volcanic centers in 11 western states that have the potential for future eruptions.

Name	Location	Feet
Africa		
Kilimanjaro	Tanzania	19,340
Cameroon	Cameroons	13,354
Teide (Tenerife) (1909)	Canary Is.	12,198
Nyirangongo (1977)	Zaire	11,400
Nyamuragira (1982)	Zaire	10,028
Fogo (1951)	Cape Verde Is.	9,281
Karthala (1977)	Comoro Is.	8,000
Piton de la Fournaise (1981)	Reunion Is.	5,981
Erta-Ale (1973)	Ethiopia	1,650
Antarctica		
Erebus (1979)	Ross Island	12,450
Big Ben (1960)	Heard Island	9,007
Melbourne	Victoria Land	8,500
Deception Island (1970)	South Shetland Islands	1,890
Asia-Oceania		
Klyuchevskaya (1974)	USSR	15,584
Kerintji (1968)	Sumatra	12,467
Fuji	Japan	12,388
Rindjani (1966)	Indonesia	12,224
Tolbachik (1941)	USSR	12,080
Semeru (1981)	Java	12,060
Ichinskaya	USSR	11,880
Kronotskaya (1923)	USSR	11,575
Koryakskaya (1957)	USSR	11,339
Slamet (1967)	Java	11,247
Raung (1945)	Java	10,932
Shiveluch (1964)	USSR	10,771
Dempo (1940)	Sumatra	10,364
Ardjuno-Welirang	Java	10,354
Agung (1964)	Bali	10,308
Sundoro (1906)	Java	10,285
Tjiremai (1938)	Java	10,098
On-Take (1980)	Japan	10,049
Mayon (1978)	Philippines	9,991
Papandajan (1925)	Java	9,802
Gede (1949)	Java	9,705
Zhupanovsky (1959)	USSR	9,705
Apo	Philippines	9,690
Merapi (1982)	Java	9,551
Bezymianny (1981)	USSR	9,514
Marapi (1981)	Sumatra	9,485
Tambora (1913)	Indonesia	9,353
Ruapehu (1982)	New Zealand	9,175
Peuetsagoe (1921)	Sumatra	9,121
Avachinskaya (1945)	USSR	9,026
Balbi	Solomon Is.	9,000
Geureudong	Sumatra	8,497
Asama (1973)	Japan	8,300
Sumbing (1921)	Sumatra	8,225
Tandikat (1914)	Sumatra	8,166
Niigata Yakeyama (1974)	Japan	8,111
Yake Dake (1963)	Japan	8,064

Name	Location	Feet
Canlaon	Philippines	8,015
Sinabung	Sumatra	7,913
Bromo (1950)	Java	7,848
Idjen (1936)	Java	7,828
Alaid (1972)	Kuril Is.	7,662
Asama (1982)	Japan	7,626
Ulawun (1980)	New Britain	7,532
Ngauruhoe (1975)	New Zealand	7,515
Guntur	Java	7,379
Bamus	New Britain	7,338
Chokai (1974)	Japan	7,300
Galunggung (1918)	Java	7,113
Amburombu (1969)	Indonesia	7,051
Sorikmerapi (1917)	Sumatra	7,037
Butak Petarangan (1939)	Java	6,890
Sibajak	Sumatra	6,870
Tokachi (1962)	Japan	6,813
Azuma (1978)	Japan	6,700
Tangkuban Prahu (1967)	Java	6,637
Tongariro	New Zealand	6,458
Zheltovskaya (1923)	USSR	6,401
Catarman (1952)	Philippines	6,371
Kaba (1941)	Sumatra	6,358
Sangeang Api (1966)	Indonesia	6,351
Nasu (1977)	Japan	6,210
Tiatia (1973)	Kuril Islands	6,013
Manam (1982)	Papua New Guinea	6,000
Soputan (1968)	Celebes	5,994
Siau (1976)	Indonesia	5,853
Kelud (1967)	Java	5,679
Batur (1968)	Bali	5,636
Ternate (1963)	Indonesia	5,627
Lewotobi (1935)	Indonesia	5,591
Kirisima (1982)	Japan	5,577
Lamongan	Java	5,482
Keli Mutu (1968)	Indonesia	5,460
Akita Komaga take (1970)	Japan	5,449
Lli Boleng (1950)	Indonesia	5,443
Gamkonora (1981)	Indonesia	5,364
Aso (1981)	Japan	5,223
Lewotobi Laki-Laki (1968)	Indonesia	5,217
Lokon-Empung (1970)	Celebes	5,187
Bulusan (1980)	Philippines	5,115
Sarycheva (1976)	Kuril Islands	4,960
Me-akan (1966)	Japan	4,931
Ibu (1911)	Indonesia	4,921
Karkar (1981)	Papua New Guinea	4,920
Karymskaya (1976)	USSR	4,869
Lopevi (1960)	New Hebrides	4,755
Ambrym (1979)	New Hebrides	4,376
Mahawu	Celebes	4,367
Awu (1968)	Indonesia	4,350
Ili Lewotolo (1920)	Indonesia	4,348
Tongkoko	Celebes	3,770
Ili Werung (1948)	Indonesia	3,678
Komaga take (1942)	Japan	3,669
Sakurazima (1982)	Japan	3,668
Langila (1982)	New Britain	3,586
Dukono (1971)	Indonesia	3,566
Lamington (1952)	Papua New Guinea	3,500
Lolobau (1905)	New Britain	3,058
Suwanosezima (1981)	Japan	2,640
O-Sima (1977)	Japan	2,550
Usu (1978)	Japan	2,400
White Island (1981)	New Zealand	1,075
Taal (1977)	Philippines	984
Central America—Caribbean		
Tajumulco	Guatemala	13,845
Tacana	Guatemala	13,428
Acatenango (1972)	Guatemala	12,992
Fuego (1980)	Guatemala	12,582
Santiaguito (Santa Maria) (1982)	Guatemala	12,362
Atitlan	Guatemala	11,565
Irazu (1967)	Costa Rica	11,260
San Pedro	Guatamala	9,921
Poas (1981)	Costa Rica	8,930
Pacaya (1982)	Guatemala	8,346
Izalco (1966)	El Salvador	7,749
San Miguel (1976)	El Salvador	6,994
Rincon de la Vieja (1968)	Costa Rica	6,234
El Viejo (San Cristobal) (1981)	Nicaragua	5,840
Ometepe (Concepcion) (1978)	Nicaragua	5,106
Arenal (1981)	Costa Rica	5,092
La Soufriére	Guadeloupe	4,813
Pelée (1932)	Martinique	4,583
Momotombo (1952)	Nicaragua	4,199
Conchagua (1947)	El Salvador	4,100
Soufriere (1979)	St. Vincent	4,048
Telica (1982)	Nicaragua	3,409
South America		
Guallatiri (1960)	Chile	19,882
Lascar (1968)	Chile	19,652
Cotopaxi (1975)	Ecuador	19,347
El Misti	Peru	19,098
Tupungatito (1980)	Chile	18,504
Tolima (1943)	Colombia	18,002
Sangay (1976)	Ecuador	17,159
Tungurahua (1944)	Ecuador	16,512
Cotacachi (1955)	Ecuador	16,204
Guagua Pichincha (1981)	Ecuador	15,696
Purace (1977)	Colombia	15,604
Lautaro (1960)	Chile	11,098
Llaima (1979)	Chile	10,239
Villarrica (1980)	Chile	9,318
Hudson (1973)	Chile	8,580
Shoshuenco (1960)	Chile	7,743
Puyehue (1960)	Chile	7,349
Calbuco (1961)	Chile	6,611
Alcedo (1970)	Galapagos Is.	3,599
Mid-Pacific		
Mauna Kea	Hawaii	13,796
Mauna Loa (1978)	Hawaii	13,680
Kilauea (1981)	Hawaii	4,077
Mid-Atlantic Ridge		
Beerenberg (1970)	Jan Mayen Is.	7,470
Tristan da Cunha (1962)	Tristan da Cunha Is.	6,760
Askja (1961)	Iceland	4,954
Hekla (1981)	Iceland	4,892
Katla (1918)	Iceland	3,182
Leirhnukur (1975)	Iceland	2,145
Krafla (1981)	Iceland	2,145
Surtsey (1967)	Iceland	568
Europe		
Etna (1981)	Italy	11,053
Vesuvius (1944)	Italy	4,190
Stromboli (1975)	Italy	3,038
Thera (1956)	Greece	1,824
Vulcano	Italy	1,637
North America		
Citlaltepec	Mexico	18,700
Popocatepetl (1920)	Mexico	17,887
Rainier	Washington	14,410
Wrangell	Alaska	14,163
Colima (1982)	Mexico	14,003
Torbert (1953)	Alaska	11,413
Spurr (1953)	Alaska	11,069
Baker	Washington	10,779
Lassen (1915)	California	10,457
Redoubt (1966)	Alaska	10,197
Iliamna (1978)	Alaska	10,092
Mt. St. Helens (1982)	Washington	9,677
Shishaldin (1981)	Aleutian Is.	9,387
Veniaminof	Alaska	8,225
Pavlof (1981)	Aleutian Is.	8,215
Griggs	Alaska	7,600
Paricutin (1952)	Mexico	7,451
El Chichon (1982)	Mexico	7,300
Mageik (1912)	Alaska	7,244
Douglas	Alaska	7,064
Chiginagak	Alaska	7,031
Katmai (1962)	Alaska	6,715
Kukak	Alaska	6,700
Makushin (1980)	Aleutian Is.	6,680
Pogromni (1964)	Alaska	6,568
Martin (1960	Alaska	6,050
Trident 1963)	Alaska	6,010
Tanaga	Aleutian Is.	5,925
Great Sitkin (1974)	Aleutian Is.	5,710
Cleveland (1951)	Aleutian Is.	5,675
Gareloi (1982)	Aleutian Is.	5,334
Korovin	Aleutian Is.	4,852
Kanaga	Aleutian Is.	4,416
Aniakchak	Alaska	4,400
Akutan (1980)	Aleutian Is.	4,275
Kiska (1969)	Aleutian Is.	4,275
Augustine (1976)	Alaska	3,927
Little Sitkin	Aleutian Is.	3,897
Okmok (1958)	Aleutian Is.	3,519
Seguam (1977)	Alaska	3,458

Highest and Lowest Continental Altitudes

Source: National Geographic Society, Washington, D.C.

Continent	Highest point	Feet elevation	Lowest point	Feet below sea level
Asia	Mount Everest, Nepal-Tibet	29,028	Dead Sea, Israel-Jordan	1,312
South America	Mount Aconcagua, Argentina	22,834	Valdes Peninsula, Argentina	131
North America	Mount McKinley, Alaska	20,320	Death Valley, California	282
Africa	Kilimanjaro, Tanzania	19,340	Lake Assal, Djibouti	512
Europe	Mount El'brus, USSR	18,510	Caspian Sea, USSR	92
Antarctica	Vinson Massif	16,864	Unknown	...
Australia	Mount Kosciusko, New South Wales	7,310	Lake Eyre, South Australia	52

Height of Mount Everest

Mt. Everest was considered to be 29,002 ft. tall when Edmund Hillary and Tenzing Norgay scaled it in 1953. This triangulation figure had been accepted since 1850. In 1954 the Surveyor General of the Republic of India set the height at 29,028 ft., plus or minus 10 ft. because of snow. The National Geographic Society accepts the new figure, but many mountaineering groups still use 29,002 ft.

High Peaks in United States, Canada, Mexico

Name	Place	Feet
McKinley	Alas	20,320
Logan	Can	19,850
Citlaltepec (Orizaba)	Mexico	18,700
St. Elias	Alas-Can	18,008
Popocatepetl	Mexico	17,887
Foraker	Alas	17,400
Iztaccihuatl	Mexico	17,343
Lucania	Can	17,147
King	Can	16,971
Steele	Can	16,644
Bona	Alas	16,550
Blackburn	Alas	16,390
Kennedy	Alas	16,286
Sanford	Alas	16,237
South Buttress	Alas	15,885
Wood	Can	15,885
Vancouver	Alas-Can	15,700
Churchill	Alas	15,638
Fairweather	Alas-Can	15,300
Zinantecatl (Toluca)	Mexico	15,016
Hubbard	Alas-Can	15,015
Bear	Alas	14,831
Walsh	Can	14,780
East Buttress	Alas	14,730
Matlalcueyetl	Mexico	14,636
Hunter	Alas	14,573
Alverstone	Alas-Can	14,565
Browne Tower	Alas	14,530
Whitney	Cal	14,494
Elbert	Col	14,433
Massive	Col	14,421
Harvard	Col	14,420
Rainier	Wash	14,410
Williamson	Cal	14,375
Blanca	Col	14,345
La Plata	Col	14,336
Uncompahgre	Col	14,309
Crestone	Col	14,294
Lincoln	Col	14,286
Grays	Col	14,270
Antero	Col	14,269
Torreys	Col	14,267
Castle	Col	14,265
Quandary	Col	14,265
Evans	Col	14,264
Longs	Col	14,256
McArthur	Can	14,253
Wilson	Col	14,246
White	Cal	14,246
North Palisade	Cal	14,242
Shavano	Col	14,229
Belford	Col	14,197
Princeton	Col	14,197
Crestone Needle	Col	14,197
Yale	Col	14,196
Bross	Col	14,172
Kit Carson	Col	14,165
Wrangell	Alas	14,163
Shasta	Cal	14,162
Sill	Cal	14,162
El Diente	Col	14,159
Maroon	Col	14,156
Tabeguache	Col	14,155
Oxford	Col	14,153
Sneffels	Col	14,150
Point Success	Wash	14,150
Democrat	Col	14,148
Capitol	Col	14,130
Liberty Cap	Wash	14,112
Pikes Peak	Col	14,110
Snowmass	Col	14,092
Windom	Col	14,087
Russell	Cal	14,086
Eolus	Col	14,084
Columbia	Col	14,073
Augusta	Alas-Can	14,070
Missouri	Col	14,067
Humboldt	Col	14,064
Bierstadt	Col	14,060
Sunlight	Col	14,059
Split	Cal	14,058
Nauhcampatepetl (Cofre de Perote)	Mexico	14,049
Handies	Col	14,048
Culebra	Col	14,047
Langley	Cal	14,042
Lindsey	Col	14,042
Middle Palisade	Cal	14,040
Little Bear	Col	14,037
Sherman	Col	14,036
Redcloud	Col	14,034
Tyndall	Cal	14,018
Pyramid	Col	14,018
Wilson Peak	Col	14,017
Muir	Cal	14,015
Wetterhorn	Col	14,015
North Maroon	Col	14,014
San Luis	Col	14,014
Huron	Col	14,005
Holy Cross	Col	14,005
Colima	Mexico	14,003
Sunshine	Col	14,001
Grizzly	Col	14,000
Barnard	Cal	13,990
Stewart	Col	13,980
Keith	Cal	13,977
Ouray	Col	13,971
Le Conte	Cal	13,960
Meeker	Col	13,911
Kennedy	Can	13,905

South America

Peak, Country	Feet
Aconcagua, Argentina	22,834
Ojos del Salado, Arg.-Chile	22,572
Bonete, Argentina	22,546
Tupungato, Argentina-Chile	22,310
Pissis, Argentina	22,241
Mercedario, Argentina	22,211
Huascaran, Peru	22,205
Llullaillaco, Argentina-Chile	22,057
El Libertador, Argentina	22,047
Cachi, Argentina	22,047
Yerupaja, Peru	21,709
Galan, Argentina	21,654
El Muerto, Argentina-Chile	21,457
Sajama, Bolivia	21,391
Nacimiento, Argentina	21,302
Illimani, Bolivia	21,201
Coropuna, Peru	21,083
Laudo, Argentina	20,997
Ancohuma, Bolivia	20,958
Ausangate, Peru	20,945
Toro, Argentina-Chile	20,932
Illampu, Bolivia	20,873
Tres Cruces, Argentina-Chile	20,853
Huandoy, Peru	20,852
Parinacota, Bolivia-Chile	20,768
Tortolas, Argentina-Chile	20,745
Ampato, Peru	20,702
Condor, Argentina	20,669
Salcantay, Peru	20,574
Chimborazo, Ecuador	20,561
Huancarhuas, Peru	20,531
Famatina, Argentina	20,505
Pumasillo, Peru	20,492
Solo, Argentina	20,492
Polleras, Argentina	20,456
Pular, Chile	20,423
Chani, Argentina	20,341
Aucanquilcha, Chile	20,295
Juncal, Argentina-Chile	20,276
Negro, Argentina	20,184
Quela, Argentina	20,128
Condoriri, Bolivia	20,095
Palermo, Argentina	20,079
Solimana, Peru	20,068
San Juan, Argentina-Chile	20,049
Sierra Nevada, Arg.-Chile	20,023
Antofalla, Argentina	20,013
Marmolejo, Argentina-Chile	20,013
Chachani, Peru	19,931
Licancabur, Argentina-Chile	19,425

The highest point in the West Indies is in the Dominican Republic, Pico Duarte (10,417 ft.)

Africa, Australia, and Oceania

Peak, country	Feet
Kilimanjaro, Tanzania	19,340
Kenya, Kenya	17,058
Margherita Pk., Uganda-Zaire	16,763
Jaja, New Guinea	16,500
Trikora, New Guinea	15,585
Mandala, New Guinea	15,420
Ras Dashan, Ethiopia	15,158

Peak, country	Feet
Meru, Tanzania	14,979
Wilhelm, New Guinea	14,793
Karisimbi, Zaire-Rwanda	14,787
Elgon, Kenya-Uganda	14,178
Batu, Ethiopia	14,131
Guna, Ethiopia	13,881
Gughe, Ethiopia	13,780

Peak, country	Feet
Toubkal, Morocco	13,665
Kinabalu, Malaysia	13,455
Kerinci, Sumatra	12,467
Cook, New Zealand	12,349
Teide, Canary Islands	12,198
Semeru, Java	12,060
Kosciusko, Australia	7,310

Europe

Peak, country	Feet
Alps	
Mont Blanc, Fr. It.	15,771
Monte Rosa (highest peak of group), Switz.	15,203
Dom, Switz.	14,911
Liskamm, It., Switz.	14,852
Weisshorn, Switz.	14,780
Taschhorn, Switz.	14,733
Matterhorn, It., Switz.	14,690
Dent Blanche, Switz.	14,293
Nadelhorn, Switz.	14,196
Grand Combin, Switz.	14,154
Lenzpitze, Switz.	14,088
Finsteraarhorn, Switz.	14,022
Castor, Switz.	13,865
Zinalrothorn, Switz.	13,849
Hohberghorn, Switz.	13,842
Alphubel, Switz.	13,799
Rimpfischhorn, Switz.	13,776
Aletschorn, Switz.	13,763
Strahlhorn, Switz.	13,747
Dent D'Herens, Switz.	13,686

Peak, county	Feet
Breithorn, It., Switz.	13,665
Bishorn, Switz.	13,645
Jungfrau, Switz.	13,642
Ecrins, Fr.	13,461
Monch, Switz.	13,448
Pollux, Switz.	13,422
Schreckhorn, Switz.	13,379
Ober Gabelhorn, Switz.	13,330
Gran Paradiso, It.	13,323
Bernina, It., Switz.	13,284
Fiescherhorn, Switz.	13,283
Grunhorn, Switz.	13,266
Lauteraarhorn, Switz.	13,261
Durrenhorn, Switz.	13,238
Allalinhorn, Switz.	13,213
Weissmies, Switz.	13,199
Lagginhorn, Switz.	13,156
Zupo, Switz.	13,120
Fletschhorn, Switz.	13,110
Adlerhorn, Switz.	13,081
Gletscherhorn, Switz.	13,068
Schalihorn, Switz.	13,040
Scerscen, Switz.	13,028

Peak, country	Feet
Eiger, Switz.	13,025
Jagerhorn, Switz.	13,024
Rottalhorn, Switz.	13,022
Pyrenees	
Aneto, Sp.	11,168
Posets, Sp.	11,073
Perdido, Sp.	11,007
Vignemale, Fr., Sp.	10,820
Long, Sp.	10,479
Estats, Sp.	10,304
Montcalm, Sp.	10,105
Caucasus (Europe-Asia)	
El'brus, USSR	18,510
Shkara, USSR	17,064
Dykh Tau, USSR	17,054
Kashtan Tau, USSR	16,877
Dzhangi Tau, USSR	16,565
Kazbek, USSR	16,558

Asia

Peak	Country	Feet
Everest	Nepal-Tibet	29,028
K2 (Godwin Austen)	Kashmir	28,250
Kanchenjunga	India-Nepal	28,208
Lhotse I (Everest)	Nepal-Tibet	27,923
Makalu I	Nepal-Tibet	27,824
Lhotse II (Everest)	Nepal-Tibet	27,560
Dhaulagiri	Nepal	26,810
Manaslu I	Nepal	26,760
Cho Oyu	Nepal-Tibet	26,750
Nanga Parbat	Kashmir	26,660
Annapurna I	Nepal	26,504
Gasherbrum	Kashmir	26,470
Broad	Kashmir	26,400
Gosainthan	Tibet	26,287
Annapurna II	Nepal	26,041
Gyachung Kang	Nepal-Tibet	25,910
Disteghil Sar	Kashmir	25,868
Himalchuli	Nepal	25,801
Nuptse (Everest)	Nepal-Tibet	25,726
Masherbrum	Kashmir	25,660
Nanda Devi	India	25,645
Rakaposhi	Kashmir	25,550
Kamet	India-Tibet	25,447
Namcha Barwa	Tibet	25,445
Gurla Mandhata	Tibet	25,355
Ulugh Muz Tagh	Sinkiang-Tibet	25,340

Peak	Country	Feet
Kungur	Sinkiang	25,325
Tirich Mir	Pakistan	25,230
Makalu II	Nepal-Tibet	25,120
Minya Konka	China	24,900
Kula Gangri	Bhutan-Tibet	24,784
Changtzu (Everest)	Nepal-Tibet	24,780
Muz Tagh Ata	Sinkiang	24,757
Skyang Kangri	Kashmir	24,750
Communism Peak	USSR	24,590
Jongsang Peak	India-Nepal	24,472
Pobedy Peak	Sinkiang-USSR	24,406
Sia Kangri	Kashmir	24,350
Haramosh Peak	Pakistan	24,270
Istoro Nal	Pakistan	24,240
Tent Peak	India-Nepal	24,165
Chomo Lhari	Bhutan-Tibet	24,040
Chamlang	Nepal	24,012
Kabru	India-Nepal	24,002
Alung Gangri	Tibet	24,000
Baltoro Kangri	Kashmir	23,990
Mussu Shan	Sinkiang	23,890
Mana	India	23,860
Baruntse	Nepal	23,688
Nepal Peak	India-Nepal	23,500
Amne Machin	China	23,490
Gauri Sankar	Nepal-Tibet	23,440

Peak	Country	Feet
Badrinath	India	23,420
Nunkun	Kashmir	23,410
Lenina Peak	USSR	23,405
Pyramid	India-Nepal	23,400
Api	Nepal	23,399
Pauhunri	India-Tibet	23,385
Trisul	India	23,360
Kangto	India-Tibet	23,260
Nyenchhen Thanglha	Tibet	23,255
Trisuli	India	23,210
Pumori	Nepal-Tibet	23,190
Dunagiri	India	23,184
Lombo Kangra	Tibet	23,165
Saipal	Nepal	23,100
Macha Pucchare	Nepal	22,958
Numbar	Nepal	22,817
Kanjiroba	Nepal	22,580
Ama Dablam	Nepal	22,350
Cho Polu	Nepal	22,093
Lingtren	Nepal-Tibet	21,972
Khumbutse	Nepal-Tibet	21,785
Hlako Gangri	Tibet	21,266
Mt. Grosvenor	China	21,190
Thagchhab Gangri	Tibet	20,970
Damavand	Iran	18,606
Ararat	Turkey	16,804

Antarctica

Peak	Feet
Vinson Massif	16,864
Tyree	16,290
Shinn	15,750
Gardner	15,375
Epperly	15,100
Kirkpatrick	14,855
Elizabeth	14,698
Markham	14,290
Bell	14,117
Mackellar	14,098
Anderson	13,957
Bentley	13,934
Kaplan	13,878

Peak	Feet
Andrew Jackson	13,750
Sidley	13,720
Ostenso	13,710
Minto	13,668
Miller	13,650
Long Gables	13,620
Dickerson	13,517
Giovinetto	13,412
Wade	13,400
Fisher	13,386
Fridtjof Nansen	13,350
Wexler	13,202
Lister	13,200

Peak	Feet
Shear	13,100
Odishaw	13,008
Donaldson	12,894
Ray	12,808
Sellery	12,779
Waterman	12,730
Anne	12,703
Press	12,566
Falla	12,549
Rucker	12,520
Goldthwait	12,510
Morris	12,500
Erebus	12,450

Peak	Feet
Campbell	12,434
Don Pedro Christophersen	12,355
Lysaght	12,326
Huggins	12,247
Sabine	12,200
Astor	12,175
Mohl	12,172
Frankes	12,064
Jones	12,040
Gjelsvik	12,008
Coman	12,000

How Deep Is the Ocean?

Principal ocean depths. **Source:** Defense Mapping Agency Hydrographic/Topographic Center

Name of area	Location		Depth Meters	Depth Fathoms	Depth Feet
Pacific Ocean					
Mariana Trench	11°25'N	142°10'E	11,776	6,439	38,635
Philippine Trench	09°49'N	126°52'E	11,497	6,287	37,720
Tonga Trench	23°16'S	174°45'W	11,313	6,186	37,116
Izu Trench	30°45'N	142°30'E	11,232	6,142	36,850
Kermadec Trench	31°45'S	176°59'W	10,585	5,788	34,728
Kuril Trench	44°11'N	150°32'E	10,570	5,780	34,678
New Britain Trench	06°35'S	153°52'E	9,649	5,276	31,657
Bonin Trench	23°52'N	143°55'E	9,088	4,969	29,816
Japan Trench	38°13'N	144°31'E	8,887	4,859	29,157
Palau Trench	07°42'N	135°12'E	8,526	4,662	27,972
Peru-Chile Trench	23°28'S	71°23'W	8,439	4,615	27,687
Yap Trench	08°37'N	138°03'E	8,398	4,592	27,552
Aleutian Trench	51°08'N	174°48'E	8,161	4,462	26,775
New Hebrides Trench	20°36'S	168°37'E	7,916	4,329	25,971
Ryukyu Trench	24°30'N	127°11'E	7,802	4,266	25,597
Mid. America Trench	13°57'N	93°35'W	6,796	3,716	22,297
Atlantic Ocean					
Puerto Rico Trench	19°46'N	68°03'W	9,460	5,173	31,037
So. Sandwich Trench	55°43'S	25°59'W	8,658	4,734	28,406
Romanche Gap	0°13'S	18°31'W	8,090	4,424	26,542
Cayman Trench	18°50'N	81°38'W	8,083	4,420	26,519
Brazil Basin	03°31'S	22°47'W	6,789	3,712	22,274
Indian Ocean					
Java Trench	10°15'S	109°50'E	7,542	4,124	24,744
Diamantina Trench	34°56'S	102°32'E	7,391	4,041	24,249
Ob' Trench	09°45'S	67°18'E	6,640	3,631	21,785
Vema Trench	32°47'S	98°44'E	5,938	3,247	19,482
Agulhas Basin	45°20'S	26°50'E	5,907	3,230	19,380
Arctic Ocean					
Eurasia Basin	78°16'N	04°W	4,914	2,687	16,122
Mediterranean Sea					
Ionian Basin	36°32'N	21°23'E	5,275	2,884	17,306

Ocean Areas and Average Depths

Four major bodies of water are recognized by geographers and mapmakers. They are: the Pacific, Atlantic, Indian, and Arctic oceans. The Atlantic and Pacific oceans are considered divided at the equator into the No. and So. Atlantic; the No. and So. Pacific. The Arctic Ocean is the name for waters north of the continental land masses in the region of the Arctic Circle.

	Sq. miles	Avg. depth in feet
Pacific Ocean	64,186,300	13,739
Atlantic Ocean	33,420,000	12,257
Indian Ocean	28,350,500	12,704
Arctic Ocean	5,105,700	4,362
South China Sea	1,148,500	4,802
Caribbean Sea	971,400	8,448
Mediterranean Sea	969,100	4,926
Bering Sea	873,000	4,893
Gulf of Mexico	582,100	5,297
Sea of Okhotsk	537,500	3,192
Sea of Japan	391,100	5,468
Hudson Bay	281,900	305
East China Sea	256,600	620
Andaman Sea	218,100	3,667
Black Sea	196,100	3,906
Red Sea	174,900	1,764
North Sea	164,900	308
Baltic Sea	147,500	180
Yellow Sea	113,500	121
Persian Gulf	88,800	328
Gulf of California	59,100	2,375

The Malayan Sea is not considered a geographical entity but a term used for convenience for waters between the South Pacific and the Indian Ocean.

Continental Statistics

Source: National Geographic Society, Washington, D.C.

Continents	Area (sq. mi.)	% of Earth	Population (est.)	% World total	Highest point (in feet)	Lowest point
Asia	16,999,000	29.7	2,738,718,000	59.7	Everest, 29,028	Dead Sea, −1,312
Africa	11,688,000	20.4	498,000,000	10.9	Kilimanjaro, 19,340	Lake Assal, −512
North America	9,366,000	16.3	381,000,000	8.3	McKinley, 20,320	Death Valley, −282
South America	6,881,000	12.0	252,000,000	5.5	Aconcagua,22,834	Valdes Penin., −131
Europe	4,017,000	7.0	690,282,000	15.1	El'brus, 18,510	Caspian Sea, −92
Australia	2,966,000	5.2	15,000,000	0.3	Kosciusko, 7,310	Lake Eyre, −52
Antarctica	5,100,000	8.9			Vinson Massif, 16,864	Not Known
Est. World Population			4,585,000,000			

Important Islands and Their Areas

Source: National Geographic Society, Washington, D.C.

Figure in parentheses shows rank among the world's 10 largest islands; some islands have not been surveyed accurately; in such cases estimated areas are shown.

Location-Ownership

Area in square miles

Arctic Ocean

Canadian

Axel Heiberg	16,671
Baffin (5)	195,928
Banks	27,038
Bathurst	6,194
Devon	21,331
Ellesmere (10)	75,767
Melville	16,274
Prince of Wales	12,872
Somerset	9,570
Southampton	15,913
Victoria (9)	83,896

USSR

Franz Josef Land	8,000
Novaya Zemlya (two is.)	35,000
Wrangel	2,800

Norwegian

Svalbard	23,940
Nordaustlandet	5,410
Spitsbergen	15,060

Atlantic Ocean

Anticosti, Canada	3,066
Ascension, UK	34
Azores, Portugal	902
Faial	67
Sao Miguel	291
Bahamas	5,353
Bermuda Is., UK	20
Block, Rhode Island	10
Canary Is., Spain	2,808
Fuerteventura	668
Gran Canaria	592
Tenerife	795
Cape Breton, Canada	3,981
Cape Verde Is.	1,750
Faeroe Is., Denmark	540
Falkland Is., UK	4,700
Fernando de Noronha Archipelago, Brazil	7
Greenland, Denmark (1)	840,000
Iceland	39,769
Long Island, N. Y.	1,396
Bioko Is. Equatorial Guinea	785
Madeira Is., Portugal	307
Marajo, Brazil	15,528
Martha's Vineyard, Mass.	91
Mount Desert, Me.	108
Nantucket, Mass.	46
Newfoundland, Canada	42,030
Prince Edward, Canada	2,184
St. Helena, UK	47
South Georgia, UK	1,450
Tierra del Fuego, Chile and Argentina	18,800
Tristan da Cunha, UK	40

British Isles

Great Britain, mainland (8)	84,200
Channel Islands	75
Guernsey	24
Jersey	45
Sark	2
Hebrides	2,744
Ireland	32,599
Irish Republic	27,136
Northern Ireland	5,463
Man	227
Orkney Is.	390
Scilly Is.	6
Shetland Is.	567
Skye	670
Wight	147

Baltic Sea

Aland Is., Finland	581
Bornholm, Denmark	227
Gotland, Sweden	1,164

Caribbean Sea

Antigua	108
Aruba, Netherlands	75
Barbados	166
Cuba	44,218
Isle of Youth	1,182
Curacao, Netherlands	171
Dominica	290
Guadeloupe, France	687
Hispaniola, Haiti and Dominican Republic	29,530
Jamaica	4,244
Martinique, France	425
Puerto Rico, U.S.	3,515
Tobago	116
Trinidad	1,864
Virgin Is., UK	59
Virgin Is., U.S.	132

Indian Ocean

Andaman Is., India	2,500
Madagascar (4)	226,658
Mauritius	720
Pemba, Tanzania	380
Reunion, France	969
Seychelles	171
Sri Lanka	25,332
Zanzibar, Tanzania	640

Persian Gulf

Bahrain	258

Mediterranean Sea

Balearic Is., Spain	1,936
Corfu, Greece	229
Corsica, France	3,365
Crete, Greece	3,186
Cyprus	3,572
Elba, Italy	86
Euboea, Greece	1,409
Malta	122
Rhodes, Greece	542
Sardinia, Italy	9,262
Sicily, Italy	9,822

Pacific Ocean

Aleutian Is., U.S.	6,821
Adak	289
Amchitka	121
Attu	388
Kanaga	135
Kiska	110
Tanaga	209
Umnak	675
Unalaska	1,064
Unimak	1,600
Canton, Kiribati*	4
Caroline Is., U.S. trust terr.	472
Christmas, Kiribati*	94
Diomede, Big, USSR	11
Diomede, Little, U.S.	2
Easter, Chile	69
Fiji	7,056
Vanua Levu	2,242
Viti Levu	4,109
Funafuti, Tuvalu*	2
Galapagos Is., Ecuador	3,043
Guadalcanal, UK	2,500
Guam	209
Hainan, China	13,000
Hawaiian Is., U.S.	6,450
Hawaii	4,037
Oahu	593
Hong Kong, UK	29
Japan	145,809
Hokkaido	30,144
Honshu (7)	87,805
Iwo Jima	8
Kyushu	14,114
Okinawa	459
Shikoku	7,049
Kodiak, U.S.	3,670
Marquesas Is., France	492
Marshall Is., U.S. trust terr.	70
Bikini*	2
Nauru	8
New Caledonia, France	6,530
New Guinea (2)	306,000
New Zealand	103,883
Chatham	372
North	44,035
South	58,305
Stewart	674
Northern Mariana Is.	184
Philippines	115,831
Leyte	2,787
Luzon	40,880
Mindanao	36,775
Mindoro	3,790
Negros	4,907
Palawan	4,554
Panay	4,446
Samar	5,050
Quemoy	56
Sakhalin, USSR	29,500
Samoa Is.	1,177
American Samoa	77
Tutuila	52
Samoa (Western)	1,101
Savaii	670
Upolu	429
Santa Catalina, U.S.	72
Tahiti, France	402
Taiwan	13,823
Tasmania, Australia	26,178
Tonga Is.	270
Vancouver, Canada	12,079
Vanuatu	5,700

East Indies

Bali, Indonesia	2,147
Borneo, Indonesia-Malaysia, UK (3)	280,100
Celebes, Indonesia	69,000
Java, Indonesia	48,900
Madura, Indonesia	2,113
Moluccas, Indonesia	28,766
New Britain, Papua New Guinea	14,093
New Ireland, Papua New Guinea	3,707
Sumatra, Indonesia (6)	165,000
Timor	11,570

***Atolls:** Bikini (lagoon area, 230 sq. mi., land area 2 sq. mi.), U.S. Trust Territory of the Pacific Islands; Canton (lagoon 20 sq. mi., land 4 sq. mi.), Kiribati; Christmas (lagoon 140 sq. mi., land 94 sq. mi.), Kiribati; Funafuti (lagoon 84 sq. mi., land 2 sq. mi.), Tuvalu.

Australia, often called an island, is a continent. Its mainland area is 2,939,975 sq. mi.

Islands in minor waters; Manhattan (22 sq mi.) Staten (59 sq. mi.) and Governors (173 acres), all in New York Harbor, U.S.; Isle Royale (209 sq. mi.), Lake Superior, U.S.; Manitoulin (1,068 sq. mi.), Lake Huron, Canada; Pinang (110 sq. mi.), Strait of Malacca, Malaysia; Singapore (239 sq. mi.), Singapore Strait, Singapore.

Major Rivers in North America

Source: U.S. Geological Survey

River	Source or Upper Limit of Length	Outflow	Miles
Alabama	Gilmer County, Ga.	Mobile River	735
Albany	Lake St. Joseph, Ont., Can.	James Bay	610
Allegheny	Potter County, Pa.	Ohio River	325
Altamaha-Ocmulgee	Junction of Yellow and South Rivers, Newton County, Ga.	Atlantic Ocean	392
Apalachicola-Chattahoochee	Towns County, Ga.	Gulf of Mexico, Fla.	524
Arkansas	Lake County, Col.	Mississippi River, Ark.	1,459
Assiniboine	Eastern Saskatchewan	Red River	450
Attawapiskat	Attawapiskat, Ont., Can.	James Bay	465
Big Black (Miss.)	Webster County, Miss.	Mississippi River	330
Black (N.W.T.)	Contwoyto Lake	Chantrey Inlet	600
Brazos	Junction of Salt and Double Mountain Forks, Stonewall County, Tex.	Gulf of Mexico	870
Canadian	Las Animas County, Col.	Arkansas River, Okla.	906
Cedar (Iowa)	Dodge County, Minn.	Iowa River, Ia.	329
Cheyenne	Junction of Antelope Creek and Dry Fork, Converse County, Wyo.	Missouri River	290
Churchill	Methy Lake	Hudson Bay	1,000
Cimarron	Colfax County, N.M.	Arkansas River, Okla.	600
Clark Fork-Pend Oreille	Silver Bow County, Mon.	Columbia River, B.C.	505
Colorado (Ariz.)	Rocky Mountain National Park, Col. (90 miles in Mexico)	Gulf of Cal., Mexico	1,450
Colorado (Texas)	West Texas	Matagorda Bay	840
Columbia	Columbia Lake, British Columbia	Pacific Ocean, bet. Ore. and Wash.	1,243
Columbia, Upper	Columbia Lake, British Columbia	To mouth of Snake River	890
Connecticut	Third Connecticut Lake, N.H.	L.I. Sound, Conn.	407
Coppermine (N.W.T.)	Lac de Gras	Coronation Gulf (Atlantic Ocean)	525
Cumberland	Letcher County, Ky.	Ohio River	720
Delaware	Schoharie County, N.Y.	Liston Point, Delaware Bay	390
Fraser	Near Mount Robson (on Continental Divide)	Strait of Georgia	850
Gila	Catron County, N.M.	Colorado River, Ariz.	630
Green (Ut.-Wyo.)	Junction of Wells and Trail Creeks, Sublette County, Wyo.	Colorado River, Ut.	730
Hamilton (Lab.)	Lake Ashuanipi	Atlantic Ocean	600
Hudson	Henderson Lake, Essex County, N.Y.	Upper N.Y. Bay, N.Y.,-N.J.	306
Illinois	St. Joseph County, Ind.	Mississippi River	420
James (N.D.-S.D.)	Wells County, N.D.	Missouri River, S.D.	710
James (Va.)	Junction of Jackson and Cowpasture Rivers, Botetourt County, Va.	Hampton Roads	340
Kanawha-New	Junction of North and South Forks of New River, N.C.	Ohio River	352
Kentucky	Junction of North and Middle Forks, Lee County, Ky.	Ohio River	259
Klamath	Lake Ewauna, Klamath Falls, Ore.	Pacific Ocean	250
Koyukuk	Endicott Mountains, Alaska	Yukon River	470
Kuskokwim	Alaska Range	Kuskokwim Bay	680
Liard	Southern Yukon, Alaska	Mackenzie River	693
Little Missouri	Crook County, Wyo.	Missouri River	560
Mackenzie	Great Slave Lake	Arctic Ocean	900
Milk	Junction of North and South Forks, Alberta Province	Missouri River, Mon.	625
Minnesota	Big Stone Lake, Minn.	Mississippi River, St. Paul, Minn.	332
Mississippi	Lake Itasca, Minn.	Mouth of Southwest Pass	2,348
Mississippi, Upper	Lake Itasca, Minn.	To mouth of Missouri R.	1,171
Mississippi-Missouri-Red Rock	Source of Red Rock, Beaverhead Co., Mon.	Mouth of Southwest Pass	3,710
Missouri	Junction of Jefferson, Madison, and Gallatin Rivers, Madison County, Mon.	Mississippi River	2,315
Missouri-Red Rock	Source of Red Rock, Beaverhead Co., Mon.	Mississippi River	2,533
Mobile-Alabama-Coosa	Gilmer County, Ga.	Mobile Bay	780
Nelson (Manitoba)	Lake Winnipeg	Hudson Bay	410
Neosho	Morris County, Kan.	Arkansas River, Okla.	460
Niobrara	Niobrara County, Wyo.	Missouri River, Neb.	431
North Canadian	Union County, N.M.	Canadian River, Okla.	760
North Platte	Junction of Grizzly and Little Grizzly Creeks, Jackson County, Col.	Platte River, Neb.	618
Ohio	Junction of Allegheny and Monongahela Rivers, Pittsburgh, Pa.	Mississippi River, Ill.-Ky.	981
Ohio-Allegheny	Potter County, Pa.	Mississippi River	1,306
Osage	East-central Kansas	Missouri River, Mo.	500
Ottawa	Lake Capimitchigama	St. Lawrence	790
Ouachita	Polk County, Ark.	Red River, La.	605
Peace	Stikine Mountains, B.C.	Slave River	1,195
Pearl	Neshoba County, Miss.	Gulf of Mexico, Miss.-La.	411
Pecos	Mora County, N.M.	Rio Grande, Tex.	735
Pee Dee-Yadkin	Watauga County, N.C.	Winyah Bay, S.C.	435
Pend Oreille	Near Butte, Mon.	Columbia River	490
Platte	Junction of North and South Platte Rivers, Neb.	Missouri River, Neb.	310
Porcupine	Ogilvie Mountains, Alaska	Yukon River, Alaska	460
Potomac	Garrett County, Md.	Chesapeake Bay	383
Powder	Junction of South and Middle Forks, Wyo.	Yellowstone River, Mon.	375
Red (Okla.-Tex.-La.)	Curry County, N.M.	Mississippi River	1,270
Red River of the North	Junction of Otter Tail and Bois de Sioux Rivers, Wilkin County, Minn.	Lake Winnipeg, Manitoba	545

River	Source or Upper Limit of Length	Outflow	Miles
Republican	Junction of North Fork and Arikaree River, Neb.	Kansas River, Kan.	445
Rio Grande	San Juan County, Col.	Gulf of Mexico	1,885
Roanoke	Junction of North and South Forks, Montgomery County, Va.	Albemarle Sound, N.C.	380
Rock (Ill.-Wis.)	Dodge County, Wis.	Mississippi River, Ill.	300
Sabine	Junction of South and Caddo Forks, Hunt County, Tex.	Sabine Lake, Tex.-La.	380
Sacramento	Siskiyou County, Cal.	Suisun Bay	377
St. Francis	Iron County, Mo.	Mississippi River, Ark.	425
St. Lawrence	Lake Ontario	Gulf of St. Lawrence (Atlantic Ocean)	800
Salmon (Idaho)	Custer County, Ida.	Snake River, Ida.	420
San Joaquin	Junction of South and Middle Forks, Madera County, Cal.	Suisun Bay	350
San Juan	Silver Lake, Archuleta County, Col.	Colorado River, Ut.	360
Santee-Wateree-Catawba	McDowell County, N.C.	Atlantic Ocean, S.C.	538
Saskatchewan, North	Rocky Mountains	Lake Winnipeg	1,100
Saskatchewan, South	Rocky Mountains	Lake Winnipeg	1,205
Savannah	Junction of Seneca and Tugaloo Rivers, Anderson County, S.C.	Atlantic Ocean, Ga.-S.C.	314
Severn (Ontario)	Sandy Lake	Hudson Bay	610
Smoky Hill	Cheyenne County, Col.	Kansas River, Kan.	540
Snake	Teton County, Wyo.	Columbia River, Wash.	1,038
South Platte	Junction of South and Middle Forks, Park County, Col.	Platte River, Neb.	424
Susitna	Alaska Range	Cook Inlet	300
Susquehanna	Otsego Lake, Otsego County, N.Y.	Chesapeake Bay, Md.	444
Tallahatchie	Tippah County, Miss.	Yazoo River, Miss.	301
Tanana	Wrangell Mountains	Yukon River, Alaska	620
Tennessee	Junction of French Broad and Holston Rivers	Ohio River, Ky.	652
Tennessee-French Broad	Bland County, Va.	Ohio River	900
Tombigbee	Prentiss County, Miss.	Mobile River, Ala.	525
Trinity	North of Dallas, Tex.	Galveston Bay, Tex.	360
Wabash	Darke County, Oh.	Ohio River, Ill.-Ind.	529
Washita	Hemphill County, Tex.	Red River, Okla.	500
White (Ark.-Mo.)	Madison County, Ark.	Mississippi River	720
Willamette	Douglas County, Ore.	Columbia River	270
Wind-Bighorn	Junction of Wind and Little Wind Rivers, Fremont Co., Wyo. (Source of Wind R. is Togwotee Pass, Teton Co., Wyo.)	Yellowstone R., Mon.	336
Wisconsin	LeVieux Desert, Vilas County, Wis.	Mississippi River	430
Yellowstone	Park County, Wyo.	Missouri River, N.D.	671
Yukon	Junction of Lewes and Pelly Rivers, Yukon	Bering Sea, Alaska	1,770

Flows of Largest U.S. Rivers

Source: U.S. Geological Survey (average discharges for the period 1941-70). Ranked according to average discharge in cubic feet per second (cfs) at mouth.

Rank	River	Average discharge	Length[a] (miles)	Drainage area	Most distant source	Maximum discharge at gauging station farthest downstream	Date
1	Mississippi	[b]640,000	[c]3,710	[d]1,247,300	Beaverhead Co., Mont.	2,080,000	2-17-37
2	Columbia	262,000	1,243	258,000	Columbia Lake, B.C.	1,240,000	June 1894
3	Ohio	258,000	1,306	203,900	Potter Co., Pa.	1,850,000	2-1-37
4	St. Lawrence	[e]243,000	—	[e]302,000	—	[f]350,000	July 1973
5	Yukon	[g]240,000	1,770	327,600	Coast Mountains, B.C.	1,030,000	6-22-64
6	[h]Atchafalaya	183,000	135	95,105	Curry Co., N. Mex.	—	—
7	Missouri	76,300	2,533	529,400	Beaverhead Co., Mont.	892,000	June 1844
8	Tennessee	[m]64,000	900	40,910	Bland Co., Va.	500,000	2-17-48
9	Red	[i]62,300	1,270	93,244	Curry Co., N. Mex.	233,000	4-17-45
10	Kuskokwim	62,000	680	49,000	Alaska Range, Alas.	392,000	6-5-64
11	Mobile	61,400	780	43,800	Gilmer, Co., Ga.	—	—
12	Snake	50,000	1,038	109,000	Teton Co., Wyo.	409,000	June 1894
13	Arkansas	45,100	1,459	160,600	Lake Co., Col.	536,000	5-27-43
14	Copper	[j]43,000	280	24,000	Alaska Range, Alas.	265,000	7-15-71
15	Tanana	[k]41,000	620	44,000	Wrangell Mtn., Alas.	186,000	8-18-67
16	Susitna	[l]40,000	300	20,000	Alaska Range, Alas.	197,000	6-16-77
17	Susquehanna	37,190	444	27,570	Otsego Co., N.Y.	1,080,000	6-23-72
18	Willamette	35,660	270	11,200	Douglas Co., Ore.	500,000	12-4-1861
19	Alabama	32,400	735	22,600	Gilmer Co., Ga.	267,000	3-7-61
20	White	32,100	720	28,000	Madison Co., Ark.	343,000	4-17-45
21	Wabash	30,400	529	33,150	Darke Co., Oh.	428,000	3-30-13
22	Pend Oreille	29,900	490	25,820	Near Butte, Mont.	171,300	6-13-48
23	Tombigbee	27,300	525	20,100	Prentiss Co., Miss.	286,000	4-22-79
24	Cumberland	[m]26,900	720	18,080	Letcher Co., Ky.	209,000	3-16-75
25	Stikine	[n]26,000	310	20,000	Stikine Range, B.C.	219,000	8-12-76
26	Sacramento	—	377	27,100	Siskiyou Co., Cal.	[o]322,000	12-25-64
27	Apalachicola	24,700	524	19,600	Towns Co., Ga.	293,000	3-20-29
28	Illinois	22,800	420	27,900	St. Joseph Co., Ind.	123,000	May 1943
29	Koyukuk	[p]22,000	470	32,400	Endicott Mtns., Alas.	266,000	6-6-64
30	Porcupine	[q]20,000	460	45,000	Ogilvie Mtns., Alas.	299,000	5-24-73

(a) Because river lengths and methods of measurement may change from time to time, the length figures given are subject to revision; (b) about 25 percent of flow occurs in the Atchafalaya River; (c) the length from mouth to source of the Mississippi River in Minnesota is 2,348 miles; (d) at Baptiste Collete Bayou, Louisiana; (e) at international boundary lat. 45°; (f) maximum monthly discharge; (g) period

1957-70; (h) continuation of Red River; (i) flow of Ouachita River added; (j) period 1956-69; (k) period 1962-69; (l) based on records of Chulitna, Talkeetna, and Yetna rivers; (m) period 1931-60; (n) period 1954-63; summer records only; (o) discharge of American River not included (p) period 1960-69; (q) period 1964-69; (r) at Liston Point on Delaware Bay.

Large Rivers in Canada

Source: "Inland Waters Directorate," Environment Canada

(Ranked according to average discharge in cubic feet per second (cfs). Figures indicate discharge and drainage to river mouths.

Rank	River	Average discharge	Length (miles	Drainage area (sq. mi.)
1	St. Lawrence (to Nicolet)	355,000	1,900	396,000[1]
2	Mackenzie	350,000	2,635	690,000
3	Fraser	128,000	850	89,900[2]
4	Columbia (International Boundary)	102,000	498	59,700[3]
5	Nelson	100,000	1,600	437,000[4]
6	Kokosak	85,500	543	51,500
7	Yukon (International Boundary)	83,000	714	115,000[5]
8	Ottawa	70,500	790	56,500
9	Saguenay (to head of Peribonea)	62,200	434	34,000
10	Skeena	62,100	300	21,200

(1) Including 195,000 sq. mi. in U.S. (2) Including diversion. (3) Including 20,000 sq. mi. in U.S. (4) Including 69,500 sq. mi. in U.S. (5) Including 9,000 sq. mi. in U.S.

Principal World Rivers

Source: National Geographic Society, Washington, D.C. (length in miles)

River	Outflow	Lgth	River	Outflow	Lgth	River	Outflow	Lgth
Albany	James Bay	610	Indus	Arabian Sea	1,800	Red River of N.	Lake Winnipeg	545
Amazon	Atlantic Ocean	4,000	Irrawaddy	Bay of Bengal	1,337	Rhine	North Sea	820
Amu	Aral Sea	1,578	Japura	Amazon River	1,750	Rhone	Gulf of Lions	505
Amur	Tatar Strait	2,744	Jordan	Dead Sea	200	Rio de la Plata	Atlantic Ocean	150
Angara	Yenisey River	1,151	Kootenay	Columbia River	485	Rio Grande	Gulf of Mexico	1,885
Arkansas	Mississippi	1,459	Lena	Laptev Sea	2,734	Rio Roosevelt	Aripuana	400
Back	Arctic Ocean	605	Loire	Bay of Biscay	634	Saguenay	St. Lawrence R.	434
Brahmaputra	Bay of Bengal	1,800	Mackenzie	Arctic Ocean	2,635	St. John	Bay of Fundy	418
Bug, Southern	Dnieper River	532	Madeira	Amazon River	2,013	St. Lawrence	Gulf of St. Law.	800
Bug, Western	Wisla River	481	Magdalena	Caribbean Sea	956	Salween	Andaman Sea	1,500
Canadian	Arkansas River	906	Marne	Seine River	326	Sao Francisco	Atlantic Ocean	1,988
Chang Jiang	E. China Sea	3,964	Mekong	S. China Sea	2,600	Saskatchewan	Lake Winnipeg	1,205
Churchill, Man.	Hudson Bay	1,000	Meuse	North Sea	580	Seine	English Chan.	496
Churchill, Que.	Atlantic Ocean	532	Mississippi	Gulf of Mexico	2,348	Shannon	Atlantic Ocean	230
Colorado	Gulf of Calif.	1,450	Missouri	Mississippi	2,533	Snake	Columbia River	1,038
Columbia	Pacific Ocean	1,243	Murray-Darling	Indian Ocean	2,310	Sungari	Amur River	1,150
Congo	Atlantic Ocean	2,900	Negro	Amazon	1,400	Syr	Aral Sea	1,370
Danube	Black Sea	1,776	Nelson	Hudson Bay	1,600	Tajo, Tagus	Atlantic Ocean	626
Dnieper	Black Sea	1,420	Niger	Gulf of Guinea	2,590	Tennessee	Ohio River	652
Dniester	Black Sea	877	Nile	Mediterranean	4,145	Thames	North Sea	215
Don	Sea of Azov	1,224	Ob-Irtysh	Gulf of Ob	3,362	Tiber	Tyrrhenian Sea	252
Drava	Danube River	447	Oder	Baltic Sea	567	Tigris	Shatt al-Arab	1,180
Dvina, North	White Sea	824	Ohio	Mississippi	975	Tisza	Danube River	600
Dvina, West	Gulf of Riga	634	Orange	Atlantic Ocean	1,300	Tocantins	Para River	1,677
Ebro	Mediterranean	565	Orinoco	Atantic Ocean	1,600	Ural	Caspian Sea	1,575
Elbe	North Sea	724	Ottawa	St. Lawrence R.	790	Uruguay	Rio de la Plata	1,000
Euphrates	Shatt al-Arab	1,700	Paraguay	Parana River	1,584	Volga	Caspian Sea	2,194
Fraser	Str. of Georgia	850	Parana	Rio de la Plata	2,485	Weser	North Sea	454
Gambia	Atlantic Ocean	700	Peace	Slave River	1,195	Wisla	Bay of Danzig	675
Ganges	Bay of Bengal	1,560	Pilcomayo	Paraguay River	1,000	Yellow (See Huang)		
Garonne	Bay of Biscay	357	Po	Adriatic Sea	405	Yenisey	Kara Sea	2,543
Hsi	S. China Sea	1,200	Purus	Amazon River	2,100	Yukon	Bering Sea	1,979
Huang	Yellow Sea	2,903	Red	Mississippi	1,270	Zambezi	Indian Ocean	1,700

Famous Waterfalls

Source: National Geographic Society, Washington, D.C.

The earth has thousands of waterfalls, some of considerable magnitude. Their importance is determined not only by height but volume of flow, steadiness of flow, crest width, whether the water drops sheerly or over a sloping surface, and in one leap or a succession of leaps. A series of low falls flowing over a considerable distance is known as a cascade.

Sete Quedas or Guaira is the world's greatest waterfall when its mean annual flow (estimated at 470,000 cusecs, cubic feet per second) is combined with height. A greater volume of water passes over Boyoma Falls (Stanley Falls), though not one of its seven cataracts, spread over nearly 60 miles of the Congo River, exceeds 10 feet.

Estimated mean annual flow, in cusecs, of other major waterfalls are: Niagara, 212,200; Paulo Afonso, 100,000; Urubupunga, 97,000; Iguazu, 61,000; Patos-Maribondo, 53,000; Victoria, 38,400; and Kaieteur, 23,400.

Height = total drop in feet in one or more leaps. † = falls of more than one leap; * = falls that diminish greatly seasonally; ** = falls that reduce to a trickle or are dry for part of each year. If river names not shown, they are same as the falls. R. = river; L. = lake; (C) = cascade type.

Name and location	Ht.
Africa	
Angola	
Duque de Braganca, Lucala R.	344
Ruacana, Cuene R.	406
Ethiopia	
Dal Verme, Dorya R.	98
Fincha	508
Tesissat, Blue Nile R.	140
Lesotho	
*Maletsunyane	630
Zimbabwe-Zambia	
*Victoria, Zambezi R.	343
South Africa	
*Augrabies, Orange R.	480
Howick, Umgeni R.	364
† Tugela	2,014
Highest fall	597
Tanzania-Zambia	
*Kalambo	726
Uganda	
Kabalega (Murchison) Victoria Nile R.	130
Asia	
India—*Cauvery	330
*Gokak, Ghataprabha R.	170
*Jog (Gersoppa), Sharavathi R.	830

Name and location	Ht.
Japan	
*Kegon, Daiya R.	330
Laos	
Khon Cataracts, Mekong R. (C)	70
Australasia	
Australia	
New South Wales	
† Wentworth	614
Highest fall	360
Wollomombi	1,100
Queensland	
Coomera	210
Tully	885
† Wallaman, Stony Cr.	1,137
Highest fall	937
New Zealand	
Bowen	540
Helena	890
Stirling	505
† Sutherland, Arthur R.	1,904
Highest fall	815
Europe	
Austria—† Gastein	492
Highest fall	280
† *Golling, Schwarzbach R.	250
† Krimml	1,312
France—*Gavarnie	1,385
Great Britain—Scotland	
Glomach	370
Wales	
Cain	150
Rhaiadr	240
Iceland—Detti	144
† Gull, Hvita R.	105
Italy—Frua, Toce R. (C)	470
Norway	
Mardalsfossen (Northern)	1,535
† Mardalsfossen (Southern)	2,149
† **Skjeggedal, Nybuai R.	1,378
**Skykje	984
Vetti, Morka-Koldedola R.	900
Voring, Bjoreio R.	597
Sweden	
† Handol	427
† Tannforsen, Are R.	120
Switzerland	
† Diesbach	394
Giessbach (C)	984
Handegg, Aare R.	150
Iffigen	120
Pissevache, Salanfe R.	213
† Reichenbach	656
Rhine	79
† Simmen	459
Staubbach	984
† Trummelbach	1,312
North America	
Canada	
Alberta	
Panther, Nigel Cr.	600
British Columbia	
† Della	1,443
† Takakkaw, Daly Glacier	1,200
Northwest Territories	
Virginia, S. Nahanni R.	294
Quebec	
Montmorency	274
Canada—United States	
Niagara: American	182
Horseshoe	173
United States	
California	
*Feather, Fall R.	640
Yosemite National Park	
*Bridalveil	620
*Illilouette	370
*Nevada, Merced R.	594
**Ribbon	1,612
**Silver Strand, Meadow Br.	1,170
*Vernal, Merced R.	317
† **Yosemite	2,425
Yosemite (upper)	1,430
Yosemite (lower)	320
Yosemite (middle) (C)	675
Colorado	
† Seven, South Cheyenne Cr.	300
Hawaii	
Akaka, Kolekole Str.	442
Idaho	
**Shoshone, Snake R.	212
Twin, Snake R.	120
Kentucky	
Cumberland	68
Maryland	
*Great, Potomac R. (C)	71
Minnesota	
**Minnehaha	53
New Jersey	
Passaic	70
New York	
*Taughannock	215
Oregon	
† Multnomah	620
Highest fall	542
Tennessee	
Fall Creek	256
Washington	
Mt. Rainier Natl. Park	
Narada, Paradise R.	168
Sluiskin, Paradise R.	300
Palouse	197
**Snoqualmie	268
Wisconsin	
*Big Manitou, Black R. (C)	165
Wyoming	
Yellowstone Natl. Pk. Tower	132
*Yellowstone (upper)	109
*Yellowstone (lower)	308
Mexico	
El Salto	218
**Juanacatlan, Santiago R.	72
South America	
Argentina-Brazil	
Iguazu	230
Brazil	
Glass	1,325
Patos-Maribondo, Grande R.	115
Paulo Afonso, Sao Francisco R.	275
Urubupunga, Parana R.	40
Brazil-Paraguay	
Sete Quedas	
Parana R.	130
Colombia	
Catarata de Candelas, Cusiana R.	984
*Tequendama, Bogota R.	427
Ecuador	
*Agoyan, Pastaza R.	200
Guyana	
Kaieteur, Potaro R.	741
Great, Kamarang R.	1,600
† Marina, Ipobe R.	500
Highest fall	300
Venezuela—	
† *Angel	3,212
Highest fall	2,648
Cuquenan	2,000

Notable Deserts of the World

Arabian (Eastern), 70,000 sq. mi. in Egypt between the Nile river and Red Sea, extending southward into Sudan.

Atacama, 600 mi. long area rich in nitrate and copper deposits in N. Chile.

Black Rock, 1,000 sq. mi. barren plain in NW Nev.

Death Valley, 2,936 sq. mi. in E. Cal. and SW Nev. Contains lowest point below sea level (282 ft.) in western hemisphere.

Gibson, 250,000 sq. mi. in the interior of W. Australia.

Gobi, 500,000 sq. mi. in Mongolia and China.

Great Sandy, 150,000 sq. mi. in W. Australia.

Great Victoria, 250,000 sq. mi. in W. and S. Australia.

Kalahari, 225,000 sq. mi. in southern Africa.

Kara-Kum, 110,000 sq. mi. in Turkmen, SSR.

Kavir (Dasht-e-Kavir), great salt waste in central Iran some 400 mi. long.

Kyzyl-Kum, 100,000 sq. mi. in Kazakh and Uzbek; SSRs.

Libyan, 600,000 sq. mi. in the Sahara extending from Lybia through SW Egypt into Sudan.

Lut (Dasht-e-Lut), 20,000 sq. mi. in E. Iran.

Mojave, 15,000 sq. mi. in S. Cal.

Nafud (An Nafud), 50,000 sq. mi. near Jawf in Saudi Arabia.

Namib, long narrow area extending 800 miles along SW coast of Africa.

Nubian, 120,000 sq. mi. in the Sahara in NE Sudan.

Painted Desert, section of high plateau in N. Ariz. extending 150 mi.

Rub al-Khali (Empty Quarter), 250,000 sq. mi. in the south Arabian Peninsula. World's largest continuous sand area.

Sahara, 3,320,000 sq. mi. in N. Africa extending westward to the Atlantic. Largest tropical and climatic desert in the world.

Simpson, 120,000 sq. mi. in central Australia.

Sonoran, 120,000 sq. mi. in SW Ariz. and SE Cal. extending into Mexico.

Syrian, 100,000 sq. mi. arid wasteland extending over much of N. Saudi Arabia, E. Jordan, S. Syria, and W. Iraq.

Taklamakan, 125,000 sq. mi. in Sinkiang Province, China.

Thar (Great Indian), 100,000 sq. mi. arid area extending 400 mi. along India-Pakistan border.

The Great Lakes

Source: National Ocean Survey, U.S. Commerce Department

The Great Lakes form the largest body of fresh water in the world and with their connecting waterways are the largest inland water transportation unit. Draining the great North Central basin of the U.S., they enable shipping to reach the Atlantic via their outlet, the St. Lawrence R., and also the Gulf of Mexico via the Illinois Waterway, from Lake Michigan to the Mississippi R. A third outlet connects with the Hudson R. and thence the Atlantic via the N. Y. State Barge Canal System. Traffic on the Illinois Waterway and the N.Y. State Barge Canal System is limited to recreational boating and small shipping vessels.

Only one of the lakes, Lake Michigan, is wholly in the United States; the others are shared with Canada. Ships carrying grain, lumber and iron ore move from the shores of Lake Superior to Whitefish Bay at the east end of the lake, thence through the Soo (Sault Ste. Marie) locks, through the St. Mary's River and into Lake Huron. To reach the steel mills at Gary, and Port of Indiana and South Chicago, Ill., ore ships move west from Lake Huron to Lake Michigan through the Straits of Mackinac.

Lake Huron discharges its waters into Lake Erie through a narrow waterway, the St. Clair R., Lake St. Clair (both included in the drainage basin figures) and the Detroit R. Lake St. Clair, a marshy basin, is 26 miles long and 24 miles wide at its maximum. A ship channel has been dredged through the lake.

Lake Superior is 600 feet above mean water level at Point-au-Pere, Quebec, on the International Great Lakes Datum (1955). From Duluth, Minn., to the eastern end of Lake Ontario is 1,156 mi.

	Superior	Michigan	Huron	Erie	Ontario
Length in miles	350	307	206	241	193
Breadth in miles	160	118	183	57	53
Deepest soundings in feet	1,330	923	750	210	802
Volume of water in cubic miles	2,900	1,180	850	116	393
Area (sq. miles) water surface—U.S.	20,600	22,300	9,100	4,980	3,560
Canada	11,100	.....	13,900	4,930	3,990
Area (sq. miles) entire drainage basin—U.S.	16,900	45,600	16,200	18,000	15,200
Canada	32,400	.....	35,500	4,720	12,100
Total Area (sq. miles) U.S. and Canada	**81,000**	**67,900**	**74,700**	**32,630**	**34,850**
Mean surface above mean water level at Point-au-Pere, Quebec, aver. level in feet (1900-1981)	600.58	578.23	578.23	570.38	244.70
Latitude, North	46° 25′	41° 37′	43° 00′	41° 23′	43° 11′
	49° 00′	46° 06′	46° 17′	42° 52′	44° 15′
Longitude, West	84° 22′	84° 45′	79° 43′	78° 51′	76° 03′
	92° 06′	88° 02′	84° 45′	83° 29′	79° 53′
National boundary line in miles	282.8	None	260.8	251.5	174.6
United States shore line (mainland only) miles	863	1,400	580	431	300

Largest Lake in Each Province and Territory of Canada

Source: "Inland Waters Directorate," Environment Canada.

Province	Largest within:	Largest partly in:	Shared with:	Origin	Area (sq. miles)	Ft. above sea level
Alberta	Claire			Natural	555	700
		Athabasca	Saskatchewan	Natural	3,066	700
British Columbia	Williston			Manmade	640	2,180
Manitoba	Winnipeg			Natural	9,417	713
Newfoundland	Smallwood Reservoir			Manmade	2,520	S.L.
New Brunswick	Grand			Natural	70	4
Northwest Territories	Great Bear			Natural	12,096	512
Nova Scotia	Bras d'Or			Natural	424	Tidal
Ontario	Nipigon			Natural	1,872	1,050
		Huron	U.S.	Natural	15,241	580
Prince Edward Island	Forest Hill Pond			Manmade	.7	50
Quebec	Mistassinl			Natural	902	1,230
Saskatchewan	Reindeer			Natural	2,560	1,106
		Athabasca	Alberta	Natural	3,066	700
Yukon Territory	Kluane			Natural	158	2,563

Lakes of the World

Source: National Geographic Society, Washington, D.C.

A lake is a body of water surrounded by land. Although some lakes are called seas, they are lakes by definition. The Caspian Sea is bounded by the Soviet Union and Iran and is fed by eight rivers.

Name	Continent	Area sq. mi.	Length mi.	Depth feet	Elev. feet
Caspian Sea	Asia-Europe	143,244	760	3,363	−92
Superior	North America	31,700	350	1,333	600
Victoria	Africa	26,828	250	270	3,720
Aral Sea	Asia	24,904	280	220	174
Huron	North America	23,000	206	750	579
Michigan	North America	22,300	307	923	579
Tanganyika	Africa	12,700	420	4,823	2,534
Baykal	Asia	12,162	395	5,315	1,493
Great Bear	North America	12,096	192	1,463	512
Malawi	Africa	11,150	360	2,280	1,550
Great Slave	North America	11,031	298	2,015	513
Erie	North America	9,910	241	210	570
Winnipeg	North America	9,417	266	60	713
Ontario	North America	7,550	193	802	245
Balkhash	Asia	7,115	376	85	1,115
Ladoga	Europe	6,835	124	738	13
Chad	Africa	6,300	175	24	787
Maracaibo	South America	5,217	133	115	Sea level
Onega	Europe	3,710	145	328	108
Eyre	Australia	3,600	90	4	−52
Volta	Africa	3,276	250	....	....
Titicaca	South America	3,200	122	922	12,500
Nicaragua	North America	3,100	102	230	102
Athabasca	North America	3,064	208	407	700
Reindeer	North America	2,568	143	720	1,106
Turkana	Africa	2,473	154	240	1,230
Issyk Kul	Asia	2,355	115	2,303	5,279
Torrens	Australia	2,230	130	....	92
Vanern	Europe	2,156	91	328	144
Nettilling	North America	2,140	67	....	95
Winnipegosis	North America	2,075	141	38	830
Albert	Africa	2,075	100	168	2,030
Kariba	Africa	2,050	175	390	1,590
Nipigon	North America	1,872	72	540	1,050
Gairdner	Australia	1,840	90	....	112
Urmia	Asia	1,815	90	49	4,180
Manitoba	North America	1,799	140	12	813

Notable Bridges in North America

Source: State Highway Engineers: Canadian Civil Engineering — ASCE

Asterisk (*) designates railroad bridge. Span of a bridge is distance (in feet) between its supports.

Suspension

Year	Bridge	Location	Longest span
1964	Verrazano-Narrows	New York, N.Y.	4,260
1937	Golden Gate	San Fran. Bay, Cal.	4,200
1957	Mackinac	Sts. of Mackinac	3,800
1931	Geo. Washington	Hudson River	3,500
1952	Tacoma	Washington	2,800
1936	[1]Transbay	San Fran. Bay, Cal.	2,310
1939	Bronx-Whitestone	East R., N.Y.C.	2,300
1970	Pierre Laporte	Quebec	2,190
1951	Del. Memorial	Wilmington, Del.	2,150
1968	Del. Mem. (new)	Wilmington, Del.	2,150
1957	Walt Whitman	Phila., Pa.	2,000
1929	Ambassador	Detroit-Canada	1,850
1961	Throgs Neck	Long Is. Sound	1,800
1926	Benjamin Franklin	Philadelphia	1,750
1924	Bear Mt., N.Y.	Hudson River	1,632
1952	[2]Wm. Preston Lane Mem.	Sandy Point, Md.	1,600
1903	Williamsburg	East R., N.Y.C.	1,600
1969	Newport	Narragansett Bay, R.I.	1,600
1883	Brooklyn	East R., N.Y.C.	1,595
1939	Lions Gate	Burrard Inlet, B.C.	1,550
1930	Mid-Hudson, N.Y.	Poughkeepsie	1,500
1964	Vincent Thomas	Los Angeles Harbor	1,500
1909	Manhattan	East R., N.Y.C.	1,470
1936	Triborough	East R., N.Y.C.	1,380
1931	St. Johns	Portland, Ore.	1,207
1929	Mount Hope	Rhode Island	1,200
1939	Deer Isle	Maine	1,080
1931	Maysville (Ky.)	Ohio River	1,060
1867	Cincinnati	Ohio River	1,057
1971	Dent	Clearwater Co., Ida.	1,050
1900	Miampimi	Mexico	1,030
1849	Wheeling, W. Va.	Ohio River	1,010

Cantilever

Year	Bridge	Location	Longest span
1917	Quebec	Quebec	1,800
1970	Commodore Barry	Chester, Pa.	1,644
1958	New Orleans, La.	Mississippi R.	1,575
1936	Transbay	San Fran. Bay	1,400
1968	Baton Rouge, La.	Mississippi R.	1,235
1955	Nyack-Tarrytown	Hudson River	1,212
1930	Longview, Wash.	Columbia River	1,200
1909	Queensboro	East R., N.Y.C.	1,182
1927	Carquinez Strait	California	1,100
1958	Parallel Span	"	1,100
1930	Jacques Cartier	Montreal, P.Q.	1,097
1968	Isaiah D. Hart	Jacksonville, Fla.	1,088
1957	[3]Richmond	San Fran. Bay, Cal.	1,070
1929	Grace Memorial	Charleston, S.C.	1,050
1963	Newburgh-Beacon	Hudson, R., N.Y.	1,000
1975	Caruthersville, Mo.	Mississippi R.	920
1977	Saint Marys	Saint Marys, W. Va.	900
1969	Silver Memorial	Pt. Pleasant, W. Va.	900
1940	Natchez	Mississippi R.	875
1938	Blue Water	Pt. Huron, Mich.	871
1972	Vicksburg	Mississippi River	870
1954	Sunshine Skyway	St. Petersburg, Fla.	864
1940	*Baton Rouge	Mississippi R.	848
1899	*Cornwall	St. Lawrence R.	843
1940	Greenville	Mississippi R.	840
1961	Helena, Ark.	Mississippi R.	840
1963	Brent Spence	Covington, Ky.	831
1963	Cincinnati, Oh.	Ohio River	830
1956	Earl C. Clements	Ohio R., Ill-Ky.	825[8]
1930	*Vicksburg	Mississippi R.	825
1929	Louisville	Ohio River	820
1961	Campbellton-Cross Point	New Brunswick-Quebec	815
1943	Jeff'rson Barr'ks., Mo.	Mississippi R.	804
1950	Maurice J. Tobin	Boston, Mass.	800
1935	Rip Van Winkle	Catskill, N.Y.	800
1938	Cairo	Ohio River, Ill.-Ky.	800
1940	Ludlow Ferry	Potomac R.	800
1932	Washington Mem.	Seattle, Wash.	800
1936	McCullough	Coos Bay, Ore.	793
1935	[4]Huey P Long	New Orleans	790
1916	*Memphis (Harahan)	Mississippi R.	790
1892	*Memphis	Mississippi R.	790
1949	Memphis-Arkansas	Mississippi R.	790
1904	*Mingo Jct., W. Va.	Ohio River	769
1910	*Beaver, Pa.	Ohio River	767
1966	[5]S.N. Pearman	Charleston, S.C.	760
1940	Owensboro	Ohio River	750
1911	Sewickley, Pa.	Ohio River	750
1928	Outerbridge, N.Y.-N.J.	Arthur Kill	750
1964	Sunshine, Don'ville	Mississippi, La.	750

Simple Truss

Year	Bridge	Location	Longest span
1977	Chester	Chester, W. Va.	746
1917	*Metropolis	Ohio River	720
1929	Irvin S. Cobb	Ohio River-Ill.-Ky.	716
1922	*Tanana River	Nenana, Alaska	700
1933	*Henderson	Ohio River-Ind.-Ky.	665
1967	I-77, Ohio River	Marietta, Oh.	650
1917	MacArthur, Ill.-Mo.	St. Louis	647
1919	Louisville	Ohio River	644
1933	Atchafalaya	Morgan City, La.	608
1924	*Castleton	Hudson River	598
1889	*Cincinnati	Ohio River	542
1951	Allegheny River	Allegheny Co., Pa.	533
1914	Pittsburgh	Allegheny R.	531
1930	*Martinez	California	528
1967	Tanana River	Alaska	500
1974	Fort Hill, I-64	Charleston, W. Va.	465

Steel Truss

Year	Bridge	Location	Longest span
1940	Gov. Nice Mem.	Potomac River, Md.	800
1975	I-24	Tenn R., Ky.	720
1938	US-62, Ky.	Green River	700
1952	US-62, Ky.	Cumberland River	700
1940	Jamestown	Jamestown, R.I.	640
1940	Greenville	Mississippi R., Ark.	640
1949	Memphis	Mississippi R., Ark.	621
1938	US-22	Delaware River, N.J.	540
1972	Mississippi River	Muscatine, Ia.	512
1896	Newport	Ohio River, Ky.	511
1931	US-60	Cumberland R., Ky.	500
1958	Lake Oahe	Mobridge, S.D.	500
1958	Lake Oahe	Gettysburg, S.D.	500
1910	McKinley, St. Louis	Mississippi River	500
1963	Millard E. Tydings	Susquehanna R., Md.	490
1955	Four Bears	Missouri R., N.D.	475
1930	Lake Champlain	Lake Champlain, N.Y.	434
1947	Mayo	Suwanee R., Fla.	420
1929	Clarendon	White River, Ark.	400
1931	US-60	Tennessee R., Ky.	400

Continuous Truss

Year	Bridge	Location	Longest span
1966	Astoria, Ore.	Columbia R.	1,232
1966	Marquam	Willamette R., Ore.	1,044
1969	Miss. R.	Dyersburg, Tenn.	900
1969	Irondequoit Bay	Rochester, N.Y.	891
1943	Dubuque, Ia.	Mississippi R.	845
1953	John E. Mathews	Jacksonville, Fla.	810
1957	Kingston-Rhinecliff	Hudson R., N.Y.	800
1918	*Sciotoville	Ohio River	775
1974	Betsy Ross	Philadelphia, Pa.	729
1929	Madison-Milton	Ohio River	727
1966	Matthew E. Welsh	Mauckport	707[6]
1962	Champlain	Montreal, P.Q.	707
1975	Girard Point	Philadelphia, Pa.	700
1929	Chain of Rocks	Mississippi R.	699
1966	Braga	Taunton R., Mass.	682
1938	Port Arthur-Orange	Texas	680
1929	*Cincinnati	Ohio River	675
1928	Cape Girardeau, Mo.	Mississippi R.	672
1946	Chester, Ill.	Mississippi R.	670
1930	Quincy, Ill.	Mississippi R.	628
1959	US 181, over harbor	Corpus Christi, Tex.	620
1934	Bourne	Cape Cod Canal	616
1935	Sagamore	Cape Cod Canal	616
1965	Clarion River	Clarion Co., Pa.	612
1957	Blatnik	Duluth, Minn.	600
1965	Rio Grande Gorge	Taos, N.M.	600
1941	Columbia River	Kettle Falls, Wash.	600
1954	Columbia River	Umatilla, Ore.	600
1954	Columbia River	The Dalles, Ore.	576
1962	W. Br. Feather River	Oroville, Cal.	576
1936	Meredosia	Illinois River	567
1936	Mark Twain Mem.	Hannibal, Mo.	562
1957	Mackinac	Mackinac Straits, Mich.	560
1937	Homestead	Pittsburgh	553
1961	Ship Canal	Seattle, Wash.	552

Year	Bridge	Location	Longest span
1932	Pulaski Skyway	Passaic R., N.J.	550
1973	I-95, Thames River	New London, Conn.	540
1927	Ross Island	Portland, Ore.	535
1958	Interstate	Portland, Ore.	531
1936	South Omaha	Missouri R, Neb.-Ia.	525
1932	Savanna, Ill.-Sabula	Mississippi R.	520
1962	Columbia River	Beebe, Wash.	520
1970	Snake River	Central Ferry, Wash.	520

Continuous Box and Plate Girder

Year	Bridge	Location	Longest span
1967	San Mateo-Hayward No. 2	San Fran. Bay, Cal.	750
1963	Gunnison River	Gunnison, Col.	720
1969	San Diego-Coronado	San Diego Bay, Cal.	660[7]
1973	Ship Channel	Houston, Tex.	630
1967	Poplar St.	St. Louis, Mo.	600
1977	US-64, Tennessee R.	Savannah, Tenn.	525
1965	McDonald-Cartier	Ottawa, Ont.	520
1971	Lake Koocanusa	Lincoln Co., Mon.	500
1972	Sitka Harbor	Sitka, Alaska	450
1974	I-430	Arkansas R.	430
1972	I-635, Kansas City	Missouri R., Kan.-Mo.	425
1967	Chattanooga	Tennessee R., Tenn.	420
1978	Snake River	Clarkston, Wash.	420
1975	Yukon River	North Slope Road, Alas.	410
1972	I-75, Tennessee River	Loudon, Co., Tenn	400
1941	Susquehanna	Susquehanna R., Md.	400
1963	Lake Charles B'Pass	Louisiana	399
1957	Conn. Turnpike	Quinnipiac R.	387
1960	Route 34	New Haven, Conn.	379
1971	S.H. No. 1	Pendleton, Ark.	377
1960	Tennessee River	Chattanooga, Tenn.	375
1966	I-80, LeClaire, Ia.	Mississippi	370
1971	Sacramento R.	Bryte, Cal.	370
1963	I-40, Tennessee River	Benton Co., Tenn.	365
1967	San Mateo Creek	Hillsborough, Cal.	360
1950	US-62, Kentucky Dam	Tennessee R., Ky.	350
1961	Whiskey Creek	Trinity Co., Cal.	350
1972	Franklin Falls	Snoq'lmie Pass, Wash.	350
1971	Don Pedro Reserv	Tuolumne Co., Cal.	350

Continuous Plate

Year	Bridge	Location	Longest span
1965	New Chain of Rocks	Mississippi R., Ill.	5,411[9]
1973	Great Congress Gty.	Schenectady, N.Y.	1,870
1971	Congress St.	Troy, N.Y.	1,420
1967	Mississippi River	LaCrescent, Minn.	450
1966	I-480	Missouri R., Ia.-Neb.	425
1970	I-435	Missouri R., Mo.	425
1972	I-80	Missouri R., Ia.-Neb.	425
1971	St. Croix River	Hudson, Minn.	390
1968	Lafayette St.	St. Paul, Minn.	362
1970	Green River	Hendersonville, N.C.	350
1974	Mississippi R.	Prairie du Chien, Wisc.	350
1969	Fort Smith	Arkansas River	340
1964	Lexington Ave.	St. Paul, Minn.	340

I-Beam Girder

Year	Bridge	Location	Longest span
1941	US-31E	Rolling Fork R., Ky.	340
1948	US-27	Licking River, Ky.	316
1947	US-31E	Green River, Ky.	316
1941	US-62	Rolling Fork, Ky.	240
1942	Licking River	Owingsville, Ky.	240
1954	Fuller Warren	Jacksonville, Fla.	224

Steel Arch

Year	Bridge	Location	Longest span
1977	New River Gorge	Fayetteville, W. Va.	1,700
1931	Bayonne, N.J.	Kill Van Kull	1,652
1972	Fremont	Portland, Ore.	1,255
1964	Port Mann	British Columbia	1,200
1959	Glen Canyon	Colorado River	1,028
1967	Trois-Rivieres	St. Lawrence R., P.Q.	1,100
1962	Lewiston-Queenston	Niagara River, Ont.	1,000
1976	Perrine	Twin Falls, Ida.	993
1917	*Hell Gate	East R., N.Y.C.	977
1941	Rainbow	Niagara Falls	950
1972	I-40, Mississippi R.	Memphis, Tenn.	900[10]
1970	Lake Quinsigamond	Worcester, Mass.	849
1966	Charles Braga	Somerset, Mass.	840
1967	Lincoln Trail	Ohio R., Ind.-Ky.	825
1961	Sherman Minton	Louisville, Ky.	800
1936	Henry Hudson	Harlem River	800
1936	French King	Conn. R. (Rt. 2, Mass.)	782
1931	West End	Pittsburgh	778
1972	Piscataqua R.	I-95, N.H.-Me.	756
1979	SR 156, Tennessee R.	So. Pittsburgh, Tenn.	750
1963	Cold Spring Canyon	Santa Barbara, Cal.	700
1973	I-24, Paducah, Ky.	Ohio River	700

Concrete Arch

Year	Bridge	Location	Longest span
1971	Selah Creek (twin)	Selah, Wash.	549
1968	Cowlitz River	Mossyrock, Wash.	520
1931	Westinghouse	Pittsburgh	425
1923	Cappelen	Minneapolis	400
1930	Jack's Run	Pittsburgh	400
1973	Elwha River	Port Angeles, Wash.	380
1931	Bixby Creek	Monterey Coast, Cal.	330
1953	Arroyo Seco	Pasadena, Cal.	320
1927	Mendota	Ft. Snelling, Minn.	304

Twin Concrete Trestle

Year	Bridge	Location	Longest span
1963	Slidell, La.	L. Pontchartrain	28,547[9]

Concrete Slab Dam

Year	Bridge	Location	Longest span
1927	Conowingo Dam	Maryland	4,611
1952	John H. Kerr Dam	Roanoke River, Va.	2,785
1936	Hoover Dam	Boulder City, Nev.	1,324

Drawbridges

Vertical Lift

Year	Bridge	Location	Longest span
1959	*Arthur Kill	N.Y.-N.J.	558
1935	*Cape Cod Canal	Massachusetts	544
1960	*Delair, N.J.	Delaware River	542
1937	Marine Parkway	New York City	540
1931	Burlington, N.J.	Delaware R.	534
1912	*A-S-B Fratt	Kansas City	428
1945	*Harry S. Truman	Kansas City	427
1932	*M-K-T R.R.	Missouri R.	414
1969	Wilm'gtn Mem.	Wilmington, N.C.	408
1930	Aerial	Duluth, Minn.	386
1941	Main St.	Jacksonville, Fla.	386
1962	Burlington	Ontario	370
1922	*Cincinnati	Ohio River	365
1967	Benj. Harrison Mem.	James River, Va.	363
1961	Corpus Christi Harbor	Corpus Christi, Tex.	344[4]
1962	Sand Island Access	Oahu, Hawaii	340
1941	U.S. 1&9, Passaic R.	Newark, N.J.	332
1929	Carlton	Bath-Woolwich, Me.	328
1930	*Martinez	California	328
1960	St. Andrews Bay	Panama City, Fla.	327
1929	*Penn-Lehigh	Newark Bay	322
1920	*Chattanooga	Tennessee R.	310
1936	Triboro, N.Y.C.	Harlem River	310
1936	Hardin	Illinois River	309
1960	Sacramento River	Rio Vista, Cal.	306
1957	Claiborne Ave.	New Orleans	305
1927	Cochrane	Mobile, Ala.	300
1928	James River	Newport News	300
1929	San Mateo	California	300
1926	*Missouri Pacific	Kragen, Ark.	300

Bascule

Year	Bridge	Location	Longest span
1926	Fort Madison	Mississippi R.	525[4]
1969	Pearl River	Slidell, La.	482
1916	Keokuk Municipal	Mississippi R., Ia.	377
1917	SR-8, Tennessee River	Chattanooga, Tenn.	306
1940	Lorain, Ohio	Black River	300
1958	Morrison	Portland, Ore.	285
1969	Elizabeth River	Chesapeake, Va.	281
1957	Craig Memorial	I-280, Toledo, Oh.	245
1952	Downtown	Norfolk, Va.	230

Swing Bridges

Year	Bridge	Location	Longest span
1950	Douglass Memorial	Anac'tia R., Wash. D.C.	386
1945	Lord Delaware	Mattaponi River, Va.	252
1957	Eltham	Pamunkey River, Va.	237
1939	Chickahominy River	Route 5, Va.	222
1930	Nansemond River	Route 125, Va.	200

Swing Span

Year	Bridge	Location	Longest span
1908	*Willamette R.	Portland, Ore.	521
1903	*East Omaha	Missouri R.	519
1952	Yorktown	York River, Va.	500
1897	*Duluth, Minn.	St. Louis Bay	486
1899	*C.M.&N.R.R.	Chicago	474
1897	Sioux City, Ia.	Missouri R. (Nebr.-Ia.)	470
1914	*Coos Bay	Oregon	458

Floating Pontoon

Year	Bridge	Location	Longest span
1963	Evergreen Pt.	Seattle, Wash.	7,518
1940	Lacey V. Murrow	Seattle	6,561
1961	Hood Canal	Pt. Gamble, Wash.	6,471

(1) The Transbay Bridge has 2 spans of 2,310 ft. each. (2) A second bridge in parallel will be completed. (3) The Richmond Bridge has twin spans 1,070 ft. each. (4) Railroad and vehicular bridge. (5) Two spans each 760 ft. (6) Two spans each 707 ft. (7) Two spans each 660 ft. (8) Two spans each 825 ft. (9) Total length of bridge. (10) Two spans each 900 ft.

Construction Details of Large and Unusual Bridges

Verrazano-Narrows Bridge, between Staten Island and Brooklyn, N.Y., has a suspension span of 4,260 ft., exceeding the Golden Gate Bridge, San Francisco, by 60 ft. One level in use Nov., 1964, second opened Jun. 28, 1969. The name is a compromise; it spans the Narrows and commemorates a visit to New York Harbor in Apr., 1524, deduced from certain notes left by Giovanni da Verrazano, Italian navigator sailing for Francis I of France.

Allegheny River Bridge (Interstate 80) near Emlenton, Pa., 270 ft. above the water, tallest in eastern U.S., a continuous truss, 688 ft. long, 1968.

Angostura, suspension type, span 2,336 feet, 1967 at Ciudad Bolivar, Venezuela. Total length, 5,507.

Charles Braga Bridge over Taunton River between Fall River and Somerset, Mass. It is 5,780 feet long.

Bendorf Bridge on the Rhine River, 5 mi. n. of Coblenz, completed 1965, is a 3-span cement girder bridge, 3,378 ft. overall length, 101 ft. wide, with the main span 682 ft.

Burro Creek Bridge with 4 spans over Burro Creek on highway 93 near Kingman, Ariz. Main span steel truss 680 ft. Others plate girder, 110 and 2 of 85 ft. 1966.

Champlain Bridge at Montreal crossing the St. Lawrence River was opened 1962. It is 4 miles long.

Chesapeake Bay Bridge-Tunnel, opened Apr. 15, 1964 on US-13, connects Virginia Beach-Norfolk with the Eastern Shore of Virginia. Shore to shore, 17.6 miles. Twelve miles of trestles, 4 man-made islands, 2 mile-long tunnels, and 2 bridges.

Cross Bay Parkway Bridge (N.Y.), 3,000 feet long with 6 traffic lanes, 11 eight foot wide precast, prestressed concrete T girders to support spans 130 feet long each with main span 275 feet.

Delaware Memorial Bridge over Delaware River near Wilmington. A twin suspension bridge paralleling the original 250 ft. upstream has a 2,150-ft. main span suspended from 440-ft. towers.

Eads Bridge across the Mississippi R. between St. Louis and E. St. Louis, built in 1874 has 4 main spans 1,520 ft., 2,502 ft., and 1,118 ft. crossing Miss. R., a railroad and a road.

Evergreen Point Bridge, Wash. consists of 33 floating concrete pontoons weighing 4,700 tons each, held in place by 77 ton crete anchors. Pontoon structure is 6,561 ft. long; with approaches bridge is 12,596 ft. long.

Fremont Bridge. Part of Stadium Freeway, Portland, Ore., crossing Willamette R. 1,255 ft. steel arch span with two 452 ft. flanking steel arch spans. 1971.

Frontenac Bridge, Quebec, suspension, span 2,190 ft., open 1970.

Gladesville Bridge at Sydney, Australia, has the longest concrete arch in the world (1,000 ft. span).

George Washington Bridge, New York City, 4th longest suspension bridge in the world, spans the Hudson River between W. 178th St., Manhattan, and Ft. Lee, N.J.; 4,760 ft. between anchorages, two levels, 14 traffic lanes. Triborough Bridge connects Manhattan, the Bronx, and Queens; project comprises a suspension bridge, a vertical lift bridge, and a fixed bridge, all connected by long viaducts. The famous Brooklyn Bridge over the East River, connecting Manhattan and Brooklyn, was completed in 1883, breaking all previous records by spanning 1,595 ft.

Golden Gate Bridge, crossing San Francisco Bay, has the second longest single span, 4,200 ft.

Hampton Roads Bridge-Tunnel, Va. A crossing completed in 1957 consisting of 2 man-made islands, 2 concrete trestle bridges, and one tunnel, under Hampton Roads with a length of 7,479 ft. A parallel facility with a 7,315 ft. tunnel is now open to traffic.

Hood Canal Floating Bridge, Wash., 23 floating concrete pontoons 4,980 tons each. Roadway is supported on crete T-beam sections mounted on pontoons 20 feet above canal. Floating section is 6,471 ft. long, overall 7,866 ft. Closed Feb. 13, 1979; severe storm damage.

Humber Bridge, with a suspension span of 4,626 ft., the longest in the world, crosses the Humber estuary 5 miles west of the city of Kingston upon Hull, England. Unique in a large suspension bridge are the towers of reinforced concrete instead of steel.

International Bridge, a series of 8 arch and truss bridges crossing St. Mary's and the Soo Locks between Mich. and Ontario. Two-mile toll completed 1962.

Lacy V. Murrow Floating Bridge, Wash., 25 floating pontoons of 4,558 tons each. Bridge with approaches is 8,583 ft.

Lake Pontchartrain Twin Causeway, a twin-span crete trestle bridge and 24-mile link within metropolitan New Orleans that connects the north and south shore. First span opened 1956, second 1969.

Lavaca Bay Causeway, Tex., 2.2 miles long, consisting of one 260 ft. continuous plate girder unit and 194 precast, prestressed concrete spans of 60 ft. length. 1961.

Newport Bridge between Newport and Jamestown, R.I. Total length 11,248 ft., a main suspension span of 1,600 feet, 2 side spans each 688 feet long. It has U.S.A.'s first prefabricated wire strands.

New York City bridges, *see Verrazano-Narrows Bridge and George Washington Bridge above.*

Ogdensburg-Prescott Internat'l Bridge across the St. Lawrence River from Ogdensburg, N.Y., to Johnston, Ont., opened 1970, is 13,510 ft. long with approaches and 7,260 ft. between abutments.

Oland Island Bridge in Sweden was completed in 1972. It is 19,882 feet long, Europe's longest.

Oosterscheldebrug, opened Dec. 15, 1965, is a 3.125-mile causeway for automobiles over a sea arm in Zeeland, the Netherlands. It completes a direct connection between Flushing and Rotterdam.

Poplar St. Bridge over the Mississippi at St. Louis, a 5-span continuous orthotropic deck plate girder bridge, longest span 600 ft. Eight lanes, 2,165 ft. long.

Quebec Road, suspension, span 2,190 feet, 1969, Quebec, Canada.

Rio-Niteroi, Guanabara Bay, Brazil, under construction, will be world's longest continuous box and plate girder bridge, 8 miles, 3,363 feet long, with a center span of 984 feet and a span on each side of 656 feet.

Robert Opie Norris Bridge, Rappahannock R. between Greys Pt. and White Stone, Va. 9,989 ft. long. Main spans are two 144 foot cantilever truss spans with a 360 foot truss span suspended between them.

Rockville Bridge, world's longest 4-track stone arch bridge, 3,810 ft., with 48 arches. Part of the Consolidated Rail Corp. system west of Harrisburg, Pa. It contains 440 million lbs. of stone, 100,000 cubic yds. of masonry and crosses the Susquehanna Riv. to Rockville, Pa.

Royal Gorge Bridge, 1,053 ft. above the Arkansas River in Colorado, is the highest bridge above water. Opened Dec. 8, 1929, it is 1,260 ft. long with a main span of 880 ft., width 18 ft.

San Mateo-Hayward Bridge across San Francisco Bay is first major orthotropic bridge in U.S. It is 6.7 miles long, 4.9 mile low-level concrete trestle and 1.8 miles high-level steel bridge.

Seven Mile Bridge is the longest of an expanse of bridges connecting the Florida Keys. It was built by the Florida East Coast Railway between 1904 and 1916, now a state highway.

Shenandoah River Bridges, one spans the south fork, 1,924 ft. long, the other the north fork, 1,090 ft. long. Warren County, Va.

Straits of Mackinac Bridge, completed in 1957, is the longest suspension bridge between anchorages and with approaches extends nearly 5 mi. between Mackinaw City and St. Ignace, Mich.

Sunshine Skyway, a 15-mile-long bridge-causeway with twin roadbeds that crosses Tampa Bay at St. Petersburg, Fla., a system of twin bridges 864 feet long and 4 smaller bridges with 6 causeways. The main span of the south bound bridge was torn away May 9, 1980, when support tower was hit by a cargo ship.

Tagus River Bridge near Lisbon, Portugal, longest suspension bridge outside the United States, has a 3,323-ft. main span. Opened Aug. 6, 1966, it was named Salazar Bridge for the former premier.

Thomas A. Edison Memorial Bridge (causeway) across Sandusky Bay between Martin Point and Danbury, Oh., is 2.67 miles long. The main bridge is 2,044 feet long.

Thousand Island Bridge, St. Lawrence River. American span 800 ft.; Canadian 750 ft.

Union St. Bridge in Woodstock, Vt., a timber lattice truss with a span of 122 feet built in 1969 using old time procedure of hand drilled holes and wooden pegs.

Vancouver Bridge, Canada's longest railway lift span connecting Vancouver and North Vancouver over Burrard Inlet. It is in 3 sections, the longest 493 ft. Spans are part of a project that includes a 2-mile tunnel under Vancouver Hts.

Woodrow Wilson Memorial Bridge across the Potomac River at Alexandria, Va., is over a mile long.

Zoo Bridge across the Rhine at Cologne, with steel box girders, has a main span of 850 ft.

The Interstate Highway 610 crossing of the Houston Ship Channel in Texas is 6,300 feet in length and consists of various lengths of prestressed concrete beam and slab approach spans and a 1,233 foot main unit of two 471'6" plate girder units and one 290 ft. simple span.

Underwater Vehicular Tunnels in North America

(3,000 feet in length or more)

Name	Location	Waterway	Lgth. Ft.
Bart Trans-Bay Tubes (Rapid Transit)	San Francisco, Cal.	S.F. Bay	3.6 miles
Brooklyn-Battery	New York, N.Y.	East River	9,117
Holland Tunnel	New York, N.Y.	Hudson River	8,557
Lincoln Tunnel	New York, N.Y.	Hudson River	8,216
Baltimore Harbor Tunnel	Baltimore, Md.	Patapsco River	7,650
Hampton Roads	Norfolk, Va.	Hampton Roads	7,479
Queens Midtown	New York, N.Y.	East River	6,414
Thimble Shoal Channel	Cape Henry, Va.	Chesapeake Bay	5,738
Sumner Tunnel	Boston, Mass.	Boston Harbor	5,650
Chesapeake Channel	Cape Charles, Va.	Chesapeake Bay	5,450
Louis-Hippolyte Lafontaine Tunnel	Montreal, Que.	St. Lawrence River	5,280
Detroit-Windsor	Detroit, Mich.	Detroit River	5,135
Callahan Tunnel	Boston, Mass.	Boston Harbor	5,046
Midtown Tunnel	Norfolk, Va.	Elizabeth River	4,194
Baytown Tunnel	Baytown, Tex.	Houston Ship Channel	4,111
Posey Tube	Oakland, Cal.	Oakland Estuary	3,500
Downtown Tunnel	Norfolk, Va.	Elizabeth River	3,350
Webster St.	Alameda, Cal.	Oakland Estuary	3,350
Bankhead Tunnel	Mobile, Ala.	Mobile River	3,109
I-10 Twin Tunnel	Mobile, Ala.	Mobile River	3,000

Land Vehicular Tunnels in U.S.

(over 1,200 feet in length.)

Name	Location	Lgth. Ft.
Eisenhower Memorial	Route 70, Col.	8,941
Copperfield	Copperfield, Ut.	6,989
Allegheny (twin)	Penna. Turnpike	6,070
Liberty Tubes	Pittsburgh, Pa.	5,920
Zion Natl. Park	Rte. 9, Utah.	5,766
East River Mt. (twin)	Interstate 77, W. Va.-Va.	5,661
Tuscarora (twin)	Penna. Turnpike	5,326
Kittatinny (twin)	Penna. Turnpike	4,727
Lehigh	Penna. Turnpike	4,379
Blue Mountain (twin)	Penna. Turnpike	4,339
Wawona	Yosemite Natl. Park	4,233
Squirrel Hill	Pittsburgh, Pa.	4,225
Big Walker Mt.	Route I-77, Va.	4,200
Fort Pitt	Pittsburgh, Pa.	3,560
Mall Tunnel	Dist. of Columbia.	3,400
Caldecott	Oakland, Cal.	3,371
Cody No. 1	U.S. 14, 16, 20, Wyo.	3,224
Kalihi	Honolulu, Ha.	2,780
Memorial	W. Va. Tpke. (I-77).	2,669
Cross-Town	178 St. N.Y.C.	2,414
F.D. Roosevelt Dr.	81-89 Sts. N.Y.C.	2,400
Dewey Sq.	Boston, Mass.	2,400
Battery Park	N.Y.C.	2,300
Battery St.	Seattle, Wash.	2,140
Big Oak Flat	Yosemite Natl. Park	2,083
Carlin	I-80, Nev.	1,993
Prudential	Boston, Mass.	1,980
Internatl. Underpass	Los Angeles, Cal.	1,910
Street-Car	Providence, R.I.	1,793
Broadway	San Francisco, Cal.	1,616
9th Street Expy.	Washington, D.C.	1,610
F.D. Roosevelt Dr.	42-48 Sts. N.Y.C.	1,600
Lowry Hill	Minneapolis.	1,496
Wheeling	Interstate 70, W. Va.	1,490
Mt. Baker Ridge (3)	Seattle, Wash.	1,466
Knowls Creek	Lane County, Ore.	1,430
Mule Pass.	Near Bisbee, Ariz.	1,400
Arch Cape	Oregon Coast Hwy. 9	1,228
Queen Creek	Superior, Ariz.	1,200
West Rock	New Haven, Conn.	1,200

World's Longest Railway Tunnels

Source: Railway Directory & Year Book 1980. Tunnels over 4.9 miles in length.

Tunnel	Date	Miles	Yds	Operating railway	Country
Dai-shimizu	1979	13	1,384	Japanese National	Japan
Simplon No. 1 and 2	1906, 1922	12	546	Swiss Fed. & Italian St.	Switz.-Italy
Kanmon	1975	11	1,093	Japanese National	Japan
Apennine	1934	11	881	Italian State	Italy
Rokko	1972	10	158	Japanese National	Japan
Gotthard	1882	9	552	Swiss Federal	Switzerland
Lotschberg	1913	9	130	Bern-Lotschberg-Simplon	Switzerland
Hokuriku	1962	8	1,079	Japanese National	Japan
Mont Cenis (Frejus)	1871	8	847	Italian State	France-Italy
Shin-Shimizu	1961	8	675	Japanese National	Japan
Aki	1975	8	161	Japanese National	Japan
Cascade	1929	7	1,388	Burlington Northern	U.S.
Flathead	1970	7	1,319	Great Northern	U.S.
Keijo	1970	7	88	Japanese National	Japan
Lierasen	1973	6	1,135	Norwegian State	Norway
Santa Lucia	1977	6	656	Italian State	Italy
Arlberg	1884	6	643	Austrian Federal	Austria
Moffat	1928	6	366	Denver & Rio Grande Western	U.S.
Shimizu	1931	6	44	Japanese National	Japan
Kvineshei	1943	5	1,107	Norwegian State	Norway
Bigo	1975	5	927	Japanese National	Japan
Rimutaka	1955	5	816	New Zealand Gov.	New Zealand
Ricken	1910	5	603	Swiss Federal	Switzerland
Kaimai	1978	5	873	New Zealand Gov.	New Zealand
Grenchenberg	1915	5	575	Swiss Federal	Switzerland
Otira	1923	5	559	New Zealand Gov.	New Zealand
Tauern	1909	5	546	Austrian Federal	Austria
Haegebostad	1943	5	462	Norwegian State	Norway
Ronco	1889	5	272	Italian State	Italy
Hauenstein (Lower)	1916	5	90	Swiss Federal	Switzerland
Connaught	1916	5	34	Canadian Pacific	Canada
Karawanken	1906	4	1,677	Austrian Federal	Austria-Yugo.
Kobe	1972	4	1,671	Japanese National	Japan
New Tanna	1964	4	1,658	Japanese National	Japan

STATES AND OTHER AREAS OF THE U.S.

Sources: Population: Bureau of the Census (July, 1981 provisional estimates, including armed forces personnel in each state but excluding such personnel stationed overseas); area: Geography Division, Bureau of the Census; Value added by manufacture: Bureau of the Census; lumber production: Commerce Department; mineral production: Bureau of Mines; commercial fishlandings: Marine Fisheries Service; per capita income: Bureau of Economic Analysis, Commerce Department; forested land: Department of Agriculture, Forest Service; unemployment: Bureau of Labor Statistics; energy production: Energy Department; education: Education Department; construction valuation: Dodge Construction Potentials, McGraw-Hill Information Systems Company. All other information comes from sources in the individual states.

Alabama

Heart of Dixie, Cotton State

People. Population (1981): 3,917,000; **rank:** 22. **Pop. density:** 77.2 per sq. mi. **Urban** (1980): 60%. **Racial distrib.** (1980): 73.7% White; 26.3% Black; Hispanic 33,100. **Major ethnic groups:** German, English, Italian, Polish. **Net migration** (1970-79): +75,000.

Geography. Total area: 51,609 sq. mi.; **rank:** 29. **Land area:** 50,708 sq. mi. **Acres forested land:** 21,361,100. **Location:** in the east south central U.S., extending N-S from Tenn. to the Gulf of Mexico; east of the Mississippi River. **Climate:** long, hot summers; mild winters; generally abundant rainfall. **Topography:** coastal plains inc. Prairie Black Belt give way to hills, broken terrain; highest elevation, 2,407 ft. **Capital:** Montgomery.

Economy. Principal industries: pulp and paper, apparel, textiles, primary metals, lumber and wood, food processing, fabricated metals, automotive tires. **Principal manufactured goods:** cast iron and plastic pipe, ships, paper products, chemicals, steel, mobile homes, fabrics, poultry processing. **Value added by manufacture** (1978): $9.7 bln. **Agriculture: Chief crops:** soybeans, cotton, peanuts, corn, hay, wheat, pecans, peaches, potatoes, tomatoes. **Livestock:** 1.95 mln. cattle; 540,000 hogs/pigs; 19 mln. poultry. **Timber/lumber** (1979): pine, hardwoods; 1.56 bln. bd. ft. **Minerals** (1979): natural gas, bituminous coal, crude petroleum, accounting for 80% of the $1.9 bln. total mineral value for raw materials. Also, cement and stone. **Commercial fishing** (1980): $51 mln. **Chief ports:** Mobile. **Value of construction** (1981): $1.7 bln. **Employment distribution:** 26.8% manuf.; 20.1% trade; 15.6% serv. **Per capita income** (1981): $8,200. **Unemployment** (1981): 10.7%. **Tourism** (1981): tourists spent $2.5 bln.

Finance. No. banks (1980): 318; **No. savings assns.** (1981): 50.

Federal government. No. federal civilian employees (Mar. 1981): 56,160. **Avg. salary:** $21,558. **Notable federal facilities:** George C. Marshall NASA Space Center, Huntsville; Maxwell AFB, Montgomery; Ft. Rucker, Ozark; Ft. McClellan, Anniston; Natl. Fertilizer Development Center, Muscle Shoals.

Energy. Electricity production (1981, mwh, by source): Hydroelectric: 6.01 mln. Mineral: 45.1 mln. Nuclear: 23.6 mln.

Education. No. schools: 1,582 elem. and second.; 58 higher ed. **Avg. salary, public school teachers** (1980): $13,312.

State data. Motto: We dare defend our rights. **Flower:** Camellia. **Bird:** Yellowhammer. **Tree:** Southern pine. **Song:** Alabama. **Entered union** Dec. 14, 1819; rank, 22d. **State fair** at: Birmingham; Oct. 7–16.

History. First Europeans were Spanish explorers in the early 1500s. The French made the first permanent settlement, on Mobile Bay, 1701-02; later, English settled in the northern areas. France ceded the entire region to England at the end of the French and Indian War, 1763, but Spanish Florida claimed the Mobile Bay area until U. S. troops took it, 1813. Gen. Andrew Jackson broke the power of the Creek Indians, 1814, and they were removed to Oklahoma. The Confederate States were organized Feb. 4, 1861, at Montgomery, the first capital.

Tourist attractions. Jefferson Davis' "first White House" of the Confederacy; Ivy Green, Helen Keller's birthplace at Tuscumbia; statue of Vulcan near Birmingham; George Washington Carver Museum at Tuskegee Institute; Alabama Space and Rocket Center at Huntsville.

At Russell Cave National Monument, near Bridgeport, may be seen a detailed record of occupancy by humans from about 10,000 BC to 1650 AD.

Famous Alabamians include Hank Aaron, Tallulah Bankhead, Hugo L. Black, George Washington Carver, Nat King Cole, William C. Handy, Helen Keller, Harper Lee, Joe Louis, John Hunt Morgan, Jesse Owens, Booker T. Washington, Hank Williams.

Chamber of Commerce: 468 S. Perry St., P.O. Box 76, Montgomery, AL 36101.

Alaska

No official nickname

People. Population (1981): 412,000; **rank:** 50. **Pop. density:** 0.72 per sq. mi., **Urban** (1980): 64.3%. **Major ethnic groups:** Anglo-Saxons, Alaska natives (Eskimos, Aleuts and Indians). **Net migration** (1970-81): +36,781.

Geography. Total area: 586,412 sq. mi.; **rank:** 1. **Land area:** 569,600 sq. mi. **Acres forested land:** 119,114,900. **Location:** NW corner of North America, bordered on east by Canada. **Climate:** SE, SW, and central regions, moist and mild; far north extremely dry. Extended summer days, winter nights, throughout. **Topography:** includes Pacific and Arctic mountain systems, central plateau, and Arctic slope. Mt. McKinley, 20,320 ft., is the highest point in North America. **Capital:** Juneau.

Economy. Principal industries: oil, gas, tourism. **Principal manufactured goods:** fish products, lumber and pulp, furs. **Value added by manufacture** (1978): $546.8 mln. **Agriculture: Chief crops:** barley, hay, silage, potatoes, lettuce, milk, eggs. **Livestock:** 8,300 cattle; 1,000 hogs/pigs; 6,500 sheep; 28,000 poultry. **Timber/lumber:** spruce, yellow cedar, hemlock. **Minerals** (1979): crude petroleum, natural gas, sand and gravel. Total mineral production valued at $5.7 bln. **Commercial fishing** (1980): $560 mln. **Chief ports:** Anchorage, Dutch Harbor, Seward, Skagway, Juneau, Sitka, Valdez, Wrangell. **International airports at:** Anchorage, Fairbanks, Ketchikan, Juneau. **Value of construction** (1981): $1.08 bln. **Employment distribution:** 34.6% gvt.; 17.8% serv. 9% transp. **Per capita income** (1981): $14,190. **Unemployment** (1981): 9.3%. **Tourism** (1980): out-of-state visitors spent $260 mln.

Finance. No. banks: (1980): 12; **No. savings assns.:** (1981): 4.

Federal government. No. federal civilian employees (Mar. 1981): 13,149. **Avg. salary:** $24,687.

Energy. Electricity production (1981, mwh, by source): Hydroelectric: 590,311 Mineral: 2.6 mln.

Education. No. schools: 420 elem. and second.; 16 higher ed. **Avg. salary, public school teachers** (1980): $26,173.

State data. Motto: North to the future. **Flower:** Forget-me-not. **Bird:** Willow ptarmigan. **Tree:** Sitka spruce. **Song:** Alaska's Flag. **Entered union:** Jan. 3, 1959; rank, 49th. **State fair at:** Palmer; late Aug.—early Sept.

History. Vitus Bering, a Danish explorer working for Russia, was the first European to land in Alaska, 1741. Alexander Baranov, first governor of Russian America, set up headquarters at Archangel, near present Sitka, in 1799. Secretary of State William H. Seward in 1867 bought Alaska from Russia for $7.2 million, a bargain some called "Seward's Folly." In 1896 gold was discovered and the famed Gold Rush was on.

Tourist attractions: Glacier Bay National Park, Denali National Park, one of North America's great wildlife sanctuaries, Pribilof Islands fur seal rookeries, restored St. Michael's Russian Orthodox Cathedral, Sitka.

Famous Alaskans include Carl Eielson, Ernest Gruening, Joe Juneau, Sydney Laurence, James Wickersham.

Chamber of Commerce: 134 3rd., Juneau, AK 99801.

Arizona

Grand Canyon State

People. Population (1981): 2,794,000; **rank:** 29. **Pop. density:** 24.6 per sq. mi. **Urban** (1980): 83.8% **Racial distrib. (1980):** 82.4% White; 2.7% Black; 14.8% Other (includes American Indians); Hispanic 440,915. **Major ethnic groups:** Mexican, German, English, Italian. **Net migration** (1970-79): +464,000.

Geography. Total area: 113,909 sq. mi.; **rank:** 6. **Land area:** 113,417 sq. mi. **Acres forested land:** 18,493,900. **Location:** in the southwestern U.S. **Climate:** clear and dry in the southern regions and northern plateau; high central areas have heavy winter snows. **Topography:** Colorado plateau in the N, containing the Grand Canyon; Mexican Highlands running diagonally NW to SE; Sonoran Desert in the SW. **Capital:** Phoenix.

Economy: Principal industries: manufacturing, tourism, mining, agriculture. **Principal manufactured goods:** electronics, printing and publishing, foods, primary and fabricated metals, aircraft and missiles, apparel. **Value added by manufacture** (1980): $5.58 bln. **Agriculture: Chief crops:** cotton, sorghum, barley, corn, wheat, sugar beets, citrus fruits. **Livestock:** 1.14 mln. cattle; 99,000 hogs/pigs; 490,000 sheep; 565,000 poultry. **Timber/lumber** (1978): pine, fir, spruce; 383 mln. bd. ft. **Minerals** (1980): copper (prod. valued at $1.7 bln. 71% of total mineral production), gold, silver, molybdenum, sand and gravel, lime. **International airports at:** Phoenix, Tucson, Yuma. **Value of construction** (1981): $3.1 bln. **Employment distribution** (1981): 24% trade, 19% gvt., 21% serv., 16% manuf. **Per capita income** (1981): $9,693. **Unemployment** (1981): 6.1% **Tourism** (1980): tourists spent $4.0 bln.

Finance. No. banks: (1980): 35; **No. savings assns.** (1981): 12.

Federal government: No. federal civilian employees (Mar. 1981): 31,422. **Avg. salary:** $19,778. **Notable federal facilities:** Williams, Luke, Davis-Monthan AF bases; Ft. Huachuca Army Base; Yuma Proving Grounds.

Energy. Electricity production (1981, mwh, by source): Hydroelectric: 6.8 mln.; Mineral: 33.8.

Education. No. schools: 1,053 elem. and second.; 23 higher ed. **Avg. salary, public school teachers** (1980): $15,835.

State data. Motto: Ditat Deus (God enriches). **Flower:** Blossom of the Seguaro cactus. **Bird:** Cactus wren. **Tree:** Paloverde. **Song:** Arizona. **Entered union** Feb. 14, 1912; rank, 48th. **State fair** at: Phoenix; late Oct.–early Nov.

History. Marcos de Niza, a Franciscan, and Estevan, a black slave, explored the area, 1539. Eusebio Francisco Kino, Jesuit missionary, taught Indians Christianity and farming, 1690-1711, left a chain of missions. Spain ceded Arizona to Mexico, 1821. The U. S. took over at the end of the Mexican War, 1848. The area below the Gila River was obtained from Mexico in the Gadsden Purchase, 1854. Long Apache wars did not end until 1886, with Geronimo's surrender.

Tourist attractions. The Grand Canyon of the Colorado, an immense, vari-colored fissure 217 mi. long, 4 to 13 mi. wide at the brim, 4,000 to 5,500 ft. deep; the Painted Desert, extending for 30 mi. along U.S. 66; the Petrified Forest; Canyon Diablo, 225 ft. deep and 500 ft. wide; Meteor Crater, 4,150 ft. across, 570 ft. deep, made by a prehistoric meteor. Also, London Bridge at Lake Havasu City.

Famous Arizonans include Cochise, Geronimo, Barry Goldwater, Zane Grey, George W. P. Hunt, Helen Jacobs, Percival Lowell, William H. Pickering, Morris Udall, Stewart Udall, Frank Lloyd Wright.

Chamber of Commerce: 2701 E. Camelback Rd. Phoenix, AZ 85016.

Arkansas

Land of Opportunity

People. Population (1981): 2,296,000; **rank:** 33. **Pop. density:** 44.2 per sq. mi. **Urban** (1980): 51.5%. **Racial distrib.** (1980): 66.1% White; 16.3% Black; Hispanic 17,873. **Major ethnic groups:** German, English, Italian, Polish. **Net migration** (1970-80): +231,371.

Geography. Total area: 53,104 sq. mi.; **rank:** 27. **Land area:** 51,945 sq. mi. **Acres forested land:** 18,281,500. **Location:** in the west south-central U.S. **Climate:** long, hot summers, mild winters; generally abundant rainfall. **Topography:** eastern delta and prairie, southern lowland forests, and the northwestern highlands, which include the Ozark Plateaus. **Capital:** Little Rock.

Economy. Principal industries: manufacturing, agriculture, tourism. **Principal manufactured goods:** poultry products, forestry products, aluminum, electric motors, transformers, garments, shoes, bricks, fertilizer, petroleum products. **Value added by manufacture** (1978): $5.5 bln. **Agriculture: Chief crops:** soybeans, rice, cotton, hay, wheat, sorghum, tomatoes, strawberries. **Livestock:** 2.05 mln. cattle; 720,000 hogs/pigs; 6.35 mln. poultry. **Timber/lumber** (1979): oak, hickory, gum, cypress, pine; 75 mln. bd. ft. **Minerals** (1979): bauxite, bromine, and vanadium prod. 1st in U.S. Also natural gas, crude petroleum. Total mineral production valued at $667.9 mln. **Commercial fishing** (1980): $5.2 mln. **Chief ports:** Little Rock, Pine Bluff, Osceola, Helena, Fort Smith, Van Buren, Camden. **Value of construction** (1981): $1.22 bln. **Employment distribution:** 25.9% manuf.; 19.8% trade; 14.2% serv.; 8.1% agric. **Per capita income** (1981): $8,042. **Unemployment** (1981): 9.1% **Tourism** (1981): out-of state visitors spent $1.6 bln.

Finance. No. banks (1980): 262; **No. savings assns.** (1981): 70.

Federal government. No. federal civilian employees (Mar. 1981): 16,250. **Avg. salary:** $19,114. **Notable federal facilities:** Nat'l. Center for Toxicological Research, Jefferson; Pine Bluff Arsenal.

Energy. Electricity production (1981, mwh, by source): Hydroelectric: 1.2 mln.; Mineral: 15.0 mln.; Nuclear: 9.1 mln.

Education. No. schools: 1,286 elem. and second.; 34 higher ed. **Avg. salary, public school teachers** (1980): $12,419.

State data. Motto: Regnat Populus (The people rule). **Flower:** Apple Blossom. **Bird:** Mockingbird. **Tree:** Pine. **Song:** Arkansas. **Entered union:** June 15, 1836; rank, 25th. **State fair at:** Little Rock; late Sept.- early Oct.

History. First European explorers were de Soto, 1541, Jolliet, 1673; La Salle, 1682. First settlement was by the French under Henri de Tonty, 1686, at Arkansas Post. In 1762 the area was ceded by France to Spain, then back again in 1800, and was part of the Louisiana Purchase by the U.S. in 1803. Arkansas seceded from the Union in 1861, only after the Civil War began, and more than 10,000 Arkansans fought on the Union side.

Tourist attractions. Hot Springs National Park, water ranging from 95° to 147°F; Blanchard Caverns, near Mountain View, are among the nation's largest; Crater of Diamonds, near Murfreesboro, only U.S. diamond mine; Buffalo Natl. River.

Famous Arkansans include Hattie Caraway, "Dizzy" Dean, Orval Faubus, James W. Fulbright, Douglas MacArthur, John L. McClellan, James S. McDonnel, Winthrop Rockefeller, Edward Durell Stone, Archibald Yell.

Chamber of Commerce: 911 Wallace Bldg., Little Rock, AR 72201.

California

Golden State

People. Population (1981): 24,196,000; **rank:** 1. **Pop. density:** 154.7 per sq. mi. **Urban** (1980): 91.3%. **Racial distrib.** (1980): 76.1% White; 7.6% Black; 16.1% Other (includes American Indians, Asian Americans, and Pacific Islanders); Hispanic 4,543,770. **Major ethnic groups:** English, German, Italian, Russian. **Net migration** (1970-80): +1,462,000.

Geography. Total area 158,693 sq. mi.; **rank:** 3. **Land area:** 156,361 sq. mi. **Acres forested land:** 40,152,100. **Location:** on western coast of the U.S. **Climate:** moderate temperatures and rainfall along the coast; extremes in the interior. **Topography:** long mountainous coastline; central valley; Sierra Nevada on the east; desert basins of the southern interior; rugged mountains of the north. **Capital:** Sacramento.

Economy. Principal industries: agriculture, aerospace, manufacturing, construction, recreation. **Principal manufactured goods:** foods, primary and fabricated metals, machinery, electric and electronic equipment, chemicals and allied products. **Value added by manufacture** (1978): $62.5 bln. **Agriculture: Chief crops:** cotton, grapes, dairy products, lettuce, eggs, tomatoes, nursery products, nuts, apricots, avocados, citrus fruits, barley, rice, olives. **Livestock** (1980): 4.6 mln. cattle; 180,000 hogs/pigs; 1 mln. sheep; 83.1 mln. poultry. **Timber/lumber** (1979): fir, pine, redwood, oak; 3.9 bln. bd. ft. **Minerals** (1977): crude petroleum, natural gas, and natural gas liquids 69% of total value mineral production, $4.1 bln. **Commercial fishing** (1980): $323.3 mln. **Chief ports:** Long Beach, San Diego, Oakland, San Francisco, Sacramento, Stockton. **International airports at:** Los Angeles, San Francisco. **Value of construction** (1981): $17.19 bln. **Employment distribution** (1980): 23.0% trade; 20.0% serv.; 17.9% gvt. **Per capita income** (1981): $12,057. **Unemployment** (1981): 7.4% **Tourism** (1976): out-of-state visitors spent $12.4 bln.

Finance. Notable industries: banking, insurance, real estate, investment. **No. banks** (1980): 296; **No. savings assns.** (1981): 188.

Federal government. No. federal civilian employees (Mar. 1981): 259,460. **Avg. salary:** $20,826. **Notable federal facilities:** Vandenberg, Beale, Travis, McClellan AF bases, San Francisco Mint.

Energy. Electricity production (1981, mwh, by source): Hydroelectric: 29.8 mln.; Mineral: 91.3 mln.; Nuclear: 3.2 mln.

Education. No. schools: 9,023 elem. and second.; 262 higher ed. **Avg. salary, public school teachers** (1980): $19,450.

State Data. Motto: Eureka (I have found it). **Flower:** Golden poppy. **Bird:** California valley quail. **Tree:** California redwood. **Song:** I Love You, California. **Entered Union** Sept. 9, 1850; rank, 31st. **State fair** at: Sacramento; late Aug.—early Sept.

History. First European explorers were Cabrillo, 1542, and Drake, 1579. First settlement was the Spanish Alta California mission at San Diego, 1769, first in a string founded by Franciscan Father Junipero Serra. U. S. traders and settlers arrived in the 19th century and staged the abortive Bear Flag Revolt, 1846; the Mexican War began later in 1846 and U.S. forces occupied California; Mexico ceded the province to the U.S., 1848, the same year the Gold Rush began.

Tourist attractions. Scenic regions are Yosemite Valley; Lassen and Sequoia-Kings Canyon national parks; Lake Tahoe; the Mojave and Colorado deserts; San Francisco Bay; and Monterey Peninsula. Oldest living things on earth are believed to be a stand of Bristlecone pines in the Inyo National Forest, est. to be 4,600 years old. The world's tallest tree, the Howard Libbey redwood, 362 ft. with a girth of 44 ft., stands on Redwood Creek, Humboldt County.

Also, Palomar Observatory; Disneyland; J. Paul Getty Museum, Malibu; Tournament of Roses and Rose Bowl.

Famous Californians include Luther Burbank, John C. Fremont, Bret Harte, Wm. R. Hearst, Jack London, Aimee Semple McPherson, John Muir, William Saroyan, Junipero Serra, Leland Stanford, John Steinbeck, Earl Warren.

Chamber of Commerce: 455 Capitol Mall, Sacramento, CA 95814.

Colorado

Centennial State

People. Population (1981): 2,965,000; **rank:** 27. **Pop. density:** 28.6 per sq. mi. **Urban** (1980): 80.6%. **Racial distrib.** (1980): 88.9% White; 3.5% Black; Hispanic 339,300. **Major ethnic groups:** German, Russian, English, Italian. **Net migration** (1970-80): +668,811.

Geography. Total area: 104,247 sq. mi.; **rank:** 8. **Land area:** 103,766 sq. mi. **Acres forested land:** 22,271,000. **Location:** in west central U.S. **Climate:** low relative humidity, abundant sunshine, wide daily, seasonal temperatures ranges; alpine conditions in the high mountains. **Topography:** eastern dry high plains; hilly to mountainous central plateau; western Rocky Mountains of high ranges alternating with broad valleys and deep, narrow canyons. **Capital:** Denver.

Economy. Principal industries: manufacturing, government, mining, tourism, agriculture, aerospace, electronics equipment. **Principal manufactured goods:** computer equipment, instruments, foods, machinery, aerospace products, rubber, steel. **Value added by manufacture** (1979): $6.14 bln. **Agriculture: Chief crops:** corn, wheat, hay, sugar beets, barley, potatoes, apples, peaches, pears, soy beans. **Livestock** (1979): 3.1 mln. cattle; 330,000 hogs/pigs; 795,000 sheep; 6,450,000 poultry. **Timber/lumber** (1979): oak, ponderosa pine, Douglas fir; 330.8 mln. bd. ft. **Minerals** (1980): molybdenum, uranium, coal, natural gas, petroleum. Total mineral production valued at $2.3 bln. **International airports at:** Denver. **Value of construction** (1981): $4.38 bln. **Employment distribution** (1979): 21.2% trade; 17.1% serv.; 16.7% gvt.; 12.8% manuf. **Per capita income** (1981): $11,142. **Unemployment** (1981): 5.5%. **Tourism** (1979): out-of-state visitors spent $890 mln.

Finance. No. banks (1980): 442; **No. savings assns.** (1981): 46.

Federal government. No. federal civilian employees (Mar. 1981): 42,576. **Avg. salary:** $21,485. **Notable federal facilities:** U.S. Air Force Academy; U.S. Mint; Ft. Carson, Lowry AFB; Solar Energy Research Institute; U.S. Rail Transport. Test Center; N. Amer. Aerospace Defense Command.

Energy. Electricity production (1981, mwh, by source): Hydroelectric: 1.4 mln.; Mineral: 23.3 mln.; Nuclear: 748,931.

Education. No. schools: 1,435 elem. and second.; 41 higher ed. **Avg. salary, public school teachers** (1979): $16,205.

State data. Motto: Nil Sine Numine (Nothing without Providence). **Flower:** Rocky Mountain columbine. **Bird:** Lark bunting. **Tree:** Colorado blue spruce. **Song:** Where the Columbines Grow. Entered union Aug. 1, 1876; rank 38th. **State fair** at: Pueblo; last week in Aug.

History. Early civilization centered around Mesa Verde 2,000 years ago. The U.S. acquired eastern Colorado in the Louisiana Purchase, 1803; Lt. Zebulon M. Pike explored the area, 1806, discovering the peak that bears his name. After the Mexican War, 1846-48, U.S. immigrants settled in the east, former Mexicans in the south.

Tourist attractions. Rocky Mountain National Park; Garden of the Gods; Great Sand Dunes and Dinosaur national monuments; Pikes Peak and Mt. Evans highways; Mesa Verde National Park (pre-historic cliff dwellings); 35 major ski areas. The Grand Mesa tableland comprises Grand Mesa Forest, 659,584 acres, with 200 lakes stocked with trout.

Famous Coloradans include Frederick Bonfils, William N. Byers, M. Scott Carpenter, Jack Dempsey, Douglas Fairbanks, Lowell Thomas, Byron R. White, Paul Whiteman.

Tourist information: Dept. of Local Affairs, 1313 Sherman St., Denver, CO 80203.

Connecticut

Constitution State, Nutmeg State

People. Population (1981): 3,134,000; **rank:** 25. **Pop. density:** 644.6 per sq. mi. **Urban** (1980): 78.8% **Racial distrib.** (1980): 90.0% White; 6.9% Black; Hispanic 124,499. **Major ethnic groups:** Italian, Polish, English, Irish. **Net migration** (1970-79): −37,000.

Geography. Total area: 5,009 sq. mi.; **rank:** 48. **Land area:** 4,862 sq. mi. **Acres forested land:** 1,860,800. **Location:** New England state in the northeastern corner of the U.S. **Climate:** moderate; winters avg. slightly below freezing, warm, humid summers. **Topography:** western upland, the Berkshires, in the NW, highest elevations; narrow central lowland N-S; hilly eastern upland drained by rivers. **Capital:** Hartford.

Economy. Principal industries: manufacturing, retail trade, government, services. **Principal manufactured goods:** aircraft engines and parts, submarines, copper wire and tubing, silverware, helicopters, bearings, cutlery, machine tools. **Value added by manufacture** (1978): $12.2 bln. **Agriculture: Chief crops:** tobacco, hay, apples, potatoes, nursery stock. **Livestock:** 103,000 cattle; 12,000 hogs/pigs; 5,400 sheep; 6.0 mln. poultry. **Timber/lumber** (1980): oak, birch, beech, maple; 73 mln. bd. ft. **Minerals** (1980): stone, sand and gravel. Total mineral production valued at $62.8 mln. **Commercial fishing** (1980): $4.67 mln. **Chief ports:** New Haven, Bridgeport, New London. **International airports at:** Windsor Locks. **Value of construction** (1981): $1.82 bln. **Employment distribution:** 31% manuf.; 19% serv. **Per capita income** (1981): $12,995. **Unemployment** (1981): 6.2%. **Tourism** (1981): out-of-state visitors spent $1.8 bln.

Finance. Notable industries: insurance, finance, banking. **No. banks** (1980): 64; **No. savings assns.** (1981): 39.

Federal Government. No. federal civilian employees (Mar. 1981): 16,600. **Avg. salary:** $20,580. **Notable federal facilities:** U.S. Coast Guard Academy; U.S. Navy Submarine Base.

Energy Electricity production (1981, mwh, by source): Hydroelectric: 253,743; Mineral: 10.9 mln.; Nuclear: 12.7 mln.

Education. No. schools: 1,408 elem. and second.; 47 higher ed. **Avg. salary, public school teachers** (1979): $16,475.

State data. Motto: Qui Transtulit Sustinet (He who transplanted still sustains). **Flower:** Mountain laurel. **Bird:** American robin. **Tree:** White oak. **Song:** Yankee Doodle Dandy. **Fifth** of the 13 original states to ratify the Constitution, Jan. 9, 1788.

History. Adriaen Block, Dutch explorer, was the first European visitor, 1614. By 1634, settlers from Plymouth Bay started colonies along the Connecticut River and in 1637 defeated the Pequot Indians. In the Revolution, Connecticut men fought in most major campaigns and turned back British raids on Danbury and other towns, while Connecticut privateers captured British merchant ships.

Tourist attractions. Mark Twain House, Hartford; Yale University's Art Gallery, Peabody Museum, all in New Haven; Mystic Seaport, Mystic, a recreated 19th century seaport village; P.T. Barnum Museum, Bridgeport.

Famous "Nutmeggers" include Ethan Allen, Phineas T. Barnum, Samuel Colt, Jonathan Edwards, Nathan Hale, Katharine Hepburn, Isaac Hull, J. Pierpont Morgan, Israel Putnam, Harriet Beecher Stowe, Mark Twain, Noah Webster, Eli Whitney.

Tourist Information: State Dept. of Economic Development, 210 Washington St., Hartford, CT 06106.

Delaware

First State, Diamond State

People. Population (1981): 598,000; **rank:** 47. **Pop. density:** 301.7 per sq. mi. **Urban** (1980): 70.6%. **Racial distrib.** (1980): 82.0% White; 16.1% Black; Hispanic 9,671. **Major ethnic groups:** Italian, English, Polish, German. **Net migration** (1970-80): +7,470.

Geography. Total area: 2,057 sq. mi.; **rank:** 49. **Land area:** 1,982 sq. mi. **Acres forested land:** 391,800. **Location:** occupies the Delmarva Peninsula on the Atlantic coastal plain. **Climate:** moderate. **Topography:** Piedmont plateau to the N, sloping to a near sea-level plain. **Capital:** Dover.

Economy. Principal industries: chemistry, agriculture, poultry, shellfish, tourism, auto assembly, food processing, transportation equipment. **Principal manufactured goods:** nylon, apparel, luggage, foods, autos, processed meats and vegetables, railroad and aircraft equipment. **Value added by manufacture** (1978): $2.01 bln. **Agriculture: Chief crops:** soybeans, corn, potatoes, mushrooms, greenhouse and dairy products, grain, hay. **Livestock:** 31,000 cattle; 50,000 hogs/pigs; 1,700 sheep; 850,000 poultry. **Timber/Lumber:** 408 mln. bd. ft. **Minerals** (1978): Sand and gravel. Total mineral production valued at $2.2 mln. **Commercial fishing** (1980): $4.6 mln. **Chief ports:** Wilmington. **International airports at:** Philadelphia/Wilmington. **Value of construction** (1981): $496 mln. **Employment distribution:** 72.7% non-manufacturing; 27.3% manuf. **Per capita income** (1981): $11,279. **Unemployment** (1981): 7.9%. **Tourism** (1979): out-of-state visitors spent $358.5 mln.

Finance. No. banks (1980): 20; **No. savings assns.** (1981): 15.

Federal government. No. federal civilian employees (Mar. 1981): 4,177. **Avg. salary:** $20,193. **Notable federal facilities:** Dover Air Force Base, Federal Wildlife Refuge, Bombay Hook.

Energy. Electricity production (1981, mwh, by source): Mineral: 8.3 mln.

Education. No. schools: 254 elem. and second.; 10 higher ed. **Avg. salary, public school teachers** (1980): $16,148.

State data. Motto: Liberty and independence. **Flower:** Peach blossom. **Bird:** Blue hen chicken. **Tree:** American holly. **Song:** Our Delaware. **First** of original 13 states to ratify the Constitution, Dec. 7, 1787. **State fair** at: Harrington; end of July.

History. The Dutch first settled in Delaware near present Lewes, 1631, but were wiped out by Indians. Swedes settled at present Wilmington, 1638; Dutch settled anew, 1651, near New Castle and seized the Swedish settlement, 1655, only to lose all Delaware and New Netherland to the British, 1664.

Tourist attractions. Ft. Christina Monument, the site of founding of New Sweden; John Dickinson "Penman of the Revolution" home, Dover; Henry Francis du Pont Winterthur Museum; Hagley Museum, Wilmington; Old Swedes (Trinity Parish) Church, erected 1698, is the oldest Protestant church in the U.S. still in use.

Famous Delawareans include Thomas F. Bayard, Henry Seidel Canby, E. I. du Pont, John P. Marquand, Howard Pyle, Caesar Rodney.

Chamber of Commerce: 1102 West St., Wilmington, DE 19081.

Florida

Sunshine State

People. Population (1981): 10,183,000; **rank:** 7. **Pop. density:** 188.3 per sq. mi. **Urban** (1980): 84.3%. **Racial distrib.** (1980): 83.9% White; 13.7% Black; Hispanic 858,158. **Major ethnic groups:** German, English, Italian, Russian. **Net migration** (1970-81): +3,281,954.

Geography: Total area: 58,560 sq. mi.; **rank:** 22. **Land area:** 54,136 sq. mi. **Acres forested land:** 17,932,900. **Location:** peninsula jutting southward 500 mi. bet. the Atlantic and the Gulf of Mexico. **Climate:** subtropical N of Bradenton-Lake Okeechobee-Vero Beach line; tropical S of line. **Topography:** land is flat or rolling; highest point is 345 ft. in the NW. **Capital:** Tallahassee.

Economy. Principal industries: services, trade, gvt., agriculture, tourism, manufacturing, aerospace, food processing, chemical, finance, insurance, real estate, construction. **Principal manufactured goods:** metal products, paper, electronics equip., transp. equipment. **Value added by manufacture** (1980): $11.2 bln. **Agriculture: Chief crops:** citrus fruits, vegetables, sugarcane, avocados, watermelons, peanuts, cotton, tobacco, strawberries, peaches. **Livestock** (1981): 2.8 mln. cattle; 370,000 hogs/pigs; 4,500 sheep; 12 mln. poultry. **Timber/lumber** (1980): pine, oak, cypress, palm; 468 mln. bd. ft. **Minerals** (1979): petroleum, stone, phosphate rock. Total mineral production valued at $1.9 bln. **Commercial fishing** (1981): $124.8 mln. **Chief ports:** Tampa, Jacksonville, Miami, Pensacola. **International airports at:** Miami, Tampa, Jacksonville, Orlando, Ft. Lauderdale, W. Palm Beach. **Value of construction** (1981): $12.29 bln. **Per capita income** (1981): $10,050. **Unemployment** (1981): 6.8% **Tourism** (1981): out-of-state visitors spent $18 bln.

Finance. No. banks (1980): 565; **No. savings assns.** (1981): 128.

Federal government. No. federal civilian employees (Mar. 1981): 71,727. **Avg. salary:** $20,853. **Notable federal facilities:** John F. Kennedy Space Center, Cape Canaveral; Eglin Air Force Base.

Energy. Electricity production (1981, mwh, by source): Hydroelectric: 179,901; Mineral: 84.4 mln.; Nuclear: 14.5 mln.

Education. No. schools: 2,695 elem. and second.; 77 higher ed. **Avg. salary, public school teachers** (1980): $14,149.

State data. Motto: In God we trust. **Flower:** Orange blossom. **Bird:** Mockingbird. **Tree:** Sabal palmetto palm. **Song:** Swanee River. **Entered union** Mar. 3, 1845; rank, 27th. **State fair** at: Tampa; Feb.

History. First European to see Florida was Ponce de Leon, 1513. France established a colony, Fort Caroline, on the St. Johns River, 1564; Spain settled St. Augustine, 1565, and Spanish troops massacred most of the French. Britain's Francis Drake burned St. Augustine, 1586. Britain held the area briefly, 1763-83, returning it to Spain. After Andrew Jackson led a U.S. invasion, 1818, Spain ceded Florida to the U.S., 1819. The Seminole War, 1835-42, resulted in removal of most Indians to Oklahoma. Florida seceded from the Union, 1861, was readmitted, 1868.

Tourist attractions. Miami, with the nation's greatest concentration of luxury hotels at Miami Beach; St. Augustine, oldest city in U.S.; Walt Disney World, an entertainment and vacation development near Orlando, Kennedy Space Center, Cape Canaveral.

Everglades National Park, 3d largest of U.S. national parks, preserves the beauty of the vast Everglades swamp. Castillo de San Marcos, St. Augustine, is a national monument. Also, the Ringling Museum of Art, and the Ringling Museum of the Circus, both in Sarasota; Sea World, and Circus World, Orlando; Busch Gardens, Tampa.

Famous Floridians include Henry M. Flagler, James Weldon Johnson, MacKinlay Kantor, Henry B. Plant, Marjorie Kinnan Rawlings, Joseph W. Stilwell, Charles P. Summerall.

Chamber of Commerce: P.O. Box 5497, Tallahassee, FL 32301.

Georgia

Empire State of the South, Peach State

People. Population (1981): 5,574,000; **rank:** 12. **Pop. density:** 96.0 per sq. mi. **Urban** (1980): 62.4%. **Racial distrib.** (1980): 72.2% White; 26.8% Black; Hispanic 61,261. **Major ethnic groups:** German, English, Russian, Italian. **Net migration** (1970-79): +128,000.

Geography. Total area: 58,876 sq. mi.; **rank:** 21. **Land area:** 58,073 sq. mi. **Acres forested land:** 25,256,100. **Location:** South Atlantic state. **Climate:** maritime tropical air masses dominate in summer; continental polar air masses in winter; east central area drier. **Topography:** most southerly of the Blue Ridge Mtns. cover NE and N central; central Piedmont extends to the fall line of rivers; coastal plain levels to the coast flatlands. **Capital:** Atlanta.

Economy. Principal industries: manufacturing, forestry, agriculture, chemicals. **Principal manufactured goods:** textiles, transportation equipment, foods, clothing, paper and wood products, chemical products, cigarettes. **Value added by manufacture** (1978): $13.9 bln. **Agriculture: Chief crops:** cotton, peanuts, tobacco, pecans, peaches, rye, corn, soybeans. **Livestock** (1978): 1.85 mln. cattle; 1.59 mln. hogs/pigs; 3,200 sheep; 38.6 mln. poultry. **Timber/lumber** (1978): pine, hardwood; 1.3 bln. bd. ft. **Minerals** (1978): clay, crushed stone, and cement accounted for 91% of the total mineral production (valued at $577 mln.). **Commercial fishing** (1980): $20.1 mln. **Chief ports:** Savannah, Brunswick. **International airports at:** Atlanta. **Value of construction** (1981): $3.8 bln. 3.8 bln. Employment distribution: 25.2% manuf.; 22% trade; 14.2% serv. **Per capita income** (1981): $8,960. **Unemployment** (1981): 6.4% **Tourism** (1979): tourists spent $2.2 bln.

Finance. No. banks (1980): 435; **No. savings assns.** (1981): 88.

Federal government. No. federal civilian employees (Mar. 1981): 70,030. **Avg. salary:** $20,709. **Notable federal facilities:** Robins AFB; Fts. Benning, Gordon, McPherson; Nat'l. Law Enforcement Training Ctr., Glynco.

Energy. Electricity production (1981, mwh, by source): Hydroelectric: 2.3 mln.; Mineral: 52.4 mln.; Nuclear: 7.2 mln.

Education. No. schools: 2,057 elem. and second.; 82 higher ed. **Avg. salary, public school teachers** (1980): $14,027.

State data. Motto: Wisdom, justice and moderation. **Flower:** Cherokee rose. **Bird:** Brown thrasher. **Tree:** Live oak. **Song:** Georgia On My Mind. **Fourth** of the 13 original states to ratify the Constitution, Jan. 2, 1788.

History. Gen. James Oglethorpe established the first settlements, 1733, for poor and religiously-persecuted Englishmen. Oglethorpe defeated a Spanish army from Florida at Bloody Marsh, 1742. In the Revolution, Georgians seized the Savannah armory, 1775, and sent the munitions to the Continental Army; they fought seesaw campaigns with Cornwallis' British troops, twice liberating Augusta and forcing final evacuation by the British from Savannah, 1782.

Tourist attractions. The Little White House in Warm Springs where Pres. Franklin D. Roosevelt died Apr. 12, 1945, 2,500-acre Callaway Gardens, Jekyll Island State Park, the restored 1850s farming community of Westville; Dahlonega, site of America's first gold rush; Stone Mountain, and Six Flags Over Georgia.

Okefenokee in the SE is one of the largest swamps in the U.S., a wetland wilderness and peat bog covering 660 sq. mi. A large part of it is a National Wildlife Refuge, a home for wild birds, alligators, bear, deer.

Famous Georgians include James Bowie, Erskine Caldwell, Lucius D. Clay, Ty Cobb, John C. Fremont, Joel Chandler Harris, Martin Luther King Jr., Sidney Lanier, Margaret Mitchell, Joseph Wheeler.

Chamber of Commerce: 1200 Commerce Bldg., Atlanta, GA 30303.

Hawaii

Aloha State

People. Population (1981): 981,000; **rank:** 40. **Pop. density:** 152.7 per sq. mi. **Urban** (1980): 86.5%. **Racial distrib.** (1980): 33.0% White; 1.7% Black; 65.1% Other (includes Asian Americans and Pacific Islanders); Hispanic 71,479. **Major ethnic groups:** Caucasian, Japanese, part-Hawaiian, Filipino, Chinese. **Net migration.** (1970-80): +36,200.

Geography. Total area: 6,450 sq. mi.; **rank:** 47. **Land area:** 6,425 sq. mi. **Acres forested land:** 1,986,000. **Location:** Hawaiian Islands lie in the North Pacific, 2,397 mi. SW from San Francisco. **Climate:** temperate, mountain regions cooler; Mt. Waialeale, on Kauai, wettest spot in the U.S. annual rainfall 486.1 in. **Topography:** islands are tops of a chain of submerged volcanic mountains; active volcanoes: Mauna Loa, Kilauea. **Capital:** Honolulu.

Economy. Principal industries: tourism, government, sugar refining, agriculture, aquaculture, fishing, motion pictures, manufacturing. **Principal manufactured goods:** sugar, canned pineapple, clothing, foods. **Value added by manufacture** (1978): $598.2 mln. **Agriculture: Chief crops:** sugar, pineapples, macadamia nuts, fruits, coffee, vegetables, melons, and floriculture. **Livestock:** 220,000 cattle; 57,000 hogs/pigs; 1.3 mln. poultry. **Minerals** (1979): Portland cement, stone. Total mineral production valued at $55 mln. **Commercial fishing** (1980): $11.87 mln. **Chief ports:** Honolulu, Port Allen, Kahului, Hilo. **International airports at:** Honolulu. **Value of construction** (1981): $9.2 mln. **Employment distribution:** 26% serv.; 23.4% gvt.; 22.6% trade. **Per capita income** (1981): $11,096. **Unemployment** (1981): 5.4%. **Tourism** (1981): visitors spent $3.2 bln.

Finance. No. banks (1980): 12; **No. savings assns.** (1981): 7.

Federal government. No. federal civilian employees (Mar. 1981): 23,572. **Avg. salary:** $21,773. **Notable federal facilities:** Pearl Harbor Naval Shipyard; Hickam AFB; Schofield Barracks.

Energy. Electricity production (1981, mwh, by source): Hydroelectric: 13,723; Mineral: 6.5 mln.

Education. No. schools: 322 elem. and second.; 12 higher ed. **Avg. salary, public school teachers** (1980): $18,339.

State data. Motto: The life of the land is perpetuated in righteousness. **Flower:** Hibiscus. **Bird:** Hawaiian goose. **Tree:** Candlenut. **Song:** Hawaii Ponoi. **Entered union** Aug. 21, 1959; rank, 50th. **State fair** at: Honolulu; late May through mid-June.

History. Polynesians from islands 2,000 mi. to the south settled the Hawaiian Islands, probably about 700 A.D. First European visitor was British Capt. James Cook, 1778. Missionaries arrived, 1820, taught religion, reading and writing. King Kamehameha III and his chiefs created the first Constitution and a Legislature which set up a public school system. Sugar production began in 1835, it became the dominant industry. In 1893, Queen Liliuokalani was deposed, followed, 1894, by a republic headed by Sanford B. Dole. Annexation by the U.S. came in 1898.

Tourist attractions. Natl. Memorial Cemetery of the Pacific, USS Arizona Memorial, Pearl Harbor; Hawaii Volcanoes, Haleakala National Parks, Polynesian Cultural Center, Diamond Head, Waikiki Beach, Oahu.

Famous Islanders include John A. Burns, Father Joseph Damien, Sanford B. Dole, Wallace R. Farrington, Hiram L. Fong, Daniel K. Inouye, Duke Kahanamoku, King Kamehameha The Great, Queen Kaahumanu, Queen Liliuokalani, Bernice Pauahi Bishop, Bette Midler.

Chamber of Commerce: Dillingham Bldg., 735 Bishop St., Honolulu, HI 96813.

Idaho

Gem State

People. Population (1981): 959,000; **rank:** 41. **Pop. density:** 11.6 per sq. mi. **Urban** (1980): 54.0%. **Racial distrib.** (1980): 95.5% White; 0.3% Black; Hispanic 36,615. **Major ethnic groups:** English, German, Swedish, Norwegian. **Net migration** (1970-80): +129,000.

Geography. Total area: 83,557 sq. mi.; **rank:** 13. **Land area:** 82,677 sq. mi. **Acres forested land:** 21,726,600. **Location:** Pacific Northwest-Mountain state bordering on British Columbia. **Climate:** tempered by Pacific westerly winds; drier, colder, continental clime in SE; altitude an important factor. **Topography:** Snake R. plains in the S; central region of mountains, canyons, gorges (Hells Canyon, 7,000 ft., deepest in N.A.); subalpine northern region. **Capital:** Boise.

Economy. Principal industries: agriculture, manufacturing, tourism, lumber, mining, electronics. **Principal manufactured goods:** processed foods, lumber and wood products, chemical products, primary metals, fabricated metal products, machinery. **Value added by manufacture** (1980): $1.8 bln. **Agriculture: Chief crops:** potatoes, peas, sugar beets, alfalfa seed, wheat, hops, barley, plums and prunes, mint, onions, corn, cherries, apples, trout. **Livestock:** 1.99 mln. cattle; 175,000 hogs/pigs; 512,000 sheep; 1.023 mln. poultry. **Timber/lumber** (1978): yellow, white pine; Douglas fir; white spruce; 2.0 bln. bd. ft. **Minerals** (1979): silver, phosphate rock, lead, zinc, sand and gravel. Total mineral production valued at $415 mln. **Commercial fishing** (1979): $35,000. **Chief ports:** Lewiston. **International airports at:** Boise. **Value of construction** (1981) $653 mln. **Employment distribution:** 20% trade; 15% serv., 13% manuf.; 9% agric. **Per capita income** (1981): $8,906. **Unemployment** (1981): 7.6%. **Tourism** (1981): out-of-state visitors spent $1 bln.

Finance. No. banks (1980): 26; **No. savings assns.** (1981): 9.

Federal government. No. federal civilian employees (Mar. 1981): 8,374. **Avg. salary:** $20,814. **Notable federal facilities:** Ida. Nat'l. Engineering Lab, Idaho Falls; Nat'l. Reactor Testing Sta., Upper Snake River Plains.

Energy. Electricity production (1981, mwh, by source): Hydroelectric: 9.5 mln.; Mineral: 1,333.

Education: No. schools: 596 elem. and second.; 9 higher ed. **Avg. salary, public school teachers** (1980): $13,615.

State data. Motto: Esto Perpetua (It is perpetual). **Flower:** Syringa. **Bird:** Mountain bluebird. **Tree:** White pine. **Song:** Here We Have Idaho. **Entered union** July 3, 1890; rank, 43d. **State fair** at: Boise and Coeur d'Alene; late Aug.—early Sept.

History. Exploration of the Idaho area began with Lewis and Clark, 1805-06. Next came fur traders, setting up posts, 1809-34, and missionaries, establishing missions, 1830s-1850s. Mormons made their first permanent settlement at Franklin, 1860. Idaho's Gold Rush began that same year, and brought thousands of permanent settlers. Strangest of the Indian Wars was the 1,300-mi. trek in 1877 of Chief Joseph and the Nez Perce tribe, pursued by troops that caught them a few miles short of the Canadian border. In 1890, Idaho adopted a progressive Constitution and became a state.

Tourist attractions. Hells Canyon, deepest gorge in N.A.; Craters of the Moon; Sun Valley, year-round resort in the Sawtooth Mtns.; Crystal Falls Cave; Shoshone Falls; Lava Hot Springs; Lake Pend Oreille; Lake Coeur d'Alene.

Famous Idahoans include William E. Borah, Fred T. Dubois, Chief Joseph, Sacagawea.

Chamber of Commerce: P.O. Box 389, Boise, ID 83701.

Illinois

The Inland Empire

People. Population (1981): 11,462,000; **rank:** 5. **Pop. density:** 205.6 per sq. mi. **Urban** (1980): 83.3%. **Racial distrib.** (1980): 80.7% White; 14.6% Black; Hispanic 635,525. **Major ethnic groups:** German, Polish, Italian, English, Russian. **Net migration** (1970-79): −542,000.

Geography. Total area: 56,400 sq. mi.; **rank:** 24. **Land area:** 55,748 sq. mi. **Acres forested land:** 3,810,400. **Location:** east-north central state; western, southern, and eastern boundaries formed by Mississippi, Ohio, and Wabash Rivers, respectively. **Climate:** temperate; typically cold, snowy winters, hot summers. **Topography:** prairie and fertile plains throughout; open hills in the southern region. **Capital:** Springfield.

Economy. Principal industries: manufacturing, wholesale and retail trade, finance, insurance, real estate, agricultural, services. **Principal manufactured goods:** machinery, electric and electronic equipment, foods, primary and fabricated metals, chemical products, printing and publishing. **Value added by manufacture** (1978): $44.8 bln. **Agriculture: Chief crops:** corn, soybeans, wheat, oats, hay. **Livestock** (1980): 2.65 mln. cattle; 6.95 mln. hogs/pigs; 184,000 sheep; 6.9 mln. poultry. **Timber/lumber** (1978): cottonwood, gum, walnut; 221 mln. bd. ft. **Minerals** (1977): mineral fuels (coal, natural gas, petroleum) accounted for 75% of the total $1.7 bln. mineral production. Also stone, sand and gravel, cement. **Commercial fishing** (1980): $2.0 mln. **Chief ports:** Chicago. **International airports at:** Chicago. **Value of construction** (1981): $4.8 bln. **Employment distribution:** 24% manuf.; 23% trade; 20% serv.; 2% agric. **Per capita income** (1981): $11,479. **Unemployment** (1981) 8.5%. **Tourism** (1980): out-of-state visitors spent $4.0 bln.

Finance. Notable industries: insurance, real estate. **No. banks** (1980): 1,260; **No. savings assns.** (1981): 342.

Federal government. No. federal civilian employees (Mar. 1981): 86,599. **Avg. salary:** $20,584. **Notable federal facilities:** Fermi Nat'l. Accelerator Lab; Argonne Nat'l. Lab; Ft. Sheridan; Rock Island; Great Lakes, Rantoul, Scott Field.

Energy. Electricity production (1981, mwh, by source): Hydroelectric: 116,848; Mineral: 69.3 mln.; Nuclear: 29.5 mln.

Education. No. schools: 5,592 elem. and second.; 154 higher ed. **Avg. salary, public school teachers** (1980): $17,781.

State data. Motto: State sovereignty—national union. **Flower:** Native violet. **Bird:** Cardinal. **Tree:** White oak. **Song:** Illinois. **Entered union** Dec. 3, 1818; rank, 21st. **State fair** at: Springfield; early Aug.

History. Fur traders were the first Europeans in Illinois, followed shortly, 1673, by Jolliet and Marquette, and, 1680, La Salle, who built a fort near present Peoria. First settlements were French, at Fort St. Louis on the Illinois River, 1692, and Kaskaskia, 1700. France ceded the area to Britain, 1763; Amer. Gen. George Rogers Clark, 1778, took Kaskaskia from the British without a shot. Defeat of Indian tribes in Black Hawk War, 1832, and railroads in 1850s, inspired immigration.

Tourist attractions: Lincoln shrines at Springfield, New Salem, Sangamon; Cahokia Mounds, E. St. Louis; Starved Rock State Park; Crab Orchard Wildlife Refuge; Mormon settlement at Nauvoo; Fts. Kaskaskia, Chartres, Massac (parks).

Famous Illinoisans include Jane Addams, William Jennings Bryan, Stephen A. Douglas, James T. Farrell, Ernest Hemingway, Edgar Lee Masters, Carl Sandburg, Adlai Stevenson, Frank Lloyd Wright.

Tourist Information: Illinois Dept. of Commerce and Community Affairs, 222 South College, Springfield, IL 62706.

Indiana

Hoosier State

People. Population (1981): 5,468,000; **rank:** 13. **Pop. density:** 151.5 per sq. mi. **Urban** (1980): 64.2%. **Racial distrib.** (1980): 91.1 White; 7.5% Black; Hispanic 87,020. **Major ethnic groups:** German, Polish, English, Mexican. **Net migration** (1970-79): −150,000.

Geography. Total area: 36,291 sq. mi.; **rank:** 38. **Land area:** 36,097 sq. mi. **Acres forested land:** 3,942,900. **Location:** east north-central state; Lake Michigan on northern border. **Climate:** 4 distinct seasons with a temperate climate. **Topography:** hilly southern region; fertile rolling plains of central region; flat, heavily glaciated north; dunes along Lake Michigan shore. **Capital:** Indianapolis.

Economy: Principal industries: manufacturing, wholesale and retail trade, agriculture, government, services. **Principal manufactured goods:** primary and fabricated metals, transportation equipment, electrical and electronic equipment, non-electrical machinery, chemical products, foods. **Value added by manufacture** (1978): 25.6 bln. **Agriculture: Chief crops:** corn, wheat, soybeans, hay. **Livestock** (1980): 1.85 mln. cattle; 4.9 mln. hogs/pigs; 165,000 sheep; 20.5 mln. poultry. **Timber/lumber** (1977): oak, tulip, beech, sycamore; 166 mln. bd. ft. **Minerals** (1979): mineral fuels, esp. coal; sand, gravel, stone; total $829.0 mln. mineral production. **Commercial fishing** (1980): $112,000. **Chief ports:** Lake Michigan facility, east of Gary, Southwind Maritime Centre at Mt. Vernon. **International airports at:** Indianapolis. **Value of construction** (1981): $2.37 bln. **Employment distribution** (1981): 31.1% manuf.; 22.2% trade; 16.1% serv. **Per capita income** (1981): $9,656. **Unemployment** (1981). 10.1%. **Tourism** (1979): tourists spent $2.1 bln.

Finance. No. banks (1980): 407; **No. savings assns.** (1981): 135.

Federal government. No. federal civilian employees (Mar. 1981): 33,926 **Avg. salary:** $20,002. **Notable federal facilities:** Naval Avionics Ctr.; Ft. Benjamin Harrison; Grissom AFB; Navy Weapons Support Ctr., Crane.

Energy. Electricity production (1981 mwh, by source): Hydroelectric: 508,684; Mineral: 67.3 mln.

Education. No. schools: 2,540 elem. and second.; 66 higher ed. **Avg. salary, public school teachers** (1980): $15,078.

State data. Motto: Crossroads of America. **Flower:** Peony. **Bird:** Cardinal. **Tree:** Tulip poplar. **Song:** On the Banks of the Wabash, Far Away. **Entered union** Dec. 11, 1816; rank, 19th. **State fair** at: Indianapolis; mid-Aug.

History: Pre-historic Indian Mound Builders of 1,000 years ago were the earliest known inhabitants. A French trading post was built, 1731-32, at Vincennes and La Salle visited the present South Bend area, 1679 and 1681. France ceded the area to Britain, 1763. During the Revolution, American Gen. George Rogers Clark captured Vincennes, 1778, and defeated British forces 1779; at war's end Britain ceded the area to the U.S. Miami Indians defeated U.S. troops twice, 1790, but were beaten, 1794, at Fallen Timbers by Gen. Anthony Wayne. At Tippecanoe, 1811, Gen. William H. Harrison defeated Tecumseh's Indian confederation.

Tourist attractions. Lincoln, George Rogers Clark memorials; Wyandotte Cave; Vincennes, Tippecanoe sites; Indiana Dunes; Hoosier Nat'l. Forest; Benjamin Harrison Home.

Famous "Hoosiers" include Ambrose Burnside, Hoagy Carmichael, Eugene V. Debs, Theodore Dreiser, Paul Dresser, Cole Porter, Gene Stratton Porter, Ernie Pyle, James Whitcomb Riley, Booth Tarkington, Lew Wallace, Wendell L. Willkie, Wilbur Wright.

Chamber of Commerce: Board of Trade Building, Indianapolis, IN 46204.

Iowa

Hawkeye State

People. Population (1981): 2,899,000; **rank:** 28. **Pop. density:** 51.8 per sq. mi. **Urban** (1980): 58.6%. **Racial distrib.** (1980): 97.4% White; 1.4% Black; Hispanic 15,852. **Major ethnic groups:** German, Scandinavian, English, Dutch. **Net migration** (1970-80): −60,491.

Geography. Total area: 56,290 sq. mi.; **rank:** 25. **Land area:** 55,941 sq. mi. **Acres forested land:** 1,561,300. **Location:** Midwest state bordered by Mississippi R. on the E and Missouri R. on the W. **Climate:** humid, continental.

Topography: Watershed from NW to SE; soil especially rich and land level in the N central counties. **Capital:** Des Moines.

Economy. Principal industries: manufacturing, agriculture. **Principal manufactured goods:** tires, farm machinery, electronic products, appliances, office furniture, chemicals, fertilizers, auto accessories. **Value added by manufacture** (1978): $9.8 bln. **Agriculture: Chief crops:** silage and grain corn, soybeans, oats, hay. **Livestock** (1980): 2.7 mln. cattle; 23.4 mln. hogs/pigs; 313,000 sheep; 7.9 mln. poultry. **Timber/lumber:** red cedar. **Minerals** (1980): cement, stone, and sand and gravel accounted for 93% of the total $248 mln. production. **Commercial fishing** (1980): $900,000 **Value of construction** (1981): 1.25 bln. **Employment distribution:** 25.4% trade; 22.1% manuf.; 18.9% serv.; 18.8% gvt. **Per capita income** (1981): $10,149. **Unemployment** (1981): 6.9%. **Tourism** (1978): tourists spent $1.27 bln.

Finance. No. banks (1980): 657; **No. savings assns.** (1981): 65.

Federal government. No. federal civilian employees (Mar. 1981): 14,054. **Avg. salary:** $20,056.

Energy. Electricity production (1981, mwh, by source): Hydroelectric: 980,277; Mineral: 19.4 mln.; Nuclear: 2.2 mln.

Education. No. schools: 2,153 elem. and second.; 62 higher ed. **Avg. salary, public school teachers** (1980): $15,340.

State data. Motto: Our liberties we prize and our rights we will maintain. **Flower:** Wild rose. **Bird:** Eastern goldfinch. **Tree:** Oak. **Song:** The Song of Iowa. **Entered union** Dec. 28, 1846; rank, 29th. **State fair** at: Des Moines; mid-to-late Aug.

History. A thousand years ago several groups of prehistoric Indian Mound Builders dwelt on Iowa's fertile plains. Marquette and Jolliet gave France its claim to the area, 1673. It became U.S. territory through the 1803 Louisiana Purchase. Indian tribes were moved into the area from states further east, but by mid-19th century were forced to move on to Kansas. Before and during the Civil War, Iowans strongly supported Abraham Lincoln and became traditional Republicans.

Tourist attractions. Herbert Hoover birthplace and library, West Branch; Effigy Mounds Nat'l. Monument, Marquette, a pre-historic Indian burial site; Davenport Municipal Art Gallery's collection of Grant Wood's paintings and memorabilia.

Famous Iowans include James A. Van Allen, Marquis Childs, Buffalo Bill Cody, Susan Glaspell, James Norman Hall, Harry Hansen, Billy Sunday, Carl Van Vechten, Henry Wallace, Meredith Willson, Grant Wood.

Tourist information: Travel Development Council, 250 Jewett Bldg., Des Moines, IA 50319.

Kansas

Sunflower State

People. Population (1981): 2,383,000; **rank:** 32. **Pop. density:** 29.1 per sq. mi. **Urban** (1980): 66.7%. **Racial distrib.** (1980): 91.7% White; 5.3% Black; Hispanic 63,333. **Major ethnic groups:** German, Russian, English, Mexican. **Net migration** (1970-80): −20,334.

Geography. Total area: 82,264 sq. mi.; **rank:** 14. **Land area:** 81,787 sq. mi. **Acres forested land:** 1,344,400. **Location:** West North Central state, with Missouri R. on E. **Climate:** temperate but continental, with great extremes bet. summer and winter. **Topography:** hilly Osage Plains in the E; central region level prairie and hills; high plains in the W. **Capital:** Topeka.

Economy. Principal industries: agriculture, machinery, mining, aerospace. **Principal manufactured goods:** processed foods, aircraft, petroleum products, farm machinery. **Value added by manufacture** (1978): $6.1 bln. **Agriculture: Chief crops:** wheat, sorghum, corn, hay. **Livestock:** 6.0 mln. cattle; 1.77 mln. hogs/pigs; 200,000 sheep; 2.26 mln. poultry. **Timber/lumber:** oak, walnut. **Minerals** (1980): petroleum, natural gas liquids, cement, salt, stone, sand and gravel. Total mineral production $3.5 bln. **Commercial fishing** (1980): $39,000 **Chief ports:** Kansas City. **International airports at:** Wichita. **Value of construction** (1981): $1.28 bln. **Employment distribution** (1981): 19.6% trade; 16.1% manuf.; 16.0% gvt.; 14.9% serv. **Per capita income** (1981): $10,870. **Unemployment** (1981): 4.2%. **Tourism** (1978): out-of-state visitors spent $1.1 bln.

Finance. No. banks (1980): 620; **No. savings assns.** (1981): 77.

Federal government. No. federal civilian employees (Mar. 1981): 18,773. **Avg. salary:** 20,224. **Notable federal facilities:** McConnell AFB; Fts. Riley, Leavenworth.

Energy. Electricity production (1981, mwh, by source): Hydroelectric: 7,614; Mineral: 24.5 mln..

Education. No. schools: 1,801 elem. and second.; 52 higher ed. **Avg. salary, public school teachers** (1980): $13,690.

State data. Motto: Ad Astra per Aspera (To the stars through difficulties). **Flower:** Native sunflower. **Bird:** Western meadowlark. **Tree:** Cottonwood. **Song:** Home on the Range. **Entered union** Jan. 29, 1861; rank, 34th. **State fair** at: Hutchinson; 2d week of Sept.

History. Coronado marched through the Kansas area, 1541; French explorers came next. The U.S. took over in the Louisiana Purchase, 1803. In the pre-war North-South struggle over slavery, so much violence swept the area it was called Bleeding Kansas. Railroad construction after the war made Abilene and Dodge City terminals of large cattle drives from Texas.

Tourist attractions. Eisenhower Center and "Place of Meditation," Abilene; Agricultural Hall of Fame and National Ctr., Bonner Springs, displays farm equipment; Dodge City; Ft. Scott.

Famous Kansans include Thomas Hart Benton, John Brown, Walter P. Chrysler, Amelia Earhart, Cyrus Holliday, Gen. Hugh Johnson, Walter Johnson, Alf Landon, Brock Pemberton, Robert Stroud.

Chamber of Commerce: 500 First National Tower, One Townsite Plaza, Topeka, KS 66603.

Kentucky

Bluegrass State

People. Population (1981): 3,662,000 **rank:** 24. **Pop. density:** 92.4 per sq. mi. **Urban** (1980): 50.9% **Racial Distrib.** (1980): 92.3% White; 7.1% Black; Hispanic (1970): 11,112. **Major ethnic groups:** German, English, Italian, Irish. **Net migration** (1970-79): +91,000.

Geography. Total area: 40,395 sq. mi.; **rank:** 37. **Land area:** 39,650 sq. mi. **Acres forested land:** 12,160,800. Location: east south central state, bordered on N by Illinois, Indiana, Ohio; on E by West Virginia and Virginia; in S by Tennessee; on W by Missouri. **Climate:** moderate, with plentiful rainfall. **Topography:** mountainous in E; rounded hills of the Knobs in the N; Bluegrass, heart of state; wooded rocky hillsides of the Pennyroyal; Western Coal Field; the fertile Purchase the SW. **Capital:** Frankfort.

Economy. Principal industries: manufacturing, coal mining, construction, agriculture. **Principal manufactured goods:** whiskey, textiles, cigarettes, steel products, trucks. **Value added by manufacture** (1978): $10.8 bln. **Agriculture: Chief crops:** tobacco, soybeans, corn, wheat, hay, fruit. **Livestock:** 2.7 mln. cattle; 1.3 mln. hogs/pigs; 21,000 sheep; 3.5 mln. chickens. **Timber/lumber** (1977): hardwoods, pines; 412 mln. bd. ft. **Minerals** (1979): fossil fuels accounted for 98% of the total $4 bln. mineral production. **Commercial fishing** (1978): $923,000. **Chief ports:** Paducah, Louisville, Covington, Owensboro, Ashland. **International airports at:** Covington. **Value of construction** (1981): $3.42 bln. **Employment distribution:** manuf. 23.9%; trade 21.5%; gvt. 18.5%; serv. 16.4%. **Per capita income** (1981): $8,455. **Unemployment** (1981): 8.4%. **Tourism** (1978): tourists spent $1.2 bln.

Finance. No. banks (1980): 345; **No. savings assns.** (1981): 90.

Federal government. No. federal civilian employees (Mar. 1981): 30,441. **Avg. salary:** $19,123. **Notable federal facilities:** U.S. Gold Bullion Depository; Ft. Knox; Addiction Research Center and Federal Correction Institution, Lexington.

Energy. Electricity production (1981, mwh, by source): Hydroelectric: 2.6 mln.; Mineral: 57.5 mln..

Education. No. schools: 1,677 elem. and second.; 42 higher ed. **Avg. salary, public school teachers** (1980): $14,480.

State data. Motto: United we stand, divided we fall. **Flower:** Goldenrod. **Bird:** Cardinal. **Tree:** Kentucky coffee tree. **Song:** My Old Kentucky Home. **Entered union** June 1, 1792; rank, 15th. **State fair** at: Louisville.

History. Kentucky was the first area west of the Alleghenies settled by American pioneers; first permanent settlement, Harrodsburg, 1774. Daniel Boone blazed the Wilderness Trail through the Cumberland Gap and founded Boonesboro, 1775. Indian attacks, spurred by the British, were unceasing until, during the Revolution, Gen. George Rogers Clark captured British forts in Indiana and Illinois, 1778. In 1792, after Virginia dropped its claims to the region, Kentucky became the 15th state.

Tourist attractions. Kentucky Derby and accompanying festivities, Louisville; Land Between the Lakes Nat'l. Recreation Area encompassing Kentucky Lake and Lake Barkley; Mammoth Cave with 150 mi. of passageways, 200-ft. high rooms, blind fish, and Echo River, 360 ft. below ground; Old Ft. Harrod State Park; Lincoln birthplace, Hodgenville; My Old Kentucky Home, Bardstown.

Famous Kentuckians include Muhammad Ali, Alben Barkley, Daniel Boone, Louis D. Brandeis, Kit Carson, Henry Clay, Jefferson Davis, John Fox Jr., Thomas Hunt Morgan, Elizabeth Madox Roberts, Col. Harland Sanders, Robert Penn Warren.

Chamber of Commerce: Versailles Rd., P.O. Box 817, Frankfort, KY 40601.

Louisiana

Pelican State

People. Population (1981): 4,308,000; **rank:** 18. **Pop. density:** 95.9 per sq. mi. **Urban** (1980): 68.7%. **Racial distrib.** (1980): 69.2% White; 29.4% Black; Hispanic 99,105. **Major ethnic groups:** Italian, German, English, French. **Net migration** (1970-79): +34,000.

Geography. Total area: 48,523 sq. mi.; **rank:** 31. **Land area:** 44,930 sq. mi. **Acres forested land:** 14,558,100. **Location:** south central Gulf Coast state. **Climate:** subtropical, affected by continental weather patterns. **Topography:** lowlands of marshes and Mississippi R. flood plain; Red R. Valley lowlands; upland hills in the Florida Parishes; average elevation, 100 ft. **Capital:** Baton Rouge.

Economy. Principal industries: wholesale and retail trade, government, manufacturing, construction, transportation, mining. **Principal manufactured goods:** chemical products, foods, transportation equipment, electronic equipment, apparel, petroleum products. **Value added by manufacture** (1978): $10.8 bln. **Agriculture: Chief crops:** soybean, sugarcane, rice, corn, cotton, sweet potatoes, melons, pecans. **Livestock:** 1.45 mln. cattle; 130,000 hogs/pigs; 9,900 sheep; 3.2 mln. poultry. **Timber/lumber** (1978): pines, hardwoods, oak; 2.2 bln. bd. ft. **Minerals** (1978): mineral fuels (natural gas, liquified petroleum gases, crude petroleum, natural gasoline and cycle products), sulfur, lime, salt, sand and gravel. Total mineral production valued at $12 bln. **Commercial fishing** (1980): $177.9 mln. **Chief ports:** New Orleans, Baton Rouge, Lake Charles, S. Louisiana Port Commission at La Place. **International airports at:** New Orleans. **Value of construction** (1981): $3.77 bln. **Employment distribution:** 28% trade; 23% gvt.; 22% serv.; 15% manuf.; 12% constr. **Per capita income** (1981): $9,486. **Unemployment** (1981): 8.4%. **Tourism** (1980): out-of-state visitors spent $2.15 bln.

Finance. Notable industries: finance, insurance, real estate. **No. banks** (1980): 269; **No. savings assn.** (1981): 128.

Federal government. No. federal civilian employees (Mar. 1981): 27,396. **Avg. salary:** $19,355. **Notable federal facilities:** Barksdale, England, Ft. Polk military bases; Strategic Petroleum Reserve, New Orleans; Michoud Assembly Plant, New Orleans; U.S. Public Service Hospital, Carville.

Energy. Electricity production (1981, mwh, by source): Mineral: 44.1 mln.

Education. No. schools: 1,878 elem. and second.; 32 higher ed. **Avg. salary, public school teachers** (1980): $13,770.

State data. Motto: Union, justice and confidence. **Flower:** Magnolia. **Bird:** Eastern brown pelican. **Tree:** Cypress. **Song:** Give Me Louisiana. **Entered union** Apr. 30, 1812; rank, 18th. **State fair** at: Shreveport; Oct.

History. The area was first visited, 1530, by Cabeza de Vaca and Panfilo de Narvaez. The region was claimed for France by LaSalle, 1682. First permanent settlement was by French at Fort St. Jean Baptiste (now Natchitoches), 1717. France ceded the region to Spain, 1762, took it back, 1800, and sold it to the U.S., 1803, in the Louisiana Purchase. During the Revolution, Spanish Louisiana aided the Americans. Admitted to statehood, 1812, Louisiana was the scene of the Battle of New Orleans, 1815.

Louisiana Creoles are descendants of early French and/or Spanish settlers. About 4,000 Acadians, French settlers in Nova Scotia, Canada, were forcibly transported by the British to Louisiana in 1755 (an event commemorated in Longfellow's *Evangeline*) and settled near Bayou Teche; their descendants became known as Cajuns. Another group, the Islenos, were descendants of Canary Islanders brought to Louisiana by a Spanish governor in 1770. Traces of Spanish and French survive in local dialects.

Tourist attractions. Mardi Gras, French Quarter, Superdome, Dixieland jazz, all New Orleans; Battle of New Orleans site; Longfellow-Evangeline Memorial Park.

Famous Louisianians include Louis Armstrong, Pierre Beauregard, Judah P. Benjamin, Braxton Bragg, Grace King, Huey Long, Leonidas K. Polk, Henry Miller Shreve, Edward D. White Jr.

Chamber of Commerce: P.O. Box 3988, Baton Rouge, LA 70821.

Maine

Pine Tree State

People. Population (1981): 1,133,000; **rank:** 39. **Pop. density:** 36.6 per sq. mi. **Urban** (1980): 47.5% **Racial distrib.** (1980): 98.3% White; 0.3% Black; Hispanic: 5,005. **Major ethnic groups:** English, Irish, Italian, German, French. **Net migration** (1970-80): +75,389.

Geography. Total area: 33,215 sq. mi.; **rank:** 39. **Land area:** 30,920 sq. mi. **Acres forested land:** 17,718,300. **Location:** New England state at northeastern tip of U.S. **Climate:** Southern interior and coastal, influenced by air masses from the S and W; northern clime harsher, avg. +100 in. snow in winter. **Topography:** Appalachian Mtns. extend through state; western borders have rugged terrain; long sand beaches on southern coast; northern coast mainly rocky promontories, peninsulas, fjords. **Capital:** Augusta.

Economy. Principal industries: manufacturing, services, trade, government, agriculture, fisheries, forestry. **Principal manufactured goods:** paper and wood products, textiles, leather, processed foods. **Value added by manufacture** (1978): $2.6 bln. **Agriculture: Chief crops:** potatoes ($139.8 mln.), apples, blueberries, sweet corn, peas, beans. **Livestock:** 131,000 cattle; 20,000 hogs/pigs; 13,000 sheep; 9.2 mln. poultry. **Timber/lumber** (1979): pine, spruce, fir; 409 mln. bd. ft. **Minerals** (1980): sand and gravel, cement, zinc, stone, copper. Total mineral production valued at $49.7 mln. **Commercial fishing** (1980): $92.7 mln. **Chief ports:** Searsport, Portland. **International airports at:** Portland, Bangor. **Value of con-**

struction (1981): $424 mln. **Employment distribution** (1980): 27% manuf.; 21.3% trade; 19.8% gvt.; 19.2% serv. **Per capita income** (1981): $8,655. **Unemployment** (1981): 7.2% **Tourism** (1979): out-of-state visitors spent more than $500 mln.

Finance. No. banks (1980): 41; **No. savings assns.** (1981): 19.

Federal government. No. federal civilian employees (Mar. 1981): 7,046. **Avg. salary:** $19,768. **Notable federal facilities:** Kittery Naval Shipyard; Brunswick Naval Air Station; Loring Air Force Base.

Energy. Electricity production (1981, mwh, by source): Hydroelectric: 1.9 mln.; Mineral: 2.2 mln.; Nuclear: 5.2 mln.

Education. No. schools: 847 elem. and second.; 27 higher ed. **Avg. salary, public school teachers** (1980): $12,450.

State data. Motto: Dirigo (I direct). **Flower:** White pine cone and tassel. **Bird:** Chickadee. **Tree:** Eastern white pine. **Song:** State of Maine Song. **Entered union** Mar. 15, 1820; rank, 23d.

History. Maine's rocky coast was explored by the Cabots, 1498-99. French settlers arrived, 1604, at the St. Croix River; English, 1607, on the Kennebec. In 1691, Maine was made part of Massachusetts. In the Revolution, a Maine regiment fought at Bunker Hill; a British fleet destroyed Falmouth (now Portland), 1775, but the British ship Margaretta was captured near Machiasport. In 1820, Maine broke off from Massachusetts, became a separate state.

Tourist attractions. Acadia Nat'l. Park, Bar Harbor, on Mt. Desert Is.; Bath Iron Works and Marine Museum; Boothbay (Harbor) Railway Museum; Sugarloaf/USA Ski Area; Ogunquit, Portland, York.

Famous "Down Easters" include James G. Blaine, Cyrus H.K. Curtis, Hannibal Hamlin, Longfellow, Sir Hiram and Hudson Maxim, Edna St. Vincent Millay, Kate Douglas Wiggin, Ben Ames Williams.

Chamber of Commerce: 477 Congress St., Portland, ME 04111.

Maryland

Old Line State, Free State

People. Population (1981): 4,263,000; rank: 19. **Pop. density:** 430.9 per sq. mi. **Urban** (1980): 80.3% **Racial distrib.** (1980): 74.9% White; 22.7% Black; Hispanic 64,740. **Major ethnic groups:** German, Italian, Russian, English, Polish. **Net migration** (1970-80): +48,000.

Geography. Total area: 10,577 sq. mi.; **rank:** 42. **Land area:** 9,891 sq. mi. **Acres forested land:** 2,653,200. **Location:** Middle Atlantic state stretching from the Ocean to the Allegheny Mtns. **Climate:** continental in the west; humid subtropical in the east. **Topography:** Eastern Shore of coastal plain and Maryland Main of coastal plain, piedmont plateau, and the Blue Ridge, separated by the Chesapeake Bay. **Capital:** Annapolis.

Economy. Principal industries: food, manufacturing, tourism. **Principal manufactured goods:** food and kindred products, primary metals, electric and electronic equipment. **Value added by manufacture** (1978): $7.7 bln. **Agriculture: Chief crops:** tobacco, corn, soybeans. **Livestock:** 380,000 cattle; 235,000 hogs/pigs; 18,000 sheep; 1.87 mln. poultry. **Timber/lumber** (1978): hardwoods; 213.1 mln. bd. ft. **Minerals** (1978): coal, stone, sand and gravel. Total value of mineral production, $217 mln. **Commercial fishing** (1980): $44.7 mln. **Chief ports:** Baltimore. **International airports at:** Baltimore. **Value of construction** (1981): 2.55 bln. **Employment distribution:** 24% government; 23.8% wholesale and retail trade; 19.9% services and mining. **Per capita income** (1981): $11,534. **Unemployment** (1981): 7.3%. **Tourism** (1980): tourists spent $13 bln.

Finance. No. banks (1980): 102; **No. savings assns.** (1981): 61.

Federal government. No. federal civilian employees (Mar. 1981): 118,647. **Avg. salary:** $23,078. **Notable federal facilities:** U.S. Naval Academy, Annapolis; Natl. Agric. Research Cen.; Ft. George C. Meade, Aberdeen Proving Ground.

Energy. Electricity production (1981, mwh, by source): Hydroelectric: 1.43 mln.; Mineral: 17.2 mln.; Nuclear: 11.5 mln.

Education. No. schools: 1,681 elem. and second.; 54 higher ed. **Avg. salary, public school teachers** (1980): $17,589.

State data. Motto. Fatti Maschii, Parole Femine (Manly deeds, womanly words). **Flower:** Black-eyed susan. **Bird:** Baltimore oriole. **Tree:** White oak. **Song:** Maryland, My Maryland. **Seventh** of the original 13 states to ratify Constitution, Apr. 28, 1788. **State fair** at: Timonium; end-Aug. to Sept. 7.

History. Capt. John Smith first explored Maryland, 1608. William Claiborne set up a trading post on Kent Is. in Chesapeake Bay, 1631. Britain granted land to Cecilius Calvert, Lord Baltimore, 1632; his brother led 200 settlers to St. Marys River, 1634. The bravery of Maryland troops in the Revolution, as at the Battle of Long Island, won the state its nickname, The Old Line State. In the War of 1812, when a British fleet tried to take Fort McHenry, Marylander Francis Scott Key, 1814, wrote *The Star-Spangled Banner.*

Tourist Attractions. Racing events include the Preakness, at Pimlico track, Baltimore; the International at Laurel Race Course; the John B. Campbell Handicap at Bowie. Also Annapolis yacht races; Ocean City summer resort; restored Ft. McHenry, Baltimore, near which Francis Scott Key wrote *The Star-Spangled Banner;* Antietam Battlefield, 1862, near Hagerstown; South Mountain Battlefield, 1862; Edgar Allan Poe house, Baltimore; The State House, Annapolis, 1772, the oldest still in use in the U.S.

Famous Marylanders include Benjamin Banneker, Francis Scott Key, H.L. Mencken, William Pinkney, Upton Sinclair, Roger B. Taney, Charles Willson Peale.

Chamber of Commerce: 60 West St., Annapolis, MD 21401.

Massachusetts

Bay State, Old Colony

People. Population (1981): 5,773,000; **rank:** 11. **Pop. density:** 737.7 per sq. mi. **Urban** (1980): 83.8% **Racial distrib.** (1980): 93.4% White; 3.8% Black; Hispanic 141,043. **Major ethnic groups:** Canadian, Italian, Irish, English, Polish. **Net migration** (1970-79): −145,225.

Geography. Total area: 8,257 sq. mi.; **rank:** 45. **Land area:** 7,826 sq. mi. **Acres forested land:** 2,952,300. **Location:** New England state along Atlantic seaboard. **Climate:** temperate, with colder and drier clime in western region. **Topography:** jagged indented coast from Rhode Island around Cape Cod; flat land yields to stony upland pastures near central region and gentle hilly country in west; except in west, land is rocky, sandy, and not fertile. **Capital:** Boston.

Economy. Principal industries: manufacturing, services, trade, construction. **Principal manufactured goods** (1980): electronics, machinery, instruments, fabricated metals, printing and publishing. **Value added by manufacture** (1978): $18.6 bln. **Agriculture: Chief crops:** nursery, greenhouse products, misc. vegetables, apples, tobacco, corn, potatoes. **Livestock** (1981): 103,000 cattle; 49,000 hogs/pigs; 9,632 sheep; 23,600 horses, ponies; 1.8 mln. poultry. **Timber/lumber** (1980): white pine, oak, other hard woods; 240 mln. bd. ft. **Minerals** (1979): sand and gravel, stone. Total value of mineral production $92.5 mln. **Commercial fishing** (1980): $178.6 mln. **Chief ports:** Boston, Fall River, Salem, Gloucester. **International airport at:** Boston. **Value of construction** (1981): $3.16 bln. **Employment distribution** (1980): 26.0% manuf.; 23.0% serv.; 22.2% trade. **Per capita income** (1981): $11,158. **Unemployment** (1981): 6.4%. **Tourism** (1980): out-of-state visitors spent $3.0 bln.

Finance. No. banks (1980): 140; **No. savings assns.** (1981): 29.

Federal government. No. federal civilian employees (Mar. 1981): 49,600. **Avg. salary:** $20,383. **Notable federal facilities:** Ft. Devens; U.S. Customs House, Boston; Q.M. Laboratory, Natick.

Energy. Electricity production (1981, mwh, by source): Hydroelectric: 367,523; Mineral: 28.2 mln.; Nuclear: 4.3 mln.

Education. No. schools: 2,838 elem. and second.; 119 higher ed. **Avg. salary, public school teachers** (1980): $17,000.

State data. Motto: Ense Petit Placidam Sub Libertate Quietem (By the sword we seek peace, but peace only under liberty). **Flower:** Mayflower. **Bird:** Chickadee. **Tree:** American elm. **Song:** All Hail to Massachusetts. **Sixth** of the original 13 states to ratify Constitution, Feb. 6, 1788.

History. The Pilgrims, seeking religious freedom, made their first settlement at Plymouth, 1620; the following year they gave thanks for their survival with the first Thanksgiving Day. Indian opposition reached a high point in King Philip's War, 1675-76, won by the colonists. Demonstrations against British restrictions set off the "Boston Massacre," 1770, and Boston "tea party," 1773. First bloodshed of the Revolution was at Lexington, 1775.

Tourist attractions. Cape Cod with Provincetown artists' colony; Berkshire Music Festival, Tanglewood; Boston "Pops" concerts; Museum of Fine Arts, Arnold Arboretum, both Boston; Jacob's Pillow Dance Festival, West Becket; historical Shaker Village, Old Sturbridge, Lexington, Concord, Salem, Plymouth Rock.

Famous "Bay Staters" include Samuel Adams, Louisa May Alcott, Horatio Alger, Clara Barton, Emily Dickinson, Emerson, Hancock, Hawthorne, Oliver W. Holmes, Winslow Homer, Elias Howe, Samuel F.B. Morse, Poe, Revere, Sargent, Thoreau, Whistler, Whittier.

Chamber of Commerce: None.

Michigan

Great Lake State, Wolverine State

People. Population (1981): 9,204,000; **rank:** 8. **Pop. density:** 162.0 per sq. mi. **Urban** (1980): 70.7%. **Racial distrib.** (1980): 84.9% White; 12.9% Black; Hispanic 162,388. **Major ethnic groups:** Polish, German, English, Italian. **Net migration** (1970-79): +376,518.

Geography. Total area: 58,216 sq. mi.; **rank:** 23. **Land area:** 56,817 sq. mi. **Acres forested land:** 19,270,400. **Location:** east north central state bordering on 4 of the 5 Great Lakes, divided into an Upper and Lower Peninsula by the Straits of Mackinac, which link lakes Michigan and Huron. **Climate:** well-defined seasons tempered by the Great Lakes. **Topography:** low rolling hills give way to northern tableland of hilly belts in Lower Peninsula; Upper Peninsula is level in the east, with swampy areas; western region is higher and more rugged. **Capital:** Lansing.

Economy. Principal industries: manufacturing, mining, agriculture, food processing, tourism, fishing. **Principal manufactured goods:** automobiles, machine tools, chemicals, foods, primary metals and metal products, plastics. **Value added by manufacture** (1978): $41.8 bln. **Agriculture: Chief crops:** corn, winter wheat, soybeans, dry beans, oats, hay, sugar beets, honey, asparagus, sweet corn, apples, cherries, grapes, peaches, blueberries, flowers. **Livestock:** 1.38 mln. cattle; 1.1 mln. hogs/pigs; 124,000 sheep; 8.3 mln. poultry. **Timber/lumber** (1977): hickory, ash, oak, hemlock; 350 mln. bd. ft. **Minerals** (1981): crude petroleum, natural gas. Total mineral production valued at $1.3 bln. **Commercial fishing** (1980): $4.8 mln. **Chief ports:** Detroit, Muskegon, Sault Ste. Marie. **International airports at:** Detroit. **Value of construction** (1981): $3.3 bln. **Employment distribution:** 29% manuf.; 19% serv.; **Per capita income** (1981): $11,009. **Unemployment** (1981): 12.3%. **Tourism** (1980): out-of-state visitors spent $3.9 bln.

Finance. No. banks (1980): 376; **No. savings assns.** (1981): 59.

Federal government. No. federal civilian employees (Mar. 1981): 44,282. **Avg. salary:** $20,472. **Notable federal facilities:** Isle Royal, Sleeping Bear Dunes national parks.

Energy. Electricity production (1981, mwh, by source): Hydroelectric: 1.1 mln; Mineral: 57.4 mln.; Nuclear: 17.1 mln.

Education. No. schools: 4,785 elem. and second.; 96 higher ed. **Avg. salary, public school teachers** (1980): $19,456.

State data. Motto: Si Quaeris Peninsulam Amoenam Circumspice (If you seek a pleasant peninsula, look about you). **Flower:** Apple blossom. **Bird:** Robin. **Tree:** White pine. **Song:** Michigan, My Michigan. **Entered union** Jan. 26, 1837; rank, 26th. **State fair** at: Detroit, Aug. 27–Sept. 6; Upper Peninsula (Escanaba) Aug. 17–22.

History. French fur traders and missionaries visited the region, 1616, set up a mission at Sault Ste. Marie, 1641, and a settlement there, 1668. The whole region went to Britain, 1763. During the Revolution, the British led attacks from the area on American settlements to the south until Anthony Wayne defeated their Indian allies at Fallen Timbers, Ohio, 1794. The British returned, 1812, seized Ft. Mackinac and Detroit. Oliver H. Perry's Lake Erie victory and William H. Harrison's troops, who carried the war to the Thames River in Canada, 1813, freed Michigan once more.

Tourist attractions. Henry Ford Museum, Greenfield Village, reconstruction of a typical 19th cent. American village, both in Dearborn; Michigan Space Ctr., Jackson; Tahquamenon *(Hiawatha)* Falls; DeZwaan windmill and Tulip Festival, Holland; "Soo Locks," St. Marys Falls Ship Canal, Sault Ste. Marie.

Famous Michiganders include George Custer, Paul de Kruif, Thomas Dewey, Edna Ferber, Henry Ford, Edgar Guest, Betty Hutton, Robert Ingersoll, Will Kellogg, Danny Thomas, Stewart Edward White.

Chamber of Commerce: 200 N. Washington Sq., Suite 400, Lansing, MI 48933.

Minnesota

North Star State, Gopher State

People. Population (1981): 4,094,000; **rank:** 21. **Pop. density:** 51.6 per sq. mi. **Urban** (1980): 66.9%. **Racial distrib.** (1980): 96.5% White; 1.3% Black; Hispanic 32,124. **Major ethnic groups:** German, Swedish, Norwegian. **Net migration** (1970-80): +8,600.

Geography. Total area: 84,068 sq. mi.; **rank:** 12. **Land area:** 79,289 sq. mi. **Acres forested land:** 16,709,200. **Location:** north central state bounded on the E by Wisconsin and Lake Superior, on the N by Canada, on the W by the Dakotas, and on the S by Iowa. **Climate:** northern part of state lies in the moist Great Lakes storm belt; the western border lies at the edge of the semi-arid Great Plains. **Topography:** central hill and lake region covering approx. half the state; to the NE, rocky ridges and deep lakes; to the NW, flat plain; to the S, rolling plains and deep river valleys. **Capital:** St. Paul.

Economy. Principal industries: agri business, forest products, mining, manufacturing, tourism. **Principal manufactured goods:** food processing, non-electrical machinery, chemicals, paper, electric and electronic equipment, printing and publishing, instruments, fabricated metal products. **Value added by manufacture** (1978): $10.9 bln. **Agriculture: Chief crops:** corn, soybeans, wheat, sugar beets, sunflowers, barley. **Livestock** (1982): 3.9 mln. cattle; 4.3 mln. hogs/pigs; 335,000 sheep; 39.3 mln. poultry. **Timber/lumber:** needle-leaves and hardwoods. **Minerals** (1980): iron ore (95% of the total $1.74 bln. of mineral production), sand and gravel, stone. **Commercial fishing** (1980): $2.12 **Chief ports:** Duluth, St. Paul, Minneapolis. **International airports at:** Minneapolis-St. Paul. **Value of construction** (1981): $2.66 bln. **Employment distribution** (1981): 25% trade; 20.6% manuf.; 21.7% serv.; 17.8% gvt. **Per capita income** (1981):

$10,747. **Unemployment** (1981): 5.5%. **Tourism** (1980): out-of-state visitors spent $2 bln.

Finance. No. banks: (1980): 764; **No. savings assns.** (1981): 53.

Federal government. No. federal civilian employees (Mar. 1981): 23,609. **Avg. salary:** $20,749.

Energy. Electricity production (1981, mwh, by source): Hydroelectric: 793,495; Mineral: 20.5 mln.; Nuclear: 10.2 mln.

Education. No. schools: 2,173 elem. and second.; 65, higher ed. **Avg. salary, public school teachers** (1980): $16,750.

State data. Motto: L'Etoile du Nord (The star of the north). **Flower:** Pink and white lady's-slipper. **Bird:** Common loon. **Tree:** Red pine. **Song:** Hail! Minnesota. **Entered union** May 11, 1858; rank, 32d. **State fair** at: Saint Paul; end-Aug. to early Sept.

History. Fur traders and missionaries from French Canada opened the region in the 17th century. Britain took the area east of the Mississippi, 1763. The U.S. took over that portion after the Revolution and in 1803 bought the western area as part of the Louisiana Purchase. The U.S. built present Ft. Snelling, 1820, bought lands from the Indians, 1837. Sioux Indians staged a bloody uprising, 1862, and were driven from the state.

Tourist attractions. Minnehaha Falls, Minneapolis, inspiration for Longfellow's *Hiawatha;* Voyageurs Nat'l. Park, a water wilderness along the Canadian border; Mayo Clinic, Rochester; St. Paul Winter Carnival; the "land of 10,000 lakes" actually has 12,034 lakes over 10 acres in size; many water and winter sports and activities throughout the state.

Famous Minnesotans include F. Scott Fitzgerald, Cass Gilbert, Hubert Humphrey, Sister Elizabeth Kenny, Sinclair Lewis, Paul Manship, E. G. Marshall, William and Charles Mayo, Walter F. Mondale, Charles Schulz, Harold Stassen, Thorstein Veblen.

Tourist Information: Minnesota Dept. of Energy, Planning & Development, 101 Capitol Square Bldg., 550 Cedar St., St. Paul, MN 55101.

Mississippi

Magnolia State

People. Population (1981): 2,531,000; **rank:** 31. **Pop. density:** 53.0 per sq. mi. **Urban** (1980): 47.3%. **Racial distrib.** (1980): 64.1% White; 35.2% Black; Hispanic (1970): 8,182. **Major ethnic groups:** German, Italian, English. **Net migration** (1970-79): +7,000.

Geography. Total area: 47,716 sq. mi.; **rank:** 32. **Land area:** 47,296 sq. mi. **Acres forested land:** 16,715,600. **Location:** south central state bordered on the W by the Mississippi R. and on the S by the Gulf of Mexico. **Climate:** semi-tropical, with abundant rainfall, long growing season, and extreme temperatures unusual. **Topography:** low, fertile delta bet. the Yazoo and Mississippi rivers; loess bluffs stretching around delta border; sandy Gulf coastal terraces followed by piney woods and prairie; rugged, high sandy hills in extreme NE followed by black prairie belt. Pontotoc Ridge, and flatwoods into the north central highlands. **Capital:** Jackson.

Economy. Principal industries: manufacturing, food processing, seafood, government, wholesale and retail trade, agriculture. **Principal manufactured goods:** apparel, transportation equipment, lumber and wood products, foods, electrical machinery and equipment. **Value added by manufacture** (1978): $5.9 bln. **Agriculture: Chief crops:** soybeans, cotton, rice. 60 **Livestock:** 1.80 mln. cattle; 410,000 hogs/pigs; 4,500 sheep; 10.18 mln. poultry. **Timber/lumber** (1978): pine, oak, hardwoods; 1.3 bln. bd. ft. **Minerals** (1977): crude petroleum and natural gas (85% of total $499 mln. value of mineral production), sand and gravel. **Commercial fishing** (1980): $26.6 mln. **Chief ports:** Pascagoula, Vicksburg, Gulfport, Natchez. **Value of construction** (1981): $1.34 bln. **Employment distribution:** 22.9% manuf.; 19.4% gvt.; 16.9% trade; 12.5% serv. **Per capita income** (1981): $7,256. **Unemployment** (1981): 8.3%. **Tourism** (1976): out-of-state visitors spent $850.5 mln.

Finance. No. banks (1980): 178; **No. savings assns.** (1981): 58.

Federal government. No. federal civilian employees (Mar. 1981): 24,557. **Avg. salary:** $20,092. **Notable federal facilities:** Columbus, Keesler AF bases; Meridian Naval Air Station, NASA/NOAA International Earth Sciences Center.

Energy. Electricity production (1981, mwh, by source): Mineral 14.8 mln.

Education. No. schools: 1,234 elem. and second.; 46 higher ed. **Avg. salary, public school teachers** (1980): $11,900.

State data. Motto: Virtute et Armis (By valor and arms). **Flower:** Magnolia. **Bird:** Mockingbird. **Tree:** Magnolia. **Song:** Go, Mississippi! **Entered union** Dec. 10, 1817; rank, 20th. **State fair** at: Jackson; Fall.

History. De Scto explored the area, 1540, discovered the Mississippi River, 1541. La Salle traced the river from Illinois to its mouth and claimed the entire valley for France, 1682. First settlement was the French Ft. Maurepas, near Ocean Springs, 1699. The area was ceded to Britain, 1763; American settlers followed. During the Revolution, Spain seized part of the area and refused to leave even after the U.S. acquired title at the end of the Revolution, finally moving out, 1798. Mississippi seceded 1861. Union forces captured Corinth and Vicksburg and destroyed Jackson and much of Meridian.

Tourist attractions. Vicksburg National Military Park and Cemetery, other Civil War sites; Natchez Trace; Indian mounds; estate pilgrimage at Natchez; Mardi Gras and blessing of the shrimp fleet, Aug., both in Biloxi.

Famous Mississippians include Dana Andrews, William Faulkner, Lucius O.C. Lamar, Elvis Presley, Leontyne Price, Hiram Revels, Eudora Welty.

Chamber of Commerce: P.O. Box 1849, Jackson, MS 39205.

Missouri

Show Me State

People. Population (1981): 4,941,000; **rank:** 15. **Pop. density:** 71.6 per sq. mi. **Urban** (1980): 68.1%. **Racial distrib.** (1980): 88.3% White; 10.4% Black; Hispanic 51,667. **Major ethnic groups:** German, Italian, English, Russian. **Net migration** (1970-80): +10,726.

Geography. Total area: 69,686 sq. mi.; **rank:** 19. **Land area:** 68,995 sq. mi. **Acres forested land:** 12,876,000. **Location:** West North central state near the geographic center of the conterminous U.S.; bordered on the E by the Mississippi R., on the NW by the Missouri R. **Climate:** continental, susceptible to cold Canadian air, moist, warm Gulf air, and drier SW air. **Topography:** Rolling hills, open, fertile plains, and well-watered prairie N of the Missouri R.; south of the river land is rough and hilly with deep, narrow valleys; alluvial plain in the SE; low elevation in the west. **Capital:** Jefferson City.

Economy. Principal industries: agriculture, manufacturing, aerospace, tourism. **Principal manufactured goods:** transportation equipment, food and related products, electrical and electronic equipment, chemicals. **Value added by manufacture** (1978): $15.0 bln. **Agriculture: Chief crops:** soybeans, corn, wheat, cotton. **Livestock:** 5.4 mln. cattle; 4.6 mln. hogs/pigs; 123,000 sheep; 7.7 mln. poultry. **Timber/lumber:** oak, hickory. **Minerals** (1980): lead, fire clay, zinc, barite, lime cement. Total value of mineral production $1.2 bln. **Commercial fishing** (1980) $220,000. **Chief ports:** St. Louis, Kansas City. **International airports at:** St. Louis, Kansas City. **Value of construction** (1981): $2.55 bln. **Employment distribution:** 24% trade; 23% serv.; 22% manuf.; 17% gvt.; 7% transp. **Per capita income** (1981): $9,876. **Unemployment** (1981): 7.7%. **Tourism** (1982): out-of-state visitors spent $3.9 bln.

Finance. Notable industries: banking. **No. banks** (1980): 731; **No. savings assns.** (1981); 105.

Federal government: No. federal civilian employees (Mar. 1981): 57,652. **Avg. salary:** $20,260. **Notable fed-**

eral facilities: Federal Reserve banks, St. Louis, Kansas City; Ft. Leonard Wood, Rolla.

Energy. Electricity production (1981 mwh, by source): Hydroelectric: 669,081; Mineral: 48.1 mln.

Education. No. schools: 2,763 elem. and second.; 84 higher ed. **Avg. salary, public school teachers** (1980): $13,847.

State data. Motto: Salus Populi Suprema Lex Esto (The welfare of the people shall be the supreme law). **Flower:** Hawthorn. **Bird:** Bluebird. **Tree:** Dogwood. **Song:** Missouri Waltz. **Entered union** Aug. 10, 1821; rank, 24th. **State fair** at: Sedalia; 3d week in Aug.

History. DeSoto visited the area, 1541. French hunters and lead miners made the first settlement, c. 1735, at Ste. Genevieve. The U.S. acquired Missouri as part of the Louisiana Purchase, 1803. The fur trade and the Santa Fe Trail provided prosperity; St. Louis became the "jump-off" point for pioneers on their way West. Pro- and anti-slavery forces battled each other there during the Civil War.

Tourist attractions. Mark Twain State Park, Florida; Tom Sawyer and Huckleberry Finn statues, Hannibal; Jesse James birthplace, Excelsior Springs; Pony Express Museum, St. Joseph. The Harry S. Truman Library, near Independence, contains presidential papers and memorabilia. Mr. Truman is buried in the library courtyard.

Famous Missourians include Zoe Akins, Thomas Hart Benton, Omar Bradley, George Washington Carver, Thomas Dooley, T. S. Eliot, Bernarr Macfadden, J. C. Penney; John J. Pershing, Joseph Pulitzer, Sara Teasdale, Mark Twain.

Chamber of Commerce: 400 E. High St., P.O. Box 149, Jefferson City, MO 65101.

Montana

Treasure State

People. Population (1981): 793,000; **rank:** 45. **Pop. density:** 5.45 per sq. mi. **Urban** (1980): 52.9%. **Racial distrib.** (1980): 94.0% White; 0.2% Black; 5.6% Other (includes American Indians); Hispanic 9,974. **Major ethnic groups:** German, Norwegian, Russian, English. **Net migration** (1970-79): +38,000.

Geography. Total area: 147,138 sq. mi.; **rank:** 4. **Land area:** 145,587 sq. mi. **Acres forested land:** 22,559,300. **Location:** Mountain state bounded on the E by the Dakotas, on the S by Wyoming, on the S/SW by Idaho, and on the N by Canada. **Climate:** colder, continental climate with low humidity. **Topography:** Rocky Mtns. in western third of the state; eastern two-thirds gently rolling northern Great Plains. **Capital:** Helena.

Economy. Principal industries: agriculture, mining, manufacturing, tourism. **Principal manufactured goods:** petroleum products, primary metals and minerals, lumber and wood products, farm machinery, processed foods. **Value added by manufacture** (1978): $850 mln. **Agriculture: Chief crops:** wheat, cattle, barley, sheep, sugar beets, hay, flax, oats. **Livestock** (1982): 2.9 mln. cattle; 200,000 hogs/pigs; 616,000 sheep; 940,000 poultry. **Timber/lumber** (1977): Douglas fir, pines, larch; 1.3 bln. bd. ft. **Minerals** (1978): mineral fuels (71% of the total $719 mln. mineral production), copper, silver. **International airports at:** Great Falls. **Value of construction** (1981): 2.0 bln. **Employment distribution** (1981): 20.8% trade; 19.9% gvt.; 16.0% serv.; 8.6% agric; 6.6% manuf. **Per capita income** (1981): $9,676. **Unemployment** (1981): 6.9%. **Tourism** (1980): out-of-state visitors spent $510 mln.

Finance. No. banks (1980): 166; **No. savings assns.** (1981): 13.

Federal government. No. federal civilian employees (Mar. 1981): 9,561. **Avg. salary:** $20,847. **Notable federal facilities:** Malmstrom AFB; Ft. Peck, Hungry Horse, Libby, Yellowtail dams.

Energy. Electricity production (1981, mwh, by source): Hydroelectric: 11.3 mln; Mineral: 2.4 mln.

Education. No. schools: 876 elem. and second.; 13 higher ed. **Avg. salary, public school teachers** (1980): $14,540.

State data. Motto: Oro y Plata (Gold and silver). **Flower:** Bitterroot. **Bird:** Western meadowlark. **Tree:** Ponderosa pine. **Song:** Montana. **Entered union** Nov. 8, 1889; rank, 41st. **State fair** at: Great Falls; end July to early Aug.

History. French explorers visited the region, 1742. The U.S. acquired the area partly through the Louisiana Purchase, 1803, and partly through the explorations of Lewis and Clark, 1805-06. Fur traders and missionaries established posts in the early 19th century. Indian uprisings reached their peak with the Battle of the Little Big Horn, 1876. The coming of the Northern Pacific Railway, 1883, brought population growth.

Tourist attractions. Glacier National Park, on the Continental Divide, is a scenic and recreational wonderland, with 60 glaciers, 200 lakes, and many trout streams.

Also, Museum of the Plains Indian, Blackfeet Reservation near Browning; Custer Battlefield National Cemetery; Flathead Lake, in the NW, Lewis and Clark Cavern, Morrison Cave State Park, near Whitehall.

There are 7 Indian reservations, covering over 5 million acres; tribes are Blackfeet, Crow, Confederated Salish & Kootenai, Assiniboine, Gros Ventre, Sioux, Northern Cheyenne, Chippewa, Cree. Population of the reservations is approximately 25,500.

Famous Montanans include Gary Cooper, Marcus Daly, Chet Huntley, Will James, Myrna Loy, Mike Mansfield, Jeannette Rankin, Charles M. Russell, Brent Musberger.

Chamber of Commerce: 110 Neil Ave., P.O. Box 1730, Helena, MT 59601.

Nebraska

Cornhusker State

People. Population (1981): 1,577,000; **rank:** 36. **Pop. density:** 20.6 per sq. mi. **Urban** (1980): 62.9%. **Racial distrib.** (1980): 94.9% White; 3.1% Black; Hispanic 28,020. **Major ethnic groups:** German, Czechoslovakian, Swedish, Russian. **Net migration** (1970-80): −12,600.

Geography. Total area: 77,227 sq. mi.; **rank:** 15. **Land area:** 76,483 sq. mi. **Acres forested land:** 1,029,100. **Location:** West North Central state with the Missouri R. for a N/NE border. **Climate:** continental semi-arid. **Topography:** till plains of the central lowland in the eastern third rising to the Great Plains and hill country of the north central and NW. **Capital:** Lincoln.

Economy. Principal industries: agriculture, food processing, manufacturing. **Principal manufactured goods:** foods, machinery, electric and electronic equipment, primary and fabricated metal products, chemicals. **Value added by manufacture** (1978): $3.2 bln. **Agriculture: Chief crops:** corn, soy beans, hay, wheat, sorghum, beans, popcorn, oats, potatoes, sugar beets. **Livestock:** 7.25 mln. cattle; 4.1 mln. hogs/pigs; 225,000 sheep; 4.15 mln. poultry. **Minerals** (1980): cement, sand and gravel, natural gas liquids, petroleum. Total mineral production valued at $271.8 mln. **Commercial fishing** (1980): $28,000. **Chief ports:** Omaha, Sioux City, Brownville, Blair, Plattsmouth, Nebraska City. **Value of construction** (1981): $771 mln. **Employment distribution:** 21.0% trade; 16.9% gvt.; 15.6% serv.; 12.2% manuf. **Per capita income** (1981): $10,296. **Unemployment** (1981): 4.1%. **Tourism** (1980): out-of-state visitors spent $1 bln.

Finance. No. banks (1980): 464; **No. savings assns.** (1981): 32.

Federal government. No. federal civilian employees (Mar. 1981): 12,301. **Avg. salary:** $20,630. **Notable federal facilities:** Strategic Air Command Base, Omaha.

Energy. Electricity production (1981, mwh, by source): Hydroelectric: 1.2 mln.; Mineral: 8.9 mln.; Nuclear: 5.9 mln.

Education. No. schools: 1,993 elem. and second.; 31 higher ed. **Avg. salary, public school teachers** (1980): $13,519.

State data. Motto: Equality before the law. **Flower:** Goldenrod. **Bird:** Western meadowlark. **Tree:** Cottonwood. **Song:** Beautiful Nebraska. **Entered union** Mar. 1, 1867; rank, 37th. **State fair** at: Lincoln; Sept. 2-11.

History. Spanish and French explorers and fur traders visited the area prior to the Louisiana Purchase, 1803. Lewis and Clark passed through, 1804-06. First permanent settlement was Bellevue, near Omaha, 1823. Many Civil War veterans settled under free land terms of the 1862 Homestead Act; struggles followed between homesteaders and ranchers.

Tourist attractions. Boys Town, founded by Fr. Flanagan, west of Omaha, is a self-contained community of under-privileged and homeless boys. Arbor Lodge State Park, Nebraska City, is a memorial to J. Sterling Morton, founder of Arbor Day. Buffalo Bill Ranch State Historical Park, North Platte, contains Cody's home and memorabilia of his Wild West Show.

Also, Pioneer Village, Minden; Oregon Trail, landmarks, Scotts Bluff National Mountain and Chimney Rock Historic Site.

Famous Nebraskans include Fred Astaire, Charles W. and William Jennings Bryan, Willa Cather, Michael and Edward A. Cudahy, Loren Eiseley, Rev. Edward J. Flanagan, Henry Fonda, Rollin Kirby, Harold Lloyd, Malcolm X, Roscoe Pound.

Chamber of Commerce: 1008 Terminal Bldg., Lincoln, NE 68508.

Nevada

Sagebrush State, Battle Born State

People. Population (1981): 845,000; **rank:** 44. **Pop. density:** 7.7 per sq. mi. **Urban** (1980): 85.3%. **Racial distrib.** (1980): 87.5% White; 6.3% Black; Hispanic 53,786. **Major ethnic groups:** Italian, German, English, Mexican. **Net migration** (1970-80): +312,000.

Geography. Total area: 110,540 sq. mi.; **rank:** 7. **Land area:** 109,889 sq. mi. **Acres forested land:** 7,683,300. **Location:** Mountain state bordered on N by Oregon and Idaho, on E by Utah and Arizona, on SE by Arizona, and on SW/W by California. **Climate:** semi-arid. **Topography:** rugged N-S mountain ranges; southern area is within the Mojave Desert; lowest elevation, Colorado R. Canyon, 470 ft. **Capital:** Carson City.

Economy. Principal industries: tourism, mining, manufacturing, lumber, government, agriculture, warehousing, trucking. **Principal manufactured goods:** gaming devices, electronics, chemicals, forest products, stone-clay-glass products. **Value added by manufacture** (1978): $660.1 mln. **Agriculture: Chief crops:** alfalfa, barley, wheat, oats, cotton. **Livestock:** 570,000 cattle; 8,000 hogs/pigs; 133,000 sheep; 14,000 poultry. **Timber/lumber** (1977): pine, fir, spruce; 19 mln. bd. ft. **Minerals** (1979): gold (3d largest in U.S. with 26% of total output), copper, sand and gravel. Total mineral production valued at $251.2 mln. **International airports at** Las Vegas, Reno. **Value of construction** (1981): $1.2 bln. **Employment distribution:** 42% serv.; 20% trade; 14% gvt. **Per capita income** (1981): $11,633. **Unemployment** (1981): 7.1% **Tourism** (1980): out-of-state visitors spent $2.4 bln.

Finance. No. banks (1980): 11; **No. savings assns.** (1981): 8.

Federal government. No. federal civilian employees (Mar. 1981): 8,235. **Avg. salary:** $21,213. **Notable federal facilities:** Nevada Test Site.

Energy. Electricity production (1981, mwh, by source): Hydroelectric: 1.7 mln.; Mineral: 13.9 mln. .

Education. No. schools: 287 elem. and second.; 6 higher ed. **Avg. salary, public school teachers** (1980): $16,191.

State data. Motto: All for our country. **Flower:** Sagebrush. **Bird:** Mountain bluebird. **Tree:** Single-leaf pinon. **Song:** Home Means Nevada. **Entered union** Oct. 31, 1864; rank, 36th. **State fair** at Reno; early Sept.

History. Nevada was first explored by Spaniards in 1776. Hudson's Bay Co. trappers explored the north and central region, 1825; trader Jedediah Smith crossed the state, 1826 and 1827. The area was acquired by the U.S., in 1848, at the end of the Mexican War. First settlement, Mormon Station, now Genoa, was est. 1849. In the early 20th century, Nevada adopted progressive measures such as the initiative, referendum, recall, and woman suffrage.

Tourist attractions. Legalized gambling provided the impetus for the development of resort areas Lake Tahoe, Reno, and Las Vegas. Ghost towns, rodeos, trout fishing, water sports and hunting important.

Notable are Helldorado Week in May, Las Vegas; Basque Festival, Elko; Reno Rodeo, 4th of July; Valley of Fire State Park, Overton; Death Valley, on the California border; Lehman Caves National Monument.

Famous Nevadans include Walter Van Tilburg Clark, Sarah Winnemucca Hopkins, John William MacKay, Pat McCarran, William Morris Stewart.

Chamber of Commerce: 133 No. Sierra St., Reno, NV 89104, and 2301 E. Sahara Ave., Las Vegas, NV 89501.

New Hampshire

Granite State

People. Population (1981): 936,000; **rank:** 43. **Pop. density:** 103.7 per sq. mi. **Urban** (1980): 52.2%. **Racial distrib.** (1980): 98.8% White; 0.4% Black; Hispanic 5,587. **Major ethnic groups:** English, Irish, French, Polish, Italian, German. **Net migration** (1970-79): +101,000.

Geography. Total area: 9,304 sq. mi.; **rank:** 44. **Land area:** 9,027 sq. mi. **Acres forested land:** 5,013,500. **Location:** New England state bounded on S by Massachusetts, on W by Vermont, on N/NW by Canada, on E by Maine and the Atlantic O. **Climate:** highly varied, due to its nearness to high mountains and ocean. **Topography:** low, rolling coast followed by countless hills and mountains rising out of a central plateau. **Capital:** Concord.

Economy. Principal industries: manufacturing, communications, trade, agriculture, mining. **Principal manufactured goods:** leather products, wood and paper products, electrical equipment, machinery, minerals, fabricated metal products. **Value added by manufacture** (1978): $2.7 bln. **Agriculture: Chief crops:** vegetables, dairy products, greenhouse products, hay, apples. **Livestock:** 70,000 cattle; 9,900 hogs/pigs; 8,500 sheep; 950,000 poultry. **Timber/lumber** (1978): white pine, hemlock, oak, birch; 240 mln. bd. ft. **Minerals** (1979): sand and gravel. Total mineral production valued at $23.2 mln. **Commercial fishing** (1980): $5.2 mln. **Chief ports:** Portsmouth. **Value of construction** (1981): $545 mln. **Employment distribution:** 29.2% manuf.; 22.4% trade; 19.2% serv. **Per capita income** (1981): $10,073. **Unemployment** (1981): 5.0%. **Tourism** (1981): out-of-state visitors spent $700 mln.

Finance. Notable industries: insurance, banking. **No. banks** (1980): 76; **No. savings assns.** (1981): 15.

Federal government. No. federal civilian employees (Mar. 1981): 13,702. **Avg. salary:** $20,262. **Notable federal facilities:** Pease Air Base, Newington.

Energy. Electricity production (1981, mwh, by source): Hydroelectric: 1.2 mln.; Mineral: 4.4 mln.

Education: No. schools: 561 elem. and second.; 24 higher ed. **Avg. salary, public school teachers** (1980): $13,342.

State data. Motto: Live free or die. **Flower:** Purple lilac. **Bird:** Purple finch. **Tree:** White birch. **Song:** Old New Hampshire. **Ninth** of the original 13 states to ratify the Constitution, June 21, 1788.

History. First explorers to visit the New Hampshire area were England's Martin Pring, 1603, and Champlain, 1605. First settlement was Little Harbor, near Rye, 1623. Indian raids were halted, 1759, by Robert Rogers' Rangers. Before the Revolution, New Hampshire men seized a British fort at Portsmouth, 1774, and drove the royal governor out, 1775. Three regiments served in the Continental Army and scores of privateers raided British shipping.

Tourist attractions. Mt. Washington, highest peak in Northeast, hub of network of trails; Lake Winnipesaukee; White Mt. Natl. Forest; Crawford, Franconia, Pinkham notches in White Mt. region—Franconia famous for the Old Man of the Mountains, described by Hawthorne as the Great Stone Face; the Flume, a spectacular gorge; the aerial tramway on Cannon Mt; the MacDowell Colony, Peterborough, summer haven for writers, composers, artists.

Famous New Hampshirites include Salmon P. Chase, Ralph Adams Cram, Mary Baker Eddy, Daniel Chester French, Robert Frost, Horace Greeley, Sarah Buell Hale, Augustus Saint-Gaudens, Daniel Webster.

Tourist Information: Department of Resources and Economic Development, Office of Vacation Travel, P.O. Box 856, Concord, NH 03301.

New Jersey

Garden State

People. Population (1981): 7,404,000; **rank:** 9. **Pop. density:** 944.9 per sq. mi. **Urban** (1980): 89.0%. **Racial distrib.** (1980): 83.2% White; 12.5% Black; Hispanic 491,867. **Major ethnic groups:** Italian, German, Polish. **Net migration** (1970-80): −120,700.

Geography. Total area: 7,836 sq. mi.; **rank:** 46. **Land area:** 7,521 sq. mi. **Acres forested land:** 1,928,400. **Location:** Middle Atlantic state bounded on the N and E by New York and the Atlantic O., on the S and W by Delaware and Pennsylvania. **Climate:** moderate, with marked difference bet. NW and SE extremities. **Topography:** Appalachian Valley in the NW also has highest elevation, High Pt., 1,801 ft.; Appalachian Highlands, flat-topped NE-SW mountain ranges; Piedmont Plateau, low plains broken by high ridges (Palisades) rising 400-500 ft.; Coastal Plain, covering three-fifths of state in SE, gradually rises from sea level to gentle slopes. **Capital:** Trenton.

Economy. Principal industries: manufacturing, trade, services. **Principal manufactured goods:** chemicals, food, fabricated metals, electrical and electronic equipment, petroleum prods. **Value added by manufacture** (1978): $40.5 bln. **Agriculture: Chief crops:** tomatoes, blueberries, cranberries, corn, peaches, grains, hay. **Livestock:** 100,000 cattle; 95,000 hogs/pigs; 9,700 sheep; 1.34 mln. poultry. **Timber/lumber** (1977): pine, white cedar, oak, elm; 22.9 mln. bd. ft. **Minerals** (1978): sand and gravel, stone, zinc. Total value of mineral production, $118 mln. **Commercial fishing** (1980): $49.88 mln. **Chief ports:** Newark, Elizabeth, Hoboken, Ameri-Port (Delaware R.). **International airports at:** Newark. **Value of construction** (1981): $3.47 bln. **Employment distribution** (1981): 22.3% trade, 21.7% manuf.; 20.6% serv.; 17.0% gvt. **Per capita income** (1981): $12,115. **Unemployment** (1981): 7.3%. **Tourism** (1981): tourists spent $7.5 bln.

Finance. Notable industries: banking, insurance. **No. banks** (1980): 169; **No. savings assns.** (1981): 160.

Federal government. No. federal civilian employees (Mar. 1981): 61,355. **Avg. salary:** $20,923. **Notable federal facilities:** McGuire AFB Fort Dix; Fort Monmouth; Picatinny Arsenal; Lakewood Naval Air Station, Lakehurst Naval Air Engineering Center.

Energy. Electricity production (1981, mwh, by source): Mineral: 20.3 mln.; Nuclear: 11.7 mln.

Education. No. schools: 3,164 elem. and second.; 63 higher ed. **Avg. salary, public school teachers** (1980): $17,075.

State Data. Motto: Liberty and prosperity. **Flower:** Purple violet. **Bird:** Eastern goldfinch. **Tree:** Red oak. **Third** of the original 13 states to ratify the Constitution, Dec. 18, 1787. **State fair** at: Great Adventure, Jackson Twp.; 2d week of Sept.

History. The Lenni Lenape (Delaware) Indians had mostly peaceful relations with European colonists who arrived after the explorers Verrazano, 1524, and Hudson, 1609. The Dutch were first; when the British took New Netherland, 1664, the area between the Delaware and Hudson Rivers was given to Lord John Berkeley and Sir George Carteret. New Jersey was the scene of nearly 100 battles, large and small, during the Revolution, including Trenton, 1776, Princeton, 1777, Monmouth, 1778.

Tourist attractions. Grover Cleveland birthplace, Caldwell; Walt Whitman Poetry Center, Camden; Edison Lab National Monument, West Orange; numerous Revolutionary historic sites; Great Adventure amusement park; 127 miles of Atlantic Ocean beaches; Miss America Pageant, Atlantic City; legalized casino gambling, inaugurated 1978, in Atlantic City.

Famous New Jerseyites include Aaron Burr, James Fenimore Cooper, Stephen Crane, Thomas Edison, Alexander Hamilton, Joyce Kilmer, Gen. George McClellan, Thomas Paine, Molly Pitcher, Paul Robeson, Walt Whitman, Alexander Woolcott.

Chamber of Commerce: 5 Commerce St., Newark, NJ 07102.

New Mexico

Land of Enchantment

People. Population (1981): 1,328,000; **rank:** 38. **Pop. density:** 10.9 per sq. mi. **Urban** (1980): 72.1%. **Racial distrib.** (1980): 75.1% White; 1.8% Black; 15.3% Other (includes American Indians); Hispanic 476,089. **Major ethnic groups:** Spanish, Indian, English. **Net migration** (1970-80): +165,000.

Geography. Total area: 121,666 sq. mi.; **rank:** 5. **Land area:** 121,412 sq. mi. **Acres forested land:** 18,059,800. **Location:** southwestern state bounded by Colorado on the N, Oklahoma, Texas, and Mexico on the E and S, and Arizona on the W. **Climate:** dry, with temperatures rising or falling 5°F with every 1,000 ft. elevation. **Topography:** eastern third, Great Plains; central third Rocky Mtns. (85% of the state is over 4,000 ft. elevation); western third high plateau. **Capital:** Santa Fe.

Economy. Principal industries: extractive industries, tourism, agriculture. **Principal manufactured goods:** foods, electrical machinery, apparel, lumber, printing, transportation equipment. **Value added by manufacture** (1978): $794.9 mln. **Agriculture: Chief crops:** wheat, hay, sorghum, grain, onions, cotton, corn. **Livestock:** 1.72 mln. cattle; 72,000 hogs/pigs; 578,000 sheep; 1.21 mln. poultry. **Timber/lumber** (1978): Ponderosa pine, Douglas fir; 199 mln. bd. ft. **Minerals** (1978): perlite, potassium salts, uranium each ranked first in U.S. production. Also copper, molybdenum, natural gas, natural gas liquids, pumice, crude petroleum. Total value of mineral production, $3.4 bln. **International airports at:** Albuquerque. **Value of construction** (1981): $1.35 bln. **Employment distribution:** 23.0% serv.; 18.0% agric.; 10% manuf.; 8.9% gvt. **Per capita income** (1981): $8,654. **Unemployment** (1981): 7.3%. **Tourism** (1980): out-of-state visitors spent $1.46 bln.

Finance. No. banks (1980): 90; **No. savings assns.** (1981): 33.

Federal government. No. federal civilian employees (Mar. 1981): 24,495. **Avg. salary:** $20,304. **Notable federal facilities:** Kirtland, Cannon, Holloman AF bases; Los Alamos Scientific Laboratory; White Sands Missile Range.

Energy. Electricity production (1981, mwh, by source): Hydroelectric: 87,978; Mineral: 22.9 mln. .

Education. No. schools: 694 elem. and second.; 19 higher ed. **Avg. salary, public school teachers** (1980): $14,674.

State data. Motto: Crescit Eundo (It grows as it goes). **Flower:** Yucca. **Bird:** Roadrunner. **Tree:** Pinon. **Song:** O, Fair New Mexico, Asi Es Nuevo Mexico. **Entered union** Jan. 6, 1912; rank, 47th. **State fair** at: Albuquerque; mid-Sept.

History. Franciscan Marcos de Niza and a black slave Estevan explored the area, 1539, seeking gold. First settlements were at San Juan Pueblo, 1598, and Santa Fe, 1610. Settlers alternately traded and fought with the Apaches, Comanches, and Navajos. Trade on the Santa Fe Trail to Missouri started 1821. The Mexican War was declared May, 1846, Gen. Stephen Kearny took Santa Fe, August. In the 1870s, cattlemen staged the famed Lincoln County War in which Billy (the Kid) Bonney played a leading role. Pancho Villa raided Columbus, 1916.

Tourist Attractions. Carlsbad Caverns, a national park, has caverns on 3 levels and the largest natural cave "room" in the world, 1,500 by 300 ft., 300 ft. high; White Sands Natl. Monument, the largest gypsum deposit in the world.

Pueblo ruin from 100 AD, Chaco Canyon; Acoma, the "sky city," built atop a 357-ft. mesa; 19 Pueblo, 4 Navajo, and 2 Apache reservations. Also, ghost towns, dude ranches, skiing, hunting, and fishing.

Famous New Mexicans include Billy (the Kid) Bonney, Kit Carson, Peter Hurd, Archbishop Jean Baptiste Lamy, Bill Mauldin, Georgia O'Keeffe, Kim Stanley, Lew Wallace.

Tourist information: New Mexico Travel Division, Bataan Bldg., Sante Fe, N.M. 87503 (800-545-2040).

New York

Empire State

People. Population (1981): 17,602,000; **rank:** 2. **Pop. density:** 368.0 per sq. mi. **Urban** (1980): 84.6%. **Racial distrib.** (1980): 79.5% White; 13.68% Black; Hispanic (1980): 1,659,245. **Major ethnic groups:** Italian, Russian, Polish, German. **Net migration** (1970-80): −1,431,132.

Geography. Total area: 49,576 sq. mi.; **rank:** 30. **Land area:** 47,831 sq. mi. **Acres forested land:** 17,218,400. **Location:** Middle Atlantic state, bordered by the New England states, Atlantic Ocean, New Jersey and Pennsylvania, Lakes Ontario and Erie, and Canada. **Climate:** variable; the SE region moderated by the ocean. **Topography:** highest and most rugged mountains in the NE Adirondack upland; St. Lawrence-Champlain lowlands extend from Lake Ontario NE along the Canadian border; Hudson-Mohawk lowland follows the flows of the rivers N and W, 10-30 mi. wide; Atlantic coastal plain in the SE; Appalachian Highlands, covering half the state westward from the Hudson Valley, include the Catskill Mtns., Finger Lakes; plateau of Erie-Ontario lowlands. **Capital:** Albany.

Economy. Principal industries: manufacturing, finance, communications, tourism, transportation, services. **Principal manufactured goods:** books and periodicals, clothing and apparel, pharmaceuticals, machinery, instruments, toys and sporting goods, electronic equipment, automotive and aircraft components. **Value added by manufacture** (1978): $48.3 bln. **Agriculture: Chief crops:** potatoes, apples, corn, grapes, onions, hay. **Products:** milk, eggs, maple syrup, nursery products, poultry, wines. **Livestock:** 1.78 mln. cattle; 175,000 hogs/pigs; 69,000 sheep; 13.8 mln. poultry. **Timber/lumber** (1979): saw log production; 596 mln. bd. ft. **Minerals** (1978): natural gas, sand and gravel, stone, peat, clay. First in emery, ilmenite production. Total value mineral production, $438 mln. **Commercial fishing** (1980): $45.06 mln. **Chief ports:** New York, Buffalo, Albany. **International airports at:** New York, Buffalo, Syracuse, Massena, Ogdensburg, Watertown. **Value of construction** (1981): $6.46 bln. **Employment distribution:** 1.6% agric.; 21% manuf.; 33% serv.; 19% trade. **Per capita income** (1981): $11,440. **Unemployment** (1981): 7.6%. **Tourism** (1979): tourists spent $7 bln.

Finance. Notable industries: banking, trade, security and commodity brokerage and exchange, insurance, real estate. **No. banks** (1980): 224; **No. savings assns.** (1981): 105.

Federal government. No. federal civilian employees (Mar. 1981): 133,908. **Avg. salary:** $19,947. **Notable federal facilities:** West Point Military Academy; Merchant Marine Academy; Ft. Drum; Griffiss, Plattsburgh AF bases; Watervliet Arsenal.

Energy. Electricity production (1981, mwh, by source): Hydroelectric: 25.7 mln.; Mineral: 62.7 mln.; Nuclear: 17.4 mln.

Education: No. schools: 6,025 elem. and second.; 286 higher ed. **Avg. salary, public school teachers** (1980): $19,800.

State data. Motto: Excelsior (Ever upward). **Flower:** Rose. **Bird:** Bluebird. **Tree:** Sugar maple. **Eleventh** of the original 13 states to ratify the Constitution, July 26, 1788. **State fair** at: Syracuse, Aug. 28 to Sept. 6.

History. In 1609 Henry Hudson discovered the river that bears his name and Champlain explored the lake, far upstate, which was named for him. Dutch built posts near Albany 1614 and 1624; in 1626 they settled Manhattan. A British fleet seized New Netherland, 1664. Ninety-two of the 300 or more engagements of the Revolution were fought in New York, including the Battle of Bemis Heights-Saratoga, a turning point of the war.

Tourist attractions. New York City; Adirondack and Catskill mtns.; Finger Lakes, Great Lakes; Thousand Islands; Niagara Falls; Saratoga Springs racing and spas; Philipsburg Manor, Sunnyside, the restored home of Washington Irving, The Dutch Church of Sleepy Hollow, all in North Tarrytown; Corning Glass Center and Steuben factory, Corning; Fenimore House, National Baseball Hall of Fame and Museum, both in Cooperstown; Ft. Ticonderoga overlooking lakes George and Champlain.

The Franklin D. Roosevelt National Historic Site, Hyde Park, includes the graves of Pres. and Mrs. Roosevelt, the family home since 1867, the Roosevelt Library. Sagamore Hill, Oyster Bay, the Theodore Roosevelt estate, includes his home.

Famous New Yorkers include Peter Cooper, George Eastman, Julia Ward Howe, Charles Evans Hughes, Henry and William James, Herman Melville, Alfred E. Smith, Elizabeth Cady Stanton, Walt Whitman.

Chamber of Commerce: 150 State St., Albany, NY 12207.

North Carolina

Tar Heel State, Old North State

People. Population (1981): 5,953,000; **rank:** 10. **Pop. density:** 122.0 per sq. mi. **Urban** (1980): 42.9%. **Racial distrib.** (1980): 75.8% White; 22.4% Black; Hispanic (1980): 56,607. **Major ethnic groups:** German, English. **Net migration** (1970-80): +393,369.

Geography. Total area: 52,586 sq. mi.; **rank:** 28. **Land area:** 48,798 sq. mi. **Acres forested land:** 20,043,300. **Location:** South Atlantic state bounded by Virginia, South Carolina, Georgia, Tennessee, and the Atlantic O. **Climate:** sub-tropical in SE, medium-continental in mountain region; tempered by the Gulf Stream and the mountains in W. **Topography:** coastal plain and tidewater, two-fifths of state, extending to the fall line of the rivers; piedmont plateau, another two-fifths, 200 mi. wide of gentle to rugged hills; southern Appalachian Mtns. contains the Blue Ridge and Great Smoky mtns. **Capital:** Raleigh.

Economy. Principal industries: manufacturing, agriculture, tobacco, tourism. **Principal manufactured goods:** textiles, tobacco products, electrical/electronic equip., chemicals, furniture, food products, non-electrical machinery. **Value added by manufacture** (1978): $20.6 bln. **Agriculture: Chief crops:** tobacco, soybeans, corn, peanuts, small sweet potatoes, grains, vegetables, fruits. **Livestock:** 1.16 mln. cattle; 2.46 mln. hogs/pigs; 8,000 sheep; 19.3 mln. poultry. **Timber/lumber** (1979): yellow pine, oak, hickory, poplar, maple. 1.5 bln. bd. ft. **Minerals** (1980): stone, feldspar, lithium minerals, sand and gravel, scrap mica. Total mineral production valued at $361 mln. **Commercial fishing** (1980): $68.8 mln. **Chief ports:** Morehead City, Wilmington. **Value of construction** (1981): $3.35 bln. **Employment distribution:** 34.5% manuf.; 19.8% trade; 17.2% gvt.; 14.3% serv. **Per capita income** (1981): $8,679. **Unemployment** (1981): 6.4%. **Tourism** (1981): out-of-state visitors spent $2.7 bln.

Finance. No. banks (1980): 80; **No. savings assns.** (1981): 137.

Federal government. No. federal civilian employees (Mar. 1981): 35,178. **Avg. salary:** $19,661. **Notable federal facilities:** Ft. Bragg; Camp LeJeune Marine Base; U.S. EPA Research and Development Labs, Cherry Point Marine Corps Air Station.

Energy. Electricity production (1981, mwh, by source): Hydroelectric: 2.9 mln.; Mineral: 62.8 mln.; Nuclear: 6.2 mln.

Education. No. schools: 2,274 elem. and second.; 126 higher ed. **Avg. salary, public school teachers** (1980): $14,355.

State data. Motto: Esse Quam Videri (To be rather than to seem). **Flower:** Dogwood. **Bird:** Cardinal. **Tree:** Pine. **Song:** The Old North State. **Twelfth** of the original 13 states to ratify the Constitution, Nov. 21, 1789. **State fair** at: Raleigh; mid-Oct.

History. The first English colony in America was the first of 2 established by Sir Walter Raleigh on Roanoke Is., 1585 and 1587. The first group returned to England; the second, the "Lost Colony," disappeared without trace. Permanent settlers came from Virginia, c. 1660. Roused by British repressions, the colonists drove out the royal governor, 1775; the province's congress was the first to vote for independence; ten regiments were furnished to the Continental Army. Cornwallis' forces were defeated at Kings Mountain, 1780, and forced out after Guilford Courthouse, 1781.

Tourist attractions. Cape Hatteras and Cape Lookout national seashores; Great Smoky Mtns. (half in Tennessee); Guilford Courthouse and Moore's Creek parks, Revolutionary battle sites; Bennett Place, NW of Durham, where Gen. Joseph Johnston surrendered the last Confederate army to Gen. Wm. Sherman; Ft. Raleigh, Roanoke Is., where Virginia Dare, first child of English parents in the New World, was born Aug. 18, 1587; Wright Brothers National Memorial, Kitty Hawk.

Famous North Carolinians include Richard J. Gatling, Billy Graham, Wm. Rufus King, Dolley Madison, Edward R. Murrow, Enos Slaughter, Moses Waddel.

Tourist information: Division of Travel & Tourism Development, P.O. Box 25249, Raleigh, NC 27611.

North Dakota

Sioux State, Flickertail State

People. Population (1981): 658,000; **rank:** 46. **Pop. density:** 9.5 per sq. mi. **Urban** (1980): 48.8%. **Racial distrib.** (1980): 95.8% White; 0.39% Black; Hispanic (1980): 3,903. **Major ethnic groups** Norwegian, Russian, German. **Net migration** (1970-80): −16,983.

Geography. Total area: 70,665 sq. mi.; **rank:** 17. **Land area:** 69,273 sq. mi. **Acres forested land:** 421,800. **Location:** West North Central state, situated exactly in the middle of North America, bounded on the N by Canada, on the E by Minnesota, on the S by South Dakota, on the W by Montana. **Climate:** continental, with a wide range of temperature and moderate rainfall. **Topography:** Central Lowland in the E comprises the flat Red River Valley and the Rolling Drift Prairie; Missouri Plateau of the Great Plains on the W. **Capital:** Bismarck.

Economy. Principal industries: agriculture, manufacturing. **Principal manufactured goods:** farm equipment, processed foods. **Value added by manufacture** (1978): $485 mln. **Agriculture: Chief crops:** spring wheat, durum, barley, rye, flaxseed, oats, potatoes, soybeans, sugarbeets, sunflowers, hay. **Livestock:** 1.8 mln. cattle; 265,000 hogs/pigs; 262,000 sheep; 1.5 mln. poultry. **Minerals** (1980): petroleum (70% of the total $935.8 mln. output value), natural gas, natural gas liquids, lignite, salt, lime. **Commercial fishing** (1980): $111,000. **International airports at:** Fargo, Grand Forks, Bismarck, Minot. **Value of construction** (1981): $513 mln. **Employment distribution:** 16.8% agric.; 15.6% serv.; 4.9% manuf. **Per capita income** (1981): $10,525. **Unemployment** (1981): 5.0%. **Tourism** (1979): out-of-state visitors spent $196 mln.

Finance No. banks (1980): 178; **No. savings assns.** (1981): 11.

Federal government. No. federal civilian employees (Mar. 1981): 6,688. **Avg. salary:** $19,746. **Notable federal facilities:** Strategic Air Command bases at Minot, Grand Forks; Northern Prairie Wildlife Research Center; Garrison Dam; Theodore Roosevelt Natl. Park; Grand Forks Energy Research Center; Ft. Union Natl. Historic Site.

Energy. Electricity production (1981, mwh, by source): Hydroelectric: 2.3 mln.; Mineral: 13.8 mln.

Education. No. schools: 831 elem. and second.; 16 higher ed. **Avg. salary, public school teachers** (1980): $13,263.

State data. Motto: Liberty and union, now and forever, one and inseparable. **Flower:** Wild prairie rose. **Bird:** Western Meadowlark. **Tree:** American elm. **Song:** North Dakota Hymn. **Entered union** Nov. 2, 1889; rank, 39th. **State fair** at: Minot; 3d week in July.

History. Pierre La Verendrye was the first French fur trader in the area, 1738, followed later by the English. The U.S. acquired half the territory in the Louisiana Purchase, 1803. Lewis and Clark built Ft. Mandan, spent the winter of 1804-05 there. In 1818, American ownership of the other half was confirmed by agreement with Britain. First permanent settlement was at Pembina, 1812. Missouri River steamboats reached the area, 1832; the first railroad, 1873, bringing many homesteaders. The state was first to hold a presidential primary, 1912.

Tourist attractions. International Peace Garden, a 2,200-acre tract extending across the border into Manitoba, commemorates the friendly relations between the U.S. and Canada; 65,000-acre Theodore Roosevelt National Park, Badlands, contains the president's Elkhorn Ranch; Ft. Abraham Lincoln State Park and Museum, S of Mandan.

Famous North Dakotans include Maxwell Anderson, Angie Dickinson, John Bernard Flannagan; Louis L'Amour, Peggy Lee, Eric Sevareid, Vilhjalmur Stefansson, Lawrence Welk.

Chamber of Commerce: P.O. Box 2467, Fargo, ND 58102.

Ohio

Buckeye State

People. Population (1981): 10,781,000; **rank:** 6. **Pop. density:** 263.1 per sq. mi. **Urban** (1980): 73.3%. **Racial distrib.** (1980): 88.8% White; 9.9% Black; Hispanic (1980): 119,880. **Major ethnic groups:** German, Italian, Polish, English. **Net migration** (1970-80): −548,772.

Geography. Total area: 41,222 sq. mi.; **rank:** 35. **Land area:** 40,975 sq. mi. **Acres forested land:** 6,146,600. **Location:** East North Central state bounded on the N by Michigan and Lake Erie; on the E and S by Pennsylvania, West Virginia; and Kentucky; on the W by Indiana. **Climate:** temperate but variable; weather subject to much precipitation. **Topography:** generally rolling plain; Allegheny plateau in E; Lake [Erie] plains extend southward; central plains in the W. **Capital:** Columbus.

Economy. Principal industries: manufacturing, tourism, government, trade. **Principal manufactured goods:** transportation equipment, machinery, primary and fabricated metal products. **Value added by manufacture** (1978): $47.6 bln. **Agriculture: Chief crops:** corn, hay, winter wheat, oats, soybeans. **Livestock** (1981): 1.82 mln. cattle; 2.2 mln. hogs/pigs; 310,000 sheep; 14.2 mln. poultry. **Timber/lumber** (1978): oak, ash, maple, walnut, beech; 444 mln. bd. ft. **Minerals** (1979): mineral fuels (82% of the total $1.76 bln. value of mineral production), clays, sand and gravel, stone, gypsum. **Commercial fishing** (1980): $3.35 mln. **Chief ports:** Cleveland, Toledo, Cincinnati, Ashtabula. **International airports at:** Cleveland, Cincinnati, Columbus, Dayton. **Value of construction** (1981): $4.8 bln. **Employment distribution:** 26% manuf.; 20.6% trade; 18.6% serv.; 14.8% gvt. **Per capita income** (1981): $10,371. **Unemployment** (1981): 9.6%.

Tourism (1978): out-of-state visitors spent $4.2 bln.

Finance. Notable industries: banking, insurance. **No. banks** (1980): 385; **No. savings assns.** (1981): 271.

Federal government. No. federal civilian employees (Mar. 1981): 77,528. **Avg. salary:** $21,625. **Notable federal facilities:** Wright Patterson, Rickenbacker AF bases; Defense Construction Supply Center; Lewis Research Ctr.; Portsmouth Gaseous Diffusion Plant; Mound Laboratory.

Energy. Electricity production (1981, mwh, by source): Hydroelectric: 5,545; Mineral: 107.3 mln.; Nuclear: 4.4 mln.

Education. No. schools: 4,943 elem. and second.; 133 higher ed. **Avg. salary, public school teachers** (1980): $15,187.

State data. Motto: With God, all things are possible. **Flower:** Scarlet carnation. **Bird:** Cardinal. **Tree:** Buckeye. **Song:** Beautiful Ohio. **Entered union** Mar. 1, 1803; rank, 17th. **State fair** at: Columbus; mid-Aug.

History. LaSalle visited the Ohio area, 1669. American fur-traders arrived, beginning 1685; the French and Indians sought to drive them out. During the Revolution, Virginians defeated the Indians, 1774, but hostilities were renewed, 1777. The region became U.S. territory after the Revolution. First organized settlement was at Marietta, 1788. Indian warfare ended with Anthony Wayne's victory at Fallen Timbers, 1794. In the War of 1812, Oliver H. Perry's victory on Lake Erie and William H. Harrison's invasion of Canada, 1813, ended British incursions.

Tourist attractions. Memorial City Group National Monuments, a group of 24 prehistoric Indian burial mounds; Neil Armstrong Air and Space Museum, Wapakoneta; Air Force Museum, Dayton; Pro Football Hall of Fame, Canton; birthplaces, homes, and memorials to Ohio's 6 U.S. presidents: Wm. Henry Harrison, U.S. Grant, Garfield, Hayes, McKinley, Harding.

Famous Ohioans include Sherwood Anderson, Neil Armstrong, George Bellows, Ambrose Bierce, Paul Laurence Dunbar, Thomas Edison, John Glenn, Bob Hope, Eddie Rickenbacker, John D. Rockefeller Sr. and Jr., Gen. Wm. Sherman, Orville Wright.

Chamber of Commerce: 17 S. High St., 8th Fl., Columbus, OH 43215.

Oklahoma

Sooner State

People. Population (1981): 3,100,000; **rank:** 26. **Pop. density:** 45.1 per sq. mi. **Urban** (1980): 67.3%. **Racial distrib.** (1980): 85.8% White; 6.76% Black; 5.6% Amer. Ind. **Major ethnic groups:** German, English, Mexican. **Net migration** (1970-80): +292,164.

Geography. Total area: 69,919 sq. mi.; **rank:** 18. **Land area:** 68,782 sq. mi. **Acres forested land:** 8,513,300. **Location:** West South Central state bounded on the N by Colorado and Kansas; on the E by Missouri and Arkansas; on the S and W by Texas and New Mexico. **Climate:** temperate; southern humid belt merging with colder northern continental; humid eastern and dry western zones. **Topography:** high plains predominate the W, hills and small mountains in the E; the east central region is dominated by the Arkansas R. Basin, and the Red R. Plains, in the S. **Capital:** Oklahoma City.

Economy. Principal industries: mineral and energy exploration and production, manufacturing, agriculture. **Principal manufactured goods:** oil field machinery and equipment, non-electrical machinery, food and kindred products, fabricated metal products. **Value added by manufacture** (1978): $5.2 bln. **Agriculture: Chief crops:** wheat, cotton lint, sorghum grain, peanuts, hay, soybeans, cotton seed, barley, oats, pecans. **Livestock:** 5.4 mln. cattle; 350,000 hogs/pigs; 95,000 sheep; 51 mln. poultry. **Timber/lumber** (1979): pine, oaks, hickory; 288 mln. bd. ft. **Minerals** (1979): mineral fuels (95% of the total $4 bln. mineral production), gypsum, sand and gravel, stone, feldspar, pumice. **Commercial fishing** (1979): $2.8 mln. **Chief ports:** Catoosa, Muskogee. **International airports at:** Oklahoma City, Tulsa. **Value of construction** (1981): $2.84 bln. **Employment distribution** (1981): 24.2% trade; 18.1% gvt.; 18.1% serv.; 16.4% manuf. **Per capita income** (1981): $10,210. **Unemployment** (1981): 3.6%. **Tourism** (1981): tourists spent $3 bln.

Finance. No. banks (1980): 503; **No. savings assns.** (1981): 55.

Federal government. No. federal civilian employees (Mar. 1981): 41,040. **Avg. salary:** $20,152. **Notable federal facilities:** Federal Aviation Agency and Tinker AFB, both Oklahoma City; Ft. Sill, Lawton; Altus AFB, Altus; Vance AFB, Enid.

Energy. Electricity production (1981, mwh, by source): Hydroelectric: 1.1 mln.; Mineral: 42.9 mln.

Education. No. schools: 1,929 elem. and second.; 43 higher ed. **Avg. salary, public school teachers** (1980): $13,210.

State data. Motto: Labor Omnia Vincit (Labor conquers all things). **Flower:** Mistletoe. **Bird:** Scissortailed flycatcher. **Tree:** Redbud. **Song:** Oklahoma! **Entered union** Nov. 16, 1907; rank, 46th. **State fair** at: Oklahoma City; last week of Sept.

History. Part of the Louisiana Purchase, 1803, Oklahoma was known as Indian Territory (but was not given territorial government) after it became the home of the "Five Civilized Tribes"—Cherokee, Choctaw, Chickasaw, Creek, and Seminole—1828-1846. The land was also used by Comanche, Osage, and other Plains Indians. As white settlers pressed west, land was opened for homesteading by runs and lottery, the first run taking place Apr. 22, 1889. The most famous run was to the Cherokee Outlet, 1893.

Tourist attraction. Will Rogers Memorial, Claremore, contains his collections of saddles, ropes, trophies; his tomb is there. Also, National Cowboy Hall of Fame, Oklahoma City; restored Ft. Gibson Stockade, near Muskogee, the Army's largest outpost in Indian lands; Indian powwows; rodeos; fishing; hunting; Ouachita National Forest.

Famous Oklahomans include Carl Albert, Woody Guthrie, Gen. Patrick J. Hurley, Karl Jansky, Mickey Mantle, Wiley Post, Oral Roberts, Will Rogers, Maria Tallchief, Jim Thorpe.

Chamber of Commerce: 4020 N. Lincoln Blvd., Oklahoma City, OK 73105.

Oregon

Beaver State

People. Population (1981): 2,651,000; **rank:** 30. **Pop. density:** 27.6 per sq. mi. **Urban** (1980): 67.9%. **Racial distrib.** (1980): 94.5% White; 1.4% Black; Hispanic (1980): 65,883. **Major ethnic groups:** German, Scandinavian, English, Russian. **Net migration** (1970-81): +395,149.

Geography. Total area: 96,981 sq. mi.; **rank:** 10. **Land area:** 96,184 sq. mi. **Acres forested land:** 29,810,000. **Location:** Pacific state, bounded on N by Washington; on E by Idaho; on S by Nevada and California; on W by the Pacific. **Climate:** coastal mild and humid climate; continental dryness and extreme temperatures in the interior. **Topography:** Coast Range of rugged mountains; fertile Willamette R. Valley to E and S; Cascade Mtn. Range of volcanic peaks E of the valley; plateau E of Cascades, remaining two-thirds of state. **Capital:** Salem.

Economy. Principal industries: manufacturing, forestry, food processing, agriculture, tourism. **Principal manufactured goods:** lumber, foods, instruments, machinery, fabricated metals, primary metals, paper, transportation equipment. **Value added by manufacture** (1978): $7.1 bln. **Agriculture: Chief crops:** wheat, hay, potatoes, rye grass, onions, pears, barley, snapbeans, sweet corn, cherries. **Livestock:** 1.90 mln. cattle; 78,000 hogs/pigs; 560,000 sheep; 7.13 mln. poultry. **Timber/lumber** (1978): Douglas fir, hemlock, ponderosa pine; 7.5 bln. bd. ft. **Minerals** (1979): nickel, crushed stone, sand

and gravel, cement, clays, diatomite, lime, pumice, talc. Total mineral production valued at $150 mln. **Commercial fishing** (1980): $55.75 mln. **Chief ports:** Portland, Astoria, Newport, Coos Bay. **International Airports at:** Portland. **Value of construction** (1981): $2.05 bln. **Employment distribution:** 24.9% trade; 19.9% manuf.; 19.8% govt.; 18.9% serv. **Per capita income** (1981): $9,991. **Unemployment** (1981): 9.9%. **Tourism** (1981): out-of-state visitors spent $1.27 bln.

Finance: No. banks (1980): 82; **No. savings assns.** (1981): 26.

Federal government. No. federal civilian employees (Mar. 1981): 21,972. **Avg. salary:** $21,199. **Notable federal facilities:** Bonneville Power Administration.

Energy: Electricity production (1981, mwh, by source): Hydroelectric: 32.1 mln.; Mineral: 1.7 mln.; Nuclear: 6.4 mln.

Education. No. schools: 1,421 elem. and second.; 43 higher ed. **Avg. salary, public school teachers** (1980): $16,015.

State data. Motto: The union. **Flower:** Oregon grape. **Bird:** Western meadowlark. **Tree:** Douglas fir. **Song:** Oregon, My Oregon. **Entered union** Feb. 14, 1859; rank, 33d. **State fair** at: Salem; end-Aug. to early Sept.

History. American Capt. Robert Gray discovered and sailed into the Columbia River, 1792; Lewis and Clark, traveling overland, wintered at its mouth 1805-06; fur traders followed. Settlers arrived in the Willamette Valley, 1834. In 1843 the first large wave of settlers arrived via the Oregon Trail. Early in the 20th century, the "Oregon System," reforms which included the initiative, referendum, recall, direct primary, and woman suffrage, was adopted.

Tourist attractions. John Day Fossil Beds National Monument; Columbia River Gorge; Mt. Hood & Timberline Lodge; Crater Lake National Park, deepest lake in the U.S. (1,932 ft.) in a former volcano, 6 mi. in diameter; Oregon Dunes National Recreation Area; Ft. Clatsop National Memorial includes a replica of the fort in which Lewis and Clark spent the winter of 1805-06. Oregon Caves National Monument contains stone waterfalls. Also skiing, annual Pendleton Round-Up.

Famous Oregonians include Ernest Bloch, Childe Hassam, Ernest Haycox, Chief Joseph, Edwin Markham, Dr. John McLoughlin, Joaquin Miller, Linus Pauling, John Reed, Alberto Salazar, William Simon U'Ren.

Chamber of Commerce: 220 Cottage St., N.E., Salem, OR 97301.

Pennsylvania

Keystone State

People. Population (1981): 11,871,000; **rank:** 4. **Pop. density:** 264.0 per sq. mi. **Urban** (1980): 69.3%. **Racial distrib.** (1980): 89.7% White; 8.8% Black; Hispanic (1980): 154,004. **Major ethnic groups:** Italian, Polish, German, English. **Net migration** (1970-79): −478,000.

Geography. Total area: 45,333 sq. mi.; **rank:** 33. **Land area:** 44,966 sq. mi. **Acres forested land:** 16,825,900. **Location:** Middle Atlantic state, bordered on the E by the Delaware R., on the S by the Mason-Dixon Line; on the W by West Virginia and Ohio; on the N/NE by Lake Erie and New York. **Climate:** continental with wide fluctuations in seasonal temperatures. **Topography:** Allegheny Mtns. run SW to NE, with Piedmont and Coast Plain in the SE triangle; Allegheny Front a diagonal spine across the state's center; N and W rugged plateau falls to Lake Erie Lowland. **Capital:** Harrisburg.

Economy. Principal industries: steel, travel, health, apparel, machinery, food & agriculture. **Principal manufactured goods:** primary metals, foods, fabricated metal products, non-electrical machinery, electrical machinery. **Value added by manufacture** (1979): $40.5 bln. **Agriculture: Chief crops:** corn, hay, mushrooms, apples, potatoes, winter wheat, oats, vegetables, tobacco, grapes. **Livestock:** 1.9 mln. cattle; 870,000 hogs/pigs; 85,000 sheep; 20.9 mln. poultry. **Timber/lumber** (1978): pine, spruce, oak, maple; 558 mln. bd. ft. **Minerals** (1978): bituminous coal, anthracite, sand & gravel, limestone. **Commercial fishing** (1980): $312,000. **Chief ports:** Philadelphia, Pittsburgh, Erie. **International airports at:** Philadelphia, Pittsburgh, Erie, Harrisburg. **Value of construction** (1981): $4.77 bln. **Employment distribution:** 27.9% manuf.; 20.8% trades; 20.4% serv.; 15.3% gvt. **Per capita income** (1981): $10,373. **Unemployment** (1981): 8.4%. **Tourism** (1980): out-of-state visitors spent $6.4 bln.

Finance. No. banks (1980): 362; **No. savings and loan assns.** (1981): 239.

Federal government. No. federal civilian employees (Mar. 1981): 114,592. **Avg. salary.** $19,804. **Notable federal facilities:** Army War College, Carlisle; Ships Control Ctr., Mechanicsburg; New Cumberland Army Depot; Philadelphia Navy Yard, Philadelphia.

Energy. Electricity production (1981, mwh, by source): Hydroelectric: 658,833; Mineral: 101.7 mln. Nuclear: 14.3 mln.

Education. No. schools: 5,451 elem. and second.; 178 higher ed. **Avg. salary, public school teachers** (1980): $16,700.

State data. Motto: Virtue, liberty and independence. **Flower:** Mountain laurel. **Bird:** Ruffed grouse. **Tree:** Hemlock. **Second** of the original 13 states to ratify the Constitution, Dec. 12, 1787. **State fair** at: Harrisburg; 2d week in Jan.

History. First settlers were Swedish, 1643, on Tinicum Is. In 1655 the Dutch seized the settlement but lost it to the British, 1664. The region was given by Charles II to William Penn, 1681, Philadelphia (brotherly love) was the capital of the colonies during most of the Revolution, and of the U.S., 1790-1800. Philadelphia was taken by the British, 1777; Washington's troops encamped at Valley Forge in the bitter winter of 1777-78. The Declaration of Independence, 1776, and the Constitution, 1787, were signed in Philadelphia.

Tourist attractions. Independence Hall, Liberty Bell, Carpenters Hall, all in Philadelphia; Valley Forge; Gettysburg battlefield; Amish festivals, Lancaster Cty., Hershey Chocolate World; Pocono Mtns.; Delaware Water Gap; Longwood Gardens, near Kennett Square; Pine Creek Gorge; hunting, fishing, winter sports.

Famous Pennsylvanians include Marian Anderson, Maxwell Anderson, Andrew Carnegie, Stephen Foster, Benjamin Franklin, George C. Marshall, Andrew W. Mellon, Robert E. Peary, Mary Roberts Rinehart, Betsy Ross.

Chamber of Commerce: 222 N. 3d St., Harrisburg, PA 17101.

Rhode Island

Little Rhody, Ocean State

People. Population (1981): 953,000; **rank:** 41. **Pop. density:** 908.5 per sq. mi. **Urban** (1980): 87.0% **Racial distrib.** (1980): 94.6% White; 2.9% Black; Hispanic (1980): 19,707. **Major ethnic groups:** Italian, English, Irish. **Net migration** (1970-79): −27,000.

Geography. Total area: 1,214 sq. mi.; **rank:** 50. **Land area:** 1,049 sq. mi. **Acres forested land:** 404,200. **Location:** New England state. **Climate:** invigorating and changeable. **Topography:** eastern lowlands of Narragansett Basin; western uplands of flat and rolling hills. **Capital:** Providence.

Economy. Principal industries: manufacturing, services. **Principal manufactured goods:** costume jewelry, machinery, textiles, electronics, silverware. **Value added by manufacture** (1978): $2.9 bln. **Agriculture: Chief crops:** potatoes, apples, corn. **Livestock:** 10,000 cattle; 8,700 hogs/pigs; 2,100 sheep; 260,000 poultry. **Timber/lumber:** oak, chestnut. **Minerals** (1980): gem stones, sand and gravel, stone. Total value mineral production, $7.5 mln. **Commercial fishing** (1980): $46.1 mln. **Chief ports:** Providence, Newport, Tiverton. **Value of construction** (1981): $380 mln. **Employment distribution** (1980): 32.1% manuf.; 20.8% serv.; 20.4% trade. **Per capita income** (1981): $10,466. **Unemployment** (1981):

7.6%. **Tourism** (1980): out-of-state visitors spent $375 mln.

Finance. Notable industries: banking, insurance. **No. banks** (1980): 17; **No. savings assns.** (1981): 5.

Federal government. No. federal civilian employees (Mar. 1981): 7,983. **Avg. salary:** $20,736. **Notable federal facilities:** Naval War College.

Energy. Electricity production (1981, mwh, by source): Mineral: 818,730.

Education. No. schools: 431 elem. and second.; 13 higher ed. **Avg. salary, public school teachers** (1980): $17,929.

State data. Motto: Hope. **Flower:** Violet. **Bird:** Rhode Island red. **Tree:** Red maple. **Song:** Rhode Island. **Thirteenth** of original 13 states to ratify the Constitution, May 29, 1790. **State fair** at: E. Greenwich; mid-Aug.

History. Rhode Island is distinguished for its battle for freedom of conscience and action, begun by Roger Williams, founder of Providence, who was exiled from Massachusetts Bay Colony in 1636, and Anne Hutchinson, exiled in 1638. Rhode Island gave protection to Quakers in 1657 and to Jews from Holland in 1658.

The colonists broke the power of the Narragansett Indians in the Great Swamp Fight, 1675, the decisive battle in King Philip's War. British trade restrictions angered the colonists and they burned the British revenue cutter Gaspee, 1772. The colony declared its independence May 4, 1776. Gen. John Sullivan and Lafayette won a partial victory, 1778, but failed to oust the British.

Tourist attractions. Newport mansions; summer resorts and water sports; Touro Synagogue, Newport, 1763; first Baptist Church in America, Providence, 1638; Gilbert Stuart birthplace, Saunderstown; Narragansett Indian Fall Festival.

Famous Rhode Islanders include Ambrose Burnside, George M. Cohan, Nelson Eddy, Jabez Gorham, Nathanael Greene, Christopher and Oliver La Farge, Matthew C. and Oliver Perry, Gilbert Stuart.

Chamber of Commerce: 206 Smith St., Providence, RI 02908.

South Carolina

Palmetto State

People. Population (1981): 3,167,000; **rank:** 24. **Pop. density:** 104.8 per sq. mi. **Urban** (1980): 54.1%. **Racial distrib.** (1980): 68.8% White; 30.4% Black; Hispanic (1980): 33,414. **Major ethnic groups:** German, English. **Net migration** (1970-80): +272,967.

Geography. Total area: 31,055 sq. mi.; **rank:** 40. **Land area:** 30,203.37 sq. mi. **Acres forested land:** 12,249,400. **Location:** south Atlantic coast state, bordering North Carolina on the N; Georgia on the SW and W; the Atlantic O. on the E, SE and S. **Climate:** humid sub-tropical. **Topography:** Blue Ridge province in NW has highest peaks; piedmont lies between the mountains and the fall line; coastal plain covers two-thirds of the state. **Capital:** Columbia.

Economy: Principal industries: tourism, textiles, apparel, chemical, agriculture, manufacturing. **Principal manufactured goods:** textiles, chemicals and allied products, non-electrical machinery, apparel and related products. **Value added by manufacture** (1978): $9.4 bln. **Agriculture: Chief crops:** tobacco, soybeans, corn, cotton, peaches, hay, vegetables. **Livestock** (1980): 625,000 cattle; 700,000 hogs/pigs; 9.49 mln. poultry. **Timber/lumber** (1979): pine, oak; 1.2 bln. bd. ft. **Minerals** (1980): cement, stone, limestone, granite, sand and gravel, clays; vermiculite, kaolin, both 2d in U.S. production. Total mineral production valued at $210 mln. **Commercial fishing** (1980): $20.5 mln. **Chief ports:** Charleston, Georgetown, Port Royal. **International airports at:** Charleston, Greenville-Spartanburg, Myrtle Beach, Columbia, Florence. **Value of construction** (1981): $2.1 bln. **Employment distribution** (1981): 32.4% manuf.; 19% gvt.; 13.9% serv. **Per capita income** (1981): $8,050. **Unemployment** (1981): 8.4%. **Tourism** (1979): out-of-state visitors spent $2.2 bln.

Finance. No. banks (1980): 85; **No. savings assns.** (1981): 70.

Federal government: No. federal civilian employees (Mar. 1981): 28,219. **Avg. Salary:** $19,618. **Notable federal facilities:** Polaris Submarine Base; Barnwell Nuclear Power Plant; Ft. Jackson.

Energy. Electricity production (1981, mwh, by source): Hydroelectric: 1.2 mln.; Mineral: 22.7 mln.; Nuclear: 17.3 mln.

Education. No. schools: 1,329 elem. and second.; 61 higher ed. **Avg. salary, public school teachers** (1980): $12,947.

State data. Motto: Dum Spiro Spero (While I breathe, I hope). **Flower:** Carolina jessamine. **Bird:** Carolina wren. **Tree:** Palmetto. **Song:** Carolina. **Eighth** of the original 13 states to ratify the Constitution, May 23, 1788. **State fair** at: Columbia; Oct. 16-25.

History. The first English colonists settled, 1670, on the Ashley River, moved to the site of Charleston, 1680. The colonists seized the government, 1775, and the royal governor fled. The British took Charleston, 1780, but were defeated at Kings Mountain that year, and at Cowpens and Eutaw Springs, 1781. In the 1830s, South Carolinians, angered by federal protective tariffs, adopted the Nullification Doctrine, holding a state can void an act of Congress. The state was the first to secede and, in 1861, Confederate troops fired on and forced the surrender of U. S. troops at Ft. Sumter, in Charleston Harbor, launching the Civil War.

Tourist attractions. Restored historic Charleston harbor area and Charleston gardens: Middleton Place, Magnolia, Cypress; other gardens at Brookgreen, Edisto, Glencairn; state parks; coastal islands; shore resorts such as Myrtle Beach; fishing and quail hunting; Ft. Sumter National Monument, in Charleston Harbor; Charleston Museum, est. 1773, is the oldest museum in the U.S..

Famous South Carolinians include James F. Byrnes, John C. Calhoun, DuBose Heyward, James Longstreet, Francis Marion, Charles Pinckney, John Rutledge, Thomas Sumter.

Chamber of Commerce: 1002 Calhoun St., Columbia, SC 29201.

South Dakota

Coyote State, Sunshine State

People. Population (1981): 686,000; **rank:** 45. **Pop. density:** 9.0 per sq. mi. **Urban** (1980): 46.4%. **Racial distrib.** (1980): 92.6% White; 0.31% Black; 7.1% Other (includes American Indians); Hispanic (1980): 4,028. **Major ethnic groups:** German, Norwegian, Russian. **Net migration** (1970-81): −24,511.

Geography. Total area: 77,047 sq. mi.; **rank:** 16. **Land area:** 75,955 sq. mi. **Acres forested land:** 1,702,000. **Location:** West North Central state bounded on the N by North Dakota; on the E by Minnesota and Iowa; on the S by Nebraska; on the W by Wyoming and Montana. **Climate:** characterized by extremes of temperature, persistent winds, low precipitation and humidity. **Topography:** Prairie Plains in the E; rolling hills of the Great Plains in the W; the Black Hills, rising 3,500 ft. in the SW corner. **Capital:** Pierre.

Economy: Principal industries: agriculture, tourism, manufacturing. **Principal manufactured goods:** processed meats, electrical appliances, occupational health and safety products, computer sub-assemblies. **Value added by manufacture** (1978): $726.1 mln. **Agriculture: Chief crops:** corn; spring, durum, winter wheat; barley, oats, rye, flax, sorghum, soybeans, sunflowers, millet. **Livestock** (1981): 3.9 mln. cattle; 1.71 mln. hogs/pigs; 780,000 sheep; 2.0 mln. poultry. **Timber/lumber** (1979): ponderosa pine; 190 mln. bd. ft. **Minerals** (1980 est.): gold (1st in U.S.), crude oil, stone, sand and gravel. Total value mineral production, $238.3 mln. **Commercial fishing** (1980): $340,000. **Value of construction** (1981): $351 mln. **Employment distribution:** 15.5% serv.; 12.3%

agric.; 7.7% manuf. **Per capita income** (1981): $8,793. **Unemployment** (1981): 5.1%. **Tourism** (1979): out-of-state visitors spent $415 mln.

Finance. No. banks (1980): 153; **No. savings assns.** (1981): 16.

Federal government. No. federal civilian employees (Mar. 1981): 8,288. **Avg. salary:** $19,392. **Notable federal facilities:** Bureau of Indian Affairs, Ellsworth AFB, Corp of Engineers.

Energy. Electricity production (1981, mwh, by source): Hydroelectric: 5.3 mln.; Mineral: 2.7 mln.

Education: No. schools: 869 elem. and second.; 18 higher ed. **Avg. salary, public school teachers** (1980): $12,350.

State data. Motto: Under God, the people rule. **Flower:** Pasque flower. **Bird:** Ringnecked pheasant. **Tree:** Black Hills spruce. **Song:** Hail, South Dakota. **Entered union** Nov. 2, 1889; rank, 40th. **State fair** at: Huron; early Sept.

History. Les Verendryes explored the region, 1742-43. Lewis and Clark passed through the area, 1804 and 1806. First white American settlement was at Fort Pierre, 1817. Gold was discovered, 1874, on the Sioux Reservation; miners rushed in. The U.S. first tried to stop them, then relaxed its opposition. Custer's defeat by the Sioux followed; the Sioux relinquished the land, 1877 and the "great Dakota Boom" began, 1879. A new Indian uprising came in 1890, climaxed by the massacre of Indian families at Wounded Knee.

Tourist attractions. Needles Highway through the Black Hills; Badlands National Park "moonscape"; Custer State Park's bison and burro herds; Ft. Sisseton, a restored army frontier post of 1864; the "Great Lakes of South Dakota," reservoirs created behind Oahe, Big Bend, Ft. Randall, and Gavins Point dams on the Missouri R.

Mount Rushmore, in the Black Hills, has an altitude of 6,200 ft. Sculptured on its granite face are the heads of Washington, Jefferson, Lincoln, and Theodore Roosevelt. These busts by Gutzon Borglum are proportionate to men 465 ft. tall. Rushmore is visited by about 2 million persons annually.

Famous South Dakotans include Crazy Horse, Alvin H. Hansen, Dr. Ernest O. Lawrence, Sacagawea, Sitting Bull.

Chamber of Commerce: P.O. Box 190, Pierre, SD 57501.

Tennessee

Volunteer State

People. Population (1981): 4,612,000; **rank:** 17. **Pop. density:** 111.6 per sq. mi. **Urban** (1980): 60.4%. **Racial distrib.** (1980): 83.5% White; 15.8% Black; Hispanic (1980): 34,081. **Major ethnic groups:** German, English, Italian. **Net migration** (1970-80): +231,925.

Geography. Total area: 42,244 sq. mi.; **rank:** 34. **Land area:** 41,328 sq. mi. **Acres forested land:** 13,160,500. **Location:** East South Central state bounded on the N by Kentucky and Virginia; on the E by North Carolina; on the S by Georgia, Alabama, and Mississippi; on the W by Arkansas and Missouri. **Climate:** humid continental to the N; humid sub-tropical to the S. **Topography:** rugged country in the E; the Great Smoky Mtns. of the Unakas; low ridges of the Appalachian Valley; the flat Cumberland Plateau; slightly rolling terrain and knobs of the Interior Low Plateau, the largest region; Eastern Gulf Coastal Plain to the W, is laced with meandering streams; Mississippi Alluvial Plain, a narrow strip of swamp and flood plain in the extreme W. **Capital:** Nashville.

Economy. Principal industries: trade, services, construction; transp., commun., public utilities; finance, ins., real estate. **Principal manufactured goods:** apparel, chemicals, electrical mach., food prods., non-elec. mach., fabricated metal prods., primary and fabricated metals, foods, electrical and electronic machinery, transportation equipment, apparel. **Value added by manufacture** (1978): $14.0 bln. **Agriculture: Chief crops:** soybeans, tobacco, cotton, wheat, corn, nursery stock. **Livestock:** 2.4 mln. cattle; 1.1 mln. hogs/pigs; 11,000 sheep; 5.7 mln. poultry. **Timber/lumber** (1979): red oak, white oak, yellow poplar, hickory; 684 mln. bd. ft. **Minerals** (1978): bituminous coal, stone, zinc, ball clay, cement. Total value mineral production, $347.5 mln. **Commercial fishing** (1978): $2.4 mln. **Chief ports:** Memphis, Nashville, Chattanooga. **International airports at:** Memphis. **Value of construction** (1981): $2.56 bln. **Employment distribution:** 26.4% manuf.; 19.4% trade; 16.1% govt.; 16.0% serv. **Per capita income** (1981): $8,604. **Unemployment** (1981): 9.1%. **Tourism** (1979): out-of-state visitors spent $1.7 bln.

Finance. Notable industries: insurance. **No. banks** (1980): 353; **No. savings assns.** (1981): 92.

Federal government. No. federal civilian employees (Mar. 1981): 66,317. **Avg. salary:** $20,877. **Notable federal facilities:** Tennessee Valley Authority; Oak Ridge Nat'l. Laboratories.

Energy: Electricity production (1981, mwh, by source): Hydroelectric: 5.9 mln.; Mineral: 48.3 mln.; Nuclear: 4.7 mln.

Education. No. schools: 1,856 elem. and second.; 76 higher ed. **Avg. salary, public school teachers** (1980): $13,158.

State data. Motto: Agriculture and commerce. **Flower:** Iris. **Bird:** Mockingbird. **Tree:** Tulip poplar. **Song:** The Tennessee Waltz. **Entered union** June 1, 1796; rank, 16th. **State fair** at: Nashville; 3d week of Sept.

History. Spanish explorers first visited the area, 1541. English traders crossed the Great Smokies from the east while France's Marquette and Jolliet sailed down the Mississippi on the west, 1673. First permanent settlement was by Virginians on the Watauga River, 1769. During the Revolution, the colonists helped win the Battle of Kings Mountain, N.C., 1780, and joined other eastern campaigns. The state seceded from the Union 1861, and saw many engagements of the Civil War, but 30,000 soldiers fought for the Union.

Tourist attractions. Natural wonders include Reelfoot Lake, the reservoir basin of the Mississippi R. formed by the 1811 earthquake; Lookout Mountain, Chattanooga; Fall Creek Falls, 256 ft. high; Great Smoky Mountains National Park.

Also, the Hermitage, 13 mi. E of Nashville, home of Andrew Jackson; the homes of presidents Polk and Andrew Johnson; the Parthenon, Nashville, a replica of the Parthenon of Athens; the Grand Old Opry, Nashville.

Famous Tennesseans include Davy Crockett, David Farragut, William C. Handy, Sam Houston, Cordell Hull, Grace Moore, Dinah Shore, Alvin York.

Tourist Information: Tourist Development Office, 601 Broadway, Nashville, TN 37202.

Texas

Lone Star State

People. Population (1981): 14,766,000 **rank:** 3. **Pop. density:** 56.3 per sq. mi. **Urban** (1980): 79.6%. **Racial distrib.** (1980): 78.6% White; 12.0% Black; Hispanic (1980): 2,985,643. **Major ethnic groups:** Mexican, German. **Net migration** (1970-79): +1,045,000.

Geography: Total area: 267,338 sq. mi.; **rank:** 2. **Land area:** 262,134 sq. mi. **Acres forested land:** 23,279,300. **Location:** Southwestern state, bounded on the SE by the Gulf of Mexico; on the SW by Mexico, separated by the Rio Grande; surrounding states are Louisiana, Arkansas, Oklahoma, New Mexico. **Climate:** extremely varied; driest region is the Trans-Pecos; wettest is the NE. **Topography:** Gulf Coast Plain in the S and SE; North Central Plains slope upward with some hills; the Great Plains extend over the Panhandle, are broken by low mountains; the Trans-Pecos is the southern extension of the Rockies. **Capital:** Austin.

Economy. Principal industries: petroleum, manufacturing, construction. **Principal manufactured goods:** machinery, transportation equipment, foods, refined petroleum, apparel. **Value added by manufacture** (1978): $36.4 bln. **Agriculture: Chief crops:** cotton, grain sorghum, grains, vegetables, citrus and other fruits, pecans, peanuts. **Livestock:** 13.7 mln. cattle; 930,000 hogs/pigs; 2.36 mln. sheep; 13.3 mln. poultry. **Timber/lumber** (1978): pine, cypress; 950 mln. bd. ft. **Minerals** (1978): petroleum, natural gas, natural gas liquids, cement, sulfur, stone, sand and gravel, lime, salt; total $19.9 bln. **Commercial fishing** (1980): $153.9 mln. **Chief ports:** Houston, Galveston, Brownsville, Beaumont, Port Arthur, Corpus Christi. **Major International airports at:** Houston, Dallas/Ft. Worth, San Antonio. **Value of construction** (1981): $16.1 bln. **Employment distribution:** 18% manuf.; 17% serv.; 6% transp. **Per capita income** (1981): $10,743. **Unemployment** (1981): 5.3%. **Tourism** (1979): out-of-state visitors spent $4.8 bln.

Finance. No. banks (1980): 1,427; **No. savings assns.** (1981): 311.

Federal government. No. federal civilian employees (Mar. 1981): 132,865. **Avg. salary:** $20,068. **Notable federal facilities:** Fort Hood (Killeen).

Energy. Electricity production (1981, mwh, by source): Hydroelectric: 1.1 mln.; Mineral: 206 mln.

Education. No. schools: 5,953 elem. and second.; 147 higher ed. **Avg. salary, public school teachers** (1980): $14,157.

State data. Motto: Friendship. **Flower:** Bluebonnet. **Bird:** Mockingbird. **Tree:** Pecan. **Song:** Texas, Our Texas. **Entered union** Dec. 29, 1845; rank, 28th. **State fair** at: Dallas; mid-Oct.

History. Pineda sailed along the Texas coast, 1519; Cabeza de Vaca and Coronado visited the interior, 1541. Spaniards made the first settlement at Ysleta, near El Paso, 1682. Americans moved into the land early in the 19th century. Mexico, of which Texas was a part, won independence from Spain, 1821; Santa Anna became dictator, 1835. Texans rebelled; Santa Anna wiped out defenders of the Alamo, 1836. Sam Houston's Texans defeated Santa Anna at San Jacinto and independence was proclaimed the same year. In 1845, Texas was admitted to the Union.

Tourist attractions. Padre Island National Seashore; Big Bend, Guadalupe Mtns. national parks; The Alamo; Ft. Davis; Six Flags Amusement Park. Named for Pres. Lyndon B. Johnson are a state park, a natl. historic site marking his birthplace, boyhood home, and ranch, all near Johnson City, and a library in Austin.

Famous Texans include Stephen Austin, James Bowie, Carol Burnett, J. Frank Dobie, Sam Houston, Howard Hughes, Mary Martin, Chester Nimitz, Katharine Ann Porter, Sam Rayburn.

Chamber of Commerce: 1004 International Life Bldg., Austin, TX 78701.

Utah

Beehive State

People. Population (1981): 1,518,000; **rank:** 36. **Pop. density:** 18.5 per sq. mi. **Urban** (1980): 84.4%. **Racial distrib.** (1980): 95% White; —% Black; Hispanic (1980): 60,302. **Major ethnic groups:** Hispanics, Amer. Indian, Asian. **Net migration** (1970-80): +149,000.

Geography. Total area: 84,916 sq. mi.; **rank:** 11. **Land area:** 82,096 sq. mi. **Acres forested land:** 15,557,400. **Location:** Middle Rocky Mountain state; its southeastern corner touches Colorado, New Mexico, and Arizona, and is the only spot in the U.S. where 4 states join. **Climate:** arid; yet the SW has a semitropical climate. **Topography:** high Colorado plateau is cut by brilliantly-colored canyons of the SE; broad, flat, desert-like Great Basin of the W; the Great Salt Lake and Bonneville Salt Flats to the NW; Middle Rockies in the NE run E-W; valleys and plateaus of the Wasatch Front. **Capital:** Salt Lake City.

Economy. Principal industries: mining, manufacturing, tourism, trade, services, transportation. **Principal manufactured goods:** guided missiles and parts, electronic components, food products, primary metals, electrical and transportation equipment. **Value added by manufacture** (1978 est.): $2.3 bln. **Agriculture: Chief crops:** wheat, hay, apples, peaches, barley, alfalfa seed. **Livestock:** 875,000 cattle; 58,000 hogs/pigs; 660,000 sheep; 2.5 mln. poultry. **Timber/lumber:** aspen, spruce, pine. **Minerals** (1980): crude oil, copper, coal, uranium, gold, natural gas, vanadium, silver, zinc, lead, iron ore, lime, salt. Total value of mineral production valued at $2.0 bln. **International airports at:** Salt Lake City. **Value of construction** (1981): $1.1 bln. **Employment distribution:** (1981) 23.4% trade; 22.4% govt., 18.6% serv.; 16.0% manuf. **Per capita income** (1981): $8,307. **Unemployment** (1981): 6.7%. **Tourism** (1978): out-of-state visitors spent $220 mln.

Finance. No. banks (1980): 78; **No. savings assns.** (1981): 15.

Federal government. No. federal civilian employees (Mar. 1981): 33,722. **Avg. salary:** $19,731. **Notable federal facilities:** Hill AFB; Tooele Army Depot, IRS Western Service Center.

Energy. Electricity production (1981, mwh, by source): Hydroelectric: 623,003; Mineral: 11.1 mln.

Education. No. schools: 574 elem. and second.; 14 higher ed. **Avg. salary, public school teachers** (1980): $14,965.

State data. Motto: Industry. **Flower:** Sego lily. **Bird:** Seagull. **Tree:** Blue spruce. **Song:** Utah, We Love Thee. **Entered union** Jan. 4, 1896; rank, 45th. **State fair** at: Salt Lake City; Sept.

History. Spanish Franciscans visited the area, 1776, the first white men to do so. American fur traders followed. Permanent settlement began with the arrival of the Mormons, 1847. They made the arid land bloom and created a prosperous economy, organized the State of Deseret, 1849, and asked admission to the Union. This was not achieved until 1896, after a long period of controversy over the Mormon Church's doctrine of polygamy, which it discontinued in 1890.

Tourist attractions. Temple Square, Mormon Church hdqtrs., Salt Lake City; Great Salt Lake; fishing streams; lakes and reservoirs, numerous winter sports; campgrounds. Natural wonders may be seen at Zion, Canyonlands, Bryce Canyon, Arches, and Capitol Reef national parks; Dinosaur, Rainbow Bridge, Timpanogas Cave, and Natural Bridges national monuments. Also Lake Powell and Flaming Gorge Dam.

Famous Utahans include Maude Adams, Ezra Taft Benson, John Moses Browning, Philo Farnsworth, Osmond Family, Ivy Baker Priest, George Romney, Brigham Young, Loretta Young.

Tourist information: Division of Travel Development, Council Hall, Salt Lake City, UT 84114.

Vermont

Green Mountain State

People. Population (1981): 516,000; **rank:** 48. **Pop. density:** 55.7 per sq. mi. **Urban** (1980): 33.8%. **Racial distrib.** (1980): 99.0% White; 0.22% Black; Hispanic (1980): 3,304. **Major ethnic groups:** English, Italian, German. **Net migration** (1970-80): +66,724.

Geography. Total area: 9,609 sq. mi.; **rank:** 43. **Land area:** 9,267 sq. mi. **Acres forested land:** 4,511,700. **Location:** northern New England state. **Climate:** temperate, with considerable temperature extremes; heavy snowfall in mountains. **Topography:** Green Mtns. N-S backbone 20-36 mi. wide; avg. altitude 1,000 ft. **Capital:** Montpelier.

Economy. Principal industries: manufacturing, tourism, agriculture, mining, government. **Principal manufactured goods:** machine tools, furniture, scales, books, computer components, skis, fishing rods. **Value added by manufacture** (1978): $1.38 bln. **Agriculture: Chief crops:** apples, maple syrup, silage corn, hay; also, dairy products. **Livestock:** 355,000 cattle; 9,000 hogs/pigs; 11,000 sheep; 325,000 poultry. **Timber/lumber:** pine, spruce, fir, hemlock. **Minerals** (1979): stone; asbestos (2d in U.S.); talc (1st in U.S.); sand and gravel; gemstones; dimension granite, marble, and slate (2d in U.S.). Total value mineral production, $49.5 mln. **International airports at:** Burlington. **Value of construction** (1981): $246 mln. **Employment distribution:** 22% manuf.; 19% serv.; 15% retail trade. **Per capita income** (1980): $8,654. **Unemployment** (1981): 5.7%. **Tourism** (1980): out-of-state visitors spent $450 mln.

Finance. No. banks (1980): 29; **No. savings assns.** (1981): 5.

Federal government. No. federal civilian employees (Mar. 1981): 3,229. **Avg. salary:** $20,317.

Energy. Electricity production (1981, mwh, by source): Hydroelectric: 932,798; Mineral: 40,442; Nuclear: 3.6 mln.

Education. No. schools: 443 elem. and second.; 21 higher ed. **Avg. salary, public school teachers** (1980): $12,750.

State data. Motto: Freedom and unity. **Flower:** Red clover. **Bird:** Hermit thrush. **Tree:** Sugar maple. **Song:** Hail, Vermont. **Entered union** Mar. 4, 1791; rank, 14th. **State fair** at: Rutland; early Sept.

History. Champlain explored the lake that bears his name, 1609. First American settlement was Ft. Dummer, 1724, near Brattleboro. Ethan Allen and the Green Mountain Boys captured Ft. Ticonderoga, 1775; John Stark defeated part of Burgoyne's forces near Bennington, 1777. In the War of 1812, Thomas MacDonough defeated a British fleet on Champlain off Plattsburgh, 1814.

Tourist attractions. Year-round outdoor sports, esp. hiking, camping and skiing; there are over 56 ski areas in the state. Popular are the Shelburne Museum; Rock of Ages Tourist Center, Graniteville; Vermont Marble Exhibit, Proctor; Bennington Battleground; Pres. Coolidge homestead, Plymouth; Maple Grove Maple Museum, St. Johnsbury.

Famous Vermonters include Ethan Allen, Adm. George Dewey, John Dewey, Stephen A. Douglas, Dorothy Canfield Fisher, James Fisk.

Chamber of Commerce: P.O. Box 37, Montpelier, VT 05602.

Virginia

Old Dominion

People. Population (1981): 5,430,000; **rank:** 14. **Pop. density:** 136.5 per sq. mi. **Urban** (1980): 66.0% **Racial distrib.** (1980): 79.1% White; 18.9% Black; Hispanic (1980): 79,873. **Major ethnic groups:** English, German, Italian. **Net migration** (1970-80): +348,200.

Geography. Total area: 40,817 sq. mi.; **rank:** 36. **Land area:** 39,780 sq. mi. **Acres forested land:** 16,417,400. **Location:** South Atlantic state bounded by the Atlantic O. on the E and surrounded by North Carolina, Tennessee, Kentucky, West Virginia, and Maryland. **Climate:** mild and equable. **Topography:** mountain and valley region in the W, including the Blue Ridge Mtns.; rolling piedmont plateau; tidewater, or coastal plain, including the eastern shore. **Capital:** Richmond.

Economy. Principal industries: government, trade, manufacturing, tourism, agriculture. **Principal manufactured goods:** textiles, food processing, apparel, transportation equipment, chemicals. **Value added by manufacture** (1978): $11.9 bln. **Agriculture: Chief crops:** tobacco, soybeans, peanuts, corn. **Livestock:** 1.62 mln. cattle; 670,000 hogs/pigs; 172,000 sheep; 104 mln. poultry. **Timber/lumber** (1977): pine and hardwoods; 957 mln. bd. ft. **Minerals** (1977): bituminous coal, stone, cement, lime, sand and gravel, zinc. Total value mineral production, $1.3 bln. **Commercial fishing** (1980): $85 mln. **Chief ports:** Hampton Roads. **International airports at:** Norfolk, Dulles, Richmond, Newport News. **Value of construction** (1981): $3.45 bln. **Employment distribution:** 19% manuf.; 21% trade; 19% serv.; 24% gvt. **Per capita income** (1981): $10,445. **Unemployment** (1981): 6.1%. **Tourism** (1978): out-of-state visitors spent $2.4 bln.

Finance. No. banks (1980): 230; **No. savings assns.** (1981): 86.

Federal government. No. federal civilian employees (Mar. 1981): 133,664. **Avg. salary:** $22,273. **Notable federal facilities:** Pentagon; Naval Sta., Norfolk; Naval Air Sta., Norfolk, Virginia Beach; Naval Shipyard, Portsmouth; Marine Corps Base, Quantico; Langley AFB; NASA at Langley.

Energy. Electricity production (1981, mwh, by source): Hydroelectric: 337,508; Mineral: 19.3 mln.; Nuclear: 17.8 mln.

Education. No. schools: 2,031 elem. and second.; 72 higher ed. **Avg. salary, public school teachers** (1980): $14,025.

State data. Motto: Sic Semper Tyrannis (Thus always to tyrants). **Flower:** Dogwood. **Bird:** Cardinal. **Tree:** Dogwood. **Song:** Carry Me Back to Old Virginia. **Tenth** of the original 13 states to ratify the Constitution, June 26, 1788. **State fair** at: Richmond; late Sept.-early Oct.

History. English settlers founded Jamestown, 1607. Virginians took over much of the government from royal Gov. Dunmore in 1775, forcing him to flee. Virginians under George Rogers Clark freed the Ohio-Indiana-Illinois area of British forces. Benedict Arnold burned Richmond and Petersburg for the British, 1781. That same year, Britain's Cornwallis was trapped at Yorktown and surrendered.

Tourist attractions. Colonial Williamsburg; Busch Gardens; Wolf Trap Farm, near Falls Church; Arlington National Cemetery; Mt. Vernon, home of George Washington; Jamestown Festival Park; Yorktown; Jefferson's Monticello, Charlottesville; Robert E. Lee's birthplace, Stratford Hall, and grave, at Lexington; Appomattox; Shenandoah National Park; Blue Ridge Parkway; Virginia Beach.

Famous Virginians include Richard E. Byrd, James B. Cabell, Patrick Henry, Joseph E. Johnston, Robert E. Lee, Meriwether Lewis and William Clark, John Marshall, Edgar Allan Poe, Walter Reed, Booker T. Washington.

Chamber of Commerce: 611 E. Franklin St., Richmond, VA 23219.

Washington

Evergreen State

People. Population (1981): 4,217,000; **rank:** 20. **Pop. density:** 63.3 per sq. mi. **Urban** (1980): 73.5%. **Racial distrib.** (1980): 91.4% White; 2.5% Black; Hispanic (1980): 119,986. **Major ethnic groups:** German, English, Norwegian. **Net migration** (1970-81): +549,000.

Geography. Total area: 68,192 sq. mi.; **rank:** 20. **Land area:** 66,570 sq. mi. **Acres forested land:** 23,181,000. **Location:** northwestern coastal state bordered by Canada on the N; Idaho on the E; Oregon on the S; and the Pacific O. on the W. **Climate:** mild, dominated by the Pacific O. and protected by the Rockies. **Topography:** Olympic Mtns. on NW peninsula; open land along coast to Columbia R.; flat terrain of Puget Sound Lowland; Cascade Mtns. region's high peaks to the E; Columbia Basin in central portion; highlands to the NE; mountains to the SE. **Capital:** Olympia.

Economy. Principal industries: transp. equip., lumber and wood products, agriculture, food products. **Principal manufactured goods:** aircraft, lumber and plywood, pulp and paper, aluminum, fruits and vegetables. **Value added by manufacture** (1978): $10.4 bln. **Agriculture: Chief crops:** Wheat, apples, potatoes, hay, barley, hops, pears. **Livestock** (1981): 1.45 mln. cattle; 100,000 hogs/pigs; 80,000 sheep; 6,598 mln. poultry. **Timber/lumber** (1981): Douglas fir, hemlock, cedar, pine; 4.3 bln. bd. ft. **Minerals** (1977): cement, coal, sand and gravel, stone. Total value mineral production, $216 mln. **Commercial fishing** (1980): $85.5 mln. **Chief ports:** Seattle, Tacoma, Vancouver, Kelso-Longview. **International airports at:** Seattle/-Tacoma, Spokane, Boeing Field. **Value of construction** (1981): $3.64 bln. **Employment distribution:** 24% trade;

20% govt.; 20% serv.; 19% manuf. **Per capita income** (1981): $11,266. **Unemployment** (1981): 9.5%. **Tourism** (1980): out-of-state visitors spent $2.7 bln.

Finance. No. banks (1980): 103; **No. savings assns.** (1981): 47.

Federal government. No. federal civilian employees (Mar. 1981): 54,231. **Avg. salary:** $21,471. **Notable federal facilities:** Bonneville Power Admin.; Ft. Lewis; McChord AFB; Hanford Nuclear Reservation; Bremerton Naval Shipyards.

Energy. Electricity production (1981, mwh, by source): Hydroelectric: 93.6 mln.; Mineral: 7.0 mln.; Nuclear: 2.0 mln.

Education. No. schools: 1,933 elem. and second.; 49 higher ed. **Avg. salary, public school teachers** (1980): $18,815.

State data. Motto. Alki (By and by). **Flower:** Western rhododendron. **Bird:** Willow goldfinch. **Tree:** Western hemlock. **Song:** Washington, My Home. **Entered union** Nov. 11, 1889; rank, 42d.

History. Spain's Bruno Hezeta sailed the coast, 1775. American Capt. Robert Gray sailed up the Columbia River, 1792. Canadian fur traders set up Spokane House, 1810; Americans under John Jacob Astor established a post at Fort Okanogan, 1811. Missionary Marcus Whitman settled near Walla Walla, 1836. Final agreement on the border of Washington and Canada was made with Britain, 1846, and gold was discovered in the state's northeast, 1855, bringing new settlers.

Tourist attractions. Mt. Rainier, Olympic, North Cascades national parks; Mt. St. Helens; Pacific beaches; Puget Sound; Indian culture; outdoor year-round sports; rodeos.

Famous Washingtonians include Bing Crosby, William O. Douglas, Mary McCarthy, Edward R. Murrow, Theodore Roethke, Marcus Whitman, Minoru Yamasaki.

Chamber of Commerce: P.O. Box 658, Olympia, WA 98507.

West Virginia

Mountain State

People. Population (1981): 1,952,000. **rank:** 34. **Pop. density:** 81.1 per sq. mi. **Urban** (1980): 36.2. **Racial distrib.** (1980): 96.1% White; 3.3% Black; Hispanic (1980): 12,707. **Major ethnic groups:** Italian, English, German. **Net migration** (1970-79): +28,000.

Geography. Total area: 24,181 sq. mi.; **rank:** 41. **Land area:** 24,070 sq. mi. **Acres forested land:** 11,668,600. **Location:** South Atlantic state bounded on the N by Ohio, Pennsylvania, Maryland; on the S and W by Virginia, Kentucky, Ohio; on the E by Maryland and Virginia. **Climate:** humid continental climate except for marine modification in the lower panhandle. **Topography:** ranging from hilly to mountainous; Allegheny Plateau in the W, covers two-thirds of the state; mountains here are the highest in the state, over 4,000 ft. **Capital:** Charleston.

Economy. Principal industries: mining, mineral and chemical production, primary metals and stone, clay, and glass prods., agriculture. **Principal manufactured goods:** machinery, hardwood prods., fabricated metals, basic organic chemicals, aluminum, steel. **Value added by manufacture** (1978): $4.4 bln. **Agriculture: Chief crops:** apples, peaches, hay, tobacco, corn. **Chief products:** milk, eggs, honey. **Livestock:** 620,000 cattle; 52,000 hogs/pigs; 110,000 sheep; 24.7 mln. poultry. **Timber/lumber:** oak, yellow poplar, hickory, walnut, cherry. **Minerals** (1977): bituminous coal, natural gas, crude petroleum, clay, cement, lime, salt. Total value mineral production $3.7 billion. **Commercial fishing** (1980): $21,000. **Chief port:** Huntington. **Value of construction** (1981): $685 mln. **Per capita income** (1981): $8,334. **Unemployment** (1980): 9.4%. **Tourism** (1981): out-of-state visitors spent $1.1 bln.

Finance. No. banks (1980): 237; **No. savings assns.** (1981): 28.

Federal government. No. federal civilian employees (Mar. 1981): 13,006. **Avg. salary:** $20,045. **Notable federal facilities:** National Radio Astronomy Observatory, Green Bank; Bureau of Public Debt. Bldg., Parkersburg; Natl. Park, Harper's Ferry; Correctional Institution for Women, Alderson.

Energy. Electricity production (1980, mwh, by source): Hydroelectric: 423,784; Mineral: 70.3 mln.; Nuclear: —.

Education. No. schools: 1,317 elem. and second.; 28 higher ed. **Avg. salary, public school teachers** (1980): $13,000.

State Data. Motto: Montani Semper Liberi (Mountaineers are always free) **Flower:** Big rhododendron. **Bird:** Cardinal. **Tree:** Sugar maple. **Songs:** The West Virginia Hills; This Is My West Virginia; West Virginia, My Home, Sweet Home. **Entered union** June 20, 1863; rank, 35th. **State fair** at: Fairlea; 3d week in Aug.

History. Early explorers included George Washington, 1753, and Daniel Boone. The area became part of Virginia and often objected to rule by the eastern part of the state. When Virginia seceded, 1861, the Wheeling Conventions repudiated the act and created a new state, Kanawha, subsequently changed to West Virginia. It was admitted to the Union as such, 1863.

Tourist attractions. Harpers Ferry National Historic Park has been restored to its condition in 1859, when John Brown seized the U.S. Armory. Still standing is the fire-engine house in which Brown and a score of followers were besieged and captured by a force of U.S. Marines under Col. Robert E. Lee.

Also Science and Cultural Center, Charleston; White Sulphur and Berkeley Springs mineral water resorts; state parks and forests; trout fishing; turkey, deer, and bear hunting.

Famous West Virginians include Newton D. Baker, Pearl Buck, John W. Davis, Thomas "Stonewall" Jackson, Dwight Whitney Morrow, Michael Owens.

Chamber of Commerce: P.O. Box 2789, Charleston, WV 25330.

Wisconsin

Badger State

People. Population (1981): 4,742,000; **rank:** 16. **Pop. density:** 87.1 per sq. mi. **Urban** (1980): 64.2%. **Racial distrib.** (1980): 94.4% White; 3.8% Black; Hispanic (1980): 62,981. **Major ethnic groups:** German, Norwegian, Italian. **Net migration** (1970-80): +9,000.

Geography. Total area: 56,154 sq. mi.; **rank:** 26. **Land area:** 54,464 sq. mi. **Acres forested land:** 14,907,700. **Location:** North central state, bounded on the N by Lake Superior and Upper Michigan; on the E by Lake Michigan; on the S by Illinois; on the W by the St. Croix and Mississippi rivers. **Climate:** long, cold winters and short, warm summers tempered by the Great Lakes. **Topography:** narrow Lake Superior Lowland plain met by Northern Highland which slopes gently to the sandy crescent Central Plain; Western Upland in the SW; 3 broad parallel limestone ridges running N-S are separated by wide and shallow lowlands in the SE. **Capital:** Madison.

Economy. Principal industries: manufacturing, trade, services, government, transportation, communications, agriculture, tourism. **Principal manufactured goods:** machinery, foods, fabricated metals, transportation equipment, paper and wood products. **Value added by manufacture** (1978): $18.8 bln. **Agriculture: Chief crops:** corn, beans, beets, peas, hay, oats, cabbage, cranberries. **Chief products:** milk, cheese. **Livestock:** 4.6 mln. cattle, 1.8 mln. milk cows; 1.68 mln. hogs/pigs; 127,000 sheep; 10.5 mln. poultry. **Timber/lumber:** maple, birch, oak, evergreens. **Minerals** (1980): sand and gravel and crushed stone, dimension stone, taconite, lime. Total value mineral production $142.5 mln. **Commercial fishing** (1980): $5.9 mln. **Chief ports:** Superior, Milwaukee, Green Bay, La Crosse, Kenosha. **International airports at:** Milwaukee. **Value of construction** (1981): $2.12 bln. **Employment distribution** (1980): 28.8% manuf.; 22.6% trade; 18.8% serv.; 16.5% gvt. **Per capita income** (1981): $10,056. **Unemployment** (1981): 7.8%. **Tourism** (1979): out-of-state visitors spent $2.4 bln.

Finance. Notable industries: insurance. **No. banks** (1980): 641; **No. savings assns.** (1981): 103.

Federal government. No. federal civilian employees (Mar. 1981): 21,346. **Avg. salary:** $19,814. **Notable federal facilities:** Ft. McCoy.

Energy. Electricity production (1981, mwh, by source): Hydroelectric: 1.8 mln.; Mineral: 25.4 mln.; Nuclear: 9.7 mln.

Education. No. schools: 3,096 elem and second.; 62 higher ed. **Avg. salary, public school teachers** (1980): $18,180.

State data. Motto: Forward. **Flower:** Wood violet. **Bird:** Robin. **Tree:** Sugar maple. **Song:** On, Wisconsin! **Entered union** May 29, 1848; rank, 30th. **State fair** at: West Allis; mid-Aug.

History. Jean Nicolet was the first European to see the Wisconsin area, arriving in Green Bay, 1634; French missionaries and fur traders followed. The British took over, 1763. The U.S. won the land after the Revolution but the British were not ousted until after the War of 1812. Lead miners came next, then farmers. Railroads were started in 1851, serving growing wheat harvests and iron mines.

Tourist attractions. Old Wade House and Carriage Museum, Greenbush; Villa Louis, Prairie du Chien; Circus World Museum, Baraboo; Wisconsin Dells; Door County peninsula; Chequamegon and Nicolet national forests; Lake Winnebago; numerous lakes for water sports, ice boating and fishing; skiing and hunting.

Famous Wisconsinites include Edna Ferber, King Camp Gillette, Harry Houdini, Robert LaFollette, Alfred Lunt, Joseph R. McCarthy, Spencer Tracy, Thorstein Veblen, Orson Welles, Thornton Wilder, Frank Lloyd Wright.

Tourist information: Wisconsin Assn. of Manufacturers and Commerce, 111 E. Wisconsin Ave., Milwaukee, WI 53202.

Wyoming

Equality State

People. Population (1981) 492,000; **rank:** 49. **Pop. density:** 5.1 per sq. mi. **Urban** (1980): 62.7%. **Racial distrib.** (1980): 95.0% White; 0.71% Black; Hispanic (1980): 24,499. **Major ethnic groups:** German, English, Russian. **Net migration** (1970-79): +77,000.

Geography. Total area: 97,914 sq. mi.; **rank:** 9. **Land area:** 97,203 sq. mi. **Acres forested land:** 10,028,300. **Location:** Mountain state lying in the high western plateaus of the Great Plains. **Climate:** semi-desert conditions throughout; true desert in the Big Horn and Great Divide basins. **Topography:** the eastern Great Plains rise to the foothills of the Rocky Mtns.; the Continental Divide crossed the state from the NW to the SE. **Capital:** Cheyenne.

Economy. Principal industries: mining, minerals, agriculture, forestry, tourism. **Principal manufactured goods:** refined petroleum products, foods, wood products, stone, clay and glass products. **Value added by manufacture** (1981): $425.6 mln. **Agriculture: Chief crops:** wheat, beans, barley, oats, sugar beets, hay. **Livestock:** 1.34 mln. cattle; 32,000 hogs/pigs; 1.05 mln. sheep; 70,000 poultry. **Timber/lumber** (1979): aspen, yellow pine; 200 mln. bd. ft. **Minerals** (1978): petroleum, sodium carbonate, coal, uranium, natural gas; total $2.6 bln. value of mineral production. **International airports at:** Casper. **Value of construction** (1981): $578 mln. **Employment distribution:** 16% trade; 14% serv.; 12% mining. **Per capita income** (1981): $11,780. **Unemployment** (1981): 4.1%. **Tourism** (1980): out-of-state visitors spent $600 mln.

Finance. No. banks (1980): 103; **No. savings and loan assns.** (1981): 12.

Federal government. No. federal civilian employees (Mar. 1981): 5,468. **Avg. salary:** $20,444. **Notable federal facilities:** Warren AFB; Laramie Energy Research Ctr.

Energy. Electricity production (1981, mwh, by source): Hydroelectric: 840,888, Mineral: 25.6 mln.

Education. No. schools: 411 elem. and second.; 8 higher ed. **Avg. salary, public school teachers** (1980): $17,537.

State data. Motto: Equal Rights. **Flower:** Indian paintbrush. **Bird:** Meadowlark. **Tree:** Cottonwood. **Song:** Wyoming. **Entered union** July 10, 1890; rank, 44th. **State fair** at: Douglas; end of Aug.

History. Francés Francois and Louis Verendrye were the first Europeans, 1743. John Colter, American, was first to traverse Yellowstone Park, 1807-08. Trappers and fur traders followed in the 1820s. Forts Laramie and Bridger became important stops on the pioneer trail to the West Coast. Indian wars followed massacres of army detachments in 1854 and 1866. Population grew after the Union Pacific crossed the state, 1869. Women won the vote, for the first time in the U.S., from the Territorial Legislature, 1869.

Tourist attractions. Yellowstone National Park, 3,472 sq. mi. in the NW corner of Wyoming and the adjoining edges of Montana and Idaho, the oldest U.S. national park, est. 1872, has some 10,000 geysers, hot springs, mud volcanoes, fossil forests, a volcanic glass (obsidian) mountain, the 1,000-ft.-deep canyon and 308-ft.-high waterfall of the Yellowstone River, and a wide variety of animals living free in their natural habitat.

Also, Grand Teton National Park, with mountains 13,000 ft. high; National Elk Refuge, covering 25,000 acres; Devils Tower, a cluster of rock columns 865 ft. high; Fort Laramie and surrounding areas of pioneer trails; Buffalo Bill Museum, Cody; Cheyenne Frontier Days Celebration, last full week in July, the state's largest rodeo, and world's largest purse.

Famous Wyomingites include James Bridger, Buffalo Bill Cody, Nellie Tayloe Ross.

Tourist information: Travel Commission, Etchepare Circle, Cheyenne, WY 82002.

District of Columbia

Area: 67 sq. mi. **Population:** (1981): 631,000. **Motto:** Justitia omnibus, Justice for all. **Flower:** American beauty rose. **Tree:** Scarlet oak. **Bird:** Wood thrush. The city of Washington is coextensive with the District of Columbia.

The District of Columbia is the seat of the federal government of the United States. It lies on the west central edge of Maryland on the Potomac River, opposite Virginia. Its area was originally 100 sq. mi. taken from the sovereignty of Maryland and Virginia. Virginia's portion south of the Potomac was given back to that state in 1846.

The 23d Amendment, ratified in 1961, granted residents the right to vote for president and vice president for the first time and gave them 3 members in the Electoral College. The first such votes were cast in Nov. 1964.

Congress, which has legislative authority over the District under the Constitution, established in 1878 a government of 3 commissioners appointed by the president. The Reorganization Plan of 1967 substituted a single commissioner (also called mayor), assistant, and 9-member City Council. Funds were still appropriated by Congress; residents had no vote in local government, except to elect school board members.

In Sept. 1970, Congress approved legislation giving the District one delegate to the House of Representatives. The delegate could vote in committee but not on the House floor. The first was elected 1971.

In May 1974 voters approved a charter giving them the right to elect their own mayor and a 13-member city council; the first took office Jan. 2, 1975. The district won the right to levy its own taxes but Congress retained power to veto council actions, and approve the city's annual budget.

Proposals for a "federal town" for the deliberations of the Continental Congress were made in 1783, 4 years before the adoption of the Constitution that gave the Confederation a national government. Rivalry between northern and southern delegates over the site appeared in the First Congress, 1789. John Adams, presiding officer of the Senate, cast the deciding vote of that body for Germantown, Pa. In 1790 Congress compromised by making Philadelphia the temporary capital for 10 years. The Virginia members of the House wanted a capital on the eastern bank of the Potomac; they were defeated by the Northerners, while the Southerners defeated the Northern attempt to have the nation assume the war debts of the 13 original states, the Assumption Bill fathered by Alexander Hamilton. Hamilton and Jefferson arranged a compromise: the Virginia men voted for the Assumption Bill, and the Northerners conceded the capital to the Potomac. President Washington chose the site in Oct. 1790 and persuaded landowners to sell their holdings to the government at £25, then about $66, an acre. The capital was named Washington.

Washington appointed Pierre Charles L'Enfant, a French engineer who had come over with Lafayette, to plan the capital on an area not over 10 mi. square. The L'Enfant plan, for streets 100 to 110 feet wide and one avenue 400 feet wide and a mile long, seemed grandiose and foolhardy. But Washington endorsed it. When L'Enfant ordered a wealthy landowner to remove his new manor house because it obstructed a vista, and demolished it when the owner refused, Washington stepped in and dismissed the architect. The official map and design of the city was completed by Benjamin Banneker, a distinguished black architect and astronomer, and Andrew Ellicott.

On Sept. 18, 1793, Pres. Washington laid the cornerstone of the north wing of the Capitol. On June 3, 1800, Pres. John Adams moved to Washington and on June 10, Philadelphia ceased to be the temporary capital. The City of Washington was incorporated in 1802; the District of Columbia was created as a municipal corporation in 1871, embracing Washington, Georgetown, and Washington County.

Outlying U.S. Areas

Commonwealth of Puerto Rico

(Estado Libre Asociado de Puerto Rico)

People. Population (1980): 3,187,566. **Pop. density:** 928 per sq. mi. **Urban** (1975): 61.8%. **Racial distribution:** 99% Hispanic. **Net migration** (1981): −10,460.

Geography. Total area: 3,435 sq. mi. **Land area:** 3,421 sq. mi. **Location:** island lying between the Atlantic to the N and the Caribbean to the S; it is easternmost of the West Indies group called the Greater Antilles, of which Cuba, Hispaniola, and Jamaica are the larger units. **Climate:** mild, with a mean temperature of 76°. **Topography:** mountainous throughout three-fourths of its rectangular area, surrounded by a broken coastal plain; highest peak is Cerro de Punta, 4,389 ft. **Capital:** San Juan.

Economy. Principal industries: manufacturing. **Principal manufactured goods:** petrochemicals; pharmaceuticals; food products, apparel. **Value added by manufacture** (1981): $5.0 bln. **Agriculture: Chief crops:** sugar; coffee; plantains; bananas; yams; taniers; pineapples; pidgeon peas; peppers; tomatoes; pumpkins; coriander; lettuce; tobacco. **Livestock** (1981): 488,600 cattle; 241,213 pigs; 7.5 mln. poultry. **Minerals** (1980): cement, crushed stone, sand and gravel, lime. Total value mineral production, $157.5 mln. **Commercial fishing** (1981): $6.0 mln. **Chief ports/river shipping:** San Juan, Ponce, Mayaguez, Guáyanillá, Yabucoa, Aguirre. **International airports at:** San Juan. **Value of construction** (1981): $1.4 bln. **Employment distribution:** 24% gvt.; 19% manuf.; 19% trade; 19% serv. **Per capita income** (1981): $3,502. **Unemployment** (1981): 18.0%. **Tourism** (1981): No. out-of-area visitors: 1 mln.; $608.5 mln. spent.

Finance. Notable industries: life insurance, mortgage banks, credit unions, retirement fund systems. **Financial institutions** (1981): No. banks: 19; No. savings and loan assns. (1981): 20; Other: 4 retirement fund systems; over 100 credit unions.

Federal government. No. federal civilian employees (1981): 11,097. **Federal payroll** (1981): $211.0 mln. **Notable federal facilities:** U.S. Naval Station at Roosevelt Roads; U.S. Army Salinas Training Area and Ft. Allen; Sabana SECA Communications Center (U.S. Navy).

Energy. Production (1981): Hydroelectric: 12,875 mln. Kwh.

Education. No. schools: 1,803 elem. and second.; 43 higher ed. **Avg. salary, public school teachers** (1981): $8,400.

Misc. Data. Motto. Joannes Est Nomen Ejus (John is his name). **Flower:** Maga. **Bird:** Reinita. **Tree:** Ceiba. **Song:** La Borinquena.

History: Puerto Rico (or Borinquen, after the original Arawak Indian name Boriquen), was discovered by Columbus, Nov. 19, 1493. Ponce de Leon conquered it for Spain, 1509, and established the first settlement at Caparra, across the bay from San Juan.

Sugar cane was introduced, 1515, and slaves were imported 3 years later. Gold mining petered out, 1570. Spaniards fought off a series of British and Dutch attacks; slavery was abolished, 1873. The U.S. took the island during the Spanish-American War, 1898, without any major battle.

General tourist attractions: Ponce Museum of Art; forts El Morro and San Cristobal; Old Walled City of San Juan; Arecibo Observatory; Cordillera Central and state parks; El Yunque Rain Forest; San Juan Cathedral; Porta Coeli Chapel and Museum of Religious Art, San German; Condado Convention Center; Casa Blanca, Ponce de Leon family home, Puerto Rican Family Museum of 16th and 17 centuries and now Fine Arts Centers.

Cultural facilities, festivals, etc.: Festival Casals classical music concerts, mid-June; Puerto Rico Symphony Orchestra at Music Conservatory; Botanical Garden and Museum of Anthropology, Art, and History at the University of Puerto Rico; Institute of Puerto Rican Culture, at the Dominican Convent.

The Commonwealth of Puerto Rico is a self-governing part of the U.S. with a primary Hispanic culture. Puerto Ricans are U.S. citizens and about 1.5 million now live in the continental U.S., although since 1974, a reverse migration flow has resulted in net immigration to the island.

The current commonwealth political status of Puerto Rico gives the island's citizens virtually the same control over their internal affairs as the fifty states of the U.S. However, they do not vote in national elections, although they do vote in national primary elections.

Puerto Rico is represented in Congress solely by a resident commissioner who has a voice but no vote, except in committees.

No federal income tax is collected from residents on income earned from local sources in Puerto Rico.

Puerto Rico's famous "Operation Bootstrap" begun in the late 1940s succeeded in changing the island from "The Poorhouse of the Caribbean" to an area with the highest per capita income in Latin America. This pioneering program encouraged manufacturing and the development of the tourist trade by selective tax exemption, low-interest loans, and other incentives. Despite the marked success of Puerto Rico's development efforts over an extended period of time, per capita income in Puerto Rico is low in comparison to that of the U.S. In calendar year 1981, net transfer payments from the U.S. government to individuals and governments in Puerto Rico totalled $2,739.4 bln., or 23% of the Gross Domestic Product of $11,105 bln.

Famous Puerto Ricans include: Pablo Casals, Orlando Cepeda, Roberto Clemente, Jose Feliciano, Luis A. Ferre, Jose Ferrer, Dona Felisa Rincon de Gautier, Luis Munoz Marin, Rita Moreno, Adm. Horacio Rivero.

Chamber of Commerce: 100 Tetuan P.O.B. S3789, San Juan, PR 00904.

Guam

Pearl of the Pacific

People. Population (1980): 106,000. **Pop. density:** 521.5 per sq. mi. **Urban** (1970): 25.5%. Native Guamanians, ethnically called chamorros, are basically of Indonesian stock, with a mixture of Spanish and Filipino. In addition to the offical language, they speak the native Chamorro.

Geography. Total area: 209 sq. mi. land, 30 mi. long and 4 to 8.5 mi. wide. **Location:** largest and southernmost of the Mariana Islands in the West Pacific, 3,700 mi. W of Hawaii. **Climate:** tropical, with temperatures from 70° to 90°F; avg. annual rainfall, about 70 in. **Topography:** coralline limestone plateau in the N; southern chain of low volcanic mountains sloping gently to the W, more steeply to coastal cliffs on the E; general elevation, 500 ft.; highest pt., Mt. Lamlam, 1,334 ft. **Capital:** Agana.

Economy. Principal industries: contruction, light manufacturing, tourism, petroleum refining, banking. **Principal manufactured goods:** textiles, foods, petroleum products. **Value added by manufacture:** $187.5 million/yr. **Agriculture: Chief crops:** cabbages, eggplants, cucumber, long beans, tomatoes, bananas, coconuts, watermelon, yams, canteloupe, papayas, maize, sweet potatoes. **Livestock:** 1,011 cattle; 9,842 hogs/pigs; 108,862 poultry. **Commercial fishing:** $187,000. **Chief ports:** Apra Harbor. **International airports at:** Tamuning. **Value of construction** (1980): $80.61 mln. **Employment distribution:** 45% gvt.; 13% construct.; 3% manufacturing; 12% services; 18% trade. **Per capita income** (1979): $4,769. **Unemployment** (1980): 10%. **Tourism** (1980): No. out-of-area visitors: 300,000.

Finance. Notable industries: insurance, real estate, finance. **No. banks:** 13; **No. savings and loan assns.:** 2.

Federal government. No. federal employees (1980): 6,600. **Notable federal facilities:** Andersen AFB; other naval and air bases.

Education. No. public schools: 27 elementary; 9 secondary; 1 higher education. **Avg. salary, public school teachers** (1979): $12,684.

Misc. Data. Flower: Puti Tai Nobio (Bougainvillea). **Bird:** Toto (Fruit dove). **Tree:** Ifit (Intsiabijuga). **Song:** Stand Ye Guamanians.

History. Magellan arrived in the Marianas Mar. 6, 1521, and called them the Ladrones (thieves). They were colonized in 1668 by Spanish missionaries who renamed them the Mariana Islands in honor of Maria Anna, queen of Spain. When Spain ceded Guam to the U.S., it sold the other Marianas to Germany. Japan obtained a League of Nations mandate over the German islands in 1919; in Dec. 1941 it seized Guam; the island was retaken by the U.S. in July 1944.

Guam is under the jurisdiction of the Interior Department. It is administered under the Organic Act of 1950, which provides for a governor and a 21-member unicameral legislature, elected biennially by the residents who are American citizens but do not vote for president.

Beginning in Nov., 1970, Guamanians elected their own governor, previously appointed by the U.S. president. He took office in Jan. 1971. In 1972 a U.S. law gave Guam one delegate to the U.S. House of Representatives; the delegate may vote in committee but not on the House floor.

General tourist attractions. annual mid-Aug. Merizo Water Festival; Tarzan Falls; beaches; water sports, duty-free port shopping.

Virgin Islands

St. John, St. Croix, St. Thomas

People. Population (1980): 95,000. **Pop. density:** 757.6 per sq. mi. **Urban** (1970): 25%. **Racial distribution:** 15% White; 85% Black. **Major ethnic groups:** West Indian, Chachas. **Net migration** (1977): +9,000.

Geography. Total area: 133 sq. mi.; **Land area:** 132 sq. mi. **Location:** 3 larger and 50 smaller islands and cays in the S and W of the V.I. group (British V.I. colony to the N and E) which is situated 70 mi. E of Puerto Rico, located W of the Anegada Passage, a major channel connecting the Atlantic O. and the Caribbean Sea. **Climate:** subtropical; the sun tempered by gentle trade winds; humidity is low; average temperature, 78° F. **Topography:** St. Thomas is mainly a ridge of hills running E and W, and has little tillable land; St. Croix rises abruptly in the N but slopes to the S to flatlands and lagoons; St. John has steep, lofty hills and valleys with little level tillable land. **Capital:** Charlotte Amalie, St. Thomas.

Economy. Principal industries: tourism, rum, petroleum refining, bauxite processing, watch assembly, textiles. **Principal manufactured goods:** rum, textiles, pharmaceuticals, perfumes. **Gross Domestic Product** (1977): $500 million. **Agriculture: Chief crops:** truck garden produce. **Minerals:** sand, gravel. **Chief ports:** Cruz Bay, St. John; Frederiksted and Christiansted, St. Croix; Charlotte Amalie, St. Thomas. **International airports on:** St. Thomas, St. Croix. **Value of construction** (1976): $42,303,000. **Per capita income** (1978): $5,367. **Unemployment** (Dec. 1981): 7.0%. **Tourism** (1980): No. out-of-area visitors: 1,172,113; $355 mln. spent. **No. banks** (1979): 6.

Education: No. public schools: 33 elem. and second.; 1 higher education. **Avg. salary, public school teachers** (1980): $13,575.

Misc. data. Flower: Yellow elder or yellow cedar. **Bird:** Yellow breast. **Song:** Virgin Islands March.

History. The islands were discovered by Columbus in 1493, who named them for the virgins of St. Ursula, the sailor's patron saint. Spanish forces, 1555, defeated the Caribes and claimed the territory; by 1596 the native population was annihilated. First permanent settlement in the U.S. territory, 1672, by the Danes; U.S. purchased the islands, 1917, for defense purposes.

The inhabitants have been citizens of the U.S. since 1927. Legislation originates in a unicameral house of 15 senators, elected for 2 years. The governor, formerly appointed by the U.S. president, was popularly elected for the first time in Nov. 1970. In 1972 a U.S. law gave the Virgin Islands one delegate to the U.S. House of Representatives; the delegate may vote in committee but not in the House.

General tourist attractions. Megen Bay, St. Thomas; duty-free shopping; Virgin Islands National Park, 14,488 acres on St. John of lush growth, beaches, Indian relics, and evidence of colonial Danes.

Chamber of Commerce: for St. Thomas and St. John: P.O. Box 324, St. Thomas, VI 00801; for St. Croix: 17 Church St., Christiansted, St. Croix, VI 00820.

American Samoa

Capital: Fagatogo, Island of Tutuila. **Area:** 76 sq. mi. **Population:** (1978 est.) 31,171. **Motto:** Samoa Muamua le Atua (In Samoa, God Is First). **Song:** Amerika Samoa. **Flower:** Paogo (Ula-fala). **Plant:** Ava.

Blessed with spectacular scenery and delightful South Seas climate, American Samoa is the most southerly of all lands under U. S. ownership. It is an unincorporated territory consisting of 6 small islands of the Samoan group: **Tutuila, Aunu'u, Manu'a Group (Ta'u, Olosega and Ofu),** and **Rose.** Also administered as part of American Samoa is **Swain's Island,** 210 mi. to the NW, acquired by the U.S. in 1925. The islands are 2,600 mi. SW of Honolulu.

American Samoa became U. S. territory by a treaty with the United Kingdom and Germany in 1899. The islands were ceded by local chiefs in 1900 and 1904.

Samoa (Western), comprising the larger islands of the Samoan group, was a New Zealand mandate and UN Trusteeship until it became an independent nation Jan. 1, 1962 *(see Index.)*

Tutuila and Annu'u have an area of 52 sq. mi. Ta'u has an area of 17 sq. mi., and the islets of Ofu and Olosega, 5 sq. mi. with a population of a few thousand. Swain's Island has nearly 2 sq. mi. and a population of about 100.

About 70% of the land is bush. Chief products and exports are fish products, copra, and handicrafts. Taro, bread-fruit, yams, coconuts, pineapples, oranges, and bananas are also produced.

Formerly under jurisdiction of the Navy, since July 1, 1951, it has been under the Interior Dept. On Jan. 3, 1978, the first popularly elected Samoan governor and lieutenant governor were inaugurated. Previously, the governor was appointed by the Secretary of the Interior. American Samoa has a bicameral legislature and an elected delegate to appear before U.S. agencies in Washington. In 1980 the Territory will elect a non-voting delegate to Congress.

The American Samoans are of Polynesian origin. They are nationals of the U.S.; there are more than 15,000 in Hawaii and 90,000 on the U.S. west coast.

Minor Caribbean Islands

Quita Sueño Bank, Roncador and Serrana, lie in the Caribbean between Nicaragua and Jamaica. They are uninhabited. U.S. claim to the islands was relinquished in a treaty with Colombia, which entered into force on Sept. 17, 1981.

Navassa lies between Jamaica and Haiti, covers about 2 sq. mi., is reserved by the U.S. for a lighthouse and is uninhabited.

Wake, Midway, Other Islands

Wake Island, and its sister islands, **Wilkes** and **Peale,** lie in the Pacific Ocean on the direct route from Hawaii to Hong Kong, about 2,000 mi. W of Hawaii and 1,290 mi. E of Guam. The group is 4.5 mi. long, 1.5 mi. wide, and totals less than 3 sq. mi.

The U.S. flag was hoisted over Wake Island, July 4, 1898, formal possession taken Jan. 17, 1899; Wake has been administered by the U.S. Air Force since 1972. Population (1980) was 300.

The **Midway Islands,** acquired in 1867, consist of 2, **Sand** and **Eastern,** in the North Pacific 1,150 mi. NW of Hawaii, with area of about 2 sq. mi., administered by the Navy Dept. Population (1975 est.) was 2,256.

Johnston Atoll, SW of Hawaii, area 1 sq. mi., pop. 300 (1978), is under Air Force control, and **Kingman Reef,** S of Hawaii, is under Navy control.

Howland, Jarvis, and **Baker Islands** south of the Hawaiian group, uninhabited since World War II, are under the Interior Dept.

Palmyra is an atoll SW of Hawaii, 4 sq. mi. Privately owned, it is under the Interior Dept.

Islands Under Trusteeship

The U. S Trust Territory of the Pacific Islands, also called Micronesia, includes 3 major archipelagoes: the **Caroline Islands, Marshall Islands,** and **Mariana Islands** (except **Guam:** see above). There are 2,141 islands, 98 of them inhabited. Total land area is 687 sq. mi., but the islands are scattered over 3 million sq. mi. in the western Pacific N of the equator and E of the Philippines. Population (1980 est.): 116,662.

The Marianas

In process of becoming a U.S. commonwealth were the Northern Mariana Islands, which since 1947 have been part of the Trust Territory of the Pacific Islands, assigned to U.S. administration by the United Nations. The Northern Marianas comprise all the Marianas except Guam, stretching N-S in a 500-mi. arc of tropical islands east of the Philippines and southeast of Japan.

Residents of the islands on June 17, 1975, voted 78% in favor of becoming a commonwealth of the U.S. rather than continuing with the Carolines and Marshalls in the U.S.-UN Trusteeship. On Mar. 24, 1976, U.S. Pres. Ford signed a congressionally-approved commonwealth covenant giving the Marianas control of domestic affairs and giving the U.S. control of foreign relations and defense, and the right to maintain military bases on the islands. The full force of commonwealth status will come into effect at the termination of the trusteeship.

Pres. Carter, on Oct. 24, 1977, approved the Constitution of the Northern Mariana Islands with the effective date of Jan. 9, 1978. In December 1977, the voters of the Northern Marianas elected a governor, lieutenant governor, and members of a bicameral legislature for the new government.

Ferdinand Magellan was the first European to visit the Marianas, 1521. Spain, Germany, and Japan held the islands in turn until World War II when the U.S. seized them in bitter battles on 2 of the main islands, Saipan and Tinian.

Population in 1980 was estimated at 16,600, mostly on Saipan. English is the official language, Roman Catholicism the major religion. The people are descendants of the early Chamorros, Spanish, Japanese, Filipinos, and Mexicans. Land area is 181.9 sq. mi.

Tourism is an important industry; visitors are mostly from Japan. Crops include coconuts, breadfruit, melons and tomatoes.

The Carolines and Marshalls

In 1885, many of the Carolines, Marshalls, and Marianas were claimed by Germany. Others, held by Spain, were sold to Germany at the time of the Spanish-American War, 1898. After the outbreak of World War I, Japan took over the 3 archipelagoes; following that war, League of Nations mandates over them were awarded to Japan.

After World War II, the United Nations assigned them, 1947, as a Trust Territory to be administered by the U.S. They were placed, 1951, under administration of the U.S. Interior Dept.

There is a high commissioner, appointed by the U.S. president. Saipan is the headquarters of the administration. The Congress of Micronesia, an elected legislature with limited powers, held its first meeting, 1965.

In 1969, a commission of the Congress of Micronesia recommended that Micronesia be given internal self-government in free association with the U.S. All the Micronesian entities now have their own locally-elected governments.

A U.S. offer of commonwealth status was rejected by Micronesian leaders in 1970.

The U.S. and three Trust Territory negotiating commissions representing, respectively, the Marshall Islands, Palau, and the Federated States of Micronesia, comprised of Truk, Yap, Ponape and Kosrae, are negotiating a free association arrangement: the three Micronesian areas would enjoy full self-government; the U.S. would retain responsibility for defense. The final subsidiary clauses of a compact of free association, initialled in late 1980, are being negotiated by the 3 Micronesian governments and the U.S.

Among the noted islands are the former Japanese strongholds of **Palau, Peleliu, Truk,** and **Yap** in the Carolines; **Bikini** and **Eniwetok,** where U.S. nuclear tests were staged, and **Kwajalein,** another World War II battle scene, all in the Marshalls.

Many of the islands are volcanic with luxuriant vegetation; others are of coral formation. Only a few are self-sustaining. Principal exports are copra, trochus shells, fish products, handicrafts, and vegetables.

Disputed Pacific Islands

In the central Pacific, S and SW of Hawaii lie 25 islands that were claimed by the U.S.; 18 of them were also claimed by the United Kingdom and 7 by New Zealand. **Kiribati** achieved its independence from the U.K. in July, 1979.

The **Tuvalu (Ellice) Islands,** including Funafuti, Nukufetau, Nukulailai, and Nurakita, became independent of the UK, Oct. 1, 1978.

The **Cook Islands,** including Danger, Manahiki, Rakahanga, and Penrhyn (Tongareva), are self-governing in free association with New Zealand. **Tokelau** is a New Zealand territory.

The U.S. signed a treaty with Kiribati on Sept. 20, 1979; with Tuvalu on Feb. 7, 1979; and with the Cook Islands and New Zealand for Tokelau on Dec. 2, 1980. These treaties relinquished U.S. claim to the disputed islands. They are all awaiting action by the U.S. Senate.

NORTH AMERICAN CITIES

Their History, Business and Industry, Educational Facilities, Cultural Advantages, Tourist Attractions and Transportation

Akron, Ohio

The World Almanac is sponsored in the Akron area by the Akron Beacon Journal, 44 E. Exchange Street, Akron, OH 44328; (216) 375-8111; a Knight-Ridder newspaper; founded 1839; circulation 163,409 daily, 225,667 Sunday; Paul Poorman editor and vice president, James V. Gels, vice president and general manager.

Population: 237,177 (city), 660,233 (SMSA); 5th in state; total employed (Apr., 1982) 255,400; average household effective buying income $21,190.
Area: 56 sq. mi. (city), 413 sq. mi. (metro) on Ohio Canal, 30 mi. so. of Lake Erie; founded 1825; Summit Co. seat.
Industry: home plants of Firestone, Goodyear, Goodrich, General and Goodyear Aerospace employ 24,960; other products mfd. in area include auto bodies, salt, clay, matches, rubber toys, road building equipment, missile components.
Transportation: Akron-Canton Airport served by 2 major carriers; Akron Muni Airport; Conrail covers 9 former private rail and trunk lines; birthplace of trucking industry, served by 79 motor common carriers; metro transit system; Greyhound and Continental Trailways; 3 taxicab firms; city bisected east-west and north-south by interstate highway systems.
Communications: 11 TV, 3 cablevision, and 19 radio stations; 2 public broadcast TV outlets.
New construction: over $193 million in private investments in 1981 by Goodyear Tire, Goodyear Aerospace, Rockwell, General Tire, Firestone, B.F. Goodrich, Monsanto and others.
Federal facilities: downtown federal office bldg.; Army Reserve Center; Navy-Marine Reserve Center.
Medical facilities: 7 major hospitals including specialized children's treatment center; State of Ohio Fallsview Psychiatric Hospital; Northeast Ohio Univ. College of Medicine.
Education: Univ. of Akron and School of Law; Kent State Univ.; Firestone Conservatory of Music.
Sports: NBA Cleveland Cavaliers play in nearby Richfield Township Coliseum; Firestone Country Club, home of the $400,000 World Series of Golf; 35,000-seat Akron Rubber Bowl; Derby Downs, home of the All-American Soap Box Derby; home of the annual PBA $200,000 Firestone Tournament of Champions.
Cultural attractions: E. J. Thomas Performing Arts Center; Blossom Music Center, summer home of the Cleveland Orchestra; Stan Hywet mansion; Akron Art Institute; Akron Symphony Orchestra, Akron Civic Theater, Ohio Ballet.
Other attractions: Akron Zoological Park; John Brown Home; Simon Perkins Mansion; Railway Museum, Hale Farm, Quaker Sq., Cuyahoga Nat. Recreation Area.
Birthplace of: Hugh Downs, Vaughn Monroe, Thurman Munson, Ara Parseghian.
Further information: Akron Regional Development Board, or Akron-Summit Convention and Visitors Bureau, both 1 Cascade Plaza, Akron, OH 44308.

Albuquerque, New Mexico

The World Almanac is sponsored in the Albuquerque area by The Albuquerque Tribune, 717 Silver Avenue S.W., Albuquerque, NM 87102; phone (505) 842-2371; founded June 22, 1922 by Carl Magee; a Scripps-Howard Newspaper since Sept. 24, 1923; circulation 46,000; editor William Tanner; sponsors Tribune Annual Spelling Bee.

Population: 331,767 (city), 419,700 (county), 448,798 (SMSA); first in state; total employed 190,900 (1980).
Area: 87.1 sq. mi. on Rio Grande and interstates 40, 25, and U.S. 66; Bernalillo County seat.
Industry: electronics with Signetics, Sperry Flight Systems, GTE-Lenkurt, Gulton, Sparton, Sandia Laboratories, General Electric, Digital Equipment Corp., Motorola, Honeywell, Intel; medical with Ethicon; clothing with Levi Strauss, Pioneer Wear.
Commerce: retail sales $2.2 billion; per capita income $8,760; financial resources $2.5 billion in 13 banks, $1.5 billion in 6 savings and loan assns.
Transportation: Santa Fe Railway, Amtrak; Continental Trailways and Greyhound bus lines; Albuquerque Int'l Airport, hub for 10 airlines, average 632 air movements daily.
Communications: 5 TV, 21 radio stations, 3 TV cable systems.
New construction: value of building permits $201 million in 1981, down 16% from 1980.
Medical facilities: 9 major hospitals.
Cultural facilities: symphony orchestra, light opera, 55 art galleries, 5 museums, 8 library branches, 16 theaters.
Educational facilities: Univ. of New Mexico, Univ. of Albuquerque, Technical-Vocational Institute; 109 public schools.
Recreational facilities: Sandia Peak ski area with longest tramway in North America; Rio Grande Zoo, Cibola National Forest, 12 golf courses, 31 swimming pools, 118 free city tennis courts, 102 private courts, 165 city parks.
Convention facilities: downtown convention center with underground parking facility and 300-room hotel; 107 motels and hotels.
Sports: Dukes baseball, Univ. of New Mexico athletic activities, Annual World Balloon Fiesta.
History: founded Feb. 7, 1706; named for Duke of Albuquerque, viceroy of New Spain.
Birthplace of: Al and Bobby Unser.
Further information: Chamber of Commerce, 401 2d NW, Albuquerque, NM 87102.

Allentown, Pennsylvania

The World Almanac is sponsored in the Allentown-Bethlehem-Easton area by Call-Chronicle Newspapers, 101 North 6th Street, Allentown, PA 18105; phone (215) 820-6500; Call founded 1883, daily circulation The Morning Call 118,662, Weekender 118,058, Sunday 156,512; publisher Bernard C. Stinner, president Roy Follett, exec. editor Lawrence J. Hymans; sponsors newspaper-in-the-classroom, newsprint recycling, college finance seminars, forum 1040, youth run.

Population: Allentown 103,758, Bethlehem 70,419, Easton 25,800, SMSA 637,109, 3d in state; total employed 278,300.
Area: 1,490 sq. mi. (metro) in eastern Pa. at Lehigh and Delaware rivers; Lehigh County seat.
Industry: Bethlehem Steel Corp., 2d largest in U.S.; home offices for Mack Truck Inc., Air Products & Chemicals, Martin Guitar, Rodale Press, New Jersey Zinc Co., Allen Products (ALPO); area leads in textile production; transistor developed in Western Electric here. Other industries include Kraft Foods, F.&M. Schaefer Brewing Co., American Can Co. (Dixie), Durkee Foods.
Commerce: 3d largest Pa. market; metro retail sales over $2.7 billion; average family buying power $23,200.
Transportation: 3 major rail lines, 5 bus lines; 9 federal and

state highways intersect area; jet airport serves some 600,000 passengers annually on 5 airlines.
Communications: 4 TV and 12 radio stations.
Medical facilities: 6 major hospitals.
Cultural facilities: Allentown Art Museum (including Kress Renaissance and Baroque collection), Bethlehem Bach Choir, Allentown Symphony, 7 theater groups (plus summer and college theater groups); Allentown Band is oldest continuing concert band in U.S.; Pa. Stage Co.; Ballet Guild.
Educational facilities: 10 colleges including Lehigh Univ., Moravian, Muhlenberg, Cedar Crest, Lafayette, and Allentown Business School. 65 private and parochial schools.
Other attractions: center of "Pennsylvania Dutch" area, covered bridges; 1,400-acre park system; 1,170-acre game preserve, pre-Cambrian mountain range, access to Appalachian Trail, many historic houses, Allentown Fair, Kutztown Folk Festival, Liberty Bell Shrine, Bavarian Festival at Barnesville. Drum Corps Int'l Eastern Championship; new Hilton Hotel (contains $25 million art collection including large collection of Norman Rockwell prints).
Sports: fishing, game hunting, auto racing at Pocono Raceway, Lehigh Valley Jets basketball, Olympic bicycle velodrome at Trexlertown, Pennsylvania Stoners soccer.
History: settled in 1600s by Germans seeking religious freedom; Allentown founded 1762; hiding place for Liberty Bell during Revolutionary War; GAR founded Flag Day here 1906; one of 5 First Defender Companies in Civil War.
Further information: Chambers of Commerce in Allentown: 462 Walnut Street, 18105; Bethlehem: 11 W. Market Street, 18018; Easton: 157 S. 4th Street, 18042.

Amarillo, Texas

The World Almanac is sponsored in the Amarillo area by the Amarillo Globe-News, 900 S. Harrison, Amarillo, TX 79166; phone (806) 376-4488; a division of the Southwestern Newspapers Corp., and publisher of Daily News, Globe-Times and Sunday News-Globe; James L. Whyte, vice president and general manager; Jerry Huff, executive editor.

Population: 149,230 city, 173,550 SMSA; total employed 87,000; 4.5% unemployed.
Area: 82 sq. mi. in central panhandle of Texas at junction of Interstate 40 and 27 in Potter and Randall counties; Potter County seat.
Industry: 3-state hub of $10.4 billion agribusiness market including wheat, beef, and produce, value $2.9 billion; ASARCO, Inc. copper refinery, Santa Fe Rail welding plant; Bell Helicopter, Levi Strauss, Iowa Beef Processors, Amarillo Gear, oil and gas, coal burning electricity plant, and Owens-Corning Fiberglas plant.
Commerce: wholesale-retail center for 5-state area; retail sales $1.023 billion; bank resources $1.58 billion, 6 savings and loan assns.
Transportation: served by 7 airlines; 2 railroads, 4 bus lines, 21 truck lines; 2 interstate, 4 federal, and one state highway intersect Amarillo.
Communications: 4 TV, 12 radio stations.
Medical facilities: 9 hospitals including VA facilities in metro area; mental health centers, speech and hearing center; cancer center (Texas Tech Univ. Medical School branch.
Culture, recreation: Amarillo Symphony, fine arts complex, civic center complex and convention center, 2 dinner theaters, Amarillo Theatre Center (55th year of operation), Alibates National Monument, Lake Meredith, Wonderland Amusement Park and Storyland Zoo, Palo Duro Canyon State Park, Cal Farley's Boys Ranch, summer musical drama "Texas"; regional history museum, Discovery Center Planetarium, 46 parks, central library and 3 branches, 2 colleges, state vocational-technical school, National Helium Monument.
Sports: drag racing, stock car racing; Gold Sox baseball; rodeo, motorcycle racing.
History: settled 1887 as railroad crew camp, incorporated 1892; named for yellow lake clay.
Birthplace of: Cyd Charisse, Carolyn Jones.
Further information: Amarillo Chamber of Commerce, 1000 S. Polk, Amarillo, TX 79101.

Anchorage, Alaska

The World Almanac is sponsored in the Anchorage area by The Anchorage Times, 820 W. 4th Avenue, Anchorage, AK 99501, or P.O. Box 40, Anchorage, AK 99510; phone (907) 279-5622; founded 1915; circulation 48,000(E), 60,000(S); editor-publisher Robert B. Atwood; sponsors Alaska State Spelling Bee, Kodak Photo Contest.

Population: city, borough unified in 1975; total population of new municipality is 173,992.
Area: 927 sq. mi. (census district), at head of Cook Inlet on south central coast.
Industry and commerce: business center for most of Alaska; aviation, oil companies, railroading, shipping, wholesaling, retailing, and national defense activities are largest elements in area's economy.
Transportation: Anchorage International Airport is major refueling stop on transpolar flights; thousands of small planes make city one of country's busiest air traffic centers with 5 airports and 25% of world's seaplanes in area; headquarters of Alaska Railroad; $12 million port.
Communications: 4 TV and 11 radio stations; 2 daily newspapers.
Medical facilities: 3 hospitals.
Federal facilities: Elmendorf AFB, Ft. Richardson.
Cultural facilities: annual Festival of Music; 4 theater groups; fine arts museum; community concert organization, opera company, civic symphony.
Educational facilities: 57 elementary and secondary schools enroll 37,000; Univ. of Alaska, Alaska Pacific Univ.
Recreation: 2 major alpine ski areas; cross-country skiing and bicycling; annual Fur Rendezvous with dogsled races; Iditarod dogsled race to Nome; Chugach National Forest.
Convention facilities: 7 major hotels and motels offer more than 2,800 rooms.
History: founded 1915 as headquarters for Alaska Railroad; twice winner of All America city award, for coping with rapid growth, and for swift recovery from catastrophic 1964 earthquake.
Further information: Chamber of Commerce, 415 F Street; or Convention and Visitors Bureau, 201 E 3d Avenue, both Anchorage, AK 99501.

Atlanta, Georgia

The World Almanac is sponsored in the Atlanta area by The Atlanta Journal and Constitution, 72 Marietta Street, Atlanta, GA 30303; phone (404) 526-5151; circulation, The Atlanta Constitution (morn.) 208,289, The Atlanta Journal (eve.) 184,237, combined daily 392,526, Saturday WEEKEND 411,359, Sunday Journal and Constitution 499,084; member Million Market Newspapers, Inc.; sponsor: The Atlanta Journal 500, The Phillips Collection, The Southern Living Cooking School.

Population: 425,022 (city), 2,010,368 (SMSA), first in state; total employed 931,000 (metro, 1980).
Area: 136 sq. mi. in north central Georgia, on Piedmont plateau of Blue Ridge foothills, 1,050 ft above sea level; 4,326 sq. mi. in 15-county metro area; state capital and Fulton County seat.
Industry: 431 of Fortune 500 firms operate in Atlanta; Ford, 2 GM assembly plants, Lockheed-Ga. Co.; home base for

Coca-Cola, Fuqua, Ind., Delta Air Lines, Equifax, Genuine Parts, Gold Kist, Rollins, Inc., National Service Industries, Life of Georgia.
Commerce: financial, retail, wholesale center of Southeast; massive Merchandise Mart has 2d largest wholesale showroom in U.S. under one roof; 6th Federal Reserve District hdqtrs.; 74 banks with resources of $9.7 billion (15-county metro); 20 savings and loan associations with 180 branches in metro area with deposits of $5.4 billion (1980).
Transportation: founded as railroad center; now served by 7 lines of 2 systems; Greyhound and Trailways bus terminal used by 3 companies with 205 buses in and out daily; 19 passenger carriers, 12 freight only carriers; more than 1,700 scheduled flights daily; single-plane service to 156 cities from Hartsfield International Airport, direct flights to 10 international cities; 2d busiest airport in world, 37.6 million passengers and no. one transfer hub in nation's domestic air route pattern. Metropolitan Atlanta Rapid Transit Authority; under construction is 52.9 mi. rapid rail, 8 mi. of rapid busways coordinated with street bus operations; 6 legs of 3 interstate hwys. intersecting 100-acre downtown interchange; 63 mi. hwy. encircles city.
Communications: 8 TV stations, 41 radio stations, 8 cable TV companies; Protestant Radio and TV Center; largest Bell System toll-free dialing area; one of nation's 5 TV and radio network control centers; 8 daily newspapers.
New construction: $2.1 billion MARTA rapid transit system, $100 million Georgia Pacific office bldg., $37.7 million Georgia Power office bldg., $100 million Southern Bell office bldg, Marathon Bldg., Palace Hotel, Downtown Days Inn, World Congress Center expansion, Memorial Arts Center, total private constr. permits (1981) $1.3 billion.
Medical facilities: 56 hospitals with over 11,000 beds (metro), VA hospital; national Center for Disease Control of U.S. Pub. Health Dept., National Cancer Center at Emory Univ. Med. School.
Federal facilities: 37,200 federal, non-military employees (1980); Ft. McPherson, hdqtrs. U.S. Army Forces Command; Ft. Gillem; Dobbins AFB; NAS Atlanta.
Cultural facilities: Memorial Arts Center with museum, symphony orchestra, ballet, School of Art; Civic Center with auditorium-theater-exhibition hall; Callanwolde, multi-use arts center; 29 degree-granting colleges including Ga. Tech, Ga. State Univ., Emory Univ.
Sports: NBA Hawks; NFL Falcons; NL Braves; World Championship Tennis, college football's Peach Bowl, PGA Atlanta Classic, Peachtree Road Race, The Atlanta Open International Tennis Championships, The Atlanta Journal 500; road, sports car racing, motocross.
Convention facilities: 1,128,000 convention delegates in 1981; Ga. World Congress Center has largest single display room in U.S. equal to 8 football fields; simultaneous translation facilities; 40,000 hotel/motel rooms, most downtown.
History: named 1845; chartered 1847; burned by Union Gen. Sherman 1864.
Birthplace of: James Dickey, Walt Frazier, Martin Luther King Jr., Gladys Knight, Brenda Lee, Margaret Mitchell, Bert Parks, Jerry Reed.
Further information: Chamber of Commerce, 1300 N. Omni International, Atlanta, GA 30302.

Augusta, Georgia

The World Almanac is sponsored in the Augusta area by the Chronicle-Herald, 725 Broad Street, Augusta, GA 30903; phone (404) 724-0851; Chronicle established in 1785, circulation 57,308, Herald 18,559, Sunday, 83,831; William S. Morris III publisher, E.B. Skinner general manager, David L. Playford managing editor, Herald; W.H. Eanes managing editor, Chronicle.

Population: 47,532 (city), 320,574 (SMSA).
Area: 1,695 sq. mi. (metro: Richmond, Columbia counties, Ga.; Aiken County, S.C.) straddling Savannah River; Augusta County seat.
Industry: diversified; Continental forest industries Du Pont, Procter & Gamble, Lily-Tulip, Olin, Dymo, Monsanto, Columbia Nitrogen, A.E.C., TRW Corp., Owens-Corning, Kendall, Textron, Kimberly-Clark, Hall Printing, G.D. Searle.
Commerce: wholesale, retail center of 17 counties in 2 states; 1980 taxable sales $1.6 billion; per capita income $6,666, household buying income $19,812; 7 banks, 5 savings-loan assns.; distribution center.
Transportation: 5 railroads, 26 truck lines, 2 airlines at modern airport and in-city field for executive planes; Interstate 20, other federal highways.
Communications: 3 TV and 13 radio stations.
Medical facilities: 9 major hospitals, including Eisenhower Memorial at Ft. Gordon, Medical College of Georgia.
Federal facilities: Ft. Gordon and Savannah River (AEC) Plant.
Cultural facilities: Augusta College, Medical College of Ga., Paine College, Univ. of S.C. at Aiken; museum, art gallery, arts council with 25 affiliates; Augusta Symphony, Augusta Opera Assn., Augusta Ballet Co.
Recreational facilities: hunting, fishing, boating, camping; 7 golf courses; home of Masters Golf Tournament; and the Atlantic Coast Cutting Horse Futurity.
Convention facilities: 14,570 sq. ft. exhibition hall, 23,000 sq. ft. arena.
History: founded and named for wife of Prince of Wales 1735; capital of Georgia 1778.
Birthplace of: James Brown, Jasper Johns, Joseph Wheeler, Frank Yerby.
Further information: Chamber of Commerce of Greater Augusta, 600 Broad Street Plaza, Augusta, GA 30902.

Bakersfield, California

The World Almanac is sponsored in the Bakersfield and Kern County area by The Bakersfield Californian mornings and Sunday), 1707 Eye Street, Bakersfield, CA 93302; phone (805) 395-7500; founded 1866 as Havilah Courier, christened The Bakersfield Californian 1897; circulation: 75,000 daily, 85,000 Sunday; president Berenice Fritts Koerber, publisher Donald H. Fritts, executive director Alfred T. Fritts, chief executive officer J.K. Stanners.

Population: 105,611 city, 227,806 metro, 412,474 Kern County.
Area: approximately 8,060 square miles in Kern County of which Bakersfield is county seat; in California's San Joaquin Valley.
Industry: oil, gas, agriculture, military; oil valuation $976 million; total agriculture production $799.4 million; Edwards AFB and China Lake Naval Test Station in eastern Kern County.
Commerce: retail sales in Kern $1.5 billion; total bank deposits $1.640 billion.
Transportation: 2 railroads, 3 airlines, 2 bus lines, Interstate 5, Highway 99.
Communications: 3 TV and 12 radio stations; CATV from Los Angeles.
Cultural facilities: symphony orchestra, Cunningham Art Gallery; 4-year state college, city college; community theater.
History: Kern County organized April 2, 1866, from portions of Los Angeles and Tulare counties; discovery of gold on Kern River in 1851 brought influx of settlers; oil discovered in 1865, with major boom in 1909; gold mining town of Havilah first county seat, moved to Bakersfield in 1875.
Birthplace of: Michael Deaver, Merle Haggard, Dennis Ralston.

Baltimore, Maryland

The World Almanac is sponsored in the Baltimore area by The Baltimore Sunpapers, 501 N. Calvert St., Baltimore, Md. 21202; phone (301) 332-6000; founded in 1837; published by the A. S. Abell Publishing Company; publishes The Sun, The Evening Sun and The Sunday Sun; daily circulation 345,876; Sunday 374,405; president and publisher John R. Murphy, managing editor The Sun James I. Houck, managing editor The Evening Sun John M. Lemmon; The Sun has 8 foreign bureaus in addition to its Washington Bureau, and a West Coast correspondent; news & feature stories from all 3 papers are syndicated nationally by The Field News Service.

Population: 786,755 (city), 2,166,308 (SMSA); first in state; 9th in U.S.; 983,033 metro employed.
Area: 91 sq. mi. (city), 2,225 sq. mi. (metro) in central Maryland on Patapsco R., a tributary of Chesapeake Bay.
Industry: steel production, electronic equipment, food processing, transportation equipment, chemical products.
Commerce: $16.7 billion effective buying income in city and 5 surrounding counties; average household EBI $24,174, retail sales over $10.3 billion in 1980; 14 regional shopping malls, over 250 shopping centers, 9 department stores.
Transportation: Baltimore-Washington International Airport; passenger terminal can handle 11 million passengers a year; Harbor Tunnel, Francis Scott Key Bridge; Amtrak; state authorized buses; subway system under construction; major interstate highways allow overnight trucking service to 67 million people; Chessie & Conrail systems.
Port facilities: nation's 3d largest port; responsible for 170,000 jobs and $4 billion in annual economic impact on state; World Trade Center focal point of port commerce; leading cargoes: ores, coal, petroleum products, grains.
New construction: Central business district rebuilt in last 20 years featuring Charles Center, Hopkins Plaza, Inner Harbor; Inner Harbor area includes: Hyatt Regency Hotel, National Aquarium, Harborplace, Mt. Royal District; Md. Concert Center, renovation of Lyric Theatre, Md. Institute College of Art; Coldspring, New Town, 375-acre city neighborhood development.
Convention facilities: $50-million Inner Harbor Baltimore Convention Center with 115,000 sq. ft. unobstructed exhibition space, 41,000 sq. ft. of meeting space divisible into 26 rooms; Civic Center: 35 meeting rooms, 111,000 sq. ft. exhibit space; downtown hotels, approx. 2,100 rooms.
Cultural facilities: Baltimore Symphony Orchestra, Baltimore Ballet Co., Baltimore Opera Co., Baltimore Museum of Art, Walters Art Gallery, Md. Science Center, Morris Mechanic Theatre, Center Stage, Arena Players, Merriweather Post Pavilion, Md. Historical Society.
Educational facilities: 42 metro colleges & universities including Johns Hopkins Univ. and School of Medicine; Univ. of Md. Professional Schools, Towson State Univ., Morgan State Univ., Peabody Conservatory of Music, U.S. Naval Academy, Goucher College.
Sports & Recreation: Orioles (baseball), Colts (NFL football), Blast (indoor soccer); horse racing at Timonium, Bowie, Laurel, Pimlico (home of Preakness); steeplechase racing features Md. Hunt Cup; Chesapeake Bay offers fishing, boating, yachting, waterfowl hunting; ocean and ski resorts within 3-hour drive.
Communications: 3 daily newspapers (morning, 2 evening), 2 Sunday; 5 TV stations (4 commercial, 1 PBS) plus several cable TV companies operating in the metro area; 33 radio stations.
Other attractions: City Fair, Timonium State Fair in Sept.; Preakness Festival Week in May; ethnic, craft, music festivals through summer; Ft. McHenry Historic Shrine where Francis Scott Key wrote "Star Spangled Banner;" Constellation, first ship in U.S. Navy; Baltimore and Ohio Transportation Museum; Edgar Allen Poe home and grave; Babe Ruth house; Washington Monument; Baltimore Streetcar Museum; Cloisters Children's Museum; 142-acre zoo in Druid Hill Park; Little Italy; restored early 19th century rowhouses in Fells Point, Bolton Hill, Seton Hill, Otterbein, Barre Circle; Top of the World observation center; Shot Tower; Lacrosse Hall of Fame; St. Elizabeth Seton's House; Pride of Baltimore clipper ship; Lexington Market.
History: founded in 1729 by members of the Calvert family, the Lords of Baltimore; one of the 13 original colonies; nation's first railroad (Baltimore & Ohio) built to counter competition from new Erie Canal. Baltimore "firsts" include: first umbrella in U.S.; first investment banking house in U.S.; first commercial ice cream factory; first dental college in the world; first trolleycar & longest service line; Notre Dame, first Catholic women's college; first typesetting machine (Merganthaler); first telegraph line (Morse) set up from Baltimore to Washington; first Ouija board invented.
Birthplace of: Spiro Agnew, Eubie Blake, Billie Holiday, Al Kaline, Thurgood Marshall, H.L. Mencken, Babe Ruth, Upton Sinclair, Leon Uris.
Further information: Baltimore Economic Development Corp., 22 Light Street; Baltimore Promotion Council, 1102 St. Paul Street both 21202; Baltimore Convention Bureau, 1 West Pratt Street, Convention Plaza, 21201.

Baton Rouge, Louisiana

The World Almanac is sponsored in the Baton Rouge area by the Morning Advocate and State-Times, 525 Lafayette Street, Baton Rouge, LA 70802 (mailing address: P.O. Box 588, Baton Rouge, LA 70821), phone (504) 383-1111; founded 1842; combined daily circulation 117,506, Sunday 122,058; president: Charles P. Manship Jr.; publisher: Douglas L. Manship; vice president of news and production: Richard Palmer; vice president of business and advertising: Charles Garvey; executive editor all newspapers: Jim Hughes; managing editors: Jack Clark (Morning Advocate), Don Buchanan (State-Times), Art Adams (Sunday Advocate).

Population: 219,486 (city), 495,888 (SMSA); total 1981 SMSA employment 206,000.
Area: 73.4 sq. mi. (city), 472.1 sq. mi (parish), on east bank of Mississippi River, 80 mi. northeast of New Orleans; state capital and East Baton Rouge Parish seat.
Industry: northern anchor of 100-mile long petrochemical complex along the Mississippi River.
Commerce: marketing center for major trade area of over 625,000; bank resources $3.2 billion; 7 banks, 8 savings and loan associations.
Transportation: major transfer point on southern federal interstate system; one airport with 5 airlines; 2 bus lines; 4 railroad trunk lines; Port of Baton Rouge is 4th largest in U.S. with over 80 million tons in 1981.
Communications: 5 TV and 13 radio stations; 2 daily newspapers, 5 weeklies.
Cultural facilities: 6 museums, 4 theaters, symphony, planetarium, observatory, 15 art galleries.
Convention facilities: "Riverside Centroplex" civic center, maximum exhibit space 72,000 sq. ft., maximum seating of 12,000 in Centroplex arena; LSU Assembly Center, seating 15,000; Felton G. Clark Activity Center, seating 9,000.
Educational facilities: Louisiana State Univ., founded 1860, center of 8-campus system; Southern Univ., largest Negro land-grant educational institution in the world, founded 1880, center of 3-college system.
Sports: home of LSU Tigers and Southern Jaguars home stadium; football, baseball, basketball, track.
Other attractions: state capitol building, city-parish zoo and arboretum; 113 public parks; major recreational rivers and lakes.
History: called "le Baton Rouge" (French for "red stick") by members of Iberville's exploratory expedition (St. Patrick's Day, 1699) because of presence of a red pole marking boundary between hunting grounds of Houmas and Bayougoula Indians; first white settlement circa 1719; scene of Revolutionary War battle (1779), 1810 revolt which culminated with the region passing from Spanish and into

American hands, and a Civil War battle (1862). Parish is also the location of Port Hudson, scene of the longest continuous siege (48 days) during the Civil War; incorporated 1817; state capital 1849-1862, 1882-present.

Birthplace of: Bob Pettit.

Further information: Chamber of Commerce, P.O. Box 1868, Baton Rouge, LA 70821; Baton Rouge Area Conv. Bureau, P.O. Box 3202, Baton Rouge, LA 70821.

Billings, Montana

The World Almanac is sponsored in the Billings area by the Billings Gazette, 401 N. Broadway, Billings, MT 59101; phone (406) 657-1200; founded 1885; member of Lee Enterprises, Inc. since 1960; circulation daily 61,796, Sunday 63,161; publisher George D. Remington, editor Richard J. Wesnick.

Population: 66,798 (city) 108,035 (county), first in state; total employed 55,603, 6.4% unemployment.

Area: south central Montana on Yellowstone River, 125 mi. from Yellowstone Park; Yellowstone County seat.

Industry: 3 oil refineries, beet sugar refinery, 2 packing plants, 3d largest livestock auction yards in U.S., center for northern Great Plains coal industry; headquarters for oil, minerals and gas companies and related services; district headquarters Burlington Northern Railroad.

Commerce: wholesale-retail center for eastern Montana, northern Wyoming; retail sales (1981) $725.6 million; 9 banks, 2 savings and loan assns., average spendable family income $20,655.

Transportation: 4 airlines, one railroad, 2 bus lines, 98 motor carriers, interstates 90 and 94; Metro city bus transit.

Communications: 3 TV and 10 radio stations; one weekly, one daily newspaper.

Medical facilities: 2 hospitals, 478 beds, 108 dentists, 200 doctors, 5 nursing homes, Northern Rockies Regional Cancer Treatment Center, Regional Mental Health Center.

Cultural facilities: 13 art galleries, symphony orchestra, 2 western museums, studio theater, theater of performing arts, liberal arts college, private (church related) college, 90 churches, vo-tech program, sheltered workshop, 37 public schools, 10 parochial schools, Center for Handicapped Children, Migrant Children's Program.

Other attractions: big game hunting, fishing, boating, skiing within one hour's drive; snowmobiling, bicycling, saddle clubs; auto & motorcylce clubs, 23 city parks; 2,800 hotel/motel rooms, Metra civic center for sports and concerts; 6 golf courses.

History: founded 1882 with arrival of Northern Pacific Railroad; named after Frederic Billings, then NP president; now largest city in 500-mile radius.

Further information: Tourist Information Bureau, Billings Chamber of Commerce, P.O. Box 2519, Billings, MT 59103.

Binghamton, New York

The World Almanac is sponsored in the Binghamton area by The Evening Press and The Sun-Bulletin, Vestal Parkway East, Binghamton, NY 13902; phone (607) 798-1234; circulation: evening 65,873, Sunday 82,820, morning 27,640, Saturday morning and holidays 72,068; president and publisher Fred G. Eaton, executive editor William F. Mungo Jr., managing editor/features-opinion Michael G. Doll, managing editor/news David J. Mack.

Population: 55,860 (city), 301,274 (metro area), 8th among state metro areas; total employed 144,700.

Area: 10.98 sq. mi. at junction of Chenango and Susquehanna rivers; 715 sq. mi. in county; Broome County seat.

Industry: IBM, computers; Singer Co., transportation equipment products and simulators; Endicott Johnson Corp., shoes; General Electric, aircraft electronic equipment; Savin, copiers; Universal Instruments, production assembly equipment; Frito Lay, snack foods; Crowley Food, dairy food processing; Amphenol Cadre, electronic equipment; Chenango Industries, electronic assembly; Maple-Vail Book Manufacturing Group, printing and publication; Anitec Image Corp., graphic paper, film, chemicals for photographic industry; Ozalid Corp., diazo sensitized materials, duplicating machines, microfilm equipment; Automation Services, electrical components and computer subassemblies.

Commerce: national headquarters of Security and Columbian Mutual Life Insurance Cos.; 12 banks.

Transportation: 6 airlines, major being USAir, out of Edwin A. Link Field; intersection Interstates 81 & 88 and Route 17; Conrail and Delaware & Hudson freight rail carriers; Greyhound, Short Line, Trailways, Chenango Valley bus lines.

Communications: 4 TV stations, 4 AM, 4 FM radio stations.

Medical facilities: 4 major hospitals.

Cultural facilities: Roberson Center for the Arts and Sciences, Binghamton Museum of Fine Arts, Kopernik Observatory; Tri-Cities Opera, Binghamton Symphony & Choral Society, BC Pops; SUNY-Binghamton—Cider Mill Playhouse, Harpur Jazz & Wind Ensemble, Univ. Orchestra & Chorus, Univ. Art Gallery; Broome Community College.

Other attractions: Veterans Memorial Arena, Oakdale Mall, municipal parks zoo, 2 major state parks on outskirts of city; 4 county parks.

Sports: Binghamton Whalers American Hockey League team; BC Open golf tournament.

History: settled 1800; became rail center by 1848, with roads replacing old Chenango Canal that fed Erie Canal; named for Philadelphia patriot and multi-millionaire William Bingham.

Further information: Broome County Convention and Visitors Bureau, 84 Court Street, Binghamton, NY 13902.

Birmingham, Alabama

The World Almanac is sponsored in the Birmingham area by The Birmingham Post-Herald, 2200 Fourth Avenue N., Birmingham, AL 35202; phone (205) 325-2222; Post founded 1921 by Scripps-Howard Newspapers; Herald founded 1887; circulation, 75,630; editor Angus McEachran, vice president W. H. Metz, managing editor David Brown; major public service projects include Goodfellow Christmas Fund.

Population: 284,413 (city), 834,067 (SMSA); employment 343,100 (metro, 1980).

Area: 89 sq. mi. in north central Alabama; state's largest city; Jefferson County seat.

Industry: heavy manufacturing in metals; U.S. Steel, formerly area's largest employer, has ceased operations; U.S. Pipe and Foundry and American Cast Iron Pipe Co. are in top 10 employers; So. Central Bell's 5-state headquarters.

Commerce: wholesale-retail center for Alabama; retail sales (1981) $5.5 billion; 14 banks (county), 6 bank holding companies, 7 savings and loan assns.

Transportation: 5 major rail freight lines, Amtrak; Greyhound and Continental Trailways bus lines; Eastern, American, Delta, United, Republic and USAir air lines with modern airport terminal; 75 truck line terminals; 3 interstate highways, I-59 complete, I-65 and I-20 under construction.

Communications: 2 daily newspapers, 3 commercial TV stations, 16 commercial radio stations, one PBS TV and one PBS radio outlet.

Medical facilities: Univ. of Alabama in Birmingham Medi-

al Center covers 60 sq. blocks; heart surgery team brings atients from all over the world; VA hospital, in same comlex, is the base of organ transplant program; Baptist Medial Centers have 2 major hospitals; 13 other hospitals.
ultural facilities: symphony orchestra; Oscar Wells Muum of Art; Civic Opera; 4 resident civic theaters; 2 resient ballet companies.
ducation: Samford Univ., Birmingham-Southern, Miles, nd Daniel Payne colleges; Jefferson State and Lawson State ınior colleges.
onvention facilities: civic center with exhibition hall, theaer, music hall, and coliseum; several convention hotels and notels in civic center area.
ports: nicknamed "Football Capital of the South" for Jniv. of Alabama and Auburn Univ. games played at muicipal stadium, Legion Field.
Other attractions: world's 2d largest cast iron statue, Vulcan, god of the forge, overlooks Birmingham from Red Mt. as a symbol of the steel industry; Arlington Shrine, housed federal troops during Civil War; Botanical Gardens complex; Jimmie Morgan Zoo; extensive city park system.
History: chartered 1871; soon became known as the "Magic City" because of its rapid growth brought on by the presence of the 3 ingredients in steelmaking — coal, iron ore, and lime; mining died out in recent years and most iron ore is now imported by ship and barge to Birmingport on Warrior River from South America; coal mining, in decline since the 1940s, is on the upswing.
Birthplace of: Mel Allen, Charles O. Finley, Lionel Hampton, Kate Jackson, Walker Percy.
Further information: Chamber of Commerce, 2027 First Avenue N., Birmingham, AL 35202.

Bismarck, North Dakota

The World Almanac is sponsored in western North Dakota by the Bismarck Tribune, 707 Front Avenue, Bisnarck, ND 58501; phone (701) 223-2500; founded 1873 as weekly, became daily 1881; circ. 29,750; pubsher Sanders Hook, editor Charles W. Walk, advertising manager James H. Hewitson; major awards include ulitzer Prize Gold Medal, 1937.

opulation: 44,485, 2d in state; total employed 24,010.
rea: 18.5 sq. mi on Missouri River; state capital and urleigh County seat.
ndustry: agriculture, printing, trucking, farm machinery, tate government, electric power, manufacturing, concrete roducts, railroad, insurance, livestock sales, lignite coal.
ommerce: retail trade area radius 100 miles, serving 50,000 people; retail sales (1981) $322 million; bank depos-s (1981) $922 million; 6 banks, 5 building and loan assns.
ransportation: 2 rail lines; airport, hub for 5 airlines; 6 ruck lines, 4 bus lines, U.S. Highways 18 and 83, I-94.
ommunications: one daily newspaper; 4 AM, 3 FM radio tations, 3 TV stations.
ew construction: 1981 building permits $45.5 million.
ledical facilities: 2 hospitals, 453 bed capacity, served by 20 MDs.
ederal facilities: federal buildings house 20 offices; 14th adar Bomb Scoring Detachment.
Cultural facilities: Bismarck Junior College, Mary College; 72,000-volume public library, state library, Elan Gallery, Heritage Center.
Recreation: 30 parks with over 1,450 acres, indoor artificial ice arena, 3 golf courses, 5 swimming pools, playgrounds, tennis courts, YMCA, duck and game hunting, fishing, nearby Fort Lincoln State Park.
Convention facilities: 8,000 seat Civic Center; 1,480 rooms in 18 motels, 5 banquet and meeting facilities for groups 200-1,200.
Other attractions: Dakota Zoo, Garrison Dam, United Tribes of North Dakota Educational Technical Center, state capitol.
History: founded 1872 as Edwinton, a rail town; name changed to Bismarck in 1873 to encourage German investment capital.
Further information: Chamber of Commerce, 412 Sixth Street, Bismarck, ND 58501.

Bloomington, Illinois

The World Almanac is sponsored in Bloomington-Normal and central Illinois by The Daily Pantagraph, 301 V. Washington Street, Bloomington, IL 61701; phone (309) 829-9411; founded 1837 by Jesse W. Fell; circuation 52,509; president Davis U. Merwin; publisher Peter E. Thieriot; editor Harold Liston; business manager loyd S. Combs; managing editor Bill Wills.

opulation: 87,500 Bloomington-Normal, 119,149 (McLean County); mid-way between Chicago and St. Louis in central llinois.
ndustry: over 50 industries in county, among major insurnce cities in U.S., home offices of State Farm, Country Companies, Union Auto; leads nation in corn and soybean roduction with 1,789 farms in county.
ommerce: 1980 metro retail sales $560 million; per houseold income $24,489; per household retail sales, $13,148.
ransportation: B-N Airport, 4 bus lines, 6 federal and state ighways, 4 railroads, Amtrak, 35 interstate and 23 intratate motor carriers; Britt Airways.
ommunications: 6 radio stations.
ledical facilities: 3 hospitals; Watson-Gailey Foundation Eye Bank.
Cultural facilities: Illinois Wesleyan Univ. in Bloomington; Illinois State Univ. in Normal; 81 churches; home of American Passion Play; B-N Symphony, community players.
History: incorporated 1850; site of A. Lincoln's "Lost Speech" and David Davis mansion; state historical shrine; city's Stevenson family has produced 3 generations of leadership; vice president Adlai E.; governor, presidential candidate and UN Ambassador, Adlai E. II; and former U.S. Senator Adlai E. III.
Birthplace of: Hoagy Carmichael.
Further information: Association of Commerce and Industry of McLean County, 210 S. East Street, Bloomington, IL 61701.

Boise, Idaho

The World Almanac is sponsored in the Boise area by the Idaho Statesman, 1200 N. Curtis Road, Boise, ID 33704; phone (208) 377-6200; founded 1864 as Tri-Weekly; daily circulation 56,920, Sunday 70,288; pubisher Gary F. Sherlock, managing editor Rod Sandeed; a Gannett newspaper.

Population: 154,735 (city division, 1980), 173,036 (metro rea), first in state; total employed 84,500 (metro).
Area: 1,054 sq. mi. on Boise River at foot of Salmon River Mountains; state capital and Ada County seat.
Industry: mobile home and recreational trailer production; Hewlett-Packard; world headquarters Boise Cascade Corp., Morrison-Knudsen Co., and Albertson Food Stores.
ommerce: wholesale and retail center for southwest Idaho; retail sales $2.5 billion (1980); bank resources $707 million in 6 banks with 27 branches; 4 savings and loan associations, and 7 insurance company offices.
Transportation: 3 major airlines, 2 feeder airlines, one rail freight line, 4 bus lines, 17 common carrier truck lines; Amtrak.
Communications: 4 TV and 9 radio stations.
Medical facilities: 3 major hospital complexes including a

Veteran's Administration facility.
Cultural facilities: Boise Philharmonic Orchestra, art gallery, state museum, Boise Little Theatre, public library, Boise State Univ.
Other attractions: 33 parks, Southwestern Idaho Fairgrounds, 2 major recreational lakes, scenic mountain areas; Bogus Basin ski resort offers one of the world's longest illuminated ski runs.
History: founded 1863; named derived from "les bois" (th trees), a description for area used by French fur trappers i 1811.
Further information: Boise Chamber of Commerce, P. C Box 2368, or Department of Commerce and Developmen Idaho Statehouse, both Boise, ID 83701.

Boston, Massachusetts

The World Almanac is sponsored in the Boston area by the Boston Herald American, 300 Harrison Ave Boston, MA 02106; phone (617) 426-3000. The Herald American was established June 19, 1972; daily circu lation 221,630, Sunday 234,038; publisher James T. Dorris, general manager Dennis Mulligan, editor Donal Forst.

Population: 562,994 (city), 2,759,800 (SMSA).
Area: 46 sq. mi. on Massachusetts Bay; state capital and Suffolk County seat.
Commerce: northeast center for finance and insurance; home office for 50 insurance companies; banking center for New England with total commercial banking deposits of $42.356 billion (1981); accounts for 40% of the nation's mutual fund holdings; retail center for northern New England; major center for electronics, publishing and high-tech ind.
Transportation: terminating point for 2 railroads, Amtrak and Boston & Maine; MBTA (Massachusetts Bay Transportation Authority) provides surface and subway transportation for metropolitan Boston; Massachusetts Port Authority (operates Logan International Airport and the Port of Boston (shipping); 5 interstate highways.
Communications: 21 newspapers (3 daily, 19 weekly), 8 TV and 33 radio stations.
New construction: Copley Place, Lafayette Place, Waterfront Hotel and building rehabilitation, Quincy Market (incl. Faneuil Hall restoration), and the Ritz Carlton hotel/condominium complex.
Medical facilities: health care is Boston's largest industry in terms of dollars invested; major institutions: Mass. General, Children's, and New England medical centers; Boston City, Beth Israel, Deaconess hospitals; Harvard, Boston Univ., and Tufts medical schools; Lahey Clinic.
Federal facilities: 50 federal agencies employ 45,700 (military facilities not included).
Cultural facilities: Boston Public Library, the Boston Athenaeum, Boston Symphony Orchestra; Boston Pops; Boston Opera Co.; Boston Ballet; Museum of Fine Arts; Museum of Science/Hayden Planetarium; New England Aquarium; Museum of Transportation; Children's Museum.
Educational facilities: 16 degree-granting institutions in th city and 47 in the metro area, including Harvard, Bosto College, Boston Univ., Tufts, M.I.T., Brandeis, Univ. c Mass., Suffolk, Emmanuel, Simmons, and Wentworth Inst.
Recreation: 2,327 acres of city recreation area, includes his toric Boston Common and Public Garden; Metropolita District Commission provides extensive facilities, includin beaches and harbor islands.
Convention facilities: 58 hotels (31 in Boston area and 2 suburban) equipped to handle conventions; exhibition hall include Commonwealth Pier Exhibition Hall with 168,00 sq. ft. and the John B. Hynes Veterans Auditorium in Pru dential Center with 154,000 sq. ft. and auditorium seatin 5,800. These facilities will all be enlarged by 1983.
Sports: AL Red Sox (baseball), NBA Celtics (basketball NFL New England Patriots (football), NHL Bruin (hockey).
Other attractions: Quincy Market (a reconstruction of th historic Boston marketplace), Faneuil Hall, the "Freedor Trail", a 1½ mile walk through historic Boston; Beacon Hi and Back Bay historical districts; U.S.S. Constitution - "Ol Ironsides" - the oldest commissioned ship in the U.S. Navy.
Nicknames: The Hub (of the Universe), Bean Town.
History: capital city of commonwealth, founded 1630; fror 1770, Boston was scene of many events leading to America Revolution, including Boston Tea Party on Dec. 16, 177 incorporated Feb. 23, 1822.
Birthplace of: Ralph Waldo Emerson, Arthur Fiedler, Ben jamin Franklin, Jack Lemmon, Robert Lowell, Edgar Alle Poe, John L. Sullivan, Donna Summer, Paul Revere, Bar bara Walters.
Further information: Boston Chamber of Commerce, 12 High Street, Boston, MA 02110.

Bridgeport, Connecticut

The World Almanac is sponsored in the Bridgeport area by The Bridgeport Post (eve.), The Telegran (morn.), and The Sunday Post; published by The Post Publishing Co., 410 State Street, Bridgeport, CT 0660 (203) 333-0161; circulation Post 72,910, Telegram 17,886, Sunday Post 92,399; John E. Pfriem president an general manager, Charles A. Betts managing editor.

Population: 142,546, largest in state; planning region 300,897; 9-town district labor force 551,305.
Area: 17.5 sq. mi. on north shore of Long Island Sound at mouth of the Pequonnock R.; Fairfield County Seat.
Industry: "Industrial Capital of Connecticut;" products include machine tools, ammunition, wiring devices, brass goods, valves, electrical apparatus and appliances; nearby are Sikorsky Aircraft and Avco Lycoming; corporate headquarters: Warnaco, General Electric in Fairfield; Raybestos-Manhattan, and American Chain & Cable in Trumbull.
Commerce: retail sales $2 billion (1980); downtown renewal includes 64-store shopping complex with Gimbels and Sears stores, 2,000-car parking garage, U.S. Courthouse; $50 million development in planning stage, will include 300-room hotel, executive conference center, cultural and media center.
Transportation: railroad station served by Amtrak, adjacent to multi-transportation center and 500-car parking garage; city served by Conn. Turnpike (Interstate 95); Merritt Parkway (Conn. 15); U.S. 1 (Boston Post Road); municipal Si korsky Memorial Airport; Conrail; 2 national bus lines summer ferry to Port Jefferson, N.Y.
Medical facilities: 3 general hospitals, state mental health center; municipal convalescent hospital; major Easter Sea rehabilitation center.
Cultural facilities: Univ. of Bridgeport, Fairfield Univ., Sa cred Heart Univ., Housatonic Comm. College; Museum c Art, Science, Industry; P. T. Barnum museum; symphon orchestra; city-supported downtown cabaret theater; Ameri can Shakespeare theater in adjoining town of Stratford.
Recreational facilities: "The Park City" has 1,200 acres c parks, including Seaside with 2-mile shoreline; zoo, munici pal indoor ice-skating rink, 9,000-capacity Jai Alai fronton summertime community-wide Barnum Festival.
Birthplace of: Edwin Land, Robert Mitchum.
Further information: Bridgeport Area Chamber of Com merce, 180 Fairfield Avenue, Bridgeport, CT 06604.

Bristol, Tennessee-Virginia

The World Almanac is sponsored in the Bristol, Tenn.-Va. area by the Bristol Herald Courier, PO Box 609 Bristol, VA 24203; phone (703) 669-2181; published by Bristol Newspapers, Inc.

Population: 42,500 (23,000 Bristol Tenn., 19,500 Bristol Va.). A civilian labor force 39,620, 36,630 employed.

Area: 30 sq. mi. (cities combined).
Commerce: wholesale and retail center for SW Va.; retail sales in the 6 county market area is $1.9 billion with a market population of 390,200. Average household income $15,650 in 1981.
Industry: Bristol Steel and Iron, Reynolds Metals, Beecham Laboratories pharmaceuticals, Sperry Univac, Raytheon Corp., Westinghouse, United Coal Co. corporate headquarters, Electrolux, Burlington Industries.
Transportation: Norfolk & Western and Southern railways; 12 motor freight lines; Tri-City Airport serviced by Piedmont, Republic, US Air, Atlanta Sunbird Airlines; Greyhound, Trailways buses; located on Interstate 81.
Communications: 3 TV stations, cablevision; 9 radio stations; Bristol Herald Courier (morning) and Bristol Virginia-Tennessean (afternoon) newspapers.
Medical facilities: Bristol Memorial Hospital with 422 beds; 160 doctors and family care facilities of E. Tenn. St. Univ. Medical School; regional mental health center; regional speech and hearing center.
Cultural facilities: 2 community theaters, nearby Barter Theatre at Abingdon; Bristol Ballet Co. (ranked 2d best regional company of South and 3d in nation); Bristol Concert Choir; art museum; 756-seat United Coal Co. Humanities Center; Bristol Country Music Fdn.; Appalachian Music Museum, Appalachian Music Days; Train-station Marketplace (National Register of Historic Places); Tennessee's oldest drug store; site of first country music recording for national distribution (birthplace of commercial country music 1927); Rocky Mount State Historic Site.
Education: cities maintain separate public school systems with 2 high schools, 2 junior high schools, 13 elementary schools; Sullins Academy (a private school); Catholic parochial school; Virginia Intermont, King, Bristol colleges; E. Tenn. St. Univ. in nearby Johnson City.
Recreation: 24 city parks covering 2,000 acres, 200-acre Steele Creek Park and lake in Tenn. along with 1,200-acre Slagle Creek land, Va.'s 450-acre Sugar Hollow Recreation Area; 2 public swimming pools, 24 tennis courts; 2 city stadiums for football and 2 for baseball, 7,000-seat Viking Hall basketball and civic center; senior citizen center,; Bristol Caverans; TVA's South Holston and Boone reservoirs.
Sports: Tiger baseball; auto racing complex, incl. Bristol Intl. Raceway (NASCAR) and Thunder Valley Dragway, headquarters of Intl. Hot Rod Assn.
History: began as Fort Shelby during pioneer days; a center for iron works during the Revolution and a railroad center during the Civil War. Boundary between the cities is the state line down the middle of the main street in the business district.
Further information: Greater Bristol Area Chamber of Commerce, 510 W. Cumberland St., Bristol, VA 24201; phone (703) 669-2141.

Buffalo, New York

The World Almanac is sponsored in the Buffalo area by The Buffalo Evening News, One News Plaza, P.O. Box 100, Buffalo, NY 14240; phone (716) 849-4444; circulation 266,000, Sunday 204,000; Warren E. Buffett chairman; Henry Z. Urban publisher and president; Stanford Lipsey vice chairman; Murray B. Light editor and vice president; Richard K. Feather vice president.

Population: 357,870 (city), 1,241,434 (SMSA), 3d in state; hub of broad 8 county area with population of 1,714,400.
Area: 49.6 sq. mi. city, 1,567 sq. mi. metro, at western end of N.Y. State on Lake Erie, Niagara River, and U.S.-Can. boundary; Erie County seat; metro area includes Niagara Falls, Lockport, Tonawanda, N. Tonawanda, Lackawanna.
Industry: 1,063 manufacturing establishments, headquarters for Rich Products, Buffalo Forge, Trico Products, Fisher-Price Toys; large plants for Republic Steel, Bethlehem Steel, Chevrolet, Ford, Westinghouse, Union Carbide.
Commerce: wholesale and financial center for western N.Y.; retail sales $5.5 billion (metro); average income per household after taxes (metro) $15,947; distribution center for northeastern U.S. and Canada; $6.5 billion in trade between U.S. and Canada handled each year; 13 commercial banks, 8 savings banks, 4 savings and loans.
Transportation: Greater Buffalo Int. Airport served by 6 airlines with over 3 million passengers, 160,000 flights (1981); 6 major railroads, 22 freight terminals; about 350 motor carriers; highway system includes New York State Thruway and Kensington Expressway. Direct highway and rail to all of Canada; water service to Great Lakes-St. Lawrence Seaways system, overseas, and Atlantic seaboard.
Communications: 2 major Buffalo newspapers, 3 additional dailies and one Sunday in surrounding cities; 5 TV, 22 AM and FM radio stations; 5 cable systems.
Cultural facilities: Buffalo Philharmonic in Kleinhans Music Hall; Albright-Knox Art Gallery; Studio Arena theater; Shea's Theater; Museum of Science; Historical Museum; Zoological Gardens (23 acres); Shaw Festival at Niagara-on-the-Lake, Ontario; performing arts center (Artpark) in Lewiston.
Educational facilities: State Univ. at Buffalo (largest unit of state univ.); Niagara Univ., Canisius College; 5 other colleges; several 2-year institutions.
Convention facilities: Memorial Auditorium seats up to 17,000, new Buffalo convention center seats up to 20,000; Niagara Falls Convention Center seats up to 12,000; additional facilities available at several hotels and motels.
Sports: Bills football (NFL), Rich Stadium; Sabres hockey (NHL), Stallions soccer (MISL), War Memorial Auditorium; Bison baseball (AA), War Memorial Stadium.
Recreation: abundant facilities for all year around sports and activities; near both U.S. and Canada vacationlands.
Other attractions: Niagara Falls and river areas from Buffalo to Lake Ontario; Robert Moses and Adam Beck hydro stations; St. Lawrence Seaway, Welland Canal locks, aquarium (Niagara Falls), Our Lady of Victory Basilica (Lackawanna); Old Fort Niagara; Letchworth and Allegany parks; Darien Lake Fun Country; Naval Park; Buffalo Raceway
Birthplace of: Harold Arlen, Richard Hofstadter, Bob Lanier, Bob Smith, Warren Spahn.
Further information: Chamber of Commerce, 107 Delaware, Buffalo, NY 14202.

Calgary, Alberta, Canada

The World Almanac is sponsored in Calgary and southern Alberta by the Calgary Sun, 830 - 10th Avenue S.W., Calgary, Alberta, T2R 0B1; phone (1-403) 263-7730; known as the Calgary Albertan for 78 years up to Aug. 1, 1980; daily circulation 60,000, Sunday circulation 64,000; publisher Hartley Steward, managing editor Les Pyette, general manager Paul Whitlock.

Population: 560,618.
Area: 235 sq. mi.; elevation 3,440 feet in the foothills of the Rockies, 150 miles north of the Alberta-Montana border.
Industry: 526 oil and gas companies, 519 service and supply companies, 358 energy industry consultant firms, 400 data processing firms, and over 1,000 industrial plants in city; meatpacking, transportation, and fertilizer industries also play a prominent part; manufacturing payroll (1979) $442 million; trading area population over one million; more industrial info. available from Bruce McDonald, director, Business Development, P.O. Box 2100, Calgary, Alberta.
Commerce: retail sales (1979) $3.25 billion; gross income of market area (1979) $7.71 billion; per capita spending in market area (1979) $3,200; no sales or gasoline tax.
Transportation: 2 railways; Greyhound Canadian headquarters; International Airport served by 9 airlines.
Communications: 3 TV stations, 2 cable companies; 5 FM, 5 AM radio stations; 2 daily and 4 weekly newspapers.
Medical facilities: 7 major hospitals, 5 auxiliary hospitals, and one tuberculosis center.

New construction: $1.5 billion in construction in 1980 as oil and gas boom continues.
Cultural facilities: 2,700 seat auditorium; Glenbow Museum; QR Arts Centre; Centennial Planterium; symphony orchestra; performing arts center under construction; live theater groups; ballet troupe; opera company, synchronized swimming group.
Education: 254 schools from elementary through senior high school; Univ. of Calgary, Alberta Vocational Centre, Mount Royal College, Southern Alberta Institute of Technology.
Recreation: One hour drive to 4 major ski resorts in Rocky Mountains; 22 ice arenas, 223 athletic parks, 2 ski areas within city, 14 golf courses.
Sports: Calgary Flames (NHL); Calgary Stampede in July attracts one million people over 10 days; Stampeders, Canadian Football League; Calgary Canucks, Alberta Junior Hockey League; Calgary Wranglers, Western Hockey League; Calgary Expos, baseball; Calgary Outlaws, semi-pro soccer.
Other attractions: Heritage Park reconstructs pioneer life on a lake; Calgary Zoo; Dinosaur Park with life-size models; Calgary Tower; more than 1,500 restaurants.
History: began as R.C.M.P. outpost in 1875; railroad arrived in 1883 as population reached 1,800; discovery of oil during 1914 in Turner Valley started Calgary on road to become Canada's oil capital.
Further information: Chamber of Commerce, 517 Centre Street; Calgary Tourist and Convention Association 1300 - 6th Avenue S.W., Calgary, Alberta.

Charleston, West Virginia

The World Almanac is sponsored in the Charleston area by The Charleston Gazette, 1001 Virginia Street, East, Charleston, WV 25301; phone (304) 348-5140; circulation (morn.) 54,739. (Sun.) 105,796; founded 1873 as the Kanawha Chronicle, became The Charleston Gazette 1898; W. E. Chilton III publisher; Don Marsh editor.

Population: 63,968 (city), 231,414 (county), most populous city, county in state; county labor force, 125,900.
Area: 29.3 sq. mi. at meeting place of the Kanawha and Elk rivers; state capital. Kanawha County seat.
Industry: manufacturing including chemicals and fabricated metals; coal, glass, petroleum products, alloys.
Commerce: wholesale, retail center for West Virginia, So. Ohio, E. Kentucky; county retail sales, $1.3 billion; average family income $23,875.
Transportation: 2 rail freight lines, Amtrak, bus lines, state's busiest airport; barge lines, 3 interstate highways.
Communications: 4 TV and 10 radio stations.
Medical facilities: 6 hospitals, 2 of them major complexes.
Cultural facilities: modern civic center and auditorium, Sunrise Cultural and Art Center, symphony orchestra, Community Music Assn., Light Opera Guild, Kanawha Players, State Museum & Cultural Center, Univ. of Charleston.
Other attractions: Coonskin Park, Kanawha State Forest, 6 golf courses, public tennis, International League baseball.
History: first settlement, Fort Lee, 1788; Virginia Assembly established Charles Town 1794; named Charleston 1818.
Further information: Charleston Regional Chamber of Commerce and Development, 818 Virginia Street, East, Charleston, WV 25301.

Charlotte, North Carolina

The World Almanac is sponsored in the Charlotte area by The Charlotte Observer, 600 S. Tryon Street, Charlotte, NC 28233; phone (704) 379-6300; founded 1886 as Charlotte Chronicle; changed to Charlotte Daily Observer, March 1892; sold to Knight Newspapers Inc. 1955; circulation 169,222 daily, 241,802 Sunday; president and publisher Rolfe Neill; editor Rich Oppel.

Population: 314,447 (city), 404,270 (Mecklenburg County), 1.3 million (12-county metro area); labor force 375,400.
Area: 123.4 sq. mi. in Piedmont section of N.C., a plateau extending from the Appalachians to the Coastal Plains.
Industry: over 900 manufacturing companies, chemicals, textiles, food prods., machinery, printing, publishing.
Commerce: major trucking center, photographic and data processing center, 1,800 wholesale firms with $11.4 billion sales; retail sales $5.2 billion (Mecklenburg County); average household income $24,368; 15 banks, 11 mortgage banks, 6 building and loan associations.
Transportation: 120 trucking firms; 2 major railway lines; 4 bus lines; 4 airlines with 189 air movements per day.
Communications: 5 TV and 14 radio stations.
Medical facilities: an outstanding center in Southeast, 7 hospitals including 3 large general.
Cultural facilities: Opera Assn.; Charlotte Symphony Orchestra; Oratorio Society; Mint Museum (art); Nature Museum; Spirit Square (facility for all art activities under one roof); over 400 churches; Discovery Place (museum).
Education: Univ. of N.C.-Charlotte; Davidson College; Johnson C. Smith Univ.; Queens College; Central Piedmont Community College; Kings College; Hamilton College.
Convention facilities: Charlotte Coliseum-Auditorium, Civic Center, Trade Mart, Merchandise Mart.
Sports: Charlotte Motor Speedway (NASCAR) with World 600 and National 500 races; Charlotte Observer Marathon; Carolina Lightnin' (pro soccer); Charlotte Orioles (pro baseball), World Series Invt. Golf Tournament.
Other attractions: 2 major recreational lakes; Carowinds (family theme park); climate — four distinct seasons, avg. daily max. temp. 71.2, yearly avg. temp. 60.5; Festival in the Park; Southern Living Show, Spring Fest.
History: incorporated 1768, named for Queen Charlotte of England; played major role in American Revolution; was gold mining capital of country before 1849; U.S. Mint built in 1836 to serve gold mining industry.
Birthplace of: Billy Graham.
Further information: Chamber of Commerce, P.O. Box 32785, Charlotte, NC 28232; phone (704) 377-6911.

Chattanooga, Tennessee

The World Almanac is sponsored in the Chattanooga area by the Chattanooga News-Free Press, 400 E. 11th Street, Chattanooga, TN 37401; phone (615) 756-6900; circulation 67,000 daily, 130,000 Sunday; publisher Roy McDonald, president Frank McDonald, senior vice president Everett Allen, vice president and editor Lee Anderson, secretary J. W. Hoback, treasurer Clifford Welch.

Population: 169,565 (city), 420,873 (SMSA); 4th in state; 174,100 employed in labor force.
Area: 2,146 sq. mi. metropolitan shopping area at juncture of Tennessee River and north Georgia boundary line; Hamilton County seat.
Industry: about 600 manufacturers employ 50,200, producing more than 1,500 products including principal textiles, fabricated metals, chemicals, primary metals, food products, machinery, apparel, paper products, and leather goods; receipts added by manufacture approximately $1.3 billion.
Commerce: wholesale and retail center; wholesale sales over $2 billion, bank assets $1.2 billion; 18 banks, 2 mortgage banks, 5 savings and loan assns., 2 major life insurance cos.
Transportation: 2 major freight lines, 2 bus lines, 16 federal and state highways; modern municipal airport.
New construction: multi-million-dollar TVA office complex and related downtown redevelopment; arena at Univ. of Tenn. at Chattanooga.
Communications: one cable TV, 5 TV, 18 radio stations; 2 newspapers.

Medical facilities: speech and hearing rehabilitation center; children and adults rehabilitation and education center; Willie D. Miller Eye Center; 14 major hospital complexes including 3 psychiatric facilities.
Cultural facilities: Univ. of Tenn. at Chattanooga; 3 liberal arts colleges; state tech community college; state vocational-tech school; symphony orchestra; opera assn., civic chorus, community concert assn., Boys Choir, conservatory of music, Little Theatre, programs and performances at the Tivoli Theater, Memorial Auditorium and Miller Park.
Other attractions: multi-million dollar vacation complex; Chattanooga Choo-Choo, in one of the world's largest restaurants, in restored railroad terminal; recreational lakes, mountains, and museums.
History: explored by DeSoto 1540, settled 1828 at Ross's Landing, incorporated 1839.
Birthplace of: Jimmy Blanton, Bessie Smith, Roscoe Tanner.
Further information: Chattanooga Convention and Visitors Bureau, Civic Forum, Greater Chattanooga Area Chamber of Commerce, Chattanooga, TN.

Chicago, Illinois

The World Almanac is sponsored in the Chicago area by the Chicago Tribune, 435 N. Michigan Avenue, Chicago, IL 60611; phone (312) 222-3232; founded 1847; circulation daily 770,798, Sunday 1,107,574; publisher Stanton R. Cook, editor James D. Squires; major awards include 9 Pulitzer prizes won by staff members.

Population: 3,005,072 (city), 2d largest city in nation; 5,253,190 (Cook County); 7,102,328 (SMSA); 3,419,300 in resident labor force; est. 19% of U.S. population dwells within a 300 mile radius, 31% within 500 miles.
Area: 228.124 sq. mi. (city); 4,657 sq. mi. (metro area).
Industry: metro area is a leader in production of steel, metal products, sausages, cookies, candy, metal furniture, mattresses, envelopes, boxes, inorganic chemicals, soap, paint, gaskets, cans, saws, screws, bolts, barrels, machine tools, blowers, switchgear, radios, TV's, communications equipment, railroad equipment, and surgical appliances, scientific and engineering instruments; Chicago (SCA) produces a gross metro product of $120.1 billion, 4.1% of GNP.
Commerce: 15,026 manufacturers in Chicago with sales over $70 billion; 51,399 retailers in metro area with sales over $35.8 billion in 1981; 14,012 wholesalers in metro area with sales over $74.4 billion (1977); 62,765 service establishments in the area do an $8.9 billion business (1977); median household income $22,597; Midwest Stock Exchange; 7th Federal Reserve District Bank; world's leading grain futures market; Chicago Board of Trade; Mercantile Exchange, Mid Amer. Commodity Exchange.
Transportation: 3 major airports with 34 passenger carriers handle over 39.1 million passengers, 826,103 aircraft movements; O'Hare is one of the world's busiest and largest airports handling 828,530 tons of freight and mail; 391,676 trucks registered in the metro area; 51 million tons of manufactured goods shipped out yearly; Chicago trucks service more than 54,000 communities; over 12 major highways; 3d largest interstate highway system in nation. Railways ship 512 million tons; 90,000 freight cars per week, 40,000 passengers daily through Union Station; ships carry 72,000,000 tons of cargo in and out of metro area.
New construction: $181 million in industrial construction on 75 projects in 1981; $991 million in residential construction activity; $1.0 billion in commercial construction on 620 projects; site of the tallest building in the world: Sears Tower with 110 stories.
Convention facilities: 674 conventions, 184 trade shows, 14,248 corporate meetings, 2.6 million total attendance; $1 billion income generated.
Educational facilities: 95 institutions of higher learning, including Univ. of Chicago, Illinois Institute of Tech., Loyola Univ., Univ. of Illinois, DePaul, Northwestern.
Recreation: 131 forest preserves, 572 city parks, 147 golf courses, 15 athletic parks and race tracks; 35 museums, zoos, and permanent exhibitions; 88 swimming pools, 31 beaches.
Cultural facilities: Art Institute, Museum of Contemporary Art, Museum of Science and Industry; Shedd Aquarium; Adler Planetarium; Lincoln Park and Brookfield zoos; Museum of Natural Sciences; Historical Society; Chicago Symphony Orch.; Lyric Opera, Schubert, Goodman, Arie Crown Theaters.
Sports: NFL Bears, AL White Sox, NL Cubs, NHL Black Hawks, NBA Bulls, NASL Sting.
History: Indians named the area Checagou after area's strong-smelling wild onions; incorporated as a city 1837 with population of 4,170.
Further information: Visitors Bureau and Information Center, Association of Commerce and Industry, 130 S. Michigan Avenue, Chicago, IL 60603.

Cincinnati, Ohio

The World Almanac is sponsored in the Cincinnati area by The Cincinnati Post, a Scripps-Howard Newspaper, 800 Broadway, Cincinnati, OH 45202; phone (513) 352-2000; founded in 1881 by Alfred and Walter Wellman; evening circulation 147,560; editor William R. Burleigh.

Population: 385,457 (city), 1,392,394 (SMSA), 2d in state.
Area: 2,154 sq. mi. (metro) in SW Ohio, SE Ind., and 3 N. central counties in Ky.; Hamilton County seat.
Industry: home of Procter & Gamble, Federated, Kroger, Kenner, Armco Steel, U.S. Shoe, Western Southern, Union Central & Ohio National Life Insurance, Baldwin Piano and Organ, Cincinnati Milacron, Dubois Chemical, Senco Products, Stearns & Foster, Totes, Gibson Cards, GM, Ford, and GE plants; production of jet engines, playing cards, chemicals, cosmetics, machine tools, belts, clothing; printing and publishing.
Communications: 6 TV stations; subscription and cable TV available in some areas; 12 AM, 25 FM radio stations; 28 weekly, 2 daily newspapers.
New construction: Good Samaritan Hospital, 19-story, 507-bed tower is scheduled for completion in 1986; Hyatt Regency is scheduled to break ground for a 500-room downtown hotel; Jewish hospital renovation and addition of 300 beds; Netherland Hilton $25 million renovation; Ford plans to start developing 'a small city' in Clermont county; Public Library addition; expansion of elevated walkways.
Medical facilities: 30 hospitals with 9,652 beds; 192 physicians per 100,000 population; Children's Hospital Medical Center; UC Medical Center where Sabin oral polio vaccine was discovered; Shriners Burn Institute and VA Hospital.
Cultural facilities: Art Museum, Historical Society, Symphony Orchestra, Krohn Conservatory, Lloyd Library, May Festival, Taft Museum, Cincinnati Opera, Arts Consortium, Cincinnati Ballet, Museum of Natural History, Contemporary Arts Center, Playhouse in the Park, UC Observatory, and Northern Kentucky Arts Council.
Educational facilities: Cincinnati, Xavier, Northern Kentucky univs.; Cincinnati Bible, Mount St. Joseph, Edgecliff, Hebrew Union, St. Gregory, Thomas More colleges; 8 technical and 2-year colleges; 47 vocational schools.
Convention facilities: numerous hotels, motels, and restaurants; Convention and Exposition Center; Music Hall; Cincinnati Gardens; Emery and Taft auditoriums; Riverfront Stadium and Riverfront Coliseum.
Sports: Reds NL baseball, Bengals NFL football, Suds softball, River Downs and Latonia race tracks; College Football Hall of Fame.
Other attractions: Cincinnati Zoo, Fountain Square Plaza, Americana and Kings Island amusement parks, Delta Queen and New Mississippi Queen excursion boats.
Birthplace of: Eddie Arcaro, Doris Day, James Levine, Tyrone Power, Roy Rogers, Pete Rose, Roger Staubach, Robert A. Taft, William Howard Taft.
Further information: Chamber of Commerce, 120 West 5th Street, Cincinnati, OH 45202; phone (513) 579-3100.

Cleveland, Ohio

The World Almanac is sponsored in the Cleveland area by The Plain Dealer, 1801 Superior Avenue, Cleveland, Ohio 44114; (216) 344-4500; founded 1842; a Newhouse Newspaper; circulation, morning 405,842 Sunday 448,259; Thomas Vail, publisher and editor; Roy O. Kopp, business manager; David L. Hopcraft, executive editor; major awards include National Press Club Washington Correspondent award, Heywood Brour Award, and Ohio Associated Press Award.

Population: 573,822 (city), 1,895,997 (SMSA), first in state; total employed 905,000 (non-agricultural).

Area: 1,519 sq. mi., SMSA 4 county area; along southern shore of Lake Erie, east and west of Cuyahoga River; Cuyahoga County seat.

Industry: within 600 miles are 12 of the top 20 U.S. markets, 55% of U.S. population, 64% of U.S. manufacturing plants, 74% of top Fortune Magazine 1,000 U.S. industrial corporate headquarters; no single industry dominates economy—metal and steel products are mainstays; machinery and tools, fabricated metal products, primary metals, automotive products. Important industries include electric motors, petroleum, rubber, plastic, stone clay and glass, chemicals, paints, wearing apparel, measuring instruments, electronic components; food products is $15 billion a year business. Retail sales are more than $8.5 billion; median household income $18,865.

Transportation: Hopkins Airport with 6 million passengers each year; Burke Lakefront Airport, 5 minutes from public square and capable of handling intermediate jets; Port of Cleveland visited by more than 23 overseas steamship lines and Great Lakes fleet; Cleveland is only U.S. city with airport-to-downtown rail service; Amtrak train service.

Communications: Plain Dealer, morning daily plus Sunday; numerous foreign language newspapers; 6 TV stations; 17 AM and 22 FM radio stations.

New construction: $200 million Sohio Bldg., $100 million Republic Steel continuous casting plant; $45 million Superior Square office building; $37 million Ohio Bell office building; new corporate headquarters buildings for Scott & Fetzer, Nordson, Ridge Tool, and TRW, $38 million Union Carbide building.

Cultural facilities: Cleveland Orchestra; Play House, na tion's oldest and largest resident professional theater; Museum of Art; Karamu House for interracial arts; Westerr Reserve Historical Society; Health Museum; Natural Science Museum; Cultural Gardens; zoo; Blossom Music Center Garden Center; Sea World; aquarium.

Educational facilities: Case Western Reserve Univ., Cuyahoga Community College, John Carroll Univ., Notre Dame Ursuline, and Dyke colleges; Cleveland State Univ.

Sports: NFL Browns, American League Indians, NBA Cavaliers; golfing, horse and car racing, boating, polo.

Other attractions: Convention Center is largest city-owned facility in U.S., public library is 5th in size of collection in U.S.; Public Square, marked by 52-story Terminal Tower "The Forest City" is encircled by 18,500 acres of parks Cleveland Clinic, known for medical research, attracts patients throughout the world; University Hospitals of Cleveland has largest research and care center for cystic fibrosis in country; center of a regional renal transplant program; Metropolitan General Hospital is noted for its neurological and burn clinic; many nationality restaurants.

History: settlement established in summer, 1796 by Gen Moses Cleaveland, was capital of the Western Reserve, became a city in 1836.

Birthplace of: Jim Backus, Howard Da Silva, Ruby Dee Joel Grey, Hal Holbrook, Burgess Meredith.

Further information: Greater Cleveland Growth Assn., 69C Union Commerce Building, Cleveland, OH 44115; phone (216) 621-3300. Convention Visitor's Bureau, 1301 E. 6th Street, Cleveland, OH 44114; phone (216) 621-4110.

Columbia, South Carolina

The World Almanac is sponsored in the Columbia area by Columbia Newspapers, Inc., P.O. Box 1333, Columbia, SC 29202; phone (803) 771-6161; circulation, The State (am) 106,054; The Columbia Record (pm) 31,414; The State (Sun.) 129,139 (ABC 3/31/81); Ben R. Morris, publisher and president; R. Sidney Crim general manager; James W. Holton Jr., assistant general manager and advertising director; William E. Rone editorial page editor, The State; H. Harrison Jenkins, editorial page editor, The Columbia Record; Thomas N McLean, executive editor, The State and The Columbia Record.

Population: 99,296 (1980 census), city corporate limits; 2-county metro area (Richland and Lexington) 408,176.

Area: 1,465 sq. mi. (metro area); center of South Carolina near confluence of Broad and Saluda rivers (at Columbia).

Government: state capital with about 100 state agencies, 19 federal agencies; government employees total more than 31,000; Fort Jackson military post employs over 20,000.

Industry: more than 50 national firms such as General Electric, Allied Chemical, Continental Can, Burlington, Litton, Sony, United Tech., Bendix, M. Lowenstein, Rockwell Int., Square D, Westinghouse, Colite Ind., Nassau Recycle, Michelin, Mepco Electra, Canron Ltd.; fibers, heavy equipment, electronics, textiles, fertilizer, cement products, and tires. Columbia (SMSA) industrial wages for fiscal 1979 exceeded $314 million; total industrial capital invested exceeded $876 million in fiscal 1979.

Commerce: retail sales (metro, 1980) over $1.67 billion; total effective buying income was $3.01 billion, while the average effective buying income per household was $21,936; 11 commercial (main) banking institutions.

Transportation: Metropolitan Airport with 2 airlines and freight service; 3 rail freight lines, Amtrak; 46 major freight companies; 3 interstate, 6 federal, and 6 state highways.

Communications: 4 TV and 14 radio stations.

Medical facilities: 6 general hospitals, including moderi Richland Memorial; William S. Hall Psychiatric Institute; 2 state mental hospitals.

Cultural facilities: Town Theatre, the oldest continuous community theater in nation; 3 other theaters; Museum o Art and Sciences; Gibbes Planetarium; Township Auditorium, Dreher Auditorium with Philharmonic Orchestra, City Ballet, Lyric Theatre and Choral Society; Fraser Hall.

Recreation facilities: 13 golf courses; city park system; 7 municipal pools; wide range of hunting activities; Riverbanks Zoological Park; Lake Murray, water sports.

Sports: Williams-Brice Stadium, home of Univ. of South Carolina Fighting Gamecock football team; Carolina Coliseum for basketball, conventions.

Educational facilities: 31,000-student Univ. of South Carolina; 4 private colleges; Technical Education Center; Lutheran Seminary.

History: established 1786 as state capital; burned in 1865 by Union General Sherman.

Further information: Chamber of Commerce, 1308 Laure Street, Columbia, SC 29202.

Columbus, Georgia — Phenix City, Alabama

The World Almanac is sponsored in the Columbus, Ga. - Phenix City, Ala., area by the Columbus Enquirer and the Columbus Ledger, 17 W. 12th Street, Columbus, GA 31994; phone (404) 324-5526; combined daily circulation 65,494, Sunday 70,841; Enquirer founded 1828, awarded Pulitzer Prize 1926; Ledger founded 1886, awarded Pulitzer Prize 1955. Published by the R. W. Page Corporation; Glenn Vaughn, president and publisher; Bill Brown, vice-president and executive editor; Rick Kaspar, vice-president and general manager Joe Rivais, vice-president and production director. Owned by Knight-Ridder Newspapers, Inc.

Population: 170,108 (Columbus); 27,012 (Phenix City); 239,400 (metro); 98,600 employed (metro).
Area: 1,100 sq. miles (metro: Muscogee and Chattahoochee counties, Ga.; Russell County, Ala.) on the Chattahoochee R.
Industry: major textile production center: Fieldcrest Mills, Inc., Bibb Company, Swift Textiles, Westpoint Pepperell, Columbus Mills; Lummus Industries, Columbus Foundries, Interstate Brands, Union Carbide, TRW, Inc.; Internat'l. hqs. Tom's Foods, Ltd. and Burnham Van Service; lumber products, beverages, concrete, bakery goods, and paper.
Commerce: center of west Georgia—east Alabama finance, agriculture, textiles, hydroelectric power; metro retail sales $972.2 million; avg. household buying income $19,953; 9 banks, 6 savings and loan associations.
Federal facilities: Ft. Benning, world's largest infantry school, $483.1 million annual disbursements.
Transportation: 2 rail, 2 bus lines; Delta, Atlantic Southeastern airlines; 33 truck lines; Chattahoochee R. is navigable.
Communications: 3 TV and 10 radio stations.
New construction: 180-room Hilton Hotel; Ft. Benning expansion; 417-bed hospital to replace Medical Center; North By-pass; expansions for Swift Textiles, Southeast Canners, SCM Corp.; Pratt-Whitney aircraft plant.
Medical facilities: 5 hospitals.
Cultural facilities: Museum of Arts and Sciences, Springer and Three Arts Theaters, Bradley Memorial Library; Columbus College, Chattahoochee Valley Comm. College.
Sports: Astros, Southern baseball league.
History: Columbus founded 1828; gained early prominence as shipping center for cotton, fish; birthplace of Coca-Cola formula. Phenix City founded 1883, growing from a Creek Indian trading post.
Birthplace of: Harvey Glance, Carson McCullers, George Foster Peabody.
Further information: Columbus Chamber of Commerce, P.O. Box 1200, Columbus, GA 31902, or Phenix City-Russell County Chamber of Commerce, P.O. Box 1326, Phenix City, AL 36867.

Columbus, Ohio

The World Almanac is sponsored in the Columbus area by the Columbus Citizen-Journal, 34 S. Third Street, Columbus, OH 43216; phone (614) 461-5000; Citizen founded 1899, Journal 1811; circ. 114,266 a.m. daily except Sun.; owned by E. W. Scripps Co.; editor Richard R. Campbell, general manager Gregory A. Dembski, managing editor Seymour Raiz.

Population: 564,871 (city), 1,088,973 (SMSA); 2d in state; total employed in SMSA 518,700.
Area: 183.1 sq. mi. city, 552 sq. mi. county, in central Ohio at the confluence of Olentangy and Scioto Rivers; state capital and Franklin County seat.
Industry: highly diversified; 1,015 manufs. in county (1981) including General Motors, Rockwell International, Western Electric, Borden, R. G. Barry; planes, missiles, refrigerators, mining mach., telephones, auto parts; home office of Battelle Memorial Inst. with world-wide research lab.
Commerce: wholesale, retail center for central, southern Ohio, parts of W. Va., Ky. Retail sales, $4.9 billion; financial assets of 9 banks, 19 savings and loan assns. $40.7 billion; 50 insurance co. home offices, assets $9.4 billion; per capita income (county) $8,341.
Transportation: 150 truck lines, 4 intercity bus lines, 3 railroads, 12 airlines using Port Columbus International with 684 air movements daily; OSU's Don Scott Field capable of handling intermediate jets; 22 major highways.
Communications: 5 TV stations, 19 radio stations and 4 cable TV companies incl. QUBE, the first 2-way system; 2 daily, 19 weekly, 6 monthly newspapers.
Medical facilities: 12 hospitals, med. centers; Children's Hospital; Ohio St. Univ. Col. of Medicine.
Cultural facilities: Ohio Theatre, Palace Theatre, OSU Mershon Aud., symphony orchestra, Cultural Arts Center, Bicentennial Park; art museums, Columbus Museum of Art and Sculpture Garden; Players Theatre, 3 professional and 11 community theaters, 4 ballet cos.; public library, 22 branches; Center of Science and Industry, Ohio Historical Center, 19th century village; Columbus Zoo.
Other attractions: Ohio Expositions Center; German Village, Victorian Village, Ohio Center for conventions; Franklin Park Conserv., The Centrum, Park of Roses; Ohio Railway Museum, 252 parks, boating, floating amphitheater.
Educational facilities: Ohio State, Capital Univ. and Theo. Sem., Franklin Univ., Ohio Dominican Col., Columbus Col. of Art & Design, Columbus Tech. Inst., Ohio Inst. of Tech., Otterbein Col.
New construction: Amer. Electric Power hdqtrs., $90 mil.; John W. Galbreath & Co.'s Hyatt and Capitol Square Office Building, $88.6 mil.; Huntington Center, $100 mil.; new state office tower, $140 mil.
Federal facilities: Defense Construction Supply Center; Confederate cemetery, federal office bldg., Ft. Hayes.
Sports: Ohio Stadium and Franklin County Stadium; Clippers (baseball), Pacesetters (women's football), Beulah Park (thoroughbreds), Scioto Downs (harness); Muirfield Memorial golf tournament; NHRA Spring Nationals.
History: founded 1812 as state capital, named for Christopher Columbus.
Birthplace of: Ketti Frings, Archie Griffin, Curtis Lemay, Jack Nicklaus, Eddie Rickenbacker, Arthur Schlesinger Jr., James Thurber.
Further information: Chamber of Commerce, P. O. Box 1527, Columbus, OH 43216.

Corpus Christi, Texas

The World Almanac is sponsored in the Corpus Christi area by The Caller and The Times, P.O. Box 9136, Corpus Christi, TX 78408; Caller (a.m.) founded 1883; Times (p.m.) founded 1911; merged 1929; Caller circulation 62,339, Times 24,107, Sunday 89,188; publisher Edward H. Harte; general manager Stephen W. Sullivan; executive editor Robert E. Rhodes; Caller managing editor John R. Thomas; Times managing editor Bill Duncan.

Population: 231,999
Area: 328 sq. mi. (226 water), 210 miles SW of Houston on Corpus Christi Bay; Nueces County seat.
Industry: oil refineries; offshore oil rig fabrication; chemical, petrochemical, synthetics, aluminum, and zinc plants.
Commerce: Port of Corpus Christi handled 50.3 million tons in 1981; economic hub of South Texas; farming, ranching, oil and gas production, commercial fishing, tourist trade; 15 banks have deposits in excess of $1.5 billion.
Transportation: 5 airlines, 2 bus lines, 3 freight railroads.
Communications: 2 daily newspapers, 5 TV stations (one public service, one Spanish), plus cable television.
New construction: Permits issued for $207 million in 1982.
Medical facilities: 10 hospitals, including a children's center, with more than 1,400 beds.
Federal facilities: Corpus Christi Naval Air Station is headquarters for Naval Air Training Command; Corpus Christi Army Depot is Army's only complete helicopter overhaul plant; combined payroll more than $141 million.
Cultural facilities: Corpus Christi Museum, Art Museum of South Texas, Museum of Oriental Cultures, symphony, Little Theatre, Del Mar College, Corpus Christi State Univ., Corpus Christi Bayfront Plaza Audit. and Conv. Center.
Recreation: Public beaches and fishing piers on the Bay and along Gulf of Mexico on Mustang Island and in 88-mile-long Padre Island National Seashore; surf and charter boat fishing; sailing, city marina with launching ramps; large tennis center, 3 private tennis clubs, 6 golf courses.
History: Spanish explorer Alonzo de Pineda discovered Corpus Christi Bay in 1519; Blas Maria de la Garza Falcon established San Petronilla Ranch on Petronilla Creek about 1765; city grew from a frontier trading post established in 1839; city incorporated February 16, 1852.
Birthplace of: Farrah Fawcett.
Further information: Corpus Christi Chamber of Commerce, P.O. Box 640, Corpus Christi, TX 78403.

Dallas, Texas

The World Almanac is sponsored in Dallas by The Dallas Morning News, Communications Center, Dallas, TX 75265; phone (214) 745-8222; published by the oldest business in Texas, the News was founded in 1842 by Samuel Bangs; circulation, 380,981 Sunday, 308,649 daily; publisher Joe M. Dealey, president James M. Moroney Jr., vice president, executive editor Burl Osborne. Winner of numerous national awards including Freedoms Foundation, National Headliner and Business in the Arts. Sponsors Teen-age Citizenship Tribute, Fly-the-Flag program, Spelling Bee, Science Fair, Sports Show, Involved Citizen Award, etc.

Population: 904,078 (city), (7th in nation); 1,556,390 (county), Dallas-Fort Worth SMSA 2,964,342; total employed 1.6 million with 5.2% unemployment.
Area: 900 sq. mi. astride Trinity River in north Texas about 75 miles south of Oklahoma border; elevation from 450 to 750 feet; Dallas County seat.
Industry: banking and insurance capital of the Southwest, Dallas ranks 3d among U.S. cities in the number of million-dollar-net-worth companies with 1,120 such firms; 2,994 manufacturing plants shipped $234 million worth of goods during 1980—principally oil field machinery, electronics, food, apparel, soaps and detergents.
Commerce: a $5.5 billion wholesale market; Dallas ranks first nationally in giftware, home furnishing and floor covering wholesaling, 2d in apparel and toys. Metro retail sales totaled $15.7 billion in 1981, while estimated buying income reached $28.4 billion.
Transportation: Dallas-Fort Worth and Love Field airports. In 1981 DF/W was 4th in the world in air carrier operations with 445,781 and 23.5 million passengers enplaned; Love Field's air carrier operations totaled 104,684 and 1.9 million passengers enplaned. City is served by 21 major and 7 commuter and 12 freight air lines, 8 railroads, 2 transcontinental bus lines, 45 motor freight lines, 4 taxi companies with 1,000 cabs. Dallas Transit System serves 126,000 people daily on 106 lines, 587 route miles.
Communications: 2 metropolitan daily newspapers, numerous suburban dailies, 4 commercial VHF TV stations, public television, 21 UHF stations, 16 AM and 21 FM radio stations, 2 city magazines.
New construction: $2.03 billion in building permits in 1981; projects include $116 million Southwestern Bell Telephone Co. Bldg., $108 million Southland Investment Bldg. in Las Colinas, $85 million Arco Bldg., $40 million Dallas Convention Center addition, $40 million Lincoln Plaza, $35 million Cadillac-Fairview Bldg.
Medical facilities: 42 hospitals with 9,100 beds, 403 bassinets. Baylor University Medical Center consistently ranks in the top 10 among the country's "super hospitals."
Cultural facilities: symphony orchestra, civic opera, summer musicals, civic ballet, Shakespeare Festival; drama at Dallas Theater Center, Theater Three, Greenville Ave. Theater, Repertory Theater, and 4 dinner theaters; 7 museums; SMU's Owens Fine Arts Center with a collection of paintings and sculpture; numerous art galleries.
Education: 150,448 students attend 33 colleges and universities within 33 miles of Dallas; Southern Methodist Univ., the Univ. of Texas at Dallas, Univ. of Dallas, North Texas State, Univ. of Texas at Arlington, Baylor Univ. College of Dentistry, Southwestern Medical School; the Dallas Community College, over 40,000 students on 7 campuses.
Convention facilities: 3 major convention centers, including expanded Dallas Convention Center with more combined meeting-exhibit space (611,000 sq. ft.) than any other in U.S.; 24,923 air-conditioned hotel rooms. Dallas always among nation's top 3 convention cities. In 1981, 1.54 million people attended 1,661 conventions.
Sports: professional sports include football, baseball, basketball, tennis, golf, hockey, soccer, and rodeo. Cotton Bowl is site of annual New Year's Day football game.
Other attractions: Six Flags Over Texas, Dallas Zoo, Reunion Arena, International Wildlife Park; Fair Park is home of State Fair of Texas 16 days each October; Dallas Arts Museum, The Science Place, Museum of Natural History; Hall of State; Garden Center and Music Hall; excellent lakes, golf courses, parks, luxury hotels, and restaurants.
History: first settler was Tennessee frontiersman John Neely Bryan who established a trading post and plotted the townsite in 1844; incorporated 1856; named for Vice-President George Mifflin Dallas. Since 1931, the city has had council-manager form of government. Spectacular population growth began after World War II, when aircraft manufacturing augmented an economy that had been built first on cotton, then on oil, banking, and insurance; diversified economic expansion fed the growth into the 1980s.
Birthplace of: Ernie Banks, Robbie Benson, Morgan Fairchild, Trini Lopez, Harold Marcus, Stephen Stills, Lee Trevino.
Further information: Dallas Chamber of Commerce, Fidelity Union Tower, Dallas, TX 75201.

Dayton, Ohio

The World Almanac is sponsored in the Dayton area by The Journal Herald, 37 S. Ludlow Street, Dayton, OH 45402; phone (513) 225-2421; founded as Dayton Repertory; circulation 105,183; executive editor Arnold Rosenfeld, mng. editor William Worth, editorial page editor William Wild, "Day" section editor Mickey Davis.

Population: 203,588 (city), 826,891 (SMSA), 4th in state; total employed 341,800.
Area: 1,708 sq. mi. (SMSA), 465 sq. mi. (Montgomery County), 55 sq. mi. (City).
Industry: NCR Corp., General Motors (Delco Moraine, Delco Products, Delco Air, Inland Mfg., new small diesel truck plant, Harrison Radiator Div.); Frigidaire, Standard Register, Monarch Marking Systems, Mead Corp., Duriron Co., Inc., Monsanto Research Corp., Ohio Bell, Dayton Newspaper, Inc. (publishers of The Journal Herald and the Dayton Daily News), Dayton Power and Light; more than 800 other manufacturing facilities.
Commerce: retail sales $3.3 billion; average effective buying household income $22,115.
Transportation: 2 airports, 7 airlines, 2 trunk rail systems, 4 bus lines, county wide Dayton Regional Transit Authority.
Communications: 5 TV, 8 radio stations.
Medical facilities: 12 hospitals, including Wright Patterson AFB Hospital and a VA facility.
Federal facilities: Wright Patterson AFB, HQ. for Air Force Logistics Command and Aero. Systems Div.; Defense Electronics Supply Center, federal building, VA center.
Convention facilities: modern downtown convention and exhibition center.
New construction: downtown Arcade, Gem City Savings Assoc. headquarters, Amphitheater (part of the Miami River Corridor Project), Courthouse Plaza (includes dept. store, bank bldg., Mead Tower world headquarters, and 2 restaurants), General Motors small diesel truck plant, Wright State Business School, expansion of Sinclair Community College, Marriott Hotel, and expansion of the Salem Mall.
Educational facilities: Univ. of Dayton (law school), Wright State Univ. (med. school and new business school); Sinclair, Miami Jacobs Jr. colleges; United Theolgical Seminary, Central State Univ., Wilberforce Univ., Wittenberg Univ., Cederville, Wilmington, Antioch colleges, Air Force Inst. of Tech., Capital Univ. Without Walls, Central Michigan Univ. (WPAFB), Christian Inst. of Tech., Dayton Bible College, International Broadcasting School, Kettering Col. of Med. Arts, and Sawyer Col.
Cultural facilities: Dayton Art Inst., Philharmonic Orch., opera, ballet, contemporary dance co.; 4 amateur theatrical groups, 2 professional cos.; Diehl band shell, River Corridor Amphitheater, Deeds Carillon, dinner theater.
Sports: Amateur Trapshoot national headquarters, college sports, Bogie Busters Pro/Am golf tourn. for Muscular Sclerosis; Dayton Hydroglobe, 5 amateur soccer teams.

Other attractions: Air Force Museum, Carillon Park, Aviation Hall of Fame, Dayton Air Fair, Old Courthouse Museum, A World A'Fair, Dayton River Corridor Festival, Paul Lawrence Dunbar Home, Wright Bros. Memorial, Oregon Historic District, Cox Arboretum, Aullwood Audubon Center and Farm, Wegerzyn Center.
Birthplace of: Erma Bombeck, Irving Babbitt, Moses Malone, Mike Schmidt, Martin Sheen, Jonathan Winters, Orville Wright.
Further information: Dayton Area Chamber of Commerce, Suite 1980, Winters Bank Tower, 40 North Main Street, Dayton, OH 45423.

Denver, Colorado

The World Almanac is sponsored in the Denver area by the Rocky Mountain News, 400 W. Colfax Ave., Denver, CO 80204; phone (303) 892-5000; founded 1859 by William N. Byers; circulation daily 312,873, Sunday 335,665; editor Ralph Looney, general manager William W. Fletcher; sponsors Colorado-Wyoming Spelling Bee, Golden Wedding Anniversary Party, and Huck Finn Day.

Population: 491,396 (city), 1,615,442 (SMSA), first in state; total employed 820,574 (SMSA).
Area: 116.4 sq. mi. on S. Platte R. at edge of Great Plains near Rocky Mts.; state capital, Denver Co. seat.
Industry: Mountain Bell, employing 21,000 statewide; Adolph Coors Cos., 6th largest U.S. brewer of beer, also makes glass and metal containers and ceramic parts; Storage Tech. Corp., manuf. of computer memory parts; Martin Marietta Corp., aerospace research and prod.; Gates Rubber Co., maker of v-belts and hose; Samsonite Corp.
Commerce: largest distribution center in the region; bank deposits $9.3 billion; 126 banks, 16 savings and loan assns.; 76 insurance co. home offices statewide.
Transportation: 5 major rail freight lines, Amtrak; Continental and Greyhound bus lines; 3 interstate highways intersect city; Stapleton International Airport has 1,300 flights daily, 7th busiest in world, served by 19 airlines, home of Frontier Airlines, United Airlines Flight Training Ctr.
Medical facilities: largest medical center between Kansas City and San Francisco; Univ. of Colo. Health Sciences Center; National Jewish Hospital; Children's Asthma Research Inst. and Hospital (CARIH); 34 hospitals.
Communications: 2 newspapers; 7 TV, 35 radio stations.
Federal facilities: largest complex of federal laboratory facilities outside Washington, D.C., with 33,000 fed. employees; site of Lowry AFB, U.S. Mint, Dept. of Energy's Rocky Flats nuclear weapons plant and Solar Energy Research Inst., Air Force Accounting and Finance Ctr., Fitzsimmons Army Medical Ctr., Army's Rocky Mountain Arsenal.
Cultural facilities: symphony orchestra; several nonprofessional orchestras and choral groups; Denver Art Museum; Denver Center for the Performing Arts; 24 other theater cos.; 100,000 sq. ft. convention complex; 9,000-seat Red Rocks outdoor amphitheater.
Educational facilities: Univ. of Colorado (campuses in Boulder, Denver and Colorado Springs); Univ. of Denver; Colorado School of Mines; Metropolitan State, Loretto Heights and Regis cols.; Illiff School of Theology; Univ. of Colo. Health Sciences Center.
Recreational facilities: 209 parks, including 20,000 acres in mountains (most in nation); 44 golf courses in metro area; 3 amusement parks; numerous ski areas.
Sports: pro teams include NFL Broncos; Bears, American Association baseball; NBA Nuggets; CHL Flames; MISL Avalanche; Denver Gold, U.S Football League.
Other attractions: State Capitol, Colorado Heritage Center, City Park Zoo; Museum of Natural History; Gates Planetarium; Botanic Gardens.
History: founded 1858 with discovery of gold; fast became supply center for mountain mining camps; named for territorial governor.
Birthplace of: Ward Bond, Mary Chase, Douglas Fairbanks, Pat Hingle, Paul Whiteman.
Further information: Denver Chamber of Commerce, 1301 Welton St., 80204; Denver and Colorado Convention and Visitors Bureau, 225 W. Colfax Ave., 80202.

Des Moines, Iowa

The World Almanac is sponsored in Iowa by the Des Moines Register, 715 Locust Street, Des Moines, IA 50304; phone (515) 284-8000; founded 1849; circulation daily Register 248,000, Sunday Register 397,000; board chairman David Kruidenier; president Michael Gartner; executive vice president and publisher Gary Gerlach; editor James Gannon; major awards include 12 Pulitzer prizes.

Population: 191,003 (city), 337,814 (SMSA).
Area: 66 sq. mi., at juncture of Raccoon and Des Moines rivers, so. central Iowa. State capital and Polk Cnty. seat.
Industry: considered to be 2d largest insurance center in U.S. (56 home companies) and 2d largest tire center with Firestone, Armstrong plants; publishing center — Meredith Co., Better Homes and Gardens, Wallace-Homestead, Wall Street Journal plant, others; farm implements — North American headquarters of Massey Ferguson, John Deere; lawn and garden equipment, sporting goods, food products, cosmetics, dental equipment, automotive accessories, concrete forms, nozzles, tools; 700 wholesale and jobbing firms; Standard Oil credit card center, bulk mail center.
Commerce: retail sales in metro area $2.106 billion (1981); per capita income $9,235 (1981); average household income, $24,175.
Transportation: enlarged in-city airport, 6 major airlines; 4 bus lines, 4 railroads, 69 truck lines; highways 80 and 35.
New construction: downtown high rise condos, apts., and large downtown office bldg. with 9-story atrium.
Communications: 13 radio, 4 TV stations, cablevision.
Medical facilities: 9 hospitals with 2,700 beds.
Cultural facilities: art center, Center of Science and Industry, community playhouse, drama workshop, Drake Univ., symphony orchestra, Grand View, Area Community, and 2 bible colleges; Univ. of Osteopathic Medicine and Health Sciences, Civic Center Theater, Botanical Center.
Recreation: 1,400 acres of parks, 9 public golf courses, 10 public pools, tennis, YWCA, YMCA; 5,000-acre reservoir.
Other attractions: AAA baseball, Drake Relays, Missouri Valley and Big Eight (Iowa State U.) conferences; 15,000-seat auditorium; boys and girls state basketball tournaments, State Fair, Living History Farms, Children's Zoo, 36-story Ruan Center, tallest in Iowa, Terrace Hill (Governor's Mansion), state capitol and state historical bldg.
History: founded 1843 as a fort to protect rights of Indians; incorporated 1853, became Iowa capital 1857.
Birthplace of: Cloris Leachman, Sada Thompson.
Further information: Chamber of Commerce, 8th and High Streets, Des Moines, IA 50309.

Detroit, Michigan

The World Almanac is sponsored in the Detroit area by The Detroit News, 615 W. Lafayette, Detroit, MI 48231; phone (313) 222-2095; founded 1873 by James E. Scripps; circulation daily 629,392, Sunday 825,384; published by The Evening News Association: president, Peter B. Clark; senior vice-president, Richard M. Spitzley; The Detroit News: president and publisher, Robert C. Nelson; vice-president and general manager, Gene R. Arehart; and editor, William E. Giles. Awarded the 1982 Pulitzer Prize Gold Medal for Meritorious Public Service. Sponsors more than 30 community service programs including: Science Fair, Spelling Bee, Bicycle Marathon, Book & Author Luncheons and Golden Gloves Boxing.

Population: 1,203,339 (city) first in state, 6th in U.S.; 4,344,139 (SMSA).
Area: 139.6 sq. mi. on the Detroit River, a Great Lakes connecting link and the world's busiest inland waterway; Wayne County seat.
Industry: "The Motor City"; area plants produce 25% of the nation's cars and trucks, employing more than 195,100. Nonautomotive manufacturing and nonmanufacturing firms employ more than 1.2 million; other products are machine tools, iron products, metal stampings, hardware, industrial chemicals, drugs, paint, wire products.
Commerce: metro median income per household $19,710 (1978); area retail sales $18.8 billion (1979).
Transportation: served by 10 railroads, over 220 intercity truck lines, 19 airlines, and 25 steamship lines serving more than 40 countries.
Communications: 8 TV and 50 radio stations.
New construction: 2.4 acre, Phase II of Renaissance Center, $65 million twin office towers; 3.4 acre, $48 million West Clinical Service Bldg. of Henry Ford Hospital; 3.7 acre, $53 million New Center office-retail bldg.; 21 acre, $42 million Wayne County Jail.
Cultural facilities: symphony orchestra, International Institute, Meadow Brook music and drama programs, Institute of Arts, concert band, and the Freedom Festival, celebrating Canada Day, July 1, and U.S. Independence Day, July 4.
Educational facilities: 13 colleges and universities in metro area including Wayne State Univ., Univ. of Detroit, and branches of the Univ. of Michigan and Michigan State.
Convention facilities: Cobo Hall and Convention Arena with 500,000 sq. ft. of exhibit space; Joe Louis Arena with 33,000 sq. ft. of exhibition space; more than 23,000 rooms in 350 hotels and motels in greater Detroit (Wayne, Oakland, Macomb counties).
Sports: Tigers baseball (American League), Express (NASL), NFL Lions, NHL Red Wings, NBA Pistons; 6 winter skiing areas within short driving distance.
Other attractions: Chrysler, Ford, American Motors, and General Motors auto plants; Henry Ford Museum and Greenfield Village, Cranbrook Institute (science museum and arts), Belle Isle, zoo, public library, historical museum, and Fort Wayne Military Museum.
History: founded 1701 by the Frenchman Cadillac as a strategic frontier fort and trading post, ceded to the British in 1763 and turned over to the U.S. in 1796 as a village of 2,500; reoccupied by the British for a year in the War of 1812. Completion of the Erie Canal in 1825 opened a cheap water transport route from New York to the Northwest and made Detroit an important commercial center. R. E. Olds built Detroit's first auto factory in 1899; and Henry Ford, who handbuilt his first car in 1896, formed his first company in 1899, and the present Ford Motor Co. in 1903.
Birthplace of: Nelson Algren, Ralph Bunche, Ellen Burstyn, Francis Ford Coppola, George Gervin, Marlo Thomas, Lily Tomlin, Robert Wagner.
Further information: Greater Detroit Chamber of Commerce, 150 Michigan Avenue; and Detroit Public Information Dept., City-County Bldg., both Detroit, MI 48226; and Detroit Convention Bureau, 100 Renaissance Center, Detroit, MI 48243.

Dubuque, Iowa

The World Almanac is sponsored in the Dubuque area by the Dubuque Telegraph Herald (Mon.-Fri. evenings; Sunday Mornings), 8th and Bluff Streets, P.O. Box 688, Dubuque, IA 52001; phone (319) 588-5611; founded 1836; circulation 39,073 daily, 41,938 Sunday; publisher Norman R. McMullin, executive editor Stephen M. Kent, advertising director Dan Grady.

Population: 62,321 city, 93,637 SMSA.
Area: 23.7 sq. mi. in Dubuque County on the Mississippi River on the eastern boundry of the state; Dubuque County seat; 183 miles west of Chicago; 310 miles north of St. Louis
Commerce: retail sales $423 million (1980), median household income $22,217 (1980).
Medical facilities: 3 hospitals with 697 beds; Iowa's 2d largest medical clinic.
Industry: agriculture, meat processing, industrial tractor manufacturing, millwork, oil handling equipment, pumps, plumbing goods, furniture, paper containers, snow removal equipment, metal tanks and fittings, sheet metal goods; iron, copper, brass, and aluminum castings; medical laboratory equipment, insulation board, chemicals, insecticides, chemical fertilizer, textbook publishing.
Transportation: Illinois Central Gulf, Milwaukee Road, Burlington Northern railroads; 16 motor truck cos., 3 interstate bus lines, intracity bus lines; barge transportation; airport 6.5 miles south of city by Mississippi Valley and Mid-Continent airlines, 2 charter services; 5 air freight cos.; city is served by U.S. highways 20, 52, 61, 151.
Communications: One television station, CATV; 2 AM, 3 FM radio stations; daily, weekly labor, and weekly Catholic newspapers.
Federal facilities: U.S. Post Office and court house; Corps of Engineers Lock and Dam; U.S. Coast Guard.
Cultural facilities: 8 art galleries, symphony orchestra, community theater groups, Carnegie-Stout Public Library.
Education: 13 public elementary schools; 2 public junior high schools; 2 public high schools; 10 parochial elementary schools, one parochial high school; Univ. of Dubuque; Clarke, Loras colleges; vocational-technical school; nurses training school.
Recreation: 24 parks, YM-YWCA, 6 golf courses in county; 3 public swimming pools, 2 nature preserves, ski area; boating, fishing, water skiing, cross country skiing, downhill skiing, ice skating, racquetball.
Convention facilities: Five Flags Civic Center; 17 hotels and motels, 71 restaurants, 22 fast food services; 14 night clubs.
Sports: Blues, Merchants, and Pilots semi-pro baseball; Fighting Saints hockey; city league softball, basketball, volleyball, horseshoes.
Other attractions: 4th Street cable railway, Shot Tower; riverboat museum; Farmers' Market held every Saturday May-October, selling homegrown and homemade products; Pickett's Brewery, only one in Iowa; architecture from 1870-1910 period; Trappist Monastery 12 miles SW of city.
History: founded by Julien Dubuque who mined lead in the area in 1785; area has been under 5 different flags throughout its history; local government organized in 1837, city charter adopted 1841, council-manager-ward form of government adopted 1980; keystone of the tri-state area of Ia., Ill., and Wis.
Further information: Dubuque Area Chamber of Commerce, 880 Locust Street, Dubuque, IA 52001; phone (319) 583-8246; or Dubuque Information and Referral Service, 1358 Central Avenue, Dubuque, IA 52001, phone (319) 557-8800.

Edmonton, Alberta, Canada

The World Almanac is sponsored in central and northern Alberta by the Edmonton Journal, 10006 - 101 Street, P.O. Box 2421, Edmonton, Alberta, T5J 2S6; phone (403) 425-9120; founded November 11, 1903. A division of Southam Press Limited; circulation 200,192; publisher J. Patrick O'Callaghan; editor Stephen Hume; assistant editor William Thorsell; sponsor Learn to ski, swim, canoe, run, pan gold, play golf, tennis, racquetball, and Shape Up Fitness programs; Recipe Contest, Literary Awards, Newspaper in Education.

Population: 521,205 city (1981), 702,299 metro (1981); capital of the province of Alberta, largest Alberta city, 5th in Canada; total metro employed 363,300 (1981).
Area: 263 sq. mi. on North Saskatchewan River. 2nd largest city in area in Canada.
Industry: 2d largest refining center in Canada, 12,000 pro-

ducing wells; petrochemical facilities include plastics, fertilizers, man made fibers, steel tube mills, 2nd largest meat processing center in Canada; serves 2 major oil sands plants to the north; prosperous mixed farming area.
Commerce: major supply center for Northwest Territories, Yukon, northeastern B.C. and Canadian Arctic; origin and terminus of 5 oil and natural gas pipelines east and west; retail sales (metro 1981) $7.3 billion; mfg. shipments (metro 1981) $5.9 billion; trading area population 1.25 million.
Transportation: crossroads of Yellowhead, Alaska, and Mackenzie highways; Canadian National, Canadian Pacific; Northern Alberta, Great Slave, and Alberta Resources railroads; 4 airports, 7 airlines, 304,349 itinerant movements in 1980; Light Rail Transit System.
Communications: 19 radio stations including one French station; 4 TV stations including one French station, 2 cable TV and FM radio networks.
New construction: over $1.503 billion in building permits issued in metro area in 1981.
Medical facilities: 6 general and 5 auxiliary hospitals, 4 extended care centers, 2 rehabilitation centers, 13 nursing homes.
Cultural facilities: Edmonton Symphony Orchestra, Edmonton Art Gallery, Centennial Library plus 11 public libraries, Provincial Museum and Archives, Canada's Aviation Hall of Fame, Convention Centre, Univ. of Alberta (Canada's 3d largest), Northern Alberta Inst. of Tech. (Canada's largest tech. col.), Grant McEwan Community Col., Alberta and Edmonton ballet companies. Canada's most active professional theater, housed in the Citadel Theatre complex; Northern Light professional theaters; Stage West dinner theater; Edmonton Opera, Northern Alberta Jubilee Auditorium, Queen Elizabeth Planetarium, Muttart Conservatory.
Other attractions: Klondike Days, annual celebration of the 1898 Yukon gold rush held in mid-July; August Heritage Festival; Valley Zoo, Fort Edmonton, John Janzen Nature Centre, Capital City Recreation Park (largest of it's kind in North America), 12 public parks; Alberta Wildlife Park, Polar Park, Elk Island National Park and many lakes nearby.
Sports: CFL Eskimos, NHL Oilers, NASL Drillers, PCL Trappers; 18,000 seat Coliseum, 61,000 seat Commonwealth Stadium, aquatic center, velodrome, shooting range and lawn bowling greens; Kinsmen Fieldhouse indoor track; 9 public sports fields; 13 indoor swimming pools, 5 outdoor pools, 16 indoor ice arenas, 10 golf courses, horse racing. City will host 1983 World Student Games in July.
History: Fort Edmonton built in 1795, named after town now a borough of London, England; oil discovered at Leduc (20 miles south) in 1947 rocketed the city into prominence as one of the world's leading petrochemical centers.
Birthplace of: Dave Babych, Thomas Chong, Mark Messier.
Further information: Chamber of Commerce, 600 Sun Life Place, 10123 - 99 Street, Edmonton, Alberta; City of Edmonton Tourist Information, 10145 - 100 Street, Edmonton, Alberta; or City of Edmonton Business Development Dept., 2410 Oxford Tower, Edmonton Centre, 10235 - 101 Street, Edmonton, Alberta.

El Paso, Texas

The World Almanac is sponsored in the El Paso area by the El Paso Herald-Post, 401 Mills Avenue, El Paso, TX, 79999; phone (915) 546-6100; Herald founded in 1881, Post 1922, merged (under Scripps-Howard) 1931; circulation 33,000; Harry Moskos, editor, Ron Royhab, managing editor.

Population: 479,448 (El Paso), plus twin city Juarez, Mex., 600,000.
Area: 239 sq. miles on the western tip of Texas where the Rio Grande cuts the boundaries of Texas, New Mexico, and Mexico at the foot of the Rockies (including Franklin Mountains); El Paso County seat.
Industry: manufacturing payroll $335.2 million (1980), employment 35,600; clothing largest employer with BTK Industries, Farah, Sun Apparel, Blue Bell; Juarez-El Paso inbond industries at 96 and 36,700 employed including electronic and others such as RCA, GTE Sylvania, Allen Bradley; home of El Paso Natural Gas, Asarco Inc., Tony Lama Boots, Phelps Dodge, Standard and Texaco refineries, Old El Paso (Pet Foods) and Ashley's of Texas canned Mexican foods; nut processing, cattle, pecans, cotton and other agriculture. Foreign trade zone at El Paso Intl. Airport.
Commerce: Wholesale-retail center for West Texas, southern New Mexico, northern Mexico; retail sales, (1980) $1.7 billion, 22 banks, 6 savings and loans; exports (1980) $1.7 billion, imports $1.4 billion.
Transportation: 5 major rail lines, 8 bus lines, 9 major highways; gateway to Mexico, busiest crossing point in the U.S. with more than 77 million crossings a year; International Airport with seven airlines with 234,036 flights including military, 955,159 passengers, 14,757 tons air cargo in 1980.
Communications: 6 TV and 23 radio stations.
New construction: 1981 building permits totaled $213,196,639.
Medical facilities: 16 hospitals with 2,429 beds; area cancer treatment center; University of Texas System School of Nursing, Texas Tech University School of Medicine.
Federal facilities: Ft. Bliss (U.S. Army Air Defense Center, Allied Students Missile Center, Sgts. Major Academy), William Beaumont Army Medical Center and MacGregor Range, Holloman Air Force Base in New Mexico.
Cultural facilities: University of Texas at El Paso, El Paso Community College, El Paso Symphony, Art, History and Archeological museums including the Kress Collection at the El Paso Museum of Art, Ballet El Paso, theater groups, Chamizal National Memorial Theatre and McKelligon Canyon Pavilion; civic-convention center, public libraries.
Other attractions: annual Sun Carnival and Sun Bowl football game; Terry Bradshaw Cancer Treatment Center Tournament, Tigua Indian Community arts and crafts center, missions that pre-date those of California; Old Mesilla Art Colony; horse racing in nearby New Mexico, horse and dog racing in Juarez; ProNaf museum and restaurants in Juarez; zoo, Museum of History, Wilderness Park Museum, Hueco Tanks State Park; Guadalupe Mountains and Big Bend National Parks within 300 miles; skiing in Ruidoso, N.M., Carlsbad Caverns within 200 miles; exotic Juarez, Mexico and Pancho Villa Country.
Birthplace of: Vikki Carr, Tom Mix, Debbie Reynolds, Fulton J. Sheen.
Further information: Convention and Visitors Bureau, 5 Civic Center Plaza, El Paso, TX, 79901.

Erie, Pennsylvania

The World Almanac is sponsored in the Erie area by The Erie Daily Times, 205 W. 12th Street, Erie, PA 16501; phone (814) 456-8531; founded in 1888; circulation 74,000 daily, 92,000 Sunday; Edward M. Mead, Michael Mead, co-publishers; executive editor Joseph Meagher, managing editor Len Kholos.

Population: 119,123 (city), 279,780 (county), 3d in state; total employed 51,500 (city), 113,300 (county).
Area: 19.53 sq. mi. at tip of NW Pa.; Erie County seat.
Commerce: county produces $269 million in exports, highest per capita in Pennsylvania; Erie's retail sales total more than $855 million; tourism—5 miles of beaches, fishing, boating; winter sports with 6 county parks and Presque Isle State Park offering camping, hiking trails, tennis courts, picnic areas, and ball fields; seaport—60 or more oceangoing vessels each year; over 506 industrial plants produce machinery and parts, iron and steel forgings, hardware, meters, plastics, paper (Hammermill), furniture, toys; General Electric produces Amtrak passenger trains.
New construction: John E. Lampe marina, public facility which will provide 250 boat stalls, launching ramps, and include a 30 acre park; Erie Insurance Exchange expansion, $33 million; So. Shore Towers Apts., $5 mil.
Transportation: 5 railroads, Boston-Chicago Amtrak line; airport; 35 trucking companies, 4 bus lines.
Cultural facilities: Penn State Univ. extension; Gannon,

Mercyhurst, and Villa Maria colleges; Philharmonic Society, Council of the Arts; theater groups; Erie County Field House for plays, entertainment, and sports; work begun on $8 million Erie Civic Center.
Convention facilities: Erie Hilton, 2 Holiday Inns, 90 other hotels and motels with over 3,200 rooms.
Medical facilities: Hamot Medical Center, Saint Vincent Health Center, VA hospital, Medi-Center, Millcreek Community Hospital, Erie County Geriatric Center, Corry Memorial Hospital, Shriners' Hospital for Crippled Children, Union City Memorial Hospital, Doctors' Osteopathic Hospital, Fairview Medical Center.
History: named after Eriez Indians; site of building of ship Niagara with which Oliver Hazard Perry defeated British in 1813 in Lake Erie battle.
Birthplace of: Fred Biletnikoff, Harry Burleigh.
Further information: Chamber of Commerce, 1006 State, Erie, PA 16501.

Evansville, Indiana

The World Almanac is sponsored in southwestern Indiana, western Kentucky, and southeastern Illinois by the Evansville Press, P.O. Box 454, Evansville, IN 47703; phone (812) 464-7600; founded July 2, 1906, by E.W. Scripps and J.C. Harper; circulation 45,600; editor William W. Sorrels, managing editor Tom Tuley.

Population: 130,496 (city), 309,408 (SMSA); 4th in state.
Area: 47 sq. mi. at bend of Ohio River in southwest corner of state; Vanderburgh County seat.
Industry: Whirlpool Corp. plants (refrigeration and air conditioning); Mead Johnson & Co. (pharmaceutical division of Bristol-Myers Co.); Alcoa Warrick Operations (aluminum) just east of city; 283 manufacturing firms.
Commerce: retail sales $775.6 million (1981); effective buying income per household $16,247 (1981); home offices of CrediThrift of America, Inc.; 4 banks, 6 savings and loan.
Transportation: world headquarters of Atlas Van Lines; 4 railroads, 5 commercial barge lines, 3 interstate bus lines; Air Illinois, Allegheny, Britt, Comair, Eastern air lines.
Communications: 2 daily, 1 weekly newspaper; 4 TV and 8 radio stations.
New construction: more than $3 billion in commercial and industrial expansion underway including downtown Riverview Commerce Centre bank, hotel and Coal Exchange office building; 120-store Eastland Mall.
Medical facilities: 4 general and mental hospitals; branch of Indiana University Medical School.
Cultural facilities: Philharmonic Orchestra, Museum of Arts and Science, Mesker Zoo, Univ. of Evansville, Indiana State Univ., Evansville; Angel Mounds State Memorial.
Other attractions: new 150-passenger "Spirit of Evansville" riverboat, Willard Library.
Sports: Evansville Triplets baseball of American Assn. (AAA), farm team of Detroit Tigers.
Birthplace of: Sidney Catlett, Ron Glass, Bob Griese, Paul Splittorff.
Further information: Chamber of Commerce, Southern Securities Building, Evansville, IN 47708.

Everett, Washington

The World Almanac is sponsored in Snohomish & Island County by The Herald, P.O. Box 930, Everett, WA 98206, (206) 339-3000; founded in 1891; circulation 58,986 evening, Saturday morning, 59,017 Sunday. Published by The Daily Herald Company, a division of The Washington Post Company. Publisher and president Christopher M. Little; executive editor Joann Byrd; vice president of marketing Larry L. Hanson; vice president of operations Donald R. Palmer.

Population: 54,413 (city), 337,720 (county), 3d in state; 1,607,469 (SMSA).
Area: 37 square miles (city), on Puget Sound, 28 miles north of Seattle, Snohomish County seat.
Commerce: (County) Retail sales $1.5 billion.
Industry: manufacturing: aircraft Boeing plant, electronics John Fluke, Hewlett-Packard, Eldec; forest - Scott Paper, Weyerhaeuser, E.A. Nord.
Communications: 3 radio stations, 1 cable station.
Transportation: highways; I-5, U.S. 99, I-405, U.S. 2. Auto freight rail, major transcontinental line, ocean shipping, Snohomish County Airport.
Education: Everett Community College, Edmonds Community College.
Recreations: large marina, 3 golf courses, 24 tennis courts, 22 city parks. Skiing, fishing, Civic Auditorium, Memorial Stadium.
Convention facilities: three hotel convention facilities (county).
Medical facilities: 2 hospitals (city).
History: incorporated in 1893, became county seat 1894.
Further information: Everett Area Chamber of Commerce, 26 & Wetmore, Everett WA 98201.

Fort Myers, Florida

The World Almanac is sponsored in the Fort Myers area by the Fort Myers News-Press, 2442 Anderson Avenue, Fort Myers, FL 33901; phone (813) 335-0200; founded in 1931 as merger of the 47-year-old Weekly Press and 11-year-old Tropical News, acquired by Gannett Co. Inc. in 1971; circulation 62,000 daily and 73,000 Sunday; executive editor Ron Thornburg; publisher Paul Flynn; editorial page editor Homer Pyle.

Population: 36,625 (city); 205,266 (county); fastest growing SMSA in nation; 73,000 employed.
Area: 25.44 square miles on southwest Florida gulf coast, south of Sarasota and north of Naples; county seat.
Commerce: wholesale-retail sector of the economy provides largest number of jobs in county and is largest single source of income. Retail sales (1980, county) $1.1 billion. Construction, real estate and tourism are other major industries. 2 largest manufacturers are Fort Myers News-Press and Ohio Medical Products. 2 largest employers are United Telephone Co. and Lee Memorial Hospital. Largest agricultural crop is flowers. Three enclosed malls with fourth under construction. Captran Resorts International, pioneer in time-sharing resorts in U.S. based here. Nearly one-quarter of population is retirement aged. 1980 assessed property value $5.3 billion. 1981 median family income $18,900. Bank and S&L deposits (1980) $1.9 billion.
Communications: 11 radio; 3 local TV; 1 local educational TV station to broadcast this year; one daily regional newspaper; 14 daily and weekly, paid and free circulation papers.
Educational facilities: Edison Community College; University of South Florida upper division branch; Vocational-Technical School; K-12 enrollment 30,184.
Transportation: 9 airlines; 2 cross-country and 1 countrywide bus service; railroad freight service; 9 taxicab companies; limited-use shipping port.
Cultural facilities: Lee Civic Center, 9,000 seats; Fort Myers Exhibition Hall; 10 public libraries.
Medical facilities: Lee Memorial Hospital (publicly owned); Fort Myers Community Hospital; Cape Coral Hospital; Lehigh Acres General Hospital.
Recreational facilities: 23 golf courses; Naples-Fort Myers Kennel Club (greyhound racing); Terry Park, home of Fort Myers Royals minor league baseball (Class A) and Kansas

City Royals spring training camp; 51 city and county parks; sandy beach islands accessible by boat or car; 54 city and county tennis courts; 1 city raquetball club; 30 campsites.
Other attractions: Thomas A. Edison Winter Home; Nature Center of Lee County; Shell Factory; J.N. Ding Darling Wildlife Refuge.
History: established 1850 as outpost against Seminole attacks on settlers. First word of sinking of battleship Maine was heard at telegraph office here. Southernmost battle of civil war fought here 1865.
Further information: Chamber of Commerce, 2254 Edwards Drive, Fort Myers, FL 33901.

Fort Wayne, Indiana

The World Almanac is sponsored in the Fort Wayne area by the Journal-Gazette, 600 W. Main Street, Fort Wayne, IN 46802; phone (219) 461-8333; established June 14, 1899 by consolidation of The Journal and The Daily Gazette; circulation daily 56,953, Sundays 106,401; president-publisher Richard G. Inskeep; secretary-treasurer Naomi Erb; editor Craig Klugman.

Population: 172,196 (city), 380,439 (SMSA); total employed 163,800 (metro).
Area: 51.96 sq. mi. at confluence of St. Joseph, St. Mary's, and Maumee rivers in NE Ind.; Allen County seat. Allen County is largest of Indiana's 92 counties (671 sq. mi.), and has greatest number of farms in state, 1,858.
Industry: General Electric and International Harvester largest employers; Magnavox, Essex International, and Central Soya home offices; several firms manufacture about 85% of world's diamond wire dies.
Commerce: wholesale and retail center for northeastern Indiana, southeastern Michigan, northwestern Ohio; retail sales (metro) over $1.784 billion; bank deposits $1.715 billion; 5 banks, 4 savings-and-loan assns.; E. B. I. per household (metro) $24,442; 6 life insurance companies, including Lincoln National Life, based here.
Transportation: 2 major rail freight lines, Amtrak; motor freight lines including home-based North American Van, Elway Express, Scott, and Transport Motor; I-69 connects city with Indianapolis and Indiana Toll Road; U.S. 30 dual lane to Chicago; municipal airport; United, Delta, Piedmont, Air Wisconsin airlines.
Communications: 10 radio, 5 TV stations, 35 cable stations.
Medical facilities: 4 hospitals including VA.
Cultural facilities: Philharmonic Orchestra; Fine Arts and Performing Arts complex; 7 univ. and colleges; 3 museums; Foellinger outdoor theater, art museum under construction.
Sports: War Memorial Coliseum; annual Mad Anthony celebrities golf.
Other attractions: replica of 3d Fort Wayne (1815); children's zoo, 88 parks and playgrounds, 19 golf courses, 37 shopping centers, $4 mil. plant conservatory and botanical gardens under constr.
History: first white settlement in Indiana (circa 1692).
Birthplace of: Bill Blass, Carole Lombard, George Jean Nathan.
Further information: Chamber of Commerce, 826 Ewing Street, Ft. Wayne, IN 46802.

Fort Worth, Texas

Population: city 385,141 (5th in state), county 860,880, Ft. Worth/Dallas SMSA 2,964,342; 465,842 total employed with 6.1% unemployment.
Area: 861 sq. mi. on the Trinity River in north central Texas, about 50 miles from Oklahoma border; Tarrant County seat.
Commerce: diversified manufacturing, including aerospace, plants, food and beverage, mobile homes, autos, medical industries; 1,651 manufacturers; agribusiness related industry produces over $28.3 million in agriculture products a year.
Transportation: Dallas-Fort Worth regional airport 24 minutes driving time from downtown; 4th in the world (1981) in air carrier operations with 445,781; 23.5 passengers; 9 major railroads, Amtrak; 41 motor carriers; city-owned local bus service, 2 transcontinental, 2 intrastate bus lines.
Communications: one daily newspaper; 26 area radio stations, 8 area TV stations; weekly and monthly publications, including Fort Worth Magazine.
Medical facilities: 31 hospitals with 4,700 beds; 2 children's hospitals with 200 beds, 4 government hospitals.
Federal facilities: 14 federal agencies; Carswell AFB.
Cultural facilities: Casa Manana, America's first permanent musical arena theater; community theater; symphony, opera, ballet; Texas Boys Choir and Texas Girls Choir; Van Cliburn Piano Competition; Kimbell Art Museum, Amon Carter Museum of Western Art, Fort Worth Museum of Science & History, Fort Worth Art Center.
Education: 8 colleges and universities with more than 53,000 students; 27 other colleges and campuses within 50-mile radius with over 97,000 students; Texas Christian Univ., Univ. of Texas at Arlington; Texas Wesleyan College; Texas College of Osteopathic Medicine; 3 campuses of Tarrant County Junior College; Southwestern Baptist Theological Seminary.
Recreation: Forest Park, Heritage Park, Fort Worth Zoological Park, Trinity Park, Botanic Gardens, Japanese Garden, Water Garden Park; 9 municipal golf courses.
Convention facilities: Tarrant County Convention Center; Will Rogers Memorial Center; 219 conventions (1981); 63 hotels and motels with 6,000 rooms.
Sports attractions: Dallas Cowboys football, Texas Rangers baseball, Fort Worth Texans hockey; Colonial National Golf Tournament; TCU football.
Other attractions: Six Flags Over Texas, Fat Stock Show and Rodeo, Miss Texas Pageant, Log Cabin Village, North Fort Worth western historical area; Cowtown Rodeo weekly; Pate Museum of Transportation.
History: Founded 1849 as a frontier Army post on the Chisholm Trail; later became major railhead.
Birthplace of: Larry Hagman, Sandra Haynie, Roger Miller, Byron Nelson, Fess Parker, Rex Reed, Johnny Rutherford.
Further information: Chamber of Commerce, 700 Throckmorton, Fort Worth, TX 76102.

Fresno, California

The World Almanac is sponsored in the Fresno area by The Fresno Bee, 1626 E Street, Fresno, CA 93786; phone (209) 441-6111; founded 1922; circulation daily 137,699 Sunday 156,376; president C. K. McClatchy, editor C. K. McClatchy, executive editor George Gruner, managing editor Don Slinkard.

Population: 218,202 (city), 515,013 (county); total employed 266,800.
Area: one of largest counties in the state, 3,819,456 acres; located in center of the state; Fresno County seat.
Agriculture: leading county in U.S. in farm production, number of farms, and annual value of agriculture production; state's leading county in total value and production of plums, grapes, cantaloupes, barley, turkeys, peaches, boysenberries, figs, nectarines, cotton, alfalfa seed.
Industry: 600 diversified manufacturing establishments; food processing is major industry; 2d in importance is production of beverages, primarily wine, brandy, and spirits; metro retail sales over $2.3 billion.
Transportation: 7 airlines; Amtrak; freeways connect to all major metropolitan areas in California; served by 23 common truck carriers, one interstate bus line, and 2 mainline railroads with freight handling facilities; U.S. port of entry.
Communications: one public and 6 commercial TV stations, 5 cable TV services, 18 commercial radio stations, and 2 public radio stations.
Medical facilities: 6 general hospitals including a VA installation; a surgical center and a medical school under con-

struction.
Cultural facilities: community philharmonic, opera, ballet and theater; Fresno Art Center, Meux Home Museum, Discovery Center, Kearney Museum, downtown malls with one of the best outdoor art displays in the West.
Recreation: Western Hockey League team, California Baseball League team; golf, tennis, swimming; Yosemite, Sequoia, and Kings Canyon national parks with groves of giant Sequoia trees plus facilities for all sports.
Other attractions: Duncan Water Gardens, Underground Gardens; Roeding Park with city zoo and children's Storyland; nationally famous rodeo, county fair.
Convention facilities: William Saroyan Theatre seats 2,361; Exhibit Hall facilities can accommodate up to 3,500; 11 meeting rooms, exhibit space of 59,000 sq. ft; Selland Arena has capacity of 7,500; 5,000 hotel and motel rooms.
History: area explored by the Spaniards in the early 1800s and visited by fur trappers before 1840; gold miners came in the 1850s; county created Apr. 19, 1856, from parts of Mariposa, Merced, and Tulare counties.
Birthplace of: Mike Connors, Sam Peckinpah, William Saroyan, Tom Seaver.
Further information: Fresno City & County Chamber of Commerce, P.O. Box 1469, Fresno, CA 93721.

Greenville, South Carolina

The World Almanac is sponsored in the Greenville County area by The Greenville News and Greenville Piedmont (daily a.m. and p.m. and combined weekend editions), P.O. Box 1688, 305 S. Main Street, Greenville, SC 29602; phone (803) 298-4100; circulation 107,936 daily, 106,017 Sunday (Mar. 1979); chairman of the board and publisher J. Kelly Sisk, president and co-publisher Rhea T. Eskew, executive editor John S. Pittman.

Population: 58,242 city, 287,913 county, 562,934 SMSA; 292,340 SMSA labor force, 9.5% SMSA unemployment.
Area: 789 sq. mi. in county; Greenville is county seat; in South Carolina's Piedmont area; county includes 7 incorporated areas.
Industry: textiles, apparel, tires, fiber production, chemicals, machinery, electronics, food.
Commerce: 1980 retail sales in SMSA $2.39 billion; 1979 bank debits in SMSA $23.8 billion; 1980 per capita income $8,201 county.
Transportation: 2 airports, 2 airlines, 2 bus lines, 3 railroads; Interstate 85, US highways 25, 29, 123, 276.
Communications: 5 TV, 15 radio stations, 2 cable TV services; 2 daily, 3 weekly newspapers.
New construction: $1.07 billion industrial development and expansion from 1960 to May 1982, creating more than 33,000 jobs; $30 million downtown hotel-convention center to be completed in 1982; $15 million Bausch & Lomb manuf. plant, $20 million highrise office bldng.
Cultural facilities: Greenville County Museum of Art, Greenville Little Theatre, Warehouse Theatre, Bob Jones Univ. Classic Players, Furman Univ. Guild, Greenville Symphony Orchestra, Bob Jones Univ. Art Museum; 2 four-year univs., two-year college, technical col.; more than 400 churches representing 26 faiths.
Medical facilities: 9 hospitals, St. Francis Community Hospital, Shriners Hospital for Crippled Children.
Sports: Furman Univ. in Southern Conference, nearby Clemson Univ. in Atlantic Coast Conference; 3 stock car tracks in county; boating in upstate lakes.
History: county created by General Assembly 1786, city named Pleasantburg in 1797, Greenville in 1831.
Birthplace of: Charles Townes.
Further information: Greater Greenville Chamber of Commerce, 24 Cleveland Street, P.O. Box 10048, Greenville, SC 29603; (803) 242-1050.

Halifax, Nova Scotia, Canada

The World Almanac is sponsored in Nova Scotia by The Chronicle-Herald and The Mail-Star, 1650 Argyle Street, Halifax, Nova Scotia; phone (902) 426-2811; circulation Chronicle (morning) 71,961, Mail-Star (aft.) 57,037; publisher Graham W. Dennis, president Fred G. Mounce, general manager Frank Huelin, managing editor Ken Foran, treasurer W.D. Coleman.

Population: 280,000, labor force 126,000.
Area: 24.19 sq. mi. on S.E. coast of province; capital city.
Industry: leading industrial area in Atlantic Canada; oil refineries, electronic equipment manufacturers, ship yards, metal works, breweries, and fish processing; one of Canada's most diversified scientific research centers.
Commerce: financial center of region, head offices of all major banks; retail sales over $1 billion, average family income $22,743 (1980): government employs 47,401.
Transportation: 1 passenger-freight line; 11 container lines; container port with 5 sea-shore cranes handled containers with tonnage of 1.8 million (1980); about 347,000 tons break bulk cargo and 10.9 million tons bulk cargo; international airport handled 1.6 million passengers (1980).
Communications: 5 radio, 2 TV stations; 3 daily newspapers.
New construction: building permits issued for over $500 million worth of construction for last 3 years.
Education: 12 universities, colleges, tech-voc schools, 9 research institutes; 48 common and 4 private schools.
Medical facilities: 9 hospitals (3 teaching).
Cultural facilities: Atlantic Symphony Orchestra. Rebecca Cohn Auditorium, 6 museums, bus and water tours.
Parks: 3 major parks (403 acres).
Sports: Halifax Voyageurs of the AHL.
History: founded in 1749 by the English; meeting place of first legislative assembly in Canada (1758).
Birthplace of: Charles Huggins, Ruby Keeler.
Further information: Halifax Visitors and Convention Bureau, Suite 508, Market Mall, Scotia Square, Halifax, Nova Scotia B3J 3A5; phone (902) 426-8736.

Hartford, Connecticut

The World Almanac is sponsored in the Hartford metro area by The Hartford Courant (mornings and Sunday), 285 Broad Street, Hartford, CT 06115; phone (203) 241-6200; founded 1764; circulation: 208,845 daily, 290,254 Sunday; publisher and chief executive officer Keith L. McGlade, vice president and treasurer Richard H. King, vice president and director of advertising Raymond A. Jansen Jr., vice president and editor Mark Murphy.

Population: 136,392 city, 726,036 SMSA, 807,766 Hartford County.
Area: approx. 1,524 sq. mi. in metro area.
Industry: insurance, government, defense.
Commerce: retail sales in metro area $4.3 billion; total bank deposits $9.404 billion.
Transportation: 2 railroads, 24 airlines, 8 bus lines; interstate highways I91 (north and south), I84 (east and west) cross in city.
Communications: 3 TV, 20 radio stations; cable TV.
Cultural facilities: Hartford Symphony, Connecticut Opera, Wadsworth Atheneum, Hartford Stage Company, Hartford Ballet, Mark Twain House, Children's Museum.
Educational facilities: Trinity College, Univ. of Hartford, Univ. of Conn. Law School, School of Social Work, and Hartford Branch; Greater Hartford and Manchester community colleges.
Sports: NHL Whalers play in Hartford Civic Center.
History: founded 1636 by Thomas Hooker and group of settlers from Newtown (Cambridge), Mass., became Connecti-

cut's capitol city 1665.
Birthplace of: John Gregory Dunne, Totie Fields, Katharine Hepburn, J.P. Morgan, Bill Rodgers, Thomas Tryon, Edward Bennett Williams.
Further information: Chamber of Commerce, 250 Constitution Plaza, Hartford, CT 06103.

Honolulu, Hawaii

The World Almanac is sponsored in Hawaii by The Honolulu Advertiser, P.O. Box 3110, Honolulu, HI 96802; phone (808) 537-2977; founded July 2, 1856, as Pacific Commercial Advertiser by Henry M. Whitney; circulation 83,721 mornings, 201,301 Sunday; president and publisher Thurston Twigg-Smith, editor-in-chief George Chaplin, executive editor Buck Buchwach, managing editor Mike Middlesworth; awards from American Political Science Assn., American Assn. for the Advancement of Science, others.

Population: 762,565; 79% of state population; total employed (civilian only) 329,100.
Area: 596.3 sq. mi., encompassing Oahu Island; state capital.
Commerce: major destination for U.S., Japanese tourists; average daily visitor census 96,095 in 1981; tourists spent $3.2 billion in 1981; sugarcane and pineapple major agriculture export crops; retail sales (statewide) $6.7 billion; total personal income $9.76 billion (1980); per capita personal income $11,096; Pacific basin business and financial center.
Transportation: dependent on ships, planes for most goods; passengers arrive mostly by air; 22 airlines serve airport, 10 domestic carriers, 12 foreign, 5 inter-island.
Communications: 5 TV, 23 radio stations; 2 major daily newspapers.
Medical facilities: 22 civilian acute care hospitals, one military acute care hospital, 20 specialty hospitals; Univ. of Hawaii School of Medicine.
Federal facilities: 7 major military bases, including Pearl Harbor Naval Base.
Cultural facilities: statewide public school system, 230 schools; 146 private schools; 9-campus Univ. of Hawaii; main campus at Manoa in Honolulu; university stresses oceanography, tropical environment problems and resources, tsunami research, volcanology, inter-race relations; East-West Center, Inc., at Manoa; Bernice Pauahi Bishop Museum for studies of Pacific cultures; Polynesian Cultural Center showcases native dances, music, arts; Honolulu Academy of Arts, Iolani Palace.
Recreation: surfing, swimming, sailing, fishing, football, basketball, baseball.
Other attractions: Waikiki Beach, extinct volcano Diamond Head, Arizona Memorial, balmy weather, tradewinds, multi-racial population, cultural diversity, Polynesian heritage.
History: Honolulu ("sheltered bay" in Hawaiian) was a small village when first westerners called aboard 2 British ships in 1786, 8 years after Capt. James Cook became first known European to discover Hawaiian Islands.
Birthplace of: Hiram Fong, Charlie Hough, Daniel Inouye, Bette Midler.
Further information: Hawaii Visitors Bureau, 2270 Kalakaua Avenue, Honolulu, HI 96815.

Houston, Texas

The World Almanac is sponsored in the Southwest by The Houston Post, 4747 Southwest Freeway, Houston, TX 77001; phone (713) 621-7000; founded in 1836; circulation daily 376,879, Saturday 400,060, Sunday 440,135; Oveta Culp Hobby, chairman of the board and editor; William P. Hobby, president; awards include Pulitzer Prize, Grand Prix, Editor & Publisher; community events sponsored: Educational Services, Science Engineering Fair, Scholastic Art Awards, Scholastic Writing Awards, travel shows, Houston Post Family Night at the Shrine Circus, the Ice Capades, the Harlem Globetrotters, the Avon Championship Tennis Circuit and the Southern Living Cooking Show.

Population: (city) 1,594,086, (SMSA) 2,891,146 total employed (SMSA) 1.5 million; highest average annual pay of any metro area in the Southwest.
Area: 556 sq. mi. (city) on upper center Gulf Coast prairies, 49 ft. above sea level; Harris County seat; connected to Gulf of Mexico by 50-mile inland waterway, the Ship Channel.
Industry: nation's leading manufacturer in petrochemicals; headquarters for world's oil-related industries, with 360 internationally active companies; important in machinery manufacturing and chemicals and allied products; a leading supplier of petrochemicals and synthetic rubber; produces millions of dollars worth of agricultural products.
Commerce: Houston-Galveston SCSA leads South and Southwest in retail sales volume; average spendable family income $25,265; 10th across nation in median family income; 233 metro banks; 53 foreign banks.
Transportation: Port of Houston (1st among nation's ports in volume of goods transported internationally and 2nd in total cargo) connects with 250 world ports by over 200 steamship lines, hosts over 5,000 ships yearly; 25 airlines, 2 airports; 5 rail systems; 50 common-carrier truck lines; 210-mile freeway system; 1,016-mile bus transit system.
Communications: 2 daily newspapers; 29 radio stations; 5 commercial, one educational TV station.
New construction: new construction leader for 3rd year in a row; broke $2 billion barrier for new construction.
Medical facilities: Texas Medical Center includes 26 institutions; Harris County has 59 hospitals (including VA) with 16,401 beds, 30 ambulances, 3 Life Flight helicopters.
Federal facilities: Lyndon B. Johnson Space Center, $202 million manned-spacecraft center; Ellington AFB.
Cultural facilities: $3 mil. Alley Theatre and Miller Outdoor Theatre; Houston Symphony Orchestra, Houston Grand Opera, Houston Ballet Foundation perform in $7.5 million Jones Hall for Performing Arts; 30 major art galleries inc. Museum of Fine Arts and Contemporary Art Museum; Houston Public Library, 26 branches, 4 bookmobiles; Harris County Public Library, 17 branches, 2 bookmobiles.
Education: 29 univers. including Rice, Univ. of Houston, Texas Southern; 7 medical schools including Baylor Col. of Medicine and Univ. of Texas Health Science Center; Houston Independent School District, 7th largest in nation.
Recreational facilities: 272 parks, 5 golf courses, 42 swimming pools, 3 tennis centers with 54 courts and 82 neighborhood courts; Astroworld 65-acre amusement park; botanical garden arboretum, Hermann Park and Zoo; 55 community centers, 70 county parks, 70 miles of Gulf beaches.
Convention facilities: 668 major conventions held in Houston in 1981; hotels and motels have 31,906 rooms; the Astrodome can seat 60,000 for conventions; downtown locations include Albert Thomas Convention Center; Music Hall; Sam Houston Coliseum; Exposition Hall.
Sports: Astros baseball, Oilers football, Rockets basketball; sports events centers are Astrodome and Summit.
Scientific facilities: one of the top 10 science centers in the nation; over 80 research firms.
History: founded 1836 by J.K. and A.C. Allen, city eventually encompassed Old Harrisburg which was an 1826 townsite laid out by John Harris; named for Gen Sam Houston, commander of the Texas Army, which won independence from Mexico for the Republic of Texas Apr. 21, 1836. Houston was first president of the Republic, later governor of the state of Texas; both Houston and Harrisburg were for brief periods capitals of the republic.
Birthplace of: Allen Drury, Howard Hughs, A.J. Foyt, Barbara Jordan, Ann Miller, Kenny Rogers, Jaclyn Smith, B.J. Thomas.
Further information: Houston Convention and Visitor Council, 1522 Main St.; Houston Chamber of Commerce, 1100 Milam, both Houston, TX 77002.

Huntington, West Virginia

The World Almanac is sponsored in the Huntington-Ashland-Ironton area by The Herald-Dispatch (morn.), Huntington Publishing Company, 946 Fifth Avenue, Huntington, WV 25701; member of the Gannett Group; circulation 48,538 Sunday 50,483; publisher and president Harold E. Burdick, controller Ed Burns, executive editor C. Donald Hatfield.

Population: 63,684 (city), 315,000 (5-county metro area).
Area: 15.86 sq. mi., on Ohio River near where West Virginia, Ohio, and Kentucky meet; seat of Cabell Co.
Industry: center for coal transport and for hand-crafted glass; leading industries are Ashland Oil, Armco Steel Co., Huntington Alloys, Inc.; 200 plants, 400 products.
Commerce: largest port for inland vessels in U.S. handles nearly 20 million tons per year, moved by 7 freight companies; 1980 retail sales in metro area, 1.3 billion dollars.
Transportation: Tri-State Airport, is served by 2 airlines and 2 commuter airlines; Amtrak; 18 truck lines; urban bus transport system; 2 interstate bus lines.
Cultural: The Huntington Galleries museum, The Huntington Chamber Orchestra, Marshall Artist Series, Community Players, Musical Arts Guild, and River Cities Summer Scene.
Medical: 6 general hospitals with 1,800 total beds; 3 specialty hospitals including a VA hospital.
Educational: Public and private schools. Home of Marshall University including the College of Medicine.
Financial: Eleven banks and 4 savings and loans, with assets of over $1 billion.
Communications: 3 commercial, 1 educational, 4 cable TV; 14 radio stations and one daily newspaper.
Library services: New county library opened in downtown Huntington in 1980 with over 200,000 volumes. Additionally the Marshall Univ. library makes its facilities available.
Recreation: Six parks, covering 700 acres. Four state parks within an hour's drive. 12 public and private golf courses. 16 movie theaters. The Huntington Civic Center, an 11,000 seat auditorium for concerts, conventions and trade shows. City Auditorium; Memorial Field House; Cam Henderson Center. Boating, sailing, swimming, on the Ohio River, Beech Fork Dam, Cabwaylingo State Park. Skiing, hunting, fishing, and camping in nearby Appalachian and Allegheny Mountains. Camden Park, is on the outskirts of Huntington.
Conventions: Full convention facilities available: new civic center, new Holiday Inn (downtown) guest-convention complex, and nearly 1800 motel rooms.
Birthplace of: Peter Marshall.
Further Information: Chamber of Commerce, 522 Ninth Street, Huntington, WV 25701.

Indianapolis, Indiana

The World Almanac is sponsored in the Indianapolis area by The Indianapolis Star, The Indianapolis News, 307 N. Pennsylvania Street, Indianapolis, IN 46204; phone (317) 633-1240. News founded 1869, Star 1903; circulation daily Star, 222,799, daily News, 140,440, Sunday Star, 364,917; publisher Eugene S. Pulliam; president William A. Dyer Jr; Star editor John H. Lyst; News editor Dr. Harvey C. Jacobs; Pulitzer prizes-News, Star; Nat'l. Headliners first prize-Star.

Population: 700,807 (city), 1,161,539 (SMSA); total employed 559,900.
Area: 379.4 sq. mi.; geographic center of state; state capital and Marion County seat.
Industry: 1,520 manufacturers; plane and auto engines, electronics, pharmaceuticals, machinery.
Commerce: commercial center for Indiana; retail sales $5.9 bil.; per capita personal income $9,100; 6 banks with resources over $7.4 bil.; home offices of over 60 insurance cos.
Transportation: 10 passenger and 2 cargo airlines; Indianapolis Intl. Airport; 5 rail freight lines; Amtrak; 3 interstate bus lines; 57 truck lines; 7 interstate freeway routes.
Communications: 6 TV stations and 18 radio stations.
New construction: over $390 mil. under construction 1982.
Medical facilities: 17 hospitals, over 6,800 beds.
Federal facilities: Fort Harrison incl. Army Finance and Accounting Center, U.S.A. Admin. Center.
Cultural facilities: Museum of Art, Oldfields Museum of Decorative Arts; Indiana State Museum; Indianapolis Zoo; Children's Museum; Conner Prairie Pioneer Settlement and Museum of Indiana Heritage; Clowes Hall; Civic Theatre, oldest amateur group; repertory theater; Starlight Musicals.
Education facilities: Butler Univ., Indiana Central Univ., Marian Col., Christian Theological and St. Mauer's seminaries, Purdue-Indiana Univ. at Indianapolis, Indiana Univ. medical center, nation's largest.
Recreation facilities: 13,000 park acres; 16 swimming pools; 12 golf courses; 18,000-seat domed arena; 10,000-seat sports center with 24 tennis courts; Veladrome; natatorium; track & field stadium.
Convention facilities: Indiana Convention-Exposition Center, Indiana State Fairgrounds.
Sports: home of the Pacers NBA; minor league baseball, soccer, hockey.
Other attractions: Indianapolis 500; Hoosier 100; annual National Drag Racing championships; U.S. open Clay Court championships.
History: important before Civil War, with nation's first union railway station (1853); home of James Whitcomb Riley, Booth Tarkington, and President Benjamin Harrison.
Birthplace of: Eli Lilly, Richard Luger, Steve McQueen, Jane Pauley, Booth Tarkington, Kurt Vonnegut Jr.
Additional information: Indianapolis Chamber of Commerce, 320 N. Meridian Street, Indianapolis, IN 46204.

Jacksonville, Florida

The World Almanac is sponsored in the Jacksonville area by The Florida Times-Union and the Jacksonville Journal, One Riverside Avenue, Jacksonville, FL 32202; phone (904) 359-4111; circulation, Times-Union 154,753, Journal 44,933, combined Saturday 173,082, combined Sunday 199,779; publisher J.J. Daniel, president John A. Tucker; Journal won Pulitzer prize for photography in 1967.

Population: (1981) 524,700 county, 747,000 metro; total employment 236,000 (1981).
Area: 827 sq. mi., includes nearly all of Duval Co. in northeast Florida; under one consolidated government.
Industry: diversified economy; banking, medical and insurance center.
Commerce: emphasis on finance distribution; home or regional hq. for 35 insurance companies; 1980 retail sales $2.6 billion; effective buying income per household $19,458.
Transportation: 3 major railroads and Amtrak; over 40 truck lines; 8 airlines averaging 110 air movements daily; 2 interstate bus lines; the South Atlantic's major domestic distribution center, handled 15.6 million tons in 1979.
Communications: 6 TV stations, 2 cable TV systems, 21 radio stations, 2 daily newspapers.
New construction: $502.3 million in permits issued 1981.
Medical facilities: 13 general hospitals and one naval hospital with total of 3,300 beds.
Federal facilities: 3 naval stations including the 2d largest naval complex on East Coast add $700 million yearly to the economy.
Cultural facilities: Cummer Art Gallery, Jacksonville Art Museum, Museum of Arts and Sciences, Brest Planetarium, Marine Science Center, Jacksonville Symphony, Opera Repertory, Ballet Guild, 6 community theaters.
Education: Univ. of North Florida, Jacksonville Univ., Ed-

ward Waters, Florida Junior, and Jones colleges.
Sports: Gator Bowl; $540,000 Tournament Players Championships golf tournament; Jacksonville Univ. basketball and baseball; Murjani tennis tournament; pro football, soccer, and baseball, greyhound racing.
Other attractions: civic auditorium, coliseum, Jacksonville Zoo, Fort Caroline, Kingsley Plantation; 8 miles of public beaches, Mayport Jazz Festival.
History: founded in 1822 by Isaiah Hart; named for Andrew Jackson; fire in 1901 destroyed 2,368 buildings, left 10,000 homeless; city, county governments merged 1968.
Birthplace of: Pat Boone.
Further information: Chamber of Commerce, 3 Independent Drive, P.O. Drawer 329, Jacksonville, FL 32201.

Kalamazoo, Michigan

The World Almanac is sponsored in the Kalamazoo area by The Kalamazoo Gazette, 401 S. Burdick, Kalamazoo, MI 49007; phone (616) 345-3511; founded 1833; circulation daily 60,609, Sunday 68,540; owned and operated by Booth Newspapers, Inc.; president Werner Veit, editor Daniel M. Ryan, manager Ralph H. Bastien Jr.

Population: 79,722 (city), 211,921 (county); total employed (Kalamazoo-Portage SMSA) 134,700.
Area: located equidistant to two of the largest metro areas in nation — Chicago and Detroit, 140 miles away; Kalamazoo County seat.
Industry: paper-making is the traditional industry with 5 large plants; Fisher Body Division body stamping plant; Upjohn Co., pharmaceuticals.
Commerce: shopping center for large part of southwestern Michigan; in 1959, city became first in country to close downtown streets and create a pedestrian mall, now known as "Mall City;" 7 banks with combined assets in 1980 of $1.17 billion, 2 savings and loan assns. with assets over $600 million.
Communications: daily newspaper, one TV, 9 radio stations.
Transportation: 2 railroads provide freight service, Amtrak passenger service; 34 general carriers provide trucking services; airport with freight and passenger service; 3 bus lines.
Cultural facilities: 5 auditoriums offering music and theatrical performances; 5 live arts theaters, art center, symphony orchestra, Kalamazoo Civic Players.
Educational facilities: 3 colleges and one university.
Other attractions: Kalamazoo Nature Center, 83 lakes (county), National Junior Tennis Championships, 2 major hospitals, Kalamazoo Hilton Convention Center, IHL Kalamazoo Wings (hockey).
Birthplace of: Edna Ferber, Thomas Schippers.
Further information: Kalamazoo County Chamber of Commerce, 500 W. Crosstown, Kalamazoo, MI 49008, phone (616) 381-4000.

Kansas City, Missouri

Population: 448,159 (city), 1,381,829 (SMSA); total employed 616,100 (SMSA).
Area: 3,341 sq. mi., SMSA, at confluence of Missouri and Kansas rivers in Jackson, Clay, and Platte counties.
Industry: world's food capital, estimated sales from farming and agriculture $7.5 billion in 1981; top employers: U.S. government, TWA, General Motors, Bendix, Hallmark Cards, Western Electric; among the top 5 cities in flour production and grain elevator capacity; ranks 1st in Foreign-Trade Zone space and underground storage facilities.
Commerce: total retail sales for 1981 over $8 billion; bank deposits 8.3 billion; the center of a 7-county metro area.
Transportation: 20 airlines at Kansas City International Airport; 191 truck lines and several barge companies; city is one of the nation's major rail centers.
Communications: 6 TV stations, 14 AM, 18 FM radio stations, 5 daily newspapers.
New construction: Shubrooks, Inc., Frankona American Life, DeLaval Agricultural Division, and Kemper Insurance, established headquarters in Kansas City; one million square-foot warehouse by W.W. Grainger, Inc. will open in 1982. Existing firms expanding include: TWA, Hallmark, North Supply, Wilcox Electric, United Telecom, and Panhandle Eastern.
Cultural facilities: Starlight Theater; William Rockhill Nelson Gallery of Art, with one of the largest Oriental collections outside China; Performing Arts Foundation presents festival events; Univ. of Missouri at Kansas City; Rockhurst Col.; Kansas City Art Inst.; Univ. of Kansas Medical Center. Linda Hall Library is one of the largest technical reference libraries in the nation.
Recreational facilities: more than 100 parks over 5,345 acres, including Swope Park, 2nd largest in nation, with zoo.
Sports: The American Royal Livestock and Horse Show; home of the NFL Chiefs, American League Royals, NBA Kings, MISL Comets.
History: French trading post established in 1821 by Francois Chouteau. Became trade and transportation center as the Oregon and Santa Fe trails spread westward. As agricultural production boomed, it became an important market and distribution center for crops.
Further information: The Chamber of Commerce of Greater Kansas City, 600 CharterBank Center, 920 Main Street, Kansas City, MO 64105.

Kitchener-Waterloo, Ontario, Canada

The World Almanac is sponsored in the Kitchener-Waterloo area by the Kitchener-Waterloo Record, 225 Fairway Road S., Kitchener, Ont. N2G 4E5; phone (519) 894-2231; founded 1878; circulation 75,916; president and general manager Paul J. Motz, vice-president and publisher K. A. Baird

Population: 138,271 (Kitchener), 54,157 (Waterloo), 306,775 (Waterloo region); total employed 150,000.
Area: 51.74 sq. mi. (Kitchener) and 25.47 sq. mi. (Waterloo), 65 miles west of Toronto.
Industry: highly diversified industry (500 companies), rubber, plastics, electronics, metal fabrication, brewing, distilling, meat packing, footwear, furniture, food processing, automotive components; Budd Canada Inc., largest autoframe manufacturer in Canada; Arrow Shirt Co., largest shirt making facility under one roof in Canada. Annual gross product exceeds $2.27 billion.
Agricultural: hog and dairy area; Waterloo region's 1,678 farms (242,291 acres) accounted for $120 million production in 1978.
Commerce: wholesale and retail center for area; metro retail sales (1981) $1.25 billion; 10 banks, 67 branches; 14 trust companies, 23 branches; 41 life insurance offices, 29 other insurance offices; Waterloo, "The Hartford of Canada," head office for 6 insurance companies.
Transportation: 2 major rail lines, 34 truck lines, on Ontario's key highway 401; Waterloo-Wellington Airport; 45 mi. from Toronto International.
Communications: one TV and 4 radio stations; one daily, one weekly newspaper.
Medical facilities: 2 major hospitals.
Cultural facilities: symphony orchestra, Kitchener-Waterloo Art Gallery, Doon Pioneer Village; Centre in the Square, 28 mi. from Stratford, home of the Shakespearian Festival.
Educational facilities: Univ. of Waterloo, Wilfrid Laurier Univ., Conestoga College.
Other attractions: nationally-known farmers market; Canada's largest Oktoberfest; Woodside, national historic park, boyhood home of W. L. Mackenzie King.
History: founded 1807 by Pennsylvania German settlers; retains strong Germanic flavor.
Further information: Kitchener Chamber of Commerce, 67 King East; Waterloo Chamber of Commerce, 5 Bridgeport Road W.

Knoxville, Tennessee

The World Almanac is sponsored by The Knoxville News-Sentinel, 204 W. Church Avenue, Knoxville, TN 37901; Sentinel founded in 1886, News in 1921 by Scripps-Howard Newspapers; Sentinel purchased by Scripps-Howard in 1926 and combined with News; circulation 100,626 daily, 158,654 Sunday; president and general manager Roger A. Daley, editor Ralph L. Millett Jr., managing editor Harold E. Harlow.

Population: 183,139 (city), 319,298 (county), 476,517 (metro area), 3d in state; 216,000 total employed in metro area.
Area: 77.6 sq. mi. (city), 528 sq. mi. (county), located almost exact center of that portion of U.S. lying east of the Miss. River and south of Great Lakes; Knox Co. seat.
Industry: chemicals and primary metals; 51 diversified major industries (coal and zinc mining, marble quarrying, meat packing, electronics, steel fabrication, industrial controls eqpt., furniture, auto safety eqpt., refuse eqpt., apparel), with Aluminum Co. of America, Union Carbide Corp. Nuclear Div. at Oak Ridge; headquarters for Magnovox Consumer Electronics Corp., Matsushita (Panasonic), London Fog, Levi Strauss, Allied Chemicals, Robertshaw-Fulton Controls, Rohm & Haas.
Commerce: wholesale and retail trade center of a multi-county area in east Tennessee, Virginia, Kentucky, and North Carolina; county retail sales (1981) $2.0 billion.
Transportation: 5 airlines, 2 commuter airlines. 2 interstate bus lines, 44 motor freight carriers; L & N and Southern railroads; interstate highways I-40 and I-75 intersect in heart of city; Tennessee River barges.
New construction: downtown renewal continues, $200 million expended since 1972; $225 million in Interstate improvements; Art and Architecture bldg. completed; $24 million sewer plant; Neyland Stadium (football) enclosed north end, increased seating to 92,000; London Fog plant ($24 million), Panasonic plant underway.
Cultural facilities: Univ. of Tennessee, Knoxville Col., Knoxville Symphony Orchestra, Knoxville Civic Opera, 13 museums, art gallery, auditorium-coliseum; city-county library (621,487 volumes), Zoological Park, Univ. community theater, Clarence Brown Theater, choral society, opera workshop, Lamar House-Bijou Theater.
Sports: Univ. of Tennessee (all major collegiate sports), Knoxville College; Knoxville pro baseball; Golden Gloves boxing arena.
Other attractions: site of 1982 World's Fair on theme "Energy Turns The World"; Great Smoky Mountains National Park, 39 miles from Knoxville; within 30 miles of Knoxville, 8 TVA lakes providing fishing, boating, swimming; Oak Ridge, 22 miles from Knoxville; American Museum of Atomic Energy and Oak Ridge Nat. Lab; Dogwood Arts Festival held each Apr.
Birthplace of: James Agee, Joseph Wood Krutch.
Further Information: Greater Knoxville Chamber of Commerce, P.O. Box 2229, Knoxville, TN 37901.

Las Vegas, Nevada

The World Almanac is sponsored in the Las Vegas area by the Las Vegas Review-Journal, P.O. Box 70, 1111 W. Bonanza, Las Vegas, NV 89125; phone (702) 383-0211; founded as a weekly in 1909; purchased 1956 by Donald W. Reynolds, present publisher; member Donrey Media Group; circulation 92,993 weekdays, 104,120 Sundays; general manager Earl Johnson.

Population: 164,674 (city), 462,218 (SMSA), first in state; labor force 258,400, total employment 237,300 (county, '81 annual avg.).
Area: 55 sq. mi. (city), 275 sq. mi. (metro), near center of broad desert valley in southern Nevada; 290 mi. NE of Los Angeles, 283 mi. NW of Phoenix; Clark County seat.
Industry: 24 hr. tourism, gaming, manufacturing (stone, clay, glass, food, chemicals), warehousing, mining.
Commerce: total taxable sales $3.6 billion (county, 1981); average spendable family income $21,888; 6 commercial banks, $3.4 billion total deposits; 7 savings & loans with $1.9 billion savings deposits.
Transportation: McCarran Int'l Airport with 9.5 million passengers in 1981; 15 major carriers, 5 commuter lines, 23 air freight carriers; Union Pacific RR; Amtrak; 15 truck lines; 6 major van lines; 3 intercity bus lines; U.S. highways 93 & 95, Interstate 15.
Communications: 5 TV stations (4 commercial, one PBS); 14 AM, 4 FM radio stations, one PBS; 3 daily newspapers.
Medical facilities: 8 hospitals, 1,774 beds; 20 convalescent and rest homes; 56 clinics.
Federal facilities: Nellis AFB, largest tactical fighter training base in world with 7.5 million acres combined air and ground area, home of Thunderbirds USAF Air Demonstration Squadron; Water & Power Resources Service, responsible for water in 17 western states.
Education: 78 elementary, 18 jr. high, 14 high schools, 2 spec. ed., one vo-tech, 32 private schools; Clark Cnty. Community Col.; Univ. of Nevada (UNLV).
Cultural facilities: Clark Co. Dist. Library; James R. Dickinson (Univ.) Library with Nevada gaming collections. Las Vegas Art League and Museum; Reed Whipple Cultural Arts Center; Judy Bayley Theatre; Artemus W. Ham Concert Hall; Las Vegas Civic Symphony; Nevada Dance Theatre; City Museum of Archeology; Southern Nevada Museum and Cultural Center; Rainbow Co. Children's Theatre.
Recreation: Lake Mead, Lake Mojave, Hoover Dam, Tule Springs, Valley of Fire, Red Rock Canyon area, Toiyabe National Forest (Mt. Charleston), Rogers Springs, Desert Nat'l Wildlife Range, Colorado River, skiing, boating, fishing, swimming, hiking, camping.
Sports: amateur and professional competition in tennis, golf, auto racing, bowling, basketball, boccie ball, boxing; UNLV sports; Caesars Grand Prix; Mint 400 Off Road race, Sahara Invitational golf, Alan King tennis classic, WCT Challenge Cup, Pizza Hut basketball invitational.
History: first recorded group to enter the Las Vegas Valley was Antonio Armijo's party in early 1839. Las Vegas, Spanish for "The Meadows," first settled by Europeans in June 1855 by a 30-man Mormon group under William Bringhurst; city of Las Vegas founded May 15, 1905, as a result of public land auction by the railroad.
Further information: Las Vegas Chamber of Commerce, 2301 E. Sahara Avenue, Las Vegas, NV 89104; Las Vegas Convention/Visitors Authority, 711 E. Desert Inn Road, Las Vegas, NV 89109.

Lethbridge, Alberta, Canada

The World Almanac is sponsored in the Lethbridge area by The Lethbridge Herald, 504 7th Street S., Lethbridge, Alberta; phone (403) 328-4411; founded as a daily in 1907; circulation weekdays 28,980, Saturdays 31,231; publisher Don Doram, managing editor Klaus Pohle.

Population: 54,624.
Area: 25 sq. mi.; located on Oldman River, 60 miles north of Montana border, 130 miles south of Calgary.
Industry: based on agriculture; three packing plants slaughtered 30% of the cattle slaughtered in Alberta; more than one million acres of irrigated farms produce sugar beets, market and processing vegetables, grains; much larger dryland area growing grains, grass and rapeseed; vast ranching and cattle-feeding operations; brewery, distillery, flour mill, food processing plants, oilseed processing plants; foundry, recreation vehicle, mobile home, truck body, boat and farm machinery manufacturing.

Commerce: 1981 retail sales $482 million, 17% more than 1980; 7 banks, 7 trust companies, 3 credit unions, 11 finance companies: 5 major shopping malls; distributing center for area of 155,000 people.
Transportation: CP Rail, 2 bus lines, depots for 50 trucking firms, regional airline to major Alberta cities.
Communications: one newspaper; 2 TV, 3 radio stations.
New construction: building permits totalled $91.6 million in 1981, compared with $88.3 million in 1980; relocation of CP railyards will free 135 acres for redevelopment.
Medical facilities: 2 general hospitals (plans for new 330-bed hospital), one long-term care hospital, 3 nursing homes, 4 senior citizens retirement lodges.
Education and culture: Lethbridge Agriculture Centre is Canada's 2d largest; Univ. of Lethbridge, Lethbridge Comm. College; Alexander Galt Museum, Nikka Yuko Centennial Japanese Garden, Fort Whoop-Up, replica of historic fort; Lethbridge Symphony Orchestra and Chorus, Bowman Arts Centre, Yates Memorial Centre.
Other attractions: 4 large parks, 5 artificial ice arenas, 3 golf courses, 3 indoor and 2 outdoor swim pools, Sportsplex (arena), exhibition grounds, Sick's Brewery Gardens.
Sports: Lethbridge Dodgers, farm team of L.A. Dodgers; Broncos, Western Canada Jr. Hockey League; Dusters, Continental Basketball Association franchise.
History: early coal-mining town; Coalbanks, renamed Lethbridge Oct. 16, 1885, after coal co. official; a whiskey-trader's depot, Fort Whoop-Up was booming 5 mi. southwest of Lethbridge in 1860s; first settlers came 15 years later, many from the U.S., others from Europe.
Birthplace of: Conrad Bain.
Further information: Lethbridge Chamber of Commerce, 200 Commerce House, 529 6th Street S., Lethbridge, T1J 2E1; Travel and Convention Association of Southern Alberta, 2805 Scenic Drive, Lethbridge; Economic Development Directorate, City Hall, Lethbridge.

Lexington, Kentucky

The World Almanac is sponsored in central and eastern Kentucky by the Lexington Herald-Leader Co., publishers of the Lexington Leader (afternoon daily, circulation 33,660), the Lexington Herald (morning daily, circulation 71,589), and the Sunday Herald-Leader (circulation 113,889), all Knight-Ridder newspapers; publisher and chairman Creed Black; vice-president and general manager Lewis Owens; vice-president and Herald editor John Carroll; vice-president and Leader editor Steve Wilson; vice-president of production Phil Eaton.

Population: 204,165; 316,098 SMSA.
Area: 283 sq. mi.; 2d largest city in Kentucky, located in central Kentucky, 80 miles east of Louisville, 84 miles south of Cincinnati; Fayette County seat.
Industry: shipping and wholesale center for central and eastern Kentucky; livestock and general farming area; horse breeding and sales; leaf tobacco production and market.
Commerce: (1980) retail sales urban-county $1.3 billion, SMSA $1.6 billion; effective buying income per household $22,000; 8 commercial banks with $1.3 billion in deposits; 4 savings and loan assns. with assets of $255 million; 9 mortgage companies.
Transportation: Chesapeake and Ohio, Southern, Louisville and Nashville railroads; 30 motor freight companies; Frontier, Delta, Piedmont, USAir, Air Kentucky airlines; Lex-Tran city bus service.
Communications: newspapers: Lexington Herald (morn.), Lexington Leader (eve.), Sunday Herald-Leader; 3 commercial TV stations, one state educational TV network; CATV; 4 AM, 3 FM radio stations.
New construction: (1980) 4,150 building permits totalling $210 million.
Medical facilities: 4 general hospitals (incl. Univ. of Kentucky Medical Center), 1,505 beds; 5 specialized hospitals with 1,714 beds; 950 physicians, 2,146 registered nurses; 607 LPN's, 222 dentists, 16 optometrists, 250 pharmacists.
Cultural facilities: Lexington Council of the Arts; Lexington Philharmonic Orchestra; Kentucky Guild of Artists and Craftsmen; Lexington Ballet Co.; Studio Players; Univ. of Kentucky School of Fine Arts; Lexington Opera House; Ashland, home of Henry Clay; Blue Grass Trust for Historic Preservation.
Religion. 197 churches and synagogues representing 34 denominations.
Education: 34 elementary schools; 10 junior, 5 senior high schools; 6 parochial schools; Univ. of Kentucky; Transylvania Univ.; Lexington Theological Seminary; Lexington Baptist College; Lexington Technical Institute; Episcopal Theological Seminary; 9 business and secretarial schools.
Sports and Recreation: Keeneland (thoroughbred racing); The Red Mile (harness racing); Kentucky Horse Park; Univ. of Kentucky basketball and football; 65 neighborhood playgrounds and community parks; 22 motion picture theaters; 8 private country clubs; 4 public golf courses.
Convention facilities: Lexington Convention Center including 23,000-seat Rupp Arena; 32 hotels and motels with 4,500 rooms.
History: incorporated as a township in May of 1781; a leading manufacturing center of the early West for hemp goods, nails, and gunpowder; early site of cotton and furniture factories, breweries and distilleries; known as "Athens of the West" due to Transylvania Univ., first institution of higher learning west of the Allegheny Mountains.
Birthplace of: John Y. Brown.
Further information: Greater Lexington Chamber of Commerce, 421 North Broadway, Lexington, KY 40508.

Little Rock, Arkansas

The World Almanac is sponsored in the Little Rock area by the Arkansas Gazette, 112 West Third Street, Little Rock, AR 72201; phone (501) 371-3700; founded 1819 at Arkansas Post, A.T., by Wm. E. Woodruff, moved to Little Rock 1821; circulation 128,396 daily, 154,790 Sunday; Hugh B. Patterson Jr., publisher and president; William F. McIlwain, editor; Carrick H. Patterson, managing editor; J. O. Powell, editorial page editor; John T. Meriwether, vice president and general manager.

Population: (January, 1982) 170,200 (city), 404,500 (SMSA); 176,100 employed (metro, Feb. 1982).
Area: 90.8 sq. mi. (city), 781.0 sq. mi. (county); state capital and Pulaski County seat.
Industry: (metro) 350 manufacturing plants, employing 30,000 persons; Alcoa, Archer-Daniels Midland, Armstrong Rubber, Club Products, CPC International, General Electric, Jacuzzi, Maybelline, Remington Arms, Siemens-Allis, Teletype, 3-M Company, Timex and Westinghouse.
Commerce: retail sales (1980) $1.8 billion; bank resources (Jan. 1979) $2 billion; 14 banks, 7 building & loan associations, 5 old line insurance companies.
Transportation: Two freight railroads, Amtrak passenger service, 5 trunk airlines, 2 feeder airlines, 3 interstate bus lines, one inter-city bus line, 64 truck lines, 10 common carrier barge lines. Highway system includes 5 Interstate highways, 4 U.S. highways and 11 state highways.
Communications: 3 commercial TV, one ETV, 20 radio stations; 4 daily, 5 weekly newspapers.
Medical facilities: 12 hospitals including UA Medical Sciences campus, 2 VA hospitals, and Ark. State Hospital.
Federal facilities: Little Rock AFB, Tactical Airlift Wing; Camp Joseph T. Robinson, Arkansas National Guard headquarters and training center; U.S. National Guard Bureau's Non-Commissioned Officers Institute.
Education: Univ. of Arkansas at Little Rock with Schools of Law, Medicine, Nursing, and Pharmacy; UA Graduate Institute of Technology; Philander Smith, Shorter and Arkan-

sas Baptist colleges; 120 public and 50 private schools.
Cultural facilities: Arkansas Arts Center, Arkansas Opera Theatre, Arkansas Repertory Theatre, Arkansas Symphony Orchestra, Ballet Arkansas, Broadway Theatre Series, Barton Coliseum, Museum of Science and Natural History, Robinson Auditorium convention center-hotel complex; Statehouse Convention Center-hotel complex; three major public libraries.
History: French explorer Bernard de la Harpe led a party up the Arkansas River in 1722. The name Little Rock evolved through usage and was first commonly used to describe the area in the early 1800's.
Birthplace of: Brooks Robinson.
Further information: Greater Little Rock Chamber of Commerce, One Spring Street; Little Rock Bureau for Conventions and Visitors, Markham and Broadway; Arkansas Dept. of Parks & Tourism, One State Capitol Mall; all Little Rock, AR 72201.

Los Angeles, California

The World Almanac is sponsored in Los Angeles by the Los Angeles Herald Examiner, 1111 S. Broadway, Los Angeles, CA 90015, phone (213) 744-8000; Los Angeles Examiner founded 1903 by Wm. R Hearst, merged Los Angeles Herald Express 1962; circulation 281,533 daily, 307,124 Sunday; Francis L. Dale publisher, Mary Anne Dolan editor, N.S. Hayden president, Theodore P. Grassl general manager, David W. Feldman director of sales.

Population: 2,979,500 (city-Jan. '81), 7,497,200 (county-July '80), 5-county urban area 11.5 million; first in state, 2d urban area in U.S.; total civilians employed 3,366,400 (county '80); labor force 3,603,100 (county '80).
Area: 463.7 sq. mi. on Pacific, 418 mi. south of San Francisco, 145 mi. north of Mexico; Los Angeles County seat; one of 81 cities in county.
Industry: leading aerospace industry with 7 of the top 10 defense contractors in the nation located in the area; center of entertainment industry with more than 600 firms in movie and television entertainment work. Women's clothing, sportswear, electronics, rubber tires, printing, furniture, paper, autos, auto parts, chemicals, manufacturing. Work force (county, '80): agriculture, forestry, and fishing 21,029; mining 12,900; construction 119,200; transport and utilities 198,700; trade 817,700 (268,500 wholesale, 549,200 retail); finance, insurance, and real estate 233,100; services 830,700; government 492,100; manufacturing 916,000; 2d largest county in mfg. activity. Among top 20 counties in U.S. in agricultural production; farm income $210.8 million (county '81); livestock (dairy, eggs, meat) production $60.2 million (county '81); sea fish harvested 490.4 million pounds (county '77).
Commerce: total taxable retail sales $45.7 billion (county '80); median household income $19,998 (city '81); 138 banks, with 1,510 branches, 72 savings and loans with 963 branches (city '81); bank deposits $42.8 billion, S&L savings $41.6 billion (city '81).
Transportation: Santa Fe, Union Pacific, Southern Pacific railroads; Amtrak; Continental, Greyhound bus lines; Southern California Rapid Transit District serving 2,100 square mi. with 2,400 buses plus other local and intercity bus lines; Airport Transit Bus and Gray Line tours; 4.8 million vehicles (county Feb. '82), one of largest concentrations in nation—3,720,450 autos, 703,159 trucks, 238,019 trailers, 169,238 motorcycles; 156.6 mi. freeway (city), 491.2 mi. (county); 57 commercial airlines serving Los Angeles International Airport, 503,389 takeoffs and landings, 32.7 million passengers, 903,584 tons cargo ('81); 9 other airports; more than 46 miles of commercial waterfront in Los Angeles-Long Beach Harbor. 8,600 ships pass through the Harbor each year carrying 90 million tons of cargo valued at $26 billion.
Communications: 19 TV stations (10 UHF, 9 VHF), 71 radio stations, 65 commercial; more than 90 newspapers in English and foreign languages, 14 publishing daily (county).
New construction: residential building permits 21,380 units: single family 6,184; multiple 15,196 (county, '81).
Medical facilities: 822 hospitals and clinics with 80,252 beds, including 180 general care hospitals, 39,154 beds, 22 psychiatric, 2,076 beds, 409 nursing homes, 38,665 beds (county, Mar. '78).
Educational facilities: 1,156 elementary, 190 jr. high, 153 sr. high, 77 continuation, 66 adult, approx. 800 private all levels (county '80); 61 libraries (city) plus 91 others in the county; UCLA, Univ. Southern Cal., California Institute of Technology; Loyola, Marymount, Pepperdine universities; Claremont, Woodbury, Occidental, Whittier, Mt. St. Mary colleges; 21 community colleges; campuses of California State University-Los Angeles, Long Beach, Northridge, Dominguez Hills.
Cultural facilities: 1,838 churches, Huntington Art Gallery and Library, Hollywood Bowl, Greek Theater, Music Center, Mark Taper Forum, Ahmanson Theater, Huntington Hartford Theater, Griffith Park Planetarium, Mt. Wilson and Mt. Palomar observatories; Los Angeles Museum, County Art Museum, UCLA Botanical Gardens, La Brea Tar Pits and natural history museum, Southwest Museum.
Recreational facilities: more than 300 city parks and recreation centers, plus 122 county parks; 14 public golf courses, 15 public beaches within 35 miles of city center; ocean, mountains, desert, lakes, forests; Disneyland, Marineland, Knott's Berry Farm, Lion Country Safari, Universal Movie Studio tour.
Convention facilities: approx. 20,000 hotel rooms (city), 50,000 (county); large convention center.
Sports: collegiate sports including Rose Bowl; pro teams in baseball (Dodgers), basketball (Lakers), hockey (Kings), soccer (Aztecs).
History: discovered 1542 by Portuguese navigator Juan Rodriguez Cabrillo; Mission San Gabriel founded Sept., 1771; city formally founded Sept. 4, 1781 by Spanish colonial governor as El Pueblo de Nuestra Senora la Reina de los Angeles de Porciuncula; inc. April 4, 1850.
Further information: Chamber of Commerce, P.O. Box 3696, Terminal Annex, Los Angeles, CA 90051.

Louisville, Kentucky

The World Almanac is sponsored in Kentucky and southern Indiana by The Courier-Journal and The Louisville Times, 525 West Broadway, Louisville, KY 40202; phone (502) 582-4011; Courier-Journal founded 1868, Times 1884; Courier circulation 182,843, Times 143,121, Sunday 324,624; chairman of the board Barry Bingham Sr., editor and publisher Barry Bingham Jr.; major awards include 8 Pulitzer prizes.

Population: 298,451 (city), 901,970 (SMSA); first in state; total employed 379,600 (SMSA).
Area: 65.2 sq. mi. (city), 1,392 sq. mi. (metro); on southern bank of Ohio River.
Industry and Commerce: 14th in total industrial shipments; famous for baseball bats, cigarettes, railroad repair shops, electrical appliances, farm machinery, motor vehicles, plumbing fixtures, and whiskey; 1,011 manufacturing firms; est. retail sales (Jefferson Co., 1981) $4.238 billion.
Transportation: 6 trunk-line railroads, one terminal railroad, 125 inter-city truck lines; 5 barge lines; 3 bus lines; 9 airlines, and 2 municipal airports.
Communications: 20 radio and 4 TV stations, 2 educational, 3 cable.
Medical facilities: 21 hospitals, 6,000 total beds.
Cultural facilities: Louisville Orchestra, Kentucky Opera Assn., Art Center Assn., J.B. Speed Art Museum; 20 private art galleries, Macauley Theatre, Actors Theatre, The Children's Theatre, Louisville Civic Ballet, Louisville-Jefferson County Youth Orchestra, The Louisville Free Public Library (20 branches); 700 churches, 40 denominations.
Education: 10 colleges and universities, 3 business colleges

and technical schools in area.
New construction: Three major projects downtown are under way: a $31 million Performing Arts Center will be completed in September 1983, a $50 million headquarters building for Humana Inc. will be completed in 1985 as will a $40 million revitalization effort named the Broadway Project.
Recreation: 158 public parks, more than 7,000 acres.
Convention facilities: Kentucky Fair & Exposition Center, largest ground-level exhibit hall and auditorium complex in North America with 650,000 sq. ft., 20,000-plus seating, parking for 27,000 cars; 100,000 sq. ft. Commonwealth Convention Center in downtown Louisville; Louisville Gardens, downtown, handles up to 7,000.
Sports: Kentucky Derby, held annually at Churchill Downs since 1875; Louisville Downs harness racing; Louisville Redbirds, AAA professional baseball team, the Kentucky Bourbons professional softball team.
Other: Belle of Louisville excursion steamboat; Churchill Downs Museum; Louisville Zoo, American Printing House for the Blind; Kentucky Railway Museum; Museum of History and Science; Cave Hill Cemetery, new downtown Galleria complex.
History: founded by explorer George Rogers Clark in 1778; named after King Louis XVI of France.
Birthplace of: Muhammad Ali, Louis Brandeis, William Conrad, Irene Dunne, Paul Hornung, Wes Unseld.
Further information: Louisville Area Chamber of Commerce, 300 West Liberty, Louisville, KY 40202.

Lubbock, Texas

The World Almanac is sponsored in the Lubbock area by the Lubbock Avalanche-Journal, 8th Street and Avenue J, Lubbock, TX 79408; phone (806) 762-8844; founded 1900 as Leader, became Avalanche 1908, daily 1921; Plains Journal weekly founded 1923, consolidated 1926; circulation (morn.) 57,514, (eve.) 14,161, (Sat.) 66,966, (Sun.) 79,989; member Southwestern Newspaper Corp.; general manager Robert Norris, editor Jay Harris.

Population: 173,979 (city), 211,861 (SMSA); 100,210 total employed.
Area: 82.2 sq. mi.; center of South Plains territory of northwest Texas; Lubbock County seat.
Industry: vegetable oils, cotton seed flour, grain sorghum, livestock, petroleum, sand and gravel; 250 manufacturing companies.
Commerce: wholesale and retail center for west Texas and eastern New Mexico; retail sales $2.306 billion; bank resources $1.203 billion; 9 banks.
Transportation: 13 motor freight carriers; 2 major railroads, bus line; Lubbock International Airport, with 5 major airlines averaging 80 flights per day; 6 major highways.
Communications: 5 TV and 16 radio stations.
Medical facilities: 7 hospitals, Lubbock State School for Mentally Retarded; Texas Tech Medical School.
Federal facilities: Reese AFB, federal building, Federal Aviation Admin., and National Weather Service, U.S. Customs port of entry.
Cultural facilities: symphony orchestra, Theatre Centre; Museum of Texas Tech Univ., Moody Planetarium; Ranching Heritage Center (authentic ranch houses dating to 1835), Lubbock Christian College; Texas Tech Univ., Lubbock Cultural Affairs Council, Lubbock Garden & Arts Center.
Recreational facilities: 55 city parks, 3,000 acres, Mackenzie State Park, state's largest, with Prairie Dog Town; Buffalo Lakes, Canyon Lakes-Parks; 3,200-seat Municipal Auditorium, 10,000-seat Municipal Coliseum, annual Panhandle South Plains Fair; Lubbock Memorial Civic Center, modern convention facility including 44,000 sq. ft. exhibit hall with banquet facilities for 1,400, auditorium seating 1,400.
Sports: Texas Tech, and Lubbock Christian college sports; Tech Jones Stadium, indoor rodeos.
Birthplace of: Mac Davis, Buddy Holly.
Further information: Chamber of Commerce, P.O. Box 561, Lubbock, TX 79408.

Lynchburg, Virginia

The World Almanac is sponsored in the Lynchburg area by The News and the Daily Advance, P.O. Box 131, Lynchburg, Va., 24505; phone (804) 237-2941; published by Carter Glass & Sons, Publishers, Inc.

Population: 66,743 (city)
Area: 50 sq. miles
Commerce: retail sales $418,986,741 (1981)
Industry: Babcock & Wilcox, nuclear energy; General Electric, communications systems; Lynchburg Foundry, metal castings; C.B. Fleet, pharmaceuticals; Craddock-Terry, shoes; Limitorque Corp., machinery manufacturer; Simplimatic Engineering; Meredith Burda, rotogravure printing.
Transportation: 20 trucking firms, airport served by Piedmont and Air Virginia airlines; Southern, N&W, and C&O railroads and Amtrak; metropolitan bus fleet.
Communications: WSET television, cable, 12 radio stations; The News and The Daily Advance newspapers.
New construction: $50,575,711 in 1981.
Medical facilities: Virginia Baptist Hospital with 313 beds and Lynchburg General Hospital with 270 beds and a 110-bed extended care facility; cooperative agreement between the hospitals prevents duplication of services.
Cultural facilities: Fine Arts Center which offers drama, music, and visual arts year round, Point of Honor Museum, Old Courthouse, Dabney Scott House, Adams House, Miller-Claytor House, Anne Spencer House, Monument Terrace, all historic landmarks; 94 churches representing some 30 faiths; Thomas Road Baptist Church (18,000 members), one of the nations's largest.
Education: 2 public high schools, 3 junior high schools, 14 elementary schools, pupil-teacher Holy Cross elementary and high school (Catholic), Lynchburg Christian Academy (grades 1-12) affiliated with Thomas Road Baptist Church; Central Virginia Community Col. (2 year), Lynchburg Col., Randolph-Macon Women's Col. and Liberty Baptist Col.
Recreation: 9 parks, Blackwater Creek Natural Area, 12 horseshoe pits, 2 swimming pools, 39 tennis courts, City Stadium with baseball capacity of 4,126 and football capacity of 14,200, 5 golf courses, 7 playgrounds, public library with 100,000 items, 6 senior citizen centers.
Sports: Lynchburg Mets baseball team (Carolina League), full range of intercollegiate sports including football (Liberty Baptist College), baseball, basketball, soccer, swimming, tennis, wrestling, track; Lynchburg 10-Miler for distance runners attracts over 4,000 from across the country each September; Central Virginia Invitational Tennis Tourn. is one of the top amateur events of the East Coast.
Birthplace of: Carter Glass, Samuel Untermyer.
History: Began as a tobacco trading center in the early 1800s; named after John Lynch.

Macon, Georgia

The World Almanac is sponsored in the Macon area by the Macon Telegraph and News, 120 Broadway, Macon, Georgia 31213; phone (912) 744-4200; acquired by Knight-Ridder Newspapers, Inc., 1969; circulation Telegraph (morning) 52,878; News (evening) 19,064; Saturday 68,207; Sunday 85,266. Publisher Bert Struby, general manager Edmund E. Olson, executive editor Billy Watson, News editor Ed Corson.

Population: 116,860 city, 254,623 metro, 4th in state; metro civilian labor force 109,426.
Area: 52 square miles, 6 miles northwest of geographical center of Georgia; Bibb County seat.

Industry: Brown and Williamson Tobacco Corp.; Armstrong World Inds., Inc., acoustical tile plant; The Bibb Co., textile industry leader; The Keebler Co., cracker manuf. plant; Georgia Kraft Company, container board manuf.; YKK, Inc., zipper manuf.; Levi Strauss and Co., clothing manuf.; Bassett Furniture Inds., furniture manuf.; Gulf Apparel Corp.; The Macon Telegraph Publishing Company, daily newspaper publisher; Boeing Machine Products, Inc., cargo handling systems; Colonial Baking Co.; Weyerhaeuser Co., wood products; Inland Container Corp. and Packaging Corp. of America, corrugated containers.
Transportation: Central of Georgia; Southern; Georgia; Seaboard; Atlanta/West Point; L&N and Western railroads. 33 motor freight carriers. Intercity bus lines, Greyhound and Trailways. Delta, Atlantic-Southeast, and Atlanta Express airlines.
Medical facilities: 5 hospitals located in Macon with 1,088 beds; the Macon-Bibb County Public Health Dept.
Federal facilities: Robins AFB including Warner Robins Air Logistics Center, 16 miles from Macon, is Georgia's largest employer.
Educational facilities: Wesleyan Col., nation's oldest col. for women; Mercer Univ. with law school and med. school; Macon Jr. Col.
Other attractions: Ocmulgee National Monument is largest archeological development east of the Mississippi disclosing 6 different Indian group occupancies and restored Indian mounds and lodges; $4.5 million coliseum seats 10,000.
History: Fort Hawkins established in 1806; chartered in 1823; named for Nathaniel Macon of North Carolina.
Birthplace of: Melvyn Douglas, Sidney Lanier, Otis Redding, Little Richard.
Further information: Macon Chamber of Commerce, 305 Coliseum Drive, Macon, GA 31201.

Madison, Wisconsin

The World Almanac is sponsored in Madison by Madison Newspapers, Inc., publisher of The Capital Times and the Wisconsin State Journal, 1901 Fish Hatchery Road, Madison, WI 53713; phone (608) 252-6100; circulation, Wisconsin State Journal (morn.) 72,246, The Capital Times (eve.) 31,895, combined daily 107,141, Sunday Wisconsin State Journal 124,795.

Population: 170,616 (city), 323,109 (SMSA), 2d in state; metro work force 176,000.
Area: 52 sq. mi. (city), 1,194 sq. mi. (metro/county) in south central Wisconsin; state capital and Dane County seat.
Commerce: home office of 29 insurance firms, 375 industrial firms, 28 banks, 10 savings and loans; 25 major shopping areas; 1980 retail sales $1.5 billion; average effective buying income $22,500; city has AAA financial rating.
Transportation: Dane County Regional Airport serving 700,000 passengers and 5 million lbs. of freight; 5 airlines, 3 railroads, 2 interstate highways (I-90, I-94); 4 bus lines, 30 common carriers, city owned bus system.
Communications: 3 commercial, one public, and 2 cable TV stations, commercial (8 AM and 9 FM) radio stations; 2 daily and 17 weekly newspapers (metro/county).
Medical facilities: 5 hospitals including Univ. of Wis. and VA; 21 major clinics, approx. 1,200 physicians.
Federal facilities: Forest Products Laboratory, National Fish and Wildlife Laboratory.
Cultural facilities: Dane County Coliseum, Madison Civic Center, 2 art centers, 2 museums, dinner playhouse, 11 drama groups, ballet company, symphony and 7 other music organizations; approx. 330 churches representing 45 denominations.
Education: Univ. of Wisconsin; Edgewood, Madison Business, Madison Area Technical colleges; 35 elementary, 10 middle, 4 high schools, 14 parochial, one vocational-technical; 7 city and 32 university libraries.
Recreation: 5 lakes with total of 18,000 acres of water surface, approx. 4,700 acres of parks; Vilas Zoo, Univ. of Wis. Arboretum, 9 golf courses.
Convention facilities: Dane County Coliseum, 5 major hotels, 55 supper clubs; Greater Madison Convention Bureau (425 W. Washington, Madison, WI 53703).
Sports: Univ. of Wisconsin in Big Ten, football, basketball, hockey and other major sports.
Other attractions: weekly Farmer's Market (May-Oct.), World Dairy Exposition headquarters, annual Winter Spirit Festival, All-American city.
Birthplace of: John Bardeen, Philip F. La Follette, Wayne Morse, Thorton Wilder.
Further information: Greater Madison Chamber of Commerce, 625 W. Washington Avenue, Madison, WI 53701.

Memphis, Tennessee

The World Almanac is sponsored in the Memphis area by The Memphis Press-Scimitar, 495 Union Avenue, Memphis, TN 38101; phone (901) 529-2500; Scimitar founded 1880 by G.P.M. Turner; Press 1906 by Scripps-McRae League, predecessor of Scripps-Howard Newspapers; circulation 97,007; editor Milton R. Britten, managing editor Van Pritchartt Jr.

Population: 646,356 (city), 909,767 (SMSA); first in state; 364,400 employed.
Area: 290 sq. mi. on east bank of the Mississippi River; Shelby County seat.
Industry: extensive cotton marketing-warehousing and processing of cotton seed into vegetable oil products; headquarters of Holiday Inns Inc., Federal Express Co. (air freight), and Conwood Corp. (tobacco and food products); other large industries include Schering-Plough (drugs), and Firestone (tires).
Commerce: wholesale-retail center for large parts of Tennessee, Arkansas, and Mississippi; retail sales (1981) $4.5 billion; bank deposits $2.6 billion; 9 banks, 5 savings-loan assns.; per capita personal income $8,392.
Transportation: 14 airlines, 42 air freight companies, 5.2 million air passengers (1980); 6 trunk line railroads, 108 motor freight lines, 6 barge lines.
Communications: 5 TV and 24 radio stations, 2 daily newspapers.
Medical facilities: 15 hospitals housing 7,108 beds, 10 full-time clinics, 1,799 doctors, 519 dentists, 30 long-term care facilities housing 4,184 beds.
Federal facilities: Naval Air Station, Naval Air Technical Training Center, Defense Depot Memphis, and Air Force's 164th Air Transport Group.
Cultural facilities: Memphis Symphony Orchestra, opera theater, Theatre Memphis, Brooks Art Gallery, Chucalissa Indian Village & Museum, Memphis Museum; annual performances of Metropolitan Opera.
Educational facilities: Memphis State Univ., Southwestern, LeMoyne-Owen, Christian Brothers colleges; U-T Center for Health Sciences, Shelby State Comm. College, State Technical Institute, Southern College of Optometry, Memphis Academy of Arts, Mid-South Bible College; 160 public elementary-secondary schools, 100 private schools, 22 public library branches offer 1.5 million volumes.
Recreational facilities: Meeman-Shelby Forest state park, 197 other parks, 21 golf courses, 16 public swimming pools, 13 country clubs.
Convention facilities: Cook Convention Center, 1.3 million sq. ft, seating 17,000; 59 hotels & motels with 9,115 total rooms.
Sports: Liberty Bowl, home of Memphis State Univ. football, site of Liberty Bowl game; Mid-South Coliseum, home of MSU basketball team; Memphis Chicks, Southern League baseball; Danny Thomas Memphis Classic golf tournament; Memphis Americans, professional indoor soccer team; U. S. National Indoor Tennis Championships.
Other attractions: Cotton Carnival each May; Mid-South Fair each Sept., Libertyland theme park, Beale St., home of

the blues where composer W. C. Handy lived; Mid-America Mall; Graceland, home and burial site of Elvis Presley.
History: DeSoto, exploring Mississippi River, stopped here in 1541; Ft. Adams est. in 1797; Memphis inc. in 1826; yellow fever in 1878 nearly depopulated city, but its population grew back to 64,589 in 1890.
Birthplace of: Aretha Franklin, George Hamilton, Bill Madlock, Ellis Rabb.
Further information: Memphis Area Chamber of Commerce, 555 Beale Street, Memphis, TN 38103.

Mexico City (Ciudad de Mexico), Mexico

Population: 15,000,000 (1980 est. metro. area).
Area: about 53 sq. mi. within the 573 sq. mi. Federal District (Distrito Federal; population, 1980 est. 9.3 million); in central Mexico at an altitude of 7,349 ft.
Industry and commerce: capital of Mexico; the political and economic hub of the nation; manufactures include steel, automobiles, appliances, textiles, rubber goods, furniture, and electrical equipment; marketing center of Mexico.
Transportation: center of modern highway and rail system; 25-mi. subway system is being extended and will eventually extend to 50 miles; served by most international air lines, Mexico City is 4 hrs. by jet from New York and 3 hrs. from Los Angeles.
Communications: major media center for Mexico and parts of Latin America; major film center.
Cultural facilities: cultural capital of Latin America: Palace of Fine Arts and Ballet Folklorico; National Palace (Diego Rivera murals); National University with over 90,000 students; National Museum of Anthropology; Polyforum Cultural Siqueiros, containing world's largest mural; 4 symphony orchestras; city is an architectural exhibit of Aztec ruins, baroque cathedrals, ultra-modern buildings.
Other attractions: Xochimilco with the "floating gardens" and gondolas; Chapultepec Castle, palace of the French-supported Emperor and Empress of Mexico, Maximilian and Carlota; 22-ton Aztec Calendar Stone; 2 volcanoes, Popocatepetl (17,887 ft.) and Iztaccihuatl (17,343 ft.); sports centers.
History: traditionally founded 1321 by Aztecs, city was called Tenochtitlan; captured by Spanish under Cortez in 1519 and again in 1521; occupied by the U.S. in 1847 and by the French from 1863 to 1867.
Further information: Mexican National Tourist Council, Mariano Escobedo 726, Mexico, D.F., or 405 Park Avenue, NY 10022; or 9701 Wilshire Boulevard, Beverly Hills, CA 90212.

Miami, Florida

The World Almanac is sponsored in the Miami area by The Miami Herald, 1 Herald Plaza, Miami, FL 33101; phone (305) 350-2111; founded Dec. 1, 1910, by Frank B. Shutts; circulation (1981) 444,860 daily, 545,898 Sunday; chairman James L. Knight, executive editor John McMullan, editor Jim Hampton, managing editor Heath Meriweather; newspaper or staff writers have won or shared in 6 Pulitzer prizes, and numerous other honors.

Population: 346,931 (city), 1,573,817 (SMSA); first in state; total employed in metro area, 621,100 (1980 average).
Area: 53.8 sq. mi. land and water, on Biscayne Bay at mouth of Miami River in southeast Florida; largest of 28 municipalities in Dade County; Dade County seat.
Industry: 5,000 light manufacturing plants; tourism and aviation are mainstays of economy; 779 hotels and motels with 60,069 rooms handle 15 million visitors a year; aviation hub with Eastern (largest industrial employer) headquarter base; winter agriculture center.
Commerce: center of Latin American finance and commerce with more than 100 banks, 16 savings and loan associations, 14 foreign banks, and 15 Edge Act banks; largest concentration of international banks outside New York; annual retail sales total nearly $5 billion; Port of Miami is the largest cruise center in world with 24 liners and 1.7 million passengers (1980); 2 duty-free trade zones, with one million sq. ft. of space.
Transportation: Miami International, served by 109 air carriers, handled more than 22 million travelers in 1980; Seaboard Coast Line, Amtrak, and all-freight Fla. East Coast Railroads operate in Miami, as do Greyhound and Trailways buses; 65 truck lines.
Communications: 6 commercial and 5 educational or closed-circuit TV stations; 31 radio stations.
New construction: $6.8 billion investment in structures incl. $1.2 billion People Mover; downtown Knight Convention Center, The World Trade Center, hotels, office towers, condominiums, restaurants, and stores.
Medical facilities: 41 hospitals, 11,894 beds; 5,362 beds at 39 nursing homes in metro area; 2,975 members of Dade County Medical Association; VA hospital, Jackson Memorial Hospital one of area's leading research facilities.
Federal facilities: Homestead AFB south of Miami with some 8,000 Air Force, Army, and Navy personnel; Federal Aviation Administration; Coast Guard bases; 2 federal hospitals; oceanographic center; 13,700 U.S. employees.
Cultural facilities: Philharmonic, Opera Guild, and other musical groups perform regularly; 18 auditoriums, resident and touring theatrical productions, 6 major art museums; 29 public libraries; 12 playhouses and 60 night clubs and theater restaurants, some in major hotels; New World Contemporary Festival of the Arts scheduled for June, 1982, headed by Rudolph Bing, sponsored by Greater Miami Opera Assn.
Educational facilities: 6 colleges and universities, plus 3 campuses of Miami-Dade Community College; Univ. of Miami is largest independent institution of higher learning in southeast; Florida International Univ.; public school system has 229,858 students and is the 5th largest in nation.
Recreational facilities: 14 miles of public beach on ocean and bay; 365 parks and playgrounds, 11 stadiums and grandstands, 45 golf courses, 57 marinas with 37,000 boats registered; 105 movie houses, 100 miles of bikeways, 28 bowling alleys.
Convention facilities: Miami Beach convention hall can handle largest conventions; 300 conventions brought more than 86,000 delegates to Miami in 1979; 570 conventions brought 290,000 delegates to Miami Beach in same year.
Sports: pro football Miami Dolphins and Univ. of Miami play in Orange Bowl, which seats 75,000; stadium also hosts Orange Bowl game, Orange Blossom Classic; Miami Stadium is spring home of Baltimore Orioles; parimutuel wagering at 5 horse and greyhound tracks, jai-alai frontons.
Other attractions: balmy subtropical climate with mean annual temperature of 75.3 degrees; 600 Protestant churches; 53 Catholic churches, 55 synagogues; city is bilingual with over 500,000 Latin American residents; one of nation's largest Jewish communities; marine stadium features powerboat and regatta racing; Everglades National Park, 40 miles south of Miami, is virgin wilderness.
History: America's newest big city, Miami had only 3 houses in 1895 in a community called Fort Dallas. Julia Tuttle persuaded Henry Flagler to extend his railroad south from West Palm Beach to stimulate Miami development; city was incorporated in 1896, when railroad arrived.
Further information: Metro-Dade Department of Tourism, 234 West Flagler Street, Miami, FL 33130.

Milwaukee, Wisconsin

The World Almanac is sponsored in the Milwaukee area by The Milwaukee Journal, 333 W. State Street, P.O. Box 661, Milwaukee, WI 53201; telephone (414) 224-2000; founded 1882 by Lucius W. Nieman; circulation 304,917 daily, 461,267 Sunday; chairman of the board Donald B. Abert; president, Journal Co. Thomas J.

McCollow; president, Newspapers, Inc. and publisher Warren J. Heyse; senior vice-president and editor Richard H. Leonard; major awards include 2 Pulitzer prizes to the newspaper and 3 to staff members.

Population: 633,185 (city), 1,399,400 (SMSA); city 16th and metro area 28th in the U.S.; total employment 683,700 (metro area).
Area: 95.8 sq. mi. on shore of Lake Michigan, Milwaukee County seat.
Industry: county 15th in U.S. volume of industrial production, more than $9 billion (1981); 29% of workers employed in manufacturing; large U.S. producer of diesel and gasoline engines, outboard motors, motorcycles, tractors, padlocks; major producer of electrical equipment, mining, and construction machinery (SMSA); graphic arts and food processing are largest non-durable goods employers; home to 10 "Fortune 500" industries.
Commerce: wholesale and retail trade center for Wisconsin, upper Michigan; total retail sales $6.4 billion (SMSA); wholesale trade $15 billion (SMSA); Median household effective buying income $22,204 (SMSA); metro area is home of 99 banks, 38 savings and loan assns. and 153 credit unions.
Transportation: 4 major rail lines; Amtrak; 7 airlines provide direct service to East and West coasts, the South, Southeast, Southwest and Florida for more than three million passengers annually using General Mitchell Field which has international air arrivals facility; 19 U.S. and foreign flag ship lines use Milwaukee's St. Lawrence Seaway port which handles more than 4.2 million tons annually including 1.8 million tons overseas cargo; Port of Milwaukee, gateway for as many as 350 cities in 31 states and overseas ports except for the Far East; Milwaukee SMSA exports more than $2 billion worth of goods annually; 4 inter-city bus lines, 130 motor freight carriers, I-94, I-43, 5 federal and 14 state highways intersect Milwaukee.
Communications: morning, evening, and Sunday metropolitan newspapers, 5 commercial and 2 educational TV stations; 11 cable and/or pay TV companies, 23 AM and FM radio stations.
Medical facilities: 28 major hospitals and medical centers, including 600-bed VA hospital and a regional burn center.
Cultural facilities: Milwaukee Symphony, Repertory Theater, opera and operetta companies, Mid-America Ballet; Milwaukee Art Center, Milwaukee museum, 4th largest in U.S.; Univ. of Wisconsin-Milwaukee, Marquette Univ., Medical College of Wisconsin, 8 other colleges and vocational schools; 3-theater Performing Arts Center; complete convention, exhibition arena-auditorium complex; Mitchell Park Conservatory, Milwaukee County Stadium, and Milwaukee County Zoo are parts of 13,000 acre Milwaukee County park system.
Sports: Brewers (American League), Bucks (NBA); Admirals (Int. Hockey League); Marquette Univ., Univ. Wisconsin-Milwaukee; Green Bay Packers (NFL) play 3 home games at Milwaukee County Stadium.
History: founded by Solomon Juneau (1818), one of many French trappers in area in early 1800s; incorporated as town 1837, as city 1846, 2 years prior to Wisconsin statehood.
Birthplace of: Woody Herman, Polly Fisher, Alfred Lunt, Pat O'Brien, William Rehnquist, Henry Reuss, Spencer Tracy, Gene Wilder.
Further information: Metropolitan Milwaukee Association of Commerce, 756 N. Milwaukee Street, Milwaukee, WI 53202.

Minneapolis, Minnesota

Population: 370,951 (city), 2,109,207 (SMSA); first in state, 35th in nation; total employed (city, 1981) 72% of adult pop.
Area: 59 sq. mi. (city), 4,000 sq. mi. (10-county metro area) around St. Anthony Falls near junction of Minnesota and Mississippi rivers; Hennepin County seat.
Industry: diverse; major electronics-computer manufacturing center including Honeywell, Control Data, Medtronics; headquarters for nation's 4 largest grain millers, including General Mills, Pillsbury, and International Multifoods.
Commerce: $25,000 median household income; $5.8 billion total retail sales metro area (1980); 24 commercial banks, 6 savings and loan assns.; headquarters for Ninth Federal Reserve District; world trade center, 12th among U.S. metro areas in exports; Mpls. Grain Exchange.
Transportation: 5 trunk railroads; 150 trucking firms; 5 major barge lines headquartered in city; Mpls.-St. Paul International Airport, averaging 600 flights daily.
Communications: 4 commercial, 2 educational TV stations; 39 radio stations.
Medical facilities: 21 hospitals, including a leading heart hospital at Univ. of Minn.
Federal facilities: Farm Credit Administration regional office; FBI regional office; EPA district office, area headquarters HUD.
Cultural facilities: Minnesota Orchestra, 7 art galleries-museums, Tyrone Guthrie Theatre, Walker Art Center, Univ. of Minnesota, Orchestra Hall, Inst. of Arts.
Sports: Minnesota Twins (American League), Minnesota Vikings (NFL), Minnesota North Stars (NHL).
Other attractions: 153 parks, 22 lakes; 57-story IDS Tower; Minnehaha Falls; Mpls. Aquatennial celebration in July.
History: first visited in 1680s by Fr. Louis Hennepin who discovered and named St. Anthony Falls on the Mississippi River; French fur traders used the area in 18th century; inc. 1871. Falls became power source for lumber and milling operations in 19th century.
Birthplace of: James Arness, Lew Ayres, William Benton, Arlene Dahl, Jean Paul Getty, Harrison Salisbury, Charles Schulz, Mike Todd.
Further information: Greater Minneapolis Chamber of Commerce Information, 15 S. 5th Street, Minneapolis, MN 55402; (612) 370-9132.

Mobile, Alabama

The World Almanac is sponsored in the Mobile area by The Mobile Press Register, 304 Government Street, Mobile, AL 36630; phone (205) 433-1551; circulation, Register (morn.) 51,415, Press (eve.) 51,383, Sunday, 98,186; Register founded 1813, Press 1928. William J. Hearin publisher and president, Fallon Trotter executive editor, John Fay associate executive editor.

Population: 200,452 (city), 439,941 (SMSA); (metro), 2d city in state; total employed (metro) 171,000.
Area: 142 sq. mi. on Mobile Bay; Mobile County seat.
Industry: $300 million-plus Alabama State Docks and the growing oil and natural gas fields in Mobile County have attracted varied industry to city; Mobile fields produce 2.8 million barrels of oil, 3.8 million barrels of condensate and millions of cubic feet of natural gas annually; other industry includes paper, timber, chemicals, paints, aircraft engines, shipbuilding, and metals.
Commerce: wholesale-retail center for large portion of southwest Alabama and southeast Mississippi; county retail sales more than $1.8 billion (1981).
Transportation: 4 railroads; one of the great river systems; 4 major airlines, 55 truck lines, and 135 shipping lines.
Communications: 3 TV, 15 radio stations; cable TV.
Medical facilities: Univ. of South Alabama Medical Center, Cancer Research Center, and 6 modern hospitals.
Cultural facilities: Municipal Auditorium-Theater complex seats 16,000; art gallery, museum, amateur theater, public library and branches; Univ. of South Alabama, Spring Hill and Mobile colleges, and Bishop State Junior College.
Military facilities: Coast Guard base and Coast Guard aviation training center.
Annual attractions: Azalea Trail Run, America's Junior Miss, Senior Bowl football game, Mardi Gras, Historic Homes Tour.
History: founded in 1702 by Jean Baptiste Le Moyne; 6 flags have flown over city since then.
Birthplace of: Hank Aaron, Willie McCovey, Amos Otis.
Further information: Chamber of Commerce, P.O. Box 2187, Mobile, AL 36652.

Montgomery, Alabama

The World Almanac is sponsored in the Montgomery area by the Advertiser-Journal, 200 Washington Street, Montgomery, AL 36102; phone (205) 262-1611; Advertiser founded 1828, Journal 1881; circulation Advertiser (morn) 47,823, Journal (eve) 25,013, combined Sunday 75,446; publisher Jim Martin.

Population: 178,157 (city), 272,687 (SMSA).
Area: 128.98 sq. mi. (city), 442 sq. mi. (county); state capital; Montgomery County seat.
Industry: machinery manufacture, glass products, textiles, refrigeration equipment, furniture, food products, paper, and fertilizers; industrial park in East Montgomery.
Commerce: wholesale retail center for 13 counties in central Alabama; SMSA retail sales $1.109 billion; average spendable income $20,924, per capita income $8,324; 7 banks, 5 savings and loan assns.; state docks, 37 trucking lines, 6 insurance co. home offices.
Transportation: 5 major railroads, 3 airlines, 2 national bus lines, one city bus line; interstates 65 and 85 intersect in the city; Alabama River navigable to the Gulf of Mexico.
Communications: 2 daily, 2 weekly newspapers; 4 TV, 14 radio stations; cable TV.
Medical facilities: 5 general hospitals, VA hospital, Air Force hospital, area mental health hospital, private hospital.
Federal facilities: Maxwell AFB, houses the Air Univ., Gunter Air Force station.
Cultural facilities: Art Guild, Civic Ballet, Little Theatre, Community Concert Series, Museum of Fine Arts, Tumbling Waters Flag Museum; 14 theaters, 19 recreational facilities, city zoo; 5 major colleges and universities.
Sports: Blue Gray Football Classic; Southeastern Championship Rodeo; George Lindsay Celebrity Golf Tournament, American Express Tennis Tournament, Blue Gray Tennis Tournament, Alabama River Run, Alabama River Raft Race, Barbara Mandrell Golf Tournament.
Other attractions: river boat makes regularly scheduled excursions of the Alabama River; State Capitol housed Confederate offices; White House of Confederacy, home of Jefferson Davis; Hank Williams grave site, Dexter Avenue Baptist Church; Fort Tolouse, antebellum town with many colonial mansions and churches.
History: inc. 1819; site of inauguration of Jefferson Davis as president of the Confederate States of America, Feb. 18, 1861.
Birthplace of: Nat "King" Cole, Bart Starr, Toni Tennille, Willie Wilson.
Further information: Chamber of Commerce, P.O. Box 79, Montgomery, AL 36192.

Montreal, Quebec, Canada

The World Almanac is sponsored in Montreal area by The Gazette, a Southam newspaper, 250 St. Antoine Street, Montreal H2Y 3R7, Quebec, Canada; phone (514) 282-2222; founded 1778 by Fleury Mesplet; circulation 210,000 daily; publisher Robert McConnell, editor Mark Harrison, managing editor Mel Morris, editorial page editor Joan Fraser; sponsors Christmas fund; 18 National Newspaper awards in last 8 years.

Population: 1,214,300 (city), 2,761,000 (metro); the 3d largest French-speaking city in the world, 67% French origin, 12% Anglo-Saxon, 21% other origins; Canada's largest urban center.
Area: 68 sq. mi. on an island of 190 sq. mi. in the St. Lawrence River where the Ottawa and Richelieu rivers flow into it at the head of the St. Lawrence Seaway; metro area extends over 1,000 sq. mi.; the 769 ft. Mount Royal dominates the Island which averages 100 ft. above sea level.
Industry: Canada's industrial hub ($7 billion, value of shipments of goods of own manufacturer).
Commerce: total effective buying income $15 billion, headquarters of many of Canada's financial institutions, home of the Montreal and Canadian stock exchanges; about 75% of countries have consulates or representatives in Montreal.
Transportation: St. Lawrence Seaway, Port of Montreal; 14 miles long, 42 miles of harbor with 140 berths; Mirabel jetport with multi-million electric train link to downtown planned for late 1980's; existing Metro has been expanded to 51 miles; world headquarters of Air Canada, International Civil Aviation Organization, and International Air Transport Association serving 2 major airports; headquarters of Canadian National and Canadian Pacific railways.
Communications: 4 TV stations, 21 radio stations, 4 daily newspapers; headquarters for Bell Canada, CN-CP Telecommunications.
Educational facilities: Concordia University, McGill University, Universite de Montreal, Universite de Quebec.
Cultural facilities: Place des Arts with 3,000 seat hall and 2 theaters, attracting the finest forms of artistic, cultural, and musical entertainment; the Montreal Museum of Fine Arts, the Musee de l'Art Contemporain; some of the world's most beautiful churches, including the Mary Queen of The World Basilica, a half-size replica of St. Peter's in Rome.
Sports: Olympic complex including a 56,000 permanent seat stadium, home of the National Baseball League Expos, the Canadian Football League Concorde, and the National Soccer Assn. Manic; 7,200 seat Velodrome, 2 50-meter pools, 25-meter diving pool, and a scuba diving pool — 15-meter depth; the Montreal Forum, home of the NHL Canadiens.
Recreational facilities: within an hour of the Laurentien and Eastern townships skiing, hunting, and fishing areas; over 5,000 restaurants; over 100 cinemas, 19 museums, 13 city libraries, the Montreal Botanical Gardens, St. Helen's Island Park, Dow Planetarium, Montreal Municipal Golf Course.
Convention facilities: over 15,000 hotel and motel rooms; full facilities for conventions; new Montreal Convention Centre scheduled for completion in July 1983.
Medical facilities: over 80 hospitals with 26,000 beds, including the renowned Montreal Neurological Institute, and the Montreal Children's Hospital.
History: Montreal was first visited by Jacques Cartier in 1535; founded under the name of Ville Marie in 1642; Old Montreal, some 1,000 acres in all, is the largest such restoration in North America and retains the general atmosphere of the 18th century.
Further information: Convention and Visitor's Bureau of Greater Montreal, 1270 Sherbrooke Street W., H3G 1H7; The Montreal Tourist Bureau, 85 Notre Dame Street East, Montreal, Quebec.

Nashville, Tennessee

The World Almanac is sponsored in Nashville by The Tennessean, 1100 Broadway, Nashville, TN 37202; phone (615) 255-1221; founded as The Tennessean in 1907 but incorporated publications date to 1812; member of the Gannett Group; circulation daily 127,296, Sunday 246,081; president, editor and publisher John Seigenthaler; 3 Pulitzer prizes, 8 Headliner awards, 5 Sigma Delta Chi awards.

Population: 477,811 in unified metro government, 2d in state.
Area: 533 sq. mi., on Cumberland River, in north central part of state; state capital and Davidson County seat.
Industry: music (over 50% of U.S. singles are recorded in 40 studio complexes); clothing, headquarters of Genesco; insurance, 2 of largest U.S. companies located here; world's largest glass plant; chemicals, printing (especially religious materials), aerostructures, tires, air conditioning, heating equipment, and tourism.
Commerce: retail center for middle Tennessee, south Kentucky; retail sales $2.8 billion; bank resources over $4 billion in 8 banks, 100 branches.
Transportation: 9 U.S. highways and 6 branches of the inter-

state system radiate from Nashville; 13 commercial airlines with over 200 daily flights; 2 railroads; bus service, over 100 motor freight lines.
Communications: 5 TV stations (one public), and 22 AM and FM radio stations.
Medical facilities: 18 hospitals, 2 medical schools, VA hospital, speech-hearing center.
Cultural: symphony orchestra; replica of Parthenon with art gallery; public and state libraries; botanic garden and fine arts center, 3 community theaters, performing arts center.
Educational facilities: 16 colleges and universities; 129 public schools, 42 private schools.
Convention facilities: 10,000-seat auditorium; Opryland convention center.
Other attractions: Grand Ole Opry, Opryland U.S.A. (theme park featuring music); Country Music Hall of Fame; Hermitage (home of Andrew Jackson); Belle Meade antebellum mansion, Cumberland Museum & Science Cntr.
Recreation facilities: water sports, outdoor activity on Old Hickory and Percy Priest lakes.
History: settled in 1780 as a fort in then western North Carolina; incorporated, 1784, with first written charter west of Alleghenies.
Birthplace of: Julian Bond.
Further information: Chamber of Commerce, 161 4th Avenue N., Nashville, TN 37219.

New Haven, Connecticut

The World Almanac is sponsored in the greater New Haven area by the New Haven Register (founded 1812) and the New Haven Journal-Courier (founded 1755); circulation Register (eve.) 95,967, Sunday 138,896, Journal-Courier (morn.) 37,505; chairman of the board, chief executive officer Lionel S. Jackson; president and publisher Lionel S. Jackson Jr.; vp and general manager Edward J. Murphy; editor Don W. Sharpe; managing editor (Register) Richard W. Odermatt; managing editor (Journal-Courier) John O. Bailey.

Population: 126,109 (city), 416,053 (SMSA), 2d in state.
Area: 21.1 sq. mi. southern coast of Conn. on north shore of Long Island Sound; New Haven County seat.
Industry: 1,000 firms in immediate area; principal products are guns, hardware, rubber goods, paper products, machinery, and tools, transportation, finance, health serv.
Commerce: wholesale-retail center for southern Conn., total retail sales (1981) $2.9 billion; serves 735,433 people with EBI of $24,427; busy harbor, 12 mil. tons each year.
Transportation: Conrail, Amtrak Cosmopolitan turbotrain; 25 major truck lines; 14 federal and state highways; Tweed-New Haven Airport served by 3 commuter airlines, limo service to New York and Hartford airports; bus line.
Communications: VHF, 2 UHF TV, 6 radio stations.
Medical facilities: Yale Medical Center, Yale-New Haven Hospital; Hospital of St. Raphael, Community Health Center Plan and West Haven Veterans Hospital.
Cultural facilities: Yale Univ. Library with over 6 million books, one of the world's largest collections; Yale's Peabody Museum of Natural History, art gallery, and Beinecke Rare Book Library; The Yale Center for British Art, New Haven Colony Historical Society, cultural center, Yale Rep., Shubert and Long Wharf Theatres; New Haven Symphony, Woolsey Hall.
Educational facilities: Yale Univ. and graduate schools; Albertus Magnus, Southern Conn. State, South Central Community, Quinnipiac, Greater New Haven State Technical colleges; Univ. of New Haven, Stone Business Col.
Recreational facilities: Yale Bowl, Payne-Whitney Gym, Ingalls Rink, The Coliseum; 15 parks, scenic drives, West Rock Nature Center; 7 golf courses, 6 skating rinks.
Convention facilities: convention center with hotel.
Sports: AHL Nighthawks (hockey), West Haven A's (AA Eastern League baseball).
History: founded 1638 by Puritans; named after Newhaven in England; incorporated 1638, became a part of Conn. 1662; first mayor was Roger Sherman, signer of Declaration of Independence.
Birthplace of: Jerry Bock, Al Capp, Norman Lear, Robert Moses, George Murphy, Benjamin Spock.
Further information: Greater New Haven Chamber of Commerce, 195 Church Street, New Haven, CT. 06506.

New Orleans, Louisiana

The World Almanac is sponsored in New Orleans by The Times-Picayune-The States-Item, 3800 Howard Avenue, New Orleans, LA 70140; phone (504) 586-3560; founded 1837; editor Charles A. Ferguson; sponsors the Crescent City Classic, Doll and Toy Fund.

Population: (March 1982) 468,200 (city), 1,186,725 (SMSA); first in state; total employed, 480,200 (metro area as of May 1979).
Area: 363.5 sq. mi. of which 199.4 are land.
Industry: Port of New Orleans, 2d largest in nation; volume of business for 1979-80 was record $12.5 billion; tourist business is 2d largest, with $1.3 billion spent in metro area in 1980.
Commerce: trade center for lower Mississippi Valley; metro area bank deposits $5.69 billion as of Dec. 1980; metro savings and loan assets of $4.14 billion as of Mar. 1981; average household income 1980, $23,144; retail sales $4.97 billion in 1980.
Transportation: rail hub with direct lines north, east, and west; Amtrak passenger service to Chicago, Los Angeles; Southern railway to New York; New Orleans International Airport serves airlines, Lakefront Airport commercial aviation; cruise ships to Mexico and Caribbean.
New construction: HEAL Complex, Sheraton Hotel, 1555 Poydras-Exxon, Piazza D'Italia, Canal St. Ferry Terminal, Commodity Exchange, Chevron Place, Texaco Center, Poydras Center, 1615 Poydras, Intercontinental Hotels.
Communications: 4 commercial TV stations and educational channel; 20 radio stations.
Medical facilities: major medical center with 2 schools of medicine; one dental school; Charity Hospital 2d largest in nation; Ochsner Medical Institutions.
Federal facilities: hdqtrs. 5th U. S. Circuit Court of Appeals and 8th Naval District; regional office U. S. Census Bureau, field office U. S. Dept. Agriculture Marketing Service.
Recreation: City Park, 1500 acres with golf, tennis, boating; Audubon Park, 250 acres with golf, tennis, and zoo; Pontchartrain Beach Amusement Park, large lakeside amusement center.
Convention facilities: 22,000 rooms in major hotels; 160,000 sq. ft. exhibition space in Superdome, 134,000 sq. ft. in Rivergate, and 32,500 sq. ft. Municipal Auditorium.
Cultural facilities: Theater for the Performing Arts seats 2,317 for operas, concerts; Municipal Auditorium seats up to 8,000 for special events; museums include New Orleans Museum of Art, Louisiana State Museum, Historic New Orleans Collection, and many small galleries.
Educational facilities: Tulane Univ., Univ. of New Orleans, Loyola Univ., Dillard, Southern Univ. in New Orleans, Xavier, St. Mary's Dominican.
Other attractions: Louisiana Superdome seats 75,000; French Quarter is historic tourist attraction.
Sports: Saints (NFL); Sugar Bowl game on New Year's day.
History: named after the Duke of Orleans, founded in swamp within crescent of the Mississippi River 100 miles from Gulf of Mexico by Jean Baptiste Le Moyne, Sieur de Bienville, in 1718; became capital of Louisiana Territory in 1722, when Adrien de Pauger laid out what is now the French Quarter; became part of U.S. with Louisiana Purchase in 1803.
Birthplace of: Louis Armstrong, Pierre Beauregard, Truman Capote, Lillian Hellman, Al Hirt, Louis Prima, Rusty Staub, Andrew Young.
Further information: Chamber of Commerce of New Orleans Area, 301 Camp Street; Greater New Orleans Tourist and Convention Commission, 334 Royal Street, both New Orleans, LA 70130.

New York City, New York

The World Almanac is sponsored in the greater New York City metropolitan area by the New York Daily News, 220 E. 42d Street, New York, NY 10017, phone (212) 949-1234. New York News Inc. founded June 26, 1919 by Joseph Medill Patterson; circulation daily 1,540,000; Sunday 2,043,000; president and publisher Robert M. Hunt; vice president and editor James G. Wieghart; executive vice president and general manager Henry K. Wurzer; managing editor William L. Umstead; associate editor John J. Smee. Pulitzer Prizes for editorial writing, news photography, cartoon, international and local investigative reporting; sponsors Golden Gloves, National Spelling Bee championship for New York City, and other major school athletic, cultural, and educational events as community service programs.

Population: 7,071,030 (city), 16,558,400 (consolidated area, 20 counties); first in state and nation; total employed 3,244,300 (1981, consolidated area); average household EBI (consol. area): $25,863.

Area: 300 sq. mi. at mouth of Hudson River; embraces 5 boroughs — Manhattan, Bronx, Brooklyn, Queens, and Staten Island.

Industry: nation's leader in manufacturing and service industries; produces 10.8% of America's apparel, 7.4% of printing and publishing; 11,321 manufacturing establishments (1980).

Commerce: nation's richest port, handling annual 50 million long tons of maritime cargo; Wall Street, world's largest financial center, with New York and American stock exchanges; wholesale-retail center for New York, New Jersey and southwestern Connecticut; retail sales $66.7 billion (1981); 202 commercial banks, deposits $153.4 billion; 82 savings banks, resources $44.2 billion (1980); World Trade Center, twin 110-story towers.

Transportation: Kennedy International Airport with over 13 million overseas air travelers, handled 787,042 tons of import-export air tonnage (1981); served by 83 scheduled air carriers; LaGuardia Airport served by more than 35 scheduled airlines; 4 heliports. Conrail, Amtrak railroads; 2 major rail terminals, Penn and Grand Central stations; 34 bus carriers; subway network covers every borough except Staten Island; ferry and the 4,260-ft. Verrazano-Narrows Bridge (world's longest suspension span) link Staten Island to Manhattan and Brooklyn; 18 bridges connect Manhattan with other boroughs, George Washington Bridge to New Jersey; 4 tunnels under the Hudson and East rivers.

Communications: 15 TV stations (6 commercial, 2 educational, one municipal, 2 Spanish, 4 CATV); 39 AM and FM radio stations; WPIX-TV and WPIX-FM are broadcast affiliates of The News.

Medical facilities: over 100 hospitals, 5 major medical research centers specialize in cancer, heart diseases, sickle cell anemia, and other research; Sloan-Kettering Institute for Cancer Research; 4 VA hospitals.

Federal facilities: Fort Wadsworth, Staten Island; Governors Island, many federal agencies represented in buildings at Federal Plaza and 90 Church St.

Educational facilities: 29 univers. and cols. including medical cols., law schools, cols. of pharmacy, cols. of dentistry, institutes of art and architecture; 1,000 schools in the public school system; 879 private schools; public libraries total 201.

Cultural facilities: Lincoln Center for the Performing Arts (Philharmonic, cols., Company, Metropolitan Opera, and other theatrical arts), Carnegie Hall, Brooklyn Academy of Music. Broadway and Off-Broadway alliance for varied theatrical productions; outdoor Delacorte Theatre in Central Park; 65 museums including American Museum of Natural History, Metropolitan Museum of Art, Museum of the Performing Arts, Museum of Modern Art, Whitney Museum, and South Street Seaport Museum.

Other attractions: United Nations; botanic gardens in the Bronx and Brooklyn; Central Park and Prospect Park; Bronx Zoo and 4 other zoos; Hayden Planetarium; The Cloisters; N.Y. Aquarium in Coney Island.

Sports: NBA Knicks, Nets; NHL Rangers and Stanley Cup Champion Islanders; NL Mets and NFL Jets play in Shea Stadium; AL Yankees play in Yankee Stadium; NFL Giants and NASL Cosmos play in Giants Stadium in nearby E. Rutherford, N.J.; Madison Square Garden hosts sports, concerts, ice shows, other events. Thoroughbred racing at Belmont and Aqueduct; harness racing at Roosevelt, Yonkers, and the Meadowlands; area has off-track betting.

History: discovered by Giovanni da Verrazano in 1524; in 1626 Peter Minuit bought the island from the Manhattan Indians for about $24 in goods and trinkets; settlement named New Amsterdam. In 1664, British troops occupied city without resistance and named it New York in honor of the Duke of York, brother of the King. On Jan. 1, 1898, Manhattan and large areas to the NE, E, and S were consolidated into one city of New York.

Birthplace of: Kareem Abdul-Jabbar, Lauren Bacall, Humphrey Bogart, William F. Buckley, James Cagney, Lena Horne, Henry James, Sandy Koufax, James A. Michener, Eugene O'Neill, Theodore Roosevelt, Beverly Sills, Barbra Streisand.

Further information: Convention and Visitors Bureau, 2 Columbus Circle, New York, NY.

Newport News, Hampton, Williamsburg, Virginia

The World Almanac is sponsored in the Virginia Peninsula area by the Daily Press, Inc., publishers of the Daily Press (mornings and Sunday) and The Times-Herald (evenings except Sunday), 7505 Warwick Boulevard, Newport News, VA 23607; phone (804) 244-8421; The Daily Press, Inc., also operates an AM and FM radio station, WGH, broadcasting popular and classical music.

Population: 363,817 (SMSA).

Area: Newport News, Hampton, and Williamsburg are the key cities in the Newport News—Hampton SMSA that borders Hampton Roads, one of the great waterways of the world, connecting the James River to Chesapeake Bay, and ultimately, to the Atlantic Ocean.

Industry: economic base of the area is the shipbuilding industry; Newport News Shipbuilding is a major contractor to the U.S. Navy and to private-sector shipowners and operators, and is reputed to be the largest shipyard in the world; it employs more than 25,000 production workers at its facility along the James River. Hampton Roads area is the most important coal port in the world; it gathers coal from the Appalachian Mountains and redistributes it by ship to ports around the world; area also is a major source of seafood, particularly crabs and oysters that are plentiful in Chesapeake Bay and its tributary rivers.

Commerce: manufacturing shipments in 1980 exceeded $2.6 billion; in addition to shipbuilding, the principal industries are meat-packing, oil refining, and a complex of technical industries associated with NASA space activities; personal income in 1980 in excess of $3.4 billion, or $8,711 per capita; retail sales (excluding autos, gasoline, and liquor) in excess of $1.4 billion.

Federal facilities: located in the area are the Tactical Command of the U.S. Air Force, Naval Supply and Weapons stations, the Army's training and transportation commands and the training center of the U.S. Coast Guard; NASA's Langley Research Center also maintains an installation on the Peninsula.

Other attractions: based on Colonial Williamsburg, and with the additional attractions of Jamestown, Yorktown, and Busch Gardens, a theme park utilizing the concept of "The Old Country"; tourism is a major industry; one million tourists visited Colonial Williamsburg in 1980.

Birthplace of: Pearl Bailey, Ella Fitzgerald, William Styron.

History: Peninsula selected by the first colonists as evidenced by the Jamestown settlement of 1607; site of the first capital of Colonial Virginia and the intellectual center of the American Revolution; during the World Wars, area was a major staging area for troops moving overseas and for fleets using Hampton Roads as a base of operations.

Oakland, California

Population: 339,288 (city), employed in Oakland, 179,236.
Area: 53.4 sq. mi.; Alameda County seat.
Industry: food processing, fabricated metal products, transportation equipment, chemicals and paint; Port of Oakland is 2d in containerized cargo; home base for Kaiser Ind.
Commerce: 9,401 retail and wholesale outlets (1981) with taxable sales of $1.9 billion; median income for family, $11,997 per annum.
Transportation: western terminus for Southern Pacific, Santa Fe, and Western Pacific railroads; International Airport is major airfreight terminal and center for supplemental air carriers; Bay Area Rapid Transit, underground, underwater 75-mile subway connecting 15 communities.
Medical facilities: 9 hospitals include Children's Hospital Medical Center, Kaiser Found., and the Veterans Admin.
New construction: Pacific Telephone Bldg; Wells Fargo Bldg.; Clorox Bldg.; 16–square–block city center project and major downtown garage in Phase III of construction; Oakland Convention Center; Hyatt Regency Hotel.
Cultural facilities: museum, half garden, half gallery design, has divisions of natural science, history, and art; symphony, Chinese Community Cultural Center.
Educational facilities: Univ. of California at Berkeley, Mills College, College of Holy Names, Cal. State, Hayward; Chabot, California College of Arts and Crafts, Peralta Community College.
Recreational facilities: 26,000–acre regional park system serving the East Bay; zoo in 100-acre Knowland State Park; Lake Merritt Park includes botanical garden, wildfowl refuge, natural science center, and Children's Fairyland.
Sports: Athletics (baseball), Golden State Warriors (basketball).
Other attractions: Oakland Coliseum, over 50,000 capacity, for theatrical entertainment, exhibits, conventions, and circus; Jack London Square.
History: area explored in 1772, settled in 1850; incorporated as town in 1852, as city in 1854.
Birthplace of: Max Baer Jr., Don Budge, Buster Crabbe, Robert Culp, Sidney Howard, Al Hrabosky, Rod McKuen, Edward Meese, Jack Soo.
Further information: Chamber of Commerce, 1320 Webster Street, Oakland, CA 94612.

Oklahoma City, Oklahoma

The World Almanac is sponsored in the Oklahoma City area by The Daily Oklahoman and Oklahoma City Times, 500 N. Broadway, Oklahoma City, OK 73125; phone (405) 232-3311; morning Oklahoman founded 1894; evening Times in 1888; Oklahoma Publishing Co., acquired Oklahoman 1903, Times 1916; circulation Oklahoman 187,876, Times 87,352, Saturday Oklahoman & Times 229,866, Sunday Oklahoman 297,187; editor and publisher Edward L. Gaylord, managing editor Jim Standard.

Population: (1981) 407,500 (city) 843,700 (SMSA); largest in state, 3.3% unemployed 1981 (SMSA).
Area: 650 sq. mi. (city), 700 sq. mi. (county), 3,491 sq. mi. (metro area); located in state's center on Canadian River; elev. 1,276 feet; state capital and Oklahoma Co. seat.
Industry: state's industry, finance, government, energy and agribusiness hub; Oklahoma City Air Logistics Center at Tinker AFB employs 16,000 civilians, 5,000 military; General Motors assembly plant employs 5,700, Western Electric employs 5,500; national hdqtrs. for Kerr-McGee, Hertz, Wilson Foods, Inc., Federal Aviation Agency, T.G. & Y. Stores, Lee Way Motor Freight, Macklanburg-Duncan, Scrivner, Inc., C. R. Anthony, Cain's Coffee Co., Dolese Bros., Globe Life and Accident Insurance, Star Manufacturing Co., Oklahoma Pub. Co., Sirloin Stockade, Braums Ice Cream, L. S. B. Ind., CMI Corp., and Fleming Foods; home of the Interstate Oil Compact Commission.
Commerce: marketing center; median household income $21,200, effective buying income $9.3 billion, consumer retail sales $4.5 billion (metro); banking with $9 billion resources, savings and loans with $1.7 billion in assets.
Transportation: interstate highways 35, 40, 44, and 240; federal highways U. S. 62, 66, 77, 81, 270, and 277; 5 major bus lines; the Santa Fe, Frisco, and Katy railroads provide rail freight service; 41 truck lines; 8 major airlines service Will Rogers World Airport, plus 3 commuter lines.
Communications: 3 metro daily newspapers, 8 weekly newspapers; 24 radio, 7 TV stations, one education TV channel, 3 subscription TV channels, cable TV.
New construction: building permits $646 million (metro); $360 million in new construction has been completed in the Central Business District Project 1-A, most of which is linked by an all-weather pedestrian system, the Metro Concourse; first units of luxury townhouses and apartments begun, $300 million in construction projected.
Medical facilities: Oklahoma Health Center, incl. Univ. of Oklahoma medical schools, VA and 3 other hospitals; Oklahoma Medical Research Foundation and Dean McGee Eye Institute; 18 hospitals, 9 community health clinics.
Cultural facilities: National Cowboy Hall of Fame and Western Heritage Center; Oklahoma Art Center; Artsannex; Artsplace II, Oklahoma Museum of Art, Omniplex, Kirkpatrick Planetarium, Oklahoma Symphony Orchestra, Ballet Oklahoma, Oklahoma Heritage Center, National Softball Hall of Fame, Oklahoma Historical Society, 45th Infantry Division Museum, Firefighters Museum, Field Trial Hall of Fame, Lyric Theater, Oklahoma Theater Center, Oklahoma County libraries with 11 branches and 5 bookmobiles.
Education: 18 institutions of higher education in or near city; Univ. of Oklahoma Health Sciences Center, Oklahoma City Univ., Oklahoma Christian College, Oklahoma State Univ. Tech. Inst., South Oklahoma City Junior College, Midwest Christian College (city); Oscar Rose Junior College, Central State Univ., Univ. of Oklahoma, Bethany Nazarene College, Hillsdale Free Baptist College, St. Gregory's College, Oklahoma Baptist Univ. (metro); 7 vo-tech schools, 138 elementary, 63 secondary schools, 13 private schools.
Recreation: Lakes; Lake Thunderbird and Little River State Park (metro); 132 municipal parks, 11 gymnasiums, 24 recreation centers, Oklahoma City Zoo, Martin Park Nature Center, 28 golf courses, 84 public tennis courts, 60 public playgrounds, 12 municipal ball diamonds.
Convention facilities: Myriad Convention Center seats 26,700 in arena; Civic Center Music Hall; State Fairgrounds Arena; 84 hotels and motels with 8,750 rooms.
Sports: Univ. of Oklahoma in Big 8 Conference; 89ers baseball, Stars hockey.
Annual events: National Finals Rodeo, 7 horse shows, Miss Rodeo America Pageant, Festival of the Arts, State Fair of Oklahoma, Oklahoma City Powwow, National Academy of Western Art Exhibition and Western Heritage Awards, Junior Livestock Show and Exposition.
History: settled by land run April 22, 1889; became state capital in 1910.
Birthplace of: Johnny Bench, Ralph Ellison, Bobby Murcer, Dale Robertson, Jimmy Rushing.
Further information: Oklahoma City Chamber of Commerce, One Santa Fe Plaza, Oklahoma City, OK 73102.

Omaha, Nebraska

Population: (1981) 313,911 city, 569,614 SMSA; first in state; 261,250 civilian labor force.
Area: eastern Nebraska, 92 sq. miles of rolling hills on west bank of Missouri River; Douglas County seat.
Industry: $3.7 billion annual shipments; Western Electric, 600 others employ 36,000; food processing center: 4th largest livestock market in salable receipts.
Commerce: major trade center, $1.7 billion retail sales; 3,000 retail, 1,200 wholesale firms; $21,344 income per household; 25 banks, $4.1 billion assets; 6 savings & loans, $2.7 billion assets; 4th largest insurance center in U.S., 44 principal admin. offices; hqs. Union Pacific, Northwestern Bell,

ConAgra, Valmont, Peter Kiewit Sons, Hinky Dinky, Brandis, Richman Gordman, Mutual of Omaha & Guarantee Mutual.

Transportation: 8 major airlines; 4th largest rail center, served by 6 major railroads, transcontinental Amtrak; 98 truck lines Interstate highways 80 and 29, 2 intercity bus lines, 5 barge lines; 3.3 million tons carried on Missouri River annually; port of entry, foreign trade zone.

Communications: 6 TV channels, 19 radio stations, cable TV.

Medical Facilities: 16 hospitals, 6,334 beds; 2 medical (University of Nebraska & Creighton University), one dental, 7 nursing schools, Eppley Inst. for Cancer Research.

Federal Facilities: Strategic Air Command's global headquarters, Army Corps of Engineers, Federal Reserve branch.

Cultural Facilities: Orpheum performing arts center, symphony, opera, ballet, 17 theater groups, 15 museums.

Educational Facilities: 3 universities, 6 colleges educate 32,000 students; 30 adult education schools.

Recreation: 6,000 acres of public parks include 140 tennis courts, 30 pools, 17 golf courses, 3 marinas, ice rinks.

Sports: Omaha Royals baseball, Ak-Sar-Ben horse racing, NCAA College World Series.

Other Attractions: 1,300 acre Fontenelle Forest, Henry Doorly Zoo, Boys Town, President Ford's Birthplace, Gen. Dodge House, Western Heritage Museum, Aerospace Museum, downtown's Old Market; unique 60,000-member Ak-Sar-Ben civic organization, Schramm Aquarium. Ranked 10th among 50 largest U.S. cities in quality of life.

History: Lewis & Clark, 1804; Mormon settlement, 1846; capitol of Nebraska territory 1855-67.

Birthplace of: Fred Astaire, Marlon Brando, Montgomery Clift, Gerald Ford, Bob Gibson, Melvin Laird, Nick Nolte, Paul Williams, Malcolm X.

Further Information: Greater Omaha Chamber of Commerce, 1606 Douglas, Omaha, Nebraska 68102.

Orange County, California

The World Almanac is sponsored in Orange County by The Orange County Register, 625 N. Grand Avenue, Santa Ana, CA 92711; phone (714) 835-1234; circulation combined daily 254,562 Sunday 289,078; founded in 1905, purchased in 1935 by R.C. Hoiles, founder of Freedom Newspapers Inc., a 31-daily newspaper group; R.D. Threshie, publisher; Richard Wallace, general mgr.; Larry Burkhart, dir. of mktg; Carolyn Charkey, mgr. of public relations; Chris Anderson, editor; Howard Grothe, v.p. advertising; Mell Killpatrick, production mgr.; Tom Peterson, dir. of circulation.

Population: 1,931,570, 2d most populous county in the state, compares with 212,364 in 1950, 2.5 million projected for 1990; county encompasses 26 cities.

Area: 511,040 acres in S. California from Pacific O. inland 25 miles to Cleveland Natl. Forest; 42-mile coastline from Long Beach to San Clemente and Camp Pendleton.

Commerce and Industry: median income (1980) $25,900 (The Register's Consumer Attitude Survey); total personal income (1980 est.) $20.1 billion; taxable retail sales (1981 est.) $14.1 billion; 1980 automobile purchases: $2.6 billion; 1980 general merchandise: $1.36 billion; 1980 eating and drinking places. Unemployment rate 4.7% in 1981; among major employers in Orange Co. are Rockwell International, Beckman Instruments, Alpha Beta and Disneyland.

New construction: 14,000 permits were issued for homes in 1980; the median price of a single family home was $122,000 (1980); vacancy factor was 1.8 percent during the year.

Transportation: 8 major freeways, including main Los Angeles-San Diego artery; transit district with countywide routes including freeway commuter buses and Dial-A-Ride in some areas; John Wayne Airport, nation's 3d busiest airport with 524,750 tower operations in 1981.

Communications: local UHF-TV station, 7 VHF-TV stations regionally, over 40 radio stations.

Federal facilities: Marine Corps Air Station at El Toro, Los Alamitos Naval Air Station, Seal Beach Naval Weapons Station, Santa Ana Marine Corps Lighter-Than-Air Station (now used for helicopters, once for dirigibles), federal building in Santa Ana, General Services Administration building-national archives center in Laguna Niguel, Cleveland National Forest, Marine Corps Camp Pendleton in nearby San Diego County.

Medical facilities: Univ. of Cal. medical school at Irvine, 65 hospitals and convalescent hospitals.

Recreation: 781 acres of beaches, more than 13,000 acres for regional parks, 141 scenic sea cliffs, 3 yacht basins, 3 fishing lakes, wilderness campgrounds, 35 golf courses, 21-mile equestrian and bicycle trail along Santa Ana River.

Other attractions: Disneyland, Knott's Berry Farm amusement park, Lion Country Safari, Movieland Wax Museum, Los Alamitos Racetrack; motorcycle park, auto raceway, Laguna Beach Art Festival-Pageant of Masters, Santa Ana Zoo, air and car museums, Anaheim Stadium.

Convention facilities: Anaheim Convention Center, Disneyland Convention Center, hotels in Anaheim, Buena Park, Costa Mesa, Irvine, Newport Beach, Santa Ana.

Sports: (AL) Cal. Angels, (NASL) Cal. Surf, (NFL) L.A. Rams; interscholastic sports.

Cultural-Educational facilities: 2 major public univ., one private liberal arts col., 7 community cols., multiple trade and special interest schools, 507 public K-12 schools; 237 private and church K-12 schools; city and county libraries, symphony orchestra society; 2 master chorales, 6 ballet companies, 32 community theater groups, repertory theater, 4 art museums.

History: first Spanish expedition 1769 by Capt. Gaspar de Portola, who recorded first reported earthquake in the state; county formed March 11, 1889 from Los Angeles County. Swallows traditionally return each year to Mission San Juan Capistrano on March 19.

Further information: Anaheim Visitor and Convention Center Bureau, 800 W. Katella Avenue, Anaheim, CA, Orange County Chamber of Commerce, One City Boulevard W., Orange, CA.

Orlando, Florida

The World Almanac is sponsored in the Orlando area by The Orlando Sentinel, 633 N. Orange Ave., Orlando, FL 32802; phone (305) 420-5000; Sentinel and Evening Star founded as dailies in 1913; merged in 1931; acquired by Tribune Company of Chicago in 1965; combined to create "all day" newspaper in 1973; circulation (ABC Newspaper Publisher's Statement 6 months ending March 31, 1981) 207,621 weekdays, 203,171 Saturday, 249,974 Sunday; president and publisher Harold R. Lifvendahl, editor David Burgin.

Population: 128,394 (city), 694,645 (SMSA); 4th fastest-growing city over 500,000 population; metro employed 331,938, unemployment rate 6.3.

Area: 44 sq. mi. (city); 2,822 sq. mi. (metro); elevation 20 ft. to 190 ft.; only major inland Florida city; Orange County seat.

Commerce: regional transportation, communications, distribution, retail, financial, education, and agriculture center for central Florida; Orlando Foreign Trade Zone; 1981 metro retail sales $4.0 billion; retail sales per household rank 16th among cities over 500,000 population; insurance center with 9 regional and 3 national home offices; regional offices for Southern Bell and United Telephone; 31 banks, $2.7 billion in 1981 deposits; 18 savings and loan associations, $2.0 billion in 1981 deposits.

Industry: over 800 manufacturers with 35,000 employees; emerging electronics center (Martin Marietta, Western Electric, Stromberg-Carlson, Westinghouse, NCR, Piezo, Burroughs); citrus-processing and packing; food processing; packaging; marine and boat manufacturing.

Agriculture: center for vegetables, foliage plants, and citrus products; over one third of Florida's citrus groves located in surrounding east central Florida region.

Tourism: number one tourist destination in the world; Walt

Disney World with annual attendance of 14 million; Sea World; EPCOT; Six Flag's Stars Hall of Fame; Mystery Fun House; Wet 'n Wild; Wings and Wheels Museum; Church Street Station; Lake Buena Vista; Cypress Gardens; Kennedy Space Center; Ringling Brothers and Barnum & Bailey Circus World; Daytona Beach.
Conventions: major national convention city; over 1,700 conventions in 1981 drawing 395,000 delegates; convention expenditures over $93 million; 33,000 first class hotel and motel rooms; Orange County Civic Center with 325,000 sq. ft. of exhibit space scheduled to open in early 1983.
Transportation: Orlando International Airport handled 6.5 million passengers in 1981, major U.S. hub airport, new $300 million terminal, 14 commercial airlines; 3 full service general aviation airports; Seaboard Coastline Railroad, Amtrak; Greyhound and Trailways bus lines; 33 common carrier truck lines; 8 freight forwarding companies; Port Canaveral, Jacksonville, Tampa nearest sea ports; I-4 and Florida Turnpike provide access to I-75 and I-95.
Communications: 6 television stations (3 network, 2 independent, 1 public); 25 radio stations (13 AM, 12 FM); 9 cablevision systems with 90,000 subscribers.
New construction: over $3.7 billion in major commercial projects scheduled during next 3 to 5 years. 1981 metro residential building permits 11,177.
Education: Univ. of Central Florida, Valencia Community College, Seminole Community College, Rollins College.
Federal facilities: Orlando Naval Training Center supporting 29 commands and activities including Naval Nuclear Power School, military personnel 12,500, civilian personnel 3,000; total local federal disbursements $370 million.
Medical facilities: over 4,000 beds in 17 hospitals including Orlando Regional Medical Center and Florida Hospital.
Cultural facilities: Florida Symphony Orchestra, Loch Haven Art Center, John Young Science Center, Orange County Historical Museum, Central Florida Civic Theater, Central Florida Zoological Park, Orlando Public Library System, Morse Gallery of Art.
Sports: Tangerine Bowl football game in 50,000 seat stadium; Minnesota Twins spring training site; Univ. of Central Florida Knights (football, basketball, soccer); Rollins College Tarheels (basketball, soccer); Bay Hill Classic, Walt Disney World National Team Championship, Florida Lady Citrus golf tournaments; Golden South Classic AAU track and field meet; Silver Spurs Rodeo (semi-annual); Ben White Raceway; Sanford-Orlando Kennel Club; Orlando-Seminole Jai-Alai Fronton; Daytona International Speedway.
History: area first settled in 1830's; Orange County established 1845; Orlando incorporated 1875; named for Col. Orlando J. Rees killed in Seminole Indians War.
Additional information: Orlando Area Chamber of Commerce, P.O. Box 1234, Orlando, FL 32802.

Ottawa, Ontario, Canada

Population: (1981) 295,163 (city), 717,978 (metro region including greater Ottawa 546,849 and the city of Hull, Que. 56,225); Canada's 12th largest city, linked with neighboring Hull by 5 bridges; labor force (Ottawa-Hull) 368,000.
Area: 42.5 sq. mi. (city), 1,100 sq. mi. (region) on Ontario-Quebec border at the Chaudiere Falls on the Ottawa River; national capital.
National Capital Region: Ottawa and Hull, occupying 1,800 sq. mi. of eastern Ontario and western Quebec, form the National Capital Region of Canada, administered by the National Capital Commission (NCC), created by Parliament in 1959, which deals directly with 2 provincial governments, 2 regional governments, and 57 municipal jurisdictions.
Industry: major employer (100,294) is the federal government; tourism provides 14,000 jobs; Bell Canada largest private employer.
Commerce: 1980 retail sales $2.8 billion; 1980 per capita disposable income $9,735; 3d largest convention site in Canada with capacity for 5,000; 6,000 hotel-motel rooms; exhibit space 60,000 sq. ft. in 3 major hotels, 120,000 sq. ft. in the Civic Centre and 75,700 sq. ft. in the Nepean Sports- plex.
Transportation: Ottawa International Airport, 15 minutes from downtown, ranks as the nation's 10th busiest, more than 100 scheduled flights daily by 7 airlines; surface transportation provided by VIA rail and intercity bus service.
Communications: 2 daily (one in French), 4 weekly newspapers; 6 TV and 14 radio stations.
Education facilities: Carleton Univ., the bi-lingual Univ. of Ottawa, and Algonquin Community College.
Medical facilities: 11 hospitals, many include a public psychiatric unit; bed capacity over 4,000.
Cultural facilities: $45 million National Arts Centre with 2,300-seat opera house-concert hall, and an 800-seat theater; Ottawa Little Theatre.
National museums: Nat. Gallery of Canada, Museum of Man, Museum of Natural Sciences, Museum of Science and Tech., Canadian War Museum, Nat. Aero. Collection.
Sports: Ottawa Rough Riders, CFL; Ottawa 67's hockey.
Other attractions: gothic-style Parliament buildings, housing Canada's House of Commons and Senate; in summer, Changing the Guard ceremony 2 militia regiments; Peace Tower, memorial to Canada's war dead; Central Canada Exhibition; Ottawa's oldest building, the Bytown Museum; Royal Mint; Rideau Canal provides boating in summer, the longest skating rink in the world; 5 miles of the Rideau Canal from downtown to Carleton Univ.; the Experimental Farm, 1,200 working acres in the heart of Ottawa; Winter Fair; 80 camping and trailer parks, 7 beaches; mountain lake recreation facilities; Gatineau Park (88,218 acres).
History: founded 1827 as Bytown, inc. as Ottawa 1855; named after Outaouac (or Outaouais Indian tribe); chosen as Canada's capital in 1857 by Queen Victoria.
Further information: Canada's Capital Visitors Bureau, 7th Floor, 222 Queen Street, Ottawa, Ont. K1P 5V9.

Pensacola, Florida

The World Almanac is sponsored in the Pensacola area by the Pensacola News-Journal, One News Journal Plaza, Pensacola FL 32501; phone (904) 433-0041; predecessor The Floridian founded in 1821, first daily News 1899, Journal 1898, merged 1924; combined circulation daily 68,800, Sunday 71,699; member Gannett Group; publisher Clifford W. Barnhart, editor J. Earle Bowden.

Population: 57,619 (city), 238,391 (county), 295,325 (metro area).
Area: southern end of 759 sq. mi. Escambia County at westernmost edge of Florida panhandle.
Industry: Monsanto Corp., St. Regis Pulp & Paper Co., Vanity Fair, American Cyanamid, Armstrong Cork, Westinghouse, Air Products, Reichhold Chemicals.
Labor force: civilian 121,600, military 13,220.
Commerce: retail sales $1.1 billion; average family income $17,555; effective buying income over $1.7 billion.
Transportation: 3 airlines, 2 railroads, 2 bus lines, 16 truck lines, intercoastal waterway, interstate 10, 4 U.S. highways.
Communications: 5 TV, 14 radio stations.
New construction: Monsanto expansion, Ellyson Field industrial park development, downtown mall, St. Regis Paper Co. expansion, port expansion, downtown Hilton.
Medical facilities: Baptist, University, West Florida, U.S. Naval, and Sacred Heart Hospitals.
Federal facilities: Naval Air Station, Corry Field, Saufley Field, Whiting Field, carrier USS Lexington.
Cultural facilities: public library, Historical Museum, T.T. Wentworth Museum, Hispanic Museum, Transportation Museum, Museum of Naval Aviation, Saenger Theater, Art Association, Arts Council, Inc., Oratorio Society, Pensacola Symphony, Little Theater.
Educational facilities: Univ. of West Florida, Pensacola Junior College.
Recreation facilities: Pensacola Beach, 9 golf courses, greyhound park, stock car raceway.
Sports: Pensacola Open, American Amateur Golf Classic, Virginia Slims tennis, International Bill Fishing Tournament, intercollegiate sports; pari-mutuel greyhound racing; American Amateur Tennis Classic, Fiesta Road Run, Sertoma Run, Palafox Place Run.

Events: Fiesta of Five Flags, Mardi Gras, Seafood Festival, Great Gulfcoast Art Festival, July 4th celebration.
Birthplace of: Jacqueline Cochran, Nancy Dussault, Charles Percy.
Further information: Pensacola Area Chamber of Commerce, 117 West Garden Street, Pensacola, FL 32593; phone (904) 438-4081; Pensacola-Escambia Development Comm., 803 N. Palafox, Pensacola, FL 32501; phone (904) 433-3065.

Philadelphia, Pennsylvania

The World Almanac is sponsored in the Philadelphia area by The Philadelphia Inquirer, 400 N. Broad Street, Philadelphia, PA 19101; phone (215) 854-2000; est. 1829, lineage traced to Pennsylvania Packet, founded 1771; circulation 564,223 daily, 1,040,991 Sunday; Pulitzer prizes 1975, 1976, 1977, 1978, 1979, 1980; published by Philadelphia Newspapers, Inc.; president Sam S. McKeel; executive editor Eugene L. Roberts Jr.; editor Edwin Guthman; managing editor Gene Foreman; sponsors Delaware Valley Science Fair; Phillies tickets, Spelling Bee, Book & Author luncheons, Old Newsboys' Day, Phila. Distance Run, Head of the Schuylkill Regatta. PNI also publishes the Philadelphia Daily News, afternoon tabloid, at same address; founded 1925; circulation 304,659; editor F. Gilman Spencer; executive editor Zachary Stalberg; managing editor Tom Livingston; sponsors Broad St. Run, city Double Dutch Jumprope Contest.

Population: 1,688,210 (city), 4,700,996 (SMSA), 5.9 million (14-co. RTA); 6.8 million (18-co. ADI); employment 2.0 million (metro).
Area: 130 sq. mi. (city), 3,553 sq. mi. (metro); located in southeastern Pa. on Delaware and Schuylkill rivers; 90 mi. from N.Y.C., 136 mi. from Wash., D.C., 60 mi. from Atlantic City; Phila. is county seat (city and co. coextensive).
Industry: over 90% of all U.S. basic industries represented; major center for textiles and apparel, food processing, petroleum (3d largest oil refining region on East Coast), printing and publishing, instruments, chemicals and pharmaceuticals, finance and insurance; companies headquartered in metro area include Sun Co., IU International, Campbell Soup, Scott Paper, Rohm & Haas, Crown Cork & Seal, Pennwalt, CertainTeed, SmithKline Beckman, Thiokol, Penn Mutual Life, INA, ARA Services, Alco Standard, Arco Chemical.
Commerce: 58 comm. banks (metro), $21.5 billion deposits; 7 mutual savings banks, $11.4 billion; retail sales (metro) $19.9 billion; median household income (metro) $24,738.
Transportation: biggest freshwater port in world (50 mi. waterfront); 72-acre Free Trade Zone; 2d in intl. cargo among N. Atlantic U.S. ports (65.7 million tons in 1981); 2 modern marine terminals for containerized cargo; rail service by Conrail, Chessie System, and Amtrak; over 250 truck lines; vast highway network, 6 bridges in metro area between Pa. and N.J.; Phila. Intl. Airport handled over 9 million passengers in 1981 and 102,840 tons of freight through Cargo City facility; area transit (SEPTA) conveyed 231.6 million passengers on subway, el, rail commuter, bus, and streetcar lines in 1981.
Communications: 2 daily newspapers: Inquirer, Daily News; 24 AM, 29 FM; 6 comm. TV stations, one subscription station; cable TV.
New construction: 1981 building permits: 428.8 mil., $308 million center-city RR commuter tunnel; $200 million Gallery II project on Market St. East (125-store mall, 31-story office bldg., and dept. store); $125 million One Logan Sq. complex (incl. 375-room, world-class Four Seasons Hotel); 450-room Hershey Phila. Hotel; 312-room Hotel Rittenhouse; Intl. Airport high-speed line.
Medical facilities: 124 hospitals (metro); 6 medical schools, 2 dental schools, 2 pharmacy schools.
Federal facilities: Phila. Naval Base; Defense Industrial Supply Ctr.; Defense Personnel Support Ctr.; U.S. Navy Aviation Supply Office Compound; Veterans Adm. Ctr.; Internal Revenue Serv. Ctr.; U.S. Mint; Ft. Dix, McGuire AFB, Willow Grove Naval Air Station (metro).
Cultural facilities: Phila. Orchestra; Pa. Ballet; Opera Co. of Phila.; Acad. of Music; Phila. Museum of Art; Franklin Inst.; Pa. Acad. of the Fine Arts; Rodin Museum; Univer. Museum; Acad. of Natural Sciences; Port of History Museum; Barnes Fdtn.; Mann Music Center; Robin Hood Dell East; theaters: Walnut St. (oldest in U.S.); Forrest; community, campus and summer theaters.
Educational facilities: 88 degree-granting insts. in metro area; some 600 academic and ind. labs.
Convention facilities: Civic Center with 383,000 sq. ft. of air-cond. exhibit space; 13,000-seat Convention Hall; over 500 motels/hotels (metro) with 15,000+ first-class rooms.
Recreational facilities: over 8,600 acres of parks inc. 4,516-acre Fairmount Park (largest city park in U.S.); close to Atlantic City, Atlantic Ocean beaches, Pocono Mtns.
Sports: NL Phillies, NFL Eagles and Army-Navy football game (Veterans Stadium); MISL Fever, NBA 76ers and NHL Flyers (Spectrum); Penn Relays (Franklin Field); sculling races (Schuylkill R.); area horse racing (Keystone, Liberty Bell, Brandywine, Del. Park, Atlantic City); Philadelphia Independence Marathon.
Other attractions: Old City district and Benjamin Franklin Parkway centers of interest; many historic bldgs. preserved, restored or reconstructed; Penn's Landing waterfront dev.; Afro-American Museum; City Hall; Elfreth's Alley; Franklin Court; Society Hill; Fairmount Park mansions; zoo (America's first); Mummers Parade (Jan. 1); Freedom Festival; Super Sunday festival (Oct.); nearby attractions incl. Longwood Gardens, Great Adventure.
History: Wm. Penn founded his "Greene Countrie Towne" as Quaker colony in 1682; gave it Greek name that means "City of Brotherly Love"; national capital 1790-1800; historic shrines incl. Independence Hall, Liberty Bell, Carpenters' Hall, Franklin's grave, Betsy Ross House, Gloria Dei Church, Christ Church, USS Olympia, Olde Fort Mifflin; Valley Forge, Gettysburg, Trenton, and Princeton nearby.
Birthplace of: Marian Anderson, Roy Campenella, Wilt Chamberlin, Alexander Haig, Mario Lanza, Jim McKay.
Further information: Victor Kendrick, Office of City Representative, 1660 Municipal Services Bldg., Phila., PA 19107, phone (215) 686-3655; Phila. Tourist Bureau, 1525 J.F. Kennedy Boulevard, Phila., PA 19102; phone (215) 568-1976.

Phoenix, Arizona

The World Almanac is sponsored in the Phoenix area by The Phoenix Gazette, 120 East Van Buren Street, Phoenix, AZ 85004; phone (602) 271-8000; founded October 28, 1880, as Arizona Gazette by Charles H. McNeil; circulation 106,220, publisher Darrow Tully, managing editor Lynne Holt. The Gazette sponsors Music Memory Programs, Family Symphony Concerts, Phoenix Giants' bat boy contest, Youth Night at the Phoenix Suns, tennis clinic, cactus show, and other events.

Population: (1981) 810,000 (City of Phoenix), 1,533,583 (SMSA); capital and largest city in state; total employed 652,400.
Industry: electronic equip. manufacturers. Second largest in the country. Honeywell and Motorola each employ more than 7,000; Arizona divisions of the Garrett Corp., Sperry Flight Systems, and Mountain Bell each employ more than 5,000; other major employers are American Express, Amerco, Arizona Public Service, Courier Terminal Systems, General Electric, General Semi-conductor, Goodyear Aerospace, Greyhound, Intel, International Metal Products, ITT Courier Terminal Systems, Marathon Steel, Phoenix Newspapers Inc., Reynolds Metals, Salt River Project, Siemens Corporation, Spring City Knitting Co., Tanner Prestressed

Architectural Concrete, Ind., United Metro, and Western Electric Cable.
Commerce: Wholesale-retail center for state; retail sales (1981) $9.5 billion for the Phoenix Metro area, effective household buying income $21,477; bank and S&L assets $26.4 billion; 18 banks and 7 S&Ls.
Transportation: transportation center of the Southwest; Sky Harbor International Airport served by 16 major airlines, more than 6.6 million passengers (1981); 5 smaller airports in other areas of the county; 3 railroads; 2 transcontinental bus lines; 10 transcontinental truck lines; 25 heavy equipment haulers; 34 interstate and 39 intrastate truck lines; 7 air cargo firms.
Communications: 8 TV and 36 radio stations.
New construction: (1981) 22,479 new residential building permits; total value of building permits, $1.5 billion.
Medical facilities: Barrow Neurological Institute; 27 general care hospitals. Veterans' Hospital; other special services.
Cultural facilities: art museum, public library, symphony orchestra, Indian museums, zoo, botanical gardens, community and professional theaters; Civic Plaza convention center; Gammage Auditorium.
Federal facilities: Luke AFB, Williams AFB.
Educational facilities: Arizona State Univ., American Graduate School of International Management, Grand Canyon Col., DeVry Institute of Tech., Arizona Tech, Univ. of Phoenix, Lamson Business Col., Maricopa Technical Col. (vocational), six community colleges, 15 public and parochial high schools, and 66 elementary schools.
Sports: 72 golf courses and $300,000 Phoenix Open; inland surfing beach; ice skating rinks; amusement park; pro basketball and baseball teams; auto, greyhound, and horse racing; annual Fiesta Bowl football game.
Other attractions: Frank Lloyd Wright's Taliesin West; Paolo Soleri's Arcosanti; Dons' Club guided tours of Arizona; full calendar of events including state and county fairs and rodeos, horse shows, regattas, polo tournaments.
History: founded 1870, on site of ancient Indian settlement; the Hohokam tribe, which flourished ca. 500-1200 A.D., developed an intricate system of irrigation canals which form the base of the canal system in use today.
Birthplace of: Lynda Carter, Barry Goldwater.
Further information: Phoenix and Valley of the Sun Convention and Visitors Bureau, 2701 E. Camelback Road, Phoenix, AZ 85016; or Phoenix Metropolitan Chamber of Commerce, 34 W. Monroe, Suite 900, Phoenix, AZ 85003.

Pittsburgh, Pennsylvania

The World Almanac is sponsored in the Pittsburgh area by The Pittsburgh Press, 34 Boulevard of the Allies, Pittsburgh, PA 15230; phone (412) 263-1100; founded June 23, 1884, as Evening Penny Press by Thomas J. Keenan; circulation 250,000 daily, 650,000 Sunday; editor John Troan, business manager William A. Holcombe, managing editor Ralph Brem; sponsors Press Old Newsboys Fund for Children's Hospital which raised $2.3 million in 1981.

Population: 423,938 (city), 2,244,620 (4-county metro area), 2d in state and 31st in nation; metro area labor force of 1,035,800 (Apr. 1981), unemployment was 10% (Mar. 1982).
Area: 55.5 sq. mi at juncture of Allegheny and Monongahela rivers which form Ohio River; Allegheny County seat; altitude, 702 feet.
Industry: one-fifth of nation's steelmaking capacity; western Pennsylvania mines produce 40 million tons of bituminous coal annually; 6,000 different products made in area; home of world's first full-scale nuclear power plant; world's largest manufacturers of aluminum, steel rolls, rolling mill machinery, air brakes, plate and window glass, and safety equipment; 3d largest headquarters city in nation.
Commerce: retail sales (Allegheny County, 1981) $5.0 billion; average household effective buying income (Allegheny County) $20,000.
Transportation: 15 scheduled airlines handled 10.1 million passengers on 276,000 flights at International Airport (1981); 7 railroads; Continental Trailways and Greyhound bus lines; over 400 common carriers; Port Authority Transit vehicles carried 103 million passengers (1981) over 166 routes, 5 trolley lines and 1 incline; 9 major highways serve the city; a 4.5 mile busway opened in 1977, and another 6.8 mile busway and $480 million 10.5 mile light rail trolley system, incl. a downtown subway, are under construction.
Communications: 2 daily newspapers; 6 TV (including country's first educational station) and 25 radio stations.
New construction: through Renaissance II, the city will increase its office space by more than 25% and spend approximately $4.5 billion in construction and development during the next 5 years; $32 million convention center opened in 1981; headquarters for PPG Industries and Dravo Corp. in addition to Riverfront Center and Oxford Center are under construction; Greater Pittsburgh International Airport planning expansion. Station Square, Allegheny River Edge Park, and Grant Street East expansion underway.
Medical facilities: 20 hospitals include Univ. of Pittsburgh Health and Medical complex where Dr. Jonas Salk developed polio vaccine; VA installation.
Federal facilities: Federal Building contains scores of U.S. government offices (information center: 412/644-3456); Army base at Oakdale; Air Force base.
Cultural facilities: Heinz Hall is home of the opera co., ballet, civic light opera, youth symphony and symphony orchestra; 4 community theaters, one legitimate theater; Frick Art Museum; Carnegie Museum and Art Gallery, home of the Pittsburgh International series, a biennial one-man art show offering a $55,000 prize; American Wind Symphony.
Educational facilities: Univ. of Pittsburgh, Duquesne Univ., Point Park, Chatham, Carlow, Robert Morris, and La Roche colleges; Carnegie-Mellon Univ., Community College of Allegheny Co.; 18 Carnegie public libraries, 3 bookmobiles, community libraries.
Sports: NL Pirates, NFL Steelers; NHL Penquins, NISL Spirit.
Other attractions: Highland Park Zoo, children's zoo, Twilight Zoo, aquarium, aviary, Buhl Planetarium, Allegheny Observatory, Phipps Conservatory, Fort Pitt Museum; 2 amusement parks; 2 operating passenger inclines; folk festival; Three Rivers Arts Festival every June; harness racing; river cruises; Civic Arena; Three Rivers Stadium.
History: first hunters and trappers came through in 1714; city dates from Nov. 25, 1758, when English forces under Brig. Gen. John Forbes occupied the ruins of Fort Duquesne, which French soldiers had burned and abandoned, and built a new and bigger fortress called Fort Pitt. When incorporated in 1816, it already had a reputation as a "Smoky City" from factories and coal-burning homes. Massive "Renaissance Plan" has cleared the skies and rebuilt the heart of the city during the past 30 years.
Birthplace of: Henry Steele Commager, Billy Conn, Erroll Garner, Martha Graham, George S. Kaufman, Gene Kelly, John Unitas.
Further information: Chamber of Commerce, 411 Seventh Avenue, Pittsburgh, PA 15219; Convention and Visitors Bureau, 200 Roosevelt Boulevard, Pittsburgh, PA 15222.

Portland, Maine

The World Almanac is sponsored in the Portland area by the Maine Sunday Telegram, 390 Congress, Portland, ME 04104; phone (207) 775-5811; published by Guy Gannett Publishing Co., founded 1921; circulation 126,403; publisher Jean Gannett Hawley, editor John K. Murphy; also publishes morning Press Herald, circulation 57,981 and Evening Express, 30,258.

Population: 61,572 (city), 183,457 (SMSA) (metro area), first in state; total employed 94,200 (SMSA).
Area: 21.6 sq. mi.; peninsula on Casco Bay; Cumberland County seat.
Industry: One of Atlantic Coast's busiest oil shipping centers, east terminus Montreal pipeline; fishing fleet base, sea-

ood shipping center; landbased products: printed materials, netal, processed food, electronic parts, paper, ship overhauling.
Commerce: tourist center, regional retail-wholesale hub, arge shopping complex, 1,485 retail, 350 wholesale, 600 service enterprises; retail sales (1980) $448.2 million.
Transportation: municipal jetport, Delta, Bar Harbor, Maine Air airlines; 3 rail freight lines, integrated bus system, Greyhound, Michaud Trailways bus terminals, 35 truck lines; Maine Turnpike, interstate 95 and 295 highways connect to all New England; deep water anchorage, auto ferries year round to Yarmouth, Nova Scotia.
Communications: 3 TV, 5 AM, 6 FM stations.
New construction: art museum, housing for elderly, fish processing complex; export-import pier, condominiums, regional shopping center expansion, insurance co. headquarters expansion, Bath Iron Works drydock and overhaul facility.
Medical facilities: medical center, 2 hospitals.
Cultural facilities: symphony orch., Kotzschmar organ, one of world's largest; public, historical libraries; Victorian art museums; Henry Longfellow home (1785); branch Univ. of Maine, Westbrook College, art, vocational, and business schools; Portland Headlight, oldest lighthouse in country.
Recreation: 18-hole municipal golf course, 9 others in area; scenic cruises; swimming, tennis, fishing within easy travel; scenic parks.
Conventional facilities: civic center, 3 large assembly halls, meeting rooms in modern hotels and motels.
Sports: Maine Mariners hockey (AHL).
Birthplace of: Cyrus Curtis, Stephen King, Linda Lavin, Henry Wadsworth Longfellow, Thomas Reed.
Further information: Tourist Bureau, 142 Free Street, Portland, ME.

Portland, Oregon

The World Almanac is sponsored in the Portland area by The Oregon Journal, 1320 SW Broadway, Portland, OR 97201; phone (503) 221-8275; founded Mar. 11, 1902; circulation 109,107; editor Donald J. Sterling Jr., managing editor Peter Thompson.

Population: 366,383 (city), 1,026,144 (SMSA), first in state; total employed, 583,100.
Area: 80 sq. mi., at junction of Columbia and Willamette rivers; Multnomah County seat.
Industry: electrical and electronic industries along with lumber and wood products, food, and paper; ranks first in manufacture of logging, lumbering equipment; home of Louisiana-Pacific (forest products), Tektronix (oscilloscopes), Omark (saw cutting chain), Hyster (lifts, hoists, lumber handling), White Stag, Pendleton, Jantzen (clothing).
Commerce: wholesale-retail center for large part of Oregon, SW Washington; retail sales metro area (1980), $6.29 billion; 18 banks, 9 savings and loan associations, 1 savings bank.
Transportation: 3 major rail freight lines, Amtrak; Greyhound, Trailways buses; 10th largest freshwater port in U.S., with 27-mile frontage, 29 marine berths; 13 million tons of cargo pass over docks annually; more than 2,200 ships visit annually; hub for 13 airlines, air freight service.
Communications: 5 TV and 30 radio stations.
Medical facilities: 17 major hospitals, Oregon Health Sciences University Hospital, VA hospital.
Cultural facilities: art museum, Oregon Symphony Orchestra, Opera Assn., Oregon Historical Society, Portland State Univ., Univ. of Portland, and Lewis & Clark, Reed, Warner Pacific, Judson Baptist, and Concordia colleges.
Other attractions: annual Rose Festival, Rose Show; park system includes Washington Park, Hoyt Arboretum International Rose Test Garden, Amer. Rhododendron Soc. Test Garden, Washington Park Zoo, Oregon Museum of Science and Industry, Forestry Center; Forest Park is largest forest area in a U.S. city's limits. Analysis of 243 population centers in mid-1970s named Portland as "America's Most Liveable City."
Sports: Trail Blazers of the NBA play at the Memorial Coliseum; Timbers (soccer) and Beavers (baseball) play at Civic Stadium.
History: chartered 1851 with population of 821; named after Portland, Me., rather than Boston, Mass., on flip of coin by 2 early citizens.
Birthplace of: Leon Ames, James Beard, Dick Fosbury, Brett Musburger, Linus Pauling, Jane Powell, John Reed, Sally Struthers.
Further information: Chamber of Commerce, 824 SW 5th, Portland, OR 97204.

Providence, Rhode Island

The World Almanac is sponsored in the Providence area by The Providence Journal-Bulletin, 75 Fountain Street, Providence, RI 02902; phone (401) 277-7000; Journal founded 1829, Bulletin 1863, Sunday Journal 1883; circulation, Journal (morn.) 78,634, Bulletin (eve.) 139,687, Sunday Journal 230,800; chairman & chief executive officer John C. A. Watkins, publisher & president Michael P. Metcalf, senior v.p.-operations & admin. Charles P. O'Donnell, v.p. and exec. editor Charles McC. Hauser.

Population: 156,804 (city), 867,800 (metro); total employed 104,964.
Area: 18.91 sq. mi., at the head of Narragansett Bay in Providence County; state capital.
Industry: jewelry, silverware, plated ware, costume jewelry are largest industries; Textron is based in Providence, 937 manufacturing companies in the city.
Commerce: wholesale-retail center for entire state; retail sales $3.1 billion (metro); median household effective buying income $19,228 (metro); home of Narragansett Capital, largest small business investment company in nation; 2 savings and loan assns., 2 mutual savings banks, one cooperative bank, 6 commercial banks.
Transportation: Amtrak; 3 bus lines; 45 locally-based common carriers and contract truckers; 11 major highways link Providence to every corner of R.I.; 5 major airlines out of T. F. Green Airport in Warwick (15 min. away); port is 3d largest in New England with 25 wharves and docks, 10.5 miles of commercial waterfront on the bay.
Communications: 3 TV and 8 radio stations.
Medical facilities: 7 hospitals; one VA hospital.
Cultural facilities: Trinity Square Repertory Co., R. I. Philharmonic, R. I. School of Design Museum; R. I. Historical Society.
Education: Brown Univ., founded 1764, is 7th oldest college in nation; 7-year M.D. program inaugurated 1973; Providence and R. I. colleges, and R. I. School of Design.
Recreation: one of America's most attractive recreational areas centers around Providence; 69 salt water beaches, 23 fresh water beaches, 50 golf and country clubs, 5 ski areas, 31 yacht clubs, 28 parks, all within 45 minutes of city.
Convention facilities: R.I. Civic Center (seats 12,000).
Sports: America's Cup races since 1930; Newport-Bermuda race starts at Newport every other year.
Other attractions: largest collection of original early American homes of any city; located along Benefit St., they have been preserved by the Providence Preservation Society.
History: founded 1636 by Roger Williams; incorporated 1832; official state name is "Rhode Island and Providence Plantations."
Birthplace of: George M. Cohan, Nelson Eddy, Bobby Hackett, Edwin O'Connor, Leonard Woodcock.
Further information: Chamber of Commerce, 10 Dorrance Street, Providence, RI 02903.

Quebec City, Quebec, Canada

Population: 186,088 (city), 480,500 (metro); oldest city in Canada (1608) and the capital of the province of Quebec.
Area: 30 sq. mi.; natural citadel on north shore of St. Lawrence River at confluence with St. Charles River; 400 miles from Gulf of St. Lawrence; 167 miles east of Montreal; older part is built on a cliff 360 ft. above the St. Lawrence.
Industry: some 300 industrial firms, ranging from primary industry products to a variety of consumer products, employ over 16,000 people; food and beverage, leather footwear and leather products, textiles, apparel, wood products, pulp and paper, printing and publishing, iron and steel products, nonferrous metal and chemical products.
Commerce: total effective buying income $3 billion; Quebec harbor, one of the busiest seaports of Canada, accommodates the largest ocean-going vessels with year-round facilities, an important container terminal; Provincial Government, with more than 15,000 employees, is the largest single employer and consumer in the city.
Transportation: Canadian Pacific and Canadian National railroads; Air Canada, Quebecair, Nordair; bus center.
Communications: 3 TV stations (2 French, one English); 6 radio stations (French), 2 newspapers (French).
Medical facilities: 5 large general hospitals.
Cultural facilities: historic character, cultural appeal and natural beauty make tourism important area of economic activity; annual "Carnaval" in Feb. is internationally known; annual summer festival (July) changes the city into an open theater for numerous artistic events; Expo-Quebec, an annual provincial exhibition (industrial, commercial, and agricultural), draws over 500,000 people a year.
Educational facilities: Laval University, the first in North America; Quebec University; 3 colleges.
Sports: home of NHL Nordiques.
Other attractions: only walled city in North America with fortifications standing today as they were 125 years ago; the Citadel, built from 1823-1832, contains within its walls 25 buildings, including the summer residence of Governor-General of Canada, Parliament buildings (1886), Quebec Museum, Battlefield Park, Ursulines Museum, Seminary (1663), Talon cellars, Notre Dame des Victoires Church, and Tresor Street.
History: founded 1608 by French explorer Samuel de Champlain; cradle of French civilization in America; once the key to the interior of the North American continent.

Raleigh, North Carolina

The World Almanac is sponsored in eastern North Carolina by The News and Observer and The Raleigh Times, 215 S. McDowell Street, Raleigh, NC 27602; phone (919) 829-4500; circulation N&O (morn.) 129,240, Times (eve.) 33,338 N&0 Sunday 170,317; publisher Frank Daniels Jr., editorial director Claude Sitton, editor Times A.C. Snow, managing editor N&O Bob Brooks, Times Mike Yopp.

Population: 149,771 (city), 300,833 (county), 525,059 (SMSA area of Wake, Orange, and Durham counties); 3d in stated; 156,865 employed (Wake County), 275,000 (metro).
Area: 55 sq. mi. in the geographical center of the state where Piedmont joins coastal plains; alt. 363 ft., temperate climate; state capital and Wake County seat.
Commerce: retail center of eastern N.C.; 1981 retail sales $1.878 billion (city), $2.499 billion (Wake County), $3.676 billion (metro); 16 banks, and 7 savings and loans; average annual income per household $26,613.
Education: 9 colleges; North Carolina State Univ. (Raleigh), Univ. of North Carolina (Chapel Hill), and Duke Univ. (Durham) form Research Triangle; Triangle Park employs 18,000 in all areas of research including toxicological, pharmaceutical, development of telecommunications fiber, environmental, engineering, and humanities research; metro area has more Ph.Ds per capita than anywhere in the world.
Transportation: 2 rail and 5 bus lines, Amtrak; 275 motor freight companies; airport has 7 airlines carrying 868,216 passengers per year; one interstate, 4 U.S. and 2 state highways into city; city mass transit bus system.
Communications: 5 TV and 15 radio stations; 2 daily newspapers and 10 weeklies.
New construction: $166 million 1981).
Medical facilities: 6 hospitals (1,894 beds); major state mental hospital; 516 Wake County doctors, 173 dentists.
Convention facilities: 35 motels, 3,783 rooms; Civic Center seats 10,000; Dorton Arena, 8,110; Memorial Auditorium, 2,289; Reynolds Coliseum, 12,700; Jane S. McKimmon Center, 3,000.
Cultural facilities: 3 museums, state fairgrounds, state symphony, community college and professional theater groups.
Recreation: 5,200-acre Umstead State Park, Lake Wheeler with 650 acres of water and 60 acres of land; B. Everett Jordon Lake Carter Stadium (45,600 seats); 13 year-round recreation areas or city parks; 600 restaurants.
Sports: ACC football and basketball; pro golf and tennis; annual track and field meets; annual horse shows; 2 major dog shows; annual speedboat regatta; college sports.
History: city of Raleigh was established in 1792 in honor of Sir Walter Raleigh; Andrew Johnson birthplace; Oakwood Historic District preserves large Victorian neighborhoods.
Further information: Raleigh Chamber of Commerce, 411 S. Salisbury Street, Raleigh, NC 27602; phone (919) 833-3005.

Regina, Saskatchewan, Canada

The World Almanac is sponsored in southern Saskatchewan by The Leader-Post, 1964 Park Street, Regina, Sask., S4P 3GA, phone (306) 565-8211; founded 1883 by Nicholas Flood Davin; circulation 69,670; president Michael Sifton, Toronto; executive vice-president Max Macdonald; editor W. Ivor Williams; associate editor C.E.W. Bell; managing editor J.M.F. Swan; business manager William Duffus; advertising manager George Crawford; MacLaren Trophy for editorial page reproduction excellence.

Population: 164,313, first in province; labor force, 87,000.
Area: 42.7 sq. mi., 100 miles north of Canada-U.S. border; provincial capital.
Industry: over 295 manufacturing industries; gross production value (1980) $690 million, 34% of Saskatchewan total.
Commerce: service center for oil, potash; grain production area; retail sales (1981) $933.9 million, 24.27% of province.
Transportation: 2 rail lines, 5 airlines, 3 bus lines, and 125 trucking companies; main Trans-Canada highway bisects; city-run transit system.
Communications: 3 TV, 8 radio stations, cable television.
Medical facilities: 4 major hospitals, 1,510 beds.
Cultural facilities: Saskatchewan Centre of Arts, multipurpose theater-convention center with: Jubilee theater (seats 450) stage, ballroom, reception hall and dining room; Centennial theater (seats 2,029); Hanbidge Hall convention area, 12,200 square feet, 9 meeting rooms, seats 1,600; Regina Symphony; Globe Repertory; Museum Natural History; Norman Mackenzie Art Gallery; RCMP Museum.
Educational facilities: Regina University; 14 collegiates; 97 elementary, 7 specialized schools; Wascana Institute of Applied Arts and Sciences.
Recreation facilities: Saskatchewan Roughriders (Canadian pro football); 175 parks and playgrounds; 8 golf courses; 6 swimming pools; 9 indoor ice rinks.
Other attractions: Wascana Centre, 2,300-acre development, with man-made lake, public buildings, parks, recreation in heart of city; home of Canadian Western Agribition, Canada's major international livestock show.
History: founded 1882, and since that time headquarters for RCMP training depot.
Further information: Regina Chamber of Commerce, 2145 Albert Street, Regina, Sask.

Reno, Nevada

The World Almanac is sponsored in the northern Nevada area by the Nevada State Journal and Reno Evening Gazette, 955 Kuenzli Street, P.O. Box 22000, Reno, NV 89520; phone (702) 786-8989; Journal founded 1870, Gazette founded 1876; combined daily circulation 56,548, Sunday 53,601; publisher Maurice Hickey.

Population: 100,756 (city), 193,623 (county), including Sparks, 2d largest in the state; 1982 labor force 124,000.
Area: 36.8 sq. mi. (including Stead annexation) in northwestern part of the state at the eastern foot of the Sierra Nevadas; Washoe County seat.
Industry: gross gaming revenue for county $507.9 million (1981); warehousing continued to grow because of Nevada's liberal free port law with est. 25 million sq. ft. in the county.
Commerce: taxable sales in SMSA (Washoe County) for 1981, $1.7 billion; assessed valuation (city) $1.5 billion; bank resources $4.04 billion.
Transportation; 17 motor freight lines, 3 freight railroads, Amtrak, 3 commercial bus lines, 11 airlines; airport handled (1981) 2.2 million passengers; U.S. 395 and Interstate 80.
Communications: 4 TV, 12 radio stations, 2 CATV, one satellite TV.
New construction: 1,621 units totaling $27.3 million assessed valuation (1981).
Medical facilities: 4 hospitals, including VA.
Educational facilities: Univ. of Nevada, Reno, Truckee Meadow Comm. College; public schools with 30,709 students, private/parochial schools with 1,400 students.
Cultural facilities: 1,428 seat Pioneer Theater Aud., Atmospherium Planetarium, 8,000 seat Centennial Coliseum, and 350,000 volume library; national air races; Reno Rodeo ($320,000 purse, richest in U.S.); Nevada Historical Society, Nevada Opera Guild, Reno Philharmonic Orch.; Sierra Nevada Museum of Art, Sierra Arts Found., Reno Little Theatre.
Recreation: 24-hour gambling; world's largest gambling casino; 21 ski resorts within a 1½ hour drive; Lake Tahoe and Pyramid Lake offering fishing, boating, swimming, sunbathing, medium game-hunting, camping; historic Virginia City mining town and tourist attraction within 1/2 hour drive.
Sports: Reno Padres minor league baseball.
History: established 1868 with public auction of land by Central Pacific Railroad Co., known prior as Lake's Crossing; named after Civil War hero General Jesse L. Reno.
Birthplace of: Paul Laxalt.
Further information: Chamber of Commerce, P.O. Box 3499, Reno, NV 89505; Marketing Department, Reno Newspapers, Inc. P.O. Box 22000, Reno, NV 89520.

Richmond, Virginia

The World Almanac is sponsored in the Richmond area by the Richmond Times-Dispatch and News Leader, 333 E. Grace Street, Richmond, VA 23219; phone (804) 649-6000; Times-Dispatch founded 1850 by James A Cowardin, circulation 135,335 daily, 218,804 Sunday; News Leader founded 1896 by Joseph Bryan, circulation 113,983; chairman D. Tennant Bryan; publisher J. Stewart Bryan III; vice chairman Alan S. Donnahoe; president James S. Evans; executive editor Alf Goodykoontz; Times-Dispatch managing editor Marvin Garrette; News Leader managing editor J.A. Finch.

Population: 219,214 (city), 591,719 (metro area), total employed (non-agricultural) 313,676.
Area: 62.5 sq. mi. (city), located at fall line of James River, 90 miles from Atlantic Ocean; independent city.
Industry: tobacco, with 12,600 workers, and chemicals, with 7,700 are leaders in employment; Philip Morris cigarette plant is world's largest and most modern; printing, publishing, manufacture of paper and allied products, and food.
Commerce: wholesale-retail center for central Virginia; retail sales $2.52 billion in 1979, per capita income $9,741, median effective buying income $19,447, total income (SMSA) $6 billion.
Transportation: 4 major railroads, 5 intercity bus lines, 4 commercial air lines, 3 commuter air lines, 69 motor truck lines; 3 interstate, 6 U.S., and 9 state highways; deepwater terminal accessible to ocean-going ships.
Communications: 5 TV, 26 radio stations; 2 cable TV stations.
Medical facilities: Medical College of Virginia known worldwide for heart and kidney transplants, medical research; 21 other hospitals, including McGuire VA Hospital.
Federal facilities: Defense General Supply Center, Fifth Federal Reserve Bank, U. S. Fourth Circuit Court, Ft. Lee (Quartermaster Corps).
Cultural facilities: Va. Museum and Theater with professional artists make city a center for dramatic, other performing arts; other drama groups; symphony orchestra.
Educational facilities: Virginia Commonwealth Univ. has state's largest enrollment; Univ. of Richmond, Virginia Union Univ., Union Theological Seminary (Presbyterian), Randolph-Macon College.
Recreational facilities: coliseum for athletic, entertainment events; city-owned Mosque auditorium, Parker Field, City Stadium, numerous parks.
Convention facilities: large downtown hotels near Mosque and Coliseum.
Sports: Braves (IL baseball); national ranked track and tennis events.
Other attractions: St. John's Church, scene of Patrick Henry's "Liberty or Death" speech; Virginia Capitol, designed by Thomas Jefferson; White House of the Confederacy; Civil War battlefields.
History: exploration here in 1607 by Capt. John Smith, first settlement 1609, incorporated as town 1742, made Va. capital 1779, Confederate Capital 1861-65; burned 1781 by Benedict Arnold, and 1865 when cotton, tobacco stockpiles fire set by fleeing Confederates spread to city; damaged by floods 1771, 1969, 1972.
Birthplace of: Arthur Ashe, Warren Beatty, Ellen Glasgow, Freeman Gosden, Shirley MacLaine, Fran Tarkenton.
Further information: Chamber of Commerce, 201 E. Franklin Street, Richmond, VA 23219.

Roanoke, Virginia

The World Almanac is sponsored in the Roanoke area by the Roanoke Times & World-News, 201-203 Campbell Avenue, Roanoke, VA 24010; phone (703) 981-3100; Times founded 1886, World-News founded 1889; Barton W. Morris Jr., president and publisher; circulation combined daily 117,094, Sunday 119,083.

Population: 100,427 (city), 223,578 (SMSA); labor force 112,910.
Area: 43.25 sq. mi.; SMSA includes Roanoke City, Salem City; Roanoke, Craig, Botetourt counties; located at southern extremity of Shenandoah Valley midway between Maryland and Tennessee.
Industry: 19% of work force in manufacturing; leading firms are General Electric, Eaton Corp., ITT, Singer, Burlington Industries, Mohawk Rubber, Ingersoll Rand.
Commerce: headquarters Shenandoah Life Ins. Co., Estate Life Ins. Co., Appalachian Power Co., Advance Stores, Mick or Mack Groceries; Regional Allstate Ins. Co. offices; Kroger (central warehouse); retail sales metro area (1981) $1.196 billion; average household effective buying income $19,459 (metro area); retail center for 20 counties and parts of W. Va. and N.C.

Transportation: Norfolk & Western Railway Co. headquarters; 2 airlines; Trailways and Greyhound buses; Amtrak north-south Washington, D.C.-West Va.; 30 interstate trucking firms with terminals; highways interstate 81, spur 581, US 11, 460, 220, 221, Blue Ridge Parkway.
Communications: 3 TV and 13 radio stations.
Medical facilities: 4 general, 4 specialty hospitals, VA facility; state hospital.
Cultural facilities: 2 civic centers with aud., coliseums and exhibit halls; symphony orchestra, art center, theaters; Roanoke, Hollins, Virginia Western Community, Nat. Business colleges; Va. Polytechnic Inst. and State Univ.; concert and lecture series.
Other attractions: Mill Mt. Park rising 1,000 ft. in center of city; children's zoo; Transportation and Historical Museum, Smith Mt., Fairy Stone and Claytor Lakes state parks; Natural Bridge, Dixie Caverns, Peaks of Otter.

Sports: baseball; school sports, winter skiing nearby; public recreation and parks programs.

History: formerly named Big Lick, Roanoke, an Indian word for shell money, became a city in 1884 with the linking of the Shenandoah Valley Railroad with Norfolk and Western Railroad.
Birthplace of: Wayne Newton, John Payne.
Further information: Roanoke Valley Chamber of Commerce, 14 West Kirk Avenue, P.O. Box 20, Roanoke, VA 24001.

Rochester, New York

The World Almanac is sponsored in the Rochester area by Gannett Rochester Newspapers, 55 Exchange Street, Rochester, NY 14614; phone (716) 232-7100; circulation Democrat and Chronicle (morn.) 133,095, Times-Union (eve.) 116,082, Democrat and Chronicle (Sunday) 243,371, (Saturday) 197,526; publisher George Dastyck, executive editor Robert Giles, director of advertising Peter Stegner. Times-Union reporters awarded a 1972 Pulitzer prize; Gannett News Service awarded 1980 Pulitzer prize.

Population: 241,741 (city), 972,000 (SMSA).
Area: 675 sq. mi. (Monroe County) straddling Genesee River on Lake Ontario, 2,966 sq. mi. (metro); Monroe County seat.
Industry: world leader in production of photographic, optical, and scientific instruments with Eastman Kodak (59,582 employees), Xerox (14,918), and Bausch & Lomb (4,000), all founded in Rochester; other fields include machinery, food products, apparel, printing and publishing.
Commerce: retail sales (1980) $4.5 billion; 20 commercial and savings banks; 1980 average household effective buying income $25,553 (metro area).
Transportation: Monroe County Airport with 8 major airlines and several freight companies; rail freight service by 4 lines, Amtrak; Greyhound, Trailways, Blue Bird bus lines; Rochester Transit Service; port of Rochester; over 75 motor freight firms.
Communications: 5 TV and 23 radio stations.
New construction: Eastman Kodak, 2 manufacturing plants; Strong Museum, convention center, Marketplace mall.
Medical facilities: one of the nation's most advanced health care centers; 8 general hospitals including Strong Memorial.
Cultural facilities: Eastman Theater, part of Univ. of Rochester's Eastman School of Music, and home of the Philharmonic Orchestra; Memorial Art Gallery; Museum and Science Center, including Strasenburgh Planetarium; George Eastman House of Photography; 3 theater companies.
Educational facilities: 8 private and 2 public 4-year colleges; 3 community colleges.
Recreational facilities: Finger Lakes area with 13 parks, summer and winter sports, golf, tennis, bowling; 16-park Monroe County System including Seneca Park Zoo, Highland Park, Lilac Festival.
Convention facilities: 2d largest used site in NY; War Memorial 7,500 cap., Dome Arena 5,000 cap.; 4,600 hotel & motel rooms; convention center under constr.
Sports: International League Red Wings, Baltimore Orioles farm team; AHL Amerks, NASL Lancers; Continental Basketball Assn. Zeniths, American Pro Softball League Express; thoroughbred racing and Finger Lake race track (Canandaigua).
Birthplace of: Philip Barry, Cab Calloway, Walter Hagen, Garson Kanin, Chuck Mangione, Mitch Miller, Hugh O'Brian.
Further information: Chamber of Commerce, 55 St. Paul Street, 14604; Convention and Visitors Bureau, 120 E. Main Street, 14614.

Rockford, Illinois

The World Almanac is sponsored in the Rockford area by the Rockford Newspapers, Inc., 99 E. State Street, Rockford, IL 61105; phone (815) 987-1200; publisher of the Rockford Register Star (daily 77,000) and Sunday Register Star, (85,000); publisher Gary L. Watson; member of the Gannett Group.

Population: 139,712 (city), 250,884 (county); 134,353 work force (county).
Area: 38.104 sq. mi. (city) on Rock River in extreme north central Illinois; Winnebago County seat; 519 sq. mi. (county).
Industry: more than 700 manufacturing establishments; products include machine tools (Sundstrand, Ingersoll Milling Machine, Barber-Colman, Greenlee Bros.), screws and bolts (Rockford Products, Elco, Camcar, National Lock), pharmaceuticals (Warner-Lambert, American Chicle), and paints (Valspar); Chrysler Corp. assembly plant is in nearby Belvidere.
Commerce: retail "magnet" for northern Ill. and southern Wis.; 31 shopping centers including Mall at CherryVale (108 stores); retail sales (1981) $954 million (city); 16 commercial banks, resources (1981) $1.174 billion; 5 savings and loan assns., resources (1981) $781.3 million.
Transportation: 4 rail freight lines, 3 bus lines, 39 truck lines; U.S. 51 and 20, interstate 90, Ill. 70, 2 and 173.
Communications: 4 TV, 6 radio stations, 1 public ser. sta., 1 cable TV; 4 weekly newspapers, one daily newspaper.
Medical facilities: 3 hospitals, 2 public supported extended care facilities.
Cultural facilities: Metro Centre, symphony orchestra, concert band, civic theater, 3 choral organizations, 6 legitimate theaters.
Education: 58 public schools (K-12), 32 parochial and private schools (K-12); Rockford College, Rock Valley College (2 years, liberal arts), UI-Rockford School of Medicine, Rockford Business College (2 years).
Recreation: 26 forest preserves, over 125 parks totaling 3,000 acres; one state park, 7 public golf courses, 3 country club courses, 106 public tennis courts, 7 private tennis courts, 2 indoor tennis facilities, 2 private platform tennis facilities, 3 public swimming pools, 7 private swim clubs, 80 baseball diamonds; Riverview Ice House; 4 roller skating rinks.
Agriculture: 192,000 acres tillable farmland (est. value $390 million); 2,400 persons on 925 commercial farms.
Other attractions: Children's Farm, Time Museum, Tinker Swiss Cottage, Rockford Museum, John Erlander Home, Burpee Natural History Museum, Burpee Art Museum, Rockford Council for the Arts and Sciences.
History: founded in 1834 by Germanicus Kent and Thatcher Blake beside fording place across Rock River; incorporated in 1852.
Birthplace of: John Anderson, James Breasted, Julia Lathrop, Janet Lynn.
Further information: Rockford Area Chamber of Commerce: 815 E. State Street, Rockford, IL 61101.

Sacramento, California

The World Almanac is sponsored in the Sacramento area by The Sacramento Bee, 21st & Q, Sacramento, CA 95816; phone (916) 446-9211; founded 1857; circulation daily 219,216, Sunday 244,841; president C. K. McClatchy, editor C. K. McClatchy, executive editor Frank McCulloch, managing editor Mike Kidder.

Population: 275,741 (city), 783,381 (county), 1,010,989 (SMSA); total employed 444,900 (SMSA).
Area: 94 sq. mi. (city), 997 sq. mi. (county), 85 mi. northeast of San Francisco in Sacramento Valley, at junction of Sacramento and American rivers; state capital and Sacramento County seat.
Industry: 475 manufacturing plants including Campbell Soup, Procter & Gamble, Cal. Almond Growers Exchange, Del Monte, Teichert Construction, Aerojet-General, Hewlett-Packard, Computer Sciences Corp., and Cal. Farm Bureau Federation, United Grocers, Tandy Corporation in Woodland, General Electric Medical Systems Div., American Hospital Supply, Shugart Associates, Second Foundation, Signetics Corp, GTE Data Services, Cable Data.
Commerce: wholesale-retail center for Sacramento Valley; total retail sales $5.4 billion in 1981.
Transportation: 3 county operated airports, including metropolitan airport, plus numerous private airports; Port of Sacramento with direct link to Pacific; 2 mainline transcontinental rail carriers; junction 4 major highways.
Communications: 6 TV and 23 radio stations.
New construction: restoration of Old Sacramento as historical project, Christofer Centre, Park Plaza Center, Corporate Center, Capitol Bank of Commerce, California Center, Franklin Electric, Consolidated Freightways Regional Center, Madison West Business Center, Fuller Industrial Park, Roseville Industrial Park, Bradshaw Technology Center.
Medical facilities: 14 full-service hospitals, Univ. of California Medical School in nearby Davis.
Federal facilities: 2 large air force bases, army depot, many regional federal offices.
Cultural facilities: Sacramento Community Center complex; symphony orchestra, ballet co., 10 live theaters (including the Music Circus, an in-the-round summer stock theater), the Crocker Art Gallery, and many art shows.
Education: California State Univ.-Sacramento, McGeorge College of Law, the nearby Univ. of California-Davis, and 4 community colleges.
Recreation: zoo, 95 public parks, 74 playgrounds, 8 public and 4 private golf courses, fishing, hunting, boating, camping, hiking, and skiing in nearby high Sierras; Golden Bear harness racing, American River Parkway bicycle trail, nearby Lake Tahoe.
Other attractions: Sutter's fort, State Capitol, Governor's Mansion, Old Sacramento historical area, Railway Museum; annual events: Camellia Festival, Dixieland Jazz Festival, Golden West track & field meet, Pig Bowl.
History: first permanent settlement founded by John Augustus Sutter Sr. in 1839; James Marshall discovered gold at Sutter's Mill in 1848, 35 mi. northeast, gateway to the Mother Lode Country; Pony Express and Central Pacific Railroad were part of early history.
Birthplace of: Joan Didion, Kathy Hammond.
Further information: Sacramento Metropolitan Chamber of Commerce, 917 7th Street, P.O. Box 1017; phone (916) 443-3771; or Sacramento Area Commerce & Trade Organization, 917 7th Street, P.O. Box 1132, phone (916) 444-2144; both Sacramento, CA 95805.

St. Louis, Missouri

The World Almanac is sponsored in the St. Louis area by the St. Louis Post-Dispatch, 900 N. Tucker Boulevard, St. Louis, MO 63101; phone (314) 622-7000; founded Dec. 12, 1878 by Joseph Pulitzer; circulation 238,099 Mondays through Fridays; 443,422 Sundays (average for 6 months ending March 31, 1981); editor and publisher Joseph Pulitzer Jr., associate editor Michael E. Pulitzer, managing editor David Lipman, contributing editor Evarts A. Graham Jr., vice president and general manager of newspaper operations Glenn Christopher; major awards include 5 Pulitzer prizes to the newspaper and 11 to staff members.

Population: 453,085 (city), 974,815 (county), 2,344,912 (SMSA), 12th in nation in payroll employment (964,600, first quarter, 1982).
Area: 4,935 sq. mi. (metro) just south of confluence of Missouri and Mississippi rivers.
Industry: 2d to Detroit in auto and truck assembly with Ford, GM, and Chrysler plants; headquarters of McDonnell Douglas, aerospace manufacturer; Interco, largest shoe company in U.S.; Anheuser-Busch, world's largest brewer; Monsanto, General Dynamics, Ralston-Purina, Pet, Inc., Chromalloy American, Consolidated Aluminum, Emerson Electric, Brown Group; 3,215 manufacturing concerns employ 224,300 (first quarter of 1982); ranks 10th in nation in number of "Fortune 500" company headquarters.
Commerce: $10.1 billion retail sales (1981 metro); $19,997 median family income; more than 220 banking institutions, total deposits $7.2 billion (Apr., 1982).
Transportation: 11 major airlines with 10 million passenger movements (1981); 2d largest rail center in U.S.; 17 trunk line railroads; largest inland port in U.S. handled 21.6 millions tons of cargo in 1979; 9 major highways, 14 motor-bus lines, 350 motor freight lines, 14 barge lines.
Communications: 6 TV and 35 radio stations.
New construction: industrial and commercial contracts totaled $650 million, and residential $339.4 million (1981); Lambert International Airport expansion; $40 million computer center for McDonnell-Douglas; $50 million IBM office project.
Medical facilities: 65 hospitals (metro) with 14,651 beds; Washington Univ. and St. Louis Univ. medical schools and affiliated hospitals provide treatment in many areas.
Federal facilities: Military Personnel Records Center, Defense Mapping Agency Aerospace Center, Army Troop Support and Aviation Material Readiness Command, Army Aviation Research & Development Command, Army Logistics Management Systems Agency, Postal Service Data Processing Center, Scott AFB.
Cultural facilities: Art Museum; Museum of Science and Natural History; restored historic homes; symphony orchestra; Loretto-Hilton Repertory Theatre; St. Louis Opera Theater (3-week summer season), American Theater; 4 dinner theaters; Laumeier Sculpture Garden; Municipal Theatre (Muny Opera) offers Broadway shows in big outdoor theater in Forest Park.
Educational facilities: 4 major universities: Washington, St. Louis, Univ. of Missouri at St. Louis, and Southern Illinois Univ. at Edwardsville; 26 colleges and seminaries with over 200 other private schools.
Convention facilities: 16,000 hotel rooms; 90,000 sq. ft. exhibit space in Kiel Auditorium; 240,000 sq. ft. exhibit space in Cervantes Convention Center.
Sports: Busch Stadium home of the Cardinal baseball and football teams; St. Louis Blues (NHL); horse racing at Fairmont Park; St. Louis Steamers, indoor soccer.
Recreational facilities: Jefferson National Expansion Memorial with 630-foot Gateway Arch on riverfront; 1,326-acre Forest Park with 3 golf courses, ball fields, floral displays, zoo, McDonnell Planetarium, Steinberg skating rink and Jefferson Memorial displaying Lindbergh trophies; National Museum of Transport; Six Flags, St. Louis; Grant's Farm with President Grant's cabin and animal displays; Missouri Botanical Garden with floral displays, Japanese garden and advanced research display greenhouse, the Climatron; excursion boats, show boat, minesweeper, Army Corps of Engineers museum on riverfront; Dental Health Theater with world's largest model teeth; Maryland Plaza/-Central West End, a collection of art galleries, shops, night spots and entertainment; Westport Plaza; the Magic House, a 15-room mansion with scientific "magic" for children.

Other attractions: Downtown area contains significant architecture including Eads Bridge, Old Post Office, Union Station, Old Courthouse, Old Cathedral, Spanish International Pavilion which now contains a hotel tower; Louis Sullivan's Wainwright Building refurbished as a state office building; and restoration of Laclede's Landing area on riverfront north of Gateway Arch.
History: named for French King Louis IX by fur trapper Pierre Laclede whose trading post became major fur market and gateway to the West; starting point of Lewis and Clark expedition and other explorations.

Birthplace of: Yogi Berra, Grace Bumbry, Redd Foxx, Betty Grable, Dick Gregory, Phyllis Schlafly, Roy Wilkins, Shelly Winters.

Further information: Convention and Visitors Bureau, 500 N. Broadway, or Regional Commerce and Growth Assn., 10 S. Broadway, both St. Louis, Mo.

St. Paul, Minnesota

The World Almanac is sponsored in the St. Paul area by the St. Paul Dispatch and Pioneer Press, 55 E. 4th Street, St. Paul, MN 55101; phone (612) 222-5011; founded 1849 as Minnesota Pioneer by James Goodhue; circulation, Pioneer Press (morn M-F) 106,168; Dispatch (eve M-F) 117,212; Pioneer Press/Dispatch (morn Sat.) 179,894; Sunday Pioneer Press, 248,468; Bernard H. Ridder Jr., chairman, executive committee, Knight-Ridder Newspapers, Inc.; publisher Thomas L. Carlin, vice president/editor John R. Finnegan, executive editor David Hall, editor Ronald Clark. First newspaper published in Minnesota.

Population: 270,230 (city); 2,109,207 (SMSA) 2d in state; total employed (city, 1981) 69% of all adults.
Area: 55 sq. mi. in eastern Minnesota on banks of Mississippi River close to Minnesota and Wisconsin vacationlands; state capital and Ramsey County seat.
Industry: West Publishing, world's largest law book publisher; international center for electronics and computer technology; Union Stockyards is largest livestock center in nation. Headquarters 3M Co., Am. Hoist & Derrick Co., Burlington Northern RR, Univac, Brown & Bigelow, Whirlpool, Economics Laboratory, Hoerner-Waldorf Corp., St. Paul Companies (insurance), West Publishing.
Commerce: retail sales (1981) $3.8 billion; median household income, $24,500; 25 banks, 6 savings and loan assns.
Transportation: 5 major and 2 regional rail lines, Amtrak; 21 intercity truck firms, 37 terminals; 3 interstate bus lines; 730-mile public transit system; metro. airport, hub of 8 commercial airlines, headquarters for Northwest and Republic airlines, averages 600 air movements per day; Downtown Airport; 60 firms operate barges on Mississippi River.
Communications: 4 commercial and 2 educational TV stations; 29 radio stations.
Medical facilities: 12 private hospitals; a 611 bed community hospital and research center: St. Paul-Ramsey Hospital.
Federal facilities: Ft. Snelling; regional headquarters for Health and Human Services, IRS, FCC, Immigration and Naturalization Service; U.S. District Court.
Cultural facilities: St. Paul Chamber Orchestra, St. Paul City Ballet, Chimera Theatre, Science Museum of Minn. & Omnitheater. Univ. of Minnesota Institute of Agriculture, Hamline Univ., St. Thomas, St. Catherine, Bethel, Concordia, and Macalester colleges, and William Mitchell College of Law; 80 public schools and 61 private schools.
Recreational facilities: more than 900 lakes in metro area, 438 tennis courts, 148 swimming beaches, 513 parks, 50 golf courses, 27 ski centers; 100 miles of hiking and biking trails.
Convention facilities: Civic Center with 101,000 sq. ft. exhibit space, seating for 35,000 in 4 main buildings, 15 meeting halls; 50 hotels and motels.
Other attractions: Winter Carnival in Jan., Como Park Zoo and Conservatory; onyx statue of Indian God of Peace in City Hall, Minnesota Historical Society Museums, Arts & Science Center, Fort Snelling State Park.
History: once called "Pig's Eye" for first settler, Pierre "Pig's Eye" Parrant; changed to St. Paul when Father Lucien Galtier built St. Paul's Chapel 1841; became town 1847, city 1854.
Birthplace of: Warren Burger, William Demarest, F. Scott Fitzgerald, Kate Millett, DeWitt Wallace, Dave Winfield.
Further information: St. Paul Area Chamber of Commerce, 701 North Central Tower, 445 Minnesota Street, St. Paul, MN 55101.

St. Petersburg, Florida

The World Almanac is sponsored in Florida's Suncoast Area by the St. Petersburg Times and Evening Independent, 490 1st Avenue So., St. Petersburg, FL 33701; phone (813) 893-8111; Times founded 1884, Independent 1908; circulation Times (morn.) 235,418. Independent (evening) 38,584. Sunday Times 292,499; Eugene C. Patterson, editor of the Times and president of the Times Publishing Co.; Robert Stiff, editor, the Independent. John B. Lake, executive vice president and publisher, the Times Publishing Co.

Population: 236,893 (city), 743,301 (Pinellas County), 1,550,035 (SMSA); Pinellas County (Mar. 1982) employment 275,300 (unemployment) 7.1%.
Industry and commerce: 3 million tourists in 1981; General Electric, Honeywell, Sperry, Eckerd Drugs, Jim Walter Research, All-State Insurance regional office, GTE, Paradyne Corp., ECI, Aircraft Porous Media, VRN, Silor Optical; ABA Industries, county 1981 retail sales $3.9-billion.
Transportation: U.S. 19, 41 and 98 link city to rest of gulf-coast Florida; interstates 175, 75 and 4 link St. Petersburg with Tampa, Orlando, and east coast; Tampa International Airport; other airports are St. Petersburg-Clearwater International and Albert Whitted; Amtrak, Seaboard Coast Line railroads; Greyhound and Trailways bus lines.
Communications: 8 TV, 46 radio stations.
Convention and tourist facilities: nearly 72,000 units house visitors; Bayfront Center seats 8,250 in arena, 2,250 in auditorium; Pinellas restaurants can serve 110,400 people at one time; Disney World 2 hours away.
Medical facilities: 18 major hospitals with 4,687 beds.
Cultural facilities: Museum of Fine Arts, Dali Museum, Gulf Coast Symphony, Historical Museum, community theaters. Eckerd College Free Institutions Forums; varied musical, theatrical and dance events at Bayfront Center complex.
Educational facilities: Univ. of South Florida's downtown Bayboro Campus, Stetson College of Law, Eckerd College, St. Petersburg Junior College, with 3 campuses.
Recreational facilities: 76 parks on 1,800 acres, many with recreational buildings, pools, tennis courts, boat ramps, and picnic areas; municipal and private marinas; deep sea fishing, golf courses, baseball fields.
Sports: St. Louis Cardinals and New York Mets spring training site; greyhound racing, baseball, jai alai, horse racing, NFL football, basketball, pro tennis, boat racing, NASL soccer; LPGA-PGA team golf, LPGA S&H Green Stamps golf classic.
Additional information: St. Petersburg Chamber of Commerce, 225 4th Street S., St. Petersburg, FL 33701.

Salem, Oregon

The World Almanac is sponsored in the Salem area by the Statesman-Journal Newspaper, 280 Church Street NE, P.O. Box 13009, Salem, OR 97309; phone (503) 399-6611; publisher of the morning Statesman-Journal; daily circulation 63,014, Sunday 62,999; John H. McMillan, publisher.

Population: 89,233 (city), 249,895 (SMSA),
Area: 32 sq. mi. on the Willamette River in the center of the bountiful Willamette Valley 50 miles south of Portland; 61 miles from Pacific Ocean; state capital, Marion County seat.
Industry: government (over 14,500 state employees), agriculture (over 100 crops), food processing — 2d in nation for fruit, berries, and vegetables; over 14 canneries produced over 10 million cases of canned goods and 260 million pounds of frozen foods; lumber and lumber products; manufacturing (batteries, radios, metal products, feeds, paints, textiles, food processing cans); pulp and paper mill.
Commerce: retail sales (1980) $992 million; med. household income (1980) $16,460; 9 banks, 7 savings & loan assns.
Transportation: 2 rail freight lines, Amtrak; Greyhound, Trailways bus lines, 20 truck lines, Air Oregon.
Communications: one public TV, 6 radio stations, one daily newspaper, one farm weekly newspaper.
Medical facilities: hospital with 2 units, General and Memorial.
Cultural facilities: symphony orchestra, art association, little theater, Bush House museum, Deepwood, Mission Mill museum, Northwest History collection, Willamette Univ., Civic Center.
Education: metro area includes 108 public schools — 89 elementary, 12 junior highs, 20 high schools, and 15 parochial schools; State Schools for the Blind and Deaf, Chemeketa Community College, Willamette Univ., Western Baptist College, and Oregon College of Education.
Recreation: back-packing, fishing, golf, snow and water skiing, camping, 44 parks in 5 mile radius; hunting for deer, elk, and fowl; Bush Pasture Park; within one hour drive Mt. Hood, Detroit Lake, Oregon Coast, Mt. Jefferson; 9 golf courses in 15 mile radius; 70 tennis courts in area.
Sports: Salem Angels baseball, Northwest League.
History: founded in 1842 by Methodist missionary, Jason Lee.
Further information: Chamber of Commerce, P.O. Box 231, Salem, OR 97308.

Salt Lake City, Utah

The World Almanac is sponsored in the Salt Lake City area by the Salt Lake Tribune, 143 S. Main Street, Salt Lake City, UT 84111; phone (801) 237-2045; founded Apr. 15, 1871; circulation 114,800 daily, 183,580 Sunday; publisher John W. Gallivan; editor Will Fehr; 1957 Pulitzer Prize; civic projects, statewide civic beautification awards; Sub for Santa program; Community Christmas Tree Plantings; Spring Garden Festival; Ski Race; No Champs Tennis and Golf tournaments, Newspaper in Education; Old Fashioned 4th of July.

Population: 163,033 (city), 619,066 (county), 935,280 (SMSA); first in state; 79% of state pop. lives in Wasatch Front Counties of Salt Lake, Davis, Utah, and Weber; state capital and Salt Lake County seat.
Area: nestled in a vast valley (elev. 4,327 ft.) surrounded by Wasatch and Oquirrh mountains.
Industry: labor force (metro area, 1981 est.) 290,433; average unemployment rate 6.3%; effective buying income $3.9 billion (county, 1979); per family income (county, 1980) $19,500 total construction value (county, 1980) $344.9 million; major employers are Hill AFB (30 miles north), Univ. of Utah, Brigham Young Univ., Granite School District, Kennecott Copper Corp., American Express, local defense industries; county has over 900 manufacturing plants; metro area major center for electronics, apparel manufacturing, mining, smelting, refining, distribution, warehousing center of Mountain West; area becoming center for energy resources development operations.
Transportation: 16 air lines, free-trade zone, International Airport; 22 freight carriers; geographic center of 11 western states; hub of central transcontinental highway system; 3 railroads, all major western truck, bus lines.
Communications: 2 daily newspapers, 4 commercial TV stations, 3 cable TV, 2 public TV, Home Box Office TV; 18 radio stations.
New construction: Sheraton Hotel, $62 million; $28 million, 480-room Marriott Hotel; $16.5 million expansion of Salt Palace convention, exhibit center; two 23-story residential condominiums, state office bldg.; 13-story bank bldg, first phase of $410 million Triad Center.
Medical facilities: 10 hospitals, including Univ. of Utah Medical Center, major research in transplant surgery.
Educational facilities: Univ. of Utah; Westminster, Utah Technical, and LDS Business colleges.
Cultural facilities: Utah Symphony Orchestra, Mormon Tabernacle Choir, Ballet West, Utah Opera Co., Ririe-Woodbury Co., Repertory Dance Theatre, 2 cultural arts halls.
Other attractions: Temple Square, home of 4 million-member Church of Jesus Christ of Latter-Day Saints (Mormons); Salt Palace Civic Auditorium; 700 acres in 22 parks, 25 playgrounds, 10 golf courses, 100 tennis courts; near Great Salt Lake (7 times more salty than ocean); Hogle Zoological Gardens, Kennecott Copper's Bingham mine.
Sports: 9 major ski resorts; Golden Eagles (Central Hockey League), Salt Lake Gulls baseball; Bonneville Salt Flats, Univ. of Utah in major NCAA sports; Utah Jazz (NBA).
History: founded July 24, 1847 by Brigham Young and contingent of pioneers.
Birthplace of: William Haywood, Loretta Young.
Further information: Chamber of Commerce, 19 E. 2d So.; Utah Travel Council, Council Hall; Salt Lake Valley Visitors and Convention Bureau, West Temple at First South, all Salt Lake City, UT.

San Antonio, Texas

The World Almanac is sponsored in the San Antonio area by the S. A. Express (morning) and S. A. News (evening), P.O. Box 2171, San Antonio, TX 78297; phone (512) 225-7411; circulation daily, Express 84,879, News 75,512, Sunday Express-News 193,635; chairman K. Rupert Murdoch, publisher and editor Charles O. Kilpatrick; Express-News Corp. is a division of News America, Inc.

Population: 785,410 city, 988,800 county, total employed 432,950.
Area: 1,247 sq. mi. (Bexar County); 2 1/2 hours from Gulf Coast and Mexican border.
Industry: 5 military bases include Kelly AFB, largest employer; fast-growing medical industry; diverse manufacturing, tourism, construction, trade, and service industries.
Commerce: center for 100 mile radius retail trade area, livestock production; retail sales (1981) $16.1 billion.
Federal facilities: Kelly AFB, hq. AF Air Security Service; Randolph AFB, hq. Air Training Command & AF Personnel Center; Brooks AFB, hq. AF Aerospace Medical Division; Lackland AFB with Wilford Hall USAF Medical Center; Fort Sam Houston, hq. 5th Army, & Army Health Services Command, Brooke Army Medical Center.
Medical facilities: Univ. of Texas Medical, Dental, Nursing schools; Audie Murphy VA Hospital; Southwest Research Institute; Southwest Foundation of Res. and Educ.
Transportation: International Airport, Stinson air field, 11 major airlines; 3 rail freight, Amtrak; 6 bus lines; 44 common-carrier truck lines; 576 miles of freeway and state highways.
Educational facilities: Univ. of Texas at San Antonio; Trinity, St. Mary's, and Our Lady of the Lake universities; Incarnate Word College; 2 jr. colleges, San Antonio, St. Philip's; permanent extension of National Univ. of Mexico.
Convention facilities: Convention Center with large arena, theater, exhibit, meeting space.
Cultural facilities: symphony orchestra; Institute of Texan Cultures, Mexican Cultural Institute, Witte Museum, McNay Art Institute, San Antonio Museum of Art.
Sports: Spurs (NBA), Dodgers minor league baseball, S.A. Bulls minor league football; livestock show and rodeo, Texas Open PGA Tournament, Avon Ladies Tennis Tournament.

Other attractions: historic Alamo, Spanish missions of San Jose, Concepcion, Capistrano, Espada; Hemis Fair Plaza with 750-foot observation tower-restaurant; downtown River Walk; zoo; Fiesta San Antonio, Folklife Festival.

Birthplace of: Carol Burnett, Joan Crawford, Paula Prentiss.

Further information: Greater San Antonio Chamber of Commerce, 602 E. Commerce, P. O. Box 1628, San Antonio, TX 78296.

San Bernardino, California

The World Almanac is sponsored in the San Bernardino area by the Sun, 399 North D Street, San Bernardino, CA 92401; phone (714) 889-9666; Sun founded 1894; daily circulation 79,982, Sunday 87,187; member Gannett chain; publisher William Honeysett, advertising director William Ridenour, editor Wayne C. Sargent.

Population: 129,000 (city, 1982 est.), 1,675,800 (2-cnty. metro area, 1982 est.).

Area: 47.22 sq. mi. at base of Cajon Pass, 58 miles east of Los Angeles; San Bernardino County seat.

Industry: business and industrial firms include Celotex-Marley, Scott Paper (foam div.), Captive Plastics, Culligan, Hanford Foundry, Knudsen Dairy, Mode O'Day, Pepsi Cola and Seven-Up bottling plants, Santa Fe Railway, TRW Systems, and Terry Industries.

Commerce: trading center for 20,189 sq. mi. San Bernardino county, largest in the nation; retail sales (1980) $970 million; 7 banks, 19 branches; 11 savings and loan assns.; 2 major shopping center complexes, each parking over 5,000 cars.

Transportation: Santa Fe, Southern Pacific, and Union Pacific rail lines, Amtrak; Greyhound and Continental bus lines; major interstate highways; nearby Ontario International Airport.

Communications: 15 radio and one VHF educational TV station; access to 5 Los Angeles channels.

Medical facilities: 3 major hospitals with 995 beds; major research and training center for heart surgery and hip and knee replacement surgery.

Federal facilities: Norton Air Force Base.

Cultural facilities: symphony orchestra, Civic Light Opera, nearby Redlands Bowl (summer concerts); National Orange Show with orange festival every spring; Convention Center-Exhibit Hall complex.

Educational facilities: California State College, junior college, 3 major universities nearby.

New construction: 6 redevelopment project areas with commercial and industrial development sites.

Sports: Little League Western Regional Headquarters.

History: founded 1852 by Mormons who purchased land from Spanish grant holders.

Birthplace of: Gene Hackman, Bob Lemon, Paul McCloskey.

Further information: Chamber of Commerce, 546 West 6th Street, San Bernardino, CA 92401.

San Diego, California

The World Almanac is sponsored in San Diego by The San Diego Union and The Tribune (Copley Newspapers), P.O. Box 191, San Diego, CA 92112; phone (714) 299-3131; Union founded 1868 (pioneer daily of Southwest); circulation, Union (morn.) 207,411, Tribune (eve.) 125,507, Sunday Union 327,939; publisher Helen K. Copley, general manager Al De Bakcsy, Union editor Gerald L. Warren, Tribune editor Neil Morgan.

Population: 876,504 (city), 1,859,623 (SMSA); total civilian employment 727,200.

Area: (county) 4,255 sq. mi.; 70 mi. Pacific Coast, San Clemente to Mexican border.

Industry: The 1981 estimated San Diego Gross Regional Product, the total output of all goods and services, was $27.6 billion with manufacturing contributing the greatest percentage, nearly 32%. Corporations with bases or divisions include Bendix, Burroughs, Control Data, Cubic, General Dynamics, Gulf, Honeywell, International Harvester's Solar division, NCR Corp., Pacific Southwest Airlines, Rohr, Sea World, Teledyne Ryan, TraveLodge, Van Camp sea food, Foodmaker (Jack-in-the-Box); aerospace, rapid transit design and manufacture, oceanography, nuclear energy, medicine important; also shipbuilding, tuna fishing, clothing, ocean shipping; among top 20 counties in farm products (avocados, cut flowers, eggs); Marine Corps Recruit Depot, Naval Training Center, North Island and Miramar Naval Air Stations, Naval Electronics Lab and Undersea Center, Marine Corps base at Camp Pendleton.

Transportation: freeway system is state's 2d largest; Amtrak, 11 airlines, bus lines; primary airport Lindbergh Field.

Communications: some 30 TV and radio stations.

Medical facilities: Salk Institute for Biological Studies, Scripps Clinic & Research Foundation; Naval Hospital; many hospitals.

Education and Cultural facilities: San Diego State Univ., U.S. International Univ., Univ. of San Diego, Univ. of California, San Diego (3 colleges and Scripps Institution of Oceanography), Point Loma College; symphony; Old Globe Theatre (functioning reproduction of Shakespeare's Globe Theatre); opera; ballet; Fine Arts and Timken galleries; La Jolla Museum of Contemporary Art.

Other attractions: world famous zoo and wild animal park; Balboa Park, central 1,400 acres containing museums, zoo, Fleet Space Theatre (computerized planetarium); Mission Bay Park includes Sea World; "Old San Diego" state historical park; "Star of India" ship-museum; neighboring Mexico (Tijuana); 70 miles of beaches.

Sports: NFL Chargers; NL Padres; NBA Clippers; NASL Sockers; Holiday Bowl; Andy Williams Open golf tournament; racing at Del Mar, Caliente (Mexico).

Other attractions: climate sunny; summer and winter resort; avg. temp. 68° summer, 57° winter, rainfall mainly December to March; famous "place names" include La Jolla (part of San Diego); 70 golf courses including Torrey Pines; large convention facilities; off-shore "whale watching."

History: area discovered 1542 by Cabrillo, founded in 1769 by Father Junipero Serra.

Birthplace of: Florence Chadwick, Maureen Connolly, Robert Duvall, Nanette Fabray, Graig Nettles, Charlene Tilton, Larry Wilcox, Ted Williams.

Further information: San Diego Chamber of Commerce, 110 West "C", Suite 1600, San Diego, CA 92101.

San Francisco, California

The World Almanac is sponsored in the San Francisco-Oakland area by The San Francisco Examiner, P.O. Box 3100, Rincon Annex, San Francisco, CA 94119; phone (415) 777-2424; founded June 12, 1865; circulation daily Examiner, 160,000; Sunday Examiner & Chronicle, 690,000; president R. A. Hearst, general manager Jim Sevrens; major awards: Pulitzer Prize, Freedoms Foundation, California Newspaper Publisher's Assn.; Examiner sponsors Golden Gloves, Bay to Breakers Race, Opera in the Park, Senior Citizens Christmas Camp.

Population: 678,974, 3,226,867 (SMSA); total employed 332,976 (city).

Area: 44.6 sq. mi. on the northern tip of a peninsula; San Francisco County seat.

Industry: food products, printing, publishing, fabricated metal products; west's financial capital and administrative center for many of the nation's leading corporations; West Coast operations' headquarters for a majority of the federal agencies; finance, insurance, and real estate; a major port of the Pacific Coast.

Commerce: wholesale-retail employment 106,500; services 152,900; manufacturing 50,100; total wholesale and retail outlets 26,436, taxable sales $5.3 billion; 40 banks with 157 branches; 25 savings and loans with 39 branches; total deposits in banks $32.4 billion.
Transportation: 40 major airlines serve the Bay Area; International Airport processed 20.9 million passengers, 317,952 metric tons of freight (1981); Municipal Railway (intra-city); AC-Transit and Bay Area Rapid Transit System (BART) to East Bay cities; Greyhound bus and Southern Pacific Railroad to Peninsula areas; Golden Gate Bridge District bus and ferry service to Marin County; Port of San Francisco services available: LASH, BULK, general cargo, containerization and barge service.
Communications: 2 major newspapers; 118 others serving the Bay Area; 45 radio stations, 7 TV channels received directly, one cable TV system.
Medical facilities: 24 gen. hospitals with over 7,406 beds, 5 spec. hospitals with over 1,935 beds; 3,033 physicians/surgeons and 772 dentists; Univ. of Cal. Medical Center.
Cultural facilities: Louise M. Davies Symphony Hall, San Francisco Opera, Spring Opera, Western Opera Theater, symphony, ballet, Civic Light Opera, American Conservatory Theater, Japanese Cultural Center, Chinese Cultural Center, International Film Festival; 3 museums, 29 libraries, 540 churches, and 136 theaters.
Educational facilities: 97 public elementary schools; 17 junior high, 11 high schools, and 965 special schools with a combined enrollment of 59,884; Univ. of California, San Francisco; California State Univ., Univ. of San Francisco, and City College of San Francisco.
Recreational facilities: 120 parks and many miniparks, 78 playgrounds, 6 golf courses, numerous tennis courts, 10 swimming pools, 5½ miles of ocean beach, one lake, one fishing pier, Marina small craft harbor and 3 yacht clubs.
Convention facilities: 102 hotels and motels with over 20,000 rooms, 650,000 sq. ft. George R. Moscone Convention Center.
Sports: Candlestick Park, home of the NL Giants and NFL 49ers; pro teams in all major sports.
Other attractions: zoo and 1,013-acre Golden Gate Park containing the California Academy of Sciences, De Young Museum, Japanese Tea Garden, and Arboretum; cable cars, Fisherman's Wharf, Chinatown, the Ferry Building.
History: San Francisco Bay discovered 1769 by Sgt. Jose Ortega; pueblo of Yerba Buena est. 1834, renamed San Francisco on January 3, 1847; inc. April 15, 1850.
Birthplace of: Gracie Allen, David Belasco, Jerry Brown, Jim Corbett, Isadora Duncan, Clint Eastwood, Robert Frost, Jack London, Johnny Mathis, Robert S. MacNamara, O.J. Simpson, Irving Stone, Natalie Wood.
Further information: Chamber of Commerce, 465 California Street, San Francisco, CA 94104; San Francisco Convention Bureau, 1390 Market Street, San Francisco, CA 94102.

San Jose, California

The World Almanac is sponsored in the San Jose area by the Mercury and News, 750 Ridder Park Drive, San Jose, CA 95190; phone (408) 920-5000; Mercury founded June 20, 1851, News July 23, 1883; combined daily circulation 223,107, Sunday Mercury News 270,497; president and publisher P. Anthony Ridder, editor Robert Ingle.

Population: 636,550 (city), 1,340,600 (metro area coextensive with Santa Clara County); total employed 749,000 (metro, March '82).
Area: broad alluvial 832,256-acre valley at south end of San Francisco Bay; Santa Clara County seat.
Industry: largest county in northern Cal. for manufacturing employment and total wages; called "Silicon Valley" due to high technology semiconductor and other electronics firms; IBM, Hewlett-Packard, Varian Assocs., Intel Corp., National Semiconductor, Memorex, Amdahl, Lockheed Missles & Space, Rolm, Tandem Computers, Apple Computer; diversity shown by Ford Motor Co., Spectra Physics, FMC Corp., Syntex; county a major producer of cut flowers; over 50 wineries, many distributing world wide.
Commerce: leading retail trade center of northern Cal., $7.5 billion in 1981; 141 shopping centers; 1st nationally in median household income among U.S. metro areas; 80% of all households earn $15,000 plus annually, 60% earn $25,000 plus, 13% earn $50,000 plus (metro).
Transportation: Municipal Airport served by 12 major airlines, 3 commuter carriers; highway system interconnected with inter-state in north-south, east-west directions; Southern Pacific and Western Pacific railroads; county transit buses link to Bay Area Rapid Transit.
Education: San Jose State, Santa Clara, and Stanford universities, plus several community colleges; 61% of adult population is college educated (metro).
Cultural facilities: 100–year–old Symphony, Civic Light Opera, Actors Repertory, Dance and Musical theaters; 2,700–seat Center for Performing Arts; Flint Center; San Jose Historical Museum; Rosicrucian Egyptian Museum, Planetarium, Art Gallery; De Saisset Gallery and Museum; Montalvo Center for the Arts; Triton Museum of Art; New Almaden Mercury Mining Museum.
Sports: Earthquakes (soccer); Expos (minor league baseball); 8 reservoirs with boat ramps, 1 with camping; 2 outlets to S. F. Bay for ocean sports; Amer. and Nat. league football and baseball franchses nearby.
Other attractions: Japanese Tea Gardens; Lick Observatory; Winchester Mystery House; Marriott's Great America.
History: founded 1777, first civil settlement in Cal.; county is one of 27 original in state; first public school in state, San Jose Granary, 1795; first state capital, Dec. 15, 1849.
Birthplace of: Peggy Fleming, Amadeo Giannini, Farley Granger, Carney Lansford, Jesse Lasky, Jim Plunkett.
Further information: Chamber of Commerce Metro-San Jose, One Paseo de San Antonio, San Jose, CA 95113; phone (408) 998-7000.

San Juan, Puerto Rico

The World Almanac is sponsored in Puerto Rico by The San Juan Star, GPO Box 4187, San Juan, PR 00936; phone (809) 782-4200; founded Nov. 2, 1959; circulation 50,000 daily; 55,000 Sunday; president & general manager John A. Zerbe Jr.; vice president & editor Andrew T. Viglucci; major awards include 1961 Pulitzer Prize for editorial writing; APME citations 1960, 1965; staff awards include 1970 IAPA Mergenthaler Award, 1971, 1972, 1974 and 1977 Overseas Press Club Award; 1975 National Spelling Bee Champion.

Population: 432,973 (city); 1,300,000 (metro area), first in commonwealth.
Area: 47 sq. mi.
Industry: seat of Puerto Rico's tourism industry with 12 luxury hotels and more than 100 high rise condominiums. City is also the commercial and shipping hub of the island and the Caribbean and major stop for dozens of cruise ships. Major industries are electronics, pharmaceuticals, computers and computer equipment and banking services. Center of the island's rum industry with the Bacardi distillery, the largest in the world, on San Juan Bay. More than 80 per cent of all rum sold in the U.S. is Puerto Rican rum.
Transportation: San Juan International Airport (SJU) handles more than 6 million passengers a year with four major U.S. airlines and a dozen foreign lines; Isla Grande airport handles general aviation.
Education: seat of the Rio Piedras Campus of the Univ. Of Puerto Rico, the public university system, InterAmerican Univ., UPR Medical Sciences campus and UPR Law School, Sacred Heart Univ., World Univ. and several junior and regional colleges.
Cultural facilities and events: The Casals Festival, guided for 18 years by the late Maestro Casals, is an annual June event bringing together some of the world's finest musicians;

Pro-Arte Musical sponsors major concerts; Symphony Orchestra; two opera companies; two ballet companies; and several theater companies. A $10 million Center for Performing Arts; the Institute of Puerto Rican Culture; ancient Spanish forts in Old San Juan are Palacio de Santa Catalina (Governor's Mansion), San Felipe del Morro and San Cristobal; Pablo Casals Museum and art galleries and museums throughout Old San Juan.
Communications: 5 daily newspapers; 4 commercial television stations, 1 government-operated PBS TV network; cable TV and Home Box Office; 25 radio stations.
Sports: 25,000 seat Bithorn Stadium for Winter League baseball; 18,000-seat Sixto Escobar Track Stadium; 10,000-seat Roberto Clemente Coliseum; 20,000-seat El Comandante Race Track; several other sports facilities built for VIII Pan American Games which San Juan hosted in 1979.
Convention facilities: Condado Convention Center seats 5,000 for meetings, 3,000 for meals. Other convention facilities at various hotels.
New construction: several bank and office towers as well as high-rise condominiums.
History: discovered by Columbus on his 2d voyage (Nov. 19, 1493), colonized by Juan Ponce de Leon, Puerto Rico's first Spanish governor; ceded by Spain to U.S. in Treaty of Paris after Spanish-American War of 1898; since 1952 a commonwealth freely associated with the U.S., free market with U.S., common currency, common citizenship.
Further information: Chamber of Commerce, 100 Tetuan St., Old San Juan; Tourism Co. Banco de Santander Bldg., Old San Juan.

Santa Ana, California

See Orange County, California

Saskatoon, Saskatchewan, Canada

The World Almanac is sponsored in central and northern Saskatchewan by the Saskatoon Star-Phoenix, 204 Fifth Avenue North, Saskatoon, Sask. S7K 2P1; phone (306) 652-9200; Daily Star and Phoenix founded in 1906 and 1902 respectively, merged in 1928 into the Star-Phoenix; circulation 55,000; publisher, Michael C. Sifton; executive vice-president, James K. Struthers.

Population: 158,000, 2d in province; per capita income $10,508.
Area: 45.38 sq. mi. on the South Saskatchewan River in the central part of the province.
Industry: retail, wholesale, distribution hub for primary trading area of 250,000 and secondary area of 510,000; center of the provinces $2 billion plus mining industry, primary potash (1981, $1 billion), oil (1981 production 7.3 million cubic metres), uranium (1981 sales $250 million); other industries include agriculture (1981 cash receipts $3.8 billion), meat packing, construction, light manufacturing, and high technology electronics including fibre optics.
Commerce: 1981 retail sales totalled $876.5 million or $5,425 per capita (41% above national average); 10 year average unemployment rate varied from 3.5% to 8.5%; job opportunities grow at a rate of 3.5% to 4% per year.
Transportation: 4 scheduled airlines, 2 railways, 3 bus lines, several air charter services and numerous freight carriers; airport is the fastest growing in Canada and has international status with flights to the U.S.; Yellowhead highway is easiest access through Rockies from prairies to Pacific.
Communications: one daily newspaper, 2 local TV stations, cable TV with community channel and 4 U.S. stations; 8 radio stations, one farm weekly, one community weekly.
Medical facilities: 3 major hospitals with 1,231 beds; essential health care costs are covered by a government-run medicare program; University Hospital is a teaching hospital.
Educational facilities: Univ. of Saskatchewan, famed for agriculture, space, physics, medicine, veterinary colleges; Kelsey Institute of Applied Arts & Sciences, School for the Deaf, School for Retarded Children, French School.
Cultural facilities: Centennial Auditorium, multi-purpose theater (2,000 seats), convention center (1,800 seats); Western Development Museum houses North America's largest display of antique cars, farm implements, and 1910 Pioneer Village; Mendel Art Gallery; John Diefenbaker Centre, Saskatoon Symphony Orchestra; 4 theater cos.
Recreation: 2,494 acres of parkland, wild animal farm, 5 golf courses, 5 swimming pools, 5 indoor ice rinks, man-made ski mountain, skeet range; variety of resort areas are within easy driving distance.
History: founded 1882 as a Temperance colony, incorporated 1906; named after Saskatoon berry found on banks of river; close to battle sites of the Riel rebellion of 1885.
Further information: Board of Trade, 308 24th Street East, Saskatoon, Sask. S7K 4R2.

Savannah, Georgia

The World Almanac is sponsored in the Savannah area by the Savannah News-Press, 111 West Bay Street, Savannah GA 31402; phone (912) 236-9511; publisher of the Savannah Morning News and Evening Press; combined circulation 77,030 daily, 72,961 Sunday; Donald E. Harwood, general manager; Wallace M. Davis Jr., executive editor; Gene Stewart, advertising director.

Population: 141,634 (city), 225,581 (SMSA); SMSA civilian labor force 99,706.
Area: 57 sq. mi. on Savannah River, 18 mi. from Atlantic Ocean; Chatham County seat.
Industry: world's largest pulp-to-paper container plant owned by Union Camp Corp.; Savannah Sugar Refining Corp., nation's 3d largest seller; jet aircraft manufacturer (Gulf Stream American Aviation Corp.); tea packaging (Tetley); fertilizer materials, ship repair, titanium dioxide production (American Cyanamid).
Commerce: hub of "Coastal Empire" economic center of Ga. and 3 S. Carolina counties; the Southeast's leading foreign trade port between Baltimore and New Orleans; served by 97 steamship lines, 36 deep water terminals; retail sales (1980) $1.3 billion; 7 commercial banks, 42 branches; 4 savings and loan assns, 12 branches.
Transportation: 4 rail freight lines, Seaboard Coastline, Southern, Central of Georgia, and Savannah-Atlanta; Amtrak; Greyhound and Trailways bus lines, 74 truck lines; Delta, Eastern, Dolphin Airways; intercoastal waterway.
Communications: Savannah News-Press, Inc. (daily and Sunday), 4 weekly papers; 4 TV and 14 radio stations.
New construction: Ga. Port Authority's port expansion; Mulberry Inn, Days Inn, Oglethorpe Mall expansion.
Medical facilities: 4 hospitals, Medical Arts Center.
Federal facilities: U. S. Customs House, Ft. Stewart/Hunter assigned the 24th Infantry Division, 19,367 troops, 280,000 acres, 35 mi. so. of city.
Cultural facilities: Savannah Art Assn., Savannah Symphony, Ballet Guild, Little Theatre, Telfair Academy of Arts and Sciences, Kennedy Fine Arts Center, SSC; Fine Arts Bldg., ASC; Maritime Museum, Fort Pulaski National Monument and Military Museum, Civic Center.
Education: Armstrong St. and Savannah St. colleges, units of the Univ. System of Georgia; Savannah Col. of Art & Design; 60 public, 3 vocational-tech, 18 parochial, 10 private, 3 business schools; Skidaway Inst. of Oceanography.
Recreation: 18 theaters; 7 golf courses, 33 tennis courts; 71 squares, parks, playgrounds; 3 sports fields; 2 recreation centers; 2 stadiums; 4 fishing piers, 12 boat ramps.
Convention facilities: 8,000 seat auditorium at Civic Center.
Sports: Braves Southern League baseball; Savannah Speed-

way; SSC Tigers, ASC Pirates.
Annual events: St. Patrick's Day Parade, Oktober Festival, Blessing of the Fleet, Night in Olde Savannah, Arts Festival, Farmer's Market, Christmas Parade, Garden Club Show.
Other attractions: Savannah Science, Ships of the Sea, and Antique Car museums; Fort Jackson, Fort Pulaski, Fort Screven and Tybee Museum, Fort McAllister; downtown historic section; river cruises.
History: mother city of Ga.; Gen. James Oglethorpe and 120 followers settled last of 13 original colonies here; site of Revolutionary War battle, end of Gen. Sherman's Civil War "March to the Sea"; much of the old city is a national historic landmark, largest in the country.
Birthplace of: Conrad Aiken, Charles Coburn, John C. Fremont, Stacy Keach, Johnny Mercer, Flannery O'Connor.
Further information: Savannah Area Chamber of Commerce, Savannah Visitors Center, 301 W. Broad Street, Savannah, GA 31402; phone (912) 233-3069.

Seattle, Washington

Population: (1982 est.) 492,000 (city), 1,667,800 (SMSA); first in state; total employed (metro) 774,300.
Area: 91.6 sq. mi. between Puget Sound and Lake Washington; King County seat.
Industry: headquarters for Boeing, 70,395 employees, world's largest manufacturer of commercial jet aircraft; Port of Seattle; Seattle-Tacoma airport; nation's 2d largest containerized-shipping seaport; 42,360 employer units; transport products, retail trade, insurance, banking, shipbuilding, forest products, agricultural goods and tourism.
Commerce: business center for western Wash. and Alaska; major import-export center for Far East; total taxable retail sales (1981) $4.51 billion; per capita income (1980) $9,300; EBI (1981) $18,904; 41 commercial and savings banks with 310 branches.
Transportation: 3 transcontinental railroads, Amtrak; International Airport served by 27 scheduled airlines, 5 commuter airlines, handled 9.1 million passengers (1981); ferries serve Puget Sound, Canada, and Alaska.
Communications: 5 daily newspapers in metro area; 7 TV, 23 AM and 19 FM stations.
New construction: $387.7 mil. tot. building permit value (1981).
Medical facilities: 27 hospitals, including Univ. of Wash. Health Sciences Center, Northwest Kidney Center, and Fred Hutchinson Cancer Research Center.
Educational facilities: Four 4-year colleges: Univ. of Wash., Seattle Univ., Univ. of Puget Sound, Pac. Lutheran Univ. and Seattle Pacific Univ.; 11 community colleges.
Federal facilities: 13th Naval Dist. Hdqts.; Pacific Marine center, National Oceanic & Atmospheric Admin.; 13th Coast Guard Dist. Hdqts.; many regional offices, 37-story federal office bldg.
Cultural facilities: symphony orchestra, opera association, art museum and 10 other museums, 92 art galleries, 6 professional theater companies.
Recreation: major boating center; salmon and trout fishing; several nearby ski areas; Mt. Rainier, North Cascades, and Olympic National parks within 2-hour drive.
Sports: Kingdome, concrete-dome stadium, home of NFL Seahawks, AL Mariners, NBA SuperSonics and NASL Sounders.
Other attractions: Seattle Center, site of 1962 world's fair, has 14,000-seat coliseum, 3,100-seat opera house, playhouse, arena, Space Needle, and Pacific Science Center; Seattle Aquarium, Woodland Park Zoo.
History: settled 1851, named for an Indian chief who befriended the settlers; virtually destroyed by fire in 1889, quickly rebuilt; Alaska Gold Rush of 1897 spurred growth of Seattle to its status as the Northwest's principal city.
Birthplace of: Max Brand, Carol Channing, Judy Collins, Jimi Hendrix, Gypsy Rose Lee, Mary McCarthy, Minoru Yamasaki.
Further information: Chamber of Commerce, 215 Columbia Street, Seattle, WA 98104, or Convention and Visitors Bureau, 1815 7th Avenue, 98101.

Sioux Falls, South Dakota

The World Almanac is sponsored in the Sioux Falls area by the Argus Leader, 200 S. Minnesota Avenue, Sioux Falls, SD 57102; phone (605) 331-2200, a Gannett newspaper; founded in 1881; circulation 43,694 daily (A.M.), 54,275 Sunday; publisher and president Larry Fuller.

Population: 81,182 (city), 109,432 (metro); largest in state.
Area: 36 sq. mi. in southeastern South Dakota, located at junction of interstates 29 and 90; Minnehaha County seat.
Industry and Commerce: Sioux Falls stockyards are largest in the U.S.; John Morrell & Co. is the largest employer with 3,200 employees; there are 7 commercial banks, 5 savings and loan assns.; wholesale and retail center for South Dakota, parts of Minnesota and Iowa; yearly retail sales over $6.69 million.
Transportation: served by 5 major highways, 4 bus lines, and 3 rail lines; Joe Foss Field with modern terminal is within 2 miles of business district and has 3 major airlines.
Communication: daily and weekly newspaper, 3 TV and 10 radio stations; state headquarters for Northwestern Bell Telephone Co.
Medical facilities: 4 hospitals with over 1,040 beds, including the Royal C. Johnson Memorial Hospital for war veterans and Crippled Children's Hospital and School.
Federal facilities: Earth Resources Observation Systems Data Center of the U.S. Dept. of Interior.
Cultural and Educational facilities: public library, convention center, Civic Fine Arts Assn., Sioux Falls Symphony, Community Playhouse, Augustana College, Sioux Falls College, North American Baptist Seminary, the SD School for the Deaf, vocational school, 2 business schools, 2 nurses training schools, 28 public and 9 parochial schools; 96 churches.
Recreation: 52 parks, 4 swimming pools, 3 municipal golf courses, Great Plains Zoo, 10,000-seat Arena, 4,000-seat Coliseum, Packer Stadium.
Further information: Chamber of Commerce, 127 E. 10th Street, Sioux Falls, SD 57101.

Spokane, Washington

The World Almanac is sponsored in the Spokane area by the Spokane Daily Chronicle, P.O. Box 2168, Spokane, WA 99210; phone (509) 455-6933; founded 1881; circulation 58,028 evening, Mon.-Sat.; published by Cowles Publishing Co., William H. Cowles, 3rd, president; Donald Gormley, general manager; E. Curtiss Pierson, managing editor.

Population: 171,300 (city), 352,700 (county); 2d in state; total employed 135,400.
Area: 52.12 sq. mi. centrally located in eastern Washington, 18 miles from the Idaho border, 110 miles south of Canadian border; Spokane County seat.
Industry: heavily based on service industries and wholesale and retail trade with 447 manufacturing establishments; 2,541 retail, 730 wholesale, and 2,965 establishments dealing with services; annual payrolls in Spokane County $1.583 billion; effective buying income (1981) for Spokane County $3.1 billion; Kaiser Aluminum and Chemical Corp. has 2 plants, a reduction plant and a rolling mill; area industries include forest products, silver, lead, zinc, and other mining; agriculture, poultry, dairy and meat products, flour and cereals, livestock, processed foods; commercial truck trailer bodies, electrical fixtures, electronic keyboard manufacturing, and plastic products.
Commerce: retail, transportation, and medical center of an

80,000 sq. mi. inland market in eastern Washington, northern Idaho, and western Montana, known as the Inland Empire with a population of more than 1.4 million; retail sales in the Inland Empire $5.9 billion, metro area $1.6 billion; 8 commercial banks, 2 mutual savings banks, and 5 savings and loan associations.
Transportation: 3 transcontinental railroads, Amtrak; public bus system; International Airport served by 5 major airlines and 2 commuter airlines; 2 airways for small aircraft; 25 motor freight lines.
Communications: 2 daily newspapers; 3 commercial, one public, cable, TV; 11 AM, 10 FM radio stations; 1 magazine; 2 weekly newspapers.
Convention facilities: Riverpark Center, legacy of Expo '74, 2,700 seat opera house and 40,000 sq. ft. convention center; Spokane Coliseum capacity 8,000 with 45,000 sq. ft. exhibit space; hotels and motels have 3,000 guest rooms.
Medical facilities: 6 major hospitals, 7 specialized hospitals, and Fairchild AFB hospital; one of the highest ratios of private physicians to population in nation.
Education facilities: one college, 2 universities, and 2 community colleges; 50 elementary, 3 special schools (handicap), 17 junior high schools and senior high schools.
Federal facilities: Fairchild AFB, federal office bldg.
Cultural facilities: symphony orchestra, opera house, 2 museums, Civic Theater, arboretum, Walk in the Wild Zoo, Pacific Northwest Indian Center; community concerts, music and allied arts festival, Spokane Interplayers Ensemble.
Recreation: 76 lakes within a 50-mile radius of the city; 12 indoor and 8 outdoor theaters; 11 city swimming pools, 55 public tennis courts, 12 golf courses, 99 public parks, 12 national parks and 15 national forests within a day's drive; 4 snow ski resorts within a 2 hour drive; power and sail boating, hunting, and fishing.
Sports: Spokane Indians, farm club for California Angels; 35,000 seat Albi football stadium; Playfair horse race track; 8,000 seat Spokane Coliseum for basketball, hockey, and boxing; Chiefs Senior Hockey Club.
Other attractions: city-center Riverfront Park, site of Expo '74 World's Fair, includes IMAX theater, ice rink, children's zoo, gondola ride over river falls, antique carousel, train ride, outdoor amphitheaters; average annual rainfall 17.19 inches.
History: Lewis and Clark expedition of 1804-06 through area; first permanent settlers in 1871 attracted to river and falls where they built a house and a sawmill; 2 sq. mi. city of 1,000 people inc. 1881 as Spokan Falls; after Washington gained statehood in 1889, city name changed to Spokane.
Further information: Spokane Area Chamber of Commerce, P.O. Box 2147, Spokane, WA 99210.

Springfield, Illinois

The World Almanac is sponsored in the Springfield area by The State Journal-Register (morn. and eve.), oldest newspaper in Illinois, 330 South Ninth Street, P.O. Box 219, Springfield, IL 62705, phone (217) 788-1300; circulation 72,477 (Sunday); John P. Clarke, publisher; Edward H. Armstrong, editor; Patrick Coburn, managing editor.

Population: 100,100 (city), 186,104 (SMSA), 4th in state; total employed (annual average) 91,136.
Area: 46.86 square miles on Sangamon River in center of state; state capital and Sangamon County seat.
Commerce: state and federal offices; 11 banks, 8 savings and loan associations, 10 insurance company home offices; 154 national, regional, and state associations; 30 civic clubs, 74 social service organizations; 41 women's organizations; annual retail sales $780 million.
Transportation: 5 railroads, 69 truck carriers, one airport, nearby barge facilities.
Communications: 2 TV stations, 8 radio stations.
Medical facilities: 3 hospitals with 1,629 beds; 358 doctors, 97 dentists, 17 chiropractors, 36 clinics, 29 licensed nursing homes, the Springfield Regional Trauma Center.
Cultural facilities: municipal band, opera, symphony, chorus, Theatre Guild, state museum, Lincoln historical sites, New Salem State Park, Old State Capitol, art associations, summer theater, Springfield Ballet Company, Illinois Country Opry, Clayville renovated stagecoach stop, arts and crafts festivals, Oliver Parks Telephone Museum, Lincoln Library, Lincoln Memorial Garden, Nelson Recreation Center, Henson Robinson Zoo, Sangamon State University Auditorium, Prairie Capital Convention Center, community arts council.
Education: Lincoln Land Community College, Sangamon State University, Springfield College in Illinois, Southern Illinois University School of Medicine, Capital Area Vocational School.
Recreation: 40 parks, swimming, boating, Lake Springfield, 4 golf courses, tennis courts, 2,410 acres in parks.
Special events: Illinois State Fair, Old Capitol Art Fair, International Carillon Festival, Midwest Charity Horse Show, LPGA Rail Golf Classic, Springfield Cardinals baseball, Springfield Kings hockey, Ethnic Festival, Autumnfest, Photo Fair, Old Capitol Sound and Light Show, Lincoln-Fest, NCAA Division II Soccer Tournament.
Birthplace of: Vachel Lindsay, Charles Post.
Further information: Greater Springfield Chamber of Commerce, 3 Old State Capitol Plaza, Springfield, IL.

Springfield, Massachusetts

The World Almanac is sponsored in the Springfield area by The Morning Union, the evening Daily News and The Sunday Republican, 1860 Main Street, Springfield, MA 01103, phone (413) 788-1000; Union founded 1864, Daily News 1880, Republican 1824; circulation, Union 72,415, Daily News 75,559, Republican 142,383; publisher David Starr, Union-Republican editor Arnold S. Friedman, Daily News editor Richard C. Garvey.

Population: 152,319 (city), 530,373 (SMSA); 2d in state, 76,081 employed in city.
Area: 33.1 sq. mi. in SW part of state; I-91 and I-90 cross near city; Hampden County seat.
Industry: 231 manufacturing plants produce boxes, children's games, wallets, handguns, plastics, envelopes, hair shampoo, chemicals, paper; among major employers: Monsanto, Milton Bradley, Smith & Wesson, Breck.
Commerce: metro retail sales $1.88 billion; avg. household spendable income $14,703; Mass. Mutual Life Ins. Co. is one of the largest in U.S.; Baystate West, a combined high-rise shopping mall, office-hotel complex.
Transportation: Amtrak, 2 rail lines, 5 bus lines; Bradley International Airport (Hartford-Springfield) 18 miles south; major truck depot.
Communications: 3 TV, 9 radio stations.
Medical facilities: 6 major hospital complexes.
Educational facilities: 21 accredited colleges and universities include Amherst, American International, Hampshire, Mount Holyoke, Univ. of Massachusetts, Our Lady of the Elms, Smith, Springfield, Western New England (and Law School), Williams, Westfield State, North Adams State, Holyoke and Greenfield community colleges, Springfield Technical Community College.
Cultural facilities: State West Theater, Civic Center and Symphony Hall, quadrangle complex; 2 museums of art, library, natural history museum including planetarium; 145 churches and 7 synagogues; 155 parks; Eastern States Exposition, Tanglewood Music Festival.
Sports: Indians (AHL) hockey; Holyoke Millers baseball; Basketball Hall of Fame; Tip-Off Tourney opens college basketball season in U.S.
History: founded 1636 by William Pynchon; first U.S. musket developed at city's armory (now a U.S. landmark) 1795.
Birthplace of: Creighton Abrams, Chester Bowles, Theodor "Dr. Seuss" Geisel, Lawrence O'Brien, Eleanor Powell.
Further information: Chamber of Commerce, 1500 Main Street, Springfield, MA 01103.

Stockton, California

The World Almanac is sponsored in the San Joaquin County area by the Stockton Record (eves. and Saturday and Sunday mornings), 530 E. Market Street, Stockton, CA 95202; phone (209) 943-6397; founded in 1895; circulation 57,140 daily, 56,342 Sunday; president and publisher Robert P. Uecker, executive editor Philip Bookman, managing editor James S. Hushaw.

Population: 149,779 city, 347,342 county; total county employment 141,200 to 167,200 in 1981.
Area: 1,440 sq. mi. county, 35.13 sq. mi. city; located 80 mi. east of San Francisco; San Joaquin County seat.
Industry: agriculture, $165 million countywide in 1981; food processing, light manufacturing, Port of Stockton, Sharpe Army Depot, Rough and Ready Island Naval Station.
Commerce: $1.0 billion taxable retail sales city, $1.9 billion county wide in 1981.
New construction: $75 million (city) in 1981
Medical facilities: San Joaquin General Hospital, Dameron, St. Joseph's, Oak Park Community, Stockton State (for mental and physically disabled).
Cultural facilities: 110 churches, Univ. of the Pacific (private), Delta College (2-year public), Humphreys College (private); Pioneer Museum and Haggin Galleries, city/-county library, Stockton Civic Theater, Stockton Symphony, ballet troupe, 3 dinner theaters, Stockton Civic Auditorium.
Recreation: city-operated programs include softball leagues, soccer, 3 public golf courses, several private clubs offering golf, tennis, swimming, racquetball, boating facilities; access to 1,000 miles of San Joaquin-Sacramento River Delta waterways.
Convention facilities: Stockton Civic Auditorium, Hilton Hotel, Holiday Inn
History: founded 1844 by Capt. Charles M. Weber and inc. 1850; San Joaquin County established 1850; city was major transshipment point between San Francisco and the Central Sierra mines during Gold Rush era; most early commerce and industry centered around servicing mining activities.
Birthplace of: Brian Goodell.
Further information: Greater Stockton Chamber of Commerce, 1105 N. El Dorado Street, Stockton, CA 95202; phone (209) 466-7066.

Syracuse, New York

The World Almanac is sponsored in the Syracuse area by the Herald-Journal, Clinton Square, P.O. Box 4915, Syracuse, NY, 13221; phone (315) 470-0011; founded Jan. 15, 1877, by Arthur Jenkins; circulation 112,194 daily, 232,703 Sunday Herald-American Post Standard; president Stephen Rogers, editor and publisher Stephen A. Rogers, editor William D. Cotter; sponsors Christmas toy fund.

Population: 170,105 (city), 642,547 (SMSA), (metro), 6th in state; 280,100 employed.
Area: 25.82 sq. mi. near center of state; interstate routes 90 and 81 intersect at Syracuse.
Industry: some 500 manufacturing plants produce electrical and non-electrical machinery, primary metals, food, transportation equipment, chemicals, pharmaceuticals, paper, candles, china; Schlitz brewery, world's largest ever built at one time, located in suburban Lysander; Miller brewery north of city; major employers: General Electric, Carrier Corp., Crucible Steel, Crouse-Hinds, Allied Industries.
Commerce: retail sales (1981 est.) $2.7 billion; average household spendable income (1981 est.) $22,500.
Transportation: 2 rail freight lines, Amtrak; 3 bus lines, 164 truck lines; 10 airlines.
Communications: 4 TV, 16 radio stations.
Medical facilities: 4 major hospital complexes.
Cultural facilities: Syracuse Univ., State Univ. College of Environmental Science and Forestry, and Le Moyne, Maria Regina, and Onondaga Community colleges; Everson Museum of Art; symphony; $22 million county center.
Sports: Syracuse Univ. football at new 52,000-seat Carrier dome; Chiefs (baseball).
History: first explored 1615 by French; salt deposits led to area development, known as "Salt City;" "crossroads" since Indian days; became city 1847.
Birthplace of: Theodore Hesburgh, Rod Serling, Lee Shubert, Jimmy Van Heusen.
Further information: Chamber of Commerce, One MONY Plaza, Syracuse, NY 13202.

Tacoma, Washington

The World Almanac is sponsored in the Tacoma area by the Tacoma News Tribune, 1950 South State St., P.O. Box 11000, Tacoma, WA 98411; phone (206) 597-8511; founded in 1907; circulation 106,730 daily, 112,076 Sunday; publisher Elbert H. Baker, II, president and general manager William G. Robinson.

Population: 160,100 (city), 504,500 (SMSA); 2nd in state; total employed 159,800.
Area: 47.66 sq. miles, located in W. Washington between Puget Sound and the Cascades; Pierce County seat.
Industry: wood and paper products, metal and chemical plants. Other major employers: military; federal, state and local government; boat building; services; Boeing; Weyerhaeuser; agriculture also prominent. Largest port in Washington State.
Commerce: total retail sales (1981) $2.07 billion, median household income (1981) $20,669.
Transportation: two transcontinental railway lines; belt-line railway; Seattle-Tacoma Intl. Airport; Tacoma Industrial Airport; tug and barge; steamship.
Communications: 1 daily newspaper; 2 local TV, 3 network TV, 1 public TV; cable TV; 28 AM and 25 FM stations.
New construction: downtown district under renovation; cultural, historical and hotel construction under way.
Medical facilities: 9 hospitals.
Education facilities: two 4-year colleges: Pacific Lutheran University and University of Puget Sound, Law School; 2 community colleges; 2 voc.-tech. schools.
Federal facilities: 4th largest Army base: Fort Lewis Army Base; McChord AFB; U.S. Geodetic Survey Facility.
Cultural facilities: Symphony; Washington State Historical Museum; professional theaters; Tacoma opera; Cultural Center; Philharmonic; Tacoma Art Museum.
Recreation: boating and sailing among islands of southern Puget Sound; skiing; fishing; camping; hiking; climbing.
Sports: Tacoma Twins baseball; Tacoma Dome-largest wood-domed structure in the world.
Other attractions: Mt. Rainier, 2nd highest peak in continental U.S.; Nisqually Wildlife Area; Pt. Defiance Park and Zoo; Northwest Trek Wildlife Preserve.
Further information: Chamber of Commerce, P.O. Box 1933, Tacoma, WA 98401.

Tallahassee, Florida

The World Almanac is sponsored in the north Florida-south Georgia Panhandle area by The Tallahassee Democrat, 227 N. Magnolia Drive, Tallahassee, FL 32302; phone (904) 599-2100; founded 1905; circulation 51,900 (morn), 62,100 Sunday; member Knight-Ridder Newspapers, Inc., J. Carrol Dadisman, president and publisher; Walker Lundy, vice president and executive editor.

Population: 81,548 (city) 157,076 (SMSA); total employment 73,500 (city); 79,700 (SMSA).
Area: 26.14 sq. mi. between Gulf of Mexico and Georgia line; state capital and Leon County seat.
Commerce: 41% of economic base is state and local government; small manufacturers 4.0%; agriculture only 0.7% of economic base; retail-wholesale center serving 17 county area; 3 shopping malls and 23 shopping centers; retail sales (1980 Leon County) $707 million; effective buying income per household $20,831; 13 commercial banks (resources, $543 million) and 5 savings & loan (resources 3.5 billion).
Transportation: 3 major airlines, 4 commuter flight services, one railroad, 10 motor carriers.
Communications: 13 radio, 2 local TV stations, one local educational TV station.
Educational facilities: Florida State Univ., Florida A & M Univ., Tallahassee Community College, Lively Area Vocational Tech School.
Convention facilities: Tallahassee-Leon County Civic Center, a 300,000 sq. ft. complex opened in 1981; Florida State Conference Center, 32,000 sq. ft., open Jan. 1983.
Medical facilities: Tallahassee Memorial Regional Medical Center, Capital Medical Center, Sunland Center (HRS), Ambulatory Centre of Tallahassee.
Recreational facilities: 6 recreation centers, 11 playgrounds, 75 ball fields, 30 tennis courts; salt water fishing in Gulf of Mexico; bass fishing in Lake Jackson; deer, dove, quail, duck, geese hunting; 4 golf courses, PGA Tallahassee Open Invitational.
Other attractions: college athletic events at Florida State Univ. and Florida A & M; symphony, ballet, repertory theater, opera, touring plays, and art exhibits; 1845 historic capital and 22-story capital tower; Apalachicola National Forest; Junior Museum; Wakulla Springs, Maclay Gardens State Park, LeMoyne Art Gallery, Natural Bridge State Historic Memorial, Florida State Univ. "Flying High" Circus.
History: est. as state capital 1823; Tallahassee means "old town" or "deserted fields" in Creek; area prospered with large plantations and antebellum mansions, many still standing.
Further information: Chamber of Commerce, P.O. Box 1639, Tallahassee, FL 32302; phone (904) 224-8116.

Tampa, Florida

The World Almanac is sponsored in the Tampa Bay area by The Tampa Tribune and The Tampa Times, 202 S. Parker Street, Tampa, FL 33606; phone (813) 272-7711; Times founded in 1893, Tribune 1894; combined circulation 211,305; R.F. Pittman, Jr., publisher; J.F. Urbanski, vice president/general manager; J. Clendinen, chairman of editorial board; P. Hogan, Tribune managing editor; B. Witwer, Times managing editor.

Population: 272,700 (city), 1,605,000 (SMSA); total employed in county 279,000 (civilian, non-agricultural).
Area: 84.45 sq.mi. (city) 1,062.0 sq.mi. (county) on Gulf of Mexico, halfway between the northern edge and southern tip of Florida; Hillsborough County seat.
Industry: Port of Tampa is the closest U.S. deepwater port to the Panama Canal and among the largest in the nation: total tonnage for 1981 reached 45 million; principal export cargo is phosphate; Bone Valley Formation, 30% of world's phosphate production; cigar manufacturing; strong shrimp industry, Singleton; beer breweries (Anheuser-Busch and Joseph Schlitz); Florida Steel Corp.; other industries include Jim Walter Corp.; General Telephone; Florida Mining & Materials; Lykes Brothers; Critikon Corp. (a division of Johnson & Johnson); American Shipbuilding; Badger American (Raytheon); General Electric; General Mills; Honeywell; Reynolds Metals; and Shrine of North America.
Commerce: (1980) county retail sales $3.3 billion; 28 banks with total deposits (1981) of $2.6 billion; 6 savings and loans (1981) $1.6 billion.
Transportation: 5 bus lines, 2 railroads, Seaboard Coast Line and Amtrak; 46 trucking lines; junction of I-75 and I-4; Tampa International Airport, 7.1 million passengers in 1981; 17 major airlines; 10 regional airlines; Port of Tampa, 140 steamship lines.
Convention facilities: Curtis Hixon Hall, 7,400 capacity main hall plus 10 other rooms; Tampa hotels and motels have over 11,000 guest rooms and over 125 meeting/banquet rooms with seating from 25 to 1,000.
New construction: Tampa City Center, Westbank, Metropolitan Tower, Paragon Plaza Phase II, Saturn Condominium Project, Landmark Hotel, Tampa International Airport expansion, Busch Gardens expansion, Austin Center, Hyde Park—AMLEA Project, Kings Point Development, One Laurel Place Condominium, Monte Carlo Condominium, Atrium Condominium, Harbour Island Project, Tampa Sports Authority Complex, University of Tampa Sports Center, Tampa General Hospital expansion, Tampa Corporate Center, Hilton Hotel, Hyatt Regency Hotel, Critikon Headquarters (a division of Johnson & Johnson), harbor dredging and extension of Crosstown Expressway. Total of $665.6 million construction underway.
Medical facilities: 7 major hospitals.
Cultural facilities: Florida Gulf Coast Symphony; The Tampa Museum; Tampa Theater; Tampa Ballet Company; Hillsborough County Museum of Science and Industry; community theater; Gasparilla Art Fair.
Education: University of South Florida; University of Tampa; Florida College, Tampa College, Hillsborough Community College.
Other attractions: Busch Gardens; Adventure Island water theme park, Lowry Park Zoo; Ybor City (Latin Quarter); annual Gasparilla Pirate Invasion; 87 parks; 31 recreation areas, site of Florida State Fair.
Sports: NFL Tampa Bay Buccaneers with 71,500 seat stadium; NASL (Soccer) Tampa Bay Rowdies, Tampa Tarpons (farm team for Cincinnati Reds); Cincinnati Reds spring training site; thoroughbred horse racing at Tampa Bay Downs; greyhound racing, jai-alai.
History: Fort Brooke est. 1824 on site of present Tampa; inc. 1885.
Birthplace of: Cannonball Adderley, Steve Garvey, Butterfly McQueen, Lou Piniella, Mel Tillis.
Further information: Greater Tampa Chamber of Commerce, 801 E. Kennedy Boulevard, Tampa, FL 33602; phone (813) 228-7777.

Toledo, Ohio

The World Almanac is sponsored in the Toledo area by The Blade, 541 Superior Street, Toledo, OH 43660; phone (419) 245-6000; founded 1835; circulation 166,859 daily, 211,117 Sunday; publishers Paul Block Jr. and William Block; assistant to the publishers William Day; editor Bernard Judy; executive editor Albert Cross; managing editor Joseph O'Conor.

Population: 354,635 (city), 791,137 (SMSA); total employed 288,800.
Area: 85.3 sq. mi. at juncture of Maumee River and Lake Erie in northwestern Ohio; Lucas County seat.
Industry: glass, headquarters for Owens-Illinois, Owens Corning & Libbey-Owens-Ford; automotive parts, largest producer in nation, home of Amer. Motors Jeep, Toledo Scale, and Schindler Haughton Elevator; one of the largest petroleum refining centers between Chicago and the East Coast.
Commerce: Port of Toledo is one of the prime bulk shipping ports on the Great Lakes, handling vast quantities of grain, coal, iron ore, and petroleum products; ranks 3d on Great Lakes and 20th in U.S.; total retail sales $3.60 billion; spendable income per household $26,400.
Transportation: 7 railroads, 9 major airlines, 100 motor freight lines, 2 interstate bus lines; 13 major highways converge here, permitting the rapid flow of goods to almost 60%

of the nation's consumers.
New construction: $94 million Owens-Illinois world headquarters, $10 million Toledo Trust Co. office bldg.
Communications: 4 TV, 13 radio stations and one cablevision company.
Medical facilities: 10 major hospital complexes, including the Medical College of Ohio Hospital.
Cultural facilities: Museum of Art with largest display of antique glass in the world; Peristyle used for the performing arts; symphony, opera company.
Education: Univ. of Toledo and its Community and Technical College; Michael J. Owens Technical College; Bowling Green State Univ.; Monroe Community College.
Other attractions: Municipal Zoo among top 10 in the nation; modern 2,500 seat Masonic Auditorium, Great Hall.
Sports: Mud Hens, farm club of the Minnesota Twins, at the Lucas County Recreation Center.
History: founded in 1837; took its name from sister city, Toledo, Spain.
Birthplace of: Gloria Steinem, Art Tatum.
Further information: Convention and Vistors Bureau, 218 Huron, Toledo, OH 43604.

Toronto, Ontario, Canada

The World Almanac is sponsored in the metropolitan Toronto area by The Toronto Star, One Yonge Street, Toronto, Ontario, M5E 1E6; phone (416) 367-2000; established 1892, Joseph E. Atkinson, publisher, 1899-1948; circulation daily 484,856, Saturday, 801,492, Sunday, 434,915; chairman and publisher Beland H. Honderich; executive vice-president David Jolley; editor-in-chief, George Radwanski. Canada's largest newspaper in circulation, display and classified advertising lineage; winner of 47 national newspaper awards and sponsor of the Santa Claus Fund and Fresh Air fund.

Population: 592,746 (city), 2,120,271 (metro); largest city in Canada, 9th in North America; labor force 1.8 million.
Area: 241 sq. mi. on northwest shore of Lake Ontario; provincial capital.
Industry: Canada's leading commercial and industrial center; 6,300 manufacturing establishments; principal industries: slaughtering and meat packing, clothing, printing and publishing, machinery, electrical goods, furniture, food products, rubber goods, sheet metal products.
Commerce: retail sales (1981) $12.7 billion; headquarters for Eaton's and Simpson's, Canada's largest department stores; head offices of 24 trust companies and 12 federally chartered banks, including 57 foreign bank subsidiaries; Toronto Stock Exchange, 3d in N.A., traded shares worth $25 billion 1981; per cap disposable income $10,614.
Transportation: Transit Commission carries 392 million passengers annually on 764 miles of routes including 34 miles of subway; 2.2 million tons of cargo unloaded from 142 ships (1981) at this major Great Lakes port; 54 airlines handle 14.8 million passengers annually at International Airport.
Communications: 7 TV stations including educational and French-language channels; 10 AM and 8 FM radio stations; 3 daily newspapers, 42 foreign language newspapers.
New construction: value of building permits (1981) $1.1 billion; $54-million expansion-renovation of Royal Ontario Museum; $74-million convention center will seat 10,000; $80-million downtown housing-commercial development.
Medical facilities: 40 active-treatment hospitals including renowned Hospital for Sick Children; special treatment centers: Clark Institute for Psychiatry, Addiction Research Centre, Ontario Crippled Children's Centre, Ontario Centre for the Deaf.
Cultural facilities: 69 alternate and cabaret theater groups, including Canada's largest children's theater; National Ballet of Canada and Canadian Opera Company perform in 3,200-seat O'Keefe Centre; symphony orchestra and Mendelssohn Choir at 2,700-seat Roy Thomson Hall, opened September 1982; touring shows at Royal Alexandra Theatre; 83 public libraries, Henry Moore collection of sculptures and drawings in Art Gallery of Ontario.
Education: York and Toronto Univs.; Ryerson Polytechnical Inst., 4 cols. of applied arts and tech., 2 teachers' cols., Royal Conservatory of Music, Ontario Col. of Art, Osgoode Hall Law School.
Recreation: Canadian National Exhibition, world's biggest annual fair; Ontario Place, 100 acres of offshore islands with restaurants, marina, and 1,000-seat Cinesphere for film showings; Toronto Islands have 3 yacht clubs, 560 acres of beaches and picnic grounds; Harborfront, 86-acre sports, arts, and entertainment park.
Convention facilities: Canada's top convention center; 277,188 visitors attended 636 conventions in 1981 and spent $120 million; total rooms, 19,000.
Sports: 10 public golf courses; thoroughbred and harness racing; NHL Maple Leafs play in 16,435-seat Gardens; Blue Jays AL baseball, Argonauts CFL football and Blizzard NASL soccer play in 54,000-seat Exhibition Stadium.
Other attractions: Ontario Science Centre, designed for participation and involvement; Black Creek Pioneer Village, living displays of Upper Canada; McMichael collection of paintings by Canada's famed Group of Seven; Metro Zoo has 500 species roaming 5 continental areas covering 700 acres; Canada's Wonderland, 400-acre amusement park; CN Tower, world's tallest free-standing structure; Eaton Centre downtown galleria contains 300 shops.
History: town of York founded 1793 on site of French fort as capital of British colony of Upper Canada; incorporated as city 1834 and named Toronto from Indian word for meeting place.
Birthplace of: Walter Huston, Beatrice Lillie, Raymond Massey, Brad Park, Lester Pearson, Mary Pickford, Christopher Plummer, Morley Safer.
Further information: Convention and Visitors Association, Toronto Eaton Centre, Toronto, Ontario M5B 2H1.

Tucson, Arizona

The World Almanac is sponsored in the Tucson area by The Arizona Daily Star, 4850 S. Park Avenue, PO Box 26807, Tucson, AZ 85726; phone (602) 294-4433; founded 1877 as a weekly; Michael E. Pulitzer, editor and publisher; Frank E. Johnson, executive managing editor; Stephen E. Auslander, editorial page editor, Frank Delehanty, business manager; Thomas J. Foust, director, special services; Star sponsors Sportsmen's Fund for less-chance youngsters.

Population: 354,400 est. (city), 567,900 est. (county) 191,100 employed in county out of total civilian labor force of 218,000.
Area: Sonoran Desert of southern Arizona, elev. 2,500 ft.; Santa Catalina Mts. immediately N and E reach 9,000 ft.; Pima County seat; 60 miles from Mexico.
Industry: Hughes Aircraft, IBM, Gates Learjet, Davis Monthan AFB, aircraft reclamation plants handling surplus craft from DM AFB; electronics, light manufacturing, tourism; center of the "copper circle"—Anaconda, Duval, American Smelting and Refining, Kennecott, Magma, Pima, and other mining operations.
Transportation: International Airport served by most major airlines, with Cochise Airlines within Arizona, and AeroMexico to and from Mexico; 3 smaller airports; 2 national, one local bus line; Southern Pacific Railroad; trucks.
Communications: 2 newspapers; 5 TV and 18 radio stations.
Medical facilities: 9 hospitals including Arizona Health Sciences Center which has teaching hospital.
Climate: dry, mild; freezing temperatures are rare in winter; summer brings some rain and temperature of 100 deg. F.
Culture: Univ. of Arizona, Pima Community College; Tucson Museum of Art, Tucson Symphony, Arizona Theater Co., Tucson Metropolitan Ballet; many musical, drama, and dance groups, dinner theater; Ariz. Opera Co., Southern Arizona Light Opera Company, Tucson Boys Chorus; Los Changuitos Feos mariachi group provide local flavor, plus many ethnic groups.

Convention facilities: convention center accommodates 10,000 theater-style in arena, sit-down functions 5,000, meeting-rooms 1,000 theater-style, music hall 2,300; contiguous exhibit space 64,000 sq. ft. adjacent to hotel.
Sports: Toros, Pacific Coast League farm team of Houston Astros; Cleveland Indians spring training site; Tucson Open golf tournament; various pro tennis tournaments; UA is a member of PAC 10 athletic conference.
Other attractions: Kitt Peak National Observatory is 60 miles from Tucson; UA Flandrau Planetarium, many other astronomical observatories; nationally famous rodeo in Feb.; Arizona-Sonora Desert Museum; Old Tucson; Tucson Festival in Apr., Saguaro National Monument; Nogales, 60 miles away, is nearest major border city in Mexico.
History: Presidio of Tucson est. 1775; Mission San Xavier del Bac founded nearby by Rev. Eusebio Francisco Kino SJ, who first visited area in 1692.
Birthplace of: Barbara Eden, Linda Ronstadt.
Further information: Tucson Metrop. Chamber of Commerce, PO Box 991, Tucson, AZ 85702; Metropolitan Tucson Convention and Visitors Bureau, 120 W. Broadway, PO Box 3028, Tucson, AZ 85702.

Tulsa, Oklahoma

The World Almanac is sponsored in the Tulsa area by The Tulsa Tribune, 318 S. Main, Tulsa, OK 74102; phone (918) 582-8400; founded 1904 as The Tulsa Democrat (renamed the Tulsa Tribune in 1920); circulation 78,000; editor Jenkin Lloyd Jones; managing editor Gordon Fallis; executive editor Jenkin Lloyd Jones Jr.

Population: 360,919 (city), 678,627 (SMSA); 344,400 employed.
Area: 185,405 sq. mi. on Arkansas River at 96th meridian in Tulsa, Osage, and Rogers counties.
Industry: (1981) manufacturing, which includes aerospace, metal fabrication, and oil, provides jobs for 20% of the SMSA work force; 63,900 mfg. employees, including 42,585 production workers, total payroll $1.32 billion; of these totals 45,632 worked in the city earning $913 million; retail employees 17% SMSA workers, and the service industry employs 20%; top employers are American Airlines, Cities Service, McDonnell Douglas, Rockwell International, Combustion Engineering.
Commerce: retail sales (1981) $2.74 billion; 27 banks, 5 savings and loans; per capita income $10,156.
Transportation: (1981) Tulsa Port of Catoosa, nation's most inland port, head of Arkansas Verdigris navigation channel, barge tonnage 1.85 million tons; 4 rail freight lines, 2 regional bus lines, 2 national bus lines, 30 truck lines, 14 airlines with 2,256,497 passenger movements.
Communications: 2 daily newspapers, 5 TV, 14 radio stations.
New construction: (1981) building permits valued at $607.6 million.
Medical facilities: 5 gen. hospitals, City of Faith med. center, Osteopathic Col., Univ. of Oklahoma med. school branch.
Federal facilities: District Corps of Engineers, hq. Southwestern Power Admin.
Cultural facilities: Univ. of Tulsa, Oral Roberts Univ., Tulsa Junior College; Philharmonic, opera, civic ballet, 4 art museums including Philbrook Art Center, Thomas Gilcrease Inst. of American History and Art, Rebecca and Gershon Fenster Gallery of Jewish Art, the Alexandre Hogue Gallery; American Theater Co.
Convention facilities: 463 conventions in 1981.
Sports: Tulsa Roughnecks pro soccer; Tulsa Ice Oilers pro hockey in Central Hockey League; Tulsa Twisters team rodeo; Tulsa Drillers, farm team for Texas Rangers; intercollegiate athletics; 4 public and 7 country club golf courses.
Birthplace of: Blake Edwards, Jennifer Jones, Daniel Patrick Moynihan, Tony Randall.
Further information: Metropolitan Tulsa Chamber of Commerce, 616 S. Boston Avenue, Tulsa, OK 74119.

Vancouver, British Columbia, Canada

The World Almanac is sponsored in the Vancouver area by The Vancouver Sun, 2250 Granville Street, Vancouver, B.C., V6H 3G2; phone (604) 732-2111; founded 1886; circulation, Mon.-Thurs. 230,145; Fri. 272,754; Sat. 278,813; publisher Clark Davey, director of marketing Michael J.B. Alexandor; sponsors world's largest free Salmon Derby, Sun Family Pops Concerts, Sun Tournament of Soccer Champions, and many other community services.

Population: 414,281 (city), 1,268,183 (metro area); first in province, 3d in Canada.
Area: 44 sq. mi. on the Pacific coast at the mouth of the north arm of the Fraser River; scenic beauty of the city accented by the towering, snowcapped Coast Mountains to the north and rich agricultural land to the east and south.
Industry: 98 miles of waterfront, stretching up Burrard Inlet, the largest cargo port on the Pacific and Canada's 2d busiest, with 49.5 million tons handled in 1981; major cargos: grain, lumber, coal, mineral ore, chemicals, and manufactured goods; tourism a major industry with an estimated 11.2 million visitors bringing in $970 million in 1981.
Commerce: retail sales $6.2 billion in 1981; value of shares traded on the Vancouver exchange $1.6 billion in 1981.
Transportation: western terminus of Canada's 2 national railways, Canadian National Railway and Canadian Pacific; headquarters of provincially operated British Columbia Railway, which is linked to the U.S. by Amtrak along the Burlington Northern Railway right-of-way; 3 major long-distance bus carriers, Provincial Stage Lines, Trailways, and Greyhound; International Airport served by 8 major airlines handled more than 7.3 million passengers in 1981.
Communications: 12 AM, 7 FM radio stations; 4 local TV stations; also U.S. network TV outlets.
Medical facilities: General and St. Paul's are largest hospitals; also Shaughnessy and the New Children's in Vancouver, Royal Columbian in New Westminster, Burnaby General, Lion's Gate in North Vancouver, and Riverview Psychiatric Hospital.
Cultural facilities: symphony orchestra, opera assn., several professional theater groups, Centennial and Maritime Museums and Art Gallery; Queen Elizabeth Theatre and The Orpheum are the major art facilities.
Other attractions: Pacific National Exhibition, Gastown, Chinatown, the H.R. MacMillan Planetarium, Bloedel Conservatory, Granville Island Public Market, aquarium; 1,000-acre Stanley Park, zoo, Capilano Suspension Bridge, VanDusen Botanical Garden, Park & Tilford Garden, Lynn Canyon Ecology Centre, Heritage Village; 18 golf courses, Grouse Mountain, Cypress Bowl, and Mount Seymour ski areas; Univ. of British Columbia, Simon Fraser Univ.; 18 beaches, fresh and salt water fishing.
Sports: B.C. Lions (CFL football); Canucks (NHL hockey); Whitecaps (NASL soccer); Vancouver Canadians (PCL baseball); Exhibition Park racetrack (thoroughbreds); Cloverdale Raceway (harness racing).
History: discovered by Spaniards, first mapped 1791; taken possession by Capt. George Vancouver for British 1792; Hudson's Bay Co. post established early 1800s; city incorporated 1886.
Birthplace of: Yvonne De Carlo, S. I. Hayakawa, Margaret Trudeau.
Further information: Chamber of Commerce, 1177 West Hastings, Vancouver, B.C.

Washington, District of Columbia

The World Almanac is sponsored in the Washington, D.C. area by *The Journal* Newspapers, 475 School Street SW; phone (703) 750-2000. The group includes The Montgomery Journal, The Prince George's Journal, The Fairfax Journal, The Arlington Journal, and The Alexandria Journal, which have been publishing daily since Sept. 14, 1981. John Greenwald, editorial director.

Population: 637,651 (city), 3,045,399 (SMSA) including D.C. and parts of Md. and Va. (1980 Census).
Area: 67 square miles (city), 2,812 (metro) at head of tidewater of Potomac River, 30 miles from Chesapeake Bay, 130 miles from Atlantic Ocean, 240 miles from NYC.
Industry: U. S. Capital, federal government employs 345,456 civilian (March 1982) and 60,186 military personnel (Sept. 1981). Total employment 1,536,620 (1980 Census). Leading industries: government-related activities, law, journalism, professional and trade assns., unions, lobbying organizations, high technology (particularly computer science) provide another large portion of employment base; tourism second major industry to local and federal government.
Transportation: circumferential highway; 101-mile rapid rail system, 39 miles and 44 stations; extensive local bus service; long-distance rail and bus service (Amtrak from Alexandria, Va., Washington's Union Station, and Beltsville, Md.); Washington National, Dulles International and Baltimore-Washington International airports.
Commerce: metro area per-capita income, $12,871 (1980); area retail sales $17.7 billion. First large convention center scheduled to open downtown in December 1982.
Communications: several national magazines, news bureaus of major newspapers, wire services, and TV networks, 21 FM, 19 AM radio stations, 8 television stations; 3 major daily newspapers (The Washington Post, The Journals and The Washington Times), more than 40 weekly newspapers. Cable television service in suburbs of Arlington, Alexandria in Virginia and Prince George's County in Maryland. Variety of other pay television services available.
Educational facilities: George Washington, American, Catholic, District of Columbia, and Georgetown Universities; and Gallaudett Col. (for the deaf); nearby, George Mason Univ. and Univ. of Maryland. More than 24 out-of-area universities maintain Washington-area campuses.
Medical facilities: major medical research center; National Institutes of Health, Walter Reed Hospital, Bethesda Naval Medical Center; about 40 general and 3 teaching hospitals.
Cultural facilities: Kennedy Center with 4 performance halls. Wolf Trap Farm Park in nearby Vienna, Va., and Merriweather Post Pavillion in Columbia, Md., for outdoor theater. Also Arena Stage, Ford's Theater, National Theater and numerous community theater groups; Smithsonian Institution; Corcoran Gallery of Art; numerous private museums, D.C. Public Library with 24 branches, suburban public library systems.
Sports: Professional teams include: basketball (Bullets), hockey (Capitals) football (Redskins); minor league baseball (Alexandria Dukes).
History: named for George Washington and Christopher Columbus; Georgetown in the District of Columbia first settled 1665, then annexed by the city when D.C. created as seat of federal government by Act of Congress 1790. Originally included land that is now Arlington County, Va., but that section was retroceded to Virginia after the Civil War.
Birthplace of: Edward Albee, Elgin Baylor, Carl Bernstein, John Foster Dulles, Duke Ellington, Goldie Hawn, Helen Hayes, J. Edgar Hoover, Roger Mudd.
Further information: Convention and Visitors Association, 1575 I Street NW, Suite 250, Washington, D.C. 20005.

West Palm Beach, Florida

The World Almanac is sponsored in Palm Beach County by Palm Beach Newspapers, Inc., 2751 South Dixie Highway, West Palm Beach, FL 33405; phone (305) 837-4100; publisher of The Post and The Evening Times; combined daily circulation 128,600; Sunday, The Post 155,600.

Population: 62,530 (city), 615,165 (metro); total labor force 245,400.
Area: 43.6 sq. mi. (city), 2,023 sq. mi. (metro), in southeast top of Fla.'s "Gold Coast."
Industry: Pratt & Whitney Aircraft, IBM, U.S. Sugar Corp., Atlantic Sugar Assoc., Gulf & Western Food Products Co., Duda & Sons Corp, Assoc. farms, Rinker Materials Corp., Solitron Devices, Inc., Perry Oceanographics Inc., Rel, Inc., Southern Bell, Florida Power & Light, tourism.
Commerce: 52 general service banks, 16 savings and loans, total assets $6.45 billion (1980); retail sales $3.60 billion (1980), per capita EBI $8,936 (1980).
Transportation: Palm Beach Intl. Airport; 2 rail freight lines, Amtrak; Greyhound, Trailways bus lines; Palm Beach County Transportation Authority (bus); Sunshine Lines 15 truck lines; Port of Palm Beach for freight shipping.
Communications: 3 TV, 14 radio stations, cable TV; 3 daily newspapers, one winter-season daily, 6 weeklies, society journal magazine, 7 special publications.
Medical facilities: 11 hospitals, 1 under construction, 2,832 beds now, with additional hospital the total will be 2,992.
Cultural facilities: Society of Four Arts, Henry Morrison Flagler Museum, Norton Gallery & School of Art, Morikami Museum and Park; 4 community, 2 legitimate, 3 college theaters; West Palm Beach Auditorium, Lion Country Safari.
Education: Florida Atlantic Univ. (Jr. & Sr.), Palm Beach Jr. College, North & South Tech. Ed. centers, Palm Beach Atlantic College.
Sports: West Palm Beach Expos minor league baseball; Atlanta Braves spring training site; greyhound racing, jai-alai fronton, Gold Coast Barracudas semi-pro football, 100 golf courses, 2 polo fields, county fairgrounds, auto race track; tennis, water sports, and hunting.
History: founded late 1800's by workers and business people associated with the construction of the Royal Poinciana Hotel in Palm Beach by Henry Morrison Flagler who set aside 48 homesites on the shore of Lake Worth; inc. 1894.
Further information: Area Planning Board of Palm Beach County, 2300 Palm Beach Lakes Boulevard, West Palm Beach, FL 33407; Chamber of Commerce, 501 N. Flagler Drive, West Palm Beach, FL 33401.

Wichita, Kansas

The World Almanac is sponsored in the Wichita area by the Wichita Eagle and Beacon Publishing Co., Inc., 825 East Douglas, Wichita, KS 67202; phone (316) 268-6000; founded 1872 as weeklies, became dailies 1884, consolidated 1961; combined to form single morning publication (Wichita Eagle-Beacon) Oct. 1, 1980; circulation 124,171 daily, 183,080 Sunday; Norman Christiansen, president and publisher; Peter Ridder, general manager; Davis Merritt Jr., executive editor; Clark Hoyt, managing editor.

Population: 1980 census (city) 279,272, first in state; (SMSA) 410,121; employment (1982 first quarter average) 201,750.
Area: (city) 105.25 sq. mi. at juncture of Arkansas and Little Arkansas rivers; Sedgwick County seat.
Industry: 60% of free world general aviation aircraft is manufactured in Wichita; aircraft employment in area: Beech 3,850, Boeing 15,425, Cessna 7,205, Gates Learjet 2,850; other fields: meat processing, flour milling, grain storage, petroleum refining, natural gas, chemicals; largest non-aero manufacturer employer, Coleman Co.
Commerce: wholesale-retail center for large part of Kansas and northern Oklahoma; metro (SMSA) retail sales (1981) $2.5 billion; bank resources $2.6 billion.
Transportation: 4 major rail freight lines, Continental Trailways bus line, 72 truck lines, 9 major highways; Jabara Airport, Mid-Continent Airport, 8 airlines, 62 flights daily, averages 600 air movements per day; National Flying Farmers headquarters.
Communications: 4 TV, 7 AM and 6 FM radio stations; cable TV.
Medical facilities: world's largest speech and hearing rehabilitation center (Institute of Logopedics); 6 hospital complexes including VA installation; 710 doctors.

Federal facilities: McConnell AFB, VA regional office.
Educational facilities: Wichita State Univ., Univ. of Kansas School of Medicine-Wichita, Friends Univ., Kansas Newman College; 91 elementary, 17 jr. high, 13 high schools; 18 special, 17 vocational schools.
Convention facilities: facilities include Kansas Coliseum, 189,000 sq. ft., seating capacity 12,200; Century II Civic Center, 100,000 sq. ft., seating capacity 10,000.
Cultural facilities: Wichita Symphony Orchestra; Omnisphere (planetarium), Wichita Art Museum, Wichita Art Assn. and Childrens Theater, Wichita Music Theater, Crown Uptown Dinner Theater, Marple Theater, Ulrich Museum of Art, American Theatre League, Metropolitan Ballet Co., Mid-America Dance Co., Repertory Arts Assn., Wichita Choral Society, community theater, city library, mid-America All Indian Center; 376 churches.
Other Attractions: Sedgwick County Zoo, FantaSea water amusement park, Joyland Amusement Park, Cow Town (restoration of 1872 Wichita), historical museum; 70 city parks (over 2,895 acres), 2 county parks, recreation lakes, Lake Afton Observatory; National Junior Livestock Show, Wichita River Festival, Wichita Jazz Festival.
Sports: Wichita Aeros, Montreal Expos farm team; Wichita Wind (CHL), Edmonton Oiler farm team; Wichita Wings (MISL); National Baseball Congress; 12 golf courses, 198 tennis courts, auto racing, polo, raquetball, track and field.
History: founded 1870, became railhead (shipping point) for cattle herds driven up Chisholm Trail; named after Wichita Indians.
Birthplace of: Stan Kenton, Jim Ryun, Gale Sayers.
Further information: Chamber of Commerce, 350 West Douglas, Wichita, KS 67202.

Wilmington, Delaware

The World Almanac is sponsored in Delaware by The News-Journal Company, Wilmington, DE 19899; phone (302) 573-2000; publisher of The Morning News, Evening Journal (combined daily circulation 127,687), The News Journal (Saturdays and holidays, circulation 114,027) and the Sunday News Journal (circulation 114,798), member Gannett Group; president and publisher, Brian Donnelly; executive editor, Sidney H. Hurlburt; editor of the editorial page, J. Donald Brandt.

Population: 70,195 (Wilmington), 526,300 (1981 SMSA); Wilmington is the largest city in the state.
Area: 15.1 square miles at the confluence of the Brandywine, Christina, and Delaware rivers.
Industry: one of the largest chemical and petrochemical centers in the U.S.; autos, utilities, steel; about 400 manufacturing firms; insurance firms, banks, holding companies.
Commerce: port is major auto importing center; retail sales (SMSA 1981) $2.3 billion, est. (1981 av. household EBI in SMSA) $24,352; state has 12 state-chartered commercial banks, 14 state-chartered savings and loans, 6 national banks, 2 mutual savings banks, 2 federally-chartered savings and loans, 2 non-deposit trust companies.
Transportation: 2 major freight railway lines, 1 commercial railway line, 3 bus lines, 206 commercial and private freight carriers, 1 airport.
Communications: one public TV station, 6 radio stations.
Medical facilities: Wilmington Medical Center; St. Francis, Riverside Hospital; Alfred I. duPont Institute for children with orthopedic handicaps, several mental hospitals.
Federal facilities: Dover AFB (Dover).
Cultural attractions: Grand Opera House, Winterthur Museum, Hagley Museum, Old Brandywine Village, Willingtown Square, Fort Christina Park, Delaware Symphony Orchestra, Opera Delaware Society, Wilmington Drama League, Museum of Natural History; Fort Delaware; Wilmington Institute Free Library, The Playhouse.
Education: Univ. of Delaware (Newark); Delaware State College (Dover); Delaware Technical and Community College, Brandywine Junior College, Delaware Law School (Wilmington), Wilmington Col.
Sports: horse racing at Delaware Park, Brandywine Raceway, Dover Downs, Harrington Raceway (Harrington); auto racing at Dover Downs; Univ. of Delaware football.
Other attractions: Rehoboth Beach; Longwood Gardens and Brandywine River Museum (both in nearby PA); Delaware Art Museum (Wilmington); historic old New Castle; old Dover; Ashland Nature Center; several state parks and recreational areas.
Convention facilities: Wilmington has 4 major hotels.
History: founded as Fort Christina in 1638; named for Queen of Sweden; name changed to Willington in 1731 and then to Wilmington in 1739 in honor of the Earl of Wilmington; it is the first city in the first state of the union.
Birthplace of: Valerie Bertinelli, J.P. Marquand, Randy White.
Further information: Delaware State Chamber of Commerce, 1102 West Street, Wilmington, DE 19801; The News-Journal Co., Market Research/Public Service Dept., Wilmington, DE 19899.

Windsor, Ontario, Canada

The World Almanac is sponsored in Windsor and a large part of southwestern Ontario including Essex, Kent and Lambton counties, by The Windsor Star (ave. circ. 91,000), 167 Ferry Street, Windsor, Ontario, N9A 4M5, a division of Southam Inc.; published daily since 1890 (present name since 1957); publisher Gordon Bullock, general manager A.H. Fast, editor Carl Morgan.

Population: 197,000 (city) 249,500 (metro), 315,000 (county of Essex); total employed 108,000 (metro).
Area: 46.24 sq. mi. (city), 316.93 sq. mi. (metro), 718.97 sq. mi. (Essex County); one mile across Detroit River from Detroit, Mich.; largest Canadian city on U.S.-Canadian border.
Industry: (1981) investment into manufacturing sector was in excess of $725 million; over 700 manufacturers produce products valued at $4 billion per year. General Motors of Canada Transmission Plant, expanded Windsor Trim Plant, established a data processing research facility in Windsor. Ford Motor Company new V-6 Engine Plant and Aluminum Casting Plant. Kelsey Hayes, Gulf & Western, National Auto Rad and Champion Spark Plug serve automotive markets in the U.S. and Canada. Windsor is the "home of Canadian Club" and a major food and beverage processing center; Green Giant, Chun-King, Dainty Rice, Windsor Packers, H.J. Heinz and Holiday Juice; city is the machine tool center of Canada; chemical industry produces paints and lacquers, metal working compounds, pharmaceuticals and vitamin preparations.
Commerce: Retail sales (metro) $870 million; ave. wkly. earnings $343.60; 5th. largest manufacturing center in Canada; 10 banks, 82 branches, 15 trust companies, 26 finance companies; 34 credit unions.
Transportation: 6 major railways, 2 major airlines (Nordair, Air Canada); linked to Detroit by vehicular tunnel, rail tunnel and suspension bridge; western terminus Highway 401; over 50 major freight carriers; deep water port; bonded warehouse facilities, municipal bus line, 4 intercity bus lines.
Communications: daily newspaper; 6 radio stations; one TV outlet; access to Detroit's 50 radio and 6 TV outlets; monthly magazine.
New Construction: (city) 517 dwelling units; (metro) 618 dwelling units; (Essex & Kent Counties) 761 dwelling units (1981). Windsor has a program of commercial and residential downtown renewal. Currently underway is the City Centre project, which will include a 320 room luxury hotel, an office tower, an apartment tower, retail space, a cinema and parking structure.
Medical Facilities: 4 major hospitals, regional children's center; handicapped children's rehabilitation center.
Educational facilities: Univ. of Windsor, St. Clair College of Applied Arts & Technology.
Cultural facilities: Cleary Auditorium and Convention Cen-

tre; Art Gallery of Windsor, Windsor Symphony Orchestra; Multicultural Council of Windsor; Univ. of Windsor Players; Windsor Light Opera Assn; Windsor Public Library; Essex Hall Theatre; Ontario Film Theatre.
Other Attractions: Hiram Walker Historical Museum, Fort Malden Historic Park & Museum, Jackson Park Sunken Gardens; Dieppe Gardens, Coventry Gardens and Peace Fountain; Willistead Manor House; Fox Creek Conservation Area, Heritage Village, Windsor Raceway, Bob-Lo Island Amusement Park, Great Lakes resort area, Ojibway Park, Point Pelee Provincial Park; site of International Freedom Festival and Multicultural Carousel of Nations Festival.
Sports: Windsor Spitfire Hockey Team, Windsor Minor Lacrosse Assn., Windsor Yacht Club, several marinas; 7 public golf courses; 2 public curling rinks, 96 parks and playgrounds.
Birthplace of: Dorothy Collins.
History: originally established by Ottawa and Huron Indians; first permanent white settlement established around 1750; site of War of 1812 between Americans and the British; in 1836, citizens chose the name Windsor; became a city with a population of 11,000 in 1892.
Further Information: Chamber of Commerce, 500 Riverside Drive West, Tourist Information, 80 Chatham Street East, Windsor Essex County Development Commission, Place Goyeau, all Windsor, Ontario.

Winnipeg, Manitoba, Canada

The World Almanac is sponsored in the Winnipeg area by the Winnipeg Free Press, 300 Carlton Street, Winnipeg, Man., Canada; phone (204) 943-9331; founded 1872; daily circulation 180,174; publisher Don Nicol, editor John Dafoe, managing editor Murray Burt; the newspaper and its staff have received numerous journalism awards.

Population: 584,842.
Area: 235 sq. mi. surrounding the junction of Red and Assiniboine rivers, near center of North America; capital of the province of Manitoba.
Industry: manufacturing and agriculture are the largest source of jobs; 1,025 establishments, 53,000 employees; value of factory shipments $2.35 billion.
Commerce: retail sales over $1.9 billion in 1979; Winnipeg Commodity Exchange only gold futures market in Canada; headquarters Canada Grains Council, Canadian Grain Commission, Canadian Wheat Board.
Transportation: International Airport served by 10 airlines; 2 national railways, Via-Rail passenger service; one rail line to U.S.; 5 national and regional bus lines; trucking hub.
Communications: 10 TV channels, 4 stations; 11 radio stations.
New construction: valued at $274.5 million in 1981.
Medical facilities: one of Canada's largest medical teaching centers; research in immunology, transplant-tissue rejection, cancer, blood diseases, respiratory diseases, endocrinology, neo-natal, pre-natal medicine; of Manitoba's 85 active treatment hospitals, 13 are in Winnipeg, including 2 major teaching centers plus Univ. of Manitoba Rh Inst.; 300-plus bed Seven Oaks Hospital opened in 1980.
Federal facilities: passport office, Canada mint.
Cultural facilities: art gallery, Royal Winnipeg Ballet, contemporary dancers, Winnipeg Symphony Orchestra, Manitoba Chamber Orchestra, Manitoba Opera Assn., Manitoba Theatre Center, Cercle Moliere, Museum of Man and Nature, summer Rainbow Stage, Manitoba theater workshop, over 12 amateur theater groups.
Educational facilities: Univ. of Manitoba with 4 affiliated colleges; Univ. of Winnipeg, Red River Community College.
Sports: Blue Bombers (Canadian Football League), Winnipeg Jets (National Hockey League), Assiniboia Downs.
Convention facilities: downtown Winnipeg Convention Center handles up to 5,000 delegates.
Other attractions: major zoo in Assiniboine Park; Red River exhibition, multi-cultural Folklorama festival each summer; folk festival in Birds Hill Park; French Canadian winter carnival in St. Boniface; planetarium.
History: first colony, Lord Selkirk Settlers, 1812; inc. Nov. 8, 1873; in 1972, city government replaced 7 cities, 4 urban municipalities, one town and a metropolitan government.
Additional information: Chamber of Commerce, 400-177 Lombard Avenue, Tourist Information, 101 Legislative Building, and Tourist and Convention Association of Manitoba, 226-375 York Avenue.

Winston-Salem, North Carolina

The World Almanac is sponsored in the Piedmont Triad area by the Winston-Salem Journal and The Sentinel, 418-420 N. Marshall Street, Winston-Salem, NC 27102; phone (919) 727-7211; Sentinel founded 1856, Journal 1897; brought under same ownership in 1926; now an affiliate of Media General Inc.; general manager Thomas E. Waldrop, publisher Joe Doster.

Population: 131,885 (city), 243,683 (county); work force in county 163,000.
Area: 61.34 sq. mi. (city), 419 sq. mi. (county), in north central N.C.; Forsyth County seat.
Industry: R. J. Reynolds Industries with diversified interests in tobacco, food, shipping, oil, and packaging; Western Electric Co., Westinghouse, Jos. Schlitz brewery, Hanes Corp., Hanes Dye and Finishing Co., Brenner Industries, Wachovia Corp., and Bahnson Co.
Commerce: total retail sales county (1980 est.) $2.0 billion, part of the Piedmont Triad, with Greensboro and High Point comprise a growing part of Piedmont part of N.C.
Transportation: headquarters for Piedmont Airlines at Smith Reynolds Airport; city also served by 4 airlines at Greensboro-High Point-Winston-Salem regional airport; 2 bus lines; 54 carriers of various types.
Communications: 4 TV, 10 radio stations; cable TV.
New construction: Journal and Sentinel newspapers building $10 million addition.
Medical facilities: Bowman Gray School of Medicine of Wake Forest Univ.; Baptist, Forsyth Memorial, and Medical Park hospitals; other treatment centers.
Cultural facilities: one of the nation's first arts councils formed in 1949; Winston Square, Sawtooth Bldg. and Stevens Center comprise downtown cultural center; N.C. School of the Arts, Wake Forest Univ., Salem College, Winston-Salem State Univ.; Old Salem, restoration of town between 1766 and 1830.
Recreation: more than 50 public parks, 10 community centers, 10 public pools; boating and fishing at Winston and Salem lakes; 17 golf courses including Tanglewood.
Convention facilities: Winston-Salem Hyatt hotel complex sits across street from Benton Convention Center; hotels and motels offer more than 2,400 rooms in area.
Sports: Red Sox, farm club of Boston Red Sox; stock car racing; Wake Forest football at Groves stadium; Winston-Salem State football at Bowman Gray Stadium; college basketball at Memorial Coliseum.
History: Salem founded 1766 by the Moravian Church; Winston founded 1849 as ind. city; cities merged in 1913.
Further information: Chamber of Commerce, P.O. Box 1408, Winston-Salem, NC 27102.

Worcester, Massachusetts

Population: (1980 census), 161,799 city; 646,352 county; 372,940 SMSA.
Commerce: retail sales $797 million (city), 2.8 million (county); EBI per household $19,414 (1980).

Industry: (county) 5,169 retail establishments, 4,696 service businesses, and 1,505 manufacturers.
New construction: 31 projects, totaling more than $100 million, have been completed or are presently underway in downtown Worcester.
Communications: 1 TV, 8 radio stations; Worcester Telegram and Evening Gazette, Worcester Magazine.
Education: 7 colleges and universities, 1 medical school, 1 veterinary school, 1 post doctoral research and teaching institute, 1 industrial tech. inst.
Medical facilities: 14 general and 5 long-term hospitals; new $125 million U-Mass. Med. School, Teaching Hospital.
Cultural facilities: Worcester Art Museum, American Antiquarian Society, Craft Center, Worcester Historical Museum, Worcester Science Center, Higgins Armory, Old Sturbridge Village, Mechanics Hall, E.M. Loew's Center for the Performing Arts, New England Repertory Theatre. Worcester Foothills Theatre Co.
History: First settled in 1674, named and resettled in 1684. Permanently settled in 1713. Incorporated as a town in 1722, as a city in 1848.
Further information: Worcester Area Chamber of Commerce, or Worcester County Convention and Visitors Bureau, 350 Mechanics Tower, Worcester, Mass. 01608.

Yakima, Washington

The World Almanac is sponsored in the Yakima SMSA by the Yakima Herald-Republic (published daily and Sunday), 114 North Fourth Street, Yakima, WA 98909; phone (509) 248-1251; founded 1903 as the Yakima Republic, given present name in 1970; circulation (Dec., 1981) daily 39,661, Sunday 43,665; publisher James E. Barnhill. The Yakima Herald-Republic is a division of Harte-Hanks Communications, Inc.

Population: 49,825 city, 172,508 SMSA.
Area: 11.78 sq. mi. in south central Washington, 142 miles southeast of Seattle, 146 miles south of Canadian border; altitude 1,052 ft., Yakima County seat.
Industry: food processing, agriculture, timber; first in the nation in production of apples, hops, mint; first in number of fruit trees.
Commerce: (1981) retail sales $768.4 million (SMSA); E.B.I. per household (1981) $20,187; postal receipts (1980) $4 million.
Transportation: Republic Airlines and Cascade Airways; Burlington Northern, Union Pacific railroads; Greyhound; interstate 82, highways 12 and 97.
Communications: daily, weekly newspapers; 4 TV, 10 radio stations.
New construction: 843 building permits totalling over $34 million issued in 1979.
Medical facilities: 3 hospitals with 460 beds, 150 physicians, 11 osteopaths, 64 dentists, 13 optometrists; cardiac surgery at St. Elizabeth's Hospital.
Federal facilities: U.S. Army Firing Center, 409 permanent personnel, trains active and reserve units on 263,131 acres; U.S. Army, Marine, and Navy reserve facilities; U.S. Postal Service regional center.
Cultural facilities: Yakima Valley Museum, Yakima Valley Regional Library, Allied Arts Council, Yakima Symphony, Little Theater, Capitol Theater; over 95 churches.
Education: Yakima Valley College, J. M. Perry Institute, Yakima Business College; City College; 7 public school districts in and around city, 7 parochial schools, St. Elizabeth Health Sciences Library.
Sports and Recreation: 12 theaters, 5 drive-ins; historic trolleys; hunting and fishing; skiing in Cascade Mountains 45 minutes from city; 4 golf courses, 30 tennis courts, 9 swimming pools, 31 parks; auto racing, horse racing; youth baseball, softball; Central Washington State Fair, Washington State Open Horse Show.
Convention facilities: Yakima Convention Center, over 1,400 motel units.
History: founded Jan. 27, 1886 as North Yakima on route of Northern Pacific Railroad.
Further information: Greater Yakima Chamber of Commerce, P.O. Box 1490, or Yakima V&C Bureau, 10 North 8th Street, both Yakima, WA 98907.

Youngstown, Ohio

The World Almanac is sponsored in the Youngstown area by The Vindicator, Vindicator Square, Youngstown, OH 44503; phone (216) 747-1471; founded 1863 by J. H. Odell; Wm. F. Maag began daily Sept. 25, 1889; daily circulation 101,978, Sunday 152,930; president, publisher, Betty J.H. Brown; general manager William Mittler; managing editor Ann N. Przelomski.

Population: 115,436 (city), 529,887 (SMSA).
Area: 35 sq. mi. in northeastern Ohio at juncture of Ohio Turnpike, I-80, and Ohio Rt. 11; Mahoning County seat.
Industry: no longer a strong iron and steel center, still some production with Jones & Laughlin Steel Corp., Republic Steel; local steel supplied to big nearby plants of General Motors Packard Electric Div. in Warren and GMAD plant in Lordstown, where Chevrolet vans and other GM models are assembled; GF Business Equipment sells office furnishings world wide; Commercial Shearing does world-wide tunnel frame and hydraulics business; other fabricators use local steel, rubber.
Commerce: wholesale-retail center for large area of northeast Ohio, western Pennsylvania; retail sales of metro area (est.) over $2.1 billion; (est.) value added by manufacturing $2.6 billion; average spendable family income $20,006.
Transportation: truck transport center with 105 motor freight terminals; rail lines; airport served by United Airlines, BAS, Allegheny Commuter; headquarters for Beckett Aviation, largest fleet of executive aircraft in U.S.
Communications: 4 TV stations, all major networks and PBS; 9 radio stations.
Medical facilities: Northeastern Ohio Univ. College of Medicine, 6 large hospitals in area.
Federal facilities: U.S. Air Force Reserve base flying transports at airport; regional post office; army and navy reserve centers.
Cultural facilities: symphony orchestra with downtown bldg.; ballet guild, Youngstown Playhouse in own modern bldg., Butler Institute of American Art.
Educational facilities: Youngstown State Univ. with graduate program; Penn-Ohio Junior College; Youngstown College of Business and Professional Drafting; 52 public and parochial schools; branches of Kent State Univ. in nearby Warren, Salem, and East Liverpool.
Recreational facilities: 10 parks, 44 playgrounds, golf course, 6 swimming pools; Mill Creek Park with 2,383 acres; 4 large reservoirs in area for recreation, many golf courses.
Birthplace of: Arnold Palmer.
Further information: Youngstown Area Chamber of Commerce, 200 Wick Bldg., Youngstown, OH 44503.

Washington, Capital of the U.S.

The Capitol

The United States Capitol has presented an entirely new east central front since 1961. That portion was extended 32 ft. 6 in. and reproduced in Georgia marble. The extension added 100 rooms and cost $11.4 million. The original wall of Virginia sandstone became an inner wall.

Dr. William Thornton, an amateur architect, submitted a plan for the Capitol in the spring of 1793 that won him $500 and a city lot. The design consisted of a center section topped with a low dome; on either side were wings to accommodate the House and

Senate that measured about 126 ft. by 120 ft. George Washington laid the cornerstone Sept. 18, 1793; in Nov. 1800 Congress met in that north or Senate wing.

The south, or House wing, was completed in 1807 under the direction of Benjamin H. Latrobe. At the time the Capitol was burned by the British in 1814 the Capitol consisted of these 2 wings joined by a wooden walkway. The interiors were gutted by the fire and nearly 5 years were needed to rebuild the Capitol. It was occupied again in 1819; the central portion with its low copper-covered wooden dome was completed in 1829 by the 3d architect of the Capitol, Charles Bulfinch.

The present Senate and House wings and the iron dome were designed and constructed by Thomas U. Walter, the 4th architect of the Capitol, between 1851-1863. The House moved into its chamber Dec. 16, 1857 and the Senate Jan. 4, 1859. These moves enabled the Supreme Court to occupy the Old Senate Chamber from 1860-1935 when it moved into its own building. The Old Hall of the House became National Statuary Hall. Those original House and Senate chambers have been restored and are open to the public.

The present cast iron dome at its greatest exterior measures 135 ft. 5 in., and it is topped by the bronze Statue of Freedom that stands 19½ ft. and weighs 14,985 pounds. On its base are the words "E Pluribus Unum (Out of Many One). The sculptor was Thomas Crawford and the cost, including casting, $23,796. The Rotunda, covered by the huge dome, measures 96 ft. in diameter. Looking upward 180 ft. into the "eye" of the dome one sees the huge fresco, "Apotheosis of Washington," by Constantino Brumidi.

Office Buildings for Members

Members of Congress meet constituents and transact other business in 5 office buildings on Capitol Hill, 2 for the Senate and 3 for the House. The original Senate building, the Richard Brevard Russell Office Building, was completed in 1909, enlarged in 1933; the second Senate building, the Everett McKinley Dirksen Office Building, was constructed in 1958.

The original House building (1908) was named for former Speaker Joseph G. Cannon (R. Ill.), the second (1933) for former Speaker Nicholas Longworth (R. Oh.), and the third (1964) for former Speaker Sam Rayburn (D. Tex.). The Rayburn Building has underground transportation to the Capitol.

Hours for Visiting

The Capitol is normally open from 9 a.m. to 4:30 p.m. daily, closed Christmas, New Year's Day, and Thanksgiving Day.

Tours through the Capitol, including the House and Senate Galleries, are conducted from 9 a.m. to 4 p.m. without charge.

The White House

The White House, the president's residence, stands on 18 acres on the south side of Pennsylvania Avenue, between the Treasury and the Executive Office Building. The main building 168 by 85-1/2 ft., has 6 floors, with the East Terrace, 135 by 35 ft., leading to the East Wing, a 3-story building, 139 by 82 ft., used for offices and as an entrance for tours. The West Terrace, 174 by 35 ft., contains offices and press facilities, and leads to the West Wing, 3 stories high, 148 by 98 ft., erected in 1902 and enlarged several times since.

The White House was designed by James Hoban, an Irish-born architect, in a competition that paid $500. President Washington chose the site, which was included on the plan of the Federal City prepared by the French engineer, Major Pierre L'Enfant. The cornerstone was laid Oct. 13, 1792. President Washington never lived in the house. President John Adams entered in Nov. 1800, and Mrs. Adams hung her washing in the uncompleted East Room.

The walls are of sandstone, quarried at Aquia Creek, Va. The exterior walls were painted, causing the building to be termed the "White House." On Aug. 24, 1814, during Madison's administration, the house was burned by the British. James Hoban rebuilt it by Oct. 1817, for President Monroe to move in.

The south portico was added in 1824 and the north portico in 1829. In 1948 President Truman had a second-floor balcony built into the south portico. In 1948 he had Congress authorize complete rebuilding because the White House was unsafe. Reconstruction cost $5,761,000. The interior was completely removed, new underpinning 24 ft. deep was placed under the outside walls and a steel frame was built to support the interior.

Visiting Hours

The White House is open from 10 a.m. to 12 noon, Tuesday through Friday, except on Thanksgiving, Christmas, and New Year. Also Saturdays, 10 a.m. to 2 p.m. Jun. 1 through Labor Day, and 10 a.m. to noon Labor Day through May 31. Only the public rooms on the ground floor and state floor may be visited.

President's Guest House

Blair House, the President's Guest House, fronts on Pennsylvania Ave., northwest of the White House grounds. It is supervised by the Dept. of State and is the official residence of heads of state who visit Washington. Built 1824, it was the home of Francis Preston Blair (1791-1876), political leader and Lincoln advisor.

Other Centers of Interest

Arlington National Cemetery

Arlington National Cemetery, on the former Custis estate in Virginia, is the site of the **Tomb of the Unknown Soldier** and the final resting place of John Fitzgerald Kennedy, president of the United States, who was buried there Nov. 25, 1963. A torch burns day and night over his grave. The remains of his brother Sen. Robert F. Kennedy (N.Y.) were interred on June 8, 1968, in an area adjacent. Many other famous Americans are also buried at Arlington, as well as American soldiers from every major war.

Arlington National Cemetery, administered by the Department of the Army, was established June 15, 1864, on land originally the estate of George Washington Parke Custis.

The Unknown Soldier of World War I was entombed on the east front of the Arlington Memorial Amphitheater Nov. 11, 1921. The tomb is inscribed: *Here rests in honored glory an American soldier known but to God.* The body had been chosen at Chalons-sur-Marne from unidentified dead in Europe. On Memorial Day, May 30, 1958, 2 unidentified servicemen, one of whom died in World War II and one in the Korean War, were placed in crypts beside the first.

As of May 1, 1981, a total of 181,209 interments had been made in Arlington National Cemetery. Among the unknown dead are 2,111 who died on the battlefields of Virginia in the Civil War and 167 who lost their lives when the battleship Maine was blown up in Havana Harbor Feb. 15, 1898. The total of unknown dead interred in Arlington National Cemetery is 4,724.

Arlington House, The Robert E. Lee Memorial

On a hilltop above the cemetery, stands Arlington House, the Robert E. Lee Memorial, which from 1955 to 1972 was officially called the Custis-Lee Mansion. The house has a portico 60 ft. wide, with 8 Doric columns, and faces the Potomac. With its 2 wings the house extends 140 ft. It was built by George Washington Parke Custis, grandson of Martha Washington and father of Mary Ann Randolph Custis, who married Lee in this house in 1831. Here Lee wrote his resignation from the U.S. Army, Apr. 20, 1861. The house became a military headquarters and was confiscated by the government. The U.S. Supreme Court restored it to the legal heir, George Washington Custis Lee, grandson of the builder, who sold the entire estate (including the mansion) to the Government in 1883 for $150,000. The mansion and grounds are administered by the National Park Service of the Dept. of the Interior.

U.S. Marine Corps War Memorial

North of the National Cemetery, approximately 350 yards, stands the bronze statue of the raising of the United States flag on Iwo Jima, executed by Felix de Weldon from the photograph by Joe Rosenthal, and presented to the nation by members and friends of the U.S. Marine Corps, at a cost of $850,000. It was dedicated Nov. 10, 1954, and is under the administration of the Dept. of the Interior, National Park Service.

Folger Shakespeare Library

The Folger Shakespeare Library on Capitol Hill, Washington, D. C., is a research institution devoted to the advancement of learning in the background of Anglo-American civilization in the 16th and 17th centuries and in most aspects of the continental Renaissance. It has the largest collection of Shakespeareana in the world with 79 copies of the First Folio. Its collection of English books printed before 1640 is the largest in the Western Hemisphere. The library owns approximately 250,000 books and manuscripts, about half of them rare. It is also the home of a professional acting company and chamber music ensemble.

The library was founded and endowed by Henry Clay Folger, a former president of the Standard Oil Co. of New York, and his wife, Emily Jordan Folger. The exhibition gallery and replica Elizabethan Theatre are open free 10 a.m. to 4 p.m. daily; closed federal holidays and on Sundays after Labor Day to April 15.

Library of Congress

Established by and for Congress in 1800, the Library of Congress has extended its services over the years to other Government agencies and other libraries, to scholars, and to the general public, and it now serves as the national library. Three buildings, the Thomas Jefferson Bldg. (1897), John Adams Bldg. (1939) and James Madison Bldg. (1980), cover 64.6 acres of floor space. The library also occupies 2 other buildings in the metropolitan area.

Dr. Daniel J. Boorstin became the 12th Librarian of Congress Nov. 12, 1975. Today the library's collections contain more than 74 million items, including more than 18 million volumes and pamphlets.

The library's exhibit halls are open to the public. Guided tours are given every hour from 9 a.m. through 4 p.m. Monday through Friday. Arrangements for groups should be made in advance with the Tour Coordinator.

Thomas Jefferson Memorial

The Thomas Jefferson Memorial stands on the south shore of the Tidal Basin in West Potomac park. It is a circular stone structure, with Vermont marble on the exterior and Georgia white marble inside and combines architectural elements of the dome of the Pantheon in Rome and the rotunda designed by Jefferson for the University of Virginia. The central circular chamber, 86¼ ft. in diameter, is dominated by a 19-ft. tall full-length figure of Thomas Jefferson by the American sculptor Rudulph Evans. The architects were John Russell Pope and his associates Otto R. Eggers and Daniel P. Higgins. The Memorial was dedicated by President F. D. Roosevelt Apr. 13, 1943, the 200th anniversary of Jefferson's birth.

The memorial is open daily from 8 a.m. to midnight, except Christmas Day. An elevator and curb ramps for the handicapped are in service.

John F. Kennedy Center

John F. Kennedy Center for the Performing Arts, designated by Congress as the National Cultural Center and the official memorial in Washington to President Kennedy, opened September 8, 1971. The white marble building, designed by Edward Durell Stone, houses a 2,300-seat Opera House, a 2,750-seat Concert Hall, the 1,150-seat Eisenhower Theater, the 513-seat Terrace Theater, the 224-seat American Film Institute Theater, a 100-seat laboratory theater, and 3 restaurants. Tours are available daily, free of charge, between 10:00 a.m. and 1:15 p.m.

Lincoln Memorial

The Lincoln Memorial in West Potomac Park, on the axis of the Capitol and the Washington Monument, consists of a large marble hall enclosing a heroic statue of Abraham Lincoln in meditation sitting on a large armchair. It was dedicated on Memorial Day, May 30, 1922. The Memorial was designed by Henry Bacon. The statue was made by Daniel Chester French. Murals and ornamentation on the bronze ceiling beams are by Jules Guerin.

The memorial, built on bedrock, is of white Colorado-Yule marble. There are 2 Doric columns at the entrance and 36 others in the colonnade.

The seated figure of Lincoln is 19 ft. from head to foot and the classic armchair is 12½ ft. tall. Over the back of the chair a flag is draped in marble. On the north wall is inscribed the Second Inaugural Address. On the south wall is the Gettysburg Address.

The memorial is open daily from 8 a.m. to midnight, except Christmas Day. A new elevator for the handicapped is in service.

Mount Vernon

Mount Vernon on the south bank of the Potomac, 16 miles below Washington, D. C., is part of a large tract of land in northern Virginia which was originally included in a royal grant made to Lord Culpepper, who in 1674 granted 5,000 acres to Nicholas Spencer and John Washington.

The present house is an enlargement of one apparently built on the site of an earlier one by John's grandson, Augustine Washington, who lived there 1735-1738. His son Lawrence came there in 1743, when he renamed the plantation Mount Vernon in honor of Admiral Vernon under whom he had served in the West Indies. Lawrence Washington died in 1752 and was succeeded as proprietor of Mount Vernon by his half-brother, George Washington.

Washington brought his wife, Martha Dandridge Custis, to Mount Vernon in 1759, having previously enlarged the house from 1-½ to 2-½ stories. During the Revolution Washington visited Mount Vernon only twice, on the way to and from Yorktown in 1781. In 1789 he left to become president and lived in New York and Philadelphia, with brief visits to the plantation. He came back in 1797 and died in Mount Vernon Dec. 14, 1799. He was buried in the old family vault. He had made plans for a new burial vault and this was built in 1831. Both his remains and those of Martha, who died in 1802, were transferred there.

In 1853 Miss Ann Pamela Cunningham of South Carolina organized the Mount Vernon Ladies' Assn., which bought the mansion and 200 acres, since extended to just under 500 acres. The Association reassembled original Washington furniture and repaired the buildings.

National Arboretum

The National Arboretum, one of Washington's great showplaces, occupies 444 acres in the northeastern section of the city. The National Herb Garden and National Bonsai Collection are special attractions in the nation's only federally-supported gardens.

The Arboretum is open every day of the year except Christmas.

National Archives

The Declaration of Independence, the Constitution of the United States, and the Bill of Rights are on permanent display in the National Archives Exhibition Hall. They are sealed in glass-and-bronze cases. The National Archives also holds the permanently valuable federal records of the United States government.

The National Archives and Records Service is a part of the General Services Administration. Through the Office of Presidential Libraries it administers the Herbert Hoover Library at West Branch, Iowa, the Franklin D. Roosevelt Library at Hyde Park, N.Y., the Harry S. Truman Library at Independence, Mo., the Dwight D. Eisenhower Library at Abilene, Kan., the John Fitzgerald Kennedy Library at Boston, Mass., the Lyndon Baines Johnson Library at Austin, Tex., and the Gerald Ford Library to be built in Ann Arbor, Mich., and museum to stand in Grand Rapids.

National Gallery of Art

The National Gallery of Art, situated in an area bounded by Constitution Avenue and the Mall, between Third and Seventh Streets, was established by Joint Resolution of Congress Mar. 24, 1937, and opened Mar. 17, 1941.

The collections comprise gifts of over 300 donors (none of the works were acquired with Government funds) and cover the American and various European schools of art from the 13th century to the present.

The building was erected with funds given by Andrew W. Mellon, who also gave his collection of 126 paintings and 26 pieces of sculpture, which included such masterpieces as Raphael's Alba Madonna, the Niccolini-Cowper Madonna, and St. George and the Dragon, van Eyck's Annunciation, Botticelli's Adoration of the Magi, and 9 Rembrandts.

Open daily except Christmas and New Year's, from 10 a.m. to 5 p.m. Monday through Saturday and noon to 9 p.m. Sunday. Summer, 10 a.m. to 9 p.m., noon to 9 p.m. on Sunday.

The Pentagon

The Pentagon, headquarters of the Department of Defense, is the world's largest office building, with 3 times the floor space of the Empire State Building in New York. Situated in Arlington, Va., it houses more than 23,000 employees in offices that occupy 3,707,745 square feet.

The Pentagon was completed Jan. 15, 1943, at a cost of about $83 million. It covers 34 acres, is 5 stories high and consists of 5 rings of buildings connected by 10 corridors, with a 5-acre pentagonal court in the center. Total length of the corridors is 17½ miles.

Tours are available Monday through Friday (excluding federal holidays), from 9 a.m. to 3:30 p.m.

Smithsonian Institution

The Smithsonian Institution is one of the world's great historical, scientific, educational, and cultural establishments. It comprises numerous facilities, mostly in Wash., D.C. It was founded by an Act of Congress in 1846, pursuant to a bequest of James Smithson, a British scholar-scientist, to the United States.

Among the Smithsonian's components are the Anacostia Neighborhood Museum, Arts and Industries Building, Freer Gallery of Art, Hirshhorn Museum and Sculpture Garden, Natl. Museum of American History, Natl. Museum of Natural History, Natl. Museum of Man, Natl. Air and Space Museum, Natl. Museum of American Art, Museum of African Art, Natl. Portrait Gallery, Natl. Zoological Park, Smithsonian Associates, Smithsonian Institution Traveling Exhibition Service.

Washington Monument

The Washington Monument is a tapering shaft or obelisk of white marble, 555 ft., 5-⅛ inches in height and 55 ft., 1-½ inches square at base. Eight small windows, 2 on each side, are located at the 500-ft. level, where Washington points of interest are indicated.

The capstone was placed Dec. 6, 1884. The monument was dedicated Feb. 21, 1885, and opened Oct. 9, 1888. It weighs 81,120 tons. It is dressed with white Maryland marble in 2-ft. courses. Set into the interior wall are 190 memorial stones from states, foreign countries, and organizations. An iron stairway has 50 landings and 898 steps. A modern elevator takes sightseers to the 500-ft. level in one minute.

The Monument is open 7 days a week, 9 a.m. to 5 p.m., 8 a.m. to 12 midnight in the summer. It is closed Christmas Day.

Notable Tall Buildings in North American Cities

Height from sidewalk to roof, including penthouse and tower if enclosed as integral part of structure; actual number of stories beginning at street level. Asterisks (*) denote buildings still under construction Jan. 1983.

City	Hgt. ft.	Stories
Akron, Oh.		
First National Tower	**330**	28
Akron Center	**321**	24
Albany, N.Y.		
Office Tower, So. Mall	**589**	44
State Office Building	**388**	34
Agency (4 bldgs.), So. Mall	**310**	23
Atlanta, Ga.		
Peachtree Center Plaza Hotel	**723**	71
Georgia Pacific Tower	**697**	51
Southern Bell Telephone,	**677**	47
First National Bank, 2 Peachtree	**556**	44
Equitable Building, 100 Peachtree	**453**	34
101 Marietta Tower, 101 Marietta St.	**446**	36
Peachtree Summit No. 1	**406**	31
North Avenue Tower, 310 North Ave.	**403**	26
Tower Place, 3361 Piedmont Road	**401**	29
National Bank of Georgia	**390**	32
Richard B. Russell, Federal Bldg.	**383**	26
Atlanta Hilton Hotel	**383**	32
Peachtree Center Harris Bldg.	**382**	31
Southern Bell Telephone	**380**	...
Trust Company Bank	**377**	28
Coastal States Insurance	**377**	27
Peachtree Center Cain Building	**376**	30
Peachtree Center Building	**374**	31
Life of Georgia Tower	**371**	29
Georgia Power Tower, 333 Piedmont	**349**	24
Peachtree Center South	**332**	27
Gas Light Tower, 235 Peachtree	**331**	27
Hyatt Regency Hotel, 265 Peachtree	**330**	23
100 Colony Square, 1175 Peachtree	**328**	25
Georgia Power Building	**318**	22
Colony Square Hotel, 180 14th St.	**310**	28
Austin, Tex.		
Austin National Bank	**328**	26
American Bank	**313**	21
State Capitol	**309**	...
Univ. of Texas Admin. Bldg.	**307**	29
Baltimore, Md.		
U.S. Fidelity & Guaranty Co.	**529**	40
Maryland National Bank Bldg.	**509**	34
World Trade Center Bldg.	**405**	32
Saint-Paul Apartments Bldg.	**385**	37
Arlington Federal S & L Bldg.	**370**	28
Blaustein Bldg.	**370**	30
Charles Plaza Apts. So.	**350**	31
Charles Center South	**330**	26
Tower Bldg.	**330**	16
Baltimore Arts Tower	**319**	15
First National Bank of Maryland	**315**	22
Lord Baltimore Hotel	**315**	24
Mercantile-Safe Deposit and Trust Co.	**315**	21
Charles Plaza Apts. No.	**315**	28
Baton Rouge, La.		
State Capitol	**460**	34
American Bank Bldg.	**310**	25
Birmingham, Ala.		
First Natl. Southern Natural Bldg.	**390**	30
South Central Bell Hdqts. Bldg.	**390**	30
City Federal Bldg.	**325**	27
Boston, Mass.		
John Hancock Tower	**790**	60
Prudential Tower	**750**	52
Boston Co. Bldg., Court St.	**605**	41
Federal Reserve Bldg.	**604**	32
First National Bank of Boston	**591**	37
Shawmut Bank Bldg.	**520**	38
Sixty State St.	**509**	38
One Post Office Sq.	**507**	40
Employers Commercial Employees Bldg.	**507**	40
New England Merch. Bank Bldg.	**500**	40
U.S. Custom House	**496**	32
John Hancock Bldg.	**495**	26
State St. Bank Bldg.	**477**	34
One Hundred Summer St.	**450**	33
McCormack Bldg.	**401**	22
Keystone Custodian Funds	**400**	32
Saltonstall Office Bldg.	**396**	22
Harbor Towers (2 bldgs.)	**396**	40
John F. Kennedy Bldg.	**387**	24
Longfellow Towers (2 bldgs.)	**380**	38
Federal Bldg. & Post Office	**345**	22
Suffolk County Courthouse	**330**	19
Jamaicaway Towers	**320**	30
Sheraton-Boston Hotel	**310**	29
Buffalo, N.Y.		
Marine Midland Center	**529**	40
City Hall	**378**	32
Rand Bldg., not incl. 40-ft. beacon	**351**	29
Main Place Tower	**350**	26
One M&T Plaza	**317**	21
Liberty Bank	**305**	23
Calgary, Alta.		
Calgary Tower	**626**	...
Scotia Centre	**504**	38
Nova Bldg., 801 7th Ave. SW	**500**	37
Two Bow Valley Square	**468**	39
Fifth & Fifth Bldg.	**460**	35
Oxford Square North	**463**	34
Shell Tower	**460**	34
Oxford Square South	**449**	33
Four Bow Valley Square	**441**	37
Esso Plaza (twin towers)	**435**	34
Family Life Bldg.	**410**	33
Pan Canadian Bldg., 150 9th Ave. SW	**410**	28
Norcen Tower	**408**	33
Sun Oil Bldg.	**397**	34
Western Centre	**385**	40
Three Bow Valley Square	**382**	33
Mobil Tower	**369**	29
Sun Life Bldg. (twin towers)	**374**	28
A.G.T. Tower, 411 1st St. SE.	**366**	28
One Palliser Square	**350**	28
Mount Royal House	**330**	34
Standard Life Bldg.	**327**	25
Place Concorde (twin towers)	**321**	36
Bow Valley Inn	**320**	25
Charlotte, N.C.		
NCNB Plaza, 101 S. Tryon	**503**	40
First Union Plaza	**433**	32
Wachovia Center, 400 S. Tryon	**420**	32
Southern National Center,	**300**	22
Chicago, Ill.		
Sears Tower (world's tallest)	**1,454**	110
Standard Oil (Indiana)	**1,136**	80
John Hancock Center	**1,127**	100
Water Tower Place (a)	**859**	74
First Natl. Bank	**850**	60
Three First National Plaza	**775**	57
*One Magnificent Mile	**770**	58
Huron Apts	**723**	56
IBM Bldg.	**695**	52
Daley Center	**662**	31
Lake Point Tower	**645**	70
Board of Trade, incl. 81 ft. statue	**605**	44
Prudential Bldg., 130 E. Randolph	**601**	41
Antenna tower, 311 ft., makes total	**912**	...
1000 Lake Shore Plaza Apts.	**590**	55
Marina City Apts., 2 buildings	**588**	61
Mid Continental Plaza	**580**	50
Pittsfield, 55 E. Washington St.	**557**	38
Kemper Insurance Bldg.	**555**	45
Newberry Plaza, State & Oak	**553**	56
One South Wacker Dr.	**550**	40
Harbor Point	**550**	54
LaSalle Natl. Bank, 135 S. LaSalle St.	**535**	44
One LaSalle Street	**530**	49
111 E. Chestnut St.	**529**	56
River Plaza, Rush & Hubbard	**524**	56
Pure Oil, 35 E. Wacker Drive	**523**	40
United Ins. Bldg., 1 E. Wacker Dr.	**522**	41
Lincoln Tower, 75 E. Wacker Dr.	**519**	42
Carbide & Carbon, 230 N. Mich.	**503**	37
Walton Colonnade	**500**	44
LaSalle-Wacker, 221 N. LaSalle St.	**491**	41
Amer. Nat'l. Bank, 33 N. LaSalle St.	**479**	40
Bankers, 105 W. Adams St.	**476**	41
Brunswick Bldg.	**475**	37
Continental Companies	**475**	45
American Furniture Mart	**474**	24

City	Hgt. ft.	Stories
333 Wacker Dr.	472	36
Sheraton Hotel, 505 N. Mich. Ave.	471	42
Playboy Bldg., 919 N. Mich. Ave.	468	37
188 Randolph Tower	465	45
Tribune Tower, 435 N. Mich. Ave.	462	36
Chicago Marriott, Mich. & Ohio Sts.	460	45

(a) World's tallest reinforced concrete bldg.

Cincinnati, Oh.

City	Hgt. ft.	Stories
Carew Tower	568	49
Central Trust Tower	504	33
Netherland Hilton	372	31
Dubois Tower, 5th & Walnut	423	32
Central Trust Center	355	27
First Natl. Bank Center	351	26
Stouffer's North Tower	350	33
Kroger Bldg.	320	25
Federated Bldg.	317	21

Cleveland, Oh.

City	Hgt. ft.	Stories
Terminal Tower	708	52
Erieview Plaza Tower	529	38
Justice Center, 1250 Ontario	420	26
Federal Bldg.	419	32
National City Complex	410	35
Cleveland Trust Tower No. 1	383	29
*Medical Mutual Bldg.	380	31
Ohio-Bell Telephone	365	24
Cleveland State Univ. Towers	319	21
Central Natl. Bank Bldg.	305	21
Diamond Shamrock Bldg.	300	23
CEI Bldg.	300	22

Columbus, Oh.

City	Hgt. ft.	Stories
James A. Rhodes (State Office Tower), 30 E. Broad	624	41
LeVeque Tower, 50 W. Broad	555	47
One Nationwide Plaza	485	40
Borden Bldg., 180 E. Broad	438	34
Columbus Center, 100 E. Broad	357	24
Ohio Bell Bldg., 150 E. Gay St.	346	26
88 E. Broad St.	324	20
BancOhio Plaza, 155 E. Broad	317	25

Dallas, Tex.

City	Hgt. ft.	Stories
*Main Centre, 901 Main St.	939	73
First International Bldg.	710	56
Arco Tower, 1601 Bryan St.	660	49
Thanksgiving Tower, 1600 Pacific Ave.	645	50
*Two Dallas Centre	635	50
First National Bank	625	52
Republic Bank Tower	598	50
First City Center, 1700 Pacific Ave.	595	49
*SW Bell Admin. Tower	580	37
*One Lincoln Plaza	579	45
Olympia York, 1999 Bryan St.	562	37
Reunion Tower	560	50
Southland Life Tower	550	42
Diamond Shamrock, 717 N. Harwood St.	550	34
2001 Bryan St.	512	40
San Jacinto Tower	456	33
Republic Bank Bldg., not incl. 150-ft. ornamental tower	452	36
One Main Place	445	34
LTV Tower	434	31
Mercantile Natl. Bank Bldg., not incl. 115-ft. weather beacon	430	31
Mobil Bldg.	430	31
Mart Hotel	400	29
Fidelity Union Tower	400	33
One Dallas Centre	386	30
Southwestern Bell Toll Bldg.	372	22
Court House & Fedl. Office Bldg.	362	16
Mercantile Dallas Bldg.	360	22
Sheraton Hotel	352	38
Plaza of The America's (E. Tower)	344	26
Hyatt Hotel, 303 Reunion Blvd.	343	30
Elm Place, 1005-09 Elm St.	341	22
Main Tower	336	26
Dallas Galleria Tower	333	26
Plaza of the America's (N. & S. towers)	332	25
Park Central No. 3	327	20
Adolphus Tower	327	27
Bell Telephone Bldg.	326	23

Dayton, Oh.

City	Hgt. ft.	Stories
Winters Bank Bldg.	404	30
Mead Tower, 10 W. 2d St.	365	28
Centre City Office Bldg.	297	21
Hulman Bldg.	295	23
Grant-Deneau Bldg.	290	22

Denver, Col.

City	Hgt. ft.	Stories
*Republic Plaza	714	56
*City Center Four	706	54
*United Bank of Denver	697	52
Arco Tower	600	42
Anaconda Tower	580	40
One Denver Place	467	35
Amoco Bldg., 17th Ave. & Broadway	450	36
Brooks Towers, 1020 15th St.	420	42
First of Denver Plaza	415	32
*Stellar Plaza	410	32
17th Street Plaza	406	32
Energy Center 1	404	29
Colorado Nat'l. Bank, 17th & Curtis	389	26
First National Bank	385	28
Security Life Bldg.	384	33
*Centennial Plaza	374	31
Energy Plaza, 1125 17th St.	370	28
*Downtown Plaza	368	30
Lincoln Center	366	30
Denver Natl. Bank Plaza	363	29
Western Fed. Savings	357	27
Colorado State Bank	352	26
Executive Tower	350	30
Larimer Place	335	32
410 Building	335	24
Mountain Bell, 17th & Curtis	330	21
D&F Tower	330	20
Great West Plaza (twin towers)	325	29
Prudential Tower Plaza	322	25
Barclay Towers	314	30

Des Moines, Ia.

City	Hgt. ft.	Stories
Ruan Center	457	36
Financial Center, 7th & Walnut	345	25
Marriott Hotel, 700 Grand Ave.	340	33
Equitable Bldg.	318	19

Detroit, Mich.

City	Hgt. ft.	Stories
Detroit Plaza Hotel	720	71
City Natl. Bank Bldg., 637 Griswold	557	47
15000 Town Center Dr.	554	40
Guardian, 500 Griswold	485	40
Renaissance Center (4 bldgs.)	479	39
Book Tower, 1227 Wash. Blvd.	472	35
13000 Town Center Dr.	443	32
Cadillac Tower, 51 Cadillac Sq.	437	40
David Stott, 1150 Griswold	436	38
Mich. Cons. Gas Co. Bldg.	430	32
Fisher, W. Grand Blvd. & 2d St.	420	28
J. L. Hudson Bldg.	397	28
McNamara Federal Office Bldg.	393	27
Detroit Bank & Trust Bldg., 6438 Woodward	374	27
American Center	374	27
Top of Troy Bldg.	374	27
Detroit Bank & Trust Bldg., 211 W. Fort.	370	28
Edison Plaza	365	25
Woodward Tower	358	34
Buhl, 535 Griswold	350	26
Ford Bldg.	346	25
Michigan Bell Telephone	340	19
1st Federal Savings & Loan	338	23
Pontchartrain Motor Hotel	336	23
Commonwealth Bldg.	325	25
1300 Lafayette East	325	30

Edmonton, Alta.

City	Hgt. ft.	Stories
AGT Tower, 10020-100 St.	441	34
CCB Tower, 10124-103 Ave.	410	34
Principal Plaza, 10303 Jasper Ave.	370	30
CN Tower, 1004-104 Ave.	365	26
Toronto Dominion Tower	325	27
Oxford Tower	325	29
Sun Life Bldg.	320	25
Edmonton House	315	34

Fort Wayne, Ind.

City	Hgt. ft.	Stories
One Summit Square, 911 S. Calhoun	442	27
Ft. Wayne Natl. Bank	339	26
Lincoln Natl. Bank	312	23

Fort Worth, Tex.

City	Hgt. ft.	Stories
*Center Tower II	546	38
*1st United Tower	536	40
Continental Plaza	525	40
1st City Bank Tower	475	33
Ft. Worth Natl. Bank	454	37
Continental Natl. Bank Bldg.	380	30

City	Hgt. ft.	Stories
Continental Life	307	24
First National Bank, 500 W. 7th	300	21
One Tandy Center	300	20
Two Tandy Center	300	20
Hamilton, Ont.		
Century Twenty One	418	43
Stelco Tower	339	25
The Olympia	321	33
Harrisburg, Pa.		
State Office Tower #2	334	21
City Towers	291	25
Hartford, Conn.		
Travelers Ins. Co. Bldg.	527	34
Hartford Plaza	420	22
Hartford Natl. Bank & Trust	360	26
One Commercial Plaza	349	27
One Financial Plaza, 755 Main	335	26
One Corporate Center	305	23
Honolulu, Ha.		
Ala Moana Hotel	390	38
Pacific Trade Center	360	30
Ala Nanala Apt.	350	41
Honolulu Tower	350	40
Lakeside Development	350	40
Tapa Tower	350	35
Discovery Bay	350	42
Hyatt Regency Waikiki	350	39
Hemmeter Center	350	39
Mehelani Waikiki Lodge	350	43
Regency Tower, 2525 Date St.	350	42
Regency Tower #2	350	43
Yacht Harbor Towers	350	40
Canterbury Place	350	40
Iolani Towers	350	38
Diamond Head Tower	350	38
Ala Wai Sunset	350	44
Century Center	350	41
Pacific Beach Hotel	350	43
Waikiki Ala Wai Waterfront	350	43
Waikiki Lodge II	350	43
*Lakeside Development, Ala Makahala Pl.	349	40
Chateau Waikiki	349	39
Rainbow Plaza	348	37
Waikiki Beach Tower	347	39
2121 Ala Wai Blvd.	347	41
*Lakeside Development, Ala Poha Pl.	346	40
*Lakeside Development, Ala Napunani	346	40
Royal Kuhio	346	39
Century Square	344	36
Houston, Tex.		
Texas Commerce Tower	997	75
Allied Bank Plaza, 1000 Louisiana	992	71
*Transco Tower	899	64
*Main Place, 1201 Main	803	60
*RepublicBank Center	780	56
First International Plaza	748	55
*1600 Smith St.	729	54
Gulf Tower, 1301 McKinney	725	52
One Shell Plaza (not incl. 285 ft. TV tower)	714	50
*Four Allen Center	692	50
Capital Natl. Bank Plaza	685	50
One Houston Center	678	47
First City Tower	662	47
1100 Milam Bldg.	651	47
Exxon Bldg.	606	44
*The America Tower	577	42
*Marathon Oil Tower	572	41
Two Houston Center	570	40
Dresser Tower	550	40
*1415 Louisiana Tower	550	44
Pennzoil, 700 Milam (2 bldgs.)	523	36
Two Allen Center	521	36
Entex Bldg.	518	35
Tenneco Bldg.	502	33
Conoco Tower	465	32
One Allen Center	452	34
Summit Tower West	441	31
Coastal Tower	441	31
Four Leafs Towers (2 bldgs.)	439	40
Gulf Bldg.	428	37
*Central Tower (4 Oaks Place)	420	30
First City Natl. Bank	410	32
Houston Lighting & Power	410	27
Neils Esperson Bldg.	409	31
Hyatt Regency Houston	401	34
*Park Central	390	28
Houston Natural Gas Bldg.	386	28
Amoco Center, 501 Westlake Blvd.	382	28
Bank of the Southwest	369	24
*Resource Centre 1	352	26
Sheraton-Lincoln Hotel	352	28
*Allied Bank Tower (4 Oaks Place)	351	25
*West Tower (4 Oaks Place)	351	25
Two Shell Plaza	341	26
American General Life	337	25
*ParkWest Tower One	337	25
Transco	333	25
Four Seasons Hotel, 1300 Lamar	330	29
Allied Chemical Bldg.	328	25
609 Fannin Bldg.	325	22
Holiday Inn	325	30
Hull, Que.		
Les Terrasses De La Chaudiere	383	30
Place Du Portage, Phase 1	333	24
Indianapolis, Ind.		
American United Life Ins. Co.	533	37
Indiana Natl. Bank Tower	504	37
City-County Bldg.	377	26
Merchants Plaza/Hyatt Regency Hotel	328	26
Indiana Bell Telephone	320	20
Blue Cross-Blue Shield Bldg.	302	18
Jacksonville, Fla.		
Independent Life & Acccident Ins. Co.	535	37
Gulf Life Ins. Co. Bldg.	432	28
Prudential Ins. Co. of America	295	22
Kansas City, Mo.		
Kansas City Power and Light Bldg.	476	32
City Hall	443	29
Federal Office Bldg.	413	35
Commerce Tower	402	32
Southwest Bell Telephone Bldg.	394	27
Pershing Road Associates	352	28
A. T. & T. Long Line Bldg.	331	20
Bryant Bldg.	319	26
Federal Reserve Bldg.	311	21
City Center Square, 1100 Main	302	30
Holiday Inn	300	28
Las Vegas, Nev.		
Las Vegas Hilton	375	30
MGM Grand	362	26
Landmark Hotel	356	31
Sundance Hotel	322	33
Little Rock, Ark.		
First National Bank	454	33
Worthen Bank & Trust	375	28
Union National Bank	331	24
Tower Bldg.	300	18
Los Angeles, Cal.		
First Interstate Bank	858	62
Security Pacific Natl. Bank	738	55
Crocker Center, 313 S. Grand	718	53
Atlantic Richfield Plaza (2 bldgs.)	699	52
"J" Square, 444 S. Flower	625	49
Crocker-Citizen Plaza	620	42
Century Plaza Towers (2 bldgs.)	571	44
Union Bank Square	516	41
City Hall	454	28
Equitable Life Bldg.	454	34
Occidental Life Bldg.	452	32
Mutual Benefit Life Ins. Bldg.	435	31
Broadway Plaza	414	33
1900 Ave. of Stars	398	27
1 Wilshire Bldg.	395	28
The Evian, 10490 Wilshire Blvd.	390	31
Bonaventure Hotel, 404 S. Figueroa	367	35
Cal. Fed. Savings & Loan Bldg.	363	28
Century City Office Bldg.	363	26
Bunker Hill Towers	349	32
International Industries Plaza	347	24
City Natl. Bank Bldg.	344	24
Wilshire West Plaza	327	24
Louisville, Ky.		
First Natl. Bank	512	40
Citizen's Plaza	420	30
Galt House	325	25
United Kentucky Bldg.	312	24

City	Hgt. ft.	Stories
Memphis, Tenn.		
100 N. Main Bldg.	**430**	37
Commerce Square	**396**	31
Sterick Bldg.	**365**	31
Clark, 5100 Poplar	**365**	32
First Natl. Bank Bldg.	**332**	25
Hyatt Regency	**329**	28
Miami, Fla.		
One Biscayne Corp.	**456**	40
First Federal Savings & Loan	**375**	32
Dade County Court House	**357**	28
New World Center	**340**	30
Plaza Venetia	**332**	33
Flagler Center Bldg.	**318**	25
Milwaukee, Wis.		
First Wis. Center & Office Tower	**625**	42
City Hall	**350**	9
Wisconsin Telephone Co.	**313**	19
Minneapolis, Minn.		
IDS Center	**775**	57
Multifoods Tower	**715**	52
Pillsbury Bldg., 200 S. 6th St.	**552**	40
Foshay Tower, not including 163-ft. antenna tower	**447**	32
*Amfac Hotel	**440**	32
Hennepin County Government Center	**403**	24
First Natl. Bank Bldg.	**366**	28
Municipal Building	**355**	14
North Western Bell Telephone	**350**	26
100 Washington Square	**340**	22
Cedar-Riverside	**337**	39
Dain Tower	**311**	26
Montreal, Que.		
Place Victoria	**624**	47
Place Ville Marie	**616**	42
Canadian Imperial Bank of Commerce	**604**	43
Le Complexe Desjardins		
La Tour du Sud	**498**	40
La Tour du L'Est	**428**	32
La Tour du Nord	**355**	27
La Tour Laurier	**425**	36
C.I.L. House	**429**	32
Chateau Champlain Hotel	**420**	38
Port Royal Apts.	**400**	33
Royal Bank Tower	**397**	22
Sun Life Bldg.	**390**	26
Banque Canadienne National	**390**	32
Place du Canada	**372**	33
Hydro Quebec	**360**	27
Alexis Nihon Plaza	**331**	33
Nashville, Tenn.		
Natl. Life & Acc. Ins. Co.	**452**	31
Nashville Life & Casualty Tower	**409**	30
James K. Polk State Office Bldg.	**392**	32
First American Natl. Bank	**354**	28
Hyatt Regency	**300**	28
Newark, N.J.		
National Newark & Essex Bank	**465**	36
Raymond-Commerce	**448**	36
Park Plaza Bldg.	**400**	26
Prudential Corporate Bldg.	**369**	27
Prudential Ins. Co., 753 Broad St.	**360**	26
Western Electric Bldg.	**359**	31
Gateway 1	**359**	31
American Insurance Company	**326**	21
New Orleans, La.		
One Shell Square	**697**	51
Plaza Tower	**531**	45
Marriott Hotel	**450**	42
Canal Place One	**439**	32
Bank of New Orleans	**438**	31
Int'l. Trade Mart Bldg.	**407**	33
225 Baronne St.	**362**	28
Hyatt-Regency Hotel, Poydras Plaza	**360**	25
Hibernia Bank Bldg.	**355**	23
1250 Poydras Plaza	**341**	24
New Orleans Hilton, Intl. River Center	**340**	29
American Bank Bldg.	**330**	23
Pan American Life Bldg.	**323**	27
New York, N.Y.		
World Trade Center (2 towers)	**1,350**	110
Empire State, 34th St. & 5th Ave.	**1,250**	102
TV tower, 222 ft., makes total	**1,472**	...
Chrysler, Lexington Ave. & 43d St.	**1,046**	77
American International Bldg., 70 Pine St.	**950**	67
40 Wall Tower	**927**	71
Citicorp Center	**914**	46
RCA Bldg., Rockefeller Center	**850**	70
1 Chase Manhattan Plaza	**813**	60
Pan Am Bldg., 200 Park Ave.	**808**	59
Woolworth, 233 Broadway	**792**	60
1 Penn Plaza	**764**	57
Exxon, 1251 Ave. of Americas	**750**	54
1 Liberty Plaza	**743**	50
Citibank	**741**	57
One Astor Plaza	**730**	54
Union Carbide Bldg., 270 Park Ave.	**707**	52
General Motors Bldg.	**705**	50
Metropolitan Life, 1 Madison Ave.	**700**	50
500 5th Ave.	**697**	60
9 W. 57th St.	**688**	50
Chem. Bank, N.Y. Trust Bldg.	**687**	50
55 Water St.	**687**	53
Chanin, Lexington Ave. & 42d St.	**680**	56
Gulf & Western Bldg.	**679**	44
Marine Midland Bldg., 140 Bway.	**677**	52
McGraw Hill, 1221 Ave. of Am.	**674**	51
Lincoln, 60 E. 52d Street	**673**	53
1633 Broadway	**670**	48
725 5th Ave.	**664**	60
American Brands, 245 Park Ave.	**648**	47
*A. T. & T. Tower, 570 Madison Ave.	**648**	37
General Electric, 570 Lexington	**640**	50
Irving Trust, 1 Wall St.	**640**	50
345 Park Ave.	**634**	44
Grace Plaza, 1114 Ave. of Am.	**630**	50
1 New York Plaza	**630**	50
Home Insurance Co. Bldg.	**630**	44
N.Y. Telephone, 1095 Ave. of Am.	**630**	40
888 7th Ave.	**628**	42
1 Hammarskjold Plaza	**628**	50
Waldorf-Astoria, 301 Park Ave.	**625**	47
Burlington House, 1345 Ave. of Am.	**625**	50
Olympic Tower, 645 5th Ave.	**620**	51
10 E. 40th St.	**620**	48
101 Park Ave.	**618**	50
New York Life, 51 Madison Ave.	**615**	40
Penney Bldg., 1301 Ave. of Am.	**609**	46
IBM, 590 Madison Ave.	**603**	41
560 Lexington Ave.	**600**	46
Celanese Bldg., 1211 Ave. of Am.	**592**	45
U.S. Court House, 505 Pearl St.	**590**	37
Federal Bldg., Foley Square	**587**	41
Time & Life, 1271 Ave. of Am.	**587**	47
Cooper Bregstein Bldg., 1250 Bway.	**580**	40
1185 Ave. of Americas	**580**	42
Municipal, Park Row & Centre St.	**580**	34
1 Madison Square Plaza	**576**	42
Westvaco Bldg. 299 Park Ave.	**574**	42
Socony Mobil Bldg., East 42d St.	**572**	45
Sperry Rand Bldg., 1290 Ave. of Am.	**570**	43
600 3d Ave.	**570**	42
Helmsley Bldg., 230 Park Ave.	**565**	35
1 Bankers Trust Plaza	**565**	40
Palace Hotel, Madison & 51st St.	**563**	51
30 Broad St.	**562**	48
Sherry-Netherland, 5th Ave. & 59th St.	**560**	40
Continental Can, 633 3d Ave.	**557**	39
Sperry & Hutchinson, 330 Madison	**555**	39
Galleria, 117 E. 57th St.	**552**	57
Interchem Bldg., 1133 Ave. of Am.	**552**	45
151 E. 44th St.	**550**	42
N.Y. Telephone, 323 Bway.	**550**	45
919 3d Ave.	**550**	47
Burroughs Bldg., 605 3d Ave.	**550**	44
Bankers Trust, 33 E. 48 St.	**547**	41
Transportation Bldg., 225 Bway.	**546**	45
Equitable, 120 Broadway	**545**	42
1 Brooklyn Bridge Plaza	**540**	42
Equitable Life, 1285 Ave. of Am.	**540**	42
Ritz Tower, Park Ave. & 57th St.	**540**	41
Bankers Trust, 6 Wall St.	**540**	39
1166 Ave. of Americas	**540**	44
1700 Broadway	**533**	41
Downtown Athletic Club, 19 West St.	**530**	45
Nelson Towers, 7th Ave. & 34th St.	**525**	45
767 3d Ave.	**525**	39
Hotel Pierre, 5th Ave. & 61st St.	**525**	44
House of Seagram, 375 Park Ave.	**525**	38
*7 World Trade Center	**525**	40
Random House, 825 3d Ave.	**522**	40

City	Hgt. ft.	Stories
3 Park Ave.	522	42
North American Plywood, 800 3d Ave.	520	41
Du Mont Bldg., 515 Madison Ave.	520	42
26 Broadway	520	31
Newsweek Bldg., 444 Madison Ave.	518	43
Sterling Drug Bldg., 90 Park Ave.	515	41
First National City Bank	515	41
Bank of New York, 48 Wall St.	513	32
Navarre, 512 7th Ave.	513	43
Williamsburgh Savings Bank, Bklyn.	512	42
ITT—American, 437 Madison Ave.	512	40
International, Rockefeller Center	512	41
1407 Broadway Realty Corp.	512	44
United Nations, 405 E. 42 St.	505	39
Park Vendome Tower	505	48
Oakland, Cal.		
Ordway Bldg., 2150 Valdez St.	404	28
Kaiser Bldg.	390	28
Clorox Bldg.	330	24
City Hall	319	15
Tribune Tower	305	21
Oklahoma City, Okla.		
Liberty Tower	500	36
First National Bank	493	33
City National Bank Tower	440	32
First Oklahoma Tower	425	31
Kerr-McGee Center	393	30
Mid America Plaza	362	19
*Penn Bank Tower	321	21
Fidelity Plaza	310	15
Southwestern Bell Telephone	303	15
Omaha, Neb.		
Woodmen Tower	469	30
Northwestern Bell Telephone Hdqrs.	334	16
Masonic Manor	320	22
First Natl. Bank	295	22
Ottawa, Ont.		
Place de Ville, Tower C	368	29
R.H. Coats Bldg.	326	27
Place Bell Canada	318	26
DBS Tower	308	26
Holiday Inn	308	28
Parliament Bldgs., Peace Tower	303	...
Philadelphia, Pa.		
City Hall Tower, incl. 37-ft. statue of Wm. Penn	548	7
Fidelity Mutual Life Ins. Bldg.	531	38
1818 Market St.	500	40
Phila. Saving Fund Society	490	39
Central Penn Natl. Bank	490	36
Centre Square (2 towers)	490/416	38/32
Industrial Valley Bank Bldg.	482	32
Philadelphia National Bank	475	25
Two Girard Plaza	450	30
2000 Market St. Bldg.	435	29
Atlantic Richfield Tower, Centre Square	412	33
Fidelity Bank Bldg.	405	30
Lewis Tower, 15th & Locust	400	33
1500 Locust St.	390	44
Academy House, 1420 Locust St.	390	37
Philadelphia Electric Co.	384	27
INA Annex, 1600 Arch St.	383	27
Penn Mutual Life	375	20
The Drake, 15th & Spruce	375	33
Medical Tower, 255 So. 17th	364	33
State Bldg., 1400 Spring Garden	351	18
United Engineers, 17th & Ludlow	344	20
Land Title, Broad & Chestnut	344	22
Packard, 15th & Chestnut	340	25
Inquirer Building	340	18
Dorchester	339	32
Franklin-Plaza Hotel	333	30
Suburban Station Bldg.	330	21
Phoenix, Ariz.		
Valley National Bank	483	40
Arizona Bank Downtown	407	31
First National Bank	372	27
United Bank Plaza, 3334 N. Central	356	27
First Federal Savings Bldg.	341	26
Hyatt Regency	317	20
Regency Apts.	297	21
Great Western Bank Plaza	295	20
Pittsburgh, Pa.		
U.S. Steel Bldg.	841	64
Dravo Tower	725	54
PPG Tower	623	40
One Oxford Centre	615	46
Gulf, 7th Ave. and Grant St.	582	44
University of Pittsburgh	535	42
Mellon Bank Bldg.	520	41
1 Oliver Plaza	511	39
Grant, Grant St. at 3rd Ave.	485	40
Koppers, 7th Ave. and Grant	475	34
Equibank Bldg.	445	34
Pittsburgh National Bldg.	424	30
Alcoa Bldg., 425 Sixth Ave.	410	30
Liberty Tower	358	29
Westinghouse Bldg.	355	23
Oliver, 535 Smithfield St.	347	25
Gateway Bldg. No. 3	344	24
Centre City Tower	341	26
Federal Bldg., 1000 Liberty Ave.	340	23
Bell Telephone, 416 7th Ave.	339	21
Hilton Hotel	333	22
Frick, 437 Grant St.	330	20
Portland, Ore.		
First Natl. Bank of Oregon	538	41
Georgia Pacific Bldg.	367	27
Providence, R.I.		
Industrial National Bank	420	26
Rhode Island Hospital Trust Tower	410	30
40 Westminster Bldg.	301	24
Richmond, Va.		
James Monroe Bldg.	450	29
City Hall (incl. penthouse)	425	17
*United Virginia Bank Bldg.	400	24
Federal Reserve Bank	393	26
First & Merchants Natl. Bank	333	25
One James River Plaza	305	22
Rochester, N.Y.		
Xerox Tower	443	30
Lincoln First Tower	390	26
Eastman Kodak Bldg.	360	19
First Federal Bank Plaza	305	22
St. Louis, Mo.		
Gateway Arch	630	...
Mercantile Trust Bldg.	550	37
Centerre Bldg.	515	35
Laclede Gas. Bldg., 8th & Olive	400	30
S.W. Bell Telephone Bldg.	398	31
Civil Courts	387	13
Queeny Tower	321	24
Counsel House Plaza	320	30
Park Plaza Hotel	310	30
Pierre Laclede Tower	309	24
Stauffer's Riverfront Inn, 3rd St.	301	22
St. Paul, Minn.		
First Natl. Bank Bldg., incl. 100-ft. sign	517	32
Osborn Bldg.	368	20
Kellogg Square Apts.	366	32
Northwestern Bell Telephone Bldg.	340	15
American National Bank Bldg.	335	25
North Central Tower	328	27
Minn. Mutual Life Center	315	21
St. Paul Cathedral	307	...
Conwed Tower	305	25
Salt Lake City, Ut.		
L.D.S. Church Office Bldg.	420	30
Beneficial Life Tower	351	27
City & County Bldg.	290	...
San Antonio, Tex.		
Tower of the Americas	622	...
Tower Life	404	30
Nix Professional Bldg.	375	23
Natl. Bank of Commerce	310	24
First Natl. Bank Tower	302	20
Frost Bank Tower	300	21
San Diego, Cal.		
California First Bank	388	27
Columbia Centre	379	27
Imperial Bank	355	24
Wells Fargo Bldg.	348	20
Wickes Bldg.	340	25
Financial Square	339	24
Central Federal	320	22
Union Bank	320	22

City	Hgt. ft.	Stories
Little America Westgate Hotel	303	19
San Francisco, Cal.		
Transamerica Pyramid	853	48
Bank of America	778	52
Embarcadero Center, No. 4	570	45
Security Pacific Bank	569	45
One Market Plaza, Spear St.	565	43
Wells Fargo Bldg.	561	43
Standard Oil, 575 Market St.	551	39
Shaklee Bldg., 444 Market	537	38
Aetna Life	529	38
First & Market Bldg.	529	38
Metropolitan Life	524	38
Hilton Hotel	493	46
Pacific Gas & Electric	492	34
Union Bank	487	37
Pacific Insurance	476	34
Bechtel Bldg., Fremont St.	475	33
333 Market Bldg.	474	33
Hartford Bldg.	465	33
Mutual Benefit Life	438	32
Russ Bldg.	435	31
Pacific Telephone Bldg.	435	26
Embarcadero Center, No. 3	412	31
Levi Strauss	412	31
Cal. State Automobile Assn.	399	29
Alcoa Bldg.	398	27
St. Francis Hotel	395	32
Shell Bldg.	386	29
595 Market Bldg.	379	30
Del Monte	378	28
Great Western Savings	359	26
Union Square Hyatt House Hotel	355	35
Equitable Life Bldg.	355	25
Fox Plaza	354	29
International Bldg.	350	22
450 Sutter Street	343	26
Cathedral Apts.	340	21
Royal Towers	330	24
Fairmont Hotel	330	29
Seattle, Wash.		
*Columbia Center	954	76
Seattle-1st Natl. Bank Bldg.	609	50
Space Needle	605	...
*First Interstate Center	574	48
Seafirst 5th Ave. Plaza	543	42
Bank of Cal., 900 4th Ave.	536	42
Rainer Bank Tower, 4th & Univ.	514	42
Smith Tower	500	42
Federal Office Bldg.	487	37
Pacific Northwest Bell	466	33
One Union Square	456	38
1111 3d Ave. Bldg.	454	35
Washington Plaza Second Tower	448	44
Westin Bldg., 2001 6th Ave.	409	34
Washington Plaza	397	40
Financial Center	389	30
Daon Bldg., 840 Olive Way	381	19
Sheraton Seattle Hotel	371	34
Fourth & Blanchard Bldg.	360	24
Park Hilton Hotel	352	33
First Hill Plaza	344	33
Safeco Plaza	325	22
Norton Bldg.	310	21
Springfield, Mass.		
Valley Bank Tower	370	29
Chestnut Towers	290	34
Tampa, Fla.		
Tampa City Center	537	39
First Financial Tower	458	36
Exchange Natl. Bldg.	280	22
Toledo, Oh.		
Owens-Illinois Corp. Headquarters	411	32
Owens-Corning Fiberglas Tower	400	30
Ohio Citizens Bank Bldg.	368	27

City	Hgt. ft.	Stories
City-County State Office Bldg.	300	22
Toronto, Ont.		
CN Tower, World's tallest self-supporting structure	1,821	...
First Canadian Place	952	72
Commerce Court West	784	57
Toronto-Dominion Tower (TD Centre)	758	56
Royal Trust Tower (TD Centre)	600	46
Royal Bank Plaza—South Tower	589	41
Manulife Centre	545	53
*Confederation Square	540	37
Two Bloor West	486	34
Exchange Tower	480	36
Commerce Court North	476	34
Simpson Tower	473	33
Sun Life Centre	470	35
Cadillac-Fairview Bldg., 10 Queen St.	465	36
Palace Pier (2 bldgs.)	452	46
Continental Bank Bldg.	450	35
Sheraton Centre	443	43
Hudson's Bay Centre	442	35
Leaside Towers (2 bldgs.)	423	44
Commercial Union Tower (TD Centre)	420	32
Maple Leaf Mills Tower	419	30
Plaza 2 Hotel	415	41
*Sun Life Bldg., 150 King St.	410	28
Royal York Hotel	399	27
390 Bay St.	394	31
Royal Bank Plaza—North Tower	387	26
Eaton Tower	385	29
*Maclean-Hunter Bldg.	380	30
Harborside Apts.	380	39
Harbour Castle Hilton, East	374	35
Travellers Tower	369	27
*360 Sun Life, 200 King St.	360	24
York Centre	360	27
3 Massey Square	354	38
Harbour Castle Hilton, West	353	35
Mowat Block	349	24
Toronto Professional Tower	346	26
L'Apartel at Harbour Square	344	36
Sutton Place Hotel	340	32
Richmond-Adelaide Centre	340	27
50 Cordova Ave.	340	36
Tulsa, Okla.		
Bank of Oklahoma Tower	667	52
City of Faith (clinic)	648	60
1st National Tower	516	41
4th Natl. Bank of Tulsa	412	33
320 South Boston Bldg.	400	24
Cities Service Bldg.	388	28
Univ. Club Tower	377	32
Philtower	343	24
Vancouver, B.C.		
Harbour Centre (incl. 100 ft. pylon)	581	32
Royal Bank Tower	468	37
Scotiabank Tower	451	36
Canada Trust Tower, 1055 Melville	454	35
T-D Bank Tower	410	31
200 Granville Square	403	30
Bentall III, 595 Burrand	399	31
Sheraton-Landmark Hotel	394	41
Hyatt Regency Vancouver	357	36
Hotel Vancouver	352	22
Oceanic Plaza	342	26
Board of Trade Tower	342	26
MacMillan-Bloedel Bldg.	340	28
Guinness Tower	328	23
Marine Bldg.	321	21
Winnipeg, Man.		
Richardson Bldg., 375 Main	406	32
Commodity Exchange Tower	393	32
55 Nassau St.	356	38
Winston-Salem, N.C.		
Wachovia Bldg.	410	30
Reynolds Bldg.	315	21

Tall Buildings in Other Cities

Figures denote number of stories. Height in feet is in parentheses.

Cape Canaveral, Fla., Vehicle Assembly Bldg., 40 (552); Allentown, Pa., Power & Light Bldg., 23 (320); Amarillo, Tex., American Natl. Bank, 33 (374); Bethlehem, Pa., Martin Tower, 21 (332); Charleston, W. Va., Kanawha Valley Bldg., 20 (384); Cuyahoga Falls, Oh., Cathedral Tower Restaurant, 60 (554); Frankfort, Ky., Capital Plaza Office Tower, 28 (338); Galveston, Tex., American National Ins., 20 (358); Greenville, S.C., Daniel Bldg., 22 (305); Halifax, N.S., Fenwick Towers, 31 (300); Knoxville, Tenn., United American Bank, 30 (400); Lansing, Mich., Michigan Natl. Tower, 25 (300, not including antenna tower); Lexington, Ky., Kinkaid Tower, 22 (333); Lincoln, Neb., State Capitol (432); Mobile, Ala., First Natl. Bank, 33 (420); New Haven, Conn., Knights of Columbus Hqs. (319); Niagara Falls, Ont., Skylon, (520); Syracuse, N.Y., State Tower, 22 (315); Tallahassee, Fla., State Capitol Tower, 22 (345).

HISTORY

Memorable Dates in U.S. History

1492

Christopher Columbus and crew sighted land **Oct. 12** in the present-day Bahamas.

1497

John Cabot explored northeast coast to Delaware.

1513

Juan Ponce de Leon explored Florida coast.

1524

Giovanni da Verrazano led French expedition along coast from Carolina north to Nova Scotia; entered New York harbor.

1539

Hernando de Soto landed in Florida **May 28**; crossed Mississippi River, **1541.**

1540

Francisco Vazquez de Coronado explored Southwest north of Rio Grande. Hernando de Alarcon reached Colorado River, Don Garcia Lopez de Cardenas reached Grand Canyon. Others explored California coast.

1565

St. Augustine, Fla. founded by Pedro Menendez. Razed by Francis Drake **1586.**

1579

Francis Drake claimed California for Britain. Metal plate, found **1936**, thought to be left by Drake, termed probable hoax **1979.**

1607

Capt. John Smith and 105 cavaliers in 3 ships landed on Virginia coast, started first permanent English settlement in New World at **Jamestown, May 13.**

1609

Henry Hudson, English explorer of Northwest Passage, employed by Dutch, sailed into New York harbor in **Sept.**, and up Hudson to Albany. The same year, **Samuel de Champlain** explored Lake Champlain just to the north.

Spaniards settled **Santa Fe., N.M.**

1619

House of Burgesses, first representative assembly in New World, elected **July 30** at Jamestown, Va.

First Negro laborers — indentured servants — in English N. American colonies, landed by Dutch at Jamestown in **Aug.** Chattel slavery legally recognized, **1650.**

1620

Plymouth Pilgrims, Puritan separatists from Church of England, some living in Holland, left Plymouth, England **Sept. 15** on Mayflower. Original destination Virginia, they reached Cape Cod **Nov. 19**, explored coast; 103 passengers landed **Dec. 21** (Dec. 11 Old Style) at Plymouth. Mayflower Compact was agreement to form a government and abide by its laws. Half of colony died during harsh winter.

1624

Dutch left 8 men from ship New Netherland on **Manhattan Island** in **May.** Rest sailed to Albany.

1626

Peter Minuit bought Manhattan for Dutch from Man-a-hat-a Indians **May 6** for trinkets valued at $24.

1634

Maryland founded as Catholic colony with religious tolerance.

1636

Harvard College founded **Oct. 28**, now oldest in U.S., Grammar school, compulsory education established at Boston.

Roger Williams founded Providence, R.I., **June**, as a democratically ruled colony with separation of church and state. Charter was granted, **1644.**

1654

First Jews arrived in New Amsterdam.

1660

British Parliament passed **Navigation Act**, regulating colonial commerce to suit English needs.

1664

Three hundred **British troops Sept. 8 seized New Netherland** from Dutch, who yield peacefully. Charles II granted province of New Netherland and city of New Amsterdam to brother, Duke of York; both renamed New York. The Dutch recaptured the colony **Aug. 9, 1673**, but ceded it to Britain **Nov. 10, 1674.**

1676

Nathaniel Bacon led planters against autocratic British Gov. Berkeley, burned Jamestown, Va. Bacon died, 23 followers executed.

Bloody **Indian war** in New England ended **Aug. 12.** King Philip, Wampanoag chief, and many Narragansett Indians killed.

1682

Robert Cavelier, Sieur de La Salle, claimed lower Mississippi River country for France, called it Louisiana **Apr. 9.** Had French outposts built in Illinois and Texas, **1684.** Killed during mutiny **Mar. 19, 1687.**

1683

William Penn signed treaty with Delaware Indians and made payment for Pennsylvania lands.

1692

Witchcraft delusion at Salem (now Danvers) Mass. inspired by preaching; 19 persons executed.

1696

Capt. William Kidd, American hired by British to fight pirates and take booty, becomes pirate. Arrested and sent to England, where he was hanged **1701.**

1699

French settlements made in Mississippi, Louisiana.

1704

Indians attacked Deerfield, Mass. **Feb. 28-29**, killed 40, carried off 100.

Boston News Letter, first regular newspaper, started by John Campbell, postmaster. (*Publick Occurences* was suppressed after one issue **1690.**)

1709

British-Colonial troops captured French fort, Port Royal, Nova Scotia, in **Queen Anne's War 1701-13.** France yielded Nova Scotia by treaty **1713.**

1712

Slaves revolted in New York **Apr. 6.** Six committed suicide, 21 were executed. Second rising, **1741;** 13 slaves hanged, 13 burned, 71 deported.

1716

First theater in colonies opened in Williamsburg, Va.

1728

Pennsylvania Gazette founded by Samuel Keimer in Philadelphia. Benjamin Franklin bought interest **1729.**

1732

Benjamin Franklin published first *Poor Richard's Almanac;* published annually to 1757.

1735

Freedom of the press recognized in New York by acquittal of John Peter Zenger, editor of *Weekly Journal*, on charge of libeling British Gov. Cosby by criticizing his conduct in office.

1740-41

Capt. Vitus Bering, Dane employed by Russians, reached Alaska.

1744

King George's War pitted British and colonials vs. French. Colonials captured Louisburg, Cape Breton Is. **June 17, 1745.** Returned to France **1748** by Treaty of Aix-la-Chapelle.

1752

Benjamin Franklin, flying kite in thunderstorm, proved

lightning is electricity **June 15**; invented lightning rod.

1754

French and Indian War (in Europe called 7 Years War, started 1756) began when French occupied Ft. Duquesne (Pittsburgh). British moved Acadian French from Nova Scotia to Louisiana **Oct. 1755.** British captured Quebec **Sept. 18, 1759** in battles in which French Gen. Montcalm and British Gen. Wolfe were killed. Peace signed **Feb. 10 1763.** French lost Canada and American Midwest. British tightened colonial administration in North America.

1764

Sugar Act placed duties on lumber, foodstuffs, molasses and rum in colonies.

1765

Stamp Act required revenue stamps to help defray cost of royal troops. Nine colonies, led by New York and Massachusetts at Stamp Act Congress in New York **Oct. 7-25, 1765,** adopted Declaration of Rights opposing taxation without representation in Parliament and trial without jury by admiralty courts. Stamp Act **repealed Mar. 17, 1766.**

1767

Townshend Acts levied taxes on glass, painter's lead, paper, and tea. In **1770** all duties except on tea were repealed.

1770

British troops fired **Mar. 5** into Boston mob, killed 5 including **Crispus Attucks,** a Negro, reportedly leader of group; later called **Boston Massacre.**

1773

East India Co. tea ships turned back at Boston, New York, Philadelphia in **May.** Cargo ship burned at Annapolis **Oct. 14,** cargo thrown overboard at **Boston Tea Party Dec. 16.**

1774

"Intolerable Acts" of Parliament curtailed Massachusetts self-rule; barred use of Boston harbor till tea was paid for.

First Continental Congress held in Philadelphia **Sept. 5-Oct. 26;** protested British measures, called for civil disobedience.

Rhode Island abolished slavery.

1775

Patrick Henry addressed Virginia convention, **Mar. 23** said "Give me liberty or give me death."

Paul Revere and William Dawes on night of **Apr. 18** rode to alert patriots that British were on way to Concord to destroy arms. At Lexington, Mass. **Apr. 19** Minutemen lost 8 killed. On return from Concord British took 273 casualties.

Col. Ethan Allen (joined by Col. Benedict Arnold) captured Ft. **Ticonderoga, N.Y. May 10;** also Crown Point. Colonials headed for **Bunker Hill,** fortified Breed's Hill, Charlestown, Mass., repulsed British under Gen. William Howe twice before retreating **June 17;** British casualties 1,000; called Battle of Bunker Hill. Continental Congress **June 15** named **George Washington** commander-in-chief.

1776

France and Spain each agreed **May 2** to provide one million livres in arms to Americans.

In Continental Congress **June 7,** Richard Henry Lee (Va.) moved "that these united colonies are and of right ought to be free and independent states." Resolution adopted July 2. **Declaration of Independence** approved **July 4.**

Col. Moultrie's batteries at **Charleston, S.C.** repulsed British sea attack **June 28.**

Washington, with 10,000 men, lost **Battle of Long Island Aug. 27,** evacuated New York.

Nathan Hale executed as spy by British **Sept. 22.**

Brig. Gen. Arnold's **Lake Champlain** fleet was defeated at Valcour **Oct. 11,** but British returned to Canada. Howe failed to destroy Washington's army at **White Plains Oct. 28.** Hessians captured Ft. Washington, Manhattan, and 3,000 men **Nov. 16;** Ft. Lee, N.J. **Nov. 18.**

Washington in Pennsylvania, recrossed **Delaware River Dec. 25-26,** defeated 1,400 Hessians at Trenton, N.J. **Dec. 26.**

1777

Washington defeated Lord Cornwallis at **Princeton Jan. 3.** Continental Congress adopted Stars and Stripes. *See Flag article.*

Maj. Gen. John Burgoyne with 8,000 from Canada captured **Ft. Ticonderoga July 6.** Americans beat back Burgoyne at Bemis Heights **Oct. 7** and cut off British escape route. Burgoyne surrendered 5,000 men at **Saratoga N.Y. Oct. 17.**

Marquis de Lafayette, aged 20, made major general.

Articles of Confederation and Perpetual Union adopted by Continental Congress **Nov. 15**

France recognized independence of 13 colonies **Dec. 17.**

1778

France signed treaty of aid with U.S. **Feb. 6.** Sent fleet; British evacuated Philadelphia in consequence **June 18.**

1779

John Paul Jones on the *Bonhomme Richard* defeated *Serapis* in British North Sea waters **Sept. 23.**

1780

Charleston, S.C. fell to the British **May 12,** but a British force was defeated near **Kings Mountain, N.C. Oct. 7** by militiamen.

Benedict Arnold found to be a traitor **Sept. 23.** Arnold escaped, made brigadier general in British army.

1781

Bank of North America incorporated in Philadelphia **May 26.**

Cornwallis, harrassed by U.S. troops, retired to **Yorktown, Va.** Adm. De Grasse landed 3,000 French and stopped British fleet in Hampton Roads. Washington and Rochambeau joined forces, arrived near Williamsburg **Sept. 26.** When siege of Cornwallis began **Oct. 6,** British had 6,000, Americans 8,846, French 7,800. **Cornwallis surrendered Oct. 19.**

1782

New **British** cabinet agreed **in March** to **recognize U.S.** independence. Preliminary agreement signed in Paris **Nov. 30.**

1783

Massachusetts Supreme Court **outlawed slavery** in that state, noting the words in the state Bill of Rights "all men are born free and equal."

Britain, U.S. signed **peace treaty Sept. 3** (Congress ratified it **Jan. 14, 1784).**

Washington ordered army disbanded Nov. 3, bade farewell to his officers at Fraunces Tavern, N.Y. City **Dec. 4.**

Noah Webster published *American Spelling Book,* great bestseller.

1784

First successful daily newspaper, **Pennsylvania Packet & General Advertiser,** published **Sept. 21.**

1786

Delegates from 5 states at **Annapolis, Md. Sept. 11-14** asked Congress to call convention in Philadelphia to write practical constitution for the 13 states.

1787

Shays's Rebellion, of debt-ridden farmers in Massachusetts, failed **Jan. 25.**

Northwest Ordinance adopted **July 13** by Continental Congress. Determined government of Northwest Territory north of Ohio River, west of New York; 60,000 inhabitants could get statehood. Guaranteed freedom of religion, support for schools, no slavery.

Constitutional convention opened at Philadelphia **May 25** with George Washington presiding. Constitution adopted by delegates **Sept. 17;** ratification by 9th state, New Hampshire, **June 21, 1788,** meant adoption; declared in effect **Mar. 4, 1789.**

1789

George Washington chosen president by all electors voting (73 eligible, 69 voting, 4 absent); John Adams, vice president, 34 votes. **Feb. 4.** First Congress met at Federal Hall, N.Y. City; regular sessions began **Apr. 6.** Washington inaugurated there **Apr. 30.** Supreme Court created by Federal Judiciary Act **Sept. 24.**

1790

Congress met in Philadelphia **Dec. 6,** new temporary Capital.

1791

Bill of Rights went into effect **Dec. 15.**

1792

Gen. **"Mad" Anthony Wayne** made commander in Ohio-Indiana area, trained "American Legion"; established string of forts. Routed Indians at Fallen Timbers on Maumee River **Aug. 20, 1794,** checked British at Fort Miami, Ohio.

1793

Eli Whitney invented **cotton gin,** reviving southern slavery.

1794

Whiskey Rebellion, west Pennsylvania farmers protesting liquor tax of **1791,** was suppressed by 15,000 militiamen **Sept. 1794.** Alexander Hamilton used incident to establish authority of the new federal government in enforcing its laws.

1795

U.S. bought peace from **Algiers and Tunis** by paying $800,000, supplying a frigate and annual tribute of $25,000 **Nov. 28.**

Gen. Wayne signed peace with Indians at Fort Greenville.

Univ. of North Carolina became first operating state university.

1796

Washington's Farewell Address as president delivered **Sept. 19.** Gave strong warnings against permanent alliances with foreign powers, big public debt, large military establishment and devices of "small, artful, enterprising minority" to control or change government.

1797

U.S. **frigate United States** launched at Philadelphia **July 10;** Constellation at Baltimore **Sept. 7;** Constitution (Old Ironsides) at Boston **Sept. 20.**

1798

War with France threatened over French raids on U.S. shipping and rejection of U.S. diplomats. Congress voided all treaties with France, ordered Navy to capture French armed ships. Navy (45 ships) and 365 privateers captured 84 French ships. USS Constellation took French warship Insurgente **1799.** Napoleon stopped French raids after becoming First Consul.

1801

Tripoli declared war June 10 against U.S., which refused added tribute to commerce-raiding Arab corsairs. Land and naval campaigns forced Tripoli to conclude **peace June 4, 1805.**

1803

Supreme Court, in **Marbury v. Madison** case, for the first time overturned a U.S. law **Feb. 24.**

Napoleon, who had recovered Louisiana from Spain by secret treaty, sold all of **Louisiana,** stretching to Canadian border, to U.S., for $11,250,000 in bonds, plus $3,750,000 indemnities to American citizens with claims against France. U.S. took title **Dec. 20.** Purchases doubled U.S. area.

1804

Lewis and Clark expedition ordered by Pres. Jefferson to explore what is now northwest U.S. Started from St. Louis **May 14;** ended **Sept. 23, 1806.** Sacajawea, an Indian woman, served as guide.

Vice Pres. **Aaron Burr,** after long political rivalry, **shot Alexander Hamilton** in a duel **July 11** in Weehawken, N.J.; Hamilton died the next day.

1807

Robert Fulton made first practical steamboat trip; left N.Y. City **Aug. 17,** reached Albany, 150 mi., in 32 hrs.

1808

Slave importation outlawed. Some 250,000 slaves were illegally imported **1808-1860.**

1811

William Henry Harrison, governor of Indiana, defeated Indians under the Prophet, in battle of Tippecanoe **Nov. 7.**

Cumberland Road begun at Cumberland, Md.; became important route to West.

1812

War of 1812 had 3 main causes: Britain seized U.S. ships trading with France; Britain seized 4,000 naturalized U.S. sailors by **1810;** Britain armed Indians who raided western border. U.S. stopped trade with Europe **1807** and **1809.** Trade with Britain only was stopped, **1810.**

Unaware that Britain had raised the blockade 2 days before, **Congress declared war June 18** by a small majority. The West favored war, New England opposed it. The British were handicapped by war with France.

U.S. naval victories in **1812** included: USS Essex captured Alert **Aug. 13;** USS Constitution destroyed Guerriere **Aug. 19;** USS Wasp took Frolic **Oct. 18;** USS United States defeated Macedonian off Azores **Oct. 25;** Constitution beat Java **Dec. 29.** British captured Detroit **Aug. 16.**

1813

Commodore **Oliver H. Perry** defeated British fleet at Battle of Lake Erie, **Sept. 10.** U.S. victory at Battle of the Thames, Ont., **Oct. 5,** broke Indian allies of Britain, and made Detroit frontier safe for U.S. But Americans failed in Canadian invasion attempts. York (Toronto) and Buffalo were burned.

1814

British landed in Maryland in August, defeated U.S. force **Aug. 24, burned Capitol** and White House. Maryland militia stopped British advance **Sept. 12.** Bombardment of Ft. McHenry, Baltimore, for 25 hours, **Sept. 13-14,** by British fleet failed; Francis Scott Key wrote words to **Star Spangled Banner.**

U.S. won naval Battle of **Lake Champlain Sept. 11.** Peace treaty signed at Ghent **Dec. 24.**

1815

Some 5,300 British, unaware of peace treaty, attacked U.S. entrenchments near **New Orleans, Jan. 1.** British had over 2,000 casualties, Americans lost 71.

U.S. flotilla finally ended piracy by **Algiers, Tunis, Tripoli** by **Aug. 6.**

1816

Second Bank of the U.S. chartered.

1817

Rush-Bagot treaty signed **Apr. 28-29;** limited U.S., British armaments on the Great Lakes.

1819

Spain cedes **Florida** to U.S. **Feb. 22.**

American steamship Savannah made first part steam-powered, part sail-powered crossing of Atlantic, Savannah, Ga. to Liverpool, Eng., 29 days.

1820

Henry Clay's **Missouri Compromise** bill passed by Congress **May 3.** Slavery was allowed in Missouri, but not elsewhere west of the Mississippi River north of 36° 30′ latitude (the southern line of Missouri). Repealed **1854.**

1821

Emma Willard founded Troy Female Seminary, first U.S. women's college.

1823

Monroe Doctrine enunciated **Dec. 2,** opposing European intervention in the Americas.

1824

Pawtucket, R.I. **weavers strike** in first such action by women.

1825

Erie Canal opened; first boat left Buffalo **Oct. 26,** reached N.Y. City **Nov. 4.** Canal cost $7 million but cut travel time one-third, shipping costs nine-tenths; opened Great Lakes area, made N.Y. City chief Atlantic port.

John Stevens, of Hoboken, N.J., built and operated first experimental **steam locomotive** in U.S.

1828

South Carolina **Dec. 19** declared the right of state **nullification of federal laws,** opposing the "Tariff of Abominations."

Noah Webster published his *American Dictionary of the English Language.*

Baltimore & Ohio first U.S. passenger railroad, was begun **July 4.**

1830

Mormon church organized by Joseph Smith in Fayette, N.Y. **Apr. 6.**

1831

Nat Turner, Negro slave in Virginia, led local slave rebellion, killed 57 whites in **Aug.** Troops called in, Turner captured, tried, and hanged.

1832

Black Hawk War (Ill.-Wis.) **Apr.-Sept.** pushed Sauk and Fox Indians west across Mississippi.

South Carolina convention passed **Ordinance of Nullification in Nov.** against permanent tariff, threatening to withdraw from the Union. Congress **Feb. 1833** passed a compromise tariff act, whereupon South Carolina repealed its act.

1833

Oberlin College, first in U.S. to adopt coeducation; refused to bar students on account of race, **1835.**

1835

Texas proclaimed right to secede from Mexico; Sam Houston put in command of Texas army, **Nov. 2-4.**

Gold discovered on **Cherokee land** in Georgia. Indians forced to cede lands **Dec. 20** and to cross Mississippi.

1836

Texans besieged in Alamo in San Antonio by Mexicans under Santa Anna **Feb. 23-Mar. 6**; entire garrison killed. Texas independence declared, **Mar. 2.** At San Jacinto **Apr. 21** Sam Houston and Texans defeated Mexicans.

Marcus Whitman, H.H. Spaulding and wives reached Fort Walla Walla on Columbia River, Oregon. **First white women to cross plains.**

Seminole Indians in Florida under Osceola began attacks **Nov. 1,** protesting forced removal. The unpopular 8-year war ended **Aug. 14, 1842;** Indians were sent to Oklahoma. War cost the U.S. 1,500 soldiers.

1841

First emigrant **wagon train for California,** 47 persons, left Independence, Mo. **May 1,** reached Cal. **Nov. 4.**

Brook Farm commune set up by New England transcendentalist intellectuals. Lasts to **1846.**

1842

Webster-Ashburton Treaty signed **Aug. 9,** fixing the U.S.-Canada border in Maine and Minnesota.

First use of **anesthetic** (sulphuric ether gas).

Settlement of Oregon begins via **Oregon Trail.**

1844

First message over first **telegraph line** sent **May 24** by inventor Samuel F.B. Morse from Washington to Baltimore: "What hath God wrought!"

1845

Texas Congress **voted for annexation** to U.S. **July 4.** U.S. Congress admits Texas to Union **Dec. 29.**

1846

Mexican War. Pres. James K. Polk ordered Gen. Zachary Taylor to seize disputed Texan land settled by Mexicans. After border clash, U.S. declared war **May 13;** Mexico **May 23.** Northern Whigs opposed war, southerners backed it.

Bear flag of Republic of California raised by American settlers at Sonoma **June 14.**

About 12,000 U.S. troops took Vera Cruz Mar. 27, 1847, Mexico City Sept. 14, 1947. By **treaty, Feb. 1848,** Mexico ceded claims to Texas, California, Arizona, New Mexico, Nevada, Utah, part of Colorado. U.S. assumed $3 million American claims and paid Mexico $15 million.

Treaty with Great Britain **June 15** set **boundary in Oregon** territory at 49th parallel (extension of existing line). Expansionists had used slogan "54° 40′ or fight."

Mormons, after violent clashes with settlers over polygamy, left Nauvoo, Ill. for West under Brigham Young, settled **July 1847 at Salt Lake City, Utah.**

Elias Howe invented **sewing machine.**

1847

First **adhesive U.S. postage stamps** on sale **July 1;** Benjamin Franklin 5¢, Washington 10¢.

Ralph Waldo Emerson published first book of poems; **Henry Wadsworth Longfellow** published *Evangeline.*

1848

Gold discovered Jan. 24 in California; 80,000 prospectors emigrate in **1849.**

Lucretia Mott and Elizabeth Cady Stanton lead **Seneca Falls, N.Y. Women's Rights Convention July 19-20.**

1850

Sen. Henry Clay's **Compromise of 1850** admitted California as 31st state **Sept. 9,** slavery forbidden; made Utah and New Mexico territories without decision on slavery; made Fugitive Slave Law more harsh; ended District of Columbia slave trade.

1851

Herman Melville's *Moby Dick,* **Nathaniel Hawthorne's** *House of the Seven Gables* published.

1852

Uncle Tom's Cabin, by **Harriet Beecher Stowe,** published.

1853

Commodore Matthew C. Perry, U.S.N., received by Lord of Toda, Japan **July 14; negotiated treaty to open Japan** to U.S. ships.

1854

Republican party formed at Ripon, Wis. **Feb. 28.** Opposed Kansas-Nebraska Act (became law **May 30**) which left issue of slavery to vote of settlers.

Henry David Thoreau published *Walden.*

1855

Walt Whitman published *Leaves of Grass.*

First railroad train crossed Mississippi on the river's first bridge, Rock Island, Ill.-Davenport, Ia. **Apr. 21.**

1856

Republican party's first nominee for president, **John C. Fremont,** defeated. Abraham Lincoln made 50 speeches for him.

Lawrence, Kan. sacked **May 21** by slavery party; abolitionist **John Brown** led anti-slavery men against Missourians at **Osawatomie, Kan. Aug. 30**

1857

Dred Scott decision by U.S. Supreme Court **Mar. 6** held, 6-3, that a Negro slave did not become free when taken into a free state, Congress could not bar slavery from a territory, and Negroes could not be citizens.

1858

First **Atlantic cable** completed by Cyrus W. Field **Aug. 5;** cable failed **Sept. 1.**

Lincoln-Douglas debates in Illinois **Aug. 21-Oct. 15.**

1859

First commercially productive **oil well,** drilled near Titusville, Pa., by Edwin L. Drake **Aug. 27.**

Abolitionist **John Brown** with 21 men seized U.S. Armory at **Harpers Ferry (then Va.) Oct. 16.** U.S. Marines captured raiders, killing several. Brown was hanged for treason by Virginia **Dec. 2.**

1860

New England shoe-workers, 20,000, strike, win higher wages.

Abraham Lincoln, Republican, elected president in 4-way race.

First **Pony Express** between Sacramento, Cal. and St. Joseph, Mo. started **Apr. 3;** service ended **Oct. 24, 1861** when first transcontinental telegraph line was completed.

1861

Seven southern states set up **Confederate States of America Feb. 8,** with Jefferson Davis as president. Confederates fired on **Ft. Sumter** in Charleston, S.C. **Apr. 12,** captured it **Apr. 14.**

President **Lincoln called for 75,000 volunteers Apr. 15.** By **May,** 11 states had seceded. Lincoln blockaded southern ports **Apr. 19,** cutting off vital exports, aid.

Confederates repelled Union forces at first **Battle of Bull Run July 21.**

First **transcontinental telegraph** was put in operation.

1862

Homestead Act was approved **May 20;** it granted free

family farms to settlers.

Land Grant Act approved **July 7,** providing for public land sale to benefit agricultural education; eventually led to establishment of state university systems.

Union forces were victorious in western campaigns, took **New Orleans.** Battles in East were inconclusive.

1863

Lincoln issued **Emancipation Proclamation Jan. 1,** freeing "all slaves in areas still in rebellion."

The entire **Mississippi River** was in Union hands by **July 4.** Union forces won a major victory at **Gettysburg, Pa. July 1-July 4.** Lincoln read his **Gettysburg Address Nov. 19.**

Draft riots in N.Y. City killed about 1,000, including Negroes who were hung by mobs **July 13-16.** Rioters protested provision allowing money payment in place of service. Such payments were ended 1864.

1864

Gen. Sherman marched through Georgia, taking Atlanta **Sept. 1,** Savannah **Dec. 22.**

Sand Creek massacre of Cheyenne and Arapaho Indians **Nov. 29** in a raid by 900 cavalrymen who killed 150-500 men, women, and children; 9 soldiers died. The tribes were awaiting surrender terms when attacked.

1865

Robert E. Lee surrendered 27,800 Confederate troops to Grant at Appomattox Court House, Va. **Apr. 9.** J.E. Johnston surrendered 31,200 to Sherman at Durham Station, N.C. **Apr. 18.** Last rebel troops surrendered **May 26.**

President **Lincoln was shot Apr. 14** by John Wilkes Booth in Ford's Theater, Washington; died the following morning. Booth was reported dead **Apr. 26.** Four co-conspirators were hung **July 7.**

Thirteenth Amendment, abolishing slavery, took effect **Dec. 18.**

1866

First post of the **Grand Army of the Republic** formed **Apr. 6;** was a major national political force for years. Last encampment, **Aug. 31, 1949,** attended by 6 of the 16 surviving veterans.

Ku Klux Klan formed secretly in South to terrorize Negros who voted. Disbanded **1869-71.** A second Klan was organized **1915.**

Congress took control of southern Reconstruction, backed freedmen's rights.

1867

Alaska sold to U.S. by Russia for $7.2 million **Mar. 30** through efforts of Sec. of State William H. Seward.

Horatio Alger published first book, *Ragged Dick.*

The **Grange** was organized **Dec 4,** to protect farmer interests.

1868

The World Almanac, a publication of the *New York World,* appeared for the first time.

Pres. **Andrew Johnson** tried to remove Edwin M. Stanton, secretary of war; was impeached by House **Feb. 24** for violation of Tenure of Office Act; acquitted by Senate **March-May.** Stanton resigned.

1869

Financial **"Black Friday"** in New York **Sept. 24;** caused by attempt to "corner" gold.

Transcontinental railroad completed; golden spike driven at Promontory, Utah **May 10** marking the junction of Central Pacific and Union Pacific.

Knights of Labor formed in Philadelphia. By **1886,** it had 700,000 members nationally.

Woman suffrage law passed in Territory of Wyoming **Dec. 10.**

1871

Great fire destroyed Chicago Oct. 8-11; loss est. at $196 million.

1872

Amnesty Act restored civil rights to citizens of the South **May 22** except for 500 Confederate leaders.

Congress founded first national park — **Yellowstone** in Wyoming.

1873

First U.S. **postal card** issued **May 1.**

Banks failed, panic began in **Sept.** Depression lasted 5 years.

"Boss" William Tweed of N.Y. City convicted of stealing public funds. He died in jail in **1878.**

Bellevue Hospital in N.Y. City started the first **school of nursing.**

1875

Congress passed **Civil Rights Act Mar. 1** giving equal rights to Negroes in public accommodations and jury duty. Act invalidated in **1883** by Supreme Court.

First **Kentucky Derby** held **May 17** at Churchill Downs, Louisville, Ky.

1876

Samuel J. Tilden, Democrat, received majority of popular votes for president over **Rutherford B. Hayes,** Republican, but 22 electoral votes were in dispute; issue left to Congress. Hayes given presidency **in Feb., 1877** after Republicans agree to end Reconstruction of South.

Col. **George A. Custer** and 264 soldiers of the 7th Cavalry killed **June 25** in "last stand," Battle of the Little Big Horn, Mont., in Sioux Indian War.

Mark Twain published *Tom Sawyer.*

1877

Molly Maguires, Irish terrorist society in Scranton, Pa. mining areas, broken up by hanging of 11 leaders for murders of mine officials and police.

Pres. Hayes sent troops in violent national **railroad strike.**

1878

First commercial **telephone** exchange opened, New Haven, Conn. **Jan. 28.**

1879

F.W. Woolworth opened his first five-and-ten store in Utica, N.Y. **Feb. 22.**

Henry George published *Progress & Poverty,* advocating single tax on land.

1881

Pres. **James A. Garfield shot** in Washington, D.C. **July 2;** died **Sept. 19.**

Booker T. Washington founded Tuskegee Institute for Negroes.

Helen Hunt Jackson published *A Century of Dishonor* about mistreatment of Indians.

1883

Pendleton Act, passed **Jan. 16,** reformed federal civil service.

Brooklyn Bridge opened **May 24.**

1886

Haymarket riot and bombing, evening of **May 4,** followed bitter labor battles for 8-hour day in Chicago; 7 police and 4 workers died, 66 wounded. Eight anarchists found guilty. Gov. John P. Altgeld denounced trial as unfair.

Geronimo, Apache Indian, finally surrendered **Sept. 4.**

American Federation of Labor (AFL) formed **Dec. 8** by 25 craft unions.

1888

Great blizzard in eastern U.S. **Mar. 11-14;** 400 deaths.

1889

Johnstown, Pa. flood May 31; 2,200 lives lost.

1890

First execution by **electrocution:** William Kemmler **Aug. 6** at Auburn Prison, Auburn, N.Y., for murder.

Battle of **Wounded Knee, S.D. Dec. 29,** the last major conflict between Indians and U.S. troops. About 200 Indian men, women, and children, and 29 soldiers were killed.

Castle Garden closed as N.Y. immigration depot; **Ellis Island** opened **Dec. 31,** closed **1954.**

Sherman Antitrust Act begins federal effort to curb monopolies.

Jacob Riis published *How the Other Half Lives,* about city slums.

1892

Homestead, Pa., strike at Carnegie steel mills; 7 guards and 11 strikers and spectators shot to death **July 6;** setback for unions.

1893

Financial panic began, led to 4-year depression.

1894

Thomas A. **Edison's kinetoscope** (motion pictures) (invented **1887**) given first public showing **Apr. 14** in N.Y. City.

Jacob S. Coxey led 500 unemployed from the Midwest into Washington, D.C. **Apr. 29.** Coxey was arrested for trespassing on Capitol grounds.

1896

William Jennings Bryan delivered "Cross of Gold" speech at Democratic National Convention in Chicago **July 8.**

Supreme Court, in **Plessy v. Ferguson,** approved racial segregation under the "separate but equal" doctrine.

1898

U.S. **battleship Maine** blown up **Feb. 15** at Havana, 260 killed.

U.S. blockaded Cuba Apr. 22 in aid of independence forces. Spain declared **war Apr. 24.** U.S. destroyed Spanish fleet in Philippines **May 1,** took Guam **June 20.**

Puerto Rico taken by U.S. **July 25-Aug. 12.** Spain agreed **Dec. 10** to cede Philippines, Puerto Rico, and Guam, and approved independence for Cuba.

U.S. annexed independent republic of **Hawaii.**

1899

Filipino insurgents, unable to get recognition of independence from U.S., started guerrilla war **Feb. 4.** Crushed with capture **May 23, 1901** of leader, Emilio Aguinaldo.

U.S. declared **Open Door Policy** to make China an open international market and to preserve its integrity as a nation.

John Dewey published *School and Society,* backing progressive education.

1900

Carry Nation, Kansas anti-saloon agitator, began raiding with hatchet.

U.S. helped suppress **"Boxers"** in Peking.

1901

Pres. William **McKinley was shot Sept. 6** by an anarchist, Leon Czolgosz; died **Sept. 14.**

1903

Treaty between U.S. and Colombia to have U.S. dig **Panama Canal** signed **Jan. 22,** rejected by Colombia. Panama declared independence with U.S. support **Nov. 3;** recognized by Pres. Theodore Roosevelt **Nov. 6.** U.S., Panama signed canal treaty **Nov. 18.**

Wisconsin set first **direct primary** voting system **May 23.**

First **automobile trip** across U.S. from San Francisco to New York **May 23-Aug. 1.**

First successful flight in heavier-than-air mechanically propelled airplane by **Orville Wright Dec. 17** near Kitty Hawk, N.C., 120 ft. in 12 seconds. Fourth flight same day by **Wilbur Wright,** 852 ft. in 59 seconds. Improved plane patented **May 22, 1906.**

Jack London published *Call of the Wild.*

Great Train Robbery, pioneering film, produced.

1904

Ida Tarbell published muckraking *History of Standard Oil.*

1905

First **Rotary Club** of local businessmen founded in Chicago.

1906

San Francisco earthquake and fire **Apr. 18-19** left 452 dead, $350 million damages.

Pure Food and Drug Act and Meat Inspection Act both passed **June 30.**

1907

Financial panic and depression started **Mar. 13.**

First round-world cruise of U.S. **"Great White Fleet";** 16 battleships, 12,000 men.

1909

Adm. Robert E. Peary reached **North Pole Apr. 6** on 6th attempt, accompanied by Matthew Henson, a black, and 4 Eskimos.

National Conference on the Negro convened **May 30,** leading to founding of the National Association for the Advancement of Colored People.

1910

Boy Scouts of America founded **Feb. 8.**

1911

Supreme Court dissolved **Standard Oil Co.**

First **transcontinental airplane flight** (with numerous stops) by C.P. Rodgers, New York to Pasadena, **Sept. 17-Nov. 5;** time in air 82 hrs., 4 min.

1912

U.S. sent marines **Aug. 14** to **Nicaragua,** which was in default of loans to U.S. and Europe.

1913

N.Y. Armory Show introduced modern art to U.S. public **Feb. 17.**

U.S. blockaded Mexico in support of revolutionaries.

Charles Beard published his *Economic Interpretation of the Constitution.*

Federal Reserve System was authorized **Dec. 23,** in a major reform of U.S. banking and finance.

1914

Ford Motor Co. raised basic wage rates from $2.40 for 9-hr. day to $5 for 8-hr. day **Jan. 5.**

When U.S. sailors were arrested at Tampico **Apr. 9,** Atlantic fleet was sent to **Veracruz,** occupied city.

Pres. Wilson proclaimed **U.S. neutrality** in the European war **Aug. 4.**

The **Clayton Antitrust Act** was passed **Oct. 15,** strengthening federal anti-monopoly powers.

1915

First **telephone talk,** New York to San Francisco, **Jan. 25** by Alexander Graham Bell and Thomas A. Watson.

British ship **Lusitania** sunk **May 7** by German submarine; 128 American passengers lost (Germany had warned passengers in advance). As a result of U.S. campaign, Germany issued apology and promise of payments **Oct. 5.** Pres. Wilson asked for a military fund increase **Dec. 7.**

U.S. troops landed in **Haiti July 28.** Haiti became a virtual U.S. protectorate under **Sept. 16** treaty.

1916

Gen. John J. **Pershing entered Mexico** to pursue Francisco (Pancho) Villa, who had raided U.S. border areas. Forces withdrawn **Feb. 5, 1917.**

Rural Credits Act passed **July 17,** followed by Warehouse Act. **Aug. 11;** both provided financial aid to farmers.

Bomb exploded during **San Francisco** Preparedness Day parade **July 22,** killed 10. Thomas J. Mooney, labor organizer, and Warren K. Billings, shoe worker, were convicted; both pardoned in **1939.**

U.S. bought **Virgin Islands** from Denmark **Aug. 4.**

U.S. established military government in the **Dominican Republic Nov. 29.**

Trade and loans to **European Allies** soared during the year.

John Dewey published *Democracy in Education.*

Carl Sandburg published *Chicago Poems.*

1917

Germany, suffering from British blockade, declared almost unrestricted **submarine warfare Jan. 31.** U.S. cut diplomatic ties with Germany **Feb. 3,** and formally declared war **Apr. 6.**

Conscription law was passed **May 18.** First U.S. troops arrived in Europe **June 26.**

The 18th **(Prohibition)** Amendment to the Constitution was submitted to the states by Congress **Dec. 18.** On **Jan. 16, 1919,** the 36th state (Nebraska) ratified it. Franklin D. Roosevelt, as 1932 presidential candidate, endorsed repeal; 21st Amendment repealed 18th; ratification completed **Dec. 5, 1933.**

1918

Over one million **American troops** were in Europe by **July**. War ended **Nov. 11.**

Influenza epidemic killed an estimated 20 million worldwide, 548,000 in U.S.

1919

First **transatlantic flight,** by U.S. Navy seaplane, left Rockaway, N.Y. **May 8,** stopped at Newfoundland, Azores, Lisbon **May 27.**

Boston police strike Sept. 9; National Guard breaks strike.

Sherwood Anderson published *Winesburg, Ohio.*

About 250 **alien radicals** were deported **Dec. 22.**

1920

In national **Red Scare,** some 2,700 Communists, anarchists, and other radicals were arrested **Jan.-May.**

Senate refused **Mar. 19** to ratify the **League of Nations Covenant.**

Nicola Sacco, 29, shoe factory employee and radical agitator, and **Bartolomeo Vanzetti,** 32, fish peddler and anarchist, accused of killing 2 men in Mass. payroll holdup **Apr. 15.** Found guilty **1921.** A 6-year worldwide campaign for release on grounds of want of conclusive evidence and prejudice failed. Both were executed **Aug. 23, 1927.** Vindicated July 19, 1977 by proclamation of Mass. Gov. Dukakis.

First regular licensed **radio broadcasting** begun **Aug. 20.**

Wall St., N.Y. City, **bomb** explosion killed 30, injured 100, did $2 million damage **Sept. 16.**

Sinclair Lewis' *Main Street,* **F. Scott Fitzgerald's** *This side of Paradise* published.

1921

Congress sharply curbed **immigration,** set national quota system **May 19.**

Joint Congressional resolution declaring **peace with Germany, Austria, and Hungary** signed **July 2** by Pres. Harding; treaties were signed in **Aug.**

Limitation of Armaments Conference met in Washington **Nov. 12 to Feb. 6, 1922.** Major powers agreed to curtail naval construction, outlaw poison gas, restrict submarine attack on merchantmen, respect integrity of China. Ratified **Aug. 5, 1925.**

Ku Klux Klan began revival with violence against blacks in North, South, and Midwest.

1922

Violence during **coal-mine strike** at Herrin, Ill., **June 22-23** cost 36 lives, 21 of them non-union miners.

Reader's Digest founded.

1923

First **sound-on-film motion picture,** "Phonofilm" was shown by Lee de Forest at Rivoli Theater, N.Y. City, beginning in **April.**

1924

Law approved by Congress **June 15** making all **Indians citizens.**

Nellie Tayloe Ross elected governor of Wyoming **Nov. 9** after death of her husband **Oct. 2;** installed **Jan. 5, 1925,** first woman governor. **Miriam (Ma) Ferguson** was elected governor of Texas **Nov. 9;** installed **Jan. 20, 1925.**

George Gershwin wrote *Rhapsody in Blue.*

1925

John T. Scopes found guilty of having taught evolution in Dayton, Tenn. high school, fined $100 and costs **July 24.**

1926

Dr. Robert H. Goddard demonstrated practicality of **rockets Mar. 16** at Auburn, Mass. with first liquid fuel rocket; rocket traveled 184 ft. in 2.5 secs.

Air Commerce Act passed, providing federal aid for airlines and airports.

1927

About 1,000 **marines landed in China Mar. 5** to protect property in civil war. U.S. and British consulates looted by nationalists **Mar. 24.**

Capt. **Charles A. Lindbergh** left Roosevelt Field, N.Y. **May 20** alone in plane Spirit of St. Louis on first New York-Paris nonstop flight. Reached Le Bourget airfield **May 21,** 3,610 miles in 33 ½ hours.

The Jazz Singer, with **Al Jolson,** demonstrated part-talking pictures in N.Y. City **Oct. 6.**

Show Boat opened in New York **Dec. 27.**

O. E. Rolvaag published *Giants in the Earth.*

1929

"St. Valentine's Day massacre" in Chicago **Feb. 14;** gangsters killed 7 rivals.

Farm price stability aided by **Agricultural Marketing Act,** passed **June 15.**

Albert B. Fall, former sec. of the interior, was convicted of accepting a bribe of $100,000 in the leasing of the **Elk Hills (Teapot Dome)** naval oil reserve; sentenced **Nov. 1** to $100,000 fine and year in prison.

Stock Market crash Oct. 29 marked end of postwar prosperity as stock prices plummeted. Stock losses for 1929-31 estimated at $50 billion; worst American depression began.

Thomas Wolfe published *Look Homeward, Angel.* **William Faulkner** published *The Sound and the Fury.*

1930

London **Naval Reduction Treaty** signed by U.S., Britain, Italy, France, and Japan **Apr. 22;** in effect **Jan. 1, 1931;** expired **Dec. 31, 1936.**

Hawley-Smoot Tariff signed; rate hikes slash world trade.

1931

Empire State Building opened in N.Y. City **May 1.**

Pearl Buck published *The Good Earth.*

1932

Reconstruction Finance Corp. established **Jan. 22** to stimulate banking and business. Unemployment stood at 12 million.

Charles Lindbergh Jr. kidnaped Mar. 1, found dead **May 12.**

Bonus March on Washington **May 29** by World War I veterans demanding Congress pay their bonus in full. Army, under Gen. Douglas MacArthur, disbanded the marchers on Pres. Hoover's orders.

1933

All **banks in the U.S. were ordered closed** by Pres. Roosevelt **Mar. 6.**

In the "100 days" special session, **Mar. 9—June 16,** Congress passed **New Deal** social and economic measures.

Gold standard dropped by U.S.; announced by Pres. Roosevelt **Apr. 19,** ratified by Congress **June 5.**

Prohibition ended in the U.S. as 36th state ratified 21st Amendment **Dec. 5.**

U.S. foreswore armed intervention in **Western Hemisphere** nations **Dec. 26.**

1934

U.S. troops pull out of **Haiti Aug. 6.**

1935

Comedian **Will Rogers** and aviator Wiley Post **killed Aug. 15** in Alaska plane crash.

Social Security Act passed by Congress **Aug. 14.**

Huey Long, Senator from Louisiana and national political leader, was **assassinated Sept. 8.**

Porgy and Bess, **George Gershwin** opera on American Negro theme, opened **Oct. 10** in N.Y. City.

Committee for Industrial Organization (CIO) formed to expand industrial unionism **Nov. 9.**

1936

Boulder Dam completed.

Margaret Mitchell published *Gone With the Wind.*

1937

Amelia Earhart Putnam, aviator, and co-pilot Fred Noonan lost **July 2** near Howland Is. in the Pacific.

Pres. Roosevelt asked for 6 additional Supreme Court justices; **"packing" plan** defeated.

Auto, steel labor unions won first big contracts.

1938

Naval Expansion Act passed **May 17.**

National minimum wage enacted **June 28.**

Orson Welles radio dramatization of *War of the Worlds* caused nationwide scare **Oct. 30.**

1939

Pres. Roosevelt asked **defense budget hike Jan. 5, 12.**

N.Y. World's Fair opened **Apr. 30,** closed **Oct. 31;** reopened **May 11, 1940,** and finally closed **Oct. 21.**

Einstein alerts FDR to **A-bomb** opportunity in **Aug. 2** letter.

U.S. declares its neutrality in European war **Sept. 5.**

Roosevelt proclaimed a limited **national emergency Sept. 8,** an unlimited emergency **May 27, 1941.** Both ended by Pres. Truman **Apr. 28, 1952.**

John Steinbeck published *Grapes of Wrath.*

1940

U.S. authorized sale of **surplus war material** to Britain **June 3;** announced transfer of 50 overaged destroyers **Sept. 3.**

First **peacetime draft** approved **Sept. 14.**

Richard Wright published *Native Son.*

1941

The **Four Freedoms** termed essential by Pres. Roosevelt in speech to Congress **Jan. 6;** freedom of speech and religion, freedom from want and fear.

Lend-Lease Act signed **Mar. 11,** providing $7 billion in military credits for Britain. Lend-Lease for USSR approved in **Nov.**

U.S. occupied **Iceland July 7.**

The **Atlantic Charter,** 8-point declaration of principles, issued by Roosevelt and Winston Churchill **Aug. 14.**

Japan attacked **Pearl Harbor,** Hawaii, 7:55 a.m. **Dec. 7,** 19 ships sunk or damaged, 2,300 dead. U.S. declared war on Japan **Dec. 8,** on Germany and Italy **Dec. 11** after those countries declared war.

1942

Federal government forcibly moved 110,000 **Japanese-Americans** (including 75,000 U.S. citizens) from West Coast to detention camps. Exclusion lasted 3 years.

Battle of **Midway June 3-6** was Japan's first major defeat.

Marines landed on **Guadalcanal Aug. 7;** last Japanese not expelled until **Feb. 9, 1943.**

U.S., Britain invaded North Africa **Nov. 8.**

First **nuclear chain reaction** (fission of uranium isotope U-235) produced at Univ. of Chicago, under physicists Arthur Compton, Enrico Fermi, others **Dec. 2.**

1943

All war contractors barred from **racial discrimination May 27.**

Pres. Roosevelt signed **June 10** the pay-as-you-go income tax bill. Starting **July 1** wage and salary earners were subject to a **paycheck withholding** tax.

Race riot in Detroit June 21; 34 dead, 700 injured. Riot in Harlem section of N.Y. City; 6 killed.

U.S. troops invaded Italy **Sept. 9.**

Marines advanced in **Gilbert Is. in Nov.**

1944

U.S., Allied forces invaded Europe at **Normandy June 6.**

G.I. Bill of Rights signed **June 22,** providing veterans benefits.

U.S. forces landed on **Leyte,** Philippines **Oct. 20.**

1945

Yalta Conference met in the Crimea, USSR, **Feb. 3-11.** Roosevelt, Churchill, and Stalin agreed Russia would enter war against Japan.

Marines landed on **Iwo Jima Feb. 19;** U.S. forces invaded **Okinawa Apr. 1.**

Pres. Roosevelt, 63, died of cerebral hemorrhage in Warm Springs, Ga. **Apr. 12.**

Germany surrendered May 7.

First **atomic bomb,** produced at Los Alamos, N.M., exploded at Alamogordo, N.M. **July 16.** Bomb dropped on **Hiroshima Aug. 6,** on **Nagasaki Aug. 9.** Japan surrendered **Aug. 15.**

U.S. forces entered **Korea** south of 38th parallel to displace Japanese **Sept. 8.**

Gen. Douglas MacArthur took over supervision of Japan **Sept. 9.**

1946

Strike by 400,000 **mine workers** began **Apr. 1;** other industries followed.

Philippines given independence by U.S. **July 4.**

1947

Truman Doctrine: Pres. Truman asked Congress to aid Greece and Turkey to combat Communist terrorism **Mar. 12.** Approved **May 15.**

United Nations Security Council voted unanimously **Apr. 2** to place under **U.S. trusteeship** the Pacific islands formerly mandated to Japan.

Jackie Robinson on Brooklyn Dodgers **Apr. 11,** the first black to play in major league baseball.

Taft-Hartley Labor Act curbing strikes was vetoed by Truman **June 20;** Congress overrode the veto.

Proposals later known as the **Marshall Plan,** under which the U.S. would extend aid to European countries, were made by Sec. of State George C. Marshall **June 5.** Congress authorized some $12 billion in next 4 years.

1948

USSR began a land **blockade of Berlin's** Allied sectors **Apr. 1.** This blockade and Western counter-blockade were lifted **Sept. 30, 1949,** after British and U.S. planes had lifted 2,343,315 tons of food and coal into the city.

Organization of American States founded **Apr. 30.**

Alger Hiss, former State Dept. official, indicted Dec. 15 for perjury, after denying he had passed secret documents to Whittaker Chambers for transmission to a communist spy ring. His second trial ended in conviction **Jan. 21, 1950,** and a sentence of 5 years in prison.

Kinsey Report on Sexuality in the Human Male published.

1949

U.S. troops withdrawn from **Korea June 29.**

North Atlantic Treaty Organization **(NATO)** established **Aug. 24** by U.S., Canada, and 10 West European nations, agreeing that "an armed attack against one or more of them in Europe and North America shall be considered an attack against all."

Mrs. I. Toguri D'Aquino **(Tokyo Rose** of Japanese wartime broadcasts) was sentenced **Oct. 7** to 10 years in prison for treason. Paroled **1956,** pardoned **1977.**

Eleven leaders of **U.S. Communist party** convicted **Oct. 14,** after 9-month trial in N.Y. City, of advocating violent overthrow of U.S. government. Ten defendants sentenced to 5 years in prison each and the 11th, to 3 years. Supreme Court upheld the convictions **June 4, 1951.**

1950

U.S. **Jan 14** recalled all consular officials from **China** after the latter seized the American consulate general in Peking.

Masked bandits robbed **Brink's Inc.,** Boston express office, **Jan. 17** of $2.8 million, of which $1.2 million was in cash. Case solved **1956,** 8 sentenced to life.

Pres. Truman authorized production of **H-bomb Jan. 31.**

United Nations asked for troops to restore Korea peace **June 25.**

Truman ordered Air Force and Navy to Korea **June 27** after North Korea invaded South. Truman approved ground forces, air strikes against North **June 30.**

U.S. sent 35 military advisers to **South Vietnam June 27,** and agreed to provide military and economic aid to anti-Communist government.

Army seized all railroads Aug. 27 on Truman's order to prevent a general strike; roads returned to owners in **1952.**

U.S. forces landed at Inchon Sept. 15; UN force took Pyongyang **Oct. 20,** reached China border **Nov. 20,** China sent troops across border **Nov. 26.**

Two members of a **Puerto Rican nationalist** movement tried to kill Pres. Truman **Nov. 1.** (see Assassinations)

U.S. **Dec. 8** banned shipments to **Communist China** and to Asiatic ports trading with it.

1951

Sen. **Estes Kefauver** led Senate investigation into organized crime. Preliminary report **Feb. 28** said gambling take was over $20 billion a year.

Julius Rosenberg, his wife, Ethel, and Morton Sobell, all U.S. citizens, were found guilty **Mar. 29** of conspiracy to commit wartime espionage. Rosenbergs sentenced to death, Sobell to 30 years. Rosenbergs **executed June 19, 1953.** Sobell released **Jan. 14, 1969.**

Gen. Douglas MacArthur was removed from his Korea command **Apr. 11** for making unauthorized policy statements.

Korea cease-fire talks began in July; lasted 2 years. **Fighting ended July 27, 1953.**

Tariff concessions by the U.S. to the Soviet Union, Communist China, and all communist-dominated lands were suspended **Aug. 1.**

The U.S., **Australia,** and **New Zealand** signed a mutual security pact **Sept. 1.**

Transcontinental television inaugurated **Sept. 4** with Pres. Truman's address at the Japanese Peace Treaty Conference in San Francisco.

Japanese Peace Treaty signed in San Francisco **Sept. 8** by U.S., Japan, and 47 other nations.

J.D. Salinger published *Catcher in the Rye.*

1952

U.S. **seizure of nation's steel mills** was ordered by Pres. Truman **Apr. 8** to avert a strike. Ruled illegal by Supreme Court **June 2.**

Peace contract between West Germany, U.S., Great Britain, and France was signed **May 26.**

The last racial and ethnic barriers to naturalization were removed, **June 26-27,** with the passage of the **Immigration and Naturalization Act of 1952.**

First **hydrogen device** explosion **Nov. 1** at Eniwetok Atoll in Pacific.

1953

Pres. Eisenhower announced **May 8** that U.S. had given France $60 million for **Indochina War.** More aid was announced in **Sept.** In **1954** it was reported that three fourths of the war's costs were met by U.S.

1954

Nautilus, first atomic-powered submarine, was launched at Groton, Conn. **Jan. 21.**

Five members of Congress were wounded in the House **Mar. 1** by **4 Puerto Rican independence supporters** who fired at random from a spectators' gallery.

Sen. Joseph McCarthy led televised hearings **Apr. 22-June 17** into alleged Communist influence in the Army.

Racial segregation in public schools was unanimously ruled unconstitutional by the Supreme Court **May 17,** as a violation of the 14th Amendment clause guaranteeing equal protection of the laws.

Southeast Asia Treaty Organization **(SEATO)** formed by collective defense pact signed in Manila **Sept. 8** by the U.S., Britain, France, Australia, New Zealand, Philippines, Pakistan, and Thailand.

Condemnation of **Sen. Joseph R. McCarthy** (R., Wis.) voted by Senate, 67-22 **Dec. 2** for contempt of a Senate elections subcommittee, for abuse of its members, and for insults to the Senate during his Army investigation hearings.

1955

U.S. agreed **Feb. 12** to help train **South Vietnamese** army.

Supreme Court ordered **"all deliberate speed"** in integration of public schools **May 31.**

A **summit meeting** of leaders of U.S., Britain, France, and USSR took place **July 18-23** in Geneva, Switzerland.

Rosa Parks refused **Dec. 1** to give her seat to a white man on a bus in Montgomery, Ala. Bus segregation ordinance declared unconstitutional by a federal court following boycott and NAACP protest.

Merger of America's 2 largest labor organizations was effected **Dec. 5** under the name American Federation of Labor and Congress of Industrial Organizations. The merged **AFL-CIO** had a membership estimated at 15 million.

1956

Massive resistance to Supreme Court desegregation rulings was called for **Mar. 12** by 101 Southern congressmen.

Federal-Aid **Highway Act** signed **June 29,** inaugurating interstate highway system.

First transatlantic **telephone cable** went into operation **Sept. 25.**

1957

Congress approved first **civil rights bill** for Negroes since Reconstruction **Apr. 29,** to protect voting rights.

National Guardsmen, called out by Arkansas Gov. Orval Faubus **Sept. 4,** barred 9 Negro students from entering previously all-white Central High School in **Little Rock.** Faubus complied **Sept. 21** with a federal court order to remove the National Guardsmen. The Negroes entered school **Sept. 23** but were ordered to withdraw by local authorities because of fear of mob violence. Pres. Eisenhower sent federal troops **Sept. 24** to enforce the court's order.

Jack Kerouac published *On the Road,* beatnik journal.

1958

First U.S. earth satellite to go into orbit, **Explorer I,** launched by Army **Jan. 31** at Cape Canaveral, Fla.; discovered Van Allen radiation belt.

Five thousand U.S. Marines sent to **Lebanon** to protect elected government from threatened overthrow **July-Oct.**

First domestic **jet airline** passenger service in U.S. opened by National Airlines **Dec. 10** between New York and Miami.

1959

Alaska admitted as 49th state **Jan. 3; Hawaii** admitted **Aug. 21.**

St. Lawrence Seaway opened **Apr. 25.**

The George Washington, first U.S. ballistic-missile submarine, launched at Groton, Conn. **June 9.**

N.S. Savannah, world's first atomic-powered merchant ship, launched **July 21** at Camden, N.J.

Soviet Premier **Khrushchev** paid unprecedented visit to U.S. **Sept. 15-27,** made transcontinental tour.

1960

A wave of **sit-ins** began **Feb. 1** when 4 Negro college students in Greensboro, N.C. refused to move from a Woolworth lunch counter when they were denied service. By **Sept. 1961** more than 70,000 students, whites and blacks, had participated in sit-ins.

U.S. launched first **weather satellite,** Tiros I, **Apr. 1.**

Congress approved a strong **voting rights act Apr. 21.**

A U-2 reconnaisance plane of the U.S. was shot down in the Soviet Union **May 1.** The incident led to cancellation of an imminent Paris summit conference.

Mobs attacked U.S. embassy in **Panama Sept. 17** in dispute over flying of U.S. and Panamanian flags.

U.S. announced **Dec. 15** it backed rightist group in **Laos,** which took power the next day.

1961

The U.S. severed diplomatic and consular relations with **Cuba Jan. 3,** after disputes over nationalizations of U.S. firms, U.S. military presence at Guantanamo base, etc.

Invasion of Cuba's **"Bay of Pigs" Apr. 17** by Cuban exiles trained, armed, and directed by the U.S., attempting to overthrow the regime of Premier Fidel Castro, was repulsed.

Commander Alan B. Shepard Jr. was rocketed from Cape Canaveral, Fla., 116.5 mi. above the earth in a Mercury capsule **May 5** in the first U.S. manned sub-orbital space flight.

1962

Lt. Col. John H. Glenn Jr. became the first American in orbit **Feb. 20** when he circled the earth 3 times in the Mercury capsule **Friendship 7.**

Pres. Kennedy said **Feb. 14** U.S. military advisers in Vietnam would fire if fired upon.

Supreme Court **Mar. 26** backed **one-man one-vote** apportionment of seats in state legislatures.

First U.S. **communications satellite** launched in **July.**

James Meredith became first black student at Univ. of Mississippi **Oct. 1** after 3,000 troops put down riots.

A Soviet **offensive missile buildup in Cuba** was revealed **Oct. 22** by Pres. Kennedy, who ordered a naval and air quarantine on shipment of offensive military equipment to the island. Kennedy and Soviet Premier Khrushchev reached agreement **Oct. 28** on a formula to end the crisis. Kennedy announced **Nov. 2** that Soviet missile bases in Cuba were being dismantled.

Rachel Carson's *Silent Spring* launched environmentalist movement.

1963

Supreme Court ruled **Mar. 18** that all **criminal defendants** must have counsel and that illegally acquired evidence was not admissible in state as well as federal courts.

Supreme Court ruled, 8-1, **June 17** that laws requiring **recitation of the Lord's Prayer** or Bible verses in public schools were unconstitutional.

A limited **nuclear test-ban treaty** was agreed upon **July 25** by the U.S., Soviet Union and Britain, barring all nuclear tests except underground.

Washington demonstration by 200,000 persons **Aug. 28** in support of **Negro demands** for equal rights. Highlight was speech in which Dr. Martin Luther King said: "I have a dream that this nation will rise up and live out the true meaning of its creed, 'We hold these truths to be self-evident: that all men are created equal.' "

South Vietnam Pres. **Ngo Dinh Diem assassinated Nov. 2;** U.S. had earlier withdrawn support.

Pres. John F. Kennedy was shot and fatally wounded by an assassin **Nov. 22** as he rode in a motorcade through downtown Dallas, Tex. Vice Pres. Lyndon B. Johnson was inaugurated president shortly after in Dallas. Lee Harvey Oswald was arrested and charged with the murder. Oswald was shot and fatally wounded **Nov. 24** by Jack Ruby, 52, a Dallas nightclub owner, who was convicted of murder **Mar. 14, 1964** and sentenced to death. Ruby died of natural causes **Jan. 3, 1967** while awaiting retrial.

U.S. troops in **Vietnam** totalled over 15,000 by year-end; aid to South Vietnam was over $500 million in **1963.**

1964

Panama suspended relations with U.S. **Jan. 9** after riots. U.S. offered **Dec. 18** to negotiate a new canal treaty.

Supreme Court ordered **Feb. 17** that **congressional districts** have equal populations.

U.S. reported **May 27** it was sending military planes to **Laos.**

Omnibus **civil rights bill** passed **June 29** banning discrimination in voting, jobs, public accommodations, etc.

Three **civil rights workers** were reported missing in Mississippi **June 22;** found buried **Aug. 4.** Twenty-one white men were arrested. On **Oct. 20, 1967,** an all-white federal jury convicted 7 of conspiracy in the slayings.

U.S. Congress **Aug. 7** passed **Tonkin Resolution,** authorizing presidential action in Vietnam, after North Vietnam boats reportedly attacked 2 U.S. destroyers **Aug. 2.**

Congress approved War on Poverty bill **Aug. 11.**

The **Warren Commission** released **Sept. 27** a report concluding that Lee Harvey Oswald was solely responsible for the Kennedy assassination.

1965

Pres. Johnson in **Feb.** ordered continuous **bombing of North Vietnam** below 20th parallel.

Some 14,000 U.S. troops sent to **Dominican Republic** during civil war **Apr. 28.** All troops withdrawn by following year.

New **Voting Rights Act** signed **Aug. 6.**

Los Angeles riot by blacks living in **Watts** area resulted in death of 35 persons and property damage est. at $200 million **Aug. 11-16.**

Water Quality Act passed **Sept. 21** to meet pollution, shortage problems.

National origins quota system of **immigration** abolished **Oct. 3.**

Massive **electric power failure** blacked out most of northeastern U.S, parts of 2 Canadian provinces the night of **Nov. 9-10.**

U.S. forces in **South Vietnam** reached 184,300 by year-end.

1966

U.S. forces began firing into **Cambodia May 1.**

Bombing of Hanoi area of North Vietnam by U.S. planes began **June 29.** By **Dec. 31,** 385,300 U.S. troops were stationed in South Vietnam, plus 60,000 offshore and 33,000 in Thailand.

Medicare, government program to pay part of the medical expenses of citizens over 65, began **July 1.**

Edward Brooke (R, Mass.) elected **Nov. 8** as first Negro U.S. senator in 85 years.

1967

Black representative **Adam Clayton Powell** (D, N.Y.) was denied **Mar. 1** his seat in Congress because of charges he misused government funds. Reelected in 1968, he was seated, but fined $25,000 and stripped of his 22 years' seniority.

Pres. Johnson and Soviet Premier Aleksei Kosygin met **June 23 and 25** at **Glassboro State College** in N.J.; agreed not to let any crisis push them into war.

Black riots in **Newark, N.J. July 12-17** killed some 26, injured 1,500; over 1,000 arrested. In Detroit, Mich., **July 23-30** at least 40 died; 2,000 injured, and 5,000 left homeless by rioting, looting, burning in city's black ghetto. Quelled by 4,700 federal paratroopers and 8,000 National Guardsmen.

Thurgood Marshall sworn in **Oct. 2** as first black U.S. Supreme Court Justice. Carl B. Stokes (D, Cleveland) and Richard G. Hatcher (D, Gary, Ind.) were elected first black mayors of major U.S. cities **Nov. 7.**

By **December** 475,000 U.S. troops were in **South Vietnam,** all North Vietnam was subject to bombing. Protests against the war mounted in U.S. during year.

1968

USS Pueblo and 83-man crew seized in Sea of Japan **Jan. 23** by North Koreans; 82 men released **Dec. 22.**

"Tet offensive": Communist troops attacked Saigon, 30 province capitals **Jan. 30,** suffer heavy casualties.

Pres. Johnson **curbed bombing** of North Vietnam **Mar. 31.** Peace talks began in Paris **May 10.** All bombing of North is halted **Oct. 31.**

Martin Luther King Jr., 39, assassinated Apr. 4 in Memphis, Tenn. James Earl Ray, an escaped convict, pleaded guilty to the slaying, was sentenced to 99 years.

Sen. Robert F. Kennedy (D, N.Y.) 42, **shot June 5** in Hotel Ambassador, Los Angeles, after celebrating presidential primary victories. Died **June 6.** Sirhan Bishara Sirhan, Jordanian, convicted of murder.

1969

Expanded four-party **Vietnam peace talks** began **Jan. 18.** U.S. force peaked at 543,400 in April. Withdrawal started **July 8.** Pres. Nixon set Vietnamization policy **Nov. 3.**

A car driven by **Sen. Edward M. Kennedy** (D, Mass.) plunged off a bridge into a tidal pool on Chappaquiddick Is., Martha's Vineyard, Mass. **July 18.** The body of Mary Jo Kopechne, a 28-year-old secretary, was found drowned in the car.

U.S. astronaut **Neil A. Armstrong,** 38, commander of the Apollo 11 mission, became the first man to **set foot on the moon July 20.** Air Force Col. Edwin E. Aldrin Jr. accompanied Armstrong.

Anti-Vietnam War **demonstrations reached peak** in U.S.; some 250,000 marched in Washington, D.C. **Nov. 15.**

Massacre of hundreds of civilians at **Mylai, South Vietnam** in 1968 incident was reported **Nov. 16.**

1970

United Mine Workers official **Joseph A. Yablonski,** his wife, and their daughter were found shot **Jan. 5** in their Clarksville, Pa. home. UMW chief W. A. (Tony) Boyle was later convicted of the killing.

A federal jury **Feb. 18** found the defendants in the **"Chicago 7"** trial innocent of conspiring to incite riots during the 1968 Democratic National Convention. However, 5 were convicted of crossing state lines with intent to incite riots.

Millions of Americans participated in anti-pollution demonstrations **Apr. 22** to mark the first **Earth Day.**

U.S. and South Vietnamese forces crossed **Cambodian** borders **Apr. 30** to get at enemy bases. Four students were killed **May 4** at **Kent St.** Univ. in Ohio by National Guardsmen during a protest against the war.

Two **women generals,** the first in U.S. history, were named by Pres. Nixon **May 15.**

A **postal reform** measure was signed **Aug. 12,** creating an independent U.S. Postal Service, thus relinquishing governmental control of the U.S. mails after almost 2 centuries.

1971

Charles Manson, 36, and 3 of his followers were found guilty **Jan. 26** of first-degree murder in the 1969 slaying of actress Sharon Tate and 6 others.

U.S. air and artillery forces aided a 44-day incursion by South Vietnam forces into **Laos** starting **Feb. 8.**

A Constitutional Amendment lowering the **voting age to** 18 in all elections was approved in the Senate by a vote of 94-0 **Mar. 10.** The proposed 26th Amendment got House approval by a 400-19 vote **Mar. 23.** Thirty-eighth state ratified **June 30.**

A court-martial jury Mar. 29, convicted **Lt. William L. Calley Jr.** of premeditated murder of 22 South Vietnamese at Mylai on **Mar. 16, 1968.** He was sentenced to life imprisonment **Mar. 31.** Sentence was reduced to 20 years **Aug. 20.**

Publication of classified **Pentagon papers** on the U.S. involvement in Vietnam was begun **June 13** by the New York Times. In a 6-3 vote, the U.S. Supreme Court **June 30** upheld the right of the Times and the Washington Post to publish the documents under the protection of the First Amendment.

U.S., Japan signed treaty **June 17** for return of **Okinawa**, seized during World War II.

Pres. Nixon began a sweeping new economic program **Aug. 15** imposing a 90-day **wage, price, and rent freeze.** He also devalued the dollar by cutting its tie with gold.

More than 1,000 N.Y. State troopers and police stormed the **Attica State Correctional Facility** where 1,200 inmates held 38 guards hostage **Sept. 13,** ending a 4-day rebellion in the maximum-security prison; 9 hostages, 28 convicts killed in the assault.

U.S. bombers struck massively in North Vietnam for 5 days starting **Dec. 26,** in retaliation for alleged violations of agreements reached prior to the 1968 bombing halt. U.S. forces at year-end were down to 140,000.

1972

Pres. Nixon arrived in **Peking Feb. 21** for an 8-day visit to China, which he called a "journey for peace." The unprecedented visit ended with a joint communique pledging that both powers would work for "a normalization of relations."

By a vote of 84 to 8, the Senate approved **Mar. 22** a Constitutional Amendment banning **discrimination against women** because of their sex and sent the measure to the states for ratification.

North Vietnamese forces launched the biggest attacks in 4 years across the demilitarized zone **Mar. 30.** The U.S. responded **Apr. 15** by resumption of bombing of Hanoi and Haiphong after a 4-year lull.

Nixon announced **May 8** the mining of **North Vietnam ports.** Last U.S. combat troops left **Aug. 11.**

Alabama Gov. George C. Wallace, campaigning at a Laurel, Md. shopping center **May 15, was shot** and seriously wounded as he greeted a large crowd. Arthur H. Bremer, 21, was sentenced Aug. 4 to 63 years for shooting Wallace and 3 bystanders.

In the first visit of a U.S. president to Moscow, Nixon arrived **May 22** for a week of summit talks with Kremlin leaders which culminated in a landmark **strategic arms pact.**

Five men were arrested **June 17** for breaking into the offices of the Democratic National Committee in the **Watergate** office complex in Washington, D.C.

The White House announced **July 8** that the U.S. would sell to the USSR at least $750 million of **American wheat,** corn, and other grains over a period of 3 years. But the USSR bought most of it in 1st year.

1973

Five of seven defendants in the **Watergate** break-in trial pleaded guilty **Jan. 11 and 15,** and the other 2 were convicted **Jan. 30.**

The Supreme Court ruled 7-2, **Jan. 22,** that a state may not prevent a woman from having an **abortion** during the **first 6 months of pregnancy,** invalidating abortion laws in Texas and Georgia, and, by implication, overturning restrictive abortion laws in 44 other states.

Four-party **Vietnam peace pacts** were signed in Paris **Jan. 27,** and North Vietnam released some 590 U.S. prisoners by **Apr. 1.** Last U.S. troops left **Mar. 29.**

The **end of the military draft** was announced **Jan. 27** by Defense Sec. Melvin R. Laird.

China and the U.S. agreed **Feb. 22** to set up permanent liaison offices in each other's country.

Some 200-300 members of the militant American Indian Movement **Feb. 27** seized the trading post and church at historic **Wounded Knee** on the Oglala Sioux Reservation in South Dakota.

Top **Nixon aides** H.R. Haldeman, John D. Ehrlichman, and John W. Dean, and Attorney General Richard Kleindienst **resigned Apr. 30** amid charges of White House efforts to obstruct justice in the Watergate case.

The Senate Armed Services Committee **July 16** began a probe into allegations that the U.S. Air Force had made 3,500 secret **B-52 raids into Cambodia** in **1969** and **1970.**

John Dean, former Nixon counsel, told Senate hearings **June 25** that Nixon, his staff and campaign aides, and the Justice Department all had conspired to cover up Watergate facts. Nixon refused July 23 to release **tapes** of relevant White House conversations. Some tapes were turned over to the court **Nov. 26.**

The U.S. officially ceased bombing in **Cambodia** at midnight **Aug. 14** in accord with a June Congressional action.

Vice Pres. Spiro T. Agnew Oct. 10 resigned and pleaded "nolo contendere" (no contest) to charges of tax evasion on payments made to him by Maryland contractors. Agnew was sentenced to 3 years probation and fined $10,000. Gerald Rudolph Ford **Oct. 12** became first appointed vice president under the 25th Amendment; sworn in **Dec. 6.**

A total ban on **oil exports** to the U.S. was imposed by Arab oil-producing nations **Oct. 19-21** after the outbreak of an Arab-Israeli war. The ban was lifted **Mar. 18, 1974.**

Atty. Gen. Elliot Richardson resigned, and his deputy William D. Ruckelshaus and Watergate Special Prosecutor Archibald Cox were fired by Pres. Nixon **Oct. 20** when Cox threatened to secure a judicial ruling that Nixon was violating a court order to turn tapes over to Watergate case Judge John Sirica.

Leon Jaworski, conservative Texas Democrat, was named **Nov. 1** by the Nixon administration to be special prosecutor to succeed Archibald Cox.

Congress overrode **Nov. 7** Nixon's veto of the **war powers** bill which curbed the president's power to commit armed forces to hostilities abroad without Congressional approval.

1974

Herbert W. Kalmbach, Pres. Nixon's personal lawyer and fundraiser, pleaded guilty **Feb. 25** to promising a contributor an ambassadorship for a $100,000 contribution.

Impeachment hearings were opened **May 9** against Nixon by the House Judiciary Committee.

John D. Ehrlichman and 3 **White House "plumbers"** were found guilty **July 12** of conspiring to violate the civil rights of Dr. Lewis Fielding, formerly psychiatrist to Pentagon Papers leaker Daniel Ellsberg, by breaking into his Beverly Hills, Cal. office.

The U.S. Supreme Court ruled, 8-0, **July 24** that Nixon had to turn over **64 tapes** of White House conversations sought by Watergate Special Prosecutor Leon Jaworski.

The House Judiciary Committee, in televised hearings **July 24-30,** recommended 3 **articles of impeachment** against Nixon. The first, voted 27-11 **July 27,** charged Nixon with taking part in a criminal conspiracy to obstruct justice in the Watergate cover-up. The second, voted 28-10 **July 29,** charged he "repeatedly" failed to carry out his constitutional oath in a series of alleged abuses of power. The third, voted 27-17 **July 30,** accused him of unconstitutional defiance of committee subpoenas. The House of Representatives voted without debate **Aug. 20,** by 412-3, to accept the committee report, which included the recommended impeachment articles.

Nixon resigned Aug. 9. His support began eroding **Aug. 5** when he released 3 tapes, admitting he originated plans to have the FBI stop its probe of the Watergate break-in for political as well as national security reasons.

An **unconditional pardon** to ex-Pres. Nixon for all federal crimes that he "committed or may have committed" while president was issued by Pres. Gerald Ford **Sept. 8.**

Charges that the Central Intelligence Agency **(CIA)** abused its powers by massive domestic operations were published **Dec. 21.**

1975

Found guilty of **Watergate** cover-up charges **Jan. 1** were ex-Atty. Gen. John N. Mitchell, ex-presidential advisers H.R. Haldeman and John D. Ehrlichman.

U.S. civilians were evacuated from **Saigon Apr. 29** as communist forces completed takeover of South Vietnam.

U.S. merchant ship **Mayaguez** and crew of 39 seized by Cambodian forces in Gulf of Siam **May 12.** In rescue operation, U.S. Marines attacked Tang Is., planes bombed air base; Cambodia surrendered ship and crew; U.S. losses were 15 killed in battle and 23 dead in a helicopter crash.

Congress voted $405 million for South **Vietnam refugees May 16;** 140,000 were flown to the U.S.

Illegal **CIA operations,** including records on 300,000 persons and groups, infiltration of agents into black, anti-war and political movements, monitoring of overseas phone calls, mail surveillance, and drug-testing, were described by a "blue-ribbon" panel headed by Vice Pres. Rockefeller **June 10.** Information on assassination plots against foreign leaders was ordered withheld by Pres. Ford.

William L. Calley's court-martial conviction for the murder of 22 Vietnamese, overturned in lower courts, was reinstated by the U.S. Court of Appeals in New Orleans **Sept. 10.**

FBI agents captured **Patricia (Patty) Hearst,** kidnaped **Feb. 4, 1974,** in San Francisco **Sept. 18** with others. She was indicted for bank robbery; a San Francisco jury convicted her **Mar. 20, 1976.**

1976

Payments abroad of $22 million in bribes by Lockheed Aircraft Corp. to sell its planes were revealed **Feb. 4** by a Senate subcommittee. Lockheed admitted payments in Japan, Turkey, Italy, and Holland.

The U.S. celebrated its **Bicentennial July 4,** marking the 200th anniversary of its independence with festivals, parades, and N.Y. City's Operation Sail, a gathering of tall ships from around the world viewed by 6 million persons.

A mystery ailment **"legionnaire's disease"** killed 29 persons who attended an American Legion convention **July 21-24** in Philadelphia. The cause was found to be a bacterium, it was reported **June 18, 1977.**

The Viking II lander set down on **Mars'** Utopia Plains **Sept. 3,** following the successful landing by Viking I **July 20.**

1977

Pres. Jimmy Carter **Jan. 27** pardoned most Vietnam War **draft evaders,** who numbered some 10,000.

Convicted murderer **Gary Gilmore** was executed by Utah firing squad **Jan. 17,** in the first exercise of capita punishment anywhere in the U.S. since **1967.** Gilmore ha opposed all attempts to delay the execution.

Carter signed an act **Aug. 4** creating a new Cabinet-leve **Energy Department.**

Carter announced **Sept. 21** that budget director **Be Lance,** a personal friend, had resigned due to pressure ove his disputed private financial practices.

1978

Sen. Hubert H. Humphrey (D., Minn.), 66, lost a battl with cancer **Jan. 13,** after 32 years of public service, includ ing 4 years as vice-president of the United States.

U.S. Senate voted **Apr. 18** to turn over the **Panama Cana** to Panama on Dec. 31, 1999, by a vote of 68-32, ending sev eral months of heated debate; an earlier vote **(Mar. 16)** ha given approval to a treaty guaranteeing the area's neutrali after the year 2000.

California voters **June 6** approved (by a 65% majority the **Proposition 13** initiative to cut property taxes in th state by 57%, thus severely limiting government spending.

The U.S. Supreme Court **June 28** voted 5-4 not to allow firm quota system in affirmative action plans and ordere that **Alan Bakke** be admitted to a California medical schoo Bakke, a white, had contended that he was a victim of "re verse discrimination"; the Court did uphold affirmative ac tion programs that were more "flexible" in nature.

The **House Select Committee on Assassinations** opene hearings **Sept. 6** into assassinations of Pres. Kennedy an Martin Luther King Jr.; the committee recessed **Dec. 30** af ter concluding conspiracies likely in both cases, but with n further hard evidence for further prosecutions.

Congress passed the **Humphrey-Hawkins "full employ ment" Bill Oct. 15,** which set national goal of reducing un employment to 4% by 1983, while reducing inflation to 3 in same period; Pres. Carter signed bill, **Oct. 27.**

1979

A major accident occurred, **Mar. 28,** at a nuclear reacto on **Three Mile Island** near Middletown, Pa. Radioactiv gases escaped through the plant's venting system and a larg hydrogen gas bubble formed in the top of the reactor con tainment vessel.

In the worst disaster in U.S. aviation history, an Ameri can Airlines **DC-10 jetliner** lost its left engine and crashe shortly after takeoff in Chicago, **May 25,** killing 275 people.

Pope John Paul II, Oct. 1-6, visited the U.S. and rea firmed traditional Roman Catholic teachings.

The federal government announced, **Nov. 1,** a $1.5 billio loan-guarantee plan to aid the nation's 3d largest auto maker, **Chrysler Corp.,** which had reported a loss of $460. million for the 3d quarter of 1979.

Some 90 people, including 63 Americans, were taken hos tage, **Nov. 3,** at the **American embassy in Teheran,** Iran, b militant students who demanded the return of former Sha Mohammad Reza Pahlavi, who was undergoing medica treatment in New York City.

1980

Citing "an extremely serious threat to peace," Pres. Carte announced, **Jan. 4,** a series of **punitive measures against th USSR,** most notably an embargo on the sale of grain an high technology, in retaliation for the Soviet invasion of A ghanistan.

Eight Americans were killed and 5 wounded, **Apr. 24,** i an ill-fated attempted to **rescue the hostages** held by Irania **militants** at the U.S. Embassy in Teheran.

Wreaking death and general devastation on southweste Washington and northern Oregon, **Mt. St. Helens erupte May 18,** in a violent blast estimated to be 500 times as pow erful as the Hiroshima atomic bomb. The blast, followed b others on **May 25** and **June 12,** left 25 confirmed dead, a least 40 missing, and economic losses estimated at nearly $ billion.

In protest of the Soviet Union's invasion of Afghanista the **U.S. Olympic Committee** voted, **Apr. 12,** not to atten the Moscow Summer Olympics.

In a sweeping victory, **Nov. 4, Ronald Wilson Reagan** was lected 40th President of the United States, defeating incum-ent Jimmy Carter. The stunning GOP victory extended to he U.S. Congress where Republicans gained control of the enate and wrested 33 House seats from the Democrats.

Former Beatle **John Lennon** was shot and killed, **Dec. 8,** utside his apartment building on New York City's Upper Vest Side. Charged in the slaying was Mark David Chap-nan, a professed Beatle fan and former psychiatric patient.

1981

Minutes after the **inauguration of Pres. Ronald Reagan, Jan. 20,** the **52 Americans** who had been held **hostage in ran** for 444 days were flown to freedom following an agree-nent in which the U.S. agreed to return to Iran $8 billion in rozen assets.

President Reagan was **shot in the chest** by a would-be as-assin, **Mar. 30,** in Washington, D.C., as he walked to his imousine following an address at the Washington Hilton. The alleged assailant, **John W. Hinckley, Jr.,** fired several hots before he was overpowered by police and secret service gents. Also wounded in the shooting were presidential ress secretary **James S. Brady,** who was struck above the eft eye and critically injured, secret service agent Timothy J. McCarthy, and police officer Thomas K. Delahanty.

The world's first reusable spacecraft, the **Space Ship Co-umbia,** was sent into space, **Apr. 12,** and completed its suc-essful mission 2 days later, speeding out of orbit and glid-ng to a safe unassisted landing on the desert near Edwards Air Force Base, Cal. Some minor difficulties were encoun-ered during the flight, most notably the loss of **17 heat-shielding tiles,** but NASA officials termed the mission "100% successful." **Columbia's second flight,** launched **Nov. 12,** was cut short when one of the craft's electricity-producing fuel cells malfunctioned shortly after lift-off.

Wayne B. Williams, a 23-year-old black free-lance pho-tographer, was indicted, **July 17,** in the murders of 2 of the **28 young blacks killed in the Atlanta area** during the 2-year period beginning July 1979.

Both houses of Congress passed, **July 29,** President Rea-gan's **tax-cut legislation.** The bill, the largest tax cut in the nation's history, was expected to reduce taxes by $37.6 billion in fiscal year 1982, and would save taxpayers $750 billion over the next 5 years. On **July 31,** following an intensive lobbying effort by the Reagan Administration, the House and Senate gave final approval to the president's **package of budget cuts,** reducing the level of federal spending to $695 billion from the previously planned $730 billion level.

Federal air traffic controllers, Aug. 3, began an **illegal nationwide strike** after their union rejected the government's final offer for a new contract. President Reagan warned the workers that if they did not return to work by 11:00 a.m., **Aug. 5,** they would be fired, but most of the 13,000 striking controllers defied the back-to-work order.

California agricultural experts admitted, **July 9,** that the hundreds of thousands of **Mediterranean fruit flies** released in the state and thought to be sterile, were, in fact, fertile. The result was an increase in the reproductive rate among the insects that threatened the state's $1-billion produce crop. Following a series of **sprayings and quarantines,** officials announced, **Sept. 9,** that no fertile flies had been found in the state since **Sept. 3,** but it would not be known until late spring 1982 whether or not the fly had been eradicated.

In a 99-0 vote, the Senate confirmed, **Sept. 21,** the appointment of **Sandra Day O'Connor** as an **associate justice of the U.S. Supreme Court.** She was the first woman appointed to that body. Justice O'Connor took her seat, **Sept. 25.**

By a vote of 52 to 48, the Senate, **Oct. 28, approved the sale** of **Airborne Warning and Control System** (AWACS) radar surveillance planes and other air-combat equipment to Saudi Arabia. The House, **Oct. 14,** had rejected, by an overwhelming 301-to-111 count, the Reagan administration's proposal, but by law only the **concurrent opposition** of both houses of Congress could block the sale.

President Reagan ordered a series of **sanctions against the new Polish military government, Dec. 23,** in response to the imposition of martial law that had occurred in that country. This was followed, **Dec. 29,** by **reprisals against the Soviet Union** for its alleged role in the crackdown.

For events of 1982 and late 1981, See Chronology

Paleontology: The History of Life

All dates are approximate, and are subject to change based on new fossil finds or new dating techniques; but the sequence of events is generally accepted. Dates are in years before the present.

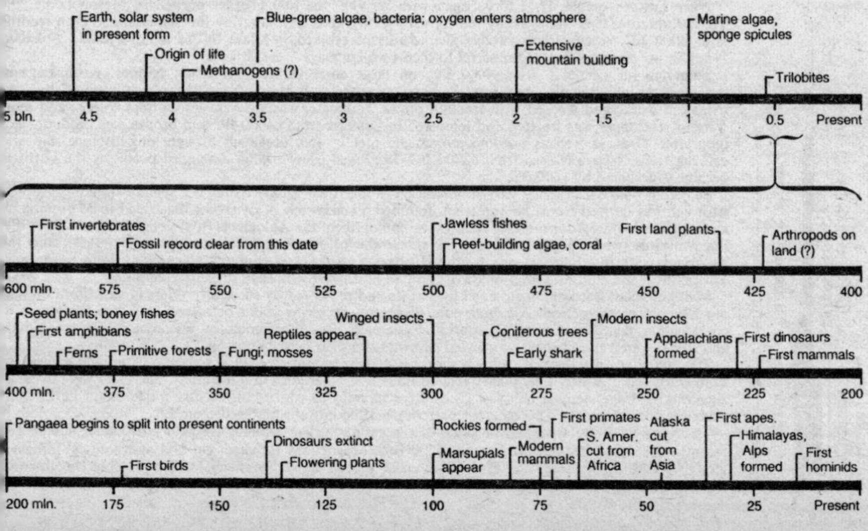

WORLD HISTORY

by Barry Youngerman

Prehistory: Our Ancestors Take Over

Homo sapiens. The precise origins of *homo sapiens*, the species to which all humans belong, are subject to broad speculation based on a small number of fossils, genetic and anatomical studies, and the geological record. But nearly all scientists agree that we evolved from ape-like primate ancestors in a process that began millions of years ago.

Current theories say the first hominid (human-like primate) was *Ramapithecus*, who emerged 12 million years ago. Its remains have been found in Asia, Europe, and Africa. Further development was apparently limited to Africa, where 2 lines of hominids appeared some 5 or 6 million years ago. One was *Australopithecus*, a tool-maker and social animal, who lived from perhaps 4 to 3 million years ago, and then apparently became extinct.

The 2nd was a human line, *Homo habillus*, a large-brained specimen that walked upright and had a dextrous hand. *Homo habillus* lived in semi-permanent camps and had a food-gathering and sharing economy.

Homo erectus, our nearest ancestor, appeared in Africa perhaps 1.75 million years ago, and began spreading into Asia and Europe soon after. It had a fairly large brain and a skeletal structure similar to ours. *Homo erectus* learned to control fire, and probably had primitive language skills. The final brain development to *Homo sapiens* and then to our sub-species *Homo sapiens sapiens* occurred between 500,000 and 50,000 years ago, over a wide geographic area and in many different steps and recombinations. All humans of all races belong to this sub-species.

The spread of mankind into the remaining habitable continents probably took place during the last ice age up to 100,000 years ago: to the Americas across a land bridge from Asia, and to Australia across the Timor Straits.

Earliest cultures. A variety of cultural modes — in tool-making, diet, shelter, and possibly social arrangements and spiritual expression, arose as early mankind adapted to different geographic and climatic zones.

Three basic tool-making traditions are recognized by archeologists as arising and often coexisting from one million years ago to the near past: the *chopper tradition*, found largely in E. Asia, with crude chopping tools and simple flake tools; the *flake tradition*, found in Africa and W. Europe, with a variety of small cutting and flaking tools, and the *biface tradition*, found in all of Africa, W. and S. Europe and S. Asia, producing pointed hand axes chipped on both faces. Later biface sites yield more refined axes and a variety of other tools, weapons, and ornaments using bone, antler and wood as well as stone.

Only sketchy evidence remains for the different stages in man's increasing control over the environment. Traces of 400,000-year-old covered wood shelters have been found at Nice, France. Scraping tools at Neanderthal sites (200,000-30,000 BC in Europe, N. Africa, the Middle East and Central Asia) suggest the treatment of skins for clothing. Sites from all parts of the world show seasonal migration patterns and exploitation of a wide range of plant and animal food sources.

Painting and decoration, for which there is evidence at the Nice site, flourished along with stone and ivory sculpture after 30,000 years ago; 60 caves in France and 30 in Spain show remarkable examples of wall painting. Other examples have been found in Africa. Proto-religious rites are suggested by these works, and by evidence of ritual cannibalism by Peking Man, 500,000 BC, and of ritual burial with medicinal plants and flowers by Neanderthals at Shanidar in Iraq.

The Neolithic Revolution. Sometime after 10,000 BC among widely separated human communities, a series of dramatic technological and social changes occurred that are summed up as the Neolithic Revolution. The cultivation of previously wild plants encouraged the growth of permanent settlements. Animals were domesticated as a work force and food source. The manufacture of pottery and cloth began. These techniques permitted a huge increase in world population and in human control over the earth.

No region can safely claim priority as the "inventor" of these techniques. Dispersed sites in Cen. and S. America, S.E. Europe, and the Middle East show roughly contemporaneous (10-8,000 BC) evidence of one or another "neolithic" trait. Dates near 6-3,000 BC have been given for E. and S. Asian, W. European, and sub-Saharan African neolithic remains. The variety of crops — field grains, rice, maize, and roots, and the varying mix of other traits suggest that the revolution occurred independently in all these regions.

History Begins: 4000 - 1000 BC

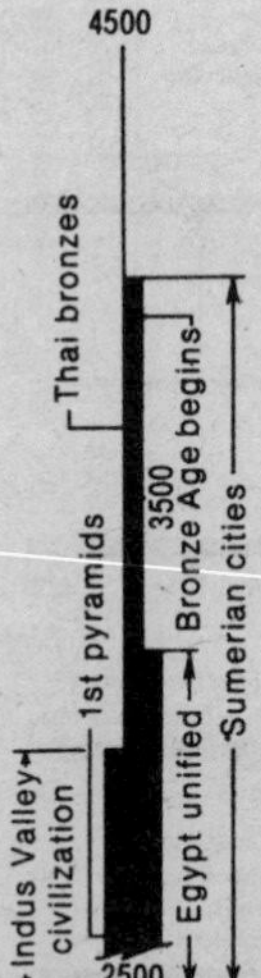

Near Eastern cradle. If history began with writing, the first chapter opened in Mesopotamia, the Tigris-Euphrates river valley. Clay tablets with pictographs were used by the Sumerians to keep records after 4000 BC. A **cuneiform** (wedge shaped) script evolved by 3000 BC as a full syllabic alphabet. Neighboring peoples adapted the script to their own language.

Sumerian life centered, from 4000 BC, on large cities (Eridu, Ur, Uruk, Nippur, Kish, Lagash, organized around temples and priestly bureaucracies, with the surrounding plains watered by vast irrigation works and worked with traction plows. Sailboats, wheeled vehicles, potters wheels, and kilns were used. Copper was smelted and tempered in Sumeria from c4000 BC and bronze was produced not long after. Ores, as well as precious stones and metals were obtained through long-distance ship and caravan trade. Iron was used from c2000 BC. Improved ironworking, developed partly by the **Hittites** became widespread by 1200 BC.

Sumerian political primacy passed among cities and their kingly dynasties. Semitic-speaking peoples with cultures derived from the Sumerian, founded a succession of dynasties that ruled in Mesopotamia and neighboring areas for most of 1800 years; among them the **Akkadians** (first under Sargon c2350 BC) the Amorites (whose laws, codified by **Hammurabi**, c1792-1750 BC, have Biblical parallels), and the Assyrians, with interludes of rule by the Hittites, Kassites, and Mitanni, all possibly Indo-Europeans. The political and cultural center of gravity shifted northwest with each successive empire.

Mesopotamian learning, maintained by scribes and preserved by successive rulers in vast libraries, was not abstract or theoretical. Algebraic and geometric problems could be solved on a practical basis in construction, commerce, or administration. Systematic lists of astronomical phenomena, plants, animals and stones were kept; medical texts listed ailments and their herbal cures.

The Sumerians worshipped anthropomorphic gods representing natural forces — Anu, god of heaven Enlil (Ea), god of water. Epic poetry related these and other gods in a hierarchy. Sacrifices were made at **ziggurats** — huge stepped temples. Gods were thought to control all events, which could be foretold using oracular materials. This religious pattern persisted into the first millenium BC.

The Syria-Palestine area, site of some of the earliest urban remains (Jericho, 7000 BC), and of the recently uncovered **Ebla** civilization (fl. 2500 BC), experienced Egyptian cultural and political influence along with Mesopotamian. The **Phoenician** coast was an active commercial center. A phonetic alphabet was invented here before 1600 BC. It became the ancestor of all European, Middle Eastern, Indian, S.E

.sian, Ethiopian, and Korean alphabets.

Regional commerce and diplomacy were aided by the use of Akkadian as a *lingua franca,* later ꞏplaced by Aramaic.

Egypt. Agricultural villages along the Nile were united by 3300 BC into two kingdoms, Upper and ower Egypt, unified under the Pharaoh Menes c3100 BC; Nubia to the south was added 2600 BC. A ational bureaucracy supervised construction of canals and monuments (**pyramids** starting 2700 BC). rilliant First Dynasty achievements in architecture, sculpture and painting, set the standards and forms r all subsequent Egyptian civilization and are still admired. **Hieroglyphic writing** appeared by 3400 BC, ecording a sophisticated literature including romantic and philosophical modes after 2300 BC.

An ordered hierarchy of gods, including totemistic animal elements, was served by a powerful riesthood in Memphis. The pharaoh was identified with the falcon god Horus. Later trends were the elief in an afterlife, and the quasi-monotheistic reforms of **Akhenaton** (c1379-1362 BC).

After a period of conquest by Semitic Hyksos from Asia (c1700-1500 BC), the New Kingdom stablished an empire in Syria. Egypt became increasingly embroiled in Asiatic wars and diplomacy. ventually it was conquered by Persia in 525 BC, and it faded away as an independent culture.

India. An urban civilization with a so-far-undeciphered writing system stretched across the Indus 'alley and along the Arabian Sea c3000-1500 BC. Major sites are Harappa and **Mohenjo-Daro** in akistan, well-planned geometric cities with underground sewers and vast granaries. The entire region 500,000 sq. mi.) may have been ruled as a single state. Bronze was used, and arts and crafts were highly eveloped. Religious life apparently took the form of fertility cults.

Indus civilization was probably in decline when it was destroyed by **Aryan invaders** from the orthwest, speaking an Indo-European language from which all the languages of Pakistan, north India nd Bangladesh descend. Led by a warrior aristocracy whose legendary deeds are recorded in the **Rig 'eda,** the Aryans spread east and south, bringing their pantheon of sky gods, elaborate priestly Brahmin) ritual, and the beginnings of the caste system; local customs and beliefs were assimilated by he conquerors.

Europe. On Crete, the bronze-age **Minoan civilization** emerged c2500 BC. A prosperous economy and ichly decorative art (e.g. at Knossos palace) was supported by seaborne commerce. Mycenae and other ities in Greece and Asia Minor (e.g. **Troy**) preserved elements of the culture to c1100 BC. Cretan Linear script, c2000-1700 BC, is undeciphered; Linear B, c1300-1200 BC, records a Greek dialect.

Possible connection between Minoan-Mycenaean monumental stonework, and the great megalithic ionuments and tombs of W. Europe, Iberia, and Malta (c4000-1500 BC) is unclear.

China. Proto-Chinese neolithic cultures had long covered northern and southeastern China when the rst large political state was organized in the north by the **Shang dynasty** c1500 BC. Shang kings called hemselves Sons of Heaven, and presided over a cult of human and animal sacrifice to ancestors and ature gods. The Chou dynasty, starting c1100 BC, expanded the area of the Son of Heaven's dominion, ut feudal states exercised most temporal power.

A writing system with 2,000 different characters was already in use under the Shang, with **pictographs** ater supplemented by phonetic characters. The system, with modifications, is still in use, despite changes n spoken Chinese.

Technical advances allowed urban specialists to create fine ceramic and jade products, and bronze asting after 1500 BC was the most advanced in the world.

Bronze artifacts have recently been discovered in northern Thailand dating to 3600 BC, hundreds of ears before similar Middle Eastern finds.

Americas. Olmecs settled on the Gulf coast of Mexico, 1500 BC, and soon developed the first ivilization in the Western Hemisphere. Temple cities and huge stone sculpture date to 1200 BC. A udimentary calendar and writing system existed. Olmec religion, centering on a jaguar god, and art orms influenced all later Meso-American cultures.

Neolithic ceremonial centers were built on the Peruvian desert coast, c2000 BC.

Classical Era of Old World Civilizations

Greece. After a period of decline during the Dorian Greek invasions (1200-1000 BC), Greece and the Aegean area developed a unique civilization. Drawing upon Mycenaean traditions, Mesopotamian earning (weights and measures, lunisolar calendar, astronomy, musical scales), the Phoenician alphabet modified for Greek), and Egyptian art, the revived **Greek city-states** saw a rich elaboration of ntellectual life. Long-range commerce was aided by metal coinage (introduced by the Lydians in Asia Minor before 700 BC); colonies were founded around the Mediterranean and Black Sea shores (Cumae in taly 760 BC, Massalia in France c600 BC).

Philosophy, starting with Ionian speculation on the nature of matter and the universe (Thales 634-546), and including mathematical speculation (Pythagoras c580-c500), culminated in Athens in the ationalist idealism of **Plato** (c428-347) and **Socrates** (c470-399); the latter was executed for alleged mpiety. Aristotle (384-322) united all fields of study in his system. The arts were highly valued. Architecture culminated in the **Parthenon** in Athens (438, sculpture by Phidias); poetry and drama Aeschylus 525-456) thrived. Male beauty and strength, a chief artistic theme, were enhanced at the gymnasium and the national games at Olympia.

Ruled by local tyrants or oligarchies, the Greeks were never politically united, but managed to resist nclusion in the Persian Empire (Darius defeated at Marathon 490 BC, Xerxes at Salamis, Plataea 479 BC). Local warfare was common; the **Peloponnesian Wars,** 431-404 BC, ended in Sparta's victory over Athens. Greek political power waned, but classical Greek cultural forms spread thoughout the ancient world from the Atlantic to India.

Hebrews. Nomadic Hebrew tribes entered Canaan before 1200 BC, settling among other Semitic peoples speaking the same language. They brought from the desert a **monotheistic faith** said to have been evealed to Abraham in Canaan c1800 BC and to Moses at Mt. Sinai c1250 BC, after the Hebrews' scape from bondage in Egypt. David (ruled 1000-961 BC) and Solomon (ruled 961-922 BC) united the Hebrews in a kingdom that briefly dominated the area. Phoenicians to the north established colonies

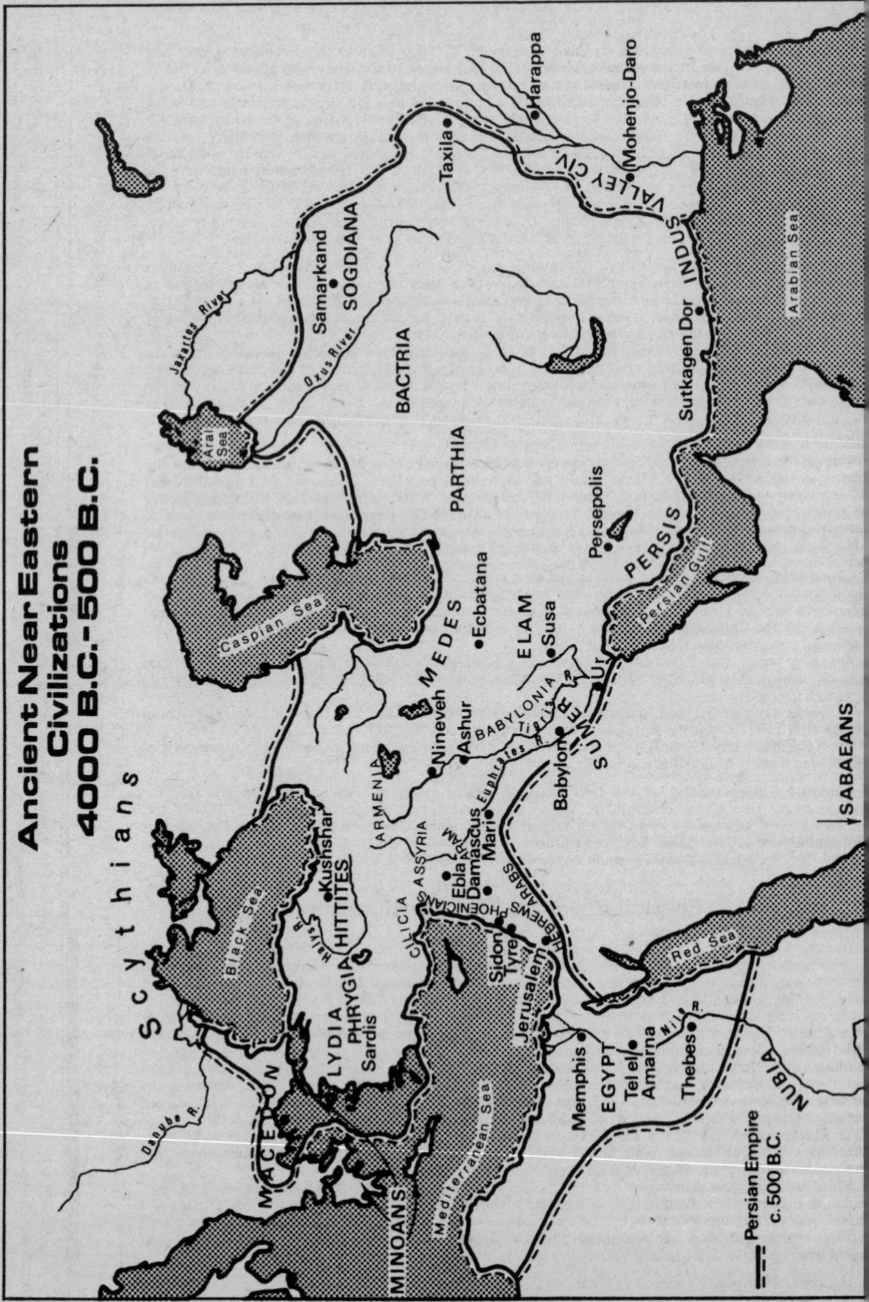
Ancient Near Eastern
Civilizations
4000 B.C.-500 B.C.
Scythians
Danube R.
MACEDON
MINOANS
Black Sea
LYDIA
PHRYGIA
Sardis
Halys R.
HITTITES
Kushshar
CILICIA
ASSYRIA
ARMENIA
Mediterranean Sea
Sidon
Tyre
Jerusalem
PHOENICIANS
HEBREWS
ARABS
Ebla
Damascus
Mari
ARAM
Nineveh
Ashur
Euphrates R.
Tigris R.
BABYLONIA
Babylon
SUMER
Ur
MEDES
Ecbatana
ELAM
Susa
Caspian Sea
PARTHIA
Persepolis
PERSIS
Persian Gulf
Aral Sea
Jaxartes River
Oxus River
Samarkand
SOGDIANA
BACTRIA
Sutkagen Dor
INDUS VALLEY CIV.
Taxila
Harappa
Mohenjo-Daro
Arabian Sea
Red Sea
SABAEANS
Memphis
EGYPT
Tel el Amarna
Nile R.
Thebes
NUBIA
Persian Empire
c. 500 B.C.

:ound the E. and W. Mediterranean (**Carthage** c814 BC) and sailed into the Atlantic.

A temple in Jerusalem became the national religious center, with sacrifices performed by a hereditary ·iesthood. Polytheistic influences, especially of the fertility cult of Baal, were opposed by **prophets** :lijah, Amos, Isaiah).

Divided into **two kingdoms** after Solomon, the Hebrews were unable to resist the revived Assyrian npire, which conquered Israel, the northern kingdom in 722 BC. Judah, the southern kingdom, was onquered in 586 BC by the Babylonians under Nebuchadnezzar II. But with the fixing of most of the iblical canon by the mid-fourth century BC, and the emergence of rabbis, arbiters of law and custom, ıdaism successfully survived the loss of Hebrew autonomy. A Jewish kingdom was revived under the fasmoneans (168-42 BC).

China. During the **Eastern Chou** dynasty (770-256 BC), Chinese culture spread east to the sea and outh to the Yangtze. Large feudal states on the periphery of the empire contended for pre-eminence, but ontinued to recognize the Son of Heaven (king), who retained a purely ritual role enriched with courtly ıusic and dance. In the Age of Warring States (403-221 BC), when the first sections of the **Great Wall** 'ere built, the Ch'in state in the West gained supremacy, and finally united all of China.

Iron tools entered China c500 BC, and casting techniques were advanced, aiding agriculture. Peasants wned their land, and owed civil and military service to nobles. Cities grew in number and size, though arter remained the chief trade medium.

Intellectual ferment among noble scribes and officials produced the Classical Age of Chinese literature ıd philosophy. **Confucius** (551-479 BC) urged a restoration of a supposedly harmonious social order of ıe past through proper conduct in accordance with one's station and through filial and ceremonial piety. he *Analects,* attributed to him, are revered throughout East Asia. **Mencius** (d. 289 BC) added the view ıat the Mandate of Heaven can be removed from an unjust dynasty. The Legalists sought to curb the ıpposed natural wickedness of people through new institutions and harsh laws; they aided the Ch'in rise) power. The Naturalists emphasized the balance of opposites — yin, yang — in the world. **Taoists** ought mystical knowledge through meditation and disengagement.

India. The political and cultural center of India shifted from the Indus to the Ganges River Valley. uddhism, Jainism, and mystical revisions of orthodox Vedism all developed around 500-300 BC. The *'panishads,* last part of the *Veda,* urged escape from the illusory physical world. Vedism remained the reserve of the priestly Brahmin caste. In contrast, **Buddhism,** founded by Siddarta Gautama (c563-c483 C), appealed to merchants in the growing urban centers, and took hold at first (and most lastingly) on ıe geographic fringes of Indian civilization. The classic Indian epics were composed in this era: The *amayana* around 300 BC, the *Mahabharata* over a period starting 400 BC.

Northern India was divided into a large number of monarchies and aristocratic republics, probably erived from tribal groupings, when the Magadha kingdom was formed in Bihar c542 BC. It soon ecame the dominant power. The **Maurya dynasty,** founded by Chandragupta c321 BC, expanded the ngdom, uniting most of N. India in a centralized bureaucratic empire. The third Mauryan king, **Asoka** uled c274-236) conquered most of the subcontinent: he converted to Buddhism, and inscribed its tenets ı pillars throughout India. He downplayed the caste system and tried to end expensive sacrificial rites.

Before its final decline in India, Buddhism developed the popular worship of heavenly Bodhisatvas nlightened beings), and produced a refined architecture (stupa—shrine—at Sanchi 100 AD) and ulpture (Gandhara reliefs 1-400 AD).

Persia. Aryan peoples (Persians, Medes) dominated the area of present Iran by the beginning of the rst millenium BC. The prophet **Zoroaster** (born c628 BC) introduced a dualistic religion in which the rces of good (Ahura Mazda, Lord of Wisdom) and evil (Ahiram) battle for dominance; individuals are dged by their actions and earn damnation or salvation. Zoroaster's hymns (*Gathas*) are included in the *vesta,* the Zoroastrian scriptures. A version of this faith became the established religion of the Persian mpire, and probably influenced later monotheistic religions.

Africa. Nubia, periodically occupied by Egypt since the third millenium, ruled Egypt c750-661, and ırvived as an independent Egyptianized kingdom (**Kush;** capital Meroe) for 1,000 years.

The Iron Age Nok culture flourished c500 BC-200 AD on the Benue Plateau of **Nigeria.**

Americas. The Chavin culture controlled north Peru from 900-200 BC. Its ceremonial centers, aturing the jaguar god, survived long after. Chavin architecture, ceramics, and textiles influenced other eruvian cultures.

Mayan civilization began to develop in Central America in the 5th century BC.

Great Empires Unite the Civilized World: 400 BC - 400 AD

Persia and Alexander. Cyrus, ruler of a small kingdom in Persia from 559 BC, united the Persians and edes within 10 years, conquered Asia Minor and Babylonia in another 10. His son Cambyses and andson **Darius** (ruled 522-486) added vast lands to the east and north as far as the Indus Valley and entral Asia, as well as Egypt and Thrace. The whole empire was ruled by an international bureaucracy ıd army, with Persians holding the chief positions. The resources and styles of all the subject vilizations were exploited to create a rich syncretic art.

The Hellenized kingdom of Macedon, which under Phillip II dominated Greece, passed to his son **lexander** in 336 BC. Within 13 years, Alexander conquered all the Persian dominions. Imbued by his tor Aristotle with Greek ideals, Alexander encouraged Greek colonization, and Greek-style cities were unded throughout the empire (e.g. Alexandria, Egypt). After his death in 323 BC, wars of succession vided the empire into three parts — **Macedon,** Egypt (ruled by the **Ptolemies**), and the **Seleucid** npire.

In the ensuing 300 years (the **Hellenistic Era**), a cosmopolitan Greek-oriented culture permeated the cient world from W. Europe to the borders of India, absorbing native elites everywhere.

Hellenistic philosophy stressed the private individual's search for happiness. The Cynics followed ogenes (c372-287), who stressed satisfaction of animal needs and contempt for social convention. Zeno 335-c263) and the Stoics exalted reason, identified it with virtue, and counseled an ascetic disregard for sfortune. The Epicureans tried to build lives of moderate pleasure without political or emotional

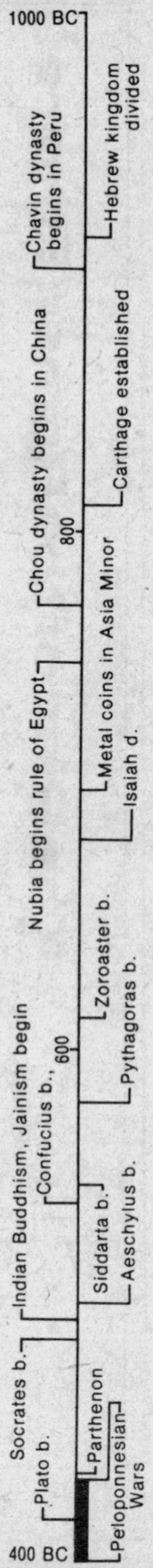

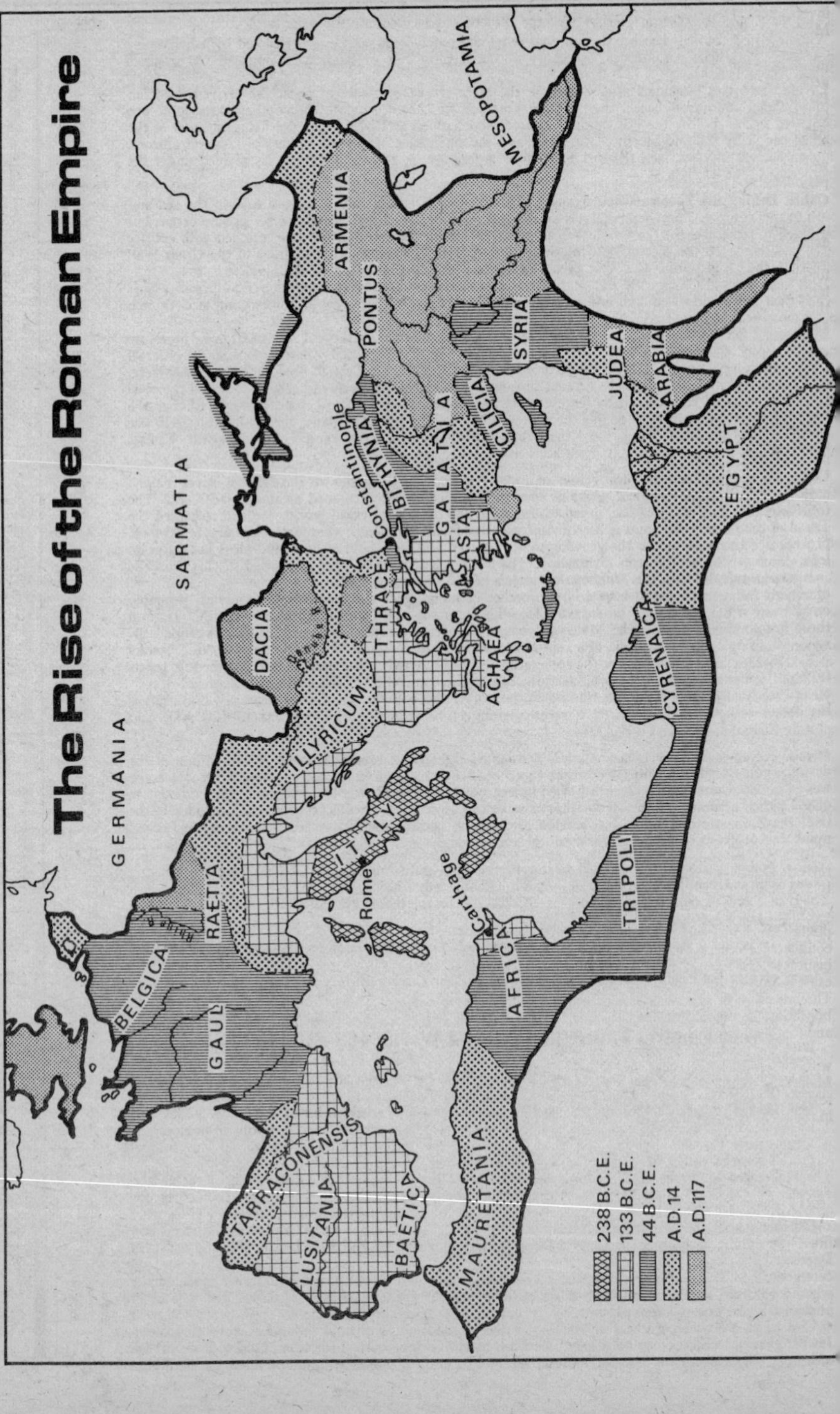
The Rise of the Roman Empire
GERMANIA
SARMATIA
MESOPOTAMIA
ARMENIA
PONTUS
SYRIA
JUDEA
ARABIA
CILICIA
GALATIA
BITHYNIA
Constantinople
ASIA
EGYPT
DACIA
THRACE
ACHAEA
CYRENAICA
ILLYRICUM
ITALY
Rome
Carthage
RAETIA
BELGICA
GAUL
AFRICA
TRIPOLI
TARRACONENSIS
LUSITANIA
BAETICA
MAURETANIA
238 B.C.E.
133 B.C.E.
44 B.C.E.
A.D. 14
A.D. 117

involvement. Hellenistic arts imitated life realistically, especially in sculpture and literature (comedies of Menander, 342-292).

The sciences thrived, especially at Alexandria, where the Ptolemies financed a great library and museum. Fields of study included mathematics (**Euclid's** geometry, c300 BC; Menelaus' non-Euclidean geometry, c100 AD); astronomy (heliocentric theory of Aristarchus, 310-230 BC; Julian calendar 45 BC; Ptolemy's *Almagest,* c150 AD); geography (world map of Eratosthenes, 276-194 BC); hydraulics (**Archimedes,** 287-212 BC); medicine (Galen, 130-200 AD), and chemistry. Inventors refined uses for siphons, valves, gears, springs, screws, levers, cams, and pulleys.

A restored Persian empire under the **Parthians** (N. Iranian tribesmen) controlled the eastern Hellenistic world 250 BC-229 AD. The Parthians and the succeeding Sassanian dynasty (229-651) fought with Rome periodically. The **Sassanians** revived Zoroastrianism as a state religion, and patronized a nationalistic artistic and scholarly renaissance.

Rome. The city of Rome was founded, according to legend, by Romulus in 753 BC. Through military expansion and colonization, and by granting citizenship to conquered tribes, the city annexed all of Italy south of the Po in the 100-year period before 268 BC. The Latin and other Italic tribes were annexed first, followed by the Etruscans (a civilized people north of Rome) and the Greek colonies in the south. With a large standing army and reserve forces of several hundred thousand, Rome was able to defeat Carthage in the 3 **Punic Wars,** 264-241, 218-201, 149-146 (despite the invasion of Italy by Hannibal, 218), thus gaining Sicily and territory in Spain and North Africa.

New provinces were added in the East, as Rome exploited local disputes to conquer Greece and Asia Minor in the 2d century BC, and Egypt in the first (after the defeat and suicide of **Antony and Cleopatra,** 30 BC). All the Mediterranean civilized world up to the disputed Parthian border was now Roman, and remained so for 500 years. Less civilized regions were added to the Empire: Gaul (conquered by Julius Caesar, 56-49 BC), Britain (43 AD) and Dacia NE of the Danube (117 AD).

The original aristocratic republican government, with democratic features added in the fifth and fourth centuries BC, deteriorated under the pressures of empire and class conflict (**Gracchus** brothers, social reformers, murdered 133, 121; slave revolts 135, 73). After a series of civil wars (Marius vs. Sulla 88-82, Caesar vs. Pompey 49-45, triumvirate vs. Caesar's assassins 44-43, Antony vs. Octavian 32-30), the empire came under the rule of a deified monarch (first emperor, **Augustus,** 27 BC-14 AD). Provincials (nearly all granted citizenship by Caracalla, 212 AD) came to dominate the army and civil service. Traditional Roman law, systematized and interpreted by independent jurists, and local self-rule in provincial cities were supplanted by a vast tax-collecting bureaucracy in the 3d and 4th centuries. The legal rights of women, children, and slaves were strengthened.

Roman innovations in **civil engineering** included water mills, windmills, and rotary mills, and the use of cement that hardened under water. Monumental architecture (baths, theaters, apartment houses) relied on the arch and the dome. The network of roads (some still standing) stretched 53,000 miles, passing through mountain tunnels as long as 3.5 miles. Aqueducts brought water to cities, underground sewers removed waste.

Roman art and literature were derivative of Greek models. Innovations were made in sculpture (naturalistic busts and equestrian statues), decorative wall painting (as at Pompeii), satire (Juvenal, 60-127), history (Tacitus 56-120), prose romance (Petronius, d. 66 AD). Violence and torture dominated mass public amusements, which were supported by the state.

India. The **Gupta** monarchs reunited N. India c320 AD. Their peaceful and prosperous reign saw a revival of Hindu religious thought and Brahmin power. The old Vedic traditions were combined with devotion to a plethora of indigenous deities (who were seen as manifestations of Vedic gods). **Caste lines** were reinforced, and Buddhism gradually disappeared. The art (often erotic), architecture, and literature of the period, patronized by the Gupta court, are considered to be among India's finest achievements (Kalidasa, poet and dramatist, fl. c400). Mathematical innovations included the use of zero and decimal numbers. Invasions by White Huns from the NW destroyed the empire c550.

Rich cultures also developed in S. India in this era. Emotional Tamil religious poetry aided the Hindu revival. The Pallava kingdom controlled much of S. India c350-880, and helped spread Indian civilization to S.E. Asia.

China. The Ch'in ruler Shih Huang Ti (ruled 221-210 BC), known as the First Emperor, centralized political authority in China, standardized the written language, laws, weights, measures, and coinage, and conducted a census, but tried to destroy most philosophical texts. The **Han dynasty** (206 BC-220 AD) instituted the Mandarin bureaucracy, which lasted for 2,000 years. Local officials were selected by examination in the Confucian classics and trained at the imperial university and at provincial schools. The invention of **paper** facilitated this bureaucratic system. Agriculture was promoted, but the peasants bore most of the tax burden. Irrigation was improved; water clocks and sundials were used; astronomy and mathematics thrived; landscape painting was perfected.

With the expansion south and west (to nearly the present borders of today's China), trade was opened with India, S.E. Asia, and the Middle East, over sea and caravan routes. Indian missionaries brought Mahayana Buddhism to China by the first century AD, and spawned a variety of sects. Taoism was revived, and merged with popular superstitions. Taoist and Buddhist monasteries and convents multiplied in the turbulent centuries after the collapse of the Han dynasty.

The One God Triumphs: 1-750 AD

Christianity. Religions indigenous to particular Middle Eastern nations became international in the first 3 centuries of the Roman Empire. Roman citizens worshipped **Isis** of Egypt, **Mithras** of Persia, **Demeter** of Greece, and the great mother **Cybele** of Phrygia. Their cults centered on mysteries (secret ceremonies) and the promise of an afterlife, symbolized by the death and rebirth of the god. Judaism, which had begun as the national cult of Judea, also spread by emigration and conversion. It was the only ancient religion west of India to survive.

Christians, who emerged as a distinct sect in the second half of the 1st century AD, revered **Jesus,** a Jewish preacher said to have been killed by the Romans at the request of Jewish authorities in Jerusalem c30 AD. They considered him the Savior (Messiah, or Christ) who rose from the dead and could grant

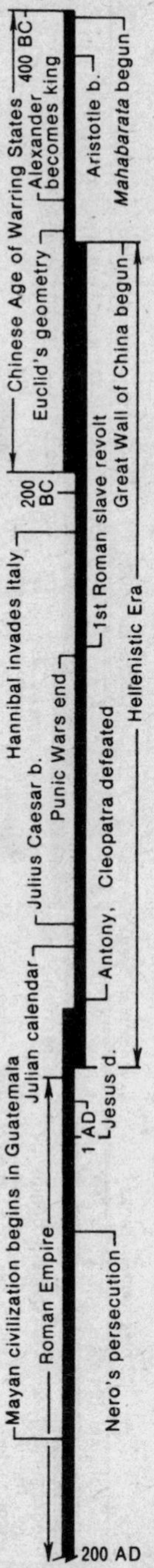

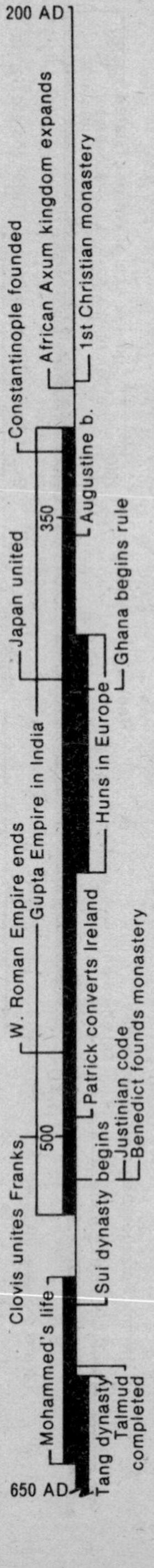

eternal life to the faithful, despite their sinfulness. They believed he was an incarnation of the one god worshipped by the Jews, and that he would return soon to pass final judgment on the world. The missionary activities of such early leaders as **Paul of Tarsus** spread the faith, at first mostly among Jews or among quasi-Jews attracted by the Pauline rejection of such difficult Jewish laws as circumcision. Intermittent persecution, as in Rome under Nero in 64 AD, on grounds of suspected disloyalty, failed to disrupt the Christian communities. Each congregation, generally urban and of plebeian character, was tightly organized under a leader (bishop) elders (presbyters or priests), and assistants (deacons). Stories about Jesus (the Gospels) and the early church (Acts) were written down in the late first and early 2d centuries, and circulated along with letters of Paul. An authoritative canon of these writings was not fixed until the 4th century.

A school for priests was established at Alexandria in the second century. Its teachers (**Origen** c182-251) helped define Christian doctrine and promote the faith in Greek-style philosophical works. Pagan Neoplatonism was given Christian coloration in the works of Church Fathers such as Augustine (354-430). Christian hermits, often drawn from the lower classes, began to associate in monasteries, first in Egypt (St. Pachomius c290-345), then in other eastern lands, then in the West (**St. Benedict's rule**, 529). Popular adoration of saints, especially Mary, mother of Jesus, spread.

Under **Constantine** (ruled 306-337), Christianity became in effect the established religion of the Empire. Pagan temples were expropriated, state funds were used to build huge churches and support the hierarchy, and laws were adjusted in accordance with Christian notions. Pagan worship was banned by the end of the fourth century, and severe restrictions were placed on Judaism.

The newly established church was rocked by doctrinal disputes, often exacerbated by regional rivalries both within and outside the Empire. Chief heresies (as defined by church councils backed by imperial authority) were **Arianism,** which denied the divinity of Jesus; **Donatism,** which rejected the convergence of church and state and denied the validity of sacraments performed by sinful clergy; and the **Monophysite** position denying the dual nature of Christ.

Judaism. First century Judaism embraced several sects, including: the **Sadducees,** mostly drawn from the Temple priesthood, who were culturally Hellenized; the **Pharisees,** who upheld the full range of traditional customs and practices as of equal weight to literal scriptural law, and elaborated synagogue worship; and the **Essenes,** an ascetic, millenarian sect. Messianic fervor led to repeated, unsuccessful rebellions against Rome (66-70, 135). As a result, the Temple was destroyed, and the population decimated.

To avoid the dissolution of the faith, a program of codification of law was begun at the academy of Yavneh. The work continued for some 500 years in Palestine and Babylonia, ending in the final redaction of the **Talmud** (c600), a huge collection of legal and moral debates, rulings, liturgy, Biblical exegesis, and legendary materials.

Islam. The earliest Arab civilization emerged by the end of the 2d millenium BC in the watered highlands of Yemen. Seaborne and caravan trade in frankincense and myrrh connected the area with the Nile and Fertile Crescent. The Minaean, Sabean (Sheba), and Himyarite states successively held sway. By Mohammed's time (7th century AD), the region was a province of Sassanian Persia. In the North, the **Nabataean kingdom** at Petra and the kingdom of Palmyra were first Aramaicized and then Romanized and finally absorbed like neighboring Judea into the Roman Empire. Nomads shared the central region with a few trading towns and oases. Wars between tribes and raids on settled communities were common and were celebrated in a poetic tradition that by the 6th century helped establish a classic literary Arabic.

In 611 **Mohammed,** a wealthy 40-year-old Arab of Mecca, had a revelation from Allah, the one true god, calling on him to repudiate pagan idolatry. Drawing on elements of Judaism and Christianity, and eventually incorporating some Arab pagan traditions (such as reverence for the black stone at the kaaba shrine in Mecca), Mohammed's teachings, recorded in the **Koran,** forged a new religion, Islam (submission to Allah). Opposed by the leaders of Mecca, Mohammed made a *hejira* (migration) to Medina to the north in 622, the beginning of the Moslem lunar calendar. He and his followers defeated the Meccans in 624 in the first *jihad* (holy war), and by his death (632), nearly all the Arabian peninsula accepted his religious and secular leadership.

Under the first two **caliphs** (successors) Abu Bakr (632-34) and Oman (634-44), Moslem rule was confirmed over Arabia. Raiding parties into Byzantine and Persian border areas developed into campaigns of conquest against the two empires, which had been weakened by wars and by disaffection among subject peoples (including Coptic and Syriac Christians opposed to the Byzantine orthodox church). Syria, Palestine, Egypt, Iraq, and Persia all fell to the inspired Arab armies. The Arabs at first remained a distinct minority, using non-Moslems in the new administrative system, and tolerating Christians, Jews, and Zoroastrians as self-governing "Peoples of the Book," whose taxes supported the empire.

Disputes over the succession, and puritan reaction to the wealth and refinement that empire brought to the ruling strata, led to the growth of schismatic movements. The followers of Mohammed's son-in-law Ali (assassinated 661) and his descendants became the founders of the more mystical **Shi'ite** sect, still the largest non-orthodox Moslem sect. The Karijites, puritanical, militant, and egalitarian, persist as a minor sect to the present.

Under the **Ummayad** caliphs (661-750), the boundaries of Islam were extended across N. Africa and into Spain. Arab armies in the West were stopped at Tours in 732 by the Frank **Charles Martel.** Asia Minor, the Indus Valley, and Transoxiana were conquered in the East. The vast majority of the subject population gradually converted to Islam, encouraged by tax and career privileges. The Arab language supplanted the local tongues in the central and western areas, but Arab soldiers and rulers in the East eventually became assimilated to the indigenous languages.

New Peoples Enter History: 400-900

Barbarian invasions. Germanic tribes infiltrated S and E from their Baltic homeland during the 1st millenium BC, reaching S. Germany by 100 BC and the Black Sea by 214 AD. Organized into large federated tribes under elected kings, most resisted Roman domination and raided the empire in time of civil war (Goths took Dacia 214, raided Thrace 251-269). German troops and commanders came to dominate the Roman armies by the end of the 4th century. **Huns,** invaders from Asia, entered Europe 372, driving more Germans into the western empire. Emperor Valens allowed Visigoths to cross e Danube 376. Huns under Attila (d. 453) raided Gaul, Italy, Balkans. The western empire, weakened overtaxation and social stagnation, was overrun in the 5th century. Gaul was effectively lost 406-7, ain 409, Britain 410, Africa 429-39. Rome itself was sacked 410 by Visigoths under Alaric, 455 by ndals. The last western emperor, Romulus Augustulus, was deposed 476 by the Germanic chief loacer.

Celts. Celtic cultures, which in pre-Roman times covered most of W. Europe, were confined almost tirely to the British Isles after the Germanic invasions. **St. Patrick** completed the conversion of Ireland 457-92). A strong monastic tradition took hold. Irish monastic missionaries in Scotland, England, and e continent (Columba c521-597; Columban c543-615) helped restore Christianity after the Germanic vasions. The monasteries became renowned centers of classic and Christian learning, and presided over e recording of a Christianized Celtic mythology, elaborated by secular writers and bards. An intricate corative art style developed, especially in book illumination (Lindisfarne Gospels, c700, Book of Kells, h century).

Successor states. The Visigoth kingdom in Spain (from 419) and much of France (to 507) saw a ntinuation of much Roman administration, language, and law (Breviary of Alaric 506), until its struction by the Moslems, 711. The Vandal kingdom in Africa, from 429, was conquered by the yzantines, 533. Italy was ruled in succession by an Ostrogothic kingdom under Byzantine suzerainty 9-554, direct Byzantine government, and the German Lombards (568-774). The latter divided the ninsula with the Byzantines and the papacy under the dynamic reformer Pope Gregory the Great 90-604) and his successors.

King Clovis (ruled 481-511) united the Franks on both sides of the Rhine, and after his conversion to thodox Christianity, defeated the Arian Burgundians (after 500) and Visigoths (507) with the support the native clergy and the papacy. Under the **Merovingian** kings a feudal system emerged: power was agmented among hierarchies of military landowners. Social stratification, which in late Roman times d acquired legal, hereditary sanction, was reinforced. The Carolingians (747-987) expanded the ngdom and restored central power. **Charlemagne** (ruled 768-814) conquered nearly all the Germanic nds, including Lombard Italy, and was crowned Emperor by Pope Leo III in Rome in 800. A nturies-long decline in commerce and the arts was reversed under Charlemagne's patronage. He elcomed Jews to his kingdom, which became a center of Jewish learning (Rashi 1040-1105). He onsored the "Carolingian Renaissance" of learning under the Anglo-Latin scholar Alcuin (c732-804), ho reformed church liturgy.

Byzantine Empire. Under Diocletian (ruled 284-305) the empire had been divided into 2 parts to cilitate administration and defense. Constantine founded **Constantinople,** 330, (at old Byzantium) as a lly Christian city. Commerce and taxation financed a sumptuous, orientalized court, a class of reditary bureaucratic families, and magnificent urban construction (Hagia Sophia, 532-37). The city's rtifications and naval innovations (Greek fire) repelled assaults by Goths, Huns, Slavs, Bulgars, Avars, rabs, and Scandinavians. Greek replaced Latin as the official language by c700. Byzantine art, a solemn, cral, and stylized variation of late classical styles (mosaics at S. Vitale, Ravenna, 526-48) was a starting int for medieval art in E. and W. Europe.

Justinian (ruled 527-65) reconquered parts of Spain, N. Africa, and Italy, codified Roman law (*codex stinianus,* 529, was medieval Europe's chief legal text), closed the Platonic Academy at Athens and dered all pagans to convert. Lombards in Italy, Arabs in Africa retook most of his conquests. The aurian dynasty from Anatolia (from 717) and the Macedonian dynasty (867-1054) restored military and mmercial power. The Iconoclast controversy (726-843) over the permissibility of images, helped ienate the Eastern Church from the papacy.

Arab Empire. Baghdad, founded 762, became the seat of the **Abbasid** Caliphate (founded 750), while mmayads continued to rule in Spain. A brilliant cosmopolitan civilization emerged, inaugurating an rab-Moslem golden age. Arab lyric poetry revived; Greek, Syriac, Persian, and Sanskrit books were anslated into Arabic, often by Syriac Christians and Jews, whose theology and Talmudic law, spectively, influenced Islam. The arts and music flourished at the court of **Harun al-Rashid** (786-809), lebrated in *The Arabian Nights.* The sciences, medicine, and mathematics were pursued at Baghdad, ordova, and Cairo (founded 969). Science and Aristotelian philosophy culminated in the systems of vicenna (980-1037), Averroes (1126-98), and Maimonides (1135-1204), a Jew; all influenced later hristian scholarship and theology. The Islamic ban on images encouraged a sinuous, geometric corative tradition, applied to architecture and illumination. A gradual loss of Arab control in Persia rom 874) led to the capture of Baghdad by Persians, 945. By the next century, Spain and N. Africa were led by Berbers, while Turks prevailed in Asia Minor and the Levant. The loss of political power by the liphs allowed for the growth of non-orthodox trends, especially the mystical **Sufi** tradition (theologian hazali, 1058-1111).

Africa. Immigrants from Saba in S. Arabia helped set up the **Axum** kingdom in Ethiopia in the 2d ntury (their language, Ge'ez, is preserved by the Ethiopian Church). In the 4th century, when the ngdom became Christianized, it defeated Kushite Meroe and expanded into Yemen. Axum was the nter of a vast ivory trade; it controlled the Red Sea coast until c1100. Arab conquest in Egypt cut xum's political and economic ties with Byzantium.

The Iron Age entered W. Africa by the end of the 1st millenium BC. **Ghana,** the first known b-Saharan state, ruled in the upper Senegal-Niger region c400-1240, controlling the trade of gold from ines in the S to trans-Sahara caravan routes to the N. The **Bantu** peoples, probably of W. African igin, began to spread E and S perhaps 2000 years ago, displacing the Pygmies and Bushmen of central

Japan. The advanced Neolithic Yayoi period, when irrigation, rice farming, and iron and bronze sting techniques were introduced from China or Korea, persisted to c400 AD. The myriad Japanese ates were then united by the **Yamato** clan, under an emperor who acted as the chief priest of the imistic **Shinto** cult. Japanese political and military intervention in Korea by the 6th century quickened Chinese cultural invasion, bringing Buddhism, the Chinese language (which long remained a literary d governmental medium), Chinese ideographs and Buddhist styles in painting, sculpture, literature, and chitecture (7th c. Horyu-ji temple at Nara). The Taika Reforms, 646, tried to centralize Japan cording to Chinese bureaucratic and Buddhist philosophical values, but failed to curb traditional panese decentralization. A nativist reaction against the Buddhist **Nara period** (710-94) ushered in the

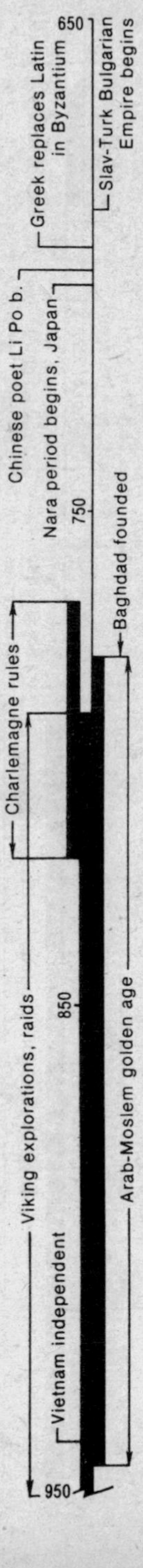

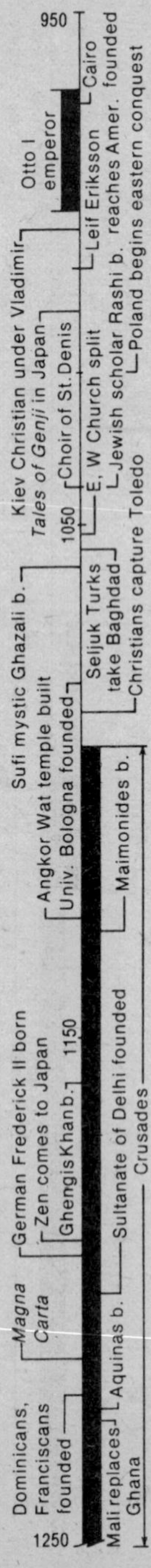

Heian period (794-1185) centered at the new capital, Kyoto. Japanese elegance and simplicity modifi Chinese styles in architecture, scroll painting, and literature; the writing system was also simplified. T courtly novel *Tale of Genji* (1010-20) testifies to the enhanced role of women.

Southeast Asia. The historic peoples of southeast Asia began arriving some 2500 years ago from Chi and Tibet, displacing scattered aborigines. Their agriculture relied on rice and tubers (yams), which th may have introduced to Africa. Indian cultural influences were strongest; literacy and Hindu a Buddhist ideas followed the southern India-China trade route. From the southern tip of Indochina, t kingdom of **Funan** (1st-7th centuries) traded as far west as Persia. It was absorbed by Chenla, its conquered by the **Khmer Empire** (600-1300). The Khmers, under Hindu god-kings (Suryavarman 1113-c1150), built the monumental Angkor Wat temple center for the royal phallic cult. The **Nam-V** kingdom in Annam, dominated by China and Chinese culture for 1,000 years, emerged in the 10 century, growing at the expense of the Khmers, who also lost ground in the NW to the ne highly-organized **Thai** kingdom. On Sumatra, the **Srivijaya** Empire at Palembang controlled vital s lanes (7th to 10th centuries). A Buddhist dynasty, the Sailendras, ruled central **Java** (8th-9th centurie building at Borobudur one of the largest stupas in the world.

China. The short-lived Sui dynasty (581-618) ushered in a period of commercial, artistic, and scienti achievement in China, continuing under the **T'ang** dynasty (618-906). Such inventions as the magne compass, gunpowder, the abacus, and printing were introduced or perfected. Medical innovatio included cataract surgery. The state, from the cosmopolitan capital, Ch'ang-an, supervised foreign tra which exchanged Chinese silks, porcelains, and art works for spices, ivory, etc., over Central Asi caravan routes and sea routes reaching Africa. A golden age of poetry bequeathed tens of thousands works to later generations (Tu Fu 712-70, Li Po 701-62). Landscape painting flourished. Commercial a industrial expansion continued under the **Northern Sung** dynasty (960-1126), facilitated by paper mon and credit notes. But commerce never achieved respectability; government monopolies expropriat successful merchants. The population, long stable at 50 million, doubled in 200 years with t introduction of early-ripening rice and the double harvest. In art, native Chinese styles were revived.

Americas. An Indian empire stretched from the Valley of Mexico to Guatemala, 300-600, centering the huge city **Teotihuacan** (founded 100 BC). To the S, in Guatemala, a high **Mayan** civilizati developed, 150-900, around hundreds of rural ceremonial centers. The Mayans improved on Olm writing and the calendar, and pursued astronomy and mathematics (using the idea of zero). In America, a widespread pre-Inca culture grew from **Tiahuanaco** near Lake Titicaca (Gateway of the Su c700).

Christian Europe Regroups and Expands: 900-1300

Scandinavians. Pagan Danish and Norse **(Viking)** adventurers, traders, and pirates raided the coasts the British Isles (Dublin founded c831), France, and even the Mediterranean for over 200 years beginni in the late 8th century. Inland settlement in the W was limited to Great Britain (King Canute, 994-103 and Normandy, settled under Rollo, 911, as a fief of France. Other Vikings reached Iceland (87 Greenland (c986), and probably N. America (Leif Eriksson c1000). Norse traders **(Varangians)** develop Russian river commerce from the 8th-11th centuries, and helped set up a state at Kiev in the late 9 century. Conversion to Christianity occurred during the 10th century, reaching Sweden 100 years lat Eleventh century Norman bands conquered S. Italy and Sicily. Duke **William of Normandy** conquer England, 1066, bringing continental feudalism and the French language, essential elements in la English civilization.

East Europe. Slavs inhabited areas of E. Central Europe in prehistoric times, and reached most of th present limits by c850. The first Slavic states were in the Balkans (Slav-Turk **Bulgarian Empi** 680-1018) and Moravia (628). Missions of St. Cyril (whose Greek-based Cyrillic alphabet is still used S. and E. Slavs) converted Moravia, 863. The Eastern Slavs, part-civilized under the overlordship of t Turkish-Jewish **Khazar** trading empire (7th-10th centuries), gravitated toward Constantinople by the 9 century. The **Kievan state** adopted Eastern Christianity under Prince Vladimir, 989. King Boleslav (992-1025) began **Poland's** long history of eastern conquest. The Magyars **(Hungarians)** in Europe sin 896, accepted Latin Christianity, 1001.

Germany. The German kingdom that emerged after the breakup of Charlemagne's Empire remainec confederation of largely autonomous states. The Saxon Otto I, king from 936, established the **H Roman Empire** of Germany and Italy in alliance with Pope John XII, who crowned him emperor, 962; defeated the Magyars, 955. Imperial power was greatest under the **Hohenstaufens** (1138-1254), desp the growing opposition of the papacy, which ruled central Italy, and the Lombard League citi Frederick II (1194-1250) improved administration, patronized the arts; after his death German influe was removed from Italy.

Christian Spain. From its northern mountain redoubts, Christian rule slowly migrated south throu the 11th century, when Moslem unity collapsed. After the capture of **Toledo** (1085), the kingdoms Portugal, Castile, and Aragon undertook repeated crusades of reconquest, finally completed in 14 Elements of Islamic civilization persisted in recaptured areas, influencing all W. Europe.

Crusades. Pope Urban II called, 1095, for a crusade to restore Asia Minor to Byzantium and conq the Holy Land from the Turks. Some 10 crusades (to 1291) succeeded only in founding 4 tempor Frankish states in the Levant. The 4th crusade sacked Constantinople, 1204. In Rhineland (109 England (1290), France (1306), Jews were massacred or expelled, and wars were launched agai Christian heretics (**Albigensian** crusade in France, 1229). Trade in eastern luxuries expanded, led by t Venetian naval empire.

Economy. The agricultural base of European life benefitted from improvements in **plow design** c10 and by draining of lowlands and clearing of forests, leading to a rural population increase. Towns grew N. Italy, Flanders, and N. Germany (Hanseatic League). Improvements in **loom design** permitted fact textile production. **Guilds** dominated urban trades from the 12th century. Banking (centered in Ita 12th-15th century) facilitated long-distance trade.

The Church. The split between the Eastern and Western churches was formalized in 1054. W. a

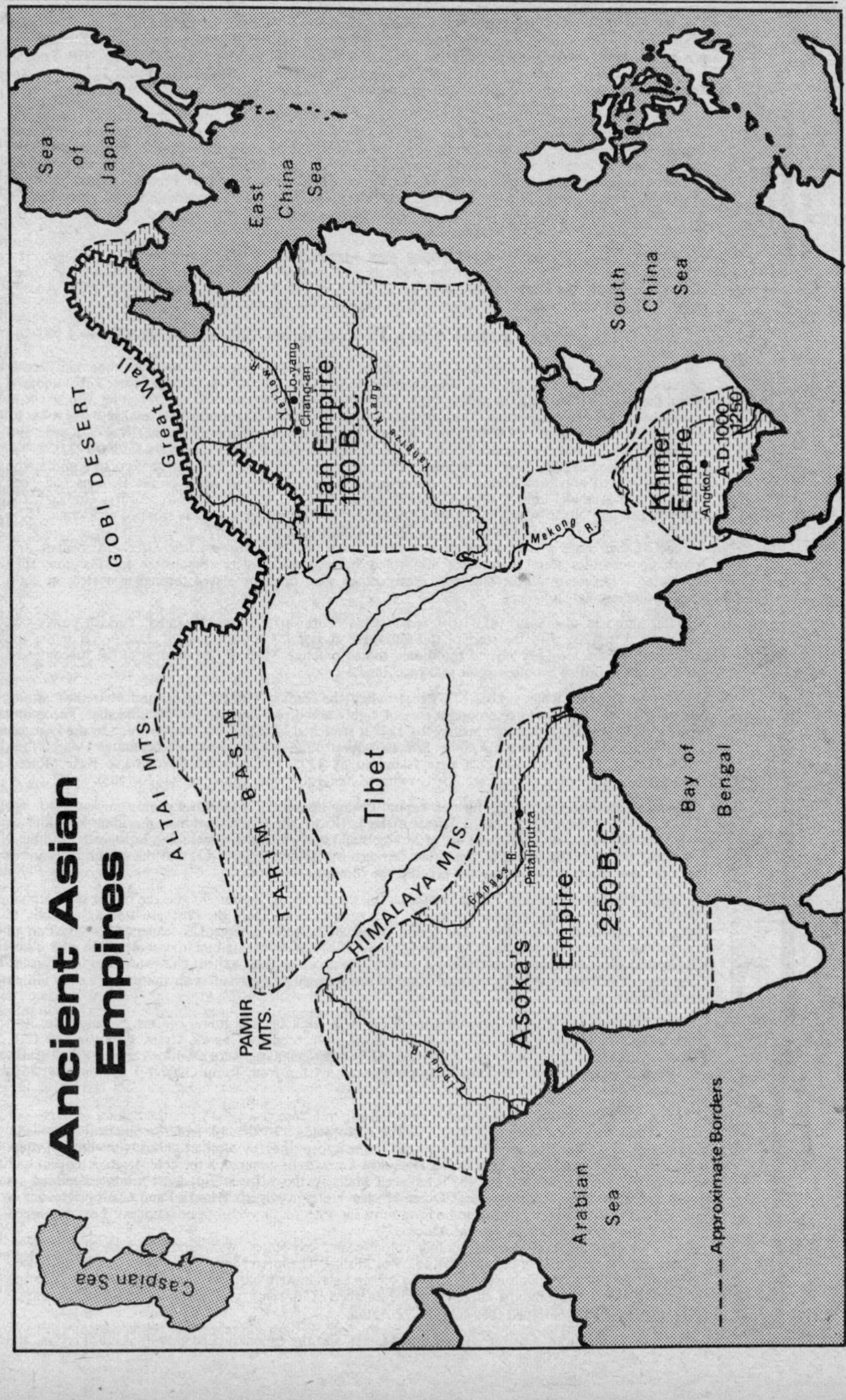

Ancient Asian Empires
Caspian Sea
Arabian Sea
Approximate Borders
PAMIR MTS.
Indus R.
Asoka's Empire 250 B.C.
ALTAI MTS.
TARIM BASIN
HIMALAYA MTS.
Ganges R.
Pataliputra
Bay of Bengal
Tibet
GOBI DESERT
Great Wall
Yellow R.
Chang-an
Lo-yang
Han Empire 100 B.C.
Yangtze Kiang
Mekong R.
Khmer Empire
Angkor
A.D.1000-1250
South China Sea
East China Sea
Sea of Japan

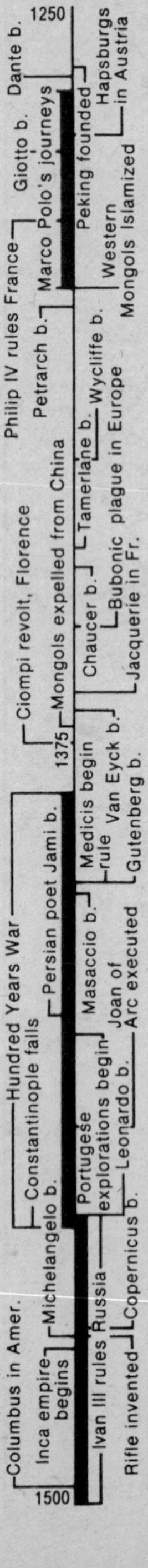

Central Europe was divided into 500 bishoprics under one united hierarchy, but conflicts between secular and church authorities were frequent (German **Investiture Controversy,** 1075-1122). Clerical power was first strengthened through the international monastic reform begun at Cluny, 910. Popular religious enthusiasm often expressed itself in heretical movements (Waldensians from 1173), but was channelled by the **Dominican** (1215) and **Franciscan** (1223) friars into the religious mainstream.

Arts. Romanesque architecture (11th-12th centuries) expanded on late Roman models, using the rounded arch and massed stone to support enlarged basilicas. Painting and sculpture followed Byzantine models. The literature of **chivalry** was exemplified by the epic (Chanson de Roland, c1100) and by courtly love poems of the troubadours of Provence and minnesingers of Germany. **Gothic architecture** emerged in France (choir of St. Denis, c1040) and spread as French cultural influence predominated in Europe. Rib vaulting and pointed arches were used to combine soaring heights with delicacy, and freed walls for display of stained glass. Exteriors were covered with painted relief sculpture and elaborate architectural detail.

Learning. Law, medicine, and philosophy were advanced at independent **universities** (Bologna, late 11th century), originally corporations of students and masters. Twelfth century translations of Greek classics, especially Aristotle, encouraged an analytic approach. Scholastic philosophy, from Anselm (1033-1109) to Aquinas (1225-74) attempted to reconcile reason and revelation.

Apogee of Central Asian Power; Islam Grows: 1250-1500

Turks. Turkic peoples, of Central Asian ancestry, were a military threat to the Byzantine and Persian Empires from the 6th century. After several waves of invasions, during which most of the Turks adopted Islam, the **Seljuk Turks** took Baghdad, 1055. They ruled Persia, Iraq, and, after 1071, Asia Minor, where massive numbers of Turks settled. The empire was divided in the 12th century into smaller states ruled by Seljuks, Kurds (**Saladin** c1137-93), and Mamelukes (a military caste of former Turk, Kurd, and Circassian slaves), which governed Egypt and the Middle East until the Ottoman era (c1290-1922).

Osman I (ruled c1290-1326) and succeeding sultans united Anatolian Turkish warriors in a militaristic state that waged holy war against Byzantium and Balkan Christians. Most of the Balkans had been subdued, and Anatolia united, when **Constantinople fell,** 1453. By the mid-16th century, Hungary, the Middle East, and North Africa had been conquered. The Turkish advance was stopped at Vienna, 1529, and at the naval battle of Lepanto, 1571, by Spain, Venice, and the papacy.

The Ottoman state was governed in accordance with orthodox Moslem law. Greek, Armenian, and Jewish communities were segregated, and ruled by religious leaders responsible for taxation; they dominated trade. State offices and most army ranks were filled by slaves through a system of child conscription among Christians.

India. Mahmud of Ghazni (971-1030) led repeated Turkish raids into N. India. Turkish power was consolidated in 1206 with the start of the **Sultanate at Delhi.** Centralization of state power under the early Delhi sultans went far beyond traditional Indian practice. Moslem rule of most of the subcontinent lasted until the British conquest some 600 years later.

Mongols. Genghis Khan (c1162-1227) first united the feuding Mongol tribes, and built their armies into an effective offensive force around a core of highly mobile cavalry. He and his immediate successors created the largest land empire in history; by 1279 it stretched from the east coast of Asia to the Danube, from the Siberian steppes to the Arabian Sea. East-West trade and contacts were facilitated (Marco Polo c1254-1324). The western Mongols were Islamized by 1295; successor states soon lost their Mongol character by assimilation. They were briefly reunited under the Turk Tamerlane (1336-1405).

Kublai Khan ruled China from his new capital Peking (founded 1264). Naval campaigns against Japan (1274, 1281) and Java (1293) were defeated, the latter by the Hindu-Buddhist maritime kingdom of Majapahit. The **Yuan** dynasty made use of Mongols and other foreigners (including Europeans) in official posts, and tolerated the return of Nestorian Christianity (suppressed 841-45) and the spread of Islam in the South and West. A native reaction expelled the Mongols, 1367-68.

Russia. The Kievan state in Russia, weakened by the decline of Byzantium and the rise of the Catholic Polish-Lithuanian state, was overrun by the Mongols, 1238-40. Only the northern trading republic of Novgorod remained independent. The grand dukes of Moscow emerged as leaders of a coalition of princes that eventually defeated the Mongols, by 1481. With the fall of Constantinople, the **Tsars** (Caesars) at Moscow (from Ivan III, ruled 1462-1505) set up an independent Russian Orthodox Church. Commerce failed to revive. The isolated Russian state remained agrarian, with the peasant class falling into serfdom.

Persia. A revival of Persian literature, using the Arab alphabet and literary forms, began in the 10th century (epic of Firdausi, 935-1020). An art revival, influenced by Chinese styles, began in the 12th. Persian cultural and political forms, and often the Persian language, were used for centuries by Turkish and Mongol elites from the Balkans to India. Persian mystics from Rumi (1207-73) to Jami (1414-92) promoted **Sufism** in their poetry.

Africa. Two Berber dynasties, imbued with Islamic militance, emerged from the Sahara to carve out empires from the Sahel to central Spain — the **Almoravids,** c1050-1140, and the fanatical **Almohads,** c1125-1269. The Ghanaian empire was replaced in the upper Niger by Mali, c1230-c1340, whose Moslem rulers imported Egyptians to help make **Timbuktu** a center of commerce (in gold, leather, slaves) and learning. The Songhay empire (to 1590) replaced Mali. To the S, forest kingdoms produced refined art works (Ife terra cotta, **Benin** bronzes). Other Moslem states in Nigeria (Hausas) and Chad originated in the 11th century, and continued in some form until the 19th century European conquest. Less developed Bantu kingdoms existed across central Africa.

Some 40 Moslem Arab-Persian trading colonies and city-states were established all along the E. African coast from the 10th century (Kilwa, Mogadishu). The interchange with Bantu peoples produced the **Swahili** language and culture. Gold, palm oil, and slaves were brought from the interior, stimulating the growth of the Monamatapa kingdom of the Zambezi (15th century). The Christian Ethiopian empire (from 13th century) continued the traditions of Axum.

Southeast Asia. Islam was introduced into Malaya and the Indonesian islands by Arab, Persian, and

Indian traders. Coastal Moslem cities and states (starting before 1300), enriched by trade, soon dominated the interior. Chief among these was the **Malacca** state, on the Malay peninsula, c1400-1511.

Arts and Statecraft Thrive in Europe: 1350-1600

Italian Renaissance & humanism. Distinctive Italian achievements in the arts in the late Middle Ages (Dante, 1265-1321, Giotto, 1276-1337) led to the vigorous new styles of the Renaissance (14th-16th centuries). Patronized by the rulers of the quarreling petty states of Italy (Medicis in Florence and the papacy, c1400-1737), the plastic arts perfected realistic techniques, including **perspective** (Masaccio, 1401-28, Leonardo 1452-1519). Classical motifs were used in architecture and increased talent and expense were put into secular buildings. The Florentine dialect was refined as a national literary language (Petrarch, 1304-74). Greek refugees from the E strengthened the respect of humanist scholars for the classic sources (Bruni 1370-1444). Soon an international movement aided by the spread of **printing** (Gutenberg c1400-1468), **humanism** was optimistic about the power of human reason (Erasmus of Rotterdam, 1466-1536, Thomas More's *Utopia*, 1516) and valued individual effort in the arts and in politics (Machiavelli, 1469-1527).

France. The French monarchy, strengthened in its repeated struggles with powerful nobles (Burgundy, Flanders, Aquitaine) by alliances with the growing commercial towns, consolidated bureaucratic control under Philip IV (ruled 1285-1314) and extended French influence into Germany and Italy (popes at Avignon, France, 1309-1417). The **Hundred Years War**, 1338-1453, ended English dynastic claims in France (battles of Crécy, 1346, Poitiers, 1356; Joan of Arc executed, 1431). A French Renaissance, dating from royal invasions of Italy, 1494, 1499, was encouraged at the court of Francis I (ruled 1515-47), who centralized taxation and law. French vernacular literature consciously asserted its independence (La Pleiade, 1549).

England. The evolution of England's unique political institutions began with the Magna Carta, 1215, by which King John guaranteed the privileges of nobles and church against the monarchy and assured jury trial. After the Wars of the Roses (1455-85), the **Tudor dynasty** reasserted royal prerogatives (Henry VIII, ruled 1509-47), but the trend toward independent departments and ministerial government also continued. English trade (wool exports from c1340) was protected by the nation's growing maritime power (**Spanish Armada** destroyed, 1588).

English replaced French and Latin in the late 14th century in law and literature (Chaucer, 1340-1400) and English translation of the Bible began (Wycliffe, 1380s). Elizabeth I (ruled 1558-1603) presided over a confident flowering of poetry (Spenser, 1552-99), drama (**Shakespeare,** 1552-1616), and music.

German Empire. From among a welter of minor feudal states, church lands, and independent cities, the **Hapsburgs** assembled a far-flung territorial domain, based in Austria from 1276. The family held the title Holy Roman Emperor from 1452 to the Empire's dissolution in 1806, but failed to centralize its domains, leaving Germany disunited for centuries. Resistance to Turkish expansion brought Hungary under Austrian control from the 16th century. The Netherlands, Luxembourg, and Burgundy were added in 1477, curbing French expansion.

The Flemish painting tradition of naturalism, technical proficiency, and bourgeois subject matter began in the 15th century (Jan Van Eyck, 1366-1440), the earliest northern manifestation of the Renaissance. **Durer** (1471-1528) typified the merging of late Gothic and Italian trends in 16th century German art. Imposing civic architecture flourished in the prosperous commercial cities.

Spain. Despite the unification of Castile and Aragon in 1479, the 2 countries retained separate governments, and the nobility, especially in Aragon and Catalonia, retained many privileges. Spanish lands in Italy (Naples, Sicily) and the Netherlands entangled the country in European wars through the mid-17th century, while explorers, traders, and conquerors built up a Spanish empire in the Americas and the Philippines.

From the late 15th century, a **golden age** of literature and art produced works of social satire (plays of Lope de Vega, 1562-1635; Cervantes, 1547-1616), as well as spiritual intensity (El Greco, 1541-1614; Velazquez, 1599-1660).

Black Death. The bubonic plague reached Europe from the E in 1348, killing as much as half the population by 1350. Labor scarcity forced a rise in wages and brought greater freedom to the peasantry, making possible **peasant uprisings** (Jacquerie in France, 1358, Wat Tyler's rebellion in England, 1381). In the *ciompi* revolt, 1378, Florentine wage earners demanded a say in economic and political power.

Explorations. Organized European maritime exploration began, seeking to evade the Venice-Ottoman monopoly of eastern trade and to promote Christianity. Expeditions from Portugal beginning 1418 explored the west coast of Africa, until **Vasco da Gama** rounded the Cape of Good Hope in 1497 and reached India. A Portuguese trading empire was consolidated by the seizure of Goa, 1510, and Malacca, 1551. Japan was reached in 1542. Spanish voyages (**Columbus,** 1492-1504) uncovered a new world, which Spain hastened to subdue. Navigation schools in Spain and Portugal, the development of large sailing ships (carracks), and the invention of the rifle, c1475, aided European penetration.

Mughals and Safavids. East of the Ottoman empire, two Moslem dynasties ruled unchallenged in the 16th and 17th centuries. The Mughal empire in India, founded by Persianized Turkish invaders from the NW under Babur, dates from their 1526 conquest of Delhi. The dynasty ruled most of India for over 200 years, surviving nominally until 1857. **Akbar** (ruled 1556-1605) consolidated administration at his glorious court, where Urdu (Persian-influenced Hindi) developed. Trade relations with Europe increased. Under Shah Jahan (1629-58), a secularized art fusing Hindu and Moslem elements flourished in miniature painting and architecture (**Taj Mahal**). Sikhism, founded c1519, combined elements of both faiths. Suppression of Hindus and Shi'ite Moslems in S India in the late 17th century weakened the empire.

Fanatical devotion to the Shi'ite sect characterized the Safavids of Persia, 1502-1736, and led to hostilities with the Sunni Ottomans for over a century. The prosperity and strength of the empire are evidenced by the mosques at its capital, **Isfahan.** The dynasty enhanced Iranian national consciousness.

China. The Ming emperors, 1368-1644, the last native dynasty in China, wielded unprecedented personal power, while the Confucian bureaucracy began to suffer from inertia. European trade (Portugese

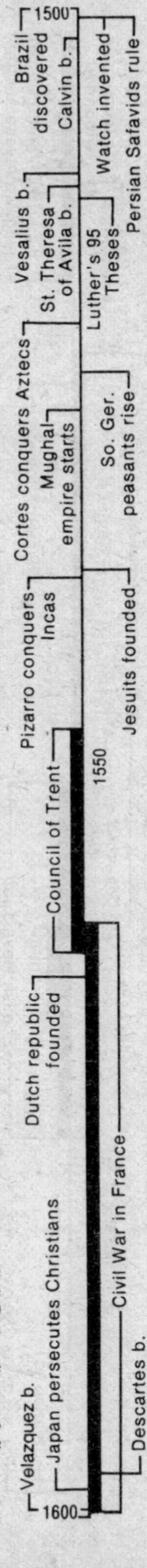

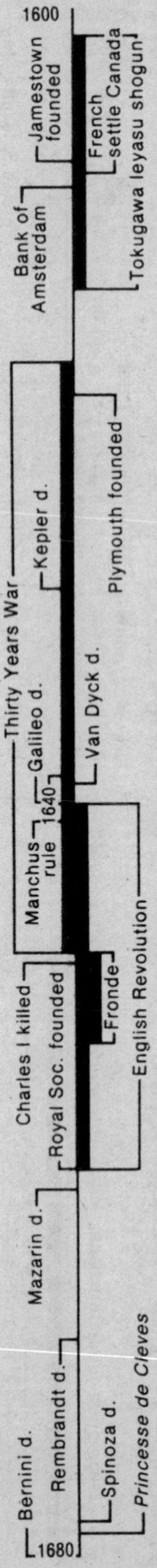

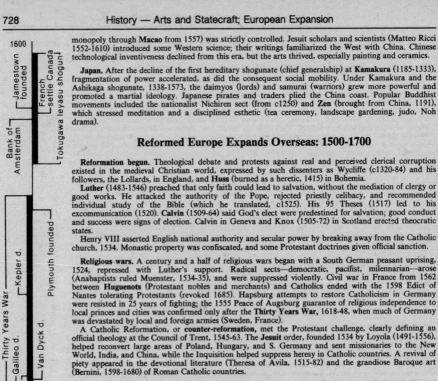

monopoly through **Macao** from 1557) was strictly controlled. Jesuit scholars and scientists (Matteo Ricci 1552-1610) introduced some Western science; their writings familiarized the West with China. Chinese technological inventiveness declined from this era, but the arts thrived, especially painting and ceramics.

Japan. After the decline of the first hereditary shogunate (chief generalship) at **Kamakura** (1185-1333), fragmentation of power accelerated, as did the consequent social mobility. Under Kamakura and the Ashikaga shogunate, 1338-1573, the daimyos (lords) and samurai (warriors) grew more powerful and promoted a martial ideology. Japanese pirates and traders plied the China coast. Popular Buddhist movements included the nationalist Nichiren sect (from c1250) and **Zen** (brought from China, 1191), which stressed meditation and a disciplined esthetic (tea ceremony, landscape gardening, judo, Noh drama).

Reformed Europe Expands Overseas: 1500-1700

Reformation begun. Theological debate and protests against real and perceived clerical corruption existed in the medieval Christian world, expressed by such dissenters as Wycliffe (c1320-84) and his followers, the Lollards, in England, and **Huss** (burned as a heretic, 1415) in Bohemia.

Luther (1483-1546) preached that only faith could lead to salvation, without the mediation of clergy or good works. He attacked the authority of the Pope, rejected priestly celibacy, and recommended individual study of the Bible (which he translated, c1525). His 95 Theses (1517) led to his excommunication (1520). **Calvin** (1509-64) said God's elect were predestined for salvation; good conduct and success were signs of election. Calvin in Geneva and Knox (1505-72) in Scotland erected theocratic states.

Henry VIII asserted English national authority and secular power by breaking away from the Catholic church, 1534. Monastic property was confiscated, and some Protestant doctrines given official sanction.

Religious wars. A century and a half of religious wars began with a South German peasant uprising, 1524, repressed with Luther's support. Radical sects—democratic, pacifist, millennarian—arose (Anabaptists ruled Muenster, 1534-35), and were suppressed violently. Civil war in France from 1562 between **Huguenots** (Protestant nobles and merchants) and Catholics ended with the 1598 Edict of Nantes tolerating Protestants (revoked 1685). Hapsburg attempts to restore Catholicism in Germany were resisted in 25 years of fighting; the 1555 Peace of Augsburg guarantee of religious independence to local princes and cities was confirmed only after the **Thirty Years War,** 1618-48, when much of Germany was devastated by local and foreign armies (Sweden, France).

A Catholic Reformation, or **counter-reformation,** met the Protestant challenge, clearly defining an official theology at the Council of Trent, 1545-63. The **Jesuit** order, founded 1534 by Loyola (1491-1556), helped reconvert large areas of Poland, Hungary, and S. Germany and sent missionaries to the New World, India, and China, while the Inquisition helped suppress heresy in Catholic countries. A revival of piety appeared in the devotional literature (Theresa of Avila, 1515-82) and the grandiose Baroque art (Bernini, 1598-1680) of Roman Catholic countries.

Scientific Revolution. The late nominalist thinkers (Ockham, c1300-49) of Paris and Oxford challenged Aristotelian orthodoxy, allowing for a freer scientific approach. But metaphysical values, such as the Neoplatonic faith in an orderly, mathematical cosmos, still motivated and directed subsequent inquiry. **Copernicus** (1473-1543) promoted the heliocentric theory, which was confirmed when Kepler (1571-1630) discovered the mathematical laws describing the orbits of the planets. The Christian-Aristotelian belief that heavens and earth were fundamentally different collapsed when **Galileo** (1564-1642) discovered moving sunspots, irregular moon topography, and moons around Jupiter. He and **Newton** (1642-1727) developed a mechanics that unified cosmic and earthly phenomena. To meet the needs of the new physics, Newton and Leibnitz (1646-1716) invented calculus, Descartes (1596-1650) invented analytic geometry.

An explosion of observational science included the discovery of blood circulation (Harvey, 1578-1657) and microscopic life (Leeuwenhoek, 1632-1723), and advances in anatomy (Vesalius, 1514-64, dissected corpses) and chemistry (Boyle, 1627-91). Scientific research institutes were founded: Florence, 1657, London **(Royal Society),** 1660, Paris, 1666. Inventions proliferated (Savery's steam engine, 1696).

Arts. Mannerist trends of the high Renaissance **(Michelangelo,** 1475-1564) exploited virtuosity, grace, novelty, and exotic subjects and poses. The notion of artistic genius was promoted, in contrast to the anonymous medieval artisan. Private connoisseurs entered the art market. These trends were elaborated in the 17th century **Baroque** era, on a grander scale. Dynamic movement in painting and sculpture was emphasized by sharp lighting effects, use of rich materials (colored marble, gilt), realistic details. Curved facades, broken lines, rich, deep-cut detail, and ceiling decoration characterized Baroque architecture, especially in Germany. Monarchs, princes, and prelates, usually Catholic, used Baroque art to enhance and embellish their authority, as in royal portraits by Velazquez (1599-1660) and Van Dyck (1599-1641).

National styles emerged. In France, a taste for rectilinear order and serenity (Poussin, 1594-1665), linked to the new rational philosophy, was expressed in classical forms. The influence of **classical values** in French literature (tragedies of Racine, 1639-99) gave rise to the "battle of the Ancients and Moderns." New forms included the essay (Montaigne, 1533-92) and novel (*Princesse de Cleves,* La Fayette, 1678).

Dutch painting of the 17th century was unique in its wide social distribution. The Flemish tradition of undemonstrative realism reached its peak in **Rembrandt** (1606-69) and Vermeer (1632-75).

Economy. European economic expansion was stimulated by the new trade with the East, New World gold and silver, and a doubling of population (50 mln. in 1450, 100 mln. in 1600). New business and financial techniques were developed and refined, such as joint-stock companies, insurance, and letters of credit and exchange. The Bank of Amsterdam, 1609, and the Bank of England, 1694, broke the old monopoly of private banking families. The rise of a business mentality was typified by the spread of clock towers in cities in the 14th century. By the mid-15th century, portable clocks were available; the first watch was invented in 1502.

By 1650, most governments had adopted the **mercantile system,** in which they sought to amass metallic wealth by protecting their merchants' foreign and colonial trade monopolies. The rise in prices and the new coin-based economy undermined the craft guild and feudal manorial systems. Expanding industries, such as clothweaving and mining, benefitted from technical advances. Coal replaced disappearing wood as the chief fuel; it was used to fuel new 16th century blast furnaces making cast iron.

New World. The **Aztecs** united much of the Mesoamerican culture area in a militarist empire by 1519, from their capital, Tenochtitlan (pop. 300,000), which was the center of a cult requiring enormous levels of ritual human sacrifice. Most of the civilized areas of S. America were ruled by the centralized **Inca Empire** (1476-1534), stretching 2,000 miles from Ecuador to N.W. Argentina. Lavish and sophisticated traditions in pottery, weaving, sculpture, and architecture were maintained in both regions.

These empires, beset by revolts, fell in 2 short campaigns to gold-seeking Spanish forces based in the Antilles and Panama. **Cortes** took Mexico, 1519-21; **Pizarro** Peru, 1531-35. From these centers, land and sea expeditions claimed most of N. and S. America for Spain. The Indian high cultures did not survive the impact of Christian missionaries and the new upper class of whites and mestizos. In turn, New World silver, and such Indian products as potatoes, tobacco, corn, peanuts, chocolate, and rubber exercised a major economic influence on Europe. While the Spanish administration intermittently concerned itself with the welfare of Indians, the population remained impoverished at most levels, despite the growth of a distinct South American civilization. European diseases reduced the native population.

Brazil, which the Portuguese discovered in 1500 and settled after 1530, and the Caribbean colonies of several European nations developed a plantation economy where sugar cane, tobacco, cotton, coffee, rice, indigo, and lumber were grown commercially by slaves. From the early 16th to the late 19th centuries, some 10 million Africans were transported to **slavery** in the New World.

Netherlands. The urban, Calvinist northern provinces of the Netherlands rebelled against Hapsburg Spain, 1568, and founded an oligarchic mercantile republic. Their strategic control of the Baltic grain market enabled them to exploit Mediterranean food shortages. Religious refugees — French and Belgian Protestants, Iberian Jews — added to the cosmopolitan commercial talent pool. After Spain absorbed Portugal in 1580, the Dutch seized Portuguese possessions and created a vast, though generally short-lived commercial empire in Brazil, the Antilles, Africa, India, Ceylon, Malacca, Indonesia, and Taiwan, and challenged or supplanted Portuguese traders in China and Japan.

England. Anglicanism became firmly established under Elizabeth I after a brief Catholic interlude under "Bloody Mary," 1553-58. But religious and political conflicts led to a rebellion by Parliament, 1642. Roundheads (Puritans) defeated Cavaliers (Royalists); Charles I was beheaded, 1649. The new **Commonwealth** was ruled as a military dictatorship by Cromwell, who also brutally crushed an Irish rebellion, 1649-51. Conflicts within the Puritan camp (democratic Levelers defeated 1649) aided the Stuart restoration, 1660, but Parliament was permanently strengthened and the peaceful **"Glorious Revolution"**, 1688, advanced political and religious liberties (writings of Locke, 1632-1704). British privateers (Drake, 1540-96) challenged Spanish control of the New World, and penetrated Asian trade routes (Madras taken, 1639). N. American colonies (Jamestown, 1607, Plymouth, 1620) provided an outlet for religious dissenters.

France. Emerging from the religious civil wars in 1628, France regained military and commercial great power status under the ministries of **Richelieu** (1624-42), Mazarin (1643-61), and Colbert (1662-83). Under Louis XIV (ruled 1643-1715) royal absolutism triumphed over nobles and local *parlements* (defeat of Fronde, 1648-53). Permanent colonies were founded in Canada (1608), the Caribbean (1626), and India (1674).

Sweden. Sweden seceded from the Scandinavian Union in 1523. The thinly-populated agrarian state (with copper, iron, and timber exports) was united by the Vasa kings, whose conquests by the mid-17th century made Sweden the dominant Baltic power. The empire collapsed in the Great Northern War (1700-21).

Poland. After the union with Lithuania in 1447, Poland ruled vast territories from the Baltic to the Black Sea, resisting German and Turkish incursions. Catholic nobles failed to gain the loyalty of the Orthodox Christian peasantry in the East; commerce and trades were practiced by German and Jewish immigrants. The bloody 1648-49 cossack uprising began the kingdom's dismemberment.

China. A new dynasty, the **Manchus,** invaded from the NE and seized power in 1644, and expanded Chinese control to its greatest extent in Central and Southeast Asia. Trade and diplomatic contact with Europe grew, carefully controlled by China. New crops (sweet potato, maize, peanut) allowed an economic and population growth (300 million pop. in 1800). Traditional arts and literature were pursued with increased sophistication (*Dream of the Red Chamber,* novel, mid-18th century).

Japan. Tokugawa Ieyasu, shogun from 1603, finally unified and pacified feudal Japan. Hereditary daimyos and samurai monopolized government office and the professions. An urban merchant class grew, literacy spread, and a cultural renaissance occurred (haiku of Basho, 1644-94). Fear of European domination led to persecution of Christian converts from 1597, and stringent isolation from outside contact from 1640.

Philosophy, Industry, and Revolution: 1700-1800

Science and Reason. Faith in human reason and science as the source of truth and a means to improve the physical and social environment, espoused since the Renaissance (Francis Bacon, 1561-1626), was bolstered by scientific discoveries in spite of theological opposition (**Galileo's forced retraction,** 1633). Descartes applied the logical method of mathematics to discover "self-evident" scientific and philosophical truths, while Newton emphasized induction from experimental observation.

The challenge of reason to traditional religious and political values and institutions began with **Spinoza** (1632-77), who interpreted the Bible historically and called for political and intellectual freedom.

French philosophes assumed leadership of the **"Enlightenment"** in the 18th century. Montesquieu (1689-1755) used British history to support his notions of limited government. Voltaire's (1694-1778) diaries and novels of exotic travel illustrated the intellectual trends toward secular ethics and relativism. Rousseau's (1712-1778) radical concepts of the **social contract** and of the inherent goodness of the common man gave impetus to anti-monarchical republicanism. The *Encyclopedia,* 1751-72, edited by Diderot and d'Alembert, designed as a monument to reason, was largely devoted to practical technology.

In England, ideals of political and religious liberty were connected with empiricist philosophy and science in the followers of Locke. But the extreme **empiricism of Hume** (1711-76) and Berkeley

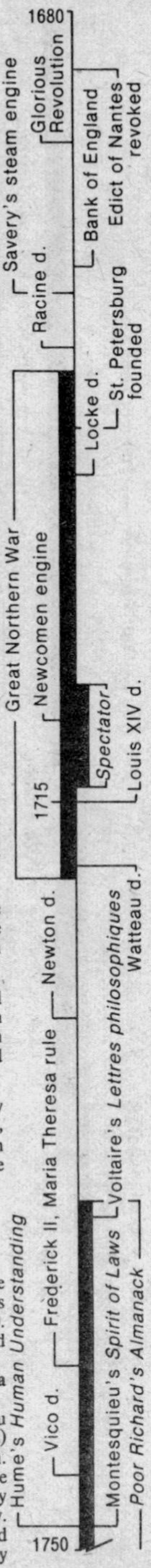

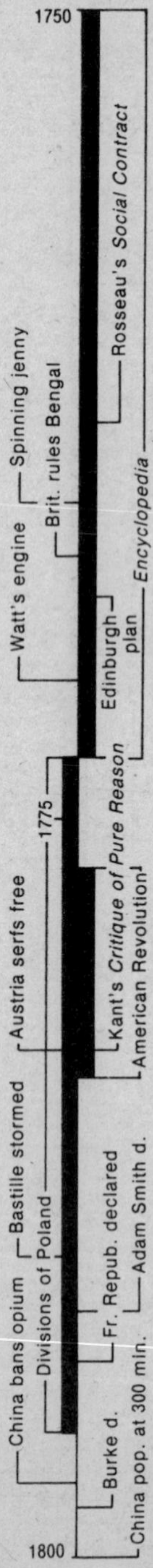

(1685-1753) posed limits to the identification of reason with absolute truth, as did the evolutionary approach to law and politics of Burke (1729-97) and the utilitarianism of Bentham (1748-1832). Adam Smith (1723-90) and other **physiocrats** called for a rationalization of economic activity by removing artificial barriers to a supposedly natural free exchange of goods.

Despite the political disunity and backwardness of most of Germany, German writers participated in the new philosophical trends popularized by Wolff (1679-1754). **Kant's** (1724-1804) **idealism,** unifying an empirical epistemology with *a priori* moral and logical concepts, directed German thought away from skepticism. Italian contributions included work on electricity by Galvani (1737-98) and Volta (1745-1827), the pioneer **historiography of Vico** (1668-1744), and writings on penal reform by Beccaria (1738-94). The American Franklin (1706-90) was celebrated in Europe for his varied achievements.

The growth of the **press** (*Spectator,* 1711-14) and the wide distribution of realistic but sentimental **novels** attested to the increase of a large bourgeois public.

Arts. Rococo art, characterized by extravagant decorative effects, asymmetries copied from organic models, and artificial pastoral subjects, was favored by the continental aristocracy for most of the century (Watteau, 1684-1721), and had musical analogies in the ornamentalized polyphony of late Baroque. The **Neoclassical** art after 1750, associated with the new scientific archeology, was more streamlined, and infused with the supposed moral and geometric rectitude of the Roman Republic (David, 1748-1825). In England, **town planning** on a grand scale began (Edinburgh, 1767).

Industrial Revolution in England. Agricultural improvements, such as the sowing drill (1701) and livestock breeding, were implemented on the large fields provided by enclosure of common lands by private owners. Profits from agriculture and from colonial and foreign trade (1800 volume, £ 54 million) were channelled through hundreds of banks and the **Stock Exchange** (founded 1773) into new industrial processes.

The Newcomen steam pump (1712) aided coal mining. Coal fueled the new efficient steam engines patented by Watt in 1769, and coke-smelting produced cheap, sturdy iron for machinery by the 1730s. The **flying shuttle** (1733) and **spinning jenny** (1764) were used in the large new cotton textile factories, where women and children were much of the work force. Goods were transported cheaply over **canals** (2,000 miles built 1760-1800).

Central and East Europe. The monarchs of the three states that dominated eastern Europe — Austria, Prussia, and Russia — accepted the advice and legitimation of philosophes in creating more modern, centralized institutions in their kingdoms, enlarged by the division of Poland (1772-95).

Under **Frederick II** (ruled 1740-86) Prussia, with its efficient modern army, doubled in size. State monopolies and tariff protection fostered industry, and some legal reforms were introduced. Austria's heterogeneous realms were legally unified under **Maria Theresa** (ruled 1740-80) and **Joseph II** (1780-90). Reforms in education, law, and religion were enacted, and the Austrian serfs were freed (1781). With its defeat in the Seven Years' War in 1763, Austria lost Silesia and ceased its active role in Germany, but was compensated by expansion to the E and S (Hungary, Slavonia, 1699, Galicia, 1772).

Russia, whose borders continued to expand in all directions, adopted some Western bureaucratic and economic policies under **Peter I** (ruled 1682-1725) and Catherine II (ruled 1762-96). Trade and cultural contacts with the West multiplied from the new Baltic Sea capital, **St. Petersburg** (founded 1703).

American Revolution. The British colonies in N. America attracted a mass immigration of religious dissenters and poor people throughout the 17th and 18th centuries, coming from all parts of the British Isles, Germany, the Netherlands, and other countries. The population reached 3 million whites and blacks by the 1770s. The small native population was decimated by European diseases and wars with and between the various colonies. British attempts to control colonial trade, and to tax the colonists to pay for the costs of colonial administration and defense clashed with traditions of local self government, and eventually provoked the colonies to rebellion. (*See American Revolution in Index.*)

French Revolution. The growing French middle class lacked political power, and resented aristocratic tax privileges, especially in light of liberal political ideals popularized by the American Revolution. Peasants lacked adequate land and were burdened with feudal obligations to nobles. Wars with Britain drained the treasury, finally forcing the king to call the **Estates-General** in 1789 (first time since 1614), in an atmosphere of food riots (poor crop in 1788).

Aristocratic resistance to absolutism was soon overshadowed by the reformist Third Estate (middle class), which proclaimed itself the **National Constituent Assembly** June 17 and took the "Tennis Court oath" on June 20 to secure a constitution. The storming of the **Bastille** July 14 by Parisian artisans was followed by looting and seizure of aristocratic property throughout France. Assembly reforms included abolition of class and regional privileges, a Declaration of Rights, suffrage by taxpayers (75% of males), and the **Civil Constitution of the Clergy** providing for election and loyalty oaths for priests. A republic was declared Sept. 22, 1792, in spite of royalist pressure from Austria and Prussia, which had declared war in April (joined by Britain the next year). Louis XVI was beheaded Jan. 21, 1793, Queen Marie Antoinette was beheaded Oct. 16, 1793.

Royalist uprisings in La Vendee and the S and military reverses led to a **reign of terror** in which tens of thousands of opponents of the Revolution and criminals were executed. Radical reforms in the **Convention** period (Sept. 1793-Oct. 1795) included the abolition of colonial slavery, economic measures to aid the poor, support of public education, and a short-lived de-Christianization.

Division among radicals (execution of Hebert, March 1794, Danton, April, and Robespierre, July) aided the ascendance of a moderate **Directory,** which consolidated military victories. **Napoleon Bonaparte** (1769-1821), a popular young general, exploited political divisions and participated in a coup Nov. 9, 1799, making himself first consul (dictator).

India. Sikh and Hindu rebels (Rajputs, Marathas) and Afghans destroyed the power of the Mughals during the 18th century. After France's defeat in the Seven Years War, 1763, Britain was the chief European trade power in India. Its control of inland **Bengal and Bihar** was recognized by the Mughal shah in 1765, who granted the **British East India Co.** (under Clive, 1727-74) the right to collect land revenue there. Despite objections from Parliament (1784 India Act) the company's involvement in local wars and politics led to repeated acquisitions of new territory. The company exported Indian textiles, sugar, and indigo.

World Population Growth 10,000 BC to 1978

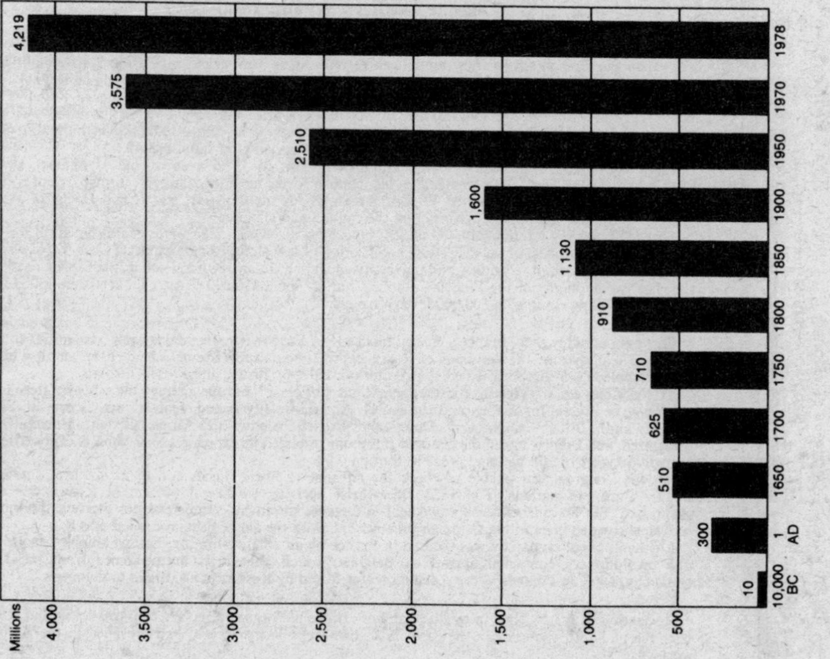

19th Century Railroad Growth in Selected Countries

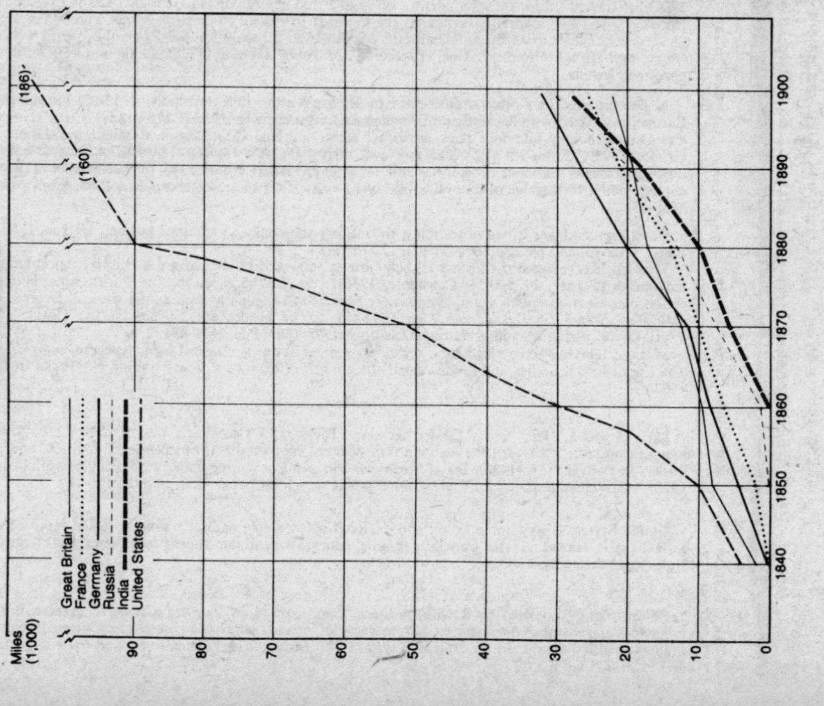

Change Gathers Steam: 1800-1840

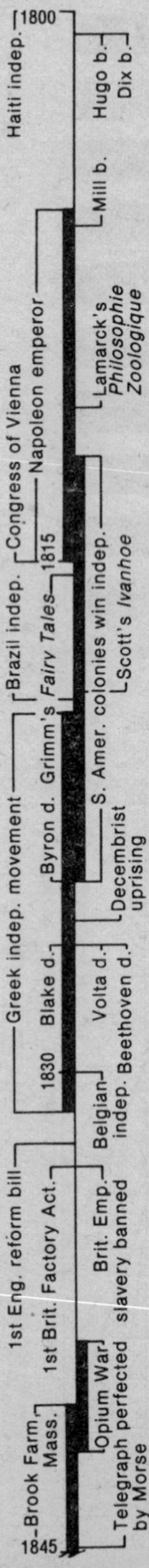

French ideals and empire spread. Inspired by the ideals of the French Revolution, and supported by the expanding French armies, new republican regimes arose near France: the **Batavian** Republic in the Netherlands (1795-1806), the **Helvetic** Republic in Switzerland (1798-1803), the **Cisalpine** Republic in N. Italy (1797-1805), the **Ligurian** Republic in Genoa (1797-1805), and the **Parthenopean** Republic in S. Italy (1799). A Roman Republic existed briefly in 1798 after Pope Pius VI was arrested by French troops. In Italy and Germany, new nationalist sentiments were stimulated both in imitation of and reaction to France (anti-French and anti-Jacobin peasant uprisings in Italy, 1796-9).

From 1804, when Napoleon declared himself emperor, to 1812, a succession of military victories (Austerlitz, 1805, Jena, 1806) extended his control over most of Europe, through puppet states (**Confederation of the Rhine** united W. German states for the first time and **Grand Duchy of Warsaw** revived Polish national hopes), expansion of the empire, and alliances.

Among the lasting reforms initiated under Napoleon's absolutist reign were: establishment of the Bank of France, centralization of tax collection, codification of law along Roman models (*Code Napoleon*), and reform and extension of secondary and university education. In an 1801 concordat, the papacy recognized the effective autonomy of the French Catholic Church. Some 400,000 French soldiers were killed in the Napoleonic Wars, along with 600,000 foreign troops.

Last gasp of old regime. France's coastal blockade of Europe (**Continental System**) failed to neutralize Britain. The disastrous 1812 invasion of Russia exposed Napoleon's overextension. After an 1814 exile at Elba, Napoleon's armies were defeated at **Waterloo,** 1815, by British and Prussian troops.

At the **Congress of Vienna,** the monarchs and princes of Europe redrew their boundaries, to the advantage of Prussia (in Saxony and the Ruhr), Austria (in Illyria and Venetia), and Russia (in Poland and Finland). British conquest of Dutch and French colonies (S. Africa, Ceylon, Mauritius) was recognized, and France, under the restored Bourbons, retained its expanded 1792 borders. The settlement brought 50 years of international peace to Europe.

But the Congress was unable to check the advance of liberal ideals and of nationalism among the smaller European nations. The 1825 **Decembrist uprising** by liberal officers in Russia was easily suppressed. But an independence movement in **Greece,** stirred by commercial prosperity and a cultural revival, succeeded in expelling Ottoman rule by 1831, with the aid of Britain, France, and Russia.

A constitutional monarchy was secured in France by an **1830 revolution;** Louis Philippe became king. The revolutionary contagion spread to **Belgium,** which gained its independence from the Dutch monarchy, 1830; to **Poland,** whose rebellion was defeated by Russia, 1830-31; and to Germany.

Romanticism. A new style in intellectual and artistic life began to replace Neo-classicism and Rococo after the mid-18th century. By the early 19th, this style, Romanticism, had prevailed in the European world.

Rousseau had begun the reaction against excessive rationalism and skepticism; in education (*Emile,* 1762) he stressed subjective spontaneity over regularized instruction. In Germany, Lessing (1729-81) and Herder (1744-1803) favorably compared the German folk song to classical forms, and began a cult of Shakespeare, whose passion and "natural" wisdom was a model for the Romantic *Sturm und Drang* (storm and stress) movement. **Goethe's** *Sorrows of Young Werther* (1774) set the model for the tragic, passionate genius.

A new interest in **Gothic architecture** in England after 1760 (Walpole, 1717-97) spread through Europe, associated with an aesthetic Christian and mystic revival (Blake, 1757-1827). Celtic, Norse, and German mythology and folk tales were revived or imitated (Macpherson's Ossian translation, 1762, Grimm's *Fairy Tales,* 1812-22). The medieval revival (Scott's *Ivanhoe,* 1819) led to a new interest in history, stressing national differences and organic growth (Carlyle, 1795-1881; Michelet, 1798-1874), corresponding to theories of natural evolution (Lamarck's *Philosophie zoologique,* 1809, Lyell's *Geology,* 1830-33).

Revolution and war fed an obsession with freedom and conflict, expressed by poets (**Byron,** 1788-1824, **Hugo,** 1802-85) and philosophers (**Hegel,** 1770-1831).

Wild gardens replaced the formal French variety, and painters favored rural, stormy, and mountainous landscapes (**Turner,** 1775-1851; **Constable,** 1776-1837). Clothing became freer, with wigs, hoops, and ruffles discarded. Originality and genius were expected in the life as well as the work of inspired artists (Murger's *Scenes from Bohemian Life,* 1847-49). Exotic locales and themes (as in "Gothic" horror stories) were used in art and literature (Delacroix, 1798-1863, **Poe,** 1809-49).

Music exhibited the new dramatic style and a breakdown of classical forms (Beethoven, 1770-1827). The use of folk melodies and modes aided the growth of distinct national traditions (Glinka in Russia, 1804-57).

Latin America. Haiti, under the former slave **Toussaint L'Ouverture,** was the first Latin American independent state, 1800. All the mainland Spanish colonies won their independence 1810-24, under such leaders as **Bolivar** (1783-1830). Brazil became an independent empire under the Portuguese prince regent, 1822. A new class of military officers divided power with large landholders and the church.

United States. Heavy immigration and exploitation of ample natural resources fueled rapid economic growth. The spread of the franchise, public education, and antislavery sentiment were signs of a widespread democratic ethic.

China. Failure to keep pace with Western arms technology exposed China to greater European influence, and hampered efforts to bar imports of opium, which had damaged Chinese society and drained wealth overseas. In the **Opium War,** 1839-42, Britain forced China to expand trade opportunities and to cede Hong Kong.

Triumph of Progress: 1840-80

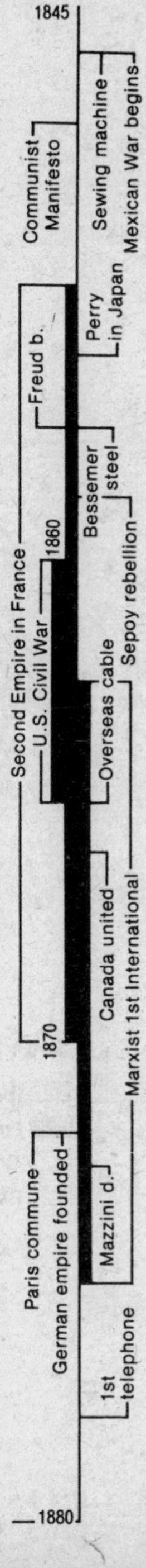

Idea of Progress. As a result of the cumulative scientific, economic, and political changes of the preceding eras, the idea took hold among literate people in the West that continuing growth and improvement was the usual state of human and natural life.

Darwin's statement of the **theory of evolution** and survival of the fittest (*Origin of Species*, 1859), defended by intellectuals and scientists against theological objections, was taken as confirmation that progress was the natural direction of life. The controversy helped define popular ideas of the dedicated scientist and ever-expanding human knowledge of and control over the world (Foucault's demonstration of earth's rotation, 1851, Pasteur's germ theory, 1861).

Liberals following Ricardo (1772-1823) in their faith that unrestrained competition would bring continuous economic expansion sought to adjust political life to the new social realities, and believed that unregulated competition of ideas would yield truth (Mill, 1806-73). In England, successive reform bills (1832, 1867, 1884) gave representation to the new industrial towns, and extended the franchise to the middle and lower classes and to Catholics, Dissenters, and Jews. On both sides of the Atlantic, reformists tried to improve conditions for the mentally ill (Dix, 1802-87), women (Anthony, 1820-1906), and prisoners. Slavery was barred in the British Empire, 1833; the United States, 1865; and Brazil, 1888.

Socialist theories based on ideas of human perfectibility or historical progress were widely disseminated. Utopian socialists like Saint-Simon (1760-1825) envisaged an orderly, just society directed by a technocratic elite. A model factory town, New Lanark, Scotland, was set up by utopian Robert Owen (1771-1858), and utopian communal experiments were tried in the U.S. (Brook Farm, Mass., 1841-7). Bakunin's (1814-76) anarchism represented the opposite utopian extreme of total freedom. Marx (1818-83) posited the inevitable triumph of socialism in the industrial countries through a historical process of class conflict.

Spread of industry. The technical processes and managerial innovations of the English industrial revolution spread to Europe (especially Germany) and the U.S., causing an explosion of industrial production, demand for raw materials, and competition for markets. Inventors, both trained and self-educated, provided the means for larger-scale production (Bessemer steel, 1856, sewing machine, 1846). Many inventions were shown at the 1851 London Great Exhibition at the Crystal Palace, whose theme was universal prosperity.

Local specialization and long-distance trade were aided by a revolution in transportation and communication. Railroads were first introduced in the 1820s in England and the U.S. Over 150,000 miles of track had been laid worldwide by 1880, with another 100,000 miles laid in the next decade. Steamships were improved (*Savannah* crossed Atlantic, 1819). The telegraph, perfected by 1844 (Morse), connected the Old and New Worlds by cable in 1866, and quickened the pace of international commerce and politics. The first commercial telephone exchange went into operation in the U.S. in 1878.

The new class of industrial workers, uprooted from their rural homes, lacked job security, and suffered from dangerous overcrowded conditions at work and at home. Many responded by organizing trade unions (legalized in England, 1824; France, 1884). The U.S. Knights of Labor had 700,000 members by 1886. The First International, 1864-76, tried to unite workers internationally around a Marxist program. The quasi-Socialist Paris Commune uprising, 1871, was violently suppressed. Factory Acts to reduce child labor and regulate conditions were passed (1833-50 in England). Social security measures were introduced by the Bismarck regime in Germany, 1883-89.

Revolutions of 1848. Among the causes of the continent-wide revolutions were an international collapse of credit and resulting unemployment, bad harvests in 1845-7, and a cholera epidemic. The new urban proletariat and expanding bourgeoisie demanded a greater political role. Republics were proclaimed in France, Rome, and Venice. Nationalist feelings reached fever pitch in the Hapsburg empire, as Hungary declared independence under Kossuth, a Slav Congress demanded equality, and Piedmont tried to drive Austria from Lombardy. A national liberal assembly at Frankfurt called for German unification.

But riots fueled bourgeois fears of socialism (Marx and Engels' 1848 *Communist Manifesto*) and peasants remained conservative. The old establishment — The Papacy, the Hapsburgs (using Croats and Romanians against Hungary), the Prussian army — was able to rout the revolutionaries by 1849. The French Republic succumbed to a renewed monarchy by 1852 (Emperor Napoleon III).

Great nations unified. Using the "blood and iron" tactics of Bismarck from 1862, Prussia controlled N. Germany by 1867 (war with Denmark, 1864, Austria, 1866). After defeating France in 1870 (loss of Alsace-Lorraine), it won the allegiance of S. German states. A new **German Empire** was proclaimed, 1871. **Italy,** inspired by Mazzini (1805-72) and Garibaldi (1807-82), was unified by the reformed Piedmont kingdom through uprisings, plebiscites, and war.

The **U.S.,** its area expanded after the 1846-47 Mexican War, defeated a secession attempt by slave states, 1861-65. The Canadian provinces were united in an autonomous **Dominion of Canada,** 1867. Control in **India** was removed from the East India Co. and centralized under British administration after the 1857-58 Sepoy rebellion, laying the groundwork for the modern Indian State. Queen Victoria was named Empress of India, 1876.

Europe dominates Asia. The Ottoman Empire began to collapse in the face of Balkan nationalisms and European imperial incursions in N. Africa (Suez Canal, 1869). The Turks had lost control of most of both regions by 1882. Russia completed its expansion south by 1884 (despite the temporary setback of the Crimean War with Turkey, Britain, and France, 1853-56) taking Turkestan, all the Caucasus, and Chinese areas in the East and sponsoring Balkan Slavs against the Turks. A succession of reformist and reactionary regimes presided over a slow modernization (serfs freed, 1861). Persian independence suffered as Russia and British India competed for influence.

China was forced to sign a series of unequal treaties with European powers and Japan. Overpopulation and an inefficient dynasty brought misery and caused rebellions (Taiping, Moslems) leaving tens of millions dead. Japan was forced by the U.S. (Commodore Perry's visits, 1853-54) and Europe to end its isolation. The Meiji restoration, 1868, gave power to a Westernizing oligarchy. Intensified empire-building gave Burma to Britain, 1824-86, and Indo-China to France, 1862-95. Christian missionary activity followed imperial and trade expansion in Asia.

Respectability. The fine arts were expected to reflect and encourage the progress of morals and

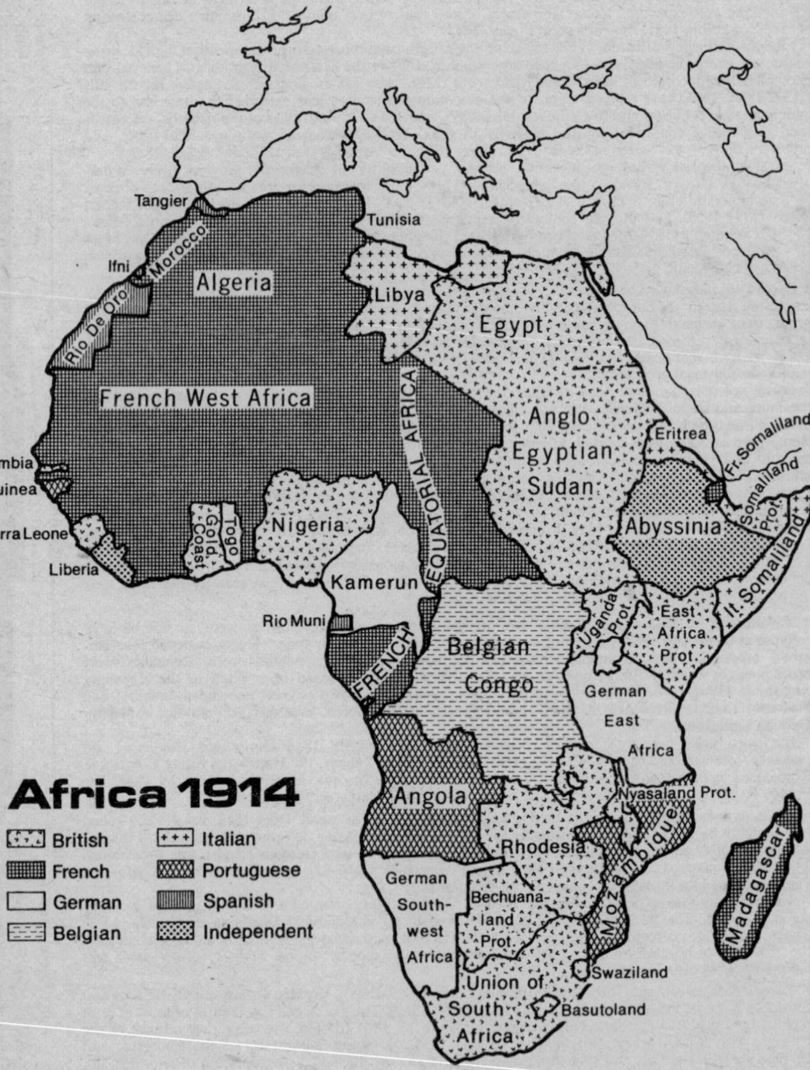

Africa 1914
British
French
German
Belgian
Italian
Portuguese
Spanish
Independent
Tangier
Tunisia
Morocco
Ifni
Algeria
Rio De Oro
Libya
Egypt
French West Africa
EQUATORIAL AFRICA
Anglo Egyptian Sudan
Eritrea
Fr. Somaliland
Somaliland Prot.
Gambia
Port. Guinea
Sierra Leone
Liberia
Gold Coast
Togo
Nigeria
Kamerun
Abyssinia
It. Somaliland
Rio Muni
FRENCH
Belgian Congo
Uganda Prot.
East Africa Prot.
German East Africa
Angola
Nyasaland Prot.
Rhodesia
Mozambique
Madagascar
German South-west Africa
Bechuana-land Prot.
Swaziland
Union of South Africa
Basutoland

manners among the different classes. "Victorian" prudery, exaggerated delicacy, and familial piety were heralded by **Bowdler's** expurgated edition of Shakespeare (1818). Government-supported mass education inculcated a work ethic as a means to escape poverty (Horatio Alger, 1832-99).

The official **Beaux Arts** school in Paris set an international style of imposing public buildings (Paris Opera, 1861-74, Vienna Opera, 1861-69) and uplifting statues (Bartholdi's *Statue of Liberty,* 1885). Realist painting, influenced by photography (Daguerre, 1837), appealed to a new mass audience with social or historical narrative (Wilkie, 1785-1841, Poynter, 1836-1919) or with serious religious, moral, or social messages (pre-Raphaelites, Millet's Angelus, 1858) often drawn from ordinary life. The **Impressionists** (Pissarro, 1830-1903, Renoir, 1841-1919) rejected the central role of serious subject matter in favor of a colorful and sensual depiction of a moment, but their sunny, placid depictions of bourgeois scenes kept them within the respectable consensus.

Realistic **novelists** presented the full panorama of social classes and personalities, but retained sentimentality and moral judgment (Dickens, 1812-70, Eliot, 1819-80, Tolstoy, 1828-1910, Balzac, 1799-1850).

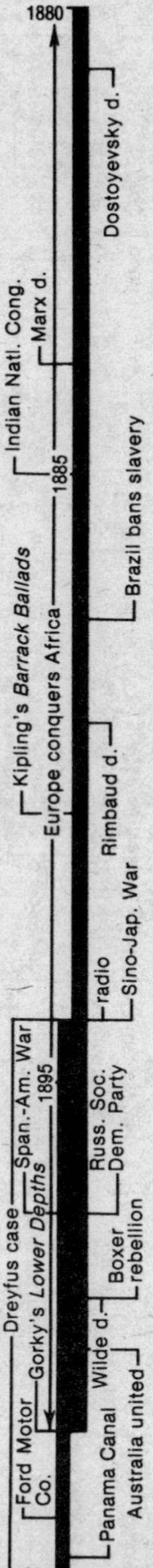

Veneer of Stability: 1880-1900

Imperialism triumphant. The vast **African** interior, visited by European explorers (Barth, 1821-65, Livingstone, 1813-73) was conquered by the European powers in rapid, competitive thrusts from their coastal bases after 1880, mostly for domestic political and international strategic reasons. W. African Moslem kingdoms (Fulani), Arab slave traders (Zanzibar), and Bantu military confederations (Zulu) were alike subdued. Only Christian Ethiopia (defeat of Italy, 1896) and Liberia resisted successfully. France (W. Africa) and Britain ("Cape to Cairo," Boer War, 1899-1902) were the major beneficiaries. The ideology of "the white man's burden" (Kipling, *Barrack Room Ballads,* 1892) or of a "civilizing mission" (France) justified the conquests.

West European foreign capital investments soared to nearly $40 billion by 1914, but most was in E. Europe (France, Germany) the Americas (Britain) and the white colonies. The foundation of the modern interdependent world economy was laid, with cartels dominating raw material trade.

An industrious world. Industrial and technological proficiency characterized the 2 new great powers — **Germany** and the **U.S.** Coal and iron deposits enabled Germany to reach second or third place status in iron, steel, and shipbuilding by the 1900s. German electrical and chemical industries were world leaders. The U.S. post-civil war boom (interrupted by "panics," 1884, 1893, 1896) was shaped by massive immigration from S. and E. Europe from 1880, government subsidy of railroads, and huge private monopolies (Standard Oil, 1870, U.S. Steel, 1901). The **Spanish-American War,** 1898 (Phillipine rebellion, 1899-1901) and the Open Door policy in China (1899) made the U.S. a world power.

England led in **urbanization** (72% by 1890), with **London** the world capital of finance, insurance, and shipping. Electric subways (London, 1890), sewer systems (Paris, 1850s), parks, and bargain department stores helped improve living standards for most of the urban population of the industrial world.

Asians assimilate. Asian reaction to European economic, military, and religious incursions took the form of imitation of Western techniques and adoption of Western ideas of progress and freedom. The Chinese "self-strengthening" movement of the 1860s and 70s included rail, port, and arsenal improvements and metal and textile mills. Reformers like **K'ang Yu-wei** (1858-1927) won liberalizing reforms in 1898, right after the European and Japanese "scramble for concessions."

A universal education system in Japan and importation of foreign industrial, scientific, and military experts aided Japan's unprecedented rapid modernization after 1868, under the authoritarian Meiji regime. Japan's victory in the **Sino-Japanese War,** 1894-95, put Formosa and Korea in its power.

In India, the British alliance with the remaining princely states masked reform sentiment among the Westernized urban elite; higher education had been conducted largely in English for 50 years. The **Indian National Congress,** founded in 1885, demanded a larger government role for Indians.

"Fin-de-siecle" sophistication. Naturalist writers pushed realism to its extreme limits, adopting a quasi-scientific attitude and writing about formerly taboo subjects like sex, crime, extreme poverty, and corruption (Flaubert, 1821-80, Zola, 1840-1902, Hardy, 1840-1928). Unseen or repressed psychological motivations were explored in the clinical and theoretical works of **Freud** (1856-1939) and in the fiction of Dostoevsky (1821-81), James (1843-1916), Schnitzler (1862-1931) and others.

A contempt for bourgeois life or a desire to shock a complacent audience was shared by the French **symbolist** poets (Verlaine, 1844-96, Rimbaud, 1854-91), neo-pagan English writers (Swinburne, 1837-1909), continental dramatists (Ibsen, 1828-1906) and satirists (Wilde, 1854-1900). **Nietzsche** (1844-1900) was influential in his elitism and pessimism.

Post-impressionist art neglected long-cherished conventions of representation (Cezanne, 1839-1906) and showed a willingness to learn from primitive and non-European art (Gauguin, 1848-1903, Japanese prints).

Racism. Gobineau (1816-82) gave a pseudo-biological foundation to modern racist theories, which spread in the latter 19th century along with **Social Darwinism,** the belief that societies are and should be organized as a struggle for survival of the fittest. The Medieval period was interpreted as an era of natural Germanic rule (Chamberlain, 1855-1927) and notions of superiority were associated with German national aspirations (Treitschke, 1834-96). **Anti-Semitism,** with a new racist rationale, became a significant political force in Germany (Anti-Semitic Petition, 1880), Austria (Lueger, 1844-1910), and France (Dreyfus case, 1894-1906).

Last Respite: 1900-1909

Alliances. While the peace of Europe (and its dependencies) continued to hold (1907 **Hague Conference** extended the rules of war and international arbitration procedures), imperial rivalries, protectionist trade practices (in Germany and France), and the escalating arms race (British *Dreadnought* battleship launched, Germany widens Kiel canal, 1906) exacerbated minor disputes (German-French Moroccan "crises", 1905, 1911).

Security was sought through alliances: **Triple Alliance** (Germany, Austria-Hungary, Italy) renewed

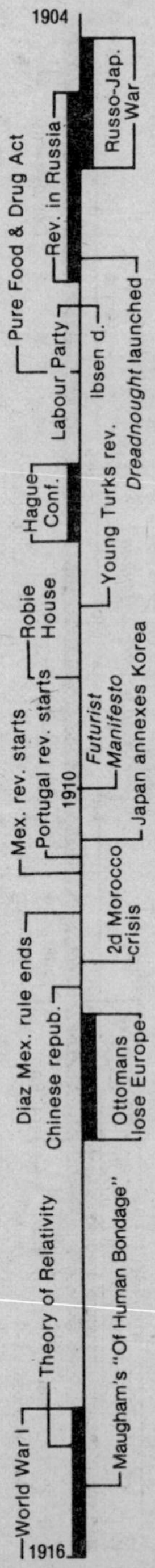

1902, 1907; Anglo-Japanese Alliance, 1902; Franco-Russian Alliance, 1899; **Entente Cordiale** (Britain, France) 1904; Anglo-Russian Treaty, 1907; German-Ottoman friendship.

Ottomans decline. The inefficient, corrupt Ottoman government was unable to resist further loss of territory. Nearly all European lands were lost in 1912 to Serbia, Greece, Montenegro, and Bulgaria. Italy took Libya and the Dodecanese islands the same year, and Britain took Kuwait, 1899, and the Sinai, 1906. The **Young Turk** revolution in 1908 forced the sultan to restore a constitution, introduced some social reform, industrialization, and secularization.

British Empire. British trade and cultural influence remained dominant in the empire, but constitutional reforms presaged its eventual dissolution: the colonies of **Australia** were united in 1901 under a self-governing commonwealth. **New Zealand** acquired dominion status in 1907. The old Boer republics joined Cape Colony and Natal in the self-governing **Union of South Africa** in 1910.

The 1909 Indian Councils Act enhanced the role of elected province legislatures in **India.** The Moslem League, founded 1906, sought separate communal representation.

East Asia. Japan exploited its growing industrial power to expand its empire. Victory in the 1904-05 war against Russia (naval battle of Tsushima, 1905) assured Japan's domination of **Korea** (annexed 1910) and Manchuria (took Port Arthur 1905).

In China, central authority began to crumble (empress died, 1908). Reforms (Confucian exam system ended 1905, modernization of the army, building of railroads) were inadequate and secret societies of reformers and nationalists, inspired by the Westernized **Sun Yat-sen** (1866-1925) fomented periodic uprisings in the south.

Siam, whose independence had been guaranteed by Britain and France in 1896, was split into spheres of influence by those countries in 1907.

Russia. The population of the Russian Empire approached 150 million in 1900. Reforms in education, law, and local institutions (*zemstvos*), and an industrial boom starting in the 1880s (oil, railroads) created the beginnings of a modern state, despite the autocratic tsarist regime. Liberals (1903 Union of Liberation), Socialists (Social Democrats founded 1898, Bolsheviks split off 1903), and populists (Social Revolutionaries founded 1901) were periodically repressed, and national minorities persecuted (anti-Jewish pogroms, 1903, 1905-6).

An industrial crisis after 1900 and harvest failures aggravated poverty in the urban proletariat, and the 1904-05 defeat by Japan (which checked Russia's Asian expansion) sparked the revolution of 1905-06. A **Duma** (parliament) was created, and an agricultural reform (under Stolypin, prime minister 1906-11) created a large class of landowning peasants (kulaks).

The world shrinks. Developments in transportation and communication and mass population movements helped create an awareness of an interdependent world. Early **automobiles** (Daimler, Benz, 1885) were experimental, or designed as luxuries. Assembly-line mass production (Ford Motor Co., 1903) made the invention practicable, and by 1910 nearly 500,000 motor vehicles were registered in the U.S. alone. **Heavier-than-air flights** began in 1903 in the U.S. (Wright brothers), preceded by glider, balloon, and model plane advances in several countries. Trade was advanced by improvements in **ship design** (gyrocompass, 1907), speed (Lusitania crossed Atlantic in 5 days, 1907), and reach (Panama Canal begun, 1904).

The first transatlantic **radio** telegraphic transmission occurred in 1901, 6 years after Marconi discovered radio. Radio transmission of human speech had been made in 1900. Telegraphic transmission of photos was achieved in 1904, lending immediacy to news reports. **Phonographs,** popularized by Caruso's recordings (starting 1902) made for quick international spread of musical styles (ragtime). **Motion pictures,** perfected in the 1890s (Dickson, Lumiere brothers), became a popular and artistic medium after 1900; newsreels appeared in 1909.

Emigration from crowded European centers soared in the decade: 9 million migrated to the U.S., and millions more went to Siberia, Canada, Argentina, Australia, South Africa, and Algeria. Some 70 million Europeans emigrated in the century before 1914. Several million Chinese, Indians, and Japanese migrated to Southeast Asia, where their urban skills often enabled them to take a predominant economic role.

Social reform. The social and economic problems of the poor were kept in the public eye by realist fiction writers (Dreiser's *Sister Carrie,* 1900; Gorky's *Lower Depths,* 1902; Sinclair's *Jungle,* 1906), journalists (U.S. **muckrakers** — Steffens, Tarbell) and artists (Ashcan school). Frequent labor strikes and occasional assassinations by anarchists or radicals (Austrian Empress, 1898; King Umberto I of Italy, 1900; U.S. Pres. McKinley, 1901; Russian Interior Minister Plehve, 1904; Portugal's King Carlos, 1908) added to social tension and fear of revolution.

But democratic reformism prevailed. In Germany, Bernstein's (1850-1932) **revisionist Marxism,** downgrading revolution, was accepted by the powerful Social Democrats and trade unions. The British Fabian Society (the Webbs, Shaw) and the Labour Party (founded 1906) worked for reforms such as social security and union rights (1906), while women's suffragists grew more militant. U.S. **progressives** fought big business (Pure Food and Drug Act, 1906). In France, the 10-hour work day (1904) and separation of church and state (1905) were reform victories, as was universal suffrage in Austria (1907).

Arts. An unprecedented period of experimentation, centered in France, produced several new **painting** styles: fauvism exploited bold color areas (Matisse, *Woman with Hat,* 1905); expressionism reflected powerful inner emotions (the Brücke group, 1905); cubism combined several views of an object on one flat surface (Picasso's *Demoiselles,* 1906-07); futurism tried to depict speed and motion (Italian Futurist Manifesto, 1910). **Architects** explored new uses of steel structures, with facades either neo-classical (Adler and Sullivan in U.S.); curvilinear Art Nouveau (Gaudi's Casa Mila, 1905-10); or functionally streamlined (Wright's Robie House, 1909).

Music and **Dance** shared the experimental spirit. Ruth St. Denis (1877-1968) and Isadora Duncan (1878-1927) pioneered modern dance, while Diaghilev in Paris revitalized classic ballet from 1909. Composers explored atonal music (Debussy, 1862-1918) and dissonance (Schönberg, 1874-1951), or revolutionized classical forms (Stravinsky, 1882-71), often showing jazz or folk music influences.

War and Revolution: 1910-1919

War threatens. Germany under Wilhelm II sought a political and imperial role consonant with its industrial strength, challenging Britain's world supremacy and threatening France, still resenting the loss of Alsace-Lorraine. Austria wanted to curb an expanded Serbia (after 1912) and the threat it posed to its own Slav lands. Russia feared Austrian and German political and economic aims in the Balkans and Turkey. An accelerated arms race resulted: the German standing army rose to over 2 million men by 1914. Russia and France had over a million each, Austria and the British Empire nearly a million each. Dozens of enormous battleships were built by the powers after 1906.

The **assassination of Austrian Archduke Ferdinand** by a Serbian, June 28, 1914, was the pretext for war. The system of alliances made the conflict Europe-wide; Germany's invasion of Belgium to outflank France forced Britain to enter the war. Patriotic fervor was nearly unanimous among all classes in most countries.

World War I. German forces were stopped in France in one month. The rival armies dug **trench networks.** Artillery and improved machine guns prevented either side from any lasting advance despite repeated assaults (600,000 dead at **Verdun,** Feb.-July 1916). Poison gas, used by Germany in 1915, proved ineffective. Over one million U.S. troops tipped the balance after mid-1917, forcing Germany to sue for peace.

In the East, the Russian armies were thrown back (battle of **Tannenberg,** Aug. 20, 1914) and the war grew unpopular. An allied attempt to relieve Russia through Turkey failed (**Gallipoli** 1916). The new Bolshevik regime signed the capitulatory Brest-Litovsk peace in March, 1918. Italy entered the war on the allied side, Apr. 1915, but was pushed back by Oct. 1917. A renewed offensive with Allied aid in Oct.-Nov. 1918 forced Austria to surrender.

The British Navy successfully blockaded Germany, which responded with submarine U-boat attacks; **unrestricted submarine warfare** against neutrals after Jan. 1917 helped bring the U.S. into the war. Other battlefields included Palestine and Mesopotamia, both of which Britain wrested from the Turks in 1917, and the African and Pacific colonies of Germany, most of which fell to Britain, France, Australia, Japan, and South Africa.

From 1916, the civilian population and economy of both sides were mobilized to an unprecedented degree. Over 10 million soldiers died (May 1917 French mutiny crushed). *For further details, see 1978 and earlier editions of The World Almanac.*

Settlement. At the **Versailles conference** (Jan.-June 1919) and in subsequent negotiations and local wars (Russian-Polish War 1920), the map of Europe was redrawn with a nod to U.S. Pres. Wilson's principle of self-determination. Austria and Hungary were separated and much of their land was given to Yugoslavia (formerly Serbia), Romania, Italy, and the newly independent Poland and Czechoslovakia. Germany lost territory in the West, North, and East, while Finland and the Baltic states were detached from Russia. Turkey lost nearly all its Arab lands to British-sponsored Arab states or to direct French and British rule.

A huge **reparations** burden and partial demilitarization were imposed on Germany. Wilson obtained approval for a League of Nations, but the U.S. Senate refused to allow the U.S. to join.

Russian revolution. Military defeats and high casualties caused a contagious lack of confidence in Tsar Nicholas, who was forced to abdicate, Mar. 1917. A liberal provisional government failed to end the war, and massive desertions, riots, and fighting between factions followed. A moderate socialist government under Kerensky was overthrown in a violent **coup by the Bolsheviks** in Petrograd under Lenin, who disbanded the elected Constituent Assembly, Nov. 1917.

The Bolsheviks brutally suppressed all opposition and ended the war with Germany, Mar. 1918. **Civil war** broke out in the summer between the Red Army, including the Bolsheviks and their supporters, and monarchists, anarchists, nationalities (Ukrainians, Georgians, Poles) and others. Small U.S., British, French and Japanese units also opposed the Bolsheviks, 1918-19 (Japan in Vladivostok to 1922). The civil war, anarchy, and pogroms devastated the country until the 1920 Red Army victory. The wartime total monopoly of political, economic, and police power by the Communist Party leadership was retained.

Other European revolutions. An unpopular monarchy in **Portugal** was overthrown in 1910. The new republic took severe anti-clerical measures, 1911.

After a century of Home Rule agitation, during which **Ireland** was devastated by famine (one million dead, 1846-47) and emigration, republican militants staged an unsuccessful uprising in Dublin, Easter 1916. The execution of the leaders and mass arrests by the British won popular support for the rebels. The Irish Free State, comprising all but the 6 northern counties, achieved dominion status in 1922.

In the aftermath of the world war, radical revolutions were attempted in Germany (**Spartacist** uprising Jan. 1919), **Hungary** (Kun regime 1919), and elsewhere. All were suppressed or failed for lack of support.

Chinese revolution. The Manchu Dynasty was overthrown and a republic proclaimed, Oct. 1911. First president Sun Yat-sen resigned in favor of strongman Yuan Shih-k'ai. Sun organized the parliamentarian **Kuomintang** party.

Students launched protests May 4, 1919 against League of Nations concessions in China to Japan. Nationalist, liberal, and socialist ideas and political groups spread. The **Communist Party** was founded 1921. A communist regime took power in Mongolia with Soviet support in 1921.

India restive. Indian objections to British rule erupted in nationalist riots as well as in the non-violent tactics of Gandhi (1869-1948). Nearly 400 unarmed demonstrators were shot at **Amritsar,** Apr. 1919. Britain approved limited self-rule that year.

Mexican revolution. Under the long Diaz dictatorship (1876-1911) the economy advanced, but Indian and mestizo lands were confiscated, and concessions to foreigners (mostly U.S.) damaged the middle class. A **revolution in 1910** led to civil wars and U.S. intervention (1914, 1916-17). Land reform and a more democratic constitution (1917) were achieved.

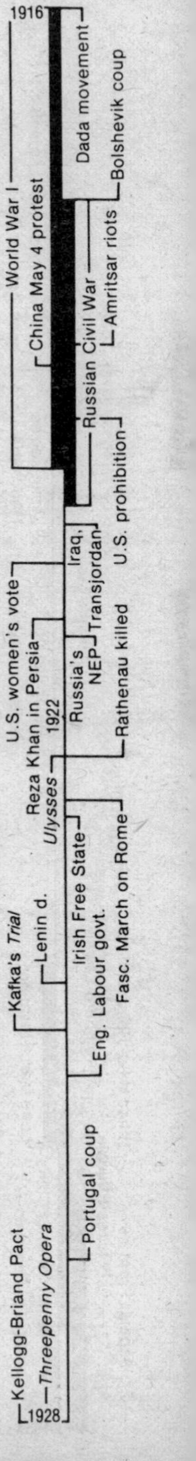

The Aftermath of War: 1920-29

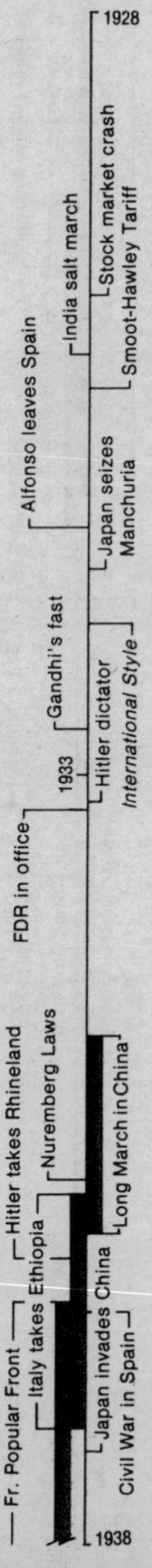

U.S. Easy credit, technological ingenuity, and war-related industrial decline in Europe caused a long economic boom, in which ownership of the new products — autos, phones, radios — became democratized. Prosperity, an increase in women workers, women's suffrage (1920) and drastic change in fashion (flappers, mannish bob for women, clean-shaven men), created a wide perception of social change, despite prohibition of alcoholic beverages (1919-33). Union membership and strikes increased. Fear of radicals led to Palmer raids (1919-20) and Sacco/Vanzetti case (1921-27).

Europe sorts itself out. Germany's liberal **Weimar constitution** (1919) could not guarantee a stable government in the face of rightist violence (Rathenau assassinated 1922) and Communist refusal to cooperate with Socialists. Reparations and allied occupation of the Rhineland caused staggering inflation which destroyed middle class savings, but economic expansion resumed after mid-decade, aided by U.S. loans. A sophisticated, innovative culture developed in architecture and design (Bauhaus, 1919-28), film (Lang, *M,* 1931), painting (Grosz), music (Weill, *Threepenny Opera,* 1928), theater (Brecht, *A Man's a Man,* 1926), criticism (Benjamin), philosophy (Jung), and fashion. This culture was considered decadent and socially disruptive by rightists.

England elected its first labor governments (Jan. 1924, June 1929). A 10-day general strike in support of coal miners failed, May 1926. In **Italy,** strikes, political chaos and violence by small Fascist bands culminated in the Oct. 1922 Fascist March on Rome, which established Mussolini's dictatorship. Strikes were outlawed (1926), and Italian influence was pressed in the Balkans (Albania a protectorate 1926). A conservative dictatorship was also established in **Portugal** in a 1926 military coup.

Czechoslovakia, the only stable democracy to emerge from the war in Central or East Europe, faced opposition from Germans (in the Sudetenland), Ruthenians, and some Slovaks. As the industrial heartland of the old Hapsburg empire, it remained fairly prosperous. With French backing, it formed the Little Entente with Yugoslavia (1920) and **Romania** (1921) to block Austrian or Hungarian irredentism. **Hungary** remained dominated by the landholding classes and expansionist feeling. Croats and Slovenes in **Yugoslavia** demanded a federal state until King Alexander proclaimed a dictatorship (1929). Poland faced nationality problems as well (Germans, Ukrainians, Jews); Pilsudski ruled as dictator from 1926. The Baltic states were threatened by traditionally dominant ethnic Germans and by Soviet-supported communists.

An economic collapse and famine in **Russia,** 1921-22, claimed 5 million lives. The New Economic Policy (1921) allowed land ownership by peasants and some private commerce and industry. Stalin was absolute ruler within 4 years of Lenin's 1924 death. He inaugurated a brutal collectivization program 1929-32, and used foreign communist parties for Soviet state advantage.

Internationalism. Revulsion against World War I led to pacifist agitation, the Kellogg-Briand Pact renouncing aggressive war (1928), and **naval disarmament** pacts (Washington, 1922, London, 1930). But the League of Nations was able to arbitrate only minor disputes (Greece-Bulgaria, 1925).

Middle East. Mustafa Kemal (Ataturk) led **Turkish** nationalists in resisting Italian, French, and Greek military advances, 1919-23. The sultanate was abolished 1922, and elaborate reforms passed, including secularization of law and adoption of the Latin alphabet. Ethnic conflict led to persecution of **Armenians** (over 1 million dead in 1915, 1 million expelled), Greeks (forced Greek-Turk population exchange, 1923), and Kurds (1925 uprising).

With evacuation of the Turks from **Arab** lands, the puritanical Wahabi dynasty of eastern Arabia conquered present Saudi Arabia, 1919-25. British, French, and Arab dynastic and nationalist maneuvering resulted in the creation of two more Arab monarchies in 1921: Iraq and Transjordan (both under British control), and two French mandates: Syria and Lebanon. Jewish immigration into British-mandated **Palestine,** inspired by the Zionist movement, was resisted by Arabs, at times violently (1921, 1929 massacres).

Reza Khan ruled **Persia** after his 1921 coup (shah from 1925), centralized control, and created the trappings of a modern state.

China. The Kuomintang under **Chiang Kai-shek** (1887-1975) subdued the warlords by 1928. The Communists were brutally suppressed after their alliance with the Kuomintang was broken in 1927. Relative peace thereafter allowed for industrial and financial improvements, with some Russian, British, and U.S. cooperation.

Arts. Nearly all bounds of subject matter, style, and attitude were broken in the arts of the period. **Abstract** art first took inspiration from natural forms or narrative themes (Kandinsky from 1911), then worked free of any representational aims (Malevich's suprematism, 1915-19, Mondrian's geometric style from 1917). The **Dada** movement from 1916 mocked artistic pretension with absurd collages and constructions (Arp, Tzara, from 1916). Paradox, illusion, and psychological taboos were exploited by **surrealists** by the latter 1920s (Dali, Magritte). Architectural schools celebrated industrial values, whether vigorous abstract constructivism (Tatlin, *Monument to 3rd International,* 1919) or the machined, streamlined **Bauhaus** style, which was extended to many design fields (Helvetica type face).

Prose writers explored revolutionary narrative modes related to dreams (Kafka's *Trial,* 1925), internal monologue (Joyce's *Ulysses,* 1922), and word play (Stein's *Making of Americans,* 1925). Poets and novelists wrote of modern alienation (Eliot's *Waste Land,* 1922) and aimlessness (Lost Generation).

Sciences. Scientific specialization prevailed by the 20th century. Advances in knowledge and technological aptitude increased with the geometric increase in the number of practitioners. Physicists challenged common-sense views of causality, observation, and a mechanistic universe, putting science further beyond popular grasp (Einstein's general theory of relativity, 1915; Bohr's quantum mechanics, 1913; Heisinger's uncertainty principle, 1927).

Rise of the Totalitarians: 1930-39

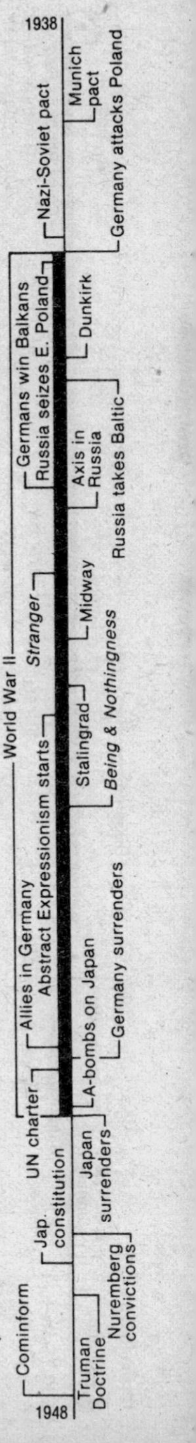

Depression. A worldwide financial panic and economic depression began with the Oct. 1929 U.S. stock market crash and the May 1931 failure of the Austrian Credit-Anstalt. A credit crunch caused international bankruptcies and **unemployment:** 12 million jobless by 1932 in the U.S., 5.6 million in Germany, 2.7 million in England. Governments responded with **tariff restrictions** (Smoot-Hawley Act 1930; Ottawa Imperial Conference, 1932) which dried up world trade. Government public works programs were vitiated by deflationary budget balancing.

Germany. Years of agitation by violent extremists was brought to a head by the Depression. Nazi leader **Hitler** was named chancellor by Pres. Hindenburg Jan. 1933, and given dictatorial power by the Reichstag in Mar. Opposition parties were disbanded, strikes banned, and all aspects of economic, cultural, and religious life brought under central government and Nazi party control and manipulated by sophisticated propaganda. Severe persecution of Jews began (**Nuremberg Laws** Sept. 1935). Many Jews, political opponents and others were sent to concentration camps (Dachau, 1933) where thousands died or were killed. Public works, renewed conscription (1935), arms production, and a 4-year plan (1936) ended unemployment.

Hitler's expansionism started with reincorporation of the Saar (1935), occupation of the **Rhineland** (Mar. 1936), and annexation of Austria (Mar. 1938). At **Munich,** Sept. 1938, an indecisive Britain and France sanctioned German dismemberment of Czechoslovakia.

Russia. Urbanization and education advanced. Rapid industrialization was achieved through successive **5-year-plans** starting 1928, using severe labor discipline and mass forced labor. Industry was financed by a decline in living standards and exploitation of agriculture, which was almost totally collectivized by the early 1930s (*kolkhoz,* collective farm; *sovkhoz,* state farm, often in newly-worked lands). Successive **purges** increased the role of professionals and management at the expense of workers. Millions perished in a series of man-made disasters: elimination of kulaks (peasant land-owners), 1929-34; severe famine, 1932-33; party purges (Great Purge, 1936-38); suppression of nationalities; and poor conditions in labor camps.

Spain. An industrial revolution during World War I created an urban proletariat, which was attracted to socialism and anarchism; Catalan nationalists challenged central authority. The 5 years after King Alfonso left Spain, Apr. 1931, were dominated by tension between intermittent leftist and anti-clerical governments and clericals, monarchists and other rightists. Anarchist and communist rebellions were crushed, but a July, 1936, extreme right rebellion led by Gen. Francisco Franco and aided by Nazi Germany and Fascist Italy succeeded, after a 3-year **civil war** (over 1 million dead in battles and atrocities). The war polarized international public opinion.

Italy. Despite propaganda for the ideal of the Corporate State, few domestic reforms were attempted. An entente with Hungary and Austria, Mar. 1934, a pact with Germany and Japan, Nov. 1937, and intervention by 50-75,000 troops in Spain, 1936-39, sealed Italy's identification with the fascist bloc (anti-Semitic laws after Mar. 1938). Ethiopia was conquered, 1935-37, and **Albania** annexed, Jan. 1939, in conscious imitation of ancient Rome.

East Europe. Repressive regimes fought for power against an active opposition (liberals, socialists, communists, peasants, Nazis). Minority groups and Jews were restricted within national boundaries that did not coincide with ethnic population patterns. In the destruction of **Czechoslovakia, Hungary** occupied southern Slovakia (Mar. 1938) and Ruthenia (Mar. 1939), and a pro-Nazi regime took power in the rest of Slovakia. Other boundary disputes (e.g. Poland-Lithuania, Yugoslavia-Bulgaria, Romania-Hungary) doomed attempts to build joint fronts against Germany or Russia. Economic depression was severe.

East Asia. After a period of liberalism in **Japan,** nativist militarists dominated the government with peasant support. Manchuria was seized, Sept. 1931-Feb. 1932, and a puppet state set up (Manchukuo). Adjacent Jehol (inner Mongolia) was occupied in 1933. China proper was invaded July 1937; large areas were conquered by Oct. 1938.

In **China** Communist forces left Kuomintang-besieged strongholds in the South in a Long March (1934-35) to the North. The Kuomintang-Communist civil war was suspended Jan. 1937 in the face of threatening Japan.

The democracies. The Roosevelt Administration, in office Mar. 1933, embarked on an extensive program of social reform and economic stimulation, including protection for labor unions (heavy industries organized), social security, public works, wages and hours laws, assistance to farmers. Isolationist sentiment (1937 Neutrality Act) prevented U.S. intervention in Europe, but military expenditures were increased in 1939.

French political instability and polarization prevented resolution of economic and international security questions. The **Popular Front** government under Blum (June 1936-Apr. 1938) passed social reforms (40-hour week) and raised arms spending. National coalition governments ruled Britain from Aug. 1931, brought some economic recovery, but failed to define a consistent foreign policy until Chamberlain's government (from May 1937), which practiced deliberate **appeasement** of Germany and Italy.

India. Twenty years of agitation for autonomy and then for independence (Gandhi's **salt march,** 1930) achieved some constitutional reform (extended provincial powers, 1935) despite Moslem-Hindu strife. Social issues assumed prominence with peasant uprisings (1921), strikes (1928), Gandhi's efforts for untouchables (1932 "fast unto death"), and social and agrarian reform by the provinces after 1937.

Arts. The streamlined, geometric design motifs of Art Deco (from 1925) prevailed through the 1930s. Abstract art flourished (Moore sculptures from 1931) alongside a new realism related to social and political concerns (**Socialist Realism** the official Soviet style from 1934; Mexican muralists Rivera, 1886-1957, and Orozco, 1883-1949), which was also expressed in fiction and poetry (Steinbeck's *Grapes of Wrath,* 1939; Sandburg's *The People, Yes,* 1936). Modern architecture (*International Style,* 1932) was unchallenged in its use of man-made materials (concrete, glass), lack of decoration, and monumentality (Rockefeller Center, 1929-40). U.S.-made films captured a world-wide audience with their larger-than-life fantasies (*Gone with the Wind,* 1939).

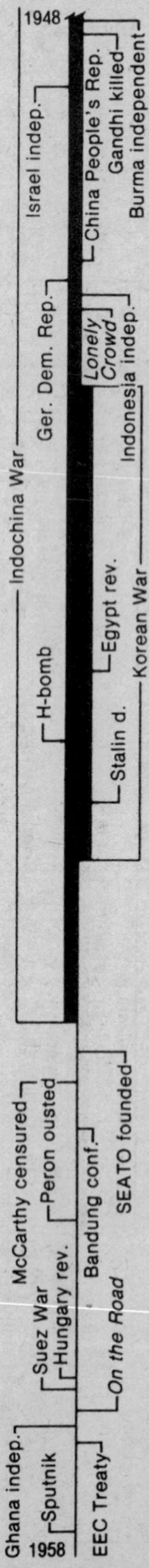

War, Hot and Cold: 1940-49

War in Europe. The Nazi-Soviet non-agression pact (Aug. '39) freed Germany to attack Poland (Sept.). Britain and France, who had guaranteed Polish independence, declared war on Germany. Russia seized East Poland (Sept.), attacked Finland (Nov.) and took the Baltic states (July '40). Mobile German forces staged **"blitzkrieg"** attacks Apr.-June, '40, conquering neutral Denmark, Norway, and the low countries and defeating France; 350,000 British and French troops were evacuated at **Dunkirk** (May). The Battle of Britain, June-Dec. '40, denied Germany air superiority, German-Italian campaigns won the Balkans by Apr. '41. Three million Axis troops **invaded Russia** June '41, marching through the Ukraine to the Caucasus, and through White Russia and the Baltic republics to Moscow and Leningrad.

Russian winter counterthrusts, '41-'42 and '42-'43 stopped the German advance (Stalingrad Sept. '42-Feb. '43). With British and U.S. Lend-Lease aid and sustaining great casualties, the Russians drove the Axis from all E. Europe and the Balkans in the next 2 years. Invasions of N. Africa (Nov. '42), Italy (Sept. '43), and Normandy (June '44) brought U.S., British, Free French and allied troops to Germany by spring '45. Germany surrendered May 7, 1945.

War in Asia-Pacific. Japan occupied Indochina Sept. '40, dominated Thailand Dec. '41, attacked Hawaii, the Philippines, Hong Kong, Malaya Dec. 7, 1941. Indonesia was attacked Jan. '42, Burma conquered Mar. 42. Battle of **Midway** (June '42) turned back the Japanese advance. "Island-hopping" battles (Guadalcanal Aug. '42-Jan. '43, **Leyte Gulf** Oct. '44, Iwo Jima Feb.-Mar. '45, Okinawa Apr. '45) and massive bombing raids on Japan from June '44 wore out Japanese defenses. Two U.S. atom bombs, dropped Aug. 6 and 9, forced Japan to surrender Aug. 14, 1945. *For further details, see 1978 and earlier editions of The World Almanac.*

Atrocities. The war brought 20th-century cruelty to its peak. Nazi murder camps (Auschwitz) systematically killed 6 million Jews. Gypsies, political opponents, sick and retarded people, and others deemed undesirable were murdered by the Nazis, as were vast numbers of Slavs, especially leaders. German bombs killed 70,000 English civilians. Some 100,000 Chinese civilians were killed by Japanese forces in the capture of Nanking. Severe retaliation by the Soviet army, E. European partisans, Free French and others took a heavy toll. U.S. and British bombing of Germany killed hundreds of thousands, as did U.S. bombing of Japan (80-200,000 at Hiroshima alone). Some 45 million people lost their lives in the war.

Home front. All industries were reoriented to war production and support, and rationing was universal. Science was harnessed for the war effort, yielding such innovations as radar, jet planes, and synthetic materials. Unscathed U.S. industry, partly staffed by women, helped decide the war.

Settlement. The United Nations charter was signed in San Francisco June 26, 1945 by 50 nations. The International Tribunal at Nuremberg convicted 22 German leaders for war crimes Sept. '46, 23 Japanese leaders were convicted Nov. '48. Postwar border changes included large gains in territory for the USSR, losses for Germany, a shift westward in Polish borders, and minor losses for Italy. Communist regimes, supported by Soviet troops, took power in most of E. Europe, including Soviet-occupied Germany (GDR proclaimed Oct. '49). Japan lost all overseas lands.

Recovery. Basic political and social changes were imposed on Japan and W. Germany by the western allies (Japan constitution Nov. '46, W. German basic law May '49). U.S. Marshall Plan aid ($12 billion '47-'51) spurred W. European economic recovery after a period of severe inflation and strikes in Europe and the U.S. The British Labour Party introduced a national health service and nationalized basic industries in 1946.

Cold War. Western fears of further Soviet advances (Cominform formed Oct. '47, Czechoslovakia coup, Feb. '48, Berlin blockade Apr.'48-Sept. '49) led to formation of NATO. Civil War in Greece and Soviet pressure on Turkey led to U.S. aid under the Truman Doctrine (Mar. '47). Other anti-communist security pacts were the Org. of American States (Apr. '48) and Southeast Asia Treaty Org. (Sept. '54). A new wave of Soviet purges and repression intensified in the last years of Stalin's rule, extending to E. Europe (Slansky trial in Czechoslovakia, 1951). Only Yugoslavia resisted Soviet control (expelled by Cominform, June '48; U.S. aid, June '49).

China, Korea. Communist forces emerged from World War II strengthened by the Soviet takeover of industrial Manchuria. In 4 years of fighting, the Kuomintang was driven from the mainland; the People's Republic was proclaimed Oct. 1, 1949. Korea was divided by Russian and U.S. occupation forces. Separate republics were proclaimed in the 2 zones Aug.-Sept. '48.

India. India and Pakistan became independent dominions Aug. 15, 1947. Millions of Hindu and Moslem refugees were created by the partition; riots, 1946-47, took hundreds of thousands of lives; Gandhi himself was assassinated Jan. '48. Burma became completely independent Jan. '48; Ceylon took dominion status in Feb.

Middle East. The UN approved partition of Palestine into Jewish and Arab states. Israel was proclaimed May 14, 1948. Arabs rejected partition, but failed to defeat Israel in war, May '48-July '49. Immigration from Europe and the Middle East swelled Israel's Jewish population. British and French forces left Lebanon and Syria, 1946. Transjordan occupied most of Arab Palestine.

Southeast Asia. Communists and others fought against restoration of French rule in Indochina from 1946; a non-communist government was recognized by France Mar. '49, but fighting continued. Both Indonesia and the Philippines became independent, the former in 1949 after 4 years of war with Netherlands, the latter in 1946. Philippine economic and military ties with the U.S. remained strong; a communist-led peasant rising was checked in '48.

Arts. New York became the center of the world art market; abstract expressionism was the chief mode (Pollock from '43, de Kooning from '47). Literature and philosophy explored existentialism (Camus' *Stranger*, 1942, Sartre's *Being and Nothingness*, 1943). Non-western attempts to revive or create regional styles (Senghor's Negritude, Mishima's novels) only confirmed the emergence of a universal culture. Radio and phonograph records spread American popular music (swing, bebop) around the world.

The American Decade: 1950-59

Polite decolonization. The peaceful decline of European political and military power in Asia and Africa accelerated in the 1950s. Nearly all of **N. Africa** was freed by 1956, but France fought a bitter war to retain Algeria, with its large European minority, until 1962. **Ghana,** independent 1957, led a parade of new black African nations (over 2 dozen by 1962) which altered the political character of the UN. Ethnic disputes often exploded in the new nations after decolonization (UN troops in Cyprus 1964; **Nigeria** civil war 1967-70). Leaders of the new states, mostly sharing socialist ideologies, tried to create an Afro-Asian bloc (Bandung Conf. 1955), but Western economic influence and U.S. political ties remained strong (Baghdad Pact, 1955).

Trade. World trade volume soared, in an atmosphere of monetary stability assured by international accords (**Bretton Woods** 1944). In Europe, economic integration advanced (**European Economic Community** 1957, European Free Trade Association 1960). Comecon (1949) coordinated the economies of Soviet-bloc countries.

U.S. Economic growth produced an abundance of consumer goods (9.3 million motor vehicles sold, 1955). Suburban housing tracts changed life patterns for middle and working classes (Levittown 1946-51). **Eisenhower's** landside election victories (1952, 1956) reflected consensus politics. Censure of McCarthy (Dec. '54) curbed the political abuse of anti-communism. A system of alliances and military bases bolstered U.S. influence on all continents. Trade and payments surpluses were balanced by overseas investments and foreign aid ($50 billion, 1950-59).

USSR. In the "thaw" after Stalin's death in 1953, relations with the West improved (evacuation of Vienna, Geneva summit conf., both 1955). Repression of scientific and cultural life eased, and many prisoners were freed or rehabilitated culminating in **de-Stalinization** (1956). Khrushchev's leadership aimed at consumer sector growth, but farm production lagged, despite the virgin lands program (from 1954). The 1956 Hungarian revolution, the 1960 U-2 spy plane episode, and other incidents renewed East-West tension and domestic curbs.

East Europe. Resentment of Russian domination and Stalinist repression combined with nationalist, economic and religious factors to produce periodic violence. East Berlin workers rioted in 1953, Polish workers rioted in Poznan, June 1956, and a broad-based revolution broke out in Hungary, Oct. 1956. All were suppressed by Soviet force or threats (at least 7,000 dead in Hungary). But Poland was allowed to restore private ownership of farms, and a degree of personal and economic freedom returned to Hungary. Yugoslavia experimented with worker self-management and a market economy.

Korea. The 1945 division of Korea left industry in the North, which was organized into a militant regime and armed by Russia. The South was politically disunited. Over 60,000 North Korean troops invaded the South June 25, 1950. The U.S., backed by the UN Security Council, sent troops. UN troops reached the Chinese border in Nov. Some 200,000 Chinese troops crossed the Yalu River and drove back UN forces. Cease-fire in July 1951 found the opposing forces near the original 38th parallel border. After 2 years of sporadic fighting, an armistice was signed July 27, 1953. U.S. troops remained in the South, and U.S. economic and military aid continued. The war stimulated rapid economic recovery in Japan. *For details, see 1978 and earlier editions of The World Almanac.*

China. Starting in 1952, industry, agriculture, and social institutions were forcibly collectivized. As many as several million people were executed as Kuomintang supporters or as class and political enemies. The Great Leap Forward, 1958-60, unsuccessfully tried to force the pace of development by substituting labor for investment.

Indochina. Ho's forces, aided by Russia and the new Chinese Communist government, fought French and pro-French Vietnamese forces to a standstill, and captured the strategic Dienbienphu camp in May, 1954. The Geneva Agreements divided Vietnam in half pending elections (never held), and recognized Laos and Cambodia as independent. The U.S. aided the anti-Communist Republic of Vietnam in the South.

Middle East. Arab revolutions placed leftist, militantly nationalist regimes in power in Egypt (1952) and Iraq (1958). But Arab unity attempts failed (United Arab Republic joined Egypt, Syria, Yemen 1958-61). Arab refusal to recognize Israel (Arab League economic blockade began Sept. 1951) led to a permanent state of war, with repeated incidents (Gaza, 1955). Israel occupied Sinai, Britain and France took the Suez Canal, Oct. 1956, but were replaced by the UN Emergency Force. The Mossadegh government in Iran nationalized the British-owned oil industry May 1951, but was overthrown in a U.S.-aided coup Aug. 1953.

Latin America. Dictator Juan Peron, in office 1946, enforced land reform, some nationalization, welfare state measures, and curbs on the Roman Catholic Church, but crushed opposition. A Sept. 1955 coup deposed Peron. The 1952 revolution in Bolivia brought land reform, nationalization of tin mines, and improvement in the status of Indians, who nevertheless remained poor. The Batista regime in Cuba was overthrown, Jan. 1959, by Fidel Castro, who imposed a communist dictatorship, aligned Cuba with Russia, improved education and health care. A U.S.-backed anti-Castro invasion (Bay of Pigs, Apr. 1961) was crushed. Self-government advanced in the British Caribbean.

Technology. Large outlays on research and development in the U.S. and USSR focussed on military applications (H-bomb in U.S. 1952, USSR 1953, Britain 1957, intercontinental missiles late 1950s). Soviet launching of the Sputnik satellite, Oct. 1957, spurred increases in U.S. science education funds (National Defense Education Act).

Literature and letters. Alienation from social and literary conventions reached an extreme in the theater of the absurd (Beckett's *Waiting for Godot* 1952), the "new novel" (Robbe-Grillet's *Voyeur* 1955), and avant-garde film (Antonioni's *L'Avventura* 1960). U.S. Beatniks (Kerouac's *On the Road* 1957) and others rejected the supposed conformism of Americans (Riesman's *Lonely Crowd* 1950).

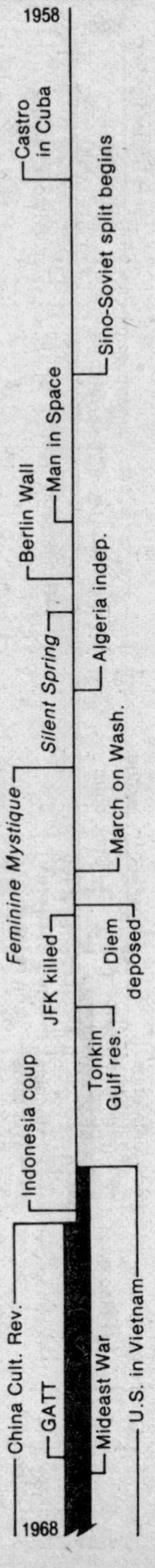

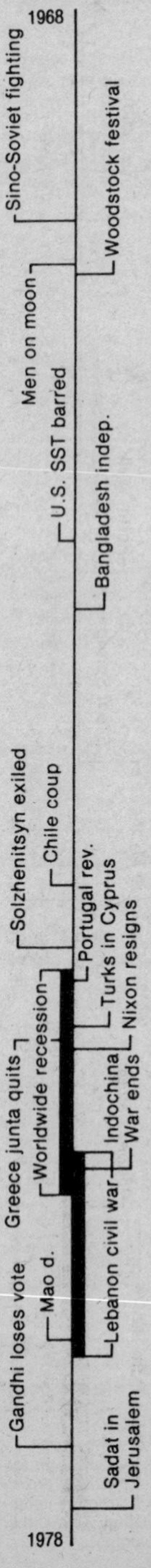

Rising Expectations: 1960-69

Economic boom. The longest sustained economic boom on record spanned almost the entire decade in the capitalist world; the closely-watched GNP figure doubled in the U.S. 1960-70, fueled by Vietnam War-related budget deficits. The **General Agreement on Tariffs and Trade,** 1967, stimulated West European prosperity, which spread to peripheral areas (Spain, Italy, E. Germany). Japan became a top economic power ($20 billion exports 1970). Foreign investment aided the industrialization of Brazil. Soviet 1965 economic reform attempts (decentralization, material incentives) were limited; but growth continued.

Reform and radicalization. A series of political and social reform movements took root in the U.S., later spreading to other countries with the help of ubiquitous U.S. film and television programs and heavy overseas travel (2.2 million U.S. passports issued 1970). Blacks agitated peaceably and with partial success against segregation and poverty (1963 March on Washington, 1964 **Civil Rights Act**); but some urban ghettos erupted in extensive riots (Watts, 1965; Detroit, 1967; King assassination, Apr. 4, 1968). New concern for the poor (Harrington's *Other America,* 1963) led to Pres. Johnson's **"Great Society"** programs (Medicare, Water Quality Act, Higher Education Act, all 1965). Concern with the **environment** surged (Carson's *Silent Spring,* 1962). **Feminism** revived as a cultural and political movement (Friedan's *Feminine Mystique,* 1963, National Organization for Women founded 1966) and a movement for homosexual rights emerged (Stonewall riot, in NYC, 1969).

Opposition to U.S. involvement in Vietnam, especially among university students (**Moratorium** protest Nov. '69) turned violent (Weatherman Chicago riots Oct. '69). New Left and Marxist theories became popular, and membership in radical groups swelled (Students for a Democratic Society, Black Panthers). Maoist groups, especially in Europe, called for total transformation of society. In France, students sparked a nationwide strike affecting 10 million workers May-June '68, but an electoral reaction barred revolutionary change.

Arts and styles. The boundary between fine and popular arts were blurred by Pop Art (Warhol) and rock musicals (Hair, 1968). Informality and exaggeration prevailed in fashion (beards, miniskirts). A non-political "counterculture" developed, rejecting traditional bourgeois life goals and personal habits, and use of marijuana and hallucinogens spread (Woodstock festival Aug. '68). Indian influence was felt in music (Beatles), religion (Ram Dass), and fashion.

Science. Achievements in space (men on moon July '69) and electronics (lasers, integrated circuits) encouraged a faith in scientific solutions to problems in agriculture ("green revolution"), medicine (heart transplants 1967) and other areas. The harmful effects of science, it was believed, could be controlled (1963 nuclear weapon test ban treaty, 1968 non-proliferation treaty).

China. Mao's revolutionary militance caused disputes with Russia under "revisionist" Khrushchev, starting 1960. The two powers exchanged fire in 1969 border disputes. China used force to capture areas disputed with India, 1962. The "Great Proletarian Cultural Revolution" tried to impose a utopian egalitarian program in China and spread revolution abroad; political struggle, often violent, convulsed China 1965-68.

Indochina. Communist-led guerrillas aided by N. Vietnam fought from 1960 against the S. Vietnam government of Ngo Dinh Diem (killed 1963). The U.S. military role increased after the 1964 Tonkin Gulf incident. U.S. forces peaked at 543,400, Apr. '69. Massive numbers of N. Viet troops also fought. Laotian and Cambodian neutrality were threatened by communist insurgencies, with N. Vietnamese aid, and U.S. intrigues. *For details, see 1978 and earlier editions of The World Almanac.*

Third World. A bloc of authoritarian leftist regimes among the newly independent nations emerged in political opposition to the U.S.-led Western alliance, and came to dominate the conference of nonaligned nations (Belgrade 1961, Cairo 1964, Lusaka 1970). Soviet political ties and military bases were established in Cuba, Egypt, Algeria, Guinea, and other countries, whose leaders were regarded as revolutionary heros by opposition groups in pro-Western or colonial countries. Some leaders were ousted in coups by pro-Western groups—Zaire's Lumumba (killed 1961), Ghana's Nkrumah (exiled 1966), and Indonesia's Sukarno (effectively ousted 1965 after a Communist coup failed).

Middle East. Arab-Israeli tension erupted into a brief war June 1967. Israel emerged as a major regional power. Military shipments before and after the war brought much of the Arab world into the Soviet political sphere. Most Arab states broke U.S. diplomatic ties, while Communist countries cut their ties to Israel. Intra-Arab disputes continued: Egypt and Saudi Arabia supported rival factions in a bloody Yemen civil war 1962-70; Lebanese troops fought Palestinian commandos in 1969.

East Europe. To stop the large-scale exodus of citizens, E. German authorities built a fortified wall across Berlin Aug. '61. Soviet sway in the Balkans was weakened by Albania's support of China (USSR broke ties Dec. '61) and Romania's assertion of industrial and foreign policy autonomy in 1964. Liberalization in Czechoslovakia, spring 1968, was crushed by troops of 5 Warsaw Pact countries. West German treaties with Russia and Poland, 1970, facilitated the transfer of German technology and confirmed post-war boundaries.

Disillusionment: 1970-79

U.S.: Caution and neoconservatism. A relatively sluggish economy, energy and resource shortages (natural gas crunch 1975, gasoline shortage 1979), and environmental problems contributed to a **"limits of growth"** philosophy that affected politics (Cal. Gov. Brown). Suspicion of science and technology killed or delayed major projects (supersonic transport dropped 1971, DNA recombination curbed 1976, Seabrook A-plant protests 1977-78) and was fed by the Three Mile Island nuclear reactor accident in Mar. '79.

Mistrust of big government weakened support for government reform plans among liberals. School busing and racial quotas were opposed (**Bakke decision** June '78); the Equal Rights Amendment for women languished; civil rights for homosexuals were opposed (Dade County referendum June '77).

U.S. defeat in **Indochina** (evacuation Apr. '75), revelations of Central Intelligence Agency misdeeds (Rockefeller Commission report June '75), and the **Watergate** scandals (Nixon quit Aug. '74) reduced faith in U.S. moral and material capacity to influence world affairs. Revelations of Soviet crimes (Solzhenitsyn's *Gulag Archipelago* from 1974) and Russian intervention in Africa aided a revival of anti-Communist sentiment.

Economy sluggish. The 1960s boom faltered in the 1970s; a severe recession in the U.S. and Europe 1974-75 followed a huge oil price hike Dec. '73. Monetary instability (U.S. cut ties to gold Aug. '71), the decline of the dollar, and **protectionist** moves by industrial countries (1977-78) threatened trade. Business investment and spending for research declined. Severe inflation plagued many countries (25% in Britain, 1975; 18% in U.S., 1979).

China picks up pieces. After the 1976 deaths of Mao and Chou, a power struggle for the leadership succession was won by pragmatists. A nationwide purge of orthodox Maoists was carried out, and the "**Gang of Four**", led by Mao's widow Chiang Ching, was arrested.

The new leaders freed over 100,000 political prisoners, and reduced public adulation of Mao. Political and trade ties were expanded with Japan, Europe, and the U.S. in the late 1970's, as relations worsened with Russia, Cuba, and Vietnam (4-week invasion by China in 1979). Ideological guidelines in industry, science, education, and the armed forces, which the ruling faction said had caused chaos and decline, were reversed (bonuses to workers, Dec. '77; exams for college entrance, Oct. '77). Severe restrictions on cultural expression were eased (Beethoven ban lifted Mar. '77).

Europe. European unity moves (EEC-EFTA trade accord 1972) faltered as economic problems appeared (Britain floated pound 1972; France floated franc 1974). Germany and Switzerland curbed guest workers from S. Europe. Greece and Turkey quarreled over Cyprus (Turks intervened 1974) and Aegean oil rights.

All of non-Communist Europe was under democratic rule after free elections were held in **Spain** June '76, 7 months after the death of Franco. The conservative, colonialist regime in **Portugal** was overthrown Apr. '74. In **Greece,** the 7-year-old military dictatorship yielded power in 1974. Northern Europe, though ruled mostly by Socialists (**Swedish** Socialists unseated 1976, after 44 years in power), turned conservative. The **British** Labour government imposed wage curbs 1975, and suspended nationalization schemes. Terrorism in **Germany** (1972 Munich Olympics killings) led to laws curbing some civil liberties. **French** "new philosophers" rejected leftist ideologies, and the shaky Socialist-Communist coalition lost a 1978 election bid.

Religion back in politics. The improvement in Moslem countries' political fortunes by the 1950s (with the exception of Central Asia under Soviet and Chinese rule), and the growth of Arab oil wealth, was followed by a resurgence of traditional piety. **Libyan** dictator Qaddafi mixed strict Islamic laws with socialism in his militant ideology and called for an eventual Moslem return to Spain and Sicily. The illegal Moslem Brotherhood in **Egypt** was accused of violence, while extreme Moslem groups bombed theaters, 1977, to protest secular values.

In **Turkey,** the National Salvation Party was the first Islamic group to share power (1974) since secularization in the 1920s. Religious authorities, such as Ayatollah Ruholla Khomeini, led the **Iranian** revolution and religiously motivated Moslems took part in the insurrection in Saudi Arabia that briefly seized the Grand Mosque in Mecca in 1979. Moslem puritan opposition to **Pakistan** Pres. Bhutto helped lead to his overthrow July '77. However, Moslem solidarity could not prevent Pakistan's eastern province (**Bangladesh**) from declaring independence, Dec. '71, after a bloody civil war.

Moslem and Hindu resentment against coerced sterilization in **India** helped defeat the Gandhi government, which was replaced Mar. '77 by a coalition including religious Hindu parties and led by devout Hindu Desai. Moslems in the southern **Philippines,** aided by Libya, conducted a long rebellion against central rule from 1973.

Evangelical Protestant groups grew in numbers and prosperity in the U.S. ("**born again**" Pres. Carter elected 1976), and the Catholic charismatic movement obtained respectability. A revival of interest in Orthodox Christianity occurred among **Russian** intellectuals (Solzhenitsyn). The secularist **Israeli** Labor party, after decades of rule, was ousted in 1977 by conservatives led by Begin, an observant Jew; religious militants founded settlements on the disputed West Bank, part of Biblically-promised Israel. U.S. Reform Judaism revived many previously discarded traditional practices.

The Buddhist Soka Gakkai movement launched the Komeito party in Japan, 1964, which became a major opposition party in 1972 and 1976 elections.

Old-fashioned religious wars raged intermittently in **N. Ireland** (Catholic vs. Protestant, 1969-) and **Lebanon** (Christian vs. Moslem, 1975-), while religious militancy complicated the Israel-Arab dispute (1973 Israel-Arab war. In spite of a **1979 peace treaty between Egypt and Israel** which looked forward to a resolution of the Palestinian issue, increased religious militancy on the West Bank made such a resolution seem unlikely.

Latin America. Repressive conservative regimes strengthened their hold on most of the continent, with the violent coup against the elected Allende government in **Chile,** Sept. '73, the 1976 military coup in **Argentina,** and coups against reformist regimes in **Bolivia,** 1971 and 1979, and **Peru,** 1976. In Central America, increasing liberal and leftist militancy led to the ouster of the Somoza regime of Nicaragua in 1979 and civil conflict in El Salvador.

Indochina. Communist victory in Vietnam, Cambodia, and Laos by May '75 did not bring peace. Attempts at radical social reorganization left over one million dead in Cambodia during 1975-78 and caused hundreds of thousands of ethnic Chinese and others to flee Vietnam ("boat people," 1979). The Vietnamese invasion of Cambodia swelled the refugee population and contributed to widespread starvation in that devastated country.

Russian expansion. Soviet influence, checked in some countries (troops ousted by Egypt 1972) was projected further afield, often with the use of Cuban troops (Angola 1975- , Ethiopia 1977-), and aided by a growing navy, merchant fleet, and international banking ability. Detente with the West — 1972 Berlin pact, 1970 strategic arms pact (**SALT**) — gave way to a more antagonistic relationship in the late 1970s, exacerbated by the Soviet invasion of Afghanistan in 1979.

Africa. The last remaining European colonies were granted independence (**Spanish Sahara** 1976, **Djibouti** 1977) and, after 10 years of civil war and many negotiation sessions, a black government took over Zimbabwe (Rhodesia) in 1979; white domination remained in **S. Africa.** Great power involvement in local wars (Russia in **Angola, Ethiopia;** France in **Chad, Zaire, Mauritania**) and the use of tens of thousands of Cuban troops was denounced by some African leaders as neocolonialism. Ethnic or tribal clashes made Africa the chief world locus of sustained warfare in the late 1970s.

Arts. Traditional modes in painting, architecture, and music, pursued in relative obscurity for much of the 20th century, returned to popular and critical attention in the 1970s. The pictorial emphasis in neorealist and photorealist painting, the return of many architects to detail, decoration, and traditional natural materials, and the concern with ordered structure in musical composition were, ironically, novel experiences for artistic consumers after the exhaustion of experimental possibilities. However, these more conservative styles coexisted with modernist works in an atmosphere of variety and tolerance.

100 Years Ago

1883 saw some important milestones in the area of rail transportation. Europe's first transcontinental train, the luxurious Orient Express, departed for Constantinople from Paris' Gare de l'Est, Oct. 4. Actually, because no direct rail link to Constantinople existed at the time, passengers rode the new train to the Bulgarian border, ferried across the Danube, rode a less elaborate train to Varna on the Black Sea, and from there sailed to Turkey.

A "last spike" ceremony, Sept. 8, in Gold Creek (Montana Territory), marked the completion of The Northern Pacific Railroad after 13 years of work.

Also in 1883, U.S. railroads adopted the standard time system with Eastern, Central, Rocky Mountain, and Pacific time zones.

Civil Service Commission Established

Congress passed, January 16, the Pendleton Civil Service Reform Act that provided for competitive examinations for positions in the federal government through the establishment of a Civil Service Commission. By establishing a merit system for appointments and promotions, the new law sharply reduced the procurement of federal jobs using contacts and connections with elected officials—the so-called "spoils system."

1883 was the peak year of immigration to the United States from the countries of Denmark, Norway, Sweden, Switzerland, the Netherlands, and China.

Over 11 million died in the worldwide cholera pandemic that broke out in 1883.

Brooklyn Bridge Opens

Twelve people were trampled to death in the excitement of the dedication ceremonies as the Brooklyn bridge opened May 24. The bridge's designer, John Augustus Roebling, had died in 1869 from tetanus after his leg was crushed by a ferryboat while he worked on the bridge. Construction of the great span had been carried on by his son, Washington Augustus. Washington, now crippled, half-paralyzed, and made partially blind from caisson disease (the "bends"), observed the dedication ceremonies from his house on Brooklyn's Columbia Heights.

Scientific Advances

Using nitrocellulose, French chemist Hilaire Bernigaud, comte de Chardonnet, invented the first artificial silk.

Telegraph service between the United States and Brazil began 100 years ago.

Robert Koch developed a preventive inoculation against anthrax, and also identified the comma bacillus, the cause of Asiatic cholera.

English engineer Hiram Stevens Maxim invented the first fully automatic machine gun, the first gun to use the recoil energy of each bullet to eject the spent cartridge, insert the new round, and fire.

Six hundred cannery workers lost their jobs when the first successful pea-podder machine was installed at Owasco, New York.

Buffalo Bill Show Introduced

Buffalo Bill's Wild West Show, complete with riding, target shooting, and showmanship, introduced to America an open-air spectacle that would be a favorite for the next 20 years. Promoter William Frederick Cody was a former buffalo hunter and cavalry scout famous for having killed and scalped the Cheyenne leader Yellow Hand in a duel. In 1885, markswoman Annie Oakley (born Phoebe Mozee), "The Peerless Lady Wing-Shot," would join the show. Sioux chieftain Sitting Bull would also become one of the show's added attractions.

Former circus performers Benjamin Franklin Keith and George H. Batchelder opened the Keith & Batchelder's Dime Museum in Boston. The pair assembled for their exhibit a group of sideshow attractions as a means of supporting themselves during the slack winter months when the circus was not touring. Features included tattooed ladies, wild men of Borneo, sword swallowers, snake charmers, Circassian beauties, and the cow that allegedly kicked over the lantern that started the Chicago fire.

Arts, Literature & Publishing

Thus Spake Zarathustra (*Also Sprach Zarathustra*), Friedrich Wilhelm Nietzsche's philosophical work, was published in the first of four parts.

Christine Nilsson sang the role of Marguerite in Gounod's opera *Faust* at the opening of New York's Metropolitan Opera House, Oct. 22.

Treasure Island, the adventure novel by Robert Louis Stevenson that included the pirate song, "Fifteen men on a dead man's chest—/ Yo-ho-ho, and a bottle of rum!. . ." was published in 1883.

Henrik Ibsen's *An Enemy of the People* (*En Folkefiende*) was first performed at Oslo's Christiania Theater January 13, 1883.

Husitska, a dramatic orchestral work by Antonin Dvorak, was first performed at Prague's Bohemian Theater. Symphony No. 3 in F major by Johannes Brahms was performed in Vienna.

The hymns, "When the Mists Have Rolled Away," by Ira David Sankey, verses by Annie Herbert; and "Till We Meet Again" ("God Be With You") by William Gould Tomer, verses by Jeremiah Eames Rankin, were introduced.

Mark Twain's *Life on the Mississippi*, the first manuscript submitted in typewritten form, was published.

Indiana poet James Whitcomb Riley of the *Indianapolis Journal* published his work, *The Old Swimmin' Hole and 'Leven More Poems*, a volume that included "When the Frost is on the Punkin!"

Grit, the weekly magazine for rural readers, began publication in 1883. Over the next 94 years, the magazine would grow to a circulation of more than 5 million.

The New York World, with a circulation of 15,000 and losing $40,000 a year, was acquired by Joseph Pulitzer of the *St. Louis Post-Dispatch* from Jay Gould. Pulitzer would make the paper profitable.

The *Ladies Home Journal* began publication in 1883, as did *Life* magazine. *Science* magazine, founded by telephone pioneer Alexander Graham Bell and his father-in-law G.G. Hubbard, also began in 1883. The magazine would become the organ of the American Association for the Advancement of Science.

Business

Bernard H. Kroger, 23, a grocery salesman, opened a 17-foot-front store in Cincinnati called the Great Western Tea Company. Kroger put up $372 in capital, and a partner invested $350. Later that year Kroger bought out the partner for $1,550. The B.H. Kroger Company would have 4 stores by mid-1885, and would eventually grow to more than 1,250 stores in 20 states.

Oscar F. Mayer, in partnership with his brother Gottfried, opened a Chicago retail shop to sell fresh and cured meats, marking the beginning of Oscar Mayer wieners.

Births and Deaths

The list of notable persons born in 1883 includes Italian dictator Benito Mussolini, Austrian novelist Franz Kafka, English economist John Maynard Keynes, German-American architect Walter Gropius, and French painter Maurice Utrillo. Karl Marx died in 1883, as did Russian novelist Ivan Turgenev, French artists Gustave Dore and Edouard Manet, and the German opera composer Richard Wagner.

Some Notable Marine Disasters Since 1850

(Figures indicate estimated lives lost)

1854, Mar.—City of Glasgow; British steamer missing in North Atlantic; 480.

1854, Sept. 27—Arctic; U.S. (Collins Line) steamer sunk in collision with French steamer Vesta near Cape Race; 285-351.

1856, Jan. 23—Pacific; U.S. (Collins Line) steamer missing in North Atlantic; 186-286.

1858, Sept. 23—Austria; German steamer destroyed by fire in North Atlantic; 471.

1863, Apr. 27—Anglo-Saxon; British steamer wrecked at Cape Race; 238.

1865, Apr. 27—Sultana; a Mississippi River steamer blew up near Memphis, Tenn; 1,400.

1869, Oct. 27—Stonewall; steamer burned on Mississippi River below Cairo, Ill.; 200.

1870, Jan. 25—City of Boston; British (Inman Line) steamer vanished between New York and Liverpool; 177.

1870, Oct 19—Cambria; British steamer wrecked off northern Ireland; 196.

1872, Nov. 7—Mary Celeste; U.S. half-brig sailed from New York for Genoa; found abandoned in Atlantic 4 weeks later in mystery of sea; crew never heard from; loss of life unknown.

1873, Jan. 22—Northfleet; British steamer foundered off Dungeness, England; 300.

1873, Apr. 1—Atlantic; British (White Star) steamer wrecked off Nova Scotia; 585.

1873, Nov. 23—Ville du Havre; French steamer, sunk after collision with British sailing ship Loch Earn; 226.

1875, May 7—Schiller; German steamer wrecked off Scilly Isles; 312.

1875, Nov. 4—Pacific; U.S. steamer sunk after collision off Cape Flattery; 236.

1878, Sept. 3—Princess Alice; British steamer sank after collision in Thames; 700.

1878, Dec. 18—Byzantin; French steamer sank after Dardanelles collision; 210.

1881, May 24—Victoria; steamer capsized in Thames River, Canada; 200.

1883, Jan. 19—Cimbria; German steamer sunk in collision with British steamer Sultan in North Sea; 389.

1887, Nov. 15—Wah Yeung; British steamer burned at sea; 400.

1890, Feb. 17—Duburg; British steamer wrecked, China Sea; 400.

1890, Sept. 19—Ertogrul; Turkish frigate foundered off Japan; 540.

1891, Mar. 17—Utopia; British steamer sank in collision with British ironclad Anson off Gibraltar; 562.

1895, Jan. 30—Elbe; German steamer sank in collision with British steamer Craithie in North Sea; 332.

1895, Mar. 11—Reina Regenta; Spanish cruiser foundered near Gibraltar; 400.

1898, Feb. 15—Maine; U.S. battleship blown up in Havana Harbor; 266.

1898, July 4—La Bourgogne; French steamer sunk in collision with British sailing ship Cromartyshire off Nova Scotia; 549.

1904, June 15—General Slocum; excursion steamer burned in East River, New York City; 1,030.

1904, June 28—Norge; Danish steamer wrecked on Rockall Island, Scotland; 620.

1906, Aug. 4—Sirio; Italian steamer wrecked off Cape Palos, Spain; 350.

1908, Mar. 23—Matsu Maru; Japanese steamer sank in collision near Hakodate, Japan; 300.

1909, Aug. 1—Waratah; British steamer, Sydney to London, vanished; 300.

1910, Feb. 9—General Chanzy; French steamer wrecked off Minorca, Spain; 200.

1911, Sept. 25—Liberté; French battleship exploded at Toulon; 285.

1912, Apr. 14-15—Titanic; British (White Star) steamer hit iceberg in North Atlantic; 1,503.

1912, Sept. 28—Kichemaru; Japanese steamer sank off Japanese coast; 1,000.

1914, May 29—Empress of Ireland; British (Canadian Pacific) steamer sunk in collision with Norwegian collier in St. Lawrence River; 1,014.

1915, May 7—Lusitania; British (Cunard Line) steamer torpedoed and sunk by German submarine U. 20 off Ireland; 1,198.

1915, July 24—Eastland; excursion steamer capsized in Chicago River; 812.

1916, Feb. 26—Provence; French cruiser sank in Mediterranean; 3,100.

1916, Mar. 3—Principe de Asturias; Spanish steamer wrecked near Santos, Brazil; 558.

1916, Aug. 29—Hsin Yu; Chinese steamer sank off Chinese coast; 1,000.

1917, Dec. 6—Mont Blanc, Imo; French ammunition ship and Belgian steamer collided in Halifax Harbor; 1,600.

1918, Apr. 25—Kiang-Kwan Chinese steamer sank in collision off Hankow; 500.

1918, July 12—Kawachi; Japanese battleship blew up in Tokayama Bay; 500.

1918, Oct. 25—Princess Sophia; Canadian steamer sank off Alaskan coast; 398.

1919, Jan. 17—Chaonia; French steamer lost in Straits of Messina, Italy; 460.

1919, Sept. 9—Valbanera; Spanish steamer lost off Florida coast; 500.

1921, Mar. 18—Hong Kong; steamer wrecked in South China Sea; 1,000.

1922, Aug. 26—Niitaka; Japanese cruiser sank in storm off Kamchatka, USSR; 300.

1927, Oct. 25—Principessa Mafalda; Italian steamer blew up, sank off Porto Seguro, Brazil; 314.

1934, Sept. 8—Morro Castle; U.S. steamer, Havana to New York, burned off Asbury Park, N.J.; 125.

1939, May 23—Squalus; U.S. submarine sank off Portsmouth, N.H.; 26.

1939, June 1—Thetis; British submarine, sank in Liverpool Bay; 99.

1942, Feb. 18—Truxton and Pollux; U.S. destroyer and cargo ship ran aground, sank off Newfoundland; 204.

1942, Oct. 2—Curacao; British cruiser sank after collision with liner Queen Mary; 335.

1947, Jan. 19—Himera; Greek steamer hit a mine off Athens; 392.

1947, Apr. 16—Grandcamp; French freighter exploded in Texas City, Tex., Harbor, starting fires; 510.

1952, Apr. 26—Hobson and Wasp; U.S. destroyer and aircraft carrier collided in Atlantic; 176.

1953, Jan. 31—Princess Victoria; British ferry foundered off northern Irish coast; 134.

1954, Sept. 26—Toya Maru; Japanese ferry sank in Tsugaru Strait, Japan; 1,172.

1956, July 26—Andrea Doria and Stockholm; Italian liner and Swedish liner collided off Nantucket; 51.

1957, July 14—Eshghabad; Soviet ship ran aground in Caspian Sea; 270.

1961, Apr. 8—Dara; British liner burned in Persian Gulf; 212.

1961, July 8—Save; Portuguese ship ran aground off Mozambique; 259.

1963, Apr. 10—Thresher; U.S. Navy atomic submarine sank in North Atlantic; 129.

1964, Feb. 10—Voyager, Melbourne; Australian destroyer sank after collision with Australian aircraft carrier Melbourne off New South Wales; 82.

1968, Jan. 25—Dakar; Israeli submarine vanished in Mediterranean; 69.

1968, Jan. 27—Minerve; French submarine vanished in Mediterranean; 52.

1968, May 21—Scorpion; U.S. nuclear submarine sank in Atlantic near Azores; 99.

1969, June 2—Evans; U.S. destroyer cut in half by Australian carrier Melbourne, S. China Sea; 74.

1970, Mar. 4—Eurydice; French submarine sank in Mediterranean near Toulon; 57.

1970, Dec. 15—Namyong-Ho; South Korean ferry sank in Korea Strait; 308.

1974, May 1— Motor launch capsized off Bangladesh; 250.

1974, Sept. 26— Soviet destroyer burned and sank in Black Sea; est. 200.

1975, Aug. 9— Two Chinese riverboats collided and sank near Canton; c.500.

1976, Oct. 20—George Prince and Frosta; ferryboat and Norwegian tanker collided on Mississippi R. at Luling, La.; 77.

1976, Dec. 25—Patria; Egyptian liner caught fire and sank in the Red Sea; c. 100.

1977, Jan. 11—Grand Zenith; Panamanian-registered tanker sank off Cape Cod, Mass.; 38.

1977, Jan. 17—Spanish freighter collided with launch in Barcelona, Spain harbor; 46.

1979, Jan. 8—Betelgeuse; French oil tanker exploded in Bantry Bay, Ire.; 50.

1979, Aug. 14—23 yachts competing in Fastnet yacht race sunk or abandoned during storm in S. Irish Sea; 18.

1980, Jan. 28—Blackthorn; U.S. Coast Guard vessel sunk in collision with oil tanker in Tampa Bay; 23.

1981, Jan. 27—Tamponas II; Indonesian passenger ship caught fire and sank in Java Sea; 580.

1981, May 26—Nimitz; U.S. Marine combat jet crashed on deck of U.S. aircraft carrier; 14.

Major Earthquakes

Magnitude of earthquakes (Mag.), distinct from deaths or damage caused, is measured on the Richter scale, on which each higher number represents a tenfold increase in energy measured in ground motion. Adopted in 1935, the scale has been applied in the following table to earthquakes as far back as reliable seismograms are available.

	Date	Place	Deaths	Mag.
526	May 20	Syria, Antioch	250,000	N.A.
856	....	Greece, Corinth	45,000	"
1057	....	China, Chihli	25,000	"
1268	....	Asia Minor, Cilicia	60,000	"
1290	Sept. 27	China, Chihli	100,000	"
1293	May 20	Japan, Kamakura	30,000	"
1531	Jan. 26	Portugal, Lisbon	30,000	"
1556	Jan. 24	China, Shaanxi	830,000	"
1667	Nov.	Caucasia, Shemaka	80,000	"
1693	Jan. 11	Italy, Catania	60,000	"
1730	Dec. 30	Japan, Hokkaido	137,000	"
1737	Oct. 11	India, Calcutta	300,000	"
1755	June 7	Northern Persia	40,000	"
1755	Nov. 1	Portugal, Lisbon	60,000	8.75*
1783	Feb. 4	Italy, Calabria	30,000	N.A.
1797	Feb. 4	Ecuador, Quito	41,000	N.A.
1822	Sept. 5	Asia Minor, Aleppo	22,000	N.A.
1828	Dec. 28	Japan, Echigo	30,000	"
1868	Aug. 13-15	Peru and Ecuador	40,000	"
1875	May 16	Venezuela, Colombia	16,000	"
1896	June 15	Japan, sea wave	27,120	"
1906	Apr. 18-19	Cal., San Francisco	452	8.3
1906	Aug. 16	Chile, Valparaiso	20,000	8.6
1908	Dec. 28	Italy, Messina	83,000	7.5
1915	Jan. 13	Italy, Avezzano	29,980	7.5
1920	Dec. 16	China, Gansu	100,000	8.6
1923	Sept. 1	Japan, Tokyo	99,330	8.3
1927	May 22	China, Nan-Shan	200,000	8.3
1932	Dec. 26	China, Gansu	70,000	7.6
1933	Mar. 2	Japan	2,990	8.9
1934	Jan. 15	India, Bihar-Nepal	10,700	8.4
1935	May 31	India, Quetta	30,000	7.5
1939	Jan. 24	Chile, Chillan	28,000	8.3
1939	Dec. 26	Turkey, Erzincan	30,000	7.9
1946	Dec. 21	Japan, Honshu	2,000	8.4
1948	June 28	Japan, Fukui	5,131	7.3
1949	Aug. 5	Ecuador, Pelileo	6,000	6.8
1950	Aug. 15	India, Assam	1,530	8.7
1953	Mar. 18	NW Turkey	1,200	7.2
1956	June 10-17	N. Afghanistan	2,000	7.7
1957	July 2	Northern Iran	2,500	7.4
1957	Dec. 13	Western Iran	2,000	7.1
1960	Feb. 29	Morocco, Agadir	12,000	5.8
1960	May 21-30	Southern Chile	5,000	8.3
1962	Sept. 1	Northwestern Iran	12,230	7.1
1963	July 26	Yugoslavia, Skopje	1,100	6.0
1964	Mar. 27	Alaska	114	8.5
1966	Aug. 19	Eastern Turkey	2,520	6.9
1968	Aug. 31	Northeastern Iran	12,000	7.4
1970	Mar. 28	Western Turkey	1,086	7.4
1970	May 31	Northern Peru	66,794	7.7
1971	Feb. 9	Cal., San Fernando Valley	65	6.5
1972	Apr. 10	Southern Iran	5,057	6.9
1972	Dec. 23	Nicaragua	5,000	6.2
1974	Dec. 28	Pakistan (9 towns)	5,200	6.3
1975	Sept. 6	Turkey (Lice, etc.)	2,312	6.8
1976	Feb. 4	Guatemala	22,778	7.5
1976	May 6	Northeast Italy	946	6.5
1976	June 26	New Guinea, Irian Jaya	443	7.1
1976	July 28	China, Tangshan	800,000	8.2
1976	Aug. 17	Philippines, Mindanao	8,000	7.8
1976	Nov. 24	Eastern Turkey	4,000	7.9
1977	Mar. 4	Romania, Bucharest, etc.	1,541	7.5
1977	Aug. 19	Indonesia	200	8.0
1977	Nov. 23	Northwestern Argentina	100	8.2
1978	June 12	Japan, Sendai	21	7.5
1978	Sept. 16	Northeast Iran	25,000	7.7
1979	Sept. 12	Indonesia	100	8.1
1979	Dec. 12	Colombia, Ecuador	800	7.9
1980	Oct. 10	Northwestern Algeria	4,500	7.3
1980	Nov. 23	Southern Italy	4,800	7.2

(*) estimated from earthquake intensity. (N.A.) not available.

Floods, Tidal Waves

Date		Location	Deaths
1887	....	Huang He River, China	900,000
1889	May 31	Johnstown, Pa.	2,200
1900	Sept. 8	Galveston, Tex.	5,000
1903	June 15	Heppner, Ore.	325
1911	....	Chang Jiang River, China	100,000
1913	Mar. 25-27	Ohio, Indiana	732
1915	Aug. 17	Galveston, Tex.	275
1928	Mar. 13	Collapse of St. Francis Dam, Santa Paula, Cal.	450
1928	Sept. 13	Lake Okeechobee, Fla.	2,000
1931	Aug.	Huang He River, China	3,700,000
1937	Jan. 22	Ohio, Miss. Valleys	250
1939	....	Northern China	200,000
1947	....	Honshu Island, Japan	1,900
1951	Aug.	Manchuria	1,800
1953	Jan. 31	Western Europe	2,000
1954	Aug. 17	Farahzad, Iran	2,000
1955	Oct. 7-12	India, Pakistan	1,700
1959	Nov. 1	Western Mexico	2,000
1959	Dec. 2	Frejus, France	412
1960	Oct. 10	Bangladesh	6,000
1960	Oct. 31	Bangladesh	4,000
1962	Feb. 17	German North Sea coast	343
1962	Sept. 27	Barcelona, Spain	445
1963	Oct. 9	Dam collapse, Vaiont, Italy	1,800
1966	Nov. 4-6	Florence, Venice, Italy	113
1967	Jan. 18-24	Eastern Brazil	894
1967	Mar. 19	Rio de Janeiro, Brazil	436
1968	Aug. 7-14	Gujarat State, India	1,000
1968	Oct. 7	Northeastern India	780
1969	Mar. 17	Mundau Valley, Alagoas, Brazil	218
1969	Aug. 25	Western Virginia	189
1969	Sept. 15	South Korea	250
1969	Oct. 1-8	Tunisia	500
1970	May 20	Central Romania	160
1970	July 22	Himalayas, India	500
1971	Feb. 26	Rio de Janeiro, Brazil	130
1972	Feb. 26	Buffalo Creek, W. Va.	118
1972	June 9	Rapid City, S.D.	236
1972	Aug. 7	Luzon Is., Philippines	454
1974	Mar. 29	Tubaro, Brazil	1,000
1974	Aug. 12	Monty-Long, Bangladesh	2,500
1975	Jan. 11	Southern Thailand	131
1976	June 5	Teton Dam collapse, Ida.	11
1976	July 31	Big Thompson Canyon, Col.	130
1976	Nov. 17	East Java, Indonesia	136
1977	July 19-20	Johnstown, Pa.	68
1978	June-Sept.	Northern India	1,200
1979	Jan.-Feb.	Brazil	204
1979	July	Lomblem Is., Indonesia	539
1979	Aug. 11	Morvi, India	5,000-15,000
1980	Feb. 13-22	So. Cal., Ariz.	26
1981	Apr.	Northern China	550
1981	July	Sichuan, Hubei Prov., China	1,300
1982	Jan. 23	Nr. Lima, Peru	600

Some Major Tornadoes Since 1925

Source: National Climatic Center, NOAA, U.S. Commerce Department

Date			Place	Deaths
1925	Mar.	18	Mo., Ill. Ind.	689
1926	Nov.	25	Belleville to Portland, Ark.	53
1927	Apr.	12	Rock Springs, Tex.	74
1927	May	9	Arkansas, Poplar Bluff, Mo.	92
1927	Sept.	29	St. Louis, Mo.	72
1929	Apr.	25	SE-Central Ga.	40
1930	May	6	Hill & Ellis Co., Tex.	41
1932	Mar.	21	Ala. (series of tornadoes)	268

Date			Place	Deaths
1936	Apr.	5	Tupelo, Miss.	216
1936	Apr.	6	Gainesville, Ga.	203
1938	Sept.	29	Charleston, S.C.	32
1942	Mar.	16	Central to NE Miss.	75
1942	Apr.	27	Rogers & Mayes Co., Okla.	52
1944	June	23	Oh., Pa., W. Va., Md.	150
1945	Apr.	12	Okla.-Ark.	102
1947	Apr.	9	Tex., Okla. & Kan.	169
1948	Mar.	19	Bunker Hill & Gillespie, Ill.	33
1949	Jan.	3	La. & Ark.	58
1952	Mar.	21	Ark., Mo., Tenn. (series)	208
1953	May	11	Waco, Tex.	114
1953	June	8	Flint to Lakeport, Mich.	116
1953	June	9	Worcester and vicinity, Mass.	90
1953	Dec.	5	Vicksburg, Miss.	38
1955	May	25	Udall, Kan.	80
1957	May	20	Kan., Mo.	48
1958	June	4	Northwestern Wisconsin	30
1959	Feb.	10	St. Louis, Mo.	21
1960	May	5, 6	SE Oklahoma, Arkansas	30
1965	Apr.	11	Ind., Ill., Oh., Mich., Wis.	271
1966	Mar.	3	Jackson, Miss.	57
1966	Mar.	3	Mississippi, Alabama	61
1967	Apr.	21	Illinois	33
1968	May	15	Arkansas	34
1969	Jan.	23	Mississippi	32
1971	Feb.	21	Mississippi delta	110
1973	May	26-7	South, Midwest (series)	47
1974	Apr.	3-4	Ala., Ga., Tenn., Ky., Oh.	350
1977	Apr.	1	Southeast Bangladesh	600
1977	Apr.	4	Ala., Miss., Ga.	22
1978	Apr.	16	Orissa, India	500
1979	Apr.	10	Tex., Okla.	60
1980	June	3	Grand Island, Neb. (series)	4
1982	Mar.	2-4	South, Midwest (series)	17
1982	May	29	So. Ill.	15

Hurricanes, Typhoons, Blizzards, Other Storms

Names of hurricanes and typhoons in italics—H.—hurricane; T.—typhoon

Date	Location	Deaths
1888 Mar. 11-14	Blizzard, Eastern U.S.	400
1900 Sept. 8	H., Galveston, Tex.	6,000
1926 Sept. 16-22	H., Fla., Ala.	372
1926 Oct. 20	H., Cuba	600
1928 Sept. 12-17	H., W. Indies, Fla.	4,000
1930 Sept. 3	H., San Domingo	2,000
1938 Sept. 21	H., New England	600
1942 Oct. 15-16	H., Bengal, India	11,000
1944 Sept. 12-16	H., N.C. to New Eng.	389
1953 Sept. 25-27	T., Vietnam, Japan	1,300
1954 Aug. 30	H. *Carol,* Northeast U.S.	68
1954 Oct. 12-13	H. *Hazel,* Eastern, U.S., Haiti	347
1955 Aug. 12-13	H. *Connie,* Carolinas, Va., Md.	43
1955 Aug. 18-19	H. *Diane,* Eastern U.S.	400
1955 Sept. 19	H. *Hilda,* Mexico	200
1955 Sept. 22-28	H. *Janet,* Caribbean	500
1956 Feb. 1-29	Blizzard, Western Europe	1,000
1957 June 27-30	H. *Audrey,* La., Tex.	430
1958 Feb. 15-16	Blizzard, NE U.S.	171
1959 Sept. 17-19	T. *Sarah,* Far East	2,000
1959 Sept. 26-27	T. *Vera,* Honshu, Japan	4,466
1960 Sept. 4-12	H. *Donna,* Caribbean, E. U.S.	148
1961 Oct. 31	H. *Hattie,* Br. Honduras	400
1962 Feb. 17	Flooding, German Coast	343
1962 Sept. 27	Flooding, Barcelona, Spain	445
1963 May 28-29	Windstorm, Bangladesh	22,000
1963 Oct. 4-8	H. *Flora,* Cuba, Haiti	6,000
1964 Oct. 4-7	H. *Hilda,* La., Miss., Ga.	38
1964 June 30	T. *Winnie,* N. Philippines	107
1964 Sept. 5	T. *Ruby,* Hong Kong and China	735
1964 Sept. 14	Flooding, central S. Korea	563
1964 Nov. 12	Flooding, S. Vietnam	7,000
1965 May 11-12	Windstorm, Bangladesh	17,000
1965 June 1-2	Windstorm, Bangladesh	30,000
1965 Sept. 7-10	H. *Betsy,* Fla., Miss., La.	74
1965 Dec. 15	Windstorm, Bangladesh	10,000
1966 June 4-10	H. *Alma,* Honduras, SE U.S.	51
1966 Sept. 24-30	H. *Inez,* Carib., Fla., Mex.	293
1967 July 9	T. *Billie,* Japan	347
1967 Sept. 5-23	H. *Beulah,* Carib., Mex., Tex.	54
1967 Dec. 12-20	Blizzard, Southwest, U.S.	51
1968 Nov. 18-28	T. *Nina,* Philippines	63
1969 Aug. 17-18	H. *Camille,* Miss., La.	256
1970 July 30-Aug. 5	H. *Celia,* Cuba, Fla., Tex.	31
1970 Aug. 20-21	H. *Dorothy,* Martinique	42
1970 Sept. 15	T. *Georgia,* Philippines	300
1970 Oct. 14	T. *Sening,* Philippines	583
1970 Oct. 15	T. *Titang,* Philippines	526
1970 Nov. 13	Cyclone, Bangladesh	(est.) 300,000
1971 Aug. 1	T. *Rose,* Hong Kong	130
1972 June 19-29	H. *Agnes,* Fla. to N.Y.	118
1972 Dec. 3	T. *Theresa,* Philippines	169
1973 June-Aug.	Monsoon rains in India	1,217
1974 June 11	Storm *Dinah,* Luzon Is., Philip.	71
1974 July 11	T. *Gilda,* Japan, S. Korea	108
1974 Sept. 19-20	H. *Fifi,* Honduras	2,000
1974 Dec. 25	Cyclone leveled Darwin, Aus.	50
1975 Sept. 13-27	H. *Eloise,* Caribbean, NE U.S.	71
1976 May 20	T. *Olga,* floods, Philippines	215
1977 July 25, 31	T. *Thelma,* T. *Vera,* Taiwan	39
1978 Oct. 27	T. *Rita,* Philippines	c. 400
1979 Aug. 30-Sept. 7	H. *David,* Caribbean, E U.S.	1,100
1980 Aug. 4-11	H. *Allen,* Caribbean, Texas	272
1981 Nov. 25	T. *Irma,* Luzon Is., Philip.	176

Record Oil Spills

Name, place	Date	Cause	Tons
Ixtoc I oil well, southern Gulf of Mexico	June 3, 1979	Blowout	600,000
Atlantic Empress & Aegean Captain, off Trinidad & Tobago	July 19, 1979	Collision	300,000
Amoco Cadiz, near Portsall, France	March 16, 1978	Grounding	223,000
Torrey Canyon, off Land's End, England	March 18, 1967	Grounding	119,000
Sea Star, Gulf of Oman	Dec. 19, 1972	Collision	115,000
Urquiola, La Coruna, Spain	May 12, 1976	Grounding	100,000
Hawaiian Patriot, northern Pacific	Feb. 25, 1977	Fire	99,000
Othello, Tralhavet Bay, Sweden	March 20, 1970	Collision	60,000-100,000
Jacob Maersk, Porto do Leixoes, Portugal	Jan. 29, 1975	Grounding	84,000
Wafra, Cape Agulhas, South Africa	Feb. 27, 1971	Grounding	63,000
Epic Colacotroni, Caribbean	May, 1975	Grounding	57,000

Other Notable Oil Spills

Source: Conservation Division, U.S. Geological Survey, U.S. Interior Department

Name, place	Date	Cause	Gallons
World Glory, off South Africa	June 13, 1968	Hull failure	13,524,000
Keo, off Massachusetts	Nov. 5, 1969	Hull failure	8,820,000
Storage tank, Sewaren, N.J.	Nov. 4, 1969	Tank rupture	8,400,000
Ekofisk oil field, North Sea	Apr. 22, 1977	Well blowout	8,200,000
Argo Merchant, Nantucket, Mass.	Dec. 15, 1976	Grounding	7,700,000
Pipeline, West Delta, La.	Oct. 15, 1967	Dragging anchor	6,720,000
Tanker off Japan	Nov. 30, 1971	Ship broke in half	6,258,000

Explosions

Date			Location	Deaths
1910	Oct.	1	Los Angeles Times Bldg.	21
1913	Mar.	7	Dynamite, Baltimore harbor	55
1915	Sept.	27	Gasoline tank car, Ardmore, Okla.	47
1917	Apr.	10	Munitions plant, Eddystone, Pa.	133
1917	Dec.	6	Halifax Harbor, Canada	1,654
1918	May	18	Chemical plant, Oakdale, Pa.	193
1918	July	2	Explosives, Split Rock, N.Y.	50
1918	Oct.	4	Shell plant, Morgan Station, N.J.	64
1919	May	22	Food plant, Cedar Rapids, Ia.	44
1920	Sept.	16	Wall Street, New York, bomb	30
1924	Jan.	3	Food plant, Pekin, Ill.	42
1928	April	13	Dance hall, West Plains, Mo.	40
1937	Mar.	18	New London, Tex., school	294
1940	Sept.	11	Hercules Powder, Kenvil, N.J.	51
1942	June	5	Ordnance plant, Elwood, Ill.	49
1944	Apr.	14	Bombay, India, harbor	700
1944	July	17	Port Chicago, Cal., pier	322
1944	Oct.	21	Liquid gas tank, Cleveland	135
1947	Apr.	16	Texas City, Tex., pier	561
1948	July	28	Farben works, Ludwigshafen, Ger.	184
1950	May	19	Munitions barges, S. Amboy, N. J.	30
1956	Aug.	7	Dynamite trucks, Cali, Colombia	1,100
1958	Apr.	18	Sunken munitions ship, Okinawa	40
1958	May	22	Nike missiles, Leonardo, N.J.	10
1959	Apr.	10	World War II bomb, Philippines	38
1959	June	28	Rail tank cars, Meldrin, Ga.	25
1959	Aug.	7	Dynamite truck, Roseburg, Ore.	13
1959	Nov.	2	Jamuri Bazar, India, explosives	46
1959	Dec.	13	Dortmund, Ger., 2 apt. bldgs.	26
1960	Mar.	4	Belgian munitions ship, Havana	100
1960	Oct.	25	Gas, Windsor, Ont., store	11
1962	Jan.	16	Gas pipeline, Edson, Alberta, Can.	8
1962	Oct.	3	Telephone Co. office, N. Y. City	23
1963	Jan.	2	Packing plant, Terre Haute, Ind.	16
1963	Mar.	9	Dynamite plant, S. Africa	45
1963	Mar.	9	Steel plant, Belecke, W. Germany	19
1963	Aug.	13	Explosives dump, Gauhiti, India	32
1963	Oct.	31	State Fair Coliseum, Indianapolis	73
1964	July	23	Bone, Algeria, harbor munitions	100
1965	Mar.	4	Gas pipeline, Natchitoches, La.	17
1965	Aug.	9	Missile silo, Searcy, Ark.	53
1965	Oct.	21	Bridge, Tila Bund, Pakistan	80
1965	Oct.	30	Cartagena, Colombia	48
1965	Nov.	24	Armory, Keokuk, Ia.	20
1966	Oct.	13	Chemical plant, La Salle, Que.	11
1967	Feb.	17	Chemical plant, Hawthorne, N.J.	11
1967	Dec.	25	Apartment bldg., Moscow	20
1968	Apr.	6	Sports store, Richmond, Ind.	43
1970	Apr.	8	Subway construction, Osaka, Japan	73
1971	June	24	Tunnel, Sylmar, Cal.	17
1971	June	28	School, fireworks, Pueblo, Mex.	13
1971	Oct.	21	Shopping center, Glasgow, Scot.	20
1973	Feb.	10	Liquified gas tank, Staten Is., N.Y.	40
1975	Dec.	27	Chasnala, India, mine	431
1976	Apr.	13	Lapua, Finland, munitions works	45
1977	Nov.	11	Freight train, Iri, S. Korea	57
1977	Dec.	22	Grain elevator, Westwego, La.	35
1978	Feb.	24	Derailed tank car, Waverly, Tenn.	12
1978	July	11	Propylene tank truck, Spanish coastal campsite	150
1980	Oct.	23	School, Ortuella, Spain	64
1981	Feb.	13	Sewer system, Louisville, Ky.	0
1982	Apr.	7	Tanker truck, tunnel, Oakland, Cal.	7
1982	Apr.	25	Antiques exhibition, Todi, Italy	33

Fires

Date			Location	Deaths
1845	May		Theater, Canton, China	1,670
1871	Oct.	8	Chicago, $196 million loss	250
1871	Oct.	8	Peshtigo, Wis., forest fire	1,182
1876	Dec.	5	Brooklyn (N.Y.), theater	295
1877	June	20	St. John, N. B., Canada	100
1881	Dec.	8	Ring Theater, Vienna	850
1887	May	25	Opera Comique, Paris	200
1887	Sept.	4	Exeter, England, theater	200
1894	Sept.	1	Hinckley, Minn., forest fire	413
1897	May	4	Charity bazaar, Paris	150
1900	June	30	Hoboken, N. J., docks	326
1902	Sept.	20	Church, Birmingham, Ala.	115
1903	Dec.	30	Iroquois Theater, Chicago	602
1908	Jan.	13	Rhoads Theater, Boyertown, Pa.	170
1908	Mar.	4	School, Collinwood, Oh.	176
1911	Mar.	25	Triangle factory, N. Y. City	145
1913	Oct.	14	Colliery, Mid Glamorgan, Wales	439
1918	Apr.	13	Norman Okla., state hospital	38
1918	Oct.	12	Cloquet, Minn., forest fire	400
1919	June	20	Mayaguez Theater, San Juan	150
1923	May	17	School, Camden, S. C.	76
1924	Dec.	24	School, Hobart, Okla.	35
1929	May	15	Clinic, Cleveland, Oh.	125
1930	Apr.	21	Penitentiary, Columbus, Oh.	320
1931	July	24	Pittsburgh, Pa., home for aged	48
1934	Dec.	11	Hotel Kerns, Lansing, Mich.	34
1938	May	16	Atlanta, Ga., Terminal Hotel	35
1940	Apr.	23	Dance hall, Natchez, Miss.	198
1942	Nov.	28	Cocoanut Grove, Boston	491
1942			Hostel, St. John's, Newfoundland	100
1943	Sept.	7	Gulf Hotel, Houston	55
1944	July	6	Ringling Circus, Hartford	168
1946	June	5	LaSalle Hotel, Chicago	61
1946	Dec.	7	Winecoff Hotel, Atlanta	119
1946	Dec.	12	New York, ice plant, tenement	37
1949	Apr.	5	Hospital, Effingham, Ill.	77
1950	Jan.	7	Davenport, Ia., Mercy Hospital	41
1953	Mar.	29	Largo, Fla., nursing home	35
1953	Apr.	16	Chicago, metalworking plant	35
1957	Feb.	17	Home for aged, Warrenton, Mo.	72
1958	Mar.	19	New York City loft building	24
1958	Dec.	1	Parochial school, Chicago	95
1958	Dec.	16	Store, Bogota, Colombia	83
1959	June	23	Resort hotel, Stalheim, Norway	34
1960	Mar.	12	Pusan, Korea, chemical plant	68
1960	July	14	Mental hospital, Guatemala City	225
1960	Nov.	13	Movie theater, Amude, Syria	152
1961	Jan.	6	Thomas Hotel, San Francisco	20
1961	May	15	Tenement, Hong Kong	25
1961	Dec.	8	Hospital, Hartford, Conn.	16
1961	Dec.	17	Circus, Niteroi, Brazil	323
1963	May	4	Theater, Diourbel, Senegal	64
1963	Nov.	18	Surfside Hotel, Atlantic City, N.J.	25
1963	Nov.	23	Rest home, Fitchville, Oh.	63
1963	Dec.	29	Roosevelt Hotel, Jacksonville, Fla.	22
1964	May	8	Apartment building, Manila	30
1964	Dec.	18	Nursing home, Fountaintown, Ind.	20
1965	Mar.	1	Apartment, LaSalle, Canada	28
1966	Mar.	11	Numata, Japan, 2 ski resorts	31
1966	Aug.	13	Melbourne, Australia, hotel	29
1966	Sept.	12	Anchorage, Alaska, hotel	14
1966	Oct.	17	N. Y. City bldg. (firemen)	12
1966	Dec.	7	Erzurum, Turkey, barracks	68
1967	Feb.	7	Restaurant, Montgomery, Ala.	25
1967	May	22	Store, Brussels, Belgium	322
1967	July	16	State prison, Jay, Fla.	37
1968	Jan.	9	Brooklyn, N. Y., tenement	13
1968	Feb.	26	Shrewsbury, England, hospital	22
1968	May	11	Vijayawada, India, wedding hall	58
1968	Nov.	18	Glasgow, Scotland, factory	24
1969	Jan.	26	Victoria Hotel, Dunnville, Ont.	13
1969	Dec.	2	Nursing home, Notre Dame, Can.	54
1970	Jan.	9	Nursing home, Marietta, Oh.	27
1970	Mar.	20	Hotel, Seattle, Wash.	19
1970	Nov.	1	Dance hall, Grenoble, France	145
1970	Nov.	5	Nursing home, Pointe-aux-Trembles, Que.	17
1970	Dec.	20	Hotel, Tucson, Arizona	28
1971	Mar.	6	Psychiatric clinic, Burghoezli, Switzerland	28
1971	Apr.	20	Hotel, Bangkok, Thailand	24
1971	Oct.	19	Nursing home, Honesdale, Pa.	15
1971	Dec.	25	Hotel, Seoul, So. Korea	162
1972	May	13	Osaka, Japan, nightclub	116
1972	July	5	Sherborne, England, hospital	30
1973	Feb.	6	Paris, France, school	21
1973	Nov.	6	Fukui, Japan, train	28
1973	Nov.	29	Kumamoto, Japan, department store	107
1973	Dec.	2	Seoul, Korea, theater	50
1974	Feb.	1	Sao Paulo, Brazil, bank building	189
1974	June	30	Port Chester, N. Y., discotheque	24

Date			Location	Deaths
1974	Nov.	3	Seoul, So. Korea, hotel discotheque	88
1975	Dec.	12	Mina, Saudi Arabia, tent city	138
1976	Oct.	24	Bronx, N.Y., social club	25
1977	Feb.	25	Rossiya Hotel, Moscow	45
1977	May	28	Southgate, Ky., nightclub	164
1977	June	9	Abidjan, Ivory Coast nightclub	41
1977	June	26	Columbia, Tenn., jail	42
1977	Nov.	14	Manila, PI, hotel	47
1978	Jan.	28	Kansas City, Coates House Hotel	16
1979	Dec.	31	Chapais, Quebec, social club	42
1980	May	20	Kingston, Jamaica, nursing home	157
1980	Nov.	21	MGM Grand Hotel, Las Vegas	84
1980	Dec.	4	Stouffer Inn, Harrison, N.Y.	26
1981	Jan.	9	Keansburg, N.J., boarding home	30
1981	Feb.	10	Las Vegas Hilton	8
1981	Feb.	14	Dublin, Ireland, discotheque	44

Major U.S. Railroad Wrecks

Source: Office of Safety, Federal Railroad Administration

Date			Location	Deaths
1876	Dec.	29	Ashtabula, Oh.	92
1880	Aug.	11	Mays Landing, N. J.	40
1887	Aug.	10	Chatsworth, Ill.	81
1888	Oct.	10	Mud Run, Pa.	55
1896	July	30	Atlantic City, N. J.	60
1903	Dec.	23	Laurel Run, Pa.	53
1904	Aug.	7	Eden, Col.	96
1904	Sept.	24	New Market Tenn.	56
1906	Mar.	16	Florence, Col.	35
1906	Oct.	28	Atlantic City, N. J.	40
1906	Dec.	30	Washington, D. C.	53
1907	Jan.	2	Volland, Kan.	33
1907	Jan.	19	Fowler, Ind.	29
1907	Feb.	16	New York, N.Y.	22
1907	Feb.	23	Colton, Cal.	26
1907	July	20	Salem, Mich.	33
1910	Mar.	1	Wellington, Wash.	96
1910	Mar.	21	Green Mountain, Ia.	55
1911	Aug.	25	Manchester, N. Y.	29
1912	July	4	East Corning, N. Y.	39
1912	July	5	Ligonier, Pa.	23
1914	Aug.	5	Tipton Ford, Mo.	43
1914	Sept.	15	Lebanon, Mo.	28
1916	Mar.	29	Amherst, Oh.	27
1917	Feb.	27	Mount Union, Pa.	20
1917	Sept.	28	Kellyville, Okla.	23
1917	Dec.	20	Shepherdsville, Ky.	46
1918	June	22	Ivanhoe, Ind.	68
1918	July	9	Nashville, Tenn.	101
1918	Nov.	2	Brooklyn, N. Y., Malbone St. Tunnel	97
1919	Jan.	12	South Byron, N. Y.	22
1919	July	1	Dunkirk, N. Y.	12
1919	Dec.	20	Onawa, Maine	23
1921	Feb.	27	Porter, Ind.	37
1921	Dec.	5	Woodmont, Pa.	27
1922	Aug.	5	Sulphur Spring, Mo.	34
1922	Dec.	13	Humble, Tex.	22
1925	June	16	Hackettstown, N. J.	50
1925	Oct.	27	Victoria, Miss.	21
1926	Sept.	5	Waco, Col.	30
1928	Aug.	24	I.R.T. subway, Times Sq., N. Y.	18
1938	June	19	Saugus, Mont.	47
1939	Aug.	12	Harney, Nev.	24
1940	Aug.	19	Little Falls, N. Y.	31
1940	July	31	Cuyahoga Falls, Oh.	43
1943	Aug.	29	Wayland, N. Y.	27
1943	Sept.	6	Frankford Junction, Philadelphia, Pa.	79
1943	Dec.	16	Between Rennert and Buie, N. C.	72
1944	July	6	High Bluff, Tenn.	35
1944	Aug.	4	Near Stockton, Ga.	47
1944	Sept.	14	Dewey, Ind.	29
1944	Dec.	31	Bagley, Utah	50
1945	Aug.	9	Michigan, N. D.	34
1946	Apr.	25	Naperville, Ill.	45
1947	Feb.	18	Gallitzin, Pa.	24
1950	Feb.	17	Rockville Centre, N. Y.	31
1950	Sept.	11	Coshocton, Oh.	33
1950	Nov.	22	Richmond Hill, N. Y.	79
1951	Feb.	6	Woodbridge, N. J.	84
1951	Nov.	12	Wyuta, Wyo.	17
1951	Nov.	25	Woodstock, Ala.	17
1953	Mar.	27	Conneaut, Oh.	21
1956	Jan.	22	Los Angeles, Cal.	30
1956	Feb.	28	Swampscott, Mass.	13
1956	Sept.	5	Springer, N. M.	20
1957	June	11	Vroman, Col.	12
1958	Sept.	15	Elizabethport, N. J.	48
1960	Mar.	14	Bakersfield, Cal.	14
1962	July	28	Steelton, Pa.	19
1966	Dec.	28	Everett, Mass.	13
1971	June	10	Salem, Ill.	11
1972	Oct.	30	Chicago, Ill.	45
1977	Feb.	4	Chicago, Ill., elevated train	11

World's worst train wreck occurred Dec. 12, 1917, Modane, France, passenger train derailed, 543 killed.

Some Notable Aircraft Disasters Since 1937

Date			Aircraft	Site of accident	Deaths
1937	May	6	German zeppelin Hindenburg	Burned at mooring, Lakehurst, N.J.	36
1944	Aug.	23	U.S. Air Force B-24	Hit school, Freckelton, England	76[1]
1945	July	28	U.S. Army B-25	Hit Empire State bldg., N.Y.C.	14[1]
1947	May	30	Eastern Air Lines DC-4	Crashed near Port Deposit, Md.	53
1952	Dec.	20	U.S. Air Force C-124	Fell, burned, Moses Lake, Wash.	87
1953	Mar.	3	Canadian Pacific Comet Jet	Karachi, Pakistan	11[2]
1953	June	18	U.S. Air Force C-124	Crashed, burned near Tokyo	129
1955	Nov.	1	United Air Lines DC-6B	Exploded, crashed near Longmont, Col.	44[3]
1956	June	20	Venezuelan Super-Constellation	Crashed in Atlantic off Asbury Park, N.J.	74
1956	June	30	TWA Super-Const., United DC-7	Collided over Grand Canyon, Arizona	128
1960	Dec.	16	United DC-8 jet, TWA Super-Const.	Collided over N.Y. City	134[4]
1962	Mar.	4	Br. Caledonian Airlines DC-7C	Crashed near Douala, Cameroon	111
1962	Mar.	16	Flying Tiger Super-Const.	Vanished in Western Pacific	107
1962	June	3	Air France Boeing 707 jet	Crashed on takeoff from Paris	130
1962	June	22	Air France Boeing 707 jet	Crashed in storm, Guadeloupe, W.I.	113
1963	June	3	Chartered Northw. Airlines DC-7	Crashed in Pacific off British Columbia	101
1963	Nov.	29	Trans-Canada Airlines DC-8F	Crashed after takeoff from Montreal	118
1965	May	20	Pakistani Boeing 720-B	Crashed at Cairo, Egypt, airport	121
1966	Jan.	24	Air India Boeing 707 jetliner	Crashed on Mont Blanc, France-Italy	117
1966	Feb.	4	All-Nippon Boeing 727	Plunged into Tokyo Bay	133
1966	Mar.	5	BOAC Boeing 707 jetliner	Crashed on Mount Fuji, Japan	124
1966	Dec.	24	U.S. military-chartered CL-44	Crashed into village in So. Vietnam	129[1]
1967	Apr.	20	Swiss Britannia turboprop	Crashed at Nicosia, Cyprus	126
1967	July	19	Piedmont Boeing 727, Cessna 310	Collided in air, Hendersonville, N.C.	82
1968	Apr.	20	S. African Airways Boeing 707	Crashed on takeoff, Windhoek, SW Africa	122
1968	May	3	Braniff International Electra	Crashed in storm near Dawson, Tex.	85
1969	Mar.	16	Venezuelan DC-9	Crashed after takeoff from Maracaibo, Venezuela	155[5]
1969	Mar.	20	United Arab Ilyushin-18	Crashed at Aswan airport, Egypt	87
1969	June	4	Mexican Boeing 727	Rammed into mountain near Monterrey, Mexico	79
1969	Dec.	8	Olympia Airways DC-6B	Crashed near Athens in storm	93
1970	Feb.	15	Dominican DC-9	Crashed into sea on takeoff from Santo Domingo	102

Date	Aircraft	Site of accident	Deaths
1970 July 3	British chartered jetliner	Crashed near Barcelona, Spain	112
1970 July 5	Air Canada DC-8	Crashed near Toronto International Airport	108
1970 Aug. 9	Peruvian turbojet	Crashed after takeoff from Cuzco, Peru	101[1]
1970 Nov. 14	Southern Airways DC-9	Crashed in mountains near Huntington, W. Va.	75[6]
1971 July 30	All-Nippon Boeing 727 and Japanese Air Force F-86	Collided over Morioka, Japan	162[7]
1971 Aug. 11	Soviet Aeroflot Tupolev-104	Crashed at Irkutsk airport, USSR	97
1971 Sept. 4	Alaska Airlines Boeing 727	Crashed into mountain near Juneau, Alaska	111
1972 Aug. 14	E. German Ilyushin-62	Crashed on take-off East Berlin	156
1972 Oct. 13	Aeroflot Ilyushin-62	E. German airline crashed near Moscow	176
1972 Dec. 3	Chartered Spanish airliner	Crashed on take-off, Canary Islands	155
1972 Dec. 29	Eastern Airlines Lockheed Tristar	Crashed on approach to Miami Int'l. Airport	101
1973 Jan. 22	Chartered Boeing 707	Burst into flames during landing, Kano Airport, Nigeria	176
1973 Apr. 10	British Vanguard turboprop	Crashed during snowstorm at Basel, Switzerland	104
1973 June 3	Soviet Supersonic TU-144	Exploded in air near Goussainville, France	14[8]
1973 July 11	Brazilian Boeing 707	Crashed on approach to Orly Airport, Paris	122
1973 July 31	Delta Airlines jetliner	Crashed, landing in fog at Logan Airport, Boston	89
1973 Dec. 23	French Caravelle jet	Crashed in Morocco	106
1974 Jan. 31	Pan American Boeing 707 jet	Crashed in Pago Pago, American Samoa	96
1974 Mar. 3	Turkish DC-10 jet	Crashed at Ermenonville near Paris	346
1974 Apr. 23	Pan American 707 jet	Crashed in Bali, Indonesia	107
1974 Sept. 8	TWA 707 jet	Crashed in Ionian Sea off Greece, after bomb explosion Arab guerrilla group claimed responsibility	80
1974 Dec. 1	TWA-727	Crashed in storm, Upperville, Va.	92
1974 Dec. 4	Dutch-chartered DC-8	Crashed in storm near Colombo, Sri Lanka	191
1975 Apr. 4	Air Force Galaxy C-58	Crashed near Saigon, So. Vietnam, after takeoff with load of orphans	172
1975 June 24	Eastern Airlines 727 jet	Crashed in storm, JFK Airport, N.Y. City	113
1975 Aug. 3	Chartered 707	Hit mountainside, Agadir, Morocco	168
1976 Sept. 10	British Airways Trident, Yugoslav DC-9	Collided near Zagreb, Yugoslavia	176
1976 Sept. 19	Turkish 727	Hit mountain, southern Turkey	155
1976 Oct. 6	Cuban DC-8	Crashed near Barbados after bomb explosion	73
1976 Oct. 12	Indian Caravelle jet	Crashed after takeoff, Bombay airport	95
1976 Oct. 13	Bolivian 707 cargo jet	Crashed in Santa Cruz, Bolivia	100[9]
1976 Dec. 28	Aeroflot TU-104	Crashed at Moscow's Sheremetyevo airport	72
1977 Jan. 13	Aeroflot TU-104	Exploded and crashed at Alma-Ata, Central Asia	90
1977 Mar. 27	KLM 747, Pan American 747	Collided on runway, Tenerife, Canary Islands	581
1977 Nov. 19	TAP Boeing 727	Crashed on Madeira	130
1977 Dec. 4	Malaysian Boeing 737	Hijacked, then exploded in mid-air over Straits of Johore	100
1977 Dec. 13	U.S. DC-3	Crashed after takeoff at Evansville, Ind.	29[10]
1978 Jan. 1	Air India 747	Exploded, crashed into sea off Bombay	213
1978 Mar. 16	Bulgarian TU-134	Crashed at Vratsa, Bulgaria	73
1978 Sept. 25	Boeing 727, Cessna 172	Collided in air, San Diego, Cal.	150
1978 Nov. 15	Chartered DC-8	Crashed near Colombo, Sri Lanka	183
1979 May 25	American Airlines DC-10	Crashed after takeoff at O'Hare Intl. Airport, Chicago	275[11]
1979 Aug. 17	Two Soviet Aeroflot jetliners	Collided over Ukraine	173
1979 Oct. 31	Western Airlines DC-10	Mexico City Airport	74
1979 Nov. 26	Pakistani Boeing 707	Crashed near Jidda, Saudi Arabia	156
1979 Nov. 28	New Zealand DC-10	Crashed into mountain in Antarctica	257
1980 Mar. 14	Polish Ilyushin 62	Crashed making emergency landing, Warsaw	87[12]
1980 Aug. 19	Saudi Arabian Tristar	Burned after emergency landing, Riyadh	301
1981 Dec. 1	Yugoslavian DC-9	Crashed into mountain in Corsica	174
1982 Jan. 13	Air Florida Boeing 737	Crashed into Potomac River after takeoff	78
1982 July 9	Pan-Am Boeing 727	Crashed after takeoff in Kenner, La.	153[13]

(1) Including those on the ground and in buildings. (2) First fatal crash of commercial jet plane. (3) Caused by bomb planted by John G. Graham in insurance plot to kill his mother, a passenger. (4) Including all 128 aboard the planes and 6 on ground. (5) Killed 84 on plane and 71 on ground. (6) Including 43 Marshall U. football players and coaches. (7) Airliner-fighter crash, pilot of fighter parachuted to safety, was arrested for negligence. (8) First supersonic plane crash killed 6 crewmen and 8 on the ground; there were no passengers. (9) Crew of 3 killed; 97, mostly children, killed on ground. (10) Including U. of Evansville basketball team. (11) Highest death toll in U.S. aviation history. (12) Including 22 members of U.S. boxing team. (13) Including 8 on ground.

Principal U.S. Mine Disasters

Source: Bureau of Mines, U.S. Interior Department

Note: Prior to 1968, only disasters with losses of 50 or more lives are listed; since 1968, all disasters in which 5 or more people were killed are listed. Only fatalities to mining company employees are included. All Bituminous-coal mines unless otherwise noted.

Date	Location	Deaths
1855 Mar.	Coalfield, Va.	55
1867 Apr. 3	Winterpock, Va.	69
1869[1] Sept. 6	Plymouth, Pa.	110
1883 Feb. 16	Braidwood, Ill.	69
1884 Jan. 24	Crested Butte, Col.	59
1884 Mar. 13	Pocahontas, Va.	112
1891 Jan. 27	Mount Pleasant, Pa.	109
1892 Jan. 7	Krebs, Okla.	100
1895 Mar. 20	Red Canyon, Wy.	60
1896[1] June 28	Pittston, Pa.	58
1900 Jan. 1	Scofield, Ut.	200
1902 May 19	Coal Creek, Tenn.	184
1902 July 10	Johnstown, Pa.	112
1903 June 30	Hanna, Wy.	169
1904 Jan. 25	Cheswick, Pa.	179
1905 Feb. 20	Virginia City, Ala.	112
1907 Jan. 29	Stuart W. Va.	84
1907 Dec. 6	Monongah, W. Va.	361
1907 Dec. 16	Yolande, Ala.	57
1907 Dec. 19	Jacobs Creek, Pa.	239
1908 Mar. 28	Hanna, Wy.	59
1908 Nov. 28	Marianna, Pa.	154
1908 Dec. 29	Switchback, W. Va.	50
1909 Jan. 12	Switchback, W. Va.	67
1909 Nov. 13	Cherry, Ill.	259
1910 Jan. 31	Primero, Col.	75
1910 May 5	Palos, Ala.	90
1910 Oct. 8	Starkville, Col.	56
1910 Nov. 8	Delagua, Col.	79
1911 Apr. 7	Throop, Pa.	72
1911 Apr. 8	Littleton, Ala.	128
1911 Dec. 9	Briceville, Tenn.	84
1912 Mar. 20	McCurtain, Okla.	73
1912 Mar. 26	Jed, W. Va.	83
1913 Apr. 23	Finleyville, Pa.	96
1913 Oct. 22	Dawson, N.M.	263
1914 Apr. 28	Eccles, W. Va.	181
1914 Oct. 27	Royalton, Ill.	52
1915 Mar. 2	Layland, W. Va.	112
1917 Apr. 27	Hastings, Col.	121
1917[2] June 8	Butte, Mon.	163
1917 Aug. 4	Clay, Ky.	62
1919[1] June 5	Wilkes-Barre, Pa.	92
1922 Nov. 6	Spangler, Pa.	77

Date	Location	Deaths
1922 Nov. 22	Dolomite, Ala.	90
1923 Feb. 8	Dawson, N.M.	120
1923 Aug. 14	Kemmerer, Wy.	99
1924 Mar. 8	Castle Gate, Ut.	171
1924 Apr. 28	Benwood, W. Va.	119
1925 Feb. 20	Sullivan, Ind.	52
1925 May 27	Coal Glen, N.C.	53
1925 Dec. 10	Acmar, Ala.	53
1926 Jan. 13	Wilburton, Okla.	91
1926[2] Nov. 3	Ishpeming, Mich.	51
1927 Apr. 30	Everettville, W. Va.	97
1928 May 19	Mather, Pa.	195
1929 Dec. 17	McAlester, Okla.	61
1930 Nov. 5	Millfield, Oh.	79
1932 Dec. 23	Moweagua, Ill.	54
1940 Jan. 10	Bartley, W. Va.	91
1940 Mar. 16	St. Clairsville, Oh.	72
1940 July 15	Portage, Pa.	63
1942 May 12	Osage, W. Va.	56
1943 Feb. 27	Washoe, Mon.	74
1944 July 5	Belmont, Oh.	66
1947 Mar. 25	Centralia, Ill.	111
1951 Dec. 21	West Frankfort, Ill.	119
1968[3] Mar. 6	Calumet, La.	21
1968 Nov. 20	Farmington, W. Va.	78
1970 Dec. 30	Hyden, Ky.	38
1972[2] May 2	Kellogg, Ida	91
1976 Mar. 9, 11	Oven Fork, Ky.	26
1977 Mar. 1	Tower City, Pa.	9
1981 Apr. 15	Redstone, Col.	15
1981 Dec. 7	Topmost, Ky.	8
1981 Dec. 8	nr. Chattanooga, Tenn.	13
1982 Jan. 20	Floyd County, Ky.	7

(1) Anthracite mine. (2) Metal mine. (3) Nonmetal mine.

World's worst mine disaster killed 1,549 workers in Honkeiko Colliery in Manchuria Apr. 25, 1942.

Historic Assassinations Since 1865

1865—Apr. 14. U. S. Pres. Abraham Lincoln, shot in Washington, D. C.; died Apr. 15.

1881—Mar. 13. Alexander II, of Russia—July 2. U. S. Pres. James A. Garfield, Washington; died Sept. 19.

1900—July 29. Umberto I, king of Italy.

1901—Sept. 6. U. S. Pres. William McKinley in Buffalo, N. Y., died Sept. 14. Leon Czolgosz executed for the crime Oct. 29.

1913—Feb. 23. Mexican Pres. Francisco, I, Madero and Vice Pres. Jose Pino Suarez.—Mar. 18. George, king of Greece.

1914—June 28. Archduke Francis Ferdinand of Austria-Hungary and his wife in Sarajevo, Bosnia (later part of Yugoslavia), by Gavrilo Princip.

1916—Dec. 30. Grigori Rasputin, politically powerful Russian monk.

1918—July 12. Grand Duke Michael of Russia, at Perm.—July 16. Nicholas II, abdicated as czar of Russia; his wife, the Czarina Alexandra, their son, Czarevitch Alexis, and their daughters, Grand Duchesses Olga, Tatiana, Marie, Anastasia, and 4 members of their household were executed by Bolsheviks at Ekaterinburg.

1920—May 20. Mexican Pres. Gen. Venustiano Carranza in Tlaxcalantongo.

1922—Aug. 22. Michael Collins, Irish revolutionary.

1923—July 20. Gen. Francisco "Pancho" Villa, ex-rebel leader, in Parral, Mexico.

1928—July 17. Gen. Alvaro Obregon, president-elect of Mexico, in San Angel, Mexico.

1933—Feb. 15. In Miami, Fla. Joseph Zangara, anarchist, shot at Pres.-elect Franklin D. Roosevelt, but a woman seized his arm, and the bullet fatally wounded Mayor Anton J. Cermak, of Chicago, who died Mar. 6. Zangara was electrocuted on Mar. 20, 1933.

1934—July 25. In Vienna, Austrian Chancellor Engelbert Dollfuss by Nazis.

1935—Sept. 8. U. S. Sen. Huey P. Long, shot in Baton Rouge, La., by Dr. Carl Austin Weiss, who was slain by Long's bodyguards.

1940—Aug. 20. Leon Trotsky (Lev Bronstein), 63, exiled Russian war minister, near Mexico City. Killer identified as Ramon Mercador del Rio, a Spaniard, served 20 years in Mexican prison.

1948—Jan. 30. Mohandas K. Gandhi, 78, shot in New Delhi, India, by Nathuran Vinayak Godse.—Sept. 17. Count Folke Bernadotte, UN mediator for Palestine, ambushed in Jerusalem.

1951—July 20. King Abdullah ibn Hussein of Jordan.

1956—Sept. 21. Pres. Anastasio Somoza of Nicaragua, in Leon; died Sept. 29.

1957—July 26. Pres. Carlos Castillo Armas of Guatemala, in Guatemala City by one of his own guards.

1958—July 14. King Faisal of Iraq; his uncle, Crown Prince Abdul Illah, and July 15, Premier Nuri as-Said, by rebels in Baghdad.

1959—Sept. 25. Prime Minister Solomon Bandaranaike of Ceylon, by Buddhist monk in Colombo.

1961—Jan. 17. Ex-Premier Patrice Lumumba of the Congo, in Katanga Province—May 30. Dominican dictator Rafael Leonidas Trujillo Molina shot to death by assassins near Ciudad Trujillo.

1963—June 12. Medgar W. Evers, NAACP's Mississippi field secretary, in Jackson, Miss.—Nov. 2. Pres. Ngo Dinh Diem of the Republic of Vietnam and his brother, Ngo Dinh Nhu, in a military coup.—Nov. 22. U. S. Pres. John F. Kennedy fatally shot in Dallas, Tex.; accused Lee Harvey Oswald murdered while awaiting trial.

1965—Jan. 21. Iranian premier Hassan Ali Mansour fatally wounded by assassin in Teheran; 4 executed.—Feb. 21. Malcolm X, black nationalist, fatally shot in N. Y. City; 3 sentenced to life.

1966—Sept. 6. Prime Minister Hendrik F. Verwoerd of South Africa stabbed to death in parliament at Capetown.

1968—Apr. 4. Rev. Dr. Martin Luther King Jr. fatally shot in Memphis, Tenn.; James Earl Ray sentenced to 99 years.—June 5. Sen. Robert F. Kennedy (D-N. Y.) fatally shot in Los Angeles; Sirhan Sirhan, resident alien, convicted of murder.

1971—Nov. 28. Jordan Prime Minister Wasfi Tal, in Cairo, by Palestinian guerrillas.

1973—Mar. 2. U. S. Ambassador Cleo A. Noel Jr., U. S. Charge d'Affaires George C. Moore and Belgian Charge d'Affaires Guy Eid killed by Palestinian guerrillas in Khartoum, Sudan.

1974—Aug. 15. Mrs. Park Chung Hee, wife of president of So. Korea, hit by bullet meant for her husband.—Aug. 19. U. S. Ambassador to Cyprus, Rodger P. Davies, killed by sniper's bullet in Nicosia.

1975—Feb. 11. Pres. Richard Ratsimandrava, of Madagascar, shot in Tananarive.—Mar. 25. King Faisal of Saudi Arabia shot by nephew Prince Musad Abdel Aziz, in royal palace, Riyadh.—Aug. 15. Bangladesh Pres. Sheik Mujibur Rahman killed in coup.

1976—Feb. 13. Nigerian head of state, Gen. Murtala Ramat Mohammed, slain by self-styled "young revolutionaries."

1977—Mar. 16. Kamal Jumblat, Lebanese Druse chieftain, was shot near Beirut.—Mar. 18. Congo Pres. Marien Ngouabi shot in Brazzaville.

1978—July 9. Former Iraqi Premier Abdul Razak Al-Naif shot in London.

1979—Feb. 14. U.S. Ambassador Adolph Dubs shot and killed by Afghan Moslem extremists in Kabul.—Mar. 30. British Tory MP Airey Neave killed when bomb in his car exploded. IRA claimed responsibility.—Aug. 27. Lord Mountbatten, WW2 hero, and 2 others were killed when a bomb exploded on his fishing boat off the coast of Co. Sligo, Ire. The IRA claimed responsibility. —Oct. 26. So. Korean President Park Chung Hee and 6 bodyguards fatally shot by Kim Jae Kyu, head of Korean CIA, and 5 aides in Seoul.

1980—Apr. 12. Liberian President William R. Tolbert slain in military coup.—Sept. 17. Former Nicaraguan President Anastasio Somoza Debayle and 2 others shot in Paraguay.

1981—Aug. 30. Iranian President Mohammed Ali Raji and Premier Mohammed Jad Bahonar killed by bomb in Teheran.—Oct. 6. Egyptian President Anwar El-Sadat fatally shot by a band of commandos while reviewing a military parade in Cairo.

Assassination Attempts

1910—Aug. 6. N. Y. City Mayor William J. Gaynor shot and seriously wounded by discharged city employee.

1912—Oct. 14. Former U. S. President Theodore Roosevelt shot and seriously wounded by demented man in Milwaukee.

1950—Nov. 1. In an attempt to assassinate President Truman, 2 members of a Puerto Rican nationalist movement—Griselio Torresola and Oscar Collazo—tried to shoot their way into Blair House. Torresola was killed, and a guard, Pvt. Leslie Coffelt was fatally shot. Collazo was convicted Mar. 7. 1951 for the murder of Coffelt.

1970—Nov. 27. Pope Paul VI unharmed by knife-wielding assailant who attempted to attack him in Manila airport.

1972—May 15. Alabama Gov. George Wallace shot in Laurel, Md. by Arthur Bremer; seriously crippled.

1972—Dec. 7. Mrs. Ferdinand E. Marcos, wife of the Philippine president, was stabbed and seriously injured in Pasay City, Philippines.

1975—Sept. 5. Pres. Gerald R. Ford was unharmed when a Secret Service agent grabbed a pistol aimed at him by Lynette (Squeaky) Fromme, a Charles Manson follower, in Sacramento.

1975—Sept. 22. Pres. Gerald R. Ford escaped unharmed when Sara Jane Moore, a political activist, fired a revolver at him.

1980—Apr. 14. Indian Prime Minister Indira Gandhi was unharmed when a man threw a knife at her in New Delhi.

1981—Jan. 16. Irish political activist Bernadette Devlin McAliskey and her husband were shot and seriously wounded by 3 members of a protestant paramilitary group in Co. Tyrone, Ire.

1981—Mar. 30. Pres. Ronald Reagan, Press Secy. James Brady, Secret Service agent Timothy J. McCarthy, and Washington, D.C. policeman Thomas Delahanty were shot and seriously wounded by John W. Hinckley Jr. in Washington, D.C.

1981—May 13. Pope John Paul II and 2 bystanders were shot and wounded by Mehmet Ali Agca, an escaped Turkish murderer, in St. Peter's Square, Rome.

1982—May 12. Pope John Paul II was unharmed when a man with a knife was overpowered by security guards, in Fatima, Portugal.

1982—June 3. Israel's ambassador to Britain Shlomo Argov was shot and seriously wounded by Arab terrorists in London.

Major Kidnapings

Edward A. Cudahy Jr., 16, in Omaha, Neb., **Dec. 18, 1900.** Returned Dec. 20 after $25,000 paid. Pat Crowe confessed.

Robert Franks, 13, in Chicago, **May 22, 1924**, by 2 youths, Richard Loeb and Nathan Leopold, who killed boy. Demand for $10,000 ignored. Loeb died in prison, Leopold paroled 1958.

Charles A. Lindbergh Jr., 20 mos. old, in Hopewell, N.J., **Mar. 1, 1932;** found dead May 12. Ransom of $50,000 was paid to man identified as Bruno Richard Hauptmann, 35, paroled German convict who entered U.S. illegally. Hauptmann passed ransom bill and $14,000 marked money was found in his garage. He was convicted after spectactular trial at Flemington, and electrocuted in Trenton, N.J., prison, Apr. 3. 1936.

William A. Hamm Jr., 39, in St. Paul, **June 15, 1933.** $100,000 paid. Alvin Karpis given life, paroled in 1969.

Charles F. Urschel, in Oklahoma City, **July 22, 1933.** Released July 31 after $200,000 paid. George (Machine Gun) Kelly and 5 others given life.

Brooke L. Hart, 22, in San Jose, Cal. Thomas Thurmond and John Holmes arrested after demanding $40,000 ransom. When Hart's body was found in San Francisco Bay, **Nov. 26, 1933**, a mob attacked the jail at San Jose and lynched the 2 kidnappers.

George Weyerhaeuser, 9, in Tacoma, Wash., **May 24, 1935.** Returned home June 1 after $200,000 paid. Kidnappers given 20 to 60 years.

Charles Mattson, 10, in Tacoma, Wash., **Dec. 27, 1936.** Found dead Jan. 11, 1937. Kidnaper asked $28,000, failed to contact.

Arthur Fried, in White Plains, N.Y., **Dec. 4, 1937.** Body not found. Two kidnapers executed.

Robert C. Greenlease, 6, taken from school **Sept. 28, 1953**, and held for $600,000. Body found Oct. 7. Mrs. Bonnie Brown Heady and Carl A. Hall pleaded guilty and were executed.

Peter Weinberger, 32 days old, Westbury, N.Y., **July 4, 1956**, for $2,000 ransom, not paid. Child found dead. Angelo John LaMarca, 31, convicted, executed.

Cynthia Ruotolo, 6 wks old, taken from carriage in front of Hamden, Conn. store **Sept. 1, 1956.** Body found in lake.

Lee Crary, 8 in Everett, Wash., **Sept. 22, 1957**, $10,000 ransom, not paid. He escaped after 3 days, led police to George E. Collins, who was convicted.

Eric Peugeot, 4, taken from playground at St. Cloud golf course, Paris, **Apr. 12, 1960.** Released unharmed 3 days later after payment of undisclosed sum. Two sentenced to prison.

Frank Sinatra Jr., 19, from hotel room in Lake Tahoe, Cal., **Dec. 8, 1963.** Released **Dec. 11** after his father paid $240,000 ransom. Three men sentenced to prison; most of ransom recovered.

Barbara Jane Mackle, 20, abducted **Dec. 17, 1968**, from Atlanta, Ga., motel, was found unharmed 3 days later, buried in a coffin-like wooden box 18 inches underground, after her father had paid $500,000 ransom; Gary Steven Krist sentenced to life, Ruth Eisenmann-Schier to 7 years; most of ransom recovered.

Anne Katherine Jenkins, 22, abducted **May 10, 1969**, from her Baltimore apartment, freed 3 days later after her father paid $10,000 ransom.

Mrs. Roy Fuchs, 35, and 3 children held hostage 2 hours, **May 14, 1969**, in Long Island, N. Y., released after her husband, a bank manager, paid kidnapers $129,000 in bank funds; 4 men arrested, ransom recovered.

C. Burke Elbrick, U.S. ambassador to Brazil, kidnaped by revolutionaries in Rio de Janeiro **Sept. 4, 1969;** released 3 days later after Brazil yielded to kidnaper's demands to publish manifesto and release 15 political prisoners.

Patrick Dolan, 18, found shot to death near Sao Paulo, Brazil, **Nov. 5, 1969**, after he was kidnaped and $12,500 paid.

Sean M. Holly, U.S. diplomat, in Guatemala **Mar. 6, 1970;** freed 2 days later upon release of 3 terrorists from prison.

Lt. Col. Donald J. Crowley, U.S. air attache, in Dominican Republic **Mar. 24, 1970;** released after government allowed 20 prisoners to leave the country.

Count Karl von Spreti, W. German ambassador to Guatemala, **Mar. 31, 1970;** slain after Guatemala refused demands for $700,000 and release of 22 prisoners.

Pedro Eugenio Arambaru, former Argentine president, by terrorists **May 29, 1970;** body found July 17.

Ehrenfried von Holleben, W. German ambassador to Brazil, by terrorists **June 11, 1970;** freed after release of 40 prisoners.

Daniel A. Mitrione, U.S. diplomat, **July 31, 1970**, by terrorists in Montevideo, Uruguay; body found Aug. 10 after government rejected demands for release of all political prisoners.

James R. Cross, British trade commissioner, **Oct. 5, 1970**, by French Canadian separatists in Quebec; freed Dec. 3 after 3 kidnapers and relatives flown to Cuba by government.

Pierre Laporte, Quebec Labor Minister, by separatists **Oct. 10, 1970;** body found Oct. 18.

Giovanni E. Bucher, Swiss ambassador **Dec. 7, 1970**, by revolutionaries in Rio de Janeiro; freed Jan. 16, 1971, after Brazil released 70 political prisoners.

Geoffrey Jackson, British ambassador, in Montevideo, **Jan. 8, 1971**, by Tupamaro terrorists. Held as ransom for release of imprisoned terrorists, he was released Sept. 9, after the prisoners escaped.

Ephraim Elrom, Israel consul general in Istanbul, **May 17, 1971.** Held as ransom for imprisoned terrorists, he was found dead May 23.

Mrs. Virginia Piper, 49 abducted **July 27, 1972**, from her home in suburban Minneapolis; found unharmed near Duluth 2 days later after her husband paid $1 million ransom to the kidnapers.

Victor E. Samuelson, Exxon executive, **Dec. 6, 1973**, in Campana, Argentina, by Marxist guerrillas, freed Apr. 29, 1974, after payment of record $14.2 million ransom.

J. Paul Getty 3d, 17, grandson of the U.S. oil mogul, released **Dec. 15, 1973**, in southern Italy after $2.8 million ransom paid.

Patricia (Patty) Hearst, 19, taken from her Berkeley, Cal., apartment **Feb. 4, 1974.** Symbionese Liberation Army demanded her father, Randolph A. Hearst, publisher, give millions to poor. Hearst offered $2 million in food; the Hearst Corp. offered $4 million worth. Kidnapers objected to way food was distributed. Patricia, in message, said she had joined SLA; she was identified by FBI as taking part in a San Francisco bank holdup, **Apr. 15;** she claimed, in message, she had been coerced. Again identified by FBI in a store holdup, **May 16**, she was classified by FBI as "an armed, dangerous fugitive." FBI, **Sept. 18, 1975**, captured Patricia and others in San Francisco; they were indicted on various charges. Patricia for bank robbery. A San Francisco jury convicted her, **Mar. 20, 1976.** She was released from prison under executive clemency, **Feb. 1, 1979.** In 1978, William and Emily Harris were sentenced to 10 years to life for the Hearst kidnaping.

J. Reginald Murphy, 40, an editor of *Atlanta* (Ga.) *Constitution*, kidnaped **Feb. 20, 1974**, freed **Feb. 22** after payment of $700,000 ransom by the newspaper. Police arrested William A. H. Williams, a contractor; most of the money was recovered.

J. Guadalupe Zuno Hernandez, 83, father-in-law of Mexican President Luis Echeverria Alvarez, seized by 4 terrorists **Aug. 28, 1974;** government refused to negotiate; he was released **Sept. 8.**

E. B. Reville, Hepzibah, Ga., banker, and wife Jean, kidnaped **Sept. 30, 1974.** Ransom of $30,000 paid. He was found alive; Mrs. Reville was found dead of carbon monoxide fumes in car trunk **Oct. 2.**

Jack Teich, Kings Point, N,Y., steel executive, seized **Nov. 12, 1974;** released **Nov. 19** after payment of $750,000.

Samuel Bronfman, 21, heir to Seagram liquor fortune, allegedly abducted **Aug. 9, 1975**, in Purchase, N.Y.; $2.3 million ransom paid. FBI and N.Y.C. police found Samuel **Aug. 17** in Brooklyn, N.Y., apartment, recovered ransom, and arrested Mel Patrick Lynch and Dominic Byrne. Two found not guilty of kidnap, but convicted of extortion after they claimed Sam masterminded ransom plot.

Hanns-Martin Schleyer, a West German industrialist, was kidnaped in Cologne, **Sept. 5, 1977** by armed terrorists. Schleyer was found dead, **Oct. 19**, in an abandoned car shortly after 3 jailed terrorist leaders of the Baader-Meinhof gang were found dead in their prison cells near Stuttgart, West Germany.

Aldo Moro, former Italian premier, kidnaped in Rome, **Mar. 16, 1978**, by left-wing terrorists. Five of his bodyguards killed during abduction. Moro's bullet-ridden body was found in a parked car, **May 9**, in Rome. Six members of the Red Brigades arrested, charged, June 5, with complicity in the kidnaping.

James L. Dozier, a U.S. Army general, kidnapped from his apartment in Verona, Italy, **Dec. 17, 1981**, by members of the Red Brigades terrorist organization. He was rescued, **Jan. 28, 1982**, by Italian police.

ASTRONOMY AND CALENDAR

Edited by Dr. Kenneth L. Franklin, Astronomer
American Museum-Hayden Planetarium

Celestial Events Highlights, 1983

(All times are Greenwich Mean Time)

This year may be noteworthy for the 19 occultations of planets by the moon, and of no bright stars. The actual occultation may not be visible from your location, but treat such a notice as a close encounter of the two bodies. If you wish to take pictures of some of these celestial events, mark them on your calendar. Notice Mars in particular. There are 6 near misses at least, plus 2 in September, and on Dec. 17, Venus will be 0°.2 north of Saturn in the morning sky. Note that the moon is about 0°.5 across.

By early spring, Venus will begin its appearance in the western sky at sunset, leaving our view by midsummer. Its place will be taken by Jupiter and Saturn which have joined the beautiful goddess during the spring. Mars is lost virtually all year, and, of course, dizzy little Mercury plays its usual leap frog with the sun: now here, now there, and always difficult to locate.

A total solar eclipse in June is of interest, because of its duration, more than 5 minutes, and location, Java. Many tours are already booked by eclipse-watching hobbyists.

The Perseid meteor shower, as noted here in the last few years, continues to offer its August display and may be even better. We are still (mid-1982) waiting for the rediscovery of comet Swift-Tuttle, the parent body of this shower. The recent inclusion of fire balls in the display has been considered as a harbinger of this "hairy star".

January, 1983

Mercury moves through interior conjunction this month and will be out of sight.

Venus moves out of the evening twilight and may be conspicuous low in the western sky after sunset on exceptionally clear days.

Mars moves from Capricornus into Aquarius this month, but is too faint to be seen easily in the evening twilight.

Jupiter is the bright object on the border between Libra and Scorpius in the eastern dawn twilight.

Saturn rises before Jupiter and is east of Spica, in Virgo.

Moon is at apogee on the 14th, occults Neptune on the 12th, and is at perigee on the 28th.

Jan. 2—Earth at perihelion, 91.4 million miles from the sun.

Jan. 3—Quadrantid meteor shower fine after midnight.

Jan. 6—Mercury stationary, begins retrograde motion.

Jan. 16—Mercury in interior conjunction.

Jan. 19—Sun enters Capricornus.

Jan. 27—Mercury stationary, resumes direct motion.

February

Mercury is 26° west of the sun at greatest elongation on the 8th, located in the southeast before dawn.

Venus continues to be more conspicuous in the western evening twilight.

Mars leaves Aquarius for Pisces but is difficult to see low in the western evening twilight.

Jupiter, bright in the eastern dawn twilight, enters Ophiuchus.

Saturn remains in Virgo looking like a bright star.

Moon occults Neptune on the 8th, is at apogee on the 10th, and at perigee on the 25th.

Feb. 7—Pluto stationary, begins retrograde motion.

Feb. 8—Mercury at greatest western elongation, 26° from sun.

Feb. 13—Saturn stationary, begins retrograde motion.

Feb. 16—Sun enters Aquarius.

March

Mercury is at superior conjunction on the 26th, thus lost to view all month.

Venus is much more prominent in the western evening twilight.

Mars is moving rapidly and inconspicuously through Pisces, lost in the western evening twilight.

Jupiter, in Ophiuchus, is stationary and beings its retrograde motion on the 28th.

Saturn looks like a bright star in eastern Virgo, very close to the moon on the 30th.

Moon occults Jupiter on the 6th, Neptune on the 7th, is at apogee on the 9th, at perigee on the 25th, and passes close to Saturn on the 30th.

Mar. 6—Moon occults Jupiter.

Mar. 11—Sun enters Pisces.

Mar. 21—Vernal equinox; spring begins.

Mar. 26—Mercury in superior conjunction.

Mar. 28—Jupiter stationary, begins retrograde motion.

April

Mercury remains too close to the sun (20° at greatest elongation) to be seen easily in the western evening twilight.

Venus should be no problem to see as it remains after sunset in the western twilight.

Mars is now lost until late summer.

Jupiter is backing through Ophiuchus, brighter than any star in the sky.

Saturn is approaching Spica from the east.

Moon occults Jupiter on the 2nd, is at apogee on the 6th, at perigee on the 21st, passes close to Saturn on the 26th, and occults Jupiter again on the 29th.

Apr. 2—Moon occults Jupiter.

Apr. 18—Sun enters Aries; Pluto at opposition.

Apr. 21—Mercury at greatest elongation, 20° east of the sun; Saturn at opposition.

Apr. 22—Lyrid meteor shower best after moon sets.

Apr. 29—Moon occults Jupiter.

May

Mercury passes through interior conjunction this month so is lost to view in the sun's glare.

Venus and the crescent moon are quite close together on the evening of the 15th, making a good photo opportunity.

Mars is still lost to view beyond the sun.

Jupiter is in the sky all night long, brighter than any star, only 0°.8 north of Uranus on the 16th providing a good pointer to Uranus, and very close to the full moon on the 26th, a remarkable photo opportunity.

Saturn is close to the moon on the 23rd, another great photo opportunity.

Moon is at apogee on the 13th, is close to Venus on the 16th, Saturn on the 23rd, and occults Jupiter on the 26th.

May 2—Mercury stationary, begins retrograde motion.

May 4, 5—Eta Aquarid meteor shower suffers from last quarter moon.

May 12—Mercury in interior conjunction.

May 13—Sun enters Taurus.

May 16—Venus close to moon; Jupiter close to Uranus.

May 23—Saturn close to moon.
May 26—Moon occults Jupiter.
May 27—Jupiter at opposition.

June

Mercury may be seen north of east in the morning twilight early in the month.

Venus is a delight in the western evening twilight only 1°.5 south of the 3-day crescent moon on the 14th.

Mars is in conjunction with the sun on the 3rd, thus completely lost from view.

Jupiter clearly dominates the night sky in Scorpius.

Saturn is beginning to fade as it still approaches Spica in Virgo.

Moon is at apogee on the 1st, occults Mercury on the 9th, eclipses the sun on the 11th, at perigee on the 13th, occults Jupiter on the 22nd, is eclipsed on the 25th, and is at apogee on the 28th.

June 3—Mars in conjunction with the sun.
June 8—Mercury at greatest elongation, 24° west of the sun.
June 9—Moon occults Mercury.
June 11—Total solar eclipse.
June 16—Venus at greatest elongation, 45° from the sun.
June 19—Neptune at opposition.
June 20—Sun enters Gemini.
June 21—Solstice; summer begins.
June 22—Moon occults Jupiter.
June 25—Partial lunar eclipse.

July

Mercury is lost in the sun all month.

Venus at its brightest in the western evening sky rapidly moves closer to the horizon at sunset.

Mars is still effectively lost until month's end when it begins to move out of the eastern dawn twilight.

Jupiter dominates the late evening sky after Venus sets.

Saturn begins to move away from Spica, still looking like a first magnitude star.

Moon is at perigee on the 11th, is close to Jupiter on the 18th, and at apogee on the 26th.

July 2—Saturn stationary, resumes direct motion.
July 6—Earth at aphelion, 94.4 million miles from the sun.
July 9—Mercury in superior conjunction.
July 14—Pluto stationary, resumes direct motion.
July 19—Venus at greatest brilliancy.
July 20—Sun enters Cancer.
July 29—Jupiter stationary, resumes direct motion; Delta Aquarid meteor shower bothered by waning gibbous moon.

August

Mercury is technically visible in the western evening twilight all month, achieving greatest elongation on the 19th, 27° east of the sun.

Venus is stationary on the 1st, and at interior conjunction on the 25th, thus visible in the west at dusk only the first week of the month.

Mars looking like a 2nd magnitude reddish star in the eastern dawn sky moves from Gemini into Cancer.

Jupiter is prominent in the south at dusk in the constellation Libra.

Saturn is west of Jupiter in Virgo looking like a 1st magnitude star.

Moon passes close to Mars on the 7th, is at perigee on the 8th at new moon (watch for extreme tides), passes close to Saturn on the 13th, Jupiter on the 16th, and is at apogee on the 22nd.

Aug. 1—Venus is stationary, beginning its retrograde motion.
Aug. 10—Sun enters Leo.
Aug. 11-13—Perseid meteor shower is free of moonlight and may be good these nights. Watch for rare fireballs.
Aug. 14—Uranus is stationary, resuming its direct motion.
Aug. 19—Mercury at greatest elongation, 27° east of the sun.
Aug. 25—Venus in interior conjunction.

September

Mercury is in interior conjunction at mid-month, hence lost to view for the entire period.

Venus becomes increasingly prominent in the eastern sky before dawn.

Mars leaves Cancer and passes less than a degree north of Regulus in Leo on the 29th.

Jupiter is 1°.3 south of the moon on the 16th moving into Scorpius from Libra, then into Ophiuchus by month's end.

Saturn, still looking like a 1st magnitude star in Virgo, is 1°.7 south of the moon on the 10th.

Moon is at perigee on the 6th, passes close to Saturn on the 10th, occults Jupiter on the 12th, and is at apogee on the 18th.

Sept. 1—Mercury is stationary, beginning its retrograde motion.
Sept. 8—Neptune is stationary, resuming its direct motion.
Sept. 12—Moon occults Jupiter.
Sept. 14—Venus is stationary, resuming its direct motion.
Sept. 15—Mercury is in interior conjunction.
Sept. 16—Sun enters Virgo.
Sept. 23—Autumnal equinox; Autumn begins.
Sept. 24—Mercury is stationary resuming its direct motion; Jupiter is 0°.4 North of Uranus.
Sept. 28—Mars is 0°.9 north of Regulus.

October

Mercury is at greatest elongation 18° west of the sun, on the 1st, virtually the only chance at a sighting in the eastern dawn all month.

Venus clearly dominates the dawn sky all month, passing Mars on the 28th.

Mars remains in Leo this month and, still looking like a 2nd magnitude star, passes brilliant Venus by 1°.7 on the 28th.

Jupiter is occulted by the crescent moon on the 10th, but out of view of the western hemisphere.

Saturn might be visible early in the month as a 1st magnitude star to sharp eyes seeking it in the western evening twilight, but it is in conjunction with the sun on the 31st.

Moon is at perigee on the 4th, passes close to Saturn on the 7th, occults Uranus and Jupiter on the 10th, and is at apogee on the 16th.

Oct. 1—Venus at greatest brilliancy; Mercury at greatest elongation, 18° west of the sun.
Oct. 10—Moon occults Uranus and Jupiter.
Oct. 21 —Orionid meteor shower spoiled by full moon.
Oct. 23—Pluto in conjunction with the sun.
Oct. 28—Venus 1°.7 south of Mars.
Oct. 30—Sun enters Libra.

November

Mercury is lost in the sun's glare nearly all month.

Venus still dominates the morning sky.

Mars, brightening slightly, moves into Virgo.

Jupiter looks like a bright star in the western evening twilight, being occulted by the crescent moon on the 7th.

Saturn reappears in the eastern dawn by the end of the month, but is still difficult to find.

Moon is at perigee on the 1st, occults Uranus on the 6th, Jupiter on the 7th, is at apogee on the 13th, and is at perigee again on the 26th.

Nov. 4—Venus at greatest elongation, 47° west of the sun.
Nov. 6—Moon occults Uranus.
Nov. 7—Moon occults Jupiter.
Nov. 22—Sun enters Scorpius.
Nov. 29—Sun enters Ophiuchus.

December

Mercury may be found in the evening western twilight most of this month.

Venus is still the brightest planet or star in the morning sky, passing 0°.2 North of Saturn on the 27th.

Mars remains in Virgo passing 4° north of Spica on the 28th.

Jupiter is lost in the solar glare all month.

Saturn is becoming more prominent in the eastern dawn sky, passing 0°.2 south of Venus on the 17th.

Moon occults Saturn on the 2nd, eclipses the sun on the 4th, occults Mercury on the 6th, is at apogee on the 11th, is penumbrally eclipsed on the 20th, is at perigee on the 22nd, occults Saturn on the 29th, Venus on the 30th, and Uranus on the 31st.

Dec. 2—Uranus in conjunction with the sun; moon occults Saturn.

Dec. 4—Annular eclipse of the sun.

Dec. 6—Moon occults Mercury.

Dec. 13—Mercury at greatest elongation, 21° east of the sun; Geminid meteor shower, famous for fireballs, not hurt by 1st quarter moon.

Dec. 14—Jupiter in conjunction with the sun.

Dec. 16—Sun enters Sagittarius.

Dec. 17—Venus 0°.2 north of Saturn.

Dec. 20—Penumbral lunar eclipse.

Dec. 21—Neptune in conjunction with the sun; Mercury stationary, begins retrograde motion.

Dec. 22—Winter solstice; winter begins.

Dec. 24—Moon occults Saturn.

Dec. 30—Moon occults Venus.

Dec. 31—Mercury in interior conjunction; moon occults Uranus.

Planets and the Sun

The planets of the solar system, in order of their mean distance from the sun, are Mercury, Venus, Earth, Mars, Jupiter, Saturn, Uranus, Neptune and Pluto. Both Uranus and Neptune are visible through good field glasses, but Pluto is so distant and so small that only large telescopes or long exposure photographs can make it visible.

Since Mercury and Venus are nearer to the sun than is the earth, their motions about the sun are seen from the earth as wide swings first to one side of the sun and then to the other, although they are both passing continuously around the sun in orbits that are almost circular. When their passage takes them either between the earth and the sun, or beyond the sun as seen from the earth, they are invisible to us. Because of the laws which govern the motions of planets about the sun, both Mercury and Venus require much less time to pass between the earth and the sun than around the far side of the sun, so their periods of visibility and invisibility are unequal.

The planets that lie farther from the sun than does the earth may be seen for longer periods of time and are invisible only when they are so located in our sky that they rise and set about the same time as the sun when, of course, they are overwhelmed by the sun's great brilliance. None of the planets has any light or radiant heat of its own but each shines only by reflecting sunlight from its surface. Mercury and Venus, because they are between the earth and the sun, show phases very much as the moon does. The planets farther from the sun are always seen as full, although Mars does occasionally present a slightly gibbous phase — like the moon when not quite full.

The planets move rapidly among the stars because they are very much nearer to us. The stars are also in motion, some of them at tremendous speeds, but they are so far away that their motion does not change their apparent positions in the heavens sufficiently for anyone to perceive that change in a single lifetime. The very nearest star is about 7,000 times as far away as the most distant planet.

Visible Planets of the Solar System

Mercury, Venus, Mars, Jupiter and Saturn

Mercury

Mercury, nearest planet to the sun, is the second smallest of the nine planets known to be orbiting the sun. Its diameter is 3,100 miles and its mean distance from the sun is 36,000,000 miles.

Mercury moves with great speed in its journey about the sun, averaging about 30 miles a second to complete its circuit in 88 of our days. Mercury rotates upon its axis over a period of nearly 59 days, thus exposing all of its surface periodically to the sun. It is believed that the surface passing before the sun may have a temperature of about 800° F., while the temperature on the side turned temporarily away from the sun does not fall as low as might be expected. This night temperature has been described by Russian astronomers as "room temperature" — possibly about 70°. This would contradict the former belief that Mercury did not possess an atmosphere, for some sort of atmosphere would be needed to retain the fierce solar radiation that strikes Mercury. A shallow but dense layer of carbon dioxide would produce the "greenhouse" effect, in which heat accumulated during exposure to the sun would not completely escape at night. The actual presence of a carbon dioxide atmosphere is in dispute.

This uncertainty about conditions upon Mercury and its motion arise from its shorter angular distance from the sun as seen from the earth, for Mercury is always too much in line with the sun to be observed against a dark sky, but is always seen during either morning or evening twilight.

Mariner 10 made 3 passes by Mercury in 1974 and 1975. A large fraction of the surface was photographed from varying distances, revealing a degree of cratering similar to that of the moon. An atmosphere of hydrogen and helium may be made up of gases of the solar wind temporarily concentrated by the presence of Mercury. The discovery of a weak but permanent magnetic field was a surprise. It has been held that both a fluid core and rapid rotation were necessary for the generation of a planetary magnetic field. Mercury may demonstrate these conditions to be unnecessary, or the field may reveal something about the history of Mercury.

Venus

Venus, slightly smaller than the earth, moves about the sun at a mean distance of 67,000,000 miles in 225 of our days. Its synodical revolution — its return to the same relationship with the earth and the sun, which is a result of the combination of its own motion and that of the earth — is 584 days. Every 19 months, then, Venus will be nearer to the earth than any other planet of the solar system. The planet is covered with a dense, white, cloudy atmosphere that conceals whatever is below it. This same cloud reflects sunlight efficiently so that when Venus is favorably situated, it is the third brightest object in the sky, exceeded only by the sun and the moon.

Spectral analysis of sunlight reflected from Venus' cloud tops has shown features that can best be explained by identifying the material of the clouds as sulphuric acid (oil of vitriol). Infrared spectroscopy from a balloon-borne telescope nearly 20 miles above the earth's surface gave indications of a small amount of water vapor present in the same region of the atmosphere of Venus. In 1956, radio astronomers at the Naval Research Laboratories in Washington, D. C., found a temperature for Venus of about 600° F., in marked contrast to minus 125° F., previously found at the cloud tops. Subsequent radio work confirmed a high temperature and produced evidence for this temperature to be associated with the solid body of Venus. With this peculiarity in mind, space scientists devised experiments for the U.S. space probe Mariner 2 to perform when it flew by in 1962. Mariner 2 confirmed the high temperature and the fact that it pertained to the ground rather than to some special activity of the atmosphere. In addition, Mariner 2 was unable to detect any radiation belts similar to the earth's so-called Van Allen belts. Nor was it able to detect the existence of a magnetic field even as weak as 1/100,000 of that of the earth.

In 1967, a Russian space probe, Venera 4, and the American Mariner 5 arrived at Venus within a few hours of each other. Venera 4 was designed to allow an instrument package to land gently on the planet's surface via parachute. It ceased transmission of information in about 75 minutes when the temperature it read went above 500° F. After considerable controversy, it was agreed that it still had 20 miles to go to reach the surface. The U.S. probe, Mariner 5, went around the dark side of Venus at a distance of about 6,000 miles. Again, it detected no significant magnetic field but its radio signals passed to earth through Venus' atmosphere twice — once on the night side and once on the day side. The results are startling. Venus' atmosphere is nearly all carbon dioxide and must exert a pressure at the planet's surface of up to 100 times the earth's normal sea-level pressure of one atmosphere. Since the earth and Venus are about the same size, and were presumably formed at the same time by the same general process from the same mixture of chemical elements, one is faced with the question: which is the planet with the unusual history — earth or Venus?

Radar astronomers using powerful transmitters as well as sensitive receivers and computers have succeeded in determining the rotation period of Venus. It turns out to be 243 days clockwise — in other words, contrary to the spin of most of the other planets and to its own motion around the sun. If it were exactly 243.16 days, Venus would always present the same face toward the earth at every inferior conjunction. This rate and sense of rotation allows a "day" on Venus of 117.4 earth days. Any part of Venus will receive sunlight on its clouds for over 58 days and will be in darkness for 58 days. Recent radar observations have shown surface features below the clouds. Large craters, continent-sized highlands, and extensive, dry "ocean" basins have been identified.

Mariner 10 passed Venus before traveling on to Mercury in 1974. The carbon dioxide molecule found in such abundance in the atmosphere is rather opaque to certain ultraviolet wavelengths, enabling sensitive television cameras to take pictures of the Venusian cloud cover. Photos radioed to earth show a spiral pattern in the clouds from equator to the poles.

In December, 1978, two U. S. Pioneer probes arrived at Venus. One went into orbit about Venus, the other split into 5 separate probes targeted for widely-spaced entry points to sample different conditions. The instrumentation ensemble was selected on the basis of previous missions that had shown the range of conditions to be studied. The probes confirmed expected high surface temperatures and high winds aloft. Winds of about 200 miles per hour, there, may account for the transfer of heat into the night side in spite of the low rotation speed of the planet. Surface winds were light at the time, however. Atmosphere and cloud chemistries were examined in detail, providing much data for continued analysis. The probes detected 4 layers of clouds and more light on the surface than expected solely from sunlight. This light allowed Russian scientists to obtain at least two photos showing rocks on the surface. Sulphur seems to play a large role in the chemistry of Venus, and reactions involving sulphur may be responsible for the glow. To learn more about the weather and atmospheric circulation on Venus, the orbiter takes daily photos of the daylight side cloud cover. It confirms the cloud pattern and its circulation shown by Mariner 10. The ionosphere shows large variability. The orbiter's radar operates in 2 modes: one, for ground elevation variability, and the second for ground reflectivity in 2 dimensions, thus "imaging" the surface. Radar maps of the entire planet that show the features mentioned above have been produced.

Mars

Mars is the first planet beyond the earth, away from the sun. Mars' diameter is about 4,200 miles, although a determination of the radius and mass of Mars by the space-probe, Mariner 4, which flew by Mars on July 14, 1965 at a distance of less than 6,000 miles, indicated that these dimensions were slightly larger than had been previously estimated. While Mars' orbit is also nearly circular, it is somewhat more eccentric than the orbits of many of the other planets, and Mars is more than 30 million miles farther from the sun in some parts of its year than it is at others. Mars takes 687 of our days to make one circuit of the sun, traveling at about 15 miles a second. Mars rotates upon its axis in almost the same period of time that the earth does — 24 hours and 37 minutes. Mars' mean distance from the sun is 141 million miles, so that the temperature on Mars would be lower than that on the earth even if Mars' atmosphere were about the same as ours. The atmosphere is not, however, for Mariner 4 reported that atmospheric pressure on Mars is between 1% and 2% of the earth's atmospheric pressure. This thin atmosphere appears to be largely carbon dioxide. No evidence of free water was found.

There appears to be no magnetic field about Mars. This would eliminate the previous conception of a dangerous radiation belt around Mars. The same lack of a magnetic field would expose the surface of Mars to an influx of cosmic radiation about 100 times as intense as that on earth.

Deductions from years of telescopic observation indicate that 5/8ths of the surface of Mars is a desert of reddish rock, sand, and soil. The rest of Mars is covered by irregular patches that appear generally green in hues that change through the Martian year. These were formerly held to be some sort of primitive vegetation, but with the findings of Mariner 4 of a complete lack of water and oxygen, such growth does not appear possible. The nature of the green areas is now unknown. They may be regions covered with volcanic salts whose color changes with changing temperatures and atmospheric conditions, or they may be gray, rather than green. When large gray areas are placed beside large red areas, the gray areas will appear green to the eye.

Mars' axis of rotation is inclined from a vertical to the plane of its orbit about the sun by about 25° and therefore Mars has seasons as does the earth, except that the Martian seasons are longer because Mars' year is longer. White caps form about the winter pole of Mars, growing through the winter and shrinking in summer. These polar caps are now believed to be both water ice and carbon dioxide ice. It is the carbon dioxide that is seen to come and go with the seasons. The water ice is apparently in many layers with dust between them, indicating climatic cycles.

The canals of Mars have become more of a mystery than they were before the voyage of Mariner 4. Markings forming a network of fine lines crossing much of the surface of Mars have been seen there by men who have devoted much time to the study of the planet, but no canals have shown clearly enough in previous photographs to be universally accepted. A few of the 21 photographs sent back to earth by Mariner 4 covered areas crossed by canals. The pictures show faint, ill-defined, broad, dark markings, but no positive identification of the nature of the markings.

Mariners 6 & 7 in 1969 sent back many more photographs of higher quality than those of the pioneering Mariner 4. These pictures showed cratering similar to the earlier views, but in addition showed 2 other types of terrain. Some regions seemed featureless for many square miles, but others were chaotic, showing high relief without apparent organization into mountain chains or craters.

Mariner 9, the first artificial body to be placed in an orbit about Mars, has transmitted over 10,000 photographs covering 100% of the planet's surface. Preliminary study of these photos and other data shows that Mars resembles no other planet we know. Using terrestrial terms, however, scientists describe features that seem to be clearly of volcanic origin. One of these features is Nix Olympica, apparently a caldera whose outer slopes are over 300 miles in diameter. Some features may have been produced by cracking (faulting) of the surface and the sliding of one region over or past another. Many craters seem to have been produced by impacting bodies such as may have come from the nearby asteroid belt. Features near the south pole may have been produced by glaciers that are no longer present. Flowing water, nonexistent on Mars at the present time, probably carved canyons, one 10 times longer and 3 times deeper than the Grand Canyon.

Although the Russians landed a probe on the Martian surface, it transmitted for only 20 seconds. In 1976, the U.S. landed 2 Viking spacecraft on the Martian surface. The landers had devices aboard to perform chemical analyses of the soil in search of evidence of life. The results have been inconclusive. The 2 Viking orbiters have returned the best pictures yet of Martian topographic features. Many features can be explained only if Mars once had large quantities of flowing water.

Mars' position in its orbit and its speed around that orbit in relation to the earth's position and speed bring Mars fairly close to the earth on occasions about two years apart and then move Mars and the earth too far apart for accurate observation and photography. Every 15-17 years, the close approaches are especially favorable to close observation.

Mars has 2 satellites, discovered in 1877 by Asaph Hall. The outer satellite, Deimos, revolves around Mars in about 31 hours. The inner satellite, Phobos, whips around Mars in a little more than 7 hours, making 3 trips around the planet each Martian day. Mariner and Viking photos show these bodies to be irregularly shaped and pitted with numerous craters. Phobos also shows a system of linear grooves, each about 1/3-mile across and roughly parallel. Phobos measures about 8 by 12 miles and Deimos about 5 by 7.5 miles in size.

Jupiter

Jupiter is the largest of the planets. Its equatorial diameter is 88,000 miles, 11 times the diameter of the earth. Its polar diameter is about 6,000 miles shorter. This is an equilibrium condition resulting from the liquidity of the planet and its extremely rapid rate of rotation: a Jupiter day is only 10 earth hours long. For a planet this size, this rotational speed is amazing, and it moves a point on Jupiter's equator at a speed of 22,000 miles an hour, as compared with 1,000 miles an hour for a point on the earth's equator. Jupiter is at an average distance of 480 million miles from the sun and takes almost 12 of our years to make one complete circuit of the sun.

The only directly observable chemical constituents of Jupiter's atmosphere are methane (CH_4) and ammonia (NH_3), but it is reasonable to assume the same mixture of elements available to make Jupiter as to make the sun. This would mean a large fraction of hydrogen and helium must be present also, as well as water (H_2O). The temperature at the tops of the clouds may be about minus 260° F. The clouds are probably ammonia ice crystals, becoming ammonia droplets lower down. There may be a space before water ice crystals show up as clouds: in turn, these become water droplets near the bottom of the entire cloud layer. The total atmosphere may be only a few hundred miles in depth, pulled down by the surface gravity (= 2.64 times earth's) to a relatively thin layer. Of course, the gases become denser with depth until they may turn into a slush or a slurry. Perhaps there is no surface — no real interface between the gaseous atmosphere and the body of Jupiter. Pioneers 10 and 11 provided evidence for considering Jupiter to be almost entirely liquid hydrogen. Long before a rocky core about the size of the earth is reached, hydrogen mixed with helium becomes a liquid metal at very high temperature. Jupiter's cloudy atmosphere is a fairly good reflector of sunlight and makes it appear far brighter than any of the stars.

Fourteen of Jupiter's 16 or more satellites have been found through earth-based observations. Four of the moons are large and bright, rivaling our own moon and the planet Mercury in diameter, and may be seen through a field glass. They move rapidly around Jupiter and their change of position from night to night is extremely interesting to watch. The other satellites are much smaller and in all but one instance much farther from Jupiter and cannot be seen except through powerful telescopes. The 4 outermost satellites are revolving around Jupiter clockwise as seen from the north, contrary to the motions of the great majority of the satellites in the solar system and to the direction of revolution of the planets around the sun. The reason for this retrograde motion is not known, but one theory is that Jupiter's tremendous gravitational power may have captured 4 of the minor planets or asteroids that move about the sun between Mars and Jupiter, and that these would necessarily revolve backward. At the great distance of these bodies from Jupiter — some 14 million miles — direct motion would result in decay of the orbits, while retrograde orbits would be stable. Jupiter's mass is more than twice the mass of all the other planets put together, and accounts for Jupiter's tremendous gravitational field and so, probably, for its numerous satellites and its dense atmosphere.

In December, 1973, Pioneer 10 passed about 80,000 miles from the equator of Jupiter and was whipped into a path taking it out of our solar system in about 50 years. In December, 1974, Pioneer 11 passed within 30,000 miles of Jupiter, moving roughly from south to north, over the poles.

Photographs from both encounters were useful at the time but were far surpassed by those of Voyagers I and II. Thousands of high resolution multi-color pictures show rapid variations of features both large and small. The Great Red Spot exhibits internal counterclockwise rotation. Much turbulence is seen in adjacent material passing north or south of it. The satellites Amalthea, Io, Europa, Ganymede, and Callisto were photographed, some in great detail. Each is individual and unique, with no similarities to other known planets or satellites. Io has active volcanoes that probably have ejected material into a doughnut-shaped ring enveloping its orbit about Jupiter. This is not to be confused with the thin flat disk-like ring closer to Jupiter's surface. Now that such a ring has been seen by the Voyagers, older uncertain observations from Earth can be reinterpreted as early sightings of this structure.

Saturn

Saturn, last of the planets visible to the unaided eye, is almost twice as far from the sun as Jupiter, almost 900 million miles. It is second in size to Jupiter but its mass is much smaller. Saturn's specific gravity is less than that of water. Its diameter is about 71,000 miles at the equator; its rotational speed spins it completely around in a little more than 10 hours, and its atmosphere is much like that of Jupiter, except that its temperature at the top of its cloud layer is at least 100° lower. At about 300° F. below zero, the ammonia would be frozen out of Saturn's clouds. The theoretical construction of Saturn resembles that of Jupiter; it is either all gas, or it has a small dense center surrounded by a layer of liquid and a deep atmosphere.

Until Pioneer 11 passed Saturn in September 1979 only 10 satellites of Saturn were known. Since that time, the situation is quite confused. Added to data interpretations from the fly-by are earth-based observations using new techniques while the rings are edge-on and virtually invisible. It was hoped that the Voyager I and II fly-bys would help sort out the system. It is now believed that Saturn has at least 22 satellites, some sharing orbits. The Saturn satellite system is still confused.

Saturn's ring system begins about 7,000 miles above the visible disk of Saturn, lying above its equator and extending about 35,000 miles into space. The diameter of the ring system visible from Earth is about 170,000 miles; the rings are estimated to be no thicker than 10 miles. In 1973, radar observation showed the ring particles to be large chunks of material averaging a meter on a side.

Voyager I and II observations showed the rings to be considerably more complex than had been believed, so much so that interpretation will take much time. To the untrained eye, the Voyager photographs could be mistaken for pictures of a colorful phonograph record.

Uranus

Voyager II, after passing Saturn in August 1981, heads for a rendezvous with Uranus in 1986. Uranus, discovered by Sir William Herschel on Mar. 13, 1781, lies at a distance of 1.8 billion miles from the sun, taking 84 years to make its circuit around our star. Uranus has a diameter of about 32,000 miles and spins once in some 15.5 hours. One of the most fascinating features of Uranus is how far it is tipped over. Its north pole lies 98° from being directly up and down to its orbit plane. Thus, its seasons are extreme. If the sun rises at the north pole, it will stay up for 42 years; then it will set and the north pole will be in darkness (and winter) for 42 years.

Uranus has 5 satellites (known to date) whose orbits lie in the plane of the planet's equator. In that plane there are also 9 rings, discovered in 1978. Virtually invisible from Earth, the rings were found by observers watching Uranus pass before a star. As they waited, they saw their photoelectric equipment register a short eclipse of the star, then another, and another. Then the planet occulted the star as expected. After the star came out from behind Uranus, the star winked out several more times. Subsequent observations and analyses indicate 9 narrow, nearly opaque, rings circling Uranus.

The structure of Uranus is subject to some debate. Basically, however, it may have a rocky core surrounded by a thick icy mantle on top of which is a crust of hydrogen and helium that gradually becomes an atmosphere. Perhaps Voyager II will shed some light on this problem.

Neptune

Neptune, currently the most distant planet from the sun (until 1999), lies at an average distance of 2.8 billion miles. Having a diameter of about 31,000 miles and a rotation period of 18.2 hours, it is a virtual twin of Uranus. It is significantly more dense than Uranus, however, and this increases the debate over its internal structure. Neptune circles the sun in 164 years in a nearly circular orbit.

Neptune has 3 satellites, the third being found in 1981. The largest, Triton, is in a retrograde orbit suggesting that it was captured rather than being co-eval with Neptune. Triton is sufficiently large to raise significant tides on Neptune which will one day, say 100 million years from now, cause Triton to come close enough to Neptune for it to be torn apart. Nereid was found in 1949, and is in a long looping orbit suggesting it, too, was captured. The orbit of the third body is under analysis at this writing. Observations made in 1968 but not interpreted until 1982 suggest that Neptune, too, has a ring system.

As with the other giant planets, Neptune is emitting more energy than it receives from the sun. These excesses are thought to be cooling from internal heat sources and from the heat of the formation of the planets.

Little is known of Neptune beyond its distance, but Voyager II, if all continues to operate, will send us pictures and observations in 1989.

Pluto

Although Pluto on the average stays about 3.6 billion miles from the sun, its orbit is so eccentric that it is now approaching its minimum distance of 2.7 billion miles, less than the current distance of Neptune. Thus Pluto, until 1999, is temporarily planet number 8 from the sun. At its mean distance, Pluto takes 247.7 years to circumnavigate the sun. Until recently that was about all that was known of Pluto.

About a century ago, a hypothetical planet was believed to lie beyond Neptune and Uranus. Little more than a guess, a mass of one Earth was assigned to the mysterious body and mathematical searches were begun. Amid some controversy about the validity of the predictive process, Pluto was found nearly where it was predicted to be. It was found by Clyde Tombaugh at the Lowell Observatory in Flagstaff, Ariz., in 1930.

At the U.S. Naval Observatory, also in Flagstaff, on July 2, 1978, James Christy obtained a photograph of Pluto that was distinctly elongated. Repeated observations of this shape and its variation were convincing evidence of the discovery of a satellite of Pluto. Now named Charon, it may be 500 miles across, at a distance of over 10,000 miles, and taking 6.4 days to move around Pluto, the same length of time Pluto takes to rotate once. Gravitational laws allow these interactions to give us the mass of Pluto as 0.0017 of the Earth and a diameter of 1,500 miles. This makes the density about the same as that of water.

It is now clear that Pluto, the body found by Tombaugh, could not have influenced Neptune and Uranus to go astray. Theorists are again at work looking for a new planet X.

Greenwich Sidereal Time for 0^h GMT, 1983

(Add 12 hours to obtain Right Ascension of Mean Sun)

Date		h	m	Date		h	m	Date		h	m	Date		h	m
Jan.	1	06	40.3		11	13	14.6	July	10	19	09.4	Oct.	8	01	04.2
	11	07	19.8		21	13	54.0		20	19	48.8		18	01	43.7
	21	07	59.2	May	1	14	33.4		30	20	28.3		28	02	23.1
	31	08	38.6		11	15	12.9	Aug.	9	21	07.7	Nov.	7	03	02.5
Feb.	10	09	18.0		21	15	52.3		19	21	47.1		17	03	41.9
	20	09	57.4		31	16	31.7		29	22	26.5		27	04	21.3
Mar.	2	10	36.9	June	10	17	11.1	Sept.	8	23	05.9	Dec.	7	05	00.8
	12	11	16.3		20	17	50.1		18	23	45.4		17	05	40.2
	22	11	55.7		30	18	30.0		28	00	24.8		27	06	19.6
Apr.	1	12	35.1												

Astronomical Signs and Symbols

⊙	The Sun	⊕	The Earth	♅	Uranus	□	Quadrature
☾	The Moon	♂	Mars	♆	Neptune	☍	Opposition
☿	Mercury	♃	Jupiter	♇	Pluto	☊	Ascending Node
♀	Venus	♄	Saturn	☌	Conjunction	☋	Descending Node

Two heavenly bodies are in "conjunction" (☌) when they are due north and south of each other, either in Right Ascension (with respect to the north celestial pole) or in Celestial Longitude (with respect to the north ecliptic pole). If the bodies are seen near each other, they will rise and set at nearly the same time. They are in "opposition" (☍) when their Right Ascensions differ by exactly 12 hours, or their Celestial Longitudes differ by 180°. One of the two objects in opposition will rise while the other is setting. "Quadrature" (□) refers to the arrangement when the coordinates of two bodies differ by exactly 90°. These terms may refer to the relative positions of any two bodies as seen from the earth, but one of the bodies is so frequently the sun that mention of the sun is omitted; otherwise both bodies are named. The geocentric angular separation between sun and object is termed "elongation." Elongation is limited only for Mercury and Venus; the "greatest elongation" for each of these bodies is noted in the appropriate tables and is approximately the time for longest observation. When a planet is in its "ascending" (☊) or "descending" (☋) node, it is passing northward or southward, respectively, through the plane of the earth's orbit, across the celestial circle called the ecliptic. The term "perihelion" means nearest to the sun, and "aphelion," farthest from the sun. An "occultation" of a planet or star is an eclipse of it by some other body, usually the moon.

Planetary Configurations, 1983

Greenwich Mean Time (0 designates midnight; 12 designates noon)

Mo	D.	h.	m.		
Jan.	2	16	-		⊕ at perihelion
	6	18	-		☿ stationary
	7	10		☌ ☿ ♀	☿ 2° N
	7	12	-	☌ ♄ ☽	♄ 2° S
	9	22	-	☌ ♃ ☽	♃ 2° S
	15	19	-	☌ ♀ ☽	♀1°.8 N
	16	03	-	☌ ☿ ☉	Inferior
	17	04	-	☌ ♂ ☽	♂ 3° N
	27	10	-		☿ stationary
Feb	3	21	-	☌ ♄ ☽	♄ 2° S
	6	13	-	☌ ♃ ☽	♃ 1°.5 S
	8	20	-		☿ Gr elong 26° W of ☉
	10	15	-	☌ ☿ ☽	☿ 2° N
	13	08	-		♄ stationary
	15	02	-	☌ ♀ ☽	♀ 4° N
	15	06	-	☌ ♂ ☽	♂ 5° N
	17	05	-	☌ ♃ *	♃ 5° N of Antares
	18	22	-	☌ ♀ ♂	♀ 0°.5 S
Mar.	3	06	-	☌ ♄ ☽	♄ 1°.7 S
	6	03	-	☌ ♃ ☽	♃ 1° S; occultation
	16	06	-	☌ ♂ ☽	♂ 5° N
	17	06	-	☌ ♀ ☽	♀ 5° N
	21	04	39		Vernal equinox; Spring begins
	26	11	-	☌ ☿ ☉	Superior
	28	01	-		♃ stationary
	30	14	-	☌ ♄ ☽	♄ 1°.5 S
Apr.	2	13	-	☌ ♃ ☽	♃ 0°.6 S; occultation
	9	12	-	☌ ☿ ♂	☿ 1°.4 N
	14	15	-	☌ ☿ ☽	☿ 6° N
	16	07	-	☌ ♀ ☽	♀ 4° N
	18	18	-	☍ ♇ ☉	
	21	08	-		☿ Gr elong 20° E of ☉
	21	19	-	☍ ♄ ☉	
	22	13	-	☌ ♀ *	♀ 7° N of Aldebaran
	26	19	-	☌ ♄ ☽	♄ 1°.6 S
	29	19	-	☌ ♃ ☽	♃ 0°.6 S; occultation
May	2	04	-		☿ stationary
	6	06	-	☌ ♃ *	♃ 6° N of Antares
	12	17	-	☌ ☿ ☉	Inferior
	16	01	-	☌ ♀ ☽	♀ 1°.5 N
	23	23	-	☌ ♄ ☽	♄ 1°.8 S
	24	23	-		☿ stationary
	26	21	-	☌ ♃ ☽	♃ 0°.8 S; occultation
	27	22	-	☍ ♃ ☉	
	29	01	-	☍ ♅ ☉	
	31	05	-	☌ ♀ *	♀ 4° S of Pollux
June	3	11	-	☌ ♂ ☉	
	8	06	-		☿ Gr elong 24° W of ☉
	9	10	-	☌ ☿ ☽	☿ 0°.8 S; occultation
	11	05	-	☌ ☽ ☉	Total solar eclipse
	14	11	-	☌ ♀ ☽	♀ 1°.5 S
	16	07	-		♀ Gr elong 45° E of ☉
	19	17	-	☍ ♆ ☉	
	20	03	-	☌ ♄ ☽	♄ 2° S
	21	06	-	☌ ☿ *	☿ 4° N of Aldebaran
	21	23	09		Summer solstice; Summer begins
	22	21	-	☌ ♃ ☽	♃ 1°.2 S; occultation
	25	09	-	☍ ☽ ☉	Lunar eclipse
July	2	13	-		♄ stationary
	6	10	-		⊕ at aphelion
	9	16	-	☌ ☿ ☉	Inferior
	9	23	-	☌ ♀ *	♀ 0°.7 S of Regulus
	13	08	-	☌ ♀ ☽	♀ 6° S
	17	09	-	☌ ♀ ☽	♀ 2° S
	19	15	-		♀ Gr brilliancy
	19	23	-	☌ ♃ ☽	♃ 1°.4 S
	29	13	-		♃ stationary
Aug.	1	02	-	☌ ☿ *	☿ 0°.4 N of Regulus
	1	12	-		♀ stationary
	4	12	-	☌ ♂ *	♂ 6° S of Pollux
	6	06	-	☌ ☿ ♀	☿ 6° N
	7	12	-	☌ ♂ ☽	♂ 1°.8 S
	10	01	-	☌ ♀ ☽	♀ 12° S
	10	11	-	☌ ☿ ☽	☿ 6° S
	13	18	-	☌ ♄ ☽	♄ 1°.9 S
	16	06	-	☌ ♃ ☽	♃ 1°.3 S
	19	16	-		☿ Gr elong 27° E of ☉
	25	05	-	☌ ♀ ☉	Inferior
Sept.	1	19	-		☿ stationary
	5	02	-	☌ ♂ ☽	♂ 3° S
	5	14	-	☌ ♀ ☽	♀ 13° S
	7	20	-	☌ ☿ ☽	☿ 10° S
	10	07	-	☌ ♄ ☽	♄ 1°.7 S
	12	18	-	☌ ♃ ☽	♃ 0°.9 S; occultation
	14	08	-		♀ stationary
	14	19	-	☌ ♀ ♂	♀ 9° S
	15	16	-	☌ ☿ ☉	Inferior
	23	14	42		Autumnal equinox; Autumn begins
	24	01	-		☿ stationary
	24	22	-	☌ ♃ ♅	♃ 0°.4 N
	28	21	-	☌ ♂ *	♂ 0°.9 N of Regulus
Oct	1	07	-		♀ Gr brilliancy
	1	10	-		☿ Gr elong 18° W of ☉
	3	07	-	☌ ♀ ☽	♀ 9° S
	3	16	-	☌ ♂ ☽	♂ 4° S
	5	03	-	☌ ☿ ☽	☿ 4° S
	7	07	-	☌ ♀ *	♀ 4° S of Regulus
	7	23	-	☌ ♄ ☽	♄ 1°,4 S
	10	08	-	☌ ♅ ☽	♅ 1°.0 S; occultation
	10	11	-	☌ ♃ ☽	♃ 0°.4 S; occultation
	13	01	-	☌ ♃ *	♃ 5° N of Antares
	23	11	-	☌ ♇ ☉	
	28	13	-	☌ ♀ ♂	♀ 1°.7 S
	30	17	-	☌ ☿ ☉	Superior
	31	06	-	☌ ♄ ☉	
Nov	1	04	-	☌ ♂ ☽	♂ 4° S
	1	06	-	☌ ♀ ☽	♀ 5° S
	4	20	-		♀ Gr elong 47° W of ☉
	6	20	-	☌ ♅ ☽	♅ 0°.7 S; occultation
	7	07	-	☌ ♃ ☽	♃ 0°.2 N; occultation
	20	07	-	☌ ☿ *	☿ 3° N of Antares
	26	06	-	☌ ☿ ♃	☿ 3° S
	29	15	-	☌ ♀ *	♀ 4° N of Spica
	29	15	-	☌ ♂ ☽	♂ 4° S
Dec	2	03	-	☌ ♅ ☉	
	2	04	-	☌ ♄ ☽	♄ 0°.9 S; occultation
	4	12	-	☌ ☽ ☉	Annular solar eclipse
	6	03	-	☌ ☿ ☽	☿ 0°.9 S; occultation
	13	21	-		☿ Gr elong 21° E of ☉
	14	13	-	☌ ♃ ☉	
	17	11	-	☌ ♀ ♄	♀ 0°.2 N
	20	02	-	☍ ☽ ☉	Penumbral eclipse
	21	10	-	♂ ♆ ☉	
	22	10	30		Winter solstice; Winter begins
	27	08	-	☌ ♂ *	♂ 4° N of Spica
	28	00	-	☌ ♂ ☽	♂ 3° S
	29	16	-	☌ ♄ ☽	♄ 0°.6 S; occultation
	30	19	-	☌ ♀ ☽	♀ 0°.7 N; occultation
	31	08	-	☌ ☿ ☉	Inferior
	31	18	-	☌ ♅ ☽	♅ 0°.4 S; occultation

Planetary Configurations, 1984

Mo	D.	h.	m.		
Jan.	3	22	-		⊕ at perihelion
	8	03	-	☌ ♀ *	♀ 7° N of Antares
	11	01	-		☿ stationary
	22	05	-		☿ Gr elong 24° W of ☉
	25	09	-	☌ ♂ ☽	♂ 1°.6 S
	26	01	-	☌ ♄ ☽	♄ 0°.2 S; occultation
	27	02	-	☌ ♀ ♃	♀ 0°.8 N
	29	16	-	☌ ♃ ☽	♃ 1°.8 N
	29	22	-	☌ ♀ ☽	♀ 3° N
	30	21	-	☌ ☿ ☽	☿ 3° N
Feb.	15	13	-	☌ ♂ ♄	♂ 0°.8 S
	22	09	-	☌ ♄ ☽	♄ 0°.3 N; occultation

Mo	D. h. m.			
	22 14	-	☌ ♂ ☽	♂ 0°.3 S; occultation
	24 10	-	☌ ♅ ☽	♅ 0°.2 N; occultation
	25 06	-		♄ stationary
	26 08	-	☌ ♃ ☽	♃ 2° N
	29 03	-	☌ ♀ ☽	♀ 4° N
Mar	8 17	-	☌ ☿ ☉	Superior
	20 10 25			Vernal equinox; Spring begins
	20 18	-	☌ ♄ ☽	♄ 0°.6 N; occultation
	21 13	-	☌ ♂ ☽	♂ 0°.5 N; occultation
	24 21	-	☌ ♃ ☽	♃ 3° N
	30 12	-	☌ ♀ ☽	♀ 4° N

Mo	D. h. m.			
Apr.	3 00	-	☌ ☿ ☽	☿ 6° N
	3 03	-		☿ Gr elong 19° E of ☉
	5 02	-		♂ stationary
	12 00	-		☿ stationary
	17 01	-	☌ ♄ ☽	♄ 0°.6 N; occultation
	17 23	-	☌ ♂ ☽	♂ 0°.04 N; occultation
	19 03	-	☌ ♅ ☽	♅ 0°.6 N; occultation
	20 16	-	☍ ♇ ☉	
	21 09	-	☌ ♃ ☽	♃ 3° N
	22 05	-	☌ ☿ ☉	Inferior
	29 20	-		♃ stationary
	30 00	-	☌ ☿ ♀	☿ 0°.7 N

Rising and Setting of Planets, 1983

Greenwich Mean Time (0 designates midnight)

1983		20° N. Latitude Rise	Set	30° N. Latitude Rise	Set	40° N. Latitude Rise	Set	50° N. Latitude Rise	Set	60° N. Latitude Rise	Set
						Venus, 1983					
Jan	6	7:49	18:43	8:09	18:24	8:33	17:59	9:08	17:24	10:08	16:24
	16	7:57	19:00	8:13	18:44	8:34	18:23	9:03	17:54	9:51	17:06
	26	8:01	19:17	8:13	19:04	8:29	18:48	8:51	18:26	9:27	17:51
Feb	5	8:02	19:32	8:11	19:23	8:21	19:12	8:36	18:57	8:59	18:34
	15	8:01	19:46	8:05	19:41	8:11	19:36	8:18	19:28	8:30	19:17
	25	7:54	19:54	7:54	19:54	7:54	19:54	7:55	19:54	7:55	19:54
Mar	7	7:52	20:07	7:48	20:11	7:42	20:17	7:35	20:24	7:24	20:35
	17	7:50	20:20	7:41	20:29	7:30	20:40	7:16	20:54	6:53	21:17
	27	7:49	20:33	7:36	20:46	7:20	21:03	6:58	21:25	6:22	22:00
Apr	6	7:50	20:48	7:34	21:04	7:12	21:26	6:43	21:55	5:54	22:44
	16	7:54	21:02	7:34	21:22	7:08	21:48	6:33	22:24	5:29	23:27
	26	8:01	21:17	7:38	21:39	7:09	22:08	6:28	22:50	5:11	24:06
May	6	8:09	21:30	7:45	21:54	7:14	22:25	6:30	23:09	5:04	24:35
	16	8:19	21:41	7:55	22:05	7:24	22:36	6:39	23:21	5:12	24:48
	26	8:30	21:48	8:07	22:11	7:37	22:40	6:55	23:23	5:35	24:42
Jun	5	8:39	21:50	8:18	22:11	7:51	22:38	7:13	23:16	6:06	24:23
	15	8:46	21:48	8:28	22:06	8:05	22:29	7:32	23:01	6:38	23:56
	25	8:49	21:40	8:34	21:55	8:15	22:14	7:49	22:39	7:06	23:22
Jul	5	8:46	21:26	8:34	21:38	8:20	21:52	8:00	22:12	7:29	22:43
	15	8:37	21:05	8:28	21:14	8:18	21:24	8:04	21:38	7:42	22:00
	25	8:18	20:37	8:12	20:42	8:06	20:49	7:57	20:58	7:42	21:12
Aug	4	7:46	19:57	7:43	20:01	7:38	20:05	7:33	20:10	7:25	20:19
	14	6:59	19:06	6:56	19:08	6:54	19:11	6:50	19:15	6:44	19:21
	24	5:57	18:06	5:54	18:09	5:51	18:12	5:46	18:16	5:39	18:23
Sep	3	4:52	17:07	4:48	17:11	4:43	17:16	4:35	17:24	4:24	17:35
	13	3:59	16:20	3:53	16:26	3:45	16:33	3:35	16:43	3:20	16:59
	23	3:24	15:49	3:17	15:56	3:08	16:05	2:55	16:17	2:37	16:36
Oct	3	3:03	15:28	2:55	15:36	2:46	15:45	2:34	15:57	2:14	16:17
	13	2:52	15:15	2:45	15:22	2:37	15:30	2:25	15:41	2:08	15:59
	23	2:48	15:06	2:43	15:11	2:36	15:17	2:28	15:24	2:14	15:39
Nov	2	2:49	14:59	2:46	15:02	2:42	15:05	2:37	15:10	2:30	15:18
	12	2:53	14:53	2:53	14:54	2:52	14:54	2:52	14:54	2:52	14:55
	22	2:59	14:49	3:02	14:46	3:06	14:43	3:11	14:38	3:18	14:30
Dec	2	3:08	14:46	3:14	14:40	3:22	14:32	3:33	14:22	3:49	14:06
	12	3:18	14:45	3:28	14:36	3:40	14:24	3:56	14:07	4:22	13:42
	22	3:31	14:47	3:44	14:34	4:00	14:17	4:22	13:55	4:57	13:20
						Mars, 1983					
Jan	6	9:02	20:15	9:16	20:01	9:33	19:44	9:57	19:20	10:35	18:42
	16	8:49	20:10	9:00	19:59	9:14	19:45	9:34	19:26	10:04	18:55
	26	8:35	20:05	8:44	19:56	8:54	19:46	9:09	19:31	9:32	19:08
Feb	5	8:20	19:59	8:26	19:53	8:34	19:46	8:44	19:36	8:59	19:20
	15	8:05	19:53	8:08	19:50	8:12	19:45	8:18	19:40	8:26	19:32
	25	7:49	19:47	7:49	19:46	7:50	19:45	7:51	19:44	7:53	19:42
Mar	7	7:30	19:37	7:28	19:39	7:25	19:41	7:22	19:45	7:17	19:50
	17	7:14	19:30	7:09	19:35	7:03	19:40	6:56	19:48	6:44	20:00
	27	6:58	19:23	6:51	19:30	6:42	19:39	6:30	19:51	6:11	20:10
Apr	6	6:42	19:16	6:33	19:25	6:21	19:38	6:04	19:54	5:38	20:20
	16	6:27	19:09	6:15	19:21	6:00	19:36	5:40	19:56	5:07	20:29
	26	6:13	19:01	5:58	19:16	5:40	19:34	5:16	19:58	4:36	20:38
May	6	5:59	18:54	5:42	19:11	5:22	19:31	4:53	20:00	4:06	20:47
	16	5:46	18:47	5:27	19:05	5:05	19:28	4:33	20:00	3:38	20:54
	26	5:33	18:40	5:13	18:59	4:49	19:24	4:14	19:59	3:13	21:00
June	5	5:22	18:32	5:01	18:53	4:34	19:19	3:56	19:57	2:50	21:04
	15	5:11	18:24	4:49	18:46	4:21	19:13	3:42	19:53	2:31	21:04
	25	5:00	18:15	4:38	18:37	4:10	19:05	3:29	19:46	2:15	21:00
July	5	4:50	18:05	4:28	18:28	3:59	18:56	3:19	19:36	2:04	20:51
	15	4:40	17:54	4:18	18:16	3:50	18:44	3:10	19:24	1:58	20:37
	25	4:31	17:43	4:09	18:04	3:42	18:31	3:03	19:10	1:54	20:19
Aug	4	4:21	17:30	4:00	17:50	3:35	18:16	2:58	18:53	1:54	19:57
	14	4:11	17:16	3:52	17:35	3:28	17:59	2:53	18:34	1:55	19:32
	24	4:01	17:01	3:43	17:19	3:21	17:41	2:50	18:12	1:57	19:05
Sep	3	3:50	16:45	3:34	17:01	3:14	17:21	2:46	17:49	2:00	18:36
	13	3:39	16:28	3:25	16:42	3:07	17:00	2:42	17:25	2:02	18:05
	23	3:30	16:13	3:17	16:25	3:02	16:41	2:41	17:02	2:06	17:36

		20° N. Latitude		30° N. Latitude		40° N. Latitude		50° N. Latitude		60° N. Latitude	
		Rise	Set	Rise	Set	Rise	Set	Rise	Set	Rise	Set
Oct	3	3:18	15:54	3:07	16:05	2:54	16:18	2:36	16:36	2:08	17:04
	13	3:05	15:35	2:57	15:43	2:46	15:54	2:32	16:08	2:09	16:31
	23	2:52	15:15	2:46	15:21	2:37	15:29	2:26	15:40	2:09	15:58
Nov	2	2:39	14:54	2:34	14:59	2:28	15:05	2:21	15:12	2:09	15:24
	12	2:25	14:34	2:22	14:36	2:19	14:39	2:15	14:44	2:08	14:50
	22	2:10	14:12	2:10	14:13	2:09	14:14	2:08	14:15	2:06	14:17
Dec	2	1:56	13:51	1:57	13:50	1:58	13:48	2:01	13:46	2:04	13:43
	12	1:40	13:30	1:44	13:26	1:48	13:22	1:53	13:17	2:01	13:09
	22	1:25	13:08	1:30	13:03	1:36	12:57	1:44	12:48	1:57	12:35

Jupiter, 1983

		20° N. Latitude		30° N. Latitude		40° N. Latitude		50° N. Latitude		60° N. Latitude	
		Rise	Set	Rise	Set	Rise	Set	Rise	Set	Rise	Set
Jan.	6	3:33	14:33	3:51	14:15	4:13	13:53	4:44	13:22	5:36	12:30
	16	3:02	14:01	3:20	13:43	3:43	13:20	4:14	12:48	5:08	11:55
	26	2:30	13:28	2:48	13:09	3:11	12:46	3:44	12:14	4:39	11:19
Feb.	5	1:57	12:54	2:16	12:36	2:39	12:12	3:12	11:39	4:08	10:43
	15	1:23	12:20	1:42	12:01	2:06	11:37	2:39	11:04	3:36	10:07
	25	0:49	11:45	1:08	11:26	1:32	11:02	2:05	10:28	3:03	9:31
Mar.	7	0:13	11:08	0:32	10:49	0:56	10:25	1:30	9:51	2:28	8:53
	17	23:35	10:31	23:55	10:12	0:19	9:48	0:53	9:14	1:51	8:15
	27	22:57	9:52	23:16	9:33	23:40	9:09	0:14	8:35	1:12	7:36
Apr.	6	22:17	9:12	22:36	8:53	22:59	8:29	23:34	7:55	0:32	6:57
	16	21:35	8:31	21:54	8:12	22:18	7:48	22:52	7:14	23:50	6:16
	26	20:53	7:49	21:12	7:30	21:36	7:06	22:09	6:32	23:06	5:35
May	6	20:09	7:06	20:28	6:47	20:51	6:23	21:25	5:50	22:21	4:53
	16	19:24	6:22	19:43	6:03	20:06	5:40	20:39	5:07	21:35	4:11
	26	18:39	5:37	18:58	5:19	19:21	4:56	19:54	4:23	20:49	3:28
June	5	17:54	4:53	18:13	4:35	18:35	4:12	19:08	3:40	20:02	2:45
	15	17:10	4:09	17:28	3:51	17:50	3:28	18:22	2:56	19:15	2:03
	25	16:25	3:25	16:43	3:07	17:06	2:45	17:37	2:14	18:30	1:21
July	5	15:42	2:42	16:00	2:25	16:22	2:03	16:53	1:32	17:45	0:39
	15	15:00	2:01	15:18	1:43	15:40	1:21	16:11	0:50	17:03	23:58
	25	14:20	1:20	14:37	1:02	14:59	0:40	15:30	0:10	16:22	23:18
Aug.	4	13:40	0:41	13:58	0:23	14:20	0:01	14:51	23:30	15:43	22:38
	14	13:02	0:02	13:20	23:45	13:42	23:22	14:14	22:51	15:06	21:59
	24	12:26	23:25	12:44	23:07	13:06	22:45	13:38	22:13	14:31	21:20
Sep.	3	11:50	22:49	12:08	22:31	12:31	22:08	13:03	21:36	13:57	20:42
	13	11:16	22:14	11:34	21:55	11:57	21:32	12:30	21:00	13:25	20:05
	23	10:43	21:40	11:02	21:22	11:25	20:58	11:58	20:25	12:54	19:29
Oct.	3	10:11	21:07	10:30	20:48	10:54	20:24	11:27	19:51	12:25	18:53
	13	9:39	20:34	9:59	20:15	10:23	19:51	10:57	19:17	11:56	18:18
	23	9:08	20:02	9:28	19:43	9:53	19:18	10:28	18:43	11:28	17:43
Nov.	2	8:38	19:31	8:58	19:11	9:23	18:46	9:59	18:10	11:00	17:09
	12	8:08	19:00	8:28	18:40	8:54	18:14	9:30	17:38	10:33	16:35
	22	7:38	18:30	7:59	18:09	8:25	17:43	9:01	17:06	10:06	16:02
Dec.	2	7:09	17:59	7:30	17:39	7:56	17:12	8:33	16:35	9:39	15:30
	12	6:40	17:29	7:01	17:08	7:27	16:42	8:05	16:04	9:11	14:58
	22	6:10	16:59	6:31	16:38	6:58	16:12	7:36	15:34	8:43	14:26

Saturn, 1983

		20° N. Latitude		30° N. Latitude		40° N. Latitude		50° N. Latitude		60° N. Latitude	
		Rise	Set	Rise	Set	Rise	Set	Rise	Set	Rise	Set
Jan	6	1:25	12:55	1:33	12:46	1:44	12:35	1:59	12:20	2:22	11:57
	16	0:47	12:17	0:56	12:08	1:07	11:57	1:22	11:42	1:46	11:19
	26	0:10	11:39	0:19	11:30	0:30	11:19	0:45	11:04	1:09	10:40
Feb	5	23:31	11:00	23:40	10:51	23:51	10:40	0:07	10:25	0:30	10:01
	15	22:52	10:21	23:01	10:12	23:12	10:01	23:27	9:46	23:51	9:22
	25	22:12	9:42	22:21	9:33	22:32	9:22	22:47	9:07	23:10	8:43
Mar	7	21:31	9:01	21:40	8:52	21:51	8:41	22:06	8:27	22:29	8:04
	17	20:50	8:20	20:58	8:12	21:09	8:01	21:24	7:47	21:46	7:24
	27	20:08	7:39	20:16	7:31	20:27	7:20	20:41	7:06	21:03	6:44
Apr	6	19:26	6:58	19:34	6:49	19:44	6:39	19:58	6:25	20:19	6:04
	16	18:43	6:16	18:51	6:08	19:01	5:58	19:14	5:44	19:35	5:24
	26	18:00	5:34	18:08	5:26	18:18	5:16	18:31	5:03	18:51	4:43
May	6	17:18	4:52	17:25	4:44	17:35	4:35	17:47	4:22	18:07	4:03
	16	16:35	4:10	16:43	4:03	16:52	3:54	17:04	3:41	17:23	3:22
	26	15:53	3:29	16:00	3:22	16:09	3:13	16:21	3:01	16:40	2:42
June	5	15:12	2:48	15:19	2:41	15:28	2:32	15:39	2:20	15:58	2:02
	15	14:31	2:07	14:38	2:00	14:46	1:51	14:58	1:40	15:16	1:22
	25	13:51	1:27	13:58	1:20	14:06	1:11	14:18	1:00	14:36	0:42
July	5	13:11	0:47	13:18	0:40	13:27	0:32	13:38	0:20	13:56	0:02
	15	12:32	0:08	12:39	0:01	12:48	23:52	13:00	23:40	13:18	23:22
	25	11:54	23:29	12:01	23:22	12:10	23:13	12:22	23:01	12:41	22:43
Aug	4	11:17	22:51	11:24	22:44	11:33	22:35	11:45	22:23	12:05	22:03
	14	10:40	22:14	10:47	22:06	10:57	21:57	11:09	21:44	11:29	21:24
	24	10:03	21:37	10:11	21:29	10:21	21:19	10:34	21:06	10:55	20:45
Sep	3	9:28	20:59	9:36	20:52	9:46	20:42	10:00	20:28	10:21	20:07
	13	8:52	20:23	9:01	20:15	9:11	20:05	9:25	19:50	9:48	19:28
	23	8:18	19:48	8:27	19:39	8:37	19:28	8:52	19:13	9:15	18:50
Oct	3	7:43	19:12	7:52	19:03	8:04	18:51	8:19	18:36	8:43	18:12
	13	7:09	18:36	7:18	18:27	7:30	18:15	7:46	17:59	8:11	17:34
	23	6:34	18:01	6:44	17:51	6:57	17:39	7:13	17:22	7:39	16:56
Nov	2	6:00	17:25	6:10	17:15	6:23	17:03	6:40	16:45	7:07	16:18
	12	5:26	16:50	5:37	16:39	5:50	16:26	6:08	16:09	6:36	15:40
	22	4:52	16:15	5:03	16:04	5:16	15:50	5:35	15:32	6:04	15:03
Dec	2	4:17	15:39	4:28	15:28	4:42	15:14	5:01	14:55	5:31	14:25
	12	3:43	15:03	3:54	14:52	4:08	14:38	4:28	14:18	4:59	13:47
	22	3:07	14:27	3:19	14:16	3:34	14:01	3:54	13:41	4:25	13:09

Star Tables

These tables include stars of visual magnitude 2.5 and brighter. Co-ordinates are for the epoch Jan. 0.916, 1983. Where no parallax figures are given, the trigonometric parallax figure is smaller than the margin for error and the distance given is obtained by indirect methods. Stars of variable magnitude designated by v.

To find the time when the star is on meridian, subtract R.A.M.S. of the sun table on page 758 from the star's right ascension, first adding 24h to the latter, if necessary. Mark this result P.M., if less than 12h; but if greater than 12, subtract 12h and mark the remainder A.M.

Star	Magnitude	Parallax ″	Light yrs.	Right ascen. h. m.	Declination ° ′
α Andromedae (Alpheratz)	2.06	0.02	90	0 07.5	+29 00
β Cassiopeiae	2.26v	0.07	45	0 08.3	+59 03
α Phoenicis	2.39	0.04	93	0 25.5	−42 24
α Cassiopeiae (Schedir)	2.22	0.01	150	0 39.5	+56 27
β Ceti	2.02	0.06	57	0 42.7	−18 05
γ Cassiopeiae	2.13v	0.03	96	0 55.7	+60 38
β Andromedae	2.02	0.04	76	1 08.8	+35 32
α Eridani (Achernar)	0.51	0.02	118	1 37.1	−57 19
γ Andromedae	2.14		260	2 02.8	+42 15
α Arietis	2.00	0.04	76	2 06.2	+23 23
α Ursae Min. (Pole Star)	1.99v		680	2 14.5	+89 11
o Ceti	2.00v	0.01	103	2 18.5	−3 03
β Persei (Algol)	2.06v	0.03	105	3 07.1	+40 53
α Persei	1.80	0.03	570	3 23.1	+49 48
α Tauri (Aldebaran)	0.86v	0.05	68	4 34.9	+16 29
β Orionis (Rigel)	0.14v		900	5 13.7	−8 13
α Aurigae (Capella)	0.05	0.07	45	5 15.4	+45 59
γ Orionis (Bellatrix)	1.64	0.03	470	5 24.2	+6 20
β Tauri (El Nath)	1.65	0.02	300	5 25.2	+28 36
δ Orionis	2.20v		1500	5 31.1	−0 19
ε Orionis	1.70		1600	5 35.4	−1 13
ζ Orionis	1.79	0.02	1600	5 39.9	−1 57
κ Orionis	2.06	0.01	2100	5 46.9	−9 40
α Orionis (Betelgeuse)	0.41v		520	5 54.2	+7 24
β Aurigae	1.86	0.04	88	5 58.3	+44 57
β Canis Majoris	1.96	0.01	750	6 22.0	−17 57
α Carinae (Canopus)	−0.72	0.02	98	6 23.6	−52 41
γ Geminorum	1.93	0.03	105	6 36.7	+16 25
α Canis Majoris (Sirius)	−1.47	0.38	8.7	6 44.4	−16 42
ε Canis Majoris	1.48		680	6 58.0	−28 57
δ Canis Majoris	1.85		2100	7 07.7	−26 22
η Canis Majoris	2.46		2700	7 23.4	−29 16
α Geminorum (Castor)	1.97	0.07	45	7 33.5	+31 56
α Canis Minoris (Procyon)	0.37	0.29	11.3	7 38.4	+5 16
β Geminorum (Pollux)	1.16	0.09	35	7 44.3	+28 04
ζ Puppis	2.23		2400	8 03.0	−39 57
γ Velorum	1.88		520	8 09.0	−47 17
ε Carinae	1.90		340	8 22.2	−59 27
δ Velorum	1.95	0.04	76	8 44.2	−54 39
λ Velorum	2.24	0.02	750	9 07.4	−43 22
β Carinae	1.67	0.04	86	9 13.0	−69 39
ι Carinae	2.25		750	9 16.6	−59 12
κ Velorum	2.49	0.01	470	9 21.6	−54 56
α Hydrae	1.98	0.02	94	9 26.8	−8 35
α Leonis (Regulus)	1.36	0.04	84	10 07.5	+12 03
γ Leonis	1.99	0.02	90	10 19.0	+19 56
β Ursae Majoris (Merak)	2.37	0.04	78	11 00.8	+56 28
α Ursae Majoris (Dubhe)	1.81	0.03	105	11 02.7	+61 51
β Leonis (Denebola)	2.14	0.08	43	11 48.2	+14 40
γ Ursae Majoris (Phecda)	2.44	0.02	90	11 52.9	+53 47
α Crucis	1.39		370	12 25.6	−63 00
γ Crucis	1.69		220	12 30.2	−57 00
γ Centauri	2.17		160	12 40.6	−48 52
β Crucis	1.28v		490	12 46.7	−59 36
ε Ursae Majoris (Alioth)	1.79v	0.01	68	12 53.3	+56 03
ζ Ursae Majoris (Mizar)	2.26	0.04	88	13 23.2	+55 01
α Virginis (Spica)	0.91v	0.02	220	13 24.3	−11 04
ε Centauri	2.33v		570	13 38.8	−53 23
η Ursae Majoris (Alkaid)	1.87		210	13 46.9	+49 24
β Centauri	0.63v	0.02	490	14 02.6	−60 18
θ Centauri	2.04	0.06	55	14 05.7	−36 17
α Bootis (Arcturus)	−0.06	0.09	36	14 14.9	+19 16
η Centauri	2.39v		390	14 34.4	−42 05
α Centauri	0.01	0.75	4.3	14 38.4	−60 46
α Lupi	2.32v		430	14 40.8	−47 19
ε Bootis	2.37	0.01	103	14 44.2	+27 09
β Ursae Minoris	2.07	0.03	105	14 50.7	+74 14
α Coronae Borealis	2.23v	0.04	76	15 34.0	+26 46
δ Scorpii	2.34		590	15 59.3	−22 34
α Scorpii (Antares)	0.92v	0.02	520	16 28.4	−26 24
α Trianguli Australis	1.93	0.02	82	16 46.9	−69 00
ε Scorpii	2.28	0.05	66	16 49.0	−34 16
η Ophiuchi	2.43	0.05	69	17 09.4	−15 42
λ Scorpii	1.60v		310	17 32.5	−37 06
α Ophiuchi	2.09	0.06	58	17 34.1	+12 34
θ Scorpii	1.86	0.02	650	17 36.1	−42 59
κ Scorpii	2.39v		470	17 41.3	−39 01
γ Draconis	2.21	0.02	108	17 56.2	+51 29
ε Sagittarii	1.81	0.02	124	18 23.0	−34 24
α Lyrae (Vega)	0.04	0.12	26.5	18 36.4	+38 46
σ Sagittarii	2.12		300	18 54.2	−26 19
α Aquilae (Altair)	0.77	0.20	16.5	19 50.0	+8 49
γ Cygni	2.22		750	20 21.6	+40 12
α Pavonis	1.95		310	20 24.3	−56 47
α Cygni (Deneb)	1.26		1600	20 40.8	+45 13
ε Cygni	2.46	0.04	74	20 45.5	+33 54
α Cephei	2.44	0.06	52	21 18.2	+62 31
ε Pegasi	2.38		780	21 43.4	+9 48
α Gruis	1.76	0.05	64	22 07.2	−47 03
β Gruis	2.17v		280	22 41.7	−46 58
α Piscis Austrinis (Fomalhaut)	1.15	0.14	22.6	22 56.7	−29 43
β Pegasi	2.50v	0.02	210	23 02.9	+27 59
α Pegasi	2.50	0.03	109	23 03.9	+15 07

Astronomical Constants; Speed of Light

The following astronomical constants were adopted in 1968, in accordance with the resolutions and recommendations of the International Astronomical Union (Hamburg 1964): Velocity of light, 299,792.5 kilometers per second, or about 186,282.3976 statute miles per second: solar parallax, 8′.794: constant of nutation, 9′.210; and constant of aberration, 20′.496.

Aurora Borealis and Aurora Australis

The Aurora Borealis, also called the Northern Lights, is a broad display of rather faint light in the northern skies at night. The Aurora Australis, a similar phenomenon, appears at the same time in southern skies. The aurora appears in a wide variety of forms. Sometimes it is seen as a quiet glow, almost foglike in character; sometimes as vertical streamers in which there may be considerable motion; sometimes as a series of luminous expanding arcs. There are many colors, with white, yellow, and red predominating.

The auroras are most vivid and most frequently seen at about 20 degrees from the magnetic poles, along the northern coast of the North American continent and the eastern part of the northern coast of Europe. They have been seen as far south as Key West and as far north as Australia and New Zealand, but rarely.

While the cause of the auroras is not known beyond question, there does seem to be a definite correlation between auroral displays and sun-spot activity. It is thought that atomic particles expelled from the sun by the forces that cause solar flares speed through space at velocities of 400 to 600 miles per second. These particles are entrapped by the earth's magnetic field, forming what are termed the Van Allen belts. The encounter of these clouds of the solar wind with the earth's magnetic field weakens the field so that previously trapped particles are allowed to impact the upper atmosphere. The collisions between solar and terrestrial atoms result in the glow in the upper atmosphere called the aurora. The glow may be vivid where the lines of magnetic force converge near the magnetic poles.

The auroral displays appear at heights ranging from 50 to about 600 miles and have given us a means of estimating the extent of the earth's atmosphere.

The auroras are often accompanied by magnetic storms whose forces, also guided by the lines of force of the earth's magnetic field, disrupt electrical communication.

The Planets and the Solar System

Planet	Mean daily motion "	Orbital velocity miles per sec.	Sidereal revolution days	Synodical revolution days	Dist. from sun in millions of mi. Max.	Min.	Dist. from Earth in millions of mi. Max.	Min.	Light at[1] perihelion	aphelion
Mercury . .	14732.420	29.75	87.9693	115.9	43.403	28.597	136	50	10.58	4.59
Venus . . .	5767.668	21.76	224.7009	583.9	67.726	66.813	161	25	1.94	1.89
Earth	3548.192	18.51	365.2564	—	94.555	91.445	—	—	1.03	0.97
Mars	1886.519	14.99	686.9796	779.9	154.936	128.471	248	35	0.524	0.360
Jupiter . . .	298.993	8.12	4332.1248	398.9	507.046	460.595	600	368	0.0408	0.0336
Saturn . . .	119.718	5.99	10825.863	378.1	937.541	838.425	1031	745	0.01230	0.00984
Uranus . . .	41.978	4.23	30676.15	369.7	1859.748	1699.331	1953	1606	0.00300	0.00250
Neptune . .	21.493	3.38	59911.13	367.5	2821.686	2760.386	2915	2667	0.00114	0.00109
Pluto	14.116	2.95	90824.2	366.7	4551.386	2756.427	4644	2663	0.00114	0.00042

Light at perihelion and aphelion is solar illumination in units of mean illumination at Earth.

Planet	Mean longitude of:* ascending node °	'	"	perihelion °	'	"	Inclination* of orbit to ecliptic °	'	"	Mean distance**	Eccentricity of orbit	Mean longitude at the epoch* °	'	"
Mercury. . . .	48	06	43	77	09	50	7	00	16	0.387100	0.205630	111	13	00
Venus	76	30	54	131	33	36	3	23	40	0.723330	0.006788	176	09	15
Earth				102	28	59				0.999990	0.016734	292	45	52
Mars	49	24	47	335	44	38	1	51	00	1.523633	0.093382	260	50	43
Jupiter	100	16	44	14	51	43	1	18	21	5.20488	0.047777	193	46	07
Saturn.	113	30	22	95	26	20	2	29	10	9.57501	0.053616	183	50	50
Uranus	73	59	49	175	01	05	0	46	20	19.2930	0.050521	233	41	36
Neptune . . .	131	31	59	42	16	48	1	46	23	30.1733	0.004505	263	59	39
Pluto	110	02	17	223	14	31	17	08	11	39.9022	0.256387	211	50	01

*Consistent for the standard Epoch: 1981 July 15.0 Ephemeris Time **Astronomical units

Sun and planets	Semi-diameter at unit distance ' "	at mean least dist. ' "	in miles mean s.d.	Volume ⊕=1.	Mass. ⊕=1.	Density ⊕=1.	Axial rotation d.	h.	m.	s.	Gravity at surface ⊕=1.	Reflecting power Pct.	Probable temperature °F.
Sun	15 59.62	___	432560	1303730	332830	0.26	24	16	48		27.9	___	+10,000
Mercury . . .	3.37	5.45	1505	0.054	0.0554	0.98	59				0.37	0.06	+ 620
Venus	8.46	30.50	3762	0.880	0.8150	0.94	244.3	(R)			0.88	0.72	+ 900
Earth	___	___	3960	1.000	1.000	1.00		23	56	4	1.00	0.39	+ 72
Moon	2.40	16 43.00	1080	0.020	0.0123	0.61	27	7	43	12	0.17	0.07	– 10
Mars	4.68	8.94	2107	0.149	0.1075	0.72		24	37	23	0.38	0.16	– 10
Jupiter	98.37	23.43	44270	1316.	317.84	0.24		9	50	30	2.64	0.70	– 240
Saturn	82.80	9.76	37300	755.	95.147	0.13		10	14		1.15	0.75	– 300
Uranus	32.90	1.80	15200	52.	14.54	0.29		10	49	(R)	1.15	0.90	– 340
Neptune . . .	31.10	1.06	15600	57.	17.23	0.30		18	12		1.12	0.82	– 370
Pluto*	1.80	0.06	800	0.008	0.0016	0.19	6	9			0.04	0.14	? ?

*Much of this information is too new to be verified, but observers at the U.S. Naval Observatory have derived values similar to these after having discovered that Pluto has a satellite. It apparently revolves about Pluto in a period equal to Pluto's rotation period. (R) retrograde of Venus and Uranus.

Four Eclipses in 1983

Greenwich Mean Time

First Eclipse

A total eclipse of the sun, June 11, partial phases visible in Southern Indian Ocean, South East Asia, Philippines, most of Micronesia, Melanesia, and Australia. Path of totality includes Java, Southern Celebes and Southern New Guinea.

Circumstances of the Eclipse

Eclipse begins	June 11	02:09.5
Central Eclipse begins . . .	June 11	03:11.3
Central eclipse at local apparent moon	June 11	04:33.4
Central eclipse ends	June 11	06:14.1
Eclipse ends	June 11	07:15.8

Second Eclipse

A partial eclipse of the moon, June 25, the beginning of the umbral phase visible in extreme eastern Australia, New Zealand, Antarctica, the Pacific Ocean, South America, North America except the northern part, and the Western Atlantic Ocean. The end of the umbral phase visible in South America except the north eastern part, North America except the north eastern part, Antarctica, the Pacific Ocean, New Zealand, and Australia except the extreme north western part.

Circumstances of the eclipse

Moon enters penumbra . .	June 25	05:43.0
Moon enters umbra	June 25	07:14.4
Middle of eclipse	June 25	08:22.3
Moon leaves umbra	June 25	09:33.1
Moon leaves penumbra . .	June 25	11:01.6

Magnitude of eclipse: 0.339

Third Eclipse

An annular eclipse of the sun, December 4, the partial phases visible throughout eastern Atlantic ocean, north eastern South America, British Isles, central and southern Europe through Turkey, and the African continent. The path of annularity begins in the Atlantic Ocean, hits land in Gabon and ends in north east Somalia.

Circumstances of the Eclipse

Eclipse begins	Dec. 4	09:41.0
Central eclipse begins . . .	Dec. 4	10:47.5
Central eclipse at local apparent moon	Dec. 4	12:19.6
Central eclipse ends	Dec. 4	14:13.3
Eclipse ends	Dec. 4	15:19.9

Fourth Eclipse

A penumbral eclipse of the moon, December 19-20, the beginning of which will be visible in South America except the southern tip, North America, the Arctic regions, Greenland, the Atlantic Ocean, Africa, Europe, Asia except the far eastern part, and the western Indian Ocean. The end will be visible in Africa except the eastern part, Europe, South America, the Atlantic Ocean, North America, the Arctic region, the eastern part of the Pacific Ocean, and extreme western and northern Asia.

Circumstances of the Eclipse

Moon enters penumbra . .	Dec. 19	23:45.9
Middle of eclipse	Dec. 20	01:49.0
Moon leaves penumbra . .	Dec. 20	03:52.3

Penumbral magnitude 0.914

Morning and Evening Stars 1983

Greenwich Mean Time

	Morning	Evening
Jan.	Mercury (from 16) Jupiter Saturn	Mercury (to 16) Venus Mars
Feb.	Mercury Jupiter Saturn	Venus Mars
Mar.	Mercury (to 26) Jupiter Saturn	Mercury (from 26) Venus Mars
April	Jupiter Saturn (to 21)	Mercury Venus Mars Saturn (from 21)
May	Mercury (from 12) Jupiter (to 27)	Mercury (to 12) Venus Mars Jupiter (from 27) Saturn
June	Mercury Mars (from 3)	Venus Mars (to 3) Jupiter Saturn
July	Mercury (to 9) Mars	Mercury (from 9) Venus Jupiter Saturn
Aug.	Venus (from 25) Mars	Mercury Venus (to 25) Jupiter Saturn
Sept.	Mercury (from 15) Venus Mars	Mercury (to 15) Jupiter Saturn
Oct.	Mercury (to 30) Venus Mars Saturn (from 31)	Mercury (from 30) Jupiter Saturn (to 31)
Nov.	Venus Mars Saturn	Mercury Jupiter
Dec.	Mercury (from 31) Venus Mars Jupiter (from 14) Saturn	Mercury (to 31) Jupiter (to 14)

Astronomical Twilight—Meridian of Greenwich

Date 1983	20° Begin	20° End	30° Begin	30° End	40° Begin	40° End	50° Begin	50° End	60° Begin	60° End
	h m	h m	h m	h m	h m	h m	h m	h m	h m	h m
Jan. 1	5 16	**6 50**	5 30	**6 35**	5 45	**6 21**	6 00	**6 07**	6 18	**5 49**
11	5 19	**6 56**	5 33	**6 43**	5 46	**6 30**	6 00	**6 17**	6 15	**6 01**
21	5 21	**7 01**	5 32	**6 51**	5 43	**6 40**	5 55	**6 30**	6 06	**6 18**
Feb. 1	5 21	**7 07**	5 29	**6 58**	5 38	**6 51**	5 45	**6 44**	5 51	**6 38**
11	5 18	**7 11**	5 24	**7 05**	5 29	**7 01**	5 32	**6 59**	5 32	**7 01**
21	5 13	**7 15**	5 17	**7 12**	5 17	**7 12**	5 16	**7 14**	5 09	**7 23**
Mar. 1	5 08	**7 18**	5 08	**7 19**	5 06	**7 21**	4 59	**7 29**	4 44	**7 45**
11	5 00	**7 21**	4 58	**7 24**	4 50	**7 32**	4 38	**7 46**	4 12	**8 12**
21	4 52	**7 24**	4 45	**7 32**	4 33	**7 44**	4 14	**8 04**	3 37	**8 43**
Apr. 1	4 42	**7 28**	4 31	**7 39**	4 14	**7 57**	3 47	**8 25**	2 53	**9 21**
11	4 32	**7 32**	4 18	**7 47**	3 56	**8 09**	3 20	**8 47**	2 03	**10 10**
21	4 23	**7 36**	4 04	**7 54**	3 37	**8 23**	2 52	**9 11**	0 37	**11 47**
May 1	4 14	**7 41**	3 52	**8 04**	3 19	**8 37**	2 22	**9 39**		
11	4 08	**7 46**	3 41	**8 13**	3 03	**8 53**	1 49	**10 09**		
21	4 02	**7 52**	3 32	**8 22**	2 48	**9 07**	1 13	**10 46**		
June 1	3 58	**7 58**	3 26	**8 30**	2 36	**9 20**	0 21	**11 52**		
11	3 56	**8 03**	3 22	**8 36**	2 29	**9 30**				
21	3 57	**8 06**	3 22	**8 40**	2 28	**9 35**				
July 1	3 59	**8 07**	3 25	**8 41**	2 30	**9 35**				
11	4 03	**8 06**	3 30	**8 39**	2 40	**9 30**				
21	4 08	**8 03**	3 39	**8 33**	2 52	**9 18**	1 12	**11 23**		
Aug. 1	4 15	**7 56**	3 48	**8 23**	3 09	**9 01**	1 49	**10 20**		
11	4 20	**7 50**	3 56	**8 13**	3 22	**8 46**	2 21	**9 46**		
21	4 24	**7 41**	4 05	**8 01**	3 34	**8 27**	2 47	**9 15**		
Sept. 1	4 29	**7 31**	4 14	**7 46**	3 51	**8 08**	3 13	**8 43**	1 40	**10 02**
11	4 32	**7 20**	4 20	**7 33**	4 02	**7 50**	3 33	**8 16**	2 36	**9 12**
21	4 35	**7 11**	4 26	**7 19**	4 14	**7 31**	3 52	**7 52**	3 11	**8 31**
Oct. 1	4 38	**7 02**	4 33	**7 05**	4 25	**7 13**	4 10	**7 28**	3 41	**7 54**
11	4 40	**6 53**	4 40	**6 53**	4 35	**6 58**	4 26	**7 05**	4 07	**7 23**
21	4 43	**6 47**	4 45	**6 44**	4 45	**6 43**	4 41	**6 46**	4 32	**6 55**
Nov. 1	4 46	**6 41**	4 52	**6 34**	4 56	**6 30**	4 58	**6 27**	4 56	**6 27**
11	4 50	**6 38**	4 59	**6 28**	5 06	**6 21**	5 13	**6 14**	5 17	**6 08**
21	4 55	**6 36**	5 06	**6 25**	5 16	**6 15**	5 26	**6 04**	5 37	**5 52**
Dec. 1	5 00	**6 37**	5 13	**6 24**	5 25	**6 11**	5 38	**5 58**	5 53	**5 42**
11	5 06	**6 40**	5 20	**6 26**	5 34	**6 12**	5 48	**5 57**	6 06	**5 38**
21	5 11	**6 45**	5 25	**6 30**	5 39	**6 16**	5 55	**6 00**	6 15	**5 40**
31	5 15	**6 50**	5 30	**6 35**	5 44	**6 21**	6 00	**6 06**	6 18	**5 48**

Largest Telescopes Are in Northern Hemisphere

Most of the world's major astronomical installations are in the northern hemisphere, while many of astronomy's major problems are found in the southern sky. This imbalance has long been recognized and is being remedied.

In the northern hemisphere the largest reflector is the 236-inch mirror at the Special Astrophysical Observatory in the Caucasus in the Soviet Union. The largest reflectors in the U.S. include 3 in California: at Palomar Mtn., 200 inches; at Lick Observatory, Mt. Hamilton, 120 inches; and at Mt. Wilson Observatory, 100 inches. Also in the U.S. are a 158 inch reflector at Kitt Peak, Arizona, dedicated in June 1973, and a 107-inch telescope at the McDonald Observatory on Mt. Locke in Texas. A telescope at the Crimean Astrophysical Observatory in the Soviet Union has a 104-inch mirror.

Placed in service in 1975 were three large reflectors for the southern hemisphere. Associated Universities for Research in Astronomy (AURA), the operating organization of Kitt Peak National Observatory, dedicated the 158-inch reflector (twin of the telescope on Kitt Peak) at Cerro Tololo International Observatory, Chile; the European Southern Observatory has a 141-inch reflector at La Silla, Chile; and the Anglo-Australian telescope, 152 inches in diameter, is at Siding Spring Observatory in Australia.

Optical Telescopes

Optical astronomical telescopes are of two kinds, refracting and reflecting. In the first, light passes through a lens which brings the light rays into focus, where the image may be examined after being magnified by a second lens, the eyepiece, or directly photographed.

The reflector consists of a concave parabolic mirror, generally of Pyrex or now of a relatively heat insensitive material, cervit, coated with silver or aluminum, which reflects the light rays back toward the upper end of the telescope, where they are either magnified and observed by the eyepiece or, as in the case of the refractors, photographed. In most reflecting telescopes, the light is reflected again by a secondary mirror and comes to a focus after passing through a hole in the side of the telescope, where the eye-piece or camera is located, or after passing through a hole in the center of the primary mirror.

World's Largest Refractors

Location and diameter in inches

Yerkes Obs., Williams Bay, Wis.	40
Lick Obs., Mt. Hamilton, Cal.	36
Astrophys. Obs., Potsdam, E. Germany	32
Paris Observatory, Meuden, France	32
Allegheny Obs., Pittsburgh, Pa.	30
Univ. of Paris, Nice, France	30
Royal Greenwich Obs., Herstmonceux, England	28
Union Obs., Johannesburg, South Africa	26.5
Universitats-Sternwarte, Vienna, Austria	26.5
University of Virginia	26
Obs., Academy of Sciences, Pulkova, USSR	26
Astronomical Obs., Belgrade, Yugoslavia	26
Leander McCormick Obs., Charlottesville, Va.	26
Obs. Mitaka, Tokyo-to, Japan	26
US Naval Obs., Washington, D.C.	26
Mt. Stromlo Obs., Canberra, Australia	26

World's Largest Reflectors

Special Astrophysical Obs., Zelenchukskaya, USSR	236
Palomar Obs., Palomar Mtn., Cal.	200, 100, 60
Whipple Obs. (SAO), Mt. Hopkins, Ariz.	176*, 60
Kitt Peak National Obs., Tucson, Ariz.	158, 84, 60
Cerro Tololo, Chile	158, 60
Siding Spring, Australia	153
La Silla, Chile	141, 60
Lick Obs., Mt. Hamilton, Cal.	120
McDonald Obs., Fort Davis, Tex.	107, 82
Crimean Astrophys. Obs., Nauchny, USSR	104
Byurakan Obs., Armenia S.S.R.	102
Royal Greenwich Obs., Herstmonceux, England	98
Steward Obs., Tucson, Ariz.	90
Mauna Kea Obs., Univ. of Hawaii, Ha.	88, 84
Shemakha Astroph. Obs., Azerbaijan S.S.R.	79
Saint Michel l'Observatoire, (Basses Alpes), Fr.	77
Haute Provence, France	76, 60
Tokyo Obs., Japan	74
Mt. Stromlo, Australia	74
David Dunlap Obs., Ont., Canada	74
Helwan Obs., Helwan, Egypt	74
Astrophys. Obs., Kamogata, Okayama-ken, Japan	74
Sutherland, South Africa	74
Dominion Astrophys. Obs., Victoria, B.C.	73
Perkins Obs., Flagstaff, Ariz.	72
Obs., Padua Univ., Asiago, Italy	72
Agassiz Station Harvard Obs., Cambridge, Mass.	61
National Obs., Bosque Alegre Sta., Argentina	61
U.S. Naval Obs., Flagstaff, Ariz.	61
Catalina Mtn., Ariz.	61
Arizona Univ. Obs., Tucson, Ariz.	60
Boyden Obs., Bloemfontein, South Africa	60
Mt. Haleakala, Ha.	60
Figl Astroph. Obs., Vienna, Austria	60
Mt. Wilson Obs., Pasadena, Cal.	60

*Multiple mirror telescope, equivalent aperture.

Major U.S. Planetariums

Academy Planetarium, U.S. Air Force Academy
Adler Planetarium, Chicago, Ill.
American Museum-Hayden Planetarium, N.Y.C.
Buhl Planetarium, Pittsburgh, Pa.
Charles Hayden Planetarium, Boston, Mass.
Einstein Spacearium, Washington, D.C.
Fels Planetarium, Philadelphia, Pa.
Fernbank Science Center Planetarium, Altanta, Ga.
Griffith Planetarium, Los Angeles, Cal.
La. Arts and Science Planetarium, Baton Rouge, La.
McDonnell Planetarium, St. Louis, Mo.
Morehead Planetarium, Chapel Hill, N.C.
Morrison Planetarium, San Francisco, Cal.
Robert T. Longway Planetarium, Flint, Mich.
Strassenburgh Planetarium, Rochester, N.Y.

The Sun

The sun, the controlling body of our solar system, is a star whose dimensions cause it to be classified among stars as average in size, temperature, and brightness. Its proximity to the earth makes it appear to us as tremendously large and bright. A series of thermo-nuclear reactions involving the atoms of the elements of which it is composed produces the heat and light that make life possible on earth.

The sun has a diameter of 864,000 miles and is distant, on the average, 92,900,000 miles from the earth. It is 1.41 times as dense as water. The light of the sun reaches the earth in 499.012 seconds or slightly more than 8 minutes. The average solar surface temperature has been measured by several indirect methods which agree closely on a value of 6,000° Kelvin or about 10,000° F. The interior temperature of the sun is about 35,000,000 F.°.

When sunlight is analyzed with a spectroscope, it is found to consist of a continuous spectrum composed of all the colors of the rainbow in order, crossed by many dark lines. The "absorption lines" are produced by gaseous materials in the atmosphere of the sun. More than 60 of the natural terrestrial elements have been identified in the sun, all in gaseous form because of the intense heat of the sun.

Spheres and Corona

The radiating surface of the sun is called the **photosphere,** and just above it is the **chromosphere.** The chromosphere is visible to the naked eye only at times of total solar eclipses, appearing then to be a pinkish-violet layer with occasional great prominences projecting above its general level. With proper instruments the chromosphere can be seen or photographed whenever the sun is visible without waiting for a total eclipse. Above the chromosphere is the **corona,** also visible to the naked eye only at times of total eclipse. Instruments also permit the brighter portions of the corona to be studied whenever conditions are favorable. The pearly light of the corona surges millions of miles from the sun. Iron, nickel, and calcium are believed to be principal contributors to the composition of the corona, all in a state of extreme attenuation and high ionization that indicates temperatures on the order of a million degrees Fahrenheit.

Sunspots

There is an intimate connection between sunspots and the corona. At times of low sunspot activity, the fine streamers of the corona will be much longer above the sun's equator than over the polar regions of the sun, while during high sunspot activity, the corona extends fairly evenly outward from all regions of the sun, but to a much greater distance in space. Sunspots are dark, irregularly-shaped regions whose diameters may reach tens of thousands of miles. The average life of a sunspot group is from two to three weeks, but there have been groups that have lasted for more than a year, being carried repeatedly around as the sun rotated upon its axis. The record for the duration of a sunspot is 18 months. Sunspots reach a low point every 11.3 years, with a peak of activity occurring irregularly between two successive minima.

The sun is 400,000 times as bright as the full moon and gives the earth 6 million times as much light as do all the other stars put together. Actually, most of the stars that can be easily seen on any clear night are brighter than the sun.

The Zodiac

The sun's apparent yearly path among the stars is known as the **ecliptic.** The zone 16° wide, 8° on each side of the ecliptic, is known as the **zodiac.** Inside of this zone are the apparent paths of the sun, moon, earth, and major planets. Beginning at the point on the ecliptic which marks the position of the sun at the vernal equinox, and thence proceeding eastward, the zodiac is divided into twelve signs of 30° each, as shown herewith.

These signs are named from the twelve constellations of the zodiac with which the signs coincided in the time of the astronomer Hipparchus, about 2,000 years ago. Owing to the precession of the equinoxes, that is to say, to the retrograde motion of the equinoxes along the ecliptic, each sign in the zodiac has, in the course of 2,000 years, moved backward 30° into the constellation west of it; so that the sign Aries is now in the constellation Pisces, and so on. The vernal equinox will move from Pisces into Aquarius about the middle of the 26th century. The signs of the zodiac with their Latin and English names are as follows:

Spring	1.	♈ Aries.	The Ram.
	2.	♉ Taurus.	The Bull.
	3.	♊ Gemini.	The Twins.
Summer	4.	♋ Cancer.	The Crab.
	5.	♌ Leo.	The Lion.
	6.	♍ Virgo.	The Virgin.
Autumn	7.	♎ Libra.	The Balance.
	8.	♏ Scorpio.	The Scorpion.
	9.	♐ Sagittarius.	The Archer.
Winter	10.	♑ Capricorn.	The Goat.
	11.	♒ Aquarius.	The Water Bearer.
	12.	♓ Pisces.	The Fishes.

The Moon

The moon completes a circuit around the earth in a period whose mean or average duration is 27 days 7 hours 43.2 minutes. This is the moon's sidereal period. Because of the motion of the moon in common with the earth around the sun, the mean duration of the lunar month — the period from one new moon to the next new moon — is 29 days 12 hours 44.05 minutes. This is the moon's synodical period.

The mean distance of the moon from the earth according to the American Ephemeris is 238,857 miles. Because the orbit of the moon about the earth is not circular but elliptical, however, the maximum distance from the earth that the moon may reach is 252,710 miles and the least distance is 221,463 miles. All distances are from the center of one object to the center of the other.

The moon's diameter is 2,160 miles. If we deduct the radius of the moon, 1,080 miles, and the radius of the earth, 3,963 miles from the minimum distance or perigee, given above, we shall have for the nearest approach of the bodies' surfaces 216,420 miles.

The moon rotates on its axis in a period of time exactly equal to its sidereal revolution about the earth — 27.321666 days. The moon's revolution about the earth is irregular because of its elliptical orbit. The moon's rotation, however, is regular and this, together with the irregular revolution, produces what is called "libration in longitude" which permits us to see first farther around the east side and then farther around the west side of the moon. The moon's variation north or south of the ecliptic permits us to see farther over first one pole and then the other of the moon and this is "libration in latitude." These two libration effects permit us to see a total of about 60% of the moon's surface over a period of time. The hidden side of the moon was photographed in 1959 by the Soviet space vehicle Lunik III. Since then many excellent pictures of nearly all of the moon's surface have been transmitted to earth by Lunar Orbiters launched by the U.S.

The tides are caused mainly by the moon, because of its proximity to the earth. The ratio of the tide-raising power of the moon to that of the sun is 11 to 5.

Harvest Moon and Hunter's Moon

The Harvest Moon, the full moon nearest the Autumnal Equinox, ushers in a period of several successive days when the moon rises soon after sunset. This phenomenon gives farmers in temperate latitudes extra hours of light in which to harvest their crops before frost and winter come. The 1983 Harvest Moon falls on Sept. 22. Harvest moon in the south temperate latitudes falls on Mar. 28.

The next full moon after Harvest Moon is called the Hunter's Moon, accompanied by a similar phenomenon but less marked; — Oct. 21, northern hemisphere; Apr. 27, southern hemisphere.

Moon's Perigee and Apogee, 1983

Perigee								Apogee							
Day		GMT	EST	Day		GMT	EST	Day		GMT	EST	Day		GMT	EST
Jan	28	11	06	July	11	10	05	Jan	14	05	00	June	28	23	18
Feb	25	22	17	Aug	8	19	14	Feb	10	08	03	July	26	07	02
Mar	25	22	17	Sept	6	05	00	Mar	9	23	18	Aug	22	09	04
Apr	21	08	03	Oct	4	11	06	Apr	6	18	13	Sept	18	17	12
May	16	16	11	Nov	1	03	22*	May	4	13	08	Oct	16	08	03
June	13	06	01	Nov	26	02	21*	June	1	08	03	Nov	13	03	22*
				Dec	22	18	13					Dec	11	01	20*

*Previous day

The Earth: Size, Computation of Time, Seasons

Size and Dimensions

The earth is the fifth largest planet and the third from the sun. Its mass is 6 sextillion, 588 quintillion short tons. Using the parameters of an ellipsoid adopted by the International Astronomical Union in 1964 and recognized by the International Union of Geodesy and Geophysics in 1967, the length of the equator is 24,901.55 miles, the length of a meridian is 24,859.82 miles, the equatorial diameter is 7,926.41 miles, and the area of this reference ellipsoid is approximately 196,938,800 square miles.

The earth is considered a solid, rigid mass with a dense core of magnetic, probably metallic material. The outer part of the core is probably liquid. Around the core is a thick shell or mantle of heavy crystalline rock which in turn is covered by a thin crust forming the solid granite and basalt base of the continents and ocean basins. Over broad areas of the earth's surface the crust has a thin cover of sedimentary rock such as sandstone, shale, and limestone formed by weathering of the earth's surface and deposition of sands, clays, and plant and animal remains.

The temperature in the earth increases about 1°F. with every 100 to 200 feet in depth, in the upper 100 kilometers of the earth, and the temperature near the core is believed to be near the melting point of the core materials under the conditions at that depth. The heat of the earth is believed to be derived from radioactivity in the rocks, pressures developed within the earth, and original heat (if the earth in fact was formed at high temperatures).

Atmosphere of the Earth

The earth's atmosphere is a blanket composed of nitrogen, oxygen, and argon, in amounts of about 78, 21, and 1% by volume. Also present in minute quantities are carbon dioxide, hydrogen, neon, helium, krypton, and xenon.

Water vapor displaces other gases and varies from nearly zero to about 4% by volume. The height of the **ozone** layer varies from approximately 12 to 21 miles above the earth. Traces exist as low as 6 miles and as high as 35 miles. Traces of methane have been found.

The atmosphere rests on the earth's surface with the weight equivalent to a layer of water 34 ft. deep. For about 300,000 ft. upward the gases remain in the proportions stated. Gravity holds the gases to the earth. The weight of the air compresses it at the bottom, so that the greatest density is at the earth's surface. Pressure, as well as density, decreases as height increases because the weight pressing upon any layer is always less than that pressing upon the layers below.

The temperature of the air drops with increased height until the **tropopause** is reached. This may vary from 25,000 to 60,000 ft. The atmosphere below the tropopause is the **troposphere;** the atmosphere for about twenty miles above the tropopause is the **stratosphere,** where the temperature generally increases with height except at high latitudes in winter. A temperature maximum near the 30-mile level is called the **stratopause.** Above this boundary is the **mesosphere** where the temperature decreases with height to a minimum, the **mesopause,** at a height of 50 miles. Extending above the mesosphere to the outer fringes of the atmosphere is the **thermosphere,** a region where temperature increases with height to a value measured in thousands of degrees Fahrenheit. The lower portion of this region, extending from 50 to about 400 miles in altitude, is characterized by a high ion density, and is thus called the **ionosphere.** The outer region is called **exosphere;** this is the region where gas molecules traveling at high speed may escape into outer space, above 600 miles.

Latitude, Longitude

Position on the globe is measured by means of meridians and parallels. Meridians, which are imaginary lines drawn around the earth through the poles, determine **longitude.** The meridian running through Greenwich, England, is the **prime meridian of longitude,** and all others are either east or west. Parallels, which are imaginary circles parallel with the equator, determine **latitude.** The length of a degree of longitude varies as the cosine of the latitude. At the equator a degree is 69.171 statute miles; this is gradually reduced toward the poles. Value of a longitude degree at the poles is zero.

Latitude is reckoned by the number of degrees north or south of the equator, an imaginary circle on the earth's surface everywhere equidistant between the two poles. According to the IAU Ellipsoid of 1964, the length of a degree of latitude is 68.708 statute miles at the equator and varies slightly north and south because of the oblate form of the globe; at the poles it is 69.403 statute miles.

Computation of Time

The earth rotates on its axis and follows an elliptical orbit around the sun. The rotation makes the sun appear to move across the sky from East to West. It determines day and night and the complete rotation, in relation to the sun, is called the **apparent** or **true solar day.** This varies but an average determines the **mean solar day** of 24 hours.

The mean solar day is in universal use for civil purposes. It may be obtained from apparent solar time by correcting observations of the sun for the equation of time, but when high precision is required, the mean solar time is calculated from its relation to sidereal time. These relations are extremely complicated, but for most practical uses, they may be considered as follows:

Sidereal time is the measure of time defined by the diurnal motion of the vernal equinox, and is determined from observation of the meridian transits of stars. One complete rotation of the earth relative to the equinox is called the **sidereal day.** The **mean sidereal day** is 23 hours, 56 minutes, 4.091 seconds of mean solar time.

The **Calendar Year** begins at 12 o'clock midnight precisely local clock time, on the night of Dec. 31-Jan. 1. The day and the calendar month also begin at midnight by the clock. The interval required for the earth to make one absolute revolution around the sun is a **sidereal year;** it consisted of 365 days, 6 hours, 9 minutes, and 9.5 seconds of mean solar time (approximately 24 hours per day) in 1900, and is increasing at the rate of 0.0001-second annually.

The **Tropical Year,** on which the return of the seasons depends, is the interval between two consecutive returns of the sun to the vernal equinox. The tropical year consists of 365 days, 5 hours, 48 minutes, and 46 seconds in 1900. It is decreasing at the rate of 0.530 seconds per century.

In 1956 the unit of time interval was defined to be identical with the second of **Ephemeris Time,** 1/31,556,925.9747 of the tropical year for 1900 January 0d 12th hour E.T. A physical definition of the second based on a quantum transition of cesium (atomic second) was adopted in 1964. The atomic second is equal to 9,192,631,770 cycles of the emitted radiation. In 1967 this atomic second was adopted as the unit of time interval for the Intern'l System of Units.

The Zones and Seasons

The five zones of the earth's surface are Torrid, lying between the Tropics of Cancer and Capricorn; North Temperate, between Cancer and the Arctic Circle; South Temperate, between Capricorn and the Antarctic Circle; The Frigid Zones, between the polar Circles and the Poles.

The inclination or tilt of the earth's axis with respect to the sun determines the seasons. These are commonly marked in the North Temperate Zone, where spring begins at the vernal equinox, summer at the summer solstice, autumn at the autumnal equinox and winter at the winter solstice.

In the South Temperate Zone, the seasons are reversed. Spring begins at the autumnal equinox, summer at the winter solstice, etc.

If the earth's axis were perpendicular to the plane of the earth's orbit around the sun there would be no change of seasons. Day and night would be of nearly constant length and there would be equable conditions of temperature. But the axis is tilted 23° 27′ away from a perpendicular to the orbit and only in March and September is the axis at right angles to the sun.

The points at which the sun crosses the equator are the equinoxes, when day and night are most nearly equal. The points at which the sun is at a maximum distance from the equator are the solstices. Days and nights are then most unequal.

In June the North Pole is tilted 23° 27′ toward the sun and the days in the northern hemisphere are longer than the nights, while the days in the southern hemisphere are shorter than the nights. In December the North Pole is tilted 23° 27′ away from the sun and the situation is reversed.

The Seasons in 1983

In 1983 the 4 seasons will begin as follows: add one hour to EST for Atlantic Time; subtract one hour for Central, two hours for Mountain, 3 hours for Pacific, 4 hours for Yukon, 5 hours for Alaska-Hawaii and six hours for Bering Time. Also shown in Greenwich Mean Time.

		Date	GMT	EST
Vernal Equinox	**Spring**	Mar. 21	04:39	23.39*
Summer Solstice	**Summer**	June 21	23:09	18:09
Autumnal Equinox	**Autumn**	Sept. 23	14:42	09:42
Winter Solstice	**Winter**	Dec. 22	10:30	05:30

*Previous day

Poles of The Earth

The geographic (rotation) poles, or points where the earth's axis of rotation cuts the surface, are not absolutely fixed in the body of the earth. The pole of rotation describes an irregular curve about its mean position.

Two periods have been detected in this motion: (1) an annual period due to seasonal changes in barometric pressure, load of ice and snow on the surface and to other phenomena of seasonal character; (2) a period of about 14 months due to the shape and constitution of the earth.

In addition there are small but as yet unpredictable irregularities. The whole motion is so small that the actual pole at any time remains within a circle of 30 or 40 feet in radius centered at the mean position of the pole.

The pole of rotation for the time being is of course the pole having a latitude of 90° and an indeterminate longitude.

Magnetic Poles

The **north magnetic pole** of the earth is that region where the magnetic force is vertically downward and the **south magnetic pole** that region where the magnetic force is vertically upward. A compass placed at the magnetic poles experiences no directive force.

There are slow changes in the distribution of the earth's magnetic field. These changes were at one time attributed in part to a periodic movement of the magnetic poles around the geographical poles, but later evidence refutes this theory and points, rather, to a slow migration of "disturbance" foci over the earth.

There appear shifts in position of the magnetic poles due to the changes in the earth's magnetic field. The center of the area designated as the north magnetic pole was estimated to be in about latitude 70.5° N and longitude 96° W in 1905; from recent nearby measurements and studies of the secular changes, the position in 1970 is estimated as latitude 76.2° N and longitude 101° W. Improved data rather than actual motion account for at least part of the change.

The position of the south magnetic pole in 1912 was near 71° S and longitude 150° E; the position in 1970 is estimated at latitude 66° S and longitude 139.1° E.

The direction of the horizontal components of the magnetic field at any point is known as magnetic north at that point, and the angle by which it deviates east or west of true north is known as the magnetic declination, or in the mariner's terminology, the **variation of the compass.**

A compass without error points in the direction of magnetic north. (In general this is *not* the direction of the magnetic north pole.) If one follows the direction indicated by the north end of the compass, he will travel along a rather irregular curve which eventually reaches the north magnetic pole (though not usually by a great-circle route). However, the action of the compass should not be thought of as due to any influence of the distant pole, but simply as an indication of the distribution of the earth's magnetism at the place of observation.

Rotation of The Earth

The speed of rotation of the earth about its axis has been found to be slightly variable. The variations may be classified as:

(A) **Secular.** Tidal friction acts as a brake on the rotation and causes a slow secular increase in the length of the day, about 1 millisecond per century.

(B) **Irregular.** The speed of rotation may increase for a number of years, about 5 to 10, and then start decreasing. The maximum difference from the mean in the length of the day during a century is about 5 milliseconds. The accumulated difference in time has amounted to approximately 44 seconds since 1900. The cause is probably motion in the interior of the earth.

(C) **Periodic.** Seasonal variations exist with periods of one year and six months. The cumulative effect is such that each year the earth is late about 30 milliseconds near June 1 and is ahead about 30 milliseconds near Oct. 1. The maximum seasonal variation in the length of the day is about 0.5 millisecond. It is believed that the principal cause of the annual variation is the seasonal change in the wind patterns of the Northern and Southern Hemispheres. The semiannual variation is due chiefly to tidal action of the sun, which distorts the shape of the earth slightly.

The secular and irregular variations were discovered by comparing time based on the rotation of the earth with time based on the orbital motion of the moon about the earth and of the planets about the sun. The periodic variation was determined largely with the aid of quartz-crystal clocks. The introduction of the cesium-beam atomic clock in 1955 made it possible to determine in greater detail than before the nature of the irregular and periodic variations.

Moonrise Tonight

If your editors were to take perverse delight in scaring you into believing that determining moonrise tonight were a difficult process, we would tell you that the problem simply involves making a few subtractions and taking a few proportions in order to perform double interpolation twice. Although this description may sound complicated, the actual process is easy to do, especially with the little pocket calculators that seem ubiquitous today. The first major step adjusts the figures in the tables on page — and — to your place in the world. These answers are permanent and need never to be determined again, one set for each place on the globe. The second major part requires taking the proper 4 numbers from the following tables and playing with them. The third major step involves calculating a few nit-picking details that fine tune your answers to your clock. Then you are ready to step outside and amaze your friends.

Note, however, that your results apply to a sea horizon seen from sea level. If you have mountains around you, rising (or first sighting) can be much later, and setting (or last sighting) can be much earlier than you calculate. If you live on a peak, the opposite may occur. Make your calculations, then observe the true circumstances and write down the differences for your place. Make your corrections for each event you want.

Now let's help the people in Amarillo, Texas, watch the moon rise on May 26.

I. Where in the world is Amarillo, Texas? (See pp. 770-771).
Latitude: 35° 12′ 27″ N; Longitude: 101° 50′ 04″ W.

A. Convert the latitude and longitude to decimals: 27″ ÷ 60 = 0′.45; 12′ + 0′.45 = 12.′ 45; 12.′ 45 ÷ 60 = 0°.2075; 35° + 0°.2075 = 35°.2075. 04″ ÷ 60 = 0′.0667; add 50′ = 50′.0667, ÷ 60 = 0°.8344, add 101° = 101°.8344.

B. Note tables give values for each 10 degrees of latitude. What fraction is Amarillo in its latitude interval?

35°.2075 − 30° = 5.2075 of 10°, or **0.521**.

C. What fraction of the world is Amarillo west of Greenwich where the calculations are made for the tables?
101.8344 ÷ 360 = **0.2829**.

D. When do sky events take place in Amarillo as opposed to the time the clock reads? The difference is 4 minutes per degree. If you are East of the clock meridian, it will happen earlier where you are. MST is based on the 105 West meridian.
101.8344-105° = −3.° 1656
−3.1656 × 4 = −12.66 minutes. Call it **13 minutes** earlier than the event at the 105° meridian.

E. Write these 3 numbers on this page now (and in all succeeding editions of this book). If you move from Amarillo you must do this first step for your new home, but only once for each new place. If you don't live in Amarillo, do Amarillo's calculations and get **these** answers. Then, when you have mastered this exercise, do the calculations using the appropriate figures for your home.

II. When is moonrise on May 26 for the Amarillo latitude on the Greenwich meridian?

A. May 26: 18:46 at 30°; 19:08 at 40°.
19:08 − 18:46 = 22 minutes later at 40° than at 30°.
How much to prorate or apportion for Amarillo? Recall your answer from I, B: 0.52.
22 × 0.52 = 11 minutes later than 30°, thus 18:57.

B. Repeat for May 27:
May 27: 19:44 for 30°; 20:11 for 40°.
20:11 − 19:44 = 27 minutes later at 40° than at 30°.
27 × 0.52 = 14 minutes later than 30°, thus 19:58.

III. But Amarillo is only 0.283 (Answer from I,C) of the world away from Greenwich, and should need only 0.283 of the change from May 26 to May 27 at Amarillo's latitude. Thus, 19:58 − 18:57 = 61 minutes.
61 × 0.283 = 17 minutes after 18:57, or 19:14 at Amarillo.

IV. But what should Amarillo's clock read?
Since East means earlier, and Amarillo is 13 minutes earlier (Ans. I,D) 19:14 − 13 = 19:01; or subtracting 12 hours, 7:01 pm MST (or 8:01 MDT).

V. Special consideration should be made for Amarillo, which sits on a wide flat peak 3,685 feet above sea level: rising of the sun or moon can be 5 minutes earlier and settings 5 minutes later than these calculations. Your best bet is to make the calculations and correct for actual sighting times, and write these corrections on this page.

Table A: Latitude Adjustment

Lat. \ Diff in Min.	10	20	30	40	50	60	70	80	90	100	110	120
0° 20	0	1	1	1	2	2	2	3	3	3	4	4
40	1	1	2	3	3	4	5	5	6	7	7	8
1 00	1	2	3	4	5	6	7	8	9	10	11	12
20	1	3	4	5	7	8	9	11	12	13	15	16
40	2	3	5	7	8	10	12	13	15	17	18	20
2 00	2	4	6	8	10	12	14	16	18	20	22	24
20	2	5	7	9	12	14	16	19	21	23	26	28
40	3	5	8	11	13	16	19	21	24	27	29	32
3 00	3	6	9	12	15	18	21	24	27	30	33	36
20	3	7	10	13	17	20	23	27	30	33	37	40
40	4	7	11	15	18	22	26	29	33	37	40	44
4 00	4	8	12	16	20	24	28	32	36	40	44	48
20	4	9	13	17	22	26	30	35	39	43	48	52
40	5	9	14	19	23	28	33	37	42	47	51	56
5 00	5	10	15	20	25	30	35	40	45	50	55	60
20	5	11	16	21	27	32	37	43	48	53	59	64
40	6	11	17	23	28	34	40	45	51	57	62	68
6 00	6	12	18	24	30	36	42	48	54	60	66	72
20	6	13	19	25	32	38	44	51	57	63	70	76
40	7	13	20	27	33	40	47	53	60	67	73	80
7 00	7	14	21	28	35	42	49	56	63	70	77	84
20	7	15	22	29	37	44	51	59	66	73	81	88
40	8	15	23	31	38	46	54	61	69	77	84	92
8 00	8	16	24	32	40	48	56	64	72	80	88	96
20	8	17	25	33	42	50	58	67	75	83	92	100
40	9	17	26	35	43	52	61	69	78	87	95	104
9 00	9	18	27	36	45	54	63	72	81	90	99	108
20	9	19	28	37	47	56	65	75	84	93	103	112
40	10	19	29	39	48	58	68	77	87	97	106	116

Table B: Longitude Adjustment

Long. \ Diff. in Min.	10	20	30	40	50	60	70	80	90	100	110	120
50°	1	3	4	6	7	8	10	11	12	14	15	17
55	2	3	5	6	8	9	11	12	14	15	17	18
60	2	3	5	7	8	10	12	13	15	17	18	20
65	2	4	5	7	9	11	13	14	16	18	20	22
70	2	4	6	8	10	12	14	16	18	19	21	23
75	2	4	6	8	10	12	15	17	19	21	23	25
80	2	4	7	9	11	13	16	18	20	22	24	27
85	2	5	7	9	12	14	16	19	21	24	26	28
90	2	5	8	10	12	15	18	20	22	25	28	30
95	3	5	8	11	13	16	18	21	24	26	29	32
100	3	6	8	11	14	17	19	22	25	28	31	33
105	3	6	9	12	15	18	20	23	26	29	32	35
110	3	6	9	12	15	18	21	24	28	31	34	37
115	3	6	10	13	16	19	22	26	29	32	35	38
120	3	7	10	13	17	20	23	27	30	33	37	40
125	4	7	10	14	17	21	24	28	31	35	38	42
130	4	7	11	14	18	22	25	29	32	36	40	43
135	4	8	11	15	19	22	26	30	34	38	41	45
140	4	8	12	16	19	23	27	31	35	39	43	47
145	4	8	12	16	20	24	28	32	36	40	44	48
150	4	8	12	17	21	25	29	33	38	42	46	50
155	4	9	13	17	22	26	30	34	39	43	47	52
160	4	9	13	18	22	27	31	36	40	44	49	53
165	5	9	14	18	23	28	32	37	41	46	50	55
170	5	9	14	19	24	28	33	38	42	47	52	57

Latitude, Longitude, and Altitude of North American Cities

Source: National Oceanic and Atmospheric Administration, U.S. Commerce Department for geographic positions.
Source for Canadian cities: Geodetic Survey of Canada, Dept. of Energy, Mines, and Resources.
Altitudes U.S. Geological Survey and various sources. *Approx. altitude at downtown business area U.S.; in Canada at city hall except where (a) is at tower of major airport.

City	Lat. N °	′	″	Long. W °	′	″	Alt.* feet
Abilene, Tex.	32	27	05	99	43	51	1710
Akron, Oh.	41	05	00	81	30	44	874
Albany, N.Y.	42	39	01	73	45	01	20
Albuquerque, N.M.	35	05	01	106	39	05	4,945
Allentown, Pa.	40	36	11	75	28	06	255
Alert, N.W.T.	82	29	50	62	21	15	95
Altoona, Pa.	40	30	55	78	24	03	1,180
Amarillo, Tex.	35	12	27	101	50	04	3,685
Anchorage, Alas.	61	10	00	149	59	00	118
Ann Arbor, Mich.	42	16	59	83	44	52	880
Asheville, N.C.	35	35	42	82	33	26	1,985
Ashland, Ky.	38	28	36	82	38	23	536
Atlanta, Ga.	33	45	10	84	23	37	1,050
Atlantic City, N.J.	39	21	32	74	25	53	10
Augusta, Ga.	33	28	20	81	58	00	143
Augusta, Me.	44	18	53	69	46	29	45
Austin, Tex.	30	16	09	97	44	37	505
Bakersfield, Cal.	35	22	31	119	01	18	400
Baltimore, Md.	39	17	26	76	36	45	20
Bangor, Me.	44	48	13	68	46	18	20
Baton Rouge, La.	30	26	58	91	11	00	57
Battle Creek, Mich.	42	18	58	85	10	48	820
Bay City, Mich.	43	36	04	83	53	15	595
Beaumont, Tex.	30	05	20	94	06	09	20
Belleville, Ont.	44	09	42	77	23	11	257
Bellingham, Wash.	48	45	34	122	28	36	60
Berkeley, Cal.	37	52	10	122	16	17	40
Bethlehem, Pa.	40	37	16	75	22	34	235
Billings, Mon.	45	47	00	108	30	04	3,120
Biloxi, Miss.	30	23	48	88	53	00	20
Binghamton, N.Y.	42	06	03	75	54	47	865
Birmingham, Ala.	33	31	01	86	48	36	600
Bismarck, N.D.	46	48	23	100	47	17	1,674
Bloomington, Ill.	40	28	58	88	59	36	800
Boise, Ida.	43	37	07	116	11	58	2,704
Boston, Mass.	42	21	24	71	03	25	21
Bowling Green, Ky.	36	59	41	86	26	33	510
Brandon, Man.	49	51	00	99	57	00	1,265(a)
Brantford, Ont.	43	07	30	80	15	30	705(a)
Brattleboro, Vt.	42	51	06	72	33	48	300
Bridgeport, Conn.	41	10	49	73	11	22	10
Brockton, Mass.	42	05	02	71	01	25	130
Brownsville, Tex.	25	54	07	97	29	58	35
Buffalo, N.Y.	42	52	52	78	52	21	585
Burlington, Ont.	43	19	33	79	47	57	284
Burlington, Vt.	44	28	34	73	12	46	110
Butte, Mon.	46	01	06	112	32	11	5,765
Calgary, Alta.	51	02	46	114	03	24	3,427
Cambridge, Mass.	42	22	01	71	06	22	20
Camden, N.J.	39	56	41	75	07	14	30
Canton, Oh.	40	47	50	81	22	37	1,030
Carson City, Nev.	39	10	00	119	46	00	4,680
Cedar Rapids, Ia.	41	58	01	91	39	53	730
Central Islip, N.Y.	40	47	24	73	12	00	80
Champaign, Ill.	40	07	05	88	14	48	740
Charleston, S.C.	32	46	35	79	55	53	9
Charleston, W.Va.	38	21	01	81	37	52	601
Charlotte, N.C.	35	13	44	80	50	45	720
Charlottetown, P.E.I.	46	14	07	63	07	49	31
Chattanooga, Tenn.	35	02	41	85	18	32	675
Cheyenne, Wy.	41	08	09	104	49	07	6,100
Chicago, Ill.	41	52	28	87	38	22	595
Churchill, Man.	58	45	15	94	10	00	94(a)
Cincinnati, Oh.	39	06	07	84	30	35	550
Cleveland, Oh.	41	29	51	81	41	50	660
Colorado Springs	38	50	07	104	49	16	5,980
Columbia, Mo.	38	57	03	92	19	46	730
Columbia, S.C.	34	00	02	81	02	00	190
Columbus, Ga.	32	28	07	84	59	24	265
Columbus, Oh.	39	57	47	83	00	17	780
Concord, N.H.	43	12	22	71	32	25	290
Corpus Christi, Tex.	27	47	51	97	23	45	35
Dallas, Tex.	32	47	09	96	47	37	435
Dartmouth, N.S.	44	39	50	63	34	08	24
Davenport, Ia.	41	31	19	90	34	33	590
Dawson, Yukon	64	03	30	139	26	00	1,211(a)
Dayton, Oh.	39	45	32	84	11	43	574
Daytona Beach, Fla.	29	12	44	81	01	10	7
Decatur, Ill.	39	50	42	88	56	47	682
Denver, Col.	39	44	58	104	59	22	5,280
Des Moines, Ia.	41	35	14	93	37	00	805
Detroit, Mich.	42	19	48	83	02	57	585
Dodge City, Kan.	37	45	17	100	01	09	2,480
Dubuque, Ia.	42	29	55	90	40	08	620
Duluth, Minn.	46	46	56	92	06	24	610
Durham, N.C.	36	00	00	78	54	45	405
Eau Claire, Wis.	44	48	31	91	29	49	790
Edmonton, Alta.	53	32	43	113	29	21	2,186
El Paso, Tex.	31	45	36	106	29	11	3,695
Elizabeth, N.J.	40	39	43	74	12	59	21
Enid, Okla.	36	23	40	97	52	35	1,240
Erie, Pa.	42	07	15	80	04	57	685
Eugene, Ore.	44	03	16	123	05	30	422
Eureka, Cal.	40	48	08	124	09	46	45
Evansville, Ind.	37	58	20	87	34	21	385
Fairbanks, Alas.	64	48	00	147	51	00	448
Fall River, Mass.	41	42	06	71	09	18	40
Fargo, N.D.	46	52	30	96	47	18	900
Flagstaff, Ariz.	35	11	36	111	39	06	6,900
Flint, Mich.	43	00	50	83	41	33	750
Ft. Smith, Ark.	35	23	10	94	25	36	440
Fort Wayne, Ind.	41	04	21	85	08	26	790
Fort Worth, Tex.	32	44	55	97	19	44	670
Fredericton, N.B.	45	57	47	66	38	38	29
Fresno, Cal.	36	44	12	119	47	11	285
Gadsden, Ala.	34	00	57	86	00	41	555
Gainesville, Fla.	29	38	56	82	19	19	175
Gallup, N.M.	35	31	30	108	44	30	6,540
Galveston, Tex.	29	18	10	94	47	43	5
Gary, Ind.	41	36	12	87	20	19	590
Grand Junction, Col.	39	04	06	108	33	54	4,590
Grand Rapids, Mich.	42	58	03	85	40	13	610
Great Falls, Mon.	47	29	33	111	18	23	3,340
Green Bay, Wis.	44	30	48	88	00	50	590
Greensboro, N.C.	36	04	17	79	47	25	839
Greenville, S.C.	34	50	50	82	24	01	966
Guelph, Ont.	43	32	35	80	14	54	1,065
Gulfport, Miss.	30	22	04	89	05	36	20
Halifax, N.S.	44	38	54	63	34	30	60
Hamilton, Ont.	43	15	20	79	52	30	329
Hamilton, Oh.	39	23	59	84	33	47	600
Harrisburg, Pa.	40	15	43	76	52	59	365
Hartford, Conn.	41	46	12	72	40	49	40
Helena, Mon.	46	35	33	112	02	24	4,155
Hilo, Hawaii	19	43	30	155	05	24	40
Holyoke, Mass.	42	12	29	72	36	36	115
Honolulu, Ha.	21	18	22	157	51	35	21
Houston, Tex.	29	45	26	95	21	37	40
Hull, Que.	45	25	42	75	42	41	185
Huntington, W.Va.	38	25	12	82	26	33	565
Huntsville, Ala.	34	44	18	86	35	19	640
Indianapolis, Ind.	39	46	07	86	09	46	710
Iowa City, Ia.	41	39	37	91	31	53	685
Jackson, Mich.	42	14	43	84	24	22	940
Jackson, Miss.	32	17	56	90	11	06	298
Jacksonville, Fla.	30	19	44	81	39	42	20
Jersey City, N.J.	40	43	50	74	03	56	20
Johnstown, Pa.	40	19	35	78	55	03	1,185
Joplin, Mo.	37	05	26	90	42	11	990
Juneau, Alas.	58	18	12	134	24	30	50
Kalamazoo, Mich.	42	17	29	85	35	14	755
Kansas City, Kan.	39	07	04	94	38	24	750
Kansas City, Mo.	39	04	56	94	35	20	750
Kenosha, Wis.	42	35	43	87	50	11	610
Key West, Fla.	24	33	30	81	48	12	5
Kingston, Ont.	44	13	53	76	28	48	264
Kitchener, Ont.	43	26	58	80	29	12	1,100
Knoxville, Tenn.	35	57	39	83	55	07	890
Lafayette, Ind.	40	25	11	86	53	39	550
Lancaster, Pa.	40	02	25	76	18	29	355
Lansing, Mich.	42	44	01	84	33	15	830
Laredo, Tex.	27	30	22	99	30	30	440
La Salle, Que.	45	25	30	73	39	30	110
Las Vegas, Nev.	36	10	20	115	08	37	2,030
Laval, Que.	45	33	05	73	44	42	142
Lawrence, Mass.	42	42	16	71	10	08	65
Lethbridge, Alta.	49	41	38	112	49	58	2,985
Lexington, Ky.	38	02	50	84	29	46	955
Lihue, Ha.	21	58	48	159	22	30	210
Lima, Oh.	40	44	35	84	06	20	865
Lincoln, Neb.	40	48	59	96	42	15	1,150
Little Rock, Ark.	34	44	42	92	16	37	286
London, Ont.	42	59	17	81	14	03	822
Long Beach, Cal.	33	46	14	118	11	18	35
Lorain, Oh.	41	28	05	82	10	49	610
Los Angeles, Cal.	34	03	15	118	14	28	340
Louisville, Ky.	38	14	47	85	45	49	450
Lowell, Mass.	42	38	25	71	19	14	100
Lubbock, Tex.	33	35	05	101	50	33	3,195

City	Lat. N °	'	"	Long. W °	'	"	Alt.* Feet
Macon, Ga.	32	50	12	83	37	36	335
Madison, Wis.	43	04	23	89	22	55	860
Manchester, N.H.	42	59	28	71	27	41	175
Marshall, Tex.	32	33	00	94	23	00	410
Memphis, Tenn.	35	08	46	90	03	13	275
Meriden, Conn.	41	32	06	72	47	30	190
Mexico City, Mexico	19	25	45	99	07	00	7,347
Miami, Fla.	25	46	37	80	11	32	10
Milwaukee, Wis.	43	02	19	87	54	15	635
Minneapolis, Minn.	44	58	57	93	15	43	815
Minot, N.D.	48	14	09	101	17	38	1,550
Mississauga, Ont.	43	33	00	79	35	00	260(a)
Mobile, Ala.	30	41	36	88	02	33	5
Moline, Ill.	41	30	31	90	30	49	585
Moncton, N.B.	46	05	18	64	46	41	38
Montgomery, Ala.	32	22	33	86	18	31	160
Montpelier, Vt.	44	15	36	72	34	41	485
Montreal, Que.	45	30	33	73	33	14	90
Moose Jaw, Sask.	50	23	34	105	32	04	1,784
Muncie, Ind.	40	11	28	85	23	16	950
Nashville, Tenn.	36	09	33	86	46	55	450
Natchez, Miss.	31	33	48	91	23	30	210
Newark, N.J.	40	44	14	74	10	19	55
New Bedford, Mass.	41	38	13	70	55	41	15
New Britain, Conn.	41	40	08	72	46	59	200
New Haven, Conn.	41	18	25	72	55	30	40
New Orleans, La.	29	56	53	90	04	10	5
New York, N.Y.	40	45	06	73	59	39	55
Niagara Falls, N.Y.	43	05	34	79	03	26	570
Niagara Falls, Ont.	43	06	22	79	03	51	590
Nome, Alas.	64	30	00	165	25	00	25
Norfolk, Va.	36	51	10	76	17	21	10
North Bay, Ont.	46	18	35	79	27	45	670
Oakland, Cal.	37	48	03	122	15	54	25
Ogden, Ut.	41	13	31	111	58	21	4,295
Oklahoma City	35	28	26	97	31	04	1,195
Omaha, Neb.	41	15	42	95	56	14	1,040
Orlando, Fla.	28	32	42	81	22	38	70
Oshawa, Ont.	43	53	46	78	51	57	350
Ottawa, Ont.	45	26	24	75	41	42	185
Paducah, Ky.	37	05	13	88	35	56	345
Pasadena, Cal.	34	08	44	118	08	41	830
Paterson, N.J.	40	55	01	74	10	21	100
Pensacola, Fla.	30	24	51	87	12	56	15
Peoria, Ill.	40	41	42	89	35	33	470
Peterborough, Ont.	44	18	32	78	19	13	673
Philadelphia, Pa.	39	56	58	75	09	21	100
Phoenix, Ariz.	33	27	12	112	04	28	1,090
Pierre, S.D.	44	22	18	100	20	54	1,480
Pittsburgh, Pa.	40	26	19	80	00	00	745
Pittsfield, Mass.	42	26	53	73	15	14	1,015
Pocatello, Ida.	42	51	38	112	27	01	4,460
Port Arthur, Tex.	29	52	30	93	56	15	10
Portland, Me.	43	39	33	70	15	19	25
Portland, Ore.	45	31	06	122	40	35	77
Portsmouth, N.H.	43	04	30	70	45	24	20
Portsmouth, Va.	36	50	07	76	18	14	10
Prince Rupert, B.C.	54	19	00	130	19	00	125(a)
Providence, R.I.	41	49	32	71	24	41	80
Provo, Ut.	40	14	06	111	39	24	4,550
Pueblo, Col.	38	16	17	104	36	33	4,690
Quebec City, Que.	46	48	51	71	12	30	163
Racine, Wis.	42	43	49	87	47	12	630
Rapid City, S.D.	44	04	52	103	13	11	3,230
Raleigh, N.C.	35	46	38	78	38	21	365
Reading, Pa.	40	20	09	75	55	40	265
Regina, Sask.	50	27	02	104	36	30	1,894(a)
Reno, Nev.	39	31	27	119	48	40	4,490
Richmond, Va.	37	32	15	77	26	09	160
Roanoke, Va.	37	16	13	79	56	44	905
Rochester, Minn.	44	01	21	92	28	03	990
Rochester, N.Y.	43	09	41	77	36	21	515
Rockford, Ill.	42	16	07	89	05	48	715
Sacramento, Cal.	38	34	57	121	29	41	30
Saginaw, Mich.	43	25	52	83	56	05	595
St. Catharines, Ont.	43	09	30	79	14	30	362(a)
St. Cloud, Minn.	45	34	00	94	10	24	1,040
Saint John, N.B.	45	16	22	66	03	48	27
St. John's, Nfld.	47	34	00	52	43	30	200(a)
St. Joseph, Mo.	39	45	57	94	51	02	850
St. Louis, Mo.	38	37	45	90	12	22	455
St. Paul, Minn.	44	57	19	93	06	07	780
St. Petersburg, Fla.	27	46	18	82	38	19	20
Salem, Ore.	44	56	24	123	01	59	155
Salina, Kan.	38	50	36	97	36	46	1,229
Salt Lake City, Ut.	40	45	23	111	53	26	4,390
San Angelo, Tex.	31	27	39	100	26	03	1,845
San Antonio, Tex.	29	25	37	98	29	06	650
San Bernardino, Cal.	34	06	30	117	17	28	1,080
San Diego, Cal.	32	42	53	117	09	21	20
San Francisco, Cal.	37	46	39	122	24	40	65
San Jose, Cal.	37	20	16	121	53	24	90
San Juan, P.R.	18	27	00	66	04	15	35
Santa Barbara, Cal.	34	25	18	119	41	55	100
Santa Cruz, Cal.	36	58	18	122	01	18	20
Santa Fe, N.M.	35	41	11	105	56	10	6,950
Sarasota, Fla.	27	20	05	82	32	30	20
Saskatoon, Sask.	52	07	49	106	39	35	1,587
Sault Ste. Marie, Ont.	46	30	24	84	20	04	589
Savannah, Ga.	32	04	42	81	05	37	20
Schenectady, N.Y.	42	48	42	73	55	42	245
Scranton, Pa.	41	24	32	75	39	46	725
Seattle, Wash.	47	36	32	122	20	12	10
Sheboygan, Wis.	43	45	03	87	42	52	630
Sherbrooke, Que.	45	24	00	71	53	30	625(a)
Sheridan, Wy.	44	47	55	106	57	10	3,740
Shreveport, La.	32	30	46	93	44	58	204
Sioux City, Ia.	42	29	46	96	24	30	1,110
Sioux Falls, S.D.	43	32	35	96	43	35	1,395
Somerville, Mass.	42	23	15	71	06	07	13
South Bend, Ind.	41	40	33	86	15	01	710
Spartanburg, S.C.	34	57	03	81	56	06	875
Spokane, Wash.	47	39	32	117	25	33	1,890
Springfield, Ill.	39	47	58	89	38	51	610
Springfield, Mass.	42	06	21	72	35	32	85
Springfield, Mo.	37	13	03	93	17	32	1,300
Springfield, Oh.	39	55	38	83	48	29	980
Stamford, Conn.	41	03	09	73	32	24	35
Steubenville, Oh.	40	21	42	80	36	53	660
Stockton, Cal.	37	57	30	121	17	16	20
Sudbury, Ont.	46	29	24	80	59	24	917(a)
Superior, Wis.	46	43	14	92	06	07	630
Sydney, N.S.	46	08	30	60	11	00	50
Syracuse, N.Y.	43	03	04	76	09	14	400
Tacoma, Wash.	47	14	59	122	26	15	110
Tallahassee, Fla.	30	26	30	84	16	56	150
Tampa, Fla.	27	56	58	82	27	25	15
Terre Haute, Ind.	39	28	03	87	24	26	496
Texarkana, Tex.	33	25	48	94	02	30	324
Thunder Bay, Ont.	48	22	56	89	14	46	616
Toledo, Oh.	41	39	14	83	32	39	585
Topeka, Kan.	39	03	16	95	40	23	930
Toronto, Ont.	43	39	10	79	23	00	300
Trenton, N.J.	40	13	14	74	46	13	35
Trois-Rivieres, Que.	46	21	00	72	33	00	115(a)
Troy, N.Y.	42	43	45	73	40	58	35
Tucson, Ariz.	32	13	15	110	58	08	2,390
Tulsa, Okla.	36	09	12	95	59	34	804
Urbana, Ill.	40	06	42	88	12	06	....
Utica, N.Y.	43	06	12	75	13	33	415
Vancouver, B.C.	49	18	56	123	04	44	141
Victoria, B.C.	48	25	43	123	21	48	57
Waco, Tex.	31	33	12	97	08	00	405
Walla Walla, Wash.	46	04	08	118	20	24	936
Washington, D.C.	38	53	51	77	00	33	25
Waterbury, Conn.	41	33	13	73	02	31	260
Waterloo, Ia.	42	29	40	92	20	20	850
West Palm Beach, Fla.	26	42	36	80	03	07	15
Wheeling, W. Va.	40	04	03	80	43	20	650
Whitehorse, Yukon	60	43	15	135	03	15	2,305(a)
White Plains, N.Y.	41	02	00	73	45	48	220
Wichita, Kan.	37	41	30	97	20	16	1,290
Wichita Falls, Tex.	33	54	34	98	29	28	945
Wilkes-Barre, Pa.	41	14	32	75	53	17	640
Wilmington, Del.	39	44	46	75	32	51	135
Wilmington, N.C.	34	14	14	77	56	58	35
Windsor, Ont.	42	18	56	83	02	10	603
Winnipeg, Man.	49	53	56	97	08	23	762
Winston-Salem, N.C.	36	05	52	80	14	42	860
Worcester, Mass.	42	15	37	71	48	17	475
Yakima, Wash.	46	36	09	120	30	39	1,060
Yellowknife, N.W.T.	62	28	15	114	22	00	674(a)
Yonkers, N.Y.	40	55	55	73	53	54	10
York, Pa.	39	57	35	76	43	36	370
Youngstown, Oh.	41	05	57	80	39	02	840
Yuma, Ariz.	32	42	54	114	37	24	160
Zanesville, Oh.	39	56	18	82	00	30	720

World Cities

City	Lat. °	'	"	Long. °	'	"	Alt.
London, UK (Greenwich)	51	30	00N	0	0	0	245
Paris, France	48	50	14N	2	20	14E	300
Berlin, Germany	52	32	00N	13	25	00E	110
Rome, Italy	41	53	00N	12	30	00E	95
Warsaw, Poland	52	15	00N	21	00	00E	360
Moscow, USSR	55	45	00N	37	42	00E	394
Athens, Greece	37	58	00N	23	44	00E	300
Jerusalem, Israel	31	47	00N	35	13	00E	2,500
Johannesburg, So. Afr.	26	10	00S	28	02	00E	5,740
New Delhi, India	28	38	00N	77	12	00E	770
Peking, China	39	54	00N	116	28	00E	600
Rio de Janeiro, Brazil	22	53	43S	43	13	22W	30
Tokyo, Japan	35	45	00N	139	45	00E	30
Sydney, Australia	33	52	00S	151	12	00E	25

1st Month — January, 1983 — 31 days

Greenwich Mean Time

NOTE: Light figures indicate Sun. **Dark** figures indicate **Moon.** *Degrees are North Latitude.*

CAUTION: Must be converted to local time. For instruction see page 768.

Day of month week year	Sun on Meridian **Moon Phase** h m s	Sun's Declination ° ′	20° Rise Sun **Moon** h m	20° Set Sun **Moon** h m	30° Rise Sun **Moon** h m	30° Set Sun **Moon** h m	40° Rise Sun **Moon** h m	40° Set Sun **Moon** h m	50° Rise Sun **Moon** h m	50° Set Sun **Moon** h m	60° Rise Sun **Moon** h m	60° Set Sun **Moon** h m
1 Sa	12 03 10	−23 04	06 35	17 32	06 56	17 11	07 22	16 45	7 59	16 08	9 02	15 05
1			**19 57**	**8 30**	**19 39**	**08 51**	**19 15**	**09 16**	**18 42**	**09 51**	**17 45**	**10 50**
2 Su	12 03 38	−22 59	06 35	17 32	06 56	17 12	07 22	16 46	07 59	16 09	09 02	15 06
2			**21 02**	**09 25**	**20 48**	**09 41**	**20 30**	**10 01**	**20 05**	**10 29**	**19 24**	**11 13**
3 Mo	12 04 06	−22 54	06 35	17 33	06 56	17 13	07 22	16 47	07 59	16 10	09 01	15 08
3			**22 04**	**10 13**	**21 54**	**10 25**	**21 42**	**10 39**	**21 26**	**10 58**	**21 00**	**11 29**
4 Tu	12 04 34	−22 48	06 36	17 34	06 56	17 14	07 22	16 48	07 58	16 12	09 00	15 09
4			**23 02**	**10 56**	**22 57**	**11 03**	**22 52**	**11 11**	**22 44**	**11 23**	**22 32**	**11 40**
5 We	12 05 01	−22 42	06 36	17 34	06 57	17 14	07 22	16 48	07 58	16 13	9 00	15 10
5			**23 57**	**11 36**	**23 57**	**11 38**	**23 58**	**11 40**	**23 58**	**11 44**	**23 59**	**11 49**
6 Th	12 05 28	−22 35	06 36	17 35	06 57	17 15	07 22	16 49	07 58	16 14	08 59	15 12
6	**04 00** ☾			**12 14**		**12 11**		**12 08**		**12 03**		**11 57**
7 Fr	12 05 54	−22 28	06 36	17 36	06 57	17 16	07 22	16 50	07 58	16 15	08 58	15 14
7			**00 50**	**12 51**	**00 55**	**12 44**	**01 02**	**12 35**	**01 10**	**12 23**	**01 24**	**12 05**
8 Sa	12 06 20	−22 21	06 36	17 37	06 57	17 16	07 22	16 51	07 57	16 16	08 57	15 16
8			**01 43**	**13 29**	**01 52**	**13 17**	**02 04**	**13 03**	**02 21**	**12 44**	**02 47**	**12 14**
9 Su	12 06 46	−22 13	06 37	17 37	06 57	17 17	07 22	16 52	07 57	16 18	08 56	15 18
9			**02 35**	**14 08**	**02 49**	**13 52**	**03 06**	**13 33**	**03 30**	**13 07**	**04 09**	**12 26**
10 Mo	12 07 11	−22 04	06 37	17 38	06 57	17 18	07 22	16 53	07 56	16 19	08 55	15 20
10			**03 27**	**14 49**	**03 44**	**14 31**	**04 06**	**14 07**	**04 37**	**13 35**	**05 29**	**12 41**
11 Tu	12 07 35	−21 55	6 37	17 38	06 57	17 19	7 22	16 54	7 56	16 20	08 54	15 22
11			**4 19**	**15 33**	**04 40**	**15 12**	**05 05**	**14 46**	**05 41**	**14 09**	**06 45**	**13 04**
12 We	12 07 59	−21 46	06 37	17 39	06 57	17 20	7 22	16 55	07 55	16 22	08 52	15 24
12			**5 11**	**16 20**	**5 33**	**15 58**	**06 01**	**15 30**	**06 41**	**14 49**	**07 53**	**13 37**
13 Th	12 08 23	−21 37	06 38	17 40	06 57	17 20	07 21	16 56	07 55	16 23	08 51	15 26
13			**6 01**	**17 10**	**06 24**	**16 47**	**06 53**	**16 19**	**07 34**	**15 38**	**08 48**	**14 24**
14 Fr	12 08 46	−21 26	06 38	17 40	06 57	17 21	07 21	16 57	07 54	16 24	08 50	15 28
14	**05 08** ●		**06 49**	**18 00**	**07 11**	**17 39**	**07 39**	**17 12**	**08 18**	**16 34**	**09 28**	**15 25**
15 Sa	12 09 08	−21 16	06 38	17 41	06 57	17 22	07 21	16 58	07 53	16 26	08 48	15 30
15			**07 35**	**18 52**	**07 55**	**18 33**	**08 20**	**18 09**	**08 55**	**17 35**	**09 56**	**16 36**
16 Su	12 09 29	−21 05	06 38	17 42	06 56	17 23	07 20	17 00	07 52	16 27	08 47	15 32
16			**08 17**	**19 43**	**08 34**	**19 27**	**08 56**	**19 07**	**09 26**	**18 40**	**10 14**	**17 53**
17 Mo	12 09 50	−20 54	06 38	17 42	06 56	17 24	07 20	17 01	07 52	16 28	08 46	15 35
17			**08 57**	**20 34**	**09 11**	**20 22**	**09 28**	**20 07**	**09 51**	**19 46**	**10 28**	**19 12**
18 Tu	12 10 10	−20 42	06 38	17 43	06 56	17 25	07 19	17 02	07 51	16 30	08 44	15 37
18			**09 34**	**21 25**	**09 44**	**21 17**	**09 56**	**21 07**	**10 12**	**20 53**	**10 38**	**20 32**
19 We	12 10 29	−20 30	06 38	17 43	06 56	17 26	07 19	17 03	07 50	16 32	08 42	15 40
19			**10 10**	**22 15**	**10 16**	**22 11**	**10 23**	**22 07**	**10 32**	**22 01**	**10 46**	**21 52**
20 Th	12 10 48	−20 17	06 38	17 44	06 56	17 26	07 18	17 04	07 49	16 34	08 40	15 42
20			**10 46**	**23 06**	**10 47**	**23 07**	**10 48**	**23 08**	**10 50**	**23 10**	**10 53**	**23 13**
21 Fr	12 11 06	−20 04	06 38	17 44	06 55	17 27	07 18	17 06	07 48	16 35	08 39	15 44
21			**11 22**	**23 59**	**11 18**		**11 14**		**11 09**		**11 01**	
22 Sa	12 11 23	−19 51	06 38	17 45	06 55	17 28	07 17	17 07	07 47	16 37	08 37	15 47
22	**05 33** ☽		**12 00**		**11 52**	**00 05**	**11 42**	**00 12**	**11 29**	**00 21**	**11 09**	**00 37**
23 Su	12 11 39	−19 38	06 38	17 46	06 55	17 29	07 16	17 08	07 46	16 38	08 35	15 50
23			**12 41**	**0 54**	**12 29**	**01 05**	**12 14**	**01 18**	**11 53**	**01 36**	**11 20**	**02 04**
24 Mo	12 11 55	−19 24	06 38	17 47	06 55	17 30	07 16	17 09	07 44	16 40	08 33	15 52
24			**13 28**	**01 53**	**13 11**	**02 08**	**12 50**	**02 27**	**12 22**	**02 53**	**11 36**	**03 36**
25 Tu	12 12 09	−19 09	06 37	17 47	06 54	17 31	07 15	17 10	07 43	16 42	08 31	15 43
25			**14 20**	**02 55**	**14 00**	**03 14**	**13 34**	**03 38**	**12 59**	**04 12**	**11 59**	**05 09**
26 We	12 12 23	−18 54	06 37	17 48	06 54	17 32	07 14	17 11	07 42	16 43	08 29	15 57
26			**15 19**	**04 00**	**14 57**	**04 22**	**14 28**	**04 49**	**13 48**	**05 29**	**12 38**	**06 38**
27 Th	12 12 36	−18 39	06 37	17 48	06 54	17 33	07 13	17 12	07 41	16 45	08 27	16 00
27			**16 24**	**05 06**	**16 01**	**05 28**	**15 33**	**05 57**	**14 52**	**06 38**	**13 39**	**07 52**
28 Fr	12 12 49	−18 24	06 36	17 49	06 53	17 34	07 12	17 14	07 40	16 46	08 24	16 02
28	**22 26** ○		**17 32**	**06 09**	**17 11**	**06 30**	**16 45**	**06 57**	**16 08**	**07 36**	**15 04**	**08 42**
29 Sa	12 13 00	−18 08	06 36	17 50	06 53	17 34	07 12	17 15	07 38	16 48	08 22	16 04
29			**18 39**	**07 07**	**18 23**	**07 26**	**18 02**	**07 49**	**17 32**	**08 20**	**16 43**	**09 13**
30 Su	12 13 11	−17 52	06 36	17 50	06 52	17 35	07 11	17 16	07 37	16 50	08 20	16 07
30			**19 45**	**08 00**	**19 33**	**08 14**	**19 18**	**08 31**	**18 57**	**08 55**	**18 24**	**09 33**
31 Mo	12 13 21	−17 36	06 36	17 51	06 52	17 36	07 10	17 17	07 36	16 52	08 18	16 10
31			**20 47**	**08 47**	**20 40**	**08 56**	**20 32**	**09 08**	**20 20**	**09 23**	**20 02**	**09 46**

2nd Month February, 1983 28 Days

Greenwich Mean Time

NOTE: Light figures indicate Sun. **Dark** figures indicate **Moon.** *Degrees are North Latitude.*

CAUTION: Must be converted to local time. For instruction see page 768.

Day of month week year	Sun on meridian **Moon phase**	Sun's Declination	20° Rise Sun **Moon**	20° Set Sun **Moon**	30° Rise Sun **Moon**	30° Set Sun **Moon**	40° Rise Sun **Moon**	40° Set Sun **Moon**	50° Rise Sun **Moon**	50° Set Sun **Moon**	60° Rise Sun **Moon**	60° Set Sun **Moon**
	h m s	° ′	h m	h m	h m	h m	h m	h m	h m	h m	h m	h m
1 Tu	12 13 30	−17 19	06 36	17 52	06 51	17 36	07 09	17 18	07 34	16 54	08 16	16 12
32			**21 46**	**09 30**	**21 44**	**09 34**	**21 42**	**09 39**	**21 39**	**09 46**	**21 35**	**09 56**
2 We	12 13 38	−17 02	06 35	17 52	06 51	17 37	07 08	17 20	07 33	16 55	08 13	16 15
33			**22 42**	**10 10**	**22 45**	**10 09**	**22 49**	**10 08**	**22 55**	**10 07**	**23 04**	**10 05**
3 Th	12 13 45	−16 45	06 35	17 53	06 50	17 38	07 07	17 21	07 32	16 57	08 11	16 18
34			**23 36**	**10 49**	**23 44**	**10 43**	**23 54**	**10 36**		**10 27**		**10 13**
4 Fr	12 13 52	−16 27	06 35	17 54	06 49	17 39	07 06	17 22	07 30	16 59	08 08	16 21
35	**19 17** ☾			**11 27**		**11 17**		**11 05**	**00 08**	**10 48**	**00 30**	**10 22**
5 Sa	12 13 58	−16 10	06 34	17 54	06 48	17 40	07 05	17 24	07 28	17 00	08 06	16 24
36			**00 29**	**12 06**	**00 42**	**11 52**	**00 57**	**11 35**	**01 19**	**11 11**	**01 54**	**10 33**
6 Su	12 14 03	−15 51	06 34	17 55	06 48	17 41	07 04	17 25	07 27	17 02	08 04	16 26
37			**01 22**	**12 47**	**01 39**	**12 30**	**01 59**	**12 08**	**02 28**	**11 37**	**03 16**	**10 44**
7 Mo	12 14 07	−15 33	06 34	17 55	06 47	17 42	07 03	17 26	07 25	17 04	08 01	16 29
38			**02 15**	**13 31**	**02 34**	**13 10**	**02 59**	**12 45**	**03 34**	**12 09**	**04 34**	**11 07**
8 Tu	12 14 11	−15 14	06 34	17 56	06 46	17 43	07 02	17 27	07 24	17 06	07 58	16 32
39			**03 07**	**14 17**	**03 28**	**13 55**	**03 56**	**13 27**	**04 35**	**12 47**	**05 45**	**11 36**
9 We	12 14 13	−14 55	06 33	17 56	06 46	17 44	07 01	17 28	07 22	17 07	07 56	16 34
40			**03 57**	**15 05**	**04 20**	**14 43**	**04 49**	**14 14**	**05 30**	**13 33**	**06 44**	**12 18**
10 Th	12 14 15	−14 36	06 33	17 57	06 45	17 44	07 00	17 29	07 20	17 08	07 53	16 36
41			**04 46**	**15 56**	**05 09**	**15 34**	**05 37**	**15 06**	**06 17**	**14 26**	**07 29**	**13 15**
11 Fr	12 14 16	−14 17	06 32	17 57	06 44	17 45	06 59	17 30	07 19	17 10	07 50	16 39
42			**05 33**	**16 47**	**05 53**	**16 27**	**06 20**	**16 02**	**06 56**	**15 26**	**08 00**	**14 24**
12 Sa	12 14 17	−13 57	06 32	17 58	06 43	17 46	06 58	17 31	07 17	17 12	07 48	16 42
43			**06 16**	**17 39**	**06 34**	**17 22**	**06 57**	**17 01**	**07 29**	**16 31**	**08 21**	**15 40**
13 Su	12 14 16	−13 37	06 31	17 58	06 42	17 46	06 57	17 32	07 16	17 14	07 45	16 44
44	**00 32** ●		**06 57**	**18 30**	**07 11**	**18 17**	**07 30**	**18 00**	**07 55**	**17 37**	**08 36**	**17 00**
14 Mo	12 14 15	−13 17	06 31	17 59	06 42	17 47	06 55	17 34	07 14	17 15	07 42	16 47
45			**07 35**	**19 21**	**07 46**	**19 12**	**07 59**	**19 01**	**08 18**	**18 45**	**08 47**	**18 20**
15 Tu	12 14 13	−12 57	06 30	17 59	06 41	17 48	06 54	17 35	07 12	17 17	07 40	16 50
46			**08 11**	**20 12**	**08 18**	**20 07**	**08 26**	**20 01**	**08 38**	**19 53**	**08 55**	**19 40**
16 We	12 14 11	−12 36	06 29	18 00	06 40	17 49	06 53	17 36	07 10	17 19	07 37	16 52
47			**08 47**	**21 03**	**08 49**	**21 03**	**08 52**	**21 02**	**08 56**	**21 02**	**09 03**	**21 01**
17 Th	12 14 07	−12 15	06 28	18 00	06 39	17 50	06 52	17 38	07 08	17 20	07 34	16 55
48			**09 22**	**21 55**	**09 20**	**21 59**	**09 18**	**22 05**	**09 15**	**22 12**	**09 10**	**22 23**
18 Fr	12 14 03	−11 54	06 28	18 01	06 38	17 50	06 50	17 39	07 06	17 22	07 32	16 58
49			**09 59**	**22 48**	**09 53**	**22 57**	**09 45**	**23 09**	**09 34**	**23 24**	**09 18**	**23 48**
19 Sa	12 13 58	−11 33	06 27	18 01	06 37	17 51	06 49	17 40	07 04	17 24	07 29	17 00
50			**10 39**	**23 44**	**10 27**	**23 58**	**10 14**		**09 55**		**09 27**	
20 Su	12 13 53	−11 12	06 26	18 02	06 36	17 52	06 48	17 41	07 02	17 26	07 26	17 02
51	**17 32** ☽		**11 22**		**11 06**		**10 47**	**00 15**	**10 21**	**00 38**	**09 40**	**01 17**
21 Mo	12 13 47	−10 50	06 26	18 02	06 35	17 52	06 46	17 42	07 00	17 28	07 24	17 05
52			**12 10**	**00 43**	**11 51**	**01 01**	**11 27**	**01 23**	**10 54**	**01 54**	**09 58**	**02 47**
22 Tu	12 13 40	−10 29	06 25	18 03	06 34	17 53	06 44	17 43	06 59	17 29	07 21	17 08
53			**13 04**	**01 45**	**12 42**	**02 06**	**12 15**	**02 32**	**11 36**	**03 10**	**10 28**	**04 16**
23 We	12 13 32	−10 07	06 25	18 03	06 33	17 54	06 43	17 44	06 57	17 31	07 18	17 10
54			**14 04**	**02 48**	**13 41**	**03 10**	**13 12**	**03 39**	**12 31**	**04 20**	**11 17**	**05 34**
24 Th	12 13 24	−09 45	06 24	18 03	06 32	17 55	06 42	17 45	06 55	17 33	07 15	17 13
55			**15 08**	**03 50**	**14 46**	**04 13**	**14 19**	**04 41**	**13 39**	**05 21**	**12 29**	**06 33**
25 Fr	12 13 15	−09 23	06 24	18 04	06 31	17 56	06 40	17 46	06 53	17 34	07 12	17 16
56			**16 15**	**04 49**	**15 56**	**05 10**	**15 32**	**05 35**	**14 58**	**06 11**	**14 00**	**07 11**
26 Sa	12 13 06	−09 01	06 23	18 04	06 30	17 56	06 38	17 48	06 51	17 36	07 09	17 18
57			**17 21**	**05 44**	**17 07**	**06 00**	**16 48**	**06 21**	**16 23**	**06 49**	**15 41**	**07 35**
27 Su	12 12 56	−08 38	06 22	18 04	06 29	17 57	06 37	17 49	06 49	17 38	07 06	17 21
58	**08 58** ○		**18 26**	**06 34**	**18 16**	**06 45**	**18 04**	**07 00**	**17 48**	**07 20**	**17 22**	**07 50**
28 Mo	12 12 45	−08 16	06 21	18 04	06 28	17 58	06 36	17 50	06 47	17 40	07 03	17 24
59			**19 27**	**07 19**	**19 23**	**07 26**	**19 17**	**07 34**	**19 10**	**07 45**	**18 59**	**08 02**

3rd Month **March, 1983** **31 Days**

Greenwich Mean Time

NOTE: Light figures indicate Sun. **Dark** figures indicate **Moon.** *Degrees are North Latitude.*

CAUTION: Must be converted to local time. For instruction see page 768.

Day of month week year	Sun on meridian **Moon phase** h m s	Sun's Declination ° ′	20° Rise Sun **Moon** h m	20° Set Sun **Moon** h m	30° Rise Sun **Moon** h m	30° Set Sun **Moon** h m	40° Rise Sun **Moon** h m	40° Set Sun **Moon** h m	50° Rise Sun **Moon** h m	50° Set Sun **Moon** h m	60° Rise Sun **Moon** h m	60° Set Sun **Moon** h m
1 Tu	12 12 34	−07 53	06 20	18 05	06 27	17 58	06 34	17 51	06 45	17 41	07 00	17 26
60			**20 26**	**08 01**	**20 27**	**08 03**	**20 28**	**08 05**	**20 30**	**08 07**	**20 33**	**08 11**
2 We	12 12 23	−07 30	06 20	18 05	06 26	17 59	06 32	17 52	06 43	17 42	06 57	17 28
61			**21 23**	**08 41**	**21 29**	**08 38**	**21 37**	**08 34**	**21 47**	**08 28**	**22 03**	**08 19**
3 Th	12 12 11	−07 07	06 19	18 06	06 25	18 00	06 31	17 53	06 41	17 44	06 54	17 31
62			**22 18**	**09 21**	**22 29**	**09 13**	**22 43**	**09 03**	**23 02**	**08 49**	**23 32**	**08 28**
4 Fr	12 11 58	−06 44	06 18	18 06	06 24	18 01	06 30	17 54	06 39	17 46	06 51	17 34
63			**23 13**	**10 01**	**23 28**	**09 48**	**23 47**	**09 33**		**09 11**		**08 38**
5 Sa	12 11 45	−06 21	06 18	18 07	06 22	18 02	06 28	17 56	06 36	17 48	06 48	17 36
64				**10 43**		**10 26**		**10 05**	**00 14**	**09 37**	**00 57**	**08 50**
6 Su	12 11 32	−05 58	06 17	18 07	06 21	18 02	06 26	17 57	06 34	17 49	06 46	17 38
65	**13 16** ☾		**00 07**	**11 26**	**00 26**	**11 06**	**00 49**	**10 42**	**01 23**	**10 07**	**02 19**	**09 08**
7 Mo	12 11 18	−05 35	06 16	18 07	06 20	18 03	06 25	17 58	06 32	17 51	06 43	17 41
66			**01 00**	**12 12**	**01 22**	**11 50**	**01 49**	**11 22**	**02 27**	**10 43**	**03 35**	**09 34**
8 Tu	12 11 04	−05 12	06 15	18 07	06 19	18 04	06 24	17 59	06 30	17 53	06 40	17 44
67			**01 52**	**13 00**	**02 15**	**12 37**	**02 44**	**12 08**	**03 25**	**11 27**	**04 40**	**10 11**
9 We	12 10 49	−04 48	06 14	18 08	06 18	18 04	06 22	18 00	06 28	17 54	06 37	17 46
68			**02 42**	**13 50**	**03 05**	**13 27**	**03 34**	**12 59**	**04 15**	**12 18**	**05 30**	**11 04**
10 Th	12 10 34	−04 25	06 13	18 08	06 16	18 05	06 20	18 01	06 26	17 56	06 34	17 48
69			**03 29**	**14 41**	**03 51**	**14 20**	**04 18**	**13 54**	**04 57**	**13 16**	**06 05**	**12 09**
11 Fr	12 10 19	−04 01	06 12	18 08	06 15	18 05	06 19	18 02	06 24	17 58	06 31	17 51
70			**04 13**	**15 33**	**04 33**	**15 15**	**04 57**	**14 52**	**05 31**	**14 19**	**06 28**	**13 24**
12 Sa	12 10 03	−03 38	06 11	18 08	06 14	18 06	06 18	18 03	06 22	18 00	06 28	17 54
71			**04 55**	**16 24**	**05 11**	**16 10**	**05 31**	**15 51**	**05 59**	**15 26**	**06 44**	**14 43**
13 Su	12 09 47	−03 14	06 10	18 08	06 13	18 06	06 16	18 04	06 20	18 01	06 25	17 56
72			**05 34**	**17 16**	**05 46**	**17 05**	**06 02**	**16 52**	**06 23**	**16 33**	**06 56**	**16 04**
14 Mo	12 09 31	−02 51	06 10	18 09	06 12	18 07	06 14	18 05	06 17	18 02	06 22	17 58
73	**17 43** ●		**06 11**	**18 07**	**06 19**	**18 01**	**06 30**	**17 53**	**06 43**	**17 42**	**07 05**	**17 26**
15 Tu	12 09 14	−02 27	06 09	18 09	06 11	18 08	06 13	18 06	06 15	18 04	06 19	18 01
74			**06 47**	**18 59**	**06 51**	**18 57**	**06 56**	**18 55**	**07 02**	**18 52**	**07 12**	**18 48**
16 We	12 08 58	−02 03	06 08	18 10	06 10	18 08	06 11	18 07	06 13	18 06	06 16	18 04
75			**07 23**	**19 51**	**07 22**	**19 54**	**07 22**	**19 58**	**07 21**	**20 03**	**07 19**	**20 11**
17 Th	12 08 41	−01 39	06 08	18 10	06 08	18 09	06 10	18 08	06 10	18 07	06 13	18 06
76			**08 00**	**20 44**	**07 54**	**20 52**	**07 48**	**21 02**	**07 39**	**21 15**	**07 26**	**21 36**
18 Fr	12 08 24	−01 16	06 07	18 11	06 07	18 10	06 08	18 09	06 08	18 08	06 10	18 08
77			**08 38**	**21 40**	**08 29**	**21 52**	**08 16**	**22 08**	**08 00**	**22 29**	**07 35**	**23 04**
19 Sa	12 08 06	−00 52	06 06	18 11	06 06	18 10	06 06	18 10	06 06	18 10	06 07	18 11
78			**09 20**	**22 38**	**09 06**	**22 55**	**08 48**	**23 16**	**08 24**	**23 45**	**07 46**	
20 Su	12 07 49	−00 28	06 05	18 11	06 05	18 11	06 04	18 11	06 04	18 12	06 04	18 13
79			**10 06**	**23 38**	**09 48**	**23 58**	**09 25**		**08 54**		**08 02**	**00 34**
21 Mo	12 07 31	−00 05	06 04	18 12	06 04	18 12	06 03	18 12	06 02	18 14	06 01	18 16
80			**10 57**		**10 36**		**10 09**	**00 24**	**09 32**	**01 00**	**08 26**	**02 04**
22 Tu	12 07 13	+00 19	06 03	18 12	06 02	18 12	06 02	18 13	06 00	18 15	05 58	18 18
81	**02 25** ☽		**11 54**	**00 39**	**11 31**	**01 02**	**11 02**	**01 30**	**10 21**	**02 11**	**09 06**	**03 25**
23 We	12 06 55	+00 43	06 02	18 12	06 01	18 13	06 00	18 14	05 58	18 17	05 55	18 20
82			**12 55**	**01 40**	**12 32**	**02 03**	**12 04**	**02 32**	**11 22**	**03 14**	**10 08**	**04 29**
24 Th	12 06 37	+01 06	06 01	18 12	06 00	18 14	05 58	18 15	05 56	18 18	05 52	18 22
83			**13 59**	**02 39**	**13 38**	**03 00**	**13 12**	**03 27**	**12 35**	**04 06**	**11 31**	**05 12**
25 Fr	12 06 19	+01 30	06 00	18 12	05 58	18 14	05 56	18 16	05 54	18 20	05 48	18 25
84			**15 04**	**03 33**	**14 47**	**03 52**	**14 25**	**04 15**	**13 56**	**04 47**	**13 06**	**05 39**
26 Sa	12 06 00	+01 54	06 00	18 13	05 57	18 15	05 55	18 17	05 51	18 22	05 45	18 28
85			**16 07**	**04 23**	**15 55**	**04 37**	**15 40**	**04 55**	**15 19**	**05 19**	**14 45**	**05 57**
27 Su	12 05 42	+02 17	05 59	18 13	05 56	18 15	05 53	18 19	05 49	18 23	05 42	18 30
86			**17 09**	**05 09**	**17 02**	**05 18**	**16 53**	**05 30**	**16 41**	**05 45**	**16 23**	**06 09**
28 Mo	12 05 24	+02 41	05 58	18 13	05 55	18 16	05 52	18 20	05 47	18 24	05 39	18 32
87	**19 27** ○		**18 08**	**05 52**	**18 07**	**05 56**	**18 05**	**06 01**	**18 02**	**06 08**	**17 58**	**06 18**
29 Tu	12 05 06	+03 04	05 57	18 14	05 54	18 16	05 50	18 21	05 44	18 26	05 36	18 35
88			**19 06**	**06 33**	**19 10**	**06 32**	**19 15**	**06 30**	**19 21**	**06 29**	**19 31**	**06 26**
30 We	12 04 47	+03 28	05 56	18 14	05 52	18 17	05 48	18 22	05 42	18 28	05 33	18 38
89			**20 03**	**07 13**	**20 12**	**07 07**	**20 23**	**06 59**	**20 38**	**06 49**	**21 02**	**06 34**
31 Th	12 04 29	+03 51	05 55	18 14	05 51	18 18	05 47	18 23	05 40	18 29	05 30	18 40
90			**21 00**	**07 33**	**21 13**	**07 32**	**21 30**	**07 29**	**21 53**	**07 11**	**22 31**	**06 43**

4th Month **April, 1983** **30 Days**

Greenwich Mean Time

NOTE: Light figures indicate Sun. **Dark** figures indicate **Moon.** *Degrees are North Latitude.*

CAUTION: Must be converted to local time. For instruction see page 768.

Day of month week year	Sun on meridian **Moon phase** h m s	Sun's Declination ° ′	20° Rise Sun **Moon** h m	20° Set Sun **Moon** h m	30° Rise Sun **Moon** h m	30° Set Sun **Moon** h m	40° Rise Sun **Moon** h m	40° Set Sun **Moon** h m	50° Rise Sun **Moon** h m	50° Set Sun **Moon** h m	60° Rise Sun **Moon** h m	60° Set Sun **Moon** h m
1 Fr	12 04 11	+04 14	05 54	18 14	05 50	18 18	05 45	18 24	05 38	18 31	05 27	18 42
91			**21 55**	**08 35**	**22 13**	**08 20**	**22 35**	**08 01**	**23 06**	**07 35**	**23 58**	**06 54**
2 Sa	12 03 53	+04 37	05 54	18 14	05 49	18 19	05 44	18 25	05 36	18 32	05 24	18 45
92			**22 50**	**09 18**	**23 11**	**08 59**	**23 37**	**08 36**		**08 03**		**07 09**
3 Su	12 03 35	+05 00	05 53	18 15	05 48	18 19	05 42	18 26	05 34	18 34	05 21	18 48
93			**23 24**	**10 04**		**09 42**		**09 15**	**00 14**	**08 37**	**01 19**	**07 30**
4 Mo	12 03 17	+05 23	05 52	18 15	05 47	18 20	05 40	18 27	05 32	18 36	05 18	18 50
94				**10 52**	**00 06**	**10 29**	**00 35**	**10 00**	**01 16**	**09 18**	**02 31**	**08 03**
5 Tu	12 03 00	+05 46	05 51	18 15	05 46	18 21	05 38	18 28	05 30	18 38	05 15	18 52
95	**08 38** ☾		**00 35**	**11 42**	**00 58**	**11 19**	**01 28**	**10 49**	**02 10**	**10 07**	**03 28**	**08 50**
6 We	12 02 42	+06 09	05 50	18 16	05 44	18 22	05 37	18 29	05 28	18 39	05 12	18 54
96			**01 24**	**12 33**	**01 46**	**12 11**	**02 15**	**11 43**	**02 55**	**11 03**	**04 08**	**09 52**
7 Th	12 02 25	+06 32	05 49	18 16	05 43	18 22	05 36	18 30	05 25	18 40	05 09	18 57
97			**02 09**	**13 25**	**02 30**	**13 05**	**02 56**	**12 40**	**03 32**	**12 05**	**04 35**	**11 04**
8 Fr	12 02 08	+06 54	05 48	18 16	05 42	18 23	05 34	18 31	05 23	18 42	05 06	18 49
98			**02 52**	**14 16**	**03 10**	**14 00**	**03 32**	**13 39**	**04 02**	**13 11**	**04 53**	**12 23**
9 Sa	12 01 52	+07 17	05 47	18 16	05 41	18 24	05 32	18 32	05 21	18 44	05 03	19 02
99			**03 31**	**15 08**	**03 46**	**14 55**	**04 03**	**14 40**	**04 27**	**14 18**	**05 05**	**13 43**
10 Su	12 01 35	+07 39	05 47	18 17	05 40	18 24	05 31	18 33	05 19	18 45	05 00	19 04
100			**04 09**	**15 59**	**04 19**	**15 51**	**04 32**	**15 41**	**04 48**	**15 27**	**05 15**	**15 05**
11 Mo	12 01 19	+08 01	05 46	18 17	05 38	18 25	05 30	18 34	05 17	18 46	04 57	19 06
101			**04 45**	**16 51**	**04 51**	**16 47**	**04 58**	**16 43**	**05 08**	**16 37**	**05 22**	**16 27**
12 Tu	12 01 03	+08 24	05 45	18 17	05 37	18 25	05 28	18 35	05 15	18 48	04 54	19 09
102			**05 21**	**17 43**	**05 23**	**17 44**	**05 24**	**17 46**	**05 26**	**17 48**	**05 29**	**17 51**
13 We	12 00 47	+08 45	05 44	18 17	05 36	18 26	05 26	18 36	05 13	18 50	04 51	19 12
103	**07 58** ●		**05 58**	**18 37**	**05 55**	**18 43**	**05 50**	**18 51**	**05 44**	**19 01**	**05 35**	**19 18**
14 Th	12 00 32	+09 07	05 43	18 18	05 35	18 26	05 25	18 37	05 10	18 51	04 48	19 14
104			**06 37**	**19 33**	**06 28**	**19 44**	**06 18**	**19 58**	**06 04**	**20 17**	**05 43**	**20 47**
15 Fr	12 00 17	+09 29	05 42	18 18	05 34	18 27	05 24	18 38	05 08	18 52	04 45	19 16
105			**07 18**	**20 31**	**07 05**	**20 47**	**06 49**	**21 07**	**06 27**	**21 34**	**05 53**	**22 19**
16 Sa	12 00 02	+09 50	05 42	18 18	05 33	18 27	05 22	18 39	05 06	18 54	04 42	19 19
106			**08 03**	**21 32**	**07 40**	**21 52**	**07 24**	**22 16**	**06 55**	**22 51**	**06 06**	**23 52**
17 Su	11 59 48	+10 12	05 41	18 19	05 32	18 28	05 20	18 40	05 04	18 56	04 39	19 22
107			**08 54**	**22 34**	**08 33**	**22 56**	**08 07**	**23 25**	**07 30**		**06 28**	
18 Mo	11 59 34	+10 33	05 40	18 19	05 31	18 28	05 19	18 41	05 02	18 58	04 36	19 24
108			**09 49**	**23 35**	**09 26**	**23 59**	**08 57**		**08 16**	**00 05**	**07 02**	**01 18**
19 Tu	11 59 21	+10 54	05 40	18 20	05 30	18 29	05 18	18 42	05 00	18 59	04 34	19 26
109			**10 49**		**10 25**		**09 56**	**00 28**	**09 14**	**01 11**	**07 56**	**02 28**
20 We	11 59 07	+11 15	05 39	18 20	05 29	18 30	05 16	18 43	04 58	19 01	04 31	19 29
110	**08 58** ☽		**11 51**	**00 34**	**11 29**	**00 57**	**11 02**	**01 25**	**10 23**	**02 05**	**09 13**	**03 17**
21 Th	11 58 55	+11 35	05 38	18 20	05 28	18 30	05 14	18 44	04 56	19 02	04 28	19 32
111			**12 54**	**01 29**	**12 36**	**01 49**	**12 13**	**02 14**	**11 40**	**02 49**	**10 44**	**03 47**
22 Fr	11 58 42	+11 56	05 38	18 21	05 26	18 31	05 13	18 45	04 54	19 04	04 25	19 34
112			**13 56**	**02 19**	**13 42**	**02 35**	**13 25**	**02 55**	**13 00**	**03 22**	**12 20**	**04 06**
23 Sa	11 58 30	+12 16	05 37	18 21	05 25	18 32	05 12	18 46	04 53	19 06	04 22	19 36
113			**14 57**	**03 05**	**14 48**	**03 16**	**14 36**	**03 30**	**14 21**	**03 49**	**13 56**	**04 18**
24 Su	11 58 19	+12 36	05 36	18 21	05 24	18 32	05 10	18 47	04 51	19 07	04 19	19 39
114			**15 56**	**03 47**	**15 52**	**03 54**	**15 47**	**04 02**	**15 40**	**04 12**	**15 30**	**04 28**
25 Mo	11 58 08	+12 56	05 35	18 21	05 23	18 33	05 09	18 48	04 49	19 08	04 16	19 42
115			**16 53**	**04 28**	**16 54**	**04 29**	**16 56**	**04 30**	**16 58**	**04 32**	**17 02**	**04 35**
26 Tu	11 57 57	+13 16	05 35	18 27	05 22	18 34	05 08	18 49	04 47	19 10	04 14	19 44
116			**17 50**	**05 07**	**17 56**	**05 03**	**18 04**	**04 58**	**18 15**	**04 52**	**18 33**	**04 43**
27 We	11 57 47	+13 35	05 34	18 22	05 22	18 34	05 06	18 50	04 45	19 12	04 11	19 46
117	**06 31** ○		**18 46**	**05 47**	**18 57**	**05 38**	**19 12**	**05 27**	**19 31**	**05 13**	**20 03**	**04 50**
28 Th	11 57 37	+13 54	05 33	18 22	05 21	18 35	05 05	18 51	04 43	19 13	04 08	19 49
118			**19 42**	**06 27**	**19 58**	**06 14**	**20 18**	**05 57**	**20 46**	**05 35**	**21 32**	**05 00**
29 Fr	11 57 28	+14 13	05 32	18 22	05 20	18 36	05 04	18 52	04 41	19 14	04 05	19 52
119			**20 38**	**07 10**	**20 58**	**06 53**	**21 22**	**06 31**	**21 57**	**06 01**	**22 57**	**05 12**
30 Sa	11 57 19	+14 32	05 32	18 23	05 19	18 36	05 02	18 53	04 40	19 16	04 02	19 54
120			**21 33**	**07 55**	**21 55**	**07 34**	**22 23**	**07 09**	**23 03**	**06 32**		**05 30**

5th Month May, 1983 31 days

Greenwich Mean Time

NOTE: Light figures indicate Sun. **Dark** figures indicate **Moon.** *Degrees are North Latitude.*

CAUTION: Must be converted to local time. For instruction see page 768.

Day of month week year	Sun on meridian **Moon phase** h m s	Sun's Declination ° ′	20° Rise Sun **Moon** h m	20° Set Sun **Moon** h m	30° Rise Sun **Moon** h m	30° Set Sun **Moon** h m	40° Rise Sun **Moon** h m	40° Set Sun **Moon** h m	50° Rise Sun **Moon** h m	50° Set Sun **Moon** h m	60° Rise Sun **Moon** h m	60° Set Sun **Moon** h m
1 Su	11 57 11	+14 50	05 31	18 23	05 18	18 37	05 01	18 54	04 38	19 18	04 00	19 5
121			**22 26**	**08 43**	**22 50**	**08 20**	**23 19**	**07 51**		**07 10**	**00 16**	**05 5**
2 Mo	11 57 04	+15 08	05 31	18 24	05 17	18 38	05 00	18 55	04 36	19 19	03 57	19 5
122			**23 17**	**09 33**	**23 40**	**09 09**		**08 39**	**00 02**	**07 56**	**01 21**	**06 3**
3 Tu	11 56 57	+15 26	05 30	18 24	05 16	18 38	04 59	18 56	04 34	19 20	03 54	20 0
123				**10 24**		**10 01**	**00 09**	**09 32**	**00 52**	**08 50**	**02 09**	**07 3**
4 We	11 56 50	+15 44	05 30	18 24	05 15	18 39	04 58	18 57	04 32	19 22	03 52	20 0
124			**00 04**	**11 16**	**00 26**	**10 55**	**00 53**	**10 28**	**01 32**	**09 50**	**02 40**	**08 4**
5 Th	11 56 44	+16 02	05 29	18 25	05 14	18 40	04 56	18 58	04 31	19 24	03 49	20 0
125	**03 43** ☾		**00 48**	**12 07**	**01 07**	**11 49**	**01 31**	**11 27**	**02 05**	**10 55**	**03 01**	**10 0**
6 Fr	11 56 39	+16 19	05 28	18 25	05 13	18 40	04 55	18 59	04 29	19 25	03 46	20 0
126			**01 28**	**12 59**	**01 44**	**12 44**	**02 04**	**12 26**	**02 31**	**12 01**	**03 15**	**11 2**
7 Sa	11 56 34	+16 36	05 28	18 26	05 12	18 41	04 54	19 00	04 27	19 26	03 44	20 1
127			**02 06**	**13 49**	**02 18**	**13 39**	**02 33**	**13 27**	**02 53**	**13 09**	**03 25**	**12 4**
8 Su	11 56 30	+16 52	05 27	18 26	05 12	18 42	04 52	19 01	04 26	19 28	03 41	20 1
128			**02 43**	**14 40**	**02 50**	**14 35**	**03 00**	**14 28**	**03 13**	**14 18**	**03 32**	**14 0**
9 Mo	11 56 27	+17 09	05 27	18 27	05 11	18 42	04 51	19 02	04 24	19 30	03 38	20 1
129			**03 18**	**15 32**	**03 21**	**15 31**	**03 25**	**15 30**	**03 31**	**15 28**	**03 39**	**15 2**
10 Tu	11 56 24	+17 25	05 26	18 27	05 10	18 43	04 50	19 03	04 22	19 31	03 36	20 1
130			**03 54**	**16 25**	**03 53**	**16 29**	**03 51**	**16 34**	**03 49**	**16 41**	**03 45**	**16 5**
11 We	11 56 21	+17 41	05 26	18 27	05 10	18 44	04 49	19 04	04 20	19 32	03 34	20 2
131			**04 32**	**17 21**	**04 26**	**17 30**	**04 18**	**17 41**	**04 08**	**17 56**	**03 52**	**18 2**
12 Th	11 56 20	+17 56	05 26	18 28	05 09	18 44	04 48	19 05	04 19	19 34	03 31	20 2
132	**19 25** ●		**05 12**	**18 19**	**05 01**	**18 33**	**04 47**	**18 50**	**04 29**	**19 14**	**04 00**	**19 5**
13 Fr	11 56 18	+18 11	05 25	18 28	05 09	18 45	04 47	19 06	04 18	19 36	03 28	20 2
133			**05 57**	**19 20**	**05 41**	**19 39**	**05 21**	**20 02**	**04 55**	**20 34**	**04 12**	**21 2**
14 Sa	11 56 18	+18 26	05 25	18 28	05 08	18 45	04 46	19 07	04 16	19 37	03 26	20 2
134			**06 46**	**20 24**	**06 26**	**20 45**	**06 02**	**21 13**	**05 27**	**21 52**	**04 30**	**23 0**
15 Su	11 56 18	+18 41	05 24	18 28	05 07	18 46	04 45	19 08	04 15	19 38	03 24	20 3
135			**07 41**	**21 28**	**07 18**	**21 51**	**06 50**	**22 21**	**06 10**	**23 03**	**04 59**	
16 Mo	11 56 18	+18 55	05 24	18 29	05 07	18 46	04 44	19 09	04 14	19 40	03 22	20 3
136			**08 41**	**22 29**	**08 17**	**22 52**	**07 48**	**23 21**	**07 05**		**05 46**	**00 2**
17 Tu	11 56 19	+19 09	05 23	18 29	05 06	18 47	04 44	19 10	04 12	19 42	03 19	20 3
137			**09 44**	**23 26**	**09 21**	**23 47**	**08 53**		**08 12**	**00 03**	**06 58**	**01 1**
18 We	11 56 21	+19 23	05 23	18 30	05 05	18 48	04 43	19 11	04 11	19 43	03 17	20 3
138			**10 48**		**10 28**		**10 03**	**00 14**	**09 28**	**00 51**	**08 27**	**01 5**
19 Th	11 56 23	+19 36	05 23	18 30	05 04	18 48	04 42	19 12	04 10	19 44	03 15	20 3
139	**14 17** ☽		**11 51**	**00 18**	**11 35**	**00 35**	**11 15**	**00 57**	**10 48**	**01 27**	**10 03**	**02 1**
20 Fr	11 56 25	+19 49	05 22	18 31	05 04	18 49	04 41	19 12	04 08	19 46	03 12	20 4
140			**12 51**	**01 05**	**12 40**	**01 18**	**12 27**	**01 34**	**12 08**	**01 55**	**11 39**	**02 2**
21 Sa	11 56 29	+20 01	05 22	18 31	05 03	18 50	04 40	19 13	04 07	19 47	03 10	20 4
141			**13 49**	**01 47**	**13 44**	**01 55**	**13 37**	**02 05**	**13 27**	**02 19**	**13 12**	**02 3**
22 Su	11 56 32	+20 14	05 22	18 32	05 03	18 50	04 39	19 14	04 06	19 48	03 08	20 4
142			**14 46**	**02 27**	**14 45**	**02 30**	**14 45**	**02 34**	**14 44**	**02 39**	**14 42**	**02 4**
23 Mo	11 56 37	+20 26	05 22	18 32	05 02	18 51	04 38	19 15	04 05	19 49	03 06	20 4
143			**15 41**	**03 06**	**15 46**	**03 04**	**15 52**	**03 01**	**15 59**	**02 58**	**16 12**	**02 5**
24 Tu	11 56 41	+20 37	05 22	18 32	05 02	18 52	04 38	19 16	04 04	19 50	03 04	20 5
144			**16 36**	**03 44**	**16 46**	**03 37**	**16 58**	**03 29**	**17 14**	**03 17**	**17 40**	**03 0**
25 We	11 56 46	+20 48	05 21	18 33	05 01	18 52	04 37	19 17	04 03	19 52	03 02	20 5
145			**17 32**	**04 23**	**17 46**	**04 12**	**18 04**	**03 58**	**18 28**	**03 38**	**19 08**	**03 0**
26 Th	11 56 52	+20 59	05 21	18 33	05 01	18 53	04 37	19 18	04 02	19 53	03 00	20 5
146	**18 48** ○		**18 27**	**05 05**	**18 46**	**04 49**	**19 08**	**04 29**	**19 41**	**04 02**	**20 35**	**03 1**
27 Fr	11 56 58	+21 10	05 21	18 34	05 01	18 54	04 36	19 19	04 01	19 54	02 58	20 5
147			**19 23**	**05 48**	**19 44**	**05 29**	**20 11**	**05 05**	**20 49**	**04 31**	**21 58**	**03 3**
28 Sa	11 57 05	+21 20	05 20	18 34	05 00	18 54	04 36	19 20	04 00	19 56	02 56	20 5
148			**20 17**	**06 35**	**20 40**	**06 13**	**21 10**	**05 45**	**21 52**	**05 05**	**23 09**	**03 5**
29 Su	11 57 12	+21 30	05 20	18 35	05 00	18 55	04 35	19 20	03 59	19 57	02 55	21 0
149			**21 09**	**07 24**	**21 33**	**07 01**	**22 03**	**06 31**	**22 46**	**05 48**		**04 3**
30 Mo	11 57 20	+21 39	05 20	18 35	05 00	18 55	04 34	19 21	03 58	19 58	02 53	21 0
150			**21 58**	**08 15**	**22 21**	**07 52**	**22 49**	**07 22**	**23 30**	**06 39**	**00 05**	**05 2**
31 Tu	11 57 28	+21 48	05 20	18 35	05 00	18 56	04 34	19 22	03 57	19 59	02 52	21 0
151			**22 43**	**09 07**	**23 04**	**08 45**	**23 29**	**08 17**		**07 37**	**00 43**	**06 2**

6th Month — June, 1983 — 30 days

Greenwich Mean Time

NOTE: Light figures indicate Sun. **Dark** figures indicate **Moon.** *Degrees are North Latitude.*

CAUTION: Must be converted to local time. For instruction see page 768.

Day of month week year	Sun on meridian **Moon phase** h m s	Sun's Declination ° ′	20° Rise Sun **Moon** h m	20° Set Sun **Moon** h m	30° Rise Sun **Moon** h m	30° Set Sun **Moon** h m	40° Rise Sun **Moon** h m	40° Set Sun **Moon** h m	50° Rise Sun **Moon** h m	50° Set Sun **Moon** h m	60° Rise Sun **Moon** h m	60° Set Sun **Moon** h m
1 We	11 57 36	+21 57	05 20	18 36	05 00	18 56	04 34	19 22	03 56	20 00	02 50	21 06
152			**23 25**	**09 59**	**23 42**	**09 39**		**09 15**	**00 06**	**08 40**	**01 08**	**07 40**
2 Th	11 57 45	+22 05	05 20	18 36	04 59	18 57	04 33	19 23	03 56	20 01	02 48	21 08
153				**10 50**		**10 34**	**00 04**	**10 14**	**00 34**	**09 46**	**01 23**	**08 59**
3 Fr	11 57 55	+22 13	05 20	18 36	04 59	18 57	04 33	19 24	03 55	20 02	02 47	21 10
154	**21 07** ☾		**00 03**	**11 41**	**00 17**	**11 29**	**00 34**	**11 14**	**00 57**	**10 53**	**01 34**	**10 19**
4 Sa	11 58 04	+22 20	05 20	18 36	04 59	18 58	04 32	19 24	03 54	20 03	02 46	21 12
155			**00 40**	**12 31**	**00 50**	**12 23**	**01 02**	**12 14**	**01 18**	**12 00**	**01 42**	**11 40**
5 Su	11 58 14	+22 27	05 20	18 37	04 59	18 58	04 32	19 25	03 54	20 04	02 44	21 13
156			**01 15**	**13 21**	**01 20**	**13 18**	**01 27**	**13 14**	**01 36**	**13 09**	**01 49**	**13 01**
6 Mo	11 58 25	+22 34	05 20	18 37	04 58	18 59	04 31	19 26	03 53	20 04	02 43	21 14
157			**01 50**	**14 13**	**01 51**	**14 14**	**01 52**	**14 17**	**01 53**	**14 19**	**01 55**	**14 24**
7 Tu	11 58 36	+22 40	05 20	18 38	04 58	18 59	04 31	19 26	03 53	20 05	02 42	21 16
158			**02 26**	**15 06**	**02 22**	**15 13**	**02 17**	**15 21**	**02 11**	**15 32**	**02 01**	**15 50**
8 We	11 58 47	+22 46	05 20	18 38	04 58	19 00	04 31	19 27	03 52	20 06	02 41	21 17
159			**03 05**	**16 03**	**02 56**	**16 14**	**02 45**	**16 29**	**02 31**	**16 49**	**02 09**	**17 20**
9 Th	11 58 58	+22 52	05 20	18 38	04 58	19 00	04 31	19 27	03 52	20 06	02 40	21 18
160			**03 47**	**17 03**	**03 33**	**17 19**	**03 17**	**17 40**	**02 54**	**18 08**	**02 18**	**18 55**
10 Fr	11 56 10	+22 57	05 20	18 39	04 58	19 01	04 31	19 28	03 51	20 07	02 40	21 20
161			**04 34**	**18 06**	**04 16**	**18 27**	**03 54**	**18 52**	**03 23**	**19 28**	**02 33**	**20 32**
11 Sa	11 59 22	+23 02	05 20	18 39	04 58	19 01	04 31	19 28	03 51	20 08	02 39	21 21
162	**04 37** ●		**05 27**	**19 12**	**05 06**	**19 35**	**04 39**	**20 04**	**04 01**	**20 45**	**02 56**	**22 01**
12 Su	11 59 34	+23 06	05 20	18 39	04 58	19 01	04 31	19 29	03 51	20 09	02 38	21 22
163			**06 27**	**20 16**	**06 03**	**20 40**	**05 34**	**21 10**	**04 51**	**21 53**	**03 35**	**23 11**
13 Mo	11 59 47	+23 10	05 20	18 40	04 58	19 02	04 30	19 29	03 50	20 10	02 38	21 23
164			**07 31**	**21 17**	**07 08**	**21 40**	**06 38**	**22 07**	**05 56**	**22 47**	**04 38**	**23 56**
14 Tu	11 59 59	+23 13	05 20	18 40	04 58	19 02	04 30	19 30	03 50	20 10	02 37	21 24
165			**08 37**	**22 13**	**08 16**	**22 32**	**07 49**	**22 55**	**07 11**	**23 28**	**06 04**	
15 We	12 00 12	+23 16	05 20	18 40	04 58	19 02	04 30	19 30	03 50	20 11	02 36	21 25
166			**09 42**	**23 03**	**09 25**	**23 17**	**09 03**	**23 35**	**08 33**		**07 42**	**00 22**
16 Th	12 00 25	+23 19	05 20	18 40	04 58	19 02	04 30	19 30	03 50	20 11	02 36	21 26
167			**10 45**	**23 47**	**10 32**	**23 57**	**10 17**		**09 55**	**00 00**	**09 21**	**00 38**
17 Fr	12 00 38	+23 21	05 20	18 40	04 58	19 03	04 30	19 31	03 50	20 12	02 36	21 26
168	**19 46** ☽		**11 45**		**11 37**		**11 28**	**00 09**	**11 16**	**00 25**	**10 56**	**00 49**
18 Sa	12 00 50	+23 23	05 21	18 41	04 59	19 03	04 31	19 31	03 50	20 12	02 35	21 26
169			**12 42**	**00 28**	**12 40**	**00 33**	**12 37**	**00 39**	**12 33**	**00 46**	**12 28**	**00 57**
19 Su	12 01 03	+23 25	05 21	18 41	04 59	19 04	04 31	19 32	03 50	20 12	02 35	21 27
170			**13 37**	**01 07**	**13 40**	**01 07**	**13 44**	**01 06**	**13 49**	**01 05**	**13 57**	**01 04**
20 Mo	12 01 16	+23 26	05 21	18 41	04 59	19 04	04 31	19 32	03 50	20 12	02 35	21 27
171			**14 32**	**01 45**	**14 40**	**01 40**	**14 49**	**01 33**	**15 03**	**01 24**	**15 24**	**01 11**
21 Tu	12 01 30	+23 26	05 22	18 41	04 59	19 04	04 32	19 32	03 50	20 12	02 36	21 27
172			**15 26**	**02 23**	**15 39**	**02 13**	**15 54**	**02 01**	**16 16**	**01 44**	**16 52**	**01 18**
22 We	12 01 42	+23 27	05 22	18 42	05 00	19 04	04 32	19 33	03 51	20 13	02 36	21 28
173			**16 21**	**03 03**	**16 38**	**02 49**	**16 59**	**02 31**	**17 28**	**02 06**	**18 18**	**01 28**
23 Th	12 01 55	+23 26	05 22	18 42	05 00	19 04	04 32	19 33	03 51	20 13	02 36	21 28
174			**17 16**	**03 45**	**17 36**	**03 27**	**18 01**	**03 04**	**18 38**	**02 33**	**19 41**	**01 40**
24 Fr	12 02 08	+23 26	05 22	18 42	05 00	19 04	04 32	19 33	03 51	20 13	02 36	21 28
175			**18 10**	**04 30**	**18 32**	**04 09**	**19 01**	**03 42**	**19 42**	**03 05**	**20 57**	**01 59**
25 Sa	12 02 21	+23 25	05 23	18 42	05 00	19 04	04 33	19 33	03 52	20 13	02 37	21 28
176	**08 32** ○		**19 03**	**05 18**	**19 26**	**04 55**	**19 56**	**04 26**	**20 39**	**03 44**	**21 59**	**02 28**
26 Su	12 02 34	+23 23	05 23	18 43	05 01	19 05	04 33	19 33	03 52	20 13	02 37	21 27
177			**19 53**	**06 08**	**20 16**	**05 45**	**20 45**	**05 15**	**21 27**	**04 32**	**22 43**	**03 12**
27 Mo	12 02 46	+23 21	05 23	18 43	05 01	19 05	04 33	19 33	03 52	20 13	02 38	21 27
178			**20 39**	**07 00**	**21 01**	**06 37**	**21 28**	**06 09**	**22 06**	**05 27**	**23 12**	**04 12**
28 Tu	12 02 59	+23 19	05 23	18 43	05 01	19 05	04 33	19 33	03 52	20 13	02 39	21 26
179			**21 22**	**07 52**	**21 41**	**07 32**	**22 04**	**07 06**	**22 37**	**06 29**	**23 31**	**05 24**
29 We	12 03 11	+23 16	05 24	18 43	05 01	19 05	04 34	19 33	03 53	20 13	02 40	21 26
180			**22 02**	**08 44**	**22 17**	**08 26**	**22 36**	**08 04**	**23 02**	**07 34**	**23 43**	**06 42**
30 Th	12 03 23	+23 13	05 24	18 43	05 02	19 05	04 34	19 33	03 53	20 13	02 40	21 25
181			**22 39**	**09 34**	**22 50**	**09 21**	**23 04**	**09 04**	**23 23**	**08 40**	**23 52**	**08 02**

7th Month — July, 1983 — 31 Days

Greenwich Mean Time

NOTE: Light figures indicate Sun. **Dark** figures indicate **Moon.** *Degrees are North Latitude.*

CAUTION: Must be converted to local time. For instruction see page 768.

Day of month week year	Sun on meridian **Moon phase** h m s	Sun's Declination °	20° Rise Sun **Moon** h m	20° Set Sun **Moon** h m	30° Rise Sun **Moon** h m	30° Set Sun **Moon** h m	40° Rise Sun **Moon** h m	40° Set Sun **Moon** h m	50° Rise Sun **Moon** h m	50° Set Sun **Moon** h m	60° Rise Sun **Moon** h m	60° Set Sun **Moon** h m
1 Fr	12 03 35	+23 10	05 24	18 43	05 02	19 05	04 34	19 33	03 54	20 13	02 41	21 25
182			**23 14**	**10 24**	**23 21**	**10 15**	**23 29**	**10 03**	**23 41**	**09 47**	**23 59**	**09 21**
2 Sa	12 03 47	+23 06	05 24	18 43	05 02	19 05	04 35	19 33	03 55	20 12	02 42	21 24
183			**23 48**	**11 14**	**23 51**	**11 09**	**23 54**	**11 02**	**23 58**	**10 54**		**10 41**
3 Su	12 03 58	+23 01	05 24	18 44	05 03	19 05	04 36	19 32	03 56	20 12	02 44	21 24
184	**12 12** ☾			**12 03**		**12 03**		**12 03**		**12 02**	**00 05**	**12 01**
4 Mo	12 04 09	+22 57	05 25	18 44	05 04	19 05	04 36	19 32	03 56	20 12	02 45	21 23
185			**00 23**	**12 55**	**00 21**	**12 59**	**00 18**	**13 05**	**00 15**	**13 12**	**00 10**	**13 23**
5 Tu	12 04 20	+22 52	05 25	18 44	05 04	19 05	04 37	19 32	03 57	20 11	02 46	21 22
186			**00 59**	**13 48**	**00 52**	**13 58**	**00 44**	**14 09**	**00 33**	**14 25**	**00 17**	**14 50**
6 We	12 04 31	+22 46	05 26	18 44	05 04	19 05	04 38	19 32	03 58	20 11	02 48	21 21
187			**01 38**	**14 45**	**01 27**	**14 59**	**01 13**	**15 17**	**00 54**	**15 41**	**00 25**	**16 21**
7 Th	12 04 41	+22 40	05 26	18 44	05 05	19 04	04 38	19 32	03 59	20 10	02 49	21 20
188			**02 22**	**15 46**	**02 06**	**16 05**	**01 47**	**16 28**	**01 20**	**17 00**	**00 36**	**17 56**
8 Fr	12 04 51	+22 34	05 27	18 43	05 05	19 04	04 39	19 31	04 00	20 10	02 50	21 18
189			**03 12**	**16 50**	**02 52**	**17 12**	**02 27**	**17 40**	**01 52**	**18 19**	**00 54**	**19 30**
9 Sa	12 05 00	+22 27	05 27	18 43	05 06	19 04	04 39	19 31	04 01	20 09	02 52	21 17
190			**04 08**	**17 56**	**03 45**	**18 20**	**03 17**	**18 49**	**02 36**	**19 32**	**01 24**	**20 51**
10 Su	12 05 09	+22 20	05 27	18 43	05 06	19 04	04 40	19 30	04 02	20 08	02 54	21 16
191	**12 18** ●		**05 11**	**19 00**	**04 47**	**19 23**	**04 17**	**19 52**	**03 34**	**20 34**	**02 15**	**21 48**
11 Mo	12 05 18	+22 13	05 28	18 43	05 07	19 04	04 40	19 30	04 03	20 08	02 56	21 14
192			**06 18**	**20 00**	**05 55**	**20 21**	**05 27**	**20 46**	**04 46**	**21 22**	**03 33**	**22 23**
12 Tu	12 05 26	+22 05	05 28	18 43	05 07	19 03	04 41	19 29	04 04	20 07	02 57	21 12
193			**07 26**	**20 54**	**07 06**	**21 11**	**06 42**	**21 31**	**06 08**	**21 59**	**05 10**	**22 44**
13 We	12 05 34	+21 57	05 28	18 43	05 08	19 03	04 42	19 29	04 05	20 06	02 59	21 11
194			**08 32**	**21 42**	**08 17**	**21 54**	**07 59**	**22 08**	**07 34**	**22 27**	**06 53**	**22 57**
14 Th	12 05 42	+21 48	05 28	18 43	05 08	19 03	04 43	19 28	04 06	20 05	03 01	21 10
195			**09 35**	**22 26**	**09 26**	**22 33**	**09 14**	**22 40**	**08 58**	**22 51**	**08 33**	**23 06**
15 Fr	12 05 48	+21 39	05 29	18 42	05 09	19 02	04 44	19 28	04 07	20 04	03 02	21 08
196			**10 35**	**23 07**	**10 31**	**23 08**	**10 26**	**23 09**	**10 19**	**23 11**	**10 09**	**23 14**
16 Sa	12 05 55	+21 30	05 30	18 42	05 09	19 02	04 44	19 27	04 08	20 03	03 04	21 06
197			**11 32**	**23 45**	**11 33**	**23 41**	**11 35**	**23 37**	**11 37**	**23 30**	**11 41**	**23 21**
17 Su	12 06 01	+21 20	05 30	18 42	05 10	19 02	04 45	19 27	04 09	20 02	03 06	21 05
198	**02 50** ☽		**12 27**		**12 34**		**12 42**		**12 53**	**23 50**	**13 10**	**23 28**
18 Mo	12 06 06	+21 10	05 30	18 42	05 10	19 02	04 46	19 26	04 10	20 01	03 08	21 03
199			**13 22**	**00 24**	**13 33**	**00 15**	**13 47**	**00 04**	**14 07**		**14 38**	**23 36**
19 Tu	12 06 11	+20 59	05 30	18 42	05 11	19 01	04 46	19 26	04 12	20 00	03 10	21 01
200			**14 17**	**01 03**	**14 32**	**00 50**	**14 52**	**00 34**	**15 19**	**00 11**	**16 05**	**23 48**
20 We	12 06 15	+20 49	05 31	18 41	05 11	19 01	04 47	19 25	04 13	19 59	03 12	20 59
201			**15 11**	**01 44**	**15 30**	**01 27**	**15 55**	**01 06**	**16 29**	**00 36**	**17 29**	
21 Th	12 06 18	+20 38	05 31	18 41	05 12	19 00	04 48	19 24	04 14	19 58	03 14	20 57
202			**16 05**	**02 28**	**16 27**	**02 08**	**16 55**	**01 42**	**17 35**	**01 06**	**18 47**	**00 04**
22 Fr	12 06 21	+20 26	05 32	18 41	05 12	19 00	04 49	19 23	04 15	19 57	03 16	20 55
203			**16 58**	**03 15**	**17 21**	**02 52**	**17 51**	**02 23**	**18 34**	**01 43**	**19 53**	**00 30**
23 Sa	12 06 24	+20 14	05 32	18 40	05 13	18 59	04 50	19 22	04 16	19 56	03 18	20 52
204			**17 49**	**04 04**	**18 12**	**03 40**	**18 42**	**03 11**	**19 24**	**02 27**	**20 43**	**01 08**
24 Su	12 06 26	+20 02	05 32	18 40	05 13	18 59	04 50	19 22	04 18	19 54	03 21	20 50
205	**23 27** ○		**18 36**	**04 55**	**18 58**	**04 32**	**19 26**	**04 03**	**20 06**	**03 20**	**21 16**	**02 03**
25 Mo	12 06 27	+19 50	05 33	18 40	05 14	18 58	04 51	19 21	04 19	19 53	03 23	20 48
206			**19 20**	**05 47**	**19 40**	**05 26**	**20 05**	**04 59**	**20 39**	**04 20**	**21 37**	**03 12**
26 Tu	12 06 28	+19 37	05 33	18 40	05 15	18 58	04 52	19 20	04 20	19 52	03 25	20 46
207			**20 01**	**06 39**	**20 17**	**06 20**	**20 38**	**05 57**	**21 06**	**05 24**	**21 51**	**04 28**
27 We	12 06 28	+19 24	05 34	18 39	05 16	18 57	04 53	19 19	04 22	19 50	03 28	20 44
208			**20 39**	**07 30**	**20 51**	**07 15**	**21 07**	**06 56**	**21 28**	**06 30**	**22 01**	**05 48**
28 Th	12 06 27	+19 10	05 34	18 39	05 16	18 57	04 54	19 18	04 23	19 49	03 30	20 41
209			**21 14**	**08 20**	**21 23**	**08 09**	**21 33**	**07 56**	**21 47**	**07 37**	**22 08**	**07 07**
29 Fr	12 06 26	+18 56	05 34	18 39	05 17	18 56	04 55	19 17	04 24	19 48	03 32	20 39
210			**21 48**	**09 09**	**21 52**	**09 03**	**21 57**	**08 55**	**22 04**	**08 44**	**22 14**	**08 27**
30 Sa	12 06 25	+18 42	05 34	18 38	05 17	18 55	04 56	19 16	04 26	19 46	03 34	20 36
211			**22 22**	**09 58**	**22 22**	**09 56**	**22 21**	**09 54**	**22 21**	**09 51**	**22 20**	**09 46**
31 Su	12 06 22	+18 28	05 34	18 38	05 18	18 55	04 57	19 15	04 27	19 45	03 36	20 34
212			**22 57**	**10 48**	**22 52**	**10 51**	**22 46**	**10 54**	**22 38**	**10 59**	**22 25**	**11 06**

8th Month August, 1983 31 Days

Greenwich Mean Time

NOTE: Light figures indicate Sun. **Dark** figures indicate **Moon.** *Degrees are North Latitude.*

CAUTION: Must be converted to local time. For instruction see page 768.

Day of month week year	Sun on meridian **Moon phase** h m s	Sun's Declination ° ′	20° Rise Sun **Moon** h m	20° Set Sun **Moon** h m	30° Rise Sun **Moon** h m	30° Set Sun **Moon** h m	40° Rise Sun **Moon** h m	40° Set Sun **Moon** h m	50° Rise Sun **Moon** h m	50° Set Sun **Moon** h m	60° Rise Sun **Moon** h m	60° Set Sun **Moon** h m
1 Mo	12 06 19	+18 13	05 35	18 37	05 18	18 54	04 58	19 14	04 28	19 44	03 39	20 32
213			**23 34**	**11 39**	**23 24**	**11 47**	**23 12**	**11 56**	**22 57**	**12 09**	**22 32**	**12 28**
2 Tu	12 06 16	+17 58	05 35	18 37	05 19	18 53	04 59	19 13	04 30	19 42	03 41	20 29
214	**00 52** ☾			**12 33**		**12 45**	**23 43**	**13 01**	**23 19**	**13 21**	**22 42**	**13 55**
3 We	12 06 12	+17 43	05 36	18 36	05 20	18 52	05 00	19 12	04 31	19 40	03 44	20 26
215			**00 14**	**13 31**	**00 00**	**13 47**		**14 08**	**23 47**	**14 37**	**22 56**	**15 26**
4 Th	12 06 07	+17 27	05 36	18 36	05 20	18 52	05 00	19 11	04 32	19 38	03 46	20 24
216			**01 00**	**14 31**	**00 41**	**14 52**	**01 19**	**15 18**		**15 54**	**23 18**	**16 58**
5 Fr	12 06 02	+17 11	05 37	18 35	05 21	18 51	05 01	19 10	04 34	19 37	03 48	20 22
217			**01 51**	**15 35**	**01 30**	**15 58**	**01 03**	**16 27**	**00 24**	**17 09**	**23 57**	**18 25**
6 Sa	12 05 56	+16 55	05 37	18 35	05 22	18 50	05 02	19 09	04 35	19 35	03 51	20 19
218			**02 50**	**16 39**	**02 26**	**17 03**	**01 56**	**17 33**	**01 14**	**18 16**		**19 34**
7 Su	12 05 50	+16 39	05 37	18 34	05 22	18 49	05 03	19 08	04 36	19 34	03 53	20 16
219			**03 54**	**17 41**	**03 31**	**18 03**	**03 01**	**18 31**	**02 19**	**19 11**	**01 01**	**20 19**
8 Mo	12 05 43	+16 22	05 38	18 34	05 23	18 48	05 04	19 06	04 38	19 32	03 56	20 14
220	**19 18** ●		**05 02**	**18 39**	**04 41**	**18 58**	**04 15**	**19 21**	**03 27**	**19 53**	**02 30**	**20 46**
9 Tu	12 05 36	+16 05	05 38	18 33	05 24	18 47	05 05	19 05	04 40	19 30	03 58	20 12
221			**06 11**	**19 31**	**05 54**	**19 45**	**05 32**	**20 02**	**05 03**	**20 26**	**04 13**	**21 02**
10 We	12 05 27	+15 48	05 38	18 32	05 24	18 46	05 06	19 04	04 41	19 29	04 00	20 09
222			**07 17**	**20 18**	**07 05**	**20 27**	**06 51**	**20 37**	**06 30**	**20 52**	**05 58**	**21 13**
11 Th	12 05 19	+15 30	05 38	18 32	05 25	18 45	05 07	19 03	04 42	19 27	04 02	20 06
223			**08 20**	**21 01**	**08 14**	**21 04**	**08 06**	**21 08**	**07 56**	**21 14**	**07 39**	**21 22**
12 Fr	12 05 09	+15 13	05 38	18 31	05 25	18 44	05 08	19 02	04 44	19 25	04 05	20 04
224			**09 21**	**21 42**	**09 20**	**21 40**	**09 19**	**21 37**	**09 18**	**21 34**	**09 16**	**21 29**
13 Sa	12 05 00	+14 55	05 39	18 31	05 26	18 44	05 09	19 00	04 46	19 23	04 08	20 01
225			**10 19**	**22 21**	**10 23**	**22 14**	**10 29**	**22 06**	**10 37**	**21 54**	**10 50**	**21 36**
14 Su	12 04 49	+14 36	05 39	18 30	05 26	18 43	05 10	18 59	04 47	19 21	04 10	19 58
226			**11 15**	**23 01**	**11 25**	**22 50**	**11 37**	**22 35**	**11 54**	**22 15**	**12 21**	**21 44**
15 Mo	12 04 38	+14 18	05 40	18 29	05 27	18 42	05 11	18 58	04 48	19 19	04 12	19 55
227	**12 47** ☽		**12 11**	**23 43**	**12 25**	**23 27**	**12 43**	**23 07**	**13 09**	**22 39**	**13 50**	**21 55**
16 Tu	12 04 27	+13 59	05 40	18 28	05 28	18 41	05 12	18 56	04 50	19 18	04 15	19 52
228			**13 06**		**13 25**		**13 48**	**23 42**	**14 21**	**23 07**	**15 16**	**22 09**
17 We	12 04 14	+13 40	05 40	18 28	05 28	18 40	05 13	18 54	04 52	19 16	04 18	19 49
229			**14 01**	**00 26**	**14 22**	**00 06**	**14 49**		**15 28**	**23 42**	**16 37**	**22 31**
18 Th	12 04 02	+13 21	05 41	18 27	05 29	18 39	05 14	18 53	04 53	19 14	04 20	19 46
230			**14 54**	**01 12**	**15 18**	**00 50**	**15 47**	**00 22**	**16 30**		**17 48**	**23 05**
19 Fr	12 03 49	+13 02	05 41	18 26	05 30	18 38	05 15	18 52	04 54	19 12	04 22	19 43
231			**15 46**	**02 00**	**16 09**	**01 37**	**16 39**	**01 07**	**17 23**	**00 24**	**18 43**	**23 55**
20 Sa	12 03 35	+12 43	05 42	18 26	05 30	18 37	05 16	18 50	04 56	19 10	04 24	19 40
232			**16 34**	**02 51**	**16 57**	**02 27**	**17 25**	**01 58**	**18 06**	**01 15**	**19 20**	
21 Su	12 03 21	+12 23	05 42	18 25	05 31	18 36	05 17	18 49	04 58	19 08	04 27	19 38
233			**17 19**	**03 43**	**17 40**	**03 21**	**18 05**	**02 53**	**18 42**	**02 13**	**19 44**	**01 00**
22 Mo	12 03 06	+12 03	05 42	18 24	05 31	18 35	05 18	18 48	04 59	19 06	04 29	19 35
234			**18 01**	**04 35**	**18 18**	**04 15**	**18 40**	**03 50**	**19 10**	**03 16**	**19 59**	**02 15**
23 Tu	12 02 51	+11 43	05 42	18 23	05 32	18 34	05 19	18 46	05 00	19 04	04 32	19 32
235	**14 59** ○		**18 39**	**05 26**	**18 53**	**05 10**	**19 10**	**04 50**	**19 33**	**04 22**	**20 10**	**03 35**
24 We	12 02 35	+11 23	05 42	18 22	05 32	18 32	05 20	18 45	05 02	19 02	04 34	19 29
236			**19 15**	**06 16**	**19 25**	**06 04**	**19 37**	**05 49**	**19 53**	**05 28**	**20 18**	**04 55**
25 Th	12 02 19	+11 02	05 43	18 22	05 33	18 31	05 20	18 44	05 04	19 00	04 36	19 26
237			**19 50**	**07 06**	**19 55**	**06 58**	**20 02**	**06 49**	**20 10**	**06 35**	**20 24**	**06 15**
26 Fr	12 02 03	+10 41	05 43	18 21	05 33	18 30	05 21	18 42	05 05	18 58	04 39	19 23
238			**20 24**	**07 55**	**20 24**	**07 52**	**20 25**	**07 48**	**20 27**	**07 43**	**20 29**	**07 34**
27 Sa	12 01 46	+10 21	05 43	18 20	05 34	18 29	05 22	18 40	05 06	18 56	04 41	19 20
239			**20 58**	**08 45**	**20 54**	**08 46**	**20 50**	**08 48**	**20 44**	**08 50**	**20 35**	**08 54**
28 Su	12 01 29	+10 00	05 44	18 20	05 34	18 28	05 23	18 39	05 08	18 54	04 44	19 17
240			**21 33**	**09 35**	**21 25**	**09 41**	**21 15**	**09 49**	**21 01**	**09 59**	**20 41**	**10 15**
29 Mo	12 01 11	+09 39	05 44	18 19	05 35	18 27	05 24	18 38	05 10	18 52	04 46	19 14
241			**22 11**	**10 27**	**21 59**	**10 38**	**21 43**	**10 51**	**21 22**	**11 10**	**20 49**	**11 39**
30 Tu	12 00 53	+09 17	05 44	18 18	05 35	18 26	05 25	18 36	05 11	18 50	04 48	19 11
242			**22 54**	**11 22**	**22 37**	**11 37**	**22 16**	**11 56**	**21 47**	**12 23**	**21 00**	**13 07**
31 We	12 00 35	+08 56	05 44	18 17	05 36	18 25	05 26	18 34	05 12	18 48	04 50	19 08
243	**11 22** ☾		**23 41**	**12 20**	**23 21**	**12 39**	**22 55**	**13 04**	**22 19**	**13 38**	**21 17**	**14 37**

9th Month — September, 1983 — 30 Days

Greenwich Mean Time

NOTE: Light figures indicate Sun. **Dark** figures indicate **Moon.** *Degrees are North Latitude.*

CAUTION: Must be converted to local time. For instruction see page 768.

Day of month week year	Sun on meridian **Moon phase** h m s	Sun's Declination ° ′	20° Rise Sun **Moon** h m	20° Set Sun **Moon** h m	30° Rise Sun **Moon** h m	30° Set Sun **Moon** h m	40° Rise Sun **Moon** h m	40° Set Sun **Moon** h m	50° Rise Sun **Moon** h m	50° Set Sun **Moon** h m	60° Rise Sun **Moon** h m	60° Set Sun **Moon** h m
1 Th	12 00 17	+08 34	05 44	18 16	05 36	18 24	05 27	18 32	05 14	18 46	04 53	19 05
244				**13 21**		**13 43**	**23 43**	**14 11**	**23 01**	**14 52**	**21 47**	**16 05**
2 Fr	11 59 58	+08 13	05 45	18 15	05 37	18 22	05 28	18 31	05 16	18 43	04 56	19 02
245			**00 35**	**14 23**	**00 12**	**14 46**		**15 17**	**23 57**	**16 00**	**22 37**	**17 20**
3 Sa	11 59 39	+07 51	05 45	18 14	05 38	18 21	05 29	18 29	05 17	18 41	04 58	18 59
246			**01 35**	**15 24**	**01 11**	**15 47**	**00 41**	**16 17**		**16 59**	**23 54**	**18 14**
4 Su	11 59 19	+07 29	05 45	18 14	05 38	18 20	05 30	18 28	05 18	18 39	05 00	18 56
247			**02 40**	**16 22**	**02 17**	**16 43**	**01 49**	**17 09**	**01 08**	**17 45**		**18 47**
5 Mo	11 59 00	+07 07	05 45	18 13	05 39	18 18	05 31	18 26	05 20	18 36	05 02	18 53
248			**03 47**	**17 16**	**03 28**	**17 33**	**03 04**	**17 53**	**02 29**	**18 21**	**01 30**	**19 07**
6 Tu	11 58 40	+06 44	05 45	18 12	05 40	18 17	05 32	18 24	05 22	18 34	05 05	18 50
249			**04 54**	**18 05**	**04 40**	**18 17**	**04 21**	**18 31**	**03 56**	**18 50**	**03 15**	**19 20**
7 We	11 58 20	+06 22	05 45	18 11	05 40	18 16	05 33	18 23	05 23	18 32	05 07	18 47
250	**02 35** ●		**05 59**	**18 51**	**05 50**	**18 57**	**05 39**	**19 04**	**05 24**	**19 14**	**04 59**	**19 29**
8 Th	11 57 59	+06 00	05 45	18 10	05 41	18 15	05 34	18 21	05 24	18 30	05 10	18 44
251			**07 02**	**19 33**	**06 59**	**19 34**	**06 55**	**19 34**	**06 49**	**19 35**	**06 41**	**19 36**
9 Fr	11 57 39	+05 37	05 46	18 09	05 41	18 14	05 34	18 20	05 26	18 28	05 12	18 41
252			**08 03**	**20 14**	**08 05**	**20 09**	**08 08**	**20 03**	**08 12**	**19 55**	**08 18**	**19 43**
10 Sa	11 57 18	+05 14	05 46	18 08	05 42	18 12	05 35	18 18	05 28	18 26	05 14	18 38
253			**09 02**	**20 55**	**09 10**	**20 45**	**09 19**	**20 33**	**09 33**	**20 16**	**09 54**	**19 51**
11 Su	11 56 58	+04 52	05 46	18 07	05 42	18 11	05 36	18 16	05 29	18 24	05 17	18 35
254			**10 00**	**21 37**	**10 13**	**21 23**	**10 29**	**21 04**	**10 51**	**20 39**	**11 27**	**20 00**
12 Mo	11 56 37	+04 29	05 46	18 06	05 43	18 10	05 37	18 14	05 30	18 22	05 19	18 32
255			**10 57**	**22 21**	**11 15**	**22 02**	**11 36**	**21 39**	**12 07**	**21 07**	**12 58**	**20 12**
13 Tu	11 56 15	+04 06	05 46	18 05	05 43	18 08	05 38	18 13	05 32	18 20	05 22	18 29
256			**11 54**	**23 07**	**12 14**	**22 45**	**12 41**	**22 18**	**13 18**	**21 39**	**14 24**	**20 31**
14 We	11 55 54	+03 43	05 47	18 04	05 44	18 07	05 39	18 12	05 34	18 17	05 24	18 26
257	**02 24** ☽		**12 29**	**23 55**	**13 12**	**23 32**	**13 41**	**23 02**	**14 23**	**22 19**	**15 41**	**21 01**
15 Th	11 55 33	+03 20	05 47	18 03	05 44	18 06	05 40	18 10	05 35	18 15	05 26	18 23
258			**13 41**		**14 05**		**14 36**	**23 52**	**15 20**	**23 08**	**16 42**	**21 46**
16 Fr	11 55 12	+02 57	05 47	18 02	05 44	18 05	05 41	18 08	05 36	18 13	05 28	18 20
259			**14 31**	**00 46**	**14 54**	**00 22**	**15 24**		**16 06**		**17 24**	**22 47**
17 Sa	11 54 50	+02 34	05 47	18 01	05 45	18 04	05 42	18 06	05 38	18 10	05 31	18 17
260			**15 17**	**01 37**	**15 39**	**01 15**	**16 06**	**00 46**	**16 44**	**00 04**	**17 51**	
18 Su	11 54 29	+02 11	05 48	18 01	05 46	18 02	05 43	18 05	05 40	18 08	05 34	18 14
261			**16 00**	**02 29**	**16 18**	**02 09**	**16 42**	**01 43**	**17 14**	**01 06**	**18 09**	**00 00**
19 Mo	11 54 07	+01 47	05 48	18 00	05 46	18 01	05 44	18 03	05 41	18 06	05 36	18 11
262			**16 39**	**03 21**	**16 54**	**03 04**	**17 13**	**02 42**	**17 39**	**02 11**	**18 20**	**01 19**
20 Tu	11 53 46	+01 24	05 48	17 59	05 47	18 00	05 45	18 02	05 42	18 04	05 38	18 08
263			**17 16**	**04 12**	**17 27**	**03 58**	**17 41**	**03 41**	**17 59**	**03 18**	**18 28**	**02 40**
21 We	11 53 25	+01 01	05 48	17 58	05 47	17 58	05 46	18 00	05 44	18 02	05 40	18 05
264			**17 51**	**05 02**	**17 58**	**04 53**	**18 06**	**04 41**	**18 17**	**04 26**	**18 34**	**04 01**
22 Th	11 53 03	+00 38	05 49	17 57	05 48	17 57	05 47	17 58	05 46	17 59	05 43	18 02
265	**06 36** ○		**18 25**	**05 52**	**18 27**	**05 47**	**18 30**	**05 41**	**18 34**	**05 33**	**18 39**	**05 21**
23 Fr	11 52 42	+00 14	05 49	17 56	05 48	17 56	05 48	17 57	05 47	17 57	05 45	17 59
266			**18 59**	**06 41**	**18 57**	**06 41**	**18 54**	**06 41**	**18 50**	**06 41**	**18 44**	**06 41**
24 Sa	11 52 21	−00 09	05 49	17 55	05 49	17 55	05 49	17 55	05 48	17 55	05 47	17 56
267			**19 34**	**07 32**	**19 27**	**07 37**	**19 19**	**07 42**	**19 07**	**07 51**	**18 50**	**08 03**
25 Su	11 52 00	−00 32	05 49	17 54	05 50	17 54	05 50	17 54	05 50	17 53	05 50	17 53
268			**20 12**	**08 24**	**20 00**	**08 33**	**19 46**	**08 45**	**19 27**	**09 01**	**18 57**	**09 27**
26 Mo	11 51 39	−00 56	05 50	17 53	05 50	17 52	05 51	17 52	05 52	17 51	05 52	17 50
269			**20 52**	**09 18**	**20 36**	**09 32**	**20 17**	**09 50**	**19 50**	**10 14**	**19 06**	**10 54**
27 Tu	11 51 18	−01 19	05 50	17 52	05 51	17 51	05 52	17 50	05 53	17 49	05 54	17 47
270			**21 38**	**10 15**	**21 18**	**10 33**	**20 53**	**10 56**	**20 19**	**11 29**	**19 21**	**12 24**
28 We	11 50 58	−01 43	05 50	17 51	05 52	17 50	05 53	17 48	05 54	17 47	05 56	17 44
271			**22 28**	**11 14**	**22 06**	**11 35**	**21 37**	**12 03**	**20 56**	**12 42**	**19 44**	**13 53**
29 Th	11 50 38	−02 06	05 50	17 50	05 52	17 48	05 54	17 46	05 56	17 44	05 59	17 40
272	**20 05** ☾		**23 25**	**12 14**	**23 00**	**12 38**	**22 30**	**13 08**	**21 46**	**13 51**	**20 25**	**15 12**
30 Fr	11 50 18	−02 29	05 51	17 50	05 53	17 47	05 55	17 45	05 58	17 42	06 02	17 37
273				**13 14**		**13 38**	**23 32**	**14 08**	**22 49**	**14 52**	**21 30**	**16 12**

10th Month **October, 1983** **31 Days**

Greenwich Mean Time

NOTE: Light figures indicate Sun. **Dark** figures indicate **Moon.** *Degrees are North Latitude.*

CAUTION: Must be converted to local time. For instruction see page 768.

Day of month week year	Sun on meridian **Moon phase** h m s	Sun's Declination ° ′	20° Rise Sun **Moon** h m	20° Set Sun **Moon** h m	30° Rise Sun **Moon** h m	30° Set Sun **Moon** h m	40° Rise Sun **Moon** h m	40° Set Sun **Moon** h m	50° Rise Sun **Moon** h m	50° Set Sun **Moon** h m	60° Rise Sun **Moon** h m	60° Set Sun **Moon** h
1 Sa	11 49 58	−02 53	05 51	17 49	05 53	17 46	05 56	17 43	05 59	17 40	06 04	17 34
274			**00 26**	**14 11**	**00 02**	**14 34**		**15 02**		**15 41**	**22 57**	**16 50**
2 Su	11 49 39	−03 16	05 51	17 48	05 54	17 45	05 57	17 41	06 00	17 38	06 06	17 31
275			**01 30**	**15 05**	**01 09**	**15 24**	**00 42**	**15 47**	**00 04**	**16 20**		**17 13**
3 Mo	11 49 20	−03 39	05 52	17 47	05 54	17 44	05 58	17 40	06 02	17 36	06 08	17 28
276			**02 35**	**15 55**	**02 18**	**16 09**	**01 57**	**16 26**	**01 27**	**16 50**	**00 37**	**17 27**
4 Tu	11 49 01	−04 02	05 52	17 46	05 55	17 42	05 58	17 38	06 04	17 33	06 11	17 25
277			**03 40**	**16 41**	**03 28**	**16 49**	**03 13**	**17 00**	**02 53**	**17 15**	**02 20**	**17 37**
5 We	11 48 43	−04 25	05 52	17 45	05 55	17 41	05 59	17 37	06 05	17 31	06 13	17 22
278			**04 43**	**17 24**	**04 36**	**17 27**	**04 28**	**17 31**	**04 18**	**17 36**	**04 01**	**17 44**
6 Th	11 48 24	−04 49	05 52	17 44	05 56	17 40	06 00	17 36	06 06	17 29	06 16	17 19
279	**11 16** ●		**05 44**	**18 05**	**05 43**	**18 03**	**05 43**	**18 00**	**05 42**	**17 56**	**05 41**	**17 51**
7 Fr	11 48 07	−05 12	05 52	17 44	05 56	17 39	06 02	17 34	06 08	17 27	06 18	17 16
280			**06 44**	**18 46**	**06 49**	**18 39**	**06 56**	**18 29**	**07 04**	**18 17**	**07 18**	**17 57**
8 Sa	11 47 50	−05 35	05 53	17 43	05 57	17 38	06 03	17 32	06 10	17 25	06 20	17 14
281			**07 44**	**19 28**	**07 54**	**19 16**	**08 07**	**19 00**	**08 25**	**18 39**	**08 54**	**18 05**
9 Su	11 47 33	−05 58	05 53	17 42	05 58	17 37	06 04	17 31	06 11	17 23	06 23	17 11
282			**08 43**	**20 12**	**08 58**	**19 55**	**09 17**	**19 34**	**09 45**	**19 04**	**10 29**	**18 16**
10 Mo	11 47 16	−06 20	05 53	17 41	05 58	17 36	06 05	17 30	06 13	17 21	06 26	17 08
283			**09 41**	**20 58**	**10 01**	**20 37**	**10 25**	**20 11**	**11 00**	**19 35**	**12 01**	**18 31**
11 Tu	11 47 00	−06 43	05 54	17 40	05 59	17 34	06 06	17 28	06 14	17 18	06 28	17 05
284			**10 38**	**21 47**	**11 01**	**21 24**	**11 29**	**20 54**	**12 11**	**20 12**	**13 26**	**18 56**
12 We	11 46 45	−07 06	05 54	17 40	06 00	17 33	06 07	17 26	06 16	17 16	06 30	17 02
285			**11 33**	**22 38**	**11 57**	**22 13**	**12 28**	**21 43**	**13 12**	**20 58**	**14 36**	**19 34**
13 Th	11 46 29	−07 28	05 54	17 39	06 00	17 32	06 08	17 25	06 18	17 14	06 33	16 59
286	**19 42** ☽		**12 25**	**23 30**	**12 49**	**23 06**	**13 20**	**22 36**	**14 04**	**21 52**	**15 26**	**20 31**
14 Fr	11 46 15	−07 51	05 54	17 38	06 01	17 31	06 09	17 24	06 19	17 12	06 36	16 56
287			**13 13**		**13 36**		**14 04**	**23 33**	**14 45**	**22 53**	**15 58**	**21 41**
15 Sa	11 46 01	−08 13	05 54	17 37	06 02	17 30	06 10	17 22	06 21	17 10	06 38	16 53
288			**13 57**	**00 22**	**14 17**	**00 00**	**14 42**		**15 18**	**23 58**	**16 18**	**23 00**
16 Su	11 45 47	−08 36	05 55	17 36	06 02	17 29	06 21	17 20	06 22	17 08	06 40	16 50
289			**14 38**	**01 14**	**14 54**	**00 55**	**15 15**	**00 31**	**15 44**		**16 30**	
17 Mo	11 45 34	−08 58	05 55	17 35	06 03	17 28	06 12	17 19	06 24	17 06	06 43	16 47
290			**15 15**	**02 05**	**15 28**	**01 50**	**15 44**	**01 31**	**16 05**	**01 05**	**16 39**	**00 21**
18 Tu	11 45 22	−09 20	05 56	17 35	06 04	17 27	06 13	17 18	06 26	17 04	06 46	16 44
291			**15 51**	**02 56**	**15 59**	**02 45**	**16 10**	**02 31**	**16 24**	**02 12**	**16 45**	**01 42**
19 We	11 45 10	−09 41	05 56	17 34	06 04	17 26	06 14	17 16	06 27	17 02	06 48	16 42
292			**16 25**	**03 45**	**16 29**	**03 39**	**16 34**	**03 31**	**16 40**	**03 20**	**16 50**	**03 03**
20 Th	11 44 59	−10 03	05 57	17 34	06 05	17 25	06 15	17 14	06 28	17 00	06 50	16 39
293			**16 59**	**04 35**	**16 58**	**04 34**	**16 58**	**04 31**	**16 57**	**04 28**	**16 55**	**04 24**
21 Fr	11 44 48	−10 25	05 57	17 33	06 05	17 24	06 16	17 13	06 30	16 58	06 53	16 36
294	**21 53** ○		**17 34**	**05 26**	**17 29**	**05 29**	**17 22**	**05 33**	**17 13**	**05 38**	**17 00**	**05 46**
22 Sa	11 44 38	−10 46	05 57	17 32	06 06	17 23	06 17	17 12	06 32	16 56	06 56	16 33
295			**18 11**	**06 18**	**18 01**	**06 26**	**17 48**	**06 36**	**17 32**	**06 49**	**17 06**	**07 11**
23 Su	11 44 29	−11 07	05 58	17 32	06 07	17 22	06 18	17 10	06 34	16 54	06 58	16 30
296			**18 51**	**07 12**	**18 36**	**07 25**	**18 18**	**07 41**	**17 53**	**08 03**	**17 14**	**08 39**
24 Mo	11 44 20	−11 28	05 58	17 31	06 07	17 21	06 19	17 08	06 35	16 53	07 00	16 28
297			**19 35**	**08 09**	**19 16**	**08 26**	**18 53**	**08 48**	**18 20**	**09 18**	**17 26**	**10 10**
25 Tu	11 44 12	−11 49	05 58	17 30	06 08	17 20	06 20	17 07	06 37	16 51	07 03	16 25
298			**20 25**	**09 08**	**20 02**	**09 29**	**19 35**	**09 56**	**18 55**	**10 34**	**17 46**	**11 41**
26 We	11 44 05	−12 10	05 58	17 29	06 09	17 19	06 21	17 06	06 39	16 49	07 06	16 22
299			**21 19**	**10 09**	**20 55**	**10 33**	**20 25**	**11 02**	**19 41**	**11 46**	**18 20**	**13 06**
27 Th	11 43 58	−12 31	05 59	17 28	06 10	17 18	06 22	17 04	06 40	16 47	07 08	16 20
300			**22 19**	**11 09**	**21 55**	**11 33**	**21 24**	**12 04**	**20 40**	**12 49**	**19 17**	**14 12**
28 Fr	11 43 53	−12 51	05 59	17 28	06 10	17 17	06 24	17 03	06 42	16 45	07 10	16 17
301			**23 21**	**12 07**	**22 59**	**12 30**	**22 31**	**12 59**	**21 50**	**13 41**	**20 37**	**14 56**
29 Sa	11 43 48	−13 11	06 00	17 27	06 11	17 16	06 25	17 02	06 44	16 43	07 13	16 14
302	**03 37** ☾			**13 01**		**13 21**	**23 42**	**13 46**	**23 09**	**14 22**	**22 12**	**15 21**
30 Su	11 43 44	−13 31	06 00	17 27	06 12	17 15	06 26	17 01	06 46	16 41	07 16	16 11
303			**00 25**	**13 50**	**00 06**	**14 06**		**14 26**		**14 53**	**23 52**	**15 37**
31 Mo	11 43 40	−13 51	06 01	17 26	06 12	17 14	06 27	17 00	06 47	16 40	07 18	16 08
304			**01 27**	**14 35**	**01 13**	**14 46**	**00 56**	**15 00**	**00 31**	**15 18**		**15 47**

11th Month November, 1983 30 Days

Greenwich Mean Time

NOTE: Light figures indicate Sun. **Dark** figures indicate **Moon.** *Degrees are North Latitude.*

CAUTION: Must be converted to local time. For instruction see page 768.

Day of month week year	Sun on meridian **Moon phase** h m s	Sun's Declination ° ′	20° Rise Sun **Moon** h m	20° Set Sun **Moon** h m	30° Rise Sun **Moon** h m	30° Set Sun **Moon** h m	40° Rise Sun **Moon** h m	40° Set Sun **Moon** h m	50° Rise Sun **Moon** h m	50° Set Sun **Moon** h m	60° Rise Sun **Moon** h m	60° Set Sun **Moon** h m
1 Tu	11 43 38	−14 10	06 02	17 26	06 13	17 14	06 28	16 58	06 48	16 38	07 20	16 06
305			**02 29**	**15 18**	**02 20**	**15 24**	**02 09**	**15 31**	**01 54**	**15 40**	**01 31**	**15 56**
2 We	11 43 36	−14 30	06 02	17 25	06 14	17 13	06 29	16 57	06 50	16 36	07 23	16 03
306			**03 29**	**15 58**	**03 26**	**15 59**	**03 22**	**15 59**	**03 16**	**16 00**	**03 08**	**16 00**
3 Th	11 43 35	−14 49	06 02	17 25	06 15	17 12	06 30	16 56	06 52	16 34	07 26	16 00
307			**04 28**	**16 38**	**04 30**	**16 33**	**04 33**	**16 27**	**04 38**	**16 19**	**04 44**	**16 06**
4 Fr	11 43 35	−15 08	06 03	17 24	06 16	17 12	06 32	16 55	06 54	16 33	07 28	15 58
308	**22 21 ●**		**05 27**	**17 19**	**05 35**	**17 09**	**05 45**	**16 56**	**05 58**	**16 39**	**06 20**	**16 13**
5 Sa	11 43 35	−15 26	06 03	17 24	06 16	17 11	06 33	16 54	06 55	16 32	07 30	15 56
309			**06 26**	**18 02**	**06 39**	**17 47**	**06 55**	**17 28**	**07 18**	**17 02**	**07 56**	**16 21**
6 Su	11 43 37	−15 44	06 04	17 23	06 17	17 10	06 34	16 53	06 57	16 30	07 33	15 53
310			**07 25**	**18 48**	**07 43**	**18 28**	**08 05**	**18 04**	**08 37**	**17 30**	**09 31**	**16 34**
7 Mo	11 43 39	−16 03	06 04	17 23	06 18	17 09	06 35	16 52	06 59	16 28	07 36	15 50
311			**08 24**	**19 36**	**08 45**	**19 13**	**09 12**	**18 45**	**09 51**	**18 05**	**11 01**	**16 53**
8 Tu	11 43 42	−16 20	06 05	17 22	06 18	17 08	06 36	16 51	07 00	16 27	07 38	15 48
312			**09 21**	**20 27**	**09 45**	**20 02**	**10 15**	**19 32**	**10 59**	**18 47**	**12 21**	**17 25**
9 We	11 43 46	−16 38	06 06	17 22	06 19	17 08	06 38	16 50	07 02	16 26	07 41	15 46
313			**10 15**	**21 19**	**10 40**	**20 55**	**11 11**	**20 24**	**11 56**	**19 39**	**13 22**	**18 14**
10 Th	11 43 51	−16 55	06 06	17 22	06 20	17 07	06 39	16 49	07 04	16 24	07 44	15 43
314			**11 06**	**22 12**	**11 30**	**21 49**	**12 00**	**21 20**	**12 43**	**20 38**	**14 01**	**19 20**
11 Fr	11 43 57	−17 12	06 07	17 22	06 21	17 06	06 40	16 48	07 06	16 22	07 46	15 41
315			**11 52**	**23 05**	**12 14**	**22 45**	**12 41**	**22 19**	**13 19**	**21 42**	**14 26**	**20 38**
12 Sa	11 44 03	−17 29	06 07	17 21	06 22	17 06	06 41	16 47	07 07	16 21	07 49	15 38
316	**15 49 ☽**		**12 34**	**23 57**	**12 53**	**23 40**	**13 16**	**23 19**	**13 47**	**22 49**	**14 40**	**21 59**
13 Su	11 44 10	−17 45	06 08	17 21	06 23	17 05	06 42	16 46	07 08	16 20	07 52	15 36
317			**13 13**		**13 28**		**13 46**		**14 10**	**23 56**	**14 50**	**23 20**
14 Mo	11 44 18	−18 01	06 08	17 21	06 24	17 05	06 43	16 45	07 10	16 18	07 54	15 34
318			**13 49**	**01 37**	**13 59**	**01 29**	**14 12**	**00 18**	**14 29**		**14 56**	
15 Tu	11 44 27	−18 17	06 08	17 21	06 25	17 04	06 44	16 44	07 12	16 17	07 56	15 32
319			**14 23**	**01 37**	**14 29**	**01 29**	**14 37**	**01 18**	**14 46**	**01 04**	**15 01**	**00 41**
16 We	11 44 37	−18 32	06 09	17 20	06 26	17 04	06 46	16 44	07 14	16 16	07 59	15 30
320			**14 57**	**02 26**	**14 58**	**02 23**	**15 00**	**02 18**	**15 02**	**02 11**	**15 06**	**02 01**
17 Th	11 44 48	−18 47	06 09	17 20	06 26	17 03	06 47	16 43	07 15	16 14	08 02	15 28
321			**15 31**	**03 16**	**15 28**	**03 17**	**15 24**	**03 19**	**15 19**	**03 20**	**15 11**	**03 23**
18 Fr	11 44 59	−19 02	06 10	17 20	06 27	17 03	06 48	16 42	07 17	16 13	08 04	15 26
322			**16 07**	**04 08**	**15 59**	**04 14**	**15 49**	**04 21**	**15 36**	**04 31**	**15 16**	**04 46**
19 Sa	11 45 12	−19 16	06 11	17 20	06 28	17 02	06 49	16 41	07 18	16 12	08 06	15 24
323			**16 46**	**05 02**	**16 34**	**05 13**	**16 18**	**05 26**	**15 56**	**05 44**	**15 23**	**06 14**
20 Su	11 45 25	−19 31	06 12	17 20	06 28	17 02	06 50	16 40	07 20	16 11	08 09	15 22
324	**12 29 ○**		**17 30**	**05 58**	**17 12**	**06 14**	**16 51**	**06 33**	**16 21**	**07 01**	**15 33**	**07 46**
21 Mo	11 45 39	−19 44	06 12	17 19	06 29	17 01	06 51	16 40	07 22	16 10	08 12	15 20
325			**18 18**	**06 58**	**17 57**	**07 18**	**17 31**	**07 43**	**16 53**	**08 18**	**15 49**	**09 20**
22 Tu	11 45 53	−19 58	06 13	17 19	06 30	17 01	06 52	16 39	07 23	16 09	08 14	15 18
326			**19 12**	**08 00**	**18 49**	**08 23**	**18 19**	**08 52**	**17 36**	**09 34**	**16 18**	**10 51**
23 We	11 46 09	−20 11	06 14	17 19	06 31	17 01	06 53	16 38	07 24	16 08	08 16	15 16
327			**20 12**	**09 02**	**19 47**	**09 27**	**19 16**	**09 58**	**18 31**	**10 43**	**17 07**	**12 07**
24 Th	11 46 25	−20 23	06 14	17 19	06 32	17 00	06 54	16 38	07 26	16 07	08 18	15 14
328			**21 15**	**10 02**	**20 51**	**10 26**	**20 22**	**10 56**	**19 40**	**11 40**	**18 22**	**12 59**
25 Fr	11 46 42	−20 35	06 15	17 19	06 33	17 00	06 56	16 38	07 28	16 06	08 21	15 13
329			**22 18**	**10 58**	**21 58**	**11 19**	**21 33**	**11 46**	**20 57**	**12 24**	**19 54**	**13 29**
26 Sa	11 47 00	−20 44	06 15	17 19	06 34	17 00	06 57	16 37	07 29	16 05	08 23	15 11
330			**23 21**	**11 49**	**23 06**	**12 06**	**22 46**	**12 28**	**22 19**	**12 58**	**21 33**	**13 47**
27 Su	11 47 19	−20 59	06 16	17 19	06 35	17 00	06 58	16 37	07 30	16 04	08 25	15 10
331	**10 50 ☾**			**12 35**		**12 48**	**23 58**	**13 03**	**23 40**	**13 25**	**23 12**	**13 58**
28 Mo	11 47 38	−21 10	06 16	17 19	06 36	17 00	06 59	16 37	07 32	16 04	08 28	15 08
332			**00 22**	**13 17**	**00 12**	**13 25**		**13 34**		**13 46**		**14 05**
29 Tu	11 47 58	−21 21	06 17	17 19	06 36	17 00	07 00	16 36	07 34	16 03	08 30	15 06
333			**01 21**	**13 57**	**01 16**	**13 59**	**01 10**	**14 02**	**01 01**	**14 06**	**00 47**	**14 11**
30 We	11 48 19	−21 31	06 18	17 19	06 37	17 00	07 01	16 36	07 35	16 02	08 32	15 05
334			**02 19**	**14 36**	**02 19**	**14 33**	**02 19**	**14 29**	**02 20**	**14 24**	**02 21**	**14 17**

12th Month — December, 1983 — 31 days

Greenwich Mean Time

NOTE: Light figures indicate Sun. **Dark** figures indicate **Moon.** *Degrees are North Latitude.*

CAUTION: Must be converted to local time. For instruction see page 768.

Day of month / week / year	Sun on meridian / Moon phase (h m s)	Sun's Declination (° ′)	20° Rise Sun / Moon (h m)	20° Set Sun / Moon (h m)	30° Rise Sun / Moon (h m)	30° Set Sun / Moon (h m)	40° Rise Sun / Moon (h m)	40° Set Sun / Moon (h m)	50° Rise Sun / Moon (h m)	50° Set Sun / Moon (h m)	60° Rise Sun / Moon (h m)	60° Set Sun / Moon (h m)
1 Th	11 48 41	−21 41	06 18	17 19	06 38	17 00	07 02	16 36	07 36	16 02	08 34	15 04
335			**03 16**	**15 15**	**03 22**	**15 07**	**03 29**	**14 57**	**03 39**	**14 43**	**03 54**	**14 23**
2 Fr	11 49 03	−21 50	06 19	17 20	06 38	17 00	07 03	16 36	07 38	16 01	08 36	15 02
336			**04 13**	**15 56**	**04 24**	**15 43**	**04 38**	**15 27**	**04 57**	**15 04**	**05 28**	**14 30**
3 Sa	11 49 26	−21 59	06 20	17 20	06 39	17 01	07 04	16 35	07 39	16 01	08 38	15 01
337			**05 11**	**16 39**	**05 27**	**16 22**	**05 47**	**16 00**	**06 15**	**15 29**	**07 01**	**14 40**
4 Su	11 49 50	−22 08	06 20	17 20	06 40	17 00	07 05	16 35	07 40	16 00	08 40	15 00
338	**12 26 ●**		**06 10**	**17 26**	**06 30**	**17 05**	**06 55**	**16 38**	**07 31**	**16 00**	**08 34**	**14 55**
5 Mo	11 50 14	−22 16	06 21	17 20	06 41	17 00	07 06	16 35	07 41	16 00	08 42	14 59
339			**07 08**	**18 16**	**07 31**	**17 52**	**08 00**	**17 22**	**08 42**	**16 39**	**09 59**	**15 20**
6 Tu	11 50 39	−22 24	06 22	17 20	06 42	17 00	07 07	16 35	07 42	16 00	08 44	14 58
340			**08 04**	**19 08**	**08 28**	**18 43**	**08 59**	**18 12**	**09 44**	**17 27**	**11 10**	**16 01**
7 We	11 51 04	−22 31	06 22	17 21	06 42	17 00	07 08	16 35	07 44	15 59	08 45	14 57
341			**08 57**	**20 01**	**09 21**	**19 38**	**09 52**	**19 07**	**10 36**	**18 23**	**11 59**	**17 01**
8 Th	11 51 30	−22 38	06 23	17 21	06 43	17 00	07 09	16 35	07 45	15 59	08 47	14 56
342			**09 45**	**20 55**	**10 08**	**20 33**	**10 37**	**20 06**	**11 17**	**19 26**	**12 30**	**18 15**
9 Fr	11 51 54	−22 44	06 24	17 21	06 44	17 00	07 10	16 35	07 46	15 59	08 48	14 56
343			**10 30**	**21 48**	**10 49**	**21 29**	**11 14**	**21 06**	**11 49**	**20 33**	**12 48**	**19 36**
10 Sa	11 52 23	−22 50	06 24	17 22	06 44	17 00	07 10	16 35	07 47	15 58	08 50	14 55
344			**11 10**	**22 39**	**11 26**	**22 24**	**11 46**	**22 06**	**12 14**	**21 40**	**12 59**	**20 58**
11 Su	11 52 50	−22 56	06 25	17 22	06 45	17 01	07 11	16 35	07 48	15 58	08 52	14 54
345			**11 46**	**23 28**	**11 59**	**23 18**	**12 14**	**23 05**	**12 34**	**22 47**	**13 06**	**22 19**
12 Mo	11 53 17	−23 01	06 25	17 22	06 46	17 01	07 12	16 35	07 49	15 58	08 53	14 54
346	**13 09 ☽**		**12 21**		**12 29**		**12 39**		**12 52**	**23 54**	**13 12**	**23 38**
13 Tu	11 53 45	−23 06	06 26	17 22	06 47	17 01	07 13	16 35	07 50	15 58	08 54	14 54
347			**12 54**	**00 17**	**12 58**	**00 11**	**13 02**	**00 04**	**13 08**		**13 16**	
14 We	11 54 13	−23 10	06 26	17 22	06 48	17 02	07 14	16 36	07 51	15 58	08 56	14 54
348			**13 28**	**01 06**	**13 27**	**01 05**	**13 25**	**01 03**	**13 23**	**01 01**	**13 21**	**00 58**
15 Th	11 54 42	−23 14	06 27	17 23	06 48	17 02	07 14	16 36	07 51	15 58	08 57	14 53
349			**14 02**	**01 56**	**13 56**	**02 00**	**13 49**	**02 04**	**13 40**	**02 10**	**13 25**	**02 19**
16 Fr	11 55 11	−23 17	06 27	17 23	06 49	17 02	07 15	16 36	07 52	15 58	08 58	14 53
350			**14 39**	**02 48**	**14 29**	**02 56**	**14 16**	**03 07**	**13 58**	**03 21**	**13 31**	**03 44**
17 Sa	11 55 40	−23 20	06 28	17 24	06 50	17 02	07 16	16 36	07 53	15 58	08 59	14 53
351			**15 20**	**03 43**	**15 05**	**03 56**	**14 46**	**04 13**	**14 21**	**04 36**	**13 40**	**05 13**
18 Su	11 56 09	−23 22	06 28	17 24	06 50	17 03	07 16	16 36	07 54	15 59	09 00	14 54
352			**16 07**	**04 41**	**15 47**	**04 59**	**15 23**	**05 22**	**14 49**	**05 53**	**13 53**	**06 47**
19 Mo	11 56 38	−23 24	06 29	17 25	06 51	17 03	07 17	16 37	07 54	15 59	09 00	14 54
353			**16 59**	**05 43**	**16 36**	**06 05**	**16 08**	**06 32**	**15 27**	**07 11**	**14 15**	**08 22**
20 Tu	11 57 08	−23 25	06 30	17 25	06 51	17 04	07 17	16 37	07 55	16 00	09 01	14 54
354	**02 00 ○**		**17 58**	**06 47**	**17 33**	**07 11**	**17 02**	**07 41**	**16 18**	**08 26**	**14 55**	**09 48**
21 We	11 57 38	−23 26	06 30	17 26	06 52	17 04	07 18	16 37	07 56	16 00	09 02	14 54
355			**19 02**	**07 56**	**18 38**	**08 14**	**18 07**	**08 45**	**17 23**	**09 30**	**16 01**	**10 53**
22 Th	11 58 07	−23 26	06 31	17 26	06 52	17 05	07 18	16 38	07 56	16 01	09 02	14 55
356			**20 07**	**08 50**	**19 46**	**09 12**	**19 19**	**09 41**	**18 40**	**10 21**	**17 31**	**11 32**
23 Fr	11 58 37	−23 26	06 32	17 27	06 53	17 05	07 19	16 38	07 57	16 01	09 03	14 56
357			**21 13**	**09 44**	**20 56**	**10 03**	**20 34**	**10 27**	**20 03**	**11 00**	**19 12**	**11 54**
24 Sa	11 59 07	−23 26	06 32	17 27	06 53	17 06	07 19	16 39	07 57	16 02	09 03	14 56
358			**22 16**	**10 33**	**22 04**	**10 47**	**21 48**	**11 05**	**21 27**	**11 29**	**20 54**	**12 07**
25 Su	11 59 37	−23 25	06 32	17 28	06 54	17 06	07 20	16 40	07 57	16 02	09 03	14 57
359			**23 16**	**11 17**	**23 09**	**11 26**	**23 01**	**11 38**	**22 50**	**11 53**	**22 32**	**12 16**
26 Mo	12 00 07	−23 24	06 33	17 28	06 54	17 07	07 20	16 40	07 58	16 03	09 04	14 58
360	**18 52 ☾**			**11 58**		**12 02**		**12 06**		**12 13**		**12 22**
27 Tu	12 00 36	−23 22	06 33	17 29	06 55	17 07	07 21	16 41	07 58	16 03	09 04	14 58
361			**00 14**	**12 37**	**00 13**	**12 35**	**00 11**	**12 34**	**00 09**	**12 31**	**00 06**	**12 28**
28 We	12 01 06	−23 19	06 33	17 29	06 55	17 08	07 21	16 42	07 58	16 04	09 04	14 59
362			**01 11**	**13 15**	**01 15**	**13 05**	**01 20**	**13 01**	**01 27**	**12 50**	**01 38**	**12 33**
29 Th	12 01 36	−23 16	06 34	17 30	06 55	17 09	07 21	16 43	07 58	16 05	09 04	15 00
363			**02 07**	**13 55**	**02 17**	**13 43**	**02 28**	**13 29**	**02 44**	**13 10**	**03 10**	**12 40**
30 Fr	12 02 05	−23 13	06 34	17 30	06 56	17 10	07 22	16 44	07 58	16 06	09 04	15 02
364			**03 04**	**14 36**	**03 18**	**14 20**	**03 36**	**14 00**	**04 01**	**13 33**	**04 42**	**12 48**
31 Sa	12 02 34	−23 09	06 35	17 31	06 56	17 10	07 22	16 44	07 59	16 07	09 03	15 03
365			**04 01**	**15 21**	**04 19**	**15 01**	**04 43**	**14 35**	**05 16**	**14 00**	**06 13**	**13 01**

Perpetual Calendar

The number shown for each year indicates which Gregorian calendar to use. For 1583-1802, or for Julian calendar, see page 783. For years 1803-1820, use numbers for 1983-2000, respectively.

1821....2	1847....6	1873....4	1899....1	1925....5	1951....2	1977....7	2003....4	2029....2	2055....6
1822....3	1848...14	1874....5	1900....2	1926....6	1952...10	1978....1	2004...12	2030....3	2056...14
1823....4	1849....2	1875....6	1901....3	1927....7	1953....5	1979....2	2005....7	2031....4	2057....2
1824...12	1850....3	1876...14	1902....4	1928....8	1954....6	1980...10	2006....1	2032...12	2058....3
1825....7	1851....4	1877....2	1903....5	1929....3	1955....7	1981....5	2007....2	2033....7	2059....4
1826....1	1852...12	1878....3	1904...13	1930....4	1956....8	1982....6	2008...10	2034....1	2060..12
1827....2	1853....7	1879....4	1905....1	1931....5	1957....3	1983....7	2009....5	2035....2	2061..7
1828...10	1854....1	1880...12	1906....2	1932...13	1958....4	1984....8	2010....6	2036...10	2062..1
1829....5	1855....2	1881....7	1907....3	1933....1	1959....5	1985....3	2011....7	2037....5	2063..2
1830....6	1856...10	1882....1	1908...11	1934....2	1960...13	1986....4	2012....8	2038....6	2064..10
1831....7	1857....5	1883....2	1909....6	1935....3	1961....1	1987....5	2013....3	2039....7	2065..5
1832....8	1858....6	1884...10	1910....7	1936...11	1962....2	1988...13	2014....4	2040....8	2066..6
1833....3	1859....7	1885....5	1911....1	1937....6	1963....3	1989....1	2015....5	2041....3	2067..7
1834....4	1860....8	1886....6	1912....9	1938....7	1964...11	1990....2	2016...13	2042....4	2068..8
1835....5	1861....3	1887....7	1913....4	1939....1	1965....6	1991....3	2017....1	2043....5	2069..3
1836...13	1862....4	1888....8	1914....5	1940....9	1966....7	1992...11	2018....2	2044...13	2070..4
1837....1	1863....5	1889....3	1915....6	1941....4	1967....1	1993....6	2019....3	2045....1	2071..5
1838....2	1864...13	1890....4	1916...14	1942....5	1968....9	1994....7	2020...11	2046....2	2072..13
1839....3	1865....1	1891....5	1917....2	1943....6	1969....4	1995....1	2021....6	2047....3	2073..1
1840...11	1866....2	1892...13	1918....3	1944...14	1970....5	1996....9	2022....7	2048...11	2074..2
1841....6	1867....3	1893....1	1919....4	1945....2	1971....6	1997....4	2023....1	2049....6	2075..3
1842....7	1868...11	1894....2	1920...12	1946....3	1972...14	1998....5	2024....9	2050....7	2076..11
1843....1	1869....6	1895....3	1921....7	1947....4	1973....2	1999....6	2025....4	2051....1	2077..6
1844....9	1870....7	1896...11	1922....1	1948...12	1974....3	2000...14	2026....5	2052....9	2078..7
1845....4	1871....1	1897....6	1923....2	1949....7	1975....4	2001....2	2027....6	2053....4	2079..1
1846....5	1872....9	1898....7	1924...10	1950....1	1976...12	2002....3	2028...14	2054....5	2080..9

1

JANUARY

S	M	T	W	T	F	S
1	2	3	4	5	6	7
8	9	10	11	12	13	14
15	16	17	18	19	20	21
22	23	24	25	26	27	28
29	30	31				

FEBRUARY

S	M	T	W	T	F	S
			1	2	3	4
5	6	7	8	9	10	11
12	13	14	15	16	17	18
19	20	21	22	23	24	25
26	27	28				

MARCH

S	M	T	W	T	F	S
			1	2	3	4
5	6	7	8	9	10	11
12	13	14	15	16	17	18
19	20	21	22	23	24	25
26	27	28	29	30	31	

APRIL

S	M	T	W	T	F	S
						1
2	3	4	5	6	7	8
9	10	11	12	13	14	15
16	17	18	19	20	21	22
23	24	25	26	27	28	29
30						

MAY

S	M	T	W	T	F	S
	1	2	3	4	5	6
7	8	9	10	11	12	13
14	15	16	17	18	19	20
21	22	23	24	25	26	27
28	29	30	31			

JUNE

S	M	T	W	T	F	S
				1	2	3
4	5	6	7	8	9	10
11	12	13	14	15	16	17
18	19	20	21	22	23	24
25	26	27	28	29	30	

JULY

S	M	T	W	T	F	S
						1
2	3	4	5	6	7	8
9	10	11	12	13	14	15
16	17	18	19	20	21	22
23	24	25	26	27	28	29
30	31					

AUGUST

S	M	T	W	T	F	S
		1	2	3	4	5
6	7	8	9	10	11	12
13	14	15	16	17	18	19
20	21	22	23	24	25	26
27	28	29	30	31		

SEPTEMBER

S	M	T	W	T	F	S
					1	2
3	4	5	6	7	8	9
10	11	12	13	14	15	16
17	18	19	20	21	22	23
24	25	26	27	28	29	30

OCTOBER

S	M	T	W	T	F	S
1	2	3	4	5	6	7
8	9	10	11	12	13	14
15	16	17	18	19	20	21
22	23	24	25	26	27	28
29	30	31				

NOVEMBER

S	M	T	W	T	F	S
			1	2	3	4
5	6	7	8	9	10	11
12	13	14	15	16	17	18
19	20	21	22	23	24	25
26	27	28	29	30		

DECEMBER

S	M	T	W	T	F	S
					1	2
3	4	5	6	7	8	9
10	11	12	13	14	15	16
17	18	19	20	21	22	23
24	25	26	27	28	29	30
31						

2

JANUARY

S	M	T	W	T	F	S
	1	2	3	4	5	6
7	8	9	10	11	12	13
14	15	16	17	18	19	20
21	22	23	24	25	26	27
28	29	30	31			

FEBRUARY

S	M	T	W	T	F	S
				1	2	3
4	5	6	7	8	9	10
11	12	13	14	15	16	17
18	19	20	21	22	23	24
25	26	27	28			

MARCH

S	M	T	W	T	F	S
				1	2	3
4	5	6	7	8	9	10
11	12	13	14	15	16	17
18	19	20	21	22	23	24
25	26	27	28	29	30	31

APRIL

S	M	T	W	T	F	S
1	2	3	4	5	6	7
8	9	10	11	12	13	14
15	16	17	18	19	20	21
22	23	24	25	26	27	28
29	30					

MAY

S	M	T	W	T	F	S
		1	2	3	4	5
6	7	8	9	10	11	12
13	14	15	16	17	18	19
20	21	22	23	24	25	26
27	28	29	30	31		

JUNE

S	M	T	W	T	F	S
					1	2
3	4	5	6	7	8	9
10	11	12	13	14	15	16
17	18	19	20	21	22	23
24	25	26	27	28	29	30

JULY

S	M	T	W	T	F	S
1	2	3	4	5	6	7
8	9	10	11	12	13	14
15	16	17	18	19	20	21
22	23	24	25	26	27	28
29	30	31				

AUGUST

S	M	T	W	T	F	S
			1	2	3	4
5	6	7	8	9	10	11
12	13	14	15	16	17	18
19	20	21	22	23	24	25
26	27	28	29	30	31	

SEPTEMBER

S	M	T	W	T	F	S
						1
2	3	4	5	6	7	8
9	10	11	12	13	14	15
16	17	18	19	20	21	22
23	24	25	26	27	28	29
30						

OCTOBER

S	M	T	W	T	F	S
	1	2	3	4	5	6
7	8	9	10	11	12	13
14	15	16	17	18	19	20
21	22	23	24	25	26	27
28	29	30	31			

NOVEMBER

S	M	T	W	T	F	S
				1	2	3
4	5	6	7	8	9	10
11	12	13	14	15	16	17
18	19	20	21	22	23	24
25	26	27	28	29	30	

DECEMBER

S	M	T	W	T	F	S
						1
2	3	4	5	6	7	8
9	10	11	12	13	14	15
16	17	18	19	20	21	22
23	24	25	26	27	28	29
30	31					

3

JANUARY

S	M	T	W	T	F	S
		1	2	3	4	5
6	7	8	9	10	11	12
13	14	15	16	17	18	19
20	21	22	23	24	25	26
27	28	29	30	31		

FEBRUARY

S	M	T	W	T	F	S
					1	2
3	4	5	6	7	8	9
10	11	12	13	14	15	16
17	18	19	20	21	22	23
24	25	26	27	28		

MARCH

S	M	T	W	T	F	S
					1	2
3	4	5	6	7	8	9
10	11	12	13	14	15	16
17	18	19	20	21	22	23
24	25	26	27	28	29	30
31						

APRIL

S	M	T	W	T	F	S
	1	2	3	4	5	6
7	8	9	10	11	12	13
14	15	16	17	18	19	20
21	22	23	24	25	26	27
28	29	30				

MAY

S	M	T	W	T	F	S
			1	2	3	4
5	6	7	8	9	10	11
12	13	14	15	16	17	18
19	20	21	22	23	24	25
26	27	28	29	30	31	

JUNE

S	M	T	W	T	F	S
						1
2	3	4	5	6	7	8
9	10	11	12	13	14	15
16	17	18	19	20	21	22
23	24	25	26	27	28	29
30						

JULY

S	M	T	W	T	F	S
	1	2	3	4	5	6
7	8	9	10	11	12	13
14	15	16	17	18	19	20
21	22	23	24	25	26	27
28	29	30	31			

AUGUST

S	M	T	W	T	F	S
				1	2	3
4	5	6	7	8	9	10
11	12	13	14	15	16	17
18	19	20	21	22	23	24
25	26	27	28	29	30	31

SEPTEMBER

S	M	T	W	T	F	S
1	2	3	4	5	6	7
8	9	10	11	12	13	14
15	16	17	18	19	20	21
22	23	24	25	26	27	28
29	30					

OCTOBER

S	M	T	W	T	F	S
		1	2	3	4	5
6	7	8	9	10	11	12
13	14	15	16	17	18	19
20	21	22	23	24	25	26
27	28	29	30	31		

NOVEMBER

S	M	T	W	T	F	S
					1	2
3	4	5	6	7	8	9
10	11	12	13	14	15	16
17	18	19	20	21	22	23
24	25	26	27	28	29	30

DECEMBER

S	M	T	W	T	F	S
1	2	3	4	5	6	7
8	9	10	11	12	13	14
15	16	17	18	19	20	21
22	23	24	25	26	27	28
29	30	31				

4

JANUARY

S	M	T	W	T	F	S
			1	2	3	4
5	6	7	8	9	10	11
12	13	14	15	16	17	18
19	20	21	22	23	24	25
26	27	28	29	30	31	

FEBRUARY

S	M	T	W	T	F	S
						1
2	3	4	5	6	7	8
9	10	11	12	13	14	15
16	17	18	19	20	21	22
23	24	25	26	27	28	

MARCH

S	M	T	W	T	F	S
						1
2	3	4	5	6	7	8
9	10	11	12	13	14	15
16	17	18	19	20	21	22
23	24	25	26	27	28	29
30	31					

APRIL

S	M	T	W	T	F	S
		1	2	3	4	5
6	7	8	9	10	11	12
13	14	15	16	17	18	19
20	21	22	23	24	25	26
27	28	29	30			

MAY

S	M	T	W	T	F	S
				1	2	3
4	5	6	7	8	9	10
11	12	13	14	15	16	17
18	19	20	21	22	23	24
25	26	27	28	29	30	31

JUNE

S	M	T	W	T	F	S
1	2	3	4	5	6	7
8	9	10	11	12	13	14
15	16	17	18	19	20	21
22	23	24	25	26	27	28
29	30					

JULY

S	M	T	W	T	F	S
		1	2	3	4	5
6	7	8	9	10	11	12
13	14	15	16	17	18	19
20	21	22	23	24	25	26
27	28	29	30	31		

AUGUST

S	M	T	W	T	F	S
					1	2
3	4	5	6	7	8	9
10	11	12	13	14	15	16
17	18	19	20	21	22	23
24	25	26	27	28	29	30
31						

SEPTEMBER

S	M	T	W	T	F	S
	1	2	3	4	5	6
7	8	9	10	11	12	13
14	15	16	17	18	19	20
21	22	23	24	25	26	27
28	29	30				

OCTOBER

S	M	T	W	T	F	S
			1	2	3	4
5	6	7	8	9	10	11
12	13	14	15	16	17	18
19	20	21	22	23	24	25
26	27	28	29	30	31	

NOVEMBER

S	M	T	W	T	F	S
						1
2	3	4	5	6	7	8
9	10	11	12	13	14	15
16	17	18	19	20	21	22
23	24	25	26	27	28	29
30						

DECEMBER

S	M	T	W	T	F	S
	1	2	3	4	5	6
7	8	9	10	11	12	13
14	15	16	17	18	19	20
21	22	23	24	25	26	27
28	29	30	31			

5

JANUARY

S	M	T	W	T	F	S
				1	2	3
4	5	6	7	8	9	10
11	12	13	14	15	16	17
18	19	20	21	22	23	24
25	26	27	28	29	30	31

FEBRUARY

S	M	T	W	T	F	S
1	2	3	4	5	6	7
8	9	10	11	12	13	14
15	16	17	18	19	20	21
22	23	24	25	26	27	28

MARCH

S	M	T	W	T	F	S
1	2	3	4	5	6	7
8	9	10	11	12	13	14
15	16	17	18	19	20	21
22	23	24	25	26	27	28
29	30	31				

APRIL

S	M	T	W	T	F	S
			1	2	3	4
5	6	7	8	9	10	11
12	13	14	15	16	17	18
19	20	21	22	23	24	25
26	27	28	29	30		

MAY

S	M	T	W	T	F	S
					1	2
3	4	5	6	7	8	9
10	11	12	13	14	15	16
17	18	19	20	21	22	23
24	25	26	27	28	29	30
31						

JUNE

S	M	T	W	T	F	S
	1	2	3	4	5	6
7	8	9	10	11	12	13
14	15	16	17	18	19	20
21	22	23	24	25	26	27
28	29	30				

JULY

S	M	T	W	T	F	S
			1	2	3	4
5	6	7	8	9	10	11
12	13	14	15	16	17	18
19	20	21	22	23	24	25
26	27	28	29	30	31	

AUGUST

S	M	T	W	T	F	S
						1
2	3	4	5	6	7	8
9	10	11	12	13	14	15
16	17	18	19	20	21	22
23	24	25	26	27	28	29
30	31					

SEPTEMBER

S	M	T	W	T	F	S
		1	2	3	4	5
6	7	8	9	10	11	12
13	14	15	16	17	18	19
20	21	22	23	24	25	26
27	28	29	30			

OCTOBER

S	M	T	W	T	F	S
				1	2	3
4	5	6	7	8	9	10
11	12	13	14	15	16	17
18	19	20	21	22	23	24
25	26	27	28	29	30	31

NOVEMBER

S	M	T	W	T	F	S
1	2	3	4	5	6	7
8	9	10	11	12	13	14
15	16	17	18	19	20	21
22	23	24	25	26	27	28
29	30					

DECEMBER

S	M	T	W	T	F	S
		1	2	3	4	5
6	7	8	9	10	11	12
13	14	15	16	17	18	19
20	21	22	23	24	25	26
27	28	29	30	31		

6 1982

JANUARY

S	M	T	W	T	F	S
					1	2
3	4	5	6	7	8	9
10	11	12	13	14	15	16
17	18	19	20	21	22	23
24	25	26	27	28	29	30
31						

FEBRUARY

S	M	T	W	T	F	S
	1	2	3	4	5	6
7	8	9	10	11	12	13
14	15	16	17	18	19	20
21	22	23	24	25	26	27
28						

MARCH

S	M	T	W	T	F	S
	1	2	3	4	5	6
7	8	9	10	11	12	13
14	15	16	17	18	19	20
21	22	23	24	25	26	27
28	29	30	31			

APRIL

S	M	T	W	T	F	S
				1	2	3
4	5	6	7	8	9	10
11	12	13	14	15	16	17
18	19	20	21	22	23	24
25	26	27	28	29	30	

MAY

S	M	T	W	T	F	S
						1
2	3	4	5	6	7	8
9	10	11	12	13	14	15
16	17	18	19	20	21	22
23	24	25	26	27	28	29
30	31					

JUNE

S	M	T	W	T	F	S
		1	2	3	4	5
6	7	8	9	10	11	12
13	14	15	16	17	18	19
20	21	22	23	24	25	26
27	28	29	30			

JULY

S	M	T	W	T	F	S
				1	2	3
4	5	6	7	8	9	10
11	12	13	14	15	16	17
18	19	20	21	22	23	24
25	26	27	28	29	30	31

AUGUST

S	M	T	W	T	F	S
1	2	3	4	5	6	7
8	9	10	11	12	13	14
15	16	17	18	19	20	21
22	23	24	25	26	27	28
29	30	31				

SEPTEMBER

S	M	T	W	T	F	S
			1	2	3	4
5	6	7	8	9	10	11
12	13	14	15	16	17	18
19	20	21	22	23	24	25
26	27	28	29	30		

OCTOBER

S	M	T	W	T	F	S
					1	2
3	4	5	6	7	8	9
10	11	12	13	14	15	16
17	18	19	20	21	22	23
24	25	26	27	28	29	30
31						

NOVEMBER

S	M	T	W	T	F	S
	1	2	3	4	5	6
7	8	9	10	11	12	13
14	15	16	17	18	19	20
21	22	23	24	25	26	27
28	29	30				

DECEMBER

S	M	T	W	T	F	S
			1	2	3	4
5	6	7	8	9	10	11
12	13	14	15	16	17	18
19	20	21	22	23	24	25
26	27	28	29	30	31	

7

1983

JANUARY

S	M	T	W	T	F	S
						1
2	3	4	5	6	7	8
9	10	11	12	13	14	15
16	17	18	19	20	21	22
23	24	25	26	27	28	29
30	31					

FEBRUARY

S	M	T	W	T	F	S
		1	2	3	4	5
6	7	8	9	10	11	12
13	14	15	16	17	18	19
20	21	22	23	24	25	26
27	28					

MARCH

S	M	T	W	T	F	S
		1	2	3	4	5
6	7	8	9	10	11	12
13	14	15	16	17	18	19
20	21	22	23	24	25	26
27	28	29	30	31		

APRIL

S	M	T	W	T	F	S
					1	2
3	4	5	6	7	8	9
10	11	12	13	14	15	16
17	18	19	20	21	22	23
24	25	26	27	28	29	30

MAY

S	M	T	W	T	F	S
1	2	3	4	5	6	7
8	9	10	11	12	13	14
15	16	17	18	19	20	21
22	23	24	25	26	27	28
29	30	31				

JUNE

S	M	T	W	T	F	S
			1	2	3	4
5	6	7	8	9	10	11
12	13	14	15	16	17	18
19	20	21	22	23	24	25
26	27	28	29	30		

JULY

S	M	T	W	T	F	S
					1	2
3	4	5	6	7	8	9
10	11	12	13	14	15	16
17	18	19	20	21	22	23
24	25	26	27	28	29	30
31						

AUGUST

S	M	T	W	T	F	S
	1	2	3	4	5	6
7	8	9	10	11	12	13
14	15	16	17	18	19	20
21	22	23	24	25	26	27
28	29	30	31			

SEPTEMBER

S	M	T	W	T	F	S
				1	2	3
4	5	6	7	8	9	10
11	12	13	14	15	16	17
18	19	20	21	22	23	24
25	26	27	28	29	30	

OCTOBER

S	M	T	W	T	F	S
						1
2	3	4	5	6	7	8
9	10	11	12	13	14	15
16	17	18	19	20	21	22
23	24	25	26	27	28	29
30	31					

NOVEMBER

S	M	T	W	T	F	S
		1	2	3	4	5
6	7	8	9	10	11	12
13	14	15	16	17	18	19
20	21	22	23	24	25	26
27	28	29	30			

DECEMBER

S	M	T	W	T	F	S
				1	2	3
4	5	6	7	8	9	10
11	12	13	14	15	16	17
18	19	20	21	22	23	24
25	26	27	28	29	30	31

8

1984

JANUARY

S	M	T	W	T	F	S
1	2	3	4	5	6	7
8	9	10	11	12	13	14
15	16	17	18	19	20	21
22	23	24	25	26	27	28
29	30	31				

FEBRUARY

S	M	T	W	T	F	S
			1	2	3	4
5	6	7	8	9	10	11
12	13	14	15	16	17	18
19	20	21	22	23	24	25
26	27	28	29			

MARCH

S	M	T	W	T	F	S
				1	2	3
4	5	6	7	8	9	10
11	12	13	14	15	16	17
18	19	20	21	22	23	24
25	26	27	28	29	30	31

APRIL

S	M	T	W	T	F	S
1	2	3	4	5	6	7
8	9	10	11	12	13	14
15	16	17	18	19	20	21
22	23	24	25	26	27	28
29	30					

MAY

S	M	T	W	T	F	S
		1	2	3	4	5
6	7	8	9	10	11	12
13	14	15	16	17	18	19
20	21	22	23	24	25	26
27	28	29	30	31		

JUNE

S	M	T	W	T	F	S
					1	2
3	4	5	6	7	8	9
10	11	12	13	14	15	16
17	18	19	20	21	22	23
24	25	26	27	28	29	30

JULY

S	M	T	W	T	F	S
1	2	3	4	5	6	7
8	9	10	11	12	13	14
15	16	17	18	19	20	21
22	23	24	25	26	27	28
29	30	31				

AUGUST

S	M	T	W	T	F	S
			1	2	3	4
5	6	7	8	9	10	11
12	13	14	15	16	17	18
19	20	21	22	23	24	25
26	27	28	29	30	31	

SEPTEMBER

S	M	T	W	T	F	S
						1
2	3	4	5	6	7	8
9	10	11	12	13	14	15
16	17	18	19	20	21	22
23	24	25	26	27	28	29
30						

OCTOBER

S	M	T	W	T	F	S
	1	2	3	4	5	6
7	8	9	10	11	12	13
14	15	16	17	18	19	20
21	22	23	24	25	26	27
28	29	30	31			

NOVEMBER

S	M	T	W	T	F	S
				1	2	3
4	5	6	7	8	9	10
11	12	13	14	15	16	17
18	19	20	21	22	23	24
25	26	27	28	29	30	

DECEMBER

S	M	T	W	T	F	S
						1
2	3	4	5	6	7	8
9	10	11	12	13	14	15
16	17	18	19	20	21	22
23	24	25	26	27	28	29
30	31					

9

JANUARY

S	M	T	W	T	F	S
	1	2	3	4	5	6
7	8	9	10	11	12	13
14	15	16	17	18	19	20
21	22	23	24	25	26	27
28	29	30	31			

FEBRUARY

S	M	T	W	T	F	S
				1	2	3
4	5	6	7	8	9	10
11	12	13	14	15	16	17
18	19	20	21	22	23	24
25	26	27	28	29		

MARCH

S	M	T	W	T	F	S
					1	2
3	4	5	6	7	8	9
10	11	12	13	14	15	16
17	18	19	20	21	22	23
24	25	26	27	28	29	30
31						

APRIL

S	M	T	W	T	F	S
	1	2	3	4	5	6
7	8	9	10	11	12	13
14	15	16	17	18	19	20
21	22	23	24	25	26	27
28	29	30				

MAY

S	M	T	W	T	F	S
			1	2	3	4
5	6	7	8	9	10	11
12	13	14	15	16	17	18
19	20	21	22	23	24	25
26	27	28	29	30	31	

JUNE

S	M	T	W	T	F	S
						1
2	3	4	5	6	7	8
9	10	11	12	13	14	15
16	17	18	19	20	21	22
23	24	25	26	27	28	29
30						

JULY

S	M	T	W	T	F	S
	1	2	3	4	5	6
7	8	9	10	11	12	13
14	15	16	17	18	19	20
21	22	23	24	25	26	27
28	29	30	31			

AUGUST

S	M	T	W	T	F	S
				1	2	3
4	5	6	7	8	9	10
11	12	13	14	15	16	17
18	19	20	21	22	23	24
25	26	27	28	29	30	31

SEPTEMBER

S	M	T	W	T	F	S
1	2	3	4	5	6	7
8	9	10	11	12	13	14
15	16	17	18	19	20	21
22	23	24	25	26	27	28
29	30					

OCTOBER

S	M	T	W	T	F	S
		1	2	3	4	5
6	7	8	9	10	11	12
13	14	15	16	17	18	19
20	21	22	23	24	25	26
27	28	29	30	31		

NOVEMBER

S	M	T	W	T	F	S
					1	2
3	4	5	6	7	8	9
10	11	12	13	14	15	16
17	18	19	20	21	22	23
24	25	26	27	28	29	30

DECEMBER

S	M	T	W	T	F	S
1	2	3	4	5	6	7
8	9	10	11	12	13	14
15	16	17	18	19	20	21
22	23	24	25	26	27	28
29	30	31				

10

JANUARY

S	M	T	W	T	F	S
		1	2	3	4	5
6	7	8	9	10	11	12
13	14	15	16	17	18	19
20	21	22	23	24	25	26
27	28	29	30	31		

FEBRUARY

S	M	T	W	T	F	S
					1	2
3	4	5	6	7	8	9
10	11	12	13	14	15	16
17	18	19	20	21	22	23
24	25	26	27	28	29	

MARCH

S	M	T	W	T	F	S
						1
2	3	4	5	6	7	8
9	10	11	12	13	14	15
16	17	18	19	20	21	22
23	24	25	26	27	28	29
30	31					

APRIL

S	M	T	W	T	F	S
		1	2	3	4	5
6	7	8	9	10	11	12
13	14	15	16	17	18	19
20	21	22	23	24	25	26
27	28	29	30			

MAY

S	M	T	W	T	F	S
				1	2	3
4	5	6	7	8	9	10
11	12	13	14	15	16	17
18	19	20	21	22	23	24
25	26	27	28	29	30	31

JUNE

S	M	T	W	T	F	S
1	2	3	4	5	6	7
8	9	10	11	12	13	14
15	16	17	18	19	20	21
22	23	24	25	26	27	28
29	30					

JULY

S	M	T	W	T	F	S
		1	2	3	4	5
6	7	8	9	10	11	12
13	14	15	16	17	18	19
20	21	22	23	24	25	26
27	28	29	30	31		

AUGUST

S	M	T	W	T	F	S
					1	2
3	4	5	6	7	8	9
10	11	12	13	14	15	16
17	18	19	20	21	22	23
24	25	26	27	28	29	30
31						

SEPTEMBER

S	M	T	W	T	F	S
	1	2	3	4	5	6
7	8	9	10	11	12	13
14	15	16	17	18	19	20
21	22	23	24	25	26	27
28	29	30				

OCTOBER

S	M	T	W	T	F	S
			1	2	3	4
5	6	7	8	9	10	11
12	13	14	15	16	17	18
19	20	21	22	23	24	25
26	27	28	29	30	31	

NOVEMBER

S	M	T	W	T	F	S
						1
2	3	4	5	6	7	8
9	10	11	12	13	14	15
16	17	18	19	20	21	22
23	24	25	26	27	28	29
30						

DECEMBER

S	M	T	W	T	F	S
	1	2	3	4	5	6
7	8	9	10	11	12	13
14	15	16	17	18	19	20
21	22	23	24	25	26	27
28	29	30	31			

11

JANUARY

S	M	T	W	T	F	S
			1	2	3	4
5	6	7	8	9	10	11
12	13	14	15	16	17	18
19	20	21	22	23	24	25
26	27	28	29	30	31	

FEBRUARY

S	M	T	W	T	F	S
						1
2	3	4	5	6	7	8
9	10	11	12	13	14	15
16	17	18	19	20	21	22
23	24	25	26	27	28	29

MARCH

S	M	T	W	T	F	S
1	2	3	4	5	6	7
8	9	10	11	12	13	14
15	16	17	18	19	20	21
22	23	24	25	26	27	28
29	30	31				

APRIL

S	M	T	W	T	F	S
			1	2	3	4
5	6	7	8	9	10	11
12	13	14	15	16	17	18
19	20	21	22	23	24	25
26	27	28	29	30		

MAY

S	M	T	W	T	F	S
					1	2
3	4	5	6	7	8	9
10	11	12	13	14	15	16
17	18	19	20	21	22	23
24	25	26	27	28	29	30
31						

JUNE

S	M	T	W	T	F	S
	1	2	3	4	5	6
7	8	9	10	11	12	13
14	15	16	17	18	19	20
21	22	23	24	25	26	27
28	29	30				

JULY

S	M	T	W	T	F	S
			1	2	3	4
5	6	7	8	9	10	11
12	13	14	15	16	17	18
19	20	21	22	23	24	25
26	27	28	29	30	31	

AUGUST

S	M	T	W	T	F	S
						1
2	3	4	5	6	7	8
9	10	11	12	13	14	15
16	17	18	19	20	21	22
23	24	25	26	27	28	29
30	31					

SEPTEMBER

S	M	T	W	T	F	S
		1	2	3	4	5
6	7	8	9	10	11	12
13	14	15	16	17	18	19
20	21	22	23	24	25	26
27	28	29	30			

OCTOBER

S	M	T	W	T	F	S
				1	2	3
4	5	6	7	8	9	10
11	12	13	14	15	16	17
18	19	20	21	22	23	24
25	26	27	28	29	30	31

NOVEMBER

S	M	T	W	T	F	S
1	2	3	4	5	6	7
8	9	10	11	12	13	14
15	16	17	18	19	20	21
22	23	24	25	26	27	28
29	30					

DECEMBER

S	M	T	W	T	F	S
		1	2	3	4	5
6	7	8	9	10	11	12
13	14	15	16	17	18	19
20	21	22	23	24	25	26
27	28	29	30	31		

12

JANUARY

S	M	T	W	T	F	S
				1	2	3
4	5	6	7	8	9	10
11	12	13	14	15	16	17
18	19	20	21	22	23	24
25	26	27	28	29	30	31

FEBRUARY

S	M	T	W	T	F	S
1	2	3	4	5	6	7
8	9	10	11	12	13	14
15	16	17	18	19	20	21
22	23	24	25	26	27	28
29						

MARCH

S	M	T	W	T	F	S
	1	2	3	4	5	6
7	8	9	10	11	12	13
14	15	16	17	18	19	20
21	22	23	24	25	26	27
28	29	30	31			

APRIL

S	M	T	W	T	F	S
				1	2	3
4	5	6	7	8	9	10
11	12	13	14	15	16	17
18	19	20	21	22	23	24
25	26	27	28	29	30	

MAY

S	M	T	W	T	F	S
						1
2	3	4	5	6	7	8
9	10	11	12	13	14	15
16	17	18	19	20	21	22
23	24	25	26	27	28	29
30	31					

JUNE

S	M	T	W	T	F	S
		1	2	3	4	5
6	7	8	9	10	11	12
13	14	15	16	17	18	19
20	21	22	23	24	25	26
27	28	29	30			

JULY

S	M	T	W	T	F	S
				1	2	3
4	5	6	7	8	9	10
11	12	13	14	15	16	17
18	19	20	21	22	23	24
25	26	27	28	29	30	31

AUGUST

S	M	T	W	T	F	S
1	2	3	4	5	6	7
8	9	10	11	12	13	14
15	16	17	18	19	20	21
22	23	24	25	26	27	28
29	30	31				

SEPTEMBER

S	M	T	W	T	F	S
			1	2	3	4
5	6	7	8	9	10	11
12	13	14	15	16	17	18
19	20	21	22	23	24	25
26	27	28	29	30		

OCTOBER

S	M	T	W	T	F	S
					1	2
3	4	5	6	7	8	9
10	11	12	13	14	15	16
17	18	19	20	21	22	23
24	25	26	27	28	29	30
31						

NOVEMBER

S	M	T	W	T	F	S
	1	2	3	4	5	6
7	8	9	10	11	12	13
14	15	16	17	18	19	20
21	22	23	24	25	26	27
28	29	30				

DECEMBER

S	M	T	W	T	F	S
			1	2	3	4
5	6	7	8	9	10	11
12	13	14	15	16	17	18
19	20	21	22	23	24	25
26	27	28	29	30	31	

13

JANUARY

S	M	T	W	T	F	S
					1	2
3	4	5	6	7	8	9
10	11	12	13	14	15	16
17	18	19	20	21	22	23
24	25	26	27	28	29	30
31						

FEBRUARY

S	M	T	W	T	F	S
	1	2	3	4	5	6
7	8	9	10	11	12	13
14	15	16	17	18	19	20
21	22	23	24	25	26	27
28	29					

MARCH

S	M	T	W	T	F	S
		1	2	3	4	5
6	7	8	9	10	11	12
13	14	15	16	17	18	19
20	21	22	23	24	25	26
27	28	29	30	31		

APRIL

S	M	T	W	T	F	S
					1	2
3	4	5	6	7	8	9
10	11	12	13	14	15	16
17	18	19	20	21	22	23
24	25	26	27	28	29	30

MAY

S	M	T	W	T	F	S
1	2	3	4	5	6	7
8	9	10	11	12	13	14
15	16	17	18	19	20	21
22	23	24	25	26	27	28
29	30	31				

JUNE

S	M	T	W	T	F	S
			1	2	3	4
5	6	7	8	9	10	11
12	13	14	15	16	17	18
19	20	21	22	23	24	25
26	27	28	29	30		

JULY

S	M	T	W	T	F	S
					1	2
3	4	5	6	7	8	9
10	11	12	13	14	15	16
17	18	19	20	21	22	23
24	25	26	27	28	29	30
31						

AUGUST

S	M	T	W	T	F	S
	1	2	3	4	5	6
7	8	9	10	11	12	13
14	15	16	17	18	19	20
21	22	23	24	25	26	27
28	29	30	31			

SEPTEMBER

S	M	T	W	T	F	S
				1	2	3
4	5	6	7	8	9	10
11	12	13	14	15	16	17
18	19	20	21	22	23	24
25	26	27	28	29	30	

OCTOBER

S	M	T	W	T	F	S
						1
2	3	4	5	6	7	8
9	10	11	12	13	14	15
16	17	18	19	20	21	22
23	24	25	26	27	28	29
30	31					

NOVEMBER

S	M	T	W	T	F	S
		1	2	3	4	5
6	7	8	9	10	11	12
13	14	15	16	17	18	19
20	21	22	23	24	25	26
27	28	29	30			

DECEMBER

S	M	T	W	T	F	S
				1	2	3
4	5	6	7	8	9	10
11	12	13	14	15	16	17
18	19	20	21	22	23	24
25	26	27	28	29	30	31

14

JANUARY

S	M	T	W	T	F	S
						1
2	3	4	5	6	7	8
9	10	11	12	13	14	15
16	17	18	19	20	21	22
23	24	25	26	27	28	29
30	31					

FEBRUARY

S	M	T	W	T	F	S
		1	2	3	4	5
6	7	8	9	10	11	12
13	14	15	16	17	18	19
20	21	22	23	24	25	26
27	28	29				

MARCH

S	M	T	W	T	F	S
			1	2	3	4
5	6	7	8	9	10	11
12	13	14	15	16	17	18
19	20	21	22	23	24	25
26	27	28	29	30	31	

APRIL

S	M	T	W	T	F	S
						1
2	3	4	5	6	7	8
9	10	11	12	13	14	15
16	17	18	19	20	21	22
23	24	25	26	27	28	29
30						

MAY

S	M	T	W	T	F	S
	1	2	3	4	5	6
7	8	9	10	11	12	13
14	15	16	17	18	19	20
21	22	23	24	25	26	27
28	29	30	31			

JUNE

S	M	T	W	T	F	S
				1	2	3
4	5	6	7	8	9	10
11	12	13	14	15	16	17
18	19	20	21	22	23	24
25	26	27	28	29	30	

JULY

S	M	T	W	T	F	S
						1
2	3	4	5	6	7	8
9	10	11	12	13	14	15
16	17	18	19	20	21	22
23	24	25	26	27	28	29
30	31					

AUGUST

S	M	T	W	T	F	S
		1	2	3	4	5
6	7	8	9	10	11	12
13	14	15	16	17	18	19
20	21	22	23	24	25	26
27	28	29	30	31		

SEPTEMBER

S	M	T	W	T	F	S
					1	2
3	4	5	6	7	8	9
10	11	12	13	14	15	16
17	18	19	20	21	22	23
24	25	26	27	28	29	30

OCTOBER

S	M	T	W	T	F	S
1	2	3	4	5	6	7
8	9	10	11	12	13	14
15	16	17	18	19	20	21
22	23	24	25	26	27	28
29	30	31				

NOVEMBER

S	M	T	W	T	F	S
			1	2	3	4
5	6	7	8	9	10	11
12	13	14	15	16	17	18
19	20	21	22	23	24	25
26	27	28	29	30		

DECEMBER

S	M	T	W	T	F	S
					1	2
3	4	5	6	7	8	9
10	11	12	13	14	15	16
17	18	19	20	21	22	23
24	25	26	27	28	29	30
31						

Julian and Gregorian Calendars; Leap Year

Calendars based on the movements of sun and moon have been used since ancient times, but none has been perfect. The Julian calendar, under which western nations measured time until 1582 A.D., was authorized by Julius Caesar in 46 B.C., the year 709 of Rome. His expert was a Greek, Sosigenes. The Julian calendar, on the assumption that the true year was 365 1/4 days long, gave every fourth year 366 days. The Venerable Bede, an Anglo-Saxon monk, announced in 730 A.D. that the 365 1/4-day Julian year was 11 min., 14 sec. too long, making a cumulative error of about a day every 128 years, but nothing was done about it for over 800 years.

By 1582 the accumulated error was estimated to have amounted to 10 days. In that year Pope Gregory XIII decreed that the day following Oct. 4, 1582, should be called Oct. 15, thus dropping 10 days.

However, with common years 365 days and a 366-day leap year every fourth year, the error in the length of the year would have recurred at the rate of a little more than 3 days every 400 years. So 3 of every 4 centesimal years (ending in 00) were made common years, not leap years. Thus 1600 was a leap year, 1700, 1800 and 1900 were not, but 2000 will be. Leap years are those divisible by 4 except centesimal years, which are common unless divisible by 400.

The Gregorian calendar was adopted at once by France, Italy, Spain, Portugal and Luxembourg. Within 2 years most German Catholic states, Belgium and parts of Switzerland and the Netherlands were brought under the new calendar, and Hungary followed in 1587. The rest of the Netherlands, along with Denmark and the German Protestant states made the change in 1699-1700 (German Protestants retained the old reckoning of Easter until 1776).

The British Government imposed the Gregorian calendar on all its possessions, including the American colonies, in 1752. The British decreed that the day following Sept. 2, 1752, should be called Sept. 14, a loss of 11 days. All dates preceding were marked O.S., for Old Style. In addition New Year's Day was moved to Jan. 1 from Mar. 25. (e.g., under the old reckoning, Mar. 24, 1700 had been followed by Mar. 25, 1701.) George Washington's birth date, which was Feb. 11, 1731, O.S., became Feb. 22, 1732, N.S. In 1753 Sweden too went Gregorian, retaining the old Easter rules until 1844.

In 1793 the French Revolutionary Government adopted a calendar of 12 months of 30 days each with 5 extra days in September of each common year and a 6th extra day every 4th year. Napoleon reinstated the Gregorian calendar in 1806.

The Gregorian system later spread to non-European regions, first in the European colonies, then in the independent countries, replacing traditional calendars at least for official purposes. Japan in 1873, Egypt in 1875, China in 1912 and Turkey in 1917 made the change, usually in conjunction with political upheavals. In China, the republican government began reckoning years from its 1911 founding — e.g., 1948 was designated the year 37. After 1949, the Communists adopted the Common, or Christian Era year count, even for the traditional lunar calendar.

In 1918 the revolutionary government in Russia decreed that the day after Jan. 31, 1918, Old Style, would become Feb. 14, 1918, New Style. Greece followed in 1923. (In Russia the Orthodox Church has retained the Julian calendar, as have various Middle Eastern Christian sects.) For the first time in history, all major cultures have one calendar.

To change from the Julian to the Gregorian calendar, add 10 days to dates Oct. 5, 1582, through Feb. 28, 1700; after that date add 11 days through Feb. 28, 1800; 12 days through Feb. 28, 1900; and 13 days through Feb. 28, 2100.

A century consists of 100 consecutive calendar years. The 1st century consisted of the years 1 through 100. The 20th century consists of the years 1901 through 2000 and will end Dec. 31, 2000. The 21st century will begin Jan. 1, 2001.

Julian Calendar

To find which of the 14 calendars printed on pages 784-785 applies to any year, starting Jan. 1, under the Julian system, find the century for the desired year in the three left-hand columns below; read across. Then find the year in the four top rows; read down. The number in the intersection is the calendar designation for that year.

Year (last two figures of desired year)

				01	02	03	04	05	06	07	08	09	10	11	12	13	14	15	16	17	18	19	20	21	22	23	24	25	26	27	28
				29	30	31	32	33	34	35	36	37	38	39	40	41	42	43	44	45	46	47	48	49	50	51	52	53	54	55	56
				57	58	59	60	61	62	63	64	65	66	67	68	69	70	71	72	73	74	75	76	77	78	79	80	81	82	83	84
Century			00	85	86	87	88	89	90	91	92	93	94	95	96	97	98	99													
0	700	1400	12	7	1	2	10	5	6	7	8	3	4	5	13	1	2	3	11	6	7	1	9	4	5	6	14	2	3	4	12
100	800	1500	11	6	7	1	9	4	5	6	14	2	3	4	12	7	1	2	10	5	6	7	8	3	4	5	13	1	2	3	11
200	900	1600	10	5	6	7	8	3	4	5	13	1	2	3	11	6	7	1	9	4	5	6	14	2	3	4	12	7	1	2	10
300	1000	1700	9	4	5	6	14	2	3	4	12	7	1	2	10	5	6	7	8	3	4	5	13	1	2	3	11	6	7	1	9
400	1100	1800	8	3	4	5	13	1	2	3	11	6	7	1	9	4	5	6	14	2	3	4	12	7	1	2	10	5	6	7	8
500	1200	1900	14	2	3	4	12	7	1	2	10	5	6	7	8	3	4	5	13	1	2	3	11	6	7	1	9	4	5	6	14
600	1300	2000	13	1	2	3	11	6	7	1	9	4	5	6	14	2	3	4	12	7	1	2	10	5	6	7	8	3	4	5	13

Gregorian Calendar

Pick desired year from table below or on page 784 (for years 1800 to 2059). The number shown with each year shows which calendar to use for that year, as shown on pages 784-785 (The Gregorian calendar was inaugurated Oct. 15, 1582. From that date to Dec. 31, 1582, use calendar 6.)

1583-1802

1583 . . 7	1603 . . 4	1623 . . 1	1643 . . 5	1663 . . 2	1683 . . 6	1703 . . 2	1723 . . 6	1743 . . 3	1763 . . 7	1783 . . 4
1584 . . 8	1604 . 12	1624 . . 9	1644 . 13	1664 . 10	1684 . 14	1704 . 10	1724 . 14	1744 . 11	1764 . . 8	1784 . 12
1585 . . 3	1605 . . 7	1625 . . 4	1645 . . 1	1665 . . 5	1685 . . 2	1705 . . 5	1725 . . 2	1745 . . 6	1765 . . 3	1785 . . 7
1586 . . 4	1606 . . 1	1626 . . 5	1646 . . 2	1666 . . 6	1686 . . 3	1706 . . 6	1726 . . 3	1746 . . 7	1766 . . 4	1786 . . 1
1587 . . 5	1607 . . 2	1627 . . 6	1647 . . 3	1667 . . 7	1687 . . 4	1707 . . 7	1727 . . 4	1747 . . 1	1767 . . 5	1787 . . 2
1588 . 13	1608 . 10	1628 . 14	1648 . 11	1668 . . 8	1688 . 12	1708 . . 8	1728 . 12	1748 . . 9	1768 . 13	1788 . 10
1589 . . 1	1609 . . 5	1629 . . 2	1649 . . 6	1669 . . 3	1689 . . 7	1709 . . 3	1729 . . 7	1749 . . 4	1769 . . 1	1789 . . 5
1590 . . 2	1610 . . 6	1630 . . 3	1650 . . 7	1670 . . 4	1690 . . 1	1710 . . 4	1730 . . 1	1750 . . 5	1770 . . 2	1790 . . 6
1591 . . 3	1611 . . 7	1631 . . 4	1651 . . 1	1671 . . 5	1691 . . 2	1711 . . 5	1731 . . 2	1751 . . 6	1771 . . 3	1791 . . 7
1592 . 11	1612 . . 8	1632 . 12	1652 . . 9	1672 . 13	1692 . 10	1712 . 13	1732 . 10	1752 . 14	1772 . 11	1792 . . 8
1593 . . 6	1613 . . 3	1633 . . 7	1653 . . 4	1673 . . 1	1693 . . 5	1713 . . 1	1733 . . 5	1753 . . 2	1773 . . 6	1793 . . 3
1594 . . 7	1614 . . 4	1634 . . 1	1654 . . 5	1674 . . 2	1694 . . 6	1714 . . 2	1734 . . 6	1754 . . 3	1774 . . 7	1794 . . 4
1595 . . 1	1615 . . 5	1635 . . 2	1655 . . 6	1675 . . 3	1695 . . 7	1715 . . 3	1735 . . 7	1755 . . 4	1775 . . 1	1795 . . 5
1596 . . 9	1616 . 13	1636 . 10	1656 . 14	1676 . 11	1696 . . 8	1716 . 11	1736 . . 8	1756 . 12	1776 . . 9	1796 . 13
1597 . . 4	1617 . . 1	1637 . . 5	1657 . . 2	1677 . . 6	1697 . . 3	1717 . . 6	1737 . . 3	1757 . . 7	1777 . . 4	1797 . . 1
1598 . . 5	1618 . . 2	1638 . . 6	1658 . . 3	1678 . . 7	1698 . . 4	1718 . . 7	1738 . . 4	1758 . . 1	1778 . . 5	1798 . . 2
1599 . . 6	1619 . . 3	1639 . . 7	1659 . . 4	1679 . . 1	1699 . . 5	1719 . . 1	1739 . . 5	1759 . . 2	1779 . . 6	1799 . . 3
1600 . 14	1620 . 11	1640 . . 8	1660 . 12	1680 . . 9	1700 . . 6	1720 . . 9	1740 . 13	1760 . 10	1780 . 14	1800 . . 4
1601 . . 2	1621 . . 6	1641 . . 3	1661 . . 7	1681 . . 4	1701 . . 7	1721 . . 4	1741 . . 1	1761 . . 5	1781 . . 2	1801 . . 5
1602 . . 3	1622 . . 7	1642 . . 4	1662 . . 1	1682 . . 5	1702 . . 1	1722 . . 5	1742 . . 2	1762 . . 6	1782 . . 3	1802 . . 6

The Julian Period

How many days have you lived? To determine this, you must multiply your age by 365, add the number of days since your last birthday until today, and account for all leap years. Chances are your answer would be wrong. Astronomers, however, find it convenient to express dates and long time intervals in days rather than in years, months and days. This is done by placing events within the Julian period.

The Julian period was devised in 1582 by Joseph Scaliger and named after his father Julius (not after the Julian calendar). Scaliger had Julian Day (JD) #1 begin at noon, Jan. 1, 4713 B. C., the most recent time that three major chronological cycles began on the same day — 1) the 28-year solar cycle, after which dates in the Julian calendar (e.g., Feb. 11) return to the same days of the week (e.g., Monday); 2) the 19-year lunar cycle, after which the phases of the moon return to the same dates of the year; and 3) the 15-year indiction cycle, used in ancient Rome to regulate taxes. It will take 7980 years to complete the period, the product of 28, 19, and 15.

Noon of Dec. 31, 1982, marks the beginning of JD 2,445,335; that many days will have passed since the start of the Julian period. The JD at noon of any date in 1983 may be found by adding to this figure the day of the year for that date, which is given in the left hand column in the chart below. Simple JD conversion tables are used by astronomers.

Days Between Two Dates

Table covers period of two ordinary years. Example—Days between Feb. 10, 1982 and Dec. 15, 1983; subtract 41 from 714; answer is 673 days. For leap year, such as 1984, one day must be added.

Date	Jan.	Feb.	Mar.	April	May	June	July	Aug.	Sept.	Oct.	Nov.	Dec.
1	1	32	60	91	121	152	182	213	244	274	305	335
2	2	33	61	92	122	153	183	214	245	275	306	336
3	3	34	62	93	123	154	184	215	246	276	307	337
4	4	35	63	94	124	155	185	216	247	277	308	338
5	5	36	64	95	125	156	186	217	248	278	309	339
6	6	37	65	96	126	157	187	218	249	279	310	340
7	7	38	66	97	127	158	188	219	250	280	311	341
8	8	39	67	98	128	159	189	220	251	281	312	342
9	9	40	68	99	129	160	190	221	252	282	313	343
10	10	41	69	100	130	161	191	222	253	283	314	344
11	11	42	70	101	131	162	192	223	254	284	315	345
12	12	43	71	102	132	163	193	224	255	285	316	346
13	13	44	72	103	133	164	194	225	256	286	317	347
14	14	45	73	104	134	165	195	226	257	287	318	348
15	15	46	74	105	135	166	196	227	258	288	319	349
16	16	47	75	106	136	167	197	228	259	289	320	350
17	17	48	76	107	137	168	198	229	260	290	321	351
18	18	49	77	108	138	169	199	230	261	291	322	352
19	19	50	78	109	139	170	200	231	262	292	323	353
20	20	51	79	110	140	171	201	232	263	293	324	354
21	21	52	80	111	141	172	202	233	264	294	325	355
22	22	53	81	112	142	173	203	234	265	295	326	356
23	23	54	82	113	143	174	204	235	266	296	327	357
24	24	55	83	114	144	175	205	236	267	297	328	358
25	25	56	84	115	145	176	206	237	268	298	329	359
26	26	57	85	116	146	177	207	238	269	299	330	360
27	27	58	86	117	147	178	208	239	270	300	331	361
28	28	59	87	118	148	179	209	240	271	301	332	362
29	29	—	88	119	149	180	210	241	272	302	333	363
30	30	—	89	120	150	181	211	242	273	303	334	364
31	31	—	90	—	151	—	212	243	—	304	—	365

Date	Jan.	Feb.	Mar.	April	May	June	July	Aug.	Sept.	Oct.	Nov.	Dec.
1	366	397	425	456	486	517	547	578	609	639	670	700
2	367	398	426	457	487	518	548	579	610	640	671	701
3	368	399	427	458	488	519	549	580	611	641	672	702
4	369	400	428	459	489	520	550	581	612	642	673	703
5	370	401	429	460	490	521	551	582	613	643	674	704
6	371	402	430	461	491	522	552	583	614	644	675	705
7	372	403	431	462	492	523	553	584	615	645	676	706
8	373	404	432	463	493	524	554	585	616	646	677	707
9	374	405	433	464	494	525	555	586	617	647	678	708
10	375	406	434	465	495	526	556	587	618	648	679	709
11	376	407	435	466	496	527	557	588	619	649	680	710
12	377	408	436	467	497	528	558	589	620	650	681	711
13	378	409	437	468	498	529	559	590	621	651	682	712
14	379	410	438	469	499	530	560	591	622	652	683	713
15	380	411	439	470	500	531	561	592	623	653	684	714
16	381	412	440	471	501	532	562	593	624	654	685	715
17	382	413	441	472	502	533	563	594	625	655	686	716
18	383	414	442	473	503	534	564	595	626	656	687	717
19	384	415	443	474	504	535	565	596	627	657	688	718
20	385	416	444	475	505	536	566	597	628	658	689	719
21	386	417	445	476	506	537	567	598	629	659	690	720
22	387	418	446	477	507	538	568	599	630	660	691	721
23	388	419	447	478	508	539	569	600	631	661	692	722
24	389	420	448	479	509	540	570	601	632	662	693	723
25	390	421	449	480	510	541	571	602	633	663	694	724
26	391	422	450	481	511	542	572	603	634	664	695	725
27	392	423	451	482	512	543	573	604	635	665	696	726
28	393	424	452	483	513	544	574	605	636	666	697	727
29	394	—	453	484	514	545	575	606	637	667	698	728
30	395	—	454	485	515	546	576	607	638	668	699	729
31	396	—	455	—	516	—	577	608	—	669	—	730

Lunar Calendar, Chinese New Year, Vietnamese Tet

The ancient Chinese lunar calendar is divided into 12 months of either 29 or 30 days (compensating for the fact that the mean duration of the lunar month is 29 days, 12 hours, 44.05 minutes). The calendar is synchronized with the solar year by the addition of extra months at fixed intervals.

The Chinese calendar runs on a sexagenary cycle, i.e., 60 years. The cycles 1876-1935 and 1936-1995, with the years grouped under their twelve animal designations, are printed below. The Year 1983 is found in the twelfth column, under Pig, and is known as a "Year of the Pig." Readers can find the animal name for the year of their birth, marriage, etc., in the same chart. (Note: the first 3-7 weeks of each of the western years belong to the previous Chinese year and animal designation.)

Both the western (Gregorian) and traditional lunar calendars are used publicly in China, and two New Year's celebrations are held. On Taiwan, in overseas Chinese communities, and in Vietnam, the lunar calendar has been used only to set the dates for traditional festivals, with the Gregorian system in general use.

The four-day Chinese New Year, Hsin Nien, and the three-day Vietnamese New Year festival, Tet, begin at the first new moon after the sun enters Aquarius. The day may fall, therefore, between Jan. 21 and Feb. 19 of the Gregorian calendar. Jan. 25, 1982 marks the start of the new Chinese year. The date is fixed according to the date of the new moon in the Far East. Since this is west of the International Date Line the date may be one day later than that of the new moon in the United States.

Rat	Ox	Tiger	Hare (Rabbit)	Dragon	Snake	Horse	Sheep (Goat)	Monkey	Rooster	Dog	Pig
1876	1877	1878	1879	1880	1881	1882	1883	1884	1885	1886	1887
1888	1889	1890	1891	1892	1893	1894	1895	1896	1897	1898	1899
1900	1901	1902	1903	1904	1905	1906	1907	1908	1909	1910	1911
1912	1913	1914	1915	1916	1917	1918	1919	1920	1921	1922	1923
1924	1925	1926	1927	1928	1929	1930	1931	1932	1933	1934	1935
1936	1937	1938	1939	1940	1941	1942	1943	1944	1945	1946	1947
1948	1949	1950	1951	1952	1953	1954	1955	1956	1957	1958	1959
1960	1961	1962	1963	1964	1965	1966	1967	1968	1969	1970	1971
1972	1973	1974	1975	1976	1977	1978	1979	1980	1981	1982	1983
1984	1985	1986	1987	1988	1989	1990	1991	1992	1993	1994	1995

Chronological Eras, 1983

The year 1983 of the Christian Era comprises the latter part of the 207th and the beginning of the 208th year of the independence of the United States of America.

Era	Year	Begins in 1983		Era	Year	Begins in 1983	
Byzantine	7492	Sept.	14	Japanese	2643	Jan.	1
Jewish	5744	Sept. (sunset)	8	Grecian (Seleucidae)	2295	Sept. or Oct.	14 14
Olympiads (Third year of Olympiad 690)	2759	July	1	Diocletian	1700	Sept.	12
Roman (Ab Urbe Condita)	2736	Jan.	14	Indian (Saka)	1905	Mar.	22
Nabonassar (Babylonian)	2732	Apr.	28	Mohammedan (Hegira)	1404	Oct.	8

Chronological Cycles, 1983

Dominical Letter	B	Golden Number (Lunar Cycle)	VIII	Roman Indiction	6
Epact	16	Solar Cycle	4	Julian Period (year of)	6696

Standard Time Differences — North American Cities

At 12 o'clock noon, Eastern Standard Time, the standard time in N.A. cities is as follows:

Akron, Oh.	12.00	Noon	Frankfort, Ky.	12.00	Noon	Pierre, S.D.	11.00	A.M.
Albuquerque, N.M.	10.00	A.M.	Galveston, Tex.	11.00	A.M.	Pittsburgh, Pa.	12.00	Noon
Atlanta, Ga.	12.00	Noon	Grand Rapids, Mich.	12.00	Noon	Portland, Me.	12.00	Noon
Austin, Tex.	11.00	A.M.	Halifax, N.S.	1.00	P.M.	Portland, Ore.	9.00	A.M.
Baltimore, Md.	12.00	Noon	Hartford, Conn.	12.00	Noon	Providence, R.I.	12.00	Noon
Birmingham, Ala.	11.00	A.M.	Helena, Mon.	10.00	A.M.	*Regina, Sask.	11.00	A.M.
Bismarck, N.D.	11.00	A.M.	*Honolulu, Ha.	7.00	A.M.	Reno, Nev.	9.00	A.M.
Boise, Ida.	10.00	A.M.	Houston, Tex.	11.00	A.M.	Richmond, Va.	12.00	Noon
Boston, Mass.	12.00	Noon	*Indianapolis, Ind.	12.00	Noon	Rochester, N.Y.	12.00	Noon
Buffalo, N.Y.	12.00	Noon	Jacksonville, Fla.	12.00	Noon	Sacramento, Cal.	9.00	A.M.
Butte, Mon.	10.00	A.M.	Juneau, Alas.	9.00	A.M.	St. John's, Nfld.	1.30	P.M.
Calgary, Alta.	10.00	A.M.	Kansas City, Mo.	11.00	A.M.	St. Louis, Mo.	11.00	A.M.
Charleston, S.C.	12.00	Noon	Knoxville, Tenn.	12.00	Noon	St. Paul, Minn.	11.00	A.M.
Charleston, W.Va.	12.00	Noon	Lexington, Ky.	12.00	Noon	Salt Lake City, Ut.	10.00	A.M.
Charlotte, N.C.	12.00	Noon	Lincoln, Neb.	11.00	A.M.	San Antonio, Tex.	11.00	A.M.
Charlottetown, P.E.I.	1.00	P.M.	Little Rock, Ark.	11.00	A.M.	San Diego, Cal.	9.00	A.M.
Chattanooga, Tenn.	12.00	Noon	Los Angeles, Cal.	9.00	A.M.	San Francisco, Cal.	9.00	A.M.
Cheyenne, Wy.	10.00	A.M.	Louisville, Ky.	12.00	Noon	Santa Fe, N.M.	10.00	A.M.
Chicago, Ill.	11.00	A.M.	*Mexico City	11.00	A.M.	Savannah, Ga.	12.00	Noon
Cleveland, Oh.	12.00	Noon	Memphis, Tenn.	11.00	A.M.	Seattle, Wash.	9.00	A.M.
Colorado Spr., Col.	10.00	A.M.	Miami, Fla.	12.00	Noon	Shreveport, La.	11.00	A.M.
Columbus, Oh.	12.00	Noon	Milwaukee, Wis.	11.00	A.M.	Sioux Falls, S.D.	11.00	A.M.
Dallas, Tex.	11.00	A.M.	Minneapolis, Minn.	11.00	A.M.	Spokane, Wash.	9.00	A.M.
*Dawson, Yuk.	9.00	A.M.	Mobile, Ala.	11.00	A.M.	Tampa, Fla.	12.00	Noon
Dayton, Oh.	12.00	Noon	Montreal, Que.	12.00	Noon	Toledo, Oh.	12.00	Noon
Denver, Col.	10.00	A.M.	Nashville, Tenn.	11.00	A.M.	Topeka, Kan.	11.00	A.M.
Des Moines, Ia.	11.00	A.M.	New Haven, Conn.	12.00	Noon	Toronto, Ont.	12.00	Noon
Detroit, Mich.	12.00	Noon	New Orleans, La.	11.00	A.M.	*Tucson, Ariz.	10.00	A.M.
Duluth, Minn.	11.00	A.M.	New York, N.Y.	12.00	Noon	Tulsa, Okla.	11.00	A.M.
El Paso, Tex.	10.00	A.M.	Nome, Alas.	6.00	A.M.	Vancouver, B.C.	9.00	A.M.
Erie, Pa.	12.00	Noon	Norfolk, Va.	12.00	Noon	Washington, D.C.	12.00	Noon
Evansville, Ind.	11.00	A.M.	Okla. City, Okla.	11.00	A.M.	Wichita, Kan.	11.00	A.M.
Fairbanks, Alas.	7.00	A.M.	Omaha, Neb.	11.00	A.M.	Wilmington, Del.	12.00	Noon
Flint, Mich.	12.00	Noon	Peoria, Ill.	11.00	A.M.	Winnipeg, Man.	11.00	A.M.
*Fort Wayne, Ind.	12.00	Noon	Philadelphia, Pa.	12.00	Noon			
Fort Worth, Tex.	11.00	A.M.	*Phoenix, Ariz.	10.00	A.M.			

*Cities with an asterisk do not observe daylight savings time. During much of the year, it is necessary to add one hour to the cities which do observe daylight savings time to get the proper time relation.

Standard Time Differences—World Cities

The time indicated in the table is fixed by law and is called the legal time, or, more generally, Standard Time. Use of Daylight Saving Time varies widely. *Indicates morning of the following day. At 12.00, Eastern Standard Time, the standard time (in 24-hour time) in foreign cities is as follows:

Alexandria	19 00	Copenhagen	18 00	Lima	12 00	Santiago (Chile)	13 00
Amsterdam	18 00	Dacca	23 00	Lisbon	18 00	Seoul	2 00*
Athens	19 00	Delhi	22 30	Liverpool	17 00	Shanghai	1 00*
Auckland	5 00*	Dublin	17 00	London	17 00	Singapore	00 30*
Baghdad	20 00	Gdansk	18 00	Madrid	18 00	Stockholm	18 00
Bangkok	0 00	Geneva	18 00	Manila	1 00*	Sydney (Australia)	3 00*
Belfast	17 00	Havana	12 00	Melbourne	3 00*	Tashkent	23 00
Berlin	18 00	Helsinki	19 00	Montevideo	14 00	Teheran	20 30
Bogota	12 00	Ho Chi Minh City	1 00*	Moscow	20 00	Tel Aviv	19 00
Bombay	22 30	Hong Kong	1 00*	Nagasaki	2 00*	Tokyo	2 00*
Bremen	18 00	Istanbul	19 00	Oslo	18 00	Valparaiso	13 00
Brussels	18 00	Jakarta	0 00	Paris	18 00	Vladivostok	3 00*
Bucharest	19 00	Jerusalem	19 00	Peking	1 00*	Vienna	18 00
Budapest	18 00	Johannesburg	19 00	Prague	18 00	Warsaw	18 00
Buenos Aires	14 00	Karachi	22 00	Rangoon	23 30	Wellington (N.Z.)	5 00*
Calcutta	22 30	Le Havre	18 00	Rio De Janeiro	14 00	Yokohama	2 00*
Cape Town	19 00	Leningrad	20 00	Rome	18 00	Zurich	18 00
Caracas	13 00						

Standard Time, Daylight Saving Time, and Others

Source: Defense Mapping Agency Hydrographic Center; Department of Transportation; National Bureau of Standards; U.S. Naval Observatory

Standard Time

Standard time is reckoned from Greenwich, England, recognized as the Prime Meridian of Longitude. The world is divided into 24 zones, each 15° of arc, or one hour in time apart. The Greenwich meridian (0°) extends through the center of the initial zone, and the zones to the east are numbered from 1 to 12 with the prefix "minus" indicating the number of hours to be subtracted to obtain Greenwich Time.

Westward zones are similarly numbered, but prefixed "plus" showing the number of hours that must be added to get Greenwich Time. While these zones apply generally to sea areas, it should be noted that the Standard Time maintained in many countries does not coincide with zone time. A graphical representation of the zones is shown on the Standard Time Zone Chart of the World published by the Defense Mapping Agency Hydrographic Center, Washington, DC 20390.

The United States and possessions are divided into eight Standard Time zones, as set forth by the Uniform Time Act of 1966, which also provides for the use of Daylight Saving Time therein. Each zone is approximately 15° of longitude in width. All places in each zone use, instead of their own local time, the time counted from the transit of the "mean sun" across the Standard Time meridian which passes near the middle of that zone.

These time zones are designated as Atlantic, Eastern, Central, Mountain, Pacific, Yukon, Alaska-Hawaii, and Bering, and the time in these zones is basically reckoned from the 60th, 75th, 90th, 105th, 120th, 135th, 150th, 165th meridians west of Greenwich. The line wanders to conform to local geographical regions. The time in the various zones is earlier than Greenwich Time by 4, 5, 6, 7, 8, 9, 10, and 11 hours respectively.

24-Hour Time

24-hour time is widely used in scientific work throughout the world. In the United States it is used also in operations of the Armed Forces. In Europe it is used in preference to the 12-hour a.m. and p.m. system. With the 24-hour system the day begins at midnight and hours are numbered 0 through 23.

International Date Line

The Date Line is a zig-zag line that approximately coincides with the 180th meridian, and it is where each calendar day begins. The date must be advanced one day when crossing in a westerly direction and set back one day when crossing in an easterly direction.

The line is deflected between north latitude 48° and 75°, so that all Asia lies to the west of it.

Daylight Saving Time

Daylight Saving Time is achieved by advancing the clock one hour. Under the Uniform Time Act, which became effective in 1967, all states, the District of Columbia, and U.S. possessions were to observe Daylight Saving Time beginning at 2 a.m. on the last Sunday in April and ending at 2 a.m. on the last Sunday in October. Any state could, by law, exempt itself; a 1972 amendment to the act authorized states split by time zones to take that into consideration in exempting themselves. Arizona, Hawaii, Puerto Rico, the Virgin Islands, American Samoa, and part of Indiana are now exempt. Some local zone boundaries in Kansas, Texas, Florida, Michigan, and Alaska have been modified in the last several years by the Dept. of Transportation, which oversees the act. To conserve energy Congress put most of the nation on year-round Daylight Saving Time for two years effective Jan. 6, 1974 through Oct. 26, 1975; but a further bill, signed in October, 1974, restored Standard Time from the last Sunday in that month to the last Sunday in February, 1975. At the end of 1975, Congress failed to renew this temporary legislation and the nation returned to the older end-of April to end-of October DST system.

Legal or Public Holidays, 1983

Technically there are no national holidays in the United States; each state has jurisdiction over its holidays, which are designated by legislative enactment or executive proclamation. In practice, however, most states observe the federal legal public holidays, even though the President and Congress can legally designate holidays only for the District of Columbia and for federal employees.

Federal legal public holidays are: New Year's Day, Washington's Birthday, Memorial Day, Independence Day, Labor Day, Columbus Day, Veterans Day, Thanksgiving, and Christmas.

Chief Legal or Public Holidays

When a holiday falls on a Sunday or a Saturday it is usually observed on the following Monday or preceding Friday. For some holidays, government and business closing practices vary. In most states, the office of the Secretary of State can provide details of holiday closings.

Jan. 1 (Saturday) — New Year's Day. All the states.

Feb. 12 (Saturday) — Lincoln's Birthday. Alas., Fla., Ill., Ind., Kan., Md., Mich., N.M., Pa., Ut., Vt., Wash., W. Va. It is celebrated in Ariz., Del., Ore. on Feb. 7.

Feb. 21 (3d Monday in Feb.) — Washington's Birthday. All the states. In several states the holiday is called Presidents' Day or Washington-Lincoln Day.

Apr. 1 — (Good Friday). Observed in all the states. A legal or public holiday in Conn., Del., Fla., Ha., Ind., Ky., La., Md., N.D., N.J., Tenn., and W.V.

May 30 (last Monday in May) — Memorial Day. All the states except Miss. and S.C.

July 4 (Monday) — Independence Day. All the states.

Sept. 5 (1st Mon. in Sept.) — Labor Day. All the states.

Oct. 10 (2d Mon. in Oct.) — Columbus Day. Ariz., Cal.; Col., Conn., D.C., Del., Fla., Ga., Ha., Ida., Ill., Ind., Kan., Me., Mass., Mich., Minn., Mo., Mont., Nev., N.H., N.J., N.M., N.Y., N.C., Oh., Pa., R.I., S.D., Tenn., Tex., Ut., Vt., Va., W.Va., Wis., Wyo., P.R. Observed on Oct. 12 in Md. and Okla.

Nov. 8 (1st Tues after 1st Mon. in Nov.) — General Election Day. Conn., D.C., Ind., Ky., Mo., Mont., N.J., N.Y., N.C., Pa., Tex., Va.

Nov. 11 (Friday) — Armistice Day (Veterans' Day). All the states.

Nov. 24 (4th Thurs. in Nov.) — Thanksgiving Day). All the states. The day after Thanksgiving is also celebrated as a full or partial holiday in some states.

Dec. 25 (Sunday) — Christmas. All the states.

Other Legal or Public Holidays

Dates are for 1983 observance, when known.

Jan. 9 — Volunteer Fireman Day (2d Sunday in Jan.). In New Jersey.

Jan. 15 — Martin Luther King's Birthday. D.C., Fla., Ill., Md., Mass., Mich., Minn., N.J., Oh., Pa., S.C. In Va. on Jan. 1. Many schools and black groups in other states also observe the day.

Jan. 19 — Robert E. Lee's Birthday. Ala., Ark., Fla., Ga., La., Miss., N.C., S.C. Lee-Jackson Day in Va. Confederate Heroes Day in Tex.

Feb. 14 — Admission Day. In Ore.

Mar. 2 — Texas Independence Day. In that state.

Mar. 1 — Town Meeting Day (1st Tuesday in Mar.). In Vt.

Mar. 25 — Maryland Day. In that state.

Mar. 26 — Prince Jonah Kuhio Kalanianaole Day. In Ha.

Mar. 29 — Seward's Day. In Alas.

Apr. 12 — Anniversary of signing Halifax Resolves. In N.C.

Apr. 19 — Patriot's Day. In Mass., Me.

Apr. 26 — Confederate Memorial Day. In Fla., Ga., Miss.

May 4 — Independence Day. In R.I.

May 10 — Confederate Memorial Day. In N.C.

May 18 — Primary Election Day. In Pa.

June 3 — Confederate Memorial Day. In La. Jefferson Davis's Birthday in Fla., Ga. Celebrated in Miss. on the first Mon. in June (June 6 in 1983).

June 11 — King Kamehameha I Day. In Ha.

June 14 — Flag Day. Observed in all states; A legal holiday in Pa.

June 17 — Bunker Hill Day. In Boston and Suffolk County, Mass.

June 25 — Pioneer Day. In Utah

July 25 — Constitution Day. In Puerto Rico.

Aug. 1 — Colorado Day. In that state.

Aug. 8 — Victory Day (2d Monday in August). In Ariz.

Aug. 16 — Bennington Battle Day. In Vt.

Aug. 19 — Admission Day (3d Friday in August). In Ha.

Aug. 27 — Lyndon Johnson's Birthday. In Tex.

Sept. 9 — Admissions Day. In Cal.

Sept. 12 — Defenders' Day. In Md.

Sept. 14 — Primary Election Day. In Wis.

Oct 10 — Pioneer Day (2d Monday in Oct.). In S.D.

Oct. 18 — Alaska Day. In that state.

Oct. 31 — Nevada Day. In that state.

Nov. 1 — All Saints' Day. In La.

Days Usually Observed

American Indian Day (Sept. 23 in 1983). Always fourth Friday in September.

Arbor Day. Tree-planting day. First observed April 10, 1872, in Nebraska. Now observed in every state in the Union except Alaska (often on the last Friday in April). A legal holiday in Utah (always last Friday in April), and in Nebraska (April 22).

Armed Forces Day (May 21 in 1983). Always third Saturday in that month, by presidential proclamation. Replaced Army, Navy, and Air Force Days.

Bill of Rights Day, Dec. 15. By Act of Congress. Bill of Rights took effect Dec. 15, 1791.

Bird Day. Often observed with Arbor Day.

Child Health Day (Oct. 3 in 1983). Always first Monday in October, by presidential proclamation.

Citizenship Day, Sept. 17. President Truman, Feb. 29, 1952, signed bill designating Sept. 17 as annual Citizenship Day. It replaced I Am An American Day, formerly 3rd Sunday in May and Constitution Day, formerly Sept. 17.

Easter Monday (Apr. 4 in 1983). A statutory day in Canada.

Easter Sunday (Apr. 3 in 1983).

Elizabeth Cady Stanton Day, Nov. 12. Birthday of pioneer leader for equal rights for women.

Epiphany (Jan. 6 in 1982). Observed in Puerto Rico.

Father's Day (June 19 in 1983). Always third Sunday in that month.

Flag Day, June 14. By presidential proclamation. It is a legal holiday in Pennsylvania.

Forefathers' Day, Dec. 21. Landing on Plymouth Rock, in 1620. Is celebrated with dinners by New England societies especially "Down East."

Four Chaplains Memorial Day, Feb. 3.

Gen. Douglas MacArthur Day, Jan. 26. A memorial day in Arkansas.

Gen. Pulaski Memorial Day, Oct. 11. Native of Poland and Revolutionary War hero; died (Oct. 11, 1779) from wounds received at the seige of Savannah, Ga. Observed officially in Indiana.

Georgia Day, Feb. 12. Observed in that state. Commemorates landing of first colonists in 1733.

Grandparent's Day (Sept. 11 in 1983). Always first Sunday after Labor Day. Legislated in 1979.

Groundhog Day, Feb. 2. A popular belief is that if the groundhog sees his shadow this day, he returns to his burrow and winter continues 6 weeks longer.

Halloween, Oct. 31. The evening before All Saints or All-Hallows Day. Informally observed in the U.S. with masquerading and pumpkin-decorations. Traditionally an occasion for children to play pranks.

Loyalty Day, May 1. By act of Congress.

May Day. Name popularly given to May 1st. Celebrated as Labor Day in most of the world, and by some groups in the U.S. Observed in many schools as a Spring Festival.

Minnesota Day, May 11. In that state.

Mother's Day (May 8 in 1983). Always second Sunday in that month. First celebrated in Philadelphia in 1908. Mother's Day has become an international holiday.

National Day of Prayer. By presidential proclamation each year on a day other than a Sunday.

National Freedom Day, Feb. 1. To commemorate the signing of the Thirteenth Amendment, abolishing slavery, Feb. 1, 1865. By presidential proclamation.

National Maritime Day, May 22. First proclaimed 1935 in commemoration of the departure of the SS Savannah, from Savannah, Ga., on May 22, 1819, on the first successful transatlantic voyage under steam propulsion. By presidential proclamation.

Pan American Day, Apr. 14. In 1890 the First International Conference of American States, meeting in Washington, was held on that date. A resolution was adopted which resulted in the creation of the organization known today as the Pan American Union. By presidential proclamation.

Primary Election Day. Observed usually only when presidential or general elections are held.

Reformation Day, Oct. 31. Observed by Protestant groups.

Sadie Hawkins Day (Nov. 12 in 1983). First Saturday after November 11.

St. Patrick's Day, Mar. 17. Observed by Irish Societies, especially with parades.

St. Valentine's Day, Feb. 14. Festival of a martyr beheaded at Rome under Emperor Claudius. Association of this day with lovers has no connection with the saint and probably had its origin in an old belief that on this day birds begin to choose their mates.

Susan B. Anthony Day, Feb. 15. Birthday of a pioneer crusader for equal rights for women.

United Nations Day, Oct. 24. By presidential proclamation, to commemorate founding of United Nations.

Verrazano Day, Apr. 7. Observed by New York State, to commemorate the probable discovery of New York harbor by Giovanni da Verrazano in April, 1524.

Victoria Day (May 23 in 1983). Birthday of Queen Victoria, a statutory day in Canada, celebrated the first Monday before May 25.

Frances Willard Day, Sept. 28. Observed in Minnesota to honor the educator and temperance leader.

Will Rogers Day, Nov. 4. In Oklahoma.

World Poetry Day, Oct. 15.

Wright Brothers Day, Dec. 17. By presidential designation, to commemorate first successful flight by Orville and Wilbur Wright, Dec. 17, 1903.

Other Holidays, Anniversaries, Events — 1983

Feb. 11 (Fri.) — National Inventors' Day.
Feb. 16 — Ash Wednesday.
Feb. 17, 1933 — Newsweek magazine is founded.
Mar. 4, 1933 — Chicago World's Fair opens, celebrating "Century of Progress," and fan-dancer Sally Rand attracts thousands.
Mar. 12, 1933 — Pres. Franklin D. Roosevelt begins radio "fireside chats."
Mar. 18, 1933 — The Tennessee Valley Authority Act is passed by Congress.
Mar. 24, 1883 — Brooklyn Bridge opens.
Mar. 29 (Tues.) — Passover begins.
Apr. 1 — April Fool's Day.
Apr. 1 — Good Friday.
June 24 (Fri.) — San Juan Day in Puerto Rico. St. Jean Day in Quebec.
June 26 (Sun.) — United Nations Charter Day.
July 1 (Fri.) — Canada Day.
July 14 (Thurs.) — Bastille Day in France.
July 25 (Mon.) — Puerto Rico Constitution Day.
July 31, 1933 — "Jack Armstrong, the All-American Boy" begins on Chicago's KBBM-radio, sponsored by 9-year-old Wheaties, "the Breakfast of Champions."
Aug. 6 (Sat.) — Hiroshima Day.
Aug. 7, 1933 — "Alley Oop" cartoon strip by V.T. Hamlin introduced.
Sept. 8, 1933 — Northern Pacific Railroad completed.
Sept. 8 (Thurs.) — Rosh Hashanah.
Sept. 17 (Sat.) — Yom Kippur.
Oct. 4, 1883 — The Orient Express, Europe's first transcontinental train, takes its first run.
Nov. 5 (Sat.) — Guy Fawkes Day in Britain.
Nov. 19 (Sat.) — Discovery of Puerto Rico Day.
Dec. 1 (Thurs.) — Chanukkah.
Dec. 12 (Mon.) — Fiesta of Our Lady of Guadalupe in Mexico.
Dec. 27 (Tues.) — Boxing Day in the British Commonwealth of Nations.

Wind Chill Table

Source: National Oceanic and Atmospheric Administration, U.S. Commerce Department

Both temperature and wind cause heat loss from body surfaces. A combination of cold and wind makes a body feel colder than the actual temperature. The table shows, for example, that a temperature of 20 degrees Fahrenheit, plus a wind of 20 miles per hour, causes a body heat loss equal to that in minus 10 degrees with no wind. In other words, the wind makes 20 degrees feel like minus 10.

Top line of figures shows actual temperatures in degrees Fahrenheit. Column at left shows wind speeds.

MPH	35	30	25	20	15	10	5	0	−5	−10	−15	−20	−25	−30	−35	−40	−45
5	33	27	21	19	12	7	0	−5	−10	−15	−21	−26	−31	−36	−42	−47	−52
10	22	16	10	3	−3	−9	−15	−22	−27	−34	−40	−46	−52	−58	−64	−71	−77
15	16	9	2	−5	−11	−18	−25	−31	−38	−45	−51	−58	−65	−72	−78	−85	−92
20	12	4	−3	−10	−17	−24	−31	−39	−46	−53	−60	−67	−74	−81	−88	−95	−103
25	8	1	−7	−15	−22	−29	−36	−44	−51	−59	−66	−74	−81	−88	−96	−103	−110
30	6	−2	−10	−18	−25	−33	−41	−49	−56	−64	−71	−79	−86	−93	−101	−109	−116
35	4	−4	−12	−20	−27	−35	−43	−52	−58	−67	−74	−82	−89	−97	−105	−113	−120
40	3	−5	−13	−21	−29	−37	−45	−53	−60	−69	−76	−84	−92	−100	−107	−115	−123
45	2	−6	−14	−22	−30	−38	−46	−54	−62	−70	−78	−85	−93	−102	−109	−117	−125

(Wind speeds greater than 45 mph have little additional chilling effect.)

Temperature-Humidity (Discomfort) Index

The temperature-humidity index, THI, is a measure of summertime human discomfort resulting from the combined effects of temperature and humidity. (The THI may be calculated by adding wet-bulb and dry-bulb temperatures, multiplying the sum by 0.4 and adding 15.)

The following chart shows the combinations of temperature degrees and humidity percentages which produce discomfort for most persons (the equivalent of a THI value of 75) and those which produce acute discomfort for almost everyone (equivalent to a THI of 80).

Discomfort temp.-humid.	Acute discomfort temp.-humid.	Discomfort temp.-humid.	Acute discomfort temp.-humid.	Discomfort temp.-humid.	Acute discomfort temp.-humid.
75°—100%	81°—100%	82°—49%	88°—54%	90°—14%	96°—20%
76°— 91%	82°— 93%	83°—43%	89°—49%	91°—10%	97°—16%
77°— 82%	83°— 86%	84°—38%	90°—43%	92°— 7%	98°—13%
78°— 75%	84°— 78%	85°—33%	91°—38%	93°— 5%	99°—11%
79°— 68%	85°— 71%	86°—29%	92°—34%	94°— 3%	100°— 8%
80°— 61%	86°— 65%	87°—25%	93°—30%	95°— 1%	101°— 6%
81°— 55%	87°— 59%	88°—20%	94°—26%	96°— 1%	102°— 3%
		89°—17%	95°—23%	97°— 1%	103°— 1%

From 95 degrees up there is discomfort at any humidity. When the temperature is over 102 degrees there is acute discomfort at any humidity.

Tides and Their Causes

Source: National Oceanic and Atmospheric Administration, U.S. Commerce Department

The tides are a natural phenomenon involving the alternating rise and fall in the large fluid bodies of the earth caused by the combined gravitational attraction of the sun and moon. The combination of these two variable force influences produce the complex recurrent cycle of the tides. Tides may occur in both oceans and seas, to a limited extent in large lakes, the atmosphere, and, to a very minute degree, in the earth itself. The period between succeeding tides varies as the result of many factors and force influences.

The tide-generating force represents the difference between (1) the centrifugal force produced by the revolution of the earth around the common center-of-gravity of the earth-moon system and (2) the gravitational attraction of the moon acting upon the earth's overlying waters. Since, on the average, the moon is only 238,857 miles from the earth compared with the sun's much greater distance of 93,000,000 miles, this closer distance outranks the much smaller mass of the moon compared with that of the sun, and the moon's tide-raising force is, accordingly, 2 1/5 times that of the sun.

The effect of the tide-generating forces of the moon and sun acting tangentially to the earth's surface (the so-called "tractive force") tends to cause a maximum accumulation of the waters of the oceans at two diametrically opposite positions on the surface of the earth and to withdraw compensating amounts of water from all points 90° removed from the positions of these tidal bulges. As the earth rotates beneath the maxima and minima of these tide-generating forces, a sequence of two high tides, separated by two low tides, ideally is produced each day.

Twice in each lunar month, when the sun, moon, and earth are directly aligned, with the moon between the earth and the sun (at new moon) or on the opposite side of the earth from the sun (at full moon), the sun and the moon exert their gravitational force in a mutual or additive fashion. Higher high tides and lower low tides are produced. These are called *spring* tides. At two positions 90° in between, the gravitational forces of the moon and sun — imposed at right angles—tend to counteract each other to the greatest extent, and the range between high and low tides is reduced. These are called *neap* tides. This semi-monthly variation between the spring and neap tides is called the *phase inequality*.

The inclination of the moon's orbit to the equator also produces a difference in the height of succeeding high tides and in the extent of depression of succeeding low tides which is known as the *diurnal inequality*. In extreme cases, this phenomenon can result in only one high tide and one low tide each day.

The actual amount of the uplift of the waters in the deep ocean may amount to only one or two feet. However, as this tide approaches shoal waters and its effects are augmented the tidal range may be greatly increased. In Nova Scotia along the narrow channel of the Bay of Fundy, the range of tides or difference between high and low waters, may reach 43 1/2 feet or more (under spring tide conditions) due to resonant amplification.

At New Orleans, the periodic rise and fall of the tide varies with the state of the Mississippi, being about 10 inches at low stage and zero at high. The Canadian Tide Tables for 1972 gave a maximum range of nearly 50 feet at Leaf Basin, Ungava Bay.

In every case, actual high or low tide can vary considerably from the average due to weather conditions such as strong winds, abrupt barometric pressure changes, or prolonged periods of extreme high or low pressure.

The Average Rise and Fall of Tides

Places	Ft.	In.	Places	Ft.	In.	Places	Ft.	In.
Baltimore, Md.	1	1	Mobile, Ala.	1	6	San Diego, Cal.	4	1
Boston, Mass.	9	6	New London, Conn.	2	7	Sandy Hook, N.J.	4	7
Charleston, S.C.	5	2	Newport, R.I.	3	6	San Francisco, Cal.	4	0
Colon, Panama	1	1	New York, N.Y.	4	6	Savannah, Ga.	7	5
Eastport, Me.	18	2	Old Pt. Comfort, Va.	2	6	Seattle, Wash.	7	7
Galveston, Tex.	1	5	Philadelphia, Pa.	5	11	Tampa, Fla.	2	10
Halifax, N.S.	4	5	Portland, Me.	9	0	Vancouver, B.C.	10	6
Key West, Fla.	1	4	St. John's, Nfld.	2	7	Washington, D.C.	2	11

Speed of Winds in the U.S.

Source: National Oceanic and Atmospheric Administration, U.S. Commerce Department

Miles per hour — average through 1980. High through 1980. Wind velocities in true values.

Station	Avg.	High	Station	Avg.	High	Station	Avg.	High
Albuquerque, N.M.	9.0	90	Helena, Mont.	7.9	73	New York, N.Y.(c)	9.4	70
Anchorage, Alas.	6.8	61	Honolulu, Ha.	11.8	67	Omaha, Neb.	10.7	109
Atlanta, Ga.	9.1	70	Jacksonville, Fla.	8.3	82	Pensacola, Fla.	8.3	53
Bismarck, N.D.	10.4	72	Key West, Fla.	11.3	84	Philadelphia, Pa.	9.6	73
Boston, Mass.	12.6	61	Knoxville, Tenn.	7.2	36	Pittsburgh, Pa.	9.3	58
Buffalo, N.Y.	12.2	91	Little Rock, Ark.	8.1	65	Portland, Ore.	7.9	88
Cape Hatteras, N.C.	11.4	(b)110	Louisville, Ky.	8.4	61	Rochester, N.Y.	9.8	73
Chattanooga, Tenn.	6.2	37	Memphis, Tenn.	9.1	46	St. Louis, Mo.	9.6	60
Chicago, Ill.	10.3	58	Miami, Fla.	9.2	(a)74	Salt Lake City, Ut.	8.8	71
Cincinnati, Oh.	7.1	49	Minneapolis, Minn.	10.5	92	San Diego, Cal.	6.7	56
Cleveland, Oh.	10.8	74	Mobile, Ala.	9.1	(b)63	San Francisco, Cal.	10.5	58
Denver, Col.	9.0	56	Montgomery, Ala.	6.7	72	Savannah, Ga.	8.0	66
Detroit, Mich.	10.2	46	Mt. Washington, N.H.	35.0	231	Spokane, Wash.	8.7	59
Fort Smith, Ark.	7.6	60	Nashville, Tenn.	8.0	35	Toledo, Oh.	9.5	72
Galveston, Tex.	11.0	(d)100	New Orleans, La.	8.2	(b)98	Washington, D.C.	9.3	78

(a) Highest velocity ever recorded in Miami area was 132 mph, at former station in Miami Beach in September, 1926.
(b) Previous location. (c) Data for Central Park, Battery Place data through 1960, avg. 14.5, high 113. (d) Recorded before anemometer blew away. Estimated high 120.

The Meaning of "One Inch of Rain"

An acre of ground contains 43,560 square feet. Consequently, a rainfall of 1 inch over 1 acre of ground would mean a total of 6,272,640 cubic inches of water. This is equivalent of 3,630 cubic feet.

As a cubic foot of pure water weights about 62.4 pounds, the exact amount varying with the density, it follows that the weight of a uniform coating of 1 inch of rain over 1 acre of surface would be 226,512 pounds, or about 113 short tons. The weight of 1 U.S. gallon of pure water is about 8.345 pounds. Consequently a rainfall of 1 inch over 1 acre of ground would mean 27,143 gallons of water.

National Weather Service Watches and Warnings

Source: National Weather Service, NOAA, U.S. Commerce Department

National Weather Service forecasters issue a Tornado Watch for a specific area where it is reasonably possible that tornadoes may occur during the valid time of the watch. A Watch is to alert people to watch for tornado activity and listen for a Tornado Warning. A Tornado Warning means that a tornado has been sighted or indicated by radar, and that safety precautions should be taken at once. A Hurricane Watch means that an existing hurricane poses a threat to coastal and inland communities in the area specified by the Watch. A Hurricane Warning means hurricane force winds and/or dangerously high water and exceptionally high waves are expected in a specified coastal area within 24 hours.

Tornado—A violent rotating column of air pendant from a thundercloud, usually recognized as a funnel-shaped vortex accompanied by a loud roar. With rotating winds est. up to 300 mph., it is the most destructive storm. Tornado paths have varied in length from a few feet to nearly 300 miles (avg. 5 mi.); diameter from a few feet to over a mile (average 220 yards); average forward speed, 25-40 mph.

Cyclone—An atmospheric circulation of winds rotating counterclockwise in the northern hemisphere and clockwise in the southern hemisphere. Tornadoes, hurricanes, and the lows shown on weather maps are all examples of cyclones having various sizes and intensities. Cyclones are usually accompanied by precipitation or stormy weather.

Hurricane—A severe cyclone originating over tropical ocean waters and having winds 74 miles an hour or higher. (In the western Pacific, such storms are known as typhoons.) The area of strong winds takes the form of a circle or an oval, sometimes as much as 500 miles in diameter. In the lower latitudes hurricanes usually move toward the west or northwest at 10 to 15 mph. When the center approaches 25° to 30° North Latitude, direction of motion often changes to northeast, with increased forward speed.

Blizzard—A severe weather condition characterized by low temperatures and by strong winds bearing a great amount of snow (mostly fine, dry snow picked up from the ground). The National Weather Service specifies, for blizzard, a wind of 35 miles an hour or higher, temperatures 20°F. or lower, and sufficient falling and/or blowing snow to reduce visibility to less than 1/4 of a mile. For "severe blizzard" wind speeds of 45 mph or more, temperature near or below 10°F., and visibility reduced by snow to near zero.

Monsoon—A name for seasonal winds (derived from Arabic "mausim," a season). It was first applied to the winds over the Arabian Sea, which blow for six months from northeast and six months from southwest, but it has been extended to similar winds in other parts of the world. The monsoons are strongest on the southern and eastern sides of Asia.

Flood—The condition that occurs when water overflows the natural or artificial confines of a stream or other body of water, or accumulates by drainage over low-lying areas.

National Weather Service Marine Warnings and Advisories

Small Craft Advisory: A Small Craft Advisory alerts mariners to sustained (exceeding two hours) weather and/or sea conditions either present or forecast, potentially hazardous to small boats. Hazardous conditions may include winds of 18 to 33 knots and/or dangerous wave or inlet conditions. It is the responsibility of the mariner, based on his experience and size or type of boat, to determine if the conditions are hazardous. When a mariner becomes aware of a Small Craft Advisory, he should immediately obtain the latest marine forecast to determine the reason for the Advisory.

Gale Warning indicates that winds within the range 34 to 47 knots are forecast for the area.

Storm Warning indicates that winds 48 knots and above, no matter how high the speed, are forecast for the area. However, if the winds are associated with a tropical cyclone (hurricane), the storm warning indicates that winds within the range 48 to 63 knots are forecast.

Hurricane Warning indicates that winds 64 knots and above are forecast for the area.

Primary sources of dissemination are commercial radio, TV, U.S. Coast Guard Radio stations, and NOAA VHF-FM broadcasts. These broadcasts on 162.40 and 162.55 MHz can usually be received 20-40 miles from the transmitting antenna site, depending on terrain and quality of the receiver used. Where transmitting antennas are on high ground, the range is somewhat greater, reaching 60 miles or more.

Men's Names Added to Hurricane List

U.S. government agencies responsible for weather and related communications have used girls' names to identify major tropical storms since 1953. A U.S. proposal that both male and female names be adopted for hurricanes, starting in 1979, was accepted by a committee of the World Meteorological Organization.

Names assigned to Atlantic hurricanes, 1983 — Alicia, Barry, Chantal, Dean, Erin, Felix, Gabrielle, Hugo, Iris, Jerry, Karen, Luis, Marilyn, Noel, Opal, Pable, Roxanne, Sebastien, Tanya, Van, Wendy.

Names assigned to Eastern Pacific hurricanes, 1983 — Adolph, Barbara, Cosme, Dalilia, Erick, Flossie, Gil, Henriette, Ismael, Juliette, Kiko, Lorena, Manuel, Narda, Octave, Priscilla, Raymond, Sonia, Tico, Velma, Winnie.

Explanation of Normal Temperatures

Normal temperatures listed in the tables on pages 794 and 796 are based on records of the National Weather Service for the 30-year period from 1941-1970 inclusive. To obtain the average maximum or minimum temperature for any month, the daily temperatures are added; the total is then divided by the number of days in that month.

The normal maximum temperature for January, for example, is obtained by adding the average maximums for Jan., 1941, Jan., 1942, etc., through Jan., 1970. The total is then divided by 30. The normal minimum temperature is obtained in a similar manner by adding the average minimums for each January in the 30-year period and dividing by 30. The normal temperature for January is one half of the sum for the normal maximum and minimum temperatures for that month. The mean temperature for any one day is one-half the total of the maximum and minimum temperatures for that day.

Monthly Normal Temperature and Precipitation

Source: National Oceanic and Atmospheric Administration, U.S. Commerce Department

These normals are based on records for the 30-year period 1941 to 1970 inclusive. See explanation on page 793. For stations that did not have continuous records from the same instrument site for the entire 30 years, the means have been adjusted to the record at the present site.

Airport station; *city office stations. T, temperature in Fahrenheit; P, precipitation in inches; L, less than .05 inch.

Station	Jan. T.	Jan. P.	Feb. T.	Feb. P.	Mar. T.	Mar. P.	Apr. T.	Apr. P.	May T.	May P.	June T.	June P.	July T.	July P.	Aug. T.	Aug. P.	Sept. T.	Sept. P.	Oct. T.	Oct. P.	Nov. T.	Nov. P.	Dec. T.	Dec. P.
Albany, N.Y.	22	2.2	24	2.1	33	2.6	47	2.7	58	3.3	68	3.0	72	3.1	70	2.9	62	3.1	51	2.6	40	2.8	26	2.9
Albuquerque, N.M.	35	0.3	40	0.4	46	0.5	56	0.5	65	0.5	75	0.5	79	1.4	77	1.3	70	0.8	58	0.8	45	0.3	36	0.5
Anchorage, Alas.	12	0.8	18	0.8	24	0.6	35	0.6	46	0.6	55	1.1	58	2.1	56	2.3	48	2.4	35	1.4	21	1.0	13	1.1
Asheville, N.C.	38	3.4	39	3.6	46	4.7	56	3.5	64	3.3	71	4.0	74	4.9	73	4.5	67	3.6	57	3.3	46	2.9	39	3.6
Atlanta, Ga.	42	4.3	45	4.4	51	5.8	61	4.6	69	3.7	76	3.7	78	4.9	78	3.5	72	3.2	62	2.5	51	3.4	44	4.2
Baltimore, Md.	33	2.9	35	2.8	43	3.7	54	3.1	64	3.6	72	3.8	77	4.1	75	4.2	69	3.1	57	2.8	46	3.1	35	3.3
Barrow, Alas.	-15	0.2	-19	0.2	-15	0.2	-1	0.2	19	0.2	33	0.4	39	0.9	38	1.0	30	0.6	15	0.6	-1	0.3	-12	0.2
Birmingham, Ala.	44	4.8	47	5.3	53	6.2	63	4.6	71	3.6	77	4.0	80	5.2	79	4.3	74	3.6	63	2.6	52	3.7	45	5.2
Bismarck, N.D.	8	0.5	14	0.4	25	0.7	43	1.4	54	2.2	64	3.6	71	2.2	69	2.0	58	1.3	47	0.8	29	0.6	16	0.5
Boise, Ida.	29	1.5	36	1.2	41	1.0	49	1.1	57	1.3	65	1.1	75	0.2	72	0.3	63	0.4	52	0.8	40	1.3	32	1.4
Boston, Mass.	29	3.7	30	3.5	38	4.0	49	3.5	59	3.5	68	3.2	73	2.7	71	3.5	65	3.2	55	3.0	45	4.5	33	4.2
Buffalo, N.Y.	24	2.9	24	2.6	32	2.9	45	3.2	55	3.0	66	2.2	70	2.9	68	3.5	62	3.3	52	3.0	40	3.7	28	3.0
Burlington, Vt.	17	1.7	19	1.7	29	1.9	43	2.6	55	3.0	65	3.5	70	3.5	67	3.7	59	3.1	49	2.7	37	2.9	23	2.2
Caribou, Me.	11	2.0	13	2.1	24	2.2	37	2.4	50	3.0	60	3.4	65	4.0	62	3.8	54	3.5	44	3.3	31	3.5	16	2.6
Charleston, S.C.	49	2.9	51	3.3	57	4.8	65	3.0	72	3.8	78	6.3	80	8.2	80	6.4	75	5.2	66	3.1	56	2.1	49	3.1
Chicago, Ill.	24	1.9	27	1.6	37	2.7	50	3.8	60	3.4	71	4.0	75	4.1	74	3.1	66	3.0	55	2.6	40	2.2	29	2.1
Cincinnati, Oh.*	32	3.4	34	3.0	43	4.1	55	3.9	64	4.0	73	3.9	76	4.0	75	3.0	68	2.7	58	2.2	45	3.1	34	2.9
Cleveland, Oh.	27	2.6	28	2.2	36	3.1	48	3.5	58	3.5	68	3.3	71	3.5	70	3.0	64	2.8	54	2.6	42	2.8	30	2.4
Columbus, Oh.	28	2.9	30	2.3	39	3.4	51	3.7	61	4.1	70	4.1	74	4.2	72	2.9	65	2.4	54	1.9	42	2.7	31	2.4
Dallas-Ft. Worth, Tex.	45	1.8	49	2.4	55	2.5	65	4.3	73	4.5	81	3.1	85	1.8	85	2.3	78	3.2	68	2.7	56	2.0	48	1.8
Denver, Col.	30	0.6	33	0.7	37	1.2	48	1.9	57	2.6	66	1.9	73	1.8	72	1.3	63	1.1	52	1.1	39	0.8	33	0.4
Des Moines, Ia.	19	1.1	24	1.1	34	2.3	50	2.9	61	4.2	71	4.9	75	3.3	73	3.3	64	3.1	54	2.1	38	1.4	25	1.1
Detroit, Mich.	26	1.9	27	1.8	35	2.3	48	3.1	58	3.4	69	3.0	73	3.0	72	3.0	65	2.3	54	2.5	41	2.3	30	2.2
Dodge City, Kan.	31	0.5	35	0.6	41	1.1	54	1.7	64	3.1	74	3.3	79	3.1	78	2.6	69	1.7	58	1.7	43	0.6	33	0.5
Duluth, Minn.	9	1.2	12	0.9	24	1.8	39	2.6	49	3.4	59	4.4	66	3.7	64	3.8	54	3.1	45	2.3	28	1.7	14	1.4
Eureka, Cal.*	47	7.4	48	5.2	48	4.8	50	3.0	53	2.1	55	0.7	56	0.1	57	0.3	57	0.7	54	3.2	52	5.8	49	6.6
Fairbanks, Alas.	-12	0.6	-3	0.5	10	0.5	29	0.3	47	0.7	59	1.4	61	1.9	55	2.2	44	1.1	25	0.7	3	0.7	-10	0.7
Fresno, Cal.	45	1.8	50	1.7	54	1.6	60	1.2	67	0.3	74	0.1	81	L	78	L	74	0.1	64	0.4	54	1.2	46	1.7
Galveston, Tex.*	54	3.0	56	2.7	61	2.6	69	2.6	76	3.2	81	4.1	83	4.4	83	4.4	80	5.6	73	2.8	64	3.2	57	3.7
Grand Junction, Col.	27	0.6	34	0.6	41	0.8	52	0.8	62	0.6	71	0.6	79	0.5	75	1.1	67	0.8	55	0.9	40	0.6	30	0.6
Gr. Rapids, Mich.	23	1.9	25	1.5	33	2.5	47	3.4	57	3.2	67	3.4	72	3.1	70	2.5	62	3.3	52	2.6	39	2.8	27	2.2
Hartford, Conn.	25	3.3	27	3.2	36	3.8	48	3.8	58	3.5	68	3.5	73	3.4	70	3.9	63	3.6	53	3.0	41	4.3	28	4.1
Helena, Mon.	18	0.6	25	0.4	31	0.7	43	0.9	52	1.8	59	2.4	68	1.0	66	1.0	56	1.0	45	0.6	32	0.6	23	0.6
Honolulu, Ha.	72	4.4	72	2.5	73	3.2	75	1.4	77	1.0	79	0.3	80	0.6	81	0.8	80	0.7	79	1.5	77	3.0	74	3.7
Houston, Tex.	52	3.6	55	3.5	61	2.7	69	3.5	76	5.1	81	4.5	83	4.1	83	4.4	79	4.7	71	4.1	61	4.0	55	4.0
Huron, S.D.	13	0.4	18	0.8	29	1.1	46	2.0	57	2.8	67	3.8	74	2.2	72	2.0	61	1.8	50	1.5	32	0.7	19	0.5
Indianapolis, Ind.	28	2.9	31	2.4	40	3.8	52	3.9	62	4.1	72	4.2	75	3.7	73	2.8	66	2.9	56	2.5	42	3.1	31	2.7
Jackson, Miss.	47	4.5	50	4.6	56	5.6	66	4.7	73	4.4	79	3.4	82	4.3	81	3.6	76	3.0	66	2.2	55	3.9	49	5.0
Jacksonville, Fla.	55	2.8	56	3.6	61	3.6	68	3.1	74	3.2	79	6.3	81	7.4	81	7.9	78	7.8	71	4.5	61	1.8	55	2.6
Juneau, Alas.	24	3.9	28	3.4	32	3.6	39	3.0	47	3.3	53	2.9	56	4.7	54	5.0	49	6.9	42	7.9	33	5.5	27	4.5
Kansas City, Mo.	27	1.3	32	1.3	41	2.6	54	3.5	64	4.3	73	5.6	78	4.4	77	3.8	68	4.2	58	3.2	42	1.5	31	1.5
Knoxville, Tenn.	41	4.7	43	4.7	50	4.9	60	3.6	68	3.3	76	3.6	78	4.7	77	3.2	72	2.8	61	2.7	49	3.6	42	4.5
Lander, Wyo.	20	0.5	26	0.7	31	1.2	43	2.4	53	2.6	61	1.9	71	0.6	69	0.4	58	1.1	47	1.2	32	0.9	23	0.5
Little Rock, Ark.	40	4.2	43	4.4	50	4.9	62	5.3	70	5.3	78	3.5	81	3.4	81	3.0	73	3.6	62	3.0	50	3.9	42	4.1
Los Angeles, Cal.*	57	3.0	58	2.8	59	2.2	62	1.3	65	0.1	68	L	73	L	74	L	73	0.2	68	0.3	63	2.0	58	2.2
Louisville, Ky.	33	3.5	36	3.5	44	5.1	56	4.1	65	4.2	73	4.1	77	3.8	76	3.0	69	2.9	58	2.4	45	3.3	36	3.3
Marquette, Mich.*	18	1.5	20	1.5	27	1.9	40	2.6	50	2.9	60	3.4	66	3.1	66	3.0	57	3.5	49	2.4	34	3.0	24	2.0
Memphis, Tenn.	41	4.9	44	4.7	51	5.1	63	5.4	71	4.4	79	3.5	82	3.5	80	3.3	74	3.0	63	2.6	51	3.9	43	4.7
Miami, Fla.	67	2.2	68	2.0	71	2.1	75	3.6	78	6.1	81	9.0	82	6.9	83	6.7	82	8.7	78	8.2	72	2.7	68	1.6
Milwaukee, Wis.	19	1.6	23	1.1	31	2.2	45	2.8	54	2.9	65	3.6	70	3.4	69	2.7	61	3.0	51	2.0	37	2.0	24	1.8
Minneapolis, Minn.	12	0.7	17	0.8	28	1.7	45	2.0	57	3.4	67	3.9	72	3.7	70	3.1	60	2.7	50	1.8	32	1.2	19	0.9
Mobile, Ala.	51	4.7	54	4.8	59	7.1	68	5.6	75	4.5	80	6.1	82	8.9	82	6.9	78	6.6	69	2.6	59	3.4	53	5.9
Moline, Ill.	22	1.7	26	1.3	36	2.6	51	3.8	61	3.9	71	4.4	75	4.6	73	3.4	65	3.8	54	2.7	39	1.9	27	1.8
Nashville, Tenn.	38	4.8	41	4.4	49	5.0	60	4.1	69	4.1	77	3.4	80	3.8	79	3.2	72	3.1	61	2.2	48	3.5	40	4.5
Newark, N.J.	31	2.9	33	3.0	41	3.9	52	3.4	62	3.6	71	3.0	76	4.0	75	4.3	68	3.4	58	2.8	46	3.6	35	3.5
New Orleans, La.	53	4.5	56	4.8	61	5.5	69	4.2	75	4.2	80	4.7	82	6.7	82	5.3	78	5.6	70	2.3	60	3.9	55	5.1
New York, N.Y.*	32	2.7	33	2.9	41	3.7	52	3.3	62	3.5	72	3.0	77	3.7	75	4.0	68	3.3	59	2.9	47	3.8	36	3.5
Nome, Alas.	6	0.9	5	0.8	7	0.8	19	0.7	35	0.7	46	1.0	50	2.4	49	3.6	42	2.4	29	1.4	16	1.0	4	0.7
Norfolk, Va.	41	3.4	41	3.3	48	3.4	58	2.7	67	3.3	75	3.6	78	5.7	77	5.9	72	4.2	62	3.1	52	2.9	42	3.1
Okla. City, Okla.	37	1.1	41	1.3	48	2.1	60	3.5	68	5.2	77	4.2	82	2.7	81	2.6	73	3.6	62	2.6	49	1.4	40	1.3
Omaha, Neb.	23	0.8	28	1.0	37	1.6	52	3.0	63	4.1	72	4.9	77	3.7	76	4.0	66	3.3	56	1.9	40	1.1	28	0.8
Parkersburg, W.Va.*	33	3.1	35	2.8	43	3.8	55	3.5	64	3.6	72	4.0	75	4.3	74	3.3	67	2.8	57	2.1	45	2.5	35	2.8
Philadelphia, Pa.	32	2.8	34	2.6	42	3.7	53	3.3	63	3.4	72	3.7	77	4.1	75	4.1	68	3.0	57	2.5	46	3.4	35	3.3
Phoenix, Ariz.	51	0.7	55	0.6	60	0.8	68	0.3	76	0.1	85	0.1	91	0.8	89	1.2	84	0.7	72	0.5	60	0.5	53	0.8
Pittsburgh, Pa.	28	2.8	29	2.4	38	3.6	50	3.4	60	3.6	69	3.5	72	3.8	70	3.2	64	2.5	53	2.5	41	2.5	31	2.5
Portland, Me.	22	3.4	23	3.5	32	3.6	43	3.3	53	3.3	62	3.1	68	2.6	66	2.6	59	3.1	49	3.3	39	4.9	26	4.1
Portland, Ore.	38	5.9	43	4.1	46	3.6	51	2.2	57	2.1	62	1.6	67	0.5	67	0.8	62	1.6	54	3.6	45	5.6	41	6.0
Providence, R.I.	28	3.5	29	3.5	37	4.0	47	3.7	57	3.5	66	2.7	72	2.9	70	3.9	63	3.3	54	3.3	43	4.5	32	4.1
Raleigh, N.C.	41	3.2	42	3.3	49	3.4	60	3.1	67	3.3	74	3.7	78	5.1	77	4.9	71	3.8	60	2.8	50	2.8	41	3.1
Rapid City, S.D.	22	0.5	26	0.6	31	1.0	45	2.1	55	2.8	64	3.7	73	2.1	72	1.5	61	1.2	50	0.9	35	0.5	27	0.4
Reno, Nev.	32	1.2	37	0.9	40	0.7	47	0.5	55	0.7	62	0.4	69	0.3	67	0.2	60	0.2	50	0.4	40	0.7	33	1.1
Richmond, Va.	38	2.9	39	3.0	47	3.4	58	2.8	67	3.4	74	3.5	78	5.6	76	5.1	70	3.6	59	2.9	49	3.2	39	3.2
St. Louis, Mo.	31	1.9	35	2.1	43	3.0	57	3.9	66	3.9	75	4.4	79	3.7	77	2.9	70	2.9	59	2.8	45	2.5	35	2.0
Salt Lake City, Ut.	28	1.3	33	1.2	40	1.6	49	2.1	58	1.5	66	1.3	77	0.7	75	0.9	65	0.7	52	1.2	39	1.3	30	1.4
San Antonio, Tex.	51	1.7	55	2.1	61	1.5	70	2.5	76	3.1	82	2.8	85	1.7	85	2.4	79	3.7	71	2.8	60	1.8	53	1.5
San Diego, Cal.	55	1.9	57	1.5	58	1.6	61	0.8	63	0.2	66	0.1	70	L	71	0.1	70	0.1	66	0.3	61	1.3	57	1.7
San Francisco, Cal.	48	4.4	51	3.0	53	2.5	55	1.6	58	0.4	62	0.1	63	L	63	L	64	0.2	61	1.0	55	2.3	50	4.0
San Juan, P.R.	75	3.7	75	2.5	76	2.0	78	3.4	79	6.5	81	5.6	81	6.4	81	7.0	81	6.1	81	5.6	79	5.5	77	4.7
Sault Ste. Marie, Mich.*	14	1.9	15	1.5	24	1.7	38	2.2	49	3.0	59	3.3	64	2.6	63	3.1	55	3.9	46	2.9	33	3.3	20	2.4
Savannah, Ga.	50	2.9	52	2.9	58	4.4	66	2.9	73	4.2	79	5.9	81	7.9	81	6.5	76	5.6	67	2.8	57	1.9	50	3.3
Seattle, Wash.	38	5.8	42	4.2	44	3.6	49	2.5	55	1.7	60	1.5	65	0.7	64	1.1	60	2.0	52	3.9	45	5.9	41	5.9
Spokane, Wash.	25	2.5	32	1.7	38	1.5	46	1.1	55	1.5	62	1.4	70	0.4	68	0.6	60	0.8	48	1.4	36	2.2	29	2.4
Springfield, Mo.	33	1.7	37	2.2	44	3.0	57	4.3	65	4.9	74	4.7	78	3.6	77	2.9	69	4.1	59	3.4	46	2.3	36	2.5
Syracuse, N.Y.	24	2.7	25	2.8	33	3.0	47	3.1	57	3.0	67	3.1	72	3.1	70	3.5	63	2.7	53	3.1	41	3.3	28	3.1
Tampa, Fla.	60	2.3	62	2.9	66	3.9	72	2.1	77	2.4	81	6.5	82	8.4	82	8.0	81	6.4	75	2.5	67	1.8	62	2.2
Trenton, N.J.*	32	2.8	33	2.7	41	3.8	52	3.2	62	3.4	71	3.2	76	4.7	74	4.2	67	3.2	57	2.5	46	3.3	35	3.3
Washington, D.C.	36	2.6	37	2.5	45	3.3	56	2.9	66	3.7	75	3.5	79	4.1	77	4.7	71	3.1	60	2.7	48	2.9	37	3.0
Wilmington, Del.	32	2.9	34	2.8	42	3.7	52	3.2	62	3.4	71	3.2	76	4.3	74	4.0	68	3.4	57	2.6	46	3.5	35	3.3

Annual Climatological Data

Source: National Oceanic and Atmospheric Administration, U.S. Commerce Department

1980		Temperature °F				Precipitation[1]			Sleet or snow			Fastest Wind		No. of days			
Station	Elev. ft.	Highest	Date	Lowest	Date	Total (in.)	Greatest in 24 hrs.	Date	Total (in.)	Greatest in 24 hours.	Date	MPH	Date	Clear*	Cloudy*	Prec. .01 in. or more	Snow, sleet 1 in. or more
Albany, N.Y.	275	94	7/21	−20	12/25	32.59	3.11	8/5	46.2	11.8	11/17	40	12/24	78	191	117	11
Albuquerque, N.M.	5311	105	7/18	15	11/18	8.87	1.75	8/13	14.2	7.4	12/8	52	4/11	161	93	50	3
Anchorage, Alas.	114	75	7/20	−23	12/17	19.17	1.18	5/28	50.7	12.3	1/31	59	1/29	62	250	130	13
Asheville, N.C.	2140	95	7/17	9	3/13	40.83	2.55	5/17	13.8	3.7	3/1	35	9/23	122	139	110	5
Atlanta, Ga.	1010	105	7/17	11	3/3	46.94	3.77	5/22	4.4	2.7	3/1	38	3/21	118	147	115	2
Baltimore, Md.	148	102	7/16	5	12/26	34.71	1.71	10/24	14.4	4.7	3/1	47	6/29	119	137	116	6
Barrow, Alas.	31	64	8/5	−52	1/16	4.42	0.49	6/4	22.5	2.0	10/5	47	8/29	—	—	77	7
Birmingham, Ala.	620	106	7/13	11	3/3	61.47	—	—	0.3	—	—	—	—	—	—	111	0
Bismarck, N.D.	1647	101	7/10	−28	1/9	16.39	1.81	10/15	30.0	6.4	1/5	54	8/29	97	163	80	9
Boise, Ida.	2838	106	7/22	−7	1/27	15.21	1.00	5/25	12.2	2.4	11/23	40	3/15	110	182	101	3
Boston, Mass.	15	99	7/21	−7	12/25	29.39	1.84	10/25	18.5	5.3	2/16	48	10/25	111	141	105	5
Buffalo, N.Y.	705	89	7/21	−10	12/25	38.31	2.69	8/2	64.4	5.0	3/21	48	12/2	43	207	179	23
Burlington, Va.	332	93	6/25	−26	12/26	30.89	2.18	7/29	61.4	10.0	3/14	37	1/11	48	211	158	14
Charleston, S.C.	40	100	7/13	15	3/3	40.92	4.57	7/25	5.1	3.8	12/26	35	7/5	108	154	102	2
Charleston, W. Va.	1016	97	7/16	0	3/3	47.81	2.62	7/8	38.0	7.3	3/1	35	8/1	69	111	149	13
Chicago, Ill.	607	102	7/7	−8	12/25	38.66	2.76	8/16	51.5	3.9	2/25	55	7/16	75	177	145	22
Cincinnati, Oh.	869	97	7/8	−11	3/3	37.13	2.61	7/8	33	8.1	2/29	35	7/8	95	186	120	11
Cleveland, Oh.	777	97	7/15	−5	2/3	32.61	1.93	8/2	52.9	6.6	2/15	39	1/11	44	226	149	18
Columbus, Oh.	812	97	7/20	−5	12/25	37.42	2.14	6/1	31.6	6.1	11/17	43	1/11	72	180	133	12
Concord, N.H.	342	98	6/25	−21	12/21	27.06	2.43	8/1	42.8	9.4	11/17	42	1/12	88	158	110	9
Dallas, Tex.	551	113	6/27	15	3/2	22.08	3.44	9/28	1.6	1.2	2/9	32	2/29	151	113	56	1
Denver, Co.	5283	100	8/6	−5	2/8	13.67	1.58	4/23	53.8	6.4	2/7	44	7/9	122	133	85	18
Des Moines, Ia.	938	102	7/30	−9	2/1	25.09	2.17	8/15	32.3	7.4	10/27	50	7/4	99	153	95	11
Detroit, Mich.	633	93	7/15	−8	12/25	37.24	1.73	6/2	38.2	5.9	3/7	40	7/16	79	183	143	10
Dodge City, Kan.	2582	108	7/15	−8	1/31	19.80	1.85	6/18	36.3	8.6	3/23	49	5/26	147	132	72	9
Duluth, Minn.	1428	95	7/10	−24	1/9	25.57	3.38	9/3	56.3	11.7	1/6	39	12/12	83	182	129	17
Fairbanks, Alas.	436	85	8/12	−50	1/13	7.88	0.69	6/30	43.1	4.0	1/5	32	6/20	69	216	107	13
Fresno, Cal.	328	111	7/26	28	12/12	10.28	1.82	2/19	—	—	—	30	4/20	186	107	41	0
Galveston, Tex.	7	96	8/23	26	3/2	34.58	2.67	7/28	T	T	2/2	42	11/25	—	—	96	0
Grand Rapids, Mich.	784	94	7/20	−4	12/27	36.90	2.35	8/16	59.7	5.3	12/29	29	1/11	54	209	146	21
Helena, Mont.	3828	94	7/28	−25	1/6	17.05	1.61	9/11	41.7	6.2	1/5	42	7/22	75	192	100	17
Honolulu, Ha.	7	91	10/6	56	1/26	26.90	3.71	12/14	—	—	—	35	1/8	67	104	115	0
Houston, Tex.	96	107	8/23	22	3/2	38.99	3.56	10/17	1.4	1.4	2/2	30	2/7	122	149	92	1
Huron, S.D.	1281	106	8/6	−18	1/9	18.15	1.77	7/5	21.8	4.9	3/28	49	7/3	109	151	84	8
Indianapolis, Ind.	792	100	7/15	−7	3/2	34.86	2.57	8/14	29.3	4.3	2/28	46	6/2	88	182	120	11
Jackson, Miss.	291	106	7/16	15	3/3	63.06	8.20	4/11	T	T	12/26	32	8/3	139	139	97	0
Jacksonville, Fla.	26	102	7/13	23	3/3	39.53	2.73	7/23	T	T	3/2	38	4/8	100	142	108	0
Juneau, Alas.	12	83	6/5	−7	1/5	61.88	1.64	10/16	89.1	13.4	12/7	—	—	—	—	234	24
Kansas City, Mo.	973	106	7/30	−8	2/12	31.79	3.67	12/6	26.7	4.5	2/7	60	8/10	127	144	96	11
Lander, Wyo.	5563	95	7/29	−27	1/29	11.02	1.42	5/10	112.8	14.2	3/30	66	5/25	111	144	65	26
Little Rock, Ark.	257	109	7/17	14	12/25	38.22	—	—	3.2	—	—	—	—	—	—	84	1
Los Angeles, Cal.	97	98	6/28	43	12/14	21.60	3.37	2/13	0	0	—	46	5/23	159	100	40	0
Louisville, Ky.	477	101	7/16	1	3/3	37.89	2.50	10/17	18.2	6.8	1/30	48	8/3	104	166	115	4
Marquette, Mich.	1415	92	4/22	−22	1/9	33.92	2.12	4/8	150.4	7.6	1/6	44	1/7	—	—	182	58
Memphis, Tenn.	258	108	7/13	16	2/1	54.43	4.76	6/23	3.6	1.2	2/8	35	8/9	147	137	88	1
Miami, Fla.	7	95	10/1	32	3/3	57.34	4.16	4/6	—	—	—	52	5/25	74	116	113	0
Milford, Ut.	5028	101	7/22	1	2/9	12.27	1.00	9/9	34.9	4.9	1/18	47	5/23	173	97	76	17
Milwaukee, Wis.	672	98	7/7	−6	12/25	33.41	2.47	6/5	64.1	6.2	12/1	52	9/9	75	200	134	22
Minneapolis, Minn.	834	100	7/11	−15	1/9	21.77	2.54	6/4	47.6	6.6	4/8	46	6/5	99	167	106	17
Mobile, Ala.	211	103	7/15	23	3/3	78.12	8.65	4/12	T	T	3/2	35	5/25	122	142	117	0
Moline, Ill.	582	97	7/15	−12	12/25	36.49	3.25	8/16	42.3	7.1	4/14	52	7/5	106	147	125	14
Nashville, Tenn.	590	104	7/16	2	3/3	34.92	3.29	5/16	10.0	3.7	2/5	35	2/25	125	154	104	4
New Orleans, La.	4	102	8/22	25	3/3	73.09	7.95	4/12	T	T	3/2	35	4/13	93	162	103	0
New York, N.Y.	132	99	7/21	−1	12/25	38.81	3.45	7/29	9.1	3.2	3/13	52	10/25	92	134	99	3
Nome, Alas.	13	71	7/18	−35	1/16	16.96	0.86	7/26	60.7	4.1	2/8	37	2/5	92	206	148	25
Norfolk, Va.	24	104	8/1	9	2/11	38.38	4.13	8/15	41.9	12.4	2/6	40	3/3	117	141	112	7
Oklahoma City, Okla.	1285	110	8/2	8	12/25	24.35	2.73	5/15	5.8	4.0	11/17	45	4/7	152	122	61	2
Omaha, Neb.	1309	102	7/14	−15	1/31	30.34	—	—	19.7	—	—	—	—	—	—	78	8
Philadelphia, Pa.	5	99	7/21	1	12/25	38.80	3.85	10/25	15.5	5.1	1/4	49	7/22	101	151	113	5
Phoenix, Ariz.	1110	115	7/28	35	2/10	6.06	0.82	2/14	—	—	—	55	7/21	215	76	41	0
Pittsburgh, Pa.	1137	98	7/20	−1	3/2	39.46	2.27	7/8	37.9	8.8	11/17	39	12/2	56	204	153	14
Portland, Me.	43	93	8/8	−20	12/26	33.88	3.02	4/9	45.9	8.9	11/17	42	1/12	100	151	120	11
Portland, Ore.	21	101	7/21	13	1/29	42.41	2.17	12/24	12.4	7.5	1/8	36	3/12	64	231	155	4
Providence, R.I.	51	100	7/21	−10	12/25	36.11	3.41	3/21	17.4	4.1	11/17	36	10/26	104	143	113	8
Raleigh, N.C.	434	98	8/1	6	12/26	35.64	3.38	1/25	21.4	9.0	3/2	35	7/17	127	150	110	7
Rapid City, S.D.	3162	106	7/29	−15	1/29	17.18	2.51	6/14	41.5	5.3	12/30	55	10/9	115	135	93	17
Reno, Nev.	4404	104	7/26	12	12/10	9.20	1.20	1/12	19.6	5.7	2/20	65	12/3	151	134	63	8
Richmond, Va.	164	101	7/16	5	12/26	41.13	3.45	10/18	38.8	13.3	1/5	42	8/5	115	153	113	9
Rochester, N.Y.	547	94	7/21	−12	12/25	34.32	2.98	10/25	98.8	7.0	12/24	43	1/12	52	211	170	32
St. Louis, Mo.	535	107	7/15	−2	12/25	27.48	2.09	9/16	34.4	6.9	11/26	45	2/25	114	149	97	10
Salt Lake City, Ut.	4221	101	7/28	−4	1/31	17.19	1.01	1/13	55.7	10.7	1/28	59	1/10	127	150	100	16
San Antonio, Tex.	788	105	6/27	19	3/2	24.23	3.16	9/6	T	T	11/25	35	8/10	118	128	80	0
San Diego, Cal.	13	95	6/28	44	11/19	14.96	2.14	1/28	0	0	—	56	1/29	135	101	48	0
San Francisco, Cal.	8	97	10/1	31	1/30	18.34	1.92	2/18	T	T	3/5	40	3/31	164	114	55	0
Sault Ste Mane. Mich.	721	88	5/23	−25	12/25	29.98	1.86	4/8	153.3	11.6	12/10	35	12/17	68	214	167	39
Savannah, Ga.	46	104	7/13	20	2/3	37.84	2.96	3/12	T	T	12/27	35	3/21	101	158	106	0
Seattle, Wash.	400	87	8/10	15	1/29	35.60	1.60	11/20	11.7	5.1	1/7	43	1/42	52	233	147	4
Sioux City, Ia.	1095	106	7/7	−16	1/31	17.71	1.41	8/9	21.8	3.0	10/27	61	9/20	105	144	85	10
Spokane, Wash.	2357	101	7/22	−6	1/7	17.03	1.08	12/2	32.0	5.0	1/4	42	4/28	56	215	111	13
Springfield, Mo.	1268	105	7/30	−4	2/12	27.36	1.67	6/22	33.1	16.1	2/7	43	4/7	130	144	86	6
Syracuse, N.Y.	410	93	7/21	−22	12/25	32.08	1.73	10/25	114.1	8.9	1/25	50	1/12	48	218	184	33
Tampa, Fla.	19	94	8/7	29	3/3	40.60	2.35	4/14	T	T	3/3	29	7/24	89	129	113	0
Trenton, N.J.	56	100	7/21	2	12/25	34.16	2.67	10/25	17.9	3.8	1/4	47	3/18	86	154	110	7
Washington, D.C.	10	103	7/16	12	12/26	29.32	1.61	10/24	20.1	5.2	1/4	50	9/14	101	155	110	6
Williston, N.D.	1899	109	7/10	−34	12/24	10.80	1.09	9/11	38.7	8.3	1/5	39	6/23	111	145	84	19
Wilmington, Del.	74	98	9/2	2	12/25	33.92	2.56	10/25	13.9	3.9	1/4	39	3/18	107	155	112	5

*To get partly cloudy days deduct the total of clear and cloudy days from 365 (1 yr.). T—trace. (1) Date shown is the starting date of the storm (in some cases it lasted more than one day).

Normal Temperatures, Highs, Lows, Precipitation

Source: National Oceanic and Atmospheric Administration, U.S. Commerce Department

These normals are based on records for the thirty-year period 1941-1970. (See explanation on page 793.) The extreme temperatures (through 1980) are listed for the stations shown and may not agree with the states records shown on page 797.

Airport stations; * designates city office stations. The minus (−) sign indicates temperatures below zero. Fahrenheit thermometer registration.

State	Station	Normal temperature — January Max.	January Min.	July Max.	July Min.	Extreme temperature — Highest	Lowest	Normal annual precipitation (inches)
Alabama	Mobile	61	41	91	73	104	7	66.98
Alabama	Montgomery	58	37	91	72	105	5	49.86
Alaska	Juneau	29	18	64	48	90	−22	54.67
Arizona	Phoenix	65	38	105	78	118	17	7.05
Arkansas	Little Rock	50	29	93	70	109	−5	48.52
California	Los Angeles*	67	47	83	64	110	28	14.05
California	San Francisco	55	41	71	54	106	20	19.53
Colorado	Denver	44	16	87	59	104	−30	15.51
Connecticut	Hartford	33	16	84	61	102	−26	43.37
Delaware	Wilmington	40	24	86	66	102	−6	40.25
Dist. of Col.	Washington	44	28	88	69	103	1	38.89
Florida	Jacksonville	65	45	90	72	105	12	54.47
Florida	Key West	76	66	89	80	95	46	39.99
Florida	Miami	76	59	89	76	98	31	59.80
Georgia	Atlanta	51	33	87	69	105	−3	48.34
Hawaii	Honolulu	79	65	87	73	93	53	22.90
Idaho	Boise	37	21	91	59	111	−23	11.50
Illinois	Chicago-Midway	32	17	84	65	104	−19	34.44
Indiana	Indianapolis	36	20	85	65	104	−20	38.74
Iowa	Des Moines	28	11	85	65	105	−24	30.85
Iowa	Dubuque	26	9	82	61	99	−28	40.27
Kansas	Wichita	41	21	92	70	113	−12	30.58
Kentucky	Louisville	42	25	87	66	105	−20	43.11
Louisiana	New Orleans	62	44	90	73	102	14	56.77
Maine	Portland	31	12	79	57	103	−39	40.80
Maryland	Baltimore	42	25	87	67	102	−7	40.46
Massachusetts	Boston	36	23	81	65	102	−12	42.52
Michigan	Detroit-City	32	19	83	63	105	−16	30.96
Michigan	Sault Ste. Marie*	22	6	75	53	98	−35	31.70
Minnesota	Minn.-St. Paul	21	3	82	61	104	−34	25.94
Mississippi	Jackson	58	36	93	71	106	6	49.19
Missouri	St. Louis	40	23	88	69	107	−14	35.89
Montana	Helena	28	8	84	52	105	−42	11.38
Nebraska	Omaha	33	12	89	66	114	−22	30.18
Nevada	Winnemucca	41	16	91	51	106	−34	8.47
New Hampshire	Concord	31	10	83	57	102	−37	36.17
New Jersey	Atlantic City	41	24	85	65	106	−11	45.46
New Mexico	Albuquerque	47	24	92	65	105	−17	7.77
New Mexico	Roswell	55	21	95	64	107	−9	10.61
New York	Albany	30	13	84	60	100	−28	33.36
New York	New York-La Guardia	38	26	84	69	107	−2	41.61
No. Carolina	Charlotte	52	32	88	69	104	−3	42.72
No. Carolina	Raleigh	51	30	88	67	105	−1	42.54
No. Dakota	Bismarck	19	−3	84	57	109	−44	16.16
Ohio	Cincinnati-Abbe	40	24	87	66	109	−17	40.03
Ohio	Cleveland	33	20	82	61	103	−19	34.99
Oklahoma	Oklahoma City	48	26	93	70	110	−4	31.37
Oregon	Portland	44	33	79	55	107	−3	37.61
Pennsylvania	Harrisburg	38	23	87	65	107	−8	36.47
Pennsylvania	Philadelphia	40	24	87	67	104	−5	39.93
Rhode Island	Block Island	37	25	76	63	92	−4	40.51
So. Carolina	Charleston	60	37	39	71	103	8	52.12
So. Dakota	Huron	23	2	87	61	112	−39	19.44
So. Dakota	Rapid City	34	10	86	59	110	−27	17.12
Tennessee	Nashville	48	29	90	69	107	−15	46.00
Texas	Amarillo	49	23	91	66	108	−14	20.28
Texas	Galveston*	59	48	87	79	101	8	42.20
Texas	Houston	63	42	94	73	107	17	48.19
Utah	Salt Lake City	37	19	93	61	107	−30	15.17
Vermont	Burlington	26	8	81	59	101	−30	32.54
Virginia	Norfolk	49	32	87	70	104	5	44.68
Washington	Seattle-Tacoma	43	33	75	54	99	0	38.79
Washington	Spokane	31	20	84	55	108	−25	17.42
West Virginia	Parkersburg*	41	24	86	65	106	−27	38.44
Wisconsin	Madison	25	8	81	59	104	−37	30.25
Wisconsin	Milwaukee	27	11	80	59	101	−24	29.07
Wyoming	Cheyenne	38	15	84	55	100	−34	14.65
Puerto Rico	San Juan	82	69	87	75	97	60	59.15

Mean Annual Snowfall (inches) based on record through 1980: Boston, Mass. 42; Sault Ste. Marie, Mich., 113; Albany, N.Y. 65.2; Rochester, N.Y. 89.2; Burlington, Vt., 78.6; Cheyenne, Wyo., 53.3; Juneau, Alas. 105.8.

Wettest Spot: Mount Waialeale, Ha., on the island of Kauai, is the rainiest place in the world, according to the National Geographic Society, with an average annual rainfall of 460 inches.

Highest Temperature: A temperature of 136° F. observed at Azizia, Tripolitania in Northern Africa on Sept. 13, 1922, is generally accepted as the world's highest temperature recorded under standard conditions.

The record high in the United States was 134° in Death Valley, Cal., July 10, 1913.

Lowest Temperature: A record low temperature of −126.9° F. (−88.3° C.) was recorded at the Soviet Antarctic station Vostok on Aug. 24, 1960.

The record low in the United States was −80° at Prospect Creek, Alas., Jan. 23, 1971.

The lowest official temperature on the North American continent was recorded at 81 degrees below zero in February, 1947, at a lonely airport in the Yukon called Snag.

These are the meteorological champions—the official temperature extremes—but there are plenty of other claimants to thermometer fame. However, sun readings are unofficial records, since meteorological data to qualify officially must be taken on instruments in a sheltered and ventilated location.

Record Temperatures by States Through 1980

Source: National Oceanic and Atmospheric Administration, U.S. Commerce Department

State	Lowest °F	Highest	Latest date	Station	Approximate elevation in feet
Alabama	−27		Jan. 30, 1966	New Market	725
		112	*Sept. 5, 1925*	*Centerville*	*345*
Alaska	−79.8		Jan. 23, 1971	Prospect Creek Camp	1,100
		100	*June 27, 1915*	*Fort Yukon*	**419*
Arizona	−40		Jan. 7, 1971	Hawley Lake	8,180
		127	*July 7, 1905*	*Parker*	*345*
Arkansas	−29		Feb. 13, 1905	Pond	1,250
		120	*Aug. 10, 1936*	*Ozark*	*396*
California	−45		Jan. 20, 1937	Boca	5,532
		134	*July 10, 1913*	*Greenland Ranch*	*−178*
Colorado	−60		Feb. 1, 1951	Taylor Park	9,206
		118	*July 11, 1888*	*Bennett*	*5,484*
Connecticut	−32		Feb. 16, 1943	Falls Village	585
		105	*July 22, 1926*	*Waterbury*	*409*
Delaware	−17		Jan. 17, 1893	Millsboro	20
		110	*July 21, 1930*	*Millsboro*	*20*
Dist. of Col.	−15		Feb. 11, 1899	Washington	112
		106	*July 20, 1930*	*Washington*	*112*
Florida	−2		Feb. 13, 1899	Tallahassee	193
		109	*June 29, 1931*	*Monticello*	*207*
Georgia	−17		Jan. 27, 1940	CCC Camp F-16	1,000
		113	*May 27, 1978*	*Greenville*	*860*
Hawaii	14		Jan. 2, 1961	Haleakala, Maui	9,750
		100	*Apr. 27, 1931*	*Pahala*	*850*
Idaho	−60		Jan. 16, 1943	Island Park Dam	6,285
		118	*July 28, 1934*	*Orofino*	*1,027*
Illinois	−35		Jan. 22, 1930	Mount Carroll	817
		117	*July 14, 1954*	*E. St. Louis*	*410*
Indiana	−35		Feb. 2, 1951	Greensburg	954
		116	*July 14, 1936*	*Collegeville*	*672*
Iowa	−47		Jan. 12, 1912	Washta	1,157
		118	*July 20, 1934*	*Keokuk*	*614*
Kansas	−40		Feb. 13, 1905	Lebanon	1,812
		121	*July 24, 1936*	*Alton (near)*	*1,651*
Kentucky	−34		Jan. 28, 1963	Cynthiana	719
		114	*July 28, 1930*	*Greensburg*	*581*
Louisiana	−16		Feb. 13, 1899	Minden	194
		114	*Aug. 10, 1936*	*Plain Dealing*	*268*
Maine	−48		Jan. 19, 1925	Van Buren	510
		105	*July 10, 1911*	*North Bridgton*	*450*
Maryland	−40		Jan. 13, 1912	Oakland	2,461
		109	*July 10, 1936*	*Cumberland and Frederick*	*623-325*
Massachusetts	−34		Jan. 18, 1957	Birch Hill Dam	840
		107	*Aug. 2, 1975*	*Chester and New Bedford*	*120-640*
Michigan	−51		Feb. 9, 1934	Vanderbilt	785
		112	*July 13, 1936*	*Mio*	*963*
Minnesota	−59		Feb. 16, 1903	Pokegama Dam	1,280
		114	*July 6, 1936*	*Moorhead*	*904*
Mississippi	−19		Jan. 30, 1966	Corinth	420
		115	*July 29, 1930*	*Holly Springs*	*600*
Missouri	−40		Feb. 13, 1905	Warsaw	700
		118	*July 14, 1954*	*Warsaw and Union*	*687-560*
Montana	−70		Jan. 20, 1954	Rogers Pass	5,470
		117	*July 5, 1937*	*Medicine Lake*	*1,950*
Nebraska	−47		Feb. 12, 1899	Camp Clarke	3,700
		118	*July 24, 1936*	*Minden*	*2,169*
Nevada	−50		Jan. 8, 1937	San Jacinto	5,200
		122	*June 23, 1954*	*Overton*	*1,240*
New Hampshire	−47		Jan. 1934	Mt. Washington	6,262
		106	*July 4, 1911*	*Nashua*	*125*
New Jersey	−34		Jan. 5, 1904	River Vale	70
		110	*July 10, 1936*	*Runyon*	*18*
New Mexico	−50		Feb. 1, 1951	Gavilan	7,350
		116	*July 14, 1934*	*Orogrande*	*4,171*
New York	−52		Feb. 9, 1934	Stillwater Reservoir	1,670
		108	*July 22, 1926*	*Troy*	*35*
North Carolina	−29		Jan. 30, 1966	Mt. Mitchell	6,525
		109	*Sept. 7, 1954*	*Weldon*	*81*
North Dakota	−60		Feb. 15, 1936	Parshall	1,929
		121	*July 6, 1936*	*Steele*	*1,857*
Ohio	−39		Feb. 10, 1899	Milligan	800
		113	*July 21, 1934*	*Gallipolis (near)*	*673*
Oklahoma	−27		Jan. 18, 1930	Watts	958
		120	*July 26, 1943*	*Tishmoningo*	*670*
Oregon	−54		Feb. 10, 1933	Seneca	4,700
		119	*Aug. 10, 1938*	*Pendleton*	*1,074*
Pennsylvania	−42		Jan. 5, 1904	Smethport	1,469
		111	*July 10, 1936*	*Phoenixville*	*100*
Rhode Island	−23		Jan. 11, 1942	Kingston	100
		104	*Aug. 2, 1975*	*Providence*	*51*
South Carolina	−20		Jan. 18, 1977	Caesar's Head	3,100
		111	*June 28, 1954*	*Camden*	*170*
South Dakota	−58		Feb. 17, 1936	McIntosh	2,277
		120	*July 5, 1936*	*Gannvalley*	*1,750*

State	Lowest °F	Highest	Latest date	Station	Approximate elevation in feet
Tennessee	−32		Dec. 30, 1917	Mountain City	2,471
		113	*Aug. 9, 1930*	*Perryville*	*377*
Texas	−23		Feb. 8, 1933	Seminole	3,275
		120	*Aug. 12, 1936*	*Seymour*	*1,291*
Utah	−50		Jan. 5, 1913	Strawberry Tunnel	7,650
		116	*June 28, 1892*	*Saint George*	*2,880*
Vermont	−50		Dec. 30, 1933	Bloomfield	915
		105	*July 4, 1911*	*Vernon*	*310*
Virginia	−29		Feb. 10, 1899	Monterey	3,008
		110	*July 15, 1954*	*Balcony Falls*	*725*
Washington	−48		Dec. 30, 1968	Mazama	2,120
	−48		Dec. 30, 1968	Winthrop	1,755
		118	*Aug. 5, 1961*	*Ice Harbor Dam*	*475*
West Virginia	−37		Dec. 30, 1917	Lewisburg	2,200
		112	*July 10, 1936*	*Martinsburg*	*435*
Wisconsin	−54		Jan. 24, 1922	Danbury	908
		114	*July 13, 1936*	*Wisconsin Dells*	*900*
Wyoming	−63		Feb. 9, 1933	Moran	6,770
		114	*July 12, 1900*	*Basin*	*3,500*

Canadian Normal Temperatures, Highs, Lows, Precipitation

Source: Atmospheric Environment Service, Environment Canada

These normals are based on varying periods of record over the thirty-year period 1941 to 1970 inclusive. Extreme temperatures are based on varying periods of record for each station through 1981. Airport station; * designates city office stations. The minus (−) sign indicates temperatures below zero. Celsius thermometer registration.

Province	Station	Temperature: Normal, January Max.	January Min.	July Max.	July Min.	Extreme: Highest	Lowest	Precipitation normal annual (millimeters)
Alberta	Calgary	−5	−17	24	10	36	−45	437
Alberta	Edmonton (Industrial Airport)	−10	−19	23	12	34	−48	446
British Columbia	Prince George	−7	−16	22	8	34	−50	621
British Columbia	Victoria	6	2	20	11	35	−16	657
British Columbia	Vancouver	5	0	22	13	33	−18	1068
Manitoba	Churchill	−24	−31	17	7	33	−45	397
Manitoba	Winnipeg	−13	−23	26	14	41	−45	535
Newfoundland	Gander	−2	−10	22	11	36	−27	1078
Newfoundland	St. John's	−1	−7	20	10	31	−23	1511
New Brunswick	Fredericton	−4	−14	26	13	37	−37	1060
New Brunswick	Moncton	−3	−13	25	13	37	−32	1099
New Brunswick	Saint John	−2	−13	22	11	34	−37	1400
Nova Scotia	Halifax	−2	−10	23	13	34	−26	1396
Nova Scotia	Sydney	−1	−8	23	13	35	−25	1341
Ontario	Ottawa	−6	−16	26	15	38	−36	851
Ontario	Sudbury	−8	−18	25	13	36	−38	835
Ontario	Toronto	−1	−8	27	17	41	−33	790
Ontario	Windsor	−1	−8	28	17	38	−26	836
Prince Edward Island	Charlottetown	−3	−11	23	14	34	−28	1128
Quebec	Montreal	−5	−14	26	16	36	−38	941
Quebec	Quebec City	−7	−16	25	13	36	−36	1089
Quebec	Val-d'Or	−11	−23	23	11	34	−44	902
Saskatchewan	Prince Albert	−15	−27	25	11	38	−50	389
Saskatchewan	Regina	−12	−23	26	12	43	−50	398
Northwest Territories	Alert*	−28	−36	7	1	20	−49	156
Northwest Territories	Yellowknife	−24	−33	21	11	32	−51	250
Yukon Territory	Dawson*	−25	−32	22	9	35	−58	325
Yukon Territory	Whitehorse*	−15	−23	20	8	34	−52	260

Canadian Low and High Temperature Records Through 1981

Source: Atmospheric Environment Service, Environment Canada

Province	Lowest °C	Highest	Latest date	Station	Approximate elevation in meters
Alberta	−61		Jan. 11, 1911	Fort Vermillion	278
		42	*July 12, 1886*	*Medicine Hat*	721
British Columbia	−59		Jan. 31, 1947	Smith River	673
		44	*July 17, 1941*	*Chinock Cove*	404
		44	*July 17, 1941*	*Lillooet*	290
		44	*July 17, 1941*	*Lytton*	183
Manitoba	−53		Jan. 9, 1899	Norway House	219
		44	*July 12, 1936*	*Emerson*	241
Newfoundland	−49		Mar. 7, 1968	Twin Falls	457
		42	*Aug. 11, 1914*	*Northwest River*	61
New Brunswick	−47		Feb. 1, 1955	Sisson Dam	278
		39	*Aug. 19, 1935*	*Rexton*	6
Nova Scotia	−41		Jan. 31, 1920	Upper Stewiacke	23
		38	*Aug. 19, 1935*	*Collegeville*	76
Ontario	−58		Jan. 23, 1935	Iroquois Falls	244
		42	*July 13, 1936*	*Fort Frances*	354
Prince Edward Island	−37		Jan. 26, 1884	Kilmahumaig	6
		37	*Aug. 19, 1935*	*Charlottetown*	22
Quebec	−54		Feb. 5, 1923	Doucet	376
		40	*Aug. 15 1928*	*Bark Lake*	365
Saskatchewan	−57		Feb. 1, 1893	Prince Albert	436
		45	*July 5, 1937*	*Midale*	582
		45	*July 5, 1937*	*Yellow Grass*	579
North West Territories	−57		Dec. 26, 1917	Fort Smith	202
		39	*July 18, 1941*	*Fort Smith*	207
Yukon Territory	−63		Feb. 3, 1947	Snag	586
		35	*June 18, 1950*	*Mayo*	495

Canadian Normal Temperature and Precipitation

Source: Atmospheric Environment Service, Environment Canada

Normal refers to the mean daily temperature and total monthly precipitation based on varying periods of record over the thirty-year period 1941 to 1970 inclusive. In most cases no adjustment factor was used.

Airport station; *designates city office stations. T, temperature in Celsius; P, precipitation in millimeters.

Station	Jan. T.	Jan. P.	Feb. T.	Feb. P.	Mar. T.	Mar. P.	Apr. T.	Apr. P.	May T.	May P.	June T.	June P.	July T.	July P.	Aug. T.	Aug. P.	Sept. T.	Sept. P.	Oct. T.	Oct. P.	Nov. T.	Nov. P.	Dec. T.	Dec. P.
Calgary, Alta.	−11	17	−7	20	−4	20	3	30	9	50	13	92	17	68	15	56	11	35	6	19	−3	16	−8	15
Charlottetown, P.E.I.	−7	111	−7	95	−3	85	2	82	9	82	14	83	18	73	18	93	14	86	9	97	3	126	−4	116
Churchill, Man.	−28	14	−27	13	−20	18	−11	24	−2	28	6	40	12	49	12	58	6	52	−1	40	−12	40	−22	20
Dawson, Yukon*	−29	19	−23	16	−14	13	−2	9	8	22	14	37	16	53	13	51	6	28	−3	27	−17	25	−25	26
Edmonton, Alta.	−15	25	−11	20	−5	17	4	23	11	37	15	75	18	83	16	72	11	36	5	19	−4	19	−11	21
Fredericton, N.B.	−9	95	−8	93	−2	69	4	74	11	81	16	79	19	88	18	88	13	82	8	88	2	109	−6	114
Frobisher Bay, N.W.T.	−26	24	−25	28	−22	21	−14	22	−3	23	4	38	8	53	7	58	2	43	−5	42	−12	37	−20	26
Halifax, N.S.	−6	137	−7	128	−2	104	3	108	9	99	15	79	18	80	18	108	14	95	9	118	4	163	−3	179
Hamilton, Ont.*	−5	66	−4	60	0	66	7	78	13	72	19	71	22	72	21	77	17	71	11	69	5	67	−2	67
Kitchener, Ont.*	−7	61	−6	56	−1	71	7	71	13	83	18	81	21	89	20	79	16	73	10	71	3	78	−4	74
London, Ont.	−6	76	−6	65	−1	72	7	78	12	75	18	81	21	81	20	73	16	79	10	74	3	83	−4	87
Moncton, N.B.	−8	107	−8	100	−3	93	3	84	10	80	15	91	19	80	18	80	14	73	8	91	2	113	−5	109
Montreal, Que.	−10	76	−9	71	−2	71	6	74	13	67	19	83	21	85	20	87	15	80	9	75	2	87	−7	86
Ottawa, Ont.	−11	60	−10	57	−3	61	6	68	12	70	18	73	21	81	19	82	15	79	9	66	1	79	−8	77
Quebec City, Que.	−12	86	−11	77	−4	69	3	75	11	81	16	102	19	108	18	103	13	106	7	82	0	100	−9	101
Regina, Sask.	−17	18	−14	17	−8	18	3	23	11	41	15	83	19	58	18	50	12	36	5	19	−5	18	−13	16
Saint John, N.B.	−7	145	−8	131	−3	105	3	112	9	102	14	95	17	89	16	99	13	103	8	110	3	154	−5	157
St. John's, Nfld.	−4	145	−4	156	−2	133	1	114	6	99	10	89	15	83	15	113	12	112	7	139	4	161	−1	167
Saskatoon, Sask.	−19	18	−15	18	−9	17	3	21	11	34	15	57	19	53	17	45	11	33	5	19	−6	19	−14	18
Sault Ste. Marie, Ont.	−11	81	−11	55	−5	57	3	56	9	85	15	88	18	72	18	67	13	95	8	79	1	106	−6	94
Toronto, Ont.	−4	63	−4	57	1	66	8	67	13	73	19	63	22	81	21	67	17	61	11	62	5	67	−2	64
Vancouver, B.C.	2	147	4	117	6	94	9	61	12	48	15	45	17	30	17	37	14	61	10	122	6	141	4	165
Victoria, B.C.	4	107	6	76	7	49	9	34	12	21	14	21	16	12	16	20	14	33	11	74	7	95	5	115
Whitehorse, Yukon.	−19	19	−13	14	−8	15	0	11	7	14	12	29	14	33	12	36	8	29	1	20	−9	22	−16	20
Windsor, Ont.	−4	55	−3	52	1	66	8	81	14	83	20	84	22	83	21	82	17	61	12	63	4	62	−2	64
Winnipeg, Man.	−18	24	−16	19	−8	26	3	37	11	57	17	80	20	80	19	74	13	53	7	35	−4	27	−14	23
Yellowknife, N.W.T.	−29	14	−26	12	−19	12	−8	10	4	14	12	17	16	33	14	36	7	28	−1	31	−14	24	−24	19

Canadian Annual Climatological Data

Source: Atmospheric Environment Service, Environment Canada

Station		Temperature (Celsius)				Precipitation			Snowfall			Fastest wind		No. of days	
1980	Elev. meters	Highest	Date D/Mo.	Lowest	Date D/Mo.	Total (mm)	Greatest in 24 hrs.	Date D/Mo.	Total (cm)	Greatest in 24 hrs.	Date D/Mo.	Km/h	Date D/Mo.	Precip., measurable	Snow, measurable
Calgary, Alta.	1084	29.7	sev.	−34.1	6/12	446.0	38.2	23/5	146.3	12.0	sev.	100	25/5	124	56
Charlottetown, P.E.I.	55	30.1	26/6	−28.1	26/12	1081.7	50.4	17/7	229.8	16.5	23/1	111	27/11	186	71
Churchill, Man.	29	28.2	29/4	−38.6	12/1	482.0	39.0	21/8	212.2	13.8	16/12	104	sev.	179	114
Dawson, Yukon	369	32.9	6/6	−53.8	sev.	348.8	28.8	14/8	80.9	10.2	29/10	56	21/4	111	38
Edmonton, Alta.	671	30.5	22/7	−33.6	9/1	552.4	52.5	28/8	151.9	17.0	23/3	83	24/1	127	53
Fredericton, N.B.	20	34.8	26/6	−30.4	22/12	1159.2	66.4	30/7	209.7	28.2	18/11	93	16/3	170	51
Frobisher, N.W.T.	34	22.4	17/8	−37.5	23/2	401.1	30.2	6/6	279.0	19.4	7/4	126	12/1	160	126
Halifax, N.S.	145	30.1	24/8	−23.3	25/12	1332.6	58.0	30/12	168.3	22.1	23/1	109	12/1	165	47
Hamilton, Ont.	237	31.4	19/7	−26.8	25/12	801.9	32.9	21/3	82.2	6.2	8/3	104	11/1	148	50
Moncton, N.B.	71	31.8	26/6	−28.4	26/12	1155.9	48.6	3/12	230.4	25.5	sev.	78	11/3	186	58
Montreal, Que.	36	31.3	24/6	−32.4	25/12	911.7	48.8	22/7	139.4	19.8	14/3	102	12/1	159	54
Ottawa, Ont.	114	32.4	25/7	−31.6	25/12	890.3	44.8	21/3	198.6	15.4	22/2	82	7/1	134	69
Quebec, Que.	73	30.2	25/6	−32.2	25/12	1157.3	58.9	20/9	238.7	26.0	14/3	85	sev.	186	78
Regina, Sask.	577	37.2	22/5	−38.0	24/12	279.6	21.2	23/6	91.2	9.0	7/4	98	13/1	115	61
St. John, N.B.	109	29.4	24/8	−30.9	26/12	1392.2	76.4	18/3	223.3	19.6	18/11	93	12/1	177	55
St. John's, Nfld.	140	26.8	30/7	−19.7	11/1	1826.9	66.4	16/8	279.6	33.6	11/1	120	6/11	248	83
Saskatoon, Sask.	501	35.2	10/7	−35.6	sev.	288.8	20.2	3/9	111.4	8.4	3/12	98	10/7	111	58
Sault Ste. Marie, Ont.	192	32.7	25/6	−31.4	25/12	805.3	35.3	13/6	336.2	26.0	20/12	102	26/10	184	92
Thunder Bay, Ont.	199	34.8	22/5	−31.6	3/2	796.3	44.7	13/9	245.8	36.2	6/1	78	22/4	133	58
Toronto, Ont.	111	31.3	26/6	−23.9	25/12	784.5	37.8	14/4	103.2	18.4	8/3	104	sev.	158	46
Vancouver, B.C.	2	26.1	10/8	−12.2	6/12	1418.5	45.4	1/9	41.0	12.6	5/12	85	17/8	173	12
Victoria, B.C.	69	28.1	21/7	−7.5	29/1	744.8	38.6	9/12	44.0	13.5	7/1	113	12/1	136	9
Waterloo/Wellington, Ont.	314	32.0	19/7	−27.2	25/12	779.3	43.0	28/7	133.0	21.2	8/3	87	11/1	146	66
Whitehorse, Yukon	703	30.0	6/6	−45.2	28/12	280.9	16.2	16/9	154.9	27.0	25/12	85	16/11	125	65
Windsor, Ont.	190	34.0	15/7	−18.3	25/12	957.1	50.8	31/8	99.6	9.2	29/12	107	16/7	152	47
Winnipeg, Man.	239	37.0	22/5	−35.2	29/2	405.3	25.7	3/8	101.4	18.6	10/1	102	1/10	108	53
Yellowknife, N.W.T.	205	26.1	26/7	−42.4	12/1	258.4	16.8	29/10	121.8	13.0	23/1	70	17/12	105	60

Speed of Winds in Canada

Source: Atmospheric Environment Service, Environment Canada

Kilometers-per-hour average in most cases is for the period of record 1955 to 1972. High is based on varying periods of record dependent on the origin of the station through 1981.

Station	Avg.	High	Station	Avg.	High	Station	Avg.	High
Calgary, Alta.	21.4	105	London, Ont.	16.4	101	Sault Ste. Marie, Ont.	15.3	89
Charlottetown, P.E.I.	19.3	103	Moncton, N.B.	18.7	100	Thunder Bay, Ont.	14.2	81
Churchill, Man.	25.2	126	Montreal, Que.	15.8	82	Toronto, Ont.	17.2	90
Dawson, Yukon.	6.7	52	Ottawa, Ont.	15.1	87	Vancouver, B.C.	12.1	89
Edmonton, Alta.	14.9	71	Quebec City, Que.	16.7	109	Victoria, B.C.	17.7	109
Fredericton, N.B.	14.2	81	Regina, Sask.	21.5	97	Whitehorse, Yukon	15.1	81
Frobisher Bay, N.W.T.	16.6	129	Saint John, N.B.	19.0	97	Windsor, Ont.	17.1	92
Halifax, N.S.	18.3	97	Saint John's, Nfld.	24.3	137	Winnipeg, Man.	19.3	90
Hamilton, Ont.	12.8	66	Saskatoon, Sask.	17.9	105	Yellowknife, N.W.T.	16.1	72

ENVIRONMENT

Estimated Incremental Pollution Control Expenditures

Source: Council on Environmental Quality (billions of 1980 dollars). Does not include research, conservation, and enhancement programs.

Pollutant/source	1980 O&M[1]	1980 Annual Capital costs[2]	1980 Total annual costs[3]	1989 O&M[1]	1989 Annual Capital costs[2]	1989 Total annual costs[3]	Cumulative 1980-89 O&M[1]	Cumulative 1980-89 Capital costs[2]	Cumulative 1980-89 Total costs[3]
Air pollution									
Public	1.3	.3	1.6	2.2	.5	2.7	17.2	4.0	21.2
Private									
Mobile	3.5	5.3	8.8	3.3	11.3	14.6	33.1	88.2	121.3
Industrial	2.2	2.5	4.7	3.3	4.5	7.8	28.1	36.0	64.1
Electric utilities	4.8	1.9	6.7	6.4	3.3	19.7	56.3	26.7	83.0
Subtotal	**11.8**	**10.0**	**21.8**	**15.2**	**19.6**	**34.8**	**134.7**	**154.9**	**289.6**
Water pollution									
Public	1.8	4.6	6.4	3.6	10.8	14.4	27.1	63.6	90.7
Private									
Industrial	3.7	2.8	6.5	5.9	4.9	10.8	45.8	37.1	82.9
Electric utilities	.1	.4	.5	.3	.4	.7	2.2	3.9	6.1
Subtotal	**5.6**	**7.8**	**13.4**	**9.8**	**16.1**	**25.9**	**75.1**	**104.6**	**179.7**
Solid Waste									
Public	.05	.05	.05	.5	.3	.8	2.8	2.2	5.0
Private	.05	.05	.05	1.0	.8	1.8	7.0	4.8	11.8
Subtotal	**.05**	**.05**	**.05**	**1.5**	**1.1**	**2.5**	**9.8**	**7.0**	**16.8**
Toxic Substances	.1	.2	.3	.5	.7	1.2	3.9	5.0	8.9
Drinking Water	.05	.05	.05	.1	.3	.4	1.4	1.5	2.9
Noise	.05	.1	.1	.6	1.1	1.7	2.8	4.7	7.5
Pesticides	.1	.05	.1	.1	.05		1.3	.05	1.3 .1
Land Reclamation	.3	1.2	1.5	.3	1.3	1.6	4.1	12.5	16.6
Total	**17.9**	**19.3**	**37.3**	**28.1**	**40.2**	**68.2**	**233.1**	**290.2**	**523.3**

(1) Operating and maintenance costs. (2) Interest and depreciation. (3) O&M plus capital costs. (4) Incremental costs are those made in response to federal legislation beyond those that would have been made in the absence of that legislation.

Investment for Pollution Control by U.S. Industries

Source: Bureau of Economic Analysis, U.S. Commerce Department
(billions of dollars)

New plant and equipment expenditures by U.S. nonfarm business: total and for pollution abatement

	1981 Total expenditures[1]	1981 Pollution abatement Total	1981 Pollution abatement Air	1981 Pollution abatement Water	1981 Pollution abatement Solid waste	Planned 1982 Total expenditures[1]	Planned 1982 Pollution abatement Total	Planned 1982 Pollution abatement Air	Planned 1982 Pollution abatement Water	Planned 1982 Pollution abatement Solid waste
Total nonfarm business	321.49	8.93	4.97	3.04	.92	345.11	9.37	4.91	3.43	1.03
Manufacturing	126.79	5.42	2.69	2.10	.63	136.81	5.78	2.67	2.44	.67
Durable goods	61.84	1.97	1.09	.70	.18	67.24	2.19	1.14	.82	.23
Primary metals[2]	8.12	.78	.54	.19	.05	8.74	.85	.54	.24	.07
Blast furnaces, steel works	3.17	.49	.33	.13	.02	4.07	.51	.30	.18	.03
Nonferrous metals	3.46	.23	.16	.05	.03	2.95	.26	.17	.06	.03
Fabricated metals	2.96	.07	.02	.04	(*)	3.33	.07	.02	.04	.01
Electrical machinery	10.31	.18	.08	.07	.02	12.60	.24	.11	.10	.03
Machinery, except elec.	13.22	.15	.05	.09	.01	14.91	.18	.06	.10	.01
Transportation equipment[2]	18.39	.46	.20	.21	.06	18.59	.49	.19	.23	.07
Motor vehicles	10.08	.35	.16	.16	.04	9.49	.38	.16	.18	.04
Aircraft	6.43	.10	.03	.05	.02	7.25	.10	.03	.05	.03
Stone, clay, and glass	3.14	.16	.12	.03	.01	3.18	.17	.12	.03	.02
Other durables[3]	5.69	.16	.07	.07	.02	5.89	.19	.10	.07	.03
Nondurable goods	64.95	3.46	1.60	1.40	.45	69.58	3.59	1.53	1.63	.44
Food including beverage	8.22	.30	.13	.14	.04	8.07	.27	.12	.13	.02
Textiles	1.56	05	.03	.02	(*)	1.52	.05	.02	.03	(*)
Paper	6.72	.38	.16	.12	.11	6.75	.48	.25	.17	.06
Chemicals	13.60	.88	.38	.36	.14	15.38	.97	.39	.43	.15
Petroleum	26.56	1.76	.88	.74	.14	28.96	1.72	.71	.83	.19
Rubber	1.77	.04	.02	.02	.01	2.03	.06	.02	.02	.01
Other nondurables[4]	6.53	.04	.02	.01	.01	6.87	.04	.02	.01	.01
Nonmanufacturing	194.70	3.51	2.28	.94	.29	208.30	3.59	2.24	.99	.36
Mining	16.86	.46	.18	.18	.10	18.33	.61	.23	.24	.14
Transportation	12.05	.09	.04	.04	.01	13.53	.13	.06	.06	.01
Railroad	4.24	.04	.02	.02	(*)	4.55	.06	.03	.03	(*)
Air	3.81	.01	.01	(*)	(*)	4.15	.02	.01	.01	(*)
Other	4.00	.05	.02	.02	(*)	4.83	.06	.02	.03	(*)
Public utilities	38.40	2.80	1.98	.67	.15	40.20	2.71	1.88	.65	.18
Electric	29.74	2.71	1.91	.65	.15	31.77	2.63	1.82	.63	.18
Gas and other	8.65	.09	.06	.03	(*)	8.43	.07	.05	.02	(*)
Trade and services	86.33	.11	.05	.04	.03	90.48	.10	.05	.03	.03
Communication and other[5]	41.06	.03	.02	.01	(*)	45.75	.04	.03	.01	.01

(1) Consists of final estimates taken from the quarterly surveys of total new plant and equipment and, for 1982, plans based on the 1981 fourth-quarter survey taken in late January and February 1982. (2) Includes industries not shown separately. (3) Consists of lumber, furniture, instruments, and miscellaneous. (4) Consists of apparel, tobacco, leather, and printing-publishing. (5) Consists of communication; construction; social services and membership organizations; and forestry, fisheries, and agricultural services. *Less than $5 million.

Environmental Quality Index

Wildlife: Last year most of the nation's hard-won conservation laws came under the harsh scrutiny of the Reagan Administration's pledge to cut back on federal regulations and make massive budget cuts. Among the hardest hit were programs dealing with wetlands acquisition and protection. At a time when the states were being asked to assume more of the regulatory responsibility, a National Wildlife Federation survey revealed that 21 of the nation's 50 state fish and wildlife agencies lacked the funds needed to keep their conservation programs running effectively.

On the plus side of the conservation ledger, Interior Secretary James Watt strongly supported a congressional move to end federal expenditures for developing thousands of miles of fragile barrier islands along the Atlantic and Gulf coasts. And the Supreme Court upheld key strip-mining curbs administered by the Office of Surface Mining. Unfortunately, the perennial problem of habitat loss persisted— in 1981, 40 square miles of wetlands were lost in Louisiana alone.

The old problem of chemical poisoning again reared its ugly head when Kepone levels in Virginia's James River increased, and the powerful pesticide endrin was discovered in birds after it was sprayed on 260,000 acres of wheat in the West. Furthermore, the EPA moved to free up the use of the controversial compound 1080, banned since 1972, to kill coyotes and other predators. Summing up, NWF Director Alan Wentz warned that unless controls on pesticides were tightened, "we may be returning to an era of indiscriminate chemical use—with resultant damage to wildlife."

Minerals: Worldwide oil production increased slightly. However, consumption decreased significantly, and as a result, the nation was well supplied with oil over much of 1981. In the first 6 months of the year, imports plummeted 20 percent, and prices at the pump actually dropped.

Some analysts attributed the turnabout to the skyrocketing prices that followed oil decontrol in February. Environmentalists argued that Americans had reacted to steadily climbing petroleum prices and had begun to conserve energy long before decontrol took place. Indications were that the government's recent emphasis on conservation and promotion of renewable energy sources was showing results. However, the Reagan Administration apparently didn't see it that way.

Reagan budget proposals included an 86 percent cut in the federal government's energy conservation program. The impact was felt in weatherization programs for low-income families, state energy conservation programs (almost all of which came to a halt) and perhaps most significantly, on the nation's solar energy development efforts which were cut by some 70 percent.

The administration's approach to achieving national energy independence was to propose opening up more federal lands and offshore areas—including the fragile George's Bank off the coast of New England—to coal, oil and other mineral development. Conservationists were left to wonder why, given the urgent need for national energy independence, the administration all but abandoned the solar and energy conservation programs.

Air: The Clean Air Act is one of the nation's oldest environmental laws, as well as the most far-reaching, the costliest, and the most controversial. Thus, environmentalists weren't surprised when the administration targeted this legislation for budget cutting.

That the act has been effective is beyond dispute; the Council on Environmental Quality reported that the Clean Air Act was saving 14,000 lives and over $21 billion in health, property and other damages each year. Critics of the law focused on its cost, complaining that it impedes energy development, slows industrial growth, fuels inflation and eliminates jobs. The administration seemed to agree with the critics, and to boost economic growth proposed an easing of rules. Among the suggested changes: postponing federal deadlines for improved pollution control in the nation's most polluted areas; weakening requirements for coal scrubbing devices; modifying standards for pollution control in national parks; and doubling the permissible levels of certain automobile pollutants (even though auto makers were already meeting the tougher standards).

The other unsolved problem, one that particularly concerned environmentalists, was that of "acid rain." This problem has spread rapidly in recent years, compounded by the increasing use of tall smokestacks by power plants. Experts feared that the situation would worsen as the nation began to use more coal. The Clean Air Act had no provisions to control the long-range pollutants that contribute to acid rain, but an amendment was proposed to address this problem. The administration was openly opposed to controls on the grounds that not enough information about the situation was available, but the National Academy of Sciences warned that the problem was so serious that sulphur emissions should be cut by at least 50 percent to protect human health.

Water: The task of water cleanup has proven to be extremely complicated, due to pollution runoff into surface waters and toxic contamination of underground supplies, which is difficult to monitor and control. Thirty-seven states reported that some of their waters would be unable to meet the law's "fishable and swimmable" mandates by 1983 because of "nonpoint problems," pollution from uncontrolled sources. In addition, more than a third of the new municipal treatment facilities did not meet legal standards and were incapable of handling the variety of toxic wastes that passed through them. Cuts in federal funding only exacerbated these problems. Moreover, the problem of the safe disposal of hazardous wastes remained, yet the administration's 1982 budget cut preliminary investigation and cleanup from 1,300 to 900 sites.

One of the biggest problems in 1981 concerned quantity rather than quality. A drought hit some 42 states, causing record low water levels in several. In addition, many experts pointed to waste and mismanagement as the cause of water shortages.

Forests: The high interest rates that devastated the housing industry kept a tight lid on timber demand, continuing a trend of several years. In a dozen western states, 138 of 750 sawmills closed down, throwing 30,000 people out of work. This was "conservation" of a sort but, nearly everyone agreed, for the wrong reason.

Experts predicted, however, that beyond the current recession, the pressure for increased harvesting on forestlands would be as strong as ever. And there would be pressure to cut more of the slower-growing, older trees. Environmentalists contended that this would have an adverse effect on wildlife, increase siltation of streams and rivers and diminish watershed protection.

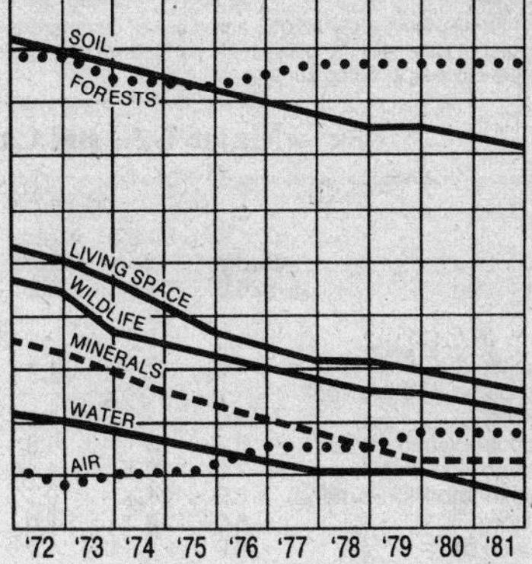

Soil: Once again in 1981, the nation's most serious soil problem was erosion, and the most alarming agricultural issue was the continued loss of farmland to development. Although the demand for increased food production continued to grow both at home and abroad, protection of America's cropland remained woefully inadequate. Last year, the Soil Conservation Service reported that erosion was 35 percent worse than in the Dust Bowl days of the 1930s. In the past, approximately 5 million tons of topsoil were lost to farmlands each year; in 1981, the figure approached 8 million tons. The problem has stemmed not from weather, but rather from the failure of farmers to use antierosion measures. New development continued to gobble up or isolate around 3 million acres of agricultural land, as it has in the recent past.

Living Space: The most worrisome living-space issue continued to be too many people and not enough room. The rapid growth in country dwellers and the counties adjacent to major cities increased demands on inadequately funded mass transit systems, schools and sewage-treatment facilities, and decreased open green space.

These factors, coupled with the nation's economic downturn, placed tremendous pressure on federally owned lands. The issue became one of how much control the government should exercise over public land. There were some positive developments for environmentalists last year—most notably, President Reagan's opposition to basing the MX missile system in Nevada and Utah, and, with the near-completion of the interstate highway system, the end of feverish roadway-construction—but 1981 was on balance a gloomy year for America's living space. Unfortunately, conservationists feared, 1982 might be even worse.

U.S. Forest Land by State and Region

Source: Forest Service, U.S. Agriculture Department, 1979.

State or region	Land area (1,000 acres)	Area forested (1,000 acres)	Percent forested
Connecticut	3,081	1,861	60
Maine	19,729	17,718	90
Massachusetts	5,007	2,952	59
New Hampshire	5,731	5,013	87
Rhode Island	664	404	61
Vermont	5,907	4,512	76
New England	**40,119**	**32,460**	**81**
Delaware	1,233	392	32
Maryland	6,289	2,653	42
New Jersey	4,775	1,928	40
New York	30,357	17,218	57
Pennsylvania	28,592	16,826	59
West Virginia	15,334	11,669	76
Mid Atlantic	**87,813**	**50,686**	**58**
Michigan	30,634	19,270	63
Minnesota	50,382	16,709	33
North Dakota	43,939	422	1
South Dakota	48,381	1,702	4
Wisconsin	34,616	14,908	43
Lake States	**207,952**	**53,011**	**25**
Illinois	35,442	3,810	11
Indiana	22,951	3,943	17
Iowa	35,634	1,561	4
Kansas	52,127	1,344	3
Kentucky	25,282	12,161	48
Missouri	43,868	12,876	29
Nebraska	48,828	1,029	2
Ohio	26,121	6,147	24
Central	**241,425**	**42,871**	**18**
Alabama	32,231	21,361	66
Arkansas	33,091	18,282	55
Florida	33,994	17,040	50
Georgia	36,796	25,256	69
Louisiana	28,409	14,558	51
Mississippi	29,930	16,716	56
North Carolina	30,956	20,043	65
Oklahoma	43,728	8,513	19
South Carolina	19,143	12,249	64
Tennessee	26,290	13,161	50
Texas	167,283	23,279	14
Virginia	25,286	16,417	65
South	**474,906**	**185,514**	**39**
Alaska	362,485	119,145	33
California	99,847	40,152	48
Hawaii	4,109	1,986	40
Oregon	61,356	29,810	49
Washington	42,456	23,181	55
Pacific Coast	**570,253**	**214,274**	**38**
Arizona	72,580	18,494	25
Colorado	66,283	22,271	34
Idaho	52,676	21,726	41
Montana	92,826	22,559	24
Nevada	70,295	7,683	11
New Mexico	77,669	18,060	23
Utah	52,505	15,557	30
Wyoming	62,055	10,028	16
Rocky Mountain	**546,959**	**136,378**	**25**
Total U.S.	**2,169,427**	**[1]715,194**	**33**

(1) Of this total, 482,486,000 acres are of commercial quality (137 million acres are government owned); 20,664,000 acres are productive but reserved (land set aside by statute); 4,626,000 acres are deferred for possible reserve status; and 228,782,000 acres are unproductive or awaiting survey.

Major U.S. and Canadian Public Zoological Parks

Source: World Almanac questionnaire, 1982; budget, metro population, and attendance are in millions. (A) designates Park has not provided up-to-date information. (b) includes capital improvements.

Zoo	Budget-	Metro pop.	Attendance	Acres	Species	Major Attractions
San Diego	$20.0	1.8	3.2	100	750	Loalas, pygmy chimps, Skyfari aerial tramway, parrots, koalas (breeding colony), red pandas.
Bronx (N.Y.C.) (A)	16.0	11.5	2.0	252	600	Wild Asia, children's zoo, Reptile House.
Brookfield (Chicago)	14.5	7.1	1.8	200	500	Porpoise show, predator ecology, baboon island.
San Diego (Wild Animal Park) (A)	10.0	1.7	1.0	1,800	293	Canine show, bird and elephant show, monorail.
National (Wash. D.C.)	9.2	3.1	3.3	168	395	Lion/Tiger complex, Beaver Valley, giant pandas.
Toronto	7.6	2.1	1.1	710	395	Canadian Domain ride, exotic plants and birds.
Washington Pk (Portland)	6.5 [b]	1.1	0.7	62	125	Asian elephants, musk oxen, Humboldt penguins.
St. Louis	6.0	2.3	2.0	83	633	Big cat country, herpetarium, primate house.
Milwaukee	6.0	1.3	1.2	185	560	Monkey island, moose yard, predator/prey exhibit.
Oklahoma City	5.5	0.8	0.6	110	435	African plains, Patagonian cliffs, Galapagos Isl.
Calgary	5.2	0.65	0.75	150	350	Exotic vertebrates, prehistoric park, tropical conservatory.
Philadelphia (A)	5.5	5.0	1.1	42	525	Reptiles, African plains, hummingbirds.
Minnesota	5.0	2.0	1.0	500	325	Whale, dolphin and bird shows; X-country skiing.
Los Angeles	3.9	8.0	1.5	113	472	Koalas, white tigers, children's zoo.
Woodland Pk (Seattle)	2.9	1.4	0.8	90	327	Nocturnal house, N.E. waterfowl habitat.
Houston	2.8	2.9	1.9	46	526	Gorilla habitat, tropical bird house, Kipp aquarium.
Cleveland	2.5	2.4	0.6	130	382	Primate and cat bldg., pachyderm building.
Columbus	2.5	1.3	0.6	90	633	Gorilla and reptile collection, giraffe complex.
Denver	2.5	1.7	1.0	76	336	Bird world, Bighorn and Dall sheep exhibit.
Lincoln Park (Chicago)	2.4	7.1	4.0	35	410	Great apes, farm in the zoo, snow leopards.
San Francisco	2.3	3.2	0.8	75	325	Gorilla world, insect zoo, white tigers.
Buffalo	2.3	1.2	0.4	24	234	Rhino yard, tropical gorilla exhibit, children's zoo.
San Antonio	2.2	1.1	0.9	50	730	Dioramas, rare antelopes, white rhinoceros, gelada baboons.
Phoenix	2.2	1.5	0.7	125	288	Arabian oryx herd, Orangutans, Arizona exhibit.
Dallas	2.0	0.9	0.6	50	550	Okapi, bongo antelope, Grevy's zebra.
Arizona-Sonora Desert Museum (Tucson)	2.0	0.5	0.4	11	260	Earth science center, sunset desert demo.
Memphis	2.0	0.9	0.6	36	339	Great apes, aquarium, hooved stock.
Albuquerque	1.9	0.4	0.4	50	900	Rain forest exhibit, reptile house.
Baltimore	1.7	1.5	0.4	142	281	Largest black-footed penguin colony in U.S.
Columbia, S.C.	1.7	0.4	0.3	151	190	Polar bears, rain forest exhibit.
Pittsburgh	1.5	1.0	0.6	75	374	Twilight zoo, AquaZoo, Children's zoo train.
Toledo	1.2	0.8	0.4	33	369	Freshwater aquarium, greenhouse, botanical gardens.

Mammals: Orders and Major Families

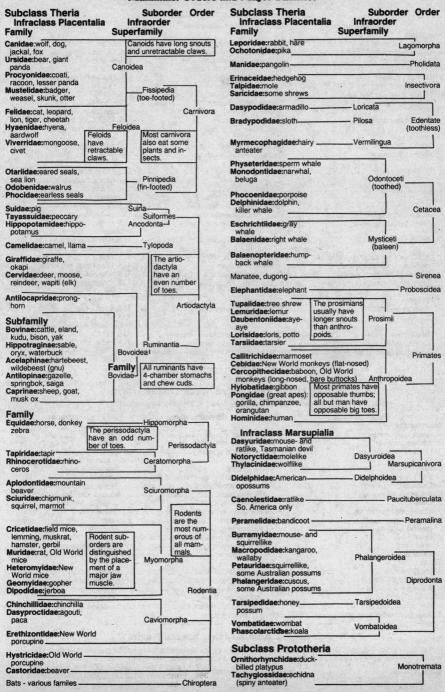

Subclass Theria
Infraclass Placentalia

Family	Superfamily	Suborder / Infraorder	Order
Canidae: wolf, dog, jackal, fox	Canoidea	Fissipedia (toe-footed)	Carnivora
Ursidae: bear, giant panda	Canoidea	Fissipedia (toe-footed)	Carnivora
Procyonidae: coati, racoon, lesser panda	Canoidea	Fissipedia (toe-footed)	Carnivora
Mustelidae: badger, weasel, skunk, otter	Canoidea	Fissipedia (toe-footed)	Carnivora
Felidae: cat, leopard, lion, tiger, cheetah	Feloidea	Fissipedia (toe-footed)	Carnivora
Hyaenidae: hyena, aardwolf	Feloidea	Fissipedia (toe-footed)	Carnivora
Viverridae: mongoose, civet	Feloidea	Fissipedia (toe-footed)	Carnivora
Otariidae: eared seals, sea lion		Pinnipedia (fin-footed)	Carnivora
Odobenidae: walrus		Pinnipedia (fin-footed)	Carnivora
Phocidae: earless seals		Pinnipedia (fin-footed)	Carnivora
Suidae: pig	Suina	Suiformes	Artiodactyla
Tayassuidae: peccary	Suina	Suiformes	Artiodactyla
Hippopotamidae: hippopotamus	Ancodonta	Suiformes	Artiodactyla
Camelidae: camel, llama		Tylopoda	Artiodactyla
Giraffidae: giraffe, okapi		Ruminantia	Artiodactyla
Cervidae: deer, moose, reindeer, wapiti (elk)		Ruminantia	Artiodactyla
Antilocapridae: pronghorn	Bovoidea	Ruminantia	Artiodactyla
Subfamily (Family Bovidae)			
Bovinae: cattle, eland, kudu, bison, yak	Bovoidea	Ruminantia	Artiodactyla
Hippotraginae: sable, oryx, waterbuck	Bovoidea	Ruminantia	Artiodactyla
Acelaphinae: hartebeest, wildebeest (gnu)	Bovoidea	Ruminantia	Artiodactyla
Antilopinae: gazelle, springbok, saiga	Bovoidea	Ruminantia	Artiodactyla
Caprinae: sheep, goat, musk ox	Bovoidea	Ruminantia	Artiodactyla
Family			
Equidae: horse, donkey zebra		Hippomorpha	Perissodactyla
Tapiridae: tapir		Ceratomorpha	Perissodactyla
Rhinocerotidae: rhinoceros		Ceratomorpha	Perissodactyla
Aplodontidae: mountain beaver		Sciuromorpha	Rodentia
Sciuridae: chipmunk, squirrel, marmot		Sciuromorpha	Rodentia
Cricetidae: field mice, lemming, muskrat, hamster, gerbil		Myomorpha	Rodentia
Muridae: rat, Old World mice		Myomorpha	Rodentia
Heteromyidae: New World mice		Myomorpha	Rodentia
Geomyidae: gopher		Myomorpha	Rodentia
Dipodidae: jerboa		Myomorpha	Rodentia
Chinchillidae: chinchilla		Caviomorpha	Rodentia
Dasyproctidae: agouti, paca		Caviomorpha	Rodentia
Erethizontidae: New World porcupine		Caviomorpha	Rodentia
Hystricidae: Old World porcupine			Rodentia
Castoridae: beaver			Rodentia
Bats - various familes			Chiroptera

> Canoids have long snouts and unretractable claws.

> Feloids have retractable claws.

> Most carnivora also eat some plants and insects.

> The artiodactyla have an even number of toes.

> All ruminants have 4-chamber stomachs and chew cuds.

> The perissodactyla have an odd number of toes.

> Rodent suborders are distinguished by the placement of a major jaw muscle.

> Rodents are the most numerous of all mammals.

Family	Suborder / Infraorder	Order
Leporidae: rabbit, hare		Lagomorpha
Ochotonidae: pika		Lagomorpha
Manidae: pangolin		Pholidata
Erinaceidae: hedgehog		Insectivora
Talpidae: mole		Insectivora
Saricidae: some shrews		Insectivora
Dasypodidae: armadillo	Loricata	Edentate (toothless)
Bradypodidae: sloth	Pilosa	Edentate (toothless)
Myrmecophagidae: hairy anteater	Vermilingua	Edentate (toothless)
Physeteridae: sperm whale	Odontoceti (toothed)	Cetacea
Monodontidae: narwhal, beluga	Odontoceti (toothed)	Cetacea
Phocoenidae: porpoise	Odontoceti (toothed)	Cetacea
Delphinidae: dolphin, killer whale	Odontoceti (toothed)	Cetacea
Eschrichtiidae: gray whale	Mysticeti (baleen)	Cetacea
Balaenidae: right whale	Mysticeti (baleen)	Cetacea
Balaenopteridae: humpback whale	Mysticeti (baleen)	Cetacea
Manatee, dugong		Sirenea
Elephantidae: elephant		Proboscidea
Tupaiidae: tree shrew	Prosimii	Primates
Lemuridae: lemur	Prosimii	Primates
Daubentoniidae: aye-aye	Prosimii	Primates
Lorisidae: loris, potto	Prosimii	Primates
Tarsiidae: tarsier	Prosimii	Primates
Callitrichidae: marmoset	Anthropoidea	Primates
Cebidae: New World monkeys (flat-nosed)	Anthropoidea	Primates
Cercopithecidae: baboon, Old World monkeys (long-nosed, bare buttocks)	Anthropoidea	Primates
Hylobatidae: gibbon	Anthropoidea	Primates
Pongidae (great apes): gorilla, chimpanzee, orangutan	Anthropoidea	Primates
Hominidae: human	Anthropoidea	Primates

> The prosimians usually have longer snouts than anthropoids.

> Most primates have opposable thumbs; all but man have opposable big toes.

Infraclass Marsupialia

Family	Superfamily	Order
Dasyuridae: mouse- and ratlike, Tasmanian devil	Dasyuroidea	Marsupicanivora
Notoryctidae: molelike	Dasyuroidea	Marsupicanivora
Thylacinidae: wolflike	Dasyuroidea	Marsupicanivora
Didelphidae: American opossums	Didelphoidea	Marsupicanivora
Caenolestidae: ratlike So. America only		Paucituberculata
Peramelidae: bandicoot		Peramalina
Burramyidae: mouse- and squirrellike	Phalangeroidea	Diprodonta
Macropodidae: kangaroo, wallaby	Phalangeroidea	Diprodonta
Petauridae: squirrellike, some Australian possums	Phalangeroidea	Diprodonta
Phalangeridae: cuscus, some Australian possums	Phalangeroidea	Diprodonta
Tarsipedidae: honey possum	Tarsipedoidea	Diprodonta
Vombatidae: wombat	Vombatoidea	Diprodonta
Phascolarctidae: koala	Vombatoidea	Diprodonta

Subclass Prototheria

Family	Order
Ornithorhynchidae: duck-billed platypus	Monotremata
Tachyglossidae: echidna (spiny anteater)	Monotremata

Some Endangered Species in North America

Source: U.S. Fish and Wildlife Service, U.S. Interior Department

Common name	Scientific name	Range
Mammals		
Virginia big-eared bat	Plecotus townsendii virginianus	U.S. (Ky., W.V., Va.)
Columbian white-tailed deer	Odocoileus virginianus leucurus	U.S. (Wash., Ore.)
San Joaquin kit fox	Vulpes macrotis mutica	U.S. (Cal.)
Salt marsh harvest mouse	Reithrodontomys raviventris	U.S. (Cal.)
Florida panther	Felis concolor coryi	U.S. (La., Ark. east to S.C., Fla.)
Utah prairie dog	Cynomys parvidens	U.S. (Ut.)
Morro Bay kangaroo rat	Dipodomys heermanni morroensis	U.S. (Cal.)
Delmarva Peninsula fox squirrel	Sciurus niger cinereus	U.S. (DelMarVa Peninsula to SE Pa.)
West Indian manatee	Trichechus manatus	U.S. (SE), Caribbean, So. Amer.
Red wolf	Canis rufus	U.S. (Southeast to Tex.)
Birds		
Masked bobwhite (quail)	Colinus virginianus ridgwayi	U.S. (Ariz.), Mexico
California condor	Gymnogyps californianus	U.S. (Ore., Cal.), Mexico (Baja Calif.)
Whooping crane	Grus americana	U.S. (Rky. Mntns. east to Carolinas), Canada, Mexico
Eskimo curlew	Numenius borealis	Alaska and N. Canada to Argentina
Bald eagle	Haliaeetus leucocephalus	U.S. (most states), Canada
American peregrine falcon	Falco peregrinus anatum	Canada to Mexico
Aleutian Canada goose	Branta canadensis leucopareia	U.S. (Ark., Cal., Ore., Wash.), Japan
Brown pelican	Pelecanus occidentalis	U.S. (Carolinas to Tex., Cal.), West Indies, C. and S. America
Attwater's greater prairie chicken	Tympanuchus cupido attwateri	U.S. (Tex.)
Bachman's warbler (wood)	Vermivora bachmanii	U.S. (Southeastern), Cuba
Kirtland's warbler (wood)	Dendroica kirtlandii	U.S., Canada, Bahama Is.
Ivory-billed woodpecker	Campephilus principalis	U.S. (Southcentral and Southeast), Cuba
Reptiles		
American alligator**	Alligator mississippiensis	U.S. (Southeast)
American crocodile	Crocodylus acutus	U.S. (Fla.), Mexico, South and Central America, Carribean
Island night lizard*	Xantusia (-Klauberina) riversiana	U.S. (Cal.)
Eastern indigo snake*	Drymarchon corais couperi	U.S. (Ala., Fla., Ga., Miss., S.C.)

*Threatened rather than endangered. **Endangered except where listed as threatened.

Some Other Endangered Species in the World

Source: U.S. Fish and Wildlife Service, U.S. Interior Department

Common name	Scientific name	Range
Mammals		
Giant sable antelope	Hippotragus niger variani	Angola
African elephant*	Loxodonta africana	Africa
Saudi Arabian gazelle	Gazella dorcas saudiya	Israel, Iraq, Jordan, Saudi Arabia, Syria, Kuwait
Brown hyena	Hyaena brunnea	Southern Africa
Red kangaroo*	Macropus (-Megaleia) rufs	Australia
Leopard**	Panthera pardus	Africa, India, SE Asia
Black howler monkey*	Alouatta pigra	Mexico, Guatemala, Belize
Ocelot	Felis pardalis	C. and S. America
Thin-spined porcupine	Chaetomys subspinosus	Brazil
Tiger	Panthera tigris	Asia
Banded hare wallaby	Lagostrophus fasciatus	Australia
Gray whale	Eschrichtius robustus	N. Pacific Ocean
Wild yak	Bos grunniens mutus	China (Tibet), India
Mountain zebra	Equus zebra zebra	South Africa
Birds		
Indigo macaw	Anodorhynchus leari	Brazil
West African ostrich	Struthio camelus spatzi	Spanish Sahara
Anjouan scops owl	Otus rutilus capnodes	Indian Ocean: Comoro Island
Golden parakeet	Aratinga guarouba	Brazil
Australian parrot	Geopsittacus occidentalis	Australia

*Threatened rather than endangered. **Threatened in South Africa.

Young of Animals Have Special Names

The young of many animals, birds and fish have come to be called by special names. A young eel, for example, is an elver. Many young animals, of course, are often referred to simply as infants, babies, younglets, or younglings.

bunny: rabbit.
calf: cattle, elephant, antelope, rhino, hippo, whale, etc.
cheeper: grouse, partridge, quail.
chick, chicken: fowl.
cockerel: rooster.
codling, sprag: codfish.
colt: horse (male).
cub: lion, bear, shark, fox, etc.

cygnet: swan.
duckling: duck.
eaglet: eagle.
elver: eel.
eyas: hawk, others.
fawn: deer.
filly: horse (female).
fingerling: fish generally.
flapper: wild fowl.
fledgling: birds generally.
foal: horse, zebra, others.
fry: fish generally.
gosling: goose.
heifer: cow.
joey: kangaroo, others.
kid: goat.
kit: fox, beaver, rabbit, cat.
kitten, kitty, catling: cats, other fur-bearers.
lamb, lambkin, cosset, hog: sheep.
leveret: hare.
nestling: birds generally.
owlet: owl.
parr, smolt, grilse: salmon.
piglet, shoat, farrow, suckling: pig.
polliwog, tadpole: frog.
poult: turkey.
pullet: hen.
pup: dog, seal, sea lion, fox.
puss, pussy: cat.
spike, blinker, tinker: mackerel.
squab: pigeon.
squeaker: pigeon, others.
whelp: dog, tiger, beasts of prey.
yearling: cattle, sheep, horse, etc.

Speeds of Animals

Source: Natural History magazine, March 1974.

Animal	Mph	Animal	Mph	Animal	Mph
Cheetah	70	Mongolian wild ass	40	Human	27.89
Pronghorn antelope	61	Greyhound	39.35	Elephant	25
Wildebeest	50	Whippet	35.50	Black mamba snake	20
Lion	50	Rabbit (domestic)	35	Six-lined race runner	18
Thomson's gazelle	50	Mule deer	35	Wild turkey	15
Quarterhorse	47.5	Jackal	35	Squirrel	12
Elk	45	Reindeer	32	Pig (domestic)	11
Cape hunting dog	45	Giraffe	32	Chicken	9
Coyote	43	White-tailed deer	30	Spider (Tegenaria atrica)	1.17
Gray fox	42	Wart hog	30	Giant tortoise	0.17
Hyena	40	Grizzly bear	30	Three-toed sloth	0.15
Zebra	40	Cat (domestic)	30	Garden snail	0.03

Most of these measurements are for maximum speeds over approximate quarter-mile distances. Exceptions are the lion and elephant, whose speeds were clocked in the act of charging; the whippet, which was timed over a 200-yard course; the cheetah over a 100-yard distance; man for a 15-yard segment of a 100-yard run (of 13.6 seconds); and the black mamba, six-lined race runner, spider, giant tortoise, three-toed sloth, and garden snail, which were measured over various small distances.

Gestation, Longevity, and Incubation of Animals

Longevity figures were supplied by Ronald T. Reuther. They refer to animals in captivity; the potential life span of animals is rarely attained in nature. Maximum longevity figures are from the Biology Data Book, 1972. Figures on gestation and incubation are averages based on estimates by leading authorities.

Animal	Gestation (day)	Average longevity (years)	Maximun longevity (yrs., mos.)
Ass	365	12	35-10
Baboon	187	20	35-7
Bear: Black	219	18	36-10
Grizzly	225	25	—
Polar	240	20	34-8
Beaver	122	5	20-6
Buffalo (American)	278	15	—
Bactrian camel	406	12	29-5
Cat (domestic)	63	12	28
Chimpanzee	231	20	44-6
Chipmunk	31	6	8
Cow	284	15	30
Deer (white-tailed)	201	8	17-6
Dog (domestic)	61	12	20
Elephant (African)	—	35	60
Elephant (Asian)	645	40	70
Elk	250	15	26-6
Fox (red)	52	7	14
Giraffe	425	10	33-7
Goat (domestic)	151	8	18
Gorilla	257	20	39-4
Guinea pig	68	4	7-6
Hippopotamus	238	25	—
Horse	330	20	46
Kangaroo	42	7	—

Animal	Gestation (day)	Average longevity (years)	Maximum longevity (yrs., mos.)
Leopard	98	12	19-4
Lion	100	15	25-1
Monkey (rhesus)	164	15	—
Moose	240	12	—
Mouse (meadow)	21	3	—
Mouse (dom. white)	19	3	3-6
Opossum (American)	14-17	1	—
Pig (domestic)	112	10	27
Puma	90	12	19
Rabbit (domestic)	31	5	13
Rhinoceros (black)	450	15	—
Rhinoceros (white)	—	20	—
Sea lion (California)	350	12	28
Sheep (domestic)	154	12	20
Squirrel (gray)	44	10	—
Tiger	105	16	26-3
Wolf (maned)	63	5	—
Zebra (Grant's)	365	15	—

Incubation time (days)

Chicken	21
Duck	30
Goose	30
Pigeon	18
Turkey	26

A Collection of Animal Collectives

The English language boasts an abundance of names to describe groups of things, particularly pairs or aggregations of animals. Some of these words have fallen into comparative disuse, but many of them are still in service, helping to enrich the vocabularies of those who like their language to be precise, who tire of hearing a group referred to as "a bunch of," or who enjoy the sound of words that aren't overworked.

band of gorillas
bed of clams, oysters
bevy of quail, swans
brace of ducks
brood of chicks
cast of hawks
cete of badgers
charm of goldfinches
chattering of choughs
cloud of gnats
clowder of cats
clutch of chicks
clutter of cats
colony of ants
congregation of plovers
covey of quail, partridge
cry of hounds
down of hares
drift of swine
drove of cattle, sheep
exaltation of larks
flight of birds
flock of sheep, geese
gaggle of geese
gam of whales
gang of elks
grist of bees
herd of elephants
hive of bees
horde of gnats
husk of hares
kindle or **kendle** of kittens
knot of toads
leap of leopards
leash of greyhounds, foxes
litter of pigs
mob of kangaroos
murder of crows
muster of peacocks
mute of hounds

nest of vipers
nest, nide of pheasants
pack of hounds, wolves
pair of horses
pod of whales, seals
pride of lions
school of fish
sedge or **siege** of cranes
shoal of fish, pilchards
skein of geese
skulk of foxes
sleuth of bears
sounder of boars, swine
span of mules
spring of teals
swarm of bees
team of ducks, horses
tribe or **trip** of goats
troop of kangaroos, monkeys
volery of birds
watch of nightingales
wing of plovers
yoke of oxen

Major Venomous Animals

Snakes

Coral snake - 2 to 4 ft. long, in Americas south of Canada; bite is nearly painless; very slow onset of paralysis, difficulty breathing; mortality high without anti-venin.

Rattlesnake - 2 to 8 ft. long, throughout W. Hemisphere. Rapid onset of symptoms of severe pain, swelling; mortality low, but amputation of affected limb is sometimes necessary; anti-venin. Probably high mortality for Mojave rattler.

Cottonmouth water moccasin - less than 6 ft. long, wetlands of southern U.S. from Virginia to Texas. Rapid onset of symptoms of severe pain, swelling; mortality low, but tissue destruction, caused by the venom's effect on the blood, can be extensive; anti-venin.

Copperhead - less than 4 ft. long, from New England to Texas; pain and swelling; very seldom fatal.

Fer-de-lance - up to 7 ft. long, Martinique only; venom attacks nerves and blood; probably high mortality.

Bushmaster - up to 9 ft. long, jungles of C. and S. America; few bites recorded; probably low mortality.

Yellow-beard - up to 7 ft. long, from tropical Mexico to Brazil; severe tissue damage common; low mortality; anti-venin.

Asian pit vipers - from 2 to 5 ft. long throughout Asia; reactions and mortality vary but most bites cause tissue damage and mortality is generally low.

Sharp-nosed pit viper - up to 5 ft. long, in eastern China and Indo-China; the most toxic of Asian pit vipers; very rapid onset of swelling and tissue damage, internal bleeding; moderate mortality; anti-venin.

Boomslang - under 6 ft. long, in African savannahs; rapid onset of nausea and dizziness, often followed by slight recovery and then sudden death from internal hemorrhaging; bites rare, mortality high; anti-venin.

European vipers - from 1 to 3 ft. long; bleeding and tissue damage; mortality low; anti-venins.

Puff adder - up to 5 ft. long, fat; south of the Sahara and throughout the Middle East; rapid large swelling, great pain, dizziness; moderate mortality often from internal bleeding; anti-venin.

Gaboon viper - over 6 ft. long, fat; 2-inch fangs; south of the Sahara; massive tissue damage, internal bleeding; mortality rate not clear.

Saw-scaled or carpet viper - up to 2 ft. long, in dry areas from India to Africa; severe bleeding, fever; high mortality, venom 3 times more toxic than common cobra's; anti-venin.

Desert horned viper - in dry areas of Africa and western Asia; swelling and tissue damage; low mortality; anti-venin.

Russel's viper or tic-palonga - over 5 ft. long, throughout Asia; internal bleeding; mortality rate not clear; bite reports common; anti-venin.

Black mamba - up to 14 ft. long, fast-moving; S. and C. Africa; rapid onset of dizziness, difficulty breathing, erratic heart-beat; mortality high, nears 100% without anti-venin.

Kraits - in S. Asia; rapid onset of sleepiness; numbness; kraits are among the most lethal snakes in the world with up to 50% mortality even with anti-venin treatment.

Common or Asian cobra - 4 to 8 ft. long, throughout S. Asia; considerable tissue damage, sometimes paralysis; mortality probably not more than 10%; anti-venin.

King cobra - up to 16 ft. long, large hood; throughout S. Asia; rapid swelling, dizziness, loss of consciousness, difficulty breathing, erratic heart-beat; mortality varies sharply with amount of venom involved, most bites involve non-fatal amounts; anti-venin.

Yellow or Cape cobra - 7 ft. long, in southern Africa; most toxic venom of any cobra; rapid onset of swelling, breathing and cardiac difficulties; mortality high without treatment; anti-venin.

Ringhals, or spitting, cobra - 5 ft. and 7 ft. long; southern Africa; squirt venom through holes in front of fangs as a defense; venom is severely irritating and can cause blindness.

Australian brown snakes - very slow onset of symptoms of cardiac or respiratory distress; moderate mortality; anti-venin.

Tiger snake - 2 to 6 ft. long, S. Australia; pain, numbness, mental disturbances with rapid onset of paralysis; may be the most deadly of all land snakes though anti-venin is quite effective.

Death adder - less than 3 ft. long, Australia; rapid onset of faintness, cardiac and respiratory distress; at least 50% mortality without anti-venin.

Taipan - up to 11 ft. long, in Australia and New Guinea; rapid paralysis with severe breathing difficulty; mortality nears 100% without anti-venin.

Sea snakes - throughout Pacific and Indian oceans except NE Pacific; almost painless bite, variety of muscle pain, paralysis; mortality rate about 15%, many bites are not envenomed; some anti-venins.

Notes: Not all snake bites by venomous snakes are actually envenomed; for a variety of reasons, the snake may be temporarily lacking in venom or fail to inject it. Any animal bite, however, carries the danger of tetanus and no bite by a venomous snake should go untreated. Anti-venins are not certain cures; they are only an aid in the treatment of bites. Mortality rates above are for envenomed bites; low mortality, up to 5% result in death; moderate, up to 15%; high, over 15%. Even in cases in which the victim recovers fully, prolonged hospitalization and extensive, continuous medical procedures are usually required.

Lizards

Gila monster - up to 30 inches long with heavy body and tail, in high desert in southwest U.S. and N. Mexico; immediate severe pain followed by vomiting, thirst, difficulty swallowing, weakness approaching paralysis; mortality very low with medical treatment, otherwise high; anti-venin.

Mexican beaded lizard - similar to Gila monster, Mexican west-coast; reaction and mortality rate similar to Gila monster; anti-venin.

Insects

Ants, bees, wasps, hornets, etc. All have global distribution. Usual reaction is piercing pain in area of sting. Never directly fatal, except in cases of massive multiple stings. Many people suffer allergic reactions - swelling, rashes, partial paralysis –and a few may die within minutes from severe sensitivity to the venom (anaphylactic shock).

Spiders, scorpions

Black widow - small, round-bodied with hour-glass marking; the widow and its relatives are found around the world in tropical and temperate zones; sharp pain, weakness, clammy skin, muscular rigidity, breathing difficulty and, in small children, convulsions; low mortality.

Brown recluse or fiddleback - small, oblong body; can be found anywhere in U.S. today; slow onset of pain and severe ulceration at place of bite; in severe cases fever, nausea, and stomach cramps; ulceration may last months; very low mortality.

***Atrax* spiders** - several varieties, often large, found in Australia; slow onset of breathing and circulation difficulties; low mortality.

Tarantulas - large, hairy spiders found around the world; American tarantulas, and probably all others, are **harmless,** though their bite may cause some pain and swelling.

Scorpions - crab-like body with stinger in tail, various sizes, many varieties throughout tropical and subtropical areas; various symptoms may include severe pain spreading from the wound, numbness, severe emotional agitation, cramps; severe reactions include vomiting, diarrhea, respiratory failure; moderate, perhaps high, mortality, particularly in children; anti-venins.

Sea Life

Sea wasps - jellyfish, with tentacles up to 30 ft. long, in the South Pacific; very rapid onset of circulatory problems; high mortality largely because of the speed of toxic reaction; anti-venin.

Portuguese man-of-war - jellyfish-like, with tentacles up to 70 ft. long, in most warm water areas; immediate severe pain; not fatal, though shock may cause death in a rare case.

Octopi - global distribution, usually in warm waters; all varieties produce venom but only a few can cause death; rapid onset of paralysis with breathing difficulty.

Stingrays - several varieties of differing sizes, found in tropical and temperate seas and some fresh water; severe pain, rapid onset of nausea, vomiting, breathing difficulties; wound area may ulcerate, gangrene may appear; seldom fatal.

Stonefish - brownish fish which lies motionless as a rock on bottom in shallow water; throughout S. Pacific and Indian oceans; extraordinary pain, rapid paralysis; low mortality.

Cone-shells - molluscs in small, beautiful shells in the S. Pacific and Indian oceans; shoot barbs into victims; paralysis; low mortality.

American Kennel Club Registrations

	Rank 1981	1981	Rank 1980	1980
Poodles	1	93,050	1	95,250
Cocker Spaniels	2	83,504	3	76,113
Doberman Pinschers	3	77,387	2	79,908
German Shepherd Dogs	4	60,976	4	58,865
Labrador Retrievers	5	58,569	5	52,398
Golden Retrievers	6	48,473	6	44,100
Miniature Schnauzers	7	35,912	8	34,962
Beagles	8	35,655	7	35,091
Dachshunds	9	33,560	9	33,881
Shetland Sheepdogs	10	29,481	10	28,325
Yorkshire Terriers	11	25,698	11	24,665
Lhasa Apsos	12	25,424	12	24,477
English Springer Span.	13	22,574	14	21,370
Collies	14	20,843	13	21,477
Siberian Huskies	15	20,465	15	20,884
Shih-Tzu	16	19,547	17	17,957
Chow Chows	17	18,511	24	14,589
Pekingese	18	18,366	16	18,859
Pomeranians	19	17,926	18	17,341
Brittany Spaniels	20	17,411	20	17,146
Basset Hounds	21	17,262	19	17,151
Chihuahuas	22	16,495	21	16,239
Boxers	23	15,574	23	14,901
Great Danes	24	13,311	25	14,330
Boston Terriers	25	11,681	26	11,636
Irish Setters	26	10,972	22	14,938
German Shorthaired Pointers	27	10,542	28	10,670
Old English Sheepdogs	28	9,697	27	10,758
Samoyeds	29	8,307	29	8,430
Maltese	30	7,775	31	7,324
Alaskan Malamutes	31	7,154	30	7,642
West Highland White Terriers	32	7,033	33	6,824
Bulldogs	33	6,933	34	6,712
Airedale Terriers	34	6,918	32	6,898
Rottweilers	35	6,524	44	4,701
Cairn Terriers	36	6,346	35	6,561
Scottish Terriers	37	6,202	36	6,334
Pugs	38	6,097	40	5,731
Keeshonden	39	5,848	38	6,081
Dalmatians	40	5,482	41	5,585
Afghan Hounds	41	5,337	37	6,122
Norwegian Elkhounds	42	4,899	42	5,374
St. Bernards	43	4,885	39	5,908
Weimaraners	44	4,469	43	4,714
Chesapeake Bay Retr.	45	4,071	46	3,828
Fox Terriers (Smooth and Wire)	46	3,832	45	3,866
Bichons Frises	47	3,268	47	2,651
Silky Terriers	48	2,701	48	2,640
Akitas	49	2,660	50	2,279
Welsh Corgis (Pembroke)	50	2,482	49	2,445
Newfoundlands	51	2,309	51	2,147
Miniature Pinschers	52	2,034	53	1,817
Vizslas	53	1,980	52	1,837
Bloodhounds	54	1,730	54	1,709
Bouviers des Flandres	55	1,669	57	1,389
Great Pyrenees	56	1,603	62	1,267
Schipperkes	57	1,535	56	1,462
Basenjis	58	1,455	59	1,348
Whippets	59	1,383	60	1,323
American Staffordshire Terriers	60	1,369	64	1,228
Mastiffs	61	1,367	66	1,198
English Cocker Spaniels	62	1,356	63	1,232
Borzois	63	1,307	61	1,309
Rhodesian Ridgebacks	64	1,243	70	1,168
English Setters	65	1,184	58	1,370
Gordon Setters	66	1,171	69	1,170
Irish Wolfhounds	67	1,143	67	1,192
German Wirehaired Pointers	68	1,088	68	1,171

	Rank 1981	1981	Rank 1980	1980
Bull Terriers	69	1,053	65	1,222
Soft-Coated Wheaten Terriers	70	970	71	981
Bullmastiffs	71	908	72	918
Standard Schnauzers	72	751	76	648
Papillons	73	732	78	613
Welsh Terriers	74	724	74	748
Bearded Collies	75	723	75	653
Belgian Sheepdogs	76	711	79	584
Salukis	77	686	77	627
Australian Terriers	78	679	73	770
Giant Schnauzers	79	567	82	540
Italian Greyhounds	80	562	81	560
Australian Cattle Dogs	81	544	55	1,685
Kerry Blue Terriers	82	532	80	576
Manchester Terriers	83	511	83	492
Pointers	84	456	84	427
Bernese Mountain Dogs	85	450	87	380
Tibetan Terriers	86	434	86	387
Belgian Tervuren	87	405	85	422
Japanese Chin	88	382	89	373
Bedlington Terriers	89	380	92	336
Welsh Corgis (Cardigan)	90	333	91	361
American Water Span.	91	332	90	363
Pulik	92	319	88	375
Black and Tan Coonhounds	93	284	93	333
Staffordshire Bull Terriers	94	282	95	260
Lakeland Terriers	95	258	97	219
Irish Terriers	96	250	94	305
Border Terriers	97	249	98	207
Kuvaszok	98	244	99	197
Briards	99	234	96	250
Flat-Coated Retrievers	100	208	101	194
Norwich Terriers	100	208	102	190
Brussels Griffons	102	199	104	170
Skye Terriers	102	199	103	171
French Bulldogs	104	184	104	170
Welsh Springer Spaniels	105	180	107	148
Dandie Dinmont Terriers	106	179	99	197
Komondorok	107	156	109	135
Scottish Deerhounds	108	155	106	155
Norfolk Terriers	109	150	113	95
Greyhounds	110	123	108	137
Wirehaired Pointing Griffons	110	123	109	135
Sealyham Terriers	112	114	112	108
Affenpinschers	113	105	115	85
Irish Water Spaniels	114	101	111	114
English Toy Spaniels	115	81	117	76
Clumber Spaniels	116	78	114	90
Ibizan Hounds	117	64	118	68
Belgian Malinois	118	60	120	48
American Foxhounds	119	57	119	51
Curly-Coated Retrievers	120	54	116	79
Field Spaniels	121	42	121	32
Otter Hounds	122	34	123	29
Harriers	123	22	121	32
Sussex Spaniels	124	12	124	10
English Foxhounds	125	1	125	0
Total Registrations:		**1,033,849**		**1,011,799**

Dogs Registered by Groups	**1981**	**1980**
Sporting breeds	268,950	253,649
Hound breeds	106,400	107,100
Working breeds	293,099	294,050
Terrier breeds	74,350	73,550
Toy breeds	118,700	114,450
Non-sporting breeds	172,350	169,000
	1,033,849	**1,011,799**

Cat Breeds

There are 27 cat breeds recognized: abyssinian, american shorthair, balinese, birman, bombay, burmese, colorpoint shorthair, egyptian mau, exotic shorthair, havana brown, himalayan, japanese bobtail, korat, leopard cat, lilac foreign shorthair, maine coon cat, manx, ocicat, oriental shorthair, persian, rex, russian blue, scottish fold, siamese, sphynx, turkish angora, wirehair shorthair.

WEIGHTS AND MEASURES

Source: National Bureau of Standards, U.S. Commerce Department

U.S. Moving, Inch by 25.4 mm, to Metric System

On July 2, 1971, following the report of a metric conversion study committee, Commerce Secy. Maurice H. Stans recommended a gradual U.S. changeover during a 10-year period at the end of which the U.S. would be predominantly, but not exclusively, on the metric system. The Metric Conversion Act of 1975, signed Dec. 23, 1975, declared a national policy of coordinating voluntary increasing use of the Metric System and established a U. S. Metric Board to coordinate the change over.

Currently conversion to metric is confined to the following industries: automotive, construction and farm equipment, computer, and bottling. In addition, with encouragement of the U.S. Education Department, our school systems are emphasizing teaching of the metric system.

The International System of Units

Two systems of weights and measures exist side by side in the United States today, with roughly equal but separate legislative sanction: the U.S. Customary System and the International (Metric) System. Throughout U.S. history, the Customary System (inherited from, but now different from, the British Imperial System) has been, as its name implies, customarily used; a plethora of federal and state legislation has given it, through implication, standing as our primary weights and measures system. However, the Metric System (incorporated in the scientists' new SI or Systeme International d'Unites) is the only system that has ever received specific legislative sanction by Congress. The "Law of 1866" reads:

It shall be lawful throughout the United States of America to employ the weights and measures of the metric system; and no contract or dealing, or pleading in any court, shall be deemed invalid or liable to objection because the weights or measures expressed or referred to therein are weights or measures of the metric system.

Over the last 100 years, the Metric System has seen slow, steadily increasing use in the United States and, today, is of importance nearly equal to the Customary System.

On Feb. 10, 1964, the National Bureau of Standards issued the following bulletin:

> Henceforth it shall be the policy of the National Bureau of Standards to use the units of the International System (SI), as adopted by the 11th General Conference on Weights and Measures (October 1960), except when the use of these units would obviously impair communication or reduce the usefulness of a report.

What had been the Metric System became the International System (SI), a more complete scientific system.

Seven units have been adopted to serve as the base for the International System as follows: **length**—meter; **mass**—kilogram; **time**—second; **electric current**—ampere; **thermodynamic temperature**—kelvin; **amount of substance**—mole; and **luminous intensity**—candela.

Prefixes

The following prefixes, in combination with the basic unit names, provide the multiples and submultiples in the International System. For example, the unit name "meter," with the prefix "kilo" added, produces "kilometer," meaning "1,000 meters."

Prefix	Symbol	Multiples and submultiples	Equivalent	Prefix	Symbol	Multiples and submultiples	Equivalent
exa	E	10^{18}	quintillionfold	deci	d	10^{-1}	tenth part
peta	P	10^{15}	quadrillionfold	centi	c	10^{-2}	hundredth part
tera	T	10^{12}	trillionfold	milli	m	10^{-3}	thousandth part
giga	G	10^{9}	billionfold	micro	mu	10^{-6}	millionth part
mega	M	10^{6}	millionfold	nano	n	10^{-9}	billionth part
kilo	k	10^{3}	thousandfold	pico	p	10^{-12}	trillionth part
hecto	h	10^{2}	hundredfold	femto	f	10^{-15}	quadrillionth part
deka	da	10	tenfold	atto	a	10^{-18}	quintillionth part

Tables of Metric Weights and Measures

Linear Measure

10 millimeters (mm)	= 1 centimeter (cm)
10 centimeters	= 1 decimeter (dm) = 100 millimeters
10 decimeters	= 1 meter (m) = 1,000 millimeters
10 meters	= 1 dekameter (dam)
10 dekameters	= 1 hectometer (hm) = 100 meters
10 hectometers	= 1 kilometer (km) = 1,000 meters

Area Measure

100 square millimeters (mm^2)	= 1 square centimeter (cm^2)
10,000 square centimeters	= 1 square meter (m^2) = 1,000,000 square millimeters
100 square meters	= 1 are (a)
100 ares	= 1 hectare (ha) = 10,000 square meters
100 hectares	= 1 square kilometer (km^2) = 1,000,000 square meters

Fluid Volume Measure

10 milliliters (mL)	= 1 centiliter (cL)
10 centiliters	= 1 deciliter (dL) = 100 milliliters
10 deciliters	= 1 liter (L) = 1,000 milliliters
10 liters	= 1 dekaliter (daL)
10 dekaliters	= 1 hectoliter (hL) = 100 liters
10 hectoliters	= 1 kiloliter (kL) = 1,000 liters

Cubic Measure

1,000 cubic millimeters (mm^3)	= 1 cubic centimeter (cm^3)
1,000 cubic centimeters	= 1 cubic decimeter (dm^3) = 1,000,000 cubic millimeters
1,000 cubic decimeters	= 1 cubic meter (m^3) = 1 stere = 1,000,000 cubic centimeters = 1,000,000,000 cubic millimeters

Weight

10 milligrams (mg)	= 1 centigram (cg)
10 centigrams	= 1 decigram (dg) = 100 milligrams
10 decigrams	= 1 gram (g) = 1,000 milligrams
10 grams	= 1 dekagram (dag)
10 dekagrams	= 1 hectogram (hg) = 100 grams
10 hectograms	= 1 kilogram (kg) = 1,000 grams
1,000 kilograms	= 1 metric ton (t)

Table of U.S. Customary Weights and Measures

Linear Measure

12 inches (in)	= 1 foot (ft)
3 feet	= 1 yard (yd)
5 1/2 yards	= 1 rod (rd), pole, or perch (16 1/2 feet)
40 rods	= 1 furlong (fur)=220 yards=660 feet
8 furlongs	= 1 survey mile (mi) = 1,760 yards = 5,280 feet
3 miles	= 1 league = 5,280 yards = 15,840 feet
6076.11549 feet	= 1 International Nautical Mile

Liquid Measure

When necessary to distinguish the liquid pint or quart from the dry pint or quart, the word "liquid" or the abbreviation "liq" should be used in combination with the name or abbreviation of the liquid unit.

4 gills	= 1 pint (pt) = 28.875 cubic inches
2 pints	= 1 quart (qt) = 57.75 cubic inches
4 quarts	= 1 gallon (gal) = 231 cubic inches = 8 pints = 32 gills

Area Measure

Squares and cubes of units are sometimes abbreviated by using "superior" figures. For example. ft^2 means square foot, and ft^3 means cubic foot.

144 square inches	= 1 square foot (ft^2)
9 square feet	= 1 square yard (yd^2) = 1,296 square inches
30 1/4 square yards	= 1 square rod (rd^2) = 272 1/4 square feet
160 square rods	= 1 acre = 4,840 square yards = 43,560 square feet
640 acres	= 1 square mile (mi^2)
1 mile square	= 1 section (of land)
6 miles square	= 1 township = 36 sections = 36 square miles

Cubic Measure

1 cubic foot (ft^3)	= 1,728 cubic inches (in^3)
27 cubic feet	= 1 cubic yard (yd^3)

Gunter's or Surveyors' Chain Measure

7.92 inches (in)	= 1 link
100 links	= 1 chain (ch) = 4 rods = 66 feet
80 chains	= 1 survey mile (mi) = 320 rods = 5,280 feet

Troy Weight

24 grains	= 1 pennyweight (dwt)
20 pennyweights	= 1 ounce troy (oz t) = 480 grains
12 ounces troy	= 1 pound troy (lb t) = 240 pennyweights = 5,760 grains

Dry Measure

When necessary to distinguish the dry pint or quart from the liquid pint or quart, the word "dry" should be used in combination with the name or abbreviation of the dry unit.

2 pints (pt)	= 1 quart (qt) = 67.2006 cubic inches
8 quarts	= 1 peck (pk) = 537.605 cubic inches = 16 pints
4 pecks	= 1 bushel (bu) = 2,150.42 cubic inches = 32 quarts

Avoirdupois Weight

When necessary to distinguish the avoirdupois ounce or pound from the troy ounce or pound, the word "avoirdupois" or the abbreviation "avdp" should be used in combination with the name or abbreviation of the avoirdupois unit.

(The "grain" is the same in avoirdupois and troy weight.)

27 11/32 grains	= 1 dram (dr)
16 drams	= 1 ounce (oz) = 437 1/2 grains
16 ounces	= 1 pound (lb) = 256 drams = 7,000 grains
100 pounds	= 1 hundredweight (cwt)°
20 hundredweights	= 1 ton = 2,000 pounds°

In "gross" or "long" measure, the following values are recognized.

112 pounds	= 1 gross or long hundredweight°
20 gross or long hundredweights	= 1 gross or long ton = 2,240 pounds°

°When the terms "hundredweight" and "ton" are used unmodified, they are commonly understood to mean the 100-pound hundredweight and the 2,000-pound ton, respectively: these units may be designated "net" or "short" when necessary to distinguish them from the corresponding units in gross or long measure.

Tables of Equivalents

In this table it is necessary to distinguish between the "international" and the "survey" foot. The international foot, defined in 1959 as exactly equal to 0.3048 meter, is shorter than the old survey foot by approximately 6 parts in 10 million. The survey foot is still used in data expressed in feet in geodetic surveys within the U.S. In this table the survey foot is italicized.

When the name of a unit is enclosed in brackets thus, [1 hand], this indicates (1) that the unit is not in general current use in the United States, or (2) that the unit is believed to be based on "custom and usage" rather than on formal definition.

Equivalents involving decimals are, in most instances, rounded off to the third decimal place except where they are exact, in which cases these exact equivalents are so designated.

Lengths

1 angstrom (A)	0.1 nanometer (exactly); 0.000 1 micron (exactly); 0.000 000 1 millimeter (exactly); 0.000 000 004 inch
1 cable's length	120 fathoms (exactly); 720 *feet* (exactly); 219 meters
1 centimeter (cm)	0.3937 inch
1 chain (ch) (Gunter's or surveyors)	66 *feet* (exactly); 20.1168 meters
1 chain (engineers)	100 feet; 30.48 meters (exactly)
1 decimeter (dm)	3.937 inches
1 degree (geographical)	364,566.929 feet; 69.047 miles (avg.); 111.123 kilometers (avg.)
-of latitude	68.078 miles at equator; 69.043 miles at poles
-of longitude	69.171 miles
1 dekameter (dam)	32.808 feet
1 fathom	6 *feet* (exactly); 1.8288 meters (exactly)
1 foot (ft)	0.3048 meters (exactly)
1 furlong (fur)	10 chains (surveyors) (exactly); 660 *feet* (exactly); 1/8 survey mile (exactly); 201.168 meters
[1 hand] (height measure for horses from ground to top of shoulders)	4 inches
1 inch (in)	2.54 centimeters (exactly)
1 kilometer (km)	0.621 mile; 3,281.5 feet
1 league (land)	3 survey miles (exactly); 4.828 kilometers
1 link (Gunter's or surveyors)	7.92 inches (exactly); 0.201 meter
1 link engineers	1 foot; 0.305 meter
1 meter (m)	39.37 inches; 1.094 yards
1 micron (u) [the Greek letter mu]	0.001 millimeter (exactly); 0.000 039 37 inch
1 mil	0.001 inch (exactly); 0.025 4 millimeter (exactly)
1 mile (mi) (survey or land)	5,280 *feet* (exactly); 1.609 kilometers
1 international nautical mile (INM)	1.852 kilometers (exactly); 1.150779 survey miles; 6,076.11549 feet
1 millimeter (mm)	0.039 37 inch
1 nanometer (nm)	0.001 micron (exactly); 0.000 000 039 37 inch
1 pica (typography)	12 points
1 point (typography)	0.013 837 inch (exactly); 0.351 millimeter
1 rod (rd), pole, or perch	16 1/2 *feet* (exactly); 5.029 meters
1 yard (yd)	0.9144 meter (exactly)

Areas or Surfaces

1 acre	43,560 square *feet* (exactly); 4,840 square yards; 0.405 hectare
1 are (a)	119.599 square yards; 0.025 acre

(continued)

1 bolt (cloth measure):	
length	100 yards (on modern looms)
width	42 inches (usually, for cotton) 60 inches (usually, for wool)
1 hectare (ha)	2.471 acres
[1 square (building)]	100 square feet
1 square centimeter (cm^2)	0.155 square inch
1 square decimeter (dm^2)	15.500 square inches
1 square foot (ft^2)	929.030 square centimeters
1 square inch (in^2)	6.4516 square centimeters (exactly)
1 square kilometer (km^2)	247.105 acres 0.386 square mile
1 square meter (m^2)	1.196 square yards 10.764 square feet
1 square mile (mi^2)	258.999 hectares
1 square millimeter (mm^2)	0.002 square inch
1 square rod (rd^2) sq. pole, or sq. perch	25.293 square meters
1 square yard (yd^2)	0.836 square meter

Capacities or Volumes

1 barrel (bbl) liquid	31 to 42 gallons°

°There are a variety of "barrels," established by law or usage. For example: federal taxes on fermented liquors are based on a barrel of 31 gallons: many state laws fix the "barrel for liquids" as 31 ½ gallons; one state fixes a 36-gallon barrel for cistern measurement; federal law recognizes a 40-gallon barrel for "proof spirits"; by custom, 42 gallons comprise a barrel of crude oil or petroleum products for statistical purposes, and this equivalent is recognized "for liquids" by 4 states.

1 barrel (bbl), standard, for fruits, vegetables, and other dry commodities except dry cranberries	7,056 cubic inches 105 dry quarts 3.281 bushels, struck measure
1 barrel (bbl), standard, cranberry	5,826 cubic inches 86 45/64 dry quarts 2.709 bushels, struck measure
1 board foot (lumber measure)	a foot-square board 1 inch thick
1 bushel (bu) (U.S.) (struck measure)	2,150.42 cubic inches (exactly) 35.238 liters
[1 bushel, heaped (U.S.)]	2,747.715 cubic inches 1.278 bushels, struck measure°

°Frequently recognized as 1¼ bushels, struck measure.

[1 bushel (bu) (British Imperial) (struck measure)]	1.032 U.S. bushels struck measure 2,219.36 cubic inches
1 cord (cd) firewood	128 cubic feet (exactly)
1 cubic centimeter (cm^3)	0.061 cubic inch
1 cubic decimeter (dm^3)	61.024 cubic inches
1 cubic inch (in^3)	0.554 fluid ounce 4.433 fluid drams 16.387 cubic centimeters
1 cubic foot (ft^3)	7.481 gallons 28.317 cubic decimeters
1 cubic meter (m^3)	1.308 cubic yards
1 cubic yard (yd^3)	0.765 cubic meter
1 cup, measuring	8 fluid ounces (exactly) ½ liquid pint (exactly)
[1 dram, fluid (fl dr) (British)]	0.961 U.S. fluid dram 0.217 cubic inch 3.552 milliliters
1 dekaliter (dal)	2.642 gallons 1.135 pecks
1 gallon (gal) (U.S.)	231 cubic inches (exactly) 3.785 liters 0.833 British gallon 128 U.S. fluid ounces (exactly)
[1 gallon (gal) British Imperial]	277.42 cubic inches 1.201 U.S. gallons 4.546 liters 160 British fluid ounces (exactly)
1 gill (gi)	7.219 cubic inches 4 fluid ounces (exactly) 0.118 liter
1 hectoliter (hl)	26.418 gallons 2.838 bushels
1 liter (l) (1 cubic decimeter exactly)	1.057 liquid quarts 0.908 dry quart 61.025 cubic inches
1 milliliter (ml) (1 cu cm exactly)	0.271 fluid dram 16.231 minims 0.061 cubic inch
1 ounce, liquid (U.S.)	1.805 cubic inches 29.573 milliliters 1.041 British fluid ounces
[1 ounce, fluid (fl oz) (British)]	0.961 U.S. fluid ounce 1.734 cubic inches 28.412 milliliters
1 peck (pk)	8.810 liters
1 pint (pt), dry	33.600 cubic inches 0.551 liter
1 pint (pt), liquid	28.875 cubic inches (exactly) 0.473 liter
1 quart (qt) dry (U.S.)	67.201 cubic inches 1.101 liters 0.969 British quart
1 quart (qt) liquid (U.S.)	57.75 cubic in (exactly) 0.946 liter 0.833 British quart
[1 quart (qt) (British)]	69.354 cubic inches 1.032 U.S. dry quarts 1.201 U.S. liquid quarts
1 tablespoon	3 teaspoons°(exactly) 4 fluid drams ½ fluid ounce (exactly)
1 teaspoon	⅓ tablespoon°(exactly) 1⅓ fluid drams°

°The equivalent "1 teaspoon—1⅓ fluid drams" has been found by the bureau to correspond more closely with the actual capacities of "measuring" and silver teaspoons than the equivalent "1 teaspoon—1 fluid dram" which is given by many dictionaries.

Weights or Masses

1 assay ton°° (AT)	29.167 grams

°°Used in assaying. The assay ton bears the same relation to the milligram that a ton of 2,000 pounds avoirdupois bears to the ounce troy; hence the weight in milligrams of precious metal obtained from one assay ton of ore gives directly the number of troy ounces to the net ton.

1 bale (cotton measure)	500 pounds in U.S. 750 pounds in Egypt
1 carat (c)	200 milligrams (exactly) 3.086 grains
1 dram avoirdupois (dr avdp)	27 11/32 (=27.344) grains 1.772 grams
gamma, see microgram	
1 grain	64.799 milligrams
1 gram	15.432 grains 0.035 ounce, avoirdupois
1 hundredweight, gross or long°°° (gross cwt)	112 pounds (exactly) 50.802 kilograms
1 hundredweight, net or short (cwt. or net cwt.)	100 pounds (exactly) 45.359 kilograms
1 kilogram (kg)	2.205 pounds
1 microgram (μg [The Greek letter mu in combination with the letter g])	0.000001 gram (exactly)
1 milligram (mg)	0.015 grain
1 ounce, avoirdupois (oz avdp)	437.5 grains (exactly) 0.911 troy ounce 28.350 grams
1 ounce, troy (oz t)	480 grains (exactly) 1.097 avoirdupois ounces 31.103 grams
1 pennyweight (dwt)	1.555 grams
1 pound, avoirdupois (lb avdp)	7,000 grains (exactly) 1.215 troy pounds 453.592 37 grams (exactly)
1 pound, troy (lb t)	5,760 grains (exactly) 0.823 avoirdupois pound 373.242 grams
1 ton, gross or long°°° (gross ton)	2,240 pounds (exactly) 1.12 net tons (exactly) 1.016 metric tons

°°°The gross or long ton and hundredweight are used commercially in the United States to only a limited extent, usually in restricted industrial fields. These units are the same as British "ton" and "hundredweight."

1 ton, metric (t)	2,204.623 pounds 0.984 gross ton 1.102 net tons
1 ton, net or short (sh ton)	2,000 pounds (exactly) 0.893 gross ton 0.907 metric ton

Tables of Interrelation of Units of Measurement

Units of length and area of the international and survey measures are included in the following tables. Units unique to the survey measure are italicized. See pg 809, Tables of Equivalents, 1st para.

1 international foot = 0.999 998 survey foot (exactly)
1 survey foot = 1200/3937 meter (exactly)
1 international foot = 12 × 0.0254 meter (exactly)

Bold face type indicates exact values

Units of Length

Units	Inches	*Links*	Feet	Yards	*Rods*	*Chains*	Miles	cm	Meters
1 inch=	**1**	0.126 263	0.083 333	0.027 778	0.005 051	0.001 263	0.000 016	**2.54**	**0.025 4**
1 *link*=	**7.92**	**1**	**0.66**	**0.22**	**0.04**	**0.01**	**0.000 125**	20.117	0.201 168
1 foot=	**12**	1.515 152	**1**	0.333 333	0.060 606	0.015 152	0.000 189	**30.48**	**0.304 8**
1 yard=	**36**	4.545 45	**3**	**1**	0.181 818	0.045 455	0.000 568	**91.44**	**0.914 4**
1 *rod*=	**198**	**25**	**16.5**	**5.5**	**1**	**0.25**	**0.003 125**	502.92	5.029 2
1 *chain*=	**792**	**100**	**66**	**22**	**4**	**1**	**0.012 5**	2011.68	20.116 8
1 mile=	**63 360**	**8000**	**5280**	**1760**	**320**	**80**	**1**	**160 934.4**	**1609.344**
1 cm=	0.3937	0.049 710	0.032 808	0.010 936	0.001 988	0.000 497	0.000 006	**1**	**0.01**
1 meter=	39.37	4.970 960	3.280 840	1.093 613	0.198 838	0.049 710	0.000 621	**100**	**1**

Units of Area

Units	Sq. inches	*Sq. links*	Sq. feet	Sq. yards	*Sq. rods*	*Sq. chains*
1 sq. inch=	**1**	.015 942 3	0.006 944	0.000 771 605	0.000 025 5	0.000 001 594
1 sq. *link*=	62.726 4	**1**	**0.435 6**	**0.0484**	**0.0016**	**0.000 1**
1 sq. foot=	**144**	2.295 684	**1**	0.111 111 1	0.003 673 09	0.000 229 568
1 sq. yard=	**1296**	20.661 16	**9**	**1**	0.033 057 85	0.002 066 12
1 sq. *rod*=	**39 204**	**625**	**272.25**	**30.25**	**1**	**0.062 5**
1 sq. *chain*=	**627 264**	**10 000**	**4 356**	**484**	**16**	**1**
1 *acre*=	**6 272 640**	**100 000**	**43 560**	**4 840**	**160**	**10**
1 sq. mile=	**4 014 489 600**	**64 000 000**	**27 878 400**	**3 097 600**	**102 400**	**6400**
1 sq. cm=	0.155 000 3	0.002 471 05	0.001 076	0.000 119 599	0.000 003 954	0.000 000 247
1 sq. meter=	1550.003	24.710 44	10.763 91	1.195 990	0.039 536 70	0.002 471 044
1 *hectare*=	15 500 031	247 104	107 639.1	11 959.90	395.367 0	24.710 44

Units	*Acres*	Sq. miles	Sq. cm	Sq. meters	*Hectares*
1 sq. inch=	0.000 000 159 423	0.000 000 000 249 10	**6.451 6**	**0.000 645 16**	0.000 000 065
1 sq. *link*=	**0.000 01**	**0.000 000 015 625**	404.685 642 24	0.040 468 56	0.000 004 047
1 sq. foot=	0.000 022 956 84	0.000 000 035 870 06	929.034 1	0.092 903 41	0.000 009 290
1 sq. yard=	0.000 206 611 6	0.000 000 322 830 6	**8 361.273 6**	**0.836 127 36**	0.000 083 613
1 sq. *rod*=	**0.006 25**	**0.000 009 765 625**	252 929.5	25.292 95	0.002 529 295
1 sq. *chain*=	**0.1**	**0.000 156 25**	4 046 873	404.687 3	0.040 468 73
1 *acre*=	**1**	**0.001 562 5**	40 468 73	4 046.873	0.404 687 3
1 sq. mile=	**640**	**1**	25 899 881 103	2 589 988.11	258.998 811 034
1 sq. cm=	0.000 000 024 711	0.000 000 000 038 610	**1**	**0.000 1**	**0.000 000 01**
1 sq. meter=	0.000 247 104 4	0.000 000 386 102 2	**10 000**	**1**	**0.0001**
1 *hectare*=	2.471 044	0.003 861 006	**100 000 000**	**10 000**	**1**

Units of Mass Not Greater than Pounds and Kilograms

Units	Grains	Pennyweights	Avdp drams	Avdp ounces
1 grain=	**1**	0.041 666 67	0.036 571 43	0.002 285 71
1 pennyweight=	**24**	**1**	0.877 714 3	0.054 857 14
1 dram avdp=	**27.343 75**	1.139 323	**1**	**0.062 5**
1 ounce avdp=	**437.5**	18.229 17	**16**	**1**
1 ounce troy=	**480**	**20**	17.554 29	1.097 143
1 pound troy=	**5760**	**240**	210.651 4	13.165 71
1 pound avdp=	**7000**	291.666 7	**256**	**16**
1 milligram=	0.015 432	0.000 643 015	0.000 564 383	0.000 035 274
1 gram=	15.432 36	0.643 014 9	0.564 383 4	0.035 273 96
1 kilogram=	15 432.36	643.014 9	564.383 4	35.273 96

Units	Troy ounces	Troy pounds	Avdp pounds	Milligrams	Grams	Kilograms
1 grain=	0.002 083 33	0.000 173 611	0.000 142 857	**64.798 91**	**0.064 798 91**	0.000 064 799
1 pennyw't.=	**0.05**	0.004 166 667	0.003 428 571	**1555.173 84**	**1.555 173 84**	0.001 555 174
1 dram avdp=	0.056 966 15	0.004 747 179	0.003 906 25	1771.845 195	1.771 845 195	0.001 771 845
1 oz avdp=	0.911 458 3	0.075 954 86	**0.062 5**	**28 349.523 125**	**28.349 523 125**	0.028 349 52
1 oz troy=	**1**	0.083 333 333	0.068 571 43	**31 103.476 8**	**31.103 476 8**	0.031 103 48
1 lb troy=	**12**	**1**	0.822 857 1	**373 241.721 6**	**373.241 721 6**	0.373 241 722
1 lb avdp=	14.583 33	1.215 278	**1**	**453 592.37**	**453.592 37**	**0.453 592 37**
1 milligram=	0.000 032 151	0.000 002 679	0.000 002 205	**1**	**0.001**	**0.000 001**
1 gram=	0.032 150 75	0.002 679 229	0.002 204 623	**1000**	**1**	**0.001**
1 kilogram=	32.150 75	2.679 229	2.204 623	**1 000 000**	**1000**	**1**

Units of Mass Not Less than Avoirdupois Ounces

Units	Avdp oz	Avdp lb	Short cwt	Short tons	Long tons	Kilograms	Metric tons
1 oz av=	**1**	**0.0625**	**0.000 625**	**0.000 031 25**	0.000 027 902	0.028 349 523	0.000 028 350
1 lb av=	**16**	**1**	**0.01**	**0.000 5**	0.000 446 429	**0.453 592 37**	0.000 453 592
1 sh cwt=	**1 600**	**100**	**1**	**0.05**	0.044 642 86	**45.359 237**	**0.045 359 237**
1 sh ton=	**32 000**	**2000**	**20**	**1**	0.892 857 1	**907.184 74**	**0.907 184 74**
1 long ton=	**35 840**	**2240**	**22.4**	**1.12**	**1**	**1016.046 908 8**	1.016 046 909
1 kg=	35.273 96	2.204 623	0.022 046 23	0.001 102 311	0.000 984 207	**1**	**0.001**
1 metric ton=	35 273.96	2 204.623	22.046 23	1.102 311	0.984 206 5	**1000**	**1**

(continued)

Units of Volume

Units	Cubic inches	Cubic feet	Cubic yards	Cubic cm	Cubic dm	Cubic meters
1 cubic inch=	**1**	0.000 578 704	0.000 021 433	**16.387 064**	0.016 387	0.000 016 387
1 cubic foot=	**1728**	**1**	0.037 037 04	**28 316.846 592**	28.316 847	0.028 316 847
1 cubic yard=	**46 656**	**27**	**1**	**764 554.857 984**	764.554 858	0.764 554 858
1 cubic cm=	0.061 023 74	0.000 035 315	0.000 001 308	**1**	**0.001**	**0.000 001**
1 cubic dm=	61.023 74	0.035 314 67	0.001 307 951	**1 000**	**1**	**0.001**
1 cubic meter	61 023.74	35.314 67	1.307 951	**1 000 000**	**1000**	**1**

Units of Capacity (Liquid Measure)

Units	Minims	Fluid drams	Fluid ounces	Gills	Liquid pt
1 minim=	**1**	0.016 666 7	0.002 083 33	0.000 520 833	0.000 130 208
1 fluid dram=	**60**	**1**	**0.125**	**0.031 25**	**0.007 812 5**
1 fluid ounce=	**480**	**8**	**1**	**0.25**	**0.062 5**
1 gill=	**1920**	**32**	**4**	**1**	**0.25**
1 liquid pint=	**7680**	**128**	**16**	**4**	**1**
1 liquid quart=	**15 360**	**256**	**32**	**8**	**2**
1 gallon=	**61 440**	**1024**	**128**	**32**	**8**
1 cubic inch=	265.974	4.432 900	0.554 112 6	0.138 528 1	0.034 632 03
1 cubic foot=	459 603.1	7 660.052	957.506 5	239.376 6	59.844 16
1 milliliter=	16.230 73	0.270 512 18	0.033 814 02	0.008 453 506	.002 113 376
1 liter=	16 230.73	270.512 18	33.814 02	8.453 506	2.113 376

Units	Liquid quarts	Gallons	Cubic inches	Cubic feet	Liters
1 minim=	0.000 065 104 17	0.000 016 276 04	0.003 759 766	0.000 002 175 790	0.000 061 611 52
1 flu. dram=	**0.003 906 25**	**0.000 976 562 5**	0.225 585 9	0.000 130 547 4	0.003 696 691
1 fluid oz=	**0.031 25**	**0.007 812 5**	**1.804 687 5**	0.001 044 379	0.029 573 53
1 gill=	**0.125**	**0.031 25**	**7.218 75**	0.004 177 517	0.118 294 118
1 liquid pt=	**0.5**	**0.125**	**28.875**	0.016 710 07	0.473 176 473
1 liquid qt=	**1**	**0.25**	**57.75**	0.033 420 14	0.946 352 946
1 gallon=	**4**	**1**	**231**	0.133 680 6	3.785 411 784
1 cubic in.=	0.017 316 02	0.004 329 004	**1**	0.000 578 703 7	0.016 387 064
1 cubic foot=	29.922 08	7.480 519	**1728**	**1**	**28.316 846 592**
1 liter=	1.056 688	0.264 172 05	61.023 74	0.035 314 67	**1**

Units of Capacity (Dry Measure)

Units	Dry pints	Dry quarts	Pecks	Bushels	Cubic in.	Liters
1 dry pint=	**1**	**0.5**	**0.062 5**	**0.015 625**	**33.600 312 5**	0.550 610 47
1 dry quart=	**2**	**1**	**0.125**	**0.031 25**	**67.200 625**	1.101 220 9
1 peck=	**16**	**8**	**1**	**0.25**	**537.605**	8.809 767 5
1 bushel=	**64**	**32**	**4**	**1**	**2150.42**	35.239 07
1 cubic inch=	0.029 761 6	0.014 880 8	0.001 860 10	0.000 465 025	**1**	0.016 387 06
1 liter=	1.816 166	0.908 083	0.113 510 37	0.028 377 59	61.023 74	**1**

Miscellaneous Measures

Caliber—the diameter of a gun bore. In the U.S., caliber is traditionally expressed in hundredths of inches, eg. .22 or .30. In Britain, caliber is often expressed in thousandths of inches, eg. .270 or .465. Now, it is commonly expressed in millimeters, eg. the 7.62 mm. M14 rifle and the 5.56 mm. M16 rifle. Heavier weapons' caliber has long been expressed in millimeters, eg. the 81 mm. mortar, the 105 mm. howitzer (light), the 155 mm. howitzer (medium or heavy).

Naval guns' caliber refers to the barrel length as a multiple of the bore diameter. A 5-inch, 50-caliber naval gun has a 5-inch bore and a barrel length of 250 inches.

Carat, karat—a measure of the amount of alloy per 24 parts in gold. Thus 24-carat gold is pure; 18-carat gold is one-fourth alloy.

Decibel (db)—a measure of the relative loudness or intensity of sound. A 20-decibel sound is 10 times louder than a 10-decibel sound; 30 decibels is 100 times louder; 40 decibels is 1,000 times louder, etc. One decibel is the smallest difference between sounds detectable by the human ear. A 140-decibel sound is painful.

10 decibels	– a light whisper
20	– quiet conversation
30	– normal conversation
40	– light traffic
50	– typewriter, loud conversation
60	– noisy office
70	– normal traffic, quiet train
80	– rock music, subway
90	– heavy traffic, thunder
100	– jet plane at takeoff

Em—a printer's measure designating the square width of any given type size. Thus, an em of 10-point type is 10 points. An en is half an em.

Gauge—a measure of shotgun bore diameter. Gauge numbers originally referred to the number of lead balls of the gun barrel diameter in a pound. Thus, a 16 gauge shotgun's bore was smaller than a 12-gauge shotgun's. Today, an international agreement assigns millimeter measures to each gauge, eg:

Gauge	Bore diameter in mm.
6	23.34
10	19.67
12	18.52
14	17.60
16	16.81
20	15.90

Horsepower—the energy needed to lift 550 pounds one foot in one second, or to lift 33,000 pounds one foot in one minute. Equivalent to 746 watts or 2,546.0756 btu/h.

Quire—25 sheets of paper

Ream—500 sheets of paper

Electrical Units

The **watt** is the unit of power (electrical, mechanical, thermal, etc.). Electrical power is given by the product of the voltage and the current.

Energy is sold by the **joule,** but in common practice the billing of electrical energy is expressed in terms of the **kilowatt-hour,** which is 3,600,000 joules or 3.6 megajoules.

The **horsepower** is a non-metric unit sometimes used in mechanics. It is equal to 746 watts.

The **ohm** is the unit of electrical resistance and represents the physical property of a conductor which offers a resistance to the flow of electricity, permitting just 1 ampere to flow at 1 volt of pressure.

Compound Interest

Compounded Annually

Principal	Period	4%	5%	6%	7%	8%	9%	10%	12%	14%	16%
$100	1 day	0.011	0.014	0.016	0.019	0.022	0.025	0.027	0.033	0.038	0.044
	1 week	0.077	0.096	0.115	0.134	0.153	0.173	0.192	0.230	0.268	0.307
	6 mos.	2.00	2.50	3.00	3.50	4.00	4.50	5.00	6.00	7.00	8.00
	1 year	4.00	5.00	6.00	7.00	8.00	9.00	10.00	12.00	14.00	16.00
	2 years	8.16	10.25	12.36	14.49	16.64	18.81	21.00	25.44	29.96	34.56
	3 years	12.49	15.76	19.10	22.50	25.97	29.50	33.10	40.49	48.15	56.09
	4 years	16.99	21.55	26.25	31.08	36.05	41.16	46.41	57.35	68.90	81.06
	5 years	21.67	27.63	33.82	40.26	46.93	53.86	61.05	76.23	92.54	110.03
	6 years	26.53	34.01	41.85	50.07	58.69	67.71	77.16	97.38	119.50	143.64
	7 years	31.59	40.71	50.36	60.58	71.38	82.80	94.87	121.07	150.23	182.62
	8 years	36.86	47.75	59.38	71.82	85.09	99.26	114.36	147.60	185.26	227.84
	9 years	42.33	55.13	68.95	83.85	99.90	117.19	135.79	177.31	225.19	280.30
	10 years	48.02	62.89	79.08	96.72	115.89	136.74	159.37	210.58	270.72	341.14
	12 years	60.10	79.59	101.22	125.22	151.82	181.27	213.84	289.60	381.79	493.60
	15 years	80.09	107.89	139.66	175.90	217.22	264.25	317.72	447.36	613.79	826.55
	20 years	119.11	165.33	220.71	286.97	366.10	460.44	572.75	864.63	1,274.35	1,846.08

Ancient Measures

Biblical

Cubit	= 21.8 inches
Omer	= 0.45 peck 3.964 liters
Ephah	= 10 omers
Shekel	= 0.497 ounce 14.1 grams

Greek

Cubit	= 18.3 inches
Stadion	= 607.2 or 622 feet
Obolos	= 715.38 milligrams
Drachma	= 4.2923 grams
Mina	= 0.9463 pounds
Talent	= 60 mina

Roman

Cubit	= 17.5 inches
Stadium	= 202 yards
As, libra, pondus	= 325.971 grams, .71864 pounds

Weight of Water

1	cubic inch	.0360 pound
12	cubic inches	.433 pound
1	cubic foot	62.4 pounds
1	cubic foot	7.48052 U.S. gal
1.8	cubic feet	112.0 pounds
35.96	cubic feet	2240.0 pounds
1	imperial gallon	10.0 pounds
11.2	imperial gallons	112.0 pounds
224	imperial gallons	2240.0 pounds
1	U.S. gallon	8.33 pounds
13.45	U.S. gallons	112.0 pounds
269.0	U.S. gallons	2240.0 pounds

Density of Gases and Vapors

Source: National Bureau of Standards (kilograms per cubic meter)

Gas	Wgt.	Gas	Wgt.	Gas	Wgt.
Acetylene	1.171	Ethylene	1.260	Methyl fluoride	1.545
Air	1.293	Fluorine	1.696	Mono methylamine	1.38
Ammonia	.759	Helium	.178	Neon	.900
Argon	1.784	Hydrogen	.090	Nitric oxide	1.341
Arsene	3.48	Hydrogen bromide	3.50	Nitrogen	1.250
Butane-iso	2.60	Hydrogen chloride	1.639	Nitrosyl chloride	2.99
Butane-n	2.519	Hydrogen iodide	5.724	Nitrous oxide	1.997
Carbon dioxide	1.977	Hydrogen selenide	3.66	Oxygen	1.429
Carbon monoxide	1.250	Hydrogen sulfide	1.539	Phosphine	1.48
Carbon oxysulfide	2.72	Krypton	3.745	Propane	2.020
Chlorine	3.214	Methane	.717	Silicon tetrafluoride	4.67
Chlorine monoxide	3.89	Methyl chloride	2.25	Sulfur dioxide	2.927
Ethane	1.356	Methyl ether	2.091	Xenon	5.897

Temperature Conversion Table

The numbers in **bold face type** refer to the temperature either in degrees Celsius or Fahrenheit which are to be converted. If converting from degrees Fahrenheit to Celsius, the equivalent will be found in the column on the left, while if converting from degrees Celsius to Fahrenheit the answer will be found in the column on the right.

For temperatures not shown. To convert Fahrenheit to Celsius subtract 32 degrees and multiply by 5, divide by 9; to convert Celsius to Fahrenheit, multiply by 9, divide by 5 and add 32 degrees.

Celsius		Fahrenheit	Celsius		Fahrenheit	Celsius		Fahrenheit
− 273.2	**− 459.7**	....	− 17.8	**0**	32	35.0	**95**	203
− 184	**− 300**	....	− 12.2	**10**	50	36.7	**98**	208.4
− 169	**− 273**	− 459.4	− 6.67	**20**	68	37.8	**100**	212
− 157	**− 250**	− 418	− 1.11	**30**	86	43	**110**	230
− 129	**− 200**	− 328	4.44	**40**	104	49	**120**	248
− 101	**− 150**	− 238	10.0	**50**	122	54	**130**	266
− 73.3	**− 100**	− 148	15.6	**60**	140	60	**140**	284
− 45.6	**− 50**	− 58	21.1	**70**	158	66	**150**	302
− 40.0	**− 40**	− 40	23.9	**75**	167	93	**200**	392
− 34.4	**− 30**	− 22	26.7	**80**	176	121	**250**	482
− 28.9	**− 20**	− 4	29.4	**85**	185	149	**300**	572
− 23.3	**− 10**	14	32.2	**90**	194			

Water boils at 212° Fahrenheit at sea level. For every 550 feet above sea level, boiling point of water is lower by about 1° Fahrenheit. Methyl alcohol boils at 148° Fahrenheit. Average human oral temperature, 98.6° Fahrenheit. Water freezes at 32° Fahrenheit. Although "Centigrade" is still frequently used, the International Committee on Weights and Measures and the National Bureau of Standards have recommended since 1948 that this scale be called "Celsius."

Breaking the Sound Barrier; Speed of Sound

The prefix Mach is used to describe supersonic speed. It derives from Ernst Mach, a Czech-born German physicist, who contributed to the study of sound. When a plane moves at the speed of sound it is Mach 1. When twice the speed of sound it is Mach 2. When it is near but below the speed of sound its speed can be designated at less than Mach 1, for example, Mach .90. Mach is defined as "in jet propulsion, the ratio of the velocity of a rocket or a jet to the velocity of sound in the medium being considered."

When a plane passes the sound barrier—flying faster than sound travels—listeners in the area hear thunderclaps, but pilots do not hear them.

Sound is produced by vibrations of an object and is transmitted by alternate increase and decrease in pressures that radiate outward through a material media of molecules —somewhat like waves spreading out on a pond after a rock has been tossed into it.

The frequency of sound is determined by the number of times the vibrating waves undulate per second, and is measured in cycles per second. The slower the cycle of waves, the lower the sound. As frequencies increase, the sound is higher.

Sound is audible to human beings only if the frequency falls within a certain range. The human ear is usually not sensitive to frequencies of less than 20 vibrations per second, or more than about 20,000 vibrations per second—although this range varies among individuals. Anything at a pitch higher than the human ear can hear is termed ultrasonic.

Intensity or loudness is the strength of the pressure of these radiating waves, and is measured in decibels. The human ear responds to intensity in a range from zero to 120 decibels. Any sound with pressure over 120 decibels is painful.

The speed of sound is generally placed at 1,088 ft. per second at sea level at 32°F. It varies in other temperatures and in different media. Sound travels faster in water than in air, and even faster in iron and steel. If in air it travels a mile in 5 seconds, it does a mile under water in 1 second, and through iron in ⅓ of a second. It travels through ice cold vapor at approximately 4,708 ft. per sec., ice-cold water, 4,938; granite, 12,960; hardwood, 12,620; brick, 11,960; glass, 16,410 to 19,690; silver, 8,658; gold, 5,717.

Colors of the Spectrum

Color, an electromagnetic wave phenomenon, is a sensation produced through the excitation of the retina of the eye by rays of light. The colors of the spectrum may be produced by viewing a light beam refracted by passage through a prism, which breaks the light into its wave lenghts.

Customarily, the primary colors of the spectrum are thought of as those 6 monochromatic colors which occupy relatively large areas of the spectrum: red, orange, yellow, green, blue, and violet. However, Sir Isaac Newton named a 7th, indigo, situated between blue and violet on the spectrum. Aubert estimated (1865) the solar spectrum to contain approximately 1,000 distinguishable hues of which according to Rood (1881) 2 million tints and shades can be distinguished; Luckiesh stated (1915) that 55 distinctly different hues have been seen in a single spectrum.

By many physicists only 3 primary colors are recognized: red, yellow, and blue (Mayer, 1775); red, green, and violet (Thomas Young, 1801); red, green, and blue (Clerk Maxwell, 1860).

The color sensation of black is due to complete lack of stimulation of the retina, that of white to complete stimulation. The infra-red and ultra-violet rays, below the red (long) end of the spectrum and above the violet (short) end respectively, are invisible to the naked eye. Heat is the principal effect of the infra-red rays and chemical action that of the ultra-violet rays.

Common Fractions Reduced to Decimals

8ths	16ths	32ds	64ths	
			1	.015625
		1	2	.03125
			3	.046875
	1	2	4	.0625
			5	.078125
		3	6	.09375
			7	.109375
1	2	4	8	.125
			9	.140625
		5	10	.15625
			11	.171875
	3	6	12	.1875
			13	.203125
		7	14	.21875
			15	.234375
2	4	8	16	.25
			17	.265625
		9	18	.28125
			19	.296875
	5	10	20	.3125
			21	.328125
		11	22	.34375

8ths	16ths	32ds	64ths	
			23	.359375
3	6	12	24	.375
			25	.390625
		13	26	.40625
			27	.421875
	7	14	28	.4375
			29	.453125
		15	30	.46875
			31	.484375
4	8	16	32	.5
			33	.515625
		17	34	.53125
			35	.546875
	9	18	36	.5625
			37	.578125
		19	38	.59375
			39	.609375
5	10	20	40	.625
			41	.640625
		21	42	.65625
			43	.671875
	11	22	44	.6875

8ths	16ths	32ds	64ths	
			45	.703125
		23	46	.71875
			47	.734375
6	12	24	48	.75
			49	.765625
		25	50	.78125
			51	.796875
	13	26	52	.8125
			53	.828125
		27	54	.84375
			55	.859375
7	14	28	56	.875
			57	.890625
		29	58	.90625
			59	.921875
	15	30	60	.9375
			61	.953125
		31	62	.96875
			63	.984375
8	16	32	64	1.

Spirits Measures

Pony	0.5 jigger
Shot	0.666 jigger; 1.0 ounce
Jigger	1.5 shot
Pint	16 shots; 0.625 fifth
Fifth	25.6 shots; 1.6 pints; 0.8 quart; 0.75706 liter
Quart	32 shots; 1.25 fifth
Magnum	2 quarts; 2.49797 bottles (wine)

For champagne and brandy only:

Jeroboam	6.4 pints; 1.6 magnum; 0.8 gallon

For champagne only:

Rehoboam	3 magnums
Methuselah	4 magnums
Salmanazar	6 magnums
Balthazar	8 magnums
Nebuchadnezzar	10 magnums

Wine bottle (standard):

	0.800633 quart; 0.7576778 liter

Mathematical Formulas

To find the CIRCUMFERENCE of a:

ircle — Multiply the diameter by 3.14159265 (usually 3.1416).

To find the AREA of a:

ircle — Multiply the square of the diameter by .785398 (usually .7854).

ectangle — Multiply the length of the base by the height.

phere (surface) — Multiply the square of the radius by 3.1416 and multiply by 4.

Square — Square the length of one side.

Trapezoid — Add the two parallel sides, multiply by the height and divide by 2.

Triangle — Multiply the base by the height and divide by 2.

To find the VOLUME of a:

one — Multiply the square of the radius of the base by 3.1416, multiply by the height, and divide by 3.

ube — Cube the length of one edge.

ylinder — Multiply the square of the radius of the base by 3.1416 and multiply by the height.

yramid — Multiply the area of the base by the height and divide by 3.

Rectangular Prism — Multiply the length by the width by the height.

Sphere — Multiply the cube of the radius by 3.1416, multiply by 4 and divide by 3.

Playing Cards and Dice Chances

Poker Hands

Hand	Number possible	Odds against
oyal flush	4	649,739 to 1
ther straight flush	36	72,192 to 1
our of a kind	624	4,164 to 1
ull house	3,744	693 to 1
lush	5,108	508 to 1
traight	10,200	254 to 1
hree of a kind	54,912	46 to 1
wo pairs	123,552	20 to 1
ne pair	1,098,240	4 to 3 (1.37 to 1)
lothing	1,302,540	1 to 1
Total	**2,598,960**	

Dice
(probabilities on 2 dice)

otal	Odds against (Single toss)	Total	Odds against (Single toss)
	35 to 1	8	31 to 5
	17 to 1	9	8 to 1
	11 to 1	10	11 to 1
	8 to 1	11	17 to 1
	31 to 5	12	35 to 1
	5 to 1		

Dice
(Probabilities of consecutive winning plays)

No. consecutive wins	By 7, 11, or point	No. consecutive wins	By 7, 11 or point
1	244 in 495	6	1 in 70
2	6 in 25	7	1 in 141
3	3 in 25	8	1 in 287
4	1 in 17	9	1 in 582
5	1 in 34		

Pinochle Auction
(Odds against finding in "widow" of 3 cards)

Open places	Odds against	Open places	Odds against
1	5 to 1	4	3 to 2 for
2	2 to 1	5	2 to 1 for
3	Even		

Bridge

The odds—against suit distribution in a hand of 4-4-3-2 are about 4 to 1, against 5-4-2-2 about 8 to 1, against 6-4-2-1 about 20 to 1, against 7-4-1-1 about 254 to 1, against 8-4-1-0 about 2,211 to 1, and against 13-0-0-0 about 158,753,389,899 to 1.

Measures of Force and Pressure

yne = force necessary to accelerate a 1-gram mass 1 centimeter per second per second = 0.000072 poundals

oundal = force necessary to accelerate a 1-pound mass 1 foot per second per second = 13,825.5 dynes = 0.138255 newtons

ewton = force which, applied for 1 second, will give an acceleration of 1 meter per second per second to a 1-kilogram mass = 100 dynes per square centimeter = 100 microbars = 7.233 poundals

Pascal (pressure) = 1 newton per square meter = 0.020885 pound per square foot

Atmosphere (air pressure at sea level) = 2,116.102 pounds per square foot = 14.6952 pounds per square inch = 1.0332 kilograms per square centimeter = 101,323 newtons per square meter.

Large Numbers

.S.	Number of zeros	French British, German	U.S.	Number of zeros	French British, German
illion	6	million	sextillion	21	1,000 trillion
illion	9	milliard	septillion	24	quadrillion
rillion	12	billion	octillion	27	1,000 quadrillion
uadrillion	15	1,000 billion	nonillion	30	quintillion
uintillion	18	trillion	decillion	33	1,000 quintillion

Roman Numerals

	1	VI	6	XI	11	L	50	CD	400	X̲	10,000
I	2	VII	7	XIX	19	LX	60	D	500	L̲	50,000
II	3	VIII	8	XX	20	XC	90	CM	900	C̲	100,000
V	4	IX	9	XXX	30	C	100	M	1,000	D̲	500,000
/	5	D	10	XL	40	CC	200	V̲	5,000	M̲	1,000,000

NOTE: Underlining a roman numeral increases its value by a factor of 1,000.

Chemical Elements, Discoverers, Atomic Weights

Atomic weights, based on the exact number 12 as the assigned atomic mass of the principal isotope of carbon, carbon 12, are provid through the courtesy of the International Union of Pure and Applied Chemistry and Butterworth Scientific Publications.

For the radioactive elements, with the exception of uranium and thorium, the mass number of either the isotope of longest half-life (*) the better known isotope (**) is given.

Chemical element	Symbol	Atomic number	Atomic weight	Year discov.	Discoverer
Actinium	Ac	89	227*	1899	Debierne
Aluminum	Al	13	26.9815	1825	Oersted
Americium	Am	95	243*	1944	Seaborg, et al.
Antimony	Sb	51	121.75	1450	Valentine
Argon	Ar	18	39.948	1894	Rayleigh, Ramsay
Arsenic	As	33	74.9216	13th c.	Albertus Magnus
Astatine	At	85	210*	1940	Corson, et al.
Barium	Ba	56	137.34	1808	Davy
Berkelium	Bk	97	249**	1949	Thompson, Ghiorso, Seaborg
Beryllium	Be	4	9.0122	1798	Vauquelin
Bismuth	Bi	83	208.980	15th c.	Valentine
Boron	B	5	10.811a	1808	Gay-Lussac, Thenard
Bromine	Br	35	79.904b	1826	Balard
Cadmium	Cd	48	112.40	1817	Stromeyer
Calcium	Ca	20	40.08	1808	Davy
Californium	Cf	98	251**	1950	Thompson, et al.
Carbon	C	6	12.01115a	B.C.	
Cerium	Ce	58	140.12	1803	Klaproth
Cesium	Cs	55	132.905	1860	Bunsen, Kirchhoff
Chlorine	Cl	17	35.453b	1774	Scheele
Chromium	Cr	24	51.996b	1797	Vauquelin
Cobalt	Co	27	58.9332	1735	Brandt
Copper	Cu	29	63.546b	B.C.	
Curium	Cm	96	247*	1944	Seaborg, James, Ghiorso
Dysprosium	Dy	66	162.50	1886	Boisbaudran
Einsteinium	Es	99	254*	1952	Ghiorso, et al.
Erbium	Er	68	167.26	1843	Mosander
Europium	Eu	63	151.96	1901	Demarcay
Fermium	Fm	100	257*	1953	Ghiorso, et al.
Fluorine	F	9	18.9984	1771	Scheele
Francium	Fr	87	223*	1939	Perey
Gadolinium	Gd	64	157.25	1886	Marignac
Gallium	Ga	31	69.72	1875	Boisbaudran
Germanium	Ge	32	72.59	1886	Winkler
Gold	Au	79	196.967	B.C.	
Hafnium	Hf	72	178.49	1923	Coster, Hevesy
Hahnium	Ha	105	262*	1970	Ghiorso, et al.
Helium	He	2	4.0026	1868	Janssen, Lockyer
Holmium	Ho	67	164.930	1878	Soret, Delafontaine
Hydrogen	H	1	1.00797a	1766	Cavendish
Indium	In	49	114.82	1863	Reich, Richter
Iodine	I	53	126.9044	1811	Courtois
Iridium	Ir	77	192.2	1804	Tennant
Iron	Fe	26	55.847b	B.C.	
Krypton	Kr	36	83.80	1898	Ramsay, Travers
Lanthanum	La	57	138.91	1839	Mosander
Lawrencium	Lr	103	256*	1961	Ghiorso, T. Sikkeland, A.E. Larsh, and R.M. Latimer
Lead	Pb	82	207.19	B.C.	
Lithium	Li	3	6.939	1817	Arfvedson
Lutetium	Lu	71	174.97	1907	Welsbach, Urbain
Magnesium	Mg	12	24.312	1829	Bussy
Manganese	Mn	25	54.9380	1774	Gahn
Mendelevium	Md	101	258*	1955	Ghiorso, et al.
Mercury	Hg	80	200.59	B.C.	
Molybdenum	Mo	42	95.94	1782	Hjelm
Neodymium	Nd	60	144.24	1885	Welsbach
Neon	Ne	10	20.183	1898	Ramsay, Travers
Neptunium	Np	93	237*	1940	McMillan, Abelson
Nickel	Ni	28	58.71	1751	Cronstedt
Niobium[1]	Nb	41	92.906	1801	Hatchett
Nitrogen	N	7	14.0067	1772	Rutherford
Nobelium	No	102	255*	1958	Ghiorso, et al.
Osmium	Os	76	190.2	1804	Tennant
Oxygen	O	8	15.9994a	1774	Priestley, Scheele
Palladium	Pd	46	106.4	1803	Wollaston
Phosphorus	P	15	30.9738	1669	Brand
Platinum	Pt	78	195.09	1735	Ulloa
Plutonium	Pu	94	242**	1940	Seaborg, et al.
Polonium	Po	84	210**	1898	P. and M. Curie
Potassium	K	19	39.102	1807	Davy
Praseodymium	Pr	59	140.907	1885	Welsbach
Promethium	Pm	61	147**	1945	Glendenin, Marinsky, Coryell
Protactinium	Pa	91	231*	1917	Hahn, Meitner
Radium	Ra	88	226*	1898	P. & M. Curie, Bemont
Radon	Rn	86	222*	1900	Dorn
Rhenium	Re	75	186.2	1925	Noddack, Tacke, Berg
Rhodium	Rh	45	102.905	1803	Wollaston
Rubidium	Rb	37	85.47	1861	Bunsen, Kirchhoff
Ruthenium	Ru	44	101.07	1845	Klaus
Rutherfordium	Rf	104	261*	1969	Ghiorso, et al.

Chemical element	Symbol	Atomic number	Atomic weight	Year discov.	Discoverer
Samarium	Sm	62	150.35	1879	Boisbaudran
Scandium	Sc	21	44.956	1879	Nilson
Selenium	Se	34	78.96	1817	Berzelius
Silicon	Si	14	28.086a	1823	Berzelius
Silver	Ag	47	107.868b	B.C.	
Sodium	Na	11	22.9898	1807	Davy
Strontium	Sr	38	87.62	1790	Crawford
Sulfur	S	16	32.064a	B.C.	
Tantalum	Ta	73	180.948	1802	Ekeberg
Technetium	Tc	43	99**	1937	Perrier and Segre
Tellurium	Te	52	127.60	1782	Von Reichenstein
Terbium	Tb	65	158.924	1843	Mosander
Thallium	Tl	81	204.37	1861	Crookes
Thorium	Th	90	232.038	1828	Berzelius
Thulium	Tm	69	168.934	1879	Cleve
Tin	Sn	50	118.69	B.C.	
Titanium	Ti	22	47.90	1791	Gregor
Tungsten (Wolfram)	W	74	183.85	1783	d'Elhujar
Uranium	U	92	238.03	1789	Klaproth
Vanadium	V	23	50.942	1830	Sefstrom
Xenon	Xe	54	131.30	1898	Ramsay, Travers
Ytterbium	Yb	70	173.04	1878	Marignac
Yttrium	Y	39	88.905	1794	Gadolin
Zinc	Zn	30	65.37	B.C.	
Zirconium	Zr	40	91.22	1789	Klaproth

(1) Formerly Columbium. (a) Atomic weights so designated are known to be variable because of natural variations in isotopic composition. The observed ranges are: hydrogen±0.0001; boron±0.003; carbon±0.005; oxygen±0.0001; silicon±0.001; sulfur±0.003. (b) Atomic weights so designated are believed to have the following experimental uncertainties: chlorine±0.001; chromium±0.001; iron±0.003; bromine±0.001; silver±0.001; copper±0.001.

Inventions and Scientific Discoveries

Invention	Date	Inventor	Nation.
Adding machine	1642	Pascal	French
Adding machine	1885	Burroughs	U.S.
Addressograph	1892	Duncan	U.S.
Aerosol spray	1941	Goodhue	U.S.
Air brake	1868	Westinghouse	U.S.
Air conditioning	1911	Carrier	U.S.
Air pump	1650	Guericke	German
Airplane, automatic pilot	1929	Green	U.S.
Airplane, experimental	1896	Langley	U.S.
Airplane jet engine	1939	Ohain	German
Airplane with motor	1903	Wright bros.	U.S.
Airplane, hydro	1911	Curtiss	U.S.
Airship	1852	Giffard	French
Airship, rigid dirigible	1900	Zeppelin	German
Arc tube	1923	Alexanderson	U.S.
Autogyro	1920	de la Cierva	Spanish
Automobile, differential gear	1885	Benz	German
Automobile, electric	1892	Morrison	U.S.
Automobile, exp'mtl	1875	Marcus	Austrian
Automobile, gasoline	1887	Daimler	German
Automobile, gasoline	1892	Duryea	U.S.
Automobile magneto	1897	Bosch	German
Automobile muffler	...	Maxim, H.P.	U.S.
Automobile self-starter	1911	Kettering	U.S.
Automobile, steam	1889	Roper	U.S.
Babbitt metal	1839	Babbitt	U.S.
Bakelite	1907	Baekeland	Belg., U.S.
Balloon	1783	Montgolfier	French
Barometer	1643	Torricelli	Italian
Bicycle, modern	1884	Starley	English
Bifocal lens	1780	Franklin	U.S.
Block signals, railway	1867	Hall	U.S.
Bomb, depth	1916	Tait	U.S.
Bottle machine	1903	Owens	U.S.
Braille printing	1829	Braille	French
Burner, gas	1855	Bunsen	German
Calculating machine	1823	Babbage	English
Camera—see also Photography			
Camera, Kodak	1888	Eastman, Walker	U.S.
Camera, Polaroid Land	1948	Land	U.S.
Car coupler	1873	Janney	U.S.
Carburetor, gasoline	1876	Daimler	German
Card time recorder	1894	Cooper	U.S.
Carding machine	1797	Whittemore	U.S.
Carpet sweeper	1876	Bissell	U.S.
Cash register	1879	Ritty	U.S.
Cathode ray tube	1878	Crookes	English
Cellophane	1911	Brandenberger	Swiss
Celluloid	1870	Hyatt	U.S.
Cement, Portland	1845	Aspdin	English
Chronometer	1735	Harrison	English
Circuit breaker	1925	Hilliard	U.S.
Clock, pendulum	1657	Huygens	Dutch
Coaxial cable system	1929	Affel, Espensched	U.S.
Coke oven	1893	Hoffman	Austrian
Compressed air rock drill	1871	Ingersoll	U.S.
Comptometer	1887	Felt	U.S.
Computer, automatic sequence	1939	Aiken et al.	U.S.
Condenser microphone (telephone)	1920	Wente	U.S.
Corn, hybrid	1917	Jones	U.S.
Cotton gin	1793	Whitney	U.S.
Cream separator	1880	DeLaval	Swedish
Cultivator, disc	1878	Mallon	U.S.
Cystoscope	1877	Nitze	German
Dental plate, rubber	1855	Goodyear	U.S.
Diesel engine	1895	Diesel	German
Dynamite	1866	Nobel	Swedish
Dynamo, continuous current	1860	Picinotti	Italian
Dynamo, hydrogen cooled	1915	Schuler	U.S.
Electric battery	1800	Volta	Italian
Electric fan	1882	Wheeler	U.S.
Electrocardiograph	1903	Einthoven	Dutch
Electroencephalograph	1929	Berger	German
Electromagnet	1824	Sturgeon	English
Electron spectrometer	1944	Deutsch, Elliott, Evans	U.S.
Electron tube multigrid	1913	Langmuir	U.S.
Electroplating	1805	Brugnatelli	Italian
Electrostatic generator	1929	Van de Graaff	U.S.
Elevator brake	1852	Otis	U.S.
Elevator, push button	1922	Larson	U.S.
Engine, automobile	1879	Benz	German
Engine, coal-gas 4-cycle	1877	Otto	German
Engine, compression ignition	1883	Daimler	German
Engine, electric ignition	1880	Benz	German
Engine, gas, compound	1926	Eickemeyer	U.S.
Engine, gasoline	1872	Brayton, Geo.	U.S.
Engine, gasoline	1886	Daimler	German
Engine, steam, piston	1705	Newcomen	English
Engine, steam, piston	1769	Watt	Scottish
Engraving, half-tone	1893	Ives	U.S.

Invention	Date	Inventor	Nation.
Filament, tungsten	1915	Langmuir	U.S.
Flanged rail	1831	Stevens	U.S.
Flatiron, electric	1882	Seeley	U.S.
Furnace (for steel)	1861	Siemens	German
Galvanometer	1820	Sweigger	German
Gas discharge tube	1922	Hull	U.S.
Gas lighting	1792	Murdoch	Scottish
Gas mantle	1885	Welsbach	Austrian
Gasoline (lead ethyl)	1922	Midgley	U.S.
Gasoline, cracked	1913	Burton	U.S.
Gasoline, high octane	1930	Ipatieff	Russian
Geiger counter	1913	Geiger	German
Glass, laminated safety	1909	Benedictus	French
Glider	1853	Cayley	English
Gun, breechloader	1811	Thornton	U.S.
Gun, Browning	1916	Browning	U.S.
Gun, magazine	1875	Hotchkiss	U.S.
Gun, silencer	1909	Maxim, H.P.	U.S.
Guncotton	1846	Schoenbein	German
Gyrocompass	1911	Sperry	U.S.
Gyroscope	1852	Foucault	French
Harvester-thresher	1888	Matteson	U.S.
Helicopter	1939	Sikorsky	U.S.
Hydrometer	1768	Baume	French
Ice-making machine	1851	Gorrie	U.S.
Iron lung	1928	Drinker, Slaw	U.S.
Kaleidoscope	1817	Brewster	English
Kinetoscope	1887	Edison	U.S.
Lacquer, nitrocellulose	1921	Flaherty	U.S.
Lamp, arc	1879	Brush	U.S.
Lamp, incandescent	1879	Edison	U.S.
Lamp, incand., frosted	1924	Pipkin	U.S.
Lamp, incand., gas	1916	Langmuir	U.S.
Lamp, Klieg	1911	Kliegl, A.&J.	U.S.
Lamp, mercury vapor	1912	Hewitt	U.S.
Lamp, miner's safety	1816	Davy	English
Lamp, neon	1915	Claude	French
Lathe, turret	1845	Fitch	U.S.
Launderette	1934	Cantrell	U.S.
Lens, achromatic	1758	Dollond	English
Lens, fused bifocal	1908	Borsch	U.S.
Leydenjar (condenser)	1745	von Kleist	German
Lightning rod	1752	Franklin	U.S.
Linoleum	1860	Walton	English
Linotype	1885	Mergenthaler	U.S.
Lock, cylinder	1865	Yale	U.S.
Locomotive, electric	1851	Vail	U.S.
Locomotive, exp'mtl	1801	Trevithick	English
Locomotive, exp'mtl	1812	Fenton et al.	English
Locomotive, exp'mtl	1813	Hedley	English
Locomotive, exp'mtl	1814	Stephenson	English
Locomotive practical	1829	Stephenson	English
Locomotive, 1st U.S.	1830	Cooper, P.	U.S.
Loom, power	1785	Cartwright	English
Loudspeaker, dynamic	1924	Rice, Kellogg	U.S.
Machine gun	1861	Gatling	U.S.
Machine gun, improved	1872	Hotchkiss	U.S.
Machine gun (Maxim)	1883	Maxim, H.S.	U.S., Eng.
Magnet, electro	1828	Henry	U.S.
Mantle, gas	1885	Welsbach	Austrian
Mason jar	1858	Mason, J.	U.S.
Match, friction	1827	John Walker	English
Mercerized textiles	1843	Mercer, J.	English
Meter, induction	1888	Shallenberger	U.S.
Metronome	1816	Malzel	Austrian
Micrometer	1636	Gascoigne	English
Microphone	1877	Berliner	U.S.
Microscope, compound	1590	Janssen	Dutch
Microscope, electronic	1931	Knoll, Ruska	German
Microscope, field ion	1951	Mueller	Germany
Monitor, warship	1861	Ericsson	U.S.
Monotype	1887	Lanston	U.S.
Motor, AC	1892	Tesla	U.S.
Motor, induction	1887	Tesla	U.S.
Motorcycle	1885	Daimler	German
Movie machine	1894	Jenkins	U.S.
Movie, panoramic	1952	Waller	U.S.
Movie, talking	1927	Warner Bros.	U.S.
Mower, lawn	1868	Hills	U.S.
Mowing machine	1831	Manning	U.S.
Neoprene	1930	Carothers	U.S.
Nylon synthetic	1930	Carothers	U.S.
Nylon	1937	Du Pont lab	U.S.
Oil cracking furnace	1891	Gavrilov	Russian
Oil filled power cable	1921	Emanueli	Italian
Oleomargarine	1868	Mege-Mouries	French
Ophthalmoscope	1851	Helmholtz	German
Paper machine	1809	Dickinson	U.S.
Parachute	1785	Blanchard	French
Pen, ballpoint	1888	Loud	U.S.
Pen, fountain	1884	Waterman	U.S.
Pen, steel	1780	Harrison	English
Pendulum	1581	Galileo	Italian
Percussion cap	1814	Shaw	U.S.
Phonograph	1877	Edison	U.S.
Photo, color	1892	Ives	U.S.
Photo film, celluloid	1887	Goodwin	U.S.
Photo film, transparent	1878	Eastman, Goodwin	U.S.
Photoelectric cell	1895	Elster	German
Photographic paper	1898	Baekeland	U.S.
Photography	1835	Talbot	English
Photography	1837	Daguerre	French
Photography	1839	Niepce	French
Photophone	1880	Bell	U.S.
Phototelegraphy	1925	Bell Labs	U.S.
Piano	1709	Cristofori	Italian
Piano, player	1863	Fourneaux	French
Pin, safety	1849	Hunt	U.S.
Pistol (revolver)	1835	Colt	U.S.
Plow, cast iron	1797	Newbold	U.S.
Plow, disc	1896	Hardy	U.S.
Pneumatic hammer	1890	King	U.S.
Powder, smokeless	1863	Schultze	German
Printing press, rotary	1846	Hoe	U.S.
Printing press, web	1865	Bullock	U.S.
Propeller, screw	1804	Stevens	U.S.
Propeller, screw	1837	Ericsson	Swedish
Punch card accounting	1884	Hollerith	U.S.
Radar	1922	Taylor, Young	U.S.
Radio amplifier	1907	De Forest	U.S.
Radio beacon	1928	Donovan	U.S.
Radio crystal oscillator	1918	Nicolson	U.S.
Radio receiver, cascade tuning	1913	Alexanderson,	U.S.
Radio receiver, heterodyne	1913	Fessenden	U.S.
Radio transmitter triode modulation	1914	Alexanderson	U.S.
Radio tube-diode	1905	Fleming	English
Radio tube oscillator	1915	De Forest	U.S.
Radio tube triode	1907	De Forest	U.S.
Radio, signals	1895	Marconi	Italian
Radio, magnetic detector	1902	Marconi	Italian
Radio FM 2-path	1929	Armstrong	U.S.
Rayon	1883	Swan	English
Razor, electric	1931	Schick	U.S.
Razor, safety	1895	Gillette	U.S.
Reaper	1834	McCormick	U.S.
Record, cylinder	1887	Bell, Tainter	U.S.
Record, disc	1887	Berliner	U.S.
Record, long playing	1948	Goldmark	U.S.
Record, wax cylinder	1888	Edison	U.S.
Refrigerants, low-boiling fluorine compound	1930	Midgely and co-workers	U.S.
Refrigerator car	1868	David	U.S.
Resin, synthetic	1931	Hill	English
Rifle, repeating	1860	Spencer	U.S.
Rocket engine	1929	Goddard	U.S.
Rubber, vulcanized	1839	Goodyear	U.S.
Saw, band	1808	Newberry	English
Saw, circular	1777	Miller	English
Searchlight, arc	1915	Sperry	U.S.
Sewing machine	1846	Howe	U.S.
Shoe-sewing machine	1860	McKay	U.S.
Shrapnel shell	1784	Shrapnel	English
Shuttle, flying	1733	Kay	English
Sleeping-car	1858	Pullman	U.S.
Slide rule	1620	Oughtred	English
Soap, hardwater	1928	Bertsch	German
Spectroscope	1859	Kirchoff, Bunsen	German
Spectroscope (mass)	1918	Dempster	U.S.
Spinning jenny	1767	Hargreaves	English
Spinning mule	1779	Crompton	English
Steamboat, exp'mtl	1783	Jouffroy	French

Invention	Date	Inventor	Nation.
Steamboat, exp'mtl	1785	Fitch	U.S.
Steamboat, exp'mtl	1787	Rumsey	U.S.
Steamboat, exp'mtl	1788	Miller	Scottish
Steamboat, exp'mtl	1803	Fulton	U.S.
Steamboat, exp'mtl	1804	Stevens	U.S.
Steamboat, practical	1802	Symington	Scottish
Steamboat, practical	1807	Fulton	U.S.
Steam car	1770	Cugnot	French
Steam turbine	1884	Parsons	English
Steel	1856	Bessemer	English
Steel alloy	1891	Harvey	U.S.
Steel alloy, high-speed	1901	Taylor, White	U.S.
Steel, electric	1900	Heroult	French
Steel, manganese	1884	Hadfield	English
Steel, stainless	1916	Brearley	English
Stereoscope	1838	Wheatstone	English
Stethoscope	1819	Laennec	French
Stethoscope, binaural	1840	Cammann	U.S.
Stock ticker	1870	Edison	U.S.
Storage battery, rechargeable	1859	Plante	French
Stove, electric	1896	Hadaway	U.S.
Submarine	1891	Holland	U.S.
Submarine, even keel	1894	Lake	U.S.
Submarine, torpedo	1776	Bushnell	U.S.
Tank, military	1914	Swinton	English
Tape recorder, magnetic	1899	Poulsen	Danish
Telegraph, magnetic	1837	Morse	U.S.
Telegraph, quadruplex	1874	Edison	U.S.
Telegraph, railroad	1887	Woods	U.S.
Telegraph, wireless high frequency	1896	Marconi	Italian
Telephone	1876	Bell	U.S.-Can.
Telephone amplifier	1912	De Forest	U.S.
Telephone, automatic	1891	Stowger	U.S.
Telephone, radio	1902	Poulsen, Fessenden	U.S.
Telephone, radio	1906	De Forest	U.S.
Telephone, radio, l. d	1915	AT&T	U.S.
Telephone, recording	1898	Poulseon	Danish
Telephone, wireless	1899	Collins	U.S.
Telescope	1608	Lippershey	Neth.
Telescope	1609	Galileo	Italian
Telescope, astronomical	1611	Kepler	German
Teletype	1928	Morkrum, Kleinschmidt	U.S.
Television, iconoscope	1923	Zworykin	U.S.
Television, electronic	1927	Farnsworth	U.S.
Television, (mech. scanner)	1926	Baird	Scottish
Thermometer	1593	Galileo	Italian
Thermometer	1710	Reaumur	French
Thermometer, mercury	1714	Fahrenheit	German
Time recorder	1890	Bundy	U.S.
Time, self-regulator	1918	Bryce	U.S.
Tire, double-tube	1845	Thomson	English
Tire, pneumatic	1888	Dunlop	Irish
Toaster, automatic	1918	Strite	U.S.
Tool, pneumatic	1865	Law	English
Torpedo, marine	1804	Fulton	U.S.
Tractor, crawler	1900	Holt	U.S.
Transformer A.C.	1885	Stanley	U.S.
Transistor	1947	Shockley, Brattain, Bardeen	U.S.
Trolley car, electric	1884-87	Van DePoele, Sprague	U.S.
Tungsten, ductile	1912	Coolidge	U.S.
Turbine, gas	1899	Curtis, C.G.	U.S.
Turbine, hydraulic	1849	Francis	U.S.
Turbine, steam	1896	Curtis, C.G.	U.S.
Type, movable	1450	Gutenberg	German
Typewriter	1868	Soule, Glidden	U.S.
Vacuum cleaner, electric	1907	Spangler	U.S.
Washer, electric	1907	Hurley Co.	U.S.
Welding, atomic hydrogen	1924	Langmuir, Palmer	U.S.
Welding, electric	1877	Thomson	U.S.
Wind tunnel	1923	Munk	U.S.
Wire, barbed	1874	Glidden	U.S.
Wire, barbed	1875	Haisn	U.S.
X-ray tube	1913	Coolidge	U.S.
Zipper	1891	Judson	U.S.

Discoveries and Innovations: Chemistry, Physics, Biology, Medicine

	Date	Discoverer	Nation.
Acetylene gas	1892	Wilson	U.S.
ACTH	1949	Armour & Co.	U.S.
Adrenalin	1901	Takamine	Japanese
Aluminum, electrolytic process	1886	Hall	U.S.
Aluminum, isolated	1825	Oersted	Danish
Analine dye	1856	Perkin	English
Anesthesia, ether	1842	Long	U.S.
Anesthesia, local	1885	Koller	Austrian
Anesthesia, spinal	1898	Bier	German
Anti-rabies	1885	Pasteur	French
Antiseptic surgery	1867	Lister	English
Antitoxin, diphtheria	1891	Von Behring	German
Argyrol	1901	Barnes	U.S.
Arsphenamine	1910	Ehrlich	German
Aspirin	1889	Dresser	German
Atabrine	...	Mietzsch, et al.	German
Atomic numbers	1913	Moseley	English
Atomic theory	1803	Dalton	English
Atomic time clock	1947	Libby	U.S.
Atom-smashing theory	1919	Rutherford	English
Aureomycin	1948	Duggar	U.S.
Bacitracin	1945	Johnson, et al.	U.S.
Bacteria (described)	1676	Leeuwenhoek	Dutch
Barbital	1903	Fischer	German
Bleaching powder	1798	Tennant	English
Blood, circulation	1628	Harvey	English
Bordeaux mixture	1885	Millardet	French
Bromine from sea	1924	Edgar Kramer	U.S.
Calcium carbide	1888	Wilson	U.S.
Calculus	1670	Newton	English
Camphor synthetic	1896	Haller	French
Canning (food)	1804	Appert	French
Carbomycin	1952	Tanner	U.S.
Carbon oxides	1925	Fisher	German
Chlorine	1810	Davy	English
Chloroform	1831	Guthrie, S.	U.S.
Chloromycetin	1947	Burkholder	U.S.
Classification of plants and animals	1735	Linnaeus	Swedish
Cocaine	1860	Niermann	German
Combustion explained	1777	Lavoisier	French
Conditioned reflex	1914	Pavlov	Russian
Conteben	1950	Belmisch, Mietzsch, Domagk	German
Cortisone	1936	Kendall	U.S.
Cortisone, synthesis	1946	Sarett	U.S.
Cosmic rays	1910	Gockel	Swiss
Cyanimide	1905	Frank, Caro	German
Cyclotron	1930	Lawrence	U.S.
DDT (not applied as insecticide until 1939)	1874	Zeidler	German
Deuterium	1932	Urey, Brickwedde, Murphy	U.S.
DNA (structure)	1951	Crick; Watson; Wilkins	English; U.S.; English
Electric resistance (law)	1827	Ohm	German
Electric waves	1888	Hertz	German
Electrolysis	1852	Faraday	English
Electromagnetism	1819	Oersted	Danish
Electron	1897	Thomson, J.	English
Electron diffraction	1936	Thomson, G.; Davisson	English; U.S.
Electroshock treatment	1938	Cerletti, Bini	Italian
Erythromycin	1952	McGuire	U.S.
Evolution, natural selection	1858	Darwin	English
Falling bodies, law	1590	Galileo	Italian

	Date	Discoverer	Nation.
Gases, law of combining volumes	1808	Gay-Lussac	French
Geometry, analytic	1619	Descartes	French
Gold (cyanide process for extraction)	1887	MacArthur, Forest	British
Gravitation, law	1687	Newton	English
Holograph	1948	Gabor	British
Human heart transplant	1967	Barnard	S. African
Indigo, synthesis of	1880	Baeyer	German
Induction, electric	1830	Henry	U.S.
Insulin	1922	Banting, Best, Macleod	Canadian
Intelligence testing	1905	Binet, Simon	French
Isinazid	1952	Hoffman-La-Roche	U.S.
		Domagk	German
Isotopes, theory	1912	Soddy	English
Laser (light amplification by stimulated emission of radiation)	1958	Townes, Schawlow	U.S.
Light, velocity	1675	Roemer	Danish
Light, wave theory	1690	Huygens	Dutch
Lithography	1796	Senefelder	Bohemian
Lobotomy	1935	Egas Moniz	Portuguese
LSD-25	1943	Hoffman	Swiss
Mendelian laws	1866	Mendel	Austrian
Mercator projection (map)	1568	Mercator (Kremer)	Flemish
Methanol	1925	Patard	French
Milk condensation	1853	Borden	U.S.
Molecular hypothesis	1811	Avogadro	Italian
Motion, laws of	1687	Newton	English
Neomycin	1949	Waksman, Lechevalier	U.S.
Neutron	1932	Chadwick	English
Nitric acid	1648	Glauber	German
Nitric oxide	1772	Priestley	English
Nitroglycerin	1846	Sobrero	Italian
Oil cracking process	1891	Dewar	U.S.
Oxygen	1774	Priestley	English
Ozone	1840	Schonbein	German
Paper, sulfite process	1867	Tilghman	U.S.
Paper, wood pulp, sulfate process	1884	Dahl	German
Penicillin	1929	Fleming	English
practical use	1941	Florey, Chain	English
Periodic law and table of elements	1869	Mendeleyev	Russian
Planetary motion, laws	1609	Kepler	German
Plutonium fission	1940	Kennedy, Wahl, Seaborg, Segre	U.S.
Polymixin	1947	Ainsworth	English
Positron	1932	Anderson	U.S.
Proton	1919	Rutherford	English
Psychoanalysis	1900	Freud	Austrian
Quantum theory	1900	Planck	German
Quasars	1963	Matthews, Sandage	U.S.
Quinine synthetic	1918	Rabe	German
Radioactivity	1896	Becquerel	French
Radium	1898	Curie, Pierre	French
		Curie, Marie	Pol.-Fr.
Relativity theory	1905	Einstein	German
Reserpine	1949	Jal Vaikl	Indian
Salvarsan (606)	1910	Ehrlich	German
Schick test	1913	Schick	U.S.
Silicon	1823	Berzelius	Swedish
Streptomycin	1945	Waksman	U.S.
Sulfadiazine	1940	Roblin	U.S.
Sulfanilamide	1934	Domagk	German
Sulfanilamide theory	1908	Gelmo	German
Sulfapyridine	1938	Ewins, Phelps	English
Sulfathiazole	...	Fosbinder, Walter	U.S.
Sulfuric acid	1831	Phillips	English
Sulfuric acid, lead	1746	Roebuck	English
Terramycin	1950	Finlay, et al.	U.S.
Tuberculin	1890	Koch	German
Uranium fission (theory)	1939	Hahn, Meitner, Strassmann	German
		Bohr	Danish
		Fermi	Italian
		Einstein, Pegran, Wheeler	U.S.
Uranium fission, atomic reactor	1942	Fermi, Szilard	U.S.
Vaccine, measles	1954	Enders, Peebles	U.S.
Vaccine, polio	1953	Salk	U.S.
Vaccine, polio, oral	1955	Sabin	U.S.
Vaccine, rabies	1885	Pasteur	French
Vaccine, smallpox	1796	Jenner	English
Vaccine, typhus	1909	Nicolle	French
Van Allen belts, radiation	1958	Van Allen	U.S.
Vitamin A	1913	McCollum, Davis	U.S.
Vitamin B	1916	McCollum	U.S.
Vitamin C	1912	Holst, Froelich	Norwegian
Vitamin D	1922	McCollum	U.S.
Wassermann test	1906	Wassermann	German
Xerography	1938	Carlson	U.S.
X-ray	1895	Roentgen	German

Copyright Law of The United States

Source: Copyright Office, Library of Congress

Original works of authorship in any tangible medium of expression are entitled to protection under the copyright law (Title 17 of the United States Code). The law came into effect on January 1, 1978 (Public Law 94-553, 90 Stat. 2541); it superseded the Copyright Act of 1909, as amended. Before the 1976 Act, there had been only three general revisions of the original copyright law of 1790, namely those of 1831, 1870, and 1909.

Categories of Works

Copyright protection under the new law extends to original works of authorship fixed in any tangible medium of expression, now known or later developed, from which they can be perceived, reproduced, or otherwise communicated, either directly or with the aid of a machine or device. Works of authorship include books, periodicals and other literary works, musical compositions with accompanying lyrics, dramas and dramatico-musical compositions, pantomimes and choreographic works, motion pictures and other audiovisual works, and sound recordings.

The owner of a copyright is given the exclusive right to reproduce the copyrighted work in copies or phonorecords and distribute them to the public by sale, rental, lease, or lending. The owner of a copyright also enjoys the exclusive right to make derivative works based upon the copyrighted work, to perform the work publicly if it be a literary, musical, dramatic, or choreographic work, a pantomime, motion picture, or other audiovisual work, and in the case of literary, musical, dramatic, and choreographic works, pantomimes, and pictorial, graphic, or sculptural works, including the individual images of a motion picture or other audiovisual work, to display the copyrighted work publicly. All of these rights are subject to certain specified exceptions, including the so-called judicial doctrine of "fair use," which is included in the law for the first time.

The act also provides special provisions permitting compulsory licensing for the recording and distribution of phonorecords of nondramatic musical compositions, noncommercial transmissions by public broadcasters of published musical, pictorial, sculptural, and graphic works, performances of copyrighted nondramatic music by means of jukeboxes, and the secondary transmission of copyrighted works on cable television systems.

Single National System

The law establishes a single national system of statutory protection for all copyrightable works fixed in tangible form, whether published or unpublished. Before Jan. 1, 1978 unpublished works were entitled to protection under the common law of the various states while published works came under the Federal statute.

Registration of a claim to copyright in any work, whether published or unpublished, may be made voluntarily at any time during the copyright term by the owner of the copyright or of any exclusive right in the work. Registration is not a condition of copyright protection, but is a prerequisite to an infringement suit. Subject to certain exceptions, the remedies of statutory damages and attorney's fees are not available for those infringements occurring before registration. Even if registration is not made, copies or phonorecords of works published in the U.S. with notice of copyright are required to be deposited for the collections of the Library of Congress. This deposit requirement is not a condition of protection, but does render the copyright owner subject to penalties for failure to deposit after a demand by the Register of Copyrights.

Duration of Copyright

For works created on or after Jan. 1, 1978, copyright subsists from their creation for a term consisting of the life of the author and 50 years after the author's death. For works made for hire, and for anonymous and pseudonymous works (unless the author's identity is revealed in Copyright Office records), the term is 100 years from creation or 75 years from first publication, whichever is shorter.

The law retains for works that were under statutory protection on January 1, 1978, the 28 year term of copyright from first publication (or from registration in some cases), renewable by certain persons for a second term of protection of 47 years. Copyrights in their first 28-year term on Jan. 1, 1978, have to be renewed in order to be protected for the full maximum term of 75 years. Copyrights in their second term on Jan. 1, 1978 were automatically extended to last for a total term of 75 years.

For works that had been created before the law came into effect but had neither been published nor registered for copyright before Jan. 1, 1978, the term of copyright is generally computed in the same way as for new works: the life-plus-50 or 75/100-year terms will apply. However, all works in this category are guaranteed at least 25 years of statutory protection. The law specifies that copyright in a work of this kind will not expire before Dec. 31, 2002, and if the work is published before that date the term is extended by another 25 years, through the end of the year 2027.

Notice of Copyright

Under the 1909 copyright law the copyright notice was the most important requirement for obtaining copyright protection for a published work. For published works, all copies had to bear the prescribed notice from the time of first publication. If a work was published before Jan. 1, 1978 without the required notice, copyright protection was lost permanently and cannot be regained.

The present copyright law requires a notice on copies or phonorecords of sound recordings that are distributed to the public. Errors and omissions, however, do not immediately result in forfeiture of the copyright and can be corrected within prescribed time limits. Innocent infringers misled by an omission or error in the notice generally are shielded from liability.

The notice of copyright required on all visually perceptible copies published in the U.S. or elsewhere under the 1976 Act consists of the symbol © (the letter C in a circle), the word "Copyright," or the abbreviation "Copr.," and the year of first publication, and the name of the owner of copyright in the work. Example: © 1981 JOHN DOE

The notice must be affixed in such manner and location as to give reasonable notice of the claim of copyright.

The notice of copyright prescribed for all published phonorecords of sound recordings consists of the symbol ℗ (the letter P in a circle), the year of first publication of the sound recording, and the name of the owner of copyright in the sound recording, placed on the surface of the phonorecord, or on the phonorecord label or container in such manner and location as to give reasonable notice of the claim of copyright. Example: ℗ 1981 DOE RECORDS, INC.

Manufacturing Requirements

The requirements in the manufacturing clause in the copyright law mandating that certain works be manufactured in the U.S. gradually narrowed until they were totally eliminated on July 1, 1982, after a legislative extension was vetoed by President Ronald Reagan. Under the 1909 Act certain works had to be manufactured in the U.S. to receive copyright protection; the 1978 Copyright Act did not make manufacture in the U.S. a condition of protection and reduced the scope of the provisions. The 1978 Act also provided for the phase-out of the manufacturing clause, which finally occurred on July 1, 1982.

International Protection

The U.S. has copyright relations with more than 70 countries, under which works of American authors are protected in those countries, and the works of their authors are protected in the U.S. The basic feature of this protection is "national treatment," under which the alien author is treated by a country in the same manner that it treats its own authors. Relations exist by virtue of bilateral agreements or through the Buenos Aires Convention or the Universal Copyright Convention. U.S. legislation implementing the latter convention, which became effective Sept. 16, 1955, gives the works of foreign authors the benefit of exemptions from the manufacturing requirements of the U.S. copyright law, provided the works are first published abroad with a copyright notice including the symbol © , the name of the copyright owner and the year date of first publication, and that the work either is by an "author" who is a citizen or subject of a foreign country which belongs to the Convention or is first published in a foreign member country. Conversely, works of U.S. authors are exempt from certain burdensome requirements in particular foreign member countries.

Works published on or after Jan. 1, 1978, are subject to protection under the copyright statute if, on the date of first publication, one or more of the authors is a national or domiciliary of the U.S., or is a national, domiciliary, or sovereign authority of a foreign nation that is a party to a copyright treaty to which the United States is also a party, or is a stateless person, regardless of domicile, or if the work is first published either in the U.S. or in a foreign nation that, on the date of first publication is a party to the Universal Copyright Convention. All unpublished works are protected here regardless of the citizenship or domicile of the author.

A U.S. author may obtain copyright protection in all countries that are members of the Universal Copyright Convention (UCC). In member countries, where no formalities are required, the works of U.S. authors are protected automatically. Member countries whose laws impose formalities protect U.S. works if all published copies bear a convention notice which consists of the symbol ©, together with the name of the copyright owner and the year date of publication. Example: © JOHN DOE 1981.

Further information and application forms may be obtained free of charge by writing to the Information and Publications Section LM-455, Copyright Office, The Library of Congress, Washington, D.C. 20559.

Copyright registration application forms may be ordered on a 24-hour basis by calling (202) 287-9100.

SPORTS OF 1982

Olympic Games Records

The modern Olympic Games, first held in Athens, Greece, in 1896, were the result of efforts by Baron Pierre de Coubertin, a French educator, to promote interest in education and culture, also to foster better international understanding through the universal medium of youth's love of athletics.

His source of inspiration for the Olympic Games was the ancient Greek Olympic Games, most notable of the four Panhellenic celebrations. The games were combined patriotic, religious, and athletic festivals held every four years. The first such recorded festival was that held in 776 B.C., the date from which the Greeks began to keep their calendar by "Olympiads," or four-year spans between the games.

The first Olympiad is said to have consisted merely of a 200-yard foot race near the small city of Olympia, but the games gained in scope and became demonstrations of national pride. Only Greek citizens — amateurs — were permitted to participate. Winners received laurel, wild olive, and palm wreaths and were accorded many special privileges. Under the Roman emperors, the games deteriorated into professional carnivals and circuses. Emperor Theodosius banned them in 394 A.D.

Baron de Coubertin enlisted 9 nations to send athletes to the first modern Olympics in 1896; now more than 100 nations compete. Winter Olympic Games were started in 1924.

In 1980, 62 nations, including the United States, Canada, W. Germany, and Japan, refused to participate in the games in protest against the Soviet invasion of Afghanistan.

Sites and Unofficial Winners of Games

1896 Athens (U.S.)
1900 Paris (U.S.)
1904 St. Louis (U.S.)
1906 Athens (U.S.)*
1908 London (U.S.)
1912 Stockholm (U.S.)
1920 Antwerp (U.S.)
1924 Paris (U.S.)
1928 Amsterdam (U.S.)
1932 Los Angeles (U.S.)
1936 Berlin (Germany)
1948 London (U.S.)
1952 Helsinki (U.S.)
1956 Melbourne (USSR)
1960 Rome (USSR)
1964 Tokyo (U.S.)
1968 Mexico City (U.S.)
1972 Munich (USSR)
1976 Montreal (USSR)
1980 Moscow (USSR)
1984 Los Angeles (scheduled)

*Games not recognized by International Olympic Committee. Games 6 (1916), 12 (1940), and 13 (1944) were not celebrated. East and West Germany began competing separately in 1968.

Olympic Games Champions, 1896—1980

(*Indicates Olympic Records)

Track and Field — Men

60-Meter Run

1900	Alvin Kraenzlein, United States	7s*
1904	Archie Hahn, United States	7s*

100-Meter Run

1896	Thomas Burke, United States	12s
1900	Francis W. Jarvis, United States	10.8s
1904	Archie Hahn, United States	11s
1908	Reginald Walker, South Africa	10.8s
1912	Ralph Craig, United States	10.8s
1920	Charles Paddock, United States	10.8s
1924	Harold Abrahams, Great Britain	10.6s
1928	Percy Williams, Canada	10.8s
1932	Eddie Tolan, United States	10.3s
1936	Jesse Owens, United States	10.3s
1948	Harrison Dillard, United States	10.3s
1952	Lindy Remigino, United States	10.4s
1956	Bobby Morrow, United States	10.5s
1960	Armin Hary, Germany	10.2s
1964	Bob Hayes, United States	10.0s
1968	Jim Hines, United States	9.9s*
1972	Valeri Borzov, USSR	10.14s
1976	Hasely Crawford, Trinidad	10.06s
1980	Allan Wells, Great Britain	10.25s

200-Meter Run

1900	Walter Tewksbury, United States	22.2s
1904	Archie Hahn, United States	21.6s
1908	Robert Kerr, Canada	22.4s
1912	Ralph Craig, United States	21.7s
1920	Allan Woodring, United States	22s
1924	Jackson Scholz, United States	21.6s
1928	Percy Williams, Canada	21.8s
1932	Eddie Tolan, United States	21.2s
1936	Jesse Owens, United States	20.7s
1948	Mel Patton, United States	21.1s
1952	Andrew Stanfield, United States	20.7s
1956	Bobby Morrow, United States	20.6s
1960	Livio Berruti, Italy	20.5s
1964	Henry Carr, United States	20.3s
1968	Tommie Smith, United States	19.8s*
1972	Valeri Borzov, USSR	20.00s
1976	Donald Quarrie, Jamaica	20.23s
1980	Pietro Mennea, Italy	20.19s

400-Meter Run

1896	Thomas Burke, United States	54.2s
1900	Maxey Long, United States	49.4s
1904	Harry Hillman, United States	49.2s
1908	Wyndham Halswelle, Great Britain, walkover	50s
1912	Charles Reidpath, United States	48.2s
1920	Bevil Rudd, South Africa	49.6s
1924	Eric Liddell, Great Britain	47.6s
1928	Ray Barbuti, United States	47.8s
1932	William Carr, United States	46.2s
1936	Archie Williams, United States	46.5s
1948	Arthur Wint, Jamaica, B W I	46.2s
1952	George Rhoden, Jamaica, B W I	45.9s
1956	Charles Jenkins, United States	46.7s
1960	Otis Davis, United States	44.9s
1964	Michael Larrabee, United States	45.1s
1968	Lee Evans, United States	43.8s*
1972	Vincent Matthews, United States	44.66s
1976	Alberto Juantorena, Cuba	44.26s
1980	Viktor Markin, USSR	44.60s

800-Meter Run

1896	Edwin Flack, Great Britain	2m. 11s
1900	Alfred Tysoe, Great Britain	2m. 1.4s
1904	James Lightbody, United States	1m. 56s
1908	Mel Sheppard, United States	1m. 52.8s
1912	James Meredith, United States	1m. 51.9s
1920	Albert Hill, Great Britain	1m. 53.4s
1924	Douglas Lowe, Great Britain	1m. 52.4s
1928	Douglas Lowe, Great Britain	1m. 51.8s
1932	Thomas Hampson, Great Britain	1m. 49.8s
1936	John Woodruff, United States	1m. 52.9s
1948	Mal Whitfield, United States	1m. 49.2s
1952	Mal Whitfield, United States	1m. 49.2s
1956	Thomas Courtney, United States	1m. 47.7s
1960	Peter Snell, New Zealand	1m. 46.3s
1964	Peter Snell, New Zealand	1m. 45.1s
1968	Ralph Doubell, Australia	1m. 44.3s
1972	Dave Wottle, United States	1m. 45.9s
1976	Alberto Juantorena, Cuba	1m. 43.50s*
1980	Steve Ovett, Great Britain	1m. 45.40s

1,500-Meter Run

1896	Edwin Flack, Great Britain	4m. 33.2s
1900	Charles Bennett, Great Britain	4m. 6s

1904	James Lightbody, United States	4m. 5.4s
1908	Mel Sheppard, United States	4m. 3.4s
1912	Arnold Jackson, Great Britain	3m. 56.8s
1920	Albert Hill, Great Britain	4m. 1.8s
1924	Paavo Nurmi, Finland	3m. 53.6s
1928	Harry Larva, Finland	3m. 53.2s
1932	Luigi Beccali, Italy	3m. 51.2s
1936	Jack Lovelock, New Zealand	3m. 47.8s
1948	Henri Eriksson, Sweden	3m. 49.8s
1952	Joseph Barthel, Luxemburg	3m. 45.2s
1956	Ron Delany, Ireland	3m. 41.2s
1960	Herb Elliott, Australia	3m. 35.6s
1964	Peter Snell, New Zealand	3m. 38.1s
1968	Kipchoge Keino, Kenya	3m. 34.9s*
1972	Pekka Vasala, Finland	3m. 36.3s
1976	John Walker, New Zealand	3m. 39.17s
1980	Sebastian Coe, Great Britain	3m. 38.4s

3,000-Meter Steeplechase

1920	Percy Hodge, Great Britain	10m. 0.4s
1924	Willie Ritola, Finland	9m. 33.6s
1928	Toivo Loukola, Finland	9m. 21.8s
1932	Volmari Iso-Hollo, Finland	10m. 33.4s
	(About 3,450 mtrs. extra lap by error)	
1936	Volmari Iso-Hollo, Finland	9m. 3.8s
1948	Thure Sjoestrand, Sweden	9m. 4.6s
1952	Horace Ashenfelter, United States	8m. 45.4s
1956	Chris Brasher, Great Britain	8m. 41.2s
1960	Zdzislaw Krzyszkowiak, Poland	8m. 34.2s
1964	Gaston Roelants, Belgium	8m. 30.8s
1968	Amos Biwott, Kenya	8m. 51s
1972	Kipchoge Keino, Kenya	8m. 23.6s
1976	Anders Garderud, Sweden	8m. 08.2s*
1980	Bronislaw Malinowski, Poland	8m. 09.7s

5,000-Meter Run

1912	Hannes Kolehmainen, Finland	14m. 36.6s
1920	Joseph Guillemot, France	14m. 55.6s
1924	Paavo Nurmi, Finland	14m. 31.2s
1928	Willie Ritola, Finland	14m. 38s
1932	Lauri Lehtinen, Finland	14m. 30s
1936	Gunnar Hockert, Finland	14m. 22.2s
1948	Gaston Reiff, Belgium	14m. 17.6s
1952	Emil Zatopek, Czechoslovakia	14m. 6.6s
1956	Vladimir Kuts, USSR	13m. 39.6s
1960	Murray Halberg, New Zealand	13m. 43.4s
1964	Bob Schul, United States	13m. 48.8s
1968	Mohamed Gammoudi, Tunisia	14m. 05.0s
1972	Lasse Viren, Finland	13m. 26.4s
1976	Lasse Viren, Finland	13m. 24.76s
1980	Miruts Yifter, Ethiopia	13m. 21.0s*

10,000-Meter Run

1912	Hannes Kolehmainen, Finland	31m. 20.8s
1920	Paavo Nurmi, Finland	31m. 45.8s
1924	Willie Ritola, Finland	30m. 23.2s
1928	Paavo Nurmi, Finland	30m. 18.8s
1932	Janusz Kusocinski, Poland	30m. 11.4s
1936	Ilmari Salminen, Finland	30m. 15.4s
1948	Emil Zatopek, Czechoslovakia	29m. 59.6s
1952	Emil Zatopek, Czechoslovakia	29m. 17.0s
1956	Vladimir Kuts, USSR	28m. 45.6s
1960	Pytor Bolotnikov, USSR	28m. 32.2s
1964	Billy Mills, United States	28m. 24.4s
1968	Naftali Temu, Kenya	29m. 27.4s
1972	Lasse Viren, Finland	27m. 38.4s*
1976	Lasse Viren, Finland	27m. 40.38s
1980	Miruts Yifter, Ethiopia	27m. 42.7s

Marathon

1896	Spiridon Loues, Greece	2h. 58m. 50s
1900	Michel Teato, France	2h. 59m. 45s
1904	Thomas Hicks, United States	3h. 28m. 53s
1908	John J. Hayes, United States	2h. 55m. 18.4s
1912	Kenneth McArthur, South Africa	2h. 36m. 54.8s
1920	Hannes Kolehmainen, Finland	2h. 32m. 35.8s
1924	Albin Stenroos, Finland	2h. 41m. 22.6s
1928	A.B. El Ouafi, France	2h. 32m. 57s
1932	Juan Zabala, Argentina	2h. 31m. 36s
1936	Kitei Son, Japan	2h. 29m. 19.2s
1948	Delfo Cabrera, Argentina	2h. 34m. 51.6s
1952	Emil Zatopek, Czechoslovakia	2h. 23m. 03.2s
1956	Alain Mimoun, France	2h. 25m.
1960	Abebe Bikila, Ethiopia	2h. 15m. 16.2s
1964	Abebe Bikila, Ethiopia	2h. 12m. 11.2s
1968	Mamo Wolde, Ethiopia	2h. 20m. 26.4s
1972	Frank Shorter, United States	2h. 12m. 19.8s
1976	Waldemar Cierpinski, E. Germany	2h. 09m. 55s*
1980	Waldemar Cierpinski, E. Germany	2h. 11m. 03s

10,000-Meter Cross-Country

1920	Paavo Nurmi, Finland	27m. 15s*
1924	Paavo Nurmi, Finland	32m. 54.8s

20-Kilometer Walk

1956	Leonid Spirine, USSR	1h. 31m. 27.4s
1960	Vladimir Golubnichy, USSR	1h. 34m. 7.2s
1964	Kenneth Mathews, Great Britain	1h. 29m. 34.0s
1968	Vladimir Golubnichy, USSR	1h. 35m. 58.4s
1972	Peter Frenkel, E. Germany	1h. 26m. 42.4s
1976	Daniel Bautista, Mexico	1h. 24m. 40.6s
1980	Maurizio Damilano, Italy	1h. 23m. 35.5s*

50-Kilometer Walk

1932	Thomas W. Green, Great Britain	4h. 50m. 10s
1936	Harold Whitlock, Great Britain	4h. 30m. 41.4s
1948	John Ljunggren, Sweden	4h. 41m. 52s
1952	Giuseppe Dordoni, Italy	4h. 28m. 07.8s
1956	Norman Read, New Zealand	4h. 30m. 42.8s
1960	Donald Thompson, Great Britain	4h. 25m. 30s
1964	Abdon Pamich, Italy	4h. 11m. 11.4s
1968	Christoph Hohne, E. Germany	4h. 20m. 13.6s
1972	Bern Kannenberg, W. Germany	3h. 56m. 11.6s
1980	Hartwig Gauter, E. Germany	3h. 49m. 24.0s*

110-Meter Hurdles

1896	Thomas Curtis, United States	17.6s
1900	Alvin Kraenzlein, United States	15.4s
1904	Frederick Schule, United States	16s
1908	Forrest Smithson, United States	15s
1912	Frederick Kelly, United States	15.1s
1920	Earl Thomson, Canada	14.8s
1924	Daniel Kinsey, United States	15s
1928	Sydney Atkinson, South Africa	14.8s
1932	George Saling, United States	14.6s
1936	Forrest Towns, United States	14.2s
1948	William Porter, United States	13.9s
1952	Harrison Dillard, United States	13.7s
1956	Lee Calhoun, United States	13.5s
1960	Lee Calhoun, United States	13.8s
1964	Hayes Jones, United States	13.6s
1968	Willie Davenport, United States	13.3s
1972	Rod Milburn, United States	13.24s*
1976	Guy Drut, France	13.30s
1980	Thomas Munkelt, E. Germany	13. 39s

200-Meter Hurdles

1900	Alvin Kraenzlein, United States	25.4s
1904	Harry Hillman, United States	24.6s*

400-Meter Hurdles

1900	J.W.B. Tewksbury, United States	57.6s
1904	Harry Hillman, United States	53s
1908	Charles Bacon, United States	55s
1920	Frank Loomis, United States	54s
1924	F. Morgan Taylor, United States	52.6s
1928	Lord Burghley, Great Britain	53.4s
1932	Robert Tisdall, Ireland	51.8s
1936	Glenn Hardin, United States	52.4s
1948	Roy Cochran, United States	51.1s
1952	Charles Moore, United States	50.8s
1956	Glenn Davis, United States	50.1s
1960	Glenn Davis, United States	49.3s
1964	Rex Cawley, United States	49.6s
1968	Dave Hemery, Great Britain	48.1s
1972	John Akii-Bua, Uganda	47.82s
1976	Edwin Moses, United States	47.64s*
1980	Volker Beck, E. Germany	48.70s

Standing High Jump

1900	Ray Ewry, United States	5ft. 5 in.
1904	Ray Ewry, United States	4ft. 11 in.
1908	Ray Ewry, United States	5ft. 2 in.
1912	Platt Adams, United States	5ft. 4 1-4 in.*

Running High Jump

1896	Ellery Clark, United States	5ft. 11 1-4 in.
1900	Irving Baxter, United States	6ft. 2 4-5 in.
1904	Samuel Jones, United States	5ft. 11 in.
1908	Harry Porter, United States	6ft. 3 in.
1912	Alma Richards, United States	6ft. 4 in.
1920	Richard Landon, United States	6ft. 4 1-4 in.
1924	Harold Osborn, United States	6ft. 6 in.
1928	Robert W. King, United States	6ft. 4 3-8 in.
1932	Duncan McNaughton, Canada	6ft. 5 5-8 in.
1936	Cornelius Johnson, United States	6ft. 7 15-16 in.
1948	John L. Winter, Australia	6ft. 6 in.
1952	Walter Davis, United States	6ft. 8.32 in.
1956	Charles Dumas, United States	6ft. 11 1-4 in.
1960	Robert Shavlakadze, USSR	7ft. 1 in.

1964	Valery Brumel, USSR	7ft. 1 3-4 in.
1968	Dick Fosbury, United States	7ft. 4 1-4 in.
1972	Yuri Tarmak, USSR	7ft. 3 3-4 in.
1976	Jacek Wszola, Poland	7ft. 4 1-2 in.
1980	Gerd Wessig, E. Germany	7ft. 8 3-4 in.*

Standing Broad Jump

1900	Ray Ewry, United States	10ft. 6 2-5 in.
1904	Ray Ewry, United States	11ft. 4 7-8 in.*
1908	Ray Ewry, United States	10ft. 11 1-4 in.
1912	Constantin Tsicilitras, Greece	11ft. 3-4 in.

Long Jump

1896	Ellery Clark, United States	20ft. 9 3-4 in.
1900	Alvin Kraenzlein, United States	23ft. 6 7-8 in.
1904	Myer Prinstein, United States	24ft. 1 in.
1908	Frank Irons, United States	24ft. 6 1-2 in.
1912	Albert Gutterson, United States	24ft. 11 1-4 in.
1920	William Petterssen, Sweden	23ft. 5 1-2 in.
1924	DeHart Hubbard, United States	24ft. 5 1-8 in.
1928	Edward B. Hamm, United States	25ft. 4 3-4 in.
1932	Edward Gordon, United States	25ft. 3-4 in.
1936	Jesse Owens, United States	26ft. 5 5-16 in.
1948	William Steele, United States	25ft. 8 in.
1952	Jerome Biffle, United States	24ft. 10 in.
1956	Gregory Bell, United States	25ft. 8 1-4 in.
1960	Ralph Boston, United States	26ft. 7 3-4 in.
1964	Lynn Davies, Great Britain	26ft. 5 3-4 in.
1968	Bob Beamon, United States	29ft. 2 1-2 in.*
1972	Randy Williams, United States	27ft. 1-2 in.
1976	Arnie Robinson, United States	27ft. 4 1-2 in.
1980	Lutz Dombrowski, E. Germany	28ft. 1-4 in.

400-Meter Relay

1912	Great Britain	42.4s
1920	United States	42.2s
1924	United States	41s
1928	United States	41s
1932	United States	40s
1936	United States	39.8s
1948	United States	40.6s
1952	United States	40.1s
1956	United States	39.5s
1960	Germany (U.S. disqualified)	39.5s
1964	United States	39.0s
1968	United States	38.2s
1972	United States	38.19s*
1976	United States	38.33s
1980	USSR	38.26s

1,600-Meter Relay

1908	United States	3m. 27.2s
1912	United States	3m. 16.6s
1920	Great Britain	3m. 22.2s
1924	United States	3m. 16s
1928	United States	3m. 14.2s
1932	United States	3m. 8.2s
1936	Great Britain	3m. 9s
1948	United States	3m. 10.4s
1952	Jamaica, B.W.I.	3m. 03.9s
1956	United States	3m. 04.8s
1960	United States	3m. 02.2s
1964	United States	3m. 00.7s
1968	United States	2m. 56.1s*
1972	Kenya	2m. 59.8s
1976	United States	2m. 59.52s
1980	USSR	3m. 01.1s

Pole Vault

1896	William Hoyt, United States	10ft. 9 3-4 in.
1900	Irving Baxter, United States	10ft. 9 7-8 in.
1904	Charles Dvorak, United States	11ft. 6 in.
1908	A. C. Gilbert, United States Edward Cook Jr., United States	12ft. 2 in.
1912	Harry Babcock, United States	12ft. 11 1-2 in.
1920	Frank Foss, United States	13ft. 5 in.
1924	Lee Barnes, United States	12ft. 11 1-2 in.
1928	Sabin W. Carr, United States	13ft. 9 3-8 in.
1932	William Miller, United States	14ft. 1 7-8 in.
1936	Earle Meadows, United States	14ft. 3 1-4 in.
1948	Guinn Smith, United States	14ft. 1 1-4 in.
1952	Robert Richards, United States	14ft. 11 1-8 in.
1956	Robert Richards, United States	14ft. 11 1-2 in.
1960	Don Bragg, United States	15ft. 5 1-8 in.
1964	Fred Hansen, United States	16ft. 8 3-4 in.
1968	Bob Seagren, United States	17ft. 8 1-2 in.
1972	Wolfgang Nordwig, E. Germany	18ft. 1-2 in.
1976	Tadeusz Slusarski, Poland	18ft. 1-2 in.
1980	Wladyslaw Kozakiewicz, Poland	18ft. 11 1-2 in.*

16-lb. Hammer Throw

1900	John Flanagan, United States	167ft. 4 in.
1904	John Flanagan, United States	168ft. 1 in.
1908	John Flanagan, United States	170ft. 4 1-4 in.
1912	Matt McGrath, United States	179ft. 7 1-8 in.
1920	Pat Ryan, United States	173ft. 5 5-8 in.
1924	Fred Tootell, United States	174ft. 10 1-8 in.
1928	Patrick O'Callaghan, Ireland	168ft. 7 1-2 in.
1932	Patrick O'Callaghan, Ireland	176ft. 11 1-8 in.
1936	Karl Hein, Germany	185ft. 4 in.
1948	Imre Nemeth, Hungary	183ft. 11 1-2 in.
1952	Jozsef Csermak, Hungary	197ft. 11 9-16 in.
1956	Harold Connolly, United States	207ft. 3 1-2 in.
1960	Vasily Rudenkov, USSR	220ft. 1 5-8 in.
1964	Romuald Klim, USSR	228ft. 9 1-2 in.
1968	Gyula Zsivotsky, Hungary	240ft. 8 in.
1972	Anatoli Bondarchuk, USSR	248ft. 8 in.
1976	Yuri Syedykh, USSR	254ft. 4 in.
1980	Yuri Syedykh, USSR	268ft. 4 1-2 in.*

Discus Throw

1896	Robert Garrett, United States	95ft. 7 1-2 in.
1900	Rudolf Bauer, Hungary	118ft. 2.9-10 in.
1904	Martin Sheridan, United States	128ft. 10 1-2 in.
1908	Martin Sheridan, United States	134ft. 2 in.
1912	Armas Taipale, Finland	148ft. 4 in.
	Both hands—Armas Taipale, Finland	271ft. 10 1-4 in.
1920	Elmer Niklander, Finland	146ft. 7 1-4 in.
1924	Clarence Houser, United States	151ft. 5 1-8 in.
1928	Clarence Houser, United States	155ft. 3 in.
1932	John Anderson, United States	162ft. 4 7-8 in.
1936	Ken Carpenter, United States	165ft. 7 3-8 in.
1948	Adolfo Consolini, Italy	173ft. 2 in.
1952	Sim Iness, United States	180ft. 6.85 in.
1956	Al Oerter, United States	184ft. 10 1-2 in.
1960	Al Oerter, United States	194ft. 2 in.
1964	Al Oerter, United States	200ft. 1 1-2 in.
1968	Al Oerter, United States	212ft. 6 1-2 in.
1972	Ludvik Danek, Czechoslovakia	211ft. 3 in.
1976	Mac Wilkins, United States	221ft. 5.4 in.*
1980	Viktor Rashchupkin, USSR	218ft. 8 in.

Standing Hop, Step, and Jump

1900	Ray Ewry, United States	34ft. 8 1-2 in.*
1904	Ray Ewry, United States	34ft. 7 1-4 in.

Triple Jump

1896	James Connolly, United States	45ft.
1900	Myer Prinstein, United States	47ft. 4 1-4 in.
1904	Myer Prinstein, United States	47 ft.
1908	Timothy Aheame, Great Britain	48ft. 11 1-4 in.
1912	Gustaf Lindblom, Sweden	48ft. 5 1-8 in.
1920	Vilho Tuulos, Finland	47ft. 6 7-8 in.
1924	Archie Winter, Australia	50ft. 11 1-4 in.
1928	Mikio Oda, Japan	49ft. 11 in.
1932	Chuhei Nambu, Japan	51ft. 7 in.
1936	Naoto Tajima, Japan	52ft. 5 7-8 in.
1948	Arne Ahman, Sweden	50ft. 6 1-4 in.
1952	Adhemar de Silva, Brazil	53ft. 2 9-16 in.
1956	Adhemar de Silva, Brazil	53ft. 7 1-2 in.
1960	Jozef Schmidt, Poland	55ft. 1 3-4 in.
1964	Jozef Schmidt, Poland	55ft. 3 1-4 in.
1968	Viktor Saneev, USSR	57ft. 3-4 in.*
1972	Viktor Saneev, USSR	56ft. 11 in.
1976	Viktor Saneev, USSR	56ft. 8 3-4 in.
1980	Jaak Uudmae, USSR	56ft. 11 1-8 in.

16-lb. Shot Put

1896	Robert Garrett, United States	36ft. 9 3-4 in.
1900	Robert Sheldon, United States	46ft. 3 1-8 in.
1904	Ralph Rose, United States	48ft. 7 in.
1908	Ralph Rose, United States	46ft. 7 1-2 in.
1912	Pat McDonald, United States	50ft. 4 in.
	Both hands—Ralph Rose, United States	90ft. 5 1-2 in.
1920	Ville Porhola, Finland	48ft. 7 1-8 in.
1924	Clarence Houser, United States	49ft. 2 1-2 in.
1928	John Kuck, United States	52ft. 3-4 in.
1932	Leo Sexton, United States	52ft. 6 3-16 in.
1936	Hans Woellke, Germany	53ft. 1 3-4 in.
1948	Wilbur Thompson, United States	56ft. 2 in.
1952	Parry O'Brien, United States	57ft. 1 7-16 in.
1956	Parry O'Brien, United States	60ft. 11 in.
1960	William Nieder, United States	64ft. 6 3-4 in.
1964	Dallas Long, United States	66ft. 8 1-4 in.
1968	Randy Matson, United States	67ft. 4 3-4 in.
1972	Wladyslaw Komar, Poland	69ft. 6 in.
1976	Udo Beyer, E. Germany	69ft. 3-4 in.
1980	Vladimir Kiselyov, USSR	70ft. 1-2 in.*

Javelin Throw

1908	Erik Lemming, Sweden	178ft. 7 1-2 in.
	Held in middle—Erik Lemming, Sweden	179ft. 10 1-2 in.
1912	Erik Lemming, Sweden	198ft. 11 1-4 in.
	Both hands, Julius Saaristo, Finland	358ft. 11 7-8 in.
1920	Jonni Myrra, Finland	215ft. 9 3-4 in.
1924	Jonni Myrra, Finland	206ft. 6 3-4 in.
1928	Eric Lundquist, Sweden	218ft. 6 1-8 in.
1932	Matti Jarvinen, Finland	238ft. 7 in.
1936	Gerhard Stoeck, Germany	235ft. 8 5-16 in.
1948	Kaj Rautavaara, Finland	228ft. 10 1-2 in.
1952	Cy Young, United States	242ft. 0.79 in.
1956	Egil Danielsen, Norway	281ft. 2 1-4 in.
1960	Viktor Tsibulenko, USSR	277ft. 8 3-8 in.
1964	Pauli Nevala, Finland	271ft. 2 1-2 in.
1968	Janis Lusis, USSR	295ft. 7 1-4 in.
1972	Klaus Wolfermann, W. Germany	296ft. 10 in.
1976	Miklos Nemeth, Hungary	310ft. 4 in.*
1980	Dainis Kula, USSR	299ft. 2 3-8 in.

Decathlon

1912	Hugo Wieslander, Sweden	7,724.49 pts.
1920	Helge Lovland, Norway	6,804.35 pts.
1924	Harold Osborn, United States	7,710.77 pts.
1928	Paavo Yrjola, Finland	8,053.29 pts.
1932	James Bausch, United States	8,462.23 pts.
1936	Glenn Morris, United States	7,900 pts.
1948	Robert Mathias, United States	7,139 pts.
1952	Robert Mathias, United States	7,887 pts.
1956	Milton Campbell, United States	7,937 pts.
1960	Rafer Johnson, United States	8,392 pts.
1964	Willi Holdorf, Germany	7,887 pts.
1968	Bill Toomey, United States	8,193 pts.
1972	Nikola Avilov, USSR	8,454 pts.
1976	Bruce Jenner, United States	8,618 pts.*
1980	Daley Thompson, Great Britain	8,495pts.

Former point systems used prior to 1964.

Track and Field—Women

100-Meter Run

1928	Elizabeth Robinson, United States	12.2s
1932	Stella Walsh, Poland	11.9s
1936	Helen Stephens, United States	11.5s
1948	Francina Blankers-Koen, Netherlands	11.9s
1952	Marjorie Jackson, Australia	11.5s
1956	Betty Cuthbert, Australia	11.5s
1960	Wilma Rudolph, United States	11.0s*
1964	Wyomia Tyus, United States	11.4s
1968	Wyomia Tyus, United States	11.0s*
1972	Renate Stecher, E. Germany	11.07s
1976	Annegret Richter, W. Germany	11.08s*
1980	Ludmila Kondratyeva, USSR	11.6s

200-Meter Run

1948	Francina Blankers-Koen, Netherlands	24.4s
1952	Marjorie Jackson, Australia	23.7s
1956	Betty Cuthbert, Australia	23.4s
1960	Wilma Rudolph, United States	24.0s
1964	Edith McGuire, United States	23.0s
1968	Irena Szewinska, Poland	22.5s
1972	Renate Stecher, E. Germany	22.40s
1976	Barbel Eckert, E. Germany	22.37s
1980	Barbel Wockel, E. Germany	22.03*

400-Meter Run

1964	Betty Cuthbert, Australia	52s
1968	Colette Besson, France	52s
1972	Monika Zehrt, E. Germany	51.08s
1976	Irena Szewinska, Poland	49.29s
1980	Marita Koch, E. Germany	48.88s*

800-Meter Run

1928	Lina Radke, Germany	2m. 16.8s
1960	Ludmila Shevcova, USSR	2m. 4.3s
1964	Ann Packer, Great Britain	2m. 1.1s
1968	Madeline Manning, United States	2m. 0.9s
1972	Hildegard Flack, W. Germany	1m. 58.6s
1976	Tatyana Kazankina, USSR	1m. 54.94
1980	Nadezhda Olizayrenko, USSR	1m. 53.5s*

1,500-Meter Run

1972	Ludmila Bragina, USSR	4m. 01.4s
1976	Tatyana Kazankina, USSR	4m. 05.48s
1980	Tatyana Kazankina, USSR	3m. 56.6s*

400-Meter Relay

1928	Canada	48.4s
1932	United States	47.0s
1936	United States	46.9s
1948	Netherlands	47.5s
1952	United States	45.9s
1956	Australia	44.5s
1960	United States	44.5s
1964	Poland	43.6s
1968	United States	42.8s
1972	West Germany	42.81s
1976	East Germany	42.55s
1980	East Germany	41.60s*

1,600-Meter Relay

1972	East Germany	3m. 23s
1976	East Germany	3m. 19.23s*
1980	USSR	3m. 20.02s

80-Meter Hurdles

1932	Mildred Didrikson, United States	11.7s
1936	Trebisonda Villa, Italy	11.7s
1948	Francina Blankers-Koen, Netherlands	11.2s
1952	Shirley Strickland de la Hunty, Australia	10.9s
1956	Shirley Strickland de la Hunty, Australia	10.7s
1960	Irina Press, USSR	10.8s
1964	Karen Balzer, Germany	10.5s
1968	Maureen Caird, Australia	10.3s*

100-Meter Hurdles

1972	Annelie Ehrhardt, E. Germany	12.59
1976	Johanna Schaller, E. Germany	12.77s
1980	Vera Komisova, USSR	12.56s*

High Jump

1928	Ethel Catherwood, Canada	5ft. 3 in.
1932	Jean Shiley, United States	5ft. 5 1-4 in.
1936	Ibolya Csak, Hungary	5ft. 3 in.
1948	Alice Coachman, United States	5ft. 6 1-8 in.
1952	Esther Brand, South Africa	5ft. 5 3-4 in.
1956	Mildred L. McDaniel, United States	5ft. 9 1-4 in.
1960	Iolanda Balas, Romania	6ft. 3-4 in.
1964	Iolanda Balas, Romania	6ft. 2 3-4 in.
1968	Miloslava Reskova, Czechoslovakia	5ft. 11 3-4 in.
1972	Ulrike Meyfarth, W. Germany	6ft. 3 1-4 in.
1976	Rosemarie Ackermann, E. Germany	6ft. 3 3-4 in.
1980	Sara Simeoni, Italy	6ft. 5 1-2 in.*

Discus Throw

1928	Helena Konopacka, Poland	129ft. 11 7-8 in.
1932	Lillian Copeland, United States	133ft. 2 in.
1936	Gisela Mauermayer, Germany	156ft. 3 3-16 in.
1948	Micheline Ostermeyer, France	137ft. 6 1-2 in.
1952	Nina Romaschkova, USSR	168ft. 8 1-2 in.
1956	Olga Fikotova, Czechoslovakia	176ft. 1 1-2 in.
1960	Nina Ponomareva, USSR	180ft. 8 1-4 in.
1964	Tamara Press, USSR	187ft. 10 1-2 in.
1968	Lia Manoliu, Romania	191ft. 2 1-2 in.
1972	Faina Melnik, USSR	218ft. 7 in.
1976	Evelin Schlaak, E. Germany	226ft. 4 1-2 in.
1980	Evelin Jahl, E. Germany	229ft. 6 1-4 in.*

Javelin Throw

1932	Mildred Didrikson, United States	143ft. 4 in.
1936	Tilly Fleischer, Germany	148ft. 2 3-4 in.
1948	Herma Bauma, Austria	149ft. 6 in.
1952	Dana Zatopkova, Czechoslovakia	165ft. 7 in.
1956	Inessa Janzeme, USSR	176ft. 8 in.
1960	Elvira Ozolina, USSR	183ft. 8 in.
1964	Mihaela Penes, Romania	198ft. 7 1-2 in.
1968	Angela Nemeth, Hungary	198ft. 1-2 in.
1972	Ruth Fuchs, E. Germany	209ft. 7 in.
1976	Ruth Fuchs, E. Germany	216ft. 4 in.
1980	Maria Colon, Cuba	224ft. 5 in.*

Shot Put (8lb., 13oz.)

1948	Micheline Ostermeyer, France	45ft. 1 1-2 in.
1952	Galina Zybina, USSR	50ft. 1 1-2 in.
1956	Tamara Tishkyevich, USSR	54ft. 5 in.
1960	Tamara Press, USSR	56ft. 9 7-8 in.
1964	Tamara Press, USSR	59ft. 6 1-4 in.
1968	Margitta Gummel, E. Germany	64ft. 4 in.
1972	Nadezhda Chizova, USSR	69ft.

1976	Ivanka Christova, Bulgaria	69ft. 5 in.
1980	Ilona Slupianek, E. Germany	73ft. 6 1-4 in.*

Long Jump

1948	Olga Gyarmati, Hungary	18ft. 8 1-4 in.
1952	Yvette Williams, New Zealand	20ft. 5 3-4 in.
1956	Elzbieta Krzeskinska, Poland	20ft. 9 3-4 in.
1960	Vyera Krepkina, USSR	20ft. 10 3-4 in.
1964	Mary Rand, Great Britain	22ft. 2 1-4 in.
1968	Viorica Viscopoleanu, Romania	22ft. 4 1-2 in.
1972	Heidemarie Rosendahl, W. Germany	22ft. 3 in.
1976	Angela Voigt, E. Germany	22ft. 2 1-2 in.
1980	Tatyana Kolpakova, USSR	23ft. 2 in.*

Pentathlon

1964	Irina Press, USSR	5,246 pts.
1968	Ingrid Becker, W. Germany	5,098 pts.
1972	Mary Peters, England	4,801 pts.
1976	Sigrun Siegl, E. Germany	4,745 pts.
1980	Nadyezhda Tkachenko, USSR	5,083pts.*

Former point system, 1964–1968

Swimming—Men

100-Meter Freestyle

1896	Alfred Hajos, Hungary	1:22.2
1904	Zoltan de Halmay, Hungary (100 yards)	1:02.8
1908	Charles Daniels, U.S.	1:05.6
1912	Duke P. Kahanamoku, U.S.	1:03.4
1920	Duke P. Kahanamoku, U.S.	1:01.4
1924	John Weissmuller, U.S.	59.0
1928	John Weissmuller, U.S.	58.6
1932	Yasuji Miyazaki, Japan	58.2
1936	Ferenc Csik, Hungary	57.6
1948	Wally Ris, U.S.	57.3
1952	Clark Scholes, U.S.	57.4
1956	Jon Henricks, Australia	55.4
1960	John Devitt, Australia	55.2
1964	Don Schollander, U.S.	53.4
1968	Mike Wenden, Australia	52.2
1972	Mark Spitz, U.S.	51.22
1976	Jim Montgomery, U.S.	49.99*
1980	Jorg Woithe, E. Germany	50.40

200-Meter Freestyle

1968	Mike Wenden, Australia	1:55.2
1972	Mark Spitz, U.S.	1:52.78
1976	Bruce Furniss, U.S.	1:50.29
1980	Sergei Kopliakov, USSR	1:49.81*

400-Meter Freestyle

1904	C. M. Daniels, U.S. (440 yards)	6:16.2
1908	Henry Taylor, Great Britain	5:36.8
1912	George Hodgson, Canada	5:24.4
1920	Norman Ross, U.S.	5:26.8
1924	John Weissmuller, U.S.	5:04.2
1928	Albert Zorilla, Argentina	5:01.6
1932	Clarence Crabbe, U.S.	4:48.4
1936	Jack Medica, U.S.	4:44.5
1948	William Smith, U.S.	4:41.0
1952	Jean Boiteux, France	4:30.7
1956	Murray Rose, Australia	4:27.3
1960	Murray Rose, Australia	4:18.3
1964	Don Schollander, U.S.	4:12.2
1968	Mike Burton, U.S.	4:09.0
1972	Brad Cooper, Australia	4:00.27
1976	Brian Goodell, U.S.	3:51.93
1980	Vladimir Salnikov, USSR	3:51.31*

1,500-Meter Freestyle

1908	Henry Taylor, Great Britain	22:48.4
1912	George Hodgson, Canada	22:00.0
1920	Norman Ross, U.S.	22:23.2
1924	Andrew Charlton, Australia	20:06.6
1928	Arne Borg, Sweden	19:51.8
1932	Kusuo Kitamura, Japan	19:12.4
1936	Noboru Terada, Japan	19:13.7
1948	James McLane, U.S.	19:18.5
1952	Ford Konno, U.S.	18:30.0
1956	Murray Rose, Australia	17:58.9
1960	Jon Konrads, Australia	17:19.6
1964	Robert Windle, Australia	17:01.7
1968	Mike Burton, U.S.	16:38.9
1972	Mike Burton, U.S.	15:52.58
1976	Brian Goodell, U.S.	15:02.40
1980	Vladimir Salnikov, USSR	14:58.27*

400-Meter Medley Relay

1960	United States	4:05.4
1964	United States	3:58.4
1968	United States	3:54.9
1972	United States	3:48.16
1976	United States	3:42.22*
1980	Australia	3:45.70

400-Meter Freestyle Relay

1964	United States	3:33.2
1968	United States	3:31.7
1972	United States	3:26.42*

800-Meter Freestyle Relay

1908	Great Britain	10:55.6
1912	Australia	10:11.6
1920	United States	10:04.4
1924	United States	9:53.4
1928	United States	9:36.2
1932	Japan	8:58.4
1936	Japan	8:51.5
1948	United States	8:46.0
1952	United States	8:31.1
1956	Australia	8:23.6
1960	United States	8:10.2
1964	United States	7:52.1
1968	United States	7:52.3
1972	United States	7:35.78
1976	United States	7:23.22*
1980	USSR	7:23.50

100-Meter Backstroke

1904	Walter Brack, Germany (100 yds.)	1:16.8
1908	Arno Bieberstein, Germany	1:24.6
1912	Harry Hebner, U.S.	1:21.2
1920	Warren Kealoha, U.S.	1:15.2
1924	Warren Kealoha, U.S.	1:13.2
1928	George Kojac, U.S.	1:08.2
1932	Masaji Kiyokawa, Japan	1:08.6
1936	Adolph Kiefer, U.S.	1:05.9
1948	Allen Stack, U.S.	1:06.4
1952	Yoshi Oyakawa, U.S.	1:05.4
1956	David Thiele, Australia	1:02.2
1960	David Thiele, Australia	1:01.9
1968	Roland Matthes, E. Germany	58.7
1972	Roland Matthes, E. Germany	56.58
1976	John Naber, U.S.	55.49*
1980	Bengt Baron, Sweden	56.53

200-Meter Backstroke

1964	Jed Graef, U.S.	2:10.3
1968	Roland Matthes, E. Germany	2:09.6
1972	Roland Matthes, E. Germany	2:02.82
1976	John Naber, U.S.	1:59.19*
1980	Sandor Wladar, Hungary	2:01.93

100-Meter Breaststroke

1968	Don McKenzie, U.S.	1:07.7
1972	Nobutaka Taguchi, Japan	1:04.94
1976	John Hencken, U.S.	1:03.11*
1980	Duncan Goodhew, Great Britain	1:03.34

200-Meter Breaststroke

1908	Frederick Holman, Great Britain	3:09.2
1912	Walter Bathe, Germany	3:01.8
1920	Haken Malmroth, Sweden	3:04.4
1924	Robert Skelton, U.S.	2:56.6
1928	Yoshiyuki Tsuruta, Japan	2:48.8
1932	Yoshiyuki Tsuruta, Japan	2:45.4
1936	Tetsuo Hamuro, Japan	2:42.5
1948	Joseph Verdeur, U.S.	2:39.3
1952	John Davies, Australia	2:34.4
1956	Masura Furukawa, Japan	2:34.7
1960	William Mulliken, U.S.	2:37.4
1964	Ian O'Brien, Australia	2:27.8
1968	Felipe Munoz, Mexico	2:28.7
1972	John Hencken, U.S.	2:21.55

1976	David Wilkie, Great Britain	2:15.11*
1980	Robertas Zulpa, USSR	2:15.85

100-Meter Butterfly

1968	Doug Russell, U.S.	55.9
1972	Mark Spitz, U.S.	54.27*
1976	Matt Vogel, U.S.	54.35
1980	Par Arvidsson, Sweden	54.92

200-Meter Butterfly

1956	William Yorzyk, U.S.	2:19.3
1960	Michael Troy, U.S.	2:12.8
1964	Kevin J. Berry, Australia	2:06.6
1968	Carl Robie, U.S.	2:08.7
1972	Mark Spitz, U.S.	2:00.70
1976	Mike Bruner, U.S.	1:59.23*
1980	Sergei Fesenko, USSR	1:59.76

200-Meter Individual Medley

1968	Charles Hickcox, U.S.	2:12.0
1972	Gunnar Larsson, Sweden	2:07.17*

400-Meter Individual Medley

1964	Dick Roth, U.S.	4:45.4
1968	Charles Hickcox, U.S.	4:48.4
1972	Gunnar Larsson, Sweden	4:31.98
1976	Rod Strachan, U.S.	4:23.68
1980	Aleksandr Sidorenko, USSR	4:22.89*

	Springboard Diving	Points
1908	Albert Zurner, Germany	85.5
1912	Paul Guenther, Germany	79.23
1920	Louis Kuehn, U.S.	675.00
1924	Albert White, U.S.	696.40
1928	Pete Desjardins, U.S.	185.04
1932	Michael Galitzen, U.S.	161.38
1936	Richard Degener, U.S.	161.57
1948	Bruce Harlan, U.S.	163.64
1952	David Browning, U.S.	205.29
1956	Robert Clotworthy, U.S.	159.56
1960	Gary Tobian, U.S.	170.00
1964	Kenneth Sitzberger, U.S.	159.90
1968	Bernie Wrightson, U.S.	170.15
1972	Vladimir Vasin, USSR	594.09
1976	Phil Boggs, U.S.	619.52
1980	Aleksandr Portnov, USSR	905.02

	Platform Diving	Points
1904	Dr. G.E. Sheldon, U.S.	12.75
1908	Hjalmar Johansson, Sweden	83.75
1912	Erik Adlerz, Sweden	73.94
1920	Clarence Pinkston, U.S.	100.67
1924	Albert White, U.S.	487.30
1928	Pete Desjardins, U.S.	98.74
1932	Harold Smith, U.S.	124.80
1936	Marshall Wayne, U.S.	113.58
1948	Sammy Lee, U.S.	130.05
1952	Sammy Lee, U.S.	156.28
1956	Joaquin Capilla, Mexico	152.44
1960	Robert Webster, U.S.	165.56
1964	Robert Webster, U.S.	148.58
1968	Klaus Dibiasi, Italy	164.18
1972	Klaus Dibiasi, Italy	504.12
1976	Klaus Dibiasi, Italy	600.51
1980	Falk Hoffmann, E. Germany	835.65

Swimming—Women

100-Meter Freestyle

1912	Fanny Durack, Australia	1:22.2
1920	Ethelda Bleibtrey, U.S.	1:13.6
1924	Ethel Lackie, U.S.	1:12.4
1928	Albina Osipowich, U.S.	1:11.0
1932	Helene Madison, U.S.	1:06.8
1936	Hendrika Mastenbroek, Holland	1:05.9
1948	Greta Anderson, Denmark	1:06.3
1952	Katalin Szoke, Hungary	1:06.8
1956	Dawn Fraser, Australia	1:02.0
1960	Dawn Fraser, Australia	1:01.2
1964	Dawn Fraser, Australia	59.5
1968	Jan Henne, U.S.	1:00.0
1972	Sandra Neilson, U.S.	58.59
1976	Kornelia Ender, E. Germany	55.65
1980	Barbara Krause, E. Germany	54.79*

200-Meter Freestyle

1968	Debbie Meyer, U.S.	2:10.5
1972	Shane Gould, Australia	2:03.56
1976	Kornelia Ender, E. Germany	1:59.26
1980	Barbara Krause, E. Germany	1:58.33*

400-Meter Freestyle

1924	Martha Norelius, U.S.	6:02.2
1928	Martha Norelius, U.S.	5:42.8
1932	Helene Madison, U.S.	5:28.5
1936	Hendrika Mastenbroek, Netherlands	5:26.4
1948	Ann Curtis, U.S.	5:17.8
1952	Valerie Gyenge, Hungary	5:12.1
1956	Lorraine Crapp, Australia	4:54.6
1960	Susan Chris von Saltza, U.S.	4:50.6
1964	Virginia Duenkel, U.S.	4:43.3
1968	Debbie Meyer, U.S.	4:31.8
1972	Shane Gould, Australia	4:19.04
1976	Petra Thuemer E. Germany	4:09.89
1980	Ines Diers, E. Germany	4:08.76*

800-Meter Freestyle

1968	Debbie Meyer, U.S.	9:24.0
1972	Keena Rothhammer, U.S.	8:53.68
1976	Petra Thuemer, E. Germany	8:37.14
1980	Michelle Ford, Australia	8:28.90*

100-Meter Backstroke

1924	Sybil Bauer, U.S.	1:23.3
1928	Marie Braun, Netherlands	1:22.0
1932	Eleanor Holm, U.S.	1:19.4
1936	Dina Senff, Netherlands	1:18.9
1948	Karen Harup, Denmark	1:14.4
1952	Joan Harrison, South Africa	1:14.3
1956	Judy Grinham, Great Britain	1:12.9
1960	Lynn Burke, U.S.	1:09.3
1964	Cathy Ferguson, U.S.	1:07.7
1968	Kaye Hall, U.S.	1:06.2
1972	Melissa Belote, U.S.	1:05.78
1976	Ulrike Richter, E. Germany	1:01.83
1980	Rica Reinisch, E. Germany	1:00.86*

200-Meter Backstroke

1968	Pokey Watson, U.S.	2:24.8
1972	Melissa Belote, U.S.	2:19.19
1976	Ulrike Richter, E. Germany	2:13.43
1980	Rica Reinisch, E. Germany	2:11.77*

100-Meter Breaststroke

1968	Djurdjica Bjedov, Yugoslavia	1:15.8
1972	Cathy Carr, U.S.	1:13.58
1976	Hannelore Anke, E. Germany	1:11:16
1980	Ute Geweniger, E. Germany	1:10.22*

200-Meter Breaststroke

1924	Lucy Morton, Great Britain	3:32.2
1928	Hilde Schrader, Germany	3:12.6
1932	Clare Dennis, Australia	3:06.3
1936	Hideko Maehata, Japan	3:03.6
1948	Nelly Van Vliet, Netherlands	2:57.2
1952	Eva Szekely, Hungary	2:51.7
1956	Ursula Happe, Germany	2:53.1
1960	Anita Lonsbrough, Great Britain	2:49.5
1964	Galina Prozumenschikova, USSR	2:46.4
1968	Sharon Wichman, U.S.	2:44.4
1972	Beverly Whitfield, Australia	2:41.71
1976	Marina Koshevaia, USSR	2:33.35
1980	Lina Kachushite, USSR	2:29.54*

200-Meter Individual Medley

1968	Claudia Kolb, U.S.	2:24.7
1972	Shane Gould, Australia	2:23.07*

400-Meter Individual Medley

1964	Donna de Varona, U.S.	5:18.7
1968	Claudia Kolb, U.S.	5:08.5
1972	Gail Neall, Australia	5:02.97
1976	Ulrike Tauber, E. Germany	4:42.77
1980	Petra Schneider, E. Germany	4:36.29*

100-Meter Butterfly

1956	Shelley Mann, U.S.	1:11.0
1960	Carolyn Schuler, U.S.	1:09.5
1964	Sharon Stouder, U.S.	1:04.7
1968	Lynn McClements, Australia	1:05.5
1972	Mayumi Aoki, Japan	1:03.34
1976	Kornelia Ender, E. Germany	1:00.13*
1980	Caren Metschuck, E. Germany	1:00.42

200-Meter Butterfly

1968	Ada Kok, Netherlands	2:24.7
1972	Karen Moe, U.S.	2:15.57
1976	Andrea Pollack, E. Germany	2:11.41
1980	Ines Geissler, E. Germany	2:10.44*

400-Meter Medley Relay

1960	United States	4:41.1
1960	United States	4:33.9
1968	United States	4:28.3
1972	United States	4:20.75
1976	East Germany	4:07.95
1980	East Germany	4:06.67*

400-Meter Freestyle Relay

1912	Great Britain	5:52.8
1920	United States	5:11.6
1924	United States	4:58.8
1928	United States	4:47.6
1932	United States	4:38.0
1936	Netherlands	4:36.0
1948	United States	4:29.2
1952	Hungary	4:24.4
1956	Australia	4:17.1
1960	United States	4:08.9
1964	United States	4:03.8
1968	United States	4:02.5
1972	United States	3:55.19
1976	United States	3:44.82
1980	East Germany	3:42.71*

Springboard Diving

		Points
1920	Aileen Riggin, U.S.	539.90
1924	Elizabeth Becker, U.S.	474.50
1928	Helen Meany, U.S.	78.62
1932	Georgia Coleman U.S.	87.52
1936	Marjorie Gestring, U.S.	89.27
1948	Victoria M. Draves, U.S.	108.74
1952	Patricia McCormick, U.S.	147.30
1956	Patricia McCormick, U.S.	142.36
1960	Ingrid Kramer, Germany	155.81
1964	Ingrid Engel-Kramer, Germany	145.00
1968	Sue Gossick, U.S.	150.77
1972	Micki King, U.S.	450.03
1976	Jenni Chandler, U.S.	506.19
1980	Irina Kalinina, USSR	725.91

Platform Diving

		Points
1912	Greta Johansson, Sweden	39.90
1920	Stefani Fryland-Clausen, Denmark	34.60
1924	Caroline Smith, U.S.	166.00
1928	Elizabeth B. Pinkston, U.S.	31.60
1932	Dorothy Poynton, U.S.	40.26
1936	Dorothy Poynton Hill, U.S.	33.93
1948	Victoria M. Draves, U.S.	68.87
1952	Patricia McCormick, U.S.	79.37
1956	Patricia McCormick, U.S.	84.85
1960	Ingrid Kramer, Germany	91.28
1964	Lesley Bush, U.S.	99.80
1968	Milena Duchkova, Czech.	109.59
1972	Ulrika Knape, Sweden	390.00
1976	Elena Vaytsekhouskaya, USSR	406.59
1980	Martina Jaschke, E. Germany	596.25

22d Summer Olympics

Moscow, USSR, July 19-Aug. 3, 1980

Final Medal Standings

(nations in alphabetical order)

	Gold	Silver	Bronze	Total
Australia	2	2	5	9
Austria	1	3	1	5
Belgium	1	0	0	1
Brazil	2	0	2	4
Britain	5	7	9	21
Bulgaria	8	16	16	40
Cuba	8	7	5	20
Czechoslovakia	2	2	9	13
Denmark	2	1	2	5
Ethiopia	2	0	2	4
Finland	3	1	4	8
France	6	5	3	14
Germany, East	47	36	43	126
Greece	1	0	2	3
Guyana	0	0	1	1
Holland	0	1	3	4
Hungary	7	10	15	32
India	1	0	0	1
Ireland	0	1	1	2
Italy	8	3	4	15
Jamaica	0	0	3	3
Korea, North	0	3	2	5
Lebanon	0	0	1	1
Mexico	0	1	3	4
Mongolia	0	2	2	4
Poland	3	14	14	31
Romania	6	6	13	25
Spain	1	3	2	6
Sweden	3	3	6	12
Switzerland	2	0	0	2
Tanzania	0	2	0	2
USSR	80	70	47	197
Uganda	0	1	0	1
Venezuela	0	1	0	1
Yugoslavia	2	3	4	9
Zimbabwe	1	0	0	1

Duplicate medals awarded in some events

Olympic Information

Symbol: Five rings or circles, linked together to represent the sporting friendship of all peoples. The rings also symbolize the 5 continents—Europe, Asia, Africa, Australia, and America. Each ring is a different color—blue, yellow, black, green, and red.

Flag: The symbol of the 5 rings on a plain white background.

Motto: "Citius, Altius, Fortius." Latin meaning "faster, higher, braver," or the modern interpretation "swifter, higher, stronger". The motto was coined by Father Didon, a French educator, in 1895.

Creed: "The most important thing in the Olympic Games is not to win but to take part, just as the most important thing in life is not the triumph but the struggle. The essential thing is not to have conquered but to have fought well."

Oath: An athlete of the host country recites the following at the opening ceremony. "In the name of all competitors I promise that we will take part in these Olympic Games, respecting and abiding by the rules which govern them, in the true spirit of sportsmanship for the glory of sport and the honor of our teams." Both the oath and the creed were composed by Pierre de Coubertin, the founder of the modern Games.

Flame: Symbolizes the continuity between the ancient and modern Games. The modern version of the flame was adopted in 1936. The torch used to kindle the flame is first lit by the sun's rays at Olympia, Greece, and then carried to the site of the Games by relays of runners. Ships and planes are used when necessary.

Winter Olympic Games Champions, 1924-1980

Sites and Unofficial Winners of Games

1924 Chamonix, France (Norway)
1928 St. Moritz, Switzerland (Norway)
1932 Lake Placid, N.Y. (U.S.)
1936 Garmisch-Partenkirchen (Norway)
1948 St. Moritz (Sweden)
1952 Oslo, Norway (Norway)
1956 Cortina d'Ampezzo, Italy (USSR)
1960 Squaw Valley, Cal. (USSR)
1964 Innsbruck, Austria (USSR)
1968 Grenoble, France (Norway)
1972 Sapporo, Japan (USSR)
1976 Innsbruck, Austria (USSR)
1980 Lake Placid, N.Y. (E. Germany)
1984 Sarajevo, Yugoslavia (scheduled)

Biathlon

	10 Kilometers	Time
1980	Frank Ulrich, E. Germany	32:10.69

	20 Kilometers	Time
1960	Klas Lestander, Sweden	1:33:21.6
1964	Vladimir Melanin, USSR	1:20:26.8
1968	Magnar Solberg, Norway	1:13:45.9
1972	Magnar Solberg, Norway	1:15:55.50
1976	Nikolai Kruglov, USSR	1:14:12.26
1980	Anatoly Alabyev, USSR	1:08:16.31

	40-Kilometer Relay	Time
1968	USSR, Norway, Sweden	2:13:02
1972	USSR, Finland, E. Germany	1:51:44
1976	USSR, Finland, E. Germany	1:57:55.64
1980	USSR, E. Germany, W. Germany (30 km.)	1:34:03.27

Bobsledding

4-Man Bob

	(Driver in parentheses)	Time
1924	Switzerland (Edward Scherrer)	5:45.54
1928	United States (William Fiske) (5-man)	3:20.50
1932	United States (William Fiske)	7:53.68
1936	Switzerland (Pierre Musy)	5:19.85
1948	United States (Edward Rimkus)	5:20.10
1952	Germany (Andreas Ostler)	5:07.84
1956	Switzerland (Frank Kapus)	5:10.44
1964	Canada (Victor Emery)	4:14.46
1968	Italy (Eugenio Monti) (2 races)	2:17.39
1972	Switzerland (Jean Wicki)	4:43.07
1976	E. Germany (Meinhard Nehmer)	3:40.43
1980	E. Germany (Mainhard Nehmer)	3:59.92

	2-Man Bob	Time
1932	United States (Hubert Stevens)	8:14.74
1936	United States (Ivan Brown)	5:29.29
1948	Switzerland (F. Endrich)	5:29.20
1952	Germany (Andreas Ostler)	5:24.54
1956	Italy (Dalla Costa)	5:30.14
1964	Great Britain (Antony Nash)	4:21.90
1968	Italy (Eugenio Monti)	4:41.54
1972	W. Germany (Wolfgang Zimmerer)	4:47.07
1976	E. Germany (Meinhard Nehmer)	3:40.43
1980	Switzerland (Erich Schaerer)	4:09.36

Figure Skating

Men's Singles

1908 Ulrich Sachow, Sweden
1920 Gillis Grafstrom, Sweden
1924 Gillis Grafstrom, Sweden
1928 Gillis Grafstrom, Sweden
1932 Karl Schaefer, Austria
1936 Karl Schaefer, Austria
1948 Richard Button, U.S.
1952 Richard Button, U.S.
1956 Hayes Alan Jenkins, U.S.
1960 David W. Jenkins, U.S.
1964 Manfred Schnelldorfer, Germany
1968 Wolfgang Schwartz, Austria
1972 Ondrej Nepela, Czechoslovakia
1976 John Curry, Great Britain
1980 Robin Cousins, Great Britain

Women's Singles

1908 Madge Syers, Great Britain
1920 Magda Julin-Mauroy, Sweden
1924 Heima von Szabo-Planck, Austria
1928 Sonja Henie, Norway
1932 Sonja Henie, Norway
1936 Sonja Henie, Norway
1948 Barbara Ann Scott, Canada
1952 Jeanette Altwegg, Great Britain
1956 Tenley Albright, U.S.
1960 Carol Heiss, U.S.
1964 Sjoukje Dijkstra, Netherlands
1968 Peggy Fleming, U.S.
1972 Beatrix Schuba, Austria
1976 Dorothy Hamill, U.S.
1980 Anett Poetzsch, E. Germany

Pairs

1908 Anna Hubler & Heinrich Burger, Germany
1920 Ludovika & Walter Jakobsson, Finland
1924 Helene Engelman & Alfred Berger, Austria
1928 Andree Joly & Pierre Brunet, France
1932 Andree Joly & Pierre Brunet, France
1936 Maxie Herber & Ernest Baier, Germany
1948 Micheline Lannoy & Pierre Baugniet, Belgium
1952 Ria and Paul Falk, Germany
1956 Elisabeth Schwarz & Kurt Oppelt, Austria
1960 Barbara Wagner & Robert Paul, Canada
1964 Ludmila Beloussova & Oleg Protopopov, USSR
1968 Ludmila Beloussova & Oleg Protopopov, USSR
1972 Irina Rodnina & Alexei Ulanov, USSR
1976 Irina Rodnina & Aleksandr Zaitzev, USSR
1980 Irina Rodnina & Aleksandr Zaitzev, USSR

Ice Dancing

1976 Ludmila Pakhomova & Aleksandr Gorschkov, USSR
1980 Natalya Linichuk & Gennadi Karponosov, USSR

Alpine Skiing

	Men's Downhill	Time
1948	Henri Oreiller, France	2:55.0
1952	Zeno Colo, Italy	2:30.8
1956	Anton Sailer, Austria	2:52.2
1960	Jean Vuarnet, France	2:06.0
1964	Egon Zimmermann, Austria	2:18.16
1968	Jean Claude Killy, France	1:59.85
1972	Bernhard Russi, Switzerland	1:51.43
1976	Franz Klammer, Austria	1:45.73
1980	Leonhard Stock, Austria	1:45.50

	Men's Giant Slalom	Time
1952	Stein Eriksen, Norway	2:25.0
1956	Anton Sailer, Austria	3:00.1
1960	Roger Staub, Switzerland	1:48.3
1964	Francois Bonlieu, France	1:46.71
1968	Jean Claude Killy, France	3:29.28
1972	Gustavo Thoeni, Italy	3:09.62
1976	Heini Hemmi, Switzerland	3:26.97
1980	Ingemar Stenmark, Sweden	2:40.74

	Men's Slalom	Time
1948	Edi Reinalter, Switzerland	2:10.3
1952	Othmar Schneider, Austria	2:00.0
1956	Anton Sailer, Austria	194.7 pts.
1960	Ernst Hinterseer, Austria	2:08.9
1964	Josef Stiegler, Austria	2:11.13
1968	Jean Claude Killy, France	1:39.73
1972	Francesco Fernandez Ochoa, Spain	1:49.27
1976	Piero Gros, Italy	2:03.29
1980	Ingemar Stenmark, Sweden	1:44.26

	Women's Downhill	Time
1948	Heidi Schlunegger, Switzerland	2:28.3
1952	Trude Jochum-Beiser, Austria	1:47.1
1956	Madeline Berthod, Switzerland	1:40.7
1960	Heidi Biebl, Germany	1:37.6
1964	Christi Haas, Austria	1:55.39
1968	Olga Pall, Austria	1:40.87
1972	Marie Therese Nadig, Switzerland	1:36.68
1976	Rosi Mittermaier, W. Germany	1:46.16
1980	Annemarie Proell Moser, Austria	1:37.52

	Women's Giant Slalom	Time
1952	Andrea Mead Lawrence, U.S.	2:06.8
1956	Ossi Reichert, Germany	1:56.5
1960	Yvonne Ruegg, Switzerland	1:39.9
1964	Marielle Goitschel, France	1:52.24

1968	Nancy Greene, Canada	1:51.97
1972	Marie Therese Nadig, Switzerland	1:29.90
1976	Kathy Kreiner, Canada	1:29.13
1980	Hanni Wenzel, Liechtenstein (2 runs)	2:41.66

	Women's Slalom	Time
1948	Gretchen Fraser, U.S.	1:57.2
1952	Andrea Mead Lawrence, U.S.	2:10.6
1956	Renee Colliard, Switzerland	112.3 pts.
1960	Anne Heggtveigt, Canada	1:49.6
1964	Christine Goitschel, France	1:29.86
1968	Marielle Goitschel, France	1:25.86
1972	Barbara Cochran, U.S.	1:31.24
1976	Rosi Mittermaier, W. Germany	1:30.54
1980	Hanni Wenzel, Liechtenstein	1:25.09

Nordic Skiing

Men's Cross-Country Events

	15 kilometers (9.3 miles)	Time
1924	Thorleif Haug, Norway	1:14:31
1928	Johan Grottumsbraaten, Norway	1:37:01
1932	Sven Utterstrom, Sweden	1:23:07
1936	Erik-August Larsson, Sweden	1:14:38
1948	Martin Lundstrom, Sweden	1:13:50
1952	Hallgeir Brenden, Norway	1:01:34
1956	Hallgeir Brenden, Norway	49:39.0
1960	Haakon Brusveen, Norway	51:55.0
1964	Eero Maentyranta, Finland	50:54.1
1968	Harald Groenningen, Norway	47:54.2
1972	Sven-Ake Lundback, Sweden	45:28.24
1976	Nikolai Bajukov, USSR	43:58.47
1980	Thomas Wassberg, Sweden	41:57.63

(Note: approx. 18-km. course 1924-1952)

	30 kilometers (18.6 miles)	Time
1956	Veikko Hakulinen, Finland	1:44:06.0
1960	Sixten Jernberg, Sweden	1:51:03.9
1964	Eero Maentyranta, Finland	1:30:50.7
1968	Franco Nones, Italy	1:35:39.2
1972	Vyacheslav Vedenin, USSR	1:36:31.15
1976	Sergei Savaliev, USSR	1:30:29.38
1980	Nikolai Zimyatov, USSR	1:27:02.80

	50 kilometers (31 miles)	Time
1924	Thorleif Haug, Norway	3:44:32.0
1928	Per Erik Hedlund, Sweden	4:52:03.0
1932	Veli Saarinen, Finland	4:28:00.0
1936	Elis Viklund, Sweden	3:30:11.0
1948	Nils Karlsson, Sweden	3:47:48.0
1952	Veikko Hakulinen, Finland	3:33:33.0
1956	Sixten Jernberg, Sweden	2:50:27.0
1960	Kalevi Hamalainen, Finland	2:59:06.3
1964	Sixten Jernberg, Sweden	2:43:52.6
1968	Ole Ellefsaeter, Norway	2:28:45.8
1972	Paal Tyldum, Norway	2:43:14.75
1976	Ivar Formo, Norway	2:37:30.05
1980	Nikolai Zimyatov, USSR	2:27:24.60

	40-km. Cross-Country Relay	Time
1936	Finland, Norway, Sweden	2:41:33.0
1948	Sweden, Finland, Norway	2:32:08.0
1952	Finland, Norway, Sweden	2:20:16.0
1956	USSR, Finland, Sweden	2:15:30.0
1960	Finland, Norway, USSR	2:18:45.6
1964	Sweden, Finland, USSR	2:18:34.6
1968	Norway, Sweden, Finland	2:08:33.5
1972	USSR, Norway, Switzerland	2:04:47.94
1976	Finland, Norway, USSR	2:07:59.72
1980	USSR, Norway, Finland	1:57:03.46

	Combined Cross-Country & Jumping	Points
1924	Thorleif Haug, Norway	453.800
1928	Johan Grottumsbraaten, Norway	427.800
1932	Johan Grottumsbraaten, Norway	446.200
1936	Oddbjorn Hagen, Norway	430.300
1948	Heikki Hasu, Finland	448.800
1952	Simon Slattvik, Norway	451.621
1956	Sverre Stenersen, Norway	455.000
1960	Georg Thoma, Germany	457.952
1964	Tormod Knutsen, Norway	469.280
1968	Franz Keller, W. Germany	449.040
1972	Ulrich Wehling, E. Germany	413.340
1976	Ulrich Wehling, E. Germany	423.390
1980	Ulrich Wehling, E. Germany	432.200

	Ski Jumping (90 meters)	Points
1924	Jacob Thams, Norway	227.5
1928	Alfred Andersen, Norway	230.5
1932	Birger Ruud, Norway	228.0
1936	Birger Ruud, Norway	232.0
1948	Petter Hugsted, Norway	228.1
1952	Anders Bergmann, Norway	226.0
1956	Antti Hyvarinen, Finland	227.0
1960	Helmut Recknagel, Germany	227.2
1964	Toralf Engan, Norway	230.7
1968	Vladimir Beloussov, USSR	231.3
1972	Wojiech Fortuna, Poland	219.9
1976	Karl Schnabl, Austria	234.8
1980	Jouko Tormanen, Finland	231.5

	Ski Jumping (70 meters)	Points
1964	Veikko Kankkonen, Finland	229.9
1968	Jiri Raska, Czechoslovakia	216.5
1972	Yukio Kasaya, Japan	244.2
1976	Hans Aschenbach, E. Germany	252.0
1980	Anton Innauer, Austria	266.3

Women's Events

	5 kilometers (approx. 3.1 miles)	Time
1964	Claudia Boyarskikh, USSR	17:50.5
1968	Toini Gustafsson, Sweden	16:45.2
1972	Galina Koulacova, USSR	17:00.50
1976	Helena Takalo, Finland	15:48.69
1980	Raisa Smetanina, USSR	15:06.92

	10 kilometers	Time
1952	Lydia Wideman, Finland	41:40.0
1956	Lyubov Kosyreva, USSR	38:11.0
1960	Maria Gusakova, USSR	39:46.6
1964	Claudia Boyarskikh, USSR	40:24.3
1968	Toini Gustafsson, Sweden	36:46.5
1972	Galina Koulacova, USSR	34:17.82
1976	Raisa Smetanina, USSR	30:13.41
1980	Barbara Petzold, E. Germany	30:31.54

	15-km. Cross-Country Relay	Time
1956	Finland, USSR, Sweden	1:09:01.0
1960	Sweden, USSR, Finland	1:04:21.4
1964	USSR, Sweden, Finland	59:20.2
1968	Norway, Sweden, USSR	57:30.0
1972	USSR, Finland, Norway	48:46.1
1976	USSR, Finland, E. Germany (20 km.)	1:07:49.75
1980	E. Germany, USSR, Norway (20 km.)	1:02:11.10

Ice Hockey

1920	Canada, U.S., Czechoslovakia
1924	Canada, U.S., Great Britain
1928	Canada, Sweden, Switzerland
1932	Canada, U.S., Germany
1936	Great Britain, Canada, U.S.
1948	Canada, Czechoslovakia, Switzerland
1952	Canada, U.S., Sweden
1956	USSR, U.S., Canada
1960	U.S., Canada, USSR
1964	USSR, Sweden, Czechoslovakia
1968	USSR, Czechoslovakia, Canada
1972	USSR, U.S., Czechoslovakia,
1976	USSR, Czechoslovakia, W. Germany
1980	U.S., USSR, Sweden

Luge

	Men's Singles	Time
1964	Thomas Keohler, Germany	3:26.77
1968	Manfred Schmid, Austria	2:52.48
1972	Wolfgang Scheidel, E. Germany	3:27.58
1976	Detlef Guenther, E. Germany	3:27.688
1980	Bernhard Glass, E. Germany	2:54.796

	Men's Doubles	Time
1964	Austria	1:41.62
1968	E. Germany	1:35.85
1972	Italy, E. Germany (tie)	1:28.35
1976	E. Germany	1:25.604
1980	E. Germany	1:19.331

	Women's Singles	Time
1964	Ortun Enderlein, Germany	3:24.67
1968	Erica Lechner, Italy	2:28.66
1972	Anna M. Muller, E. Germany	2:59.18
1976	Margit Schumann, E. Germany	2:50.621
1980	Vera Zozulya, USSR	2:36.537

Speed Skating

Men's Events

500 meters (approx. 547 yds.)		Time
1924	Charles Jewtraw, U.S.	0:44.0
1928	Clas Thunberg, Finland & Bernt Evensen, Norway (tie)	0:43.4
1932	John A. Shea, U.S.	0:43.4
1936	Ivar Ballangrud, Norway	0:43.4
1948	Finn Helgesen, Norway	0:43.1
1952	Kenneth Henry, U.S.	0:43.2
1956	Evgeniy Grishin, USSR	0:40.2
1960	Evgeniy Grishin, USSR	0:40.2
1964	Terry McDermott, U.S.	0:40.1
1968	Erhard Keller, W. Germany	0:40.3
1972	Erhard Keller, W. Germany	0:39.44
1976	Evgeny Kulikov, USSR	0:39.17
1980	Eric Heiden, U.S.	0:38.03

1,000 meters		Time
1976	Peter Mueller, U.S.	1:19.32
1980	Eric Heiden, U.S.	1:15.18

1,500 meters		Time
1924	Clas Thunberg, Finland	2:20.8
1928	Clas Thunberg, Finland	2:21.1
1932	John A. Shea, U.S.	2:57.2
1936	Charles Mathiesen, Norway	2:19.2
1948	Sverre Farstad, Norway	2:17.6
1952	Hjalmar Andersen, Norway	2:20.4
1956	Evgeniy Grishin, & Yuri Mikhailov, both USSR (tie)	2:08.6
1960	Roald Edgar Aas, Norway & Evgeniy Grishin, USSR (tie)	2:10.4
1964	Ants Anston, USSR	2:10.3
1968	Cornetis Verkerk, Netherlands	2:03.4
1972	Ard Schenk, Netherlands	2:02.96
1976	Jan Egil Storholt, Norway	1:59.38
1980	Eric Heiden, U.S.	1:55.44

5,000 meters		Time
1924	Clas Thunberg, Finland	8:39.0
1928	Ivar Ballangrud, Norway	8:50.5
1932	Irving Jaffee, U.S.	9:40.8
1936	Ivar Ballangrud, Norway	8:19.6
1948	Reidar Liaklev, Norway	8:29.4
1952	Hjalmar Andersen, Norway	8:10.6
1956	Boris Shilkov, USSR	7:48.7
1960	Viktor Kosichkin, USSR	7:51.3
1964	Knut Johannesen, Norway	7:38.4
1968	F. Anton Maier, Norway	7:22.4
1972	Ard Schenk, Netherlands	7:23.61
1976	Sten Stensen, Norway	7:24.48
1980	Eric Heiden, U.S.	7:02.29

10,000 meters		Time
1924	Julius Skutnabb, Finland	18:04.8
1928	Event not held, thawing of ice	
1932	Irving Jaffee, U.S.	19:13.6
1936	Ivar Ballangrud, Norway	17:24.3
1948	Ake Seyffarth, Norway	17:26.3
1952	Hjalmar Andersen, Norway	16:45.8
1956	Sigvard Ericsson, Sweden	16:35.9
1960	Knut Johannesen, Norway	15:46.6
1964	Jonny Nilsson, Sweden	15:50.1
1968	Jonny Hoeglin, Sweden	15:23.6
1972	Ard Schenk, Netherlands	15:01.3
1976	Piet Kleine, Netherlands	14:50.59
1980	Eric Heiden, U.S.	14:28.13

Women's Events

500 meters		Time
1960	Helga Haase, Germany	0:45.9
1964	Lydia Skoblikova, USSR	0:45.0
1968	Ludmila Titova, USSR	0:46.1
1972	Anne Henning, U.S.	0:43.44
1976	Sheila Young, U.S.	0:42.76
1980	Karin Enke, E. Germany	0:41.78

1,000 meters		Time
1960	Klara Guseva, USSR	1:34.1
1964	Lydia Skoblikova, USSR	1:33.2
1968	Caroline Geijssen, Netherlands	1:32.6
1972	Monika Pflug, W. Germany	1:31.40
1976	Tatiana Averina, USSR	1:28.43
1980	Natalya Petruseva, USSR	1:24.10

1,500 meters		Time
1960	Lydia Skoblikova, USSR	2:52.2
1964	Lydia Skoblikova, USSR	2:22.6
1968	Kaija Mustonen, Finland	2:22.4
1972	Dianne Holum, U.S.	2:20.85
1976	Galina Stepanskaya, USSR	2:16.58
1980	Anne Borckink, Netherlands	2:10.95

3,000 meters		Time
1960	Lydia Skoblikova, USSR	5:14.3
1964	Lydia Skoblikova, USSR	5:14.9
1968	Johanna Schut, Netherlands	4:56.2
1972	Stien Baas-Kaiser, Netherlands	4:52.14
1976	Tatiana Averina, USSR	4:45.19
1980	Bjoerg Eva Jensen, Norway	4:32.13

Winter Olympic Medal Winners in 1980

Lake Placid, N.Y., Feb. 12-24

	Gold	Silver	Bronze	Total
Austria	3	2	2	7
Bulgaria	0	0	1	1
Canada	0	1	1	2
Czechoslovakia	0	0	1	1
Finland	1	5	3	9
France	0	0	1	1
Germany, East	9	7	7	23
Germany, West	0	2	3	5
Great Britain	1	0	0	1
Hungary	0	1	0	1
Italy	0	2	0	2
Japan	0	1	0	1
Liechtenstein	2	2	0	4
Netherlands	1	2	1	4
Norway	1	3	6	10
Sweden	3	0	1	4
Switzerland	1	1	3	5
USSR	10	6	6	22
United States	6	4	2	12

Westminster Kennel Club

Year	Best-in-show	Breed	Owner
1970	Ch. Arriba's Prima Donna	Boxer	Dr. & Mrs. P. J. Pagano & Dr. Theodore S. Fickles
1971	Ch. Chinoe's Adamant James	English springer spaniel	Dr. Milton Prickett
1972	Ch. Chinoe's Adamant James	English springer spaniel	Dr. Milton Prickett
1973	Ch. Acadia Command Performance	Poodle	Mrs. Jo Ann Sering & Edward B. Jenner
1974	Ch. Gretchenhof Columbia River	German pointer	Dr. Richard Smith
1975	Ch. Sir Lancelot of Barvan	Old English sheepdog	Mr. & Mrs. Ronald Vanword
1976	Ch. Jo-Ni's Red Baron of Crofton	Lakeland terrier	Virginia Dickson
1977	Ch. Dersade Bobby's Girl	Sealyham	Dorothy Wymer
1978	Ch. Cede Higgens	Yorkshire terrier	Barbara & Charles Switzer
1979	Ch. Oak Tree's Irishtocrat	Irish water spaniel	Anne E. Snelling
1980	Ch. Sierra Cinnar	Siberian husky	Kathleen Kanzler
1981	Ch. Dhandy Favorite Woodchuck	Pug	Robert Houslohner
1982	Ch. St. Aubrey Dragonora of Elsdon	Pekingese	Anne Snelling

World Record Fish Caught by Rod and Reel

Source: International Game Fish Association.
Records confirmed to June, 1982

Saltwater Fish

Species	Weight	Where caught	Date	Angler
Albacore	88 lbs. 2 oz.	Pt. Mogan, Canary Islands	Nov. 19, 1977	Siegried Dickemann
Amberjack, greater	155 lbs. 10 oz.	Bermuda	June 24, 1981	Joseph Dawson
Barracuda, great	83 lbs.	Lagos, Nigeria	Jan. 13, 1952	K.J.W. Hackett
Bass, black sea	8 lbs. 12 oz.	Oregon Inlet, N.C.	Apr. 21, 1979	Joe W. Mizelle Sr.
Bass, giant sea	563 lbs. 8 oz.	Anacaba Island, Cal.	Aug. 20, 1968	James D. McAdam Jr.
Bass, striped	76 lbs.	Montauk, N.Y.	July 17, 1981	Roberta Rocchetta
Bluefish	31 lbs. 12 oz.	Hatteras Inlet, N.C.	Jan. 30, 1972	James M. Hussey
Bonefish	19 lbs.	Zululand, S. Africa	May 26, 1962	Brian W. Batchelor
Bonito, Atlantic	16 lbs. 12 oz.	Canary Islands	Dec. 6, 1980	Rolf Fredderies
Bonito, Pacific	23 lbs. 8 oz.	Victoria, Mahe Seychelles	Feb. 19, 1975	Anne Cochain
Cobia	110 lbs. 5 oz.	Mombasa, Kenya	Sept. 8, 1964	Eric Tinworth
Cod	98 lbs. 12 oz.	Isle of Shoals, N.H.	June 8, 1969	Alphonse Bielevich
Conger	39 lbs. 7 oz.	Pornichet-La Baule, France	May 26, 1980	Jean-Claude Guilmineau
Dolphin	87 lbs.	Papagallo Gulf, Costa Rica	Sept. 25, 1976	Manual Salazar
Drum, black	113 lbs. 1 oz.	Lewes, Del.	Sept. 15, 1975	Gerald Townsend
Drum, red	90 lbs.	Rodanthe, N.C.	Nov. 7, 1973	Elvin Hooper
Flounder, summer	22 lbs. 7 oz.	Montauk, N.Y.	Sept. 15, 1975	Charles Nappi
Halibut, Atlantic	250 lbs.	Gloucester, Mass.	July 3, 1981	Louis Sirard
Halibut, California	42 lbs.	Santa Rosa Is., Cal.	May 24, 1981	Jerry Yahiro
Halibut, Pacific	235 lbs.	Juneau, Alaska	Sept. 15, 1980	Norbert Koch
Jack, crevalle	54 lbs. 7oz.	Pt. Michel, Gabon	Jan. 15, 1982	Thomas Gibson Jr.
Jack, horse-eye	23 lbs. 2 oz.	Cancun, Mexico	Oct. 2, 1981	Norman Carpenter
Jewfish	680 lbs.	Fernandina Beach, Fla.	May 20, 1961	Lynn Joyner
Kawakawa	26 lbs.	Merimbula, Australia	Jan. 26, 1980	Wally Elfring
Mackerel, king	90 lbs.	Key West, Fla.	Feb. 16, 1976	Norton Thomton
Marlin, Atlantic blue	1,282 lbs.	St. Thomas, Virgin Islands	Aug. 6, 1977	Larry Martin
Marlin, black	1,560 lbs.	Cabo Blanco, Peru	Aug. 4, 1953	A. C. Glassell Jr.
Marlin, Pacific blue	1,153 lbs.	Guam	Aug. 21, 1969	Greg Perez
Marlin, striped	417 lbs. 8 oz.	Cavalli Islands, New Zealand	Jan. 14, 1977	Phillip Bryers
Marlin, white	181 lbs. 14 oz.	Vitoria, Brazil	Dec. 8, 1979	Evandro Luiz Caser
Permit	51 lbs. 8 oz.	Lake Worth, Fla.	Apr. 28, 1978	William M. Kenney
Pollack	16 lbs. 1 oz.	Plymouth, England	Aug. 13, 1978	Peter J. Peck
Pollock	46 lbs. 7 oz.	Brielle, N.J.	May 26, 1975	John Tomes Holton
Pompano, African	41 lbs. 8 oz.	Ft. Lauderdale, Fla.	Feb. 15, 1979	Wayne Sommers
Roosterfish	114 lbs.	La Paz, Mexico	June 1, 1960	Abe Sackheim
Runner, rainbow	33 lbs. 10 oz.	Clarion Is., Mexico	Mar. 14, 1976	Ralph A. Mikkelsen
Sailfish, Atlantic	128 lbs. 1 oz.	Luanda, Angola	Mar. 27, 1974	Harm Steyn
Sailfish, Pacific	221 lbs.	Santa Cruz Is., Ecuador	Feb. 12, 1947	C. W. Stewart
Seabass, white	83 lbs. 12 oz.	San Felipe, Mexico	Mar. 31, 1953	L.C. Baumgardner
Seatrout, spotted	16 lbs.	Mason's Beach, Va.	May 28, 1977	William Katko
Shark, blue	437 lbs.	Catherine Bay, N.S.W. Australia	Oct. 2, 1976	Peter Hyde
Shark, hammerhead	717 lbs.	Jacksonville Beach, Fla.	July 27, 1980	Richard E. Morse
Shark, man-eater or white	2,664 lbs.	Ceduna, Australia	Apr. 21, 1959	Alfred Dean
Shark, mako	1,080 lbs.	Montauk, N.Y.	Aug. 26, 1979	James Melanson
Shark, porbeagle	465 lbs.	Cornwall, England	July 23, 1976	Jorge Potier
Shark, thresher	802 lbs.	Tutukaka, New Zealand	Feb. 8, 1981	Dianne North
Shark, tiger	1,780 lbs.	Cherry Grove, S.C.	June 14, 1964	Walter Maxwell
Skipjack, black	14 lbs. 8 oz.	Baja, Mexico	May 24, 1977	Lorraine Carlton
Snapper, cubera	60 lbs. 12 oz.	Miami Beach, Fla.	Feb. 27, 1980	Richard A. Klein
Snook	53 lbs. 10 oz.	Costa Rica	Oct. 18, 1978	Gilbert Ponzi
Spearfish	90 lbs. 13 oz.	Madeira Island, Portugal	June 2, 1980	Joseph Larkin
Swordfish	1,182 lbs.	Iquique, Chile	May 7, 1953	L. Marron
Tanguigue	85 lbs. 6 oz.	Rottnest Is., W. Australia	May 5, 1978	Barry Wrightson
Tarpon	283 lbs.	Lake Maracaibo, Venezuela	Mar. 19, 1956	M. Salazar
Tautog	21 lbs. 6 oz.	Cape May, N.J.	June 12, 1954	R.N. Sheafer
Trevally, giant	116 lbs.	Pago Pago, Amer. Samoa	Feb. 20, 1978	William G. Foster
Tuna, Atlantic bigeye	375 lbs. 8 oz.	Ocean City, Md.	Aug. 26, 1977	Cecil Browne
Tuna, blackfin	42 lbs.	Bermuda	June 2, 1978	Alan J. Card
Tuna, bluefin	1,496 lbs.	Aulds Cove, Nova Scotia	Oct. 26, 1979	Ken Fraser
Tuna, dog-tooth	194 lbs.	Korea	Sept. 27, 1980	Kim Chul
Tuna, longtail	60 lbs.	Bermagui, N.S.W., Australia	Mar. 17, 1975	N.N. Webster
Tuna, Pacific bigeye	435 lbs.	Cabo Blanco, Peru	Apr. 17, 1957	Dr. Russel Lee
Tuna, skipjack	39 lbs. 15 oz.	Walker Cay, Bahamas	Jan. 21, 1952	F. Drowley
	40 lbs.	Mauritius	Apr. 19, 1971	Joseph Caboche Jr.
Tuna, southern bluefin	348 lbs. 5 oz.	Whakatane, New Zealand	Jan. 16, 1981	Rex Wood
Tuna, yellowfin	388 lbs. 12 oz.	San Benedicto Island, Mexico	Apr. 1, 1977	Curt Wiesenhutter
Tunny, little	27 lbs.	Key Largo, Fla.	Apr. 20, 1976	William E. Allison
Wahoo	149 lbs.	Cay Cay, Bahamas	June 15, 1962	John Pirovano
Weakfish	17 lbs. 14 oz.	Rye, N.Y.	May 31, 1980	William Herold
Yellowtail, California	71 lbs. 15 oz.	Alijos Rocks, Mexico	June 24, 1979	Michael Carpenter
Yellowtail, southern	111 lbs.	Bay of Islands, New Zealand	June 11, 1961	A.F. Plim

Freshwater Fish

Species	Weight	Where Caught	Date	Angler
Bass, largemouth	22 lbs. 4 oz.	Montgomery Lake, Ga.	June 2, 1932	George W. Perry
Bass, peacock	26 lbs. 8 oz.	Matevini R., Colombia	Jan. 26, 1982	Rod Neubert
Bass, redeye	8 lbs. 3 oz.	Flint River, Ga.	Oct. 23, 1977	David A. Hubbard

Species	Weight	Where caught	Date	Angler
Bass rock	3 lbs.	York River, Ont.	Aug. 1, 1974	Peter Gulgin
Bass, smallmouth	11 lbs. 15 oz.	Dale Hollow Lake, Ky.	July 9, 1955	David L. Hayes
Bass, spotted	8 lbs. 15 oz.	Lewis Smith Lake, Ala.	Mar. 18, 1978	Philip Terry Jr.
Bass, striped	59 lbs. 12 oz.	Colorado River, Ariz.	May 26, 1977	Frank Smith
Bass, white	5 lbs. 9 oz.	Colorado River, Tex.	Mar. 31, 1977	David Cordill
Bass, whiterock	20 lbs. 6 oz.	Savannah River, Ga.	May 28, 1978	Dan Wood
Bass, yellow	2 lbs. 4 oz.	Lake Monroe, Ind.	Mar. 27, 1977	Donald L. Stalker
Bluegill	4 lbs. 12 oz.	Ketona Lake, Ala.	Apr. 9, 1950	T.S. Hudson
Bowfin	21 lbs. 8 oz.	Florence, S.C.	Jan. 29, 1980	Robert Harmon
Buffalo, bigmouth	70 lbs. 5 oz.	Bastrop, La.	Apr. 21, 1980	Delbert Sisk
Buffalo, smallmouth	51 lbs.	Lawrence, Kan.	May 2, 1979	Scott Butler
Bullhead, black	8 lbs.	Lake Waccabuc, N.Y.	Aug. 1, 1951	Kani Evans
Bullhead, brown	5 lbs. 8 oz.	Veal Pond, Ga.	May 22, 1975	Jimmy Andrews
Bullhead, yellow	3 lbs.	Nelson Lake, Wis.	May 8, 1977	Mark Nessman
Burbot	18 lbs. 4 oz.	Pickford, Mich.	Jan. 31, 1980	Thomas Courtemanche
Carp	55 lbs. 5 oz.	Clearwater Lake, Minn.	July 10, 1952	Frank J. Ledwein
Catfish, blue	97 lbs.	Missouri River, S.D.	Sept. 16, 1959	E.B. Elliott
Catfish, channel	58 lbs.	Santee-Cooper Res., S.C.	July 7, 1964	W.B. Whaley
Catfish, flathead	79 lbs. 8 oz.	White River, Ind.	Aug. 13, 1966	Glenn T. Simpson
Catfish, white	17 lbs. 7 oz.	Success L., Tulare, Cal.	Nov. 15, 1981	Chuck Idell
Char, Arctic	29 lbs. 11 oz.	Arctic River, N.W.T.	Aug. 21, 1968	Jeanne P. Branson
Crappie, black	6 lbs.	Westwago, La.	Nov. 28, 1969	Lettie T. Robertson
Crappie, white	5 lbs. 3 oz.	Enid Dam, Miss.	July 31, 1957	Fred L. Bright
Dolly Varden	33 lbs. 13 oz.	Unalaklett R., Alaska	Aug. 29, 1980	Roy Lawson
Drum, freshwater	54 lbs. 8 oz.	Nickajack Lake, Tenn.	Apr. 20, 1972	Benny E. Hull
Gar, alligator	279 lbs.	Rio Grande River, Tex.	Dec. 2, 1951	Bill Valverde
Gar, Florida	21 lbs. 3 oz.	Boca Raton, Fla.	June 3, 1981	Jeff Sabol
Gar, longnose	50 lbs. 5 oz.	Trinity River, Tex.	July 30, 1954	Townsend Miller
Gar, shortnose	3 lbs. 5 oz.	Lake Francis Case, S.D.	June 9, 1977	J. Pawlowski
Grayling, Arctic	5 lbs. 15 oz.	Katseyedie River, N.W.T.	Aug. 16, 1967	Jeanne P. Branson
Huchen	70 lbs. 12 oz.	Carinthia, Austria	Jan. 1, 1980	Martin Esterl
Inconnu	33 lbs. 9 oz.	Kobuk R., Alaska	Aug. 29, 1981	John Berg
Kokanee	6 lbs. 9 oz.	Priest Lake, Ida.	June 9, 1975	Jerry Verge
Muskellunge	69 lbs. 15 oz.	St. Lawrence River, N.Y.	Sept. 22, 1957	Arthur Lawton
Muskellunge, tiger	51 lbs. 3 oz.	Lac Vieux-Desert, Wis., Mich.	July 16, 1919	John Knobla
Perch, white	4 lbs. 12 oz.	Messalonskee Lake, Me.	June 4, 1949	Mrs. Earl Small
Perch, yellow	4 lbs. 3 oz.	Bordentown, N.J.	May, 1865	Dr. C.C. Abbot
Pickerel, chain	9 lbs. 6 oz.	Homerville, Ga.	Feb. 17, 1961	Baxley McQuaig Jr.
Pike, northern	62 lbs. 8 oz.	Rickenbach, Switzerland	June 15, 1979	Jurg Notzli
Redhorse, northern	3 lbs. 11 oz.	Missouri River, S.D.	May 26, 1977	Philip Laumeyer
Redhorse, silver	5 lbs. 14 oz.	Shelbyville, Ind.	Oct. 20, 1980	Ernest Harley Jr.
	5 lbs. 14 oz.	Betsie R., Frankfort, Mich.	May 4, 1980	Darrell Hasler
Salmon, Atlantic	79 lbs. 2 oz.	Tana River, Norway	1928	Henrik Henriksen
Salmon, chinook	93 lbs.	Kelp Bay, Alas.	June 24, 1977	Howard C. Rider
Salmon, chum	27 lbs. 3 oz.	Raymond Cove, Alas.	June 11, 1977	Robert A. Jahnke
Salmon, coho	31 lbs.	Cowichan Bay, B.C.	Oct. 11, 1947	Mrs. Lee Hallberg
Salmon, pink	12 lbs. 9 oz.	Morse, Kenai rivers, Alas.	Aug. 17, 1974	Steven A. Lee
Salmon, sockeye	7 lbs. 14 oz.	American R., Alaska	July 19, 1981	Brooke Halsey Jr.
Sauger	8 lbs. 12 oz.	Lake Sakakawea, N.D.	Oct. 6, 1971	Mike Fischer
Shad, American	9 lbs. 4 oz.	Delaware River, Pa.	Apr. 26, 1979	J. Edward Whitman
	9 lbs. 4 oz.	Connecticut R., Wilson, Conn.	Apr. 20, 1981	Edward W. Cypus
Splake	16 lbs. 12 oz.	Island Lake, Col.	Sept. 14, 1973	Del Canty
Sturgeon	407 lbs.	Sacramento River, Cal.	May 10, 1979	Raymond Pihenger
Sunfish, green	2 lbs. 2 oz.	Stockton Lake, Mo.	June 18, 1971	Paul M. Dilley
Sunfish, redbreast	1 lb. 8 oz.	Suwannee River, Fla.	Apr. 30, 1977	Tommy D. Cason Jr.
Sunfish, redear	4 lbs. 8 oz.	Chase City, Va.	June 19, 1970	Maurice E. Ball
Tigerfish	46 lbs. 4 oz.	L. Tanganyika, Zambia	Oct. 10, 1981	Giorgio Cuturi
Trout, brook	14 lbs. 8 oz.	Nipigon River, Ont.	July 1916	Dr. W.J. Cook
Trout, brown	35 lbs. 15 oz.	Nahuel Huapi, Argentina	Dec. 16, 1952	Eugenio Cavaglia
Trout, cutthroat	41 lbs.	Pyramid Lake, Nev.	Dec. 1925	J. Skimmerhorn
Trout, golden	11 lbs.	Cook's Lake, Wyo.	Aug. 5, 1948	Charles S. Reed
Trout, lake	65 lbs.	Great Bear Lake, N.W.T.	Aug. 8, 1970	Larry Daunis
Trout, rainbow	42 lbs. 2 oz.	Bell Island, Alas.	June 22, 1970	David Robert White
Trout, tiger	20 lbs. 13 oz.	Lake Michigan, Wis.	Aug. 12, 1978	Pete Friedland
Walleye	25 lbs.	Old Hickory Lake, Tenn.	Aug. 1, 1960	Mabry Harper
Warmouth	2 lbs. 2 oz.	Douglas Swamp, S.C.	May 19, 1973	Willie Singletary
Whitefish, lake	13 lbs. 5 oz.	Meaford, Ont.	Apr. 19, 1981	Wayne Caswell
Whitefish, mountain	5 lbs.	Athabasca River, Alta.	June 3, 1963	Orville Welch
Whitefish, round	3 lbs. 4 oz.	Leland Harbor, Mich.	Nov. 2, 1977	Vernon Bauer

Intercollegiate Rowing Association Championship

Lake Onondaga, Syracuse, N.Y. (3 miles)

Year	Winner	Time	Year	Winner	Time	Year	Winner	Time
1962	Cornell	17:02.9	1969	Penn (a)	6:30.4	1976	California (a)	6:31.0
1963	Cornell	17:24.0	1970	Washington (a)	6:39.3	1977	Cornell (a)	6:32.4
1964	California (a)	6:31.1	1971	Cornell (a)	6:06.0	1978	Syracuse (a)	6:39.5
1965	Navy	16:51.3	1972	Penn (a)	6:22.6	1979	Brown (a)	6:26.4
1966	Wisconsin	16:03.4	1973	Wisconsin (a)	6:21.0	1980	Navy (a)	6:46.0
1967	Penn	16:15.9	1974	Wisconsin (a)	6:33.0	1981	Cornell (a)	5:57.3
1968	Penn (a)	6:15.6	1975	Wisconsin (a)	6:08.2	1982	Cornell (a)	5:57.5

(a) race at 2,000 meters

College Basketball

Final Conference Standings, 1981–82

Big East

Team	Conference W	Conference L	All Games W	All Games L
Villanova	11	3	20	6
Georgetown	10	4	23	6
St. John's	9	5	19	7
Boston College	8	6	18	8
Syracuse	7	7	15	11
Connecticut	7	7	17	9
Seton Hall	2	12	11	15
Providence	2	12	10	16

ECAC South

Team	Conference W	Conference L	All Games W	All Games L
James Madison	10	1	23	5
Richmond	6	4	17	10
Old Dominion	5	4	18	11
William & Mary	6	5	15	12
Navy	2	4	12	13
George Mason	2	7	13	13
E. Carolina	2	8	10	16

North

Team	Conference W	Conference L	All Games W	All Games L
Northeastern	8	1	22	6
Canisius	7	2	19	7
Niagara	7	2	18	10
Boston Univ.	6	2	19	8
Holy Cross	4	4	16	11
Maine	3	7	7	19
Colgate	2	6	8	17
Vermont	2	8	10	16
New Hampshire	2	9	9	18

Metro-South
Metro Division

Team	Conference W	Conference L	All Games W	All Games L
Fairleigh Dickinson	10	3	14	11
Long Island	10	4	20	9
St. Francis, NY	8	6	10	15
Siena	8	7	15	12
Marist	6	9	12	14
Wagner	1	14	4	22

South Division

Team	Conference W	Conference L	All Games W	All Games L
Robert Morris	9	5	17	12
Baltimore	8	6	15	12
Towson St.	7	7	10	17
Loyola, Md.	7	7	11	16
St. Francis, Pa.	3	11	6	20

East Coast
Eastern Section

Team	Conference W	Conference L	All Games W	All Games L
Temple	11	0	19	6
St. Joseph's	10	1	22	4
American	8	3	19	7
LaSalle	7	4	14	12
Drexel	7	4	16	10
Hofstra	4	7	11	15

Western Section

Team	Conference W	Conference L	All Games W	All Games L
West Chester	8	8	13	13
Rider	7	9	11	15
Lafayette	7	9	12	14
Delaware	6	10	9	16
Bucknell	3	13	7	19
Lehigh	3	13	9	16

Eastern Eight

Team	Conference W	Conference L	All Games W	All Games L
West Virginia	13	1	24	2
Rutgers	9	5	18	8
Pittsburgh	8	6	17	9
Geo. Washington	7	7	13	13
St. Bonaventure	7	7	13	13
Duquesne	5	9	11	15
Rhode Island	4	10	10	16
Massachusetts	3	10	7	19

Ivy League

Team	Conference W	Conference L	All Games W	All Games L
Penn	12	2	17	9
Columbia	9	5	16	10
Princeton	9	5	14	13
Yale	7	7	13	13
Cornell	7	7	10	16
Harvard	6	8	11	15
Brown	5	9	5	21
Dartmouth	1	13	7	19

Atlantic Coast

Team	Conference W	Conference L	All Games W	All Games L
N. Carolina	12	2	24	2
Virginia	12	2	27	2
Wake Forest	9	5	19	7
N. Carolina St.	7	7	21	8
Maryland	5	9	15	11
Duke	4	10	10	16
Clemson	4	10	14	12
Georgia Tech	3	11	10	15

Mid Eastern

Team	Conference W	Conference L	All Games W	All Games L
N. Carolina A&T	10	2	17	8
Howard Univ.	9	3	15	10
S. Carolina St.	7	5	10	14
Florida A&M	5	7	9	16
Delaware St.	4	8	13	12
Bethune Cookman	4	8	9	17
Md. E. Shore	3	9	6	19

Metro Atlantic

Team	Conference W	Conference L	All Games W	All Games L
St. Peter's	9	1	19	7
Fordham	8	2	17	9
Iona	7	3	21	8
Fairfield	3	7	10	16
Manhattan	3	7	11	15
Army	0	10	5	21

Mid-American

Team	Conference W	Conference L	All Games W	All Games L
Ball State	12	4	16	10
Bowling Green	10	6	16	10
N. Illinois	9	7	13	13
E. Michigan	8	8	15	11
W. Michigan	8	8	14	12
Ohio U.	8	8	13	13
Miami, Ohio	8	8	11	15
Toledo	7	9	15	11
Kent St.	6	10	10	15
C. Michigan	4	12	10	15

Metro

Team	Conference W	Conference L	All Games W	All Games L
Memphis St.	10	2	21	4
Louisville	8	4	18	8
Tulane	8	4	17	7
Virginia Tech	7	5	17	9
Cincinnati	4	8	15	11
Florida St.	4	8	10	16
St. Louis	1	11	6	20

Ohio Valley

Team	Conference W	Conference L	All Games W	All Games L
W. Kentucky	13	3	18	8
Murray State	13	3	20	6
Middle Tenn.	12	4	19	7
Morehead St.	11	5	17	9
Tennessee Tech.	8	8	12	14
Youngstown	5	11	8	18
Austin Peay	4	12	6	19
Akron	3	13	7	19
E. Kentucky	3	13	5	21

Trans America

Team	Conference W	Conference L	All Games W	All Games L
Ark-Little Rock	12	4	19	8
NW Louisiana	10	6	19	9
NE Louisiana	9	7	19	10
Centenary	9	7	17	12
Mercer	8	8	16	11
Georgia So.	8	8	13	13
Houston Bapt.	8	8	13	14
Samford	6	10	11	15
Hardin-Simmns	2	14	6	20

Missouri Valley

Team	Conference W	Conference L	All Games W	All Games L
Bradley	13	3	20	9
Tulsa	12	4	21	5
Wichita St.	12	4	23	6
New Mexico St.	10	6	16	10
Illinois St.	9	7	15	11
Drake	7	9	12	14
S. Illinois	7	9	11	15
Creighton	4	12	7	19
W. Texas St.	3	13	11	15
Indiana St.	3	13	9	17

Midwestern City

Team	Conference W	Conference L	All Games W	All Games L
Evansville	10	2	21	5
Oral Roberts	8	4	18	10
Loyola, Ill.	8	4	15	11
Oklahoma City	6	6	13	13
Detroit	6	6	10	16
Butler	3	9	7	19
Xavier, Ohio	1	11	7	19

Southland

Team	Conference W	Conference L	All Games W	All Games L
S.W. Louisiana	8	2	22	7
Lamar	7	3	22	5
Texas-Arlington	6	4	15	11
McNeese St.	4	6	13	14
Arkansas St.	3	7	15	11
Louisiana Tech.	2	8	11	15

Big Ten

Team	Conference W	Conference L	All Games W	All Games L
Minnesota	14	4	22	5
Iowa	12	6	20	7
Ohio State	12	6	21	9
Indiana	12	6	18	9
Purdue	11	7	14	13
Illinois	10	8	17	10
Michigan St.	6	12	11	17
Michigan	6	12	6	21
Northwestern	4	14	8	19
Wisconsin	3	15	6	20

Big Eight

Team	Conference W	Conference L	All Games W	All Games L
Missouri	12	2	23	3
Kansas St.	10	4	20	6
Oklahoma	8	6	17	9
Nebraska	7	7	15	11
Oklahoma St.	7	7	15	11
Iowa St.	5	9	10	16
Kansas	4	10	13	13
Colorado	3	11	11	15

Southeastern

Team	Conference W	Conference L	All Games W	All Games L
Kentucky	13	5	20	6
Tennessee	13	5	18	8
Alabama	12	6	20	6
Louisiana St.	11	7	14	12
Mississippi	11	7	16	10
Georgia	10	8	16	10
Auburn	7	11	13	13
Vanderbilt	7	11	14	12
Mississippi St.	4	14	8	18
Florida	2	16	5	21

Southern

Team	Conference W	Conference L	All Games W	All Games L
Tenn.-Chat.	15	1	24	3
W. Carolina	11	5	18	8
Davidson	9	7	13	14
E. Tennessee St.	8	8	13	14
Marshall	8	8	16	11
Furman	7	9	11	15
The Citadel	7	9	14	12
Appalachian St.	6	10	11	15
VMI	1	15	1	25

Southwest

Team	Conference W	Conference L	All Games W	All Games L
Arkansas	12	4	21	5
Houston	11	5	20	6
Texas A&M	10	6	17	9
Baylor	9	7	16	10
TCU	9	7	12	12
Texas Tech	8	8	16	10
Texas	6	10	16	10
Rice	6	10	15	14
SMU	1	15	6	20

Southwestern Athletic

Team	Conference W	Conference L	All Games W	All Games L
Jackson St.	10	2	18	8
Alcorn St.	10	2	19	6
Texas Southern	8	4	19	7
Grambling St.	6	6	11	15
Mississippi Valley	4	8	5	19
Southern Univ.	3	9	7	17
Prairie View	1	11	3	21

	Conference W	Conference L	All Games W	All Games L
Big Sky				
Idaho	13	1	24	2
Montana	10	4	17	9
Nev.-Reno	9	5	18	7
Weber St.	6	8	15	12
Boise St.	6	8	12	14
Idaho St.	5	9	14	12
Montana St.	5	9	11	18
N. Arizona	2	12	6	20
Pacific Coast Athletic				
Fresno St.	13	1	24	2
Cal-Irvine	10	4	21	5
Fullerton St.	9	5	16	13
San Jose St.	7	7	13	12
Long Beach St.	7	7	11	15
Cal-Santa Barbara	5	9	10	16
Pacific	3	11	7	19
Utah St.	2	12	4	22
Pacific-10				
Oregon St.	16	2	23	4
UCLA	14	4	21	6
Southern Cal.	13	5	19	8
Washington	11	7	18	9
Washington St.	10	8	16	14
California	8	10	14	13
Arizona St.	8	10	13	14
Oregon	4	14	9	18
Arizona	4	14	9	18
Stanford	2	16	7	20

	Conference W	Conference L	All Games W	All Games L
Sun Belt				
Ala.-Birmingham	9	1	23	5
Virginia Comm.	7	3	17	11
Jacksonville	5	5	14	13
South Florida	4	6	16	11
N.C.-Charlotte	3	7	15	12
S. Alabama	2	8	12	16
West Coast Athletic				
Pepperdine	14	0	21	6
San Francisco	11	3	25	5
Portland	9	5	17	10
Santa Clara	7	7	16	11
Gonzaga	7	7	15	12
San Diego	4	10	11	15
St. Mary's	3	11	11	16
Loyola, Cal.	1	13	3	24
Western Athletic				
Wyoming	14	2	22	6
San Diego St.	11	5	20	8
Texas-El Paso	11	5	20	8
Brigham Young	9	7	17	12
Hawaii	9	7	17	10
New Mexico	7	9	14	14
Utah	6	10	11	17
Air Force	3	13	8	19
Colorado St.	2	14	8	19

Major Independents

	W	L
DePaul	26	1
Marquette	21	8
Dayton	19	8
New Orleans	18	8
Nevada-Las Vegas	19	9
Cleveland St.	17	10
SE Louisiana	16	11
So. Mississippi	15	11
North Texas St.	15	12
Penn St.	15	12
Tennessee St.	13	11
E. Illinois	14	13
Ill.-Chicago Circle	14	13
W. Illinois	14	13
Wis.-Green Bay	14	13
Baptist	13	13
S. Carolina	14	15
N. Car.-Wilmington	13	14
No. Iowa	12	15
Stetson	12	15
Campbell	11	16
Notre Dame	10	17
U.S. International	9	18
Valparaiso	9	18
Texas-San Antonio	8	19
Nicholls St.	6	20
Pan American	5	20
Utica College	4	22
Georgia St.	4	23

NCAA Basketball Championships in 1982

East

First round—James Madison 55, Ohio State 48; St. John's 66, Penn 56; Northeastern 63, St. Joseph's (Pa.) 62; Wake Forest 74, Old Dominion 57.

Second round—North Carolina 52, James Madison 50; Alabama 69, St. John's 68; Villanova 76, Northeastern 72; Memphis State 56, Wake Forest 55.

Semifinals—North Carolina 74, Alabama 69; Villanova 70, Memphis State 66.

Championship—North Carolina 70, Villanova 60.

Midwest

First round—Boston College 70, San Francisco 66; Kansas State 77, Northern Illinois 68; Houston 94, Alcorn State 84; Marquette 67, Evansville 62.

Second round—Boston College 82, De Paul 75; Kansas State 65, Arkansas 64; Houston 78, Tulsa 74; Missouri 73, Marquette 69.

Semifinals—Boston College 69, Kansas State 65; Houston 79, Missouri 78.

Championship—Houston 99, Boston College 92.

Mideast

First round—Tennessee 61, SW Louisiana 57; Indiana 94, Robert Morris 62; Middle Tennessee 50, Kentucky 44; Tenn.-Chattanooga 58, North Carolina State 51.

Second round—Virginia 54, Tennessee 51; Ala.-Birmingham 80, Indiana 70; Louisville 81, Middle Tennessee 56; Minnesota 62, Tenn.-Chattanooga 61.

Semifinals—Ala.-Birmingham 68, Virginia 66; Louisville 67, Minnesota 61.

Finals—Louisville 75, Ala.-Birmingham 68.

West

First round—Wyoming 61, Southern Cal. 58; West Virginia 102; North Carolina A & T 72; Iowa 70, NE Louisiana 63; Pepperdine 99, Pitt 88.

Second round—Georgetown 51, Wyoming 43; Fresno State 50, West Virginia 46; Idaho 69, Iowa 67; Oregon State 70, Pepperdine 51.

Semifinals—Georgetown 58, Fresno State 40; Oregon State 60, Idaho 42.

Finals—Georgetown 69, Oregon State 45.

National Semifinals

North Carolina 68, Houston 63; Georgetown 50, Louisville 46.

Championship

North Carolina 63, Georgetown 62.

NCAA Division I Champions

Year	Champion	Year	Champion	Year	Champion	Year	Champion
1939	Oregon	1950	CCNY	1961	Cincinnati	1972	UCLA
1940	Indiana	1951	Kentucky	1962	Cincinnati	1973	UCLA
1941	Wisconsin	1952	Kansas	1963	Loyola (Chi.)	1974	No. Carolina State
1942	Stanford	1953	Indiana	1964	UCLA	1975	UCLA
1943	Wyoming	1954	La Salle	1965	UCLA	1976	Indiana
1944	Utah	1955	San Francisco	1966	Texas Western	1977	Marquette
1945	Oklahoma A&M	1956	San Francisco	1967	UCLA	1978	Kentucky
1946	Oklahoma A&M	1957	North Carolina	1968	UCLA	1979	Michigan State
1947	Holy Cross	1958	Kentucky	1969	UCLA	1980	Louisville
1948	Kentucky	1959	California	1970	UCLA	1981	Indiana
1949	Kentucky	1960	Ohio State	1971	UCLA	1982	North Carolina

NCAA Division II Champions

Year	Champion	Year	Champion	Year	Champion	Year	Champion
1966	Kentucky Wesleyan	1971	Evansville	1975	Old Dominion	1979	North Alabama
1967	Winston-Salem	1972	Roanoke	1976	Puget Sound	1980	Virginia Union
1968	Kentucky Wesleyan	1973	Kentucky Wesleyan	1977	Tennessee-Chattanooga	1981	Florida Southern
1969	Kentucky Wesleyan	1974	Morgan State	1978	Cheyney State	1982	Univ. of D.C.
1970	Philadelphia Textile						

National Invitation Tournament Champions

Year	Champion	Year	Champion	Year	Champion	Year	Champion
1938	Temple	1950	CCNY	1961	Providence	1972	Maryland
1939	Long Island Univ.	1951	Brigham Young	1962	Dayton	1973	Virginia Tech
1940	Colorado	1952	LaSalle	1963	Providence	1974	Purdue
1941	Long Island Univ.	1953	Seton Hall	1964	Bradley	1975	Princeton
1942	West Virginia	1954	Holy Cross	1965	St. John's	1976	Kentucky
1943	St. John's	1955	Duquesne	1966	Brigham Young	1977	St. Bonaventure
1944	St. John's	1956	Louisville	1967	Southern Illinois	1978	Texas
1945	De Paul	1957	Bradley	1968	Dayton	1979	Indiana
1946	Kentucky	1958	Xavier (Ohio)	1969	Temple	1980	Virginia
1947	Utah	1959	St. John's	1970	Marquette	1981	Tulsa
1948	St. Louis	1960	Bradley	1971	North Carolina	1982	Bradley
1949	San Francisco						

Figure Skating Champions

National Champions			World Champions	
Men	**Women**	**Year**	**Men**	**Women**
Richard Button	Tenley Albright	**1952**	Richard Button, U.S.	Jacqueline du Bief, France
Hayes Jenkins	Tenley Albright	**1953**	Hayes Jenkins, U.S.	Tenley Albright, U.S.
Hayes Jenkins	Tenley Albright	**1954**	Hayes Jenkins, U.S.	Gundi Busch, W. Germany
Hayes Jenkins	Tenley Albright	**1955**	Hayes Jenkins, U.S.	Tenley Albright, U.S.
Hayes Jenkins	Tenley Albright	**1956**	Hayes Jenkins, U.S.	Carol Heiss, U.S.
Dave Jenkins	Carol Heiss	**1957**	Dave Jenkins, U.S.	Carol Heiss, U.S.
Dave Jenkins	Carol Heiss	**1958**	Dave Jenkins, U.S.	Carol Heiss, U.S.
Dave Jenkins	Carol Heiss	**1959**	Dave Jenkins, U.S.	Carol Heiss, U.S.
Dave Jenkins	Carol Heiss	**1960**	Alain Giletti, France	Carol Heiss, U.S.
Bradley Lord	Laurence Owen	**1961**	none	none
Monty Hoyt	Barbara Roles Pursley	**1962**	Don Jackson, Canada	Sjoukje Dijkstra, Neth.
Tommy Litz	Lorraine Hanlon	**1963**	Don McPherson, Canada	Sjoukje Dijkstra, Neth.
Scott Allen	Peggy Fleming	**1964**	Manfred Schnelldorfer, W. Germany	Sjoukje Dijkstra, Neth.
Gary Visconti	Peggy Fleming	**1965**	Alain Calmat, France	Petra Burka, Canada
Scott Allen	Peggy Fleming	**1966**	Emmerich Danzer, Austria	Peggy Fleming, U.S.
Gary Visconti	Peggy Fleming	**1967**	Emmerich Danzer, Austria	Peggy Fleming, U.S.
Tim Wood	Peggy Fleming	**1968**	Emmerich Danzer, Austria	Peggy Fleming, U.S.
Tim Wood	Janet Lynn	**1969**	Tim Wood, U.S.	Gabriele Seyfert, E. Germany
Tim Wood	Janet Lynn	**1970**	Tim Wood, U.S.	Gabriele Seyfert, E. Germany
John Misha Petkevich	Janet Lynn	**1971**	Ondrej Nepela, Czech.	Beatrix Schuba, Austria
Ken Shelley	Janet Lynn	**1972**	Ondrej Nepela, Czech.	Beatrix Schuba, Austria
Gordon McKellen Jr.	Janet Lynn	**1973**	Ondrej Nepela, Czech.	Karen Magnussen, Canada
Gordon McKellen Jr.	Dorothy Hamill	**1974**	Jan Hoffmann, E. Germany	Christine Errath, E. Germany
Gordon McKellen Jr.	Dorothy Hamill	**1975**	Sergei Volkov, USSR	Dianne de Leeuw, Neth.-U.S.
Terry Kubicka	Dorothy Hamill	**1976**	John Curry, Gt. Britain	Dorothy Hamill, U.S.
Charles Tickner	Linda Fratianne	**1977**	Vladimir Kovalev, USSR	Linda Fratianne, U.S.
Charles Tickner	Linda Fratianne	**1978**	Charles Tickner, U.S.	Anett Potzsch, E. Germany
Charles Tickner	Linda Fratianne	**1979**	Vladimir Kovalev, USSR	Linda Fratianne, U.S.
Charles Tickner	Linda Fratianne	**1980**	Jan Hoffmann, E. Germany	Anett Potzsch, E. Germany
Scott Hamilton	Elaine Zayak	**1981**	Scott Hamilton, U.S.	Denise Biellmann, Switzerland
Scott Hamilton	Rosalynn Sumners	**1982**	Scott Hamilton, U.S.	Elaine Zayak, U.S.

World Pairs and Dancing Champions in 1982

Sabine Baess and Tassilo Thierbach of E. Germany won the 1982 world pairs figure skating championship in Copenhagen, Denmark. Jayne Torwill and Christopher Dean of Great Britain triumphed in ice dancing.

Canadian National Figure Skating Champions

Year	Men	Women	Year	Men	Women
1965	Donald Knight	Petra Burka	1974	Toller Cranston	Lynn Nightingale
1966	Donald Knight	Petra Burka	1975	Toller Cranston	Lynn Nightingale
1967	Donald Knight	Valerie Jones	1976	Toller Cranston	Lynn Nightingale
1968	Jay Humphrey	Karen Magnussen	1977	Ron Shaver	Lynn Nightingale
1969	Jay Humphrey	Linda Carbonetto	1978	Brian Pockar	Heather Kemkaran
1970	David McGillivray	Karen Magnussen	1979	Brian Pockar	Janet Morissey
1971	Toller Cranston	Karen Magnussen	1980	Brian Pockar	Heather Kemkaren
1972	Toller Cranston	Karen Magnussen	1981	Brian Orser	Tracey Wainman
1973	Toller Cranston	Karen Magnussen	1982	Brian Orser	Kay Thomson

U.S. Amateur Boxing Championships in 1982

Charlotte, N.C., Apr. 12-17, 1982

106 lbs.—Mario Lesperance, Vallejo, Cal.
112 lbs.—Steve McCrory, Detroit, Mich.
119 lbs.—Floyd Favors, Capitol Hts., Md.
125 lbs.—Orlando Johnson, Chicago, Ill.
132 lbs.—Pernell Whitaker, Norfolk, Va.
139 lbs.—Henry Hughes, Cleveland, Oh.
147 lbs.—Mark Breland, New York, N.Y.
156 lbs.—Dennis Milton, New York, N.Y.
165 lbs.—Michael Grogan, Atlanta, Ga.
178 lbs.—Bennie Heard, Augusta, Ga.
201 lbs.—Elmer Martin, U.S. Navy
Over 201 lbs.—Tyrone Biggs, Philadelphia, Pa.

Koch Wins Nordic World Cup Championship

Bill Koch became the first U.S. nordic skier to capture the overall title in the Nordic World Cup championships in 1982.

National Hockey League, 1981-82

Final Standings

Wales Conference

Patrick Division

	W	L	T	Pts	GF	GA
N.Y. Islanders	54	16	10	118	385	250
N.Y. Rangers	39	27	14	92	316	306
Philadelphia	38	31	11	87	325	313
Pittsburgh	31	36	13	75	310	337
Washington	26	41	13	65	319	338

Adams Division

	W	L	T	Pts	GF	GA
Montreal	46	17	17	109	360	223
Boston	43	27	10	96	323	285
Buffalo	39	26	15	93	307	273
Quebec	33	31	16	82	356	345
Hartford	21	41	18	60	264	351

Campbell Conference

Norris Division

	W	L	T	Pts	GF	GA
Minnesota	37	23	20	94	346	288
Winnipeg	33	33	14	80	319	332
St. Louis	32	40	8	72	315	349
Chicago	30	38	12	72	332	363
Toronto	20	44	16	56	298	380
Detroit	21	47	12	54	271	350

Smythe Division

	W	L	T	Pts	GF	GA
Edmonton	48	17	15	111	417	295
Vancouver	30	33	17	77	290	286
Calgary	29	34	17	75	334	345
Los Angeles	24	41	15	63	314	369
Colorado	18	49	13	49	241	362

Stanley Cup Playoff Results

N.Y. Rangers defeated Philadelphia 3 games to 1.
Boston defeated Buffalo 3 games to 1.
Vancouver defeated Calgary 3 games to 0.
St. Louis defeated Winnipeg 3 games to 1.
Chicago defeated Minnesota 3 games to 1.
N.Y. Islanders defeated Pittsburgh 3 games to 2.
Quebec defeated Montreal 3 games to 2.
Los Angeles defeated Edmonton 3 games to 2.
Vancouver defeated Los Angeles 4 games to 1.
N.Y. Islanders defeated N.Y. Rangers 4 games to 2.
Quebec defeated Boston 4 games to 3.
Chicago defeated St. Louis 4 games to 2.
N.Y. Islanders defeated Quebec 4 games to 0.
Vancouver defeated Chicago 4 games to 1.
N.Y. Islanders defeated Vancouver 4 games to 0.

Leading Scorers

Player, team	GP	G	A	Pts
Gretzky, Edmonton	80	92	120	212
Bossy, N.Y. Islanders	80	64	83	147
P. Stastny, Quebec	80	46	93	139
Maruk, Washington	80	60	76	136
Trottier, N.Y. Islanders	80	50	79	129

Player, team	GP	G	A	Pts
Savard, Chicago	80	32	87	119
Dionne, Los Angeles	78	50	67	117
Smith, Minnesota	80	43	71	114
Ciccarelli, Minnesota	76	55	52	107
Taylor, Los Angeles	78	39	67	106

Goaltending Leaders

Goalie, team	GP	MIN	GA	Avg
Rick Wamsley, Montreal	38	2206	101	2.75
Bill Smith, N.Y. Islanders	46	2685	133	2.97
Roland Melanson, N.Y. Islanders	36	2115	114	3.23
Grant Fuhr, Edmonton	48	2847	157	3.31
Richard Brodeur, Vancouver	52	3010	168	3.35
Marco Baron, Boston	44	2515	144	3.44

Goalie, team	GP	MIN	GA	Avg
Gilles Meloche, Minnesota	51	3026	175	3.47
Don Edwards, Buffalo	62	3500	205	3.51
Rogie Vachon, Boston	38	2165	132	3.66
Pete Peeters, Philadelphia	44	2591	160	3.71
Steve Weeks, N.Y. Rangers	49	2852	179	3.77
Michel Dion, Pittsburgh	62	3580	226	3.79

Stanley Cup Champions

1928	New York	1939	Boston	1950	Detroit	1961	Chicago	1972	Boston
1929	Boston	1940	New York	1951	Toronto	1962	Toronto	1973	Montreal
1930	Montreal	1941	Boston	1952	Detroit	1963	Toronto	1974	Philadelphia
1931	Montreal	1942	Toronto	1953	Montreal	1964	Toronto	1975	Philadelphia
1932	Toronto	1943	Detroit	1954	Detroit	1965	Montreal	1976	Montreal
1933	New York	1944	Montreal	1955	Detroit	1966	Montreal	1977	Montreal
1934	Chicago	1945	Toronto	1956	Montreal	1967	Toronto	1978	Montreal
1935	Montreal Maroons	1946	Montreal	1957	Montreal	1968	Montreal	1979	Montreal
1936	Detroit	1947	Toronto	1958	Montreal	1969	Montreal	1980	N.Y. Islanders
1937	Detroit	1948	Toronto	1959	Montreal	1970	Boston	1981	N.Y. Islanders
1938	Chicago	1949	Toronto	1960	Montreal	1971	Montreal	1982	N.Y. Islanders

Conn Smythe Trophy (MVP in Playoffs)

1965 Jean Beliveau, Montreal
1966 Roger Crozier, Detroit
1967 Dave Keon, Toronto
1968 Glenn Hall, St. Louis
1969 Serge Savard, Montreal
1970 Bobby Orr, Boston
1971 Ken Dryden, Montreal
1972 Bobby Orr, Boston
1973 Yvan Cournoyer, Montreal
1974 Bernie Parent, Philadelphia
1975 Bernie Parent, Philadelphia
1976 Reg Leach, Philadelphia
1977 Guy Lafleur, Montreal
1978 Larry Robinson, Montreal
1979 Bob Gainey, Montreal
1980 Bryan Trottier, N.Y. Islanders
1981 Butch Goring, N.Y. Islanders
1982 Mike Bossy, N.Y. Islanders

NHL All Star Team, 1982

First team	Position	Second team
Billy Smith, N.Y. Islanders	Goalie	Grant Fuhr, Edmonton
Doug Wilson, Chicago	Defense	Paul Coffey, Edmonton
Ray Bourque, Boston	Defense	Brian Engblom, Montreal
Wayne Gretzky, Edmonton	Center	Bryan Trottier, N.Y. Islanders
Mike Bossy, N.Y. Islanders	Right Wing	Rick Middleton, Boston
Mark Messier, Edmonton	Left Wing	John Tonelli, N.Y. Islanders

Individual Scoring
(40 or More Games Played)

Boston Bruins

	GP	G	A	Pts	PIM
Rick Middleton	75	51	43	94	12
Barry Pederson	80	44	48	92	53
Peter McNab	80	36	40	76	19
Ray Bourque	65	17	49	66	51
Brad Park	75	14	42	56	82
Terry O'Reilly	70	22	30	52	213
Steve Kasper	73	20	31	51	72
Keith Crowder	71	23	21	44	101
Wayne Cashman	64	12	31	43	59
Tom Fergus	61	15	24	39	12
Mike O'Connell	80	5	34	39	75
Don Marcotte	69	13	22	35	14
Normand Leveille	65	14	19	33	49
Bruce Crowder	63	16	11	27	31
Stan Jonathan	67	6	17	23	57
Mike Gillis	53	9	8	17	54
Mike Milbury	51	2	10	12	71
Brad McCrimmon	78	1	8	9	83
Larry Melnyk	48	0	8	8	84

Buffalo Sabres

	GP	G	A	Pts	PIM
Mike Foligno	82	33	44	77	177
Gilbert Perreault	62	31	42	73	40
Dale McCourt	78	33	36	69	18
John Van Boxmeer	69	14	54	68	62
Yvon Lambert	77	25	39	64	38
Jean F. Sauve	69	19	36	55	46
Tony McKegney	73	23	29	52	41
Craig Ramsay	80	16	35	51	8
Lindy Ruff	79	16	32	48	194
Ric Seiling	57	22	25	47	58
Alan Haworth	57	21	18	39	30
Andre Savard	62	18	20	38	24
Mike Ramsey	80	7	23	30	56
Richie Dunn	72	7	19	26	73
Steve Patrick	41	8	8	16	64
Larry Playfair	77	6	10	16	258
Brent Peterson	61	10	5	15	49
Bill Hait	65	2	9	11	44

Calgary Flames

	GP	G	A	Pts	PIM
Mel Bridgman	72	33	54	87	141
Lanny McDonald	71	40	42	82	57
Guy Chouinard	64	23	57	80	12
Pekka Rautakallio	80	17	51	68	40
Jim Peplinski	74	30	37	67	115
Kevin Lavallee	75	32	29	61	30
Paul Reinhart	62	13	48	61	17
Willi Plett	78	21	36	57	288
Kent Nilsson	41	26	29	55	8
Ken Houston	70	22	22	44	91
Jamie Hislop	80	16	25	41	35
Phil Russell	71	4	25	29	110
Gary McAdam	46	12	15	27	18
Denis Cyr	45	12	10	22	13
Dan Labraaten	43	10	12	22	6
Bob Murdoch	73	3	17	20	76
Steve Konroyd	63	3	14	17	78
Bill Clement	69	4	12	16	28
Charles Bourgeois	54	2	13	15	112

Chicago Black Hawks

	GP	G	A	Pts	PIM
Denis Savard	80	32	87	119	82
Doug Wilson	76	39	46	85	54
Tom Lysiak	71	32	50	82	84
Al Secord	80	44	31	75	303
Tim Higgins	74	20	30	50	85
Grant Mulvey	73	30	19	49	141
Rich Preston	75	15	28	43	30
Doug Crossman	70	12	28	40	24
Reg Kerr	59	11	28	39	39
Terry Ruskowski	60	7	30	37	120
Darryl Sutter	40	23	12	35	31
Ted Bulley	59	12	18	30	120
Bob Murray	45	8	22	30	48
Peter Marsh	57	10	18	28	47
Keith Brown	33	4	20	24	26
Bill Gardner	69	8	15	23	20
Dave Hutchison	66	5	18	23	246
Greg Fox	79	2	19	21	137
Rick Paterson	48	4	7	11	8

Colorado Rockies

	GP	G	A	Pts	PIM
Don Lever	82	30	39	69	26
Bob MacMillan	80	22	39	61	41
Brent Ashton	80	24	36	60	26
Steve Tambellini	79	29	30	59	14
Rob Ramage	80	13	29	42	201
Merlin Malinowski	69	13	28	41	32
Aaron Broten	58	15	24	39	6
Dwight Foster	70	12	19	31	41
Bob Miller	56	11	20	31	27
Dave Cameron	66	11	12	23	103
Paul Gagne	59	10	12	22	17
Joe Micheletti	41	5	17	22	32
Stan Weir	61	5	16	21	23
Bob Lorimer	79	5	15	20	68
Joe Cirella	65	7	12	19	52
Kevin Maxwell	46	6	9	15	52
Joel Quenneville	64	5	10	15	55
Veli Pekka Ketola	44	9	5	14	4
Graeme Nicolson	41	2	7	9	51
Mike Kitchen	63	1	8	9	60
John Wensink	57	5	3	8	152

Detroit Red Wings

	GP	G	A	Pts	PIM
Mark Osborne	80	26	41	67	61
Reed Larson	80	21	39	60	112
Mike Blaisdell	80	23	32	55	48
Walt McKechnie	74	18	37	55	35
John Ogrodnick	80	28	26	54	28
Willie Huber	74	15	30	45	98
Danny Gare	59	20	24	44	99
Mark Kirton	74	14	28	42	62
Vaclav Nedomansky	68	12	28	40	22
Greg Smith	69	10	22	32	79
Eric Vail	58	14	15	29	35
Paul Woods	75	10	17	27	48
Derek Smith	61	9	15	24	12
Don Murdoch	49	9	13	22	23
Jim Schoenfeld	52	8	11	19	99
Ted Nolan	41	4	13	17	45
John Barrett	69	1	12	13	93

Edmonton Oilers

	GP	G	A	Pts	PIM
Wayne Gretzky	80	92	120	212	26
Glenn Anderson	80	38	67	105	71
Paul Coffey	80	29	60	89	106
Mark Messier	78	50	38	88	119
Jari Kurri	71	32	54	86	32
Dave Lumley	66	32	42	74	96
Risto Siltanen	63	15	48	63	24
Matti Hagman	72	21	38	59	18
Pat Hughes	68	24	22	46	99
Kevin Lowe	80	9	31	40	63
Dave Hunter	63	16	22	38	63
Laurie Boschman	65	11	22	33	187
Lee Fogolin	80	4	25	29	154
Brett Callighen	46	8	19	27	28
Dave Semenko	59	12	12	24	194
Garry Lariviere	62	1	21	22	41
Garry Unger	46	7	13	20	69
Charlie Huddy	41	4	11	15	48

Hartford Whalers

	GP	G	A	Pts	PIM
Blaine Stoughton	80	52	39	91	57
Pierre Larouche	67	34	37	71	12
Doug Sulliman	77	29	40	69	39
Ron Francis	59	25	43	68	51
Mark Howe	76	8	45	53	18
Garry Howatt	80	18	32	50	242
Rick Meagher	65	24	19	43	51
Chris Kotsopoulos	68	13	20	33	147

	GP	G	A	Pts	PIM
Blake Wesley	78	9	18	27	123
Don Nachbaur	77	5	21	26	117
Warren Miller	74	10	12	22	68
Dave Keon	78	8	11	19	6
Mark Renaud	48	1	17	18	39
Paul Shmyr	66	1	11	12	134
Jack McIlhargey	50	1	5	6	60
Russ Anderson	56	1	4	5	183

Los Angeles Kings

	GP	G	A	Pts	PIM
Marcel Dionne	78	50	67	117	50
Dave Taylor	78	39	67	106	130
Jim Fox	77	30	38	68	23
Larry Murphy	79	22	44	66	95
Steve Bozek	71	33	23	56	68
Mark Hardy	77	6	39	45	130
Charlie Simmer	50	15	24	39	42
Greg Terrion	61	15	22	37	23
Dan Bonar	79	13	23	36	111
Doug Smith	80	16	14	30	64
Ian Turnbull	54	11	17	28	89
Steve Jensen	45	8	19	27	19
John Kelly	70	12	11	23	100
Jerry Korab	50	5	13	18	91
Dean Hopkins	41	2	13	15	102
Dave Lewis	64	1	13	14	75
Jay Wells	60	1	8	9	145

Minnesota North Stars

	GP	G	A	Pts	PIM
Bobby Smith	80	43	71	114	84
Dino Ciccarelli	76	55	52	107	138
Neal Broten	73	38	59	97	42
Steve Payne	74	33	44	77	76
Craig Hartsburg	76	17	60	77	115
Al MacAdam	79	18	43	61	37
Steve Christoff	69	26	30	56	14
Brad Palmer	72	22	23	45	18
Tom McCarthy	40	12	30	42	36
Tim Young	49	10	31	41	67
Gordie Roberts	79	4	30	34	119
Brad Maxwell	51	10	21	31	96
Mark Johnson	56	12	13	25	40
Kent Erik Andersson	70	9	12	21	18
Anders Hakansson	72	12	4	16	29
Fred Barrett	69	1	15	16	89
Curt Giles	74	3	12	15	87
Jack Carlson	57	8	4	12	103
Bill Nyrop	42	4	8	12	35

Montreal Canadiens

	GP	G	A	Pts	PIM
Keith Acton	78	36	52	88	88
Guy Lafleur	66	27	57	84	24
Mark Napier	80	40	41	81	14
Mario Tremblay	80	33	40	73	66
Pierre Mondou	73	35	33	68	57
Larry Robinson	71	12	47	59	41
Steve Shutt	57	31	24	55	40
Doug Jarvis	80	20	28	48	20
Bob Gainey	79	21	24	45	24
Rejean Houle	51	11	32	43	34
Rod Langway	66	5	34	39	116
Doug Wickenheiser	56	12	23	35	43
Doug Risebrough	59	15	18	33	116
Brian Engblom	76	4	29	33	76
Mark Hunter	71	18	11	29	143
Robert Picard	62	2	26	28	106
Chris Nilan	49	7	4	11	204
Gilbert Delorme	60	3	8	11	55

N.Y. Islanders

	GP	G	A	Pts	PIM
Mike Bossy	80	64	83	147	22
Bryan Trottier	80	50	79	129	88
John Tonelli	80	35	58	93	57
Clark Gillies	79	38	39	77	75
Denis Potvin	60	24	37	61	83
Bob Bourne	76	27	26	53	77
Duane Sutter	77	18	35	53	100
Mike McEwen	73	10	39	49	50
Bob Nystrom	74	22	25	47	103
Brent Sutter	43	21	22	43	114

	GP	G	A	Pts	PIM
Stefan Persson	70	6	37	43	99
Anders Kallur	58	18	22	40	18
Wayne Merrick	68	12	27	39	20
Tomas Jonsson	70	9	25	34	51
Butch Goring	67	15	17	32	10
Billy Carroll	72	9	20	29	32
Dave Langevin	73	1	20	21	82
Ken Morrow	75	1	18	19	56
Gord Lane	51	0	13	13	98

N.Y. Rangers

	GP	G	A	Pts	PIM
Mike Rogers	80	38	65	103	43
Ron Duguay	72	40	36	76	82
Mark Pavelich	79	33	43	76	67
Ed Johnstone	68	30	28	58	57
Don Maloney	54	22	36	58	73
Reijo Ruotsalainen	78	18	38	56	27
Dave Maloney	64	13	36	49	105
Robbie Ftorek	49	9	33	42	28
Barry Beck	60	9	29	38	111
Dave Silk	64	15	20	35	39
Mikko Leinonen	53	11	19	30	18
Mike Allison	48	7	15	22	74
Tom Laidlaw	79	3	18	21	104
Andre Dore	56	4	16	20	64
Nick Fotiu	70	8	10	18	151
Carol Vadnais	50	5	6	11	45
Ed Hospodar	41	3	8	11	152
Peter Wallin	40	2	9	11	12
Tom Younghans	50	4	5	9	17

Philadelphia Flyers

	GP	G	A	Pts	PIM
Kenny Linseman	79	24	68	92	275
Brian Propp	80	44	47	91	117
Bill Barber	80	45	44	89	85
Ron Flockhart	72	33	39	72	44
Darryl Sittler	73	32	38	70	74
Bobby Clarke	62	17	46	63	154
Ray Allison	51	17	37	54	104
Tim Kerr	61	21	30	51	138
Reggie Leach	66	26	21	47	18
Ilkka Sinisalo	66	15	22	37	22
Behn Wilson	59	13	23	36	135
Paul Holmgren	41	9	22	31	183
Bob Hoffmeyer	57	7	20	27	142
Brad Marsh	83	2	23	25	116
Al Hill	41	6	13	19	58
Glen Cochrane	63	6	12	18	329
Tom Gorence	66	5	8	13	8
Jimmy Watson	76	3	9	12	99
Fred Arthur	74	1	7	8	47

Pittsburgh Penguins

	GP	G	A	Pts	PIM
Rick Kehoe	71	33	52	85	8
Randy Carlyle	73	11	64	75	131
Pat Boutette	80	23	51	74	230
Paul Gardner	59	36	33	69	28
Mike Bullard	75	37	27	64	91
George Ferguson	71	22	31	53	45
Rick MacLeish	74	19	28	47	44
Paul Baxter	76	9	34	43	407
Greg Malone	78	15	24	39	125
Pat Price	77	7	31	38	322
Peter Lee	74	18	16	34	98
Gregg Sheppard	58	11	10	21	35
Ron Stackhouse	76	2	19	21	102
Pat Graham	42	6	8	14	55
Marc Chorney	60	1	6	7	63
Barry Melrose	64	1	5	6	186

Quebec Nordiques

	GP	G	A	Pts	PIM
Peter Stastny	80	46	93	139	91
Real Cloutier	67	37	60	97	34
Marian Stastny	74	35	54	89	27
Michel Goulet	80	42	42	84	48
Anton Stastny	68	26	46	72	16
Dale Hunter	80	22	50	72	272
Wilf Paiement	77	25	46	71	221
Marc Tardif	75	39	31	70	55
Mario Marois	71	11	32	43	161

	GP	G	A	Pts	PIM
Jacques Richard	59	15	26	41	77
Dave Pichette	67	7	30	37	152
Alain Cote	79	15	16	31	82
Pat Hickey	61	15	15	30	36
Pierre Lacroix	68	4	23	27	74
Pierre Aubry	62	10	13	23	27
Normand Rochefort	72	4	14	18	115
Andre Dupont	60	4	12	16	100
Wally Weir	62	3	5	8	173
Jean Hamel	40	1	6	7	32

St. Louis Blues

	GP	G	A	Pts	PIM
Bernie Federko	74	30	62	92	70
Blake Dunlop	77	25	53	78	32
Brian Sutter	74	39	36	75	239
Jorgen Pettersson	77	38	31	69	28
Perry Turnbull	79	33	26	59	161
Joe Mullen	45	25	34	59	4
Mike Zuke	76	13	40	53	41
Wayne Babych	51	19	25	44	51
Jack Brownschidle	80	5	33	38	26
Mike Crombeen	71	19	8	27	32
Larry Patey	70	14	12	26	97
Guy Lapointe	55	1	25	26	76
Rick LaPointe	71	2	20	22	127
Rik Wilson	48	3	18	21	24
Ed Kea	78	2	14	16	62
Bill Baker	49	3	8	11	67
Jim Pavese	42	2	9	11	101
Ralph Klassen	45	3	7	10	6

Toronto Maple Leafs

	GP	G	A	Pts	PIM
Rick Vaive	77	54	35	89	157
Bill Derlago	75	34	50	84	42
John Anderson	69	31	26	57	30
Borje Salming	69	12	44	56	170
Bob Manno	72	9	41	50	67
Terry Martin	72	25	24	49	39
Miroslav Frycer	59	24	23	47	78
Rene Robert	55	13	24	37	37
Rocky Saganiuk	65	17	16	33	49
Jim Benning	74	7	24	31	46
Normand Aubin	43	14	12	26	22
Dan Maloney	44	8	7	15	71
Trevor Johansen	59	4	10	14	73
Fred Boimistruck	57	2	11	13	32
Jim Korn	70	2	10	12	148
Bob McGill	68	1	10	11	263
Ron Zanussi	43	0	8	8	14
Barry Melrose	64	1	5	6	186

Vancouver Canucks

	GP	G	A	Pts	PIM
Thomas Gradin	76	37	49	86	32
Stan Smyl	80	34	44	78	144
Ivan Boldirev	78	33	40	73	45
Curt Fraser	79	28	39	67	175
Ivan Hlinka	72	23	37	60	16
Tony Currie	60	23	25	78	19
Lars Molin	72	15	31	46	10
Kevin McCarthy	71	6	39	45	84
Darcy Rota	51	20	20	40	139
Dave Williams	77	17	21	38	341
Blair MacDonald	59	18	15	33	20
Jim Nill	69	10	14	24	132
Lars Lindgren	75	5	16	21	74
Per-Olov Brasar	53	6	12	18	6
Gary Lupul	41	10	7	17	26
Ron Delorme	59	9	8	17	177
Harold Snepsts	68	3	14	17	153
Marc Crawford	40	4	8	12	29
Colin Campbell	47	0	8	8	131

Washington Capitals

	GP	G	A	Pts	PIM
Dennis Maruk	80	60	76	136	128
Ryan Walter	78	38	49	87	142
Mike Gartner	80	35	45	80	121
Bobby Carpenter	80	32	35	67	69
Chris Valentine	60	30	37	67	92
Bengt Gustafsson	70	26	34	60	40
Darren Veitch	67	9	44	53	54
Greg Theberge	57	5	32	37	49
Bobby Gould	76	21	13	34	73
Rick Green	65	3	25	28	93
Terry Murray	74	3	22	25	60
Doug Hicks	61	3	21	24	66
Gaetan Duchesne	74	9	14	23	46
Torrie Robertson	54	8	13	21	204
Glen Currie	43	7	7	14	14
Timo Blomquist	44	1	11	12	62
Randy Holt	61	2	6	8	259

Winnipeg Jets

	GP	G	A	Pts	PIM
Dale Hawerchuk	80	45	58	103	47
Morris Lukowich	77	43	49	92	102
Dave Christian	80	25	51	76	28
David Babych	79	19	49	68	92
Paul MacLean	74	36	25	61	106
Willy Lindstrom	74	32	27	59	33
Lucien DeBlois	65	25	27	52	87
Thomas Steen	73	15	29	44	42
Bengt Lundholm	66	14	30	44	10
Normand Dupont	62	13	25	38	22
Doug Smail	72	17	18	35	55
Larry Hopkins	41	10	15	25	22
Tim Watters	69	2	22	24	97
Tim Trimper	74	8	8	16	100
Don Spring	78	0	16	16	21
Craig Levie	40	4	9	13	48
Bryan Maxwell	45	1	9	10	110
Serge Savard	47	2	5	7	26

WHA Champions and Trophy Winners

Avco World Trophy
Playoff winner

1973	New England Whalers
1974	Houston Aeros
1975	Houston Aeros
1976	Winnipeg Jets
1977	Quebec Nordiques
1978	Winnipeg Jets
1979	Winnipeg Jets

Gordie Howe Trophy
MVP

1973	Bobby Hull, Winnipeg
1974	Gordie Howe, Houston
1975	Bobby Hull, Winnipeg
1976	Marc Tardif, Quebec
1977	Robbie Ftorek, Phoenix
1978	Marc Tardif, Quebec
1979	Dave Dryden, Edmonton

Hunter Trophy
Leading scorer

1973	Andre Lacroix, Philadelphia
1974	Mike Walton, Minnesota
1975	Andre Lacroix, San Diego
1976	Marc Tardif, Quebec
1977	Real Cloutier, Quebec
1978	Marc Tardif, Quebec
1979	Real Cloutier, Quebec

NCAA Hockey Champions

1948	Michigan
1949	Boston College
1950	Colorado College
1951	Michigan
1952	Michigan
1953	Michigan
1954	Rensselaer Poly
1955	Michigan
1956	Michigan
1957	Colorado College
1958	Denver
1959	North Dakota
1960	Denver
1961	Denver
1962	Michigan Tech
1963	North Dakota
1964	Michigan
1965	Michigan Tech
1966	Michigan State
1967	Cornell
1968	Denver
1969	Denver
1970	Cornell
1971	Boston Univ.
1972	Boston Univ
1973	Wisconsin
1974	Minnesota
1975	Michigan Tech
1976	Minnesota
1977	Wisconsin
1978	Boston Univ.
1979	Minnesota
1980	North Dakota
1981	Wisconsin
1982	North Dakota

NHL Trophy Winners

Ross Trophy
Leading scorer

1982	Wayne Gretzky, Edmonton
1981	Wayne Gretzky, Edmonton
1980	Marcel Dionne, Los Angeles
1979	Bryan Trottier, N.Y. Islanders
1978	Guy Lafleur, Montreal
1977	Guy Lafleur, Montreal
1976	Guy Lafleur, Montreal
1975	Bobby Orr, Boston
1974	Phil Esposito, Boston
1973	Phil Esposito, Boston
1972	Phil Esposito, Boston
1971	Phil Esposito, Boston
1970	Bobby Orr, Boston
1969	Phil Esposito, Boston
1968	Stan Mikita, Chicago
1967	Stan Mikita, Chicago
1966	Bobby Hull, Chicago
1965	Stan Mikita, Chicago
1964	Stan Mikita, Chicago

Norris Trophy
Best defenseman

1982	Doug Wilson, Chicago
1981	Randy Corlyle, Pittsburgh
1980	Larry Robinson, Montreal
1979	Denis Potvin, N.Y. Islanders
1978	Denis Potvin, N.Y. Islanders
1977	Larry Robinson, Montreal
1976	Denis Potvin, N.Y. Islanders
1975	Bobby Orr, Boston
1974	Bobby Orr, Boston
1973	Bobby Orr, Boston
1972	Bobby Orr, Boston
1971	Bobby Orr, Boston
1970	Bobby Orr, Boston
1969	Bobby Orr, Boston
1968	Bobby Orr, Boston
1967	Harry Howell, N.Y. Rangers
1966	Jacques Laperriere, Montreal
1965	Pierre Pilote, Chicago
1964	Pierre Pilote, Chicago

Calder Trophy
Best rookie

1982	Dale Hawerchuk, Winnipeg
1981	Peter Stastny, Quebec
1980	Ray Bourque, Boston
1979	Bob Smith, Minnesota
1978	Mike Bossy, N.Y. Islanders
1977	Willi Plett, Atlanta
1976	Bryan Trottier N.Y. Islanders
1975	Eric Vail, Atlanta
1974	Denis Potvin, N.Y. Islanders
1973	Steve Vickers, N.Y. Rangers
1972	Ken Dryden, Montreal
1971	Gil Perreault, Buffalo
1970	Tony Esposito, Chicago
1969	Danny Grant, Minnesota
1968	Derek Sanderson, Boston
1967	Bobby Orr, Boston
1966	Brit Selby, Toronto
1965	Roger Crozier, Detroit
1964	Jacques Laperriere, Montreal

Hart Trophy
MVP

1982	Wayne Gretzky, Edmonton
1981	Wayne Gretzky, Edmonton
1980	Wayne Gretzky, Edmonton
1979	Bryan Trottier, N.Y. Islanders
1978	Guy Lafleur, Montreal
1977	Guy Lafleur, Montreal
1976	Bobby Clarke, Philadelphia
1975	Bobby Clarke, Philadelphia
1974	Phil Esposito, Boston
1973	Bobby Clarke, Philadelphia
1972	Bobby Orr, Boston
1971	Bobby Orr, Boston
1970	Bobby Orr, Boston
1969	Phil Esposito, Boston
1968	Stan Mikita, Chicago
1967	Stan Mikita, Chicago
1966	Bobby Hull, Chicago
1965	Bobby Hull, Chicago
1964	Jean Beliveau, Montreal

Vezina Trophy
Leading goalie(1)

1982	Billy Smith, N.Y. Islanders
1981	Sevigny, Herron, Larocque, Montreal
1980	Edwards, Sauve, Buffalo
1979	Dryden, Larocque, Montreal
1978	Dryden, Larocque, Montreal
1977	Dryden, Larocque, Montreal
1976	Ken Dryden, Montreal
1975	Bernie Parent, Philadelphia
1974	Tony Esposito, Chicago
	Bernie Parent, Philadelphia
1973	Ken Dryden, Montreal
1972	Esposito, Smith, Chicago
1971	Giacomin, Villemure, N.Y. Rangers
1970	Tony Esposito, Chicago
1969	Hall, Plante, St. Louis
1968	Worsley, Vachon, Montreal
1967	Hall, De Jordy, Chicago
1966	Hodge, Worsley, Montreal
1965	Sawchuck, Bower, Toronto
1964	Charlie Hodge, Montreal

Lady Byng Trophy
Sportsmanship

1982	Rick Middleton, Boston
1981	Rick Kehoe, Pittsburgh
1980	Wayne Gretzky, Edmonton
1979	Bob MacMillan, Atlanta
1978	Butch Goring, Los Angeles
1977	Marcel Dionne, Los Angeles
1976	Jean Ratelle, Boston
1975	Marcel Dionne, Detroit
1974	John Bucyk, Boston
1973	Gilbert Perreault, Buffalo
1972	Jean Ratelle, N.Y. Rangers
1971	John Bucyk, Boston
1970	Phil Goyette, St. Louis
1969	Alex Devecchio, Detroit
1968	Stan Mikita, Chicago
1967	Stan Mikita, Chicago
1966	Alex Devecchio, Detroit
1965	Bobby Hull, Chicago
1964	Ken Wharram, Chicago

Frank Selke Trophy (best defensive forward)—1978-81, Bob Gainey, Montreal; 1982, Steve Kasper, Boston.
(1) Most valuable goalie beginning in 1982.

Curling Champions

Source: North American Curling News

World Champions

Year	Country, skip
1966	Canada, Ron Northcott
1967	Scotland, Chuck Hay
1968	Canada, Ron Northcott
1969	Canada, Ron Northcott
1970	Canada, Don Duguid
1971	Canada, Don Duguid
1972	Canada, Crest Melesnuk
1973	Sweden, Kjell Oscarius
1974	United States, Bud Somerville
1975	Switzerland, Otto Danieli
1976	United States, Bruce Roberts
1977	Sweden, Ragnar Kamp
1978	United States, Bob Nichols
1979	Norway, Kristian Soerum
1980	Canada, Rich Folk
1981	Switzerland, Jurg Tanner
1982	Canada, Al Hackner

U.S. Men's Champions

Year	State, skip
1966	North Dakota, Joe Zbacnik
1967	Washington, Bruce Roberts
1968	Wisconsin, Bud Somerville
1969	Wisconsin, Bud Somerville
1970	North Dakota, Art Tallackson
1971	North Dakota, Dale Dalziel
1972	North Dakota, Bob LaBonte
1973	Massachusetts, Barry Blanchard
1974	Wisconsin, Bud Somerville
1975	Washington, Ed Risling
1976	Minnesota, Bruce Roberts
1977	Minnesota, Bruce Roberts
1978	Wisconsin, Bob Nichols
1979	Minnesota, Scotty Baird
1980	Minnesota, Paul Pustover
1981	Wisconsin, Somerville-Nichols
1982	Wisconsin, Steve Brown

U.S. Ladies Champions

Year	State, skip
1978	Wisconsin, Sandy Robarge
1979	Washington, Nancy Langley
1980	Washington, Sharon Kozai
1981	Washington, Nancy Langley
1982	Illinois, Ruth Schwenker

NCAA Wrestling Champions

Year	Champion
1963	Oklahoma
1964	Oklahoma State
1965	Iowa State
1966	Oklahoma State
1967	Michigan State
1968	Oklahoma State
1969	Iowa State
1970	Iowa State
1971	Oklahoma State
1972	Iowa State
1973	Iowa State
1974	Oklahoma
1975	Iowa
1976	Iowa
1977	Iowa State
1978	Iowa
1979	Iowa
1980	Iowa
1981	Iowa
1982	Iowa

National Basketball Association, 1981-82

Final Standings

Eastern Conference

Atlantic Division

Club	W	L	Pct	GB
Boston	63	19	.768	.....
Philadelphia	58	24	.707	5
New Jersey	44	38	.537	19
Washington	43	39	.524	20
New York	33	49	.402	31

Central Division

Club	W	L	Pct	GB
Milwaukee	55	27	.671	.....
Atlanta	42	40	.512	13
Detroit	39	43	.476	16
Indiana	35	47	.427	20
Chicago	34	48	.415	21
Cleveland	15	67	.183	40

Western Conference

Midwest Division

Club	W	L	Pct	GB
San Antonio	48	34	.585	.....
Denver	46	36	.561	2
Houston	46	36	.561	2
Kansas City	30	52	.366	18
Dallas	28	54	.341	20
Utah	25	57	.305	23

Pacific Division

Club	W	L	Pct.	GB
Los Angeles	57	25	.695	.....
Seattle	52	30	.634	5
Phoenix	46	36	.561	11
Golden State	45	37	.549	12
Portland	42	40	.512	15
San Diego	17	65	.207	40

NBA Playoff Results

Washington defeated New Jersey 2 games to 0.
Philadelphia defeated Atlanta 2 games to 0.
Seattle defeated Houston 2 games to 1.
Phoenix defeated Denver 2 games to 1.
Boston defeated Washington 4 games to 1.
Philadelphia defeated Milwaukee 4 games to 2.
Los Angeles defeated Phoenix 4 games to 0.
San Antonio defeated Seattle 4 games to 1.
Philadelphia defeated Boston 4 games to 3.
Los Angeles defeated San Antonio 4 games to 0.
Los Angeles defeated Philadelphia 4 games to 2.

NBA Champions 1947-1982

	Regular season		Playoffs	
Year	Eastern Conference	Western Conference	Winner	Runner-up
1947	Washington	Chicago	Philadelphia	Chicago
1948	Philadelphia	St. Louis	Baltimore	Philadelphia
1949	Washington	Rochester	Minneapolis	Washington
1950	Syracuse	Minneapolis	Minneapolis	Syracuse
1951	Philadelphia	Minneapolis	Rochester	New York
1952	Syracuse	Rochester	Minneapolis	New York
1953	New York	Minneapolis	Minneapolis	New York
1954	New York	Minneapolis	Minneapolis	Syracuse
1955	Syracuse	Ft. Wayne	Syracuse	Ft. Wayne
1956	Philadelphia	Ft. Wayne	Philadelphia	Ft. Wayne
1957	Boston	St. Louis	Boston	St. Louis
1958	Boston	St. Louis	St. Louis	Boston
1959	Boston	St. Louis	Boston	Minneapolis
1960	Boston	St. Louis	Boston	St. Louis
1961	Boston	St. Louis	Boston	St. Louis
1962	Boston	Los Angeles	Boston	Los Angeles
1963	Boston	Los Angeles	Boston	Los Angeles
1964	Boston	San Francisco	Boston	San Francisco
1965	Boston	Los Angeles	Boston	Los Angeles
1966	Philadelphia	Los Angeles	Boston	Los Angeles
1967	Philadelphia	San Francisco	Philadelphia	San Francisco
1968	Philadelphia	St. Louis	Boston	Los Angeles
1969	Baltimore	Los Angeles	Boston	Los Angeles
1970	New York	Atlanta	New York	Los Angeles

	Atlantic	Central	Midwest	Pacific	Winner	Runner-up
1971	New York	Baltimore	Milwaukee	Los Angeles	Milwaukee	Baltimore
1972	Boston	Baltimore	Milwaukee	Los Angeles	Los Angeles	New York
1973	Boston	Baltimore	Milwaukee	Los Angeles	New York	Los Angeles
1974	Boston	Capital	Milwaukee	Los Angeles	Boston	Milwaukee
1975	Boston	Washington	Chicago	Golden State	Golden State	Washington
1976	Boston	Cleveland	Milwaukee	Golden State	Boston	Phoenix
1977	Philadelphia	Houston	Denver	Los Angeles	Portland	Philadelphia
1978	Philadelphia	San Antonio	Denver	Portland	Washington	Seattle
1979	Washington	San Antonio	Kansas City	Seattle	Seattle	Washington
1980	Boston	Atlanta	Milwaukee	Los Angeles	Los Angeles	Philadelphia
1981	Boston	Milwaukee	San Antonio	Phoenix	Boston	Houston
1982	Boston	Milwaukee	San Antonio	Phoenix	Los Angeles	Philadelphia

NBA All League Team in 1982

First team	Position	Second team
Julius Erving, Philadelphia	Forward	Alex English, Denver
Larry Bird, Boston	Forward	Bernard King, Golden State
Moses Malone, Houston	Center	Robert Parish, Boston
Gus Williams, Seattle	Guard	Magic Johnson, Los Angeles
George Gervin, San Antonio	Guard	Sidney Moncrief, Milwaukee

Final Statistics

Individual Scoring Leaders

(Minimum: 70 games played or 1400 points)

	G	Pts	Avg
Gervin, San Antonio	79	2551	32.3
Malone, Houston	81	2520	31.1
Dantley, Utah	81	2457	30.3
English, Denver	82	2082	25.4
Erving, Philadelphia	81	1974	24.4
Abdul-Jabbar, Los Angeles	76	1818	23.9
Williams, Seattle	80	1875	23.4
King, Golden State	79	1833	23.2
Free, Golden State	78	1789	22.9
Bird, Boston	77	1761	22.9
Issel, Denver	81	1852	22.9
Long, Detroit	69	1514	21.9
Tripucka, Detroit	82	1772	21.6
Vandeweghe, Denver	82	1760	21.5
Vincent, Dallas	81	1732	21.4
Wilkes, Los Angeles	82	1734	21.1
Thompson, Portland	79	1642	20.8
Mitchell, San Antonio	84	1726	20.5
R. Williams, New Jersey	82	1674	20.4
Parish, Boston	80	1590	19.9

Field Goal Percentage Leaders

(Minimum: 300 FG made)

	FG	FGA	Pct
Gilmore, Chicago	546	837	.652
S. Johnson, Kansas City	395	644	.613
B. Williams, New Jersey	513	881	.582
Abdul-Jabbar, Los Angeles	753	1301	.579
Natt, Portland	515	894	.576
Dantley, Utah	904	1586	.570
King, Golden State	740	1307	.566
B. Jones, Philadelphia	416	737	.564
Cartwright, New York	390	694	.562
Ruland, Washington	420	749	.561

Free Throw Percentage Leaders

(Minimum: 125 FT made)

	FG	FGA	Pct
Macy, Phoenix	152	169	.899
Criss, San Diego	141	159	.887
Long, Detroit	238	275	.865
Gervin, San Antonio	555	642	.864
Bird, Boston	328	380	.863
Silas, Cleveland	246	286	.860
Newlin, New York	126	147	.857
Vandeweghe, Denver	347	405	.857
Grevey, Washington	165	193	.855
Sikma, Seattle	447	523	.855

3-Pt. Field Goal Leaders

(Minimum: 25 made)

	FG	FGA	Pct
Russell, New York	25	57	.439
Toney, Philadelphia	25	59	.424
Macy, Phoenix	39	100	.390
Winters, Milwaukee	36	93	.387
Buse, Indiana	73	189	.386
Dunleavy, Houston	33	86	.384
Aguirre, Dallas	25	71	.352
Grevey, Washington	28	82	.341
Bratz, San Antonio	46	138	.333
Hassett, Golden State	71	214	.332

Assist Leaders

(Minimum: 70 games or 400 assists)

	G	No	Avg
Moore, San Antonio	79	762	9.6
E. Johnson, Los Angeles	78	743	9.5
Cheeks, Philadelphia	79	667	8.4
Archibald, Boston	68	541	8.0
Nixon, Los Angeles	82	652	8.0
Thomas, Detroit	72	565	7.8
Green, Utah	81	630	7.8
Huston, Cleveland	78	590	7.6
Ransey, Portland	78	555	7.1
Richardson, New York	82	572	7.0

Rebound Leaders

(Minimum: 70 games or 800 rebounds)

	G	Tot	Avg
Malone, Houston	81	1188	14.7
Sikma, Seattle	82	1038	12.7
B. Williams, New Jersey	82	1005	12.3
Thompson, Portland	79	921	11.7
Lucas, New York	80	903	11.3
Smith, Golden State	74	813	11.0
Bird, Boston	77	837	10.9
Parish, Boston	80	866	10.8
Gilmore, Chicago	82	835	10.2
Robinson, Phoenix	74	721	9.7

Steals Leaders

(Minimum: 70 games or 125 steals)

	G	No	Avg
E. Johnson, Los Angeles	78	208	2.67
Cheeks, Philadelphia	79	209	2.65
Richardson, New York	82	213	2.60
Buckner, Milwaukee	70	174	2.49
R. Williams, New Jersey	82	199	2.43
Green, Utah	81	185	2.28
Williams, Seattle	80	172	2.15
Thomas, Detroit	72	150	2.08
Moore, San Antonio	79	163	2.06
Buse, Indiana	82	164	2.00

Blocked Shots Leaders

(Minimum: 70 games or 100 blocked shots)

	G	No	Avg
Johnson, San Antonio	75	234	3.12
Rollins, Atlanta	79	224	2.84
Abdul-Jabbar, Los Angeles	76	207	2.72
Gilmore, Chicago	82	221	2.70
Parish, Boston	80	192	2.40
McHale, Boston	82	185	2.26
Williams, Indiana	82	178	2.17
Tyler, Detroit	82	160	1.95
C. Jones, Philadelphia	81	146	1.80
Erving, Philadelphia	81	141	1.74

1982 NBA Player Draft

The following are the first round picks of the National Basketball Assn.

Los Angeles—James Worthy, North Carolina
San Diego—Terry Cummings, DePaul
Utah—Dominique Wilkins, Georgia
Dallas—Bill Garnett, Wyoming
Kansas City—LaSalle Thompson, Texas
New York—Trent Tucker, Minnesota
Chicago—Quintin Dailey, San Francisco
Indiana—Clark Kellogg, Ohio State
Detroit—Cliff Levingston, Wichita State
Atlanta—Keith Edmonson, Purdue
Portland—Lafayette Lever, Arizona State
Cleveland—John Bagley, Boston College
New Jersey—Eric Floyd, Georgetown
Golden State—Lester Conner, Oregon State
Phoenix—David Thirdkill, Bradley
Houston—Terry Teagle, Baylor
Kansas City—Brooke Steppe, Georgia Tech
Detroit—Ricky Pierce, Rice
Denver—Rob Williams, Houston
Milwaukee—Paul Pressey, Tulsa
New Jersey—Eddie Phillips, Alabama
Philadelphia—Mark McNamara, California
Boston—Darren Tillis, Cleveland State

NBA Team Statistics in 1981-82

Offense

Team	Field Goals Made	Field Goals Att	Field Goals Pct	Free Throws Made	Free Throws Att	Free Throws Pct	Rebounds Off	Rebounds Def	Rebounds Tot	Scoring Pts	Scoring Avg
Denver	3980	7656	.520	2371	2978	.796	1149	2443	3592	10371	126.5
Los Angeles	3919	7585	.517	1549	2161	.717	1258	2505	3763	9400	114.6
San Antonio	3698	7613	.486	1812	2335	.776	1253	2537	3790	9272	113.1
Boston	3657	7334	.499	1817	2457	.740	1253	2489	3742	9180	112.0
Philadelphia	3616	6974	.518	1846	2471	.747	1031	2389	3420	9119	111.2
Detroit	3561	7391	.482	1938	2581	.751	1298	2345	3643	9112	111.1
Utah	3679	7446	.494	1714	2282	.751	1147	2362	3509	9094	110.9
Golden State	3646	7349	.496	1709	2382	.717	1282	2452	3734	9092	110.9
Portland	3629	7187	.505	1719	2387	.720	1142	2355	3497	9006	109.8
San Diego	3552	7101	.500	1693	2341	.723	1131	2196	3327	8896	108.5
Milwaukee	3544	7015	.505	1753	2329	.753	1167	2415	3582	8890	108.4
Seattle	3505	7178	.488	1747	2362	.740	1103	2544	3647	8795	107.3
Kansas City	3604	7284	.495	1551	2158	.719	1086	2276	3362	8785	107.1
New Jersey	3501	7227	.484	1714	2354	.728	1194	2320	3514	8746	106.7
Chicago	3369	6728	.501	1951	2545	.767	1125	2525	3650	8743	106.6
New York	3523	7178	.491	1603	2171	.738	1168	2273	3441	8707	106.2
Phoenix	3508	7140	.491	1635	2157	.758	1123	2517	3640	8705	106.2
Houston	3504	7366	.476	1622	2225	.729	1403	2284	3687	8680	105.9
Dallas	3390	7224	.469	1740	2366	.735	1213	2228	3441	8575	104.6
Washington	3400	7168	.474	1626	2105	.772	1047	2583	3630	8485	103.5
Cleveland	3405	7334	.464	1628	2179	.747	1190	2170	3360	8463	103.2
Indiana	3332	7164	.465	1612	2176	.741	1141	2372	3513	8379	102.2
Atlanta	3210	6776	.474	1833	2387	.768	1135	2368	3503	8281	101.0

Defense

Allowed by	Field Goals Made	Field Goals Att	Field Goals Pct	Rebounds Off	Rebounds Def	Rebounds Tot	Miscellaneous Steals	Miscellaneous Blk Sh	Scoring Pts	Scoring Avg	Scoring Dif
Atlanta	3150	6709	.470	1135	2388	3523	578	434	8237	100.5	+0.5
Washington	3362	7229	.465	1110	2516	3626	624	543	8413	102.6	+0.9
Phoenix	3350	7186	.466	1158	2366	3524	775	360	8422	102.7	+3.5
Milwaukee	3297	7066	.467	1172	2155	3327	720	350	8441	102.9	+5.5
Seattle	3411	7407	.461	1241	2420	3661	660	311	8456	103.1	+4.1
Indiana	3470	7062	.491	1204	2598	3802	678	397	8532	104.0	−1.9
Philadelphia	3371	7083	.476	1289	2344	3633	702	470	8649	105.5	+5.7
Boston	3490	7429	.470	1193	2247	3440	681	367	8657	105.6	+6.4
Houston	3566	7180	.497	1170	2304	3474	678	353	8683	105.9	+0.0
New Jersey	3343	6934	.482	1142	2346	3488	832	539	8690	106.0	+0.7
Chicago	3659	7388	.495	1134	2225	3359	807	469	8909	108.6	−2.0
New York	3541	7018	.505	1125	2366	3491	703	358	8926	108.9	−2.7
Dallas	3530	6953	.508	1108	2361	3469	643	509	8938	109.0	−4.4
Portland	3637	7293	.499	1221	2367	3588	708	427	8957	109.2	+0.6
Los Angeles	3745	7679	.488	1275	2255	3530	718	435	9001	109.8	+4.9
Golden State	3555	7250	.490	1112	2407	3519	661	393	9007	109.8	+1.0
Kansas City	3493	6984	.500	1171	2552	3723	707	450	9039	110.2	−3.1
San Antonio	3566	7385	.483	1141	2434	3585	611	429	9083	110.8	+2.3
Cleveland	3608	7044	.512	1125	2529	3654	655	480	9161	111.7	−8.5
Detroit	3749	7362	.509	1159	2434	3593	782	581	9187	112.0	−0.9
San Diego	3739	7105	.526	1033	2276	3309	772	487	9502	115.9	−7.4
Utah	3835	7530	.509	1253	2599	3852	663	420	9558	116.6	−5.7
Denver	4265	8142	.524	1358	2459	3817	749	569	10328	126.0	+0.5

NBA Most Valuable Player

1956 Bob Pettit, St. Louis
1957 Bob Cousy, Boston
1958 Bill Russell, Boston
1959 Bob Pettit, St. Louis
1960 Wilt Chamberlain, Philadelphia
1961 Bill Russell, Boston
1962 Bill Russell, Boston
1963 Bill Russell, Boston
1964 Oscar Robertson, Cincinnati
1965 Bill Russell, Boston
1966 Wilt Chamberlain, Philadelphia
1967 Wilt Chamberlain, Philadelphia
1968 Wilt Chamberlain, Philadelphia
1969 Wes Unseld, Baltimore
1970 Willis Reed, New York
1971 Lew Alcindor, Milwaukee
1972 Kareem Abdul-Jabbar (Alcindor), Milwaukee
1973 Dave Cowens, Boston
1974 Kareem Abdul-Jabbar, Milwaukee
1975 Bob McAdoo, Buffalo
1976 Kareem Abdul-Jabbar, Los Angeles
1977 Kareem Abdul-Jabbar, Los Angeles
1978 Bill Walton, Portland
1979 Moses Malone, Houston
1980 Kareem Abdul-Jabbar, Los Angeles
1981 Julius Erving, Philadelphia
1982 Moses Malone, Houston

NBA Rookie of the Year

1954 Don Meineke, Ft. Wayne
1955 Ray Felix, Baltimore
1956 Maurice Stokes, Rochester
1957 Tom Heinsohn, Boston
1958 Woody Sauldsberry, Philadelphia
1959 Elgin Baylor, Minnesota
1960 Wilt Chamberlain, Philadelphia
1961 Oscar Robertson, Cincinnati
1962 Walt Bellamy, Chicago
1963 Terry Dischinger, Chicago
1964 Jerry Lucas, Cincinnati
1965 Willis Reed, New York
1966 Rick Barry, San Francisco
1967 Dave Bing, Detroit
1968 Earl Monroe, Baltimore
1969 Wes Unseld, Baltimore
1970 Lew Alcindor, Milwaukee
1971 Dave Cowens, Boston; Geoff Petrie, Portland (tie)
1972 Sidney Wicks, Portland
1973 Bob McAdoo, Buffalo
1974 Ernie DiGregorio, Buffalo
1975 Keith Wilkes, Golden State
1976 Alvan Adams, Phoenix
1977 Adrian Dantley, Buffalo
1978 Walter Davis, Phoenix
1979 Phil Ford, Kansas City
1980 Larry Bird, Boston
1981 Darrell Griffith, Utah
1982 Buck Williams, New Jersey

NBA Scoring Leaders

Year	Scoring champion	Pts	Avg
1947	Joe Fulks, Philadelphia	1,389	23.2
1948	Max Zaslofsky, Chicago	1,007	21.0
1949	George Mikan, Minneapolis	1,698	28.3
1950	George Mikan, Minneapolis	1,865	27.4
1951	George Mikan, Minneapolis	1,932	28.4
1952	Paul Arizin, Philadelphia	1,674	25.4
1953	Neil Johnston, Philadelphia	1,564	22.3
1954	Neil Johnston, Philadelphia	1,759	24.4
1955	Neil Johnston, Philadelphia	1,631	22.7
1956	Bob Pettit, St. Louis	1,849	25.7
1957	Paul Arizin, Philadelphia	1,817	25.6
1958	George Yardley, Detroit	2,001	27.8
1959	Bob Pettit, St. Louis	2,105	29.2
1960	Wilt Chamberlain, Philadelphia	2,707	37.9
1961	Wilt Chamberlain, Philadelphia	3,033	38.4
1962	Wilt Chamberlain, Philadelphia	4,029	50.4
1963	Wilt Chamberlain, San Francisco	3,586	44.8
1964	Wilt Chamberlain, San Francisco	2,948	36.5
1965	Wilt Chamberlain, San Fran., Phila.	2,534	34.7
1966	Wilt Chamberlain, Philadelphia	2,649	33.5
1967	Rick Barry, San Francisco	2,775	35.6
1968	Dave Bing, Detroit	2,142	27.1
1969	Elvin Hayes, San Diego	2,327	28.4
1970	Jerry West, Los Angeles	2,309	31.2
1971	Lew Alcindor, Milwaukee	2,596	31.7
1972	Kareem Abdul-Jabar (Alcindor), Milwaukee	2,822	34.8
1973	Nate Archibald, Kansas City-Omaha	2,719	34.0
1974	Bob McAdoo, Buffalo	2,261	30.6
1975	Bob McAdoo, Buffalo	2,831	34.5
1976	Bob McAdoo, Buffalo	2,427	31.1
1977	Pete Maravich, New Orleans	2,273	31.1
1978	George Gervin, San Antonio	2,232	27.2
1979	George Gervin, San Antonio	2,365	29.6
1980	George Gervin, San Antonio	2,585	33.1
1981	Adrian Dantley, Utah	2,452	30.7
1982	George Gervin, San Antonio	2,551	32.3

NBA All-Defensive Team in 1982

First team	Position	Second team
Bobby Jones, Philadelphia	Forward	Larry Bird, Boston
Dan Roundfield, Atlanta	Forward	Lonnie Shelton, Seattle
Caldwell Jones, Philadelphia	Center	Jack Sikma, Seattle
Michael Cooper, Las Angeles	Guard	Quinn Buckner, Milwaukee
Dennis Johnson, Phoenix	Guard	Sidney Moncrief, Milwaukee

Basketball Hall of Fame

Springfield, Mass.

Players
Arizin, Paul
Baylor, Elgin
Beckman, John
Borgmann, Bennie
Brennan, Joseph
Barlow, Thomas
Chamberlain, Wilt
Cooper, Charles
Cousy, Bob
Davies, Bob
DeBernardi, Forrest
Dehnert, Dutch
Endacott, Paul
Foster, Bud
Friedman, Max
Fulks, Joe
Gale, Lauren
Gola, Tom
Greer, Hal
Gruenig, Ace
Hagan, Cliff
Hanson, Victor
Holman, Nat
Hyatt, Chuck
Johnson, William
Krause, Moose
Kurland, Bob
Lapchick, Joe
Lucas, Jerry
Luisetti, Hank
Martin, Slater
McCracken, Branch
McCracken, Jack
Macauley, Ed
Mikan, George
Murphy, Stretch
Page, Pat
Pettit, Bob
Phillip, Andy
Pollard, Jim
Ramsey, Frank
Reed, Willis
Robertson, Oscar
Roosma, John S.
Russell, Honey
Russell, Bill
Schayes, Adolph
Schmidt, Ernest
Schommer, John
Sedran, Barney
Sharman, Bill
Steinmetz, Christian
Thompson, Cat
Vandivier, Fuzzy
Wachter, Edward
West, Jerry
Wooden, John

Coaches
Auerbach, Red
Barry, Sam
Blood, Ernest
Cann, Howard
Carlson, Dr. H. C.
Carnevale, Ben
Case, Everett
Dean, Everett
Diddle, Edgar
Drake, Bruce
Gaines, Clarence
Gill, Slats
Hickey, Edgar
Hobson, Howard
Iba, Hank
Julian, Alvin
Keaney, Frank
Keogan, George
Lambert, Ward
Litwack, Harry
Loeffler, Kenneth
Lonborg, Dutch
McCutchan, Arad
McGuire, Frank
McLendon, John
Meyer, Ray
Meanwell, Dr. W. E.
Newell, Pete
Rupp, Adolph
Sachs, Leonard
Shelton, Everett
Wooden, John

Referees
Enright, James
Hepbron, George
Hoyt, George
Kennedy, Matthew
Nucatola, John
Quigley, Ernest
Shirley, J. Dallas
Tobey, David
Walsh, David

Contributors
Allen, Phog
Bee, Clair
Brown, Walter
Bunn, John
Douglas, Bob
Duer, Al O.
Fisher, Harry
Gottlieb, Edward
Gulick, Dr. L. H.
Harrison, Lester
Hepp, Dr. Ferenc
Hickox, Edward
Hinkle, Tony
Irish, Ned
Jones, R. W.
Kennedy, Walter
Liston, Emil
Mokray, Bill
Morgan, Ralph
Morgenweck, Frank
Naismith, Dr. James
O'Brien, John
Olsen, Harold
Podoloff, Maurice
Porter, H. V.
Reid, William
Ripley, Elmer
St. John, Lynn
Saperstein, Abe
Schabinger, Arthur
Stagg, Amos Alonzo
Taylor, Chuck
Tower, Oswald
Trester, Arthur
Wells, Clifford

Teams
First Team
Original Celtics
Buffalo Germans
Renaissance

American Basketball Association, 1968-1976

Champions

	Regular season		Playoffs	
Year	Eastern division	Western division	Winner	Runner-up
1968	Pittsburgh	New Orleans	Pittsburgh	New Orleans
1969	Indiana	Oakland	Oakland	Indiana
1970	Indiana	Denver	Indiana	Los Angeles
1971	Virginia	Indiana	Utah	Kentucky
1972	Kentucky	Utah	Indiana	New York
1973	Carolina	Utah	Indiana	Kentucky
1974	New York	Utah	New York	Utah
1975	Kentucky	Denver	Kentucky	Indiana
1976	Denver		New York	Denver

Professional Sports Directory

Baseball

Commissioner's Office
75 Rockefeller Plaza
New York, NY 10019

National League

National League Office
1 Rockefeller Plaza
New York, NY 10020

Atlanta Braves
PO Box 4064
Atlanta, GA 30302

Chicago Cubs
Wrigley Field
Chicago, IL 60613

Cincinnati Reds
100 Riverfront Stadium
Cincinnati, OH 45202

Houston Astros
Astrodome
P.O. Box 288
Houston, TX 77001

Los Angeles Dodgers
Dodger Stadium
1000 Elysian Park Ave.
Los Angeles, CA 90012

Montreal Expos
PO Box 500, Station M
Montreal, Que. H1V 3P2

New York Mets
William A. Shea Stadium
Roosevelt Ave. & 126th St.
Flushing, NY 11368

Philadelphia Phillies
PO Box 7575
Philadelphia, PA 19101

Pittsburgh Pirates
600 Stadium Circle
Pittsburgh, PA 15212

St. Louis Cardinals
Busch Memorial Stadium
250 Stadium Plaza
St. Louis, MO 63102

San Diego Padres
PO Box 2000
San Diego, CA 92120

San Francisco Giants
Candlestick Park
San Francisco, CA 94124

American League

American League Office
280 Park Ave.
New York, NY 10017

Baltimore Orioles
Memorial Stadium
Baltimore, MD 21218

Boston Red Sox
24 Yawkey Way
Boston, MA 02215

California Angels
Anaheim Stadium
2000 State College Blvd.
Anaheim, CA 92803

Chicago White Sox
Comiskey Park
324 W. 35th St.
Chicago, IL 60616

Cleveland Indians
Cleveland Stadium
Cleveland, OH 44114

Detroit Tigers
Tiger Stadium
Detroit, MI 48216

Kansas City Royals
Harry S. Truman Sports Complex
PO Box 1969
Kansas City, MO 64141

Milwaukee Brewers
Milwaukee County Stadium
Milwaukee, WI 53214

Minnesota Twins
Hubert H. Humphrey Metrodome
501 Chicago Ave. So.
Minneapolis, MN 44415

New York Yankees
Yankee Stadium
Bronx, NY 10451

Oakland A's
Oakland Coliseum
Oakland, CA 94621

Seattle Mariners
419 2d Ave.
Seattle, WA 98104

Texas Rangers
Arlington Stadium
PO Box 1111
Arlington, TX 76010

Toronto Blue Jays
Box 7777
Adelaide St. PO
Toronto, Ont. M5C 2K7

National Basketball Association

League Office
Olympic Tower
645 5th Ave.
New York, NY 10022

Atlanta Hawks
100 Techwood Drive NW
Atlanta, GA 30303

Boston Celtics
Boston Garden
North Station
Boston, MA 02114

Chicago Bulls
333 North Michigan Ave.
Chicago, IL 60601

Cleveland Cavaliers
The Coliseum
PO Box 355
Richfield, OH 44286

Dallas Mavericks
Reunion Arena
777 Sports St.
Dallas, TX 75207

Denver Nuggets
McNichols Sports Arena
1635 Clay St.
Denver, CO 80204

Detroit Pistons
Pontiac Silverdome
1200 Featherstone
Pontiac, MI 48057

Golden State Warriors
Oakland Coliseum
Oakland, CA 94621

Houston Rockets
The Summit
Houston, TX 77046

Indiana Pacers
Market Square Center
151 N. Delaware
Indianapolis, IN 46204

Kansas City Kings
1800 Genessee
Kansas City, MO 64102

Los Angeles Lakers
The Forum
3900 W. Manchester Blvd.
or PO Box 10
Inglewood, CA 90306

Milwaukee Bucks
901 North 4th St.
Milwaukee, WI 53203

New Jersey Nets
185 E. Union Ave.
E. Rutherford, NJ 07073

New York Knickerbockers
Madison Square Garden Center
4 Pennsylvania Plaza
New York, NY 10001

Philadelphia 76ers
Veterans Stadium
PO Box 25040
Philadelphia, PA 19147

Phoenix Suns
Funk's Greyhound Bldg.
2910 N. Central
Phoenix, AZ 85012

Portland Trail Blazers
Lloyd Bldg.
700 NE Multnomah St.
Portland, OR 97232

San Antonio Spurs
HemisFair Arena
P.O. Box 530
San Antonio, TX 78292

San Diego Clippers
San Diego Sports Arena
3500 Sports Arena Blvd.
San Diego, CA 92110

Seattle SuperSonics
419 Occidental South
Seattle, WA 98104

Utah Jazz
Salt Palace
100 SW Temple
Salt Lake City, UT 84101

Washington Bullets
1 Harry S. Truman Dr.
Landover, MD 20786

National Hockey League

League Headquarters
960 Sun Life Bldg.
Montreal, Quebec H3B 2W2

Boston Bruins
150 Causeway St.
Boston, MA 02114

Buffalo Sabres
Memorial Auditorium
Buffalo, NY 14202

Calgary Flames
P.O. Box 1540
Station M
Calgary, Alta. T2P 3B9

Chicago Black Hawks
1800 W. Madison St.
Chicago, IL 60612

Detroit Red Wings
600 Civic Center Drive
Detroit, MI 48226

Edmonton Oilers
Northlands Coliseum
Edmonton, Alta. T5B 4M9

Hartford Whalers
One Civic Center Plaza
Hartford, CT 06103

Los Angeles Kings
PO Box 10
The Forum
Inglewood, CA 90306

Minnesota North Stars
7901 Cedar Ave. S.
Bloomington, MN 55420

Montreal Canadiens
2313 St. Catherine St., West
Montreal, Quebec H3H 1N2

New Jersey Devils
Brendan Byrne Arena
E. Rutherford, NJ 07073

New York Islanders
Nassau Coliseum
Uniondale, NY 11553

New York Rangers
Madison Square Garden
4 Pennsylvania Plaza
New York, NY 10001

Philadelphia Flyers
The Spectrum
Pattison Place
Philadelphia, PA 19148

Pittsburgh Penguins
Civic Arena
Pittsburgh, PA 15219

Quebec Nordiques
5555 3ieme Ave. Ouest
Charlesbourg, Que. G1H 6R1

St. Louis Blues
5700 Oakland Ave.
St. Louis, MO 63110

Toronto Maple Leafs
60 Carlton St.
Toronto, Ont. M5B 1L1

Vancouver Canucks
100 North Renfrew St.
Vancouver, B.C. V5K 3N7

Washington Capitals
Capital Centre
Landover, MD 20786

Winnipeg Jets
15-1430 Maroons Road
Winnipeg, Man. R3G 0L5

National Football League

League Office
410 Park Avenue
New York, NY 10022

Atlanta Falcons
Suwanee Road
Suwanee, GA 30174

Baltimore Colts
P.O. Box 2000
Owings Mills, MD 21117

Buffalo Bills
1 Bills Drive
Orchard Park, NY 14127

Chicago Bears
55 E. Jackson
Chicago, IL 60604

Cincinnati Bengals
200 Riverfront Stadium
Cincinnati, OH 45202

Cleveland Browns
Cleveland Stadium
Cleveland, OH 44114

Dallas Cowboys
6116 North Central Expressway
Dallas, TX 75206

Denver Broncos
5700 Logan St.
Denver, CO 80216

Detroit Lions
1200 Featherstone Rd.
Box 4200
Pontiac, MI 48057

Green Bay Packers
1265 Lombardi Ave.
Green Bay, WI 54303

Houston Oilers
P.O. Box 1516
Houston, TX 77001

Kansas City Chiefs
1 Arrowhead Drive
Kansas City, MO 64129

Los Angeles Rams
2327 W. Lincoln Ave.
Anaheim, CA 92801

Miami Dolphins
3550 Biscayne Blvd.
Miami, FL 33137

Minnesota Vikings
9520 Viking Dr.
Eden Prairie, MN 55344

New England Patriots
Schaefer Stadium
Foxboro, MA 02035

New Orleans Saints
1500 Poydras St.
New Orleans, LA 70112

New York Giants
Giants Stadium
E. Rutherford, NJ 07073

New York Jets
598 Madison Ave.
New York, NY 10022

*Oakland Raiders
7850 Edgewater Drive
Oakland, CA 94621

Philadelphia Eagles
Veterans Stadium
Philadelphia, PA 19148

Pittsburgh Steelers
Three Rivers Stadium
Pittsburgh, PA 15212

St. Louis Cardinals
200 Stadium Plaza
St. Louis, MO 63102

San Diego Chargers
P.O. Box 20666
San Diego, CA 92120

San Francisco 49ers
711 Nevada St.
Redwood City, CA 94061

Seattle Seahawks
5305 Lake Washington Blvd.
Kirkland, WA 98033

Tampa Bay Buccaneers
1 Buccaneer Place
Tampa, FL 33607

Washington Redskins
PO Box 17247
Dulles Intl. Airport
Washington, DC 20041

*Will play in Los Angeles in 1982.

North American Soccer League

League Office
1133 Ave. of the Americas
New York, NY 10036

Chicago Sting
Suite 1525
333 N. Michigan Ave.
Chicago, IL 60601

Edmonton Drillers
Suite 200
10736-107 Ave.
Edmonton, Alta. T5H 0W6

Ft. Lauderdale Strikers
1350 North East 56th St.
Ft. Lauderdale, FL 33334

Jacksonville Tea Men
1245 East Adams St.
Ft. Lauderdale, FL 32202

Le Manic de Montreal
1259 Berri St.
Montreal, Que. H2L 4C7

New York Cosmos
44 E. 50th St.
New York, NY 10022

Portland Timbers
910 Southwest 18th
Portland, OR 97205

San Diego Sockers
9449 Friars Road
San Diego, CA 92108

San Jose Earthquakes
800 Charcot Ave.
San Jose, CA 95131

Seattle Sounders
419 Occidental South
Seattle, WA 98104

Tampa Bay Rowdies
2222 N. Westshore Blvd.
Tampa, FL 33607

Toronto Blizzard
Exhibition Stadium
Toronto, Ont. M6K 3C3

Tulsa Roughnecks
PO Box 35190
Tulsa, OK 75135

Vancouver Whitecaps
3683 E. Hastings St.
Vancouver, B.C. V5K 2B1

Canadian Interuniversity Athletic Union Champions

Men

	Basketball	Football	Hockey	Soccer	Swimming, Diving	Volleyball	Wrestling
1978	St. Mary's	Queen's	Alberta	Manitoba	Waterloo	Manitoba	O.U.A.A.
1979	St. Mary's	Acadia	Alberta	Alberta	Waterloo	Saskatchewan	O.U.A.A.
1980	Victoria	Alberta	Alberta	New Brunswick	Toronto	Manitoba	Lakehead
1981	Victoria	Acadia	Moncton	McGill	Toronto	Alberta	Guelph
1982	Victoria		Moncton		Calgary	Calgary	Guelph

Women

	Basketball	Field Hockey	Swimming, Diving	Volleyball	Gymnastics	Track & Field
1978	Laurentian	British Columbia	Acadia	British Columbia	—	—
1979	Laurentian	Toronto	Toronto	Saskatchewan	Alberta	—
1980	Victoria	York	Toronto	Saskatchewan	York	—
1981	Victoria	Toronto	Toronto	Saskatchewan	McMaster	Western Ont.
1982	Victoria		Toronto	Dalhousie	Manitoba	Western Ont.

Kentucky Derby

Churchill Downs, Louisville, Ky.; inaugurated 1875; distance 1-1/4 miles; 1-1/2 miles until 1896. 3-year olds. Times—seconds in fifths.

Year	Winner	Jockey	Trainer	Wt.	Second	Winner's share	Time
1908	Stone Street	A. Pickens	J. W. Hall	117	Sir Cleges	$4,850	2:15.1
1909	Wintergreen	V. Powers	C. Mack	117	Miami	4,850	2:08.1
1910	Donau	F. Herbert	G. Ham	117	Joe Morris	4,850	2:06.2
1911	Meridian	G. Archibald	A. Ewing	117	Governor Gray	4,850	2:05.
1912	Worth	C. H. Shilling	F. M. Taylor	117	Duval	4,850	2:09.2
1913	Donerail	R. Goose	T. P. Hayes	117	Ten Point	5,475	2:04.4
1914	Old Rosebud	J. McCabe	F. D. Weir	114	Hodge	9,125	2:03.2
1915	Regret*	J. Notter	J. Rowe Sr.	112	Pebbles	11,450	2:05.2
1916	George Smith	J. Loftus	H. Hughes	117	Star Hawk	16,600	2:04.3
1917	Omar Khayyam	C. Borel	C. T. Patterson	117	Ticket	9,750	2:04.
1918	Exterminator	W. Knapp	H. McDaniel	114	Escoba	14,700	2:10.4
1919	Sir Barton	J. Loftus	H. G. Bedwell	112	Billy Kelly	20,825	2:09.4
1920	Paul Jones	T. Rice	W. Garth	126	Upset	30,375	2:09.
1921	Behave Yourself	C. Thompson	H. J. Thompson	126	Black Servant	38,450	2:04.1
1922	Morvich	A. Johnson	F. Burlew	126	Bet Mosie	46,775	2:04.3
1923	Zev	E. Sande	D. J. Leary	126	Martingale	53,600	2:05.2
1924	Black Gold	J. D. Mooney	H. Webb	126	Chilhowee	52,775	2:05.1
1925	Flying Ebony	E. Sande	W. B. Duke	126	Captain Hal	52,950	2:07.3
1926	Bubbling Over	A. Johnson	H. J. Thompson	126	Bagenbaggage	50,075	2:03.4
1927	Whiskery	L. McAtee	F. Hopkins	126	Osmand	51,000	2:06.
1928	Reigh Count	C. Lang	B. S. Michell	126	Misstep	55,375	2:10.2
1929	Clyde Van Dusen	L. McAtee	C. Van Dusen	126	Naishapur	53,950	2:10.4
1930	Gallant Fox	E. Sande	J. Fitzsimmons	126	Gallant Knight	50,725	2:07.3
1931	Twenty Grand	C. Kurtsinger	J. Rowe Jr.	126	Sweep All	48,725	2:01.4
1932	Burgoo King	E. James	H. J. Thompson	126	Economic	52,350	2:05.1
1933	Brokers Tip	D. Meade	H. J. Thompson	126	Head Play	48,925	2:06.4
1934	Cavalcade	M. Garner	R. A. Smith	126	Discovery	28,175	2:04.
1935	Omaha	W. Saunders	J. Fitzsimmons	126	Roman Soldier	39,525	2:05.
1936	Bold Venture	I. Hanford	M. Hirsch	126	Brevity	37,725	2:03.3
1937	War Admiral	C. Kurtsinger	G. Conway	126	Pompoon	52,050	2:03.1
1938	Lawrin	E. Arcaro	B. A. Jones	126	Dauber	47,050	2:04.4
1939	Johnstown	J. Stout	J. Fitzsimmons	126	Challedon	46,350	2:03.2
1940	Gallahadion	C. Bierman	R. Waldron	126	Bimelech	60,150	2:05.
1941	Whirlaway	E. Arcaro	B. A. Jones	126	Staretor	61,275	2:01.2
1942	Shut Out	W. D. Wright	J. M. Gaver	126	Alsab	64,225	2:04.2
1943	Count Fleet	J. Longden	G. D. Cameron	126	Blue Swords	60,275	2:04.
1944	Pensive	C. McCreary	B. A. Jones	126	Broadcloth	64,675	2:04.1
1945	Hoop, Jr.	E. Arcaro	I. H. Parke	126	Pot o'Luck	64,850	2:07.
1946	Assault	W. Mehrtens	M. Hirsch	126	Spy Song	96,400	2:06.3
1947	Jet Pilot	E. Guerin	T. Smith	126	Phalanx	92,160	2:06.3
1948	Citation	E. Arcaro	B. A. Jones	126	Coaltown	83,400	2:05.2
1949	Ponder	S. Brooks	B. A. Jones	126	Capot	91,600	2:04.1
1950	Middleground	W. Boland	M. Hirsch	126	Hill Prince	92,650	2:01.3
1951	Count Turf	C. McCreary	S. Rutchick	126	Royal Mustang	98,050	2:02.3
1952	Hill Gail	E. Arcaro	B. A. Jones	126	Sub Fleet	96,300	2:01.3
1953	Dark Star	H. Moreno	E. Hayward	126	Native Dancer	90,050	2:02.
1954	Determine	R. York	W. Molter	126	Hasty Road	102,050	2:03.
1955	Swaps	W. Shoemaker	M. A. Tenney	126	Nashua	108,400	2:01.4
1956	Needles	D. Erb	H. L. Fontaine	126	Fabius	123,450	2:03.2
1957	Iron Liege	W. Hartack	H. A. Jones	126	Gallant Man	107,950	2:02.1
1958	Tim Tam	I. Valenzuela	H. A. Jones	126	Lincoln Road	116,400	2:05.
1959	Tomy Lee	W. Shoemaker	F. Childs	126	Sword Dancer	119,650	2:02.1
1960	Venetian Way	W. Hartack	V. Sovinski	126	Bally Ache	114,850	2:02.2
1961	Carry Back	J. Sellers	J. A. Price	126	Crozier	120,500	2:04.
1962	Decidedly	W. Hartack	H. Luro	126	Roman Line	119,650	2:00.2
1963	Chateaugay	B. Baeza	J. Conway	126	Never Bend	108,900	2:01.4
1964	Northern Dancer	W. Hartack	H. Luro	126	Hill Rise	114,300	2:00.
1965	Lucky Debonair	W. Shoemaker	F. Catrone	126	Dapper Dan	112,000	2:01.1
1966	Kauai King	D. Brumfield	H. Forrest	126	Advocator	120,500	2:02.
1967	Proud Clarion	R. Ussery	L. Gentry	126	Barbs Delight	119,700	2:00.3
1968	Dancer's Image (a)	R. Ussery	H. Forrest	126	Forward Pass	122,600	2:02.1
1969	Majestic Prince	W. Hartack	J. Longden	126	Arts and Letters	113,200	2:01.4
1970	Dust Commander	M. Manganello	D. Combs	126	My Dad George	127,800	2:03.2
1971	Canonero II	G. Avila	J. Arias	126	Jim French	145,500	2:03.1
1972	Riva Ridge	R. Turcotte	L. Laurin	126	No Le Hace	140,300	2:01.4
1973	Secretariat	R. Turcotte	L. Laurin	126	Sham	155,050	1:59.2
1974	Cannonade	A. Cordero	W. C. Stephens	126	Hudson County	274,000	2:04.
1975	Foolish Pleasure	J. Vasquez	L. Jolley	126	Avatar	209,611	2:02.
1976	Bold Forbes	A. Cordero	L. Barrera	126	Honest Pleasure	165,200	2:01.3
1977	Seattle Slew	J. Cruquet	W. H. Turner Jr.	126	Run Dusty Run	214,700	2:02.1
1978	Affirmed	S. Cauthen	L. Barrera	126	Alydar	186,900	2:01.1
1979	Spectacular Bid	R. Franklin	G. Delp	126	General Assembly	228,650	2:02.2
1980	Genuine Risk*	J. Vasquez	L. Jolley	126	Rumbo	250,550	2:02
1981	Pleasant Colony	J. Velasquez	J. Campo	126	Woodchopper	317,200	2:02
1982	Gato del Sol	E. Delahoussaye	E. Gregson	126	Laser Light	428,850	2:02.2

(a) Dancer's Image was disqualified from purse money after tests disclosed that he had run with a pain-killing drug, phenylbutazone, in his system. All wagers were paid on Dancer's Image. Forward Pass was awarded first place money.

The Kentucky Derby has been won five times by two jockeys, Eddie Arcaro, 1938, 1941, 1945, 1948 and 1952; and Bill Hartack, 1957, 1960, 1962, 1964 and 1969; and three times by each of three jockeys, Isaac Murphy, 1884, 1890, and 1891; Earle Sande, 1923, 1925 and 1930, and Willie Shoemaker, 1955, 1959, 1965. *Regret and Genuine Risk are the only fillies to win the Derby.

Preakness

Pimlico, Baltimore, Md.; inaugurated 1873; 1 3-16 miles, 3 yr. olds. Time—seconds in fifths.

Year	Winner	Jockey	Trainer	Wt.	Second	Winner's share	Time
1944	Pensive	C. McCreary	B.A. Jones	126	Platter	$60,075	1:59.1
1945	Polynesian	W.D. Wright	M. Dixon	126	Hoop Jr.	66,170	1:58.4
1946	Assault	W. Mehrtens	M. Hirsch	126	Lord Boswell	96,620	2:01.2
1947	Faultless	D. Dodson	H.A. Jones	126	On Trust	98,005	1:59
1948	Citation	E. Arcaro	H.A. Jones	126	Vulcan's Forge	91,870	2:02.2
1949	Capot	T. Atkinson	J.M. Gaver	126	Palestinian	79,985	1:56
1950	Hill Prince	E. Arcaro	J.H. Hayes	126	Middleground	56,115	1:59.1
1951	Bold	E. Arcaro	P.M. Burch	126	Counterpoint	83,110	1:56.2
1952	Blue Man	C. McCreary	W.C. Stephens	126	Jampol	86,135	1:57.2
1953	Native Dancer	E. Guerin	W.C. Winfrey	126	Jamie K	65,200	1:57.4
1954	Hasty Road	J. Adams	H. Trotsek	126	Correlation	91,600	1:57.2
1955	Nashua	E. Arcaro	J. Fitzsimmons	126	Saratoga	67,550	1:54.3
1956	Fabius	W. Hartack	H.A. Jones	126	Needles	84,250	1:58.2
1957	Bold Ruler	E. Arcaro	J. Fitzsimmons	126	Iron Liege	65,250	1:56.1
1958	Tim Tam	I. Valenzuela	H.A. Jones	126	Lincoln Road	97,900	1:57.1
1959	Royal Orbit	W. Harmatz	R. Cornell	126	Sword Dancer	136,200	1:57
1960	Bally Ache	R. Ussery	H.J. Pitt	126	Victoria Park	121,000	1:57.3
1961	Carry Back	J. Sellers	J.A. Price	126	Globemaster	126,200	1:57.3
1962	Greek Money	J.L. Rotz	V.W. Raines	126	Ridan	135,800	1:56.1
1963	Candy Spots	W. Shoemaker	M.A. Tenney	126	Chateaugay	127,500	1:56.1
1964	Northern Dancer	W. Hartack	H. Luro	126	The Scoundrel	124,200	1:56.4
1965	Tom Rolfe	R. Turcotte	F.Y. Whiteley Jr.	126	Dapper Dan	128,100	1:56.1
1966	Kauai King	D. Brumfield	H. Forrest	126	Stupendous	129,000	1:55.2
1967	Damascus	W. Shoemaker	F.Y. Whiteley Jr.	126	In Reality	141,500	1:55.1
1968	Forward Pass	I. Valenzuela	H. Forrest	126	Out of the Way	142,700	1:56.4
1969	Majestic Prince	W. Hartack	J. Longden	126	Arts and Letters	129,500	1:55.3
1970	Personality	E. Belmonte	J.W. Jacobs	126	My Dad George	151,300	1:56.1
1971	Canonero II	G. Avila	J. Arias	126	Eastern Fleet	137,400	1:54
1972	Bee Bee Bee	E. Nelson	D.W. Carroll	126	No Le Hace	135,300	1:55.3
1973	Secretariat	R. Turcotte	L. Laurin	126	Sham	129,900	1:54.2
1974	Little Current	M. Rivera	L. Rondinello	126	Neopolitan Way	156,000	1:56.3
1975	Master Derby	D. McHargue	W.E. Adams	126	Foolish Pleasure	158,100	1:56.2
1976	Elocutionist	J. Lively	P.T. Adwell	126	Play The Red	129,700	1:55
1977	Seattle Slew	J. Cruguet	W.H. Turner Jr.	126	Iron Constitution	138,600	1:54.2
1978	Affirmed	S. Cauthen	L. Barrera	126	Alydar	136,200	1:54.2
1979	Spectacular Bid	R. Franklin	G. Delp	126	Golden Act	165,300	1:54.1
1980	Codex	A. Cordero	D.W. Lucas	126	Genuine Risk	180,600	1:54.1
1981	Pleasant Colony	J. Velasquez	J. Campo	126	Bold Ego	270,800	1:54.3
1982	Aloma's Ruler	J. Kaenel	J. Lenzini	126	Linkage	209,990	1:55.2

Belmont Stakes

Elmont, N.Y.; inaugurated 1867; 1 ½ miles, 3 year olds. Time—seconds in fifths.

Year	Winner	Jockey	Trainer	Wt.	Second	Winner's share	Time
1944	Bounding Home	G.L. Smith	M. Brady	126	Pensive	$55,000	2:32.1
1945	Pavot	E. Arcaro	O. White	126	Wildlife	52,675	2:30.1
1946	Assault	W. Mehrtens	M. Hirsch	126	Natchez	75,400	2:30.4
1947	Phalanx	R. Donoso	S. Veitch	126	Tide Rips	78,900	2:29.2
1948	Citation	E. Arcaro	H.A. Jones	126	Better Self	77,700	2:28.1
1949	Capot	T. Atkinson	J.M. Gaver	126	Ponder	60,900	2:30.1
1950	Middleground	W. Boland	M. Hirsch	126	Lights Up	61,350	2:28.3
1951	Counterpoint	D. Gorman	S. Veitch	125	Battlefield	82,000	2:29
1952	One Count	E. Arcaro	O. White	126	Blue Man	82,400	2:30.1
1953	Native Dancer	E. Guerin	W.C. Winfrey	126	Jamie K.	82,500	2:28.3
1954	High Gun	E. Guerin	M. Hirsch	126	Fisherman	89,000	2:30.4
1955	Nashua	E. Arcaro	J. Fitzsimmons	126	Blazing Count	83,700	2:29
1956	Needles	D. Erb	H. Fontaine	126	Career Boy	83,600	2:29.4
1957	Gallant Man	W. Shoemaker	J. Nerud	126	Inside Tract	77,300	2:26.3
1958	Cavan	P. Anderson	T.J. Barry	126	Tim Tam	73,440	2:30.1
1959	Sword Dancer	W. Shoemaker	J.E. Burch	126	Bagdad	93,525	2:28.2
1960	Celtic Ash	W. Hartack	T.J. Barry	126	Venetian Way	96,785	2:29.3
1961	Sherluck	B. Baeza	H. Young	126	Globemaster	104,900	2:29.1
1962	Jaipur	W. Shoemaker	W.F. Mulholland	126	Admiral's Voyage	109,550	2:28.4
1963	Chateaugay	B. Baeza	J.P. Conway	126	Candy Spots	101,700	2:30.1
1964	Quadrangle	M. Ycaza	J.E. Burch	126	Roman Brother	110,850	2:28.2
1965	Hail to All	J. Sellers	E. Yowell	126	Tom Rolfe	104,150	2:28.2
1966	Amberoid	W. Boland	L. Laurin	126	Buffle	117,700	2:29.3
1967	Damascus	W. Shoemaker	F.Y. Whiteley Jr.	126	Cool Reception	104,950	2:28.4
1968	Stage Door Johnny	H. Gustines	J.M. Gaver	126	Forward Pass	117,700	2:27.1
1969	Arts and Letters	B. Baeza	J.E. Burch	126	Majestic Prince	104,050	2:28.4
1970	High Echelon	J.L. Rotz	J.W. Jacobs	126	Needles N Pens	115,000	2:34
1971	Pass Catcher	W. Blum	E. Yowell	126	Jim French	97,710	2:30.2
1972	Riva Ridge	R. Turcotte	L. Laurin	126	Ruritania	93,950	2:28
1973	Secretariat	R. Turcotte	L. Laurin	126	Twice A Prince	90,120	2:24
1974	Little Current	M. Rivera	L. Rondinello	126	Jolly Johu	101,970	2:29.1
1975	Avatar	W. Shoemaker	A.T. Doyle	126	Foolish Pleasure	116,160	2:28.1
1976	Bold Forbes	A. Cordero	Laz Barrera	126	McKenzie Bridge	116,850	2:29
1977	Seattle Slew	J. Cruguet	W.H. Turner Jr.	126	Run Dusty Run	109,080	2:29.3
1978	Affirmed	S. Cauthen	Laz Barrera	126	Alydar	110,580	2:26.4
1979	Coastal	R. Hernandez	D.A. Whiteley	126	Golden Act	161,400	2:28.3
1980	Temperence Hill	E. Maple	J. Cantey	126	Genuine Risk	176,220	2:29.4
1981	Summing	G. Martens	Luis Barrera	126	Highland Blade	170,580	2:29
1982	Conquistador Cielo	L. Pincay	W. Stephens	126	Gato Del Sol	159,720	2:28.1

Triple Crown Turf Winners, Jockeys, and Trainers

(Kentucky Derby, Preakness, and Belmont Stakes)

Year	Horse	Jockey	Trainer
1919	Sir Barton	J. Loftus	H. G. Bedwell
1930	Gallant Fox	E. Sande	J. Fitzsimmons
1935	Omaha	W. Sanders	J. Fitzsimmons
1937	War Admiral	C. Kurtsinger	G. Conway
1941	Whirlaway	E. Arcaro	B.A. Jones
1943	Count Fleet	J. Longden	G.D. Cameron
1946	Assault	Mehrtens	M. Hirsch
1948	Citation	E. Arcaro	H.A. Jones
1973	Secretariat	R. Turcotte	L. Laurin
1977	Seattle Slew	J. Cruguet	W.H. Turner Jr.
1978	Affirmed	S. Cauthen	L.S. Barrera

Annual Leading Money-Winning Horses

Year	Horse	Dollars
1944	Pavot	179,040
1945	Busher	273,735
1946	Assault	424,195
1947	Armed	376,325
1948	Citation	709,470
1949	Ponder	321,825
1950	Noor	346,940
1951	Counterpoint	250,525
1952	Crafty Admiral	277,255
1953	Native Dancer	513,425
1954	Determine	328,700
1955	Nashua	752,550
1956	Needles	440,850
1957	Round Table	600,383
1958	Round Table	662,780
1959	Sword Dancer	537,004
1960	Bally Ache	455,045
1961	Carry Back	565,349
1962	Never Bend	402,969
1963	Candy Spots	604,481
1964	Gun Bow	580,100
1965	Buckpasser	568,096
1966	Buckpasser	669,078
1967	Damascus	817,941
1968	Forward Pass	546,674
1969	Arts and Letters	555,604
1970	Personality	444,049
1971	Riva Ridge	503,263
1972	Droll Roll	471,633
1973	Secretariat	860,404
1974	Chris Evert	551,063
1975	Foolish Pleasure	716,278
1976	Forego	491,701
1977	Seattle Slew	641,370
1978	Affirmed	901,541
1979	Spectacular Bid	1,279,334
1980	Temperance Hill	1,130,452
1981	John Henry	1,148,800

Annual Leading Jockey—Money Won

Year	Jockey	Dollars
1950	Eddie Arcaro	1,410,160
1951	Willie Shoemaker	1,329,890
1952	Eddie Arcaro	1,859,591
1953	Willie Shoemaker	1,784,187
1954	Willie Shoemaker	1,876,760
1955	Eddie Arcaro	1,864,796
1956	Bill Hartack	2,343,955
1957	Bill Hartack	3,060,501
1958	Willie Shoemaker	2,961,693
1959	Willie Shoemaker	2,843,133
1960	Willie Shoemaker	2,123,961
1961	Willie Shoemaker	2,690,819
1962	Willie Shoemaker	2,916,844
1963	Willie Shoemaker	2,526,925
1964	Willie Shoemaker	2,649,553
1965	Braulio Baeza	2,582,702
1966	Braulio Baeza	2,951,022
1967	Braulio Baeza	3,088,888
1968	Braulio Baeza	2,835,108
1969	Jorge Velasquez	2,542,315
1970	Laffit Pincay Jr.	2,626,526
1971	Laffit Pincay Jr.	3,784,377
1972	Laffit Pincay Jr.	3,225,827
1973	Laffit Pincay Jr.	4,093,492
1974	Laffit Pincay Jr.	4,251,060
1975	Braulio Baeza	3,695,198
1976	Angel Cordero Jr.	4,709,500
1977	Steve Cauthen	6,151,750
1978	Darrel McHargue	6,029,885
1979	Laffit Pincay Jr.	8,193,535
1980	Chris McCarron	7,663,300
1981	Chris McCarron	8,397,604

Leading Money-Winning Horses

As of Aug., 1982

Horse, year foaled	Sts.	1st	2d	3d	Dollars
John Henry, 1975	65	30	12	7	3,569,610
Spectacular Bid, 1976	30	26	2	1	2,781,607
Affirmed, 1975	29	22	5	1	2,393,818
Kelso, 1957	63	39	12	2	1,977,896
Forego, 1970	57	34	9	7	1,938,957
Round Table, 1954	66	43	8	5	1,749,869
Excellor, 1973	33	15	5	6	1,654,002
Temperence Hill, 1977	31	11	4	2	1,567,650
Dahlia, 1970	48	15	3	7	1,543,139
Buckpasser, 1963	31	25	4	1	1,462,014
Allez France, 1970	21	13	3	1	1,386,146
Secretariat, 1970	21	16	3	1	1,316,808
Nashua, 1952	30	22	4	1	1,288,565
Ancient Title, 1970	57	24	11	9	1,252,791
Susan's Girl, 1969	63	29	14	11	1,251,667

U.S. Thoroughbred Records

Furlongs	Horse, age, weight	Track, state	Date	Time
5	Zip Pocket, 3, 122	Turf Paradise, Ariz.	Apr. 22, 1967	0:55.2
	Big Volume, 4, 120	Fresno District Fair, Cal.	Oct. 15, 1977	0:55.2
5½	Zip Pocket, 3, 129	Turf Paradise, Ariz.	Nov. 19, 1967	1:01.2
6 (¾ mile)	Grey Papa, 6, 116	Longacres, Wash.	Sept. 4, 1972	1:07.1
6½	Best Hitter, 4, 114	Longacres, Wash.	Aug. 24, 1973	1:13.4
	Trooper Seven, 4, 122	Longacres, Wash.	Aug. 10, 1980	1:13.4
7	Rich Cream, 5, 118	Hollywood, Cal.	May 28, 1980	1:19.2
8 (1 mile)	Dr. Fager, 4, 134	Arlington, Ill.	Aug. 24, 1968	1:32.1
8½	Swaps, 4, 130	Hollywood, Cal.	June 23, 1956	1:39
9	Secretariat, 3, 124	Belmont, N.Y.	Sept. 15, 1973	1:45.2
9½	Riva Ridge, 4, 127	Aqueduct, N.Y.	July 4, 1973	1:52.2
10	Spectacular Bid, 4, 126	Santa Anita, Cal.	Feb. 3, 1980	1:57.4
10½	Tempted, 4, 128	Aqueduct, N.Y.	Oct. 12, 1959	2:09
11	Man o' War, 3, 126	Belmont, N.Y.	June 12, 1920	2:14.1
12 (1½ miles)	Secretariat, 3, 126	Belmont, N.Y.	June 9, 1973	2:24
13	Swaps, 4, 130	Hollywood, Cal.	July 25, 1956	2:38.1
14	Noor, 5, 117	Santa Anita, Cal.	Mar. 4, 1950	2:52.4
16 (2 miles)	Kelso, 7, 124	Aqueduct, N.Y.	Oct. 31, 1964	3:19.1

Eclipse Awards in 1981

Sponsored by the Thoroughbred Racing Assn., Daily Racing Form, and the National Turf Writers Assn.

Horse of the Year—John Henry
Best 2-year-old colt—Deputy Minister
Best 2-year-old filly—Before Dawn
Best 3-year-old colt—Pleasant Colony
Best 3-year-old filly—Wayward Lass
Best colt, horse, or gelding (4-year-olds & up)—John Henry
Best filly or mare (4-year-olds & up)—Relaxing
Best male turf horse—John Henry
Best turf filly or mare—De La Rose
Best sprinter—Guilty Conscience
Best steeplechase horse—Zaccio
Best trainer—Ron McAnally
Best jockey—Bill Shoemaker
Best apprentice jockey—Richard Migliore
Best owner—Dotsam Stable
Best breeder—Golden Chance Farm

Lacrosse Champions in 1982

World Lacrosse Championship

At Baltimore, Md., June 25—United States 22, Australia 14.

3d Place

At Baltimore, Md., June 24—Canada 20, England 19.

U.S. Club Lacrosse Association Championship

At Baltimore, Md., June 12—Maryland L.C. 17, Long Island L.C. 14.

NCAA Division I Championship

At Charlottesville, Va., May 29—North Carolina 7, Johns Hopkins 5.

Semi-finals

North Carolina 15, Cornell 8; Johns Hopkins 13, Virginia 9.

Quarter-finals

Cornell 11, Army 9; North Carolina 16, Navy 2; Virginia 15, Adelphi 7; Johns Hopkins 14, Maryland 9.

NCAA Division III Championship

At Geneva, N.Y., May 23—Hobart 9, Washington College 8 (O.T.).

All-Star College Game

At Geneva, N.Y., June 5—North 14, South 9.

Junior College Lacrosse Championship

At Selden, N.Y., May 9—Nassau (N.Y.) C.C. 14, Farmingdale (N.Y.) 8.

Women AIAW Collegiate Lacrosse Championship

Division I—Temple 3, Maryland 2.
Division II—Delaware 10, Lehigh 8.
Division III—Millersville St. (Pa.) 10, Lynchburg (Va.) 3.

Women AIAW Division I All-Star Team

Attack: Francesca DenHartog (Harvard), Candy Finn (Penn State), Marie Schmucker (Temple), Betsy Williams (Penn State), Penny Johnson (Ohio Univ.), Sharon Watson (Maryland).
Defense: Nancy Lock (Pennsylvania), Barb Jordan (Penn State), Roni Pack (Temple), Lynne Baysinger (Maryland), Cathy Gamble (Temple), Chris Paradia (William and Mary).
Goalie: Debby Kelley (Temple), Leslie Campbell (Pennsylvania).

Coach of the Year

USILA Division I—Paul Doherty, Adelphi University.
USILA Division III—Bryan Matthews, Washington College.
Note: No Division II competition.

USILA Division I All America Team

Attack: Jeff Cook (Johns Hopkins), Mike Burnett (UNC), Jim Wilkerson (Md.).
Midfield: Al Ray (Rutgers), Rick Giusto (Va.), Peter Voelkel (UNC), Jeff Homire (UNC).
Defense: Mike Sotir (Va.), George McGeeney (UMBC), John Haus (UNC).
Goal: Tom Sears (UNC).
Note: 4 midfielders selected for the 3 midfield positions.

USILA Division III All America Team

Attack: Jeffrey Kauffman (Washington), Paul Goldsmith (Roanoke), Peter Jenkins (Washington).
Midfield: Mark Darcangelo (Hobart), Dickie Grieves (Washington), Larry Grimaldi (Hobart).
Defense: Mark Fowler (Salisbury St., Md.), Kevin Martin (Hobart), Kevin O'Connor (Washington).
Goal: Guy Van Arsdale (Hobart).

U.S. National Alpine Championships in 1982

Men's Downhill—Cregg Hegg, U.S.
Men's Slalom—Francois Jodoin, Canada
Men's Giant Slalom—not run
Women's Downhill—Cindy Oak, U.S.
Women's Slalom—Tamara McKinney, U.S.
Women's Giant Slalom—not run

The World Cup Winners

	Men		Women		Nation's Cup
1967	Jean Claude Killy, France	1967	Nancy Greene, Canada	1967	France
1968	Jean Claude Killy, France	1968	Nancy Greene, Canada	1968	France
1969	Karl Schranz, Austria	1969	Gertrud Gabl, Austria	1969	Austria
1970	Karl Schranz, Austria	1970	Michele Jacot, France	1970	France
1971	Gustavo Thoeni, Italy	1971	Annemarie Proell, Austria	1971	France
1972	Gustavo Thoeni, Italy	1972	Annemarie Proell, Austria	1972	France
1973	Gustavo Thoeni, Italy	1973	Annemarie Proell, Austria	1973	Austria
1974	Piero Gros, Italy	1974	Annemarie Proell, Austria	1974	Austria
1975	Gustavo Thoeni, Italy	1975	Annemarie Proell, Austria	1975	Austria
1976	Ingemar Stenmark, Sweden	1976	Rose Mittermaier, W. Germany	1976	Italy
1977	Ingemar Stenmark, Sweden	1977	Lise-Marie Morerod, Austria	1977	Austria
1978	Ingemar Stenmark, Sweden	1978	Hanni Wenzel, Liechtenstein	1978	Austria
1979	Peter Luescher, Switzerland	1979	Annemarie Proell Moser, Austria	1979	Austria
1980	Andreas Wenzel, Liechtenstein	1980	Hanni Wenzel, Liechtenstein	1980	Austria
1981	Phil Mahre, U.S.	1981	Marie-Theres Nadig, Switzerland	1981	Switzerland
1982	Phil Mahre, U.S.	1982	Erika Hess, Switzerland	1982	Austria

Professional Sports Arenas

The seating capacity of sports arenas can vary depending on the event being presented. The figures below are the normal seating capacity for basketball. (*) indicates hockey seating capacity.

Name, location	Capacity
Allen County War Memorial, Ft. Wayne	*8,022
Arizona Veteran's Memorial Coliseum, Phoenix	12,660-*12,474
Astrohall, Houston	10,000
Baltimore Civic Center	13,043-*10,200
Boston Garden	15,320-*14,673
Buffalo Memorial Auditorium	17,900-*16,433(a)
Byrne Arena, E. Rutherford, N.J.	20,000-*19,100
Capital Centre, Landover, Md.	19,035-*18,130
Charlotte Coliseum	11,666-*9,575
Checkerdome, St. Louis	20,000-*17,968
Chicago Stadium	17,374-*17,100
Cincinnati Gardens	11,650-*10,606
Cobo Hall, Detroit	11,147
The Coliseum, Richfield Township, Oh.	19,548
Convention Center, San Antonio	10,146
Cow Palace, San Francisco	14,500-*12,195
Fairgrounds Coliseum, Indianapolis	9,479
Freedom Hall, Louisville, Ky.	16,613
Greensboro Coliseum	15,500-*13,280
Halifax Metro Centre	*9,549
Hampton Roads Coliseum, Va.	10,000-*8,200
Hartford Civic Center	*14,510
HemisFair Arena, San Antonio	15,693
Hersheypark Arena, Pa.,	*7,286
International Amphitheatre, Chicago	9,000
Jefferson County Coliseum, Birmingham, Ala.	*16,753
Joe Louis Sports Arena, Detroit	*19,275
Kansas Coliseum, Wichita	*8,906
Kemper Memorial Arena, Kansas City	16,642
Kiel Auditorium, St. Louis	10,574
Kingdome, Seattle	40,192
Los Angeles Forum	17,505-*16,005
Los Angeles Sports Arena	15,333-*11,325
Louisiana Superdome	47,284
Madison Square Garden, New York	19,591-*17,500
Maple Leaf Gardens, Toronto	17,000-*16,485(a)
Market Square Arena, Indianapolis	17,032-*15,861
McNichols Sports Arena, Denver,	17,251-*16,399
Met. Sports Center, Bloomington, Minn.	*15,184
Mid-South Coliseum, Memphis	11,065
Milwaukee Arena	10,938-*8,000
Mobile Municipal Auditorium	13,100
Montreal Forum	*16,074
Myriad, Oklahoma City	*13,263
Nashville Municipal Auditorium	*9,000
Nassau Veterans Memorial Coliseum, Uniondale, N.Y.	*15,160
Norfolk Scope, Va.	10,600-*9,364
Northlands Coliseum, Edmonton	*17,490
Oakland Coliseum Arena	13,237
Olympia Stadium, Detroit	*16,673
Omaha Civic Auditorium	9,144
The Omni, Atlanta	15,785-*15,191
Ottawa Civic Center	*9,355
Pacific Coliseum, Vancouver, B.C.	*15,613
Penn Palestra, Philadelphia	9,200
Pittsburgh Civic Arena	*16,033
Portland Memorial Coliseum	12,666-*10,500
Providence Civic Center	11,619-*10,730
Quebec Coliseum	*15,250
Reunion Arena, Dallas	17,761
Richmond Coliseum, Va.	10,700-*8,400
Riverfront Coliseum, Cincinnati	*15,794
St. Paul Civic Center, Minn.	*15,594
Salt Palace, Salt Lake City	12,143-*10,640
San Diego Sports Arena	13,841-*13,039
Seattle Center Coliseum	14,098
Silverdome, Pontiac, Mich.	22,366
Spectrum, Philadelphia	18,276-*17,077
Springfield Civic Center, Mass.	*7,455
Stampede Corral, Calgary, Alta	*6,492
The Summit, Houston	15,676-*15,256
Tarrant County Convention Center, Ft. Worth	13,500
Tingley Coliseum, Albuquerque	*12,000
Uline Arena, Washington, D. C.	11,000
Veterans Memorial Audit., Des Moines	15,000
Winnipeg Arena	*15,250
Winston-Salem Memorial Coliseum	9,020

(a) includes standees

James E. Sullivan Memorial Trophy Winners

The James E. Sullivan Memorial Trophy, named after the former president of the AAU and inaugurated in 1930, is awarded annually by the AAU to the athlete who "by his or her performance, example and influence as an amateur, has done the most during the year to advance the cause of sportmanship."

Year	Winner	Sport
1930	Bobby Jones	Golf
1931	Barney Berlinger	Track
1932	Jim Bausch	Track
1933	Glen Cunningham	Track
1934	Bill Bonthron	Track
1935	Lawson Little	Golf
1936	Glenn Morris	Track
1937	Don Budge	Tennis
1938	Don Lash	Track
1939	Joe Burk	Rowing
1940	Greg Rice	Track
1941	Leslie MacMitchell	Track
1942	Cornelius Warmerdam	Track
1943	Gilbert Dodds	Track
1944	Ann Curtis	Swimming
1945	Doc Blanchard	Football
1946	Arnold Tucker	Football
1947	John Kelly Jr	Rowing
1948	Robert Mathias	Track
1949	Dick Button	Skating
1950	Fred Wilt	Track
1951	Rev. Robert Richards	Track
1952	Horace Ashenfelter	Track
1953	Dr. Sammy Lee	Diving
1954	Mal Whitfield	Track
1955	Harrison Dillard	Track
1956	Patricia McCormick	Diving
1957	Bobby Joe Morrow	Track
1958	Glenn Davis	Track
1959	Parry O'Brien	Track
1960	Rafer Johnson	Track
1961	Wilma Rudolph Ward	Track
1962	James Beatty	Track
1963	John Pennel	Track
1964	Don Schollander	Swimming
1965	Bill Bradley	Basketball
1966	Jim Ryun	Track
1967	Randy Matson	Track
1968	Debbie Meyer	Swimming
1969	Bill Toomey	Track
1970	John Kinsella	Swimming
1971	Mark Spitz	Swimming
1972	Frank Shorter	Track
1973	Bill Walton	Basketball
1974	Rick Wohlhuter	Track
1975	Tim Shaw	Swimming
1976	Bruce Jenner	Track
1977	John Naber	Swimming
1978	Tracy Caulkins	Swimming
1979	Kurt Thomas	Gymnastics
1980	Eric Heiden	Speed Skating
1981	Carl Lewis	Track

American Power Boat Assn. Gold Cup Champions

Year	Boat	Driver
1970	Miss Budweiser	Dean Chenoweth
1971	Miss Madison	Jim McCormick
1972	Atlas Van Lines	Bill Muncey
1973	Miss Budweiser	Dean Chenoweth
1974	Pay'N Pak	George Henley
1975	Pay 'N Pak	George Henley
1976	Miss U.S.	Tom D'Eath
1977	Atlas Van Lines	Bill Muncey
1978	Atlas Van Lines	Bill Muncey
1979	Atlas Van Lines	Bill Muncey
1980	Miss Budweiser	Dean Chenoweth
1981	Miss Budweiser	Dean Chenoweth
1982	Atlas Van Lines	Chip Hanauer

Annual Results of Major Bowl Games

(Note: Dates indicate the year that the game was played).

Rose Bowl, Pasadena

1902 Michigan 49, Stanford 0
1916 Wash. State 14, Brown 0
1917 Oregon 14, Pennsylvania 0
1918-19 Service teams
1920 Harvard 7, Oregon 6
1921 California 28, Ohio State 0
1922 Wash. & Jeff. 0, California 0
1923 So. California 14, Penn State 3
1924 Navy 14, Washington 14
1925 Notre Dame 27, Stanford 10
1926 Alabama 20, Washington 19
1927 Alabama 7, Stanford 7
1928 Stanford 7, Pittsburgh 6
1929 Georgia Tech 8, California 7
1930 So. California 47, Pittsburgh 14
1931 Alabama 24, Wash. State 0
1932 So. California 21, Tulane 12
1933 So. California 35, Pittsburgh 0
1934 Columbia 7, Stanford 0
1935 Alabama 29, Stanford 13
1936 Stanford 7, So. Methodist 0
1937 Pittsburgh 21, Washington 0
1938 California 13, Alabama 0
1939 So. California 7, Duke 3
1940 So. California 14, Tennessee 0
1941 Stanford 21, Nebraska 13
1942 Oregon St. 20, Duke 16
(at Durham)
1943 Georgia 9, UCLA 0
1944 So. California 29, Washington 0
1945 So. California 25, Tennessee 0
1946 Alabama 34, So. California 14
1947 Illinois 45, UCLA 14
1948 Michigan 49, So. California 0
1949 Northwestern 20, California 14
1950 Ohio State 17, California 14
1951 Michigan 14, California 6
1952 Illinois 40, Stanford 7
1953 So. California 7, Wisconsin 0
1954 Mich. State 28, UCLA 20
1955 Ohio State 20, So. California 7
1956 Mich. State 17, UCLA 14
1957 Iowa 35, Oregon St. 19
1958 Ohio State 10, Oregon 7
1959 Iowa 38, California 12
1960 Washington 44, Wisconsin 8
1961 Washington 17, Minnesota 7
1962 Minnesota 21, UCLA 3
1963 So. California 42, Wisconsin 37
1964 Illinois 17, Washington 7
1965 Michigan 34, Oregon St. 7
1966 UCLA 14, Mich. State 12
1967 Purdue 14, So. California 13
1968 Southern Cal. 14, Indiana 3
1969 Ohio State 27, Southern Cal 16
1970 Southern Cal 10, Michigan 3
1971 Stanford 27, Ohio State 17
1972 Stanford 13, Michigan 12
1973 So. California 42, Ohio State 17
1974 Ohio State 42, So. California 21
1975 So. California 18, Ohio State 17
1976 UCLA 23, Ohio State 10
1977 So. California 14, Michigan 6
1978 Washington 27, Michigan 20
1979 So. California 17, Michigan 10
1980 So. California 17, Ohio State 16
1981 Michigan 23, Washington 6
1982 Washington 28, Iowa 0

Orange Bowl, Miami

1933 Miami (Fla.) 7, Manhattan 0
1934 Duquesne 33, Miami (Fla.) 7
1935 Bucknell 26, Miami (Fla.) 0
1936 Catholic U. 20, Mississippi 19
1937 Duquesne 13, Miss. State 12
1938 Auburn 6, Mich. State 0
1939 Tennessee 17, Oklahoma 0
1940 Georgia Tech 21, Missouri 7
1941 Miss. State 14, Georgetown 7
1942 Georgia 40, TCU 26
1943 Alabama 37, Boston Col. 21
1944 LSU 19, Texas A&M 14
1945 Tulsa 26, Georgia Tech 12
1946 Miami (Fla.) 13, Holy Cross 6
1947 Rice 8, Tennessee 0
1948 Georgia Tech 20, Kansas 14
1949 Texas 41, Georgia 28
1950 Santa Clara 21, Kentucky 13
1951 Clemson 15, Miami (Fla.) 14
1952 Georgia Tech 17, Baylor 14
1953 Alabama 61, Syracuse 6
1954 Oklahoma 7, Maryland 0
1955 Duke 34, Nebraska 7
1956 Oklahoma 20, Maryland 6
1957 Colorado 27, Clemson 21
1958 Oklahoma 48, Duke 21
1959 Oklahoma 21, Syracuse 6
1960 Georgia 14, Missouri 0
1961 Missouri 21, Navy 14
1962 LSU 25, Colorado 7
1963 Alabama 17, Oklahoma 0
1964 Nebraska 13, Auburn 7
1965 Texas 21, Alabama 17
1966 Alabama 39, Nebraska 28
1967 Florida 27, Georgia Tech 12
1968 Oklahoma 26, Tennessee 24
1969 Penn State 15, Kansas 14
1970 Penn State 10, Missouri 3
1971 Nebraska 17, Louisiana St. 12
1972 Nebraska 38, Alabama 6
1973 Nebraska 40, Notre Dame 6
1974 Penn State 16, Louisiana St. 9
1975 Notre Dame 13, Alabama 11
1976 Oklahoma 14, Michigan 6
1977 Ohio State 27, Colorado 10
1978 Arkansas 31, Oklahoma 6
1979 Oklahoma 31, Nebraska 24
1980 Oklahoma 24, Florida St. 7
1981 Oklahoma 18, Florida St. 17
1982 Clemson 22, Nebraska 15

Sugar Bowl, New Orleans

1935 Tulane 20, Temple 14
1936 TCU 3, LSU 2
1937 Santa Clara 21, LSU 14
1938 Santa Clara 6, LSU 0
1939 TCU 15, Carnegie Tech 7
1940 Texas A&M 14, Tulane 13
1941 Boston Col. 19, Tennessee 13
1942 Fordham 2, Missouri 0
1943 Tennessee 14, Tulsa 7
1944 Georgia Tech 20, Tulsa 18
1945 Duke 29, Alabama 26
1946 Oklahoma A&M 33, St. Mary's 13
1947 Georgia 20, No. Carolina 10
1948 Texas 27, Alabama 7
1949 Oklahoma 14, No. Carolina 6
1950 Oklahoma 35, LSU 0
1951 Kentucky 13, Oklahoma 7
1952 Maryland 28, Tennessee 13
1953 Georgia Tech. 24, Mississippi 7
1954 Georgia Tech 42, West Virginia 19
1955 Navy 21, Mississippi 0
1956 Georgia Tech 7, Pittsburgh 0
1957 Baylor 13, Tennessee 7
1958 Mississippi 39, Texas 7
1959 LSU 7, Clemson 0
1960 Mississippi 21, LSU 0
1961 Mississippi 14, Rice 6
1962 Alabama 10, Arkansas 3
1963 Mississippi 17, Arkansas 13
1964 Alabama 12, Mississippi 7
1965 LSU 13, Syracuse 10
1966 Missouri 20, Florida 18
1967 Alabama 34, Nebraska 7
1968 LSU 20, Wyoming 13
1969 Arkansas 16, Georgia 2
1970 Mississippi 27, Arkansas 22
1971 Tennessee 34, Air Force 13
1972 Oklahoma 40, Auburn 22
*1972 (Dec.) Oklahoma 14, Penn State 0
1973 Notre Dame 24, Alabama 23
1974 Nebraska 13, Florida 10
1975 Alabama 13, Penn State 6
1977 (Jan.) Pittsburgh 27, Georgia 3
1978 Alabama 35, Ohio State 6
1979 Alabama 14, Penn State 7
1980 Alabama 24, Arkansas 9
1981 Georgia 17, Notre Dame 10
1982 Pittsburgh 24, Georgia 20
*Penn St. awarded game by forfeit

Cotton Bowl, Dallas

1937 TCU 16, Marquette 6
1938 Rice 28, Colorado 14
1939 St. Mary's 20, Texas Tech 13
1940 Clemson 6, Boston Col. 3
1941 Texas A&M 13, Fordham 12
1942 Alabama 29, Texas A&M 21
1943 Texas 14, Georgia Tech 7
1944 Randolph Field 7, Texas 7
1945 Oklahoma A&M 34, TCU 0
1946 Texas 40, Missouri 27
1947 Arkansas 0, LSU 0
1948 So. Methodist 13, Penn State 13
1949 So. Methodist 21, Oregon 13
1950 Rice 27, No. Carolina 13
1951 Tennessee 20, Texas 14
1952 Kentucky 20, TCU 7
1953 Texas 16, Tennessee 0
1954 Rice 28, Alabama 6
1955 Georgia Tech 14, Arkansas 6
1956 Mississippi 14, TCU 13
1957 TCU 28, Syracuse 27
1958 Navy 20, Rice 7
1959 TCU 0, Air Force 0
1960 Syracuse 23, Texas 14
1961 Duke 7, Arkansas 6
1962 Texas 12, Mississippi 7
1963 LSU 13, Texas 0
1964 Texas 28, Navy 6
1965 Arkansas 10, Nebraska 7
1966 LSU 14, Arkansas 7
1967 Georgia 24, So. Methodist 9
1968 Texas A&M 20, Alabama 16
1969 Texas 36, Tennessee 13
1970 Texas 21, Notre Dame 17
1971 Notre Dame 24, Texas 11
1972 Penn State 30, Texas 6
1973 Texas 17, Alabama 13
1974 Nebraska 19, Texas 3
1975 Penn State 41, Baylor 20
1976 Arkansas 31, Georgia 10
1977 Houston 30, Maryland 21
1978 Notre Dame 38, Texas 10
1979 Notre Dame 35, Houston 34
1980 Houston 17, Nebraska 14
1981 Alabama 30, Baylor 2
1982 Texas 14, Alabama 12

Sun Bowl, El Paso

1936 Hardin Simmons 14, New Mex. St. 14
1937 Hardin-Simmons 34, Texas Mines 6
1938 West Virginia 7, Texas Tech 6
1939 Utah 26, New Mexico 0
1940 Catholic U. 0, Arizona St. 0
1941 Western Reserve 26, Arizona St. 13
1942 Tulsa 6, Texas Tech 0
1943 2d Air Force 13, Hardin-Simmons 7
1944 Southwestern (Tex.) 7, New Mexico 0
1945 Southwestern (Tex.) 35, U. of Mex. 0
1946 New Mexico 34, Denver 24
1947 Cincinnati 38, Virginia Tech 6
1948 Miami (O.) 13, Texas Tech 12
1949 West Virginia 21, Texas Mines 12
1950 Texas Western 33, Georgetown 20
1951 West Texas St. 14, Cincinnati 13
1952 Texas Tech 25, Col. Pacific 14
1953 Col. Pacific 26, Miss. Southern 7
1954 Texas Western 37, Miss. Southern 14
1955 Texas Western 47, Florida St. 20
1956 Wyoming 21, Texas Tech 14
1957 Geo. Washington 13, Tex. Western 0
1958 Louisville 34, Drake 20
1959 Wyoming 14, Hardin-Simmons 6
1960 New Mexico St. 28, No. Texas St. 8
1961 New Mexico St. 20, Utah State 13
1962 Villanova 17, Wichita 9
1963 West Texas St. 15, Ohio U. 14
1964 Oregon 21, So. Methodist 14
1965 Georgia 7, Texas Tech 0
1966 Texas Western 13, TCU 12
1967 Wyoming 28, Florida St. 20
1968 UTex El Paso 14, Mississippi 7
1969 Auburn 34, Arizona 10
1969 (Dec.) Nebraska 45, Georgia 6
1970 Georgia Tech. 17, Texas Tech. 9
1971 LSU 33, Iowa State 15
1972 North Carolina 32, Texas Tech 28
1973 Missouri 34, Auburn 17
1974 Mississippi St. 26, No. Carolina 24
1975 Pittsburgh 33, Kansas 19
1977 (Jan.) Texas A&M 37, Florida 14
1977 (Dec.) Stanford 24, Louisiana St. 14
1978 Texas 42, Maryland 0
1979 Washington 14, Texas 7
1980 Nebraska 31, Mississippi St. 17
1981 Oklahoma 40, Houston 14

Gator Bowl, Jacksonville

1946 Wake Forest 26, So. Carolina 14
1947 Oklahoma 34, N.C. State 13
1948 Maryland 20, Georgia 20
1949 Clemson 24, Missouri 23
1950 Maryland 20, Missouri 7
1951 Wyoming 20, Wash. & Lee 7
1952 Miami (Fla.) 14, Clemson 0
1953 Florida 14, Tulsa 13
1954 Texas Tech 35, Auburn 13
1955 Auburn 33, Baylor 13
1956 Vanderbilt 25, Auburn 13
1957 Georgia Tech 21, Pittsburgh 14
1958 Tennessee 3, Texas A&M 0
1959 Mississippi 7, Florida 3
1960 Arkansas 14, Georgia Tech 7
1961 Florida 13, Baylor 12
1962 Penn State 30, Georgia Tech 15
1963 Florida 17, Penn State 7
1964 No. Carolina 35, Air Force 0
1965 Florida St. 36, Oklahoma 19
1966 Georgia Tech 31, Texas Tech 21
1967 Tennessee 18, Syracuse 12
1968 Penn State 17, Florida St. 17
1969 Missouri 35, Alabama 10
1969 (Dec.) Florida 14, Tenn. 13
1971 (Jan.) Auburn 35, Mississippi 28
1972 Georgia 7, N. Carolina 3
1973 Auburn 24, Colorado 3
1973 (Dec.) Tex. Tech. 28, Tenn. 19
1974 Auburn 27, Texas 3
1975 Maryland 13, Florida 0
1976 Notre Dame 20, Penn State 9
1977 Pittsburgh 34, Clemson 3
1978 Clemson 17, Ohio State 15
1979 No. Carolina 17, Michigan 15
1980 Pittsburgh 37, So. Carolina 9
1981 No. Carolina 31, Arkansas 27

Bluebonnet Bowl, Houston

1959 Clemson 23, TCU 7
1960 Texas 3, Alabama 3
1961 Kansas 33, Rice 7
1962 Missouri 14, Georgia Tech 10
1963 Baylor 14, LSU 7
1964 Tulsa 14, Mississippi 7
1965 Tennessee 27, Tulsa 6
1966 Texas 19, Mississippi 0
1967 Colorado 31, Miami (Fla.) 21
1968 SMU 28, Oklahoma 27
1969 Houston 36, Auburn 7
1970 Oklahoma 24, Alabama 24
1971 Colorado 29, Houston 17
1972 Tennessee 24, Louisiana St. 17
1973 Houston 47, Tulane 7
1974 N. Carolina St. 31, Houston 31
1975 Texas 38, Colorado 21
1976 Nebraska 27, Texas Tech 24
1977 USC 47, Texas A&M 28
1978 Stanford 25, Georgia 22
1979 Purdue 27, Tennessee 22
1980 No. Carolina 16, Texas 7
1981 Michigan 33, UCLA 14

Peach Bowl, Atlanta

1968 LSU 31, Florida St. 27
1969 West Virginia 14, S. Carolina 3
1970 Arizona St. 48, N. Carolina 26
1971 Mississippi 41, Georgia Tech. 18
1972 N. Carolina St. 49, W. Va. 13
1973 Georgia 17, Maryland 16
1974 Vanderbilt 6, Texas Tech. 6
1975 W. Virginia 13, No. Carolina St. 10
1976 Kentucky 21, North Carolina 0
1977 N. Carolina St. 24, Iowa St. 14
1978 Purdue 41, Georgia Tech. 21
1979 Baylor 24, Clemson 18
1981 (Jan.) Miami 20, Virginia Tech. 10
1982 West Virginia 26, Florida 6

Tangerine Bowl, Orlando

1968 Richmond 49, Ohio 42
1969 Toledo 56, Davidson 33
1970 Toledo 40, William & Mary 12
1971 Toledo 28, Richmond 3
1972 Tampa 21, Kent State 18
1973 Miami, Ohio 16, Florida 7
1974 Miami, Ohio 21, Georgia 10
1975 Miami, Ohio 20, South Carolina 7
1976 Okla. St. 49, Brigham Young 21
1977 Florida St. 40, Texas Tech 17
1978 N. Carolina St. 30, Pittsburgh 17
1979 Louisiana St. 34, Wake Forest 10
1980 Florida 35, Maryland 20
1981 Missouri 19, So. Mississippi 17

Fiesta Bowl, Phoenix

1971 Arizona St. 45, Florida St. 38
1972 Arizona St. 49, Missouri 35
1973 Arizona St. 28, Pittsburgh 7
1974 Okla. St. 16, Brigham Young 6
1975 Arizona St. 17, Nebraska 14
1976 Oklahoma 41, Wyoming 7
1977 Penn St. 42, Arizona St. 30
1978 UCLA 10, Arkansas 10
1979 Pittsburgh 16, Arizona 10
1980 Penn St. 31, Ohio St. 19
1981 Penn St. 26, USC 10

Liberty Bowl, Memphis

1959 Penn State 7, Alabama 0
1960 Penn State 41, Oregon 12
1961 Syracuse 15, Miami 14
1962 Oregon State 6, Villanova 0
1963 Miss. State 16, N.C. State 12
1964 Utah 32, West Virginia 6
1965 Mississippi 13, Auburn 7
1966 Miami (Fla.) 14, Va. Tech 7
1967 N.C. State 14, Georgia 7
1968 Mississippi 34, Va. Tech 17
1969 Colorado 47, Alabama 33
1970 Tulane 17, Colorado 3
1971 Tennessee 14, Arkansas 13
1972 Georgia Tech 31, Iowa State 30
1973 No. Carolina St. 31, Kansas 18
1974 Tennessee 7, Maryland 3
1975 USC 20, Texas A&M 0
1976 Alabama 36, UCLA 6
1977 Nebraska 27, N. Carolina 17
1978 Missouri 20, Louisiana St. 15
1979 Penn St. 9, Tulane 6
1980 Purdue 28, Missouri 25
1981 Ohio State 31, Navy 28

Other Bowl Games in 1981

Amos Alonzo Stagg Bowl—Widener 17, Dayton 10.
California Bowl—Toledo 27, San Jose St. 25.
Independence Bowl—Texas A&M 33, Oklahoma St. 16.
Garden State Bowl—Tennessee 28, Wisconsin 21.
Holiday Bowl—Brigham Young 38, Washington St. 36.
Hall of Fame Bowl—Mississippi St. 10, Kansas 0.
Palm Bowl—Texas St. 42, North Dakota 13.
Pioneer Bowl—Idaho St. 34, Eastern Kentucky 23.

College Football Teams

Division I Teams

Team	Nickname	Team colors	Conference	Coach	1981 record (W-L-T)
Air Force	Falcons	Blue & silver	Western Athletic	Ken Hatfield	4-7-0
Akron	Zips	Blue & Gold	Ohio Valley	Jim Dennison	5-5-0
Alabama	Crimson Tide	Crimson & white	Southeastern	Paul Bryant	9-2-1
Alcorn State	Braves	Purple & gold	Southwestern	Marino Casem	5-5-0
Appalachian State	Mountaineers	Black & gold	Southern	Mike Working	3-7-1
Arizona	Wildcats	Red & blue	Pacific Ten	Larry Smith	6-5-0
Arizona State	Sun Devils	Maroon & gold	Pacific Ten	Darryl Rogers	9-2-0
Arkansas	Razorbacks	Cardinal & white	Southwest	Lou Holtz	8-4-0
Arkansas State	Indians	Scarlet & black	Southland	Lawrence Lacewell	6-5-0
Army	Cadets	Black, gold, gray	Independent	Ed Cavanaugh	3-7-1
Auburn	Tigers	Orange & blue	Southeastern	Pat Dye	5-6-0
Austin Peay State	Governors	Red & white	Ohio Valley	Emory Hale	5-5-0
Ball State	Cardinals	Cardinal & white	Mid-American	Dwight Wallace	4-7-0
Baylor	Bears	Green & gold	Southwest	Grant Teaff	5-6-0
Bethune-Cookman	Wildcats	Maroon & gold	Mid-Eastern	Bobby Frazier	7-4-0
Boise State	Broncos	Orange & Blue	Big Sky	Jim Criner	10-3-0
Boston College	Eagles	Maroon & gold	Independent	Jack Bicknell	5-6-0
Boston Univ.	Terriers	Scarlet & white	Yankee	Rick Taylor	6-5-0
Bowling Green St.	Falcons	Orange & brown	Mid-American	Denny Stolz	5-5-1
Brigham Young	Cougars	Royal blue & white	Western Athletic	LaVell Edwards	11-2-0
Brown	Bruins, Bears	Brown, cardinal, white	Ivy	John Anderson	3-7-0
Bucknell	Bisons	Orange & blue	Independent	Bob Curtis	4-6-0
California	Golden Bears	Blue & gold	Pacific Ten	Joe Kapp	2-9-0
Central Michigan	Chippewas	Maroon & gold	Mid-American	Herb Deromedi	7-4-0
Cincinnati	Bearcats	Red & black	Independent	Mike Gottfried	6-5-0
Citadel	Bulldogs	Blue & white	Southern	Art Baker	7-3-1
Clemson	Tigers	Purple & orange	Atlantic Coast	Danny Ford	12-0-0
Colgate	Red Raiders	Maroon	Independent	Fred Dunlap	7-3-0
Colorado State	Rams	Green & gold	Western Athletic	Leon Fuller	0-12-0
Colorado	Buffaloes	Silver, gold & blue	Big Eight	Bill McCartney	3-8-0
Columbia	Lions	Blue & white	Ivy	Bob Naso	1-9-0
Connecticut	Huskies	Blue & white	Yankee	Walt Nadzak	4-7-0
Cornell	Big Red	Carnelian & white	Ivy	Bob Blackman	3-7-0
Dartmouth	Big Green	Dartmouth green & white	Ivy	Joe Yukica	6-4-0
Davidson	Wildcats	Red & black	Independent	Ed Farrell	4-6-0
Delaware	Fightin' Blue Hens	Blue & gold	Independent	Harold Raymond	9-3-0
Delaware State	Hornets	Red & blue	Mid-Eastern	Joe Purzycki	2-9-0
Drake	Bulldogs	Blue & white	Missouri Valley	Chuck Shelton	10-1-0
Duke	Blue Devils	Royal blue & white	Atlantic Coast	Red Wilson	6-5-0
East Carolina	Pirates	Purple & gold	Independent	Ed Emory	5-6-0
East Tennessee St.	Buccaneers	Blue & gold	Southern	Jack Carlisle	6-5-0
Eastern Illinois	Panthers	Blue & Gray	Mid-Continent	Darrell Mudra	6-5-0
Eastern Kentucky	Colonels	Maroon & white	Ohio Valley	Roy Kidd	12-2-0
Eastern Michigan	Hurons	Green & white	Mid-American	Mike Stock	0-11-0
Florida	Gators	Orange & blue	Southeastern	Charley Pell	7-5-0
Florida A&M	Rattlers	Orange & green	Mid-Eastern	Rudy Hubbard	7-4-0
Florida State	Seminoles	Garnet & gold	Independent	Bobby Bowden	6-5-0
Fresno State	Bulldogs	Cardinal & blue	Pacific Coast	Jim Sweeney	5-6-0
Fullerton, Cal. State	Titans	Blue, orange, white	Pacific Coast	Gene Murphy	3-8-0
Furman	Palidans	Purple & white	Southern	Dick Sheridan	8-3-0
Georgia	Bulldogs	Red & black	Southeastern	Vince Dooley	10-2-0
Georgia Tech	Yellow Jackets	Old gold & white	Atlantic Coast	Bill Curry	1-10-0
Grambling State	Tigers	Black & gold	Southwestern	Eddie Robinson	6-4-1
Harvard	Crimson	Crimson	Ivy	Joe Restic	5-4-1
Hawaii	Rainbow Warriors	Green & white	Western Athletic	Dick Tomey	9-2-0
Holy Cross	Crusaders	Royal purple	Independent	Rick Carter	6-5-0
Houston	Cougars	Scarlet & white	Southwest	Bill Yeoman	7-4-1
Howard	Bison	Blue & white	Mid-Eastern	Floyd Keith	6-4-0
Idaho	Vandals	Silver & gold	Big Sky	Dennis Erickson	3-8-0
Idaho State	Bengals	Orange & black	Big Sky	Dave Kragthorpe	12-1-0
Illinois	Fighting Illini	Orange & blue	Big Ten	Mike White	7-4-0
Illinois State	Redbirds	Red & white	Missouri Valley	Bob Otolski	3-7-0
Indiana	Fightin' Hoosiers	Cream & crimson	Big Ten	Lee Corso	3-8-0
Indiana State	Sycamores	Blue & white	Missouri Valley	Dennis Raetz	5-5-1
Iowa	Hawkeyes	Old gold & black	Big Ten	Hayden Fry	8-4-0
Iowa State	Cyclones	Cardinal & gold	Big Eight	Donnie Duncan	5-5-1
Jackson State	Tigers	Blue & white	Southwestern	W.C. Gorden	9-2-1
James Madison	Dukes	Purple & gold	Independent	Challace McMillin	3-8-0
Kansas	Jayhawks	Crimson & blue	Big Eight	Don Fambrough	8-4-0
Kansas State	Wildcats	Purple & white	Big Eight	Jim Dickey	2-9-0
Kent State	Golden Flashes	Blue & gold	Mid-American	Ed Chiebek	4-7-0
Kentucky	Wildcats	Blue & white	Southeastern	Jerry Clairborne	3-8-0
Lafayette	Leopards	Maroon & white	Independent	Bill Russo	9-2-0
Lamar	Cardinals	Red & white	Southland	Ken Stephens	4-6-1
Lehigh	Engineers	Brown & white	Independent	John Whitehead	8-3-0
Long Beach, Cal. State	Forty-Niners	Brown & gold	Pacific Coast	Dave Currey	2-8-0
Louisiana State	Fighting Tigers	Purple & gold	Southeastern	Jerry Stovall	3-7-1
Louisiana Tech	Bulldogs	Red & blue	Southland	Billy Brewer	4-6-1
Louisville	Cardinals	Red, black, white	Independent	Bob Weber	5-6-0
Maine	Black Bears	Blue & white	Yankee	Ron Rogerson	3-7-1

Team	Nickname	Team colors	Conference	Coach	1981 record (W-L-T)
Marshall	Thundering Herd	Green & white	Southern	Sonny Randle	2-9-0
Maryland	Terps	Red, white, black & gold	Atlantic Coast	Bobby Ross	4-6-1
Massachusetts	Minutemen	Maroon & white	Yankee	Robert Pickett	6-3-0
McNeese State	Cowboys	Blue & gold	Southland	Hubert Boales	7-3-1
Memphis State	Tigers	Blue & gray	Independent	Rex Dockery	1-10-0
Miami (Fla.)	Hurricanes	Orange, green, white	Independent	Howard Schnellenberger	9-2-0
Miami (Ohio)	Redskins	Red & white	Mid-American	Tom Reed	8-2-1
Michigan	Wolverines	Maize & blue	Big Ten	Bo Schembechler	9-3-0
Michigan State	Spartans	Green & white	Big Ten	Frank Waters	5-6-0
Middle Tennessee St.	Blue Raiders	Blue & white	Ohio Valley	Boots Donnelly	6-5-0
Minnesota	Gophers	Maroon & gold	Big Ten	Joe Salem	6-5-0
Mississippi	Rebels	Red & blue	Southeastern	Steve Sloan	4-6-1
Mississippi State	Bulldogs	Maroon & white	Southeastern	Emory Bellard	8-4-0
Miss. Valley State	Delta Devils	Green & white	Southwestern	Archie Cooley	4-6-1
Missouri	Tigers	Old gold & black	Big Eight	Warren Powers	8-4-0
Montana	Grizzlies	Copper, silver, gold	Big Sky	Larry Donovan	7-3-0
Montana State	Bobcats	Blue & gold	Big Sky	Doug Graber	3-7-0
Morehead State	Eagles	Blue & gold	Ohio Valley	Steve Loney	1-9-0
Murray State	Racers	Blue & gold	Ohio Valley	Frank Beamer	8-3-0
Navy	Midshipmen	Navy blue & gold	Independent	Gary Tranquill	7-4-1
Nebraska	Cornhuskers	Scarlet & cream	Big Eight	Tom Osborne	9-3-0
Nevada-Las Vegas	Rebels	Scarlet & gray	Pacific Coast	Harvey Hyde	6-6-0
Nevada-Reno	Wolf Pack	Silver & blue	Big Sky	Chris Ault	7-4-0
New Hampshire	Wildcats	Blue & white	Yankee	Bill Bowes	7-3-0
New Mexico	Lobos	Cherry & silver	Western Athletic	Joe Morrison	4-7-1
New Mexico State	Aggies	Crimson & white	Missouri Valley	Gil Krueger	3-8-0
Nicholls St.	Colonels	Red & grey	Independent	William Jackson	5-5-1
North Carolina	Tar Heels	Blue & white	Atlantic Coast	Dick Crum	10-2-0
North Carolina A & T	Aggies	Blue & gold	Mid-Eastern	Maurice Forte	3-8-0
North Carolina State	Wolfpack	Red & white	Atlantic Coast	Monte Kiffin	4-7-0
North Texas State	Mean Green, Eagles	Green & white	Southland	Bob Tyler	2-9-0
Northeast Louisiana	Indians	Maroon & gold	Southland	Pat Collins	5-6-0
Northeastern	Huskies	Red & black	Independent	Pat Pawlak	3-7-0
Northern Arizona	Lumberjacks	Blue & gold	Big Sky	Joe Harper	4-7-0
Northern Illinois	Huskies	Cardinal & black	Mid-American	Bill Mallory	3-8-0
Northern Iowa	Panthers	Purple & Old Gold	Mid-Continent	Stan Sheriff	5-6-0
Northwestern	Wildcats	Purple & white	Big Ten	Dennis Green	0-11-0
Northwestern State	Demons	Burnt orange, purple, white	Independent	A.L. Williams	4-6-0
Notre Dame	Fighting Irish	Gold & blue	Independent	Gerry Faust	5-6-0
Ohio State	Buckeyes	Scarlet & gray	Big Ten	Earle Bruce	9-3-0
Ohio Univ	Bobcats	Green & white	Mid-American	Brian Burke	5-6-0
Oklahoma	Sooners	Crimsom & cream	Big Eight	Barry Switzer	7-4-1
Oklahoma State	Cowboys	Orange & black	Big Eight	Jimmy Johnson	7-5-0
Oregon	Ducks	Green & yellow	Pacific Ten	Rich Brooks	2-9-0
Oregon State	Beavers	Orange & black	Pacific Ten	Joe Avezzano	1-10-0
Pacific	Tigers	Orange & black	Pacific Coast	Bob Toledo	5-6-0
Penn State	Nittany Lions	Blue & white	Independent	Joe Paterno	10-2-0
Pennsylvania	Red & Blue, Quakers	Red & blue	Ivy	Jerry Berndt	1-9-0
Pittsburgh	Panthers	Gold & blue	Independent	Serafino Fazio	11-1-0
Prairie View A & M	Panthers	Purple & gold	Southwestern	Jim McKinley	2-8-0
Princeton	Tigers	Orange & black	Ivy	Frank Navarro	5-4-1
Purdue	Boilermakers	Old gold & black	Big Ten	Leon Bertnett	5-6-0
Rhode Island	Rams	Blue & white	Yankee	Bob Griffin	6-6-0
Rice	Owls	Blue & gray	Southwest	Ray Alborn	4-7-0
Richmond	Spiders	Red & blue	Independent	Dal Shealy	4-7-0
Rutgers	Scarlet Knights	Scarlet	Independent	Frank Burns	5-6-0
San Diego State	Aztecs	Scarlet & black	Western Athletic	Doug Scovil	6-5-0
San Jose State	Spartans	Blue, gold & white	Pacific Coast	Jack Elway	9-3-0
South Carolina	Fighting Gamecocks	Garnet & black	Independent	Richard Bell	6-6-0
South Carolina State	Bulldogs	Garnet & blue	Mid-Eastern	Bill Davis	10-3-0
Southeastern La.	Lions	Green & gold	Independent	Oscar Lofton	8-3-0
Southern	Jaguars	Blue & gold	Southwestern	Otis Washington	3-8-0
Southern California	Trojans	Cardinal & gold	Pacific Ten	John Robinson	9-3-0
Southern Illinois	Salukis	Maroon & white	Missouri Valley	Rey Dempsey	7-4-0
Southern Methodist	Mustangs	Red & blue	Southwest	Bobby Collins	10-1-0
Southern Mississippi	Golden Eagles	Black & gold	Independent	Jim Carmody	9-2-1
Southwestern La.	Ragin' Cajuns	Vermillion & white	Independent	Sam Robertson	1-9-1
Stanford	Cardinals	Cardinal & white	Pacific Ten	Paul Wiggin	4-7-0
Syracuse	Orangemen	Orange	Independent	Dick MacPherson	4-6-1
Temple	Owls	Cherry & white	Independent	Wayne Hardin	5-5-0
Tennessee	Volunteers	Orange & white	Southeastern	John Majors	8-4-0
Tenn.-Chattanooga	Moccasins	Navy blue & gold	Southern	Bill Oliver	7-3-1
Tennessee State	Tigers	Blue & white	Independent	John A. Merritt	9-3-0
Tennessee Tech	Golden Eagles	Purple & gold	Ohio Valley	Don Wade	6-5-0
Texas	Longhorns	Orange & white	Southwest	Fred Akers	10-1-1
Texas-Arlington	Mavericks	Royal blue & white	Southland	Bud Elliott	6-5-0
Texas-El Paso	Miners	Orange & white	Western Athletic	Bill Yung	1-10-0
Texas A & M	Aggies	Maroon & white	Southwest	Jackie Sherrill	7-5-0
Texas Christian	Horned Frogs	Purple & white	Southwest	F.A. Dry	2-7-2
Texas Southern	Tigers	Maroon & gray	Southwestern	Joe Redmond	4-6-1
Texas Tech	Red Raiders	Scarlet & black	Southwest	Jerry Moore	1-9-1
Toledo	Rockets	Blue & gold	Mid-American	Dan Simrell	9-3-0
Tulane	Green Wave	Olive green & sky blue	Independent	Vince Gibson	6-5-0

Team	Nickname	Team colors	Conference	Coach	1981 record (W-L-T)
Tulsa	Golden Hurricane	Blue, red, gold	Missouri Valley	John Cooper	6-5-0
UCLA	Bruins	Navy blue & gold	Pacific Ten	Terry Donahue	7-4-1
Utah State	Aggies	Navy blue & white	Pacific Coast	Bruce Snyder	5-5-1
Utah	Utes	Crimson & white	Western Athletic	Chuck Stobart	8-2-1
Vanderbilt	Commodores	Black & gold	Southeastern	George MacIntyre	4-7-0
Virginia	Cavaliers	Orange & blue	Atlantic Coast	George Welsh	1-10-0
VMI	Keydets	Red, white & yellow	Southern	Bob Thalman	6-3-1
Virginia Tech	Gobblers	Orange & marroon	Independent	Bill Dooley	7-4-0
Wake Forest	Demon Deacons	Old gold & black	Atlantic Coast	Al Groh	4-7-0
Washington	Huskies	Purple & gold	Pacific Ten	Don James	10-2-0
Washington State	Cougars	Crimson & gray	Pacific Ten	Jim Walden	8-3-1
Weber State	Wildcats	Purple & white	Big Sky	Mike Price	7-4-0
West Texas State	Buffaloes	Maroon & white	Missouri Valley	Don Davis	7-4-0
West Virginia	Mountaineers	Old gold & blue	Independent	Don Nehlen	9-3-0
Western Carolina	Catamounts	Purple & gold	Southern	Bob Waters	4-7-0
Western Illinois	Leathernecks	Purple & Gold	Mid-Continent	Pete Rodriguez	5-6-0
Western Kentucky	Hilltoppers	Red & white	Independent	Jimmy Feix	6-5-0
Western Michigan	Broncos	Brown & gold	Mid-American	Jack Harbaugh	6-5-0
Wichita State	Shockers	Yellow & black	Missouri Valley	Willie Jeffries	4-6-1
William & Mary	Indians	Green, gold, silver	Independent	Jimmye Laycock	5-6-0
Wisconsin	Badgers	Cardinal & white	Big Ten	Dave McClain	7-5-0
Wyoming	Cowboys	Brown & yellow	Western Athletic	Al Kincaid	8-3-0
Yale	Bulldogs, Elis	Yale blue & white	Ivy	Carmen Cozza	9-1-0
Youngstown St.	Penguins	Scarlet & white	Ohio Valley	Bill Narduzzi	7-4-0

Selected Division 2 and 3 Teams

Alma	Scots	Maroon & cream	Michigan	Phil Brooks	2-7-0
Amherst	Lord Jeffs	Purple & white	Little Three	James Ostendarp	5-3-0
Baldwin-Wallace	Yellow Jackets	Brown & gold	Ohio	Bob Packard	8-2-0
Beloit	Buccaneers	Gold & blue	Midwest	Ed DeGeorge	4-5-0
Bowdoin	Polar Bears	White	CCB	Jim Lentz	2-6-0
Butler	Bulldogs	Blue & white	Heartland	Bill Sylvester	3-7-0
Carleton	Knights	Maize & blue	Midwest	Bob Sullivan	7-2-0
Cheyney State	Wolves	Blue & white	Pennsylvania	Andy Hinson	2-8-0
Chico, Cal. St.	Wildcats	Cardinal & white	Far Western	Dick Trimmer	5-5-0
Coast Guard	Cadets, Bears	Blue & white	Independent	Larry Rutledge	3-6-0
Coe	Kohawks	Crimson & gold	Midwest	Roger Schlegel	7-2-0
Concordia	Cougars	Maroon & gold	Minn. IAC	Conrad Aumann	11-0-2
Dayton	Flyers	Red & blue	Independent	Mike Kelly	12-2-0
Denison	Big Red	Red & white	Ohio	Keith Piper	3-6-0
Duquesne	Dukes	Red & blue	Independent	Dan McCann	4-5-0
Emory & Henry	Wasps	Blue & gold	Old Dominion	Lou Wacker	0-8-1
Evansville	Purple Aces	Purple & white	Heartland	Randy Rodgers	3-8-0
John Carroll	Blue Streaks	Blue & gold	Presidents Athletic	Don Stupica	3-6-0
Kalamazoo	Hornets	Orange & black	Michigan	Ed Baker	3-6-0
Kenyon	Lords	Purple & white	Ohio	Tom McHugh	5-4-0
Knox	Siwash	Purple & gold	Midwest	Joe Campanelli	2-7-0
Lawrence	Vikings	Navy & white	Midwest	Ron Roberts	9-0-0
Middlebury	Panthers	Blue & white	Independent	Mickey Heinecken	7-1-0
Millsaps	Majors	Purple & white	Independent	Harper Davis	7-2-0
Morgan State	Bears	Blue & orange	Independent	Tom Morris	4-5-0
Mt. Union	Purple Raiders	Purple & white	Ohio	Ken Wable	5-4-0
Muhlenberg	Mules	Cardinal & gray	Middle Atlantic	Ralph Kirchenheiter	3-6-0
North Dakota State	Bison	Yellow & green	North Central	Don Morton	10-3-0
North Dakota	Sioux	Green & white	North Central	Pat Behrns	6-4-0
Northern Michigan	Wildcats	Old gold & green	Independent	Bill Rademacher	10-0-0
Ohio Northern	Polar Bears	Orange & black	Ohio	A. Wallace Hood	6-3-0
Ohio Wesleyan	Battling Bishops	Red & black	Ohio	Jack Fouts	4-5-0
Olivet	Comets	Red & white	Michigan	Ron Lynch	2-5-1
Puget Sound	Loggers	Green & gold	Independent	Ron Simonson	10-1-0
Ripon	Redmen	Crimson & white	Midwest	Larry Terry	7-2-0
Rochester	Yellow Jackets	Yellow & blue	Independent	Pat Stark	4-4-1
St. Cloud State	Huskies	Red & black	North Central	Mike Simpson	4-6-1
St. Lawrence	Saints	Scarlet & brown	ICAC	Andy Talley	5-4-0
St. Norbert	Green Knights	Green & gold	Independent	Larry Van Alstine	2-7-0
St. Olaf	Oles	Black & gold	Minn. IAC	Tom Porter	4-7-0
Santa Clara	Broncos	Cardinal & white	Independent	Pat Malley	2-8-0
Slippery Rock	Rockets, The Rock	Green & white	Pennsylvania	Don Ault	2-7-0
So. Dakota State	Jackrabbits	Yellow & blue	North Central	Wayne Haensel	4-6-0
South Dakota	Coyotes	Red & white	North Central	Dave Triplett	5-6-0
Swarthmore	Little Quakers	Garnet	Middle Atlantic	Tom Lapinski	7-2-0
Thiel	Tomcats	Blue & gold	President's Athletic	David Lyon	4-4-1
Towson State	Tigers	Gold & white	Independent	Phil Albert	5-5-0
Trenton State	Lions	Blue & gold	New Jersey State	Eric Hamilton	5-4-1
Tufts	Jumbos	Blue & brown	Independent	Vic Gatto	5-2-1
Upsala	Vikings	Blue & gray	Middle Atlantic	Vince Caprano	4-6-0
Valparaiso	Crusaders	Brown & gold	Heartland	Bill Koch	1-9-0
Wash. & Jeff.	Presidents	Red & black	Presidents Athletic	John Luckhardt	2-7-0
Wash. & Lee	Generals	Royal blue, white	Old Dominion	Gary Fallon	8-2-0
Wayne State	Tartars	Green & gold	Great Lakes	Dave Farris	4-5-0
Wesleyan	Cardinals	Red & black	Little Three	Bill MacDermott	4-3-1
West Chester St.	Golden Rams	Purple & gold	Independent	Otto Kneidinger	8-3-0
Wilkes	Colonels	Navy & gold	Middle Atlantic	Bill Unsworth	0-9-0
Williams	Ephmen	Purple	Little Three	Robert Odell	3-5-0
Wittenberg	Tigers	Red & white	Ohio	Dave Maurer	8-2-0
Wooster	Fighting Scots	Black & gold	Ohio	Jim Kapp	4-5-0

College Football Conference Champions

Atlantic Coast

1968	No. Carolina St.
1969	So. Carolina
1970	Wake Forest
1971	North Carolina
1972	North Carolina
1973	No. Carolina St.
1974	Maryland
1975	Maryland
1976	Maryland
1977	North Carolina
1978	Clemson
1979	No. Carolina St.
1980	North Carolina
1981	Clemson

Ivy League

1968	Yale, Harvard
1969	Princeton, Dartmouth, Yale
1970	Dartmouth
1971	Dartmouth, Cornell
1972	Dartmouth
1973	Dartmouth
1974	Yale, Harvard
1975	Harvard
1976	Yale, Brown
1977	Yale
1978	Dartmouth
1979	Yales
1980	Yale
1981	Yale, Dartmouth

Big Eight

1968	Kansas, Oklahoma
1969	Missouri, Nebraska
1970	Nebraska
1971	Nebraska
1972	Nebraska
1973	Oklahoma
1974	Oklahoma
1975	Oklahoma, Nebraska
1976	Oklahoma, Colorado, Oklahoma State
1977	Oklahoma
1978	Nebraska, Oklahoma
1979	Oklahoma
1980	Oklahoma
1981	Nebraska

Big Ten

1968	Ohio State
1969	Michigan, Ohio State
1970	Ohio State
1971	Michigan
1972	Ohio State, Michigan
1973	Ohio State, Michigan
1974	Ohio State, Michigan
1975	Ohio State
1976	Michigan, Ohio State
1977	Michigan, Ohio State
1978	Michigan St., Michigan
1979	Ohio State
1980	Michigan
1981	Iowa, Ohio State

Mid-America

1968	Ohio Univ.
1969	Toledo
1970	Toledo
1971	Toledo
1972	Kent State
1973	Miami
1974	Miami
1975	Miami
1976	Ball State
1977	Miami
1978	Ball State
1979	Central Michigan
1980	Central Michigan
1981	Toledo

Missouri Valley

1968	Memphis State
1969	Memphis State
1970	Louisville
1971	Memphis State
1972	Louisville, W. Texas, Drake
1973	No. Texas St., Tulsa
1974	Tulsa
1975	Tulsa
1976	Tulsa, N. Mexico St.
1977	W. Texas St.
1978	N. Mexico St.
1979	W. Texas St.
1980	Tulsa, Wichita St.
1981	Drake, Tulsa

Southeastern

1968	Georgia
1969	Tennessee
1970	Louisiana State
1971	Alabama
1972	Alabama
1973	Alabama
1974	Alabama
1975	Alabama
1976	Georgia
1977	Alabama
1978	Alabama
1979	Alabama
1980	Georgia
1981	Georgia, Alabama

Southwest

1968	Texas, Arkansas
1969	Texas
1970	Texas
1971	Texas
1972	Texas
1973	Texas
1974	Baylor
1975	Texas A&M, Texas, Arkansas
1976	Houston
1977	Texas
1978	Houston
1979	Houston, Arkansas
1980	Baylor
1981	SMU

Pacific Ten

1968	USC
1969	USC
1970	Stanford
1971	Stanford
1972	USC
1973	USC
1974	USC
1975	UCLA, Cal.
1976	USC
1977	Washington
1978	USC
1979	USC
1980	Washington
1981	Washington

Southern

1968	Richmond
1969	Richmond, Davidson
1970	William & Mary
1971	Richmond
1972	East Carolina
1973	East Carolina
1974	VMI
1975	Richmond
1976	East Carolina
1977	Tenn.-Chattanooga
1978	Tenn.-Chattanooga, Furman
1979	Tenn.-Chattanooga
1980	Furman
1981	Furman

Western Athletic

1968	Wyoming
1969	Arizona State
1970	Arizona State
1971	Arizona State
1972	Arizona State
1973	Arizona State, Arizona
1974	Brigham Young
1975	Arizona State
1976	Wyoming, Brigham Young
1977	Brigham Young, Arizona St.
1978	Brigham Young
1979	Brigham Young
1980	Brigham Young
1981	Brigham Young

Pacific Coast

1969	San Diego State
1970	Long Beach State
1972	San Diego State
1973	San Diego State
1974	San Diego State
1975	San Jose State
1976	San Diego State
1977	Fresno State
1978	Utah St., San Jose St.
1979	San Jose St.
1980	Long Beach State
1981	San Jose State

National College Football Champions

The NCAA recognizes as unofficial national champion the team selected each year by the AP (poll of writers) and the UPI (poll of coaches). When the polls disagree both teams are listed. The AP poll originated in 1936 and the UPI poll in 1950.

1936	Minnesota
1937	Pittsburgh
1938	Texas Christian
1939	Texas A&M
1940	Minnesota
1941	Minnesota
1942	Ohio State
1943	Notre Dame
1944	Army
1945	Army
1946	Notre Dame
1947	Notre Dame
1948	Michigan
1949	Notre Dame
1950	Oklahoma
1951	Tennessee
1952	Michigan State
1953	Maryland
1954	Ohio State, UCLA
1955	Oklahoma
1956	Oklahoma
1957	Auburn, Ohio State
1958	Louisiana State
1959	Syracuse
1960	Minnesota
1961	Alabama
1962	Southern Cal.
1963	Texas
1964	Alabama
1965	Alabama, Mich. State
1966	Notre Dame
1967	Southern Cal.
1968	Ohio State
1969	Texas
1970	Nebraska, Texas
1971	Nebraska,
1972	Southern Cal.
1973	Notre Dame, Alabama
1974	Oklahoma, So. Cal.
1975	Oklahoma
1976	Pittsburgh
1977	Notre Dame
1978	Alabama, So. Cal.
1979	Alabama
1980	Georgia
1981	Clemson

Outland Awards

Honoring the outstanding interior lineman selected by the Football Writers' Association of America.

1946	George Connor, Notre Dame, T
1947	Joe Steffy, Army, G
1948	Bill Fischer, Notre Dame, G
1949	Ed Bagdon, Michigan St., G
1950	Bob Gain, Kentucky, T
1951	Jim Weatherall, Oklahoma, T
1952	Dick Modzelewski, Maryland, T
1953	J. D. Roberts, Oklahoma, G
1954	Bill Brooks, Arkansas, G
1955	Calvin Jones, Iowa, G
1956	Jim Parker, Ohio State, G
1957	Alex Karras, Iowa, T
1958	Zeke Smith, Auburn, G
1959	Mike McGee, Duke, T
1960	Tom Brown, Minnesota, G
1961	Merlin Olsen, Utah State, T
1962	Bobby Bell, Minnesota, T
1963	Scott Appleton, Texas, T
1964	Steve Delong, Tennessee, T
1965	Tommy Nobis, Texas, G
1966	Loyd Phillips, Arkansas, T
1967	Ron Yary, Southern Cal, T
1968	Bill Stanfill, Georgia, T
1969	Mike Reid, Penn State, DT
1970	Jim Stillwagon, Ohio State, LB
1971	Larry Jacobson, Nebraska, DT
1972	Rich Glover, Nebraska, MG
1973	John Hicks, Ohio State, G
1974	Randy White, Maryland, DE
1975	Leroy Selmon, Oklahoma, DT
1976	Ross Browner, Notre Dame, DE
1977	Brad Shearer, Texas, DT
1978	Greg Roberts, Oklahoma, G
1979	Jim Ritcher, No. Carolina St., C
1980	Mark May, Pittsburgh, OT
1981	Dave Rimington, Nebraska, C

College Football Stadiums

School	Capacity
Alabama, Univ. of (Bryant-Denny Stad.), University	59,000
Arizona State Univ. (Sun Devil), Tempe	70,330
Arizona, Univ. of (Arizona Stad.), Tucson	57,000
Arkansas, Univ. of (Razorback Stad.) Fayetteville	41,500
Auburn Univ. (Jordan Hare Stad.), Auburn, Ala.	71,863
Baylor Univ. Stad., Waco, Tex.	48,500
Boston Coll. (Alumni Stad.), Boston, Mass.	32,000
Bowling Green State Univ. (Doyt Perry Field), Oh.	23,272
Brigham Young Univ. Stad., Provo, Ut.	35,700
Cal., Univ. of (Memorial Stad.), Berkeley	76,780
Cincinnati, Univ. of (Nippert), Oh.	25,270
Citadel (Johnson Hagood Stad.), Charleston, S.C.	22,500
Clemson Univ. (Memorial Stad.), S.C.	53,440
Colorado St. Univ. (Hughes Stad.), Ft. Collins	30,000
Colorado, Univ. of (Folsom Field), Boulder	52,005
Columbia Univ. (Baker Field), N.Y., N.Y.	32,000
Cornell (Schoellkopf Crescent), Ithaca, N.Y.	27,000
Dartmouth Coll. (Memorial Field), Hanover, N.H.	20,416
Delaware, Univ. of (Delaware Stad.), Newark	22,004
Duke Univ., (Wade Stad.), Durham, N.C.	40,078
E. Carolina Univ. (Ficklen Stad.), Greenville, N.C.	35,000
Florida State, (Campbell Stad.), Tallahassee	51,095
Florida, Univ. of (Florida Field), Gainesville	62,800
Fresno State (Bulldog Stad.), Cal.	30,000
Georgia Tech. (Grant Field), Atlanta	58,121
Georgia, Univ. of (Sanford Stad.), Athens	76,000
Harvard Stad., Boston, Mass.	37,289
Hawaii, Univ. of (Aloha Stad.), Honolulu	50,000
Holy Cross (Fitton Field), Worcester, Mass.	25,000
Illinois, Univ. of (Memorial Stad.), Champaign	71,229
Indiana St. (Memorial Stad.), Terre Haute	20,500
Indiana Univ. (Memorial Stad.), Bloomington	52,354
Iowa State Stad., Ames	50,000
Iowa, Univ. of (Kinnick Stad.), Iowa City	60,200
Kansas State Univ. Stad., Manhattan	42,000
Kansas, Univ. of (Memorial Stad.), Lawrence	51,500
Kent State Univ. (Dix Stad.), Kent, Oh.	30,200
Kentucky, Univ. of (Commonwealth), Lexington	58,000
La. State Univ. (Tiger Stad.), Baton Rouge	76,092
Louisiana Tech. Univ. (Joe Aillet Stad.), Ruston	22,500
Maryland, Univ. of (Byrd), College Park	45,000
Memphis State (Liberty Bowl), Tenn.	50,180
Michigan State Univ. (Spartan Stad.), E. Lansing	76,000
Michigan, Univ. of (Mich. Stad.), Ann Arbor	101,701
Minnesota, Univ. of (Memorial Stad.), Minneapolis	56,725
Mississippi St. Univ. (Scott Field)	35,000
Mississippi, Univ. of (Hemingway Stad.), University	41,500
Missouri, Univ. of (Faurot Field), Columbia	75,000
Nebraska, Univ. of (Memorial Stad.), Lincoln	73,531
Nevada-Las Vegas, Univ. of (Silver Bowl)	32,000
New Mexico State Univ. (Memorial Stad.), Las Cruces	30,000
New Mexico, Univ. Stad., Albuquerque	30,646
North Carolina St. U. (Carter-Finley Stad.), Raleigh	45,600
North Carolina, Univ. of (Kenan Stad.), Chapel Hill	49,500
Northern Illinois Univ. (Huskie Stad.), DeKalb	20,257
Northwestern Univ. (Dyche Stad.), Evanston, Ill.	49,256
Notre Dame Stad., South Bend, Ind.	59,075
Ohio State Univ. (Ohio Stad.), Columbus	83,112
Oklahoma State (Lewis Stad.), Stillwater	50,817
Oklahoma, Univ. of (Owen Field), Norman	74,777
Oregon St. Univ. (Parker Stad.), Corvallis	40,593
Oregon, Univ. of (Autzen Stad.), Eugene	42,000
Pacific, Univ. of the (Pacific Memorial), Stockton, Cal.	30,000
Penn. State Univ. (Beaver Stad.), University Park	83,770
Penn., Univ. of (Franklin Field), Phila.	60,546
Pittsburgh, Univ. of (Pitt. Stad.), Pa.	56,500
Princeton, (Palmer Stad.), Princeton, N.J.	45,725
Purdue, (Ross-Ade Stad.), Lafayette, Ind.	69,250
Rice Stad., Houston, Texas	70,000
Rutgers Stad., New Brunswick, N.J.	23,000
So. Carolina, Univ. of (Williams-Brice), Columbia	54,406
So. Illinois Univ. (McAndrew Stad.), Carbondale	20,100
So. Miss., Univ. of (Roberts Stad.), Hattiesburg	33,000
Southwestern La., Univ. of (Cajun Field), Lafayette	24,610
Stanford Stad., Stanford, Cal.	84,892
Syracuse Univ., (Carrier Dome), N.Y.	50,000
Tenn., Univ. of (Neyland Stad.), Knoxville	91,246
Texas A. & M. Univ. (Kyle Field), College Station	70,016
Texas Christian Univ. (TCU-Amon Carter Stad.) Ft. Worth	46,000
Texas-El Paso (Sun Bowl)	30,000
Texas Tech. Univ. (Jones Stad.), Lubbock	47,000
Texas, Univ. of (Memorial Stad.), Austin	80,000
Tulsa, Univ. of (Skelly Stad.), Okla.	40,235
U.S. Air Force Acad. (Falcon Stad.), Col.	49,668
U.S. Military Academy (Michie Stad.), West Point, N.Y.	39,480
U.S. Naval Academy (Navy-Marine Corps Mem. Stad.) Annapolis, Md.	28,000
Utah State Univ. (Romney Stad.), Logan	30,000
Utah, Univ. of (Robert Rice Stad.), Salt Lake City	30,000
Vanderbilt (Dudley Stad.), Nashville	41,000
Virginia Tech. (Lane Stad.), Blacksburg	52,500
Virginia, Univ. of (Scott Stad.), Charlottesville	42,000
Wake Forest (Groves Stad.), Winston-Salem, N.C.	30,500
Wash. State Univ. (Clarence D. Martin), Pullman	40,000
Washington, Univ. of (Husky Stad.), Seattle	59,800
West Va. Univ. (Mountaineer Field), Morgantown	50,000
Western Mich. Univ. (Waldo Stad.), Kalamazoo	24,500
Wichita State Univ. (Cessna Stad.), Kan.	31,500
Wisconsin, Univ. of (Camp Randall), Madison	7[illegible],280
Wyoming, Univ. of (Memorial), Laramie	33,500
Yale Bowl, New Haven, Conn.	70,874

All-Time Division 1-A Percentage Leaders

(Classified as Division 1 for last 15 years; including bowl games; ties computed as half won and half lost.)

						Bowl Games		
	Years	Won	Lost	Tied	Pct	W	L	T
Notre Dame	93	621	172	39	.770	7	3	0
Yale (A)	109	718	203	53	.764	0	0	0
Michigan	102	632	209	31	.743	6	7	0
Alabama	87	585	199	42	.734	18	14	3
Texas	89	605	219	30	.726	15	11	2
Princeton (A)	112	642	235	48	.720	0	0	0
Southern Cal.	89	544	201	48	.716	20	7	0
Oklahoma	87	554	207	49	.714	16	6	1
Ohio State	92	562	224	48	.703	7	9	0
Harvard (A)	107	643	264	47	.699	1	0	0
Penn State	95	568	255	39	.682	12	6	2
Tennessee	85	536	239	45	.681	12	12	0
Nebraska	92	557	267	39	.668	11	9	0
Miami (O.) (B)	93	487	240	36	.662	5	1	0
Dartmouth (A)	100	534	267	40	.659	0	0	0
Army	92	518	263	49	.654	1	0	0
Louisiana State	88	496	268	42	.641	10	11	1
Minnesota	98	500	276	40	.637	1	2	0
Arizona State	69	364	203	20	.637	6	4	1
Michigan State	85	451	263	39	.625	2	2	0
Georgia	88	494	290	49	.622	10	10	1
Pennsylvania (A)	105	617	369	40	.621	0	1	0
Washington	92	459	273	47	.619	5	5	1
Colorado	92	476	293	31	.614	4	6	0
Stanford	75	419	256	45	.613	7	5	1

(A) Moving to Division 1-AA. (B) Classification undetermined.

Longest Division 1-A Winning Streaks

Wins	Team	Years	Ended by	Score
47	Oklahoma	1953-57	Notre Dame	7-0
39	Washington	1908-14	Oregon State	0-0
37	Yale	1890-93	Princeton	6-0
37	Yale	1887-89	Princeton	10-0
35	Toledo	1969-71	Tampa	21-0
34	Pennsylvania	1894-96	Lafayette	6-4
31	Oklahoma	1948-50	Kentucky	13-7
31	Pittsburgh	1914-18	Cleveland Naval Reserve	10-9
31	Pennsylvania	1896-98	Harvard	10-0
30	Texas	1968-70	Notre Dame	24-11
29	Michigan	1901-03	Minnesota	6-6
28	Alabama	1978-80	Mississippi State	6-3
28	Oklahoma	1973-75	Kansas	23-3
28	Michigan State	1950-53	Purdue	6-0
27	Nebraska	1901-04	Colorado	6-0
26	Cornell	1921-24	Williams	14-7
26	Michigan	1903-05	Chicago	2-0
25	Michigan	1946-49	Army	21-7
25	Army	1944-46	Notre Dame	0-0
25	Southern Cal	1931-33	Oregon State	0-0

Heisman Trophy Winners

Awarded annually to the nation's outstanding college football player.

1935 Jay Berwanger, Chicago, HB
1936 Larry Kelley, Yale, E
1937 Clinton Frank, Yale, QB
1938 David O'Brien, Tex. Christian, QB
1939 Nile Kinnick, Iowa, QB
1940 Tom Harmon, Michigan, HB
1941 Bruce Smith, Minnesota, HB
1942 Frank Sinkwich, Georgia, HB
1943 Angelo Bertelli, Notre Dame, QB
1944 Leslie Horvath, Ohio State, QB
1945 Felix Blanchard, Army, FB
1946 Glenn Davis, Army, HB
1947 John Lujack, Notre Dame, QB
1948 Doak Walker, SMU, HB
1949 Leon Hart, Notre Dame, E
1950 Vic Janowicz, Ohio State, HB
1951 Richard Kazmaier, Princeton, HB
1952 Billy Vessels, Oklahoma, HB
1953 John Lattner, Notre Dame, HB
1954 Alan Ameche, Wisconsin, FB
1955 Howard Cassady, Ohio St., HB
1956 Paul Hornung, Notre Dame, QB
1957 John Crow, Texas A & M, HB
1958 Pete Dawkins, Army, HB
1959 Billy Cannon, La. State, HB
1960 Joe Bellino, Navy, HB
1961 Ernest Davis, Syracuse, HB
1962 Terry Baker, Oregon State, QB
1963 Roger Staubach, Navy, QB
1964 John Huarte, Notre Dame, QB
1965 Mike Garrett, USC, HB
1966 Steve Spurrier, Florida, QB
1967 Gary Beban, UCLA, QB
1968 O. J. Simpson, USC, RB
1969 Steve Owens, Oklahoma, RB
1970 Jim Plunkett, Stanford, QB
1971 Pat Sullivan, Auburn, QB
1972 Johnny Rodgers, Nebraska, RB-R
1973 John Cappelletti, Penn State, RB
1974 Archie Griffin, Ohio State, RB
1975 Archie Griffin, Ohio State, RB
1976 Tony Dorsett, Pittsburgh, RB
1977 Earl Campbell, Texas, RB
1978 Billy Sims, Oklahoma, RB
1979 Charles White, USC, RB
1980 George Rogers, So. Carolina, RB
1981 Marcus Allen, USC, RB

Sports on Television

Source: Sports 1981, A.C. Nielsen Co.

	Household rating %	% Viewing audience			
		Men	Women	Teens	Children
Football					
NFL Superbowl	49.1	45	34	9	12
ABC-NFL (Monday evening)	21.7	59	30	6	5
CBS-NFL	17.5	56	28	8	8
NBC-NFL	13.9	56	29	7	8
College bowl games	14.1	53	33	8	6
College All-Star games	11.6	53	37	4	6
NCAA regular season	12.0	57	28	6	9
Baseball					
World Series	30.0	49	39	5	7
All-Star game	20.1	NA	NA	NA	NA
Regular season	6.5	54	32	6	8
Horse racing					
Average all	13.8	45	42	4	9
Basketball					
NBA average	6.5	56	28	10	6
NCAA average	7.9	54	28	10	8
Bowling					
Pro tour	8.5	44	40	7	9
Auto racing	6.5	48	34	8	10
Golf					
Average all tournaments	4.9	50	39	5	6
Tennis					
Wimbledon	6.0	42	40	11	7
Tournament average	4.7	44	41	8	7
Multi-sports series					
ABC Wide World of Sports	9.7	48	34	9	9
CBS Sports Spectacular	6.4	53	31	5	11
Sportsworld	6.6	49	33	5	13

National Football League

Final 1981 Standings

National Conference

Eastern Division

	W	L	T	Pct	PF	PA
Dallas	12	4	0	.750	367	277
Philadelphia	10	6	0	.625	368	221
New York	9	7	0	.563	295	257
Washington	8	8	0	.500	347	349
St. Louis	7	9	0	.438	315	408

Central Division

	W	L	T	Pct	PF	PA
Tampa Bay	9	7	0	.563	315	268
Detroit	8	8	0	.500	397	322
Green Bay	8	8	0	.500	324	361
Minnesota	7	9	0	.438	325	369
Chicago	6	10	0	.375	253	324

Western Division

	W	L	T	Pct	PF	PA
San Francisco	13	3	0	.813	357	250
Atlanta	7	9	0	.438	426	355
Los Angeles	6	10	0	.375	303	351
New Orleans	4	12	0	.250	207	378

American Conference

Eastern Division

	W	L	T	Pct	PF	PA
Miami	11	4	1	.719	345	275
New York	10	5	1	.656	355	287
Buffalo	10	6	0	.625	311	276
Baltimore	2	14	0	.125	259	533
New England	2	14	0	.125	322	370

Central Division

	W	L	T	Pct	PF	PA
Cincinnati	12	4	0	.750	421	304
Pittsburgh	8	8	0	.500	356	297
Houston	7	9	0	.438	281	355
Cleveland	5	11	0	.313	276	375

Western Division

	W	L	T	Pct	PF	PA
San Diego	10	6	0	.625	478	390
Denver	10	6	0	.625	321	289
Kansas City	9	7	0	.563	343	290
Oakland	7	9	0	.438	273	343
Seattle	6	10	0	.375	322	388

NFC playoffs—New York Giants 27, Philadelphia 21; Dallas 38, Tampa Bay 0; San Francisco 38, New York Giants 24; San Francisco 28, Dallas 27.

AFC playoffs—Buffalo 31, New York Jets 27; Cincinnati 28, Buffalo 21; San Diego 41, Miami 38; Cincinnati 27, San Diego 7.

Championship game—San Francisco 26, Cincinnati 21.

San Francisco Defeats Cincinnati in Super Bowl

The San Francisco 49ers won their first Super Bowl championship by defeating the Cincinnati Bengals 26-21 at the Silverdome in Pontiac, Mich.

Score by Periods

San Francisco	7	13	0	6—26
Cincinnati	0	0	7	14—21

Scoring

San Francisco—Montana one yd. run (Wersching kick).
San Francisco—Cooper 11 yd. pass from Montana (Wersching kick).
San Francisco—Wersching 22 yd. field goal.
San Francisco—Wersching 26 yd. field goal.
Cincinnati—Anderson 5 yd. run (Breech kick).
Cincinnati—Ross 4 yd. pass from Anderson (Breech kick).
San Francisco—Wersching 40 yd. field goal.
San Francisco—Wersching 23 yd. field goal.
Cincinnati—Ross 3 yd. pass from Anderson (Breech kick).

Individual Statistics

Rushing—San Francisco, Cooper 9-34, Ring 5-17, Montana 6-18, Patton 17-55, J. Davis 2-5, Clark 1-minus 2; Cincinnati, Johnson 14-36, Alexander 5-17, Anderson 4-15, A. Griffin 1-4.

Passing—San Francisco, Montana 14-22-0-157; Cincinnati, Anderson 25-34-2-300.

Receiving—San Francisco, Patton 1-6, Clark 4-45, Solomon 4-52, Young 1-14, Cooper 2-15, Ring 1-3, Wilson 1-22; Cincinnati, Curtis 3-42, Ross 11-104, Johnson 2-8, Collinsworth 5-107, Alexander 2-3, Kreider 2-36.

Interceptions—San Francisco, Hicks, 1-27, Wright 1-25.

Punt returns—San Francisco, Hicks, 1-6; Cincinnati, Fuller 4-35.

Kickoff returns—San Francisco, Lawrence 1-17, Hicks 1-23, Clark 1-0; Cincinnati, Verser 5-52, A. Griffin 1-0, Frazier 1-0.

Punting—San Francisco, Miller 4-46.3; Cincinnati, McInally 3-43.7.

Team Statistics

	San Fran.	Cincinnati
Total first downs	20	24
Rushing	9	7
Passing	9	13
Penalty	2	4
Third-down efficiency	8-15	6-12
Total yards	275	356
Yards Rushing	127	72
Yards Passing	148	284
Passes	14-22-0	25-34-2
Punts	4-46.3	3-43.7
Total ret. yards	98	87
Punt returns	1-6	4-35
Kickoff returns	3-40	7-52
Interceptions returns	2-52	0-0
Penalties	8-65	8-57
Time of possession	32:13	27:47

Super Bowl

Year	Winner	Loser	Site
1967	Green Bay Packers, 35	Kansas City Chiefs, 10	Los Angeles Coliseum
1968	Green Bay Packers, 33	Oakland Raiders, 14	Orange Bowl, Miami
1969	New York Jets, 16	Baltimore Colts, 7	Orange Bowl, Miami
1970	Kansas City Chiefs, 23	Minnesota Vikings, 7	Tulane Stadium, New Orleans
1971	Baltimore Colts, 16	Dallas Cowboys, 13	Orange Bowl, Miami
1972	Dallas Cowboys, 24	Miami Dolphins, 3	Tulane Stadium, New Orleans
1973	Miami Dolphins, 14	Washington Redskins, 7	Los Angeles Coliseum
1974	Miami Dolphins, 24	Minnesota Vikings, 7	Rice Stadium, Houston
1975	Pittsburgh Steelers, 16	Minnesota Vikings, 6	Tulane Stadium, New Orleans
1976	Pittsburgh Steelers, 21	Dallas Cowboys, 17	Orange Bowl, Miami
1977	Oakland Raiders, 32	Minnesota Vikings, 14	Rose Bowl, Pasadena
1978	Dallas Cowboys, 27	Denver Broncos, 10	Superdome, New Orleans
1979	Pittsburgh Steelers, 35	Dallas Cowboys, 31	Orange Bowl, Miami
1980	Pittsburgh Steelers, 31	Los Angeles Rams, 19	Rose Bowl, Pasadena
1981	Oakland Raiders, 27	Philadelphia Eagles, 10	Superdome, New Orleans
1982	San Francisco 49ers, 26	Cincinatti Bengals, 21	Silverdome, Pontiac, Mich.

National Football League Champions

Year	East Winner (W.L.T.)	West Winner (W.L.T.)	Playoff
1933	New York Giants (11-3-0)	Chicago Bears (10-2-1)	Chicago Bears 23, New York 21
1934	New York Giants (8-5-0)	Chicago Bears (13-0-0)	New York 30, Chicago Bears 13
1935	New York Giants (9-3-0)	Detroit Lions (7-3-2)	Detroit 26, New York 7
1936	Boston Redskins (7-5-0)	Green Bay Packers (10-1-1)	Green Bay 21, Boston 6
1937	Washington Redskins (8-3-0)	Chicago Bears (9-1-1)	Washington 28, Chicago Bears 21
1938	New York Giants (8-2-1)	Green Bay Packers (8-3-0)	New York 23, Green Bay 17
1939	New York Giants (9-1-1)	Green Bay Packers (9-2-0)	Green Bay 27, New York 0
1940	Washington Redskins (9-2-0)	Chicago Bears (8-3-0)	Chicago Bears 73, Washington 0
1941	New York Giants (8-3-0)	Chicago Bears (10-1-1)(a)	Chicago Bears 37, New York 9
1942	Wash. Redskins (10-1-1)	Chicago Bears (11-0-0)	Washington 14, Chicago Bears 6
1943	Wash. Redskins (6-3-1)(a)	Chicago Bears (8-1-1)	Chicago Bears, 41, Washington 21
1944	New York Giants (8-1-1)	Green Bay Packers (8-2-0)	Green Bay 14, New York 7
1945	Wash. Redskins (8-2-0)	Cleveland Rams (9-1-0)	Cleveland 15, Washington 14
1946	New York Giants (7-3-1)	Chicago Bears (8-2-1)	Chicago Bears 24, New York 14
1947	Philadelphia Eagles (8-4-0)(a)	Chicago Cardinals (9-3-0)	Chicago Cardinals 28, Philadelphia 21
1948	Philadelphia Eagles (9-2-1)	Chicago Cardinals (11-1-0)	Philadelphia 7, Chicago Cardinals 0
1949	Philadelphia Eagles (11-1-0)	Los Angeles Rams (8-2-2)	Philadelphia 14, Los Angeles 0
1950	Cleveland Browns (10-2-0)(a)	Los Angeles Rams (9-3-0)(a)	Cleveland 30, Los Angeles 28
1951	Cleveland Browns (11-1-0)	Los Angeles Rams (8-4-0)	Los Angeles 24, Cleveland 17
1952	Cleveland Browns (8-4-0)	Detroit Lions (9-3-0)(a)	Detroit 17, Cleveland 7
1953	Cleveland Browns (11-1-0)	Detroit Lions (10-2-0)	Detroit 17, Cleveland 16
1954	Cleveland Browns (9-3-0)	Detroit Lions (9-2-1)	Cleveland 56, Detroit 10
1955	Cleveland Browns (9-2-1)	Los Angeles Rams (8-3-1)	Cleveland 38, Los Angeles 14
1956	New York Giants (8-3-1)	Chicago Bears (9-2-1)	New York 47, Chicago Bears 7
1957	Cleveland Browns (9-2-1)	Detroit Lions (8-4-0)(a)	Detroit 59, Cleveland 14
1958	New York Giants (9-3-0)(a)	Baltimore Colts (9-3-0)	Baltimore 23, New York 17(b)
1959	New York Giants (10-2-0)	Baltimore Colts (9-3-0)	Baltimore 31, New York 16
1960	Philadelphia Eagles (10-2-0)	Green Bay Packers (8-4-0)	Philadelphia 17, Green Bay 13
1961	New York Giants (10-3-1)	Green Bay Packers (11-3-0)	Green Bay 37, New York 0
1962	New York Giants (12-2-0)	Green Bay Packers (13-1-0)	Green Bay 16, New York 7
1963	New York Giants (11-3-0)	Chicago Bears (11-1-2)	Chicago 14, New York 10
1964	Cleveland Browns (10-3-1)	Baltimore Colts (12-2-0)	Cleveland 27, Baltimore 0
1965	Cleveland Browns (11-3-0)	Green Bay Packers (10-3-1)(a)	Green Bay 23, Cleveland 12
1966	Dallas Cowboys (10-3-1)	Green Bay Packers (12-2-0)	Green Bay 34, Dallas 27

(a) Won divisional playoff. (b) Won at 8:15 sudden death overtime period.

Year	Conference	Division	Winner (W-L-T)	Playoff
1967	East	Century	Cleveland (9-5-0)	Dallas 52, Cleveland 14
		Capitol	Dallas (9-5-0)	
	West	Central	Green Bay (9-4-1)	Green Bay 28, Los Angeles 7
		Coastal	Los Angeles (11-1-2)(a)	Green Bay 21, Dallas 17
1968	East	Century	Cleveland (10-4-0)	Cleveland 31, Dallas 20
		Capitol	Dallas (12-2-0)	
	West	Central	Minnesota (8-6-0)	Baltimore 24, Minnesota 14
		Coastal	Baltimore (13-1-0)	Baltimore 34, Cleveland 0
1969	East	Century	Cleveland (10-3-1)	Cleveland 38, Dallas 14
		Capitol	Dallas (11-2-1)	
	West	Central	Minnesota (12-2-0)	Minnesota 23, Los Angeles 20
		Coastal	Los Angeles (11-3-0)	Minnesota 27, Cleveland 7
1970	American	Eastern	Baltimore (11-2-1)	Baltimore 17, Cincinnati 0
		Central	Cincinnati (8-6-0)	Oakland 21, Miami 14
		Western	Oakland (8-4-2)	Baltimore 27, Oakland 17
	National	Eastern	Dallas (10-4-0)	Dallas 5, Detroit 0
		Central	Minnesota (12-2-0)	San Francisco 17, Minnesota 14
		Western	San Francisco (10-3-1)	Dallas 17, San Francisco 10
1971	American	Eastern	Miami (10-3-1)	Miami 27, Kansas City 24
		Central	Cleveland (9-5-0)	Baltimore 20, Cleveland 3
		Western	Kansas City (10-3-1)	Miami 21, Baltimore 0
	National	Eastern	Dallas (11-3-0)	Dallas 20, Minnesota 12
		Central	Minnesota (11-3-0)	San Francisco 24, Washington 20
		Western	San Francisco (9-5-0)	Dallas 14, San Francisco 3
1972	American	Eastern	Miami (14-0-0)	Miami 20, Cleveland 14
		Central	Pittsburgh (11-3-0)	Pittsburgh 13, Oakland 7
		Western	Oakland (10-3-1)	Miami 21, Pittsburgh 17
	National	Eastern	Washington (11-3-0)	Washington 16, Green Bay 3
		Central	Green Bay (10-4-0)	Dallas 30, San Francisco 28
		Western	San Francisco (8-5-1)	Washington 26, Dallas 3
1973	American	Eastern	Miami (12-2-0)	Miami 34, Cincinnati 16
		Central	Cincinnati (10-4-0)	Oakland 33, Pittsburgh 14
		Western	Oakland (9-4-1)	Miami 27, Oakland 10
	National	Eastern	Dallas (10-4-0)	Dallas 27, Los Angeles 16
		Central	Minnesota (12-2-0)	Minnesota 27, Washington 20
		Western	Los Angeles (12-2-0)	Minnesota 27, Dallas 10
1974	American	Eastern	Miami (11-3-0)	Oakland 28, Miami 26
		Central	Pittsburgh (10-3-1)	Pittsburgh 32, Buffalo 14
		Western	Oakland (12-2-0)	Pittsburgh 24, Oakland 13
	National	Eastern	St. Louis (10-4-0)	Minnesota 30, St. Louis 14
		Central	Minnesota (10-4-0)	Los Angeles 19, Washington 10
		Western	Los Angeles (10-4-0)	Minnesota 14, Los Angeles 10
1975	American	Eastern	Baltimore (10-4-0)	Pittsburgh 28, Baltimore 10
		Central	Pittsburgh (12-2-0)	Oakland 31, Cincinnati 28
		Western	Oakland (11-3-0)	Pittsburgh 16, Oakland 10
	National	Eastern	St. Louis (11-3-0)	Dallas 17, Minnesota 14

(continued)

(continued)

Year	Conference	Division	Winner (W-L-T)	Playoff
		Central	Minnesota (12-2-0)	Los Angeles 35, St. Louis 23
		Western	Los Angeles (12-2-0)	Dallas 37, Los Angeles 7
1976	American	Eastern	Baltimore (11-3-0)	Pittsburgh 40, Baltimore 14
		Central	Pittsburgh (10-4-0)	Oakland 24, New England 21
		Western	Oakland (13-1-0)	Oakland 24, Pittsburgh 12
	National	Eastern	Dallas (11-3-0)	Minnesota 35, Washington 20
		Central	Minnesota (11-2-1)	Los Angeles 14, Dallas 12
		Western	Los Angeles (10-3-1)	Minnesota 24, Los Angeles 13
1977	American	Eastern	Baltimore (10-4-0)	Oakland 37, Baltimore 31
		Central	Pittsburgh (9-5-0)	Denver 34, Pittsburgh 21
		Western	Denver (12-2-0)	Dallas 37, Chicago 7
	National	Eastern	Dallas (12-2-0)	Minnesota 14, Los Angeles 7
		Central	Minnesota (9-5-0)	Denver 20, Oakland 17
		Western	Los Angeles (10-4-0)	Dallas 23, Minnesota 6
1978	American	Eastern	New England (11-5-0)	Pittsburgh 33, Denver 10
		Central	Pittsburgh (14-2-0)	Houston 31, New England 14
		Western	Denver (10-6-0)	Pittsburgh 34, Houston 5
	National	Eastern	Dallas (12-4-0)	Dallas 27, Atlanta 20
		Central	Minnesota (8-7-1)	Los Angeles 34, Minnesota 10
		Western	Los Angeles (12-4-0)	Dallas 28, Los Angeles 0
1979	American	Eastern	Miami (10-6-0)	Houston 17, San Diego 14
		Central	Pittsburgh (12-4-0)	Pittsburgh 34, Miami 14
		Western	San Diego (12-4-0)	Pittsburgh 27, Houston 13
	National	Eastern	Dallas (11-5-0)	Tampa Bay 24, Philadelphia 17
		Central	Tampa Bay (10-6-0)	Los Angeles 21, Dallas 19
		Western	Los Angeles (9-7-0)	Los Angeles 9, Tampa Bay 0
1980	American	Eastern	Buffalo (11-5-0)	San Diego 20, Buffalo 14
		Central	Cleveland (11-5-0)	Oakland 14, Cleveland 12
		Western	San Diego (11-5-0)	Oakland 34, San Diego 27
	National	Eastern	Philadelphia (12-4-0)	Philadelphia 31, Minnesota 16
		Central	Minnesota (9-7-0)	Dallas 30, Atlanta 27
		Western	Atlanta (12-4-0)	Philadelphia 20, Dallas 7
1981	American	Eastern	Miami (11-4-1)	San Diego 41, Miami 38
		Central	Cincinnati (12-4-0)	Cincinnati 28, Buffalo 21
		Western	San Diego (10-6-0)	Cincinnati 27, San Diego 7
	National	Eastern	Dallas (12-4-0)	Dallas 38, Tampa Bay 0
		Central	Tampa Bay (9-7-0)	San Francisco 38, N.Y. Giants 24
		Western	San Francisco (13-3-0)	San Francisco 28, Dallas 27

NEA All-NFL Team in 1981

Chosen by team captains, player representatives, and head coaches of the 28 NFL teams in a poll conducted by Newspaper Enterprise Assn.

First team	Offense	Second team
James Lofton, Green Bay	Wide receiver	Frank Lewis, Buffalo
Alfred Jenkins, Atlanta	Wide receiver	Steve Watson, Denver
Kellen Winslow, San Diego	Tight end	Joe Senser, Minnesota
Anthony Munoz, Cincinnati	Tackle	Mike Kenn, Atlanta
Marvin Powell, N.Y. Jets	Tackle	Pat Donovan, Dallas
John Hannah, New England	Guard	Herbert Scott, Dallas
Randy Cross, San Francisco	Guard	Ed Newman, Miami
Mike Webster, Pittsburgh	Center	Rich Saul, Los Angeles
Ken Anderson, Cincinnati	Quarterback	Joe Montana, San Francisco
Billy Sims, Detroit	Running back	George Rogers, New Orleans
Tony Dorsett, Dallas	Running back	Joe Cribbs, Buffalo
Nick Lowery, Kansas City	Placekicker	Ed Murray, Detroit

First team	Defense	Second team
Joe Klecko, N.Y. Jets	End	Mark Gastineau, N.Y. Jets
Ed Jones, Dallas	End	Fred Dean, San Francisco
Randy White, Dallas	Tackle	Fred Smerlas, Buffalo
Doug English, Detroit	Tackle	Bob Baumhower, Miami
Jack Lambert, Pittsburgh	Middle linebacker	Randy Gradishar, Denver
Bob Swenson, Denver	Linebacker	Rod Martin, Oakland
Lawrence Taylor, N.Y. Giants	Linebacker	Matt Blair, Minnesota
Ronnie Lott, San Francisco	Cornerback	Gary Green, Kansas City
Mark Haynes, N.Y. Giants	Cornerback	Roynell Young, Philadelphia
Gary Barbaro, Kansas City	Safety	Gary Fencik, Chicago
Nolan Cromwell, Los Angeles	Safety	Dwight Hicks, San Francisco
Tom Skladany, Detroit	Punter	Pat McInally, Cincinnati

George Halas Trophy Winners

The Halas Trophy, named after football coach George Halas, is awarded annually to the outstanding defensive player in football in a poll conducted by Murray Olderman of Newspaper Enterprise Assn.

1966	Larry Wilson, St. Louis
1967	Deacon Jones, Los Angeles
1968	Deacon Jones, Los Angeles
1969	Dick Butkus, Chicago
1970	Dick Butkus, Chicago
1971	Carl Eller, Minnesota
1972	Joe Greene, Pittsburgh
1973	Alan Page, Minnesota
1974	Joe Greene, Pittsburgh
1975	Curley Culp, Houston
1976	Jerry Sherk, Cleveland
1977	Harvey Martin, Dallas
1978	Randy Gradishar, Denver
1979	Lee Roy Selmon, Tampa Bay
1980	Lester Hayes, Oakland
1981	Joe Klecko, N.Y. Jets

National Football Conference Leaders

(National Football League prior to 1970)

Passing

Player, team	Atts	Com	YG	TD	Year
Rudy Bukich, Chicago	312	176	2,641	20	**1965**
Bart Starr, Green Bay	251	156	2,257	14	**1966**
Sonny Jurgensen, Washington	508	288	3,747	31	**1967**
Earl Morrall, Baltimore	317	182	2,909	26	**1968**
Sonny Jurgensen, Washington	422	274	3,102	22	**1969**
John Brodie, San Francisco	378	223	2,941	24	**1970**
Roger Staubach, Dallas	211	126	1,882	15	**1971**
Norm Snead, N.Y. Giants	325	196	2,307	17	**1972**
Roger Staubach, Dallas	286	179	2,428	23	**1973**
Sonny Jurgensen, Washington	167	107	1,185	11	**1974**
Fran Tarkenton, Minnesota	425	273	2,294	25	**1975**
James Harris, Los Angeles	158	91	1,460	8	**1976**
Roger Staubach, Dallas	361	210	2,620	18	**1977**
Roger Staubach, Dallas	413	231	3,190	25	**1978**
Roger Staubach, Dallas	461	267	3,586	27	**1979**
Ron Jaworski, Philadelphia	451	257	3,529	27	**1980**
Joe Montana, San Francisco	488	311	3,565	19	**1981**

Pass-Receiving

Player, team	Ct	YG	TD
Dave Parks, San Francisco	80	1,344	12
Charlie Taylor, Washington	72	1,119	12
Charlie Taylor, Washington	70	990	9
Clifton McNeil, San Francisco	71	944	7
Dan Abramowicz, New Orleans	73	1,015	7
Dick Gordon, Chicago	71	1,026	13
Bob Tucker, Giants	59	791	4
Harold Jackson, Philadelphia	62	1,048	4
Harold Carmichael, Philadelphia	67	1,116	9
Charles Young, Philadelphia	63	696	3
Chuck Foreman, Minnesota	73	691	9
Drew Pearson, Dallas	58	806	6
Ahmad Rashad, Minnesota	51	681	2
Rickey Young, Minnesota	88	704	5
Ahmad Rashad, Minnesota	80	1,156	9
Earl Cooper, San Francisco	83	567	4
Dwight Clark, San Francisco	85	1,105	4

Scoring

Player, team	TD	PAT	FG	Pts	Year
Gale Sayers, Chicago	22	0	0	132	**1965**
Bruce Gossett, Los Angeles	0	29	28	113	**1966**
Jim Bakken, St. Louis	0	36	27	117	**1967**
Leroy Kelly, Cleveland	20	0	0	120	**1968**
Fred Cox, Minnesota	0	43	26	121	**1969**
Fred Cox, Minnesota	0	35	30	125	**1970**
Curt Knight, Washington	0	27	29	114	**1971**
Chester Marcol, Green Bay	0	29	33	128	**1972**
David Ray, Los Angeles	0	40	30	130	**1973**
Chester Marcol, Green Bay	0	19	25	94	**1974**
Chuck Foreman, Minnesota	22	0	0	132	**1975**
Mark Moseley, Washington	0	31	22	97	**1976**
Walter Payton, Chicago	16	0	0	96	**1977**
Frank Corrall, Los Angeles	0	31	29	118	**1978**
Mark Moseley, Washington	0	39	25	114	**1979**
Ed Murray, Detroit	0	35	27	116	**1980**
Ed Murray, Detroit	0	46	25	121	**1981**

Rushing

Player, team	Yds	Atts	TD
Jimmy Brown, Cleveland	1,544	289	17
Gale Sayers, Chicago	1,231	229	8
Leroy Kelly, Cleveland	1,205	235	11
Leroy Kelly, Cleveland	1,239	248	16
Gayle Sayers, Chicago	1,032	236	8
Larry Brown, Washington	1,125	237	5
John Brockington, Green Bay	1,105	216	4
Larry Brown, Washington	1,216	285	8
John Brockington, Green Bay	1,144	265	3
Larry McCutcheon, Los Angeles	1,109	236	3
Jim Otis, St. Louis	1,076	269	5
Walter Payton, Chicago	1,390	311	13
Walter Payton, Chicago	1,852	339	14
Walter Payton, Chicago	1,395	333	11
Walter Payton, Chicago	1,610	369	14
Walter Payton, Chicago	1,460	317	15
George Rogers, New Orleans	1,674	378	13

American Football Conference Leaders

(American Football League prior to 1970)

Passing

Player, team	Atts	Com	YG	TD	Year
Jack Hadl, San Diego	348	174	2,798	20	**1965**
Len Dawson, Kansas City	284	159	2,527	26	**1966**
Daryle Lamonica, Oakland	425	220	3,228	30	**1967**
Len Dawson, Kansas City	224	131	2,109	17	**1968**
Greg Cook, Cincinnati	197	106	1,845	15	**1969**
Daryle Lamonica, Oakland	356	179	2,516	22	**1970**
Bob Griese, Miami	263	145	2,089	19	**1971**
Earl Morrall, Miami	150	83	1,360	11	**1972**
Ken Stabler, Oakland	260	163	1,997	14	**1973**
Ken Anderson, Cincinnati	328	213	2,667	18	**1974**
Ken Anderson, Cincinnati	377	228	3,169	21	**1975**
Ken Stabler, Oakland	291	194	2,737	27	**1976**
Bob Griese, Miami	307	180	2,252	22	**1977**
Terry Bradshaw, Pittsburgh	368	207	2,915	28	**1978**
Dan Fouts, San Diego	530	332	4,082	24	**1979**
Brian Sipe, Cleveland	554	337	4,132	30	**1980**
Ken Anderson, Cincinnati	479	300	3,754	29	**1981**

Pass-Receiving

Player, team	Ct	YG	TD
Lionel Taylor, Denver	85	1,131	6
Lance Alworth, San Diego	73	1,383	13
George Sauer, N.Y. Jets	75	1,189	6
Lance Alworth, San Diego	68	1,312	10
Lance Alworth, San Diego	64	1,003	4
Marlin Briscoe, Buffalo	57	1,036	8
Fred Biletnikoff, Oakland	61	929	9
Fred Biletnikoff, Oakland	58	802	7
Fred Willis, Houston	57	371	1
Lydell Mitchell, Baltimore	72	544	2
Reggie Rucker, Cleveland	60	770	3
Lydell Mitchell, Baltimore	60	554	4
MacArthur Lane, Kansas City	66	686	1
Lydell Mitchell, Baltimore	71	620	4
Steve Largent, Seattle	71	1,168	8
Joe Washington, Baltimore	82	750	3
Kellen Winslow, San Diego	89	1,290	9
Kellen Winslow, San Diego	88	1,075	10

Scoring

Player, team	TD	PAT	FG	Pts	Year
Gino Cappelletti, Boston	9	27	17	132	**1965**
Gino Cappelletti, Boston	6	35	16	119	**1966**
George Blanda, Oakland	0	56	20	116	**1967**
Jim Turner, N.Y. Jets	0	43	34	145	**1968**
Jim Turner, N.Y. Jets	0	33	32	129	**1969**
Jan Stenerud, Kansas City	0	26	30	116	**1970**
Garo Yepremian, Miami	0	33	28	117	**1971**
Bobby Howfield, N.Y. Jets	0	40	27	121	**1972**
Roy Gerela, Pittsburgh	0	36	29	123	**1973**
Roy Gerela, Pittsburgh	0	33	20	93	**1974**
O.J. Simpson, Buffalo	23	0	0	138	**1975**
Toni Linhart, Baltimore	0	49	20	109	**1976**
Errol Mann, Oakland	0	39	20	99	**1977**
Pat Leahy, N.Y. Jets	0	41	22	107	**1978**
John Smith, New England	0	46	23	115	**1979**
John Smith, New England	0	51	26	129	**1980**
Jim Breech, Cincinnati	0	49	22	115	**1981**

Rushing

Player, team	Yds	Atts	TD
Paul Lowe, San Diego	1,121	222	7
Jim Nance, Boston	1,458	299	11
Jim Nance, Boston	1,216	269	7
Paul Robinson, Cincinnati	1,023	238	8
Dick Post, San Diego	873	182	6
Floyd Little, Denver	901	209	3
Floyd Little, Denver	1,133	284	6
O.J. Simpson, Buffalo	1,251	292	6
O.J. Simpson, Buffalo	2,003	332	12
Otis Armstrong, Denver	1,407	263	9
O.J. Simpson, Buffalo	1,817	329	16
O.J. Simpson, Buffalo	1,503	290	8
Mark van Eeghen, Oakland	1,273	324	7
Earl Campbell, Houston	1,450	302	13
Earl Campbell, Houston	1,697	368	19
Earl Campbell, Houston	1,934	373	13
Earl Campbell, Houston	1,376	361	10

Jim Thorpe Trophy Winners

The winner of the Jim Thorpe Trophy, named after the athletic great, is picked by Murray Olderman of Newspaper Enterprise Assn. in a poll of players from the 28 NFL teams. It goes to the most valuable NFL player and is the oldest and highest professional football award.

Year	Player, team
1955	Harlon Hill, Chicago Bears
1956	Frank Gifford, N.Y. Giants
1957	John Unitas, Baltimore Colts
1958	Jim Brown, Cleveland Browns
1959	Charley Conerly, N.Y. Giants
1960	Norm Van Brocklin, Philadelphia Eagles
1961	Y.A. Tittle, N.Y. Giants
1962	Jim Taylor, Green Bay Packers
1963	(tie) Jim Brown, Cleveland Browns, and Y.A. Tittle, N.Y. Giants
1964	Lenny Moore, Baltimore Colts
1965	Jim Brown, Cleveland Browns
1966	Bart Starr, Green Bay Packers
1967	John Unitas, Baltimore Colts
1968	Earl Morrall, Baltimore Colts
1969	Roman Gabriel, Los Angeles Rams
1970	John Brodie, San Francisco 49ers
1971	Bob Griese, Miami Dolphins
1972	Larry Brown, Washington Redskins
1973	O.J. Simpson, Buffalo Bills
1974	Ken Stabler, Oakland Raiders
1975	Fran Tarkenton, Minnesota Vikings
1976	Bert Jones, Baltimore Colts
1977	Walter Payton, Chicago Bears
1978	Earl Campbell, Houston Oilers
1979	Earl Campbell, Houston Oilers
1980	Earl Campbell, Houston Oilers
1981	Ken Anderson, Cincinnati Bengals

1981 NFL Individual Leaders

National Football Conference

Passing[1]

	Att	Comp	Pct Comp	Yards	Avg Gain	TD	Pct TD	Int	Rating Points
Montana, San Francisco	488	311	63.7	3565	7.31	19	3.9	12	88.2
White, Dallas	391	223	57.0	3098	7.92	22	5.6	13	87.5
Bartkowski, Atlanta	533	297	55.7	3829	7.18	30	5.6	23	79.2
Dickey, Green Bay	354	204	57.6	2593	7.32	17	4.8	15	79.1
Theismann, Washington	496	293	59.1	3568	7.19	19	3.8	20	77.3
Williams, Tampa Bay	471	238	50.5	3563	7.56	19	4.0	14	76.5
Simms, N.Y. Giants	316	172	54.4	2031	6.43	11	3.5	9	74.2
Jaworski, Philadelphia	461	250	54.2	3095	6.71	23	5.0	20	74.0
Hipple, Detroit	279	140	50.2	2358	8.45	14	5.0	15	73.3
Kramer, Minnesota	593	322	54.3	3912	6.60	26	4.4	24	72.8
Hart, St. Louis	241	134	55.6	1694	7.03	11	4.6	14	68.9
Haden, Los Angeles	267	138	51.7	1815	6.80	9	3.4	13	64.4
Manning, New Orleans	232	134	57.8	1447	6.24	5	2.2	11	64.0
Lomax, St. Louis	236	119	50.4	1575	6.67	4	1.7	10	60.1
Evans, Chicago	436	195	44.7	2354	5.40	11	2.5	20	51.0

Rushing

	Att	Yds	Avg	TD
Rogers, New Orleans	378	1674	4.4	13
Dorsett, Dallas	342	1646	4.8	4
Sims, Detroit	296	1437	4.9	13
Montgomery, Philadelphia	286	1402	4.9	8
Anderson, St. Louis	328	1376	4.2	9
Andrews, Atlanta	289	1301	4.5	10
Payton, Chicago	339	1222	3.6	6
Tyler, Los Angeles	260	1074	4.1	12
Brown, Minnesota	274	1063	3.9	6
Washington, Washington	210	916	4.4	4

Punt Returns

	No	Yds	Avg	TD
Irvin, Los Angeles	46	615	13.4	3
Fisher, Chicago	43	509	11.8	1
Groth, New Orleans	37	436	11.8	0
Nelms, Washington	45	492	10.9	2
Mitchell, St. Louis	42	445	10.6	1
Lee, Green Bay	20	187	9.4	1
Hicks, San Francisco	19	171	9.0	0
Martin, Detroit	52	450	8.7	1
Woerner, Atlanta	33	278	8.4	0
Payton, Minnesota	38	303	8.0	0

Receiving

	No	Yds	Avg	TD
Clark, San Francisco	85	1105	13.0	4
Brown, Minnesota	83	694	8.4	2
Andrews, Atlanta	81	735	9.1	2
Senser, Minnesota	79	1004	12.7	8
Lofton, Green Bay	71	1294	18.2	8
Jenkins, Atlanta	70	1358	19.4	13
Washington, Washington	70	558	8.0	3
Tilley, St. Louis	66	1040	15.8	3
White, Minnesota	66	1001	15.2	3
Ellis, Green Bay	65	499	7.7	3

Kickoff Returns

	No	Yds	Avg	TD
Nelms, Washington	37	1099	29.7	0
Lawrence, San Francisco	17	437	25.7	1
Smith, Atlanta	47	1143	24.3	0
Mitchell, St. Louis	55	1292	23.5	0
Wilson, New Orleans	31	722	23.3	0
Payton, Minnesota	39	898	23.0	1
Garrett, N.Y.G.-Wash.	18	401	22.3	0
Rogers, New Orleans	28	621	22.2	0
Henry, Philadelphia	25	533	21.3	0
Williams, Chicago	23	486	21.1	0

Interceptions

	No	Yds	Avg	TD
Walls, Dallas	11	133	12.1	0
Hicks, San Francisco	9	239	26.6	1
Brown, Tampa Bay	9	215	23.9	2
Thurman, Dallas	9	187	20.8	0
Allen, Detroit	9	123	13.7	0
Pridemore, Atlanta	7	221	31.6	1
Lott, San Francisco	7	117	16.7	3
Greene, St. Louis	7	111	15.9	0
Downs, Dallas	7	81	11.6	0
Murphy, Washington	7	68	9.7	0

Scoring-Kicking

	XP	XPA	FG	FGA	Pts
Murray, Detroit	46	46	25	35	121
Septien, Dallas	40	40	27	35	121
Luckhurst, Atlanta	51	51	21	33	114
Danelo, N.Y. Giants	31	31	24	38	103
Franklin, Philadelphia	41	43	20	31	101
Stenerud, Green Bay	35	36	22	24	101
Danmeier, Minnesota	34	37	21	25	97
Moseley, Washington	38	42	19	30	95
O'Donoghue, St. Louis	36	37	19	32	93
Corral, Los Angeles	36	36	17	26	87

Punting

	No	Yds	Avg
Skladany, Detroit	64	2784	43.5
Jennings, N.Y. Giants	97	4198	43.3
Swider, Tampa Bay	58	2476	42.7
Corral, Los Angeles	89	3735	42.0
Birdsong, St. Louis	69	2883	41.8
Miller, San Francisco	93	3858	41.5
Coleman, Minnesota	88	3646	41.4
White, Dallas	79	3222	40.8

Scoring-Touchdowns

	TD	Rush	Pass	Pts
Tyler, Los Angeles	17	12	5	102
Sims, Detroit	15	13	2	90
Jenkins, Atlanta	13	0	13	78
Riggins, Washington	13	13	0	78
Rogers, New Orleans	13	13	0	78
Andrews, Atlanta	12	10	2	72
Springs, Dallas	12	10	2	72
Montgomery, Philadelphia	10	8	2	60

American Conference

Passing[1]

	Att	Comp	Pct Comp	Yards	Avg Gain	TD	Pct TD	Int	Rating Points
Anderson, Cincinnati	479	300	62.6	3754	7.84	29	6.1	10	98.5
Morton, Denver	376	225	59.8	3195	8.50	21	5.6	14	90.6
Fouts, San Diego	609	360	59.1	4802	7.89	33	5.4	17	90.6
Bradshaw, Pittsburgh	370	201	54.3	2887	7.80	22	5.9	14	83.7
Zorn, Seattle	397	236	59.4	2788	7.02	13	3.3	9	82.3
Todd, N.Y. Jets	497	279	56.1	3231	6.50	25	5.0	13	81.8
Jones, Baltimore	426	244	57.3	3094	7.26	21	4.9	20	76.8
Ferguson, Buffalo	498	252	50.6	3652	7.33	24	4.8	20	74.1
Woodley, Miami	366	191	52.2	2470	6.75	12	3.3	13	69.7
Stabler, Houston	285	165	57.9	1988	6.98	14	4.9	18	69.5
Sipe, Cleveland	567	313	55.2	3876	6.84	17	3.0	25	68.3
Kenney, Kansas City	274	147	53.6	1983	7.24	9	3.3	16	63.8
Grogan, New England	216	117	54.2	1859	8.61	7	3.2	16	63.0
Cavanaugh, New England	219	115	52.5	1633	7.46	5	2.3	13	60.0
Wilson, Oakland	366	173	47.3	2311	6.31	14	3.8	19	58.8

(1) At least 192 passes needed to qualify. Leader based on percentage of completions, touchdown passes, interceptions, and average yards.

Rushing

	Att	Yds	Avg	TD
Campbell, Houston	361	1376	3.8	10
Muncie, San Diego	251	1144	4.6	19
Delaney, Kansas City	234	1121	4.8	3
Pruitt, Cleveland	247	1103	4.5	7
Cribbs, Buffalo	257	1097	4.3	3
Johnson, Cincinnati	274	1077	3.9	12
Harris, Pittsburgh	242	987	4.1	8
Collins, New England	204	873	4.3	7
King, Oakland	170	828	4.9	0
Nathan, Miami	147	782	5.3	5

Scoring-Kicking

	XP	XPA	FG	FGA	Pts
Breech, Cincinnati	49	51	22	32	115
Lowery, Kansas City	37	38	26	36	115
Leahy, N.Y. Jets	38	39	25	36	113
Benirschke, San Diego	55	61	19	26	112
von Schamann, Miami	37	38	24	31	109
Steinfort, Denver	36	37	17	30	87
Smith, New England	37	39	15	24	82
Bahr, S.F.-Clev.	34	34	15	26	79
Mike-Mayer, Buffalo	37	37	14	24	79
Fritsch, Houston	32	34	15	22	77

Receiving

	No	Yds	Avg	TD
Winslow, San Diego	88	1075	12.2	10
Largent, Seattle	75	1224	16.3	9
Ross, Cincinnati	71	910	12.8	5
Lewis, Buffalo	70	1244	17.8	4
Joiner, San Diego	70	1188	17.0	7
Chandler, N.O.-S.D.	69	1142	16.6	6
Newsome, Cleveland	69	1002	14.5	6
Collinsworth, Cincinnati	67	1009	15.1	8
Pruitt, Cleveland	65	636	9.8	4
Stallworth, Pittsburgh	63	1098	17.4	5

Kickoff Returns

	No	Yds	Avg	TD
Roaches, Houston	28	769	27.5	1
Walker, Miami	38	932	24.5	1
Tullis, Houston	32	779	24.3	1
Verser, Cincinnati	29	691	23.8	0
Brooks, San Diego	40	949	23.7	0
Murphy, Kansas City	20	457	22.9	0
Hall, Cleveland	36	813	22.6	0
Whittington, Oakland	25	563	22.5	0
Montgomery, Clev.-Oak.	17	382	22.5	0
Anderson, Pittsburgh	37	825	22.3	0

Interceptions

	No	Yds	Avg	TD
Harris, Seattle	10	155	15.5	2
Ray, N.Y. Jets	7	227	32.4	2
Harris, Kansas City	7	109	15.6	0
Blount, Pittsburgh	6	106	17.7	1
Lambert, Pittsburgh	6	76	12.7	0
Clark, Buffalo	5	142	28.4	0
Barbaro, Kansas City	5	134	26.8	0
Foley, Denver	5	81	16.2	0
Shell, Pittsburgh	5	52	10.4	0

Scoring-Touchdowns

	TD	Rush	Pass	Pts
Muncie, San Diego	19	19	0	114
Johnson, Cincinnati	16	12	4	96
Watson, Denver	13	0	13	78
Jackson, Kansas City	11	10	1	66
Campbell, Houston	10	10	0	60
Cribbs, Buffalo	10	3	7	60
Dickey, Baltimore	10	7	3	60
Largent, Seattle	10	1	9	60
Winslow, San Diego	10	0	10	60

Punt Returns

	No	Yds	Avg	TD
Brooks, San Diego	22	290	13.2	0
Johns, Seattle	16	177	11.1	0
Smith, Kansas City	50	528	10.6	0
Vigorito, Miami	36	379	10.5	1
Anderson, Pittsburgh	20	208	10.4	0
Manning, Denver	41	378	9.2	0
Hooks, Buffalo	17	142	8.4	0
Watts, Oakland	35	284	8.1	1

Punting

	No	Yds	Avg
McInally, Cincinnati	72	3272	45.4
Guy, Oakland	96	4195	43.7
Colquitt, Pittsburgh	84	3641	43.3
Cox, Cleveland	68	2884	42.4
Camarillo, New England	47	1959	41.7
Roberts, San Diego	62	2540	41.0
Orosz, Miami	83	3386	40.8
Ramsey, N.Y. Jets	81	3290	40.6

Pro Football Hall of Fame

Canton, Ohio

Herb Adderley
Lance Alworth
Doug Atkins
Morris (Red) Badgro
Cliff Battles
Sammy Baugh
Chuck Bednarik
Bert Bell
Raymond Berry
Charles Bidwell
George Blanda
Jim Brown
Paul Brown
Roosevelt Brown
Dick Butkus
Tony Canadeo
Joe Carr
Guy Chamberlin
Jack Christiansen
Dutch Clark
George Connor
Jim Conzelman
Willie Davis
Art Donovan
Paddy Driscoll
Bill Dudley
Turk Edwards
Weeb Ewbank
Tom Fears
Ray Flaherty
Len Ford
Dr. Daniel Fortmann
Bill George
Frank Gifford
Otto Graham
Red Grange
Forrest Gregg
Lou Groza
Joe Guyon
George Halas
Ed Healey
Mel Hein
Pete Henry
Arnold Herber
Bill Hewitt
Clarke Hinkle
Elroy Hirsch
Cal Hubbard
Sam Huff
Lamar Hunt
Don Hutson
Deacon Jones
Walt Kiesling
Frank (Bruiser) Kinard
Curly Lambeau
Dick (Night Train) Lane
Yale Lary
Dante Lavelli
Bobby Layne
Tuffy Leemans
Bob Lilly
Vince Lombardi
Sid Luckman
Link Lyman
Tim Mara
Gino Marchetti
George Marshall
Ollie Matson
George McAfee
Hugh McElhenny
John (Blood) McNally
Mike Michalske
Wayne Millner
Ron Mix
Lenny Moore
Marion Motley
George Musso
Bronko Nagurski
Greasy Neale
Ernie Nevers
Ray Nitschke
Leo Nomellini
Merlin Olsen
Jim Otto
Steve Owen
Clarence (Ace) Parker
Jim Parker
Joe Perry
Pete Pihos
Hugh (Shorty) Ray
Dan Reeves
Jim Ringo
Andy Robustelli
Art Rooney
Gale Sayers
Joe Schmidt
Bart Starr
Ernie Stautner
Ken Strong
Joe Stydahar
Jim Taylor
Jim Thorpe
Y.A. Tittle
George Trafton
Charlie Trippi
Emlen Tunnell
Clyde (Bulldog) Turner
Norm Van Brocklin
Steve Van Buren
Johnny Unitas
Bob Waterfield
Bill Willis
Larry Wilson
Alex Wojciechowicz

Football Stadiums

See index for major league baseball seating capacity, and college stadiums.

Name, location	Capacity
Anaheim Stadium, Anaheim, Cal.	69,000
Arrowhead Stadium, Kansas City, Mo.	78,198
Atlanta-Fulton County Stadium	60,748
Astrodome, Houston, Tex.	50,000
Baltimore Memorial Stadium	60,763
Buffalo War Memorial Stadium	46,206
Busch Memorial Stadium, St. Louis	51,392
Candlestick Park, San Francisco, Cal.	61,115
Cleveland Municipal Stadium	80,322
Cotton Bowl, Dallas, Tex.	72,000
Franklin Field, Philadelphia, Pa.	60,546
Gator Bowl, Jacksonville, Fla.	70,000
Giants Stadium, E. Rutherford, N.J.	76,891
Hubert H. Humphrey Metrodome, Minneapolis	62,212
John F. Kennedy Stadium, Philadelphia, Pa.	105,000
Robert F. Kennedy Memorial Stadium, Wash., D.C.	55,031
Kezar Stadium, San Francisco, Cal.	59,636
Kingdome, Seattle, Wash.	64,752
Ladd Memorial Stadium, Mobile, Ala.	40,605
Lambeau Field, Green Bay, Wis.	56,267
Legion Field, Birmingham, Ala.	72,000
Liberty Bowl, Memphis, Tenn.	50,180
Los Angeles Memorial Coliseum	93,761
Louisiana Superdome, New Orleans	71,330
Metropolitan Stadium, Bloomington, Minn.	48,446
Mile High Stadium, Denver, Col.	75,103
Milwaukee County Stadium	55,958
Mississippi Memorial Stadium, Jackson	61,000
Jack Murphy Stadium, San Diego	52,596
Oakland-Alameda County Coliseum	54,615
Orange Bowl, Miami, Fla.	75,459
Pontiac Silverdome, Mich.	80,638
Rich Stadium, Buffalo, N.Y.	80,020
Riverfront Stadium, Cincinnati, Oh.	59,754
Rose Bowl, Pasadena, Cal.	106,721
Rubber Bowl, Akron, Oh.	35,007
Schaefer Stadium, Foxboro, Mass.	61,297
Shea Stadium, New York, N.Y.	60,372
Soldier Field, Chicago, Ill.	64,124
Sugar Bowl, New Orleans, La.	80,982
Tampa Stadium, Tampa, Fla.	72,126
Texas Stadium, Dallas, Tex.	65,101
Three Rivers Stadium, Pittsburgh, Pa.	50,350
Veterans Stadium, Philadelphia, Pa.	71,529

Bert Bell Memorial Trophy Winners

The Bert Bell Memorial Trophy, named after the former NFL commissioner, is awarded annually to the outstanding rookies in a poll conducted by Murray Olderman of Newspaper Enterprise Assn.

1964	Charlie Taylor, Washington, WR
1965	Gale Sayers, Chicago, RB
1966	Tommy Nobis, Atlanta, LB
1967	Mel Farr, Detroit, RB
1968	Earl McCullouch, Detroit, WR
1969	Calvin Hill, Dallas, RB
1970	Raymond Chester, Oakland, TE
1971	AFC: Jim Plunkett, New England, QB
	NFC: John Brockington, Green Bay, RB
1972	AFC: Franco Harris, Pittsburgh, RB
	NFC: Willie Buchanon, Green Bay, DB
1973	AFC: Boobie Clark, Cincinnati, RB
	NFC: Chuck Foreman, Minnesota, RB
1974	Don Woods, San Diego, RB
1975	AFC: Robert Brazile, Houston, LB
	NFC: Steve Bartkowski, Atlanta, QB
1976	AFC: Mike Haynes, New England, CB
	NFC: Sammy White, Minnesota, WR
1977	Tony Dorsett, Dallas, RB
1978	Earl Campbell, Houston, RB
1979	Ottis Anderson, St. Louis, RB
1980	Billy Sims, Detroit, RB
1981	Lawrence Taylor, N.Y. Giants, LB

American Football League

Year	Eastern Division	Western Division	Playoff
1960	Houston Oilers (10-4-0)	L. A. Chargers (10-4-0)	Houston 24, Los Angeles 16
1961	Houston Oilers (10-3-1)	San Diego Chargers (12-2-0)	Houston 10, San Diego 3
1962	Houston Oilers (11-3-0)	Dallas Texans (11-3-0)	Dallas 20, Houston 17(b)
1963	Boston Patriots (8-6-1)(a)	San Diego Chargers (11-3-0)	San Diego 51, Boston 10
1964	Buffalo Bills (12-2-0)	San Diego Chargers (8-5-1)	Buffalo 20, San Diego 7
1965	Buffalo Bills (10-3-1)	San Diego Chargers (9-2-3)	Buffalo 23, San Diego 0
1966	Buffalo Bills (9-4-1)	Kansas City Chiefs (11-2-1)	Kansas City 31, Buffalo 7
1967	Houston Oilers (9-4-1)	Oakland Raiders (13-1-0)	Oakland 40, Houston 7
1968	New York Jets (11-3-0)	Oakland Raiders (12-2-0)(a)	New York 27, Oakland 23
1969	New York Jets (10-4-0)	Oakland Raiders (12-1-1)	Kansas City 17, Oakland 7(c)

(a) won divisional playoff (b) won at 2:45 of second overtime. (c) Kansas City defeated Jets to make playoffs.

All-Time Pro Football Records

NFL, AFL, and All-American Football Conference

(at start of 1982 season)

Leading Lifetime Rushers

Player	League	Yrs	Att	Yards	Avg	Player	League	Yrs	Att	Yards	Avg
Jim Brown	NFL	9	2,359	12,312	5.2	Lawrence McCutcheon	NFL	10	1,521	6,578	4.3
O.J. Simpson	AFL-NFL	11	2,404	11,236	4.7	Lydell Mitchell	NFL	9	1,675	6,534	3.9
Franco Harris	NFL	10	2,462	10,339	4.2	Earl Campbell	NFL	4	1,404	6,457	4.6
Joe Perry	AAFC-NFL	16	1,929	9,723	5.0	Floyd Little	AFL-NFL	9	1,641	6,323	3.8
Walter Payton	NFL	7	2,204	9,608	4.4	Tony Dorsett	NFL	5	1,368	6,270	4.6
Jim Taylor	NFL	10	1,941	8,597	4.4	Don Perkins	NFL	8	1,500	6,217	4.1
Larry Csonka	AFL-NFL	11	1,891	8,081	4.3	Ken Willard	NFL	10	1,622	6,105	3.8
John Riggins	NFL	10	1,861	7,536	4.0	Calvin Hill	NFL	12	1,452	6,083	4.2
Leroy Kelly	NFL	10	1,727	7,274	4.2	Chuck Foreman	NFL	8	1,556	5,950	3.8
John Henry Johnson	NFL-AFL	13	1,571	6,803	4.3	Mark van Eeghen	NFL	8	1,475	5,907	4.0

Most Yards Gained, Season — 2,003, O.J. Simpson, Buffalo Bills, 1973.
Most Yards Gained, Game — 275, Walter Payton, Chicago Bears vs. Minnesota Vikings, Nov. 20, 1977.
Most Games, 100 Yards or more, Season — 11, O.J. Simpson, Buffalo Bills, 1973; Earl Campbell, Houston Oilers, 1979.
Most Games, 100 Yards or more, Career — 58, Jim Brown, Cleveland Browns, 1957-1965.
Most Games, 200 Yards or more, Career — 6, O.J. Simpson, Buffalo Bills, 1969-1977; San Francisco 49ers, 1978-1979.
Most Touchdowns Rushing, Career — 106, Jim Brown, Cleveland Browns, 1957-1965.
Most Touchdowns Rushing, Season — 19, Jim Taylor, Green Bay Packers, 1962; Earl Campbell, Houston Oilers, 1979; Chuck Muncie, San Diego Chargers, 1981.
Most Touchdowns Rushing, Game — 6, Ernie Nevers, Chicago Cardinals vs. Chicago Bears, Nov. 8, 1929.
Most Rushing Attempts, Season — 378, George Rogers, New Orleans Saints, 1981.
Most Rushing Attempts, Game — 41, Franco Harris, Pittsburgh vs. Cincinnati, Oct. 17, 1976.
Longest run from Scrimmage — 97 yds., Andy Uram, Green Bay vs. Chicago Cardinals, Oct. 8, 1939; Bob Gage, Pittsburgh vs. Chicago Bears, Dec. 4, 1949. (Both scored touchdown).

Leading Lifetime Passers

(Minimum 1,500 attempts)

Player	League	Yrs	Att	Comp	Yds	Pts*	Player	League	Yrs	Att	Comp	Yds	Pts*
Otto Graham	AAFC-NFL	10	2,626	1,464	23,584	86.8	Frank Ryan	NFL	13	2,133	1,090	16,042	77.7
Roger Staubach	NFL	11	2,958	1,685	22,700	83.5	Ken Stabler	AFL-NFL	12	3,223	1,944	24,268	77.5
Sonny Jurgensen	NFL	18	4,262	2,433	32,224	82.8	Bob Griese	AFL-NFL	14	3,429	1,926	25,092	77.3
Len Dawson	NFL-AFL	19	3,741	2,136	28,711	82.6	Norm Van Brocklin	NFL	12	2,895	1,553	23,611	75.3
Ken Anderson	NFL	11	3,539	2,036	25,562	80.5	Sid Luckman	NFL	12	1,744	904	14,686	75.0
Fran Tarkenton	NFL	18	6,467	3,686	47,003	80.5	Brian Sipe	NFL	8	2,758	1,552	19,083	74.9
Bart Starr	NFL	16	3,149	1,808	24,718	80.3	Don Meredith	NFL	9	2,308	1,170	17,199	74.7
Bert Jones	NFL	9	2,464	1,382	17,663	79.1	Roman Gabriel	NFL	15	4,495	2,365	29,429	74.5
Dan Fouts	NFL	9	3,203	1,849	24,256	78.4	Y.A. Tittle	AAFC-NFL	17	4,395	2,427	33,070	74.4
Johnny Unitas	NFL	18	5,186	2,830	40,239	78.2	Earl Morrall	NFL	21	2,689	1,379	20,809	74.2

*Rating points based on performances in the following categories: Percentage of completions, percentage of touchdown passes, percentage of interceptions, and average gain per pass attempt.

Most Yards Gained, Season — 4,802, Dan Fouts, San Diego Chargers, 1981.
Most Yards Gained, Game — 554, Norm Van Brocklin, Los Angeles Rams vs. New York Yankees, Sept. 18, 1951 (27 completions in 41 attempts).
Most Touchdowns Passing, Career — 342, Fran Tarkenton, Minnesota Vikings, 1961-65; N.Y. Giants, 1967-71; Minnesota Vikings, 1972-78.
Most Touchdown Passing, Season — 36, George Blanda, Houston Oilers, 1961 and Y.A. Tittle, N.Y. Giants, 1963.
Most Touchdown Passing, Game — 7, Sid Luckman, Chicago Bears vs. New York Giants, Nov. 14, 1943; Adrian Burk, Philadelphia Eagles vs. Washington Redskins, Oct. 17, 1954; George Blanda, Houston Oilers vs. New York Titans, Nov. 19, 1961; Y.A. Tittle, New York Giants vs. Washington Redskins, Oct. 28, 1962; Joe Kapp, Minnesota Vikings vs. Baltimore Colts, Sept. 28, 1969.
Most Passing Attempts, Season — 609, Dan Fouts, San Diego Chargers, 1981.
Most Passing Attempts, Game — 68, George Blanda, Houston Oilers vs. Buffalo Bills, Nov. 1, 1964 (37 completions).
Most Passes Completed, Season — 360, Dan Fouts, San Diego Chargers, 1981.
Most Passes Completed, Game — 42, Richard Todd, N.Y. Jets vs. San Francisco 49ers, Sept. 21, 1980.
Most Consecutive Passes Completed — 17, Bert Jones, Baltimore Colts vs. N.Y. Jets, Dec. 15, 1974.

Leading Lifetime Receivers

Player	League	Yrs	No	Yds	Avg	Player	League	Yrs	No	Yds	Avg
Charley Taylor	NFL	13	649	9,110	14.0	Charlie Joiner	AFL-NFL	13	495	8,476	17.1
Don Maynard	AFL-NFL	15	633	11,834	18.7	Tommy McDonald	NFL	12	495	8,410	17.0
Ray Berry	NFL	13	631	9,275	14.7	Don Hutson	NFL	11	488	7,991	16.4
Fred Biletnikoff	AFL-NFL	14	589	8,974	15.2	Jackie Smith	NFL	16	488	7,991	16.4
Harold Jackson	NFL	14	571	10,246	17.9	Art Powell	AFL-NFL	10	479	8,046	16.8
Lionel Taylor	AFL	10	567	7,195	12.7	Boyd Dowler	NFL	12	474	7,270	15.4
Lance Alworth	AFL-NFL	11	542	10,266	18.9	Ahmad Rashad	NFL	9	472	6,598	14.0
Bobby Mitchell	NFL	11	521	7,954	15.3	Pete Retzlaff	NFL	11	452	7,412	16.4
Harold Carmichael	NFL	11	516	7,923	15.4	Roy Jefferson	NFL	12	451	7,539	16.7
Billy Howton	NFL	12	503	8,459	16.8	Haven Moses	AFL-NFL	14	448	8,091	18.1

Most Yards Gained, Season — 1,746, Charley Hennigan, Houston Oilers, 1961.
Most Yards Gained, Game — 303, Jim Benton, Cleveland Rams vs. Detroit Lions, Nov. 22, 1945 (10 receptions).
Most Pass Receptions, Season — 101, Charley Hennigan, Houston Oilers, 1964.
Most Pass Receptions, Game — 18, Tom Fears, Los Angeles Rams vs. Green Bay Packers, Dec. 3, 1950 (189 yards).
Most Consecutive Games, Pass Receptions — 127, Harold Carmichael, Philadelphia Eagles, 1972-1980.
Most Touchdown Passes, Career — 99, Don Hutson, Green Bay Packers, 1935-1945.
Most Touchdown Passes, Season — 17, Don Hutson, Green Bay Packers, 1942; Elroy Hirsch, Los Angeles Rams, 1951; Bill Groman, Houston Oilers, 1961.
Most Touchdown Passes, Game — 5, Bob Shaw, Chicago Cardinals vs. Baltimore Colts, Oct. 2, 1950; Kellen Winslow, San Diego vs. Oakland, Nov. 22, 1981.

Leading Lifetime Scorers

Player	League	Yrs	TD	PAT	FG	Total
George Blanda	NFL-AFL	26	9	943	335	2,002
Lou Groza	AAFC-NFL	21	1	810	264	1,608
Jim Turner	AFL-NFL	16	1	521	304	1,439
Jim Bakken	NFL	17	0	534	282	1,380
Fred Cox	NFL	15	0	519	282	1,365
Jan Stenerud	AFL-NFL	15	0	432	304	1,344
Gino Cappelletti	AFL	11	42	350	176	1,130
Don Cockroft	NFL	13	0	432	216	1,080
Garo Yepremian	AFL-NFL	14	0	444	210	1,074
Bruce Gossett	NFL	11	0	374	219	1,031
Sam Baker	NFL	15	2	428	179	977
Lou Michaels	NFL	13	1	386	187	955*
Roy Gerela	AFL-NFL	11	0	351	184	903
Bobby Walston	NFL	12	46	365	80	881
Mark Moseley	NFL	11	0	300	189	867
Pete Gogolak	AFL-NFL	10	0	344	173	863
Errol Mann	NFL	11	0	315	177	846
Don Hutson	NFL	11	105	172	7	823
Paul Hornung	NFL	9	62	190	66	760
Jim Brown	NFL	9	126	0	0	756

*Includes safety.

Most Points, Season — 176, Paul Hornung, Green Bay Packers, 1960 (15 TD's, 41 PAT's, 15 FG's).
Most Points, Game — 40, Ernie Nevers, Chicago Cardinals vs. Chicago Bears, Nov. 28, 1929 (6 TD's, 4 PAT's).
Most Touchdowns, Season — 23, O.J. Simpson, Buffalo Bills, 1975 (16 rushing, 7 pass receptions).
Most Touchdowns, Game — 6, Ernie Nevers, Chicago Cardinals vs. Chicago Bears, Nov. 28, 1929 (6 rushing); Dub Jones, Cleveland Browns vs. Chicago Bears, Nov. 25, 1951 (4 rushing, 2 pass receptions); Gale Sayers, Chicago Bears vs. San Francisco 49ers, Dec. 12, 1965 (4 rushing, 1 pass reception, 1 punt return).
Most Points After Touchdown, Season — 64, George Blanda, Houston Oilers, 1961 (65 attempts).
Most Consecutive Points After Touchdown — 234, Tommy Davis, San Francisco 49ers, 1959-1969.
Most Field Goals, Game — 7, Jim Bakken, St. Louis Cardinals vs. Pittsburgh Steelers, Sept. 24, 1967.
Most Field Goals, Season — 34, Jim Turner, New York Jets, 1968 and 1969.
Most Field Goals Attempted, Season — 49, Bruce Gossett, Los Angeles Rams, 1966; Curt Knight, Washington Redskins, 1971.
Most Field Goals Attempted, Game — 9, Jim Bakken, St. Louis Cardinals vs. Pittsburgh Steelers, Sept. 24, 1967 (7 successful).
Most Consecutive Field Goals — 20, Garo Yepremian, Miami Dolphins, 1978, New Orleans Saints, 1979.
Most Consecutive Games, Field Goal — 31, Fred Cox, Minnesota Vikings, 1968-1970.
Longest Field Goal — 63 yds., Tom Dempsey, New Orleans Saints vs. Detroit Lions, Nov. 8, 1970.
Highest Field Goal Completion Percentage, Season (14 attempts) — 91.67 Jan Stenerud, Green Bay Packers, 1981 (22 FG's in 24 attempts).

Pass Interceptions

Most Passes Had Intercepted, Game — 8, Jim Hardy, Chicago Cardinals vs. Philadelphia Eagles, Sept. 24, 1950 (39 attempts)
Most Passes Had Intercepted, Season — 42, George Blanda, Houston Oilers, 1962 (418 attempts).
Most Passes Had Intercepted, Career — 277, George Blanda, Chicago Bears, 1949-1958; Houston Oilers, 1960-1966; Oakland Raiders, 1967-1975 (4,000 attempts).
Most Consecutive Passes Attempted Without Interception — 294, Bart Starr, Green Bay Packers, 1964-1965.
Most Interceptions By, Season — 14, Dick Lane, Los Angeles Rams, 1952.
Most Interceptions By, Career — 81, Paul Krause, Washington Redskins, 1964-67; Minnesota Vikings, 1968-79.
Most Consecutive Games, Passes Intercepted By — 8, Tom Morrow, Oakland Raiders, 1962 (4), 1963 (4).
Most Touchdowns Scored via Pass Interceptions, Lifetime — 9, Ken Houston, Houston Oilers, 1967 (2); 1968 (2); 1969; 71 (4).

Punting

Highest Punting Average, Career (300 punts) — 45.10, Sam Baugh, Washington Redskins, 1937-1952 (338 punts).
Highest Punting Average, Season (20 punts) — 51.3, Sam Baugh, Washington Redskins, 1940 (35 punts).
Longest Punt — 98 yds., Steve O'Neal, New York Jets vs. Denver Broncos, Sept. 21, 1969.

Kickoff Returns

Most Yardage Returning Kickoffs, Career — 6,922, Ron Smith, Chicago Bears, 1965; Atlanta Falcons, 1966-67; Los Angeles Rams, 1968-69; Chicago Bears, 1970-72; San Diego Chargers, 1973; Oakland Raiders, 1974.
Most Yardage Returning Kickoffs, Season — 1,317, Bobby Jancik, Houston Oilers, 1963.
Most Yardage Ruturning Kickoffs, Game — 294, Wally Triplett, Detroit Lions vs. Los Angeles Rams, Oct. 29, 1950 (4 returns).
Most Touchdowns Scored via Kickoff Returns, Career — 6, Ollie Matson, Chicago Cardinals, 1952 (2), 1954, 1956, 1958 (2); Gale Sayers, Chicago Bears, 1965, 1966 (2), 1967 (3); Travis Williams, Green Bay Packers, 1967 (4), 1969; Los Angeles Rams, 1971.
Most Touchdowns Scored via Kickoff Returns, Season — 4, Travis Williams, Green Bay Packers, 1967; Cecil Turner, Chicago Bears, 1970.
Most Touchdowns Scored via Kickoff Returns, Game — 2, Tim Brown, Philadelphia Eagles vs. Dallas Cowboys, Nov. 6, 1966; Travis Williams, Green Bay Packers vs. Cleveland Browns, Nov. 12, 1967.
Most Kickoff Returns, Career — 275, Ron Smith, Chicago Bears, 1965; Atlanta Falcons, 1966-67; Los Angeles Rams, 1968-69; Chicago Bears, 1970-72; San Diego Chargers, 1973; Oakland Raiders, 1974.
Most Kickoff Returns, Season — 60, Drew Hill, Los Angeles Rams, 1981.
Longest Kickoff Return — 106 yds., Al Carmichael, Green Bay Packers vs. Chicago Bears, October 7, 1956; Noland Smith, Kansas City vs. Denver, Dec. 17, 1967; Roy Green, St. Louis Cardinals vs. Dallas Cowboys, Oct. 21, 1979 (all scored TD).

Punt Returns

Most Yardage Returning Punts, Career — 2,714, Rick Upchurch, Denver Broncos, 1975-1981.
Most Yardage Returning Punts, Season — 655, Neal Colzie, Oakland Raiders, 1975.
Most Yardage Returning Punts, Game — 207, Leroy Irvin, Los Angeles Rams vs. Atlanta Falcons, Oct. 11. 1981.
Most Touchdowns Scored via Punt Returns, Career — 8, Jack Christiansen, Detroit Lions, 1951 (4), 1952 (2), 1954, 1956.
Most Punt Returns, Career — 258, Emlen Tunnell, New York Giants, 1948-1958; Green Bay Packers, 1959-1961.
Most Punt Returns, Season — 70, Danny Reece, Tampa Bay Buccaneers, 1979.
Longest Punt Return — 98 yards, Gil LeFebvre, Cincinnati Reds vs. Brooklyn Dodgers, Dec. 3, 1933; Charles West, Minnesota Vikings vs. Washington Redskins, Nov. 3, 1968; Dennis Morgan, Dallas Cowboys vs. St. Louis Cardinals, Oct. 13, 1974 (all scored TD).

Miscellaneous Records

Most Fumbles, Season — 17, Dan Pastorini, Houston Oilers, 1973.
Most Fumbles, Game — 7, Len Dawson, Kansas City Chiefs vs. San Diego Chargers, Nov. 15, 1964.
Longest Winning Streak (regular season) — 17 games, Chicago Bears, 1933-1934.
Longest Undefeated Streak (includes tie games) — 29 games, Cleveland Browns, 1947-1949 (won 27, tied 2).
Most Seasons, Active Player — 26, George Blanda, Chicago Bears, 1949-1958; Houston Oilers, 1960-1966 and Oakland, 67-75.

1982 NFL Player Draft

The following are the first round picks of the National Football League

Team	Player	Pos.	College
1—New England	Ken Sims	DT	Texas
2—Baltimore	Johnie Cooks	LB	Mississippi St.
3—New Orleans (a)			
4—Cleveland	Chip Banks	LB	So. California
5—Baltimore	Art Schlichter	QB	Ohio State
6—Chicago	Jim McMahon	QB	Brigham Young
7—Seattle	Jeff Bryant	DE	Clemson
8—Minnesota	Darrin Nelson	RB	Stanford
9—Houston	Mike Munchak	OG	Penn State
10—Atlanta	Gerald Riggs	RB	Arizona State
11—Oakland	Marcus Allen	RB	So. California
12—Kansas City	Anthony Hancock	WR	Tennessee
13—Pittsburgh	Walt Abercrombie	RB	Baylor
14—New Orleans	Lindsay Scott	WR	Georgia
15—Los Angeles	Barry Redden	RB	Richmond
16—Detroit	Jimmy Williams	LB	Nebraska
17—St. Louis	Luis Sharpe	OT	UCLA
18—Tampa Bay	Sean Farrell	OG	Penn State
19—N.Y. Giants	Butch Woolfolk	RB	Michigan
20—Buffalo	Perry Tuttle	WR	Clemson
21—Philadelphia	Mike Quick	WR	N.C. St.
22—Denver	Gerald Willhite	RB	San Jose St.
23—Green Bay	Ron Hallstrom	OG	Iowa
24—N.Y. Jets	Bob Crable	LB	Notre Dame
25—Miami	Roy Foster	OG	So. California
26—Dallas	Rod Hill	DB	Kentucky State
27—Cincinnati	Glen Collins	DE	Mississippi St.
28—New England	Lester Williams	DT	Miami, Fla.

(a) Used pick in supplemental draft for QB Dave Wilson of Illinois, July 8, 1981.

Canadian Football League

Final 1981 Standings

Eastern Division

	W	L	T	PF	PA	Pts
Hamilton Tiger-Cats	11	4	1	414	335	23
Ottawa Rough Riders	5	11	0	306	446	10
Montreal Alouettes	3	13	0	267	518	6
Toronto Argonauts	2	14	0	241	506	4

Western Division

	W	L	T	PF	PA	Pts
Edmonton Eskimos	14	1	1	576	277	29
Winnipeg Blue Bombers	11	5	0	517	299	22
British Columbia Lions	10	6	0	438	377	20
Saskatchewan Roughriders	9	7	0	431	371	18
Calgary Stampeders	6	10	0	306	367	12

East semifinal—Ottawa 20, Montreal 16
West semifinal—British Columbia 15, Winnipeg 11
East final—Ottawa 17, Hamilton 13
West final—Edmonton 22, British Columbia 16
Championship (Grey Cup)—Edmonton 22, British Columbia 16

Canadian Football League (Grey Cup)

Winners of Eastern and Western divisions meet in championship game for Grey Cup (donated by Governor-General Earl Grey in 1909). Canadian football features 3 downs, 110-yard field, and each team can have 12 players on field at one time.

1949	Montreal Alouettes 28, Calgary Stampeders 15
1950	Toronto Argonauts 13, Winnipeg Blue Bombers 0
1951	Ottawa Rough Riders 21, Saskatchewan Roughriders 14
1952	Toronto Argonauts 21, Edmonton Eskimos 11
1953	Hamilton Tiger-Cats 12, Winnipeg Blue Bombers 6
1954	Edmonton Eskimos 26, Montreal Alouettes 25
1955	Edmonton Eskimos 34, Montreal Alouettes 19
1956	Edmonton Eskimos 50, Montreal Alouettes 27
1957	Hamilton Tiger-Cats 32, Winnipeg Blue Bombers 7
1958	Winnipeg Blue Bombers 35, Hamilton Tiger-Cats 28
1959	Winnipeg Blue Bombers 21, Hamilton Tiger-Cats 7
1960	Ottawa Rough Riders 16, Edmonton Eskimos 6
1961	Winnipeg Blue Bombers 21, Hamilton Tiger-Cats 14
1962	Winnipeg Blue Bombers 28, Hamilton Tiger-Cats 27
1963	Hamilton Tiger-Cats 21, British Columbia Lions 10
1964	British Columbia Lions 34, Hamilton Tiger-Cats 24
1965	Hamilton Tiger-Cats 22, Winnipeg Blue Bombers 16
1966	Saskatchewan Roughriders 29, Ottawa Rough Riders 14
1967	Hamilton Tiger-Cats 24, Saskatchewan Roughriders 1
1968	Ottawa Rough Riders 24, Calgary Stampeders 21
1969	Ottawa Rough Riders 29, Saskatchewan Roughriders 11
1970	Montreal Alouettes 23, Calgary Stampeders 10
1971	Calgary Stampeders 14, Toronto Argonauts 11
1972	Hamilton Tiger-Cats 13, Saskatchewan Roughriders 10
1973	Ottawa Rough Riders 22, Edmonton Eskimos 18
1974	Montreal Alouettes 20, Edmonton Eskimos 7
1975	Edmonton Eskimos 9, Montreal Alouettes 8
1976	Ottawa Rough Riders 23, Saskatchewan Roughriders 20
1977	Montreal Alouettes 41, Edmonton Eskimos 6
1978	Edmonton Eskimos 20, Montreal Alouettes 13
1979	Edmonton Eskimos 17, Montreal Alouettes 9
1980	Edmonton Eskimos 48, Hamilton Tiger-Cats 10
1981	Edmonton Eskimos 22, British Columbia Lions 16

Pro Rodeo Championship Standings in 1981

Event	Winner	Money won
All Around	Jimmie Cooper, Monument, N.M.	$105,862
Saddle Bronc	Brad Gjermundson, Marshall, N.D.	64,409
Bareback	J.C. Trujillo, Steamboat Springs, Col.	76,140
Bull Riding	Don Gay, Mexquite, Tex.	63,908
Calf Roping	Roy Cooper, Durant, Okla	94,476
Steer Wrestling	Byron Walker, Ennis, Tex.	$ 65,245
Team Roping	Walt Woodard, Stockton, Cal.	48,818
	Doyle Gellerman, Oakdale, Cal.	48,818
Steer Roping	Arnold Felts, Mutual, Okla.	36,121
Women's Barrel Racing	Lynn McKenzie, Shreveport, La.	45,314

Pro Rodeo Cowboy All Around Champions

Year	Winner	Money won
1963	Dean Oliver, Boise, Ida.	$31,329
1964	Dean Oliver, Boise, Ida.	31,150
1965	Dean Oliver, Boise, Ida.	33,163
1966	Larry Mahan, Brooks, Ore.	40,358
1967	Larry Mahan, Brooks, Ore.	51,996
1968	Larry Mahan, Salem, Ore.	49,129
1969	Larry Mahan, Brooks, Ore.	57,726
1970	Larry Mahan, Brooks, Ore.	41,493
1971	Phil Lyne, George West, Tex.	49,245
1972	Phil Lyne, George West, Tex.	60,852
1973	Larry Mahan, Dallas, Tex.	$64,447
1974	Tom Ferguson, Miami, Okla.	66,929
1975	Leo Camarillo, Oakdale, Cal.	50,300
	Tom Ferguson, Miami, Okla.	50,300
1976	Tom Ferguson, Miami, Okla.	87,908
1977	Tom Ferguson, Miami, Okla.	76,730
1978	Tom Ferguson, Miami, Okla.	103,734
1979	Tom Ferguson, Miami, Okla.	96,272
1980	Paul Tierney, Rapid City, S.D.	105,568
1981	Jimmie Cooper, Monument, N.M.	105,862

American Bowling Congress Championships in 1982

79th tournament, Baltimore, Md.

Regular Division

Individual

1. Bruce Bohm, Chicago, Ill. 288, 213, 247 — 748.
2. Terry Lekites, Alexandria, Va. 278, 222, 232 — 732.
3. (tie) Rich Wonders, Racine, Wis. 235, 252, 244 — 731; ian Fischer, Chicago, Ill. 248, 258, 225 — 731.

All Events

1. Rich Wonders, Racine, Wis. 641, 704, 731 — 2,076.
2. Darrell Lewis, Portland, Ore. 678, 627, 703 — 2,008.
3. Steve Fehr, Cincinnati, Oh. 697, 677, 623 — 1,997.

Doubles

1. Darold Meisel, Milwaukee, Wis. 232, 215, 213 — 660 & ch Wonders, Racine, Wis. 235, 211, 258 — 704; aggregate 364.
2. Gary Daroszewski, Milwaukee, Wis. 241, 212, 231 — 684 & erry Kulibert, Oshkosh, Wis. 255, 192, 214 — 661; aggregate 345.

Team

1. Carl's Bowlers Paddock, Cincinnati, Oh. — Don Scudder 226, 220, 213 — 659; Terry Saccone 197, 204, 204 — 605; Greg Nesbit 204, 203, 211 — 618; Steve Fehr 265, 242, 190 — 697; Dave Callery 215, 227, 247 — 689; aggregate 3,268.
2. Pro Bowl, Lansing, Mich. — Dave Beck 192, 191, 253 — 636; Jack Curry 232, 213, 187 — 632; Jeff Curtis 209, 193, 226 — 628; Carl White 216, 216, 233 — 665; Frank Gadaleto 227, 212, 216 — 655; aggregate 3,216.

Booster Division

Team

1. Charlotte Bowling Assn., Charlotte N.C. — Hal Kendrick 231, 233, 226 — 690; Robert Hinzman 180, 159, 177 — 516; Thomas Ballard 168, 145, 176 — 489; George House 152, 173, 186 — 511; J. Joseph Hulsart 138, 212, 178 — 528; aggregate 2,734.
2. Streator Construction, Streator, Ill. — Jack Leonard 211, 195, 212 — 618; Louis Amell 151, 177, 154 — 482; Michael James 169, 180, 169 — 518; Glenn DeLong 154, 161, 202 — 517; Ron Hedglin 212, 172, 192 — 576; aggregate 2,711.

Other Bowling Championships in 1982

U.S. Open Men, Houston, Tex., Jan. 31-Feb. 6; David Husted, ilwaukie, Ore., average 219, prize $21,000. Women, Hender-nville, Tenn., May 11-15; Shinobu Saitoh, Tokyo, Japan, aver-ge 210, prize $9,000.

National Intercollegiate Championships, Men — Baltimore, d., May 14, doubles: Myrl Serra, Arizona State and Tim Lynch, orthern Colorado; singles: Pete Peterson, Wisconsin-Parkside; all events: Myrl Serra, Arizona State. Women — St. Louis, Mo., Apr. 5; doubles: Melisa Day, Ball State and Donna Kolb, Western Ill.; singles: Melisa Day, Ball State; all events: Melisa Day, Ball State.

National Collegiate Team Championship — Orlando, Fla., April 29-May 1; Men: Washington State; Women: Erie Community College.

Bowlers with 9 or More Sanctioned 300 Games

lvin Mesger, Sullivan, Mo.	27
ave Soutar, Kansas City, Mo.	18
ick Weber Sr., St. Louis, Mo.	18
eorge Billick, Old Forge, Pa.	17
onnie Graham, Louisville, Ky.	15
on Johnson, Las Vegas, Nev.	15
ohn Wilcox Jr., Shavertown, Pa.	15
Faragalli, Wayne, N.J.	14
lanny Salazar, San Jose, Cal.	14
ennis Barnes, Oakland, Cal.	13
ay Bluth, St. Louis, Mo.	13
on Carter, Miami, Fla.	13
avid Forcier, Providence, R.I.	13
red McClain, Detroit, Mich.	13
eata Semiz, Fairfield, N.J.	13
ony Torrice, Wolcott, Conn.	13
ames Ewald Jr., Louisville, Ky.	12
asey Jones, Plymouth, Wis.	12
eith Orton, Brigham City, Ut.	12
utch Soper, Santa Ana, Cal.	12
alter Ward, Cleveland, Oh.	12
ave Williams, Sebastopol, Cal.	12
rank Clause, Old Forge, Pa.	11
ave Davis, Tinton Falls, N.J.	11
Larry Laub, San Francisco, Cal.	11
Ted Long, Windgap, Pa.	11
Edward Lubanski, Oak Park, Mich.	11
*Hank Marino, Milwaukee, Wis.	11
Norm Meyers, St. Louis, Mo.	11
Pat Patterson, St. Louis, Mo.	11
Jim Rashleger, San Carlos, Cal.	11
Ron Woolet, Louisville, Ky.	11
Ernie Schlegel, Vancouver, Wash.	11
Earl Anthony, Dublin, Cal.	10
Dan Baudoin, Belmont, Cal.	10
Dick Beattie, Detroit, Mich.	10
Larry Brott, Denver, Col.	10
Steve Carson, Oklahoma City, Okla.	10
Mike Durbin, Chagrin Falls, Oh.	10
Ken Ernske, Spring Valley, N.Y.	10
Russell Fields, San Jose, Cal.	10
Roger Fink, Lodi, Cal.	10
Al Fuscarino, Garfield, N.J.	10
Bob Handley, Shawnee Mission, Kan.	10
Robert Hart, Bay City, Mich.	10
Mickey Higham, Kansas City, Mo.	10
Gus Lampo, Endicott, N.Y.	10
George Pappas, Charlotte, N.C.	10
Skip Pavone, San Jose, Cal.	10
Jim Stefanich, Joliet, Ill.	10
Boss Bosco, Akron, Oh.	9
Roy Buckley, New Albany, Oh.	9
Richard Butler, Alton, Ill.	9
Gary Dickinson, Burleson, Tex.	9
Skee Foremsky, Conroe, Tex.	9
Lou Foxie, Paterson, N.J.	9
Jim Godman, Lorain, Oh.	9
Larry Gray, Torrance, Cal.	9
John Hatz, Littleton, Col.	9
Tom Hennessey, St. Louis, Mo.	9
Mitch Jabczenski, Taylor, Mich.	9
Dick Kumma, Vancouver, Wash.	9
Julius Lamar, Dallas, Tex.	9
Stan Marchut, Paramus, N.J.	9
Larry Miller, Youngstown, Oh.	9
Gary Rebillot, N. Canton, Oh.	9
Terry Saccone, Cincinnati, Oh.	9
Al Savas, Milwaukee, Wis.	9
Bill Spigner, Chicago, Ill.	9
Thomas Suchan, Akron, Oh.	9
Jerry Woji, Stockton, Cal.	9
Dennis Wright, Milwaukee, Wis.	9

Bowled two 300 games in official 3 game series.

Official Records of Annual ABC Tournaments

ype of record	Holder of record	Year	Score
ligh team total	Ace Mitchell Shur-Hooks, Akron	1966	3,357
ligh team game	Falstaff Beer, San Antonio	1958	1,226
ligh doubles score	John Klares-Steve Nagy, Cleveland	1952	1,453
ligh doubles game	Tommy Hudson, Akron, Ohio-Les Zikes, Chicago	1976	558
ligh singles total	Mickey Higham, Kansas City, Mo.	1977	801
ligh all events score	Jim Godman, Lorain, Oh.	1974	2,184
ligh team all events	Cook County Tobacco, Chicago, Ill.	1981	9,695
ligh life-time pin total	Bill Doehrman, Ft. Wayne	1908-1981	109,398

Record Averages for Consecutive Tournaments

lo. in row	Holder of record	Span	Games	Average
wo	Rich Wonders, Racine, Wis.	1981-82	18	229.94
hree	Jim Godman, Lorain, Oh.	1974-76	27	223.96
our	Jim Godman, Lorain, Oh.	1974-77	36	219.44
ive	Jim Godman, Lorain, Oh.	1973-77	45	216.33
en	Bob Strampe, Detroit	1961-70	111	211.10

Masters Bowling Tournament Champions

Year	Winner	Runner-up	W-L	Avg
1971	Jim Godman Lorain, Oh.	Don Johnson, Detroit	9-1	229
1972	Bill Beach, Sharon, Pa.	Jim Godman, Lorain, Oh.	8-1	220
1973	Dave Soutar, Gilroy, Cal.	Dick Ritger, Hartford, Wis.	7-0	218
1974	Paul Colwell, Tucson	Steve Neff, Sarasota, Fla.	7-0	234
1975	Ed Ressler Jr., Allentown, Pa.	Sam Flanagan, Parkersburg, W. Va.	9-1	213
1976	Nelson Burton Jr., St. Louis	Steve Carson, Oklahoma City	7-0	220
1977	Earl Anthony, Tacoma, Wash.	Jim Godman, Lorain, Oh.	7-0	218
1978	Frank Ellenburg, Mesa, Ariz.	Earl Anthony, Tacoma, Wash.	8-1	200
1979	Doug Myers, El Toro, Cal.	Bill Spigner, Hamden, Conn.	7-1	202
1980	Neil Burton, St. Louis, Mo.	Mark Roth, North Arlington, N.J.	7-1	206
1981	Randy Lightfoot, St. Charles, Mo.	Skip Tucker, Merritt Island, Fla.	7-1	218
1982	Joe Berardi, Brooklyn, N.Y.	Ted Hannahs, Zanesville, Oh.	7-0	205

All-Time Records for League and Tournament Play

Type of record	Holder of record	Year	Score	Competition
High team total	Budweiser Beer, St. Louis	1958	3,858	League
High team game	C. T. Maintenance, Berea, Oh.	1981	1,353	League
High doubles total	Nelson Burton Jr., Billy Walden, St. Louis	1970	1,614	Tournament
High doubles game	John Cotta and Steve Larson, Manteca, Cal.	1981	600	Tournament
High individual total	Albert Brandt, Lockport, N.Y.	1939	886	League
High all events score	Paul Andrews, East Moline, Ill.	1981	2,415	Tournament

* In 4-person league.

PBA Winter Tour, 1982

Date	Event	Winner	Winner's share
Jan. 9	Miller High Life Classic, Anaheim, Cal.	Guppy Troup	$23,000
Jan. 16	Showboat Invitational, Las Vegas, Nev.	James Miller	27,000
Jan. 23	Alameda Open, Alameda, Cal.	Earl Anthony	13,000
Jan. 30	Quaker State Open, Grand Prairie, Tex.	Art Trask	20,000
Feb. 6	BPAA U.S. Open, Houston, Tex.	Dave Husted	21,000
Feb. 13	Rolaids Open, Florissant, Mo.	Bill Straub	17,000
Feb. 20	True Value Open, Peoria, Ill.	Art Trask	27,000
Feb. 27	PBA National Championship, Toledo, Oh.	Earl Anthony	38,000
Mar. 6	Sunshine Open, Miami, Fla.	Bob Handley	13,000
Mar. 13	Fair Lanes Open, Washington, D.C.	Mal Alcosta	15,000
Mar. 20	Long Island Open, Garden City, N.Y.	Steve Cook	13,000
Mar. 27	Miller High Life Open, Milwaukee, Wis.	Earl Anthony	23,000
Apr. 3	King Louie Open, Overland Park, Kan.	Pete Couture	16,000
Apr. 10	Cleveland Open, Cleveland, Oh.	Art Trask	13,000
Apr. 17	Greater Hartford Open, Windsor Locks, Conn.	Pete Weber	13,000
Apr. 24	Firestone Tournament of Champions, Akron, Oh.	Mike Durbin	40,000

Leading Averages in 1981

(400 or more games in PBA tournaments)

Pos.	Name, City	Tournaments	Games	Pinfall	Average
1.	Mark Roth, Spring Lake Hts., N.J.	25	856	185,494	216.699
2.	Earl Anthony, Dublin, Cal.	32	1156	249,017	215.413
3.	Marshall Holman, Medford, Ore.	23	868	185,797	214.052
4.	Tom Baker, Buffalo, N.Y.	29	928	197,746	213.088
5.	Wayne Webb, Indianapolis, Ind.	30	1005	213,163	212.102
6.	Gary Dickinson, Burleson, Tex.	17	559	118,315	211.655
7.	Bob Handley, Fairway, Kan.	29	886	187,462	211.582
8.	Steve Martin, Kingsport, Tenn.	27	867	183,283	211.399
9.	Joe Berardi, Brooklyn, N.Y.	27	947	199,664	210.838
10.	Ernie Schlegel, Vancouver, Wash.	22	667	140,576	210.759
11.	Mike Aulby, Indianapolis, Ind.	33	906	190,882	210.687
12.	George Pappas, Charlotte, N.C.	29	917	193,190	210.676
13.	Gil Sliker, Washington, N.J.	33	1029	216,754	210.645
14.	Dave Husted, Milwaukee, Ore.	31	879	185,154	210.642
15.	Jay Robinson, Van Nuys, Cal.	33	1074	226,068	210.492

Firestone Tournament of Champions

This is professional bowling's richest tournament and has been held each year since its inception in 1965, in Akron, Oh the home of the Professional Bowlers Association. First prize in 1982 was $40,000.

Year	Winner	Year	Winner	Year	Winner	Year	Winner
1965	Billy Hardwick	1970	Don Johnson	1975	Dave Davis	1979	George Pappas
1966	Wayne Zahn	1971	Johnny Petraglia	1976	Marshall Holman	1980	Wayne Webb
1967	Jim Stefanich	1972	Mike Durbin	1977	Mike Berlin	1981	Steve Cook
1968	Dave Davis	1973	Jim Godman	1978	Earl Anthony	1982	Mike Durbin
1969	Jim Godman	1974	Earl Anthony				

Leading PBA Averages by Year

Year	Bowler	Tournaments	Average	Year	Bowler	Tournaments	Average
1962	Don Carter, St. Louis, Mo.	25	212.844	1972	Don Johnson, Akron, Oh.	30	215.290
1963	Billy Hardwick, Louisville, Ky.	26	210.346	1973	Earl Anthony, Tacoma, Wash.	29	215.799
1964	Ray Bluth, St. Louis, Mo.	27	210.512	1974	Earl Anthony, Tacoma, Wash.	28	219.394
1965	Dick Weber, St. Louis, Mo.	19	211.895	1975	Earl Anthony, Tacoma, Wash.	30	219.060
1966	Wayne Zahn, Atlanta, Ga.	27	208.663	1976	Mark Roth, New York, N.Y.	28	215.970
1967	Wayne Zahn, Atlanta, Ga.	29	212.342	1977	Mark Roth, New York, N.Y.	28	218.174
1968	Jim Stefanich, Joliet, Ill.	33	211.895	1978	Mark Roth, North Arlington, N.J.	25	219.834
1969	Bill Hardwick, Louisville, Ky.	33	212.957	1979	Mark Roth, North Arlington, N.J.	26	221.662
1970	Nelson Burton Jr., St. Louis, Mo.	32	214.908	1980	Earl Anthony, Dublin, Cal.	18	218.535
1971	Don Johnson, Akron, Oh.	31	213.977	1981	Mark Roth, Spring Lake Hts., N.J.	25	216.699

PBA Leading Money Winners

Total winnings are from PBA, ABC Masters, and BPAA All-Star tournaments only, and do not include numerous other tournaments or earnings from special television shows and matches.

Year	Bowler	Dollars	Year	Bowler	Dollars	Year	Bowler	Dollars
1960	Don Carter	22,525	1968	Jim Stefanich	67,377	1975	Earl Anthony	107,585
1961	Dick Weber	26,280	1969	Billy Hardwick	64,160	1976	Earl Anthony	110,833
1962	Don Carter	49,972	1970	Mike McGrath	52,049	1977	Mark Roth	105,583
1963	Dick Weber	46,333	1971	Johnny Petraglia	85,065	1978	Mark Roth	134,500
1964	Bob Strampe	33,592	1972	Don Johnson	56,648	1979	Mark Roth	124,517
1965	Dick Weber	47,674	1973	Don McCune	69,000	1980	Wayne Webb	116,700
1966	Wayne Zahn	54,720	1974	Earl Anthony	99,585	1981	Earl Anthony	164,735
1967	Dave Davis	54,165						

Women's International Bowling Congress Champions

Individual	All events	Year	2-woman teams	5-woman teams
Beverly Shonk, Canton, Oh. 686	Betty Morris, Stockton, Cal. 1,866	**1976**	Georgene Cordes-Shirley Sjostrom, Bloomington, Minn.; Eloise Vacco-Debbie Rainone, Cleveland Hts., Oh. (tie) 1,232	PWBA 1, Oklahoma City, Okla. 2,839
Akiko Yamaga, Tokyo, Japan 714	Akiko Yamaga, Tokyo, Japan 1,895	**1977**	Ozella Houston-Dorothy Jackson, Detroit, Mich. 1,234	Allgauer's Restaurant Chicago, Ill. 2,818
Mae Bolt, Berwyn, Ill. 709	Annese Kelly, New York, N.Y. 1,896	**1978**	Barbara Shelton-Annese Kelly, New York, N.Y. 1,211	Cook County Vending, Chicago, Ill. 2,956
Betty Morris, Stockton, Cal. 699	Betty Morris, Stockton, Cal. 1,945	**1979**	Mary Ann Deptula-Geri Beattie, Warren, Dearborn Hts., Mich. 1,314	Alpine Lanes, Euless, Tex. 3,096
Betty Morris, Stockton, Cal. 674	Cheryl Robinson, Van Nuys, Cal. 1,848	**1980**	Carol Lee-Dawn Raddatz, Hempstead, E. Northport, N.Y. 1,247	All Japan, Tokyo, Japan 3,014
Virginia Norton, So. Gate, Cal. 672	Virginia Norton, So. Gate, Cal. 1,905	**1981**	Nikki Gianulias-Donna Adamek, Vallejo, Duarte, Cal. 1,305	Earl Anthony's Dublin Bowl, Dublin Cal. 2,963
Gracie Freeman, Alexandria, Va. 652	Aleta Rzepecki, Detroit, Mich. 1,905	**1982**	Shirley Hintz-Lisa Rathgeber, Merritt Island, Palmetto, Fla.; Pat Costello-Donna Adamek, Fremont, Durant, Cal. (tie) 1,264	Zavakos Realtors, Dayton, Oh. 2,961

Most Sanctioned 300 Games

Donna Adamek, Duarte, Cal.	6	Pat Adams, Santa Cruz, Cal.	3	Kathy Lecroy, Fort Worth, Tex.	3
Betty Morris, Stockton, Cal.	5	Debbie Bennett, Akron, Oh.	3	Sylvia Martin, Philadelphia, Penn.	3
Jeanne Maiden, Willowick, Oh.	5	Pam Buckner, Reno, Nev.	3	Cindy Mason, Sunnyvale, Cal.	3
Beverly Ortner, Tucson, Ariz.	4	Toni Gillard, Beverly, Oh.	3	Ruby Thomas, Abilene, Tex.	3
Regi Hills, St. Louis, Mo	4	Letitia Johnson, Napa, Cal.	3	Carolyn Trump, Akron, Oh.	3

Table Tennis in 1981-82

U.S. National Table Tennis Closed Championship

Las Vegas, Nev., Dec. 17-20, 1981

Men's Singles — Scott Boggan, Merrick, N.Y.
Women's Singles — In Sook Bhushan, Denver, Col.
Mixed Doubles — Dan Seemiller & In Sook Bhushan, Pittsburgh Pa., & Denver, Col.
Women's Doubles — In Sook Bhushan & Kasia Gaca, Denver, Col.
Men's Doubles — Dan & Rick Seemiller, Pittsburgh, Pa.

U.S. National Table Tennis Open

Detroit, Mich., June 30-July 4, 1982

Men's Singles — Zoran Kosanovic, Canada
Women's Singles — Kayoko Kawahigashi, Japan
Mixed Doubles — Koichi Kawamura & Tomoko Tamura, Japan
Women's Doubles — Kayoko Kawahigashi & Rie Wada, Japan
Men's Doubles — Dan & Rick Seemiller, Pittsburgh, Pa.
Men's Team — Japan.
Women's Team — Korea "B"

Estimated Earnings of Athletes

The actual amount of money paid by a club to an athlete is known only to the club, the athlete, his agent, and the IRS. The following salary and earnings figures have been taken from published sources, reliable, but not official. The figures do not include outside income, such as fees for personal appearances and commercial endorsements. The earnings of boxers are difficult to determine. As much as 1/3 of their earnings may go to their managers. They also have large training expenses. Larry Holmes and Sugar Ray Leonard can earn several million dollars for a single fight.

Athlete	Dollars
Moses Malone, basketball	2,000,000
Gary Carter, baseball	2,000,000
George Foster, baseball	1,600,000
Dave Winfield, baseball	1,500,000
Pete Rose, baseball	1,300,000
Mike Schmidt, baseball	1,200,000
Fred Lynn, baseball	1,200,000
Eddie Murray, baseball	1,000,000
Nolan Ryan, baseball	1,000,000
Phil Niekro, baseball (mostly deferred payments)	1,000,000
George Brett, baseball	1,000,000
Kareem Abdul-Jabbar, basketball	1,000,000
Marquis Johnson, basketball	1,000,000
Wayne Gretzky, hockey	1,000,000
Reggie Jackson, baseball	975,000
John McEnroe, tennis (1981)	941,000
Otis Birdsong, basketball	900,000
Dave Parker, baseball	900,000
Rod Carew, baseball	900,000
Dave Concepcion, baseball	900,000
Martina Navratilova, tennis (1981)	865,437
Bobby Grich, baseball	825,000
Mitch Kupchak, basketball	800,000
Ken Griffey, baseball	800,000
Ron Guidry, baseball	800,000
Andre Dawson, baseball	800,000
James Edwards, basketball	800,000
Scott Wedman, basketball	800,000
Darrell Porter, baseball	800,000
Ron Leflore, baseball	800,000
Don Sutton, baseball	775,000
Gus Williams, basketball	750,000
Dave Collins, baseball	750,000
Steve Carlton, baseball	750,000
David Thompson, basketball	650,000-750,000
Ivan Lendl, tennis (1981)	716,037
Rick Burleson, baseball	700,000
Claudell Washington, baseball	700,000
Bruce Sutter, baseball	700,000
Tommy John, baseball	700,000
Jim Rice, baseball	700,000
Vida Blue, baseball	700,000
Julius Erving, basketball	500,000-700,000
Darrell Waltrip, auto racing (1981)	693,342
Ted Simmons, baseball	665,000
Larry Bird, basketball	650,000
Bobby Allison, auto racing (1981)	644,311
Mike Bossy, hockey	640,000
Walter Payton, football	600,000
Steve Kemp, baseball	600,000
Roy Smalley, baseball	600,000
Archie Manning, football	600,000
Keith Hernandez, baseball	600,000
Craig Swan, baseball	600,000
Marcel Dionne, hockey	600,000
Magic Johnson, basketball	600,000
Carlton Fisk, baseball	580,000
Chris Evert-Lloyd, tennis (1981)	572,162
Bill Buckner, baseball	510,000
Bert Blyleven, baseball	500,000
Tom Cousineau, football	500,000
Gorman Thomas, baseball	500,000
Ed Farmer, baseball	495,000
Sparky Lyle, baseball	480,000
Oscar Gamble, baseball	475,000
Robin Yount, baseball	470,000
Terry Bradshaw, football	470,000
Tracy Austin, tennis (1981)	453,409
Bob Lanier, basketball	450,000
Rich Gossage, baseball	450,000
Rick Cerone, baseball	440,000
Joe Rudi, baseball	440,000
Johnny Bench, baseball	420,000
Ron Jaworski, football	410,000
Tom Kite, golf (1981)	375,699
George Rogers, football	375,000
Ray Floyd, golf (1981)	359,360
Gil Perreault, hockey	350,000
Billy Sims, football	350,000
Tom Watson, golf (1981)	347,660
Lynn Swann, football	340,000
Randy White, football	318,000
Tony Esposito, hockey	300,000
Giorgio Chinaglia, soccer	283,000
Bert Jones, football	275,000
Steve Bartkowski, football	230,000
Jack Ham, football	230,000
Lee Roy Selmon, football	218,000
Beth Daniel, golf (1981)	206,977
Joanne Carner, golf (1981)	206,649
Earl Anthony, bowling (1981)	164,735

Wrestling Champions in 1982

National AAU Senior Freestyle Championships

Lincoln, Neb., Apr. 29-May 1

105.5 lbs.—Bill Rosado, Sunkist Kids.
114.5 lbs.—Bob Weaver, New York AC.
125.5 lbs.—Gene Mills, New York AC.
136.5 lbs.—Lee Roy Smith, Cowboy WC.
149.5 lbs.—Andy Rein, Wisconsin WC.
163 lbs.—Lee Kemp, Wisconsin WC.
180.5 lbs.—Bruce Kinseth, Hawkeye WC.
198 lbs.—Bill Scherr, Nebraska Olympic Club.
220 lbs.—Greg Gibson, U.S. Marines.
Heavyweight—Bruce Baumgartner, New York AC.
Team champion—New York Athletic Club.
Outstanding wrestler—Lee Roy Smith.

National AAU Senior Greco-Roman Championships

Cincinnati, Oh., May 7-8

105.5 lbs.—T.J. Jones, U.S. Navy.
114.5 lbs.—Mark Fuller, Little C Athletic Club.
125.5 lbs.—Dan Mello, U.S. Marines.
136.5 lbs.—Frank Famiano, Adirondack 3-Style Club.
149.5 lbs.—Doug Yeats, Canada.
163 lbs.—John Matthews, Michigan WC.
180.5 lbs.—Tom Press, Minnesota WC.
198 lbs.—Steve Fraser, Michigan WC.
220 lbs.—Greg Gibson, U.S. Marines.
Heavyweight—Pete Lee, Grand Rapids, Mich.
Team champion—U.S. Marine Corps.
Outstanding wrestler—Dan Mello.

World Cup Freestyle Championships

Toledo, Oh., March 27-28

105.5 lbs.—Adam Cuestas, U.S.
114.5 lbs.—Joe Gonzales, U.S.
125.5 lbs.—Sergey Beloglazov, USSR.
136.5 lbs.—Viktor Alexeev, USSR.
149.5 lbs.—Mikhail Kharachura, USSR.
163 lbs.—Lee Kemp, U.S.
180.5 lbs.—Mark Schultz, U.S.
198 lbs.—Clark Davis, Canada
220 lbs.—Magomed Magomedov, USSR.
Heavyweight—Salman Chasimikov, USSR.
Team champion—United States.

Contract Bridge Championships for North America in 1981-82

Source: American Contract Bridge League, Memphis, Tenn.

Fall Championships

San Francisco, Cal., Nov. 20-29, 1981

Reisinger Open Teams (Board-a-Match) Trophy — Chip Martel, Davis, Cal.; Peter Pender, Guerneville, Cal.; Hugh Ross, Oakland, Cal.; Lew Stansby, Castro Valley, Cal.

North American Swiss Teams — Bob Etter, Stockton, Cal.; Ann Jacobson, Stockton, Calif.; Bob Thomson, Emeryville, Cal.; Ron Beall, Oakland, Cal.

Mixed Pairs — James Zimmerman, Shaker Hts., Oh.; Esta Van Zandt, Houston, Tex.

Life Master Men's Pairs — Roger Abelson, Berkeley, Cal.; Mike Levinson, Daly City, Cal.

Life Master Women's Pairs — Edith Kemp, Miami Beach, Fla.; Nancy Gruver, Ellicott City, Md.

Spring Championships

Niagara Falls, N.Y., March 19-28, 1982

Women's Knockout Teams — Edith Kemp, Miami Beach, Fla.; Nancy Gruver, Ellicott City, Md.; Mary Jane Farell, Beverly Hills, Cal.; Randy Montin, Whittier, Cal.; Dorothy Truscott, New York, N.Y.; Stasha Cohen, New York, N.Y.

Open Pairs — Gerald Caravelli, Des Plaines, Ill.; Craig Janitschke, Lacey, Wash.

Grand National Pairs — Ivan Scope, San Francisco, Cal.; Bill Nutting, Kensington, Cal.

Men's Pairs — Harold Lilie, Valley Stream, N.Y.; David Berkowitz, Harmon Cove, N.J.

Women's Pairs — Beverly Rosenberg, Sherman Oaks, Cal.; Hermine Baron, Los Angeles, Cal.

Vanderbilt Open Team — George Rosenkranz, Mexico City, Mexico; Eddie Wold, Houston, Tex.; Jim Jacoby, Dallas, Tex.; Mike Passell, Dallas, Tex.; Eric Rodwell, W. Lafayette, Ind.; Jeff Meckstroth, Columbus, Oh.

Men's Board-A-Match Teams — Dave Berkowitz, Harmon Cove, N.J.; Al Rand, New York, N.Y.; Mathew Granovetter, New York, N.Y.; Harold Lilie, Valley Stream, N.Y.

Open Pairs — Gerald Caravelli, Des Plaines, Ill.; Craig Janitschke, Lacey, Wash.

Summer Championships

Albuquerque, N.M., July 23-Aug. 1, 1982

Spingold Master Teams — Bobby Wolff, Dallas, Tex.; Bob Hamman, Dallas, Tex.; Alan Sontag, New York, N.Y.; Mike Becker, New York, N.Y.; Peter Weichsel, Miami Beach, Fla.; Ron Rubin, Livingston, N.J.

Men's Swiss Teams — Allan Stauber, Poughkeepsie, N.Y.; Jan Janitschke, Denver, Col.; Ross Grabel, Huntington Beach, Cal.; Mike Smolen, Marina del Rey, Cal.

Women's Swiss Teams — Dorothy Truscott, New York, N.Y.; Stasha Cohen, New York, N.Y.; Edith Kemp, Miami Beach, Fla.; Nancy Gruver, Ellicott City, Md.; Mary Jane Farell, Beverly Hills, Cal.; Randi Montin, Whittier, Cal.

Grand National Open Teams —Chip Martel, Davis, Cal.; Peter Pender, Guerneville, Cal.; Hugh Ross, Oakland, Cal.; Lew Stansby, Castro Valley, Cal.; Ron Von der Porten, San Francisco, Cal.; Kyle Larsen, Walnut Creek, Cal.

Master Mixed Teams — (tie) Lynn Deas, Schenectady, N.Y.; Norb Kremer, Alexandria, Va.; Beth Palmer, Silver Spring, Md.; Bill Cole, Silver Spring, Md.; Carol Sanders, Nashville, Tenn.; Tommy Sanders, Nashville, Tenn.; Sid Lazard, New Orleans, La.; Joan Dewitt, Chicago, Ill.

Life Master Pairs — Thomas Sanders, Nashville, Tenn.; Ronald Andersen, New York, N.Y.

Non-Life Master Swiss Teams — Jay Feldman, Bill Carnes, David Rinehart, Gordon Grossetta, Norval Baran, all Tucson, Ariz.; Bill Brown, Arlington, Va.

Men's Swiss Teams — Allan Stauber, Poughkeepsie, N.Y.; Jan Janitschke, Denver, Col.; Ross Grabel, Huntington Beach, Cal.; Mike Smolen, Marina del Rey, Cal.

Women's Swiss Teams — Dorothy Truscott, New York, N.Y.; Stasha Cohen, New York, N.Y.; Edith Kemp, Miami Beach, Fla.; Nancy Gruver, Ellicott City, Md.; Mary Jane Farell, Beverly Hills, Cal.; Randi Montin, Whittier, Cal.

Chess

Chess dates back to antiquity. Its exact origin is unknown. The strongest players of their time, and therefore regarded by later generations as world champions, were Francois Philidor, France; Alexandre Deschappelles, France; Louis de la Bourdonnais, France; Howard Staunton, England; Adolph Anderssen, Germany and Paul Morphy, United States. In 1866 Wilhelm Steinitz of Czechoslovakia defeated Adolph Anderssen and claimed the title of world champion. The official world champions, since the title was first used follow:

1866-1894 Wilhelm Steinitz, Austria
1894-1921 Dr. Emanuel Lasker, Germany
1921-1927 Jose R. Capablanca, Cuba
1927-1935 Dr. Alexander A. Alekhine, Russia
1935-1937 Dr. Max Euwe, Netherlands
1937-1946 Dr. Alexander A. Alekhine, USSR
1948-1957 Mikhail Botvinnik, USSR
1957-1958 Vassily Smysolv, USSR
1958-1959 Mikhail Botvinnik, USSR
1960-1961 Mikhail Tal, USSR
1961-1963 Mikhail Botvinnik, USSR
1963-1969 Tigran Petrosian, USSR
1969-1972 Boris Spassky, USSR
1972-1975 Bobby Fischer, U.S. (a)
1975 Anatoly Karpov, USSR

(a) Defaulted championship after refusal to accept International Chess Federation rules for a championship match, April 1975.

United States Champions

Unofficial champions

1857-1871 Paul Morphy
1871-1876 George Mackenzie
1876-1880 James Mason
1880-1889 George Mackenzie
1889-1890 S. Lipschutz
1890 Jackson Showalter
1890-1891 Max Judd
1891-1892 Jackson Showalter
1892-1894 S. Lipschutz

Official champions

1894 Jackson Showalter
1894-1895 Albert Hodges
1895-1897 Jackson Showalter
1897-1909 Harry Pillsbury
1909-1936 Frank Marshall
1936-1944 Samuel Reshevsky
1944-1946 Arnold Denker
1946-1948 Samuel Reshevsky
1948-1951 Herman Steiner
1951-1954 Larry Evans
1954-1957 Arthur Bisguier
1957-1961 Bobby Fischer
1961-1962 Larry Evans
1962-1968 Bobby Fischer
1968-1969 Larry Evans
1969-1972 Samuel Reshevsky
1972-1973 Robert Byrne
1973-1974 Lubomir Kavalek, John Grefe
1974-1977 Walter Browne
1978-1980 Lubomir Kavalek
1980-1981 (tie) Larry Evans, Larry Christiansen, Walter Browne
1981 (tie) Walter Browne, Yasser Seirawan

Pocket Billiards Championship in 1982

Steve Mizerak won the 1982 World Championship of Pocket Billiards defeating Danny DiLiberto 150-80, on Aug. 22 in New York City. Jean Balukas defeated Loree-Jan Ogonowski to win her 6th women's title.

Notable Sports Personalities

Henry Aaron, b. 1934: Milwaukee-Atlanta outfielder hit record 755 home runs; led NL 4 times.
Kareem Abdul-Jabbar, b. 1947: Milwaukee, L.A. Lakers center; MVP 6 times; leading scorer twice.
Grover Cleveland Alexander, (1887-1950): pitcher won 374 NL games; pitched 16 shutouts, 1916.
Muhammad Ali, b. 1942; 3-time heavyweight champion.
Mario Andretti, b. 1940; U.S. Auto Club national champ 3 times: won Indy 500, 1969; Grand Prix champ, 1978.
Eddie Arcaro, b. 1916: jockey rode 4,779 winners including the Kentucky Derby 5 times; the Preakness and Belmont Stakes 6 times each.
Henry Armstrong, b. 1912: boxer held feather-, welter-, lightweight titles simultaneously, 1937-38.
Arthur Ashe, b. 1943: U.S. singles champ, 1968, Wimbledon champ, 1975.
Red Auerbach, b. 1917: coached Boston Celtics to 9 NBA championships.
Ernie Banks, b. 1931: Chicago Cubs slugger hit 512 NL homers: twice MVP.
Roger Bannister, b. 1929: Briton ran first sub 4-minute mile, May 6, 1954.
Rick Barry, b. 1944: NBA scoring leader, 1967; ABA, 1969.
Sammy Baugh, b. 1914: Washington Redskins quarterback held numerous records upon retirement after 16 pro seasons.
Elgin Baylor, b. 1934: L.A. Lakers forward; 1st team all-star 10 times.
Bob Beamon, b. 1946: long jumper won 1968 Olympic gold medal with record 29 ft. 2½ in.
Jean Beliveau, b. 1931: Montreal Canadiens center scored 507 goals; twice MVP.
Johnny Bench, b. 1947: Cincinnati Reds catcher; MVP twice; led league in home runs twice, RBIs 3 times.
Patty Berg, b. 1918: won over 80 golf tournaments: AP Woman Athlete-of-the-Year 3 times.
Yogi Berra, b. 1925: N.Y. Yankees catcher; MVP 3 times; played in 14 World Series.
Raymond Berry, b. 1933: Baltimore Colts receiver caught 631 passes.
Larry Bird, b. 1956: Boston Celtics forward; 1st team all-star 3 times.
George Blanda, b. 1927: quarterback, kicker; 26 years as active player, scoring record 2,002 points.
Bjorn Borg, b. 1956: led Sweden to first Davis Cup, 1975; Wimbledon champion, 5 times.
Julius Boros, b. 1920: won U.S. Open, 1952, 1963; PGA champ, 1968.
Jack Brabham, b. 1926: Grand Prix champ 3 times.
George Brett, b. 1953: Kansas City Royals 3d baseman led AL in batting, 1976, 1980; MVP, 1980.
Lou Brock, b. 1939: St. Louis Cardinals outfielder stole record 118 bases, 1974; record 937 career; led NL 8 times.
Jimmy Brown, b. 1936: Cleveland Browns fullback ran for record 12,312 career yards; MVP 3 times.
Paul "Bear" Bryant, b. 1913; college football coach set record 315 victories, 1981.
Don Budge, b. 1915: won numerous amateur and pro tennis titles, "grand slam," 1938.
Maria Bueno, b. 1939: U.S. singles champ 4 times; Wimbledon champ 3 times.
Dick Butkus, b. 1942: Chicago Bears linebacker twice chosen best NFL defensive player.
Dick Button, b. 1929: figure skater won 1948, 1952 Olympic gold medals; world titlist, 1948-52.
Walter Camp, (1859-1925): Yale football player, coach, athletic director; established many rules; promoted All-America designations.
Roy Campanella, b. 1921: Brooklyn Dodgers catcher; MVP 3 times.
Earl Campbell, b. 1955: Houston Oilers running back; NFL MVP 1978-1980.
Rod Carew, b. 1945: AL infielder won 7 batting titles; MVP, 1977.
Steve Carlton, b. 1944: NL pitcher won 20 games 5 times, Cy Young award 3 times.
Billy Casper, b. 1931: PGA Player-of-the-Year 3 times; U.S. Open champ twice.
Wilt Chamberlain, b. 1936: center scored NBA career record 31,419 points; MVP 4 times.
Bobby Clarke, b. 1949: Philadelphia Flyers center led team to 2 Stanley Cup championships: MVP 3 times.
Roberto Clemente, (1934-1972): Pittsburgh Pirates outfielder won 4 batting titles; MVP, 1966.
Ty Cobb, (1886-1961): Detroit Tigers outfielder had record .367 lifetime batting average, 4,191 hits, 12 batting titles.
Sebastian Coe, b. 1956: Briton set record in 800 meters, 1,000 meters, and mile, 1981.
Nadia Comaneci, b. 1961: Romanian gymnast won 3 gold medals, achieved 7 perfect scores, 1976 Olympics.
Maureen Connolly, (1934-1969): won tennis "grand slam," 1953; AP Woman-Athlete-of-the-Year 3 times.
Jimmy Connors, b. 1952: U.S. singles champ 4 times; Wimbledon champ twice.
James J. Corbett, (1866-1933): heavyweight champion, 1892-97; credited with being the first "scientific" boxer.
Margaret Smith Court, b. 1942: Australian won U.S. singles championship 5 times; Wimbledon champ 3 times.
Bob Cousy, b. 1928: Boston Celtics guard led team to 6 NBA championships: MVP, 1957.
Stanley Dancer, b. 1927: harness racing driver drove Hambletonian winner 3 times, Little Brown Jug winner 4 times.
Dizzy Dean, (1911-1974): colorful pitcher for St. Louis Cardinals "Gashouse Gang" in the 30s; MVP, 1934.
Jack Dempsey, b. 1895: heavyweight champion, 1919-26.
Joe DiMaggio, b. 1914: N.Y. Yankees outfielder hit safely in record 56 consecutive games, 1941; MVP 3 times.
Leo Durocher, b. 1906: colorful manager of Dodgers, Giants, and Cubs; won 3 NL pennants.
Gertrude Ederle, b. 1906: first woman to swim English Channel, broke existing men's record, 1926.
Julius Erving, b. 1950: MVP and leading scorer in ABA 3 times; NBA MVP, 1981.
Phil Esposito, b. 1942: scored record 76 goals and 152 points in 1970-71; NHL scoring leader 5 times.
Chris Evert Lloyd, b. 1954: U.S. singles champ 6 times, Wimbledon champ twice.
Ray Ewry, (1873-1937): track and field star won 8 gold medals, 1900, 1904, and 1908 Olympics.
Juan Fangio, b. 1911: Argentine World Grand Prix champion 5 times.
Bob Feller, b. 1918: Cleveland Indians pitcher won 266 games; pitched 3 no-hitters, 12 one-hitters.
Peggy Fleming, b. 1948: world figure skating champion, 1966-68; gold medalist 1968 Olympics.
Whitey Ford, b. 1928: N.Y. Yankees pitcher won record 10 World Series games.
Dick Fosbury, b. 1947: high jumper won 1968 Olympic gold medal; developed the "Fosbury Flop."
George Foster, b. 1951: NL outfielder hit 52 home runs, selected MVP, 1977; led NL RBI's, 1976-78.
Jimmy Foxx, (1907-1967): Red Sox, Athletics slugger; MVP 3 times; triple crown, 1933.
A.J. Foyt, b. 1935: won Indy 500 4 times; U.S. Auto Club champ 6 times.
Dawn Fraser, b. 1937: Australian swimmer won Olympics 100-meter freestyle 3 times.
Joe Frazier, b. 1944: heavyweight champion, 1970-73.
Lou Gehrig, (1903-1941): N.Y. Yankees 1st baseman played record 2,130 consecutive games, MVP, 1936.
George Gervin, b. 1952: leading NBA scorer, 1978-80, 1981.
Althea Gibson, b. 1927: twice U.S. and Wimbledon singles champ.
Bob Gibson, b. 1935: St. Louis Cardinals pitcher won Cy Young award twice; struck out NL record 3,117 batters.
Frank Gifford, b. 1930: N.Y. Giants back; MVP 1956.
Otto Graham, b. 1921: Cleveland Browns quarterback; all-pro 4 times.
Red Grange, b 1903: All-America at Univ. of Illinois; played for Chicago Bears, 1925-35.
Joe Greene, b. 1946: Pittsburgh Steelers lineman; twice NFL outstanding defensive player.
Wayne Gretzky, b. 1961: Edmonton Oilers center scored record 92 goals, 212 pts., 1982; MVP, 1980-82.
Lefty Grove, (1900-1975): pitcher won 300 AL games; 20-game winner 8 times.
Walter Hagen, (1892-1969): won PGA championship 5 times. British Open 4 times.
George Halas, b. 1895: founder-coach of Chicago Bears; won 5 NFL championships.
Bill Hartack, b. 1932: jockey rode 5 Kentucky Derby winners.
Doug Harvey, b. 1930: Montreal Canadiens defenseman; Norris Trophy 7 times.
Bill Haughton, b. 1923: harness racing driver won Little Brown Jug 4 times, Hambletonian 4 times.
John Havlicek, b. 1940: Boston Celtics forward scored over 26,000 NBA points.
Eric Heiden, b. 1958: speed skater won 5 1980 Olympic gold medals.
Carol Heiss, b. 1940: world champion figure skater 5 consecutive years, 1956-60; won 1960 Olympic gold medal.
Sonja Henie, (1912-1969): world champion figure skater, 1927-36; Olympic gold medalist, 1928, 1932, 1936.
Ben Hogan, b. 1912: won 4 U.S. Open championships, 2 PGA, 2 Masters.

Willie Hoppe, (1887-1959): won some 50 world billiard titles.
Larry Holmes, b. 1949: WBC Heavyweight Champ 1978- .
Rogers Hornsby, (1896-1963): NL 2d baseman batted record .424 in 1924; twice won triple crown; batting leader, 1920-25.
Paul Hornung, b. 1935: Green Bay Packers runner-placekicker scored record 176 points, 1960.
Gordie Howe, b. 1928: hockey forward holds NHL career records in goals, assists, and points; NHL MVP 6 times, leading scorer 6 times.
Carl Hubbell, b. 1903: N.Y. Giants pitcher; 20-game winner 5 consecutive years, 1933-37.
Bobby Hull, b. 1939: NHL all-star 10 times.
Catfish Hunter, b 1946: pitched perfect game, 1968; 20-game winner 5 times.
Don Hutson, b. 1913: Green Bay Packers receiver caught NFL record 99 touchdown passes.
Reggie Jackson, b. 1946: slugger led AL in home runs 3 times; MVP, 1973; hit 5 World Series home runs, 1977.
Bruce Jenner, b. 1949: decathlon gold medalist, 1976.
Jack Johnson, (1878-1946): heavyweight champion, 1910-15.
Rafer Johnson, b. 1935: decathlon gold medalist, 1960.
Walter Johnson, (1887-1946): Washington Senators pitcher won 414 games.
Bert Jones, b. 1951: quarterback; MVP, 1976.
Bobby Jones, (1902-1971); won "grand slam of golf" 1930; U.S. Amateur champ 5 times, U.S. Open champ 4 times.
Deacon Jones, b. 1938: L.A. Rams lineman; twice NFL outstanding defensive player.
Sonny Jurgensen, b. 1934: quarterback named all-pro 5 times; completed record 288 passes, 1967.
Duke Kahanamoku, (1890-1968): swimmer won 1912, 1920 Olympic gold medals in 100-meter freestyle.
Harmon Killebrew, b. 1936: Minnesota Twins slugger led AL in home runs 6 times.
Jean Claude Killy, b. 1943: French skier won 3 1968 Olympic gold medals.
Ralph Kiner, b. 1922: Pittsburgh Pirates slugger led NL in home runs 7 consecutive years, 1946-52.
Billie Jean King, b. 1943: U.S. singles champ 4 times; Wimbledon champ 6 times.
Olga Korbut, b. 1956: Soviet gymnast won 3 1972 Olympic gold medals.
Sandy Koufax, b. 1935: Dodgers pitcher won Cy Young award 3 times; lowest ERA in NL, 1962-66; pitched 4 no-hitters, one a perfect game.
Guy Lafleur, b. 1951: Montreal Canadiens forward led NHL in scoring 3 times; MVP, 1977, 1978.
Tom Landry, b. 1924: Dallas Cowboys head coach since 1960.
Rod Laver, b. 1938: Australian won tennis "grand slam," 1962, 1969; Wimbledon champ 4 times.
Sugar Ray Leonard, b. 1956: welterweight champ, 1981.
Vince Lombardi, (1913-1970): Green Bay Packers coach led, team to 5 NFL championships and 2 Super Bowl victories.
Johnny Longden, b. 1907: jockey rode 6,032 winners.
Joe Louis, (1914-1981): 1914: heavyweight champion, 1937-49.
Sid Luckman, b. 1916: Chicago Bears quarterback led team to 4 NFL championships; MVP, 1943.
Fred Lynn, b. 1952: Outfielder led AL in batting, 1979; AL MVP, 1975.
Connie Mack, (1862-1956): Philadelphia Athletics manager, 1901-50; won 9 pennants, 5 championships.
Bill Madlock, b. 1951: NL batting leader, 1975, 1976, 1981.
Moses Malone, b. 1955: NBA center was MVP 1979, 1982.
Mickey Mantle, b. 1931: N.Y. Yankees outfielder; triple crown, 1956; 18 World Series home runs.
Alice Marble, b. 1913: U.S. singles champ 4 times.
Rocky Marciano, (1923-1969): heavyweight champion, 1952-56; retired undefeated.
Roger Maris, b. 1934: N.Y. Yankees outfielder hit record 61 home runs, 1961; MVP, 1960 and 1961.
Billy Martin, b. 1928: baseball manager led N.Y. Yankees to World Series title, 1977.
Eddie Mathews, b. 1931: Milwaukee-Atlanta 3d baseman hit 512 career home runs.
Christy Mathewson, (1880-1925): N.Y. Giants pitcher won 373 games.
Bob Mathias, b. 1930: decathlon gold medalist, 1948, 1952.
Willie Mays, b. 1931: N.Y.-S.F. Giants center fielder hit 660 home runs; twice MVP.
John McEnroe, b. 1959: U.S. singles champ, 1979-81; Wimbledon champ, 1981.
John McGraw, (1873-1934): N.Y. Giants manager led team to 10 pennants, 3 championships.
Debbie Meyer, b. 1952: swimmer won 200-, 400-, and 800- meter freestyle events, 1968 Olympics.
George Mikan, b. 1924: Minneapolis Lakers center selected in a 1950 AP poll as the greatest basketball player of the first half of the 20th century.
Stan Mikita, b. 1940: Chicago Black Hawks center led NHL in scoring 4 times; MVP twice.
Archie Moore, b. 1913: world light-heavyweight champion, 1952-62.
Howie Morenz, (1902-1937): Montreal Canadiens forward chosen in a 1950 Canadian press poll as the outstanding hockey player of the first half of the 20th century.
Joe Morgan, b. 1943: National League MVP, 1975, 1976.
Thurman Munson, (1947-1979): N.Y. Yankees catcher; MVP, 1976.
Stan Musial, b. 1920: St. Louis Cardinals star won 7 NL batting titles; MVP 3 times; NL record 3,630 hits.
Bronko Nagurski, b. 1908: Chicago Bears fullback and tackle; gained over 4,000 yds. rushing.
Joe Namath, b. 1943: quarterback passed for record 4,007 yds., 1967.
Byron Nelson, b. 1912: won 11 consecutive golf tournaments in 1945; twice Masters and PGA titlist.
Ernie Nevers, (1903-1976): Stanford star selected the best college fullback to play between 1919-1969, in a poll of the Football Writers Assn.; played pro football and baseball.
John Newcombe, b. 1943: Australian twice U.S. singles champ; Wimbledon titlist 3 times.
Jack Nicklaus, b. 1940: PGA Player-of-the-Year, 1967, 1972; leading money winner 8 times.
Chuck Noll, b. 1931: Pittsburgh Steelers coach led team to 4 Super Bowl titles.
Paavo Nurmi, (1897-1973): Finnish distance runner won 6 Olympic gold medals, 1920, 1924, 1928.
Al Oerter, b. 1936: discus thrower won gold medal at 4 consecutive Olympics, 1956-68.
Bobby Orr, b. 1948: Boston Bruins defenseman; Norris Trophy 8 times; led NHL in scoring twice, assists 5 times.
Mel Ott, (1909-1958): N.Y. Giants outfielder hit 511 home runs; led NL 6 times.
Jesse Owens, (1913-1980): track and field star won 4 1936 Olympic gold medals.
Satchel Paige, (1906-1982): pitcher starred in Negro leagues, 1924-48; entered major leagues at age 42.
Arnold Palmer, b. 1929: golf's first $1 million winner; won 4 Masters, 2 British Opens.
Jim Palmer, b. 1945: Baltimore Orioles pitcher; Cy Young award 3 times; 20-game winner 7 times.
Dave Parker, b. 1951: Pittsburgh Pirates outfielder led NL in batting, 1977, 1978; MVP, 1978.
Floyd Patterson, b. 1935: twice heavyweight champion.
Walter Payton, 1954: Chicago Bears running back ran for game record 275 yards, 1977; leading NFC rusher, 1976-80.
Pele, b. 1940: Brazilian soccer star scored 1,281 goals during 22-year career.
Bob Pettit, b. 1932: first NBA player to score 20,000 points; twice NBA scoring leader.
Richard Petty, b. 1937: NASCAR national champ 6 times; 7-times Daytona 500 winner.
Laffit Pincay Jr., b. 1946: leading money-winning jockey, 1970-74, 1979.
Jacques Plante, b. 1929: goalie, 7 Vezina trophies; first goalie to wear a mask in a game.
Gary Player, b. 1935: South African won the Masters, U.S. Open, PGA, and twice the British Open.
Annemarie Proell Moser, b. 1953: Austrian skier won the World Cup championship 5 times; 1980 Olympic gold medalist.
Willis Reed, b. 1942: N.Y. Knicks center; MVP, 1970; playoff MVP, 1970, 1973.
Jim Rice, b. 1953: Boston Red Sox outfielder led AL in home runs, 1977-78; MVP 1978.
Maurice Richard, b. 1921: Montreal Canadiens forward scored 544 regular season goals, 82 playoff goals.
Branch Rickey, (1881-1965): executive instrumental in breaking baseball's color barrier, 1947; initiated farm system, 1919.
Oscar Robertson, b. 1938: guard averaged career 25.7 points per game; record 9,887 career assist; MVP, 1964.
Brooks Robinson, b. 1937: Baltimore Orioles 3d baseman played in 4 World Series; MVP, 1964.
Frank Robinson, b. 1935: slugger MVP in both NL and AL; triple crown winner, 1966; first black manager in majors.
Jackie Robinson, (1919-1972): broke baseball's color barrier with Brooklyn Dodgers, 1947; MVP, 1949.
Larry Robinson, b. 1951: Montreal Canadiens defenseman won Norris trophy, 1977, 1980.
Sugar Ray Robinson, b. 1920: middleweight champion 5 times, welterweight champion.
Knute Rockne, (1883-1931): Notre Dame football coach, 1918-31; revolutionized game by stressing forward pass.
Pete Rose, b. 1942: won 3 NL batting titles; hit safely in 44 consecutive games, 1978; set record for most NL hits, 1981.
Wilma Rudolph, b. 1940: sprinter won 3 1960 Olympic gold medals.
Bill Russell, b. 1934: Boston Celtics center led team to 11 NBA titles; MVP 5 times; first black coach of major pro sports team.

Babe Ruth, (1895-1948): N.Y. Yankees outfielder hit 60 home runs, 1927; 714 lifetime; led AL 11 times.
Johnny Rutherford, b. 1938: auto racer won Indy 500 3 times.
Nolan Ryan, b. 1947: pitcher struck out record 383 batters, 1973; pitched record 5 no-hitters.
Jim Ryun, b. 1947: runner set records for the mile and 1,500 meters, 1967.
Gene Sarazen, b. 1902: won PGA championship 3 times, U.S. Open twice; developer of sand wedge.
Gale Sayers, b. 1943: Chicago Bears back twice led NFC in rushing.
Mike Schmidt, b. 1949: Phillies 3d baseman led NL in home runs, 1974-76, 1980-81; NL MVP, 1980, 1981.
Tom Seaver, b. 1944: NL pitcher won Cy Young award 3 times.
Willie Shoemaker, b. 1931: jockey rode 3 Kentucky Derby and 5 Belmont Stakes winners; leading career money winner.
Eddie Shore, b. 1902; Boston Bruins defenseman; MVP 4 times, first-team all-star 7 times.
Al Simmons, (1902-1956): AL outfielder had lifetime .334 batting average.
O.J. Simpson, b. 1947: running back rushed for record 2,003 yds., 1973; AFC leading rusher 4 times.
George Sisler, (1893-1973): St. Louis Browns 1st baseman had record 257 hits, 1920; batted .340 lifetime.
Sam Snead, b. 1912: PGA and Masters champ 3 times each.
Peter Snell, b. 1938: New Zealand runner won 800-meter race, 1960, 1964 Olympics.
Warren Spahn, b. 1921: pitcher won 363 NL games; 20-game winner 13 times; Cy Young award, 1957.
Tris Speaker, (1885-1958): AL outfielder batted .344 over 22 seasons; hit record 793 career doubles.
Mark Spitz, b. 1950: swimmer won 7 1972 Olympic gold medals.
Amos Alonzo Stagg, (1862-1965): coached Univ. of Chicago football team for 41 years, including 5 undefeated seasons; introduced huddle, man-in-motion, and end-around play.
Willie Stargell, b. 1941: Pittsburgh Pirate slugger chosen NL, World Series MVP, 1979.
Bart Starr, b. 1934: Green Bay Packers quarterback led team to 5 NFL titles and 2 Super Bowl victories.
Roger Staubach, b. 1942: Dallas Cowboys quarterback; leading NFC passer 5 times.
Casey Stengel, (1890-1975): managed Yankees to 10 pennants, 7 championships, 1949-60.
Jackie Stewart, b. 1939: Scot auto racer retired with record 27 Grand Prix victories.
John L. Sullivan, (1858-1918): last bareknuckle heavyweight champion, 1882-1892.
Fran Tarkenton, b. 1940: quarterback holds career passing records for touchdowns, completions, yardage.
Gustave Thoeni, b. 1951: Italian 4-time world alpine ski champ.
Jim Thorpe, (1888-1953): football All-America, 1911, 1912; won pentathlon and decathlon, 1912 Olympics; played major league baseball for 6 seasons.
Bill Tilden, (1893-1953): U.S. singles champ 7 times; played on 11 Davis Cup teams.
Y.A. Tittle, b. 1926: N.Y. Giants quarterback; MVP, 1961, 1963.
Lee Trevino, b. 1939: won the U.S. and British Open championships twice.
Bryan Trottier, b. 1956: N.Y. Islanders center led team to 3 consecutive Stanley Cup championships, 1980-82.
Gene Tunney, (1897-1978): heavyweight champion, 1926-28.
Wyomia Tyus, b. 1945: sprinter won 1964, 1968 Olympic 100-meter dash.
Johnny Unitas, b. 1933: Baltimore Colts quarterback passed for over 40,000 yds.; MVP, 1957, 1967.
Al Unser, b. 1939: Indy 500 winner, 3 times.
Bobby Unser, b. 1934: Indy 500 winner, 1968, 1981, twice U.S. Auto Club national champ.
Fernando Valenzuela, b. 1960: L.A. Dodgers pitcher won Cy Young award, 1981.
Norm Van Brocklin, b. 1926: quarterback passed for game record 554 yds., 1951; MVP, 1960.
Honus Wagner, (1874-1955): Pittsburgh Pirates shortstop won 8 NL batting titles.
Joe Walcott, b. 1914: heavyweight champion, 1951-52.
Bill Walton b. 1952: led Portland Trail Blazers to NBA championship, 1977; MVP, 1978.
Tom Watson, b. 1949: leading money-winning golfer, 1977-80.
Johnny Weissmuller, b. 1903: swimmer won 52 national championships, 5 Olympic gold medals; set 67 world records.
Jerry West, b. 1938: L.A. Lakers guard had career average 27 points per game; first team all-star 10 times.
Kathy Whitworth, b. 1939: women's golf leading money winner 8 times: first woman to earn over $300,000.
Ted Williams, b. 1918: Boston Red Sox outfielder won 6 batting titles; last major leaguer to hit over .400: .406 in 1941: .344 lifetime batting average.
Helen Wills, b. 1906: winner of 7 U.S., 8 British, 4 French women's singles titles.
John Wooden, b. 1910: coached UCLA basketball team to 10 national championships.
Mickey Wright, b. 1935: won LPGA championship 4 times, Vare Trophy 5 times; twice AP Woman-Athlete-of-the-Year.
Carl Yastrzemski, b. 1939: Boston Red Sox slugger won 3 batting titles, triple crown, 1967.
Cy Young, (1867-1955): pitcher won record 511 major league games.
Babe Didrikson Zaharias, (1914-1956): track star won 2 1932 Olympic gold medals; won numerous golf tournaments.
Emil Zatopek, b. 1922: Czech distance runner won 5,000- and 10,000-meter and marathon, 1952 Olympics.

National Skeet Shooting Championships in 1982

Savannah, Ga., July 22-30, 1982

High Overall - 550 targets

Champion — Richard Boss, 550.
Women — Sheri Confer, 541.
Industry — Jim Prall, 547.
Veteran — Ken Pletcher, 531.
Sub-senior — Arthur Zongetti, 545.
Senior — Ed Scherer, 544.
Junior — Mike Tesch, 542.
Collegiate — Mike Schmidt Jr., 548.

.410 Bore - 100 targets

Champion — Mike Wooten, 100.
Women — Susan Mayes, 99.
Industry — Asa Oliver, 98.
Veteran — Ken Pletcher, 94.
Sub-senior — T. J. Maddox, 99.
Senior — C. A. Graham, 100.
Junior — Charles Lane, 99.
Collegiate — Luke Deshotels, 100.

28 Gauge - 100 targets

Champion — Don Kaufman, 100.
Women — Mary Beverly, 100.
Industry — Jim Prall, 100.
Veteran — Don Tyler, 100.
Sub-senior — Boyd Wickman, 100.
Senior — C. A. Graham, 100.
Junior — Bobby Wrenn, 100.
Collegiate — Mike Schmidt Jr., 100.

20 Gauge - 100 targets

Champion — Wayne Mayes, 100.
Women — Louise Terry, 100.
Industry — Jim Prall, 100.
Veteran — Ken Pletcher, 99.
Sub-senior — T. J. Maddox, 100.
Senior — Ed Scherer, 100.
Junior — Tal Sprinkles, 100.
Collegiate — Alexander Rhoten, 100.

12 Gauge - 250 targets

Champion — John Shima, 250.
Women — Sheri Confer, 250.
Industry — Jim Prall, 250.
Veteran — Frank Laudano, 248.
Sub-senior — Larry Drennan, 250.
Senior — R. Miller, 250.
Junior — Earl Mitchell, 249.
Collegiate — Mike Schmidt Jr., 250.

Champion of Champions - 100 targets

Champion — Bob Eads, 100.
Women — Marilyn Scola, 100.
Industry —Dave Tilden, 99.
Veteran — Barbee Ponder, 99.
Sub-senior — Don Barber, 100.
Senior — Ed Scherer, 99.
Junior — Robbie Wilson, 100.
Collegiate — Preston Douglass, 100.

World Track and Field Records

As of Sept. 1982

*Indicates pending record; a number of new records await confirmation. The International Amateur Atheletic Federation, the world body of track and field, recognizes only records in metric distances except for the mile.

Men's Records

Running

Event	Record	Holder	Country	Date	Where made
100 meters	**9.95 s.**	Jim Hines	U.S.	Oct. 14, 1968	Mexico City
200 meters	**19.72 s.**	Pietro Mennea	Italy	Sept. 12, 1979	Mexico City
400 meters	**43.86 s.**	Lee Evans	U.S.	Oct. 18, 1968	Mexico City
800 meters	**1 m., 41.72 s.**	Sebastian Coe	Gr. Britain	June 10, 1981	Florence, Italy
1,000 meters	**2 m., 12.18 s.**	Sebastian Coe	Gr. Britain	July 11, 1981	Oslo
1,500 meters	**3 m., 31.36 s.**	Steve Ovett	Gr. Britain	Aug. 27, 1980	Koblenz, W. Germany
1 mile	**3 m., 47.33 s.**	Sebastian Coe	Gr. Britain	Aug. 28, 1981	Brussels
2,000 meters	**4 m., 51.4 s.**	John Walker	New Zealand	June 30, 1976	Oslo
3,000 meters	**7 m., 32.1 s.**	Henry Rono	Kenya	June 27, 1978	Oslo
5,000 meters	***13 m., 00.42 s.**	Dave Moorcroft	Gr. Britain	July 7, 1982	Oslo
10,000 meters	**27 m., 22.47 s.**	Henry Rono	Kenya	June 11, 1978	Vienna
20,000 meters	**57 m., 24.2 s.**	Jos Hermens	Netherlands	May 1, 1976	Netherlands
25,000 meters	**1 hr., 13 m., 55.8 s.**	Toshihiko Seko	Japan	Mar. 22, 1981	New Zealand
30,000 meters	**1 hr., 29 m., 18.8 s.**	Toshihiko Seko	Japan	Mar. 22, 1981	New Zealand
3,000 meter stpl	**8 m., 05.4 s.**	Henry Rono	Kenya	May 13, 1978	Seattle

Hurdles

Event	Record	Holder	Country	Date	Where made
110 meters	**12.93 s.**	Renaldo Nehemiah	U.S.	Aug. 19, 1981	Zurich
400 meters	**47.13 s.**	Edwin Moses	U.S.	July 3, 1980	Milan, Italy

Relay Races

Event	Record	Holder	Country	Date	Where made
400 mtrs.	**38.03 s.**	National team (Collins, Riddick, Wiley, Williams)	U.S.	Sept. 3, 1977	Dusseldorf
800 mtrs. (4×200)	**1 m., 20.3 s.**	USC	U.S.	May 27, 1978	Tempe, Ariz.
1,600 mtrs. (4×400)	**2 m., 56.1 s.**	National team (Matthews, Freeman, James, Evans)	U.S.	Oct. 20, 1968	Mexico City
3,200 mtrs. (4×800)	***7 m., 03.89 s.**	National team	Gr. Britain	Sept., 1982	London

Field Events

Event	Record	Holder	Country	Date	Where made
High jump	**7 ft., 8¾ in.**	Gerd Wessig	E. Germany	Aug. 1, 1980	Moscow
Long jump	**29 ft., 2½ in.**	Bob Beamon	U.S.	Oct. 18,1968	Mexico City
Triple jump	**58 ft., 8¼ in.**	Joao de Oliveira	Brazil	Oct. 15, 1975	Mexico City
Pole vault	**19 ft., 2 in.**	Konstantin Volkov	USSR	Aug. 2, 1981	USSR
16 lb. shot put	**72 ft., 8 in.**	Udo Beyer	E. Germany	July 6, 1978	Sweden
Discus throw	**233 ft., 5 in.**	Wolfgang Schmidt	E. Germany	Aug. 9, 1978	E. Berlin
Javelin throw	**311 ft., 4 in.**	Ferenc Paragi	Hungary	Apr. 23, 1980	Tata, Hungary
16 lb. hammer throw	*** 275 ft., 6 in.**	Sergei Litvinov	USSR	May, 1982	Moscow
Decathlon	***8,744 pts.**	Daley Thompson	Gr. Britain	Sept. 8, 1982	Athens

Walking

Event	Record	Holder	Country	Date	Where made
2 hours	**17 mi., 881 yds.**	Jose Marin	Spain	Apr. 8, 1979	Barcelona
30,000 mtrs.	**2 h., 8 min.**	Jose Marin	Spain	Apr. 8, 1979	Barcelona
50,000 mtrs.	**3 hr., 41 m., 39 s.**	Raul Gonzales	Mexico	May 25, 1978	Norway

Women's Records

Running

Event	Record	Holder	Country	Date	Where made
100 meters	**10.88 s.**	Marlies Gohr	E. Germany	July 1, 1977	Dresden
200 meters	**21.71 s.**	Marita Koch	E. Germany	June 10, 1979	E. Berlin
400 meters	***48.15 s.**	Marita Koch	E. Germany	Sept. 8, 1982	Athens
800 meters	**1 m., 53.42 s.**	Nadezhda Olizarenko	USSR	July 27, 1980	Moscow
1,500 meters	**3 m., 52.47 s.**	Tatyana Kazankina	USSR	Aug. 13, 1980	Zurich
1 mile	***4 m., 18.08 s.**	Mary Decker Tabb	U.S.	July 9, 1982	Paris
3,000 meters	***8 m., 26.78 s.**	Svetlana Ulmasova	USSR	July, 1982	Kiev, USSR
5,000 meters	***15 m., 08.26 s.**	Mary Decker Tabb	U.S.	May, 1982	Eugene, Ore.
10,000 meters	***31 m., 35.3 s.**	Mary Decker Tabb	U.S.	July 17, 1982	Eugene, Ore.

Relay Races

Event	Record	Holder	Country	Date	Where made
400 mtrs. (4×100)	**41.60 s.**	National team	E. Germany	Aug. 1, 1980	Moscow
800 mtrs. (4×200)	**1 m., 28.15 s.**	National team	E. Germany	Aug. 9, 1980	E. Germany
1,600 mtrs. (4×400)	**3 m., 19.23 s.**	National team	E. Germany	July 31, 1976	Montreal
3,200 mtrs. (4×800)	**7 m., 52.35 s.**	National team	USSR	Aug. 16, 1976	USSR

Hurdles

110 meters	**12.36 s.**	Grazyna Rabsztyn	Poland	June 13, 1980	Warsaw
400 meters	**54.28 s.**	Karin Rossley	E. Germany	May 17, 1980	E. Germany

Field Events

High jump	*** 6 ft., 7½ in.**	Ulrike Meyfarth	W. Germany	Sept. 8, 1982	Athens
Shot put	**73 ft., 8 in.**	Ilona Slupianek	E. Germany	May 11, 1980	Potsdam
Long jump	***23 ft., 7½ in.**	Vali Ionescu	Romania	July, 1982	Bucharest
Discus throw	**235 ft., 7 in.**	Maria Vergova	Bulgaria	July 13, 1980	Sofia
Javelin	***237 ft., 6 in.**	Tiina Lillak	Finland	July, 1982	Helsinki
Pentathlon	**5,083 pts.**	Nadyezhda Tkachenko	USSR	July 24, 1980	Moscow

Evolution of the World Record for the One-Mile Run

The table below shows how the world record for the one-mile has been lowered in the past 117 years.

Year	Individual, country	Time	Year	Individual, country	Time
1864	Charles Lawes, Britain	**4:56**	1942	Arne Andersson, Sweden	**4:06.2**
1865	Richard Webster, Britain	**4:36.5**	1942	Gunder Haegg, Sweden	**4:04.6**
1868	William Chinnery, Britain	**4:29**	1943	Arne Andersson, Sweden	**4:02.6**
1868	W. C. Gibbs, Britain	**4:28.8**	1944	Arne Andersson, Sweden	**4:01.6**
1874	Walter Slade, Britain	**4:26**	1945	Gunder Haegg, Sweden	**4:01.4**
1875	Walter Slade, Britain	**4:24.5**	1954	Roger Bannister, Britain	**3:59.4**
1880	Walter George, Britain	**4:23.2**	1954	John Landy, Australia	**3:58**
1882	Walter George, Britain	**4:21.4**	1957	Derek Ibbotson, Britain	**3:57.2**
1882	Walter George, Britain	**4:19.4**	1958	Herb Elliott, Australia	**3:54.5**
1884	Walter George, Britain	**4:18.4**	1962	Peter Snell, New Zealand	**3:54.4**
1894	Fred Bacon, Scotland	**4:18.2**	1964	Peter Snell, New Zealand	**3:54.1**
1895	Fred Bacon, Scotland	**4:17**	1965	Michel Jazy, France	**3:53.6**
1895	Thomas Conneff, U.S.	**4:15.6**	1966	Jim Ryun, U.S.	**3:51.3**
1911	John Paul Jones, U.S.	**4:15.4**	1967	Jim Ryun, U.S.	**3:51.1**
1913	John Paul Jones, U.S.	**4:14.6**	1975	Filbert Bayi, Tanzania	**3:51**
1915	Norman Taber, U.S.	**4:12.6**	1975	John Walker, New Zealand	**3:49.4**
1923	Paavo Nurmi, Finland	**4:10.4**	1979	Sebastian Coe, Britain	**3:49**
1931	Jules Ladoumegue, France	**4:09.2**	1980	Steve Ovett, Britain	**3:48.8**
1933	Jack Lovelock, New Zealand	**4:07.6**	1981	Sebastian Coe, Britain	**3:48.53**
1934	Glenn Cunningham, U.S.	**4:06.8**	1981	Steve Ovett, Britain	**3:48.40**
1937	Sydney Wooderson, Britain	**4:06.4**	1981	Sebastian Coe, Britain	**3:47.33**
1942	Gunder Haegg, Sweden	**4:06.2**			

U.S. Track and Field Indoor Records

As of Sept., 1982

*Indicates pending record; a number of new records await confirmation. The International Amateur Federation, the world body of track and field, does not recognize world indoor records.

Men's Records

Running

Event	Record	Holder	Date	Where made
50 yards	***5.22**	Stanley Floyd	Jan. 22, 1982	Los Angeles
50 meters	**5.61**	James Sanford	Feb. 20, 1981	San Diego
60 yards	**6.04**	Stanley Floyd	Jan. 31, 1981	Dallas
60 meters	**6.38**	Houston McTear	Jan. 5, 1980	Long Beach, Cal.
100 yards	**9.54**	Harvey Glance	Feb. 16, 1980	Houston
200 meters	***21.25**	Mel Lattany	Mar. 10, 1982	Milan
300 yards	**29.27**	Terron Wright	Feb. 7, 1981	Bloomington, Ind.
300 meters	**33.33**	Cliff Wiley	Dec. 30, 1980	Saskatoon
400 meters	***46.08**	Bill Green	Feb. 8, 1981	Sherbrooke
500 yards	**54.4**	Lee Evans	Jan. 8, 30, 1971	Idaho and Maryland
500 meters	**1:01.5**	Mark Enyeart	Feb. 7, 1981	Louisville
600 yards	**1:07.6**	Marty McGrady	Feb. 27, 1970	New York City
600 meters	***1:17.60**	Fred Sowerby	Feb. 21, 1982	Newark, Del.
800 meters	**1:47.4**	Ted Nelson	Apr. 7, 1965	Berlin
1,000 yards	***2:04.7**	Don Paige	Feb. 5, 1982	Inglewood, Cal.
1,000 meters	***2:19.5**	Tom Byers	Feb. 6, 1982	Louisville
1,500 meters	**3:38.3**	Steve Scott	Feb. 20, 1981	San Diego
One mile	**3.51.8**	Steve Scott	Feb. 15, 1980	Los Angeles
2,000 meters	**4.58.6**	Steve Scott	Feb. 7, 1981	Louisville
3,000 meters	**7:45.2**	Steve Scott	Jan. 5, 1980	Long Beach, Cal.
2 miles	***8:16.8**	Doug Padilla	Feb. 19, 1982	San Diego
3 miles	**12:56.6**	Alberto Salazar	Feb. 6, 1981	New York City
5,000 meters	***13:20.55**	Doug Padilla	Feb. 12, 1982	New York City
50-yd. hurdles	***5.92**	Renaldo Nehemiah	Jan. 29, 1982	Toronto
60-m. hurdles	***6.82**	Renaldo Nehemiah	Jan. 30, 1982	Dallas

Field Events

High jump	**7 ft. 7 3/4 in.**	Jeff Woodard	Feb. 27, 1981	New York City
Pole vault	***18 ft. 10 in.**	Billy Olson	Feb. 27, 1982	Kansas City
Long jump	***28 ft. 1 in.**	Carl Lewis	Jan. 16, 1982	E. Rutherford, N.J.
Triple jump	***57 ft. 1 1/2 in.**	Willie Banks	Feb. 19, 1982	San Diego
Shot put	**72 ft. 2 3/4 in.**	George Woods	Feb. 8, 1974	Inglewood, Cal.

Women's Records

Running

50 yards	**5.83**	Evelyn Ashford	Feb., 1981	Toronto
50 meters	***6.13**	Jeannette Bolden	Feb. 21, 1981	Edmonton
60 yards	***6.54**	Evelyn Ashford	Feb. 26, 1982	New York City
60 meters	**7.04**	Evelyn Ashford	Jan. 5, 1980	Long Beach, Cal.
200 meters	**23.27**	Chandra Cheeseborough	Feb. 27, 1981	New York City
220 yards	***23.25**	Chandra Cheeseborough	Feb. 26, 1982	New York City
300 yards	**34.07**	Rosalyn Bryant	Mar. 13, 1982	Lincoln, Neb.
300 meters	***37.54**	Janet Dodson	Mar. 6, 1982	Morgantown, W.Va.
400 meters	**53.31**	Gwen Gardner	Feb. 8, 1980	New York City
440 yards	**53.92**	Rosalyn Bryant	Feb. 29, 1980	New York City
500 yards	**1:03.3**	Rosalyn Bryant	Feb. 18, 1977	San Diego
500 meters	**1:11.7**	Delisa Walton	Feb. 9, 1980	Louisville
600 yards	**1:17.38**	Delisa Walton	Mar. 13, 1982	Cedar Falls, Ia.
600 meters	**1:26.56**	Delisa Walton	Mar. 14, 1981	Pocatello, Ida.
800 meters	**1:58.9**	Mary Decker	Feb. 22, 1980	San Diego
880 yards	**1:58.9**	Mary Decker	Feb. 22, 1980	San Diego
1,000 yards	**2:23.8**	Mary Decker	Feb. 3, 1978	Inglewood, Cal.
1,000 meters	**2:40.2**	Francie Larrieu	Jan. 18, 1975	Los Angeles
1,500 meters	**4:00.8**	Mary Decker	Feb. 8, 1980	New York City
One mile	***4:20.5**	Mary Decker	Feb. 19, 1982	San Diego
3,000 meters	***8:47.3**	Mary Decker	Feb. 5, 1982	Inglewood, Cal.
2 miles	***9:37.03**	Joan Hansen	Feb. 26, 1982	New York City
50-yd. hurdles	**6.37**	Deby La Plante	Feb. 10, 1978	Toronto
50-m. hurdles	**6.95**	Candy Young	Feb. 3, 1979	Edmonton
60-yd. hurdles	***7.37**	Stephanie Hightower	Feb. 12, 1982	New York City
	***7.37**	Candy Young	Feb. 12, 1982	New York City
60-m hurdles	***8.04**	Stephanie Hightower	Mar. 10, 1982	Milan

Field Events

High Jump	***6 ft. 6 3/4 in.**	Coleen Rienstra	Feb. 13, 1982	Ottawa
Shot put	**61 ft. 2 1/4 in.**	Maren Seidler	Jan. 20, 1978	W. Germany
Long jump	***21 ft. 11 3/4 in.**	Veronica Bell	Feb. 26, 1982	New York City

Track and Field Events in 1982

Toronto Star — Maple Leaf Indoor Games

Toronto, Ont., Jan. 29, 1982

Men

50 Yds.—Emmit King, Univ. of Alabama. **Time—0:05.34.**
50-Yd. Hurdles—Renaldo Nehemiah, Athletic Attic. **Time—0:05.42.**
600 Meters—Fred Sowerby, D.C. International. **Time—1:20.00.**
1,000 Meters—Don Paige, Villanova. **Time—2:22.41.**
One Mile—Suleiman Nyambui, Tanzania. **Time—4:07.16.**
5,000 Meters—John Treacy, Ireland. **Time—13:44.17.**
High Jump—Dwight Stones, Pacific Coast Club. **2.25 meters.**
Pole Vault—Bill Olson, Pacific Coast Club. **5.71 meters.**

Women

50 Yds.—Jeanette Bolden, Wilt's A.C. **Time—0:05.80.**
50-Yd. Hurdles—Stephanie Hightower, Ohio State. **Time—0:06.50.**
600 Meters—DeAnn Gutowski, Los Angeles. **Time—1:31.40.**
800 Meters—Grace Verbeek, Hamilton, Ont. **Time—2:13.75.**
1,500 Meters—Jan Merrill, New London, Conn. **Time—4:17.46.**

USA/Mobil Outdoor Championships

Knoxville, Tenn., June 18-20, 1982

Men

100 Meters—Carl Lewis, Santa Monica TC. **Time—0:10.11.**
200 Meters—Calvin Smith, Athletic Attic. **Time—0:20.47.**
400 Meters—Cliff Wiley, unattached. **Time—0:45.05.**
800 Meters—James Robinson, Inner City AC. **Time—1:46.12.**
1,500 Meters—Steve Scott, Sub 4 TC **Time—3:34.92.**
3,000-Meter Steeplechase—Henry Marsh, Athletics West. **Time—8:22.94.**
5,000 Meters—Matt Centrowitz, New York AC. **Time—13:31.96.**
10,000 Meters—Craig Virgin, Front Runner TC. **Time—28:33.02.**
110-Meter Hurdles—Willie Gault, Athletic Attic. **Time—0:13.54.**
400-Meter Hurdles—David Patrick, Athletics West. **Time—0:48.57.**
20-Kilometer Walk—Jim Heiring, Athletic Attic. **Time—1:30:21.3.**
High Jump—Milt Ottey, Philadelphia Pioneer Club. **7 ft. 5¾ in.**
Pole Vault—(tie) Dan Ripley & Billy Olsen, both Pacific Coast Club. **18 ft. 9¼ in.**
Long Jump—Carl Lewis, Santa Monica TC. **27 ft. 10 in.**
Triple Jump—Robert Cannon, Athletic Attic. **55 ft. ¾ in.**
Shot Put—Kevin Akins, unattached. **69 ft. 9½ in.**
Discus—Luis Delis, Cuba. **225 ft. 5 in.**
Hammer—Dave McKenzie, unattached. **235 ft. 2 in.**
Javelin—Bob Roggy, Athletics West. **289 ft. 9 in.**
Team champion—Athletic Attic.

Women

100 Meters—Evelyn Ashford, Medalist TC. **Time—0:10.96.**
200 Meters—Merlene Ottey, LA Naturite TC. **Time—0:22.17.**
400 Meters—Denean Howard, LA Naturite TC. **Time—0:50.87.**
800 Meters—Delisa Walton, LA Naturite TC. **Time—2:00.91.**
1,500 Meters—Mary Decker Tabb, Athletics West. **Time—4:03.37.**
3,000 Meters—Francie Larrieu, New Balance TC. **Time—8:58.66.**
10,000 Meters—Kim Schurpfeil, Stanford TC. **Time—33:25.88.**
100-Meter Hurdles—Stephanie Hightower, LA Naturite TC. **Time—0:12.86.**
400-Meter Hurdles—Tammy Etienne, Metroplex Striders. **Time—0:56.55.**
5-Kilometer Walk—Susan Liers Westerfield, Island TC. **Time—24:56.6.**
High Jump—Debbie Brill, Pacific Coast Club. **6 ft. 4¾ in.**
Long Jump—Carol Lewis, Santa Monica TC. **22 ft. 4¼ in.**
Shot Put—Maria Sarria, Cuba. **61 ft. 8¼ in.**
Discus—Ria Stalman, LA Naturite TC. **203 ft. 10 in.**
Javelin—Lynda Hughes, Oregon. **202 ft. 3 in.**
Team champion—LA Naturite TC.

USA/Mobil Indoor Championships

New York, N.Y., Feb. 26, 1982

Men

60 Yds.—Ron Brown, Arizona St. **Time—0:06.14.**
440 Yds.—Walter McCoy, Athletic Attic. **Time—0:48.24.**
600 Yds.—Fred Sowerby, DC International. **Time—1:09.50.**
1,000 Yds.—Don Paige, Athletic Attic. **Time—2:05.81.**
One Mile—Jim Spivey, Indiana. **Time—3:57.04.**
3 Miles—Paul Cummings, New Balance TC. **Time—13:00.52.**
60-Yd. Hurdles—Tonie Campbell, unattached. **Time—0:07.13.**

2-Mile Walk—Jim Heiring, Athletic Attic. **Time—12:24.82.**
High Jump—Dwight Stones, Pacific Coast Club. **7 ft. 4½ in.**
Pole Vault—Billy Olson, Pacific Coast Club. **18 ft. 6½ in.**
Long Jump—Carl Lewis, unattached. **28 ft. ¾ in.**
Triple Jump—Keith Connor, SMU. **55 ft. 11 in.**
Shot Put—Jeff Braun, Univ. of Chicago TC. **65 ft. 10½ in.**
Team champion.—Athletic Attic.

Women

60 Yds.—Evelyn Ashford, Medalist TC. **Time—0:06.54.**
220 Yds.—Chandra Cheeseborough, Tennessee St. **Time—0:23.46.**
440 Yds.—Maxine Underwood, Boston International. **Time—0:54.55.**
880 Yds.—Leann Warren, Oregon. **Time—2:04.61.**
One Mile—Cathie Twomey, Athletics West. **Time—4:32.92.**
2 Miles—Joan Hansen, Athletics West. **Time—9:37.03.**
60-Yd. Hurdles—Stephanie Hightower, L.A. Naturite TC. **Time—0:07.38.**
One-Mile Walk—Sue Brodock, Southern Cal. RR. **Time—7:07.14.**
High Jump—Coleen Rienstra-Sommer, Wilt's AC. **6 ft. 3¼ in.**
Long Jump—Veronica Bell, Southern Cal. Cheetahs. **21 ft. 11¾ in.**
Shot Put—Marita Walton, Maryland/Ireland. **55 ft 11¾ in.**
Team champion—Tennessee State.

NCAA Indoor Championships

Pontiac, Mich., Mar. 13, 1982

60 Yds.—Rod Richardson, Texas A&M. **Time—0:06.07.**
440 Yds.—Anthony Ketcham, Houston. **Time—0:47.47.**
600 Yds.—Eugene Sanders, Mississippi Valley. **Time—1:08.51.**
880 Yds.—David Patrick, Tennessee. **Time—1:49.94.**
1,000 Yds.—John Stephens, Arkansas. **Time—2:07.37.**
One Mile—Suleiman Nyambui, Texas-El Paso. **Time—4:00.65.**
2 Miles—Suleiman Nyambui. **Time—8:38.91.**
60-Yd. High Hurdles—Tony Campbell, Southern Cal. **Time—0:07.14.**
Long Jump—Gilbert Smith, Texas-Arlington. **26 ft. 1 in.**
Pole Vault—Doug Lytle, Kansas State. **17 ft. 9¾ in.**
High Jump—Leo Williams, Navy. **7 ft. 5¾ in.**
Shot Put—Mike Lehmann, Illinois. **67 ft. 7¾ in.**
Triple Jump—Keith Connor, SMU. **55 ft. 3 in.**
Team champion—Texas-El Paso.

Water Ski Champions in 1982

Source: American Water Ski Assn.

40th Annual National Water Ski Championships

Du Quoin, Ill., Aug. 17-22, 1982

Men's Open Overall—Carl Roberge, Orlando, Fla., 3,326 points.
Men's Open Slalom—Kris LaPoint, Castro Valley, Cal., 57 buoys.
Men's Open Tricks—Cory Pickos, Eagle Lake, Fla., 9,580 points.
Men's Open Jumping—Sammy Duvall, Orlando, Fla., 185 feet.
Women's Open Overall—Cyndi Benzel, Newberry Springs, Cal., 3,186 points.
Women's Open Slalom—Deena Brush, West Sacramento, Cal., 55½ buoys.
Women's Open Tricks—Cyndi Benzel, 5,030 points.
Women's Open Jumping—Cindy Todd, Pierson, Fla., 132 feet.
Senior Men's Overall—Ken White, Bynum, Tex., 2,679 points.
Senior Men's Slalom—Mickey Wilkenson, Golden, Col., 56 buoys.
Senior Men's Tricks—Greg Wilson, St. Marys, Oh., 4,91[illegible] points.
Senior Men's Jumping—Jim Miles, Brandon, Fla., 133 feet.
Boys' Overall—Billy Allen, San Mateo, Cal., 2,782 points.
Boys' Slalom—Bill Judge, Queenstown, Md., 48½ buoys.
Boys' Tricks—Tory Baggiano, Montgomery Ala., 7,220 points.
Boys' Jumping—Chris Swann, Winter Park, Fla., 135 feet.
Senior Women's Overall—Thelma Salmas, Lantana, Fla. 3,349 points.
Senior Women's Slalom—Thelma Salmas, 44 buoys.
Senior Women's Tricks—Thelma Salmas, 3,480 points.
Senior Women's Jumping—Thelma Salmas, 99 feet.
Girls' Overall—Brenda May, Orange City, Fla., 2,938 points.
Girls' Slalom—Melanie Maxfield, Canton, Ill., 50 buoys.
Girls' Tricks—Sally Monnier, Rock Falls, Ill., 6,210 points.
Girls' Jumping—Brenda May, 103 feet.

24th Annual Masters Tournament

Callaway Gardens, Ga., July 10-11, 1982

Men's Overall—Sammy Duvall, Orlando, Fla., 2,687 points.
Men's Slalom—Bob LaPoint, Castro Valley, Cal., 53 buoys.
Men's Tricks—Sammy Duvall, 7,460 points.
Men's Jumping—Sammy Duvall, 187 feet.
Women's Overall—Cindy Todd, Pierson, Fla., 2,679 points.
Women's Slalom—Cindy Todd, 57 buoys.
Women's Tricks—Anita Carlman, Sweden, 5,420 points.
Women's Jumping—Cindy Todd, 135 feet.

Polo Records

U.S. Open

1972	Milwaukee 9, Tulsa 5
1973	Oak Brook 9, Willow Bend 4.
1974	Milwaukee 7, Houston 6.
1975	Milwaukee 14, Tulsa-Dallas 6.
1976	Willow Bend 10, Tulsa 5.
1977	Retama 11, Wilson Ranch 7.
1978	Abercrombie & Kent 7, Tulsa 6.
1979	Retama 6, Huisache 5.
1980	Southern Hills 9, Willow Bend 6.
1981	Rolex A & K 10, Retama 9.

Silver Cup

1972	Red Doors Farm 10, Sun Ranch 6.
1973	Houston 6, Willow Bend 4.
1974	Houston 7, Willow Bend 6.
1975	Lone Oak-Bunntyco 8, Tulsa 5.
1976	Wilson Ranch 10, Tulsa 8.
1977	Boca Raton 6, Houston 5.
1978	Wilson Ranch 7, Ft. Lauderdale 6.
1979	Retama 7, Willow Bend 6.
1980	Retama 9, Houston 8.
1981	Retama 10, Thunder 8.

Golf Records

United States Open

Year	Winner	Year	Winner	Year	Winner	Year	Winner
1899	Willie Smith	1920	Edward Ray	1940	Lawson Little	1963	Julius Boros
1900	Harry Vardon	1921	Jim Barnes	1941	Craig Wood	1964	Ken Venturi
1901	Willie Anderson	1922	Gene Sarazen	1942-45	(Not played)	1965	Gary Player
1902	L. Auchterlonie	1923	Bobby Jones*	1946	Lloyd Mangrum	1966	Billy Casper
1903	Willie Anderson	1924	Cyril Walker	1947	L. Worsham	1967	Jack Nicklaus
1904	Willie Anderson	1925	Willie MacFarlane	1948	Ben Hogan	1968	Lee Trevino
1905	Willie Anderson	1926	Bobby Jones*	1949	Cary Middlecoff	1969	Orville Moody
1906	Alex Smith	1927	Tommy Armour	1950	Ben Hogan	1970	Tony Jacklin
1907	Alex Ross	1928	John Farrell	1951	Ben Hogan	1971	Lee Trevino
1908	Fred McLeod	1929	Bobby Jones*	1952	Julius Boros	1972	Jack Nicklaus
1909	George Sargent	1930	Bobby Jones*	1953	Ben Hogan	1973	Johnny Miller
1910	Alex Smith	1931	Wm. Burke	1954	Ed Furgol	1974	Hale Irwin
1911	John McDermott	1932	Gene Sarazen	1955	Jack Fleck	1975	Lou Graham
1912	John McDermott	1933	John Goodman*	1956	Cary Middlecoff	1976	Jerry Pate
1913	Francis Ouimet*	1934	Olin Dutra	1957	Dick Mayer	1977	Hubert Green
1914	Walter Hagen	1935	Sam Parks Jr.	1958	Tommy Bolt	1978	Andy North
1915	Jerome Travers*	1936	Tony Manero	1959	Billy Casper	1979	Hale Irwin
1916	Chick Evans*	1937	Ralph Guldahl	1960	Arnold Palmer	1980	Jack Nicklaus
1917-18	(Not played)	1938	Ralph Guldahl	1961	Gene Littler	1981	David Graham
1919	Walter Hagen	1939	Byron Nelson	1962	Jack Nicklaus	1982	Tom Watson

*Amateur

U.S. Women's Open Golf Champions

Year	Winner	Year	Winner	Year	Winner	Year	Winner
1948	"Babe" Zaharias	1957	Betsy Rawls	1966	Sandra Spuzich	1975	Sandra Palmer
1949	Louise Suggs	1958	Mickey Wright	1967	Catherine Lacoste*	1976	JoAnne Carner
1950	"Babe" Zaharias	1959	Mickey Wright	1968	Susie Maxwell Berning	1977	Hollis Stacy
1951	Betsy Rawls	1960	Betsy Rawls	1969	Donna Caponi	1978	Hollis Stacy
1952	Louise Suggs	1961	Mickey Wright	1970	Donna Caponi	1979	Jerilyn Britz
1953	Betsy Rawls	1962	Marie Lindstrom	1971	JoAnne Carner	1980	Amy Alcott
1954	"Babe" Zaharias	1963	Mary Mills	1972	Susie Maxwell Berning	1981	Pat Bradley
1955	Fay Crocker	1964	Mickey Wright	1973	Susie Maxwell Berning	1982	Janet Alex
1956	Mrs. K. Cornelius	1965	Carol Mann	1974	Sandra Haynie		

*Amateur

Masters Golf Tournament Champions

Year	Winner	Year	Winner	Year	Winner	Year	Winner
1934	Horton Smith	1948	Claude Harmon	1960	Arnold Palmer	1972	Jack Nicklaus
1935	Gene Sarazen	1949	Sam Snead	1961	Gary Player	1973	Tommy Aaron
1936	Horton Smith	1950	Jimmy Demaret	1962	Arnold Palmer	1974	Gary Player
1937	Byron Nelson	1951	Ben Hogan	1963	Jack Nicklaus	1975	Jack Nicklaus
1938	Henry Picard	1952	Sam Snead	1964	Arnold Palmer	1976	Ray Floyd
1939	Ralph Guldahl	1953	Ben Hogan	1965	Jack Nicklaus	1977	Tom Watson
1940	Jimmy Demaret	1954	Sam Snead	1966	Jack Nicklaus	1978	Gary Player
1941	Craig Wood	1955	Cary Middlecoff	1967	Gay Brewer Jr.	1979	Fuzzy Zoeller
1942	Byron Nelson	1956	Jack Burke	1968	Bob Goalby	1980	Severiano Ballesteros
1943-1945	(Not played)	1957	Doug Ford	1969	George Archer	1981	Tom Watson
1946	Herman Keiser	1958	Arnold Palmer	1970	Billy Casper	1982	Craig Stadler
1947	Jimmy Demaret	1959	Art Wall Jr.	1971	Charles Coody		

Professional Golfer's Association Championships

Year	Winner	Year	Winner	Year	Winner	Year	Winner
1920	Jock Hutchison	1936	Denny Shute	1953	Walter Burkemo	1968	Julius Boros
1921	Walter Hagen	1937	Denny Shute	1954	Melvin Harbert	1969	Ray Floyd
1922	Gene Sarazen	1938	Paul Runyan	1955	Doug Ford	1970	Dave Stockton
1923	Gene Sarazen	1939	Henry Picard	1956	Jack Burke	1971	Jack Nicklaus
1924	Walter Hagen	1940	Byron Nelson	1957	Lionel Hebert	1972	Gary Player
1925	Walter Hagen	1941	Victor Ghezzi	1958	Dow Finsterwald	1973	Jack Nicklaus
1926	Walter Hagen	1942	Sam Snead	1959	Bob Rosburg	1974	Lee Trevino
1927	Walter Hagen	1944	Bob Hamilton	1960	Jay Hebert	1975	Jack Nicklaus
1928	Leo Diegel	1945	Byron Nelson	1961	Jerry Barber	1976	Dave Stockton
1929	Leo Diegel	1946	Ben Hogan	1962	Gary Player	1977	Lanny Wadkins
1930	Tommy Armour	1947	Jim Ferrier	1963	Jack Nicklaus	1978	John Mahaffey
1931	Tom Creavy	1948	Ben Hogan	1964	Bob Nichols	1979	David Graham
1932	Olin Dutra	1949	Sam Snead	1965	Dave Marr	1980	Jack Nicklaus
1933	Gene Sarazen	1950	Chandler Harper	1966	Al Geiberger	1981	Larry Nelson
1934	Paul Runyan	1951	Sam Snead	1967	Don January	1982	Ray Floyd
1935	Johnny Revolta	1952	James Turnesa				

Canadian Open Golf Champions

Year	Winner	Year	Winner	Year	Winner	Year	Winner
1947	Bobby Locke	1956	Doug Sanders	1965	Gene Littler	1974	Bobby Nichols
1948	C.W. Congdon	1957	George Bayer	1966	Don Massengale	1975	Tom Weiskopf
1949	E.J. Harrison	1958	Wes Ellis Jr.	1967	Billy Casper	1976	Jerry Pate
1950	Jim Ferrier	1959	Doug Ford	1968	Bob Charles	1977	Lee Trevino
1951	Jim Ferrier	1960	Art Wall, Jr.	1969	Tommy Aaron	1978	Bruce Lietzke
1952	John Palmer	1961	Jacky Cupit	1970	Kermit Zarley	1979	Lee Trevino
1953	Dave Douglas	1962	Ted Kroll	1971	Lee Trevino	1980	Bob Gilder
1954	Pat Fletcher	1963	Doug Ford	1972	Gay Brewer	1981	Peter Oosterhuis
1955	Arnold Palmer	1964	Kel Nagle	1973	Tom Weiskopf	1982	Bruce Lietzke

Professional Golf Tournaments in 1982

Date	Event	Winner	Score	Prize
Jan. 10	Tucson Open	Craig Stadler	266	$54,000
Jan. 17	Bob Hope Desert Classic, Palm Springs, Cal.	Ed Fiori	*335	50,000
Jan. 25	Phoenix Open	Lanny Watkins	263	54,000
Jan. 31	San Diego Open	Johnny Miller	270	54,000
Feb. 7	Bing Crosby National Pro-Am, Pebble Beach, Cal.	Jim Simons	274	54,000
Feb. 14	Hawaiian Open, Honolulu	Wayne Levi	277	58,500
Feb. 21	Los Angeles Open	Tom Watson	271	54,000
Feb. 28	Doral-Eastern Open, Miami, Fla.	Andy Bean	278	54,000
Mar. 8	Bay Hill Classic, Orlando, Fla.	Tom Kite	*278	54,000
Mar. 14	Inverrary Classic, Lauderhill, Fla.	Hale Irwin	269	72,000
Mar. 21	Tournament Players Championship, Ponte Vedra Beach, Fla.	Jerry Pate	280	90,000
Mar. 28	Heritage Classic, Hilton Head, S.C.	Tom Watson	*280	54,000
Apr. 4	Greater Greensboro Open, N.C.	Danny Edwards	285	54,000
Apr. 11	Masters Tournament, Augusta, Ga.	Craig Stadler	284	64,000
Apr. 18	Tournament of Champions, Carlsbad, Cal.	Lanny Watkins	280	63,000
Apr. 26	New Orleans Open	Scott Hoch	206	54,000
May 2	Byron Nelson Classic, Dallas, Tex.	Bob Gilder	266	63,000
May 9	Houston Open	Ed Sneed	*275	63,000
May 16	Colonial National Tournament, Ft. Worth, Tex.	Jack Nicklaus	373	63,000
May 23	Atlanta Classic, Atlanta, Ga.	Keith Fergus	*273	54,000
June 6	Kemper Open, Bethesda, Md.	Craig Stadler	275	72,000
June 13	Memphis Classic, Tenn.	Ray Floyd	272	72,000
June 20	U.S. Open, Pebble Beach, Cal.	Tom Watson	282	60,000
June 27	Westchester Classic, Harrison, N.Y.	Bob Gilder	261	72,000
July 4	Western Open, Oak Brook, Ill.	Tom Weiskopf	276	54,000
July 11	Greater Milwaukee Open	Calvin Peete	274	45,000
July 25	Anheuser-Busch Classic, Williamsburg, Va.	Calvin Peete	203	63,000
Aug. 1	Canadian Open, Oakville, Ont.	Bruce Lietzke	277	76,500
Aug. 8	PGA Championship, Tulsa, Okla.	Ray Floyd	272	65,000
Aug. 15	Greater Hartford Open	Tim Norris	259	54,000
Aug. 22	Buick Open, Grand Blanc, Mich.	Lanny Watkins	273	63,000
Aug. 29	World Series of Golf, Akron, Oh.	Craig Stadler	*278	100,000
Sept. 5	B.C. Open, Endicott, N.Y.	Calvin Peete	265	49,500
Sept. 12	Pleasant Valley Classic, Sutton, Mass.	Bob Gilder	271	54,000

Women

Jan. 31	Deer Creek Championship, Deerfield Beach, Fla.	Hollis Stacy	282	$18,750
Feb. 21	Bent Tree Classic, Sarasota, Fla.	Beth Daniel	276	22,500
Feb. 28	Arizona Copper Tournament, Tucson, Ariz.	Ayako Okamoto	*281	18,750
Mar. 7	Sun City Classic, Sun City, Ariz.	Beth Daniel	278	15,000
Mar. 15	Olympia Gold Tournament, City of Industry, Cal.	Sally Little	288	22,500
Mar. 21	J & B Pro-Am, Las Vegas, Nev.	Nancy Lopez-Melton	279	30,000
Mar. 28	Women's Kemper Open, Kaanapali, Hi.	Amy Alcott	286	26,250
Apr. 4	Nabisco-Dinah Shore, Rancho Mirage, Cal.	Sally Little	278	45,000
Apr. 18	Women's International, Hilton Head, S.C.	Kathy Whitworth	281	22,500
Apr. 25	Orlando Lady Classic, Orlando, Fla.	Patty Sheehan	*209	22,500
May 2	Birmingham Classic, Birmingham, Ala.	Beth Daniel	203	15,000
May 9	United Virginia Bank Classic, Suffolk, Va.	Sally Little	*208	18,750
May 16	Lady Michelob, Roswell, Ga.	Kathy Whitworth	207	22,750
May 30	Corning Classic, Corning, N.Y.	Sandra Spuzich	*280	18,750
June 6	McDonald's Open, Malvern, Pa.	JoAnne Carner	276	37,500
June 13	LPGA Championship, Kings Island, Oh.	Jan Stephenson	279	30,000
June 20	Lady Keystone Open, Hershey, Pa.	Jan Stephenson	211	30,000
June 27	Rochester International, Pittsford, N.Y.	Sandra Haynie	273	31,500
July 4	Peter Jackson Classic, Toronto, Ont.	Sandra Haynie	280	30,000
July 11	West Virginia Classic, Wheeling, W.Va.	Hollis Stacy	*209	18,750
July 18	Mayflower Classic, Indianapolis, Ind.	Sally Little	275	30,000
July 25	U.S. Women's Open, Sacramento, Cal.	Janet Alex	283	27,315
Aug. 1	Columbia Savings Classic, Denver, Col.	Beth Daniel	276	30,000
Aug. 15	WUI Classic, Jericho, N.Y.	Beth Daniel	276	18,750
Aug. 22	World Championship of Women's Golf, Shaker Heights, Oh.	JoAnne Carner	284	50,000
Aug. 29	Henredon Classic, High Point, N.C.	JoAnne Carner	*280	24,750
Sept. 12	Mary Kay Classic, Dallas, Tex.	Sandra Spuzich	206	23,250

*Won playoff.

British Open Golf Champions

Year	Winner	Year	Winner	Year	Winner	Year	Winner
1915-19	(Not played)	1934	Henry Cotton	1954	Peter Thomson	1969	Tony Jacklin
1920	George Duncan	1935	Alf Perry	1955	Peter Thomson	1970	Jack Nicklaus
1921	Jock Hutchison	1936	Alf Padgham	1956	Peter Thomson	1971	Lee Trevino
1922	Walter Hagen	1937	T.H. Cotton	1957	Bobby Locke	1972	Lee Trevino
1923	Arthur Havers	1938	R.A. Whitcombe	1958	Peter Thomson	1973	Tom Weiskopf
1924	Walter Hagen	1939	Richard Burton	1959	Gary Player	1974	Gary Player
1925	Jim Barnes	1940-45	(Not played)	1960	Ken Nagle	1975	Tom Watson
1926	Bobby Jones	1946	Sam Snead	1961	Arnold Palmer	1976	Johnny Miller
1927	Bobby Jones	1947	Fred Daly	1962	Arnold Palmer	1977	Tom Watson
1928	Walter Hagen	1948	Henry Cotton	1963	Bob Charles	1978	Jack Nicklaus
1929	Walter Hagen	1949	Bobby Locke	1964	Tony Lema	1979	Severiano Ballesteros
1930	Bobby Jones	1950	Bobby Locke	1965	Peter Thomson		
1931	Tommy Armour	1951	Max Faulkner	1966	Jack Nicklaus	1980	Tom Watson
1932	Gene Sarazen	1952	Bobby Locke	1967	Roberto de Vicenzo	1981	Bill Rogers
1933	Denny Shute	1953	Ben Hogan	1968	Gary Player	1982	Tom Watson

U.S. Amateur

ear	Winner	Year	Winner	Year	Winner	Year	Winner
915	Robert Gardner	1932	Ross Somerville	1951	Billy Maxwell	1967	Bob Dickson
916	Chick Evans Jr.	1933	George Dunlap Jr.	1952	Jack Westland	1968	Bruce Fleisher
917-18	(not played)	1934	Lawson Little	1953	Gene Littler	1969	Steve Melnyk
919	Davidson Herron	1935	Lawson Little	1954	Arnold Palmer	1970	Lanny Wadkins
920	Chick Evans Jr.	1936	John Fischer	1955	Harvie Ward	1971	Gary Cowan
921	Jesse Guilford	1937	John Goodman	1956	Harvie Ward	1972	Vinnie Giles
922	Jess Sweetser	1938	Willie Turnesa	1957	Hillman Robbins	1973	Craig Stadler
923	Max Marston	1939	Bud Ward	1958	Charles Coe	1974	Jerry Pate
924	Bobby Jones	1940	Dick Chapman	1959	Jack Nicklaus	1975	Fred Ridley
925	Bobby Jones	1941	Bud Ward	1960	Deane Beman	1976	Bill Sander
926	George Von Elm	1942-45	(not played)	1961	Jack Nicklaus	1977	John Fought
927	Bobby Jones	1946	Ted Bishop	1962	Labron Harris Jr.	1978	John Cook
928	Bobby Jones	1947	Skee Riegel	1963	Deane Beman	1979	Mark O'Meara
929	Harrison Johnston	1948	Willie Turnesa	1964	Bill Campbell	1980	Hal Sutton
930	Bobby Jones	1949	Charles Coe	1965	Robert Murphy Jr.	1981	Nathaniel Crosby
931	Francis Ouimet	1950	Sam Urzetta	1966	Gary Cowan	1982	Jay Sigel

Women's U.S. Amateur

ear	Winner	Year	Winner	Year	Winner	Year	Winner
915	Mrs. C.H. Vanderbeck	1932	Virginia Van Wie	1951	Dorothy Kirby	1967	Lou Dill
916	Alexa Stirling	1933	Virginia Van Wie	1952	Jackie Pung	1968	JoAnn Carner
917-18	(not played)	1934	Virginia Van Wie	1953	Mary Faulk	1969	Catherine Lacoste
919	Alexa Stirling	1935	Glenna C. Vare	1954	Barbara Romack	1970	Martha Wilkinson
920	Alexa Stirling	1936	Pamela Barton	1955	Pat Lesser	1971	Laura Baugh
921	Marion Hollins	1937	Mrs. J. A. Page	1956	Marlene Stewart	1972	Mary Budke
922	Glenna Collett	1938	Patty Berg	1957	JoAnne Gunderson	1973	Carol Semple
923	Edith Cummings	1939	Betty Jameson	1958	Anne Quast	1974	Cynthia Hill
924	Mrs. D.C. Hurd	1940	Betty Jameson	1959	Barbara McIntire	1975	Beth Daniel
925	Glenna Collett	1941	Mrs. Frank New	1960	JoAnne Gunderson	1976	Donna Horton
926	Mrs. G. Stetson	1942-45	(not played)	1961	Anne Q. Decker	1977	Beth Daniel
927	Mrs. M. Horn	1946	"Babe" Zaharias	1962	JoAnne Gunderson	1978	Cathy Sherk
928	Glenna Collett	1947	Louise Suggs	1963	Anne Q. Welts	1979	Carolyn Hill
929	Glenna Collett	1948	Grace Lenczyk	1964	Barbara McIntire	1980	Juli Inkster
930	Glenna Collett	1949	Dorothy Porter	1965	Jean Ashley	1981	Juli Inkster
931	Helen Hicks	1950	Beverly Hanson	1966	JoAnne Carner	1982	Juli Inkster

PGA Hall of Fame

Established in 1940 to honor those who have made outstanding contributions to the game by their lifetime playing ability.

nderson, Willie	Dudley, Edward	Hutchison Sr., Jock	Runyan, Paul
rmour, Tommy	Dutra, Olin	Jones, Bob	Sarazen, Gene
arnes, Jim	Evans, Chick	Little, W. Lawson	Shute, Denny
erg, Patty	Farrell, Johnny	Mangrum, Lloyd	Smith, Alex
oros, Julius	Ford, Doug	McDermott, John	Smith, Horton
rady, Mike	Ghezzi, Vic	McLeod, Fred	Smith, MacDonald
urke, Billy	Guldahl, Ralph	Middlecoff, Cary	Snead, Sam
urke Jr., Jack	Hagen, Walter	Nelson, Byron	Travers, Jerry
ooper, Harry	Harbert, M. R. (Chick)	Ouimet, Francis	Travis, Walter
ruickshank, Bobby	Harper, Chandler	Palmer, Arnold	de Vicenzo, Roberto
emaret, Jimmy	Harrison, E. J.	Picard, Henry	Wood, Craig
iegel, Leo	Hogan, Ben	Revolta, Johnny	Zaharias, Mildred (Babe)

PGA Leading Money Winners

ear	Player	Dollars	Year	Player	Dollars	Year	Player	Dollars
945	Byron Nelson	52,511	1958	Arnold Palmer	42,407	1971	Jack Nicklaus	244,490
946	Ben Hogan	42,556	1959	Art Wall Jr.	53,167	1972	Jack Nicklaus	320,542
947	Jimmy Demaret	27,936	1960	Arnold Palmer	75,262	1973	Jack Nicklaus	308,362
948	Ben Hogan	36,812	1961	Gary Player	64,540	1974	Johnny Miller	353,201
949	Sam Snead	31,593	1962	Arnold Palmer	81,448	1975	Jack Nicklaus	323,149
950	Sam Snead	35,758	1963	Arnold Palmer	128,230	1976	Jack Nicklaus	266,438
951	Lloyd Mangrum	26,088	1964	Jack Nicklaus	113,284	1977	Tom Watson	310,653
952	Julius Boros	37,032	1965	Jack Nicklaus	140,752	1978	Tom Watson	362,429
953	Lew Worsham	34,002	1966	Billy Casper	121,944	1979	Tom Watson	462,636
954	Bob Toski	65,819	1967	Jack Nicklaus	188,988	1980	Tom Watson	530,808
955	Julius Boros	65,121	1968	Billy Casper	205,168	1981	Tom Kite	375,699
956	Ted Kroll	72,835	1969	Frank Beard	175,223			
957	Dick Mayer	65,835	1970	Lee Trevino	157,037			

LPGA Leading Money Winners

ear	Winner	Dollars	Year	Winner	Dollars	Year	Winner	Dollars
954	Patty Berg	16,011	1964	Mickey Wright	29,800	1974	JoAnne Carner	87,094
955	Patty Berg	16,492	1965	Kathy Whitworth	28,658	1975	Sandra Palmer	94,805
956	Marlene Hagge	20,235	1966	Kathy Whitworth	33,517	1976	Judy Rankin	150,734
957	Patty Berg	16,272	1967	Kathy Whitworth	32,937	1977	Judy Rankin	122,890
958	Beverly Hanson	12,629	1968	Kathy Whitworth	48,379	1978	Nancy Lopez	189,813
959	Betsy Rawls	26,774	1969	Carol Mann	49,152	1979	Nancy Lopez	215,987
960	Louise Suggs	16,892	1970	Kathy Whitworth	30,235	1980	Beth Daniel	231,000
961	Mickey Wright	22,236	1971	Kathy Whitworth	41,181	1981	Beth Daniel	206,977
962	Mickey Wright	21,641	1972	Kathy Whitworth	65,063			
963	Mickey Wright	31,269	1973	Kathy Whitworth	82,854			

Ryder Cup Matches

United States vs. Great Britain — Professional (biennial)
Series standing — United States 20, Great Britain 3, 1 tie

Series record

1955	United States 8; Great Britain 4
1957	Great Britain 7; United States 4
1959	United States 8½; Great Britain 3½
1961	United States 14½; Great Britain 9½
1963	United States 23; Great Britain 9
1965	United States 19½; Great Britain 12½
1967	United States 23½; Great Britain 8½
1969	United States 16; Great Britain 16
1971	United States 18½; Great Britain 13½
1973	Great Britain 13; United States 10
1975	United States 21; Great Britain 11
1977	United States 12½; Great Britain 7½
1979	United States 17; Great Britain-Ireland 11
1981	United States 18½; Great Britain-Ireland 9½

International Walker Cup Golf Match

United States vs. Great Britain — Men's Amateur (biennial)
Series standing — United States, 25, Great Britain 2, 1 tie

Series record

1955	United States 10; Great Britain 2
1957	United States 10; Great Britain 2
1959	United States 9; Great Britain 3
1961	United States 11; Great Britain 1
1963	United States 9; Great Britain 3
1965	United States 11; Great Britain 11
1967	United States 13; Great Britain 7
1969	United States 10; Great Britain 8
1971	Great Britain 13; United States 11
1973	United States 14; Great Britain 10
1975	United States 15½; Great Britain 8½
1977	United States 16; Great Britain 8
1979	United States 15½; Great Britain-Ireland 8½
1981	United States 15; Great Britain-Ireland 9

International Curtis Cup Golf Match

United States vs. Great Britain (plus Ireland) — Women's Amateur (biennial)
Series standing — United States 18, Great Britain 2, 2 ties

Series record

1954	United States 6; Great Britain 3
1957	Great Britain 5; United States 4
1959	Great Britain 4½; United States 4½
1960	United States 6½; Great Britain 2½
1962	United States 8; Great Britain 1
1964	United States 10½; Great Britain 7½
1966	United States 13; Great Britain 5
1968	United States 10½; Great Britain 7½
1970	United States 11½; Great Britain 6½
1972	United States 10; Great Britain 8
1974	United States 13; Great Britain 5
1976	United States 11½; Great Britain 6½
1978	United States 12; Great Britain 6
1980	United States 13; Great Britain 5
1982	United States 14½; Great Britain 3½

Tennis

USTA National Champions

Men's Singles

Year	Champion	Final opponent
1920	Bill Tilden	William Johnston
1921	Bill Tilden	Wallace Johnston
1922	Bill Tilden	William Johnston
1923	Bill Tilden	William Johnston
1924	Bill Tilden	William Johnston
1925	Bill Tilden	William Johnston
1926	Rene Lacoste	Jean Borotra
1927	Rene Lacoste	Bill Tilden
1928	Henri Cochet	Francis Hunter
1929	Bill Tilden	Francis Hunter
1930	John Doeg	Francis Shields
1931	H. Ellsworth Vines	George Lott
1932	H. Ellsworth Vines	Henri Cochet
1933	Fred Perry	John Crawford
1934	Fred Perry	Wilmer Allison
1935	Wilmer Allison	Sidney Wood
1936	Fred Perry	Don Budge
1937	Don Budge	Baron G. von Cramm
1938	Don Budge	C. Gene Mako
1939	Robert Riggs	S. Welby Van Horn
1940	Don McNeill	Robert Riggs
1941	Robert Riggs	F. L. Kovacs
1942	F. R. Schroeder Jr.	Frank Parker
1943	Joseph Hunt	Jack Kramer
1944	Frank Parker	William Talbert
1945	Frank Parker	William Talbert
1946	Jack Kramer	Thomas Brown Jr.
1947	Jack Kramer	Frank Parker
1948	Pancho Gonzales	Eric Sturgess
1949	Pancho Gonzales	F. R. Schroeder Jr.
1950	Arthur Larsen	Herbert Flam
1951	Frank Sedgman	E. Victor Seixas Jr.
1952	Frank Sedgman	Gardnar Mulloy
1953	Tony Trabert	E. Victor Seixas Jr.
1954	E. Victor Seixas Jr.	Rex Hartwig
1955	Tony Trabert	Ken Rosewall
1956	Ken Rosewall	Lewis Hoad
1957	Malcolm Anderson	Ashley Cooper
1958	Ashley Cooper	Malcolm Anderson
1959	Neale A. Fraser	Alejandro Olmedo
1960	Neale A. Fraser	Rod Laver
1961	Roy Emerson	Rod Laver
1962	Rod Laver	Roy Emerson
1963	Rafael Osuna	F. A. Froehling 3d
1964	Roy Emerson	Fred Stolle
1965	Manuel Santana	Cliff Drysdale
1966	Fred Stolle	John Newcombe
1967	John Newcombe	Clark Graebner
1968	Arthur Ashe	Tom Okker
1969	Rod Laver	Tony Roche
1970	Ken Rosewall	Tony Roche
1971	Stan Smith	Jan Kodes
1972	Ilie Nastase	Arthur Ashe
1973	John Newcombe	Jan Kodes
1974	Jimmy Connors	Ken Rosewall
1975	Manuel Orantes	Jimmy Connors
1976	Jimmy Connors	Bjorn Borg
1977	Guillermo Vilas	Jimmy Connors
1978	Jimmy Connors	Bjorn Borg
1979	John McEnroe	Vitas Gerulaitis
1980	John McEnroe	Bjorn Borg
1981	John McEnroe	Bjorn Borg
1982	Jimmy Connors	Ivan Lendl

Men's Doubles

Year	Champions
1925	R. Norris Williams—Vincent Richards
1926	R. Norris Williams—Vincent Richards
1927	Bill Tilden—Francis Hunter
1928	George Lott—John Hennessey
1929	George Lott—John Doeg
1930	George Lott—John Doeg
1931	Wilmer Allison—John Van Ryn
1932	H. Ellsworth Vines—Keith Gledhill
1933	George Lott—Lester Stoefen
1934	George Lott—Lester Stoefen
1935	Wilmer Allison—John Van Ryn
1936	Don Budge—C. Gene Mako
1937	Baron G. von Cramm—Henner Henkel
1938	Don Budge—C. Gene Mako
1939	Adrian Quist—John Bromwich
1940	Jack Kramer—Frederick Schroeder Jr.
1941	Jack Kramer—Frederick Schroeder Jr.
1942	Gardnar Mulloy—William Talbert
1943	Jack Kramer—Frank Parker
1944	Don McNeill—Robert Falkenburg
1945	Gardnar Mulloy—William Talbert
1946	Gardnar Mulloy—William Talbert
1947	Jack Kramer—Frederick Schroeder Jr.
1948	Gardnar Mulloy—William Talbert
1949	John Bromwich—William Sidwell
1950	John Bromwich—Frank Sedgman
1951	Frank Sedgman—Kenneth McGregor
1952	Mervyn Rose—E. Victor Seixas Jr.
1953	Rex Hartwig—Mervyn Rose

Year	Champions
1954	E. Victor Seixas Jr.—Tony Trabert
1955	Kosei Kamo—Atsushi Miyagi
1956	Lewis Hoad—Ken Rosewall
1957	Ashley Cooper—Neale Fraser
1958	Hamilton Richardson—Alejandro Olmedo
1959	Neale A. Fraser—Roy Emerson
1960	Neale A. Fraser—Roy Emerson
1961	Dennis Ralston—Chuck McKinley
1962	Rafael Osuna—Antonio Palafox
1963	Dennis Ralston—Chuck McKinley
1964	Dennis Ralston—Chuck McKinley
1965	Roy Emerson—Fred Stolle
1966	Roy Emerson—Fred Stolle
1967	John Newcombe—Tony Roche
1968	Robert Lutz—Stan Smith
1969	Fred Stolle—Ken Rosewall
1970	Pierre Barthes—Nicki Pilic
1971	John Newcombe—Roger Taylor
1972	Cliff Drysdale—Roger Taylor
1973	John Newcombe—Owen Davidson
1974	Bob Lutz—Stan Smith
1975	Jimmy Connors—Ilie Nastase
1976	Marty Riessen—Tom Okker
1977	Bob Hewitt—Frew McMillan
1978	Stan Smith—Bob Lutz
1979	John McEnroe—Peter Fleming
1980	Bob Lutz—Stan Smith
1981	John McEnroe—Peter Fleming
1982	Kevin Curren—Steve Denton

Women's Singles

Year	Champion	Final opponent
1936	Alice Marble	Helen Jacobs
1937	Anita Lizana	Pauline Betz
1938	Alice Marble	Louise Brough
1939	Alice Marble	Louise Brough
1940	Alice Marble	Margaret Osborne
1941	Sarah Palfrey Cooke	Pauline Betz
1942	Pauline Betz	Jadwiga Jedrzejowska
1943	Pauline Betz	Nancye Wynne
1944	Pauline Betz	Helen Jacobs
1945	Sarah P. Cooke	Helen Jacobs
1946	Pauline Betz	Doris Hart
1947	Louise Brough	Margaret Osborne
1948	Margaret Osborne duPont	Louise Brough
1949	Margaret Osborne duPont	Doris Hart
1950	Margaret Osborne duPont	Doris Hart
1951	Maureen Connolly	Shirley Fry
1952	Maureen Connolly	Doris Hart
1953	Maureen Connolly	Doris Hart
1954	Doris Hart	Louise Brough
1955	Doris Hart	Patricia Ward
1956	Shirley Fry	Althea Gibson
1957	Althea Gibson	Louise Brough
1958	Althea Gibson	Darlene Hard
1959	Maria Bueno	Christine Truman

Year	Champion	Final opponent
1960	Darlene Hard	Maria Bueno
1961	Darlene Hard	Ann Haydon
1962	Margaret Smith	Darlene Hard
1963	Maria Bueno	Margaret Smith
1964	Maria Bueno	Carole Graebner
1965	Margaret Smith	Billie Jean Moffitt
1966	Maria Bueno	Nancy Richey
1967	Billie Jean King	Ann Haydon Jones
1968	Virginia Wade	Billie Jean King
1969	Margaret Court	Nancy Richey
1970	Margaret Court	Rosemary Casals
1971	Billie Jean King	Rosemary Casals
1972	Billie Jean King	Kerry Melville
1973	Margaret Court	Evonne Goolagong
1974	Billie Jean King	Evonne Goolagong
1975	Chris Evert	Evonne Goolagong
1976	Chris Evert	Evonne Goolagong
1977	Chris Evert	Wendy Turnbull
1978	Chris Evert	Pam Shriver
1979	Tracy Austin	Chris Evert Lloyd
1980	Chris Evert Lloyd	Hana Mandlikova
1981	Tracy Austin	Martina Navratilova
1982	Chris Evert Lloyd	Hana Mandlikova

Women's Doubles

Year	Champions
1939	Alice Marble—Mrs. Sarah P. Fabyan
1940	Alice Marble—Mrs. Sarah P. Fabyan
1941	Mrs. S. P. Cooke—Margaret Osborne
1942	A. Louise Brough—Margaret Osborne
1943	A. Louise Brough—Margaret Osborne
1944	A. Louise Brough—Margaret Osborne
1945	A. Louise Brough—Margaret Osborne
1946	A. Louise Brough—Margaret Osborne
1947	A. Louise Brough—Margaret Osborne
1948	A. Louise Brough—Mrs. M. O. du Pont
1949	A. Louise Brough—Mrs. M. O. du Pont
1950	A. Louise Brough—Mrs. M. O. du Pont
1951	Doris Hart—Shirley Fry
1952	Doris Hart—Shirley Fry
1953	Doris Hart—Shirley Fry
1954	Doris Hart—Shirley Fry
1955	A. Louise Brough—Mrs. M. O. du Pont
1956	A. Louise Brough—Mrs. M. O. du Pont
1957	A. Louise Brough—Mrs. M. O. du Pont
1958	Darlene Hard—Jeanne Arth
1959	Darlene Hard—Jeanne Arth
1960	Darlene Hard—Maria Bueno

Year	Champions
1961	Darlene Hard—Lesley Turner
1962	Maria Bueno—Darlene Hard
1963	Margaret Smith—Robyn Ebbern
1964	Billie Jean Moffitt—Karen Susman
1965	Carole C. Graebner—Nancy Richey
1966	Maria Bueno—Nancy Richey
1967	Rosemary Casals—Billie Jean King
1968	Maria Bueno—Margaret S. Court
1969	Francoise Durr—Darlene Hard
1970	M. S. Court—Judy Tegart Dalton
1971	Rosemary Casals—Judy Tegart Dalton
1972	Francoise Durr—Betty Stove
1973	Margaret S. Court—Virginia Wade
1974	Billie Jean King—Rosemary Casals
1975	Margaret Court—Virginia Wade
1976	Linky Boshoff—Ilana Kloss
1977	Betty Stove—Martina Navratilova
1978	Martina Navratilova—Billie Jean King
1979	Betty Stove—Wendy Turnbull
1980	Billie Jean King—Martina Navratilova
1981	Anne Smith—Kathy Jordan
1982	Rosemary Casals—Wendy Turnbull

Mixed Doubles

Year	Champions	Year	Champions
1955	Doris Hart—E. Victor Seixas Jr.	1969	Margaret S. Court—Marty Riessen
1956	Mrs. M. O. duPont—Ken Rosewall	1970	Margaret S. Court—Marty Riessen
1957	Althea Gibson—Kurt Nielsen	1971	Billie Jean King—Owen Davidson
1958	Mrs. M. O. duPont—Neale Fraser	1972	Margaret S. Court—Marty Riessen
1959	Mrs. M. O. duPont—Neale Fraser	1973	Billie Jean King—Owen Davidson
1960	Mrs. M. O. duPont—Neale Fraser	1974	Pam Teeguarden—Geoff Masters
1961	Margaret Smith—Robert Mark	1975	Rosemary Casals—Dick Stockton
1962	Margaret Smith—Fred Stolle	1976	Billie Jean King—Phil Dent
1963	Margaret Smith—Kenneth Fletcher	1977	Betty Stove—Frew McMillan
1964	Margaret Smith—John Newcombe	1978	Betty Stove—Frew McMillan
1965	Margaret Smith—Fred Stolle	1979	Greer Stevens—Bob Hewitt
1966	Donna Floyd Fales—Owen Davidson	1980	Wendy Turnbull—Marty Riessen
1967	Billie Jean King—Owen Davidson	1981	Anne Smith—Kevin Curren
1968	Mary Ann Eisel—Peter Curtis	1982	Anne Smith—Kevin Curren

British Champions, Wimbledon

Inaugurated 1877

Men's Singles

Year	Champion	Final opponent	Year	Champion	Final opponent
1933	Jack Crawford	Ellsworth Vines	1961	Rod Laver	Chuck McKinley
1934	Fred Perry	Jack Crawford	1962	Rod Laver	Martin Mulligan
1935	Fred Perry	Gottfried von Cramm	1963	Chuck McKinley	Fred Stolle
1936	Fred Perry	Gottfried von Cramm	1964	Roy Emerson	Fred Stolle
1937	Donald Budge	Gottfried von Cramm	1965	Roy Emerson	Fred Stolle
1938	Donald Budge	Wilfred Austin	1966	Manuel Santana	Dennis Ralston
1939	Bobby Riggs	Elwood Cooke	1967	John Newcombe	Wilhelm Bungert
1940-45	not held		1968	Rod Laver	Tony Roche
1946	Yvon Petra	Geoff E. Brown	1969	Rod Laver	John Newcombe
1947	Jack Kramer	Tom P. Brown	1970	John Newcombe	Ken Rosewall
1948	Bob Falkenburg	John Bromwich	1971	John Newcombe	Stan Smith
1949	Ted Schroeder	Jaroslav Drobny	1972	Stan Smith	Ilie Nastase
1950	Budge Patty	Fred Sedgman	1973	Jan Kodes	Alex Metreveli
1951	Dick Savitt	Ken McGregor	1974	Jimmy Connors	Ken Rosewall
1952	Frank Sedgman	Jaroslav Drobny	1975	Arthur Ashe	Jimmy Connors
1953	Vic Seixas	Kurt Nielsen	1976	Bjorn Borg	Ilie Nastase
1954	Jaroslav Drobny	Ken Rosewall	1977	Bjorn Borg	Jimmy Connors
1955	Tony Trabert	Kurt Nielsen	1978	Bjorn Borg	Jimmy Connors
1956	Lew Hoad	Ken Rosewall	1979	Bjorn Borg	Roscoe Tanner
1957	Lew Hoad	Ashley Cooper	1980	Bjorn Borg	John McEnroe
1958	Ashley Cooper	Neale Fraser	1981	John McEnroe	Bjorn Borg
1959	Alex Olmedo	Rod Laver	1982	Jimmy Connors	John McEnroe
1960	Neale Fraser	Rod Laver			

Women's Singles

Year	Champion	Year	Champion	Year	Champion	Year	Champion
1946	Pauline Betz	1956	Shirley Fry	1965	Margaret Smith	1974	Chris Evert
1947	Margaret Osborne	1957	Althea Gibson	1966	Billie Jean King	1975	Billie Jean King
1948	Louise Brough	1958	Althea Gibson	1967	Billie Jean King	1976	Chris Evert
1949	Louise Brough	1959	Maria Bueno	1968	Billie Jean King	1977	Virginia Wade
1950	Louise Brough	1960	Maria Bueno	1969	Ann Haydon-Jones	1978	Martina Navratilova
1951	Doris Hart	1961	Angela Mortimer	1970	Margaret Court	1979	Martina Navratilova
1952	Maureen Connolly	1962	Karen Hantze-Susman	1971	Evonne Goolagong	1980	Evonne Goolagong
1953	Maureen Connolly	1963	Margaret Smith	1972	Billie Jean King	1981	Chris Evert Lloyd
1954	Maureen Connolly	1964	Maria Bueno	1973	Billie Jean King	1982	Martina Navratilova
1955	Louise Brough						

French Open Champions

Year	Men	Women	Year	Men	Women
1967	Roy Emerson	Françoise Durr	**1975**	Bjorn Borg	Chris Evert
1968	Ken Rosewall	Nancy Richey	**1976**	Adriano Panatta	Sue Barker
1969	Rod Laver	Margaret Smith Court	**1977**	Guillermo Vilas	Mima Jausovec
1970	Jan Kodes	Margaret Smith Court	**1978**	Bjorn Borg	Virginia Ruzici
1971	Jan Kodes	Evonne Goolagong	**1979**	Bjorn Borg	Chris Evert Lloyd
1972	Andres Gimeno	Billie Jean King	**1980**	Bjorn Borg	Chris Evert Lloyd
1973	Ilie Nastase	Margaret Court	**1981**	Bjorn Borg	Hana Mandlikova
1974	Bjorn Borg	Chris Evert	**1982**	Mats Wilander	Martina Navratilova

Leading Tennis Money Winners in 1981

Men		Women	
John McEnroe	$941,000	Martina Navratilova	$865,437
Ivan Lendl	716,037	Chris Evert Lloyd	572,162
Jimmy Connors	395,872	Tracy Austin	453,409
Guillermo Vilas	387,261	Andrea Jaeger	392,115
Jose Luis Clerc	317,375	Pam Shriver	366,350

Davis Cup Challenge Round

Year	Result	Year	Result	Year	Result
1900	United States 5, British Isles 0	1928	France 4, United States 1	1958	United States 3, Australia 2
1901	(not played)	1929	France 3, United States 2	1959	Australia 3, United States 2
1902	United States 3, British Isles 2	1930	France 4, United States 1	1960	Australia 4, Italy 1
1903	British Isles 4, United States 1	1931	France 3, Great Britain 2	1961	Australia 5, Italy 0
1904	British Isles 5, Belgium 0	1932	France 3, United States 2	1962	Australia 5, Mexico 0
1905	British Isles 5, United States 0	1933	Great Britain 3, France 2	1963	United States 3, Australia 2
1906	British Isles 5, United States 0	1934	Great Britain 4, United States 1	1964	Australia 3, United States 2
1907	Australia 3, British Isles 2	1935	Great Britain 5, United States 0	1965	Australia 4, Spain 1
1908	Australasia 3, United States 2	1936	Great Britain 3, Australia 2	1966	Australia 4, India 1
1909	Australasia 5, United States 0	1937	United States 4, Great Britain 1	1967	Australia 4, Spain 1
1910	(not played)	1938	United States 3, Australia 2	1968	United States 4, Australia 1
1911	Australasia 5, United States 0	1939	Australia 3, United States 2	1969	United States 5, Romania 0
1912	British Isles 3, Australasia 2	1940-45	(not played)	1970	United States 5, W. Germany 0
1913	United States 3, British Isles 2	1946	United States 5, Australia 0	1971	United States 3, Romania 2
1914	Australasia 3, United States 2	1947	United States 4, Australia 1	1972	United States 3, Romania 2
1915-18	(not played)	1948	United States 5, Australia 0	1973	Australia 5, United States 0
1919	Australasia 4, British Isles 1	1949	United States 4, Australia 1	1974	South Africa (default by India)
1920	United States 5, Australasia 0	1950	Australia 4, United States 1	1975	Sweden 3, Czech. 2
1921	United States 5, Japan 0	1951	Australia 3, United States 2	1976	Italy 4, Chile 1
1922	United States 4, Australasia 1	1952	Australia 4, United States 1	1977	Australia 3, Italy 1
1923	United States 4, Australasia 1	1953	Australia 3, United States 2	1978	United States 4, Great Britain 1
1924	United States 5, Australasia 0	1954	United States 3, Australia 2	1979	United States 5, Italy 0
1925	United States 5, France 0	1955	Australia 5, United States 0	1980	Czechoslovakia 4, Italy 1
1926	United States 4, France 1	1956	Australia 5, United States 0	1981	United States 3, Argentina 1
1927	France 3, United States 2	1957	Australia 3, United States 2		

WCT World Series of Tennis in 1982

Dates	Event, city	Singles winner	Doubles winners
Jan. 19-24	Torneo Internacional de Tenis, Mexico City, Mexico	Tomas Smid	Sherwood Stewart-Ferdi Taygan
Jan. 26-31	Gold Coast Cup, Delray Beach, Fla.	Ivan Lendl	Mel Purcell-Eliot Teltscher
Feb. 9-14	Richmond Tennis Classic, Richmond, Va.	Jose Luis Clerc	Mark Edmondson-Kim Warwick
Feb. 22-28	Bitti Bergamo Memorial, Genoa, Italy	Ivan Lendl	Pavel Slozil-Tomas Smid
Mar. 8-14	Munich Cup, Munich, West Germany	Ivan Lendl	Mark Edmondson-Tomas Smid
Mar. 15-21	Strasbourg Tennis International '82, Strasbourg, France	Ivan Lendl	Wojtek Fibak-John Fitzgerald
Mar. 29-Apr. 4	Pro Championship of Switzerland	Bill Scanlon	Tom Gullikson-Sam Giammalva
Apr. 12-18	River Oaks International, Houston, Tex.	Ivan Lendl	Kevin Curren-Steve Denton
Apr. 20-26	WCT Finals, Dallas, Tex.	Ivan Lendl	

NCAA Tennis Champions

Year	Singles	College	Doubles	College
1969	Joaquin Loyo Mayo	USC	Joaquin Loyo Mayo—Marcelo Lara	USC
1970	Jeff Borowiak	UCLA	Pat Cramer—Luis Garcia	Miami (Fla.)
1971	Jimmy Connors	UCLA	Jeff Borowiak—Haroon Rahim	UCLA
1972	Dick Stockton	Trinity (Tex.)	Sandy Mayer—Roscoe Tanner	Stanford
1973	Sandy Mayer	Stanford	Sandy Mayer—Jim Delaney	Stanford
1974	John Whitlinger	Stanford	John Whitlinger—Jim Delaney	Stanford
1975	Billy Martin	UCLA	Butch Walts—Bruce Manson	USC
1976	Bill Scanlon	Trinity	Peter Fleming—Ferdi Taygan	UCLA
1977	Matt Mitchell	Stanford	Bruce Manson—Chris Lewis	USC
1978	John McEnroe	Stanford	Bruce Nichols—John Austin	UCLA
1979	Kevin Curren	Texas	Erick Iskersky—Ben McKown	Trinity
1980	Robert Van't Hof	USC	Mel Purcell—Rodney Harman	Tennessee
1981	Tim Mayotte	Stanford	Carl Richter—David Pate	Texas Christian
1982	Mike Leach	Michigan	Peter Doohan—Pat Serret	Arkansas

The America's Cup

Competition for the America's Cup grew out of the first contest to establish a world yachting championship, one of the carnival features of the London Exposition of 1851. The race, open to all classes of yachts from all over the world, covered a 60-mile course around the Isle of Wight; the prize was a cup worth about $500, donated by the Royal Yacht Squadron of England, known as the "America's Cup" because it was first won by the United States yacht America. Successive efforts of British and Australian yachtsmen have failed to win the famous trophy, which remains in the United States.

On Sept. 25, 1980, the yacht Freedom defeated the Australian challenger, Australia, for the 4th time in 5 races to keep the symbol of world sailing supremacy in the United States. Freedom was skippered by Dennis Connor of San Diego, Cal.

Winners of the America's Cup

1851	America
1870	Magic defeated Cambria, England, (1-0)
1871	Columbia (first three races) and Sappho (last two races) defeated Livonia, England, (4-1)
1876	Madeline defeated Countess of Dufferin, Canada, (2-0)
1881	Mischief defeated Atalanta, Canada, (2-0)
1885	Puritan defeated Genesta, England, (2-0)
1886	Mayflower defeated Galatea, England, (2-0)
1887	Volunteer defeated Thistle, Scotland, (2-0)
1893	Vigilant defeated Valkyrie II, England, (3-0)
1895	Defender defeated Valkyrie III, England, (3-0)
1899	Columbia defeated Shamrock, England, (3-0)
1901	Columbia defeated Shamrock II, England, (3-0)
1903	Reliance defeated Shamrock III, England, (3-0)
1920	Resolute defeated Shamrock IV, England, (3-2)
1930	Enterprise defeated Shamrock V, England, (4-0)
1934	Rainbow defeated Endeavour, England, (4-2)
1937	Ranger defeated Endeavour II, England, (4-0)
1958	Columbia defeated Sceptre, England, (4-0)
1962	Weatherly defeated Gretel, Australia, (4-1)
1964	Constellation defeated Sovereign, England, (4-0)
1967	Intrepid defeated Dame Pattie, Australia, (4-0)
1970	Intrepid defeated Gretel II, Australia, (4-1)
1974	Courageous defeated Southern Cross, Australia, (4-0)
1977	Courageous defeated Australia, Australia, (4-0)
1980	Freedom defeated Australia, Australia, (4-1)

Trotting and Pacing Records

Source: David Carr, U.S. Trotting Assn.; records to Sept. 8, 1982

Trotting Records

Asterisk (*) denotes record was made against the clock. Times—seconds in fifths.

One mile records (mile track)

All-age — *1:54.4 — Nevele Pride, Indianapolis, Ind., Aug. 31, 1969; Lindy's Crown, DuQuoin, Ill., Aug. 30, 1980.
Two-year-old — 1:56.3 — Star Investment, Lexington, Ky., Oct. 8, 1979.
Three-year-old — 1:55 — Speedy Somolli and Florida Pro, Du Quoin, Ill., Sept. 2, 1978.

(Half-mile track)

All-age — 1:56.4 — Nevele Pride, Saratoga Springs, N.Y., Sept. 6, 1969.
Two-year-old — 2:00 — Incredible Nevele, Delaware, Oh., Sept. 22, 1981.
Three-year-old — 1:58.3 — Songcan, Delaware, Oh., 1972.

(Five Eighth-mile track)

All-Age — 1:57.1 — Lindy's Crown, Wilmington, Del., July 27, 1980.
Two-year-old — 2:00.1 — Smokin Yankee, Laurel, Md., Sept. 10, 1980.
Three-year-old — 1:58 — Keystone Sister, Meadow Lands, Pa., Aug. 14, 1981.

Pacing Records

One mile records (mile track)

All-age — *1:49.1 — Niatross, Lexington, Ky., Oct. 1, 1980.
Two-year-old — 1:53.4 — Merger, Lexington, Ky., Oct. 3, 1981.
Three-year-old — *1:49.1 — Niatross, Lexington, Ky., Oct. 1, 1980.

(Half-mile track)

All age — 1:54.4 — Niatross, Delaware, Oh., Sept. 18, 1980.
Two-year-old — 1:56.1 — Tumujin, Louisville, Ky., Sept. 12, 1981.
Three-year-old — 1:54.4 — Niatross, Delaware, Oh., Sept. 18, 1980.

(Five Eighth-mile track)

All-age — 1:53.2 — Storm Damage, Washington, Pa., Aug. 6, 1980.
Two-year-old — 1:56.1 — French Chef, Columbus, Oh., Sept. 6, 1980.
Three-year-old — 1:53.2 — Storm Damage, Washington, Pa., Aug. 6, 1980.

The Hambletonian (3-year-old trotters)

Year	Winner	Driver	Purse	Year	Winner	Driver	Purse
1947	Hoot Mon	S.F. Palin	$46,267	1965	Egyptian Candor	Del Cameron	$122,245
1948	Demon Hanover	Harrison Hoyt	59,941	1966	Kerry Way	Frank Ervin	122,540
1949	Miss Tilly	Fred Egan	69,791	1967	Speedy Streak	Del Cameron	122,650
1950	Lusty Song	Del Miller	75,209	1968	Nevele Pride	Stanley Dancer	116,190
1951	Mainliner	Guy Crippen	95,263	1969	Lindy's Pride	Howard Beissinger	124,910
1952	Sharp Note	Bion Shively	87,637	1970	Timothy T	John Simpson Sr.	143,630
1953	Helicopter	Harry Harvey	117,118	1971	Speedy Crown	Howard Beissinger	128,770
1954	Newport Dream	Del Cameron	106,830	1972	Super Bowl	Stanley Dancer	119,090
1955	Scott Frost	Joe O'Brien	86,863	1973	Flirth	Ralph Baldwin	144,710
1956	The Intruder	Ned Bower	98,591	1974	Christopher T	Bill Haughton	160,150
1957	Hickory Smoke	John Simpson Sr.	111,126	1975	Bonefish	Stanley Dancer	232,192
1958	Emily's Pride	Flave Nipe	106,719	1976	Steve Lobell	Bill Haughton	263,524
1959	Diller Hanover	Frank Ervin	125,284	1977	Green Speed	Bill Haughton	284,131
1960	Blaze Hanover	Joe O'Brien	144,590	1978	Speedy Somolli	Howard Beissinger	241,280
1961	Harlan Dean	James Arthur	131,573	1979	Legend Hanover	George Sholty	300,000
1962	A.C. Os Viking	Sanders Russell	116,312	1980	Burgomeister	Bill Haughton	293,570
1963	Speedy Scot	Ralph Baldwin	115,549	1981	Shiaway St. Pat	Ray Remmen	838,000
1964	Ayres	John Simpson Sr.	115,281	1982	Speed Bowl	Tommy Haughton	875,750

Leading Drivers

Races Won

Year	Driver		Year	Driver		Year	Driver		Year	Driver	
1958	Bill Haughton	176	1964	Bob Farrington	312	1970	Herve Filion	486	1976	Herve Filion	445
1959	William Gilmour	165	1965	Bob Farrington	310	1971	Herve Filion	543	1977	Herve Filion	441
1960	Del Insko	156	1966	Bob Farrington	283	1972	Herve Filion	605	1978	Herve Filion	423
1961	Bob Farrington	201	1967	Bob Farrington	277	1973	Herve Filion	445	1979	Ron Waples	443
1962	Bob Farrington	203	1968	Herve Filion	407	1974	Herve Filion	637	1980	Herve Filion	474
1963	Donald Busse	201	1969	Herve Filion	394	1975	Daryl Buse	360	1981	Eddie Davis	404

Money Won

Year	Driver	Dollars	Year	Driver	Dollars	Year	Driver	Dollars
1957	Bill Haughton	586,950	1966	Stanley Dancer	1,218,403	1974	Herve Filion	3,474,315
1958	Bill Haughton	816,659	1967	Bill Haughton	1,305,773	1975	Carmine Abbatiello	2,275,093
1959	Bill Haughton	711,435	1968	Bill Haughton	1,654,172	1976	Herve Filion	2,241,045
1960	Del Miller	567,282	1969	Del Insko	1,635,463	1977	Herve Filion	2,551,058
1961	Stanley Dancer	674,723	1970	Herve Filion	1,647,837	1978	Carmine Abbatiello	3,344,457
1962	Stanley Dancer	760,343	1971	Herve Filion	1,915,945	1979	John Campbell	3,308,984
1963	Bill Haughton	790,086	1972	Herve Filion	2,473,265	1980	John Campbell	3,732,306
1964	Stanley Dancer	1,051,538	1973	Herve Filion	2,233,302	1981	William O'Donnell	4,065,608
1965	Bill Haughton	889,943						

Annual Leading Money-Winning Horses

Trotters

Year	Horse	Dollars	Year	Horse	Dollars	Year	Horse	Dollars
1954	Katie Key	84,867	1964	Speedy Scot	235,710	1973	Spartan Hanover	262,023
1955	Scott Frost	186,101	1965	Dartmouth	252,348	1974	Delmonica Hanover	252,165
1956	Scott Frost	85,851	1966	Noble Victory	210,696	1975	Savoir	351,385
1957	Hoot Song	114,877	1967	Carlisle	231,243	1976	Steve Lobell	338,770
1958	Emily's Pride	118,830	1968	Nevele Pride	427,440	1977	Green Speed	584,405
1959	Diller Hanover	149,897	1969	Lindy's Pride	323,997	1978	Speedy Somolli	362,404
1960	Su Mac Lad	159,662	1970	Fresh Yankee	359,002	1979	Chiola Hanover	553,058
1961	Su Mac Lad	245,750	1971	Fresh Yankee	293,960	1980	Classical Way	350,410
1962	Duke Rodney	206,113	1972	Super Bowl	437,108	1981	Shiaway St. Pat	480,095
1963	Speedy Scot	144,403						

Pacers

Year	Horse	Dollars	Year	Horse	Dollars	Year	Horse	Dollars
1954	Red Sails	66,615	1964	Race Time	199,292	1973	Sir Dalrae	307,354
1955	Adios Harry	98,900	1965	Bret Hanover	341,784	1974	Armbro Omaha	345,146
1956	Adios Harry	129,912	1966	Bret Hanover	407,534	1975	Silk Stockings	336,312
1957	Torpid	113,982	1967	Romulus Hanover	277,636	1976	Keystone Ore	539,762
1958	Belle Action	167,887	1968	Rum Customer	355,618	1977	Governor Skipper	522,148
1959	Bye Bye Byrd	199,933	1969	Overcall	373,150	1978	Abercrombie	703,260
1960	Bye Bye Byrd	187,612	1970	Most Happy Fella	387,239	1979	Hot Hitter	826,542
1961	Adios Butler	180,250	1971	Albatross	558,009	1980	Niatross	1,414,313
1962	Henry T. Adios	220,302	1972	Albatross	459,921	1981	McKinzie Almahurst	936,418
1963	Overtrick	208,833						

Harness Horse of the Year

(Chosen by the U.S. Trotting Assn. and the U.S. Harness Writers Assn.)

1948	Rodney	1957	Torpid	1966	Bret Hanover	1974	Delmonica Hanover
1949	Good Time	1958	Emily's Pride	1967	Nevele Pride	1975	Savior
1950	Proximity	1959	Bye Bye Byrd	1968	Nevele Pride	1976	Keystone Ore
1951	Pronto Don	1960	Adios Butler	1969	Nevele Pride	1977	Green Speed
1952	Good Time	1961	Adios Butler	1970	Fresh Yankee	1978	Abercrombie
1953	Hi Lo's Forbes	1962	Su Mac Lad	1971	Albatross	1979	Niatross
1954	Stenographer	1963	Speedy Scot	1972	Albatross	1980	Niatross
1955	Scott Frost	1964	Bret Hanover	1973	Sir Dalrae	1981	Fan Hanover
1956	Scott Frost	1965	Bret Hanover				

Leading Money-Winning Horses

(As of Sept. 8, 1982)

Trotters				Pacers			
Ideal du Gazeau	$2,538,324	Savoir	$1,365,145	Niatross	$2,019,213	Land Grant	$1,125,919
Bellino II	1,960,945	Fresh Yankee	1,294,252	Rambling Willie	1,961,894	Governor Skipper	1,039,756
Un De Mai	1,660,627	Hadol du Vivier	1,263,121	McKinzie Almahurst	1,496,596	Rum Customer	1,001,548
Jorky	1,537,252	Keystone Pioneer	1,071,927	Fortune Teller	1,313,175	Cardigan Bay	1,000,837
Eleazar	1,465,454	Roquepine	956,161	Albatross	1,201,470	Abercrombie	984,391

Little Brown Jug (3-year-old pacers)

Delaware, Oh.

Year	Winner	Driver	Purse	Year	Winner	Driver	Purse
1957	Torpid	John Simpson Sr.	$73,528	1970	Most Happy Fella	Stanley Dancer	$100,110
1958	Shadow Wave	Joe O'Brien	65,252	1971	Nansemond	Herve Filion	102,944
1959	Adios Butler	Clint Hodgins	76,582	1972	Strike Out	Keith Waples	104,916
1960	Bullet Hanover	John Simpson Sr.	66,510	1973	Melvin's Woe	Joe O'Brien	120,000
1961	Henry T. Adios	Stanley Dancer	70,069	1974	Ambro Omaha	Billy Haughton	132,630
1962	Lehigh Hanover	Stanley Dancer	75,038	1975	Seatrain	Ben Webster	147,813
1963	Overtrick	John Patterson Sr.	68,294	1976	Keystone Ore	Stanley Dancer	153,799
1964	Vicar Hanover	Billy Haughton	66,590	1977	Gov. Skipper	John Chapman	150,000
1965	Bret Hanover	Frank Ervin	71,447	1978	Happy Escort	Bill Popfinger	186,760
1966	Romeo Hanover	George Sholty	74,616	1979	Hot Hitter	Herve Filion	226,455
1967	Best of All	James Hackett	84,778	1980	Niatross	Clint Galbraith	207,000
1968	Rum Customer	Billy Haughton	104,226	1981	Fan Hanover(A)	Glen Garnsey	243,779
1969	Laverne Hanover	Billy Haughton	109,731	1982	Merger	John Campbell	328,900

(A) First filly to win the Little Brown Jug.

All-American Futurity in 1982

Mr. Master Bug won the All-American Futurity for quarter horses at Ruidoso Downs, N.M. The victory in the world's richest horse race was worth $1 million to owner Marvin Barnes of Ada, Okla. The 2-year-old colt was ridden by Jacky Martin and covered the 440 yards in 22.20 seconds.

Tour de France in 1982

Bernard Hinault of France won the Tour de France, the world's most prestigious bicycle endurance race, for the 4th time in 5 years on July 25, 1982. His time for the 2,180-mile race was 92 hours 8 minutes 46 seconds. Joop Zoetemelk of Holland finished second for the 6th time, including 3 times behind Hinault.

Boxing Champions by Classes

As of Sept., 1982 the only universally accepted title holders were in the middleweight and welterweight divisions. The following are the recognized champions of the World Boxing Association and the World Boxing Council.

	WBA	WBC
Heavyweight	Mike Weaver, Los Angeles, Cal.	Larry Holmes, Easton, Pa.
Light Heavyweight	Michael Spinks, St. Louis, Mo.	Dwight Braxton, Camden, N.J.
Middleweight	Marvin Hagler, Brockton, Mass.	Marvin Hagler, Brockton, Mass.
Jr. Middleweight	Davey Moore, New York, N.Y.	Wilfred Benitez, Puerto Rico
Welterweight	Sugar Ray Leonard, Palmer Park, Md.	Sugar Ray Leonard, Palmer Park, Md.
Jr. Welterweight	Aaron Pryor, Cincinnati, Oh.	Leroy Haley, Las Vegas, Nev.
Lightweight	Ray Mancini, Youngstown, Oh.	Alexis Arguello, Nicaragua
Jr. Lightweight	Sammy Serrano, Puerto Rico	Bazooka Limon, Mexico
Featherweight	Eusebio Pedroza, Panama	Juan LaPorte, New York, N.Y.
Jr. Featherweight	Leo Cruz, Dominican Republic	Wilfredo Gomez, Puerto Rico
Bantamweight	Jeff Chandler, Philadelphia, Pa.	Lupe Pintor, Mexico
Flyweight	Santos Laciar, Argentina	Prudencio Cardona, Colombia

Ring Champions by Years

*Abandoned title

Heavyweights

1882-1892	John L. Sullivan (a)
1892-1897	James J. Corbett (b)
1897-1899	Robert Fitzsimmons
1899-1905	James J. Jeffries (c)
1905-1906	Marvin Hart
1906-1908	Tommy Burns
1908-1915	Jack Johnson
1915-1919	Jess Willard
1919-1926	Jack Dempsey
1926-1928	Gene Tunney*
1928-1930	vacant
1930-1932	Max Schmeling
1932-1933	Jack Sharkey
1933-1934	Primo Carnera
1934-1935	Max Baer
1935-1937	James J. Braddock
1937-1949	Joe Louis*
1949-1951	Ezzard Charles
1951-1952	Joe Walcott
1952-1956	Rocky Marciano*
1956-1959	Floyd Patterson
1959-1960	Ingemar Johansson
1960-1962	Floyd Patterson
1962-1964	Sonny Liston
1964-1967	Cassius Clay* (Muhammad Ali) (d)
1970-1973	Joe Frazier
1973-1974	George Foreman
1974-1978	Muhammad Ali
1978-1979	Leon Spinks (e), Muhammad Ali*
1978	Ken Norton (WBC), Larry Holmes (WBC)
1979	John Tate (WBA)
1980	Mike Weaver (WBA)

(a) London Prize Ring (bare knuckle champion).

(b) First Marquis of Queensberry champion.

(c) Jeffries abandoned the title (1905) and designated Marvin Hart and Jack Root as logical contenders and agreed to referee a fight between them, the winner to be declared champion. Hart defeated Root in 12 rounds (1905) and in turn was defeated by Tommy Burns (1906) who immediately laid claim to the title. Jack Johnson defeated Burns (1908) and was recognized as champion. He clinched the title by defeating Jeffries in an attempted comeback (1910).

(d) Title declared vacant by the World Boxing Assn. and other groups in 1967 after Clay's refusal to fulfill his military obligation. Joe Frazier was recognized as champion by New York, 5 other states, Mexico, and So. America. Jimmy Ellis was declared champion by the World Boxing Assn. Frazier KOd Ellis, Feb. 16, 1970.

(e) After Spinks defeated Ali, the WBC recognized Ken Norton as champion. Norton subsequently lost his title to Larry Holmes.

Light Heavyweights

1903	Jack Root, George Gardner
1903-1905	Bob Fitzsimmons
1905-1912	Philadelphia Jack O'Brien*
1912-1916	Jack Dillon
1916-1920	Battling Levinsky
1920-1922	George Carpentier
1922-1923	Battling Siki
1923-1925	Mike McTigue
1925-1926	Paul Berlenbach
1926-1927	Jack Delaney*
1927-1929	Tommy Loughran*
1930-1934	Maxey Rosenbloom
1934-1935	Bob Olin
1935-1939	John Henry Lewis*
1939	Melio Bettina
1939-1941	Billy Conn*
1941	Anton Christoforidis (won NBA title)
1941-1948	Gus Lesnevich, Freddie Mills
1948-1950	Freddie Mills
1950-1952	Joey Maxim
1952-1960	Archie Moore
1961-1962	vacant
1962-1963	Harold Johnson
1963-1965	Willie Pastrano
1965-1966	Jose Torres
1966-1968	Dick Tiger
1968-1974	Bob Foster*, John Conteh (WBA)
1975-1977	John Conteh (WBC), Miguel Cuello (WBC), Victor Galindez (WBA)
1978	Mike Rossman (WBA), Mate Parlov (WBC), Marvin Johnson (WBC)
1979	Victor Galindez (WBA), Matthew Saad Muhammad (WBC)
1980	Eddie Mustava Muhammad (WBA)
1981	Michael Spinks (WBA), Dwight Braxton (WBC)

Middleweights

1884-1891	Jack "Nonpareil" Dempsey
1891-1897	Bob Fitzsimmons*
1897-1907	Tommy Ryan*
1907-1908	Stanley Ketchel, Billy Papke
1908-1910	Stanley Ketchel
1911-1913	vacant
1913	Frank Klaus, George Chip
1914-1917	Al McCoy
1917-1920	Mike O'Dowd
1920-1923	Johnny Wilson
1923-1926	Harry Greb
1926-1931	Tiger Flowers, Mickey Walker
1931-1932	Gorilla Jones (NBA)
1932-1937	Marcel Thil
1938	Al Hostak (NBA), Solly Krieger (NBA)
1939-1940	Al Hostak (NBA)
1941-1947	Tony Zale
1947-1948	Rocky Graziano
1948	Tony Zale, Marcel Cerdan
1949-1951	Jake LaMotta
1951	Ray Robinson, Randy Turpin, Ray Robinson*
1953-1955	Carl (Bobo) Olson
1955-1957	Ray Robinson
1957	Gene Fullmer, Ray Robinson, Carmen Basilio
1958	Ray Robinson
1959	Gene Fullmer (NBA); Ray Robinson (N.Y.)
1960	Gene Fullmer (NBA); Paul Pender (New York and Mass.)
1961	Gene Fullmer (NBA); Terry Downes (New York, Mass., Europe)

1962	Gene Fullmer, Dick Tiger (NBA), Paul Pender (New York and Mass.)*
1963	Dick Tiger (universal).
1963-1965	Joey Giardello
1965-1966	Dick Tiger
1966-1967	Emile Griffith
1967	Nino Benvenuti
1967-1968	Emile Griffith
1968-1970	Nino Benvenuti
1970-1977	Carlos Monzon*
1977-1978	Rodrigo Valdez
1978-1979	Hugo Corro
1979-1980	Vito Antuofermo
1980	Alan Minter, Marvin Hagler

Welterweights

1892-1894	Mysterious Billy Smith
1894-1896	Tommy Ryan
1896	Kid McCoy*
1900	Rube Ferns, Matty Matthews
1901	Rube Ferns
1901-1904	Joe Walcott
1904-1906	Dixie Kid, Joe Walcott, Honey Mellody
1907-1911	Mike Sullivan
1911-1915	vacant
1915-1919	Ted Lewis
1919-1922	Jack Britton
1922-1926	Mickey Walker
1926	Pete Latzo
1927-1929	Joe Dundee
1929	Jackie Fields
1930	Jack Thompson, Tommy Freeman
1931	Freeman, Thompson, Lou Brouillard
1932	Jackie Fields
1933	Young Corbett, Jimmy McLarnin
1934	Barney Ross, Jimmy McLarnin
1935-1938	Barney Ross
1938-1940	Henry Armstrong
1940-1941	Fritzie Zivic
1941-1946	Fred Cochrane
1946-1946	Marty Servo*; Ray Robinson (a)
1946-1950	Ray Robinson*
1951	Johnny Bratton (NBA)
1951-1954	Kid Gavilan
1954-1955	Johnny Saxton
1955	Tony De Marco, Carmen Basilio
1956	Carmen Basilio, Johnny Saxton, Carmen Basilio
1957	Carmen Basilio*
1958-1960	Virgil Akins, Don Jordan
1960	Benny Paret
1961	Emile Griffith, Benny Paret
1962	Emile Griffith
1963	Luis Rodriguez, Emile Griffith
1964-1966	Emile Griffith*
1966-1969	Curtis Cokes
1969-1970	Jose Napoles, Billy Backus
1971-1975	Jose Napoles
1975-1976	John Stracey (WBC), Angel Espada (WBA)
1976-1979	Carlos Palomino (WBC), Jose Cuevas (WBA)
1979	Wilfredo Benitez (WBC), Sugar Ray Leonard (WBC)
1980	Roberto Duran (WBC), Thomas Hearns (WBA), Sugar Ray Leonard (WBC)
1981	Sugar Ray Leonard

(a) Robinson gained the title by defeating Tommy Bell in an elimination agreed to by the NY Commission and the NBA. Both claimed Robinson waived his title when he won the middleweight crown from LaMotta in 1951, Gavilan defeated Bratton in an elimination to find a successor.

Lightweights

1896-1899	Kid Lavigne
1899-1902	Frank Erne
1902-1908	Joe Gans
1908-1910	Battling Nelson
1910-1912	Ad Wolgast
1912-1914	Willie Ritchie
1914-1917	Freddie Welsh
1917-1925	Benny Leonard*
1925	Jimmy Goodrich, Rocky Kansas
1926-1930	Sammy Mandell
1930	Al Singer, Tony Canzoneri
1930-1933	Tony Canzoneri
1933-1935	Barney Ross*
1935-1936	Tony Canzoneri
1936-1938	Lou Ambers
1938	Henry Armstrong
1939	Lou Ambers
1940	Lew Jenkins
1941-1943	Sammy Angott
1944	S. Angott (NBA), J. Zurita (NBA)
1945-1951	Ike Williams (NBA: later universal)
1951-1952	James Carter
1952	Lauro Salas, James Carter
1953-1954	James Carter
1954	Paddy De Marco; James Carter
1955	James Carter; Bud Smith
1956	Bud Smith, Joe Brown
1956-1962	Joe Brown
1962-1965	Carlos Ortiz
1965	Ismael Laguna
1965-1968	Carlos Ortiz
1968-1969	Teo Cruz
1969-1970	Mando Ramos
1970	Ismael Laguna, Ken Buchanan (WBA)
1971	Mando Ramos (WBC), Pedro Carrasco (WBC)
1972-1979	Roberto Duran* (WBA)
1972	Pedro Carrasco (WBC), Mando Ramos (WBC), Chango Carmona (WBC), Rodolfo Gonzalez (WBC)
1974-1976	Guts Ishimatsu (WBC)
1976-1977	Esteban De Jesus (WBC)
1979	Jim Watt (WBC), Ernesto Espana (WBA)
1980	Hilmer Kenty (WBA)
1981	Alexis Arguello (WBC), Sean O'Grady (WBA), Arturo Frias (WBA)
1982	Ray Mancini (WBA)

Featherweights

1892-1900	George Dixon (disputed)
1900-1901	Terry McGovern, Young Corbett*
1901-1912	Abe Attell
1912-1923	Johnny Kilbane
1923	Eugene Criqui, Johnny Dundee
1923-1925	Johnny Dundee*
1925-1927	Kid Kaplan*
1927-1928	Benny Bass, Tony Canzoneri
1928-1929	Andre Routis
1929-1932	Battling Battalino*
1932-1934	Tommy Paul (NBA)
1933-1936	Freddie Miller
1936-1937	Petey Sarron
1937-1938	Henry Armstrong*
1938-1940	Joey Archibald (b)
1942-1948	Willie Pep
1948-1949	Sandy Saddler
1949-1950	Willie Pep
1950-1957	Sandy Saddler*
1957-1959	Hogan (Kid) Bassey
1959-1963	Davey Moore
1963-1964	Sugar Ramos
1964-1967	Vicente Saldivar*
1968-1971	Paul Rojas (WBA), Sho Saijo (WBA)
1971	Antonio Gomez (WBA), Kuniaki Shibada (WBC)
1972	Ernesto Marcel* (WBA), Clemente Sanchez* (WBC), Jose Legra (WBC)
1973	Eder Jofre (WBC)
1974	Ruben Olivares (WBA), Alexis Arguello (WBA), Bobby Chacon (WBC)
1975	Ruben Olivares (WBC), David Kotey (WBC)
1976	Danny Lopez (WBC)
1977	Rafael Ortega (WBA)
1978	Cecilio Lastra (WBA), Eusebio Pedrosa (WBA)
1980	Salvador Sanchez (WBC)
1982	Juan LaPorte (WBC)

(b) After Petey Scalzo knocked out Archibald (Dec. 5, 1938) in an overweight match and was refused a title bout, the NBA named Scalzo champion. The NBA title succession was: Petey Scalzo, 1938-1941; Richard Lemos, 1941; Jackie Wilson, 1941-1943; Jackie Callura, 1943; Phil Terranova, 1943-1944; Sal Bartolo, 1944-1946.

History of Heavyweight Championship Bouts

*Title Changed Hands

1889—July 8—John L. Sullivan def. Jake Kilrain, 75, Richburg, Miss. Last championship bare knuckles bout.

***1892**—Sept. 7—James J. Corbett def. John L. Sullivan, 21, New Orleans. Big gloves used for first time.

1894—Jan. 25—James J. Corbett KOd Charley Mitchell, 3, Jacksonville, Fla.

***1897**—Bob Fitzsimmons def. James J. Corbett, 14, Carson City, Nev.

***1899**—June 9—James J. Jeffries def. Bob Fitzsimmons, 11, Coney Island, N.Y.

1899—Nov. 3—James J. Jeffries def. Tom Sharkey, 25, Coney Island, N.Y.

1900—May 11—James J. Jeffries KOd James J. Corbett, 23, Coney Island, N.Y.

1901—Nov. 15—James J. Jeffries KOd Gus Ruhlin, 5, San Francisco.

1902—July 25—James J. Jeffries KOd Bob Fitzsimmons, 8, San Francisco.

1903—Aug. 14—James J. Jeffries KOd James J. Corbett, 10, San Francisco.

1904—Aug. 26—James J. Jeffries KOd Jack Monroe, 2, San Francisco.

***1905**—James J. Jeffries retired, July 3—Marvin Hart KOd Jack Root, 12, Reno. Jeffries refereed and presented the title to the victor. Jack O'Brien also claimed the title.

***1906**—Feb. 23—Tommy Burns def. Marvin Hart, 20, Los Angeles.

1906—Nov. 28—Philadelphia Jack O'Brien and Tommy Burns, 20, draw, Los Angeles.

1907—May 8—Tommy Burns def. Jack O'Brien, 20, Los Angeles.

1907—July 4—Tommy Burns KOd Bill Squires, 1, Colma, Cal.

1907—Dec. 2—Tommy Burns KOd Gunner Moir, 10, London.

1908—Feb. 10—Tommy Burns KOd Jack Palmer, 4, London.

1908—March 17—Tommy Burns KOd Jem Roche, 1, Dublin.

1908—April 18—Tommy Burns KOd Jewey Smith, 5, Paris.

1908—June 13—Tommy Burns KOd Bill Squires, 8, Paris.

1908—Aug. 24—Tommy Burns KOd Bill Squires, 13, Sydney, New South Wales.

1908—Sept. 2—Tommy Burns KOd Bill Lang, 2, Melbourne, Australia.

***1908**—Dec. 26—Jack Johnson KOd Tommy Burns, 14, Sydney, Australia. Police halted contest.

1909—May 19—Jack Johnson and Jack O'Brien, 6, draw, Philadelphia.

1909—June 30—Jack Johnson and Tony Ross, 6, draw, Pittsburgh.

1909—Sept. 9—Jack Johnson and Al Kaufman, 10, draw, San Francisco.

1909—Oct. 16—Jack Johnson KOd Stanley Ketchel, 12, Colma, Cal.

1910—July 4—Jack Johnson KOd Jim Jeffries, 15, Reno, Nev. Jeffries came back from retirement.

1912—July 4—Jack Johnson def. Jim Flynn, 9, Las Vegas, N.M. Contest stopped by police.

1913—Nov. 28—Jack Johnson KOd Andre Spaul, 2, Paris.

1913—Dec. 9—Jack Johnson and Jim Johnson, 10, draw, Paris. Bout called a draw when Jack Johnson declared he had broken his arm.

1914—June 27—Jack Johnson def. Frank Moran, 20, Paris.

***1915**—April 5—Jess Willard KOd Jack Johnson, 26, Havana. Cuba.

1916—March 25—Jess Willard and Frank Moran, 10, draw, New York.

***1919**—July 4—Jack Dempsey KOd Jess Willard, Toledo, Oh. Willard failed to answer bell for 4th round.

1920—Sept. 6—Jack Dempsey KOd Billy Miske, 3, Benton Harbor, Mich.

1920—Dec. 14—Jack Dempsey KOd Bill Brennan, 12, New York.

1921—July 2—Jack Dempsey KOd George Carpentier, 4, Boyle's Thirty Acres, Jersey City, N.J. Carpentier had held the so-called white heavyweight title since July 16, 1914, in a series established in 1913, after Jack Johnson's exile in Europe late in 1912.

1923—July 4—Jack Dempsey def. Tom Gibbons, 15, Shelby, Mont.

1923—Sept. 14—Jack Dempsey KOd Luis Firpo, 2, New York.

***1926**—Sept. 23—Gene Tunney def. Jack Dempsey, 10, Philadelphia.

1927—Sept. 22—Gene Tunney def. Jack Dempsey, 10, Chicago.

1928—July 26—Gene Tunney KOd Tom Heeney, 11, New York; soon afterward he announced his retirement.

***1930**—June 12—Max Schmeling def. Jack Sharkey, 4, New York. Sharkey fouled Schmeling in a bout which was generally considered to have resulted in the election of a successor to Gene Tunney, New York.

1931—July 3—Max Schmeling KOd Young Stribling, 15, Cleveland.

***1932**—June 21—Jack Sharkey def. Max Schmeling, 15, New York.

***1933**—June 29—Primo Carnera KOd Jack Sharkey, 6, New York.

1933—Oct. 22—Primo Carnera def. Paulino Uzcudun, 15, Rome.

1934—March 1—Primo Carnera def. Tommy Loughran, 15, Miami.

***1934**—June 14—Max Baer KOd Primo Carnera, 11, New York.

***1935**—June 13—James J. Braddock def. Max Baer, 15, New York.

***1937**—June 22—Joe Louis KOd James J. Braddock, 8, Chicago.

1937—Aug. 30—Joe Louis def. Tommy Farr, 15, New York.

1938—Feb. 23—Joe Louis KOd Nathan Mann, 3, New York.

1938—April 1—Joe Louis KOd Harry Thomas, 5, New York.

1938—June 22—Joe Louis KOd Max Schmeling, 1, New York.

1939—Jan. 25—Joe Louis KOd John H. Lewis, 1, New York.

1939—April 17—Joe Louis KOd Jack Roper, 1, Los Angeles.

1939—June 28—Joe Louis KOd Tony Galento, 4, New York.

1939—Sept. 20—Joe Louis KOd Bob Pastor, 11, Detroit.

1940—February 9—Joe Louis def. Arturo Godoy, 15, New York.

1940—March 29—Joe Louis KOd Johnny Paycheck, 2, New York.

1940—June 20—Joe Louis KOd Arturo Godoy, 8, New York.

1940—Dec. 16—Joe Louis KOd Al McCoy, 6, Boston.

1941—Jan. 31—Joe Louis KOd Red Burman, 5, New York.

1941—Feb. 17—Joe Louis KOd Gus Dorzaio, 2, Philadelphia.

1941—March 21—Joe Louis KOd Abe Simon, 13, Detroit.

1941—April 8—Joe Louis KOd Tony Musto, 9, St. Louis.

1941—May 23—Joe Louis def. Buddy Baer, 7, Washington, D.C., on a disqualification.

1941—June 18—Joe Louis KOd Billy Conn, 13, New York.

1941—Sept. 29—Joe Louis KOd Lou Nova, 6, New York.

1942—Jan. 9—Joe Louis KOd Buddy Baer, 1, New York.

1942—March 27—Joe Louis KOd Abe Simon, 6, New York.

1946—June 19—Joe Louis KOd Billy Conn, 8, New York.

1946—Sept. 18—Joe Louis KOd Tami Mauriello, 1, New York.

1947—Dec. 5—Joe Louis def. Joe Walcott, 15, New York.

1948—June 25—Joe Louis KOd Joe Walcott, 11, New York.

***1949**—June 22—Following Joe Louis' retirement Ezzard Charles def. Joe Walcott, 15, Chicago, NBA recognition only.

1949—Aug. 10—Ezzard Charles KOd Gus Lesnevich, 7, New York.

1949—Oct. 14—Ezzard Charles KOd Pat Valentino, 8, San Francisco; clinched American title.

1950—Aug. 15—Ezzard Charles KOd Freddy Beshore, 14, Buffalo.

1950—Sept. 27—Ezzard Charles def. Joe Louis in latter's attempted comeback, 15, New York; universal recognition.

1950—Dec. 5—Ezzard Charles KOd Nick Barone, 11, Cincinnati.

1951—Jan. 12—Ezzard Charles KOd Lee Oma, 10, New York.

1951—March 7—Ezzard Charles def. Joe Walcott, 15, Detroit.

1951—May 30—Ezzard Charles def. Joey Maxim, light heavyweight champion, 15, Chicago.

***1951**—July 18—Joe Walcott KOd Ezzard Charles, 7, Pittsburgh.

1952—June 5—Joe Walcott def. Ezzard Charles, 15, Philadelphia.

***1952**—Sept. 23—Rocky Marciano KOd Joe Walcott, 13, Philadelphia.

1953—May 15—Rocky Marciano KOd Joe Walcott, 1, Chicago.

1953—Sept. 24—Rocky Marciano KOd Roland LaStarza, 11, New York.

1954—June 17—Rocky Marciano def. Ezzard Charles, 15, New York.

1954—Sept. 17—Rocky Marciano KOd Ezzard Charles, 8, New York.

1955—May 16—Rocky Marciano KOd Don Cockell, 9, San Francisco.

1955—Sept. 21—Rocky Marciano KOd Archie Moore, 9, New York. Marciano retired undefeated, Apr. 27, 1956.

*1956—Nov. 30—Floyd Patterson KOd Archie Moore, 5, Chicago.
1957—July 29—Floyd Patterson KOd Hurricane Jackson, 10, New York.
1957—Aug. 22—Floyd Patterson KOd Pete Rademacher, 6, Seattle.
1958—Aug. 18—Floyd Patterson KOd Roy Harris, 12, Los Angeles.
1959—May 1—Floyd Patterson KOd Brian London, 11, Indianapolis.
*1959—June 26—Ingemar Johansson KOd Floyd Patterson, 3, New York.
*1960—June 20—Floyd Patterson KOd Ingemar Johansson, 5, New York. First heavyweight in boxing history to regain title.
1961—Mar. 13—Floyd Patterson KOd Ingemar Johansson, 6, Miami Beach.
1961—Dec. 4—Floyd Patterson KOd Tom McNeeley, 4, Toronto.
*1962—Sept. 25—Sonny Liston KOd Floyd Patterson, 1, Chicago.
1963—July 22—Sonny Liston KOd Floyd Patterson, 1, Las Vegas.
*1964—Feb. 25—Cassius Clay KOd Sonny Liston, 7, Miami Beach.
1965—May 25—Cassius Clay KOd Sonny Liston, 1, Lewiston, Maine.
1965—Nov. 11—Cassius Clay KOd Floyd Patterson, 12, Las Vegas.
1966—Mar. 29—Cassius Clay def. George Chuvalo, 15, Toronto.
1966—May 21—Cassius Clay KOd Henry Cooper, 6, London.
1966—Aug. 6—Cassius Clay KOd Brian London, 3, London.
1966—Sept. 10—Cassius Clay KOd Karl Mildenberger, 12, Frankfurt, Germany.
1966—Nov. 14—Cassius Clay KOd Cleveland Williams, 3, Houston.
1967—Feb. 6—Cassius Clay def. Ernie Terrell, 15, Houston.
1967—Mar. 22—Cassius Clay KOd Zora Folley, 7, New York. Clay was stripped of his title by the WBA and others for refusing military service.
*1970—Feb. 16—Joe Frazier KOd Jimmy Ellis, 5, New York.
1970—Nov. 18—Joe Frazier KOd Bob Foster, 2, Detroit.
1971—Mar. 8—Joe Frazier def. Cassius Clay (Muhammad Ali), 15, New York.
1972—Jan. 15—Joe Frazier KOd Terry Daniels, 4, New Orleans.
1972—May 25—Joe Frazier KOd Ron Stander, 5, Omaha.
*1973—Jan. 22—George Foreman KOd Joe Frazier, 2, Kingston, Jamaica.
1973—Sept. 1—George Foreman KOd Joe Roman, 1, Tokyo.
1974—Mar. 3—George Foreman KOd Ken Norton, 2, Caracas.
*1974—Oct. 30—Muhammad Ali KOd George Foreman, 8, Zaire.
1975—Mar. 24—Muhammad Ali KOd Chuck Wepner, 15, Cleveland.
1975—May 16—Muhammad Ali KOd Ron Lyle, 11, Las Vegas.
1975—June 30—Muhammad Ali def. Joe Bugner, 15, Malaysia.
1975—Oct. 1—Muhammad Ali KOd Joe Frazier, 14, Manila.
1976—Feb. 20—Muhammad Ali KOd Jean-Pierre Coopman, 5, San Juan.
1976—Apr. 30—Muhammad Ali def. Jimmy Young, 15, Landover, Md.
1976—May 25—Muhammad Ali KOd Richard Dunn, 5, Munich.
1976—Sept. 28—Muhammad Ali def. Ken Norton, 15, New York.
1977—May 16—Muhammad Ali def. Alfredo Evangelista, 15, Landover, Md.
1977—Sept. 29—Muhammad Ali def. Earnie Shavers, 15, New York.
*1978—Feb. 15—Leon Spinks def. Muhammad Ali, 15, Las Vegas.
*1978—Sept. 15—Muhammad Ali def. Leon Spinks, 15, New Orleans. Ali retired in 1979.

(Bouts when title changed hands only)

*1978—June 9—(WBC) Larry Holmes def. Ken Norton, 15, Las Vegas.
*1980—Mar. 31—(WBA) Mike Weaver KOd John Tate, 15, Knoxville.

U.S. National Senior Judo Championships in 1982

Indianapolis, Ind., Apr. 23-24, 1982

Men

132 lbs.—Ron Conduriago, San Jose, Cal.
143 lbs.—Jimmy Martin, San Gabriel, Cal.
156 lbs.—Mike Swain, San Jose, Cal.
172 lbs.—Brett Barron, San Mateo, Cal.
189 lbs.—Robert Berland, San Jose, Cal.
209 lbs.—Leo White, Eustis, Va.
Over 209 lbs.—Doug Nelson, Williamsburg, Ky.
Open—Mitch Santa-Maria, Roselle Park, N.J.

Women

106 lbs.—Darlene Anaya, Albuquerque, N.M.
114 lbs.—Mary Lewis, Albany, N.Y.
123 lbs.—Geri Bindell, New Milford, N.J.
134 lbs.—Cindy Sovljanski, Sterling Heights, Mich.
145 lbs.—Christina Penick, San Jose, Cal.
158 lbs.—Eileen O'Connell, Bayside N.Y.
158 lbs. & over—Margaret Castro, New York, N.Y.
Open—Heidi Bauersachs, Brooklyn, N.Y.

Softball Tournament Champions in 1982

Source: Amateur Softball Assn.

Men

Super Division — Jerry's Caterers, Miami, Fla.
Major Slow Pitch — Triangle, Minneapolis, Minn.
Major Ind. Slow Pitch — Sikorsky Aircraft, Shelton, Conn.
"A" Slow Pitch — Lawson Auto Parts, Altamonte Springs, Fla.
"A" Ind. Slow Pitch — Central Telephone, Hickory, N.C.
Church — Grace Methodist Black, Oklahoma City, Okla.
16-Inch — Park Avenue Spats, Chicago, Ill.

Women

Ind. Slow Pitch — Provident Vets, Chattanooga, Tenn.
Major Slow Pitch — Stompers, Richmond, Va.
Major Fast Pitch — Raybestos Brakettes, Stratford, Conn.
"A" Fast Pitch — San Diego Astros, San Diego, Cal.
"A" Slow Pitch — Circle K Roadrunners, Phoenix, Ariz.
Church — First Baptist Church, Tallahassee, Fla.

Little League World Series in 1982

The team from Kirkland, Wash. won the 1982 Little League World Series by defeating Taiwan 6-0 at Williamsport, Pa. on Aug. 28, 1982. Cody Webster of Kirkland pitched a 2-hitter and hit the longest home run in Little League World Series history. The victory was the first for a U.S. team since Lakewood, N.J. won the championship in 1975. Taiwan has won the world title 10 times since 1969.

College World Series in 1982

The Miami Hurricanes won the 1982 College World Series by defeating the Wichita State Shockers 9-3 in the final game at Omaha, Neb. It was the Hurricanes first College World Series title.

U.S. Indoor Diving Championships in 1982

Ron Merriott won the men's one-meter and 3-meter diving titles at the U.S. indoor championships in Milwaukee, Wis. Dan Watson won the 10-meter title.

The women's titles were won by Megan Neyer (one-meter & 3-meter), and Wendy Wyland (10-meter).

World Swimming Records

As of Sept., 1982

Effective June 1, 1969, FINA recognizes only records made over a 50-meter course.

Men's Records

Freestyle

Distance	Time	Holder	Country	Where made	Date
100 Meters	**0:49.36**	Rowdy Gaines	U.S.	Austin, Tex.	Apr. 3, 1981
200 Meters	**1:48.93**	Rowdy Gaines	U.S.	Mission Viejo, Cal.	July, 1982
400 Meters	**3:49.57**	Vladimir Salnikov	USSR	Moscow	Mar., 1982
800 Meters	**7:52.82**	Vladimir Salnikov	USSR	Moscow	Feb., 1982
1,500 Meters	**14:56.37**	Vladimir Salnikov	USSR	Moscow	Mar., 1982

Breaststroke

Distance	Time	Holder	Country	Where made	Date
100 Meters	**1:02.53**	Steve Lundquist	U.S.	Indianapolis	Aug., 1982
200 Meters	**2:14.77**	Victor Davis	Canada	Ecuador	Aug. 5, 1982

Butterfly

Distance	Time	Holder	Country	Where made	Date
100 Meters	**0:53.81**	William Paulus	U.S.	Austin, Tex.	Apr. 3, 1981
200 Meters	**1:58.01**	Craig Beardsley	U.S.	Kiev, USSR	Aug. 22, 1981

Backstroke

Distance	Time	Holder	Country	Where made	Date
100 Meters	**0:55.49**	John Naber	U.S.	Montreal	July 19, 1976
200 Meters	**1:59.19**	John Naber	U.S.	Montreal	July 24, 1976

Individual Medley

Distance	Time	Holder	Country	Where made	Date
200 Meters	**2:02.78**	Alex Baumann	Canada	Heidelberg, W. Germany	July 29, 1981
400 Meters	**4:19.78**	Ricardo Prado	Brazil	Ecuador	Aug., 1982

Freestyle Relays

Distance	Time	Holder	Country	Where made	Date
400 M. (4×100)	**3:19.26**	Cavanaugh, Leamy, McCagg, Gaines	U.S.	Ecuador	Aug., 1982
800 M. (4×200)	**7:20.83**	Forrester, Furniss, Gaines, Hackett	U.S.	W. Berlin	Aug. 24, 1978

Medley Relays

Distance	Time	Holder	Country	Where made	Date
400 M. (4×100)	**3:40.84**	Carey, Lundquist, Gribble, Gaines	U.S.	Ecuador	Aug., 1982

Women's Records

Freestyle

Distance	Time	Holder	Country	Where made	Date
100 Meters	**0:54.79**	Barbara Krause	E. Germany	Moscow	July, 1980
200 Meters	**1:58.43**	Cynthia Woodhead	U.S.	San Juan, P.R.	Aug., 1979
400 Meters	**4:06.28**	Tracey Wickham	Australia	W. Berlin	Aug. 24, 1978
800 Meters	**8:24.62**	Tracey Wickham	Australia	Edmonton, Canada	Aug. 5, 1978
1,500 Meters	**16:04.49**	Kim Linehan	U.S.	Ft. Lauderdale, Fla.	Aug. 19, 1979

Breaststroke

Distance	Time	Holder	Country	Where made	Date
100 Meters	**1:08.60**	Ute Geweniger	E. Germany	Yugoslavia	Sept. 8, 1981
200 Meters	**2:28.36**	Lina Kachushite	USSR	Potsdam	Mar. 6, 1979

Butterfly

Distance	Time	Holder	Country	Where made	Date
100 Meters	**0:57.93**	Mary T. Meagher	U.S.	Brown Deer, Wis.	Aug. 16, 1981
200 Meters	**2:05.96**	Mary T. Meagher	U.S.	Brown Deer, Wis.	Aug. 13, 1981

Backstroke

Distance	Time	Holder	Country	Where made	Date
100 Meters	**1:00.86**	Rica Reinisch	E. Germany	Moscow	July, 1980
200 Meters	**2:09.91**	Cornelia Sirch	E. Germany	Ecuador	Aug. 7, 1982

Individual Medley

Distance	Time	Holder	Country	Where made	Date
200 Meters	**2:10.60**	Petra Schneider	E. Germany	Gainesville, Fla.	Jan. 8, 1982
400 Meters	**4:36.10**	Petra Schneider	E. Germany	Ecuador	July, 1982

Freestyle Relays

Distance	Time	Holder	Country	Where made	Date
400 M. (4×100)	**3:42.71**	National Team	E. Germany	Moscow	July, 1980

Medley Relays

Distance	Time	Holder	Country	Where made	Date
400 M. (4×100)	**4:05.88**	National Team	E. Germany	Ecuador	Aug., 1982

U.S. Outdoor Swimming Championships in 1982

Indianapolis, Ind., Aug. 18-21, 1982

Men

50-Meter Freestyle—Ang Pingsiong, San Luis Obispo, Cal. **Time—0:22.69.**
100-Meter Freestyle—Rowdy Gaines, Winter Haven, Fla. **Time—0:50.27.**
200-Meter Freestyle—Rowdy Gaines. **Time—1:49.64.**
400-Meter Freestyle—Bruce Hayes, Mission Viejo, Cal. **Time—3:54.80.**
800-Meter Freestyle—Tony Corbisiero, New York, N.Y. **Time—7:58.50.**
1,500-Meter Freestyle—Jeff Kostoff, Upland, Cal. **Time—15:17.77.**
100-Meter Breaststroke—Steve Lundquist, Jonesboro, Ga. **Time—1:02.53**
200-Meter Breaststroke—John Moffet, Costa Mesa, Cal. **Time—2:17.88.**
100-Meter Backstroke—Mark Rhodenbaugh, Cincinnati, Oh. **Time—0:56.90.**
200-Meter Backstroke—Steve Barnicoat, Mission Viejo, Cal. **Time—2:02.91.**
100-Meter Butterfly—David Cowell, Belpre, Oh. **Time—0:54.61.**
200-Meter Butterfly—Craig Beardsley, Gainesville, Fla. **Time—1:59.01.**
200-Meter Individual Medley—Bill Barrett, Mission Viejo, Cal. **Time—2:04.03.**
400-Meter Individual Medley—Ricardo Prado, Mission Viejo, Cal. **Time—4:22.54.**
400-Meter Freestyle Relay—Mission Viejo. **Time—3:21.89.**
800-Meter Freestyle Relay—Mission Viejo. **Time—7:29.14.**

Women

50-Meter Freestyle—Dara Torres, Beverly Hills, Cal. **Time—0:26.13.**
100-Meter Freestyle—Paige Zemina, Ft. Lauderdale, Fla. **Time—0:57.45.**
200-Meter Freestyle—Sarah Linke, Walnut Creek, Cal. **Time—2:01.25.**
400-Meter Freestyle—Tiffany Cohen, Mission Viejo, Cal. **Time—4:11.61.**
800-Meter Freestyle—Marybeth Linzmeier, Mission Viejo, Cal. **Time—8:35.48.**
1,500 Meter Freestyle—Karin Laberge, Doylestown, Pa. **Time—16:18.94.**
100-Meter Breaststroke—Kim Rhodenbaugh, Cincinnati, Oh. **Time—1:10.79.**
200-Meter Breaststroke—Beverly Acker, Richmond, Ky. **Time—2:35.45.**
100-Meter Backstroke—Sue Walsh, Hamberg, N.Y. **Time—1:02.48.**
200-Meter Backstroke—Tracy Caulkins, Nashville, Tenn. **Time—2:15.53.**
100-Meter Butterfly—Mary T. Meagher, Louisville, Ky. **Time—0:59.75.**
200-Meter Butterfly—Mary T. Meagher. **Time—2:07.14.**
200-Meter Individual Medley—Tracy Caulkins. **Time—2:15.66.**
400-Meter Individual Medley—Tracy Caulkins. **Time—4:44.26.**
400-Meter Freestyle Relay—Mission Viejo. **Time—3:49.36.**
800-Meter Freestyle Relay—Mission Viejo. **Time—8:17.00.**

U.S. Short Course Swimming Championships

Gainesville, Fla., Apr. 7-10, 1982

Men

50-Yard Freestyle—Siong Ang, Houston. **Time—0:19.86.**
100-Yard Freestyle—Rowdy Gaines, War Eagle. **Time—0:43.64.**
200-Yard Freestyle—Rowdy Gaines. **Time—1:35.17.**
500-Yard Freestyle—Jeff Kostoff, Industry Hills. **Time—4:19.38.**
1,000-Yard Freestyle—Jeff Kostoff. **Time—8:49.97.**
1,650-Yard Freestyle—Jeff Kostoff. **Time—14:52.39.**
100-Yard Backstroke—Dave Bottom, Walnut Creek. **Time—0:48.94.**
200-Yard Backstroke—Sandor Wladar, Hungary. **Time—1:45.22.**
100-Yard Breaststroke—Steve Lundquist, Mustang. **Time—0:53.84.**
200-Yard Breaststroke—John Moffet, Beach. **Time—1:59.44.**
100-Yard Butterfly—David Cowell, Mid-Ohio Valley. **Time—0:47.89.**
200-Yard Butterfly—Craig Beardsley, Florida. **Time—1:43.81.**
200-Yard Individual Medley—Roger Von Jouanne, Southern Ill. **Time—1:48.41.**
400-Yard Individual Medley—Ricardo Prado, Mission Viejo. **Time—3:47.97.**

Women

50-Yard Freestyle—Dara Torres, Tandem. **Time—0:22.44.**
100-Yard Freestyle—Jill Sterkel, Longhorn. **Time—0:48.94.**
200-Yard Freestyle—Cynthia Woodhead, Mission Viejo. **Time—1:45.46.**
500-Yard Freestyle—Tiffany Cohen, Mission Viejo. **Time—4:39.97.**
1,000-Yard Freestyle—Tiffany Cohen. **Time—9:34.61.**
1,650-Yard Freestyle—Tiffany Cohen. **Time—15:58.52.**
100-Yard Backstroke—Debbie Rosen, K.C. Blazers. **Time—0:55.49.**
200-Yard Backstroke—Tracy Caulkins, Nashville. **Time—1:57.77.**
100-Yard Breaststroke—Tracy Caulkins. **Time—1:02.41.**
200-Yard Breaststroke—Kim Rhodenbaugh, Cinn. Pepsi Marlins. **Time—2:14.17.**
100-Yard Butterfly—Jill Sterkel. **Time—0:53.20.**
200-Yard Butterfly—Mary T. Meagher, Lakeside. **Time—1:53.37.**
200-Yard Individual Medley—Tracy Caulkins. **Time—1:58.94.**
400-Yard Individual Medley—Tracy Caulkins. **Time—4:11.75.**

Major Indoor Soccer League in 1982

Final Standings

Eastern Division

Club	W	L	Pct.	GB
New York	37	7	.841	......
Pittsburgh	30	14	.682	7
Baltimore	27	17	.614	10
Buffalo	25	20	.556	12 1/2
New Jersey	17	27	.386	20
Cleveland	15	30	.333	22 1/2
Philadelphia	11	33	.250	26

Western Division

Club	W	L	Pct	GB
St. Louis	28	16	.636	......
Wichita	27	17	.614	1
Memphis	20	24	.455	8
Denver	19	25	.432	9
Phoenix	17	27	.386	11
Kansas City	14	30	.318	14

Playoff Champion—New York.

Le Mans 24-Hour Race in 1982

Jack Ickx and Derek Bell, driving a Porsche, won the 1982 Le Mans 24-hour race averaging 126.866 mph. It was a record 6th victory for Ickx.

Auto Racing

Indianapolis 500 Winners

Year	Winner	Chassis	Engine	MPH	Purse	Runner up
1948	Mauri Rose	Deidt	Offenhauser	119.814	$171,075	Bill Holland
1949	Bill Holland	Deidt	Offenhauser	121.327	179,050	Johnnie Parsons
1950	Johnnie Parsons	Kurtis Kraft	Offenhauser	124.002(a)	201,135	Bill Holland
1951	Lee Wallard	Kurtis Kraft	Offenhauser	126.244	207,650	Mike Nazaruk
1952	Troy Ruttman	Kuzma	Offenhauser	128.922	230,100	Jim Rathmann
1953	Bill Vukovich	Kurtis Kraft 500A	Offenhauser	128.740	246,300	Art Cross
1954	Bill Vukovich	Kurtis Kraft 500A	Offenhauser	130.840	269,375	Jim Bryan
1955	Bob Sweikert	Kurtis Kraft 500C	Offenhauser	128.209	270,400	Tony Bettenhausen
1956	Pat Flaherty	Watson	Offenhauser	128.490	282,052	Sam Hanks
1957	Sam Hanks	Epperly	Offenhauser	135.601	300,252	Jim Rathmann
1958	Jimmy Bryan	Epperly	Offenhauser	133.791	305,217	George Amick
1959	Rodger Ward	Watson	Offenhauser	135.857	338,100	Jim Rathmann
1960	Jim Rathmann	Watson	Offenhauser	138.767	369,150	Rodger Ward
1961	A.J. Foyt	Watson	Offenhauser	139.130	400,000	Eddie Sachs
1962	Rodger Ward	Watson	Offenhauser	140.293	426,152	Len Sutton
1963	Parnelli Jones	Watson	Offenhauser	143.137	494,031	Jim Clark
1964	A.J. Foyt	Watson	Offenhauser	147.350	506,625	Rodger Ward
1965	Jim Clark	Lotus	Ford	151.388	628,399	Parnelli Jones
1966	Graham Hill	Lola	Ford	144.317	691,809	Jim Clark
1967	A.J. Foyt	Coyote	Ford	151.207	737,109	Al Unser
1968	Bobby Unser	Eagle	Offenhauser	152.882	809,627	Dan Gurney
1969	Mario Andretti	Hawk	Ford	156.867	805,127	Dan Gurney
1970	Al Unser	P.J. Colt	Ford	155.749	1,000,002	Mark Donohue
1971	Al Unser	P.J. Colt	Ford	157.735	1,001,604	Peter Revson
1972	Mark Donohue	McLaren	Offenhauser	163.465	1,011,846	Al Unser
1973	Gordon Johncock	Eagle	Offenhauser	159.014(b)	1,011,846	Billy Vukovich
1974	Johnny Rutherford	McLaren	Offenhauser	158.589	1,015,686	Bobby Unser
1975	Bobby Unser	Eagle	Offenhauser	149.213(c)	1,101,322	Johnny Rutherford
1976	Johnny Rutherford	McLaren	Offenhauser	148.725(d)	1,037,775	A.J. Foyt
1977	A.J. Foyt	Coyote	Ford	161.331	1,116,807	Tom Sneva
1978	Al Unser	Lola	Cosworth	161.363	1,145,225	Tom Sneva
1979	Rick Mears	Penske	Cosworth	158.899	1,271,954	A.J. Foyt
1980	Johnny Rutherford	Chaparral	Cosworth	142.862	1,502,425	Tom Sneva
1981	Bobby Unser	Penske	Cosworth	139.085	1,609,375	Mario Andretti
1982	Gordon Johncock	Wildcat	Cosworth	162.026	2,067,475	Rick Mears

(a) 345 miles. (b) 332.5 miles. (c) 435 miles. (d) 255 miles. Race record—163.465 MPH, Mark Donohue, 1972.

Notable One-Mile Speed Records

Date	Driver	Car	MPH
1/26/06	Marriott	Stanley (Steam)	127.659
3/16/10	Oldfield	Benz	131.724
4/23/11	Burman	Benz	141.732
2/12/19	DePalma	Packard	149.875
4/27/20	Milton	Dusenberg	155.046
4/28/26	Parry-Thomas	Thomas Spl.	170.624
3/29/27	Seagrave	Sunbeam	203.790
4/22/28	Keech	White Triplex	207.552
3/11/29	Seagrave	Irving-Napier	231.446
2/ 5/31	Campbell	Napier-Campbell	246.086
2/24/32	Campbell	Napier-Campbell	253.96
2/22/33	Campbell	Napier-Campbell	272.109
9/ 3/35	Campbell	Bluebird Special	301.13
11/19/37	Eyston	Thunderbolt 1	311.42
9/16/38	Eyston	Thunderbolt 1	357.5
8/23/39	Cobb	Railton	368.9
9/16/47	Cobb	Railton-Mobil	394.2
8/ 5/63	Breedlove	Spirit of America	407.45
10/27/64	Arfons	Green Monster	536.71
11/15/65	Breedlove	Spirit of America	600.601
10/23/70	Gabelich	Blue Flame	622.407
10/9/79	Barrett	Budweiser Rocket	638.637*

*not recognized as official by sanctioning bodies.

World Grand Prix Champions

Year	Driver
1950	Nino Farina, Italy
1951	Juan Fangio, Argentina
1952	Alberto Ascari, Italy
1953	Alberto Ascari, Italy
1954	Juan Fangio, Argentina
1955	Juan Fangio, Argentina
1956	Juan Fangio, Argentina
1957	Juan Fangio, Argentina
1958	Mike Hawthorne, England
1959	Jack Brabham, Australia
1960	Jack Brabham, Australia
1961	Phil Hill, United States
1962	Graham Hill, England
1963	Jim Clark, Scotland
1964	John Surtees, England
1965	Jim Clark, Scotland
1966	Jack Brabham, Australia
1967	Denis Hulme, New Zealand
1968	Graham Hill, England
1969	Jackie Stewart, Scotland
1970	Jochen Rindt, Austria
1971	Jackie Stewart, Scotland
1972	Emerson Fittipaldi, Brazil
1973	Jackie Stewart, Scotland
1974	Emerson Fittipaldi, Brazil
1975	Nicki Lauda, Austria
1976	James Hunt, England
1977	Nikki Lauda, Austria
1978	Mario Andretti, U.S.
1979	Jody Scheckter, So. Africa
1980	Alan Jones, Australia
1981	Nelson Piquet, Brazil
1982	Keke Rosberg, Finland

United States Auto Club National Champions

Year	Driver
1956	Jimmy Bryan
1957	Jimmy Bryan
1958	Tony Bettenhausen
1959	Rodger Ward
1960	A. J. Foyt
1961	A. J. Foyt
1962	Rodger Ward
1963	A. J. Foyt
1964	A. J. Foyt
1965	Mario Andretti
1966	Mario Andretti
1967	A. J. Foyt
1968	Bobby Unser
1969	Mario Andretti
1970	Al Unser
1971	Joe Leonard
1972	Joe Leonard
1973	Roger McCluskey
1974	Bobby Unser
1975	A. J. Foyt
1976	Gordon Johncock
1977	Tom Sneva
1978	Tom Sneva
1979	A. J. Foyt
1980	Johnny Rutherford
1981	George Snider

Grand Prix for Formula 1 Cars in 1982

Grand Prix	Winner, car	Grand Prix	Winner, car
Austrian	Elio de Angelis, Lotus	German	Patrick Tambay, Ferrari
Belgian	John Watson, McLaren	Italian	Rene Arnoux, Renault
British	Niki Lauda, McLaren	Las Vegas	Michele Alboreto, Tyrrell
Brazilian	Nelson Piquet, Brabham	Long Beach	Niki Lauda, McLaren
Canadian	Nelson Piquet, Brabham	Monaco	Ricardo Patrese, Brabham
Detroit	John Watson, McLaren	San Marino	Didier Pironi, Ferrari
Dutch	Didier Pironi, Ferrari	South African	Alain Prost, Renault
French	Rene Arnoux, Renault	Swiss	Keke Rosberg, Williams

NASCAR Racing in 1982

Winston Cup Grand National Races

Date	Race, site	Winner	Car	Winnings
Jan. 11	Winston Western 500, Riverside, Cal.	Bobby Allison	Chevrolet	$24,600
Feb. 15	Daytona 500, Daytona Beach, Fla.	Bobby Allison	Buick	120,630
Feb. 21	Richmond 400, Richmond, Va.	Dave Marcis	Chevrolet	19,145
Mar. 14	Valleydale 500, Bristol, Tenn.	Darrell Waltrip	Buick	26,520
Mar. 21	Coca-Cola 500, Atlanta, Ga.	Darrell Waltrip	Buick	49,614
Mar. 28	Warner W. Hodgdon Carolina 500	Cale Yarborough	Buick	17,360
Apr. 18	Northwestern Bank 400, No. Wilkesboro, N.C.	Darrell Waltrip	Buick	32,300
Apr. 4	CRC Chemicals Rebel 500, Darlington, S.C.	Dale Earnhardt	Ford	31,450
Apr. 25	Virginia National Bank 500, Martinsville, Va.	Harry Gant	Buick	26,795
May 2	Winston 500, Talladega, Ala.	Darrell Waltrip	Buick	44,250
May 8	Cracker Barrel 420, Nashville, Tenn.	Darrell Waltrip	Buick	24,025
May 16	Mason-Dixon 500, Dover, Del.	Bobby Allison	Chevrolet	25,350
May 30	World 600, Harrisburg, N.C.	Neil Bonnett	Ford	50,650
June 6	Van Scoy Diamond Mine 500, Pocono, Pa.	Bobby Allison	Buick	25,500
June 13	Budweiser 400, Riverside, Cal.	Tim Richmond	Buick	21,530
June 20	Gabriel 400, Brooklyn, Mich.	Cale Yarborough	Buick	24,700
July 4	Firecracker 400, Daytona Beach, Fla.	Bobby Allison	Buick	42,100
July 10	Busch Nashville 420, Nashville, Tenn.	Darrell Waltrip	Buick	22,025
July 25	Mountain Dew 500, Pocono, Pa.	Bobby Allison	Buick	24,200
Aug. 1	Talladega 500, Talladega, Ala.	Darrell Waltrip	Buick	58,770
Aug. 22	Champion Spark Plug 400, Brooklyn, Mich.	Bobby Allison	Buick	26,900
Aug. 28	Busch 500, Bristol, Tenn.	Darrell Waltrip	Buick	22,925
Sept. 6	Southern 500, Darlington, S.C.	Cale Yarborough	Buick	34,300
Sept. 12	Wrangler Sanforset 400, Richmond, Va.	Bobby Allison	Chevrolet	25,750
Sept. 19	CRC Chemicals 500, Dover, Del.	Darrell Waltrip	Buick	29,600

Daytona 500 Winners

Year	Driver, car	Avg. MPH	Year	Driver, car	Avg. MPH
1962	Fireball Roberts, Pontiac	152.529	1973	Richard Petty, Dodge	157.205
1963	Tiny Lund, Ford	151.566	1974	Richard Petty, Dodge (c)	140.894
1964	Richard Petty, Plymouth	154.334	1975	Benny Parsons, Chevrolet	153.649
1965	Fred Lorenzen, Ford (a)	141.539	1976	David Pearson, Mercury	152.181
1966	Richard Petty, Plymouth (b)	160.627	1977	Cale Yarborough, Chevrolet	153.218
1967	Mario Andretti, Ford	146.926	1978	Bobby Allison, Ford	159.730
1968	Cale Yarborough, Mercury	143.251	1979	Richard Petty, Oldsmobile	143.977
1969	Lee Roy Yarborough, Ford	160.875	1980	Buddy Baker, Oldsmobile	177.602
1970	Pete Hamilton, Plymouth	149.601	1981	Richard Petty, Buick	169.651
1971	Richard Petty, Plymouth	144.456	1982	Bobby Allison, Buick	153.991
1972	A. J. Foyt, Mercury	161.550			

(a) 322.5 miles because of rain. (b) 495 miles because of rain. (c) 450 miles.

Leading Daytona 500 Finishers in 1982

Driver, car	Laps	Winnings	Driver, car	Laps	Winnings
Bobby Allison, Buick	200	$120,630	Ron Bouchard, Buick	198	$37,700
Cale Yarborough, Buick	200	70,725	Harry Gant, Buick	198	30,015
Joe Ruttman, Buick	200	54,820	Buddy Baker, Buick	198	40,800
Terry Labonte, Buick	199	51,975	Jody Ridley, Ford	197	28,350
Bill Elliott, Ford	198	36,125	Roy Smith, Pontiac	196	18,975

Grand National Champions (NASCAR)

Year	Driver	Year	Driver	Year	Driver	Year	Driver
1954	Lee Petty	1961	Ned Jarrett	1968	David Pearson	1975	Richard Petty
1955	Tim Flock	1962	Joe Weatherly	1969	David Pearson	1976	Cale Yarborough
1956	Buck Baker	1963	Joe Weatherly	1970	Bobby Isaac	1977	Cale Yarborough
1957	Buck Baker	1964	Richard Petty	1971	Richard Petty	1978	Cale Yarborough
1958	Lee Petty	1965	Ned Jarrett	1972	Richard Petty	1979	Richard Petty
1959	Lee Petty	1966	David Pearson	1973	Benny Parson	1980	Dale Earnhardt
1960	Rex White	1967	Richard Petty	1974	Richard Petty	1981	Darrell Waltrip

Major League Pennant Winners, 1901–1982

National League

Year	Winner	Won	Lost	Pct	Manager
1901	Pittsburgh	90	49	.647	Clarke
1902	Pittsburgh	103	36	.741	Clarke
1903	Pittsburgh	91	49	.650	Clarke
1904	New York	106	47	.693	McGraw
1905	New York	105	48	.686	McGraw
1906	Chicago	116	36	.763	Chance
1907	Chicago	107	45	.704	Chance
1908	Chicago	99	55	.643	Chance
1909	Pittsburgh	110	42	.724	Clarke
1910	Chicago	104	50	.675	Chance
1911	New York	99	54	.647	McGraw
1912	New York	103	48	.682	McGraw
1913	New York	101	51	.664	McGraw
1914	Boston	94	59	.614	Stallings
1915	Philadelphia	90	62	.592	Moran
1916	Brooklyn	94	60	.610	Robinson
1917	New York	98	56	.636	McGraw
1918	Chicago	84	45	.651	Mitchell
1919	Cincinnati	96	44	.686	Moran
1920	Brooklyn	93	60	.604	Robinson
1921	New York	94	56	.614	McGraw
1922	New York	93	61	.604	McGraw
1923	New York	95	58	.621	McGraw
1924	New York	93	60	.608	McGraw
1925	Pittsburgh	95	58	.621	McKechnie
1926	St. Louis	89	65	.578	Hornsby
1927	Pittsburgh	94	60	.610	Bush
1928	St. Louis	95	59	.617	McKechnie
1929	Chicago	98	54	.645	McCarthy
1930	St. Louis	92	62	.597	Street
1931	St. Louis	101	53	.656	Street
1932	Chicago	90	64	.584	Grimm
1933	New York	91	61	.599	Terry
1934	St. Louis	95	58	.621	Frisch
1935	Chicago	100	54	.649	Grimm
1936	New York	91	62	.597	Terry
1937	New York	95	57	.625	Terry
1938	Chicago	89	63	.586	Hartnett
1939	Cincinnati	97	57	.630	McKechnie
1940	Cincinnati	100	53	.654	McKechnie
1941	Brooklyn	100	54	.649	Durocher
1942	St. Louis	106	48	.688	Southworth
1943	St. Louis	105	49	.682	Southworth
1944	St. Louis	105	49	.682	Southworth
1945	Chicago	98	56	.636	Grimm
1946	St. Louis	98	58	.628	Dyer
1947	Brooklyn	94	60	.610	Shotton
1948	Boston	91	62	.595	Southworth
1949	Brooklyn	97	57	.630	Shotton
1950	Philadelphia	91	63	.591	Sawyer
1951	New York	98	59	.624	Durocher
1952	Brooklyn	96	57	.627	Dressen
1953	Brooklyn	105	49	.682	Dressen
1954	New York	97	57	.630	Durocher
1955	Brooklyn	98	55	.641	Alston
1956	Brooklyn	93	61	.604	Alston
1957	Milwaukee	95	59	.617	Haney
1958	Milwaukee	92	62	.597	Haney
1959	Los Angeles	88	68	.564	Alston
1960	Pittsburgh	95	59	.617	Murtaugh
1961	Cincinnati	93	61	.604	Hutchinson
1962	San Francisco	103	62	.624	Dark
1963	Los Angeles	99	63	.611	Alston
1964	St. Louis	93	69	.574	Keane
1965	Los Angeles	97	65	.599	Alston
1966	Los Angeles	95	67	.586	Alston
1967	St. Louis	101	60	.627	Schoendienst
1968	St. Louis	97	65	.599	Schoendienst

American League

Year	Winner	Won	Lost	Pct	Manager
1901	Chicago	83	53	.610	Griffith
1902	Philadelphia	83	53	.610	Mack
1903	Boston	91	47	.659	Collins
1904	Boston	95	59	.617	Collins
1905	Philadelphia	92	56	.622	Mack
1906	Chicago	93	58	.616	Jones
1907	Detroit	92	58	.613	Jennings
1908	Detroit	90	63	.588	Jennings
1909	Detroit	98	54	.645	Jennings
1910	Philadelphia	102	48	.680	Mack
1911	Philadelphia	101	50	.669	Mack
1912	Boston	105	47	.691	Stahl
1913	Philadelphia	96	57	.627	Mack
1914	Philadelphia	99	53	.651	Mack
1915	Boston	101	50	.669	Carrigan
1916	Boston	91	63	.591	Carrigan
1917	Chicago	100	54	.649	Rowland
1918	Boston	75	51	.595	Barrow
1919	Chicago	88	52	.629	Gleason
1920	Cleveland	98	56	.636	Speaker
1921	New York	98	55	.641	Huggins
1922	New York	94	60	.610	Huggins
1923	New York	98	54	.645	Huggins
1924	Washington	92	62	.597	Harris
1925	Washington	96	55	.636	Harris
1926	New York	91	63	.591	Huggins
1927	New York	110	44	.714	Huggins
1928	New York	101	53	.656	Huggins
1929	Philadelphia	104	46	.693	Mack
1930	Philadelphia	102	52	.622	Mack
1931	Philadelphia	107	45	.704	Mack
1932	New York	107	47	.695	McCarthy
1933	Washington	99	53	.651	Cronin
1934	Detroit	101	53	.656	Cochrane
1935	Detroit	93	58	.616	Cochrane
1936	New York	102	51	.667	McCarthy
1937	New York	102	52	.662	McCarthy
1938	New York	99	53	.651	McCarthy
1939	New York	106	45	.702	McCarthy
1940	Detroit	90	64	.584	Baker
1941	New York	101	53	.656	McCarthy
1942	New York	103	51	.669	McCarthy
1943	New York	98	56	.636	McCarthy
1944	St. Louis	89	65	.578	Sewell
1945	Detroit	88	65	.575	O'Neill
1946	Boston	104	50	.675	Cronin
1947	New York	97	57	.630	Harris
1948	Cleveland	97	58	.626	Boudreau
1949	New York	97	57	.630	Stengel
1950	New York	98	56	.636	Stengel
1951	New York	98	56	.636	Stengel
1952	New York	95	59	.617	Stengel
1953	New York	99	52	.656	Stengel
1954	Cleveland	111	43	.721	Lopez
1955	New York	96	58	.623	Stengel
1956	New York	97	57	.630	Stengel
1957	New York	98	56	.636	Stengel
1958	New York	92	62	.597	Stengel
1959	Chicago	94	60	.610	Lopez
1960	New York	97	57	.630	Stengel
1961	New York	109	53	.673	Houk
1962	New York	96	66	.593	Houk
1963	New York	104	57	.646	Houk
1964	New York	99	63	.611	Berra
1965	Minnesota	102	60	.630	Mele
1966	Baltimore	97	63	.606	Bauer
1967	Boston	92	70	.568	Williams
1968	Detroit	103	59	.636	Smith

National League

		East					West				
Year	Winner	W	L	Pct	Manager	Winner	W	L	Pct	Manager	Playoff winner
1969	N.Y. Mets	100	62	.617	Hodges	Atlanta	93	69	.574	Harris	New York
1970	Pittsburgh	89	73	.549	Murtaugh	Cincinnati	102	60	.630	Anderson	Cincinnati
1971	Pittsburgh	97	65	.599	Murtaugh	San Francisco	90	72	.556	Fox	Pittsburgh
1972	Pittsburgh	96	59	.619	Virdon	Cincinnati	95	59	.617	Anderson	Cincinnati
1973	N.Y. Mets	82	79	.509	Berra	Cincinnati	99	63	.611	Anderson	New York
1974	Pittsburgh	88	82	.543	Murtaugh	Los Angeles	102	60	.630	Alston	Los Angeles
1975	Pittsburgh	92	69	.571	Murtaugh	Cincinnati	108	54	.667	Anderson	Cincinnati
1976	Philadelphia	101	61	.623	Ozark	Cincinnati	102	60	.630	Anderson	Cincinnati
1977	Philadelphia	100	61	.621	Ozark	Los Angeles	98	64	.605	Lasorda	Los Angeles

Year	East Winner	W	L	Pct	Manager	West Winner	W	L	Pct	Manager	Playoff winner
1978	Philadelphia	90	72	.556	Ozark	Los Angeles	95	67	.586	Lasorda	Los Angeles
1979	Pittsburgh	98	64	.605	Tanner	Cincinnati	90	71	.559	McNamara	Pittsburgh
1980	Philadelphia	91	71	.562	Green	Houston	93	70	.571	Virdon	Philadelphia
1981(a)	Philadelphia	34	21	.618	Green	Los Angeles	36	21	.632	Lasorda	(c)
1981(b)	Montreal	30	23	.566	Williams, Fanning	Houston	33	20	.623	Virdon	Los Angeles
1982	St. Louis	92	70	.568	Herzog	Atlanta	89	73	.549	Torre	St. Louis

American League

Year	East Winner	W	L	Pct	Manager	West Winner	W	L	Pct	Manager	Playoff winner
1969	Baltimore	109	53	.673	Weaver	Minnesota	97	65	.599	Martin	Baltimore
1970	Baltimore	108	54	.667	Weaver	Minnesota	98	64	.605	Rigney	Baltimore
1971	Baltimore	101	57	.639	Weaver	Oakland	101	60	.627	Williams	Baltimore
1972	Detroit	86	70	.551	Martin	Oakland	93	62	.600	Williams	Oakland
1973	Baltimore	97	65	.599	Weaver	Oakland	94	68	.580	Williams	Oakland
1974	Baltimore	91	71	.562	Weaver	Oakland	90	72	.556	Dark	Oakland
1975	Boston	95	65	.594	Johnson	Oakland	98	64	.605	Dark	Boston
1976	New York	97	62	.610	Martin	Kansas City	90	72	.556	Herzog	New York
1977	New York	100	62	.617	Martin	Kansas City	102	60	.630	Herzog	New York
1978	New York	100	63	.613	Martin, Lemon	Kansas City	92	70	.568	Herzog	New York
1979	Baltimore	102	57	.642	Weaver	California	88	74	.543	Fregosi	Baltimore
1980	New York	103	59	.636	Howser	Kansas City	97	65	.599	Frey	Kansas City
1981(a)	New York	34	22	.607	Michael	Oakland	37	23	.617	Martin	(d)
1981(b)	Milwaukee	31	22	.585	Rodgers	Kansas City	30	23	.566	Frey, Howser	New York
1982	Milwaukee	95	67	.586	Rodgers, Kuenn	California	93	69	.574	Mauch	Milwaukee

(a) First half; (b) Second half; (c) Montreal and Los Angeles won the divisional playoffs; (d) New York and Oakland won the divisional playoffs.

Baseball Stadiums

National League

Team	Stadium	Home run distances (ft.) LF	Center	RF	Seating capacity
Atlanta Braves	Atlanta-Fulton County Stadium	330	402	330	52,785
Chicago Cubs	Wrigley Field	355	400	353	37,272
Cincinnati Reds	Riverfront Stadium	330	404	330	52,392
Houston Astros	Astrodome	340	406	340	45,000
Los Angeles Dodgers	Dodger Stadium	330	400	330	56,000
Montreal Expos	Olympic Stadium	325	404	325	58,838
New York Mets	Shea Stadium	338	410	338	55,300
Philadelphia Phillies	Veterans Stadium	330	408	330	65,454
Pittsburgh Pirates	Three Rivers Stadium	335	400	335	54,499
St. Louis Cardinals	Busch Memorial Stadium	330	414	330	50,222
San Diego Padres	Jack Murphy Stadium	330	408	330	51,362
San Francisco Giants	Candlestick Park	335	400	335	58,000

American League

Team	Stadium	LF	Center	RF	Seating capacity
Baltimore Orioles	Memorial Stadium	309	405	309	53,208
Boston Red Sox	Fenway Park	315	390	302	33,536
California Angels	Anaheim Stadium	333	404	333	67,335
Chicago White Sox	Comiskey Park	352	402	352	44,492
Cleveland Indians	Cleveland Stadium	320	400	320	74,208
Detroit Tigers	Tiger Stadium	340	440	325	52,687
Kansas City Royals	Royals Stadium	330	410	330	40,635
Milwaukee Brewers	Milwaukee County Stadium	320	402	315	53,192
Minnesota Twins	Hubert H. Humphrey Metrodome	344	407	327	54,711
New York Yankees	Yankee Stadium	312	417	310	57,545
Oakland A's	Oakland Coliseum	330	397	330	50,255
Seattle Mariners	Kingdome	316	410	316	59,438
Texas Rangers	Arlington Stadium	330	400	330	41,284
Toronto Blue Jays	Exhibition Stadium	330	400	330	43,737

Cy Young Award Winners

Year	Player, club
1956	Don Newcombe, Dodgers
1957	Warren Spahn, Braves
1958	Bob Turley, Yankees
1959	Early Wynn, White Sox
1960	Vernon Law, Pirates
1961	Whitey Ford, Yankees
1962	Don Drysdale, Dodgers
1963	Sandy Koufax, Dodgers
1964	Dean Chance, Angels
1965	Sandy Koufax, Dodgers
1966	Sandy Koufax, Dodgers
1967	(NL) Mike McCormick, Giants
	(AL) Jim Lonborg, Red Sox
1968	(NL) Bob Gibson, Cardinals
	(AL) Dennis McLain, Tigers
1969	(NL) Tom Seaver, Mets
	(AL) (tie) Dennis McLain, Tigers
	Mike Cuellar, Orioles
1970	(NL) Bob Gibson, Cardinals
	(AL) Jim Perry, Twins
1971	(NL) Ferguson Jenkins, Cubs
	(AL) Vida Blue, A's
1972	(NL) Steve Carlton, Phillies
	(AL) Gaylord Perry, Indians
1973	(NL) Tom Seaver, Mets
	(AL) Jim Palmer, Orioles
1974	(NL) Mike Marshall, Dodgers
	(AL) Jim (Catfish) Hunter, A's
1975	(NL) Tom Seaver, Mets
	(AL) Jim Palmer, Orioles
1976	(NL) Randy Jones, Padres
	(AL) Jim Palmer, Orioles
1977	(NL) Steve Carlton, Phillies
	(AL) Sparky Lyle, Yankees
1978	(NL) Gaylord Perry, Padres
	(AL) Ron Guidry, Yankees
1979	(NL) Bruce Sutter, Cubs
	(AL) Mike Flanagan, Orioles
1980	(NL) Steve Carlton, Phillies
	(AL) Steve Stone, Orioles
1981	(NL) Fernando Valenzuela, Dodgers
	(AL) Rollie Fingers, Brewers

Home Run Leaders

National League

Year		HR
1921	George Kelly, New York	23
1922	Rogers Hornsby, St. Louis	42
1923	Cy Williams, Philadelphia	41
1924	Jacques Fournier, Brooklyn	27
1925	Rogers Hornsby, St. Louis	39
1926	Hack Wilson, Chicago	21
1927	Hack Wilson, Chicago; Cy Williams, Philadelphia	30
1928	Hack Wilson, Chicago; Jim Bottomley, St. Louis	31
1929	Charles Klein, Philadelphia	43
1930	Hack Wilson, Chicago	56
1931	Charles Klein, Philadelphia	31
1932	Charles Klein, Philadelphia, Mel Ott, New York	38
1933	Charles Klein, Philadelphia	28
1934	Collins, St. Louis; Mel Ott, New York	35
1935	Walter Berger, Boston	34
1936	Mel Ott, New York	33
1937	Mel Ott, New York; Joe Medwick, St. Louis	31
1938	Mel Ott, New York	36
1939	John Mize, St. Louis	28
1940	John Mize, St. Louis	43
1941	Dolph Camilli, Brooklyn	34
1942	Mel Ott, New York	30
1943	Bill Nicholson, Chicago	29
1944	Bill Nicholson, Chicago	33
1945	Tommy Holmes, Boston	28
1946	Ralph Kiner, Pittsburgh	23
1947	Ralph Kiner, Pittsburgh; John Mize, New York	51
1948	Ralph Kiner, Pittsburgh; John Mize, New York	40
1949	Ralph Kiner, Pittsburgh	54
1950	Ralph Kiner, Pittsburgh	47
1951	Ralph Kiner, Pittsburgh	42
1952	Ralph Kiner, Pittsburgh; Hank Sauer, Chicago	37
1953	Ed Mathews, Milwaukee	47
1954	Ted Kluszewski, Cincinnati	49
1955	Willie Mays, New York	51
1956	Duke Snider, Brooklyn	43
1957	Hank Aaron, Milwaukee	44
1958	Ernie Banks, Chicago	47
1959	Ed Mathews, Milwaukee	46
1960	Ernie Banks, Chicago	41
1961	Orlando Cepeda, San Francisco	46
1962	Willie Mays, San Francisco	49
1963	Hank Aaron, Milwaukee, Willie McCovey, San Francisco	44
1964	Willie Mays, San Francisco	47
1965	Willie Mays, San Francisco	52
1966	Hank Aaron, Atlanta	44
1967	Hank Aaron, Atlanta	39
1968	Willie McCovey, San Francisco	36
1969	Willie McCovey, San Francisco	45
1970	Johnny Bench, Cincinnati	45
1971	Willie Stargell, Pittsburgh	48
1972	Johnny Bench, Cincinnati	40
1973	Willie Stargell, Pittsburgh	44
1974	Mike Schmidt, Philadelphia	36
1975	Mike Schmidt, Philadelphia	38
1976	Mike Schmidt, Philadelphia	38
1977	George Foster, Cincinnati	52
1978	George Foster, Cincinnati	40
1979	Dave Kingman, Chicago	48
1980	Mike Schmidt, Philadelphia	48
1981	Mike Schmidt, Philadelphia	31
1982	Dave Kingman, New York	37

American League

Year		HR
1921	Babe Ruth, New York	59
1922	Ken Williams, St. Louis	39
1923	Babe Ruth, New York	41
1924	Babe Ruth, New York	46
1925	Bob Meusel, New York	33
1926	Babe Ruth, New York	47
1927	Babe Ruth, New York	60
1928	Babe Ruth, New York	54
1929	Babe Ruth, New York	46
1930	Babe Ruth, New York	49
1931	Babe Ruth, Lou Gehrig, New York	46
1932	Jimmy Foxx, Philadelphia	58
1933	Jimmy Foxx, Philadelphia	48
1934	Lou Gehrig, New York	49
1935	Jimmy Foxx, Philadelphia, Hank Greenberg, Detroit	36
1936	Lou Gehrig, New York	49
1937	Joe DiMaggio, New York	46
1938	Hank Greenberg, Detroit	58
1939	Jimmy Foxx, Boston	35
1940	Hank Greenberg, Detroit	41
1941	Ted Williams, Boston	37
1942	Ted Williams, Boston	36
1943	Rudy York, Detroit	34
1944	Nick Etten, New York	22
1945	Vern Stephens, St. Louis	24
1946	Hank Greenberg, Detroit	44
1947	Ted Williams, Boston	32
1948	Joe DiMaggio, New York	39
1949	Ted Williams, Boston	43
1950	Al Rosen, Cleveland	37
1951	Gus Zernial, Chicago-Philadelphia	33
1952	Larry Doby, Cleveland	32
1953	Al Rosen, Cleveland	43
1954	Larry Doby, Cleveland	32
1955	Mickey Mantle, New York	37
1956	Mickey Mantle, New York	52
1957	Roy Sievers, Washington	42
1958	Mickey Mantle, New York	42
1959	Rocky Colavito, Cleveland, Harmon Killebrew, Washington	42
1960	Mickey Mantle, New York	40
1961	Roger Maris, New York	61
1962	Harmon Killebrew, Minnesota	48
1963	Harmon Killebrew, Minnesota	45
1964	Harmon Killebrew, Minnesota	49
1965	Tony Conigliaro, Boston	32
1966	Frank Robinson, Baltimore	49
1967	Carl Yastrzemski, Boston, Harmon Killebrew, Minn.	44
1968	Frank Howard, Washington	44
1969	Harmon Killebrew, Minnesota	49
1970	Frank Howard, Washington	44
1971	Bill Melton, Chicago	33
1972	Dick Allen, Chicago	37
1973	Reggie Jackson, Oakland	32
1974	Dick Allen, Chicago	32
1975	George Scott, Milwaukee; Reggie Jackson, Oakland	36
1976	Graig Nettles, New York	32
1977	Jim Rice, Boston	39
1978	Jim Rice, Boston	46
1979	Gorman Thomas, Milwaukee	45
1980	Reggie Jackson, New York; Ben Oglivie, Milwaukee	41
1981	Bobby Grich, California; Tony Armas, Oakland; Dwight Evans, Boston; Eddie Murray, Baltimore	22
1982	Gorman Thomas, Milwaukee; Reggie Jackson, California	39

All-time Major League Record (154-game Season)—60—Babe Ruth, New York Yankees (A), 1927. **(162-game Season)—61—**Roger Maris, New York Yankees, 1961.

Runs Batted In Leaders

National League

Year		RBI
1948	Stan Musial, St. Louis	131
1949	Ralph Kiner, Pittsburgh	127
1950	Del Ennis, Philadelphia	126
1951	Monte Irvin, New York	121
1952	Hank Sauer, Chicago	121
1953	Roy Campanella, Brooklyn	142
1954	Ted Kluszewski, Cincinnati	141
1955	Duke Snider, Brooklyn	136
1956	Stan Musial, St. Louis	109
1957	Hank Aaron, Milwaukee	132
1958	Ernie Banks, Chicago	129
1959	Ernie Banks, Chicago	143
1960	Hank Aaron, Milwaukee	126

American League

Year		RBI
1948	Joe DiMaggio, New York	155
1949	Ted Williams, Vern Stephens, Boston	159
1950	Walt Dropo, Vern Stephens, Boston	144
1951	Gus Zernial, Chicago-Philadelphia	129
1952	Al Rosen, Cleveland	105
1953	Al Rosen, Cleveland	145
1954	Larry Doby, Cleveland	126
1955	Ray Boone, Detroit, Jack Jensen, Boston	116
1956	Mickey Mantle, New York	130
1957	Roy Sievers, Washington	114
1958	Jack Jensen, Boston	122
1959	Jack Jensen, Boston	112
1960	Roger Maris, New York	112

Year		RBI
1961	Orlando Cepeda, San Francisco	142
1962	Tommy Davis, Los Angeles	153
1963	Hank Aaron, Milwaukee	130
1964	Ken Boyer, St. Louis	119
1965	Deron Johnson, Cincinnati	130
1966	Hank Aaron, Atlanta	127
1967	Orlando Cepeda, St. Louis	111
1968	Willie McCovey, San Francisco	105
1969	Willie McCovey, San Francisco	126
1970	Johnny Bench, Cincinnati	148
1971	Joe Torre, St. Louis	137
1972	Johnny Bench, Cincinnati	125
1973	Willie Stargell, Pittsburgh	119
1974	Johnny Bench, Cincinnati	129
1975	Greg Luzinski, Philadelphia	120
1976	George Foster, Cincinnati	121
1977	George Foster, Cincinnati	149
1978	George Foster, Cincinnati	120
1979	Dave Winfield, San Diego	118
1980	Mike Schmidt, Philadelphia	121
1981	Mike Schmidt, Philadelphia	91
1982	Dale Murphy, Atlanta; Al Oliver, Montreal	109

Year		RBI
1961	Roger Maris, New York	142
1962	Harmon Killebrew, Minnesota	126
1963	Dick Stuart, Boston	118
1964	Brooks Robinson, Baltimore	118
1965	Rocky Colavito, Cleveland	108
1966	Frank Robinson, Baltimore	122
1967	Carl Yastrzemski, Boston	121
1968	Ken Harrelson, Boston	109
1969	Harmon Killebrew, Minnesota	140
1970	Frank Howard, Washington	126
1971	Harmon Killebrew, Minnesota	119
1972	Dick Allen, Chicago	113
1973	Reggie Jackson, Oakland	117
1974	Jeff Burroughs, Texas	118
1975	George Scott, Milwaukee	109
1976	Lee May, Baltimore	109
1977	Larry Hisle, Minnesota	119
1978	Jim Rice, Boston	139
1979	Don Baylor, California	139
1980	Cecil Cooper, Milwaukee	122
1981	Eddie Murray, Baltimore	78
1982	Hal McRae, Kansas City	133

Batting Champions

National League

Year	Player	Club	Pct.
1920	Rogers Hornsby	St. Louis	.370
1921	Rogers Hornsby	St. Louis	.397
1922	Rogers Hornsby	St. Louis	.401
1923	Rogers Hornsby	St. Louis	.384
1924	Rogers Hornsby	St. Louis	.424
1925	Rogers Hornsby	St. Louis	.403
1926	Eugene Hargrave	Cincinnati	.353
1927	Paul Waner	Pittsburgh	.380
1928	Rogers Hornsby	Boston	.387
1929	Lefty O'Doul	Philadelphia	.398
1930	Bill Terry	New York	.401
1931	Chick Hafey	St. Louis	.349
1932	Lefty O'Doul	Brooklyn	.368
1933	Charles Klein	Philadelphia	.368
1934	Paul Waner	Pittsburgh	.362
1935	Arky Vaughan	Pittsburgh	.385
1936	Paul Waner	Pittsburgh	.373
1937	Joe Medwick	St. Louis	.374
1938	Ernie Lombardi	Cincinnati	.342
1939	John Mize	St. Louis	.349
1940	Debs Garms	Pittsburgh	.355
1941	Pete Reiser	Brooklyn	.343
1942	Ernie Lombardi	Boston	.330
1943	Stan Musial	St. Louis	.357
1944	Dixie Walker	Brooklyn	.357
1945	Phil Cavarretta	Chicago	.355
1946	Stan Musial	St. Louis	.365
1947	Harry Walker	Philadelphia	.363
1948	Stan Musial	St. Louis	.376
1949	Jackie Robinson	Brooklyn	.342
1950	Stan Musial	St. Louis	.346
1951	Stan Musial	St. Louis	.355
1952	Stan Musial	St. Louis	.336
1953	Carl Furillo	Brooklyn	.344
1954	Willie Mays	New York	.345
1955	Richie Ashburn	Philadelphia	.338
1956	Hank Aaron	Milwaukee	.328
1957	Stan Musial	St. Louis	.351
1958	Richie Ashburn	Philadelphia	.350
1959	Hank Aaron	Milwaukee	.355
1960	Dick Groat	Pittsburgh	.325
1961	Roberto Clemente	Pittsburgh	.351
1962	Tommy Davis	Los Angeles	.346
1963	Tommy Davis	Los Angeles	.326
1964	Roberto Clemente	Pittsburgh	.339
1965	Roberto Clemente	Pittsburgh	.329
1966	Matty Alou	Pittsburgh	.342
1967	Roberto Clemente	Pittsburgh	.357
1968	Pete Rose	Cincinnati	.335
1969	Pete Rose	Cincinnati	.348
1970	Rico Carty	Atlanta	.366
1971	Joe Torre	St. Louis	.363
1972	Billy Williams	Chicago	.333
1973	Pete Rose	Cincinnati	.338
1974	Ralph Garr	Atlanta	.353
1975	Bill Madlock	Chicago	.354
1976	Bill Madlock	Chicago	.339
1977	Dave Parker	Pittsburgh	.338
1978	Dave Parker	Pittsburgh	.334
1979	Keith Hernandez	St. Louis	.344
1980	Bill Buckner	Chicago	.324
1981	Bill Madlock	Pittsburgh	.341
1982	Al Oliver	Montreal	.331

American League

Year	Player	Club	Pct.
1920	George Sisler	St. Louis	.407
1921	Harry Heilmann	Detroit	.394
1922	George Sisler	St. Louis	.420
1923	Harry Heilmann	Detroit	.403
1924	Babe Ruth	New York	.378
1925	Harry Heilmann	Detroit	.393
1926	Henry Manush	Detroit	.378
1927	Harry Heilmann	Detroit	.398
1928	Goose Goslin	Washington	.379
1929	Lew Fonseca	Cleveland	.369
1930	Al Simmons	Philadelphia	.381
1931	Al Simmons	Philadelphia	.390
1932	Dale Alexander	Detroit-Boston	.367
1933	Jimmy Foxx	Philadelphia	.356
1934	Lou Gehrig	New York	.363
1935	Buddy Myer	Washington	.349
1936	Luke Appling	Chicago	.388
1937	Charlie Gehringer	Detroit	.371
1938	Jimmy Foxx	Boston	.349
1939	Joe DiMaggio	New York	.381
1940	Joe DiMaggio	New York	.352
1941	Ted Williams	Boston	.406
1942	Ted Williams	Boston	.356
1943	Luke Appling	Chicago	.328
1944	Lou Boudreau	Cleveland	.327
1945	George Stirnweiss	New York	.309
1946	Mickey Vernon	Washington	.353
1947	Ted Williams	Boston	.343
1948	Ted Williams	Boston	.369
1949	George Kell	Detroit	.343
1950	Billy Goodman	Boston	.354
1951	Ferris Fain	Philadelphia	.344
1952	Ferris Fain	Philadelphia	.327
1953	Mickey Vernon	Washington	.337
1954	Roberto Avila	Cleveland	.341
1955	Al Kaline	Detroit	.340
1956	Mickey Mantle	New York	.353
1957	Ted Williams	Boston	.388
1958	Ted Williams	Boston	.328
1959	Harvey Kuenn	Detroit	.353
1960	Pete Runnels	Boston	.320
1961	Norm Cash	Detroit	.361
1962	Pete Runnels	Boston	.326
1963	Carl Yastrzemski	Boston	.321
1964	Tony Oliva	Minnesota	.323
1965	Tony Oliva	Minnesota	.321
1966	Frank Robinson	Baltimore	.316
1967	Carl Yastrzemski	Boston	.326
1968	Carl Yastrzemski	Boston	.301
1969	Rod Carew	Minnesota	.332
1970	Alex Johnson	California	.328
1971	Tony Oliva	Minnesota	.337
1972	Rod Carew	Minnesota	.318
1973	Rod Carew	Minnesota	.350
1974	Rod Carew	Minnesota	.364
1975	Rod Carew	Minnesota	.359
1976	George Brett	Kansas City	.333
1977	Rod Carew	Minnesota	.388
1978	Rod Carew	Minnesota	.333
1979	Fred Lynn	Boston	.333
1980	George Brett	Kansas City	.390
1981	Carney Lansford	Boston	.336
1982	Willie Wilson	Kansas City	.332

National League Records in 1982

Final standings

Eastern Division

Club	W	L	Pct	GB
St. Louis	92	70	.568	—
Philadelphia	89	73	.549	3
Montreal	86	76	.531	6
Pittsburgh	84	78	.519	8
Chicago	73	89	.451	19
New York	65	97	.401	27

Western Division

Club	W	L	Pct	GB
Atlanta	89	73	.549	—
Los Angeles	88	74	.543	1
San Francisco	87	75	.537	2
San Diego	81	81	.500	8
Houston	77	85	.475	12
Cincinnati	61	101	.377	28

National League Playoffs

St. Louis 7, Atlanta 0. St. Louis 4, Atlanta 3. St. Louis 6, Atlanta 2.

Club Batting

Club	Pct	AB	R	H	HR	SB
Pittsburgh	.273	5614	724	1535	134	161
St. Louis	.264	5455	685	1439	67	200
Los Angeles	.264	5642	691	1487	138	151
Montreal	.262	5557	697	1454	133	156
Philadelphia	.260	5454	664	1417	112	128
Chicago	.260	5531	676	1436	102	132
San Diego	.257	5575	675	1435	81	165
Atlanta	.256	5507	739	1411	146	151
San Francisco	.253	5499	673	1393	133	130
Cincinnati	.251	5479	545	1375	82	131
New York	.247	5510	609	1361	97	137
Houston	.247	5440	569	1342	74	140

Club Pitching

Club	ERA	CG	IP	H	R	BB	SO
Los Angeles	3.26	37	1488	1356	612	468	932
Montreal	3.31	34	1460	1371	616	448	936
St. Louis	3.37	25	1465	1420	609	502	689
Houston	3.42	37	1446	1338	620	479	899
San Diego	3.52	20	1476	1348	658	502	765
Philadelphia	3.61	38	1456	1395	654	472	1002
San Francisco	3.64	18	1465	1507	687	466	810
Cincinnati	3.66	22	1460	1414	661	570	998
Pittsburgh	3.81	19	1466	1434	696	521	934
Atlanta	3.82	15	1463	1484	702	502	813
New York	3.88	15	1447	1508	723	582	759
Chicago	3.92	9	1447	1510	709	452	764

Individual Batting

Leaders—440 or more at bats

Player, club	Pct	AB	R	H	HR	RBI	SB
Oliver, Montreal†	.331	617	90	204	22	109	5
Madlock, Pittsburgh	.319	568	92	181	19	95	18
Durham, Chicago†	.312	539	84	168	22	90	28
L. Smith, St. Louis	.307	592	120	182	8	69	68
Buckner, Chicago†	.306	657	93	201	15	105	15
Guerrero, Los Angeles	.304	575	87	175	32	100	22
Dawson, Montreal	.301	608	107	183	23	83	39
Baker, Los Angeles	.300	570	80	171	23	88	17
Hernandez, St. Louis†	.299	579	79	173	7	94	19
Pena, Pittsburgh	.296	497	53	147	11	63	2

Individual Pitching

Leaders—162 or more innings

Pitcher, club	W	L	ERA	G	IP	H	BB	SO
Rogers, Montreal	19	8	2.40	35	277	245	65	179
Niekro, Houston	17	12	2.47	35	270	224	64	130
Andujar, St. Louis	15	10	2.47	38	265	237	50	137
Soto, Cincinnati	14	13	2.79	35	275	202	71	274
Valenzuela, Los Ang.†	19	13	2.87	37	285	247	83	199
Candelaria, Pittsburgh†	12	7	2.94	31	174	166	37	133
Sutton, Houston	13	8	3.00	27	195	169	46	139
Carlton, Philadephia†	23	11	3.10	38	295	253	86	286
Reuss, Los Angeles†	18	11	3.11	39	254	232	50	138
Krukow, Philadelphia	13	11	3.12	33	208	211	82	138

Individual Batting (at least 115 at-bats); Individual Pitching (at least 50 innings)

*Rookie; † Bats or pitches lefthanded ‡ Switch hitter

Atlanta Braves

Batting	Pct	G	AB	R	H	HR	RBI	SB
Linares	.298	77	191	28	57	2	17	5
Royster	.295	108	261	43	77	2	25	14
Harper	.287	48	150	16	43	2	16	7
Murphy	.281	162	598	113	168	36	109	23
Ramirez	.278	157	609	74	169	10	52	27
Pocorobat†	.275	56	120	5	33	2	22	0
Chambliss†	.270	157	534	57	144	20	86	7
Washington†	.266	150	563	94	150	16	80	33
Horner	.261	140	499	85	130	32	97	3
Hubbard	.248	145	532	75	132	9	59	4
Benedict	.246	118	386	34	95	3	44	4
*Whisenton†	.238	84	143	21	34	4	17	2
Butler†	.217	89	240	35	52	0	7	21

Pitching	W	L	ERA	G	IP	H	BB	SO	Sv
Garber	8	10	2.34	69	119	100	32	68	30
*Bedrosian	8	6	2.42	64	137	102	57	123	11
Perez	4	4	3.06	16	79	85	17	29	0
Niekro	17	4	3.61	35	234	225	73	144	0
Camp	11	13	3.65	51	177	199	52	68	5
Mahler	9	10	4.21	39	205	213	62	105	0
*Cowley	1	2	4.47	17	52	53	16	27	0
*Dayley†	5	6	4.54	20	71	79	25	34	0
Walk	11	9	4.87	32	164	179	59	84	0

Chicago Cubs

Batting	Pct	G	AB	R	H	HR	RBI	SB
Durham†	.312	148	539	84	168	22	90	28
Buckner†	.306	161	657	93	201	15	105	15
Morales	.284	65	116	14	33	4	30	1
Wills‡	.272	128	419	64	114	6	38	35
*Sandberg	.271	156	635	103	172	7	54	32
Woods	.269	117	245	28	66	4	30	3
Davis	.261	130	418	41	109	12	52	0
Moreland	.261	138	476	50	124	15	68	0
Bowa‡	.246	142	499	50	123	0	29	8
Johnstone†	.241	119	282	40	68	10	45	0
Henderson	.233	92	257	23	60	2	29	6
Kennedy	.219	105	242	22	53	2	25	1

Pitching	W	L	ERA	G	IP	H	BB	So	Sv
Proly	5	3	2.30	44	82	77	22	24	1
Smith	2	5	2.69	72	117	105	37	99	17
Hernandez	4	6	3.00	75	75	74	24	54	10
Jenkins	14	15	3.15	34	217	221	68	134	0
Tidrow	8	3	3.39	65	103	106	29	62	6
Campbell	3	6	3.69	62	100	89	40	71	8
Martz	11	10	4.21	28	147	157	36	40	1
Ripley	5	7	4.26	28	122	130	38	57	0
Noles	10	13	4.42	31	171	180	61	85	0
Bird	9	14	5.14	35	191	230	30	71	0

Cincinnati Reds

Batting	Pct	G	AB	R	H	HR	RBI	SB
Biittner†	.310	97	184	18	57	2	24	1
Cedeno	.289	138	492	52	142	8	57	16
Concepcion	.287	147	572	48	164	5	53	13
Krenchicki†	.283	94	187	19	53	2	21	5
Driessen†	.269	149	516	64	139	17	57	11
*Milner†	.268	113	407	61	109	4	31	18
Oester‡	.260	151	549	63	143	9	47	5
Bench	.258	119	399	44	103	13	38	1
Vail	.254	78	189	9	48	4	29	0
Trevino	.251	120	355	24	89	1	33	3
*Walker†	.218	86	239	26	52	5	22	9
*Lawless	.212	49	165	19	35	0	4	16
*Householder‡	.211	138	417	40	88	9	34	17

Pitching	W	L	ERA	G	IP	H	BB	SO	Sv.
Soto	14	13	2.79	35	257	202	71	274	0
Kern	3	5	2.84	50	76	61	48	43	2
Price†	3	4	2.85	59	72	73	32	71	3
Hume	2	6	3.11	46	63	57	21	22	17
Berenyi	9	18	3.35	34	222	208	96	157	0
Shirley†	8	13	3.60	41	152	138	73	89	0
Pastore	8	13	3.97	31	188	210	57	94	0
Harris	2	6	4.83	34	91	96	37	67	1
Leibrandt†	5	7	5.10	36	107	130	48	34	2
Seaver	5	13	5.50	21	111	136	44	62	0

Houston Astros

Batting	Pct	G	AB	R	H	HR	RBI	SB
Knight	.294	158	609	72	179	6	70	2
Thon	.276	136	496	73	137	3	36	37
Cruz†	.275	155	570	62	157	9	68	21
Garner	.274	155	588	65	161	13	83	24
Puhl†	.262	145	507	64	133	8	50	17
Ashby‡	.257	100	339	40	87	12	49	2
Reynolds†	.254	54	118	16	30	1	7	3
Scott‡	.239	132	460	43	110	1	29	18
Howe	.238	110	365	29	87	5	38	2
Heep†	.237	85	198	16	47	4	22	0
Walling†	.205	85	146	22	30	1	14	4
Pujols	.199	65	176	8	35	4	15	0
*Kincely	.188	59	133	10	25	2	12	0

Pitching	W	L	ERA	G	IP	H	BB	SO	Sv
Niekro	17	12	2.47	35	270	224	64	130	0
LaCoss	6	6	2.90	41	115	107	54	51	0
Sutton	13	8	3.00	27	195	169	46	139	0
Ryan	16	12	3.16	35	250	196	109	245	0
Smith	5	4	3.84	49	63	69	31	28	11
Ruhle	9	13	3.93	31	149	169	24	56	1
Knepper†	5	15	4.45	33	180	193	60	108	1
LaCorte	1	5	4.48	55	76	71	46	51	7

Los Angeles Dodgers

Batting	Pct	G	AB	R	H	HR	RBI	SB
Guerrero	.304	150	575	87	175	32	100	22
Baker	.300	147	570	80	171	23	88	17
Landreaux†	.284	129	461	71	131	7	50	31
Sax	.282	150	638	88	180	4	47	49
Garvey	.282	162	625	66	176	16	86	5
Russell	.274	153	497	64	136	3	46	10
Roenicke‡	.259	109	143	18	37	1	12	5
Monday†	.257	104	210	37	54	11	42	2
Cey	.254	150	556	62	141	24	79	3
Yeager	.245	82	196	13	48	2	18	0
Scioscia†	.219	129	365	31	80	5	38	2
Orta†	.217	86	115	13	25	2	8	0

Pitching	W	L	ERA	G	IP	H	BB	SO	Sv
Howe†	7	5	2.08	66	99	87	17	49	13
Niedenfuer	3	4	2.71	55	69	71	25	60	9
Valenzuela†	19	13	2.87	37	285	247	83	199	0
Forster†	5	6	3.04	56	83	66	31	52	3
Reuss†	18	11	3.11	39	254	232	50	138	0
Welch	16	11	3.36	36	235	199	81	176	0
Stewart	9	8	3.81	45	146	137	49	80	1
Hooton	4	7	4.03	21	120	130	33	51	0

Montreal Expos

Batting	Pct	G	AB	R	H	HR	RBI	SB
Oliver†	.331	160	617	90	204	22	109	5
Francona†	.321	46	131	14	42	0	9	2
Dawson	.301	148	608	107	183	23	83	39
Carter	.293	154	557	91	163	29	97	2
Raines‡	.277	156	647	90	179	4	43	78
Wallach	.268	158	596	89	160	28	97	6
Speier	.257	156	530	41	136	7	60	1
Cromartie†	.254	144	497	59	126	14	62	3
Flynn	.244	58	193	13	47	0	20	0
White‡	.243	69	115	13	28	2	13	3
Youngblood	.240	120	292	37	70	3	29	2
*Gates†	.231	36	121	16	28	0	8	0

Pitching	W	L	ERA	G	IP	H	BB	SO	Sv
Reardon	7	4	2.06	75	109	87	36	86	26
Rogers	19	8	2.40	35	277	245	65	179	0
Palmer	6	4	3.18	13	73	60	36	46	0
Lea	12	10	3.24	27	177	145	56	115	0
Sanderson	12	12	3.46	32	224	212	58	158	0
Gullickson	12	14	3.57	34	236	231	61	155	0
Fryman†	9	4	3.75	60	69	66	26	46	12
B. Smith	2	4	4.20	47	79	81	23	50	3
Burris	4	14	4.73	37	123	143	53	55	2
Schatzeder†	1	6	5.32	39	69	84	24	33	0

New York Mets

Batting	Pct	G	AB	R	H	HR	RBI	SB
Stearns	.293	98	352	46	103	4	28	17
Valentine	.288	111	337	33	97	8	48	1
Wilson‡	.279	159	639	90	178	5	55	58
Bailor	.277	110	376	44	104	0	31	20
Backman‡	.272	96	261	37	71	3	22	8
*Rajsich†	.259	80	162	17	42	2	12	1
Brooks	.249	126	457	40	114	2	40	6
Foster	.247	151	550	64	136	13	70	1
Hodges†	.246	80	228	26	56	5	27	4
Staub†	.242	112	219	11	53	3	27	0
*Gardenhire	.240	141	384	29	92	3	33	5
*Giles	.210	45	138	14	29	3	10	6
Kingman	.204	149	535	80	109	37	99	4

Pitching	W	L	ERA	G	IP	H	BB	SO	Sv
Orosco†	4	10	2.72	54	109	92	40	89	4
Allen	3	7	3.06	50	64	65	30	59	19
Swan	11	7	3.35	37	166	165	37	67	1
Lynch	4	8	3.55	43	139	145	40	51	2
*Ownbey	1	2	3.76	8	50	44	43	28	0
Falcone†	8	10	3.84	40	171	159	71	101	2
Zachry	6	9	4.05	36	137	149	57	69	1
*Puleo	9	9	4.47	36	171	179	90	98	1
Jones†	7	10	4.60	28	107	130	51	44	0
Scott	7	13	5.14	37	147	185	60	63	3

Philadelphia Phillies

Batting	Pct	G	AB	R	H	HR	RBI	SB
Gross†	.299	119	134	14	40	0	10	4
Diaz	.288	144	525	69	151	18	85	3
Maddox	.284	119	412	39	117	8	61	7
Matthews	.281	162	616	89	173	19	83	21
Schmidt	.280	148	514	108	144	35	87	14
Vukovich†	.272	123	335	41	91	6	42	2
Trillo	.271	149	549	52	149	0	39	8
Rose‡	.271	162	634	80	172	3	54	8
Robinson	.250	66	140	14	35	7	31	1
*Dernier	.249	122	370	56	92	4	21	42
DeJesus	.239	161	536	53	128	3	59	14
*Virgil	.238	49	101	11	24	3	8	0

Pitching	W	L	ERA	G	IP	H	BB	SO	Sv
R. Reed	5	5	2.66	57	98	85	24	57	14
Carlton†	23	11	3.10	38	295	253	86	286	0
Krukow	13	11	3.12	33	208	211	82	138	0
Christenson	9	10	3.47	33	223	212	53	145	0
Monge†	7	1	3.75	47	72	70	22	43	2
Ruthven	11	11	3.79	33	204	189	59	115	0
Bystrom	5	6	4.85	19	89	93	35	50	0
Farmer	2	6	4.86	47	76	66	50	58	6

Pittsburgh Pirates

Batting	Pct	G	AB	R	H	HR	RBI	SB
Madlock	.319	154	568	92	181	19	95	18
Lacy	.312	121	359	66	112	5	31	40
Pena	.296	138	497	53	147	11	63	2
Thompson†	.284	156	550	87	156	31	101	1
*Ray‡	.281	162	647	79	182	7	63	16
Easler†	.276	142	475	52	131	15	58	1
Parker†	.270	73	244	41	66	6	29	7
Berra	.263	156	529	64	139	10	61	6
Moreno†	.245	158	645	82	158	3	44	60
Davis	.228	67	145	12	33	4	17	2

Pitching	W	L	ERA	G	IP	H	BB	SO	Sv
Scurry†	4	5	**1.74**	76	103	79	64	95	14
Tekulve	12	8	**2.87**	85	128	113	46	66	20
Candelaria†	12	7	**2.94**	31	174	166	37	133	1
Sarmiento	9	4	**3.39**	35	164	153	46	81	1
McWilliams†	8	8	**3.84**	46	159	158	44	118	1
Rhoden	11	14	**4.14**	35	230	239	70	128	0
Robinson	15	13	**4.28**	38	227	213	103	165	0
Romo	9	3	**4.36**	45	86	81	36	58	1

St. Louis Cardinals

Batting	Pct	G	AB	R	H	HR	RBI	SB
L. Smith	**.307**	156	592	120	182	8	69	68
Hernandez†	**.299**	160	579	79	173	7	94	19
*McGee‡	**.296**	123	422	43	125	4	56	24
Iorg†	**.294**	102	238	17	70	0	34	0
Oberkfell†	**.289**	137	470	55	136	2	34	11
*Green	**.283**	76	166	21	47	2	23	11
Hendrick	**.282**	136	515	65	145	19	104	3
Herr‡	**.266**	135	493	83	131	0	36	25
Tenace	**.258**	66	124	18	32	7	18	1
O. Smith‡	**.248**	140	488	58	121	2	43	25
Porter†	**.231**	120	373	46	86	12	48	1
Ramsey‡	**.230**	112	256	18	59	1	21	6

Pitching	W	L	ERA	G	IP	H	BB	SO	Sv
Andujar	15	10	**2.47**	38	265	237	50	137	0
Bair	5	3	**2.55**	63	91	69	36	68	8
Sutter	9	8	**2.90**	70	102	88	34	61	36
*Stuper	9	7	**3.36**	23	136	137	55	53	0
*LaPoint†	9	3	**3.42**	42	152	170	52	81	0
Forsch	15	9	**3.48**	36	233	238	54	69	1
*Lahti	5	4	**3.81**	33	56	53	21	22	0
Mura	12	11	**4.05**	35	184	196	80	84	0
Kaat†	5	3	**4.08**	62	75	79	23	35	2
Martin†	4	5	**4.23**	24	66	56	30	21	0

San Diego Padres

Batting	Pct	G	AB	R	H	HR	RBI	SB
Kennedy†	**.295**	153	562	75	166	21	97	1
*Gwynn†	**.289**	54	190	33	55	1	17	8
Lezcano	**.289**	138	470	73	136	16	84	2
Richards†	**.286**	132	521	63	149	3	28	30
Jones†	**.283**	116	424	69	120	12	61	18
Bonilla	**.280**	45	182	21	51	0	8	0
Perkins†	**.271**	125	347	32	94	2	34	2
Flannery†	**.264**	122	379	40	100	0	30	1
*Wiggins‡	**.256**	72	254	40	65	1	15	33
Bevacqua	**.252**	64	123	15	31	0	24	
Pittman	**.250**	70	128	16	32	0	7	
Templeton‡	**.247**	141	563	76	139	6	64	[illegible]
Salazar	**.242**	145	524	55	127	8	62	[illegible]
Lefebvre†	**.238**	102	239	25	57	4	21	

Pitching	W	L	ERA	G	IP	H	BB	SO	S
*DeLeon	9	5	**2.03**	61	102	77	16	60	[illegible]
*Dravecky†	5	3	**2.57**	31	105	86	33	59	
*Show	10	6	**2.64**	47	150	117	48	88	
*Chiffer	4	3	**2.95**	51	79	73	34	48	
Lollar†	16	9	**3.13**	34	232	192	87	150	
Lucas†	1	10	**3.24**	65	97	89	29	64	[illegible]
Montefusco	10	11	**4.00**	32	184	177	41	83	
*Hawkins	2	5	**4.10**	15	63	66	27	25	
Curtis†	8	6	**4.10**	26	116	121	46	54	
Eichelberger	7	14	**4.20**	31	177	171	72	74	
Welsh†	8	8	**4.91**	28	139	146	63	48	

San Francisco Giants

Batting	Pct	G	AB	R	H	HR	RBI	S
Morgan†	**.289**	134	463	68	134	14	61	[illegible]
Smith‡	**.284**	106	349	51	99	18	56	
*Brenly	**.283**	65	180	26	51	4	15	
Kuiper†	**.280**	107	218	26	61	0	17	
*O'Malley	**.275**	92	291	26	80	2	27	
Clark	**.274**	157	563	90	154	27	103	
Bergman†	**.273**	100	121	22	33	4	14	
May†	**.263**	114	395	29	104	9	39	
*Davis‡	**.261**	154	641	86	167	19	76	[illegible]
Leonard	**.259**	80	278	32	72	9	49	[illegible]
Wohlford	**.256**	97	250	37	64	2	25	
Evans†	**.256**	141	465	64	119	16	61	
Summers†	**.248**	70	125	15	31	4	19	
Venable†	**.224**	71	125	17	28	1	7	
LeMaster	**.216**	130	436	34	94	2	30	[illegible]

Pitching	W	L	ERA	G	IP	H	BB	SO	S
Minton	10	4	**1.83**	78	123	108	42	58	[illegible]
Lavelle†	10	7	**2.67**	68	104	97	29	76	
Breining	11	6	**3.08**	54	143	146	52	98	
*Laskey	13	12	**3.14**	32	189	186	43	88	
Barr	4	3	**3.29**	53	128	125	20	36	
Holland†	7	3	**3.33**	58	129	115	40	97	
*Hammaker†	12	8	**4.11**	29	175	189	28	102	
Gale	7	14	**4.23**	33	170	193	81	102	
Martin	7	10	**4.65**	29	141	148	64	63	
*Fowlkes	4	2	**5.19**	21	85	111	24	50	

Leading Pitchers, Earned-Run Average

National League

Year	Player, club	G	IP	ERA
1964	Sandy Koufax, Los Angeles	29	223	**1.74**
1965	Sandy Koufax, Los Angeles	43	336	**2.04**
1966	Sandy Koufax, Los Angeles	41	323	**1.73**
1967	Phil Niekro, Atlanta	46	207	**1.87**
1968	Bob Gibson, St. Louis	34	305	**1.12**
1969	Juan Marichal, San Francisco	37	300	**2.10**
1970	Tom Seaver, New York	37	291	**2.81**
1971	Tom Seaver, New York	36	286	**1.76**
1972	Steve Carlton, Philadelphia	41	346	**1.98**
1973	Tom Seaver, New York	36	290	**2.07**
1974	Buzz Capra, Atlanta	39	217	**2.28**
1975	Randy Jones, San Diego	37	285	**2.24**
1976	John Denny, St. Louis	30	207	**2.52**
1977	John Candelaria, Pittsburgh	33	231	**2.34**
1978	Craig Swan, New York	29	207	**2.43**
1979	J. R. Richard, Houston	38	292	**2.71**
1980	Don Sutton, Los Angeles	32	212	**2.21**
1981	Nolan Ryan, Houston	21	149	**1.69**
1982	Steve Rogers, Montreal	35	277	**2.40**

American League

Year	Player, club	G	IP	ERA
1964	Dean Chance, Los Angeles	46	278	[illegible]
1965	Sam McDowell, Cleveland	42	274	[illegible]
1966	Gary Peters, Chicago	29	204	[illegible]
1967	Joe Horlen, Chicago	35	258	[illegible]
1968	Luis Tiant, Cleveland	34	258	[illegible]
1969	Dick Bosman, Washington	31	193	[illegible]
1970	Diego Segui, Oakland	47	162	[illegible]
1971	Vida Blue, Oakland	39	312	[illegible]
1972	Luis Tiant, Boston	43	179	[illegible]
1973	Jim Palmer, Baltimore	38	296	[illegible]
1974	Catfish Hunter, Oakland	41	318	[illegible]
1975	Jim Palmer, Baltimore	39	323	[illegible]
1976	Mark Fidrych, Detroit	31	250	[illegible]
1977	Frank Tanana, California	31	241	[illegible]
1978	Ron Guidry, New York	35	274	[illegible]
1979	Ron Guidry, New York	33	236	[illegible]
1980	Rudy May, New York	41	175	[illegible]
1981	Steve McCatty, Oakland	22	186	[illegible]
1982	Rick Sutcliffe, Cleveland	34	216	[illegible]

ERA is computed by multiplying earned runs allowed by 9, then dividing by innings pitched.

Triple Crown Winners

Players leading league in batting, runs batted in, and homers in a single season

Year	Player, team	Year	Player, team
1909	Ty Cobb, Detroit Tigers	1937	Joe Medwick, St. Louis Cardinals
1922	Rogers Hornsby, St. Louis Cardinals	1942	Ted Williams, Boston Red Sox
1925	Rogers Hornsby, St. Louis Cardinals	1947	Ted Williams, Boston Red Sox
1933	Jimmy Foxx, Philadelphia Athletics	1956	Mickey Mantle, New York Yankees
1933	Chuck Klein, Philadelphia Phillies	1966	Frank Robinson, Baltimore Orioles
1934	Lou Gehrig, New York Yankees	1967	Carl Yastrzemski, Boston Red Sox

Most Valuable Player

Baseball Writers' Association

National League

Year	Player, team	Year	Player, team	Year	Player, team
1931	Frank Frisch, St. Louis	1949	Jackie Robinson, Brooklyn	1967	Orlando Cepeda, St. Louis
1932	Charles Klein, Philadelpha	1950	Jim Konstanty, Philadelphia	1968	Bob Gibson, St. Louis
1933	Carl Hubbell, New York	1951	Roy Campanella, Brooklyn	1969	Willie McCovey, San Francisco
1934	Dizzy Dean, St. Louis	1952	Hank Sauer, Chicago	1970	Johnny Bench, Cincinnati
1935	Gabby Hartnett, Chicago	1953	Roy Campanella, Brooklyn	1971	Joe Torre, St. Louis
1936	Carl Hubbell, New York	1954	Willie Mays, New York	1972	Johnny Bench, Cincinnati
1937	Joe Medwick, St. Louis	1955	Roy Campenella, Brooklyn	1973	Pete Rose, Cincinnati
1938	Ernie Lombardi, Cincinnati	1956	Don Newcombe, Brooklyn	1974	Steve Garvey, Los Angeles
1939	Bucky Walters, Cincinnati	1957	Henry Aaron, Milwaukee	1975	Joe Morgan, Cincinnati
1940	Frank McCormick, Cincinnati	1958	Ernie Banks, Chicago	1976	Joe Morgan, Cincinnati
1941	Dolph Camilli, Brooklyn	1959	Ernie Banks, Chicago	1977	George Foster, Cincinnati
1942	Mort Cooper, St. Louis	1960	Dick Groat, Pittsburgh	1978	Dave Parker, Pittsburgh
1943	Stan Musial, St. Louis	1961	Frank Robinson, Cincinnati	1979	(tie) Willie Stargell, Pittsburgh
1944	Martin Marion, St. Louis	1962	Maury Wills, Los Angeles		Keith Hernandez, St. Louis
1945	Phil Cavarretta, Chicago	1963	Sandy Koufax, Los Angeles	1980	Mike Schmidt, Philadelphia
1946	Stan Musial, St. Louis	1964	Ken Boyer, St. Louis	1981	Mike Schmidt, Philadelphia
1947	Bob Elliott, Boston	1965	Willie Mays, San Francisco		
1948	Stan Musial, St. Louis	1966	Roberto Clemente, Pittsburgh		

American League

Year	Player, team	Year	Player, team	Year	Player, team
1931	Lefty Grove, Philadelphia	1949	Ted Williams, Boston	1967	Carl Yastrzemski, Boston
1932	Jimmy Foxx, Philadelphia	1950	Phil Rizzuto, New York	1968	Denny McLain, Detroit
1933	Jimmy Foxx, Philadelphia	1951	Yogi Berra, New York	1969	Harmon Killebrew, Minnesota
1934	Mickey Cochrane, Detroit	1952	Bobby Shantz, Philadelphia	1970	John (Boog) Powell, Baltimore
1935	Henry Greenberg, Detroit	1953	Al Rosen, Cleveland	1971	Vida Blue, Oakland
1936	Lou Gehrig, New York	1954	Yogi Berra, New York	1972	Dick Allen, Chicago
1937	Charley Gehringer, Detroit	1955	Yogi Berra, New York	1973	Reggie Jackson, Oakland
1938	Jimmy Foxx, Boston	1956	Mickey Mantle, New York	1974	Jeff Burroughs, Texas
1939	Joe DiMaggio, New York	1957	Mickey Mantle, New York	1975	Fred Lynn, Boston
1940	Hank Greenberg, Detroit	1958	Jackie Jensen, Boston	1976	Thurman Munson, New York
1941	Joe DiMaggio, New York	1959	Nellie Fox, Chicago	1977	Rod Carew, Minnesota
1942	Joe Gordon, New York	1960	Roger Maris, New York	1978	Jim Rice, Boston
1943	Spurgeon Chandler, New York	1961	Roger Maris, New York	1979	Don Baylor, California
1944	Hal Newhouser, Detroit	1962	Mickey Mantle, New York	1980	George Brett, Kansas City
1945	Hal Newhouser, Detroit	1963	Elston Howard, New York	1981	Rollie Fingers, Milwaukee
1946	Ted Williams, Boston	1964	Brooks Robinson, Baltimore		
1947	Joe DiMaggio, New York	1965	Zoilo Versalles, Minnesota		
1948	Lou Boudreau, Cleveland	1966	Frank Robinson, Baltimore		

Rookie of the Year

Baseball Writers' Association

1947—Combined selection—Jackie Robinson, Brooklyn, 1b

1948—Combined selection—Alvin Dark, Boston, N.L. ss

National League

Year	Player, team	Year	Player, team	Year	Player, team
1949	Don Newcombe, Brooklyn, p	1961	Billy Williams, Chicago, of	1973	Gary Matthews, S.F., of
1950	Sam Jethroe, Boston, of	1962	Ken Hubbs, Chicago, 2b	1974	Bake McBride, St. Louis, of
1951	Willie Mays, New York, of	1963	Pete Rose, Cincinnati, 2b	1975	John Montefusco, S.F., p
1952	Joe Black, Brooklyn, p	1964	Richie Allen, Philadelphia, 3b	1976	(tie) Butch Metzger, San Diego, p
1953	Jim Gilliam, Brooklyn, 2b	1965	Jim Lefebvre, Los Angeles, 2b		Pat Zachry, Cincinnati, p
1954	Wally Moon, St. Louis, of	1966	Tommy Helms, Cincinnati, 2b	1977	Andre Dawson, Montreal, of
1955	Bill Virdon, St. Louis, of	1967	Tom Seaver, New York, p	1978	Bob Horner, Atlanta, 3b
1956	Frank Robinson, Cincinnati, of	1968	Johnny Bench, Cincinnati c	1979	Rick Sutcliffe, Los Angeles, p
1957	Jack Sanford, Philadelphia, p	1969	Ted Sizemore, Los Angeles, 2b	1980	Steve Howe, Los Angeles, p
1958	Orlando Cepeda, S.F., 1b	1970	Carl Morton, Montreal, p	1981	Fernando Valenzuela, Los Angeles, p
1959	Willie McCovey, S.F., 1b	1971	Earl Williams, Atlanta, c		
1960	Frank Howard, Los Angeles, of	1972	Jon Matlack, New York, p		

American League

Year	Player, team	Year	Player, team	Year	Player, team
1949	Roy Sievers, St. Louis, of	1961	Don Schwall, Boston, p	1973	Al Bumbry, Baltimore, of
1950	Walt Dropo, Boston, 1b	1962	Tom Tresh, New York, if-of	1974	Mike Hargrove, Texas, 1b
1951	Gil McDougald, New York, 3b	1963	Gary Peters, Chicago, p	1975	Fred Lynn, Boston, of
1952	Harry Byrd, Philadelphia, p	1964	Tony Oliva, Minnesota, of	1976	Mark Fidrych, Detroit, p
1953	Harvey Kuenn, Detroit, ss	1965	Curt Blefary, Baltimore, of	1977	Eddie Murray, Baltimore, dh
1954	Bob Grim, New York, p	1966	Tommie Agee, Chicago, of	1978	Lou Whitaker, Detroit, 2b
1955	Herb Score, Cleveland, p	1967	Rod Carew, Minnesota, 2b	1979	(tie) John Castino, Minnesota, 3b
1956	Luis Aparicio, Chicago, ss	1968	Stan Bahnsen, New York, p		Alfredo Griffin, Toronto, ss
1957	Tony Kubek, New York, if-of	1969	Lou Piniella, Kansas City, of	1980	Joe Charboneau, Cleveland, of
1958	Albie Pearson, Washington, of	1970	Thurman Munson, New York, c	1981	Dave Reghetti, New York, p
1959	Bob Allison, Washington, of	1971	Chris Chambliss, Cleveland, 1b		
1960	Ron Hansen, Baltimore, ss	1972	Carlton Fisk, Boston, c		

American League Records in 1982

Final standings

Eastern Division

Club	W	L	Pct	GB
Milwaukee	95	67	.586	—
Baltimore	94	68	.580	1
Boston	89	73	.549	6
Detroit	83	79	.512	12
New York	79	83	.488	16
Cleveland	78	84	.481	17
Toronto	78	84	.481	17

Western Division

Club	W	L	Pct	GB
California	93	69	.574	—
Kansas City	90	72	.556	
Chicago	87	75	.537	
Seattle	76	86	.469	1
Oakland	68	94	.420	2
Texas	64	98	.395	2
Minnesota	60	102	.370	3

American League Playoffs

California 8, Milwaukee 3.
California 4, Milwaukee 2.
Milwaukee 5, California 3.
Milwaukee 9, California 5.
Milwaukee 4, California 3

Club Batting

Club	Pct	AB	R	H	HR	SB
Kansas City	**.285**	5629	784	1603	132	133
Milwaukee	**.279**	5733	891	1599	216	84
Boston	**.274**	5596	753	1536	136	42
California	**.274**	5532	814	1518	186	55
Chicago	**.273**	5575	786	1523	136	136
Detroit	**.266**	5590	729	1489	177	93
Baltimore	**.266**	5557	774	1478	179	49
Cleveland	**.262**	5559	683	1458	109	151
Toronto	**.262**	5526	651	1447	106	118
Minnesota	**.257**	5545	657	1427	148	38
New York	**.256**	5526	709	1417	161	69
Seattle	**.254**	5626	651	1431	130	131
Texas	**.249**	5445	590	1354	115	63
Oakland	**.236**	5448	691	1287	149	232

Club Pitching

Club	ERA	CG	IP	H	R	BB	SO
Detroit	**3.80**	45	1451	1371	685	554	74
California	**3.82**	40	1464	1436	670	482	72
Chicago	**3.87**	30	1439	1502	710	460	75
Seattle	**3.88**	23	1476	1431	712	547	100
Toronto	**3.95**	41	1443	1428	701	493	77
Milwaukee	**3.98**	34	1467	1514	717	511	71
Baltimore	**3.99**	38	1462	1437	687	488	71
New York	**3.99**	24	1459	1471	716	491	93
Boston	**4.03**	23	1453	1557	713	478	81
Kansas City	**4.08**	16	1431	1443	717	471	65
Cleveland	**4.11**	31	1468	1433	748	589	88
Texas	**4.28**	32	1431	1554	749	483	69
Oakland	**4.54**	42	1456	1506	819	648	69
Minnesota	**4.72**	26	1433	1484	819	643	81

Individual Batting

Leaders—440 or more at bats

Player, club	Pct	AB	R	H	HR	RBI	SB
Wilson, Kansas City‡	**.332**	585	87	194	3	46	37
Yount, Milwaukee	**.331**	635	129	210	29	114	14
Carew, California†	**.319**	523	88	167	3	44	10
Murray, Baltimore†	**.316**	550	87	174	32	110	7
Cooper, Milwaukee†	**.313**	654	104	205	32	121	2
Garcia, Toronto	**.310**	597	89	185	5	42	54
Rice, Boston	**.309**	573	86	177	24	97	0
McRae, Kansas City	**.308**	613	91	189	27	133	4
Harrah, Clveland	**.304**	602	100	183	25	78	17
Molitor, Milwaukee	**.302**	666	136	201	19	71	41

Individual Pitching

Leaders—162 or more innings

Pitcher, club	W	L	ERA	G	IP	H	BB	SO
Sutcliffe, Cleveland	14	8	**2.96**	34	216	174	98	14
Stanley, Boston	12	7	**3.10**	48	168	161	50	8
Palmer, Baltimore	15	5	**3.13**	36	227	195	63	10
Petry, Detroit	15	9	**3.22**	35	246	220	100	13
Stieb, Toronto	17	14	**3.25**	38	288	271	75	14
Vuckovich, Milwaukee	18	6	**3.34**	30	223	234	102	10
Beattie, Seattle	8	12	**3.34**	28	172	149	65	14
Bannister, Seattle†	12	13	**3.43**	35	247	225	77	20
Witt, California	8	6	**3.51**	33	179	177	47	8
Hoyt, Chicago	19	15	**3.53**	39	239	248	48	12

Individual Batting (at least 115 at-bats); Individual Pitching (at least 50 innings)

*Rookie; † Bats or pitches lefthanded ‡ Switch hitter

Baltimore Orioles

Batting	Pct	G	AB	R	H	HR	RBI	SB
Lowenstein†	**.320**	122	322	69	103	24	66	7
Murray‡	**.316**	151	550	87	174	32	110	7
Ayala	**.305**	64	128	17	39	6	24	1
Dwyer†	**.304**	71	148	28	45	6	15	2
Dauer	**.280**	158	558	75	156	8	57	0
Roenicke	**.270**	137	393	58	106	21	74	6
*Ripken	**.264**	160	598	90	158	28	93	3
Bumbry†	**.262**	150	562	77	147	5	40	10
Sakata	**.259**	135	343	40	89	6	31	7
Dempsey	**.256**	125	344	35	88	5	36	0
Singleton‡	**.251**	156	561	71	141	14	77	0
Ford	**.235**	123	421	46	99	10	43	5
Nolan†	**.233**	77	219	24	51	6	35	1
*Gulliver†	**.200**	50	145	24	29	1	5	0

Pitching	W	L	ERA	G	IP	H	BB	SO	Sv
Palmer	15	5	**3.13**	36	227	195	63	103	1
T. Martinez†	8	8	**3.41**	76	95	81	37	78	16
*Davis	8	4	**3.49**	29	100	96	28	67	0
Flanagan†	15	11	**3.97**	36	236	233	76	103	0
Stoddard	3	4	**4.02**	50	56	53	29	42	12
Stewart	10	9	**4.14**	38	139	140	62	69	5
D. Martinez	16	12	**4.21**	40	252	263	87	111	0
McGregor†	14	12	**4.61**	37	226	238	52	84	0
Grimsley†	1	2	**5.25**	21	60	65	22	18	0

Boston Red Sox

Batting	Pct	G	AB	R	H	HR	RBI	SB
*Boggs†	**.349**	104	338	51	118	5	44	
Rice	**.309**	145	573	86	177	24	97	
Nichols	**.302**	92	245	35	74	7	33	
Lansford	**.301**	128	482	65	145	11	63	
Evans	**.292**	162	609	122	178	32	98	
Remy†	**.280**	155	636	89	178	0	47	1
Yastrzemski†	**.275**	131	459	53	126	16	72	
Stapleton	**.264**	150	538	66	142	14	65	
Perez	**.260**	69	196	18	51	6	31	
Miller†	**.254**	135	409	50	104	4	38	
Gedman†	**.249**	92	289	30	72	4	26	
Hoffman	**.209**	150	469	53	98	7	49	
Allenson	**.205**	92	264	25	54	6	33	

Pitching	W	L	ERA	G	IP	H	BB	SO	Sv
Burgmeier†	7	0	**2.29**	40	102	98	22	44	
Clear	14	9	**3.00**	55	105	92	61	109	1
Stanley	12	7	**3.10**	48	168	161	50	83	1
*Aponte	2	2	**3.18**	40	85	78	25	44	
Tudor†	13	10	**3.63**	32	195	215	59	146	
Eckersley	13	13	**3.73**	33	224	228	43	127	
Rainey	7	5	**5.02**	27	129	146	63	57	
Torrez	9	9	**5.23**	31	175	196	74	84	
Ojeda†	4	6	**5.63**	22	78	95	29	52	
Hurst†	3	7	**5.77**	28	117	161	40	53	

California Angels

Batting	Pct	G	AB	R	H	HR	RBI	SB
Ro. Jackson	**.331**	53	142	15	47	2	19	0
Carew†	**.319**	138	523	88	167	3	44	10
DeCinces	**.301**	153	575	94	173	30	97	7
Lynn†	**.299**	138	472	89	141	21	86	7
Downing	**.281**	158	623	109	175	28	84	2
Re. Jackson†	**.275**	153	530	92	146	39	101	4
Beniquez	**.265**	112	196	25	52	3	24	3
Baylor	**.263**	157	608	80	160	24	93	10
Grich	**.261**	145	506	74	132	19	65	3
Boone	**.256**	143	472	42	121	7	58	0
Foli	**.252**	150	480	46	121	3	56	2
Wilfong†	**.208**	80	183	24	38	1	16	4

Pitching	W	L	ERA	G	IP	H	BB	SO	Sv
Hassler†	2	1	**2.78**	54	71	58	40	38	4
Kison	10	5	**3.17**	33	142	120	44	86	1
Sanchez	7	4	**3.21**	46	92	89	34	58	5
Aase	3	3	**3.46**	24	52	45	23	40	4
Witt	8	6	**3.51**	33	179	177	47	85	0
John†	14	12	**3.69**	37	221	239	39	68	0
Zahn†	18	8	**3.73**	34	229	225	65	81	0
Forsch	13	11	**3.87**	37	228	225	57	73	0
Goltz	8	5	**4.08**	28	86	82	32	49	3
Renko	11	6	**4.44**	31	156	163	51	81	0
Corbett	1	9	**5.13**	43	79	73	35	52	11

Chicago White Sox

Batting	Pct	G	AB	R	H	HR	RBI	SB
R. Law†	**.318**	121	336	55	107	3	32	36
Paciorek	**.312**	104	382	49	119	11	55	3
Luzinski	**.292**	159	583	87	170	18	102	1
LeFlore	**.287**	91	334	58	96	4	25	28
Kemp†	**.286**	160	580	91	166	19	98	7
V. Law	**.281**	114	359	40	101	5	54	4
Baines†	**.271**	161	608	89	165	25	105	10
Fisk	**.267**	135	476	66	127	14	65	17
Squires†	**.267**	116	195	33	52	1	21	3
Almon	**.256**	111	308	40	79	4	26	10
Bernazard‡	**.256**	137	540	90	138	11	56	11
Rodriguez	**.241**	118	257	24	62	3	31	0
Morrison	**.223**	51	166	17	37	7	19	0

Pitching	W	L	ERA	G	IP	H	BB	SO	Sv
Hickey†	4	4	**3.00**	60	78	73	30	38	6
Hoyt	19	15	**3.53**	39	239	248	48	124	0
*Barojas	6	6	**3.54**	61	106	96	46	56	21
*Escarrega	1	3	**3.67**	38	73	73	16	33	1
Koosman†	11	7	**3.84**	42	173	194	38	88	3
Dotson	11	15	**3.84**	34	196	219	73	109	0
Lamp	11	8	**3.99**	44	189	206	59	78	5
Burns†	13	5	**4.04**	28	169	168	67	116	0
Trout†	6	9	**4.26**	25	120	130	50	62	0

Cleveland Indians

Batting	Pct	G	AB	R	H	HR	RBI	SB
Harrah	**.304**	162	602	100	183	25	78	17
Thornton	**.273**	161	589	90	161	32	116	6
Hargrove†	**.271**	160	591	67	160	4	65	2
Manning†	**.270**	152	562	71	152	8	44	12
Fischlin	**.268**	112	276	34	74	0	21	9
Bannister	**.267**	101	348	40	93	4	41	18
Milbourne‡	**.257**	125	416	40	107	2	26	3
Hassey†	**.251**	113	323	33	81	5	34	3
*Hayes†	**.250**	150	527	65	132	14	82	32
*Perconte†	**.237**	93	219	27	52	0	15	9
Dilone‡	**.235**	104	379	50	89	3	25	33
Dybzinski	**.231**	80	212	19	49	0	22	3
*Bando‡	**.212**	66	184	13	39	3	16	0
*Castillo	**.208**	47	120	11	25	2	11	0

Pitching	W	L	ERA	G	IP	H	BB	SO	Sv
Spillner	12	10	**2.49**	65	133	117	45	90	21
Sutcliffe	14	8	**2.96**	34	216	174	98	142	1
Whitson	4	2	**3.26**	40	107	91	58	61	2
*Anderson	3	4	**3.35**	25	80	84	30	44	0
Barker	15	11	**3.90**	33	244	211	88	187	0
*Brennan	4	2	**4.27**	30	92	112	10	46	2
Denny	6	11	**5.01**	21	138	126	73	94	0
Waits†	2	13	**5.40**	25	115	128	57	44	0
Sorensen	10	15	**5.61**	32	189	251	55	62	0

Detroit Tigers

Batting	Pct	G	AB	R	H	HR	RBI	SB
*Johnson‡	**.316**	54	155	23	49	4	14	7
Wockenfuss	**.301**	70	193	28	58	8	32	0
*Wilson	**.292**	84	322	39	94	12	34	2
Herndon	**.292**	157	614	92	179	23	88	12
Whitaker†	**.286**	152	560	76	160	15	65	11
Parrish	**.284**	133	486	75	138	32	87	3
Gibson†	**.278**	69	266	34	74	8	35	9
Hebner†	**.274**	68	179	25	49	8	18	1
Lemon	**.266**	125	436	75	116	19	52	1
Cabell	**.261**	125	464	45	121	2	37	15
Trammell	**.258**	157	489	66	126	9	57	19
Turner†	**.248**	85	210	21	52	8	27	1
Leach†	**.239**	82	218	23	52	3	12	4
Ivie	**.232**	80	259	35	60	14	38	0
Brookens	**.231**	140	398	40	92	9	58	5
Jones	**.223**	58	139	15	31	0	14	0

Pitching	W	L	ERA	G	IP	H	BB	SO	Sv
Petry	15	9	**3.22**	35	246	220	100	132	0
*Rucker†	5	6	**3.38**	27	64	62	23	31	0
Tobik	4	9	**3.56**	51	98	86	38	63	9
Wilcox	12	10	**3.62**	29	193	187	85	112	0
*Ujdur	10	10	**3.69**	25	178	150	69	86	0
*Pashnick	4	4	**4.01**	28	94	110	25	19	0
Morris	17	16	**4.06**	37	266	247	96	135	0
Sosa	3	3	**4.43**	38	61	64	18	24	4
Underwood†	4	8	**4.73**	33	99	108	22	43	3

Kansas City Royals

Batting	Pct	G	AB	R	H	HR	RBI	SB
W. Wilson‡	**.332**	136	585	87	194	3	46	37
McRae	**.308**	159	613	91	189	27	133	4
Brett†	**.301**	144	522	101	166	21	82	6
White	**.298**	145	524	71	156	11	56	10
Otis	**.286**	125	475	73	136	11	88	9
Washington‡	**.286**	119	437	64	125	10	60	23
Aikens†	**.281**	134	466	50	131	17	74	0
*Slaught	**.278**	43	115	14	32	3	8	0
Wathan	**.270**	121	448	79	121	3	51	36
Pryor	**.270**	73	152	23	41	2	12	2
Geronimo†	**.269**	53	119	14	32	4	23	2
Martin	**.266**	147	519	52	138	15	65	1
*Concepcion	**.234**	74	205	17	48	0	15	2
*Hammond†	**.230**	46	126	14	29	1	11	0

Pitching	W	L	ERA	G	IP	H	BB	SO	Sv
Quisenberry	9	7	**2.57**	72	136	126	12	46	35
*Armstrong	5	5	**3.20**	52	112	88	43	75	6
Castro	3	2	**3.45**	21	75	72	20	37	1
Hood†	4	0	**3.51**	30	66	71	22	31	1
Blue†	13	12	**3.78**	31	181	163	80	103	0
Gura†	18	12	**4.03**	37	248	251	64	98	0
Splittorff†	10	10	**4.28**	29	162	166	57	74	0
*Black†	4	6	**4.58**	22	88	92	34	40	0
Leonard	10	6	**5.10**	21	130	145	46	58	0
Frost	6	6	**5.51**	21	81	103	30	26	0

Milwaukee Brewers

Batting	Pct	G	AB	R	H	HR	RBI	SB
Yount	**.331**	156	635	129	210	29	114	14
Cooper†	**.313**	155	654	104	205	32	121	2
Molitor	**.302**	160	666	136	201	19	71	41
Gantner†	**.295**	132	447	48	132	4	43	6
Money	**.284**	96	275	40	78	16	55	0
Simmons‡	**.269**	137	539	73	145	23	97	0
Howell†	**.260**	98	300	31	78	4	38	0
Moore	**.254**	133	456	53	116	6	45	2
Romero	**.250**	52	144	18	36	1	7	0
Edwards†	**.247**	69	178	24	44	2	14	10
Thomas	**.245**	158	567	96	139	39	112	3
Oglivie†	**.244**	159	602	92	147	34	102	3

Pitching	W	L	ERA	G	IP	H	BB	SO	Sv
Fingers	5	6	**2.60**	50	79	63	20	71	29
Slaton	10	6	**3.29**	39	117	117	41	59	6
Sutton	4	1	**3.29**	7	54	55	18	36	0
Vuckovich	18	6	**3.34**	30	223	234	102	105	0
Bernard	3	1	**3.76**	47	79	78	27	45	6
Caldwell†	17	13	**3.91**	35	258	269	58	75	0
McClure†	12	7	**4.22**	34	172	160	74	99	0
Haas	11	8	**4.47**	32	193	232	39	104	1
Lerch†	8	7	**4.97**	21	108	123	51	33	0
Medich	12	15	**5.04**	31	185	203	93	73	0
Augustine†	1	3	**5.08**	20	62	63	26	22	0

Minnesota Twins

Batting	Pct	G	AB	R	H	HR	RBI	SB
*Hrbek†	.301	140	532	82	160	23	92	3
Ward	.289	152	570	85	165	28	91	13
*Brunansky	.272	127	463	77	126	20	46	1
*Washington	.271	119	451	48	122	5	39	3
*Vega	.266	71	199	23	53	5	29	6
*Laudner	.255	93	306	37	78	7	33	0
Butera	.254	54	126	9	32	0	8	0
Hatcher	.249	84	277	23	69	3	26	0
*Mitchell†	.249	124	454	48	113	2	28	8
*Johnson†	.247	89	235	26	58	10	32	0
*Bush†	.244	55	119	13	29	4	13	0
*Faedo	.243	90	255	16	62	3	22	1
Castino	.241	117	410	48	99	6	37	2
*Gaetti	.230	145	508	59	117	25	84	0
Engle	.226	58	186	20	42	4	16	0

Pitching	W	L	ERA	G	IP	H	BB	SO	Sv
Castillo	13	11	3.66	40	218	194	85	124	0
Williams	9	7	4.22	26	153	166	55	61	0
O'Connor†	8	9	4.29	23	126	122	57	56	0
Havens†	10	14	4.31	33	208	201	80	129	0
Davis	3	9	4.42	63	106	106	47	89	22
*Felton	0	13	4.99	48	117	99	76	92	3
*Viola†	4	10	5.21	22	126	152	38	84	0
Redfern	5	11	6.58	27	94	122	51	40	0
Pacella	1	3	7.30	24	61	74	46	22	2

New York Yankees

Batting	Pct	G	AB	R	H	HR	RBI	SB
Piniella	.307	102	261	33	80	6	37	0
Mumphrey‡	.300	123	477	76	143	9	68	11
Randolph	.280	144	553	85	155	3	36	16
Winfield	.280	140	539	84	151	37	106	5
Griffey†	.277	127	484	70	134	12	54	10
Gamble†	.272	108	316	49	86	18	57	6
Wynegar‡	.267	87	277	36	74	4	28	0
Smalley‡	.255	146	499	57	127	20	67	0
Collins‡	.253	111	348	41	88	3	25	13
Mazzilli‡	.251	95	323	43	81	10	34	13
Nettles†	.232	122	405	47	94	18	55	1
Murcer†	.227	65	141	12	32	7	30	2
Cerone	.227	89	300	29	68	5	28	0
*Robertson	.220	44	118	16	26	2	9	0
Mayberry†	.218	86	248	27	54	10	30	0

Pitching	W	L	ERA	G	IP	H	BB	SO	Sv
Gossage	4	5	2.23	56	93	63	28	102	30
May†	6	6	2.89	41	106	109	14	85	3
LaRoche†	4	2	3.42	25	50	54	11	31	0
Frazier	4	4	3.47	63	111	103	39	69	1
Righetti†	11	10	3.79	33	183	155	108	163	1
Guidry†	14	8	3.81	34	222	216	69	162	0
Rawley†	11	10	4.06	47	164	165	54	111	3
Morgan	7	11	4.37	30	150	167	67	71	0
Erickson	8	8	4.61	23	111	142	29	49	1
Alexander	1	7	6.08	16	66	81	14	26	0

Oakland A's

Batting	Pct	G	AB	R	H	HR	RBI	SB
Burroughs	.277	113	285	42	79	16	48	1
R. Henderson	.267	149	536	119	143	10	51	130
Gross†	.251	129	386	43	97	9	41	3
Sexton	.245	69	139	19	34	2	14	16
Lopes	.242	128	450	58	109	11	42	28
Heath	.242	101	318	43	77	3	39	8
Meyer†	.240	120	383	28	92	8	59	1
Murphy†	.239	151	543	84	130	27	94	26
Johnson	.238	73	214	19	51	7	31	1
Armas	.233	138	536	58	125	28	89	2
Rudi	.212	71	193	21	41	5	18	0
Newman	.199	72	251	19	50	6	30	0
McKay‡	.198	78	212	25	42	4	17	6
Stanley	.193	101	228	33	44	2	17	0
Klutts	.178	55	157	10	28	0	14	0
Spencer†	.168	33	101	6	17	2	5	0

Pitching	W	L	ERA	G	IP	H	BB	SO	Sv
Underwood†	10	6	3.29	56	153	136	68	79	7
Beard	10	9	3.44	54	91	85	35	73	11
McCatty	6	3	3.99	21	128	124	70	66	0
Langford	11	16	4.21	32	237	265	49	79	0
Kingman	4	12	4.48	23	122	131	57	46	1
Norris	7	11	4.76	28	166	154	84	83	0
Owchinko†	2	4	5.21	54	102	111	52	67	3
Keough	11	18	5.72	34	209	233	101	75	0

Seattle Mariners

Batting	Pct	G	AB	R	H	HR	RBI	SB
Bochte†	.297	144	509	58	151	12	70	8
Zisk	.292	131	503	61	147	21	62	2
Essian	.275	48	153	14	42	3	20	2
Cowens	.270	146	560	72	151	20	78	11
*Castillo‡	.257	138	506	49	130	3	49	2
Simpson†	.257	105	296	39	76	2	23	8
Gray	.257	80	269	26	69	7	29	1
Sweet‡	.256	88	258	29	66	4	24	3
Henderson	.253	104	324	47	82	14	48	2
J. Cruz‡	.242	154	549	83	133	8	49	46
Brown‡	.241	79	245	29	59	4	17	28
T. Cruz	.230	136	492	44	113	16	57	2
*Maler	.226	64	221	18	50	4	26	0
*Serna	.225	65	169	15	38	3	8	0
Bulling	.221	56	154	17	34	1	8	2
Revering†	.202	98	257	25	52	8	32	0

Pitching	W	L	ERA	G	IP	H	BB	SO	Sv
Caudill	12	9	2.35	70	95	65	35	111	26
*Vande Berg†	9	4	2.37	78	76	54	32	60	5
*Stoddard	3	3	2.41	9	67	48	18	24	[illegible]
Clark†	5	2	2.75	37	114	104	58	70	[illegible]
Beattie	8	12	3.34	28	172	149	65	140	[illegible]
Bannister†	12	13	3.43	35	247	225	77	209	[illegible]
Stanton	2	4	4.16	56	71	69	21	49	7
Perry	10	12	4.40	32	216	245	54	116	0
Nelson	6	9	4.62	22	122	133	60	71	0
*Moore	7	14	5.36	28	144	159	79	73	0
Andersen	0	0	5.99	40	79	101	23	32	1

Texas Rangers

Batting	Pct	G	AB	R	H	HR	RBI	SB
Bell	.296	148	537	62	159	13	67	5
Grubb†	.279	103	308	35	86	3	26	0
*Wright‡	.264	150	557	69	147	11	50	3
Parrish	.264	128	440	59	116	17	62	5
Sample	.261	97	360	56	94	10	29	10
L. Johnson	.259	105	324	37	84	7	38	3
Sundberg	.251	139	470	37	118	10	47	2
*Richardt	.241	119	402	34	97	3	43	9
Wagner	.240	60	179	14	43	0	8	1
Stein	.239	85	184	14	44	1	16	0
*Hostetler	.232	113	418	53	97	22	67	2
Putnam†	.230	43	122	14	28	2	9	0
Flynn	.211	88	270	13	57	0	19	6
Dent	.193	105	306	27	59	1	23	0

Pitching	W	L	ERA	G	IP	H	BB	SO	Sv
Schmidt	4	6	3.20	33	109	118	25	69	6
Darwin	10	8	3.44	56	89	95	37	61	7
Matlack†	7	7	3.53	33	147	158	37	78	1
Hough	16	13	3.95	34	228	217	72	128	0
Tanana†	7	18	4.21	30	194	199	55	87	0
Mirabella†	1	1	4.80	40	50	46	22	29	3
Butcher	1	5	4.87	18	94	102	34	39	1
Comer	1	6	5.10	37	97	133	36	23	6
Honeycutt†	5	17	5.27	30	164	201	54	64	0

Toronto Blue Jays

Batting	Pct	G	AB	R	H	HR	RBI	SB
Garcia	.310	147	597	89	185	5	42	54
Bonnell	.293	140	437	59	128	6	49	14
Iorg	.285	129	417	45	119	1	36	[illegible]
Powell†	.275	112	265	43	73	3	26	[illegible]
Nordhagen	.270	72	185	12	50	1	20	[illegible]
Upshaw†	.267	160	580	77	155	21	75	[illegible]
Whitt†	.261	105	284	28	74	11	42	[illegible]
*Barfield	.246	139	394	54	97	18	58	[illegible]
Mulliniks†	.244	112	311	32	76	4	35	[illegible]
Martinez	.242	96	260	26	63	10	37	[illegible]
Griffin‡	.241	162	539	57	130	1	48	10
Moseby†	.236	147	487	51	115	9	52	11
Woods†	.234	85	201	20	47	3	24	[illegible]
Roberts	.230	71	178	13	41	2	11	[illegible]

Pitching	W	L	ERA	G	IP	H	BB	SO	Sv
Jackson	8	8	3.06	48	97	77	31	71	[illegible]
Murray	8	7	3.16	56	111	115	32	60	11
McLaughlin	8	6	3.21	44	70	54	30	49	[illegible]
Stieb	17	14	3.25	38	288	271	75	141	[illegible]
Clancy	16	14	3.71	40	266	251	77	139	[illegible]
Leal	12	15	3.93	38	249	250	79	111	0
*Gott	5	10	4.43	30	136	134	66	82	0
Bomback	1	5	6.03	16	59	87	25	22	0
Garvin†	1	1	7.25	32	58	81	26	35	0

Members of National Baseball Hall of Fame and Museum

The shrine of organized baseball, dedicated June 12, 1939, is located in Cooperstown, N. Y.

Aaron, Hank
Alexander, Grover Cleveland
Anson, Cap
Averill, Earl
Appling, Luke
Baker, Home Run
Bancroft, Dave
Banks, Ernie
Barrow, Edward G.
Beckley, Jake
Bell, Cool Papa
Bender, Chief
Berra, Yogi
Bottomley, Jim
Boudreau, Lou
Bresnahan, Roger
Brouthers, Dan
Brown (Three Finger), Mordecai
Bulkeley, Morgan C.
Burkett, Jesse C.
Campanella, Roy
Carey, Max
Cartwright, Alexander
Chadwick, Henry
Chance, Frank
Chandler, Happy
Charleston, Oscar
Chesbro, John
Clarke, Fred
Clarkson, John
Clemente, Roberto
Cobb, Ty
Cochrane, Mickey
Collins, Eddie
Collins, James
Combs, Earle
Comiskey, Charles A.
Conlan, Jocko
Connolly, Thomas H.
Connor, Roger
Coveleski, Stan
Crawford, Sam
Cronin, Joe
Cummings, Candy
Cuyler, Kiki
Dean, Dizzy
Delahanty, Ed
Dickey, Bill
DiHigo, Martin
DiMaggio, Joe
Duffy, Hugh
Evans, Billy
Evers, John
Ewing, Buck
Faber, Urban
Feller, Bob
Flick, Elmer H.
Ford, Whitey
Foster, Andrew
Foxx, Jimmy
Frick, Ford
Frisch, Frank
Galvin, Pud
Gehrig, Lou
Gehringer, Charles
Gibson, Bob
Gibson, Josh
Giles, Warren
Gomez, Lefty
Goslin, Goose
Greenberg, Hank
Griffith, Clark
Grimes, Burleigh
Grove, Lefty
Hafey, Chick
Haines, Jesee
Hamilton, Bill
Harridge, Will
Harris, Bucky
Hartnett, Gabby
Heilmann, Harry
Herman, Billy
Hooper, Harry
Hornsby, Rogers
Hoyt, Waite
Hubbard, Cal
Hubbell, Carl
Huggins, Miller
Irvin, Monte
Jackson, Travis
Jennings, Hugh
Johnson, Byron
Johnson, William (Rudy)
Johnson, Walter
Joss, Addie
Kaline, Al
Keefe, Timothy
Keeler, William
Kelley, Joe
Kelly, George
Kelly, King
Kiner, Ralph
Klein, Chuck
Klem, Bill
Koufax, Sandy
Lajoie, Napoleon
Landis, Kenesaw M.
Lemon, Bob
Leonard, Buck
Lindstrom, Fred
Lloyd, Pop
Lopez, Al
Lyons, Ted
Mack, Connie
MacPhail, Larry
Mantle, Mickey
Manush, Henry
Maranville, Rabbit
Marquard, Rube
Mathews, Eddie
Mathewson, Christy
Mays, Willie
McCarthy, Joe
McCarthy, Thomas
McGinnity, Joe
McGraw, John
McKechnie, Bill
Medwick, Joe
Mize, Johnny
Musial, Stan
Nichols, Kid
O'Rourke, James
Ott, Mel
Paige, Satchel
Pennock, Herb
Plank, Ed
Radbourne, Charlie
Rice, Sam
Rickey, Branch
Rixey, Eppa
Roberts, Robin
Robinson, Frank
Robinson, Jackie
Robinson, Wilbert
Roush, Edd
Ruffing, Red
Rusie, Amos
Ruth, Babe
Schalk, Ray
Sewell, Joe
Simmons, Al
Sisler, George
Snider, Duke
Spahn, Warren
Spalding, Albert
Speaker, Tris
Stengel, Casey
Terry, Bill
Thompson, Sam
Tinker, Joe
Traynor, Pie
Vance, Dazzy
Waddell, Rube
Wagner, Honus
Wallace, Roderick
Walsh, Ed.
Waner, Lloyd
Waner, Paul
Ward, John
Weiss, George
Welch, Mickey
Wheat, Zach
Williams, Ted
Wilson, Hack
Wright, George
Wright, Harry
Wynn, Early
Yawkey, Tom
Young, Cy
Youngs, Ross

All-Star Baseball Games, 1933-1982

Year	Winner	Score	Location	Year	Winner	Score	Location
1933	American	**4-2**	Chicago	1959	American	**5-3**	Los Angeles
1934	American	**9-7**	New York	1960	National	**5-3**	Kansas City
1935	American	**4-1**	Cleveland	1960	National	**6-0**	New York
1936	National	**4-3**	Boston	1961	National (3)	**5-4**	San Francisco
1937	American	**8-3**	Washington	1961	Called-Rain	**1-1**	Boston
1938	National	**4-1**	Cincinnati	1962	National (3)	**3-1**	Washington
1939	American	**3-1**	New York	1962	American	**9-4**	Chicago
1940	National	**4-0**	St. Louis	1963	National	**5-3**	Cleveland
1941	American	**7-5**	Detroit	1964	National	**7-4**	New York
1942	American	**3-1**	New York	1965	National	**6-5**	Minnesota
1943*	American	**5-3**	Philadelphia	1966	National (3)	**2-1**	St. Louis
1944*	National	**7-1**	Pittsburgh	1967	National (4)	**2-1**	Anaheim
1945	(not played)			1968*	National	**1-0**	Houston
1946	American	**12-0**	Boston	1969	National	**9-3**	Washington
1947	American	**2-1**	Chicago	1970*	National (2)	**5-4**	Cincinnati
1948	American	**5-2**	St. Louis	1971*	American	**6-4**	Detroit
1949	American	**11-7**	New York	1972*	National	**4-3**	Atlanta
1950	National (1)	**4-3**	Chicago	1973*	National	**7-1**	Kansas City
1951	National	**8-3**	Detroit	1974*	National	**7-2**	Pittsburgh
1952	National	**3-2**	Philadelphia	1975*	National	**6-3**	Milwaukee
1953	National	**5-1**	Cincinnati	1976*	National	**7-1**	Philadelphia
1954	American	**11-9**	Cleveland	1977*	National	**7-5**	New York
1955	National (2)	**6-5**	Milwaukee	1978*	National	**7-3**	San Diego
1956	National	**7-3**	Washington	1979*	National	**7-6**	Seattle
1957	American	**6-5**	St. Louis	1980*	National	**4-2**	Los Angeles
1958	American	**4-3**	Baltimore	1981*	National	**5-4**	Cleveland
1959	National	**5-4**	Pittsburgh	1982*	National	**4-1**	Montreal

(1) 14 innings, (2) 12 innings, (3) 10 innings, (4) 15 innings *Night game.

Major League Perfect Games Since 1900

Year	Player	Clubs	Score	Year	Player	Clubs	Score
1904	Cy Young	Boston vs. Phil. (AL)	3-0	1964	Jim Bunning	Phil. vs. N.Y. Mets (NL)	6-0
1908	Addie Joss	Cleveland vs. Chicago (AL)	1-0	1965	Sandy Koufax	Los Angeles vs. Chic. (NL)	1-0
1917	Ernie Shore (a)	Boston vs. Wash. (AL)	4-0	1968	Jim Hunter	Oakland vs. Minn. (AL)	4-0
1922	Charles Robertson	Chicago vs. Detroit (AL)	2-0	1981	Len Barker	Cleveland vs. Toronto (AL)	3-0
1956	Don Larsen (b)	N.Y. Yankees vs. Brooklyn	2-0				

(a) Babe Ruth, the starting pitcher, was ejected from the game after walking the first batter. Shore replaced him and the base-runner was out stealing. Shore retired the next 26 batters. (b) World Series.

First Game

Milwaukee	ab	r	h	bi	St. Louis	ab	r	h	bi
Molitor 3b	6	1	5	2	Herr 2b	3	0	0	0
Yount ss	6	1	4	2	L.Smith lf	4	0	0	0
Cooper 1b	4	1	0	0	Hernandez lb	4	0	0	0
Simmons c	5	1	2	1	Hendrick rf	4	0	0	0
Oglivie lf	4	1	0	0	Tenace dh	3	0	0	0
Thomas cf	4	0	1	1	Porter c	3	0	2	0
Howell dh	2	0	0	0	Green cf	3	0	0	0
Money dh	2	1	1	1	Oberfell 3b	3	0	1	0
Moore rf	5	2	2	0	O.Smith ss	3	0	0	0
Gantner 2b	4	2	2	2					
Totals	42	10	17	9	**Totals**	30	0	3	0

Milwaukee.	2	0	0	1	1	2	0	0	4—10
St. Louis	0	0	0	0	0	0	0	0	0— 0

E - Hernandez. DP - St Louis 1. LOB - Milwaukee 10, St. Louis 4. 2B - Porter, Moore, Yount. 3B - Gantner. HR - Simmons (1). S - Gantner.

Milwaukee	ip	h	r	er	bb	so
Caldwell W, 1-0	9	3	0	0	1	3
St. Louis						
Forsch L, 0-1	5 2/3	10	6	4	1	1
Kaat	1 1/3	1	0	0	1	1
LaPoint	1 2/3	3	2	2	1	0
Lahti	1/3	3	2	2	0	1

HBP - Howell by Forsch. T - 2:30. A - 53,723.

How runs were scored—Two in Brewers first: Yount singled. Cooper walked. Oglivie reached first on an error scoring Yount. Thomas singled scoring Cooper.

One in Brewers fourth: Moore doubled. Molitor singled scoring Moore.

One in Brewers fifth: Simmons hit a home run.

Two in Brewers sixth: Gantner and Molitor singled. Yount doubled scoring Gantner and Molitor.

Four in Brewers ninth: highlighted by a 2-run triple by Gantner.

Second Game

Milwaukee	ab	r	h	bi	St. Louis	ab	r	h	bi
Molitor 3b	5	1	2	0	Herr 2b	3	1	1	1
Yount ss	4	1	1	1	Oberkfell 3b	3	1	2	1
Cooper 1b	5	0	3	1	Tenace ph	1	0	0	0
Simmons c	3	1	1	1	Ramsey 3b	0	0	0	0
Oglivie lf	4	0	1	0	Hernandez 1b	3	0	0	0
Thomas cf	3	0	0	0	Hendrick rf	3	2	0	0
Howell dh	4	1	0	0	Porter c	4	0	2	2
Moore rf	4	0	2	1	L.Smith lf	3	0	0	0
Gantner 2b	3	0	0	0	lorg dh	2	0	1	0
					Green ph	1	0	0	0
					Braun ph	0	0	0	1
					McGee cf	4	1	0	0
					O.Smith ss	4	0	2	0
Totals	35	4	10	4	**Totals**	31	5	8	5

Milwaukee	0	1	2	0	1	0	0	0	0—4
St. Louis	0	0	2	0	0	2	0	1	x—5

E - Oglivie. DP - St. Louis 1. LOB - Milwaukee 8, St. Louis 7. 2B - Moore, Herr, Yount, Porter, Cooper. HR - Simmons (2). SB - Molitor (1), McGee (1), Oberkfell (1), O. Smith (1).

Milwaukee	ip	h	r	er	bb	so
Sutton	6	5	4	4	1	3
McClure L,0-1	1 1/3	2	1	1	2	2
Ladd	2/3	1	0	0	2	0
St. Louis						
Stuper	4	6	4	4	3	3
Kaat	2/3	1	0	0	0	0
Bair	2	1	0	0	0	3
Sutter W,1-0	2 1/3	2	0	0	1	1

WP - Stuper 2. T - 2:54. A - 53,723.

How runs were scored—One in Brewers second: Howell walked. Moore doubled scoring Howell.

Two in Brewers third: Molitor singled, stole second, went to third on a wild pitch, and scored on Yount's groundout. Simmons hit a home run.

Two in Cardinals third: lorg singled and was forced at second by McGee. Herr doubled scoring McGee. Oberkfell singled scoring Herr.

One in Brewers fifth: Yount doubled. Cooper singled scoring Yount.

Two in Cardinals sixth: Oberkfell singled. Hendrick walked. Porter doubled scoring Oberkfell and Hendrick.

One in Cardinals eighth: Hernandez walked and was forced at second by Hendrick. Porter singled. L. Smith walked. Braun walked scoring Hendrick.

Third Game

St. Louis	ab	r	h	bi	Milwaukee	ab	r	h	bi
Herr 2b	5	0	0	0	Molitor 3b	4	0	0	0
Oberkfell 3b	4	0	0	0	Yount ss	3	1	0	0
Hernandez 1b	4	0	0	0	Cooper 1b	4	1	1	2
Hendrick rf	2	1	1	0	Simmons c	4	0	1	0
Porter c	4	0	0	0	Oglivie lf	4	0	0	0
L.Smith lf	4	2	2	0	Thomas cf	4	0	1	0
Green lf	0	0	0	0	Howell dh	2	0	0	0
lorg dh	4	1	1	0	Money dh	1	0	0	0
McGee cf	3	2	2	4	Moore rf	3	0	0	0
O.Smith ss	3	0	0	1	Gantner 2b	3	0	2	0
Totals	33	6	6	5	**Totals**	32	2	5	2

St. Louis	0	0	0	0	3	0	2	0	1—6
Milwaukee.	0	0	0	0	0	0	0	2	0—2

E - Cooper, Gantner, Simmons, Hernandez. DP - St. Louis 1 LOB - St. Louis 4, Milwaukee 6. 2B - Gantner, L. Smith, lorg. 3B - L. Smith. HRs - McGee 2 (2), Cooper (1).

St. Louis	ip	h	r	er	bb	so
Andujar (W, 1-0)	6 1/3	3	0	0	1	3
Kaat	1/3	1	0	0	0	1
Bair	0	0	0	0	1	0
Sutter (S, 1)	2 1/3	1	2	2	1	1
Milwaukee						
Vuckovich (L, 0-1)	8 2/3	6	6	4	3	1
McClure	1/3	0	0	0	0	0

Hendrick reached base on catcher's interference in the 9th. T - 2:53. A - 56,556.

How runs were scored—Three in Cardinals fifth: L. Smith doubled. lorg reached first on an error. McGee hit a home run.

Two in Cardinals seventh: L. Smith tripled and scored on an error. McGee hit a home run.

Two in Brewers eighth: Yount walked. Cooper hit a home run.

One in Cardinals ninth: 0. Smith walked with the bases loaded.

Fourth Game

St. Louis	ab	r	h	bi	Milwaukee	ab	r	h	bi
Herr 2b	4	0	0	2	Molitor 3b	4	1	0	0
Oberkfell 3b	2	2	1	0	Yount ss	4	1	2	2
Tenace ph	1	0	0	0	Cooper 1b	4	1	2	1
Hernandez 1b	4	0	0	0	Simmons c	2	0	0	0
Hendrick rf	4	0	1	1	Thomas cf	4	0	1	2
Porter c	3	0	1	0	Oglivie lf	3	1	1	0
L. Smith lf	4	1	1	0	Money dh	4	2	2	0
lorg dh	4	0	2	1	Moore rf	4	0	1	0
Green pr	0	0	0	0	Gantner 2b	4	1	1	1
McGee cf	4	1	1	0					
O. Smith ss	3	1	1	0					
Totals	33	5	8	4	**Totals**	33	7	10	6

St. Louis	1	3	0	0	0	1	0	0	0—5
Milwaukee.	0	0	0	0	1	0	6	0	x—7

E - Gantner, Yount, LaPoint. DP - St. Louis 2, Milwaukee 2 LOB - St. Louis 6, Milwaukee 6. 2B - Oberkfell, Money, L. Smith lorg, Gantner. 3B - Oglivie. SB - McGee, Oberkfell. SF - Herr.

St. Louis	ip	h	r	er	bb	so
LaPoint	6 2/3	7	4	1	1	3
Bair L,0-1	0	1	2	2	1	0
Kaat	0	1	1	1	1	0
Lahti	1 1/3	1	0	0	1	0
Milwaukee						
Haas	5 1/3	7	5	4	2	3
Slaton W,1-0	2	1	0	0	2	1
McClure S,1	1 2/3	0	0	0	0	2

WP - Haas, Kaat. T - 3:04. A - 56,560.

How runs were scored—One in Cardinals first: Oberkfe doubled. Hendrick singled scoring Oberkfell.

Three in Cardinals second: McGee singled. O. Smith walkec Both runners advanced on a wild pitch. Herr hit a sacrifice fl scoring McGee and Smith. Oberkfell walked and stole seconc Hernandez reached first on an error scoring Oberkfell.

One in Brewers fifth: Money doubled. Moore singled. Gantne hit into a double play scoring Money.

One in Cardinals sixth: L. Smith doubled. lorg doubled scorin Smith.

Six in Brewers seventh: Oglivie reached first on an erro Money singled. Gantner doubled scoring Oglivie. Molitor walkec Yount singled scoring Money and Gantner. Cooper singled scor ing Molitor. Simmons walked. Thomas singled scoring Yount an Cooper.

Fifth Game

St. Louis	ab	r	h	bi	Milwaukee	ab	r	h	bi
L.Smith dh	5	0	2	0	Molitor 3b	4	1	1	1
Green lf	5	2	2	0	Yount ss	4	2	4	1
Hernandez 1b	4	1	3	2	Cooper 1b	4	0	1	1
Hendrick rf	5	0	3	2	Simmons c	3	0	0	1
Porter c	5	0	1	0	Oglivie lf	4	1	2	0
Ramsey pr	0	0	0	0	Thomas cf	4	0	0	0
McGee cf	5	0	1	0	Money dh	3	1	0	0
Oberkfell 3b	4	0	3	0	Moore rf	4	1	2	1
Tenace ph	1	0	0	0	Gantner 2b	4	0	1	1
Herr 2b	4	0	0	0					
O.Smith ss	3	1	0	0					
Totals	41	4	15	4	**Totals**	34	6	11	6

St. Louis	0	0	1	0	0	0	1	0	2—4
Milwaukee	1	0	1	0	1	0	1	2	x—6

E - Forsch, Gantner, Herr. DP - St. Louis 2, Milwaukee 1. LOB - St. Louis 12, Milwaukee 7. 2B - Hernandez 2, Yount, Moore, Green. 3B - Green. HR - Yount (1). SB - L.Smith.

St. Louis	ip	h	r	er	bb	so
Forsch L,0-2	7	8	4	3	2	3
Sutter	1	3	2	2	1	2
Milwaukee						
Caldwell W,2-0	8 1/3	14	4	4	2	3
McClure S,2	2/3	1	0	0	0	1

T - 3:02. A - 56,562.

How runs were scored—One in Brewers first: Yount and Cooper singled. Both advanced on a wild pitch. Simmons grounded out scoring Yount.

One in Cardinals third: Green tripled. Hernandez doubled scoring Green.

One in Brewers third: Molitor walked. Yount doubled. Cooper grounded out scoring Molitor.

One in Brewers fifth: Moore doubled. Molitor singled scoring Moore.

One in Cardinals seventh: Hendrick singled scoring O. Smith.

One in Brewers seventh: Yount hit a home run.

Two in Brewers eighth: Oglivie singled. Money walked. Moore singled scoring Oglivie. Gantner singled scoring Money.

Two in Cardinals ninth: Green doubled. Hernendez doubled scoring Green. Hendrick singled scoring Hernandez.

Sixth Game

Milwaukee	ab	r	h	bi	St. Louis	ab	r	h	bi
Molitor 3b	4	0	1	0	L.Smith lf	3	1	1	0
Yount ss	4	0	0	0	Green lf	1	1	0	0
Cooper 1b	4	0	0	0	Oberkfell 3b	5	1	0	0
Simmons c	2	0	0	0	Hernandez 1b	5	2	2	4
Yost c	0	0	0	0	Hendrick rf	5	2	2	1
Oglivie lf	4	0	1	0	Porter c	4	1	1	2
Thomas cf	3	0	0	0	Brummer c	0	0	0	0
Edwards cf	0	0	0	0	Iorg dh	4	3	3	0
Money dh	3	0	0	0	McGee cf	4	1	1	1
Moore rf	3	0	1	0	Herr 2b	3	1	2	2
Gantner 2b	3	1	1	0	O.Smith ss	4	0	0	0
Totals	30	1	4	0	**Totals**	38	13	12	10

Milwaukee	0	0	0	0	0	0	0	0	1— 1
St. Louis	0	2	0	3	2	6	0	0	x—13

E - Yount 2, Gantner 2, Oberkfell. DP - St. Louis 2. LOB - Milwaukee 4, St. Louis 3. 2B - Iorg 2, Herr, Gantner. 3B - Iorg. HR - Porter (1), Hernandez (1). SB - L. Smith. S - Herr.

Milwaukee	ip	h	r	er	bb	so
Sutton L, 0-1	4 1/3	7	7	5	0	2
Slaton	2/3	0	0	0	0	0
Medich	2	5	6	4	1	0
Bernard	1	0	0	0	0	1
St. Louis						
Stuper W, 1-0	9	4	1	1	2	2

Wild pitch - Medich 2, Stuper. Balk - Sutton. T - 2:21. A - 53,723.

How runs were scored—Two in Cardinals second: Iorg doubled. McGee reached first on an error scoring Iorg. Herr doubled scoring McGee.

Three in Cardinals fourth: Hendrick singled. Porter hit a home run. Iorg tripled. Herr hit a sacrifice bunt scoring Iorg.

Two in Cardinals fifth: L. Smith singled. Hernandez hit a home run.

Six in Cardinals sixth: highlighted by a two-run single by Hernandez.

One in Brewers ninth: Gantner scored the lone Brewer run.

Seventh Game

Milwaukee	ab	r	h	bi	St. Louis	ab	r	h	bi
Molitor 3b	4	1	2	0	L.Smith lf	5	2	3	1
Yount ss	4	0	1	0	Oberkfell 3b	3	0	0	0
Cooper 1b	3	0	1	1	Tenace ph	0	0	0	0
Simmons c	4	0	0	0	Ramsey 3b	1	1	0	0
Oglivie lf	4	1	1	1	Hernandez 1b	3	1	2	2
Thomas cf	4	0	0	0	Hendrick rf	5	0	2	1
Howell dh	3	0	0	0	Porter c	5	0	1	1
Moore rf	3	0	1	0	Iorg dh	3	0	2	0
Gantner 2b	3	1	1	0	Green ph	0	0	0	0
					Braun dh	2	0	1	1
					McGee cf	5	1	1	0
					Herr 2b	3	0	1	0
					O.Smith ss	4	1	2	0
Totals	32	3	7	2	**Totals**	39	6	15	6

Milwaukee	0	0	0	0	1	2	0	0	0—3
St. Louis	0	0	0	1	0	3	0	2	x—6

E - Andujar. LOB - Milwaukee 3, St. Louis 13. 2b - Gantner, L.Smith 2. HR - Oglivie (1). SF - Cooper.

Milwaukee	ip	h	r	er	bb	so
Vuckovich	5 1/3	10	3	3	2	3
McClure L, 0-2	1/3	2	1	1	1	0
Haas	2	1	2	2	1	1
Caldwell	1/3	2	0	0	0	0
St. Louis						
Andujar W, 2-0	7	7	3	2	0	1
Sutter S, 2	2	0	0	0	0	2

T - 2:50. A - 53,723.

How runs were scored—One in Cardinals fourth: McGee and Herr singled. L. Smith singled scoring McGee.

One in Brewers fifth: Oglivie hit a home run.

Two in Brewers sixth: Gantner doubled. Molitor singled. Gantner scored on an error. Yount singled. Cooper hit a sacrifice fly scoring Molitor.

Three in Cardinals sixth: O. Smith singled. L. Smith doubled. Tenace walked. Hernandez singled scoring O. Smith and L. Smith. Hendrick singled scoring Ramsey who had run for Tenace.

Two in Cardinals eighth: L. Smith doubled. Hernandez walked. Porter singled scoring Smith. Braun singled scoring Hernandez.

Most Home Runs in One Season

Homers	Player, team	Year	Homers	Player, team	Year
61	Roger Maris, New York (AL)	1961	51	Ralph Kiner, Pittsburgh (NL)	1947
60	Babe Ruth, New York (AL)	1927	51	John Mize, New York (NL)	1947
59	Babe Ruth, New York (AL)	1921	51	Willie Mays, New York (NL)	1955
58	Jimmy Foxx, Philadelphia (AL)	1932	50	Jimmy Foxx, Boston (AL)	1938
58	Hank Greenberg, Detroit (AL)	1938	49	Babe Ruth, New York (AL)	1930
56	Hack Wilson, Chicago (NL)	1930	49	Lou Gehrig, New York (AL)	1934
54	Babe Ruth, New York (AL)	1920	49	Lou Gehrig, New York (AL)	1936
54	Babe Ruth, New York (AL)	1928	49	Ted Kluszewski, Cincinnati (NL)	1954
54	Ralph Kiner, Pittsburgh (NL)	1949	49	Willie Mays, San Francisco (NL)	1962
54	Mickey Mantle, New York (AL)	1961	49	Harmon Killebrew, Minnesota (AL)	1964
52	Mickey Mantle, New York (AL)	1956	49	Frank Robinson, Baltimore (AL)	1966
52	Willie Mays, San Francisco (NL)	1965	49	Harmon Killebrew, Minnesota (AL)	1969
52	George Foster, Cincinnati (NL)	1977			

World Series Results, 1903-1982

1903 Boston AL 5, Pittsburgh NL 3
1904 No series
1905 New York NL 4, Philadelphia AL 1
1906 Chicago AL 4, Chicago NL 2
1907 Chicago NL 4, Detroit AL 0, 1 tie
1908 Chicago NL 4, Detroit AL 1
1909 Pittsburgh NL 4, Detroit AL 3
1910 Philadelphia AL 4, Chicago NL 1
1911 Philadelphia AL 4, New York NL 2
1912 Boston AL 4, New York NL 3, 1 tie
1913 Philadelphia AL 4, New York NL 1
1914 Boston NL 4, Philadelphia AL 0
1915 Boston AL 4, Philadelphia NL 1
1916 Boston AL 4, Brooklyn NL 1
1917 Chicago AL 4, New York NL 2
1918 Boston AL 4, Chicago NL 2
1919 Cincinnati NL 5, Chicago AL 3
1920 Cleveland AL 5, Brooklyn NL 2
1921 New York NL 5, New York AL 3
1922 New York NL 4, New York AL 0, 1 tie
1923 New York AL 4, New York NL 2
1924 Washington AL 4, New York NL 3
1925 Pittsburgh NL 4, Washington AL 3
1926 St. Louis NL 4, New York AL 3
1927 New York AL 4, Pittsburgh NL 0
1928 New York AL 4, St. Louis NL 0
1929 Philadelphia AL 4, Chicago NL 1
1930 Philadelphia AL 4, St. Louis NL 2
1931 St. Louis NL 4, Philadelphia AL 3
1932 New York AL 4, Chicago NL 0
1933 New York NL 4, Washington AL 1
1934 St. Louis NL 4, Detroit AL 3
1935 Detroit AL 4, Chicago NL 2
1936 New York AL 4, New York NL 2
1937 New York AL 4, New York NL 1
1938 New York AL 4, Chicago NL 0
1939 New York AL 4, Cincinnati NL 0
1940 Cincinnati NL 4, Detroit AL 3
1941 New York AL 4, Brooklyn NL 1
1942 St. Louis NL 4, New York AL 1
1943 New York AL 4, St. Louis NL 1
1944 St. Louis NL 4, St. Louis AL 2
1945 Detroit AL 4, Chicago NL 3
1946 St. Louis NL 4, Boston AL 3
1947 New York AL 4, Brooklyn NL 3
1948 Cleveland AL 4, Boston NL 2
1949 New York AL 4, Brooklyn NL 1
1950 New York AL 4, Philadelphia NL 0
1951 New York AL 4, New York NL 2
1952 New York AL 4, Brooklyn NL 3
1953 New York AL 4, Brooklyn NL 2
1954 New York NL 4, Cleveland AL 0
1955 Brooklyn NL 4, New York AL 3
1956 New York AL 4, Brooklyn NL 3
1957 Milwaukee NL 4, New York AL 3
1958 New York AL 4, Milwaukee NL 3
1959 Los Angeles NL 4, Chicago AL 2
1960 Pittsburgh NL 4, New York AL 3
1961 New York AL 4, Cincinnati NL 1
1962 New York AL 4, San Francisco NL 3
1963 Los Angeles NL 4, New York AL 0
1964 St. Louis NL 4, New York AL 3
1965 Los Angeles NL 4, Minnesota AL 3
1966 Baltimore AL 4, Los Angeles NL 0
1967 St. Louis NL 4, Boston AL 3
1968 Detroit AL 4, St. Louis NL 3
1969 New York NL 4, Baltimore AL 1
1970 Baltimore AL 4, Cincinnati NL 1
1971 Pittsburgh NL 4, Baltimore AL 3
1972 Oakland AL 4, Cincinnati NL 3
1973 Oakland AL 4, New York NL 3
1974 Oakland AL 4, Los Angeles NL 1
1975 Cincinnati NL 4, Boston AL 3
1976 Cincinnati NL 4, New York AL 0
1977 New York AL 4, Los Angeles NL 2
1978 New York AL 4, Los Angeles NL 2
1979 Pittsburgh NL 4, Baltimore AL 3
1980 Philadelphia NL 4, Kansas City AL 2
1981 Los Angeles NL 4, New York AL 2
1982 St. Louis NL 4, Milwaukee AL 3

All-Time Home Run Leaders

Player	HR	Player	HR	Player	HR	Player	HR	Player	HR
Hank Aaron	755	Lou Gehrig	493	Rocky Colavito	374	Joe Adcock	336	Robert Johnson	288
Babe Ruth	714	Stan Musial	475	Gil Hodges	370	Bobby Bonds	332	Hank Sauer	288
Willie Mays	660	Willie Stargell	475	Ralph Kiner	369	Hank Greenberg	331	Del Ennis	288
Frank Robinson	586	Reggie Jackson	464	Tony Perez	363	Dave Kingman	329	Rusty Staub	287
Harmon Killebrew	573	Carl Yastrzemski	442	Joe DiMaggio	361	Willie Horton	325	Frank Thomas	286
Mickey Mantle	536	Billy Williams	426	John Mize	359	Roy Sievers	318	Ken Boyer	282
Jimmy Foxx	534	Duke Snider	407	Yogi Berra	358	Reggie Smith	314	Ted Kluszewski	279
Ted Williams	521	Al Kaline	399	Lee May	354	Graig Nettles	313	Rudy York	277
Willie McCovey	521	Frank Howard	382	Dick Allen	351	Al Simmons	307	Roger Maris	275
Ed Mathews	512	Orlando Cepeda	379	Mike Schmidt	349	Rogers Hornsby	302	George Scott	271
Ernie Banks	512	Johnny Bench	377	Ron Santo	342	Chuck Klein	300	Brooks Robinson	268
Mel Ott	511	Norm Cash	377	John (Boog) Powell	339	Jim Wynn	291	Vic Wertz	266

Major League Attendance

National League

Club	1982 Attendance	1982 Average	1981 Average	Average gain/loss
Atlanta	1,801,985	23,102	10,927	+ 12,175
Chicago	1,249,278	15,814	10,101	+ 5,713
Cincinnati	1,326,534	16,792	21,446	− 4,654
Houston	1,559,005	19,488	26,426	− 6,938
Los Angeles	3,608,881	45,111	42,523	+ 2,588
Montreal	2,318,292	29,722	29,511	+ 211
New York	1,320,968	17,613	14,372	+ 3,241
Philadelphia	2,376,394	30,862	30,347	+ 515
Pittsburgh	1,030,830	13,387	11,287	+ 2,100
St. Louis	2,111,906	26,399	19,061	+ 7,338
San Diego	1,607,566	20,349	9,614	+ 10,735
San Francisco	1,200,948	15,597	12,398	+ 3,199
Totals	**21,512,587**	**22,910**	**20,030**	**+ 2,880**

American League

Club	1982 Attendance	1982 Average	1981 Average	Average gain/loss
Baltimore	1,609,702	21,753	19,325	+ 2,428
Boston	1,931,853	24,767	20,392	+ 4,375
California	2,807,360	34,659	26,695	+ 7,964
Chicago	1,567,787	20,629	20,142	+ 487
Cleveland	1,043,573	13,553	13,498	+ 55
Detroit	1,636,058	21,527	21,280	+ 247
Kansas City	2,317,225	28,965	27,221	+ 1,744
Milwaukee	1,978,896	25,370	18,214	+ 7,156
Minnesota	921,219	11,373	7,951	+ 3,422
New York	2,018,253	26,910	32,287	− 5,377
Oakland	1,735,493	22,250	25,570	− 3,320
Seattle	1,070,406	13,215	11,362	+ 1,853
Texas	1,154,432	14,800	15,742	− 942
Toronto	1,275,978	16,571	14,806	+ 1,765
Totals	**23,068,235**	**21,164**	**19,401**	**+ 1,763**

Major League Franchise Shifts and Additions

1953—Boston Braves (N. L.) became Milwaukee Braves.

1954—St. Louis Browns (A. L.) became Baltimore Orioles.

1955—Philadelphia Athletics (A. L.) became Kansas City Athletics.

1958—New York Giants (N. L.) became San Francisco Giants.

1958—Brooklyn Dodgers (N. L.) became Los Angeles Dodgers.

1961—Washington Senators (A. L.) became Minnesota Twins.

1961—Los Angeles Angels (later renamed the California Angels) enfranchised by the American League.

1961—Washington Senators enfranchised by the American League (a new team, replacing the former Washington club, whose franchise was moved to Minneapolis-St. Paul).

1962—Houston Colt .45's (later renamed the Houston Astros) enfranchised by the National League.

1962—New York Mets enfranchised by the National League.

1966—Milwaukee Braves (N. L.) became Atlanta Braves.

1968—Kansas City Athletics (A. L.) became Oakland Athletics.

1969—Two major leagues each added two teams for totals of 12 and split into two divisions. American League additions: Kansas City Royals and Seattle Pilots; National League additions: Montreal Expos and San Diego Padres.

1970—Seattle franchise shifted to Milwaukee. Club was renamed Milwaukee Brewers.

1971—Washington franchise to Dallas-Fort Worth, with field at Arlington, Tex.

1977—Toronto and Seattle enfranchised by the American League.

Major League Leaders in 1982

National League

Home Runs

Kingman, New York, 37; Murphy, Atlanta, 36; Schmidt, Philadelphia, 35; Horner, Atlanta, 32; Guerrero, Los Angeles, 32.

RBIs

Oliver, Montreal, 109; Murphy, Atlanta, 109; Buckner, Chicago, 105; Hendrick, St. Louis, 104; Clark, San Francisco, 103.

Stolen Bases

Raines, Montreal, 78; L. Smith, St. Louis, 68; Moreno, Pittsburgh, 60; Wilson, New York, 58; S. Sax, Los Angeles, 49.

Runs

L. Smith, St. Louis, 120; Murphy, Atlanta, 113; Schmidt, Philadelphia, 108; Dawson, Montreal, 107; Sandberg, Chicago, 103.

Hits

Oliver, Montreal, 204; Buckner, Chicago, 201; Dawson, Montreal, 183; J. Ray, Pittsburgh, 182; L. Smith, St. Louis, 182.

Doubles

Oliver, Montreal, 43; T. Kennedy, San Diego, 42; Dawson, Montreal, 37; Knight, Houston, 36; Buckner, Chicago, 35; L. Smith, St. Louis, 35; Cedeno, Cincinnati, 35; Garvey, Los Angeles, 35.

Triples

Thon, Houston, 10; Wilson, New York, 9; Moreno, Pittsburgh, 9; Puhl, Houston, 9; 6 tied with 8.

Pitching (17 Decisions)

P. Niekro, Atlanta, 17-4, .810, 3.61; Rogers, Montreal, 19-8, .704, 2.40; Carlton, Philadelphia, 23-11, .676, 3.10; Breining, San Francisco, 11-6, .647, 3.08; Lollar, San Diego, 16-9, .640, 3.13; Candelaria, Pittsburgh, 12-7, .632, 2.94; Forsch, St. Louis, 15-9, .625, 3.48; Reuss, Los Angeles, 18-11, .621, 3.07.

Strikeouts

Carlton, Philadelphia, 286; Soto, Cincinnati, 274; Ryan, Houston, 245; Valenzuela, Los Angeles, 199; Rogers, Montreal, 179.

American League

Home Runs

G. Thomas, Milwaukee, 39; Re. Jackson, California, 39; Winfield, New York, 37; Oglivie, Milwaukee, 34; 5 tied with 32.

RBIs

McRae, Kansas City, 133; Cooper, Milwaukee, 121; Thornton, Cleveland, 116; Yount, Milwaukee, 114; G. Thomas, Milwaukee, 112.

Stolen Bases

R. Henderson, Oakland, 130; Garcia, Toronto, 54; J. Cruz, Seattle, 46; Molitor, Milwaukee, 41; W. Wilson, Kansas City, 37.

Runs

Molitor, Milwaukee, 136; Yount, Milwaukee, 129; D. Evans, Boston, 122; R. Henderson, Oakland, 119; Downing, California, 109.

Hits

Yount, Milwaukee, 210; Cooper, Milwaukee, 205; Molitor, Milwaukee, 201; W. Wilson, Kansas City, 194; McRae, Kansas City, 189.

Doubles

Yount, Milwaukee, 46; McRae, Kansas City, 46; White, Kansas City, 45; DeCinces, California, 42; Cowens, Seattle, 39.

Triples

W. Wilson, Kansas City, 15; Herndon, Detroit, 13; Yount, Milwaukee, 12; Mumphry, New York, 10; Moseby, Toronto, 9; Bernazard, Chicago, 9; Brett, Kansas City, 9.

Pitching (17 Decisions)

Palmer, Baltimore, 15-4, .789, 3.13; Vukovich, Milwaukee, 18-6, .750, 3.34; Burns, Chicago, 13-5, .722, 4.04; Zahn, California, 18-8, .692, 3.73; Renko, California, 11-6, .647, 4.44; Sutcliffe, Cleveland, 14-8, .636, 2.96; Guidry, New York, 14-8, .636, 3.81; B. Stanley, Boston, 12-7, .632, 3.10.

Strikeouts

F. Bannister, Seattle, 209; Barker, Cleveland, 187; Righetti, Yankees, 163; Guidry, New York, 161; Tudor, Boston, 146.

U.S. Weightlifting Federation Championships in 1982

Glenbrook, Ill., May 29-30, 1982 (men); St. Charles, Ill., Apr. 4, 1982 (women)
(Note: lifts are in kilograms; one kilogram = 2.2 lbs.)

Senior Men

114 lbs.—Brian Okada, Wailuku, Hi., **170 kg.**
123 lbs.—Albert Hood, Healthrite, **215 kg.**
132 lbs.—Philip Sanderson, York BBC, **240 kg.**
148 lbs.—Don Abrahamson, Colo Connection, **285 kg.**
165 lbs.—Cal Schake, Butler WLC, **315 kg.**
181 lbs.—Curt White, York BBC, **322.5 kg.**
198 lbs.—Kevin Winter, Sports Palace, **340 kg.**
220 lbs.—Ken Clark, Sports Palace, **367.5 kg.**
242 lbs.—Jeff Michels, Sayre Park, **400 kg.**
Over 242 lbs.—Mario Martinez, Sports Palace, **380 kg.**

Senior Women

97 lbs.—Pamela Bickler, **75 kg.**
105¼ lbs.—Michelle Evris, **107.5 kg.**
114½ lbs.—Rachel Silverman, **117.5 kg.**
123¼ lbs.—Mary Beth Cervenak, **125 kg.**
132¼ lbs.—Diane Redgate, **110 kg.**
148¾ lbs.—Judy Glenney, **167.5 kg.**
165¼ lbs.—Karyn Tarter, **147.5 kg.**
181¾ lbs.—Mary Hyden, **140 kg.**
Over 181¾ lbs.—Lorna Griffin, **175 kg.**

Ten Most Dramatic Sports Events, Nov. 1981—Oct. 1982

Selected by The World Almanac sports staff

—Dwight Clark catches Joe Montana's pass with 51 seconds remaining in the game to give San Francisco a 28-27 victory over the Dallas Cowboys in the NFL Conference championship game. The 49ers go on to win the Super Bowl.

—Rickey Henderson of the Oakland A's steals his 119th base to break the major league single-season record set by Lou Brock in 1974. Henderson finishes the season with 130 stolen bases.

—The Univ. of Alabama defeats Auburn Univ. 28-27 to give Bear Bryant his 315th coaching victory. He passes Amos Alonzo Stagg to become the football coach with the most career wins.

—Keith Hernandez of the St. Louis Cardinals hits a 2-run single in the 6th inning to tie the final World Series game against the Milwaukee Brewers. The Cardinals win the game 6-3 for their first World Series championship since 1967.

—Wayne Gretzky becomes the first player in NHL history to score 200 points in a season. The Edmonton Oilers center finishes the season with 212 points and a NHL record 92 goals.

—Clemson defeats Nebraska 22-15 in the Orange Bowl. The victory gives the undefeated Tigers their first national championship.

—Larry Holmes knocks out Gerry Cooney in the 13th round to retain his WBC heavyweight title.

—Italy defeats Germany 3-1 to win the World Cup, emblematic of world soccer supremacy. The contest is witnessed on television by some 2 billion people in 130 nations.

—Gaylord Perry of the Seattle Mariners becomes the first pitcher in 19 years to win 300 major league games. At age 43, he is the oldest in history to accomplish this feat.

—Jimmy Connors wins the U.S. Open men's single title for the 4th time. He defeats Ivan Lendl in the finals.

North American Soccer League in 1982

Final Standings

Eastern Division

	W	L	GF	GA	Bonus points	Total points
New York	23	9	73	52	67	203
Montreal	19	13	60	43	49	159
Toronto	17	15	64	47	49	151
Chicago	13	19	56	67	53	129

Southern Division

	W	L	GF	GA	Bonus points	Total points
Ft. Lauderdale	18	14	64	74	57	163
Tulsa	16	16	69	57	59	151
Tampa Bay	12	20	47	77	42	112
Jacksonville	11	21	41	71	39	105

Western Division

	W	L	GF	GA	Bonus points	Total points
Seattle	18	14	72	48	60	166
San Diego	19	13	71	54	54	162
Vancouver	20	12	58	48	46	160
Portland	14	18	49	44	42	122
San Jose	11	19	47	62	38	114
Edmonton	11	21	38	65	33	93

Total Points: Win = 6 points, Loss = 0 points, Shootout Win = 4 points. Bonus points: one point is awarded for each goal scored up to a maximum of 3 per team per game. No bonus points are given for goal scored in overtime or the Shootout.

NASL Champions

Year	Champion
1967	Oakland Clippers (NPSL)
1967	Los Angeles Wolves (USA)
1968	Atlanta Chiefs
1969	Kansas City Spurs
1970	Rochester Lancers
1971	Dallas Tornado
1972	New York Cosmos
1973	Philadelphia Atoms
1974	Los Angeles Aztecs
1975	Tampa Bay Rowdies
1976	Toronto Metros
1977	New York Cosmos
1978	New York Cosmos
1979	Vancouver Whitecaps
1980	New York Cosmos
1981	Chicago Sting
1982	New York Cosmos

Leading Scorers

Player, team	Goals	Assists	Points
Giorgio Chinaglia, New York	20	15	55
Karl-Heinz Granitza, Chicago	20	9	49
Peter Ward, Seattle	18	13	49
Ricardo Alonso, Jacksonville	21	4	46
Laurie Abrahams, Tulsa	17	10	44
Neill Roberts, Toronto	17	8	42
Ace Ntsoelengoe, Toronto	14	12	40
Mark Peterson, Seattle	17	5	39
David Byrne, Toronto	8	23	39
Godfrey Ingram, San Jose	17	3	37
Alan Willey, Montreal	15	7	37
Branko Segota, Ft. Lauderdale	12	13	37

Leading Goalkeepers

Player, team	*Minutes	Goals against	Average
Tino Lettieri, Vancouver	2,496	34	1.23
Victor Nogueira, Montreal	1,653	23	1.25
Paul Hammond, Seattle	3,001	43	1.29
Bill Irwin, Portland	2,311	34	1.32
Jan Moller, Toronto	2,743	42	1.39
Volkmar Gross, San Diego	2,563	40	1.40
Hubert Birkenmeier, New York	2,560	44	1.55
Winston DuBose, Tulsa	2,960	55	1.67
Mike Hewitt, San Jose	2,727	55	1.82
Dieter Ferner, Chicago	2,579	58	2.02

*At least 1,440 minutes needed to qualify

NASL Leading Scorers

Year	Player, team	G	A	Pts
1967	Yanko Daucik, Toronto	20	8	48
1968	John Kowalik, Chicago	30	9	69
1969	Kaizer Motaung, Atlanta	16	4	36
1970	Kirk Apostolidis, Dallas	16	3	35
	Carlos Metidieri, Rochester	14	7	35
1971	Carlos Metidieri, Rochester	19	8	46
1972	Randy Horton, New York	9	4	22
1973	Kyle Rote, Jr., Dallas	10	10	30
1974	Paul Child, San Jose	15	6	36
1975	Steven David, Miami	23	6	52
1976	Giorgio Chinaglia, New York	19	11	49
1977	Steven David, Los Angeles	26	6	58
1978	Giorgio Chinaglia, New York	34	11	79
1979	Oscar Fabbiani, Tampa Bay	25	8	58
1980	Giorgio Chinaglia, New York	32	13	77
1981	Giorgio Chinaglia, New York	29	16	74
1982	Giorgio Chinaglia, New York	20	15	55

NASL Leading Goalkeepers

Year	Player, team	GP	G	Avg
1967	Mirko Stojanovic, Oakland	29	29	1.00
1968	Ataulfo Sanchez, San Diego	22	19	0.93
1969	Manfred Kammerer, Atlanta	14	1.21	
1970	Lincoln Phillips, Washington	22	21	0.95
1971	Mirko Stojanovic, Dallas	1,359	11	0.79
1972	Ken Cooper, Dallas	1,260	12	0.86
1973	Bob Rigby, Philadelphia	1,157	8	0.62
1974	Barry Watling, Seattle	1,800	16	0.80

Year	Player, team	Minutes	G	Avg
1975	Shep Messing, Boston	1,639	17	0.93
1976	Tony Chursky, Seattle	1,981	20	0.91
1977	Ken Cooper, Dallas	2,100	21	0.90
1978	Phil Parkes, Vancouver	2,650	28	0.95
1979	Phil Parkes, Vancouver	2,705	29	0.96
1980	Jack Brand, Seattle	2,975	30	0.91
1981	Arnie Mausser, Jacksonville	2,906	39	1.21
1982	Tino Lettieri, Vancouver	2,496	34	1.23

NASL All-Star Team in 1982

First team	Position	Second team
Hubert Birkenmeier, New York	Goalkeeper	Jan van Beveren, Ft. Lauderdale
Frantz Mathieu, Montreal	Defender	Barry Wallace, Tulsa
Young Jeung Cho, Portland	Defender	Jeff Durgan, New York
Peter Nogly, Tampa Bay	Defender	Carlos Alberto, New York
Andranik Eskandarian, New York	Defender	Ray Evans, Seattle
Vladislav Bogicevic, New York	Midfielder	Steve Daley, Seattle
Ace Ntsoelengoe, Toronto	Midfielder	Johan Neeskens, New York
Arno Steffenhagen, Chicago	Midfielder	Teofilo Cubillas, Ft. Lauderdale
Giorgio Chinaglia, New York	Forward	Steve Hunt, New York
Peter Ward, Seattle	Forward	Karl-Heinz Granitza, Chicago
Ricardo Alonso, Jacksonville	Forward	Pato Margetic, Chicago

The World Cup

The World Cup, emblematic of International soccer supremacy, was won by Italy on July 11, 1982, with a 3-1 victory over W. Germany. It was the 3d time Italy has won the event. Colombia is scheduled to host the 1986 tournament. Winners and sites of previous World Cup play follow:

Year	Winner	Site	Year	Winner	Site
1930	Uruguay	Uruguay	1962	Brazil	Chile
1934	Italy	Italy	1966	England	England
1938	Italy	France	1970	Brazil	Mexico City
1950	Uruguay	Brazil	1974	W. Germany	W. Germany
1954	W. Germany	Switzerland	1978	Argentina	Argentina
1958	Brazil	Sweden	1982	Italy	Spain

Rifle and Pistol Individual Championships in 1982

Source: National Rifle Assn.

National Outdoor Rifle and Pistol Championships

Pistol — MSG Bonnie D. Harmon, Ft. Benning, Ga., 2652-159X.
Civilian Pistol — William J. Allard, Bayville, N.Y., 2614-116X.
Regular Pistol — MSG Bonnie D. Harmon, Ft. Benning, Ga., 2652-159X.
Police Pistol — John L. Farley, Americus, Ga., 2591-108X.
Woman Pistol — Ruby E. Fox, Parker, Ariz., 2579-83X.
Senior Pistol — Robert V. Coghe, Tacoma, Wash., 2578-87X.
Collegiate Pistol — Bernt L. Oydna, Edgewater, Md., 2595-96X.
Junior Pistol — Kenneth O. Swanson, Birmingham, Ala., 2470-80X.
Smallbore Rifle Prone — Presley W. Kendall, Carlisle, Ky., 6395-528X.
Civilian Smallbore Rifle Prone — Presley W. Kendall, 6395-528X.
Service Smallbore Rifle Prone — Dennis E. Ghiselli, Quantico, Va., 6385-495X.
Woman Smallbore Rifle Prone — Mary E. Stidworthy, Prescott, Ariz., 6386-526X.
Senior Smallbore Rifle Prone — Richard F. Hanson, Punta Gorda, Fl., 6369-480X.
Collegiate Smallbore Rifle Prone — Mary E. Stidworthy, 6386-526X.
High Power Rifle — Middleton Tompkins, Long Beach, Cal., 2370.
High Power Rifle Civilian — Middleton Tompkins, 2370.
High Power Rifle Service — Col Kenneth J. Erdman, Canoga Park, Cal., 2358.
High Power Rifle Woman — Noma J. McCullough, Newhall, Cal., 2322.
High Power Rifle Senior — Gerritt H. Stekeur, Latham, N.Y., 2300.
High Power Rifle Collegiate — Timothy J. Holt, Billings, Mont., 2290.
High Power Rifle Junior — Chris J. Vesy, Poland, Oh., 2321.

U. S. NRA International Shooting Championships

English Match — Mike E. Anti, Jacksonville, N.C., 1785.
Smallbore Free Rifle — Roderick M. Fitz-Randolph, Jr., Palm Bay, Fla., 3480.
Air Rifle — Roderick M. Fitz-Randolph, Jr., 1785.
Ladies Air Rifle — Wanda R. Jewell, Wahiawa, Ha., 1154.
Woman Standard Rifle Prone — Mary L. Godlove, Ft. Benning, Ga., 1770.
Woman Standard Rifle Three Position — Mary L. Godlove, 1721.
Free Pistol — Eugene E. Ross, Saugus, Cal., 1658.
Air Pistol — Erich Buljung, Ft. Benning, Ga., 1727.
Woman Air Pistol — Ruby E. Fox, Parker, Ariz., 1126.
Center Fire Pistol — Donald C. Nygord, La Crescenta, Cal., 1770.
Rapid Fire Pistol — John T. McNally, Columbus, Ga., 1775.
Standard Pistol — John R. Kailer, Ft. Benning, Ga., 1731.
Woman Smallbore Pistol — Ruby E. Fox, 1750.

National Indoor Rifle and Pistol Championships

Smallbore 4-Position Rifle — Lones W. Wigger Jr., Ft. Benning, Ga., 799.
International Smallbore Rifle — Lones W. Wigger Jr., 1181.
NRA 3-Position Smallbore Rifle — Lones W. Wigger Jr., 1191.
Woman 4-Position Smallbore Rifle — Karen E. Monez, Weatherford, Tex., 799.
Woman NRA 3-Position Smallbore Rifle — Gloria K. Parmentier, Ft. Benning, Ga., 1180.
Woman International Smallbore Rifle — Marie A. Miller, Brown Deer, Wis., 1167.
Conventional Pistol — Bonnie D. Harmon, Ft. Benning, Ga., 887.
Woman Conventional Pistol — Ruby E. Fox, Parker, Ariz., 862.
International Free Pistol — Erich Buljung, Ft. Benning, Ga., 559.
Air Pistol — Dr. Darius R. Young, Winterburn, Alta., Canada, 581.
Woman International Free Pistol — Ruby E. Fox, 524.
Woman Air Pistol — Elizabeth Gathright, Afton, Va., 549.
International Standard Pistol — Dr. Darius R. Young, 582.
Woman International Standard Pistol — Lori B. Kamler, San Francisco, Cal., 548.
Air Rifle — Lones W. Wigger Jr., 589.
Woman Air Rifle — Marie A. Miller, 577.

CHRONOLOGY OF THE YEAR'S EVENTS

Reported Month by Month in 3 Categories: National, International, and General—Nov. 1, 1981 to Nov. 1, 1982

NOVEMBER

National

Haig, Allen, and Weinberger Feud — Secretary of State Alexander M. Haig Jr. charged, **Nov. 3,** that a senior White House aide was trying to undercut him. Although he did not name the aide, it was generally assumed that he was referring to Richard V. Allen, the White House national security advisor. Allen, however, announced that Haig had personally assured him that he was not the target of the complaint. On **Nov. 5,** Pres. Ronald W. Reagan called both Haig and Allen to the Oval Office and ordered them to end their feud and to find ways to stop criticizing each other. That day Secretary of Defense Caspar W. Weinberger denied Haig's statement that NATO had a plan to use a nuclear explosion as a warning to the Soviets in the event of a war in Europe. Haig had made his statement to the Senate Foreign Relations Committee. The White House issued a statement that both men were technically correct in that NATO had considered such a plan, but had not made it what was called "a military plan."

Unemployment, Producers' Prices, and Consumer Prices Up — The Labor Department announced, **Nov. 6,** that the unemployment rate reached 8 percent in October, and that this was the highest level in 6 years. It had risen from 7.5 percent in September and had jumped a full percentage point since July. Economists said that the jobless rate would continue to go up as long as the economy declined. The total unemployed in the U.S. was pegged at more than 8 million. The Producer Price Index, which applies to finished goods and is used as a rough measure of the inflation level, climbed 0.6 of 1 percent in October, the Labor Department reported, **Nov. 10.** It was the largest rise since April, and was caused by the increase in prices of 1982-model automobiles and the end of the auto rebate programs. Consumer prices in October rose only 0.4 of 1 percent, it was announced, **Nov. 24.** This was the smallest increase in 6 months, and it was generally attributed to the deflation in prices of homes.

Reagan Suffers Budget Woes — At a White House meeting, **Nov. 6,** President Reagan announced that he had given up on his plans to achieve a balanced budget by fiscal year 1984. He did, however, say that he would continue to seek $13 billion in budget cuts in addition to the $37 billion he had recommended in the spring. He ruled out additional taxes in 1982, but said he was considering increased taxes for 1983 and 1984. It was announced on **Nov. 7** that the administration was desirous of making changes in the Medicaid and Medicare programs. The proposals included an increase in Medicare premiums, a new payroll tax on federal employees to be paid to the Medicare fund, and limits on federal payments to hospitals and physicians who cared for the elderly. Donald T. Regan, the Secretary of the Treasury, announced, **Nov. 9,** that the administration had dropped its plans to raise $3 billion more in tax revenues in 1982. On **Nov. 21,** Reagan restated his determination to cut federal aid even further by asking Congress for a 12% cut in domestic spending. On **Nov. 22,** Congress passed a $428 billion stopgap financing bill designed to give the government money to carry out its services for a short period of time. Reagan vetoed the bill, **Nov. 23,** because it contained less than one-quarter of the $8.5 billion in savings that he requested, and ordered that all but essential services be shut down. Later that day, Congress approved a 3-week extension of financing at the current level until Dec. 15 and Reagan signed the extension.

Stockman in Hot Water — David A. Stockman, the director of the Office of Management and Budget, plunged into the center of a controversy its **Nov. 11** with the appearance of the December issue of *The Atlantic Monthly.* An article in the magazine, based upon a series of interviews with Stockman, revealed a lack of faith on his part in the Reagan administration's economic theories. He was quoted as saying, "We didn't think it all the way through," and "We didn't add up all the numbers." He also admitted that Pres. Reagan's mixture of spending cuts and tax cuts would lead to large budget deficits. On **Nov. 12,** Stockman confessed that he had used poor judgment and had talked too much. He offered his resignation, but it was rejected by the president.

Allen Accused — The White House announced, **Nov. 13,** that the Justice Department was investigating a $1,000 cash payment received by Richard V. Allen, the president's national security advisory. The money had come from a Japanese magazine as payment for arranging an interview with Nancy Reagan. Larry Speakes, the deputy White House press secretary, accused Allen of "intercepting" money that was to have been given to Mrs. Reagan, and Allen said that he had intended to turn the money in to the government. Allen admitted that he had received the money the previous January and that a secretary had put it in a safe in his office. He soon changed offices and forgot that he had left the cash in the safe. On **Nov. 14,** Allen acknowledged that he had received the interview request from the magazine, but he had not arranged it himself. He also denied soliciting the money. It was announced by the White House, **Nov. 18,** that a report from the FBI indicated that there was no reason to take administrative action against Allen, but he was ordered, **Nov. 19,** to review his office records on his contacts with Japanese businessmen while he was serving as the national security advisor. On **Nov. 20,** the FBI was ordered to resume its inquiry into the Allen case, since it was believed that the original study was incomplete. The administration also announced, **Nov. 21,** that the FBI was looking into the possibility that the amount of money in question was $10,000, rather than $1,000. The figure $10,000 had been written on both the envelope containing the money and on a receipt. Secretary of the Navy John F. Lehman, Jr. said, **Nov. 23,** that he had signed a statement supporting Allen's claim that he had intended to turn the $1,000 in to the government. Lehman said that he had been in Allen's office shortly after the receipt of the money, and that Allen had expressed "chagrin and amazement" that he had been given the cash. It was reported, **Nov. 25,** that Lieut. Col. Donald L. Johnson, a friend and former Allen aide, had told the FBI that he had personally counted the money and was certain that there were only 10 $100 bills in the envelope. On **Nov. 24,** Fuyuko Kamisaka, one of the writers who interviewed Mrs. Reagan, said that she had asked Allen for a receipt for the money when it was given to him. This seemed to contradict Lehman's account. Kamisaka also said that no receipt was sent by Allen. On **Nov. 28,** Tamotsu Takase, a Japanese longtime friend of Allen, said that his wife, a journalist, had been having trouble setting up an interview with Mrs. Reagan. He claimed that he decided to help her by calling on Allen, at which time he gave him "a big present." This was in addition to the $1,000 and two watches. Allen announced, **Nov. 29,** that he was taking a leave of absence from his government job until the Justice Department had completed its investigation. The Justice Department announced, **Dec. 1,** that Allen had been cleared on the charges of bribery in cash, but they were still investigating the matter of the watches.

Civil Rights Chief Fired — President Reagan dismissed the chairman of the United States Commission on Civil Rights, Arthur S. Flemming, **Nov. 16.** E. Pendleton James, the White House personnel director, indicated that Flemming had been fired because it was White House policy to remove certain people and replace them with Reagan appointees. Flemming, however, claimed that he had been dismissed because he was a strong advocate of such civil rights issues as busing and affirmative action. Flemming was replaced by Clarence M. Pendleton, a conservative Republican.

Refugee Problems Escalate — On **Nov. 25,** 125 Haitian refugees were transferred from the Krome Avenue detention center near Miami, Fla., to Fort Allen in Puerto Rico. This reduced the population at Krome Avenue to 867, but still more than the recommended capacity of the camp of 524. On **Nov. 25,** U.S. immigration officials approved the release of 703 Cuban refugees, part of a group of 125,000 Cuban refugees who came to the U.S. by sea in the spring of 1980. Of that number, 1,700 had been detained because they were suspected of being criminals. The release of the 703 refugees, plus the 441 previously released, left some 556 still in detention.

International

Polish Problems Continue — Officials of Solidarity, Poland's independent labor union, threatened, **Nov. 1,** that they would go ahead with planned strikes. They maintained that the strikes would continue until all labor disputes had been settled. As of **Nov. 1,** some 250,000 workers were out on wildcat strikes across the country, most of them protesting food shortages. The heads of the Polish Communist Party, Solidarity, and the Roman Catholic Church met in Warsaw, **Nov. 4,** in an attempt to set up a permanent body to deal with Polish problems. Attending the meeting were Gen. Wojciech Jaruzelski, head of the Communist Party; Lech Walesa, the chief of Solidarity; and Archbishop Jozef Glemp. On **Nov. 10,** coal miners went on strike in Sosnowwiec, claiming that they had been gassed by the authorities during a previous 1-hour strike. Newspaper sellers were also on strike in Silesia, students struck in Lublin, Rzeszow, and Warsaw; farmers near Siedlce were on strike. The Polish army announced, **Nov. 19,** that it was withdrawing hundreds of small military units from the countryside. The soldiers had been assigned to help curb unrest. However, they would be kept ready to return in case they were needed. Walesa appealed to all working people in Western Europe, **Nov. 20,** asking them to urge their governments to give food aid to Poland in the face of a difficult winter. If the food were provided, he pledged that Solidarity would insure public control of the distribution. The Polish Politburo instructed the Polish government, **Nov. 27,** to pass an anti-strike law. Jaruzelski indicated that the demand stemmed from concern over the mounting economic, political, and social crises. The following day, the Polish Communist Party demanded that the Parliament approve measures to curb labor unrest, including the banning of strikes, and, on **Nov. 29,** Jaruzelski himself told the Communist Party Central Committee that strikes and anarchy must be halted before they led to a state of emergency. Janusz Onyszkiewicz, a spokesman for the Warsaw regional Solidarity union, said, **Nov. 30,** that he doubted that the Communist Party and the Polish government would seriously try to ban strikes. If they did, he said, the union would ignore the ban.

Swedes Deal with Russian Submarine — Liet. Comdr. Pyotr Gushin, the captain of the Soviet submarine *Whisky 137,* was interrogated for 6 hours, **Nov. 2,** aboard a Swedish torpedo boat. The submarine had run aground near a Swedish naval base 300 miles south of Stockholm on **Oct. 26.** His explanation for this violation of a restricted zone was that he had used a faulty compass. He also demanded that the interrogations be held aboard a Soviet vessel in the future. That day Swedish navy tugs pulled the submarine off the rocks during the height of a fierce gale. On **Nov. 3,** Gushin was questioned for another 7 hours. On **Nov. 5,** the Swedish government announced that it believed there were nuclear warheads aboard the sub, but that the vessel and its crew of 56 would be released as soon as the weather permitted. On **Nov. 6,** the submarine left Swedish waters to rejoin a Soviet navy flotilla while a crowd of 4,000 gathered in downtown Stockholm to protest the Soviet intrusion into Swedish waters.

Trouble in Chad — The commander of Libya's troops in Chad announced, **Nov. 4,** that he would withdraw within 7 days, on orders from Libyan leader Col. Muammar el-Qaddafi, all his troops from that country. It was estimated that 8,000 to 9,000 men were involved in the occupation that had begun the previous December. At that time, Chad's president, Goukouni Oueddei, had asked for the troops to help him win a civil war that had gone on for 16 years. However, on **Oct. 29,** Oueddei requested the withdrawal after Chad had received pledges from France to aid its former colony following the withdrawal. The Libyan commander in Chad, Col. Radwan Salah, **Nov. 10,** predicted another civil war in Chad once his troops had withdrawn. To prevent such a possibility, he requested an inter-African peace-keeping force manned by soldiers from Zaire, Nigeria, Senegal and other African countries to come into Chad. On **Nov. 11** the U.S. government announced that it was considering a request from Nigeria to furnish transport and supplies for the 5,000 man peace-keeping force. Goukouni, on **Nov. 12,** accused the Sudan of invading his country, attacking the town of Adré as the Libyan troops were withdrawing. It was feared at the time that the peace-keeping force would not arrive until December, but on **Nov. 16,** there were some 700 Zairian soldiers of the force in Chad.

Guerrilla Fighting Continues in El Salvador — Secretary of State Alexander M. Haig Jr. announced, **Nov. 5,** that more U.S. aid for El Salvador was needed and that the U.S. was studying ways of stopping outside military support of the guerrillas. It was also disclosed that he had asked the Defense Department to examine measures for a possible blockade of Nicaragua or a show of strength in Cuban waters. On **Nov. 10,** it was announced in El Salvador that investigations by the government into the murders of 4 Roman Catholic missionaries the previous December were at a dead end. Reports of an army drive against the guerrillas in the northern part of the country, **Nov. 27,** indicated that 1,000 soldiers had captured the town of Cinquera, but that rebels were entrenched only miles way. Scores of bodies and skeletons were found in sugar fields 3 miles north of San Salvador on **Nov. 28,** and 40 National Guardsmen and National Police killed 30 guerrillas near San Miguel, **Nov. 29.**

Troubles in Ireland Continue — The Rev. Robert J. Bradford, a Unionist member of the British Parliament, was killed, **Nov. 14,** by Irish Republican Army gunmen in Belfast, Northern Ireland. He had been a critic of the Irish nationalist guerrillas. Because of the increase in violence in Northern Ireland, Britain flew in 600 more soldiers, **Nov. 18,** bringing its troop strength to some 11,000 men.

Seychelles Coup Attempt Fails — An around-the-clock curfew was put into effect on the Seychelles islands, **Nov. 27,** after a mercenary force attempted to seize the airport at Victoria. It was announced that at least 3 mercenaries had been captured. Forty-four of the attackers hijacked a plane and flew to South Africa, where they were picked up for questioning. Despite the fact that several of the men were South African, the South African government, **Nov. 28,** denied that it had backed the mercenaries. On **Dec. 2,** the South African government released 39 of the 44 mercenaries; the other 5 were charged with kidnaping and set free on bond. Also on **Dec. 2,** the deposed president of the Seychelles, James R.M. Mancham, admitted that dissident Seychellois had sought him out in September in his London home to ask him to record a broadcast to be sent out over the air after the coup. Pres. France Albert René of the Seychelles announced that the captured mercenaries might be charged with murder because a Seychellois officer was killed in the aborted coup. On **Dec. 3,** the Seychelles government asked the UN to form an inquiry into the attack and the U.S. State Department criticized the release of the prisoners in South Africa. On **Jan. 5,** South Africa charged the 45 mercenaries under that country's strict antihijack law. They faced a possible sentence of 30 years.

U.S. and Israel Sign Accord — It was announced, **Nov. 30,** that the U.S. and Israel had come to an agreement on a memorandum of understanding, which would strengthen their cooperation against threats to the Middle East. This was taken to mean threats caused by either the Soviet Union or Soviet-controlled forces. The agreement provided that the 2 countries would act cooperatively and provide each other with military assistance to cope with the security of the entire Middle East.

General

Missing Animals Found — Two animals that had been thought to be extinct were discovered in November. The Department of the Interior announced, **Nov. 6,** that a black-footed ferret had been captured in a prairie dog colony in Wyoming. On **Nov. 11,** it was reported by an ornithologist, Jared Diamond, that he had discovered a yellow-fronted gardener bowerbird in the mountains of New Guinea.

Polio Virus Developed — Scientists at the Massachusetts Institute of Technology announced, **Nov. 12,** that they had developed an artifically fabricated genetic material that had been used for the first time to produce an active, infectious polio virus. This discovery would make it possible to study the polio virus in many new ways, they said. It was also suggested that it might lead to the development of a totally new type of polio vaccine.

Columbia Orbits Again — The space shuttle Columbia blasted off on its second mission, **Nov. 12,** with 2 astronauts aboard, Col. Joe H. Engle of the Air Force and Capt. Richard H. Truly of the Navy. The mission was originally planned for 5 days, but a malfunctioning electric power unit forced a cut in time to 2 days. The shuttle landed at Edwards Air Force Base, Calif., on **Nov. 14.** After a preliminary inspection, space agency officials announced, **Nov. 15,** that the shuttle had experienced much less wear and tear on its 2d flight than it had on its first, in which 164 heat-protective tiles were ripped off. This time only 12 were missing. Because the shuttle had flown much lower than typical satellites, its radar produced sharper and clearer pictures than had been previously taken. It was felt that these radar images would be useful in discovering mineral deposits that may lie beneath such out-of-the-way places as the world's unexplored jungles.

Shrine Discovered in Spain — It was announced, **Nov. 28,** that U.S. and Spanish scientists had uncovered what may be the world's oldest shrine at El Juyo Cave near Santander. It contained a free-standing sculptured stone head with a picture of a cat on one side and a human on the other. The head was believed to be that of a supernatural being, and it was thought that the shrine was more than 14,000 years old.

Disasters — A hurricane hit India, **Nov. 2,** and 470 fishermen were reported missing . . . Two buses carrying Moslem pilgrims in Pakistan crashed, **Nov. 7,** killing 14 and injuring 59 . . . In a train-truck accident in Spain, **Nov. 9,** 11 persons were killed . . . A Mexican jet struck a mountain slope near Altamirano, **Nov. 9,** killing all 18 people aboard . . . Forty-eight people were killed in Mérida, Mexico, **Nov. 16,** when a wall collapsed at a bull ring during a political rally . . . A snowstorm, **Nov. 21,** killed 12 people in the Middle West . . . The Philippines were hit, **Nov. 26,** by a typhoon that killed 200 . . . A bomb explosion in Damascus, Syria, **Nov. 29,** killed 90 and injured 135.

DECEMBER

National

Unemployment and Prices Up — The Bureau of Labor Statistics, **Dec. 4,** set the nation's unemployment rate at 8.4 percent, up from 8 percent the previous month. The cause of the rise was attributed to an increase in layoffs in heavy industry during November. Out of a total work force of 107 million, more than 9 million were without jobs. It was announced, **Dec. 22,** that the Consumer Price Index had risen, but only 0.5 percent. This was thought to be an encouraging sign, since for the first 11 months of the year the Index had risen 9.2 percent. It was also predicted that the inflation rate for 1981 might be as low as 8.9 percent as compared to 12.4 percent in 1980. This would be the lowest level in the Index since the 6.8 percent increase in 1977.

Power of the CIA Increased — President Reagan signed an executive order, **Dec. 4,** that broadened the authority of the intelligence agencies of the U.S. to collect information from Americans at home and abroad. The Central Intelligence Agency specifically was authorized for the first time to conduct covert operations domestically. Previously, the CIA had been forbidden to collect information within the U.S. except for commercial information or data about U.S. residents and corporations believed to be acting on behalf of a foreign country. The order also permitted surveillance of U.S. citizens and corporations abroad in any counterintelligence operation, but banned assassinations by intelligence agencies.

U.S. Deficit Climbing — The Reagan administration announced, **Dec. 7,** that their estimate indicated that the federal budget deficit would climb to a record $109 billion in 1982. They further predicted deficits of $152 billion in 1983 and $162 billion in 1984. The figure of $109 billion was more than double the forecast made in September 1981. The increase seemed to be caused by a deepening recession which had cut tax revenues and increased spending for social programs such as unemployment insurance. The previous record for a national deficit was $66 billion in 1976. Despite this, the White House Chief of Staff, James A. Baker 3d, announced, **Dec. 22,** that the president would not consider selective tax increases until early in 1982.

Controllers' Job Ban Ended — President Reagan, on **Dec. 9,** ended his 3-year ban on federal employment for the air traffic controllers who had been dismissed on **Aug. 3** for striking. They would not be rehired as controllers or as employees of the Federal Aviation Administration, but would be free to apply for other government employment. Involved were 11,500 dismissed controllers. Critics, such as the leaders of the AFL-CIO, called it an empty gesture, since cutbacks in federal employment were continuing and the controllers generally lacked the qualifications for other federal jobs.

Refugee Problems Continue — The Justice Department, **Dec. 18,** made known its plans to transfer 535 Cuban refugees from Fort Chaffee, Ark., to a former Air Force base near Glasgow, Mont. These were the refugees who had arrived here in 1980 and had not been resettled because many of them had mental or emotional problems. In another trouble spot, after a weekend riot, Haitian refugees and officials at Fort Allen in Puerto Rico reached an agreement, **Dec. 23,** to ease tension at the detention camp. The 795 refugees there had refused to work, use recreational facilities, or accept Christmas entertainment. The riot broke out, **Dec. 19,** when 200 refugees protested the installation of new gates that would have reinforced segregation among various groups of Haitians. The agreement provided that no Haitian be punished for taking part in the riot. On **Dec. 24,** Haitians being held at a federal detention facility in Miami and a federal prison in Lexington, Ky., began a hunger strike. At the Krome Avenue detention camp near Miami, 727 of the 730 Haitians being held refused breakfast and lunch, and refused to talk to their guards. In Lexington, only about 30 percent had turned out for lunch. That day the Roman Catholic Archbishop of Miami, the Rev. Edward McCarthy, appealed to the president for a humane release of the Haitians. On **Dec. 29,** the 5-day hunger strike in Miami ended when the Haitians were assured that they would not be punished for not eating.

Auto Industry Troubled — The United Automobile Workers union announced, **Dec. 21,** that its General Motors and Ford councils would meet on **Jan. 8** to consider reopening discussions on renegotiating their contracts with the auto companies. They hoped that they could trade concessions in wages or fringe benefits for job security promises in the face of layoffs due to Japanese competition in the domestic car market. The auto manufacturers had had the worst sales year in more than 2 decades, and, on **Dec. 23,** it was announced that mid-December sales had fallen 22.5 percent from the previous December. The 5 U.S. car manufacturers—GM, Ford, Chrysler, American Motors and Volkswagen—had sold only slightly more than 6 million automobiles, the worst record since 1961. The result had been a heavy recession in the industrial Middle West, and it was expected that all but GM would report losses for the 2d consecutive year.

Indian Tribes Win Court Battle — The U.S. Supreme Court refused, **Dec. 26,** to hear an appeal by the State of Michigan of a lower court ruling that had upheld the rights of 3 Indian tribes to use gill nets in Lakes Michigan, Superior, and Huron. The state had banned this practice, maintaining that gill nets snare all types of fish, particularly lake trout. The state and fishing groups argued that gill netting was destroying the lake trout and whitefish populations in these 3 Great Lakes. Previously the federal district court in Grand Rapids had ruled that the Indians had the right to use the gill nets because of a 19th-century treaty with the white settlers. The ban on gill nets would still apply to non-Indian fishermen.

MX Missile Plan Changed — The Department of Defense announced, **Dec. 31,** that it had changed its plans for the deployment of the MX missile. Forty of them would be placed in existing silos on one of the 6 Minuteman missile fields in Montana, South Dakota, North Dakota, Wyoming, or Missouri. Previously, it had been expected that the missiles would be based in Missouri in silos occupied by Titan intercontential missiles, but it was decided that geological formations around those silos made them more difficult to protect.

International

More Trouble Brews in El Salvador — On **Dec. 1,** diplomatic and military sources in Argentina admitted they had been training Salvadoran intelligence officers for 2 years, in organization, infiltration, and interrogation. In addition, Argentina had given El Salvador some $15 million in aid in 1981 and was considering giving it more. On the battle front, the rebel guerrillas opened new attacks 40 miles south of the capital city of San Salvador on **Dec. 3,** recapturing the town of Cinquera. That day the town of San Miguel was also attacked; electrical towers were bombed, blacking out the city for the 70th time since June. Msgr. Arturo Rivera Damas, the acting archbishop of San Salvador, the capital city, criticized the ruling junta, **Dec. 6,** saying that it was repressing the rural citizens and using violence against the city dwellers. But, on the same day, the Organization of American States heard a resolution of support for the junta under the command of Pres. José Napoleón Duarte, which had the support of 20 of the 27 member nations. On **Dec. 15,** the Reagan administration announced that it planned to train a battalion of 1,000 Salvadoran soldiers and a group of 500-600 junior officers in the U.S. Fred C. Iklé, the undersecretary of defense for policy also stated that the Soviet Union was spending $3 billion per year to support left-wing guerrillas in Central America and that the administration would request $18 million for the training of the Salvadoran troops. Guerrillas killed 14 Salvadoran soldiers and a militiaman in 3 separate attacks **Dec. 17–19** and set a government warehouse on fire. Salvador Cayetano Carpio, the leader of the Popular Forces of Liberation, a guerrilla group, **Dec. 22,** appealed to the world for weapons to counter U.S. aid to the junta and 36 people were killed in 24 hours in the political violence in El Salvador. Guerrillas claimed to have killed 25 Salvadoran soldiers in fighting near the border of Honduras, **Dec. 29–30.**

Libyan Terrorist Plot Suspected — The Reagan administration announced, **Dec. 3,** that it had received reports that 5 terrorists trained in Libya had entered the U.S. the previous weekend on a mission to assassinate President Reagan or other senior administration officials. Agents of the FBI and the Secret Service had been sent around the country to question Americans who had ties with Libya. Among those to be questioned were veterans of the Green Berets who had worked in Libya training terrorists. Security was increased for Reagan and his top administrators. It was generally believed that the terrorists had been sent by the leader of Libya, Muammar el-Qaddafi, in retaliation for the shooting down of two Libyan planes by U.S. jets in a dogfight the previous August. Qaddafi denied the murder plot, **Dec. 5,** and, on **Dec. 7,** President Reagan and his top national security advisors met to discuss possible punitive economic and political measures against Libya, such as an embargo on oil imports or a ban on travel to Libya by Americans. On **Dec. 10,** the Immigration and Naturalization Service told Mexican border agents to be on the lookout for two assassination squads from Libya—one of them including 3 Syrians and 3 Libyans; the other composed of 2 Iranians, a Palestinian, and an East German. That day, President Reagan requested all Americans in Libya to quit the country immediately and invalidated passports for travel to that country. Several U.S. oil companies said that they would either remove all their American workers or at least fly out those who chose to go. In Brussels, Secretary of State Alexander M. Haig Jr. said, **Dec. 11,** that the U.S. had decided that it could no longer carry on business with a nation that practiced terrorism. This statement was an answer to general skepticism and opposition to the president's actions in Europe. Meanwhile, some of the 1,500 Americans in Libya expressed disagreement with the president, saying that they did not feel personally threatened. The Libyan Minister of Petroleum, Abdel-Salam Zagaar, said, **Dec. 12,** that Libya might be forced to shut down its oil fields if the Americans returned home. On **Dec. 13,** Qaddafi canceled a scheduled news conference in which he was to reply to Reagan's shutdown plans and the next day 67 Americans, employees of Mobil Oil, left the country.

Greece Limits Its NATO Role — Prime Minister Andreas Papandreou of Greece announced, **Dec. 8,** that his country was suspending its return to the NATO military command and would disengage itself from other commitments to the organization. Greece had left the military command in 1974 when the Turks had invaded Cyprus. Papandreou, in his capacity as Defense Minister for his country, announced, **Dec. 10,** that Greek armed forces would be used only to face a possible Turkish threat, although he was not planning a complete withdrawal from NATO.

Iran-Iraq War Continues — After a tour of the battlefront, Iraqi president, Saddam Hussein, announced, **Dec. 9,** that Iraqi forces appeared to have lost some ground to the Iranian army since **Nov. 29** when the town of Bustan was recaptured by the Iranians. On **Dec. 11,** the Iranian news service told of a new offensive against the Iraqis in the province of Khuzistan that had resulted in the killing of 1,000 Iraqi troops and the capture of another 200. An Iraqi communique claimed 500 Iranians dead. President Hussein, **Dec. 15,** offered an end to the war if Iran would recognize Iraq's borders. Both Iran and Iraq, **Dec. 16,** reported that their troops had made major gains in the war—the Iraqis in the Gilan Garb and Sumar regions of Iran, killing 282; and the Iranians shooting down 2 jet fighters in the Gilan Garb Heights. On **Dec. 17,** Iraq claimed to have recaptured some hilltop positions in the Gilan area.

Peruvian Elected UN Secretary General — The UN General Assembly, **Dec. 11,** elected Javier Perez de Cuellar, a Peruvian diplomat, as the 5th secretary general of the United Nations. The balloting, which had begun on **Oct. 27,** had deadlocked between the incumbent, Kurt Waldheim of Austria and Salim A. Salim of Tanzania. However, Waldheim, on **Dec. 3,** and Salim, on **Dec. 11,** withdrew from the voting, leading the way to the selection of Cuellar.

Terrorists Kill Iranian Officials — Ayatollah Abdol-Hossein Dastgheib, Ayatollah Ruhollah Khomeini's personal representative to the southern Iranian city of Shiraz, and 7 companions were killed, **Dec. 11,** in a bomb explosion in that city. Teheran radio accused the leftist guerrilla organization, People's Mujahedeen, of the attack. The deaths brought the total to more than 1,000 officials and clergymen slain since the ousting of Pres. Abolhassan Bani-Sadr in June 1981. Two more Khomeini supporters were assassinated, **Dec. 23,** in Meshed. Mojtaba Ozbaki, a member of Parliament, and Gholamali Jaaffarzadeh, the governor of Meshed, were killed by a hand grenade while traveling in an automobile. On **Dec. 28,** another member of Parliament, Mohammad Taki Behsharat, was killed by gunfire in Teheran.

President of Argentina Ousted — Pres. Roberto Eduardo Viola of Argentina was deposed, **Dec. 11,** by the ruling 3-man junta of that country. The announcement was made without explanation, although Viola had been recuperating for more than a month from a heart ailment. Gen. Leopoldo Galtieri was appointed Viola's successor and would continue to be commander of the army as well.

Golan Heights Annexed by Israel — In an abrupt move, **Dec. 14,** Prime Minister Menachem Begin pushed a measure through the Israeli Knesset to annex the Golan Heights, a strategically sensitive zone along the Syrian border. The Reagan administration immediately said that this annexation violated the Camp David peace accords, and Syria called it a declaration of war. Some of the Arab Druse inhabitants of the Heights expressed delight at the move, **Dec. 15,** since they thought it might mark the end of military occupation by the Syrians. Other residents, who consider themselves Syrians, were not pleased. Syria, on **Dec. 16,** urged the UN Security Council to impose sanctions on Israel and Israel countered that Syria had been harrassing it from the Heights. On **Dec. 17,** the Security Council voted unanimously for a resolution calling the annexation illegal and threatening to take appropriate measures if Israel did not change its mind. It also called for a meeting of the Council no later than **Jan. 5** to consider these measures if Israel failed to obey. The U.S. suspended an agreement, **Dec. 18,** with Israel for military cooperation to counter Soviet threats to the Middle East, and Begin, **Dec. 20,** accused the U.S. of treating Israel as a vassal state. He also talked of the Senate approval of the sale of Awacs planes to Saudi Arabia, referring to it as an ugly anti-Semitic campaign.

American General Kidnaped — Brig. Gen. James L. Dozier, the deputy chief of staff for logistics and administration at the Verona headquarters for allied land forces in southern

Europe, was abducted in that city, **Dec. 17.** The Red Brigades, the leftist guerilla group, admitted responsibility by telephone to the Italian news agency ANSA. A group of men broke into Dozier's apartment early in the morning, tied up his wife and carried the general away. On **Dec. 18,** Prime Minister Giovanni Spadolini ordered a major search for Dozier, but the Italian police admitted that they had not been able to turn up a trace of the missing officer. President Reagan called the kidnapers cowardly bums and vowed to do anything for the safe recovery of the general. Six antiterrorism experts from the U.S. Defense Department joined with the Italian police, **Dec. 20,** to continue the hunt. The kidnapers planted leaflets in Milan and Venice, **Dec. 21,** taunting the efforts of the police. Three people were arrested in Milian in connection with the abduction refused, **Dec. 26,** to answer questions and declared themselves to be political prisoners. A photograph of Dozier was received by the Milan bureau of ANSA, **Dec. 27,** showing him in front of a Red Brigades banner holding a sign calling for a civil war. On **Dec. 29,** it was announced that the U.S. and Italian governments had agreed not to enter into negotiations with the Red Brigades. Experts announced, **Dec. 30,** that the photograph seemed genuine and was not a montage, as had previously been suspected.

Military Coup in Ghana Overthrows Government — Jerry J. Rawlings, a former flight lieutenant in the Ghanaian

Martial Law Declared in Poland; Troops Gain Control, Dissidents Jailed

Poland's military leaders decreed a state of martial law, **Dec. 13,** restricting civil rights and suspending the operations of the independent trade union Solidarity. In the announcement, Gen. Wojciech Jaruzelski, the Polish Prime Minister and Communist Party leader, stated that a strict regime was necessary to save Poland from catastrophe and civil war. He declared what he called "a state of war," the equivalent to a state of emergency. Also banned were public gatherings and demonstrations, and a threat of internment was imposed on citizens whose loyalty to the state was suspect.

Trouble had been brewing for months. On **Dec. 1,** policemen had surrounded a firefighters' academy in Warsaw as more than 300 cadets defied demands that they end a weeklong sit-in strike. Since the firemen in Poland were a militarized force, this was considered a mutiny against the government. The strike, supported by Solidarity, sought the same rights and privileges for the cadets that other students in Poland enjoyed. On **Dec. 2,** the police raided the academy and drove out the students, most of whom went to local headquarters of Solidarity where they were reunited with their families. On **Dec. 3,** Jaruzelski pleaded for national accord backing the Communist Party while Solidarity accused the party of blocking accord by its actions at the firefighters' academy. On **Dec. 6,** the government accused Solidarity of breaking its agreements by refusing to negotiate for a national accord, and the union called for a day of protest, **Dec. 17.**

Also on **Dec. 6,** a telegram arrived signed by Pres. Leonid I. Brezhnev and Prime Minister Nikolai A. Tikhonov of the Soviet Union expressing full support for the Communist Party of Poland. The Polish authorities accused Solidarity, **Dec. 7,** of trying to overthrow the government and broadcast what it termed to be tape recordings of remarks made in a closed meeting by union leaders in the town of Radom. Lech Walesa, the chairman of Solidarity, claimed that his statements had been taken out of context.

The Polish Roman Catholic Church announced, **Dec. 8,** that it had tried to foster an understanding between the union and the government. Archbishop Jozef Glemp had appealed to both Walesa and Jaruzelski to hold a meeting to iron out their differences. But the Soviet Union charged, **Dec. 10,** that its own security was being threatened by the Polish conflict and accused the Polish Church of stirring up anti-Communist sentiment. Walesa declared that Solidarity could retreat no further in the face of governmental attacks. On **Dec. 12,** after the union leaders asked for a national referendum on the future of the Communist government, riot policemen stormed the regional headquarters of Solidarity in Warsaw.

Czechoslovakia and Hungary praised the declaration of the state of emergency, **Dec. 13,** but Secretary of State Alexander M. Haig Jr. indicated that the U.S. was seriously concerned and warned the Soviets not to interfere in Poland. On **Dec. 14,** the Polish government took control of many factories; Solidarity was able to mount only scattered strikes in protest of the crackdown. In the U.S., the Reagan administration announced that it was suspending economic assistance to Poland, including $100 million worth of feed and food grains, while CARE and the Catholic Relief Organization were preparing to ship $15 million worth of food to Poland.

Also on **Dec. 14,** the Huta Warszawa steel mill, a Solidarity stronghold and the largest factory in Warsaw, was stormed by riot policemen and soldiers, as were other industrial installations in Warsaw and other major cities, as a means of breaking up the strikes. The shipyard in Gdansk was overrun by Polish troops at dawn on **Dec. 16** and major military movements were reported in various parts of the country.

On **Dec. 16,** the U.S. restricted the movements of Polish diplomats in retaliation for the restrictions that had been placed on U.S. diplomats in Poland, where they were confined to the cities to which they were posted. The next day 8 Polish citizens deserted their ship in Nagoya, Japan, and sought political asylum.

The Polish government announced, **Dec. 17,** that 7 people had been killed and hundreds wounded in clashes with troops. The deaths occurred at a Silesian coal mine near Katowice. The report also said that 160 militiamen and 164 civilians had been injured in street disturbances in Gdansk. Strikes had been broken up in many areas, including Lodz, Cracow, and Lublin. The authorities broadcast stern warnings of swift punishment to demonstrators.

On **December 18,** the U.S. called upon Poland to free its political prisioners and to let Walsea speak to his countrymen. On **Dec. 19,** Polish authorities announced that criminal proceedings were to begin against union activists, and Pope John Paul II sent a special Vatican envoy, Archbishop Luigi Poggi, to study the problem. Poland's ambassador to Washington, Romuald Spasowski, asked for and received political asylum in the U.S., **Dec. 20.**

On **Dec. 21,** it was reported that 2,800 Polish coal miners were on strike in Silesia and Solidarity activists had barricaded themselves inside a Katowice steel mill. Thirty-nine Poles jumped ship at Walvis Bay in South-West Africa, asking for asylum in South Africa, raising the count to at least 118 defectors from ships in ports around the world. President Reagan announced some economic sanctions against the Polish government, **Dec. 23,** and said he had warned Brezhnev that he was considering economic and political measures against Moscow. The Polish ambassador to Japan, Zdzislaw Rurarz, defected and asked for political asylum in the U.S.

On **Dec. 24,** Jaruzelski, in an address to the Polish nation, said that there was still a place for independent labor unions in Poland, but the Warsaw branch of Solidarity called on workers to continue their campaign of resistance to the government. It was reported, **Dec. 25,** that 1,276 coal miners were continuing their strike from underground in the Piast coal mine in Katowice Province; they had been there since **Dec. 14.**

The Warsaw government announced, **Dec. 27,** that meat rations for all Poles except manual laborers would be reduced in January. On **Dec. 29,** President Reagan, blaming the Soviets for some of the repression in Poland, cut back Soviet-American trade and scientific exchanges. He suspended the issuance or renewal of export licenses for electronic equipment and computers, postponed discussions on a grain arrangement and a maritime agreement, barred new licenses for gas equipment including a natural gas pipeline from Siberia to Western Europe, suspended landing rights in the U.S. for *Aeroflot,* the Soviet airline, and closed the Soviet Purchasing Commission which handled orders from the USSR for American nonfarm products.

air force, overthrew the government of Hilla Limann, **Dec. 31,** in a military coup. Radio reports from Ghana's capital city, Accra, **Jan. 1,** told of rampaging armed soldiers who were looting homes and shops in celebration of the overthrow of the civilian government the day before. Limann, the former president, was being held under house arrest, and several of his deputies had been taken into custody. Rawlings warned that looters would be punished. It was reported, **Jan. 3,** that the overthrow had alarmed the governments of many African countries, both civilian and military, especially since it might strengthen the hand of Libya's leader, Col. Muammar el-Qaddafi, who was apparently a hero to Rawlings. Limann was officially arrested, **Jan. 4,** as he was apparently trying to flee the country. Rawlings also announced that all personal assets of the former president, his cabinet, and the 140 members of parliament had been frozen, as well as the assets of their wives and children and 126 others, such as businessmen and members of Limann's People's National Party. All cash withdrawals from banks were forbidden and all non-Ghanians, mostly Lebanese and Indians, were prohibited from doing business in cocoa, coffee, and groundnuts. On **Jan. 6,** the government announced that so-called people's tribunals would replace many of the courts in trying Ghanians arrested as enemies of the people since the overthrow. These tribunals would not be bound by the laws and procedures of existing courts.

General

US Steel Proposes to Buy Marathon — The United States Steel Corporation and the Marathon Oil Company announced, **Dec. 7,** that they had come to an agreement whereby the steel company would acquire the oil company for about $6.3 billion. This came in the face of an announced plan by Mobil Corporation to take over the midwest oil company. As a result, Marathon stock rose from $77 per share to $104.25. On **Dec. 9,** Mobil disclosed that it intended to buy between 15 and 25% of United States Steel. The steel company accused Mobil of trying to block its purchase of Marathon. But, on **Dec. 24,** Judge Joseph P. Kinneary of the federal district court in Columbus, Ohio, brought in a ruling that would permit US Steel to purchase Marathon for $6.3 billion on **Jan. 7.**

Court Rejects Harris's Plea — The appellate division of the New York Supreme Court, **Dec. 30,** rejected Jean S. Harris's bid for a new trial in the murder of Dr. Herman Tarnower. Harris had contended that her constitutional rights had been violated in her first trial for the murder of the diet doctor, but the court ruled that the trial had been a fair one. Harris returned to the Bedford Hills Correctional Facility in New York State, where she was serving 15 years to life.

Disasters — A Yugoslavian jetliner smashed into a mountain in Corsica, **Dec. 1,** killing 178 people aboard ... Seven ships and small fishing vessels with 40 crew members were reported scuttled or missing, **Dec. 2,** during severe storms off the coast of Japan ... Panicked sightseers in New Delhi, India, were frightened by a sudden loss of power near a shrine, **Dec. 4,** and started a stampede that killed 45 ... Eighteen coal miners were killed in explosions —5 near Topmost, Ky., on **Dec. 7,** and 13 near Whitwell, Tenn., on **Dec. 8** ... A train smashed into a bus 90 miles north of Calcutta, India, **Dec. 15,** killing 16 ... A British coaster smashed onto the rocks off the southwest coast of England, **Dec. 20,** and 16 people were declared missing ... A typhoon in the Philippines, **Dec. 26–27,** killed 7, destroyed 5,000 homes, and left 26,000 homeless.

JANUARY

National

Allen Leaves Administration — The White House announced, **Jan. 1** that Richard V. Allen, the national security advisor, was to be replaced. Allen had been on leave of absence pending the completion of an investigation conducted by Richard A. Hauser, the deputy council to the president, into criminal misconduct charges concerning the acceptance of $1,000 and 2 watches from Japanese journalists. Although Allen had been cleared, **Dec. 23,** by the Justice Dept., he tendered his resignation, **Jan. 4.** Pres. Ronald Reagan, announcing that the job of national security advisor would be upgraded and that the advisor would report directly to him, appointed William P. Clark Jr., a deputy secretary of state, to the position.

Fierce Winter Weather Makes News — Beginning **Jan. 4,** blizzards, floods, tornadoes, freezing rain, and wind battered the United States. By **Jan. 5,** at least 34 people had died as a result of the weather. A storm on the West Coast flooded towns north of San Francisco and started mud slides that caused hundreds of people to be evacuated. A storm in the northern Rocky Mountains closed roads in Utah, Washington, Oregon, Colorado, and Wyoming. Parts of the Great Lakes states were buried under a foot or more of snow, and winds were clocked at up to 90 mph. Rain and tornadoes caused flooding in Georgia, Kentucky, and the Carolinas. On **Jan. 5,** the death count in the San Francisco Bay area stood at 13, millions of dollars worth of property had been destroyed, and the Golden Gate Bridge was closed to traffic. Meanwhile, mountain passes were blocked by as much as 8 feet of snow, as the death toll across the country rose to 24. By **Jan. 7,** water shortages and thick mud were preventing effective rescue and cleanup activity in northern California. Many people were without electricity. **Jan. 10** brought record-breaking cold to the midwest, and 9 new deaths were reported. In Sault Ste. Marie, Mich., the thermometers hit 36 degrees below zero and in Fargo, N. D., the wind chill factor put the temperature at 98 degrees below zero. Hurricane-force winds came out of the Rockies, **Jan. 17,** registering some 140 mph, and destroyed houses, broke windows, and snapped off utility poles on the high plains of eastern Colorado. Ten avalanches were reported, **Jan. 22,** in Utah's ski country, and the next day Minnesota ground to a halt as it was hit by a storm that dumped 37 inches of snow on the state. Mud slides, rock slides, and flooding occurred on the Oregon coast, as snow and rain were falling throughout most of the rest of the country.

Draft Registration Continued — President Reagan announced, **Jan. 7,** that he had decided to continue the registration of young men for possible military conscription. Although one of his campaign promises had been to eliminate registration, Reagan had decided that in case of an emergency, mobilization would be sped up at least 6 weeks if young men had registered. He did, however, promise that an actual draft would not take place unless there were a severe threat to this nation. The law requires a man to register within 30 days of his 18th birthday, but Reagan said he was prepared to offer a 30-to-60-day period of grace.

Auto Industry Tries Talks — The United Automobile Workers union agreed, **Jan. 8,** to begin negotiations with General Motors and Ford concerning possible wage and benefit reductions in exchange for job security. The auto companies were experiencing their worst slump since World War II. Some 211,000 auto workers were on an indefinite layoff and another 69,000 were on temporary layoff. The companies maintained that they could not compete with imported cars, particularly those from Japan, because of higher labor costs in the U.S. GM and Ford had been threatening to shift more production facilities out of the country. The talks were suspended, **Jan. 20,** because of disagreements over job security, the size of wage and benefit concessions, and the duration of a new contract. But GM and the union had agreed in principle to reduce auto prices if the workers would make wage and benefits concessions to the company. On **Jan. 29,** GM announced that it would reduce the prices on some cars and trucks despite the failure to get concessions from the factory workers.

Unemployment and Prices Up — The nation's unemployment rate went from 8.4 percent to 8.9 percent during December, the Bureau of Labor Statistics announced, **Jan. 8.** It was estimated that 9,462,000 people were out of work, including 460,000 who had been laid off in December. The unemployment rate for adult men stood at 8 percent, a post-World War II high, and among blacks the figure was 16.1 percent. The Producer Price Index for finished goods rose 0.3 of 1 percent in December, it was announced by the Labor Department, **Jan. 15.** The increase for all of 1981 was only 7 percent. According to the Labor Department, **Jan. 22,** consumer prices rose 0.4 of 1 percent in December, and the total increase for the year was 8.9 percent, the lowest annual increase since 1977. However, medical care costs had risen 12.5 percent during 1981—the largest increase since the government began reporting medical costs in 1935. The cost of hospital rooms increased by 17 percent, and physician's fees increased by 11.7 percent.

AT&T Lawsuit Settled — The American Telephone and Telegraph Co. agreed, **Jan. 8,** to give up the 22 Bell System companies that provide most of the country's local telephone service. This was done in order to settle an anti-trust lawsuit brought against it by the Justice Department. The company would be required to give up all its wholly-owned local telephone subsidiaries, worth $80 billion, the equivalent of two-thirds of the total assets of the corporation. In return, AT&T would be permitted to go into such fields as data processing, communications between computers, and the sale of telephone and computer terminal equipment, all of which had previously been forbidden. It would also keep its long distance service. Congressional leaders indicated, **Jan. 9,** that they would try to modify the ruling in order to protect consumers from local telephone price increases, since both New York Telephone and Southern Bell Telephone had announced that they expected the cost of their services to double over the next 5 years.

Fighter Planes to Taiwan — It was announced, **Jan. 11,** by the White House that President Reagan had decided to permit the government of Taiwan to buy F-5E fighter planes from the United States, but more advanced aircraft would not be sold to the Taiwanese. Because Taiwan had asked to buy advanced fighters and China had raised objections to any sale at all, most observers termed the decision a compromise. Alan B. Romberg of the State Department said that no limit would be placed on the number of fighters to be sold, and indicated that the F-5Es might be improved later with better electronic systems and more advanced weapons.

Jet Hits Washington Bridge — A twin-engine Air Florida jetliner crashed into the crowded 14th Street Bridge in Washington, D.C., **Jan. 13.** The Boeing 737 had taken off during a snowstorm from Washington's National Airport during the height of the rush hour on the bridge connecting the District of Columbia with suburban Virginia. After crashing into the bridge and hitting several cars, the plane broke up and plunged into the Potomac River. At the time it was estimated that 12 people were dead and more than 50 missing, but it was predicted that the final death toll would be 65. A truck and at least 4 autos were sheared open by the plane. A National Park Service helicopter was one of the first at the scene, and dropped a life preserver line to victims who were floating on the water. On **Jan. 14,** the death toll was revised and put at 78, including 4 people who were killed in their cars on the bridge. Twelve bodies had been recovered from the water and emergency crews were still at work pulling bodies and parts of the plane from the water. It was suspected that ice had formed on the plane, impeding its flight. On **Jan. 15,** it was reported that the pilots of a taxiing Braniff jetliner had seen a considerable buildup of ice on the Air Florida craft just before it took off. The ice had been seen not only on the fuselage, but also on the wings. Subzero temperatures on **Jan. 17** delayed the work of the government diving teams, and it was announced that only 5 people of the 79 on the plane had survived. On **Jan. 18,** the tail section of the craft was retrieved from the water, but because the flight recorders were still missing, divers resumed their search. On **Jan. 19,** parts of the cockpit were brought up, and, on **Jan. 24,** the recorders were retrieved. First readings from the recorders indicated that the plane had taken 15 seconds longer than normal to take off. The plane had reached a maximum altitude of 317 feet and a maximum speed of 169 mph, after which the altitude and speed dropped drastically. The investigators disclosed, **Jan. 28,** that a de-icing device in the engine system of the plane had been turned off before the crash. The National Transportation Safety Board released the transcripts of the cockpit tapes **Feb. 4.** The 2 pilots had been talking repeatedly about the snowstorm and the buildup of snow on the wings of their plane.

Reagan Bars Tax Exclusion — President Reagan said, **Jan. 18,** that the Internal Revenue Service would withhold federal tax exemptions from racially imbalanced private schools until Congress acted on the issue. However, the tax-exempt status was reinstated for 2 schools that practiced discrimination—Bob Jones University and Goldsboro Christian Schools. Reagan pointed out that he was opposed to racial discrimination, but that he was sensitive to the needs of private religious schools that used religion as a criterion for admission. This action was taken after a **Jan. 8** announcement by the Treasury and Justice departments that the revenue service would no longer deny tax exemptions to segregated schools. On **Jan. 19,** Reagan admitted that he was the originator of the proposal to grant tax-exempt status to private schools that discriminate on the basis of race.

Immigration Agency Curbed — Judge Prentice Marshall of the Federal District Court in Chicago enjoined the Immigration and Naturalization Service, **Jan. 23,** from surrounding or invading factories and homes and questioning Hispanic Americans on their citizenship status. He did not forbid the service to stop people on the street to question them. The injunction also included the enjoining of agents from arresting, stopping, detaining, or interrogating Hispanic Americans by force, without valid search or arrest warrants, or without reasonable suspicion that they were illegal aliens.

Reagan Announces "New Federalism"— In his State of the Union Message, **Jan. 26,** President Reagan promised to continue to insist on his tax cut proposals that lay at the heart of his economic recovery plans. He also announced a major plan for a "new federalism" under which he would give states and cities control over federal social programs. The amount of money returned to state and local governments would be some $47 billion in federal programs. The federal government would no longer issue food stamps or make payments to poor families with dependent children. This would be taken over by local governments. In exchange, the federal government would take over the total responsibility for Medicaid. He also proposed a 10-year plan in which the states would assume responsibility for many highway, economic development, urban renewal, education, and social services from the federal government.

International

Martial Law Continues in Poland — Interior Minister Czeslaw Kiszczak addressed the Polish nation, **Jan. 1,** urging that Solidarity's pleas for resistance to military rule be rejected. On **Jan. 2,** the Polish military government removed 90 provincial and city officials from their jobs because they could not cope with their tasks in carrying out martial law. On **Jan. 5,** Capt. Wieslaw Gornicki, an advisor to Communist Party leader Wojciech Jaruzelski, said that the military government had no intention of dissolving Solidarity. Polish television announced, **Jan. 7,** that 10 former Polish party leaders were being indicted for using their positions for personal gain. It was also reported that numerous violators of martial law had been sentenced to from 3 to 6 years in prison and a loss of civil rights for an additional 2 to 4 years. The Polish government announced that supplies of food such as meat and fish would be insufficient in January and February. On **Jan. 8,** the government announced 17 people had died in disturbances and strikes. Jaruzelski, **Jan. 9,** met with Archbishop Glemp in an attempt to enlist the church's aid in support of the government, and the censorship of foreign press dispatches was ended. On **Jan. 11,** NATO condemned the Soviets for supporting the military government in Poland and warned that Western Europe might join the United States in imposing economic sanctions against the Soviet Union, possibly involving import arrangements from the Soviet Union, maritime agreements, air services agreements, Soviet commercial representation, and export credits. On **Jan. 12** the Polish government indicated that it wanted to end martial law by **Feb. 1** and that it would want Walesa to participate in labor union talks. The government announced, **Jan. 20,** a new plan for grain farmers under which they would not be allowed to purchase seed unless they had sold grain to the government. It was feared that this would soon lead to bread rationing, in addition to the rationing of meat, butter, sugar, detergents and other products already in effect. More than 100 intellectuals sent a protest petition to the government, **Jan. 21,** demanding the lifting of martial law, the release of thousands of prisoners, and an end to the repression of Solidarity. On **Jan. 25,** Jaruzelski attacked the United States for its sanctions, insisted that martial law was justified, and called for sacrifice and labor from the people of Poland. On **Jan. 27** Warsaw radio announced that the government had approved price increases on food to take effect on **Feb. 1** Milk, meat, butter, and other staples would cost three times as much as they had. In a broadcast **Jan. 31** Warsaw radio reported that more than 200 people protesting the rise in food costs had been arrested and 14 injured in clashes with police in Gdansk over the weekend.

Egyptian Cabinet Dissolved — Pres. Hosni Mubarak of Egypt dismissed his cabinet, **Jan. 2.** He named a new prime minister, Ahmed Fuad Mohieddin, and asked him to form a new government. Previously, Mubarak had held the posts of president and prime minister, and Mohieddin had been first deputy prime minister. On **Jan. 3,** the new cabinet was announced. A new interior minister, deputy prime minister and 9 other new ministers were named.

White House Increases Aid to El Salvador — The Reagan administration, **Jan. 28,** announced that the U.S. must be willing to increase aid to the Salvadoran junta government. On the previous day, Salvadoran rebels had attacked the country's biggest air force base with armor-piercing rockets and machine gun fire; 10 soldiers were killed and 18 warplanes and 4 helicopters were damaged. To make the increased aid possible, President Reagan certified, as required by Congress, that the Salvadoran government had made progress in protecting human rights. On **Jan. 30,** the increase in the amount of aid was set at $100 million and the White House indicated that further increases would be sought from Congress in the next fiscal year. During the month of January, civil strife in El Salvador had intensified. Salvadoran rebels bombed electrical installations in San Salvador, **Jan. 1,** causing a 2-hour blackout in most major cities. On **Jan. 13,** the guerrillas announced that they had captured Jocaitique, a town 100 miles northeast of the capital, after a long battle with government soldiers. They also reported attacking 2 railroad trains. An international Roman Catholic peace organization, Pax Christi International, asked, **Jan. 19,** that the Salvadoran junta government stop its policy of genocide, and pointed out that of the more than 2,000 people murdered in El Salvador since October 1979, 85 percent had been killed by the armed forces and right-wing death squads. In the United States, a crowd of nearly 200 gathered at Ft. Benning, Ga., **Jan. 24,** to protest the training of 600 Salvadoran officer candidates by the U.S. army. It was also reported that during December a massacre had occurred in the village of Mozote. Skulls and bones of dozens of bodies, burned beyond recognition, were found in some 20 mud brick huts and along a trail to the hills. In a nearby cornfield the remains of 14 people were found. Estimates of the number of dead were between 733 and 926 allegedly killed by the government soldiers.

Israelis to Compensate Sinai Settlers — The Israeli cabinet voted, **Jan. 7,** for a package of compensations to Jewish settlers who will have to leave their homes in the Sinai when the last section of the peninsula is returned to Egypt in April. About $263 million was to be divided among some 1,400 families in the Yamit area and in Sharm el-Sheik on the Red Sea. Then, on **Jan. 18,** Israel asked Egypt to alter its border on the Sinai to avoid splitting the Palestinian town of Rafah when the area is turned over to the Egyptians. The Israelis said they preferred that Rafah be totally inside Israel, but would accept a proposal to have it inside Egyptian territory. It was felt that a divided town would have a potential for terrorist infiltration and arms smuggling from Egyptian territory into the Gaza Strip.

Gibraltar Border to Reopen — Prime Minister Leopoldo Calvo Sotelo of Spain announced, **Jan. 8,** that his country would reopen the border with Gibraltar on **Apr. 20.** The border had been closed for 12 years, and was to be opened on the day that Britain and Spain began their discussions concerning the colonial status of Gibraltar. Spain claimed that Gibraltar rightfully belonged to it, while most of the 29,000 people in Gibraltar were believed to be in favor of remaining a British territory. Britain had had control of the peninsula since 1704.

Terror Increases in Guatemala — Police in Guatemala announced, **Jan. 10,** that the bodies of 50 people kidnaped from their homes 10 days previously had been found in the western part of the country. All of the dead had been residents of the town of San Francisco el Tablón, and, in addition to the kidnaping, the attackers had burned down 20 houses in the town. Ten other people had been kidnaped with the 50, but their whereabouts was unknown. On **Jan. 13,** gunmen entered the village of Libertad las Cruces, 55 miles south of Guatemala City, and killed 12 members of a single family, aged from 6 to 65, and government troops killed 23 guerrillas in fighting near San Juan de Comala, 50 miles west of the capital. The next day, gunmen killed a family of 5 in Cobán, 140 miles north of Guatemala City. Foreign Minister Leo Tindemans of Belgium protested to Guatemala, **Jan. 24,** after the disappearance of a second Belgian missionary in that country. On **Jan. 25,** terrorists attacked the town of Santa Ana Huyistla, 150 miles northwest of the capital.

Haitian Island Attacked — A group of Haitian exiles announced, **Jan. 10,** that it had captured the island of Tortuga just off the mainland of Haiti. This attempt to overthrow the government of Pres. Jean-Claude Duvalier, it was alleged, was the work of the Miami-based National Popular Haitian Party. Later in the day, the Haitian government claimed that they had landed troops on the island and the rebels had fled. A report from Miami from an exile stated that the rebels had crossed the channel between Tortuga and Haiti proper and captured the town of Port-de-Paix. On **Jan. 11,** Information Minister Jean-Marie Chanoine of Haiti reported that 3 of the exiles had been captured by government troops on Tortuga, and, on **Jan. 12,** it was reported on television that the 3 men had died of their wounds. Five other invaders were still being sought. The Haitian government announced, **Jan. 22,** that its troops had killed 8 exiles and forced 10 others to flee.

Europe Hard Hit by Frigid Weather — Europe was suffering from its worst winter in memory. On **Jan. 11,** broken ice blocked the flow of the River Vistula in Poland, causing flooding of farm land in the area. Many towns and villages in western England were isolated by snowdrifts up to 15 feet high, and Wales was virtually cut off from the rest of Britain by a snow storm that took 5 lives. The temperature hit 43 degrees below zero in Sweden and ice stopped Denmark's domestic ferry service.

Army Aide Killed in Paris — Lieut. Col. Charles Robert Ray, an American military aide, was shot dead outside his Paris home, **Jan. 18.** The Lebanese Armed Revolutionary Faction announced in Beirut that it was responsible for the assassination. Ray was killed by a single gunman as he was walking to his car. French police said that he was killed by a man who appeared to be Middle Eastern, and that only one shot had been fired, hitting Ray in the head.

Soviet Attacks Italian Communists — In an editorial in *Pravda,* the Soviet Union attacked the leadership of the Italian Communist Party, **Jan. 24.** It accused the Italians of pursuing a policy of direct aid to imperialism. It was generally believed that the attack was made because the Italian Communist leaders had said that they felt that the Soviets were imposing their will on Poland. On **Jan. 25,** the Italian Communist Party issued a policy statement that denounced Soviet actions around the world, including those in Poland, Czechoslovakia, and Afghanistan.

General Rescued by Italian Police — Antiterrorist forces raided an apartment building in Padua, Italy, **Jan. 28,** and freed U.S. Brig. Gen. James L. Dozier. The general had been held prisoner by the Red Brigades, a terrorist group, since his kidnaping, **Dec. 17.** The squad of 10 policemen broke into the apartment and captured 5 persons, one of whom was overpowered as he held a pistol to Dozier's head. They also found 5 machine-pistols, 7 hand grenades, 6 packages of plastic explosives, and various kinds of ammunition in the apartment.

General

Leukemia Advance Reported — It was announced, **Jan. 13,** that a new treatment for leukemia had been developed by doctors at the University of Washington in Seattle. The group, led by Dr. Alexander Fefer, used bone-marrow transplants on sufferers from slow-moving, chronic leukemia, a disease that had always been considered fatal. Chronic granulocytic leukemia is a form of a bone marrow disease that usually afflicts people in their thirties and forties. Half of them die in from 2 to 4 years after the disease begins. Bone marrow transplants were used on 12 victims in the early stages of the disease. All were identical twins, and received the marrow from their fellow twin to avoid tissue rejection. Two to 5 years later, 8 of the 12 were free of the disease, and only one person had died of the cancer. The bone marrow was transplanted only after massive doses of drugs and radiation had been used to kill their cancerous cells.

Disasters — Four residents of a nursing home in Clarksboro, N.J., died, **Jan. 6,** and 77 others became ill as a result of food poisoning caused by spoiled eggs used in their holiday eggnog . . . A mudslide, **Jan. 7,** in Bogotá, Colombia, killed 27 people . . . Four jets from the Thunderbirds, an Air Force stunt team, crashed in the Nevada desert, **Jan. 18,** killing all 4 pilots . . . An explosion in a Spencer, Okla., elementary school kitchen, **Jan. 19,** killed 5 children and one teacher and injured 35 other students . . . Torrential rains in the jungles of Peru caused floods that killed 600 people, **Jan. 25** . . . A bus plunged into the river near the coastal town of Tuxpan, Mexico, **Jan. 26,** killing 19 and injuring 56.

FEBRUARY

National

Auto Manufacturers' Woes Persist — General Motors Corp. announced, **Feb. 1,** that they had made a small profit of $97 million for the 4th quarter of 1981 and $333 million for the year, despite the slump in car and truck sales. The profit was achieved by extensive cost-cutting, it was reported. The Ford Motor Co., meanwhile, had run into problems in its negotiations with the United Automobile Workers union. A tentative agreement with reached, **Feb. 11,** on an "economic framework" for a new contract, but the UAW indicated that other issues needed to be resolved. According to UAW president Douglas A. Fraser, the economic framework included such concessions by the union as the elimination of the annual 3 percent pay increase for workers. The union demand to limit the amount of work done by Ford employees in foreign countries and plant closings in the U.S. were still to be discussed, as was job security. On **Feb. 14,** the International Executive Board of the UAW approved a tentative agreement with Ford. It provided for a guaranteed income until retirement for union members who were laid off after 15 years of service. In return, the workers would give up annual raises and 6 days of paid time off for the next 2 1/2 years. Cost-of-living increases would be deferred. It was expected that Ford would save as much as $1 billion during those 2 1/2 years. The company had lost $1.06 billion in 1981. Two Detroit-area locals of the UAW approved the pact, **Feb. 22,** and, on **Feb. 28,** it was announced that the contract had been overwhelmingly approved by all 91 locals of the UAW working at Ford plants. The agreement was to go into effect Mar. 1 and extend to Sept. 14, 1984. It contained a profit-sharing plan, a guaranteed income for long-time workers who were laid off, and a promise not to close any plants for 2 years. In the meantime, General Motors announced that it would permanently close 5 parts plants and temporarily shut down 2 assembly plants. GM also announced that it was negotiating with Usuzu and Suzuki in Japan for the manufacture of a subcompact automobile. If the negotiations were successful, it was estimated, it would cost the U.S. from 30,000 to 50,000 jobs. Roger B. Smith, the chairman of GM, said that if the UAW would resume talks about the company's demand for worker concessions, it might affect the decision to manufacture the cars in Japan.

Crackdowns on Slavery Reported — Three migrant crew chiefs were convicted, **Feb. 2,** in New Bern, N.C. on federal conspiracy charges of recruiting migrant workers from cities along the Eastern seaboard and holding them against their will. One of the workers, Robert Anderson of Philadelphia, died at work after he was sent to the field despite the fact that he was ill. John Lester Harris was sentenced to life imprisonment for conspiracy resulting in death, plus 3 5-year sentences for kidnapping and involuntary servitude. Dennis Warren was sentenced to 20 years on the same charges, and Richard Warren, who was acquitted on the charge of conspiracy resulting in death, received 6 months on 2 related charges. David Mussry was arrested, **Feb. 3,** in Jakarta, Indonesia on charges that he was a recruiter for a slave ring that imported Indonesians to work for wealthy Los Angeles residents. Twenty-six of those Indonesians had been discovered the previous week in raids on homes and businesses in Los Angeles.

Reagan Releases Budget Message — Pres. Ronald Reagan released his budget message, **Feb. 6,** calling for Congress to decrease the social responsibilities of the government and increase the military strength of the nation. He advocated an increase in spending of 4.5 percent, to $757.6 billion, and called for receipts of $666.1 billion, including $12.7 billion from tax increases on business and tougher tax enforcement. Gov. Richard A. Snelling of Vermont, the Republican chairman of the National Governors' Assn., warned, **Feb. 8,** that the cuts that Reagan had proposed in federally-financed domestic programs would affect the fiscal soundness of the various states. On **Feb. 2,** Caspar W. Weinberger, the U.S. Secretary of Defense, had announced that the administration planned to ask for a 1983 military budget of $260 billion, an increase of $10 billion over what had been expected. The increase was attributed to inflation, and came at a time when the administration had predicted a deficit in the overall budget of $90 billion. Reagan conceded, **Feb. 9,** that his estimated deficit was too high but he asked the critics of his budget to offer alternatives to his plan, since both Republicans and Democrats on the House Appropriations Committee had complained about the deficit. Then, on **Feb. 12,** Treasury Secretary Donald T. Regan predicted that the projected deficit would be reduced in the spring because of an upturn in the economy.

Jobless Rate Down, Consumer Prices Slightly Up — The Bureau of Labor Statistics announced, **Feb. 5,** that the unemployment rate declined 0.3 of 1 percent in January, and had gone down to 8.5 percent. More than 9 million people were still out of work, however, and Dr. Janet L. Norwood, the bureau's commissioner, saw no real improvement on the job front. The Labor Department reported, **Feb. 25,** that the Consumer Price Index for January showed an increase of only 0.3 of 1 percent. This was the smallest increase since July 1980. Although the price of food had increased, there were declines in the prices of gasoline, new cars, houses, and clothing.

Reagan Changes Mind on Missile Silos — The Reagan administration dropped its proposal to place the new MX missiles temporarily in silos reinforced to withstand nuclear attack, it was announced **Feb. 11.** The first 40 missiles would be placed in existing Minuteman silos, which had not been reinforced by concrete and steel. It was reported that not only did the administration feel that the reinforcement was not worth the money, but also would require the permission of the USSR under the terms of the Salt I treaty. The Defense Department, however, was considering other alternatives; putting them in reinforced silos in the long run; carrying them on planes in continuous flight; storing them in bases deep underground; or protecting them in their bases with defensive missiles.

Senator Williams Sentenced — Sen. Harrison A. Williams Jr. (D, NJ) was sentenced to 3 years in prison and fined $50,000, **Feb. 16.** Williams had been convicted of bribery and conspiracy in the Abscam investigation into political corruption. Williams protested his innocence and announced that he planned to appeal the conviction, which would probably require him to serve 14 months in prison before coming up for parole. He was set free on his own recognizance pending the outcome of the appeal.

Williams Found Guilty in Atlanta — Wayne B. Williams was found guilty, **Feb. 27,** of killing 2 of the 28 murdered young blacks in Atlanta. The trial had taken 9 weeks, and Williams was sentenced to 2 consecutive life terms, but would be eligible for parole after 7 years. Williams had been arrested, **May 22, 1981,** near the Jackson Parkway Bridge over the Chattahoochee River northwest of the city. Law enforcement agents had been stationed at the bridge after the bodies of several young blacks were found in the river. Shortly after he heard a loud splash, a policeman saw William's car drive away. Williams was arrested and, 2 days later, the body of Nathaniel Cater surfaced about a mile downstream from the bridge. Cater was the last person murdered in the Atlanta bloodbath. Williams was expected to appeal the verdict.

International

Egypt and Libya Open Border — On **Feb. 1,** 2 border crossings in the desert between Egypt and Libya were reopened. They had been closed 3 years previously by Libya, who was angered when Egypt signed its peace treaty with Israel. Egypt and Libya had also fought a 4-day war in

1977. Martial law, however, was still in effect along the border. The reason for the reopening, it was said, was to permit the 200,000 Egyptians who work in Libya to visit their homeland.

Salvadoran Strife Escalates — Some 500 leftist guerrillas, **Feb. 2,** attacked the town of Nueva Trinidad, 75 miles northeast of San Salvador, in El Salvador, killing about 100 people. Among the dead in the occupied town were the military chief and 11 soldiers. That same day, the town of Usulután was also attacked by guerrillas, but order was soon restored. The leftists announced that they controlled the town of Corinto and had cut electrical power to San Miguel, San Francisco Gotera, and Usulután. Salvadoran police reported that 10 people had been killed in political violence in the previous 24 hours in San Salvador, and army leaders accused the guerrillas of staging the raids to intimidate people and keep them from voting in the March elections. Also on **Feb. 2,** Secretary of State Alexander M. Haig Jr. pledged that the U.S. would do what was necessary to prevent the overthrow of the Salvadoran junta. He also indicated that the guerrillas were backed by Cuba and Nicaragua. On **Feb. 3,** the Salvadoran government released its figures on the number of people killed in the Nueva Trinidad raid, listing 150 to 200 civilians, but foreign correspondents indicated that they believed that no more than 50 were killed. It was announced, **Feb. 3,** that Honduras, Costa Rica, and El Salvador had formed an alliance to bolster El Salvador's governing junta, a move that had been encouraged by the Reagan administration. Nicaragua, Panama, and Guatemala, however, protested the formation of the alliance, since they had urged the Salvadoran government to negotiate with the guerrillas before the elections. The guerrillas carried out another attack on Usulután, **Feb. 7.** It was announced, **Feb. 9,** that 2 more suspects had been arrested for the murders of 4 American churchwomen in 1980. This brought the total of the suspects to 6. The Salvadoran government indicated that one of them had confessed. On **Feb. 10,** the 6, all of them National Guard soldiers, were turned over to a civilian court to determine whether they should be tried. U.S. officials reported, **Feb. 12,** that there were 1,000 Salvadoran troops in the U.S. taking part in basic and advanced infantry combat training conducted by the Green Berets. They were to return to their country in May. President Reagan ordered an investigation, **Feb. 12,** into the case of 5 American advisors in El Salvador who were photographed carrying M-16 rifles and .45-caliber pistols in a combat zone. Advisers were allowed to carry only side arms, and to use them only in self-defense. The following day Lieut. Col. Harry Melander, one of the advisors, was ordered by the U. S. government to leave El Salvador and the others were reprimanded. Pres. Reagan announced, **Feb. 18,** that there were no plans to send American combat troops into action in El Salvador. On **Feb. 19,** it was announced that Deane R. Hinton, the U.S. ambassador to El Salvador, had asked Secretary of State Haig to permit U.S. military advisers to carry rifles for self-protection, but U.S. officials stated that U.S. military personnel in El Salvador had been ordered not to go into combat areas where they might be attacked by guerrillas.

Turmoil Builds in Guatemala — Leftist guerrillas ambushed a military vehicle near El Chal, 150 miles northeast of Guatemala City, **Feb. 2,** killing 2 soldiers and wounding 15. Also on **Feb. 2,** 3 national policemen were killed in a machine-gun attack on a police station in the capital. On **Feb. 5,** Roberto Hirón Lemus, the editor of La Nación, a daily newspaper, was killed by machine-gun fire in Guatemala City. He was also the publicity manager for Gen. Aníbal Guevara, a presidential candidate in the March elections. On **Feb. 6,** an armed gang stopped 2 buses on a road near Panajachel, 70 miles west of the capital, and forced the passengers off the buses, set fire to the vehicles, and then opened fire on the passengers. Eight people were killed and several wounded. Police blamed leftist rebels for the atrocity. Guerrilla bands occupied 3 radio stations, **Feb. 10,** and forced announcers to broadcast a statement that Guatemala's 4 major leftist guerrilla groups were joining forces in their fight against the government. The U.S. Embassy in Guatemala City announced, **Feb. 14,** that Brother James Arnold Miller, an American missionary, had been killed outside his school in Huehuetenango. Four unidentified gunmen wearing hoods had fired submachine guns at him from a speeding car. On **Feb. 15,** armed guerrillas invaded the village of Calante in western Guatemala, decapitating 43 people, including 6 children. Col. José Vicente Martínez, the chief of the Guatemalan military reserves, was critically wounded, **Feb. 26,** in one of at least 7 rebel attacks that killed 6 soldiers and wounded 9 others that day.

Martial Law Continues in Poland — Courts in Gdansk sentenced 101 members of the Young Poland Movement, a group advocating nationalism and Roman Catholicism, to jail from 1 to 3 months, it was announced, **Feb. 4.** The students had been arrested while handing out leaflets to people who had gathered to place flowers at a monument to slain shipyard workers. That same day, 9 miners were given prison terms of 3 to 7 years for organizing a strike in Katowice in January. Great Britain ordered sanctions against Poland and the Soviet Union, **Feb. 5,** in protest of the policy of martial law in Poland. Polish diplomats, journalists, and other representatives based in Britain would have to receive permission to travel more than 25 miles away from their base cities. The British also cut off credit to Poland and cooperation between Great Britain and Poland in the areas of medicine and public health, environmental protection, agricultural research, and atomic energy. With regard to the Soviet Union, Britain said it would impose a licensing system on Soviet ships handling fish caught in British waters and renegotiate the terms of the British-Soviet treaty on merchant navigation. On **Feb. 10,** four more miners were sentenced to from 3 to 4 years in prison for organizing the Katowice miner's strike. The U.S. Senate, **Feb. 10,** approved Pres. Reagan's proposal to pay $71 million owed by Poland to U.S. banks. The administration had indicated that to force Poland into default would alarm international money markets. On **Feb. 13,** 194 people were arrested in Poznan for trying to hold a demonstration in protest of the martial law policy of the Polish government. The government also ordered all places of public entertainment in that city to be closed; gasoline stations were also closed and private automobiles were banned from the streets. Stanislaw Ciosek, a government minister, announced, **Feb. 15,** that Lech Walesa, the Solidarity leader, would remain in detention as long as Poland remained a "barrel of gunpowder." Walesa had volunteered to negotiate with the government, but only as long as he could have legal advisers present at the talks. Ciosek indicated that he had refused the offer. Polish authorities reported, **Feb. 17,** that a 2-day police sweep had turned up some 145,000 people who were guilty of offenses against the martial law rules. Of this number, 99,000 had been warned, 29,000 were given a lecture, 3,500 were held for questioning, 7,000 were fined, and 4,000 were given court summonses, with charges filed against 614 of them. In an address to a session of the Polish Communist Central Committee, **Feb. 24,** Gen. Wojciech Jaruzelski, the Polish leader, said that the continuing tension in the country was the chief cause of the maintaining of martial law. He also promised that he would not be lenient toward his opponents. In an attack upon the U.S., he complained that the Reagan administration's sanctions were having an effect on Poland's production potential. On **Feb. 27,** Poland's Roman Catholic bishops called for an end to martial law and freedom for those who were imprisoned because of martial law violations. They also asked for a national covenant in which Solidarity would be represented.

Britain Cuts Oil Price — As the surplus of world oil continued to grow larger and larger, Great Britain cut the price of its oil, **Feb. 18.** The cut in the price of North Sea oil was $1.50 per barrel, bringing the new price to $35 per barrel, or about 3 cents per gallon. That same day Iran cut its prices by $1 per barrel in hopes of increasing sales to pay for its war with Iraq.

Lévesque Gets Vote of Confidence — Premier René Lévesque of Quebec received an overwhelming vote of confidence from his Parti Québécois, **Feb. 9.** The premier, who had threatened to resign after a party convention in December was backed by 95 percent of the 290,000 party members who voted. During a party convention that ended **Feb. 14,** Lévesque had changed his mind about resignation and had announced that if his party won a majority in the next election it might clear the way for a declaration by Quebec of secession from the rest of Canada. The present Quebec government, elected in Apr. 1981, had more than 4 years to go before it legally had to call another election.

Rebellion Breaks out in Syria — It was reported, **Feb. 10,**

that for the previous 8 days, a revolt against the government had been underway in the Syrian city of Hama. The cause for the uprising apparently lay in tensions between Sunni Moslems, who make up 65 percent of the population of the city, and the minority Alawite sect, the dominant group in the government and the army. It was further reported that about 8,000 soldiers were laying siege to the city and had leveled a part of it with tanks and artillery. Diplomatic sources indicated that there may have been as many as 360 military casualties in Hama, as well as more than 1,000 civilian casualties. Syrian officials, however, denied that there had been an uprising. On **Feb. 11,** Ahmed Iskander Ahmed, the Syrian Information Officer, announced that Hama had indeed been cut off from the rest of the country, but that the reason was that the government was conducting a search campaign for weapons. The target of the search was the fundamentalist Moslem Brotherhood, a guerrilla organization that opposed the government of Pres. Hafez al-Assad. By **Feb. 14,** the main highway running through Hama had been reopened and troops were carrying out mopping-up activities. By **Feb. 18,** much of the old part of the city had been reduced to rubble, and as many as 12,000 troops were seeking members of the Brotherhood.

Iran Fights Guerrillas — Teheran radio announced, **Feb. 10,** that a 2-day sweep by security forces had resulted in the deaths of 22 major opponents of the government, among them the second in command of the People's Mujahdeen, the guerrilla group. On **Feb. 22,** a bomb exploded in the center of the capital, killing 15 and wounding 60. Iranian spokesmen indicated that the bomb had been the work of Monarchists, rather than the Mujahdeen.

Chad Warned by OAU — The Organization of African Unity announced, **Feb. 11,** that it would withdraw its peacekeeping forces from Chad by June 30 unless a cease-fire was arranged between the government and the rebels who were fighting against it. The OAU also insisted that peace negotiations begin, elections be planned, and a new constitution be written. The peacekeeping troops had been in Chad since **December 1981,** when Libyan soliders had been withdrawn, and consisted of 3,000 soldiers from Nigeria, Senegal, and Zaire.

Nkomo Ousted — Joshua Nkomo was dismissed, **Feb. 17,** from the cabinet of Zimbabwe's prime minister, Robert Mugabe. Mugabe alleged that Nkomo had been caught red handed when a cache of Soviet-made weapons was found on a farm owned by a holding company that was controlled by Nkomo and other members of his political party. About 200 demonstrators ran through the streets of the capital, Salisbury, **Feb. 20,** yelling their support of Nkomo.

War in Lebanon Goes On — Street battles that started **Feb. 19** in the Lebanese city of Tripoli resulted in the deaths of 15 persons and the wounding of 32 more. The Syrian-backed militiamen used rockets to repel attacks by Palestinian-supported groups, as both groups tried to control the main sections of the city. Fighting continued in the southern part of the country between Shiite Moslems and Palestine guerrillas aided by Lebanese leftists. The United Nations announced, **Feb. 22,** that it planned to send 1,000 peacekeeping troops to southern Lebanon to break up the guerrilla raids and prevent breakdowns in ceasefires in the border area between Lebanon and Israel. This brought the total of UN troops in Lebanon up to 7,000. There had been rumors that Israel had threatened to move against the PLO if the ceasefires were violated. On **Feb. 25,** at least 7 people were killed and 60 wounded as two car bombs went off in a busy shopping center in Beirut, and anti-Syrian groups took credit for the explosions.

Tanzanian Jetliner Hijacked — Hijackers seized a jet, **Feb. 26,** as it was flying over Tanzania and demanded the resignation of Pres. Julius K. Nyerere. It was reported that 2 hostages had been killed. The pilot was forced to fly first to Nairobi and then to Saudi Arabia. On **Feb. 27,** the plane took off from Jidda and was reported to be flying to Rome, but it later landed in Athens and then flew to London. On **Feb. 28,** the 4 terrorists surrendered to British police and the 90 hostages were released through the intervention of Oscar Kambona, a former Tanzanian foreign minister who had been exiled to Britain.

General

More of Saturn's Moons Discovered — Scientists at the Jet Propulsion Laboratory at Pasadena, Cal., announced, **Feb. 2,** that they had found 4 and possibly 6 more small moons of Saturn when photographs taken by Voyager 2 were analyzed. This brought the total number of known moons around Saturn to 21 or 23. Three of the 4 definite discoveries were found to be sharing orbits with previously known satellites—Mimas, Dione, and Tethys. The other 2 objects could have been moons, but the pictures were not clear enough to give a positive identification. If they were indeed moons, it would mean that Tethys shares its orbit with 4 other moons. The 4 moons range in diameter from 6 to 12 miles, as compared with the moons of Saturn that can be seen by earth's telescopes whose diameters range from 100 miles to the size of Titan, which is larger than the planet Mercury.

Virus Link with Leukemia Found — A team of scientists from the National Cancer Institute and 3 universities in Japan announced, **Feb. 11,** that they had found more evidence that viruses may cause human cancer. Some types of animal cancers had long been known to be caused by viruses, but there was a lack of evidence about human cancer. It was found that antibodies had formed in response to viruses in the blood of Japanese patients suffering from T-cell leukemia. Blood samples from healthy Japanese in that area of the country showed no such antibodies. These antibodies, however, had been found in the blood of 6 of 7 patients suffering from this disease. The seventh person, without the antibodies, was undergoing chemotherapy. If a virus is proved to cause a particular type of cancer, it raises the possibility that a vaccine might be developed to fight that particular type of the disease.

Surgeon General Increases Attacks on Smoking — The Surgeon General of the U.S., C. Everett Koop, announced, **Feb. 22,** that smoking is the most important health issue of our time, as he broadened the list of cancers linked to cigarette use. He added that 30% of all cancer deaths were attributed to smoking. This included deaths by cancers of the lung, larynx, esophagus, bladder, kidney, and pancreas. Koop also urged nonsmokers to stay out of smoke-filled rooms.

Disasters — A South Korean military transport plane crashed into a mountain, **Feb. 6,** killing all 53 people aboard . . . Eleven people were killed and 17 injured when a bus ran off a road and plunged 300 feet down a hillside near Lima, Peru, **Feb. 6** . . . On **Feb. 8,** 30 were killed and more than 60 injured in a Tokyo hotel fire . . . A Japan Air Lines DC-8 crashed into Tokyo Bay, **Feb. 9,** killing 17 . . . An oil-drilling rig sank in a storm off the coast of Newfoundland, **Feb. 15,** and 84 men aboard were drowned in 50-foot seas . . . A Soviet freighter sank in heavy seas in the North Atlantic, **Feb. 16;** 18 bodies and 7 survivors were found out of the crew of 40 . . . At least 15 people were killed in the collapse of a Moscow subway escalator, **Feb. 19** . . . A century-old hotel in Havana, Cuba, collapsed, **Feb. 25,** killing 6 and injuring 1.

MARCH

National

Teamsters Reach Agreement — The International Brotherhood of Teamsters ratified a contract, **Mar. 1,** freezing the basic wage levels of unionized truck drivers and warehouse workers for 2 years. Cost-of-living increases were to be given once per year instead of twice per year, as had been the case under the old contract. The reason given for the union's agreement was that the trucking industry was in financial trouble. More than 120,000 union members had been laid off during the previous year, and the contract was expected to give the members more job security.

Senate Passes Antibusing Legislation — By a vote of 57 to 37, the U.S. Senate passed a bill, **Mar. 2,** that virtually eliminated school busing for the purpose of racial integration. A rider to a bill authorizing funds for the Department of Justice stated that no money could be used to litigate school busing cases, and another rider stated that federal courts would not be permitted to issue orders to transport children more than 5 miles or 15 minutes away from home.

Reagan Stands by His Budget Plan — Pres. Ronald Reagan warned Congress, **Mar. 3**, that their proposals to rescind parts of his tax cuts would result in a continuation of the recession and would not help the plan to balance the budget. On **Mar. 6**, however, Budget Director David A. Stockman told Congress that his estimate for the deficit in the budget for the fiscal year 1983 had climbed again, to $96.4 billion, or almost $5 billion more than the previous estimate. The rise was attributed to revised estimates of the cost of the farm price support program, which had more than tripled, from $1.9 billion to $6.8 billion. The president went to Capitol Hill, **Mar. 9**, and told Senate Republicans that he was committed to his budget plan and intended to hold down taxes and spending while increasing national security. He did offer to consider any alternative plan from Congress that would meet those criteria.

U.S. Wants Caribbean Air Bases — The State Department announced, **Mar. 3**, that the U.S. government was asking for the right to use air bases in Colombia and Honduras. The announcement was understood to be part of an effort to help defend non-Communist nations in the Caribbean. The Defense Department had previously asked for $21 million for the construction of these air fields. Dean Fischer of the State Department said that the money would be spent to improve existing air bases in the 2 countries and use them for training, search and rescue, and relief flights. The agreements would be similar to those accords reached with countries in Europe, Asia, and the Middle East. It was also indicated that both countries had expressed concern to the U.S. concerning Cuban activities in the Caribbean area.

FCC Approves New TV Stations — The Federal Communications Commission issued an order, **Mar. 4**, permitting the establishment of from 3,000 to 4,000 new television stations over a 3-year period. These stations would operate at low power and would have a viewing range of only up to 10 to 15 miles from the transmitters. Because of the low power, the stations would be able to use channels that were already being used by stations in other areas. The order was looked upon as a way to increase local service to rural and inner-city areas. The new stations, however, could be linked by satellite into networks that would serve larger audiences. The FCC stated that priority in granting licenses would be given to minority and special-interest groups.

Jobless Rate Up, Producer's Prices Down, Consumer's Prices Up — According to the Labor Department's Bureau of Labor Statistics in an announcement, **Mar. 5**, the rate of unemployment in the U.S. climbed 0.3 of 1% in February to 8.8%. The increase was attributed to layoffs in heavy industry. More than 9 1/2 million people were without jobs, an increase of 280,000 since January, and 1.8 million more than in the previous July. It was announced by the Labor Department, **Mar. 12**, that producer's prices were down in February, which was the first dip since 1976. The drop in the price for finished goods was small, only slightly more than 0.1 of 1%, but some economists were predicting that inflation was slowing down. U.S. industrial output rose during February, it was revealed, **Mar. 16**. The increase of 1.6% was caused by the easing of unusually severe winter weather. The Labor Department released the figures for consumers' prices in February, on **Mar. 23**. It reported a rise of only 0.2 of 1%, and said that the cause of the slight increase was the recession and another drop in gasoline and automobile prices.

Williams Resigns — Sen. Harrison A. Williams Jr. (D, N.J.) resigned his senate seat, **Mar. 11**, in the face of a probable expulsion from that body. Williams, a 23-year veteran of the Senate, had been convicted of 9 counts of bribery and conspiracy in the Abscam investigations. In his speech announcing his resignation, however, he maintained that he did not feel that he had violated any code of ethics. He was the first senator in more than 50 years to resign in the face of allegations of misconduct.

General Motors Settles with Auto Workers — On **Mar. 15**, General Motors Corporation asked the United Automobile Workers for concessions that were almost identical to those given to the Ford Motor Company in February. Those included freezing wages at current levels for 2 1/2 years and the elimination of 9 paid holidays, plus a 15% lower pay rate for new employees. After 37 hours of negotiation, it was announced, **Mar. 21**, that the UAW and GM had reached an accord on the proposals. It was estimated that the company would save between $2 billion and $3 billion over the 29-month life of the contract. GM also promised not to close 4 plants that had been scheduled for shutdown and agreed to a profit-sharing program. The contract was scheduled to be presented to the rank and file members of the union by the middle of April.

Pentagon Announces Rise in Weapons Cost — In its quarterly update, **Mar. 19**, the Pentagon reported that there would be a record $114.5 billion increase in the estimated cost of 44 major weapons programs. These programs included warplanes, submarines, missiles, and other fighting gear, and the total cost was projected at $454.8 billion. The Pentagon cited extra capabilities and larger quantities of weapons as the reasons for the higher costs. Also, the cost of future inflation was figured into the total, which had never been done before.

International

Poland's Troubles Continue — Gen. Wojciech Jaruzelski, the Polish Communist leader, arrived in Moscow, **Mar. 1**, to hold a series of talks with Soviet leaders. While he was there, Soviet Pres. Leonid I. Brezhnev praised the measures that the Polish Communists had taken to defend their rule, but warned that a premature end to martial law would be dangerous. Jaruzelski emphasized that the decisions to impose martial law were Polish decisions and that he needed time for martial law to work. On **Mar. 2**, just before he returned to Poland, Jaruzelski stated that any further attacks on Polish Communism would be cut short. The Polish authorities announced, **Mar. 3**, that people who were interned under martial law infractions could apply to leave the country permanently and they would be permitted to take their families with them. At the time, more than 4,000 people were being held for those offenses and more than 2,500 had been released. On **Mar. 4**, about a dozen of the detainees had applied for emigration passports. The Polish government announced, **Mar. 4**, that beginning **March 15** Poles would be permitted to travel individually to other Soviet-bloc countries and foreign tourists would be permitted to enter Poland if they had an appropriate visa.

Peking Wants Improved Relationships — Chinese Prime Minister Zhao Ziyang gave his assurance, **Mar. 1**, to U.S. Pres. Ronald Reagan that the People's Republic of China was willing to try to overcome the deadlock concerning the U.S. proposal to sell arms and spare parts to Taiwan. The Chinese had long felt that there was but one China and that Taiwan was actually a province of the Peking government. Zhao said that he hoped that Sino-U.S. relations would continue to move ahead and that obstacles between the 2 nations would be overcome.

Oil Prices Decrease Further — Great Britain, **Mar. 2**, reduced the price of its North Sea oil by $4 per barrel, lowering the price to $31 per barrel. This was the second cut in a month made by the British, and experts said that Saudi Arabia, consequently, would not be able to hold to its official price of $34 per barrel—a benchmark for other OPEC prices. In an effort to prop up sagging oil prices, the OPEC nations announced, **Mar. 6**, an apparent agreement to cut production limits by more than a million barrels per day. That meant that OPEC would produce no more than 18.5 million barrels per day, as compared with 31 million barrels per day in 1979. The OPEC nations, at a meeting in Vienna, **Mar. 20**, formally agreed to cut oil production by 700,000 barrels per day, reducing the daily output to 17.5 million barrels.

Guatemala Guerrillas Form United Front — Guerrillas in Guatemala gave notice to the government, **Mar. 2**, that the 4 main groups of insurgents had joined forces and called on all opposition forces to join them. Forming a group called Guatemalan National Revolutionary Unity, they hoped to topple the regime of Gen. Romeo Lucas García, the president. The rebels were believed to have 6,000 men and women under arms. In their statement, the 4 groups alleged that 83,500 people had been killed since 1954 by security forces, 13,500 of them in 1981 alone. On **Mar. 6**, guerrillas abducted Alvaro Contreras Vélez, the publisher of the newspaper *Prensa Libre*, and planted dynamite in the car of Julio Eduardo López, the security chief for Gen. Angel Aníbal Guevara, the front-running candidate in the upcoming presidential election. López was killed in the explosion.

U.S. Asserts Nicaraguan Involvement in Salvador — When the House Appropriations Committee challenged Secretary of State Alexander M. Haig Jr., **Mar. 4,** to prove his statements that Salvadoran guerrillas were directed by foreigners, Haig announced that a Nicaraguan military man had been captured in El Salvador. He also stated that the U.S. had evidence that there was a Nicaraguan involvement in the command and control of Salvadoran guerrilla operations. Col. Carlos Reynaldo López Nuila, the director of the Salvadoran National Police, announced, **Mar. 6,** that the Nicaraguan, 19-year-old Ligdamis Anaxis Gutiérrez Espinosa, would be given a safe-conduct pass to leave El Salvador. Gutiérrez had been captured near the Guatemalan border while allegedly on his way to take command of a group of Salvadoran guerrillas after being trained as a guerrilla in Mexico. He had escaped, however, and was in the Mexico embassy in San Salvador. Gutiérrez was regarded by the Salvador police as a guerrilla leader, but would be given the pass since the Mexican government considered him to be a student enroute to school in Mexico. Pres. José Napoleón Duarte of El Salvador endorsed a police report, **Mar. 7,** that labeled Gutiérrez as a soldier sent to train Salvadoran guerrillas, stating that the Nicaraguan was beyond a doubt an agent of the Sandinista Government of Nicaragua, trained in Mexico to help to overthrow the Salvadoran government. On Mar. 9, the Reagan administration made public aerial reconnaissance photos which allegedly showed that Nicaragua, aided by Cuba and the USSR was building the largest military force in the region. In another attempt to prove that foreign countries were aiding the Salvadoran guerrillas, the State Department presented another Nicaraguan, Orlando José Tardencillas Espinosa, to the press, **Mar. 12.** Tardencillas was expected to confirm Nicaraguan and Cuban involvement in El Salvador, since he had told the Salvadoran army, and later the American Embassy in San Salvador, that he had been trained in Cuba and Ethiopia and then sent to El Salvador by the Nicaraguan Government. But, in the press conference, he said he had never been to Cuba or Ethiopia and had never seen another Nicaraguan or Cuban in El Salvador. He also denied that Nicaraguans had provided aid to Salvadoran guerrillas. Tardencillas, who claimed to be 19 years old, said that he was a revolutionary and former soldier in the Nicaraguan army during the Sandinist revolution, but deserted to join the Sandinists and rose to command 2 military districts. He later joined the Salvadoran guerrillas. He was captured and jailed in El Salvador, he stated, in 1981, and was physically and psychologically tortured. On **Mar. 13,** Tardencillas was turned over to the Nicaraguan embassy in Washington and left that day for Nicaragua.

Sadat Assassination Trial Ends — Five of the 24 Moslem fundamentalists accused of the assassination of Pres. Anwar el-Sadat of Egypt in October 1981, were sentenced to death in Cairo, **Mar. 6.** Seventeen others were also convicted and sentenced to prison terms that ranged from one year to life; two were acquitted. On **Mar. 7,** the defense attorney for one of the 5 men sentenced to death was arrested on charges of disclosing details of the closed military trial. Pres. Hosni Mubarak of Egypt approved the death sentences of 5 of the Moslem militants, **Mar. 20,** as well as the jail terms for 17 others who had been convicted. The death penalties involved the execution by firing squads for the 2 military officers condemned, and by hanging for the other 3.

South Africa Attacks Guerrillas — A major guerrilla staging post in southwestern Angola was wiped out by South African troops **Mar. 13.** It was reported that 45 soldiers from an elite South African unit killed 201 guerrillas of the South-West Africa People's Organization (SWAPO) during a 7 1/2 hour attack. However, **Mar. 20,** Angola denied the South African claim and said the staging post was actually a refugee camp.

U.S. Accuses USSR Re Poison Gas — Deputy Secretary of State Walter J. Stoessel Jr. told the Senate Foreign Relations Committee, **Mar. 8,** that the Soviets had killed at least 3,000 people in Afghanistan with poison gas and other chemical weapons. He asserted that the information had come from Afghan army defectors who had been trained in chemical warfare by the Soviet Union as well as from refugees in Pakistan who said that they had been victims of the chemical attacks. According to Stoessel, the Soviets had used irritants, incapacitants, nerve agents, phosgene oxime, and perhaps mycotoxins, mustard, lewisite, and toxic smoke. Several times before, the U.S. had accused the USSR of using chemical weapons in violation of the 1925 Geneva Protocol on Gas Warfare. Stoessel also reported that approximately 3 million Afghans had fled their country in recent months, most of them to neighboring Pakistan, and that thousands more were being held as political prisoners in Afghanistan. He also told of reports of torture and summary executions.

Libyan Oil Banned from U.S. — The Reagan administration imposed an embargo on Libyan oil imports, **Mar. 10,** as well as a curtailment of exports of high technology to that country. The reason given for the embargo was that Libya was still supporting international terrorist and subversive activities. It was felt that this move was unlikely to affect prices or supplies of petroleum products in the U.S., but that it might hurt Libya in the event that that country was unable to sell its excess supplies of oil to other countries. U.S. imports of Libyan oil had shrunk from a 1981 average of 150,000 barrels per day to 120,000 barrels per day, and the U.S. was importing only 2% of its oil from that country. Libya, however, had been exporting 25% of its oil output to the U.S.

Nicaragua Unrest Continues — The government of Nicaragua placed its armed forces on alert, **Mar. 16,** and called on the people to join the militia following the destruction of 2 bridges by counterrevolutionaries. It was also alleged that these guerrillas were supported by the U.S. A state of emergency was in effect and censorship was imposed on radio news programs and newspapers. On **Mar. 17,** Nicaragua protested to the United Nations, saying that the U.S. had violated its air space by flying planes over its air fields to take photographs. The coordinator of the Nicaraguan junta, Daniel Ortega Saavedra, requested, **Mar. 19,** that the U.N. Security Council denounce the U.S. for what he said was an imminent invasion of Nicaragua. On **Mar. 23,** it was reported that the U.S. and Nicaragua had agreed to open discussions of their differences.

Military Advisor Total Increased — The State Department announced, **Mar. 19,** that the U.S. had increased the number of its military advisors in Honduras to 100 since the beginning of 1982. The reason for the increase was reported to be the need to enhance the security of that country because of the military buildup in neighboring Nicaragua. There were more U.S. military advisors in Honduras than in any other country, it was stated. El Salvador, for example, had but 55. Along with this, military aid to that country had increased from $10 million in the 1982 fiscal year to a request for $15 million in the next fiscal year. In addition, Honduras would receive a supplementary request for $60 million, as against the request for $35 million for El Salvador. The U.S. had also sent Green Berets to help train the Hondurans in patrolling the El Salvador border.

Knesset Votes on Begin — The Israeli Parliament, the Knesset, voted, **Mar. 23,** on a motion of no confidence in Prime Minister Menachem Begin. The vote resulted in a tie, and Begin proposed that he and his cabinet should resign. The cabinet, however, rejected that proposal, and voted 12-6 to stay in office. The reason for the vote of no confidence was the government's handling of recent disorders in the West Bank. Begin's strength in the Knesset had eroded because of the defection of some right-wing legislators opposed to the final pull-out from the Sinai, which was scheduled for **Apr. 25.** As it stood, Begin's coalition controlled precisely half of the 120 seats in the governing body.

Army Officers Stage Guatemalan Coup — Dissident Guatemalan army officers, **Mar. 23,** staged a coup, ousting the regime of Gen. Romeo Lucas Garcia. Lucas was to have been replaced by Gen. Angel Anibal Guevara in July. Guevara had been elected, amid allegations of fraud, in presidential elections held on Mar. 7. Tanks and troops surrounded the presidential palace, and spokesmen announced that the recent elections had been manipulated. A conservative junta, led by retired Gen. Efraín Rios Montt, was appointed to rule the country. Lucas was reportedly taken to the airport for a flight out of the country. On **Mar. 24** the junta suspended the Guatemalan constitution and the activities of all political parties, but made no mention of future elections. In addition to being president of the junta, Rios Montt had assumed the title of Minister of Defense. Another junta member, Gen. Horacio Maldonado, was Minister of Government in charge of the security forces, and the third, Col. Jorge Luis Gordillo, was Minister of Communications and Public Works. The junta officially annulled the results of the **Mar. 7** election on **Mar. 25.** On **Mar. 27,** guerrilla leaders announced that they believed that the new junta promised no fundamental change in the government and they had resolved to carry on their fight.

Army Stages Coup in Bangladesh — Lieut. Gen. Hussain Mohammed Ershad, the Bangladesh army's chief of staff, announced, **Mar. 24,** that he had seized power and deposed the president of the country, Abdus Sattar. Ershad stated that his aim was to end corruption in public life. Sattar, who had been elected in November 1981, said in a radio broadcast that the takeover was necessary to maintain law and order, but it was reported that his voice trembled as he made his speech. Communication with the rest of the world was ended soon after the coup. Martial law was declared and the new government announced, **Mar. 26,** that several former high government officials and 200 others had been arrested on charges of corruption, misuse of power, and anti-state activities. A retired judge, A.S.M. Ahsan, was appointed president, but he was considered a mere ceremonial figure and it was thought that Ershad was the true ruler.

Strong Turnout for Salvadoran Elections — Despite continued civil strife and the absence of candidates representing leftist guerrillas, large numbers of Salvadorans turned out, **Mar. 28,** to elect El Salvador's new constituent assembly. Although, as of **Apr. 2,** returns showed the centrist Christian Democrat party, led by junta chief Jose Napoleon Duarte, holding a 40.5% plurality of the vote, the 5 minority parties had begun negotiations to form a majority coalition in the new assembly. The assembly, in turn, would have the power to appoint an interim president, write a new constitution, and call presidential elections planned for 1983. The large turnout, some 1 million of 1.3 million eligible voters, came despite rebel call for a boycott of the elections. Civil disorder had plagued El Salvador throughout the month. On **Mar. 2,** the Salvadoran army had ended its siege of Suchitoto, 20 miles northeast of San Salvador. The assault had lasted 10 days, and the army admitted that a number of guerrilla forces were still holding out. Guerrillas reported, **Mar. 7,** that government security forces had killed a total of 124 people in El Campanario and the surrounding vicinity during the month of January. On **Mar. 8,** guerrillas attacked the cities of San Vicente and San Miguel. On **Mar. 15,** leftist guerrillas claimed they had taken the town of Cuscatancingo, only 2 1/2 miles from the center of San Salvador, but military spokesmen denied the report.

General

Birds Make Comeback — The Interior Department reported, **Mar. 10,** that certain bird populations that had previously been thought to be on the verge of extinction had been increasing in numbers. The increase had occurred during the 10 years during which DDT had been banned by the government. The birds included the bald eagle, the osprey, the brown pelican, and the peregrine falcon. The government banned DDT when it was discovered that it was interfering with the reproductive process among bird populations to the extent that the birds were laying thin-shelled eggs that easily broke.

First Land Mammal Fossil Found in Antarctica — A team of scientists led by Dr. William J. Zinsmeister of Ohio State University announced, **Mar. 20,** that they had found fossil remains of the first land mammal ever discovered in Antarctica. The fossil bones were of a small marsupial, or pouched mammal, about the size of a rat. The find gave evidence for the scientific theory that marsupials, most of whom are confined to Australia, reached that continent from South America by using Antarctica as a land bridge. This, of course, was before the continents separated and drifted apart hundreds of millions of years ago.

Shuttle Makes Third Trip — The space shuttle *Columbia* was lifted into earth orbit for the 3rd time **Mar. 22.** The astronauts aboard, Col. Jack R. Lousma of the Marine Corps and Col. C. Gordon Fullerton of the Air Force, were to spend 7 days in orbit conducting scientific and engineering studies and putting the shuttle through performance tests. On **Mar. 23** their television camera failed and, after making a photographic inspection of tile damage on the shuttle's nose, they reported the tiles that were damaged were in a noncritical area. The shuttle's radio failed, **Mar. 26,** but the astronauts were able to use backup systems. On **Mar. 29,** a sandstorm at the White Sands Missile Range, the Columbia's landing site, delayed the return of the shuttle, and, on **Mar. 30,** the longest test flight of the space shuttle ended when it landed at White Sands. The mission had lasted 8 days and 5 minutes. The astronauts had demonstrated the vehicle's ability to fly under adverse thermal conditions, to serve as a platform for scientific observations, and to operate in orbit almost 3 times longer that the previous 2 missions.

Disasters — Thousands were homeless on the island of Tongo following a tropical storm, **Mar. 4** . . . Ten persons died of suffocation, **Mar. 6,** in a Houston, Tex., hotel fire . . . An Air National Guard aerial tanker collided with a light civilian plane over the desert near Phoenix, Ariz., **Mar. 13,** killing 6 . . . A train crashed into a school bus near Mineola, N.Y., **Mar. 14,** killing 9 teenagers . . . On **Mar. 14,** a series of Alpine avalanches near Grenoble, France, killed 11 and injured 20 more . . . Twenty-seven men were killed in the crash of an Illinois National Guard jet near Winder Lake, **Mar. 19** . . . In the Indian state of Andhra Pradesh, **Mar. 20,** an express passenger train killed 40 people and seriously injured 25 when it rammed into a bus . . . Fifty people were killed, **Mar. 28,** in the eruption of a volcano near Pichucalco, Mexico . . . During a large air drop exercise over the desert near Los Angeles, Calif., **Mar. 30,** 4 army paratroopers died and at least 74 were injured.

APRIL

National

Rare Spring Storm Ravages Nation — A rare spring storm hit the United States, **Apr. 1-10,** producing over 80 tornadoes, snow, floods, and high winds. The storm moved from California, across the Rockies, through the Midwest and, by **Apr. 6,** unleashed its damage on the Northeast. At least 46 people died and hundreds were injured in the blinding blizzards that dumped 16 feet of snow in the Sierras and caused wind speeds to hit 70 miles per hour in some areas and 148 miles per hour in western North Carolina. On **Apr. 9,** another storm hit the Midwest and East and brought tornadoes to Florida as the death toll reached at least 46 persons. Pres. Ronald Reagan declared Texas a major disaster area as a result of the severe storms and tornadoes that hit the state.

Jobless Rate Up and Industrial Output Down — The number of unemployed persons rose to 9% in March, the Labor Department announced, **Apr. 2.** Nearly 9.9 million people were out of work, the highest number since World War II. The rise was taken to be an indication of a continuingly sluggish economy. The unemployment rate for blacks was 18%, setting a record, and the rate for adult males, 7.9%, tied an old record. Producers' Prices were off 0.1% in March, the Labor Department reported, **Apr. 19.** This was only the 2d time in more than 6 years that this inflation measure had declined for 2 straight months. Industrial output also declined in March, it was reported by the Federal Reserve Board, **Apr. 15.** The decrease was small—0.8%—confirming that the recession was not over. The Commerce Department reported, **Apr. 21,** that the U.S. gross national product had fallen at an annual rate of 3.9% in the first quarter of the year, indicating that the recession had continued through March. But this economic downturn continued to slow the rate of inflation. On **April 23,** the Bureau of Labor Statistics announced that consumer prices had declined 0.3% in March—the first price decline in almost 17 years. The drop was caused by declines in gasoline prices and food and housing costs. It was also reported that in the first quarter, consumer prices were up only 1%.

Auto Unionists Approve GM Pact — General Motors Corporation union employees agreed by a narrow margin to a new labor contract, **Apr. 9.** Fifty-two percent of the GM workers voted for the contract, which was similar to the Ford Motor Company contract approved in February. They would give up annual pay increases of 3% and 9 annual paid holidays, as well as postpone 3 of the 4 quarterly cost of living increases. Under the contract, new employees would be hired at 80% of the wage and benefit scales given to current workers.

Military Parts to Go to Taiwan — The Reagan Administration reported, **Apr. 13,** that it would go ahead with its plan to sell $60 million worth of military spare parts to Taiwan. The parts would be used by Taiwan's air force to keep their planes flying. China made a strong protest, **Apr. 14,** against this plan, but promised that there would be no retaliation provided that the sales included no weapons.

Reagan's Tax Problems Continue — Pres. Ronald Reagan announced, **Apr. 14,** that he had not made up his mind about a suggested tax surcharge that would be used as a budget cutting compromise. House Speaker Thomas J. O'Neill had announced that if the president would agree to this heavier tax burden for the more affluent, he might give up his opposition to limiting cost of living increases on Social Security and other benefit programs. On **Apr. 15,** Reagan proposed legislation that would give income tax credits to families that pay tuition to private elementary and secondary schools. This plan would cost $100 million in 1983 and would give an additional tax credit of $500 per child to those families whose annual adjusted gross income was $50,000 or less. On **Apr. 20,** Reagan pledged to go the extra mile to compromise with Democrats on his budget, saying that he wanted to hold the federal deficit at $95 billion for the year.

U.S. Bans Cuban Travel — John M. Walker, assistant secretary of the treasury for enforcement and operations, announced, **Apr. 19,** that travel to Cuba would be curbed. Only official travel, trips by news reporters or academic researchers, and travel for family reunification would be permitted for United States citizens. The rules also applied to citizens of other countries who were trying to travel from

Argentina Seizes Falklands; Britain Task Force Retakes Islands

The Argentine governing junta announced, **Apr. 2,** that army, navy, and air force units had captured the British-held Falkland Islands, 250 miles from the southeastern tip of their country. Several thousand Argentine troops had defeated the token force 84 British marines, defending the islands. Also captured were the South Georgia and South Sandwich Islands, part of the British archipelago. U.S. President Ronald Reagan had tried by phone to persuade Argentine Pres. Leopoldo Galtieri to call off the invasion. At the UN, the British denounced Argentina by calling the invasion a wanton act.

The British government announced that a number of Royal Navy ships were heading toward the Falklands and a carrier task force was forming off the English coast. Argentina reported that between 4,000 and 5,000 men had taken part in the invasion and that Brig. Gen. Mario Benjamin Menéndez had been appointed the new governor of the islands.

On **Apr. 3,** Prime Minister Margaret Thatcher ordered a large naval task force to sail to the islands and announced that Argentina's financial assets in the UK would be frozen, a sum in the neighborhood of $1.5 billion in gold, securities, and currency deposits. New export credits to Argentina were also canceled. John Nott, the British Defense Secretary, said that the task force which would set sail **Apr. 5,** would be led by the aircraft carrier *Invincible,* and contain another carrier, destroyers, frigates, landing ships, 1,000 marine commandos and a number of other troops. It was expected that it would take the ships about 2 weeks to reach their destination. The UN Security Council, also on **Apr. 3,** demanded the withdrawal of Argentine troops from the Falklands, but Argentina declared that it would not do so.

On **Apr. 4,** the Argentine government announced that it had overrun the last British military unit on the Falklands, a small contingent of marines on the South Georgia Islands, on the previous day. Three Argentines had been killed in the battle. New rules imposed by Argentina required that the 1,800 residents of the Falklands stay indoors. Schools, banks, and businesses were closed. In London, Nott vowed that Britain would fight if peace efforts did not work out.

Lord Carrington, the British Foreign Secretary, resigned **Apr. 5,** because of his embarrassment for not having taken measures to forestall the invasion. He, along with the rest of the Thatcher government, had come under severe criticism.

On **April 7,** France, West Germany, Belgium, and Austria banned the sale of arms and military equipment to Argentina, joining the Netherlands, Switzerland, and Britain. Britain threatened to sink any Argentine ship that came within 200 miles of the Falkland Islands after **April 11.**

Secretary of State Alexander M. Haig Jr., met in London with British officials **Apr. 8,** to try to create a plan for a peaceful settlement of the situation. British officials indicated, **Apr. 9,** that time might be running out for a peaceful settlement of the Falkland situation and that only Haig had a chance of persuading the Argentinians to withdraw its troops. Haig had left London that day for Buenos Aires. On **Apr. 10,** Pres. Leopoldo Galtieri of Argentina met with Haig for 2 hours and then announced, after the meeting, that his country would fight if it were provoked by Britain. However, Argentine diplomats said that their country would not try to force its ships past the British blockade. Also on **Apr. 10,** the European Common Market declared a total ban on imports from Argentina.

The British blockade went into effect on **April 12,** but no naval engagements were reported. Haig, back in London, met for 11 hours with British leaders. He indicated that there were still several differences to be worked out, and that time was slipping away.

Prime Minister Thatcher warned the Argentine navy, **Apr. 14,** not to test the blockade or their vessels would be sunk. Haig called the situation dangerous and said that both Argentina and Great Britain would have to be more flexible in the search for a solution to the problem. Also on **Apr. 14,** the Argentine coast guard reported that 2 of its patrol boats had defied the blockade by sailing through it to the Falklands.

On **Apr. 17,** Haig conferred with Galtieri in Buenos Aires, but with no apparent success, Galtieri demanded full sovereignty over the islands. The talks ended **April 19,** and Haig flew to Washington, D.C. Thatcher, **Apr. 20,** expressed serious reservations about the peace plan that Haig had discussed with the Argentines and announced that Foreign Secretary Frances Pym would go to Washington on **Apr. 22** with a set of counterproposals, calling for a 3-stage plan for the settlement of the dispute. The plan involved the withdrawal of Argentine troops, rule by the British for a period of time while natives were given the opportunity to emigrate, and final occupation by Argentina.

The British Government reported, **Apr. 25,** that its troops had recaptured the port of Grytviken on South Georgia after a 2-hour battle. The attack had been mounted by advance troops, carried helicopter, from the task force still steaming toward the Falklands. The following day Thatcher warned that further military action might be imminent, and that the whole of South Georgia Island had been recaptured. Britain announced, **Apr. 28,** that it would impose a total, 200-mile sea and air blockade around the Falklands, to begin **Apr. 30.** Argentina imposed its own blockade around the islands on **Apr. 29.** And, on **Apr. 30,** U.S. Pres. Ronald Reagan placed the U.S. on the side of Britain by ordering limited sanctions against Argentina and offering materiel support to Britain.

The conflict heated up, **May 1,** when Argentina announced that it had repelled several British bombing runs on the islands and damaged 3 British ships, all of them frigates. The Argentines also claimed to have shot down 2 Harrier jump-jets and crippled 2 others. On **May 2,** British bombers attacked 2 airfields on the islands and bombarded Argentine shore bases on the island. One British frigate was damaged, but not seriously, by an Argentine bomber during a counterattack. A British submarine, **May 2,** torpedoed the *General Belgrano,* Argentina's only cruiser. Argentina announced, **May 3,** that the ship had been sunk, and estimated that 500 seamen had lost their lives. Argentina also claimed that the ship had been sunk 36 miles outside the blockade zone es-the U.S. to Cuba. Citing the Cuban support for enemies of U.S. allies, he pointed out that these new rules would cut down on Cuba's earnings from tourists and tighten the U.S. trade and financial embargo against Cuba.

International

Salvadoran Parties in Post-Election Deadlock — Roberto d'Aubuisson, the leader of the extreme right-wing Nationalist Republican Alliance in El Salvador, announced, **Apr. 2,** that he was planning to merge his party with the centrist Christian Democratic Party. He indicated, however, that he opposed retaining José Napoleón Duarte of the Christian Democrats as president. It was reported, also on **Apr. 2,** that Salvador Samayoa, a spokesman for the Salvadoran guerrillas, had said that the guerrillas would stand by their offer to negotiate the formation of an interim government and the elimination of the army's high command. He added, however, that if d'Aubuisson were to become president, the guerrillas would take back their offer to negotiate. On **Apr. 19,** the new Constitutent Assembly met for the first time, appointing members to committees on debate, the budget, credentials, and protocol. Meetings were held to select members of the executive branch of the government. A right-wing coalition took control of the assembly, **Apr. 22,** giving the Christian Democrats no key legislative positions, and electing Roberto d'Aubuisson as president of the assembly. The next day, Deane R. Hinton, the American ambassador to El Salvador, said that the election of the right-wing group would not affect the Reagan administration's policy toward the Salvadorans. On **Apr. 29,** the assembly elected a political centrist, Alvaro Alfredo Magaña, as the new president, ending the month-long political deadlock.

Mexican Volcano Erupts — El Chichón volcano 420

---

tablished by the British.

An Argentine jet fighter, **May 4,** set afire and disabled the British destroyer *Sheffield,* which had to be abandoned. Britain announced, **May 6,** that an effort by Peru and the U.S. to arrange a ceasefire had collapsed, and that 2 more Sea Harrier jets had been lost in the ocean. On **May 7,** the British extended the blockade zone, stating that it would treat as hostile any Argentine warship or plane found more than 12 miles from the coast of Argentina. Argentina announced, **May 9,** that some of their positions on the islands had been attacked and British planes had sunk a fishing boat, but the 50-minute attack on Stanley and Darwin had been repelled.

A **May 11** dispatch from London reported that the British had sunk an Argentine ship thought to be an oil tanker in the narrow waterway separating East and West Falkland Islands. It was announced, **May 12,** that 2 Argentine A-4 Skyhawk jet attack planes had been shot down while attacking a British warship.

British Sea Harrier jets raided the airport at Stanley again, **May 14.** The converted cruise ship *Canberra,* with 2,500 assault troops aboard, the amphibious assault ship *Fearless,* and other ships joined the British task force. British warplanes attacked 2 Argentine supply vessels, **May 16** and one had to be abandoned.

The Common Market countries voted, **May 17,** to extend for one week the sanctions imposed against Argentina in April. On **May 20,** Prime Minister Thatcher rejected a United Nations proposal for further negotiations on the Falkland dispute.

British troops established a firm beachhead at San Carlos Bay during an attack of the Falklands on **May 21,** as Royal Marine commandos and troopers of the Parachute Regiment stormed ashore in several small-scale raids and landings. Five British ships were damaged and 1 plane was missing, but the Argentines lost 17 planes during the attack. More reinforcements for the British troops poured ashore, **May 22,** and the beachhead was widened to some 60 square miles. In the landing attack, a British missile frigate was sunk with a loss of 20 men. The reinforcements brought the total to an estimated 5,000 marines and paratroopers on the beachhead. On **May 23,** Argentina announced that it had carried out a major air attack against the British ships that were supporting the beachhead, but the British reported that they shot down 6 airplanes and damged 3 others in that attack. On **May 24,** Britain reported that 7 more Argentine warplanes had been shot down as they were attacking British ships, and Argentina claimed to have beaten back a British jet air raid on Stanley.

A majority of the Common Market nations agreed, **May 24,** to extend indefinitely the sanctions that had been imposed on Argentina.

On **May 25,** U.S. Secretary of State Haig reported that the British appeared to be close to victory and Argentina's Foreign Minister, Nicanor Costa Méndez, called for the United Nations to aid in setting up a negotiated peace.

Also, on **May 25,** the Argentines launched a new attack when fighter-bombers damaged and sank the British destroyer, *Coventry.*

The U.N. Security Council, **May 26,** asked Sec. Gen. Javier Pérez de Cuéllar to revive his role in setting up peace talks and Britain announced that it would not consider a ceasefire unless Argentina withdrew its troops from the islands.

British paratroopers and marines, **May 27,** moved out of the beachhead at San Carlos Bay and launched 2 offensives against Argentinian troops. British forces captured Darwin and Goose Green, **May 28,** defeating the second largest Argentine installation in the islands—some 1,000 men. On **May 29,** Britain claimed to have taken 900 captives in the fighting. British troops in a drive toward Stanley captured Douglas and Teal Inlet, **May 30.** It was disclosed that 12 British soldiers had been killed and 32 wounded in the fighting at Goose Green. By **May 31,** the British troops were within 15 miles of Stanley, the Falkland's capital, and were fighting Argentine troops in the hills near the town.

On **June 1,** the British announced that their forces had seized vital high ground about 10 miles west of Stanley. By **June 2,** the British were within sight of Stanley and held all the important high ground around the capital.

The Argentine high command announced, **June 4,** that it had repelled a British air attack on Stanley and had bombarded the British positions to the west. Three thousand fresh infantrymen were landed from the liner Queen Elizabeth II, **June 6,** bringing the British fighting forces in the Falklands up to 8,000. There were 7,000 Argentine troops defending Stanley. On **June 7,** British troops had captured a ridge only 5 miles from the city that overlooked the air field. It was announced that up to 60 Argentine soldiers had been killed in the preceding 5 days.

As many as 50 British soldiers and sailers were killed in an air attack, **June 8.** A major battle broke out, **June 12,** near Stanley, with heavy casualties on both sides. On **June 14,** British Prime Minister Thatcher announced that the Argentine forces in Stanley had surrendered. She also indicated that Brig. John Waters, the deputy commander of the British Land forces, was negotiating surrender terms with Brig. Gen. Mario Menéndez, the commander of the Argentine troops in Stanley. On **June 16,** the British warned that hundreds of Argentine prisoners of war could die from hunger unless the Argentine government pledged to cease all hostilities. There were some 15,000 prisoners, many of whom were suffering from malnutrition, dysentery, and scabies.

Pres. Leopolo Galtieri of Argentina resigned under pressure, **June 17,** as president, commander-in-chief of the army, and member of the ruling junta. The Foreign Ministry of Argentina announced that, with the help of the British, ships would be sent to the islands to help repatriate the prisoners of war. On **June 18,** the Argentine government indicated that the Falklands' truce was still uncertain and that a total cessasion of hostilities would be reached only if Britain withdrew its forces from the islands.

On **June 19,** the British landed on the South Sandwich Islands—a dependency of the Falklands. The foreign ministers of the European Common Market decided, **June 20,** to lift their trade embargo against Argentina as Britain announced that it had captured the South Sandwich Islands, making their victory complete. On **June 22,** Maj. Gen. Reynaldo Benito Antonio Bignone was appointed president of Argentina.

miles southeast of Mexico City erupted, **Apr. 3,** spraying several villages with rock and ash. Unconfirmed reports, **Apr. 4,** set the death toll at up to 1,000 people. It was also estimated that as many as 200,000 people had fled their villages. By **Apr. 7,** the estimated number of fatalities had climbed to 5,000 and the volcano was spewing up a 30,000-foot column of ash-filled smoke and steam, and the fallout was spreading for hundreds of miles. In some areas near the volcano the ash had piled up as high as 3 feet.

Israel-Lebanon Tensions Grow — The Reagan administration announced, **Apr. 9,** that for the previous 72 hours, new Israeli military movements near the Lebanese border had been observed. The U.S. State Department expressed its concern that the Israelis might be planning an invasion into southern parts of Lebanon and appealed for restraint. Israel continued to warn of a buildup of Palestinian forces in Lebanon in violation of the ceasefire of the previous July. On **Apr. 10,** Lebanese Pres. Elias Sarkis appealed to the U.S. and Soviet ambassadors to Lebanon to intervene in helping to stop the possible invasion. The U.S. ambassador to Israel, Samuel W. Lewis, reported, **Apr. 11,** that Prime Minister Menachem Begin of Israel had indicated that the Israeli government had made no decision whether or not to begin an invasion, although there was a great deal of concern in that country over the killing of an Israeli diplomat, Yacov Barsomantov, in Paris on **Mar. 27,** allegedly by the PLO On **Apr. 20,** Israel announced that one of its planes had been fired on 2 days before over the Golan Heights, and 2 other planes had been shot at that day over Sidon, Lebanon. Syrians in Lebanon were blamed for both attacks. Israeli planes attacked Palestinian guerrilla positions south of Beirut **Apr. 21,** ending the 9-month old ceasefire. Israel, however, said that the cease-fire could continue because the raids were meant as a warning to the PLO to stop its cease-fire violations.

Internal Problems Mount in Iran — Former Foreign Minister of Iran, Sadegh Ghotbzadeh, it was announced **Apr. 10,** had been arrested and charged with plotting to assassinate Ayatollah Ruhollah Khomeini and the members of Iran's Supreme Defense Council. Ghotbzadeh had been one of the Ayatollah's closest aides in Paris during the time of exile before the overthrow of Shah Mohammed Riza Pahlavi in 1979. A behind-the-scenes power struggle was revealed, **Apr. 13,** involving the Shiite Moslem clergymen of Khomeini and even more conservative groups of holy men. Khomeini's opponents, members of the Hojatai Society, took the position that the clergy should be less involved in government. It was expected that this rift would become greater when it would come time to select a successor to Khomeini.

Israeli Attacks Shrine — Alan Harry Goodman, an Israeli soldier who had come to Israel from Baltimore, Md., shot his way into the Dome of the Rock, an Islamic Shrine in Jerusalem, **Apr. 11.** Spraying the inside of the mosque with automatic rifle fire, he killed at least 2 Arabs and wounded at least 30. Israeli policemen and border guards stormed the shrine and captured the gunman. On **Apr. 12,** violent protests against the attack on the mosque broke out in the Israeli-occupied West Bank and Gaza Strip. Soldiers who were attempting to break up the demonstrations shot 16 Arabs, and 14 Israelis and tourists were wounded by stones thrown by the protesters. United Nations delegates from the Moslem countries demanded a meeting of the UN Security Council to discuss the attack. Goodman was arraigned, **Apr. 13,** and ordered to be held for 15 days before his trial would start. King Khalid of Saudi Arabia called on Moslem everywhere to hold a strike on **Apr. 14** to protest the violence of the attack and Israel was denounced in the UN by the Moslem nations. On **Apr. 14,** at least 15 Islamic countries in Africa and Asia joined in a general strike. Businesses, airports, and banks were closed. On **Apr. 16,** 2 Palestinian Arabs were killed and 13 wounded by Israeli troops when large groups in the Gaza Strip and the West Bank attacked the soldiers in protest over the attack in the shrine.

Nicaragua Accepts U.S. Plan — The government of Nicaragua accepted an 8-point plan proposed by the Reagan administration, **Apr. 14,** as a basis for discussions between the 2 countries about improving their relations with each other. Nicaragua suggested that the negotiations begin in Mexico. Among the points that the U.S. proposed for discussion were an end to Nicaraguan interference in neighboring countries, a limit on the size of military forces, and a promise that elections would be more democratic in that country. The U.S. promised that if these points were carried out it would curb Nicaraguans in the U.S. from plotting to overthrow the Nicaraguan government and would resume financial aid to that country.

Sadat Assassins Executed — The convicted assassins of Pres. Anwar el Sadat of Egypt, 5 militant Moslem fundamentalists, were executed, **Apr. 15.** Two of them who were on active duty with the military were shot to death. The other 3, all civilians, were hanged.

More Unrest in Guatemala — Roman Catholic bishops issued a report, **Apr. 16,** in Guatemala City, Guatemala, announcing that violence in their country had driven at least 200,000 people into neighboring countries in Central America, and that the number might actually be closer to one million. On **Apr. 17,** the military announced that 67 guerrillas had been killed in various places in the country in clashes with the army. The Reagan administration reported, **Apr. 20,** that it wanted to establish closer ties with the conservative military regime in Guatemala. Stephen W. Bosworth, the deputy assistant secretary for inter-American affairs, announced that $250,000 had been requested for fiscal year 1983 for military training funds to go to Guatemala. On **Apr. 24,** the administration decided to approve the sale to that country of $4 million in helicopter spare parts.

Polish Situation Eases Slightly — Archbishop Jozef Glemp, the Roman Catholic Primate of Poland, asked, **Apr. 18,** that all women interned under martial law be released. The Polish Communist Party announced, **Apr. 21,** that it had suspended or expelled 44,500 members during March, on charges of indifference to the party's activities. On **Apr. 28,** the Polish government reported that it had ordered the release of 800 internees. The government also rescinded some of the martial law edicts, including the lifting of the curfew.

Canada Gets Constitution — Queen Elizabeth II formally transferred constitutional power from Britain to Canada **Apr. 17.** She gave Canada its constitution, and from that point on, only Canada held the power to amend it. The constitution replaced the old British North American Act of 1867, which brought into being the Canadian federation. The premiers of the 9 English-speaking provinces attended the ceremony and had lunch with the queen. René Lévesque, the premier of Quebec, whose party disapproved of the constitution, was absent, leading thousands of marchers through the streets of Montreal in protest. He indicated that independence was Quebec's only recourse in the face of the new constitution.

Israel Withdraws from Sinai — Israel withdrew the last of its soldiers from the Sinai Peninsula, **Apr. 25,** turning the territory over to Egypt. The plans for the pullout had been long in the making and tense up until the last. On **Apr. 16,** Prime Minister Menachem Begin of Israel, who had threatened to postpone the withdrawal, had received assurances from Pres. Hosni Mubarak of Egypt on questions about the post-withdrawal border that convinced him not to postpone the withdrawal. The Israeli Army, **Apr. 19,** began evicting from Yamit, in the Sinai, Jewish protesters, some of whom had promised violence against the troops. On **Apr. 21,** the Israeli Cabinet voted to withdraw from the Sinai on April 25, as required by the peace treaty with Egypt, and the army once again moved against the protesters in Yamit. They rushed into the town and stormed the fortifications, evacuating all the resisters.

General

Mount St. Helens Erupts Again — Mount St. Helens in western Washington blew steam and ash several miles into the sky in a series of 3 eruptions **Apr. 4** and **5.** On **Apr. 6,** the mountain spewed up a plume of steam 14,000 feet into the air and gas emissions were detected.

Arsonist's Conviction Reversed — A Guatemalan, Luis Marin, who had been convicted of intentionally setting fire to a White Plains, N.Y., hotel in 1980, was released **Apr. 14,** only 4 days after he had been convicted. Judge Lawrence N. Martin Jr. ruled that, despite the jury's verdict, the prosecution had not proved its case, and the charges were dismissed. Twenty-six people had died in the fire.

Disasters — All 11 people aboard a U.S. Navy plane were killed in a crash on Crete, **Apr. 2** . . . A gasoline tanker truck exploded in a tunnel in Oakland, Cal., **Apr. 7**, after colliding with a bus, setting off a fire that killed 7 . . . A volcanic eruption in Indonesia, **Apr. 10**, killed at least 6 people and rendered 40,000 homeless. . . . More than 160 were reported missing following the sinking of a ferry near Henzada, Burma, **Apr. 11** . . . Twenty-eight men in a C-130 American military cargo plane were killed in a crash in eastern Turkey, **Apr. 13** . . . A fire in the Hudson County Jail in Jersey City, N.J., killed 7 on **Apr. 14** . . . In East Chicago, Ind., **Apr. 15**, 12 workers were killed when an unfinished bridge collapsed . . . Thirty-four people were killed in an explosion and flash fire, **Apr. 25**, in an antiques exhibition in Rome, Italy . . . A drunken policeman using carbines and grenades in Seoul, South Korea, killed 62 and wounded 20 before killing himself **Apr. 27** . . . A Chinese jetliner crashed near Guilin, China, **Apr. 27**, killing all 112 people aboard.

MAY

National

U.S. Agrees to Camp Review — The State Department and the Immigration and Naturalization Service agreed, **May 3** to allow the Inter-American Commission on Human Rights to examine conditions at 2 Haitian refugee camps. The group, a subdivision of the Organization of American States, had been requesting the inspection since 1979. The 2 camps in question, where Haitians were being detained, were Fort Allen, P.R., and the Krome North camp near Miami, Fla. There were 555 Haitians at Krome and 771 at Fort Allen. Complaints of human rights violations had been registered against both camps. Verne Jervis, a spokesman for the immigration service, indicated that the detainees were free to return to Haiti at any time, but that it was necessary to hold them so that hearings could be held to determine whether they could enter the United States.

Quota Placed on Sugar Imports — Pres. Ronald Reagan announced, **May 4**, that he would impose quotas on sugar imports. This would constitute the first such quota since 1974, and was designed to save the government several hundreds of millions of dollars per year in price support money. Prices for domestic sugar would be forced up about 4 cents per pound. These increased prices would be passed on to the consumer who would bear the burden of propping up sugar prices rather than the government which would have bought and stored excess sugar under the price support program.

Turkish Consul Killed — Orhan R. Gunduz, an honorary Turkish consul and a gift shop owner, was gunned down in Somerville, Mass., **May 4**. The responsibility for the attack was claimed by a group called the Justice Commandos for the Armenian Genocide. Gunduz was the 21st Turkish diplomat to have been murdered in various places around the world since 1973, probably by Armenian nationalists who claim the Turks killed 1.5 million of their countrymen in Turkey in 1915. On **May 7**, Police Commissioner Robert J. McGuire of New York City announced that 2 Turkish officials in his city were receiving round-the-clock police protection. The State Department had requested this protection for the Turkish chief U.N. delegate and the Counsul General.

White House, GOP Leaders Agree on Budget — It was announced, **May 5** that Republican Congressional leaders and White House aides had agreed on a federal budget proposal. This proposal was tentatively passed a few hours later by the Republican-dominated Senate Budget Committee. It included a tax increase of $95 billion over the next 3 years. At the same time, it would reduce the cost of Social Security by $40 billion. The deficit for the following year would be increased to $105 billion, an increase of about $4.5 billion. On **May 21**, the Senate adopted a $784 billion budget for fiscal 1983, projecting a $116 billion deficit, the highest ever in the U.S.

Abscam Conviction Reversed — Federal District Judge William B. Bryant, **May 14**, overturned the conviction of former Rep. Richard Kelly (R, Fla.) on charges stemming from the Abscam investigation. Bryant said that, because Kelly had initially refused bribe money from FBI men posing as Arab sheiks, they should have stopped making the offer of $25,000. Kelly was 1 of 7 members of Congress to have been convicted of bribery and conspiracy in the Abscam investigation, and lawyers indicated that the reversal increased the chances that the Supreme Court would review the tactics of the operation.

Prices Up, Profits Off — The Labor Department reported, **May 14**, that producer prices had edged up 0.1 of 1% during April, continuing the trend of a significant slowdown in price increases. On **May 19**, the Commerce Department announced that corporate profits fell 17.5% during the first quarter of the year. Declining production and high interest rates were blamed for the drop. The department also revealed that the gross national product fell at an annual rate of 4.3% in the first quarter. Adding to these declines, a 0.6 of 1% drop in industrial production and a 6.4% decline in housing starts in April, the department felt that the recession was likely to continue at least through June. The Labor Department said, **May 21**, that consumer prices rose only 0.2 of 1% in April. The reasons for the slight increase were higher costs of food and housing.

Amtrak and Unions Sign Pact — The U.S. passenger railroad, Amtrak, signed a new contract with 6 unions, **May 27**. The unions involved represented maintenance workers, clerks, electrical workers, machinists, carmen, and boilermakers. It was estimated that the agreement would save the company more than $132 million over the next 3 years and possibly allow the railroad to expand. Wage and cost-of-living increases were cut back to 18.7% through July 1, 1984, and workers won the right to set up a joint labor-management productivity council.

International

Violence Grows in Guatemala — Guatemalan police and army sources announced; **May 1**, that 5 guerrillas, a policeman, and a soldier had been killed in clashes near the Mexican border and the outskirts of Guatemala City. Two civilians were also killed in the political violence. Phone calls to radio stations and newspapers indicated that a guerrilla group, the People's Army of the Poor, claimed responsibility for 2 attacks on police substations. Military authorities, **May 11**, told of a guerrilla attack on a small town in which 20 men, women, and children were massacred. Gen. Efraín Ríos Montt, the president of the 3-man ruling junta, reported, **May 19** that the reason that the junta has not asked for military and economic aid from the United States was that evangelical Christians in the U.S. had offered his country million of dollars. Rios Montt, a born-again Christian also said that he hoped to use the money to develop model villages which would be run neither as democratic nor communist societies, labeling the system "communitarianism."

Iran Recaptures Khurramshahr — Iran claimed, **May 24**, that it had recaptured the Iranian port city of Khurramshahr and had taken 30,000 Iraqi prisoners who surrendered after their commander had been killed. Diplomatic sources in Damascus, Syria, reported that the Iranian troops had been helped by large shipments of Soviet arms from Syria, with the approval of the USSR. The fighting outside Khurramahahr had begun **May 11**, following an Irani advance that had begun earlier in the month. On **May 7**, Iran had claimed that they had broken through Iraqi lines and occupied a 22-mile strip on the southern Iraq-Iran border. Iraq, **May 8**, had admitted that part of its forces in Khuzistan had retreated in order to reinforce units in the south occupying Khurramshahr. Teheran radio, **May 8**, had announced the retaking of Hoveizeh and Hamid and, on **May 9**, Jofeyr, on their way to Khurramshahr. After initiating the assault on the port city, Iran had announced, **May 23**, that a complete seige was being imposed on the Iraqis and that waterways had been damned and a bridge occupied, sealing off all means of escape. On **May 25**, Iraq admitted that Khurramshahr had fallen to Iran and that the Iranians were within striking range of Basra, Iraq's second largest city. U.S. Secretary of State Alexander M. Haig Jr. said, **May 26**, that the United States was prepared to play a more active role in making peace between the 2 countries, seeming to warn Iran that the U.S. would protect its interests in the Persian Gulf. On that same day, the Iraqis claimed that battles were still being waged around Khurramshahr and that 238 Iranians had been killed and large numbers of Iranian tanks and vehicles had been destroyed. Iran announced, **May 27**, that fierce battles were being fought in the hills of western Iran, 80 miles from the Iraqi capital of Baghdad. The report also admitted that Iraqi gunners were shelling Khurramshahr. Iraq claimed that they had killed 55 Iranians that day.

Polish Protest Against Military Rule Flares — On **May 1**, a crowd estimated at 30,000 marched through Warsaw's Old Town to show support for the Solidarity union and to protest the military rule. This was the biggest show of opposition since the beginning of martial law, 4 1/2 months before. No arrests or incidents were reported. However, on **May 3**, protesters clashed with police in Warsaw and other cities. In Warsaw, about 10,000 people had gathered to protest the military government and were set upon by policemen, carrying shields and swinging truncheons. Scores of demonstrators were beaten by police and several were struck by flares, fired by riot police as a means of protecting the Communist Party's Central Committee building. Similar though smaller incidents had occurred in Gdansk and 8 other cities. On **May 4**, the military government, in retaliation, reintroduced the curfew, cut telephone service, and imposed other restrictions on the Polish people, including the suspension of sports and cultural events and the banning of private cars from the streets. It was also reported that 1,372 people had been taken into custody—271 of them in Warsaw. Seventy-two policemen had been injured in the clashes, but no figures of the numbers of demonstrators injured were given. It was announced, **May 6**, that, because of the riots, the wife of Lech Walesa had been refused permission to see her husband. Walesa, the leader of Solidarity, had been interned since the previous December. Polish farmers, numbering some 3,000, prayed and sang together, **May 12**, at a mass marking the first birthday of the founding of the Rural Solidarity union, although the union had been banned under martial law. The mass ended without incident. Brief work stoppages were staged, **May 13**, at most of the factories in Warsaw and in other cities to protest martial law. Police charged a group of 150 to 200 young people in Warsaw's Old Town, beating them with truncheons as they tried to enter a cathedral. A group of 5,000 to 6,000 gathered at Warsaw University to stage a silent protest. Although the Polish government declared, **May 14**, that the protest actions the previous day had been a failure, Western diplomats pointed out that the suspended Solidarity union had been able to mount the first coordinated industrial disruptions since the imposition of martial law. Konstantin V. Rusakov, a member of the secretariat of the Soviet Communist Party's Central Committee, flew to Warsaw, **May 17**. He was the first senior Soviet official to visit Poland since the beginning of martial law. It was said that he had gone to assess the Polish situation first hand and report back to Moscow. On **May 22**, Poland and the Soviet Union accused the U.S. of subversion and of trying to plunge Poland into anarchy. The Polish government announced, **May 27**, that Lech Walesa had been moved from the Warsaw villa in which he had been detained for 6 months, but declined to state where he had been relocated. The Rev. Henryk Jankowski, Walesa's parish priest, announced, **May 29**, that the government had agreed to let the Solidarity leader have a brief meeting with his family on June 3.

U.S. Aid to El Salvador Under Fire — The U.S. House Foreign Affairs Committee approved, **May 12**, an administration proposal to give $60 million in military aid to the Salvadoran government. However, on **May 20**, Sen. Charles H. Percy (Rep., Ill.), in an angry statement, said that U.S. aid would be cut off from El Salvador if the land redistribution program were stopped. The chairman of the Senate Foreign Relations Committee was reacting to the suspension by the Salvadoran Constituent Assembly of the plan that sought to give tenant farmers and sharecroppers the right to acquire title to the land they work. The State Department announced, **May 24**, that they had been assured by El Salvador that the provisions of the land redistribution plan would be carried out. Even so, the Senate Foreign Relations Committee, **May 26**, called for a $100 million reduction in military aid to El Salvador. The sum was to be cut from $166.3 million to $66 million. On **May 27**, the administration warned El Salvador that it would insist on progress in the land program.

Hindus, Sikhs Clash in India — It was reported, **May 3**, that more than 350 militant Hindus and Sikhs were arrested in the Indian state of Punjab in the aftermath of religious disorders. A group named the Dai Khalsa, or Association of the Pure, had placed 2 severed cow's heads at Hindu temples. This group had been agitating for the establishment of a Sikh nation that would be separate from India, and had been staging a campaign to have the smoking of tobacco outlawed within the walled city of Amritsar, the city where the holiest Sikh shrine, the Golden Temple, is located. They felt that Hindus were blocking the passage of this law and had placed the cow's heads to irritate the Hindus, who are prohibited, as are all Indians, from slaughtering cows. Following the temple desecrations, groups of Sikhs and Hindus attacked each other in several towns in the Punjab. A man was killed and several were wounded. Shops were burned and curfews were laid down in at least 2 towns.

Violence in Ulster Continues — Security forces in Northern Ireland found more than 3,000 firebombs in Belfast, **May 5**. Most of the bombs were found in the Ardoyne section of the city at the time when the Irish Republican Army was comemorating the first anniversary of the death of the hunger striker, Robert Sands. On **May 8**, 2 police patrols were machinegunned and 5 policemen were wounded. It was believed that the attack was mounted by the IRA guerrillas. On that same day, a fireman and a woman were wounded when a bomb meant to be used against security forces exploded in Londonderry. Also, a young Catholic man burned himself with his own gasoline bomb as he was about to throw it at a police patrol. On **May 12**, a Protestant was killed in an ambush in Strabane. He was believed to be a former member of the Ulster Defense Regiment. Also, a Catholic was gunned down in a Belfast fruit store. It was thought by police that the Protestant was killed by the IRA and the Catholic by Protestant extremists.

Reagan Proposes Arms Cut Plan — Pres. Reagan proposed an arms reduction plan, **May 9**. The scheme called for a reduction by the U.S. and the Soviets of one-third of their stocks of nuclear warheads on land- and sea-based ballistic missiles. It was estimated that each country had some 7,500 missile warheads and the reduction would lower the number to about 5,000 apiece. The second phase of Reagan's plan involved the acceptance of a ceiling on the total payload of warheads by the 2 nations. Reagan also announced that he had written a letter to the Soviet leader, Leonid I. Brezhnev, suggesting that the 2 governments begin formal negotiations by the end of June. Brezhnev indicated, **May 18**, that he was ready for the talks but that Reagan's plan was one-sided in favor of the U.S. He proposed a nuclear freeze after the arms talks began. On **May 31**, Reagan announced that the U.S. and the Soviet Union would open negatiations in Geneva on June 29 on the limitation and reduction of strategic nuclear arms.

Israeli-Arab Conflict Heats Up — Israeli jets raided several Palestinian guerrilla bases south of Beirut, Lebanon, **May 9**. The Palestinians immediately retaliated by firing artillery shells into northern Israel. An artillery battle between the Israelis and Palestinians erupted shortly afterward. The Israeli air raid killed 6 people and wounded 20. No casualties were reported as a result of the artillery barrage. On **May 25** Israeli jet fighters shot down 2 Syrian MIG's over Lebanon, but the pilots were able to parachute to safety.

Another Attempt on Pope's Life — While Pope John Paul II was conducting a religious ceremony at the shrine of Fátima in Portugal, **May 12**, a young man in clerical garb moved toward him with a knife. Security guards overpowered him and it was later found that he was a Spanish priest. The 32-year-old man, Juan Fernández Krohn, was a follower of Msgr. Marcel Lefebvre, a suspended bishop who opposed the changes made by the Second Vatican Council. Fernández was brought to court, **May 14**, and charged with attempted homicide and ordered held for trial.

Spain Joins NATO — Spain formally became the 16th member of the North Atlantic Treaty Organization, **May 30**, after being accepted by the 15 other nations in the pact. Thus Spain became the first new member since West Germany joined in 1955. In joining NATO, Spain would contribute or make available to the military command an additional 34,000 troops, more than 190 war planes, and 29 warships. Joining with Norway and Denmark, however, Spain indicated that no nuclear weapons would be allowed to be stored or used within its boundaries.

General

New Drug for Acne Approved — It was announced, **May 21,** that the Food and Drug Administration had approved a new prescription drug for the most serious form of acne. Called 13-cis retinoic acid, and to be sold as Accutane, the drug caused remission of cystic acne, a disease that about 350,000 Americans suffer from. It is a disorder of the oil glands, usually in the face, and causes deep pitting and scarring.

Moon Convicted — The founder and leader of the Unification Church, the Rev. Sun Myung Moon, was convicted of tax fraud, **May 18,** in New York City. Moon had been accused of deliberately failing to report more than $100,000 of bank account interest and $50,000 in stock profits to the Internal Revenue Service. Convicted with him was one of his top aides, Takeru Kamiyami, who had been accused of conspiracy, perjury, and obstructing the investigation that led to the trial. Moon faced up to 5 years in prison for conspiracy and 3 years on each of 3 tax counts. Kamiyami's sentence could be up to 5 years imprisonment on each of his counts. They were set free on bail pending an appeal.

Man on Rampage in Maryland — Edward Thomas Mann, a former salesman for International Business Machines Corporation, drove a car through the glass lobby doors of an IBM building in Bethesda, Md., **May 28.** Once inside, he went on a shooting spree, killing 2 workers and wounding at least 10 others. Mann, wearing a mask, had been armed with 2 rifles, a shotgun, and a pistol. After 7 hours of police negotiation by telephone, he came out of an office in the building and surrendered to the police. It had taken more than 5 hours to evacuate some 700 employees in the building. It was suggested that Mann had had some kind of grievance with the company, and he was expected to be charged with murder and assault with intent to murder.

Disasters — Two methane gas explosions in a Yugoslav coal mine in Zenica killed 39, **May 12** . . . A small commercial plane crashed near Kassel, West Germany, **May 19,** killing 8 persons aboard . . . Severe flooding in China's southeastern province of Guangdong had killed 430 and marooned 450,000, it was announced **May 19** . . . An excursion boat capsized in Tianjin, China, **May 19,** and 25 people were drowned . . . Eighteen people died in a fire in a home for mentally handicapped teenagers in Aire, France, **May 25** . . . Nicaragua and Honduras announced, **May 28,** that at least 200 people had died and 65,000 were homeless after a mammoth flood . . . Flooding and landslides killed 20 and left more than 2,000 homeless in Hong Kong **May 29** . . . Twelve were killed and 100 injured, **May 29,** as tornadoes smashed through southern Illinois.

JUNE

National

Search Authority Extended — The United States Supreme Court ruled, **June 1,** that police should be permitted to search automobiles without warrants. This meant that if law enforcement officers had probable cause to search a car without a warrant, they were also at liberty to search the luggage or packages that were found inside the auto. In 1925, the Supreme Court had established a so-called "automobile exception" to the Fourth Amendment's prohibition against unreasonable searches, stating that police could stop a moving car without a warrant and search it, if they had reason to believe that it contained contraband. However, this had not included closed containers inside the automobile. The present ruling expanded that decision.

Unemployment Rate and Consumer Prices Up — The unemployment rate rose 0.1 of 1% in May, to 9.5% of the labor force, the Labor Department announced, **June 4.** However, the May increase was smaller than the 0.4 of 1% in April, and the number of people holding jobs in May rose to 100,117,000—an increase of 780,000. The reason for the increase in unemployed was given as the thousands of high school and college graduates who entered the labor market during May, as well as a decline in manufacturing activity. The Labor Department reported, **June 22,** that consumer prices had risen 1% in May. This was caused by increases in gasoline prices, plus the prices of both homes and food.

American Prisoner Returns Home — Lisa Wicher, an American teacher who had been imprisoned in China on charges of spying, arrived home in Indianapolis, Ind., **June 4.** She had been held for a week. Wicher had been in China for 2 years collecting material for a thesis on agricultural changes in China since 1969. She said that she had been arrested by 5 or 6 uniformed members of the Chinese Public Security Bureau on **May 28,** and taken to a cement room in a detention center. She was denied the right to contact the American Embassy, and was accused of stealing secret documents and spying. She spent 3 days in solitary confinement and was then ordered to leave China within 48 hours.

Nuclear Protest Held — Hundreds of thousands of demonstrators against nuclear arms crowded into New York City's Central Park, **June 12.** The line of march into the park was filled with people in a 3-mile long crowd of protestors. Participants carried signs in dozens of languages, sang songs, and clapped hands. It was estimated that the demonstration was the largest in that city's history—the estimated size of the crowd in the park was 500,000. Tens of thousands more were backed up on the parade route which started at the United Nations. Among the speakers against nuclear weapons was Coretta Scott King, the widow of the Rev. Martin Luther King Jr.

Illegal Alien Children to be Educated — The U.S. Supreme Court ruled, **June 15,** that children who are illegal aliens have a constitutional right to free public education. The decision upheld 2 rulings by the U.S. Court of Appeals which had declared unconstitutional a Texas law cutting off state funds from local school districts for educating children who had entered the U.S. illegally. The decision, therefore, guaranteed a free public education to anyone, regardless of immigration status, who lives within a state's boundaries.

Voting Rights Act Extended — The U.S. Senate, **June 18,** adopted a bill extending for another 25 years a section of the Voting Rights Act of 1965, dealing with changes in election procedures. The House had already passed this bill and it was to be sent to the president, who had promised to sign it, for his signature. The section that was extended was the part that required all or part of 22 states to submit changes in election procedures for federal approval. All of the affected areas had a history of past discrimination or low minority turnouts at the polls. Without the extension, that section would have ceased to exist on **Aug. 6.**

Hinckley Found Not Guilty — On **June 21,** John W. Hinckley Jr. was found not guilty by reason of insanity on all 13 charges of shooting Pres. Reagan and 3 others on Mar. 30, 1981. These charges ranged from attempted assassination of a president to possession of an unlicensed pistol. The trial had lasted 8 weeks, and Hinckley was the first person since 1835 to avoid conviction on charges of assassinating or attempting to assassinate a sitting president. Hinckley was sent to St. Elizabeth's Hospital in Washington, D.C. He was to remain in custody in that mental institution until such a time as the courts would rule that he was not likely to injure himself or other persons due to mental disease. Hinckley was entitled to a hearing on the release issue within 50 days. On **June 22,** the hearing date was set for **Aug. 9.** There was no reaction to the verdict from the White House.

ERA Goes Under — The leaders of the fight to ratify the Equal Rights Amendment to the Constitution admitted defeat, **June 24.** In the 10 years since Congress passed the proposed amendment, it had been ratified by 35 states—3 short of the three-quarters needed for ratification. After last-minute defeats in the Illinois and Florida state legislatures, it appeared to be impossible to add the 3 necessary states before the **June 30** deadline. (For more detailed coverage, please see p. 264.)

Haig Resigns — Secretary of State Alexander M. Haig Jr., resigned his cabinet post, **June 25.** His reasons for resigning were not explicitly clear, but he did cite a change in the administration's foreign policy from the course that he and the president had laid out earlier in the Reagan presidency. It was speculated that he might be leaving because of a disagreement over the policy to be followed in Lebanon. Pres. Reagan accepted Haig's resignation and nominated George P. Shultz, a former Secretary of the Treasury, to replace him in the State Dept.

Haitian Refugees Paroled — U.S. District Court Judge Eugene P. Spellman, **June 29,** ordered the U.S. to parole most of the 1,900 Haitians being detained in camps while awaiting asylum in the U.S. The Justice Department said it would appeal the decision and ask for a stay of the order. Spellman, in his decision, ruled that the U.S. government was guilty of violating its own procedures because it had not announced that it would incarcerate Haitians who sought to enter the country illegally.

Court Limits Book Banning — The U.S. Supreme Court ruled, **June 25,** that the First Amendment's guarantee of freedom of speech limits the right of public school administrators to remove books that they consider objectionable from school libraries. Thus, if an administrator were to be sued by students for removing certain books, he or she might be required to defend himself or herself in federal courts. Presumably the students would sue the officials for intending to deny access to ideas.

Israel Invades Lebanon; PLO Leadership Ousted

The Israeli army, **June 6,** invaded southern Lebanon by land, sea, and air with the aim of destroying Palestine Liberation Organization strongholds in the area. More than 250 tanks and armored personnel carriers, plus thousands of infantry troops fanned out across the frontier into southern Lebanon, stretching from the city of Tyre to the foothills of Mount Hermon. Several Palestine strongholds were captured.

The immediate reason for the invasion was retaliation for the attempted assassination, **June 3,** in London of Shlomo Argov, the Israeli ambassador to Britain. Israel had accused the PLO of the crime and had attacked PLO guerrilla camps in Lebanon, **June 4.** The PLO had retaliated, firing rockets and shells at northern Israel and the Israeli-backed Christian enclave in southern Lebanon. On **June 5,** Israel and the PLO had again exchanged heavy artillery fire in what was described as the worst fighting since the ceasefire between Israel and the PLO had gone into effect in July of the previous year.

Israeli tanks and infantry captured several PLO strongholds, including Beaufort Castle, **June 7.** Israeli jets fought with Syrian planes over the southern suburbs of Beirut. Nabatiye, and Hesbeya were captured. By **June 8,** the Israelis had pushed 32 miles into Lebanon, heading toward Beirut, 15 miles away. Israel claimed to have shot down 6 Syrian fighter jets.

On **June 9,** Israel claimed that its air force had shot down 22 Syrian jets and destroyed a Syrian surface-to-air missile system in the Bekaa Valley of eastern Lebanon. Syria claimed that they had lost only 16 planes and that they had shot down 19 Israeli jets. Israeli ground forces had driven to within 4 miles of Beirut.

By **June 10,** Israeli warplanes and gunboats were attacking the southern section of Beirut and tanks and jet fighters were exchanging fire with the Syrians in the Bekaa Valley. The Israelis claimed that 61 Syrian MIG's and 5 helicopters had been shot down since **June 6,** and acknowledged no losses of their own.

Also on **June 10,** U.S. Pres. Ronald Reagan sent a message to Israeli Prime Minister Menachem Begin, calling for a ceasefire and withdrawal of Israeli troops from Lebanon. Israel and Syria, **June 11,** announced ceasefires in Lebanon, but the ceasefire did not extend to the PLO, according to Israel. Israeli planes bombed a building housing the PLO military command offices in Beirut, **June 11.** Palestinians said that more than 100 people were killed in the bombings. The guerrillas were reported to be withdrawing into west Beirut. Israel claimed that they had trapped the PLO guerrillas in Beirut and had cut off all movements to the south.

Israel declared a cease-fire for the Beirut area, **June 12,** but warned the PLO to expect heavy retaliation if they continued fighting. Fighting broke out again, **June 13,** and by **June 14,** Moslem West Beirut was cut off, trapping the military and political leadership of the PLO.

As fighting continued, Pres. Reagan and Prime Minister Begin, conferring in Washington, D.C., reached an agreement that all troops—including Israeli and Syrian—should be withdrawn from Lebanon. But Begin stipulated that Israeli forces would be withdrawn only after an international force was established to enforce a 25-mile buffer zone along the Lebanese side of the Israeli border. U.S. Senators, **June 22,** confronted Begin, particularly expressing concern about the alleged use of cluster bombs on civilians by the Israeli Air Force. Israeli jets pounded Syrians and members of the PLO along the Damascus highway, **June 22** and **23,** as a new ceasefire collapsed.

On **June 23,** the U.S. House of Representatives approved a $50 million aid package to Lebanon. Israeli fighter-bombers, warships and artillery unleashed a barrage on western Beirut, **June 25,** armored units drove Syrian tanks and troops from the Beirut-Damascus highway, and Israel agreed to a new ceasefire. It was estimated, **June 26,** that 35,000 people had been killed in Lebanon since the original attack.

The Israelis issued, **June 27,** a peace proposal with 3 major points: The Israeli Army would maintain the ceasefire, but would react with full severity if it were violated by the PLO; the Lebanese army would occupy west Beirut; all members of the PLO would turn over their weapons to the Lebanese Army and leave the country. The PLO guerrillas would be permitted to leave carrying their personal weapons, Begin announced, **June 29,** in a modification of the proposal.

On **July 2,** Dr. George Habash, the head of the Popular Front for the Liberation of Palestine and a founder of the PLO, reported that the guerrillas were ready for a battle in Beirut and indicated that his peace talks with the Lebanese government and U.S. envoy Philip C. Habib had made no progress. Israeli armored troops sealed off the Moslem section in west Beirut **July 3.**

The Israeli troops, **July 4,** began to prevent food, water, and fuel from entering the part of Beirut controlled by the PLO. At that time there were about 6,000 Palestinian guerrillas in the area, along with some 500,000 Lebanese civilians.

Pres. Ronald Reagan announced, **July 6,** that he had agreed in principle to contribute a small contingent of U.S. troops as part of a multinational force to keep the peace in Beirut if a settlement were to be reached. France also indicated that it might aid in the peace keeping.

The Syrian government, **July 9,** rejected a plan to transfer the Palestinian fighters from Beirut to Syria. This was in answer to reports that U.S. and Lebanese negotiators were discussing a plan to transfer to Syria the 5,000-7,000 guerrillas being besieged in Beirut. On **July 10,** the French government announced that it had agreed in principle to send troops to Lebanon as part of an international peace keeping force.

The Reagan Administration declared, **July 16,** that it was holding up a shipment of cluster-bomb artillery shells to Israel, pending a report from the Begin government concerning the Israeli use of those bombs. The Israelis acknowledged, **July 18,** that they had been using the bombs, but asserted that their use was consistent with Israeli-American agreements on the use of such weapons.

The latest ceasefire, in effect since **July 10,** was crushed when Israel attacked eastern Lebanon and west Beirut, **July 22,** charging that a cease-fire had been violated by Syrians and Palestinians. The heavy bombing continued in west Beirut for 7 straight days until **July 28,** when a ceasefire was restored.

On **July 29,** the UN Security Council voted to demand that Israel lift its blockade of west Beirut and allow food

International

U.S. Bases Bombed — Bombs exploded at 4 U.S. military bases in West Germany, **June 1.** An organization calling itself the Revolutionary Cells Terrorist Group claimed responsibility for the explosions and stated that they were in protest against the visit of Pres. Ronald Reagan to Bonn and Berlin later in the month. The explosions ripped through officers' quarters in Hanau, Gelnhausen, and Bamberg, and an officers' mess in Frankfurt. There were no injuries, since the bombs exploded at 1:30 a.m.; damage was estimated at $120,000.

Reagan Visits Europe — Pres. Ronald Reagan arrived in Paris, France, **June 2,** for the start of a 9-day visit to Europe, vowing to seek a greater agreement about economic policies among the industrial democracies of the West. This was his first extensive European visit since becoming president, and he said he hoped to persuade European leaders that the fight against inflation should be assigned the highest priority. On **June 3,** Reagan met with French Pres. François Mitterand and discussed the war in the Falkland Islands and France's objections to U.S. policies in Central America. Reagan, admitting that the Socialist government of France was traveling different roads toward economic growth than was the U.S., nevertheless praised Mitterand for working to set a new course for France. Prime Minister

---

and other supplies inside the city. And on **July 30,** the PLO offered a plan for the withdrawal of the 6,000 guerrillas trapped in west Beirut. The plan which, for the first time, omitted earlier PLO demands for a continued military presence in Lebanon, called for the guerrillas to leave Lebanon by land over a one-month period and to be redeployed in Syria, Jordan, and Egypt.

In the fiercest shelling to date, the Israelis bombarded Beirut, **Aug. 1,** by land, sea, and air. The bombardment was halted when a cease-fire arranged by the special U.S. envoy, Philip C. Habib, went into effect. In Washington, D.C., **Aug. 2,** Pres. Reagan told the visiting Israeli Foreign Minister, Yitzhak Shamir, that the violence in Lebanon must be stopped and food and medical supplies must be sent to west Beirut.

Israeli armored units thrust into west Beirut, **Aug. 4,** as planes, gunboats and artillery bombarded the city, shattering the latest ceasefire and bringing to a halt the negotiations between the PLO, the Lebanese government, and Habib on the plan to withdraw the 6,000 PLO fighters still trapped in west Beirut. Civilian casualties were numbered in the hundreds. Pres. Reagan appealed to Prime Minister Begin to observe a ceasefire, and, on **Aug. 5,** the U.S. asked Israel to withdraw from west Beirut.

On **Aug. 6,** it was announced that the PLO and Habib had agreed on all major points regarding the PLO withdrawal, but were awaiting the agreement of Syria, Jordan, and Egypt to take in the refugees once they were evacuated. Syria and Egypt indicated, **Aug. 7,** that they would accept some of the PLO guerrillas, as did Jordan and Iraq.

The U.S. formally presented a peace plan to Israel, **Aug. 9,** that called for a multinational force to arrive as the PLO troops were being evacuated. Israel accepted the U.S. plan in principle, **Aug. 10,** but insisted that most of the guerrillas would have to leave before the peacekeeping force arrived. Syria indicated, **Aug. 14,** that it was prepared to withdraw its soldiers and the PLO guerrillas under its command from west Beirut, and, on **Aug. 15,** the Israeli Cabinet accepted the plan for the multinational peacekeeping force.

The Lebanese government decided, **Aug. 18,** to ask the U.S., France, and Italy to contribute troops to the force, and Pres. Reagan announced that the first contingent of guerrillas was scheduled to leave west Beirut by sea on **Aug. 21** and 800 U.S. marines would arrive in Beirut on **Aug. 26.** The Israeli Cabinet, **Aug. 19,** approved the evacuation plan. About 300 members of the French Foreign Legion left Corsica, **Aug. 19,** landing in Lebanon **Aug. 21,** as 397 Palestinian guerrillas left the country by ship.

A second contingent of guerrillas left Lebanon **Aug. 22.** The U.S. Marines landed in Beirut, **Aug. 25,** and, on **Aug. 27,** more than 1,300 PLO troops left Beirut for Damascus, Syria. PLO Leader Yasir Arafat left on **Aug 30,** vowing to fight again. The remaining Syrian troops and PLO guerrillas departed, **Sept. 1.** Lebanese government security forces, **Sept. 2,** took over control of the western part of Beirut. By that afternoon, people in west Beirut who had not visited the east since 1978 were able to do so.

Israeli Defense Minister Ariel Sharon announced, **Sept. 7,** that he was pressing Lebanon's president-elect Bashir Gemayel to begin negotiating a formal peace treaty in order to bolster the security on the Israel-Lebanon border.

Israeli jet fighters destroyed 4 launch vehicles for Syrian antiaircraft, **Sept. 9.** The missiles had apparently been moved into Lebanon a few days before. Then, on **Sept. 13,** Israel launched an all-day series of air strikes against Syrian and Lebanese positions in central and eastern Lebanon, and announced that 10 targets were hit and 5 Palestine command posts were destroyed.

On **Sept. 14,** President elect Bashir Gemayel was killed when a bomb explosion shattered the headquarters of his Lebanese Christian Phalangist Party in east Beirut. Gemayel was to have been sworn in as president on **Sept. 23.** Eight others were killed in the blast and some 50 were wounded.

Israeli troops and tanks, **Sept. 15,** pushed into west Beirut in a drive that they claimed was prompted by the assassination of Gemayel. Prime Minister Shafik Wazzan appealed to the troops to withdraw. The Israeli troops seized control of most of west Beirut, **Sept. 16,** after overcoming small resistance by Lebanese Moslem and leftist militiamen.

On **Sept. 17** Lebanese Christian militiamen massacred scores of Palestinian men, women, and children in refugee camps on the southern edge of west Beirut. It was reported that at least 300 people had been killed. Although it was said that no Israeli soldiers were directly involved in the killings, it was reported that the Israelis had sealed off the area and then permitted Christian militiamen and the Phalangist militia to move into the camps.

The government of Italy asked France and the United States to join it in sending a international peacekeeping force into Lebanon, **Sept. 19.** Troops from the 3 countries had previously been withdrawn after supervising the pullout of the Palestinian guerrillas. French Foreign Minister Claude Cheysson indicated that his country was ready to act, and, on **Sept. 20,** Pres. Reagan announced that the 3 countries would send their forces back to Lebanon. Amin Gemayel, the brother of the slain Lebanese president-elect, was elected to the presidency of Lebanon, **Sept. 21.**

Defense Minister Ariel Sharon admitted, **Sept. 22,** that Israel had requested and helped plan the entry of the Lebanese Phalangist forces into the Palestinian refugee camps. But he stressed that Israeli Army commanders had told the Phalangists that it was forbidden to harm the civilian population.

Amin Gemayel was sworn into the presidency, **Sept. 23.** On **Sept. 24,** amidst increasing international criticism and pressure Menachim Begin asked Israel's Supreme Court to head an inquiry into his country's involvement in the Beirut massacre. The U.S. announced, **Sept. 25,** that U.S. Marines would not land in Beirut as planned because no accord had been reached on the Israel pullback from Beirut International Airport. Some French troops had already landed, but were confined in the French embassy, the ambassador's residence, and a French cultural center.

Several hundred thousand Israelis demonstrated in Tel Aviv, **Sept. 25,** in protest over Begin's handling of the question of Israeli involvement in the massacre and calling for the resignation of both Begin and Sharon. By **Sept. 26,** the estimated death toll in the massacre had risen to about 600.

French and Italian soldiers entered the 2 refugee camps, **Sept. 27,** to take up security duties. On **Sept. 28,** Israeli troops were withdrawn from the port of Beirut, but others remained at the airport. Pres. Reagan announced that U.S. Marines would land in Beirut on **Sept. 29** and would remain there until all Syrian and Israeli troops were withdrawn from Lebanon. On **Sept. 30,** one day after the Marines had landed, 1 Marine was killed and 3 others were wounded by an accidental detonation of what might have been a cluster bomb.

Margaret Thatcher of Great Britain conferred with Reagan, **June 4,** at the American Embassy in Paris, and it was reported that she had received staunch support from him concerning the situation in the Falklands. The leaders of the 7 industrialized nations—the United States, Japan, Britain, France, West Germany, Italy, and Canada—met in Versailles, **June 5,** with the object of seeking an agreement to limit the use of cheap export credits in world trade. Reagan raised the issue of putting sharp restrictions on credits to the Soviets, but found himself at odds with the other 6 leaders. The 7 leaders did agree, however, that all developed nations, including the Soviet Union, be permitted to receive export financing at no less than 12.5% interest for short-term loans, and that there be no ceilings placed on the volume of such loans, or credit in general, to the Eastern bloc of nations. By **June 6,** the summit meeting had come to tentative agreements on 2 points, East-West trade and the handling of currency fluctuations. The conference was then interrupted by news of the fighting in the Falklands, which forced Thatcher to fly back to London for conferences, and the invasion of Lebanon by Israel. Reagan flew to Rome, **June 7,** for a 6-hour visit with Italian leaders and an audience with Pope John Paul II. Later in the day, he flew to London, England, and then went to Windsor Castle where he was greeted by Queen Elizabeth II, who provided a guard of honor on parade for him. On **June 8,** in the first speech ever made by a U.S. president to a meeting of the combined Houses of Parliament, Reagan urged that Britain and the U.S. and the world prepare a crusade for freedom by encouraging the spread of democracy into Communist countries. He also praised the British troops who were fighting in the Falklands. Reagan then traveled to Bonn, West Germany, where, on **June 9,** he urged that both the East and West agree to a ceiling of 700,000 ground troops in Europe for each alliance. He also reiterated his nation's commitment to the defense of Europe and particularly West Germany. On **June 11,** Reagan was in Berlin, where he visited the Berlin Wall. In a speech, he assured West Germany that American military forces would remain there as long as necessary to preserve the peace and protect the freedom of the people of Berlin. He also called upon the Soviets to accept a new set of concrete and practical steps to show a commitment to arms control.

Pope Ends Historic Trip to Britain — Pope John Paul II, **June 2,** ended his journey to the British Isles with a stop in Cardiff, Wales. The trip was the first ever by a pontiff to Britain. On **May 29,** he had met with the Archbishop of Canterbury and for the first time in almost 450 years the heads of the Church of Rome and the Church of England had participated together in a church ceremony. The pope's journey had also taken him to Scotland, where, **June 1,** he celebrated a mass attended, according to estimates, by one-third of all the Catholics in Scotland.

U.S. Arms Cut Plan Rejected — In an editorial, **June 3,** the Soviet Communist Party newspaper, *Pravda,* reacted to Pres. Reagan's proposal to hold conferences on the cutting of numbers of missiles in the U.S. and Soviet arsenals. Reagan had suggested that no more than half the total number of nuclear warheads on each side be on ground-based missiles. *Pravda* pointed out that about 70% of the Soviet warheads were on ground-based missiles as compared to 20% of those of the U.S. Such a reduction would force the Soviet Union to restructure its forces, while U.S. armaments would be affected to a lesser degree. It was supposed that this position would be the one that Soviet negotiators would take at the strategic arms reduction talks with the U.S. that were to begin in Geneva on **June 29.**

Election Fraud Charged in El Salvador — Dr. Jorge Bustamente, the president of El Salvador's Central Elections Council, admitted, **June 3,** that the vote total in the March elections might have included a 10% error in the number of voters. More seriously, a research study conducted by a Salvadoran university indicated, in a magazine article published **June 4,** that the official vote may have been fraudulently overestimated by 100%. The study estimated that between 600,000 and 800,000 had voted, while the official results indicated 1,551,687 votes cast. El Salvador's provisional president Alvaro Magana, **June 5,** denied the fraud charges.

Chad Capital Falls — The French Embassy in Chad reported, **June 7,** that the capital of that country, Ndjamena, had fallen to rebel forces. This ended 2 years of fighting between the Armed Forces of the North, commanded by Hissen Habré, and troops loyal to Pres. Goukouni Oueddei. The rebels had launched their offensive from the northeast after the government of Libya had withdrawn its forces from Chad the previous November.

Iraq Makes Peace Offer, Withdraws From Iran — The Iraqi government, **June 9,** in a peace offer, promised it would withdraw its troops from Iran within 2 weeks in order "to redirect its potentials to the war against Israel." On **June 10,** Iraq announced that it was observing a unilateral ceasefire and, **June 12,** despite daily artillery fire from Iran, declared that it would continue to observe the ceasefire and that Iraqi soldiers had been instructed to fire only when fired upon. Iraqi Pres. Saddam Hussein, **June 20,** said that Iraqi troops had begun withdrawing from Iranian territory and would complete their retreat within 10 days. This followed a series of Iranian victories that had driven the Iraqis out of most of the territory that they had occupied in Iran. On **June 21,** Ayatollah Ruhollah Khomeini, the leader of Iran, said that the war with Iraq would not end even if the Iraqis made a complete withdrawal.

Guatemalan Junta Ousted — Gen. Efraín Ríos Montt deposed his 2 fellow junta members, **June 9,** and named himself president of Guatemala. Ríos Montt had promised that he would be only a caretaker ruler and would not seek the presidency. The reason given for the reversal was that the 2 junta officials had been devoting more time to politics than to running the country. On **June 21,** it was announced that at least 18 people, including 2 mayors, were killed over the weekend in political violence.

Pope Travels to Argentina — In the first papal visit to Argentina in history, Pope John Paul II, **June 11,** arrived in Buenos Aires and asked Britain and Argentina to seek peace in the conflict over the Falkland Islands. Hundreds of thousands of Argentinians turned out to watch the pontiff's motorcade. On **June 12,** at the end of his visit to Argentina, the pope acknowledged the principle of Latin American unity on the issue of the Falklands, but appealed to bishops throughout the hemisphere to prevent the world from dividing into 2 separate blocs.

Fighting Continues in El Salvador — In a search-and-destroy campaign in the mountains of Chalatenango Province, Salvadoran soldiers killed 135 rebels, it was reported **June 12.** This was the first combat operation for Salvadoran soldiers who had been trained in the U.S. The operation involved at least 3,000 government troops, 960 of whom had been trained at Ft. Bragg, N.C., and 500 who had been trained at Ft. Benning, Ga. Leftist rebels battled government troops, **June 13,** in Morazán Province, and an army officer admitted that the military had suffered very heavy losses. The heaviest fighting of the war was reported, **June 14,** in Morazán, with 76 government soldiers killed, more than 100 wounded, and 31 taken prisoner. The rebels claimed to have captured 110 rifles, 25,000 bullets, machine guns, mortars, and cannons. By **June 17,** it was announced that some 5,000 soldiers, including 2 U.S. trained battalions, were advancing in Morazán. And on **June 18,** Col. Francisco Adolfo Castillo, the No. 2 man in the defense department, and Col. Salvador Beltrán Luna, the commander of an elite infantry unit, were reported to have been killed in a helicopter crash in a combat zone in Morazán, after being hit by ground fire. On **June 20,** a rebel radio broadcast denied that Castillo had been killed and claimed that he was captured. On **June 23,** it was reported that from 4 to 7 U.S. military advisers had been seen in a combat zone, carrying M-16 rifles. Both of these alleged activities were against state department regulations. The United States Embassy in El Salvador denied these reports, **June 24.** On **June 30,** the Salvadoran army began a 1000-man offensive backed by warplanes and artillery against rebels 15 miles north of San Salvador.

USSR Bars First Use of Nuclear Weapons — In a message delivered to the UN General Assembly's special session on disarmament, Soviet Foreign Minister Andrei Gromyko, **June 15,** conveyed a pledge by Soviet Pres. Leonid I. Brezhnev that the USSR would not be the first nation to use nuclear weapons. The pledge was dismissed by Reagan administration officials. Reagan, addressing the disarmament meeting, **June 17,** did not allude specifically to the Soviet pledge, but said he was "ready to take the next steps" toward arms reduction. He said, however, that wanted 'deeds, not words," from the Soviet Union.

General

Warning on Aspirin Given — Richard S. Schweiker, the Secretary of Human Services, announced, **June 4,** that he had directed the Surgeon General of the United States, Dr. C. Everett Koop, to advise doctors and parents against usng aspirin to treat children's chicken pox or flu-like symptoms. Studies had linked aspirin to Reye's Syndrome, a rare but often fatal children's disease. The disease most often affects children of 5 to 16 years of age, and 25% of the sufferers are killed by the affliction. The Center for Disease Control had discovered in a study that a total of 137 out of 144 children with the disease had previously been treated with aspirin. No connection was found between Reye's Syndrome and the use of the drug acetaminophen, which is marketed under the name Tylenol.

Disasters — Heavy flooding killed 176 and left 25,000 homeless on Indonesia's Sumatra Island, it was announced **June 3** . . . In a collision between a suburban electric train and a freight train near Madras, India, **June 3,** 15 people were killed. . . . A storm, **June 3,** in the southwestern coastal state of Orissa in India killed 200 people and wrecked thousands of homes . . . During a rainstorm, **June 8,** a Brazilian airliner crashed into a mountain near Fortaleza, killing all 137 on board . . . Eleven people were killed during an earthquake in El Salvador, **June 19** . . . An Air India jet crashed at Bombay International Airport **June 22,** killing 19 . . . Weekend windstorms killed 43 and injured 500 in the southern Brazilian state of Paraná, it was reported, **June 27.**

JULY

National

"Kiddie Porn" Barred — The United States Supreme Court upheld, 9-0, **July 2,** a New York State law prohibiting the use of children in pornographic films, photographs, or performances. The New York law also prohibited the sale of such materials. The New York Court of Appeals had previously declared the law unconstitutional on the grounds that the state could not prohibit materials that were entitled to constitutional protection from government interference, but the Supreme Court ruled that sexual exploitation and abuse of children needed to be prevented. Associate Justice Byron R. White added that child pornography was a "category of material outside the protection of the First Amendment," therefore, it could be regulated whether or not it was obscene.

Jobless Rate Remains Unchanged, Poverty Rate and Prices Up — The unemployment rate during June held at 9.5%, it was announced by the Bureau of Labor Statistics, **July 2.** This was the highest level in 40 years. Even though the rate remained the same, unemployment rose among adult men, and factory employment declined. The unemployment level among black teenagers rose to a record 52.6%. The Census Bureau reported, **July 19,** that the number of Americans officially classified as poor had increased by about 2.2 million in 1981. This increase, to 14%, gave the country its highest rate of poverty since 1967. The threshhold of poverty as set by the government was an income of $9,287 per year for a family of 4. It was also reported that 11.1% of whites, 34.2% of blacks, and 26.2% of Hispanic Americans were below that level. On **July 23,** the Labor Department reported that consumer prices rose by 1% in June, pegging the annual inflation rate in double-digit figures for the second month in a row.

Plane Crashes Near New Orleans — A Pan American World Airways jet liner crashed in Kenner, Louisiana, a suburb of New Orleans, **July 9.** The Federal Aviation Administration announced that all 143 people on board, as well as an estimated 6 people on the ground, had been killed. Several houses were also set on fire. The Boeing 727 had taken off from New Orleans and was heading for Las Vegas when the crash occurred. During the search for bodies, an 18-month-old baby girl who had miraculously survived the crash was found, but the death toll, **July 10,** was raised to an estimated 153—145 people aboard and 8 on the ground. The FAA reported that the records of cockpit-to-ground radio transmissions just before the crash showed no emergency calls or other indications of trouble. Safety experts guessed that the plane had been brought down by forces associated with rainstorms. The weather could have produced a wind shear that would have slowed the flow of air over the wings and cause the plane to lose speed, "drowning" the engines in rain. On **July 11,** it was announced that two alerts warning of hazardous wind shifts had been sent to the plane as it taxied into position, although it was not known if the pilots received them. The National Transportation Safety Board announced **July 12** the tape recorders on board the plane had been found to be defective, which would delay the analysis of the cockpit conversations. The Safety Board announced, **July 16,** that the pilot had warned his crew that the plane was "sinking" and there was a discussion of how they could avoid the disaster.

Congressional Sex Scandal Alleged — The House of Representatives, **July 13,** authorized the House Ethics Committee to conduct an investigation into allegations congressmen and their aides had been involved in homosexual activities with teen-age pages and had taken illegal drugs. The committee was given the power to recommend censure or expulsion of any congressmen found to have violated House rules. Leroy Williams, a former Congressional page, had given the Ethics Committee the names of 3 Congressmen with whom he said he had had sexual relations, plus the name of one senator for whom he had hired a male prostitute. However, on **July 9,** FBI officials reported that Williams had failed a lie detector test. Williams had given vague answers when asked about sexual relations between members of Congress and pages. The alleged scandal also involved the reports of 30 other pages who had heard of the sale of cocaine and of homosexual activities on Capitol Hill.

Haitians Freed from Detention — The first of 1,807 Haitian refugees ordered freed by a federal judge in June were released **July 23.** Immigration officials announced that they had released 17 refugees and that others would be set free when volunteer agencies provided sponsors for them. On **July 26,** a second group of 23 was released, and orientation programs for them were begun in Miami.

Gandhi Visits U.S. — Prime Minister Indira Gandhi of India arrived in the U.S., **July 27,** for talks with the Reagan administration. On **July 28** she was the guest of honor at a luncheon at the Metropolitan Museum of Art in New York City and also met with Secretary General Javier Pérez de Cuéllar at the UN. Gandhi and Pres. Reagan announced, **July 29,** that they had agreed to increase scientific, cultural, and economic cooperation between their 2 countries. They also reported that a long-standing dispute between India and the U.S. over uranium fuel had been resolved. A U.S. law had blocked shipments from the U.S. of low-enriched uranium fuel for a United States-built atomic power plant near Bombay. Reagan agreed to give India permission to buy the fuel from France instead of the U.S.

International

New President Inaugurated in Argentina — Maj. Gen. Reynaldo Bignone, a retired army officer, was sworn in as the president of Argentina, **July 1.** In his inauguration address, he said that the ban on political activity, which had been in force for the previous 6 years, would end. Promising to consult with civilian leaders regularly, he expressed hope that the country would be a true democracy, at least by March 1984. His first task was to deal with the British, who still held 650 prisoners captured during the Falkland Islands conflict. On **July 12,** Pres. Reagan lifted the economic sanctions that he had imposed on Argentina at the outbreak of the Falkland Islands War. However, the ban on sales of military equipment remained in effect, pending an investigation of the situation in the Falklands. On **July 22,** Britain eased its 200-mile sea and air blockade around the islands, but asked that Argentina keep its military ships and airplanes at least 150 miles away.

Dominican President Dead — President Antonio Guzmán of the Dominican Republic died, **July 4,** from a bullet wound in the head. The official report indicated that the bullet came from Guzmán's pistol, which had accidentally discharged. Although many speculated that he had committed suicide, this was officially denied. Vice-president Jacobo Majluta Azar was sworn in to replace Guzmán. He immediately issued a statement saying that he would transfer power to the President-elect, Salvador Jorge Blanco, as scheduled, on **Aug. 16.**

New President for Mexico — Miguel de la Madrid Hurtado was, on **July 5,** declared the winner of the presidential elections held in Mexico on **July 3.** He was the candidate of the Institutional Revolutionary Party, which had won every presidential election since 1929, and he was scheduled to succeed Pres. José López Portillo on December 1. About 70% of Mexico's 31.5 million voters had cast their ballots, and de la Madrid had received 75% of the vote.

Heavy Fighting in El Salvador — Defense Minister José Guillermo García of El Salvador announced, **July 7,** that government soldiers had killed 400 guerrilla rebels in the province of Morazán. Thirteen Salvadoran soldiers had been killed and 26 were either wounded or missing in what was the biggest campaign in the civil war. The Salvadoran Army announced, **July 11,** that 130 guerrillas had been killed and a rebel training camp destroyed in Morazán Province, near the Honduran border. On **July 16,** the International Monetary Fund, after a long debate, approved an $85 million loan to El Salvador.

Intruder in Buckingham Palace — The London *Daily Express* reported, **July 12,** that a man had broken into Buckingham Palace on **July 9,** entered the bedroom of Queen Elizabeth II, sat on her bed, and chatted with her for 10 minutes before she could call a footman to take him away. The man also had broken into the palace on one previous occasion. In the House of Commons, **July 12,** Home Secretary William Whitelaw promised that security would be beefed up at the palace, and announced that the intruder, Michael Fagan, had been arrested. Fagan's lawyer said, **July 13,** that his client had talked with the Queen about her family, and that he had been escorted out of the bedroom by a chamber-maid, rather than a footman. On **July 19,** British authorities announced that Fagan would not be prosecuted because he had not committed a criminal offense, as in Britain trespassing is a civil matter, and not a crime. Whitelaw announced, **July 21,** that the trespass had been made possible by serious errors and omissions of police procedure, and that the police simply had not responded quickly enough.

Iran Invades Iraq — Reagan Administration officials said, **July 12,** that large numbers of Iranian troops had been moved to the Iraqi border and could start an invasion at any time. On **July 14,** Iran announced that the offensive had been started and that the first line of Iraqi bunkers had been passed. Iraq identified the location of the invasion as near Basra—14 miles from the border. U.S. officials reported that the Iranians had penetrated from 6 to 10 miles into Iraq. The invasion appeared to have stalled, **July 15,** when Iraqi forces halted, and at some points, repelled, the invaders along a 10-mile front. On **July 16,** Iran began a new offensive, but the Iraqis seemed to be holding their ground. Fierce fighting in that area continued through **July 20,** when Iraq appeared to have achieved a limited but important victory by stopping the Iranian advance, forcing a standoff. On **July 21,** the Iranians attacked Baghdad by air, causing heavy damage to oil installations. Meanwhile, Iraqi jets bombed cities in the oil-rich Khuzistan Province, where 120 people were reported killed or wounded. On **July 21,** Iran launched a new drive near Basra, and, on **July 23,** Iraqi helicopter gunships shelled Iranian positions east of Basra. Iran announced, **July 24,** that it would agree to mediation of the war by Algeria, and, on **July 31,** Iraq reported that its forces had killed more than 27,000 Iranians in the 18 days of the battle near Basra.

Guatemalan Insurrection Continues — Guatemalan Army spokesmen said, **July 18,** that a female guerrilla commander and 21 other rebels had been killed near the village of Sauce, 36 miles north of Guatemala City. Captured were Soviet-made grenades, several types of guns, and land mines. The spokesmen also reported that 10 guerrillas had been killed, **July 17,** in Chinimachicaj—20 miles west of the city. Also on **July 17,** guerrillas attacked the town of Pajmujay—50 miles west of the capital, killing 42 civilians.

IRA Bombs Explode in London — Nine British soldiers were killed and 51 people wounded in a series of bombings in London, **July 20.** The first blast occurred in Hyde Park at 10:45 A.M. as the Queen's Household Cavalry was riding from their barracks to the changing of the guard ceremony at Buckingham Palace. Three members of the guard were killed and 23 onlookers were wounded. Six horses were killed and one had to be destroyed. Two hours later, a bomb exploded in Regent's Park under the park bandstand as the band of the Royal Greenjackets was giving a concert. Six musicians were killed and 28 performers and onlookers were injured. The Irish Republican Army claimed credit for the bombings.

Polish Martial Law Eased Slightly — Polish Communist Party Leader Gen. Wojciech Jaruzelski, **July 21,** announced that more than 1,200 people who had been detained under martial law would be released. Lech Walesa, the jailed leader of Solidarity, would not be one of them. Jaruzelski also indicated that martial law might be suspended by the end of the year if tensions in the country eased. He reported, however, that the proposed visit in August of Pope John Paul II to celebrate the 600th anniversary of the Black Madonna of Czestochowa would not take place. He did suggest that the papal visit might be rescheduled for 1983 if the Polish situation were to become more peaceful. On **July 22,** supporters of Solidarity were arrested at a counter-demonstration against ceremonies honoring Poland's National Day. However, the next day, Polish authorities freed at least 14 political prisoners, most of them members of Solidarity. On **July 27,** the Polish government reported that some 1,227 prisoners would be released, but that 637 would continue to be held, including Lech Walesa.

Furor over Pipeline — The French government announced, **July 22,** that it was permitting French companies to produce U.S.-licensed components for a proposed Soviet oil pipeline. The pipeline was designed to supply Western Europe with natural gas from Siberia. On **July 24,** the Italian government announced that it would honor all agreements with the Soviets to supply equipment for the pipeline. These announcements came despite a ban announced in December 1981 by U.S. Pres. Reagan on the use of American equipment on the pipeline. Reagan had issued the ban in retaliation against the USSR for its involvement with the military government of Poland. On **June 18,** he had extended the ban to the use of licenses of U.S. technology by foreign countries. The U.S. ambassador to France, Evan Galbraith, predicted that Western European countries would find it difficult to do business in the U.S. if they violated U.S. law. He also mentioned the possibility of fines and criminal penalties against the directors of those European companies.

Panamanian Leader Resigns — Under apparent pressure from the National Guard, Panamanian Pres. Aristides Royo Sanchez, **July 30,** resigned, 2 years prior to the end of his 6-year term. He was replaced, **July 31,** by Vice Pres. Ricardo de la Espriella. Royo, a leader of leftist elements in Panama had followed a foreign policy that was often critical of U.S. policy in Latin America. The new government indicated that it would espouse a more conservative policy line.

General

Starch Blockers Said to Be Dangerous — The U.S. Food and Drug Administration announced, **July 1,** that starch blockers are unapproved and considered possibly dangerous. These diet aids that had been so popular in recent months, the FDA stated, had prompted complaints of nausea, vomiting, diarrhea, and stomach pains. Experts pointed out that if the tablets worked to block the digestion of starch, as advertized, large amounts of undigested starch would reach the large intestine. Intestinal bacteria would then digest the starch and cause the symptoms mentioned. The companies manufacturing the tablets were given 10 days to file a plan for discontinuing the marketing of the pills.

Whaling Ban Voted — The International Whaling Commission voted, **July 23,** to ban all commercial whaling, effective in 1986. Some of the nations opposing the ban threatened to file exemptions to the ruling, including Japan which filed **July 24.** Eskimos and other native hunters were permitted to continue their subsistence-level hunting of the whales.

Disasters — A Soviet jetliner crashed and burned, **July 6,** outside Moscow, killing 90. . . . A Mexican train derailed and plunged down a mountain gorge, **July 11,** near Tepic, killing at least 120 people. . . . Two light planes collided in flight, **July 14,** near Praetoria, South Africa, killing 12, including 2 generals and the South African treasury secretary . . . An exploding grenade killed 6 children in Cairo, **July 22** . . . Flooding in the Japanese state of Nagasaki, which began **July 23,** killed at least 245, with 117 missing and presumed dead . . . A ship caught fire at the entrance to Manila Bay on **July 25,** and 74 crewmen were declared missing and presumed dead . . . A twin-engined plane crashed near Lindale, Tex., **July 28,** killing all 11 aboard . . . In a multiple bus and car collision near Beaune, France, **July 31,** 53 people, most of them children, were killed . . . A bus fell into a mountain gorge in northern India, **July 31,** killing 33 and injuring 27.

AUGUST

National

Court Orders Safety Devices for Autos — The United States Court of Appeals for the District of Columbia ruled, **Aug. 4,** that all new automobiles sold after September 1983 must be equipped with air bags or automatic seat belts. This was in response to the decision of the Reagan administration in October, 1981 to rescind the regulation requiring these devices to protect automobile occupants. The ruling was the result of petitions to the court by insurance companies and consumer groups, who had argued that the safety devices would save 9,000 lives per year.

Unemployment at Record High — The unemployment rate in the U.S. rose 0.3 of 1% in July, it was announced, **Aug. 6,** by the Department of Labor. This rise brought the unemployment rate to 9.8%, a post-World War II record. Some Democratic congressmen and labor leaders accused the administration of sticking to policies that were increasing hardships among working people. The number of people in the U.S. without jobs was pegged at 10,790,000, and the Bureau of Labor Statistics estimated that there were another 1.5 million discouraged workers in the country who had given up their job-hunting activities and were not included in the unemployment figure.

Immigration Law Changed — The U.S. Senate, **Aug. 17,** approved revisions in the immigration laws. The bill offered amnesty to millions of illegal aliens who entered the country before Jan. 1, 1980. In addition, all job applicants would be required to show prospective employers their identification papers in order to prove that they were either citizens or authorized aliens. The bill was passed in the wake of the arrest of some 950,000 illegal aliens during 1981. The bill also set a limit of 425,000 immigrants each year, not counting refugees, and no more than 20,000 of which could come from any one country, excluding Mexico and Canada, for which the limit was set at 40,000 each. If there were unused Canadian visa numbers, these spots could be turned over to Mexico.

Man Convicted on Draft Charges — Enten Eller, a 20-year-old college student, was convicted in Roanoke, Va., **Aug. 17,** of failing to register for the draft. This was the first trial on those charges since mandatory registration was revived in 1980. The government had estimated that of the 8.5 million men eligible for registration, 700,000 had failed to sign up. Eller cited his religious beliefs as his reason for refusing to register. The young man was put on probation and ordered to perform at least 250 hours of community service.

Congress Passes Spending Cuts — Both houses of Congress, **Aug. 18,** approved a bill to cut spending by $13.3 billion. Its intent was to reduce the federal budget deficit by $130 billion during the next 3 years. The cuts included a reduction in cost-of-living adjustments for retired federal employees under the age of 62, a $1.9 billion-cut in food stamps, and a 2-year freeze on dairy supports.

Tax Bill Approved in Reagan Victory — Both houses of Congress, **Aug. 19,** approved a $98.3 billion tax bill. This was taken as an important victory for the Reagan administration. Pres. Ronald Reagan had campaigned actively for passage of the bill, including a news conference, a nationally televised speech, and a joint plea with House Speaker Thomas P. O'Neill (D, Mass.) in the Rose Garden of the White House. More than two-thirds of the revenue raised by the bill over the next 3 years would come from business—a reversal of the 1981 tax act, which had reduced the tax burden on businesses. The provisions of the bill included a ruling that restaurants would be required to report waiters' tips, that the excise tax on cigarettes would be doubled, that the tax on telephone service would be doubled, and that the tax on airline tickets would increase from 5% to 8%. Also, financial institutions would be required to withhold 10% of the interest and dividends paid to investors.

Soviets Accept Grain Deal — Secretary of Agriculture John R. Block announced, **Aug. 20,** that the USSR had accepted the Reagan administration's offer to extend by one year its grain sales agreement. This new grain agreement was the second yearly extension of a 5-year agreement that had regulated Soviet purchases of American grain since 1979. The Soviets were required to buy at least 6 million metric tons of American corn and wheat per year, with a maximum of 8 million metric tons.

Consumer Prices Up — The Labor Department reported, **Aug. 24,** that consumer prices had risen 0.6% in July. This abatement in the monthly increase was caused by smaller rises in gasoline prices and a decline in the growth of housing costs, plus the fact that food costs tended to stabilize.

Crime Rate Down — The Federal Bureau of Investigation reported, **Aug. 27,** that the crime rate in 1981 was down 2% from the rate of the previous year. During 1981, there had been 13.3 million serious crimes committed—just about the number committed in 1980. But, because the population had increased during that time by 4 million people, the crime rate, which relates crime to population, actually decreased. Murders decreased 2.3%, aggravated assaults 1.7%, burglaries 0.5%, motor vehicle thefts 3.6%, and forcible rapes 0.7%. The only crimes to increase in percentage were robbery, by 4.6%, and larceny-theft, by 0.6%.

Former Page Recants Sex Charges — Leroy Williams, the former congressional page who had claimed that he had had homosexual relations with lawmakers, **Aug. 27,** admitted that he had lied in his accusations. Williams said he had made the claims to draw attention to abuses in the congressional page system. The Justice Department, **Aug. 31,** concluded its investigation into allegations of sexual misconduct, stating that the probe had found insufficient evidence to prosecute or continue the investigation. The House Ethics Committee investigation, however, would continue.

International

Attempted Coup in Kenya — Pres. Daniel arap Moi of Kenya announced, **Aug. 1,** that a group of junior air force officers had attempted to overthrow the civilian government of his country. The attempted coup, however, had been crushed by Kenyan army and police units. More than 300 air force personnel had been arrested. In the fighting, 145 people were killed, and $111 million worth of property was lost in the ensuing looting. A curfew was laid down in Nairobi and Nanyuki, and, on **Aug. 2,** the 2 universities in the country were closed down and armed troops began a house-to-house search for rebels who had escaped. By **Aug. 3,** it was reported that more than 1,000 air force personnel had been detained, and, on **Aug. 4,** the number of those arrested rose to more than 3,000, including the country's entire 2,100-member air force. Most of the civilians being held were arrested for looting. The government announced, **Aug. 21,** that it had formally disbanded its air force.

Soviet Pipeline Furor Grows — The British government, **Aug. 2,** ordered 4 British companies to honor their contracts with the Soviet Union to furnish equipment for the construction of the natural gas pipeline from Siberia to western Europe. This action was in defiance of the December 1981 U.S. ban on supplying U.S.-developed technology to the USSR. Twelve British companies were involved. On **Aug. 12,** European officials delivered a formal protest to Washington, alleging that the ban was an unacceptable interference in European Economic Community affairs. The papers were delivered to the Commerce and State Departments by Otto Borch, the Danish ambassador to Washington, and Roland de Kergorlay, head of the EEC delegation to the U.S. On **Aug. 24,** a federal judge refused to grant Dresser Industries, a U.S. firm, a restraining order that would have prevented the Commerce Department from punishing it for not telling its French subsidiary to defy a French government order to deliver equipment for use on the pipeline. Cabinet members recommended that Dresser France be placed on an American denial list which would prevent it from having any commercial relations with the U.S. The Reagan administration ordered trade sanctions against Creusot-Loire and Dresser France, **Aug. 26**, and put them on the temporary denial list immediately upon learning that 3 compressors built by Dresser France for Creusot-Loire had left on a French vessel bound for the Soviet Union. It was announced, **Aug. 31**, that 4 members of the U.S. Cabinet had recommended to Pres. Reagan that he soften his trade sanctions against European companies that violate his embargo.

Iran-Iraq War Deadlocked — After 2 weeks of intensive fighting, it was reported, **Aug. 4**, that the war between Iran and Iraq was deadlocked. It was estimated that since the war broke out in September 1980, nearly 80,000 troops had been killed, 200,000 had been wounded, and 45,000 had been captured. Iran announced, **Aug. 7**, that it had captured 2 Iraqi outposts inside Iran, killing 200 of the Iraqi troops near the border town of Qasr-i-Shirin. The Iranians also announced that this proved that Iraq had not withdrawn all its troops from Iran—one of the Iranian conditions for ending the war. Both Iran and Iraq reported, **Aug. 9**, that they had inflicted heavy losses on each other in fighting northeast of Basra, and, on **Aug. 19**, it was announced that Iranian troops had killed or wounded more than 50 Iraqi soldiers and damages an Iraqi oil terminal near the head of the Persian Gulf. Pres. Saddam Hussein of Iraq warned that foreign ships using ports in Iran were in danger of being attacked by Iraqi planes. Iraq reported, **Aug. 25**, that it had bombed Kharg Island in the Persian Gulf, hitting Iranian oil installations.

Italian Government Shaken Up Again — Members of the Socialist Party pulled out of the Italian government's ruling coalition, **Aug. 6**, causing a crisis in government. The withdrawal was caused by the rejection by the Chamber of Deputies of a decree that would have eliminated tax privileges for petroleum companies. The government of Prime Minister Giovanni Spadolini resigned, **Aug. 7**, because of the lack of support by the Socialists. This marked the end of the 41st Italian government since World War II. The Italian Christian Democratic Party announced, **Aug. 9**, that they would support Spadolini if he were to try to form a new government, which he attempted to do on **Aug. 11**, although the Socialists had demanded a new election rather than a reshuffling of the 5-party coalition. Spadolini announced, **Aug. 21**, that he would form a 5-party coalition pledged to economic restraint and changes in parliamentary rules. The 5 parties would be the Christian Democrats, the Liberals, the Republicans, the Social Democrats, and the Socialists. On **Aug. 23**, he announced his new cabinet, which consisted of the same parties and the same ministers as the previous cabinet.

Ankara Airport Attacked — A group of armed Armenians opened fire at the Ankara, Turkey airport, **Aug. 7**, killing 6 people in a hail of submachine gun bullets. The number of wounded was estimated at 72. The Armenian Secret Army for the Liberation of Armenia said that the attack was a protest against the Turkish occupation of Armenia, and warned that there would be more violence in other countries unless 85 Armenians imprisoned in those countries were freed. The countries cites were the U.S., Canada, France, Britain, Switzerland, and Sweden.

El Salvador Death Toll Cited as Unrest Continues — The El Salvador Human Rights Commission reported, **Aug. 6**, that the total number of people killed in the 33-month old revolution had reached 35,000—most of them civilians killed by rightist death squads. The Salvadoran government announced, **Aug. 9**, that 19 soldiers and an undetermined number of civilians had been killed during a seige of the town of Ciudad Barrios by leftists. Salvadoran jets bombarded guerrilla positions on a volcano north of El Salvador, **Aug. 11**, and, the next day, they bombed other guerrilla camps. Meanwhile, the army raided slums in San Salvador in search of rebels. The guerrillas seized the town of Guarjila **Aug. 15**, killing 9 soldiers in the process, and the leader of the Salvadoran Roman Catholic Church, Msgr. Arturo Rivera Damas, criticized the raids on the slums and demanded that the government treat its prisoners in a more humane manner. The Salvadorean Army reported, **Aug. 24**, that it had killed 119 leftist guerrillas in a sweep through northern San Vicente Province. Also on **Aug. 31**, the army reported that it had sustained a casualty count of 3,801 in the 12-month period ending June 30—a total of 21% of its personnel.

Marcos Uncovers Subversive Plan — Pres. Ferdinand E. Marcos of the Philippines announced, **Aug. 8**, that he had discovered a plan to carry out a nationwide series of strikes, bombings, and assassinations in September. He reported that he had formed a secret plainclothed police force consisting of some 1,000 men to patrol the city of Manila. A list of subversives and anti-government groups was being compiled, he said. On **Aug. 18**, Felixberto Olalia, the chairman of the radical May 1st Movement, was formally charged with inciting sedition and rebellion.

Bombing Wave Hits Paris — An attack on a kosher restaurant in Paris, France, **Aug. 9**, killed 6 and wounded 22. Police said that the attack had been carefully planned and probably involved 5 or 6 assailants. One of them threw a grenade into the restaurant, and the rest opened fire with submachine guns. The attack was believed to have been an anti-Semitic act by the Palestine Liberation Organization, and followed other bombings in the previous month. Fadel el-Dani, a PLO leader was killed by a bomb, **July 23**, and, on **July 24**, a bomb exploded in a Left Bank cafe, wounding 2 women. The latter had been the 6th bombing in Paris in 5 days. On **Aug. 11**, a bomb exploded outside a bank that had previously been Jewish-owned, and one woman was injured. The French Cabinet banned, **Aug. 18**, the extreme leftist group, Direct Action, the group that had taken the responsibility for the 3 anti-Semitic attacks. Members of the group faced up to 2 years in prison and fines of $8,700. On **Aug. 21**, a bomb planted beneath the car of the U.S. Embassy commercial counselor, Roderick Grant, exploded, killing a policeman near the Eiffel Tower. A demolition expert, he was defusing the bomb when it exploded.

Poles Continue Political Protests — A pro-Solidarity protest in Warsaw, **Aug. 10**, was dispersed by the police. The Polish government feared that it was the beginning of a promised series of protests by unionists. On **Aug. 13**, police broke up a march by thousands of Solidarity supporters in Gdansk, and similar gatherings in Warsaw, Cracow, and Wroclaw. Archbishop Jozef Glemp, the head of the Polish Roman Catholic church, **Aug. 15**, called these marches an example of "invisible hatred." He also called for a new dialogue between authorities and the people. Polish riot police used a water cannon in Warsaw, **Aug. 16**, to disperse a few hundred people who were gathered around a floral Solidarity cross. The cannon was used again in Warsaw, **Aug. 17**, against pro-Solidarity demonstrators. Sources in both Solidarity and the Church announced, **Aug. 18**, that 60 inmates, most of them members of Solidarity, were beaten when the police were called in to stop a disorder at a detention center at Kwidzyn. The water cannon was used again in Warsaw, **Aug. 21**, to disperse a crowd of several hundred protestors. And, on **Aug. 22**, in defiance of the police, hundreds of Poles gathered in Warsaw to place Solidarity banners at two memorial crosses. Polish leader Gen. Wojciech Jaruzelski vowed, **Aug. 24**, to take strong action against any new opposition activities. Archbishop Glemp in an address to over 350,000 worshippers, **Aug. 26**, demanded that Lech Walesa, the Solidarity leader, be freed. Riot policemen, equipped with water cannons and armored personnel carriers, were deployed throughout Warsaw, **Aug. 30**, in preparation for anti-government demonstrations called for, on **Aug. 31**, by Solidarity leaders. The police quelled the demonstrations, **Aug. 31** in Warsaw, with tear gas grenades. There were also reports of clashes in Gdansk, Wroclaw, Cracow, and Nowa Huta, as well as several other smaller towns.

Church Problems Arise in Nicaragua — A Managua, Nicaragua newspaper announced, **Aug. 11**, that government-backed groups had stepped up attacks on Jehovah's Witnesses, Mormons, and Seventh-Day Adventists, accusing them of having links with the U.S. Central Intelligence Agency. Sandinist Defense Committees had seized some 20 buildings used by the sects during the previous week. *La Prensa*, the country's only opposition newspaper, was closed down, **Aug. 12**, in an incident concerning a Roman Catholic priest who claimed that the police had forced him naked into the street. The paper refused to print the police version of the story, choosing instead not to publish it at all. On **Aug. 16,** an outbreak of violence occurred between Roman Catholic students and members of a pro-government youth organization over the treatment of the priest.

Police Riot in Bombay — Five people were killed in Bombay, India in the rioting and looting that followed a police demonstration, according to reports **Aug. 18.** About 9,500 of the 22,000 members of the Bombay police department halted trains on the outskirts of the city in protest over low pay and poor working conditions. Some of the commuters on the trains went on a rampage, causing heavy damage at several railroad stations and looting many nearby stores. Loyal policemen fought with their demonstrating colleagues and also with the irate commuters. A 24-hour curfew was imposed in several parts of the city, 22 policemen were arrested, 92 others were dismissed from the force, and the police union was suspended. On **Aug. 19,** Indian troops shot and killed a rioter in Bombay, and began to restore order to the city. The government also stated that nearly all of the police of that city had taken part in the revolt. On **Aug. 24** the total number of police dismissals had reached more than 300.

State of Emergency in Peru — The Peruvian government declared a state of emergency in Lima and Callao, **Aug. 20,** after a night of political violence. Left-wing extremists had blacked out Lima and firebombed and dynamited shops and government buildings. The police rounded up between 30 and 60 alleged members of an extremist group, **Aug. 21,** but it was not until **Aug. 22** that electrical power was restored to the capital city. That day, at least 26 people were killed in a gun battle in Ayacucho between leftists and the police, and, on **Aug. 23,** the police pursued the guerrillas through the Peruvian mountains. The police also reported that they had arrested 314 suspected members of a Maoist group, Sendero Luminoso, in Lima. Guerrillas attacked a police station in the Andes Mountains and planted a bomb in a Lima newspaper office, **Aug. 24.**

The Peso Falters — Bankers met with leading Mexican officials, **Aug. 19,** in Mexico City, in an effort to devise a plan to prevent the Mexican government from running out of money or defaulting on their debts. On **Aug. 20,** the U.S. government outlined a proposed package of aid to Mexico which included $1.5 billion in loans by foreign central banks and direct loans by the U.S. in the form of prepayments for crude oil and up to $1 billion in guarantees on new loans from U.S. banks. The International Monetary Fund would also supply $4.5 billion. Gov. Edmund G. Brown Jr., of California, asked Pres. Reagan for economic disaster aid for San Diego and Imperial counties, which were suffering from the devaluation of the peso which had forced citizens of border towns in Mexico to give up shopping in cities across the California border. Investment analysts calculated that U.S. investors in Mexican financial instruments had lost hundreds of millions of dollars because of the crisis, it was reported **Aug. 23.**

Spain's Assembly Dissolved — Spanish Prime Minister Leopoldo Calvo Sotelo dissolved his parliament, **Aug. 27,** and called for new elections to be held on Oct. 28. A large number of defections from his party, the Union of the Democratic Center, spurred the action. By holding the elections in one month rather than the constitutionally scheduled time in the spring of 1983, Calvo Sotelo gave his opponents less time to organize and campaign.

General

Spacewoman Sets Record — Svetlana Savitskaya, along with 2 other Soviet cosmonauts, Leonid Popov and Aleksandr Serebrov, blasted off from earth, **Aug. 16.** On **Aug. 17,** they docked the Soyuz T-5 capsule with the Soviet Salyut 7 space station that had been in orbit since **May 13.** When the mission ended **Aug. 27,** Savitskaya, the second woman to travel into space, had logged most space flight time for a woman in history.

Major Fossil Find Reported — Hidemi Ishida of Osaka University in Japan and Richard E. Leakey, the director of the National Museums of Kenya, announced in Nairobi, **Aug. 31,** that a fossil jawbone found in Ethiopia by a Kenyan fossil hunter might be as old as 8 million years, and that it had come from a human-like creature. Its importance lay in the fact that the remains of the oldest known human ancestor, a 4½-foot-tall creature that walked on 2 legs, are only 4 million years old. This new discovery might fill an important gap in the primate record.

Disasters — A truck ran off the road near Sukkur, Pakistan, **Aug. 14,** killing 27 and injuring 34 of the 70 people aboard . . . A typhoon in South Korea killed 13 and injured 100, **Aug. 4.**

SEPTEMBER

National

Pipeline Sanctions Eased — Secretary of the Treasury Donald T. Regan announced, **Sept. 1,** that the administration was prepared to ease the sanctions that it had applied against 2 French companies that had supplied the Soviet Union with natural gas pipeline equipment in defiance of a U.S. ban. The sanctions would affect only oil and gas equipment and would not bar foreign corporations from receiving U.S. products. He also reported that the sanctions would be imposed against John Brown P.L.C., a British manufacturer of pipeline turbines that were sent to the U.S.S.R. On **Sept. 4,** Italy ignored the embargo and sent 2 U.S.-designed turbine compressors to the Soviet Union. By doing so, Italy joined Britain and France in their defiance of Pres. Ronald Reagan's Siberian natural gas pipeline embargo.

Jobless Rate Unchanged — The Labor Department reported, **Sept. 3,** that the unemployment rate in the U.S. remained unchanged at 9.8% in August. This was the highest rate since 1941, and 10,805,000 people were without jobs. The Labor Department Bureau of Labor Statistics had announced, **Sept. 2,** that in the week ending **Aug. 21** the number of people filing initial claims for unemployment benefits rose to 621,000. By mid-August, more than 4 million people had filed for unemployment insurance benefits in 1982.

Lutheran, Episcopal Churches Plan Reforms — The biennial convention of the Lutheran Church in America at Louisville recommended, **Sept. 7,** that Lutherans should establish communion fellowship with the Episcopalians. This would mean that Lutherans and Episcopalians could celebrate holy communion together while using the rites of either church. Also, members of either denomination could take communion in each other's churches. The Commission on Ecumenical Relations of the Episcopal Church had already endorsed the idea. On **Sept. 8,** 3 Lutheran denominations, the Lutheran Church in America, the American Lutheran Church, and the Association of Evangelical Lutheran Churches, voted to merge to form a new church. The new Lutheran Church would become the 3rd largest Protestant denomination in the country. On **Sept. 9,** The Episcopal Church adopted a hymnal revision. Not only were some hymns dropped and some added, but lyrics were revised to eliminate male-dominated language.

Reagan Veto Overridden — The Senate voted, **Sept. 10,** to override Pres. Ronald Reagan's veto of a $14.1 billion supplementary spending bill. The House had voted to override the veto on **Sept. 9.** This was the first major defeat for the administration during the 97th Congress. One reason cited for the vote was that congressmen resented Reagan's statement that the bill was a "budget buster," when it was almost $2 billion less than he had asked for. Other reasons given were a need to reassert congressional influence over spending priorities, the lobbying of older Americans in behalf of funds in the bill, and desire to teach the White House a lesson.

Western Railroads to Merge — The Interstate Commerce Commission authorized, **Sept. 13,** the merger of 3 railroads—the Union Pacific, the Missouri Pacific, and the Western Pacific. In effect, the merger created a vast new railroad system linking the Midwest, Southwest, and Pacific Coast. The Union Pacific was to acquire the other 2 lines and would become the third-largest system in the United States, with lines from Chicago to the West Coast and south to the Gulf of Mexico. The reason given for the ruling was that it would permit more efficient single-line handling of freight traffic.

Donovan Cleared — Special Federal Prosecutor Leon Silverman announced, **Sept. 13,** that he had found no evidence to permit the prosecution of Secretary of Labor Raymond J. Donovan for organized crime connections. It had been charged that Donovan had dealt with mob-controlled subcontractors when he was a partner in a New Jersey construction company; that he had set up dummy companies to launder money; that he had given payoffs to an organized crime figure; that he had rigged sewer contracts; and that he had made illegal contributions to the Reagan presidential campaign fund. Silverman said that he had been unable to find any corroborative evidence for these charges.

Abortion Proposal Defeated — The Senate voted, **Sept. 15**, to kill a proposal that would have imposed severe restrictions on women's abortion rights. The proposal, which had Pres. Reagan's approval, would have banned the use of federal funds for abortions and would have encouraged efforts to reverse the Supreme Court's decision to permit abortions during the first 3 months of a pregnancy.

Crime Rate Stays the Same — The Justice Department reported, **Sept. 19**, that 30% of the homes in the United States had been touched by crime in 1981. The figure was unchanged from the preceding year. Nearly 25 million households experienced a crime of violence or theft. Ten percent of all households were touched by a burglary or a violent crime by a stranger, such as rape, robbery, or assault. The kinds of households that were the most vulnerable were black households, higher income households, and households in central cities.

Emergency Strike Legislation Passed — Congress voted, **Sept. 22**, to direct 26,000 locomotive engineers to end their railroad strike, accept a new contract, and return to work. Pres. Reagan signed the emergency legislation the same day. The legislation ended a 4-day strike that had affected most of the nation's rail system. The engineers were required to accept the recommendations of an emergency fact-finding board, including a substantial pay increase but not the principal demand of the strikers—a guarantee of 15% pay differential over other rail unions. Reagan had requested the action because, according to White House estimates, the 4-day strike had put nearly half a million out of work, and could have cost the economy nearly $1 billion per day.

International

Reagan Proposes Mideast Plan — Pres. Ronald Reagan called, **Sept. 1**, for a fresh start in the Middle East peace process and urged full autonomy for the Palestinians living in the Gaza Strip under Israeli occupation. He demanded a stoppage of Israeli settlement and asked that Jordan supervise the Palestinians. On **Sept. 2**, the Israeli Cabinet voted unanimously to reject Reagan's plan for Palestinian self-rule in the occupied parts of the Strip. The Israelis said they feared that the U.S. plan would lead to a Palestinian state that would present a danger to Israel's security. They also vowed to continue their program of establishing a Jewish population in the Gaza Strip. The Israelis allocated, **Sept. 5**, $18.5 million to build 3 new settlements in the occupied West Bank and approved the building of 7 others. These 10 would bring the number of such towns in the West Bank and the Gaza up to 109.

Martial Law Protest Escalates in Poland — The Polish government announced, **Sept. 1**, that 2 demonstrators had been shot and killed in Lubin in protests against government-imposed martial law held **Aug. 31.** Throughout Poland, some 4,050 people had been arrested in street fighting that marked the second anniversary of the Gdansk shipyard agreements that started the Solidarity movement. Curfews had been reimposed in some areas of the country. On **Sept. 2**, demonstrators and riot policemen clashed in Lubin for the third day in a row, the police using tear-gas, rockets, and smoke grenades; the demonstrators using rocks. Underground Solidarity leaders, **Sept. 10**, called the antigovernment demonstrations of the previous week a moral victory and hinted that more demonstrations would be held the next week. On **Sept. 12** more clashes with the police flared up. In Wroclaw, demonstrators attacked a convoy of police vehicles, throwing rocks from apartment buildings. Water cannon and tear gas were used by the police in Nowa Huta against marching protestors. It was announced, **Sept. 19**, that more than 9,000 Poles had been fined for dealing in the black market—buying and selling rationed meat, butter, cigarettes, alcohol, gasoline, soap, sugar, flour, and other basic goods.

Mexico's Financial Woes Mount — Pres. José López Portillo of Mexico announced, **Sept. 1**, that the country's private banks would be nationalized to end what he termed the "looting" of Mexico through the flight of capital. He added that exchange controls would be imposed and that banks would remain closed until **Sept. 6**, when the Bank of Mexico would assume control of them. In the United States, bankers applauded the nationalization, because the move assuaged fears that the Mexican government would not have stood behind the debts of private banks. But Mexican businessmen reacted with anger, and the head of the Bank of Mexico resigned in protest. On **Sept. 5**, the Mexican government announced that, beginning on **Sept. 6**, there would be a 2-tiered fixed exchange rate for the peso, mortgage costs would be lowered and interest paid on savings accounts would be multiplied by 4 times. The plan, it was hoped, would end the flight of money abroad, control inflation, and make nationalization more palatable.

Philippine Arrests Continue — The arrest of 23 more Philippine trade union leaders in Manila, **Sept. 1**, brought to 38 the total of people jailed or picked up for questioning since Pres. Ferdinand E. Marcos had announced that he had discovered a plot to disrupt the government. The Philippine government, **Sept. 4**, formally charged 68 people with plotting to mount an insurrection while Pres. Marcos was to be away on a visit to the U.S. later in September. Most of the people charged were labor leaders. The government charged 13 more people with plotting a rebellion, **Sept. 7.** On **Sept. 24**, some 500 opponents of Marcos demonstrated in front of the U.S. embassy in Manila, charging that he had betrayed national interests to the economic and military objectives of the United States. Six platoons of antiriot police protected the embassy.

Sicilian Murder Spurs Anti-Mafia Campaign — Gen. Carlo Alberto Dalla Chiesa, a high-ranking Italian police official, was gunned down, **Sept. 3**, in the center of Palermo, Sicily. His wife and a police escort were also killed. Chiesa was a leader in the Carabinieri, the national military police force, and had been named, **May 1**, as the prefect of Palermo. His assignment had been to take charge of the fight against the Sicilian Mafia and stamp out the heroin trade located there. The Italian government, **Sept. 6**, appointed a new prefect of Palermo, Emanuele de Francesco, and gave him sweeping new powers. Bank security regulations were set aside in order to permit Francesco to obtain information on the holdings of suspected gangsters. He was also authorized to bug the telephone calls of suspects and was to be given all reports of a secret service organization in the Prime Minister's office. On **Sept. 8**, Nando Dalla Chiesa, the general's son, charged that the men who ordered his father's death were members of the Christian Democratic Party in Sicily.

Salvadoran Leader Meets with Guerrillas — The Salvadoran government had begun an "indirect" dialogue with guerrilla leaders, western diplomats reported, **Sept. 16.** According to the reports, Salvadoran Pres. Alvaro Magana met in Costa Rica with Costa Rican Pres. Luis Alberto Monge and Guillermo Manuael Ungo, the head of the leftist Democratic Revolutionary Front that was waging civil war in El Salvador. Earlier in the month, Acting Archbishop Arturo Rivera y Damas of San Salvador, **Sept. 5**, had announced that the church had recorded more than 200 killings in El Salvador during the preceding week. He had claimed that the exact count of victims of political violence stood at 211, far above the average weekly total.

Polish Embassy in Bern Seized — A group of armed men who claimed to belong to a Polish resistance group, **Sept. 6**, seized the Polish embassy in Bern, Switzerland. They threatened to blow up the embassy if the Warsaw government did not lift the martial law regulations in Poland. Fourteen Polish diplomats and members of the embassy staff were captured, but a pregnant woman was let go. The group's leader, who claimed that he and his 2 followers had heavy weapons and about 55 pounds of explosives, gave the Polish government 48 hours to agree to his terms. On **Sept. 8**, the gunmen freed all but 5 of their hostages and extended their deadline by another 48 hours. It was also reported that the Polish government had offered to send a special group to help the Swiss government storm the embassy, but the Swiss had made no reply to the offer. After many unsuccessful discussions with the gunmen, a special Swiss police squad stormed the embassy, **Sept. 9.** Without firing a shot, they freed the 5 hostages and captured the 4 gunmen. Remote-controlled explosives concealed in a container in which food had been delivered to the embassy, blew down the front door and 20 policemen rushed in, hurling tear-gas grenades. The operation lasted only 12 minutes.

Canadian Cabinet Shaken Up — Canadian Prime Minister Pierre Elliott Trudeau, trying to avoid an escalation in the economic crisis, **Sept. 10,** directed his 4 most important cabinet ministers to change jobs. Energy Minister Marc Lalond was made Finance Minister; Allan J. MacEachen, the former Energy Minister, was made Minister of External Affairs. Mark MacGuigan shifted from Foreign Affairs to Justice, and former Justice Minister Jean Chrétien assumed the duties of the Energy Department. It was felt that Lalonde would more aggressively fight the rising unemployment rate.

Hua Ousted in China — Hua Guofeng, the chosen successor of Mao Zedong, was dropped from the Chinese leadership, **Sept. 12,** by the first session of the new Central Committee. The action was taken in the elections of members of both the new Politburo and its inner circle, the Standing Committee. Although Hua's name was not on the lists, most of the older Communist Party veterans retained their posts. Hua, the former Minister and party chairman, was, as a result, forced to accept a token seat on the new Central Committee. On **Sept. 13,** Deng Xiaoping was elected chairman of a newly formed Central Advisory Commission to the Communist Party.

Bolivian President Resigns — Pres. Guido Vildoso of Bolivia agreed to resign, **Sept. 17,** when the military commanders of that country approved a resolution asking him to surrender his office to Congress and allow it to choose a civilian as the next president. He had been in office only 58 days. The resignation was linked to a nationwide strike of workers that had begun on **Sept. 16.** The strikers had demanded Vildoso's resignation and had closed down factories, offices, airports, and other transport facilities. Vildoso had been Bolivia's 9th president in 4 years.

More Bombings in Paris — A bomb exploded in the automobile of an Israeli embassy official in Paris, France, **Sept. 17,** injuring 41 people and blowing out windows in nearby buildings. This was the 20th attack to occur in Paris since **July 20.** Responsibility for the attack was claimed by the Lebanese Revolutionary Armed Faction. On **Sept. 18,** the Paris police announced that they had arrested 14 members of a group called Direct Action and seized 2 large caches of arms and explosives—150 dynamite sticks, sodium chlorate, detonators, slow-burning cord, 2 submachine guns, a Soviet assault rifle, and an M-1 carbine.

Disasters — After drinking homemade liquor at a festival in the southern state of Kerala, India, 50 were poisoned and died, it was reported, **Sept. 4** ... A Los Angeles apartment building fire killed 19 on **Sept. 4** ... By **Sept. 9,** more than 300 people had been killed in monsoon floods in northern and eastern India ... A U.S. Army helicopter crashed in an air show near Mannheim, Ger., **Sept. 11,** killing 45 ... A typhoon tore through central Japan, **Sept. 12,** killing 11 and leaving 17 people missing and presumed dead ... A German tourist bus was hit by a Swiss train near Pfaffikon, Switzerland, **Sept. 12,** and 39 of the 41 on board the bus were killed ... A New York-bound jetliner crashed in Malaga, Spain, **Sept. 13,** and the death toll was listed at 49 ... Another typhoon hit Japan **Sept. 13,** killing at least 26 ... On **Sept. 23** the death toll from flooding and mudslides in El Salvador and Guatemala reached 1,200 and on **Sept. 25,** 60 people were killed in a mudslide in El Salvador as they were attending church services ... A Soviet jetliner crashed at Luxembourg airport, **Sept. 29,** killing 6.

OCTOBER

National

Budget Limit Proposal Defeated — The House of Representatives **Oct. 6,** defeated an administration-backed proposal to amend the Constitution by demanding a balanced federal budget. The vote 236 to 187 in favor of the proposed amendment, fell short of the two-thirds needed before it could have been sent to the states for ratification. Pres. Ronald Reagan immediately characterized the vote as a deep burning anger and urged to voters to vote against the reelection of those congressmen who had opposed the measure. Many observers felt that this vote, on the heels of the override of Reagan's veto on a $14.1 billion spending bill, indicated that his power over the Congress had weakened.

Tylenol Poisoning Outbreak Becomes Epidemic — Local authorities in Chicago, Ill., confirmed, **Oct. 2,** that the 7th victim of cyanide-filled Tylenol capsules had died. As of that time, all of the deaths had been in the Chicago area. The Food and Drug Administration had warned consumers throughout the country to stop using the Extra-Strength Tylenol capsules, and Johnson & Johnson, the manufacturer of the drug, had offered a $100,000 reward for information leading to the arrest and conviction of the person or persons responsible for the murders. More than 100 state and federal agents were working on the case. Investigators felt that the poisoned capsules were the result of a willful act and not the fault of the manufacturer. Two Kane County sheriff's deputies had found hundreds of empty Tylenol capsules on the ground in a parking lot near Des Plaines, Ill. on **Sept. 28,** along with boxes and a white powder, but the 2 men had dismissed the find at the time. However, on **Oct. 4,** federal, state, and local agents focused their attention on the lot when it was reported that the 2 officers had become sick with vomiting, headaches, and dizziness, classic symptoms of cyanide poisoning. The Cook County (Ill.) board ordered that all over-the-counter medicines sold there in the future had to have a manufacturer's seal over the opening to the bottle. On **Oct. 5,** it was reported that an Oroville, Cal., man had been poisoned after he had swallowed Tylenol capsules laced with strychnine. The man recovered and police said that there appeared to be no connection between that case and the Chicago area deaths. Johnson & Johnson announced a nation-wide recall of all Tylenol capsules and authorities characterized the killer who substituted poison for the Tylenol powder in the capsules as a "madman and" a random killer. Michael I. Schaffer, chief toxicologist of the Cook County medical examiner's office examined the main Tylenol plant at Fort Washington, Pa., and announced, **Oct. 5,** that it was highly unlikely that the contamination had occurred there. Philadelphia police reported, **Oct. 6,** that Extra-Strength Tylenol capsules containing cyanide had been found in the apartment of a student whose death had been ruled a suicide 5 months before. On **Oct. 7,** however, Illinois Attorney General Tyrone Fahner announced that his office felt that there was no connection between the Chicago and Philadelphia deaths. A Chicago man, Jerome Howard, was held on bond, **Oct. 10,** on charges that he had tried to extort $8,000 from a hospital by threatening to poison patients with cyanide in Tylenol capsules. The FBI announced, **Oct. 13,** that they had obtained a warrant for the arrest of Robert Richardson, a Chicago man accused of trying to extort $1 million from the manufacturers of Tylenol. He had threatened to put poison in more of the Extra Strength capsules. Authorities announced, **Oct. 18,** that Robert Richardson was an alias for James W. Lewis, and he and his wife, Leann, were being sought as the primary leads in the investigation of the poisonings. Another poisoned bottle of Tylenol capsules was found by Chicago investigators, on **Oct. 21,** when it was returned unopened by a consumer.

Jobless Rate Up Again — The Labor Dept. announced, **Oct. 8,** that unemployment in the U.S. had reached 10.1% of the work force in September. This was the highest monthly figure in 42 years, and a rise of 0.3 of 1% over the August figure. According to the Bureau of Labor Statistics, more than 11,260,000 people out of a total labor force in the country of 110,980,000 were out of work—an increase of some 45,000 over the previous month. It was also estimated that the number of people who were not looking for jobs because they believed none were available had reached 1.6 million. The Reagan administration feared that, since these figures were the last that would be announced before the midterm Congressional elections in November, it would have an adverse effect on Republican hopes in that election.

Loan Charges Cut — The Federal Reserve Board announced, **Oct. 8,** that it had lowered the interest rates for loans to banks from 10% to 9½%, bringing the discount rate to its lowest level since November 1978. Following the announcement, interest rates declined in the bond and treasury bill markets. Most of the country's major banks promptly lowered their prime rates from 13 1/2% to 12 3/4%. On **Oct. 12,** 4 of the nation's largest banks, The Morgan Guaranty Trust Co., The Bank of America, the Chemical Bank, and the Manufacturers Hanover Trust Co., reduced their prime lending rate to 12%.

Reagan Announces Drug Fight Plans — In a speech at the Justice Department on **Oct. 14,** Pres. Reagan announced a plan to combat organized crime in the distribution of narcotics. Concentrating on large distribution networks rather than street pushers, 12 special task forces would be formed across the country. These groups would consist of agents from the FBI, the Drug Enforcement Administration, and the U.S. Customs Service. About 900 new agents would be hired for the agencies. About 200 assistant U.S. attorneys and 400 persons for a backup staff would also be hired. The groups would be ready to start work in January. The plan would cost from $160 million to $200 million per year.

DeLorean Arrested — John Z. Delorean, the chairman of the Delorean Motor Company, was arrested in Los Angeles, Calif., **Oct. 19,** and charged with possession of more than 59 pounds of cocaine. He was also accused of being the brains behind a scheme to sell 220 pounds of cocaine, which was estimated to be worth about $24 million. His involvement with the cocaine was explained as an attempt to raise money to shore up his automobile company, which was experiencing financial difficulties. The British government had just announced that it would close his operations in Northern Ireland. He was indicted, **Oct. 29,** in Los Angeles on charges of drug trafficing and racketeering. His lawyers posted $10 million in bail.

International

Iran-Iraq War Escalates — Iraqi officials reported, **Oct. 2,** that Iran had begun an offensive into Iraqi territory on **Oct. 1,** but the Iraqi troops had repealed it and Iraqi jets and helicopter gunships had inflicted heavy damage on Iranian armored forces just east of Baghdad. Iran denied these reports and claimed that it had gained control of a road running inside Iraqi territory from Mandali north to Naft Kaneh. On **Oct. 6,** Iraq announced that its warplanes and ground forces had repelled yet another Iranian offensive near Sumar, and had killed 2,352 Iranian soldiers. Iranian artillery shelled Iraqi oil installations and docks at Chahar Cheraqh on **Oct. 7.** Both sides reported gains on **Oct. 14.** Iraq claimed that its aircraft had attacked Iran's oil export station on Kharg Island in the Persian Gulf. Iran said that it had driven off Iraqis in Western Iran. On **Oct. 15,** Iraq said that 156 Iranians had been killed in air raids, and Iran claimed that they had shot down one of the planes.

Schmidt Out as Chancellor — Helmut Schmidt, the chancellor of West Germany, was ousted in a so-called constructive no-confidence vote in Parliament, **Oct. 1,** and was replaced by Helmut Kohl, the leader of the conservative Christian Democrat Party. Kohl became the 6th chancellor of that country since the end of World War II. It was the first time in the history of the Federal Republic that a chancellor had been removed by Parliament. Schmidt had been in office for eight years and 4 months. The ouster had actually been initiated in mid-September when the Free Democrats had abandoned their 13-year-old coalition with Schmidt's Social Democratic Party. The Free Democrats had signalled at that time that they would support Kohl in a bid for the chancellorship. Schmidt, **Oct. 26,** citing ill health, said he would not run again for chancellor.

Socialists Win in Spain — The Spanish Socialist Party, **Oct. 28,** won a landslide victory in national elections, gaining a majority of seats in the Congress and putting in Felipe González, their leader, as prime minister. González would become, at the age of 40, the youngest prime minister in Europe when the new government would be formed in December.

Sweden Hunts a Submarine — Swedish Military officials announced, **Oct. 4,** that antisubmarine helicopters and ships had been searching along the coast of the Baltic Sea since **Oct. 1,** for a suspected foreign submarine. A Swedish submarine crew had spotted the foreign sub some 300 yards from a naval base on Musko Island, 20 miles south of Stockholm. The Swedish Navy announced, **Oct. 5,** that they had trapped what they suspected was a Soviet submarine and were dropping depth charges in an effort to force it to surface. On **Oct. 6,** while the search still continued, the Soviet Union suggested that the whole search might have been a hoax aimed at disrupting Scandinavian-Soviet ties. Swedish authorities reported, **Oct. 7,** that the submarine might have escaped, and admitted that there might have been a second sub in the area. On **Oct. 8,** the authorities reported that there had been a new contact with the sub, and that it was still trapped. A Soviet spy plane was reported to be criss-crossing the Baltic on **Oct. 9,** trying to make contact with the sub, and Sweden had set up a jamming station to prevent communications between the two. Again, on **Oct. 10** the Swedes admitted that there was a possibility that the submarine had escaped. On **Oct. 13** the Commander in Chief of Sweden's armed forces admitted that the search could go on indefinitely and, on **Oct. 17,** the Swedish government ordered its navy to change anti-submarine tactics as soon as a new anti-submarine weapon was delivered, probably early in July 1983.

Bolivia Gets New President — The Bolivian Congress meeting for the first time in 2 years, elected Hernán Siles Zuazo as their new president, **Oct. 5.** At the time, Siles Zuazo was in exile in Peru as a result of a military coup in 1980 in which he was prevented from taking office. A series of national strikes and large demonstrations had forced the military dictator, Gen. Guido Vildoso Calderón to step down in mid-September and allow a civilian president to be elected. Siles Zuazo had inherited an almost bankrupt nation that was technically in default after failing to pay $10.2 million to an international banking syndicate and it was feared that Bolivia would also be unable to pay $600 million in foreign debt payments due by the end of the year. On **Oct. 11** Siles Zuazo replaced the entire military command in order to place the military under the authority of the new civilian government.

Lebanon Searches for Arms, Guerrillas — The Lebanese army, **Oct. 5,** began an intensive search of downtown west Beirut to discover arms caches and to remove any PLO guerrillas who might have remained behind in civilian clothing. Businesses and streets were sealed off and an estimated 400 people were taken into custody. The U.S. state department, **Oct. 6,** cautioned the Lebanese government not to violate human rights during the searches. On **Oct. 8,** Italy called on the U.S. and France to join it in demanding that the peacekeeping authority to be strengthened in order to oversee the police search operations. Lebanese officials reported, **Oct. 14,** that 1,441 people had been arrested in the searches and tons of arms and ammunition, as well as 23,000 forged identity papers and passports, had been found.

Solidarity Outlawed — The Polish Parliament, **Oct. 8** approved a law banning Solidarity, the Polish independent trade union. Special riot policemen, known as ZOMO, were brought into Warsaw and barracked at several central hotels to guard against demonstrations. No protests occurred, however. Pres. Reagan, **Oct. 9,** announced that he was going to suspend the favorable trade status that Poland had enjoyed for 22 years, and the result would be raised tariffs on Polish exports of manufactured products. Solidarity leaders, **Oct. 10,** called for resistance to the new law banning the union in a letter smuggled out of a Warsaw prison and signed by 9 interned union officials. Workers at the Lenin Shipyard in Gdansk struck, **Oct. 11,** to protest the law, and the protest spread to other factories in the city. Clashes between demostrators and ZOMO broke out, with the protestors setting fires and the police hurling tear gas grenades. Workers at the Lenin Shipyard were still on strike, **Oct. 12** and the government ruled the shipyard "militarized"; the workers were to be treated like soldiers subject to military orders and discipline. The workers ended the strike, **Oct. 13,** but 3,000 workers walked off their jobs at a steel plant in Nowa Huta. On **Oct. 20,** the funeral for the slain worker erupted into a Pro-Solidarity rally of 10,000 people. Underground leaders of Solidarity, **Oct. 23,** called for walkouts and demonstrations to be held **Nov. 10** and for a general strike to be held in the spring of 1983.

Rome Synagogue Raided — Unidentified gunmen throwing hand grenades and firing submachine guns, **Oct. 9,** attacked members of the congregation of a synagogue i

Rome, Italy as they were leaving the building. A 2-year-old boy was killed and at least 34 people were wounded. No terrorist group took the responsibility for the attack. Ten hours after the attack, a bomb exploded outside the Syrian Embassy in Rome, and later a bomb exploded at the Islamic Center in that city.

Suzuki to Resign — Prime Minister Zenko Suzuki of Japan announced, **Oct. 12,** that he would resign shortly. He had been criticized about his economic policies, many of the criticisms coming from members of his own Liberal Democratic Party. It was expected that he would continue to serve until the election for a new leader of the party would be held in November.

General

Mary Rose Raised — The *Mary Rose*, which sank during an engagement with the French in the reign of Henry III, was raised, **Oct. 11.** Most of its oak frame was still intact. The boat was the pride of the English fleet, and was sunk a mile off Portsmouth harbor. The salvaging had cost $7 million dollars, but it was believed that the ship would contain some 17,000 artifacts that would reveal much about the era of the Tudor kings.

Disasters — A twin-engine plane crashed near Taft, Cal. **Oct. 17,** killing all 14 people aboard.

Major Actions During the 97th Congress, 1982

The 97th Congress convened, Jan. 4, 1982. Bills passed and signed, and other major actions during the session, include the following:

Standby Oil Powers. Pres. Reagan vetoed, **Mar. 20,** legislation giving him broad authority to allocate oil supplies during a shortage. The bill gave the president discretionary power to declare an energy emergency, redirect supplies, set price ceilings on petroleum products, and preempt state allocations. It did not authorize him to ration gasoline and other oil products. The bill had been passed by the Senate, **Mar. 2.** and by the House, **Mar. 3.**

Brady Bill. Pres. Reagan signed, **Apr. 13,** a bill to allow White House Press Secretary James S. Brady, who was shot in the head in an attempt on Reagan's life, to accept donations to help pay for his medical expenses. The bill had cleared both houses, **Apr. 1.** The law forbade federal employees to accept money from sources outside the government, but the new law provided an exemption for federal workers wounded in an attempt to assasinate the president, vice-president, member of Congress, or anyone else elected to one of those offices but not yet sworn in.

Federal Courts Improvement. On **Oct. 1,** Pres. Reagan signed a bill to abolish the U.S. Court of Claims, and the U.S. Court of Customs and Patent Appeals, and replace them with the U.S. Claims Court (to handle contract disputes with the federal government) and the U.S. Court of Appeals for the Federal Circuit (to handle cases dealing with customs and patents). Both courts would have federal, rather than jurisdictional, authority. The House had passed the bill, **Mar. 9,** and the Senate, **Mar. 22.**

Busing, School Prayer, Abortion Rights

School Busing. The Senate passed a bill, **Mar. 2,** that virtually eliminated school busing for the purpose of racial integration. A rider to a bill authorizing funds for the Dept. of Justice stated that no money could be used to litigate school busing cases, and another rider stated that federal courts would not be permitted to issue orders to transport children more than 5 miles or 15 minutes from home.

Public School Prayer. The Senate, **Sept. 23,** defeated a proposal by Sen. Jesse Helms (R, N.C.) to prohibit federal courts from ruling on the constitutionality of voluntary prayer in public schools.

Abortion Rights Proposal. The Senate voted, **Sept. 13,** to kill a proposal that would have imposed severe restrictions on women's abortion rights. The proposal would have banned the use of federal funds for abortions and would have encouraged efforts to reverse the Supreme Court's decision to permit abortions during the first trimester of pregnancy.

Budget Actions

Tax Bill. Both houses approved, **Aug. 19,** a $98.3 billion tax bill. This was considered an important victory for the Reagan administration.

Compromise 1983 Budget. The Senate approved, **June 23,** a compromise plan for the fiscal 1983 budget. The plan was actually a resolution, requiring approval by both houses but not by the president. It outlined fiscal policy for 1983. The House had approved the plan, created in a House-Senate conference, **June 22.** Pres. Reagan endorsed the budget measure.

Debt Ceiling Extended. Pres. Reagan signed, **June 28,** a bill that extended the federal government's borrowing authority through Sept. 30, the end of fiscal 1982. This increased the temporary debt ceiling from $1.08 trillion to $1.143 trillion. Congress had passed the bill on June 23.

Supplemental Appropriations. Pres. Reagan, **July 18,** signed a $5.4 billion supplemental appropriations bill funding several federal programs through Sept. 30, the end of the 1982 fiscal year. This ended a veto struggle with Congress, which failed to override two vetoes of previous versions and continued to send back lower appropriations levels to the White House. The original versions would have provided $8.9 billion, including a $3 billion mortgage-subsidy program. Congress then dropped this program and sent back a $5.9 billion bill, which the President vetoed minutes after receiving it. In an attempt to override the veto, **July 13,** the House fell far short of the required two-thirds majority. The final bill eliminated another $400 million, and was passed by both houses, **July 15.**

Budget Reconciliation. Congress approved a budget reconcilation bill, **Aug. 18.** The bill called for $13.3 billion in spending cuts over the next 3 years.

Reagan Veto Overridden. The Senate voted, **Sept. 10,** to override Pres. Reagan's veto of a $14.1 billion supplementary spending bill. The House had voted to override the veto, **Sept. 9.**

Balanced Budget Amendment. In a last minute showdown, **Oct. 1,** the House defeated a proposed constitutional amendment similar to that passed by the Senate, **Sept. 4,** which was aimed at balancing the federal budget. The amendment fell 46 short of the two-thirds majority necessary. It would have required Congress to pass a balanced budget in every peacetime year unless it voted by a three-fifths majority to override the requirement.

Transportation, Business Issues

Railroad Strike. Congress voted, **Sept. 22,** to direct 26,000 locomotive engineers to end their railroad strike, accept a new contract, and return to work. The Senate had passed the bill, **Sept. 21,** by a voice vote. Pres. Reagan had called for the action, **Sept. 20.**

Intercity Bus Bill. Pres. Reagan signed a bill, **Sept. 20,** giving intercity bus operators more freedom to decide prices and routes. The law provided that any capable bus operator could service any route unless the route was proven "against the public interest." Previously, before beginning a route, operators had to prove service was necessary and rates were often fixed by state regulatory agencies. Expectations were that the new law would increase bus company competition, and lower fares.

Copyright Veto. Congress overrode, **July 13,** Pres. Reagan's veto of a copyright bill that protected the American printing industry. The bill extended until 1986 the "manufacturing clause" of U.S. copyright law, which required most books and periodicals in English by U.S. authors to be printed and bound in the U.S. or Canada in order to receive full copyright protection. The bill was passed by the House, **June 15,** and by the Senate, **June 30.** The president vetoed it **July 8.** The veto, Reagan's seventh, was the first to be overridden.

Tobacco Price Support. Pres. Reagan signed, **July 20,** a bill considerably reducing government subsidies for tobacco farmers. The bill was a reaction to a mandate added to the 1981 4-year farm authorization bill requiring the tobacco program to be operated at no net cost to taxpayers. The bill obligated tobacco growers in the price support program to contribute to a fund to cover losses when the price of tobacco fell below the price-support level. The House and Senate versions differed, and the House accepted the Senate's version, **July 15.**

Defense and Other Issues

Intelligence Agents. Pres. Reagan signed a bill, **July 23,** that made it a crime to disclose the names of current U.S. intelligence agents, informers, or sources, even if the information were available in public records. It would impose penalties of up to 10 years in prison and up to $50,000 in fines for violations.

Defense Authorization. Congress approved, **Aug. 17-18,** a $178 billion compromise defense authorization bill for fiscal 1983. The compromise restored funds to build the controversial MX missile, but authorized funding for only 5 of the 9 missiles the administration had requested. The final amount was a 36% increase over the fiscal 1982 authorization.

Election Procedure Extension. The Senate adopted, **June 18,** a bill that extended for another 25 years a section of the Voting Rights Act of 1965 dealing with changes in election procedures. The section that was extended required all or part of 22 states to submit changes in election procedures for federal approval. The affected areas had a history of discrimination or low minority turnouts at the polls.

Major Decisions of the U.S. Supreme Court, 1981-2

Among the notable actions in 1981-2, the Supreme Court:

Ruled, 6-3, that police be permitted to search cars without warrants. This meant that if police had probable cause to search a car without a warrant, they were also at liberty to search luggage or packages inside the car, thus expanding the 1925 "automobile exception" to the Fourth Amendment's prohibition against unreasonable searches to include closed containers within the car (June 1).

Ruled, 5-4, that the First Amendment's guarantee of freedom of speech limited the right of public school administrators to remove books that they found objectionable from school libraries. The case involved a Nassau County, N.Y. school district whose school board had removed, in 1975, 11 books from the district's libraries (2 were later returned) because they were "obscene, anti-religious, and anti-American." The Court ruled that the students had the right to sue the school board (June 25).

Upheld, unanimously, a New York State law prohibiting the use of children in pornographic films, photographs, or performances. The Court ruled that sexual exploitation and abuse of children needed to be prevented (July 2).

Ruled, 5-4, that children who are illegal aliens have a constitutional right to a free public education. This upheld 2 rulings by the U.S. Court of Appeals, which had declared unconstitutional a Texas law cutting off state funds from local school districts for educating children who had illegally entered the U.S. (June 15).

Denied an emergency request by Mobil Corp. that U.S. Steel Corp. be prohibited from purchasing Marathon Oil Co. shares. At the same time Mobil asked for the delay, it requested that the court review a lower court's antitrust ruling against Mobil (Dec. 30, 1981).

Ruled unanimously that employees who had access to confidential company information were, in most instances, protected by federal labor law (Dec. 2).

Refused to hear an appeal of a ruling that congressional staff members could be sued for damages. The case derived from an investigation by the staff of the House Select Committee on Aging, which, along with ABC's TV news department, conducted an undercover probe into the sale of private health insurance to the elderly. One of the probe's targets sued ABC and the committee staff for invasion of privacy and illegal wiretapping. The U.S. 4th Circuit Court of Appeals, upholding a federal district court, ruled that staff members were not guaranteed absolute immunity (Nov. 16).

Refused to review a ruling that CBS did not have to relinquish transcripts and tapes of an episode of the TV show "60 Minutes" that dealt with the defunct Wild Bill's Restaurants. The tapes had been desired by former executives of the restaurant (Nov. 16).

Ruled, 8-1, that a criminal defendent could not sue a public defender under the federal Civil Rights Act of 1971 (Dec. 14).

Ruled, 8-1, that student organizations at public colleges and universities had the constitutional right to hold religious services on campus property. This was considered the court's most important recent ruling as to the church-state issue. The single dissenter, Justice Byron R. White, warned that the ruling could force the reconsideration of other cases dealing with religious activities at public institutions (Dec. 8).

Refused to review a decision enjoining students in a Guiderland, N.Y. public school from holding voluntary prayer meetings on school property before the school day (Dec 14).

Ruled, 5-3, that state law could not stop a divorced and remarried serviceman from designating his second wife as beneficiary of his military life insurance, despite his having dependent children from his first marriage (Nov. 10).

Refused to review, thus let stand, cases on insurance company liability for asbestos-related diseases among industrial workers. Some insurance companies held the "exposure" theory of liability—the idea that liability had to be shared by the insurers that covered an industrial company during the years its workers were exposed to asbestos; other insurance companies held the "manifestation" theory, which assigned liability to the insurer only at the time the disease was diagnosed. Thousands of lawsuits on this issue were pending in state and federal courts (Mar. 8).

Refused to review a decision that most Vietnam veterans injured by exposure to Agent Orange had to seek damages through state—instead of federal—courts. Several thousand veterans sought to sue manufacturers in federal court (Dec 14).

Refused to hear an appeal by the *Washington Post* of a ruling that Charles G. (BeBe) Rebozo, millionaire and close friend of former President Richard M. Nixon, could sue the newspaper for libel because of a 1973 story that he had been involved in handling stolen stock certificates. The court refused to hear Rebozo's challenge to a ruling that he was a "public figure," and thus had to prove that the Post had acted with "actual malice" by printing the story (Nov. 2).

Ruled unanimously that the Defense Dept. need not file public environmental impact statements on the possible effects of storing nuclear weapons in specific areas. This resolved a conflict between two federal laws—the National Environ. Policy Act required gov. agencies to file public statements on the environmental effects of federal projects; and a provision of the Freedom of Information Act exempted national security data from mandatory public disclosure (Dec. 1).

Ruled, 5-4, that states had to have "clear and convincing" proof of neglect or child abuse before removing children from the custody of their natural parents; anything less was considered a violation of the parents' due process rights. This struck down a provision of the New York State Family Court Act, which allowed the children removed on a "fair preponderance of evidence" of abuse (Mar. 24).

Ruled, 5-4, that a confession of a suspected criminal, even if obtained via proper police interrogation, could not be used as evidence if the subject had been arrested without valid probable cause (June 23).

Affirmed a lower court finding that Louisiana's voluntary school prayer violated the First Amendment. The law permitted public schools to set aside up to five minutes a day for classroom prayer, during which students who did not wish to take part could be excused from the classroom (Jan. 25).

Ruled unanimously that a federal law designed to encourage state energy conservation was constitutional under the federal government's authority to regulate interstate commerce. But also ruled, 5-6, that the law did not violate the Tenth Amendment, which gave the states all powers not expressly delegated to the federal government by the Constitution (June 1).

Ruled unanimously that the Census Bureau need not disclose raw census data to local and state officials. The Court held that raw data must remain confidential to protect the public's privacy (Feb. 24).

Ruled, 5-4, that no U.S. President could be sued for damages for actions he had taken while in office. This case was derived from a civil suit brought against former Pres. Richard M. Nixon by a civilian Pentagon budget analyst who had been fired after disclosing cost overruns in C-5A air transport programs. In a companion decision, ruled, 8-1, that presidential aides were entitled to "qualified immunity" from such lawsuits (June 24).

Ruled unanimously that mentally retarded people in state institutions were entitled to constitutionally protected rights under the 14th Amendment's due process clause (June 18).

Ruled unanimously that a group of Trans World Airlines female flight attendants, fired before 1971 because of pregnancy, were entitled to retroactive seniority and back pay, even though they had not filed sex discrimination complaints with the Equal Employment Opportunity Commission within the agency's 90-day deadline. In a related ruling, the court held that the flight attendants' union could not block the awarding of retroactive seniority (Feb. 24).

Deaths, Oct. 31, 1981—Nov. 1, 1982

A

Abdullah, Sheik Mohammad, 76; political leader in Kashmir for half a century; Kashmir, Sept. 8.
Ace, Goodman, 83; comedy writer and co-star of the popular *Easy Aces* radio show in the 1930s and 40s; New York City, Mar. 25.
Adams, Harriet, 89; author of some 200 children's books including many of the Nancy Drew and Hardy Boys series; Pottersville, N.J., Mar. 27.
Albertson, Jack, 74; actor whose career spanned 50 years; recipient of Tony, Oscar, and 3 Emmy awards; Hollywood Hills, Cal., Nov. 25.
Ashbrook, John M., 53; U.S. representative from Ohio since 1961; Newark, Oh., Apr. 24.

B

Bader, Sir Douglas, 72; legless British fighter pilot who downed 24 German planes, 1940-41; London, Sept. 5.
Balmain, Pierre, 68; French designer of women's clothes; Neuilly, France, June 29.
Banning, Margaret, 90; author of some 40 books and 400 short stories; Tryon, N.C., Jan. 4.
Barbour, Walworth, 74; U.S. ambassador to Israel, 1961-73; Gloucester, Mass., July 21.
Barrios, Francisco, 28; former pitcher for the Chicago White Sox; Hermosillo, Mexico, Apr. 9.
Baxter, Frank, 86; literature professor who won 7 Emmys and a Peabody Award for his TV show, "Shakespeare on TV"; San Marino, Cal., Jan. 20.
Beaumont, Hugh, 72; actor who starred in the "Leave It to Beaver" TV series; Munich, W. Germany, May 14.
Belushi, John, 33; comic actor of films and TV's "Saturday Night Live"; Hollywood, Cal., Mar. 5.
Benchley, Nathaniel, 66; humorist, novelist, and journalist; Boston, Dec. 14.
Benelli, Giovanni Cardinal, 61; Archbishop of Florence; twice a leading candidate to be elected Pope, 1978; Rome, Oct. 26.
Benet, Brenda, 36, actress who starred in the "Days of Our Lives" TV soap opera; Los Angeles, Apr. 8.
Benjamin Jr., Adam, 47; U.S. representative from Indiana since 1977; Washington, D.C., Sept. 7.
Bergman, Ingrid, 67; Swedish stage and screen actress who won 3 Oscars; London, Aug. 29.
Bettis, Valerie, 62; choreographer and dancer; New York, Sept. 26.
Bloch, Ray, 79; television orchestra conductor for Ed Sullivan, Jackie Gleason; Miami, Mar. 29.
Bloomingdale, Alfred, 66; businessman who developed the Diners Club credit card; Santa Monica, Cal., Aug. 20.
Bogart, Neil, 39; entertainment executive and producer; Los Angeles, May 8.
Boyer, Ken, 51; former St. Louis Cardinals third baseman and manager; St. Louis, Sept. 7.
Bruce, Virginia, 72; film leading lady of the 1930s and 40s; Hollywood, Cal., Feb. 24.
Buono, Victor, 43; character actor who often portrayed a villain; Apple Valley, Cal., Jan. 1.
Burnett, W.R., 82; novelist and screenwriter, *Little Caesar, Scarface;* Santa Monica, Cal., Apr. 24.
Bushmiller, Ernie, 76; cartoonist who created the "Nancy" comic strip; Stamford, Conn., Aug. 15.
Butler, Lord Richard Austen, 79; a leading British statesman for over 50 years; Essex, England, Mar. 8.
Butterfield, Lyman H., 72; historian who edited the 20-volume *Adams Papers;* Boston, Apr. 25.

C

Canham, Erwin, 77; reporter, columnist, and editor for *The Christian Science Monitor* for nearly 50 years; Agana, Guam, Jan. 3.
Carmichael, Hoagy, 82; entertainer and composer, "Stardust", "Lazy Bones"; Rancho Mirage, Cal., Dec. 27.
Carritt, David, 55; British art historian, critic, and dealer; London, Aug. 3.
Case, Clifford, 77; U.S. Senator from New Jersey; 1955-79; Washington, D.C., Mar. 5.
Cheever, John, 70; novelist and short-story writer who detailed the lives of upper-middle-class suburbanites; Ossining, N.Y., June 19.
Chenoweth, Dean, 44; 4-time national champion hydroplane driver; Pasco, Wash., July 31.
Chuikov, Marshal Vasily, 82; Soviet marshal who led troops in defense of Stalingrad during World War II; Moscow, Mar. 18.
Churchill, Sarah, 67; British actress; daughter of Winston Churchill; London, Sept. 24.
Chylak, Nestor, 59; American League umpire for 25 years; Dunmore, Pa., Feb. 17.
Cockburn, Claud, 77; British journalist and social critic; Cork, Ireland, Dec. 15.
Cody, John Cardinal, 74; Roman Catholic archbishop of Chicago since 1965; Chicago, Apr. 25.
Coleman, Lonnie, 62; author of the "Beulah Land" trilogy of novels; Savannah, Ga., Aug. 13.
Conried, Hans, 66; versatile character actor whose career in radio, television, stage, and films spanned 40 years; Burbank, Cal., Jan. 5.
Corcoran, Thomas G., 80; lawyer who was a key advisor to FDR; Washington, D.C., Dec. 6.
Corn Jr., Ira, 60; industrialist who organized the first U.S. professional bridge team; Dallas, Apr. 28.
Coslow, Sam, 79; songwriter, "My Old Flame", "Sing You Sinners"; Bronxville, N.Y., Apr. 2.
Crawford, William, 68; editorial cartoonist for Newspaper Enterprise Assn. whose work appeared in over 700 newspapers; Washington, D.C., Jan. 6.
Crisler, H.O. "Fritz", 83; former football coach and athletic director at Michigan Univ.; Ann Arbor, Mich., Aug. 19.
Curzon, Sir Clifford, 75; British classical pianist; London, Sept. 1.

D

Daniels, Jonathan, 79; journalist, novelist, and politician who served as press secretary for FDR; Hilton Head

Island, S.C., Nov. 6.
Dannay, Frederic, 76; co-author of some 35 Ellery Queen mystery novels; Larchmont, N.Y., Sept. 3.
Davis, Dr. Loyal, 86; neurosurgeon; father-in-law of President Reagan; Scottsdale, Ariz., Aug. 19.
De Graff, Robert F., 86; pioneer publisher of paperback books; Mill Neck, N.Y., Nov. 1.
del Monaco, Mario, 67; Italian operatic tenor; Venice, Oct. 16.
Demara, Ferdinand, 60; imposter in various fields; inspiration for book and film *The Great Imposter;* Anaheim, Cal., June 7.
Deutsch, Dr. Helene R., 97; Austrian-born psychoanalyst and author, *The Psychology of Women;* Cambridge, Mass., Mar. 29.
Dietrich, Noah, 92; accountant who directed the business affairs of Howard Hughes, 1925-57; Palm Springs, Cal., Feb. 15.
DiMuro, Lou, 50; American League umpire for the past 19 years; Arlington, Tex., June 6.
Drake, Tom, 64; film actor who appeared in numerous 1940s musicals; Torrance, Cal., Aug. 11.
Dubinsky, David, 90; labor leader who headed the International Ladies Garment Workers Union, 1932-66; New York, Sept. 17.
Dubos, Dr. Rene, 81; French-born scientist and author of 20 books; New York, Feb. 20.
Duffy, Clinton, 84; retired warden of San Quentin who initiated many penal reforms; Walnut Creek, Cal., Oct. 11.
Durant, Will, 96; historian and philosopher, *The Story of Civilization, The Story of Philosophy;* Los Angeles, Nov. 8.
Dwan, Allan, 96; film director whose career spanned 50 years; Woodland Hills, Cal., Dec. 21.

E

Eberly, Bob, 65; pop singer of the big band era who performed with the Dorsey brothers; Glen Burnie, Md., Nov. 17.
Eden, Dorothy, 69; author of 18 gothic-historic novels, London, Mar. 14.
Eldjarn, Kristjan, 65; president of Iceland, 1968-80; Cleveland, Oh., Sept. 13.
Engel, Lehman, 71; conductor of more than 100 Broadway musicals; New York, Aug. 29.
Enoch, Kurt, 86; pioneer in paperback publishing; Puerto Rico, Feb. 15.
Euwe, Max, 80; world chess champion in the 1930s; former president of the International Chess Federation; Amsterdam, Nov. 26.

F

Farber, Edward R., 67; inventor who is credited with the invention of the portable strobe light for still cameras; Delafield, Wis., Jan. 22.
Fassbinder, Rainer Werner, 36; German film director, *The Marriage of Maria Braun;* Munich, June 10.
Fitzgerald, Ed, 89; entertainer who with his wife, Pegeen, broadcast *The Fitzgeralds* radio show for 44 years; New York, Mar. 22.
Fonda, Henry, 77; actor who starred in over 100 stage and film roles; won 1981 Oscar for *On Golden Pond;* Los Angeles, Aug. 12.
Fortas, Abe, 71; associate justice of the U.S. Supreme Court, 1965-69; Washington, D.C., Apr. 5.
Foster, Harold R., 89; creator of the "Prince Valiant" comic strip; Spring Hill, Fla., July 25.
Fraiberg, Selma, 63; child psychoanalyst and author, *The Magic Years;* San Francisco, Dec. 19.
Frei Montalva, Eduardo, 71; president of Chile, 1964-70; Santiago, Jan. 15.
Freud, Anna, 86; psychoanalyst; daughter of Sigmund Freud; London, Oct. 9.

G

Gance, Abel, 92; French filmmaker who is best known for the 1927 film *Napoleon,* Paris, Nov. 11.
Gardner, John, 49; novelist and poet, *The Sunlight Dialogues;* Susquehanna, Pa., Sept. 14.
Garroway, Dave, 69; host of TV's "Today" show, 1952-61; Swarthmore, Pa., July 21.
Gaver, John M., 81; thoroughbred trainer who headed Greentree Stable for 38 years; Aiken, S.C., July 11.
Gemayel, Bashir, 34; president-elect of Lebanon; Beirut, Sept. 14.
George, Bill, 51; linebacker for the Chicago Bears, 1952-65; near Rockford, Ill., Sept. 30.
Ghotbzadeh, Sadegh, 46; foreign minister of Iran during the U.S. hostage crisis; Teheran, Sept. 15.
Gimbel, Sophie, 83; leading fashion designer for some 40 years; New York, Nov. 28.
Gomulka, Wladyslaw, 77; head of Poland's Communist Party, 1956-70; Poland, Sept. 1.
Goodman, Martin, 46; president of Toronto Star Newspapers Ltd.; Toronto, Dec. 20.
Gould, Glenn, 50; Canadian pianist best known for his Bach interpretations; Toronto, Oct. 4.
Princess Grace of Monaco (Grace Kelly), 52; princess of Monaco; former film actress; Monte Carlo, Sept. 14.
Greer, Sonny, 78; drummer for the Duke Ellington orchestra for over 30 years; New York, Mar. 23.
Grosvenor, Melville, B., 80; president of the National Geographic Society and editor of its magazine, 1957-67; Miami, Apr. 22.
Grumman, Leroy, 87; founder of the aeronautics corporation that bears his name; Manhasset, N.Y., Oct. 4.
Guzman Fernandez, Antonio, 71; president of the Dominican Republic; Dominican Republic, July 4.

H

Hallstein, Walter, 80; West German lawyer and diplomat who helped found the European Economic Community; Stuttgart, W. Germany, Mar. 29.
Hampton, Hope, 84; actress, opera singer, and socialite; New York, Jan. 23.
Harnwell, Gaylord P., 78; atomic physicist and educator who headed the Univ. of Pennsylvania, 1953-70; Haverford, Pa., Apr. 18.
Henry, Pat, 58; comedian who was long associated with Frank Sinatra; Las Vegas, Feb. 18.
Harman, Fred, 79; cartoonist who created the "Red Ryder" comic strip; Phoenix, Jan. 2.
Harrison, Wallace, 86; architect who played a major role in planning Rockefeller Center and Lincoln Center in New York City; New York, Dec. 2.
Hillenkoetter, Adm. Roscoe H., 85; first director of the Central Intelligence Agency, 1947-50; New York, June 18.
Holden, William, 63; actor who was a major film star for some 40 years, *Stalag 17, Sunset Boulevard;* Santa Monica, Cal., Nov. 16.
Holloway, Stanley, 91; British entertainer who created the role of Alfred Doolittle in *My Fair Lady;* London, Jan. 30.
Hopkins, Sam "Lightnin'", 69; blues singer and guitarist; Houston, Jan. 30.
Horikoshi, Jiro, 78; Japanese aeronautical engineer who designed the Zero fighter plane used in World War II; Tokyo, Jan. 11.
Hosmer, Craig, 67; U.S. representative from California, 1953-75; at sea, Oct. 11.

I

Irish, Edward S. "Ned", 76; a leading figure in the development of college and pro basketball; founded the N.Y. Knickerbockers; Venice, Fla., Jan. 21.

J

Janson, Horst W., 68; educator and author, *History of Art;* near Zurich, Switzerland, Sept. 30.
Jarman, John, 66; U.S. representative from Oklahoma, 1951-77; Oklahoma City, Jan. 15.
Jensen, Jackie, 55; outfielder for the Boston Red Sox in the 1950s; Charlottesville, Va., July 14.
Jeritza, Maria, 94; Austrian-born operatic soprano; Orange, N.J., July 10.
Jessup, Richard, 57; author of more than 60 books, *The Cincinnati Kid;* Nokomis, Fla., Oct. 22.
Johnson, Dame Celia, 73; British stage and screen actress, *Brief Encounter;* Nettlebed, England, Apr. 26.
Jones Jr., Richard L., 72; president and board chairman of *The Tulsa Tribune;* Tulsa, Jan. 27.
Jory, Victor, 79; stage and screen actor whose career spanned 40 years; Santa Monica, Cal., Feb. 12.
Jurgens, Curt, 66; actor who appeared in over 160 European and Hollywood films; Vienna, June 18.

K

Kaiser, Edgar F., 73; industrialist and presidential advisor; San Francisco, Dec. 11.
Kaufman, Murray "the K", 60; disc jockey who helped introduce the Beatles to the U.S.; Los Angeles, Feb. 21.
King, Henry, 91; director of more than 100 Hollywood films; San Fernando Valley, Cal., June 29.
King Khalid, 69; ruler of Saudi Arabia since 1975; Taif, Saudi Arabia, June 13.
Knott, Walter, 91; millionaire who established Knott's Berry Farm amusement park in California; Buena Park, Cal., Dec. 3.
Krebs, Sir Hans, 81; biochemist who won a 1953 Nobel Prize for research on food cycles; Oxford, England, Nov. 22.

L

Lamas, Fernando, 67; film actor and TV director; Los Angeles, Oct. 8.
Lembeck, Harvey, 58; character actor of stage and films; Los Angeles, Jan. 5.
Lenya, Lotte, 83; star of the German and U.S. stage; widow of composer Kurt Weill; New York, Nov. 27.
Lockridge, Richard, 83; author of mystery novels; created Mr. & Mrs. North; Tryon, N.C., June 19.
Loring, Eugene, 72; dancer and choreographer who created *Billy the Kid;* Kingston, N.Y., Aug. 30.
Lucas, Nick, 84; entertainer who starred in vaudeville and early talking films; Colorado Springs, Col., July 28.
Lynd, Helen M., 85; social psychologist, educator, and author, *Middletown,* Warren, Oh., Jan. 30.
Lynde, Paul, 55; actor who was best known for his appearances on the *Hollywood Squares,* TV show; Beverly Hills, Cal., Jan. 10.

M

MacLeish, Archibald, 89; poet, playwright, and statesman; Boston, Apr. 20.

Magee, Patrick, 58; Irish stage and screen actor; London, Aug. 14.

Manone, Joseph "Wingy", 78; one-armed jazz trumpet player; Las Vegas, July 9.

Markey, Enid, 91; actress who created the role of Jane in the first Tarzan movie, 1918; Bay Shore, N.Y., Nov. 15.

Markey, Lucille Parker, 85; owner of Calumet Farms racing stable; Lexington, Ky., July 25.

Markham, Dewey "Pigmeat", 77; vaudeville and TV comedian; New York, Dec. 13.

Marlowe, Hugh, 71; stage and screen actor whose career spanned 50 years; New York, May 2.

Marsh, Dame Ngaio, 82; New Zealand-born author of 31 mystery novels; Christchurch, New Zealand, Feb. 18.

Marx, Louis, 85; toy maker and philanthropist; Scarsdale, N.Y., Feb. 5.

McHale, Tom; 40; author of comic novels, *Farragan's Retreat;* Pembroke Pines, Fla., Mar. 30.

McNaughton, F.F., 91; founder of newspaper and radio station empire; Effingham, Ill., Dec. 29.

Mendes-France, Pierre, 75; prime minister of France in the 1950s; Paris, Oct. 18.

Merchant, Vivian, 53; British stage actress; London, Oct. 3.

Mills, Harry, 68; member of the Mills Brothers singing group; Los Angeles, June 28.

Monk, Thelonious, 64; jazz pianist and composer; Englewood, N.J., Feb. 17.

Montor, Henry, 76; American Jewish leader who helped found the United Jewish Appeal in 1938; Jerusalem, Apr. 15.

Moore, Stanford, 68; biochemist who shared the 1972 Nobel Prize for Chemistry; New York, Aug. 23.

More, Kenneth, 67; British stage and screen actor; London, July 12.

Morrow, Vic, 51; actor in films and TV since the mid-1950s, Los Angeles, July 23.

Morton, Thruston B., 74; former U.S. senator and representative from Kentucky; Louisville, Aug. 14.

Mueller, Bishop Reuben, 85; president of the National Council of Churches, 1963-66; Franklin, Ind., July 6.

N

Nashua, 30; champion thoroughbred race horse and sire; Lexington, Ky., Feb. 3.

Nesbitt, Cathleen, 93; British character actress whose career spanned 70 years; London, Aug. 2.

Nicholson, Ben, 87; British abstract artist; London, Feb. 6.

O

Oates, Warren, 52; character actor who appeared in films and on TV; Hollywood Hills, Cal., Apr. 3.

Orff, Carl, 86; West German composer and educator; Salzburg, Mar. 29.

P

Paige, Leroy "Satchel", 75?; legendary pitcher in the Negro leagues who became a major leaguer at age 42; Kansas City, Mo., June 8.

Parker, Buddy, 68; football coach who led the Detroit Lions to NFL titles in 1952 and 1953; Kaufman, Tex., Mar. 22.

Pelletier, Wilfred, 85; Canadian conductor whose career spanned 50 years; New York, Apr. 9.

Pepper, Art, 56; jazz saxophonist; Los Angeles, June 15.

Post, Wally, 52; baseball player who hit 210 home runs during 15-year major league career; St. Henry, Oh., Jan. 6.

Poulson, Norris, 87; mayor of Los Angeles, 1953-61; Orange, Cal., Sept. 25.

Praz, Mario, 85; critic, essayist, and art collector; Rome, Italy, Mar. 23.

Powell, Eleanor, 69; tap-dancing star of numerous 1930s Hollywood musicals; Beverly Hills, Cal., Feb. 11.

Primrose, William, 77; violist noted for his purity of tone; Provo, Ut., May 1.

R

Rambert, Marie, 94; major figure in the development of the British ballet; London, June 12.

Rand, Ayn, 77; philosopher and author, *The Fountainhead;* New York, Mar. 6.

Rawls, Katherine, 64; swimmer who won 33 U.S. swimming titles; Belle Glade, Fla., Apr. 8.

Ripley, Elmer, 90; basketball player and coach; New York, Apr. 29.

Ritola, Willie, 86; Finnish track star who won 5 Olympic gold medals in the 1920s; Helsinki, Apr. 24.

Robinzine, Bill, 29; former NBA forward; Kansas City, Mo.; Sept. 16.

Ryan, T. Claude, 84; pioneer aircraft manufacturer who built Lindbergh's *Spirit of St. Louis;* San Diego, Sept. 11.

S

Sackler, Howard, 52; playwright who won the 1969 Pulitzer Prize for *The Great White Hope;* Ibiza, Spain, Oct. 13.

Sanchez, Salvador, 23; WBC featherweight champion; near Mexico City, Aug. 12.

Sawyer, Joe, 75; character actor who appeared in over 300 films; Ashland, Ore., Apr. 21.

Schneider, Romy, 43, Austrian actress who appeared in more than 60 films; Paris, May 29.

Sebelius, Keith, 65; U.S. representative from Kansas, 1969-81; Norton, Kan., Sept. 5.

Seely-Brown, Horace, 73; former U.S. representative from Connecticut; Boca Raton, Fla., Apr. 9.

Seper, Franjo Cardinal, 76; prefect of the Sacred Congregation for the Doctrine of the Faith; Rome, Dec. 31.

Shehu, Gen. Mehmet, 68; Albania's prime minister since 1954; Albania, Dec. 17.

Sillman, Leonard, 72; producer of the "New Faces" reviews; New York, Jan. 23.

Simmons, Calvin, 32; musical director of the Oakland Symphony; Lake Placid, N.Y., Aug. 21.

Smith, Walter "Red", 76; sports columnist for *The New York Times* who was awarded the 1976 Pulitzer Prize for distinguished commentary; Stamford, Conn., Jan. 15.

King Sobhuza, 83; king of Swaziland for 82 years; Swaziland, Aug. 1.

Spivak, Charlie, 77; band leader who was popular in the 1940s; Greenville, S.C., Mar. 1.

Stitt, Sonny, 58; jazz saxophonist; New York, July 22.

Strasberg, Lee, 80; leading teacher of "method" acting in the U.S.; artistic director of the famed Actors Studio; New York, Feb. 17.

Stratton, Monty, 70; major league pitcher whose attempted comeback after losing a leg inspired a 1949 movie; Greenville, Tex., Sept. 29.

Struss, Karl, 95; photographer and film pioneer who won the first Oscar for cinematography in 1927; Santa Monica, Cal., Dec. 16.

Sullivan, Daniel P., 76; FBI agent who helped track down John Dillinger and the Barker-Karpis gang; Miami, July 4.

Sullivan, John L., 83; U.S. Secretary of the Navy during the Truman administration; Exeter, N.H., Aug. 8.

Sunay, Cevdet, 82; president of Turkey, 1966-73; Istanbul, May 22.

Suslov, Mikhail, 79; chief ideologist of the Soviet Communist Party; USSR, Jan. 25.

T

Theorell, Hugo, 79; Swedish biochemist who won the 1955 Nobel Prize in Medicine; Sweden, Aug. 15.

Thornton, Charles B., 68; businessman who founded and headed Litton Industries; Los Angeles, Nov. 24.

Tjader, Carl, 56; jazz vibraphonist and percussionist; Philippines, May 5.

Truman, Bess, 97; widow of Pres. Harry Truman; Independence, Mo., Oct. 18.

Tuve, Merle A., 80; physicist whose discoveries led to the development of radar and nuclear energy; Bethesda, Md., May 20.

Turnbull, Agnes, 93; novelist and short-story writer; Livingston, N.J., Jan. 31.

Twining, Gen. Nathan, 84; chairman of the joint chiefs of staff in the 1950s; Lackland AFB, Tex., Mar. 29.

Tworkov, Jack, 82; painter and art teacher; Provincetown, Mass., Sept. 4.

U

Uris, Harold, 76; skyscraper developer and philanthropist; Palm Beach, Fla., Mar. 28.

V

Villeneuve, Gilles, 30; Canadian race car driver who won 6 grand prix races; Zolder, Belgium, May 8.

Von Zell, Harry, 75; radio announcer and actor long associated with the Burns and Allen radio and TV shows; Woodland Hills, Cal., Nov. 21.

W

Wakely, Jimmy, 68; country and western singer who starred in movie westerns in the 1940s; Los Angeles, Sept. 23.

Walker, Dixie, 71; outfielder for the Brooklyn Dodgers in the 1940s; Birmingham, Ala., May 17.

Wallenberg, Marcus, 82; Swedish financier and industrialist; Stockholm, Sept. 13.

Walsh, Rev. Michael P., 70; educator who headed Boston College, Fordham Univ.; Boston, Apr. 23.

Walters, Charles, 79; director of Hollywood musicals, *Easter Parade, Lili;* Malibu, Cal., Aug. 13.

Waner, Lloyd "Little Poison", 76; Pittsburgh Pirate outfielder who was elected to the hall of fame in 1967; Oklahoma City, July 22.

Weiss, Peter, 65; German-born playwright, *Marat/Sade;* Stockholm, May 10.

Whitney, John Hay, 77; publisher, sportsman, and philanthropist; Manhasset, N.Y., Feb. 8.

Wilson, Don, 81; radio and TV announcer long associated with Jack Benny; Palm Springs, Cal., Apr. 25.

Wood, Natalie, 43; film actress who was nominated for 3 Oscars, *West Side Story;* off Santa Catalina Island, Cal., Nov. 29.

Wurf, Jerry, 62; labor leader who headed the American Federation of State, County and Municipal Employees since 1964; Washington, D.C., Dec. 10.

Z

Zaturenska, Marya, 80; Russian-born poet who was awarded the 1938 Pulitzer Prize for poetry; Shelburne Falls, Mass., Jan. 19.

Ziolkowski, Dorczak, 74; sculptor who spent 35 years carving a monument to Chief Crazy Horse; Sturgis, S.D., Oct. 20.

Zworykin, Vladimir, 92; Russian-born scientist whose achievements were pivotal in the development of television; Princeton, N.J., July 29.

VITAL STATISTICS

Source: National Center for Health Statistics, U.S. Department of Health and Human Services

January-April 1982 (Provisional Data)

Births

During the first 4 months of 1982 there were 1,165,000 live births, virtually unchanged from the first 4 months of 1981. The birth rate decreased 1% to 15.4, and the fertility rate decreased 1% to 65.2.

Marriages

For the first 4 months of 1982 a total of 634,000 marriages was reported, yielding a marriage rate of 8.4 per 1,000 population. The number of marriages and the marriage rate were 3% higher and 1% lower, respectively, than the corresponding figures for the first 4 months of 1981.

Divorces

In the 4 months from January through April, a cumulative total of 375,000 divorces was reported, and the divorce rate for the period was 4.9 per 1,000 population. For the rate this was a decrease of 3% over the level recorded in the first 4 months of 1981.

Deaths

For April 1982 the provisional count of deaths totaled 171,000, amounting to a rate of 9.0 deaths per 1,000 population. This rate was 6% higher than the rate of 8.5% for April 1981. Among the 171,000 deaths for April 1982 were 3,500 deaths at ages under 1 year, yielding an infant mortality rate of 11.9 deaths per 1,000 live births. This rate was 4% lower than the rate of 12.4 for April 1981.

The provisional death rate for the 12 months ending with March 1982, 8.5 deaths per 1,000 population, was 3.0% lower than the rate for the 12 months ending with March 1981, 8.8 deaths per 1,000 population.

Provisional Statistics
12 months ending with April

	Number 1981	Number 1982	Rate* 1981	Rate* 1982
Live births	3,627,000	3,646,000	15.9	15.8
Deaths	2,002,000	1,957,000	8.8	8.5
Natural increase	1,625,000	1,689,000	7.1	7.3
Marriages	2,392,000	2,437,000	10.5	10.6
Divorces	1,193,000	1,203,000	5.2	5.2
Infant deaths	44,600	41,900	12.3	11.5
Population base (in millions)			228.0	230.2

*Per 1,000 population

Note: Rates are based on revised population estimates.

Annual Report for the Year 1981 (Provisional Statistics)

Births

During 1981 an estimated 3,646,000 live births occurred in the United States, 1% more than in 1980. The birth rate was 15.9 live births per 1,000 population and the fertility rate was 67.6 live births per 1,000 women aged 15–44 years. These rates were 1 and unchanged respectively, compared to 1980.

The increase in the number of births and the birth rate in 1981 is a result of the growth in the number of women in the childbearing ages. The number of women in the childbearing ages increased 2% between 1980 and 1981.

As a result of natural increase, the excess of births over deaths, 1,659,000 persons were added to the population during 1981. The rate of natural increase was 7.2 persons per 1,000 population compared with 7.1 for 1980. This increase was due to the increase in the birth rate.

Deaths

The provisional count of deaths in the United States during 1981 totaled 1,987,000, resulting in a rate of 8.7 deaths per 1,000 population. This rate was the same as the rate for 1980.

Among these deaths were 42,700 deaths at ages under 1 year yielding an infant mortality rate of 11.7 deaths per 1,000 live births. This rate was 6% lower than the provisional infant mortality rate for 1980, 12.5 deaths per 1,000 live births.

Marriages and Divorces

According to provisional reports, there were 2,438,000 marriages in 1981. This represented an increase of 1% over the provisional total for 1980 and the 6th consecutive increase in the annual marriage total. The 1981 provisional marriage total was the largest annual number of marriages ever recorded in the United States, exceeding by about 25,000 the previous peak of 2,413,000 recorded in 1980.

In 1981 the provisional marriage rate was 10.6 per 1,000 population. This rate was the same as the provisional rate for 1980. This ended a decade in which the marriage rate moved slowly downward from a peak in 1972 and gradually reversed direction, starting to climb in 1978.

An estimated 1,219,000 divorces were granted in 1981. This was 37,000 (3%) more than the provisional total for 1980 and approximately 3 times more than the final total recorded for 1962.

In 1981 the provisional divorce rate was 5.3 per 1,000 population, 2% more than 1980. The divorce rate has remained relatively stable after increasing from 2.2 in 1962 to 5.4 in 1979.

Births and Deaths in the U.S.

Refers only to events occurring within the U.S., including Alaska and Hawaii beginning in 1960. Excludes fetal deaths. Rates per 1,000 population enumerated as of April 1 for 1960, and 1970; estimated as of July 1 for all other years. (p) provisional. (NA) not available. Beginning 1970 excludes births and deaths occurring to nonresidents of the U.S.

	Births				Deaths			
Year	Males	Females	Total number	Rate	Males	Females	Total number	Rate
1955	2,073,719	1,973,576	4,097,000	25.0	872,638	656,079	1,528,717	9.3
1960	2,179,708	2,078,142	4,257,850	23.7	975,648	736,334	1,711,982	9.5
1965	1,927,054	1,833,304	3,760,358	19.4	1,035,200	792,936	1,828,136	9.4
1970	1,915,378	1,816,008	3,731,386	18.4	1,078,478	842,553	1,921,031	9.5
1975	1,613,135	1,531,063	3,144,198	14.8	1,050,819	842,060	1,892,879	8.9
1980(p)[1]	NA	NA	3,598,000	15.8	NA	NA	1,986,000	8.7
1981(p)	NA	NA	3,646,000	15.9	NA	NA	1,987,000	8.7

(1) Provisional rates for 1980 recomputed using population estimates based on the 1980 enumerated population; comparable with provisional rates for 1981, not comparable with rates shown for 1975-80.

Births and Deaths by States

Source: National Center for Health Statistics, U.S. Department of Health and Human Services

State	Births 1980p	Births 1981p	Deaths 1980p	Deaths 1981p
Alabama	62,814	61,139	35,386	35,180
Alaska	9,368	9,928	1,692	1,808
Arizona	50,173	51,322	21,609	22,348
Arkansas	36,863	35,386	22,565	22,224
California	401,616	422,066	190,251	187,658
Colorado	50,279	52,654	19,503	20,053
Connecticut	34,069	37,604	26,597	25,926
Delaware	9,544	9,372	5,201	5,169
Dist. of Col.	17,835	17,801	9,165	8,846
Florida	131,923	138,204	106,815	110,894
Georgia	95,980	91,991	43,519	47,367
Hawaii	18,277	18,241	5,190	5,282
Idaho	19,495	19,379	6,431	6,612
Illinois	186,578	181,560	100,356	99,121
Indiana	87,906	84,634	46,721	48,110
Iowa	48,050	46,617	26,714	26,798
Kansas	39,330	40,239	21,399	21,157
Kentucky	60,778	58,047	33,268	33,462
Louisiana	79,202	81,995	35,626	36,289
Maine	16,095	16,482	10,857	10,382
Maryland	52,284	54,137	33,337	33,474
Massachusetts	73,355	76,075	54,773	49,899
Michigan	143,007	138,988	74,002	75,166
Minnesota	68,848	66,943	33,495	32,207
Mississippi	47,538	45,842	22,911	23,100
Missouri	79,623	77,883	49,881	49,815
Montana	13,928	13,939	6,592	6,692
Nebraska	27,851	27,155	14,681	14,322
Nevada	13,156	14,162	6,408	6,517
New Hampshire	13,648	13,501	7,547	7,577
New Jersey	91,047	92,049	64,727	66,930
New Mexico	25,661	28,262	9,080	8,871
New York	232,491	242,873	167,769	169,249
North Carolina	85,123	84,470	49,059	49,752
North Dakota	12,939	13,415	5,850	5,786
Ohio	169,359	169,986	97,779	97,840
Oklahoma	50,681	51,252	28,308	27,801
Oregon	43,998	44,425	21,793	21,857
Pennsylvania	161,025	161,356	123,400	120,060
Rhode Island	12,512	12,849	9,553	9,384
South Carolina	49,805	49,605	24,337	24,578
South Dakota	13,013	12,679	6,462	6,291
Tennessee	73,500	71,696	43,205	43,040
Texas	268,717	287,272	108,586	112,704
Utah	43,708	41,973	8,556	8,445
Vermont	7,640	7,655	4,312	4,502
Virginia	75,042	76,266	41,889	41,539
Washington	67,972	70,274	32,495	33,158
West Virginia	29,277	28,503	19,120	19,469
Wisconsin	74,470	73,518	40,972	39,832
Wyoming	9,539	10,162	3,062	2,969
Total	**3,598,000**	**3,633,826**	**1,986,000**	**1,987,512**

(p) provisional

Marriages and Divorces by States

Source: National Center for Health Statistics, U.S. Department of Health and Human Services

1981 provisional figures; divorces include reported annulments.

State	Marriages	Divorces
Alabama	47,318	26,640
Alaska	5,809	3,555
Arizona	31,784	20,988
Arkansas	26,724	18,419
California	214,708	134,370
Colorado	36,461	18,373
Connecticut	25,517	12,049
Delaware	4,561	2,921
Dist. of Col.	5,310	3,649
Florida	111,660	75,503
Georgia	70,486	35,294
Hawaii	12,309	4,256
Idaho	14,372	6,700
Illinois	109,449	52,851
Indiana	55,699	NA
Iowa	27,063	12,164
Kansas	26,254	14,430
Kentucky	35,201	17,644
Louisiana	44,139	NA
Maine	12,552	6,356
Maryland	46,840	16,054
Massachusetts	46,274	19,145
Michigan	85,814	46,407
Minnesota	37,945	15,906
Mississippi	27,530	13,143
Missouri	53,265	27,295
Montana	8,221	5,017
Nebraska	14,418	6,846
Nevada	NA	12,164
New Hampshire	9,916	5,183
New Jersey	57,555	28,923
New Mexico	17,130	10,592
New York	150,007	63,148
North Carolina	48,040	29,692
North Dakota	6,182	2,319
Ohio	99,617	58,291
Oklahoma	48,127	24,989
Oregon	22,747	17,714
Pennsylvania	92,370	39,147
Rhode Island	7,539	3,408
South Carolina	55,008	14,137
South Dakota	8,708	2,781
Tennessee	59,865	31,816
Texas	192,368	99,021
Utah	18,346	8,259
Vermont	5,207	2,350
Virginia	61,460	25,269
Washington	48,901	29,195
West Virginia	16,734	11,064
Wisconsin	40,934	18,309
Wyoming	7,052	4,152
Total	**2,311,496**	**1,157,898**

(NA) not available. Totals reflect reporting areas only.

Marriages, Divorces, and Rates in the U.S.

Source: National Center for Health Statistics, Public Health Service

Data refer only to events occurring within the United States, including Alaska and Hawaii beginning with 1960. Rates per 1,000 population.

Year	Marriages[1] No.	Marriages[1] Rate	Divorces[2] No.	Divorces[2] Rate
1890	570,000	**9.0**	33,461	**0.5**
1895	620,000	**8.9**	40,387	**0.6**
1900	709,000	**9.3**	55,751	**0.7**
1905	842,000	**10.0**	67,976	**0.8**
1910	948,166	**10.3**	83,045	**0.9**
1915	1,007,595	**10.0**	104,298	**1.0**
1920	1,274,476	**12.0**	170,505	**1.6**
1925	1,188,334	**10.3**	175,449	**1.5**
1930	1,126,856	**9.2**	195,961	**1.6**
1935	1,327,000	**10.4**	218,000	**1.7**
1940	1,595,879	**12.1**	264,000	**2.0**
1945	1,612,992	**12.2**	485,000	**[3]3.5**
1950	1,667,231	**11.1**	385,144	**2.6**
1955	1,531,000	**9.3**	377,000	**2.3**
1960	1,523,000	**8.5**	393,000	**2.2**
1965	1,800,000	**9.3**	479,000	**2.5**
1970	2,158,802	**10.6**	708,000	**3.5**
1975	2,152,662	**10.1**	1,036,000	**4.9**
1979	2,331,337	**10.6**	1,181,000	**5.4**
1980(p)[4]	2,413,000	**10.6**	1,182,000	**5.2**
1981(p)	2,438,000	**10.6**	1,219,000	**5.3**

(1) Includes estimates and marriage licenses for some states for all years. (2) Includes reported annulments. (3) Divorce rates for 1945 based on population including armed forces overseas. (4) Provisional rates for 1980 recomputed using population estimates based on the 1980 enumerated population; comparable with provisional rates for 1981, not comparable with rates shown for 1975-80. (p) provisional.

Deaths and Death Rates for Selected Causes

Source: National Center for Health Statistics, U.S. Department of Health and Human Services

1980 Cause of death (est.)	Number	Rate[1]
All causes	**1,986,000**	**892.6**
Viral hepatitis	790	0.4
Tuberculosis, all forms	1,770	0.8
Septicemia	9,230	4.1
Syphilis and its sequelae	180	0.1
All other infective and parasitic diseases	3,730	1.7
Malignant neoplasms, including neoplasms of lymphatic and hematopoietic tissues	414,320	186.3
Diabetes mellitus	34,230	15.4
Meningitis	1,320	0.6
Major cardiovascular diseases	989,690	444.9
Diseases of heart	763,060	343.0
Active rheumatic fever and chronic rheumatic heart disease	7,950	3.6
Hypertensive heart disease	22,100	9.9
Ischemic heart disease	566,930	254.9
Acute myocardial infarction	301,210	135.4
All other forms of heart disease	155,710	70.0
Hypertension	7,140	3.2
Cerebrovascular diseases	170,420	76.6
Arteriosclerosis	29,830	13.4
Other diseases of arteries, arterioles, and capillaries	19,240	8.6
Acute bronchitis and bronchiolitis	590	0.3
Influenza and pneumonia	52,720	23.7
Influenza	2,590	1.2
Pneumonia	50,130	22.5
Chronic obstructive pulmonary diseases	55,810	25.1
Chronic and unqualified bronchitis	3,940	1.8
Emphysema	14,130	6.4
Asthma	2,500	1.1
Ulcer of stomach and duodenum	5,750	2.6
Hernia and intestinal obstruction	5,430	2.4
Cirrhosis of liver	31,330	14.1
Cholelithiasis, cholecystitis, and cholangitis	3,110	1.4
Nephritis, nephrosis and nephrotic syn.	17,390	7.8
Infections of kidney	2,640	1.2
Hyperplasia of prostate	810	0.4
Congenital anomalies	13,730	6.2
Certain causes of mortality in early infancy	22,570	10.1
Symptoms and ill-defined conditions	29,130	13.1
All other diseases	112,510	50.6
Accidents	106,550	47.9
Motor vehicle accidents	54,200	24.4
Suicide	28,290	12.7
Homicide	25,090	11.3
All other external causes	3,510	1.6

Due to rounding estimates of death, figures may not add to total. Data based on a 10% sampling of all death certificates for a 12-month (Jan.-Dec.) period. (1) Rates per 100,000 population.

Principal Types of Accidental Deaths

Source: National Center for Health Statistics, U.S. Department of Health and Human Services

Year	All types	Motor vehicle	Falls	Burns	Drowning	Firearms	Machinery	Poison gases	Other poisons
1960	93,806	38,137	19,023	7,645	5,232	2,334	1,951	1,253	1,679
1965	108,004	49,163	19,984	7,347	5,485	2,344	2,054	1,526	2,110
1970	114,638	54,633	16,926	6,718	6,391	2,406	...	1,620	3,679
1975	103,030	45,853	14,896	6,071	6,640	2,380	...	1,577	4,694
1980	—	52,600	12,300	5,500	7,000	1,800	...	1,500	2,800
1981	—	50,800	11,700	4,900	6,000	1,900	...	1,700	2,600
Death rates per 100,000 population									
1960	52.1	21.2	10.6	4.3	2.9	1.3	1.1	0.7	0.9
1965	55.8	25.4	10.3	3.8	2.8	1.2	1.1	0.8	1.1
1970	56.4	26.9	8.3	3.3	3.1	1.2	...	0.8	1.8
1975	48.4	21.5	7.0	2.8	3.1	1.1	...	0.7	2.2
1980	—	23.2	5.4	2.4	3.1	0.8	...	0.7	1.2
1981	—	22.2	5.1	2.1	2.6	0.8	...	0.8	1.1

U.S. Civil Aviation Accidents

Source: National Safety Council

	accidents			accident rates: per 100,000 aircraft-hours		per million aircraft-miles	
1981[3]	total	fatal	Deaths[1]	total	fatal	total	fatal
Large airlines	24	4	4	0.366	0.061	0.009	0.002
Commuter airlines	28	9	35	2.59	0.83	0.16	0.05
On-demand air taxies	138	34	95	3.74	0.92	—	—
General aviation[2]	3,634	662	1,265	10.0	1.82	—	—

(1) Includes passengers, crew members and others. (2) Suicide and sabotage included in accident and fatality totals but excluded from rates. (3) Preliminary.

Transportation Accident Passenger Death Rates, 1980

Source: National Safety Council

Kind of transportation	Passenger miles (billions)	Passenger deaths	Rate per 100,000,000 pass. miles	1978-1980 aver. death rate
Passenger automobiles and taxis[1]	2,200.0	29,050	1.32	1.30
Passenger automobiles on turnpikes	46.1	330	0.72	0.71
Buses	85.8	130	0.15	0.15
Intercity buses[2]	17.3	23	0.13	0.05
Railroad passenger trains	11.0	4	0.04	0.07
Scheduled air transport planes (domestic)	221.2	11	0.01	0.04

(1) Drivers of passenger automobiles are considered passengers. (2) Class 1 only, representing 65 per cent of total intercity bus passenger mileage.

Motor Vehicle Traffic Deaths by State

Source: National Safety Council

Place of accidents	Number 1981	Number 1980	Death rate* 1981	Death rate* 1980
Total U.S.†	**50,800**	**52,600**	**3.3**	**3.5**
Alabama	944	947	3.2	3.3
Alaska	97	87	3.6	3.3
Arizona	916	947	4.8	5.0
Arkansas	537	587	3.2	3.6
California	5,170	5,489	3.3	3.5
Colorado	754	708	3.3	3.2
Connecticut	527	582	2.7	3.0
Delaware	112	158	2.6	3.7
Dist. of Col.	50	46	1.5	1.4
Florida	3,121	2,879	3.9	3.6
Georgia	1,418	1,506	3.2	3.5
Hawaii	150	185	2.6	3.3
Idaho	293	331	4.2	4.8
Illinois	1,852	1,994	2.8	3.1
Indiana	1,173	1,179	3.1	3.2
Iowa	610	626	3.2	3.3
Kansas	578	595	3.3	3.4
Kentucky	830	825	3.2	3.3
Louisiana	1,233	1,213	5.0	5.2
Maine	211	261	2.8	3.5
Maryland	792	782	2.7	2.8
Massachusetts	752	881	2.1	2.5
Michigan	1,589	1,774	2.5	2.9
Minnesota	763	863	2.6	3.0
Mississippi	745	697	4.4	4.2
Missouri	1,055	1,191	3.1	3.5
Montana	338	325	5.0	4.9
Nebraska	378	396	3.3	3.5
Nevada	295	346	4.8	5.7
New Hampshire	148	194	2.3	3.0
New Jersey	1,162	1,119	2.3	2.2
New Mexico	544	615	4.7	5.4
New York	2,508	2,619	3.2	3.4
North Carolina	1,497	1,519	3.6	3.7
North Dakota	166	151	3.1	2.9
Ohio	1,780	2,033	2.4	2.8
Oklahoma	1,000	972	3.6	3.5
Oregon	645	646	3.3	3.4
Pennsylvania	2,049	2,114	2.8	3.0
Rhode Island	111	128	2.0	2.4
South Carolina	846	859	3.7	3.8
South Dakota	177	228	2.8	3.7
Tennessee	1,119	1,171	3.3	3.5
Texas	4,701	4,424	4.2	4.0
Utah	364	335	3.3	3.5
Vermont	116	134	3.1	3.6
Virginia	1,012	1,045	2.6	2.7
Washington	872	985	3.0	3.4
West Virginia	439	539	4.0	5.0
Wisconsin	927	985	2.9	3.2
Wyoming	264	245	5.2	4.9

*The death rate is the number of deaths per 100 million vehicle miles. †Includes both traffic and nontraffic motor-vehicle deaths.

Accidental Injuries by Severity of Injury

Source: National Safety Council

1981 Severity of injury	Total*	Motor vehicle	Work	Home	Public[1]
Deaths*	99,000	50,800	12,300	21,000	19,500
Disabling injuries*	9,400,000	1,900,000	2,100,000	3,200,000	2,400,000
Permanent impairments	350,000	150,000	70,000	80,000	60,000
Temporary total disabilities	9,000,000	1,750,000	2,000,000	3,100,000	2,300,000
Certain Costs of Accidental Injuries, 1981 ($ billions)					
Total*	**$87.4**	**$40.6**	**$32.5**	**$9.2**	**$6.6**
Wage loss	23.3	12.5	5.1	3.4	3.5
Medical expense	11.2	3.8	3.4	2.4	1.9
Insurance administration	16.4	9.6	6.6	0.1	0.1

*Duplication between motor vehicle, work, and home are eliminated in the total column. (1) Excludes motor vehicle and work accidents in public places.

Home Accident Deaths

Source: National Safety Council

Year	Total home	Falls	Fires, burns[2]	Suffo., ingested object	Suffo., mech-anical	Poison (solid, liquid)	Poison by gas	Fire-arms	Other
1950	29,000	14,800	5,000	(1)	1,600	1,300	1,250	950	4,100
1955	28,500	14,100	5,400	(1)	1,250	1,150	900	1,100	4,600
1960	28,000	12,300	6,350	1,850	1,500	1,350	900	1,200	2,550
1965	28,500	11,700	6,100	1,300*	1,200	1,700	1,100	1,300	4,100
1970	27,000	9,700	5,600	1,800	1,100	3,000	1,100	1,400	3,300
1975	25,000	8,000	5,000	1,800	800	3,700	1,000	1,300	3,400
1980	23,000	6,700	4,400	1,800	600	2,200	900	1,100	5,300 [3]
1981	21,000	6,700	4,000	1,800	600	2,000	1,100	1,200	3,600

*Data for this year and subsequent years not comparable with previous years due to classification changes. (1) Included in Other. (2) Includes deaths resulting from conflagration, regardless of nature of injury. (3) Includes 1,000 excessive deaths due to summer heat wave.

Pedalcycle Accidents

Since 1935, the National Safety Council reports the number of pedalcycle motor vehicle deaths has almost tripled to 1,200 in 1981. The number of pedalcycles in use, 101.5 million (including sidewalk pedalcycles), is 29 times the number in 1935; so the death rate in 1981 was one-eleventh the rate in 1935. The proportion of deaths occurring to young adults and adults has steadily increased since 1960. Persons 15 years of age and older accounted for more than three-fifths the deaths in 1981 compared to about one-fifth in 1960.

Average Lifetime in the U.S.

Source: National Center for Health Statistics, U.S. Department of Health and Human Services

1980[p] Age interval	Number living[1]	Avg. life expect.[2]	1980[p] Age interval	Number living[1]	Avg. life expect.[2]
0-1	100,000	73.6	40-45	94,797	36.6
1-5	98,743	73.6	45-50	93,469	32.1
5-10	98,486	69.8	50-55	91,380	27.8
10-15	98,323	64.9	55-60	88,126	23.7
15-20	98,174	60.0	60-65	83,324	19.9
20-25	97,676	55.3	65-70	76,545	16.4
25-30	97,011	50.6	70-75	67,640	13.3
30-35	96,353	45.9	75-80	56,355	10.4
35-40	95,649	41.3	80-85	41,431	8.2
			85 and over	26,395	6.5

(1) Of 100,000 born alive, number living at beginning of age interval. (2) Average number of years of life remaining at beginning of age interval.

Years of Life Expected at Birth

Year	Total pop.	Male	Female	Year	Total pop.	Male	Female
1980[p2]	73.8	70.0	77.7	1950	68.2	65.6	71.1
1979[p]	73.8	69.9	77.8	1940	62.9	60.8	65.2
1975	72.5	68.7	76.5	1930	59.7	58.1	61.6
1970	70.8	67.1	74.7	1920[1]	54.1	53.6	54.6
1965	70.2	66.8	73.8	1910[1]	50.0	48.4	51.8
1960	69.7	66.6	73.1	1900[1]	47.3	46.3	48.3

(p) Provisional (1) Based on data for death registration states only. (2) Based on est. of the population.

Ownership of Life Insurance in the U.S. and Assets of U.S. Life Insurance Companies

Source: American Council of Life Insurance

Legal Reserve Life Insurance Companies (millions of dollars)

Year	Purchases of life insurance: Ordinary	Group	Industrial	Total	Insurance in force: Ordinary	Group	Industrial	Credit	Total	Assets
1940	7,022	747	3,318	11,087	79,346	14,938	20,866	380	115,530	30,802
1950	18,260	6,237	5,492	29,989	149,116	47,793	33,415	3,844	234,168	64,020
1960	56,183	15,328	6,906	78,417	341,881	175,903	39,563	29,101	586,448	119,576
1965	89,643	52,867*	7,302	149,812*	499,638	308,078	39,818	53,020	900,554	158,884
1970	134,802	65,381*	6,612	206,795*	734,730	551,357	38,644	77,392	1,402,123	207,254
1975	207,052	102,659*	6,741	316,452*	1,083,421	904,695	39,423	112,032	2,139,571	289,304
1978	283,067	125,129	6,015	414,211	1,425,095	1,243,994	38,080	163,081	2,870,250	389,924
1979	329,571	157,906	5,335	492,812	1,585,878	1,419,418	37,794	179,250	3,222,340	432,282
1980	385,575	183,418	3,609	572,602	1,760,474	1,579,355	35,994	165,215	3,541,038	479,210
1981	463,845	346,351*	2,136	812,332*	1,978,080	1,888,612	34,547	162,356	4,063,595	525,803

*Includes Servicemen's Group Life Insurance $27.4 billion in 1965, $16.8 billion in 1970, and $1.7 billion in 1975, and $45.6 billion in 1981, as well as $84.4 billion of Federal Employees' Group Life Insurance in 1981.

Accidental Deaths by Month and Type, 1978 and 1981

Source: National Safety Council

Month	1981 totals	1978 details by type: All types‡	Motor vehicle	Falls	Drowning†	Fires, burns*	Ingest. of food, object	Firearms	Poison (solid, liquid)	Poison by gas
Total	**99,000**	**105,561**	**52,411**	**13,690**	**7,026**	**6,163**	**3,063**	**1,806**	**3,035**	**1,737**
January	8,100	7,836	2,952	1,388	190	868	299	154	314	254
February	7,000	6,892	2,767	1,092	166	793	244	128	238	229
March	7,500	7,791	3,617	1,080	320	640	260	143	313	177
April	7,700	8,129	4,057	1,135	460	520	237	127	237	134
May	8,500	9,115	4,622	1,083	930	357	243	107	248	107
June	8,850	9,434	4,813	1,057	1,190	315	265	115	253	60
July	9,500	10,484	5,218	1,160	1,520	319	257	130	234	82
August	9,300	9,827	5,185	1,098	980	287	235	145	234	61
September	7,800	9,110	4,941	1,118	580	298	205	131	220	71
October	8,350	9,070	4,972	1,232	300	397	279	181	235	149
November	7,850	8,633	4,622	1,092	180	530	248	232	239	181
December	8,550	9,240	4,645	1,155	210	839	291	213	270	232
Average	**8,250**	**8,797**	**4,368**	**1,141**	**586**	**514**	**255**	**151**	**253**	**145**

*Includes deaths resulting from conflagration regardless of nature of injury. †Includes drowning in water transport accidents. Some totals partly estimated. ‡ Includes some deaths not shown separately.

Physical Growth Range for Children from 2 to 18 Years

Source: National Center for Health Statistics, U.S. Department of Health and Human Services

Boys

Age	Height in centimeters			Weight in kilograms		
	Shortest 5%	Median height	Tallest 5%	Lightest 5%	Median weight	Heaviest 5%
2	82.5	86.8	94.4	10.49	12.34	15.50
3	89.0	94.9	102.0	12.05	14.62	17.77
4	95.8	102.9	109.9	13.64	16.69	20.27
5	102.0	109.9	117.0	15.27	18.67	23.09
6	107.7	116.1	123.5	16.93	20.69	26.34
7	113.0	121.7	129.7	18.64	22.85	30.12
8	118.1	127.0	135.7	20.40	25.30	34.51
9	122.9	132.2	141.8	22.25	28.13	39.58
10	127.7	137.5	148.1	24.33	31.44	45.27
11	132.6	143.3	154.9	26.80	35.30	51.47
12	137.6	149.7	162.3	29.85	39.78	58.09
13	142.9	156.5	169.8	33.64	44.95	65.02
14	148.8	163.1	176.7	38.22	50.77	72.13
15	155.2	169.0	181.9	43.11	56.71	79.12
16	161.1	173.5	185.4	47.74	62.10	85.62
17	164.9	176.2	187.3	51.50	66.31	91.31
18	165.7	176.8	187.6	53.97	68.88	95.76

Girls

Age	Shortest 5%	Median height	Tallest 5%	Lightest 5%	Median weight	Heaviest 5%
2	81.6	86.8	93.6	9.95	11.80	14.15
3	88.3	94.1	100.6	11.61	14.10	17.22
4	95.0	101.6	108.3	13.11	15.96	19.91
5	101.1	108.4	115.6	14.55	17.66	22.62
6	106.6	114.6	122.7	16.05	19.52	25.75
7	111.8	120.6	129.5	17.71	21.84	29.68
8	116.9	126.4	136.2	19.62	24.84	34.71
9	122.1	132.2	142.9	21.82	28.46	40.64
10	127.5	138.3	149.5	24.36	32.55	47.17
11	133.5	144.8	156.2	27.24	36.95	54.00
12	139.8	151.5	162.7	30.52	41.53	60.81
13	145.2	157.1	168.1	34.14	46.10	67.30
14	148.7	160.4	171.3	37.76	50.28	73.08
15	150.5	161.8	172.8	40.99	53.68	77.78
16	151.6	162.4	173.3	43.41	55.89	80.99
17	152.7	163.1	173.5	44.74	56.69	82.46
18	153.6	163.7	173.6	45.26	56.62	82.47

This table simply gives a general picture for American children at specific age/dates (not the entire age range). When used as a standard, the individual variation in children's growth should not be overlooked. In most cases the height-weight relationship is probably a more valid index of weight status than a weight-for-age assessment.

Average Weight of Americans by Height and Age

Source: Society of Actuaries; from the *1979 Build and Blood Pressure Study*

The figures represent weights in ordinary indoor clothing and shoes, and heights with shoes.

Men

Height	20-24	25-29	30-39	40-49	50-59	60-69
5'2"	130	134	138	140	141	140
5'3"	136	140	143	144	145	144
5'4"	139	143	147	149	150	149
5'5"	143	147	151	154	155	153
5'6"	148	152	156	158	159	158
5'7"	153	156	160	163	164	163
5'8"	157	161	165	167	168	167
5'9"	163	166	170	172	173	172
5'10". . . .	167	171	174	176	177	176
5'11". . . .	171	175	179	181	182	181
6'0"	176	181	184	186	187	186
6'1"	182	186	190	192	193	191
6'2"	187	191	195	197	198	196
6'3"	193	197	201	203	204	200
6'4"	198	202	206	208	209	207

Women

Height	20-24	25-29	30-39	40-49	50-59	60-69
4'10". . . .	105	110	113	118	121	123
4'11". . . .	110	112	115	121	125	127
5'0"	112	114	118	123	127	130
5'1"	116	119	121	127	131	133
5'2"	120	121	124	129	133	136
5'3"	124	125	128	133	137	140
5'4"	127	128	131	136	141	143
5'5"	130	132	134	139	144	147
5'6"	133	134	137	143	147	150
5'7"	137	138	141	147	152	155
5'8"	141	142	145	150	156	158
5'9"	146	148	150	155	159	161
5'10". . . .	149	150	153	158	162	163
5'11". . . .	155	156	159	162	166	167
6'0"	157	159	164	168	171	172

The Nation's Hospitals

Source: American Hospital Association

In 1979, there were 6,988 hospitals in the United States registered by the American Hospital Association. These institutions had about 1.36 million beds and reported admitting some 37.8 million inpatients. About $79.8 billion was spent to provide services for both inpatients and outpatients.

	Hospitals		Beds		Average daily census		Admissions		Expenses ($1,000)	
State	Fed.	Non-fed.	Fed.	Non-fed.	Fed.	Non-fed.	Fed.	Non-fed.	Fed.	Non-fed.
Alabama	8	139	2,555	22,790	2,028	17,135	43,086	727,600	138,682	1,084,346
Alaska	9	17	571	1,120	299	672	16,552	37,824	44,296	105,609
Arizona	16	64	1,844	9,876	1,316	7,203	54,632	339,752	145,235	706,207
Arkansas	4	92	1,866	10,880	1,514	7,468	25,105	416,735	83,978	486,310
California	30	578	9,762	104,592	7,321	72,732	215,098	3,120,977	788,299	8,158,237
Colorado	6	93	1,762	13,264	1,436	8,933	41,878	424,920	160,655	787,725
Connecticut	5	61	960	17,484	657	13,971	18,848	440,474	66,271	1,103,503
Delaware	2	13	426	3,794	321	3,220	6,529	78,720	21,500	194,353
Dist. of Columbia	3	14	3,620	4,943	3,451	3,839	42,547	156,890	282,704	502,731
Florida	13	238	3,881	52,615	3,127	38,041	102,040	1,585,207	275,043	2,922,928
Georgia	9	180	2,792	28,290	2,168	20,115	56,291	921,033	218,092	1,388,407
Hawaii	1	26	547	3,341	430	2,574	18,320	98,832	53,155	216,609
Idaho	2	49	182	3,567	111	2,379	4,905	129,480	15,309	174,906
Illinois	10	275	5,824	67,711	4,464	51,745	72,601	1,979,208	302,285	4,546,418
Indiana	4	130	1,973	30,362	1,469	23,897	19,476	890,120	80,615	1,581,048
Iowa	3	138	1,558	19,918	1,104	13,575	19,436	557,362	76,496	875,096
Kansas	7	157	1,906	16,493	1,419	11,682	26,535	425,186	91,387	770,249
Kentucky	5	116	1,834	16,747	1,296	13,002	35,531	632,065	116,354	822,318
Louisiana	8	150	2,498	22,651	1,717	15,875	42,474	749,688	134,343	1,159,669
Maine	1	51	642	6,447	533	4,809	6,938	175,786	26,200	337,325
Maryland	9	75	2,997	22,178	2,302	18,301	48,011	525,081	225,064	1,347,651
Massachusetts	7	179	3,699	40,759	2,970	33,177	31,570	908,516	168,158	2,797,561
Michigan	8	231	2,289	47,966	1,746	37,674	36,618	1,456,308	137,061	3,408,348
Minnesota	5	178	1,683	28,949	1,347	20,924	23,519	686,125	91,287	1,302,251
Mississippi	5	111	1,764	14,719	1,466	10,970	30,935	468,435	99,603	571,342
Missouri	7	157	2,985	31,782	2,181	23,769	50,441	912,737	237,383	1,734,925
Montana	6	61	396	4,926	245	3,167	10,062	130,025	23,930	182,685
Nebraska	5	104	883	11,022	665	7,382	20,178	290,153	52,370	478,018
Nevada	4	21	263	2,989	193	2,025	7,257	112,157	23,623	236,435
New Hampshire	2	31	322	4,358	292	3,175	6,797	130,970	22,523	213,086
New Jersey	4	131	2,591	41,152	2,032	33,955	27,432	1,051,988	127,331	2,239,970
New Mexico	11	43	895	5,209	618	3,703	33,397	164,106	74,978	281,689
New York	16	342	9,762	121,678	8,100	105,316	105,525	2,656,801	498,578	7,755,744
North Carolina	9	150	2,889	30,485	2,280	23,312	50,809	889,046	151,066	1,384,203
North Dakota	5	55	414	5,506	273	3,724	11,918	134,505	23,400	204,347
Ohio	5	234	4,045	59,530	3,173	46,590	43,045	1,821,880	221,985	3,631,462
Oklahoma	12	130	1,103	16,472	802	11,328	41,971	485,741	89,108	778,354
Oregon	2	83	958	10,670	720	7,464	15,831	367,505	54,570	662,338
Pennsylvania	11	303	6,020	80,340	4,879	63,585	46,199	1,956,557	265,592	4,497,442
Rhode Island	2	19	399	5,759	307	5,002	10,515	136,452	31,798	370,362
South Carolina	7	82	1,619	15,258	1,095	11,744	40,351	440,306	108,312	637,550
South Dakota	10	59	1,146	4,448	837	2,751	20,266	123,541	55,762	156,783
Tennessee	5	162	2,807	28,564	2,254	21,977	39,412	934,382	140,029	1,361,616
Texas	24	544	8,514	71,569	6,965	50,142	178,253	2,341,653	587,166	3,596,526
Utah	2	39	487	4,634	356	3,378	12,791	197,444	35,223	294,568
Vermont	1	18	224	2,717	191	2,010	3,693	75,068	16,511	126,997
Virginia	9	125	3,115	28,744	2,451	22,250	68,688	741,890	234,845	1,351,882
Washington	11	114	2,319	13,640	1,782	9,513	51,495	543,477	151,258	884,587
West Virginia	5	73	1,134	12,971	934	9,955	18,967	394,659	65,737	582,082
Wisconsin	3	164	2,090	26,624	1,713	19,395	23,996	759,675	107,301	1,450,782
Wyoming	3	28	533	1,998	443	1,132	6,563	64,487	23,304	83,052
Total U.S.	**361**	**6,627**	**117,348**	**1,245,501**	**91,793**	**951,657**	**1,985,597**	**35,816,529**	**7,265,755**	**72,530,632**

Selected Statistics on State and County Mental Hospitals

Source: National Institute of Mental Health

Year	Total admitted	Net releases	Deaths in hospital	Residents end of year	Expense per patient[1]
1955	178,033	NA	44,384	558,922	$1,116.59
1960	234,791	NA	49,748	535,540	1,702.41
1970	393,174	394,627	30,804	338,592	5,435.38
1975	376,156	391,345	13,401	193,436	13,634.53
1977	414,703	408,667*	9,716	159,523	NA
1978	406,407	NA	9,080	153,544	NA
1979	383,323	NA	7,830	140,423	NA
1980(p)	379,766	NA	7,108	131,998	NA

*Includes estimates. NA-not available. (p)-provisional data. (1) Per average daily resident patient population.

Patients' Expenditures in Mental Hospitals

Source: National Institute of Mental Health

Based on reports of 280 state and county hospitals on the Jan., 1980, Inventory of Mental Health Facilities.

State	No. patients	Tot. expend. ($000)	State	No. patients	Tot. expend. ($000)	State	No. patients	Tot. expend. ($000)	State	No. patients	Tot. expend. ($000)
U.S.	**140,355**	**3,756,754**	Ida.	216	5,187	Mo.	3,223	86,897	Pa.	10,739	324,671
Ala.	1,911	43,994	Ill.	4,257	163,028	Mon.	337	11,336	R.I.	861	28,656
Alas.	82	7,181	Ind.	3,061	70,963	Neb.	684	24,541	S.C.	3,278	56,509
Ariz.	397	14,465	Ia.	1,139	28,874	Nev.	140	6,243	S.D.	488	8,809
Ark.	193	11,289	Kan.	1,192	34,611	N.H.	555	21,355	Tenn.	3,034	66,487
Cal.	6,563	208,403	Ky.	775	25,198	N.J.	6,293	158,621	Tex.	5,587	130,023
Col.	1,166	40,992	La.	2,284	45,955	N.M.	234	11,625	Ut.	317	7,702
Conn.	2,137	64,890	Me.	631	15,444	N.Y.	27,046	743,714	Vt.	340	8,816
Del.	609	15,651	Md.	4,086	90,054	N.C.	3,465	94,228	Va.	5,455	82,815
D.C.	2,152	100,722	Mass.	2,800	66,050	N.D.	632	11,606	Wash.	1,344	25,608
Fla.	5,653	93,062	Mich.	4,494	183,189	Oh.	6,016	171,619	W. Va.	1,892	26,414
Ga.	4,301	123,027	Minn.	2,526	52,641	Okla.	1,548	41,891	Wis.	786	39,756
Ha.	204	6,265	Miss.	1,904	27,247	Ore.	1,065	21,797	Wy.	263	6,633

Patient Care Episodes in Mental Health Facilities

Source: National Institute of Mental Health

		Inpatient services					Outpatient services	
Year	Total all facilities[1]	State & county mental hospitals	Private mental[2] hospitals	Gen. hosp. psychiatric service (non-VA)	VA psychiatric inpatient services[3]	Federally assisted comm. men. health cen.	Federally assisted comm. men. health cen.	Other
1979	[4] 6,403,915	[4] 518,695	184,919	[4] 571,725	[4] 217,507	[4] 298,897	1,949,602	[4] 2,652,570
1977	6,392,979	574,226	184,189	571,725	217,507	266,966	1,741,729	2,834,637
1975	6,409,477	598,993	165,327	565,696	214,264	246,891	1,584,968	3,033,308
1969	3,572,822	767,115	123,850	535,493	186,913	65,000	291,148	1,603,303
1965	2,636,525	804,926	125,428	519,328	115,843	—	—	1,071,000
1955	1,675,352	818,832	123,231	265,934	88,355	—	—	379,000

(1) In order to present trends on the same set of facilities over this interval, it has been necessary to exclude from this table the following: private psychiatric office practice; psychiatric service modes of all types in hospitals or outpatient clinics of federal agencies other than the VA (e.g., Public Health Service, Indian Health Service, Department of Defense Bureau of Prisons, etc.); inpatient service modes of multiservice facilities not shown in this table; all partial care episodes, and outpatient episodes of VA hospitals. (2) Includes estimates of episodes of care in residential treatment centers for emotionally disturbed children. (3) Includes Veterans Administration neuropsychiatric hospitals and Veterans Administration general hospitals with separate psychiatric inpatient settings. (4) Since 1979 data are *not* available for Veterans Administration neuropsychiatric hospital inpatient units, general hospital inpatient psychiatric units (V.A. and non-Federal), and federally funded community mental health center (CMHCs) inpatient and outpatient services, data are shown for 1978 for CMHCs and for 1977 for V.A. psychiatric inpatient settings and for separate psychiatric inpatient and outpatient services of non-Federal general hospitals.

Legal Abortions in the U.S.

Source: Center for Disease Control, U.S. Department of Health and Human Services

Legal abortions, according to selected characteristics of the patient.

	1973	1974	1975	1976	1977	1978	1979
Number	615,831	763,476	854,853	988,267	1,079,430	1,157,776	1,251,921
Age Characteristic				**Percent distribution**			
Under 20 years	32.7	32.7	33.1	32.1	30.8	30.0	30.0
20-24 years	32.0	31.8	31.9	33.3	34.5	35.0	35.4
25 years and over	35.3	35.6	35.0	34.6	34.7	34.9	34.6
Color							
White	72.5	69.7	67.8	66.6	66.4	67.0	68.9
All other	27.5	30.3	32.2	33.4	33.6	33.0	31.1
Marital status							
Married	27.4	27.4	26.1	24.6	24.3	26.4	24.7
Unmarried	72.6	72.6	73.9	75.4	75.7	73.6	75.3
Number of living children							
0	48.6	47.8	47.1	47.7	53.4	56.6	58.1
1	18.8	19.6	20.2	20.7	19.1	19.2	19.1
2	14.2	14.8	15.5	15.4	14.4	14.1	13.8
3	8.7	8.7	8.7	8.3	7.0	5.9	5.5
4	4.8	4.5	4.4	4.1	3.3	4.2*	3.5
5 or more	4.9	4.5	4.2	3.8	2.9	—	—
Location of abortion facility							
In state of residence	74.8	86.6	89.2	90.0	90.0	93.8	90.1
Out of state of residence	25.2	13.4	10.8	10.0	10.0	6.2	9.9
Period of gestation							
Under 9 weeks	36.1	42.6	44.6	47.0	51.2	53.2	52.1
9-10 weeks	29.4	28.7	28.4	28.0	27.2	26.9	27.0
11-12 weeks	17.9	15.4	14.9	14.4	13.1	12.3	12.5
13-15 weeks	6.9	5.5	5.0	4.5	3.4	4.0	4.2
16-20 weeks	8.0	6.5	6.1	5.1	4.3	3.7	3.4
21 weeks and over	1.7	1.2	1.0	0.9	0.9	0.9	0.9

*Beginning with 1978, 4 or more.

The Nation's Handicapped

Source: National Center for Health Statistics, U.S. Department of Health and Human Services

Persons with Activity Limitation due to Chronic Conditions, by percent with Selected Conditions, according to Activity Limitation Status, Age, and Sex.

1980 Activity limitation sex, and age	Number of persons limited in activity (millions)	Selected chronic condition								
		Arthritis, rheuma-tism	Heart condi-tions	Hyper-[2] tension	Diabetes	Asthma with or w/o hay fever	Impair-ments of back/ spine	Impair-ments of lower extrem-ity or hip	Visual impair-ments	Hearing impair-ments
All degrees of activity limitation		Percent of persons limited in activity because of specified condition								
Both sexes, all ages	**31.4**	**17.5**	**16.4**	**9.9**	**5.2**	**4.6**	**9.2**	**8.0**	**4.5**	**2.4**
Under 45 years	10.2	5.4	4.3	3.3	2.3	9.0	13.9	10.7	3.3	2.9
45-64	10.4	20.0	19.7	13.2	6.4	3.0	9.9	7.2	3.1	1.7
65 and over	10.8	26.5	24.5	13.1	6.7	1.8	4.0	6.4	6.9	2.6
Male, all ages	**15.5**	**11.0**	**18.0**	**7.7**	**4.3**	**4.4**	**9.1**	**9.0**	**4.6**	**2.8**
Female, all ages	**15.9**	**23.7**	**14.7**	**12.1**	**6.0**	**4.7**	**9.2**	**7.1**	**4.4**	**2.0**
Limited but not in major activity										
Both sexes, all ages	**7.6**	**12.8**	**8.5**	**6.8**	**3.6**	**7.0**	**8.9**	**11.7**	**4.8**	**3.8**
Under 45 years	3.9	4.4	3.4	2.8	1.9	10.7	11.1	14.9	3.8	3.4
45-64	2.2	16.5	13.1	11.2	5.3	3.9	9.2	9.7	3.2	3.7
65 and over	1.5	29.6	14.8	10.7	5.6	*2.1	2.6	6.2	9.9	4.9
Limited in amount or kind of major activity										
Both sexes, all ages	**15.7**	**19.9**	**15.5**	**10.6**	**5.2**	**4.7**	**10.7**	**6.6**	**3.5**	**1.9**
Under 45 years	5.1	6.6	4.1	3.5	2.9	9.2	16.5	7.4	2.9	2.7
45-64	5.4	22.6	18.6	14.3	6.4	3.1	10.6	6.1	2.5	1.1
65 and over	5.2	30.2	23.5	14.0	6.3	1.8	4.9	6.3	5.0	2.0
Unable to carry on major activity										
Both sexes, all ages	**8.1**	**17.1**	**25.5**	**11.5**	**6.5**	**2.0**	**6.5**	**7.4**	**6.1**	**2.0**
Under 45 years	1.2	3.3	8.5	4.2	*0.9	*2.5	11.6	10.9	3.4	*1.7
45-64	2.8	17.6	26.9	12.7	7.3	2.3	9.1	7.3	4.2	*1.2
65 and over	4.1	20.7	29.3	12.8	7.4	1.7	3.3	6.5	8.1	2.6

Covers civilian, noninstitutionalized population. Based on unpublished data from the National Health Interview Survey, National Center for Health Statistics, U.S. Department of Health and Human Services. (1) Ninth Revision of the International Classification of Diseases used for coding in 1979. (2) Includes all cases of hypertension regardless of other conditions. *Figure does not meet standards of reliability or precision.

Health Care Expenditures in the U.S.

Source: Health Care Financing Administration, U.S. Department of Health and Human Services

(billions of dollars)

	Total expendi-tures	Percentage of GNP	Total private	Direct payments	Private health insurance	Philanthropy and industry	Federal payments	State and local payments
1981	$286.6	9.8%	$164.1	$81.7	$73.2	$9.2	$83.9	$38.6
1980	249.0	9.5	143.6	72.1	63.6	7.8	71.1	34.3
1979	215.0	8.9	124.4	61.8	55.9	6.7	61.0	29.5
1978	189.3	8.8	109.8	54.1	49.7	6.0	53.9	25.7
1977	169.2	8.8	99.1	48.7	44.6	5.5	47.4	22.7
1976	149.7	8.7	86.7	43.0	38.1	5.0	42.6	20.4
1975	132.7	8.6	76.5	39.0	32.4	5.0	37.1	19.1
1974	116.4	8.1	69.3	36.4	27.8	5.1	30.4	16.7
1973	103.2	7.8	63.9	34.2	24.8	4.8	25.2	14.1
1972	93.5	7.9	58.1	31.0	22.3	4.7	22.9	12.5
1971	83.3	7.7	51.6	27.8	19.5	4.4	20.3	11.3
1970	74.7	7.5	46.9	26.0	17.1	3.8	17.7	10.1
1969	65.6	7.0	40.7	22.9	14.6	3.2	16.1	8.8
1968	58.2	6.7	36.1	20.5	12.9	2.7	14.1	8.0
1967	51.3	6.4	32.3	18.8	11.1	2.4	11.9	7.1
1966	46.1	6.1	32.5	19.5	10.6	1.5	7.4	6.1
1965	41.7	6.0	31.0	18.5	10.0	1.4	5.5	5.3
1960	26.9	5.3	20.3	13.0	NA[3]	NA[3]	3.0	3.6
1955	17.7	4.4	13.2	9.1	NA[4]	NA[4]	2.0	2.6
1950	12.7	4.4	9.2	7.1	NA[5]	NA[5]	1.6	1.8
1940	4.0	4.0	3.2	2.9	NA[6]	NA[6]	NA[1]	NA[1]
1929	3.6	3.5	3.2	2.8	NA[7]	NA[7]	NA[2]	NA[2]

(1) Total public spending estimated at $0.8 billion. (2) Total public spending estimated at $0.5 billion. (3) Total private spending estimated at $20.3 billion. (4) Total private spending estimated at $13.2 billion. (5) Total private spending estimated at $9.2 billion. (6) Total private spending estimated at $3.2 billion. (7) Total private spending estimated at $3.2 billion.

Suicide Rates

Source: National Center for Health Statistics, U.S. Department of Health and Human Services

(Rates per 100,000 population) (1978)

				White			All other		
Age group	**Total**	**Male**	**Female**	**Total**	**Male**	**Female**	**Total**	**Male**	**Female**
Total.	**12.5**	**19.0**	**6.3**	**13.4**	**20.2**	**6.9**	**6.9**	**11.1**	**3.1**
10-14 years . . .	0.8	1.2	0.4	0.9	1.4	0.4	0.5	0.6	0.5
15-19 years . . .	8.0	12.8	3.1	8.7	13.8	3.4	4.5	7.5	1.6
20-24 years . . .	16.9	27.4	6.4	17.5	28.1	6.7	13.8	23.3	5.0
25-29 years . . .	17.6	27.5	7.9	17.9	27.6	8.3	15.4	26.6	5.8
30-34 years . . .	15.7	23.4	8.3	16.2	23.8	8.7	12.2	20.2	5.5
35-39 years . . .	15.6	22.3	9.3	16.2	22.7	9.8	11.9	19.5	5.7
40-44 years . . .	16.1	21.4	11.0	17.2	22.4	12.2	8.4	14.2	3.7
45-49 years . . .	16.7	22.5	11.1	17.8	23.6	12.2	8.7	14.5	3.7
50-54 years . . .	17.6	24.3	11.3	18.7	25.8	12.1	8.4	11.8	5.6
55-59 years . . .	17.8	25.4	10.8	19.1	27.1	11.6	6.4	9.4	3.8
60-64 years . . .	18.6	30.1	8.4	19.7	32.0	8.8	7.6	11.9	3.9
65-69 years . . .	18.0	30.2	8.3	19.4	32.5	9.0	6.2	10.9	2.5
70-74 years . . .	20.0	37.2	7.4	21.1	39.6	7.8	7.5	13.1	3.0
75-79 years . . .	23.1	45.9	8.4	24.3	48.9	8.7	8.8	14.5	4.3
80-84 years . . .	21.8	50.6	6.0	23.2	54.4	6.3	6.9	13.2	2.9
85+ years . . .	18.6	48.3	5.1	20.0	53.1	5.2	6.3	10.3	4.1

U.S. Fires

Source: National Fire Protection Assn.

Fires attended by the public fire service (1981 estimates)

Civilian Fire Deaths and Injuries

	Deaths	Injuries
Residential (total)	5,540	20,375
One-and Two-Family Dwellings[1]	4,430	14,875
Apartments	970	4,250
Hotels and Motels	90	850
Other Residential.	50	400
Non Residential Structures[2].	220	5,325
Highway Vehicles	770	2,900
Other Vehicles[3]	70	500
All Other[4].	100	1,350
Total	**6,700**	**30,450**

Structure Fires by Property Use

	No. of fires	Property loss
Public assembly	28,500	$356,000,000
Educational.	19,500	184,000,000
Institutional	27,000	38,000,000
Residential	733,000	3,259,000,000
One-/2-family dwellings[5]	574,000	2,713,000,000
Apartments	137,000	415,000,000
Hotels, motels	11,500	99,000,000
Other residential	10,500	32,000,000
Stores and offices.	65,500	642,000,000
Industry, utility, defense[6] . .	49,000	775,000,000
Storage in structures[6]. . . .	62,000	616,000,000
Special structures	43,000	106,000,000
Total[6].	**1,027,500**	**$5,976,000,000**

(1) Includes mobile homes. (2) Includes public assembly, educational, institutional, stores and offices, industry, utility, storage, and special structure properties. (3) Includes trains, boats, ships, aircraft, farm vehicles and construction vehicles. (4) Includes properties outside with value, brush, rubbish, and other. (5) Includes mobile homes. (6) Since some fires were not reported to the NFPA, the results presented represent only a portion of the total U.S. fires.

Annual Fire Losses in the U.S.

Source: Insurance Services Office

Year	Loss	Year	Loss	Year	Loss	Year	Loss
1940	$285,878,697	1955.	$885,218,000	1970	$2,264,000,000	1979	$4,851,000,000
1945	484,274,000	1960	1,107,824,000	1975	3,560,000,000	1980	5,579,000,000
1950	648,909,000	1965	1,455,631,000	1978	4,008,000,000	1981 (est.). . .	5,625,000,000

Fire Fighters: Deaths and Injuries

Source: International Association of Fire Fighters

U.S. and Canadian professional fire fighters

	In line of duty		Occupational diseases[1]			In line of duty		Occupational diseases[1]	
Year	**Deaths**	**Injuries**	**Deaths**	**Retirement**	**Year**	**Deaths**	**Injuries**	**Deaths**	**Retirement**
1970	115	38,583	233	465	1977	79	55,562	84	828
1972	100	62,682	133	695	1978	74	46,668	61	391
1973	90	62,619	111	702	1979	70	45,070	77	348
1974	100	56,296	107	604	1980	63	46,260	98	498
1975	108	51,312	88	721					
1976	79	49,819	79	673					

(1) Includes: heart and cardiovascular diseases; lung and respiratory diseases; and other occupational diseases.

Active Federal and Non-Federal Doctors (M.D.s) by State

Source: AMA Physician Masterfile, 1980. Special Tabulations. Division of Survey and Data Resources, American Medical Association. Chicago, 1981. (Dec. 31, 1980).

	Total	Fed.	Non-fed.
Total physicians	**467,679**	**17,901**	**449,778**
Alabama	5,229	190	5,039
Alaska	627	118	509
Arizona	5,859	324	5,535
Arkansas	3,070	131	2,939
California	60,752	2,384	58,368
Canal Zone	33	21	12
Colorado	6,391	392	5,999
Connecticut	8,322	145	8,177
Delaware	1,047	46	1,001
Wash., D.C.	4,164	538	3,626
Florida	21,131	757	20,374
Georgia	8,549	489	8,060
Hawaii	2,265	245	2,020
Idaho	1,134	45	1,089
Illinois	22,228	488	21,740
Indiana	7,527	112	7,415
Iowa	3,917	70	3,847
Kansas	4,043	150	3,893
Kentucky	5,212	153	5,059
Louisiana	6,997	245	6,752
Maine	1,927	62	1,865
Maryland	13,282	1,537	11,745
Mass.	16,661	319	16,342
Michigan	15,571	224	15,347
Minnesota	8,297	147	8,150
Mississippi	3,015	218	2,797
Missouri	8,508	177	8,331
Montana	1,153	53	1,100
Nebraska	2,509	67	2,442
Nevada	1,233	62	1,171
N.H.	1,701	46	1,655
New Jersey	15,067	268	14,799
New Mexico	2,292	149	2,143
New York	49,978	873	49,105
North Carolina	9,742	388	9,354
North Dakota	956	37	919
Ohio	18,781	439	18,342
Oklahoma	4,194	163	4,031
Oregon	5,232	113	5,119
Pennsylvania	23,742	395	23,347
Puerto Rico	4,145	133	4,012
Rhode Island	2,163	61	2,102
South Carolina	4,607	245	4,362
South Dakota	884	75	809
Tennessee	7,686	226	7,460
Texas	24,058	1,487	22,571
Utah	2,570	78	2,492
Vermont	1,215	30	1,185
Virginia	10,476	794	9,682
Virgin Islands	92		92
Washington	8,450	529	7,921
West Virginia	2,857	112	2,745
Wisconsin	8,005	146	7,859
Wyoming	610	43	567
Pacific Islands	89	4	85
Outside U.S.	1,044	1,044	
Address unknown	6,390	114	6,276

U.S. Health Expenditures

Source: Health Care Financing Administration, U.S. Department of Health and Human Services

	1950	1960	1965	1970	1975	1979	1980	1981
Total (billions)	**$12.7**	**$26.9**	**$41.7**	**$74.7**	**$132.7**	**$215.0**	**$249.0**	**$286.6**
Type of expenditure								
Health services and supplies	11.7	25.2	38.2	69.3	124.3	204.5	237.1	273.5
Hospital care	3.9	9.1	13.9	27.8	52.1	86.1	100.4	118.0
Physician services	2.7	5.7	8.5	14.3	24.9	40.2	46.8	54.8
Dentist services	1.0	2.0	2.8	4.7	8.2	13.3	15.4	17.3
Nursing home care	.2	.5	2.1	4.7	10.1	17.6	20.6	24.2
Other professional services	.4	.9	1.0	1.6	2.6	4.7	5.6	6.4
Drugs and drug sundries	1.7	3.7	5.2	8.0	11.9	17.2	19.3	21.4
Eyeglasses and appliances	.5	.8	1.2	1.9	3.2	4.6	5.1	5.7
Expenses for prepayment and administration	.5	1.1	1.7	2.7	4.4	9.3	10.7	11.2
Gov't public health activities	.4	.4	.8	1.4	3.2	6.2	7.0	7.3
Other health services	.5	1.1	1.1	2.1	3.7	5.1	6.0	7.2
Research and medical facilities construction	1.0	1.7	3.5	5.4	8.4	10.5	11.8	13.1
Research	.1	.7	1.5	2.0	3.3	4.8	5.3	5.7
Construction	.8	1.0	2.0	3.4	5.1	5.7	6.5	7.5

Accidental Deaths by Age, Sex, and Type, 1978

Source: National Safety Council

	All types	Motor vehicle	Falls	Drowning	Fires, burns	Ingest. of food, object	Firearms	Poison (solid, liquid)	Poison by gas	% Male all types
All ages	**105,561**	**52,411**	**13,690**	**7,026**	**6,163**	**3,063**	**1,806**	**3,035**	**1,737**	**70**
Under 5	4,766	1,551	192	696	896	463	52	81	51	58
5 to 14	6,118	3,130	124	1,010	586	91	297	37	76	69
15 to 24	26,622	19,164	538	2,180	530	168	581	577	525	78
25 to 34	15,533	9,648	502	1,070	542	183	300	778	287	80
35 to 44	9,491	4,926	551	630	502	257	205	432	205	77
45 to 54	9,174	4,166	835	460	667	292	162	420	171	74
55 to 64	9,600	3,882	1,266	450	733	410	112	305	185	70
65 to 74	9,072	3,217	1,852	300	789	483	68	219	110	62
75 & over	15,185	2,727	7,830	230	918	716	29	186	127	47
Sex										
Male	73,881	38,139	7,181	5,875	3,786	1,765	1,566	1,800	1,260	
Female	31,680	14,272	6,509	1,151	2,377	1,298	240	1,235	477	
Percent male	70%	73%	52%	84%	61%	58%	87%	59%	73	

Canadian Motor Vehicle Traffic Deaths

Source: Statistics Canada

Province	Number 1980	Number 1981[1]
Newfoundland	86	59
Prince Edward Island	35	21
Nova Scotia	199	165
New Brunswick	214	188
Quebec	1,493	1,462
Ontario	1,508	1,438
Manitoba	176	198
Saskatchewan	265	262
Alberta	647	696
British Columbia	811	859
Yukon	12	14
Northwest Territories	14	8
Total	**5,460**	**5,370**

(1) Preliminary.

Federal Bureau of Investigation

The Federal Bureau of Investigation (FBI) is the investi- ive arm of the Department of Justice, and is located at Street and Pennsylvania Avenue, Northwest, Washing- , D.C. 20535. It investigates all violations of Federal law ept those specifically assigned to some other agency by islative action, such violations including counterfeiting, d internal revenue, postal, and customs violations. It also estigates espionage, sabotage, treason, and other matters ecting internal security, as well as kidnaping, transporta- n of stolen goods across state lines, and violations of the deral bank and atomic energy laws.

The FBI's Identification Division houses the largest fin- print repository in the world, with over 175 million fin- print cards on file. The file is utilized by law enforcement d other governmental authorities throughout the nation to ntify persons having arrest records. The file is also avail- e for humanitarian purposes, such as the identification of sons suffering from amnesia and the victims of major di- ters.

The FBI has 59 field divisions in the principal cities of the ntry. (Consult telephone directories for locations and one numbers.)

An applicant for the position of Special Agent of the FBI st be a citizen of the U.S., at least 23 and under 35 years , and a graduate of an accredited law school or of an ac- credited college or university with a major in accounting. In addition, applicants with a four-year degree from an accredited college or university with a major in other academic areas may qualify with three additional years of full-time work experience. Specialized need areas include languages, science, and financial analysis. Those appointed to the Special Agent position must complete an initial training period of 15 weeks at the FBI Academy, Quantico, Virginia.

William H. Webster, a Federal Appeals Court judge from St. Louis, was sworn in as FBI Director for a ten-year term on February 23, 1978. He replaced Clarence M. Kelley.

U.S. Crime Reports

Source: Federal Bureau of Investigation

Offense	Number 1980	% Change over[1] 1979	1976
Murder	23,044	+7.4	+22.7
Forcible Rape	82,088	+8.0	+44.7
Robbery	548,810	+17.5	+30.6
Aggravated Assault	654,957	+6.6	+33.4
Burglary	3,759,193	+13.9	+21.7
Larceny-theft	7,112,657	+8.1	+13.4
Motor Vehicle theft	1,114,651	+1.6	+16.4

[1]Percent by which the rate of crime per 100,000 population changed in 1980 as compared with 1979 and 1976.

Reported Crime, 1979-80, by Size of Place

Source: 1980 Uniform Crime Reports, Federal Bureau of Investigation

opulation group	Crime Index total	Violent crime	Property crime	Murder and non-negligent man-slaughter	Forcible rape	Robbery	Aggra-vated assault	Burglary	Larceny-theft
tal all agencies: 13,035 agencies; total population 215,162,695:									
1979	11,675,740	1,139,860	10,535,880	20,658	73,259	457,204	588,739	3,162,235	6,314,092
1980	12,780,394	1,269,614	11,510,780	22,190	79,281	538,785	629,358	3,603,666	6,829,433
Percent change	+9.5	+11.4	+9.3	+7.4	+8.2	+17.8	+6.9	+14.0	+8.2
tal cities: 9,014 cities; total population 144,107,954:									
1979	9,441,155	947,671	8,493,484	15,876	57,533	414,233	460,029	2,446,629	5,153,687
1980	10,308,831	1,060,724	9,248,107	17,116	61,747	487,976	493,885	2,779,293	5,560,636
Percent change	+9.2	+11.9	+8.9	+7.8	+7.3	+17.8	+7.4	+13.6	+7.9
cities, 250,000 and over; population 40,879,212:									
1979	3,441,042	506,775	2,934,267	9,432	29,302	274,298	193,743	946,609	1,557,083
1980	3,824,488	571,347	3,253,141	10,183	30,671	325,096	205,397	1,085,670	1,715,824
Percent change	+11.1	+12.7	+10.9	+8.0	+4.7	+18.5	+6.0	+14.7	+10.2
cities 250,000 to 499,999; population 11,873,167:									
1979	1,086,759	134,452	952,307	2,383	9,583	63,964	58,522	308,873	540,319
1980	1,215,069	152,815	1,062,254	2,601	10,438	75,225	64,551	357,469	601,957
Percent change	+11.8	+13.7	+11.5	+9.1	+8.9	+17.6	+10.3	+15.7	+11.4
1 cities, 100,000 to 249,999; population 16,182,068:									
1979	1,280,985	113,888	1,167,097	1,891	8,037	45,741	58,219	345,149	714,979
1980	1,403,069	129,167	1,273,902	2,005	9,055	53,215	64,892	395,005	771,949
Percent change	+9.5	+13.4	+9.2	+6.0	+12.7	+16.3	+11.5	+14.4	+8.0
0 cities, 50,000 to 99,999; population 19,167,339:									
1979	1,269,620	102,131	1,167,489	1,354	6,917	36,861	56,999	334,361	716,912
1980	1,363,105	115,169	1,247,936	1,448	7,386	43,529	62,806	376,289	756,324
Percent change	+7.4	+12.8	+6.9	+6.9	+6.8	+18.1	+10.2	+12.5	+5.5
8 cities, 25,000 to 49,999; population 21,244,209:									
1979	1,267,564	87,649	1,179,915	1,212	5,657	27,579	53,021	312,880	770,775
1980	1,371,668	95,730	1,275,938	1,286	6,232	31,847	56,365	355,451	824,832
Percent change	+8.2	+9.2	+8.1	+6.1	+10.2	+14.7	+6.3	+13.6	+7.0
58 cities, 10,000 to 24,999; population 24,386,270:									
1979	1,219,522	77,532	1,141,990	1,134	4,360	19,273	52,765	290,672	765,072
1980	1,303,574	84,861	1,218,713	1,229	4,816	22,473	56,343	323,950	811,657
Percent change	+6.9	+9.5	+6.7	+8.4	+10.5	+16.6	+6.8	+11.4	+6.1
91 cities under 10,000; population 22,248,856:									
1979	962,422	59,696	902,726	853	3,260	10,301	45,282	216,958	628,866
1980	1,042,927	64,450	978,477	965	3,587	11,816	48,082	242,928	680,050
Percent change	+8.4	+8.0	+8.4	+13.1	+10.0	+14.7	+6.2	+12.0	+8.1
burban area 5,473 agencies; population 80,889,416:									
1979	3,663,684	268,391	3,395,293	4,251	19,152	75,029	169,959	984,172	2,121,169
1980	3,971,152	296,384	3,674,768	4,701	21,341	89,043	181,299	1,130,075	2,255,742
Percent change	+8.4	+10.4	+8.2	+10.6	+11.4	+18.7	+6.7	+14.8	+6.3
ral area 2,952 agencies; population 31,813,942:									
1979	654,454	54,868	599,586	2,153	4,451	6,399	41,865	232,236	325,840
1980	726,588	56,947	669,641	2,262	4,890	6,952	42,843	262,234	365,118
Percent change	+11.0	+3.8	+11.7	+5.1	+9.9	+8.6	+2.3	+12.9	+12.1

Reported Crime in Metropolitan Areas, 1980

Source: Compiled by the World Almanac based on 1980 Uniform Crime Reports, F.B.I.

The 25 Standard Metropolitan Statistical Areas listed below are those that appear most frequently among the top 30 citie in per capita reported crime rate for each of 7 kinds of major crime: the 5 listed below plus aggravated assault and auto theft.

The rates are for reported crimes only; they are not an accurate index of crimes actually committed. In many metropolita areas an unknown number of crimes go unreported by victims. This is especially true of the crimes of rape, burglary, and lar ceny. Additionally, figures are often distorted for political reasons.

The number in parentheses following the city name indicates the number of categories (including auto theft and aggravate assault) in which the city appears among the top 30.

The numbers in parentheses following crime rate figures give that city's rank in that category of crime. If no number ap pears, the city is not among the top 30 in that category. The cities are listed in order of the diversity and violence of crimina activity.

Metropolitan areas	Total[1]	Violent[2]	Property[3]	Murder[4]	Rape	Robbery	Burglary	Larceny
Miami, Fla. (7)	11,581.8 (1)	1,919.5 (1)	9,662.3 (2)	32.7 (1)	67.0 (17)	995.1 (2)	3,282.5 (2)	5,452.1 (5
Atlantic City, N.J. (4)	11,481.3 (16)	858.3 (21)	10,622.9 (1)	9.5	59.2	424.1 (13)	2,548.5 (16)	7,014.4 (1
Las Vegas, Nev. (6)	10,292.3 (4)	1,148.2 (5)	9,144.2 (4)	23.4 (3)	76.2 (5)	630.7 (3)	3,608.9 (1)	4,712.3 (27
W. Palm Beach-Boca Raton, Fla. (3)	9,823.9 (22)	1,068.2 (6)	8,755.7 (5)	10.7	56.3	299.7	2,929.0 (4)	5,264.1 (10
Orlando, Fla. (4)	9,511.5 (10)	1,021.7 (7)	8,489.8 (8)	9.8	76.0 (6)	265.5	3,191.4 (3)	4,858.6 (19
Sacramento, Cal. (4)	9,373.1 (17)	709.2	8,663.9 (6)	9.0	52.5	302.4 (30)	2,559.7 (15)	5,410.6 (7
Ft. Lauderdale, Fla. (5)	9,345.4 (8)	991.0 (10)	8,354.4 (9)	17.4 (20)	54.0	471.5 (10)	2,828.8 (5)	4,867.5 (18
Daytona Beach, Fla. (3)	9,106.9 (23)	805.8	8,301.1 (10)	7.6	57.3	214.9	2,656.4 (9)	5,207.3 (11
Tallahassee, Fla. (4)	9,072.7 (11)	820.6 (29)	8,252.1 (11)	8.3	93.6 (3)	179.5	2,571.4 (14)	5,335.6 (9
Bakersfield, Cal. (5)	9,001.3 (6)	818.3 (30)	8,183.0 (13)	20.9 (7)	60.3 (29)	266.5	2,589.3 (12)	4,918.3 (15
New York, N.Y. (5)	8,952.8 (7)	1,710.6 (2)	7,242.3 (25)	21.0 (6)	43.3	1,139.7 (1)	2,660.7 (8)	3,369.2
Stockton, Cal. (4)	8,617.3 (12)	739.1	7,878.2 (14)	18.1 (16)	47.8	323.3 (27)	2,511.3 (17)	4,731.2 (24
Fresno, Cal. (6)	8,564.8 (2)	924.6 (14)	7,640.2 (16)	20.1 (9)	71.4 (12)	337.9 (23)	2,585.0 (13)	4,372.7
San Francisco-Oakland, Cal. (3)	8,540.6 (19)	1,004.6 (8)	7,536.0 (19)	11.7	64.0 (23)	520.6 (7)	2,267.5	4,571.2
Los Angeles-Long Beach, Cal. (6)	8,418.7 (3)	1,339.6 (3)	7,091.1 (30)	23.3 (4)	75.4 (8)	628.0 (4)	2,602.5 (11)	3,371.7
Savannah, Ga. (5)	8,387.7 (5)	911.8 (16)	7,475.8 (20)	16.6 (25)	99.3 (1)	303.8 (29)	2,197.2	4,916.2 (16
Denver-Boulder, Col. (3)	8,356.9 (20)	640.3	7,716.6 (15)	9.4	64.9 (17)	229.7	2,441.7 (22)	4,703.3 (29
Reno, Nev. (4)	8,286.0 (13)	656.6	7,629.3 (17)	12.9	75.3 (7)	323.4 (26)	2,371.7 (26)	4,692.3 (30
Dallas-Ft. Worth, Tex. (2)	8,270.7 (24)	751.9	7,518.8	18.1 (16)	62.8 (24)	289.4	2,335.7	4,600.6
New Orleans, La. (4)	7,890.2 (9)	986.1 (11)	6,904.1	22.3 (5)	73.8 (11)	468.7 (11)	2,177.0	2,977.4
Gainesville, Fla. (4)	NA	956.1 (12)	9,297.5 (3)	8.9	75.1	184.9 (9)	2,722.9 (6)	6,170.6 (2
Detroit, Mich. (3)	7,582.3 (21)	859.6 (20)	6,722.8	16.1 (28)	53.9	408.7 (16)	1,981.4	3,774.0
Lubbock, Tex. (2)	7,238.7 (25)	633.7	6,605.1	17.0 (23)	64.9 (17)	109.4	2,012.7	4,187.4
Memphis, Tenn. (3)	6,492.3 (18)	851.5 (23)	5,640.8	19.5 (13)	95.2 (2)	474.4 (9)	2,334.9	2,736.1
Houston, Tex. (4)	6,900.1 (15)	718.8	6,181.3	27.6 (2)	65.9 (18)	426.9 (12)	2,319.5	2,652.6

(1) Other metro areas among the top 30 in total reported crime: Phoenix (8); Tucson (13); Riverside-San Bernardino-Ontario, Cal. (22); Columbia, S.C. (23); Wilmington, N.C. (24); Tampa-St. Petersburg, Fla. (25); Great Falls, Mont. (26); Des Moines, Iowa (27); Flint, Mich. (29), and Seattle, Wash. (30).

(2) Violent crime includes murder and non-negligent manslaughter, forcible rape, robbery, and aggravated assault. Other metro areas in the top 30 in violent crime are: Baltimore, Md. (4); Newark, N.J. (9); Columbia, S.C. (13); Monroe, La. (15); Biloxi-Gulfport, Miss. (17); Lakeland-Winter Haven, Fla. (18); Kansas City-Mo.-Kan. (19); Tampa-St. Petersburg, Fla. (22); Atlanta, Ga. (24); Flint, Mich. (25); Mobile, Ala. (26); Wichita Falls, Tex. (27); Saginaw, Mich. (28).

(3) Property crime includes burglary, larceny, and auto theft. Other metro areas in the top 30 are: Phoeniz, Ariz. (7); Tucson, Ariz. (12); Des Moines, Ia. (18); Riverside-San Bernardino-Ontario, Cal. (22); Wilmington, N.C. (22); Seattle, Wash. (23); Honolulu, Ha. (24); Tampa-St. Petersburg, Fla. (26); Madison, Wis. (27); Yakima, Wash. (28); Springfield, Mo. (29).

(4) Of the top 30 cities in murder, all but 4 are in the South (13); or in Texas (9), or in California (4).

NA = Figure not available

Crime Rates by State

Source: 1980 Uniform Crime Reports, Federal Bureau of Investigation

(Rates per 100,000 population)

State	Total	Violent	Property	Murder	Rape	Robbery	Assault	Burglary	Larceny	Aut thef
Alabama	4,933.6	448.5	4,485.1	13.2	30.0	132.1	273.2	1,526.7	2,642.2	316.
Alaska	6,210.0	479.6	5,730.5	9.7	62.5	90.0	317.4	1,385.8	3,727.7	617.
Arizona	8,170.8	650.9	7,519.9	10.3	45.2	193.6	401.8	2,155.4	4,891.2	473.
Arkansas	3,811.1	335.2	3,475.9	9.2	26.7	80.9	218.4	1,119.0	2,169.8	187.
California	7,833.1	893.6	6,939.5	14.5	58.2	384.2	436.7	2,316.5	3,880.0	742.
Colorado	7,333.5	528.6	6,804.9	6.9	52.5	160.1	309.2	2,030.8	4,325.8	448.
Connecticut	5,881.7	412.5	5,469.2	4.7	21.6	218.0	168.1	1,700.6	3,089.6	678.
Delaware	6,776.6	474.8	6,301.8	6.9	24.2	137.0	306.7	1,630.5	4,216.2	455.
Florida	8,402.0	983.5	7,418.4	14.5	56.9	355.5	556.6	2,506.8	4,434.2	477.
Georgia	5,603.7	555.3	5,048.3	13.8	44.3	197.6	299.7	1,699.2	2,976.6	372.
Hawaii	7,482.3	299.5	7,182.8	8.7	34.7	190.2	65.8	1,847.5	4,732.2	612.
Idaho	4,782.2	313.4	4,468.8	3.1	22.4	46.8	241.1	1,238.9	2,993.0	236.
Illinois	5,275.3	494.3	4,781.0	10.6	26.9	217.0	239.8	1,242.7	3,039.3	498.
Indiana	4,930.4	377.8	4,552.5	8.9	33.1	141.4	194.5	1,313.3	2,807.1	432.
Iowa	4,746.7	200.4	4,546.4	2.2	14.3	54.9	129.0	1,079.5	3,219.1	247.
Kansas	5,378.8	389.3	4,989.5	6.9	31.5	113.1	237.8	1,521.4	3,196.4	271.
Kentucky	3,433.7	266.7	3,167.1	8.8	19.2	95.2	143.5	1,040.8	1,875.5	250.
Louisiana	5,453.7	665.0	4,788.8	15.7	44.5	197.0	407.8	1,523.9	2,888.4	376.
Maine	4,367.6	193.4	4,174.2	2.8	12.9	30.8	146.8	1,182.8	2,772.3	219.

State	Total	Violent	Property	Murder	Rape	Robbery	Assault	Burglary	Larceny	Auto theft
Maryland	6,630.1	852.4	5,777.7	9.5	40.1	392.7	410.1	1,698.0	3,629.2	450.5
Massachusetts . . .	6,079.1	601.3	5,477.8	4.1	27.3	235.5	334.4	1,740.4	2,685.8	1,051.6
Michigan	6,675.9	639.5	6,036.4	10.2	46.6	244.0	338.6	1,741.3	3,710.2	584.9
Minnesota.	4,799.5	227.8	4,571.7	2.6	23.2	99.1	102.9	1,246.0	3,029.9	295.9
Mississippi	3,417.2	341.9	3,075.2	14.5	24.6	81.0	221.7	1,179.1	1,717.8	178.4
Missouri.	5,433.1	554.5	4,878.6	11.1	32.6	223.6	287.2	1,668.9	2,795.1	414.6
Montana	5,024.5	222.6	4,801.9	4.0	21.0	34.0	163.6	950.6	3,529.6	321.7
Nebraska	4,305.2	224.6	4,080.6	4.4	23.2	82.2	114.7	915.4	2,921.6	243.6
Nevada	8,854.0	912.6	7,941.4	20.0	67.2	460.6	364.9	2,906.7	4,356.3	678.4
New Hampshire . .	4,679.6	179.8	4,499.8	2.5	17.3	42.0	118.0	1,312.9	2,877.0	309.9
New Jersey.	6,401.3	604.4	5,797.0	6.9	30.7	303.7	263.0	1,878.2	3,189.3	729.5
New Mexico	5,979.0	615.0	5,364.1	13.1	43.3	127.9	430.7	1,492.5	3,521.0	350.6
New York.	6,911.6	1,029.5	5,882.0	12.7	30.9	641.3	344.6	2,061.6	3,064.4	759.9
North Carolina . . .	4,640.5	455.0	4,185.5	10.6	22.7	82.3	339.4	1,422.9	2,546.4	216.1
North Dakota. . . .	2,963.7	54.0	2,909.1	1.2	9.5	7.7	35.6	488.3	2,242.2	179.2
Ohio.	5,431.4	498.3	4,933.1	8.1	34.3	223.7	232.2	1,466.3	3,040.1	426.7
Oklahoma	5,052.9	419.5	4,633.4	10.0	36.3	104.9	268.4	1,692.7	2,520.6	420.2
Oregon	6,686.9	490.4	6,196.5	5.1	41.5	152.4	291.4	1,748.4	4,087.8	360.3
Pennsylvania	3,736.3	363.9	3,372.4	6.8	23.0	177.9	156.1	1,038.5	1,915.5	418.3
Rhode Island	5,932.6	408.5	5,524.1	4.4	17.1	118.6	168.3	1,716.3	2,964.3	843.6
South Carolina . . .	5,439.2	660.0	4,779.2	11.4	37.5	118.1	493.0	1,670.0	2,803.2	306.0
South Dakota. . . .	3,243.2	126.8	3,116.3	.7	12.5	20.1	93.6	692.5	2,255.2	168.6
Tennessee	4,497.9	458.1	4,039.8	10.8	37.4	180.6	229.4	1,501.5	2,175.2	363.1
Texas	6,143.0	550.3	5,592.7	16.9	47.3	208.5	277.6	1,853.2	3,181.4	558.1
Utah.	5,880.6	303.3	5,577.3	3.8	27.7	80.2	191.7	1,321.9	3,931.8	323.6
Vermont.	4,988.5	178.8	4,809.7	2.2	29.1	38.9	108.5	1,526.7	2,988.1	294.9
Virginia	4,620.0	307.2	4,312.6	8.6	27.4	120.1	151.1	1,202.6	2,882.3	227.9
Washington.	6,915.0	464.3	6,450.7	5.5	52.7	135.1	271.0	1,862.2	4,192.9	395.6
West Virginia	2,551.6	183.7	2,367.9	7.1	15.8	48.5	112.2	738.5	1,429.8	199.7
Wisconsin.	4,798.6	182.6	4,616.8	2.9	14.9	70.7	94.1	1,079.4	3,291.4	245.2
Wyoming	4,986.4	392.6	4,593.8	6.2	28.6	44.4	313.5	903.7	3,344.9	345.2

Total Arrest Trends by Sex, 1980

Source: 1980 Uniform Crime Reports, Federal Bureau of Investigation

	Males				Females			
	Total		Under 18		Total		Under 18	
	1980	Percent change 1979-80	1980	Percent change 1979-80	1980	Percent change 1979-80	1980	Percent change 1979-80
TOTAL[1]	**7,982,339**	**+1.4**	**1,576,706**	**−6.2**	**1,501,619**	**+2.3**	**408,256**	**−5.4**
Murder and nonnegligent manslaughter.	15,814	+4.0	1,561	+5.8	2,298	−5.2	136	−20.5
Forcible rape	28,140	+.3	4,175	−3.2	254	+18.7	76	+28.8
Robbery	127,372	+5.8	38,641	+.6	9,892	+3.8	2,870	+2.4
Aggravated assault.	222,835	+.8	31,607	−5.2	31,582	+.7	5,659	−1.1
Burglary	441,905	+2.6	198,321	−5.5	29,154	−.2	13,514	−7.8
Larceny-theft	782,710	+4.4	306,450	−4.0	320,003	−2.1	108,024	−8.4
Motor vehicle theft	115,857	−10.7	51,450	−18.2	10,993	−13.5	5,790	−19.3
Arson	15,684	−1.5	7,146	−11.0	2,154	+5.2	828	−3.8
Violent crime[1]	394,161	+2.4	75,984	−2.0	44,026	+1.1	8,741	−.2
Property crime[1]	1,356,156	+2.2	563,367	−6.1	362,304	−2.3	128,156	−8.9
Crime Index total[1].	1,750,317	+2.3	639,351	−5.6	406,330	−1.9	136,897	−8.4
Other assaults	385,537	+1.6	63,221	−4.5	62,363	+3.9	16,924	(2)
Forgery and counterfeiting. . .	49,211	+3.1	6,404	−7.4	22,285	+4.3	2,769	−3.7
Fraud.	151,785	+6.9	5,262	−16.0	107,545	+12.1	2,108	−6.6
Embezzlement	5,573	−4.4	643	−15.6	2,217	+11.4	242	+5.7
Stolen property; buying, receiving, possessing	101,414	+7.9	31,007	−2.5	11,924	+6.0	3,013	−3.8
Vandalism	209,330	−2.7	104,318	−11.4	19,849	+.5	9,062	−9.8
Weapons, carrying, possessing	142,318	+2.1	22,093	−4.6	11,009	+.6	1,341	−7.9
Prost., commercialized vice . .	23,971	−8.0	809	−31.2	57,948	+3.5	2,090	−1.3
Sex offenses (except forcible rape and prostitution)	58,059	+1.5	10,185	−2.8	4,628	−3.7	767	−7.0
Drug abuse violations	451,682	+2.1	82,302	−12.8	70,107	+1.7	16,323	−11.8
Gambling	41,726	−10.4	1,649	−19.8	4,711	−3.4	82	−5.7
Offenses against family and children	44,007	−2.9	1,279	−18.8	5,150	+2.5	722	−21.6
Driving under the influence . .	1,148,856	+3.8	26,126	−1.6	119,616	+13.1	3,010	+3.8
Liquor laws	354,728	+5.6	106,989	−2.3	62,685	+8.7	31,131	+2.8
Drunkenness	962,092	−2.1	36,248	−6.3	79,734	+2.3	5,831	−5.0
Disorderly conduct	601,023	+2.0	97,006	−5.8	110,691	+3.1	20,893	−1.5
Vagrancy	24,911	−8.8	3,172	−21.2	4,103	−49.4	590	−29.2
All other offenses (except traffic)	1,366,654	+.8	229,497	−3.1	240,921	+3.9	56,658	−.9

(1) Totals will not add due to deletion of several minor arrest categories. (2) Less than one-tenth of 1 percent.

Police Roster

Source: Uniform Crime Reports

Police officers and civilian employees in large cities as of Oct. 31, 1980

City	Officer	Civilian	City	Officer	Civilian	City	Officer	Civilian
Anchorage, Alas. . .	252	82	Indianapolis, Ind. . .	969	336	Phoenix, Ariz.	1,622	640
Atlanta, Ga.	188	18	Jacksonville, Fla. . .	951	606	Pittsburgh, Pa. . . .	1,400	110
Baltimore, Md. . . .	3,171	555	Kansas City, Mo. . .	1,183	485	Portland, Ore.. . . .	654	199
Birmingham, Ala. . .	678	173	Little Rock, Ark.. . .	305	72	Rochester, N.Y.. . .	643	237
Boston, Mass.. . . .	2,108	420	Los Angeles, Cal.. .	6,587	2,562	Sacramento, Cal.. .	506	200
Bridgeport, Conn.. .	374	20	Louisville, Ky.	733	219	St. Louis, Mo.	1,950	591
Buffalo, N.Y..	1,083	136	Memphis, Tenn.. . .	1,210	451	St. Petersburg, Fla..	386	188
Chicago, Ill.	12,392	1,250	Miami, Fla..	688	306	San Antonio, Tex.. .	1,137	227
Cincinnati, Oh. . . .	997	160	Milwaukee, Wis.. . .	2,039	247	San Diego, Cal.. . .	1,380	380
Cleveland, Oh. . . .	1,877	147	Minneapolis, Minn. .	713	93	San Francisco, Cal.	63	14
Columbus, Oh. . . .	968	317	Newark, N.J.	930	259	San Jose, Cal. . . .	796	209
Dallas, Tex.	1,990	588	New Orleans, La.. .	1,397	601	Santa Ana, Cal.. . .	288	132
Denver, Col..	1,393	297	New York, N.Y. . . .	22,590	4,349	Seattle, Wash. . . .	1,036	352
Detroit, Mich.	4,166	590	Norfolk, Va.	581	121	Stockton, Cal.. . . .	235	117
Ft. Worth, Tex. . . .	692	189	Oakland, Cal.	602	271	Tampa, Fla.	520	171
Fresno, Cal..	348	120	Oklahoma City, Okl.	725	190	Toledo, Oh.	553	56
Hartford, Conn.. . .	402	66	Omaha, Neb.	540	147	Tucson, Ariz.	571	202
Honolulu, Ha.	1,484	295	Pasadena, Cal. . . .	181	103	Washington, D.C.. .	3,652	531
Houston, Tex..	3,070	831	Philadelphia, Pa. . .	7,454	863	Wichita, Kan.	397	144

1,247 Law Enforcement Officers Killed 1970-1980

Responding to disturbance calls.	193	Handling, transporting, custody of prisoners	53
Burglaries in progress or pursuing suspect.	81	Investigating suspicious persons and circumstances	109
Robberies in progress or pursuing suspect	230	Ambush	119
Attempting other arrests	262	Handling mentally deranged.	34
Civil disorders	5	Traffic pursuits and stops	161

Geographically for the period of 1970-1980 the 1,247 officers who were slain in the line of duty were divided in this fashion: Northeast 184; North Central 260; South 548; and West 211. Another 44 officers were killed in outlying territories.

Canada: Criminal Offenses and Crime Rate

Source: Statistics Canada; Canadian Centre for Justice Statistics

	1980		1981[1]		Percent change in rate
	Actual offenses	Rate[2]	Actual offenses	Rate[2]	
Total criminal code	**2,045,399**	**8,553.0**	**2,168,201**	**8,963.4**	**4.8**
Total homicide	**593**	**2.4**	**647**	**2.6**	**8.3**
Murder, 1st degree	225	0.9	272	1.1	22.2
Murder, 2nd degree.	268	1.1	327	1.3	18.2
Manslaughter	97	0.4	44	0.1	25.0
Infanticide	3	—	4	—	—
Attempted murder	**792**	**3.3**	**900**	**3.7**	**12.1**
Total Sexual offenses.	**12,787**	**53.4**	**13,313**	**55.0**	**3.0**
Rape	2,315	9.6	2,559	10.5	9.4
Indecent assaults on female.	6,535	27.3	6,723	27.7	1.5
Indecent assaults on male	1,314	5.4	1,268	5.2	−3.7
Other sexual offenses	2,623	10.9	2,763	11.4	4.6
Total crimes of violence	**155,864**	**651.7**	**162,228**	**670.6**	**2.9**
Assaults (not indecent).	117,111	489.7	121,076	500.5	2.2
Robbery	24,581	102.7	26,292	108.6	5.7
Total property crimes.	**1,334,619**	**5,580.8**	**1,429,520**	**5,909.6**	**5.9**
Breaking & entering.	349,694	1,462.2	367,250	1,518.2	3.8
Theft, motor vehicle.	93,928	392.7	96,229	397.8	1.3
Theft, over $200.	224,595	939.1	266,288	1,100.8	17.2
Theft, $200 and under	539,490	2,255.9	561,827	23,222.6	3.0
Having stolen goods	24,657	103.1	25,599	105.8	2.6
Fraud.	102,255	427.5	112,327	464.3	8.6
Total other crimes	**554,916**	**2,320.4**	**576,453**	**2,383.0**	**2.7**
Prostitution.	1,504	6.2	1,551	6.4	3.2
Gaming and betting.	2,695	11.2	2,527	10.4	−7.1
Offensive weapons	15,938	66.6	17,706	73.1	9.8
Other criminal code.	534,779	2,236.2	554,669	2,293.0	2.5
Federal statutes-drugs	74,196	310.3	75,104	310.7	0.1
Federal statutes-other[3].	45,589	190.6	45,320	187.3	−1.7
Provincial statutes[3]	452,812	1,893.4	481,232	1,989.4	5.1
Municipal by-laws[3]	74,163	310.1	80,202	331.5	6.9
Total all offenses.	**2,692,159**	**11,257.4**	**2,850,059**	**11,782.2**	**4.7**

(1) Preliminary data, subject to revision. (2) Rate per 100,000 population. (3) Excluding traffic offenses.

State and Federal Prison Population; Death Penalty

As of Dec. 31, 1981

Source: Bureau of Justice Statistics, U.S. Justice Department

		Maximum length of sentence		Death penalty		
	Prisoners	More than a year	Year or less (and unsentenced)	Under sentence of death	Executions	Death penalty
Federal institutions	28,133	22,169	5,964	0	0	Yes
State institutions	340,876	330,307	10,569	838	1	...
Male	353,482	338,160	15,314	827	1	...
Female	15,527	14,308	1,219	11	0	...
Alabama	7,441	7,300	141	16	0	Yes
Alaska	1,019	708	311	0	0	No
Arizona	5,211e	5,206	5	38	0	Yes
Arkansas	3,283	3,251	32	23	0	Yes
California	29,267	27,977	1,290	83	0	Yes
Colorado	2,772	2,770	2	1	0	Yes
Connecticut	4,647	2,995	1,652	0	0	Yes
Delaware	1,716	1,282	434	4	0	Yes
Dist. of Columbia	3,543	2,932	611	0	0	No
Florida	23,238	23,006	672	161	1	Yes
Georgia	14,030	13,693	337	91	0	Yes
Hawaii	1,202	752	450	0	0	No
Idaho	994	994	0	2	0	Yes
Illinois	13,499	13,094	405	41	0	Yes
Indiana	8,054	7,559	495	10	0	Yes
Iowa	2,713	2,713	0	0	0	No
Kansas	2,812	2,812	0	0	0	No
Kentucky	3,993	3,993	0	9	0	Yes
Louisiana	9,405	9,405	0	10	0	Yes
Maine	866	734	132	0	0	No
Maryland	9,335e	8,912	423	8	0	Yes
Massachusetts	3,779	NA	NA	0	0	Yes
Michigan	14,992	14,992	0	0	0	No
Minnesota	2,024	2,024	0	0	0	No
Mississippi	4,624	4,484	140	27	0	Yes
Missouri	6,154	6,154	0	14	0	Yes
Montana	798	798	0	3	0	Yes
Nebraska	1,633	1,522	111	12	0	Yes
Nevada	2,141	2,141	0	12	1	Yes
New Hampshire	384	384	0	0	0	Yes
New Jersey	6,958	6,691	267	0	0	No
New Mexico	1,524	1,423	101	3	0	Yes
New York	25,658	24,006	1,652	0	0	Yes
North Carolina	15,791	14,854	937	17	0	Yes
North Dakota	308	308	0	0	0	No
Ohio	14,968	14,968	0	0	0	No
Oklahoma	5,248	5,248	0	36	0	Yes
Oregon	3,282	3,279	3	0	0	No
Pennsylvania	9,357	9,277	80	11	0	Yes
Rhode Island	962	962	NA	0	0	No
South Carolina	8,527	7,998	529	21	0	Yes
South Dakota	693	662	31	0	0	Yes
Tennessee	7,883	7,883	0	21	0	Yes
Texas	31,502	31,502	0	144	0	Yes
Utah	1,140	1,126	14	3	0	Yes
Vermont	534	396	138	0	0	Yes
Virginia	9,388	9,013	375	17	0	Yes
Washington	5,336	5,336	0	0	0	Yes
West Virginia	1,312	1,312	0	0	0	No
Wisconsin	4,378	4,378	0	0	0	No
Wyoming	558	558	0	0	0	No

e-estimate, NA-figure not available

U.S. Crime Rate Up 9% in 1980

An estimated 13,295,399 Crime Index offenses, 9 percent more than during 1979, were reported to law enforcement agencies in 1980. Collectively, violent crimes were up 18 percent and property crimes rose 9 percent. All offenses increased in volume. Among the violent crimes, murder was up 7 percent; rape, 8 percent; robbery, 18 percent; and aggravated assault, 7 percent. Among property crimes, burglary increased 14 percent; larceny, 8 percent; and auto theft, 2 percent.

Crime Index Trends by Geographic Region 1980 over 1979

(rates per 100,000 population)

Region	Total	Violent	Property	Murder	Rape	Robbery	Assault	Burglary	Larceny	Auto theft
Total	+6.9	+8.5	+6.7	+5.2	+5.5	+14.8	+4.1	+11.3	+5.6	−.8
Northeast	+7.8	+11.9	+7.3	+7.9	+4.2	+19.3	+3.8	+14.1	+4.7	+2.7
North Central	+7.0	+5.9	+7.1	+2.6	+2.7	+10.8	+2.8	+12.4	+6.5	−4.0
South	+7.1	+7.5	+7.1	+.8	+6.4	+14.4	+4.0	+11.5	+5.7	−.1
West	+5.0	+7.8	+4.7	+10.8	+5.7	+13.4	+4.3	+6.6	+4.7	−1.8

POSTAL INFORMATION

U.S. Postal Service

The Postal Reorganization Act, creating a government-owned postal service under the executive branch and replacing the old Post Office Department, was signed into law by President Nixon on Aug. 12, 1970. The service officially came into being on July 1, 1971.

The new U.S. Postal Service is governed by an 11-man Board of Governors. Nine members are appointed to 9-year terms by the president with Senate approval. These 9, in turn, choose a postmaster general, who is no longer a member of the president's cabinet. The board and the new postmaster general choose the 11th member, who serves as deputy postmaster general. An independent Postal Rate Commission of 5 members, appointed by the president, recommends postal rates to the governors for their approval.

The first postmaster general under the new system was Winton M. Blount. He resigned Oct. 29, 1971, and was replaced by his deputy, E. T. Klassen, Dec. 7, 1971. Benjamin F. Bailar succeeded him Feb. 16, 1975, and was succeeded by William F. Bolger on March 15, 1978.

As of Oct. 1, 1981, there was a total of 30,242 post offices throughout the U.S. and possessions.

U.S. Domestic Rates (in effect Nov. 1, 1981)

Domestic includes the U.S., territories and possessions, APO and FPO.

First Class

Letters written, and matter sealed against inspection, 20¢ for 1st oz. or fraction, 17¢ for each additional oz. or fraction.

U.S. Postal cards; single 13¢; double 26¢; private postcards, same.

First class includes written matter, namely letters, postal cards, postcards (private mailing cards) and all other matter wholly or partly in writing, whether sealed or unsealed, except manuscripts for books, periodical articles and music, manuscript copy accompanying proofsheets or corrected proofsheets of the same and the writing authorized by law on matter of other classes. Also matter sealed or closed against inspection, bills and statements of accounts.

Greeting Cards

May be sent first class or single piece third class.

Express Mail

Express Mail Service is available for any mailable article up to 70 pounds, and guarantees delivery between major U.S. cities or your money back. Articles received by the acceptance time authorized by the postmaster at a postal facility offering Express Mail will be delivered by 3 p.m. the next day or, if you prefer, your shipment can be picked up as early as 10 a.m. the next business day. Rates include insurance, Shipment Receipt, and Record of Delivery at the destination post office.

Consult Postmaster for other Express Mail Services and rates. (The Postal Service will refund, upon application to originating office, the postage for any Express Mail shipments not meeting the service standard except for those delayed by strike or work stoppage.)

Second Class

Single copy mailings by general public 19¢ for first ounce, 35¢ for over 1 to 2 ozs., 45¢ for over 2 to 3 ozs. and 10¢ for each additional ounce up to 8 ozs. Each additional 2 ozs. over 8 ozs., add 10¢.

Third Class

Third class (limit up to but not including 16 ounces): Mailable matter not in 1st and 2d classes.

Single mailing: Greeting cards (sealed or unsealed), small parcels, printed matter, booklets and catalogs, 20¢ the first ounce, 37¢ for over 1 to 2 ozs., 54¢ for over 2 to 3 ozs., 71¢ for over 3 to 4 ozs., 85¢ for over 4 to 6 ozs., 95¢ for over 6 to 8 ozs., $1.05 for over 8 to 10 ozs., $1.15 for over 10 to 12 ozs., $1.25 for over 12 to 14 ozs., $1.35 for over 14 but less than 16 ozs.

Bulk material: books, catalogs of 24 pages or more, seeds, cuttings, bulbs, roots, scions, and plants. 45¢ per pound, 10.9¢ minimum per piece.

Other matter: newsletters, shopper's guides, advertising circulars, 45¢ per pound, 10.9¢ minimum per piece. Separate rates for some nonprofit organizations. Bulk mailing fee, $40 per calendar year. Apply to postmaster for permit. One-time fee for permit imprint, $40.

Parcel Post—Fourth Class

Fourth class or parcel post (16 ounces and over): merchandise, printed matter, etc., may be sealed, subject to inspection.

On parcels weighing less than 15 lbs. and measuring more than 84 inches, but not more than 100 inches in length and girth combined, the minimum postal charge shall be the zone charge applicable to a 15-pound parcel.

Priority Mail

First class mail of more than 12 ounces can be sent "Priority Mail (Heavy Pieces)" service. The most expeditious handling and transportation available will be used for fastest delivery.

Forwarding Addresses

The mailer, in order to obtain a forwarding address, must endorse the envelope or cover "Address Correction Requested." The destination post office then will determine whether a forwarding address has been left on file and provide it for a fee of 25¢.

Priority Mail

Packages weighing up to 70 pounds and exceeding 100 inches in length and girth combined, including written and other material of the first class, whether sealed or unsealed, fractions of a pound being charged as a full pound, except in the 1 to 5 pound weight category where half-pound weight increments apply.

Rates according to zone apply between the U.S. and Puerto Rico and Virgin Islands.

Parcels weighing less than 15 pounds, measuring over 84 inches but not exceeding 100 inches in length and girth combined are chargeable with a minimum rate equal to that for a 15 pound parcel for the zone to which addressed.

Zones	To 1 lb.	1½	2	2½	3	3½	4	4½	5*
1, 2, 3,.......	$2.24	$2.30	$2.54	$2.78	$3.01	$3.25	$3.49	3.73	$3.97
4..........	2.24	2.42	2.70	2.98	3.25	3.53	3.81	4.09	4.37
5..........	2.24	2.56	2.88	3.21	3.53	3.85	4.18	4.50	4.83
6..........	2.34	2.72	3.09	3.47	3.85	4.22	4.60	4.97	5.35
7..........	2.45	2.87	3.30	3.73	4.16	4.59	5.02	5.45	5.88
8..........	2.58	3.07	3.57	4.06	4.56	5.05	5.55	6.05	6.54

*Consult postmaster for parcels over 5 lbs.

Special Handling

Third and fourth class parcels will be handled and delivered as expeditiously as practicable (but not special delivery) upon payment, in addition to the regular postage: up to 10 lbs., 75¢; over 10 lbs., $1.30. Such parcels must be endorsed, Special Handling.

Special Delivery

First class mail up to 2 lbs. $2.10, over 2 lbs. and up to 10 lbs., $2.35; over 10 lbs. $3.00. All other classes up to 2 lbs. $2.35, over 2 and up to 10 lbs., $3.00, over 10 lbs. $3.40.

Bound Printed Matter Rates
(Fourth class single piece zone rate)

Weight		Zones							
lbs.	Local	1&2	3	4	5	6	7	8
1.5	$0.69	$0.92	$0.94	$0.97	$1.02	$1.08	$1.16	$1.19
2	.69	.93	.95	.99	1.06	1.14	1.25	1.28
2.5	.69	.93	.96	1.01	1.10	1.20	1.33	1.38
3	.69	.94	.97	1.03	1.14	1.25	1.41	1.47
3.5	.69	.94	.98	1.05	1.17	1.31	1.50	1.56
4	.69	.95	.99	1.07	1.21	1.37	1.58	1.66
4.5	.69	.95	1.00	1.09	1.25	1.42	1.67	1.75
5	.70	.96	1.02	1.12	1.29	1.48	1.75	1.85
6	.70	.96	1.04	1.16	1.36	1.59	1.92	2.03
7	.70	.97	1.06	1.20	1.44	1.71	2.09	2.22
8	.70	.98	1.08	1.24	1.51	1.82	2.25	2.41
9	.70	.99	1.10	1.28	1.59	1.94	2.42	2.59
10	.70	1.00	1.12	1.32	1.66	2.05	2.59	2.78

Zone Mileage

1 . . Up to 50	3 . . 150-300	5 . . . 600-1,000	7 . 1,400-1,800
2 . . . 50-150	4 . . 300-600	6 . . 1,000-1,400	8 . over 1,800

Domestic Mail Special Services

Registry — all mailable matter prepaid with postage at the first-class rate may be registered. The mailer is required to declare the value of mail presented for registration.

Registered Mail

	Insured	Uninsured
$0.00 to $100	$3.30	$3.25
$100.01 to $500	3.60	3.55
$500.01 to $1,000	3.90	3.85
$1,000.01 to $2,000	4.20	4.10
$2,000.01 to $3,000	4.50	4.35
$3,000.01 to $4,000	4.80	4.60
$4,000.01 to $5,000	5.10	4.85
$5,000.01 to $6,000	5.40	5.10
$6,000.01 to $7,000	5.70	5.35
$7,000.01 to $8,000	6.00	5.60
$8,000.01 to $9,000	6.30	5.85
$9,000.01 to $10,000	6.60	6.10

Consult postmaster for registry rates above $10,000.

C.O.D.: Unregistered — is applicable to 3d and 4th class matter and sealed domestic mail of any class bearing postage at the 1st class rate. Such mail must be based on bona fide orders or be in conformity with agreements between senders and addressees. **Registered** — for details consult postmaster.

Insurance — is applicable to 3d and 4th class matter. Matter for sale addressed to prospective purchasers who have not ordered it or authorized its sending will not be insured.

Insured Mail

$0.01 to $20	$0.45
20.01 to 50	0.85
50.01 to 100	1.25
100.01 to 150	1.70
150.01 to 200	2.05
200.01 to 300	3.45
300.01 to 400	4.70

Liability for insured mail is limited to $400.

Certified mail — service is available for any matter having no intrinsic value on which 1st class or air mail postage is paid. Receipt is furnished at time of mailing and evidence of delivery obtained. The fee is 75¢ ($1.00 restricted delivery) in addition to postage. Return receipt, restricted delivery, and special delivery are available upon payment of additional fees. No indemnity.

Special Fourth Class Rate
(limit 70 lbs.)

First pound or fraction, 63¢ (46¢ if 500 pieces or more of special rate matter are presorted to 5 digit ZIP code or 58¢ if 500 pieces or more are presorted to Bulk Mail Cntrs.); each additional pound or fraction through 7 pounds, 23¢; each additional pound, 14¢. Only following specific articles: books 24 pages or more, at least 22 of which are printed consisting wholly of reading matter or scholarly bibliography containing no advertisement other than incidental announcements of books; 16 millimeter films in final form (except when mailed to or from commercial theaters); printed music in bound or sheet form; printed objective test materials; sound recordings, playscripts, and manuscripts for books, periodicals, and music; printed educational reference charts; loose-leaf pages and binders therefor consisting of medical information for distribution to doctors, hospitals, medical schools, and medical students. Package must be marked "Special 4th Class Rate" stating item contained.

Library Rate (limit 70 lbs.)

First pound 32¢, each additional pound through 7 pounds, 11¢; each additional pound, 7¢. Books when loaned or exchanged between schools, colleges, public libraries, and certain non-profit organizations; books, printed music, bound academic theses, periodicals, sound recordings, other library materials, museum materials (specimens, collections), scientific or mathematical kits, instruments or other devices; also catalogs, guides or scripts for some of these materials. Must be marked "Library Rate".

Postal Union Mail Special Services

Registration — available to practically all countries. Fee $3.25. The maximum indemnity payable — generally only in case of complete loss (of both contents and wrapper) — is $25.20. To Canada only the fee is $3.55 providing indemnity for loss up to $200.

Parcel Post Rate Schedule

1 lb., not				Zones				
exceeding	Local	1 & 2	3	4	5	6	7	8
2	1.52	1.55	1.61	1.70	1.83	1.99	2.15	2.48
3	1.58	1.63	1.73	1.86	2.06	2.30	2.55	3.05
4	1.65	1.71	1.84	2.02	2.29	2.61	2.94	3.60
5	1.71	1.79	1.96	2.18	2.52	2.92	3.32	4.07
6	1.78	1.87	2.07	2.33	2.74	3.14	3.64	4.54
7	1.84	1.95	2.18	2.49	2.89	3.38	3.95	5.02
8	1.91	2.03	2.30	2.64	3.06	3.63	4.27	5.55
9	1.97	2.11	2.41	2.75	3.25	3.93	4.63	6.08
10	2.04	2.19	2.52	2.87	3.46	4.22	5.00	6.62
11	2.10	2.28	2.60	3.00	3.68	4.51	5.38	7.15
12	2.17	2.36	2.66	3.10	3.89	4.80	5.75	7.69
13	2.21	2.41	2.72	3.19	4.02	4.96	5.95	7.97
14	2.26	2.46	2.78	3.28	4.13	5.12	6.14	8.24
15	2.31	2.51	2.83	3.36	4.25	5.26	6.32	8.48
16	2.35	2.56	2.89	3.44	4.35	5.40	6.49	8.72
17	2.40	2.59	2.94	3.51	4.45	5.53	6.65	8.94
18	2.44	2.64	2.99	3.59	4.55	5.65	6.80	9.15
19	2.48	2.68	3.04	3.66	4.64	5.77	6.94	9.35
20	2.52	2.72	3.10	3.73	4.73	5.89	7.09	9.55

Consult postmaster for parcels over 20 pounds or measuring more than 84 inches, length and girth.

Return receipt —showing to whom and date delivr'd, 60¢.

Special delivery — Available to most countries. Consult post office. Fees: for post cards, letter mail, and airmail "other articles," $2.10 up to 2 pounds; over 2 to 10 pounds, $2.35; over 10 pounds, $3.00. For surface "other articles," $2.35, $3.00, and $3.40, respectively.

Marking — an article intended for special delivery service must have affixed to the cover near the name of the country of destination "EXPRESS" (special delivery) label, obtainable at the post office, or it may be marked on the cover boldly in red "EXPRESS" (special delivery).

Special handling — entitles AO surface packages to priority handling between mailing point and U.S. point of dispatch. Fees: 75¢ for packages to 10 pounds, and $1.30 for packages over 10 pounds.

Airmail — there is daily air service to practically all countries.

Prepayment of replies from other countries — a mailer who wishes to prepay a reply by letter from another country may do so by sending his correspondent one or more international reply coupons, which may be purchased at United States post offices. One coupon should be accepted in any country in exchange for stamps to prepay a surface letter of the first unit of weight to the U.S.

Post Office-Authorized 2-Letter State Abbreviations

The abbreviations below are approved by the U.S. Postal Service for use in addresses only. They do not replace the traditional abbreviations in other contexts. The official list follows, including the District of Columbia, Guam, Puerto Rico, the Canal Zone, and the Virgin Islands (all capital letters are used):

Alabama	AL	Hawaii	HI	Missouri	MO	Puerto Rico	PR
Alaska	AK	Idaho	ID	Montana	MT	Rhode Island	RI
American Samoa	AS	Illinois	IL	Nebraska	NE	South Carolina	SC
Arizona	AZ	Indiana	IN	Nevada	NV	South Dakota	SD
Arkansas	AR	Iowa	IA	New Hampshire	NH	Tennessee	TN
California	CA	Kansas	KS	New Jersey	NJ	Texas	TX
Canal Zone	CZ	Kentucky	KY	New Mexico	NM	Trust Territories	TT
Colorado	CO	Louisiana	LA	New York	NY	Utah	UT
Connecticut	CT	Maine	ME	North Carolina	NC	Vermont	VT
Delaware	DE	Maryland	MD	North Dakota	ND	Virginia	VA
Dist. of Col.	DC	Massachusetts	MA	Northern Mariana Is.	CM	Virgin Islands	VI
Florida	FL	Michigan	MI	Ohio	OH	Washington	WA
Georgia	GA	Minnesota	MN	Oklahoma	OK	West Virginia	WV
Guam	GU	Mississippi	MS	Oregon	OR	Wisconsin	WI
				Pennsylvania	PA	Wyoming	WY

Also approved for use in addressing mail are the following abbreviations:

Alley	Aly	Courts	Cts	Heights	Hts	Rural	R
Arcade	Arc	Crescent	Cres	Highway	Hwy	Square	Sq
Boulevard	Blvd	Drive	Dr	Lane	Ln	Street	St
Branch	Br	Expressway	Expy	Manor	Mnr	Terrace	Ter
Bypass	Byp	Extended	Ext	Place	Pl	Trail	Trl
Causeway	Cswy	Extension	Ext	Plaza	Plz	Turnpike	Tpke
Center	Ctr	Freeway	Fwy	Point	Pt	Viaduct	Via
Circle	Cir	Gardens	Gdns	Road	Rd	Vista	Vis
Court	Ct	Grove	Grv				

Size Standards for Domestic Mail

Minimum Size

Pieces which do not meet the following requirements are prohibited from the mails:

a. All pieces must be at least .007 of an inch thick, and

b. All pieces (except keys and identification devices) **which are 1/4 inch or less thick** must be:

(1) Rectangular in shape,

(2) At least 3 1/2 inches high, and

(3) At least 5 inches long.

Note: Pieces **greater than 1/4 inch thick** can be mailed even if they measure less than 3 1/2 by 5 inches.

Nonstandard Mail

All First-Class Mail weighing one ounce or less and all single-piece rate Third-Class mail weighing one ounce or less is nonstandard (and subject to a 9¢ surcharge in addition to the applicable postage and fees) if:

1. Any of the following dimensions are exceeded:
   Length—11 1/2 inches,
   Height—6 1/8 inches,
   Thickness—1/4 inch, or
2. The piece has a height to length (aspect) ratio which does not fall between 1 to 1.3 and 1 to 2.5 inclusive. (The aspect ratio is found by dividing the length by the height. If the answer is between 1.3 and 2.5 inclusive, the piece has a standard aspect ratio.)

Stamps, Envelopes and Postal Cards

Form	Denomination and prices
Single or sheet	1,2,3,4,5,6,10,11,12,13,14,15,16,17,18,20,25,28,30,45 & 50 cents, $1 and $5.
Book	20 at 20¢ = $4.00
Coil of 100	20 cents. (Dispenser to hold coils of 100 stamps may be purchased for 10¢ additional.)
Coils of 500	1,2,3,5,6,9,10,12,13,15,16, & 20 cents and $1.
Coil of 3,000	1,2,3,5,6,9,10,15,16,20 and 25 cents.

Postal Receipts at Large Cities

Fiscal year	Boston	Chicago	Detroit	L.A.	New York	Phila.	St. Louis	Wash., D.C.
1975	$136,453,079	$365,378,795	$84,338,282	$193,229,077	$453,905,277	$134,571,376	$85,591,774	$115,489,343
1977	173,933,702	424,045,237	102,018,571	232,293,590	528,545,213	168,521,442	107,379,762	138,050,517
1978	185,983,338	451,745,664	112,884,557	251,481,356	559,199,925	180,365,543	115,610,668	156,623,025
1979	211,082,724	506,395,438	120,690,772	273,563,824	627,445,984	211,571,818	126,031,314	175,467,893
1980	224,428,760	528,233,991	119,240,818	271,136,828	666,377,778	221,161,624	127,427,555	187,334,312
1981	256,524,082	551,988,015	121,556,041	301,159,594	741,286,845	235,116,018	142,548,957	201,191,995

Other cities for fiscal year 1981: Atlanta, $225,716,591; Baltimore, $115,490,600; Cincinnati, $93,770,132; Cleveland, $136,108,525; Columbus, $118,971,757 Dallas, $243,711,375; Denver, $120,374,500; Houston, $199,857,382; Indianapolis, $116,058,876; Kansas City, $101,249,441; Minneapolis, $170,672,133; Pittsburgh, $122,832,034; San Francisco, $180,028,721; Seattle, $113,424,903.

Air Mail, Parcel Post International Rates

Aerogrammes — 30¢ each to all countries.
Air mail postcards (single) - 28¢ to all countries except Canada and Mexico (13¢)

Country	Rate group	Air parcel post rates: First 4 oz.	Air parcel post rates: Each add'l. 4 oz. or fraction up to first 5 lbs.
Afghanistan	D	5.40	1.10
Albania	C	4.60	.90
Algeria	D	5.40	1.10
Andorra	B	3.80	.70
Angola	E	6.20	1.30
Argentina	D	5.40	1.10
Ascension	(4)	—	—
Australia	D	5.40	1.10
Austria	B	3.80	.70
Azores	C	4.60	.90
Bahamas	A	3.00	.50
Bahrain	D	5.40	1.10
Bangladesh	E	6.20	1.30
Barbados	B	3.80	.70
Belgium	E	6.20	1.30
Belize	A	3.00	.50
Benin	D	5.40	1.10
Bermuda	A	3.00	.50
Bhutan	(5)	—	—
Bolivia	B	3.80	.70
Botswana	E	6.20	1.30
Brazil	E	6.20	1.30
Brunei	D	5.40	1.10
Bulgaria	D	5.40	1.10
Burma	D	5.40	1.10
Burundi	E	6.20	1.30
Cameroon	C	4.60	.90
Canada[3,6]	(4)	—	—
Cape Verde	D	5.40	1.10
Cayman Islands	A	3.00	.50
Central African Rep.	E	6.20	1.30
Chad	D	5.40	1.10
Chile	D	5.40	1.10
China (People's Republic of)[7]	D	5.40	1.10
Colombia	B	3.80	.70
Comoros	E	6.20	1.30
Congo	D	5.40	1.10
Corsica	E	6.20	1.30
Costa Rica	A	3.00	.50
Cuba	(5)	—	—
Cyprus	D	5.40	1.10
Czechoslovakia	C	4.60	.90
Denmark	B	3.80	.70
Djibouti	E	6.20	1.30
Dominica	A	3.00	.50
Dominican Republic	A	3.00	.50
East Timor	(5)	—	—
Ecuador	B	3.80	.70
Egypt	C	4.60	.90
El Salvador	A	3.00	.50
Equatorial Guinea	D	5.40	1.10
Estonia	E	6.20	1.30
Ethiopia	D	5.40	1.10
Faeroe Islands	C	4.60	.90
Falkland Islands	D	5.40	1.10
Fiji	B	3.80	.70
Finland	D	5.40	1.10
France (Including Monaco)	E	6.20	1.30
French Guiana	C	4.60	.90
French Polynesia	D	5.40	1.10
Gabon	D	5.40	1.10
Gambia	B	3.80	.70
German Democratic Republic (East Germany)	C	4.60	.90
Germany, Federal Rep. of (West Germany)	C	4.60	.90
Ghana	D	5.40	1.10
Gibraltar	D	5.40	1.10
Great Britain	C	4.60	.90
Greece	C	4.60	.90
Greenland	D	5.40	1.10
Grenada	B	3.80	.70
Guadeloupe	A	3.00	.50
Guatemala	A	3.00	.50
Guinea	B	3.80	.70
Guinea-Bissau	B	3.80	.70

Country	Rate group	Air parcel post rates: First 4 oz.	Air parcel post rates: Each add'l. 4 oz. or fraction up to first 5 lbs.
Guyana	B	3.80	.70
Haiti	A	3.00	.50
Honduras	B	3.80	.70
Hong Kong	C	4.60	.90
Hungary	C	4.60	.90
Iceland	D	5.40	1.10
India	D	5.40	1.10
Indonesia	E	6.20	1.30
Iran	D	5.40	1.10
Iraq	D	5.40	1.10
Ireland (Eire)	C	4.60	.90
Israel	C	4.60	.90
Italy	C	4.60	.90
Ivory Coast	D	5.40	1.10
Jamaica	A	3.00	.50
Japan	E	6.20	1.30
Jordan	C	4.60	.90
Kampuchea	(5)	—	—
Kenya	D	5.40	1.10
Kiribati	B	3.80	.70
Korea, Democratic People's Rep. (North)[1]	(5)	—	—
Korea, Rep. of (South)	D	5.40	1.10
Kuwait	C	4.60	.90
Lao	E	6.20	1.30
Latvia	E	6.20	1.30
Lebanon	C	4.60	.90
Leeward Islands	A	3.00	.50
Lesotho	E	6.20	1.30
Liberia	B	3.80	.70
Libya	C	4.60	.90
Lithuania	E	6.20	1.30
Luxembourg	B	3.80	.70
Macao	C	4.60	.90
Madagascar	C	4.60	.90
Madeira Islands	B	3.80	.70
Malawi	D	5.40	1.10
Malaysia	D	5.40	1.10
Maldives	D	5.40	1.10
Mali	C	4.60	.90
Malta	C	4.60	.90
Martinique	A	3.00	.50
Mauritania	D	5.40	1.10
Mauritius	E	6.20	1.30
Mexico	A	3.00	.50
Mongolia	(5)	—	—
Morocco	C	4.60	.90
Mozambique	E	6.20	1.30
Nauru	C	4.60	.90
Nepal	D	5.40	1.10
Netherlands	C	4.60	.90
Nertherlands Antilles	A	3.00	.50
New Caledonia	D	5.40	1.10
New Zealand	D	5.40	1.10
Nicaragua	B	3.80	.70
Niger	D	5.40	1.10
Nigeria	C	4.60	.90
Norway	D	5.40	1.10
Oman	D	5.40	1.10
Pakistan	D	5.40	1.10
Panama	A	3.00	.50
Papua New Guinea	D	5.40	1.10
Paraguay	C	4.60	.90
Peru	B	3.80	.70
Philippines	D	5.40	1.10
Pitcairn Islands	B	3.80	.70
Poland	C	4.60	.90
Portugal	B	3.80	.70
Qatar	C	4.60	.90
Reunion	E	6.20	1.30
Romania	C	4.60	.90
Rwanda	D	5.40	1.10
St. Helena	B	3.80	.70
St. Lucia	A	3.00	.50
St. Pierre & Miquelon	A	3.00	.50
St. Thomas & Principe	D	5.40	1.10
St. Vincent & The Grenadines	A	3.00	.50

Country	Rate group	Air parcel post rates: First 4 oz.	Air parcel post rates: Each add'l. 4 oz. or fraction up to First 5 lbs.
Santa Cruz Islands	B	3.80	.70
Saudi Arabia	C	4.60	.90
Senegal	D	5.40	1.10
Seychelles	D	5.40	1.10
Sierre Leone	C	4.60	.90
Singapore	D	5.40	1.10
Solomon Islands	C	4.60	.90
Somalia (Southern Region).	D	5.40	1.10
Somalia (Northern Region).	(4)	—	—
South Africa	E	6.20	1.30
Spain	C	4.60	.90
Sri Lanka	D	5.40	1.10
Sudan	D	5.40	1.10
Suriname	B	3.80	.70
Swaziland	D	5.40	1.10
Sweden	D	5.40	1.10
Switzerland	B	3.80	.70
Syria	C	4.60	.90
Taiwan	C	4.60	.90
Tanzania	E	6.20	1.30
Thailand	D	5.40	1.10
Togo	D	5.40	1.10

Country	Rate group	Air parcel post rates: First 4 oz.	Air parcel post rates: Each add'l. 4 oz. or fraction up to First 5 lbs.
Tonga	B	3.80	.70
Trinidad & Tobago	B	3.80	.70
Tristan da Cunha	B	3.80	.70
Tunisia	C	4.60	.90
Turkey	C	4.60	.90
Turks & Caicos Islands	A	3.00	.50
Tuvalu (Ellice Islands)	B	3.80	.70
Uganda	D	5.40	1.10
USSR[3]	E	6.20	1.30
United Arab Emirates	D	5.40	1.10
Upper Volta	C	4.60	.90
Uruguay	B	3.80	.70
Vanuatu	B	3.80	.70
Vatican City State	C	4.60	.90
Venezuela	B	3.80	.70
Vietnam[1]	(5)	—	—
Western Samoa	B	3.80	.70
Yemen Arab Republic	D	5.40	1.10
Yemen, Peoples Democratic Republic of	D	5.40	1.10
Yugoslavia	C	4.60	.90
Zaire	D	5.40	1.10
Zambia	E	6.20	1.30
Zimbabwe	E	6.20	1.30

Miscellaneous International Rates

Letters and Letter Pkgs (Surface)

Weight steps: Over Lbs.	Over Ozs.	Through Lbs.	Through Ozs.	Canada	Mexico	All other countries
0	0	0	1	$0.20	$0.20	$0.30
0	1	0	2	.37	.37	.47
0	2	0	3	.54	.57	.64
0	3	0	4	.71	.71	.81
0	4	0	5	.88	.88	.98
0	5	0	6	1.05	1.05	1.15
0	6	0	7	1.22	1.22	1.32
0	7	0	8	1.39	1.39	1.49
0	8	0	9	1.56	1.56	2.76
0	9	0	10	1.73	1.73	2.76
0	10	0	11	1.90	1.90	2.76
0	11	0	12	2.07	2.07	2.76
0	12	1	0	2.58	2.58	2.76
1	0	1	8	3.07	3.07	3.78
1	8	2	0	3.57	3.57	4.80
2	0	2	8	4.06	4.06	5.55
2	8	3	0	4.56	4.56	6.30
3	0	3	8	5.05	5.05	7.05
3	8	4	0	5.55	5.55	7.80
4	0	4	8	6.05	...	...
4	8	5	0	6.54	...	...

Maximum limit: 60 pounds to Canada, 4 pounds to Mexico and all other countries.

Letters and Letter Pkgs (Air)

Canada and Mexico: Refer to rates listed under Letter and Letter Pkgs. (Surface). Mail paid at this rate receives First-Class service in the United States and air service in Canada and Mexico.

Colombia, Venezuela, Central America, the Caribbean Islands, Bahamas, Bermuda, St. Pierre & Miquelon: 35 cents per half ounce up to and including 2 ounces; 30 cents each additional half ounce up to and including 32 ounces; 30 cents per additional ounce over 32 ounces.

All Other Countries: 40 cents per half ounce up to and including 2 ounces; 35 cents each additional half ounce up to and including 32 ounces; 35 cents per additional ounce over 32 ounces.

Parcel Post (Surface)

Canada, Mexico, Central America, The Caribbean Islands, Bahamas, Bermuda, St. Pierre and Miquelon; $3.10 for the first 2 pounds and $1.00 each additional pound or fraction.

All Other Countries: $3.25 for the first 2 pounds and $1.05 for each additional pound or fraction.

For Parcel Post air rates, see tables, pages 973-974.

(1) Restrictions apply; consult post office. (2) To facilitate distribution and delivery, include "Union of Soviet Socialist Republics" or "USSR" as part of the address. (3) Small packets weight limit one pound to Canada. (4) No air parcel post service. (5) No parcel post service. (6) No airmail AO or parcel post to Canada; prepare and prepay all airmail packages as letter mail. (7) The continental China postal authorities will not deliver articles unless addressed to show name of the country as "People's Republic of China"; also, only acceptable spelling of capital is "Beijing."

International Mails

Weight and Dimensional Limits and Surface Rates

For air rates and parcel post see pages 973-974

Letters and letter packages: all written matter or correspondence must be sent as letter mail. Weight limit: 4 lbs. to all countries except Canada, which is 60 lbs. **Surface rates:** Canada and Mexico, 20¢ first ounce; 17¢ each additional oz. or fraction through 12 ozs.; eighth-zone priority rates for heavier weights. Countries other than Canada and Mexico, 1 oz., 30¢; over 1 to 2 ozs., 47¢; over 2 to 3 ozs., 64¢; over 3 to 4 ozs., 81¢; over 4 to 5 ozs., 98¢; over 5 to 6 ozs., $1.15; over 6 to 7 ozs., $1.32; over 7 to 8 ozs., $1.49; over 8 ozs. to 1 pound, $2.76; over 1 lb. to 1 lb., 8 ozs., $3.78; over 1 lb., 8 ozs. to 2 lbs., $4.80; over 2 lbs. to 2 lbs., 8 ozs., $5.55; over 2 lbs., 8 ozs. to 3 lbs., $6.30; over 3 lbs. to 3 lbs., 8 ozs., $7.05; over 3 lbs., 8 ozs. to 4 lbs. $7.80. **Air rates:** Canada and Mexico, 20¢ first ounce; 17¢ each additional ounce or fraction to 1 pound. Central America, Colombia, Venezuela, the Caribbean Islands, the Bahamas, Bermuda, and St. Pierre and Miquelon, 35¢ per half ounce up to and including 2 ounces; 30¢ each additional half ounce or fraction. All other countries, 40¢ per half ounce up to and including 2 ounces; 35¢ each additional half ounce or fraction. Aerogrammes, which can be folded into the form of an envelope and sent by air to all countries, are available at post offices for 30¢ each.

Note. Mail to Canada and Mexico bearing postage paid at the surface letter rate will receive first class service in the U.S. and airmail service in Canada and Mexico during the Postal Service First Class Mail Service Improvement Program.

Postcards. Surface rates to Canada and Mexico, 13¢; to all other countries, 19¢. By air, Canada and Mexico, 13¢; to all other countries, 28¢. Maximum size permitted, 6 x 4¼ in.; minimum, 5½ x 3½.

Printed matter. To Canada, Mexico and all other countries: 20¢ (Canada and Mexico) and 23¢ (all other countries) the first ounce, 37¢ for 1 to 2 ozs., 54¢ for 2 to 3 ozs., 71¢ for 3 to 4 ozs., 85¢ for 4 to 6 ozs., 95¢ for 6 to 8 ozs., $1.14 for 8 to 10 ozs., $1.36 for 10 to 12 ozs., $1.58 for 12 to 14 ozs., $1.81 for 14 to 18 ozs., $1.94 for 18 to 20 ozs., $2.07 for 20 to 22 ozs., $2.21 for 22 to 24 ozs., $2.35 for 24 to 26 ozs., $2.49 for 26 to 28 ozs., $2.62 for 28 to 30 ozs., $2.76 for 30 to 32 ozs., $3.31 for 2 lbs. to 3 lbs., $3.86 for 3 lbs. to 4 lbs. and 96¢ for each add'l 1 lb. (Consult post office for rates and conditions applying to certain publications mailed by the publishers or by registered news agents.) Consult post office for book rates.

Exceptional weight limits for printed matter. Printed matter may weigh up to 22 lbs. to Argentina, Bolivia, Brazil, Chile, Colombia, Costa Rica, Cuba, Dominican Republic, Ecuador, El Salvador, Guatemala, Haiti, Honduras, Mexico, Nicaragua, Panama, Paraguay, Peru, Spain (including Balearic Islands, and Canary Islands) Surinam, Uruguay, and Venezuela. For other countries, limit for books is 11 lbs., all other prints, 4 lbs.

Matter for the blind. Surface rate free; air service to Canada for matter prepared as letters/letter packages is at the letter rate. (For all other countries, consult postmaster.) Weight limit 15 lbs.

Small packets. Postage rates for small items of merchandise and samples; consult post office for weight limits and requirements for customs declarations. Rates: Canada, Mexico 20¢, all other countries 23¢ for the first ounce; 37¢ for 1 to 2 ozs.; 54¢ for 2 to 3 ozs.; 71¢ for 3 to 4 ozs.; 85¢ for 4 to 6 ozs.; 95¢ for 6 to 8 ozs.; $1.14 for 8 to 10 ozs.; $1.36 for 10 to 12 ozs.; $1.58 for 12 to 14 ozs.; $1.81 for 14 to 16 ozs. (Consult post office for rates for heavier packets.) For other rates, see schedule "Air Service Other Articles" under heading of International Rates for Air Mail and Surface Parcel Post, pages 973-974.

INTELPOST-A USPS International Service Offering

The U.S. Postal Service, in conjunction with several foreign countries is making available to the public a new service offering called INTELPOST. INTELPOST is an acronym for International Electronic Post.

The INTELPOST system is a very high speed digital facsimile network between the United States and participating countries. INTELPOST utilizes existing international postal acceptance and delivery mechanisms for the acceptance and distribution of the INTELPOST original and facsimile documents. The INTELPOST original document and a transmittal form are scanned by a facsimile reader operated by USPS personnel at the INTELPOST transmitting facility and sent via international satellite communications to its destination. A black and white image of the original document is printed by a facsimile printer operated by foreign postal personnel and is inserted into an INTELPOST envelope for delivery by participating postal administration personnel according to the service offerings available in the particular country.

The cost of an INTELPOST transmission is $5.00 per page including First Class (normal) delivery in the destinating foreign country. If an optional express type delivery service is available and is selected, the cost of such service will be added to the price of the message. Service is currently available to Canada, the United Kingdom and the Netherlands. Several additional countries are in the process of building INTELPOST Centers.

International Parcel Post

For rates see pages 973-974

General dimensional limits — greatest length, 3½ feet; greatest length and girth combined, 6 feet.

Prohibited articles. Before sending goods abroad the mailer should consult the post office that they will not be confiscated or returned because their importation is prohibited or restricted by the country of address.

Packing. Parcels for transmission overseas should be even more carefully packed than those intended for delivery within the continental U.S. Containers should be used which will be strong enough to protect the contents from the weight of other mail, from pressure and friction, climatic changes, and repeated handlings.

Sealing. Registered or insured parcels must be sealed. To some countries the sealing of ordinary (unregistered and uninsured) parcels is optional, and to others compulsory. Consult post office.

Customs declarations and other forms. At least one customs declaration is required for parcel post packages (surface or air) mailed to another country. In addition, to some countries, a dispatch note is required. The forms may be obtained at post offices.

Canadian Postal Rates

(in effect Jan. 1, 1982)

First class letter mail and postcards. Up to 30 grams 30¢, over 30g and up to 50g 45¢, over 50g and up to 100g 60¢, over 100g and up to 150g 80¢, over 150g and up to 200g $1, over 200g and up to 250g $1.20, over 250 and up to 300g $1.40, over 300g and up to 350g $1.60, over 350g and up to 400g $1.80, over 400g and up to 450g $2, over 450g and up to 500g $2.20.

Parcels (over 500g). **First class** (maximum 30kg) receive priority air service. **Fourth class** (maximum 16kg receive surface transmission.

The charges given below are for local (short haul) deliveries. A chart showing the cost for deliveries to all other postal zones may be obtained from your local postmaster.

Over/up to	500g/1kg-	1kg/1.5	1.5/2	2/2.5	2.5/3	3/3.5	3.5/4	4/6	6/8	8/10	10/12	12/14
1st class	$1.90	2.30	2.45	2.60	2.75	2.90	3.05	3.35	3.65	3.95	4.25	4.55
4th class	1.10	1.20	1.30	1.45	1.60	1.75	1.90	2.10	2.35	2.90	3.20	3.55

Third class. Standard addressed rates (includes greeting cards). Up to 50g 30¢ plus 15¢ for each additional 50g up to a maximum of 500g.

Premium services. Certified mail (proof of delivery service) $1 plus postage. Special delivery first class postage plus $1 per item. Money order fee (maximum $200) - 40¢.

To U.S.A., Territories and Possessions

Airmail letters and postcards, up to and including 30g 35¢, from 30g to 50g 50¢ plus 25¢ for each additional 50g up to 500g. Over 500g up to and including 1kg $6 with increases up to $52.40 for 30kg.

Surface parcel post. Up to and including 1kg $4 plus 60¢ for each additional 500g up to a maximum of 16kg.

QUICK REFERENCE INDEX

First Class Postal Rates in Brief

U.S. Domestic (in effect Nov. 1, 1981)

Letters—20¢ first ounce, 17¢ each additional ounce.
Postal cards—13¢ each (up to 4½ × 6 in.). Double cards, 26¢. Private cards, 13¢; double 26¢.

U.S. International (in effect Nov. 1, 1981)

Letters—(1) Canada (max. weight 60 lbs.) and Mexico (max. weight 4 lbs.), 20¢ first ounce, 17¢ each addl. ounce to 1 ounces; over 12 ounces to 1 pound, $2.58; over 1 pound to 1½ pounds, $3.07; over 1½ to 2 pounds, $3.57; over 2 to 2½ pounds, $4.06; over 2½ to 3 pounds, $4.56; over 3 to 3½ pounds, $5.05; over 3½ to 4 pounds, $5.55; over 4 to 4½ pounds, $6.05; over 4½ to 5 pounds, $6.54. (2) Countries other than Canada and Mexico, 1 ounce, 30¢; over 1 to 2 ounces, 47¢; over 2 to 3 ounces, 64¢; over 3 to 4 ounces, 81¢; over 4 to 5 ounces, 98¢; over 5 to 6 ounces, $1.15; over 6 to 7 ounces $1.32; and over 7 to 8 ounces, $1.49.
Air mail letters—(1) Canada, and Mexico, same as domestic surface rates. (2) Cen. America, Colombia, Venezuela, the Caribbean Is., Bahamas, Bermuda, and St. Pierre and Miquelon, 35¢ per half ounce through 2 ounces; 30¢ each addl. ½ oz through 32 ounces. (3) All other countries, 40¢ per half ounce through 2 ounces; 35¢ each addl. ½ oz. through 32 ounces.

Aerogrammes—to all countries, 30¢ each.
Postal cards—to Canada and Mexico 13¢ each. To all other countries, 19¢ each.
Air mail postcards—to Canada and Mexico 13¢ each, to other countries 28¢ each.

Canada (in effect July 1, 1982)

Letter mail and postcards—Up to 30g 30¢, 31-50g 45¢, 51-100g 60¢, 101-150g 80¢, 151-200g $1, 201-250g $1.20, 251-300g $1.40, 301-350g $1.60, 351-400g $1.80, 401-450g $2.00, 451-500g $2.20.
To U.S.A. territories and possessions—(1) **Airmail letters and postcards,** up to and including 30g 35¢, 30-50g 50¢ plus 25¢ for each additional 50g up to 500g. Over 500g up to and including 1kg $6.00 with increases up to $52.40 for a maximum of 30kg. (2) **Surface parcel post.** Up to and including 1kg $4.00 plus 60¢ for each additional 500g up to a maximum of 16g.